Caspian Sea

Lake Van

Lake Urmiah

ARTU

MITANNI

AM NAHARAIM
aran

HORITES
(HURRIANS)

Mosul • • Nineveh
• Arbela
ASSYRIA

Asshur • • Arrapkha (Kirkuk)
Nuzi •

Tirqa •

"AMMURU"

Khabur

Tigris

Euphrates

Mari •

AMEANS

• Behistun

• Ecbatana

KASSITES

ELAM

BABYLONIA

• Eshnunna

• Der

Sippar •

Babylon • • Nippur
Borsippa • • Kish

• Susa

PERSIA

RABIA

• Adab
SUMER
Shuruppak • • Umma
• Lagash

Erech (Uruk) •
Larsa •
Ur • • Eridu

Parsagarda •
Persepolis •

• Dumah

Persian Gulf

THE ANCIENT NEAR EAST

0   100   200 miles

40°   45°   50°

40

35

30

25

THE NEW JEROME BIBLICAL COMMENTARY

Love the holy Scriptures, and wisdom will love you. Love wisdom, and she will keep you safe. Honor wisdom, and she will embrace you. (St. Jerome, *Ep.* 130.20; CSEL 56.3.201)

This commentary is named after St. Jerome, the foremost Scripture scholar among the Church Fathers, a pioneer in biblical criticism.

Edited by

RAYMOND E. BROWN, S.S.

Union Theological Seminary, New York, NY

JOSEPH A. FITZMYER, S.J. (emeritus)

Catholic University of America, Washington, DC

ROLAND E. MURPHY, O.Carm. (emeritus)

The Divinity School, Duke University, Durham, NC

With a Foreword by

HIS EMINENCE CARLO MARIA CARDINAL MARTINI, S.J.

THE NEW JEROME BIBLICAL COMMENTARY

PRENTICE HALL, *Englewood Cliffs, New Jersey 07632*

Library of Congress Cataloging-in-Publication Data

The New Jerome Biblical commentary / edited by RAYMOND E. BROWN,
JOSEPH A. FITZMYER, ROLAND E. MURPHY ; with a foreword by CARLO
MARIA CARDINAL MARTINI.

   p. cm.
   Bibliography: p.
   Includes index.
   ISBN 0-13-614934-0
   1. Bible—Commentaries. I. Brown, Raymond Edward. II. Fitzmyer,
Joseph A. III. Murphy, Roland Edmund [date]
BS491.2.N485   1990
220.7—dc19   89-31382
          CIP

THE NEW JEROME BIBLICAL COMMENTARY

Editors
Raymond E. Brown, S.S.
Joseph A. Fitzmyer, S.J.
Roland E. Murphy, O.Carm.

Previously published as *The Jerome Biblical Commentary*

Nihil Obstat:
Raymond E. Brown, S.S.
Joseph A. Fitzmyer, S.J.
Roland E. Murphy, O.Carm.
Censores Deputati

Imprimatur:
Reverend William J. Kane
Vicar General for the Archdiocese of Washington
November 15, 1988

The *nihil obstat* and *imprimatur* are official declarations that a book or pamphlet is free of doctrinal or moral error. No implication is contained therein that those who have granted the *nihil obstat* and the *imprimatur* agree with the content, opinions, or statements expressed.

Editorial/production supervision: *Edith Riker*
Manufacturing buyer: *Peter Havens*
Copyediting: *Maurya P. Horgan, The Scriptorium*
Typesetting: *Paul J. Kobelski, The Scriptorium*
Lemmata from the CCD OT used with permission of the copyright owner.

Printed in the United States of America

10   9   8   7   6   5   4   3   2   1

ISBN   0-13-614934-0

PRENTICE-HALL INTERNATIONAL (UK) LIMITED, *London*
PRENTICE-HALL OF AUSTRALIA, PTY. LIMITED, *Sydney*
PRENTICE-HALL CANADA INC., *Toronto*
PRENTICE-HALL HISPANOAMERICANA, S.A., *Mexico*
PRENTICE-HALL OF INDIA PRIVATE LIMITED, *New Delhi*
PRENTICE-HALL OF JAPAN, INC., *Tokyo*
SIMON & SCHUSTER ASIA PTE. LTD., *Singapore*
EDITORA PRENTICE-HALL DO BRASIL, LTDA., *Rio de Janeiro*

"In the sacred books the Father who is in heaven meets his children with great love and speaks with them; and the force in the Word of God is so great that it remains the support and energy of the Church, the strength of faith for her children, the food of the soul, the pure and perennial source of spiritual life."

Dei Verbum (Constitution on Divine
Revelation of Vatican II) #21

CONTENTS

Part One
THE OLD TESTAMENT

Part Two
THE NEW TESTAMENT
AND TOPICAL ARTICLES

Contents

FOREWORD TO
THE NEW
JEROME BIBLICAL COMMENTARY

This comprehensive commentary on the Bible now reappears in a form about two-thirds new, born of the patient and devoted dedication of the best of English-speaking Catholic exegetes. Like a continuous thread from which knots are removed, the issues and questions, the diverse dimensions and the message presented by the biblical text are unravelled page by page, as *The New Jerome Biblical Commentary* condenses the results of modern scientific criticism with rigor and clarity. Yet this contemporary approach is achieved without neglecting the long road that Christian tradition has travelled in dedicated, constant, and loving attention to the Word of God. This is the principal route recommended by the Second Vatican Council itself, lest the path of the Christian reader of the Bible be encumbered either by an arid literalism "that kills" (2 Cor 3:6) or by a reading that drifts off into generalized spiritual applications. In fact, the biblical message is, as is Christ himself, flesh and divine Word, history and transcendence, humanity and divinity.

In reading the varied contributions to what is truly a mine of exegesis, readers can familiarize themselves with the methods and paths followed by biblical scholars. They will note that the concentration on problems of historical and literary criticism stems from serious attention to the "marvelous 'condescension'" of God in transmitting his word in human language (*Dei verbum* 13). It is precisely this route that leads us more deeply into an understanding of the message. With the daily use of a tool such as this commentary many can come to discover the inexhaustible wealth and the freshness that springs from pages of the Bible when they are duly situated in their appropriate historical and cultural context. By putting readers into direct contact with the splendor of God's Word, this commentary will also become a means of penetrating the divine mystery so that "all Christian faithful . . . [may] learn by frequent reading of the divine Scriptures the 'excelling knowledge of Jesus Christ' (Phil 3:8)" (*Dei verbum* 25).

The New Jerome Biblical Commentary will also be an instrument for rich ecumenical dialogue. Much of the progress made by biblical scholarship in the last decades and recorded in this book has been born of the intensive research of interpreters of various Christian churches, thus fulfilling what the Second Vatican Council in its decree on Ecumenism affirmed, "In dialogue itself, the sacred utterances are precious instruments in the mighty hand of God for attaining that unity which the Savior holds out to all people" (no. 21).

We rejoice, then, that through this important tool for study and reflection the Bible will more and more become for all believers the water that gives life to the spiritual aridity of human existence (Isa 55:10–11), the food that is sweeter than honey (Ps 19:11), the hammer that shatters hardened indifference (Jer 23:29), and the sword that pierces obstinate refusal (Heb 4:12). As Gregory the Great once wrote, alluding to Psalm 123, "Truly solicitous servants always pay attention to the facial expressions of their masters so as to hear and follow out commands with promptness. So too the righteous focus their minds on the presence of Almighty God and gaze upon his Scriptures as upon his countenance" (*Moralia in Job* 16.35.43; CC 143A. 824).

CARLO MARIA CARDINAL MARTINI
Archbishop of Milan, Italy

FOREWORD TO
THE JEROME BIBLICAL COMMENTARY
(1968)

I have repeatedly stated that in many ways the Second Vatican Council would not have been possible without the long and fruitful doctrinal preparation provided by Pope Pius XII. To give only one example, we may recall how three great encyclicals of Pope Pius prepared the way for the three central documents of the Council—the encyclicals *Mystici Corporis, Divino Afflante Spiritu,* and *Mediator Dei* related respectively to the constitutions on the Church, on Divine Revelation, and on the Sacred Liturgy. Moreover, the Council would not have been able to meet successfully so many problems of modern life if beforehand the truly indefatigable teaching ministry of Pius XII had not thrown light little by little on so many pressing difficulties. In the biblical field it is certain that the flourishing development of Catholic biblical studies, due in large part to the encyclical *Divino Afflante Spiritu,* was what made possible the truly biblical orientation of the conciliar documents, based, as they were, on scriptural foundations. It was precisely for this reason that the documents of Vatican II were rightly appreciated even by our non-Catholic brethren.

This development and the fruits that it has borne have fully confirmed what I wrote years ago, namely, that the encyclical *Divino Afflante Spiritu* of Pope Pius XII "is no less important than the encyclical *Providentissimus Deus* of Pope Leo XIII, which has been called the Magna Carta of biblical studies." (See "Pio XII e le scienze bibliche," *Pio XII Pont. Max. Postridie calendas martias* MDCCCLXXVI-MDCCCCLVI [Milan, 1956] 72.) I have often had occasion to note with great pleasure that the Catholics of the United States have had a large share in this development of biblical studies. It suffices to mention the Catholic Biblical Association and its magazine *The Catholic Biblical Quarterly,* along with various other initiatives undertaken by it to make Sacred Scripture better known, studied, and loved.

The present commentary on the whole Bible is another instance of this spirit, and that is why I greet it with particular pleasure. Its great value is that it is not only *about* the Bible, but that it also, as it were, brings the reader to the Word of God itself—to read it, to study it, and to meditate on it. Indeed, we can never insist enough on the advice of Pius XII that emphasizes the power and the spiritual fruitfulness of the words of Scripture: "The Word of God . . . needs no artificial devices nor human adaptation to move hearts and arouse souls. For the Sacred Pages inspired by God are in themselves rich in original meaning;

endowed with a divine power, they have their own value; adorned with heavenly beauty, of themselves they radiate light and splendor, provided only that they are so fully and accurately explained by the interpreter that all the treasures of wisdom and prudence contained therein are brought to light" (*EB* 553; *RSS*, p. 94).

The present commentary makes it possible for the Word of God to act on man in this religious and spiritual way, since it is concerned principally with expounding "the theological doctrine of the individual books and texts in relation to faith and morals" (as the encyclical directs; *EB* 551; *RSS*, p. 93). In this way the exegesis found in the commentary will not only be of use to professors of theology, but will "also be of assistance to priests in their presentation of Christian doctrine to the people and thus help all the faithful to lead a life that is holy and worthy of a Christian" (*Ibid.*).

Thus, by putting the reader himself in contact with the Written Word of God, *The Jerome Biblical Commentary* makes a real contribution toward realizing the goal firmly insisted upon in the constitution on Divine Revelation of Vatican II (#22): "It is necessary that the faithful have full access to Sacred Scripture." Nor can there be any doubt that this work will also be a fruitful contribution to the great cause of ecumenism; for as the conciliar decree on Ecumenism (#21) has said: "In the dialogue [with our non-Catholic brethren] Sacred Scripture makes an excellent tool in the powerful hand of God for the attainment of that unity which the Savior offers to all men."

I hope therefore that this work will enjoy a wide distribution. May it realize the desire with which the constitution on Divine Revelation (#26) closes: "Through the reading and study of the sacred books, let 'the word of the Lord run its course and be glorified' (2 Thes 3:1), and let the treasure of revelation entrusted to the Church increasingly fill the hearts of men."

＋ *Aug Card Bea*

AUGUSTIN CARDINAL BEA, S.J.
Member of the Pontifical Biblical Commission
President of the Secretariat for Promoting
Christian Unity

PREFACE

This work is a compact commentary on the whole Bible written by Roman Catholic scholars according to the principles of modern biblical criticism. Its predecessor, *The Jerome Biblical Commentary,* which appeared in 1968, embodied the revolution in Catholic biblical studies that took place in the two decades between the appearance of the encyclical *Divino Afflante Spiritu* of Pope Pius XII in 1943 and the closing of Vatican Council II under Pope Paul VI in 1965. The encyclical had served as a Magna Carta allowing Catholics to use literary and historical criticism that had long been suspect; the Council and Paul VI defended the results achieved by that criticism against a reactionary assault mounted after the death of Pius XII. We editors remain proud of the *JBC.* Our preface to it stated a modest goal of gathering the new insights into one place where they would be conveniently available to all who were interested. Despite the then-recent entrance of Catholics into biblical criticism, the *JBC* was judged by many non-Catholics to be the best concise commentary in English on the Bible. A circulation of some 200,000 copies, and translations into Spanish and Italian, testified to its ready acceptance.

Two more decades now have passed, and for several reasons a new commentary has become necessary. The original contributors were almost all clergy; today the number of trained Catholic scholars has multiplied, exemplifying changes in the church itself. Thus *The New Jerome Biblical Commentary* can profit from a significant proportion of lay contributors and of women. Often the *JBC* contributors were avowedly dependent on the original work of non-Catholics who had been longer in the field. Now original investigations by Catholics have greatly increased; and on the North American scene, to speak of the region we know best, Catholics and Protestants are *ex aequo* in the quality of their biblical scholarship. Such progress had to be reflected.

Not only inner-Catholic issues, however, dictated the importance of a new commentary. There have been great changes in biblical scholarship at large in the last quarter century. Archaeology pertinent to the Bible has flourished in the Holy Land and adjacent areas, and the derived information has multiplied geometrically. Theories of dating and historical reconstructions based on pre-1970 data have had to be revised drastically, particularly in regard to Israelite history before the monarchy. Manuscript discoveries and publications have brought much greater sophistication in our understanding of noncanonical works contemporary with or similar to the biblical books. Literary and contextual approaches to the Bible have been strongly emphasized, and new perspectives have been advanced in hermeneutics. The limitations in source analysis have become clear, with a resulting concentration on the final form of the text as the primary concern of scholarship. The theological depth of the biblical word has won more attention, including an appreciation of the context given to individual books by the whole canon.

From the editors' viewpoint a new work seemed advisable in response to a need felt for improving content and format, updating the bibliography, and meeting recent interests. In particular, the *NJBC* commentary articles should be easier to consult because of the added running heads indicating chapter and verse. The topical section has been enlarged by articles on Jesus and on the Early Church (including gnosticism and subapostolic church writings). Perhaps we may best summarize the amount of change resulting from the various factors just named by our estimate that *the* NJBC *is two-thirds new*. This reflects the editors' decision not to be satisfied with retouching but to produce a fresh work.

The goal and level of the *NJBC,* however, remain the same as those of the *JBC:* emphatically a *commentary* envisioning an audience of educated readers who wish to *study* the Scriptures. We hope this audience will include those interested in religion and theology on all levels who feel the need for an adequate background in the Bible. That audience has probably become more diversified since the *JBC* was written, and one may rejoice in that. Remaining especially in view, however, are seminarians and clergy who require a commentary on the Scriptures both during their formal study of theology and for preaching in their ministry. For them the present volume may well serve both as a basic text in the seminary and as a reference book in later years — as a foundation and a *vade mecum*. Some readers may ultimately progress to deeper Scripture study, wanting to consult scientific articles and even commentary series where a whole volume is dedicated to a single book of the Bible. Teachers will also wish particularized assistance. With this in mind, a deliberate attempt has been made to supply ample bibliographical guides in several languages and to introduce the reader to the technical terminology necessary for more detailed research.

In the *JBC* we editors faced an ecumenical issue in deciding that all those invited to contribute should be Roman Catholic. Even in the 1960s it was clear that Catholic and non-Catholic biblical scholars could work together and have the same approach to and interpretation of most biblical passages. Thus the decision about restricted contributorship did not reflect unworthy motives of distrust or arrogance. The wisdom of the decision was not challenged by Protestant reviewers who recognized that the *JBC* was catholic in the non-parochial sense of the word. A fortiori, cooperation between Catholics and non-Catholics would be possible today, for the intervening decades have intensified the dialogue. For instance, a non-Catholic has participated in the revision of the *NAB* New Testament sponsored by the American bishops and destined to be used in the liturgy; and many of the contributors to the *NJBC* teach in non-Catholic seminaries and universities. Nevertheless, some of the reasoning that persuaded us to follow the policy of inviting only Catholic scholars to contribute to the *JBC* is still valid, and new reasons have appeared, whence our decision to adopt the same policy for the *NJBC.*

There persists among both Catholics and Protestants a wrong image that, while Protestants have many interpretations of Scripture, Catholics have only one, dictated by church authorities. The fact that the Roman Catholic Church has never clearly pronounced on what a passage meant to the biblical author who penned it or to the audience who first read it (→ Hermeneutics, 71:80–87) is overlooked. Accordingly it is important to have a volume such as this which enables readers of all religious persuasions to see a representative group of Catholic scholars at work — not the isolated and allegedly liberal few, but almost seventy contributors who have taught Bible in every sort of university, college, and seminary in the United States, Canada, and abroad. They exemplify the range of exegetical variation to be found in any community of scholars. The scientific methods and the struggle for objectivity would be no different were the commentary written by scholars of mixed religious background.

Another reason for the decision to invite only Catholics stems from the situation of the post-Vatican II Roman Catholic Church. Authorities of our church, as is their duty, have demonstrated vigilance in investigating possible aberrations in doctrine. Several corrections of Catholic theologians have been well publicized. Many non-Catholics are not aware of papal encouragement for modern biblical studies or of affirmations by the highest authorities that there can be no return to the repressive attitudes of the early twentieth century. Accordingly they frequently ask their Catholic colleagues whether there have been signs of a repression of the biblical movement or instances of chastisement of biblical scholars by Roman offices. Ultraconservative Catholics who never accepted the changes inaugurated by Pope Pius XII and ratified by the Council have publicly expressed the hope that such a suppression would come. It remains important, therefore, to demonstrate through a critical commentary written entirely by Catholics that the ongoing freedom of biblical research is accepted within the church. That there is no atmosphere of reaction against biblical studies or oppressive scrutiny of biblical scholars is a testimony not only to continuing ecclesiastical support for the movement but also to the responsibility demonstrated for half a century by Catholic biblical scholars who employ modern methods. If overall the conclusions reached by Catholic biblical scholars have not offensively challenged doctrine, that is because they themselves have found the interplay between faith and free biblical research enriching on both sides, rather than antagonistic.

As for details that may contribute to understanding the genesis of the *NJBC,* the articles were commissioned in 1984 and, with a few exceptions (related to the death of contributors), were in the editors' hands by 1987. Although the editors sought to accord each contributor as much independence of view and method as possible, the need to achieve a certain overall unity necessitated occasional additions, subtractions, alterations of style, and a constant effort to include the latest bibliography. It would be foolish to claim that all the articles are of equal value; but we think we are realistic in judging that the *NJBC* meets the more demanding scholarly standards of the 1990s as well as the *JBC* met the standards of the 1960s — "more demanding" in the sense that Catholic biblical scholarship has had time to mature, and more is expected from it by both Catholics and non-Catholics. The task of editing a new commentary was made easier by the experience gained in editing the *JBC;* it was made more difficult by the explosion of biblical knowledge in the intervening decades. It is our fondest hope that we have produced a volume that will render service *into a new millennium,* something that the *JBC* would not have been able to do.

A few practical guides will be helpful to the reader. Because of the length of the work, a frequent use of abbreviations was necessary. A quarter hour's perusal of the table of abbreviations used for the biblical books, for the apocrypha, for the biblical languages, etc., will forestall too frequent recourse to these tables. The biblical books bear the titles now common in English, as exemplified in the *RSV.* Proper names are given in the common English (*RSV*) spelling. Chapter-and-verse enumeration follows the original language patterns, even in those books where the versions differ.

Frequent cross references to other *NJBC* articles have been supplied by means of an arrow, followed by the abbreviated title of the article to which reference is made. To facilitate this, all eighty-three articles have been numbered and broken down into sections (indicated by boldface marginal numbers); and both article and section numbers are given in references. Thus → Exodus, 3:29 means to consult *NJBC* article 3 (on Exodus), section 29. (No confusion with references to biblical books, chapter, and verses, is possible, since the presence of the arrow always indicates a cross reference to a *NJBC* article.) The index will be a help to the reader in finding additional information.

There are two types of articles: topical and commentary. Knowing that many would need background before beginning a verse-by-verse study of the Bible, the editors planned for more than twenty articles of a topical, introductory nature. Acquaintance with some of these can be very helpful to the reader in understanding the more technical details in the commentary articles. For instance, the article on Hermeneutics (art. 71) supplies a basic treatment of attitudes in approaching the Bible. The article on Canonicity (art. 66) gives a survey of the composition of biblical literature that is essential for any reader. A generous amount of space has been devoted to articles on biblical theology. Old Testament themes are traced through their different historical stages of development, and a careful distinction is made in the New Testament section among the differing theologies of the various authors. Students and teachers would do well to look over the topical articles carefully before starting the commentaries.

The structure and paragraphing of the commentary articles are determined by the outlines of the respective biblical books. The commentary generally proceeds verse by verse, and lemmata (the words of Scripture being commented upon) are supplied in italics for easy reference. The editors made the difficult decision of not requiring the contributors to comment on any one English translation of the Bible. They recognized that there are in current usage many excellent translations, for instance, the *RSV, NAB, NJB, NJV,* and *NEB;* and they wished that this commentary might be used with any of them. (Moreover, they did not wish to countenance the extravagant claims of advertising for the universal superiority of one translation, since part of the serious study of the Bible is the recognition of the limitations inherent in all translations.) The editors did insist that the lemmata faithfully represent the biblical original, whether Hebrew, Aramaic, or Greek, so that the reader using a standard translation from the original languages would be able to recognize the biblical phrases without difficulty.

We close our preface with words of thanks. We decided to reprint the Foreword that Augustin Cardinal Bea wrote for the *JBC* so that we might attest to our enduring gratitude for his services at Vatican Council II on behalf of modern biblical studies. We further asked His Eminence Carlo Cardinal Martini to grace this volume with a new Foreword. A distinguished biblical scholar himself and former rector of the Pontifical Biblical Institute, he now serves as Archbishop of Milan, one of the largest dioceses in the world in the number of parishes and priests. In this pastoral role Cardinal Martini has continued to write books and deliver sermons on biblical topics that enrich the lives of God's people. He encouraged the translation of the *JBC* into Italian; and we are most grateful for his continued support for our endeavor, as illustrated by the Foreword.

Once again, the staff of Prentice Hall has been most cooperative; and Joseph Heider, Caroline Carney, Edie Riker, Linda Albelli, and Helen Brennan deserve special acknowledgment. At The Scriptorium, where editing and typesetting were done, Maurya P. Horgan and Paul J. Kobelski, biblical scholars in their own right, made this a work of love and gave it special attention. Many others rendered service in typing, proofreading, and some of the mechanical tasks that are so necessary in a work this size. In particular, Jerry Anne Dickel, a student at Union Theological Seminary (NYC), gave much-needed assistance in indexing, as did Andrew L. Don and Joseph Hastings of Boston College. And, of course, above all we are grateful to the contributors, not only for the quality of their articles but also for cooperativeness and generosity.

RAYMOND E. BROWN, S.S.
Editor of Topical Articles

JOSEPH A. FITZMYER, S.J.
Editor of NT Commentary Articles

ROLAND E. MURPHY, O.Carm.
Editor of OT Commentary Articles

CONTRIBUTORS

Barré, Michael L., S.S., S.T.L., Ph.D., Professor of Sacred Scripture, St. Patrick's
   Seminary, Menlo Park, CA.
   Amos, Psalms

Begg, Christopher T., S.T.D., Ph.D., Associate Professor of Old Testament, The Catholic
   University of America, Washington, DC.
   2 Kings

Blenkinsopp, Joseph, D.Phil., John A. O'Brien Professor of Biblical Studies, University of
   Notre Dame, Notre Dame, IN.
   Deuteronomy

Boadt, Lawrence, C.S.P., S.S.L., S.S.D., Associate Professor of Biblical Studies,
   Washington Theological Union, Silver Spring, MD.
   Ezekiel

Bourke, Myles M., S.S.L., S.T.D., Pastor, Corpus Christi Church, New York, NY.
   Hebrews

Brown, Raymond E., S.S., S.S.L., S.T.D., Ph.D., Auburn Distinguished Professor of
   Biblical Studies, Union Theological Seminary, New York, NY.
   *Canonicity; Apocrypha; Texts and Versions; Hermeneutics; Church Pronouncements;
   Biblical Geography; Early Church; Aspects NT Thought*

Byrne, Brendan, S.J., D.Phil., Professor of New Testament, Jesuit Theological College,
   United Faculty of Theology, Parkville, Melbourne, Australia.
   Philippians

Campbell, Antony F., S.J., S.S.L., S.T.L., Ph.D., Professor of Old Testament, Jesuit
   Theological College, United Faculty of Theology, Parkville, Melbourne, Australia.
   1 Samuel

Castelot, John J., S.S.L., S.T.D., Retired Professor of Scripture, St. John's Provincial
   Seminary, Plymouth, MI.
   Religious Institutions of Israel

Ceresko, Anthony R., O.S.F.S., S.T.L., S.S.D., Associate Professor of Old Testament,
   Faculty of Theology, University of St. Michael's College, Toronto, Canada.
   Habakkuk; Jonah

Clifford, Richard J., S.J., S.T.L., Ph.D., Professor of Old Testament, Weston School of
   Theology, Cambridge, MA.
   Genesis; Exodus

Cody, Aelred, O.S.B., S.S.D., S.T.D., Elève diplômé de l'Ecole Biblique et Archéologique
   française de Jérusalem, Master of Novices and Juniors, St. Meinrad Archabbey,
   St. Meinrad, IN.
   Haggai, Zechariah, Malachi; Religious Institutions of Israel

Collins, John J., Ph.D., Professor of Hebrew Bible and Judaica, Department of Theology, University of Notre Dame, Notre Dame, IN.
Old Testament Apocalypticism and Eschatology

Collins, Raymond F., S.T.D., Professor-in-ordinary, Faculty of Theology, Catholic University of Leuven, Louvain, Belgium.
1 Thessalonians; Inspiration; Canonicity

Collins, Thomas Aquinas, O.P., S.S.B., S.T.D., Professor Emeritus of Biblical Studies, Providence College, Providence, RI.
Church Pronouncements

Coogan, Michael David, Ph.D., Professor of Religious Studies, Stonehill College, North Easton, MA.
Joshua

Couturier, Guy P., C.S.C., M.A., S.S.L., Elève diplômé de l'Ecole Biblique et Archéologique française de Jérusalem, Professor of Scripture, Faculté de Théologie, Université de Montréal, Montreal, Canada.
Jeremiah

Craven, Toni, M.A., Ph.D., Associate Professor of Old Testament, Brite Divinity School, Texas Christian University, Fort Worth, TX.
Judith

Dalton, William J., S.J., M.A., S.S.D., Professor of New Testament, Catholic Theological College, Melbourne, Australia.
1 Peter

Di Lella, Alexander A., O.F.M., S.T.L., S.S.L., Ph.D., Professor of Biblical Studies, The Catholic University of America, Washington, DC.
Daniel; Sirach

Dillon, Richard J., S.T.L., S.S.D., Associate Professor of Theology, Fordham University, Bronx, NY.
Acts of the Apostles

Donahue, John R., S.J., S.T.L., Ph.D., Professor of Sacred Scripture, Jesuit School of Theology and Graduate Theological Union, Berkeley, CA.
Aspects NT Thought

Dumm, Demetrius, O.S.B., S.S.L., S.T.D., Professor of Scripture, St. Vincent Seminary, Latrobe, PA.
Esther

Faley, Roland J., T.O.R., S.S.L., S.T.D., Executive Director, Conference of Major Superiors of Men Religious, Silver Spring, MD.
Leviticus

Fitzgerald, Aloysius, F.S.C., S.S.D., Assistant Professor of Semitic Languages, Catholic University of America, Washington, DC.
Hebrew Poetry; Baruch

Fitzmyer, Joseph A., S.J., S.T.L., S.S.L., Ph.D., Professor Emeritus of Biblical Studies, The Catholic University of America, Washington, DC.
NT Epistles; Galatians; Romans; Philemon; History of Israel; Paul; Pauline Theology

Flanagan, James W., Ph.D., Archbishop Paul J. Hallinan Professor of Catholic Studies, Case Western Reserve University, Cleveland, OH.
2 Samuel

Giblin, Charles Homer, S.J., M.A., Ph.L., S.T.L., S.S.L., S.S.D., Professor of New Testament, Fordham University, Bronx, NY.
2 Thessalonians

Guinan, Michael D., O.F.M., S.T.L., Ph.D., Professor of Semitic Languages and Old Testament, Franciscan School of Theology, Berkeley, CA.
Lamentations

Harrington, Daniel J., S.J., M.Div., Ph.D., Professor of New Testament, Weston School of Theology, Cambridge, MA.
Mark

Hartman, Louis F., C.SS.R., S.S.L, Ling.Or.L., Late Professor of Semitics, The Catholic
     University of America, Washington, DC.
     Daniel

Horgan, Maurya P., Ph.D., General Partner, The Scriptorium, Denver CO; Adjunct
     Lecturer in Biblical Literature, The Iliff School of Theology, Denver, CO.
     Colossians

Irwin, William H., C.S.B., M.A., S.T.L., S.S.D., Associate Professor, Faculty of Theology,
     University of St. Michael's College, Toronto, Canada.
     Isaiah 1–39

Jensen, Joseph, O.S.B., S.S.L., S.T.D., Associate Professor of Old Testament, The
     Catholic University of America; Executive Secretary of the Catholic Biblical
     Association, Washington, DC.
     Isaiah 1–39

Johnson, D. W., S.J., Ph.D., Associate Professor of Semitic and Egyptian Languages and
     Literatures, The Catholic University of America, Washington, DC.
     Texts and Versions

Karris, Robert J., O.F.M., S.T.L., Th.D., St. Anthony's, St. Louis, MO.
     Luke

King, Philip J., S.T.D., S.S.L., Professor of Biblical Studies, Boston College, Chestnut
     Hill, MA.
     Biblical Archaeology

Kobelski, Paul J., Ph.D., General Partner, The Scriptorium, Denver, CO; Adjunct
     Lecturer in Biblical Literature, The Iliff School of Theology, Denver, CO.
     Ephesians

Kselman, John S., S.S., S.T.L., Ph.D., Professor of Old Testament, Weston School of
     Theology, Cambridge, MA.
     Psalms; Modern OT Criticism; Modern NT Criticism

Laberge, Léo, O.M.I., S.S.D., L.Ph., L.Th., Elève titulaire de l'Ecole Biblique et
     Archéologique de Jérusalem, Professor of Old Testament, Faculty of Theology,
     Saint Paul University, Ottawa, Canada.
     Micah

Laffey, Alice L., S.S.L., S.S.D., Associate Professor of Old Testament, Department of
     Religious Studies, College of the Holy Cross, Worcester, MA.
     Ruth

Leahy, Thomas W., S.J., S.S.L., S.T.L., Ph.D., Professor of New Testament, Jesuit School
     of Theology at Berkeley, Berkeley, CA.
     James

L'Heureux, Conrad E., Ph.D., Professor of Old Testament, University of Dayton,
     Dayton, OH.
     Numbers

McCarthy, Dennis J., S.J., S.S.L., S.T.D., Late Professor of Old Testament, Pontifical
     Biblical Institute, Rome, Italy.
     Hosea

McCreesh, Thomas P., O.P., S.T.L., Ph.D., Assistant Professor of Scripture, Dominican
     House of Studies, Washington, DC.
     Proverbs

McEleney, Neil J., C.S.P., M.A., S.T.L., S.S.L., Adjunct Ordinary Professor, The Catholic
     University of America, Washington, DC.
     1–2 Maccabees

McKenzie, John L., S.T.D., Professor Emeritus of Theology, De Paul University,
     Chicago, IL.
     Aspects OT Thought

MacKenzie, R. A. F., S.J., S.S.D., Professor Emeritus of Old Testament, Regis College,
     Toronto, Canada.
     Job

Mallon, Elias D., S.T.L., Ph.D., Associate Director, Graymoor Ecumenical Institute, New
     York, NY.
     Joel, Obadiah

Meier, John P., S.S.D., S.T.L., Professor of New Testament, The Catholic University of
America, Washington, DC; Adjunct Professor, Fordham University, Bronx, NY.
Jesus

Moloney, Francis J., S.D.B., S.T.L., S.S.L., D.Phil. (Oxon), Head of the Biblical Studies
Department, Catholic Theological College, Clayton, Victoria, Australia.
Johannine Theology

Murphy, Roland E., O.Carm., S.S.L., S.T.D., George Washington Ivey Professor
Emeritus, Duke University, Durham, NC.
*Introduction to the Pentateuch; Genesis; Introduction to Wisdom Literature; Canticle; Job;
Hosea; History of Israel*

Murphy-O'Connor, Jerome, O.P., S.S.L., S.T.D., Professor of New Testament, Ecole
Biblique et Archéologique française de Jérusalem.
1 Corinthians; 2 Corinthians

Neirynck, Frans, S.T.D., Professor of New Testament, Catholic University of Leuven,
Louvain, Belgium.
Synoptic Problem

Neyrey, Jerome H., S.J., S.T.L., Ph.D., Associate Professor of New Testament, Weston
School of Theology, Cambridge, MA.
Jude; 2 Peter

North, Robert, S.J., S.T.L., S.S.D., Compiler of *Elenchus of Biblica;* Professor Emeritus of
Archaeology, Pontifical Biblical Institute, Rome, Italy.
1–2 Chronicles, Ezra, Nehemiah; Biblical Geography; Biblical Archaeology

Nowell, Irene, O.S.B., Ph.D., Associate Professor of Religious Studies, Benedictine
College, Atchison, KS.
Nahum; Tobit

O'Connell, Kevin G., S.J., Ph.D., President and Professor of Religious Studies, Le Moyne
College, Syracuse, NY.
Texts and Versions

O'Connor, M., Ph.D., Ann Arbor, MI.
Judges

Osiek, Carolyn A., R.S.C.J., M.A.T., Th.D., Professor of New Testament, Catholic
Theological Union, Chicago, IL.
Early Church

Perkins, Pheme, M.A., Ph.D., Professor of Theology, Boston College, Chestnut Hill,
MA.
John; Johannine Epistles; Apocrypha; Early Church

Saldarini, Anthony J., Ph.D., Associate Professor, Boston College, Chestnut Hill, MA.
Apocrypha

Schneiders, Sandra M., I.H.M., S.T.L., S.T.D., Associate Professor of New Testament
Studies and Spirituality, Jesuit School of Theology and Graduate Theological
Union, Berkeley, CA.
Hermeneutics

Senior, Donald, C.P., S.T.D., Professor of New Testament, Catholic Theological Union,
Chicago, IL.
Aspects NT Thought

Stuhlmueller, Carroll, C.P., S.T.L., S.S.D., Professor of Old Testament Studies, Catholic
Theological Union, Chicago, IL.
Deutero-Isaiah and Trito-Isaiah

Suelzer, Alexa, S.P., M.A., Ph.D., Professor of Theology, St. Mary-of-the-Woods
College, St. Mary-of-the-Woods, IN.
Modern OT Criticism

Vawter, Bruce, C.M., S.T.L., S.S.D., Late Professor of Scripture, De Paul University,
Chicago, IL.
Introduction to Prophetic Literature

Viviano, Benedict T., O.P., S.S.L., Ph.D., Professor of New Testament, Ecole Biblique et
Archéologique française de Jérusalem.
Matthew

Wahl, Thomas P., O.S.B., S.T.L., S.S.L., Ph.D., Associate Professor of Theology, Saint
    John's University, Collegeville, MN.
    Zephaniah

Walsh, Jerome T., S.S.L., Ph.D., Associate Professor of Biblical Studies, St. John's
    Provincial Seminary, Plymouth, MI.
    1 Kings

Wild, Robert A., S.J., S.T.L., Ph.D., Provincial, Chicago Province of the Society of Jesus;
    Associate Professor (on leave), Department of Theology, Loyola University,
    Chicago, IL.
    Pastoral Letters

Witherup, Ronald D., S.S., S.T.L., Ph.D., Associate Professor of Sacred Scripture, St.
    Patrick's Seminary, Menlo Park, CA.
    Modern NT Criticism

Wright, Addison G., S.S., M.A., S.S.L., S.T.D., Associate Professor of Scripture, Graduate
    School of Religion and Religious Education, Fordham University, Bronx, NY;
    Adjunct Professor, Marywood College, Scranton, PA.
    Qoheleth; Wisdom; History of Israel

Yarbro Collins, Adela, M.A., Ph.D., Professor, University of Notre Dame, Notre Dame,
    IN.
    Apocalypse (Revelation); Aspects NT Thought

ABBREVIATIONS, TRANSLITERATIONS

PROTOCANONICAL AND DEUTEROCANONICAL
BOOKS OF THE BIBLE

OLD TESTAMENT

Gen	Genesis	Dt-Isa	Deutero-Isaiah
Exod	Exodus	Tr-Isa	Trito-Isaiah
Lev	Leviticus	Jer	Jeremiah
Num	Numbers	Lam	Lamentations
Deut	Deuteronomy	Bar	Baruch
Josh	Joshua	Ep Jer	Epistle of Jeremiah (= Bar 6)
Judg	Judges	Ezek	Ezekiel
1-2 Sam	1-2 Samuel	Dan	Daniel
1-2 Kgs	1-2 Kings	Pr Azar	Prayer of Azariah
1-2 Chr	1-2 Chronicles		(= Dan 3:24-90)
Ezra	Ezra	Sus	Susanna (= Dan 13:1-64)
Neh	Nehemiah	Bel	Bel and the Dragon
Tob	Tobit		(= Dan 14:1-42)
Esth	Esther	Hos	Hosea
Jdt	Judith	Joel	Joel
Esth	Esther	Amos	Amos
Add Esth	Additions to Esther (107 vv	Obad	Obadiah
	in the LXX)	Jonah	Jonah
1-2 Macc	1-2 Maccabees	Mic	Micah
Job	Job	Nah	Nahum
Ps(s)	Psalm(s)	Hab	Habakkuk
Prov	Proverbs	Zeph	Zephaniah
Eccl	Ecclesiastes (Qoheleth)	Hag	Haggai
Cant	Canticle of Canticles	Zech	Zechariah
Wis	Wisdom	Dt-Zech	Deutero-Zechariah
Sir	Sirach (Ecclesiasticus)	Mal	Malachi
Isa	Isaiah		

N.B. Psalms are cited according to the Hebr (MT) psalm number and verse. The LXX and Vg (Lat) numbers of the psalms are frequently one number lower than the Hebrew, e.g., Hebr Ps 22 is Lat Ps 21. The *KJV* and *RSV* numbers of the psalm verses are frequently one number lower than the Hebrew, e.g., Hebr. Ps 22:2 is *RSV* 22:1. Note that the psalter in the *NAB* follows the numbering of psalms and verses of the MT.

NEW TESTAMENT

Matt	Matthew	1–2 Thess	1–2 Thessalonians
Mark	Mark	1–2 Tim	1–2 Timothy
Luke	Luke	Titus	Titus
John	John	Phlm	Philemon
Acts	Acts of the Apostles	Heb	Hebrews
Rom	Romans	Jas	James
1–2 Cor	1–2 Corinthians	1–2 Pet	1–2 Peter
Gal	Galatians	1–2–3 John	1–2–3 John
Eph	Ephesians	Jude	Jude
Phil	Philippians	Rev	Revelation (Apocalypse)
Col	Colossians		

APOCRYPHA OF THE OLD TESTAMENT

Adam and Eve	*Life of Adam and Eve* (see AOT 141–67)
Apoc. Abr.	*Apocalypse of Abraham*
2 Apoc. Bar.	*Syriac Apocalypse of Baruch* (→ 67:44)
3 Apoc. Bar.	*Greek Apocalypse of Baruch* (→ 67:45)
Apoc. Mos.	*Apocalypse of Moses*
As. Mos.	*Assumption of Moses* (→ 67:49)
Asc. Isa.	*Ascension of Isaiah* (see AOT 775–812)
Bib. Ant.	Pseudo-Philo, *Biblical Antiquities* (→ 67:50)
1 Enoch	*First Enoch, Ethiopic Enoch* (→ 67:7, 9–15)
2 Enoch	*Second Enoch, Slavonic Book of the Secrets of Enoch* (→ 67:7–8)
3 Enoch	*Third Enoch, Hebrew Enoch* (→ 67:7–8)
Ep. Arist.	*Epistle/Letter of Aristeas to Philocrates* (→ 67:32–33)
1 Esdr.	*Esdras A of the LXX; III Esdras of the Latin versions* (→ 67:38–39)
2 Esdr.	*IV Esdras of the Vg* (→ 67:40)
4 Ezra	*Apocalypse of Ezra* (= chaps. 3–14 of 2 Esdr.) (→ 67:41)
Jos. Asen.	*Joseph and Aseneth* (see AOT 465–503)
Jub.	*Book of Jubilees* (→ 67:16–24)
3 Macc	*Third Maccabees* (= *Ptolemaica*) (→ 67:35)
4 Macc	*Fourth Maccabees* (= *On the Supremacy of Reason*) (→ 67:36)
Mart. Isa.	*Martyrdom of Isaiah* (see OTP 2. 143–64)
Odes Sol.	*Odes of Solomon* (see AOT 683–731)
Pr Man	*Prayer of Manasseh* (→ 67:37)
Pss. Sol.	*Psalms of Solomon* (→ 67:46–48)
QL	Qumran Literature (see "Dead Sea Scrolls and Related Texts")
Sib. Or.	*Sibylline Oracles* (→ 67:51–52)
T. 12 Patr.	*Testaments of the Twelve Patriarchs* (→ 67:25–31)
T. Benj., T. Levi,	
etc.	*Testament of Benjamin, Testament of Levi,* etc. (one of the individual testaments in *T. 12 Patr.*)
Test. Abr.	*Testament of Abraham* (see AOT 393–421)

DEAD SEA SCROLLS AND RELATED TEXTS (QL)

CD	Cairo (Geniza text of the) Damascus (Document) (→ 67:87)
DSS	Dead Sea Scrolls (→ 67:78)
Hev	Naḥal Ḥever texts (→ 67:121)
Mas	Masada texts (→ 67:123)
Mird	Khirbet Mird texts (→ 67:118)
Mur	Wadi Murabba'at texts (→ 67:119)
p	Pesher (commentary) (→ 67:89)

Q	Qumran
1Q, 2Q, 3Q, etc.	Numbered caves of Qumran, yielding written material; followed by abbreviation of biblical or apocryphal book
1QapGen	*Genesis Apocryphon* of Qumran Cave 1 (→ 67:93)
1QH	*Hôdāyôt* (*Thanksgiving Hymns*) (→ 67:86)
1QIsa^{a,b}	First or second copy of Isaiah from Qumran Cave 1 (→ 68:27)
1QpHab	*Pesher on Habakkuk* from Qumran Cave 1 (→ 67:90)
1QM	*Milḥāmâ* (*War Scroll*) from Qumran Cave 1 (→ 67:88)
1QS	*Serek hayyahad* (*Rule of the Community; Manual of Discipline*) (→ 67:83)
1QSa	Appendix A (*Rule of the Congregation*) to 1QS (→ 67:84)
1QSb	Appendix B (*Blessings*) to 1QS (→ 67:85)
3Q15	Copper Roll from Qumran Cave 3 (→ 67:94)
4QFlor	*Florilegium* (or *Eschatological Midrashim*) from Qumran Cave 4 (→ 67:92)
4QMess ar	Aramaic "Messianic" text from Qumran Cave 4 (→ 67:92)
4QPrNab	*Prayer of Nabonidus* from Qumran Cave 4 (→ 25:20)
4QTestim	*Testimonia* text from Qumran Cave 4 (→ 67:91)
4QTLevi	*Testament of Levi* from Qumran Cave 4 (→ 67:26)
4QPhyl	Phylacteries from Qumran Cave 4
11QEz	The Book of Ezekiel from Qumran Cave 11 (→ 67, p. 1070)
11QJub	*The Book of Jubilees* from Qumran Cave 11 (→ 67:17)
11QMelch	Melchizedek text from Qumran Cave 11 (→ 67. p. 1070)
11QpaleoLev	Leviticus text written in paleo-Hebrew script from Qumran Cave 11 (→ 68:17, 22, 24)
11QPs^a	First copy of a psalter from Qumran Cave 11 (→ 68:31)
11QPs^b	Second copy of a psalter from Qumran Cave 11 (→ 67, p. 1070)
11QPsAp^a	First copy of a text of apocryphal psalms from Qumran Cave 11 (→ 67, p. 1070)
11QTemple	The *Temple Scroll* from Qumran Cave 11 (→ 67:95)
11QtgJob	*Targum of Job* from Qumran Cave 11 (→ 68:104)
Ag. Ap.	Josephus, *Against Apion* (→ 67:127–30)
Ant.	Josephus, *Antiquities of the Jews*
J.W.	Josephus, *Jewish War*
Life	Josephus, *Life*

APOCRYPHA OF THE NEW TESTAMENT

Acts P. Thec.	*Acts of Paul and Thecla*
Acts Pil.	*Acts of Pilate* (→ 67:71)
Apoc. Pet.	*Apocalypse of Peter* (→ 67:73)
Gos. Eb.	*Gospel of the Ebionites* (→ 67:59)
Gos. Heb.	*Gospel of the Hebrews* (→ 67:60)
Gos. Naass.	*Gospel of the Naassenes*
Gos. Naz.	*Gospel of the Nazoreans* (→ 67:61)
Gos. Pet.	*Gospel of Peter* (→ 67:72)
Gos. Thom.	*Gospel of Thomas* (→ 67:67)
Prot. Jas.	*Protevangelium of James* (→ 67:64)
SGM	*Secret Gospel of Mark* (→ 67:63)

EARLY PATRISTIC WRITINGS

Barn.	*Epistle of Barnabas* (→ 80:41)
1–2 Clem.	*First* and *Second Clement* (→ 80:37–48)
Did.	*Didache*, or *Teaching of the Twelve Apostles* (→ 80:42)
Diogn.	*Epistle to Diognetus* (→ 80:54)
HE	Eusebius, *Historia ecclesiastica*
Herm. Man.	*Shepherd of Hermas, Mandates* (→ 80:43)
Herm. Sim.	*The Shepherd of Hermas, Similitudes*
Herm. Vis.	*The Shepherd of Hermas, Visions*

Ign. *Eph.*	Ignatius of Antioch, *Letter to the Ephesians* (→ 80:39)
Magn.	*Letter to the Magnesians*
Phld.	*Letter to the Philadelphians*
Pol.	*Letter to Polycarp*
Rom.	*Letter to the Romans*
Smyrn.	*Letter to the Smyrnaeans*
Trall.	*Letter to the Trallians*
Mart. Pol.	Martyrdom of Polycarp (→ 80:56)
Pol. Phil.	Polycarp, *To the Philippians* (→ 80:40)

TARGUMIC AND RABBINICAL WORKS

Tg. Onq.	Targum Onqelos	Tg. Neof.	Targum Neofiti I
Tg. Neb.	Targum of the Prophets	Tg. Ps.-J.	Targum Pseudo-Jonathan
Tg. Ket.	Targum of the Writings	Tg. Yer. I	Targum Yerušalmi I*
Frg. Tg.	Fragmentary Targum	Tg. Yer. II	Targum Yerušalmi II*
Sam. Tg.	Samaritan Targum	Yem. Tg.	Yemenite Targum
Tg. Isa	Targum of Isaiah	Tg. Esth I, II	First or Second Targum of
Pal. Tgs.	Palestinian Targums		Esther
		* optional title	

To distinguish the same-named tractates in the Mishna, Tosepta, Babylonian Talmud, and Jerusalem Talmud, italicized *m., t., b.,* and *y.* are used before the name.

'Abot	'Abot	Nazir	Nazir
'Arak.	'Arakin	Ned.	Nedarim
'Abod. Zar.	'Aboda Zara	Neg.	Nega'im
B. Bat.	Baba Batra	Nez.	Neziqin
Bek.	Bekorot	Nid.	Niddah
Ber.	Berakot	'Ohol.	'Oholot
Besa	Besa (= Yom Ṭob)	'Or.	'Orla
Bik.	Bikkurim	Para	Para
B. Meṣ.	Baba Meṣi'a	Pe'a	Pe'a
B. Qam.	Baba Qamma	Pesaḥ.	Pesaḥim
Dem.	Demai	Qinnim	Qinnim
'Erub.	'Erubin	Qidd.	Qiddušin
'Ed.	'Eduyyot	Qod.	Qodašin
Giṭ.	Giṭṭin	Roš Haš.	Roš Haššana
Ḥag.	Ḥagiga	Sanh.	Sanhedrin
Ḥal.	Ḥalla	Šabb.	Šabbat
Hor.	Horayot	Šeb.	Šebi'it
Ḥul.	Ḥullin	Šebu.	Šebu'ot
Kelim	Kelim	Šeqal.	Šeqalim
Ker.	Keritot	Sota	Sota
Ketub.	Ketubot	Sukk.	Sukka
Kil.	Kil'ayim	Ta'an.	Ta'anit
Ma'aś.	Ma'aśerot	Tamid	Tamid
Mak.	Makkot	Tem.	Temura
Makš.	Makširin (= Mašqin)	Ter.	Terumot
Meg.	Megilla	Ṭohar.	Ṭoharot
Me'il.	Me'ila	Ṭ. Yom	Ṭebul Yom
Menaḥ.	Menaḥot	'Uq.	'Uqsin
Mid.	Middot	Yad.	Yadayim
Miqw.	Miqwa'ot	Yebam.	Yebamot
Mo'ed	Mo'ed	Yoma	Yoma (= Kippurim)
Mo'ed Qaṭ.	Mo'ed Qaṭan	Zabim	Zabim
Ma'aś. Š.	Ma'aśer Šeni	Zebaḥ.	Zebaḥim
Našim	Našim	Zer.	Zera'im

'Abot R. Nat.	'Abot de Rabbi Nathan	Pesiq. R.	Pesiqta Rabbati
'Ag. Ber.	'Aggadat Berešit	Pesiq. Rab Kah.	Pesiqta de Rab Kahana
Bab.	Babylonian	Pirqe R. El.	Pirqe Rabbi Eliezer
Bar.	Baraita	Rab.	Rabbah (following abbrevia-
Der. Er. Rab.	Derek Ereṣ Rabba		tion for biblical book: Gen.
Der. Er. Zut.	Derek Ereṣ Zuta		Rab. [with periods] = Genesis
Gem.	Gemara		Rabbah)
Kalla	Kalla	Sem.	Semahot
Mek.	Mekilta	Sipra	Sipra
Midr.	Midraš; cited with usual	Sipre	Sipre
	abbreviation for biblical book;	Sop.	Soperim
	but Midr. Qoh. = Midraš	S. 'Olam Rab.	Seder 'Olam Rabbah
	Qohelet	Talm.	Talmud
Pal.	Palestinian	Yal.	Yalqut

NAG HAMMADI TRACTATES (NHL; → 80:64–82)

Acts Pet. 12 Apost.	Acts of Peter and the Twelve Apostles	Marsanes	Marsanes
		Melch.	Melchizedek
Allogenes	Allogenes	Norea	Thought of Norea
Ap. Jas.	Apocryphon of James	On Bap. A	On Baptism A
Ap. John	Apocryphon of John	On Bap. B	On Baptism B
Apoc. Adam	Apocalypse of Adam	On Bap. C	On Baptism C
1 Apoc. Jas.	First Apocalypse of James	On Euch. A	On the Eucharist A
2 Apoc. Jas.	Second Apocalypse of James	On Euch. B	On the Eucharist B
Apoc. Paul	Apocalypse of Paul	Orig. World	On the Origin of the World
Apoc. Pet.	Apocalypse of Peter	Paraph. Shem	Paraphrase of Shem
Asclepius	Asclepius 21–29	Pr. Paul	Prayer of the Apostle Paul
Auth. Teach.	Authoritative Teaching	Pr. Thanks.	Prayer of Thanksgiving
Dial. Sav.	Dialogue of the Savior	Sent. Sextus	Sentences of Sextus
Disc. 8–9	Discourse on the Eighth and Ninth	Soph. Jes. Chr.	Sophia of Jesus Christ
		Steles Seth	Three Steles of Seth
Ep. Pet. Phil.	Letter of Peter to Philip	Teach. Silv.	Teachings of Silvanus
Eugnostos	Eugnostos the Blessed	Testim. Truth	Testimony of Truth
Exeg. Soul	Exegesis on the Soul	Thom. Cont.	Book of Thomas the Contender
Gos. Eg.	Gospel of the Egyptians	Thund.	Thunder, Perfect Mind
Gos. Phil.	Gospel of Philip	Treat. Res.	Treatise on Resurrection
Gos. Thom.	Gospel of Thomas	Treat. Seth	Second Treatise of the Great Seth
Gos. Truth	Gospel of Truth	Tri. Trac.	Tripartite Tractate
Great Pow.	Concept of Our Great Power	Trim. Prot.	Trimorphic Protennoia
Hyp. Arch.	Hypostasis of the Archons	Val. Exp.	A Valentinian Exposition
Hypsiph.	Hypsiphrone	Zost.	Zostrianos
Interp. Know.	Interpretation of Knowledge		

SERIALS, PERIODICALS, AND BOOKS FREQUENTLY CITED

AAGA	M. Black, Aramaic Approach to the Gospels and Acts (3d ed.; Oxford, 1967)
AAS	Acta apostolicae sedis
AASF	Annales academiae rerum scientiarum fennicae
AASOR	Annual of the American Schools of Oriental Research
AB	Anchor Bible
ACW	Ancient Christian Writers
AEL	M. Lichtheim, Ancient Egyptian Literature (3 vols.; Berkeley, 1975–80)
AEOT	A. Alt, Essays on Old Testament History and Religion (GC, 1957)
AER	American Ecclesiastical Review
AGJU	Arbeiten zur Geschichte des antiken Judentums und des Urchristentums
AI	R. de Vaux, Ancient Israel (London/NY, 1963)
AJBA	Australian Journal of Biblical Archaeology

AJP	*American Journal of Philology*
AJSL	*American Journal of Semitic Languages and Literatures*
ALBO	Analecta lovaniensia biblica et orientalia
AnBib	Analecta biblica
ANE	J. B. Pritchard (ed.), *Ancient Near East* (Princeton, 1965)
ANEP	J. B. Pritchard (ed.), *Ancient Near East in Pictures* (Princeton, 1954)
ANESTP	J. B. Pritchard (ed.), *Ancient Near East Supplementary Texts and Pictures* (Princeton, 1969)
ANET	J. B. Pritchard (ed.), *Ancient Near Eastern Texts* (Princeton, 1950; 3d ed. with supplement, 1978)
ANF	The Ante-Nicene Fathers
Ang	*Angelicum*
AnGreg	Analecta gregoriana
AnOr	Analecta orientalia
ANRW	W. Haase and H. Temporini (eds.), *Aufstieg und Niedergang der römischen Welt: Teil II: Principat — Religion* (Berlin, 1979–84) II/25.1, followed by page nos.
ANTF	Arbeiten zur neutestamentlichen Textforschung
Anton	*Antonianum*
AOAT	Alter Orient und Altes Testament
AOT	H. F. D. Sparks (ed.), *The Apocryphal Old Testament* (Oxford, 1984)
AP	W. F. Albright, *The Archeology of Palestine* (Harmondsworth, 1960)
Apg.	*Apostelgeschichte* (in titles of many German commentaries on Acts)
APOT	R. H. Charles (ed.), *Apocrypha and Pseudepigrapha of the Old Testament* (Oxford, 1913)
ARAB	D. D. Luckenbill (ed.), *Ancient Records of Assyria and Babylonia* (2 vols.; Chicago, 1926–27)
Arch	*Archaeology*
ARI	W. F. Albright, *Archaeology and the Religion of Israel* (Baltimore, 1953)
ASNU	Acta seminarii neotestamentici upsaliensis
ASOR	American Schools of Oriental Research
ASTI	*Annual of the Swedish Theological Institute*
ATANT	Abhandlungen zur Theologie des Alten und Neuen Testaments
AtBib	H. Grollenberg, *Atlas of the Bible* (London, 1956)
ATD	Das alte Testament deutsch
AThD	Acta theologica danica
ATNT	K. and B. Aland, *The Text of the New Testament* (GR, 1986)
ATR	*Anglican Theological Review*
Aug	*Augustinianum*
AusBR	*Australian Biblical Review*
AUSS	*Andrews University Seminary Studies*
AzT	Arbeiten zur Theologie
BA	*Biblical Archaeologist*
BAC	Biblioteca de autores cristianos
BAGD	W. Bauer, W. F. Arndt, F. W. Gingrich, and F. W. Danker, *Greek-English Lexicon of the New Testament* (2d ed.; Chicago, 1979)
BAIAS	*Bulletin of the Anglo-Israel Archaeological Society*
BANE	G. E. Wright (ed.), *The Bible and the Ancient Near East* (Fest. W. F. Albright; NY, 1961)
BAR	*Biblical Archaeologist Reader*
BARev	*Biblical Archaeology Review*
BASOR	*Bulletin of the American Schools of Oriental Research*
BBB	Bonner biblische Beiträge
BBET	Beiträge zur biblischen Exegese und Theologie
BBM	R. E. Brown, *The Birth of the Messiah* (GC, 1977)
BBVO	Berliner Beiträge zum vorderen Orient
BCCT	J. L. McKenzie (ed.), *The Bible in Current Catholic Thought* (NY, 1962)
BCH	*Bulletin de correspondance hellénique*
BDB	F. Brown, S. R. Driver, and C. A. Briggs, *Hebrew and English Lexicon of the Old Testament* (rev. ed.; Oxford, 1952)
BDF	F. Blass, A. Debrunner, and R. W. Funk, *A Greek Grammar of the New Testament* (Chicago, 1961)
Beginnings	F. J. Foakes Jackson and K. Lake (eds.), *Beginnings of Christianity* (5 vols.; London, 1920–33)
BEJ	R. E. Brown, *The Epistles of John* (AB 30; GC, 1982)
BenMon	*Benediktinische Monatsschrift*
BeO	*Bibbia e oriente*

BET	P. Benoit, *Exégèse et théologie* (4 vols.; Paris, 1961–82)
BETL	Bibliotheca ephemeridum theologicarum lovaniensium
BEvT	Beiträge zur evangelischen Theologie
BFCT	Beiträge zur Förderung christlicher Theologie
BGBE	Beiträge zur Geschichte der biblischen Exegese
BGJ	R. E. Brown, *The Gospel According to John* (AB 29, 29A; GC, 1966–70)
BHI	J. Bright, *History of Israel* (3d ed.; Phl, 1981)
BHK	R. Kittel (ed.), *Biblia Hebraica* (3d ed.; Stuttgart, 1937)
BHMCS	*The Biblical Heritage in Modern Catholic Scholarship* (Fest. B. Vawter; ed. J. J. Collins and J. D. Crossan; Wilmington, 1986)
BHS	K. Elliger and W. Rudolph (eds.), *Biblia hebraica stuttgartensia* (Stuttgart, 1967–77)
BHT	Beiträge zur historischen Theologie
Bib	*Biblica*
BibB	*Biblische Beiträge*
BibLeb	*Bibel und Leben*
BibOr	Biblica et orientalia
Bijdr	*Bijdragen*
BIOSCS	*Bulletin of the International Organization for Septuagint and Cognate Studies*
BJRL	*Bulletin of the John Rylands University Library of Manchester*
BK	*Bibel und Kirche*
BKAT	Biblischer Kommentar: Altes Testament
BL	*Book List*
BLS	Bible and Literature Series
BM	*Beth Mikra*
BMAP	E. G. Kraeling, *The Brooklyn Museum Aramaic Papyri* (New Haven, 1953)
BN	*Biblische Notizen*
BNTC	Black's New Testament Commentaries (British printing of HNTC)
BNTE	W. D. Davies and D. Daube (eds.), *The Background of the New Testament and Its Eschatology* (Fest. C. H. Dodd; Cambridge, 1954)
BO	*Bibliotheca orientalis*
BP	W. F. Albright, *The Biblical Period from Abraham to Ezra* (NY, 1963)
BPl	E. Dhorme (ed.), *Bible de la Pléiade* (2 vols.; Paris, 1956, 1959)
BR	*Biblical Research*
BSac	*Bibliotheca Sacra*
BT	*The Bible Translator*
BTB	*Biblical Theology Bulletin*
BTS	*Bible et terre sainte*
BU	Biblische Untersuchungen
BVC	*Bible et vie chrétienne*
BWANT	Beiträge zur Wissenschaft vom Alten und Neuen Testament
BWL	W. Lambert, *Babylonian Wisdom Literature* (Oxford, 1961)
ByF	*Biblia y fe*
BZ	*Biblische Zeitschrift*
BZAW	Beihefte zur *ZAW*
BZNW	Beihefte zur *ZNW*
CAH	*Cambridge Ancient History*
CahCER	*Cahiers du Cercle Ernest Renan*
CahRB	Cahiers de la Revue biblique
CAT	Commentaire de l'Ancien Testament
CATSS	Computer Assisted Tools for Septuagint Studies
CBC	Cambridge Bible Commentary
CBL	Collectanea biblica latina
CBLAA	A. J. Mattill and M. B. Mattill, *A Classified Bibliography of Literature on the Acts of the Apostles* (NTTS 7; Leiden, 1966)
CBQ	*Catholic Biblical Quarterly*
CBQMS	Catholic Biblical Quarterly—Monograph Series
CBSC	Cambridge Bible for Schools and Colleges
CBW	Cities of the Biblical World
CC	Corpus christianorum
CCL	Corpus christianorum latinorum
CentB	Century Bible
CGTC	Cambridge Greek Testament Commentary
CH	*Church History*

CHB	*Cambridge History of the Bible*
CHerm	*Corpus hermeticum*
CHJ	*Cambridge History of Judaism*
CHR	*Catholic Historical Review*
ChrTSP	L. Cerfaux, *Christ in the Theology of Saint Paul* (NY, 1959)
ChTSP	L. Cerfaux, *The Church in the Theology of Saint Paul* (NY, 1959)
CII	*Corpus inscriptionum iudaicarum*
CIL	*Corpus inscriptionum latinarum*
CINTI	W. Klassen and G. F. Snyder (eds.), *Current Issues in New Testament Interpretation* (Fest. O. Piper; NY, 1962)
CIOTS	B. S. Childs, *Introduction to the Old Testament as Scripture* (Phl, 1979)
CIS	*Corpus inscriptionum semiticarum*
CJT	*Canadian Journal of Theology*
ClR	*Clergy Review*
CMHE	F. M. Cross, *Canaanite Myth and Hebrew Epic* (Cambridge, MA, 1973)
CNT	Commentaire du Nouveau Testament
ComViat	*Communio viatorum*
ConBNT	Coniectanea biblica, New Testament
ConBOT	Coniectanea biblica, Old Testament
ConNT	Coniectanea neotestamentica
CP	*Classical Philology*
CRAIBL	*Comptes rendus de l'académie des inscriptions et belles-lettres*
CrC	*Cross Currents*
CRINT	Compendia rerum iudaicarum ad Novum Testamentum
CSCO	Corpus scriptorum christianorum orientalium
CSEL	Corpus scriptorum ecclesiasticorum latinorum
CTJ	*Calvin Theological Journal*
CTM	*Concordia Theological Monthly*
CurTM	*Currents in Theology and Mission*
DAFC	*Dictionnaire apologétique de la foi catholique* (4th ed.; Paris, 1925)
DBSup	*Dictionnaire de la Bible, Supplément* (Paris, 1928–)
DBT	X. Léon-Dufour (ed.), *Dictionary of Biblical Theology* (2d ed.; NY, 1973)
DictB	J. Hastings (ed.), *Dictionary of the Bible* (NY, 1963)
DJD	Discoveries in the Judaean Desert
DKP	K. Ziegler and W. Sontheimer (eds.), *Der kleine Pauly: Lexikon der Antike* (5 vols.; Stuttgart, 1964–75)
DOTT	D. W. Thomas (ed.), *Documents from Old Testament Times* (London, 1958)
DRev	*Downside Review*
DS	H. Denzinger and A. Schönmetzer, *Enchiridion symbolorum* (Barcelona, 1973)
DSB	Daily Study Bible
DSSHU	E. L. Sukenik (ed.), *The Dead Sea Scrolls of the Hebrew University* (Jerusalem, 1955)
DSSMM	M. Burrows (ed.), *Dead Sea Scrolls of St. Mark's Monastery* (vols. 1 and 2/2; New Haven, 1950–51)
EAEHL	M. Avi-Yonah, *et al.* (eds.), *Encyclopedia of Archaeological Excavations in the Holy Land* (EC, 1975–78)
EB	*Enchiridion biblicum* (2d ed.; Naples, 1954)
EBB	*Elenchus bibliographicus biblicus* (found in *Bib* until 1968, when it became a separate publication [Rome, 1968–])
EBib	Etudes bibliques
EDB	L. F. Hartman (ed.), *Encyclopedic Dictionary of the Bible* (NY, 1963)
EF	Erträge der Forschung
EgThéol	*Eglise et théologie*
EHAT	Exegetisches Handbuch zum Alten Testament
EHI	R. de Vaux, *The Early History of Israel* (Phl, 1978)
EHS	Europäische Hochschulschriften
EJMI	R. A. Kraft and G. W. E. Nickelsburg (eds.), *Early Judaism and Its Modern Interpreters* (Atlanta, 1986)
EKKNT	Evangelisch-katholischer Kommentar zum Neuen Testament
EncB	*Encyclopedia Biblica* (Hebr; Jerusalem, 1954)
EncJud	*Encyclopedia Judaica* (NY/Jerusalem, 1971)
ENTT	E. Käsemann, *Essays on New Testament Themes* (SBT 41; London, 1964)
EOTI	O. Eissfeldt, *The Old Testament: An Introduction* (NY, 1965)
ErIsr	Eretz Israel

ESBNT	J. A. Fitzmyer, *Essays on the Semitic Background of the New Testament* (London, 1971; SBLSBS 5; Missoula, 1974)
EspV	*Esprit et vie* (successor to *L'Ami du clergé*)
EstBib	*Estudios bíblicos*
ETL	*Ephemerides theologicae lovanienses*
ETOT	W. Eichrodt, *Theology of the Old Testament* (2 vols.; London/Phl, 1961–67)
ETR	*Etudes théologiques et religieuses*
EvQ	*Evangelical Quarterly*
EvT	*Evangelische Theologie*
EWJ	J. Jeremias, *The Eucharistic Words of Jesus* (2d ed.; London, 1966)
EWNT	H. Balz and G. Schneider (eds.), *Exegetisches Wörterbuch zum Neuen Testament* (3 vols.; Stuttgart, 1978–83)
ExpTim	*Expository Times*
FB	*Forschung zur Bibel*
FBBS	Facet Books, Biblical Series
FC	Fathers of the Church
FGL	J. A. Fitzmyer, *The Gospel according to Luke* (AB 28, 28A; GC, 1981–85)
FGT	V. Taylor, *The Formation of the Gospel Tradition* (2d ed.; London, 1935)
FOTL	The Forms of the Old Testament Literature
FrancP	Publications of the Studium biblicum franciscanum (Jerusalem)
FRLANT	Forschungen zur Religion und Literatur des Alten und Neuen Testaments
FrTS	Frankfurter theologische Studien
FSAC	W. F. Albright, *From the Stone Age to Christianity* (GC, 1957)
FTS	Freiburger theologische Studien
FZPhTh	*Freiburger Zeitschrift für Philosophie und Theologie*
GCS	Griechische christliche Schriftsteller
GHB	P. Joüon, *Grammaire de l'hébreu biblique* (2d ed.; Rome, 1947)
GKC	*Gesenius' Hebrew Grammar,* rev. E. Kautzsch; tr. A. E. Cowley (2d ed.; Oxford, 1910)
GNS	Good News Studies
GNTI	D. Guthrie, *New Testament Introduction* (3 vols.; London, 1961, 1962, 1965)
GP	F.-M. Abel, *Géographie de la Palestine* (2 vols.; 2d ed.; Paris, 1933–38)
Greg	*Gregorianum*
GS	Geistliche Schriftlesung (see Eng version, NTSR)
GTA	Göttinger theologische Arbeiten
GTJ	*Grace Theological Journal*
HAI	A. Soggin, *A History of Ancient Israel* (Phl, 1985)
HALAT	W. Baumgartner, *et al., Hebräisches und aramäisches Lexikon zum Alten Testament* (3 vols. to date; Leiden, 1967–)
HAR	*Hebrew Annual Review*
HAT	Handbuch zum Alten Testament
HBC	J. Finegan, *Handbook of Biblical Chronology* (Princeton, 1964)
HBMI	D. Knight and G. Tucker (eds.), *The Hebrew Bible and Its Modern Interpreters* (Phl, 1985)
HBT	*Horizons in Biblical Theology*
HDR	Harvard Dissertations in Religion
Herm	Hermeneia
HeyJ	*Heythrop Journal*
HibJ	*Hibbert Journal*
HJPAJC	E. Schürer, *A History of the Jewish People in the Age of Jesus Christ* (3 vols.; Edinburgh, 1973–87)
HKAT	Handkommentar zum Alten Testament
HKNT	Handkommentar zum Neuen Testament
HNT	Handbuch zum Neuen Testament
HNTC	Harper's New Testament Commentaries (American printing of BNTC)
HPH	A. Lemaire, *Histoire du peuple hébreu* (Paris, 1981)
HR	*History of Religions*
HSAT	Die heilige Schrift des Alten Testaments
HSM	Harvard Semitic Monographs
HSS	Harvard Semitic Studies
HSNTA	E. Hennecke and W. Schneemelcher, *New Testament Apocrypha* (ed. R. McL. Wilson; 2 vols.; London, 1963–65)
HST	R. Bultmann, *History of the Synoptic Tradition* (NY, 1963)
HTIBS	Historic Texts and Interpreters in Biblical Scholarship
HTKNT	Herders theologischer Kommentar zum Neuen Testament

HTR	*Harvard Theological Review*
HTS	Harvard Theological Studies
HUCA	*Hebrew Union College Annual*
HUT	Hermeneutische Untersuchungen zur Theologie
IB	G. A. Buttrick (ed.), *Interpreter's Bible* (12 vols.; Nash, 1952)
IBC	Interpretation Bible Commentary
IBS	*Irish Biblical Studies*
ICC	International Critical Commentary
IDB	G. A. Buttrick (ed.), *The Interpreter's Dictionary of the Bible* (4 vols.; Nash, 1962)
IDBSup	Supplementary volume to *IDB* (ed. K. Crim; Nash, 1976)
IEJ	*Israel Exploration Journal*
IJH	J. E. Hayes and J. M. Miller (eds.), *Israelite and Judean History* (OTL; Phl, 1977)
Int	*Interpretation*
IOVCB	C. Laymon (ed.), *Interpreters' One Volume Commentary on the Bible* (Nash, 1971)
IPLAP	B. M. Metzger, *Index to Periodical Literature on the Apostle Paul* (NTTS 1; Leiden, 1960)
IPLCG	B. M. Metzger, *Index to Periodical Literature on Christ and the Gospels* (NTTS 6; Leiden, 1966)
IR	*The Iliff Review*
IRT	Issues in Religion and Theology
ISBE	*International Standard Bible Encyclopedia* (ed. G. W. Bromiley; GR, 1979–)
ITC	International Theological Commentary
IW	*Israelite Wisdom* (Fest. S. Terrien; ed. J. Gammie, et al.; Missoula, 1978)
JAAR	*Journal of the American Academy of Religion*
JAC	Jahrbuch für Antike und Christentum
JAL	S. Zeitlin (ed.), Jewish Apocryphal Literature
JANESCU	*Journal of the Ancient Near Eastern Society of Columbia University*
JAOS	*Journal of the American Oriental Society*
JBC	R. E. Brown, et al. (eds.), *The Jerome Biblical Commentary* (EC, 1968)
JBL	*Journal of Biblical Literature*
JBR	*Journal of Bible and Religion*
JCS	*Journal of Cuneiform Studies*
JDS	Judean Desert Studies
JE	I. Singer (ed.), *Jewish Encyclopedia* (12 vols.; NY, 1901–6)
JES	*Journal of Ecumenical Studies*
JETS	*Journal of the Evangelical Theological Society*
JJS	*Journal of Jewish Studies*
JNES	*Journal of Near Eastern Studies*
JNSL	*Journal of Northwest Semitic Languages*
JNTT	J. Jeremias, *New Testament Theology* (NY, 1971)
JPOS	*Journal of the Palestine Oriental Society*
JQR	*Jewish Quarterly Review*
JQRMS	Jewish Quarterly Review Monograph Series
JR	*Journal of Religion*
JRAS	*Journal of the Royal Asiatic Society*
JRelS	*Journal of Religious Studies*
JRS	*Journal of Roman Studies*
JSHRZ	Jüdische Schriften aus hellenistisch-römischer Zeit
JSJ	*Journal for the Study of Judaism in the Persian, Hellenistic and Roman Periods*
JSNT	*Journal for the Study of the New Testament*
JSNTSup	Journal for the Study of the New Testament—Supplement Series
JSOT	*Journal for the Study of the Old Testament*
JSOTSup	Journal for the Study of the Old Testament—Supplement Series
JSS	*Journal of Semitic Studies*
JTC	*Journal for Theology and the Church*
JTS	*Journal of Theological Studies*
KAI	H. Donner and W. Röllig, *Kanaanäische und aramäische Inschriften* (3 vols.; Wiesbaden, 1962–64; 4th ed., 1979)
KAT	E. Sellin (ed.), Kommentar zum Alten Testament
KB	L. Koehler and W. Baumgartner, *Lexicon in Veteris Testamenti Libros* (2d ed.; Leiden, 1958; repr., 1985)
KD	*Kerygma und Dogma*
KINT	H. Koester, *Introduction to the New Testament* (2 vols.; Phl, 1982)
KlT	Kleine Texte

Kümmel, *INT*	W. G. Kümmel, *Introduction to the New Testament* (Nash, 1975)
LAE	A. Deissmann, *Light from the Ancient East* (2d ed.; London, 1927)
LAEg	Simpson, W. K. (ed.), *The Literature of Ancient Egypt* (2d ed.; New Haven, 1973)
LB	*Linguistica biblica*
LBib	Y. Aharoni, *The Land of the Bible* (2d ed.; Phl, 1979)
LCL	Loeb Classical Library
LD	Lectio divina
LS	*Louvain Studies*
LSB	La sacra Bibbia
LSJ	H. G. Liddell, R. Scott, and H. S. Jones, *Greek-English Lexicon* (2 vols.; 9th ed.; Oxford, 1925–40; repr. in one vol., 1966; suppl., 1968)
LSV	Lex Spiritus Vitae
LTP	*Laval théologique et philosophique*
LTQ	*Lexington Theological Quarterly*
LUA	Lunds universitets årsskrift
LumVie	*Lumière et vie*
LWks	Luther's Works (ed. J. Pelikan; St. Louis, 1955–)
MarTS	Marburger theologische Studien
McCQ	*McCormick Quarterly*
MeyerK	H. A. W. Meyer (ed.), Kritisch-exegetischer Kommentar über das Neue Testament
MGK	J. A. Montgomery, *Kings* (ed. H. Gehman; ICC; NY, 1951)
MMGB	B. M. Metzger, *Manuscripts of the Greek Bible* (Oxford, 1981)
MNT	R. E. Brown, *et al.* (eds.), *Mary in the New Testament* (Phl/NY, 1978)
MNTC	Moffatt New Testament Commentary
MOCT	J. J. Megivern (ed.), *Official Catholic Teachings: Biblical Interpretation* (Wilmington, NC, 1978): nos. = sections
MStud	*Milltown Studies*
MSU	Mitteilungen des Septuaginta-Unternehmens
MTS	Münchener theologische Studien
MTZ	*Münchener theologische Zeitschrift*
MUSJ	*Mélanges de l'université Saint-Joseph*
N-A²⁶	E. Nestle and K. Aland, *Novum Testamentum Graece* (26th ed.; Stuttgart, 1979)
NatGeog	*National Geographic*
NAWG	*Nachrichten von der Akademie der Wissenschaften in Göttingen*
NBE	Nueva Biblia Española
NCB	New Century Bible
NCCHS	R. D. Fuller, *et al.* (eds.), *New Catholic Commentary on Holy Scripture* (London, 1969)
NCE	M. R. P. McGuire, *et al.* (eds.), *New Catholic Encyclopedia* (15 vols.; NY, 1967)
NClarB	New Clarendon Bible
NClio	*La Nouvelle Clio*
NEchtB	Die neue Echter Bibel
Neot	*Neotestamentica*
NFL	*No Famine in the Land* (Fest. J. L. McKenzie; ed. J. Flanagan and A. Robinson; Missoula, 1975)
NFT	New Frontiers in Theology
NHI	M. Noth, *History of Israel* (rev. tr. P. R. Ackroyd; NY, 1960)
NHLE	*Nag Hammadi Library in English* (dir. J. M. Robinson; SF, 1977)
NHS	Nag Hammadi Studies
NICNT	New International Commentary on the New Testament
NICOT	New International Commentary on the Old Testament
NIDNTT	C. Brown (ed.), *The New International Dictionary of New Testament Theology* (3 vols.; GR, 1975–78)
NIGTC	New International Greek Testament Commentary
NovT	*Novum Testamentum*
NovTSup	Novum Testamentum, Supplements
NPNF	Nicene and Post-Nicene Fathers
NRT	*La nouvelle revue théologique*
NTA	*New Testament Abstracts*
NTAbh	Neutestamentliche Abhandlungen
NTB	C. K. Barrett, *New Testament Background: Selected Documents* (NY, 1961)
NTD	Das Neue Testament deutsch
NTM	New Testament Message

NTMI	E. J. Epp and G. W. MacRae (eds.), *The New Testament and Its Modern Interpreters* (Atlanta, 1989)
NTQT	E. Käsemann, *New Testament Questions of Today* (Phl, 1969)
NTS	*New Testament Studies*
NTSR	New Testament for Spiritual Reading
NTTS	New Testament Tools and Studies
Numen	*Numen: International Review for the History of Religions*
NumenSup	Supplement to *Numen* (Leiden)
OAB	*Oxford Annotated Bible with the Apocrypha: Expanded Version* (*RSV*; NY, 1977)
OBO	Orbis biblicus et orientalis
OBT	Overtures to Biblical Theology
OCD	N. G. L. Hammond and H. H. Scullard (eds.), *The Oxford Classical Dictionary* (2d ed.; Oxford, 1977; repr., 1984)
ODCC	F. L. Cross and E. A. Livingstone (eds.), *The Oxford Dictionary of the Christian Church* (2d ed.; Oxford, 1977; repr., 1983)
OLP	*Orientalia lovaniensia periodica*
OLZ	*Orientalische Literaturzeitung*
OOTT	T. Vriezen, *An Outline of Old Testament Theology* (Oxford, 1958)
Or	*Orientalia*
OrAnt	Oriens antiquus
OTA	*Old Testament Abstracts*
ÖTK	Ökumenischer Taschenbuch-Kommentar
OTL	Old Testament Library
OTM	Old Testament Message
OTMS	H. H. Rowley (ed.), *The Old Testament and Modern Study* (Oxford, 1951)
OTNT	H. Conzelmann, *An Outline of the Theology of the New Testament* (NY, 1969)
OTP	J. H. Charlesworth (ed.), *The Old Testament Pseudepigrapha* (2 vols.; GC, 1983–85)
OTRG	Old Testament Reading Guide
OTS	*Oudtestamentische Studiën*
OTT	G. von Rad, *Old Testament Theology* (2 vols.; Edinburgh, 1962–65)
PC	Pelican Commentaries (= Pelican Gospel Commentaries and Westminster Pelican series)
PCB	M. Black and H. H. Rowley (eds.), *Peake's Commentary on the Bible* (London, 1962)
PEFQS	*Palestine Exploration Fund, Quarterly Statement*
PEQ	*Palestine Exploration Quarterly*
PerspLA	C. H. Talbert (ed.), *Perspectives on Luke-Acts* (Danville, 1978)
PerspT	*Perspectiva Teológica*
PG	J. Migne, Patrologia graeca
PGM	K. L. Preisendanz (ed.), *Papyri graecae magicae* (3 vols.; Leipzig, 1928–41; 2d ed., 1973)
PHOE	G. von Rad, *The Problem of the Hexateuch and Other Essays* (NY, 1966)
PIBA	*Proceedings of the Irish Biblical Association*
PJ	*Palästina-Jahrbuch*
PL	J. Migne, Patrologia latina
PNT	R. E. Brown, *et al.* (eds.), *Peter in the New Testament* (Minneapolis/NY, 1973)
POTT	D. Wiseman (ed.), *Peoples of the Old Testament Times* (Oxford, 1973)
PP	E. Käsemann, *Perspectives on Paul* (Phl, 1969)
ProcCTSA	*Proceedings of the Catholic Theological Society of America*
PRS	*Perspectives in Religious Studies*
PSB	*Princeton Seminary Bulletin*
PSBib	L. Pirot, *La sainte Bible* (rev. A. Clamer; 12 vols.; Paris, 1938–64)
PSTJ	*Perkins School of Theology Journal* (succeeded by *Perkins Journal*)
PTMS	Pittsburgh Theological Monograph Series
PVTG	Pseudepigrapha Veteris Testamenti graece
PW	G. Wissowa (ed.), *Paulys Real-Encyclopädie der classischen Altertumswissenschaft* (many vols.; Stuttgart, 1893–)
PWSup	Supplement to PW
Qad	*Qadmoniot*
QD	Quaestiones disputatae
RAC	*Reallexikon für Antike und Christentum*
RAM	*Revue d'ascétique et mystique*
RB	*Revue biblique*
RBén	*Revue bénédictine*
RDTour	*Revue diocésaine de Tournai*
RechBib	Recherches bibliques

Rechtf	J. Friedrich, *et al.* (eds.), *Rechtfertigung* (Fest. E. Käsemann; Tübingen, 1976)
Recueil	*Recueil Lucien Cerfaux* (3 vols.; Gembloux, 1954–62)
REG	*Revue des études grecques*
REJ	*Revue des études juives*
RelSRev	*Religious Studies Review*
ResQ	*Restoration Quarterly*
RevExp	*Review and Expositor*
RevistB	*Revista bíblica*
RevQ	*Revue de Qumran*
RevScRel	*Revue des sciences religieuses*
RGG	*Religion in Geschichte und Gegenwart*
RHPR	*Revue d'histoire et de philosophie religieuses*
RHR	*Revue de l'histoire des religions*
RIDA	*Revue internationale des droits de l'antiquité*
RITNT	A. Richardson, *Introduction to the Theology of the New Testament* (London, 1958)
RivB	*Rivista biblica*
RNT	Regensburger Neues Testament
RR	*Review of Religion*
RSO	*Rivista degli studi orientali*
RSR	*Recherches de science religieuse*
RSS	*Rome and the Study of Scripture* (7th ed.; St. Meinrad, 1962)
R-T	A. Robert and A. Tricot, *Guide to the Bible* (vol. 1; 2d ed.; NY, 1955)
RTAM	*Recherches de théologie ancienne et médievale*
RTL	*Revue théologique de Louvain*
RTP	*Revue de théologie et de philosophie*
SAIW	J. Crenshaw (ed.), *Studies in Ancient Israelite Wisdom* (NY, 1976)
SAns	Studia anselmiana
SANT	Studien zum Alten und Neuen Testament
SB	Sources bibliques
SBA	Studies in Biblical Archaeology
SBB	Stuttgarter biblische Beiträge
SBFLA	*Studii biblici franciscani liber annuus*
SBH	G. Fohrer, *Studien zum Buche Hiobs 1956–1979* (BZAW 159; 2d ed.; Berlin, 1983)
SBLASP	Society of Biblical Literature Abstracts and Seminar Papers
SBLDS	SBL Dissertation Series
SBLMasS	SBL Masoretic Studies
SBLMS	SBL Monograph Series
SBLSBS	SBL Sources for Biblical Study
SBLSCS	SBL Septuagint and Cognate Studies
SBLSS	SBL Semeia Supplements
SBLTT	SBL Texts and Translations
SBM	Stuttgarter biblische Monographien
SBS	Stuttgarter Bibelstudien
SBT	Studies in Biblical Theology
SBU	*Symbolae biblicae upsalienses*
SC	Sources chrétiennes
ScEccl	*Sciences ecclésiastiques*
ScEs	*Science et esprit*
Scr	*Scripture*
ScrB	*Scripture Bulletin*
ScrHier	Scripta hierosolymitana
SD	Studies and Documents
SE I, II, III	*Studia Evangelica I, II, III*, etc. (= TU 73 [1959], 87 [1964], 88 [1964], 102 [1968], 103 [1968], 112 [1973])
SEA	*Svensk exegetisk årsbok*
Sef	*Sefarad*
Sem	*Semitica*
SHAW	Sitzungsberichte der Heidelberger Akademie der Wissenschaften
SHCT	Studies in the History of Christian Thought
SIPW	P. W. Skehan, *Studies in Israelite Poetry and Wisdom* (CBQMS 1; Washington, 1971)
SJLA	Studies in Judaism in Late Antiquity
SJOT	J. Simons, *Jerusalem in the Old Testament* (Leiden, 1952)
SJT	*Scottish Journal of Theology*

SKK	Stuttgarter kleiner Kommentar
SLOE	H. H. Rowley, *The Servant of the Lord and Other Essays* (London, 1952)
SNT	Studien zum Neuen Testament
SNTSMS	Society for New Testament Studies Monograph Series
SNTU	Studien zum Neuen Testament und seiner Umwelt
SOTSMS	Society for Old Testament Study Monograph Series
SP	J. Coppens, *et al.* (eds.), *Sacra pagina* (2 vols.; Gembloux, 1959)
SPat	*Studia patavina*
SPB	Studia postbiblica
SPC	*Studiorum paulinorum congressus internationalis catholicus 1961* (2 vols.; AnBib 17–18; Rome, 1963)
SQE	K. Aland, *Synopsis quattuor evangeliorum* (10th ed.; Stuttgart, 1978)
SSN	Studia semitica neerlandica
SSS	Semitic Study Series
ST	*Studia theologica*
StJud	Studia judaica: Forschungen zur Wissenschaft des Judentums
STK	*Svensk teologisk Kvartalskrift*
StLA	L. E. Keck and J. L. Martyn (eds.), *Studies in Luke-Acts* (Fest. P. Schubert; Nash, 1966)
Str-B	[H. Strack and] P. Billerbeck, *Kommentar zum Neuen Testament aus Talmud und Midrasch* (6 vols.; Munich, 1922–61)
StudB	Studia Biblica
StudBT	*Studia biblica et theologica*
StudCath	*Studia catholica*
StudNeot	Studia Neotestamentica, Studia
StudP	Studia patristica
SUNT	Studien zur Umwelt des Neuen Testaments
SVTP	Studia in Veteris Testamenti pseudepigrapha
SymBU	Symbolae biblicae upsalienses
SZ	*Stimmen der Zeit*
TA	Theologische Arbeiten
TAG	J. A. Fitzmyer, *To Advance the Gospel: New Testament Studies* (NY, 1981)
TAVO B	Tübinger Atlas der vorderen Orients, Beiträge
TBC	Torch Bible Commentaries
TBei	*Theologische Beiträge*
TBT	*The Bible Today*
TBü	Theologische Bücherei
TCGNT	B. M. Metzger, *A Textual Commentary on the Greek New Testament* (London/NY, 1971)
TD	*Theology Digest*
TDNT	G. Kittel and G. Friedrich (eds.), *Theological Dictionary of the New Testament* (10 vols.; GR, 1964–76)
TDOT	G. J. Botterweck and H. Ringgren (eds.), *Theological Dictionary of the Old Testament* (so far 5 vols.; GR, 1974–)
TEH	Theologische Existenz heute
TextS	Texts and Studies
TF	Theologische Forschung
TGl	*Theologie und Glaube*
THK	Theologischer Handkommentar
ThStud	Theologische Studien
TI	Theological Inquiries
TLZ	*Theologische Literaturzeitung*
TNT	R. Bultmann, *The Theology of the New Testament* (2 vols.; NY, 1952–55)
TOB	*Traduction oecuménique de la Bible: Edition intégrale* (Paris, 1975–77)
TOT	W. Eichrodt, *Theology of the Old Testament* (2 vols.; Phl, 1961–67)
TQ	*Theologische Quartalschrift*
TRE	G. Krause and G. Müller (eds.), *Theologische Realenzyklopedie* (30 vols.; Berlin/NY, 1976–)
TRev	*Theologische Revue*
TRu	*Theologische Rundschau*
TS	*Theological Studies*
TSL	H. Conzelmann, *The Theology of Saint Luke* (NY, 1960)
TToday	*Theology Today*
TToday	Theology Today
TTS	Trierer theologische Studien

TU	Texte und Untersuchungen
TWAT	G. J. Botterweck and H. Ringgren (eds.), *Theologisches Wörterbuch zum Alten Testament* (so far 3 vols.; Stuttgart, 1970—)
TWNT	G. Kittel and G. Friedrich (eds.), *Theologisches Wörterbuch zum Neuen Testament* (10 vols.; Stuttgart, 1932–79)
TynBul	*Tyndale Bulletin*
TynNTC	Tyndale New Testament Commentary
TynOTC	Tyndale Old Testament Commentary
TZ	*Theologische Zeitschrift*
UBSGNT	K. Aland, *et al.* (eds.), *The Greek New Testament* (United Bible Societies; 3d ed.; NY, 1975)
UF	*Ugarit-Forschungen*
UM	C. H. Gordon, *Ugaritic Manual* (Rome, 1955)
UNT	Untersuchungen zum Neuen Testament
US	*Una Sancta*
USQR	*Union Seminary Quarterly Review*
ÜSt	M. Noth, *Überlieferungsgeschichtliche Studien* (Darmstadt, 1957)
UT	C. H. Gordon, *Ugaritic Textbook* (AnOr 38; Rome, 1967)
UUA	Uppsala universitetsårsskrift
VBW	B. Mazar, *et al.* (eds.), *Views of the Biblical World* (5 vols.; NY, 1961)
VC	*Vigiliae christianae*
VD	*Verbum domini*
VF	*Verkündigung und Forschung*
VKGNT	K. Aland, *et al.* (eds.), *Vollständige Konkordanz zum griechischen Neuen Testament* (2 vols.; Berlin/NY, 1975–78)
VP	*Vivre et penser* (= *RB* 1941–44)
VS	Verbum salutis
VSpir	*Vie spirituelle*
VT	*Vetus Testamentum*
VTSup	Vetus Testamentum Supplements
WA	J. A. Fitzmyer, *A Wandering Aramean: Collected Aramaic Essays* (SBLMS 25; Missoula, 1979)
WBA	G. E. Wright, *Biblical Archaeology* (rev. ed.; Phl, 1963)
WBC	Word Biblical Commentary
WF	Wege der Forschung
WHAB	G. E. Wright (ed.), *Westminster Historical Atlas to the Bible* (Phl, 1956)
WHJP	B. Mazar, *et al.* (ed.), *The World History of the Jewish People* (New Brunswick, 1964)
WI	G. von Rad, *Wisdom in Israel* (Nash, 1972)
Wik-Schm, *ENT*	A. Wikenhauser and J. Schmid, *Einleitung in das Neue Testament* (6th ed.; Freiburg, 1977)
WLSGF	*The Word of the Lord Shall Go Forth* (Fest. D. N. Freedman; ed. C. L. Meyers and M. O'Connor; ASOR Spec. Vol. ser. 1; Winona Lake, 1983)
WMANT	Wissenschaftliche Monographien zum Alten und Neuen Testament
WO	*Die Welt des Orients*
WTJ	*Westminster Theological Journal*
WUNT	Wissenschaftliche Untersuchungen zum Neuen Testament
WZUR	*Wissenschaftliche Zeitschrift der Universität Rostock*
YGC	W. F. Albright, *Yahweh and the Gods of Canaan* (GC, 1969)
ZA	*Zeitschrift für Assyriologie*
ZAW	*Zeitschrift für die alttestamentliche Wissenschaft*
ZBG	M. Zerwick, *Biblical Greek* (Rome, 1963)
ZBK	Zürcher Bibel Kommentare
ZDMG	*Zeitschrift der deutschen morgenländischen Gesellschaft*
ZDPV	*Zeitschrift des deutschen Palästina-Vereins*
ZKG	*Zeitschrift für Kirchengeschichte*
ZKT	*Zeitschrift für katholische Theologie*
ZNW	*Zeitschrift für die neutestamentliche Wissenschaft*
ZTK	*Zeitschrift für Theologie und Kirche*

N. B. Information on where the periodicals and serials listed here are published can be found in *EBB, NTA,* or *OTA.*

TRANSLITERATION OF HEBREW AND ARAMAIC
CONSONANTS

ʾ	=	א	z	=	ז	m	=	מ ם	q	=	ק
b	=	ב	ḥ	=	ח	n	=	נ ן	r	=	ר
g	=	ג	ṭ	=	ט	s	=	ס	ś	=	שׂ
d	=	ד	y	=	י	ʿ	=	ע	š	=	שׁ
h	=	ה	k	=	כ ך	p	=	פ ף	t	=	ת
w	=	ו	l	=	ל	ṣ	=	צ			

Note: The presence or absence of *dageš lene* in the *begadkepat* letters is not shown. Consonants with *dageš forte* are written double.

VOWELS (shown as preceded by *b*)

With *matres lectionis*			Without *matres lectionis*				With *vocal šewa*	
bâ	=	בָה	bā	=	בָ	ba	=	בַ	bă	=	בֲ
bô	=	בוֹ	bō	=	בֹ	bo	=	בָ	bŏ	=	בֳ
bû	=	בוּ	bū	=	בֻ	bu	=	בֻ			
bê	=	בֵי	bē	=	בֵ	be	=	בֶ	bě	=	בְ בֶ בֵ
bî	=	בִי	bī	=	בִ	bi	=	בִ			

bāh = בָה or בֵה. baʾ = בָא (even where א is merely a *mater lectionis*).
bēh = בֵה, and beh = בֶה (although h is merely a *mater lectionis* here).
pataḥ furtivum: rûaḥ = רוּחַ.

TRANSLITERATION OF GREEK

ē	=	η	h	=	ʿ	ph	=	φ
ou	=	ου	th	=	θ	ch	=	χ
ō	=	ω	y	=	υ	ps	=	ψ
						ng	=	γγ

PLACES OF PUBLICATION

EC	Englewood Cliffs, NJ
GC	Garden City, NY
GR	Grand Rapids, MI
LA	Los Angeles, CA
Nash	Nashville, TN
NY	New York, NY
Phl	Philadelphia, PA
SF	San Francisco, CA
Freiburg	Freiburg im Breisgau, Germany
Fribourg	Freiburg/Fribourg in der Schweiz (Switzerland)

MISCELLANEOUS ABBREVIATIONS

Abp.	Archbishop
adj.	adjective
adv.	adverb
aeth.	Ethiopic version of the Bible (used in *app. crit.*)
aor.	aorist tense
app. crit.	*apparatus criticus* (the critical apparatus in biblical texts in the original languages)
Aq	Aquila (a Gk transl. of the OT)
Aram	Aramaic (when used as an adj.)
AUC	*Ab urbe condita* (from the foundation of the City [Rome]; used in ancient Roman dates)
AV	*Authorized Version* (of the Bible; = *KJV*)
b.	Babylonian Talmud (followed by the abbreviation of the name of the specific tractate)
bo	Bohairic (Coptic) version of the Bible (used in *app. crit.*)
Bp.	Bishop
CCD	*Confraternity of Christian Doctrine* (version of the Bible)
chap.	chapter
DAS	*Divino afflante Spiritu* (→ 72:20-23)
Eng	English (when used as an adj.)
Ep.	Epistle or *Epistula*
esp.	especially
Fest.	Festschrift (generic name used for any publication honoring a person; followed by the name of the person honored)
Fr	French (when used as an adj.)
gen.	genitive
Ger	German (when used as an adj.)
GesSt	*Gesammelte Studien* (collected works)
Gk	Greek (when used as an adj.)
Hebr	Hebrew (when used as an adj.)
it	Vetus itala (part of the OL version of the Bible; used in *app. crit.*)
Ital	Italian (when used as an adj.)
JB	*Jerusalem Bible* (ed. A. Jones; GC, 1966)
JBap	John the Baptist
JPSV	*Jewish Publication Society Version* (of the Bible)
KJV	*King James Version* (of the Bible; = *AV*)
KlS	*Kleine Schriften* (e.g., of A. Alt, O. Eissfeldt)
Lat	Latin (when used as an adj.)
lat	Latin versions of the Bible in general (used in *app. crit.*)
lit.	literally
l. v.	*lectio varia* (variant reading [in textual criticism])
LXX	Septuagint (Greek transl. of the OT)
m.	Mishna (followed by the abbreviation of the name of the tractate)
Midr.	Midrash (followed by the name of the specific work)
ms(s).	manuscript(s)
MT	Masoretic Text (of the Hebrew Bible)
NAB	*New American Bible* (American Catholic version)
NEB	*New English Bible* (Oxford and Cambridge version)
NHL	Nag Hammadi Literature
NIV	*New International Version* (of the Bible)
NJB	*New Jerusalem Bible* (ed. H. Wansbrough; GC, 1985)
NJV	*New Jewish Version* (of the Bible)
no(s).	number(s)
ns	new series (used for any language)
NT	New Testament
OL	Old Latin (= *Vetus Latina*)
os	old series (used for any language)
OS	Old Syriac (transl. of the Bible)
OT	Old Testament
par.	parallel passage(s) in the Synoptic Gospels
PBC	Pontifical Biblical Commission
Pesh	Peshitta (Syr version of the Bible)

pl.	plural
prep.	preposition
pron.	pronoun
ptc.	participle
RSV	*Revised Standard Version* (of the Bible)
RV	*Revised Version* (of the Bible)
sah	Sahidic (Coptic) version of the Bible (used in *app. crit.*)
Sam. Pent.	*Samaritan Pentateuch*
SBJ	*La Sainte Bible de Jérusalem* (Fr original of *JB*)
sg.	singular
sup., suppl.	supplement
syh	Syr version of the Bible, called Harclean
Sym	Symmachus (Gk transl. of the OT)
Syn	Synoptic Gospel *or* Synoptic writers
Syr	Syriac (when used as an adj.)
Tg.	*Targum* (Aram version of the OT); followed by proper name
transl.	translation
Vg	Vulgate (common Lat version of the Bible)
viz.	*videlicet* (= namely)
vs.	versus
VL	*Vetus Latina*
y.	*Jerusalem Talmud* (followed by the abbreviation of the name of the specific tractate)
*	*Prima manus* (indicates the reading of the first copyist in a biblical ms.)
→	The arrow indicates a cross reference to an article in this commentary; it is normally followed by a shortened title of the article, its number, and a marginal paragraph number (e.g., → NT Thought, 81:20)

THE NEW
JEROME BIBLICAL
COMMENTARY

PART ONE

THE

OLD TESTAMENT

Edited by

ROLAND E. MURPHY, O.Carm.

PART ONE

THE
OLD TESTAMENT

Edited by
ROLAND E. MURPHY, O.Carm.

1

INTRODUCTION TO
THE PENTATEUCH

Roland E. Murphy, O.Carm.

BIBLIOGRAPHY

1 Brueggemann, W., *The Vitality of Old Testament Traditions* (2d ed.; Atlanta, 1982). Cassuto, U., *The Documentary Hypothesis* (Jerusalem, 1961). Cazelles, H., *DBSup* 7. 736–858. Clines, D. J., *The Theme of the Pentateuch* (JSOTSup 10; Sheffield, 1978). Cross, *CMHE* 293–325. Knight, D. (ed.), *Julius Wellhausen and His* Prolegomena to the History of Israel (Semeia 25; Chico, 1982). Noth, M., *A History of Pentateuchal Traditions* (EC, 1972). Von Rad, *PHOE* 1–78. Rendtorff, R., "The Yahwist as Theologian?" *JSOT* 3 (1977) 2–10; *Die überlieferungsgeschichtliche Problem des Pentateuch* (BZAW 147; Berlin, 1977). Schmid,

H. H., *Der sogenannte Jahwist* (Zurich, 1976). Vermeylen, J., "La formation du Pentateuque à la lumière de l'exégèse historico-critique," *RTL* 12 (1981) 324–46. Whybray, R. N., *The Making of the Pentateuch* (JSOTSup 53; Sheffield, 1987).

Pentateuchal research is presented in practically every introduction to the OT, and in biblical dictionaries, but see especially D. Knight in *HBMI* 263–96; D. J. McCarthy in *BHMCS* 34–57; C. Westermann, *Genesis 1–11* (Minneapolis, 1984) 567–606, for summary and bibliography.

OUTLINE

Analysis of the Pentateuch (§ 3–14)
  (I) Terminology and Content (§ 3–4)
  (II) Authorship (§ 5–8)

  (III) Literary Forms (§ 9–10)
  (IV) Other Ways of Reading the Pentateuch (§ 11–13)
  (V) The Theological Significance of the Pentateuch (§ 14)

ANALYSIS OF THE PENTATEUCH

3 **(I) Terminology and Content.** The term "Pentateuch" is derived from the Gk *pentateuchos*, "five containers," indicating the written leather or papyrus rolls that were kept in receptacles. In this case the five rolls are the first five books of the Bible: Genesis, Exodus, Leviticus, Numbers, and Deuteronomy, to use their Greco-Latin names. In Jewish tradition these books are known by the first word(s): "In the beginning" (*běrē'šît*), etc. Together they constitute the Law (*tôrâ*, which originally meant "teaching"). The traditional division of the Hebrew Bible into Law, Prophets, and Writings (the *Těnāk*) reflects the understanding of Gen–Deut as one unit.

Because certain scholars have worked with more or less than the Pentateuch, the following terminology should also be noted. The tetrateuch (M. Noth) is made up of Gen–Num. The hexateuch (G. von Rad) embraces Gen–Josh as a unit. These terms express a particular

understanding of the formation and relationship of the books concerned.

4 A sweep of history is given from the creation of the world and humanity down to the discourses of Moses in the plains of Moab (his death and burial are recorded in Deut 34). The content can be summarized thus: primeval history (Gen 1–11); patriarchal period (Gen 12–36); Joseph story (Gen 37–50); liberation from Egypt and journey to Sinai (Exod 1–18); giving of laws at Sinai (Exod 19–Num 10); journey from Sinai to Moab (Num 10–36); three discourses of Moses in the plains of Moab, with appendixes (Deut 1–34). Particularly noteworthy is the extensive middle section, Exod 19–Num 10, which records the large chunk of Sinai legislation.

One can, of course, summarize the content of the Pentateuch in many different ways. The five central themes pointed out by M. Noth (who works with a tetrateuch) are also helpful: the patriarchal promises, guidance out of Egypt, guidance in the wilderness, the Sinai revelation, and guidance into the arable land. Or one can follow the markings of the several uses of *tōlĕdôt,* or "generations," formula which structure Genesis (2:4a, 5:1; etc.,—the P tradition). If "promise" is taken as the overarching concept (it certainly dominates the patriarchal stories), one is tempted to include Josh, which tells the story of the fulfillment of the promise of land (hence, with von Rad, a hexateuch). However, Jewish tradition has separated the Law from the (Early) Prophets. The best explanation of this is given by J. Sanders (*Torah and Canon* [Phl, 1972] 44–53). The insertion of Deut in its present place is a deliberate break in the story line of promise/fulfillment, which underlines the figure of Moses as Torah giver, the true leader for the postexilic community (Mal 3:23 [4:4]; Ezra 8:1).

5   (II) Authorship. For almost two millennia the Pentateuch was attributed to Moses as author by both Jewish and Christian tradition. Although significant questions about his authorship were raised at points along the way, it was not until the 18th cent. that the question was seriously broached. Today it is a commonplace that he did not write the Pentateuch, but as we shall see the formation of these books is still shrouded in mystery.

Certain obvious facts suggest that Mosaic authorship is not the right fit. Moses' death is recorded in Deut 34. Various formulas suggest a time after the Mosaic period ("until this day," Deut 34:6; "when the Canaanites dwelt in the land," Gen 13:7; the designation of the land E of the Jordan as "the other side," indicating the point of view of a resident of Palestine, which Moses never entered, Gen 50:10; and various anachronisms, such as the mention of Philistines, Gen 26:14–18). One of the striking features which early on prompted the investigation of the books was the alternation of the sacred name Yahweh with the generic name for divinity, Elohim. This indication of differences is relatively superficial; it has to be supported by some consistent factors that can explain the formation of the Torah. It was when the divine names came to be associated with characteristic vocabulary, narrative styles and content (hence "constants" which suggested different authorial hands), that J (for Yahwist) and E (for Elohist) began to emerge as plausible sources in the actual text. Another telling argument was the recognition of doublets (the same event related twice), such as the call of Moses (Exod 3,6), or the endangerment of the ancestress (Gen 12:9–13:1; 20:1–18; 26:1–17). The complexity of the Torah called for the recognition of various strands within it.

6 This is not the place to rehearse the complicated history of modern biblical criticism (but it should be noted that it was honed on the analysis of the Pentateuch; → OT Criticism, 69:12–50). The differences in names and vocabulary, in style and content, within the Pentateuch were noted, and they called for an explanation. Were they due to various documents, or was it a question of "fragments" that were eventually assembled? Or another possibility: Was there a basic narrative which came to be supplemented (supplementary hypothesis)? Finally, a brilliant synthesis of previous efforts was presented by Julius Wellhausen (1844–1918), and it has dominated the field ever since, despite modifications. This "documentary hypothesis" recognizes four documents in the following sequence: J (9th cent.), E (8th cent.), D (Deuteronomist, 7th cent.) and P (Priestly, postexilic). These four major *written* sources were eventually combined in the postexilic period under the guiding hand of the P tradition, and probably a redactor (R). Behind each of these JEDP sigla stands either an

individual (esp. urged in the case of Yahwist) or, more likely, a whole school. Later nuances were brought to the theory. First, there is now a tendency to date J and E earlier (10th and 9th cents.). Second, there is a recognition that these "documents" should be conceived more flexibly as "traditions," which incorporate any number of earlier oral and written traditions. Although later scholars tended to fragment J into separate sources (J1 and J2, etc.), the tendency has been to hold to the fourfold strand and to recognize the existence of previous traditions that have entered into these sources.

As a reminder that this synthesis remains only a brilliant hypothesis, recent scholarship has raised objections (summarized in *HBMI* 263–96; *JSOT* 3 [1977] 2–60). Rolf Rendtorff (*Das überlieferungsgeschichtliche Problem des Pentateuch*) can be taken as a typical and formidable example. He claims that J is not a full narrative that weaves through the Pentateuch, attributable to one or more "theologians." It is rather an editorial reworking of many individual pieces (like P, as well). The real redaction of the Pentateuch comes with a deuteronomistic editor. There were first individual stories (e.g., the different patriarchs) which were combined in a larger complex by some unifying theme (e.g., the promises). The integration of all these complexes into the final form was a definitive theological redaction under deuteronomistic influence; see R. Rendtorff, *The Old Testament* (Phl, 1986) 157–64.

The modern consensus on the formation of the Pentateuch has been breached, but not replaced. Certain views still remain as workable hypotheses. There is widespread agreement that Exod 25–Num 10 belongs to the postexilic P tradition, even though much older material is incorporated in it. The book of Deuteronomy has a unique stamp and is appropriately named D, and it was probably formed over the course of the 8th–6th cents. But the distinction between J and E has always been a bone of contention, long before the current uncertainty. The present tendency is to think more in terms of expansions of J, and to recognize the role of a redactor (R). In the *NJBC* the designations J and E are indicated in line with the received views of the present century, but they are intended to serve as guidelines for the reader, rather than as settling issues that are still under judgment.

7 It is helpful to attend to the usual characterization of the four traditions, with the proviso that these generalizations are not absolute. J is marked by lively anthropomorphisms, vivid storytelling, and creative theological vision (promise/fulfillment dynamic). J articulated the old traditions, perhaps in response to the Solomonic enlightenment (so von Rad). The Elohist remains a problem. E has been considered to be merely interpolated independent traditions, or a redaction of J that never existed on its own. It has been associated with the traditions of the northern kingdom and supposedly emphasizes morality and reflects the proper response of Israel: faith, and fear of the Lord. D is a very clear tradition, but its existence in the Pentateuch outside of Deut itself is not very clear. It insists on fear/love of God in terms of obedience to the divine commands and under threat of punishment. Its exhortatory style and its language give it a characteristic stamp, so that it is recognizable even when it appears outside the Pentateuch, as in the typical passages (Josh 1:1–9; 23:3–16) in Dtr (this is the conventional abbreviation for the deuteronomistic history contained in Josh–2 Kgs, which shows strong D influence). P is another clearly marked strand. It is concerned with questions of cult and ritual (Lev), is interested in genealogies (Gen), and in contrast to the "Name" theology of Deut (Deut 12:5,11,21) speaks of the presence of God in terms of glory and tabernacling (Exod 16:10; 40:34–38). According to F. M. Cross (*CMHE* 293–325), the P tradition never existed as an independent narrative document. Rather, it drew on its own sources to frame and systematize the JE traditions and produced the tetrateuch (Gen–Num) in the period of the exile. Particularly characteristic are its archaizing language (e.g., use of El Shaddai), the systematization of Gen by use of the *tôlĕdôt* (generations) formula, and the periodization of history by means of the covenants which perpetuated the blessing of fertility: with Noah (Gen 9:7), Abraham (17:6), and Moses (Lev 26:9). "The atonement for sin is the function of the elaborate Priestly cultus. . . . The Priestly source . . . was designed to provide overwhelming remorse in Israel and sought by the reconstruction of the age of Moses, its cult and law, to project a community of Israel in which Yahweh could return to 'tabernacle' in their land" (*CMHE* 307).

The characteristic phraseology, themes, and emphases of the traditions are brought out in the commentaries, but the reader should be forewarned of the general nature of this characterization. For details on the four sources see *IDBSup* 229–32, 259–63, 683–87, 971–75; Brueggemann, *Vitality* esp. 127–41.

8 The analysis of the formation of the Pentateuch has many implications for the rest of the OT. It is generally agreed that Gen–Deut never functioned as a complete Torah until the exilic period. Before that time, several traditions, oral and written, would have provided guidance (not to mention the collections of prophetic oracles). The home of the J tradition is usually considered to be Judah, whereas E is assigned to Israel (an affinity with Hosea). The culmination of the deuteronomic movement in the reform of Josiah (641–609) represents a tradition (D) that originated first in the north and then became important in Judah. The various law codes (of the Covenant, Exod 20:22–23:19; Holiness, Lev 17–26; Deuteronomy, Deut 12–26) have many practices in common, but they also show the development, characteristic of law, that took place over several centuries. In the case of the centralization of worship, an emphasis in Deut and Dtr, one has to remember that this was a slow development; it would be an anachronism to understand it as operative in the time of Elijah (9th cent.).

In summary, it should be noted that conclusions can be drawn from the stages through which the Pentateuch passed. Sometimes these conclusions may not really justify statements of fact about history. Thus, one may well wonder if the literary separation of the Sinai tradition from the exodus tradition, as von Rad (*PHOE* 1–26; see H. Huffmon, *CBQ* 27 [1965] 101–13) argues, finds an echo in Israelite history, so that the two traditions were originally quite disparate and only united at a much later time. It is possible to read the Pentateuch in an "interlinear" way, as it were, drawing conclusions concerning Israel's history that are quite hypothetical. Thus, a reconstruction of the nature of the tribes on the basis of data concerning the patriarchs and the "sons of Joseph" is necessarily tenuous (see the attempts of de Vaux in *EHI* 475–749; of course, the Pentateuch forms only part of the data one must work with).

It is undeniable that the Pentateuch contains old covenant traditions that formed the religious charter of the tribes that constituted the people of God. "Ethical monotheism" is not the creation of the 9th-cent. prophets, as Wellhausen claimed. Amos (3:2) and Hosea (4:1–2) judged the people on the basis of covenantal stipulations (no matter when the term covenant, or *bĕrît*, came into common usage).

9   (III) Literary Forms. The traditional acceptance of Mosaic authorship brought in its wake a rigid notion of history in the Pentateuch. Presumably everything occurred in Exod–Deut as Moses wrote it, for he would have been a firsthand witness. The equation of biblical truth with historical truth, as exemplified in this case, is a form of reductionism; it restricts the divine freedom to produce a literature that is as rich as the OT is in fact. This means that one must read the Pentateuch (not to mention the entire OT) with an awareness of the various literary forms that are contained within it. From the time of H. Gunkel's famous commentary on Genesis, scholars have been greatly preoccupied with the question of *Gattungen,* or forms, and the Pentateuch has provided innumerable examples for analysis.

(Coats, G., *Genesis* [FOTL 1; GR, 1983]. Hayes, J. H. (ed.), *Old Testament Form Criticism* [San Antonio, 1974]. Koch, K., *The Growth of the Biblical Tradition* [NY, 1969]. Tucker, G. M., *Form Criticism of the Old Testament* [Phl, 1971].)

Some genres are easier to recognize than others. Among them may be indicated the following (the list is far from exhaustive):

Laws. These take up a large portion of the Pentateuch, from Exod to Deut; see de Vaux, *AI* 143–63.

Etiology. A narrative that provides an explanation for a certain name or situation. The etiology can be wordplay (Exod 15:23, Marah), or it can be a narrative that explains an event, such as the explanation given in Gen 47:13–26 for the land tax established by Joseph.

Ritual. A description of the way in which a community is to carry out (significant) ceremonies, such as the offering of the firstfruits in Deut 26:1–11, or the prescriptions for sacrifices (Lev 1–7).

Genealogy. A list that traces ancestral descent and/or relationship. This can be linear, giving only one line of descent (10 generations from Adam through Seth to Noah, Gen 5), or it can be segmented (branching), as in the list of the sons of Jacob in Gen 46:8–27. It should be noted that ancient genealogies were not intended to be historical records. They include more than blood relationship, for they indicate the ties formed by commerce, geography, and other concerns (see R. R. Wilson, *Genealogy and History in the Biblical World* [Yale Near Eastern Researches 7; New Haven, 1977]).

Hieros logos. "Sacred words," or sacral tradition, which refer to the origin of a holy place (Gen 28:10–22; 33:18–20).

Blessing. A form of speech that imparts an efficacious power (a performative word) upon someone. When the blessing is given on the deathbed (see Deut 33), it has also been called a "testament."

Other literary genres are more problematic. Scholars differ in their understanding of myth, saga, legend, novella or short story, and some of these can be subdivided into specific types (e.g., family saga, etc.). The purpose here is to indicate the range of possibilities.

Myth. The understanding of this term varies widely. It has been defined as a narrative about gods (H. Gunkel; perhaps only Gen 6:1–4 would qualify in the OT). It is also viewed as the story that accompanies ritual. It can also designate a way of thinking, the mythopoeic quality of human thought; see H. Frankfort, *et al., The Intellectual Adventure of Ancient Man* (rev. ed., Chicago, 1977) 3–27.

Saga. G. Coats (*Genesis* 319) defines this as "a long, prose, traditional narrative having an episodic structure and developed around stereotyped themes or objects." This can be further refined as primeval (J strand in Gen 1–11), family (the Abraham story of J in Gen 12–26), heroic (Moses in the J version, Exod 3ff.)

Legend. It is difficult to distinguish this from saga (see R. Hals, *CBQ* 34 [1972] 166–76). Coats (*Genesis* 252) defines it as a "narrative concerned primarily with the wondrous, miraculous and exemplary"; it aims to edify (Gen 22:1–19; Num 25:6–12).

Story. This is a narrative with a plot that arouses interest by creating a tension and resolving it. It may supply historical knowledge, but with a certain amount of freedom; or it may be oriented simply to entertainment, employing certain folklore motifs. It may also be called a tale or novella; examples might be the Joseph story or the book of Ruth.

History. Obviously the literary genre of history as it is conceived by modern standards cannot be applied to the biblical record. Yet the Bible does supply history in various forms. It does record events of the past, but not precisely as they occurred or as a modern would record them. Chronological sequence, cause and effect relationship, and selectivity are characteristic of historiography. As a genre, history is to be found in the books of Kings, rather than in the Pentateuch, although some kind of historical memory is preserved in the patriarchal and exodus narratives.

10   Tradition history (*Überlieferungsgeschichte* or *Traditionsgeschichte*) is the technical term given by scholars to the investigation of the stages that a given unit passes through on its way to being incorporated into a consecutive narrative. Thus, one can isolate certain literary forms, whether in oral or written tradition, which have been incorporated into a larger framework. It has been supposed, e.g., that the J narrative has made use of a tradition (the flood, or the plagues), and in another remove J has been joined with P, and the result is the Torah as we have it. The study of the final form of the Torah is properly called redaction criticism (*Redaktionsgeschichte*).

The tradition-historical method can be illustrated by an analysis of the Jacob story (Gen 25–36). In contrast to the Joseph story, which runs smoothly in its description of the relationship of Joseph to his brothers, distinct cycles can be detected in the story of Jacob. These are the Jacob–Esau and the Jacob–Laban cycles; originally distinct, they were brought together. To understand the complexity, the disposition of the text should be noted. The Jacob–Esau narrative begins in the "family history" of Isaac their father, Gen 25:19, and continues in the famous deception of the old man in Gen 27. The theme of hostile twins is developed in their very birth, in their life-styles (hunter vs. shepherd), in the sale of the birthright (*bĕkōrâ*), and in the deception of Isaac in order to obtain the blessing (*bĕrākâ*). The separation of the twins is precipitated by the choice of wives. According to P (Gen 26:34–35; 27:46; 28:1–9), Esau marries Canaanites, so Jacob is sent to Paddan-aram to marry a relative. But according to J, Jacob flees to Paddan-aram to escape Esau's fury after the deception (Gen 27:41–45). The Jacob–Laban cycle (JE, Gen 29:1–31:55) stands on its own. It relates the marriage of Jacob to the daughters of the wily Laban, who forces Jacob to work for him. But Jacob the trickster succeeds in extricating himself and returning home. This adventure begins and ends with theophanies (Bethel, 28:10–22; cf. 35:9–15; Penuel, 32:23–33). The two cycles are joined in the finale, an encounter of Jacob with Esau (32:4–22; 33:1–17). The story ends (chaps. 34–36) with genealogical data about Jacob's family and Esau's descendants (Edomites).

The entire narrative is so neatly tied together that at first reading it seems to be all of a piece. But tradition history examines carefully the various connections between events: Why did Jacob go to Paddan-aram? What does this residence say about his connections with

the Arameans in the area (cf. "my father was a wandering Aramean," Deut 26:5). How does the episode of Dinah at Shechem (chap. 34) relate to the history of relations with the Shechemites? The geographical spread— Bethel, Shechem, Hebron, Penuel, Mahanaim (32:2–3) — is a very wide one, and several of these have to do with theophanies attached to these holy places. Finally, the list of Jacob's children omits Dinah (35:16–19). How is one to evaluate this genealogy? Are they merely eponymous ancestors of tribes that only later became Israel in the post-exodus period? Needless to say, it is very difficult to answer such questions that the combination of various traditions gives rise to. At the present time, the history of traditions is more successful at suggesting various traditions than explaining them. But the questions are valid. For details, see M. Noth, *Pentateuchal Traditions;* W. Rast, *Tradition History and the Old Testament* (Phl, 1972); B. W. Anderson, "Tradition and Scripture in the Community of Faith," *JBL* 100 (1981) 5–21.

11   **(IV) Other Ways of Reading the Pentateuch.** Historical-critical methodology breaks the text down into units and traditions; it attempts to get behind the existing final form to its prehistory so to speak, as in the case of the Pentateuch. There is necessarily a great deal of hypothetical reconstruction in all this, and many are left dissatisfied. However faithful the methodology, its limitations have also to be recognized and remedied by other approaches. Since the Pentateuch finally formed a unity, the Torah, what is its meaning? Are other approaches to the Torah possible?

12   (a) A LITERARY APPROACH. This applies to the entire Bible, as well as to Gen–Deut, and it is the kind of analysis that is carried on by students of literature. It can be summed up in the words of R. Alter: "By literary analysis I mean the manifold varieties of minutely discriminating attention to the artful use of language, to the shifting play of ideas, conventions, tone, sound, imagery, syntax, narrative viewpoint, compositional units, and much else; the kind of disciplined attention, in other words, which through a whole spectrum of critical approaches has illuminated, for example, the poetry of Dante, the plays of Shakespeare, the novels of Tolstoy" (*The Art of Biblical Narrative* [NY, 1981] 12–13). In contrast to the usual historical-critical concerns, this approach does not ask questions about history; it is not diachronic (through time), but synchronic (in time). Its object is not the formation of the text with its various levels through time, but an appreciation of the text as it stands, at one time. Moreover, it believes that meaning is conveyed *through* the text, that meaning cannot be arrived at without taking into account all the characteristics of the text (sounds, onomatopoeia, catch words— in short, the aesthetic functions of language that are employed to convey meaning).

Historical questions put to the text yield history; literary questions put to the text yield meaning; but both yield meaning. There is no reason to pit one against the other; they are in fact complementary. And they are both necessary for a theological interpretation of the religious literature that is the Torah. Most commentaries are heavily weighted in favor of the historical, first because this is the dominant mode, and second because the technical knowledge supplied to the reader is not easily available. A literary appreciation of the Torah has always existed; the stories of Abraham (Gen 22), Joseph (Gen 37–50), Moses (Exod 3), Balaam's ass (Num 22) have never ceased to fascinate readers, even though they are unable to articulate the reason. Here, too, much insight can be derived from studies which emphasize this precise aspect (e.g., R. Alter, *The Art of Biblical Narrative;*

L. Alonso Schökel, *Estudios de Poética Hebrea* [Barcelona, 1963]. M. L. Fishbane, *Biblical Narrative in Ancient Israel* [NY, 1985]; G. Rendsburg, *The Redaction of Genesis* [Winona Lake, 1986]; D. Robertson, *The Old Testament and the Literary Critic* [Phl, 1977]; M. Sternberg, *The Poetics of Biblical Narrative* [Bloomington, 1985]; among the older critics von Rad displayed great literary sensitivity).

13 (b) CANONICAL APPROACH. This view has been urged by B. Childs (*CIOTS* 109–35). He proposes that the interpretation of a biblical book should be worked out from its canonical shape, the final form that the Hebr text came to have about the beginning of the Christian era. In the case of the Pentateuch, the role of Moses is clearly normative by reason of the way he is presented as mediator; all the legislation is attributed to him. One cannot speak of authorship in the proper sense, but Mosaic authority has a theological function that should not be neglected in assessing the Torah. Childs understands the Torah as expressing the will of God to the covenant people, and thus as constitutive of the covenant relationship. It is a "gift of God," which also contains promise and threat (*Old Testament Theology in a Canonical Context* [Phl, 1985] 56–57).

This holistic point of view sidesteps such issues as the theology of the Yahwist (which has been incorporated into a larger message), in favor of an understanding of the Torah that became characteristic of the postexilic community. This is not law in a legalistic sense, but law as a communication of the divine will, in which the people find their joy, as Pss 19 and 119 attest and as witnessed in the later Jewish feast, *śimḥat tôrâ* (lit., "joy of the Torah").

While this approach is a welcome change from the fragmentation of the Pentateuch into hypothetical sources and traditions, it is not to be considered an exhaustive hermeneutical move. Historical criticism has revealed tensions, developments, and dynamic changes within the history of Israel, as reflected in the formation of the Pentateuch; levels of meaning buried in the text are not to be neglected in favor of a final meaning, however significant this is in itself.

14 (V) **The Theological Significance of the Pentateuch.** It is obvious that the Torah contains the foundational events and theology of the people of God. Moreover, it is not simply a theology that emerged in the Mosaic period. It is a crystallization of early and late theological views concerning the Lord and the people. Whatever be the precise solution to the origins of the Pentateuch, the recognition of various strands or traditions contributes much to a dynamic understanding of its theology. The deuteronomic view of the divine presence (the "Name" theology) is not the same as that of the Priestly tradition ("glory"). There is no need to oppose the two views; they complement each other in their approach to mystery. Here only a summary of the overall theological significance of the Pentateuch can be provided (→ OT Thought, 77:3–98).

The primeval history (Gen 1–11) marks a significant beginning in that it underscores Israel's own understanding of itself against the background of world history. The essential goodness of creation and the dramatic presentation of human disobedience are the backdrop for the divine initiative in the call of Abraham. The promise to this patriarch (Gen 12:1–3) undergirds the patriarchal narratives. Various elements (promise of a son, many descendants, a land, etc.; cf. 12:7; 15; 16:10; 17; 22:16–18; 24:7; 26:3–5,24; 28:15; 31:3; 32:10–13 [9–12]) become explicit in the reiteration of promises to the three "fathers" (cf. C. Westermann, *The Promises to the Fathers* [Phl, 1980]). The promises thus lend a distinctive stamp to the patriarchal narratives. At the same time Gen links up with Exod, when in Gen 50:24 (cf. Exod 33:1!) the dying Joseph indicates that the Lord will lead "the sons of Israel" out of Egypt into the land promised to the fathers. The references in Exod to the patriarchs and to the "god of your fathers" (Exod 3:6,16) confirm the continuity of Gen–Exod.

The deliverance from Egyptian bondage (cf. Exod 15:1–18; Deut 26:5–9) issues in the basic relationship of God and the people at Sinai. They are chosen, because they are loved (Deut 7:8), to be a holy nation (Exod 19:8), and their response is described in the Decalogue and the various law codes, and the entire Priestly legislation, which extends through Exod 25–Lev–Num 10. The Christian, in particular, might underestimate the importance of this lengthy section. Even if many prescriptions are not considered to be binding today (and what is the hermeneutical move here?), the P tradition is at the core of the Torah. Everything depends on the presence of God among the people — a presence that calls for holiness (conceived and put into practice in various laws and rituals), "because I the Lord your God am holy" (Lev 19:2). The phrase, "I am the Lord" thunders repeatedly in Lev 19 to call Israel to attention to the Holy. In Lev 26, punishment is proclaimed, but the covenant with the patriarchs cannot be wiped out (26:42–45).

The P tradition continues into Num 1–10 with its emphasis on the cult. Rendtorff (*Old Testament* 147) remarks that the cultic legislation "is as it were a delaying factor: it gives all the regulations which the Israelites need to be able to travel through the wilderness with the sanctuary in their midst as the people set apart for YHWH and made holy." The instruction to Moses "in the plains of Moab" (Num 33:50–56) is strongly deuteronomic, as it prepares for the discourses of Moses (Deut 1:1–4:43; 5:1–28:69; 29:1–30:20). Deuteronomy is a document of revival, as the discovery of the "Book of the Law" in 1 Kgs 22:8 (cf. Deut 30:10; 31:26), perhaps its first written expression, attests. The intensity of its language matches the emphasis on election and covenant theology which pervades it. Israel was to hear the eternal "today" at every moment of crisis in its life.

The marvel of the Pentateuch is that it is so many things at once: Torah, or the will of God for Israel; promise, or an adumbration of the future of the people of God; cult, or the way to worship the Holy One; a story of human rebellion and divine redemption; a call to attend to the origins of the Judeo-Christian tradition.

2

GENESIS

Richard J. Clifford, S.J.   Roland E. Murphy, O.Carm. *

BIBLIOGRAPHY

1   Anderson, B. W. (ed.), *Creation in the Old Testament* (IRT 6; Phl, 1984). Blum, E., *Die Komposition der Vätergeschichte* (WMANT 57; Neukirchen, 1984). Brueggemann, W., *Genesis* (Atlanta, 1982). Coats, G., *Genesis* (FOTL 1; GR, 1983). Cassuto, U., *A Commentary on the Book of Genesis* (2 vols.; Jerusalem, 1961, 1964). De Vaux, *EHI* 161–287. Driver, S. R., *The Book of Genesis* (10th ed; London, 1916). Fokkelman, J. P., *Narrative Art in Genesis* (Amsterdam, 1975). Gunkel, H., *Genesis* (HKAT 1.1; 3d ed.; Göttingen, 1910). Heidel, A., *The Babylonian Genesis* (Chicago, 1951). Jacob, B., *Genesis* (NY, 1974). Mazar, B. (ed.), "Patriarchs," *WHJP* 2. Noth, M., *A History of Pentateuchal Traditions* (EC, 1972). Rendsburg, G., *The Redaction of Genesis* (Winona Lake, 1986). Sarna, N. M., *Understanding Genesis* (NY, 1970). Skinner, J., *Genesis* (ICC; Edinburgh, 1930). Speiser, E. A., *Genesis* (AB 1; GC, 1964). Thompson, T. L., *The Historicity of the Patriarchal Narratives* (BZAW 133; Berlin, 1974). Van Seters, J., *Abraham in History and Tradition* (New Haven, 1975). Vawter, B., *On Genesis* (GC, 1977). Von Rad, G., *Genesis* (OTL; rev. ed.; Phl, 1972). Westermann, C., *Genesis 1–11, Genesis 12–36, Genesis 37–50* (Minneapolis, 1984–86). Attention is called to the comprehensive bibliographies contained in the commentary of C. Westermann, which are the fruit of the University of Heidelberg Genesis-Research Institute.

INTRODUCTION

2   (I) Title and Structure. Gen is the first book of the Pentateuch, a five-section compilation of diverse traditions of varied age, given its final editing in the 6th cent. BC. The Eng title is from the LXX title, which is derived from the Greek of 5:1, "this is the record of the generation (genitive of *genēsis*) of Adam." The Hebr title *bĕrē'šît* is simply the first word of the scroll, the ancient way of naming scrolls.

Gen is concerned with origins—of the world of human beings, of Israel in its ancestors. The time of the origin of a reality is a privileged moment in the ancient Near East; the original intention of Fate and the gods is clearer then than at other times. In the beginning the impress of the creating gods upon a thing is still fresh and discernible. In Mesopotamian culture, evidently the model for most of the stories in Gen 1–11, scribes explored beginnings through stories and cosmogonies, not through abstract reasoning. Most of the extant Mesopotamian cosmogonies are brief, but there are several extended compositions that collect accounts of origins: the Gilgamesh Epic, *Enuma Elish,* and the Atrahasis story. The latter is the most relevant for Gen 1–11, for it displays the same basic plot as Gen 2–9. Atrahasis begins in

the heavens with a rebellion of the lower-class gods against the higher class, which is resolved by the creation of human beings to do the maintenance the rebels refused to do. The human race then offends the gods by its explosive spread and resulting noise. (Whether the "noise" is a moral fault is disputed.) By a succession of plagues culminating in a great flood that wipes out everyone except Utnapishtim, a divine favorite, the gods finally put an end to the disturbance. From the surviving man a fresh beginning is made, this time with inbuilt safeguards against the untrammeled population growth that led to disaster. The similarity of the Atrahasis plot to Gen 2–9 is clear; equally clear is the biblical nuance in the details (see comment on chaps. 6–9). The biblical writers have produced a version of a common Mesopotamian story of the origins of the populated world, exploring major questions about God and humanity through narrative. The ancient East had a tolerance for versions, for different stories of the same event. Successive editions of the Gilgamesh Epic and of *Enuma Elish,* as well as the Bible's telling of the exodus–conquest differently in the prose passages of the Pentateuch and in the poetry of many psalms, illustrate the tolerance. The J and E

---

* The introduction and comment on 1:1–25:18 are by R. J. Clifford; the comment on 25:19–50:26 is by R. E. Murphy.

versions of the old national story are another example. Gen 2–9 seems to be introduced by Gen 1 and carried forward by Gen 10–11 (see comment on chaps. 10–11). Gen 1–11 then is a single story, an unusually sustained "philosophical" and "theological" explanation of the human race—its relation to God, its institutions (marriage, languages, ethnic and national divisions, metal working, animal husbandry, etc.), its flaws, its destiny—and of God and God's justice and abiding fidelity to the race. Modern readers, who are not used to narrative as the vehicle of serious thought, often find it difficult to appreciate the profundity and abiding relevance of these chapters. Some readers even end up concentrating their energies in defending a "literal interpretation" of esp. chaps. 1–3 against modern evolutionary theory, something that the ancient authors of Gen, with their tolerance of versions, would never have done.

It is noteworthy that Israel's Bible begins with an extended look at the world prior to Israel (Israel's ancestor Eber is mentioned only fleetingly in 10:21,25) instead of assuming that the world began when it came to be. Israel, however, saw itself as distinct from the nations, a people dwelling apart, not reckoned among the nations (Num 23:9).

The second half of Gen, 11:27–50:26, tells of Israel's origins in its ancestors. Abraham and Sarah (11:27–25:18) labor under the same divine imperatives as the nations—to continue in existence through their progeny and to possess their land (Gen 1:26–28). Their way is different, however: by direct relationship to their God in trust. The double promise of progeny and land is repeated in the story of Jacob and his sons (25:19–36:43), but the emphasis falls rather on the transmission of the blessing of the firstborn and the filling out of the number of sons to 12, the number of the Israelite tribes. It is significant that Jacob, the father of the 12, is called Israel (32:28; 35:10). The third complex of stories concerns the 12 brothers with the spotlight on Joseph (37:1–50:26). The ancient promise is repeated, but the real interest is the relationships of the brothers to each other and to Joseph, their leader-savior. How will this one family, torn by strife, maintain its unity in an alien land and relate to its chosen leader, Joseph? Psychological and family observations, not unexpectedly, mark the story. The ancestral stories adumbrate themes of later biblical literature: living with a just God's promise of increase and of land, the relations of the tribes, the relation of the leader to his people, Israel in Egypt. The question of the historicity of the ancestral stories was raised more than a century ago, and many diverse answers have been given to the question. The position taken in this commentary is that authentic stories of 2d-millennium ancestors have been revised and added to in the long course of their transmission; recovery of the "original" stories is impossible because of the lack of extrabiblical sources.

The final stage in the long process of editing seems to have been in the exile of the 6th cent., when many of Israel's venerable traditions were given final editions. The main themes of the stories had long been clearly stamped, but it was possible to underscore certain themes for the exiled population. Exilic concerns appear: the constant emphasis on the divine intent that each nation continue in existence through progeny and possession of land; the insistence that Israel in its ancestors will receive progeny and land differently from the nations; and the emphasis on God's eternal covenant with Abraham, which is like the eternal covenant with David.

3   (II) Outline.   Gen is not a random collection of colorful episodes; it is a consciously planned narrative

in which the major segments, Gen 1:1–11:26 and 11:27–50:26, are set in deliberate parallel, and in which the components of each segment artistically build up the major segments. Gen 1:11–11:26 describes the origin of the nations, showing how God created the world, a concept that in Gen means the structured community of men and women, acting freely to fulfill their divine destiny to fill the world and possess their land. In parallel but in contrast to the nations, Gen 11:27–50:26 describes the origin of Israel (in the person of ancestors), showing how God created Israel, through fulfilling for the ancestors the human destiny of progeny and land. There are three blocks of traditions in the second segment: (A) Abraham and Sarah (11:27–25:18); (B) Jacob and his sons (25:19–36:43); and (C) Joseph and his brothers (37:1–50:26).

The stories have been edited for different generations—a process that is almost impossible to describe except in general terms. J and E were most probably reductions of an originally oral epic to a written prose form. Even the written forms seem to have been supplemented. Because of the editorial complexity, this commentary does not press the investigation into sources, preferring instead simply to list the standard attributions of sources, J, E, and P. It was P, the final editor (although some postulate a later redactor), who seems to have organized the material into large blocks by the formula, "these are the generations of . . ." (Hebr *tôlĕdôt*, lit., "begettings," but the precise nuance is disputed). It introduces traditional material. The formula occurs five times in the primeval history (2:4; 5:1; 6:9; 10:1; 11:10) and five times in the origin of Israel (11:27; 25:12; 25:19; 36:1 [= v 11]; 37:2). The formula serves as a general guide through the stories.

(I) The Story of the Nations (1:1–11:26)
   (A) Preamble: Creation of the World (1:1–2:3)
   (B) The Creation of the Man and the Woman, Their Offspring, and the Spread of Civilization (2:4–4:26)
      (a) Creation of the Man and the Woman (2:4–3:24)
      (b) Cain's Murder of Abel (4:1–16)
      (c) Cain's Descendants and the Invention of Culture (4:17–24)
      (d) Seth and the Introduction of Worship (4:25–26)
   (C) The Pre-flood Generations (5:1–6:8)
      (a) Genealogy from Adam to Noah (5:1–32)
      (b) Marriage of Divine Beings with Women (6:1–8)
   (D) The Flood and the Renewed Blessing (6:9–9:29)
      (a) The Flood (6:9–9:17)
      (b) The Character of the Sons of Noah (9:18–29)
   (E) The Populating of the World and the Prideful City (10:1–11:9)
      (a) Noah's Descendants Become Landed Peoples (10:1–31)
      (b) The Prideful City with the Tower (10:32–11:9)
   (F) Genealogy from Shem to Terah (11:10–26)
(II) The Story of the Ancestors of Israel (11:27–50:26)
   (A) The Story of Abraham and Sarah (11:27–25:18)
      (a) The Family of Terah in Haran (11:27–32)
      (b) Abraham Is Called to Journey to Canaan and Is Blessed (12:1–9)
      (c) Abraham and Sarah in Danger in Egypt (12:10–13:1)
      (d) Abraham and Lot Go Their Separate Ways (13:2–18)
      (e) Abraham Defeats the Kings and Rescues Lot (14:1–24)
      (f) God Promises Abraham a Son and Land (15:1–21)
      (g) Hagar Bears Abraham a Son (16:1–16)
      (h) God's Covenant with Abraham (17:1–27)
      (i) The Guests of Abraham and Lot (18:1–19:38)
         (i) Abraham and the three guests (18:1–5)
         (ii) Abraham bargains with God (18:16–33)

COMMENTARY

(I) The Story of the Nations (1:1–11:26).
4   (A) The Preamble: Creation of the World (1:1–2:3 [P]). The account is an obvious unit, though some scholars speculate that separate accounts, e.g., eight creative acts (*Tatbericht*) and six divine commands (*Wortbericht*) have been combined to form the present text. The P formula in 2:4a, "these are the generations of . . . ," introduces 2:4b–4:26; it does not summarize chap. 1 (against many commentators). Elsewhere in Gen it is an introductory formula. 1:1–2:3 serves as a grand preface to more than one segment: it introduces 2:4b–11:26, the origin of the nations; 11:27–50:26, the origin of Israel's ancestors; and indeed the entire Pentateuch. As a preface it highlights the two themes dominating all parts and the whole: the divinely intended increase of peoples and their possession of land.

God creates the world for humans in six days and rests on the seventh, the first week of human history; the week of six work days ending in sabbath observance is thereby hallowed (Exod 31:17). The repetition of the divine command in the execution is characteristic of ancient Near Eastern literature; P uses the convention ("let there be . . ." and "God made/created . . .") here and elsewhere, notably in the building of the tabernacle (commands in Exod 25–31, execution in Exod 35–40).

In structure, the days are arranged thus:

Formless Water and Night (vv 1–2)

1. Light (day/night)	4. Lights in heaven
2. Separation of upper/ lower water	5. Fish/birds from water
3. a. Dry land (earth, seas)	6. a. Animals
b. Plants	b. Humans
7. God rests	

In W Semitic enumerations, the seventh place is often climactic; God's sabbath is therefore the climax of the story, which is primarily about God, not humans. Days 4, 5, and 6 match days 1, 2, and 3: the sun and moon mark day and night; from the waters come forth fish and birds; two things are created on the third and the sixth day, earth and plants, animals and humans.

1–3. *When God began to create heaven and earth — the earth being formless and void, with darkness over the surface of the deep, and a wind of God sweeping over the waters — then God said, "Let there be light," and there was light.* The translation "In the beginning God created the heavens and the earth" has been traditional at least since the 3d cent. BC, when the LXX translated it so, but it is unlikely. The first two Hebr words of v 1 syntactically cannot be so translated. Other biblical and ancient Near Eastern cosmogonies use a "when . . . then" construction, e.g., "*When* Yahweh God made the earth and the heaven — when no plant of the field was yet on earth . . . *— then* Yahweh God formed man from the soil of the earth . . ." (2:4–7); the 2d-millennium Akk creation poem *Enuma Elish* begins "When on high the heavens had not been named, firm ground below had not been called by name, . . . then it was that the gods were found within them" (*ANET* 60–61, lines 1–8). **2.** *formless and void:* Hebr *tōhû wābōhû.* The first word occurs 20 times in the OT, meaning without shape or form so as to be uninhabitable by humans — metaphorically, groundless or unreal. The second word, *bōhû,* occurs 3 times to form an assonant hendiadys with *tōhû. Tōhû,* possibly etymologically related to *tĕhôm,* "the deep," suggests that the earth was entirely covered by water, as in Ps 104:6, "The deep (*tĕhôm*) covered it like a garment," (see R. J. Clifford, *JBL* 100 [1981] 87–89 for the translation); the psalm resembles Gen 1 in its description of the curbing first of the deep and then of the night, so that human life might appear. *with darkness over the surface of the deep:* Two chaotic elements obstruct the emergence of the peopled cosmos — the deep and primordial night. Night is vanquished on the first day by the creation of light, and the deep on the second and third days by the separation of waters and the making of the sea. *and a wind of God sweeping over the waters:* Hebr *rûaḥ* ("air in motion"; hence, "wind," "breath," "spirit") here means wind. In *Enuma Elish,* Anu creates four winds (1.114) and Marduk uses seven additional winds when he battles Tiamat (4.42–47); Baal in the Ugaritic text has wind as one of his companions in war (*ANET* 139). The wind of God sweeping over the waters shows that chaos was never beyond God's control. **3–5.** The first day. Verse 3 is the "then-clause" in the "when–then" construction already noted under 1:1. Light is the first thing created. God names light and darkness "day" and "night," as he names the firmament "heaven," dry land "earth," and the waters "seas"; naming shows God's mastery. God does not destroy darkness, one of the two chaotic forces mentioned in v 2; he relegates it to the nighttime, where it too becomes part of the good world. Day begins with the light; night returns ("and there was evening"). (Jewish feast days, contrary to the calculation of ordinary days, begin in the evening.) God pronounces the light good, beautiful; the phrase will be repeated six times of created elements, climaxing in the seventh climactic occurrence for the whole universe (v 31). The declaration is not a deduction from human experience but a divine declaration that all of creation is good. **6–8.** The second day. God inserts an immense concave plate in the midst of the all-encompassing waters, creating a vast hollow between the upper and the lower waters. The Vg *firmamentum*, "support," translates the LXX literally; both the LXX and the Vg miss the Hebr nuance. The Hebr word is "something hammered out flat," e.g., gold leaf on a wooden statue. Here, and in all the other acts of creation, God first commands, then executes the action.

9–13. The third day. Within the great hollow between the upper and lower waters, God restricts the water to one place, the seas, so that dry land, earth, appears. A second event takes place on the third day: the earth sprouts vegetation. The meaning is probably: let the earth be covered with a fresh green mantle of verdure, seed-bearing plants, and fruit trees with seed-bearing fruit. **11.** *yielding seed according to their own kinds:* Each plant and fruit has inherent power to propagate itself; the phrase has therefore a nuance of procreation. Each species' power to propagate itself explains the sexual differentiation of humans in v 27b. **14–19.** The fourth day, corresponding to the first day. Light has already been created; the sun and the moon are to divide day from night and also to serve for "signs and appointed times," a hendiadys (two nouns for one) for the reckoning of time. **20–23.** The fifth day, corresponding to the second; sea and sky are to bring forth creatures. The seas are to swarm with living creatures, as the earth teemed with vegetative life on the third day. Birds are reckoned as coming from the sea. God creates (Hebr *bārā'*), a word occurring 50 times in the OT, always with God as its subject. **22.** *Be fruitful, increase, and fill the waters of the sea . . . the earth:* God blesses them by empowering them to propagate themselves. The verse anticipates the creation of the human in v 28. **24–32.** The sixth day has two events, corresponding to the two events of the third day. In the first event, the earth is to bring forth animals (distinguished here from birds, who come from the water), cattle, creeping things, and undomesticated beasts. The second event, the creation of the human being, is climactic by its placement and by the large number of verses assigned to it. **26.** The divine intent is expressed by "let us make a human," an echo of the language of the divine assembly; in ancient Near Eastern literature, the gods decided the fate of humankind. The Bible accepts the picture of the assembly, but Yahweh alone makes the decision (Gen 11:3,7; Deut 32:8–9; 1 Kgs 22:19–22; Isa 6; 40:1–11; Job 1–2). The origin of human beings is not simply from the waters on the earth like the plants, fishes/birds, and animals; it is "in our image, according to our likeness." The human is a statue of the deity, not by static being but by action, who will rule over all things previously created (v 26). In the ancient Near East, the king was often called the image of

the deity and was vested with God's authority; royal language is here used for the human. Mesopotamian cosmogonies ordinarily portrayed humans as slaves. Verse 27a repeats the divine command of v 26a. **27b.** *male and female he created them:* This ensures the propagation of humanity, just as the divine making of the plants in v 12, the fishes/birds of v 21, and the animals in v 25, "according to their kinds," ensures the continuance of those groups. Sexual differentiation is the humans' way of continuing in existence.

Verse 28 is tied closely to v 27b, repeating the command already given to the fishes/birds in v 22 to "be fruitful and multiply." *Subdue the earth:* The nuance of the verb is "to master," "to bring forcefully under control." Force is necessary at the beginning to make the untamed land serve humans. Humans nonetheless are to respect the environment; they are not to kill for food but are to treat all life with respect. As the rest of v 28 shows, humans are the pinnacle of the created world; the world is made for man and woman. The imperatives in v 28 are a biblical way of defining essence, like the imperatives in Exod 20:2–17; Lev 19:2; Deut 16:18–20, etc. Plants will suffice for food for humans and animals; there will be no bloodshed. The prohibition is modified in the renewal of creation after the flood (9:2–5) because of the disobedience and violence mysteriously present in the human heart. **31.** All creation *tout ensemble*, not only its component parts, is pronounced "very good," the climactic seventh divine pronouncement. There is no evil, only beauty, in the world that God makes. **2:1–3.** Heaven and earth and "all their host," a word usually used of the heavenly population but here of the denizens of earth as well, are now completed. The vb. "complete" fulfills "when God began" of creation in 1:1. God keeps the sabbath, establishing the divine order that Israel will observe by its sabbath. The day is hallowed because God made it so.

The P account of creation differs from modern scientific conceptions, which typically focus on the formation of the planet in its solar system, and leave out of consideration animate life and human culture. Ancient Near Eastern cosmogonies, on the contrary, are mainly interested in the emergence of a people; "nature" is only the environment for the human community. Ancients frequently imagined creation as a conflict between beings endowed with will, e.g., god(s), and cosmic forces like sea or primordial night. Reports of these conflicts are, not surprisingly, often in the form of narratives that vividly depict the battle and victory, from which emerges a defined human community (see R. J. Clifford, "The Hebrew Scriptures and the Theology of Creation," *TS* 46 [1985] 507–23). Gen 1 stays within the categories of the "science" of its time and attempts to see in those categories divine power and purpose, and the unique place of humans. Conflict between chaotic forces (sea, darkness), which characterizes many other biblical and ancient Near Eastern accounts, is absent. There seems even to be a polemic against such conflict cosmogonies. Creation follows effortlessly from God's mere word. Because Gen 1 is a portrait of what God intends, it is also an eschatological statement. This serene, beautiful world, in which all is ordered to humans, and humans are ordered to God, is how it will be at the end. The stories of human sin, which follow Gen 1, cannot permanently disfigure the original divine intent; God's world will triumph. Rev 21–22, the description of God's new world, appropriately draws on this chapter.

(B) The Creation of the Man and the Woman, Their Offspring, and the Spread of Civilization (2:4–4:26 [P: 2:4a] [J: 2:4b–3:24]).

5   (a) CREATION OF THE MAN AND THE WOMAN

(2:4–3:24 [J]).   The P formula "these are the generations of" in 2:4a introduces the entire complex of 2:4b–4:26. P's own preamble in 1:1–2:3 has already underscored the major themes for the reader in the traditional material thus introduced: God's effortless creating of the human race, and their divinely assigned tasks to continue in existence and take possession of their land. **2:4b–7.** *When Yahweh God made earth and heaven—before there were any shrubs of the field in the earth, before any grass of the field sprouted, for Yahweh God had not sent rain upon the earth and there was no man to till the soil (a flow rose up from the earth to water the whole surface of the earth)—then Yahweh God made the man from the dust of the earth.* For the "when-then" construction, see 1:1–3. *then:* Lit., "in the day." This does not always mean a 24-hour day. *made earth and heaven:* Prepare an environment for the human community; the focus is on people. There were no plants because there was no rain and no human tillers. The double divine name "Yahweh God" occurs only in this chapter; the precise nuance of the double name for God is unclear. According to source criticism, Yahweh is used only by the J source until Exod 3:14, when the E source begins to use it. **6.** *flow:* Sumerian *ID,* Akk *idu,* the water under the earth that wells up in rivers; this water does not apparently fertilize the earth sufficiently for plant life. **7.** The man (*hā᾽ādām*) is made from the earth (*hā᾽ădāmâ*), prompting some scholars to propose the transl. "earth creature" rather than "man," to emphasize that its origin is from the earth and that sexual differentiation does not appear until the creation of woman in v 22 (see P. Trible, *God and the Rhetoric of Sexuality* [Phl, 1978] 72–143).

8–9. There are two trees placed beyond human use— the tree of life and the tree of the knowledge of good and bad. The tree of life appears again at the end of the story (3:22) as a remaining temptation, from which danger God expels the couple. Eating it might have enabled the couple to "live forever," i.e., become gods. The story, however, is concerned with the tree of the knowledge of good and evil. Good and evil is a merism, a literary figure by which totality is expressed by the first and last in a series or by opposites; cf. Ps 139:2, "You know when I sit down and when I stand up," i.e., all my physical movement. "To know" in Hebrew is experiential and relational, not only intellectual. Eating the fruit of the tree, therefore, imparts a mastery of life and an autonomy that is inappropriate to the earth creature, created from dust. The man would cease to be finite and human. **10–14.** The river going forth from Eden to water the garden and thence dividing into the four rivers of the world, may be the "flow" in v 6; in some Ugaritic and Akk texts the high god dwells at the "source of the double deep," i.e., the source of all life-giving waters of the earth. The garden, therefore, is the locale of God. The totality of the world is symbolized by "four," as in the Akk phrase "the four quarters of the earth." The location of Pishon and Havilah in this text is unknown; this verse, Gen 10:7, and 1 Chr 1:9 locate Havilah in Cush in southern Mesopotamia, whereas according to Gen 10:26–29 and 1 Chr 1:20–23, Havilah is a descendant of Shem—therefore, to be located in the east or southeast of Arabia. Gihon is also the name of the spring of Jerusalem (1 Kgs 1:33,38), but here it flows through Cush in southern Mesopotamia. **15–17.** Verse 15 resumes v 8b with the additional remark that the earth creature is to cultivate the garden. A limit is placed on his mastery; he is not to eat of the fruit of the tree of the knowledge of good and bad. **17.** *you shall die:* "To die" here means to be cut off, excluded from community with God, as in Ezek 18 and in other P texts; the man and the woman will be driven from the garden of God, not killed. A different anthropology in early Judaism and Christianity insisted

that God made humans incorruptible (Wis 2:23; Rom 5:12), and from this arose the Christian theological tradition that death is a result of sin. In the ancient Near East, not to die would mean that one would have to become a god since only the gods were immortal.

18–24. 18. God's observation that it is not good for the earth creature to be alone leads to the creating of a helper corresponding to him. Traditional Eng "help-mate" is a corruption of the archaic "helpmeet" = "meet or fitting helper." **19–20.** God brings to the man all animals and birds so that he might name them, a part of his charge to till and to tend the garden. His naming them shows his God-given mastery over the animals; they are for him. In v 20b, the animals do not prove to be suitable companions, a sly understatement that prepares for the creation of woman in vv 21–24. Not from earth but from the man's own self is the woman fashioned, an explanation at once of sexual attraction between men and women and of the phrase "corresponding to him." The deep sleep is from God (cf. 15:12). The man acknowledges the gift of the woman. *This one at last* [in the series of animals brought before him] *is bone of my bone, flesh of my flesh. She shall be called woman, for from man she was taken:* The Hebr pun *᾽iššâ* and *᾽iš* is reproduced in Eng "woman" and "man." In the biblical perspective, the origin of a reality often defines the reality. God made marriage part of the creation.

2:25–3:7. The section begins with 2:25 (against many commentators) since 3:1, "subtle [serpent]," plays on the ostensibly similar Hebr root *᾽ārûm,* "naked" in 2:25; the episode ends in v 7, when the couple's eyes are opened not in wisdom but in shame as they become aware that they are naked. The snake is not Satan, though later traditions so interpreted it (e.g., Wis 2:24). He is simply a mischievous creature made by God, dramatically necessary to awaken in the woman a desire to eat of the forbidden fruit; he recedes into the background when his narrative function is accomplished. The snake's question in v 1b and the woman's answer in vv 2–3 are both inaccurate interpretations of the originally simple divine command in 2:16–17. **5.** *like divine beings knowing good and bad: Elohim,* the ordinary name for God in the OT, means "divine beings" when it is used with a pl. vb., as here. At the snake's deceptive assurance, the woman eats and persuades her husband to eat. Their innocence lost through disobedience, they make primitive loincloths. **8–19.** God appears at the afternoon breeze; their sin is not hid from God, to whom they are accountable. The man blames the woman (in ironic contrast to 2:23) and the woman blames the snake; just punishment will be meted out according to the order of sinning. **14–15.** The snake is cursed, condemned to crawl on its belly, eat dirt, and be forever the enemy of the woman whom he deceived and of her offspring. *he shall strike your head:* "He" refers to offspring, which is masc. in Hebrew. Christian tradition has sometimes referred it to Christ, but the literal reference is to the human descendants of Eve, who will regard snakes as enemies. **16.** Childbearing, a constituent part of woman's nature, will be attended with great pain, symbolizing the loss of original ease with oneself and one's environment. Woman's original equality with her "correspondent," the man, is part of the loss, suggesting that the subordinate place of woman in Israelite society was not intended by God, but is rather a result of human sin (Trible, *Rhetoric of Sexuality* 126–28). **12–19.** The punishment of the man, the central actor in the story, is climactic by its third position in the series and by its length. The man is not cursed, but the earth is cursed because of the man's misdeed; his tilling and tending of it will be laborious. **18.** Thorns and thistles will grow on the ground but man must still find his sustenance therefrom, enduring a hard life till he returns to the earth whence he came. **20–21.** Punishment is not the last word. In a subtle but significant gesture, the man gives another name to his wife (cf. 2:23): Eve, mother of the living. The couple's sin has not altered the divine intent to make them fruitful. God's clothing them is another conciliatory sign, an accommodation to human limitations. **22–24.** In a wonderfully ironic speech, God notes the harm done by eating the forbidden fruit and removes the couple from the occasion of the further sin of eating of the tree of life. The couple is sent out of the garden to find their way in the ordinary world.

6   (b) CAIN'S MURDER OF ABEL (4:1–16 [J]). The entire chapter, though of diverse traditions, is now a unity: the vb. "to know" introduces sections within it, vv 1–2, 9–16, 17–22, and 25–26. The number seven recurs in vv 15 and 24; Lamech is the seventh in the generation, and several words occur seven times ("Abel," "brother," "name") or 14 times ("Cain"). The chapter also continues the preceding story; disobedience and punishment continue among the children of the man and the woman. The divine names in chaps. 2–4 appear 70 times (Elohim 40 times, Yahweh Elohim 20 times, Yahweh 10 times), the 70th ("at that time people began to call on the name of Yahweh") occurring in the final verse, 4:26 (Cassuto, *Genesis* 1. 178–96).

1–2. The birth of the brothers. *knew:* Connotes concrete experience and can express sexual relations. *I have begotten a man with the help of Yahweh:* Eve exults in her procreative power given by Yahweh. There is a play on the name Cain, something like "I have gained Cain" (*NJV*); the vb. means "to create," "to beget." **2.** *she then bore Abel:* The younger son, often preferred to the older brother in biblical narrative. Abel's name needs no pun like Cain's to explain it; the significance of "(transitory) breath," is sufficiently clear. **3–8.** The murder. **4–5.** *the choice firstlings of his flock:* A hendiadys, lit., "the firstborn of his flock and from their fat parts." Most commentators believe Abel's offering was the choice part and Cain's was not, but the emphasis falls on Yahweh's inscrutable acceptance of one and not the other. **7.** *If you act rightly, acceptance [lit., lifting], but if you do not act rightly, sin is a croucher at the door [i.e., in your path]. Its intent is directed toward you, but you are to master it:* As the literal transl. shows, Yahweh's response to the distressed (not "angry") Cain is extremely difficult to understand and may be corrupt; all transls. are uncertain. **8.** *let us go into the field:* I.e., unfrequented country; this shows that Cain's murder was premeditated. The phrase has dropped out of the MT by haplography but is preserved by the ancient versions. Cain's reaction to God's circumscribing command is to hate his favored brother. **9.** Yahweh confronts Cain, and Cain disavows Abel. **10–12.** *Hark, your brother's blood cries out to me from the ground. Now you are cursed from the ground:* The earth, which drank his brother's blood, becomes the instrument of the punishment by not yielding its fruit and by being the place on which Cain wanders. Cain will be a "ceaseless wanderer" (hendiadys; lit., "a fugitive and a wanderer"). **13–15.** When Cain pleads that the effects of his sin are unbearable, God promises protection (implied in the literal "therefore") and gives him a mark. It is one of several gestures in the ✓ Bible against the practice of blood vengeance. **16.** Cain settles in the land of Nod, a play on Hebr *nād*, the participle of "to wander" of v 12.

7   (c) CAIN'S DESCENDANTS AND THE INVENTION OF CULTURE (4:17–24 [J]). **17.** *Cain knew his wife:* Shows the continuance of the line despite human sin. *she gave birth to Enoch and he built a city and named it after his son:* Enoch at the end of the MT verse seems to be a gloss; Enoch rather is the builder and Irad is the son after whom

the city is named. Irad corresponds to Mesopotamian Eridu, the first antediluvian city according to the Sumerian King List (*ANET* 265). **18.** Another Mesopotamian tradition appearing here is the seven *apkallu*'s, the seven sages prior to the flood, who were believed to have founded the elements of culture, e.g., writing, artistic skill, etc. There are seven generations in the Cainite genealogy. Echoes of a similar Canaanite and Phoenician tradition are preserved in Philo Byblos. The names in chap. 4 are the same as or variants of those in chap. 5: Cain/Kenan; Enoch/Enoch; Irad/Jared; Mehuyael/Mahalalel; Methushael/Methusalah; Lamech/Lamech. Segmented genealogies in the ancient East were generally not for conveying historical information but for determining domestic, politico-jural, and religious matters. In chap. 4, the genealogies attribute the origin of various aspects of civilization to figures of the pre-flood period, as in Mesopotamian lore, and also to show that descendants of Cain inherit the effects of the curse. Sin is increasing, preparing for the flood (see R. R. Wilson, *Genealogy and History in the Biblical World* [New Haven, 1977] 138–58). **19–22.** Lamech takes two wives, by whom he has the three sons who are the seventh in the line (→ 10 below) and the actual founders of culture. The sons' names rhyme—Jabal, Jubal, and Tubal-Cain. **23–24.** Lamech celebrates his own tendency toward violence, a sign that Cain's violence has been transmitted to his offspring. Though God's blessing of progeny is still effective, humans have polluted it, a pointer to the coming judgment in the flood.

8   (d) SETH AND THE INTRODUCTION OF WORSHIP (4:25–26 [J]). Adam and Eve give birth to another son in place of the short-lived Abel, Seth (= "to [re]place"). **26b.** *people began to call upon the name of Yahweh:* The most important cultural institution of civilization, authentic worship, was not founded by a son of the wrathful Cain, but by the replacement of the favored Abel. According to the E source, the name of Yahweh was revealed first to Moses at Sinai (Exod 3:13–15); P also places the revelation of the name in Moses' time (Exod 6:2–8).

9   (C) **The Pre-flood Generations (5:1–6:8 [P: 1–32] [J: 6:1–8]).** The P formula in 5:1, "this is the document of the generations of Adam," introduces not just the 10-member genealogy of chap. 5 (the view of nearly all commentators) but also 6:1–8 (the view of a minority). Arguments that it introduces the whole section are: the next instance of the formula in 6:9 begins a new section, the flood; "but Noah found favor in the eyes of the Lord" (6:8) sums up both the genealogy and 6:1–8; 6:5–8 refers back in several words and phrases to 5:1–2 (an instance of the device of *inclusio* by which the end of a section refers back to its beginning); the related themes of the transmission of the image of God and blessing in Adam through firstborn sons ending in Noah (and his sons), and of the general increase of the human community (Cassuto, *Genesis* 1. 249–50). The P introductory formula introduces J and E material as well as P material.

10   (a) THE GENEALOGY FROM ADAM TO NOAH (5:1–32 [P]). The 10-member linear genealogy ending in a group of three "executive" persons who act—Shem, Ham, and Japheth—resembles the seven-member linear genealogy of 4:17–22, which also ends in three executives—Jabal, Jubal, and Tubal-Cain. P seems to have used a tradition of ancestors similar to J's. See comment on 4:18. Unlike the genealogy of chap. 4, which reflects the tradition of the seven pre-flood *apkallu*'s or culture founders of Mesopotamia and Phoenicia, chap. 5 reflects the tradition of 10 kings in some Mesopotamian lists. The pre-flood list of Sumerian kings was generally eight (*ANET* 265), but lists of kings later became standardized to 10, a number that the P writer adopts

(Westermann, *Genesis 1–11* 347–51). Some Mesopotamian lists attempt to correlate the seven sages and 10 kings, even to the point of resemblance of names; the similar names in the genealogies of chaps. 4 and 5 may be imitating this feature (Wilson, *Genealogy and History* 149–52, 165–66). The great ages of the pre-flood firstborn sons resemble the ages of the pre-flood kings in the Sumerian King List, e.g., Alulim ruled 28,900 years and Alalgar ruled 36,000 years, whereas after the flood kings ruled for a much shorter time, e.g., 200 years, 960 years (*ANET* 265–66). All of the biblical ages, however, with the exception of the seventh (Enoch) and the ninth (Lamech) generations, are about 900 years, short of the divine "day" of 1,000 years (Ps 90:4). The life-spans are lowered to 120 years in 6:3 ("for he is flesh"), but the precise meaning is uncertain. The great ages express the ancient Near Eastern view that "there were giants in those days," that life was on a larger scale in the beginning than now. A different numeration is found in the LXX and in the Samaritan Pentateuch.

The purpose of the J genealogies in 4:17–22 and vv 25–26 and that of the P genealogy in chap. 5 differ. In J's Cainite genealogy, the generations transmit the arrogance of Cain, as is proved by Lamech's bloodthirsty cry (4:23–24). The fresh genealogy in 4:25–26 suggests, however, a curse-free line through Seth. The P genealogy in 5:1–2 demonstrates that the image of God and the blessing of progeny and land given to humanity in 1:26–28 was successfully transmitted through the firstborn sons down to Noah (and his sons), who is saved by the ark from the flood inflicted on the other "sons and daughters." The P genealogy shows the procreative gift of Gen 1:26–28 being exercised, just as chap. 10 will show people exercising their God-given right to land. The two genealogies, juxtaposed, illustrate both the spreading effect of human sin and God's undiminished commitment to the blessing.

5:1–5. 1. *This is the record of the generations of Adam:* Hebr *tôlĕdôt,* lit., "begettings" (only in P in the Pentateuch), is used here in its literal sense of descendants. **1b–2.** A reprise of 1:26–28. Humans were made in the image of God, and made male and female to procreate. **3.** Adam, created in the likeness of God, is able to transmit that likeness since he begets his firstborn in his own likeness and names Seth, just as God named him. **6–31.** The transmission of the divine image is through the firstborn son. The nine firstborns—Seth, Enosh, Kenan, Mahalalel, Jared, Enosh, Methuselah, Lamech, and Noah—are all described according to a fixed scheme: the age of the son before begetting his firstborn, the number of years he lived after that birth, his begetting other sons and daughters, his total life-span, and his death. Exceptions to the scheme are the seventh generation, Enoch, and the ninth, Lamech. **22.** Enoch "walked with God," i.e., lived righteously. **24.** *he was no more for God took him:* Enoch did not die like the others, but was "taken (up)" because of his righteousness. In the period from *ca.* 300 BC to AD 300, a vast extrabiblical Enoch literature developed, which celebrated his heavenly secrets (→ Apocrypha, 67:7–15). About this storied figure, the Bible gives us only a single statement. "God took him" seems deliberately elusive, like the mysterious use of the word "took" in Pss 49:15 and 73:24 and the removal of Elijah in 1 Kgs 2:11. Enoch prefigures Noah, who also "walked with God." **28–29.** Lamech fathers Noah and gives him a name. *he will give us relief* [Hebr *niḥam*] *from our work:* The Hebr vb. upon which the pun is based is not the expected *nûaḥ,* "to rest," the actual root of Noah's name. **29.** Apparently a citation of 3:17, for "Yahweh" is not otherwise used by P until Exod 6:2. Noah begets his firstborn son, Shem, ancestor of the Semites, and two other sons, Ham and Japheth. Shem is technically the firstborn, but the image of God seems to be transmitted to all three, founders of the three great races of the author's day. The three will be executives, actors, like the three at the end of the Cainite genealogy (4:22).

11 (b) MARRIAGE OF DIVINE BEINGS WITH WOMEN (6:1–8 [J]). For reasons to regard the section as part of 5:1–32, → 9 above. The J material in 6:1–8 restates the sin that will bring on the flood. **2.** *divine beings:* lit., "sons of god," i.e., members of the class of divine beings, common in religious texts of Canaan. The Bible sometimes borrowed traditional descriptions of the heavenly world without comment (cf. Deut 32:8–9 LXX; 1 Kgs 22:19–23; Job 1–2; Ps 29). The divine beings, attracted by the women's beauty, married them and sired giant offspring, the "mighty men of old" (v 4b). Comparable literatures speak of semidivine heroes of old. Though *human* sin is not expressly mentioned in vv 1–2, the divine judgment in v 3 presumes that there was actually sin. **3.** The phrase is a divine soliloquy like 3:22, by which a limit is put on humans after their rebellion (Westermann, *Genesis 1–11* 374). As in chaps. 2–3, man and woman attempt to be like gods, refusing the obedience due as finite human beings. Though the divine beings take the initiative as powerful beings, the actions of all parties constitute the breaking of the boundary between the human and the divine. Many scholars suggest that v 2 alludes to a longer myth about marriages between heavenly beings and human wives, which produced the pre-flood race of giants. The Bible is reticent about stories of the "gods"; here it alludes to such a story only to show that the mixing of heaven and earth, which had been forbidden to the first man and woman in the garden by the prohibition against eating of the tree of the knowledge of good and bad, and of the tree of life (3:22–24), is taboo. Such heavenly–earthly unions cause God to limit further the age of human beings because "he is flesh." 120 years, in comparison with the great ages of the list of ancestors in chap. 5, is a severe limit upon humans. **4.** The verse seems overloaded and confused. *the divine beings went into the daughters of men and bore [sons] to them . . . :* Perhaps continues directly v 2; v 4a, about the Nephilim, seems to be an ancient variant of "the mighty men of old" at the end of v 4. *the Nephilim:* "The fallen ones [i.e., from heaven]" are the race of giants mentioned in Num 13:33 as the giant preconquest inhabitants of Canaan; they are the children of unholy unions. The ancient inhabitants of Canaan were frequently referred to as giants (Deut 2:10–11,20–21; 3:11; Josh 12:4; 17:15). Here the fabled inhabitants are devalued as the offspring of arrogant unions.

5–8. God judges the human community. In the comparable Akk epic, Atrahasis, the gods are divided on whether to destroy humanity by plague and flood. In monotheistic Israel, the fateful decision is made by Yahweh, who is also the creator. The conflict between saving and destroying is played out within the one God, Yahweh. Some of the divine anguish is caught in the "regret" (vv 6–7) and in the Lord's looking on Noah with favor (v 8). The section looks backward to the incessant sins of the race (chaps. 3; 4; 6:1–4) and forward to the new beginning in Noah (chap. 9). It sums up the first and prepares for the flood, which is at once a destruction and a new beginning. **5.** In 1:1–2:3 God saw the beauty of the world he made, seven times pronouncing it good; now he looks on human wickedness and regrets that he made the world. *every plan devised by his mind (NJV):* Idiomatic English for the dense Hebr phrase. **7.** *I will wipe out:* A severe way of describing what God is about to do; in Judg 21:17 it is used of obliterating an entire tribe from

Israel. The rest of v 7 details the beautifully wrought creation that God is about to destroy. **8.** Like Enoch (5:21–24), who stood out from the others, Noah stands out amid the wicked race. The somber reflection and judgment end on a note of hope.

12   (D) The Flood and the Renewed Blessing (6:9–9:29).

(a) THE FLOOD (6:9–9:17 [P: 6:9–22; 7:6,11, 13–16a,17a,18–21,24; 8:1,2a,3b–5,7,13a,14–19; 9:1–17] [J: 7:1–5,7–10,12,16b,17b,22–23; 8:2b–3a,6,8–12,13b, 20–22]). The third instance of the *tôlēdôt* formula here introduces the longest of the five segments of the primeval history. This segment tells of the great flood wiping out all flesh except the righteous Noah and his family and the animals with him in the ark. The story as it now stands is coherent but has drawn on a variety of traditions; P and J material can easily be identified. According to P, two pairs of every animal came to the ark, whereas in J Noah takes seven pairs of clean animals and two pairs of unclean animals. For P the waters above and below the earth, confined there in the beginning (1:6–10), burst upon the earth (7:11), whereas in J the floodwaters were the rains lasting 40 days and nights (7:12). P has supplemented traditional material with a narrative of his own; usually P allows J (and E) to stand on their own. Despite the visibility of the old traditions, the redactor has composed an artistic unity.

Most scholars do not include "Noah's drunkenness" (9:20–29; a better title is "the character of Noah's sons"), in the flood account, preferring to include it with the settling of the three sons' descendants in chap. 10. It seems best, however, to place it with the present narrative, both because of its falling under the P rubric of 6:9 and because it limns the character of the three sons of Noah.

The flood (6:9–9:17): Traditions of a widespread flood are found among many peoples all over the world. Some of these traditions echo the biblical flood but many do not (Westermann, *Genesis 1–11* 398–406). The biblical account is within the ancient Near Eastern tradition, esp. as attested in Mesopotamian literature. The theme of the flood that destroys humankind does not seem to belong to the main body of Sumerian traditions. The preface, added to the Sumerian King List (*ANET* 265), contains the phrase "after the flood had swept over (the earth)." The phrase or a variant occurs in a hymn of Ishme-Dagan (1953–1935) and in another text of the same period. The extant bottom third of a Sumerian tablet, probably near in date to the texts just mentioned, tells of the creation of five cities, the singling out of Ziusudra (the Sumerian equivalent of Akk Utnapishtim and the biblical Noah) to build a boat to escape the flood, and his elevation to eternal life among the gods (*ANET* 42–44; M. Civil, in W. G. Lambert and A. R. Millard, *Atrahasis: The Babylonian Story of the Flood* [Oxford 1969] 138–45). In Akk literature there appear to have been two versions of the flood. The shorter one, in which the gods decree the flood and then deify the human survivor Utnapishtim (or Ziusudra or Atrahasis), is found in tablet XI of the Gilgamesh Epic and in a small Akk fragment found at Ugarit (*Ugaritica V* 167 = RS 22.421 of *ca.* 14th cent.). The latter tablet is the only record of the Mesopotamian flood tradition found outside Mesopotamia. The flood account in Gilgamesh was probably not part of the Old Babylonian version but was added by the editor of the standard Babylonian or Nineveh recension (*ca.* 1300–1200). A digest of this tradition is found in the writings of the 4th-cent. BC Babylonian priest Berossus (Lambert and Millard, *Atrahasis* 134–37). The longer version, which includes punishment of the rebellious gods and

the creation of humans to do their work, several plagues preceding the flood, and the refounding of civilization after the flood, is preserved only in the three tablets of the Atrahasis epic. The longer version has influenced the biblical account.

Though fragments had long been known, it was only in 1969 that W. G. Lambert and A. R. Millard arranged the tablets properly and published them (*Atrahasis*). In the longer version, the flood story is prefaced by the story of the rebellion of the lower class Igigi-gods against the seven great Anunnaki-gods (among whom is Anu, Enlil, and Enki), who had forced them to take care for the universe for them. The Igigi go on strike, forcing the Anunnaki to create humans to do the menial work the Igigi refused to do any longer. The human being is created from clay mixed with the blood and spirit of the slain chief rebel god. "Twelve hundred years had not passed when the land extended and the people multiplied. The land was bellowing like a bull, the god [Enlil] got disturbed with their uproar." Exactly what the noise (Akk *rigmu*) signifies in the epic is contested. Most scholars see it as some kind of moral fault, but W. L. Moran has argued persuasively that it is simply noise, the meaning of *rigmu* elsewhere. For him, the noise is the tumult of the rapidly spreading human race, a sign that the gods did not plan wisely in creating humans (*Bib* 52 [1971] 51–61; "Some Considerations of Form and Interpretation in *Atrahasis*," *Language, Literature, and History* [Fest. E. Reiner; ed. F. Rochberg-Halton; AOS 67; New Haven, 1987] 245–55). At any rate, the gods, led by Enlil, attempt to wipe out the race by a series of three plagues, each one cleverly thwarted by Enki, who tells his favorite Atrahasis the secret of escaping it. At length, the angry assembly of the gods decrees a flood and enjoins Enki from forewarning Atrahasis. Enki cleverly gets around the restriction by innocently soliloquizing before a wall, on the other side of which Atrahasis happens to sit, hearing all. Atrahasis accordingly builds a boat for his family and animals. The floods come. The gods, by now bereft of the labor supplied by the human race, turn against Enlil, whose idea it was to blot out the race. Atrahasis the survivor is at length discovered and from him the human race is renewed. This time, however, there will be checks to untrammeled population growth. Not all women will bear children; infertile women, childbirth demons, and an order of celibate women will check population and hence the noise that disturbed the gods.

Gen has transformed the story. Moral fault, not mere noise, moves the sole God to wipe out the race. God's justice leads him to except the righteous Noah from the punishment. The blessings given to Noah are an unqualified reaffirmation of the original blessings in Gen 1. The only change in the original order is God's permitting the people to kill animals for food, a change introduced for the sake of human weakness rather than divine improvidence. Unlike the gods in Atrahasis, who created by trial and error and capriciously readjusted their ill-conceived plan, Yahweh from the beginning creates with wisdom and justice. The plot of Atrahasis—creation of humans, offense to the gods, flood, re-creation—is the plot of Gen 2–9.

The flood story in Gen is narrated in a chiastic arrangement, i.e., each element in the first part is echoed and elaborated in the second part, with the center, God's remembering of Noah, expressing the main point. Chiasm ("envelope" or "sandwich" construction) is common in biblical narrative. Reprise and repetition unify the long narrative and provide the redundance necessary for an oral culture.

Introduction: Noah, a just man in an unjust generation (6:9–10)
1. Lawlessness in God's creation (6:11–12)
2. 1st divine address: Destroy! (6:13–22)
3. 2nd divine address: Enter the ark! (7:1–10)
4. Beginning of the flood (7:11–16)
5. Rising of the flood waters (7:17–23)
   GOD REMEMBERS NOAH
6. Receding of the flood waters (7:24–8:5)
7. Drying of the earth (8:6–14)
8. 3rd divine address: Leave the ark! (8:15–19)
9. God's resolve to preserve order (8:20–22)
10. 4th divine address: Covenant blessing and peace (9:1–17)

(Adapted from B. W. Anderson [*JBL* 97 (1978) 23–29]; cf. also Cassuto, *Genesis* 2. 30–33.) The redactor's masterly chiasm makes the statement.

6:9–12. A just man in an unjust world. The P formula (v 9a) customarily introduces not only the person mentioned but his immediate descendants (Shem, Ham, and Japheth). Like Enoch, seventh in the 10-member genealogy of chap. 5, Noah stands out; he is right with God, alone blameless among his peers, walking with God. The earth that God seven times declared good at the beginning has been spoiled by "lawlessness" (v 11, rather than the too specific "violence"). God sees (v 12) and, as often in the Bible, immediately acts (cf. Exod 2:25; Isa 57:18; 59:16; 63:15). **13–22.** The first divine command: Destroy. Unlike the Atrahasis epic, in which the divine assembly's response to bothersome noise is destruction for all (with only Enki dissenting), God communicates his irrevocable decision to "destroy" the earth (lit., "spoil," as humans had spoiled it). The use of the same word for humans' action (v 11) and God's destruction (v 12) suggests that God is only completing the destruction begun by humans themselves. Differentiating between the corrupt race and the righteous Noah (v 14), God commands Noah to build an ark to escape the flood. The tension between divine mercy and justice finds narrative expression here; destruction will not be the last word. **14–16.** The ark is of gopher wood, a transcription of an unknown Hebr term. *ark:* Used elsewhere in the Bible only of Moses' basket in Exod 2; it too held the hope of the people in a time of danger. It is *ca.* 450 × 75 × 45 ft.; the cubit is a standard ancient Near Eastern measure, the length from the elbow to the tip of the middle finger (about 1½ ft.). Unlike a boat, the ark is totally enclosed except for a window (v 16a, others "roof") a cubit from the top; it is covered inside and out with pitch as a protection against the vast flood. **17–18.** God now announces he is *now* (the sense of traditional "behold" in v 17) bringing a flood as the instrument of destroying the world. *flood (mabbûl):* Almost the proper name for the flood, it is used only in Gen 6–11 (both J and P) and in Ps 29:10, where it apparently designates the chaotic waters tamed by the victorious Yahweh. **18.** God's covenant with Noah is the first mentioned in the Bible. It is the first in the P scheme of four covenants (J. Wellhausen's term for the Pentateuch is *liber quatuor foederum*), the others being the covenant with Abraham (17:1–14), with Israel at Sinai (Exod 19–24), and with Phineas (Num 26:12–13). A covenant is an agreement between two parties, often oral, sworn before the gods. The god(s) who witnessed the swearing watch over its observance. The full import of the covenant will be detailed in 9:1–17. Its initiative from God is emphasized, but divine sovereignty is not compromised by the free assent of the human partner. **19–21.** For P, all creation is good (Gen 1) and the distinctions between clean and unclean will be given only at Sinai. Hence, Noah takes two of every animal "according to its kind." For the phrase, see under Gen 1:9–13,27b. J on the other hand will stipulate in 7:2 seven pairs of clean and two pairs of unclean animals, presumably envisioning the post-flood

sacrifice of 8:20 (J). **22.** Like Moses building the dwelling in Exod, Noah obeys God without question and to the last detail.

7:1–10. Second divine address: Enter! As in 6:13–22, the section begins with a command to Noah. Noah is to enter the newly built ark and take with him seven pairs of clean and two pairs of unclean animals (see comment on 6:19–21). Along with the divine intent to destroy is the divine intent to preserve alive the righteous. **11–16.** The beginning of the flood. As the flood begins — P (v 11) and J (v 12) differing as to its source — the accent on the preserving of righteous life increases. **17–23.** The rising of the flood waters. The drama is heightened by the contrast of the mighty destroying waters covering the highest mountains by 15 cubits (= 23.5 ft.), and the tiny ark, seeds of a new beginning. *all humans:* Appears dramatically in v 21, and "Noah and those with him," climactically in v 23. **7:24–8:5.** God remembers Noah. The receding of the flood waters. **7:24–8:1.** Syntax suggests a single sentence, "And when the waters had swelled 150 days, God remembered Noah. . . ." God's remembering Noah is like his remembering of his covenant with Abraham, Isaac, and Jacob at the nadir of Hebr fortunes in Egypt (Exod 2:23–25); it is the prelude to divine action in their behalf. **4.** *the mountains of Ararat:* The mountain country of ancient Urartu in NW Iraq — to the biblical writer, the highest part of the world. There is no *Mount* Ararat in the Bible. **7–8.** The drying of the earth. The 1st-cent. AD Roman author Pliny tells of Indian sailors who release birds so to follow them as they turn toward land (*Nat. Hist.* 6.83) In Gilgamesh XI.145–54 [*ANET* 94–95]), Utnapishtim releases a dove, a swallow, and a raven, and all return except the raven. **13–14.** On the first day of the first month, the world was in the state it was in on the day of creation in Gen 1. Noah had to wait another month until the earth was properly dry land as in Gen 1:9. **8:15–19.** Third divine command: Leave the ark! **20–22.** God's resolve to preserve order. In both Atrahasis and Gilgamesh (tablet XI), the gods "gathered like flies over the sacrifice" of the flood survivors because they had not been fed and cared for by their human slaves. In a similar but far less anthropomorphic gesture, Yahweh smells the pleasing odor and promises never to repeat the universal punishment. God recognizes the mysterious evil intent within humans (6:5) and resolves to be faithful to the race in spite of it. **22.** A short poem sets forth the divinely ordained pairings that make the earth humanly habitable.

9:1–17. Fourth divine address: Covenant blessings and peace. **1.** The Atrahasis story ends with a renewal of creation but with a condition: Not all women will bear children, so that the overpopulation that provoked the wrath of the gods will never occur again (III.6.41–50, fragmentary). The blessing given to Noah in 9:1 repeats the original blessing in 1:28 verbatim, and 9:6 reaffirms without qualification the human being as the image of God (cf. 1:26–27). **2–6.** There is, however, a qualification of the original blessing: the concession that the originally vegetarian humans may kill animals for food, including fish and fowl (1:29). The qualification of the original blessing is not because of divine miscalculation in the initial creative act, as in Atrahasis, but because of God's willingness to bear with sinfully violent humans (8:21). **8:20–9:17.** An impressive chiasm: (a) 8:20–22, divine promise not to destroy the earth; (b) 9:1, blessing; (c) 9:2–6, divine sovereignty over life (concretized in blood); (b′) 9:7, blessing; (a′) 9:8–17, divine promise not to destroy the earth. The several ideas are aspects of a single intent to create life. **9.** A covenant is a solemn agreement between parties, sworn before the gods who oversee oaths. In v 9 it is essentially a promise, made originally to Noah (6:18) and now extended to all living creatures. Noah's free acceptance is nonetheless presupposed. To Jews, the prohibition against eating blood binds all people (cf. Acts 15:29). Like the covenant with Abraham, this covenant has a sign: the rainbow, which will signal the end of future rainstorms before they destroy the world.

13 (b) THE CHARACTER OF THE SONS OF NOAH (9:18–29 [J]). The character of the three sons is sketched in the episode of Noah's drunkenness. **20–23.** The fault here is not with Noah — as the first cultivator of the grape he could not have known the intoxicating quality of wine — but with Ham, who looked on his father's nakedness and told his two brothers. In Lev 20:17–21, to "uncover the nakedness" means to have sexual relations, but Ham's act does not imply sexual relations. The act and the telling of it imply contempt for one's father, a serious offense. Canaan's offense prefigures the sexual license of the later Canaanites, against which Israel is repeatedly warned. Shem and Japheth respectfully back into the tent (to avoid looking on their father) and cover him with a cloak. **24–27.** The point of the story is the curse laid on Ham, who is the father of Canaan (10:6) and the blessings upon Shem and Japheth. Hinted at is the later occupation of Canaan by Israel, the descendant of Shem. **27.** *enlarge:* Hebr *yapt* plays on the name Japheth.

14 (E) The Populating of the World and the Prideful City (10:1–11:9).

(a) NOAH'S DESCENDANTS BECOME LANDED PEOPLES (10:1–31 [J: 8–19,21,25–30] [P: 1–7,20,22–23,24]). The fourth instance of the P formula (2:4; 5:1; 6:9) introduces the section on the populating of the earth. At the creation of humans in 1:26 God had commanded them to be fertile and increase, fill the earth and subdue it. Up to now, esp. in the genealogies, the emphasis has been on "multiplying"; in this section the accent falls on filling the earth. Already 9:19 spoke of the earth's being populated from the three sons of Noah; the same statement is repeated in this section (10:5,18,25,32; 11:8). The view behind the chapter is that each people has a land assigned it by God and that it is the task of each to take possession of its God-given land ("subdue" of 1:28). Deut 32:8–9 illustrates the view: "When the Most High assigned the nations their homes, / when he separated the human race, / he fixed the boundaries of peoples according to the numbers of the sons of God (LXX, Sym); / But Yahweh's portion is his people, / Jacob, his own allotment." In the Deut poem, Yahweh assigns to each of the heavenly sons of the Most High (cf. the "70 sons of El" in Ugaritic texts) a people with its land but keeps Israel as his special people. In Gen 10, the descendants of Shem, Ham, and Japheth add up to 70, a traditional aggregate number in the Bible (Judg 8:30; 9:2; Luke 10:1,17). The number 70 is arrived at by counting all the names in the chapter except Noah and his three sons and counting Sidon (vv 15,19) only once. In Gen 46:27 and Exod 1:5 Israel too numbered 70 persons. "The people of Israel occupies in the plans of Divine Providence a place resembling, on a small scale, that of all mankind; it is a small-scale world, a microcosm similar in form to the macrocosm" (Cassuto, *Genesis* 2. 180).

Contrary to the paragraph divisions of most transls., 11:1–9 directly continues chap. 10; the nations sin by refusing to go forth to possess their lands, preferring instead to band together and build a prideful city at a site of their own choosing. Israel is mentioned indirectly in chap. 10 in its ancestor Eber (cf. "Hebrew" in vv 21, 24–25). Israel's twofold task of begetting children and possessing land will begin in chap. 12 with the charge to Abraham and Sarah. As elsewhere, Israel is contrasted

with the nations, e.g, "Lo, a people dwelling alone, and not reckoning itself among the nations (Num 23:9)." The chapter has been called "the table of nations" by scholars; it is a verbal map of the world known to the author. The main principle of division seems to be geographic, secondarily ethnic and linguistic. Many of the peoples and places cannot be identified and may have been vague to the author; identifications will be given when possible. Canaan, for reasons given below, is classed as Hamitic, though on all counts it is Semitic rather than Hamitic.

10:2–5. The descendants of Japheth include non-Semitic peoples in the north, contemporary Greece and the Mediterranean islands, Turkey, and N Iraq and Iran (the Medes). *Javan:* Ionia, the name for the Gk colonies on the W coast of Greece, but here designating all Greece. *Gomer:* Cimmerians. *Madai:* Medes. Tubal and Meshech were in E Turkey, as was Togarmah (Hittite Tagarma). *Ashkenaz:* An Indo-European people; it was the medieval rabbinic name for Germany, now designating one of the great divisions of Jews comprising E European Yiddish-speaking Jews. *Elishah:* Cyprus; Alashia of cuneiform sources. *Kittim:* Seems to refer to Cyprus also. *Dodanim:* Correctly Rodanim in 1 Chr 1:7, the inhabitants of Rhodes (*d* and *r* were easily confused in some ancient scripts). **6–20.** The descendants of Ham are within an arc extending from the mid-Mediterranean through Lebanon-Palestine (both of which had long been under the aegis of Egypt), down to the Arabian peninsula. *Put:* Libya (cf. Nah 3:9; Ezek 30:5). *Cush:* In v 6 this is the upper Nile Valley and Ethiopia, but in v 8 it seems to be Cossaea, the country of the Kassites in NE Babylonia, the proper area of the Mesopotamian Nineveh (E. A. Speiser, *IDB* 3. 236). *Havilah:* The name of more than one place (Gen 2:11; 10:7,29). *Seba:* Contemporary Yemen. **8–12.** Ancient lists sometimes included anecdotes, as in the Sumerian King List (*ANET* 265–66) and as here with Nimrod. Nimrud is the name of several cities in Mesopotamia, including Nimrud, ancient Calah. Nimrod here is the first of the great kings on earth. **10.** The "mainstays" (*NJV*) of his kingdom were the great cities of Babylonia in the S and Assyria and Nineveh in the N. Like another fabled hunter, Gilgamesh, Nimrod was a mighty hunter by the grace of God. The J source (vv 8–19) characteristically is interested in founders of culture (cf. 4:17–26 and 9:20); Nimrod is the founder of the great empires that played so large a role in the ancient Near East. What historical personage, if any, Nimrod represents is unknown. (Tukulti-)Ninurta, a 13th-cent. king who was the first actually to rule effectively Babylonia and Assyria is suggested by some scholars (E. A. Speiser, "In Search of Nimrod," ErIsr 5 [1958] 32–36). **13–14.** *Pathrusim:* Dwelt in upper Egypt (cf. Isa 11:11). Caphtor rather than the "Casluhim" is the place of origin of the Philistines (cf. Amos 9:7). **15–20.** *Canaan fathered:* "Fathered" is used metaphorically, as in Phoenician coins that mention Sidon as the mother of other cities and colonies. *Heth:* The Hittites, originally in Asia Minor but also in Syria-Palestine (see comment on 23:3). **16.** *Jebusites:* The original inhabitants of Jerusalem. Some of the other names are the inhabitants of Canaan before Israel arrived (cf., e.g., Exod 3:8). **19.** The original territory extended along the Mediterranean coast from the Phoenician cities to Gaza and eastward to the region of the Dead Sea. **21–31.** The descendants of Shem inhabit the Middle East, except Egypt and the part of the Arabian Peninsula in Egypt's orbit. **21.** *Eber:* The eponymous ancestor of the Hebrews, as Aram is of the Arameans. **22.** *Elam, Asshur:* Countries in the NE and N of Mesopotamia respectively. **25.** *Peleg:* Mentioned again in the P genealogy of 11:10–26 and also in the genealogy of Jesus in Luke 3:35. The division of the human race in the time of Peleg points forward to 11:1–9, an indication of the unity of the large section. **26–30.** The 13 descendants of Joktan are generally considered to be Arab tribes. *Hazarmaveth:* Modern Ḥadramaut in S Arabia. *Sheba:* In Yemen (cf. v 7). *Ophir:* Points to the E coast of Arabia. Havilah is probably the same as in v 7.

15 (b) THE PRIDEFUL CITY WITH THE TOWER (10:32–11:9 [J]). As pointed out above under 10:1, the race refuses to go to their apportioned lands. The divine intent that the race "scatter," or repair to their God-given lands, is repeated in 9:19; 10:5,20,25,31,32. Verse 32b prefaces the story of the city with a tower in its midst (a better title for the story than "The Tower of Babel," since the people choose to dwell in a great city rather than go to their separate homelands). 11:1 is parenthetical before the main story. 11:2 follows immediately 10:32b, "As they journeyed from the east, they came upon a plain in the land of Shinar [= Babylonia according to 10:10] and settled there." Their decision to settle contravenes the divine intent to settle in various lands. **3–7.** Human plan and divine intent are effectively contrasted by "Come let us make bricks" and "Come let us go down and there confuse their language." **4.** The tower was to have its top in the heavens. Mesopotamian temple designations contain phrases like "reaching the heavens"; temples arising from the flat Babylonian plain must have seemed to distant onlookers to be piercing the heavens. *make a name for ourselves:* One more instance of human disobedience (cf. Gen 2–3; 4:1–9; 6:1–8), the refusal to accept one's place as a human in the universe under God. Abraham in 12:2 will be told by God, in contrast, "*I* will make your name great." **6.** *there will be no preventing whatever they propose to do:* There is a vestige here of the ancient Near Eastern literary motif of divine jealousy of humans, like the vestige of the divine assembly in "let us go down" (v 7). Biblical speech about God in heaven often borrows conventional phrases; the difference is the biblical assumption about the absolute sovereignty of God over the other heavenly beings. **7–9.** Yahweh's confusing of their speech is a punishment for pride; it is also a guarding against any future massed assaults on divine sovereignty. The act resembles the expulsion of the man and the woman from further contact with the tree of life, lest they eat of that tree too (3:22–23). Yahweh's will that the race go forth to possess their land is in fact carried out in v 8 but now with added vehemence because of human resistance; God scatters them because they will not freely spread abroad. **9.** *confused:* Hebr *bālal,* a play on Babel.

16 Genealogy from Shem to Terah (11:10–26 [P]). The fifth and last use of the P formula in the primeval history introduces a genealogy linking the story of the nations to the story of Israel. That the genealogy properly ends in v 26 is shown by the immediately following rubric, "These are the descendants of Terah" (v 27), which introduces the Abraham story; Gen customarily introduces the story of the son as the "generation" of his father, e.g., Gen 25:19; 37:2. Like Gen 5, the genealogy is P. It differs from that genealogy, however, in omitting the total years that each ancestor lived and omitting the anecdote about the seventh ancestor. Both genealogies end in three "executive" sons (Shem, Ham, and Japheth; Abram, Nahor, and Haran), but the father Noah is tenth whereas the father Terah is ninth. LXX adds Kenan (from 5:12) between Arpachshad and Shelah to make 10 generations, but this seems an artificial solution to the difficulty. The purpose of the genealogy is to relate Abraham, the ancestor of Israel, to Shem, the oldest son of Noah and the father of the Semites, and to equate Abraham with the righteous Noah, in whom God made a new beginning with the human race. Linear

genealogies demonstrate that the authority of the first in the genealogy resides in the last named (Wilson, *Genealogy and History* 40–45, 163–64). The blessing of progeny and land renewed to Noah and to his sons and the added promise of divine fidelity and forbearance (9:1–17) are given to Terah and his sons, as is the promise of Shem's eventual domination of Canaan (9:25–26). More proximately, Terah's family is under the divine injunction to journey toward their divinely apportioned land, the themes of 10:1–11:9. These themes will dominate the story of Abraham and Sarah.

14–15. *Eber:* Cf. 10:24–25. The ancestor of the Hebrews. **17–23.** *Peleg:* Probably a place-name in Mesopotamia. *Serug:* Corresponds to *Sarugi* in Assyrian inscriptions, a city near Haran. *Nahor: Naḫur (Til Nahiri)* in the Mari documents and elsewhere; also in the vicinity of Haran, as is Terah (*Til Turahi*). **26.** *Abram:* A dialectal variant of the name Abraham, consisting of the elements '*ab,* "father," and *rām,* "exalted," meaning "the Father (God) is exalted." See comment on 17:5.

17 (II) The Story of the Ancestors of Israel (11:27–50:26). The genealogy of Terah marks the important division in Gen between the story of the nations in 1:1–11:26 and the story of Israel in 11:27–50:26. The Bible is everywhere conscious of the difference between the nations (*gôyîm*) and Israel. Israel, of course, is part of humankind, whose increase and spread over the earth have just been told in the preceding chapters. The divine imperatives built into human society—the drive to continue in existence through numerous progeny and the drive to possess land, to have "a local habitation and a name"—pertain to them as well as to the nations. Eber, their ancestor, is, after all, a son of Shem (10:21). When the descendants of Noah become nations with land and language (10:1–11:9), the way is prepared for Israel to become a nation. When Israel's story begins, however, Abraham and Sarah possess neither children nor a land; Sarah is barren (11:30) and Abraham leaves his native land for a land only promised to him (12:1). Israel; in the person of Abraham, Isaac, Jacob, and the 12 brothers (Joseph stories), carries out the divine mandate in a manner different from the nations—as Yahweh's special people.

The historicity of the patriarchs has been especially debated since J. Wellhausen's proposal that the stories are a retrojection from the period of the monarchy (*Die Composition des Hexateuchs und die historischen Bücher* [Berlin, 1876–78]). In the following decades dominance of the literary-critical method with its focus on the J and E documents of the monarchical period reinforced scholarly skepticism about the historicity of the stories. Countering the skepticism of the literary critic, archaeological and epigraphic finds from the ancient Near East in the century since Wellhausen have produced many parallels to the names, customs, and literary genres of the stories. The individual parallels are often difficult to assess. Taken together, they do not prove the historicity of the patriarchs but rather make plausible the general setting of the stories. One solid piece of evidence is the proper names. The names Abraham, Ishmael, and Jacob are attested in 2d-millennium texts; they are not given to Israelites in the OT period. The original meanings of Abraham ("Father [= God] is exalted") and Jacob ("May God protect") have been forgotten in the wordplays based on their names in Gen, which suggests that the names and also the stories were part of a patrimony and were not invented. The patriarchs' peaceful sojourning amid the Canaanites (contrary to Israel's stormy relations with its neighbors during the monarchy) may reflect 2d-millennium conditions. It is possible that the ancestors were part of a large Amorite migration that founded dynasties in N Syria and Mesopotamia at the beginning of the 2d-millennium. Some scholars cite Hurrian legal parallels to material in Gen regarding marriage and adoption; their relevance is still under discussion. Anachronisms in the text, such as the domesticated camel and the presence of Philistines in Canaan, are simply the products of updating, to be expected in oral transmission. The general setting of the stories is compatible with what is known of 2d-millennium life in Canaan. To give a precise date for the stories is virtually impossible unless one holds that they were part of the Amorite migration at the beginning of the millennium. The narratives reflect a process of centuries, compressed into three generations. The texts themselves show a prepolitical stage prior to later Israel, which had become politically organized and sedentary. It is generally recognized, however, that the stories of Abraham, Isaac, and Jacob may have belonged to different clans and may have been linked only later to each other through genealogies.

The religion of the patriarchs is clearly distinguished by the Bible itself from that of later Israel. In Exod 3, Yahweh is revealed as the God of the Fathers, the God of Abraham, Isaac, and Jacob (Exod 3:15; cf. 6:2-4); the name Yahweh and the new act, the exodus and the Sinai covenant, mark a new stage. God is invoked by the name God of the Father(s) and by several El titles (Hebr ' ēl, Eng "God"): God Eternal (21:33), God Most High (14:18-22), God (or El) the God of Israel (33:20), God Who Sees (16:3), God of Bethel (31:13; 35:7), and El Shadday (17:1). The latter titles seem originally to have been epithets of El, the high god of the Canaanite pantheon, who was worshiped in various shrines; most of the titles in Gen are tied to a particular shrine. The patriarchs saw that the God of the Father(s) revealed to their ancestors was the same God revealed in the sanctuaries that they visited in Canaan. Hence, they were able to worship the one God of their family in the promised land (F. M. Cross, *CMHE* 1-73).

18   (A) The Story of Abraham and Sarah (11:27-25:18). The P formula introduces the story of Terah (the first of the ancestors of Israel), Abraham, and Sarah. Elsewhere the story of the son is introduced by the name of the father (cf. 25:12; 25:19; 36:1 [repeated in 36:9], 37:2).

The Abraham-Sarah stories are a collection of stories and notices of diverse origins. About the origin, growth, and arrangement of the traditions scholarly opinion varies widely according to methodologies and assumptions about the history of Israel's religion. Some observations can safely be made, however. The story begins (11:27-32) and ends (25:1-18) with genealogical notices about respectively the families of Terah and of Abraham. 12:1-9 is clearly programmatic. The Abraham-Lot cycle consists of chaps. 13-14 + 19: between these chapters promises predominate (chaps. 15, 16, 17, and 18:1-16). Chaps. 20-24 conclude the whole by telling of the fulfillment of the promise of the son and heir (21:1-7), Abraham's obedience regarding his heir (22:1-19), and his heir's marriage (chap. 24), and of the fulfillment of the promise of the land by Abraham's acquiring a small plot and a well (21:22-34; chap. 23). Throughout, short itineraries and genealogical notices attest to Abraham's "taking" of the land and of his family's spread.

Most of the traditions are from the Yahwist (J) version of a presumed oral epic of the tribal period; E is represented, according to recent studies, only in passages duplicating other narratives (20:1-18 // 12:10-13:1 // 26:1-11; 21:22-34 // 26:26-33). P's contributions are mostly brief and redactional except for chaps. 17 and 23. P designates both redactional elements and ancient records. Much recent scholarship is wary of neat attribu-

tions to the J, E, and P sources, preferring instead to see a relatively fluid Abraham tradition, subject over a long period of time to revision and supplement even in its written form (Westermann, *Genesis 12-36* 23-131, 401-4).

A notable suggestion about the structure of the stories is the rabbinic tradition of a series of ten trials and seven blessings, which Cassuto has synthesized (*Genesis* 2. 293-97). This tradition has read into all the stories the testing (chap. 22) and reiterated promises. In the first trial Abraham receives a general divine promise; after each trial he receives consolation in the form of renewed assurances, noted by parentheses below. The structure of the trials is chiastic: 1 = 10; 2-3 = 8-9; 4 = 7; 5 = 6.

Ten trials: (1) migration from country and kindred, 12:1-4 + 7 (consolation); (2) dangerous journey to Egypt (successful return to Canaan), 12:10-13:1; (3) yielding to Lot (renewed promise of land and offspring), 13:2-18; (4) rescue of Lot (Melchizedek's blessing of Abraham), chaps. 14-15; (5) danger of loss of son by Hagar (assurance that Ishmael and his own son would be a great nation), chaps. 16-17; (6) testing through circumcision (visit of three men), 18:1-15; (7) Lot in jeopardy from wickedness of neighbors (Lot saved for Abraham's sake), 18:16-19:29; (8) Abraham again in danger from a foreign king (Abraham and Sarah delivered and Isaac born in peace), 20:1-21:7; (9) birth of Isaac, meaning the departure of the firstborn (covenant with his neighbors, building of a new sanctuary at Beer-sheba, and proclamation there of Yahweh's name), 21:8-34; (10) offering of Isaac (strong renewal of promises), chap. 22.

Seven blessings: (1) seven expressions of blessings at Haran, 12:2-3; (2) explanation and specification of two points in first promise — enduring offspring and possession of the land, 12:7; (3) further on land and offspring, 13:14-17; (4) clarification of promise of children and fixing of time for the acquisition of land, chap. 15; (5) good tidings that not one but a multitude of nations will come forth from Abraham and Sarah, and that the covenant will find particular realization in the son that Sarah will bear, chap. 17; (6) in a year Sarah's giving birth to this son, chap. 18; (7) a more comprehensive and exalted blessing than all of the previous communications, given to Abraham after the attempted sacrifice of Isaac, containing, like the first blessing, seven expressions, 22:16-18.

19   (a) The Family of Terah in Haran (11:27-32 [P:11:27,31-32] [J: 28-30]). **27.** Abraham's story is entitled "the genealogy of Terah," his father. **28.** *Ur of the Chaldeans:* An ancient city on the banks of the Euphrates in S Mesopotamia, modern Tell el-Muqayyar. After a millennium of relative unimportance it underwent a revival under the Neo-Babylonian/Chaldean empire (626-539). The 6th-cent. redactor identified the city by a contemporary reference ("Chaldeans"). As Gen 24 shows, Haran in N Mesopotamia is the native place of Abraham. The best solution to the much-discussed question of Abraham's home is to take seriously the book's perspective that all the nations originated in the East (Gen 3:24; 4:16) and moved from there to their homelands (11:2). Terah's family is part of that large migration. Like the rest of humankind, they did not complete their migration but *settled* (cf. v 31 with 11:2) in Haran. It is Abraham's task to complete the migration to the divinely appointed land. **29.** *Sarai:* Like Abram, a dialectal variant of the more usual form of the name. In 17:15 God will, in view of her new role, change her name to Sarah. Haran is to be distinguished from the place-name Haran in v 31, which begins with a different Hebr consonant. **31-32.** Terah's destination had been Canaan but he settled in Haran; presumably he repeated the pattern of of the nations in 11:1–9 — he was called to migrate to one place but settled in another. Though Terah dies much later, shortly before a wife is sent for Isaac, his death is recorded here, the narrative's manner of finishing with him. The focus is now on Abraham.

20   (b) ABRAHAM IS CALLED TO JOURNEY TO CANAAN AND IS BLESSED 12:1–9 [J: 1–4a,6–9] [P: 4b–5]). Abraham is commanded by Yahweh to leave his native land (hendiadys; lit., "your country and your kindred"; cf. the similar expression 11:28). The settling in Haran (11:31) is to end for Abraham as it had for the nations in 11:8–9, in a further migration. Here, however, the movement of Abraham is not through Yahweh's "scattering" them but from a direct call to go to "a land that I will show you." **2–4.** The blessings are seven, all aspects of God's favorable regard that enhances his individual and family life. *you will be a blessing:* People will use him as a standard of blessing like 48:20; it has virtually the same meaning as v 3, "by you all the families of the earth will bless themselves" (grammatically preferable to "in you all the families shall be blessed"). **5–9.** Verse 5 is a formula of departing for a new place (cf. 11:31; 36:6; 46:6). Abraham's journey to the center of the land, Shechem, then to Bethel, and then to the Negeb, is duplicated in Jacob's journeys (33:18; 35:1,6,27; 46:1) and in the general route of the conquest under Joshua (Josh 7:2; 8:9,30). "Scripture intends to present us here, through the symbolic conquest of Abraham, with a kind of foretaste of what would happen to his descendants later" (Cassuto, *Genesis* 2. 305–6). The building of altars shows Abraham's acknowledgment of Yahweh as Lord of the land. **9.** The Hebr root idea for "journey" — "to pull up tent stakes" — suggests the transl. "he journeyed by stages to the Negeb."

21   (c) ABRAHAM AND SARAH IN DANGER IN EGYPT (12:10–13:1 [JJ]).   Famine forces Abraham and Sarah to leave the promised land temporarily ("sojourn" in v 10) for Egypt. Their going to Egypt and encounter with Pharaoh foreshadow their descendants' experience in Egypt, suggesting constant divine protection, in which Israel later must learn to trust. The story of the ancestress in danger is told again in Gen 20 in its E version with Abimelech of Gerar replacing Pharaoh, and in 26:1–11 (J) with Isaac and Rebekah instead of Abraham and Sarah. Repetition of similar events are not unusual in ancient Oriental literature. **11–13.** Abraham is aware that Sarah, though 65 (10 years younger than Abraham, 17:17), is so beautiful that she will be taken as a wife by Pharaoh. Abraham must remain alive to fulfill the promise made to him in 12:2–3. He lies to prevent his immediate death but does not foresee that Pharaoh's great power will take matters completely out of his hands. The reader knows that the newly acquired wealth is from Pharaoh, not Yahweh, and is based on Abraham's deception. **17–20.** The second act. Yahweh directly intervenes to save the honor of Sarah by afflicting Pharaoh with plagues. **13:1.** This verse is often printed in modern Bibles with the following story because it depicts Abraham's returning safely to the promised land, but it is the conclusion of the present story. Abraham shows that he does not fully trust Yahweh's promise to make of him a great nation.

22   (d) ABRAHAM AND LOT GO THEIR SEPARATE WAYS (13:2–18 [J: 2–5,7–11a,13–18] [P: 6,11b–12]). **2–4.** Abraham retraces the route that brought him over the promised land to return to the altar he built between Bethel and Ai (12:8–9). Confident of Yahweh's promise to him of "this land" (12:7), he resolves a family conflict over land, allowing Lot, the younger man, who should defer to his uncle, to choose whatever area he desires. Lot chooses the plain of the Jordan, in antiquity a luxuriant area, visibly fertile from the W highland where the two

men stood. For his trust in God's promise, Abraham's claim on the land is reaffirmed. **7.** The Canaanites are the common J designation of the inhabitants (cf. 10:19). Perizzites is another pre-Israelite people in the land, usually found in lists of six or seven peoples, but sometimes, as here, coupled with Canaanites (34:30; Judg 1:4–5). Their precise identity is unknown. The two peoples are mentioned here to highlight Abraham's bold faith that the land held by others will belong to his descendants. **8–13.** The youthful Lot makes the expected natural choice of verdant land. Later Israel recognized that this land was given to Lot's descendants (Deut 2:9,18–19). **14–18.** In contrast to Lot, who lifts his eyes and chooses for himself (vv 10–11), Abraham waits for Yahweh to tell him to lift his eyes and see the land he will receive (v 14). Abraham's visionary possession of the land foreshadows that of Moses (Deut 3:27; 34:4). Abraham is then invited to make a procession over the land that will one day be his descendants'. As noted at 12:6–9, the conquest will follow a similar route. Abraham's dwelling at Hebron foreshadows both later Israelite possession of the S and David's rule. David's house was originally from Hebron.

23   (e) ABRAHAM DEFEATS THE KINGS AND RESCUES LOT (14:1–24 [special source]).   Abraham, like his descendants, deals with world leaders, Pharaoh (12:10–13:1) and Abimelech king of Gerar (chap. 20). In this chapter he defeats a coalition of five kings from the east (the area where Israel's enemies later arose), and a king of the Canaanites recognizes him as blessed by God Most High. The historicity of vv 1–11 is controverted. Some scholars maintain that the verses are derived from an essentially historical record of the Middle Bronze Age (W. F. Albright, *YGC* 50–51; Y. Aharoni, *LBib* 140–42); others see it as late and unhistorical (M. Noth, *NHI* 124; van Seters, *Abraham* 112–20). Attempts to identify the four kings and countries (except for Shinar = Babylon, Tidal = Hittite Tudhaliya, and Elam) are speculative. The five cities together appear only here, the first four occur in Gen 10:19 and Deut 29:23. The cities are apparently at the S end of the Dead Sea, all but Bela (Zoah) destined for destruction (Gen 19:20–24; Hos 11:8). In genre the verses are an adapted report of a campaign; parallels exist in the OT and Babylonian and Assyrian royal annals (Westermann, *Genesis 12–36* 187–95; *ANET* 274–88). The campaign now is background for Abraham's heroic deed in behalf of Lot and for his blessing by Melchizedek.

1–4. A coalition of four eastern kings arrives in the W to punish five kings who had rebelled after twelve years serving as vassals. **5–11.** The noting of the years of servitude and of rebellion and punishment is typical of royal inscriptions (cf. 2 Kgs 18–19). Before punishing the five rebels the kings make a detour, punishing four peoples (vv 5–6), then three peoples of the Transjordan, the Rephaim, the Zuzim, and the Emim (cf. Deut 2:10–12,20), and finally three of the S, the Horites, the Amalekites, and Amorites (the latter possibly a S enclave of the more generally distributed people). **8–12.** The battle turns into a rout, many from the armies of Sodom and Gomorrah falling into the bitumen pits of the region and the rest fleeing to the hills. The four kings seize the goods left behind and depart. **12.** The verse links the great campaign and battle to Abraham: Lot, Abraham's nephew, is taken. The structure of v 12 imitates that of v 11: "they took the goods" // "they took Lot . . . and they departed." **13–17.** Abraham and his allies at Mamre, where he settled after allowing Lot his preference (13:8), along with 318 men pursue the victors as far N as Dan. Dividing his forces like the judge Gideon (Judg 7:16), Abraham routs the kings and rescues all the goods and his nephew. **18–20.** The king of Sodom, apparently the chief of the five armies (his name always heads the list), meets Abraham (v 17) and addresses him (v 21). His greeting is interrupted and overshadowed by the appearance of Melchizedek, king of Salem (= Jerusalem), whose dominant position in the narrative suggests that he is first of the Canaanite kings. Recognizing Abraham's great deed—winning a victory that the five local kings were not able to achieve—he sets a feast before Abraham to win the goodwill of so favored a personage. He declares him blessed, i.e., he has been made powerful by God Most High. The divine title is attested in the Ugaritic texts of the Late Bronze Age as an epithet of El, the chief god of the Canaanite pantheon, who is here identified with Yahweh. It is one of several El titles applied to Yahweh in the patriarchal stories (→ 17 above). Abraham acknowledges the blessing by giving a tenth of the recaptured booty as a tithe to Melchizedek. The episode is one of several allusions in the story to David, the later king of Jerusalem, who also exercised priestly functions (2 Sam 6:17). **21-24.** After Melchizedek's blessing, the king of Sodom returns to center stage to offer the spoil to Abraham, who, as chief warrior, had a right to it. Abraham refuses lest someone apart from his God enrich him; only his men and the allies are to be rewarded. Abraham, portrayed here with the traits of an Israelite judge or tribal hero, refuses to enrich himself because of the divine rescue effected through him. He has learned a hard lesson from his encounter with Pharaoh (12:10-13:1); only God can enrich him.

24   (f) GOD PROMISES ABRAHAM A SON AND LAND (15:1-21 [J: 1-2 *,3b-4,6 *-12,17-21] [E?: 3a,5,13-16]). The two sections, vv 1-6, in which Abraham is promised a son and heir, and vv 7-21, in which Abraham is promised a land, are meant to be read together; v 7 begins "and he said. . . ," assuming that the reader knows from vv 1-6 that Yahweh is the speaker. Some scholars believe that the unity and indeed the very composition are redactional and late; they assume that the two promises were originally separate and that narratives were secondarily constructed from statements of promises. The structure is similar in each section. Each of the two promises is not immediately accepted; the first is met with a complaint (vv 2-3) and the second with a request for a sign (v 8). The answer of God differs in each section: a sign in v 5, an oath in vv 9-21 (see Westermann, *Genesis 12-36* 216). It is difficult, however, to abstract neatly the promise from the narrative and to imagine promises existing without specific contexts. Both scenes are dramatic and concrete though highly stylized from editing. The Ugaritic texts of the Late Bronze Age attest such spare narrative, where divine promise is answered by a lament-like response of the childless parent (R. J. Clifford, "The Word of God in the Ugaritic Epics and in the Patriarchal Narratives," *The Word in the World* [Fest. F. L. Moriarty; ed. R. J. Clifford and G. W. MacRae; Cambridge MA, 1973] 7-18).

1-6. *after these things:* This marks a new episode without a necessary connection to the preceding (22:1,20; 39:7, etc.). *the word of the Lord came:* Only here and in v 4 in Gen, this expression is common in later books (1 Sam 15:10; 2 Sam 7:4; 1 Kgs 12:22) and is a sign of later editing. *do not fear:* A generalized formula, the word of a god assuring a favored one of protection. **2-3.** Abraham complains, like Kirta and Danil in the Ugaritic texts, that he is still denied the one thing that he wants—his own son to carry on his name. He will die (lit., "go," in the sense of Ps 39:14) childless and his steward (lit., "son of my house") will be his heir. **4-5.** *what comes forth from your loins:* In opposition to "son of my house" in v 3. In Ps 89:2-5, a royal lament, Yahweh's covenant loyalty to David is declared to be as firm as the heavens. Not only

is the divine promise of v 4 as firm as the heavens, but Abraham's progeny will be like the stars in number. Yahweh's answer assures Abraham of an heir and of a great people descended from him. **6.** Abraham's trust in Yahweh wins Yahweh's favor. As similar phraseology in Deut 6:25 and 24:13 (negatively stated in Ps 32:2) shows, a particular attitude is declared acceptable to God. The verse has been seen to anticipate a Pauline interpretation of faith. **7-12.** Corresponding to the promise of a son (vv 1-6) is the promise of "this land" (vv 7-12); Abraham asks for a sign (v 8 = vv 2-3) and receives a confirmation in the form of a covenant oath (preparation in vv 9-11 and the ritual itself in vv 17-21). Verses 12-16 are the timetable of the actual possession of the land. **7.** The same formula is used in Exod 20:2; Deut 5:6; and Lev 25:38, where it refers to the bringing out of Egypt. Yahweh reveals himself as the one who brought Abraham out of Ur to give him this land. Abraham asks for a confirmation. The divine answer in v 9 really means: "In order for me to show you, bring me a heifer." **9-11.** The ritual of cutting animals in two and walking between them is attested in Jer 34:18 and at Mari. The participants invoke a similar death upon themselves in case of covenant violation. Abraham waves away birds of prey, apparently bad omens. **12-16.** A deep sleep is a prelude to divine intervention (2:21). The vision clarifies "possession" of v 7: your descendants, after 400 years of servitude, will actually possess it in the fourth generation (the patriarchal generation is apparently 100 years); you will die in a ripe old age, in peace. The iniquity of the Amorites has not yet reached the point at which God must deal out punishment. Iniquity here is conceived of quantitatively. **17-21.** The rite. The smoke, oven, and flames represent God, who in an unusual gesture of condescension accepts the consequences of not fulfilling the promise; God makes a covenant with Abraham (v 18). Many scholars see this as an oath rather than a covenant because Gen 24:7; 50:24; Deut 7:8,12,13; 8:1,18, etc., speak of an oath sworn to the fathers. Extrabiblical parallels and the text itself, however, affirm this to be a covenant. In ancient Near Eastern suzerainty covenants, the suzerain can take obligations upon himself, as here. Part of the controversy about oath versus covenant stems from modern theological ideas (D. McCarthy, *Treaty and Covenant* [AnBib 21A; Rome, 1978] "Introduction"). The promise of the land rests on God's honor. **18b-21.** The boundaries, from the Brook of Egypt (Wadi el-Arish) to the Euphrates, the NW border, refer to the greatest extent of the land under David, another pointer to the great king in these stories. Most lists of inhabitants give three, six, or seven peoples; this gives 10, an indication perhaps of editorial expansion.

25   (g) HAGAR BEARS ABRAHAM A SON (16:1-16 [J: 1b-2,4-14] [P: 1a,3,15-16]). In the previous section, Abraham had been given a timetable predicting when his descendants would possess the land (15:12-16). As to the promise of a son, however, 10 years of childlessness (cf. 12:4 with 16:16) have passed without issue. Sarah takes matters into her own hands by giving Abraham her personal servant Hagar to bear the child. Sarah's initiative is narratively stated by her prominence—her gesture, her feeling of being slighted, her persecution of Hagar; Abraham has only one sentence. The second half of the story is about the other woman in the story, Hagar, and the messenger's announcement of the fate of her child. God cares directly for the afflicted Hagar, not Sarah, who has other resources.

1-6. A Nuzi text of the 15th cent. is an example of a Hurrian legal custom similar to that invoked by Sarah: "If Gilimninu bears children, Shennima shall not take another wife. But if Gilimninu fails to bear children,

Gilimninu shall get for Shennima a woman from the Lullu country (i.e., a slave girl) as concubine. In that case Gilimninu herself shall have authority over the offspring" (Speiser, *Genesis* 120). **4.** In a culture that prized mother-hood, Sarah could not but feel a loss of esteem (*RSV* "contempt" is too strong). **5-6.** She complains to Abraham, "The wrong done to me is your fault" (not *RSV* "May the wrong be on you!"). She demands justice from Abraham, i.e., to be declared in the right. Abraham takes Sarah's side and lets her have her way. Hagar runs away from the harsh treatment. **7-16.** The angel of God in most OT passages is a figure who meets human beings, gives them messages, and then departs; the figure mediates the divine word (Westermann, *Genesis 12–36* 242-44). Comparable religious literature depicts the heavenly beings as courtiers who surround the great god(s); some OT texts witness to this courtier function (1 Kgs 22:19-22; Isa 6; Job 1-2); later reflection will develop an elaborate angelology, but in Gen angels simply mediate the message of the sender. The messenger tells the fugitive pregnant woman, presumably on her way back to her native Egypt via the Shur road, to return to her mistress. She will be the mother of a great nation; the child's name will be Ishmael (lit., "May God hear/heed"), for God has heeded her suffering. Her son will be "a wild ass of a man," quarrelsome, yet dwelling "alongside" (rather than "against") his kinfolk, i.e., dwelling at the edge of the land promised to Abraham's and Sarah's child (15:18-20). **13.** She calls the God who appeared to her in the messenger "God who sees me." "See" has the sense of see and rescue (cf. Exod 2:25; Isa 58:3; 59:15; Ps 113:6). Verse 13b is corrupt, lit., "Have I not from here seen after seeing me?"—perhaps an expression of wonder that she continues to see after contact with the divine one. She names the well Beer-lahai-roi, perhaps "the well of the living one who sees (i.e., looks after) me." *Kadesh* is about 45 mi. S of Beer-sheba; *Bered* is otherwise unknown but is obviously nearby.

26 (h) GOD's COVENANT WITH ABRAHAM (17:1-27 [P]). Chap. 17 is one of two extended compositions of P about Abraham and Sarah; P gathers the major motifs of the story so far and sets them squarely within the covenant; "covenant" occurs 13 times in the chapter. There are also links to the first covenant with Noah, "Walk before me and be blameless" (v 1; cf. 6:9); to establish a covenant with Abraham and his descendants (v 7; cf. 6:9); the sign (v 11; cf. 6:12-17). In outline, vv 1-8 promise Abraham numerous progeny and land (vv 1-3a are the condensed statement, and vv 3b-8, the elaboration); vv 9-14 are the instructions for circumcision; vv 15-21 repeat the promise of a son to Sarah, prompting God's differentiating this promise from that to Ishmael; vv 22-27 narrate Abraham's carrying out of God's commands.

1. Since the birth of Isaac will be a year from the encounter (v 21), Abraham will be 100 at the birth. God introduces himself as El Shadday (etymologically probably "God, the One of the mountain"). It is P's favorite designation of God in patriarchal times (17:1; 28:3; 35:11; 43:14; 48:3). In P's scheme, God is revealed to humankind in Gen 1-11 as Elohim, to the patriarchs as El Shadday, and to Israel as Yahweh (Exod 6:3); it is an instance of P's periodizing of history. Like Noah in his generation (6:9), Abraham is to respond loyally and obediently. **2.** The initiative in the covenant is God's, but the relationship established is reciprocal, as v 1 makes clear. Covenant (Hebr *bĕrît*) implies mutuality, though the Bible may occasionally emphasize divine initiative as it does in this chapter. **4-5.** *as for me, here is my covenant:* Abraham's name is changed in view of his new task. *Abraham:* Linguistically, a dialectal variant of Abram,

which has been used in the story up to this point. By a folk etymology "Abraham" is derived from Hebr *'ab hămôn,* "father of a multitude." "Nations" and "kings" occur as a fixed pair also in Isa 41:2; 45:1; 60:3; and Jer 25:14, suggesting perhaps that P is underscoring Abraham's role in world history for the benefit of his exilic contemporaries. **7.** God establishes an eternal covenant like the eternal throne of David in 2 Sam 7:13. **8.** Land is mentioned only here in the chapter; the emphasis elsewhere is on the son and on the multitude and fruitfulness of the descendants. **9-14.** Circumcision was widely practiced in the ancient Near East—in Egypt and Canaan, but not in Assyria or Babylon or among the Philistines. Joshua circumcised all the men on the great day of arrival in Canaan (Josh 5:2-9). Circumcision became an important rite of the chosen people in the exile, denied other symbols of identity—temple, land, and king. As with the rites of Passover and Unleavened Bread in Exod 12-13, P incorporates the later ritual of circumcision into the narrative of institution so that later generations of Israelites can participate in the founder's experience. **15-21.** "Sarah" replaces "Sarai," a dialectal variant, in view of the new role. **16.** The covenant is made with Abraham, who represents the household to God; Sarah is blessed, which here (as often) means bestowing or enhancing fertility. **17-19.** Abraham laughs in incredulity, as Sarah will later (18:12), because of their advanced age, and he asks God to consider the healthy teenager Ishmael as heir. God, however, insists on the literal interpretation of his earlier promise in 15:4: not Ishmael but Isaac (lit., "May God laugh in delight, smile upon!"), a play on Abraham's laugh. Only with Abraham's own son will the covenant be made. **20-21.** Ishmael, however, will be blessed with offspring; the 12 princes descended from him are mentioned in 25:12-18. **22-27.** Abraham carries out the instructions immediately and literally, a characteristic of P style.

27 (i) THE GUESTS OF ABRAHAM AND LOT (18:1-19:38 [J]). Chaps. 18-19 form a single story; the mysterious guests visit Abraham in Mamre to promise him and Sarah a child the next year (18:1-15), and then they visit Lot in Sodom to investigate and subsequently to punish the corrupt city (19:1-29). Between the two visits, which are meant to balance each other, Abraham questions God about the justice of the act of punishing Sodom (18:16-33). At the end of the destruction in chap. 19 there is a short narrative of how Lot became the father of Moab and the Ammonites (19:30-38). The extensive narrative continues the Abraham and Lot cycle, which began in chap. 13. Lot, Abraham's nephew, allowed to choose any place he desired when their herdsmen quarreled, chose the lush area of the Jordan Valley in the direction of Zoar (13:10-11); Abraham took the less verdant land of Canaan. Chap. 13 pointed to chap. 19 by its ominous statement, "The people of Sodom were very wicked sinners against Yahweh." Throughout these chapters there is a persistent contrast between the patient and obedient old Abraham and the impetuous and foolish young Lot. By every natural measure, the young and aggressive Lot, not the old Abraham, should have been the father of Israel.

28 (i) *Abraham and the three guests* (18:1-15). **1-8.** The prefatory v 1 states that it is Yahweh who appears to Abraham, mediated by the three men of vv 2 and 16, the one speaker of vv 10,13,15,17-33, and the two messengers or angels in chap. 19. The fluidity of actors in the scene is a narrative means of describing both the nearness and the mysterious elusiveness of God. Also expressive of majesty is the initial contrast between the dozing Abraham and the purposefully journeying men, and then Abraham's frantic preparations and their commanding silence; they speak only once but authoritatively (v 5b). The entire section is a superb example of Hebr narrative art. **9–15.** The hitherto silent guests, having been served a grand meal by Abraham, now dominate the scene by their questions, all of them about Sarah. One of them avers that he will return next year (rather than "next spring"; cf. Akk *ana balat,* "next year") and Sarah will have a son (v 10). Sarah, overhearing, laughs in disbelief, just as Abraham had laughed in 17:17. Yahweh himself reiterates the promise and rebukes Sarah (vv 13–15).

29 (ii) *Abraham bargains with God* (18:16–33). Many scholars judge this section to be later than the narratives preceding and following it; the concern with God's righteousness is an exilic theme (cf. Ezek 14:12–23 and chap. 18). However its date be assessed, Abraham does not intercede for Sodom (against many commentators) but through his bold questions learns that God, the judge of the world, is indeed just, distinguishing between the righteous and the wicked, as in the case of Noah and sinful humanity in chaps. 6–9. **16.** Abraham accompanies the men from Mamre (near Hebron) to a place where they "looked down" (so the Hebr vb.) over the S end of the Dead Sea (generally presumed to be the site of Sodom and Gomorrah, and also Zoah). **17–21.** Yahweh soliloquizes (vv 17–19), asking the question whether he will hide his plans from Abraham. In the ancient Near East, a servant of the god or king was also a friend, privy to his master's plans. Yahweh's own answer is that since Abraham's people will be great among the nations the servant will receive the gift now of knowing the divine plan. Moreover, the people will "do what is just and right," and it is fitting that the founder of such a people now see God do what is right, i.e., punish only sinners. **20–21.** God announces to Abraham his plan, and the dialogue follows. **22.** The (two) men ("angels" in 19:1) accompanying Yahweh go off to investigate Sodom; Abraham stays behind to stand before Yahweh, into whose confidence he has already been taken (vv 17–21). **22.** *will you destroy the righteous with the wicked?:* Abraham wants to know whether the judge of all the world will deal justly. Abraham, though conscious of the distance between himself and God, dares to bargain with Yahweh (vv 27–32) to the point that only 10 righteous suffice to avert destruction. Ten is the natural limit in Abraham's questioning; below that number God can save the individuals within the city as will happen with Lot. **33.** God has been revealed as just in the dialogue, so each partner departs.

30 (iii) *The destruction of Sodom and the rescue of Lot* (19:1–29). **1–3.** There is a deliberate parallel drawn between Abraham's reception of the three men and Lot's reception of the two. Abraham is privileged to receive Yahweh; Lot receives only the two messengers. Abraham is promised a son; Lot is told to flee. Verses 1–11 strikingly resemble Judg 19:15–21, which suggests dependence of one passage on the other. The time sequence is evening (v 1), dawn (v 15), and sunrise (v 23). **4–11.** All the men of the town, young and old, seek to abuse sexually the two guests of Lot. There is indeed a basis for the outcry that had come up to God (18:21)! The inhabitants' crime is twofold: violation of hospitality and forbidden sexual behavior (Lev 18:22). Lot's actions are those expected of a host trying to protect his guests: his offer of his two daughters to the mob, though horrifying to modern ears, is part of that duty (v 8) as Lot sees it. Lot having failed, the two men take over their own defense by rendering the attackers incapable of finding the door. **12–14.** The angels move quickly to remove Lot before the destruction. The two sons-in-law refuse to go, setting up the story of vv 30–38. **15–16.** At dawn, the

angels must drag the dilatory Lot and his family from the doomed city. **17–22.** Once outside, the angels command the still reluctant Lot to flee to the hills, but he does not want to leave the city for the country; he persuades them to let him go to a little city (Hebr *miṣ'ār*), which came to be called Zoar (Hebr *ṣô'ar*). **23–26.** God destroys Sodom and Gomorrah and the entire plain with sulfurous fire. **26.** Lot's wife is as foolish as her husband; violating the taboo against looking on the destruction, she is turned into a pillar of salt, again preparing for the last scene of the story. The S end of Dead Sea is even today a lunar landscape, readily encouraging the popular belief that it had been destroyed by an act of God. **27–28.** A masterful picture of Abraham returning to the place of his previous encounter with Yahweh, the judge of all the earth. Abraham knows that the deed has been just. **29.** As Lot had been rescued by Abraham in chap. 14, so he is rescued again by his relation to Abraham, the just man and friend of God.

31 (iv) *Lot the father of Moab and the Ammonites* (19:30–38). **30–35.** Lot finally obeys the angels' command to flee to the hills; he and his two daughters take up residence in a cave. With Lot's wife and the daughters' prospective husbands gone, the question is raised how Lot will have descendants. As bizarre as the story is, it illustrates the Genesis theme of new life after destruction (cf. Gen 9). The narrative is highly stylized: the names of the daughters ("the older" and "the younger"), the ease with which they dupe their father, the identical description of each encounter. **36–38.** The meaning of the succinct statements of the birth is that the line of Moab and Ammon, genealogically related to Israel, stems from Lot's daughters. The ridicule of Moab and Ammon (who later became enemies of Israel) by ridiculing their birth is typically Eastern. The main thrust of the narrative, however, is to serve as a contrast between Abraham and Lot. The just Abraham waits for the Lord to give him land and a son. Lot and his household are grasping and foolish, managing only to survive. Survive they do only because of Lot's relationship to the chosen Abraham.

32 (j) ABRAHAM AND ABIMELECH (20:1–18 [E: 1b–18] [J: 1a]). Abraham's passing off Sarah as his sister to escape trouble in a foreign land is the theme of 12:10–13:1 (J), of this chapter (E), and, with a change of actors, of 26:1–11 (J). This story is not simply the E version of the ancestral wife in danger; it seems in v 2 and elsewhere to presuppose chap. 12; it is mostly dialogue about the justice of God, Abimelech's fear of the Lord, and Abraham's intercessory power. "It is a search for answers to questions which the old narrative about Abraham raised" (Westermann, *Genesis 12–36* 319). Verses 1–2 set the scene; vv 3–13 are two dialogues, one between God and Abimelech (vv 3–8) and the second between Abimelech and Abraham (vv 9–13); vv 14–18 resume the action and right the wrong.

1–2. Abraham presumably had been at Mamre ("from there"); he now surveys the farthest limit of the holy land. *The Negeb:* A general term for the large S area of Canaan; hot and dry, it has an average annual rainfall of less than eight inches. *Kadesh(-Barnea):* Contemporary Ain Qudeirat, where the Israelites camped in the wilderness period, is about 42 mi. S of Beer-sheba; Abraham is associated with a traditional hallowed place. *Shur:* A desert region, but here probably means "the way to Shur," the road to Egypt. *Gerar:* An unknown town in the region, the site of several Isaac stories (chap. 26). **3–8.** God came in a dream to warn Abimelech that Sarah was Abraham's wife. The dream is a legal process, in which God acts as judge and prosecutor; Abimelech is exonerated of blame but not cleared of the consequence of his act. In the ancient deed–consequence perspective of the story, he is, however unwittingly, still under the death sentence for the act of abduction of a man's wife. Abimelech's household has already suffered the automatic consequences of his act (vv 17–18); only his act of restoration and Abraham's intercession can undo fully its effects. The royal servants all fear the Lord when they hear the dream (v 8), thus invalidating Abraham's excuse that "there is no fear of God at all in this place" (v 11). **9–13.** Abimelech accuses Abraham of injustice. The king's questions in v 9 are rhetorical; the question about the motive (v 10) is real and is the one that Abraham answers in vv 11–13. **9.** *great sin:* In comparable Canaanite and Egyptian texts this usually means adultery (W. L. Moran, *JNES* 18 [1958] 280–81). Abraham's answer is weak. He is wrong about there being no fear of God in the place and unconvincing in his mental reservation about Sarah's being his half sister, free to marry him (2 Sam 13:13). **14–18.** Abimelech's grand gestures illustrate his integrity, obedience (cf. v 14 with vv 5–7), and awe before God's servant, Abraham. **16.** *vindication:* Lit., "covering of the eyes"; it refers to Sarah's honor, though the exact significance of the legal gesture is unknown. **17–18.** Though he has acted neither with trust in God nor with honor in comparison with Abimelech, Abraham's privileged position as "prophet" (only here in Gen) is undiminished; his intercession is successful.

33   (k) THE BIRTH OF ISAAC AND THE EXPULSION OF HAGAR AND ISHMAEL (21:1–21 [P: 1b–5] [J: 7] [E: 6,8–21]).   Though some scholars question whether the section is a unity, e.g., Westermann, who ascribes vv 1–7 to a redactor tying up the threads from 11:30 and chaps. 17 and 18 (*Genesis 12–36* 331), most correctly see the long-awaited birth of Isaac as paralleling the birth of Ishmael (chap. 16) and hence precipitating a rivalry and expulsion as in that chapter. It is true, however, that the focus of vv 1–7 is exclusively on Sarah and Isaac and the focus of vv 8–21 exclusively on Hagar and Ishmael.

Among the themes of the Abraham and Sarah story, none occupies a greater place than the promise of a son and heir to the aged and childless couple. Sarah is described at the outset as barren (11:30), and Abraham as 75 years old (12:4). The couple's childlessness contrasts strikingly with the command to the human race at creation to "be fruitful and multiply, and fill the earth" (1:28) and with the rapid expansion of the race in chaps. 1–11. Promises of offspring are regularly made to Abraham (12:2,7; 13:16; 15:1–6; chaps. 17, 18). Plays on Isaac's name (Hebr *yiṣḥaq[ʾēl]* "May God laugh in delight, smile upon") are made in 17:17 and implied in 18:12–15 in the context of the promised birth. Verses 1–7 therefore sum up this major theme and resolve the tension surrounding this aspect of God's promise to the couple. The other strand of the tension, the promise of the land, will be partially resolved in the story of Abraham's purchase of the cave at Machpelah (24:1–20). Literary-critical exegesis has regarded vv 8–21 as the E version of the J chap. 16; Elohim is used for Yahweh, and the original text assumes that Ishmael is an infant (see commentary on v 14). However valid this assumption about the origin of the story may be, the redactor has shaped the story as an integral piece within the history of Abraham. Within the chapter, vv 1–7 emphasize that the birth fulfills God's promises; among the signs of divine action are plays on the name Isaac (cf. 17:19; 18:12–15) and the circumcision (cf. 17:9–14). The very importance of the birth of Isaac sets in motion the domestic drama with its national consequences. The weaning of the child at the customary age of three (v 8; cf. de Vaux, *AI* 43, 468) means that the child has survived the threat of infant mortality and is to survive to adulthood. Isaac's survival of infancy prompts Sarah to fight for her child and her own life, which is

bound up with Isaac; Ishmael has to go. The drama of vv 8–21 thus depends on vv 1–7.

1–7. The birth of Isaac. Virtually every sentence states the fulfillment of the divine promise, a clear sign that the birth is a major turning point in the story. **1.** The parallelism of the verse, characteristic of Hebr poetry, may reflect the oral stage of the national story. **2.** Abraham had been promised a son the year before (17:21; 18:10,14). **3.** The name Isaac had been given by God in 17:19 and implied in the wordplay of 18:12–15. The name means "May God laugh in delight, smile upon," which recalls and reverses the skepticism expressed by both Abraham and Sarah when they first heard that a child would be born to them in a year's time. **4.** Abraham circumcises the eight-day-old infant according to the instructions given in 17:9–14; it is the sign of the covenant, "which you shall keep, between me and you and your descendants after you." **5.** *100 years old:* Abraham's life is neatly divided: 75 years in Ur and Haran (12:4), 25 years waiting for the child in Canaan, and 75 years in Canaan after the birth of Isaac (25:7). **6–7.** Emotionally, the section is Sarah's. She feels herself rescued from the shame (in that culture) of not being a mother and fruitful wife; she herself reverses her earlier skeptical laughter (18:12–15). In a different way, the fruitful but rejected Hagar will be rescued in the next section.

8–21. The rejected Hagar and Ishmael are rescued by an angel. **8.** The age of weaning was three years, a proof that Isaac, in an age of high infant mortality, will survive to adulthood. It is therefore a turning point. **9–11.** The peaceful playing of the two boys stirs in Sarah deep feelings of anxiety about her own son's inheritance, since both boys are sons of Abraham. Her ruthless strategy should not be judged by modern standards; she wants Isaac alone to be the heir of the grand promises. Her own future is tied up with her son's; she is fighting for her life. **9.** *with her son Isaac:* This phrase seems to have dropped out of the MT by haplography; the phrase is preserved by the LXX and the Vg. **10.** Sarah in her anger brands her rival "that slave woman and her son," not even mentioning their names. **11.** To Abraham, the natural father of Ishmael, Sarah's ultimatum causes great pain. **12–13.** God commands Abraham to obey Sarah, for it is from Sarah's child that Abraham's line will continue (lit., "be named"). Besides, from Ishmael "a great (LXX, Vg, Sam, Syr) people" will come forth (cf. the 12 princes of 25:12–18). **14–21.** God hears the cry of Ishmael. **14–15.** This story presupposes that Ishmael is of a size to be easily carried by Hagar. According to the chronology of 16:16; 21:5,8, Abraham was 86 when Ishmael was born. Since Abraham was 100 at Isaac's birth and three years of nursing have elapsed (21:5), Ishmael is at least 16 years old. The present story is from E, whereas the other chronology is from P. **16.** Some transls. (including the LXX) correct the MT (in which Hagar weeps) to "he [Ishmael] lifted up his voice and wept" on the basis of the angel's response in v 17: "God heard the voice of the child." The emendation is unnecessary, as God can hear the cry of the silent; further, such change of subject is too sudden. **17–18.** *God heard:* Hebr *wayyišmaʿ* echoes the name Ishmael. The angel, in Gen usually a means through which God speaks, tells Hagar not to fear, that God will make a great nation from him; i.e., he will survive. The response is like the oracle of salvation delivered to persons lamenting (cf. 1 Sam 1:17; Ps 12:6). **20–21.** Family and desert have been the themes of the story. God has allayed the fears of Sarah and Hagar about their families. Now the threat of the desert to Ishmael is removed; he will thrive in the desert that nearly killed him as a child. *the wilderness of Paran:* S of Canaan along the N edge of the Sinai peninsula.

34 (l) THE TREATY WITH ABIMELECH AND THE WELL AT BEER-SHEBA (21:22-34 [E]). Of the two related promises of progeny and land, that of progeny has been fulfilled in the previous scene (21:1-21). Now the claim on the land begins to be fulfilled by Abimelech's recognition of Abraham's claim on the well at Beer-sheba; Abraham's claim on the land will be further advanced by his purchase of the cave at Machpelah (chap. 23). Scholars generally recognize two layers of tradition in this story: (A) vv 22-24,27,32, the general covenant with Abimelech; (B) vv 25-26,28-30,31, Abraham's claim on the well. The first layer duplicates, perhaps even draws on, the similar story told about Isaac (26:26-31). The endings of both stories seem to have been elaborated in 21:33-34 and in 26:32-33. Both stories play on the Hebr root *šb* ʿ ("seven," "swear") and the place-name Beer-sheba. Layer B of chap. 21 has no counterpart in chap. 26. The story in chap. 21 has been edited into a single story, in which Abraham and Abimelech make a treaty (another instance of the ancestor dealing with great figures), from which Abraham gains rights over the well-known well at Beer-sheba.

22-24. *at that time:* Relates the story to what precedes, particularly to the story of Abimelech in chap. 20. The parallel 26:26-31 has to introduce Abimelech and clarify his relationship to Abraham; here the reader knows from chap. 21 Abimelech and his relationship to Abraham. Abimelech wants to make a covenant with a divinely favored person. The two men make a covenant before God. The full Hebr idiom for swearing an oath, customarily abridged as here, is "[May God (or the gods) do such and such to you] if you deal falsely with me or my kith and kin. . . ." The covenant is oral, and the keeping of it is based on the two men's sense of honor and their belief that the witnessing God (or gods) will punish the oath breaker. *not deal falsely:* A negative way of expressing covenant loyalty (Hebr *ḥesed*), the standard both partners will use in dealing with each other. Abimelech has dealt loyally with Abraham so far (cf. chap. 21); he ensures that Abraham will treat him and his land in like manner. **25-32a.** The dispute about the well. Having covenanted with Abimelech, Abraham reproaches his partner for violating the covenant in the matter of the well, which Abimelech's men had seized (v 25). Abimelech's flowery response (v 26) may be a conventional evasion of responsibility. At any rate, Abraham presents gifts, which were part of the covenant ceremony (cf. 1 Kgs 15:19; Isa 30:6; Hos 12:1). Some scholars suggest that the verse belonged originally to the covenant ceremony of vv 22-24 and have been transposed here to situate the further giving of the seven ewe lambs in vv 28-29. **30.** Abraham's giving and Abimelech's accepting of the ewe lambs witness or prove that Abimelech accepts Abraham's right to the well. Had he refused, his gesture of refusal would have meant that he did not accept Abraham's claim. **31.** *Beer-sheba:* Means by wordplay "well of the seven" and "well of the oath." **32b-33.** Abimelech as king of the Philistines is anachronistic, since the Philistines settled the coast of Palestine only in the 12 cent. The tamarisk is a small evergreen able to grow in both desert and watered areas. A sacred tamarisk in Beer-sheba is ascribed to the patriarch. Eternal God (Hebr *ʾēl ʿôlām*) is an ancient title of the god El applied to Yahweh, used at the shrine at Beer-sheba.

35 (m) GOD TESTS ABRAHAM (22:1-19 [E]). Virtually all commentators agree that this is a coherent unit; most believe that the renewed blessing in vv 15-18 was not part of the original story but rather the climactic blessing of the seven given to Abraham (→ 18 above). The story is the tenth and greatest trial of Abraham's trials; after this scene Abraham has only to buy a site for the burial of Sarah and find a wife for Isaac. The story is a masterpiece, presenting God as the Lord whose demands are absolute, whose will is inscrutable, and whose final word is grace. Abraham shows the moral grandeur of the founder of Israel, facing God, willing to obey God's word in all its mysterious harshness. Absent here are Abraham's voluble evasions (chaps. 13, 21); he is silently trusting and obedient. Enlightenment humanism has protested the command to kill the son: "There are certain cases in which man can be convinced that it cannot be God whose voice he thinks he hears; when the voice commands him to do what is opposed to the moral law, though the phenomenon seems to him ever so majestic and surpassing the whole of nature, he must count it a deception" (E. Kant, cited in Westermann, *Genesis 12-36* 354). Such a Western judgment reduces the climactic encounter between God and Abraham to an extrinsic moral demand. The father's very life is bound up with that of his child and heir; Abraham entrusts his life and his future unconditionally to the God who calls him. (Two important studies of the chapter from a philosophical and literary perspective are S. Kierkegaard, *Fear and Trembling* [Princeton, 1983]; and E. A. Auerbach, *Mimesis* [GC, 1957] 1-20).

1-3. Abraham is told by God to offer Isaac in sacrifice. **1.** *after these things:* A conventional introduction to a new section (15:1; 22:20; 39:7; 40:11). *God tested Abraham:* Only here in Gen, and only here in the Pentateuch with an individual as object; elsewhere God tests the people Israel (Exod 15:25; 16:4; Deut 8:2,16; 13:4; 33:8). The usual context of divine testing is Israel in the wilderness, tried so that its true orientation becomes manifest. This portrait of Abraham tested has come to characterize the entire cycle of Abraham to the point that rabbinic tradition sees the entire cycle as 10 tests or trials (→ 18 above); Abraham as the founding father of Israel must entrust his entire life and future to God. As with Job, the reader knows from the start what the protagonist does not: God is trying him. *here I am:* A statement of complete availability (cf. Isa 6:8). **2.** "Only son" is inaccurate, since Abraham will have other sons; already the LXX *ton agapēton* correctly interpreted the Hebr word as "favored" by God. God emphasizes in every word the value Abraham attaches to this son. *Moriah:* 2 Chr 3:1, the only other occurrence of the name, identifies Moriah as the mountain of Jerusalem where Solomon built the temple; Abraham is thus the first to worship there. Moriah plays on the Hebr word "to see" (*rāʾâ*); v 8, "God will see to . . . the offering," and v 14 with its double use of the vb. "to see to," "to provide" continue the wordplay. Abraham obeys immediately and in silence. It is up to the reader to infer a father's feelings. **4-8.** Father and son journey to the place. **4.** *on the third day:* This may be the halfway point of a seven-day journey ending in the arrival at the mountain. Abraham leaves servants and household behind alone to face God. Isaac carries the wood, and Abraham, the knife and firestone. **7-8.** In response to Isaac's question about the sacrificial animal, Abraham replies that God will "see to" (Hebr *yirʾeh*) the sheep—not a ruse but evidence of Abraham's handing everything over to God.

9-14. God sees to the sacrifice. **11.** The angel of Yahweh had called from heaven and opened the eyes of Hagar to see the well (21:17-19). The same angel now keeps Abraham from inflicting death; the angel mediates God's word and action. **12.** God's judgment in the angel's voice acknowledges Abraham's total obedience. Abraham truly fears God, for he has not withheld his favored son. He has finally learned to give up control over his own life that he might receive it as grace. **13.** A sacrificial ram is found. This reads Hebr 'aḥad, "one," "a," for senseless MT 'aḥar, "behind" (Hebr resh [*r*] and daleth [*d*] are easily confused in some ancient scripts). Infant sacrifice was widely practiced in Canaan and in the Phoenician colonies of N Africa. It was even practiced in Israel, as the OT polemic against it shows (2 Kgs 16:3; Mic 6:7), in critical times as a means of averting divine wrath. Israel recognized that the firstborn belonged to Yahweh (Exod 13:11–16; 34:19–20) but "redeemed" firstborn human beings by an alternate sacrifice. This story tells how the founder was directed by God to "redeem" his firstborn by the sacrifice of an animal. How Israel differs from its neighbors in this regard is only one aspect of this rich story; it is not the chief point. **14.** The motif of God's "seeing to" all things is doubly emphasized by the name Abraham gives to the mountain: "Yahweh will see." **15–19.** The same angel now repeats for the seventh and climactic time (cf. 12:2–3,7; 13:14–17; 15; 17; 18) the great promises in their most generous form.

36 (n) Nahor's Descendants (22:20–24 [J]). A genealogy of Nahor, Abraham's brother, who was married to Milcah. Of the three sons of Terah, the oldest, Abraham, had finally fathered Isaac (21:1–7); the youngest, Haran, who had died in Ur, had fathered Lot. Now the reader is told of Nahor and his eight children by Milcah and his four children by his concubine Reumah. The genealogy completes the information about Terah's family to the second generation (except for the additional children born to Abraham by his second wife Keturah in 25:1–6). Jacob, like Nahor, will have eight children by his wives, and four by his concubines.

20–24. *after these things:* A conventional introduction to a new episode. It refers back most naturally to 21:1–7, the birth of Isaac, since Abraham is told, "Milcah too has borne children to Nahor." Of the 12 children, the names of three also are to be place-names: Uz is the homeland of Job (Job 1:1), probably N Edom; Buz is the homeland of one of Job's friends (32:2); Hazu (and Bazu) are mentioned by the 7th-cent. Assyrian king Esarhaddon. Gen 10:23 mentions Uz as a son of Aram. Bethuel appears as a personage in 24:15 and elsewhere. Abraham's whole family is blessed.

37 (o) Abraham Buys a Burial Site for Sarah (23:1–20 [P]). One of the two great promises to Abraham and Sarah, that of progeny, has been fulfilled (21:1–7), and Abraham has proved that he accepts the child entirely as the gift of God (chap. 22). In this chapter, the other promise of God, that he will possess the land of Canaan, is symbolically fulfilled by the plot of land Abraham buys from Ephron the Hittite with unimpeachable legality. The occasion for the purchase is the need of a burial place for Sarah. Burying the dead is a motif running through the story (vv 4,6,8,11,13,19). It is unthinkable that the ancestress should be buried in alien soil. Several scholars have pointed to Neo-Babylonian dialogue contracts of the 7th to the 5th cent. as models for the transaction (de Vaux, *EHI* 255–56; van Seters, *Abraham* 98–101). The parallels are impressive though not perfect; it is likely that general ancient Near Eastern legal custom is reflected here, adapted to the local situation. The narrative is entirely P's, like chap. 17 on circumcision, and like 27:46–28:9 on marriage within one's own people—both important issues during the exile and thereafter. P may have one eye on his own exilic generation, to encourage their hopes to possess the land.

1–2. The death of Sarah. **1.** *Kiriath-arba:* Lit., "the City of Four," now Hebron, located in the S hill country of Judah—*ca.* 27 mi. SSW of Jerusalem. Abraham was buried there (25:9), as were Isaac (35:27–29) and Rebekah (49:31), and Jacob and Leah (49:29–33).

Cenotaphs to these founders are revered today in the great mosque at Hebron, Haram el-Khalil, "the Shrine of the Friend" (i.e., of God = Abraham). **2.** Abraham "bewailed" (rather than "wept") his wife in the customary loud lamentations and rituals. **3–9.** Abraham wins the assent of the area inhabitants to negotiate for the purchase. **4.** *rose up:* He was prostrate beside his wife's body in the ritual. *Hittites:* An ethnic designation with several meanings in the Bible: the inhabitants of the great 2d-millennium Hittite empire in Asia Minor and N Syria, which collapsed *ca.* 1200; residents of the Neo-Hittite kingdoms in N Syria in the first half of the 1st-millennium; a general designation for the inhabitants of Syria and Palestine, following Assyrian terminology. The term Hatti continued to be used in the Neo-Babylonian period (6th cent.) as a geographical term that included Palestine. It is in this third, extended sense that the natives of Hebron are called Hittites. The names of the "Hittites" in Gen—Ephron and Zohar—are Semitic. **4.** *resident alien:* Hendiadys; lit., "a stranger and a sojourner." He needed the natives' permission to conduct business with the same right as the natives. **6.** Abraham as "the elect of God," i.e., a highly respected person in the area, is given permission by the assembly. **10–16.** Abraham buys the field from Ephron. **10–13.** Ephron now may deal with Abraham. With fulsome Oriental courtesy (and perhaps a little humor) he offers to give the field with the cave to Abraham. Abraham as befits a man of his station insists on paying. **14.** 400 shekels seems exorbitant in comparison with the 17 shekels that Jeremiah paid for a field (Jer 32:7) and the 6,000 that Omri paid for the entire area on which Samaria was built (1 Kgs 16:24). The Babylonian standard, commonly employed all over the ancient Near East, was probably used in the transaction: one silver shekel = 8.25 grams; one talent = 60 minas = 3,600 shekels. Abraham does not bargain with Ephron, perhaps from eagerness to make an undoubted purchase and from a sense of his own and Sarah's dignity before the crowd of foreigners. **17–20.** The text emphasizes the strict legal nature of the sale.

38 (p) A Wife for Isaac (24:1–67 [J]). The story of Abraham and Sarah is drawing to a close. Sarah has died, the promise of progeny has been fulfilled with the birth of Isaac (21:1–7), and that of land with the purchase of the burial site at Machpelah, which is a pledge of the entire land. There remains only the task of seeing to his son's proper response to the promises. Isaac must take a wife from the ancestral homeland, not Canaan, and return to Canaan (vv 3–7), so that the promise may be fulfilled literally and visibly. Abraham himself ceases speaking after he charges his servant in vv 1–9 of this chapter.

The story differs from the hitherto relatively short and self-contained narratives of the cycle by its great length, which stems largely from meticulous attention to the sign (vv 12–14), its fulfillment (vv 15–20), and the servant's repetition of sign and fulfillment to Rebekah's legal guardians to win their consent (vv 34–49). By its leisurely development of a single theme, its interest in character and local color, and its mention of Laban, it points forward to the Jacob and Joseph stories. The story has eight scenes: (1) Abraham's covenant with his senior servant to find a wife for Isaac (vv 1–9); (2) the servant's request for a sign (vv 10–14); (3) Rebekah's fulfillment of the sign (vv 15–20); (4) Rebekah's statement that she is Abraham's kin (vv 21–27); (5) the servant's welcome into the household (vv 28–33); (6) the servant's confirming the sign to the household and request for their consent (vv 34–49); (7) the family's sending Rebekah on her way with a blessing (vv 50–61); (8) The marriage (vv 62–67). The scenes are of roughly comparable length except for the repetition in scene 6. The divine guidance, which in the previous stories was through appearances and speeches of Yahweh, in this story is through the exact fulfillment of a sign—the willingness of the young woman to feed the servant and his camels.

1-2. Abraham personally has experienced the promise and now must fulfill a parent's duty to arrange his son's marriage and his son's domicile. *put your hand under my thigh and I will make you swear:* In 46:26 and Exod 1:5 sons are said to come from the father's thigh (a euphemism for the male organ). The rite is not explained but may place the one who swears under the penalty of sterility if the task is not carried out. **3.** *the God of heaven and the God of earth:* Cosmic pairs, such as heaven and earth were often invoked as witnesses to covenants. Here the one God who views all will see to the servant's carrying out the agreement. Abraham is concerned for the promise of progeny and land. Intermarriage with the Canaanites was forbidden to later Israel (Deut 7:3; Ezra 10). **7.** *who took me from my father's house and my native land:* Recalls Gen 12:1, God's initial call; Abraham is here totally obedient to that call and reliant upon God. **9.** In v 49 the servant will wait upon the reply of Rebekah's family to find out if he is free from the oath. **10.** Camels are an anachronism; Israel seems to have first encountered the camel in Midianite raids of the 11th or 12th cent. (Judg 6:5). The meeting of the bride at the well is a motif found also in 29:1–14 and Exod 2:15–22. The servant appeals to God's covenant love (*ḥesed*) for Abraham, for whom he acts. A person with a task from God may ask for or be given a sign (a sample of the divine power) to assure that the task will be divinely supported; Moses is given a sign (Exod 3:12), and Gideon asks for one (Judg 6:36–40). Here the sign will be the woman's carrying out the servant's scenario of giving water to him and to his camels. **15-20.** Rebekah's fulfillment of the sign, the watering of the camels, not only confirms the divine intent; it also shows her noble and generous nature. **21-27.** Rebekah further confirms the sign by revealing that she is Abraham's kin and by inviting the servant to lodge with her family. **21.** The masterful sentence portrays a man in the midst of having his deepest question answered. **23-24.** Rebekah's statement and her invitation end the servant's wavering, causing him to give thanks (v 27), i.e., to tell publicly that God has acted according to his covenant with Abraham ("steadfast love and faithfulness") by directing his servant to the right household.

28-33. The servant is welcomed into the household. The father of Rebekah, Bethuel, being dead, the family's consent will be given by her brother Laban. Several scholars suggest that Hurrian legal practice, attested from 15th-cent. documents found at Nuzi (a site in NE Iraq), is being followed in the transaction. In a "sistership document," the servant represents Abraham, and Laban represents his sister. The emissary gives presents to the woman and "gifts" also to the family to cover the bride payment; the bride herself must give consent (cf. "I will go" in v 58) (Speiser, *Genesis* 184–85). **30.** Laban becomes hospitable when he sees the servant's gifts, a humorous contrast to his sister's spontaneous generosity and a pointer to his character in the Jacob stories (cf. 31:14–16, 36–43). **34-49.** The servant confirms the sign and asks for the household's consent. Repetition is common in ancient narrative; minor alterations add interest (cf. vv 39,41,44,48). The exact realization of the sign is designed to persuade the family that God has led the servant to their very doorstep. **49.** Do they wish to enter into a covenant with Abraham? If not, the servant will be free from his oath ("that I may turn right or left") **50-60.** The family sends Rebekah on her way with a blessing. **50.** *and Bethuel:* Generally considered a gloss, since Laban acts

throughout. **51.** The family is persuaded that the thing is from God. **53.** See comment on 24:28–33. **55.** Laban's delaying tactics point toward the Jacob stories (29:27; 30:25–28; 31:26–30). **62-67.** Isaac marries Rebekah. *Beer-lahai-roi:* The well named by Hagar (16:14) is near Kadesh, some 86 mi. SSW of Mamre (just N of Hebron), where Abraham lived. Isaac seems to be living well S of Abraham, in the general area of the Negeb. **63.** *meditate:* A guess for Isaac's activity; the word is obscure. **64.** Isaac catches Rebekah's eye even before she knows who he is, an indication of God's bringing them together. **67.** Isaac welcomes Rebekah into his house ("tent") and marries her.

39   (q) THE DESCENDANTS OF ABRAHAM (25:1–18 [J?: 1–4,5–6,11b] [P?: 7–11a,12–18]). The section consists of various notices about Abraham's descendants, grouped together to conclude the story. The section is more concerned with completeness of listing rather than with the chronological sequence of the previous chapters. According to the P chronology, Isaac was 60, and Abraham 100 years older, when Jacob and Esau were born (25:26; 21:5), so that Abraham still had 15 years of life left to him (cf. 25:7); strict adherence to chronology would have placed Abraham's death notice at the end of the chapter rather than at its beginning. Like 11:27–32, the story of Terah, this section intends to list all the descendants of Abraham as a means of concluding his story. The Jacob story ends similarly with the listing of the 12 sons (35:22–26), the death of Isaac (35:27–28), and the descendants of Esau (chap. 36). Because the verses are mostly lists, ascription of them to the documentary sources is uncertain.

40   (i) *The descendants of Abraham* (25:1–6). Strict chronology suggests that Abraham was at least 140 when he married Keturah, since Isaac was 40 when he married Rebekah (25:20) and Abraham was 100 when he fathered Isaac (21:5); his marriage to Keturah may well have taken place long before, when Sarah was alive. 1 Chr 1:32, the only other place to mention Keturah, calls her a concubine, or secondary wife. If "by his concubines" of the MT (v 6) means "by concubinage" (so A. Ehrlich, cited by Speiser, [*Genesis* 187]), then v 6 may simply sum up Keturah's children. **2.** Several of the names are Arab tribes: Medan and Midian are perhaps doublets, the latter being well known as a tribe in the Arabian desert (37:28,36; Exod 2; 18; Num 22; 25; 31; Judg 6). Ishbak and Shuah appear in Assyrian sources as Yashbuq and Suhu, located in the steppes of N Syria (van Seters, *Abraham* 61). **3.** Sheba is a people in SW Arabia; and Dedan is a people bordering on Edom, both mentioned in 10:7 as descendants of Ham. The Asshurim (not the Assyrians), the Letushim, and the Leummim are unknown peoples, missing from the parallel in 1 Chr 1:28–33. **4.** *the descendants of Midian:* Ephah, Epher, and Hanoch occur as family names in the tribes of Judah, Manasseh, and Reuben. Abida and Eldaah are attested as personal names in inscriptions of the Sabaeans, a merchant people of SW Arabia. **5-6.** Isaac is Abraham's heir; the others are sent away to the east to protect him.

41   (ii) *The death and burial of Abraham* (25:7–11). **7.** P is interested in the age of Abraham at key times. He was 75 when he left Haran, 100 when he fathered Isaac, and 175 when he died. Verses 7–8a are almost the same as 35:28–29, the death of Isaac. **8.** *gathered to his kin:* This may refer to the archaeologically attested practice of the time to place the bones in the ancestral burial place. Abraham's death, crowning a long life blessed by God with children with burial in the family plot, exemplifies the ideal death.

42   (iii) *The descendants of Ishmael* (25:12–18). Like the conclusion of the Jacob story (chap. 36), where the numerous descendants of the rejected Esau are listed, the princely descendants of the rejected Ishmael conclude the story. The names of Ishmael's wives are not given. **13.** *Nebaioth:* His sister marries Esau (28:9; 36:3). The name occurs in 8th- and 7th-cent. cuneiform texts as *Nabayāti* or *Nab'āti,* together with Qidri (= Kedar), both Arabian tribes. *Mibsam:* In 1 Chr 4:25 this is a personal name. **14.** *Dumah:* Mentioned in Isa 21:11 as a place-name in conjunction with Seir. *Massa:* Prov 31:1 mentions a king of Massa. *Tema* is a famous oasis in NW Arabia. **16.** *villages:* In the Mari texts these refer to nomadic settlements (A. Malamat, *BA* 34 [1971] 17). **18.** *Havilah-by-Shur:* See Speiser, *Genesis* 188. There were several sites named Havilah; further identification was necessary. The site is on the way to Egypt. Read 18b "They encamped (lit., "fell") alongside their kinsmen."

43 **(B) The Story of Isaac and Jacob (25:19–36:43).** The notice of Abraham's death and the two genealogies of 25:1–6,12–18 mark the end of a major section in the book. The next block is constituted by Gen 25:19–36:43, which deals with Isaac and Jacob. G. Coats (*Genesis* 177–81) classified this material as the Isaac saga (25:19–37:2), but he recognizes a major Jacob narrative; Isaac, as an independent figure has only a shadowy existence in the book. The main narrative can be conveniently synopsized (cf. Westermann, *Genesis 12–36* 406–9): Gen 27–33 contains Jacob's flight and return, and within it two conflicts—Jacob and Laban (29–31), and Leah and Rachel (29:31–30:24). There is an introduction (25:19–34, rivalry of Jacob and Esau) and a conclusion (35–36, mainly genealogical lists). Only chaps. 26 (stories about Isaac) and 34 (Dina and the Shechemites) stand apart from this narrative. The P *tôlĕdôt* formula begins 25:19, indicating the family history of Isaac, and his death is recorded in 35:19; but the subject of interest is Jacob.

The theme of the promises to the patriarchs is present, but relatively subdued (28:3–4,13–15; 35:11–12). Blessing (*bĕrākâ*) is given more emphasis. It is at the heart of the conflict between Jacob and Esau (chaps. 27, 33) and is woven into the success Jacob achieves, esp. his struggle with God (32:24–32). It is significant that the promise and blessing are communicated through the unlikely Jacob, who is not the firstborn or beloved of his father, as Esau is. The Israelite tradition preserved the memory of Jacob's devious ways; he remained a sign that the divine choice was as mysterious as it was gratuitous. M. Fishbane (*Text and Texture* [NY, 1979] 40–62) has underscored the symmetry of the Jacob cycle (25:19–35:22), and the three issues of barrenness/fertility, nonblessing/blessing, and exile/homeland; see also T. Fretheim, "The Jacob Traditions," *Int* 26 (1972) 419–36; G. Rendsburg, *Redaction* 53–69.

A complete bibliography on chaps. 25–36 is found in Westermann, *Genesis 12–36;* see the indications on "literature" on pp. 14–17.

44 **(a) THE BIRTH OF ESAU AND JACOB (25:19–34).** **19–20.** These verses have all the earmarks of the P tradition, including the *tôlĕdôt* formula ("the descendants of Isaac"). However, no genealogy follows, but only the record of Isaac's birth from his father Abraham. Also characteristic of P is Paddan-aram ("field of Aram," Hos 12:13) and Aram-naharaim (Gen 24:10). On Bethel and Laban (here called an Aramean), see 24:24,47,50. According to P chronology, Isaac married Rebekah at forty, and it is only 20 years later that her sterility is ended (v 26). **21–22.** Note that it is through the intercession of Isaac that Rebekah finally conceives. The experience of her pregnancy (interpreted as a struggle between the two children) causes Rebekah to complain: "If this be so, why then am I?" It is not clear if she is

concerned about herself or the children. Hence she goes to consult (*drš*) an oracle from the Lord at a sanctuary; Gunkel remarks that this is an anachronism for the patriarchal period. **23.** The poetic response joins present and future: the children are already struggling in the womb, but they are nations (Israel and Edom). Contrary to Israelite custom, the elder will serve the younger. The motif of twins (so identified in v 24) struggling in the womb is known in folklore (cf. also Gen 38:27–30). **25.** The firstborn is red ('admônî; hence a reference to Edom) and also hairy (*śē'îr;* a reference to Mt. Seir in Edom; cf. Gen 32:4). Oddly, he is given a name that has nothing to do with these characteristics, Esau, the meaning of which is uncertain. The "red" points to v 30, and the "hairy" to 27:11. **26.** There is a play on the root '*qb* (heel) found in Jacob's name; he is the "heel-gripper." Actually the name of Jacob (*y'qb*) is a short form of a proper name, *y'qb-'l,* "may God protect," which occurs in ancient Near Eastern sources. These wordplays are obviously loaded against Esau, but the characterization of Jacob as "heel-gripper" and one who supplants will be sharply delineated in his life. **27–28.** Further differences between the two appear: the hunter as opposed to the homebody. One can see the split in the affections of the parents as practically inevitable. At the same time, these verses anticipate the events of chap. 27.

29–34. This episode may have originally functioned as a story of shepherds prevailing over hunters. The hunter necessarily lives a more precarious and adventuresome life than the shepherd. In any case, Esau is caricatured here as an insensitive person (in contrast to his feelings about the birthright in 27:36). **29–30.** The scene is described quickly and with some humor. Esau is so hungry he calls imperiously for food; he wants to "gulp down the red stuff" that Jacob is preparing. This allows the writer to allude once again to the name Edom; cf. v 25. **31–33.** As the story flows, Jacob shows himself to be a versatile and quick thinker when he demands: "Give me your birthright." Who would expect that as an answer? Esau brushes aside the thought of the birthright because he is dying of hunger. The tough-minded Jacob seals the bargain with an oath. **35.** The "staccato succession of five verbal forms" (Speiser) further underlines the mindless behavior of Esau.

45 **(b) ISAAC STORIES (26:1–35).** Gunkel agrees with F. Delitzsch that this chapter gives the impression of a "mosaic," in which five parts can be distinguished: a journey to Gerar because of a theophany; Rebekah's adventure in Gerar; Isaac's prosperity and departure; the dispute over wells; and the treaty of Beer-sheba. **1–11.** This bland and relatively colorless presentation of the ancestress in danger is derived from Gen 12:1–10 (cf. 20:1–18), *pace* M. Noth (*Pentateuchal Traditions* 104–6). **1–2.** This famine is clearly distinguished from that mentioned in 12:10, when Abraham went to Egypt. Now Isaac is expressly forbidden to go to Egypt (v 2). He goes to Gerar from wherever he is presupposed to be (at Beer-lahai-roi? 25:11). The mention of the Philistines at this time is an anachronism, as in 21:32–34. **3–5.** The theophany makes Isaac the vehicle of the promises to Abraham of land, people, and blessing (12:1–3; 15:18). Father Abraham is clearly the model for the promises and the obedience they should call forth (note the language of D in v 5, "commandments," etc.) **6.** *Gerar:* The site cannot be identified with certainty; it seems to be about midway between Beer-sheba and Gaza. From the episode that follows it is clear that Isaac settled down here for some time. **7.** See 12:11–12 and 20:2 for the same pattern of conduct and the same motivation (beauty of the wife; but the beautiful Rebekah of v 7 is hardly the mother of two grown sons mentioned in 25:28!). Here the situation is more casual: a response to interrogation. There is no preconceived plan. **8.** The episode moves rapidly as Abimelech sees Isaac (*yiṣḥāq*) fondling (*mĕṣaḥeq*) Rebekah. **9–11.** Abimelech comes off as a person of high moral standards. His motive is that he fears that the whole community might have become guilty through any sexual mishap to Rebekah (v 10). Isaac's conduct, like that of Abraham, is selfish and cowardly, although the danger to Rebekah appears more remote.

12–14. In contrast to the way Abraham achieved wealth in 12:16 and 20:14–16, Isaac is said to prosper because of the Lord's blessing. The description befits a landowner (crops, flocks, herds) of a later period rather than a wandering patriarch. The "envy" of the Philistines leads into the following episode. Isaac will be forced to leave because of his prosperity, not because of his wife (contrast 12:19). **15.** This verse alludes perhaps to 21:25–26, and it may motivate the dismissal by Abimelech in v 16—unless v 15 is meant only as a note to v 18, to prepare for the ensuing dispute (vv 19–25) about wells. **16–17.** Despite Abimelech's command, Isaac seems not to have gone far, since he camps (hardly the term for one who appears to be a cattle rancher in vv 12–14) in the Wadi Gerar and reopens his father's wells. **19–25.** Cf. 21:25–31. Here three disputes over wells, with appropriate etiologies, are presented. The importance of wells goes without saying—they have been and still remain subjects of dispute. Esek means "quarrel"; Sitnah, "opposition." The favorable name, Rehoboth, means "wide spaces." At Beer-sheba Isaac experiences another theophany in which the blessing of future descendants is promised "for the sake of my servant Abraham" (cf. v 5). **24.** *God of your father Abraham:* → 17 above; cf. de Vaux, *EHI* 267–87. **25a.** This is a typical formula; cf. 12:7–8; 13:4. **25b.** The note about digging a well at Beer-sheba prepares for vv 32–33.

26–33. See 21:22–33. The visit from Abimelech continues vv 12–16. There Abraham was expelled; now Abimelech sues for a treaty because "Yahweh is with you." The prestige of Isaac is further indicated by the presence of the general and counsellor; this is an official state visit. **29.** The agreement amounts to a nonaggression pact, sealed by a covenant meal (v 30). The reason for this treaty with the "Philistines" is not clear, unless it reflects later experiences of the descendants of Isaac. **32–33.** This report about a well (cf. v 25b) is intended to be an explanation of Beer-sheba (well of seven/oath). **33.** *Shibah:* The form is hapax; perhaps both "oath" (*šĕbû 'â*) and "seven" (*šeba '*) are meant. The well of seven (Beer-sheba) is also the well of the oath.

34–35. This is more than a note about Esau's marriages with Hittite women (called "Canaanites" in 28:1) and the ensuing pain it caused his parents. The verses belong to P, and they are continued in 27:46; 28:1–9, where Jacob is sent to his relatives to choose a wife. The positioning here is probably "to soften the bad impression created by the ruthless and unscrupulous conduct portrayed of Rebekah and Jacob in chapter 27" (Vawter, *Genesis* 297). In the list of Esau's wives (36:1–3), Judith is missing, and Basemath is called an Ishmaelite.

46   (c) THE BLESSING OF JACOB (27:1–45 [J]). There is a sudden shift in the presentation of Isaac. Now he is old and practically blind—in effect, on his deathbed and disposed to impart his blessing (contrast 28:1–5). This chapter continues the Jacob–Esau conflict that was begun in 25:19–34. The deception of Isaac is structured in several scenes (Coats, von Rad) in terms of the actors: Isaac and Esau (vv 1–4), Rebekah and Jacob (vv 5–17), Isaac and Jacob (vv 18–29), Isaac and Esau (vv 30–40), transitional conclusion, Esau and Rebekah (vv 41–45). Isaac's blindness leads to an emphasis on the other senses:

taste, touch, hearing, and feeling. Essential to the chapter is the notion of blessing. Blessing is often given in a deathbed setting or in a simple farewell. It is to be understood as "vitality that is passed on by the one who is departing from life to the one who is continuing in life. . . . Because the blessing is concerned with vitality as a whole, the blessing cannot return or be subsequently altered" (Westerman, *Genesis 12–36* 436). Augustine's famous dictum that the transference of the blessing to Jacob was not a lie but a mystery does not do justice to the pathos of the story. Jacob *is* a liar, yet he is also the bearer of the promise and the blessing. The arguments for distinguishing more than one source (J) in vv 1–45 are not convincing.

1–5. The figure of Esau the hunter and his close relationship with his father were already evoked in 25:27. **4.** Isaac asks for "appetizing" food (the motif of taste) before he will impart the blessing. This is because of the connection between blessing and vitality. The subject of the blessing is *napšî*, "my soul" (better: "life," "vital force"). The continuation of the scene is in vv 30–31. But before that Rebekah will execute her plan.

5–17. Again, this scene recalls the past; see 25:28. The dialogue between mother and son is neatly developed: Rachel's plan, Jacob's implicit consent (will it work?), and the implementation of the plan. **7.** *that I may bless you in the presence of the Lord:* While Rachel relates what she overheard, she adds "before the Lord" to the "soul" blessing Isaac promised in v 4. The meaning is uncertain. The *NAB* and the *NJV* follow Speiser: "with the Lord's approval." **9–10.** Rebekah's plan is deceptively simple, but one wonders whether Isaac will be so decrepit as not to distinguish between goat meat and wild game (again, the motif of taste). **11–12.** Jacob has no scruples; he wants to save his own skin. The most obvious difficulty will be the contrast between his smoothness and Esau's hairiness (cf. 25:25). Now the sensual motif is feeling. Suppose Isaac feels Jacob? **13.** With a mother's ferocity Rachel invites upon herself the curse that Jacob fears; cf. Gen 16:5. **14–17.** Jacob carries out his mother's imperious demands, but she is the main actor as cook and clothes designer; there is comic relief here in picturing Jacob dressed in Esau's clothes and in goatskins; see vv 26–27 for the motif of smelling.

18–29. This scene between Jacob and his father is tension-packed, as Isaac registers a series of misgivings (vv 18,20–22,23,26). The motifs of smelling, feeling, and tasting appear. Jacob is a brazen liar (v 18). **20.** The action of the Lord in Jacob's alleged hunting is no more than the usual biblical understanding of the all-pervasive activity of God; the "right thing," so to speak, occurred (cf. Gen 24:12). Coats (*Genesis* 202) considers this statement "blasphemous." But there is no need to impose a modern point of view on the text; no ethical judgment is passed in the entire story. **21–27.** The motif of feeling is highlighted, and the blind Jacob is deceived. The mention of blessing in v 23 and more explicitly in vv 27–29 is understood by many as an indication of several sources; similarly, the "touching" in v 22 finds a doublet in the "smelling" in v 27. This is not convincing. **24.** Another challenge is answered by another lie. **25–27.** The eating and drinking are climaxed by a kiss, and the blessing is given. **27b–29.** The blessings begin with the motif of smell. This is not the smell of wild game in open fields (Esau), but the "fragrance" of the field—a fertility blessing such as would be prized by an agricultural people. **28.** The second blessing is also agricultural, and, like v 27, it presupposes a sedentary people. *dew of the heavens and fat(ness) of the earth:* In the Ugaritic Baal epic Anat washes herself in precisely this mixture (cf. *ANET* 136; *ṭl šmm* *šmn* '*rṣ*). This blessing will be reversed in v 39. **29.** The third blessing gives dominion over Esau (Edom); this clearly refers to later history when David subjugated this people. *cursed be . . . :* A countercurse, in order to cancel any curse against Jacob; it is found also in Num 24:9. *blessed be . . . :* Cf. Gen 12:3.

30–40. This is a scene of high pathos: Isaac's trembling, Esau's sobbing and pathetic pleas for a blessing. But once given, the blessing is irrevocable and not repeatable. **31–32.** These lines almost duplicate the treacherous actions and words of Jacob in vv 18–19. **33.** The reaction of Isaac registers his awful realization of what has occurred. **34–36.** Nonetheless, Esau continues pleading for some kind of blessing. Isaac's lame excuse (v 35) leads to Esau's indictment of the "heel-gripper," or supplanter, who has taken from him both birthright (*bĕkōrâ;* cf. 25:31–33) and blessing (*bĕrākâ*). Perhaps Isaac has "put aside" ('*āṣaltā*) a blessing for him? **37–38.** But Isaac has spent himself in the "soul" (cf. vv 4,19,25,31) blessing of Jacob, and nothing remains despite Esau's tears and his third plea. **39–40.** Surprisingly, Isaac now speaks in language reminiscent of vv 28–29, but this is more of an antiblessing: no fertility; strife and subservience to his brother. However, Esau (Edom) will finally throw off the yoke of his "brother"—as is reported in 2 Kgs 8:20,22.

41–45. Once again Rebekah is aware of whatever affects her favorite son. Ever resourceful, she devises a plan to save him from Esau's murderous intent. Her reasoning concerning losing both sons (v 45) presupposes that Esau would have to flee or be subject to the death penalty were he to slay Jacob. However, she overreaches herself this time. Her plan leads to the loss of Jacob, whom she will never see again. It will be some 20 years, not a "little while" (v 44), before Jacob returns.

47 (d) JACOB'S DEPARTURE FOR PADDAN-ARAM (27:46–28:9 [P]). This section continues 26:34–35 and is generally considered part of the P tradition. It disregards the Jacob–Esau rivalry of chap. 27. Jacob is not fleeing; he is departing peacefully to acquire a wife among relatives (marriage with foreigners was a great concern in the postexilic era; see Ezra 10). Jacob calmly receives, as though for the first time, a blessing from Isaac and a charge to depart. Put succinctly: according to J, Jacob flees from Esau to his relatives; according to P, he goes there with a blessing in order to choose a wife. Westermann (*Genesis 12–36* 271, 376, 446) ties this marriage theme with precultic rites of birth (chap. 17) and death (chap. 23).

27:46. Rebekah's complaint about Hittite wives (of Esau, and perhaps Jacob?) links directly with 26:35. **28:1–4.** Isaac does not appear to be the doddering old man of chap. 27. He issues a forthright prohibition against "Canaanite" wives and charges Jacob to marry within the clan. The blessing evokes the promise to Abraham (vv 3–4, progeny and land). **3.** *El Shaddai:* → 26 above; and cf. Westermann, *Genesis 12–36* 257–58. The die is cast. Jacob has become the vehicle of promise. In the words of Mal 1:3, "Jacob I have loved, but Esau I have hated." The love/hatred refers to definitive choice, not emotion; and hence Israel, not Edom, is the chosen. **2.** *Paddan-aram:* See comment on 25:20. *Bethuel, Laban:* See comment on 24:28–33. **6–9.** As if in imitation of Jacob and as reparation for his earlier marriages to "Canaanites," Esau marries a granddaughter of Abraham, Mahalath, daughter of Ishmael. In 36:2–3 Esau's wife Basemath, a daughter of Ishmael, is listed among the "Canaanites" he married; cf. 26:34.

48 (e) JACOB'S VISION AT BETHEL (28:10–22 [J, E]). This famous passage has been explained as a combination of J (vv 13,16–17) and E (vv 11–12,17–18,20–22). It is

equally possible to understand it as a narrative with expansions (vv 13–15,20–22). The story has gone through several stages. Originally it was an etiology (v 17) explaining the origin of a holy place, Bethel, which was venerated before Israel arrived in Canaan (see a similar etiology in 32:1–3). Second, J then used this story in the context of Jacob's journey and inserted the patriarchal promise (vv 13–15; cf. the promises in 26:3–5,24–25). Finally, the promise of personal safety to Jacob (v 15) was further expanded in his vow to return to the holy place (vv 21–23). Jacob's journey to Haran is framed by two theophanies, at Bethel and at Mahanaim (28:10–22; 32:1–3).

10. This verse continues 27:45; Jacob carries out his mother's command. *Haran:* In N Mesopotamia; associated with the origins of the patriarchs; cf. Gen 22:31–32; 12:4–5; 24. **11.** *a certain place:* Lit., "the place," which will be identified as Bethel (house of God). At sunset Jacob prepares for a night's rest. *under his head:* In this transl., the stone serves as a kind of pillow. The Hebr term can also be understood to mean "at his head," as a kind of protection. **12.** The dream consists of a stairway or ramp (not a "ladder") set in the ground and arching toward heaven. It is therefore a link between heaven and earth (v 17, "gateway to heaven"), comparable to stairways that are found in the Mesopotamian ziggurats. On this stairway angels (*mal'āk,* "messenger") go up and down—another sign of contact with heaven. They are to be equated with the "sons of God," the members of the heavenly court. The meaning of the dream is the contact between God and creatures on earth; the "messengers" carry out the divine will (like the Satan in Job 1–2). On the history of the interpretation of the passage, see D. Steinmetz, *CH* 55 (1986) 179–92. **13–35.** Part of the dream is the ensuing theophany: the Lord appears and renews the promises—land, descendants, and through the descendants blessings to all nations of the earth (cf. Gen 12:3; 26:3–4). Almost as important is the personal assurance given to Jacob of the divine presence and his eventual return to the (promised) land. **16–18.** Jacob's awaking from sleep leads to his acknowledgment of divine presence (v 16, not just "messengers") and his ensuing fear and awe (v 17). He designates the place as the house of God (Beth-el). It is a holy place, for God has appeared there. *gate of heaven:* Of itself this metaphor is ambiguous; is the gate open or closed? The appearance of the Lord on earth, as at Bethel, provides an approach to the continuous presence in heaven. **18.** In the morning Jacob sets up the stone of v 11 as a (sacred) pillar (*maṣṣēbâ*). This is a remarkable action in the view of the biblical condemnation of pillars (Hos 10:1–2; Mic 5:12; Deut 7:5, etc.). Stone worship (a supernal power dwells in the stone) was a widespread phenomenon in the ancient world, and sacred pillars were certainly part of Canaanite worship. The verse witnesses to a bold Israelite appropriation of the Bethel sanctuary to Israelite worship (cf. Gen 12:8; Abraham worships at Bethel). The cultic significance is further indicated by the oil libation. **19.** This verse provides the etiology for the name of the place, Bethel. The association with the name Luz (almond) is unclear. In Josh 16:2 Luz is distinguished from Bethel; apparently it came to be seen as the older name of Bethel. **20–22.** Jacob's vow (see W. Richter, *BZ* 11 [1967] 21–52) is a strange addition to the story. What the Lord has already promised (v 15) becomes a condition of the vow (v 20). Moreover, Jacob has already proclaimed the place the "house of God" (v 17); now he says the stone shall be the house of God (v 22). For another conditional vow, cf. 2 Sam 15:7–9. **22.** *this stone . . . God's house:* According to Westermann (*Genesis 12–36* 459) this can only mean: "A sanctuary shall arise from this stone."

Jacob's promise to tithe ("tenth part") agrees with the tithing that was practiced at Bethel (Amos 4:4).

There is a love/hate relationship with Bethel in the OT. It figures prominently in patriarchal narratives (here and in Gen 12:8) and in the era of the judges (Judg 20:18, 26; 21:2; 1 Sam 7:16). According to Judg 1:22–25 it was taken over from Canaanite dominion by "the house of Joseph" i.e., Ephraim. On the other hand, Jeroboam I made it a principal sanctuary for the northern kingdom (1 Kgs 12:29; 13:1–32). Moreover, Bethel is also the name of a divinity (like El Elyon, so also El Bethel; cf. Gen 31:13, "I am El Bethel, who appeared . . ."). Bethel also appears as a divine name in the Elephantine papyri of the 5th cent. (W. Beyerlin, *Near Eastern Religious Texts Relating to the Old Testament* [OTL; Phl, 1978] 255 and n. 1).

49   (f) JACOB'S MARRIAGES (29:1–30 [J, E?]). The Jacob–Laban cycle (chaps. 29–31) begins here by an adroit fit into the Jacob–Esau story. This cycle seems to be an independent tradition that functions as a story within a story (cf. Noth, *Pentateuchal Traditions* 87–101). It is generally attributed to the J tradition, and insertions from E in 30–31 have been claimed, but the case for a division between traditions is not clear-cut in this material. For the archaeological background of the cycle, see M. Morrison, *BA* 46 (1983) 155–64.

1–14. The episode of Jacob meeting Rachel at the well recalls Gen 24:11–33 (cf. Exod 2:15–22). **1.** Jacob's journey is continued from 28:10, after the Bethel episode. He is on his way to marry among his relatives, to the land of "the sons of the East (Kedem)." The phrase designates nomadic tribes of the Syro-Arabian desert, east of Canaan. **2–3.** The narrative sets the stage for Jacob's feat. It appears that the well serves a community for the watering of their sheep and is secured by a "large stone." The mention of the three flocks reclining beside the well suggests that it was only when all the shepherds were gathered together that the stone would be removed; cf. v 8. **4–6.** The dialogue between Jacob and the shepherds serves to move the action along. The reader learns from the shepherds that Haran, Jacob's goal, has been reached, and that Laban is in *šālôm*. As it were by coincidence Laban's daughter appears on the horizon with a flock. **7–9.** The characterization of Jacob in this cycle is in contrast with the homebody of 25:27. Although a stranger, he now offers advice to the shepherds about opening the well — prompted no doubt by the pending arrival of Rachel. Their answer is restrained and to the point (cf. vv 2–3). **10–11.** The sight of Rachel galvanizes Jacob into action: removing the huge stone, watering the sheep, kissing Rachel, and weeping. The quick pace in this scene is striking, and again the characterization of Jacob, "heel-gripper," appears; he knows how to seize the opportunity, but his tears are a surprising addition. **12–13.** Another scene is sketched very rapidly, and comes to rest with the note that Jacob stayed with Laban for a month (v 14b). The scene is packed with action: Jacob's explanation of his identity, Rachel's running to inform her father (leaving Jacob, apparently, to tend the sheep), Laban's running to meet Jacob, embracing, kissing, and welcoming him home. After Laban hears Jacob's story ("everything that had happened"—one wonders about what Jacob might not have told Laban), he formally proclaims him a relative (cf. Gen 2:23). This would doubtless imply residence among the family; Jacob is not simply a hired hand, but he is favored by acceptance for marriage into the family. The mention of a month's sojourn sets up the negotiation to follow.

15–20. Laban's proposal seems innocent enough, although it will soon appear that he is as wily as Jacob. He broaches the subject of wages to Jacob who should

not work "for nothing." **16–17.** The narrator explains the background to Jacob's request for Rachel. The eyes of Leah are said to be *rak,* which could mean gentle or lovely, but also dull, without lustre. In context they seem not to compare well with Rachel's beauty, which has captured Jacob. **18–19.** Laban accepts Jacob's astonishingly generous offer of seven years of service with an allusion to their kinship; everything seems to flow smoothly. **20.** *seven years . . . a few days:* One of the few references to the romantic aspect of love in the Bible (see Song of Songs)—remarkable in view of Jacob's own description of the seven years in 31:38–40. These years are presumed to elapse before the request in v 21. **21–25.** A quick tempo of events and a compact narrative continue. Now Jacob requests the hand of Rachel after seven years of service and Laban arranges for a wedding celebration of seven days (v 27; cf. Judg 4:10; Tob 11:20). **23.** The substitution of Leah for Rachel was possible because she would have been veiled, and perhaps also because of the high excitement of the occasion. **25.** The short text says everything: "And it came to pass in the morning, and behold: it (was) Leah!" **26–28.** Jacob's remonstrations make no impression on Laban. There is a delightful irony in Laban's reply. While appealing to the custom of the place in favor of the firstborn, he is also delivering a lesson to the younger brother who usurped the right of the firstborn! Perhaps he was also loath to lose Jacob's services, for he drives a hard bargain. The present celebration will serve for two marriages, Leah and Rachel, if Jacob will serve another seven years in order to have the woman that he had already worked for. **29.** The mention of the maids, Bilhah and Zilpah (v 26), prepares for 29:31–30:24. **30.** The final note about Jacob's greater love for Rachel is a harbinger of the conflict between the women, which will be obvious in chap. 30.

50   (g) JACOB'S CHILDREN (29:31–30:24 [J, E?]). This is a story within a story which mixes genealogy with the rivalry of two women. It is very difficult to distinguish the traditional sources here. More likely a redactor has expanded a basic conflict narrative with genealogical data. **29:31.** This verse lays the ground for the conflict: Leah's fertility and Rachel's sterility. The fierce desire for progeny colors the entire chapter. *Leah was hated:* Again, the verb represents choice more than emotion, although admittedly Jacob loved Rachel more (29:30), and also Leah had complied with Laban's deceitful plan. The point now is the intervention of the Lord, who makes Leah fruitful. **32.** The structure characteristic of this verse can be observed throughout the rest of the narrative: birth, naming, and explanation. Thus, Reuben (*rĕ'ûbēn:* look, a son) is explained twice: *rā'â bĕ'onyî* (he has seen my affliction); and *ye'ĕhābanî* (he will love me). The wordplays continue for each name. **33.** *has heard: šāmaʿ*; hence the name Simeon (*šimʿôn*). **34.** *be united: yillāweh;* hence the name Levi (*lēwî*) **35.** *I will praise: 'ôdeh;* hence the name Judah (*yĕhûdâ*).

30:1–2. Sterility is a profound grief for the Israelite woman; cf. 1 Sam 1:5–8. **3–6.** In her dire situation, Rachel acts as Sarah did (Gen 16:2), giving Jacob her maid Bilhah, that a son may be born. **3.** *upon my knees:* Possibly an adoption rite, or mode of delivery (de Vaux, *AI* 42,51). **6.** *God has vindicated me: dānannî;* hence the name Dan. **7–8.** *I have struggled greatly: naptûlê niptaltî;* hence the name Naphtali. **9.** Now the sterile Leah gives Zilpah to Jacob; cf. v 3. **10–11.** *good luck: gad;* hence the name. **13.** *Happy am I: bĕ'ošrî;* hence the name Asher.

14–18. The story of the mandrakes interrupts the series of births. It seems to point toward the fertility of Rachel, but it ends with Leah's giving birth. The mandrake (mandragora) was commonly understood to be an aphrodisiac and fertility potion. The Hebr term *dûdā'îm,* is connected with *dôd,* "love(r)." It is also called "love apple." The rivalry between the women is especially sharpened in this scene. Leah rejects Rachel's request (v 15) and then accepts Rachel's offer of one night with Jacob (who must apparently have shunned Leah). The words in v 16 are bitter; Jacob's services for one night are hired (*śkr*) for the mandrakes Reuben discovered. **18.** *my reward: śĕkārî;* hence the name Issachar (*yiśśākār*). **19–20.** The sixth son is born, and two wordplays are provided. *gift: zēbed,* in alliteration with *zbl; give me presents: yizbĕlēnî;* hence the name Zebulun. **21.** There is no play on the name of the girl who is born, Dinah. **22–24.** One would expect here a reference to the effect of the mandrakes. Instead it is God who intervenes in the conception of Joseph, and two wordplays are given. **23.** *has removed:* 'āsap. **24.** *may he add: yôsēp.*

The sons of Jacob/Israel can be summed up: Born of Leah: Reuben, Simeon, Levi, Judah, Issachar, Zebulun; of Zilpah: Gad and Asher; of Bilhah: Dan and Naphtali; of Rachel: Joseph and (Gen 35:18) Benjamin. These are the eponymous ancestors of the "tribes of Israel." The number 12 appears consistently, e.g., 35:23–26; 49:1–28. However, the history of the 12 tribes or groups who eventually came together to form Israel is more complicated than a genealogy. The tribal development has its own checkered history. Joseph becomes Manasseh and Ephraim (Gen 38:8–20), but this separation does not appear in Gen 49. The tribe of Simeon seems to have been assimilated into Judah, and early on Reuben practically disappears. Levi, to which no land was apportioned, loses its tribal status and serves priestly interests.

51   (h) JACOB OUTWITS LABAN (30:25–43 [J, E]). The narrative returns to the relationship between Jacob and Laban. There are several obscurities in this section. The repetitions (permission to leave, vv 25–26; Jacob's service, vv 26,29; wages, vv 28,31) have led to suggestions that two sources have been brought together, but this is not very convincing. The real difficulty is to determine what Jacob and Laban agree to in vv 32–33, and what exactly Jacob does in vv 37–42. There is no certain explanation of these verses, as can be seen from the diversity of transls. What is clear is that Jacob got the better of the deal with Laban.

30:25. Jacob's decision to return home, following upon the birth of Joseph from Rachel, appears abrupt, without any explanation. **26.** The request includes his wives and children; this implies some kind of dependence upon Laban, although Jacob has labored 14 years for the wives. Jacob is also able to lay claim to the high quality of his service (cf. also v 29). **27.** *If I have found favor in your eyes:* The main verb is not expressed (perhaps "hear me" is understood). Laban has learned by divination (*niḥaštî*) that *yhwh* has blessed him because of Jacob. **29.** In reply to Laban's offer that Jacob determine the wages for his labor, Jacob again underlines the quality of his service (cf. v 26b), and the blessing of the Lord to which Laban had alluded (v 28). **31.** The negotiation becomes rather subtle. Jacob refuses any offer from Laban, and he insinuates that he will care for the flocks. **32.** Jacob specifies as his wages all the animals that have a rare particular color (black sheep and speckled goats). **35–36.** Although he has accepted Jacob's terms, the wily Laban removes the animals specified by Jacob and assigns them to his sons (who are mentioned for the first time). A three-day journey will separate them from the apparently hapless Jacob. **37–42.** But Jacob has his own solution for breeding the animals with the rare color. The practice must reflect a popular belief about external factors influencing the process of birth. **37–39.** Any transl. is uncertain. Jacob peels down the shoots of particular trees so that the white core is revealed; these he

places in the watering troughs opposite the she-goats who were in heat. Results: striped, speckled and spotted kids are born. **40.** A difficult verse. Apparently the sheep face the striped and black (goats?) and their offspring are colored, to the profit of Jacob. **41.** This verse reverts to the practice of vv 37–39, which Jacob employs only with the stronger animals, so that the weaker ones end up belonging to Laban. **43.** Jacob prospers, whatever one thinks of the antics of vv 37–42.

52   (i) JACOB'S FLIGHT (31:1–54 [E, J]).   There is a diversity of opinion on the identification of sources in this chapter; it shows several repetitions, additions, and inconsistencies. Older critics postulated an E source as the basis (use of the name Elohim, the dream, etc.). **1–3.** Three reasons motivate Jacob's departure: the charges made by Laban's sons, a perceptible change in Laban's attitude, and a statement of the Lord (cf. v 13). **4–16.** Jacob's explanation for departing meets with approval from the two women who previously had been in conflict with each other. His explanations are very elaborate, and the text appears overloaded. The following "reasons" are given: a change in Laban's attitude (v 5); unfair treatment from Laban, despite Jacob's valiant service (vv 6–7); divine intervention (vv 5b,7b,9,10–13). There is little connection with 30:25–42; thus, the birth of certain animals as Jacob's wages (vv 8–9) is simply interpreted as a gift from God. In vv 10–13 the combination of the dream theophany with the mating of the animals (reminiscent of, but different from, 30:25–42) has never been successfully explained. The reference to the "angel of the Lord" (v 11) harks back to the appearance of God at Bethel (28:10–22). Joseph never makes a clear request to the women to depart with him. But their willingness is shown by the charges they make against Laban (vv 14–16): They are "foreigners," without inheritance, and have even been "sold" because Laban has used the money he received for them (an apparent reference to the *mōhar* or bride-price—although there was no mention of this in 29:15–30). **16.** *the wealth God reclaimed:* An allusion to the divine intervention in v 9b. This wealth belongs to them and their children (*lĕbānênû*—and not to Laban).

18. This is generally considered to be an addition from the P tradition (cf. 28:7), which also reports Jacob's arrival in Canaan in 33:18. **19.** The immediate departure, facilitated by Laban's absence at a sheep-shearing festival, does not prevent Rachel from stealing her father's *tĕrāpîm,* small cultic images of the household gods (cf. vv 25–30). **20.** *Jacob stole the heart of Laban:* Just as Rachel stole the images, Jacob deceived Laban. **21.** This verse continues the departure theme after the parenthetical remarks of vv 19–20. The direction is across the Euphrates to Gilead (see comment on vv 25–30). **22–24.** Laban's prompt reaction enables him to catch up with Jacob, but only after a divine warning not to harm him (lit., say nothing, neither good nor bad).

25–30. The place of the meeting between Jacob and Laban is not easy to determine. The MT has Jacob on a mountain (perhaps Mizpah? v 49), while Laban pitched his tents (not "kinsmen" as in MT) on Mt. Gilead, which would be S of the Jabbok River. Even the general area of Gilead would be more than a seven-day journey from Haran (cf. v 21). Laban's complaint is twofold: Jacob's stealthy departure and the theft of the household gods. **26–27.** Laban's grievance twice picks up the vb. *gnb* (steal) from v 20. Jacob has fleeced him of his daughters as though they were prisoners of war. **28–29.** Much of this seems to be a tongue-in-cheek statement, coming as it does from the likes of Laban. But there is no question that he has superior power—except for the warning (an allusion to v 24). The first and only reference to Jacob's homesickness sounds rhetorical. Now Laban can make his charge of thievery. Jacob's reply concerning his wives makes good sense (cf. Laban's claim in v 43). **32.** The best defense of his honesty is to proclaim the death penalty (unwittingly, on Rachel) and to invite a search. **33–35.** Laban's search produces no results, and the quick-witted Rachel rises to the occasion. There is an unmistakable satirical edge to the scene in vv 34–35. In her menstrual period she sits on the idols, making them unclean (Lev 15:20–23).

36–42. Now Jacob takes the offensive with his countercharges. Laban has made a futile and unjust accusation (vv 36–37), and Jacob delivers a self-righteous description of his hard 20 years in Laban's service (vv 38–41). Except for the judgment of God, Jacob claims that he would have been dismissed "empty-handed." *Fear of Isaac:* The One whom Isaac dreads; *paḥad yiṣḥāq* has also been interpreted as "kinsman of Isaac." The meaning of the phrase, which occurs only here and in v 53, is uncertain.

43–54. The Jacob–Laban cycle ends with a pact and the departure of Laban (32:1). The text does not flow smoothly. Commonly vv 46–50 are attributed to J, and 51–54 to E (e.g., Speiser, *Genesis* 248); others regard the text as merely expanded by additions. **43.** Laban begins by asserting that everything belongs to him: daughters, children, flocks. This sounds very much like a bluff in view of his sudden (and suspect) decision to do something for his daughters and grandchildren. **44.** *be a witness:* The MT is defective here. The witness cannot be the pact (*běrît,* a feminine noun) just mentioned; the *NAB* supplies "Lord." See also v 52.

45–46. These verses seem redundant. First Jacob sets up a stone as a pillar (*maṣṣēbâ*), and then orders his kinsmen to gather stones to set up a mound (*gal*), where a (covenant) meal (cf. v 54) then takes place. **47.** *Jegar-sahadutha:* Aram phrase for "mound of testimony," which is also the meaning of the Hebr term used by Jacob, "Galeed." **48–50.** There lurks behind Laban's words an etiological explanation of the mounds that are called Galeed, and also Mizpah. Mizpah is explained by "may Yahweh watch" (*yiṣep,* in alliteration with *Miṣpâ*). Mizpah in Gilead was a cult center in the time of the judges (Judg 11:11). The mound (*gal*) is to be a witness to the mutual agreement of Laban and Jacob even when they are distant from each other. Yahweh (v 49) or God (v 50) is the witness. In v 50 Jacob is obligated to treat Laban's daughters rightly and not to take other wives. **51–52.** The words of Laban suggest that the agreement is really a nonaggression pact, testified to by the mound (*gal*) and the pillar (*maṣṣēbâ*). This may well reflect an agreement between Israelites (in Gilead) and Arameans at a later time. **53.** Laban and Jacob solemnly bind themselves to the pact under oath to their respective deities, "God of Abraham and God of Nahor." On Nahor, see Gen 11:22–25,26–29; he appears as the ancestor of Aramean tribes in 22:20–24. "The God of their fathers" seems to be a later gloss. Jacob's special oath by the "Fear of Isaac" (cf. v 50) seems redundant here. **54.** The agreement is sealed by a sacrificial meal. The English Bible tradition follows the LXX and the Vg numbering by considering the next verse, 32:1 according to the MT, as v 55. Hence, the Hebr numbering in the following chapter is one digit ahead of English Bible references.

53 (j) PREPARATION FOR THE MEETING WITH ESAU (32:1–22 [J, E]). The entire chapter is one of encounters: at Mahanaim and at the Jabbok, and finally with Esau. **1.** This verse can be considered the ending of the Jacob–Laban cycle. After the colorful farewell (cf. Gen 24:60), Laban returns home. **2.** On his way forward, Jacob is met by "angels (*mal'āk*) of God" (in Gen 28:12 he saw them on the stairway). **3.** Jacob's reaction is to call them "God's encampment" (lit., "camp of God"). This is the etiological explanation of the name of the town of Mahanaim (two camps), which lies east of the Jordan. It is difficult to determine if more is intended than the mere description of the event. Does it anticipate the episode at the Jabbok (32:23–33) or encourage Jacob in the face of the meeting with Esau (see C. Houtman, *VT* 28[1978] 37–44)?

4–9. As a preliminary to the meeting with Esau, Jacob sends an embassy to his brother, which returns with news that he finds threatening. **4.** *Seir ... Edom:* These are in effect synonymous; cf. 25:30; 36:19–20. **5–6.** The message is given as the words of Jacob; it is brief and subservient, as Jacob seeks to "gain favor." The reference to his sojourn with Laban may be merely informative, but the statement about his own affluence is meant to communicate something to Esau (willingness to share? or yield to Esau the family inheritance?). **7.** The news (not really an answer from Esau) brought by the messengers is almost as taciturn as Jacob's message, and the mention of 400 men sounds ominous. **8–9.** Jacob feels threatened, and he is vulnerable because his entourage is not a war party, but family and flocks. Ever resourceful, he prepares for the worst (a kind of "triage," Semitic style) by dividing his party into two groups (*maḥaneh* — an obvious allusion to v 3). **10–13.** Jacob's prayer has a clear structure: an address to the Lord by name with epithets and including the detail about promise (v 10); self-deprecation that is intensified by the indication of what Jacob now is (v 11); petition and description of distress (v 12); motivation for the Lord to intervene, a reminder of his promise. For echoes, see 28:13–15; 31:3. **11.** His avowal of unworthiness serves also as a motif in praise of the Lord's generosity.

14–22. Many (e.g., Gunkel) regard this section as coming from the E tradition. **14a.** The note about Jacob's lodging for the night probably goes with the end of the previous narrative (cf. the end of v 22). **15–16.** This totals 550 animals, a huge gift (vv 14,19,21,22, *minḥâ* — a play on *maḥanayim?*). **17–21.** Jacob's strategy is vividly described and is designed to assuage Esau with waves of generosity at three distinct intervals. **21.** *appease:* Lit., "cover the face" — so that Esau will not see his guilt. *forgive me:* Lit., "lift my face." The five references to "face" in vv 21–22 seem to be a deliberate preparation for the episode at Penuel ("face of God"; vv 31–32).

54 (k) JACOB'S STRUGGLE WITH GOD (32:23–33 [J, E]). Gunkel has written of this famous pericope that it is "worthy of a Rembrandt" (*Genesis* 365), but it is as enigmatic as the Mona Lisa. "Recent exegesis agrees for the most part that the text of Gen. 37:32–33 cannot be separated into two literary sources but has been subsequently expanded into a unity" (Westermann, *Genesis 12–36* 515). Expansions yes, but hardly a unity. There are no fewer than three etiologies: the explanation of the name Israel (v 29), the reason for the name Penuel/Peniel (v 31), and the etiology of the food taboo (v 33). The central event, the wrestling with a "man," retains its mystery (it is not really clear who the victor is!). This appears to be an old story, with motifs well known from folklore: passage of a river, and danger from the river numen or demons; restriction to nighttime activity (cf. Hamlet, I/1: "It faded with the crowing of the cock"). In the present form of the text this mysterious story is applied to Jacob and is construed as a struggle with God. Its intention is to honor the patriarch — but how? It seems to be placed deliberately as a counterpart to the feared encounter with Esau; Jacob is truly a man of blessing, but this time he wrestles for it and receives it from God (in contrast to his cheating Esau in order to receive Isaac's blessing). The power of the narrative is that it is multi-dimensional and suggests several meanings.

23. *Jabbok:* The present-day Wadi Zerka ("blue"), which empties into the Jordan *ca.* 25 mi. N of the Dead Sea. The movements of Jacob are confusing. His adventure occurs at Penuel, N of the Jabbok. Did he cross that deep ravine with his family and possessions and then return to the N side where he is "alone" (v 25)? **24.** This verse is repetitive, and is one reason why scholars (e.g., Gunkel) suspect a mixture of sources. **25.** *a man:* So simply is the attacker identified. The mention of daybreak here and in v 27 suggests that the original identity was some demon who operates only in the night. *wrestled:* 'ābaq is a play on the name of the river, *yabbōq*. **26.** The "man" cannot overcome Jacob, but he succeeds in dislocating his thigh joint by a mere touch (magic?). **27.** Despite the move in v 26, Jacob seems to be the one in control, as his opponent pleads for release at the approach of dawn (the motif mentioned above). Jacob refuses unless the attacker will "bless" him. What is Jacob asking for? Merely something of the "supernatural power" (Westermann) of the man?

28. Instead of giving a blessing, the man inquires as to his name, which Jacob readily gives. **29.** The change of name to Israel provides an etiology. The real etymology of *yiśrā 'ēl* is unknown ("may God rule"?), but the popular explanation given here flows out of the encounter: "you have struggled" (*śārîta;* cf. also Hos 12:4). The struggle has been with ' *ĕlōhîm* and ' *ănāšîm*—with God (or, gods? elohim beings?) and humans, (Esau and Laban?) according to the explanation given by the man. In this view, Jacob, crippled as he is, has won the match, to the extent that he has "prevailed" (*wattukāl*).

30. *why do you ask my name?:* The attacker refuses to divulge the name (after inquiring of Jacob in v 29!). Underlying this knowledge of the name is the idea that possession of such knowledge brings power over the one who is named (cf. Exod 3:13–14; Judg 13:18). *he blessed him:* Jacob at least forces the blessing that he asked for (see v 27). *Contra* Speiser, the change of name (v 29) is not the blessing. **31.** The etiology of Peniel (face of God; the variant form, however it is to be explained, appears in v 32 and elsewhere, Penuel) is given. Jacob lays claim to much less than a victory: "I have survived." This explanation of the name, as well as of the event, is geared to the common OT understanding that one cannot see the face of God without incurring death (Exod 33:20; Deut 34:10; Judg 6:22–23; 13:22). Paradoxically, it is precisely those who have seen God that lived to tell the tale! The implication of this verse is to identify the "man" with God (despite Jacob's unsuccessful attempt in v 30 to discover the name). **32.** This verse harks back to v 27 after all the intermediate reflections. The dawn feared by the man (whose disappearance has not been noted), has now come, and Jacob starts his travel, limping! **33.** The etiology for a food taboo is derived from Jacob's wound. The reference to the "Israelites" betrays that this is a later interpretation which became popular. No such prohibition is to be found in the law. In addition, the precise meaning of *gyd hnšh* is uncertain: sinew or tendon of the thigh.

In its present form this remarkable episode presents a mysterious struggle of Jacob with God. The Peniel etiology identifies the "man" as God (who also attacks Moses in the equally mysterious event of Exod 4:24–26). Moreover, the change of the name to Israel, as well as the reference to Israelites in v 33, suggests a later stage in the handing down of the tradition (see also Hos 12:4–5). Did Israel see itself engaged in a fateful combat with God—such as the testing of father Abraham in Gen 22 suggests? Through it all shines the blessing that Jacob receives. In context it is an assurance to him before his oncoming confrontation with Esau.

55 (l) JACOB'S MEETING WITH ESAU (33:1–20 [J mainly?]). The Jacob–Esau story (chaps. 27–33) concludes here. The encounter Jacob feared so much ends with reconciliation in a scene that is marked by conspicuous obeisance on Jacob's part (v 3), in contrast to the simple acceptance by Esau. But reconciliation has its limits. The brothers go their separate ways (vv 13–17). **1.** *four hundred men:* An ominous note, as in 32:7. In 32:8 Joseph divided his group as a stratagem for preservation. Now he divides his family, with clear priority, in preparation for a ritual greeting (vv 6–7). **3.** Joseph himself runs forward to inaugurate very profound obeisance. Sevenfold prostration is mentioned frequently by vassals in the Amarna Letters. **4.** Esau's open and bluff reaction is genuinely affectionate. *kissed him:* Absent from the LXX, and marked with points in the MT ("puncta extraordinaria," and perhaps a midrashic interpretation, playing on *nšq/nšk,* "kiss/bite"). **5–7.** The scene is impressive; now the family does obeisance. Joseph's reply to Esau is low-key: it is by God's "favor" that he has prospered. **8.** Esau asks the meaning of Jacob's strategy of 32:8–22, when "camps" or groups were sent on ahead. Jacob explains it as an effort to win favor (cf. 32:6). **9–11.** Jacob overrides Esau's refusal to accept the gifts and repeatedly insists until Esau gives in. **10.** *to see your face is like seeing the face of God:* Perhaps an allusion to Peniel (cf. 32:31b), but the expression indicates Jacob's sincere effort to win Esau's favor, just as one seeks the face of God in order to be forgiven (cf. Job 33:26). **11.** Jacob significantly calls his gift "my blessing." Blessing was the issue in the deception of Isaac in chap. 27. Now Esau accepts; the portrayal of Esau here contrasts with that in chaps. 25, 27.

12–17. Reconciliation there may be, but Jacob, despite his continuance of obsequious language, has no intention of joining his brother. **13.** Jacob offers the reasonable excuse that his entourage would only encumber Esau's return; instead, he will join him in Seir (Edom). **15–17.** Jacob's refusal to accept a party from Esau's 400 men as a retinue to accompany him is a clear sign of his decision. He reverts to his old sly style. As v 17 indicates, he does not go in the direction of Edom, but crosses the Jordan to Succoth (modern Deir Alla) on the W bank. *booths:* Hebr *sukkōt,* the etiology for the name of the place. The patriarch has finally taken up residence within the land of promise, as the following section emphasizes. **18–20.** Jacob's destination is the area of Shechem, a famous city in Israelite history (cf. Josh 24, etc.). *šālēm 'îr šĕkem* was understood by the ancient versions to refer to a place called Salem near Shechem. Others translate *šālēm* as "safely." **19.** *pitched his tent:* This suggests Jacob's semi-nomadic life-style, despite his building a "house" in v 17. The transaction with the "sons of Hamor," apparently the leading family of Shechem, prepares for the events of chap. 34. The value of 100 "kesitahs" cannot be determined. **20.** Jacob erects an altar (according to the MT) on the land. *El, God of Israel:* Here Israel probably means the people (cf. Josh 8:30) rather than Jacob. In that case the verse claims El as the God of Israel, and not the Canaanite divinity worshiped in the area (Westermann, *Genesis 12–36* 529–31).

56 (m) THE RAPE OF DINAH (34:1–21 [J, E]). This episode has only a loose connection with Jacob; it deals with his children. Perhaps it is placed here because of the mention of Shechem in 33:18–20. But the chronology is much later; these are grown sons, and the daughter, Dinah, mentioned briefly in 30:21 and 46:15, is one of the principal participants. Indeed, more than family history seems to be reflected in this chapter; it has to do with tribal history and the relationship of later

Israel to Shechem. The analysis of sources has led to no firm conclusions (contrast Speiser with Westermann), but one can recognize inconsistencies and apparent doublets (vv 8,11, two requests for Dinah; vv 24–26, 27–29, two attacks).

1–4. The scene is quickly described: Dinah is raped by Shechem, who eventually comes to love her and wishes to marry her. He belongs to the leading family of the town, a "Hivite" (LXX, Horite). The term is used in the general sense of "Canaanite" and specifically for Horite or Hurrian. **5–7.** Jacob seems passive in the whole affair; the role of Shechem's father, Hamor, is to set things right by marriage. The reaction of Jacob's sons is expressed in language of a later date (reference to Israel; the formula, "such a thing is not done" — cf. Judg 19:30; 2 Sam 13:12). **8–10.** Hamor's offer is not only the Dinah–Shechem marriage, but intermarriage between the groups, with appropriate rights to settle in the land. **11–12.** Shechem is introduced abruptly as speaking to "her" (presumably Dinah's) father and brothers. This is a doublet of vv 8–10. No matter the *mōhar* (bride-price) or the *mattan* (a gift to the family of the bride), Shechem wants Dinah. **13–17.** The answer serves for both Shechem and Hamor, and it involves deceit. Shechem is to be bound to circumcision (v 14). In response to Hamor's offer in vv 8–11, the sons of Jacob demand circumcision of all males if there is to be any intermarriage and settlement in the land. Circumcision is viewed here as a mark of separation from others; it is not the covenantal sign that it came to be in the postexilic period. **18–19.** These verses record separately the agreement of Hamor and Shechem to the terms laid down. Throughout the narrative two things are at issue: an agreement between Shechemites and Israelites, a marriage between Shechem and Dinah. **20–24.** The transaction between Hamor and his town council deals only with the incorporation of the Israelites into the community. They agree to circumcision. **25–29.** These verses suggest two attacks: Simeon and Levi slay Hamor and Shechem and bring Dinah back; "the sons of Israel" devastate the city. **30–31.** Jacob's rebuke considers only the safety of the community. The Shechem incident only makes things more difficult for the family in the face of retaliation by "Canaanites and Perizzites" (cf. 13:7; 15:20; Perizzites are practically synonymous with Canaanites, the ancient occupants of the land). Jacob's fears are belied by 35:5. The reply of the brothers is disdainful; their code demands the shedding of blood.

The above analysis of chap. 34 raises almost as many questions as it "answers." A close reading of the text reveals two or even three variant versions of events, and one hypothesis rests upon another to explain the present form of the text. One finishes with the overall impression that a family story (the avenging of a rape) has been rewritten in the light of tribal experiences of the later Israel. It has puzzled scholars of Israel's history that Shechem is absent from the traditional story of the conquest. Yet it seems to be under Israelite control (Josh 24) and to have a close association with the Israelites (Judg 9). Hence it is tempting to read Gen 34 in an oblique way to discover some information about the tribal period, even if such a reading is fraught with uncertainties.

As an example of another approach, from a purely literary point of view (but which of course cannot escape inevitable subjective bias), the study of this chapter by M. Sternberg (*The Poetics of Biblical Narrative* [Bloomington, 1985] 441–81) deserves notice. Here one can give only a hint of the lengthy and stimulating analysis of this chapter. Sternberg begins by showing in several deft touches (Jacob's inaction; grief and anger of the brothers; etc.) how the narrative in vv 1–12 builds up sympathy for Jacob's sons in their reaction to the rape of

Dinah. In vv 13–26, the "negotiations" between the Hivites and the sons provide a cautious balancing of the two opposing parties. However, the note at the end (v 26) about the abduction of Dinah climaxes the description of the callousness of the Hivites in the negotiations. In vv 27–31 a "stabilization" takes place, where the "sons of Jacob," as distinguished from Simeon and Levi, are the perpetrators of the massacre. The final scene presents the contrast between the do-nothing and even selfish Jacob and the passionate two brothers ("Should he treat our sister like a harlot?" — the active transl. suggesting Jacob's guilt). The narrator by several rhetorical devices has elicited from the reader a certain sympathy for Simeon and Levi. Sternberg concludes with a characterization of 15 rhetorical devices (not all of them operative in chap. 34) employed in biblical narratives to affect the reactions of readers.

57   (n) JACOB AT BETHEL (35:1–15 [E, P]). The narrator has put together in this chapter a mosaic drawn from various sources (notably P in 9–13). It is a chapter of pilgrimage, of births and deaths. Jacob has finally reached home; Isaac culminates his pilgrimage in death. The beloved Rachel, for whom Jacob labored so long, dies in giving birth to Benjamin. The chapter gives a sense of closure. **1–7.** This narrative ties in with the vow Jacob made in 28:20–22 when he was fleeing from Esau. **1.** Now Jacob is to leave Shechem where he had settled and set up a pillar (cf. 33:18–20). Oddly, it is God who tells him to "go up" (the language of pilgrimage) and build an altar to El Bethel (cf. v 7). **2–4.** Jacob's preparations are for more than the building of an altar; this is a preparation for ritual worship; washing of self and clothes (Exod 19:10–11) and renunciation of foreign gods (Josh 24:14). The symbolism of such actions is obvious; a new life of service to the God of the fathers is to begin. **4.** Images of gods and earrings (crescents in honor of the moon-god?) are buried beneath a terebinth (LXX, "oak"). **5.** A "terror of God" is comparable to the fear inspired by the Lord in Exod 23:17. This verse really belongs with the Shechem incident of chap. 34 (cf. 34:30–31). **6–7.** Jacob fulfills the divine order of v 1; cf. 28:10–22. *Luz:* Cf. 28:19. *named the place El Bethel:* The place and the god worshiped there are "equated" (Westermann). El Bethel occurs also in 31:13, but it is generally interpreted in the light of LXX, "who appeared to you in" (Bethel). A. Alt (*KlS* 1. 79–88) hypothesizes that this narrative reflects a pilgrimage from Shechem to Bethel that occurred during the period of the judges when the ark was transferred from Shechem (Josh 24) to Bethel (Judg 20:26–28).

8. This is a rather stray note about a certain Deborah; she was Rebekah's nurse and hardly belongs in Jacob's group. A burial place near Bethel, at Allon-bacuth (oak of tears) was venerated, and this explanation is given (cf. Deborah's palm tree in Judg 4:5). **9–13.** This P tradition is parallel to the Bethel revelation in 28:10–22; Jacob's name is changed, and the promises of land and progeny are renewed. **14–15.** This is another strange note. The naming of Bethel is given for a third time (cf. 28:18–19; 35:7, each linked with a separate incident, a pillar and an altar), and in connection with Jacob's setting up and dedicating (another?) pillar.

58   (o) MISCELLANEOUS ITEMS (35:16–29). **16–20.** In the journey from Bethel, Rachel dies in childbirth (cf. 30:24). *Ephrath:* Near Ramah of Benjamin; cf. 1 Sam 10:2; Jer 31:15. *Ben-oni:* Means "son of my pain." *Benjamin:* Means "son of the right," and this is understood in the sense of good fortune. In terms of geography, right means south (if one faces east), and hence Benjamin, "southerner." **19.** *Bethlehem:* This is a mistaken gloss on Ephrath; cf. v 16. **20.** A pillar is set over the grave, a kind of gravestone. **21.** The journey to Mamre resumes; the location of Migdal Eder (tower of the flock) is unknown; there is no connection here with Mic 4:8. **22a.** The details of this ugly incident are not given; in fact, the text breaks off at this point. See 49:3–4. **22b–26.** This list of Jacob's sons derives from P; the systematization takes no account of the birth of Benjamin near Ephrath (vv 16–20); → 50 above). **27.** In the P tradition Jacob's trip to Paddan-aram was motivated by the desire to marry a relative (28:1–5). In 31:18 Jacob started back, and now he has arrived at his father's home. The systematization characteristic of P is evident in the chronology: although Isaac was on his deathbed in 27:1–45 (J), P has him living another eighty years beyond that (cf. 25:26; 26:34). As Isaac and Ishmael buried Abraham at the cave of Machpelah near Mamre, so Jacob and Esau bury Isaac there (49:31).

59   (p) THE DESCENDANTS OF ESAU (36:1–43). Just as the Abraham stories concluded with an Ishmaelite genealogy (25:12–18), the Jacob cycle concludes with genealogies and lists of Esau's descendants. The *tôlĕdôt* (generations/descendants) formula was used to introduce descendants of Ishmael (25:12–28) and Isaac (35:28–29). Now the formula is used to introduce material relating to Isaac's son Esau (36:1). It will be used again to introduce the family history of Isaac's son Jacob (37:2). For details, see Wilson, *Genealogy and History* (→ 7 above) esp. 167–83. The lists contain inconsistencies that betray a complicated prehistory (recall David's conquest of Edom), but the final editor has preserved them without harmonizing them.

1–5. These verses are generally attributed to P. They contain data concerning Esau's three wives and five children, but there are some conflicts with data supplied by P in 26:34 and 28:9. **1.** Esau is (the eponymous ancestor of) Edom. **4.** *Eliphaz:* Also the name of one of Job's "friends" (Job 2:10). **6–7.** These verses summarize Esau's departure from Mamre (35:27–29) to "a land" (so the MT; it is clear from v 8 that this must be Seir). The separation of the two brothers is peaceful, and the description in v 7 is reminiscent of the separation of Abraham and Lot (Gen 13:6–10). *Seir:* The ancient name for the region inhabited by the Edomites; it is glossed here as Edom (cf. Gen 25:25).

9–14. This list, introduced by the *tôlĕdôt* formula, repeats and expands vv 1–5. **9.** Now Esau is called the father of Edom (cf. v 1). **11–13.** The names of the sons of the second generation are given here, through Eliphaz and Reuel. *Amalek:* Born of Eliphaz's concubine; eponymous ancestor of the Amalekites, who figure significantly in the OT (e.g., Exod 17:8–16). If one excludes Amalek, this is a 12-"tribe" list.

15–19. Although there is a repetition of the names from vv 9–14, the opening title is significant: "These are the chiefs of the sons of Esau." This indicates a shift from family perspective to tribal and political structure. The term *'allûpîm* (rendered in the *NAB* as "clans") designates military/political leaders (cf. Ugaritic *'ulp*, "prince"). The formula about the chiefs is repeated in vv 15,17,18, and is followed by a list of names.

20–30. The opening formula (v 20, "sons of Seir") leads into a list of segmented genealogies down to the third generation. **20.** *Seir the Horite:* Although Seir is the name of a region, it is here the name of the eponymous ancestor of the "original settlers" (*NAB*) in the region (cf. Deut 2:12). Scholarly discussions about the terms Horite /Hivite/Hurrian are still in a state of flux (see de Vaux, *EHI* 136–38). The seven sons of Seir are listed in vv 20–21, and then a list of their sons follows in vv 22–27. **29–30.** Cf. 1 Chr 1:43–50. This list of the chiefs of the

Horites duplicates the list of the seven sons of Seir the Horite (vv 20–21).

31–39. This is not a genealogy but a list of Edomite kings who antedate the Israelite monarchy; see J. Bartlett, *JTS* 16 (1965) 301–14. It is characterized by the absence of any dynastic succession. There are eight kings, identified by family ("son of") and the cities in which they reigned. It is difficult to determine if these were truly kings or tribal chieftains. **37.** *Shaul:* The same name as Saul. "Rehoboth on the River" is unknown, but the river could not be the Euphrates. **39.** *Hadar:* So the MT, but probably Hadad should be read (and see Hadad the Edomite in 1 Kgs 11:14).

40–43. This is a list of the chiefs (*'allûpîm*) of Esau (glossed as "the father of Edom," v 43). Several of the eleven names have occurred earlier in the chapter (contrast Oholibamah, a place-name in v 41, but personal in v 3).

This chapter attests the feeling of relationship that existed between Israel and Edom (cf. Deut 23:8[7]: "your brother"). This relationship deteriorated badly in later years, and it is surprising to see such attention given to the Edomites here. These lists are used by historians today in an oblique fashion to throw some light on the history of Edom (see the bibliography in Westermann, *Genesis 12–36* 558).

60   (C) The Story of Joseph (37:1–50:26). G. Coats (*Genesis* 259–61; *JBL* 93 [1974] 15–21) regards chaps. 37–50 as the Jacob saga, a collection of traditions about Jacob and his sons. It is true that in a strict sense the Joseph story embraces only chaps. 37, 39–45, and parts of 46–50, where it is interwoven with the story of Jacob. But no one would deny that Joseph is the focal point, and hence chaps. 37–50 are popularly regarded as his "story" (cf. Thomas Mann's famous work, *Joseph and His Brothers*).

As in the preceding chapters, several hands have been recognized in the composition of the story: J, E, and P. It is assumed by many that the Joseph story had two forms, one in J and another in E, before these were joined and finally edited by a redactor. R. de Vaux (*EHI* 292–95) insists that these are traditions, not documents, which were put together by a single author. He describes the breakdown thus: "1. The plots made by the sons of Israel (J) or of Jacob (E) against Joseph, who is defended by Judah (J) or Reuben (E) and is sold to the Ishmaelites (J) or carried off by the Midianites (E). 2. Joseph's early period in Egypt as the slave of an anonymous Egyptian who has him put in prison when his wife denounces him (J) or as the slave of Potiphar, the commander of the guard, who puts him in charge of the prisoners (E)" (p. 293). Similar allocations to J and E are presented for the rest of the narrative. At the same time, he allows that there are clear criteria only at the beginning of the story (chap. 37), in the differentiation between Israel, Judah, and the Ishmaelites (J), as opposed to Jacob, Reuben, and the Midianites (E). In modern times most commentaries have followed this division of the material (e.g., Speiser, Vawter, von Rad), and a stout defense of the existence of sources is to be found in L. Schmidt, *Literarische Studien zur Josephsgeschichte* (BZAW 167; Berlin, 1986) 127–297.

Other studies reflect the current questioning of the documentary hypothesis (→ Pentateuch, 1:4–8), and the Joseph story has been presented without regard to the putative strands of J and E (e.g., Westermann; Coats). A careful reading of the text will challenge the reader to make a decision between these approaches. In any case, nearly everyone agrees that there is some evidence of the P tradition, esp. in chaps. 46–50.

Because of the undeniable literary quality and power of the Joseph story, there has been a tendency to attribute it to one author (whether the Yahwist or another). In that case, what purpose was the author pursuing? G. von Rad (*PHOE* 292–300) proposed the view that "the Joseph narrative is a didactic wisdom story" (p. 300), a presentation of a wise administrator, such as would emanate from the royal court school. This interpretation rests on rather fragile hypotheses: (1) the dating of the story during the "enlightenment" that supposedly characterized the Solomonic period; (2) the unlikely claim that "the narrative of *Gen.* xxxix reads as if it had been devised expressly to illustrate the warnings of the wisdom writers" (p. 295). But von Rad was correct in pointing out with others the contrast between the previous patriarchal narratives and the Joseph story. The former is a cycle, or a catena of relatively small self-contained units. It is made up of pieces derived from the cult or local holy places. On the other hand, the Joseph story has a continuous, well-turned plot. It reminds one of the court history of David in 2 Sam 10ff. It is marked with deep psychological insights into the characters and makes effective use of a knowledge of Egyptian ways. Unlike the Abraham and Jacob and Isaac stories, there are no theophanies; God is at work, but through the actions, even the sins, of human beings. Moreover, the reader of the Joseph story becomes aware of the presence of a narrator who has artfully arranged the succession of scenes and dialogues in a symmetry of ever-increasing tension. The alienation between Joseph and his brothers works itself out until there is a reconciliation (45:1–15). There is a consistent pattern of doublings (pairs of dreams, two journeys, etc.), and a literary technique of echoes (e.g., Jacob going down to Sheol, 37:35; 42:38; 44:31) and inclusions (e.g., 43:26–28).

Is a political motive also present? Westermann (*Genesis 37–50* 24–25, 248–50) claims that there is: "The narrative wants to set in relief the positive potential in the conflict over the rise of the monarchy in Israel, while at the same time making clear how the value of the family can be preserved under it" (p. 248). The transition to the monarchy is supposed to have sharpened the question: Is a brother to rule over his brothers? The Joseph story thus is correlated with the two attitudes to monarchy expressed in 1 Sam 8–12. While it warns against the misuse of royal power (shown in the experiences of the brothers, and also in Joseph's dealings with his master's wife) it emphasizes the values and importance of family life. Many readers have not found this reading of the Joseph story convincing (but see Brueggemann, *Genesis* 288–98; 335–51).

Finally there is the role played by God. The presence and blessing of the Lord are very explicit and frequent in chap. 39, and the role of God in the interpretation of dreams is underlined in 40:8 and 41:16,25,32,39. But for the most part the action of God is characterized by "radical secrecy, distance, and unrecognizableness" (G. von Rad, *God at Work in Israel* [Nash, 1980] 34). This secrecy is broken in a dramatic way in 45:5–8 and 50:20. "God meant it for good"—this interprets the entire story by pointing out the guiding action of God, however secret it had appeared in the narrative.

A broader question can be raised that is no less theological: How does the Joseph story function in the book of Genesis? B. Childs (*CIOTS* 156–58) points out that Joseph is set aside from the patriarchs. The divine promises of land and posterity that are renewed to the earlier patriarchs are not given to him as a bearer of the promise. In Gen 50:20 he refers to the patriarchal promise of the land in such a way as to separate himself from the "fathers." From the perspective of the book, "Joseph became the means of preserving the family in a foreign country (50:20), but also the means by which a new

threat to the promise of the land was realized" (p. 157). In other words, he saves the family, but at the expense of the land, since they are now in Egypt, and the oppression from a king "who knew not Joseph" is on the horizon. When one assesses chaps. 37–50 from the viewpoint of both Jacob and Joseph, one can see that they answer the question of how Jacob/Israel came to Egypt with his family; if chap. 46 followed directly on chap. 37, we would hardly know more than that Jacob went down to Egypt and recovered his lost son, Joseph. The Joseph story, in the stricter sense, is the pearl embedded in this tradition.

The literary form of the story has been variously described: *Novelle* or short story (Gunkel, *Genesis* 397; von Rad, *Genesis* 433; Coats, *Genesis* 265); didactic tale (de Vaux, *EHI* 295–96); *belles lettres*, dealing with family and God's action (Westermann, *Genesis 37–50* 25–26). The common factor in these definitions is the emphasis on story, even though it be of a special kind. It is not properly history, although the knowledge of Egyptian life and customs evidenced in the work has been put forth as an argument for history. Such evidence cannot prove the point, since it could also be found in a work of fiction. According to Gen 41:39–44; 45:8, Joseph appears to be the vizier, second only to the pharaoh. There is no such evidence in Egyptian records, and one may suspect that this glorification of Joseph is due to the author. At the same time, it is quite possible that Joseph could have attained a position that had considerable political clout. Asiatic officials are known to have been employed by pharaohs of the Middle Kingdom (de Vaux, *EHI* 298); hence Joseph's promotion must be seen as historically possible (de Vaux, *EHI* 298–301). De Vaux concludes that extrabiblical documents "would seem to point to the probable arrival in Egypt of a Semite called Joseph who rose from the status of slave to a position in which he exercised very high functions. They also show that a group of Semites probably settled in the Delta. These, of course, are the essentials of the story of Joseph and his brothers. The evidence outside the Bible does not, however enable us to establish a date for Joseph or for the coming of his 'brothers' to Egypt" (*EHI* 317). Nonetheless, a common guess is that it occurred around the period of Hyksos rule in Egypt (*ca.* 1650–1540); so Albright, *BP* 10. On the whole it seems more realistic to assume that there was more than one "descent" of Semitic groups into Egypt (cf. Deut 26:5); for further discussion see J. A. Soggin, *HAI* 109–17; *IJH* 120–48.

A complete bibliography on chaps. 37–50 is found in Westermann, *Genesis 37–50;* see the indications on "literature" on pp. 9–12, and also esp. pp. 15–30, and the supplement for Gen 1–50 on pp. 254–56.

61   (a) JOSEPH SOLD INTO EGYPT (37:1–36 [J and E]). The narrative runs fairly smoothly, although variants (even different sources) are indicated, especially by the roles of Reuben (cistern, Midianites) and of Judah (selling of Joseph to Ishmaelites). **1.** The notice of Jacob's residence follows upon 35:27–29, the report of Isaac's death. **2.** *family history:* This is the final use in Gen of the *tôlĕdôt* formula of P, but it is Joseph who is the real hero in what follows. This verse (P) suggests enmity because of Joseph's reports about four of his brothers. **3–4.** The reason for hostility is now considered to be favoritism, symbolized by the famous coat (LXX: "many-colored"). **5–11.** Still another reason for hostility is the two dreams (note pairs of dreams, as in 40:5–19 and 41:1–7) of sheaves and stars. The dreams anticipate reality (cf. 42:6, where the brothers do indeed bow) and perhaps suggest the leadership of Joseph's son Ephraim among the tribes. **10.** The implication is that Rachel is still alive, but cf. 35:19. **12.** The geography is difficult; one residing in

Hebron (v 14) would hardly pasture flocks as far N as Shechem; this is an arduous journey for Joseph to be employed as a messenger. **17.** *Dothan:* About 20 mi. N of Shechem. **18–30.** Reuben's effort to prevent a murder is to suggest deposition in a cistern (from which one may infer from v 30 he intended to deliver him). The rescue of Joseph by the Midianites (v 28) leads into the alibi of the bloody tunic. On the other hand, Judah's effort involves selling Joseph into slavery to the Ishmaelites. The result is the same: Joseph ends up in Egypt (v 36). **25.** In the context, the mention of eating is rather cold-blooded. **35.** *Sheol:* The abode of all who die, where Jacob can go "mourning" to meet his son. **36.** *Potiphar:* Means "gift of Re (the sun-god)." He is the "chief steward," who will put Joseph to work in prison (40:4).

62   (b) JUDAH AND TAMAR (38:1–39 [J]). There is no easy answer to why this story, characteristic of J, is inserted here, interrupting the Joseph narrative. It is probably an old tradition about the patriarch Judah and the clans associated with him, Shelah, Perez, and Zerah (cf. v 29; Num 26:19–22; 1 Chr 2:1ff.). The tribe of Judah seems to have been a latecomer to the tribal federation (it is not mentioned in the song of Deborah, Judg 5), but under David and Solomon it took on leadership. **1.** *about that time:* An indefinite indication, when Judah is an adult, but in context the time is the transferral of Joseph to Egypt. He is living apart, among the Canaanites. **7.** The death of Er is explained by the all-pervasive causality of the Lord; since he apparently dies young, he must have offended God—this is the mindset of ancient Israel (such a death has to be "explained"; cf. Uzzah in 2 Sam 6:7). **8.** Onan is commissioned to raise seed to his brother's wife, according to the levirate law; cf. Deut 25:5–10. **9–10.** Onan's offense is obvious; he selfishly refuses the responsibility of fulfilling his duty to his brother, as the law provided. That is the point of his offense (not what is popularly called onanism today). **11.** Dismayed by the course of events, Judah indulges in subterfuge (as he will admit in v 26). **12–23.** Tamar takes charge of things by a ruse to teach Judah of his responsibilities. No moral judgment is passed on her action; it is Judah who admits (v 26) that she is "more in the right." **15.** *harlot:* Here *zônâ*, but in vv 21–22, *qĕdēšâ*, which is specifically a temple prostitute, who would have been engaged in the religious fertility rites. **16–18.** Tamar makes Judah pay for his pleasure by obtaining his seal (an incised cylinder seal, well known in the ancient Near East, used to sign documents), cord, and staff; these will serve as an identity card (v 25). **20–23.** Judah is aware of his misconduct and is unwilling to have it become public, after his discreet questioning fails. **24–26.** Legally Tamar is considered betrothed to Shelah, who was not given to her; hence, Judah is the one to give sentence. In later law, the penalty was stoning (Deut 22:23–24; cf. Lev 21:9). Tamar's strategy catches out Judah. Her memory seems to have been regarded with honor (Ruth 4:12). **27–30.** The theme of twins who struggle with each other even from the womb was seen already in Esau and Jacob (25:22–26). There is a play on the names: Zerah is associated with red; hence the "scarlet thread" on his hand. Perez means "breach," as he broke forth to be born first. According to Ruth 4:18–22 and 2 Chr 2:5–15, he is the ancestor of David. Note the two women, Tamar and Ruth, in the Davidic genealogy.

63   (c) JOSEPH'S TEMPTATION (39:1–23 [J]). The narrative returns to the Ishmaelites of 37:29, who here sell Joseph to an unnamed Egyptian. Editorial insertion (neatly indicated by the parenthesis about Potiphar in the *NAB*) identifies him with the Potiphar of 37:36, who is a "chief steward," or commander of the guard, and has Joseph working for him in prison (40:3). The scene in

chap. 39 takes place in the home of the unnamed Egyptian, whose wife is responsible for Joseph's being imprisoned (not merely working there, v 20). **2–6.** The role of the Lord in Joseph's success is underlined; throughout the Joseph story it is presupposed, but not so openly stated as here (vv 2,5,21,23; cf. 45:5–9; 50:20). As will happen in the case of Pharaoh (41:43–45), Joseph is given charge of everything by his master; the exception of food (v 6) seems to be for religious or dietary reasons (cf. 41:32). **7–20.** For a parallel to this event, see the Egyptian "Tale of the Two Brothers" (*ANET* 23–25). Joseph's motivation is rooted in his loyalty to his master and to God (the sacred name is significantly avoided in conversation with foreigners; cf. 41:16,25,32). Joseph's cloak would be all the more incriminating if he was forced to flee naked. **21–23.** Jail is inevitable, but again Joseph begins an upward climb, as the chief jailer repeats the beneficence of the former master. The jailing of Joseph binds two traditions: punishment by the master for alleged adultery and slave work for the chief steward (Potiphar); cf. 40:4.

64   (d) JOSEPH INTERPRETS THE PRISONERS' DREAMS (40:1–23 [E]). Joseph is now a servant assisting the chief steward by caring for the cupbearer and baker who are under house arrest; but vv 3 and 15 ("prison," "dungeon") indicate his own confinement. **6–8.** Joseph's questioning leads to the subject of dreams, an important issue in the ancient world, esp. Egypt. His answer is very orthodox, perhaps a polemic against the Egyptian understanding. **9–15.** Another pair of dreams (cf. 37:5–10) is featured. The cupbearer's dream is transparently a favorable one, and Joseph's reply is in accordance: Pharaoh "will lift up your head" (v 13). Hence Joseph gives a short summary of his life (the episode of chap. 39 is passed over) and asks the cupbearer to intervene in favor of his freedom. **16–23.** The baker's dream is interpreted unfavorably by Joseph with a grim play on words; Pharaoh will indeed "lift up" (v 19) his head, only to be hanged. The dreams are verified by the actions of Pharaoh described in v 20, who "lifts up" the heads as indicated in vv 13,19. **23.** The forgetfulness of the cupbearer prepares for 41:9–13.

65   (e) JOSEPH INTERPRETS PHARAOH'S DREAMS (41:1–57 [E, J?]). Dreams and their interpretation are important in the ancient Near East, esp. when they are royal, because then they suggest a particular relationship with the divine. Pharaoh's dreams are narrated twice (vv 1–7,17–24), and the dreams are in pairs, as before (37:6–9; 40:9–19). Verses 9–13 tie together chaps. 40–41, and vv 53–57 prepare for the famine that will bring the brothers down to Egypt. **1–7.** The royal dreams are parallel (seven cows and seven ears of grain), and the interpretation is almost transparent (the lean devour the fat). Cattle and agriculture depended on the inundation of the Nile, and, were this to be suspended, famine would indeed follow. Seven is an ominous number, for weal or for woe. **8–16.** The failure of the Egyptian experts is to be expected, since interpretation comes from God (vv 16,28; cf. Exod 7–8; Dan 2). The event jogs the memory of the cupbearer (after a lapse of two years, v 1), and Joseph is summoned quickly. **16.** "Favorable answer" (*RSV, NJB*) is not adequate in view of the interpretation in vv 30–31; (see to) "Pharaoh's welfare" (*NJV, NEB*) expresses the right nuance of *šělôm par'ōh*.

17–32. Pharaoh's version of the dreams is rather dramatic and already underlines the threatening aspect (vv 19–21). Joseph interprets both as having the same meaning: seven years of abundance to be followed by seven years of famine. This is, of course, a revelation of God (vv 25,28,32,38–39). **33–36.** Joseph's advice is precisely designed to ensure Pharaoh's welfare (cf. v 16). The term "wise man" (v 33) is hardly adequate reason for a distinction of sources (as opposed to "overseers" in v 34). **37–45.** Once Pharaoh recognizes the divine spirit in Joseph, the text moves rapidly in the description of honors that he receives: authority over the palace and also over the people (v 40, the meaning of *yiššaq* is uncertain; LXX has "will obey"). Joseph is the vizier (vv 40,43), and the investiture is described: ring, fine linen robes, golden chain, and chariot (cf. the installation of Neco, *ANET* 295). The meaning of the shout "Abrek" is unknown, but it is obviously meant in homage. **45.** Joseph's Egyptian name has been interpreted, "God speaks; he lives." His wife's name designates one who belongs to the goddess Neith. This note gave rise to the famous story of her conversion to Yahwism. See "Joseph and Aseneth" in *OTP* 2. 177–247. *On:* Egyptian Anu, a center of sun worship, and later named Heliopolis, or "city of the sun." The end of v 45 concerning Joseph and the land of Egypt is lacking in the LXX and is perhaps an intrusion from v 46b. **46.** This note about Joseph's age is attributed to P. **47–49.** Joseph carries out the plan expressed in vv 35–36. **50–52.** The birth of Joseph's two sons is here placed "before the famine." There is a play on the names, indicating the experiences of their father, Joseph, in a foreign land. **53–57.** This picks up v 49, and the wisdom of Joseph's plans is verified. Not only Egypt, but the "world" is affected, and esp. Palestine (42:1–2).

66 (f) FIRST ENCOUNTER OF JOSEPH WITH HIS BROTHERS (42:1–38 [E, J]). The narrative resumes the relationship between the brothers (chap. 37), now on a different level after Joseph's extraordinary rise to power. There are several dramatic features, as the tension between the brothers and Joseph rises: Joseph's knowledge and their ignorance (vv 8,23–24); the delicate reference to the "one who is no more" (v 13) and the recurrent memory of their deed (vv 21–22); a three-day imprisonment (v 17, as they once had imprisoned him in a cistern, 37:22); the Benjamin theme, which will eventually cause them to bring him to Egypt (vv 4,13,20,38); the eerie feeling at the discovery of their money (v 28). See the insightful literary analysis of R. Alter, *The Art of Biblical Narrative* (NY, 1981) 137–40; 160–71. Coats (*Genesis* 285) divides the chapter into four panels (vv 1–5,6–26, 27–28,29–38) according to the change in location. Many scholars (e.g., Westermann) refuse to recognize two traditions in the narrative, but cf. Vawter, *Genesis* 416.

1–5. This opening scene is uneven; Jacob's rather harsh question (v 1) appears to be unmotivated; v 5, with its curious reference to "the sons of Israel" simply repeats v 3. Although arrival in Egypt is not stated, the journey to secure rations from Egypt is under way, and the Benjamin motif sounds in v 4. **6–26.** The encounter with Joseph is marked by several speeches, while the narrator emphasizes Joseph as the main figure in the story. **6.** The gesture of the brothers is a deliberate recall of the dream in 37:5–10; cf. v 9a. **7–8.** The narrator is playing off the knowledge of Joseph (and the readers) against the ignorance of the brothers. **9.** See v 6. Joseph's accusation of "spying" would not be unusual on the part of an Egyptian official, but he is obviously lying in order to put some plan into operation. From the way events develop, it would seem that he wants to prepare a haven for his family, as well as to test the humanity of these brothers who were in effect fratricides (chap. 37). **10–11.** The dialogue with Joseph shows certain ironies. *we are the sons of one man:* Indeed they are, including Joseph! **13.** To the repeated accusation, they make passing mention of Benjamin and Joseph, who are, of course, key persons in the unfolding drama. **14–16.** Joseph insists on the spying charge a third

time and develops the test: Benjamin is to come down before they are allowed to depart. **17–20.** The prison sentence is revoked after three days and a second test proposed: While one (Simeon, v 24) is to remain, the others can return; but they must also bring back the "youngest." **18.** *a God-fearing man:* It is not clear how this motivates Joseph's new command. Where some scholars would recognize two sources in this dialogue (and elsewhere), Westermann explains the narrative by the literary device of doubling (*Genesis 37–50* 109). **21–24.** A moving scene of recriminations. One learns of Joseph's anguish and pleas (unmentioned in chap. 37), while Joseph eavesdrops on their conversation. The narrator deftly waits until this moment to indicate that an interpreter had been used. Joseph's weeping is a theme that is repeated as the story continues to its climax: 43:30–31, when he sees Benjamin; 45:1–2, when he reveals himself to the brothers. **25–26.** The brothers set off with the grain, unaware of the money that has been secretly returned to their sacks.

27–28. These verses are attributed to J, because of a second discovery of the money in v 35 (after they have reached home—perhaps the E tradition). Westermann responds, rather weakly, by claiming v 35 to be a gloss. As Alter remarks, it would be naïve to think that the Hebr writer was unaware of the contrast with v 35; incorporating both versions allows him "to give a complete imaginative account of it" (p. 138). **28.** *what is this that God has done to us?:* Their whole adventure has been marked by uncanny events. Now they are the victims of entrapment; or there has been a ghastly mistake, which is even worse than entrapment. They certainly could not imagine the resolution of the problem given in 43:23! God's action will not be fully understood until 45:5,7, if then.

29–38. The final scene compresses the events and the brothers' dialogue with Joseph, omitting the three-day imprisonment and the discovery of the money in sacks, and ending on an upbeat note (v 34). But Jacob's response suggests that the whole affair is unutterably sad (vv 36–38). The (re-)discovery of the money is devastating. **35.** See comment on vv 27–28. **36.** *childless:* Jacob's cry is bitter (cf. 37:33–35): Is he to lose a third son? **37.** Reuben's offer is rash (is Jacob to be confronted with the loss of two of his grandsons as well?) but well meant; at least there is a significant change in the attitude of the brothers since chap. 37. **38.** Jacob solemnly excludes the possibility of Benjamin's leaving (but cf. 43:1–14). Jacob's mourning echoes 37:35.

67 (g) THE SECOND JOURNEY TO EGYPT (43:1– 45:28 [J, E]). Westermann points out the similarity in structure between the two journeys: (1) departure: 42:1–5—43:1–15; (2) sojourn in Egypt: 42:6–25— 43:16–34; 44:4–45:24; (3) return to the father: 42:26– 38—44:1–3; 45:25–28. The interruption of the return to Canaan occurs in 44:4–45:24, and the brothers finally go back to Jacob. Westermann also argues that the two journeys are not doublets; rather, they exemplify the principle of doubling, whereby the author increases the tension (*Genesis 37–50* 118–19). Many regard chaps. 43–44 as largely the work of J.

43:1–2. Following upon the dire condition laid down for a return to Egypt (42:36–38 E?), Jacob's seemingly casual command in v 2 is surprising, even if the supplies have been exhausted. **3–10.** Corresponding to the role of Reuben in 42:37, Judah provides leadership, rehearsing (vv 3–5) the condition (the sending of Benjamin) laid down in 42:15–20. Although his summary reply to the complaint of the old man ("Israel" in v 6) goes into more detail than chap. 42, there is no mention of the spying charge or of Simeon. Coats calls it a "manufactured alibi"

(*Genesis* 29). It is as though the old man were hearing all this for the first time. Judah's emotional assurance (v 9, "I will bear the sin/guilt forever") contrasts with the impatience shown in v 10. **11–14.** The reaction of Israel/Jacob is threefold: take along some special local products (of little use in a time of famine!); double the silver, and thus return what was put in the sacks; Benjamin can go. God Almighty (El Shadday, normally a term in P) is to care for them; there is an element of foreboding in Jacob's final lament (v 14).

15–24. In a rapid transition (v 15), the brothers are back in Egypt. The first scene is a meeting with the steward, or majordomo, while the scheming of Joseph hovers in the background. The contrast with the first encounter (42:6–17) is striking: now they are ushered into Joseph's house! **18–23.** The scene is vividly portrayed. The first reaction of the brothers is fear—what next! They immediately bring up the affair of the money in the sacks, as if to ward off punishment. The kind reply of the steward (v 23), who has doubtless been coached by Joseph in all this, could hardly be reassuring. What is going on? The role of God (contrast 42:28) in the entire narrative is underlined by the author. The liberation of Simeon is mentioned without further ado (a redactional move to harmonize J and E?). **24–34.** The second scene is comprised of vv 24–25 (the brothers are put at ease), 26–31 (Joseph's greeting), 32–34 (the meal). **26–28.** Two prostrations enclose Joseph's greeting and a pointed query about the health of Jacob. **29–31.** The intense interest in the family continues, as Joseph encounters his younger brother and is overcome with concealed emotion (the second weeping; cf. 42:24). **32–34.** The customs of the meal are noted; the fact that Egyptians are not to eat with foreigners may have been unknown to the brothers (cf. 30:6), but certainly not unsettling. However, when they are seated in seniority by this bizarre vizier, they must have been startled; that old eerie feeling should have returned. The extra large portion for Benjamin is also unusual, since honor normally goes to the oldest. The closing remark betrays nothing but celebration.

The narrative moves rapidly as Joseph's final trick is to be played, and the tension mounts once more. **44:1–6.** Joseph's instructions to his steward are as clear as they are devilish. The return of the money (v 1) is not mentioned in v 14 (did it come from the episode in 42:25ff.?). **4–5.** The MT has only two questions; perhaps one should add in v 5 with the LXX, "Why have you stolen my silver cup?" We are in the dark as to the precise mode of cup-divination; it appears to refer to patterns assumed by the liquid. No judgment is passed here or in v 15 about divination, a practice that is condemned in Lev 19:31; 20:6; Deut 18:10–11.

6–13. The brothers feel secure in protesting their innocence (as once Jacob did with Laban, Gen 31:32), but they only fall into the trap. The charge is so senseless that they pronounce death on the perpetrator and slavery for all. The reply of the steward glosses over the mention of death and seeks only slavery for the perpetrator. The narrator describes the scene in vv 12–13 with restraint.

14–34. The story is approaching the climax. **15.** *you should have known:* How much else were they ignorant of, in this crazy-quilt pattern they found themselves in! **16–17.** Judah is now the spokesman. He proclaims the hopelessness of the situation—it is impossible to prove their innocence. *God has uncovered:* Although they are innocent of stealing, their guilt as regards the "dead" Joseph (their real crime) is now being assessed—a significant admission. Again, the solidarity of the brothers is put forward; all are to be slaves. Note the change: the intended fratricides who were at one in eliminating Joseph are now at one in offering themselves in order to save Benjamin. Joseph's reply has the same thrust as that of the steward in v 10; only the perpetrator, Benjamin, is to be enslaved.

18–34. This eloquent appeal is one of the great speeches in the OT. The change of heart in the brothers is mirrored in Judah's generosity and love for all the family. Although it is a plea for the freedom of a brother, in a deeper sense it is a plea for the life of Jacob: "his father loves him" (v 20); "his father will die" (v 22); "his very life is bound up with" Benjamin (v 30). Benjamin almost disappears from sight in the pathetic description of Jacob's suffering (vv 31, 34). Jacob's favoritism, which ignited the hatred for Joseph (37:3–4), is acknowledged without envy. Judah's speech departs from the details in 42:12–16 (Joseph's inquiry about the family) and in 43:2–14 (Jacob's sending them a second time), and his pathetic plea is all the stronger for it. In a sense, his speech summarizes the heart of the Joseph story. **25–26.** Cf. 42:29; 43:3,5. **27–31.** A deft recalling of the fate of Joseph, and of the descent of Jacob to Sheol in mourning (37:35; 42:38). **32–34.** Judah's own promise to his father (43:9) is mentioned, but only in such a way as to highlight the affliction of Jacob, "if the boy were not with me."

68   **45:1–2.** Joseph's "test" has to come to an end, when he sees the profound change in his intended murderers. In a certain way, they have shown more love for Jacob than he has. For the third time the theme of weeping underlines the family scene that follows. **3.** *I am Joseph. . . . Is my father still alive?:* A marvelously simple response. The question is perhaps not logical, but it is quite on target emotionally, after the dramatic description of Jacob given by Judah in his speech. **4.** Joseph discloses his identity a second time, with the significant addition "whom you sold into Egypt"! His appeal to the dumbfounded brothers to draw closer to him is a realistic touch. **5–8.** Joseph attempts to put his brothers at ease. With that superior knowledge that is always attributed to him in the narrative, Joseph gives the theological explanation (cf. 50:20) of the entire affair: This was all God's doing, not yours. Oddly, there is no reference to the tests and his own bizarre actions, which if explained might have carried as much weight as this theology. It is not until v 15 that they feel free to speak. Nonetheless, this reference to divine providence is rightly considered by most commentators as the key to the story, *pace* Westermann (for whom it merely means that all will be well; God has acted). Joseph's explanation continues in vv 6–8, where the reference to "remnant" (*šĕ'ērît*) is puzzling. In the Pentateuch it occurs only here, but it is common in Isaiah, where it is paired with "survivors" (*pĕlēṭâ*) in 10:20; 15:9; 37:32, as also here. Jacob's family is not a "remnant" in the sense in which this is used in later prophetic tradition; hence, this may be an expansion (so Westermann, who also insists on reading v 8a after 8b). The saving of lives (v 5) refers, of course, to the aid brought to Jacob's family during the famine, which is described by Joseph in v 6. Joseph can do all this because he is "father to Pharaoh" (v 8), a title like "father of God (Pharaoh)," which is used by Ptahhotep, the vizier (*ANET* 412).

9–13. Joseph lays out the plan he has conceived; it is to be transmitted to Jacob, and speedily ("hurry" forms an *inclusio*). The interest of the narrator in moving the story along accounts for the description of the plan at this point; the brothers can hardly have recovered from the totally unexpected turn of events. There is even a certain repetition in vv 9,11 of what Joseph has just said. The design of v 12 is to assure the brothers (after Joseph's devious dealings with them in chaps. 42–44?) that he means all that he says. There is great emphasis on their seeing, and thus being reliable witnesses to Jacob that Joseph really has power (*kābôd,* "dignity"; cf. vv 8–9).

14–15. Only now, after the theological explanation and revealing of the plan they are to carry back to Jacob, does Joseph really greet his brothers. All in all, it is not surprising that a mixture of J and E has been postulated for this unusual revelation scene (cf. Gunkel, Vawter, and other commentators).

16–20. This passage is a curious aside about how Pharaoh came to know about the arrival of Joseph's brothers. It is strange for two reasons: Pharaoh tells Joseph what arrangements to make, immediately after Joseph has given his own commission to the brothers (vv 9–13). Pharaoh's words are more general ("the produce of Egypt"; "the fat of the land"), whereas Joseph has the land of Goshen in mind (v 10). Second, 46:31–47:6 gives the impression that Pharaoh receives the news about Joseph's family for the first time. Some division of sources seems applicable here.

21–24. Joseph takes over the provisioning of his brothers for their journey (the "wagons" were not mentioned in the discourse of Pharaoh in vv 17–20). The gifts are Joseph's own doing; it is interesting that the theme of the favorite sounds again: five garments for Benjamin. Jacob's needs are provided for in v 23. There is a realistic touch to Joseph's admonition that the brothers are not to quarrel!

25–28. The arrival of the brothers and their imparting the news of Joseph's existence to Jacob form another curious episode. It is as though the narrator wanted to finish the drama quickly and bring Jacob down to Egypt. **26.** The announcement is as forthright as it is sudden. It is no wonder that Jacob's "heart was cold" at the news and that he refused to believe. Perhaps one can overlook the absence of any mention by the brothers of their deceitful treatment of Jacob in 37:31–35 (the bloody coat). But the entire scene lacks the finesse that is customary with the narrator. The brothers merely communicate Joseph's message (vv 9–13). Jacob seems to be more convinced by the sight of the wagons than by anything else. At least his sons have come back, all of them alive (there is no mention of Simeon) and without the strange occurrences that marked their first return (money in the sacks, etc., cf. 42:29–35).

69   (h) JACOB'S JOURNEY TO EGYPT (46:1–30 [E, P, J]). The contrast in style between the previous chaps. and this one is obvious, because of the presence of the P genealogy in vv 6–27. **1–5.** On Jacob's journey to Egypt an intermediate stop at Beer-sheba is noted, and a theophany is recorded. This section looks backward, associating the patriarchal promises (a land, a great people) with Jacob. He is not to fear although he is going down to Egypt, for the "God of the father" goes with him. Then it looks forward; in Egypt, Israel will become great. **4.** *I will bring you back here:* A bridge between Gen and Exod is thus created; the "you" is the progeny (cf. Exod 1:7) of Jacob (note the delicate reference to Joseph closing his eyes).

6–27. Although this chapter is basically the report of Jacob's journey to Goshen to meet Joseph (v 28), the editor has chosen at this point to utilize the P genealogy, or list, of Jacob's descendants. The list has several discrepancies (for details, see the commentaries; Westermann, *Genesis* 158–161), which suggest that it is a late composition. In context it purports to describe the family at the time of Jacob's migration, but 10 sons are attributed to young Benjamin (v 21). Daughters and granddaughters are mentioned in v 7, but only one of each occurs in the list. In v 26 the number is 66. In v 27

the number 70 (Deut 10:22) is to be explained by counting Jacob, Joseph, and his two sons. The number 70 was probably intended as a round figure, but the list tries to fill it out.

28–30. The narrative of the journey resumes. Despite the uncertain text in v 28, it is clear that Israel (Jacob) meets Joseph in Goshen, where the emotional meeting is described. If the reunion with the brothers (chap. 45) is a climax to the Joseph story, so also is the reunion of Israel and Joseph. Israel is now ready for death (contrast 42:38), since he knows that Joseph lives.

70   (i) THE AUDIENCE WITH PHARAOH (46:31–47:28 [J, P, E?]). To Jacob's meeting with Pharaoh has been attached a report about Joseph's administration of taxes (vv 13–26).

46:31–34. Joseph never ceases to work out his designs. Here he schools his brothers in anticipation of their meeting with Pharaoh. The point is to secure as their own turf the region of Goshen (45:10), generally identified with the Wadi Tumilat in the eastern Nile Delta. The Israelites are shepherds, a vocation depicted as abhorred by Egyptians (v 34), although there is no confirmatory evidence for this.

47:1–6. Joseph holds up before Pharaoh the animal cultivation of his family and their current residence in Goshen (v 1). Pharaoh's questioning of the brothers appears innocent enough, and they follow Joseph's advice about the settlement in Goshen. **5–6.** Pharaoh's words are generous (cf. 45:20), and he offers to the family the possibility of providing for the royal herds.

7–12. The scene between monarch and patriarch is described briefly and solemnly. Jacob's "blessing" (*brk,* vv 7,10) probably indicates the normal greeting and bidding farewell (Speiser, *Genesis* 351). To Pharaoh's questioning, Jacob appropriately responds that his years were "few" (in comparison with the life span of Abraham and Isaac, 180 and 175 respectively) and "hard" (the reader of Gen 27–50 can attest to that!). These are called the "years of my sojourning," i.e., as a wayfarer in life. **11–12.** Joseph is again shown in action as he settles the family in what Pharaoh called "the pick of the land" (v 6), and which the writer terms "the region of Rameses," an obvious anachronism, since it was not until the 13th cent. that the region could receive this name (cf. Exod 1:11). The conclusion to this notice is to be found in vv 27–28.

13–26. Coats (*Genesis* 298) calls this insertion a "tax etiology," which explains Joseph's law about income tax (v 26, "to this day"). It ties in with 41:57 but contributes nothing to the Joseph story, and one wonders why it was inserted. Vawter (*Genesis* 449) recognizes a "dark and sardonic humor" (cf. "grateful to be Pharaoh's slaves" in v. 25!) that the Israelites who had been freed from bondage in Egypt had retained a notice that one of their own was responsible for the crown control of the land. Step by step Joseph makes the Egyptians "Pharaoh's slaves." First the money in payment for rations is exhausted (vv 14–15). This is followed by bartering livestock for bread (vv 16–17). Finally, only land and bodies remain to be exchanged for seed (vv 18–19). But the whole procedure is too slick, and commentators point to certain inconcinnities in the text (for details, see Westermann, *Genesis 37–50* 173–77), such as the reference to Canaan in vv 13–15 and the sudden transition from a request for food during famine to a request for seed for sowing. Little is known about the economic history of Egypt, but the power of Pharaoh was not to be minimized. The exemption of priests (vv 22,26) is plausible.

27–28. A summary statement (from P?) of the settlement of the family in Egypt and the number of years of Jacob's residence. The "17 years" do not fit well with the narrative (cf. 48:8–9). All along, there has been an emphasis on the aged Jacob and his impending death (cf. 46:30; 47:9). In the following section, 47:29–31, the reader is oriented to the death of Jacob, but it will not occur until 49:33.

71   (j) Jacob Adopts Joseph's Sons (47:29–48:22 [J, E, P]). A certain unity is given to the following chapters by Jacob's exaction of promises here (vv 29–31) and their fulfillment in 50:14. **47:29–31.** The atmosphere is that of the deathbed, but the death that Joseph has already referred to so many times (37:35; 42:38, etc.) will ensue only after chaps. 48–49. The request to be buried with his fathers (but cf. 40:5, the tomb that Jacob had prepared for himself) is solemnized by the oath "under the thigh" (cf. Gen 24:29). The significance of Jacob's bowing (at? toward?) "the head of the bed" is not clear (cf. 1 Kgs 1:47).

48:1–20. This is out of harmony with 47:29–31. Joseph now learns that his father is close to death, and he comes with his two sons. Jacob's vigorous reaction comes as a surprise. He appears to be ready to impart a deathbed blessing (vv 1–2), but then launches into a report of a theophany at Luz (Bethel) that legitimates the two sons of Joseph as his own (vv 5–6). The exclusion of later progeny of Joseph is peculiar, in that no other children of Joseph are ever recorded. Verses 3–7 seem to be from the P tradition. **7.** The reference to Rachel's death (cf. 35:16,19) is hard to fit into this context. **8.** This verse clearly follows upon v 2. The implication of Jacob's reaction is that the two sons are mere children and that he has not seen them before (cf. 47:27). **10.** Unless the reference to Jacob's poor sight refers to the reason for Joseph's correction in vv 17–18, it might be construed as explaining Jacob's abrupt question in v 8. The tender scene in vv 10–12 seems to refer to an adoption, indicated by the placing of the children on Jacob's knees. **13–20.** The blessing is communicated by the laying on of hands. Joseph attempts to make it easy for his father to put the right hand on Manasseh, the firstborn, but Jacob again (chap. 27) disregards primogeniture. Joseph's objection is overruled by Jacob (vv 17–19). According to the MT of v 15 the blessing is given to Joseph, although v 16 clearly indicates the two boys. The LXX reads "them" instead of "Joseph" (a harmonization?). **15–16.** The solemn blessing refers to God in three ways: (1) the God of Abraham (who was told to "walk" in God's presence, Gen 17:1) and Isaac; (2) the God who shepherded Jacob; (3) the Angel (*mal'āk*, messenger, as in Gen 16:7, a form of divine presence), who delivered (*g'l*) Jacob. The other wish is that the names of all three of the fathers "be recalled" in them. According to Gunkel this means that the two tribes should not forget that they are Israelite, although their eponymous ancestors were born in Egypt. **17–20.** The presumption behind Joseph's action (which fits better after v 14) is that the right hand gives the greater blessing. Jacob's gentle words indicate the eventual leadership of Ephraim among the tribes. Of course, Jacob was never one to set much store by the seniority of the firstborn (chap. 27). Verse 20 is really a second blessing, expressed in the terminology of Gen 12:3; when the people of Israel wish to bless themselves, they will use the model of God's blessing upon the two boys. **21–22.** Israel/Jacob gives assurance that Joseph will return to the land promised to the fathers (cf. 50:24). But his legacy to Joseph is enigmatic: *škm* (the city of Shechem? a shoulder of land?); for a complete discussion, see de Vaux, *EHI* 637–40.

72   (k) The Testament of Jacob (49:1–28). This can be viewed as a "testament" insofar as the dying Jacob announces these sayings to his children (49:28), or as a series of "blessings" (a misnomer, because not all are

blessed; cf. v 7). Westermann and Coats regard it as a collection of "tribal sayings." This is more accurate, for the passage deals not with the "sons" of Jacob but with the Israelite tribes, as do Deut 33:2–29, the so-called blessings of Moses, and Judg 5:14–18. In fact, the verses reflect the situation of the tribal federation before the monarchy. In the context of Gen they serve as a means of linking the tribes with their eponymous ancestors, and are also memorialized as statements of Jacob. But they are not in effect prophecies (except for vv 10–12). Only later did they come to be understood as bearing on "days to come" (v 1).

There is no evidence that the chapter is due to a particular tradition, such as J. The treatment of the tribes is according to the mothers: Leah at the beginning and Rachel at the end, with the slave women, Bilhah and Zilpah, between them. Both the MT and the ancient versions show considerable differences in readings. Although individual verses may go back to the period of the judges, the present form can hardly date before the time of David. The sayings point to the leadership that was assumed by Judah and by Ephraim/Manasseh, the Joseph tribes.

49:1–2. The superscription (v 1) and an introduction are prefixed to the sayings. Verse 1a provides the setting, Jacob's approaching death, and is perhaps continued in v 28. Verse 2 underscores the fact that the sayings are all addressed to the sons. **1.** *in the end of days:* Very often denotes the end-time (Isa 2:2; Mic 4:1); here it seems to refer only to the distant future—an eschatological perspective does not fit the sayings. **3–4.** Although the text is uncertain and subject to different translations, it is clear that Reuben, after being praised as firstborn and preeminent, is rejected because of his incestuous relations with Bilhah (Gen 35:22). Early on this tribe seems to have been ineffective (Judg 5:15–16), and little record of its history has survived. **5–6.** The tribes of Simeon and Levi are blamed for the violence of their eponymous ancestors against the Shechemites (Gen 34:25–31). Their punishment is to be "scattered," i.e., Simeon, as an appendage of southern Judah, was assimilated; Levi never received a portion of land like the other tribes, and only later in history was given priestly status (cf. Deut 33:8–11). The curse against them is mitigated by being directed against their furious violence. The combination of these two tribes means that there are only 11, not 12, sayings; Joseph is not separated into Ephraim and Manasseh.

8–12. The historical relationship of the tribe of Judah to the other tribes is unclear. It is certain that it rose to leadership in the time of David, and it became associated with messianic hopes (vv 10–12). **8.** *Judah are you:* As Westermann puts it, "you are what your name means, namely, 'your brothers shall praise you.'" There is a play on words: Judah and *yôdû* (they shall praise). Judah is praised by his brothers (the other tribes) for military prowess, but no other details (when, against whom) are given. Verse 9 voices similar thoughts under the image of a lion (three words for lion are used); the comparison is a common one to indicate awesome strength (cf. Num 23:24; 24:9). **10–12.** A promise rounds out the praise. Judah is to have dominion (thus the symbols of scepter and staff) until the coming of one (Judah or another?) who receives the obedience of nations. In v 10 *šylh* is a famous *crux:* until Shiloh comes? until there comes to Shiloh? No interpretation or rewriting of the term has commanded assent (see the solutions, with bibliography, summarized in Westermann, *Genesis 37–50* 231). *NAB, NJV,* and *NEB* reflect the reading *šay lōh* (see W. Moran, *Bib* 39 [1958] 405–25). What seems clear is that there is an extension of Judah's dominion. At a certain period there will be a change, indicated by the enigmatic *šylh* and the submission of nations. The perspective is that of Judah's supremacy under David, who thus would receive the "obedience" of the nations, i.e., Canaanites. **11–12.** The symbols describe paradisal conditions of blessedness and prosperity. *he tethers his donkey to the vine:* The vine is so fertile and plentiful that one can tether the animals nearby without fear that their feeding would diminish the produce. *he washes his garments in wine:* The symbolism of abundance continues; one can even wash clothes in wine, so plentiful is it. Judah remains the subject of the verbs. "Blood of the grapes" is a Canaanite (Ugaritic) expression for wine. **12.** The point of the comparison of the eyes and teeth could be the splendor and beauty of the possessor — unless the comparison continues the symbols of abundance ("dark from wine," because there is so much of it). Traditionally these famous verses (10–12) have been given a messianic meaning. This is true only in the sense that they refer to the emergence of Judah under David, who can be considered as a type of the messiah.

13. Zebulun is described in terms of geography (cf. Josh 19:10–16). There is no evidence (perhaps Deut 33:19?) that Zebulun was ever a maritime power ("ships"); it seems to have been an inland tribe between Asher and Naphtali. **14–15.** Issachar is described as strong ("raw-boned ass") but without spirit, even lazy. The tribe settled for good country at the expense of freedom, becoming a "toiling serf," apparently among the Canaanites, for it settled in the area NW of the Jordan Valley. There is perhaps an implicit play on the name: Issachar became a hireling (*'îš śākār*) instead of clinging to its independence. **16–17.** There is a play on Dan, who "does justice" (*yādîn*). Verse 17 may indicate what this justice was: punishing its enemies, just as the lowly serpent can defeat the horse and rider. Although a small tribe, Dan was capable of skirmishing and winning. It will be recalled that Dan migrated from S to N (Josh 19:40–48; Judg 18). **18.** This has to be a marginal note that some scribe or reader inserted in the middle of the sayings. It sounds like a verse from a psalm; cf. Ps 119:166. It is foolhardy to speculate on what is implied by it (*pace* Westermann, *Genesis 37–50* 235). **19.** There is a play on words for the tribe of Gad ("raid," *gdd*), which gives as good as it gets. This reflects Gad's precarious position in Transjordan, where it was subject to raids (cf. Deut 33:20–21). **20.** Asher, on the coast between Mt. Carmel and Phoenicia, is noted for its fertility (cf. Deut 33:24). "Royal dainties" suggest profitable dealings, but the point might be that Gad served Canaanite kings in the area where it was located (Judg 1:32). **21.** The metaphors for Naphtali suggest graceful mobility (hinds, fawn).

22–26. Joseph, whose sons Ephraim and Manasseh formed the strength of the northern kingdom, merits several lines (cf. Judah, vv 8–12). **22.** Any transl. of this verse is doubtful. Joseph is likened to a plant (*RSV, NEB;* cf. Gen 41:52) or a wild ass (*NAB, NJV*), depending on the interpretation of *prt* (which may also be an allusion to Ephrat or Ephraim, the predominant tribe). In any case, praise is meant, whether for fertility or strength. **23–24.** Now the issue is Joseph's successful resistance against attacking enemies. The success is attributed to the Mighty One (*'ābîr*, "bull") of Jacob, to the shepherd, the stone (*'eben*) of Israel. These designations have a Canaanite flavor (see B. Vawter, *CBQ* 17 [1955] 1–17; Westermann, *Genesis 37–50* 239). For similar blessings that come from nature, see Deut 33:13–16. This is an agricultural blessing for fertility which invokes heavens, abyss (*tĕhôm*, Gen 1:2, whose waters provide irrigation), breasts and womb (not paralleled elsewhere), and the everlasting hills (with the LXX). These blessings are to

be upon Joseph (v 26b; so also Deut 33:16b). **27.** The characterization of Benjamin as a wolf devouring its prey is in keeping with this warlike tribe (cf. Josh 5:14; Judg 3:15–30). **28.** Presumably it is the collector of the sayings who interprets them of the 12 tribes (v 28a); the rest of the verse ties in with 49:1, interpreting them as "blessings" imparted by Jacob on his deathbed.

73 (l) THE DEATHS OF JACOB AND OF JOSEPH (49:29–50:26 [P, J]). **29.** Jacob describes his impending death as being "gathered to my people" (Gen 25:8) or his kindred, "my fathers." The directions become quite explicit and redundant in the following verses. **30–32.** The reference is clearly to the cave that Abraham bought from the Hittite, in which he buried Sarah (Gen 23). Here also was buried Abraham (25:8–9), Isaac (Gen 35:29), Rebekah, and Leah. **33.** The description of Jacob's death harks back to 48:2, where he sat up in bed. He has finished the "years of my sojourning" (Gen 47:9).

50:1. This tender scene of kissing the dead is unusual in the Bible. **2–3.** The embalming of Israel/Jacob is the Egyptian process of mummification (see *IDB* 2. 96). Thereby the Egyptians thought to preserve the body for the future residence of the soul. There is no moral or theological implication in the text. The Egyptian practice was one means for the successful transferral of the body to Palestine. **4–6.** Joseph's request of Pharaoh's permission for him to depart is accompanied by a vivid description of the old man's wishes (cf. 47:29–31). **7–9.** A very impressive escort is described and is quite a contrast to the manner in which Jacob's sons will leave Egypt centuries later. **10–11.** This curious description of the mourning at Goren-Atad ("threshing floor of brambles") in Transjordan indicates a different tradition from that of burial in Canaan (vv 12–13, P version). A typical etiology is given in v 11. The name Abel-mizraim, which would really mean "stream of the Egyptians," is explained as "mourning of the Egyptians." This journey into Transjordan, when the goal is Mamre/Hebron in S Palestine, is enigmatic. Neither of the Transjordan sites can be identified. **12–13.** The report in P is very spare; there is no mention of the "tomb" (v 5); Jacob is to be buried with the patriarchs on the plot of land that was first acquired by Abraham as a pledge of the fulfillment of the promise.

15–21. Coats (*Genesis* 311–13) terms this a recapitulation of the denouement of the Joseph story. The speeches of the brothers reproduce the consternation recorded in 45:1–3. Now that Jacob has died, what will Joseph be like? **16–17.** Their message to Joseph is the first explicit request for forgiveness that is recorded, and they slyly invoke their father's command. No wonder Joseph wept. Would they ever learn? **18–20.** Their second attempt begins with a sign of abjection (cf. 44:16). Joseph does not deny their evildoing, but points to a higher factor, God's doing ("Am I in the place of God?"). Basically his answer is the same as he gave in 45:5–9.

22–26. A respectable old age and the sight of one's descendants are typical OT blessings, both of which Joseph enjoys. 110 years is an ideal life-span in the view of ancient Egypt. **22.** *Machir:* This tribe is mentioned instead of Manasseh in Judg 5:14 among the tribes of Israel. The reference to the "knees" signifies adoption (Gen 30:3; 48:12). **24.** Joseph's words are in part a repetition of 48:21 (Jacob), and a connection with the future exodus is made. God is said twice to watch over or "visit" (*pqd*) them — a divine intervention. **25.** Joseph puts the brothers under oath to bury him in the land of promise. It will be their "descendants" who carry this out (Josh 24:32). Thus, the story of the patriarchs ends on a note open to the future: Israel in Palestine.

3

EXODUS

Richard J. Clifford, S.J.

BIBLIOGRAPHY

1 Beyerlin, W., *Origins and History of the Oldest Sinaitic Traditions* (Oxford, 1965). Beer, G., *Exodus* (HAT 3; Tübingen, 1939). Cassuto, U., *A Commentary on the Book of Exodus* (Jerusalem, 1967). Childs, B. S., *The Book of Exodus* (OTL; Phl, 1974). Daniélou, J., *From Shadow to Reality: Studies in the Biblical Typology of the Fathers* (Westminster, 1960). Dillmann, A., *Die Bücher Exodus und Leviticus* (EHAT; Leipzig, 1880). Driver, S. R., *The Book of Exodus* (CBSC; Cambridge, 1918). Greenberg,

M., "Exodus," *EncJud* 6. 1050–67; *Understanding Exodus* (NY, 1969). Herrmann, S., *Israel in Egypt* (SBT 27; London, 1973). Hyatt, J. P., *Exodus* (NCB; GR, 1980). Michaeli, F., *Le livre de l'Exode* (CAT 2; Neuchâtel, 1974). Noth, M., *Exodus* (OTL; Phl, 1962). Plastaras, J., *The God of Exodus* (Milwaukee, 1966). Schmidt, W. H., *Exodus* (BKAT 2; Neukirchen, 1974–); *Exodus, Sinai und Mose* (EF 191; Darmstadt, 1983). Walzer, M., *Exodus and Revolution* (NY, 1985).

INTRODUCTION

2 Exod is the second book of the Pentateuch, a five-section compilation of diverse traditions of varying age edited by the Priestly redactor (P) in the 6th cent. BC. The Eng title Exodus is derived from the LXX and means literally "going forth (from Egypt)," one of the main events narrated. The Hebr title *'ēlleh šĕmôt*, "these are the names (of the patriarchs who came to Egypt)," is simply the first words of the book, the ancient manner of naming scrolls.

Exod must be seen as a part of the Pentateuch, since the liberation from Egypt and the establishing of the law and dwelling (tabernacle) at Mount Sinai (the contents of Exod) are only one part of a story that begins with the creation of the world in Gen and ends in Deut with Moses addressing Israel poised to conquer Canaan. The same ancient sources that make up the other books of the Pentateuch appear also in Exod: J, E, and P (the last term designating both ancient records and 6th-cent. redaction; → Pentateuch, 1:4–8). This commentary notes the sources according to the scholarly consensus, without discussing the many controverted or uncertain attributions. It emphasizes P the redactor since P is the final teller of the tale.

3 **(I) Significance.** Exod has had a powerful hold on the imagination of later biblical authors and of Jewish and Christian thinkers. The book begins with the people in an alien land, unmindful of Yahweh's promises to them, oppressed by a cruel Pharaoh acting as a "god" toward them by regulating every aspect of their life and

keeping them slaves in Egypt. Yahweh defeats Pharaoh by a series of 10 plagues and brings the people to his mountain, Sinai (an anticipation of Canaan and Zion). At Sinai he confirms Moses as their leader, gives them his laws, establishes his dwelling, and sets them on their journey to his land Canaan. In this task, Moses is the servant, anticipating in his own life (chaps. 2–4) the people's movement from Egypt to Sinai. Moses becomes the great servant of God, the model for the biblical portraits of Joshua, Jeremiah (cf. Jer 1:4–10), Second Isaiah, and Jesus. Inescapably sharing in the people's plight, he is also close to God; by his mediation he brings people and God into faithful relationship. Exod is an indelible portrait of the community of God, called from false and demeaning servitude in an alien land to journey to the promised land.

4 **(II) Outline.** P in Exod arranges his traditions into two interlocking parts: the rescue of the Hebrews in Egypt from Pharaoh (1:1–15:21) and the journey from Egypt to Sinai (12:37–40:38). The journey is in 12 stages, each stage marked by the formula "they departed from *place name a* and encamped at *place name b*." The people begin the divinely led journey while still in Egypt before the death of Pharaoh (12:37; 13:20; 14:2); the first three stages in Egypt interlock the two halves of the book. Israel did not "wander"; it was led in purposeful stages by the fire and the cloud. The seventh stage (19:1) begins the second half of the series. The people remain here from Exod 19:2 to Num 10:10, receiving from God those gifts that in antiquity make a people: a leader (Moses), law, a temple (the desert tabernacle) with its officials and rituals, and a land.

COMMENTARY

(I) The Hebrews Freed from Pharaoh in Egypt (1:1–15:21).
5 **(A) Danger (1:1–2:22).** These chapters tell a single story: how the fulfillment of Yahweh's promise to the patriarchs of progeny and of land has made a threat to Pharaoh. He controls their birth rate and makes them remain in Egypt as slave laborers, decisions contrary to the divine promise. Chap. 1 tells of the marvelous increase of the people and Pharaoh's attack; chap. 2, of the beginnings of rescue through Moses.
6 (a) ISRAEL'S CHILDREN BECOME A NUMEROUS PEOPLE IN EGYPT (1:1–7 [P]). Verses 1–5 look back to

Gen, when famine forced the family to leave the promised land and sojourn in Egypt. The 70 are named in Gen 46:8–27. The death of Joseph, the protector of the little family, and the deaths of his brothers and of the Pharaoh friendly to Joseph (v 8) are a major turning point in the story. Similar language in Judg 2:8–10 describes the turn from the conquest to the tribal period. **7.** The descendants of Israel are no longer the 12 sons and their families as in vv 1–5; they are now a people in whom the blessings of fertility promised to the patriarchs (Gen 12:1–3 and 28:13–15 among other places) are coming true.
7 (b) PHARAOH'S FIRST ASSAULT: OPPRESSIVE

LABOR (1:8–14 [J: 8–12] [P: 13–14]). The fecundity of the people threatens Pharaoh, who fears they will out-number native Egyptians on his northeast border, side with his enemies, and "go up from the land," i.e., escape. God will counter Pharaoh's plan to keep the people from their rightful land when he commissions Moses in 3:8, "I will cause them to go up from that land." **11.** If, as this commentary proposes, the exodus took place during the 19th Dynasty, in the reign of Ramses II (1290–1224), then Raamses (Egyptian *pr-Rmssw,* "house of Ramses") is almost certainly Tell el-Dab'a-Qantir (*ca.* 16 mi. S of Tanis, the capital of the 20th and 21st Dynasties, and *ca.* 24 mi. NE of Bubastis, the capital of the 22nd Dynasty). Recent excavation by the Austrian Archaeological Insti-tute has demonstrated that Ramses II founded Raamses on the site of the old Hyksos capital Avaris when the Pelusian arm of the Nile was still navigable. Raamses later lost its access to the sea through changes in the south water course, and the great city was abandoned. The Tanitic arm to the west gained in water volume at the expense of the Pelusian arm, inviting succeeding pharaohs to build Tanis (the Gk name; Hebr Zoan) and then Bubastis as capitals on the Tanitic arm; they used the abandoned Raamses as a quarry for their building projects. The substantial monuments of Ramses II found by archaeologists in Tanis and Bubastis, shown by recent excavation to be secondary to these sites, have misled many scholars to identify Raamses with Tanis. Pithom (*Pr-tm,* "house or temple of the god Atum") has not yet been identified. Neither of the two sites proposed in the Wadi Tumilat (*ca.* 25 mi. SE of Tell el-Dab'a-Qantir) — Tell el-Maskhutah and Tell el-Ratabah — is certain (on these sites and their relation to the route of the exodus, → 23 below; M. Bietak, *Tell el-Dab'a II* [Vienna, 1975] 179–221). **12–14.** Construction of the store cities does not check the population. The Hebrews' mysterious and unexpected growth frightens the Egyp-tians, who impose on them more rigorous work; "rigor" and "work" occur seven times here.

8 (c) PHARAOH'S SECOND ASSAULT: KILLING OF THE MALE CHILDREN (1:15–22 [E]). The king, having failed to thwart the blessing by oppressive labor, now instructs the midwives to the Hebr women to kill all the male children. From the context, the midwives seem to be Egyptians, not Hebrews; the phrase can be translated, "the midwives to the Hebr women." By their God-fearing refusal to commit murder, the women join the ranks of other non-Israelites in the Bible who acknowl-edge God's favor to the people: Abimelech in Gen 20:17 and Pharaoh's daughter in Exod 2:1–10. In the folkloric perspective of the story, the king addresses the mid-wives directly, without the elaborate ceremonial of royal protocol. The women have only their wit and decency, but these suffice. Pharaoh's folly is shown by his elimi-nating those whom he most needed for his royal building projects — the men; he is afflicted with the typical dementia of the doomed wicked. His decision to cast every male into the Nile prepares for the story of Moses. **9** (d) THE BIRTH OF MOSES (2:1–10 [E]). The hidden yet divinely guided origins of a great leader is a motif attested elsewhere, e.g., Sargon of Agade of the late third millennium was placed in a basket of rush (*ANET* 119). An Egyptian myth speaks of the goddess Isis concealing the infant Horus in a delta papyrus thicket to save him from death at the hands of Seth (M. Greenberg, *Understanding Exodus,* 198–99). **1–4.** The mother and sister of Moses obey Pharaoh's command to the letter: they throw the child into the Nile. Like the midwives, they do not let the tyrant's commands limit their choices or hope. The sister positions herself so that she can find out what will happen to the boy. **5–10.** In

the second half of the drama, Pharaoh's daughter spots the child and makes arrangements to bring him up at the royal court. She names him Moses, a name that the writer relates through a folk etymology to Hebrew *māšâ,* "to draw out." Moses is really a shortened Egyptian name meaning "born of"; the element is found in names like Tutmoses. Pharaoh ends up educating Moses. Yahweh's care for his people is subtle and unspoken to this point. Nonetheless, kings in their folly are overthrown.

10 (e) MOSES FLEES EGYPT AND SETTLES IN MIDIAN (2:11–22 [J]). **11–15.** Moses is conscious of being a Hebrew despite his court upbringing. With full intent ("he looked this way and that"), he kills the Egyptian oppressor, only to find that the act makes him unwelcome to his own people. He cannot give an answer to the question, "Who made you a prince and judge over us?" Moses flees to the land of the Midianites, a tribe that inhabited variously Transjordan and the south of Canaan, where his righteous acts win him a wife and where the question about who made him a judge will be answered. **16–22.** The well is the meeting place for future husbands and wives, as in Gen 24 and 29:1–14. Here Moses shows to his future family who he is: an Egyptian in Midian and their savior.

11 (B) God Commissions Moses: First Narra-tive (2:23–6:1).

(a) THE CRIES OF THE PEOPLE COME UP TO GOD (2:23–25 [P]). The one actor who has been silent up to now is dramatically introduced: God is named five times in three verses. The Pharaoh who did not know Joseph (1:8) and who persecuted the Hebrews has died, another turning point in the story, like that after the death of Jacob's sons and the friendly Pharaoh in 1:6. Moses, destined by the circumstances of birth for a great task yet unable in Egypt to effect anything for his people, dwells as a resident alien in Midian. Touched by the suffering of his people, God remembers the covenant with the ancestors, by which he promised progeny and land to this people's descendants.

12 (b) THE CALL OF MOSES AT THE MOUNTAIN OF GOD (3:1–4:17 [J: 3:1–4a,5,7–8,16–22; 4:1–16] [E: 3:4b,6,9–15; 4:17]). In chaps. 1 and 2, Pharaoh has behaved as a god toward the people; he has tried to annul both the promise of numerous progeny, by imposing harsh labor (1:8–14) and killing all the firstborn males (1:15–22), and the promise of the land, by refusing to let the people go up to their land (1:10). For the upcoming conflict God will have his servants, Moses and Aaron, and Pharaoh will have his, the magicians (7:11,22; 8:7,18–19). Dominion over the Hebrews, about whom they fight, is conceived spatially. In Egypt the people serve Pharaoh; they must leave Egypt to serve Yahweh. In Sinai (and later, Canaan), they will be Yahweh's. Moses, like other servants in the Bible, e.g., Gideon in Judg 6 and Jeremiah in Jer 1:4–10, is reluctant. His reluc-tance, expressed in four objections, must be overcome through signs and dialogue with God (3:1–12,13–22; 4:1–9,10–17). **3:1–6.** God appears to Moses on the mountain of God (called Sinai in J and P; Horeb in E and Deut). The bush (Hebr *sĕneh,* a play on Sinai) that burns but is not consumed mediates the divine voice. Moses recognizes the holiness of the place, hears his name spoken, and meets the God of the fathers. **7–12.** Verses 7–8 from the J source are duplicated by the E source in vv 9–10. God intervenes because he has seen and heard the cry of the suffering people (cf. 2:23–25) and wishes to lead them out of Egypt. Moses balks at the divine sending, "Who am I to go . . . ?" God's answer in v 12 is enigmatic. In other biblical commissions such as that to Gideon in Judg 6:36–40, the sign is a sample of divine power *prior* to its full display in the divine act; it is intended to encourage the person called to carry out the mission. Here, uniquely in the Bible, the sign is *after* the event, to validate it as divinely intended: "You shall serve God upon this mountain" (3:12; cf. 19:2). Some scholars propose that the "I will be with you" of v 12a, God's closeness to Moses shown in miracles and intercessory powers, is the sign. At any rate, Moses does not receive prior signs like ordinary prophets. **13-15.** Moses' second objection is that the people will not believe that he speaks for God; hence, he asks for the name of the mysterious voice. The divine name manifests God to the worshiper; the old name, God of the father, is not adequate for the new age. "I am who I am" is the name Yahweh transposed into the first person; it suggests here free choice and unhindered power. In the perspective of E (and of P in 6:2-7:7, esp. 6:2-4), God revealed himself as Yahweh for the first time to Moses. For J, on the other hand, people had always called upon the name of Yahweh (Gen 4:26). The etymology of the name Yahweh is disputed. It is surely a form of the verb "to be" (*hāyâ*) and probably the causative form, "cause to be, create." Some scholars suggest that it is a shortened form of a sentence name, "(God who) creates (the heavenly host)" (F. M. Cross, *CMHE* 60-75; B. S. Childs, *Exodus* 60-64; D. J. McCarthy, *CBQ* 40 [1978] 311-22). **16-22.** God reveals his plans to Moses (Amos 3:7): The elders' acceptance of his commission, Pharaoh's refusal to let them go into the wilderness to worship Yahweh, and his battle and defeat by Yahweh. Yahweh's victorious people will plunder the defeated Egyptians; vv 21-22 are a witty adaptation of the victor's taking the clothing and jewelry of a defeated army (cf. Josh 7:21; Judg 5:30; 2 Chr 20:25). It is also compensation for their unpaid labor. **4:1-9.** To Moses' third objection, that people will not believe him, God responds with three signs, demonstrations of the divine power that Moses can count on in the future. The rod-turned-snake and the Nile-turned-bloody anticipate the first plague in 7:8-24, and his leprous hand looks forward to Moses' vindication as leader in Num 12. **4:10-17.** The Lord answers Moses' fourth objection that he is not "a man of words" by declaring, "I am Yahweh," who creates the organs of perceiving and speaking; he will surely empower Moses. Moses resists the divine empowering (v 13), asking that another be sent in his place. Having responded patiently to each of Moses' objections up to this point, Yahweh finally is angered by Moses' attempt to push the mission onto someone else. A helper is given: Aaron. God will put his words into Aaron's mouth (v 15) rather than Moses' (v 12). Verse 17 speaks of the rod with which Moses will initiate the plagues, reminding the reader that Moses and Aaron act for God as well as speak for him.

13 (c) Moses Returns to Egypt (4:18-26 [J: 19-20a,21-26] [E: 18,20b]). Moses leaves Midian in order to return to Egypt and carry out the divine commission. Given leave by his father-in-law to return and informed by Yahweh that the coast is clear (vv 18-20), he is told to act and speak with the divine power (vv 21-23). Verse 21 parallels vv 22-23. The wonders will lead to Pharaoh's hardness of heart. The words "let my firstborn go" will provoke Pharaoh's refusal (interpreting v 23 as "*yet* [not *if*] you refuse . . .''). Verses 24-26 vividly illustrate the popular belief that the firstborn son is owed to Yahweh, not to Pharaoh. Whatever the origins of the story—perhaps an old story of a night demon fooled by the blood from someone other than the intended victim—its intent is to point forward to the tenth and final plague (12:29-32) and to the redemption of the Israelite firstborn (13:1-2,11-16). Like Moses' mother

and sister, who saved him by their daring and wit, Zipporah in the face of sudden danger quickly daubs her sleeping husband's penis ("feet" in v 25, a euphemism) with the blood from the circumcision of her firstborn son and so averts the danger (Childs, *Exodus* 90-107).

14 (d) Initial Acceptance by Aaron and the Elders (4:27-31 [J]). Aaron meets Moses as foretold in the commission (4:15). True to that commission, he now speaks and acts for Moses before the elders. The elders recognize that God has come to rescue them. The divine compassion and resolve (2:23-25), revealed first to Moses, then to Aaron, are now seen by the elders who represent the people. But will Pharaoh believe?

15 (e) The First Meeting with Pharaoh (5:1-6:1 [J]). Yahweh had foretold that the people would believe Moses but that Pharaoh would not (3:16-22). Pharaoh perversely interprets the people's desire to worship Yahweh in the wilderness as shirking. He accordingly forces the people to gather the straw themselves without reducing the old quota. His clever strategy divides people from leader (v 21), leading to Moses' desperate prayer in 5:22-6:1. At this moment of increased oppression and disbelief and of Moses' discouragement, there is heard the divine promise in 6:1: I will arrange things so that Pharaoh will drive you out of Egypt! The divine promise at the nadir of Hebrew fortunes in Egypt ends the first panel of the call and preparation of Moses and of the people (3:1-6:1). A parallel panel (6:2-7:7) will tell the story a second time, in a condensed way. The second panel, like the first, begins with the self-presentation of Yahweh (6:2-8) and ends with the divine promise (7:3-5). Hebr rhetoric loves parallelism—of poetic lines, of personages (Dame Wisdom // Dame Folly in Prov; here Yahweh // Pharaoh), of lengthy sections (Exod 15:1-12 // 13-18; and the two panels of 2:23-6:1 // 6:2-7:7).

16 (C) God Commissions Moses. Second Narrative (6:2-7:7 [P]). P tells again the events of 3:1-6:1 (J-E)—from the commission of Moses to initial confrontation with Pharaoh—with typical emphasis that all is divinely foreseen and controlled. The repetition shows that the preparatory period is completed; the plagues begin in 7:8. According to P, God was known to the patriarchs as El Shadday, "God Almighty" (Gen 17:1; 35:11; 48:3), and only at Sinai revealed his true name, Yahweh. He now remembers his covenantal promises to Abraham, Isaac, and Jacob to give them the land of Canaan. Land is here emphasized because dominion is conceived spatially; only when they live in Canaan (and Sinai) will the people be fully servants of Yahweh. The people do not believe (6:9), a telescoping of the more complex picture in 4:27-6:1, where the people first believe and then falter because of Pharaoh's strategy. Verses 10-13 (reprised in 6:28-7:2) compress Moses' objections and the appointment of Aaron as his spokesman in 3:1-4:17. Verse 13 is the divine answer to Moses' complaint that he is inarticulate: "So the Lord spoke to Moses *and Aaron* and instructed *them*. . . ." Verses 14-25 identify Moses and Aaron for the first time according to their lineage; identity in the ancient Near East was through family. Like Gen 46:8-27 and other biblical genealogies, the genealogy begins with Reuben, Simeon, and Levi, the oldest of Jacob's sons, but focuses on Levi and on others important in the Pentateuch: Moses and Aaron, Nadab and Abihu (Exod 24:1,9), Korah and his sons (Num 16), and Phineas (Num 25). 6:28-7:7 is a precise prediction of what will happen between God and Pharaoh, told from the divine rather than the human perspective. The phrase "I will harden Pharaoh's heart" leaves human actors out of consideration in order to highlight God's control. Other texts underscore human freedom and so phrase divine–human relations differently: e.g., "But Pharaoh hardened his heart, and would not listen to them" (8:15). In the end, the Egyptians will acknowledge that Yahweh is supreme in his act of bringing his people out of Egypt (7:5). P completes the section by giving the ages of Moses and Aaron, a device to show the definitive end of the section.

17   (D) The Ten Plagues (7:8–13:16). The third major section describes the battle between Yahweh and Pharaoh for the service of the Hebrews. "Service," in both Hebr and Eng, means both work and worship. The redactor has skillfully arranged and augmented old traditions about seven plagues (cf. the seven in Pss 78:43–51; 105:26–36 and the fact that there are only seven plagues in J) into three triplets, and the climactic tenth plague is outside the series.

1.	Blood	4. Flies	7. Hail	10. Death
2.	Frogs	5. Pestilence	8. Locusts	of
3.	Gnats	6. Fever boils	9. Darkness	firstborn

Each triplet has a similar structure. In the first plague of each triplet, God tells Moses to present himself to Pharaoh in the morning at the Nile to warn him of the danger (7:15; 8:20; 9:13); in the second, God sends Moses into Pharaoh's palace to warn him (8:1; 9:1; 10:1); and in the third, God commands Moses and Aaron to start the plagues without warning (8:16; 9:8; 10:21). Each triplet has a distinctive motif, alluded to by the charge made in the first plague: (1) the superiority of God and his agents (7:17; 8:10,18–19); (2) God's presence in the land, shown by his shielding his people's land from the plagues (8:22; 9:4,6); (3) God's incomparability (9:14), suggested also by the statement that the like of the plagues had never been seen before (9:18,24; 10:6,14). The plagues are both a punishment inflicted upon Pharaoh for his refusal to let the people go (the emphasis of J) and a demonstration of God's power in holy war (the emphasis of P; cf. M. Greenberg, *Near Eastern Studies in Honor of William Foxwell Albright* [ed. H. Goedicke; Baltimore, 1971] 243–52; R. R. Wilson, *CBQ* 41 [1979] 18–36). Attempts have been made to find natural explanations for the plagues, e.g., the bloody Nile is caused by red algae; the gnats are a natural consequence of the festering bodies of the frogs (e.g., J. L. Mihelic and G. E. Wright, *IDB* 3, 822–24), but the emphasis in the Bible is on their stunning and unrepeatable character. God's manipulation of natural elements is a narrative way of revealing his sole divinity. Instead of an objective description of the miraculous phenomenon followed by interpretive remarks, which a modern Western historian might favor, the biblical author combines event and interpretation by selecting and omitting narrative detail. The plagues are treated similarly in Pss 78 and 105.

18   (a) INTRODUCTION TO THE PLAGUES (7:8–13 [P]). The P redactor sets the stage and introduces the actors for the ten-act conflict: Yahweh and his servants Moses and Aaron *versus* Pharaoh and his servants the magicians. The servants of Pharaoh by the third plague have ceased to be rivals of Moses ("This is the finger of God," 8:15) and by the sixth plague can no longer be in his service (9:11). By the eighth plague, they have recognized that Yahweh has defeated Pharaoh (10:7). Pharaoh, however, hardens his heart (in the Bible the organ of decision) and refuses to acknowledge that Yahweh is the sole God because of his signs and wonders.

19   (b) TRIPLET I (7:14–8:19). The first plague: blood (7:14–24 [J: 14–18,20b,21a,23–24] [P: 19,20a, 21b,22]). As in the first plagues of the other triplets, God sends Moses to Pharaoh in the morning to warn him of the danger, but Pharaoh refuses to listen. Yahweh demands that Pharaoh allow the people to go into the wilderness, i.e., to leave Pharaoh's domain that they might worship him. P characteristically heightens the effects of the plague (v 19), underlining human obedience and divine foreknowledge (vv 20a,22). The second plague: frogs (7:25–8:15 [J: 7:25–8:4,8–15a] [P: 8:5–7]). Like the other second plagues in the triplets, God sends Moses into the palace to warn Pharaoh. Pharaoh, entreating Moses to pray for the removal of the frogs, is allowed to name the time of their removal to emphasize Yahweh's complete control (8:9–11). The third plague: gnats (8:16–19 [P]). In the third plague of each triplet, Yahweh commands Moses and Aaron to initiate the plague without warning. The magicians hitherto had been able to duplicate the sign but now must confess their failure, the climax of the first third of the plagues.

20   (c) TRIPLET II (8:20–9:12). The fourth plague: flies (8:20–32 [J]). The motif of God's presence with his people is sounded in the charge to Pharaoh (8:22; cf. 9:4,6). **22.** Goshen is the area in the northeast Delta where the Hebrews lived (→ Genesis, 2:70). The sign is not simply the insect swarms but also the protection of Goshen from the plague; Yahweh begins to differentiate between his own people and Egypt. **25–29.** Moses shows his cunning; he genuinely wants to worship Yahweh in the wilderness, outside of Pharaoh's domain, but he wants a three-day headstart. The fifth plague: pestilence (9:1–7 [J]). In the pestilence affecting livestock, God again makes a distinction between his people and the Egyptians. The sixth plague: fever boils (9:8–12 [P]). The concerns of P are apparent: attention to Moses' human counterparts, the magicians; to the sovereignty of the Lord, who hardens the heart of Pharaoh; and to the divinely foreseen disobedience of Pharaoh.

21   (d) TRIPLET III (9:13–10:29). The seventh plague: hail (9:13–35 [J]). The hail is part of a thunderstorm, the appropriate context for the revelation of the storm-god Yahweh. **27.** The language is forensic, not ethical: "I am guilty this time. The Lord is in the right and I and my people are in the wrong." **31.** The mention of the crops suggests an early spring date and also explains why there were crops for the locusts of the next plague (10:5). The eighth plague: locusts (10:1–20 [J]). **1–2.** Yahweh declares he has hardened Pharaoh's heart to show his power in the signs. Verses 3–4 stress the choice offered to Pharaoh, and vv 7 and 16, his willfulness. The ninth plague: darkness (10:21–29 [J]). Darkness in the Bible is terrifying, the condition of the world before it was created (Gen 1:2); human life is impossible without light. Pharaoh still tries to force the Hebrews' return by retaining their cattle (v 24), as he had earlier tried to hold their children hostage (10:10). Moses is equal to his wiles; he claims he needs the cattle for sacrifice (vv 25–26). **27–29.** Pharaoh himself decides never to see Moses again, preparing for the climax.

22   (e) THE TENTH PLAGUE: DEATH OF THE EGYPTIAN FIRSTBORN AND ACCOMPANYING RITUALS (11:1–13:16 [J: 11:1–8; 12:21–23,27b,29–39] [P: 11:9–10; 12:1–20,28,40–51; 13:1–16] [E: 12:24–27a?]). The tenth plague is climactic not only by its position outside the triplet series but also by the prefatory prediction in 11:1 that Pharaoh will at last let them go. The spoiling of the Egyptians was the last act of the scenario given to Moses in 3:21–22. That Pharaoh will drive them out (11:1), an unusually strong and reiterated phrase, echoes the last verse of the first commission narrative in 6:1, "With a strong hand he will send you forth and with a strong hand he will expel you." Further, 4:21–26 had condensed all the plagues into the tenth plague. Such references back to the divine prediction signal the completion of the rescue of the Hebrews.

Verses 4-9 are addressed to Pharaoh, as v 8 shows. Yahweh will go forth in the midst of Egypt, present more forcefully than in any other plague. Moses leaves Pharaoh in hot anger, a mark of Pharaoh's obduracy but also of Moses' increasing mastery. **12:1-20.** Before the occurrence of the climactic plague of deliverance for Egypt, P introduces the rites of the Passover lamb (vv 3-13) and of the unleavened bread, *maṣṣôt* (vv 14-20). The two rites were originally separate. The first was a rite of herders to propitiate the gods when they moved from the well-watered winter pastures to the arid summer ones. The second was a rite of farmers, a kind of spring cleaning of the previous year's old leaven. The text connects the lamb sacrifice with the exodus (vv 11-13). The unleavened bread is made a memorial of the exodus in the narrative itself (12:34) and in an accompanying instruction (13:3-10). 12:1-20 are the words of Yahweh to Moses, and vv 21-27 are the transmission of those commands to the elders, such divine commands and their transmissions being a favorite P device. P includes the rituals for the Passover lamb and the unleavened bread (12:1-28,43-51; 13:1-16) within the tenth plague, between announcement and fulfillment. Celebrated at the spring new year, the rituals enable Israelites of each succeeding generation to participate in the escape from Pharaoh's dominion (R. de Vaux, *AI* 484-93). **12:37-39.** P gives the first of his 12 rubrics for the journey; the journey to Canaan begins within Pharaoh's Egypt, an instance of Yahweh's mastery over every land.

23 **12:37.** The first stage of the journey was from Raamses to Succoth. Succoth has been identified by some scholars with Tell el-Maskhutah and with Tell el-Ratabah, two cities in the Wadi Tumilat within 10 mi. of each other and *ca.* 25 mi. SE of Raamses. Succoth is said to be a Hebr adaptation of the Egyptian *Ṯkw(t)*, the civil name of the eighth lower Egyptian nome, which *may* be Tell el-Maskhutah; the general similarity of the names, however, is not compelling evidence for an identification. Recent archaeological work, sensitive at once to archaeology, the shifting ancient drainage of the Delta, and the different identifications of the stations attested in early Judaism (e.g., Jdt, the LXX, and the targums), has offered a plausible reconstruction of the route. For the Hebrews escaping from Raamses, there was virtually only one route that avoided the Egyptian observation posts S of Lake Balah and the important fortress at Zilu astride the Way of the Philistines; that route led through the swampy regions of Lake Balah. This shallow lake has the best claim to be *Yam Sup*—lit., "Sea of Reeds" but conventionally and wrongly translated since the LXX "Red Sea." In 14:1, the people are directed back to Pi-ha-hiroth (unidentified) which is in front of Baal-Zephon. Baal-Zephon may be modern Defenne (Gk Daphne). Exod 14:4 suggests that the Hebrews turned back to Baal-Zephon deliberately to provoke Pharaoh to chase them through swampy areas of Lake Balah and set the stage for the ultimate battle and victory.

Later biblical literature identified the places on the basis of the geography of its time. Ps 78:12,43, e.g., uses the Egyptian phrase "fields of Zoan (Tanis)." Tanis was the residence of the pharaohs of the 21st Dynasty (1065-935) but is an anachronism for the 13th cent. Other books and the LXX use the geography of their time, e.g., the LXX of 1:11 identifies one of the store cities as Heliopolis, a city on the Wadi Tumilat. So a literary tradition of a northern and a southern route developed within the Bible. It seems that the northern was the actual one (→ 7 above; Biblical Geography, 73:24-29; also Bietak, *Tell el-Dabʿa II* 135-37; and W. H. Schmidt, *Exodus, Sinai und Mose* 26-28).

24 **12:38.** A mixed multitude—not only the Hebrews but others—necessitated the adaptation of the Passover for outsiders in vv 43-49. **40-42.** The 430 years probably reflects the P chronology of generations in Egypt in Gen 15:16 and presupposed in Exod 6:14-20; each generation seems to be 100 years here as befits patriarchs, and not the usual 40. This is suggested by Gen 15:13, which says that the oppression in Egypt will last 400 years, and by 15:16, which predicts that the people will come back in the fourth generation. **13:1-2, 11-16.** Like the Passover lamb and the unleavened bread in chap. 12, the customary consecration of the firstborn is connected to the exodus. Sometimes children were directly sacrificed to the gods; the practice is directly attested by the excavations of the Phoenician colony of Carthage and indirectly in mainland Phoenicia. The word "redeem" (*pdh,* vv 13,15) elsewhere means God's rescue of Israel from Egypt; here it is used in a more restricted sense of a ransom. As in 12:25-27 and Deut 6:20-25, the child's question in a family setting occasions the explanation. **16.** The metaphor of keeping the law before one's eyes was eventually taken literally and led to the later Jewish practice of wearing phylacteries. 13:3-10 parallel vv 11-16 in relating the unleavened bread to settlement in Canaan and to the law.

25 **(E) The Destruction of the Egyptian Armies and the Thanksgiving of Miriam (13:17-15:21 [P: 14:1-4,8-10*,15-18,21-23,26,28-29] [J: 13:20-22; 14:5b-6,13-14,19b-20,24-25b,27,30-31; 15:20-21] [E: 13:17-19; 14:5a,7,11-12,19a,25a] [special source 15:1-19]).** Pharaoh's grip on the enslaved Hebrews has been loosened by the ten plagues, and the tenth plague and the exodus have been ritualized for later generations. Now Pharaoh and his army must be utterly destroyed in holy war (14:28). After the great victory, the whole people sing a song of thanksgiving, like other songs in the OT in celebration of divine victories. **17-18.** The best route for the people is not the Way of the Philistines—the most direct, but guarded by the fortress at Zilu—but rather a route through the wilderness at the Sea of Reeds, a swampy area around Lake Balah, as suggested above (→ 23). **19.** In Gen 50:22-26, Joseph made his brothers swear that they would take his bones with them when God "will visit you." The transfer of the bones is a sign that "the visitation" has taken place. **20.** The second of P's stages, corresponding to Num 33:6. **14:1-4.** P's third stage, from Num 33:7, means reversing direction. None of the locations, except Baal-Zephon, probably modern Defenne (Gk Daphne), can be located. Defenne seems to be on the highway leading NE to Zilu. Yahweh brings the people back to the main road, where they will be seen and pursued by Pharaoh's army. Yahweh is provoking them so as to "get glory" (v 4), i.e., be recognized as the only powerful deity by his decisive victory over Egypt and its gods. **5-9.** Pharaoh rises to the bait. He will pursue the people, who he thinks are trapped in the wilderness (v 3). **10-14.** As Yahweh predicted in selecting the route (13:17), the people have a change of heart when they see war; they want to return to Egypt. Moses exhorts them in vv 13-14 to prepare for holy war. In holy war, the gods fought in the heavens in support of their armies on earth. Since Yahweh is the only true deity, Israel's victory is assured. The people have only to avoid panic and be confident in the coming victory. **15-31.** The battle is conceived by each source differently. According to P, Moses divided the sea by the rod and Israel walked through on dry land, the waters being a wall to their right and left. When Israel got to the other side, Moses raised his hand and the walls of water crashed in on the Egyptian army, wiping them out. According to J,

Yahweh the storm-god drove back the sea long enough for Israel to cross in the night and then the sea returned to its wonted flow in the morning. The language is like Ps 48:5–8, where Yahweh throws the kings into a panic ("discomfort" in v 24) and uses the wind as his weapon. Victory in any case belongs to Yahweh alone. The Song of the Sea (15:1–18) is an ancient thanksgiving. In the Bible one renders thanks by reciting publicly what God has done; the public report of the rescue makes known on earth the glory God has in heaven (cf. Pss 18,30,118, 138). The hymn praises Yahweh for raising the storm that overturned Pharaoh's boats and for leading the people to his holy mountain. The song gives a version of the exodus-conquest different from the prose accounts of the Pentateuch and Josh: Yahweh's storm capsizes the Egyptian boats and he leads the people immediately to his holy mountain in Canaan, his presence at their head throwing the natives into a panic. The song is divided into two panels, the annihilation of the Egyptians (vv 4–12) and the procession to the holy mountain (vv 13–18). **1–3.** Verse 21 attributes the song to Miriam rather than to Moses—a more original attribution, since well-known figures in literary tradition tended to attract to themselves other's traditions. **4–10.** Yahweh, like Baal in the Ugaritic texts, is pictured as a storm-god battling his enemies with wind, lightning, and thunder. Verse 8 should not be read as a parallel of the P account in 14:22–28; the picture rather is like Ps 107:25–27, a storm that lifts high mountains of water. **11–12.** Yahweh's victory over Egypt demonstrates that he is superior to their gods in heaven; he controls heaven, earth, and the underworld. "Earth" in v 12b is the underworld. **13–18.** The people are a victorious army on the march, fearless because their God leads them. The natives panic, offering no resistance as the people march to Yahweh's mountain shrine. "Your holy encampment" (v 13), "the mount of your heritage," and "the sanctuary" (v 17) would be understood by later generations as Jerusalem, the site of the Temple on Mount Zion. The poem however is older than David's conquest of Jerusalem in the early 10th cent. The holy mountain shrine of Yahweh might refer to the whole land as Yahweh's mountain, as in Deut 32:13; Ezek 39:4,17; etc. In Ps 78:54 the same phrase refers to Shiloh, the shrine prior to Jerusalem. The verbs in vv 16–17 are preterite, not future: "when your people, O Yahweh, crossed over the waters to Canaan." The last verse is a prayer that the royal rule of Yahweh, demonstrated in the destruction of Egypt and the leading of his people to himself, be always available to Israel (Cross, *CMHE* 112–44).

26   (F) The Journey to Sinai and Canaan after the Egyptians Have Been Destroyed (15:22–18:27).
(a) The First Test: Marah (15:22–27 [P: 22a,27] [J: 22a–25a] [special source: 25b,26]). According to the fourth of P's journey rubrics, the people leave the Sea of Reeds and go to the Wilderness of Shur. P several times collapses several place-names in Num 33 into the phrase "wilderness of PN." This is the first of many stories of Yahweh testing the people in the wilderness. God puts humans in a position where they must show their true allegiance; God may test humans but humans may not test God. All the tests in the wilderness concern either food and drink for the people or Moses' authority. At Marah (Hebr "bitter") the people cannot drink the bitter waters and "murmured." The word occurs only in Exod 15–17 and Num 14–17 (and in Josh 9:18). It means complaining against Moses and Aaron regarding the divine nurture or guidance in the wilderness. Will the people allow Yahweh to be their God by trusting that he will feed and rule them? In this first trial (other water stories are Exod 17:2–7 and Num

20:1–13), a deliberate reference is made to the first of the Egyptian plagues, the bloody waters of the Nile that the Egyptians could not drink (cf. 7:18,21,24). Egypt (in the person of the Pharaoh) hardened its heart and the plagues ensued. If Israel opens its heart, then its fate will be different from the Egyptians' for it will experience Yahweh as healer (v 26) rather than sender of plagues. As Yahweh showed his power to the Egyptians in the ten signs and wonders, so he will test Israel in the wilderness ten times (Exod 15:22–27; 16; 17:2–7; Num 11; 12; 13–14; 16; 17; 20:1–13; 21:4–9). The episode ends in well-watered abundance, a harbinger of the later happy ending of the journey.

27   (b) The Second Test: Quails and Manna (16:1–36 [P: 1–3,6–27,32–35a] [J: 4–5,28–31,35b,36]). The second test pairs manna with quails according to the frequent biblical word pair "meat//food (or bread)." The story is told also in Num 11 in another version and in Pss 105:40 and 78:17–31; in Ps 78 the quails turn out to be poisonous, killing those who had craved them. Here the quails do not figure prominently in the story and in fact are not mentioned after v 13; the story is about the manna. This omission is surprising in the light of the ominous predictions in vv 6–12. Further, the story seems to presuppose that the Tent of Meeting and the Ark were already in existence (in vv 33–34 and probably in vv 9–10); the Glory ordinarily appeared through them. The redactor has apparently placed a version of the story of quail and manna on the way to Sinai. In accord with P's view that the people heard the law at Sinai for the first time, they are not punished for transgressions, as they will be after Sinai in Num 11. Rather, P connects the manna with sabbath observance, which for him was instituted at the creation (Gen 2:2–3). **1.** The fourth of P's journey stages. None of the places can be certainly identified. **2–5.** The people murmur against Moses and Aaron but their complaint is ultimately against Yahweh; they prefer Pharaoh's sustenance in Egypt to Yahweh's in the wilderness. As in the other pre-Sinai trials (15:25; 17:5–6), Yahweh simply accedes to the request without rebuke. The people here are tested on their willingness to follow the instruction regarding the manna; sacred food must be gathered according to divine rubrics. Verses 16–27 are the P instruction corresponding to the brief J instructions in vv 4–5 and 28–30. **6–9.** The confusion in the text—the doubling of vv 6–7 in vv 8 and 12 and the sequence of actions—cannot easily be resolved. Verses 6–7 are ominous, the preface to a story that must originally have included death from the quails. In this version of the story, the people will know Yahweh, confess him as God, when they experience again the control of nature and history shown already in the plagues and the exodus. Verse 8 is best translated, "And Moses continued, 'Yes, it will be in the very giving to you in the evening of the meat to eat and in the morning of food to sate yourself because Yahweh has heard....'" After Sinai, Israel would "come near before Yahweh" (v 9) for the Tent of Meeting, but here the location is left unspecified, as is the location of the Glory in v 10. **13–30.** The quail is *coturnix coturnix*, a small migratory bird about 7½ inches long, brown or sandy with yellowish streaks. It comes to Palestine and Sinai in March or April in great flocks. It usually follows the wind, but if the wind suddenly shifts, the entire flock may be forced to land, where, exhausted, it is easily caught. Manna is the name for the bread from heaven, derived by folk etymology from *man hû'*, "What is it?" even though correct Hebr would be *mâ hû'*. Manna is the honeylike dropping from the tamarisk tree of Palestine and Sinai, which the bedouin of the Sinai call *mann*. The droppings from the tamarisk are secretions from two kinds of scale lice, which suck large quantities of liquid from the twigs in spring in order to collect nitrogen for their grubs. It contains glucose and fructose but no protein and cannot be harvested in quantity. The Bible portrays manna as miraculous; it is not an everyday occurrence. The rubrics for dealing safely with heavenly food are twice disregarded by the people (vv 20 and 27), a hint of later disobedience to the law. The violations of the sabbath earn a rebuke in vv 28–29. **31–36.** Verse 32 enables later generations of Israel to see how Yahweh led them through the wilderness. **28** (c) THE THIRD TEST: WATER (17:1–7 [P: 1] [J: 2,4–7] [E: 3]). In 15:22–27, the people could not drink the bitter water; here there is no water at all. P has telescoped the place-names of Num 33:12–13, Dophkah and Alush, into one: Rephidim. **2–4.** The people demand water and attack Moses. To Moses their quarrel is with God directly: they do not believe he can feed them, i.e., be their God in the wilderness. **5–7.** Again, there is no divine rebuke but only the command to take some of the elders and go to the rock, which, when struck with the rod, will yield abundant water. The elders represent the people and are witnesses. The final verse, "Is Yahweh present among us or not?" sums up perfectly what it means to test God. Meribah, which plays on the Hebr root *rîb*, "to quarrel," is the site of the dispute about the water at the end of the journey in Num 20:1–13. *Massâ* is derived from the Hebr vb. *nissâ*, "to test." According to Num 27:14 and Deut 32:51, Meribah is a spring at Kadesh in the Negeb. Yahweh gives bread from heaven and water from the rock to this people in the wilderness; he thus proves his mastery over the hostile environment. **29** (d) THE DEFEAT OF THE AMALEKITES (17:8–16 [J]). The Amalekites are mentioned as a fierce tribe in the vicinity of Kadesh in Gen 14:7; Num 13:29; 14:25. Moses defeats them by stretching out over them the rod he used to defeat Pharaoh. Yahweh fights for Israel only when the rod is raised. Moses' physical fatigue in v 12 prepares for 18:18; the same word describes his inability to function without sharing his authority. Joshua and Hur are introduced. Hur is mentioned elsewhere only in 24:14, unless he is also the grandfather of the Judahite artisan mentioned in Exod 31:1–2; 35:30; and 38:22 and in the genealogies in 1 Chr 2:19,20,50 and 4:1,4. Joshua, on the other hand, becomes Moses' most trusted servant and, later on, his successor. **14–16.** The Amalekites are cursed because they attempted to keep the people from their God-given heritage. Th curse is written in a document and given as a command to Joshua as military commander. Moses builds an altar to celebrate the victory and gives it an appropriate name. **30** (e) JETHRO'S BLESSING AND ADVICE (18:1–27 [E]). In vv 1–12 Jethro meets the people who had escaped from Pharaoh at the mountain, just as he had earlier met Moses the escapee near the mountain in 2:15–22. He recognizes Yahweh as the all-powerful deity in vv 10–11, another instance of a non-Israelite confessing Yahweh as the sole God because of the prosperity of his people. This story does not accord with Moses' farewell to Jethro in 4:18–26, in which Moses took his wife and sons with him to Egypt (4:20a is J, whereas chap. 18 is E). Further evidence of diversity of the traditions about Moses and the Midianites is the different names for Moses' father-in-law: Jethro here and in chap. 4, but Reuel in 2:18 and Hobab in Judg 4:11. Num 10:29 makes Hobab the son of Reuel. The Midianites were an early ally of Israel (so here) but later an enemy, as in Num 25; 31; and Judg 6–8. **2–4.** The technical term for divorce (Deut 24:1,3) is not used here; Moses had sent her home from Egypt. Her father now brings her back to Moses. The sons' names recall Moses'

early relationship to his God. **10–12.** To bless God is to recite what he has done so that the hearers may praise him and enhance his glory. Yahweh's sole divinity is proved by his defeating the great military and political power of the region, Egypt. The meal shows Jethro's bond with Israel. **13–27.** Jethro is the one who first suggests that Moses share his authority with others. The same story is told in Deut 1:9–18, where the sharing takes place *after* Sinai and at divine command. **9–27.** Moses will now bring "before God" the cases that have no precedent and teach the people the laws and teachings of God. He will continue to be their teacher, making known to them the way in which they should walk. In other words, routine cases that can be decided on precedent no longer come to Moses. In the Bible, to judge means to be partial, i.e., to rescue the innocent and oppressed party and punish the wicked. This conception of justice contrasts with the modern Western conception of justice as blind or impartial and the separation of judicial, executive, and legislative powers.

(II) Israel at Sinai (19:1–40:38).
31 **(A) Solemn Concluding of the Covenant (19:1–24:18).** In the Priestly redactor's 12-stage procession that structures Exod to Num, the seventh station is Yahweh's mountain and the twelfth is the threshold of Yahweh's land. Israel remains encamped at Sinai from Exod 19:1 to Num 10:10. Sinai is therefore central not only by the sheer bulk of law and narrative connected with it but also by its position in the journey. Chaps. 19–24 describe the theophany (19), the Ten Commandments (20:1–17), and the Covenant Code (20:22–23:18); chaps. 25–31, the dwelling and its sacred personnel mediating God's presence; and chaps. 32–34, the apostasy and covenant renewal. At Sinai, Yahweh saw the condition of the people and resolved to act (3:7–8). Now the people have seen Yahweh and his works (19:4) and they must act. Will they agree to be God's people by obeying his will and building him a dwelling? **32** (a) ISRAEL ENCOUNTERS YAHWEH AT THE MOUNTAIN (19:1–25 [P: 1,2a] [J: 2b,11b–13,18,20–25] [E: 3a,9–11a,14–19] [special source: 3b–8]). Moses makes three round trips from camp to mountain to arrange the covenant: in vv 3–8a he relays the terms to the people, who assent to it; in vv 8b–14 according to divine instruction he purifies the people; in vv 20–25 he is made sole mediator (with Aaron as assistant) with the priests and people kept at a distance. **1–2.** The first month is Nisan, the time of Passover and Unleavened Bread. The second month is the entry into the wilderness of Sin, where the manna was given (16:1); it was the time of cereal harvest. Here the third month is the feast of Weeks, Pentecost. As early as the 2nd cent. BC some Jewish groups are recorded as connecting the giving of the law with the feast of Weeks. There is no hard evidence that mainstream Judaism made the connection between law and Pentecost until the 3rd cent. AD, but the connection may be early. The location of Mount Sinai cannot be fixed with any certainty. An imposing peak in the Sinai peninsula, Jebel Musa, has been identified with Sinai since Byzantine times (→ Biblical Geography, 73:29). Ancient biblical poetry, however, suggests that the mountain dwelling of God was directly south of Canaan and speaks of his advance with an army from the south, "Yahweh came from Sinai, and dawned from Seir upon us" (Deut 33:2; cf. Judg 5:4; Ps 68:8–9). **3–8a.** Verse 3a prefaces the liturgical poem of vv 3b–8; in v 3a Moses goes up to *'ĕlōhîm*, whereas in v 3b Yahweh calls down to Moses from the mountain. **4.** The people have seen what "I did to Egypt and how I . . . brought you to myself." They must act by deciding whether to be God's people by obeying his voice and keeping his

commandment (v 5). God's bearing of the people to his land is developed in Deut 32:10-14, which also speaks of rescuing and selecting: "like an eagle he stirs up his nest, over his young he flutters. He spreads his wings, he takes him (the young), he bears him on his wings." In 3:12 God foretold that Israel would serve, i.e., worship, at this mountain. Sinai is territory sacred to Yahweh. To become Yahweh's people they must freely agree to the divine choice. The agreement is couched in traditional biblical language—obedience and keeping of covenant. "Covenant" is a biblical term for a sworn agreement between persons, ordinarily oral, to do something. It was done "before the gods," who were thought to sanction it. Treaties between nations and peoples (often personalized as covenants between the kings) were also covenants but of a special written type, called covenant formularies by some scholars. By the middle of the second millennium in the west Semitic world (and persisting until late in the first millennium), the formularies had developed into a genre, which consisted of a history of the relationship of suzerain and vassal kings, stipulations, curses and blssings consequent upon their observance, and a list of divine witnesses. The order was fluid and (apart from the blessings and curses) some items could be omitted. Was the Sinai covenant in Exod such a covenant formulary? Many scholars, such as G. E. Mendenhall and K. Baltzer, affirm that it was but solid evidence is lacking; there are no blessings and curses in the Exod covenant, nor a detailed historical prologue. The first instance of conscious Israelite adaptation of the covenant formulary seems to be Deut 5-28; see D. J. McCarthy, *Treaty and Covenant* (AnBib 21A; Rome, 1978); G. E. Mendenhall, "Covenant," *IDB* 1. 714-23; K. Baltzer, *The Covenant Formulary* (Phl, 1971). **5-6.** If Israel agrees to hear Yahweh's voice (and not that of another god), they will be his *sĕgullâ*, "possession," also used in the same sense in Deut 7:6; 14:2; 26:18; Ps 135:4. Among other meanings, biblical *sĕgullâ* in the above-cited passages and the cognate Akkadian word *sikiltu* denote the treasures of the wealthy and of kings. In an Akkadian seal the king is the *sikiltum* of the goddess, and in a Ugaritic transl. of a Hittite-Ugaritic treaty, the Hittite king tells the Ugaritic king, "Now [you belong?] to the Sun, your Lord; you are [his serva]nt, his property [*s*]*glth*" (M. Held, *JCS* 15 [1961] 11; and H. B. Huffmon and S. B. Parker, *BASOR* 184 [1966] 36-37). Verses 5-6 are best translated, against most Eng versions, "You will be my special possession out of all the peoples. Though all the earth is mine, you will be to me a kingdom of priests, and a holy nation." "Special possession" in two other similar uses is followed by the phrase "from all the peoples"; "Indeed all the earth is mine," therefore, goes with the following phrases. The three phrases of vv 5b-6a go closely with the three of v 4. "Kingdom of priests" in v 5 is unclear; semantically parallel to "holy nation," it probably means sacred among the nations, as priests are among the people. Yahweh has defeated the great power Egypt and its gods and has brought them to the safety of his precincts. If Israel accepts Yahweh as their God, they will belong to the only God (essentially the meaning of all the phrases of vv 5b-6a). **8b-19.** Yahweh initially establishes in v 8b Moses' credibility, always a concern (4:1,5,8,9; 14:31). The people's hearing the divine cloud that guided (13:21-22) and rescued them (14:19,20,24) speaking to Moses ought to convince them. Verse 9a reprises v 8b, a Hebrew way of getting back to the main thread after the word to Moses in v 9a. Consecration of the people means their separation from the profane world; clothing is to be washed of earthly grime, and sexual relations are prohibited. The entire mountain becomes sacred by the coming of

Yahweh; anyone who strays into it becomes charged with holiness. Such a dangerous person must be removed lest his contagion infect others; he is to be killed without anyone touching him, hence by stoning or by arrows. The actual theophany in vv 16-19 takes place in a storm, like other theophanies in the Bible (Exod 15:8,10; Judg 5:4-5; Pss 18:6-19; 29; 77:16-20; etc.) and in Ugaritic literature. Scholarly arguments to the contrary notwithstanding, the theophany is not a volcano; one cannot approach an active volcano. Moreover, there were no active volcanos in the area, and there is no attestation of volcanic theophanies in comparable literature. The depiction mingles later liturgical reenactment in the description of the original event (trumpet = thunder; firepot = smoke), so that later generations might celebrate the foundational event. Mount Zion in Jerusalem later became the heir of the Sinai traditions; the law was preached from there, e.g., Ps 50 and Isa 2:1-5. **20-25.** The section emphasizes how great is the distance between Yahweh and the people and underscores the mediation of Moses. Many scholars believe that 20:18-21 originally stood after 19:19. In any case 19:20-25 establishes the mediating role of Moses.

33   (b) THE TEN COMMANDMENTS (20:1-21 [E]). The Decalogue is also found in Deut 5:6-21 with slight changes; Deut gives a different reason for the observance of the sabbath and in the last commandment places the neighbor's wife before the neighbor's house. The numeration of the commandments differs slightly in the tradition; Anglican, Greek, and Reformed traditions reckon the prohibitions against false worship as two, whereas the Lutheran and Roman Catholic traditions count them as one and divide the last commandment into two. **2-6.** A strong assertion that Yahweh is the only deity for Israel. Since he defeated their former lord and master, he and no other deity is their God. The best transl. is, "I, Yahweh, am your God." Verses 3-5a forbid images, which in the ancient Near East were the ordinary means of encounter between god and worshiper. Verse 3 refers to the statues of deities in the sanctuary; excavations have revealed shrines with several images of gods in them. The aniconic tradition is ancient in Israel; no certain image of Yahweh has so far been found at any Israelite site, though a crude depiction of a god and his consort found at Kuntillat Ajrud may be Yahweh and Asherah (M. Coogan, "Canaanite Origins and Lineage: Reflections on the Religion of Ancient Israel," *Ancient Israelite Religion* [Fest. F. M. Cross; ed. P. D. Miller *et al.*; Phl, 1987] 115-24). Verse 5b resumes and expands v 2a. "Impassioned" is a better transl. than "jealous." Yahweh is passionately committed to Israel; he will see to it that all sins are punished even if the punishment is borne by the children of the parents who have committed the sin; the people consist of more than one generation. "Sin" in the Bible often denotes at once the act and the consequences of the act. The consequences, or the plight one gets into by one's sins, are sometimes described as directly sent by God and sometimes as the natural result of human actions. In this text, divine initiative is strongly stated. Those "rejecting me" (better than traditional "hating me"), after they had accepted Yahweh in the ceremony just concluded, commit a sin that will not go unpunished. Verse 6 is the positive side: those who love, who keep his commandments, will experience the divine kindness (*ḥesed*), Yahweh's covenantal love; it is a passionate commitment to his people founded in the *noblesse oblige* of the Great Suzerain. **7.** The prohibition seems to be against the false use of an oath in legal proceedings rather than a general lack of reverence for the name. **8-11.** The sabbath is a peculiarly Israelite institution; at least no satisfactory parallel in other cultures has so far been discovered. To sanctify it means to set it apart, to avoid doing the work of the weekday on it. Verses 8–10 parallel v 11; the rhythm of time was created along with all else in the first week (Gen 1:1–2:3). **12.** In a traditional and largely oral society, elders were to be respected as repositories of tradition. Parents also depended on children to care for them in old age. **13.** Only illegal killing is prohibited; Israel had the death penalty. **15.** Kidnapping is prohibited; ordinary theft is forbidden by the last commandment. **17.** As comparable inscriptions make clear, ḥāmad means conspiracy, taking steps to steal (not merely "covet"). **18–21.** The section, underscoring the popular acceptance of Moses' mediation, matches 19:20–25, where Yahweh appoints Moses to that role. The people were afraid of close contact with God, which would have swept them out of the everyday world into the divine world, i.e., would have killed them.

34   (c) THE COVENANT CODE (20:22–23:33 [E]). The Covenant Code (so called from 24:7) is given after the single event of theophany and commandment in 20:1–17. The awestruck people beg Moses to mediate any further commandments (20:19). The collection consists of apodictic statements (20:22–26; 22:18–23:19) and case law (21:2–22:17). The latter are introduced by 22:1, "These are the judgments," which are decisions to be rendered in the specific cases that follow. Exod 24:3, which distinguishes "words" and "judgments," may express this distinction, or it may express the distinction generally between the Ten Commandments and the Covenant Code. The judgments are rationally arranged, but the apodictic sayings are wide-ranging and irregular (M. Greenberg, "Some Postulates of Biblical Law," *The Jewish Expression* [ed. J. Goldin; New Haven, 1976] 18–37).

Ancient Near Eastern codes of law were not comprehensive like the Napoleonic Code or the Roman Catholic Code of Canon Law, nor apparently did they always guide local judges in applying the law—at least in Mesopotamia, where there are discrepancies between the codes and recorded daily practice. Law codes were expressions of the divine will; the famous Code of Hammurabi (reigned 1725–1686) pictures the sun-god Shamash presenting the king with the laws that are inscribed on the lower half of the stele. At the king's accession, which was believed to be a renewal of the creation order, he proclaimed just decrees; the royal law codes enshrined that proclamation. The Covenant Code is proclaimed at Israel's creation by God's regent, Moses. Like other codes, it does not aim for completeness; it offers a sample of the divine intention for Israel and establishes the mediating office of Moses.

35   (i) *Injunctions regarding the shrine* (20:22–26 [E]). Divine–human encounter is God's to regulate, as the theophany with its explicit rules (19:10–15; 20–24) vividly demonstrates. No statues of deities are permitted in Yahweh's sanctuary because he spoke from heaven, i.e., invisibly, with no form to be reproduced by a statue (cf. Deut 4:12). Altars are to be built according to divine specifications, of earth or of unhewn stone. In the whole offering an animal is completely consumed on the altar (except the skin) in expiation for sin. The purpose of the "offering of well-being" (or "peace offering," šelāmîm, in Hebr always pl.) remains unclear. Deut 12:13–14, most probably of the late 8th cent., centralizes sacrifice in one place only, but in this period there could be many altars; indeed Josh–1 Kgs speaks of sacrifices being offered in different parts of the land without any indication of violation of law. Even with many altars, God must designate the site, must make it a place where his name, his presence, is there to bless the life of the worshiper.

The last provision, in v 26, is echoed in 28:42; whatever is unbefitting to the sacred sphere is to be avoided.

36   (ii) *Judgments regarding Hebrew slaves* (21:1–11). For other legislation on slaves, see Deut 15:12–18 and Lev 25:39–55. An Israelite could be born a slave or fall into slavery through sale by the parents as debt payment (2 Kgs 4:1; Amos 2:6) or through failure to make restitution in theft (22:1). **1.** The mišpāṭîm are the decisions made by judges; they can be translated "rules" or "judgments." **2–6.** A male slave is to serve six years and in the seventh year go free in the condition in which he entered. If the slave married a slave woman, the woman remains her master's, and the children remain with her because the child's relation to the mother was considered more basic than its relation to the father. The slave had the option of remaining with his family and his master, in which case his decision was ratified in the local shrine, and his ear, the organ of obedience, was pierced at the door of his master's house. **7–11.** The statutes concern the female slave as concubine. The relationship is not of a nature to be broken off at the end of six years as was the case of the male. If she does not please the master, a member of her family may buy her back ("redeem" her); the master may not sell her outside her family (the meaning of "foreign" here). If the woman is destined for the master's son, she shall be treated like the other daughters in the household; her food, clothing, and oil are to be supplied or else she can go free. The third element, traditionally "conjugal rights," is better translated "oil," as suggested by comparative evidence (S. Paul, *JNES* 28 [1969] 48–53).

37   (iii) *Judgments concerning capital crimes* (21:12–17 [E]). The Bible distinguishes manslaughter and willful murder. In willful murder, the blood avenger (gōʾēl), the nearest kinsman, retaliates by taking the life of the murderer. The "state" cedes to the avenger the settling of the case. Cities of refuge were provided in cases of manslaughter, where the guilty party was safe from the avenger. See Num 35 and Deut 19:1–13.

38   (iv) *Judgments concerning harm or death caused by humans, animals, or through neglect* (21:18–36 [E]). **18–19.** If the man died, his attacker would be guilty of manslaughter and would have had to flee to a city of refuge (vv 12–13). It is not manslaughter if the sick man is able to walk even if only with the aid of a cane; there is a money penalty only. **20–21.** The law regards slaves differently from their masters. As long as the slave does not die on the day of his beating, the master goes unpunished, or, rather, the loss of the slave is considered punishment enough. **22–25.** The fetus has a money value, to be determined by some kind of reckoning (the last phrase cannot be exactly translated). Harm to the mother is not measured by money but by the famous *lex talionis* (Lat, "law of retaliation," a phrase derived from the Twelve Tables of *ca.* 450 BC). Other instances are found in the Code of Hammurabi (nos. 195–205 [*ANET* 175]); Lev 24:19–20; Deut 19:21. The law seems severe but it mitigates blood vengeance; vengeance is satisfied with something less than loss of life. **26–27.** As in vv 20–21, slaves are regarded differently from free Israelites; for them there is no *lex talionis*. Just as in the Code of Hammurabi (nos. 198, 210), the upper-class person pays money damages for injuring a commoner (S. Greengus, *IDBSup* 545–46). The master's person is not touched, but at least the slave goes free. **28–32.** The owner is not held liable for his goring ox unless he knew the animal was dangerous and took no corrective steps. If the family of the person killed by the ox agreed, the culpable owner could pay a fine (Hebr kōper, the price of a life; cf. 30:12; Ps 49:7), *wergild*, money offered for the life of a murdered man to appease the kinsmen. Num

35:31–32 forbids the practice. The same rule applies to "minors" but not to slaves; since they are chattel, their owner is to be recompensed at the standard price of a slave. **33–34.** Two instances of harm to animals. One case concerns a reopened or a freshly dug pit.

39   (v) *Judgments concerning burglary and theft* (22:1–4 [E]).   Some translations rearrange the verses 22:1,4,2, 3, but the verses should be read in their normal order. "The thief" in v 2 refers back to "When a man breaks in . . ." in v 1, just as "the ox" in v 28b refers back to "When an ox . . ." in v 28a, and "the one who kindled" in v 5 refers back to "When a man kindles . . ." in v 4 (*Notes on the New Translation of the Torah* [Phl, 1969] 180). Four- or fivefold restitution of stolen goods is common in law codes; David in 2 Sam 12:6 speaks of a fourfold restoration of a lamb. Verses 2–3 allow a nocturnal thief tunneling under the wall to be beaten to death with no bloodguilt upon the householder (cf. 1 Sam 25:26,33). In daylight the apprehended thief is held to restitution according to the norm in v 4: twofold restitution since the stolen goods are still on his person. If the thief cannot make restitution, he is to be sold into slavery, the money going to satisfy the householder.

40   (vi) *Judgments concerning burning another's fields* (25:5–6 [E]).   The LXX, followed by some modern translations, translates Hebr *b'r* as "to graze," but the more common and preferable meaning here is "to burn"; vv 5–6, therefore, go together and concern culpability in burning stubble, a practice of preparing fields that is still current in the East.

41   (vii) *Judgments concerning culpability for deposited property* (22:7–15 [E]).   **7–8.** Restitution is twofold for stolen deposits, as in v 4. "Come near to God" means to take a solemn oath in the local sanctuary as v 11 suggests. **9.** As the Code of Hammurabi makes clear, the person to whom the deposit was entrusted might deny that the deposit was ever made and claim that the goods were all his. If there were no records or witnesses, the case has to be decided by oath and presumably by an ordeal or judgment by which one of the two claimants was declared guilty by God. **10–11.** Culpability for the death, injury, or loss to raiders of deposited animals is settled by oath. But simple theft (v 12) is presumed here to be preventable; the trustee is liable. Attack on cattle by wild animals, as long as the carcass is there to prove it, is reckoned to be so common as to preclude restitution. **14–15.** The borrower is responsible for borrowed animals unless the owner was there. The last phrase in v 15 is not clear; probably the owner is still entitled to the hiring fee even if the animal dies.

42   (viii) *Judgments concerning the seduction of a young woman* (22:16–17 [E]).   The case is that of a man who persuades a young woman to sleep with him. Her marriage has not yet been arranged between her father and her future bridegroom (or his family). Unlike the case in Deut 22:28–29, he uses no force but persuades her. By the fact of the man's willingness to have her, she legally is now in the position of a woman whose marriage has been arranged by the bridegroom. Her father, however, can refuse his consent, in which case the man still owes the bride-price since she is no longer a virgin and hence no longer readily marriageable.

43   (ix) *Commands about various social and cultic matters* (22:18–23:19 [E]).   This is a representative group of noncasuistic laws—prohibitions, directions, and commands—some couched in the 2d pers., some without stating a penalty. Such laws are not well attested in other ancient Near Eastern law codes (though cf. Eshnunna Laws 10–11,15–16,51–52 [*ANET* 162–63]; Hammurabi Code, nos. 36,38–40 [*ANET* 167–68]; and

the Assyrian Laws A 40,57–59 [*ANET* 183–85]); they occur rather in ritual and magic texts outside the Bible and also in treaties. The preponderance of such laws in the biblical codes seems attributable to the special role of Yahweh as sole God and hence authoritative lawgiver. **18.** Belief in one God means that the aid of spirits is not be be invoked. Concern with the problem elsewhere (Deut 18:10; Jer 27:9; and other passages) shows that the problem was real in Israel. **19.** A prohibition found also in Lev 18:23; 20:15–16; Deut 27:21. **20.** Violators of the first commandment are to be proscribed (not "utterly destroyed"), i.e., set apart from the community. **21–24.** Resident aliens (*gērîm*), people living more or less permanently in a community other than their own, were often classed with widows and the fatherless as needing protection; cf. Deut 24:19–22; Jer 7:6; Ezek 22:7. As outsiders, often without clan protection, they were vulnerable and often poor (Lev 19:10 and Deut 24:14). Special access to Yahweh is their protection. **25–27.** Loans were not made for commercial purposes but to alleviate distress; to take interest on them would be to profit from another's misfortune. Laws regulated intrusive creditors (Deut 24:6,10–13). The poor were specifically protected; their outer garment, which served as their blanket at night, had to be returned to them by evening. As in vv 21–24, the compassionate God watches over the weak. Amos (2:8) accuses the wealthy of sleeping upon garments taken in pledge. **28.** The intimate link between God and the leader who acts and speaks on his behalf is affirmed elsewhere in the Pentateuch: 14:10–12,31; 16:7–8; 17:2; Num 12:8. **29–31.** Holiness (v 31) means belonging to the deity, being removed from profane life. God's total possession of the people is signified by their offering to him the firstfruits, which represent the totality. Objects are "removed" by placing them in a shrine or giving them to sacred persons; living things are "removed" by killing them. Verse 29b is literally "your fullness and your trickling." The LXX and modern translations correctly expand the ancient expression. The human firstborn are "redeemed" by an animal substitute (13:13; 34:20; etc.). Verse 31b illustrates the meaning of holiness by a single example: Israel is to eat only meat correctly slaughtered so as to dispose of the blood (Lev 17:14–16). **23:1–3.** Like Lev 19:15–16, the verses prescribe fairness for witnesses at trials. The witness is not to enter a conspiracy to give false testimony. **4–5.** This interrupts the natural connection of vv 1–3 to vv 6–9. Deut 22:1–4 states the law with characteristic additions: it substitutes "brother," i.e., kinsman, for "enemy," and it includes all lost items, not just animals. Lev 19:17–18 forbids hatred of "brother//neighbor" and counsels loving one's neighbor as oneself. Justice, i.e., the return of goods and offering necessary assistance, is due even to personal enemies, just as it is to other classes—resident aliens, widows, and the fatherless. The last phrase is obscure in Hebr but can be understood according to Deut 22:4. **6–9.** As vv 1–3 were addressed to witnesses, these verses are addressed to judges. In the ancient Near East, the gods were believed to be behind the legal system. For a judge to sentence the innocent and to acquit the guilty does not change the reality; Yahweh will not follow the human judgment but will punish the judge. Bribes, the curse of the Eastern lawcourt, are to have no place in Israel. The protection of the resident alien, stated already in 22:21, is repeated in the new context of the just lawcourt. **10–11.** The verses are obviously related to vv 12–13 by the repetition of "six . . . but (on) the seventh. . . ." It is not certain whether the practice was actually carried out in biblical times; evidence for its practice is late, in the 5th cent. (Neh 10:31; 1 Macc 6:49,53). Lev 25:2–7,

20-22 suggest that there was a common reckoning of the seventh year for all fields. The purpose stated is not agricultural but humanitarian—that the poor may eat. **12-13.** In style these verses resemble the preceding. The reasons given for observance, that the draft animals and the workers might rest, is different from that given under the third commandment. Verse 13 seems peculiarly placed. The prohibition of even the mention of other gods serves to introduce the following verses. **14-17.** The cultic calendar, here given with several miscellaneous rules, appears also in 34:18-26; Lev 23:1-44; and Deut 16:1-17 with significant variations. The feasts are pilgrimage feasts to the shrine (Hebr *ḥag*, like the Islamic *ḥajj*; R. de Vaux, *AI* 484-506). The first feast is Unleavened Bread (Hebr *maṣṣôt*), already mentioned in 12:14-20,34; 13:3-10. Here and in 34:18 the text does not connect the rites of unleavened bread and Passover lamb, unlike the P legislation in chap. 12. "Empty-handed" in v 15 refers to offering the sheaves in the shrine. The second feast is at the harvest of wheat, seven weeks after the first cereals were cut. Num 28:26 calls it Firstfruits and feast of Weeks. It is called Pentecost, "fiftieth day," in 2 Macc 12:31-32 and Tob 2:1. The third feast, Ingathering in the old Exod calendars, came later to be called the feast of Tents, commemorating the tents of the wilderness period, or simply *the* Feast in Ezek 45:25; 1 Kgs 8:2,65. It was celebrated in autumn at the end of the year; in the early period, Israel celebrated the new year in the fall. **18-19.** Supplementing the rules for the three pilgrimage feasts are four ritual regulations. The fat, the desirable part of the animal, is to be burned entirely and at once, except that around the kidneys and intestines (Lev 3:3-4). The prohibition against boiling a kid in its mother's milk is repeated verbatim in 34:26 and Deut 14:21. Why the practice is forbidden is not known; a damaged Ugaritic text may mention a similar rite (see *Bible Review* 1/3 [1985] 48-58).

44   (x) *The blessings of keeping the covenant* (23:20-33 [E]).   Ancient law codes sometimes concluded with curses and blessings, e.g., Lipit Ishtar Code (*ANET* 161), Code of Hammurabi (*ANET* 178-80), Holiness Code (Lev 26:3-45), Deut 27-28. The biblical examples show flexibility, adapting the genre to historical circumstances. Like the blessing promised to Jacob leaving Canaan, "See I am with you and will guard you wherever you walk" (Gen 28:15; cf. vv 20-22), Yahweh through the angel will be with the people and bring them to their land. The condition for the blessings is obedience during the journey to the angel, who is Yahweh himself "in a temporary descent to visibility for a special purpose" (A. McNeile, cited in Driver, *Exodus* 248), and to the first commandment after the conquest (vv 23-25). The blessings are the divine presence that gives protection on the way (vv 20-22), food and drink and good health, living out the normal life-span, assistance in the war of conquest (vv 27-30), and secure possession of a vast land (v 31). **20.** God's presence with the people, leading them to the land, is a constant theme (e.g., 32:34; 33:2-3,12,14-16; 34:9). There is a keen awareness of how an all-holy God could dwell with a sinful people. The divine presence is pictured variously: the angel, the pillar of cloud (13:21; 40:36-38), and the Ark (Num 10:33). **21.** The name manifests the person; disobedience to the angel bearing the divine name is disobedience to God. Verses 23-25a are possibly an addition, since they interrupt the list of blessings; they resemble 34:11-14. Lists of the prior inhabitants of the land, usually in lists of three, six, or seven, are frequent in the Bible; it is not easy to identify the ethnic groups named within Palestine. The name Amorites is originally

a Babylonian term, "westerners," to designate people west of Babylon. It is favored by the E source, whereas J prefers the term Canaanite. Perizzites may have meant originally "hill dwellers" and may have come to be reckoned as a gentilic. Hittite may refer to scattered Hittite families in the area; the Hittite empire in Asia Minor never reached Palestine. Hivites are probably Hurrians, an ancient group active in northern Mesopotamia in the second millennium. Jebusites are the native inhabitants of Jerusalem. **27-30.** In holy war, panic sent by the gods is an important weapon. "Hornets" in v 28 is a traditional translation since the LXX, but the real meaning is unknown. **31.** One of several descriptions of the land; others = Gen 15:18; Deut 11:24; Num 34; 1 Kgs 4:21. The southern boundaries are the northeast border of Egypt and the desert south of Palestine, the southeast coast, and northern Syria.

45   (d) THE RATIFICATION OF THE COVENANT (24:1-18 [J: 1-2,9-11] [E: 3-8,12-15a,18b], but according to others "J" and "E" in this chapter are special sources; [P: 15b-18a]).   The chap. describes the ratification in two different ways: the representatives of the people banquet with God (1-2,9-11), and the people agree to the covenant in a blood rite (3-8,12-15a). The combination of two sources may confuse the reader. Verses 3-8 follow naturally 20:22-23:33; Moses recounts to the people the Ten Commandments and the Covenant Code ("all the words of Yahweh and the judgments") that he has just heard, and the people agree to it. In vv 1-2 + 9-11, however, God commands Moses to come up to the mountain, where he already is (20:21). Similarly, v 12 fits uneasily after v 11. In the redactor's perspective, 24:1 evidently began a fresh scene, one that does not directly continue 20:21. In this perspective, Moses and the leaders are told to ascend the mountain, but before they do in v 9, they carry out the ritual in vv 3-8. **1-2.** Nadab and Abihu are the sons of Aaron (6:23). A threefold gradation is made: Moses, who alone comes near God; the elders, who ascend but do not come near; and the people, who remain in the camp. **3-8.** Moses, as tradition dictates (cf. 19:7,9,25; 34:32; etc.), immediately reports the words (= the Ten Commandments) and the judgments (= the Covenant Code) to the people, who assent to it. A solemn ritual is prepared: the words are written down, the altar and pillars are set up, the sacrifices are offered; the "service of the word" is in v 8. Part of the blood is sprinkled on the altar, which represents God, and part is preserved for the rest of the rite. The book of the covenant is the word that defines the rite. As the blood is sprinkled on the people, they share the blood with the altar, the symbol of God. Word and rite are inseparably united. Verses 9-11 continue the source in vv 1-2. According to the present arrangement of the chapter, Moses and the representatives of the people ascend the mountain to celebrate the union. The text is reticent about God's appearance; the men apparently see him from below, as through transparent sky-blue tiles. Humans may not look upon the deity lest they be swept out of the profane world in which they live, i.e., die. On this momentous occasion, however, the invited leaders are protected by the rules of hospitality; they share a meal with their divine host. "To see a great chief and eat in his place is to join his family in the root sense of that Latin word; the whole group related by blood or not which stood under the authority and protection of the father. One is united to him as a client to his patron who protects him and whom he serves" (McCarthy, *Treaty and Covenant* 266). Verses 13-14 continue the source in vv 3-8. The elders are left in charge of the camp, with Aaron and Hur taking Moses' place in the administration of justice. Verse 12b is difficult. According to v 4, Moses has already written down "all the words of Yahweh." The contents must be limited enough for Moses to carry them in two tablets (32:19); it could not have contained all of 20:22–23:33 Probably the tablets contained the divinely made copy of the Ten Commandments, whereas the "instructions and commandments" refer to additional words that Moses will be told on the mountain. Another possible solution is that "instructions and commandments" belongs at the end of the sentence after the mention of writing. Hur, mentioned as the helper of Moses in 17:10,12, but surprisingly not in v 1, was a descendant of Judah and the grandfather of Bezalel, the builder of the Tabernacle (31:2; 1 Chr 2:19). **15–18.** In P's terminology, God's presence is an enveloping cloud (cf., e.g., 40:34), a "glory" like a consuming fire, or, in this context, the storm cloud. Moses will finish his divine encounter in 31:18.

46   (B) Divine Command to Build and Maintain the Dwelling (chaps. 25–31). Chaps. 25–31 and 35–40, ascribed entirely to P either as redactor or archival source, describe the wilderness dwelling, its furniture and personnel. The designation "tabernacle" is derived from the Vg *tabernaculum,* "tent." This commentary uses "dwelling" to preserve the occasional Hebr distinction between "tent" and "dwelling" and to show the relation of the noun to the technical use of the vb. "to dwell." In chaps. 25–31, Yahweh commands Moses to build, from the freewill offerings of the people (25:1–9) first the furnishings (the ark, table, and lampstand 25:10–40), then the large tent (chap. 26) with its altar and its court (chap. 27), and then to see to the personnel of the shrine described through the vesting (chap. 28) and ordination of priests (chap. 29) and their chief procedures (chap. 30). This is concluded by the selection of the craftsmen Bezalel and Oholiab and their assistants and an affirmation of sabbath rest (chap. 31). Moses then takes the two tablets of the law down to the people (31:18). In chaps. 35–40 the divine commands are carried out more or less to the letter, though the order of building is somewhat different from the order of commands (V. Hurowitz, *JAOS* 105 [1985] 21–30).

This section is highly important, even though the mass of detail may not interest modern readers. For a great people to exist in the ancient Near East, it had to have certain essentials: a land, specific traditions (legal and narrative), a king or great leader, a god(s), and a house for the god(s). Yahweh has shown himself to be the people's God by defeating Pharaoh, and they are encamped at his mountain and about to move on to Canaan; they also have just been given a law and have a divinely appointed leader, Moses. A house for their God remains to be built, a house that ensures God's presence in their midst. The house must be designed by God, not humans; hence, the importance of the divine commands prior to construction.

47   Many scholars, following 19th-cent. scholarship, regard the dwelling as a complete retrojection into the wilderness period of the later Temple of Solomon; the P writer could not imagine a time when Israel was without the divine presence mediated by the Temple. Such a view is unlikely. The dimensions of the Solomonic Temple are not replicated exactly in the tabernacle. It is true that there is some retrojection but not of the Temple; the elaborate Davidic tent attested in 2 Sam 6:17 and 7:2 has influenced the description of an originally portable tent shrine, like the Arab *qubba,* attested among 2nd-cent. AD Nabateans. The dwelling seems too complex and heavy for easy transport, and the altar in 27:1–8 is a transposition of a later altar into desert materials. Even though the original dwelling cannot be precisely delineated, there is no uncertainty regarding the Canaanite background of the dwelling. It is an Israelite adaptation of the tent of the high god El, attested in the Ugaritic texts of the 15th–13th cents. El, bearded and wise, lives in an elaborate tent ("seven rooms, eight enclosures"), where the gods meet in solemn assembly (*m'd,* the same root as Hebr [tent of] "meeting") and make decisions that affect humankind (F. M. Cross, "The Priestly Tabernacle in the Light of Recent Research," *The Temple in Antiquity* [Provo, 1984] 91–105; R. J. Clifford, *CBQ* 33 [1971] 221–27).

48   (a) THE PEOPLE ARE TO GIVE THE MATERIAL FOR THE DWELLING (25:1–9). Yahweh tells Moses to let all Israelites, regardless of class, make freewill contributions to the sanctuary. In comparable societies, the king, as regent of the god, built the temple. Verses 3b–9 list the raw material, roughly in order of worth. 35:5b–9 repeat vv 3b–8, and 35:10–29 (without exact parallel in chaps. 25–31) go on and tell how specialist workers were recruited and how all the people contributed. **4.** Blue and purple yarns were dyed with extracts from shellfish, and crimson yarns from the female of the cochineal insect. **5.** Traditional Eng "goatskins" are in reality dolphin skins (Hebr *tĕḥašîm* = Arab *tuḥas,* "dolphin"); the dolphin was a common motif in Phoenician art. Verse 8 states the aim, that Yahweh may dwell (*šākan*) among the people. Hebr *miškān,* the noun from *šākan,* "dwelling," should be distinguished from Hebr *'ōhel,* "tent." Already the LXX had translated both *miškān* and *'ōhel* by "tent," thereby obscuring P's careful use of the archaic word "dwelling." The verb and the noun, "to dwell" and "dwelling," connote a gracious but not necessarily permanent abiding with the people, a usage carefully preserved in 1 Kgs 8. **9.** The earthly structure is to replicate the heavenly tent and its furniture and personnel, enabling the Israelite to participate in heavenly ceremonies.

49   (b) THE ARK (25:10–22; cf. 37:1–9). The ark was a box, 45″ x 27″ x 27″, with two rings on each side for carrying-poles. The box was to be a storage place for the two tablets of the law, and its top was to be a place of encounter between humans and God. A plate of pure gold was to be laid flush with the top with two cherubim whose wings touch. Cherubim were composite creatures, with physical characteristics of animals and humans, usually winged; they were often throne guardians. The golden plate covering the top of the box, to which was attached the cherubim throne, was the most sacred object in the dwelling; here God was enthroned invisibly, meeting and speaking to the people through Moses. The Hebr term *kappōret,* lit., "cover," was translated by Martin Luther as "mercy seat," with an eye on Lev 16 and the NT; this transl. is misleading. The primary meaning of the term is given by vv 21–22: a throne and meeting place of God and humans, through the word mediated by Moses.

50   (c) THE TABLE (25:23–30; cf. 37:10–16). The table, on which the bread was set out, was 35″ x 18″ x 26″; like the ark, it was portable with carrying-poles permanently attached. There seems to have been a side panel at the top and a separate frame three inches wide, both with "molding"; the lower frame held the legs in place. Upon it were set the bread and the wine (poured from the vessels) commonly set before images of the gods to honor them. In Israel gifts were continually before Yahweh to emphasize that the covenant was forever. Twelve huge loaves were arranged each sabbath in two rows on the table, consumed after their display by the priests.

51   (d) THE LAMPSTAND (25:31–40; cf. 37:17–24). The lampstand consisted of a sturdy shaft with three branches on each side. On each branch were three almond blossoms, each with calyx and petals (*RSV*: "capitals" and "flowers"). On each of the seven tips fresh oil lamps were placed in the evening by the priest (30:7–8; Lev 24:1–4) so as to burn through the night; the lampstand was on the south side within the tent, and the lamps were placed facing the center of the tent, i.e., northward (v 37). The lampstand seems to have symbolized the fertility that comes from God; it may even represent a sacred tree, a common motif of ancient Near Eastern art. The Solomonic Temple did not have the lampstand, having instead 10 different candelabra (1 Kgs 7:49). The Second Temple seems to have gone back to the old seven-branched lampstand, to judge from Zechariah's vision (Zech 4:1–6; 11–14).

52   (e) THE DWELLING (26:1–37; cf. 36:8–38). The dwelling was 45′ x 45′ x 15′, and 7′ high. Wooden frames (vv 15–30) supported four successive coverings: a linen cloth with cherubim throne-guardians interwoven into it (visible from within the tent, vv 1–6); a goat-hair tent over the linen (vv 7–13); a covering of tanned (not "dyed red") ram skins (v 14a); a covering of dolphin skin (v 14b). Within the tent, a curtain interwoven with cherubim to match the linen interior separated the Holy of Holies from the Holy (vv 31–35), and another curtain, only slightly less fine, separated the Holy from the court outside (vv 36–37). **7–14.** The bedouin today make goat-hair tents in the same way: strips of goat-hair about 30″ wide are stitched together in strips to make a rugged, waterproof tent. Here the strips are sewn into a huge sheet 45′ x 66′, slightly larger than the linen interior (42′ x 30′) of vv 1–6, which it protects. Verses 12–13 describe how the tent overhung the linen, though the verses are not easy to understand exactly: the tent probably hung down to the ground on the two sides and the back (overlapping the linen by a foot), but in front it probably overhung the entrance only slightly, forming a valance. The entrance had its own curtain (vv 36–37). **15–30.** The tent was held up by wood frames, fitted into their silver bases by tenons. The frames must have been scaffolds, allowing the intricately worked cherubim on the inmost layer to be seen. The scaffolds were strengthened by crossbars (vv 26–29). The same word, *qrš*, describes the frames of the tent of El in the Ugaritic texts. **31–35.** Curtains were placed at the entrance to the Holy of Holies and in vv 36–37 to the dwelling itself, the quality and workmanship increasing as one moved closer to the divine presence.

53   (f) THE ALTAR (27:1–8; cf. 38:1–7). The altar, 7.5′ x 7.5′ x 4.5′, was in the open court, where animal sacrifices could be burned. The altar seems to have had a step for the priest to stand on; the wood beneath the step was faced with a bronze mesh. The description is strange: a wooden altar, even if plated with bronze, would have been burned with the burnt offering. This description seems to be out of harmony with 20:24, which permits earthen altars. The altar is an instance of retrojection of the stone and bronze altar of a later time, transposed into desert material. Cf. 1 Kgs 8:64 and 2 Chr 4:1.

54   (g) THE COURT (27:9–19; cf. 38:9–20). The court was enclosed by linen cloth hung on posts with sockets of bronze; with hooks and capitals of silver; the posts had bands of silver (38:17). Its dimensions were 150′ on N and S and 75′ on W and E; it was 7.5′ high. The court faced east, on which side the cloth covered only a part on each side (vv 14–15), the middle portion being hung with the curtain of v 16. The court was considered an integral part of the dwelling, the space where public ceremonies took place.

55   (h) THE LAMP (27:20–21; no parallel in chaps. 35–40, but cf. Lev 24:1–4). Upon the seven branches

of the lampstand (25:31–40) seven small clay lamps were set up to burn through the night. The people were to supply the finest oil for burning.

56   (i) PRIESTLY VESTMENTS (28:1–43; cf. 39:1–31). The outermost part of the dwelling, the court, has been described; it is now time to describe the personnel who staffed it. Virtually the entire chapter concerns Aaron, the high priest; his sons, the priests, get only vv 40–43. In the concrete biblical perspective, office is assumed when the vestments are donned (Num 20:25–26) — hence the fascination with the priestly garments and their function. For Aaron, the high priest, was made the ephod (vv 5–14), a breastpiece (vv 15–30), a robe (vv 31–35), the gold plate for the turban (vv 36–38), a fringed tunic, turban, and sash (v 39); vv 40–43 depict the clothing of the sons. **5–14.** The ephod seems to be a close-fitting waistcoat with shoulder straps, with a decorated band (v 8) around the waist to hold it. On each shoulder piece were onyx stones with the names of the sons of Jacob, the tribes, according to the order of their birth; thus the high priest brought all Israel into the divine presence. The material of the ephod matched the material in the Holy of Holies (cf. 26:1), emphasizing the special nature of the high priest, who alone went into the Holy of Holies. **15–30.** Attached to the high priest's waistcoat was a 9″ x 9″ envelope of the same material as the ephod and the cloth interior of the Holy of Holies. Twelve stones, each representing a tribe, set in a gold filigree frame, were sewed into it. Two braided gold chains joined the pouch to the shoulder strap (vv 22–25), and two blue cords joined the bottom of the pouch to the hem, presumably at the waist of the ephod (vv 26–28); the pouch was thus held close to the body. Aaron as high priest represented all the people when he entered "before Yahweh," because he bore on his heart (cf. Deut 6:6) the 12 sons of Israel for a remembrance (v 29). The Urim and Thummim were sacred lots, each apparently assigned a designation yes or no; these lots were cast when an oracle was sought (Num 27:21). **31–35.** The high priest was to wear a sleeveless blue robe, with pomegranates and golden bells alternating, the ringing bells acting as a protection. Dangling pomegranates have been found on a cult table at Ugarit. Verses 36–38 describe a plate on which was marked "Holy to Yahweh," which the high priest wore on his turban. It functioned to remove any sin that Israelites were guilty of when offering sacrifice; evidently it attracted to itself the stain that accrued in the inmost sanctuary from tainted offerings, and it allowed that stain to be removed. Verse 39 describes the rest of the high priestly apparel without reference to symbol or function.

57   (j) THE CONSECRATION OF PRIESTS (29:1–46; cf. Lev 8).   The rite involved the sacrifice of a bull, of two rams, and of various breads, and an investiture. Consecration here means removal from profane use. Verses 1–3 name all the offerings. Moses was the consecrator, who here took the role of priest; in v 26 he received the priest's portion. **4–9a.** The investiture of Aaron and then the four priests (28:1) with the special garments described in chap. 28. Priesthood here is understood concretely — by their special clothes and their rituals, which set them apart. The "holy crown" of v 6 is the gold plate of 28:36. Aaron's sons, the priests, were dressed simply in comparison with the high priest: tunics, turbans, and sashes. Verse 9b introduces the following. "Ordain" in Hebr is "to fill the hands" (probably with sacrifices, suggested by v 24, "You shall place it all in the hand of Aaron"). **10–14.** Aaron and the sons lay their hands on the young bull, signifying either transfer of their iniquity or, more generally, their close relationship to the ritual animal. The slaying of the bull and the placing of the blood on the altar horns and base are called a sin offering; vv 36–37 specify that the sin offering purges the altar and not the priests. **19–34.** The slaughter of the ram of ordination (Hebr "the ram of the filling [of the hands]") was a type of peace offering or offering of well-being; the human offerer eats a portion of it. Blood from the ram consecrated the organs of hearing, of handling offerings, and of walking rightly on holy ground, as well as the garments (vv 20–22). The fat portion, delectable to the ancients, was burned as a soothing odor to God. Before the offerings were burned, the high priest and the priests elevated them (better transl. than "wave") to dedicate them to Yahweh (vv 22–25). Also elevated were the breast and thigh of the ram, customarily done in communion sacrifices, since they would be given to the priests (vv 26–28). Verses 29–30 interrupt the context to tell how the high priestly garments were to be passed on. **35–37.** The ordination rite was to last seven days. It seems that priests' sins were purged through the purging of the altar; as the most sacred area it attracted to itself, magnetlike, the stain of their sins. Verses 38–42a describe a typical task of the priest: the regular sacrifice of a lamb each morning and evening. Accompanying the animal offering were about 6.5 pints of select flour mixed with about 2.6 pints of fine oil and the same amount of wine. Verses 42b–46 probably followed v 37 immediately as the original conclusion before vv 38–42a. Chaps. 30–31 were added. The section emphasizes that the primary purpose of the Tent of Meeting was for Yahweh to meet with Israel, and that his presence would make the tent and all its personnel holy. Yahweh's dwelling would prove to the people that he is their God and that he brought them out of Egypt.

58   (k) APPENDIX (30:1–31:17). 29:43–46 is the natural conclusion to chaps. 25–29; it sums up what has gone before and serves as its climax. The altar of incense (30:1–10) is not mentioned where one would expect it, in chap. 25; in chaps. 27–29 the altar of burnt offering is spoken of as "*the* altar" as if there were no other altar in the dwelling. These chapters alone are not duplicated in chaps. 35–40 or are described there in a truncated way; the impression given is that chaps. 30–31 are an appendix.

59   (i) *Altar of incense* (30:1–10; cf. 37:25–29). The altar, as part of the furniture in the Tent of Meeting along with the table and the lampstand (25:23–40), was made of acacia wood and gold, with rings and poles for carrying. Incense was part of ancient court ceremonial, the fragrance being considered a luxury. The priest burned incense twice a day, when he trimmed the lamp on the menorah. **10.** "Atonement" is a less apt transl. than "purgation"; the stain of the people's sin accumulated in the sanctuary and had to be removed yearly lest the stain drive out the divine presence (J. Milgrom, *IDBSup* 78–82). Lev 16 describes the ritual.

60   (ii) *Ransom ritual during a census* (30:11–16). Among many peoples, taking a census was considered dangerous, perhaps because it exposed the people to divine jealousy. The ritual provides a way to siphon off the divine wrath from the community: money ransom. The Hebr root for ransom, *kpr,* is the same as that for purgation of sanctuary, but the noun here means simple substitution rather than purgation of sanctuary (Milgrom, *IDBSup* 80). The money was assigned to the dwelling, where it served as ransom or substitute (interpreting the verb *kappēr* in this instance as a denominative of the noun *kōper,* "ransom").

61   (iii) *The bronze laver* (30:17–21; cf. 38:8; 40:7, 30). The great washbasin for the priests to purify themselves prior to entering the tent or approaching the

altar of burnt offering was of bronze, the material of court furniture. Not to wash would be to violate the rule for conducting oneself in the holy sphere. The Solomonic Temple had 10 such lavers (1 Kgs 7:30,38,43).

62   (iv) *The anointing oil* (30:22–33; cf. 37:29a). The oil was specially blended for anointing the dwelling, its furniture, and its personnel. It rendered them holy, i.e., set apart, not profane. In U.S. weights and measures, 12.5 lbs. of myrrh and of cassia (the bark of a tree native to India, with a cinnamon scent) and 6.25 lbs. of cinnamon and aromatic cane were mixed together with slightly less than a gallon of olive oil.

63   (v) *The incense* (30:34–38; cf. 37:29b). A special blend of incense was to be burned on the altar of 30:1–11; it was "most holy," for use within the tent and therefore not to be used nonsacrally. "Sweet(-smelling) spices" is the general term for stacte (in Hebr and LXX, "that which oozes forth," probably myrrh oil), onycha (the flaps of small mollusks, which give a strong odor when burned), galbanum (a plant resin), and frankincense (the gum resin of certain trees). Salt was used for its purifying and preservative qualities, not as "seasoning," since the spices were not eaten.

64   (vi) *The selection of artisans* (31:1–11; cf. 35:30–36:7). The master artisan of the dwelling must be divinely chosen (the meaning of the Hebr idiom "call by name") and empowered. Bezalel's "wisdom" (v 3) is practical — planning and executing; artistic skill rather than theoretical knowledge. **10.** The phrase may mean "plaited garments" or "garments for service."

65   (vii) *Affirmation of the sabbath* (31:12–17; cf. 35:1–3). After the selection of the work force in 31:1–11, Yahweh affirms the command of 20:8–11 to refrain from work on the sabbath. Not even the construction of the dwelling alters the prohibition; v 13 should be translated, "*Nevertheless* you shall keep my sabbaths. . . ." The language resembles that of the exilic prophet Ezekiel (20:20). Verses 15b–16 repeat and vary vv 13–14. Verse 17 relates the sabbath to the creation of the world, as in Gen 1:1–2:3, an apt allusion because ancient temples were often depicted as part of the creation.

66   (l) THE TABLETS OF THE LAW ARE GIVEN TO MOSES (31:18 [P: 18a] [E: 18b]). The Ten Commandments are inscribed on the tablets; the rest of the commands are for oral transmission.

67   **(C) Apostasy and Renewal of the Covenant (chaps. 32–34).** Moses has been on the mountain 40 days and nights (24:18) receiving instructions on building and maintaining the dwelling, the means of God's presence for the journey to the promised land. The people refuse to accept the divine timetable and the mode of divine presence shown Moses on the mountain. They find Moses' time with God excessive and they devise new "gods who will go before us" (32:1), thereby violating the first and fundamental commandment (20:2–6) and rejecting the guiding angel (= Yahweh) in 23:20–33; they annul the covenant made in chaps. 19–24. Moses comes into the camp, breaks the tablet, and oversees punishment (32:25–29). But Moses does not allow the bond to be broken. In perhaps the most impressive and poignant depiction of a servant of God in the Hebrew Scriptures, he gives up fame and ease for himself to stay with his people, interceding effectively in their behalf (32:9–13,30–32; 33:12–13,15–17; 34:9). God relents (not archaic "repents"), agreeing first not to annihilate the whole people (32:14,33–35; 33:1–3), then to accompany them on the way (33:14,17–34:8). A new covenant is then made (chap. 34).

   The redactor of the story has retold various traditions; there are inconsistencies and duplications that scholars have long noted but have not succeeded in explaining completely. Among the inconsistencies, the Tent of Meeting is already set up, and it is *outside* the camp in 33:7–11, whereas chap. 40 reports that it is set up after the events of chaps. 32–34 and is *inside* the camp. 33:12 seems to continue v 3 or v 6 directly. Moses in 34:9 prays that Yahweh will go with the people even though that assurance has already been given in 33:14. The angel of Yahweh in 33:3,5 is exclusive of Yahweh from the context, whereas in 23:20 the angel is Yahweh. The relation between the laws of the covenant in 24:10–27 and those of the covenant in chaps. 20–23 is not clear. Some of the problems will be discussed under the appropriate verse below, but a full discussion is beyond the scope of this commentary. We may assume, however, that the redactor was generally as aware of "inconsistencies" as we are and sought to resolve them through narrative means, as will be noted below. For the whole, Deut 9:6–10:5 should be compared. Ascription of verses to sources is difficult in this section.

68   (a) THE PEOPLE MAKE NEW GODS TO GO WITH THEM (32:1–6 [E]). The people wish to start on the journey to the land without waiting for Moses to tell them how Yahweh will dwell with them. Aaron makes them "gods who will go before them" (v 1). The phrase "to go before" occurs many times in chaps. 32–34; the central question is how the all-holy God will accompany a sinful people. Aaron, in these chapters a weak accomplice in the popular rebellion, accedes and declares over the young bulls, "these are your gods who have brought you out of Egypt" (v 4). *'Ĕlōhîm* can mean "God," but, as the pl. vb. shows, it means "gods" here; worship of them violates the first commandment (20:2–7). In the story of Israel's very origins, there was apostasy (and forgiveness leading to a renewal of covenant). In ancient Near Eastern iconography bulls figure prominently either as representations of gods, e.g., Bull El in the Ugaritic texts, or as animal thrones of deities standing upon their backs. In the people's eyes, the images represent Yahweh (hence an altar is built before them), contrary to Israel's aniconic tradition. In 1 Kgs 12:28, Jeroboam I uses the same words to lead the northern kingdom into apostasy, an act that to the deuteronomistic historian nullifies the divine promise given earlier to Jeroboam's dynasty in 1 Kgs 11:31–39. Worship is offered to the false representation of Yahweh (v 6); eating and drinking before the deity are a rite of sharing the hospitality of the great one, becoming his client, a rejection of the rite in 24:11.

69   (b) YAHWEH RESOLVES TO DESTROY THE PEOPLE (32:7–14 [E]). **7–10.** Yahweh informs Moses of the people's violation of the fundamental commandment not to worship other gods (20:2–6) and of his intent to destroy them and make a new people from Moses' family. **11–14.** Moses, the true servant of his people as well as of his God, persuades Yahweh to renounce his plan by appealing to Yahweh's *noblesse oblige:* What will the Egyptians say, and what about the promise to the ancestors that their descendants will possess the land forever?

70   (c) MOSES BREAKS THE TABLETS AND PUNISHES THE PEOPLE (32:15–35 [E with editing and accretions]). **15–20.** The divine origin of the covenant is emphasized in order to render the apostasy more stark. Moses correctly sees that the singing is not the customary songs of victory or lament but of hymns of false worship. The people are made to ingest their own sin, like the curse ingested by the suspected wife in Num 5:24. **21–24.** Aaron's irresponsibility and contempt for the people contrast with Moses' obedience and willingness to sacrifice himself for them. **25–29.** The Levites inflict the

punishment, thereby consecrating themselves forever for the service of Yahweh. The ritual of consecration is told in Num 8:5–26. **30–35.** Moses, the servant, wins forgiveness for his people, a greater concession than that of vv 7–14, where he averted their total destruction. God will lead the people, not personally as previously promised but in the person of an angel. Future punishment still hangs over the people (v 30); all future punishment will somehow be related to this original apostasy. Verse 35 fits uneasily in the context, perhaps belonging originally after v 20.

71   (d) THE PEOPLE LAMENT WHEN THEY LEARN YAHWEH IS NOT WITH THEM (33:1–6 [J: 1,3] [E: 2b–4, 5–6] [other: 2a]). Moses has succeeded in bringing God to spare the people (32:7–11) and then to forgive them (32:30–34), but Yahweh himself will not go with them to the land. The angel here, unlike other uses of angel heretofore, is a being distinct from Yahweh. The all-holy God will not go in their midst. The people put off their ornaments as they engage in the ritual of lament. God, however, is open to future dealing (v 5). Precise identification of sources is difficult; vv 1,3a seem to be continued directly in vv 12–17, whereas vv 2b–4 and vv 5–6 seem to be ancient parallels.

72   (e) MOSES PLACES THE TENT OF MEETING OUTSIDE THE CAMP (33:7–11 [E]). To express the divine absence, Moses puts the tent outside the camp, although the P legislation of 25:8 and Num 2:2 place it inside the camp. According to chap. 36 the tent is constructed only later. The text anticipates its construction here in order to illustrate how God withdrew from the midst of the congregation. Many scholars, noting that the passage is from E rather than P, postulate that the original tent was outside the camp but that P has placed it inside to illustrate the ancient tradition that God was in the midst of the people. The tent is a place not only of divine presence but also of oracles; God speaks to Moses as one person speaks to another, i.e., not in dreams or sacred lots.

73   (f) THEOPHANY OF YAHWEH IN RESPONSE TO MOSES' PLEA (33:12–23 [JJ]). In v 1 Yahweh commanded Moses to "bring up" the people, and in v 3 an angel is appointed to accompany them. Now, exploiting the divine openness of v 5, "that I may consider what to do with you," Moses asks further softening of the divine wrath: "you have not let me know who will accompany me though I continue to find favor in your eyes." Verse 14 is the answer: I (lit., "my face," "presence") will go before you. As v 15 ("*your* going with us") shows—and also comparable usage in Deut 4:37 and especially 2 Sam 17:11—Yahweh himself will go. Israel's distinctiveness as a people lies in Yahweh's special presence (vv 15–16), a presence shown in the vision to Moses in vv 17–23 and in the entire recovenanting of chap. 34. **17–23.** The sign of reconciliation between God and people is effected through Moses, servant of both. The Hebr idiom in v 19, "I will have mercy on whom I have mercy," like the analogous construction in 3:14, emphasizes divine freedom (no motive is given); the divine "glory," "goodness (or beauty)," and the name "Yahweh" include mercy toward fallen Israel. Moses, like any mortal, cannot see Yahweh's face, but he at least glimpses his back.

74   (g) THE REMAKING OF THE COVENANT (34:1–35 [J]). **1–9.** As in chap. 19, Moses the covenant mediator goes to meet God on the holy mountain, hearing the divine proclamation of his mercy and justice (contrast the emphasis in 20:5–6). **10–26.** These verses *may* have been originally the J version of the Decalogue, but it is important not to allow speculative reconstruction to distract from the narrative setting. The verses are the overlord's demands: exclusive devotion to Yahweh and to those things granted by him—land and forms of

worship. The demands and grants establish a whole
society. Not every detail of Israel's new life is mentioned
here, of course, but only a representative sample (J.
Halbe, *Das Privilegrecht Jahwes: Ex 34, 10–26* [Göttingen,
1975]). **10–11a.** A legal formula now in a cultic context.
Yahweh promises to be their God, acting in their midst
so that all nations recognize his uniqueness. Verses
11b–15a, tightly structured by chiasm ("make a covenant" in vv 12a and 15a), outline the response to the
lordship proclaimed in the preceding verses. The cult
objects of the nations, stone slabs and '*ăšērîm* are to be
destroyed. The latter were apparently wooden representations of the goddess Asherah, in popular religion the
consort of El/Yahweh. Verses 15b–16 add a warning
against joining in the worship of the natives. Verses
17–26 are a compilation of directives, one set dealing
with the feast of Unleavened Bread in the spring, the
sabbaths, and sacrificial rites, and the other, with
pilgrimage feasts. Individual items have been commented upon under 23:10–19. Verses 27–35 describe
how Moses himself wrote the Ten Commandments (in
contrast to God's writing of them before (31:18; 32:16)
and how Moses' face had thereafter to be veiled lest its
radiance frighten off the people. The "Ten Words" in v
28 need not refer to the prescriptions of vv 10–26; it
probably means the original Ten Commandments of
chap. 20. The vb. "to be radiant," occurring only in this
chap., is a denominative of the noun "horn." The Vg
translated it *cornuta*, "horned"; the Lat term became the
source of artistic representations of Moses with horns
rising out of his head. In reality, Moses' radiance
expresses his privileged place as servant close to Yahweh.
**75   (D) Building of the Dwelling and the
Descent of the Glory (chaps. 35–40 [P]).** In chaps.
35–40 the divine commands given in chaps. 25–32 are
carried out, though the order of building is different
from the order of command: an exhortation to observe
the sabbath (35:1–3) prefaces the call for voluntary contributions (35:4–29) and the appointment of craftsmen

(35:30–36:7). The first section was *ended* by these events.
The dwelling is constructed (36:8–38) before, not after,
the ark and its furniture (37:1–24); the incense altar is
constructed with them (37:25–28), differently from in
the first account. Fulfillment thereafter follows the order
of command, with special items like the totals of
38:21–31. The ordination of priests (chap. 29) is carried
out not in Exod but in Lev 8. The latter part of the
manufacture is without extended parallel to the first
section; 39:32–43 shows the completion of the construction, and chap. 40, the erection of the dwelling, its
furnishing, and the descent of the Glory. (For technical
details of the dwelling, → 46–66 above.)
**76   (a) THE PEOPLE BUILD THE DWELLING (35:1–
39:43). 35:1–3.** Before describing the massive construction project, Moses emphasizes again (cf. 31:12–17)
the command to do no labor on the sabbath; not even the
holy work of constructing the dwelling interferes with
the observance. **35:4–36:7.** This section depicts the
carrying out of 25:5–9 and 31:1–11. Free and spontaneous giving is emphasized. **36:8–38.** The dwelling is
built *before* its furnishings, contrary to the order of
25:1–40. **37:1–24.** Cf. 25:10–40. Ark, table, and lampstand are constructed. **38:1–20.** The making of the altar
and court (cf. 27:1–19). Verse 8 mentions for the first
time that the bronze laver was made from women's
mirrors. **38:21–31.** A summary of the materials for the
dwelling; it has no parallel in chaps. 25–31. **39:1–31.**
The priestly vestments (cf. 28:1–45). **39:32–43.** The
individual items are brought to Moses for his inspection.
He finds them all made according to the divine
commands.
77   (b) DEDICATION RITES (40:1–38). On the first
day of the new year, nine months after the arrival at
Sinai, the dwelling is erected at divine direction (vv
2–15). When the building is finished, "the cloud covered
the tent, // the glory of Yahweh filled the dwelling." The
journey to Canaan may now begin with Yahweh leading
(cf. Num 9:15–23).

4

LEVITICUS

Roland J. Faley, T.O.R.

BIBLIOGRAPHY

1 Cazelles, H., *Lévitique* (Paris, 1951). Cholewinski, A., *Heiligkeitsgesetz und Deuteronomium* (AnBib 66; Rome, 1976). Micklem, N., *Leviticus* (IB 2; Nash, 1953) 3–134. Milgrom, J., "The Book of Leviticus," *IOVCB* (Nash, 1971) 68–84. Noth, M., *Leviticus* (rev. ed.; Phl, 1977). Porter, J. R., *Leviticus* (CBC; Cambridge, 1976). Snaith, N., *Leviticus and Numbers* (CentB; London, 1967). Vink, A., "The Date and Origin of the Priestly Code in the Old Testament," *OTS* 15 (1969) 1–144. Wenham, C., *The Book of Leviticus* (NICOT 3; GR, 1979).

INTRODUCTION

2   (I) Title. Called in Hebrew by its opening word, *Wayyiqrā', "*And he called," Leviticus derives its Eng title from the Vg transl. of the LXX *Leuitikon*. The name is appropriate, for it served as the liturgical handbook of the levitical priesthood, and at the same time it taught the Israelites the necessity of an untainted holiness in every aspect of their lives. Being almost wholly concerned with laws and rubrics, the book advances but slightly the pentateuchal narrative.

3   (II) Authorship and Nature of the Book. As in the case of the entire Pentateuch, it is impossible to speak of an "author" in any restricted sense. The book is the work of many hands engaged through the centuries in adapting the laws, rituals, and feasts to the needs of successive eras. Lev is to be ascribed to the priestly tradition (→ Pentateuch, 1:5–7). It is tied in particularly with the legislation in Exod 25–31; 35–40, upon which it follows, and its continuation can be seen in Num 1ff. Thus the legislation is attached to the dominant figure of Moses in the Sinai desert (cf. the reference to the Tent of Meeting in Exod 20:34; Lev 1:1; and Num 1:1). Although the book contains some ancient legislation, in its present form it is to be dated to the period after the return from the exile.

The sacrificial legislation of the Second Temple is presented in Lev 1–7. An extended narrative section (Lev 8–10) treats the "ordination" of Aaron and his sons, a ritual that applied to the high priest of postexilic times. The laws of purity in chaps. 11–16 doubtless contain many old practices; the legislation leads up to the climax of purification of the Day of Atonement. The so-called Holiness Code (Lev 17–26) incorporates practices from the period of the monarchy and is characterized by the solemn emphasis on holiness in chap. 19. Chapter 27 is an appendix to the Holiness Code, dealing with gifts made to the sanctuary.

4   (III) Outline. The book may be divided as follows:

(I) The Law of Sacrifice (1:1–7:38)
  (A) Types of Sacrifice (1:1–5:26)
    (a) Holocausts (1:1–17)
    (b) Cereal Offerings (2:1–16)
    (c) Peace Offerings (3:1–17)
    (d) Sin Offerings (4:1–5:13)
    (e) Guilt Offerings (5:14–26)
  (B) The Priest and Sacrifice (6:1–7:38)
    (a) The Daily Holocaust (6:1–6)
    (b) The Daily Cereal Offering (6:7–16)
    (c) Sin Offerings (6:17–23)
    (d) Guilt Offerings (7:1–10)
    (e) Peace Offerings (7:11–21,28–34)
    (f) Blood and Fat Prohibitions (7:22–27)
    (g) Conclusion (7:35–38)
(II) The Ceremony of Ordination (8:1–10:20)
  (A) Ordination of Aaron and His Sons (8:1–13)
  (B) Ordination Sacrifices (8:14–36)
  (C) Octave of the Ordination (9:1–24)
  (D) Sin of Aaron's Sons (10:1–20)
(III) Legal Purity (11:1–15:33)
  (A) Clean and Unclean Animals (11:1–47)
  (B) Childbirth (12:1–8)
  (C) Leprosy (13:1–14:57)
    (a) In Humans (13:1–46)
    (b) In Clothing (13:47–59)
    (c) Purification (14:1–32)
    (d) In Buildings (14:33–57)

COMMENTARY

5 **(I) The Law of Sacrifice (1:1–7:38).** The sacrificial ritual inaugurating the book, because of its importance in Israel's cultic life, interrupts the P tradition account of the construction and furnishing of the Lord's dwelling (Exod 25–40) and its logical sequel, the installation of the priests (Lev 8–10). This sacrificial code, edited by the Priestly school in the postexilic period and representing the flourishing liturgy of the rebuilt Temple, is actually the final stage in a history of Israelite sacrifice, which was protracted over many centuries.

(A) Types of Sacrifice (1:1–5:26). Sacrificial terminology is more complex than an initial reading of these chapters would indicate. Here, as elsewhere in the OT, the Eng word "sacrifice" is used to render a number of Hebr words, some of them indistinguishable. Moreover, in the course of centuries, certain ideas, originally connected with one or another sacrifice, were evidently lost; others merged with rites that were closely akin. In many respects, the division of sacrifice into the five main types in the ritual is less a matter of etymology than a reflection of custom and common usage.

6 (a) HOLOCAUSTS (1:1–17). The Eng term is derived from the Vg and LXX transl. of the Hebr *'ôlâ*, signifying something that ascends or rises. Whether this notion of ascent referred to the victim's ascent to the altar, or from the altar to God, or a combination of both, cannot be determined with certainty. The Gk *holokautōma*, meaning something wholly destroyed by fire, aptly expresses the essential characteristic of the sacrifice — the victim's being placed on the altar and its complete consummation.

1. *the Meeting Tent (ʾōhel môʿēd):* Here the Lord confronts Moses and presents his legislation. The P tradition account of the dwelling's plan and execution is found mainly in Exod 25–27; 35–40. The tent was primarily a place of revelation from which Yahweh as head of the covenant assembly directed the activity of his people (Exod 25:22; 29:42–43; 30:36). For the P tradition it represents the Jerusalem Temple. Moses does not enter the tent at this time, covered as it is by the cloud and filled with the Lord's glory (Exod 40:34–38). (F. M. Cross, "The Priestly Tabernacle," *BAR* 1. 201–28. M. Haran, *JSS* 5 [1960] 50–65.) The Lord immediately enunciates the first principle regarding animal sacrifice in restricting the offering to domestic animals of the bovine (bulls, cows, calves) and ovine (sheep, lambs, goats) classes. **2.** *offering (qorbān):* That which one "brings near" to God. The same root *qrb* is found in Ugaritic with the causative equivalent, "to offer in sacrifice." It is applied to various types of sacrifice, as well as to nonsacrificial offerings made to God (Neh

10:35; 13:31). The victim must be of superior condition and devoid of any physical defect.

The ritual itself (vv 3–9) comprises six steps: the presentation of the victim, the slaughter, the aspersion of the altar, the removal of skin and dissection of the victim, the washing of certain parts, and the burning. The imposition of hands in v 4 is not a rite of substitution or sin transfer since a sin-ridden victim would never have been an acceptable offering. The action denotes solidarity, closer identification between the offerer with his personal dispositions and the gift being offered. The slaughtering is done by the offerer, not the priests. In relatively few sacrifices — e.g., those offered in their own name (4:4) or in the name of the whole community (2 Chr 29:22,24,34) — did the priests slay the victim themselves. The contact between the blood, equated by the Hebrew with life itself (17:14), and the altar, which was a sign of the divine presence, brought about the victim's transition from the earthly sphere to the divine realm, in a rite performed by the priest. The altar upon which the blood was sprinkled was located before the entrance to the tent, just as the altar of holocausts was located in front of the Solomonic Temple (2 Kgs 16:14). The piecing of the victim suggests a sacred repast — all of which, in this instance, is given to the Lord. The lighting of the fire was proper only to the first sacrifice offered; thereafter it was never extinguished (6:5–6). The prepared pieces, together with the head, the fat, and the washed intestines and extremities, were placed on the altar by the priest and then burned. **9.** *sweet smelling oblation:* The term for oblation here is *ʾiššeh*, which appears also in vv 13 and 17. Still much discussed regarding etymology, it is used with reference to any offering partly or totally consumed by fire (*ʾēš*), and, as indicated by L. Moraldi (*RSO* 32 [1957] 329–30), in Lev it is an equivalent expression for the victim itself. The sacrifice's pleasant odor is an anthropomorphic expression indicating divine acceptance (Gen 8:21).

The ritual for sheep or goat holocausts (vv 10–13) differs little from the preceding. The absence of any mention of the imposition of hands or its religious value may suggest either that it is presupposed (the skinning of the animal is also omitted) or that it may be reflective of the holocaust's more primitive ritual (Judg 6:19–22; 13:16–20). **11.** *north side of the altar:* The specification is lacking in vv 1–9. The Temple's north entrance was known as the Sheep Gate (Neh 3:1).

The ceremony for the bird holocaust (vv 14–17) is carried out entirely by the priest at the altar. The head is detached, as opposed to 5:8, where it is snapped loose but not severed. Owing to the limited amount of blood, aspersion is made on only one side of the altar. This type of holocaust is not envisioned in the instructions of v 2; it is quite likely an addition to the holocaust legislation inserted at the time of the sacrificial ritual's final edition. As the customary offering of the poorer class (5:7; 12:8; 14:22,30), it represents an accommodation of the sacrificial ideal in admitting the use of animals upon which there was no real dependence for sustenance (→ Institutions, 76:67).

7 (b) CEREAL OFFERINGS (2:1–16). Much debate still surrounds the etymology of the Hebr *minḥâ*. Most probably its basic meaning is "gift, tribute," and it is so used in a noncultic context at least 37 times in the OT. Outside the Pentateuch and Ezek, it is applied to any type of sacrifice (1 Sam 2:17; Mal 2:13; 3:3ff.; 2 Chr 32:23), whereas in the former it has the more restricted meaning of an unbloody offering of vegetable products. Originally an independent sacrifice (as here), it later appears as a supplement to the holocaust and peace offering (Num 15:1–16) (→ Institutions, 76:79–80).

The present chapter treats various forms of cereal offering. The first (vv 1–3) is of pure unbaked wheat mixed with oil to which frankincense was added. Part of the offering was burned; the remainder was given to the priests. **2.** *frankincense:* A powder of fine spices (Exod 30:34–35) added as a supplement to the cereal offering. *token offering ('azkārâ):* Moraldi links this word with the causative form of the Hebr root *zkr* meaning "to make remember." Hence, it may signify either a memorial, i.e., a means of focusing God's attention on the offerer, or a pledge, i.e., the small part offered serving as a token of the whole (see G. R. Driver, *JSS* 1 [1956] 97–105). It is used only with reference to cereal or incense (24:7) offerings.

The baked cereal offering is next considered (vv 4–13). Cakes, whether fried or baked, had to be unleavened and mixed with oil. Part was burned and part was given to the priests. Leaven, because it produced fermentation, was viewed as an agent of decomposition and could not be used in sacrificial offerings. Israelite transgressions of this regulation (Amos 4:5) no doubt resulted from the influence of the Canaanites, who looked upon fermentation as a symbol of fertility. Honey, too, despite its extensive use by the ancients, was seen as a corrupting agent and, perhaps because of its animal origins, was also considered unfit for sacred use. **13.** *salt of the covenant:* The esteem for the purifying and preservative virtue of salt (Ezek 16:4; 2 Kgs 2:20–22; Matt 5:13; Mark 9:49; Col 4:6) is akin to that still found among the Arabs. Moreover, it was a sign of friendship and solidarity binding participants at a banquet (M.-J. Lagrange, *Études sur les religions sémitiques* [Paris, 1905] 251). The sacrificial salt, within the framework of a sacred repast, strongly underscored the permanence of the covenant relationship between Yahweh and his people. See Num 18:19, where the "inviolable covenant" renders the Hebr "covenant of salt."

Finally, specifications are given for the cereal sacrifices as part of the firstfruits offering (vv 14–16). The rather ambiguous phrasing of the MT seems to depict a process by which freshly cut ears of grain were roasted and then ground to obtain the grits. Oil and frankincense were added, and the offering concluded in the same manner as the cereal offering seen above.

8 (c) PEACE OFFERINGS (3:1–17). Although the ritual for the peace offering (Hebr *zebaḥ šĕlāmîm*) is clearly defined, the meaning of the Hebr term remains obscure. *Zebaḥ* means something "slain" or "slaughtered," hence, a slain sacrificial victim (Amos 5:25; Hos 3:4); *šĕlāmîm* is derived from the root *šlm* meaning "to be complete," "to be whole," or "to be in harmony." Separately, the terms *zebaḥ* and *šĕlāmîm* refer to sacrifices only partly destroyed, with part of the victim eaten by the offerers or priests (Deut 12:27; 18:3; 27:7; Gen

31:54[?]). Thus, either term could be contrasted with the completely consumed holocaust (1 Sam 15:22; Hos 6:6; Exod 20:24; Judg 20:26). This common denominator, coupled with the fluidity of sacrifical terminology, enabled the Priestly authors of Lev to interchange the terms or even unite them when speaking of those sacrifices in which the offerer shared the victim with God. The designation "peace offering" is derived from the LXX and, for most authorities, falls short of the idea. Suggested alternatives are fulfillment offering, offering of completeness, and final offering. Although the precise meaning of *šĕlāmîm* remains uncertain, "peace offering" does serve to underscore one important aspect of the sacrifice: the preservation of harmonious relations between the participants and Yahweh as portrayed especially in the shared offering. Although OT Yahwism does not admit of the Lord's "eating" the victim, the symbolism of the sharing highlights the notion of unity in spirit and sentiment. Some authors, e.g., H. Cazelles and R. de Vaux, term the offering a communion sacrifice because one of its key elements is the notion of life sharing between God and the faithful. (→ Institutions, 76:89–90).

The ritual itself allows ox, sheep, or goat offerings, either male or female. For the herd offering (vv 1–5), initial steps include the imposition of hands, the slaughter, and aspersion. Considerable discussion has centered on the purpose of the blood ritual. Does the blood here have the expiatory value found in the sin and guilt offerings? If so, how is it to be reconciled with the offerer's innocent state? According to A. Charbel (*SP* 1. 366–76), there is no atoning value connected with the blood ritual in the peace offering. Consumption of the sacred food is here an essential feature, an action clearly prohibited for anyone in a state of uncleanness (7:20–21). Since the shedding of blood is necessary to the sacrifice itself, its aspersion on the sides of the altar simply points up the sacredness of blood (life) as belonging solely to the Lord. Fat, too, was sacred to the Lord as linked with life itself and could not be eaten as sacrificial food (3:16–17; 7:22–24). Thus, the internal organs, connected with the more vital life processes—i.e., the intestines, liver, and kidneys, and all the fat attached thereto—were burned on the altar where the customary daily holocaust was offered.

The procedure for the sheep offering (vv 6–11) is the same. The only addition is the animal's tail, which in some Palestinian species is laden with fat. **11.** *food of the Lord's oblation:* "Food" is suppressed in the LXX and supplanted by "pleasing scent." Such efforts to emphasize God's transcendent nature by the avoidance of anthropomorphisms are frequent in the Greek. However, the idea of a communal banquet is basic to the *zebaḥ šĕlāmîm*, and the problem of the Lord's eating resolves itself symbolically with the burning of his portion.

The goat ritual (vv 12–17) is identical with that of the herd offering. Verse 17 is an emphatic statement on the ritual's binding character and a final prohibition regarding blood and fat. The law against eating fat was concerned only with those animals ordinarily offered in sacrifice (7:22–24); the fat of other animals could be eaten.

Chapter 3 must be studied in conjunction with 7:11–38. The laws given there regulate consumption of the sacrificial food.

9 (d) SIN OFFERINGS (4:1–5:13). The sin offering or *ḥaṭṭāʾt*, centered in the idea of expiation, could be offered for the high priest (4:1–12), the entire community (4:13–21), the prince (4:22–26), and private persons (4:27–5:13), but only in those instances where the failure was inadvertent. Parallel legislation with certain variations and in abbreviated form is found in Num 15:22–31. The Hebr *ḥaṭṭā't* signifies both sin and its consequences (Num 32:23) as well as the offering for sin; see N. Snaith, *VT* 7 (1957) 316–17. This sacrifice looked to a reestablishment of the covenant relationship between God and humanity destroyed by sin. Its two most distinctive features were the generous aspersion of the blood and the disposal of the slaughtered victim (→ Institutions 76:72–74).

In regard to the high priest (4:1–12), the proper offering was an untainted bull. As a result of his authoritative status in the community, the high priest's sin was believed to affect the people as a whole. **2.** *a person inadvertently commits a sin:* Sin was a positive violation of the covenant relationship, whether voluntary or involuntary. Israel's responsibilities were clearly enunciated in the law, and any departure therefrom disturbed the right order of things. The presence or absence of volition did not alter the objective situation. The wrong had to be righted, and even the unwitting party (with whom chap. 4 is wholly concerned) had to offer atoning sacrifice. The community shares the priest's guilt not through personal culpability as we interpret it but because the people, closely identified with their leader, were enveloped in the wide ambit of the fault's consequences (see B. Vawter, *TD* 10 [1962] 223–26). **3.** *the anointed priest:* See comment on 8:1–13. On the imposition of hands, see comment on 1:4. After the slaughter, the blood was brought into the Meeting Tent. Only in the cases of the sin offering for the priest and for the community was part of the animal victim brought into the Holy Place of the Temple. The blood was then sprinkled against the Temple veil, an act that looked to the consecration of the blood itself (see T. C. Vriezen, *OTS* 7 [1950] 201–35). The central expiatory act was the blood aspersion, which was performed on the horned corners of the altar of incense, likewise located within the Meeting Tent. The remainder was deposited outside at the base of the holocaust altar. The usual organs and fatty parts were then consumed on the altar, and the animal's remains were taken to the ash heap and burned. The priest offerer did not partake of the food, a communal privilege prohibited in view of his sinful condition.

The community as a whole could incur guilt, if an unknown person were to transgress without awareness and his culpability did not surface. The ritual (vv 13–21) was the same as that for the high priest; however, the imposition of hands was performed by the elders representing the people. The parallel legislation in Num 15:22–26 specifies two victims: a young bull as a holocaust and a he-goat as a sin offering. This directive may well be even later than that in Lev.

Next in importance is the sin offering for the prince, the lay leader of the community (vv 22–26). The term *nāśî'* is both premonarchical and postmonarchical in biblical usage, ending with Josh and recommencing with Ezek, with only rare occurrences in the intervening period. Ezekiel applies the term not only to Israel's postexilic lay leader but also to lesser foreign rulers. He thereby makes clear to the restored Jews the importance of a modest temporal outlook within the reborn community, which is to be marked by spiritual excellence. E. A. Speiser, arguing from the point of etymology and usage, sees *nāśî'* as a passive derivative from *nāśā'*, "to raise up, elevate" (*CBQ* 25 [1963] 111–17). It thus refers to a duly elected chieftain (LXX *archōn*), which, in the case of Ezek, would refer to one elected not only by the assembly but also by God, hence, a "leader." After laying his hands on the victim, a male goat, and slaughtering it on the north side of the altar of holocausts, the leader leaves the atoning blood distribution to the priest (not

the high priest), who places the blood on the hornlike protrusions of the holocaust altar and pours the remainder at its base. None of the blood is taken into the Holy Place, as in the priest's and community's offering. The priest, not personally involved in the sin, may eat of the sacred food (6:19).

The only significant difference between the sin offering of a private person (vv 27–35) and that of the leader of the community is indicative of its lesser stature: the victim could be a female goat or lamb. **35.** *with the other oblations:* The phrase signifies sacrifices regularly offered, e.g., the morning holocaust (6:1–6).

10   The first half of chap. 5 is casuistic, containing a number of "special cases" regarding the offerer and his offering. The initial section (vv 1–6) envisions certain offenses that would necessitate an atoning sacrifice. These include the withholding of evidence, presupposing some initial unawareness by a witness under oath (Deut 19:15–20) and the inadvertent actions (with subsequent unawareness) of contracting legal uncleanness or of swearing publicly to do something. Anyone guilty of such violations had first to confess his sin by a solemn and public attestation of guilt (known also from Assyrian and Babylonian sources) and then to offer the atoning sacrifice. The rite and victim are the same as for the private expiatory sacrifice (4:27–35). The term for the sacrifice in v 6 is not *ḥaṭṭā't* but *'āšām*, "guilt offering"; see vv 14–26. (For parallels in Mesopotamian sources, see M. J. Geller, *JSS* 25 [1980] 181–92.)

Verses 7–13 look to the guilty poor man, who in the aforementioned circumstances is unable to supply the animal victim. The substitute offering (*'āšām*) was a pair of turtledoves or pigeons. In either case, one of the birds was offered as a sin offering (*ḥaṭṭā't*) and the other as a holocaust. The ritual for the sin offering was a simplified version of the animal offering: the head was snapped loose but not detached, and the blood was sprinkled on one side of the altar and the rest deposited at the altar's base. The holocaust was offered in the manner prescribed in 1:14–17. Finally, an added concession was made for those even more indigent in the form of a cereal offering, consisting of one-tenth of an ephah of flour (one ephah equals about one bu.). Devoid of either incense or oil, part of the flour was burned with the regular daily sacrifices as a "token offering" (*'azkārâ;* see 2:2), the remainder going to the priest.

11   (e) GUILT OFFERINGS (5:14–26). The dominant note in this treatment of the guilt offering is atonement and remuneration, rather than ritual. The Hebr *'āšām* means both "guilt" and "guilt offering"; the verbal form *'āšēm* means "to be guilty" or "to transgress." Although this expression is clearly an oblation that seeks to right a wrong or repair an injury, the etymology of the word affords scant help in determining the distinction between the sin and guilt offerings. Equally disconcerting is the casual interchange of the two terms in the Lev ritual (see vv 7–13). Attempts to distinguish adequately between the two terms date at least to the time of Josephus (*Ant.* 3.9.3 § 230–32; cf. P. Saydon, *CBQ* 7 [1946] 393–99). The one fundamental idea proper to *'āšām* in every instance is an offense or an offering for an offense, which is imputable regardless of personal awareness. In this regard, it is identical with the sin offering. Whatever may have been the historical distinction between the two, it is obviously lost on the redactors of the Lev ritual. The terms are even used synonymously (5:6–7).

Since for private persons the guilt-offering rite does not differ from that of the sin offering, the blood was not taken into the Holy Place and the priests were permitted to partake of the victim. **15.** *ram . . . valued at two silver* *shekels:* Repeated emphasis on the guilt offering's value suggests that for this type of offering monetary commutation was possible, the fine being paid in silver (1 Sam 6:3ff.; 2 Kgs 12:17). The first category of offense treats of inadvertent action: failure to pay Temple tithes in the full amount (vv 14–16) (requiring restitution to the Temple, plus an added 20 percent) or, in general, any violation of the Lord's commands (vv 17–18). The final case (vv 20–26), implying full awareness, deals with the fraudulent retention of another's material property, whether securities, stolen goods, or discovered articles. In matters of injustice, restitution had to be made before the offering was acceptable; this included not only the restoration of the other's property but an additional one-fifth of the object's value as compensation. (→ Institutions, 76:75.)

12   (B) The Priest and Sacrifice (6:1–7:38). Much of the material here presented is concerned with sacrifices already treated in the previous section. Its separate origin from 1:1–5:26 is seen in its Mount Sinai location (7:37–38) as opposed to the Meeting Tent (1:1). In the main, this additional legislation concerns the rights and duties of the priests in their sacrificial role. Thus, Moses is told (6:1) to address his words not to the Israelites as previously (1:2; 4:1) but to Aaron and his sons.

13   (a) THE DAILY HOLOCAUST (6:1–6). Here the emphasis falls mainly on the care of the altar fire. Two daily holocausts are prescribed, one in the evening (v 2) and one in the morning (v 5), paralleling the directives of Exod 29:38–42 and Num 28:2–8. This postexilic ritual differs from that of the monarchical period with its single holocaust in the morning, clearly distinguished from the evening cereal offering (2 Kgs 16:15). Even as late as the Torah of Ezekiel, there is mention of only one daily holocaust (Ezek 46:13–15). Performed on the holocaust altar where the perpetual fire burned, the evening offering was left on the hearth through the night, and the ashes were removed in the morning and laid at the side of the altar. The priest performed this latter action wearing his sacred ceremonial garb, and only after changing to other clothes did he leave the holy confines to carry the ashes outside of the camp to a clean place worthy to serve as a depository for the sacred relics. The final verses indicate that the continuation of the fire on the altar was the priests' responsibility. Each morning firewood was added prior to the early holocaust and the other offerings of the day. The perpetual fire, a characteristic trait of Persian cult (E. Dhorme, *RB* 10 [1913] 19), served as an uninterrupted prayer of the Hebr community to the Lord.

14   (b) THE DAILY CEREAL OFFERING (6:7–16). Closely allied to chap. 2, this section serves as an adjunct to the daily holocaust legislation. Composed of two parts, it first deals with the daily *minḥâ* offered by any priest (vv 7–11), and then with the daily offering of the high priest (vv 12–16 [esp. 13 and 15]). The rite for the first (unbaked flour with oil and incense) is identical with that of the customary unbaked cereal offering (2:1–3), with the added specification that the part left over, the priestly portion, must be eaten as unleavened cakes within the court of the Meeting Tent. Since the Lord deigned to share with his priests the sanctified gift, its sacredness had to be respected and safeguarded. It was eaten only by cult personnel (male descendants of Aaron) in a clearly designated place. Similar restrictions obtained for the sin offering (6:22) and the guilt offering (7:6). **11.** *whatever touches the oblations becomes sacred:* Both cleanness and uncleanness were contagious. Sacred objects, e.g., the altar and other Temple appurtenances (Exod 30:29), could communicate their sanctity; this holiness

could be contracted by a person (even without his volition) or by other objects. Through such contact the sphere of the deity was extended, and the person (or object) could no longer be considered profane. Verses 12–16, not found in Codex Alexandrinus, contain conflicting data: an offering for the high priest's investiture (v 13; see 8:26) and a regular daily sacrifice (v 13 of the MT reads "regular" [*tāmîd*]). By the time of the editing of Lev this had become a daily sacrifice. Its assimilation to this passage on the priestly ordination ritual (v 15), which is also related to chap. 8, may have occasioned the ambiguity. Offered in the high priest's name and that of the other priests, the twice-a-day *minḥâ* was first fried and then broken into pieces and burned as a whole offering, no part being consumed by the priest.

15   (c) SIN OFFERINGS (6:17–23). As a complement to chap. 4, this added legislation emphasizes the sin offering's special sacredness, which, since it could be easily transmitted, demanded special directives regulating the use and disposal of the victim's remains. A garment stained by its blood was washed in a sacred place (v 20); the vessel in which it was cooked before eating was either destroyed or thoroughly cleansed (v 21). In this way, holiness was removed in much the same manner that impurity was, to avoid its being diffused in any way (see de Vaux, *AI* 460–61). Both the priest offerer (v 19) and his fellow priests (v 22) could eat of the sacrifice in the court of the Meeting Tent; this custom, of course, did not apply to the sin offerings of the high priest (4:1–12) or of the whole community (4:13–21), in which instances the entire victim was burned.

16   (d) GUILT OFFERINGS (7:1–10). The ritual for these, not specified previously, was basically the same as that for the sin offering of private individuals (4:27–31). The meat could be eaten by the priests under the usual conditions. Verses 7–10 delineate in summary fashion the distribution of the sacred portions for the various types of sacrifice. To the priest offerer belongs the meat of the sin and guilt offering, the animal hide of the holocaust, and the remains of the baked or fried cereal offerings. These in turn could be shared with the other priests (cf. 7:6). The ordinary flour offering, with its almost casual ritual demanding so little of the priest (2:1–2), is given to the priestly group as a whole.

17   (e) PEACE OFFERINGS (7:11–21,28–34). Taken in conjunction with the legislation in chap. 3, the section deals with a supplementary cereal offering as well as with the distribution and consumption of the peace offering. Three distinct species of peace offering are cited: the *tôdâ* or thanksgiving offering (vv 12–15), offered as an expression of gratitude for benefits received (Ps 107:22); the *nēder* or votive offering (vv 16–17), an obligatory oblation rising from a vow or promise made to the Lord; and the *nēdābâ* or freewill offering (vv 16–17), a spontaneous gift, devotional in character, required neither by law nor personal indebtedness. Although each of these has its own particular characteristics, the distinction among them is often imprecise. For the thanksgiving offering, together with the animal victim, an assortment of unleavened and leavened baked products is prescribed as a *minḥâ*. A portion of these was burned on the altar with the animal, exclusive of the leavened cakes that were prohibited (2:11; see comment on 2:4). The remainder of the cereal offering was divided among the officiating priest, the offerer, and invited participants. Because of its sacred character, the meat of the victim was to be eaten on the day of the sacrifice to avoid any contamination or spoiling. The votive and freewill offerings, otherwise identical in ritual with the preceding, prescribed more lenient ruling regarding the leftover meat: what was not eaten on the day itself could be finished on the following day; if any meat remained after that, it had to be burned. This latter regulation sought to avoid the abuses that could easily arise in a sacrificial repast permitting a rather extensive lay participation. Thus, the meat became refuse, an "abominable thing" (*piggûl*) after the second day, and if the law were violated, not only would the violator be guilty of sacrilegious conduct (cf. also 19:5–8) but also the whole offering would be deemed worthless. Because the peace offering meat lost its sacredness through contact with anything unclean between the time of offering and consumption, it was to be burned if such occurred. Finally, a state of legal purity was required of all participants in the sacred repast. To partake of the victim in a state of uncleanness from whatever cause—e.g., disease or contact with some species of unclean animal—was to incur serious guilt. This latter legislation indicates that the sacred meal could be eaten outside the Temple precincts. **20.** *shall be cut off from his people:* The phrase does not necessarily mean the death penalty, although such is the meaning in certain instances. The offender could be socially ostracized, forbidden free access to and participation in cult, and, as a result, be separated from the divine favor that fell on the community of God's people. The particulars regarding the penalty's nature and duration are not stated.

Verses 28–34 summarize the priest's action in the peace offering. The fatty portions and designated organs (3:3–4) were burned; the choice parts, the breast, and right leg, reverted to Aaron and his sons. **30–32.** *wave offering (tĕnûpâ) . . . raised offering (tĕrûmâ):* Many commentators connect these two terms with the manner of offering the victim. The former was moved to and fro before the altar (*nûp,* "to swing," "to wave"); the latter, raised aloft (*rûm,* "to be high," "to be elevated"). However, Driver claims that such a conclusion is not supported by the evidence (*JSS* 1 [1956] 100–5). Their repeated use together (7:34; 10:14,15; Num 6:20) is indicative of their affinity, but Driver notes that the motion idea is completely absent from certain instances of use, e.g., Exod 25:2; Num 8:11,13,15. Moreover, none of the ancient versions attests to any special rite in their rendering of the term. Thus, postulating a Hebr root *nwp,* meaning "to be supereminent," he sees *tĕnûpâ* as derived ultimately from Babylonian and to be rendered "special contribution" or "additional gift." *Tĕrûmâ,* best associated with the Assyrian *tarāmu,* takes its Hebr origin from the root *trm* meaning "to levy" (despite its repeated use with the causative form of *rûm*). The substantive refers to something levied or assessed. Both terms, then, can be translated "contribution," being virtually interchangeable in use and identical in application.

18 (f) BLOOD AND FAT PROHIBITIONS (7:22–27). This section represents an interruption in the peace-offering ritual; thus it is treated separately. The fatty parts of the ox, sheep, or goat, specified in 3:3,9,14, could be eaten under no circumstances whatsoever (see comment on 3:1–5). This prohibition applied even if their death proceeded from natural or violent causes, although the law allowed the use of such fat for other purposes. Moreover, it did not extend to the fat of other species of clean animals or even to the fat from other parts of the specified animals. The law forbidding blood is universal and is emphatically enunciated three times elsewhere in Lev (3:17; 17:10–14; 19:26). The sanction is separation from the community (see 7:20).

(g) CONCLUSION (7:35–38). Verse 35 loosely connects the sacrificial code with the ordination of Aaron and his sons, announced in Exod 29 and executed in Lev 8:1ff (→ Institutions 76:66–95).

(Davies, D., "An Interpretation of Sacrifice in Lev," *ZAW* 89

[1977] 381–99. De Vaux, R., *AI* 424–56; *Studies in Old Testament Sacrifice* [Cardiff, 1964]. Geller, M. J., "The Šurpu Incantations and Lev 5:1–6," *JSS* 25 [1980] 181–92. Levine, B. A., *In the Presence of the Lord* [SJLA 5; Leiden, 1974]. Milgrom, J., *Cult and Conscience* [SJLA 18; Leiden, 1976]; "Two Kinds of Ḥaṭṭa't," *VT* 26 [1976] 333–37.)

19 (II) **The Ceremony of Ordination (8:1–10:20).** The solemn rite of ordination prescribed for Aaron and his sons is carried out according to the directives of Exod 28:1–29:35; 39:1–31; 40:12–15. Anything but primitive in character, this detailed account draws upon the ordination ceremony of the high priest with its investiture and anointing (8:7–13), three sacrifices (8:14–36), and octave-day observance (chap. 9). Chapter 10 contains the only piece of fairly continuous narrative in the book, but even there a careful reading betrays its purpose—the story serves as a vehicle to present added ritual requirements.

20 (A) **Ordination of Aaron and His Sons (8:1–13).** The place of worship and its official attendants were inseparable in ancient Israel. Thus, the directives for the Lord's dwelling (Exod 25–27) are followed by those for the priests (Exod 28–29); by the same token, the present chapters form a sequel to the actual construction of the dwelling completed at the close of Exod. Yahweh first orders Moses to assemble the entire community at the entrance to the Meeting Tent together with Aaron and his four sons (see Exod 28:1). There follows a tripartite ceremony consisting of lustration, investiture, and anointing. A detailed description of the high priest's vestments is given in Exod 28–29. Worthy of special note is the regal character of his attire, e.g., the miter or turban (*miṣnepet*) (see Ezek 21:31 and the *ṣĕnip* of Isa 62:3) and the diadem (*nēzer;* see 2 Sam 1:10; 2 Kgs 11:12)—symbols of royal authority given the high priest in postmonarchical times. **8.** *Urim and Thummim:* (→ Institutions, 76:9). Given only passing mention in the P tradition, they serve at most as a symbolic relic of the past, although perhaps the reference to them is no more than an archaic one made long after they became obsolete (see de Vaux, *AI* 352–53). The anointing of the high priest is joined with that of the dwelling, the altar and its furnishings, and the basin, which served as a blood receptacle. (For the postexilic origins of priestly anointing, → Institutions, 76:13; see also R. Tournay, *RB* 67 [1960] 5–42.) After Aaron's anointing, his sons, representative of the whole priestly class, were invested in a simpler ceremony wherein no mention is made of the ephod, breastplate, or golden diadem; the turban (*migbā'â*) they received was the regular headdress of the priests, not the royal *miṣnepet*.

21 (B) **Ordination Sacrifices (8:14–36).** Cf. Exod 29:10–26. Three sacrifices, all offered by Moses, were part of the ordination rite: a sin offering (vv 14–17), a holocaust (vv 18–21), and a special ordination sacrifice (vv 22–36). The sin offering in Exod 29:10–14 makes atonement for the priests, not the altar as here. In addition, the sacrifice is almost an exact parallel to the personal sin offerings of chap. 4. The idea of eradicating any uncleanness connected with the altar is evidently an adaptation of the earlier prescription (cf. Exod 29:36–37). The victim was a young bull, whose remains were burned and not eaten. Consumption was denied even the priests because of their intimate connection with the altar. The ordination holocaust followed the sin offering with a ram specified as victim; the procedure was that prescribed in the sacrificial code (1:10–13). The final offering, that of investiture or *millu'îm* (see v 33) climaxed the ceremony and marked the formal assumption of office. It was likely viewed as an act of thanksgiving, following the main lines of the peace offering: imposition of hands, slaughter, blood aspersion, burning of the usual parts, accompanying cereal offering, and sacred meal. However, the blood was applied by Moses to the right ear, thumb, and large toe of Aaron and his sons. The same was done with both blood and oil on the occasion of a leper's purification (14:14,17,25,28). The exact significance of the extremities may well have symbolized the sanctification of the whole man just as the altar was sanctified by spreading blood on its outermost parts (8:15). H. Cazelles (*Lévitique*, on Lev 14:14) links it with the idea of service: the ears receive instruction, which the hands and feet execute. Moses, having taken the designated organs of the ram plus the right leg, together with a single sample of each type of unleavened cereal offering (7:12), handed them to Aaron and his sons, directing them to make the act of presentation (i.e., wave offering; see comment on 7:30). He then took the offering back to burn it on the altar with the holocaust. The breast was reserved for Moses as his personal portion. The final blood and oil aspersion of the priests and their vestments is viewed by some commentators as an interpolation. It disturbs the continuity of the passage (M. Noth [*Leviticus*, 72] treats it after v 24; cf. Exod 29:21), and the exact purpose of a second consecration of Aaron (even though including the vestments) is not clear. This problem is connected with the more basic question of the extent to which Aaron's sons were included in the earlier redactions of the Lev ritual, which was originally concerned principally with the high priest; in several instances the obviously intrusive mention of the other priests in connection with certain rites evidences the work of a later hand.

The cooked meat and the bread offering of this final sacrifice were to be eaten by the priests as sacred food, i.e., within the sacred confines the same day (7:15). The ordination observance was to extend over a seven-day period during which time at least the sin offering was to be repeated daily (Exod 29:36-37). During this time the newly ordained were forbidden to leave the forecourt of the Meeting Tent under penalty of death. **33.** *your ordination is to last seven days:* The literal transl. is "for seven days he will fill your hands." (For the idea of "filling the hands," → Institutions, 76:13.)

22 (C) Octave of the Ordination (9:1-24). The eighth day after the initial ceremony was marked by a series of concluding sacrifices (vv 1-21) and a theophany (vv 22-24). The octave-day ritual has Aaron himself sacrificing on behalf of the priests and the community. The section, with its emphasis on the first sacrifices of the newly ordained priest, may have initially followed Exod 40, where priesthood and dwelling are established. If chaps. 1-8 represent a later cultic amplification, then the date in v 1, "on the eighth day," brings chap. 9 into line with the conclusion of chap. 8. With the community assembled, Aaron, in his sin offering, followed the same ritual previously employed by Moses (8:14-17), inasmuch as he had not yet formally entered the Holy Place. The remains, unable to be eaten by the priests, were burned outside the camp. The holocaust that followed was offered in the usual way. The sacrifices for the community were then executed by Aaron with his sons' assistance. The preparatory rites left to the "layman" in chaps. 1 and 3 are here performed by the priests. **16.** *other than the morning holocaust:* An anachronism showing the liturgical rather than historical concern of the editor is evident. The daily holocaust was offered only after the priests had undertaken their duties (6:1-6). The people's cereal and peace offerings were the last offered.

The ceremony is solemnly concluded in vv 22-24 with the high priest's blessing (Num 6:23-26) and his initial entrance into the Meeting Tent with Moses, pointing up his singular right of access to the dwelling of

Yahweh. The second blessing (v 23) may arise from fusion with another tradition, wherein both Moses and Aaron blessed the people as opposed to the blessing of Aaron alone in v 22. The Lord's stamp of approbation upon the proceedings takes the form of a theophany similar to that marking the completion of the dwelling (Exod 40:34-38). **23.** *the glory of the Lord:* The *kĕbôd Yahweh* was particularly manifest in unusual signs and phenomena, clearly indicative of might and transcendence: e.g., the desert cloud (Exod 16:10), the cloud and fire on Sinai (Exod 24:15-17), and the cloud encircling the dwelling (Exod 40:34-35). (See "Glory," *EDB* 867.) In the present instance, his glory takes the form of fire issuing from the Meeting Tent and consuming the already burning offerings on the altar to the awe of the onlookers. The meaning of the theophany is clear: the ordination proceedings and the sacrifices of the priest are approved as sacred and acceptable to the Lord.

23 (D) Sin of Aaron's Sons (10:1-20). The tragic episode of the death of Aaron's two sons, Nadab and Abihu (vv 1-7), transcends the interests of mere narration and emphasizes the importance of strict adherence to ritual legislation. Tucked appropriately within chap. 10 is an added body of laws for the priests (vv 8-15), and the chapter closes with the puzzling dialogue between Moses and Aaron (vv 16-20).

During the time of the octave-day celebration, Nadab and Abihu offered an illicit incense offering for which they suffered a fiery death in the Lord's presence. It is difficult to determine the exact nature of their sin. The suggestion that their sacrifice was offered outside of the prescribed times lacks sufficient evidence. Cazelles (*Lévitique*, on 10:1) proposes that the account follows an earlier tradition of chaps. 8-9 in which only Aaron had received priestly consecration; thus, the sons were performing these ceremonial acts without being priests. On the other hand, Haran (*VT* 10 [1960] 115) sees the key to the solution in the "strange" or "profane" fire (*'ēš zārâ*) of v 1. The sons had taken their fire from a place outside the altar area, whereas the censer fire was to be taken from the altar itself (16:12). It is only in connection with this "profane fire" that their sin is elsewhere recalled (Num 3:4; 26:61). It may also be that the later cultic exclusion of a priestly group (connected with Nadab and Abihu) is here presented in terms of a primitive sinful act.

Moses' commentary on the event takes the form of a short distich in which words of the Lord, otherwise unknown, are quoted. Its rather loose connection with the context and its poetic character argue strongly for an independent source, possibly an encomium on the priesthood. Both Yahweh's sacredness (*qōdeš*) and his glory (*kābôd*) seek external manifestation: the latter in signs and wonders as exemplified in the theophany of 9:23-24; the former in similar marvels (Num 20:13; 27:14), in the people themselves (19:2), and, in a special way, in his priests—"those who approach me"—whose holiness should be unsurpassed (Exod 19:22; Lev 21:17,21; Ezek 42:13-15). In the present context, however, the verse is being used reproachfully, explaining the severe punishment that has been meted out. God's sacredness is manifest through the swift and definitive removal of evil from his midst, i.e., the death of the two priests; his glory, so often restricted to loving signs of his power and might, is here revealed in a frightening and awesome manner (cf. Ezek 28:22). In the face of the tragedy, Aaron remained silent while Mishael and Elzaphan, Aaron's cousins (Exod 6:18,22), were summoned to remove the bodies in the tunics in which they died, without funeral solemnities, to a spot outside the camp. The priests were strictly prohibited from indulging in customary mourning observances. Tokens of mourning also indicated a state of uncleanness (13:45), which would arise in this instance from contact with the dead. By reason of their sacred position, the priests were not to become unclean through contact with a corpse, the only exception being death in the immediate family of the ordinary priest (21:1–4), an exception not extended to the head priest (21:10–11). In the present case, because of the seriousness of the violation, not even Aaron's remaining sons were permitted to participate even remotely in the burial rites. This whole episode underscores the importance of observing even the minutiae of ritual detail.

The legal material in vv 8–15 is not brought into relation with the untimely death of the two priests. So that they would be able to exercise their duties responsibly, especially in distinguishing the multiple categories of the clean and unclean, and be fit to instruct the people in the law, the priests were forbidden the use of any alcoholic beverage prior to the exercise of their office (Ezek 44:21). The prohibition is presented as given by the Lord himself. The following passage on the sacrificial repast resumes the octave-day ritual abruptly terminated in 9:21, allowance being made for the intervening data by the reference to Aaron's "surviving sons" in 10:12. The cereal offering, as most sacred, was to be eaten by the priests alone, near the altar. The contributed portions of the community's peace offering, the leg and breast, however, could be eaten by male or female members of the priests' families in any place not tainted by uncleanness; regulations regarding this participation are given in 22:10–16.

In the concluding pericope, Moses' anger is aroused upon learning that the people's sin offering (9:15) had been burned and not eaten. Yet this was the very procedure that was demanded for such a sin offering (4:21), since neither the priests nor the community could eat of it. The key to the solution lies in 6:23. One could not partake of any sacrifice in which some of the blood had been brought into the sanctuary, a requisite for the sin offering of the priests and the community. Thus, the priests were forbidden to eat the sin offering of the people, not because it was offered in their own name (as, e.g., in 9:8ff.) but because its blood had been sprinkled before the sanctuary veil. It was precisely this action that was lacking in Aaron's sacrifice prior to the formal entry into the Meeting Tent, which is indicated as having taken place after the octave-day sacrifices. Therefore, the meat should have been eaten by the priests; in fact, it was considered part of the rite of expiation. Aaron's response is a plea of moral uncleanness; he lacked the necessary integrity required of anyone partaking of such a sacrifice. Affected by his dead sons' sinful deed and, in Hebr thought, a sharer in their guilt, he did not enjoy a state of holiness compatible with the sin-offering repast. The response appeases Moses' anger.

(De Vaux, *AI* 345–405. Haran, M., "The Use of Incense in Ancient Israelite Ritual," *VT* 10 [1960] 113–29. Laughlin, J. C. H., "The 'Strange Fire' of Nadab and Abihu," *JBL* 95 [1976] 559–65. Lohse, E., *Die Ordination im Spätjudentum und im Neuen Testament* [Göttingen, 1951].)

24   (III) Legal Purity (11:1–15:33). The third major division is concerned with the various ways in which a state of uncleanness could arise and the means of regaining the state of purity. The purity code treats of four major categories: clean and unclean animals (11:1–47), childbirth (12:1–8), leprosy (13:1–14:57), and sexual uncleanness (15:1–33). Each, except the second, has its own conclusion. The laws, although edited in postexilic Israel, have a distinctly archaic ring.

Basically, the distinction between the clean and unclean was related to cult, for it was in terms of service

to Yahweh, either in active worship or simply in being his covenanted people, that integrity was demanded. To be unclean was to lack holiness, and such was viewed not as a moral condition but as a state of being, incompatible with the holiness of Yahweh and hence prohibitive of any contact with him. Parallel legislation on legal cleanness is found in Deut 14:3–20.

25   (A) Clean and Unclean Animals (11:1–47). The list is concerned with large land animals (vv 1–8), sea life (vv 9–12), winged creatures (vv 13–23), and small animals (vv 29–38). The classification is popular rather than scientific and sheds no real light on the ultimate reasons for the clean and unclean distinction. Extensive discussion has centered on the reasons for the distinctions made, a summary of which is given by W. H. Gispen (*OTS* 5 [1948] 193–94). Since the definitive answer lies in a past so remote that it was probably known not even by the editors, whose classification gives no indication, we are probably on safest ground to view the distinction primarily along cultic lines (see Noth, *Leviticus* 92). The animals immediately excluded from the Hebr diet were those hallowed in pagan worship as enjoying a role in sacrifice, magic, or superstitious practice—e.g., the pig, used in sacrifice to the Babylonian god Tammuz. By the same token, despite the dearth of information, it is not unlikely that other reasons, such as hygiene and natural abhorrence, also affected Hebr custom and legislation.

The dietary legislation is directed to both Moses and Aaron, the latter now enjoying added prestige after his ordination. With regard to the larger animals (vv 1–8), the law is first stated positively: Only those animals that were split-hoofed and cud chewing could be eaten. This would permit beef, lamb, and considerable wild game. As the subsequent classification indicates, the distinction was based solely on external similarities. The rock badger and the hare, although excluded on one count, could actually have been eliminated on two because they are not ruminants, despite the fact that their mastication process suggests the action of chewing the cud. That the list is by no means exhaustive gives credence to the view that the exclusion of these animals rested ultimately on some other basis. The prohibition extended to consumption as well as to contact with the dead animals, but simple contact with them while living was not forbidden.

Only aquatic animals having both fins and scales could be eaten (vv 9–12); although no examples are given, such forms as the eel would be excluded, but fish in general could be eaten. Contact with their dead bodies was also prohibited.

There is no general norm governing the prohibition of birds in vv 13–19, only an enumeration of the unclean species. The identification of some of these remains uncertain, since the exact meaning of the Hebr terms cannot be determined. We are at a loss to determine why they were rejected, the only possible clue being that they are preponderantly carnivorous.

**26   ** The section on insects (vv 20–23) begins and concludes with an unqualified rejection of all winged quadrupeds (the "other" of v 23 is not present in the Hebrew). The interpolation in vv 21–22 was introduced as an exception in favor of certain members of the grasshopper family, classified popularly in terms of the strong hind legs on which they leap. This exception may have arisen from the general respect that prevailed for their skill and ingenuity, reflected in their rather frequent appearance in Oriental art.

The brief excursus on uncleanness through contact in vv 24–28 is abruptly inserted and only indirectly connected with the main theme. The central thought here is not with eating the animals but with the distinction between touching and lifting the animals previously treated. Contact with any of these lifeless forms resulted in uncleanness for the entire day, cleanness being restored, it would seem, by the day's termination, despite the mention of a sin offering required in such circumstances in 5:2,6. If one picked up the carcass or any part thereof, one's clothing became unclean through contact and was to be washed. This law reflects the ancients' dread of contact with the dead, which implied some form of undesired communication. It seemingly did not apply to sea life or birds.

Legislation on contact rather than consumption is continued in the following pericope (vv 29–38) treating of rodents and lizards, which were never eaten. The identification of the various species in v 30 remains largely uncertain: e.g., "mole" renders the Hebr *tinšemet,* also used for one of the bird species (owl?) in v 18. Anyone touching the corpse was unclean until evening. Moreover, uncleanness was communicated to anything on which or into which the dead body fell, examples of which are given along casuistic lines: one's personal effects (clothing, etc.), household furnishings (pottery, ovens), and moistened grain. To remove impurity, pottery and earthenware utensils were destroyed; personal articles were washed and considered unclean for the day. Liquid was considered a carrier of impurity; for this reason everything in the water-filled vessel was contaminated (v 34), as was all cultivated grain that had been moistened before the mishap (v 38). Fresh water (v 36), however, whether earth water or rain water, removed all impurities (Num 19:17ff.; Zech 13:1). Thus, springs and cisterns remained clean despite the accident.

Another digression appears in vv 39–40 with legislation regarding animals ordinarily edible. Such were forbidden if they died a natural death; a touch resulted in day-long uncleanness, and any closer contact (carrying, eating) made one's clothing unclean as well.

Another popular dietary classification resumes the discussion of reptiles in vv 41–45, going beyond the species of vv 29–30 in its all-embracing character. This abhorrence of reptiles, no doubt, derived at least partially from the Hebr attitude toward the snake (Gen 3:14) and the cultic role it played in pagan fertility rites. Motivation for avoidance of such creatures is strongly positive: the holiness of Yahweh himself demands it.

The chapter closes with a recapitulation like that closing the sacrifice ritual (7:37ff.), extending to all the creature categories that have been treated.

27   (B) Childbirth (12:1–8). The remainder of the material on legal purity is concerned with cases of temporary uncleanness (→ Institutions, 76:101–103), beginning with the most important, childbirth. Viewed as a cause of impurity by numerous ancient peoples, this state of uncleanness arose neither from the act of conception nor from the delivery as such, but rather from the loss of blood connected with the latter (vv 4a,5b,7b). The woman's vitality, linked with her blood, was diminished by childbirth, and by that token she was objectively separated from Yahweh, the source of life, until her former integrity was restored. The uncleanness was more pronounced during the period immediately following birth—i.e., the first 7 days after a male birth, the first 14 after a female—during which time her impurity was as contagious as during the time of menstruation (15:19–24). After this initial period, a general lack of integrity, prohibiting any contact with the sacred, continued for an additional 33 days after the birth of a boy, and 66 after the birth of a girl. The birth of a male resulted in "lesser uncleanness," probably because of the greater strength and vitality connected with the male.

At the end of the designated period, the woman effected her own purification through the offering of atoning sacrifices in the form of a holocaust (lamb) and a sin offering (pigeon or turtledove). The offering was the same for a male or female birth. A bird offering (either a turtledove or pigeon) was permitted for both sacrifices if the women belonged to the poorer class. The oblation of the Virgin Mary on the occasion of her purification was this simple offering of the poor (Luke 2:22–24).

28   (C) Leprosy (13:1–14:57). The references to leprosy in the OT are numerous, e.g., Exod 4:6; Num 12:10–15; 2 Sam 3:29; 2 Kgs 5:1,27; 7:3; 15:5. Although leprosy as we know it today was certainly not unknown to the ancients, the Hebr *ṣāraʿat* (Vg *lepra*) is not so restricted in its use, including various forms of skin disease. This section is not concerned with Hansen's disease but with temporary disorders, the symptoms of which are given in 13:1–44, and all of which are curable. Primitive hygiene considered such maladies highly contagious and demanded the stricken person's isolation; in Lev, however, although hygienic concerns cannot be excluded, it was the lack of bodily integrity necessary for the worship of Yahweh that resulted in religious and social ostracism. Corrupting agents present in clothing and buildings—e.g., mildew, mold, and moss—because of their apparent likeness to skin diseases, likewise rendered such objects "leprous" and unclean. In all such cases, it was the presence of the evil force of corruption that necessitated protective legislation. Because so much of the material on legal purity and the means to regain it is absent from the preexilic literature, de Vaux sees here a mass borrowing and incorporation of material from various sources, rooted in archaic beliefs and superstitions, by the purity-conscious writers of the P code (de Vaux, *AI* 463–64).

29   (a) In Humans (13:1–46). The popular character of the described disorders makes it impossible to determine the exact nature of the illness cited. Not every skin disease made one unclean, but only those considered active and, therefore, infectious. Such malignancy manifested itself in different ways: through spreading (vv 7, 22,27,35); through sores, which penetrated the skin with discoloring of the surrounding hair (vv 3,20,25,30); and through an open sore ("raw flesh") (vv 10,15,42). Ordinary skin blotches, scabs resulting from boils or burns, scalp disorders, face eruptions, and baldness were not signs of impurity so long as they were devoid of infectious symptoms. Whiteness of the skin, the aftermath of a skin disease, was a sign of healing and indicated cleanness (vv 13,16–17,38–39).

The determination of the disease's active or inactive state belonged to the priest, who exercised his function not as a physician (no treatment was prescribed) but as a judge and interpreter of the law, whose favorable decision was required before purification rites permitting reentry into the community could be initiated. When a case was doubtful, a period of quarantine was imposed, lasting in some cases a week (vv 21,26) or at most a fortnight (vv 4ff.,31ff.). During the time of his uncleanness the diseased person had to remain outside the city, giving notice of his condition to the unsuspecting through the customary signs indicative of his state: torn garments, long, flowing hair, covered beard (Ezek 24:17), and the repeated cry "Unclean!"

30   (b) In Clothing (13:47–59). The evil force of corruption was also seen to be present in mildewed clothing, textiles, or leather goods, rendering them unclean. After the priest's initial inspection, the object was isolated for seven days (vv 47–50); if during that time the corruption spread, it was to be burned; if not, it was washed and quarantined for another week (vv 51–54). If with the next inspection the infection had not at least diminished, the object was destroyed; if the growth seemed to be vanishing, it was excised, and the article could be used again providing the growth did not reappear. If there was no sign of the mildew left at all, the article was declared clean and restored to former use after a second washing (vv 55–58).

31 (c) PURIFICATION (14:1–32). The treatment of the various forms of uncleanness, to be resumed in 14:33–57, is here interrupted by the purification ritual for a leprous person. It was actually composed of two ceremonies: an archaic rite symbolizing liberation from the evil spirit (vv 2–9) followed by sacrificial rites.

The unusual ceremony in 14:2–9 reflects a primitive idea that linked physical illness with a winged evil demon, which had to be exorcised for health to be restored. The priest, as sole arbiter in the matter, met the person outside the camp. If he appeared to be healed, the priest ordered him to slay one of two clean birds and mix its blood with spring water (see comment on 11:36). Taking the other bird, a piece of cedar, some red yarn, and a sprig of hyssop, the priest immersed them all in the water and blood, sprinkled the man seven times to purify him, and then released the living bird. The lustral waters drew their purifying powers from being both fresh and reddened by the bird's blood. Since the color red had an inherent power to frighten evil spirits, this was likely the significance of the crimson yarn, colored by dyestuffs derived from insects (see also the red-heifer rites, Num 19). Both the cedar and the hyssop (the latter actually a form of caper, true hyssop not being found in Palestine) were used for sacred aspersions (Num 19:18; Ps 51:9). It is possible that the yarn bound the hyssop sprig to the cedar to form an aspergillum (Cazelles) although the text is not so explicit and they are evidently not so arranged in Num 19:6. The release of the bird symbolized the departure of the evil spirit. The liberated sufferer completed this initial phase of his purification by washing his garments and shaving all his hair, in which the relics of the disease might still be concealed. Although readmitted to the community, complete reintegration was delayed for a week, during which time he remained out-of-doors for fear of contaminating his dwelling, which would require added purification rites. At the end of the seven days, he shaved, washed his body and clothing once again, and thereby regained his former state of purity.

Verses 10–32 represent a later complementary feature of purification, linked historically with the sacrificial liturgy of the Second Temple. On the eighth day after the inauguration of purification, official cultic readmittance was gained by the formerly diseased person whose state of objective separation from the Lord had not yet been completely overcome. The offerings consisted of a male lamb as a guilt offering, a ewe as a sin offering, and another male lamb as a holocaust, plus a cereal offering (flour mixed with oil) and a separate log of oil (about one pt.). The priest took the guilt offering and the oil and presented them as a "contribution" to the Lord (see comment on wave offering, 7:30). Because of its sacred character, the lamb was slaughtered in the sanctuary court where the holocaust and sin-offering victims were killed. Then, taking some of the victim's blood, the priest anointed the man's right ear, thumb, and big toe, doing the same with the oil after he first consecrated it by sprinkling it toward the Lord's dwelling. The remainder of the oil in his hand was placed on the man's head. The marked similarities here with the ceremonies for the ordination of the priests (8:12,23–24; Exod 29:20) have led some authors (e.g., Cazelles, *Lévitique*, on 14:14) to view this action as a rededication rite by which the leper is reintegrated into the holy community in terms of service. De Vaux, on the other hand, sees the anointing solely in terms of purification (*AI* 463). Blood had

axiomatic expiatory value (17:11; 8:15; Exod 30:10), and the oil anointing had its counterpart in rites for the liberation of slaves, known to us from Mesopotamian and Ugaritic contracts. With the offering of the prescribed sacrifices, cleanness was finally attained.

A commutation was granted in favor of the poor leper (vv 21–32); his offering consisted of a male lamb as a guilt offering, a smaller portion of flour mixed with oil, a log of oil, and either two turtledoves or two pigeons for the sin offering and the holocaust. With the exception of these modifications, the ceremonial procedure was the same as that of a man in ordinary circumstances.

32 (d) IN BUILDINGS (14:33–57). Because of their external resemblance to human skin disease, certain forms of fungus, such as moss, when found on buildings were believed to have made them "leprous." **34.** *if I put a leprous infection:* The phrase reflects the Hebr attitude of overlooking secondary causes in attributing all things to God as the ultimate cause. Uncleanness was present only when the fungus was active, a factor determined by the priest's inspection; however, even before judgment was passed, the house was completely emptied of its furnishings if it even bore the appearance of contagious infection (vv 33–36). If in the priest's judgment the growth gave evidence of penetrating the surface of the wall or its color strongly suggested malignancy, a seven-day quarantine was imposed on the dwelling to allow time for greater certainty in the matter (vv 37–38). To enter the house during quarantine was to incur uncleanness for the day; more intimate contact, e.g., eating or sleeping therein, resulted in impurity of both person and clothing (vv 46–47; cf 11:24–28). If at the end of the week the priest's reinspection verified the active character of the leprosy, the affected stones were removed and, together with all the plaster scraped from the walls, carried to an unclean place beyond the city (vv 39–41). The house could be repaired but had to be demolished completely if the growth reappeared (a procedure paralleling the treatment of clothing, 13:55–57). If the corrosive condition did not recur, the house was declared clean (vv 42–48).

The house was purified (vv 49–53) in the same way as the leprous man (14:1–9), the ancient "bird" ritual alone sufficing with no accompanying sacrifice required. Chapter 14 closes with a general summary of the disorders treated and the purpose of the preceding casuistry—i.e., the discernment of legal purity (vv 54–57).

33 (D) Sexual Uncleanness (15:1–33). Not only was there a certain aura of mystery surrounding the faculty of generation, but also a loss of vitality, a diminution of the life principle, was indicated in the loss of seed by a man or blood by a woman. Either resulted in a state of unworthiness precluding any active role in Israel's cultic life. The concern here is not with moral culpability. Moreover, the isolation demanded was not a punitive measure; it prevented the spread of impurity through contact. Although hygienic reasons, known from Babylonian and Egyptian sources, underlie much of the legislation, the emphasis here is clearly cultic (v 31); therefore, its rather primitive medical outlook, often based on popular assumption, should not be surprising.

Uncleanness in men, treated in vv 2–17, could arise in various ways. The abnormal flow (Hebr *zob*) of vv 2–15 is, in all probability, a reference to genital excretions resulting from gonorrhea. The sufferer communicated his impurity to other people contacted, furniture on which he lay or sat, saddles on which he rode, and household articles that he touched. Anyone brought into contact with the man himself or any object he had infected had to wash himself and his garments and remain unclean until evening; clay vessels were destroyed and wooden articles were rinsed. At the termination of his illness, he waited seven days before effecting his purification with the usual lustrations. His social reintegration was gained on the eighth day with the public offering of the two turtledoves or pigeons as an atoning sin offering and holocaust. The second cause of male impurity (vv 16-17) was the loss of semen, whether voluntary or not. His unclean state lasted the day and demanded only that he wash himself and any piece of cloth or leather stained by the seed. In Deut 23:11 is the added directive of absenting oneself from the community.

Verse 18 is transitional, linking the two sections on impurity in men and women. Legal impurity resulted from sexual relations between man and woman whether the act was licit or illicit. The law was concerned with the male's loss of vitality and with the woman's uncleanness springing from contact with the male semen. The resultant state was short-lived—of one day's duration—and the only ritual required was the bath. This cultic unworthiness arising from sexual intercourse was common among the ancients, and its antiquity in Israel is reflected in 1 Sam 21:4-5.

Female impurity (vv 19-30) arose from either menstruation (vv 19-24) or an abnormal flow of blood outside the customary time or beyond the usual length of the period (vv 25-30). At the time of menstruation the impurity lasted for seven days, during which time uncleanness could be communicated to persons and objects in much the same way as in the case of the man with a chronic flow. The exact sense of v 23 in both the MT and the LXX is difficult to determine, but the following is recommended as the closest rendering of the Hebrew: "If there be an object on the bed or seat where she lies, in touching it, one makes himself unclean until evening." A man approaching a menstruating woman sexually contracted her uncleanness, remained in it for a week, and was capable of transmitting it during that time. The stricter penalty imposed for the same act in 20:18 proceeds from an independent tradition more concerned (as the context indicates) with the moral aspects of the case. In menstrual irregularity, the woman remained unclean and in a contagious condition during the time of the flow of blood. Since this was a true illness and not a purely natural phenomenon, its more serious character demanded cultic purification on the eighth day after its cessation with the bird oblations as sin offering and holocaust. Verse 31 is significant for the chapter as well as the entire section on legal purity. The interests of cult lay at the heart of the clean and unclean legislation, any defilement of the Lord's dwelling being punishable by death (→ Institutions, 76:105-107).

(Gispen, W. H., "The Distinction between Clean and Unclean," *OTS* 5 [1948] 190-96. Milgrom, J., "The Biblical Diet Laws as an Ethical System," *Int* 17 [1963] 288-301. Wilkinson, J., "Leprosy and Leviticus: The Problem of Description and Identification," *SJT* 30 [1977] 153-69; "Leprosy and Leviticus: A Problem of Semantics," *SJT* 31 [1978] 153-66.)

34   (IV) The Day of Atonement (16:1-34). The detailed treatment of Yom Kippur is appropriately situated after the sacrificial ritual and the code of legal purity, both of which serve as background material for an understanding of the feast itself (→ Institutions, 76:147-150). The ritual is given first (vv 1-28), followed by directives on certain peripheral features of the feast, e.g., fast and rest (vv 29-34). This annual observance, so important in postexilic Israel, is never mentioned in the preexilic literature, and, as it is presented here, the ceremonies of the day represent a combination of distinct rites, brought together in a rather loosely edited chapter (note the doublets in vv 6 and 11, 9b and 15, and 4 and 32).

In outlining the ritual (vv 1-28), the Lord addresses Moses alone, who is, in turn, to convey the message to Aaron. The reference to the death of Aaron's sons in v 1 has no chronological value, serving only as an artificial link for the incorporation of the Yom Kippur material. The feast's solemnity is immediately underscored by the announcement that only with the celebration of this feast each year could the high priest pass behind the veil screening the Holy of Holies and enter the Holy Place. **2.** *in front of the propitiatory (kapporet):* The golden cover over the Ark (Exod 25:17-22) is indicated. Since the Ark itself was never recovered after the exile, the propitiatory alone remained in the Holy of Holies, which accounts for the emphasis given it in chap. 16. Because the glory of Yahweh was there made manifest (Exod 40:34; Num 7:89), entrance at any other time would result in death because of one's inability to stand before the resplendent divine presence.

The first of the combined rites was the sin offering of a bull for the priests' transgressions and a goat for the sins of the people (vv 3a,5). Bathed and clothed in sacred linen, the high priest took the blood of the slaughtered bull together with the glowing censer and incense into the Holy of Holies, where he incensed the propitiatory to obscure the divine presence and sprinkled it with the bull's blood to signify its consecration to the Lord (vv 3b-4,6,11-14). The same procedure was followed for the people's sin offering (vv 9,15). In this way, the sins of the priests and people were expiated.

Verse 16, however, introduces another theme: atonement for ritual transgressions that had affected the Lord's dwelling itself (Ezek 45:18-20). It was accomplished by a blood aspersion within the sanctuary (here identified with the aspersions of the sin offering) and a second sprinkling and blood application at the altar (probably of holocausts) outside. This rite (vv 16-19), which has been joined to the Kippur ceremony, was clearly an act of atonement for the sacred places. However, the question has been posed whether the blood action within the Holy of Holies, after the two rites were joined, was then expiatory or consecrating, for the sprinkling before the propitiatory (v 14b), like the customary sprinkling before the veil (cf. 4:6), although it looked to atonement for the priests or the people, was in itself a consecrative act. Moreover, according to Vriezen (*OTS* 7 [1950] 232), the aspersion of the propitiatory itself (v 14a) was actually the highest form of blood dedication and so, too, was originally a consecration act, reaching to the very place where Yahweh was enthroned. Hence, it retains the same sense here as in other passages where blood was sprinkled toward the Lord. Although this sense seems to have been lost early in favor of the expiatory idea of cleansing the sacred place (see v 16), its original purpose was to dedicate the atoning blood to God in a most special way.

Still another rite (vv 20-26), of unquestionably ancient vintage, was blended into the Day of Atonement liturgy. Its earliest reference is found in the mention of the two male goats (vv 5,7-10). One of these, "for the Lord," became the people's sin offering, whereas the latter, "for Azazel," became the bearer of the community's guilt. With the purification of the sanctuary completed (v 20), the priest imposed hands on the remaining goat and confessed the people's sins, thus bringing about a transmission of the sins to the goat. Carrying its evil burden, it was led off to a desert place by an attendant, who became unclean in the execution of his task. The evil was thus removed from the people's midst. The name Azazel occurs only in chap. 16. Driver (*JSS* 1 [1956] 97-98) identifies it with a place-name meaning "rugged rocks" or "precipice," from the root 'zz (Arabic 'azâzu(n), "rough ground"). De Vaux finds the argument unconvincing in terms of the personal parallelism demanded by the context: one goat for Yahweh and one for Azazel. With most modern commentators, he explains the term as the name of a supernatural being, a devil whose customary haunt was the desert (Isa 34:14; also *1 Enoch* 9:6; 10:4–8; cf. de Vaux, *AI* 509; H. Tawil, *ZAW* 92 [1980] 43–59). The Vg, following the LXX, refers to it as "the goat sent out" (*caper emissarius*), whence the Eng escape goat or scapegoat. The idea of sin transference to animals is found among the primitive customs of various peoples even today (see J. G. Frazer, *The Golden Bough* [NY, 1951] 626–27), and certain ancient Babylonian and Hittite parallels have been the object of a comparative study by S. Landersdorfer (*BZ* 19 [1931] 20–28). The most evident biblical parallel is the liberated bird of the leper's purification (14:7).

To conclude the ceremony (vv 23–38), before offering the two holocausts the high priest removed his linen vestments, infected by contact with the sinful animal, and vested in his ordinary ceremonial attire after bathing in a sacred place. The fat of the bull and the goat offered earlier was burned with the holocaust; the remaining parts were destroyed outside the camp. No part of the common sin offering was eaten. Unlike the man in v 26 whose lustrations were for impurity contracted, the person's washing in v 28 was to prevent the diffusion of holiness received from the sacred sacrificial victims.

The conclusion (vv 29–34), reflecting the feast's evolution, i.e., a fixed calendar and "universal" observance, sets the date for Kippur on the tenth day of the seventh month, Tishri (our September–October period). Both Israelite and non-Israelite residents were to fast and desist from any form of work on this "most solemn sabbath," or day of rest. This fast is the only one prescribed in the entire Torah. Verse 34 mentions only personal atonement as the purpose of the feast, whereas v 33 gives preeminence to expiation of the Temple.

(Aartun, K., "Studien zum Gesetz über den grossen Versöhnungstag Lv 16 mit Varianten," *ST* 34 [1980] 73–109. Auerbach, E., "Neujahrs- und Versöhnungsfest in den biblischen Quellen," *VT* 8 [1958] 337–43. Frazer, J. G., *The Scapegoat* [London, 1913]. Kaupel, H., *Die Dämonen im Alten Testament* [Augsburg, 1930] 81–91. Löhr, M., *Das Ritual von Lev 16* [Berlin, 1925].)

35 (V) The Law of Holiness (17:1–26:46). The name (first given by A. Klostermann in 1877) derives from the emphasis on holiness (19:2; 20:7–8). This section is a compilation of earlier laws, ritual and ethical, which were finally codified just before the exile (or perhaps during the exile; the issue depends on the way chap. 26 is interpreted). Like Deut 12–26, the Holiness Code has its own literary unity, beginning with regulations regarding the sanctuary and sacrifice and concluding with "blessings and curses." But the collection itself is marked by an almost disconcerting diversity of material, its sole unifying feature lying in its emphasis on the holiness of Yahweh. This consideration serves as the springboard for its demands of the Israelites, who, in every aspect of their lives, are to be holy as their Lord (19:2; 20:26). It must be noted, however, that the holiness solicited here exceeds mere legal purity and embraces moral rectitude as well, without which holiness is incomplete. It is this characteristic underscoring of the transcendent sanctity of Yahweh that will have such a marked effect on the entire P tradition.

(Cholewinski, A., *Heiligkeitsgesetz und Deuteronomium.* Elliott-Binns, L. E., "Some Problems of the Holiness Code," *ZAW* 67 [1955] 26–40. Zimmerli, W., "'Heiligkeit' nach dem sogenannten Heiligkeitsgesetz," *VT* 30 [1980] 439–512.)

36 (A) Sacredness of Blood (17:1–16). Originally, the slaughter of clean animals, even for profane use, was considered a sacrificial act. The shedding of blood, as an act of dominion over life itself, was the exercise of a divine prerogative and could not be viewed as legitimate unless the life was first restored to God. For this reason, all such killings were reserved for a place of cult (1 Sam 14:32–35). This requirement apparently presented no great difficulty as long as local sanctuaries were allowed, but with the centralization of cult under Josiah (621), such a law became impossible. It was mitigated in Deut 12:15–16,20–25 to a simple act of reverence for the slaughtered animal's blood.

It is surprising that the older law should be resurrected in 17:3–7 at a time after the Josian reform. Twofold motivation is given: the sacredness of blood (v 4) and the avoidance of idolatrous practices (v 7). The interests of both were best served by regulating the slaughtering procedure. Verse 5 indicates that the animals were first to be brought to the Meeting Tent and there offered to the Lord; otherwise, there resulted the guilt of bloodshed and consequent separation from the community (see 7:20). **7.** *satyrs:* The word denotes demons popularly identified with wild goats making their haunts in ruins and desert places, as Azazel (16:8). Because of the historical situation in the post-Josian period, the place designated for the killing could only have been the Jerusalem Temple. The law would have been so totally impractical in the postexilic period that it must be dated with the Holiness Code itself in the period of Jerusalem's last days. Since it would hardly have been included simply as a relic of the past with no practical import, it may represent a hopeful ideal of the Jerusalem clergy opposed to the deuteronomic freedom in the matter, or, as Noth suggests (*Leviticus* 131), an actual revival of the custom because of continued idolatrous practices in Jerusalem of the type Josiah had once attempted to correct (2 Kgs 23:8). In addressing itself most explicitly to the ordinary killing of edible animals, the law included, of course, all forms of properly cultic sacrifices as well.

The following pericope in vv 8–12 repeats the same directives of vv 3–7 with two additional features. The prohibition against local sacrifices included the holocaust (v 8b), and the law was directed to both Israelite and non-Israelite residents of the country, who as part of the community were bound by such regulations. Blood had a special sacredness as a means of atonement; specifically, failure to offer it in the cases of chap. 7 incurs the guilt of bloodshed. The illegal slaughter of animals (murder), as in vv 3–4, was atoned for by the offering of the blood (v 11). The law forbidding the Hebrew to partake of bloody meat was safeguarded by sacrificial centralization.

Two remaining possibilities, directed to Israelites and all other residents, are treated in vv 13–16 and concern the animal caught during a hunt and the animal dying of natural or violent causes. In the former instance, the animal could be eaten only after the blood was disposed of in a manner similar to that prescribed for general slaughter in Deut 12. In the second case, the animal was unclean and was therefore prohibited; anyone eating thereof contracted uncleanness and had to undergo a purification rite to be free of guilt (11:39–40).

37 (B) Sacredness of Sex (18:1–30). The chapter, chiefly concerned with sexual matters, is formed around a series of apodictic laws, which prohibit relations within determined degrees of consanguinity and affinity (vv 6–17) and outlaw certain other forms of aberrant behavior (vv 18–23). This material is introduced by an exhortation addressed to all the Israelites (vv 1–5) and is concluded with similar injunctions (vv 24–30). The sacredness surrounding the act that communicates human life prohibited sexual contact with those already allied by blood, or any close relationship, since such, especially in the former case, would be tantamount to union with one's own flesh.

The introduction (vv 1-5) carries a tone of exceptional seriousness with emphasis on the necessity of an observance that was to be the very antithesis of Canaanite practice. The reference to the Egyptians in v 3 (not mentioned in the conclusion) was included to lend authenticity to the law's purported historical setting in the desert when the only culture known to Israel would have been that of Egypt. The life to which observance leads in v 5 is the "good life," that sign of Yahweh's favor identified with the possession of the promised land.

The laws for sexual conduct within the clan (vv 6-18) are introduced in v 6 by a general prohibition regarding relations and a fortiori marriage with blood kin, although certain cases of affinity also form part of the code. Specifically, the forbidden degrees, which are not necessarily all-inclusive as here listed, embraced son and mother (v 7); father and granddaughter (v 10), in the direct line; and brother and sister (v 9), in the collateral line. The "sister" in this latter verse refers either to a full sister, one "born in your own household," or to a half sister from a previous marriage of the mother, one "born elsewhere," which clearly distinguishes the sense from that of v 11. More remotely, union was forbidden between brother and half sister (v 11), and nephew and aunt (vv 12-13). Restricted by reason of affinity were son and stepmother (v 8), father-in-law and daughter-in-law (v 15), nephew and aunt by marriage (v 14), and brother-in-law and sister-in-law (v 16). Verse 17 forbade union or marriage with the daughter or granddaughter of a woman with whom one had had relations.

The usual transl. and interpretation of v 18 envisions an anti-incest law forbidding simultaneous marriage with two sisters. On the possibility of its being an antidivorce and antipolygamy law, see A. Tosato, *CBQ* 46 (1984) 199-214.

A number of sexual abuses are excluded by the apodictic decrees of vv 19-23. These include intercourse during the uncleanness of menstruation (v 19; cf. 15:24), sodomy among men (v 22), and bestiality indulged in by man or woman (v 23; cf. Exod 22:18). An extraneous law in v 21 (perhaps suggested by the term seed [offspring] in the Hebrew of v 20) forbade the pagan practice of child sacrifice, directed by the Canaanites to the worship of the god Molech (cf. 20:2-5); see 2 Kgs 23:10; Jer 7:31; 32:35; 2 Kgs 16:3; 21:6; Ezek 16:20-21.

Removal from the land, the same punishment meted out to the Canaanites for their sexual wantonness, serves as the threatening sanction for native Israelites as well as for resident aliens (vv 24-30). Since the sacred land, which had been defiled, could never digest such abuses, it is depicted as discharging the Canaanite evil, to be repeated if necessary in the case of an unfaithful Israel. Personal sanction in v 29 takes the form of the offender's severance from the community without the specific delineations given elsewhere, e.g., death for sodomy (20:13), bestiality (20:15), and child sacrifice (20:2).

(Bigger, S. F., "The Family Laws of Lev 18 in Their Setting," *JBL* 98 [1979] 187-203. Halbe, J., "Die Reihe der Inzestverbote, Lev 18:7-18," *ZAW* 92 [1980] 60-88.)

**38		(C) Various Rules of Conduct (19:1-37).** This miscellaneous collection of laws on worship, justice, charity, and chastity, with its clearly primitive character, is of particular interest as a mirror of preexilic cultic and social life. In its dependence on the Decalogue and its own subsequent influence on postexilic legislation, it serves as an important link between the earlier and later stages of Israelite law. The chapter forms a unit with its own introduction (vv 1-2) and conclusion (vv 36b-37), which anchor the diversified contents in respect for the holiness of Yahweh.

Priority is given reverence for parents, observance of the sabbath, and avoidance of idolatry (vv 3-4), all represented in the Decalogue (Exod 20:2-6,8,12; Deut 5:6-10,12-16). The rules regarding the peace offering (vv 5-8) are substantially the same as in 7:15-19; this passage, however, points up the intimate connection between oblations and consumption, the eating of the offering after the set time limit making the whole sacrifice a profanation.

The law regarding the harvest (vv 9-10) forbade such thoroughness in gleaning as would leave nothing in the fields or vineyards for the needy (23:22; Deut 24:19-22; Ruth 2). The charitable motivation given this procedure is an early Hebr adaptation of a pre-Israelite custom of leaving something of the harvest to honor the deity responsible for the soil's fertility, a motive clearly excluded by the concluding affirmation in v 10b.

Verses 11-18 are centered mainly on one's responsibility to practice justice and charity in social dealings. The influence of the Decalogue is again pronounced: the prohibition in v 12 against profaning the divine name by perjury (more restricted than the Decalogue's general law of respect for God's name, Exod 20:7; Deut 5:11); and the law against any form of lying and deception in v 11b (broader than that of the Decalogue, which looks to court testimony, Exod 20:16; Deut 5:20). The precept regarding theft (v 11a), as in Exod 20:15 and Deut 5:19, was concerned with the deprivation of another's personal liberty—i.e., kidnapping (cf. Exod 21:16, Hebr "anyone stealing a man . . ."; Deut 24:7)—and was thus clearly distinguished from the law regarding another's goods in v 13a (see A. Alt, *KlS* 1. 333-40). The strong were not to take advantage of the weak by cheating or stealing (v 13a), withholding wages (v 13b; cf. Deut 24:14-15), or other forms of unkind treatment (v 14). **14.** *you shall not curse the deaf:* The curse, once uttered, was irrevocable and effective whether heard by the accursed or not.

Court proceedings (vv 15-16), presided over by the elders or senior members of the clan, were to be marked by strict adherence to the interests of justice, which forbade either favoring the mighty or showing compassion to the weak. In a negative way, the individual Israelite was to uphold justice by refraining from any falsification about a person made to members of the judicial body, and in a positive way, he was bound to bring to light evidence that might save the life of the one accused.

The demands of charity (vv 17-18) precluded a spirit of enmity, revenge, and grudge-bearing and required that fraternal correction be made when necessary. **17b.** *do not incur sin because of him:* Sin would lie in the failure to correct in terms of the seriousness of the responsibility to do so (Ezek 3:18-19; 33:8-9; cf. also Matt 18:15). The most celebrated passage in Lev (v 18b) proposes self-love as the measure of charity toward a fellow countryman. According to the teaching of Christ (Matt 22:37-39; Mark 12:30-31; wherein "neighbor" is taken in its widest possible extension), this lofty precept, taken together with Deut 6:5, sums up the whole of the Law and the Prophets (see A. Fernandez, *VD* 1 [1921] 27-28).

39		The law against crossbreeding and cross-semination in v 19 (cf. Deut 22:9) is seen by Noth (*Leviticus* 142) as a very ancient, probably pre-Israelite, regulation. Heterogeneous coupling was evidently considered a perversion of the divinely established order, and the prohibition was gradually extended to the use of different fibers in sewing, the yoking of different animals, and even transvestism (cf. Deut 22:11,10,5).

In vv 20–22 the woman with whom one has relations is still unmarried although "destined for" or "betrothed to" another man. Her state of slavery made marriage impossible before freedom was granted (cf. Exod 21:7–11; see Noth, *Leviticus* 142–43). There was to be an unspecified compensation after inquiry. The offended party was the slave girl's master, whose property she was. The presentation of a guilt offering is prescribed for the male offender.

Just as the male child did not properly belong to Yahweh until the time of his circumcision (Gen 17:9–14), so by analogy the fruit of a tree produced prior to the firstfruits offering was termed uncircumcised (vv 23–25). Not before the fourth year, when the fruit was truly well developed and worth eating, could it be offered to the Lord as a token of thanks. Hence, the people were forbidden to eat the fruit any time prior to the fifth year.

The older laws of vv 26–31 were prompted mainly by the dangers arising from the cultic practices of Israel's neighbors. Besides the oft-mentioned prohibition of blood (17:10–12), likewise prohibited were the following: divination and magic arts as attempts to plumb divine secrets or to control events; the mourning customs of the Canaanites—cutting of hair, body lacerations, tattooing—probably viewed as means of warding off the departed spirit by changing the appearance to avoid recognition; the abandonment of a daughter to cult prostitution, which, because of its link with the pagan fertility rites, would degrade the sacredness of the land itself; and consultation with mediums or fortune-tellers to commune with the dead or foresee the future (Exod 22:17; Deut 18:11; 1 Sam 28:1–25). In a positive way, faithful observance included respect for the sabbath and the sacredness of the sanctuary, wherein religious syncretism often led to profanation (Deut 23:18–19; Hos 4:14).

In regard to charity and justice (vv 32–36a), respect was to be shown the senior members of the community, and all attitudes of economic superiority were to be avoided in dealing with dependent foreigners, who could not possess land and had no clan ties. The given motive for this charity, recalling the days of Egyptian bondage, has a deuteronomic ring (Deut 10:19; 5:15) and is probably a secondary addition. Correct scales, weights, and measuring containers (the ephah, approx. one bu.; the hin, approx. one gal.) were to be used in all commercial transactions (Deut 25:13–16; Ezek 45:10).

40   (D) Penalties (20:1–27). There is a marked affinity between chaps. 18 and 20; the present concern is the sanctions attached to many of the aforementioned crimes. The attraction between the two chapters results from their common material rather than from any direct literary dependence, since chap. 20, like 18 and 19, forms a complete unit introduced originally by the exhortation in vv 7–8, followed by the list of crimes and penalties, and concluded in vv 22–26. Thus, vv 2–6 and 27 should be considered secondary additions.

Child sacrifice to Molech (vv 2–5; cf. 18:21) was punished by death (stoning), executed by the community or, if they failed to do so, by the Lord himself. Note the solidarity concept of the family's sharing in the man's guilt (v 5a), an idea to be greatly altered in postexilic religious thought. Also in the line of cult, v 6 sanctions with death the previous mandate (19:31) against consulting diviners.

After the customary parenesis in vv 7–8 (wherein Yahweh is both the reason and the cause of holiness), the kernel of the chapter in vv 9–21 imposes sanctions for the sexual abuses of chap. 18. Prior to this, however, first place is given to the matter of uttering maledictions

against one's parents (v 9), a precept included implicitly within the general scope of the law in 19:3. In the sexual sphere, death for both offenders was prescribed in the following cases: adultery (v 10; 18:20; Deut 22:22); relations between son and stepmother (v 11; 18:8) and father-in-law and daughter-in-law (v 12; 18:15); sodomy (v 13; 18:22); simultaneous marriage with a mother and daughter (v 14; 18:17; Deut 27:23), in which case the three offenders were burned; bestiality (vv 15–16; 18:23; Exod 22:18; Deut 27:21), wherein the animal also bears objective guilt in the wrongdoing; and relations between brother and sister (v 17; 18:9; Deut 27:22), with a menstruating woman (v 18; 18:19), and between nephew and aunt (v 19; 18:12–13). The death occurred either by human intervention (vv 10–16) or divine action, viz., a premature death (vv 17–19). In the case of sexual misbehavior with an aunt by marriage (v 20; 18:14) or marriage with a sister-in-law (v 21; 18:16; Mark 6:18), a substitute for the humanly executed death penalty took the form of a childless marriage, divinely decreed, depriving a man of the all-important continuance of his life and name through his progeny (Num 27:2–4; Deut 25:6; Ruth 4:10). Verse 21 does not contradict the levirate law (Deut 25:5ff.), since the latter looked to marriage with a sister-in-law only after the death of a brother who had died childless.

The conclusion (vv 22–26) closely parallels 18:24–30 with its admonitions and promises centered on observance of the Lord's decrees. Verse 25, ill fitting the context, seems to be an addition suggested by the "separation" idea in v 24; on the subject of clean and unclean animals, see chap. 11. Equally problematic is the abrupt addition in v 27, which complements v 6. The meaning, however, is clear. Not only were those consulting diviners reprobate, but also to be stoned were those who professionally practiced such arts and thus induced others to idolatrous conduct (cf. Deut 13:7ff.; 17:2ff.).

41   (E) Priestly Sanctity (21:1–24). Chapters 21–22 are concerned mainly with cultic regulations directed principally to the priests. Chapter 21 can be divided, according to content, into directives concerning all the priests (vv 1–9) and the main priest of the community (vv 10–15) in the first part, and sacerdotal impediments (vv 16–23) in the second part.

Contact with the dead (e.g., in preparing and moving the corpse) rendered any Israelite unclean (Num 19:11–19; 31:19, 24). Although it was permitted for the people to contract such uncleanness with good reason, such was not the case for the priests, impurity being ordinarily incompatible with their lofty office. As vv 2–4 indicate, however, exception was made in the case of a death in the priest's immediate family (see comment on 10:6–7; (Ezek 44:25–27). The sense of v 4 is extremely obscure in both the MT and the LXX. The MT reads: "A husband shall not make himself unclean among his people"; "the people" perhaps refers to the priest's in-laws. The *NAB* emends the text so that it is elaborative of v 3; a married sister, now "one flesh" with her husband, was no longer joined to the family of her birth. Certain funeral customs (vv 5–6), derived from pagan sources and prohibited for all Israelites (19:27–28), were especially outlawed for the priests. **6.** *the food of their God:* See comment on 3:11.

As to marriage (vv 7–8), the priest was required to marry a virgin, widows not being explicitly excluded. The latter is allowed by Ezek 44:22 only when it is the widow of a priest. The case in v 9 has only a loose connection with the preceding, imposing the death penalty upon the sinning daughter of a priest; the principal evil resided in the sacrilegious nature of the act, since, by reason of family solidarity, the priest would share in his daughter's guilt.

Verses 10–15 contain special directives for the main priest of the community. The Hebr phrase "the priest most exalted among his brothers" is a descriptive designation and not the same as the title high priest, arising in the postexilic period (Hag 1:1; Zech 3:1; and common in the later P tradition). However, the phrase does indicate a unified priesthood, hierarchically structured, at a time after the cultic reform of Josiah (621), thus paving the way for the later title. The mention of the anointing in v 10 provides no definitive argument for the preexilic existence of such a custom, because we lack information on the present passage's time of final editing. The community's main priest was prohibited any contact with the dead whatsoever, even close relatives, and so would never be in a position to practice accepted forms of mourning: the loosening of the hair (not "baring the head"; cf. 10:6) and tearing of the garments—neither of which is to be confused with the totally prohibited practices of v 5. He was not permitted to leave the sanctuary for burial rites (10:7). In selecting a spouse, he was to choose only a virgin, with widows excluded, and his wife was to be "from his own people"—i.e., the tribe of Levi (LXX *ek tou genous autou*)—lest the purity of the levitical strain be in any way debased in this most important family.

Integrity of the whole man was demanded of cultic functionaries. Physical imperfection was, then, an impediment to the exercise of the priestly office in a descendant of Aaron (vv 16–23). Inasmuch as the animals offered to Yahweh were to be flawless (1:3,10; 22:22–25), the same was required of priests. The list of impediments in vv 18–20 contains a number of rare terms, only the general meaning of which can be determined. Since a priest was not unclean because of such a defect, he was permitted to partake of the various sacrificial repasts, but, as long as his impediment remained, he could approach neither the sanctuary veil nor the altar of holocausts, i.e., act in any priestly capacity. Finally, in v 24, Moses relays the message to the priests and, as a matter of concern (cf. v 8), to all the Israelites as well.

42   (F) Rules on Sacrifice (22:1–33). The first section (vv 1–16) deals with the right of participation in the sacrificial food, and v 2 serves as its introduction; the second part (vv 17–30) treats of acceptable victims; vv 31–33 serve as a general conclusion.

Disregard for the sacred character of an offering was disregard for the very person of Yahweh (v 2). Therefore, the eating of those parts of the victim designated for the priests (6:19–23; 7:7–10; 7:28–34) was to follow prescribed procedure and to be carried out only when the participants were in a state of cleanness under the usual penalty of extirpation. The same rule applied equally to all Israelites in those instances where they were participants (7:20–21), but the priests' rights in the matter were, of course, more extensive. In vv 4–8, priests were excluded who suffered from "leprosy" (see comment on chaps 13–14), who had abnormal genital excretions (see comment on 15:2–15), who had experienced an emission of semen (see 15:16), or who had come in contact with any unclean person or thing. The more transient nature of the last category (uncleanness lasting only the day) conceded the restoration of rights with the usual lustration, probably equally true for the emission of seed (15:16). Disqualified also were those who ate an animal not properly slain (7:24; 11:39–40; 17:15; Ezek 4:14). Disregard of these precepts would result in death (v 9), the manner (whether by divine or human intervention) remaining undetermined.

Only members of the priest's family were allowed to eat the victim (10:14). Excluded in vv 10–14 are the following: any ordinary layman (*zār*, "a stranger"), i.e., one in no way affiliated with the sacerdotal family; a priest's tenant (*tôšāb*), i.e., a resident alien or settler economically dependent on an Israelite landowner, similar to but not the social equal of the more common type of alien, the *gēr*, who was more integrated into Israelite life; and a hired servant (*śākîr*), a wage earner employed for a definite job. Slaves, however, were part of the household, whether purchased or born to slaves in the house (although the latter category, *yĕlîdê bayit*, may be broader in scope, embracing all personnel attached to a house as slaves, who, without necessarily living therein, had certain responsibilities to their lord; cf. Gen 14:14). The priest's daughter, married to a layman, belonged to the lay household and was therefore excluded. If she was left without husband and childless, her rights were restored; if a mother, she is still supported by her husband's household and is not eligible.

A layman inadvertently eating the sacrificial food incurred objective guilt and was held to make restitution according to the estimated value plus an added one-fifth as a penalty for his oversight. Verses 15–16 enjoin the priests not to allow abuses in these matters, which would result in profanation, and not to allow prohibited parties to eat the sacrifice, which would result in the priests' incurring punishable guilt.

The section on unacceptable victims (vv 17–30) is presented for the layman's information and is more primitive than that found in chaps. 1–7. The main distinction is between holocausts (v 18) and peace offerings (*šĕlamîm*, v 21), either of which could be offered under the title of a votive offering—arising from a vow or promise—or a freewill offering—spontaneous and independent of any previous commitment. As in the sacrificial code (chaps. 1–7), the animal victims destined for such oblations had to be unblemished. An exception is introduced in v 23 (which when compared with the universal tone of the preceding verses would seem to be a secondary addition) in allowing certain defects in the freewill offering, since such was offered purely from motives of devotion. The special reference to the animal's genitals in v 24 portrays Semitic reverence for the procreative faculty.

The offering from the herd or the flock was unacceptable before the eighth day after birth (v 27), the same law being found in the book of the covenant (Exod 22:29) with reference to the firstborn animal. This prohibition is accounted for in terms of the young's complete dependence on its parent during this time, and because, like the undeveloped fruit (19:23–24), such offspring, not yet ready for human consumption, were not fit offerings for the Lord. The prohibition against the simultaneous slaughter of the ox or sheep with its young (v 28) is enigmatic but may well carry a polemic note against Canaanite practices of honoring the fertility deity by sacrificing the offspring together with its parent, the source of its life. The third form of peace offering, the thanksgiving sacrifice, heretofore unmentioned in the chapter but found together with the votive and freewill offerings in the sacrificial code (see comment on 7:11–21), must be eaten on the day of the sacrifice itself (v 30), a rule stated with equal force in 7:15.

43   (G) The Liturgical Year (23:1–44). In its more primitive form as part of the original code, the chapter treated solely of the three main annual feasts—Passover and Unleavened Bread (vv 4–8), Pentecost (vv 16–21), and Booths (vv 34–36)—and had its own conclusion (vv 37–38). Compare Exod 23:14–17; 34:18, 22–23; Deut 16:1–17. Later editors of the Holiness Code have added the sabbath precept (v 3), the rubrics of vv

10–15, the Day of Acclamation (vv 23–25), the Day of Atonement (vv 26–32), the added directives for Booths (vv 39–43), and a new conclusion (vv 44). For a summary treatment of the feasts described here, → Institutions, 76:122–138.

44 (a) PASSOVER AND UNLEAVENED BREAD (23:4–14). Celebrated on the evening of the 14th of the first month, Nisan (March–April), this most solemn commemoration of the exodus is found in its historical setting in Exod 12. There, as here, Passover is joined to the feast of Unleavened Bread (*maṣṣôt*). The latter commenced the day after the Pasch and continued for seven days, with a solemn gathering and complete abstention from work on the first and last days and determined sacrifices offered each day within the week (Num 28:16–25). It was an agricultural feast, likely taken over from the Canaanites by the Hebrews, to honor Yahweh, Lord of the harvest, at the time of the spring ingathering of the barley. Originally Passover and Unleavened Bread were completely distinct feasts, but their celebration at approximately the same time, and the making of passover, like Unleavened Bread, a pilgrimage feast (Deut 16:5ff.) at the time of the deuteronomic reform (621), resulted in a merger of the two. As stated in v 6b, the bread of *maṣṣôt* was devoid of leaven, i.e., without any admixture of remains from the previous year's harvest. Thus, with bread made entirely from the fresh grain, the feast marked a new beginning as, during the first week, the initial gleanings were eaten and special daily sacrifices were offered.

Prior to its merger with Passover, the feast of Unleavened Bread had no fixed date, since it began at the time of the ripened harvest. This situation is reflected in vv 9–14, which present the ritual procedure for firstfruit offerings. The feast began on a sabbath with the observances mentioned in v 7. On the day following the sabbath, the beginning of the work week, the landowner gave a sheaf of grain to the priest, which was in turn "waved" (see comment on 7:30) as an offering before the Lord. Moreover, a community oblation was made, consisting of a lamb holocaust plus a cereal-and-drink offering. Before this presentation to the Lord, it was forbidden to use any of the grain for the ordinary purposes of the harvest produce (v 14). This first sheaf ritual is a postexilic addition of earlier material to the Holiness Code. Since by the time of its insertion the date of Unleavened Bread was no longer variable — long since joined to Passover, which fell always on 15 Nisan — the sabbath reference in v 11, although the cause of much discussion in later Judaism, is probably converted into a reference to the day of the feast itself, a day of sabbath (complete rest) although not *the* sabbath.

45 (b) PENTECOST (23:15–21). Known also as the feast of Weeks, this second of the three great feasts of pilgrimage (*ḥāg*) was celebrated seven weeks after Unleavened Bread (Gk *pentēkostos*, "fiftieth"; see comment on 25:10). After the Passover-Unleavened Bread linkage, Pentecost also had a fixed date; it had formerly been determined by the harvest and was thus variable. The lack of unanimity in later Judaism on the exact date of the feast arose from the diverse interpretations of the sabbath reference in vv 11 and 15. Also of pre-Israelite origin, the feast lasted only one day, with a religious assembly and the presentation of offerings. The latter consisted of two loaves of bread from the harvester (the only instance of leaven being prescribed for ritual use) and from the community as a whole, first a holocaust of seven lambs, one bull, and two rams, with cereal offerings and libation, and then a goat as a sin offering and two lambs as a peace offering. **20.** *the priest shall wave:* See comment on 7:30. The offerings prescribed in Num

28:26–31, from a later ritual, are slightly different. Subsequent tradition made this feast a commemoration of the giving of the law on Sinai 50 days after the exodus (Exod 19:1).

The precept in v 22, providing for the needs of the poor and the alien, suggested perhaps by the harvest context, is an addition to the primitive text, which treated wholly of festive observance; see comment on 19:9–10.

46 (c) NEW YEAR'S DAY (23:23–25). This name for the feast (*rô'š haššānâ*) was unknown before the beginning of the Christian era; it is not so called in Josephus or Philo but was common by the time of the Mishnah. Such a designation is found neither in the present verses nor elsewhere in the OT. Moreover, with the adoption of the Babylonian calendar before the exile (which is clearly the one followed in this chapter), the year's beginning was in the spring, Nisan, not in Tishri (September–October), the seventh month and the date indicated in v 24. An account of festive observance on this day in Neh 8:1–12 makes no mention of it as a New Year's celebration; in Num 29:1–6 it is called the Day of Acclamation (or Trumpets). Nevertheless, since the seventh month was a most important one for feasts, its solemn inauguration in this manner may well have been the relic of a former feast when, according to the earlier calendar, the year began in the autumn. Cazelles admits the distinct possibility of such a fall feast honoring Yahweh as creator and king and dating from the monarchical period (*DBSup* 6. 620–45). It is on this feast that S. Mowinckel places his much-discussed annual celebration of the "enthronement" of Yahweh (*He That Cometh* [Oxford, 1956] 21–95). According to the directives here given, the day was marked by complete rest and a solemn convocation (Neh 8:1–12), announced by blasts of the silver trumpets (Num 10:1–10) as a formal reminder. The sacrifices ordered for the day are listed in Num 29:2–5.

47 (d) DAY OF ATONEMENT (23:26–32). This was the second autumn feast, celebrated nine days later. For the detailed ritual, see chap. 16. This, too, is a postexilic addition to the chapter, emphasizing the fast and abstention from work connected with the observance (16:29–31). The reckoning of a day from one evening to the next (v 32) was a result of Mesopotamian influence and became an Israelite commonplace from about the time of the exile.

48 (e) FEAST OF BOOTHS (23:33–36,39–43). Called also Tabernacles, Tents, Ingathering, or simply the Hebr *sukkôt,* this was the last of the three major and most ancient Israelite feasts. Like the feasts of Unleavened Bread and Pentecost, it was a pilgrimage feast made annually to central sanctuaries but, by the time of the final edition of Lev, celebrated only in Jerusalem. With this agricultural feast of Canaanite origin, the Israelites thankfully closed the grape and olive harvest in the fall on the 15th day of the seventh month (Tishri), five days after the Day of Atonement. It lasted one week with solemn assembly and abstention from work on the opening day and on the concluding (eighth) day after the week-long observance. Special sacrifices were carefully delineated for each day of the octave (Num 29:12–38). Verses 39–43, deriving from a later hand and inserted after the original conclusion in vv 37–38, present slight variations, especially regarding the gathering of fruit and branches (v 40), for a purpose not clearly specified. According to later rabbinical, and evidently correct, interpretation, these were used for joyful processions (cf. 2 Macc 10:6–8) and not, in the present case, as materials for constructing booths (see G. W. MacRae, *CBQ* 22 [1960] 271–72). Verses 42–43 point up the feast's significance; the building of huts, undoubtedly an ancient fruit-harvest custom, was incorporated by the Israelites into the framework of their sacred history, commemorating the time they dwelt in such constructions during their desert sojourn.

49 (H) Additional Legislation (24:1–23). The material treated here is rubrical (vv 1–9) and moral (vv 10–23) in content and clearly interrupts the calendar theme of chaps. 23 and 25. For the detailed description of the Temple lampstand (vv 1–4), see Exod 25:31–40. The injunction given to Moses in vv 2–3 repeats Exod 27:20–21.

The Temple showbread or *leḥem happānîm* (bread of the countenance or divine presence), treated in vv 5–9, consisted of 12 cakes made of pure wheat, which were placed in two rows on the gold-plated wooden table before the Holy of Holies (Exod 25:23–30). An incense offering, placed on the table with the bread, was burned on the altar when the loaves were replaced each sabbath; this practice gave the bread offering a certain sacrificial character, the incense actually being a token oblation (*'azkārâ*) for the bread itself (see comment on 2:2). Unlike the setting in pagan cult where such was simply a meal for the deity, the communal character of the act, symbolized by the sharing of food with Yahweh, served to remind the Israelites of the perpetuity of the covenant he had made with the 12 tribes (v 8). As something sacred and received by the Lord, the bread was eaten only by the priests under circumscribed conditions (cf. 1 Sam 21:3–6).

The blasphemy incident (vv 10–16,23), the only piece of narrative in the Holiness Code, actually serves as a backdrop for the law enunciated in vv 15–16. This casuistic setting (see also Num 15:32–36) is presented as a precedent in the light of which similar cases were to be judged. The gravity of the act rests both in reviling God and in the accompanying profanation of the sacred Name (v 16; cf. Exod 20:7). Despite his Israelite mother, the man in question was still considered an alien, a fact that would give this law considerable exilic and postexilic relevance. Moses receives the Lord's decision: death by stoning for any blasphemer, native or alien. The imposition of hands in v 14 is the same as the scapegoat ritual in chap. 16. All who had heard the blasphemy shared in its objective malice; here it is recommunicated to the offender. The entire community, Israelite and foreigner alike, participate in the malefactor's execution apart from the sacred confines of the camp (cf. J. Gabel and C. Wheeler in *VT* 30 [1980] 227–29).

Verses 17–22 treat of the law of retaliation (*lex talionis*), which, limiting retaliation to the seriousness of the crime, was the common procedure in ancient criminal cases—e.g., in the Code of Hammurabi (*ANET* 163–80; cf. also laws 200, 210, 219, 245, and 263). The law formerly stated in Exod 21:23–25 here includes foreigners as well as Israelites.

50 (I) The Holy Years (25:1–55). In addition to the rest for human and beast provided by the weekly sabbath (Exod 20:8–11; Deut 5:12–15), the land itself was to have a year of reprieve at stated intervals. Ancient oriental custom left the land uncultivated to assure its future fertility; in Israelite hands, the practice took on added meaning in focusing attention on the sole proprietorship of Yahweh, an idea central to the sabbatical (vv 1–7) and jubilee (vv 8–55) years.

51 (a) Sabbatical Year (25:2–7). Cultivation of field and vineyard was to be terminated after the sixth year; they were to be left untouched for the year following. **4.** *during the seventh year:* Neither here nor in Exod 23:10–11 does the text indicate whether the date was fixed and universal or variable depending on the

beginning of one's land tenure. Correlative legislation required the freeing of slaves after six years of service, "in the seventh year" (Exod 21:2–6). However, Deut 15, wherein the sabbatical legislation includes both the liberation of slaves and the relaxation of debts, leaves no doubt that the seventh year of remission was fixed (cf. 15:7–11). During the year, planting, pruning, and harvesting for storage were forbidden; the spontaneous growth was taken as needed by the owner and all his dependents without discrimination.

52 (b) Jubilee Year (25:8–55). The grand sabbatical derives its name from the trumpet (Hebr *yôbēl,* "ram," "ram's horn") sounded to inaugurate the year (v 9). It, too, had a fixed date (vv 15–16), coinciding with the seventh sabbatical. **10.** *in this fiftieth year:* The reference is a *crux interpretum.* Some authors (M. Noth, R. North, A. Jirku) see here a broad reference to the forty-ninth year; others (R. de Vaux), the fiftieth year, or year after the seventh sabbatical, hence a two-year fallow. The text's obscurity occasioned equal diversity of interpretation in antiquity (cf. J. T. Milik, *VD* 28 [1950] 165–66). A calendar with new year in the spring would place Atonement in mid-year. By using an accepted method of counting by inclusion, both the first and last half year could be counted separately, making 50 years. The seventh sabbatical was itself a jubilee, a special year of remission (see R. North, *Sociology of the Biblical Jubilee* [Rome, 1954] 109–34). The year was to begin on the Day of Atonement (the tenth day of Tishri) and was a period of emancipation in which, in addition to the usual sabbatical observance (vv 11–12), all alienated property was returned to its original owner (v 10).

The specific stipulations of vv 13–17 point to the fixed jubilee date. Since in any property transaction there was prime concern with the number of years the field would yield crops to the investor's benefit, the years remaining before the next jubilee with its reversion of property determined the sale price. The law of land return strongly emphasizes the inalienable character of family holdings.

A reassuring note is struck in vv 18–22 in response to an understandable concern about survival during sabbatical (or jubilee) years. The promise of sufficient provisions is linked with the oft-repeated assurance of abundance in return for fidelity (vv 18–19). So copious would be the produce of the sixth year that it would suffice for the seventh, as well as the eighth (replanting) and ninth (new harvest) years.

53 General precepts related to the ideal set forth in the jubilee legislation (vv 23–55) constitute the remainder of chap. 25, with the basic principle set forth in v 23: The land belongs to the Lord and is entrusted to the Israelites as a result of the covenant. Strictly speaking, they were not owners but tenants with the right of use and usufruct, and any permanent sale of land was in excess of the tenant's right. Therefore, an impoverished Israelite forced to sell was faced with three possibilities (vv 24–28): reacquisition of the family land in the name of the poor man by a relative acting as a *gō'ēl;* reacquisition by the poor man himself on the occasion of later good fortune (with proportionate reduction made from the original sale price); or reversion at the time of the jubilee.

The transition from clan settlements to town life weakened family ties with landholdings. In addition, such walled towns, originally Canaanite in many instances, were further from the Israelite ideal. Thus, privileges were restricted (vv 29–31). The possibility of redemption lasted only one year, and the home was not repossessed at the jubilee. The village settlements (without walls) were more closely allied to the adjoining farmland; alienated property therein did not have the one-year restriction and enjoyed the jubilee benefits.

The special property rights of the Levites were to be respected (vv 32–34). In their cities (not exclusively theirs, but places where they had their own holdings; cf. Josh 21) they had the unrestricted right of house redemption at any time prior to the jubilee release. Any attached land, allotted to the Levites and therefore appropriated by the Lord in a special way, could never be sold.

Deference was to be shown an indigent fellow Israelite (vv 35–38); he was to receive the same courtesy extended to non-Israelite inhabitants, i.e., residence without landed property. To demand interest from him in any form was prohibited, although such was allowed in the case of a non-Israelite debtor (Deut 23:21).

It was likewise forbidden for Israelites to make slaves of their fellow countrymen (vv 39–43), since the people, like the land, were properly Yahweh's own possession and could not become the property of another. The needy man, remaining free, could become an economic dependent (*tôšāb*)—e.g., by working the land for his keep—or he could become a wage earner (*šākîr*), but only until the time of the jubilee in either case. This law is a modification of earlier legislation, which permitted Israelites to become slaves of their own people, at least for a limited length of time (Exod 21:2–11; Deut 15:12–18). According to vv 44–46, the Hebrews were allowed slaves of foreign origin procured either outside the country or from among the resident aliens. Such individuals lost their freedom and became personal property to the extent that they could be willed to one's heirs. Since the law forbade the enslavement of one Israelite to another, there remained the question of a Hebrew who "sold" himself to a resident foreigner (vv 47–55). In such a case, the former was to be treated respectfully as a wage earner (v 53) and not as a slave. During his time as such, he could be redeemed by either a relative or himself. In the latter case the payment was determined in terms of the years of service left before the next jubilee by a distribution of the original sale price over the years, with proportionate deductions made for past years' services. The cost of redemption depended on the years (many or few) before the next jubilee. If he and his offspring were not liberated beforehand, they were released at the jubilee.

The question arises how these jubilee directives (land return, resolution of debts, liberation of slaves) could have been practically carried out in any advanced state of social development. In truth, the OT records no historical observance of the jubilee. The reference to it in Ezek 46:17 (and possibly in Isa 61:1–2) is in a future ideal context, which is probably the key to the jubilee itself. Although we cannot exclude the possibility of its being observed in the early years of the land's occupation, its presence here is best explained as a social blueprint, founded on the deeply religious concepts of justice and equality, which strove to apply the simple sabbatical principle to a society that had become more economically complex. It was drawn up and added to the Holiness Code in the period after the exile. Although not realized in the letter, its spirit of appreciation for personal rights and human dignity synthesizes much of OT teaching.

54   **(J) Sanctions (26:1–46).** The Code of Holiness terminates with the promise of blessings for fidelity to its precepts (vv 3–13) and punishment for their disregard (vv 14–39), sharing this type of conclusion with the Deuteronomic code (Deut 28) and the book of the covenant (Exod 23:20–33); however, the latter contains only blessings. In this respect the law codes follow the vassal treaty form of the 2d millennium in which a superior political power concluded the terms of his written agreement with curses and blessings. The apparent dependence in certain ideas and expressions on Ezek strongly suggests a later edited form.

A final admonition precedes the benedictions in vv 1–2, negatively by enjoining avoidance of idolatry in any form and positively by urging recognition of Yahweh's sole dominion through sabbath observance and respect for his presence among them (19:1–4). The blessings (vv 2–13) center chiefly on fertility of the soil (vv 3–5,10), with the abundant yield of the harvest presented in vivid, if exaggerated, imagery (cf. Amos 9:13). The people's future is described as a life of peace and accord with the forces of nature and easy victory over their foes (vv 6–8), abundant offspring (v 9), and crowned with the inestimable blessing of the Lord's presence (v 12). Such favor is viewed wholly in terms of the Sinai alliance (v 9b), the outcome of their deliverance from Egyptian bondage (v 13).

The sanctions for disregard of the law (vv 14–39), more numerous and detailed than the blessings, clearly reflect the chapter's period of composition during Judah's critical last years. The predicted chastisements are set forth in a rising crescendo, in a style similar to that of the Egyptian plagues (Exod 7:14–11:10). A reverse in many ways of the promised blessings, the threats include disease, the destruction of crops by overrunning hordes (vv 16–17), and agricultural failure from lack of rain (vv 18–20). **18.** *sevenfold:* Seven was the perfect number; hence, complete and comprehensive destruction is indicated. There would be also the return of wild beasts to decimate the population and its livestock (vv 21–22). The ominous pace is stepped up with the threatened simultaneous attack of enemy, disease, and famine (vv 23–26). **25.** *the sword, the avenger of my covenant:* We have here the reverse of v 9b. Punishment, like favor, was not arbitrary but was demanded by the very terms of the covenant. **26.** *ten women will need but one oven:* Ordinarily each family had its own oven; during the catastrophe there would be but one-tenth the normal supply of bread.

Obstinacy in sin launches the final measure (vv 27–35). Famine will reduce them to cannibalism, the consumption of their own offspring (v 29; Deut 28:53; Jer 19:9; Ezek 5:10; 2 Kgs 6:28ff.), and they will suffer a destruction of their sites of pagan cult (v 30), their cities, and their sanctuaries (v 31) so frightening as to appall even their invaders (v 32). Dispersion and exile will be their lot (v 33). In the actual historical context of the chapter's composition, the disregard of the more primitive sabbatical legislation is noteworthy (vv 34–35; see comment on 25:1–7). The defenseless lot of those dispersed in foreign lands will be one of constant apprehension and terror; finally they will be lost in their pagan surroundings (vv 36–39). Just as their unity as a people hinges on the presence of Yahweh in their midst (cf. vv 11–13), when he turns his back on them they quickly lose their national identity.

Yet the punishment will not be terminal but medicinal (vv 40–45). Despite Israel's infidelity, Yahweh will, in the last analysis, remain always true to the covenant made with the patriarchs and faithful to the land, an integral part of the promise (v 42). Moreover, the abandonment of the land would not be viewed as a chastisement of the sacred soil; this was to be its opportunity for a renewal of its life-giving forces, formerly precluded through disregard of the sabbatical (v 43). The notion of survival, for at least part of the population, in view of the covenant, is a most important OT theme; its expression here is strikingly similar to Ezek 16:53–63.

55   (VI) Redemption of Votive Offerings (27:1-34). This appendix modifies a number of its laws in the light of later practice. Any vow carried with it a solemn obligation of fulfillment (Num 30:2-3; Deut 23:22-24), but gradually in postexilic times the tendency grew to convert personal and real property commitments into their monetary equivalents. Regulations regarding such commutation are given detailed treatment here.

From early times it was possible to vow a person to the Lord, i.e., to the sanctuary, where his services would be used for liturgical ceremonies (1 Sam 1:11). Since, after the exile, such functions were performed solely by the Levites, it seems to have been customary to redeem persons so dedicated. Such was the normal procedure for the consecrated firstborn (Exod 13:2,12-13). Verses 1-8 specify the amount to be paid, and the sum was determined by the person's capacity to work. Thus the highest figure was for a man between 20 and 60 with proportionately descending values placed on a woman, a young man, a young girl, the elderly, and male and female children. The exact worth of a shekel cannot be determined accurately (cf. G. J. Wenham, *ZAW* 90 [1978] 264-65). These determined sums were not invariable; in extenuating circumstances the priest could arrive at a satisfactory figure (v 8).

In the case of animal offerings (vv 9-13), a distinction is made between the clean—i.e., fit for sacrifice (see comment on 1:2)—and the unclean animal. In the former case (vv 9-10), the offering made the animal sacred, and no form of exchange or commutation was permitted. If substitution with another animal were attempted, the offerer would suffer the loss of both. In the latter case (vv 11-13), since such were presented simply as a nonsacrificial gift, the priest determined the animal's value, to which a 20 percent tax was affixed if redemption were sought later.

Real property in the form of buildings or land could also be vowed (vv 14-24). The priest determined a house's worth, which served as the exchange price with the added 20 percent (vv 14-15). In the case of land (vv 16-24), hereditary property was distinguished from that acquired by purchase. Should a man vow part of his patrimony, the field's monetary value would be put at 50 shekels for each portion of the land capable of yielding one homor (about 11 bu.) of barley. The Hebrew of v 16 reads: "Your valuation shall be in accord with the amount of its seed [crop]; the seed [crop] of a homor of barley at 50 silver shekels." De Vaux contends that if this verse were to be interpreted as a reference to the seed sown, the price of the field would be absurdly low (*AI* 198-99). The customary valuation was in terms of the

harvest (cf. 25:16b). Since the consecration was temporary, expiring at the time of the jubilee, the land was assessed at full value only when donated at the beginning of a jubilee period; if the land was donated sometime later, the value was determined solely by the prejubilee years remaining (vv 17-18). With the price thus established, the field could be redeemed prior to the jubilee by paying the fixed sum plus an additional one-fifth (v 19). Priestly rights were protected against transfer of ownership in the interim; if such occurred, all rights of redemption ceased, and at the time of the jubilee the field became the property of the priests (vv 20-21). **21.** *doomed (ḥērem):* It may be read "to separate," "to set aside," "to leave exclusively for the Lord." In its earliest OT use, it was applied to the fruits of war, set aside for the Lord by being destined for doom and destruction. By extension, anything vowed to the Lord could be said to be "doomed." In the case of property acquired (vv 22-24), another man's patrimony could be vowed, with payment made at once to the sanctuary based on the field's estimated value in terms of the remaining prejubilee years. At the time of the jubilee it reverted to the original owner. All monetary transactions were to follow the official Temple standard (v 25).

Every firstborn male animal belonged to the Lord by right (Exod 13:2,12; 34:19; Num 18:15) and thus could not become the object of a vow (vv 26-27). The clean animals were sacrificed (Num 18:17), whereas the unclean could be redeemed or sold by the priests. Money is the only term of exchange here, no mention being made of the animal substitution elsewhere allowed in certain cases (Exod 13:13; 34:20).

Likewise the exclusive property of the Lord (in the adverse sense of "doomed"; see comment on v 21) were those persons or things under one's domain with which contact was forbidden, especially idolaters and their goods (Exod 22:19; Deut 13:13-19). Because such evil was worthy of extinction, the malefactors and their goods were to be set aside for the Lord (doomed) and could be neither sold nor redeemed (vv 28-29).

The practice of tithing (vv 30-33) provided for the needs of the Levites (Num 18:21,24) as well as of the poor (Deut 26:12); this 10 percent of all farm produce was not considered a voluntary offering. Redemption, however, was permitted for grain and fruit tithes at determined value plus 20 percent. Only clean animals were taken as tithes. They were chosen by a process of impartial selection, and attempted substitution resulted in the loss of the original and its substitute. Verse 34 is the book's second conclusion (cf. 26:46), an addendum to the appendix linking its material with the Sinai legislation.

5

NUMBERS

Conrad E. L'Heureux

BIBLIOGRAPHY

1 Budd, P. J., *Numbers* (WBC 5; Waco, 1984). Burns, R. J., *Exodus, Leviticus, Numbers* (OTM 3; Wilmington, 1983). Coats, G. W., *Rebellion in the Wilderness* (Nash, 1968). Fritz, V., *Israel in der Wüste* (Marburg, 1970). W. Harrelson, "Guidance in the Wilderness," *Int* 13 (1959) 24-36. Kellermann, D., *Die Priesterschrift von Numeri 1:1 bis 10:10* (Berlin, 1970). Noth, M., *Numbers: A Commentary* (OTL; London, 1968). Snaith, N. H., *Leviticus and Numbers* (NCB; London, 1967). Sturdy, J., *Numbers* (CBC; Cambridge, 1976). De Vaulx, J., *Les Nombres* (SB; Paris, 1972).

INTRODUCTION

2 **(I) Title and Composition.** The Eng title of the book goes back to the designation *arithmoi* given to it in the ancient Gk transl. This Gk word, meaning "numbers," was apparently chosen in reference to the census figures in chaps. 1 and 26 as well as arithmetical data elsewhere in the book. It has the disadvantage of accentuating what is, after all, a relatively small percentage of a work that also contains extensive narrative, poetry, and legal materials. The Hebr designation *bĕmidbar*, "in the wilderness," is a prep. phrase taken from the first verse of the book and reflects a more comprehensive view of its contents.

3 The problems of authorship and redactional history are part of the overall question of the first five books (→ Pentateuch, 1:4-8). As for what concerns Num in particular, we may note that there is a very heavy preponderance of Priestly (P) material including 1:1-10:28; 15; 17-19; 26-31; and 33-36. Earlier, non-Priestly material is found in 10:29-12:16 and 21-24. The remaining chapters have both Priestly and earlier components.

Within the Priestly sections, it is often possible to discern passages that are relatively later than the main P composition. Many analysts employ the hypothesis that a foundational Priestly work (PG) received a series of supplements (PS) later in the redactional history of the Pentateuch. Such, however, is not the only possible approach, and a major commentary by P. Budd argues that the whole can be understood as essentially the work of one Priestly "author," who shaped the book of Num with at least a degree of independence from the other books of the Pentateuch. These issues cannot be settled at present, and in the following commentary we shall be content simply to point out the contributions that a scholarly consensus regards as belonging to the later layers of Priestly work.

The earlier, non-Priestly materials were subdivided into J and E (and sometimes additional sources) by the classical Pentateuchal criticism. Within Num, however, the distinction between J and E is particularly difficult to establish. There is a tendency within recent publications to refer to all the earlier material as J or Yahwist. At present, the wisest course is to practice a great deal of caution regarding these matters.

4 **(II) Historicity.** It is generally agreed by historians that the final canonical presentation of Israel's story as a march of all twelve tribes from Egypt, through the wilderness, around the Dead Sea, ending with a massive invasion of Canaan from the east, constitutes a great simplification of what actually happened. The exact position one takes regarding this issue of how Israel came to exist in the settled land (→ History, 75:55-56) will largely determine how one approaches the historicity of Num. There is no doubt that this literature, especially P, is much more concerned with later problems of theology and community organization than with presenting objective history. In the middle of the 20th century there was a tendency among scholars, especially those influenced by W. F. Albright, to argue in favor of historicity on the basis of archaeological discoveries. The trend toward the end of the century is to be much more skeptical of the support allegedly provided by archaeology. Although there are undoubtedly ancient traditions preserved in Num, they have been so extensively reworked for later purposes that one must be exceedingly cautious in drawing conclusions about presettlement history based on the data preserved in the book.

5   (III) Theological Concepts. A major function of Num in its final Priestly form is to provide validation of the religious practice and organization of postexilic Judaism by tracing its institutions back to the time of Moses and the wilderness wandering. As such, the work may be seen as theological apologetic supporting the claims of the group that came into power during the restoration period. On a deeper level, Num exhibits the Priestly conviction that the great blessing which God bestows upon his people is the very fact that, as the Holy One, he dwells among his people. The whole cultic system is a divine gift that allows for atonement of human sin. Only this ritual means of reconciliation makes it possible for human beings to live in proximity to the tabernacling God without being destroyed by the awesome and terrifying power of holiness. The encampment of the tribes around the tent in the wilderness foreshadows the settlement that will eventually take place within the land. The dynamic orientation toward this land embodies the final goal to which Israel is called and toward which the whole Priestly work points (see W. Brueggemann, *The Land* [Phl, 1977]). The account of the wilderness period, then, provides an occasion to document God's plan for and care of his people. At the same time, both the Priestly and the earlier traditions employed the stories of the wilderness period as a way of providing typical or paradigmatic examples of how the people sin and rebel against God and his appointed representatives.

Perhaps the most enduring religious teaching of Num is that it is indeed possible to be God's people while still on the march, not yet at home. Whether one thinks of the life journey of each person toward individuation and wholeness or of the corporate experience of the community of believers, the place where Israel stands in Num is the place where all believers find themselves. Liberated from slavery, they journey toward the land of promise. The hardship and responsibility of freedom often incline the faithful to resist their own progress and long for the comfort of subservience. The example of ancient Israel can motivate them to fidelity as they continue moving on to the land to which they are called.

6   (IV) Outline. Earlier scholars often described Num as a collection of disconnected parts that lacked any logical order. More recent commentaries, especially those of Budd and de Vaulx, have demonstrated that it is indeed possible to find underlying principles of organization. Nonetheless, the construction of an outline remains difficult and reflects decisions that are sometimes rather arbitrary. The following has been heavily influenced by the outline presented in de Vaulx (*Nombres* 427–31).

(I) Organization of the Community before Its Departure from Sinai (1:1–10:10)
   (A) Census and Organization of the Community (1:1–4:49)
     (a) The First Census (1:1–47)
     (b) Distinctive Role of the Levites (1:48–54)
     (c) Layout of the Camp and Order of the March (2:1–34)
     (d) Organization of the Priestly Hierarchy (3:1–51)
     (e) Census and Responsibilities of the Levites (4:1–49)
   (B) Purity of the Camp and the Community (5:1–6:27)
     (a) Exclusion of the Impure (5:1–4)
     (b) Restitution for Offenses against Neighbor (5:5–10)

     (c) Ordeal for a Woman Suspected of Adultery (5:11–31)
     (d) The Nazirite Vow (6:1–21)
     (e) The Priestly Blessing (6:22–27)
   (C) Cultic Preparations for the Departure from Sinai (7:1–10:10)
     (a) Offerings Made by Tribal Representatives (7:1–89)
     (b) The Lampstand (8:1–4)
     (c) Purification of the Levites (8:5–26)
     (d) Concerning Passover (9:1–14)
     (e) The Cloud (9:15–23)
     (f) The Trumpets (10:1–10)

(II) March through the Desert: Sinai to the Plains of Moab (10:11–21:35)
   (A) From Sinai to the Desert of Paran (10:11–12:16)
     (a) Departure from Sinai (10:11–28)
     (b) Hobab and the Ark (10:29–36)
     (c) Taberah (11:1–3)
     (d) The Quail, the Seventy Elders, Eldad and Medad (11:4–35)
     (e) Miriam and Aaron Rebel against Moses (12:1–16)
   (B) At the Threshold of the Promised Land (13:1–15:41)
     (a) Exploration of the Promised Land and Setback (13:1–14:45)
     (b) Various Cultic Ordinances (15:1–41)
   (C) Revolt of Korah, Dathan, and Abiram; Status and Role of Priests (16:1–19:22)
     (a) Revolt of Korah, Dathan, and Abiram (16:1–35)
     (b) The Covering for the Altar (17:1–5 [RSV 16:36–40])
     (c) The Intercession of Aaron (17:6–15 [RSV 16:41–50])
     (d) Aaron's Staff (17:16–28 [RSV 17:1–13])
     (e) The Dues of the Priests and Levites (18:1–32)
     (f) The Red Heifer and the Water of Purification (19:1–22)
   (D) From Kadesh to the Plains of Moab (20:1–21:35)
     (a) The Waters of Meribah (20:1–13)
     (b) Negotiations with the King of Edom (20:14–21)
     (c) Death of Aaron (20:22–29)
     (d) Battle with the Canaanites at Hormah (21:1–3)
     (e) The Fiery Serpents (21:4–9)
     (f) Itinerary Stages through Transjordan (21:10–20)
     (g) The Defeat of Sihon and Og (21:21–35)

(III) On the Plains of Moab: Preparation for Entry into the Land (22:1–36:13)
   (A) The Story of Balaam (22:1–24:25)
     (a) Balaq Sends for Balaam (22:1–21)
     (b) Balaam's Ass (22:21–35)
     (c) Meeting of Balaam and Balaq (22:36–40)
     (d) First Oracle at Bamoth Baal (22:41–23:12)
     (e) Second Oracle at Mt. Pisgah (23:13–26)
     (f) Third Oracle on Peor (23:27–24:9)
     (g) Fourth Oracle of Balaam (24:10–19)
     (h) Concluding Oracles (24:20–25)
   (B) Apostasy at Baal Peor (25:1–18)
   (C) Preparation for Conquest and Division of the Land (25:19–36:13)
     (a) The Second Census (25:19–26:65)
     (b) The Daughters of Zelophehad (27:1–11)
     (c) Commissioning of Joshua (27:12–23)
     (d) The Ritual Calendar (28:1–30:1)
     (e) Vows Made by Women (30:2–17)
     (f) The Holy War against Midian (31:1–54)
     (g) Settlement of Gad and Reuben (32:1–42)
     (h) Overview of the Desert Itinerary (33:1–49)
     (i) Apportionment of the Land of Canaan (33:50–35:34)
     (j) The Daughters of Zelophehad (36:1–13)

COMMENTARY

7 **(I) Organization of the Community before Its Departure from Sinai (1:1–10:10).** The first part of Num describes the events and legislation that constituted Israel as an organized sacral community under the priestly hierarchy. Even though they are not yet in possession of the promised land, they are fully equipped to function as the worshiping community of Yahweh. By thus illustrating that it is possible to be God's people on the march, the Priestly traditionists offered hope to exilic and postexilic Jews as well as a message of enduring significance for the self-understanding of the Christian community.

(A) Census and Organization of the Community (1:1–4:49). In preparation for departure, a census is taken of adult males able to bear arms. These are divided into four regiments each consisting of three tribes, and the order of their encampment around the Tent of Meeting is specified. The text clarifies the relationship between priests and Levites and describes their respective duties regarding the Tent of Meeting.

8 (a) THE FIRST CENSUS (1:1–47). As frequently occurs in Priestly narratives, the structure revolves around a command from God (vv 2–4) and the account of its execution (vv 17–19). Within this framework we find the list of tribal leaders and the census list. It is quite likely that both of these lists are older than the narrative context, but their exact age and provenience are uncertain. The order in which the tribes were listed in the Priestly account of Gen 35:23–26 corresponded to the order in which the twelve sons of Jacob were born to their mothers. Here in Num 1:32–35, however, Joseph is divided into the two subtribes Ephraim and Manasseh to make up for the fact that Levi is no longer counted as one of the twelve. Furthermore, Naphtali and Asher have exchanged positions. M. Noth argued (*Numbers* 18–19) that the personal names occurring here are of an ancient type and that we have a list of the tribal representatives (*nĕśî'îm;* see E. A. Speiser, *CBQ* 25 [1963] 111–17) who functioned in the amphictyonic organization of Israel during the period of the Judges. Unfortunately, there are many uncertainties in evaluating the age of the names (see Budd, *Numbers* 4–6). The results of the census are reported in repetitious and stereotypical formulas (vv 20–46), with only minor inconsistencies as one goes from tribe to tribe. The sequence of tribes is identical to the list of leaders (vv 5–15) except that Gad is placed with its proper regiment in anticipation of 2:10–16. Critical scholars are unanimous in viewing the numbers given in this list as impossibly high and have proposed a number of theories to account for them. (1) Albright suggested (*JPOS* 5 [1925] 17–54) that we have a record of a census taken at a later period, specifically, a variant of the census taken by David according to 2 Sam 24:1–9. However, the numbers seem too high even for the time of David. (2) Others take the total figure of 603,550 as an example of gematria, i.e., play on the numerical value of the letters in certain words: the consonants in *bny yśr'l,* "sons of Israel," add up to 603, and those in *kl r'š,* "every head" add up to 550 if the quiescent *aleph* in *r'š* is ignored. However, there is no evidence that the letters of the alphabet had these numerical values during the period in which the Priestly authors worked. (3) G. Mendenhall (*JBL* 77 [1958] 52–66) built upon the fact that the Hebr word for "thousand," *'elep* sometimes refers to a subdivision

within a tribe (e.g., Judg 6:15 and Mic 5:1). If the same word in our passage were taken to mean something like "contingent," then the total given for Reuben, e.g., could be read as "46 contingents with a total of 500 men," instead of "46,500 men." This approach leads to results that are difficult to explain, for on its reckoning, the contingents from the tribe of Gad averaged 14 men while those from Simeon had only 5! In any case, the total given in v 46 requires that the word *'elep* be taken in its numerical sense. (4) Budd (*Numbers* 8–9) points to the fact that the Priestly writers were aware of older Yahwistic traditions which gave a round number of 600,000, presumably for the total population of the exodus generation (Exod 12:37; Num 11:21). On the other hand, the Priestly calculation of the amount of silver required for the bases and hooks of the tabernacle came to 301,775 shekels (Exod 38:26–28). Using the postexilic rate of a one-half shekel tax for each adult male leads to the figure 603,550. Having reached this total, the priests would have distributed the number among the twelve tribes in proportions that seemed plausible to them.

9 (b) DISTINCTIVE ROLE OF THE LEVITES (1:48–54). This redactional passage anticipates matters that will be developed in 2:1–34 and 3:1–4:49. The Priestly conception of the Levites, emphasizing their distinctiveness in contrast to both the lay tribes and the sons of Aaron, marks the culmination of a long development of thought (→ Institutions, 76:18–20); see A. H. J. Gunneweg, *Leviten und Priester* [FRLANT 89; Göttingen, 1965]; and A. Cody, *A History of Old Testament Priesthood* [AnBib 35; Rome, 1969]). **50.** *the dwelling of the testimony:* This rare expression occurs three times here and also in Exod 38:21 and Num 10:11. The Hebr word *miškān* focuses on the tabernacle's function as "dwelling place" of the Lord. *'ēdūt,* "testimony," refers to the tablets of the law. **53.** The circle of specially purified Levites protects the lay community from danger which would come from unauthorized contact with the holiness of the sanctuary. The concept of wrath (Hebr *qeṣep*) preserves a vestige of a primitive religious thought in which the sacred is an impersonal, irrational power that threatens to destroy those who have not been properly prepared to handle it (cf. 1 Sam 6:19; 2 Sam 6:6–8; Num 8:19).

10 (c) LAYOUT OF THE CAMP AND ORDER OF THE MARCH (2:1–34). The list in vv 3–31 combines information from the two lists of 1:5–15 and 1:20–47. It is introduced by vv 1–2, and vv 32–34 are a summary and comment. The order of tribes corresponds to that in 1:20–47 except that the three tribes of the Judah group are listed first because they have the position of honor to the east of the tabernacle. **17.** The position of the tabernacle in the middle of the camp reflects a central theological concern of the P tradition. The great blessing which is the goal of Yahweh's interaction with Israel is God's dwelling with his people. This tabernacling of God foreshadows the theology of John 1:14. Older pentateuchal tradition placed the tent outside the camp as in Exod 33:7.

11 (d) ORGANIZATION OF THE PRIESTLY HIERARCHY (3:1–51). The preeminence of the sons of Aaron in postexilic life requires that they be mentioned (vv 1–4) before the Levites, who are really the main topic of the chapter. In contrast to Exod 6:16–25 and Num 26:57–61, the fact that Aaron was descended from Levi

through Kohath is passed over in silence in order to
highlight the distinction between priests and Levites. On
Nadab and Abihu, see Lev 10:1–5. In vv 5–10, the relationship of Levites to priests is defined in a manner that
insists on the superiority of the latter. In contrast to Ezek
44:11–16, there is no hint that the subordination of the
Levites is a punishment. The dignity of the levitical office
is emphasized in vv 11–13 by the theological explanation
(based on Exod 13:11–16 [J]) that sees them as a
substitute for the firstborn. Some commentators find a
tension between the concept that the Levites belong to
the Lord and the statement in v 8 that they are given to
Aaron. In vv 14–39, we have a divine command (vv
14–15) followed by an execution report (v 16) introducing a genealogy of the Levites (cf. Exod 6:16–25).
This is elaborated with additional information including
census figures for males one month and older; position
of encampment; names of clan leaders and detailed
responsibilities of the Gershonites, Kohathites, and
Merarites—the three principal levitical groups of the
postexilic period. The intention of vv 40–51 is to
guarantee that the postexilic custom of monetary
redemption of the firstborn not be invalidated by the
levitical substitution of vv 11–13. As was the case for the
other tribes in 1:20–46, the total figure of 22,000 Levites
is impossibly large, and in this case the explanation based
on *'elep* as "contingent" rather than "thousand" will not
work. On the other hand, the total of 22,273 firstborn
for the lay tribes fits poorly with the 603,550 total in
1:46. There would have to be about 40 sons in each
family!

12   (e) Census and Responsibilities of the
Levites (4:1–49). A second census of the Levites counts
those who are of age for active service in the sanctuary.
The specification of 30 to 50 years contrasts with Num
8:23–26, where the span is 25 to 50. Other texts speak
of levitical service beginning at 20 (1 Chr 23:24; 2 Chr
31:17; Ezra 3:8). Within the census report is inserted
information about the responsibilities of each group of
Levites, especially in connection with the transport of
the sanctuary. Special emphasis is put on the fact that
Levites may not touch or even look upon the holiest
objects, which are carefully wrapped by the Aaronids
before being carried by the Kohathites. Just as the cordon
of Levites around the sanctuary protects the lay tribes
from dangerous exposure to holiness, the sons of Aaron
protect the Levites (vv 15,19–20). Both the effort to limit
access of the Kohathites and the statement of v 18 in
behalf of their rights probably reflect attempts to resolve
conflicts between rival priestly claims which arose in the
postexilic period.

13   (B) Purity of the Camp and the Community (5:1–6:27). The account of the community's
organization in preparation for departure from Sinai is
interrupted by a short collection of rather diverse legal
materials relating to purity within the camp.

(a) Exclusion of the Impure (5:1–4). Lev
13–14 dealt extensively with the diagnosis of skin
diseases and the uncleanness which they cause, specifying exclusion from the camp as a consequence (Lev
13:46). The present passage adds bodily discharges (cf.
Lev 15) and contact with a corpse as reasons for expulsion. The origin of the sense of abhorrence connected
with these phenomena is only partly understood (see M.
Douglas, *Purity and Danger* [London, 1966]). From
Christian and humanistic perspectives, it is difficult to
understand how sickness and closeness to God could be
mutually exclusive. **2.** Hebr *ṣārûaʿ*, traditionally translated "leprous," refers to a variety of skin diseases,
especially those involving open sores.

14   (b) Restitution for Offenses against
Neighbor (5:5–10). Restoration of harmony between
persons through restitution is an additional requirement
for maintenance of purity and order within God's community. The passage depends on Lev 5, though it adds
the stipulation that if the injured person has died with no
surviving heir, the restitution is to be made to the priest.
15   (c) Ordeal for a Woman Suspected of
Adultery (5:11–31). A ritual procedure provides the
means of convicting or exculpating a wife suspected of
unfaithfulness (see W. McKane, *VT* 30 [1980] 474–92;
T. Frymer-Kensky, *VT* 34 [1984] 11–26; J. Milgrom,
VT 35 [1985] 368–69). The lack of smoothness in the
text and the presence of repetitions suggest that two
originally separate rituals have been combined (de
Vaulx, *Nombres* 93–95). One involved the drinking of the
bitter waters; the other combined a grain offering with
a curse. The woman was proved guilty if these procedures led to ill effects. Since this would occur only if
the woman's psychological state induced physiological
reactions, the ritual itself was harmless. On the other
hand, the practice demonstrates the double standard of
patriarchal societies in which a man has the right to
submit his wife to a humiliating procedure. **18.** *the waters
of bitterness:* The phrase can also be translated "waters of
testing," which would fit somewhat better in vv 24 and
27, where the construction is different (cf. D. Pardee, *VT*
35 [1985] 112–15). **21.** *your thigh fall away and your body
swell:* Perhaps a euphemism for miscarriage.
16   (d) The Nazirite Vow (6:1–21). Dedication
to God as a Nazirite was a lifelong commitment, perhaps
originally connected with the holy war (→ Institutions,
76:111). The postexilic Priestly legislation transformed
the institution into a means whereby any person could
take on a special religious dedication of self for a specified
span of time. In case of contact with a corpse (vv 9–12),
the period of the vow began anew after the Nazirite had
undergone a purification ritual. The regulation here
seems to ignore the exclusion from the camp stipulated
in 5:1–3 and the water ritual of 19:11–13, depending
instead on Lev 12–15. The ritual accompanying the
conclusion of the vow (vv 13–20) exhibits contacts both
in content and in formulation with Lev 6–7; 12–15.
17   (e) The Priestly Blessing (6:22–27). The
Priestly blessing (cf. Lev 9:22–23) reflects God's
response to the maintenance of purity and the generous
voluntary dedication of the community as provided for
in 5:1–6:21. The Hebr text of the blessing itself probably
preserves preexilic oral tradition and exhibits polished
poetic style (cf. Ps 67:1; Sir 50:20–21; and see P. D.
Miller, *Int* 29 [1975] 240–51; D. N. Freedman, *NFL*
35–48; M. Fishbane, *JAOS* 103 [1983] 115–21; P. A. H.
de Boer, *VT* 32 [1982] 3–13). The right of invoking
Yahweh's name upon the community is here reserved to
the sons of Aaron, a postexilic development that restricted
earlier practice (cf. 2 Sam 6:18; 1 Kgs 8:14; Deut 10:8;
21:5). **25.** The concept of the shining of God's face or
presence perhaps had its original setting within the
liturgical theophany. **26.** The lifting of God's face is a
favorable gesture (cf. Pss 4:7; 33:18; 34:16). In times of
distress, it was believed that God had "hidden his face"
and abandoned his people (see Deut 31:18; Pss 30:8;
44:25; 104:29). *peace:* Hebr *šālôm* has a broader and richer
meaning more adequately reflected by the Eng words
"wholeness" and "well-being."

(C) Cultic Preparations for the Departure
from Sinai (7:1–10:10).
18   (a) Offerings Made by Tribal Representatives (7:1–89). The dedication of the tabernacle took
place on the first day of the first month of the second year
(Exod 40:17), a month prior to the date given for the

census in Num 1:1. The offerings that had been made at that time are formulated in terms that presume information given in Num 1–4, and their placement here presents them as the community's commitment to the priestly theocracy as described in earlier chapters of Num. The passage comes from one of the latest phases in the redaction of Num and presents an idealized reconstruction with extraordinarily lavish offerings over a period of twelve days. **89.** The verse reports the fulfillment of the promise made in Exod 25:22, but fits awkwardly in the context. Perhaps its placement here is due to the conviction that God's self-revelation over the propitiatory which covered the Ark became possible after the consecration of the altar was completed by the offering of the sacrifices listed in vv 10–88.

19 (b) THE LAMPSTAND (8:1–4). Aaron executes the command of Exod 27:21 and Lev 24:2–4 (see also Exod 30:8) that he and his sons should care for the lamps and the lampstand. The information contained here recapitulates material elaborated in Exod 25:31–40 and 37:17–24. See C. L. Meyers, *The Tabernacle Menorah* (AASOR 2; Missoula, 1976).

20 (c) PURIFICATION OF THE LEVITES (8:5–26). The Levites undergo a ritual of purification that is analogous to the ordination of priests and shows some contacts with Exod 29 and Lev 8 (see also Lev 14:7–8). The theological understanding of the role of the Levites is based on 3:5–13. **10.** Laying on of hands is absent from Exod 29 and Lev 8 and thus is not an ordination rite. It should rather be understood in terms of the laying of hands on the head of the sacrificial victim in the case of sin offerings (Lev 4:4,15,24,29,33). The Levites are offered to God as substitutes for the people (see M. C. Sansom, *ExpTim* 94 [1983] 323–26). **23.** In contrast to 4:23, the age of entry into service is set at 25, perhaps reflecting the practice of a historical period in which a shortage of personnel required a lowering of the age requirement.

21 (d) CONCERNING PASSOVER (9:1–14). As in a number of other passages (27:1–11; 36:1–12) a narrative about a specific case raises a juridical problem which is taken before the Lord, whose decision provides a general rule for the future. The problem arises because persons impure through contact with a corpse would be unable to celebrate Passover (→ Institutions, 76:123–127). The difficulty is resolved by providing for a second Passover, one month later, which would also meet the needs of persons who missed the first one because of travel. The regulations summarized in this passage are based on Exod 12. The Passover motif connects with the preceding chapter, which dealt with the Levites as substitutes for the firstborn (cf. Ezra 6:16–22). **1.** The date provided takes us back one month before the date of the census in 1:1. **13.** Lest the exceptions allowed for in this regulation encourage laxity, a penalty of excommunication is provided for failure to observe the Passover of the first month whenever possible. **14.** The resident alien (*gēr*) is allowed to partake of the Passover; contrast the restrictions in Exod 12:43,45.

22 (e) THE CLOUD (9:15–23). Immediately prior to the account of departure from Sinai we find information regarding the cloud that gave guidance on the journey (9:15–23) and the silver trumpets that signaled the beginning of the march (10:1–10). The older J and E traditions knew of the guidance provided by the pillar of cloud by day and the pillar of fire by night, as well as the pillar's function signaling God's presence in the tent (Exod 13:21–22; 14:19–20,24; 33:7–11). The Priestly tradition incorporates these elements and links them with its theology of the divine presence: the transcendent God manifests himself in the form of his glory (*kābôd*), which is both signified and concealed by the cloud (Exod 16:10; 24:15–18; 40:34–35; cf. 1 Kgs 8:10–11). The description of the movements of the cloud takes up and elaborates Exod 40:36–40. The constant vigilance required by the unpredictability in the movement of the cloud suggests the universal need for sensitivity to the subtle promptings which provide guidance in the spiritual journey.

23 (f) THE TRUMPETS (10:1–10). After discussion of the cloud, a second means of signaling the people is mentioned: the trumpet of beaten metal which, in postexilic times, replaced in part the earlier ram's horn. When both trumpets are sounded, the community assembles at the Tent, whereas a single trumpet summons just the chiefs (vv 3–4). On the other hand, a different manner of blowing the trumpets provides a signal for setting out on the march (vv 5–7). This "alarm" is designated by the Hebr word *tĕrû ʿâ*, which is used elsewhere for the terror-inspiring battle cry (Josh 6:5; 1 Sam 17:20) which also accompanied movement of the Ark (1 Sam 4:5; 2 Sam 6:15). The two modalities will also be characteristic after Israel has settled in the land: the first manner will announce liturgical convocation (cf. 29:1); the alarm modality will be used in warfare (vv 9–10).

(II) The March through the Desert: Sinai to the Plains of Moab (10:11–21:35).

(A) From Sinai to the Desert of Paran (10:11–12:16).

24 (a) DEPARTURE FROM SINAI (10:11–28). The Israelites set out following the cloud, in keeping with 9:15–23, and with the four groups of three tribes each in the order and with the leaders previously listed in 2:1–34. The discrepancy between 2:17 and 10:17–21 regarding the order of groups in the march is usually taken as an indication of different redactional layers within the Priestly material (so de Vaulx, *Nombres* 141–43). **12.** The itinerary formula here is part of a chain of references to the stations on the way from Egypt to the land of promise. The series provides organizational structure for material in Exod and Num. See G. W. Coats, *CBQ* 34 (1972) 135–52; J. T. Walsh, *CBQ* 39 (1977) 20–33; G. I. Davies, *The Way of the Wilderness* (SOTSMS 5; Cambridge, 1979) and *VT* 33 (1983) 1–13.

25 (b) HOBAB AND THE ARK (10:29–36). This section interrupts and contradicts the preceding material. Most notably, the statement of v 33 that the Ark went before the people to seek a place for them conflicts with the view in vv 11–28 that the cloud went before the people whereas the Ark was carried between the second and third groups of tribes. For the first time in the book of Num we have material that does not belong to Priestly tradition. Most scholars agree that the section is to be assigned to J. **29.** The Hebr word translated "father-in-law," i.e., *ḥōtēn*, can be taken as referring to Hobab (in agreement with Judg 4:11) or to Reuel (in agreement with Exod 2:18). To complicate matters further, the father-in-law of Moses is called Jethro in Exod 3:1; 4:18; 18:1. Various attempts have been made to harmonize these passages (W. F. Albright, *CBQ* 25 [1963] 1–11; T. C. Mitchell, *VT* 19 [1969] 93–112). **31–32.** Presumably, Hobab accepts the second invitation (see Judg 1:16). **35–36.** The transl. of these verses is made difficult by the presence of archaic orthography and possible textual corruption. The fragments of archaic liturgical poetry (cf. Ps 68:2) reflect the custom of carrying the Ark in procession (Ps 132:8; 2 Sam 6:3–5,12–17; 1 Kgs 8:3–11) especially as a palladium of war which accompanied the army (Jos 3:6; 6:12–13; 1 Sam 4:1–11).

26 (c) TABERAH (11:1–3). In form, we have an etiological tale that accounts for the place name Taberah (burning) by telling of the burning anger of the Lord which broke out there. (See B. S. Childs, *VT* 24 [1974] 387-97; F. W. Golka, *VT* 26 [1976] 410-28.) As to content, the story belongs to a whole series of narratives relating the disaffection from or rebellion against God and Moses which took place during the wilderness wandering (cf. Exod 14:10-14; 15:22-26; 17:1-7; Num 11:4-35; 12; 13-14; 16-17; 20:1-13). These passages, generally assigned to the J source, depict the generation that came out of Egypt as rebels who rejected Yahweh. See P. Buis, *VT* 28 (1978) 257-70; Coats, *Rebellion*; S. J. DeVries, *JBL* 87 (1968) 51-58; A. C. Tunyogi, *JBL* 81 (1962) 385-90; H. Seebass, *VT* 28 (1978) 214-23.

27 (d) THE QUAIL, THE SEVENTY ELDERS, ELDAD AND MEDAD (11:4-35). In earliest tradition, the story of the quail, based on a natural phenomenon observable in the Sinai Peninsula (see J. Gray, *VT* 4 [1954] 148-54), was remembered in a positive light as illustrating God's gracious concern for his people (cf. Ps 105:40-41; Exod 16:4-16). The story was transformed, presumably by J, so that the request for meat appeared as rebellion and God's answer became a bitterly ironic form of punishment. The account of the seventy elders is only loosely attached to the quail story, and many scholars attribute it to E because of its interest in prophecy. **4.** *the rabble:* Cf. the "mixed multitude" of Exod 12:38. **7-9.** The manna is capable of natural explanation; see F. S. Bodenheimer, *BA* 10 (1947) 1-6. **25.** Prophecy is here understood as an ecstatic or charismatic phenomenon as in 1 Sam 10:10-13; 19:20-24. **26-29.** The acknowledgment of Eldad and Medad's prophetic charism by Moses, against the objections of Joshua, serves to protect the independence of the prophetic office from those who would subject it to institutional control. In contrast to the Priestly understanding, the tabernacle is here assumed to be located outside the camp. **34.** *Kibroth-hattaavah:* The place name means "the graves of craving."

28 (e) MIRIAM AND AARON REBEL AGAINST MOSES (12:1-16). Vv 1 and 10-15 deal with opposition to Moses for marrying a Cushite woman, an episode that originally involved only Miriam. God punished her by inflicting a skin disease. In vv 2-8, however, Aaron and Miriam make a rather different claim: they should have equal authority with Moses. This issue is settled by a decree from God which affirms the uniqueness and superiority of Moses as mediator of revelation. Both elements may derive from J, though some scholars assign at least part of the chapter (especially the material dealing with prophecy) to E. **1.** *Cushite:* In 2 Kgs 19:9 as well as a handful of prophetic passages, Cush refers to Ethiopia. See, however, Hab 3:7, where Cushan is associated with Midian, and cf. Exod 2:15-22. **3.** The meekness or humility of Moses contrasts with the self-assertion of Aaron and Miriam, who would push themselves forward into positions of power. The pl. form of the Hebr word used here ('*ănāwîm*) refers to the pious, humble folk who constitute the ideal religious type in texts such as Pss 25:9; 37:11. See A. Gelin, *The Poor of Yahweh* (Collegeville, 1964); G. W. Coats in *Art and Meaning: Rhetoric in Biblical Literature* (ed. D. J. A. Clines *et al.*; Sheffield, 1982) 97-107. **6-8.** The poetry contains a number of problems of text and translation (J. Kselman, *VT* 26 [1976] 500-4). *mouth to mouth:* The expression occurs nowhere else in the Hebr Bible. Like Exod 33:11 and Deut 34:10 it refers to the unique intimacy of Moses' communication with God. **12.** See A. Cooper, *JJS* 32 (1981) 56-64.

(B) At the Threshold of the Promised Land (13:1-15:41).

29 (a) EXPLORATION OF THE PROMISED LAND AND SETBACK (13:1-14:45). Scouts are sent from Kadesh, in the south, to explore the promised land prior to invasion.

Their report leads to rebellion against the authority of God and Moses, outright rejection of the gift of the land, and a proposal to reverse the exodus. The event constitutes a major turning point in its final literary form as well as at the level of the underlying P and J sources (cf. Deut 1:6-46). On the theological issues, see K. Sakenfeld, *CBQ* 37 (1975) 317-30.

The P version of the story (13:1-17a,21,25,26*,32-33; 14:1a,2-3,5-10,26-38) has the exploration going as far north as modern Lebanon, the spies returning an "evil report" about the land itself, and both Caleb and Joshua opposing the negative majority. The theme of possession of the land was especially significant for the P tradition because of the historical situation after the destruction of Jerusalem in 587. The J account (13:17b-20,22-24, 27-31; 14:1b,4,11-25,39-45) limits the exploration to the area around Hebron; it has the spies bring a favorable report about the land itself and the fruit it produces, but counters that with the terrifying size and might of its inhabitants; and J features Caleb as the only hero. Furthermore, the J elements contain hints of material that is older from a tradition-historical point of view. In all likelihood the Calebite traditions preserved here and in Josh 14:6-15; 15:13-19; Judg 1:11-20 originally told of a successful invasion from the south and the settlement of the Hebron area by various tribal groups associated with Caleb. See W. Beltz, *Die Kaleb-Traditionen im Alten Testament* (BWANT 98; Stuttgart, 1964); M. Noth, *A History of Pentateuchal Traditions* (EC, 1972) 133-36; and S. McEvenue, *Bib* 50 (1969) 453-65.

17. *the Negeb:* → Biblical Geography, 73:82-86. **21.** *Rehob:* See 2 Sam 10:6. *Lebo-hamath:* A city near the source of the Orontes River in modern Lebanon. **22.** *Hebron:* About 20 mi. S of Jerusalem, this city is important in the patriarchal traditions and was the capital of David in the early years of his reign. *Anak:* The phrase usually translated "descendants of Anak" can be so construed only with difficulty. Actually, the reference appears to be to an elite warrior guild analogous to the votaries of Rapha in 2 Sam 21:18,20,22 (C. L'Heureux, *BASOR* 221 [1976] 83-85; P. K. McCarter, *II Samuel* [AB 9; GC, 1984] 449-50). **23.** *Eshcol:* The Hebr word means "cluster (of grapes)." **26.** *Kadesh:* (→ Biblical Geography, 73:85). **33.** *Nephilim:* According to Gen 6:1-4, these legendary giants were born when heavenly beings had intercourse with human women. The words "the sons of Anak, who come from the Nephilim," are absent from the Greek and apparently constitute a relatively late gloss designed to harmonize this P verse with the J account in v 28.

14:5. As in 17:10 (RSV 16:45) the prostration of Moses and Aaron is an act of intercession designed to ward off God's wrath. **6.** *tore their garments:* A customary expression of grief, as in Gen 37:34 and elsewhere. **7.** Joshua and Caleb give a favorable report on the land, contradicting the "evil report" brought by the other spies according to 13:32. **9.** Hebr *ṣēl,* "shadow," is a metaphor for the protection afforded by the gods. **10.** The "glory," usually concealed by the cloud (cf. Num 9:15-23), is a shining splendor that serves as the visible manifestation of Yahweh when he reveals himself to his people (cf. Exod 16:6-7,10; Num 17:7 [RSV 16:42]). **11.** The sin of the people is a lack of what the Hebrew designates with a form of the vb. *he'ĕmîn,* frequently translated "to believe." The word refers to a sense of trust, confidence, and security that the Lord, who is fully able to fulfill his commitments, intends. **25.** They are to set out by the way of *yam sûf,* traditionally translated "Red Sea," though it means "Sea of Reeds." Presumably the highway toward the Gulf of Aqabah is meant. **45.** *Hormah:* Cf. the story in Num 21:1-3.

30   (b) Various Cultic Ordinances (15:1–41). These regulations are generally late and stem from the final stages of Priestly redaction. The specification of cereal and drink offerings which are to accompany animal sacrifice (vv 1–16) are an adaptation of Ezek 46:4–7,11,13–15 (cf. also Lev 7:11–14 and Exod 29:39–41). Emphasis on the law's application to foreigners living in the land supports late dating of the material (see P. Grelot, *VT* 6 [1956] 174–89). The second ordinance (vv 17–21) requires an offering taken from *'ărîsōt*, a rare Hebr word which may mean dough, kneading trough, or a certain kind of flour. The first-fruits regulation (vv 17–21) may be intended as the specific requirement occasioning discussion of what to do in case of violation of this and any other ordinance (vv 22–31). The assertion that there can be no sacrificial atonement for willful sins (vv 30–31) highlights the enormity of the crimes reported in the preceding and following chapters. Moreover, the story of those who gathered sticks on the Sabbath (vv 32–36; see A. Phillips, *VT* 19 [1969] 125–28 and J. Weingreen, *VT* 16 [1966] 361–64) provides a concrete example of a willful offense. These interconnections demonstrate that the ordinances collected here are not arbitrarily thrown together. Furthermore, the location of the stick-gathering episode "in the wilderness" (v 32) explains the insertion of this complex within the wandering period. The small collection is aptly concluded by the ordinance concerning tassels (vv 37–41), which are intended as a constant reminder of God's law, a reminder that might help obviate such disastrous violations as are reported in chaps. 13–14 and 16–17. See S. Bertman, *BA* 24 (1961) 119–28.

(C) Revolt of Korah, Dathan, and Abiram; Status and Role of Priests (16:1–19:22).
31   (a) Revolt of Korah, Dathan, and Abiram (16:1–35). See F. Ahuis, *Autorität im Umbruch* (Stuttgart, 1983); J. Magonet, *JSOT* 24 (1982) 3–25. Two elements have been combined in this chapter. A P narrative (vv 1a,2*,3–11,16–24,27a,35) relates the rebellion of Korah and 250 associates. In a test to determine whose incense offering is accepted by the Lord, Aaron prevails over Korah and his followers, who are then destroyed by fire (cf. Nadab and Abihu, Lev 10:1–2). The second element, usually assigned to J (vv 1b,12–15,25–34) reports that two Reubenites—Dathan and Abiram—challenge the leadership of Moses and are punished supernaturally when the earth swallows them up. Indeed Dathan and Abiram are mentioned without any reference to Korah in Deut 11:6 and Ps 106:16–17. The redactional process has interwoven the stories in such a way that Korah is mentioned within the Dathan and Abiram story (vv 27 and 32) and Dathan and Abiram are named within the Korah account (v 24). It is possible that the P account itself results from the fusion of two primitively separate traditions. The issue in vv 3–7 is whether lay persons are prevented from offering incense because they are less holy. This theme could have originally been connected with the 250 lay persons mentioned in vv 2,17,35. Verses 8–11, on the other hand, center on whether Korah, a Levite, is equal to the priests in dignity and authority. The final Priestly form of the story served as a way of settling controversies that arose between priests and Levites in the postexilic period. In fact, a group of Levites descended from Korah is prominent in 1–2 Chr (→ Institutions, 76:20,24) and appears in the superscription of Pss 42, 44–49, 84–85, 87–88 (see G. Wanke, *Die Zionstheologie der Korachiten* [BZAW 97; Berlin, 1966]). The Priestly version of the rebellion serves to limit whatever claims the Korah group was putting forth in its own behalf (cf. 4:17–21). **2.** The 250

come from the whole congregation or assembly, not the tribe of Levi. **3.** Appealing to the tradition reflected in Exod 19:6 that holiness and priesthood are characteristic of all Israel, the group of lay persons rebels against the hierarchical structure. **5.** *his congregation:* The use in connection with Korah of the special term *'ēdâ*, P's regular designation for the "congregation" of God's people, implies that a rival "church" had been established. The reference reflects some stage in the conflicts among rival priestly factions which lie behind the formulation of the story. *whom he will allow to come near:* The causative form of the vb. *qrb* is a technical term referring to the right of access to the divine presence in the cult (Jer 30:21; Lev 7:35, etc.). **6.** *censers:* These were flat fire-pans unlike censers used liturgically today. **13.** *flowing with milk and honey:* The rebels' application of this description to Egypt indicates a rejection of the land of promise and a reversal of the whole enterprise of the exodus. **15.** *Do not accept their offering:* Since the Dathan and Abiram motif does not involve the question of sacrifice, the expression here simply means "Do not favor them." Budd (*Numbers* 187) points to Gen 4:4–5 for the sense. The apologia of Moses is stereotypical (cf. 1 Sam 8:16; 12:3). **19.** *the glory:* (→ 22 above). **22.** The prostration is linked with intercession as in 14:5 and 17:10. **24.** *the tabernacle of Korah:* Here and in v 27 the Hebrew employs the word *miškān*, the regular term for the sacred tabernacle. The reference to a rival shrine set up by Korah supports the idea that the story was used in the polemic against parties who planned or actually carried out programs in conflict with priestly orthodoxy. **30.** The rebels are swallowed alive by Sheol, the underworld (→ OT Thought, 77:170).
32   (b) The Covering for the Altar (17:1–5 [*RSV* 16:36–40]). The mention of Eleazar in vv 2,4 supports the view that this supplement to the Priestly stratum of the preceding chapter is relatively late. The account seems to contradict the Priestly passages in Exod 27:2 and 38:2 which states that the altar was covered with bronze from the very start.
33   (c) The Intercession of Aaron (17:6–15 [*RSV* 16:41–50]). Another Priestly supplement to Num 16, this account does not seem to go back to an independent oral tradition but to be based completely on the information provided in the preceding chapter. The passage follows the structure of the murmuring stories and reinforces the exclusive right of the Aaronids to offer incense. The account reflects power struggles concerning cultic issues during the postexilic period (cf. 2 Chr 26:16–21). The only other account in Num of an intercessory act that stops an act of divine punishment while it is in progress is Num 21:4–9, the closest parallel to the present passage. **10.** *fell on their faces:* See discussion of 14:5. **11.** *make atonement for them:* This is the only passage where the offering of incense is in itself adequate to effect atonement (but see Lev 16:11–14). **11.** *the wrath:* See discussion of 1:53.
34   (d) Aaron's Staff (17:16–28 [*RSV* 17:1–13]). Here too we find a late Priestly additon to the cycle of murmuring stories. Against the customary practice of P (Num 1:5–14,20–42,47, etc.), this account treats Levi as one of the twelve tribes. It therefore seems to be an adaptation of an older tradition which intended to highlight the special position of the Levites compared to the eleven other tribes. The Priestly form that we now have, however, insists that it was Aaron's name that was written on the rod of Levi. The blossoming of the rod of Levi is thus employed to the advantage of the Aaronids rather than the Levites. (See G. J. Wenham, *ZAW* 93 [1981] 280–81). We are reminded once again of the extent to which propagandistic motives were at work in the Priestly shaping of pentateuchal material. The

concluding verses (27–28) contain the anguished cry of the people who have witnessed how the divine "wrath," a terrifying and destructive supernatural power, breaks out upon persons who transgress upon sacred domain (16:31–35; 17:9–15). How will they survive the grave danger created by the presence of the sanctuary within their midst? The question sets the stage for the next chapter.

35   (e) THE DUES OF THE PRIESTS AND LEVITES (18:1–32). How the sanctuary of Yahweh could be served without subjecting the people to the destructive "wrath" which could break out had actually been solved already in earlier parts of Num. In 18:1–7 the Priestly author needs only to summarize what had been set out in 1:47–54; 3:4; 8:19. The priests absorb the risk of contact with the altar. The Levites have a less intense exposure, but they too play a part in protecting the lay community from contact with the sanctuary. This crucial function of the clergy is stated in the expression *nāśā' 'āwôn* (18:1), "to bear iniquity." The priests (and to a lesser extent the Levites) "bear the iniquity" in the sense that they protect the community by taking the danger upon themselves. They are unharmed by it because they have been set aside by God for just this purpose.

The itemization of offerings that go to the clergy builds upon information given elsewhere (Lev 6:11,22; 7:6; Ezek 44:29; Num 5:9). Similarly, the differentiation between the portions to be eaten only by priests and those which are shared with their families repeats the regulations of Lev except that ambiguity in Exod 29:28 and Lev 7:34 is clarified in the sense of permitting the priest's whole family to share in the offerings mentioned there. Next, the redemption of the firstborn humans is taken up (cf. 3:11–51; → 11 above). Here the payment of five shekels in redemption occurs as the norm, thus providing additional support for the priests. The firstborn of unclean animals may be redeemed (B. Gershon, *JQR* 68 [1977] 1–15).

Next, provision is made for the Levites. Since they do not own land (see, however, Num 35:1–8), they are to be supported by receiving the tithes of the other Israelites (cf. Deut 10:9; 18:1–5), which they may treat as ordinary food (v 32). However, the Levites must in turn give the priests a tithe of what they have received, thus acknowledging the hierarchical structure of the clergy.

2. *so they may be joined to you:* The vb. employed (*lwh*) forms a pun on the name Levi (cf. Gen 29:34). **14.** In the ancient institution of holy war, persons, livestock, and things which were placed under the ban (Hebr *ḥerem*) were totally destroyed (Num 21:1–3; Deut 7:1–2; etc.). Here they may be given to the priests instead. **19.** *a covenant of salt:* Salt is apparently a means of referring to the shared meal which was part of sealing a covenant (see Gen 31:51–54). The expression here, also found in 2 Chr 13:5, means an agreement that was binding in perpetuity.

36   (f) THE RED HEIFER AND THE WATER OF PURIFICATION (19:1–22). Though it is unknown in early texts, the idea that contact with a corpse caused ritual impurity became accepted in the postexilic period and is often reflected in the Priestly corpus (Lev 22:4; Num 5:2; Num 9:6–10; cf. Ezek 44:25). The process of purification from this contamination is alluded to elsewhere (e.g., Num 31:19; Ezek 44:25–26) but only in this chapter is the ritual with the water of purification described (vv 17–20). The chapter consists exclusively of Priestly material, but it is far from being a smooth and unified account: e.g., the legal statements in participial form in vv 11–13a seem unconnected with what precedes (vv 1–10) and follows (vv 14–20). The ritual with the red heifer (vv 1–9), not mentioned anywhere else in the OT (though cf.

Deut 21:1–9) is peculiar in several respects (see J. Milgrom, *VT* 31 [1981] 62–72), and the account itself is only loosely connected with what follows. Whatever the original intent of the ritual, in its present form the main purpose of the procedure is to obtain the ashes for the lustral water.

2. *red heifer:* The Hebr word actually means "cow," but the stipulation that it shall not have borne the yoke supports the likelihood that a young cow is meant. The color may be a symbolic reminder of blood or of earth. **6.** *hyssop:* The twigs of this plant were used for ceremonial sprinkling. **9.** The red heifer is here referred to as a sin offering (Hebr *ḥaṭṭā't*), one of the main categories of sacrifice according to the Priestly system in Lev. **20.** Cf. vv 11–13. **21.** Cf. vv 7,8,10.

(D) From Kadesh to the Plains of Moab (20:1–21:35).

37   (a) THE WATERS OF MERIBAH (20:1–13). The account of water miraculously provided from the rock was found in a J version in Exod 17:1–7. We now have another version which has a new twist: the incident included a sin of Moses and Aaron, which is the reason why they never entered the land of promise. The present account is substantially P, though some analysts find an E component, especially the notice about Miriam's death. In any case, the story serves a major function in the P work. To the sin of the people (Num 13–14) and of the Levites (chaps. 16–17) is now added the sin of the two leaders. There has been considerable discussion of the exact nature of this transgression (E. Arden, *JBL* 76 [1957] 50–52; P. Buis, *VT* 24 [1974] 268–85; A. S. Kapelrud, *JBL* 76 [1957] 242; T. W. Mann, *JBL* 98 [1979] 481–94; M. Margoliot, *JQR* 74 [1983] 196–228). Of the many suggestions that have been made, two have the greatest plausibility. The first argues that Moses had been instructed by God (v 8) to speak to the rock, but instead he struck it with the rod. Indeed, he struck it twice, apparently not trusting that God could work the miracle simply through the words. This interpretation is supported by the fact that the absence of instructions to strike the rock in the divine speech of v 8 must be a deliberate omission in view of the J parallel (Exod 17:6), which was clearly known to P. Another possibility is linked with the statement of Ps 106:32–33 that Moses had spoken "rash words" in this connection, suggesting that the words of Moses in v 10 constitute the problem. Perhaps the speech implies that Moses and Aaron have the power to bring water from the rock without giving credit to God. Or perhaps the anger exhibited by the speech prevents the act of divine mercy from being seen for what it truly is as a manifestation of God's holiness. **1.** *first month:* The year is not given, but according to 33:38, the death of Aaron, which follows in 20:22–29, occurred in the fortieth year of the exodus. **3.** *the people contended:* The use of the verb *rîb* forms a pun with "Meribah," which leads to an explicit etiological comment in Exod 17:7. *our brothers:* Those who had died according to 16:35 and 17:14. **8.** *the rod:* According to v 9 it was taken "from before Yahweh." It therefore seems that the rod of 17:16–26 is meant, though one might also think of Exod 14:16. **12.** *you did not trust:* However one solves the problem of the exact nature of the transgression, theologically it amounted to a lack of trust in God (see comment on 14:11). *to sanctify me:* The use of the vb. *qdš* here and in v 13 plays upon the place-name Kadesh.

38   (b) NEGOTIATIONS WITH THE KING OF EDOM (20:14–21): The passage is definitely not Priestly, and analysts variously assign it to J and E. A number of more recent works see a strong deuteronomistic redactional influence on the passage (J. R. Bartlett, *JSOT* 4 [1977] 2–27). Sturdy (*Numbers* 141–42) holds that the account is relatively late and modeled on the challenge to Moab in 21:21–24. It was created to fill the gap in the older traditions which did not mention contact with Edom in the accounts of the march through the wilderness. **14.** *your brother:* Edom is descended from Esau, the twin brother of Jacob/Israel (Gen 25:24–26). **15–16.** Compare the short historical credo in Deut 6:20–25; 26:5–9; Josh 24:2–13. *he sent an angel:* See Exod 14:19; 23:20. **17.** *the King's Highway:* → Biblical Geography, 73:31.

39   (c) DEATH OF AARON (20:22–29). The Priestly tradition recounts the death of Aaron, which is explicitly linked to the preceding story of the sin of Moses and Aaron at Meribah. The mountaintop location and the thirty days of mourning are modeled on the preexisting account of the death of Moses (Deut 34:1–12). **22.** *Mount Hor:* The location is unknown. Cf. Deut 10:6. **26.** For the priestly robes, see Lev 8:7–9.

40   (d) BATTLE WITH THE CANAANITES AT HORMAH (21:1–3). We have a fragment, preserved by J, of old Calebite or Judean traditions relating a successful invasion from the south (cf. Judg 1:17; → 29 above). The passage marks a significant turning point. From here on, the Israelites are no longer defeated by enemies but march on victoriously. **1.** The mention of the king of Arad is widely regarded as a gloss. Arad (Y. Aharoni and R. Amiran, *BA* 31 [1968] 1–32; → Biblical Archaeology, 74:83), indeed, seems to be much too far to the north in view of the fact that from 20:14–21 and 21:4 we expect Israel to be moving south from Kadesh. The location of the Way of Atharim is uncertain, but see Y. Aharoni, *IEJ* 17 (1962) 1–17. **2.** The causative form of the vb. *ḥrm*, "to utterly destroy," "devote to the ban" (→ 35 above), is linked etymologically to the place-name Hormah, the location of which is uncertain (see V. Fritz, *ZDPV* 91 [1975] 30–45).

41   (e) THE FIERY SERPENTS (21:4–9). Except for the itinerary notice in v 4a, there are no signs of P. The tendency among scholars today is to assign the story to J, though many have found the presence of E. The story provides an etiology for the bronze serpent present in the Jerusalem Temple, to which the people used to offer incense (K. R. Joines, *JBL* 87 [1968] 245–56; H. H. Rowley, *JBL* 58 [1939] 113–41). According to 2 Kgs 18:4, this cult object was destroyed during the reforms of Hezekiah along with other objects thought to be incompatible with Yahwistic faith. In the present passage, the J author does not seem opposed to the bronze serpent, though he probably intends to describe its proper use, deliberately avoiding the mention of incense offerings (see Budd, *Numbers* 233–35). **5.** The complaint disparages manna (cf. 11:6). **6.** *fiery serpents:* The term *śĕrāpîm* is in apposition with the word for snakes. If we are correct in connecting it with the root *śrp*, "to burn," the designation may refer to a burning sensation produced by the bite of this type of serpent. The sg. of what is apparently the same word occurs in v 8 as well as in Deut 8:15; Isa 14:29; 30:6. It is not clear whether this is the same word as the *śĕrāpîm* in the vision of Isaiah (Isa 6:2,6; K. R. Joines, *JBL* 86 [1967] 410–15).

42   (f) ITINERARY STAGES THROUGH TRANSJORDAN (21:10–20). The passage is structured as an itinerary list (→ 24 above); vv 10–11a come from P (cf. 33:41–49), and vv 12–20 are variously assigned to J and E, including glosses based on Judg 11:18 and other sources (de Vaulx, *Nombres* 241). Few of the sites can be identified with any degree of confidence. Two fragments of archaic poetry supplement the itinerary. The first is quoted from an otherwise unknown source referred to as "the Book of the Wars of Yahweh" (cf. "the Book of Jashar" in Josh 10:13; 2 Sam 1:18). It was preserved because it supported a particular understanding of the boundaries of Moab.

See D. L. Christensen, *CBQ* 36 (1974) 359–60. The song concerning the well, on the other hand, was connected with a story, no longer preserved, which involved Moses. See Albright, *YGC* 44; D. N. Freedman, *ZAW* 72 (1960) 101–7; *NFL* 44–46.

43   (g) THE DEFEAT OF SIHON AND OG (21:21–35). The Sihon material (vv 21–32) is generally assigned to J or to J and E, and the passage on Og (vv 33–35) seems to be derived from Deut 3:1–3. A number of studies, however, have argued that the whole section is a late deuteronomistic compilation (see J. van Seters, *JBL* 91 [1972] 182–97; 99 [1980] 117–19; Budd, *Numbers* 243–46). The poem in vv 27–30 may be quite old (P. Hanson, *HTR* 61 [1968] 297–320; D. N. Freedman, *ZAW* 72 [1960] 101–7; *NFL* 46). Indeed, some believe it was originally an Amorite victory song boasting of triumph over Moab. It would have been taken over by Israel as a means of countering Moabite claims to territory north of the Arnon (cf. Judg 11:12–28). The parallel between Num 21:28–29 and Jer 48:45–46 might be due to the latter's dependence on the former. Some, however, have taken it to indicate that the poem in Num is quite late. See further J. R. Bartlett, *PEQ* 101 (1969) 94–100; *VT* 20 (1970) 257–77; *JBL* 97 (1978) 347–51; W. A. Sumner, *VT* 18 (1968) 216–28.

(III) On the Plains of Moab: Preparation for Entry into the Land (22:1–36:13).

44   **(A) The Story of Balaam (22:1–24:25).** This self-contained unit is only loosely connected to the story of the march around Moab and the intent to reach the land of promise, and it displays inner inconsistencies. Notably, the character of Balaam is depicted in two sharply divergent ways. (See G. W. Coats, *BR* 18 [1973] 21–29; *Semeia* 24 [1982] 53–79). In the story of Balaam's ass (22:22–33), Balaam stubbornly proceeds against the will of God and obtusely fails to understand what is clear to his donkey. In what precedes and follows, however, he is a model of piety, not taking a single step before carefully consulting with the Lord. These and other indications have led source critics to attribute 22:2–21 (reworked in part by a later editor) and the two oracles of 23 to E, whereas 22:22–35 and the two oracles of 24 would be J (de Vaulx, *Nombres* 253–62). The failure of the divine names in these chapters consistently to follow the expected source-critical patterns—an issue complicated by frequent lack of agreement between Greek and Hebrew (Budd, *Numbers* 261–62)—has led several more recent scholars to hesitate about solving the problems along conventional literary-critical lines. In particular, the study of linguistic, orthographic, and poetic features of the four oracles by W. F. Albright (*JBL* 63 [1944] 207–53) supported a common origin for all four oracles.

"Balaam the son of Beor, the man who is a seer of the gods," is also the principal character in Aram texts discovered in 1967 during the excavation of Deir Alla in Jordan (J. Hoftijzer and G. van der Kooij, *Aramaic Texts from Deir 'Alla* [Leiden, 1976]; J. Hackett, *The Balaam Text from Deir 'Alla* [Chico, 1984]; A. Lemaire, *BARev* 11/5 [1985] 26–39). Inscribed on white plaster walls in red and black ink, these 8th-cent. BC texts indicate that Balaam received a message of impending doom during the night, probably in a dream. The biblical stories about Balaam (see also Num 31:8,16; Deut 23:5–6; Jos 13:22; 24:9–10; Mic 6:5; Neh 13:2) reflect more broadly disseminated Near Eastern traditions from the period of Israel's monarchy.

45   (a) BALAQ SENDS FOR BALAAM (22:1–21). **1.** The P framework of Num establishes the setting for chaps. 22–36 in the plains of Moab, just north of the Dead Sea on the eastern side of the Jordan. **3–4.** These verses seem to ignore that Balaq was already introduced in v 2. Moreover, the mention of Midian points to the conflicting tradition, also reflected in 22:36-39, that Balaam was associated with regions to the south of Moab rather than north. **5.** Pethor, on the Euphrates River, known from Egyptian and Assyrian sources, was close to the modern border between Syria and Turkey. **7.** The presentation of an honorarium to a seer was the standard practice (1 Sam 9:7; 1 Kgs 14:3; 2 Kgs 8:8). **8.** Balaam receives a revelation in a dream, as frequently in the Bible (e.g., Gen 37:5-11; 1 Kgs 3:5-14; Matt 1:18-21) as well as Near Eastern literature in general, including the Deir Alla texts. **18.** The acknowledgment by Balaam that his words of curse or blessing are absolutely dependent on the will of God contradicts Balaq's assumption that powerful magic can be bought if the price is high enough. Balaam was certainly not a worshiper of Yahweh; nonetheless, the Israelite traditionists believed that it was the God of Israel who worked through the foreign seer.

46 (b) BALAAM'S ASS (22:21-35). See H. Rouillard, *RB* 87 (1980) 5-36, 211-41. Apart from its opening and closing verses, which are redactional in nature, the passage is independent of the rest of the Balaam narrative. The divine displeasure at Balaam's journey seems to ignore the permission given in v 20, and the Moabite envoys are no longer in evidence. Furthermore, Balaam, less perceptive than his ass and stubborn in his blindness, appears in an unfavorable light, which contrasts with the overall context. **22.** The angel of the Lord (*mal'ak yhwh*) serves as a mediator of divine revelation in passages that seek to protect the divine transcendence by avoiding direct contact between God and human beings. In such passages, nevertheless, the *mal'ak yhwh* sometimes speaks and is spoken of as if identical with God (see v 32 and cf. Gen 16:7-12; Judg 6:11-24; Zech 3:1-5). **28.** The speaking of Balaam's ass is comparable to the talking serpent in Gen 3:1-5, which supports the attribution of the present passage to the J source.

47 (c) MEETING OF BALAAM AND BALAQ (22:36-40). **36.** Whether or not the city of Ir is the same as the Ar mentioned in 21:15, and whether or not its association with the river Arnon is original (Noth, *Numbers* 180-81), its exact location is uncertain. On all counts, however, it would appear to be considerably south of Balaam's destination, the plains of Moab. Perhaps we have the remains of a tradition that thought of Balaam as coming from the south rather than the north, a connection particularly at home in materials that place a negative judgment on the foreign seer (see 31:8,16). **39.** The location of Kiriath-huzoth is unknown. **40.** Balaq's slaughter of animals for eating as a sign of hospitality differs in intent from the sacrifices mentioned in 23:1-2, 14,29-30.

48 (d) FIRST ORACLE AT BAMOTH BAAL (22:41-23:12). **41.** *Bamoth-baal* means "the high places of Baal" and might not be a proper name (cf. 21:20). *the extremity of the people:* Apparently meaning just a small part (cf. v 13). Either there were too many of them to be seen at once, or Balaq had chosen this vantage point because he did not want Balaam to see how many there really were. **2.** There is a tension between v 2 and v 4 regarding who offered the sacrifices. The Hebrew has an extra "Balaq and Balaam" before the vb. "to offer," added as a gloss to smooth over the difficulty. Balaq might have hoped that the lavishness of the offerings would get him what he wanted, but Balaam knows that all depends on the will of God. **5.** For the word placed in the prophet's mouth, see Jer 1:9. **7.** Hebrew *māšāl*, usually "proverb," "parable," apparently means "oracle," "poem" here.

Aram: Syria, extending as far as the Euphrates, thus including the home of Balaam as defined in 22:5. *eastern mountains:* The ranges in the Syrian desert. **9.** *a people that dwells apart:* Cf. Lev 20:24 and esp. Deut 33:28. **10.** *who could number the dust-cloud of Israel:* Reflects the ideas in Gen 13:6; 15:5; 28:14. Hebrew *roba'*, "one-fourth," is emended on the basis of the Assyrian *turbu'tu* (de Vaulx, *Nombres* 276). Balaam's wish for himself is to be as blessed as are the descendants of Abraham and Jacob (cf. Gen 12:3; 22:18; 28:14).

49 (e) SECOND ORACLE AT MT. PISGAH (23:13-26). The framework of the passage closely parallels the structure of 22:41-23:12. **13.** The Hebrew seems to mean that just as in the case of the first oracle (22:41) Balaam can see only part of Israel. By taking the vb. *tir'eh* as an imperf. referring to what had happened before, de Vaulx (*Nombres* 278) believes that on the second occasion Balaam sees the whole of Israel. A similar conclusion is reached by different means in Noth, *Numbers* 184-85. **18.** The Hebrew reads "listen to me." A change of vocalization yields the preferable "listen to my testimony." **19.** The word for God in this verse is Hebr *'ēl*, which occurs in other Semitic languages as both a common noun and as the name of El, the father of the gods and the head of the pantheon (C. L'Heureux, *Rank Among the Canaanite Gods* [Missoula, 1979] 49-67). According to Hackett (*Balaam Text* 33, 58-60, 85-87) El is the chief God in the Deir Alla text. The immutability of God's will is affirmed also in 1 Sam 15:29. **20.** *I have been summoned to bless:* Slight emendation of the Hebrew is based on the ancient versions. **21-22.** *One does not see misfortune in Israel:* The vb. is impersonal. The reference is to the absence not of moral fault but of curse and fated evil. The *tĕrû'â* was the battle cry which accompanied the procession of the Ark (1 Sam 4:5; 2 Sam 6:15). It can also refer to royal acclamations such as "Long live the king!" (2 Sam 16:16; 1 Kgs 1:25,34,39; 2 Kgs 11:12). The kingship of God is associated with the exodus as in Exod 15:18 and Deut 33:2-5. **22.** The Hebrew says that God is like a "buffalo horn" (i.e., symbol of power) for Israel. It is preferable to take the symbol as applying to Israel rather than to God, as in Deut 33:17. This verse is repeated in 24:8. **23.** *For now it will be told to Israel what the Lord is doing:* Hebr *kā'ēt* is read as *kî 'attâ*, "for now," and *pā'al*, "he did," is repointed to *pô'ēl*, "is doing." The statement introduces v 24 (de Vaulx, *Nombres* 280). **24.** The same metaphor occurs in Deut 33:20 and Mic 5:7.

50 (f) THIRD ORACLE ON PEOR (23:27-24:9). Conventional source-critical analysis attributes the third and fourth oracles to J and sees 24:1b-2 as the original J introduction. The JE redactor would have composed 23:27-24:1a in order to assimilate the third oracle to the pattern of the first two (E). **28.** *Peor:* A mountain overlooking the plains of Moab, though the exact location is unknown. Hebr *yĕšîmōn* is a rare word which refers to the wilderness of Judah in 1 Sam 23:19. **1.** *he did not seek divinatory signs as he had previously:* On the first two occasions Balaam had gone off to a height by himself, whereas this time he faces Israel and immediately pronounces his oracles. It is not clear what were the "divinatory signs" associated with the first two oracles. **2.** *the spirit of God came upon him:* In contrast to the first two oracles, Balaam is here described as an ecstatic or charismatic prophet overcome by the divine spirit (cf. 1 Sam 10:5-6,10-11; 19:18-24; 1 Kgs 22:24). **4.** *the oracle of the one who hears the words of God:* Many scholars would insert the matching colon "and who shares what the Most High knows," as in v 16. *the Almighty:* The divine name *šadday* occurs in the Aram pl. form as a synonym for "gods" in the Deir Alla texts (Hackett, *Balaam Text* 85-89). *whose eyes are unveiled when he* *collapses:* The ecstatic prophet experienced visions as he fell to the ground, overcome by the spirit (cf. 1 Sam 19:24). **6.** The first two words in Hebrew mean literally, "like streams/valleys that are stretched out." One would have expected the name of some kind of tree. *NAB* drops several words of this verse as dittographic. **7.** He will enjoy abundant irrigation, thus agricultural plenty. There is perhaps a play on the word "seed" suggesting abundance of both seminal fluid and progeny. *Agag:* See 1 Sam 15:8,20,32. This reference suggests the early monarchical period for the date of this oracle. **8–9.** Cf. Gen 49:9 and Gen 12:3; 27:29.

51   (g) FOURTH ORACLE OF BALAAM (24:10–19). **10.** The clapping of hands is a sign of derision in Lam 2:15. **11.** Even Balaq recognizes that it is Balaam's fidelity to Yahweh that has prevented him from meeting his royal client's expectations. **17.** *star . . . scepter:* Symbols of the monarchy. The oracle is a piece of court apologetic legitimizing the reign of David by claiming that his rise and his conquest of Moab had been foreseen by the famous pagan prophet Balaam. *and the skulls of the Suteans:* The reuse of the passage by Jer 48:45 allows us to restore "skull" (Hebr *qdqd*) for the corrupt *qrqr.* The Suteans were a tribal people mentioned in Egyptian texts of the 2nd millennium. No longer understood, the reference was reinterpreted by the MT as "sons of Seth." **18–19.** These verses, referring to the subjugation of Edom by David, have been seriously disturbed in the course of transmission. A widely accepted reconstruction was proposed by W. F. Albright (*JBL* 63 [1944] 207–33).

52   (h) CONCLUDING ORACLES (24:20–25). The Balaam pericope is rounded off with brief oracles against various peoples, including the Amalekites and the Kenites. De Vaulx suggests that Asshur refers not to the mighty Assyrian empire but to a tribe mentioned in Gen 25:3,18; 2 Sam 2:9; and elsewhere (*Nombres* 295–97). The Kittim would be the Philistines. The fact that all the peoples mentioned here would thus be associated with the area south of Judah perhaps supports the tradition reflected in 22:36 that Balaam's home was in the south rather than the north.

53   (B) Apostasy at Baal Peor (25:1–18). Sexual promiscuity with Moabite women leads to worship of a foreign god, an act of apostasy which is then punished at the command of Moses (vv 1–5). The incident constitutes a final act in a series of rebellions in the wilderness (Budd, *Numbers* 281–83) and serves as solemn reminder of the peril of cultic infidelity (cf. Hos 9:10; Deut 4:3–4). The narrative is not entirely consistent within itself. There are many different opinions as to whether and how the passage is to be divided into J and E components.

A second section, vv 6–18, focusing on a single Israelite man, a Midianite woman, and the intervention of Phinehas, clearly belongs to P. The account serves to legitimize the position of the descendants of Phinehas within the priestly hierarchy and idealizes the priestly duty of protecting the purity of the community by decisive action in times of crisis (cf. the role of the Levites in Exod 32:25–29).

1. *Shittim:* On the east bank of the Jordan, opposite Jericho. **2.** Sexual involvement led to participation in foreign rites, which included feasting and, if we are to believe the evidence of Ps 106:28–31, sacrifices to the dead. **3.** *Israel yoked himself to Baal of Peor:* The Hebr vb. used here is rare, but the meaning is determined on the evidence of the common cognate noun, which means "yoke." The activity of the Israelite men amounted to the establishment of covenantal ties with the Baal worshiped at Peor (cf. 23:28). A sexual double entendre may

also be intended. **4.** The exact form of public execution is not clear (cf. 2 Sam 21:1–6). **5.** For the role of the judges, see Exod 18:21–27. **6.** *brought the Midianite woman to his family:* The reference could be simply to marriage without any suggestion of improper cultic activity. Within the context, the lamenting before the Tent of Meeting can only refer to rituals connected with the events reported in vv 1–5. **8.** Phinehas goes after the couple in a place called *qubbâ,* a word that occurs nowhere else in Biblical Hebrew. It may refer to a tent-shrine (S. C. Reif, *JBL* 90 [1971] 200–6), perhaps part of the Tent of Meeting itself. The woman's presence would therefore have been specifically cultic. Such an interpretation can be supported by understanding the place where she was pierced (Hebr *qōbātâ*) as "her shrine." However, the latter word does occur in one other place, Deut 18:3, where it refers to a part of the belly. *the plague was stopped:* Hebr *maggēpâ* probably refers to disease (G. Mendenhall, *The Tenth Generation* [Baltimore, 1973] 105–21) rather than the killing of v 5. The fact that this plague was not mentioned previously is one of several indications that the story has been abridged during the editorial process. **12.** *covenant of peace:* See Isa 54:10; Mal 2:5. **14–15.** The names of the offenders are appended in what seems to be a later addition. Cozbi's father, Zur, is mentioned in Num 31:8. The passage perhaps intends to throw unfavorable light on the descendants of Zimri. **16–18.** The conclusion prepares for the war against Midian in Num 31.

(C) **Preparation for Conquest and Division of the Land (25:19–36:13).**

54   (a) THE SECOND CENSUS (25:19–26:65). The imminent apportionment of the land is to take into consideration the relative size of each tribe. Since the census of 1:1–47, however, the generation which rebelled in the wilderness (14:29–30) has died and others perished in the plague mentioned in 25:8,18. A new census is therefore provided by P. The grand total of 601,730 compares to 603,550 in chap. 1. As to the individual tribes, Num 26 shows a significant decrease for Simeon and an increase for Manasseh and Benjamin in comparison with chap. 1. The numbers for the other tribes differ less sharply.

8–10. The basic schema of the list is supplemented with information that is all based on Num 16 except for the name "Nemuel," which might have slipped in accidentally from 26:12. **11.** The precision is necessitated by the fact that descendants of Korah continued to exercise sacred functions at a later period. **19.** Cf. Gen 38:7–10. **20.** *the sons of Perez:* The fourth and fifth clans are regarded as subdivisions of Perez in order to harmonize with Gen 38, where Judah had only three surviving sons. **29.** *Machir was the father of Gilead:* The intrusion of this stereotypical formula (Josh 17:1; 1 Chr 7:14) led to an alteration of the original schema so that the eponymous ancestors of six of the clans appear as great grandchildren rather than children of Manasseh. Cf. the list in Josh 17:1–3 and see H. Seebass, *VT* 32 (1982) 496–503. **31.** *Shechem:* This important town joined the Israelite confederation by treaty (see Josh 24) and was incorporated into the tribal list of Manasseh. **33.** The mention of Zelophehad prepares for 27:1–11 and 36:1–13. The name Tirzah is that of a well-known town, and it is possible that the four others were originally place-names too. **36.** Eran, a part of the clan of the Shuthelites, eventually became independent. **40.** Arad and Naaman split off from Bela. **52–56.** The census is linked to the principle of territorial apportionment according to tribal size. It is not clear how this rule can be reconciled with the process of casting lots referred to in v 56 (cf. Num 33:54; 34:13; Josh 14:1–5; 18:2–10, etc.). **58.** The three-clan list of v

57 represents the normative postexilic conception. The five clan names in v 58a, on the other hand, perhaps derive from a much older source. The Libnites and Hebronites are inhabitants of the priestly towns, Libna and Hebron. The Mushites may have claimed Moses as an ancestor. The Mahlites might be connected with Mahlah, daughter of Zelophehad (26:33; 27:1; 36:11). For 58b–61, cf. Exod 2:1; 6:18–20 and Lev 10:1–2.

55 (b) THE DAUGHTERS OF ZELOPHEHAD (27:1–11). Earlier legislation recognized inheritance only through sons (Deut 21:15–17). In a case where the deceased left no sons, the levirate marriage (Deut 25:5–10) would provide a male heir. In the case of Zelophehad's daughters (cf. 26:33), the levirate marriage is apparently not possible, presumably because the wife is deceased also. As in similar passages (Lev 24:10–22; Num 9:6–14; 15:32–36), the particular historical case is brought to Moses and presented to God. The decision rendered serves as a binding precedent for the future. The legal refinement resulting from the consideration of a difficult case thus provides for situations not adequately covered by earlier law. These passages all stem from a very late stage in the Priestly redaction of the Pentateuch. **3.** *he died for his own sin:* Like the rest of the desert generation, he died because of the judgment rendered in 14:20–23. Had he participated in the even more serious sin of Korah, he would have lost any right to bequeath real estate (cf. 1 Kgs 21:8–15). **4.** The intention, as in the law of jubilee (Lev 25), is to keep property within the family. **7.** The command is executed in Josh 17:3–6. A further specification concerning the marriages entered into by these women is found in Num 36. **8–11.** A modern perspective on the rights of women finds only partial satisfaction in this law. Women are granted a measure of legal dignity, but the land passed on through them will return to patriarchal patterns in the next generation.

56 (c) COMMISSIONING OF JOSHUA (27:12–23). Moses will die before entry into the land because of his sin at Meribah (20:2–13; cf. Deut 32:48–52; 34:1–9). This Priestly narrative is structured on the same pattern as the account of the death of Aaron and the commissioning of Eleazar in 20:22–29. In the case of Joshua, the emphasis lies on his role as military leader and his subordination to the high priest. The death of Moses, mentioned in vv 12–13 as if it were imminent, remains in suspense until the end of Deut. **12.** *the mountain of Abarim:* A vague reference to the Transjordanian mountains facing Jericho. Deut 32:49 and 34:1 give the further specification that Moses died on Mt. Nebo. **21.** The Urim and Thummim were sacred objects used to determine the will of God (→ Institutions, 76:9).

57 (d) THE RITUAL CALENDAR (28:1–30:1). The oldest ritual calendars (Exod 23:14–17; 34:18–26; Deut 16:17) dealt with the three great pilgrimage feasts of Passover/Unleavened Bread, Weeks, and Ingathering/Tabernacles (→ Institutions, 76:122–138). The present passage is the end product of a long development, which included the phases represented in Lev 23:1–38 and Ezek 45:18–46:15. In the exhaustive overview of Num 28–29, all previous legislation, including the regulations for the daily offering (Exod 29:38–42) and for drink and cereal offerings (Num 15:1–12) has been synthesized by a late Priestly redactor. **1–8.** The daily offerings made morning and evening, also known as the perpetual holocaust, go back as early as the monarchical period (1 Kgs 18:29,36; 2 Kgs 3:20; 16:15). **9–10.** The author is not interested in the character of the Sabbath as a day of rest (→ Institutions, 76:118–121) but only in the sacrifices for that day, which are double the daily offering. Here and throughout chaps. 28–29 the quantities differ from the

requirements stipulated by Ezekiel (see Ezek 46:4). The sacrifices in Ezek, however, were to be offered by the prince (*nāśîʾ*), and the author of Num 28–29 probably thought of them as supplementary to the offerings presented by the community. **16–25.** The family celebration of the Passover meal (Exod 12:21–27) is left unmentioned as the Priestly author focuses on the Temple cult. **26.** *the day of firstfruits:* A unique designation for what is usually called the feast of Weeks. **29:1.** The festival of the first day of the seventh month is called "the day of *tĕrûʿâ*." The Hebr word may refer to the blowing of trumpets, as seems to be the case in the parallel passage of Lev 23:24. In fact, Num 10:10 specifies the blowing of trumpets on the first day of every month. **7–11.** Surprisingly, the tenth day of the seventh month is not called Day of Atonement as it is in Lev 23:27. **12.** The feast of Ingathering or Tabernacles (*sukkôt*), named after the custom of dwelling in huts (Lev 23:39–43), was the harvest celebration of the fall and a time of great rejoicing. Its importance is attested by the lavish offerings prescribed for the eight-day period.

58 (e) VOWS MADE BY WOMEN (30:2–17). The section on vows made by women is generally recognized as a relatively late component of the Priestly material. The general principle is that vows are binding. An unmarried woman's vow can be annulled by her father if he acts on the day he first hears of it. If a woman made a vow before marriage, even if her father let it stand, it can still be annulled later by her husband if he acts on the day he hears of it. A widow or divorced woman has the same rights and obligations concerning vows as a man does. The husband has right of annulment over vows made by his wife after their marriage, but a husband who annuls his wife's vows at a time later than the day he hears of it bears the guilt for the default.

The OT laws concerning vows fail to satisfy modern standards of equal rights for men and women. These laws do, of course, recognize that a woman can make binding vows. They even guard against completely arbitrary interference by limiting the man's right of annulment to the day on which he becomes cognizant of the vow. In the final analysis, however, women are patronizingly treated as subordinates who must be protected against their own lack of responsible judgment.

59 (f) THE HOLY WAR AGAINST MIDIAN (31:1–54). A holy war is launched against the Midianites in retaliation for their part in the Baal Peor incident (25:16–18). The Midianite towns are destroyed and the adult males killed. Moses is angered that the women and children have been spared, so all but the virgin girls are slaughtered. After purification rites are carried out (D. P. Wright, *VT* 35 [1985] 213–23), the booty is equally divided between combatants and noncombatants. Each of the two groups gives a percentage to the priests and Levites. Finally the officers contribute the gold objects they had looted to the sanctuary.

The story belongs to a relatively late stage of the Priestly tradition. The text alludes to the Balaam narrative (Num 22–24), which it ties in with the Baal Peor incident (Num 25) by making Balaam responsible for instigating the apostasy (31:8,16). Num 31:2 alludes to 27:12–23. The mention of trumpets (31:6) and the description of purification rites (31:19–24) illustrate earlier legislation in Num 10:1–10 and 19:11–22 respectively. De Vaulx (*Nombres* 352–59) points out many allusions to and dependencies on other texts such as Judg 21:1–12; Judg 6–8; and 1 Sam 30:24–25. This evidence of the anthological style leads de Vaulx to characterize the chapter as essentially midrashic in nature. The author has taken up the tradition of the "day of Midian" (Isa 9:3; Ps 83:10), which originally pertained to the defeat of the

Midianites by Gideon (Judg 6–8) and created an idealized version of this victory projected back to the time of Moses. The resultant story functions as a typical representation of God's vengeance (v 3) against his enemies and points to the eschatological victory of God rather than a factual historical event. This conclusion dovetails with the skepticism aroused by the unrealistic elements within the story itself: the enormous quantity of booty, the impossibility of reconciling annihilation of Midianites with their invasion of Israel just a few generations later (Judg 6:1–6), and the conflict with older traditions of harmony between Moses and Midian (Exod 18:1–27; Num 10:28–32).

Our modern distress at the genocide depicted in this chapter is alleviated in part by the knowledge that these events did not really happen. Nonetheless, the fact that the human extermination envisaged here could even be contemplated in an idealized narrative indicates the magnitude of the hermeneutical task which must be undertaken before the Bible can be applied in a way that makes contemporary theological sense.

60   (g) SETTLEMENT OF GAD AND REUBEN (32:1–42). Gad and Reuben request permission to settle in Transjordan because the land is suitable for their livestock. Moses interprets this proposal as a dire threat to the projected invasion of Canaan. Gad and Reuben agree that having made their families and cattle secure, they will join the invasionary force, returning to Transjordan only after Canaan has been secured. Moses officially grants Gad and Reuben (along with half of Manasseh) title to lands in Transjordan. These traditions served to explain how it had come about that some of the Israelite tribes occupied territory outside of Canaan proper. At the same time, the cohesiveness of the twelve tribes as forming one people is strongly affirmed. Conventional source-critical analysis cannot be carried out satisfactorily. If J and E elements are present, they have been thoroughly reworked in the process of redaction.

3. Of the places listed here and in vv 34–37, all those which can be identified lay between the Arnon and the Jabbok. Ataroth, Dibon, Nebo, Kiriathaim and Baal-Meon are mentioned in the 9th-cent. Moabite inscription of King Mesha (*ANET* 320–21). Heshbon was the site of a major excavation project which began in 1968 and was directed by S. Horn (*IDBSup* 410–11). **9.** The reference to the exploration of the land seems to reflect the limited view of J in 13:22–24 and to ignore the P concept of 13:21 that the spies penetrated to the northern extremities of Canaan. **28.** The awareness of the position of Eleazar (20:25–28) and the commissioning of Joshua (27:12–23) reflect Priestly concerns. **33.** The reader is not prepared to expect the introduction of Manasseh at this point. **34–38.** The list of cities belonging to Gad and Reuben comes from very old traditions (perhaps pre-monarchical) and is the tradition-historical starting point in the development of this chapter. **39–42.** Supplementary information related to Deut 3:14–15; Josh 13:8–13,31; and Judg 8:11.

61   (h) Overview of the Desert Itinerary (33:1–49). The list in Num 33 itemizes the stations in the journey from Egypt to the plains of Moab (→ 24 above). Most of the place-names cannot be identified with any known geographical locations. Many of the identifications proposed by scholars are tentative and some are highly dubious. Standardized formulas are employed to introduce the points of departure and of arrival. A number of features in the list are characteristic of the P tradition. Notably, all of the geographical locations mentioned in the Priestly account of the wilderness wandering are included in the present list, with the sole exception of Paran. The list includes some names found

in the J stratum but not in P, although some important JE place-names are omitted. The names in vv 30b–34a occur only in Deut 10:6–7. Finally, there are sixteen names that occur nowhere else in the Pentateuch. M. Noth (*PJ* 36 [1940] 5–28) proposed that some of the latter places lay along an ancient pilgrim route to Sinai (which he located in northwest Arabia). A completely different approach is taken by G. I. Davies (*Way of the Wilderness*) and Budd (*Numbers* 352–53). They suggest that the itinerary originated in deuteronomistic circles.

62   (i) APPORTIONMENT OF THE LAND OF CANAAN (33:50–35:34). This long section, consisting of five Yahweh speeches (33:50–56; 34:1–12; 34:16–29; 35:1–8; 35:9–34) and a speech of Moses (34:13–15) stems from the later stages of Priestly redaction of Num. De Vaulx (*Nombres* 382) views the whole of 33:50–36:13 as a small legislative code of laws relating to the division of the land tied together by an inclusio in its first and last verses.

In 33:50–56 the Priestly redactors have synthesized material from older Pentateuchal sources (Exod 23:20–32; 34:10–16; Deut 7:2–5; 12:2–3) on the drastic measures necessary to forestall the negative influences of Canaanite religion. A conditional curse is linked to failure to annihilate the Canaanites; cf. Lev 26:14–40; Deut 28:15–68; Josh 23:12–13.

The boundaries of the land to be apportioned are then defined (34:1–15) in the idealized dimensions reflected by the expression "from Lebo-hamath to the wadi of Egypt" (1 Kgs 8:65; 2 Chr 7:8; cf. Num 13:21). Another tradition had an even more extensive territory in mind, one that would extend to the Euphrates (Gen 15:18). A more realistic formulation is found in the expression "from Dan to Beersheba," which occurs frequently in Judg, Sam, and Kgs. The closest parallel to the present passage is Ezek 47:13–20. The S frontier (vv 3–5) is equivalent to the S boundary of the tribe of Judah as described in Josh 15:1–4. The location of many of the sites mentioned here is uncertain. Essentially, the boundary started at the S tip of the Dead Sea, dipped down to Kadesh (modern Ain Qudeis) and curved back up to coincide with the River of Egypt (Wadi el-Arish). The W border is ideally set at the Mediterranean, ignoring the fact that the coast was occupied by the Philistines (so also Deut 11:24; Jos 1:4; 15:12,47; 17:9; 19:29). **7–9.** The only definition of the N boundary comparable to that in vv 7–9 is Ezek 47:15–17 (see also 48:1–2). None of the places can be identified with certainty. Details about proposed identifications are given by de Vaulx (*Nombres* 386–87). The S part of the E frontier is simply the Jordan Valley. Its N part is poorly understood because the places named in this connection cannot be located. A harmonizing redactional addition in vv 13–15 takes account of the Transjordanian traditions of chap. 32.

According to 34:16–29, the apportionment of the land is to take place under the direction of Joshua and Eleazar in agreement with Josh 14:1; 19:51 (cf. Num 27:15–23). They are to be assisted by a representative (*nāśî'*) from each of ten tribes. Gad and Reuben are omitted because their settlement in Transjordan has already been determined. The appointment of representatives parallels the arrangements made for the census (1:4–16) and the exploration of the land (13:1–16).

Since the Levites have no tribal allotment of land, the other tribes are to give over to them 48 residence cities with adjacent pasture lands (35:1–8; see B. Mazar in *Congress Volume: Oxford, 1959* [VTSup 7; Leiden, 1960] 193–205). These places are not owned by the tribe of Levi. They simply have the use of them and, apparently, are not the sole inhabitants of the designated cities. The account here is probably based upon Josh 21:1–42 (see also Lev 25:32–34), which contains the list of cities involved. Some scholars believe the idea of levitical cities is a utopian fabrication of the postexilic priesthood. Others think that there must have been some factual institution of the monarchical period which was later reinterpreted by the Priestly tradition. The many divergent theories about the exact nature of such an institution are surveyed by Budd (*Numbers* 371–76). The exact reconstruction will depend on how one understands the more general history of the Levites and their relationship with the priests (→ Institutions, 76:18–20). It is not clear how the measurements in vv 4–5 were to be taken nor how the information in the two verses is to be reconciled.

Regulations governing the cities of refuge, which relate to Josh 20:1–9 in the same way as Num 35:1–8 does to Josh 21:1–42, follow naturally upon discussion of the levitical cities (cf. 35:6). The existence of places of asylum is based on ancient institutions (1 Kgs 1:50–53; 2:28–31; Exod 21:12–24; Deut 19:1–13) which placed restrictions on the practice of blood vengeance by the relative of a person who had been killed. The Israelite legislation on this subject demonstrates an effort to reconcile the old sacral concept that bloodshed required vengeance with the ethical principle that a person involved in accidental homicide did not deserve death. The idea that confinement to the city of refuge ended with the death of the high priest (v 28) may be an adaptation of an older principle of general amnesty at the death of a king and the inauguration of a new reign. Some authors find here a suggestion that the death of the high priest, as a representative sacred person, somehow makes atonement in the place of the accidental homicide. Verses 31–32 prohibit payment of money to substitute for the death penalty in case of voluntary or involuntary manslaughter, a practice documented in other ancient law codes. The high value of human life as well as the egalitarian tendency of the OT legal tradition precluded such monetary payments in exchange for a life. In vv 33–34, the theological seriousness of the issue of bloodshed is strongly highlighted in terms of the central theme of Num: The purity of the land must be maintained because the Holy God dwells there among his people.

63 (j) THE DAUGHTERS OF ZELOPHEHAD (36:1–13). A final Priestly section may be taken as a supplement to 27:1–11. In the latter passage, it was recognized that women in a family without a male heir had the right to inherit property. Here, as a kind of afterthought, the problem arises that if the women marry, the property might eventually pass to another tribe, a situation that would apparently have become permanent as a result of an otherwise undocumented provision of the law of jubilee (Lev 25:8–34; cf. Lev 27:16–25). To avoid this eventuality, they are enjoined to marry within their own tribe (cf. Tob 6:12; 7:1–13). The last verse (13) is apparently a conclusion to the whole final section of the book, which deals with the apportionment of the land.

6

DEUTERONOMY

Joseph Blenkinsopp

BIBLIOGRAPHY

1 *General survey:* Eissfeldt, *EOTI* 171-82, 219-33. Weiser, *OTIFD* 125-35.

Older commentaries: Bertholet, A., *Deuteronomium* (KHAT; Tübingen, 1899). Driver, S. R., *Deuteronomy* (ICC; Edinburgh, 1903). Steuernagel, C., *Das Deuteronomium* (HAT; Göttingen, 1923).

Recent commentaries: Craigie, P. C., *The Book of Deuteronomy* (NICOT; GR, 1976). Mayes, A. D. H., *Deuteronomy* (NCB; London, 1979). Phillips, A., *Deuteronomy* (CBC; Cambridge, 1973). Von Rad, G., *Deuteronomy* (OTL; Phl, 1966). Wright, G. E., "Deuteronomy," *IB* 2. 311-57.

Significant recent studies: Alt, A., "Die Heimat des Deuteronomiums," *KlS* 2. 250-75; "The Origins of Israelite Law," *AEOT* 81-132. Baltzer, K., *The Covenant Formulary* (Phl, 1971). Blenkinsopp, J., *Prophecy and Canon* (Notre Dame, 1977) 24-53. Braulik, G., *Testament des Mose. Das Buch Deuteronomium* (Stuttgart, 1976). Carmichael, C. M., *The Laws of Deuteronomy* (Ithaca, 1974). Clements, R. E., "Deuteronomy and the Jerusalem Cult Tradition," *VT* 15 (1965) 300-12. Le Déaut, R., *Deutéronome: Targum du Pentateuque* 4 (Paris, 1980). Levenson, J., "Who inserted the book of the Torah?" *HTR* 68 (1975) 203-33. Lindars, B., "Torah in Deuteronomy," *Words and Meanings*

(ed. P. R. Ackroyd and B. Lindars; Cambridge, 1968) 117-36. Lohfink, N., *Das Hauptgebot* (AnBib 20; Rome, 1963); "Deuteronomy," *IDBSup* 229-32. McCarthy, D. J., *Treaty and Covenant* (AnBib 21A; 2d ed.; Rome, 1978); *Old Testament Covenant* (Oxford, 1972). Mayes, A. D. H., *The Story of Israel between Settlement and Exile* (GR, 1983). Mendenhall, G. E., "Covenant Forms in Israelite Traditions," *BA* 17 (1954) 49-76. Minette de Tillesse, G., "Sections 'tu' et sections 'vous' dans le Deutéronome," *VT* 12 (1962) 29-87. Nicholson, E. W., *Deuteronomy and Tradition* (Oxford, 1967). Noth, M., *The Deuteronomistic History* (JSOTSup 15; Sheffield, 1981); *A History of Pentateuchal Traditions* (EC, 1972). Perlitt, L., *Bundestheologie im Alten Testament* (WMANT 36; Berlin, 1969). Phillips, A., *Ancient Israel's Criminal Law* (Oxford, 1970). Polzin, R., *Moses and the Deuteronomist* (NY, 1980). Seitz, G., *Redaktionsgeschichtliche Studien zum Deuteronomium* (BWANT 93; Stuttgart, 1971). Von Rad, G., *Studies in Deuteronomy* (London, 1953). Wevers, J. W., *Text History of the Greek Deuteronomy* (Göttingen, 1978). Weinfeld, M., *Deuteronomy and the Deuteronomic School* (Oxford, 1972). Würthwein, E., "Die Josianische Reform und das Deuteronomium," *ZTK* 73 (1976) 395-423.

INTRODUCTION

2 **(I) Title, Place in Canon.** Deut is the fifth and last book of the Pentateuch or "five fifths of the Torah." The title comes to us via the Latin from the LXX title *deuteronomion,* "second law," from the Greek of 17:18, the Hebr text of which says, however, that the king must write for himself a copy of the law. The title is not, however, entirely inappropriate since the D law was intended to supersede the so-called Covenant Code (Exod 20:23-23:19). In Jewish tradition the title is simply "words" (*dĕbārîm*) from the opening verse. The book was ascribed to Moses, though it was conceded that the account of his death in the final chapter came from another hand (*b. B. Bat.* 14b-15a).

A fivefold Torah, with Deut a separate book, is not attested before the Roman period (Josephus, *Ag. Ap.* 1.37-41). While there is continuity with Num, the last chapters of which also contain laws given "in the plains of Moab" (Num 36:13), there are also indications of the

deuteronomic law, with prologue and epilogue, as a distinct, authoritative, and public text which must not be tampered with (4:2; 12:32), which must be taught (6:7, etc.), made publicly available (31:9-13,24-26), and which was originally published under royal auspices (17:18). Moreover, it is Deut that speaks consistently for the first time not of laws but the Law (see Lindars, "Torah"), and it is this Law which is generally referred to in the historical corpora (e.g., 2 Kgs 14:6 quoting Deut 24:16). The appearance of the law book, therefore, marks an important stage in the formation of the canon. At some point in the postexilic period the book was incorporated into the P narrative by means of the date at 1:3, of a type not attested elsewhere in the book but common in P (esp. Num 33:38, the death of Aaron), and the account of the death of Moses preceded by the commissioning of Joshua (32:48-52; 34:1,7-9). Comparison with Num 27:12-23, an earlier parallel P narrative, suggests that the death of Moses was transferred to its present position after Deut had been incorporated into the narrative structure. By this means the entire Pentateuch was rounded off at Moses' death and the history of founding events was thus restricted to the period up to but excluding the occupation of the land.

3 (II) Formation of Deut. Although almost all scholars admit that Deut reached its present form as a result of a long process of formation, there is no consensus on the interpretation of the internal criteria (lexical, stylistic, thematic) on which the history of the process has to be based. Von Rad's claim (*PHOE* 33–40) that the form of the book reflects a covenant ceremony at the tribal sanctuary of Shechem is suggestive but flawed, and in any case leaves much unexplained. Equally suggestive has proved to be the international treaty analogy (Mendenhall, *BA* 17 [1954] 49–76; McCarthy, *Old Testament Covenant; et al.*) esp. when confined to the Assyrian vassal treaties and to specific features in Deut (e.g., the curses in chap. 28); but it too falls short as an overall explanation. Linguistic and thematic parallels with Dtr, composed no earlier than *ca.* 560 in its final form, suggest that epoch for the decisive phase in the redaction of the book. There would be considerable agreement that the bulk of chaps. 1–4, 27, and 29–30 was added at that time together with a further expansion of the legal material in chaps. 12–26. While recapitulating and remolding themes in the older narrative tradition, the historical prologue in chaps. 1–3 may be viewed as part of a large-scale exilic-deuteronomistic work including a narrative of founding events in the Mosaic period, a collection of updated laws, a history of the kingdoms and a collection of edited prophetic material. Indications, now also widely accepted, of a first draft of the history in the late Judean period, strengthen the hypothesis of an earlier editorial stage of Deut at that time, consisting principally of the bulk of chaps. 5–11 and 28 as a framework for the laws.

A pivotal point in Pentateuchal studies has been the belief, traceable to Wilhelm de Wette in the early 19th cent., that the law book found during repair of the Temple in Josiah's reign (*ca.* 621) was an earlier edition of our Deut (2 Kgs 22:3–10). Although some features of the book support the origin or at least promulgation of Deut in that period (e.g., the nationalist ethos expressed in the rules for warfare and the native character of key institutions such as the monarchy and prophecy) Josiah was not the first to attempt centralization of cult (see 2 Kgs 18:4,22) nor was this the first time that the Temple was restored (see 2 Kgs 12:4–16). It is also possible that the account of the restoration and discovery of the book is a free composition of the Deuteronomists to explain the religious infidelity of the previous two reigns and the contrasting religious zeal of Josiah. It would, in any case, be reasonable to trace the origins of the book to the movement of religious reform—which also involved political emancipation—emerging sporadically throughout the history of Judah, a movement that must have received new impetus and motivation from the destruction of the northern kingdom.

Although the preaching and the formulation of the laws in Deut have been deeply influenced by prophets both Judean and Ephraimite, there is little probability to the hypothesis that prophets authored the book. A better case (argued by A. Bentzen and G. von Rad) can be made for levitical priests unattached to the Jerusalem Temple, but we know too little of their functions under the monarchy to advance beyond a mere possibility. That the legal material was drafted by scribes (suggested by the criticism of their activity in Jer 8:8–9) seems quite likely

(see in particular Weinfeld, *Deuteronomy*), but this function hardly amounts to authorship. We simply do not have the information to answer this question with any assurance.

4 (III) Theology of Deut. The composite nature of the book would require that we trace the development of ideas within it. All we can do here is indicate some of the leading ideas. Deut is, first of all, a law book, a point often neglected in Christian scholarship. The care to regulate life by law, one of the chief characteristics of Judaism, is seen in the adaption of an ancient legal tradition to new situations (e.g., changes in the legislation governing slavery). The D law recapitulates the message of the great prophets (e.g., "justice, only justice you shall pursue," 16:20). In some respects a utopian program, it comes down strongly on the side of the disadvantaged classes, e.g., widows, fatherless, and aliens. The purpose of the law is to outline a level of moral performance compatible with the self-revelation of Israel's God and Israel's high calling (e.g., 4:32–40). Although the covenant certainly goes back to ancient ideas and events, its mature formulation is found for the first time in Deut. While closely connected with the Horeb covenant (see esp. chaps. 1–3), the covenant in Moab is at the same time a new covenant (e.g., 28:69) corresponding to the needs of a new situation (cf. Jer 31:31–34 edited by the same school). One of its most important consequences is the association between people and land, a permanent aspect of Jewish self-understanding often underestimated by Christians. Israel is a holy people (e.g., 7:6; 14:2) which expresses its fidelity to the one God in the *Shema*, "Hear, O Israel" (6:4–9). At the risk of oversimplifying, the message of Deut can be summarized as: one God, one people, one sanctuary. It is understandable, therefore, that this most theological book of the OT has had an enormous influence on both Judaism and Christianity.

5 (IV) Outline.
(I) First Address of Moses: From Horeb to Moab (1:1–4:49)
  (A) Introduction to the Address (1:1–5)
  (B) Command to Occupy the Land (1:6–8)
  (C) Tribal and Judicial Organization (1:9–18)
  (D) The Stay at Kadesh (1:19–46)
  (E) Passage through Edom, Moab, Ammon (2:1–25)
  (F) Conquest of Heshbon and Bashan (2:26–3:11)
  (G) Settlement of Transjordanian Tribes (3:12–22)
  (H) Moses' Unanswered Prayer (3:23–29)
  (I) Prologue to the Promulgation of and Instruction in the Law (4:1–14)
  (J) On the Danger of Idolatry (4:15–31)
  (K) The Unique Vocation of Israel (4:32–40)
  (L) Appendix: Cities of Refuge (4:41–43)
  (M) Conclusion to the First Address (4:44–49)
(II) Second Address: Homiletic Introduction to the Law Book (5:1–11:32)
  (A) Summons (5:1–5)
  (B) The Decalogue (5:6–21)
  (C) Sequel to the Decalogue (5:22–6:3)
  (D) A Law for Life in the Land (6:4–25)
  (E) Command to Destroy the Peoples of Canaan and Their Cults (7:1–11)
  (F) Prosperity in the Land Assured by Fidelity to the Law (7:12–26)
  (G) Historical Recollection a Counter to the Temptations of the Land (8:1–20)
  (H) Occupation of the Land the Work of God, Not Israel (9:1–6)
  (I) Apostasy at Horeb (9:7–24)
  (J) Intercession of Moses; Second Covenant (9:25–10:11)

COMMENTARY

6 (I) First Address of Moses: From Horeb to Moab (1:1–4:49).

(A) Introduction to the Address (1:1–5). In its original form (1a,5) it introduced the discourse on the law (5:1), "the words" of 1:1 referring to commandments (cf. 5:22). It has been much expanded with topographical detail and a P date (v 3; →2 above). **1b–2.** This topographical gloss locates the address in the Arabah E of Jordan in the area of the Dead Sea. The locations of Dizahab, Laban, Suph, and Tophel are unknown. According to Num 33:17 Hazeroth was two days' trek from Sinai. Paran is in the E Sinai (Num 10:11–12; 13:3,26) and Kadesh at its northern extremity. There is evidently some confusion here about the location of the address (for Tophel, see H. Cazelles, *VT* 9 [1959] 412–15; for the location of Horeb, see G. I. Davies, *PQR* 111 [1979] 87–101; for the Kadesh traditions, see H. H. Rowley, *From Joseph to Joshua* [Oxford, 1948] 104–5; and M. Newman, *The People of the Covenant* [NY, 1962] 72–101). **3.** According to P, therefore, Moses died six months after Aaron (cf. Num 33:38). **4.** A summary of the traditions in Num 21:21–35 (cf. Deut 2:26–3:11). **5.** *beyond the Jordan:* This links with v 1a after the insertion of vv 1b–4, and "this Torah" refers back to "the words" the exposition of which has to wait until 5:1ff. or perhaps 12:1ff.

7 (B) Command to Occupy the Land (1:6–8). There follows not legal exposition but a history of events from Horeb to Moab in the form of reminiscence: the occupation is the result of a divine mandate following on the ancestral promise. **7.** *Amorites:* A generic term for the people of the central hill country. *Canaanites:* The people of the coastal region (cf. Num 13:29). The extent reflects the greater Israel of the Davidic–Solomonic kingdom.

8 (C) Tribal and Judicial Organization (1:9–18). A conflation of Num 11:14–17, the imposition of hands on the elders at the Tent, and Exod 18:13–27, the subdelegation of authority on the advice of Moses' father-in-law; here the latter is not mentioned and the appointment takes place after the giving of the law. **13–14.** Wisdom is needed for governing and judging; cf. 16:9 and the near parallel Exod 23:8. **15.** The term "commanders" (*śārîm*) and decimal division suggest military organization; "officers" (*šōṭĕrîm*), usually associated with elders and judges (Num 11:16; Deut 16:18; 29:9; 31:28;

Josh 8:33), had a scribal (cf. Akk *šāṭāru*, "to write") and an administrative function not clearly definable. **16.** The distinction is between fellow Israelite (*'aḥ,* "brother") and resident alien (*gēr*), the latter the object of special protection under the law. **17.** The creation of a central judiciary, presupposed by D legislation (17:8–13), may date to the reign of Jehoshaphat (see comment on 17:8–13).

9 (D) The Stay at Kadesh (1:19–46). The first stage of the journey is from Horeb to Kadesh-barnea, an oasis *ca.* 80 km. S of Beer-sheba (but see Num 13:26; 33:36). It represents a settlement phase of indeterminate length with which traditions in Num 12–20 are associated. It appears also to have played a part in the development of the early legal traditions (cf. 33:8–11; Num 20:13). **20–21.** The divine mandate to possess the land, of central importance for Deut, is repeated. **22–25.** The sending ahead of patrols follows Num 13–14, but in a much-abbreviated form. The suggestion here comes from the people (cf. Num 13:1) and is approved by Moses. **24.** Eshcol means "bunch of grapes"; cf. the theme of the miraculous fertility of the land in Num 13:23–24. **26–28.** The people refuse to continue, accusing Yahweh of intent to destroy them. The Anakim (giants) were a non-Semitic group settled around Hebron; they were probably Hurrian to judge by the names in Josh 15:13–14. **29–40.** Moses' counterexhortation expounds the familiar D theme of the consequences of infidelity and adumbrates the holy war motif. **31a.** The sudden change to sg. and awkward syntax suggest an addition. For Israel as Yahweh's son, see also Hos 11:1; Exod 4:22; Deut 8:5; 14:1; 32:6. **36.** A compressed version of the traditions about Caleb the Kenizzite, eponymous ancestor of an originally non-Israelite, probably Hurrian group (cf. Num 13:30; 14:6–7; 32:12; Josh 14:6–15; 15:13–19 = Judg 1:11–15). **37.** Unlike the tradition in Num 20 and its P version (Num 27:14; cf. Deut 32:51–52), Deut insists that Moses was punished for the people's sin, not for his own (see also 3:26; 4:21). **41–46.** This account of the abortive invasion from the S follows Num 14:39–45. It ends with a return to the Kadesh oasis.

10 (E) Passage through Edom, Moab, Ammon (2:1–25). 1–8a. The passage through Edom follows Num 20:14–21 but does not speak of Edom's refusal. The first stage consists of peaceful infiltration.

7. The sudden change to the sg. suggests an addition; the chronology also contradicts 2:14. **8a.** *brethren:* This implies kinship with Edom, perhaps also treaty relationship; cf. Num 20:14; Deut 23:7 and the Jacob-Esau cycle in Gen 25:19ff. **8b-15.** For the passage through Moab, see Num 21:4-20. Ar appears to have been the chief city; its location is unknown. **9.** *the sons of Lot:* Cf. Gen 19:30-38, an example of political satire. **10-12.** One of several antiquarian notes added to this section. Emim and Zamzummim are local variants of Rephaim (see Gen 14:5). *Horites:* Hurrians rather than troglodytes (cf. Gen 14:6). **14-15.** A new, untainted generation had to arise before the occupation, perhaps reflecting the situation of the exilic Deuteronomist; 38 years from the first deportation in 598 would take one down to the time of writing (→ 3 above). **20-23.** Another antiquarian gloss. *Caphtor* is probably Crete and Caphtorites the Sea Peoples (see most recently J. Strange, *Caphtor/Keftiu: A New Investigation* [Leiden, 1980]). **25.** In sg., possibly added as a peroration to this address.

11   (F) Conquest of Heshbon and Bashan (2:26-3:11). A somewhat abbreviated version of Num 21:21-35. The fate of the two kings came to be celebrated in liturgical hymn (Pss 135:11; 136:19-20). **26.** *Heshbon:* Perhaps Tell Ḥesbân, ca. 25 km. E of the Jordan. **27.** *the road:* The great caravan route called "the King's Highway" (Num 21:22) E of the Jordan from the Red Sea to Damascus and beyond. These negotiations do not fit very well with the divine command (2:24) and perhaps come from a different source. **30.** For this theological motif see Exod 4:2; Isa 6:10. **32.** *Jahaz:* A Moabite city which occurs with Aroer on the 9th-cent. Mesha stele. (For this part of the story see J. van Seters, *JBL* 99 [1980] 177ff.) **34-35.** The vowing of the subjugated peoples to extermination is not in accord with the D regulations, which require the execution only of captive males (Deut 20:13-14). That this atrocious practice was only too real is confirmed by the Mesha stele (*ANET* 320). **37.** *you:* In sg.; see comment on 2:25. **3:1.** Bashan is the broad, fertile land N of Ammon, famous for good pasture (cf. Amos 4:1; Mic 7:14). Here the account in Num 21:33-35 is somewhat expanded. *Edrei:* Perhaps Edreʿât, ca. 70 km. E of the Jordan, at the southern limits of Bashan. **9.** Another antiquarian gloss. *Sirion:* Occurs in the Ras Shamra texts; in Ps 29:6 it is parallel with Lebanon. *Senir:* Cf. Cant 4:8: 1 Chr 5:23. **11.** Another note, alluding to a well-known feature in the vicinity of Rabbah (Amman), probably a fallen megalith or large (*ca.* 13' x 6') and regular basalt slab.

12   (G) Settlement of Transjordanian Tribes (3:12-22). A much-abbreviated version of Num 32 (cf. Josh 13:8-13,15-31) dealing with Reuben, Gad, and the half-tribe of Manasseh. Reuben and Gad were the first to become sedentary, but the encroachments of Moab and Ammon rendered their situation precarious (cf. Gen 49:3-4,19; Deut 33:6) The postulate of tribal unity and solidarity required that they participate in the conquest, which Josh 22:1-9 asserts that they did; but the taunt directed at Reuben (Judg 5:15-16) and the absence of allusion to Gad in the Song of Deborah point in a different direction. Their location E of the Jordan remained problematic (see, e.g., Josh 22:10-34). **13b-14.** A reminiscence of the conquest of Argob-Bashan by Jair (Judg 10:3-5). Geshur and Maacah lay farther to the N in the Golan. **15.** Perhaps intended as a correction to vv 12-13 (cf. Num 32:39); Machir is a Manassite clan (Judg 5:14). **17.** *Chinnereth:* Tell el-Oreimeh on the NW shore of the lake of that name, commanding the Ginnosar valley and the important route passing through it. **20.** The idea of rest (*mĕnûḥâ*), i.e., secure possession of the land, is a key idea in Deut (cf. 12:9; 25:19; Ps 95:11). It seems to have

been at one time associated with the ark (Num 10:33). **21-22.** Continuity between the work of Moses and that of Joshua, based on charismatic succession, is a dominant D theme (cf. 31:7-8; Josh 1:1-18).

13   (H) Moses' Unanswered Prayer (3:23-29). Not in the source, but reminiscent of Num 14:13-25. **24.** *your mighty hand:* Traditional exodus language, much used in Deut. The rhetorical question is a mark of the D style (cf. 4:7-8,33-34). The theme of Yahweh's incomparability, similar to Dt-Isa (40:12-14,18,25; etc.), suggests the exilic situation. **26.** Moses is punished on account of the people's sin (see also 1:37; 4:21); P, in keeping with Ezekiel's teaching on personal accountability, imputes wrongdoing to Moses himself (Num 20:12; 27:13-14; Deut 32:50-52). **27.** *Pisgah:* An alternative name for Nebo (see 34:1; Num 21:20; 23:14); cf. Mt. Abarim in P (Num 27:12; Deut 32:49). Nothing in the context suggests that the viewing, here and in 34:1-3, implies legal title to the land. Explicit allusion to the promise suggests a parallel with Gen 13:14-15: not Abraham but his descendants will possess the land. This promise was of great concern to the generation of the return from exile. **28.** The charge to Joshua is repeated later (31:7-8,14-15; 34:9). **29.** *Beth-peor:* Site of a Transjordanian Baal sanctuary (cf. 4:3; Num 25:1-9) near Pisgah (Josh 13:20). The topographical juxtaposition suggests the countering of alien cults of the land and the contrast of the Mosaic with the post-Mosaic epoch.

14   (I) Prologue to the Promulgation of and Instruction in the Law (4:1-14). The connection between this section and the preceding is not original, for it assumes that instruction in the law has just been imparted (vv 1,5). It is possible that at one time 31:1-8 and the narrative strand following came immediately after 3:29 (von Rad, *Deuteronomy* 45, 48). **1.** *hear (šĕmaʿ):* A standard D opening for a liturgical address (5:1; 6:1,3, 4; 9:7). *statute (ḥōq):* A positive legal decree. *ordinance (mišpāṭ):* A judicial decision on the basis of case law. In Deut, Moses is preeminently a teacher (1:5; 4:5; 5:31; 6:1), pointing to the origin of the D legal instruction in the levitical-priestly teaching office. Law observance is an essential condition for secure possession of the land. **2.** The injunction not to alter the wording of a public text is an indication of "canonical" status; cf. the Code of Hammurabi (*ANET* 178). **3-4.** This passing allusion to the Baal-peor incident (Num 25:1-9) means that Moses is addressing the survivors; a situation appropriate for those who had resisted assimilation during the exilic age. **6-8.** Observance of the D law is to be Israel's wisdom (*ḥokmâ*) and discernment (*bînâ*), i.e., the equivalent of the wisdom tradition of other nations; an important step on the way to the identification of Torah with wisdom (Sir 24). The idea of a God who is near is important for the theology of the book; cf. 30:11-14 on the accessibility of the law. The injunction to perpetuate the memory of the founding events through education is basic to the D program (cf. 6:4-9,20-25; 11:19. **10.** *gather the people:* The vb. *haqhēl* (also 31:12,28) is a denominative form from *qāhāl*, cultic assembly, the Greek of which (*ekklēsia*) leads to the early Christian use of the term. **11-12.** The fire is symbolic of the numinous presence of the covenant God; the absence of a form (*tĕmûnâ*) is in keeping with the aniconic ideology of the book. **13.** In Deut covenant is closely associated with law, the "Ten Words" in particular. The binding force of covenant is expressed in the phrase "sworn covenant" into which one enters (29:12,14). *the Ten Words:* Elsewhere only at Exod 34:28 and Deut 10:4. The brief Decalogue did not require two tablets; two copies are probably meant, as was customary in vassal treaties.

15   (J) On the Danger of Idolatry (4:15–31).
This commentary on the prohibition of images includes
images of human beings and any other creatures (vv
15–18). The rejection of cults associated with such
images, esp. those of Baal and Asherah, was a central
point of reform under the monarchy (esp. 2 Kgs 23:4–7,
15). **17–18.** Theriomorphic deities were especially characteristic of Egyptian religion; see e.g., Ezek 8:10–12.
19. Astral cults may indicate Assyrian or Neo-Babylonian
provenience; cf. 2 Kgs 23:4,11. **20.** *iron furnace:* A D
expression (cf. 1 Kgs 8:51; Jer 11:4) for oppression in
Egypt. *special possession:* Used here of the people; at 4:38,
of the land. **23–24.** The peroration brings one back to the
opening allusion to Horeb. Yahweh as a "devouring
fire" (also 9:3) is taken from prophetic usage (Isa 29:6;
30:27,30). The title "jealous God" (*'ēl qannâ*) is ancient
(cf. Exod 20:5; 34:14; and Ugaritic parallels) and is
generally associated with the Decalogue (Deut 5:9; 6:15;
cf. 32:16,21). It implies rejection of the syncretic option
and therefore of divided cultic allegiance. **25–31.** An
address to the exiled community explaining the cause of
the disaster and prescribing a solution (cf. Josh 23:15–
16; 2 Kgs 17:7–23). The appeal to heaven and earth as
witnesses contains a faint echo of the witness of deities
to treaty making. **28.** Typical anti-idolatry polemic; cf.
Isa 40:19–20; 44:18–20; etc. **29.** This is the kernel of the
author's advice to the exilic community; cf. the similar
Jer 29:10–14 (edited by D), which refers explicitly to
exile. The "seek" passages in Amos (5:4–5,6–7,14–15)
may be from the same milieu. **30.** *you will return:* "Turning" or conversion (*tĕšûbâ*), often playing on the idea of
physical return, is a key concept from the time of the
exile. **31.** The peroration; cf. 4:24.
**16   (K) The Unique Vocation of Israel (4:32–
40).** One of the rhetorical high points of the book. **32.**
For the sapiential tradition, in evidence here, it is
axiomatic to seek guidance in the past and from the
created order. Use of the vb. *bārā'*, "create," again points
to the exilic age (cf. Isa 45:12,18). **34.** Using exodus
language, the author links the unique vocation of Israel
with the uniqueness of Yahweh; cf. also Dt-Isa. **35.** This
confession of faith (cf. 4:39) is attested in Dt-Isa (e.g.,
43:11; 44:6; 45:5,6; etc.). **37–38.** Israel's existence as a
moral community rests on a shared historical memory:
ancestors, exodus, occupation of the land. *with his own
presence:* Lit., "face" (*pānîm*); cf. Exod 33:14. The preacher
has forgotten that Moses is speaking prior to the
occupation. **40.** The peroration, forming an inclusion
with 4:1.
17   (L) Appendix: Cities of Refuge (4:41–43).
A very late addition designed to complete the account of
the settlement E of the Jordan (3:12–22). Taking off
from Deut 19:1–13, it understands the three additional
cities alluded to there as established for the Transjordanian tribes, following the detailed stipulations of Num
35:9–34 and Josh 20:1–9. The names are taken from this
last passage. The cities were intended only for those who
committed unintentional homicide.
**18   (M) Conclusion to the First Address (4:44–
49).** Close correspondence to 1:1–5 suggests an inclusion, rounding off the address. Both suggest that the
address at one time included laws (see 4:5 and cf. the
concluding formula in Num 36:13). **45.** *testimonies:* Also
in 6:17,20; (*'ēdôt*) has association with witnessing,
perhaps in the covenant context (cf. Akk *adē*, "treaty").
Elsewhere the tablets of the law are called "tablets of
testimony" (Exod 31:18) or simply "testimony" (Num
17:4). **46–49.** The conclusion has been expanded topo-
graphically as has the introduction. **46.** *Beth-peor:* See
comment on 3:29. **49.** *the slopes of Pisgah:* Also at 3:17;

perhaps Ras es-Siyaqhah, the nearest hill to Nebo, location of Moses' death (34:1).

(Begg, C., "The Literary Criticism of Deut 4,1–40," *ETL* 56
[1980] 10–55. Braulik, G., *Die Mittel deuteronomischer Rhetorik
erhoben aus Dt 4,1–40* [AnBib 68; Rome, 1978]; also *Bib* 59
[1978] 351–83. Mayes, A. D. H., "Deuteronomy 4 and the
Literary Criticism of Deuteronomy," *JBL* 100 [1981] 23–51;
also *IBS* 2 [1980] 67–83. Mittmann, S., *Dt 1,1–6,3 literarkritisch
und traditionsgeschichtlich untersucht* [BZAW 139; Göttingen,
1975].)

**19   (II) Second Address: Homiletic Introduc-
tion to the Law Book (5:1–11:32).**
        (A) Summons (5:1–5). Continuation of
historical reminiscence focusing on the Horeb covenant
reactualized for the present generation; cf. 4:10–14,
where covenant (*bĕrît*) is identified with the Decalogue.
The Decalogue in 5:6–21 is therefore presented as a
quotation. According to Deut, it was promulgated
through Moses and written by Yahweh on tablets (5:22),
and the promulgation of the "statutes and ordinances"
was delayed because of the terror inspired by the
theophany. Deut exploits this delay to introduce its
updated law in Moab on the eve of entry into the land.
20   (B) The Decalogue (5:6–21). This version
differs slightly from Exod 20:1–17 (see commentary on
individual stipulations); both go back to a common
Vorlage. The balance of probability favors a
deuteronomic origin influenced by the prophetic ethic
(e.g., Hos 4:2; Jer 7:9). At least the argument for antiquity based on the Hittite suzerainty treaties cannot be
sustained. For the text, the Nash Papyrus and the
Qumran phylacteries are important (H. Schneider, *BZ* 3
[1959] 18–31). **6.** Perhaps to be construed, "I, Yahweh,
am your God. . . ." What follows is a self-disclosure
formula, not a historical prologue analogous to the
treaty form. **7.** *before me:* May also be translated "against
me" or "in preference to me." If "before me," the allusion
would be to the images of other deities erected in
Yahweh's shrine (cf. Ezek 8:3). **8.** *graven image:* See
4:15–18. The image functions to make the deity present
and available. **9.** *jealous God:* See 4:24. The old belief in
guilt solidarity (Exod 34:7; Num 14:18) is here modified
by the phrase "of those who hate me." For the D rejection of collective imputability, see 24:16; 2 Kgs 14:6. **11.**
in vain: I.e., inappropriately, for evil purposes, e.g., perjury or magical invocation. Both the image and the name
could be manipulated for magical purposes. **12–15.** The
sabbath command is the longest; the motivation is
humanitarian (cf. Exod 23:12), unlike Exod 20:8–11,
which ties in with creation in the P manner. **16.** The
importance of a proper parent–child relationship is
emphasized in Deut (cf. 4:9; 6:7; etc.). **17.** The vb. *rāṣaḥ*
covers deliberate and accidental homicide but not capital
punishment and the killing of animals for food, both
practiced in Israel. **18.** In some LXX mss. and the Nash
Papyrus this stipulation follows v 16, dealing as it does
with the family. "Adultery" covers betrothal as well as
marriage. For a more detailed application, see 22:13–29.
19. The vb. *gānab*, "steal," applies to both property and
persons; for the latter, see Exod 21:16; Deut 24:7. **20.**
Witnessing in judicial proceedings was of crucial importance in a society with inadequate means of crime detection; see also 19:15–21. **21.** In Catholic tradition there
are two distinct commandments, but comparison with
Exod 20:17 suggests one only. The Exod version
concerns the household with all it contains including the
wife. Deut, however, puts the wife in a separate
category with a distinct verb—a modest but significant
advance.

21 **(C) Sequel to the Decalogue (5:22-6:3).**
22. *he added no more:* Only the Decalogue was given at
Horeb/Sinai, accompanied by the theophany (cf. 4:10-
12). Yahweh himself wrote the commandments (cf.
4:13; Exod 31:18; 32:16; 34:1), or, according to another
tradition, Moses did the writing (Exod 24:4; 34:27-28).
23-27. The assembly ("all the heads of your tribes" may
be a gloss) requests that henceforth Moses act as
mediator (cf. 4:33). This request follows Exod 20:18-20
closely but here serves to justify the later promulgation
of the laws. There is no evidence for a specific office of
covenant mediator in the time of the kingdoms. The task
was discharged by different categories at different times,
including the prophet (cf. Deut 18:15-19). **29.** The
Horeb community is the model for Israel in any age; cf.
4:40. **6:1-3.** That this is the conclusion to a distinct
address may be seen by comparison with 4:44-49: both
begin with "and," and in both cases the following section
begins with a call to listen. **2-3.** The final clause (to "that
it may go well with you") reverts to the sg. and may be
a later expansion. This description of the land, flowing
with milk and honey, occurs often in Deut (11:9; 26:9,
15; 27:3; 31:20); it may be borrowed from Canaanite
poetry of the Late Bronze Age (e.g., *ANET* 140).
22 **(D) A Law for Life in the Land (6:4-25).**
4. The call to hear (also 5:1; 9:1; 20:3; 27:9), paralleled
in the sapiential books (e.g., Prov 1:8), introduces the
command to love Yahweh alone. The transl. "Yahweh is
our God, Yahweh alone" makes better sense than its
alternative (as *RSV*). It is therefore not an affirmation of
monotheism but of exclusive devotion to Yahweh, a
dominant theme in Deut. In due course the *Shema* (Deut
6:4-9; 11:13-21; Num 15:37-41) became the principal
Jewish confession of faith, one that Jesus identified as the
greatest commandment (Matt 22:36-38). As in the
vassal treaties, the vb. "love" carries the political connotation of covenant fidelity (W. Moran, *CBQ* 25
[1963] 77-87). **7.** The laws ("words") must be taught to
children and be the object of total involvement (cf. Ps
1:2). **8.** This injunction, with Exod 13:9,16 and Deut
11:18, gave rise to the wearing of phylacteries (*těfillîn*;
attested from the late Second Temple period; see Matt
23:5 and the Murabba'at phylacteries), which were
pouches containing these texts worn on the forehead and
left forearm. **9.** The *mězûzâ*, "doorpost," came to refer to
the container with biblical texts affixed to the right-hand
doorpost of a house. **10-19.** Perhaps a later insertion
from the same circle as 4:1-40. **10-11.** The list of acqui-
sitions (cf. Josh 24:13) derives from an ancient blessing
formula; for the corresponding curse, see 28:30 and
Amos 5:11. **15.** For the end of the verse, cf. Amos 9:8.
16. Referring to the murmuring at Massah (Exod 17:1-7;
Num 20:2-13), the name derived from the vb. *nissâ*,
"test," "put to the proof." Massah is associated with
Meribah (cf. the vb. *rîb*, "contend"), and both are associated with Kadesh. One of the quotations attributed to
Jesus in the temptation scene (Matt 4:7). **20-25.** Continues the thought of 6:7, teaching children the laws,
perhaps with reference to phylacteries and mezuza. For
the question and answer form, see Exod 12:26-27;
13:8-9,14-16.
23 **(E) Command to Destroy the Peoples of
Canaan and Their Cults (7:1-11).** Whenever composed, this section would have served the purposes of the
more integrationist elements in exile and after the return.
Avoidance of marriage with natives was an important
plank in the programs of Ezra (Ezra 9-10) and Nehemiah
(Neh 13) **1.** The standard list of indigenous peoples. Of
the score or so occurrences of the list, only Gen 15:20;
Josh 3:10; 24:11 have seven members. Canaanites,
Amorites, or Hittites come first, and Jebusites generally

last. *Hittites:* Ethnic remnants of the Hittite empire, which
came to an end *ca.* 1200 BC. *Girgashites:* Cf. Gen 10:16; a
Ugaritic personal name Girgishi may be connected.
Amorites, Canaanites: See 1:7. *Perizzites:* Unknown, but
the termination *-izzi* is Hurrian (cf. Kenizzites). *Hivites:*
Hurrian-related enclaves around Shechem (Gen 34:2)
and Gibeon (Josh 9:7,19). *Jebusites:* The pre-Israelite
population of Jerusalem (cf. 2 Sam 5:6-7). **2.** *utterly
destroy:* Devote to the deity; see 2:34-35. The revival of
this ancient custom, at least as an aspiration, under Josiah
is understandable in view of his anti-Assyrian policy; see
also Deut 20. **5.** 7:1-5 is very close to Exod 34:11-16
and v 5 to Exod 34:13; cf. also the account of Josiah's
reforms, esp. 2 Kgs 23:6,12,14-15. *pillars (maṣṣēbôt):*
Commemorative steles generally to a fertility deity.
Asherim (ʾăšērîm): Asherah, the consort of El but also
associated with Baal in the Ras Shamra texts, was represented by cult objects, probably stylized representations
of the female figure. That her cult had its devotees in
Israel is amply attested in the OT (e.g., Jer 44:15-19) and
now in the Kuntillat 'Ajrud inscriptions (→ Biblical
Archaeology, 74:118). **6.** A distillation of the D doctrine
of election; cf. also 14:2, where holiness implies separation. *own possession (sĕgullâ):* A term taken from property
law used in Deut to express the special relationship of
Israel with Yahweh (14:2; 26:18). The love of God for
the ancestors (4:37; 10:15) and for later Israel (7:8,13;
23:5) is a prophetic theme, esp. in Hos and Jer, perhaps
connected with treaty terminology (see 6:4). **11.** Recalls
the peroration of the previous section (6:25).
24 **(F) Prosperity in the Land Assured by
Fidelity to the Law (7:12-26).** **12-15.** The list of
blessings, involving especially the productivity of
nature, was already well established (cf. Hos 2:5,8-9).
There is probably a play on words in the terms *dāgān*,
"grain," *šeger*, "increase," and *ʿaštěrôt*, "young," all fertility
deities in the Ras Shamra texts. **17.** The question-answer
form is characteristic of D parenesis; cf. 6:20-25. The
close affinity with Exod 23:23-33 continues. **20.** *hornets:*
A transl. based on the versions (cf. Exod 23:28; Josh
24:12). **22.** The same reason for delay in the conquest
occurs in Exod 23:29. Other explanations: the measure
of the natives' iniquity is not yet full (Gen 15:16); some
are left over to test Israel's faith (Judg 2:22-23). **23.** *great
confusion:* The preternatural panic induced by the deity
(1 Sam 4:7; 5:9,11; 7:10), a motif of the holy war. **25-26.**
abomination: A D term reserved mostly for Canaanite cult
objects and practices (17:4; 18:9-13; 22:5; etc.). Introducing idols into the house puts the owner under the ban
(*ḥērem*).
25 **(G) Historical Recollection a Counter to
the Temptations of the Land (8:1-20).** **1.** *the commandment (miṣwâ):* A later usage referring to the law as
a whole. **2.** Another example of drawing lessons from
the remote past, characteristic of the exilic period. The
themes are divine guidance and providence, and the
wilderness (exilic) experience as a humbling and testing
of Israel; cf. 6:16 and the function of false prophecy
(13:3). **3.** A homiletic development of the manna narrative (Exod 16: Num 11:16-23), which shows the importance of living by the word of God (H. Brunner, *VT*
8 [1958] 428-29); cf. the development of the same theme
in Isa 40-55 and Matt 4:1-11. **5.** For the sapiential theme
of divine discipline, see also 1:31; 4:36. **7-10.** This self-
contained hymnlike praise of the land begins and ends
with the gift of the "good land" and in between lists its
five attributes; "land" occurs seven times. **9.** Iron and
copper are not mined W of the Jordan, but there is
copper in the Wadi Arabah region S of the Dead Sea (cf.
Job 28:1-5). **11-20.** The theme is the danger of amnesia
with characteristic inclusion (vv 11,19); cf. 6:10-12 and

Hos 13:6. Once again we see the strong connection between historical memory and social ethic. **15.** *fiery serpents:* Cf. Num 21:6-9; *śārāp* (fiery one) occurs elsewhere as a winged mythological creature of serpentine form (Isa 6:1-7; 14:29; 30:6), but the link with scorpions suggests rather the effect of its bite. **17.** Quoting the opposition is a prophetic technique (Isa 10:8-11; 14:13-14). **18.** Deut returns often to the promissory covenant with the ancestors reinterpreted as conditional on law observance. **19.** *I solemnly warn you:* A judicial formula reminiscent of the language of vassal treaties.

26 (H) Occupation of the Land the Work of God, Not Israel (9:1-6). **1.** For the opening, see 4:1; 6:4. **4-6.** Another inclusion. The moral turpitude of the natives as the cause of dispossession is a common theme (cf. Gen 15:16). Note that here Israel does not occupy the land by virtue of its righteousness; cf. the quite different view in 6:18-19.

27 (I) Apostasy at Horeb (9:7-24). The pericope is unified by allusion to provocation and rebellion at the beginning and the end, but the thought is continued in the following section and is bound together with an inclusion (40 days and nights; 9:25; 10:10). Both encapsulate the theme of the possession of the land (9:6; 10:11). **7.** The apostasy is set within a larger history of infidelity beginning with the exodus (cf. Ezek 20). At this point there is another change from sg. to pl. **9-11.** The giving of the stone tablets, written with the finger of God during a 40-day fast on the mountain, follows Exod 24:12,18; 32:16; 34:28. **10.** *the day of the assembly:* See 4:10. **12-14.** Follows Exod 32:7-10, but see also Num 14:12. *molten image (massēkâ):* "Molten calf" in Exod (cf. 2 Kgs 17:16), reflecting the cult established at Bethel and Dan by Jeroboam (1 Kgs 12:26-33). Deut, however, sees the Horeb apostasy as paradigmatic for the entire history of Israel. **15.** Follows Exod 32:15-16 omitting the role of Joshua. **16.** A much briefer version of Exod 32:1-6. The calf (bull) had overt fertility associations, as is clear from the reference to orgiastic rites in Exod 32:6. **17.** The breaking of the tablets is a solemn juridical act performed *coram populo* signifying that Yahweh no longer considered himself bound by the agreement. The analogy is with vassal-treaty procedures rather than the Egyptian execration texts of the early second millennium. **20.** This is the only allusion to Aaron in Deut, and it is not favorable. It is absent from Exod 32, which records instead Aaron's lame excuse for his role in the apostasy. **21.** Omits the drinking of the cursed water by the people (Exod 32:20; cf. Num 5:16-28). **22-24.** Though integrated with the section, these verses appear to have been added; they refer back to 9:7, and v 25 takes up again from v 18. **22.** *Taberah:* Location unknown; Num 11:1-3 provides an etiological explanation. *Kibroth-hattaavah:* Location unknown; explained as "graves of craving" (?) in Num 11:4-32. **24.** Forms an inclusion with 9:7. For "I knew you," which is strange coming from Moses, read "Yahweh knew you" with the Samaritan Pentateuch.

28 (J) Intercession of Moses, Second Covenant (9:25-10:11). **25-29.** The prayer begins and ends with reference to Israel as Yahweh's people and heritage (see 4:20). Intercessory prayer is a prophetic function (e.g., Jer 14:11: 15:1), and, in Deut, Moses is the protoprophet (18:15; 34:10). The appeal to remember the ancestors foreshadows the rabbinic concept of their merit. The prayer is similar to Exod 32:11-14, which, however, takes place on the mountain; Exod 34:9 corresponds chronologically and refers to Israel as "heritage." **10:1-11.** The sequel to the Horeb apostasy is important as legitimating the Mosaic origin of the D law. The narrative follows Exod 34 omitting the "cultic

decalogue" (34:11-26) and insisting that the second copy of the Decalogue was identical with the first (10:1-4). We have already been told that only the Decalogue was promulgated at Horeb (5:22); thus the D law was intended to replace the Covenant Code (Exod 20:22-23:19). The sequence of events is somewhat confused; Moses wrote "the words" and put them in the ark (v 2) before making the ark and the tablets (v 3). **1.** *an ark of wood:* Deut closely associates the ark with the Decalogue; hence "the ark of the covenant" (10:8; 31:9, 25,26; Josh 3:8; etc.). **5.** As with international treaties, a copy had to be deposited in a sanctuary and read publicly from time to time (cf. 31:9-13). **6-9.** The intent of this clearly secondary passage is to dissociate Levites from the Aaron-inspired apostasy (Aaron died before the institution of the levitical priesthood; cf. Exod 32:25-29). **6.** *Beeroth Bene-jaakan:* "The wells of the sons of Jaakan," an unidentified site in the Kadesh region; cf. Num 33:31-32. *Moserah:* Cf. Moseroth (Num 33:30-31). In the P version Aaron died at Mt. Hor (Num 20:22-29). **7.** *Gudgodah:* Cf. Hor-haggidgad (Num 33:32-33), another caravan stop on the way to Kadesh. **8-9.** A description of the functions of Levites or levitical priests in Deut, where as yet there is no distinction between first- and second-order clergy (cf. 18:7). Deut may here preserve a recollection of Aaronites serving at the Bethel sanctuary (1 Kgs 12:31).

29 (K) Election and Its Consequences (10:12-11:1). **12.** The initial injunction is repeated in 11:1, forming another inclusion. The opening "and now" introduces moral requirements (cf. 4:1). **14.** The universal power of Israel's God is contrasted with the particular choice of his people (cf. Isa 40-55). **16.** Circumcision of the heart (also 30:6), a metaphor for conversion, appears to derive from Jer 4:4; 9:26. **19.** Probably added. Resident aliens (*gērîm*) were the subject of attention in the laws, often on the basis of Israel's status in Egypt; see esp. Exod 22:21; 23:9; Deut 24:17-18; Lev 19:33-34. **22.** *seventy persons:* As in Gen 46:27 and Exod 1:5 (both P) 70 is a schematic figure; cf. the 70 members of the Canaanite pantheon and the 70 elders (Exod 24:1,9; Num 11:16-25). That Israel will become as numerous as the stars (also 1:10) recalls the promise to Abraham (Gen 15:5).

30 (L) Remember Your Past! (11:2-25). **2.** The syntax of this long sentence is difficult; a vb. may have fallen out, so that we should read, "Know today that (I am not addressing) your children. . . ." But there is still the problem that the exodus generation had died out (2:14). The main point is that the memory of these events is to be kept alive after the occupation, a point that would not be lost on a generation that had grown old in the Babylonian Exile. These historical experiences are represented as a form of divine discipline (*mûsār*). **2-7.** This recounting probably draws on a liturgical tradition; cf. Pss 105, 106, 135 and esp. 78, which also enjoins teaching children (vv 5-6). **4.** *to this day:* This may refer obliquely to the condition of Egypt at the time of writing; either during the time of Neo-Babylonian supremacy or, less probably, after the Persian invasion of 525. **6.** *Dathan and Abiram:* Cf. Ps 106:16-18 and Num 16, a later conflation of this incident with the rebellion of Kohathite Levites against Aaronite supremacy. **8-12.** Recapitulates major themes treated to date: observance as a condition for possessing the land, the goodness of the land, the promise to the ancestors. **10.** The contrast is between irrigation, on which fertility depended in Egypt, and rainfall in the promised land. **13.** *my commandments:* The divine first person in the MT vv 14-15 should be retained. The author has forgotten that Moses is speaking. The thought in 13-17 is similar to

Hos 2:8-13. (On 11:10-15, see W. Vischer, *RHPR* 44 [1964] 102-9.) **22.** Cf. similar language in 10:20. **24.** The language is that of political dominion; the borders are those of the "greater Israel" of David and Solomon, which must have been to the forefront during the brief national resurgence under Josiah and remained an object of aspiration or nostalgia thereafter (e.g., Isa 55:3-5; 60:8-14; Ps 72). If the wilderness and Lebanon are taken together, they refer to boundaries to the N and NE, though we would expect "from the wilderness to Lebanon," i.e., from S to N. The Western Sea is the Mediterranean; cf. 1:6-8; Josh 1:3-4. **25.** Holy war language; cf. 2:25; 7:24.

31   (M) The Two Ways: Blessing and Curse (11:26-32). The section begins and ends with the phrase "I set before you this day." By speaking of moral decision in the sharpest terms, it appropriately concludes the parenesis of chaps. 1-11 and leads into the law of chaps. 12-26. **26.** *this day:* Emphasizes the actuality of decision. For the Two Ways, see 30:15-20; Ps 1; 1QS 4; *Did.* 1:1; Matt 7:13-14. Blessings and curses, alluded to briefly in previous chapters (e.g., 7:12-15), are specified in vv 27-28. **29-30.** These verses revert to the sg. and interfere with the peroration; they probably form "bookends" with chap. 27 (both deal with a covenant ceremony at Shechem). **30.** A confusing topographical note, since it seems to locate Gerizim and Ebal in the Jordan Valley rather than in the central highlands. There is no evidence for a Gilgal near Shechem, so the ancient shrine between Jericho and the Jordan must be intended; cf. the conflation of Gilgal and Shechem traditions in chap. 27. *the oak of Moreh:* Lit., "the oak (terebinth) of the teacher or oracle giver" (also Gen 12:6-7). The MT has the pl., perhaps to avoid the implication of cult associated with a sacred tree.

(Begg, C. T., "The Tables (Deut. x) and the Lawbook (Deut. xxxi)," *VT* 33 [1983] 96-97. Crump, W., "Dt. 7: A Covenant Sermon," *ResQ* 17 [1974] 222-35. Garcia Lopez, F., *Analyse littéraire de Deutéronome V-XI* [Jerusalem, 1978]; "Yahvé, fuente última de vida: análisis de Dt 8," *Bib* 62 [1981] 21-54; "Un peuple consacré: analyse critique de Deutéronome vii," *VT* 32 [1982] 438-63. Merendino, R. P., "Zu Dt. v-vii: Eine Klärung," *VT* 31 [1981] 80-83. On the *Shema* text: Höffken, P., *BZ* 28 [1984] 88-93. Horowitz, H. L., *Judaism* 24 [1975] 476-81. McBride, S. D., *Int* 27 [1973] 273-306. Peter, M., *BZ* 24 [1980] 252-62. Willoughby, B. E., *ResQ* 20 [1977] 73-87.)

32   (III) The Law Book (12:1-26:15). That this section has passed through several stages of editing will be apparent from the first pericope, the sanctuary law. It is not simply a law code since the parenetic and exhortatory tone of chaps. 1-11 carries over especially into the early paragraphs. It is as much a program for the future as a collection of laws, e.g., the section on offices in the community (16:18-18:22) and such utopian statements as "there shall be no poor among you" (15:4). Several suggestions have been made about the order in which the legal material has been arranged. If the original intention was to follow the order of the Decalogue, subsequent editing has introduced considerable disturbance. More probably several factors must be taken into account, including theme, literary form, and word association.

33   (A) The Sanctuary Law (12:1-27). Both the book of the covenant (Exod 20-23) and Deut open with the sanctuary law, perhaps because that is where the law was deposited. **1.** The title links with the preceding verse and introduces the entire collection (cf. 26:16 immediately following). **2-3.** The command to destroy non-Yahwistic cult places frequently occurs in the parenesis (e.g., 7:5) and is presupposed in Dtr (e.g.,

2 Kgs 18:4; 23:14-15), where its observance or nonobservance functions as a basic criterion of evaluation (e.g., 1 Kgs 11;13,36; 12:28-31; 14:23). Hezekiah did remove these "high places" (2 Kgs 18:4,22); Manasseh reestablished them (21:3); and Josiah once again destroyed them (23:5,8-9,15,19-20). **5-7.** Although 12:2-7 may come from an exilic or a postexilic stage, the divine choice of a sanctuary is an old idea, first clearly attested with Shiloh and the ark (Judg 21; 1 Sam 1; Jer 7:12,14; Ps 78:60). With David's removal of the ark to Jerusalem, that city became the chosen place par excellence. That Yahweh has put his name there signifies ownership and is perhaps also intended to discourage materialistic ideas about divine presence (cf. 1 Kgs 8:27-30). **5.** *and make his habitation there:* On this "name theology," see von Rad, *Studies in Deuteronomy* 37ff. **6.** For the different kinds of offering, see de Vaux, *AI* 415ff. **8-12.** The repetition of the injunction to sacrifice at the sanctuary chosen by Yahweh is perhaps from the same source as the first edition of the history. The command originally implied only participation in the pilgrimage feasts (cf. 16:16-17); the move from a central to a sole sanctuary arises from the need to eliminate centers of Canaanite cult, historically more an aspiration than a reality. The sanctuary law clearly supersedes the corresponding Exod 20:24-26. **9.** For the key terms "rest" and "inheritance," see 3:20; 4:21. **12.** The sacrificial system therefore also had a humanitarian and social security aspect. *the Levite within your gates:* A priestly class scattered in towns around the country and dependent on tithing; see further 18:1-8. **13-19.** Another version of the law, this time in the sg., probably the original nucleus of the pericope. Restriction of sacrifice to one place implied the secularization of butchering elsewhere. The status of both the sacrificers and the victims (clean or unclean) is therefore irrelevant, the only restriction being the Noachic law of draining the blood (cf. Gen 9:4). **19.** "Take heed" forms an inclusion with 12:13. **20-27.** This clarification of the preceding permission applies only to those too distant from the central sanctuary. The addition is often taken as a reflection of Josiah's reconquest of the north, but it is difficult to see how it could have applied before the return from exile.

(Halpern, B., "The Centralization Formula in Deuteronomy," *VT* 31 [1981] 20-38. Lohfink, N., "Zur deuteronomischen Zentralisationsformel," *Bib* 65 [1984] 297-329. Maag, V., "Erwägungen zur deuteronomistischen Kultzentralisation," *VT* 6 [1956] 10-18. Milgrom, J., "Profane Slaughter and a Formulaic Key to the Composition of Deuteronomy," *HUCA* 47 [1976] 1-17. Nicholson, E., "The Centralisation of the Cult in Dt," *VT* 13 [1963] 380-89. Weippert, H., "Der Ort den Jahwe erwählen wird, um dort seinen Namen wohnen zu lassen: die Geschichte einer alttestamentlichen Formel," *BZ* 24 [1980] 76-92.)

34   (B) Dispositions concerning Apostasy (12:28-13:18). Connected thematically with the preceding, this section also is bound together with an inclusion (12:28; 13:18). **29-31.** Parenetic introduction (cf. 7:1). **30.** On the seductive character of Canaanite cults, see also 7:16. In the context of religious thinking in antiquity the question would be quite natural; cf. the situation in Samaria after the Assyrian conquest (2 Kgs 17:24-28). **31b.** *abominable thing:* See 7:25-26. The practice of dedicating children to a deity by burning, attested in Phoenicia and Carthage, was practiced in Israel intermittently under the monarchy (2 Kgs 16:3; 17:17,31; 21:6; etc.). The deity is sometimes alluded to as Molech, a vocalization of *melek*, "king," according to *bōšet*, "shame"; cf. Lev 18:21; 20:2-5; 2 Kgs 23:10; Jer 32:35; and perhaps Isa 30:33. For a different explanation, see de Vaux, *AI* 444-46. Though abolished by Josiah, the practice continued during the last critical decades of Judah's existence (Jer 7:31; Ezek 16:21; etc.). The first of three instances of apostasy couched in a form similar to the casuistic laws (cf. Ezek 14:12-20; 18:5-18). The first testifies to the problematic nature of prophecy in the last decades of the monarchy and thereafter. **1.** The dream, usually recognized as a legitimate means of revelation, fell into disrepute toward the end of the monarchy (e.g., Jer 23:25-28,32; 27:9; 29:8). **2.** Advocacy of alien deities disqualifies even a successful prophet; cf. 18:20. **3.** For false prophecy as a test, see 1 Kgs 22:19-23. **6.** *you shall purge the evil from your midst:* A formulaic expression almost always used with the death penalty (17:7; 19:19; 21:21; 22:21,24: 24:7), and probably from ancient judicial usage relating to actions that contaminate the entire community. **6-11.** The fanatical campaign of Deut against apostasy is especially in evidence here; even close friends and relatives are to be denounced and put to death (cf. 17:2-7). **9.** *you shall kill him:* Following the LXX, a slight consonantal change gives "you must certainly denounce him." **12-17.** The case of a city: If guilt is established after judicial inquiry, it is to be put under the ban. **13.** *base fellows:* Lit., "sons of Belial"; cf. 1 Sam 10:27. The name can be construed to mean "worthless," but its origin is obscure. In postbiblical Jewish and early Christian writings it occurs (with a variant Beliar) as a name for Satan.

35   (C) Purity Laws (14:1-21). 1. *sons of Yahweh:* See 1:31; 32:5,19. The incisions and shaving of hair are mourning rites; cf. Jer 16:6; 41:5, where both occur together. For allusions to ritual shaving, see Amos 8:10; Isa 15:2; 22:12; Ezek 7:18. "The dead" may refer to the dying god Baal (cf. Aqhat I iv 11; 1 Kgs 18:28). **3.** See 7:25. **4-20.** Though lists of clean and unclean animals are an ancient component of priestly lore, this tabulation has been inserted at a rather late date, copied from the source on which Lev 11 has drawn, perhaps from Lev 11 itself or a nonextant variant. The rationale for these distinctions may include natural revulsion, apparent anomalies, and pagan cultic use. In addition, some feed on carrion and are therefore unclean by association. **4-5.** This list of 10 is not in Lev 11. **6-8.** Cf. Lev 11:3-7. Jewish tradition offers no rationale for this favoring of cloven-hoofed ruminants. The prohibition of pork, which was to attain confessional status (e.g., 2 Macc 6:18-20), was due not to fear of trichinosis but to fear of the use of the pig in pagan rituals (cf. Isa 65:4-5; 66:17; 1 Macc 1:47). **9-10.** Crustaceans were probably linked with reptiles, which were taboo. **12-18.** Cf. the practically identical list of 20 unclean birds in Lev 11:13-19; some identifications are uncertain (see G. R. Driver, *PEQ* 87 [1955] 5ff., and *NEB*). Several feed on carrion or eat bloody flesh; others (ostrich, bat, hoopoe) may have been disqualified as anomalous. **19.** Winged insects are taboo; cf. Lev 11:20-23, which exempts locust, cricket, and grasshopper. **20.** Forms an inclusion with 14:11, thus rounding off the list. **21.** The prohibition against eating anything that dies of itself follows on the need to drain the blood (Gen 9:4; Lev 11:40; Deut 12:16). Note that by the time of the Holiness Code (Lev 17-26), the resident alien (*gēr*) is also bound by this law (Lev 17:15). The prohibition against boiling a kid in its mother's milk is also at the end of the Covenant Code (Exod 23:19) and the second covenant (Exod 34:26). The context suggests a prohibited ritual, perhaps alluded to in a Ugaritic text (but see *Bible Review* 1 [1985] 48-55; 56-58).

36   (D) Periodic Religious Duties (14:22-16:17). Tithes, sabbatical year, firstlings, and pilgrim feasts are also grouped together in Exod 23:10-19 and for the most part in Exod 34:18-26. The section begins and ends with offerings to the sanctuary. **14:22-29.**

Tithing, the payment of one-tenth in support of a sanctuary, was an ancient practice and not confined to Israel (Gen 14:20; 28:22; Amos 4:4). With the offering of firstfruits and the seventh-year release it acknowledged Yahweh's ownership of the land. **22-23.** Produce and livestock are tithed; the itemization suggests Sukkoth as the occasion. Characteristically, it is meant to have a pedagogic character. **24-26.** Commuting to cash, i.e., uncoined ingots and the like, was a means of solving the problem of transportation. Practically, however, it must have been the rule rather than the exception unless the measure is seen to be utopian. Surprisingly, nothing is said here about support of Temple personnel. **28-29.** The tithe of the third year is assigned to the disadvantaged, an innovation characteristic of Deut. See further 26:12-15; Lev 27:30-33; Num 18:21-32 (P). **15:1-6.** As often in this section, the law of remission is given a new application, i.e., remission of debts and manumission from servitude incurred for debts (cf. Exod 23:10-11; Lev 25:1-7). Both aspects of the law remained in force (e.g., Neh 10:32; 1 Macc 6:49,53). **2-3.** The law applies to the Israelite ("his brother" is a gloss on "neighbor"; cf. 15:7). **4.** The utopian ideal of the abolition of poverty; but see the more realistic statement in v 11. **7-11.** An appendix directed against the abuse of withholding loans in view of the approaching seventh year, framed in a typical D homiletic context. **11.** Cf. Matt 26:11. **12-18.** An interesting modification and updating of the Covenant Code (Exod 21:2-6): "Hebrew" now means simply "Israelite"; male and female are on the same footing; the man can keep his family without opting for perpetual bondage; ample provision must be made for the manumitted slave. **15.** A typical motivation clause; cf. 5:15, etc. **17.** A symbolic act, the ear signifying obedience; perhaps also with the purpose of attaching a metal tag. **18.** According to Exod 21:32 a slave cost 30 shekels; therefore, at that time the annual wage of the hired servant was 10 shekels (de Vaux, *AI* 76). **19-23.** The setting aside of the firstborn originally involved humans as well as animals (Exod 22:28-29; cf. 13:14-15; 34:19-20). **21-22.** Blemished animals remained in the profane sphere; see 12:13-19. **16:1-17.** Earlier calendric regulations are in Exod 23:14-17; 34:18-24, and the later P versions in Lev 23:5-8; Num 28:16-29:39; cf. Ezek 45:18-25. Distinctive of Deut is the pilgrim character of the festivals. **1-8.** Deut combines Unleavened Bread, the only spring ritual in Exod, with Passover, an ancient apotropaic rite associated with transhumation, first celebrated as a pilgrim feast under Josiah (2 Kgs 23:21-23). **1.** *Abib:* Later Nisan, corresponding to March-April. **3.** The haste with which Israel left Egypt is the historicizing reason for the absence of leaven; but unleavened bread was the ordinary fare of the nomad. Note that Passover is a memorial service (cf. Exod 12:14; 1 Cor 11:24). **7.** In Exod 12:9 (P) the animal must be roasted; boiling is expressly excluded, perhaps because of pagan associations (see 14:21). **8.** Since the six days of Unleavened Bread, leading to a solemn assembly, contradicts 16:3, it may represent a later development. **9-12.** The feast of Weeks was later more precisely calculated as 50 days (Lev 23:15-16); hence Pentecost. It corresponds with the wheat harvest (Exod 23:16; 34:22). **10.** *feast:* Originally pilgrimage (cf. Islamic *ḥajj*). For the theme of rejoicing at the festivals, see also 12:7, 12,18; 14:26. **12.** Connection with the memory of slavery in Egypt was suggested by inclusion of the resident alien. In the later Second Temple period the festival came to memorialize the giving of the law. **13-15.** The feast of Tabernacles is "ingathering" in the older calendars (Exod 23:16; 34:22), the great clan festival of the early period (Judg 21:19; 1 Sam 1:3), associated with covenant and law (cf. Deut 31:10–13; Neh 7:73–8:18). The *sukkôt,* "booths," also came to recall the sojourn in the wilderness (Lev 23:42–43). **16–17.** A summary, taken from older formulations (cf. Exod 23:17; 34:23) and adapted to D requirements. Its greater antiquity is apparent in its inconsistency with the foregoing calendar, which includes Passover and does not restrict the requirement to males.

37   (E) Offices and Functions (16:18–18:22). The section deals with judges and judicial procedures (16:18–20; 17:2–13), the monarchy (17:14–20), priests (18:1–8), and prophets (18:9–22). Condemnation of cultic offenses (16:21–17:1) may have been suggested by the anti-apostasy measures that follow (17:2–7). **16:18.** These judges may have been local administrators who, beginning with Jehoshaphat in the 9th cent. (2 Chr 19:5), took over the functions of elders. **19.** Three apodictic commands based on Exod 23:2–3,6–8. The substitution of "wise" for "officials" shows the sapiential character of Deut. **20.** A clear indication that the D program drew on the teaching of the great prophets (e.g., Mic 6:6–8). **21–22.** Two anti-Canaanite measures, certainly ancient since they presuppose a multiplicity of Yahweh-altars; cf. Exod 20:24. **17:1.** Prohibition of disqualified animals; cf. 15:21. This is the first of several "abomination" laws concerned with cultic irregularities (18:12; 22:5; 23:18), which were eventually extended to non-cultic offenses (24:4; 25:16). **3.** Worship of heavenly bodies is characteristically but not exclusively Mesopotamian. **6–7.** A basic principle of testimony aimed at discouraging perjury. For the final "purge formula," see 13:5. **8–13.** The central judiciary, which also served as a court of ultimate appeal, was adumbrated earlier (1:17). Dealing with disputed matters of criminal law, it was composed of a lay judge and one or more priests. According to 2 Chr 19:8–11 Jehoshaphat set up this institution under the chief priest and the governor of Judah. **14–17.** A "mirror for kings," reflected in Israel's history (1 Sam 8:4–22; 10:26–11:8). The basic requirements: The king must be chosen by Yahweh, i.e., have prophetic support, and be a native Israelite. **16.** The horse was a symbol of pride, the war engine par excellence; cf. Isa 2:7; Mic 5:10. The royal harem also served as a kind of status symbol. **18–20.** The main point is that the king is also subject to the law, a kind of constitutional monarch. The passage bears directly on the discovery of the law book and Josiah's reaction to it (2 Kgs 22:3–13). At his accession the king is to make a copy (*mišneh*), not a second law as in the LXX. Deut is aware of historical abuses but is not opposed to monarchy, not even hereditary monarchy ("his children"). **18:1–5.** Prerogatives of the levitical priesthood. According to Deut it was established at Horeb to have charge of the ark, conduct divine service, pronounce judgment and instruct in the law (10:8–9; 17:9,12,18; 18:5; 21:15; 24:8; 31:9,25; 33:8–11). The distinction between priest and Levite is unknown except in the late strand of 27:14, where the Levites pronounce the curse. On principle, all Levites are qualified to discharge priestly functions, but since they have no territorial base (10:9), many have to depend on charity (12:12). To the extent that it succeeded, the Josian centralization program must have restricted their opportunities for employment, though Levites cannot simply be identified as the priests of the high places. (See J. G. McConville, *Law and Theology in Deuteronomy* [Sheffield, 1984] 124–53.) **3.** The portions in the later P legislation (Lev 7:31–36; Num 18:18) are, predictably, more generous. **6–8.** If a Levite comes to the central sanctuary with a desire to serve as priest and succeeds in doing so, he qualifies for

the same portions (different in *RSV*). There is probably no connection with 2 Kgs 23:9: the Levites are not the priests of the high places and it is not a question of seeking employment. **8.** The last phrase is obscure; it probably refers to inherited property, which does not disqualify the aspirant from claiming his portions. **9–14.** Inappropriate forms of mediation are contrasted with prophecy after the manner of Moses—another example of the anti-Canaanism of Deut. **10.** See 12:31. **10b–11.** These verses give eight different terms for divinatory practice, which is in evidence especially in times of crisis, e.g., the reign of Manasseh (2 Kgs 21:6). **15–22.** Prophecy is Israel's form of mediation. The (probably exilic) author wishes to find a place for prophecy in the ideal commonwealth. *prophet:* The term is used distributively, i.e., prophets will be "raised up" as the occasion requires. The true prophet is called by Yahweh, is a native Israelite, and is a continuator of the prophetic office of Moses (cf. Exod 33:11; Num 12:1–8; Hos 12:13). This important verse was interpreted eschatologically in Judaism (Mal 4:5–6; 1QS 9) and early Christianity (e.g., John 1:21; 6:14; Acts 3:22–23; 7:37). **16–17.** Prophecy originated in the request for mediation at Horeb (5:23–28). **18.** *I will put my words in his mouth:* This is reminiscent of the prophetic call of Moses (Exod 4,12, 15–16) and Jer (1:9), but "my words" may also include commandments. In the history there is a close connection between prophecy and law (e.g., 2 Kgs 17:13–15). **20.** The death penalty threatens the non-Yahwistic prophet and the one not commissioned by Yahweh (cf. Jer 23:9–32; 28:16–17). **21–22.** As in 13:1–5, the criteria for the discernment of prophetic spirits reflect the crisis of prophecy under the late monarchy. Correct prediction is insufficient by itself and not necessarily helpful to the prophet's contemporaries.

(Abba, R., "Priests and Levites in Deuteronomy," *VT* 27 [1977] 257–67. Ben-Barak, Z., "The Religious-Prophetic Background of the 'Law of the King' in Dt," *Shnaton* 1 [1975] 33–44. Blenkinsopp, J., *A History of Prophecy in Israel* [Phl, 1983] 138–46. Lohfink, N., "Hos 11,5 als Bezugstext von Dtn 17,16," *VT* 31 [1981] 226–28. Rofé, A., "The Law about the Organization of Justice in Dt (16:18–20; 17:8–13)," *BM* 21 [1975] 199–210. Teeple, H. M., *The Mosaic Eschatological Prophet* [Phl, 1957].)

38   (F) Homicide and Related Matters (19:1–21). 21:1–9, on expiation for undetected murder, may have belonged here since it interrupts the rules on warfare. **1–3.** The three cities of refuge (cf. 4:41–43) are to be spaced evenly through the land, and there is to be ready access to them; see also Josh 20:1–9; Num 35:9–34. The institution probably developed from the practice of seeking refuge in a sanctuary (Exod 21:13–14; 1 Kgs 1:51; 2:28–34). **4–7.** The cities provide protection in the case of manslaughter where no malice aforethought can be proved. The distinction between intentional and unintentional killing is clearer than in the Covenant Code (Exod 21:13–14). **6.** *the avenger of blood:* The next-of-kin (*gō'ēl*) on whom fell the duty of avenging the death (cf. 2 Sam 14:11) rather than an official charged with apprehending the murderer illegitimately claiming sanctuary (see Phillips, *Deuteronomy* 129–30). **8–10.** The three additional cities necessitated by further conquest cannot be W of the Jordan since the three already designated account for the entire country from the Galilee to the Hebron plateau. The allusion is then to the Transjordanian cities in Josh 20:1–9 (cf. Deut 4:41–43). **10.** The shedding of innocent blood pollutes the land and brings bloodguilt upon it (cf. Gen 4:10–12). **14.** The apodictic law forbidding the removal of land markers, presented in typical D language, is connected with the preceding by catchwords (*gĕbûl*, "territory," "landmark"; *rēaʿ*, "neighbor"). Moving these markers and thus stealing land is a common complaint in the prophetic (Hos 5:10; Mic 2:2) and sapiential literature (Job 24:2; Prov 22:28; 23:10) **15.** The general rule requiring at least two witnesses is first enunciated (cf. 17:6). **16–19.** This apparent contradiction to the general rule should be read as an amendment dealing with the special cases of treason or apostasy (*sārâ*, cf. 13:6; Jer 28:16; 29:32; etc.), in which one witness sufficed subject to rigorous investigation by the central judiciary (17:8–13). **19.** The false witness is subject to the same penalty as for the crime in question. For the "purge formula," see 13:5; 17:7. **21.** *your eye shall not pity:* Cf. 7:16; 13:8. The talion law occurs also in the other codes (Exod 21:23–25) and in a contaminated form in Lev 24:17–20. It was not implemented in Israelite judicial practice, with the exception of murder (cf. Gen 9:6; Lev 24:17), but was prominent in Mesopotamian and, much later, Roman law. The idea was to restrict indiscriminate vendetta by applying a rough principle of equity, but it has acquired a bad reputation by a mistaken reading of Matt 5:38.

39 (G) Rules for the Conduct of War (20:1–21:14). As noted earlier, 21:1–9 is out of place; 21:10–14, dealing with women prisoners of war, may have been moved in order to be placed with the law about two wives (21:15–17), with which it has obvious connections. Concern with war (see also 23:9–14; 24:5; 25:17–19) can be seen in the light of the nationalist revival under Josiah. The idea of divinely sanctioned warfare, even wholesale slaughter of civilians, needless to say, cannot be endorsed theologically. **1.** This draws on the ancient idea of Yahweh as warrior god (e.g., Exod 15:3), closely associated with the ark and the title "Yahweh of the hosts." **2–4.** The priest's war speech; cf. 9:1–3; 31:3–6. **5.** One of the tasks of the "officers" (see 1:15) was recruitment to the levy. **5–7.** These three exemptions are certainly predeuteronomic, based on ancient taboos (W. Herrmann, *ZAW* 70 [1958] 215–20). Here, however, their intent is humanitarian, esp. with regard to newlyweds (cf. 24:5). To the three blessings correspond the curses in 28:30 (cf. Amos 5:11). **8.** An addition, indicated by the separate introduction; cf. the reduction of Gideon's army (Judg 7:3). **10–18.** Regulations for the treatment of captured cities outside the land (vv 10–15) and within it (vv 16–18), a distinction applied to the Gibeonites (Josh 9; J. Blenkinsopp, *CBQ* 28 [1966] 207ff.). **17.** On the list of nations, see 7:1. **19–20.** Fruit trees are not to be cut down during a protracted siege; consistent with the general ecological concern of Deut, this perhaps represents the viewpoint of the "people of the land" under the later monarchy. Most armies were not so discriminating; see, e.g., 2 Kgs 3:19. **21:1–9.** Undetected murder pollutes the area in which it took place. In a Ugaritic poem Danil curses the scene of his son's murder by a party unknown (Aqhat I iii 46–49). **2.** *judges:* An addition, or perhaps correction for "elders." The elders formed a kind of town council. The urban emphasis in Deut is noteworthy. **3–6.** The unworked animal and unplowed and unsown valley are typical of this kind of ritual (cf. 1 Sam 6:7). It is not a sacrifice; the animal plays the part of the guilty party (cf. the scapegoat ritual, Lev 16:20–22). **8.** The prayer for forgiveness may not be native to this context; "forgive" (*kappēr*), as in Yom Kippur, probably had the meaning "cover" (cf. the *kappōret* or cover for the ark (Lev 16:2; etc.). **10–14.** Female prisoners of war. Unless the war was against outside enemies, the outcome would be at odds with the prohibition of marrying native women (7:3). **12.** These acts represent the end of her former life. **13.** The normal period for mourning is seven days;

exceptionally, Moses and Aaron were mourned for thirty days (Deut 34:8; Num 20:29). **14.** Though her master may divorce her, she may not be sold into slavery; characteristically, Deut provides some mitigation of the condition of the oppressed and disadvantaged.

40 (H) Miscellaneous Laws (21:15–23:1). It is difficult to detect any logical arrangement or common theme here, except that the section begins and ends with sexual and familial mores. Casuistic and apodictic forms alternate, both being about equally represented. **21:15–17.** A casuistic law ("if a man . . .") which guarantees the right of primogeniture even if the mother is not favored by her husband; paternal discretion (as, e.g., in Gen 48:13–14) is excluded. **17.** *double portion:* For this practice in the Near East, see I. Mendelsohn, *BASOR* 156 [1959] 38–40. It was applied metaphorically in prophetic succession (2 Kgs 2:9). **18–21.** The law concerning the recalcitrant son is in casuistic form and ends with the purge formula (see 13:5). Referral to the elders rather than to the judges, as we might expect from 16:18, limits the jurisdiction of the paterfamilias. Both parents must be present in keeping with the laws of testimony (17:6; 19:15). **20.** *a glutton and a drunkard:* Perhaps a gloss inspired by Prov 23:21. The son in question is a young adult (see also 5:16; Exod 21:15). **22–23.** In certain cases, exposure could follow execution both as a deterrent and to indicate the heinousness of the crime (see Josh 8:29; 10:26–27; 2 Sam 4:12). **23.** Paul uses this verse in an accommodated sense in Gal 3:13 (see M. Wilcox, *JBL* 96 [1977] 85–99). **22:1–4.** Two apodictic laws dealing with assistance to Israelites. The command to return a straying animal is expanded with two codicils dealing with cases of particular difficulty and extending the law to any lost property. As for the second case, two would be required to get a fallen animal on its feet. This represents an extension of Exod 23:4–5, which deals only with the case of an adversary at law. It goes beyond the law on theft (Exod 20:15; Deut 5:19) requiring twofold restitution for a stolen animal (Exod 22:9; cf. Code of Hammurabi § 8, *ANET* 166, where the requirement is tenfold). **5.** An apodictic law forbidding transvestism. Its application is in the cultic sphere, arising from Canaanite practice associated with a bisexual deity or from cultic prostitution involving both sexes (cf. 23:17–18; Lev 18:22; 20:13). **6–7.** Casuistic form with characteristic D motivation clause. The injunction to spare the mother bird is inspired by ecological rather than humanitarian considerations, i.e., preservation of the food supply. **8.** Flat roofs were used for sleeping and other activities (e.g., 2 Kgs 4:10). The fear of bloodguilt is especially strong at the outset of any operation (cf. 20:5–7). **9–11.** Three brief apodictic laws dealing with forbidden commingling developed in the Mishnaic treatise 'Erubin. **9.** Sowing a crop between the rows of vines is forbidden. According to Lev 19:23–24 fruit could not be harvested from trees during the first three years. The fourth year's crop went to the sanctuary and only in the fifth year was it desacralized, available for use. The present law exempts such crops from this rule. **10.** The reason may be to avoid hardship for the weaker animal. Lev 19:19 forbids mating such animals. **11.** *mingled stuff:* This occurs only here and in Lev 19:19; the precise meaning is unknown. **12.** Connected with the preceding by subject matter. In Num 15:37–41 the tassels or fringes were to remind the wearer of the duty of law observance. Here no reason is given and perhaps none was known. **13.** There follow five casuistic laws dealing with sexual mores. The husband's tactic is to recover the marriage price paid to the bride's parents. **14.** *tokens of virginity:* Either a stained garment or bed covering as proof that the hymen had been ruptured or similar indications that menstruation had taken place shortly before consummation of the marriage. The principal issue was the economic rights of the parties involved. **18–19.** The penalty consisted of a whipping, payment of a fine double the bride-price (cf. 22:29), and marriage without the option of divorce. For the severe penalties in Assyrian law, see *ANET* 181. **21.** *folly (nĕbālâ):* An ancient term for a serious disorder, usually of a sexual nature, affecting the entire community (Gen 34:7; Judg 19:23–24; 20:6,10; 2 Sam 13:12). **22.** The law covers a betrothed as well as a married woman (cf. 5:18). The death penalty is also imposed in the Code of Hammurabi (§ 129, *ANET* 171, 181) and the Assyrian laws, though both leave some discretionary action to the husband (in which respect, cf. Hos 2:5; Jer 3:8). **23–24.** With respect to rape, presumption of guilt holds for the city, not the country, as in the Assyrian laws (*ANET* 181, 185); cf. Hammurabi (§ 130, *ANET* 171). **25–27.** Analogy with a treacherous and murderous attack is suggested; cf. 19:11. **28–29.** *virgin (bĕtûlâ):* More precisely, a sexually mature female. Once again, the main concern is with the economic rights of the father. The penalty for the seducer is the same as in Exod 22:16–17, except that the bride-price is now fixed at 50 silver shekels and the father may no longer veto the marriage: cf. the similar Assyrian law (*ANET* 185). **23:1.** Formally, this law belongs with the apodictic commands that follow. It prohibits sexual relations with one of the father's women (cf. 27:20,23; Lev 18:7–8; 20:11). *uncover his father's skirt:* To cover with the skirt or kilt (Ruth 3:9; Ezek 16:8) indicated the intention to marry: the opposite would therefore imply violation of the father's sexual rights.

(Bellefontaine, E., "Deut 21:18–21: Reviewing the Case of the Rebellious Son," *JSOT* 13 [1979] 13–31. Callaway, P. R., "Deut 21:18–21: Proverbial Wisdom and Law," *JBL* 103 [1984] 341–52. Carmichael, C. M., "Uncovering a Major Source of Mosaic Law: The Evidence of Deut 21:15–22:5," *JBL* 101 [1982] 505–20. Davies, E. W., "Inheritance Rights and the Hebrew Levirate Marriage," *VT* 31 [1981] 138–44. Phillips, A., "Uncovering the Father's Skirt," *VT* 30 [1980] 38–43. Watson, P., "A Note on the 'Double Portion' of Dt 21:17 and 2 Kgs 2:9," *ResQ* 8 [1965] 70–75.)

41   (I) Humanitarian and Cultic Laws (23:2–25:19). 23:2–9. A series of five apodictic laws concerning qualifications for membership in the assembly (*qĕhal yhwh*). The basic issue was aptitude for participation in the cult, on which civic status to some extent depended. Whatever the age of these laws, they were operative in the postexilic Judean community (Neh 13:1–9). **2.** The sexually mutilated are excluded, as they are a fortiori from the priesthood (Lev 21:17–21); this was also the rule at Qumran (1QSa 2:4–9). **3.** *bastard:* In the only other occurrence in the OT, Zech 9:6, the term *mamzēr* alludes to the hybrid population of Ashdod; cf. Nehemiah's action against intermarriage with women of that city (Neh 13:23–27). **4–7.** Ammonites and Moabites were excluded *in perpetuum,* an exception to the remarkable openness of early Judaism to proselytes—itself controversial, as may be seen in the case of Ruth the Moabite. **8–9.** Third-generation Edomites and Egyptians are eligible as proselytes. Edom's close relationship, perhaps cemented by treaty (see M. Fishbane, *JBL* 89 [1970] 313–18), may explain their status. **10–15.** Cultic purity in the camp: Involuntary nocturnal emission renders unclean (Lev 15:1–18); a place is to be designated outside the camp for toilet facilities. **14.** *anything indecent ('erwat dābār):* See 24:1. **16–17.** The fugitive slave is not to be extradited, a provision that goes against the ancient Near Eastern legal tradition (e.g., Hammurabi § 15–16, 19; *ANET* 166–67). **18–19.** Cultic prostitution of both sexes was

associated with fertility rites and was taken over by Israel after the occupation (e.g., 1 Kgs 14:24; Amos 2:7; Hos 4:14). The term "dog," not necessarily pejorative, is here a contemptuous allusion to a catamite, just as the hierodule is referred to as a "whore." **20–21.** This law differs from Exod 22:24–25 in two respects: it applies to all Israelites; it allows the practice in dealing with foreigners. Usury is a frequent subject of complaint in the didactic literature (e.g., Prov 22:7). **25–26.** Two brief casuistic laws in favor of the poor and the wayfarer, and forestalling abuses (cf. Matt 12:1–8). **24:1–4.** Not a divorce law, as the Vg mistranslates it, but a stipulation that the husband who divorces his wife may not take her back after she has remarried, whether her second husband has also divorced her or is deceased. **1.** *some indecency:* Lit., "the nakedness of a thing," a physical rather than a moral defect, and certainly not adultery, which was punishable by death. The grounds for divorce continued to be an issue in the rabbinic schools and early Christianity (e.g., Matt 19:3–9). The *bill of divorce* probably indemnified the wife, as in Hammurabi § 137–41 (*ANET* 172) and the Assyrian laws (*ANET* 183). **5.** Another casuistic law extending the exemption in 20:7 to any form of public service. **6.** Cf. the pledge laws in 24:10–13. A debtor may not be deprived of anything essential to livelihood. **7.** Kidnapping for the slave trade is forbidden in the Decalogue and subject to the death penalty in the Covenant Code (Exod 21:16), as in Hammurabi § 14 (*ANET* 166). **8–9.** *leprosy:* More generic than leprosy; see E. V. Hulse, *PEQ* 107 (1975) 87–105. For the punishment of Miriam, see Num 12:9–15. **10–13.** Continuation of laws regarding lending (see also 23:20–21; 24:6,17); a modified form of Exod 22:25–26. For the poor the usual pledge was the outer garment, which must be returned at nightfall (cf. Amos 2:8; Job 22:6). **14–15.** The day laborer must be paid promptly on a daily basis. **16.** This judicial principle (cf. 2 Kgs 14:6) is based on the theological premise about the divine administration of justice (cf. Jer 31:29; Ezek 18:5–18); see 5:9. Corporate liability survived only in exceptional cases in Deut (13:12–18; 21:1–9). **17–18.** The first of these two prohibitions is based on Exod 23:6, but cf. the curse in Deut 27:19. The second is a special instance of 24:12–13. **19–22.** Three brief injunctions concerning the forgotten sheaf, the olive and grape harvests. Gleaning rights were a significant element in Deut's "social security system." **25:1–3.** Corporal punishment must be carried out in the presence of a judge and must not exceed 40 strokes—later 39 to avoid inadvertently exceeding the limit (2 Cor 11:24). The same maximum appears in the Middle Assyrian laws (*ANET* 181). **4.** An example of Deut's concern for animal welfare, applied figuratively in 1 Cor 9:9 and 1 Tim 5:18. **5–10.** Levirate marriage is limited here to an unmarried brother (unlike the case of Jacob and Tamar, Gen 38). The idea was to preserve the family estate and secure the surrogate immortality guaranteed by a male heir. The later provisions for daughters to inherit hastened the demise of this law (Num 27:1–11). **7–10.** Handing over a sandal symbolized transfer of property rights (cf. Ruth 4:7–8). The idea seems to be that the defaulter will also be dispossessed and will be known contemptuously as "the discalced." **11–12.** The case of indecent assault by a wife whose husband is losing a fist fight; cf. the similar provision in the Assyrian laws (*ANET* 181). **13–16.** Use of false weights is often denounced in the prophetic (Amos 8:5; Hos 12:8–9; Mic 6:10–12) and sapiential literature (Prov 11:1; 16:11; 20:23). **17–19.** The command to destroy Amalek, which is not really a law, may have served as an inclusion to the section beginning at 23:2, rounding off the treatment of neighboring peoples. Hostility between Israel and Amalek is an important theme in the early part of the history (1 Sam 15:1–33; 30:1–20; 2 Sam 8:12; cf. Exod 17:8–16).

(Carmichael, C. M., "A Ceremonial Crux," *JBL* 96 [1977] 321–36. Eslinger, L., "The Case of an Immodest Lady Wrestler in Dt XXV 11–12," *VT* 31 [1981] 269–81 Noonan, J. T., "The Muzzled Ox," *JQR* 70 [1979–80] 172–7.)

42 (J) Offering of the Firstfruits (26:1–15). This corresponds to the sanctuary law at the beginning (12:1–14), with which it has several verbal parallels. It also celebrates the fulfillment of the territorial promise in function of which the law is to be obeyed. **1.** For this type of opening, cf. 6:10; 7:1; 11:29; 17:14; 18:9. **2.** Cf. 12:5,11,14. **3.** *the priest who is in office at that time:* Cf. 17:9; 19:17, referring to the central judiciary. **5.** *wandering:* Or perhaps "doomed to perish." While this kind of recital probably borrows from the cult, von Rad's view of the passage as the oldest Israelite "credo," deriving from the liturgy at Gilgal and forming the nucleus of the hexateuchal narrative is now widely abandoned (see von Rad, *Deuteronomy* 157–61). **5–7.** The pattern of oppression, cry for help, divine action in response to prayer is typically deuteronomic (cf. Judg 3:7–11). **10–11.** The priest has no role here, as he has none in 14:22–27; hence 26:3–4 may be a later variant. **12.** On the third year tithe, see 14:28–29. **14.** This threefold negative confession is probably not native to this context. *the dead:* Perhaps the vegetation deity (see 14:1) in whose honor funerary meals were eaten. **15.** The same form as the (exilic) prayer of Solomon at the dedication of the Temple (1 Kgs 8:43).

43 (IV) Conclusion to the Giving of the Law (26:16–28:69). The second address of Moses continues uninterrupted through 26:16–19 and is resumed and concluded with the blessings and curses in chap. 28. 28:69 (29:1 Eng) is the finale to the entire discourse including the law (chaps. 12–26). The passage dealing with the Shechem covenant tradition (27:1–14) has been spliced in to match 11:26–32 immediately preceding the law. The list of apodictic curses (27:14–26), from a quite different source, corresponds to a form of covenant making known from Second Temple texts (Neh 10:31).

44 (A) Reciprocal Commitment (26:16–19). The threefold repetiton of "this day" and the solemn declarations suggest an actual covenant ritual (e.g., 2 Kgs 23:1–3). **17.** *you have declared:* The causative of the verb *'āmar*, only here, has the technical sense of acknowledging a statement as juridically binding. For the statements, cf. the covenant formula in Hos 2:25; Jer 31:33. **18.** *possession:* See 7:6. **18–19.** These verses appear to be based on Exod 19:4–6.

45 (B) The Shechem Covenant Ritual (27:1–26). 1–8. A conflation of a Shechem covenant tradition (vv 4,5,8; cf. Josh 8:30–35) with a Gilgal tradition (vv 2–3,6–7; cf. Josh 4:1–10), blended in typically D fashion. **4.** *Ebal:* The twin peak of Gerizim to the N, associated with the curse. **5.** The altar is to be built according to stipulations in Exod 20:25, but it is not clear whether it was thought to be in conformity with Deut 12. **8.** Repeats 27:3a with the addition of "very plainly." **9–10.** From a separate source in which levitical priests, not elders, are alongside Moses; perhaps the continuation of 26:16–19. **11–13.** Here Moses alone speaks. The division into two groups of six tribes each is a further elaboration; cf. 11:26–30 and Josh 8:33–34. The curses are pronounced on Ebal because it lies to the N. The six tribes on Ebal are all located either to the N or E of the Jordan. **14–26.** That the chapter is composite is seen in the different roles of levitical priests (v 9), the tribe of Levi (v 12), and the Levites (v 14). This last is

the only place in Deut where Levites as *clerus minor* appear, suggesting a Second Temple date (cf. Neh 8:7–8). The 12 paragraphs are not strictly curses (the threatened evil is not specified) but apodictic legal formulations. Absence of blessings is due to editorial juxtaposition of vv 11–13 and vv 14–26, of different provenience. With the exception of the first and last, the form is "Cursed be he" (*'ārûr . . .*) + relative clause in participial form + Amen of the people. The first and last may have been added to tally with the number of the tribes. **15.** *Cursed:* The anathema functioned to put the offender outside the community by making it impossible for him to participate in cult without cursing himself. **16.** Of the ten following, five condemn offenses listed in Deut and four occur only in Lev 17–26. This distribution suggests comparison with Neh 10:30 (entering into a curse and an oath) and a time when pentateuchal law was well on its way to final consolidation. On the obligation of honoring parents, see 5:16; 21:18–21. **17.** See 19:14. **18.** Lev 19:14; not in Deut. **19.** See 24:17. **20.** See 22:30 and Lev 18:7–8; a similar provision in Hammurabi § 154–58 (*ANET* 172–73). **21.** See Lev 18:23; 20:15. Bestiality was apparently practiced in certain cults to promote fertility by sympathetic magic. **22.** See Lev 18:6–18; 20:11–21. **23.** See Lev 18:8; 20:14. **24.** See 21:1–9. **25.** The case of the hired killer is not dealt with in Deut, but cf. Ezek 22:12. **26.** A redactional finale referring to the D law.

46 (C) Blessings and Curses (28:1–69). The continuation and conclusion of the second address (5:1–28:69), interrupted by chap. 27. Analogies are the curses that are especially in evidence in Assyrian vassal treaties and those appended to collections of laws. **1–2.** Continues and overlaps with 26:19. **3–6.** Five blessings (*bārûk . . .*), to which correspond the five curses of vv 15–19. They deal for the most part with agrarian life. **7–14.** Six pronouncements of blessing, formally quite different, beginning "Yahweh will . . ." + action benefiting the recipient of the blessing. **7.** Cf. 28:25. **9–10.** *a people holy to himself:* Cf. 26:18–19. To invoke the name of the deity over a person, place, or thing signified ownership. **11.** Cf. 28:51. **13–14.** *the head and not the tail:* Cf. vv 44–45 and Isa 9:14 with the postexilic gloss in the following verse. **15–19.** These curses form a mirror image to vv 1–6. **20–46.** Corresponding to vv 7–14 but much more elaborate. **20.** Roughly parallel to 28:8, where the phrase "in all that you undertake" also occurs. The change to divine 1st pers. at the end probably comes from a later expansion. **21.** The language is typically D and exilic; cf. 4:25–31; 29:28. **22–23.** These seven afflictions may represent different stages of grave sickness. **25–26.** Cf. 28:7; Jer 34:17. One of the worst disasters possible was to remain unburied (e.g., Jer 7:33; 34:20). **27.** The meaning of these terms is uncertain. *boils of Egypt:* Refers to the sixth plague (Exod 9:6–12). **28–29.** Perhaps alluding to the ninth plague, darkness (Exod 10:21–29). **33.** At this point, allusion to the Babylonian conquest begins to emerge. **36–44.** The climax in this series reflects the experience of deportation and exile. **37.** Cf. 1 Kgs 9:7; Jer 18:16; etc. **45–46.** The ending of the series of curses in vv 15–44; their fulfillment is now inevitable, not contingent on disobedience to the law. **47–57.** A prophecy *ex eventu* of the disaster of 587 and its sequel. The many parallels with Jer are to be explained in large part by the exilic deuteronomic redaction of the book (cf. Jer 4:13; 5:15–17; 19:9; 28; etc.). **58–68.** In this last section the threats are again conditional. Retrospective allusion to "this book" suggests that the passage concluded Deut at one editorial stage. **60.** The plagues of Egypt will afflict unfaithful Israel (cf. 28:27). Infidelity involves a reversal of exodus and of the

Abrahamic promise. **62.** Cf. 1:10; Gen 15:5. *few in number:* Cf. 4:27; 26:5. **64.** Cf. 4:27–28. **68.** The source for this promise is unknown; at 17:16 there is a command not to return to Egypt. **69.** (Eng 29:1). A conclusion rather than an introduction; cf. Lev 26:46; 27:34; Num 36:13. The covenant in the land of Moab is a second covenant after all, since the law revealed to Moses alone at Horeb was promulgated and accepted there.

47   **(V) Third Address (29:1–30:20; Eng 29:2–30:20).** Divisions are speculative since there are no introductory formulas between 29:1 and 31:1. In effect a sermon, probably originating in the emerging institution of the synagogue, it must be exilic at the earliest (see 29:27). Its purpose was exhortation and instruction.

48   **(A) Lessons to be Learned from History (29:1–8). 1.** *all Israel:* The ancient designation for the tribal assembly in cult or war; in updated terms, the early Jewish synagogue congregation. The following recital corresponds to the historical prologue in the disparity treaties, but it is unlikely that it was modeled directly on it. **1–2.** Cf. Exod 19:4; Josh 24:5–7; Neh 9:9–12. **3.** The community is slow to learn the lesson; cf. Isa 42:18–20 and similar complaints. **5.** See 8:4. **6.** Perhaps inadvertently, the preacher here has Yahweh speaking in the 1st person. **6–7.** A summary of 2:26–3:22. The covenant in question is the second covenant of Deut (28:69) addressed to the postcatastrophe community.

49   **(B) Charge to the Covenanting Community (29:9–28).** For the official character of the opening paragraph, in which the participants are designated, cf. Neh 10:1–30. Deut is referred to as a book (v 26). **9–10.** The congregation consists of tribal heads (or leaders and judges; see C. Begg, *ETL* 58 [1982] 87–105), elders, officers (see 1:15), adult males, children who had attained the age of discretion, wives, "hewers of wood and drawers of water." The last named was the lowest category of Temple servants or *nĕtînîm* (Ezra 2:43; Neh 7:50; cf. Josh 9:21,23,27). For the important role of elders during the exile, see Ezek 14:1; 20:1; etc. **11.** *sworn covenant:* The occasion is therefore the sealing of the covenant. The curse is associated with covenant only in this section (29:11,13,18–20; 30:7; cf. 1 Kgs 8:31; Neh 10:30). **13–14.** The preacher is at pains to stress the vital link between present and past; cf. 5:3. **16–17.** The beginning of a long admonition about the danger of foreign cults. These terms for idols, "abomination" (*šiqqûṣ*) and "ordure" (*gillul*) occur only here in Deut. **17.** *poisonous and bitter fruit:* Borrowed from Amos (5:7; 6:12). **18.** *to sweep away the moist and the dry:* The exact meaning is unknown, but this is probably a quotation, meaning that the recalcitrant one can take it all in his stride. **19.** *the book:* Deut itself inclusive of chap. 28; cf. Neh 13:1–3. **22.** The cities of the plain are listed together in Gen 10:19 and 14:2; Sodom and Gomorrah in Gen 19; Amos 4:11; etc.; Admah and Zeboiim in Hos 11:2. **21–27.** A rather sudden transition from the individual idolater to the fate of the people and the land. The question-and-answer form is characteristic of the D parenetic style; cf. 1 Kgs 9:8–9; Jer 5:19; 16:10–13; 22:8–9, and a remarkably similar form in the chronicles of Ashurbanipal (*ANET* 300). **27.** The exilic situation is here explicitly presupposed. **28.** The contrast between the things hidden and revealed has a sapiential flavor and parallels the conclusion to the next paragraph (30:11–14). It enjoins concentration on observance of the divine law rather than speculation, including the apocalyptic kind, about divine intentions (cf. Job 28:28).

50   **(C) Reversal of Fortune (30:1–14). 1–2.** Blessing and curse are now understood serially. Reflection on the disasters that have happened leads to

conversion—note the frequent occurrence of the verb *šûb*, "return," "be converted"; cf. 4:29–31; 1 Kgs 8:46–50. **3.** *restore your fortunes:* The phrase *šûb šĕbût* plays on the verb *šûb*, "return," and *šābâ*, "take captive." The theme of the ingathering of the dispersed occurs frequently in exilic and early postexilic texts (e.g., Jer 29:14; 32:37; Ezek 20:34,41; Isa 43:5; 54:7; 56:8). **6.** See 10:16. The new covenant of the exilic Deuteronomist, also reflected in Jer 31:31–34, presupposes a change of heart effected by Yahweh which would make law observance a labor of love. **10.** *this book of the law:* I.e., Deut (cf. 28:58,61; 29:19,20,26). **11–14.** The law is not esoteric knowledge requiring that a chosen intermediary like Enoch ascend to heaven in order to communicate it. It is recited in the covenant festival, and God has now put the disposition to obey it in the heart (cf. Jer 31:33; Ezek 36:26–27).

51   **(D) The Two Ways (30:15–20).** Corresponds to 11:26–28. forming an apt conclusion to the address. This form of words was probably actually used at covenant-making and covenant-renewing liturgies. **16.** *if you obey the commandments of Yahweh your God:* Supplied from the LXX and demanded by the sense. **19.** On the calling of witnesses, an essential element in the treaties, see 4:26. **20.** The address ends appropriately with an allusion to the ancestral promise, a major theme in Deut.

52   **(VI) Last Will, Testament, and Death of Moses (31:1–34:12).** While Moses continues to speak, the continuity of discourse is broken here. In these last chapters the narrative style predominates, treating the following themes: (1) commissioning of Joshua (31:1–8, 14–15,23; 34:9); (2) dispositions with regard to the law book (31:9–13,24–29; 32:45–47); (3) the Song of Moses (31:16–22,30; 32:1–44); (4) blessings on the tribes (chap. 33); (5) death of Moses (32:48–52; 34:1–8). The book is rounded off with a conclusion to the Pentateuch as a whole (34:10–12). Of these sections (1), (2), and part of (5) belong to the deuteronomic-exilic corpus, having connections with chaps. 1–3 and Josh. Most of (5) is from an editor in the P tradition and style who incorporated the book into the Pentateuch; (3) and (4) represent the latest stage of expansion together with the final verses, which should be studied in tandem with the final verses of prophets (Mal 3:23–24).

53   **(A) Commissioning of Joshua (31:1–8). 1.** *Moses continued to speak:* If one reads with the LXX and Qumran (DJD 1. 60) "Moses finished speaking," the verse could have concluded the previous section. Actually, 31:1–8 connects well with 3:23–29. **2.** The day is that of Moses' death (cf. 1:3 P). The age fits the P schema (cf. Exod 7:7; Num 33:38–39). *go out and come in:* Lead (cf. Num 27:17 P). The failure of Moses to cross the Jordan is a prominent theme in 1–3. **4.** See 2:26–3:11. **5.** Refers to 7:1–5. **6.** Cf. Josh 1:6–9. **7–8.** The installation of Joshua seems to follow a more or less fixed formula (see N. Lohfink, *Scholastik* 37 [1962] 32–44). The frequency of its occurrence attests to the importance of the transition from the Mosaic to the post-Mosaic age.

54   **(B) Dispositions with Respect to the Law; Joshua Commissioned (31:9–15). 10.** The septennial reading of the law is not attested elsewhere, not even in the regulations for the year of release and Sukkoth (15:1; 16:13–15). It may have been suggested by the periodic reading of treaty texts. **12.** Cf. 29:9–10. **14–15.** In 31:7–8 Moses does the commissioning, as also in the P versions, Num 27:15–23 and Deut 34:9. Here, however, Yahweh commissions at the Tent of Meeting (*'ōhel mô'ēd*), the only occasion where this oracle shrine is mentioned in Deut. A close parallel is the commissioning of the 70 elders also at the Tent (Num 11:16–17,

24–30). 31:23 may have been added as a conclusion, repeating v 7, before the insertion of 16–22.

55   (C) Introduction to the Song (31:16–23). The song was inserted parallel to the law, as testifying against faithless Israel, and for this reason both must be written down. **16.** (Sacred) prostitution signifies apostasy by metonymy (cf. Hos 2:7; 4:15). **17.** Cf. 29:23–27. **21.** *Yēṣer* means "inclination," with much the same sense in Gen 6:5; 8:21; 1 Chr 28:9; 29:18. The first two have contributed to the rabbinic idea of the evil inclination, *yēṣer hā-rāʿ.* **23.** The conclusion to vv 14–15.

56   (D) The Law Deposited in the Sanctuary (31:24–29). Takes up from 31:9–13 and is continued in 32:45–47. **28.** *this law:* Emend to "this song"; vv 28–29 refer more naturally to the song since a private reading of the law to elders and officers after the command to carry out the public reading (31:11) seems pointless. The confusion arose from the editorial adjustments made when the song was added. **26.** Just as a copy of a treaty had to be deposited in a sanctuary, so the law was to be laid beside the ark of the covenant. The Decalogue was placed inside the ark (10:1–5). **28.** On heaven and earth as witnesses, see 4:26; cf. 30:19; 32:1.

57   (E) The Song of Moses (31:30–32:44). The song was inserted at a late date because of the consonance of its theme with deuteronomic parenesis. The text has undergone extensive disturbance; the often divergent LXX finds some support in the 4Q fragments. Arguments for a very early date have been based on one or more of the following: affinity with E in the Pentateuch; archaic language; prosodic typology (according to Albright it fits between Exod 15 and Judg 5 on the one hand and 2 Sam 1 on the other). In the present state of pentateuchal studies, however, it would be risky to base much on E; the language could be said to be archaizing rather than archaic (as in Hab 3); and it is doubtful whether rigid prosodic theories translate into precise chronological sequence. Allusions in the poem (vv 7,15), the advanced theological ideas presupposed, the indications of sapiential and prophetic influence (e.g., the form of lawsuit or *rîb* pattern) would seem to suggest rather a date no earlier than the late monarchy or exilic period.

(Albright, W. F., *VT* 9 [1959] 339–46. Boston, J. R., *JBL* 87 [1968] 198–202. Cross, F. M., *The Ancient Library of Qumran* [NY, 1961] 182–84. Eissfeldt, O., *Das Lied Moses Deut. 32:1–43 und das Lehrgedicht Asaphs Psalm 78* [Leipzig, 1958]. Hidal, S., *ASTI* 11 [1977–78] 15–21. Mendenhall, G. E., *NFL* 63–74. Skehan, P. W., *CBQ* 12 [1951] 153–63; *BASOR* 136 [1954] 12–15; *JBL* 78 [1959] 21–22.)

1. Appeal to the heaven and earth as witnesses (cf. 4:26; 30:19; Jer 2:12; Ps 50:4–6) reflects the calling of deities as witnesses in the *rîb* (indictment) of a vassal after treaty violation (see J. Harvey, *Bib* 43 [1962] 172–96). **2.** *teaching (leqaḥ:* An example of sapiential vocabulary (e.g., Job 11:4; Prov 1:5; 4:2). **4.** *the Rock (haṣṣûr):* Or the Mountain, a divine title used frequently in Pss and later prophecy (e.g., Isa 44:8); cf. Ugaritic *ǵr.* **5.** One of the most difficult lines in the poem. A possible reconstruction of 5a would be, "they have dealt corruptly with him; they are not his sons on account of their impurity." **7.** Wisdom is to be sought from the elders, whose responsibility it is to transmit the tradition. **8.** *'elyôn:* A pre-Israelite divine title, perhaps Jerusalemite (Gen 14:18–22; Num 24:16). For "sons of Israel" read "sons of God" with the LXX and QL. The idea is that Elyon, high god of the Canaanite pantheon, assigned each of the 70 nations of the world (Gen 10) to one of the 70 deities of the pantheon and that Israel had the good fortune to be assigned to Yahweh (see P. Winter, *ZAW* 67 [1955]

40–48; 75 [1963] 218–23; M. Lana, *Henoch* 5 [1983] 179–207) **10–12.** The wilderness period as a time of special providence for Israel (cf. Hos 9:10; Jer 2:6). **11.** For the image, see Exod 19:4; on vv 6–12, see S. Geller, *HTR* 75 (1982) 35–36. **14.** *blood of the grape:* Cf. Gen 49:11 and "blood of trees" (*dm ʿṣm*) in Ras Shamra (Baal and Anath, II ii 43). **15.** *Jeshurun:* A title for Israel only here and 33:5,26; Isa 44:2; derived either from *yāšār,* "upright," or *šôr,* "ox"; in the context the latter seems more likely. **17.** *demons (šēdîm):* Only here and Ps 106:37, from Akk *šēdu.* **18.** *begot:* More precisely, "gave birth to," a maternal attribution. **21.** Here and following, the language is too generalized to allow identification of the hostile nation. **22.** A poetic image of divine judgment; cf. Judg 9:15,20; Amos 2:4; Jer 15:4. **26.** There is here a change of direction: Israel will not be completely destroyed because then the adversary would claim credit for it (cf. Josh 7:9; Isa 10:7). **28–29.** The concentration of sapiential language here is noteworthy. **30.**The reversal of a holy war theme. **31–33.** These verses refer to the adversary. **31.** *judges:* A rare word (*pělîlîm*), used elsewhere only at Exod 21:22 and Job 31:11; "fools" (*'ĕwîlîm*) would fit the context better. **36.** *his servants:* Also 32:43; recalls the same designation in Isa 65:8–9,13–15. **39.** The closest parallels are the frequent divine self-predications in Isa 41:4; 43:10–11,13,25. **41–42.** Cf. Isa 63:1–6. **43.** The concluding verse may be restored as follows with help of the LXX and QL:

> Rejoice with his people, O heavens
>   Adore him, all gods
> for he avenges the blood of his servants
>   and makes expiation for the land of his people.

An additional verse in the LXX, calling on the angels to worship him, probably a variant, is quoted at Heb 1:6. **58   (F) Exhortation to Observe the Law (32:45–47).** Although this appears to be the sequel to 31:9–13,24–29, according to 31:28–29 Moses was preparing to address only the leaders, and in any case the law had already been deposited in the sanctuary. Here, too, the confusion is due to the insertion of the song. **59   (G) Moses Prepares for Death (32:48–52).** The passage is from P and its continuation, now obscured by the insertion of the deathbed blessings (chap. 33), is in 34:1,7–9. It belongs to a later P editorial stage, being an expanded version of Num 27:12–14, the original place in the narrative for the death of Moses. The amalgamation of Deut with the P-edited narrative necessitated the relocation of the account of Moses' death. **48.** *that very day:* A characteristic P expression; the allusion is back to the date in 1:3. **49.** *Abarim:* See Num 27:12 (P); the P account of Aaron's death is at Num 20:22–29. **51.** Moses' fault at Kadesh is a theme of P (Num 20:1–13); the alternative version leaves him blameless (Exod 17:1–7), and nowhere is he blamed in Deut (see 3:26). It was evidently important for P to explain why Moses did not enter the land. *revere me as holy:* The vb. qdš was probably chosen because of assonance and alliteration with Kadesh (*qādēš*). **60   (H) Deathbed Blessings of Moses (33:1–29).** Its late insertion interrupts the narrative continuity between 32:52 and 34:1, but its place in the book is appropriate; cf. the last blessings of Isaac (Gen 27) and Jacob (Gen 49). The poem as a whole is later than Gen 49; Levi is no longer a secular tribe and Simeon has disappeared. The number 12 is maintained by counting Ephraim and Manasseh (Joseph's sons) separately. The greater praise bestowed on the Joseph tribes suggests an origin in the northern kingdom not later than the 8th cent. Yet the blessings could have been inserted into a psalm preserved at the beginning (vv 2–5) and end (vv 26–29).

(Caquot, A., *Sem* 32 [1982] 67–81. Christensen, D. L., *Bib* 65 [1984] 382–89. Cross, F. M. and D. N. Freedman, *JBL* 67 [1948] 191–210. Labuschagne, C. J., *OTS* 19 [1974] 97–112. Seebass, H., *VT* 27 [1977] 158–69.)

1. *man of God:* A synonym for "prophet" (cf. Josh 14:6; Ps 90:1). **2–5.** The theophanic theme is found also in Judg 5:4; Hab 3:3; Ps 68:17; etc. **2–3.** All the place-names occur in 1:1–2, though Sinai (for Horeb) occurs only here. Note that Sinai is in parallelism with Seir (Edom). The rest of vv 2–3 is uncertain; see the commentaries. **5.** Though Yahweh is not mentioned, v 5, along with v 4, probably alludes to his solemn enthronement as king of the tribes (cf. Exod 15:18; Judg 8:23; etc.). *Jeshurun:* See 32:15. If the tribal blessings were inserted into a psalm, this would be the logical place. **6.** *Reuben:* The title is missing. This Transjordanian tribe, still powerful in Gen 49:3–4 (cf. Judg 5:15b–16), was evidently in danger of extinction; the second stychos should read, "but let him be few in number." **7.** *Judah:* Here much less significant than Gen 49:8–12. Probably from a time of relatively peaceful relations between the kingdoms, the oracle assumes that Judah is cut off from the central and northern tribes. **8–11.** This oracle, the longest after Joseph, is composite, vv 9b–10 being a deuteronomic addition. Levi is no longer a secular tribe. **8.** *Urim and Thummim:* An oracular device, perhaps like dice (e.g., Num 27:21; 1 Sam 14:41), later attached to the priest's ephod garment (Exod 28:30). The testing at Massah and Meribah may refer to Moses and Aaron, both of levitical descent (Exod 15:25; 17:1–7; Deut 32:51). **9a.** The allusion appears to be to the levitical zeal displayed in the golden calf incident (Exod 32:25–29). **11.** Either the original conclusion to the Judah oracle (as argued by A. D. H. Mayes, *Deuteronomy* 404) or an allusion to internecine strife within priestly families. **12.** The verse is obscure. If *'ālāyw* is emended to *'elyôn,* following the LXX, we may read: "The beloved of Yahweh dwells securely/ Elyon encompasses him all day long." The reference to one dwelling between his shoulders at the end may allude to the ark shrine in Benjaminite territory before its transfer to Jerusalem. It is even possible that the entire saying alludes to the presence of the ark in Benjamin at a time when that tribe was still considered the southern province of the Joseph tribes. **13–17.** Fertility is the theme both here and in Gen 49:25–26. The key word *meged,* "choicest gift (of nature)" occurs five times. **13.** *with dew:* This should not be emended out (as *RSV*); as in the Ugaritic texts the contrast is between the heaven as a source of dew and the subterranean waters (*tĕhôm,* personified as a beast, the source of ground water; cf. Gen 49:25). **16.** *bush:* The same word as the burning bush in Exod 3:1–6; the emendation to "Sinai" is unsupported and unnecessary. *Nāzîr* also means "consecrated one," Nazirite, a sense supported by the allusion to Joseph's head. **17.** The bull image recalls the cults of the northern kingdom, but could also refer to a ruler; v 17b has been added by the compiler of the blessings to maintain the number 12. **18–19.** Zebulon and Issachar straddled the rich and strategically important Esdraelon Valley from the Mediterranean to the Rift Valley. The

saying alludes to a mountain shrine, either Tabor or Carmel, center of the Yahweh cult, and to profit from the caravan trade (see M. Dahood, *Or* 47 ([1978] 263–64). **20–21.** *he who enlarges Gad:* A fairly literal transl. of *marḥîb gād.* While the allusion could be to a leader now unknown, the reading *merḥab,* "wide place," "wide domain" (*NEB*), seems preferable. Gad settled on the plateau E of Jordan and gradually absorbed Reuben. Verse 21b may refer to Gad's obedience to the command to assist in the conquest (Num 32). **22.** Already settled in the north (cf. Gen 49:17), Dan had a reputation for launching attacks on travelers through the area. Bashan is not usual for the region that far north, in the Golan, but the emendation of "from Bashan" to "from a viper" (Ugaritic *bṯn*) does not fit the context (see Cross and Freedman, *JBL* 67 [1948] 208). **23.** An allusion to the rich plain of Ginnosar and the Sea of Galilee. **24–25.** Here and in Gen 49:20 the prosperity and strength of Asher, settled along the northern coastal region in direct contact with the Phoenician cities, are emphasized. **26–29.** Conclusion of the psalm. **26.** Reading *kĕ 'ēl* for *kā 'ēl* gives "There is none like the God of Jeshurun." An emendation (Cross and Freedman, *BASOR* 108 [1947] 6–7) gives "riding the heavens in his strength / riding the clouds in his glory"; cf. Ps 68:5. **27.** An obscure text; perhaps an allusion to the triumph of Yahweh over the other gods (see *NEB*) in preparation for his victorious intervention on behalf of his people. **28.** The traditional language of blessing.

61   **(I) Death of Moses; Conclusion to the Pentateuch (34:1–12).** The chapter brings together (1) the conclusion to the exilic-deuteronomic review of the Mosaic age, taking up from 3:25–29; (2) the revised P version of Moses' death, the original position of which was Num 27:12–23. **1–3.** *from the plains of Moab to Mount Nebo:* From the later P source. *Pisgah:* The D equivalent of Nebo; cf. 3:27; 4:49. The viewing of the land takes in an immense arc from S to N and then back to the starting point. **4.** See 1:37; 3:25–27; 4:21–22; etc. **6.** *he buried him:* The subject is Yahweh, though Sam. Pent. and some LXX mss. have the pl. The departure of the great prophet could not be less numinous than that of Elijah. A considerable literature developed around the fate of Moses and the location of his remains (e.g., Jude 9; *As. Mos.*). **7–9.** The conclusion of the P account of Moses' death and the succession of Joshua. **7.** For Moses' age, see 31:2; cf. Num 33:39 (Aaron). *natural force:* By analogy with Ugaritic *lḥt,* perhaps sexual vigor (W. F. Albright, *BASOR* 94 [1944] 32–35). **8.** The same mourning period as for Aaron (Num 20:29). **9.** In contrast to Num 27:18, where Joshua is appointed because he possesses spirit, here the spirit of wisdom (the ability to rule) is the result of the laying on of hands, which also entitled him to be obeyed. **10–12.** The final three verses are the finale to the Pentateuch as a whole. The point is to deny parity between Moses and the prophets, since the mediation of the latter is indirect—and this with reference to the promise of a "prophet like Moses" in 18:15–18. See J. Blenkinsopp, *Prophecy and Canon* 85–95. Verses 11–12 amplify the prophetic portrait of Moses by alluding to the signs and wonders which he wrought, esp. the plagues of Egypt; cf. 4:34; 6:22; 7:19; 11:3; 26:8; 29:1–2; Pss 105:26–27; 135:9.

7

JOSHUA

Michael David Coogan

BIBLIOGRAPHY

1 *Commentaries:* Boling, R. G. and G. E. Wright, *Joshua* (AB 6; GC, 1982). Cooke, G. A., *The Book of Joshua* (CBSC; Cambridge, 1918). Gray, J., *Joshua, Judges and Ruth* (CentB; London, 1967). Miller, J. M. and G. M. Tucker, *The Book of Joshua* (CBC; Cambridge, 1974). Noth, M., *Das Buch Josua* (HAT; 2d ed.; Tübingen, 1953). Soggin, J. A., *Joshua* (OTL; Phl, 1972).

Studies: Auld, A. G., *Joshua, Moses and the Land* (Edinburgh, 1980). Polzin, R., *Moses and the Deuteronomist* (NY, 1980). Weippert, M., *The Settlement of the Israelite Tribes in Palestine* (SBT 21; London, 1980).

For further bibliography see J. M. Miller, "Joshua, Book of," *IDBSup* 496; *CIOTS* 239–41.

INTRODUCTION

2 **(I) Text.** The textual situation is complicated; as in 1–2 Sam, there are two major traditions, represented by the MT on the one hand and LXX[B] (henceforth LXX, unless otherwise noted) on the other. The agreement of the LXX and 4QJos[a] indicates that the LXX was based on a Hebr text different from that which is represented by the MT; in many cases this text is shorter and better. Textual development continued, however, after the translation of this original Hebr text into Greek; deliberate changes, such as glosses, expansions, and corrections, continued to be introduced in both Hebr and Gk traditions, and unconscious mechanical errors occurred as well. Each case has thus to be evaluated separately, taking into account the Vg, the Syr, and other ancient versions as well.

(Auld, A. G., "Textual and Literary Studies in the Book of Joshua," *ZAW* 90 [1978] 412–17; "Joshua: The Hebrew and Greek Texts," *Studies in the Historical Books of the Old Testament* [VTSup 30; Leiden, 1979] 1–14. Greenspoon, L. J., *Textual Studies in the Book of Joshua* [Chico, 1983]. Holmes, S., *Joshua: The Hebrew and Greek Texts* [Cambridge, 1914]. Orlinsky, H. M., "The Hebrew *Vorlage* of the Septuagint of the Book of Joshua," *Congress Volume: Rome, 1968* [VTSup 17; Leiden, 1969] 187–95.)

3 **(II) Literary History.** Earlier critics had seen in Joshua a continuation of the various pentateuchal traditions, and they referred to the totality of Gen to Josh as the "Hexateuch." Since the pioneering studies of M. Noth, it has become clear that it is more appropriate to speak of a "Tetrateuch" (Gen to Num). Deut served as a kind of theological preface to Dtr (the deuterono-

mistic history, Josh to 2 Kgs) which followed. Dtr has a history of its own which more recent research has shown to be complicated. Most scholars agree that in its present form the work is largely a product of the 7th cent. (the reign of Josiah), which was revised in the exilic period in the light of the events of 587/586. The Josianic work may have drawn on earlier antecedents, perhaps from the time of Hezekiah. Within this larger context Josh has several distinctive themes.

4 **(III) The Themes of Joshua.** One of these is stated in 1:5: "As I was with Moses, I will be with you," reiterated in 3:7; 4:14. This theme is developed by having Joshua repeat many of Moses' actions; following the order of events in Josh, note the following parallels: (1) From the wilderness Moses sent spies to scout out the land (Num 13; Deut 1:19–46); from Transjordan Joshua sends spies to scout out the land near Jericho (Josh 2). (2) Under Moses' leadership the Israelites passed through the Reed Sea as on dry ground (Exod 14); under Joshua's leadership the Israelites cross the Jordan as on dry ground (Josh 3). (3) Before the exodus from Egypt, Moses and the Hebrews celebrated the Passover (Exod 12); after their entry into Canaan, Joshua and the Israelites celebrated the Passover (Josh 5:10–12). (4) In the wilderness where Moses was to lead the Israelites, he had a vision of a burning bush in which he was told, "Remove your shoes from your feet, for the place on which you are standing is holy ground" (Exod 3:5); in the territory into which Joshua leads the Israelites, he has a vision in which the commander of Yahweh's army tells him, "Remove your shoes from your feet, for the place on which you are standing is holy" (Josh 5:15). (5) Having entered the land, Joshua sends spies to Ai (Josh 7:2–5), just as Moses had sent spies into Transjordan (Num 21:32). (6) Moses, holding "God's rod," extended his hand, and while he did so, Israel prevailed over the Amalekites (Exod 17:8–13); Joshua, holding a sicklesword, extends his hand, and while he does so, Israel prevails over the inhabitants of Ai (8:18–26). (7) Before their deaths, both Moses (Deut) and Joshua (Josh 23–24) deliver farewell speeches to the Israelites. (8) Other parallels include the instruction to the people to sanctify themselves in preparation for the divine manifestation (Exod 19:10; Josh 3:5); intercession for the Israelites who had offended God (Exod 32:11–14; Num 11:2; 14:13–19; Deut 9:25–29; Josh 7:6–9); and the roles of Moses and Joshua as covenant mediators (Exod 24; Josh 24).

In addition to these parallels, there are a number of passages in which Joshua explicitly fulfills a command given by Moses. These include his instruction to Reuben, Gad, and Eastern Manasseh to join the other tribes in the military conquest of the land (1:12–18; see Num 32; Deut 3:12–20); the erection of the altar on Mt. Ebal (8:30–35; see Deut 27:1–26); the extermination of the inhabitants of the land (11:15; see Deut 20:16) and of the Anakim (11:21; see Deut 9:2); the division of the land by lot (14:2; see Num 34:13); and the establishment of the cities of asylum (20; see Num 35:9–15; Deut 19:1–10) and the cities of the Levites (21:1–42; see Num 35:1–8).

5   One consequence of these parallels and fulfillments is that Joshua is presented as little more than a kind of carbon copy of Moses, and it is thus difficult to penetrate behind the literary traditions to the historical Joshua. Unlike Moses, Joshua is the leader without flaw or hesitation; he is, in fact, deliberately portrayed as the ideal leader of Israel, one who keeps the teaching of Moses in its entirety (1:7–8; 11:15), and as such for Dtr the prototype of the ideal king of Israel, in particular, David, Hezekiah, and esp. Josiah (see R. D. Nelson, "Josiah in the Book of Joshua," *JBL* 100 [1981] 531–40). Like the ideal king of Deut 17:18, Joshua writes a copy of the teaching of Moses (8:32; these are the only two occurrences of the phrase "copy of the teaching" [Hebr *tôrâ*]). Joshua also serves as an antitype of Saul, the failed king: in contrast to Saul (1 Sam 13–15), Joshua enforces the rules of holy war (Josh 7) and keeps the oath made with the Gibeonites (Josh 9; cf. 2 Sam 21:1–14).

The existence of these parallels, esp. those that quote other passages, also suggests that Josh is a literary creation whose sources included preexisting Israelite traditions about Moses, much as the OT was a source for the Gospels' description of the life and esp. the death of Jesus. (A similar technique is used in the Elijah-Elisha cycle [1 Kgs 17–2 Kgs 13], in which Elisha, who "ministered" to Elijah [1 Kgs 19:21] as Joshua was "Moses' minister" [Josh 1:1], repeats many of the miracles performed by his predecessor.) In view of this elaborate development the most that can be said is that Joshua was an Ephraimite (see 19:50; 24:30), perhaps originally a local hero who became the focus for the idealized reconstruction of early Israel in Dtr.

6   In the composition of the narrative one of the sources that the deuteronomistic historians drew on was preexisting Priestly tradition, to be distinguished from its subsequent formulation in the pentateuchal source P. Throughout Josh, we find characteristic P terminology and emphases, and these make their way into the book at various stages in its history.

7   A final theme to be considered is the use of etiology, the explanation of various elements, esp. geographic features, known to the audiences of Josh, by means of stories connected with Joshua. These etiological narratives are generally marked by the phrase "to this day"; see 4:9; 5:9; 6:25; 7:26; 8:28,29; 9:27; 10:27; 13:13; 14:14; 15:63; 16:10. The use of the phrase implies chronological distance, the perspective of hindsight. As such, the use of the phrase confirms our earlier analysis of Josh as a narrative developed long after the events described in it. Analogous to these etiological narratives are etymological explanations also developed into episodes within the story, such as 5:3; 22:34.

8   **(IV) Joshua in Other Traditions.** In the Pentateuch Joshua is a minor figure. In J, he first appears in Exod 17:8, without introduction as though already known, as Moses' military aide, who leads the battle against Amalek. Thereafter he accompanies Moses up the mountain (Exod 24:13; 32:17), shares Moses' closeness to Yahweh (Exod 33:11), and functions as his youthfully rash advisor (Num 11:28). In both J and P, Joshua figures in the episode of the sending of the spies (Num 13–14), but he is clearly subordinate to Caleb (cf. Num 14:24,30). In P especially he is a secondary figure; his name is twice given as Hoshea (Num 13:8; Deut 32:44), and Eleazar the priest precedes him in the commands concerning the Transjordanian tribes (Num 32:28) and the distribution of the land (Num 34:17; cf. Josh 14:1; 17:4; 19:51; 21:1). Even in Deut, his role is minor; he is mentioned only in the latest parts of the book, anticipating his divine commissioning as Moses' successor (Deut 3:28; 31:14,23), and seems occasionally to have been interpolated into an already existing text after the completion of Dtr in order to harmonize Deut with Josh (Deut 1:38).

In contrast to the names of the other major biblical figures, Joshua's name, formed from the root for "salvation" (which occurs frequently in personal names) was not restricted to the son of Nun, but was also that of two other individuals named in the Bible, viz., the owner of the field in which the ark came to rest after the Philistines had sent it off (1 Sam 6:14), and a governor of Jerusalem during the reign of Josiah (2 Kgs 23:8). This suggests that in Israelite tradition the figure of Joshua was not a major one until developed by Dtr, a conclusion strengthened by the lack of reference to Joshua in the major sermonic and hymnic recitals of Israel's early history: Joshua is not mentioned in 1 Sam 12; Neh 9:6–31; Pss 78; 105; 106; 136. The same is true of many of the events in Josh: the fall of Jericho, the capture of Ai, the division of the land, and the covenant at Shechem are all unmentioned in biblical sources apart from Josh. Even in Dtr Joshua is mentioned only in Judg 1:1; 2:6–9 (see Josh 24:29–31); and 1 Kgs 16:34 (see Josh 6:26). In the postexilic period, Joshua gets scant attention, named without further comment in the genealogy of Ephraim (1 Chr 7:27) and referred to briefly in Neh 8:17. It is only in the late biblical period that Joshua and the events of Josh become frequently mentioned; see 2 Esdr 7:107; 1 Macc 2:55; Sir 46:1–8; Acts 7:45; Heb 4:8. In these passages we see the continuing development of the Joshua tradition: he was a judge (1 Macc 2:55) and a prophet (Sir 46:1).

In later Jewish tradition Joshua is an essential link in the chain of the transmission of the Torah from Moses. In Christian tradition Joshua becomes the prototype of the Christian warrior, and at various periods in history specific allusion is made to Josh as justification for extreme military action, as in the Crusades. In Pilgrim ideology especially Josh served as a model and a divine guarantee: once again a group of God's people escaped from oppression across a body of water to a "providence plantation." This conviction continued to inform American history, including the claim of "manifest destiny," and is evident in the many biblical place-names in New England and throughout the country.

9   (V) Joshua and Archaeological Evidence. The depiction of a total Israelite conquest is a retroversion to the early premonarchic period of a political fact of the monarchy. Inner-biblical evidence frequently contradicts the picture of total annihilation of the inhabitants of the land; see esp. Judg 1–2 as well as various details within Josh itself. Archaeological evidence confirms the literary analysis of the book: few if any of the major episodes in Josh can be shown to be historical. Thus, neither Jericho nor Ai nor Gibeon was occupied in the period in which most scholars would date the emergence of Israel in Canaan (*ca.* 1200). Although some of the cities said to have been destroyed by Joshua show evidence of destruction in this period, the dates vary considerably; Hazor, for example, was destroyed a century before Lachish. For the most part, then, the archaeological record contradicts the narrative. This is also true at the level of small details: there are no specific customs, geopolitical elements, or artifacts mentioned in Josh that can be dated solely to the end of the 2d millennium, and most are more at home in the first. On the other hand, Josh does reflect its time of composition. Thus, the list of levitical cities in chap. 21 cannot have been compiled before the 8th cent., since this is the period when most of them would have been in existence.

10   (VI) Intent. The book is a kind of historical-theological fiction, whose primary source was the preexisting literature of Israel. Other material, esp. the boundary lists of chaps. 13–21, was incorporated into this work in order to present a picture of the ideal Israel under ideal leadership. Various episodes are cautionary tales, depicting the consequences of failure to observe the Mosaic commands and commenting on the circumstances of the authors' own times. Underlying this literary work with its continuing development is a profound conviction: Yahweh had given Israel the land, and in order to maintain possession of it Israel had to obey his law.

11   Outline.

(I) Introduction (1:1–18)
  (A) The Commissioning of Joshua (1:1–9)
  (B) Joshua's Command to the People (1:10–11)
  (C) Instructions to the Transjordanian Tribes (1:12–18)
(II) The Conquest of the Land (2:1–12:24)
  (A) Rahab and the Spies (2:1–24)
  (B) The Crossing of the Jordan (3:1–5:1)
    (a) The Crossing (3:1–17)
    (b) Memorials to the Crossing (4:1–24)
    (c) The Reaction of the Kings (5:1)
  (C) Ceremonies at Gilgal (5:2–12)
    (a) Circumcision (5:2–9)
    (b) Passover (5:10–12)
  (D) The Destruction of Jericho (5:13–6:27)
    (a) Prelude: The Theophany (5:13–15)
    (b) Instructions (6:1–7)
    (c) The Procession and the Fall of the Walls (6:8–21)
    (d) Epilogue (6:22–26)
      (i) Rahab's family (6:22–25)
      (ii) The curse on Jericho (6:26)
    (e) Conclusion (6:27)
  (E) The Destruction of Ai (7:1–8:29)
    (a) Achan's Violation of the Ban (7:1)

    (b) The First Attack: Defeat (7:2–5)
    (c) The Discovery and Punishment of Achan's Sin (7:6–26)
    (d) The Second Attack: Victory (8:1–29)
  (F) Construction of the Altar and Reading of the Teaching on Mt. Ebal (8:30–35)
  (G) The Reaction of the Kings (9:1–2)
  (H) Covenant with Gibeon (9:3–27)
  (I) The Southern Campaign (10:1–43)
    (a) Defeat of the Coalition of Five Kings (10:1–27)
    (b) Defeat of the Major Cities (10:28–39)
    (c) Concluding Summary (10:40–43)
  (J) The Defeat of the Northern Kings (11:1–15)
  (K) Summaries (11:16–12:24)
    (a) Geographical Résumé (11:16–20)
    (b) The Anakim (11:21–22)
    (c) Final Summary (11:23)
    (d) Lists of Defeated Kings (12:1–24)
      (i) East of the Jordan (12:1–6)
      (ii) West of the Jordan (12:7–24)
(III) The Division of the Land (13:1–21:45)
  (A) Introduction (13:1–7)
  (B) East of the Jordan (13:8–33)
    (a) Introduction (13:8–14)
    (b) Reuben (13:15–23)
    (c) Gad (13:24–28)
    (d) Eastern Manasseh (13:29–31)
    (e) Conclusion (13:32–33)
  (C) West of the Jordan (14:1–19:51)
    (a) Introduction (14:1–5)
    (b) Caleb's Inheritance (Hebron) (14:6–15)
    (c) Judah (15:1–63)
      (i) Boundaries (15:1–12)
      (ii) Caleb's share (15:13–19)
      (iii) City lists (15:20–62)
      (iv) Jerusalem (15:63)
    (d) Joseph (16:1–17:18)
      (i) Introduction (16:1–4)
      (ii) Ephraim (16:5–10)
      (iii) Western Manasseh (17:1–13)
      (iv) Conclusion (17:14–18)
    (e) The Other Tribes (18:1–19:51)
      (i) Introduction (18:1–10)
      (ii) Benjamin (18:11–28)
      (iii) Simeon (19:1–9)
      (iv) Zebulun (19:10–16)
      (v) Issachar (19:17–23)
      (vi) Asher (19:24–31)
      (vii) Naphtali (19:32–39)
      (viii) Dan (19:40–48)
  (D) Conclusion (19:49–51)
    (a) Joshua's Personal Allotment (19:49–50)
    (b) Summary (19:51)
  (E) Cities of Asylum (20:1–9)
  (F) Cities of the Levites (21:1–42)
  (G) Summary (21:43–45)
(IV) Appendixes (22:1–24:33)
  (A) The Transjordanian Tribes (22:1–34)
    (a) Joshua's Dismissal (22:1–9)
    (b) The Altar West of the Jordan (22:10–34)
      (i) Construction and controversy (22:10–12)
      (ii) Negotiation (22:13–31)
      (iii) Resolution (22:32–34)
  (B) Joshua's Farewell Speech (23:1–16)
  (C) Covenant at Shechem (24:1–28)
  (D) Final Notes (24:29–33)
    (a) Joshua's Death and Burial (24:29–31)
    (b) Joseph's Reburial (24:32)
    (c) Eleazar's Death and Burial (24:33)

COMMENTARY

12   (I) Introduction (1:1–18). The book opens after the death of Moses, in the plains of Moab (see Deut 34:1), and is a direct continuation of Deut. The language is heavily deuteronomic; compare the following passages:

Josh 1:3–4 and Deut 11:24; Josh 1:5 and Deut 7:24; 31:8; Josh 1:6 and Deut 31:7; Josh 1:7 and Deut 31:23; 5:32; Josh 1:8 and Deut 29:9; Josh 1:9 and Deut 31:6; Josh 1:11 and Deut 11:31; 3:18. This thematic introduction to Josh stresses several key elements. Joshua is Moses' divinely chosen successor, and, although not given the title "Yahweh's servant" until 24:29, he will complete the work of Moses by leading the people into the land. There they are to observe the Mosaic commands, so that the land of the promise may continue to be theirs. Furthermore, as Moses had instructed, the tribes of Reuben, Gad, and Eastern Manasseh shall join their kin in the military conquest of the land. But there is more than retrospective here; Joshua as the ideal ruler of a united Israel anticipates David, who also is called Yahweh's servant (2 Sam 7:5; etc.), and David's two worthy successors, Hezekiah, who kept the commandments of Moses (2 Kgs 18:7), and Josiah, who "did not turn to the right or the left" (2 Kgs 22:2).

13   (A) The Commissioning of Joshua (1:1–9).
1. *Joshua:* Hebr *yĕhôšūaʿ*, probably meaning "Yahweh has saved," as the later variant forms of his name suggest: Hosea (*hôšēaʿ*, Num 13:8,16; Deut 32:44) and Jeshua (*yēšûaʿ*, Neh 8:17). In Greek the name is rendered *iēsous*, i.e., Jesus. *son of Nun:* Hebr *bin-nûn*. The archaic form of the word for son, occurring elsewhere in personal names only in the name Benjamin (*binyāmîn*) suggests the antiquity of the name and thus of Joshua himself. *Nun* means "fish." **2.** *the land which I am about to give to them:* This brief deuteronomic phrase (see, e.g., Deut 5:31; 32:52) summarizes the message of the book: the possession of the land is Yahweh's gift, at his initiative, and it is his activity that gives it to Israel. **4.** The boundaries of the promised land in deuteronomic tradition (see Deut 1:7; 11:24). The land is also delineated in Josh 9:1; 10:40; 11:16; 12:7–8; no two passages are identical. *wilderness:* The semidesert expanse S and E of the settled territory. *the Lebanon:* The double mountain range including its western part (the Lebanon, properly) and its eastern (the Antilebanon). *the great* [MT; LXX: *western*] *sea toward sunset:* I.e., the Mediterranean; → Biblical Geography, 73:32–33. **5.** *I will be with you:* Quoted from Exod 3:12; the promise is repeated in 3:7 and is fulfilled with the fall of Jericho (see 6:27). **6.** *inheritance:* The root *nḥl*, the standard deuteronomic terminology for the possession of the land; see further at 11:23. **8.** See Ps 1:2–3.

14   (B) Joshua's Command to the People (1:10–11). Joshua summarizes the divine promise. **10.** *the officials:* Lit., "scribes," but in various contexts it designates lesser military and civil functionaries; see also 3:2.

15   (C) Instructions to the Transjordanian Tribes (1:12–18). The prominent position of this unit at the beginning of the book indicates that Reuben, Gad, and Eastern Manasseh, the tribes that were settled E of the Jordan, constituted a special problem for the authors. In contrast to such passages as Gen 49:3–4; Judg 5:15–17, Josh presents the ideal picture of an Israel united in warfare and in worship (chap. 22), but underlying this ideal is considerable tension. **13–15.** See Deut 3:12–20, and cf. Num 32:20–27. **14.** *across the Jordan:* I.e, in Transjordan. This is an anachronism, since the Israelites will not cross the Jordan until chap. 4.

16   (II) The Conquest of the Land (2:1–12:24). The first major division of Josh describes in epic style the Israelites' assumption of complete control of the land. The narrative focuses on a few key cities, describing their defeat in a holy war in which the victory and hence the spoils of victory as well were Yahweh's. Again and again we are reminded that it was not numerical or strategic superiority that defeated Israel's enemies.

17   (A) Rahab and the Spies (2:1–24). This chapter, together with its sequel in 6:17,22–25, is a carefully developed literary unit that implies a different version of the capture of Jericho from that found in chap. 6, an interpretation confirmed by 24:11. Combining the details of these three passages we seem to have fragments of an account of a battle for the city that was ultimately won by Rahab's betrayal of her citizens from within the city. In the present form of Josh, however, it is the miraculous version of chap. 6 that dominates. Nevertheless, chap. 2 serves as a prolegomenon to the events that follow. Thus, the sending of the spies by Joshua anticipates his similar action in 7:2; Rahab's confession of faith in Yahweh and her eventual dispensation from the destruction required by the rules of holy war anticipate the similar speech and results of the Gibeonites, another group of non-Canaanites, in chap. 9; and finally, Rahab's speech also foreshadows Joshua's address in chap. 24. This episode is thus central to the overall purpose of Josh.

1. The reintroduction of Joshua by his patronymic indicates that we have an originally independent literary unit. *Shittim:* ca. 8 mi. NE of the junction of the Jordan and the Dead Sea. *Jericho:* → 25 below. *a prostitute:* Later tradition is embarrassed by Rahab's profession, and as the textual traditions developed, glosses were added to make it clear that the spies did not have sexual intercourse with her; Josephus makes her simply an innkeeper (*Ant.* 5.1.2. § 7). *they slept there:* The verb *škb* frequently has a sexual connotation, and there is a delicate double entendre here. **2.** *the Israelites:* They are apparently well known throughout the region even before their entry into the land; see also vv 9–10. **3–4.** The phrase "who came to you/me" is also suggestive; cf. Gen 6:4; 16:2; Deut 22:13; Judg 16:1; etc. Later scribes were not happy with this ambiguity and sought to clarify it with glosses; thus MT "who came to you, who came to your house" and LXX "who came to your house" in contrast to the original "who came to you," preserved in the Syr. These variants attest to the continuing tendency to rehabilitate Rahab. **6.** *flax:* Since it was the harvest season (see 3:15), the flax had been put on the flat roof of Rahab's two-story dwelling to dry. **9.** *I know:* The contrast with vv 4–5 "I do not know" emphasizes Rahab's decision to side with the spies. The profession of faith that follows is deuteronomic in tone (cf. v 9 and Deut 11:25; v 11 and Deut 4:39), as though Rahab were "rather well read in the deuteronomic traditions of the exodus and wilderness" (J. L. McKenzie, *The World of the Judges* [EC, 1966] 48). The words "and that all the inhabitants of the land melt before you" are not in the LXX and are probably an MT addition from v 24; cf. also Exod 15:15–16. **10.** *dried up:* This description of the event at the Reed Sea occurs only here, and is applied to the crossing of the Jordan in 4:23 and 5:1; a derived term, "dry ground," of the beds of the Reed Sea and the Jordan as the Israelites crossed, is used only in late sources, esp. Exod 14:16,22,29; 15:19 (P), anticipated perhaps in the account of creation in Gen 1:9–10 and in Josh 4:22. *Sihon . . . Og:* The traditional adversaries of Israel E of the Jordan; see Num 21:21–35; Josh 9:10. *Amorites:* In the late 3d and early 2d millennia, Amorite (meaning "westerner") was the term used in cuneiform sources to designate the inhabitants of northern Syria who eventually founded the first dynasty of Babylon. In the Bible the term is used loosely for the original inhabitants of the lands E and W of the Jordan, as well as for one specific group among them, in the lists of peoples (see at 3:10). *banned:* See comment on 6:17. **12.** *oath:* Again there are connections with the Gibeonite episode in chap. 9, where another non-Israelite group is exempted from the total destruction required by holy war because of an oath. **15.** There is considerable variation in the textual traditions here; the shortest and probably the best text is that of the LXX: "She let them down through the window." **17–21.** Dramatically the scene is awkward: Are the spies, now at ground level, shouting up to Rahab in the window? **17.** *this scarlet cord:* As in the Passover narrative (Exod 12:7), a red sign at an entry is apotropaic.

(Moran, W. L., "The Repose of Rahab's Israelite Guests," *Studi sull' Oriente e la Bibbia* [Fest G. Rinaldi; Genoa, 1967] 273–84. Tucker, G. M., "The Rahab Saga (Joshua 2): Some Form-Critical and Traditio-Historical Observations," *The Use of the Old Testament in the New* [Fest. W. F. Stinespring; ed. J. M. Efird; Durham, 1972] 66–86.)

18   (B) The Crossing of the Jordan (3:1–5:1). These chapters have a complicated literary history, as the many repetitions and contradictions show. Thus, in chap. 3, both the officers (vv 3–4) and Joshua (vv 5,9–13) give instructions to the people (called both the people [vv 3,5; Hebr *'am*] and the sons of Israel [v 9]), and Joshua commands the priests as well (v 6). In chap. 4 two sets of 12 stones are established as a memorial of the crossing, one on land W of the Jordan (v 8) at Gilgal (v 20), and the other in the bed of the river (v 9). The ark, the visible sign of Yahweh's presence, is called by 10 different terms in the MT, of which the most important are "the ark of the covenant [Hebr *běrît*] (of Yahweh)" (3:3; etc.), "the ark of Yahweh" (3:13), "the ark of the covenant of the lord of all the earth" (see comment on 3:11), and "the ark of the covenant" [Hebr *'ēdût*] (4:16; a Priestly term); the LXX generally differs from the MT. Various attempts have been made to unravel the literary history of the unit, from older analysis into pentateuchal sources to more recent division into various stages of Dtr, but none has won conviction. There is a multi-layered narrative here, which in its final form depicts the crossing as a stately religious ceremony (in contrast to the haste of 4:10).
19   (a) THE CROSSING (3:1–17). The account of the crossing of the Jordan is deliberately patterned after the crossing of the Reed Sea in Exod 14–15. Once again the waters stand in a "heap" (Hebr *nēd;* Exod 15:8; Josh 3:16), and once again the Israelites cross on dry ground (Exod 14:21, etc.; Josh 3:17; 4:18,22). In earlier biblical tradition, these crossings were considered reflexes of the same event; thus, Ps 114 connects sea and Jordan in parallel lines. This parallelism is rooted in Canaanite mythology, where an adversary of the storm-god Baal is called "Prince Sea" and "Judge River"; cf. also Ps 89:26. In the final form of biblical narrative, these two events bracket Israel's formative phase. The significance of the crossing of the body of water is highlighted by the further repetition in reverse order of theophany (Exod 3; Josh 5:13–15) and Passover (Exod 12; Josh 5:10).
2. *at the end of three days:* The chronology of 1:11 is continued, as though the events in chap. 2 had not occurred. **3.** *the ark of the covenant of Yahweh your God:* This precise formulation is found elsewhere only in Deut 31:26, which describes one of the functions of this cult object: it was a container for the text of teaching. *the priests, the Levites:* A characteristic deuteronomic term for the priesthood, which according to Deut 18:1 was coterminous with the tribe of Levi. **4.** Again, the episode of the sending of the spies, who would have known the route, is not alluded to. *two thousand cubits:* Approximately 3,000 ft., a considerable distance! The risks of getting too close to the ark are illustrated by 2 Sam 6:6–7. **5.** *purify yourselves:* In preparation for participation in a liturgical act (see 1 Sam 16:5; 1 Chr 15:12; 2 Chr

29:5; 35:6), or for a divine revelation (Num 11:18; Josh 7:13). **7.** The promise of 1:5 is repeated. **10.** The list of inhabitants of the land occurs some 28 times in the Bible; in Josh it recurs in 9:1; 11:3; 12:8; 24:11. A study of the various textual witnesses suggests that the list was composed of seven groups, named in generally the same order; see K. O'Connell, "The List of Seven Peoples in Canaan," *The Answers Lie Below* (Fest. L. Toombs; ed. H. O. Thompson; Lanham, 1984) 221–41. The list is stereotyped, and it is often impossible to identify the individual groups specifically. *Canaanites:* The land of Canaan in extrabiblical sources generally meant the area W of the Rift Valley from N Lebanon to the Egyptian border, but in the Bible the term Canaanite is variously used to identify all the inhabitants of the land W of the Jordan or as one group within that region, as in these lists. *Hittites:* Originally the terms designated the non-Semitic inhabitants of Anatolia, but in later Mesopotamian sources the toponym Hatti was used for the land S of the Euphrates including Israel and Judah (see *ANET* 280, 291). Numerous individuals in biblical tradition are identified as Hittites, but it is not clear what their precise ethnic origin was. *Hivites:* Often identified with the Hurrians of extrabiblical sources, the Hivites are located at such centers as Shechem (Gen 34:2) and Gibeon (Josh 9:7), as well as in the extreme N of Palestine (Josh 11:3; Judg 3:3). Again, precise ethnic identification is not possible. *Perizzites:* Their name may be derived from the word for unfortified settlement (Hebr **perez*), but little more is known. *Girgashites:* Their origins are obscure. *Amorites:* See comment on 2:10. *Jebusites:* Apart from their consistent association with Jerusalem (occasionally called Jebus; see 15:8,63), little is known of this group. **11.** *the ark of the covenant of the lord of all the earth:* An ungrammatical phrase in Hebrew, but one also found in the LXX. **12.** *twelve:* The fixed number of the tribes of Israel. Although the order and names of the components vary in different sources, probably reflecting the history of the various elements, the number 12 is standard both within and outside Israel. The command to choose 12 tribal representatives anticipates chap. 4. **13.** *the waters of the Jordan will be cut off:* This original has been doubly expanded: both the MT and the LXX add the gloss "the waters coming down from above (and they [MT]) will stand" (see v 16), and the MT continues with a phrase from v 16 (and ultimately from Exod 15:8) "in a single heap." **16.** *very far off, at Adam, the city opposite Zarethan:* Adam, identified with Tell ed-Dāmiyeh, on the E bank of the Jordan *ca.* 16 mi. N of the ford near Jericho, is mentioned in Hos 6:7, and also probably in 1 Kgs 7:46; 2 Chr 4:17; Pss 68:19; 78:60. Zarethan is generally identified with Tell es-Sa'idiyeh, *ca.* 11 mi. N of Adam; see *EAEHL* 1028–32. For this entire phrase LXX[A] reads "to the border of Kiriath-jearim" (see at 9:17), which, if not a mechanical scribal error, is another illustration of the heightening of the miracle as the tradition developed. *the sea of the Arabah, the sea of salt:* The Dead Sea, into which the Jordan flows just S of Jericho. The Arabah is the biblical term for the Rift Valley from the Sea of Galilee (see 11:2) to the Gulf of Aqabah/Eilat; → Biblical Geography, 73:69.
20   (b) MEMORIALS TO THE CROSSING (4:1–24). Again the final form of the narrative is confused, perhaps reflecting in part the vicissitudes of the stones. There appears to be two separate traditions, one of which, presumably earlier, recounts the placement of 12 stones taken from the river bottom of the W bank of the Jordan, where they serve as reminder of the miraculous crossing. The second, interwoven with the first, describes the placement of the stones in the bed of the Jordan; this rendition probably dates from a later time, when the stones

and the sanctuary of which they were a focus had fallen into oblivion.

The location of the sanctuary is given in v 19 as Gilgal. The site, whose precise location is disputed, has a long history in biblical tradition. It figures as a sanctuary in Judg 3:19-26; as the place where Saul was publicly anointed (1 Sam 11:14-15) and in subsequent episodes in the early monarchy (1 Sam 13:7-15; 15:12-33; 2 Sam 19:16,41); and as a pilgrimage shrine (Amos 4:4; 5:5; Hos 4:15; 12:12). In Josh it is the base of operations for the Israelites, and is last referred to as such in 14:6. Nevertheless, it is not always named as a point of departure, and in the present form of Josh it is not possible to outline a consistent itinerary. Thus, in 8:30-35 Israel is without explanation at Mt. Ebal, and in 18:1 (cf. 19:51; 21:2) it is at Shiloh, not Gilgal, where the division of the land takes place.

3. *where the priests' feet stood:* Omitted from the LXX, perhaps in an attempt to harmonize the two traditions (see v 9). For the use of 12 stones as a symbol of Israel, see Exod 24:4; 1 Kgs 18:31. **6.** *a sign:* Interpreted in v 7 as a "reminder." For the rest of the verse, cf. Deut 6:20; Exod 12:26; 13:8,14. **7.** Cf. Exod 12:14. **9.** The LXX clarifies by reading "other stones," a late harmonization. **10.** *quickly:* Another allusion to the exodus tradition (see Exod 12:33). **12.** The fulfillment of 1:14; → 4 above. **13.** *forty thousand:* The MT precedes the number with the word "about," perhaps aware of the different figure given in Num 26. *for battle:* An anticipation of the tradition of a battle for Jericho; → 25 below. **14.** A variation on the theme of 1:5; 3:7; 6:27. **19.** *Gilgal:* The name means "circle" and, despite the popular etymology in 5:9, is derived from the circle of stones at its sanctuary; for a similar toponym, see Gen 31:44-50.

21 (c) THE REACTION OF THE KINGS (5:1). This verse is transitional, providing a conclusion to the narrative of the crossing of the Jordan, and also an anticipatory summary of the events of the conquest which follows. The "hearing" of various groups is one of the editorial linking devices used in chaps. 1-12; cf. 9:1; 10:1; 11:1. The wording echoes 2:10-11. *Amorites:* Here, as the gloss "to the west" in the MT indicates, it is the inhabitants of the hill country who are meant; the phrase "across the Jordan" generally means the region E of the Jordan (see Deut 1:1; Josh 12:1; 13:8; etc.), but here, as in 9:1; 12:7; 22:7, it means the region to the W, hence the gloss.

22 (C) Ceremonies at Gilgal (5:2-12). The order of circumcision, Passover, theophany has been used to support the theory that underlying the present narrative is an ancient, premonarchical ceremony at Gilgal (Soggin; F. M. Cross, *CMHE* 103-5; H.-J. Kraus, *Worship in Israel* [Richmond, 1966] 152-59). To be sure, Exod 12:44-48 requires circumcision for participation in the Passover ritual, but no such connection is made in Josh. Furthermore, the theophany of "the commander of Yahweh's army" is revealed only to Joshua, not to the assembled congregation; is set at Jericho, not at Gilgal; and is closely related to the appearance of God to Moses in the burning bush (Exod 3) (→ 26 below). It seems, then, that we have here three originally independent traditions that are combined only at a late stage and do not reflect earlier cultic practice.

23 (a) CIRCUMCISION (5:2-9). Circumcision was probably originally a rite of passage, performed at the onset of sexual maturity and marking the entrance of the male into the community as an adult as well as one able to marry; see esp. Gen 34:14-24. The practice was widespread (see Jer 9:25-26) and ancient: note the specification of the use of flint knives (Exod 4:25; Josh 5:3). The narrative in its present form is an intricately

layered document, and the MT and the LXX vary considerably. **2.** *sit down and circumcise:* This is the reading of the LXX, and is illustrated by *ANEP* 629; it is original and was subsequently glossed by the phrase "a second time" (MT); after the insertion of this gloss, "sit down" (Hebr *šēb*) was redundantly misinterpreted as "again" (*šûb*, lit., "return"). **3.** *the Hill of Foreskins:* This somewhat grotesque toponym occurs only here. The etiology may mark the end of the original narrative of the circumcision; in its expanded form the etiology of Gilgal (see at v 9) concludes the unit. **4-6.** Here the LXX and the MT differ considerably, representing separate stages in the history of interpretation of the originally brief notice (vv 2-3). The MT is typically expansionistic, with much of its phraseology taken from Deut, and is later than the LXX tradition, which represents an independent expansion of the original short notice. *a land flowing with milk and honey:* This ancient formulaic description occurs only here in Josh. It summarizes the fertility of the land, where both the husbanding of sheep and goats and viticulture were relatively easy; by "milk" is meant sheep's or goat's milk, usually fermented, and "honey" (Hebr *dēbaš*) is grape juice reduced to a thick molasseslike syrup (cf. Arabic *dibs*). **9.** *the reproach of Egypt:* the precise meaning of this phrase remains obscure, but note the association of the word "reproach" with circumcision in Gen 34:14. *rolled away* [Hebr *gallôtî*] . . . *Gilgal:* An impressionistic etymology based on the similarity of the two words. This etiology is later than that implied in v 3.

24 (b) PASSOVER (5:10-12). The details of the Passover observance are not specified, but the mention of unleavened bread and the omission of the lamb suggest that we are dealing here with the older festival of Unleavened Bread (see Exod 23:15; 34:18), which only at a later date was combined with the sacrifice of the lamb. This ritual was celebrated in the evening of the fourteenth day of the first month (see 4:19) and seems to have been a communal celebration (rather than a family one), as in Deut 16:5-8 and esp. 2 Kgs 23:23 (cf. 2 Chr 30; 35:1-19); Joshua is thus a prototype of Josiah.

11. In later traditions, after the two originally separate festivals of Passover and Unleavened Bread had been combined, the former began on the fourteenth and the latter on the fifteenth day of the month. In order to reconcile the date given in v 10, scribes added the words "on the day after the Passover" here and in v 12; this gloss is in the MT but not in the LXX. *roasted grain:* Presumably freshly harvested, as in Lev 2:14; see also Josh 4:15. The narrative does not explain how the Israelites got this produce of the land. This celebration of the Passover, the first since the exodus, along with the crossing of the Jordan, closes the period of Moses and the wandering, which began with the Passover and the crossing of the Reed Sea (Exod 12-15). The conclusion of that epoch is dramatically signaled by the cessation of the miraculous manna (Exod 16; Deut 8:3). **12.** *that year:* I.e., the fortieth since the exodus; see Exod 16:35 for a similar repetition.

25 (D) The Destruction of Jericho (5:13-6:27). The crossing of the Jordan on dry ground closes the preparatory period, and now the main work of Joshua begins. The entire account of Jericho's fall is complex in its latest form in the MT. The LXX is shorter, less elaborate, and less liturgical: in it Joshua is instructed to station the army around Jericho, i.e., to surround it; then, at the sound of the trumpet, the people are to shout; as they shout, the walls will fall down and the people are to rush into the city. So far this is a purely military action, except for the spontaneous collapse of the walls. Then Joshua went to the priests and instructed them to command the people to surround the city, with the armed warriors preceding the Lord. Even though the priests are introduced at this point, there is still no mention of the ark, the seven days, and the other features familiar from the MT account. We seem therefore to have an earlier stage of the elaboration of what was originally a primarily military narrative, much like the account of the capture of Ai in chap. 8; this military action is, as we have seen, implied in the story of Rahab (chap. 2) and also in 4:13 and 24:11. Of course, in biblical tradition, military victory was ultimately Yahweh's doing, and even in our hypothetical early tradition this element would have been present. But the amplification of this earlier narrative has already begun in the LXX *Vorlage*, and the process continued until the stabilization of the MT, so that a straightforward battle narrative has become a highly stylized liturgical event. Now if the liturgical elements (the priests, the ark, the procession, the seven-day scheme) were relatively late additions, then it is misguided to see in the final form of the text a reflex of premonarchic Israelite ritual. Nevertheless, the final form of the tradition as found in the MT is not without interest. For six days the people, led by seven priests carrying seven trumpets, are to march around the city; on the seventh day they are to march around it seven times. (The fact that one of these days, perhaps the last, was the sabbath does not seem to have been a concern; contrast 1 Macc 2:32–38.) The frequency of the number seven in liturgical contexts (see *IDB* 4. 294–95) indicates how ritualized the narrative has become: the primary actors are the cultic personnel and, of course, Yahweh, present in the ark (cf. Num 10:35–36). This, then, is the "holy war" par excellence; in the final stage of the story human efforts have become inconsequential.

This is story, not history, a conclusion reinforced by the results of excavation at Jericho (Tell es-Sulṭān, *ca.* 10 mi. NW of the confluence of the Jordan and the Dead Sea); see *EAEHL* 550–64. The latest Late Bronze occupation at the site is 14th cent., and there was no subsequent settlement there until the 9th cent. In the time of Joshua, then, no one lived at Jericho. Why does the city figure so prominently? Two reasons may be given. As far back as the Neolithic period, Jericho was well fortified, and in that period especially its defenses were anomalous. There may thus have been an ancient folk tradition about Jericho's walls which underlies the present narrative. Furthermore, 1 Kgs 16:34 describes the reconstruction of the city under Ahiel (Hiel) of Bethel. This brief notice contains an ancient poetic fragment, paraphrased in Josh 6:26. The attribution of the (re)construction of a city to someone other than the reigning king is highly unusual, and it may be that Ahiel's activity was a kind of rebellious succession, disapproved of by the deuteronomistic historians, and that this event was the motivation both for the inclusion of the curse pronounced by Joshua in 1 Kgs and for the central position of Jericho in Josh. In other words, what the authors of Josh are saying is that Jericho is doomed unless it is Israelite; only if the city, like Rahab, acknowledges Yahweh (and his designated king) can it be saved.

26 (a) PRELUDE: THE THEOPHANY (5:13–15). Just as Moses' career as leader began with the theophany in the burning bush (Exod 3:1–4:17), so too Joshua as the new Moses experiences a revelation presented as a repetition of the earlier event. **13.** The specification of Jericho rather than Gilgal indicates that this passage belongs with the following account of Jericho's destruction. *a man:* As in Gen 18:2 and 32:24, the identity of the person appearing is not immediately given. *with his drawn sword in his hand:* The same phrase occurs in Num 22:23,31;

1 Chr 21:16; but here the envoy is a threat not to the recipient of the vision but to his adversaries, the inhabitants of the land. **14.** *No:* The enigmatic response, although textually suspect (LXX reads "to him [Hebr *lô*] for MT's *lō*'), is to be preferred. *I am the commander of Yahweh's army:* Elsewhere apparitions are identified either as a messenger (Hebr *mal'āk,* later translated as "angel") of God or as God himself. Deut never uses the term *mal'āk,* but in keeping with the essential superiority of Moses, to whom God appeared personally (see Exod 3:4), it is only a divine representative who appears to Joshua. *now I have come:* Perhaps intended as a fulfillment of Exod 23:23. The commander of the heavenly armies, however, is not mentioned again in Josh. **15.** The command to Joshua is an almost verbatim quotation of Exod 3:5.

27 (b) INSTRUCTIONS (6:1–7). **1.** The section opens with a parenthetical description of Jericho, apparently under siege. After v 2, the name of the city is not mentioned again until v 25, an indication of a separate tradition, perhaps even originally independent of Jericho. **3.** *surround . . . go around:* These words are used in the description of the liturgical procession in Ps 48:13. The two verbs are ambiguous and can mean both "to go around" and "to besiege." The LXX has only the first, with a clearly military connotation. **3b–4.** Missing from the LXX. **4.** *horns:* Three words (Hebr *šôpār; yôbēl; qeren*) are used here and in v 5, all of which seem to represent a musical instrument fashioned from the horn of an animal, often a ram. **5.** *at the blast of the ram's horn:* This seems to belong to an earlier stage of the tradition, for if the seven priests of v 4 (MT) were blowing on their seven horns, the signal for the people's shout could scarcely have been heard. For the use of a horn blast and shout in warfare, see Num 10:9; Judg 7:18; 2 Chr 13:14–15; for their use in liturgical contexts, see Num 10:10; 2 Sam 6:15; Ps 47:6. *shout with a great shout:* The same phrase is used in both military (1 Sam 4:5; but note the presence of the ark) and liturgical (Ezra 3:11) contexts.

28 (c) THE PROCESSION AND THE FALL OF THE WALLS (6:8–21). **17.** *ban for Yahweh:* The ban (Hebr *ḥērem;* the root means "to set apart," esp. as sacred [cf. Arabic *ḥaram,* English "harem"]) was a theoretical component of the practice of holy war according to which all spoils, inanimate and animate, animal and human, were the effective property of the deity who had won the victory. Material property was turned over to the Temple (see v 24) and the living were killed. In the legislation concerning holy war in Deut 20, the ban is to be applied only to the cities of the land of Canaan (vv 16–18); more remote cities are not subject to the ban (see Josh 9:9). In biblical narrative apart from Josh the ban is never fully practiced. It was commanded but not carried out in 1 Sam 15. In legislation it is to be applied to an idolatrous Israelite city (Deut 13:12–18). In other passages where the term (or its derived verb) is used it is applied only to the population of defeated cities (e.g., Deut 2:34–35; 3:6–7; Josh 10:28–42; 11:11–14). The practice is also attested in Moab, whose king, Mesha, claims to have banned the entire population of Israelite Nebo to the deity Chemosh (see *ANET* 320). In the present context the family of Rahab is exempt from the ban by special dispensation. The institution of the ban, like the jubilee year, seems to have been an ideal rarely if ever actually practiced. Its occurrence in Josh is another indication of the book's purpose, to present a picture of the ideal Israel living in its earliest days according to the deuteronomic law. **18.** *but as for you, keep yourselves from the ban(ned spoil), lest you desire and take:* Following the LXX. *trouble:* Hebr *'ākar.* The use of this

root anticipates and forms a link with the story of
Achan, which follows in chap. 7, and esp. with the etiology of the Valley of Achor in 7:25–26. **19.** *Yahweh's
treasury:* Some mss. and versions read "the treasury of
Yahweh's house," like the MT of v 24. In either reading,
a building of some kind is probably implied, and as the
term "house" (Hebr *bêt* in the sense of "temple") suggests,
Jerusalem is anachronistically intended (cf. 9:23). Some
have suggested rather that the sanctuary at Gilgal is
being referred to, but there is no literary evidence of
architecture there, nor is the term "treasury" used elsewhere in any narratives that describe the pre-Solomonic
period. Again, the purpose of the narrative is to describe
for its Israelite audience the ideal conduct of war, and it
is not surprising that such an anachronism is employed.
For a similar anticipation of later reality in an analogous
context, see 1 Sam 17:54.
29   (d) EPILOGUE (6:22–26).
     (i) *Rahab's family* (6:22–25). The episode in
chap. 2 concludes with another etiology. Rahab and her
extended family become part of Israel, the first example
of what seems to have been a not infrequent practice.
Thus, the Gibeonites (chap. 9; cf. Neh 7:25), Hepher (cf.
12:17; 17:2), and Ruth are illustrations of the inclusion
within the Israelite confederation of individuals and
groups who had not been part of the original nucleus,
whether that was defined by kinship or shared experience or both. That this fact was not entirely in accordance with the idealized account of origins is suggested
by the phrase "outside the camp" (v 23) and also perhaps
by the phrase "in the midst of Israel" (v 25), which, while
its plain sense suggests full incorporation, is used elsewhere of Canaanite groups whom the Israelites failed to
conquer (see 13:13; 16:10).
30   (ii) *The curse on Jericho (6:26).* The words of
the curse are adapted from 1 Kgs 16:34, which is closer
to the original poetic form: "(A)hiel the Bethelite built
Jericho; at the cost of Abiram his firstborn he founded
it, and at the cost of Segub his youngest he established
its gates." This poetic fragment does not give details
about the deaths of the sons; there is no justification for
presuming that some form of child sacrifice was involved. The 1 Kgs verse is prior: it is more complete,
preserving the name of Hiel (or Ahiel [LXX]) and his
sons, and its spelling of Jericho in Hebrew is archaic.
The mention of Jericho was introduced into the MT of
Josh 6:26 from 1 Kgs; it is missing from both the LXX
and from 4QTestim 22.
31   (e) CONCLUSION (6:27). *Yahweh was with
Joshua:* The fulfillment of 1:5. *his reputation spread throughout the land:* Anticipates 9:1.
32   **(E) The Destruction of Ai (7:1–8:29).** The
theme of this unit is not just the narrow question of
violation of the rules of holy war, but total obedience to
the teaching of Moses. As the phrase "Yahweh was
angry with the Israelites" (7:1) indicates, disobedience
led to divine punishment. This single episode in Josh of
Israelite infidelity thus anticipates one of the major
themes of Dtr, esp. in Judg.
     As R. de Vaux (*EHI* 618–19) has shown, the account
of the ultimate victory over Ai is modeled on the story
of the attack on Gibeah in Judg 20. In both narratives
there is initial defeat, followed by communal mourning
until evening; after a promise of divine help, a contingent of Israelites is sent to lie in ambush, while a
second lures the army of the city under attack out into
the open; then the ambush attacks and burns the city,
and when its defenders see it burning and turn back they
are set upon by the formerly retreating Israelites and
massacred. In these two accounts similar and even identical vocabulary is used, and examples will be pointed

out in the commentary. The major difference between
the two stories is the identity of the guilty parties: in
Josh 7–8 it is a Judahite who has committed "folly in
Israel"; in Judg 19–20 it is the Benjaminite town of
Gibeah. Ai was in Benjaminite territory, and the later
narrative in Josh may be a chauvinistic Benjaminite
account of victory, a victory won despite a Judahite's
sin, composed to counter the defeat of a Benjaminite
town at the hands of Judah (see Judg 20:18).
     There is another anticipation here as well: Achan's
violation of the ban parallels Saul's similar disobedience
in 1 Sam 13–15. Both episodes take place in Benjaminite
territory: in 1 Sam 13:4; 15:12 the Israelite camp is at
Gilgal; in Josh 7:2 the location of the camp is not given
(in the LXX; MT has the gloss "from Jericho"), and since
no move has been specified, it was presumably still at
Gilgal. The site of the battle with the Philistines ("east of
Beth-aven" [1 Sam 13:5]) parallels the location of the
ambush in Josh 8:9. Because of the violation of an oath,
lots must be taken (1 Sam 14:40–42); and in the defeat
of the Amalekites the entire population is killed except
for the king, Agag (1 Sam 15:9), just as all the inhabitants
of Ai were killed in the battle except for its king (Josh
9:23). The entire story of the defeat of Ai, therefore,
coming as it does immediately after the exceptional dispensation from the ban for Rahab and her family, is an
object lesson, perhaps inspired by the narrative of Saul's
violation of the ban, of the importance of total fidelity
to the Mosaic teaching.
     As is the case with Jericho, the archaeological history
of Ai (modern et-Tell, *ca.* 12 mi. N of Jerusalem; see
EAEHL 36–52) contradicts the biblical narrative; there
is no evidence of occupation at Ai from the late 3d millennium to the early Iron Age. The narrative itself gives
two etiologies which explain its association with the
impressive mound: the heap of stones in 8:29, and the
mound itself— "an eternal tell" (8:28). The name of the
city itself may have served as a stimulus for this connection, since according to most scholars Ai (Hebr *hā'ay*)
means "the ruin," and at the time of the composition of
Josh it was again uninhabited.
33   (a) ACHAN'S VIOLATION OF THE BAN (7:1).
the Israelites acted unfaithfully with regard to the ban: The
guilt for one individual's sin is shared by the entire community; see 7:11. The word translated "acted unfaithfully" recurs in 22:16,20,31, and is used elsewhere
only in the latest biblical traditions, esp. P, Chr, and
Ezek. *Achan:* The meaning is unknown; in some traditions (LXX; 1 Chr 2:7; Josephus) it is spelled Achar, an
alteration derived from the folk etymology in 7:26. The
complete genealogy anticipates the discovery of the
guilty party in 7:16–18: the audience already knows
precisely who it is. *Yahweh became angry with the Israelites:*
A standard deuteronomistic phrase; see Judg 2:14,20;
3:8; 10:7; 2 Kgs 13:3.
34   (b) THE FIRST ATTACK: DEFEAT (7:2–5). **2–3.**
The sending of spies a second time parallels Moses'
action in Num 21:32 as well as Moses' first spying mission in Num 13. As in the earlier case, the return of the
spies here is followed by defeat. The order of events in
Num is thus spying mission–defeat (A) followed by spying mission–victory (B), an order reversed in Joshua. **2.**
Ai: Apart from Josh, Ai is mentioned only in Gen 12:8;
13:3 to locate Abraham's camp, and in the lists of returnees in Ezra 2:28; Neh 7:32; in both cases it is associated with Bethel. *near Bethel:* The MT and some
versions read "near Beth-aven, east of Bethel," either a
gloss based on the derogatory name Beth-aven ("house
of wickedness") given to Bethel by the prophets (Amos
5:5; Hos 4:15; etc.), or an alternate reading (Bethel was
apparently sometimes called Beth-aven [see 1 Sam 13:5;

14:23; perhaps this alternate name was originally Beth-on ("house of wealth")]). Bethel is identified with modern Beitīn, *ca.* 11 mi. N of Jerusalem; see *EAEHL* 190–93. It was one of the major religious centers in Israelite tradition. Curiously, it is not named among the cities said to have been destroyed by Joshua. **5.** Because the ban has been violated, Israel has in effect become Yahweh's enemy and experiences what its enemies had previously experienced (cf. 2:11; 5:1) and also what it had itself experienced when Moses sent spies the first time (see Deut 1:28).

35   (c) THE DISCOVERY AND PUNISHMENT OF ACHAN'S SIN (7:6–26). **6.** Joshua carries out the typical ritual of mourning; see, e.g., 2 Sam 1:11; 2 Kgs 23:11; Job 1:20; 2:12; and de Vaux, *AI* 59. *the elders:* In legislation and in narrative, the heads of families who comprise the administrative and judicial authority of the town; see Josh 9:11; 20:4; 1 Kgs 21:8; Ruth 4:2; etc. The elders of Israel are mentioned in Josh 23:2; 24:1,31; and in 7:23 (LXX) and 8:10 in the continuation of the Ai narrative. **7–9.** Joshua's prayer on the occasion of Israel's distress is deliberately reminiscent of words of Moses in similar situations; see Exod 5:22–23; 32:11–13; Num 11:11–15; 14:13–19; Deut 9:26–29. As in Num 14:16 and Deut 9:28, Yahweh's concern for his own reputation is appealed to. **11.** *my covenant which I commanded them:* The first occurrence of the important biblical term "covenant" (*běrît*) apart from the phrase "the ark of the covenant"; it recurs in the Gibeonite episode (chap. 9) and in 23:16 (where a similar, and elsewhere unattested, phraseology is used), and 24:25. The more frequent term in Josh for the obligations imposed on Israel by Yahweh is *tôrâ*. **12.** *they have become a ban:* The result of Achan's violation of the ban is that all Israel is subject to destruction, a foretaste of which was given in their defeat (v 5). *I will no longer be with you:* The essence of Yahweh's relationship with Israel (see Deut 2:7; 20:1) will be disrupted (as in Num 14:43). **13.** *purify:* See comment on 3:5. **14.** The procedure for identifying the guilty party is apparently the casting of lots; in the analogous case in 1 Sam 14:40–42 the lots are identified as the cult objects Urim and Thummim, but there the choice is between two parties. As in the case of Saul's election as king (1 Sam 10:20–21), the movement is from the largest social unit, the "tribe" (*šēbeṭ*), to the individual. Here the component elements of the tribe are specified: the "clan" (*mišpāḥâ*) and the "house(hold)" (*bayit,* meaning "extended family"); for discussion, see N. K. Gottwald, *The Tribes of Yahweh* (Maryknoll, 1979) 257–59; L. E. Stager, *BASOR* 260 (Fall/Nov. 1985) 20–22. In every case the decision is explicitly Yahweh's. **15.** The penalty, capital punishment by burning, is attested elsewhere only in Gen 38:24; Lev 20:14; 21:9, always for sexual offenses. But according to Deut 13:17 all the spoil from a city that has practiced apostasy and hence is under the ban is to be burned, and so the punishment specified here is appropriate. In v 25 the actual execution is by stoning. *folly in Israel:* A technical legal term, elsewhere used only for sexual offenses (Gen 34:7; Deut 22:21; Judg 20:6,10; Jer 29:23; see also 2 Sam 13:12). Its use here is probably due to the dependence of the whole Ai episode on the account of the Benjaminite war in Judg 10–20. **19.** *give glory . . . offer praise:* That is, acknowledge the truth of Yahweh's identification of the guilty party. **20.** *a cloak of Shinar:* Apparently an import of considerable value. Shinar is a biblical term for Babylonia (see Gen 10:10; 11:2; Isa 11:11; Dan 1:2; → Biblical Geography, 73:16). *shekel:* Approximately 0.4 oz. **24.** The textual witnesses all show considerable secondary expansion here and in v 25. The addition of Achan's family and property to the execution may be based on traditions such as that found

in Num 16:32. *trouble:* The two verbs (from the Hebr root *'ākar*) play on the name of the valley, Achor (see v 26). *all Israel stoned him:* LXX; the MT adds "they burned them with fire and they stoned them with stones," an addition intended to eliminate the inconsistency with v 15, where execution by fire is decreed, and to include the elements added in v 24. Stoning was the ordinary mode of execution; on the basis of the surviving textual witnesses the inconsistency cannot be eliminated. **26.** *the Valley of Achor:* I.e., the Valley of Trouble, probably the Buqei'ah, *ca.* 3 mi. W of the Dead Sea (see *IDBSup* 5). It belonged to Judah (as did Achan); see 15:7. In prophetic visions of restoration this desolate area is to become fertile; see Hos 2:17; Isa 65:10.

36   (d) THE SECOND ATTACK: VICTORY (8:1–29). In notable contrast to the story of Jericho's defeat, the second and successful attack on Ai is not a holy war. There is no mention of the ark; the victory is the result of military tactics rather than a miraculous event in a liturgical setting; most significant, the spoil of the city is not subject to the ban, but may be distributed among the Israelites (vv 2,27). Nevertheless, it is clear that Yahweh is the ultimate agent of the victory. The successful tactic of ambush is his command (v 2), and it is he who gives the city into the hands of the Israelites (vv 1,7 [MT],18). The narrative itself is often repetitious, esp. in the MT, and it is likely that even in the shorter, earlier textual tradition represented by the LXX (with which a fragment of 4QJosª agrees), there has been reworking of an original account.

3. *thirty thousand:* The figure is at odds with v 12 (MT), an indication of how in the secondary reworking of the narrative the numbers were magnified. **9.** *between Bethel and Ai:* The location of the ambush is the same as that where Abram had pitched his tent (Gen 13:3). **10.** *the elders of Israel:* Their presence at the head of the army is another indication of the secular aspect of the narrative; in Josh 6 it was the priests who were the primary human actors. **11b–13.** The MT and the LXX diverge widely. The differences in directions (and, in the MT, in the size of the ambush [cf. v 3]) are irreconcilable and reflect variant traditions. **14.** *when the king of Ai saw it, early in the morning he quickly set out to meet Israel in battle, he and all his army:* Following the LXX. After these words MT adds "at the appointed place before the Arabah," a geographic specification that is unclear. **15b–16a.** Again the MT expands, adding "and they fled in the direction of the wilderness; and all the people who were in the city were summoned to pursue them." **17.** *in Ai:* MT adds "and Bethel," an addition that makes no sense in context, since Bethel was E of Ai, presumably not far from the ambush. **18.** *sicklesword:* A rare word (also used in 1 Sam 17:6,45), usually erroneously translated "javelin." The LXX misunderstands the stretching out of the hand-held sicklesword as a signal to the ambush, an interpretation that is improbable given the distance between the two Israelite contingents and the absence of a reference to a signal in v 7. Rather, as v 26 indicates, the outstretched hand guaranteed total defeat, as was the case with Moses' victory over the Amalekites (Exod 17:9–12); the parallel between Moses and Joshua is deliberate (→ 4 above). **20.** Cf. Judg 20:38,40. **26.** Missing from the LXX; perhaps a MT expansion. **28.** *an eternal tell, a ruin:* A tell is a mound composed of the accumulated occupational debris of a city; the term in this sense is an ancient as well as a modern archaeological designation (→ Biblical Archaeology, 74:25–27). It occurs in Deut 13:17, of an apostate city destroyed under the ban, and in Josh 11:13; Jer 30:18; 49:2. It is at least an interesting coincidence that Ai's name in Arabic is et-Tell ("the tell"); in any case it was, and remains, a large and imposing ruin, and it is this fact that underlies the narrative of its destruction in Josh 7–8, although the probable etymology of its name ("the ruin"), if known to the ancient authors, is not used explicitly. **29.** *he hanged on a tree until evening:* The same punishment, i.e., exposure of the corpse, is meted out to the five kings in 10:26 and to the sons of Rimmon in 2 Sam 4:12; legislative prescription of exposure is found in Deut 21:22–23. Although execution of the king of Ai prior to the exposure of his body is not explicitly stated, the other passages specify it and so it must be presumed here. This is not, therefore, an example of crucifixion in the proper sense, although in the case of Jesus' death the law concerning removal of the body the same day is also applied. The rest of the verse is almost identical to 10:27. *they threw it into a pit:* LXX; the MT reads "at the entrance of the gate of the city, a scribal error (reading *pth,* "entrance," for *pht,* "pit") which is then glossed. *they raised over him a large mound of stones to this day:* See 7:26. The repetition of the mound of stones served to unite the two parts of the narrative.

37   (F) Construction of the Altar and Reading of the Teaching on Mt. Ebal (8:30–35). This brief episode has no apparent connection with the preceding or following narratives; 9:1 logically follows 8:29. The original placement of the unit is not clear; the LXX places it after 9:2, and some modern scholars join it with chap. 24. Certainly it makes little sense geographically: after the successful campaign against Ai, presumably launched from their base at Gilgal, the Israelites would have had to travel N *ca.* 30 mi. to the Shechem area for the ceremony, and then immediately return to Gilgal (see 9:6) for the events described in 9:3–10:15; no such journeys are mentioned. Furthermore, in its present form this ceremony at Shechem (although the city is not mentioned by name) is clearly derived from Deut 11; 27; and 31. Finally, much of the vocabulary and phraseology is characteristically late. All evidence suggests, therefore, that this is a late addition to Josh. The ceremony itself has often been called a covenant renewal, and although there are elements of such rituals present here, the term covenant is not used; in Josh there is only one covenant ceremony between Yahweh and Israel, in chap. 24.

30. *Mt. Ebal:* Together with Mt. Gerizim on the S, it controlled the E–W pass at Shechem. In 1980 A. Zertal discovered the remains of an early Iron Age installation on Mt. Ebal (see M. D. Coogan, *PEQ* 119 [1987] 1–8). **31.** *as Moses the servant of Yahweh had commanded:* In Deut 11:29; 27:2–8, the altar was to be erected as soon as the Israelites had crossed the Jordan. This is the first point in the narrative where the fulfillment of this command is possible, since the defeat of Jericho and Ai are linked by the Achan episode, and thus to show Joshua's total fidelity to the Mosaic commands the episode is introduced here. *an altar of whole stones on which no iron had been used:* An almost verbatim quotation of Deut 27:5–6. Whole, i.e., unhewn, stones, as Exod 20:25 indicates, had not been profaned by human activity. Most altars recovered in the excavation of Israelite sites were constructed of hewn stones, as was that in the Solomonic Temple, despite the legal tradition. *they offered . . . peace offerings:* Based directly on Deut 27:6–7 (which itself is perhaps dependent on Exod 24:5). "Peace offerings" (*šĕlāmîm*) were divided among Yahweh, the priest, and the offerer (see Lev 3; 7:11–36), and hence it is implicitly a meal here. Neither here nor in Deut 27, however, is the meal specified, and thus the ceremony is not explicitly a covenant ritual. **32.** *on the stones:* Not the stones of the altar, but those which Moses had prescribed in Deut 27:2–3. The practice of writing on stones, esp.

legal material, is well attested in the ancient Near East, as the stele containing the Code of Hammurabi illustrates (*ANEP* 246). *a copy of the teaching:* This phrase occurs elsewhere only in the "law of the king" in Deut 17:18. Joshua is thus presented as the ideal ruler, the model for royal behavior. He writes a copy presumably because the original text was to be kept in the ark. The LXX interprets this copy as *deuteronomion,* perhaps meaning Deut itself. **33.** *its elders, officers, and judges:* The same parties are also present in 23:2 and 24:1. These were the administrative officials of Israel, and their mention here is anachronistic; all are found in Deut, however. *on either side of the ark:* The only passage in which the ark is explicitly located in the Shechem vicinity, but see on 24:1. *both resident alien and native-born:* The resident alien (*gēr*) had many rights in Israel (see 20:9; Lev 24:22; etc.), although rarely owned land. Nevertheless, they were apparently frequently taken advantage of, for in prophetic literature they are grouped with widows and orphans as those in special need of protection. The term "native-born" (*'ezrāh*) occurs only here in Josh, not at all in Deut, and elsewhere only in typically P material; it is generally opposed to "resident alien," and designates an Israelite with full rights. *to bless the people first:* In accordance with the order implied in Deut 11:29; 27:12–13, the blessing precedes the curse. The reason for the specification is the order found in Deut 27:15–28:68 (curses, then blessings and curses); the 12 curses in Deut 27:15–26 were apparently added at a later stage in the formation of Deut; our passage postdates that redactional addition. **34.** *the blessing and the curse:* There is no doubt that the elements of blessing and curse, found in ancient Near Eastern treaties, formed part of covenant ritual in Israel, and they are especially prominent in Lev 26 and Deut 27–28. But the authors of this passage are apparently not presenting a covenant ritual; rather they are concerned with showing Joshua's fulfillment of the instructions of Moses as found in Deut. This then is not the description of an ancient ceremony, but yet another construction based on already existing literary traditions. **35.** Resumes the themes of 1:7–8. *all the assembly of Israel:* The word "assembly" (*qāhāl*) is used only here in Josh; elsewhere it occurs in generally late sources. The precise phraseology here is found in Lev 16:17; Deut 31:30; 1 Chr 13:2; and notably in 1 Kgs 8:14,22 (= 2 Chr 6:3, 12); 8:55; 2 Chr 6:13, in the account of Solomon's dedication of the Temple, during which he blesses (cf. v 33 above) all the assembly of Israel. This may be another example of the presentation of Joshua as the prototype of the ideal king.

38   (G) The Reaction of the Kings (9:1–2). This brief passage provides a transition between the preceding and following narratives, much as 5:1 did. In contrast, however, to 5:1, here the reaction of the inhabitants of the land is to resist. This resistance will have two geographic foci, S and N, treated in chaps. 9–10 and 11 respectively. **1.** *When all the kings heard:* This picks up 6:27, and in turn anticipates 10:1 and 11:1. There follows another geographic description of the land (see at 1:4); since the next units concern campaigns N of the Negeb, the extreme S regions are not listed. *the hill country:* The central ridge of mountains extending N from the Negeb to Mt. Hermon, often subdivided (e.g., the hill country of Judah [11:21], the hill country of Ephraim [17:15], etc.). *the foothills:* Hebr *šĕpēlâ,* the area between the hill country of Judah and the coastal plain, corresponding in North America to the Appalachian piedmont. On the list of the inhabitants of the land, see comment on 3:10.

39   (H) Covenant with Gibeon (9:3–27). The literary background of this intriguing unit is complex.

Certainly in part it is derived from Deut 20:10–18, which prescribes application of the ban to cities in the land but not to those which are distant; the Gibeonites implicitly appeal to this law by claiming to be from a distant land (vv 6–9). The problem is the same as that raised by the Rahab episode: Why were there Canaanites in Israel who had not been killed as Yahweh had commanded through Moses? Rahab and her family were exempted from the ban on Jericho by special dispensation because of her protection of the spies, who had sworn to her that she and her family would live (2:19–20; 6:17, 22–25). Similarly, the Gibeonites are exempted from the ban because of the oath (9:20); like Rahab, they too had recognized the power of Yahweh (cf. 2:9–11 with 9:9–10,24). The oath is supreme and must be carried out, even if it was obtained under false pretenses. Thus, this episode continues one of the major themes of the first half of Josh, the application of the ban, a theme that unites the apparently disparate materials in chaps. 2 and 6–11.

This episode is clearly related to 2 Sam 21:1–14. There a famine is attributed to Saul's having killed the Gibeonites, identified as a subdivision of the Amorites, in violation of the oath. In response to the Gibeonites' request, seven of Saul's surviving sons are delivered to them for execution. No account of a massacre of Gibeonites by Saul has survived. The two narratives are connected; compare 2 Sam 21:2 ("the Israelites had sworn to them, but Saul sought to kill them") with Josh 9:18 ("The Israelites did not kill them because they had sworn to them"). The repeated references to Gibeon in 2 Sam and 1 Kgs make it clear that the city was a major center during the united monarchy, a conclusion confirmed by excavation (see *EAEHL* 446–50). There is, however, no evidence for major occupation in the Late Bronze Age, a fact that suggests the secondary nature of Josh 9. If this conclusion is valid, then the chapter can be interpreted as yet another example of the presentation of Joshua as prototype for the kings of Israel and Judah. Unlike Saul, whom Dtr judged negatively, but like David, the standard against which subsequent kings were compared, Joshua kept the oath made to the Gibeonites. One problem with this analysis is that it does not account for the pre-Saulide tradition of the oath. That an agreement between the Israelites and the Gibeonites existed there can be little doubt, but given the artificial character of Josh 9 it seems unlikely that it is directly based on older traditions about it.

Another element of the narrative that should be mentioned is the confusing number of participants on the Israelite side. In addition to Joshua, there are the "men of Israel" (v 6; cf. v 14) and the "leaders of the congregation" (*něśî'ê hā'ēdâ*, vv 15,18–21). The term "leaders" is a characteristically Priestly one and occurs elsewhere in Josh in 17:4; 22:14,30,32; its use here (esp. in association with the word *'ēdâ* for "congregation," another Priestly usage) is an indication of later reworking, influenced by the Priestly understanding of early Israel as a theocracy.

40   **3.** *Gibeon:* Modern el-Jib, *ca.* 6 mi. NNW of Jerusalem. According to 10:2 it was "a great city, like one of the royal cities"; it functions here as the head of a tetrapolis (see v 17). *heard:* This vb. is one of the unifying elements in the chapter and recurs in vv 9 and 16; cf. also v 1. *what Yahweh had done:* LXX; MT: "what Joshua had done." The LXX is more consistent with vv 9–10, 24; the reading of the MT is surprising and may be due to miscopying from the preceding line. **5.** The description of the condition of the Gibeonites and their provisions is reminiscent of Deut 8:4; 29:4. **6.** *make a covenant with us:* This is standard biblical terminology (lit., "cut a covenant [*běrît*]"), derived from the ancient ceremony

which involved cutting animals in two as a symbol of what would befall violators of the covenant (see Gen 15:9–21; Jer 34:18–20; *ANET* 660). The covenant here is a pact or treaty between two human parties and thus differs from the covenant between Yahweh and Israel (see 24:25), which was, however, modeled on such pacts. Of course, the pact involved an oath (see vv 18–19), and so the deity was its ultimate guarantor. Comparable pacts between superior and inferior parties, often called "suzerainty treaties," are found in 1 Sam 11:1; *ANET* 201–6, 529–41, 659–61. **7.** *Hivites:* See comment on 3:10. Shechem was another city identified with the Hivites in biblical tradition (Gen 34:2); like Gibeon, it is a major city in Josh (see chap. 24) for which no destruction at the hand of Joshua is claimed. **9–10.** Like Rahab (2:10–11), the Gibeonites are well versed in deuteronomic tradition; see Deut 1:30; 2:25; 31:4; etc. **10.** *Heshbon:* Tell Ḥesbān, *ca.* 13 mi. SW of Amman; see *EAEHL* 510–14. On the problem of lack of occupation prior to the Iron Age, see L. T. Geraty, "Heshbon: The First Casualty in the Israelite Quest for the Kingdom of God," *The Quest for the Kingdom of God* (Fest. G. E. Mendenhall; ed. H. B. Huffmon, *et al.;* Winona Lake, 1983) 239–48. *Og, king of Bashan, who lived in Ashtaroth and in Edrei:* So LXX; cf. Deut 1:4; Josh 12:4. Bashan in the N plateau of Transjordan, famous for its fertile volcanic soil and pasturage. Ashtaroth is usually identified with Tell 'Ashtarah, *ca.* 50 mi. SSW of Damascus, and Edrei with Tell Der'a, *ca.* 60 mi. S of Damascus, both of which preserve the ancient toponyms. **11.** *our elders:* Unlike other cities in Josh, no king is attributed to Gibeon. *we are your servants:* The technical language of suzerainty treaties. **14.** *the men took of their provisions:* Possibly a reference to a ceremonial meal forming part of the covenant ritual. **17.** *Chephirah:* Lit., "lioness," probably Khirbet el-Kefîreh, *ca.* 5 mi. SW of Gibeon. *Beeroth:* Means "wells" (cf. modern Beirut), perhaps Khirbet el-Burj, *ca.* 2 mi. S of Gibeon, or el-Bireh, *ca.* 4 mi. to the NE. *Kiriath-jearim:* Lit., "town of forests," also known as Baalah (15:9) and Kiriath-baal (15:60; 18:14); probably Deir el-'Azhar, on the border between Judah and Benjamin *ca.* 8 mi. WNW of Jerusalem. **18.** *murmured:* This word is used elsewhere only of the complaints of the Israelites in the wilderness, in Exod 15; 17; Num 14; 16; 17. **21.** *woodcutters and water carriers:* A specification of the legislation in Deut 20:11. In Deut 29:10 the phrase describes the resident aliens who apparently performed these functions for the Israelites. In this chapter it is not clear whom the Gibeonites served: here it is the congregation, but in v 23 it is "the house of my God," and in v 27 it is the congregation and Yahweh's altar. It is possible to reconcile these discrepancies by recalling that the term "congregation" (*'ēdâ*) properly means the cultic assembly, and hence the Gibeonites could have been special, although lowly, ritual personnel. In an impressionistic way this suits the traditions about a sanctuary of Yahweh at Gibeon (see 1 Kgs 3:4–15; 1 Chr 16:39–40; 21:29; 2 Chr 1:3–13). **23.** *the house of my God:* MT; an anachronistic reference to the Jerusalem Temple (see at 6:19). The LXX reads "for me and my God." **27.** After the words "for Yahweh's altar," the LXX has a resumptive addition. *for the place which he should choose:* The standard deuteronomic formula for the central sanctuary (Deut 12:5; etc.). On the Gibeonite episode, see J. Blenkinsopp, *Gibeon and Israel* (Cambridge, 1972).

41   **(I) The Southern Campaign (10:1–43).** In contrast to the preceding geographically localized narratives, chaps. 10 and 11 are accounts of two more extensive campaigns of Joshua, in the S and the N respectively. Both continue the theme of the implementation of the ban, which is rigorously enforced. 10:1 resumes 9:1, and there follows the account of a coalition of Amorite kings against Israel, motivated by the treaty made with Gibeon. The coalition is defeated with the help of direct divine intervention; its kings are executed as had been the king of Ai; and Joshua then proceeds to destroy the major southern cities. The chapter ends with a geographic summary vv 40–43).

42 (a) DEFEAT OF THE COALITION OF FIVE KINGS (10:1–27). **1.** *Adonizedek:* Means "(the god) Zedek is my lord"; the divine element Zedek also occurs in Melchizedek, also a king of Jerusalem (Gen 14:18). In the LXX his name is Adonibezek, which also occurs in Judg 1:5–7 as the name of a king (implicitly of Jerusalem) who was defeated at Bezek. Probably they are the same person. *Jerusalem:* The first mention of the city by this name in the Bible; in Gen 14:18 it is called Salem. Its archaeological history is complex, and excavations continue; → Biblical Geography, 73:92–94. Despite the implication here and elsewhere in Josh (except for 15:63), Jerusalem remained a Canaanite enclave until the time of David; see Judg 1:21; 19:10–12; 2 Sam 5:6–9; 1 Chr 11:4–8. **2.** The description of Gibeon's military might is surprising in the light of chap. 9. **3.** The first mention of the names of Israel's adversaries in Canaan; the kings of Jericho and Ai were nameless. The personal names, most of which are elsewhere unattested, vary significantly in the LXX. *Hebron:* One of the major cities in biblical tradition, it is *ca.* 19 mi. S of Jerusalem. Hebron is associated with the ancestors (Gen 13:18; 23:19; 35:27; 37:14) and was David's first capital (2 Sam 2:1–4; cf. 2 Sam 15:7–10). *Jarmuth:* Identified with Khirbet Yarmūq in the Judean foothills, *ca.* 18 mi. SW of Jerusalem. *Japhia:* Also the name of one of David's sons (2 Sam 5:15). *Lachish:* Tell ed-Duweir, in the Judean foothills *ca.* 28 mi. SW of Jerusalem; see *EAEHL* 735–53. *Debir:* Elsewhere always a toponym; it appears that in making use of an older list the authors of Joshua took it as a personal name; see further at v 38. *Eglon:* A city in the Judean foothills, mentioned only in Josh (10:23,34–36; 12:12; 15:39), frequently identified with Tell el-Ḥesi, although Tell Beit Mirsim and Tell ʿAiṭūn have also been proposed; also the name of a Moabite king (Judg 3:12). **6.** The Gibeonites appeal to the covenant which placed Israel under obligation. **10.** *Yahweh threw them into confusion:* The Hebr vb. *hāmam* is used almost exclusively of divine activity; see Exod 14:24; 23:27; Judg 4:15; 1 Sam 7:10. *the ascent of Beth-horon:* The major pass from the Aijalon Valley (see comment on v 13) to the hill country, and the site of frequent battles (see, e.g., 1 Macc 3:16–24); it was guarded by two cities, Upper Beth-horon and Lower Beth-horon (see 16:3,5), identified with Beit ʿŪr el-Fōqa and Beit ʿŪr et-Taḥta, *ca.* 5 mi. WNW of Gibeon. *Azekah:* Tell ez-Zakarīyeh, *ca.* 15. mi SW of Beth-horon; see *EAEHL* 141–43. **11.** *the descent of Beth-horon:* If not simply a variant tradition (cf. v 10), this may reflect the immediate topography of the region. *stones:* So 4QJosᵃ; the MT reads "great stones," and the LXX "hailstones" (anticipating the second part of the verse); both are secondary expansions. The divine control of the elements is a common feature in accounts of warfare; see Job 38:22–23. **12a.** There is considerable variation in the textual traditions of MT and LXX. **12b–13.** *"sun, be still in Gibeon, and moon in the Aijalon Valley"; and the sun was still, and the moon stood, until the nation took vengeance on its enemies:* The first part of this verse is a poetic couplet, and the second is an ancient interpretation that clarifies the unusual meaning of the word "be still" (Hebr *dôm*). Another interpretation is found at the end of v 13, which indicates that for at least some ancient readers what happened was that the day was miraculously lengthened

because the heavenly bodies stopped in their courses (see also Sir 46:4). This interpretation seems correct, taking into account the mention of the moon as well as the sun, at opposite ends of the horizon, and so the frequent attempts to explain the miracle as solar eclipse are misguided. This is, of course, Yahweh's victory, as the end of v 14 (and the LXX of v 13 ["until God took vengeance on their enemies"]) makes clear; the association of heavenly bodies with the deity who fights for Israel is a commonplace of biblical poetry (see Judg 5:20; Hab 3:11). *Aijalon Valley:* A major E–W depression from the Judean hill country to the coastal plain, dominated by the city of Aijalon (see at 19:42), for which it is named. **13b.** *is it not written in the Book of the Upright?:* Although not found in the LXX, this is an ancient gloss, a kind of footnote, indicating the source from which the poetic unit is taken. The same source is referred to in 2 Sam 1:18 and perhaps in 1 Kgs 8:53 LXX (emended). **16.** *the cave:* As in 24:26, the use of the def. art. is deliberate, indicating a locale well known to the ancient audience; cf. 1 Kgs 19:9. **18.** *stones:* Here and in v 27 the MT reads "large stones"; see comment on v 11. **24.** *your feet on the necks:* A gesture of complete subjugation; cf. 1 Kgs 5:3; Ps 110:1; *ANEP* 393; etc. **25.** See 1:6–7,9; 8:1. **26.** See comment on 8:29. **27.** *stones:* As in vv 11,18 the MT adds "large." This is the third cairn mentioned in Josh; see 7:26; 8:29.

43 (b) DEFEAT OF THE MAJOR CITIES (10:28–39). The rout of this Amorite coalition is partially contradicted by Judg 1:8–15, where the defeat of Jerusalem, Hebron, and Debir is attributed to Judah and Caleb; see also Josh 14:12–15. The phrase "and its king" has been added to several verses, often in different places in the MT and the LXX, in order to connect this summary with the preceding narrative. Although there is some overlap with the names of the cities in v 3, there are also differences in order, number, and names, and we thus have two originally independent units (or at least variant traditions) joined because of their geographic coincidence.

28. The ban is fully enforced. **29.** *Libnah:* Probably Tell Bornāṭ, *ca.* 6 mi. N of Lachish. **33.** *Gezer* (Tel Gezer, *ca.* 18 mi. WNW of Jerusalem; see *EAEHL* 428–43) was not captured or destroyed; this notice is thus consistent with 16:10; Judg 1:19; 1 Kgs 9:15–16. **38.** *Debir:* Probably Khirbet Rabud, *ca.* 13 mi. SE of Lachish; see *EAEHL* 995.

44 (c) CONCLUDING SUMMARY (10:40–43). This is a summary of the southern conquests of Joshua, mentioning in v 40 the hill country, the Negeb, and the foothills, and introducing a new term, "the slopes" (Hebr *ʾāšēdôt*), perhaps the steep decline from the Judean hill country to the Rift Valley. Verse 41 provides a second summary, by geopolitical rather than geophysical units.

40. *the Negeb:* The semidesert region S of Beer-sheba from the coastal plain to the Arabah; the term also means "the south" (→ Biblical Geography, 73:82–86). *he did not leave a survivor:* See Deut 20:16 and Josh 8:22. Here, as in 4:8 and 8:27, Joshua is fulfilling the commands of Yahweh rather than of Moses. **41.** *Kadesh-barnea:* Also called Kadesh, this was one of the traditional stopping places of the Israelites in the wilderness after the exodus. It is probably to be identified with Tell el-Qudeirat *ca.* 50 mi. SW of Beer-sheba; see *EAEHL* 697–99. *Gaza:* Near the modern city of the same name, on the coast of the Mediterranean *ca.* 50 mi. SW of Jerusalem; it was one of the cities of the Philistine pentapolis (see at 13:2). *Goshen:* Probably to be distinguished from the area in the E Nile Delta (see Gen 47:27; etc.), a general designation for the region between the Negeb and the hill country.

43. Identical to 10:15 and, like it, not found in the LXX; probably a later addition.

45   (J) The Defeat of the Northern Kings (11:1-15). This episode is a conscious parallel to chap. 10. Both open with the phrase "When . . . heard," continued by the summoning of a coalition of kings to fight the Israelites, followed by Yahweh's encouragement of Joshua ("Do not fear"). Then in both chapters the attacking coalition is defeated and their cities captured and destroyed, and each episode concludes with a summary of the conquest, chap. 10 of the south only, and chap. 11, resuming 9:1, of the entire land. We have here, therefore, a literary composition.

The primary source for the narrative is preexisting traditions related to those now found in Judg 4-5, a conclusion based on the name of the king of Hazor, Jabin (Josh 11:1; Judg 4:2). Unless it is supposed, without any real evidence, that the monarchy of Hazor used papponomy, it appears that there is only one event described in these two texts, the defeat of a Canaanite coalition. The tradition history is complex. Thus, the "water of Merom" (Josh 11:5,7) may be a variant for the "waters of Megiddo" (Judg 5:19), and the phrase "on the heights of the field" (Hebr *'al měrômê śādeh,* Judg 5:18) may be a wordplay alluding to the waters of Merom. The cumulative evidence suggests that the primary account is that in Judg, and that the Josh narrative is based on it.

This conclusion implies that there is no necessary connection between the statement that Joshua burned Hazor (vv 11,13) and the archaeological evidence for the destruction of Hazor (Tell el-Qedah, *ca.* 8 mi. N of the Sea of Galilee; see *EAEHL* 474-95) in the mid-13th cent. The date alone is problematic since it is a century before the destruction of Lachish (→ 9 above). Moreover, the archaeological evidence is anonymous: the extensive layer of ashes indicates the destruction of the city but not the cause of that event. A simple equation, then, of the two sources, is unlikely.

46   1. *Jabin:* Apart from Judg 4, the only other occurrence of this name is in Ps 83:10. *Jobab:* One of several individuals in the Bible with this name. *Madon . . . Shimron . . . Achshaph:* None of these places can be identified with any certainty, and their spellings vary in the versions. **2.** The geography of the verse is not clear, and the textual witnesses vary. *Chinneroth:* The Sea of Galilee. *Naphath-Dor:* Tel Dor is on the Mediterranean coast *ca.* 15 mi. S of Haifa; see *EAEHL* 334-37. The word *naphath* is obscure. **3.** On the names of the inhabitants of the land, see comment on 3:10. *Hermon:* The mountain at the extreme N of Israel and the southernmost part of the Antilebanon range, with an elevation of 9,232 ft. *Mizpah:* This name, which means "lookout," recurs in v 8; its location cannot be pinpointed. **5.** *the waters of Merom:* Merom is a city in the Galilee, also known from extrabiblical sources (see, e.g., *ANET* 283) and often identified as Tell el-Khureibeh or Meiron. **6.** *you shall hamstring their horses:* Cf. 2 Sam 8:4 (= 1 Chr 18:4); Gen 49:6. This action rendered the horses unusable in warfare. In biblical tradition horse-drawn chariots were not part of the military equipment of Israel until the reign of David; cf. Ps 20:8. **8.** *Great Sidon:* See 19:28 and 2 Sam 24:6 (LXX), as well as the Annals of Sennacherib (*ANET* 287), where it is mentioned alongside Little Sidon; apparently two parts of the ancient Phoenician metropolis (modern Şaida, on the Lebanese coast *ca.* 25 mi. NNE of Tyre) were thus distinguished. This area was never under Israelite control except in theory (see 13:4,6). *Misrephoth-maim:* Perhaps Khirbet el-Musherifeh, just S of Rosh Hanikra/Rās en-Naqūra on the Mediterranean coast near the modern border between Israel and Lebanon. **13.** *on their tells:* See comment on 8:28. **14.** As

in 8:2,27, the ban is applied only to the populations of the defeated cities. **15.** With a rhetorical flourish, the authors of Josh conclude their account of the conquest by reaffirming one of their major themes: Joshua's total fidelity to the divinely instituted Mosaic law (see Deut 20:16-17).

47   (K) Summaries (11:16-12:24). The account of the conquest concludes with a series of summaries, apparently from different traditions, which set the stage for the division of the land which follows.

(a) GEOGRAPHICAL RESUMÉ (11:16-20). Although this summary parallels that at the end of chap. 10, it is at the same time more general, covering all the conquered territory. **16-17.** Yet another description of the land according to its geophysical divisions. **17.** *the smooth mountain:* Or, Mt. Halak (a proper name); identified with Jebel Halaq, W of the Arabah, although this does not really suit the location given here. *Seir:* Edom, the southernmost region of Transjordan. *Baal-gad:* Mentioned only here and in 12:7; 13:5; its exact location is unknown. **18.** *for many days:* Only in 14:7,10 is an implicit duration of the conquest given. **20.** *to strengthen their hearts:* This phrase (*lĕhazzēq 'et-libbām,* often translated "to harden their hearts," occurs elsewhere only with reference to Pharaoh and the Egyptians before the exodus (Exod 4:21; etc.). Despite the theological problems the concept raises for modern readers, the viewpoint of the biblical writers must be recognized: Israel's enemies were of no account, mere puppets, as it were, in Yahweh's hands as he continued his purposes for Israel. For further discussion, see B. S. Childs, *The Book of Exodus* (Phl, 1974) 170-75.

48   (b) THE ANAKIM (11:21-22). This section is a short note concerning the Anakim, one of the terms for the pre-Israelite inhabitants of the land (see *ANET* 328), famous for their size and strength (Deut 9:2). The exclusion of three major Philistine cities (v 22) is the first indication that the conquest was not as complete as stated up to this point. As late as *ca.* 600 Gaza and Ashdod were independent of Judean control, and this note may reflect the political reality of Josiah's reign. **21.** *Anab:* Identified with Khirbet 'Anāb es-Şeghireh, *ca.* 15 mi. W of Hebron; see also *ANET* 242, 477. **22.** *Gath:* One of the five major Philistine cities, whose name means "vine-press." Its identification is disputed. *Ashdod:* Near the modern city of the same name, *ca.* 25 mi. NNE of Gaza on the Mediterranean coast; see *EAEHL* 103-19.

49   (c) FINAL SUMMARY (11:23). This verse reads as a conclusion to all that has preceded and would naturally be followed by the actual division of the land, in an edition of the work prior to the addition of chaps. 12-14. *as an inheritance:* The first occurrence in Josh of *nahălâ* (a related verbal form is used in 1:6). It is generally used of the land as Yahweh's gift to Israel, and as such is a favorite deuteronomic word; its primary sense is hereditary family property. *the land was quiet:* a deuteronomic cliché; see 14:15; Judg 3:11; etc.

50   (d) LISTS OF DEFEATED KINGS (12:1-24). The series of summaries concludes with lists naming various defeated adversaries on both sides of the Jordan. The first is a restatement of Moses' victories drawn from deuteronomic tradition, while the second is an originally independent document.

(i) *East of the Jordan* (12:1-6). A summary drawn largely from Deut 2-3. **1.** *the Wadi Arnon:* The modern Wadi Mūjib, which flows W from the Transjordanian plateau into the Dead Sea; the traditional boundary of Moab. **2.** *Aroer:* Khirbet 'Arā'ir, on the N bank of the Wadi Mūjib; see *EAEHL* 98-100. *Gilead:* The rugged, densely forested region between Bashan and Moab. Southern Gilead, assigned to Reuben and Gad (Num 32:29; Josh 13:25), corresponded to Ammon, while N Gilead (see v 5), assigned to Eastern Manasseh (13:31), was under Israelite control until *ca.* 721. *the Jabbok:* Modern Nahr ez-Zerqa, which flows from Amman N and then W to the Jordan; apparently the W boundary of Ammon. *Ammonites:* The inhabitants of the Transjordanian kingdom of Ammon (→ Biblical Geography, 73:47–49), whose name is preserved in the modern capital of Jordan, Amman. **3.** *Beth-hajeshimoth:* Perhaps Tell el-'Azeimah, *ca.* 2 mi. NE of the Dead Sea. *Pisgah:* The mountains of which the most prominent was Mt. Nebo (see Deut 34:1). **4.** The name of Og is preceded in the MT by the word "boundary," a late and erroneous addition. *the Rephaim:* In Canaanite mythology the Rephaim are the deified ancestors who looked after the well-being of their descendants; their name probably means "the healers." In biblical tradition the term is used to denote the inhabitants of the underworld (see Isa 14:9; 26:14; Job 26:5) and, as here, a group of pre-Israelite inhabitants of the land, whose size was legendary (see Deut 3:11; the LXX translates the word here and elsewhere as "giants").

51 (ii) *West of the Jordan* (12:7–24). After a geographic introduction, which moves from N to S (cf. 11:16–17, which moves from S to N), there is a list composed of defeated kings identified by the cities they ruled. In the list each entry is followed by the count "one" in the MT (but not in the major LXX mss.). The total in v 24 is 31 in the MT, but 29 in the LXX because of differences in readings, the more important of which will be noted. The first part of the list gives the cities in the order of their previous mention in Josh—thus, Jericho, Ai, Jerusalem, Hebron, Yarmuth, Lachish, Eglon—but after that there is no obvious order. Some of the places named occur nowhere else in the Bible, indicating that this list once had an independent existence.

Lists such as these are favorite devices in ancient literature. As C. M. Bowra observed, "Early poetry likes lists, whether of ancestors, or men gathered for battle, or men slain" (*Tradition and Design in the Iliad* [Oxford, 1930] 69). In addition to the tribal allotments and boundary descriptions in Josh 12–19, other biblical examples include the catalogue of tribes (Gen 49; Deut 33; Judg 5:14–18; etc.; cf. the "catalogue of ships" in book 2 of the *Iliad*), the frequent genealogies, and perhaps the prophetic "oracles against the nations." To a large extent the appeal of this material is limited for modern readers, but ancient audiences expected and enjoyed such detail. **14.** *Hormah:* A city of Judah (see 15:30) or Simeon (19:4) in the Negeb whose precise location is disputed. Its name is derived from the word for "ban" (Hebr *ḥērem*), as Num 21:3 illustrates. *Arad:* Tel 'Arad, *ca.* 12 mi. E of Beer-sheba; see *EAEHL* 74–89. Arad was destroyed by Moses according to Num 21:1–3. **15.** *Adullam:* Probably Tell esh-Sheikh Madhkūr, *ca.* 19 mi. SW of Jerusalem; a city in Judah (see 15:35). **17.** *Tappuah:* Identified with Tell esh-Sheikh Abu Zarad, *ca.* 25 mi. N of Jerusalem; it was on the border between Ephraim and Manasseh (see 16:8; 17:8). *Hepher:* Probably in Manasseh; see 17:2–3; 1 Kgs 4:10; and → 29 above. **18.** *Aphek in the Sharon:* This reading is based on the LXX. The designation "in the Sharon" distinguishes this Aphek (Rās el-'Ain [Tel Aphek]), *ca.* 30 mi. NW of Jerusalem, from the several other biblical Apheks; cf. similar specifications in vv 22–23. See *EAEHL* 70–73 and M. Kochavi, *BA* 44 (1981) 75–86. The Sharon is a highly fertile part of the coastal plain between Jaffa and Dor. **21.** *Taanach:* Tell Ta'annek, *ca.* 20 mi. N of Shechem (see *EAEHL* 1138–47); together with *Megiddo* (Tell el-Mutesellim; see *EAEHL* 830–56) it dominated the S side of the Jezreel

Valley. The mount of Megiddo (Hebr *har mĕgiddô*) gives its name to the final cataclysmic battle of Armageddon; because of its strategic position, in antiquity it was the site of many battles, including that in which King Josiah was killed (*ca.* 609). **22.** *Kedesh:* One of the several sites with this name, perhaps Tell Abu Qudeis, between Taanach and Megiddo. *Jokneam in the Carmel:* Tell Qeimūn, *ca.* 7 mi. NW of Megiddo. Carmel is the mountain which juts into the coastal plain at Haifa. **23a.** *Dor, Naphath-Dor:* See comment on 11:2. **24.** *Tirzah:* Tell el-Fār'ah (N), *ca.* 7 mi. NE of Shechem; see *EAEHL* 395–404.

52 **(III) The Division of the Land (13:1–21:45).** The second major section of Josh is the division of the land, a complex unit with a long history. Its presupposition is apparently that the land has been conquered, but in the details of the division it is clear that this is in fact not completely the case. These chapters, although dry to the modern readers, are important witnesses to the geopolitical history of Israel and are further witness to the ancient delight in lists of names. (On the textual and historical problems in the lists, → 62 below.) In general, the fullest description is of Judah's territory, and the further removed one gets from that focus the less precise the geographical details become; this confirms a date for the material largely in its present form in Josiah's reign in the late 7th cent.

53 **(A) Introduction (13:1–7).** This description of "the land that remains" is realistic; in fact, Israel controlled Philistia for only a brief period and never ruled Phoenicia. The introductory comment in v 1, that much of the land was not under Israelite control, anticipates 14:12; 15:14–15,63; 16:10; 17:12–13,15–18; Judg 1; 3:1–6, where it is clear that the conquest described in the preceding chapters was not a swift, total takeover but a gradual process, only completed in the reign of David. Nevertheless, both presentations share the viewpoint that the land in its entirety was Israel's inheritance from Yahweh, a theological assertion that served as an appropriate rallying cry in the reign of Josiah, when the full restoration to Israelite control of the territory of the Davidic empire seemed possible.

1. *old, advanced in years:* This phrase recurs in 23:1 and is used elsewhere only of Abraham (Gen 18:11 [together with Sarah]) and David (1 Kgs 1:1). **2.** *the Philistines:* Mentioned by name in Josh only here and in v 3, they are a group of "Sea Peoples" who settled in the S coastal plain of Israel and rapidly grew in power, eventually threatening the existence of the Israelite confederation. Although conquered by David, they retained some measure of autonomy and are referred to frequently in the prophets and in Assyrian sources. The Roman designation of the region as Palestine is derived from their name. According to biblical tradition Philistia comprised five city-states—Gaza, Ashdod, Ashkelon, Gath, and Ekron—ruled by "tyrants" (see v 3; the Hebr *soren is probably related to Gk tyrannos). *the Geshurites:* A group in the region of Philistia, mentioned elsewhere only in 1 Sam 27:8 and not to be confused with the Transjordanian people of the same name (cf. 12:5). **3.** *Shihor:* The eastern branch of the Nile; see Isa 23:3. *Ekron:* Tel Miqne (Khirbet el-Muqanna'), *ca.* 22 mi. W of Jerusalem. *the Ashkelonite:* Ashkelon, *ca.* 43 mi. WSW of Jerusalem, gives its name to the green onions we call "scallions." *the Avvites:* According to Deut 2:23, pre-Philistine inhabitants of the S coastal plain. **4.** The focus seems to have shifted from the southern coastal plain to the northern. *Aphek:* Probably the same Aphek mentioned in 12:18, although Afqa in central Lebanon has been proposed. **5.** *the Gebalites:* Gebal is modern Jebeil on the Lebanese coast *ca.* 35 mi. N of Beirut, called by the

Greeks Byblos, from which the word "Bible" comes. *Lebo-Hamath:* Modern Lebweh, in N Lebanon *ca.* 35 mi. E of Jebeil; the name is often mistranslated "the entrance of Hamath." **6.** The distribution by lot anticipates the actual division of the land in chaps. 14–19,21.

54   (B) East of the Jordan (13:8–33). Joshua's division of Transjordan fulfills Moses' promise in Num 32 and Deut 3:12–17, but the three territorial summaries are not directly related. In contrast to the precise delineations used for the allotments of most of the land W of the Jordan in the chapters that follow, the Transjordanian territory is described only cursorily, by listing principal cities in each tribal area. It is thus theoretically part of Israel for Dtr, but in practice Israel seldom controlled any of it; this accounts for the sketchy description. In other traditions, Transjordan was not part of the ideal land of Israel: note its omission in Num 34:1–12 and Ezek 48 (where Reuben, Gad, and Manasseh are all given portions W of the Jordan); the episode of the altar in Josh 22 may also reflect this understanding.

55   (a) INTRODUCTION (13:8–14). The summary description of the Transjordanian tribal allotment is similar to that found in 12:1–5. **9.** *Medeba:* Modern Madeba, *ca.* 20 mi. SSW of Amman; see *EAEHL* 819–23. *Dibon:* Modern Dhibān, *ca.* 33 mi. SSW of Amman; see *EAEHL* 330–33. **14.** Read, with the LXX and v 33, "Yahweh the god of Israel is their inheritance" (cf. Deut 10:9; 18:2), omitting MT's "the fire offerings of," an addition based on Deut 18:1. This note is repeated almost verbatim in v 33, and similar remarks are made in other discussions of the territories of Reuben, Gad, and Transjordanian Manasseh (14:3–4; 18:7). One possible reason for the association of the Levites with the Transjordanian tribes is their actual, as opposed to their ideal, status; for much of Israel's history the territory assigned to Reuben, Gad, and Manasseh was controlled by Moab, Ammon, and Aram. The tribal status of the Levites is clear in a number of traditions, yet from an early period their status was different from that of the other tribal groups: they had no territory of their own (see Gen 49:7). For a brief period they may have had a limited portion, taken from the allotments of other tribes (see 14:4 and esp. 21:1–42), but the general situation seems to have been that described here.

56   (b) REUBEN (13:15–23). Almost all the places mentioned in this list are in Moab and were generally under Moabite control; cf. Jer 48. **15.** *Bamoth-baal:* Lit., "the high places of Baal," a town in Moab mentioned in Num 22:41, also called Bamoth (Num 21:19–20) and Beth-bamoth (Mesha stele [*ANET* 320]); its location is uncertain. *Beth-baal-meon:* Lit., "the house [i.e., temple] of Baal-meon," also mentioned in the Mesha stele under that name and as Baal-meon, its name in Num 32:38. Identified as Ma'īn, *ca.* 22 mi. SW of Amman. **18.** All three places are also levitical cities; see 21:36–37. **20.** *Beth-peor:* The site of Israel's apostasy (Num 25), where Balaam gave one of his oracles (Num 23:28) and near which Moses was buried (Deut 34:6); also called simply Peor in 22:17. **21–22:** This summary is indirectly related to Num 31:8. **21.** *the leaders of Midian:* The only mention of Midian in Josh. It was apparently a confederation of tribes in S Transjordan, with which Israel was closely connected (by marriage, at least: see Exod 3:1; etc.) and also at odds (Num 31). As in Israel and other confederations, a Midianite leader was called a *nāśî*'. (See further Num 25:18 and → 39 above.) The names of the five leaders are also found in Num 31:8. *vassals:* Hebr *nĕsîkê;* the same designation is used of Midianite leaders in Ps 83:12, but its exact meaning is uncertain. **22.** *Balaam:* As in Num 31:8,16, Balaam is here presented as a villain, in contrast to Num 22–24. Only here and in Num 31:8 is Balaam said to have been killed by the Israelites.

57   (c) GAD (13:24–28). Gad's allotment consists of S Gilead, an area generally under Ammonite control, and apparently the E side of the entire Jordan Valley. **25.** *Jazer:* An important Transjordanian city, apparently not far from Amman, although its exact site is uncertain. *Aroer:* A different place from that named in 12:2; 13:9,16, also occurring in Judg 11:33, whose location is unknown. *Rabbah:* Modern Amman, the capital city of the Ammonites; its full name was "Rabbah [the great city] of the Ammonites." **26.** *Ramath-hamizpeh:* Lit., "the height of the lookout," perhaps to be identified with Mizpeh of Gilead (Judg 10:17; Gen 31:49; etc.). *Betonim:* Khirbet Baṭneh, *ca.* 12 mi. WNW of Amman; its name means "pistachios." *Mahanaim:* The site has not been clearly identified, but it must be near the confluence of the Jabbok and the Jordan (see Gen 32:3; 2 Sam 2:29). *Lodebar:* An emendation for MT *lidbir,* LXXᴬ *dabeir;* this place occurs elsewhere (see 2 Sam 9:4; Amos 6:13), but its location is uncertain. **27.** *the valley:* I.e., the Jordan Valley. *Beth-haram:* Listed in Num 32:36 as Beth-haran, it is generally identified with Tell Iktanu, *ca.* 17 mi. SW of Amman. *Beth-nimrah:* Probably Tell Blebil, *ca.* 17 mi. E of Amman, on the Wadi Nimrin (see Isa 15:6). *Succoth:* Lit., "booths"; often identified as Tell Deir 'Allā in the Jordan Valley *ca.* 25 mi. WNW of Amman (→ Numbers, 5:44), but the site's excavator, H. Franken, doubts this identification; see *EAEHL* 321–24. *Zaphon:* Also mentioned in Judg 12:1 and in the Amarna Letters, the location of this important town is disputed. *Chinnereth:* The Sea of Galilee.

58   (d) EASTERN MANASSEH (13:29–31). Manasseh's territory is N Gilead and Bashan, an area under Israelite control until the Assyrian conquest in 721, although at various times both the Ammonites and the Arameans occupied it (see Judg 10:8; 1 Kgs 22:3; Amos 1:3). Its perfunctory delineation is another indication of a late date for these passages dealing with Transjordan. **30.** *the settlements of Jair:* According to Num 32:41; Deut 3:14, Jair was a descendant of Manasseh, and it is this tradition which is followed here, rather than that in Judg 10:3–5, where Jair was one of the judges. **31.** *Machir:* According to the genealogies, Machir was the son of Manasseh (Gen 50:23; Num 26:29), a warrior (Josh 17:1), whose territory was E of the Jordan; in Judg 5:14, where Manasseh is not mentioned, it is a tribe, presumably W of the Jordan. From these and other brief notices various reconstructions of the history of Machir have been proposed, but the data are too meager for any certainty.

59   (e) CONCLUSION (13:32–33). 32. *the plains of Moab:* The formula is the same as that found in Num 22:1; 34:15. **33.** See comment on v 14.

60   (C) West of the Jordan (14:1–19:51).
(a) INTRODUCTION (14:1–5). 1. *Eleazar the priest:* According to Exod 6:25, the son of Aaron and the father of Phinehas; in Num he functions as Aaron's successor, just as Joshua was Moses'. It is he who commissioned Joshua (Num 27:18–23) and together with Joshua he is to preside over the allotment of the land, both E (Num 32:28) and W (Num 34:17) of the Jordan. In Josh this position is fulfilled here and in 17:4; 19:51; 21:1; and in its final form Josh concludes with the notice of Eleazar's death and burial; all of these notices are further evidence of Priestly tradition. *heads of families of tribes:* This exact expression occurs elsewhere only in Num 32:28, in the context of the allotment of the territory E of the Jordan, but similar language is used in Josh 19:51, which summarizes the sections concerned with the division of the land. The phrase suggests that a large number of people took part in the allotment, in contrast to Num

34:17–29, where there is one leader (Hebr *nāśî'*) for each tribe, but in accordance with the principle found elsewhere in Num (e.g., 33:54) that each tribe's allotment is proportionate to the number of its clans. **2.** *by lot:* With the LXX, requiring only a minor change in the MT's vocalization; see Num 34:13. The distribution by lot is a feature of the following chapters, and may be based on the way in which inherited property was divided among the heirs. **4.** A variant of Num 35:3; this is the command referred to in v 5. **5.** *they divided the land:* Although Joshua has the responsibility for the division of the land in one level of tradition (13:7; 18:10), and Joshua and Eleazar share the task in a later version, here and in 18:2 a more general phrasing is used.

61   (b) CALEB'S INHERITANCE (HEBRON) (14:6–15). This section also paradoxically concerns a group that was different; unlike the Transjordanian tribes and the Levites, however, whose inheritances were either historically dubious or nonexistent, the Calebites are mentioned here because they were not originally part of Israel; their claim to the Hebron region antedated Judah's, although they were subsequently assimilated into that tribe. The Calebite traditions are continued in 15:13–19. **6.** The mention of both Judah and Gilgal implicitly contradicts what follows. *Caleb:* Mentioned by name only here and in chap. 15, Caleb was a hero of the wilderness period and, as the spy who (along with Joshua, in later traditions) gave a true report about the land, was exempted from the sentence of death on the generation of the exodus (Num 14:24; Deut 1:36). *the Kenizzite:* Also in Num 32:12, this epithet associates Caleb with one of the pre-Israelite groups in the land (Gen 15:19, but only there in the standard list of the peoples of Canaan); this tradition is almost certainly original, and the association of Caleb with Judah is therefore secondary. The Kenizzites seem to have stemmed from Edom (see Gen 36:11), and their incorporation into Israel is another example of the assimilation of foreign elements given a post-factum genealogical legitimation. **7–10.** This summary is derived both from the narrative in Num 13–14 and esp. from Moses' recapitulation in Deut 1:19–46, although there is some independent material here. **10.** A rare chronological specification, according to which, allowing thirty-eight (or forty) years for the wanderings in the wilderness after Kadesh-barnea (see Deut 2:14; Num 14:33), the conquests of Joshua would have taken seven (or five) years. **12.** *this hill country:* If the demonstrative is taken literally, this contradicts the location at Gilgal given in v 6. *you heard on that day:* An odd remark, implying that Joshua was not one of the spies and lending some credibility to the false report; the LXX glosses "you heard this word on that day." *the Anakim are there:* In contradiction to, and apparently unaware of, 11:21–22. **15.** *Kiriath-arba:* The well-attested ancient name of Hebron (see Gen 23:2; Judg 1:10), meaning "city of (the) four." When the original sense of this name was lost, the word *'arba'* ("four") was reinterpreted as a personal name, and this Arba is then made the ancestor of the Anakim (see also 15:13; 21:11). *the land was quiet:* A verbatim repetition of 11:23, perhaps indicating the secondary character of chaps. 12–14; certainly 15:1 follows smoothly from 11:23.

62   (c) JUDAH (15:1–63). The first, and most detailed, description of tribal territory is that of Judah. It consists of two principal and perhaps originally independent parts, a boundary list (vv 1–12) and city lists (vv 20–62), separated by a passage about the Calebite portion and concluding with an antiquarian note about Jerusalem. The primacy given to Judah is an indication of the general origin of the material, i.e., in the Judean monarchy, probably after the fall of Samaria. Although the original sources were older, in their present form both the boundary and the city lists must date from the time of Josiah, since a number of the places mentioned were not established before these. This conclusion, originally formulated by A. Alt, has been repeatedly criticized, with earlier dates proposed, but it remains the most likely interpretation of admittedly complex and difficult material. Inconsistencies between the boundary lists of Judah and its adjacent tribes indicate a long history of modification and revision which cannot yet be adequately traced since the identification of ancient names with modern sites is far from complete and, for the most part, untested by excavation; in addition there are serious textual problems, with variant names occurring frequently in other biblical sources and in the LXX.

(Aharoni, Y., *LBib* 248–62, 347–56; Alt, A., "Judas Gaue unter Josia," *PJ* 21 (1925) 100–16 [= *KlS* 2. 276–88]; Cross, F. M. and G. E. Wright, "The Boundary and Province Lists of the Kingdom of Judah," *JBL* 75 (1956) 202–26.)

63   (i) *Boundaries* (15:1–12).   The detailed boundary description here and in subsequent sections is an early example of cartography. The border is described as an entity that moves along the geographical features of the landscape, occasionally resting at fixed places. On the S, E, and W the border of Judah corresponds to the traditional boundaries of Canaan, another indication of the primacy of Judah. **1.** *the wilderness of Zin:* The area around Zin, which itself is unidentified, corresponding to the E Negeb from Kadesh-barnea to the Arabah. **2–4.** The S boundary of Judah is the same as that of Canaan; see Num 34:3–5. **3.** *Akrabbim:* Lit., "scorpions"; its location is unknown. *Hezron . . . Addar:* In Num 34:4 these names are given as one, Hazar-addar (lit., "strong enclosure"); the location is unknown. *Karka:* Lit., "foundation," this place occurs only here in the Bible and its location is not known. **4.** *Azmon:* Unknown. *the Wadi of Egypt:* Not the Nile, but the Wadi el-'Arīsh, which enters the Mediterranean *ca.* 50 mi. SW of Gaza. **5–11.** This description of the N boundary of Judah from E to W corresponds to the S boundary of Benjamin from W to E (18:14–20), although the former lists more places and there are toponymic variants. **6.** *Beth-hoglah . . . Beth-ha-arabah:* Generally identified with 'Ain Ḥajlah and 'Ain el-Gharabeh, just N of the NE corner of the Dead Sea. **7.** *Debir:* Perhaps in the vicinity of the modern Wadi el-Dabr, which enters the Dead Sea near its NW corner; in any case, not the same place as Debir in 10:38, etc. *Gilgal:* 18:17 has Geliloth; in any case, not the Gilgal of 4:19, etc. *the ascent of Adummim:* Modern Tal'at ed-Damm near the Wadi Qelt ("the wadi" in this verse) on the old road from Jerusalem to Jericho (see Lk 10:30). *En-shemesh:* Generally identified as 'Ain el-Hod, *ca.* 2 mi. W of Jerusalem. *En-rogel:* Probably modern Bir-'Ayyūb, near the junction of the Kidron and Gehenna valleys. **8–9.** The border carefully skirts Jerusalem (see the ancient gloss, not found in 18:16); the text is thus aware of Jerusalem's non-Israelite status before David (cf. v 63). **8.** *valley of the son of Hinnom:* So MT and 18:16; the LXX, in accord with late usage, has "Valley of Hinnom" here and "Gehenna" in 18:16. This is the valley immediately W and S of Jerusalem, the site of illicit worship according to Jer 7:31, and in later writings used as a metaphor for the place of the punishment of the damned. *Valley of Rephaim:* SW of Jerusalem; see 2 Sam 5:18,22; 23:13; on Rephaim, see comment on 12:4. **9.** *the waters of Nephtoah:* Generally equated with Arab Lifta, Hebr Me-Neftoah, *ca.* 4 mi. NW of Jerusalem. **10.** *Mt. Seir:* Unknown; not to be confused with the Edomite region of the same name (see 11:17). *Mt. Jearim:* The second element is a common noun meaning "forests"; the place is thus probably distinct from Kiriath-jearim. *Chesalon:* Modern Kesla, *ca.* 10 mi. W of Jerusalem. *Beth-shemesh:* At this point the boundary is coterminous with that of Dan (19:40–48), which is also described from E to W but is much more detailed. Beth-shemesh (lit., "the house of the Sun[-god]"), called Ir-shemesh ("the city of the Sun") in 19:41, is Tell er-Rumeilah, in the Sorek Valley *ca.* 15 mi. W of Jerusalem; the nearby 'Ain Shems preserves the ancient name; see *EAEHL* 248–53. *Timnah:* Tell el-Batashi, *ca.* 5 mi. NW of Beth-shemesh; see *BASOR* 248 (1982) 1–36; also *EAEHL* 1204–5. **11.** *Shikkeron:* Perhaps Tell el-Fūl, *ca.* 3 mi. NW of Ekron. *Mount Baalah:* Perhaps el-Mughār, *ca.* 5 mi. NW of Ekron; called Baalath in 19:44. *Jabneel:* Later called Jabneh (2 Chr 26:6) and Jamnia (1 Macc 4:15), modern Yebnā/Yavne, *ca.* 5 mi. E of the Mediterranean in the Sorek Valley.

64   (ii) *Caleb's share* (15:13–19). A continuation of Calebite traditions (→ 61 above). After a transitional recapitulation, the passage is virtually identical to Judg 1:11–15, which is almost certainly primary. **13.** *to Joshua:* No such command is reported; contrast 14:12; Judg 1:20. **14.** *the three sons of Anak:* See Num 13:22; Judg 1:10. **15.** *Kiriath-sepher:* Lit., "the city of the book." **16.** *Achsah:* Her name means "anklet." The promise of the leader's daughter to a successful warrior is also attested in 1 Sam 17:25. **17.** *Othniel:* One of the judges (see Judg 3:9–11). In Judg 1:13 Othniel is Caleb's nephew, not his brother. **18.** *she got down:* The root *ṣnḥ* occurs elsewhere only in Judg 1:14; 4:21; its meaning is disputed. **65**   (iii) *City lists* (15:20–62). The cities are divided into 12 units, probably corresponding to administrative districts of the kingdom of Judah; cf. the similar division of Solomon's kingdom in 1 Kgs 4:7–19. **21.** *Arad:* With some LXX manuscripts, for MT's Eder. **22.** *Kinah:* Perhaps Khirbet Taiyib, *ca.* 3 mi. NNW of Arad. *Aroer:* For MT's *'ad'ādâ;* Khirbet 'Ar'arah, *ca.* 10 mi. SE of Beer-sheba; see A. Biran, *BARev* 9 (2, 1983) 28–37. **23.** *Kedesh:* Probably Kadesh-barnea. **24.** *Ziph:* Perhaps Khirbet ez-Zeifeh, *ca.* 20 mi. SE of Beer-sheba. **25.** *Hazor:* There appear to be several glosses on this common name (which means "enclosure") in both the MT and the LXX. **26.** *Moladah:* Perhaps Khirbet el-Waṭen, *ca.* 5 mi. E of Beer-sheba. **28.** *Beer-sheba:* Tel Beer-sheba (Tell es-Saba'), near the modern city of the same name; see *EAEHL* 160–68. Beer-sheba was the major city of the S and was the traditional limit of Israel's territory ("from Dan to Beer-sheba," Judg 20:1, etc.). **29.** *Baalah:* Called Balah in 19:3 and Bilhah in 1 Chr 4:29; its location is unknown. *Ezem:* Perhaps Umm el-'Aṣam, *ca.* 17 mi. SE of Beer-sheba. **30.** *Chesil:* So MT, and perhaps a scribal error; cf. LXX *baithēl;* 19:4, Bethul; 1 Chr 4:30. **31.** *Ziklag:* Probably Tell esh-Sharī'ah (Tel Sera'), *ca.* 12 mi. NW of Beer-sheba; see *EAEHL* 1059–69; and E. Oren, *BA* 45 (1982) 155–66. *Madmannah:* Called Beth-marcaboth ("house of chariots") in 19:5; perhaps Khirbet Tatrit, *ca.* 12 mi. NNE of Beer-sheba. *Sansannah:* Called Hazar-susah ("mare-enclosure") in 19:5; cf. 1 Chr 4:31; probably Khirbet esh-Shamsanīyāt, *ca.* 9 mi. NE of Beer-sheba. **32.** *Lebaoth:* 19:6 has Beth-lebaoth; cf. 1 Chr 4:31 Beth-biri. *Shilhim:* In 19:6 called Sharuhen (1 Chr 4:31 has Shaaraim), identified with Tell el-Fār'ah (S), *ca.* 22 mi. WSW of Beer-sheba; see *EAEHL* 1074–82. *En-rimmon:* Erroneously separated into two names in the MT; cf. 19:7; Neh 11:29. Perhaps Tell el-Khuweilifeh (Tel Halif), *ca.* 11 mi. N of Beer-sheba; see J. D. Seger, *BASOR* 252 (1983) 1–23. *twenty-nine:* The figure is low, even allowing for the errors noted above, an indication of additions made to the list after its initial composition. **33–44.** The foothills and Philistia. The inclusion of Philistine cities as part of Judahite territory may not cor-

respond to historical reality, but may be a projection to Josiah's time of the control exercised over that region during the united monarchy. **33.** *Eshtaol:* Assigned to Dan in 19:41. Perhaps Ishwa', *ca.* 13 mi. W of Jerusalem. *Zorah:* Modern Ṣar'ah, *ca.* 15 mi. W of Jerusalem. **34.** *Zanoah:* Probably Khirbet Zānū', *ca.* 14 mi. WSW of Jerusalem. *Tappuah:* Perhaps Beit en-Nattif, *ca.* 19 mi. SW of Jerusalem. **35.** *Socoh:* One of two cities by this name in Josh (see v 48), probably Khirbet 'Abbād, *ca.* 17 mi. WSW of Jerusalem. **36.** *Gederah:* The name is derived from the word for "wall" and is followed by a gloss or variant; elimination of the latter gives the correct total. **37.** *Migdal-gad:* Lit., "tower of fortune [or Gad]," perhaps Khirbet el-Mejdeleh, *ca.* 25 mi. SW of Jerusalem. **40.** *Lahmas:* Perhaps Khirbet el-Laḥm, *ca.* 3 mi. E of Lachish. **42.** *Ether:* Perhaps Khirbet el-'Atar, *ca.* 23 mi. WSW of Jerusalem. **43.** *Nezib:* Perhaps Khirbet Beit Naṣīb, *ca.* 17 mi. SW of Jerusalem. **44.** *Keilah:* Probably Khirbet Qilā, *ca.* 24 mi. SW of Jerusalem. *Achzib:* Perhaps Tell el-Beiḍā, *ca.* 19 mi. SW of Jerusalem. *Mareshah:* Tell Sandahanna, *ca.* 4 mi. NE of Lachish; see *EAEHL* 782–91. For several of the cities in this district, see Mic 1:14–15.

48–60. The hill country. **48.** *Shamir:* Perhaps Khirbet el-Bireh, near Khirbet es-Sumara, *ca.* 16 mi. NNE of Beer-sheba. *Jattir:* Probably Khirbet 'Attīr, *ca.* 16 mi. NE of Beer-sheba. *Socoh:* Probably Khirbet Shuweikeh, *ca.* 17 mi. NE of Beer-sheba. **49.** *Debir:* See comment on 10:38. The MT gives its alternate name as Kiriath-sannah, which may be an error for the more familiar Kiriath-sepher (so LXX; see v 15). **50.** *Eshtemoh:* Called Eshtemoa, probably the correct spelling, in 21:14; identified with es-Semū', *ca.* 19 mi. NE of Beer-sheba. *Anim:* Probably Khirbet Ghuwein et-Taḥtā, *ca.* 3 mi. S of Eshtemoa. **52.** *Arab:* Perhaps Khirbet er-Rābiyeh, *ca.* 8 mi. SSW of Hebron. *Dumah:* Perhaps ed-Dōmeh, *ca.* 9 mi. SW of Hebron. **53.** *Beth-tappuah:* Perhaps Taffūḥ, *ca.* 4 mi. W of Hebron. **54.** *Zior:* Perhaps Si'īr, *ca.* 5 mi. NNE of Hebron. **55.** *Maon:* Perhaps Tell Ma'īn, *ca.* 8 mi. SSE of Hebron. *Carmel:* Probably Khirbet el-Kirmil, *ca.* 8 mi. S of Hebron. *Ziph:* Probably Tell ez-Zīf, *ca.* 4 mi. SSE of Hebron. *Juttah:* Probably Yaṭṭā, *ca.* 6 mi. S of Hebron. **56–57.** *Zanoah of Cain:* So apparently LXX (which also gives the total as nine for MT's ten); perhaps Nebī Yaqīn, *ca.* 4 mi. SE of Hebron. **58.** *Halhul:* Probably modern Ḥalḥūl, *ca.* 3 mi. N of Hebron. *Beth-zur:* Khirbet eṭ-Ṭubeiqah, *ca.* 5 mi. N of Hebron; see *EAEHL* 263–67. *Gedor:* Probably Khirbet Jedūr, *ca.* 7 mi. N of Hebron. **59.** *Beth-anoth:* Perhaps Khirbet Beit-'Enūn, *ca.* 3 mi. NNE of Hebron. At the end of this verse the LXX preserves an additional district, that of Bethlehem, containing 11 names. **60.** This district is generally agreed to be too small; most of its major cities have been assigned to Benjamin (18:21–28). **61–62.** *Middin and Secacah and Nibshan:* Probably the three Iron II forts in the Buqei'ah; see *IDBSup* 5. **62.** *the City of Salt:* Probably Khirbet Qumrān, the ruins of the community that produced the Dead Sea Scrolls, where Iron II remains have also been found; see *EAEHL* 978. *En-gedi:* Near the modern area of the same name; see *EAEHL* 370–80.

    (iv) *Jerusalem* (15:63). Cf. Judg 1:21, and see above at 10:1. In 18:28 Jerusalem is assigned to Benjamin. **66**   (d) JOSEPH (16:1–17:18). The territory of Joseph is divided between its two ancient tribal divisions, Ephraim in the S and Manasseh in the N; together they occupy the central hill country.

    (i) *Introduction* (16:1–4). **1.** *the waters of Jericho:* The spring which waters the Jericho oasis, 'Ain es-Sulṭān. **2.** After "from Bethel" the MT adds, "to," as though Luz were a separate place rather than the older name of the city (see Gen 28:19; Josh 18:13; etc.); this is probably a misplaced gloss to v 1 (see LXX). *Archites:*

The only other biblical references to this group are in association with David's advisor Hushai (2 Sam 15:32; etc.). *Ataroth:* Called Ataroth-addar in 16:5; 18:13, its location is disputed.

(ii) *Ephraim* (16:5–10). The textual situation here is extremely confused, and it is difficult to reconstruct any original. **6.** *Michmethath:* The readings and the location are uncertain. *Taanath-shiloh:* Perhaps Khirbet Ta'nā el-Fōqā, *ca.* 5.5 mi. SE of Shechem. *Janohah:* Probably Khirbet Yānūn, *ca.* 6 mi. SE of Shechem. **7.** *Naarah:* Called Naaran in 1 Chr 7:28. **8.** *Tappuah:* See comment on 12:17. *Wadi Kana:* Its modern name is apparently the same. **67** (iii) *Western Manasseh* (17:1–13). **1–3.** Cf. Num 26:28–34 and 1 Chr 7:14–19. The Priestly character of this material is indicated in v 4 by the mention of Eleazar before Joshua and by the presence of the leaders (Hebr *něśî'îm*). **2.** Many of the names here occur in the Samaria ostraca as toponyms. **3–4.** Yahweh's command in Num 27:1–11 is fulfilled; cf. also Num 36:1–12. The names of Zelophehad's daughters are names of tribal groups or towns. **5.** *ten shares:* The word for "share" has the primary meaning "rope," for "measuring lines" were used to determine property rights. According to the figure given, each of the granddaughters received a share equal to that of a son. **7.** *Shechem:* Tell Balāṭa (see *EAEHL* 1083–94). The first mention of this city in Josh; → 37 above. **11.** *Beth-shean:* Tell el-Ḥusn, near the Jordan Valley *ca.* 24 mi. NE of Shechem; see *EAEHL* 207–29. *Ibleam:* Probably Khirbet Bel'ameh, *ca.* 16 mi. N of Shechem. For the remainder of the verse the text is confused, with additions from Judg 1:27; Josh 11:2, and elsewhere. **13.** See Judg 1:28. (iv) *Conclusion* (17:14–18). **14.** *clear for yourself:* The process of deforestation was continuous from prehistoric times into the Roman period. As human (and caprine) populations increased and technology became more advanced, more trees were cut down. See further L. E. Stager, *BASOR* 260 (1985) 4–5. *one lot and one share:* Contrast vv 1–6, in which Ephraim and Manasseh are separate, and Manasseh has 10 shares W of the Jordan. The stereotypical character of this treatment of the tribe of Joseph is thus apparent. **16.** *iron chariots:* That is, chariots whose wooden frames were plated with metal. *the Jezreel Valley:* The broad valley that extends from the Carmel range to the Jordan; → Biblical Geography, 73:105–10. It is named for the town of Jezreel (19:18), identified with Zer'în, *ca.* 9 mi. E of Megiddo. **17–18.** A variant version of vv 14–16. **68** (e) THE OTHER TRIBES (18:1–19:51). The remaining tribes are given relatively cursory treatment, with the exception of those whose borders were coterminous with Judah's; in these cases there is largely identical description of material already given, although occasionally the order of presentation is reversed. **69** (i) *Introduction* (18:1–10). **1.** *Shiloh:* This important Israelite center is identified as Khirbet Seilūn, *ca.* 19 mi. N of Jerusalem; see *EAEHL* 1098–1100. No reason is given for its introduction here, nor is there any account of a journey from Gilgal; all subsequent events seem to take place here until at least 23:1 (where no specific place is named), and probably 24:1 (Shechem). *they pitched the Tent of Meeting there:* The presence of the Tent of Meeting at Shiloh reflects 1 Sam 2:22 (MT). The terminology is Priestly. *the land was subdued:* See Num 32:22,29; Gen 1:28. **6.** The final assignment is done by lot, i.e., it is Yahweh who assigns the remaining territories. **7.** See comment on 13:14. **70** (ii) *Benjamin* (18:11–28). For the N boundary, see 16:1–3, and for the S, 15:1–12. Following the description of the border itself (vv 11–20), as with Judah

there is a list of cities. The latter includes cities also assigned to Judah, an indication of disputed territory or perhaps of lists of originally different origins. **12.** *Beth-aven:* See comment on 7:2. **13.** *Luz:* See comment on 16:2. **18.** *Beth-arabah:* So LXX; MT reads "opposite the Arabah"; see comment on 15:6. **22.** *Zemaraim:* Perhaps Rās ez-Zeimara, *ca.* 13 mi. NNE of Jerusalem. **23.** *Avvim:* Perhaps a gentilic form derived from the name Ai. *Parah:* Probably Tell el-Fāra, *ca.* 9 mi. NE of Jerusalem. *Ophrah:* Probably eṭ-Ṭaiyibeh, *ca.* 14 mi. NNE of Jerusalem. **24.** *Chephar-ammoni:* Lit., "the Ammonite village"; its location is unknown. *Geba:* Perhaps Jeba', *ca.* 9 mi. NNE of Jerusalem. **25.** *Ramah:* Probably er-Rām, *ca.* 7 mi. N of Jerusalem. **26.** *Mizpeh:* Tell en-Naṣbeh, *ca.* 8 mi. N of Jerusalem; see *EAEHL* 912–18. The name means "lookout." *Mozah:* Perhaps Qalūniyeh, *ca.* 5 mi. NE of Jerusalem. **28.** *Gibeath:* So MT; LXX reads Gibeah. Saul's home (1 Sam 11:4; etc.), identified as Tell el-Fūl, *ca.* 4 mi. N of Jerusalem; see *EAEHL* 444–46; and *AASOR* 45 (1978). *Kiriath-jearim:* With LXX. *thirteen:* So LXX, which reads Zela-ha-eleph as one name. **71** (iii) *Simeon* (19:1–9). Here too there is considerable overlap with Judah (15:21–32). **2.** *Shema:* So LXX (see 15:26); the MT reads Sheba. *thirteen:* In fact, 14 cities are named; → 51 above. **5.** *Beth-marcaboth:* See comment on 15:31. **7.** *Ether:* Some scholars distinguish this place from the one with the same name in 15:42. *Ashan:* Perhaps Khirbet 'Asan, *ca.* 2 mi. NW of Beersheba. *three:* MT reads "four," understanding En-rimmon to be two places. **9.** A kind of rationalization for the incorporation of Simeon into Judah and the latter's control of the south. **72** (iv) *Zebulun* (19:10–16). **10.** *Sadud:* With some LXX traditions and the Syr, for MT's Sarid; perhaps Tell Shadūd, *ca.* 6 mi. NE of Megiddo. **11.** *Dabbesheth:* Perhaps Tell esh-Shammām, *ca.* 6 mi. NNE of Megiddo. **12.** *Chisloth-tabor:* Called Chessuloth in v 18; probably Iksāl, *ca.* 11 mi. NE of Megiddo. *Daberath:* Probably Dabūriyeh, *ca.* 14 mi. NE of Megiddo. (On Tabor, see comment on v 22.) *Japhia:* Perhaps Yāfā, *ca.* 9 mi. NNE of Megiddo, although this location is out of place in the boundary description. **13.** *Gath-hepher:* Perhaps Khirbet ez-Zurra', *ca.* 14 mi. NNE of Megiddo. *to Rimmon:* So apparently the LXX; Rimmon is identified with Rummāneh, *ca.* 16 mi. NNE of Megiddo. *and turns:* Reading *wětā'ar.* **14.** *Hannathon:* Perhaps Tell el-Bedeiwîyeh, *ca.* 15 mi. NNE of Megiddo. *the valley of Iphthahel:* Probably Wadi el-Malik (Nahal Sippori). **15.** *Nahalal:* Perhaps Tell en-Nahl, *ca.* 9 mi. NNE of Megiddo. See Judg 1:30 for variant spellings of this and Kattath. *Bethlehem:* Probably Beit Lahm, *ca.* 11 mi. N of Megiddo. **73** (v) *Issachar* (19:17–23). **18.** *Shunem:* Probably Sōlem, *ca.* 9 mi. E of Megiddo. **19.** *Hapharaim:* Perhaps 'Affuleh, *ca.* 11 mi. E of Megiddo. *Anaharath:* Perhaps Tell el-Mukharkhash, *ca.* 17 mi. ENE of Megiddo. **20.** *Rabbith:* Called Daberath in the LXX and in 21:28 and 1 Chr 6:57; see comment on v 12. **21.** *Remeth:* Called Jarmuth in 21:29 and Ramoth in 1 Chr 6:58. *En-gannim:* Lit., "spring of gardens"; often identified with modern Jenin. *En-haddah:* Perhaps el-Ḥadatheh, *ca.* 19 mi. ENE of Megiddo. **22.** *Tabor:* Presumably a town near the noted mountain of the same name in the Jezreel Valley; → Biblical Geography, 73:111. *Beth-shemesh:* Perhaps Tell el-'Abeidīyeh, near Khirbet esh-Sheikh Shamsāwi, *ca.* 21 mi. ENE of Megiddo. **74** (vi) *Asher* (19:24–31). In contradiction to Judg and historical reality, the Phoenician cities are included in Israelite territory. For possible identifications of several of the sites mentioned, see *EAEHL* 23–25. **25.** *Hali:* Perhaps Khirbet Rās 'Ālī, *ca.* 11 mi. SSE of Acco.

Beten: Perhaps Khirbet Ibṭīn, ca. 11 mi. S of Acco. Ach-shaph: Perhaps Tell Keisān, ca. 5 mi. SE of Acco. **26.** Shihor-libnath: The meaning of this name is unclear; in the LXX it is interpreted as two separate places. The first component is a homonym of the word for the eastern branch of the Nile. **27.** Beth-ha-emek: Perhaps Tell Mīmās, ca. 6 mi. NE of Acco. Neiel: Perhaps Khirbet Ya'nīn, ca. 8 mi. ESE of Acco. Cabul: Probably modern Kābūl, ca. 9 mi. SE of Acco; it was the center of a district ceded to Tyre by Solomon (1 Kgs 9:13). **28.** Abdon: So some Hebr traditions, and 21:30; 1 Chr 6:59; perhaps Khirbet 'Abdeh, ca. 10 mi. NNE of Acco. Rehob: Perhaps Tell el-Bīr el-Gharbī, ca. 6 mi. ESE of Acco. Hammon: Perhaps Umm el-'Awāmīd, ca. 9 mi. S of Tyre. Kanah: Perhaps Qāna, ca. 8 mi. SE of Tyre. **29.** Tyre: Modern Ṣūr; the major Phoenician city during most of the Iron Age, built on an island and hence well defended; it was never under Israelite control. Hosah: Perhaps mainland Tyre (called Ushu/Uzu in extrabiblical sources); modern Tell el-Rashidiyeh. Mahalab: So a number of ancient sources; cf. Judg 1:31. Perhaps Khirbet el-Maḥālib, ca. 5 mi. NE of Tyre. Achzib: Modern Achzib (ez-Zīb), ca. 9 mi. N of Acco; see EAEHL 26–30. **30.** Acco: For MT's Um(m)ah; cf. Judg 1:31; a major coastal city N of the Carmel range; see EAEHL 14–23. Aphek: Perhaps Tell Kurdāneh, ca. 6 mi. S of Acco.

75   (vii) Naphtali (19:32–39). **33.** Heleph: Perhaps Khirbet 'Irbādeh, ca. 17 mi. NE of Megiddo. the oak at Zaanannim: Also mentioned in Judg 4:11. Adami-ha-nekeb: A composite name, understood by the LXX as two places; the second element means "the pass." Perhaps the tell near Khirbet ed-Dāmiyeh, ca. 19 mi. NE of Megiddo. Jabneel: Perhaps Khirbet Yemma, ca. 21 mi. ENE of Megiddo. Lakkum: Perhaps Khirbet el-Mansūra, SE of Jabneel. **34.** Aznot-tabor: Perhaps Khirbet Umm Jebeil, just N of Mt. Tabor. and the Jordan in the east: So LXX; MT erroneously adds "in Judah" after "and." **35.** Hammath: Called Hammath-dor in 21:32. Rakkath: Called Kartan in 21:32, perhaps by erroneous metathesis. Chinnereth: Probably Tell el-'Oreimeh, on the SW coast of the Sea of Galilee; see V. Fritz, Arch 40 (4, 1987) 42–49. **36.** Ramah: Perhaps Khirbet Zeitūn er-Rāmeh, ca. 12 mi. SW of Hazor. **37.** Kedesh: Probably Tell Qades, ca. 7 mi. NNW of Hazor. **38.** Beth-anath: Lit., "house of [the goddess] Anat." Beth-shemesh: Lit., "house of the Sun(-god)."

76   (viii) Dan (19:40–48). Ancient tradition originally located Dan in the S (cf. Judg 5:17; 13–16), and hence there is some overlap with the Judean city list. But apparently before the monarchy, the Danites migrated to the far north; cf. Judg 18. **41.** Ir-shemesh: See comment on 15:10. **42.** Shaalabbin: Perhaps Salbīt, ca. 16 mi. WNW of Jerusalem. Aijalon: Perhaps near modern Yālō, ca. 13 mi. WNW of Jerusalem. **44.** Gibbethon: Perhaps Tell el-Melāt, ca. 23 mi. WNW of Jerusalem. **45.** Jehud: Probably el-Yehūdīyeh, ca. 28 mi. NW of Jerusalem. Bene-berak: Probably at the modern town with the same Hebr name (Arab Ibn Ibrāq), ca. 31 mi. NW of Jerusalem; see EAEHL 184–86. Gath-rimmon: Often identified with Tell Jerīsheh, on the coast just N of Jaffa; see EAEHL 575–78. **46.** on the west the Jarkon: So LXX. The Jarkon is a river that enters the Mediterranean near Tel Aviv. Joppa: Modern Yaffa/Yafo, just S of Tel Aviv; see EAEHL 532–41. **47.** The text of this verse is extremely confused, and the various traditions are dependent on Judg 1:34–35; cf. Judg 18. The gist of the notice is that the relocation of Dan to the N was due to the lack of sufficient space and to Amorite opposition to expansion. Leshem: Probably a variant of the original name, Laish (Judg 18:7, etc.), meaning "lion." Dan: Identified with Tel Dan (Tell el-Qadi), at one of the sources

of the Jordan ca. 20 mi. NNW of Hazor; see EAEHL 313–21.

77   (D) Conclusion (19:49–51).

(a) JOSHUA'S PERSONAL ALLOTMENT (19:49–50). In a reciprocal action (cf. 11:23), the Israelites give Joshua his own private bequest, which will later be used as his burial place (see 24:30). **50.** No such divine command is elsewhere recorded. Timnath-serah: Called Timnath-heres in Judg 2:9; identified with Khirbet Tibnah, ca. 17 mi. SW of Shechem.

(b) SUMMARY (19:51). The conclusion, with many Priestly resonances, to the entire unit which began at 13:1.

78   (E) Cities of Asylum (20:1–9). This passage deals with the legal rights of asylum (as opposed to sanctuary [see below]). In addition to it there are three texts concerning the cities set aside for those who committed involuntary manslaughter, and all four are interrelated to such an extent that it is difficult to arrange them in chronological order. The common element is the protection of the killer from the "avenger of blood" (Hebr gō'ēl haddām), the member of the victim's family whose responsibility it was to avenge the death. Deut 19:1–13 describes in detail the conditions under which the principle of asylum is operative and mandates the designation of three easily accessible cities W of the Jordan; if the Israelites obey Moses' instruction and God increases their territory, they are to add three more cities of asylum. Deut 4:41–43 (from the latest stage of Deut), in fulfillment of Deut 19:8–10, adds the designation of three cities E of the Jordan. Num 35:9–34 provides a fuller description of the criteria for deciding between voluntary and involuntary homicide and ordains that the accused shall have his case heard by the congregation (Hebr 'ēdâ), presumably of his own city; if he is found innocent, he must return to the city of asylum and remain there until the death of the high priest. The present form of Josh 20 in the MT is contradictory: in v 4 it is the elders of the city of asylum who act as judges, but in v 6 it is the congregation. The term "congregation" and the reference to the high priest (v 6) are characteristic Priestly locutions. The LXX represents an earlier stage in the formation of the chapter, omitting vv 4–6 (except for the phrase "until he stands before the congregation for judgment" [v 6], but see v 9). Even at this earlier level of the developing tradition, however, there is a mixture of the vocabulary found separately in Num and Deut. It is possible, therefore, that Josh 20 is based primarily on the traditions now found in Num 35:9–13, and was secondarily expanded under the influence of Deut 19.

The contradictions suggest that the primary intent of Josh 20, then, was yet another demonstration of fulfillment: all that God had commanded Moses (Num) and that Moses had commanded Israel (Deut) was carried out by Joshua (v 2). If this conclusion is valid, then Josh 20 is a late text, based on earlier but still relatively late material, and it is not surprising that in biblical narrative there is no reference to the actual functioning of the cities of asylum. One of the oldest legal collections, the Covenant Code, also provides for asylum (Exod 21:13–14), but the place of asylum is the altar, and hence it deals specifically with sanctuary; this religious institution seems to have been operative in Israel, to judge from 1 Kgs 1:50; 2:28. On that basis it has been suggested that the cities of asylum were originally cities of sanctuary, that is, cities in which a major Israelite shrine was located at which the perpetrator of an inadvertent homicide could find sanctuary. The existence of a cultic center at Shechem is beyond question (see chap. 24), and one can perhaps be presumed for Kedesh and for Hebron (Gen

13:18; 18:1); but none is known at the three Transjordanian cities, and the only two instances of the actual use of sanctuary take place in Jerusalem, which is not mentioned in this chapter. It is best, therefore, not to try to harmonize Exod 21:12–14 with the passages that deal with the cities of asylum; the latter are part of the ideal constitution of Israel characteristic of Josh.

Of the six cities themselves, the three W of the Jordan, Kedesh, Shechem, and Hebron, are located by geographic region rather than by tribal territory: they are, respectively, in the hill country of Naphtali, in the hill country of Ephraim (broader than Ephraim's allotment, since Shechem is assigned to Manasseh in 17:7), and in the hill country of Judah. The Transjordanian cities, on the other hand, are doubly located, by geography and by tribe, and none is previously mentioned in Josh; all six do recur in the list of the cities of the Levites in chap. 21.

79 **2.** *asylum:* Hebr *miqlāṭ,* a rare term, used only of these cities, here and in Num 35; Josh 21, and 1 Chr 6:42,52; in Deut they are called simply "cities to which the homicide flees" (Deut 4:41–42; cf. 19:2–4). **3.** *unintentionally:* The procedure applies only to homicide by misadventure (as opposed to murder or manslaughter), as the gloss "without knowledge" in the MT indicates. **4–6a.** In the MT but missing from the LXX. **6.** *the death of the high priest:* Apparently it was an expiation for a death resulting from homicide by misadventure, substituting for the death of the perpetrator. **8.** *Bezer:* Probably Umm el-'Amad, *ca.* 8 mi. NE of Madeba, and also known as Bozrah (Jer 48:24). *Ramoth in Gilead:* Tell er-Rumeith, *ca.* 30 mi. N of Amman; see P. W. Lapp, *The Tale of the Tell* (Pittsburgh, 1975) 111–19. *Golan:* Perhaps Saḥm el-Jōlān just N of the southern border of Syria; the name is retained in modern usage ("the Golan Heights"). **9.** *resident alien:* See comment on 8:33. For this chapter, see A. G. Auld, "Cities of Refuge in Israelite Tradition," *JSOT* 10 (1978) 26–40.

80 **(F) Cities of the Levites (21:1–42).** In contrast to the statements elsewhere (→ 55 above) that the Levites received no territory of their own, in this passage, as in Num 35:1–8, the Levites are given extra-tribal allotments consisting of 48 cities with their surrounding grazing land from territories previously assigned to other tribes; a variant of this list is found in 1 Chr 6:39–66. The chapter has a complicated literary history. Following an introduction (vv 1–3), there is a summary of the allotments (vv 4–8); then there is a doublet: vv 9–12 deal exclusively with Hebron, which recurs in v 13; vv 13–40 then present a detailed list of the cities assigned to each levitical clan. According to a survey by John Peterson, most of the sites that can be identified were not settled before the 8th cent.; this is an indication of the artificial character of the list. It is also significant that all of the cities of asylum are included, although in chap. 20 they had been assigned to specific tribes.

2. See 14:4 and Num 35:1–8. **4.** *the Kohathites:* The most important priestly family; their eponymous ancestor Kohath was son of Levi and grandfather of Moses and Aaron. Their most important group, the descendants of Aaron, received their allotment from the territories closest to Jerusalem; the rest of the allotments move outward to the N from here. **6.** *Gershon:* Levi's oldest son. **7.** *Merari:* The third son of Levi; his descendants were the least important priestly group. **11.** *Hebron:* See comment on 14:15. **12.** Caleb's rights (see 14:13; 15:13) are not violated, at least in legalistic theory. **16.** *Ashan:* With LXX and 1 Chr 6:44 for MT's Ain. **18.** *Anathoth:* the hometown of Jeremiah (Jer 1:1); usually identified with Rās el-Karrūbeh, *ca.* 4 mi. NNW of Jerusalem. *Alemeth:*

With 1 Chr 6:45 (for MT's Almon); probably Khirbet 'Almīt, *ca.* 5 mi. NNW of Jerusalem. **27.** *Ashtaroth:* With 1 Chr 6:56; see comment on 9:10. **34.** *Kartah:* Often identified with Athlit, *ca.* 6 mi. S of Dor; see *EAEHL* 130–40.

81 **(G) Summary (21:43–45).** A conclusion, in typically deuteronomic language, to the entire preceding narrative. The promises of 1:2–9 have been fulfilled, and, with its allusion to 1:13–15, the passage also serves as a transition to chap. 22.

82 **(IV) Appendixes (22:1–24:33).** Josh concludes with several unrelated units, which nevertheless serve to unite the work as whole and to complete the presentation of the ideal Israel under the leadership of Joshua.

83 **(A) The Transjordanian Tribes (22:1–34).** The episode of the conflict between the Transjordanian and Cisjordanian tribes resumes 1:12–18, as chap. 23 resumes Yahweh's speech in 1:1–9; the pattern is chiastic. At the same time, the issue of the locus of legitimate worship, a characteristically deuteronomic concern, also anticipates chap. 24, where Shechem is implicitly designated as the central sanctuary for use by all the tribes; note also the employment of a stone "altar"/stele as witness in 22:27,34 and 24:26–27. But this deuteronomic material has been substantially revised by Priestly elements: the hero of the central portion (vv 9–34) is not Joshua but Phinehas, and Priestly vocabulary: *něśî'îm* (v 14), *'ēdâ* (v 12), *ma'al* (vv 16,20,22,31). In its final form, then, Josh 22 anticipates the centrifugal forces that will later threaten the confederation and the nation, and is a further elaboration of the theme of Joshua's leadership of a united Israel, a leadership that uses conciliation rather than combat to solve intra-Israelite disputes.

84 **(a) JOSHUA'S DISMISSAL (22:1–9).** This passage records the completion of the commands in 1:12–18 (→ 15 above). The Transjordanian tribes have fully participated in the conquest, and they are now dismissed to the territory which first Moses and then Joshua assigned to them (see Deut 3:12–17; Josh 12:1–6; 13:7–33). **5.** The language is heavily deuteronomic. *cling:* See Deut 13:5; etc. **8.** *spoil:* The enumeration of booty is reminiscent of the despoiling of the Egyptians just before the exodus (Exod 3:22; etc.). **9.** At this point characteristic Priestly terminology and concerns are introduced, beginning with the term "sons of Reuben/Gad" for "Reubenites/Gadites" (v 1). *Gilead:* Here equivalent to all of Transjordan. *their possession:* A Priestly term; see Num 32:5.

85 **(b) THE ALTAR WEST OF THE JORDAN (22:10–34).**

(i) *Construction and controversy (22:10–12).* The Transjordanian tribes construct an altar W of the Jordan before they cross to their allotted territory. Several issues are involved here, reflecting different stages in the formation of the narrative. The Priestly concern is with ritual purity; since the altar was itself not in unclean territory, it must be the purity of its users, the Transjordanian tribes, that is the issue. For deuteronomic tradition the altar, built by and presumably reserved for only two and one-half tribes, violated the principle of the central sanctuary (Deut 12:5–14) which actualized the unity of Israel. At still earlier levels we have what appears to be an alternate etiology for the name Gilead (cf. Gen 31:44–54), and the nullification of a claim (note the use of stones as boundary markers in the Jacob/Laban covenant [Gen 31:52]) by Reuben, Gad, and Transjordanian Manasseh to territory W of the Jordan; contrast Ezek 48:6,27: in the restored Israel even Reuben and Gad will have portions there.

10. The large altar whose construction is subsequently described is located W of the Jordan, "in the land of Canaan." **11.** *on the side of the Israelites:* A reiteration of the altar's location, with the implication that true Israel was only W of the Jordan. **12.** Cf. the similar language in Judg 20:1, another case of military action by the confederation against a member; identical language is used in Josh 18:1, in a religious context.

86   (ii) *Negotiation (22:13–31).*   **13.** The Transjordanian tribes, having constructed the altar, have continued their journey and crossed the Jordan to Gilead. *Phinehas:* The grandson of Aaron (Exod 6:25), who, in Priestly tradition, is one of the heroes of the wilderness and settlement periods. He killed the guilty parties in the P version of the Baal Peor episode (Num 25:6–18; see Josh 22:17), led the Israelites in their holy war against Midian (Num 31:6), and was the chief priest in the settlement period according to Judg 20:28. The priestly family at Shiloh continued to use his name: see 1 Sam 1:3; 4:4. **16–20.** The speech of the representatives of Israel recalls the divine punishment for two previous episodes of infidelity, both of which were cultic: the Baal Peor episode (Num 25) and the violation of the ban by Achan (Josh 7). **16.** *unfaithfulness:* See comment on 7:1. **19.** The designation of Transjordan as unclean is unparalleled (except perhaps for the implication in Ezek 48:6,27) and in direct contradiction to the designation of that region as divine bequest in 1:13; etc. Likewise, the proposal that the Transjordanian tribes leave their allotment and settle W of the Jordan is without precedent, as is the implication that Yahweh tents (Hebr *šākan*, another Priestly term) only W of the Jordan (cf., e.g., 2 Sam 11:11). **20.** *He did not perish alone:* Refers not to Achan's family, but to the Israelites who died in the first attack on Ai; see comment on 7:24. **21–29.** The response of the Transjordanian tribes is unconvincing in its casuistry; they admit to having built an altar, but claim that it was not for sacrifice but rather simply as a "witness." **24–25.** The real reason for the construction is given in this earliest layer of tradition—to stake a claim W of the Jordan. **27.** *a witness:* Hebr *'ēd;* cf. the etiology of Gilead in Gen 31:47–48. **29.** In the last of a series of oaths, the Transjordanian tribes express their deuteronomic orthodoxy. **30–31.** Phinehas and the leaders of Israel accept the explanation.

(iii) *Resolution (22:32–34).* **34.** *they called the altar "Witness":* So Syr; other traditions omit the name leaving an incomplete etiology. Cf. Exod 17:15. On this chapter, see J. A. Hackett, "Religious Traditions in Israelite Transjordan," *Ancient Israelite Religion* (Fest. F. M. Cross; ed. P. D. Miller, *et al.;* Phl, 1987) 129–31; J. S. Kloppenborg, "Joshua 22: The Priestly Editing of an Ancient Tradition," *Bib* 62 (1981) 347–71.

87   **(B) Joshua's Farewell Speech (23:1–16).** Like other major figures in Israelite tradition, Joshua delivers a speech at the end of his life; cf. Gen 49; Deut; 1 Kgs 2:1–9 (and 2 Sam 23:1–7). This final address parallels that of Yahweh in 1:1–9 and, like it, is heavily deuteronomic in tone, stressing the fulfillment of Yahweh's promises and the necessity of observance of the teaching of Moses lest the Israelites lose possession of the land that they have been given through Yahweh's victories. At one stage in the formation of Josh this chapter was presumably the conclusion of the book, preceding the notice of Joshua's death (24:29); 24:1–28 is set at Shechem, not Shiloh, and represents an independent tradition. **1.** See Deut 12:10. The second part of the verse repeats 13:1. **3.** Cf. 10:14,42. **4.** *the nations that remain:* The more realistic view; → 53 above and contrast 21:44. **5.** *he will drive them out:* See Deut 6:19; 9:4. **6.** Cf. 1:6–7. **7.** Cf. Exod 23:13; Deut 5:9. **8.** *cling:* See 22:5. **9.**

Cf. Deut 4:38; Josh 1:5; 10:8; 21:44. **10.** Cf. Deut 32:30. **11.** Cf. Deut 11:13; etc. **12.** Cf. Deut 7:3. **13.** Cf. Num 33:55. *perish from this good land:* Cf. Deut 4:26; 11:17. There is no explicit reference to exile here, although that would have been known to Israelite authors from the beginning of Assyrian expansion and to those responsible for Joshua from, e.g., Deut 4:27; 28:63–64. **14.** The same description of death is used by David (1 Kgs 2:2), another example of Joshua as the prototype of the ideal ruler. **14b.** Cf. 21:45. **15–16.** Cf. Deut 29:24–27.

88   **(C) Covenant at Shechem (24:1–8).** The last major section is an originally independent narrative of a covenant ceremony set at Shechem. Like the related material in 8:30–35, it shows Joshua fulfilling the commands of Moses in Deut 11; 27; 31. The pattern of divine address followed by an exhortation of Joshua also connects the unit with chaps. 1 and 23. The placement of the narrative here thus serves as fitting conclusion to Josh; all Israel is united under Joshua's leadership in worship of Yahweh, as they have been united in the battles of the conquest.

Much of the content is unparalleled elsewhere in biblical tradition. The summary in vv 2–13, although generally similar to other recitals of Yahweh's actions on Israel's behalf, omits Sinai and the wilderness traditions. Furthermore, it uses unique terminology ("thick darkness" [v 7]), presents a different view of the Balaam episode and the capture of Jericho, and refers to the worship of gods apart from Yahweh by Israel's ancestors in both Mesopotamia and Egypt. Unlike other covenant ceremonies, there is here no altar (cf. 8:30–31; Deut 27:6) or sacrifice (cf. Exod 24:3–8; Deut 27:7), and, most remarkably, Israel is given a choice not to worship Yahweh. Although reminiscent of Deut 30:19 (cf. also 1 Kgs 18:21), this option is here developed to an extraordinary degree.

At the same time, Josh 24 draws on and synthesizes a variety of traditions concerning Shechem, one of the most important Israelite cultic and political centers; cf. Gen 12:7; 33:20. Shechem (Tell Balāṭa) is one of the few major cities in the land whose destruction is not recorded in Josh; this silence is confirmed by archaeological evidence, for the site was continuously occupied from the Late Bronze Age into the early Iron Age. It seems, then, to have been peacefully incorporated into Israel (contrast Gen 34) and is a model of the actual processes by which Israel emerged in the land of Canaan as a confederation of originally disparate elements united not necessarily either by kinship or by shared experience (→ 29 above), but by their communal acceptance of Yahweh and concomitant allegiance to fellow Yahwists. At Shechem Israel became the people of Yahweh (see Deut 27:9). Although probably a relatively late composition attached to Josh in its final stage, this unit is thus an apt finale to the book.

(McCarthy, D. J., *Old Testament Covenant* [Oxford, 1972] 73–76. Nielsen, E., *Shechem* [Copenhagen, 1959]. van Seters, J., "Joshua 24 and the Problem of Tradition in the Old Testament," *In the Shelter of Elyon* [Fest. G. Ahlström; ed. W. B. Barrick and J. R. Spencer; Sheffield, 1984] 139–58. Wright, G. E., *Shechem* [NY, 1965].)

89   **1.** *he summoned the elders of Israel . . . and its officers:* The wording is almost identical to 23:2; see also on 8:33. *before God:* The presence of the ark is implied, although not mentioned explicitly; see 8:33. **2–4.** A summary of the events described in Gen 12–50, without any reference to the Joseph stories. **5–6.** The language is similar to 1 Sam 12:8, in another deuteronomic summary. **7.** The shift from direct speech of Yahweh to 3d-pers. narrative is found in both the MT (in this verse only) and the LXX (through v 13), evidence of a complicated redactional history that cannot be disentangled with any certainty; cf. an analogous shift in 1 Sam 12:11. This summary of the exodus event is apparently independent of other biblical traditions: note the unique word "darkness" (*ma'ăpēl*), and the unusual formulation "he brought the sea upon them." **9-10.** Again, although the basic story line is familiar, the details differ from other biblical accounts, and independent traditions are used. Note esp. the phrase "he fought with Israel": nowhere else is there a reference to a battle with Balak (cf. Deut 2:9; Judg 11:25), and the 3d-pers. reference to Israel is contextually anomalous. In addition, Balaam is negatively portrayed as one who wanted to curse Israel; cf. 13:22. **11.** *the lords of Jericho fought with you:* In direct contradiction to the battle of chap. 6; → 17 above. The title "lords" also reflects a different tradition from that in which Jericho was ruled by a king. **12.** *the hornet:* A vivid image, found elsewhere only in Exod 23:28; Deut 7:20. This may be a reification of Yahweh's messenger, who brought the people out of Egypt (Num 20:16) and through the wilderness and Transjordan (Exod 23:20; 32:34) and defeated the inhabitants of Canaan (Exod 23:23; 33:2; cf. Josh 5:14). *the twelve kings:* So LXX; MT erroneously reads "two," referring to Sihon and Og, already alluded to in v 8. *your bow . . . your sword:* For the idea, cf. Gen 48:22; Hos 1:7; etc. **13.** A recapitulation of Deut 6:10-11. The unearned bounty can also be rescinded; cf. Deut 28:30-33. **14.** Joshua's concluding exhortation. *put away:* See comment on v 23. *in Egypt:* The worship of other gods in Egypt is also mentioned in Ezek 20:5-8; 23:3,8; but is not found in pentateuchal traditions. **15.** *choose:* A choice between Yahweh and other gods is also found in 1 Kgs 18:21, but the moment of decision follows Yahweh's action in contrast to Baal's silence. Elsewhere false gods are chosen (Judg 10:14; Isa 41:24); here, remarkably, Joshua seems to be giving more than a rhetorical option. *in whose land you live:* In contrast to chaps. 1-12, and to some extent with 13-21, but in concord with Judg 1:1-3:6, the Amorites still occupy much of the land. **17.** *Yahweh is our god!:* This affirmation expresses the essence of Israel as a confederation whose principle of unity was religious: worship of Yahweh, and Yahweh alone. Having accepted Yahweh, the people are then able to include themselves as having shared in the formative experience of the exodus and in effect summarize Yahweh's words in Joshua's speech. **19.** *holy:* Holiness entails the separation of the sacred from the profane; Yahweh is holy because he does not allow worship of deities other than himself. *jealous:* The exact form occurs elsewhere only in Nah 1:2, which also explains its sense; see also Exod 20:5 (= Deut 5:9); 34:14; Deut 4:24; 6:15, and contrast Exod 34:7. **20.** A succinct summary of the deuteronomic theology. **22.** *you are witnesses against yourselves:* The first clear indication that this is a legal as well as a religious ceremony; as in our culture, witnesses were required at legal occasions (see Ruth 4:9-10; cf. Gen 23:17). The people have made a contract with Yahweh, or, as it is called in v 25, a covenant; one analogue for the covenant was the international treaty, in which the witnesses were the deities of the two parties. Here, since the contract is between the people and Yahweh, no other deities can be appealed to. The proper response to "you are witnesses" is "(we are) witnesses" (see Ruth 4:11), and it is found in the MT; LXX omits it, perhaps correctly, given the absence of an introduction to Joshua's words at the beginning of v 23.

23. *put away the foreign gods in your midst:* An almost verbatim quotation of Gen 35:2, resuming the command of v 14, and the first of three specific references to earlier Shechem traditions; the same formula occurs also in 1 Sam 7:4, and the vb. *hēsîr* is used of both Hezekiah's and Josiah's removal of heterodox worship (2 Kgs 18:4; 23:19). **25.** *a statute and an ordinance:* Hebr *ḥoq ûmišpāṭ;* the same phrase occurs in Exod 15:25b (D), and in the plural forms this is a deuteronomic cliche. **26.** *the book of the teaching of God:* The exact wording occurs only in Neh 8:18 (cf. 8:8; 10:29,30); elsewhere in Josh the teaching is either explicitly or implicitly that of Moses. *a large stone:* In contrast to 8:32, this stone is simply a memorial of the covenant, another witness (v 27); the use of the more generic "stone" (Hebr *'eben*) instead of the technical term "standing stone" (Hebr *maṣṣēbâ*) is probably to avoid any violation of Deut 16:22. Excavations at Shechem have uncovered a series of temples from the second half of the second millennium BC which had at their entrance one or more large standing stones; it is reasonable to identify these structures, or at least the latest, with the temple of Baal/El of the Covenant (Hebr *bĕrît*) (Judg 9:4,46; see Wright, *Shechem* [→ 88 above] 123-38), which also had a standing stone (*maṣṣēbâ*; Judg 9:6 [emended]). The "sanctuary" (Hebr *miqdāš*) mentioned here fits these data. *the oak:* Not just an oak, but the well-known oak, mentioned in one form or another in Gen 12:6; 35:4; Deut 11:30; Judg 9:6. It is especially the tree of Gen 35:4 (*hā'ēlâ*, "the terebinth") that is alluded to; the unique vocalization here (*hā'allâ*) may be a Masoretic effort to dissociate Joshua from that repository of heterodox cult objects. Despite the different vocalization, however, the mention of the familiar tree connects Joshua not just with Moses but also with ancestral tradition. **27.** *a witness:* Cf. the similar use of stones in Jacob's covenant with Laban (Gen 31:44-53) and in the Sinai covenant ceremony (Exod 24:4), and of the altar in 22:34. **28-31.** With some changes, esp. in order (followed here by the LXX), these verses duplicate Judg 2:6-9.

90   (D) Final Notes (24:29-33). A group of three brief burial notices conclude both the Joshua story and the larger narrative.

(a) JOSHUA'S DEATH AND BURIAL (24:29-31). There is an expanded, and probably derivative, version in Judg 2:6-10. Just as Deut ends with the death and burial of Moses, along with a summary statement of his career, so now Josh ends in an analogous way. **29.** *Yahweh's servant:* Moses' title is finally, and fittingly, applied to Joshua. *one hundred and ten years old:* The same life-span as Joseph (Gen 50:26). **31.** Cf. Deut 11:7. The theology is typically deuteronomic, and ironic: the Israelites who had not personally experienced Yahweh's actions would have difficulty in observing the teaching of Moses.

(b) JOSEPH'S REBURIAL (24:32). The notice resumes Gen 33:19. Gen 50:25 suggests that Joseph's body was mummified in Egyptian fashion (cf. Gen 50:2-3), but Exod 13:19 and this verse mention only his bones. The Hebr word *qĕśîṭâ*, usually vaguely translated "money," occurs only in Gen 33:19; Job 42:11; its meaning and value are unknown.

(c) ELEAZAR'S DEATH AND BURIAL (24:33). Eleazar the priest, already linked with Joshua (see at 14:1), is also buried in Ephraim. *Gibeah-phinehas:* Lit., "the hill of Phinehas," but almost certainly a toponym; cf. Gibeath-saul (1 Sam 11:4; etc.).

8

JUDGES

M. O'Connor

BIBLIOGRAPHY

1 Boling, R. G., *Judges* (AB 6A; GC, 1975). Burney, C. F., *The Book of Judges* (2d ed.; London, 1918). Gaster, T. H., *Myth, Legend, and Custom in the Old Testament* (NY, 1969). Gottwald, N. K., *The Tribes of Yahweh* (Maryknoll, 1979). Gray, J., *Joshua, Judges, Ruth* (NCB; 1986). Martin, J. D., *Judges* (CBC; Cambridge, 1975). Mayes, A. D. H., *Judges* (Sheffield, 1985). Mendenhall, G. E., *The Tenth Generation* (Baltimore, 1973). Moore, G. F., *Judges* (ICC; Edinburgh, 1895). O'Connor, M.,

"The Women in the Book of Judges," *HAR* 10 (1987) 277–93. Polzin, R., *Moses and the Deuteronomist* (NY, 1980). Revell, E. J., "The Battle with Benjamin (Judges xx 29–48) and Hebrew Narrative Techniques," *VT* 35 (1985) 417–33. Richter, W., *Die Bearbeitungen des "Retterbuches" in der deuteronomischen Epoche* (BBB 21; Bonn, 1964). Soggin, J. A., *Judges* (OTL; Phl, 1981). Trible, P., *Texts of Terror* (Phl, 1984). De Vaux, R., *EHI* 683–94.

INTRODUCTION

2 **(I) The Book.** Judg is one of several books concerned with the era between the death of Joshua and the rise of Saul. With Joshua's passing, the age dominated by Moses enters its decline; with Saul's rise, the age of David and the kings begins to take shape. In the dominant view of biblical history, this transition is a period of danger and uncertainty, and the experience of Israel in this period is liminal, an experience on a threshold (Lat *limen*) or border. The human paradigm of living on the threshold is puberty, and the rites of puberty are designed to prepare children for the dangers they will confront as adults, to help them cross the threshold. Rites of passage are social acknowledgments of liminality.

The book of Judg is a literary and historiographic view of liminality. It asks: How did Israel live without a great leader? And it answers: It lived, though not always well. The boundaries and thresholds that are of greatest concern are political and social. How does Israel live with marauding neighbors like the Philistines to the W or the Midianites to the S (chaps. 2–3, 6–16)? How do the followers of the old ways, the Canaanite city-dwellers, react to Israel and its innovations (chaps. 1, 4–5)? And how do groups of Israelites interact, tribe with tribe, clan with clan, village with village, region with region (chaps. 17–21)? These are the great questions that shape the narrative.

These questions are not confronted directly but through a shifting array of imaginative glosses on the image of boundary. Some of these glosses are simple.

The tent flap where Jael stands (4:20) and the window from which Sisera's mother watches (5:28) each separate the domestic and private sphere from the public world. The purest emblem of the threshold and its danger comes in the story of the Levite's concubine. The hospitality requisite to peaceful life had been ruptured (19:23; cf. 4:21; 5:26). After a night of rape and abuse, the nameless woman has crawled to the place where her husband is staying: "her hands were on the threshold" (19:27). This pivotal story is a preface to the disastrous civil war with which the book ends. In this story we can see other liminal figures: the Levite, from the only Israelite tribe which has no inheritance of land; the Ephraimite host who lives as a sojourner (19:16) among the Benjaminites; and the woman. No book of the Bible treats the role of women in society as intensively as Judg, save for Ruth, the events of which are dated to the same era (Ruth 1:1). Also in the story of the Levite's concubine we see the life and death boundary, evoked elsewhere by the extreme thirst of Sisera and Samson (4:19; 15:18), as well as by the cases of carrion contagion in the Samson saga.

The most important threshold (in the view of biblical history found in Judg) is the one that separates people from God, Israel from Yahweh. Moses is the exemplar of figures at this threshold; there is a fitting emphasis in the great stories of Exod 33–34 on the borders of the camp as the locus of divine encounter (Exod 33:7), on tent thresholds (33:8), and on God's hand screening Moses from God (33:22) and a veil screening Moses from Israel (34:35). On one side of this threshold, nearer to God, are various communicative agents, chiefly divine messengers or angels; the angels of Bochim (Judg 2:1), Gideon (6:11–24), Manoah and his wife (13:2–23), and the curser of Meroz (5:23; cf. Josh 5:13–15) are narrative explorations of the way Yahweh speaks to Israel. (The divine messengers are usually solitary; human messengers, in Judg as elsewhere in the Hebrew Bible, are plural; see 6:35; 7:24; 8:31; 11:12–19.) Signs of divine authentication, sought (6:36–40) and unsought (13:19; cf. the fire in Exod 3:2), are offered in the Gideon and Manoah stories. Another agent is an anonymous prophet (6:7–10; cf. 10:11–15). Related to the angels are manifestations of the Yahweh spirit. It descends on (3:10; 11:29), clothes (6:34), moves (13:25), or springs on (14:6,19; 15:14) several participants (cf. also 8:23; 14:4; 15:19). The dream oracle (7:13) is another communication device; a more remote channel is the lot or lottery used in the opening and closing chapters (1:2; 20:18, both for Judah).

On the other side of the divine/human threshold, nearer to Israel, are various leaders known as šōpĕṭîm, the term traditionally rendered "judges." These dozen saviors of this or that tribe or groups of tribes—these are the crucial interface between Yahweh and the people; these individuals enact the divine will and effectuate the divine plan. Deborah is a triply liminal figure, as woman, as prophet, and as judge, and the record of her days is a major episode. The middle of the book is taken up with the story of Abimelech, the anti-judge who tries illegitimately to force the transition to monarchy. The two latest judges (on a strictly historical view) are not included: Eli and Samuel are treated in 1 Sam 1–12, the preface to the monarchy. Like Ruth, the opening of 1 Sam treats the same period as Judg, but with a specialized thematic focus. The judge has failed as a type of leader for Israel (the pan-Israelite character of the judges reflects the intended comparison with the kings), and the monarchy to be initiated reluctantly by Samuel offers another type of leader, a king, of the sort found in neighboring nations. The refrain of the concluding chapters, "There was no king in Israel," looks forward to the monarchy (17:6; 18:1; 19:1; 21:25), as do Gideon's refusal and Abimelech's seizure of kingly rank, in the core section of the book. (On Joshua as a royal figure, → Joshua, 7:5).

The threshold of greatest historical interest to the writers and compilers of Judg is the Moses/monarchy threshold. Not all biblical historians saw importance in this threshold. The Chronicler, writing in the 5th cent. BC, begins the history of Israel with a brief glance at Saul (1 Chr 10) and goes on to David, showing no interest in the judges. The biblical historians who recognized the importance of the judges and put this book about them in final form were working at an earlier time, in the 6th cent. during the Babylonian Captivity. The Josianic reform, which had failed to avert the national catastrophe of 587, was an important and vivid memory (2 Kgs 23:22). The exilic editors, however, were neither the first nor the last to participate in shaping the canonical book; the liminal concerns of a variety of storytellers and scholars have formed the complex and exciting narrative.

3   **(II) The Materials of the Book.** Judg (like Gen, Exod, Num, Deut, and 1 and 2 Sam) includes a small amount of verse in a largely prose context. The prose is rich and repetitive and therefore liable to damage in transmission. The various Old Gk transls. (here cited collectively as LXX, despite their considerable diversity) provide basic data toward restoring and righting the text; the other ancient versions and, to a slight degree, the Qumran scrolls also assist in that labor (see Boling, *Judges* 38–42).

Some of the prose is of a piece with that of Deut and other parts of Dtr (Josh–2 Kgs), but much of it is not, representing more appealing and less didactic modes of storytelling. The story of Eglon (chap. 3) is vivid in its caricature of the fat king who is bested by the crafty Israelite. The threefold repetition found in fairy tales and folktales is used in Jotham's fable (9:8,10,12), Delilah's begging (16:6,10,13), and the Bethlehemite's pleading (19:5,8,9). The dialogue, as in 1 Sam, often shows linguistic features that set it off from the embedding prose narrative, though these can rarely be reflected in translation.

A number of passages are etiological stories, devoted to explaining the origin of place-names (1:17; cf. Num 21:1–3; Judg 2:5; 6:24; 15:17,19; 18:12) or, in one case, a festival (11:39–40). Two of the place-name explanations make the characteristic claim that the place is so called "to this day" (6:24; 18:12). Older generations of scholars tended to think of these stories as having been preserved strictly for their explanatory function, but that view is now regarded as an exaggeration.

The prose stories share not only the historiographic and literary concerns mentioned; they share, too, a focus on divine action in the human world. The judges or šōpēṭ-leaders, when they are said to be "raised up" by Yahweh, are thereby associated with the action of the deity, though in a sociopolitical sense. The Gideon story, combining divine revelation with judgeship, is the richest of the major cycles in the book.

4   There are only two bodies of verse: in chaps. 5 and 14–15. The spectacular and difficult Song of Deborah (106 lines) is usually regarded as the oldest part of the Bible, and there is reason to regard the eight lines of verse in the Samson story as antique (14:14,18; 15:16). Certain other passages sometimes treated as verse are in fact rhythmical prose; the most important is Jotham's fable (9:8–15), ideologically old but linguistically much of a piece with the surrounding text. Other such pieces include 1:14–15 and 6:3,8–9, as well as 16:23–24. (Boling treats all five of these as verse; O. Loretz [*UF* 7 (1975) 594–95] takes all except the last as prose.)

The combination of prose and verse accounts in chaps. 4 and 5 (as in Exod 14–15 and Gen 34; 49:5–7) provides a stereoscopic view of events. Such a double vision shapes other features of the book. The alternation of long and short records of individual judges provides a pattern of contrast. The marriage patterns of Ibzan's children (12:9) define and set off the marriage aberrations of Samson (14–16), Ibzan a token of ordinary life and Samson of extraordinary life. A pair of stereopticons is provided by the double prologue (1:1–2:5 vs. 2:6–3:6) and the double epilogue (chaps. 17–18 vs. 19–21). In two important cases our vision is enriched by stories in Gen. The sexual outrages of Sodom (Gen 19) and Gibeah (Judg 19) are offered as a pair by the Bible; the stories quote each other at every level and are manifestly interdependent, differing most crucially in their resolutions—catastrophe in the natural world (Sodom) and in the civil order (Gibeah). The sacrifice stories of Isaac and Jephthah's daughter, though similar, are not connected directly in the biblical text, though early postbiblical commentators associate them.

5   The personal names deserve special notice. Many Hebr names are linguistically transparent, i.e., comprehensible as words (cf. Eng "Smith" or "Charity"), phrases, or sentences. Such names can be used to enliven a text, though such use usually involves understanding the names outside their proper religious context; many names seem to be so used in Judg. Names with the element bārāq refer at base to the deity (cf. Amorite yabruq-ilu, "God shines *or* flashes lightning"), but for the hero Baraq (4:1), the name may be taken to refer to him, as "Lightning," or to his role in a battle involving a torrential rainstorm. Jephthah's name, a shortening of Jiptahel (Josh 19:14), means "[God] opens [the womb]," but in the story may stand as "[He, Jephthah himself] opens [the way to freedom]." A pun may be found in Jotham's name, which means "Yahweh [yô-] is perfect [tām]," but is here applied to a yātôm, "fatherless child, orphan."

6 (III) The Composition of the Book. Scholars discern three stages. (A) The core is the savior collection (*Retterbuch*), which included at first only the stories of Ehud, Deborah, and Gideon; this, like all subsequent versions of the book to some extent, was an exemplary collection (cf. the testing motif in 3:1–2). A comprehensive review of all judges was not in view; note simply the "lost" judge Bedan, mentioned only in passing in 1 Sam 12:11. The Othniel section was written as a kind of abstract or summary, and the Abimelech material was added. The five judges treated briefly (10:1–5; 12:8–15) were next added, along with the Jephthah material; and perhaps eventually all or most of the Samson stories were attached. The schematic geography of the final form was evident in this latest predeuteronomistic work. There is no more than one judge specified per tribe, and the enemies move from the N (Aram, 3:8), to the SE (Moab, 3:12) to the N again (Hazor, 4:2), then S (Midian, 6:1) and E (Ammon, 10:7), and finally to the W (Philistines, 13:1).

7 (B) The redactors of Dtr (Josh–2 Kgs) in the late 7th cent. added a prologue (2:6–3:6, esp. 2:11–19) and wrote or reshaped various bridge sections (3:7–10; 10:6–16; 13:1; 15:20; 16:31?), introducing, concluding, and drawing together the judges. The schematic and generally inflated chronology (probably pegged to 1 Kgs 6 and calculated backward from it) is also deuteronomistic (see Richter, *Retterbuches* 132–41; de Vaux, *EHI* 689–92); the four and a half centuries of the book's supposed action must actually correspond to a historical span of well under two centuries. The exilic deuteronomistic editors, working in a situation much changed from that of their predecessors, reshaped many passages in the history as a whole but did little to Judg (note 18:30).

(C) Postdeuteronomistic scholars added the first introduction to the book (1:1–2:5), which breaks the flow from Josh 24:28 to Judg 2:6, and the epilogues, chaps. 17–21, which interrupt the sequence from Judg 16:31 (Samson) to 1 Sam 1:1 (Eli, the next judge). This added material may be preexilic in origin and in fact quite ancient. It is because they fall outside the chronological sweep of Dtr that scholars refer to chaps. 17–21 (and sometimes 16) as "appendixes." These additions give the book its overall "unchronologized" shape. The location of Dan, for example, is first S (1:34), then N (5:17), again S (13:25; 18:2), then again N (18:28); it is generally thought that Dan was in fact initially southern and then migrated north. On Dtr, see M. Noth, *The Deuteronomistic History* (JSOTSup 15; Sheffield, 1981); F. M. Cross, *CMHE* 274–89; R. E. Friedman, *The Exile and Biblical Narrative* (HSM 22; Chico, 1981); Gottwald, *Tribes* 142–75.

8 (IV) The Historical and Social Setting. Josh and Judg are a major source for the reconstruction of the period between 1200 and 1050. Other sources include geographical study (→ Biblical Geography, 73:70–81), archaeological remains of the first half of the Iron I period (→ Biblical Archaeology, 74:94–111), and archaeologically inspired reconsiderations of basic geographical data (see, e.g., C. L. Meyers, *BASOR* 252 [1983] 47–59).

The major events of contemporary Palestine and Transjordan were reactions to the calamities of the Late Bronze Age; in the biblical view, the major happening was the establishment of Israel as a people ('am, 2:6,7; 5:11; 14:3; 20:2, etc.) or nation (gôy, 2:20). Josh presents the happening as a largely military event, whereas Judg 1 sees it as a slower and more complex process. The opposition between these views has been exaggerated; as noted above (→ 5), the first introduction falls outside the chronological framework of earlier editions of the book, and so its historical claims are hard to specify. The rest of Judg presents a view of Israel as a federation, an association of tribes with no ongoing central authority; interim leadership was afforded by the judges. (Efforts to associate this federation with archaic Greek amphictyonies or leagues have largely been discredited; see A. D. H. Mayes, in *IJH* 297–308; *Judges* 56–62.) The stories tell of judges leading a tribe or group of tribes; the largest group is in the Song of Deborah and includes apparently all the northern tribes but not Judah or Simeon. The editorial framework has expanded the scope of the judges' activities to all of Israel.

The social system implicit in Judges has most profitably been studied in the context of other preindustrialized social structures; early Israel was a largely agricultural and nonurban group, a peasant population. Tribal and similar structures (called by anthropologists "segmentary structures") reflect a variety of circumstances, including locale and ideology alongside kinship. The leaders that arise in such systems are temporary, and their service is based not on inherited position (as a king's is) nor on permanent structures (such as election in an oligarchy or democracy), though there has been a tendency to regard "minor judges" as officeholders (see below). Max Weber (1864–1920), the German social scientist, called the basis for such leadership "charisma," after the NT term for divine gift. Over the last several decades the notion of charismatic leadership has been vulgarized to notions of charm or popularity; nonetheless, the view of judges as charismatic leaders does reflect something of the biblical writers' view. Israel's shift away from a segmented society was prompted by a number of factors, though the biblical historians refer most often to the external pressure of the Philistines. There followed stages of a chieftainship (under Saul and David), a fully central state (under David), and an empire (under Solomon).

9 Two points of literary importance sometimes obscure the historical study: (1) The deuteronomistic cycles of sin–trouble–salvation, etc. are often dismissed as entirely artificial. Though the insistence on sin reflects a theologized view of history, the cyclic understanding is not therefore to be rejected: "The context of this framework is not necessarily [simply] the expression of a later ideological concept.... It possibly, and even probably, contains authentic reflections and preserved elements of ancient historical reality" (Malamat, "Charismatic" 155). (2) Some figures are treated at length and others quite briefly. From this diversity scholars have tried to extrapolate the notion of two classes of judges: major (charismatic leaders; military leaders) and minor (juridical leaders; elected officers). One scholar writes: "[There] are essentially two different forms of literary record and two different types of individual" (Mayes, *Judges* 17). In fact, the extrapolation from two types of *records* to two types of *people* is illegitimate (see Boling, *Judges* 7–9; E. T. Mullen, *CBQ* 44 [1982] 185–201), as is strongly suggested by the widespread disagreement about who the minor judges are. All scholars include the five judges of 10:1–5 and 12:8–15, but many add, for a variety of reasons, Jephthah, Othniel, Shamgar, or

Samson, or some combination of these. In fact, the major/minor split is not historically useful.

(On social structure in general: Flanagan, J. W., "Chiefs in Israel," *JSOT* 20 [1981] 47–73. Frick, F. S., *The Formation of the State in Ancient Israel* [Sheffield, 1985]. Gottwald, *Tribes;* "Two Models for the Origins of Ancient Israel," *The Quest for the Kingdom of God* [Fest. G. E. Mendenhall; ed. H. B. Huffmon, et al.; Winona Lake, 1983] 5–24. Herion, G. A., "The Impact of Modern and Social Science Assumptions on the Reconstruction of Israelite History," *JSOT* 34 [1986] 3–33. Lemche, N. P., *Early Israel* [VTSup 37; Leiden, 1985]. Lindars, B., "The Israelite tribes in Judges," *Studies in the Historical Books of the Old Testament* [VTSup 30; Leiden, 1979] 95–112. Malamat, A., "Charismatic Leadership in the Book of Judges," *Magnalia Dei* [Fest. G. E. Wright; ed. F. M. Cross, et al.; GC, 1976] 152–68. Mayes, A. D. H., *Israel in the Period of the Judges* [London, 1974]. Mendenhall, G. E., "Social Organization in Early Israel," *Magnalia Dei* 132–51; "Government, Israelite," *IDBSup* 372–74. On minor/major judges: Mullen, E. T., *CBQ* 44 [1982] 185–201. Rösel, H. N., *Bib* 61 [1980] 251–55; *BZ* 25 [1981] 180–203. Soggin, J. A., *VT* 30 [1980] 245–48. De Vaux, *EHI* 684, 751–74.)

10   Key terms are those from the root *šāpaṭ*, which means not "to judge" in the usual restricted sense of exercising juridical authority, but "to rule." The *šāpiṭum* at Mari and the *suffete* at Carthage were, like the Israelite *šōpēṭ*, rulers, exercising a wide variety of civil duties (including judicial functions). The Mari *šiptum* is an administrative edict or decision, as is Deborah's *mišpāṭ* summoning Baraq to war (4:5; contrast Samuel in 1 Sam 7:15–17). Ugaritic *tpt* means both "to rule" and "to decide (a case)." The *šāpaṭ* vocabulary "refers not to a judicial act of an officer in a court of law, but to an authoritative administrative edict of a person who exercises" social control with which she or he has been charged "by competent political or social authority" (Mendenhall, *Tenth Generation* 76).

The noun *šōpēṭ* is only used in the plural of people, in the introductory passage 2:16–19. A number of individuals are said to have "judged" Israel (Othniel, 3:10; Deborah, 4:5; Tola, 10:2; Jair, 10:2; Jephthah, 12:7; Ibzan, 12:8,9; Elon, 12:11; Abdon, 12:13,14; Samson, 15:20; 16:31). Both verb and noun are used in Jephthah's appeal to the Ammonite king. The other *šāpaṭ* word is *mišpāṭ*, which can refer to an administrative edict (4:5, with Revell; render thus, "The Israelites came up to her for a ruling, and so she summoned Baraq . . ."). In two other passages, *mišpāṭ* is often taken to refer to manner of life; in 13:12, it refers to the edict that governs the special child's way of life (it comes from Yahweh, though Manoah does not realize that when he inquires about it), and in 18:7 it describes certain northerners as living in the Sidonian manner or according to a Sidonian edict.

The question arises of whether "judge" should be maintained as a transl., given how manifestly misleading it is. Only one of the major modern Eng versions has dropped the term: *NJV* uses "chieftain" for *šōpēṭ*-leader and "to lead" for the verb forms (except in 3:10, "became chieftain," and in 11:27). See Cazelles, *Or* 53 (1984) 177–82.

11   **(V) Later Views of the Judges.**   Within the traditions of the Hebrew Bible the judges are of no importance outside the Former Prophets. Reflecting the canon's interest in them, both Sir 46:11–12 and Heb 11:32–34 praise them, with little attention to detail. The judges most celebrated in later tradition were Samson, as readily assimilated to Hercules as David was to Orpheus; Jephthah, because of his vow; and Deborah. As a christological figure, Samson outshone the other judges; in Gideon's dew and Samson's honeycomb Marian images were found.

The Scottish Protestant humanist and Neo-Latinist George Buchanan (1506–1582) wrote *Iephthes* (1545?), one of the earliest Renaissance tragedies, reshaping the Jephthah story around Euripides' *Iphigenia in Aulis* and naming the daughter Iphis. Shakespeare quotes a ballad about Jephthah's daughter in *Hamlet* (2.2.422–39). Buchanan's work influenced George Frederick Handel's oratorio *Jephthah* (1752). There are also oratorios by Handel on *Deborah* (1739, a work rarely performed), *Samson* (1743) and *Gideon* (1769). The greatest postbiblical treatment of any of the judges is John Milton's poem on the judge who sat "Eyeless in Gaza," *Samson Agonistes* (1671).

12   **(VI) Outline.**

(I) Prologues (1:1–3:6)
  (A) Argument (1:1–2:5)
    (a) Three Southern Tribes (1:1–21)
    (b) Six Northern Tribes (1:22–36)
    (c) Divine Rebuke (2:1–5)
  (B) Preface (2:6–3:6)
    (a) New Generation (2:6–10)
    (b) Apostasy (2:11–23)
    (c) Temptations (3:1–6)
(II) Othniel–Abimelech (3:7–9:57)
  (A) Othniel (3:7–11)
  (B) Ehud (3:12–30)
  (C) Shamgar (3:31)
  (D) Deborah and Baraq (4:1–24)
  (E) Deborah's Song (5:1–31)
  (F) Gideon's Call (6:1–40)
  (G) Gideon's Victory (7:1–22)
  (H) Gideon's Supporters (7:23–8:3)
  (I) Gideon's Critics (8:4–21)
  (J) Gideon's Ephod (8:22–28)
  (K) Gideon's Family (8:29–35)
  (L) Abimelech (9:1–57)
(III) Tola–Samson (10:1–16:31)
  (A) Tola and Jair (10:1–5)
  (B) Jephthah's Enemies (10:6–18)
  (C) Jephthah's Call (11:1–11)
  (D) Jephthah's Victory (11:12–33)
  (E) Jephthah's Daughter (11:34–40)
  (F) Jephthah's Critics (12:1–7)
  (G) Ibzan, Elon, and Abdon (12:8–15)
  (H) Samson's Birth (13:1–25)
  (I) Samson's Marriage (14:1–15:8)
  (J) Samson's Rampage (15:9–20)
  (K) Samson's Loves (16:1–22)
  (L) Samson's Death (16:23–31)
(IV) Epilogues (17:1–21:25)
  (A) Dan and Micah (17:1–18:31)
    (a) Micah's Shrine (17:1–13)
    (b) Dan's Migration (18:1–31)
  (B) From Gibeah to Shiloh (19:1–21:25)
    (a) Outrage at Gibeah (19:1–30)
    (b) Assembly at Mizpah (20:1–48)
    (c) Rape at Jabesh-gilead and at Shiloh (21:1–25)

COMMENTARY

13   **(I) Prologues (1:1–3:6).**
    (A) Argument (1:1–2:5).   The historical perspective is vast. These verses stand at the head of the book as an argument to it, summarizing the social and political situation implicit in it. The summary is cast in terms familiar from the Pentateuch and Joshua: Yahweh, having commissioned Israel to establish hegemony over a broad territory, is angry at Israel's failure to do so and

predicts dire social consequences.

14 (a) THREE SOUTHERN TRIBES (1:1-21). Judah and Simeon, tribes presented in the guise of brothers, engage natives of southern territory militarily, with some failures and some successes; one source of failure is identified—superior military hardware in the hands of enemies (1:19; cf. Josh 11:9; 17:16)—and some consequences of success are noted—the humbling of a petty monarch (1:6), the apportioning of territory to family groups (a process requiring both heroism [1:13] and bargaining [1:15]). Benjamin, the southernmost northerner, appears here in connection with Jerusalem, eventually the premier city of Judah.

1. Josh opens "after Moses' death" (Josh 1:1), and Judg opens "after Joshua's death," with Israel at Gilgal (Josh 14:6) or Shiloh (Josh 18:5). **2.** The choice of Judah to act first is made both here and in 20:18, in the last military action in the book. **5.** Cf. Josh 10:1. **6.** The king is mutilated not gratuitously but to render him incapable of further combat (cf. Gaster, *Myth, Legend, and Custom* 416). **7.** The king's statement involves the historical rule currently formulated as "What goes around comes around." There is no claim of *absolute* predictability here and no *direct* relationship between victims and agents: "According to what I did has God handled me." **7-8.** The Judahites captured Jerusalem and burned it down, according to this passage, in contrast to Josh 15:63, which claims that they did not dispossess the Jebusites (i.e., the Jerusalemites); in 1:21 the Benjaminites did not dispossess the Jebusites, a view supported by Josh 18:28, which attributes Jerusalem to Benjamin. The predominant historical view is that David captured Jerusalem (2 Sam 5:6-9). Jerusalem is not an Israelite city in its only other appearance in Judg (19:10). **12-15.** The same material is found in Josh 13-19. The donation to Caleb is also cited in Judg 1:20 (cf. Josh 14:6). Othniel's exploits as a judge (Judg 3:9-11) are not mentioned here. **13.** Marriage of first cousins is not only licit but favored in the Near East throughout history, though the term "brother" may mean "ally." **16.** The Kenite ("Smith" or "Tinker") settlement plays an important role later in Judg (4:11,17-22). **17.** Hormah ("Bantown," Boling, *Judges*). The ban (*ḥrm*) is a major subject of Josh; in Judg it is mentioned only here and in the last chapter (21:11). **18.** The Philistine cities were objects of David's attention (2 Sam 5:17-25; 8:1). **19.** This verse begins one accounting of the problem of Canaanites in the land, an accounting based on military failure. Ideological failure is cited in 2:2, whereas Josh refers to diplomatic failure (Josh 9) and social integration (Josh 2). **20.** Cf. v 10. **21.** Paralleled in Josh 15:63; cf. above on vv 7-8.

15 (b) SIX NORTHERN TRIBES (1:22-36). A catalogue of failures by most of the N tribes is preceded by a success story of Josephites seeking military intelligence and behaving responsibly toward the man who provides it, a counterpart to Rahab of Jericho (Josh 2:1-21; 6:17, 23,25; see Gottwald, *Tribes* 559-61).

22. The House of Joseph is treated only in this section; elsewhere various Josephite groups (Ephraim, Manasseh, and Machir) are separate units. **23.** *Bethel:* Cf. Josh 18:22; Judg 20:26; 21:2. **27-28.** The Manassite inheritance is similarly treated in Josh 17:11-13; the great cities of the N became Israelite during the united monarchy (1 Kgs 9:15-22). At Beth-shean, Saul's corpse was exhibited (1 Sam 31:10-11). **29.** The Ephraimite inheritance is similarly treated in Josh 16:10. **31.** Cf. 10:6; 18:7,28. **34-35.** The Amorite resistance to Dan is treated in Josh 19:47.

16 (c) DIVINE REBUKE (2:1-5). The divine messenger appears at Bochim ("Weepers") to summarize the Mosaic dispensation so far: Israel has failed to do as

Yahweh ordered and will in consequence suffer. Though couched as a rebuke, the message has the force of a prediction.

1. The divine messenger is treated as equivalent to Yahweh (cf. Gen 16:7); it moves from Gilgal (Joshua's base from Josh 4:19 to 10:43 [cf. 14:6]; one of Samuel's stations, 1 Sam 7:15) to Bochim, an unknown place.

17 (B) Preface (2:6-3:6). The narrative progress begins here, and thus the death of Joshua, implicit in 1:1, is again cited. The generational process described here is familiar from Sam and Kgs: the good leader dies and the apostasy away from which he led Israel is allowed again to fester. The good leaders, in this period called *šōpĕṭîm*, "judges," are Yahweh's creation; the apostasy is Israel's contribution. Cf. T. E. Fretheim, *Deuteronomic History* (Nash, 1983) 87-98.

18 (a) NEW GENERATION (2:6-10). The emphasis on the leader, here as elsewhere in the Bible, is muted by a balancing emphasis on the men and women from among whom the leader emerges; they at least implicitly aid and sustain the leader. Joshua had no private revelation; in the long run what he saw, those around him also saw. The great deeds of Yahweh are neglected when Joshua's generation dies off.

6,8-9. This material overlaps with the conclusion of Josh (24:28-30), an arrangement that reflects the continuity of the story; compare, e.g., 2 Chr 36:22-23 and Ezra 1:1-3. The hill country of Ephraim is mentioned in the Ehud and Deborah stories (3:27; 4:5), **10.** Death involves being gathered to one's people in the usual idiom; the phrase "to one's forebears" is unique. The verb "to gather" (*'āsap*) is used of death in a nonidiomatic threat in 18:25 (cf. the note on 19:15). The ascendancy of the "new generation . . . which did not know Yahweh" is a preface to the coming phase of history; cf. Exod 1:8. The vb. "to know" refers to the kind of acquaintance that leads to and sustains covenant relations.

19 (b) APOSTASY (2:11-23). The sum and substance of Moses' great sermon in Deut is the identification which tradition makes possible: "Yahweh our God made *with us* a covenant at Horeb" (Deut 5:2-3). Such identification failed in the generation after Joshua, and the ethic and ideology of Moses were rejected, except when *šōpĕṭ*-leaders were able, however briefly, to reinstate them.

11. The objects of apostasy are the Baals (v 11; 10:10), "other gods" (vv 12,17,19), "(some) of the gods of the peoples who were around" Israel (v 12), "Baal and the Astartes" (v 13). Baal was the storm-god of the Levant, a major deity and probably the most powerful; the term Baals refers to local manifestations of him or other similar male deities. The worship of Baal seems to have been part of the Israelite scene from Joshua down to the exile, and, at least during the reign of Ahab, Baal was recognized as the supreme deity of Israel, i.e., the northern kingdom (1 Kgs 16:31-32; cf. 18:21). Baal is a principal figure in the Ugaritic texts (*ANET* 129-42) and in various 1st-millennium inscriptions. Astarte (the name is cognate to Ishtar) is a Canaanite female deity; the combination "Baals and Astartes" is found in 10:6; 1 Sam 7:3-4; 12:10; cf. 1 Kgs 11:5. Astarte, too, figures in texts in Ugaritic and other languages related to Hebrew. The illicit worship is referred to here and often as "whoring" (*zānâ*), but most modern statements that aim to explain the fertility cult as an orgiastic nature religion find little support in extrabiblical texts and in fact reflect the beliefs of the biblical writers and literalize their rhetoric. Two points are important: (1) the orthodox Yahweh doctrine involves a single deity who is not primarily understood as sexual; (2) the orthodox doctrine is not centrally concerned with agricultural fertility and other features of economic life. There is evidence to indicate that the biblical writers recognize only the orthodox cult and the Baal cult, grouping as Baal worship much that a modern scholar might call heterodox Yahwism. **15.** The vocabulary of oppression is chiefly concerned with straitening or narrowing, i.e., squeezing (*ṣûr*, "to confine" [2:15; 9:31; 10:9; 11:7; 16:16]; *ṣûq*, "to narrow" [14:17; 16:16]; *lāḥaṣ*, "to press" [1:34; 2:18; 4:3; 6:9; 10:12]). **16.** Here and in v 18 the activity of being a *šōpēṭ*-leader and that of saving are linked. **18.** As a complement to the squeezing image, the enemies are here (and elsewhere in the book) represented as insects, those who "beat against them"; in Joel 2:8 the vb. is used of locusts (cf. 6:5). **21–22.** The ultimate explanation of the persistence of non-Israelite peoples in Israelite territory.

20 (c) TEMPTATIONS (3:1–6). The failure of identification with the Mosaic group has many explanations, but religious intermarriage is here singled out as focal. The biblical view has it that the demands of marriage take priority over other demands; here the spouse's ideology is able to blot out the Yahwistic ideology learned at home (cf. the fourth commandment, Exod 20:12 = Deut 5:16).

21 (II) Othniel–Abimelech (3:7–9:57). The initial group of judges forms a crescendo: after three short accounts (Othniel, Ehud, Shamgar) comes one two-chapter block of material (Deborah) and one four-chapter block (Gideon). The first four of these *šōpēṭ*-leaders successfully carry out their duties. Gideon, the fifth, after initial triumphs, apostatizes, and the severity of his defection is magnified in the following generation by his son Abimelech. The story of this first Israelite king is a foretaste of the disasters narrated in the epilogues (17:1–21:25).

22 (A) Othniel (3:7–11). The stories of the first three judges have a rhythm of their own: the short narratives of Othniel and Shamgar frame the longer passage about Ehud. Othniel first appears as the hero of Kiriath-sepher (1:12–15) and returns as the *šōpēṭ*-leader who successfully opposes Cushan-Double-Trouble, the risibly named Aramean king.

7. The object of illicit worship in Israel is usually called the Baals (→ 19 above); here the Israelites worship also the Asherahs; Asherah was a West Semitic goddess associated with Baal in the Ugaritic texts and with Yahweh in some 1st-millennium inscriptions. The goddess is mentioned elsewhere (1 Kgs 15:13 = 2 Chr 15:16; 1 Kgs 18:19; 2 Kgs 21:7; 23:4). See J. Day, *JBL* 105 (1986) 385–408, esp. 387–94; M. O'Connor, *VT* 37 (1987) 224–30. **8.** *Cushan-rishathaim:* Lit., "Cushan-of-the-Two-Troubles." Aram-naharaim ("Aram-of-the-Two-Rivers") is a region of the E part of modern Syria (*RSV:* "Mesopotamia"), unlikely to have been directly involved with Palestine in the Iron I period; it may be that another place-name should be read. **9.** *Savior* (*môšîaʿ*) is the term also applied to Ehud (3:15). **10.** The Yahweh spirit is said to be upon (ʿ*al*) Othniel.

23 (B) Ehud (3:12–30). The thoroughly ridiculous Eglon follows Cushan-Double-Trouble. The basic events here foreshadow those of 4:18–21: in both cases a clever Israelite sympathizer (Ehud, Jael) is able to assassinate an enemy leader (Eglon, Sisera) who has enormous material resources (Eglon's palace, Sisera's chariotry); the Israelite uses simple instruments (Ehud's dagger, Jael's tent peg) and "natural" qualities (Ehud's left-handedness, Jael's confinement as a woman). Political assassination is an effective tool here, but it is an uncertain element in foreign policy generally, as later Israelite history reveals.

15. Ehud is ʾîš ʾiṭṭēr yad-yĕmînô, "a man bound as to his right hand"; this phrase is almost universally taken to mean "a left-handed man," which, in view of the sequel, is probably correct, but the phrase itself is not clear. **16.** The short sword or dagger is worn on the right thigh on the assumption that only the left would be searched. **17.** The word *bārîʾ* and related words more often refer to fat or fattened animals than people; Eglon's name may be taken as "Calf." **20–24.** The architectural and other technical terms are difficult, though the main actions are not in doubt. King and assailant are alone together. Ehud "claps" or "drives" the sword into Eglon's belly (the verb *tāqaʿ* is used often in Judg of action with a weapon as well as with a ram's horn; see 3:27). **23–24.** Ehud goes out and closes the king in, leading the servants to think that he is "covering his feet," a double euphemism for "uncovering his private parts." **27.** The ram's horn is central to the battle of Jericho in Joshua (Josh 6) and to Gideon's attack on the Midianites (Judg 7). **28.** The Jordan fords are also the scene of 12:1–6, the Shibboleth story.

24 (C) Shamgar (3:31). The Philistines make their first appearance here, probably anachronistically (as in 10:7); in the Samson cycle they are the major enemy. Shamgar (cf. 5:6) bears a foreign, perhaps Hurrian, name.

25 (D) Deborah and Baraq (4:1–24). Deborah is the only female judge, the first of the few women known in the Bible as prophets (Miriam, Exod 15:20; Huldah, 2 Kgs 22:14–20; Noadiah, Neh 6:14), and one of the three women with whom a poem is associated (cf. Miriam; Hannah in 1 Sam 2:1–10). As a prophet (J. S. Ackerman, *BASOR* 220 [1975] 5–13), she directs her aide-de-camp, Baraq, in a battle in which the army of the enemy general is defeated. True to her warning that a woman would triumph over Sisera, it is not Baraq but Jael who kills the general, using his sleep as a cover for her attack. The prose story in chap. 4 complements the much older verse account in chap. 5, as Exod 14 complements the Song of the Sea in Exod 15.

2. Jabin, the king of Canaan, ruling at Hazor, is mentioned in Josh 11:1 with various other kings and in Ps 83:11 with Sisera. He plays no direct role in Judg 4, appearing only offstage (4:2,17,23–24), and is not mentioned in Judg 5. **3.** Sisera has ample iron chariotry, reflecting greater wealth and technical sophistication. He was thereby able to squeeze (*lāḥaṣ*) Israel. **4.** Deborah's name—she shares it with Rebecca's nurse (Gen 35:8)—may mean "Leader"; she was both a prophet (guiding Israel with divine assistance) and a *šōpēṭ* (coordinating federation activities). **6–7.** The actions of Deborah and Baraq are made similar by the use of the same Hebr vb.: he is to *draw* together troops at Mt. Tabor (in the Jezreel Valley) while she *draws* Sisera to Wadi Kishon. **8–9.** Baraq refuses to fight alone, so Deborah agrees to go along, warning him that the glory of the battle will belong to a woman (she means herself, though in the upshot the glory is Jael's). **11.** The battle narrative is interrupted briefly, as the suspense of v 8 is elaborated. **15–16.** The strategy is simple: the Zebulonite and Naphtalite forces go into battle, and Yahweh throws the opposition so far off balance (here, as in Exod 14:24, *hāmam*) that Baraq's troops win. The source of the confusion is not mentioned here—in chap. 5 it is a torrential rain. **17.** Sisera escapes—the only enemy to do so—and strays to Heber's house. He thinks he will be safe in this house allied to Jabin. Jael welcomes him, gives him milk (or something more like yoghurt), and settles her family's intermediate political status with a tent peg. The peg (compare Ehud's dagger) enters the thin and flat part of the skull; the verb *tāqaʿ*, as in 3:21,27. **22.** Baraq is too late. On Judg 4–5, see D. F. Murray, in *Studies in the*

Historical Books of the Old Testament [VTSup 30; Leiden, 1979] 155–89; P. Weimar, *Bib* 57 (1976) 38–73.

26   (E) Deborah's Song (5:1–31). This poem of 106 lines is generally viewed as the most archaic part of the Hebrew Bible and, in keeping with its antiquity, it is among the most obscure Hebr poems. Words are unknown, and aspects of grammar are uncertain. It is, for instance, not clear whether Deborah is the speaker of the poem or the person to whom it is spoken. It is plain that a battle is narrated in which Yahweh defeats Israel's opponents by making it rain—the stars are the army, as the title Yahweh Sabaot, "Lord of (Heavenly) Hosts" reveals (perhaps originally the name meant "He creates hosts").

The Song is the glory of Hebr archaic poetry, combining its two great themes of Yahweh as cosmic ruler and Israel as tribal union. Yahweh is a god who has emerged from the barren steppe (v 4); Yahweh has revealed the ability to control water, first in the crossing of the Red Sea and the Jordan in Exod 15 (vv 4–10, 14–16) and here in the control of the heavens (*šāmayim*), which produce the waters (*mayim*) that flood the Wadi Kishon (v 21). Sisera's chariotry is overcome by water (v 22) as Pharaoh's had been at the Sea; Sisera's army is as befuddled as the Philistines and the Canaanites were upon hearing of Israel's entry into the land. Yahweh's control of the heavens was manifest at Gibeon (cf. the poem in Josh 10:12–13), but here it is magnificent: the stars fight by pouring water into a dry arroyo and making it burst. Yahweh's emergence from the area S of Palestine (vv 4–5) is treated in Moses' testament (Deut 33, cf. Ps 68:8–9) and prefaces that poem's tribal catalogue, itself of a piece with Jacob's testament (Gen 49). The tribal catalogue here (vv 13–18) is truncated and obscure, but the roll call of tribes is plain.

The Song is also the despair of archaic Hebr poetry: of the 106 lines, nearly half are in some way obscure, in doubt, or deviant. Only 7 of the 30 verses are free of problematic points of grammar or lexical obscurity (vv 12,19,20,24,28,30,31).

Despite this, the main argument of the poem is clear: it is about water and glory. Yahweh brings a flood that wipes out Israel's enemies, without allowing Israel any of the glory of defending itself. All the enemies die in the flood (v 21) save for Sisera, the chief, who asks for water and finds his life reduced to water poured out on the ground, absorbed in the dirt (vv 25–27); the reduction is accomplished not by an Israelite male but by a female not previously committed to Israel; Jael, too, keeps Israel from self-glorification and receives in response a blessing (v 24).

Blessings and curses are given. The curse falls on Meroz—so cursed that the place is unknown (v 23)—for its failure to support the army of Yahweh. A blessing is offered for Jael (v 24), most blessed of women, who voted for Israel with her tent peg, seizing the off chance and making it a victory and vindication.

The vindication and retribution are Yahweh's alone (Deut 33:35). Human action counts for little: many of the men of the army are weak (the army has no equipment, v 8), and nearly all the women stay indoors. Of the several tribes summoned, a number did not show; and with the anatomy of their failures we are returned to water (vv 16–17; Gilead over the Jordan; Dan on ships; Asher on the shore; Reuben perhaps at water-holes). The Canaanite women (vv 29–30), for their part, seek the glory of spoils, hopes as ultimately pointless as they are groundless.

The manner of the poem is also plain. It is rapid and abrupt: "Listen, kings./ Give ear, potentates:/ I'll sing of Yahweh,/ I will sing,/ I'll chant of Yahweh, Israel's God"

(v 3). Again, "He asks for water./ She brings a bowl of milk./ She offers the great one yoghurt" (v 25).

The pressure of the narrative is enormous; nothing is made needlessly explicit: "Kings came and fought,/ Canaan's kings fought./ At Taanach, near Megiddo Flood/ They took no silver spoils" (v 19). No simple statement of failure is given; a nuanced allusion to one failed objective is sufficient. The connections are rarely explicit across the poem: The heavenly water and Sisera's drink of water are similar, but the economy of death and salvation by water is not worked out. The power of Sisera's troops has a noisy emblem: "Heels hammered,/ Horses galloped,/ His stallions galloped off" (v 22). The stallions are Sisera's, and the quiet echo of this rush of frightened horses is his also: "She hammers Sisera,/ She pounds his head,/ She pummels and pierces his temple" (v 26).

As the emphasis on blessings and curses suggests, one of the poem's subjects is speech itself. Deborah is called to sing (*dabbĕrî*) a song (v 12), as the poem itself is sung (v 3), and the goal is to recount the victories of Yahweh (v 11). The blessing and curse, summons and song are part of and take their constituent meaning from being enmeshed in the recitations basic to the worship of Yahweh. On the poem, see M. O'Connor, *Hebrew Verse Structure* (Winona Lake, 1980); M. D. Coogan, *CBQ* 40 (1978) 143–66; B. Lindars, *BJRL* 65 (1983) 158–75; J. G. Taylor, *JSOT* 23 (1982) 99–108.

27   (F) Gideon's Call (6:1–40). The background for the Midianite wars lies in the period of Moses' leadership; the Baal of Peor incident and the subsequent wars (Num 25, 31) lead up to the present battles (Mendenhall, *Tenth Generation* 105–9). Midian passes out of Israelite history after this incident. The prophet who explains to all Israel the reasons for the Midianite oppression (the first prophet after Moses and his siblings) is succeeded by an angel who tries to commission one specific Israelite to engage the Midianites. The angel is at first rebuked and later on God is tested over and over by Gideon/Jerubbaal (see Polzin, *Moses* 168–69, 185).

2–4. No extraordinary pattern is in view; the raiders are "merely the usual harvest-season tax collectors" (Mendenhall); as usual, taxes are collected from the poor without any particular view to their sustenance. **5.** The insect imagery begun in 2:18 continues here; see 7:12; cf. 14:8 and *ANET* 144. **8–10.** The prophet's speech (cf. 1 Sam 10:17–19) is self-contained; the theology it contains is archly echoed in Gideon's first speech (6:13). **11.** Hebr *mal'āk* means a messenger, divine or human; Yahweh's message bearers carry the same epithet as Gideon's own (v 35). The messenger and the message reflect a profound religious experience, but both in chap. 6 and in chap. 13 the divine messengers are subject to some scrutiny, and the stories have a comic edge. **25–26.** A night vision (or audition) of Yahweh follows as abruptly as the angel's appearance followed the prophet; a second altar is proposed, this one a replacement for an older cultic installation, the property of Gideon's father. The older installation included an altar dedicated to Baal and a wooden pole or stylized tree next to it, called an *'ăšērâ* and perhaps an object sacred to the goddess Asherah (see 3:7) See 1 Kgs 16:32; 2 Kgs 21:3,7. **31.** Joash, Gideon's father, seems to be an overnight convert to Yahwism; his speech is the earliest form of the deity taunt used most majestically by Elijah (1 Kgs 18:27) and most pathetically in Luke's account of the crucifixion (Luke 23:35,39; cf. Mark 15:29–32; Matt 27:39–44). **32.** The renaming represents a false etymology; a name like Jerubbaal, invoking Baal, is not anti-Baalist. The role of the father in the renaming is unusual. **34.** Here the spirit of God "clothes" the *šōpēt*-leader. **36–40.** The fleece test is of a type common in folklore, like saints stopping or causing rain in a small area (Gaster, *Myth, Legend, and Custom* 419–20) or statues of saints crying or bleeding. The distinctive mark of this episode is the reversibility of divine action (cf. *Enuma Elish* IV.21–26; *ANET* 66). As in 6:18, Gideon here sounds like a child, and the deity responds with parental patience.

28   (G) Gideon's Victory (7:1–22). Gideon has tested Yahweh, and now Yahweh proposes tests for Gideon's men, first for fear (v 3) and then for alertness (vv 4–6). A spy story follows, which offers military intelligence in the unusual form of a dream narrative. The battle is won on the basis of elementary technology: Gideon's guerrillas make themselves, with the aid of sound and light effects, seem more numerous than they are. The victory may be the one Isaiah alludes to with the phrase "the day of Midian" (Isa 9:3).

1. The name Jerubbaal is replaced by Gideon elsewhere. **2.** The concern for glory-grabbing tactics is also found in 4:9; there the contest involved two individuals, but here it is Israel that might vaunt itself over Yahweh. **3.** The first cut is easy; this is volunteer duty. **5–6.** The second cut is harder to follow. The smaller group includes "all who tongue-lap from the water as a dog laps" (v 5), i.e., "those who lap with their hands to their mouths" (v 6); these terms refer to people who use their hands as a dog uses its tongue, to pick up water and throw it in the mouth. These people (who are standing up) are judged more alert. (See Gaster, *Myth, Legend, and Custom* 420–21 for parallels; other understandings of these verses are possible, e.g., Revell, "Hebrew Narrative Techniques" 430). **9–15.** The night visit to the enemy camp settles Gideon's final doubts; Yahweh's offer of this unusual source of intelligence is the seventh step in their mutual bargaining. Similar intelligence operations take place in *Iliad* 10.194–597. **12.** Again the locustlike mass of the enemy is mentioned (see 6:5). **13.** If the dream has a symbolic reading, the cake is the agriculturalist Israel, the tent the seminomadic Midian. The explanation of the dream uses somewhat different terms; it is called a *šēber*, "breaking"; a literal clatter of breaking explodes in 7:20. **16–21.** The Israelites stand still and make enough noise to scare the Midianites into nearly random flailing.

29   (H) Gideon's Supporters (7:23–8:3). Israelite narrative permits only a limited number of participants, and therefore battles with individuals tend to be separated from those with armies. The death of Sisera thus follows the defeat of his armies, and here two stories of attacks on Midianite leaders follow the main battle account. First, two generals (not "princes") are captured: Oreb, "Raven," is killed at Raven's Rock, and Zeeb, "Wolf," at Wolf's Vat. The leaders are decapitated by a group of Israelites who support Gideon, though they were not involved in the earlier muster.

8:1. *they disputed with him violently:* "Dispute" (*rîb*) is used in Gideon's other name, Jerubbaal. **3.** Gideon's protestation of his insignificance is continued in 8:23.

30   (I) Gideon's Critics (8:4–21). A mirror image of the previous pericope, this story tells of Gideon's being thwarted by fellow Israelites in his pursuit of two Midianite leaders, here kings. The traitors who refused to help Gideon are punished en masse, while the enemy kings are punished singly. The family dynamics of the next chapter are prepared for here: the Midianite kings have killed Gideon's brothers (or kin), just as Abimelech kills Gideon's sons (his own brothers). Jether, the oldest of Gideon's sons, here plays a special role, as will Jotham, the youngest, in chap. 9.

5. The round loaves of bread requested here are like the ominous loaf of the Midianite dream (7:13), and the extreme hunger is reminiscent of the ravenous thirst of Sisera (4:19) and Samson (15:18). **14.** The Israelites capture a servant or boy (*na'ar;* the latter meaning is certain in 8:20) who is said to write for them a list of Succoth's leaders; the role of writing is anachronistic. **20.** The junior warrior image is used in David's first battle preparations (1 Sam 17:39): he cannot walk in Saul's armor.

31   (J) Gideon's Ephod (8:22–28). The ideology behind Judg here receives a clear statement. Yahweh has made Gideon a success, and the Israelites have mistaken that for a sign that Gideon should rule them. No, he says, "Yahweh rules over you" (8:22). At the same time that he announces this broad understanding of Mosaic ideology, Gideon undermines it with his plans for an ephod. The rich booty is not in itself objectionable (in contrast to the spoils Achan stole, Josh 7:21) — it is the local shrine, with a major cult object in private control, that has an ill effect.

23. The concern with Israel's usurping Yahweh's glory was first mentioned in 7:2. Here, "Gideon's words are an authentic expression of the old ideology . . . : If a military leader, judge or even farmer were blessed with success or outstanding achievement in his occupation, to claim glory or social prestige on such grounds would constitute an act of rebellion or treason" (Mendenhall, *Tenth Generation* 30).

32   (K) Gideon's Family (8:29–35). Seventy sons Gideon had, and the text adds, lest the term *bēn,* "son," be taken in a metaphorical sense ("political associate, ally"), sons who had come out of his thighs. The first of the two longest *šōpēt* stories in the book ends as its predecessors have, with recidivism and abandonment of Yahweh. In this case the consequences of the collapse of the peace are to be treated in detail.

33   (L) Abimelech (9:1–57). The disenfranchised bastard son Abimelech seizes the royal power Gideon refused, after butchering his 70 half brothers on a single stone (vv 5,18). This adventurer dies himself when a single stone is dropped on his head (v 53). Jotham, his youngest half brother, rebukes him and satirizes the uselessness of monarchy, but it is only when another adventurer, Gaal, whose name is "Odious," challenges Abimelech's hegemony in the region that the fragility of his power emerges. Abimelech and his local tenant get Gaal out and level Shechem. Not long after, however, a nameless tyrannicide at Thebez joins the ranks of Jael.

1–21. Abimelech is no judge and Shechem no ordinary Israelite city; Yahweh, the God of Israel, is never mentioned in chap. 9. Whatever the character of Shechem's relations with Israel, old institutions dominate the region, notably the kinglets (or minimonarchs) of the Amarna Age and the professional military bands alternately employed and feared by them. Jotham's parable expresses a view of politicians as ridiculous and dangerous. **1.** The "brothers" here and throughout the chapter are "kin"; the *mišpaḥâ* is not a strictly biological "clan" but a socio-political entity. **2.** The term "rule" (*māšal*) picks up from 8:22–23; the query is specious, since there is no hint that Gideon's sons sought to rule Shechem. **4.** The deity Baal-berith, "Lord of the Covenant," is unknown; it is not impossible that a heterodox or assimilationist form of Yahweh worship was involved. The mercenaries, freebooters, and soldiers of fortune Abimelech hired were doubtless young, strong, and innocent of ideological concerns. **7–21.** Jotham's fable, enunciated from a vantage point on Mt. Gerizim, conforms to the structure best known from Aesopic tales: a moral (in this case vv 16–21, one very convoluted sentence) follows the fable proper. For other ancient stories, Mesopotamian as well as Greek, of the rivalry of the trees, see Gaster, *Myth, Legend, and Custom* 423–47; note esp. the Ahiqar version of the dispute involving a pomegranate and a bramble (H. L. Ginsberg, *ANET* 429–30). The fable proper is not in verse (as *NJB* suggests) but in rhythmic and repetitive prose. **8.** The similar words *māšaḥ*, "to anoint" (vv 8,15), and *śāmaḥ*, "to rejoice" (vv 13,19), are used throughout Jotham's speech. **9.** The act of "waving" suggests not only the ceremonial pomp of kings but also vagabondage (Gen 4:12,14). **14–15.** The thornbush or bramble may claim to offer "protection" (one sense of *ṣēl*) but it hardly affords any real "shade" (the other sense), being a ground cover of the sort that propagates forest fires. **22.** It is hard to determine what sort of dominion Abimelech exercised. Shechem is under his control, but he rules through Zebul ("Prince"), either a client or tenant; Abimelech cannot be too far away if he is to collect his revenues. **23.** The three-year reign of Abimelech begins to collapse at Yahweh's instance. The first step involves greed: the Shechemites want to control by tariff and extortion the trade and traffic of their neighborhood. **26.** The second step involves rebellion: Gaal and his hangers-on recommend a change of government in their favor. After ingratiating and insinuating themselves into the scheme of things, the situation is ripe. The final feast of the fall festival was held in the local temple (probably the largest building available), and Gaal resorts to sedition (open meetings are always a threat to established authority). The speech is magnificent, from its opening rhetorical question to the closing imperative, "And I'd say (with LXX, *NAB, NEB*) 'Mass your men and come on out.'" **31.** The term *pāšaṭ*, "to charge," echoes *šāpaṭ*, "to judge." **36.** Gaal and Zebul are each probably afraid to let the other out of view. Gaal sees men coming down from the hilltop, and Zebul says they are shadows (cf. Mark 8:24); Gaal repeats that they are emerging from the navel of the world (v 37), and Zebul points out to him that in his seditious speech he made promises he is now called on to fulfill. The navel is the great mountain that joins heaven and earth; cf. Ezek 38:12,39–41. The battle with Gaal is won, but Abimelech's war to keep control has just begun. **42–45.** The battle against Shechem continues—Gaal had galvanized the bad feeling, but he did not create it. Abimelech razes Shechem and sows the area with salt, leaving it barren and devastated. **48.** Abimelech cuts down clumps of brush outside Shechem and puts them on his *šĕkem*, "shoulders." Burning to death is a fate both threatened (14:15) and enacted (15:6) in the Samson cycle. **50–54.** At Thebez, at Strong's Tower, Abimelech is crushed under one stone (the "rider" or upper of a pair of millstones). The assassin is an anonymous woman, though Abimelech, in fear of the infamy of such a death (cf. Jdt 16:6), orders his armor-bearer to finish him off (cf. 1 Sam 31:4). The request was in vain: Joab cites Abimelech as having died at a woman's hands (2 Sam 11:21). **57.** Fire plays a different role in Jotham's curse (9:20) than in the actual events (9:49).

(Boogaart, T. A., *JSOT* 32 [1985] 45–56. Campbell, E. F., in *WLSGF* 263–71. Fritz, V., *VT* 32 [1982] 129–44. Lindars, B., *JTS* 16 [1965] 315–26. Rösel, H. N., *VT* 33 [1983] 500–3.)

34   **(III) Tola–Samson (10:1–16:31).** The second half of the twelve-judge procession may be said to start after the Abimelech fiasco: seven judges follow. The Jephthah story is preceded by narratives of two minor judges, and three minor judges follow it. Samson is the twelfth judge and the most spectacular.

35   **(A) Tola and Jair (10:1–5).** The notice of Tola is plain, whereas Jair's is embellished with a pun

about his sons who rode burros ('*ăyārîm*, "donkeys") and ruled boroughs ('*ăyārîm*, for standard '*ārîm*, "cities") (*NJV*).

36   **(B) Jephthah's Enemies (10:6–18).** Though the Jephthah story is itself atypical in focusing on the leader's vow, the preface to it (and the tales of the later judges) contains the typical elements of most reconstructions of *šōpēṭ*-leadership. Apostasy, repentance (the only repentance in the book), and divine reaction create a climate in which a new leader is looked for; people talk eagerly, even urgently, about the person whom Yahweh will summon. This typical sense is, however, built around a deeply ambiguous description of divine reaction: "[Yahweh's] soul grew short *or* had grown short at Israel's work." Does this refer to the effort or toil of Israel's work for Ammon *or* its general search for a divine protector *or* specifically to its efforts toward Yahweh? Is Yahweh exasperated (cf. 16:16) or filled with compassion? Cf. R. Polzin, *Moses* 177–78; R. Haak, *JBL* 101 (1982) 161–67, esp. 165.

6. Here the foreign gods are the Baals and the Astartes; see comment on 2:11; 3:7. **7.** The Philistines are Samson's enemy, the Ammonites Jephthah's. **11–13.** Yahweh's rebuke is rhetorically complex (cf. 9:16–20); for a similar dialogue, see 1 Sam 12. **15.** The Israelites ask that Yahweh do "all that is good (*ṭôb*)" in his eyes; Jephthah is summoned from the land of Tob (*ṭôb*, 11:5). **17.** Mizpah is also important in 1 Sam 7. **18.** The anticipated leader will "begin" to turn back the enemy, as will Samson (13:5).

37   **(C) Jephthah's Call (11:1–11).** The leader set to emerge in 10:18 is a gangster or condottiere, a man who was victimized as a child for his illegitimacy (cf. Gen 21:9–21), and as an adult is set to get back his own. In times of social upheaval there are deracinated and disenfranchised men, and Jephthah knows how to manipulate them (9:4; 1 Sam 22:1–2; 25:13)—he gleans from the land (v 3) and builds a power base. Both his skills and his base make him attractive to his kin, but when they call him back, he dictates the terms of his leadership. He makes sure that Yahweh is also acquainted with how he is to be treated as both civil and military administrator.

38   **(D) Jephthah's Victory (11:12–33).** Jephthah, like any other good general, would prefer not to fight; the Ammonite monarch willingly parleys through one round but declines a second set of talks. Forced to fight, Jephthah mobilizes broad social support and with this base is able to subdue Ammon. Before going to battle, however, Jephthah has made a vow to Yahweh, unsolicited, unnecessary, and finally vain.

15–27. Jephthah offers a résumé of Israel's Transjordanian history, drawn largely from Num 20–24 (see esp. Num 20:14–21; 21:21–26; 22:1–3; Judg 11:17 includes a partial quotation of Num 21:22). **21–24.** A theology of war is highlighted here: "Yahweh, the god of Israel, gave Sihon and his troops into Israel's power. . . . Is it not the case that you possess whatever Chemosh, your god, causes to you to possess? Similarly, we possess all that Yahweh our god causes to be dispossessed before us." Jephthah argues not as a monotheist but as a henotheist—the gods are local and at base projections of the state that supports them; in strict Yahwist terms, such thinking makes Yahweh into (a) Baal. The most arresting feature of the passage is the reference to Chemosh as the Ammonite god; the usual array of the south Canaanite gods involves Yahweh for Israel, Chemosh for Moab, Milcom for Ammon, and Qaus for Edom. **26.** Such reasoning, involving "facts on the ground" and the dismissal of counterclaims as "ancient history," is familiar from many territorial disputes. **27.** Jephthah appeals,

"Let Yahweh the šōpēṭ judge (šāpaṭ)." Is Yahweh here an arbiter, an interested party (as the nationalist theology would suggest), or the relevant executive authority (as a more universalist theology might claim)? **29.** The Yahweh spirit having settled upon him, Jephthah is able to "cause Gilead and Manasseh to rebel [against Ammonite control] and then he made [the whole assembly at] Mizpah-Gilead [cf. 11:11] rebel; from Mizpah-Gilead he [or it] was in rebellion against the Ammonites" (cf. v 32). (Read γʿbr twice as a causative, with Mendenhall, *Tenth Generation* 140). **30–31.** The vow is unmotivated (it follows a tremendous popular success). The object to be dedicated is "who- [or what]ever comes out of the doors of my house"; the Hebrew does not indicate whether the object is animate or inanimate. **33.** The battle account is subordinated to the homecoming scene.

39   (E) Jephthah's Daughter (11:34–40). Jephthah suffered because his mother was a prostitute, and his pre-battle vow makes his only child, his nameless daughter, suffer. He binds over the only child in obedience to a superfluous vow and sacrifices the daughter, stopped by no divine messenger proferring a substitute victim (contrast Gen 22). Human sacrifice was practiced in biblical times by Israelites, though forbidden by law (Lev 18:21; 20:2–5; Deut 12:31; 18:10) and excoriated by prophets (Jer 7:31; Micah 6:6–7; cf. Ps 106:37); the relation of this sacrifice to Molech and demon offerings is obscure. The daughter dies childless and leaves the house of Jephthah without further issue. Her time of lamentation (or perhaps she herself) becomes a tradition and a standard for Israelite women.

34–40. A comparable daughter sacrifice is Agamemnon's offering of his daughter Iphigenia in order to obtain fair winds for the Greek fleet bound for Troy. **35.** Jephthah sees the situation immediately and reacts by rending (qāraʿ) his clothes and blaming his intended victim: "You have crippled (kāraʿ) me and you are my crumpling ('okrîm)." **36–37.** The victim twice consents: "Do to me according to what went out of your mouth," and "Let this thing be done to me"; cf. Luke 1:38. The rationale intervenes between these statements: "inasmuch as Yahweh has done for you the requirements of dominion from your enemies," i.e., Yahweh has acted as the executive authority here (šāpaṭ) and taken dominion (nāqam) over the Ammonites. (See Mendenhall, *Tenth Generation* 85.) **39.** The silence over the execution of the vow serves with the brief battle account (v 33) to contain the vow incident. **40.** The women's act is repetition or storytelling, rather than singing a dirge or lament.

40   (F) Jephthah's Critics (12:1–7). The victory of Jephthah is not only dimmed by the death of the judge's daughter; there is also conflict on a larger level, reflecting perhaps earlier population shifts. The Cisjordanian Ephraimites deny that they had abandoned the Transjordanian Gileadites, but the Gileadites, believing themselves ill-used, systematically attack the Ephraimites (cf. 8:1–3). The difference between the two groups can be measured linguistically, and a linguistic test is described. A Gileadite guard would point to a stream and ask a passerby what she or he called it: the Gileadites said šibbōlet and the Ephraimites sibbōlet (perhaps originally thibbolet; cf. P. Swiggers, *JSS* 26 [1981] 205–7; W. Weinberg, *ZAW* 92 [1980] 185–204), a difference similar to that between standard Eng *them, these,* and nonstandard *dem, dese.* **6.** In the biblical view, the regional language was Canaanite (Isa 19:18); in addition to the Ephraimite and Gileadite varieties cited here, Canaanite had a Jerusalemite form, which became the standard for biblical literature.

41   (G) Ibzan, Elon, and Abdon (12:8–15). The entry for Ibzan has an ethnographic note about

some sort of exogamy (see Gottwald, *Tribes* 305–8 on social background, and M. Tsevat, *JAOS* [1983] 322–26 for a literary parallel), and the entry for Abdon, like that for Jair (10:4), refers to "sons."

42   (H) Samson's Birth (13:1–25). The Samson cycle of stories includes extended accounts of the hero's birth and death, framing stories involving three Philistine women. The Philistine oppression continues from Samson's time through Saul's and into David's (see Gottwald, *Tribes* 410–25); no Israelite apart from Samson has close dealings with the Philistines. The fantastical element of these stories is picked up in the ark narrative (1 Sam 5). The first part of the cycle focuses on the annunciation to Manoah's barren wife of her Nazirite son and Manoah's laborious confirmation of the message. Samson's mother is an apt and responsive recipient of the word, while her husband is a dullard. Gideon combines elements of both responses, as does Samson himself. Samson is indeed the child of his parents.

2. The Danites are here a southern group; their migration to the north follows, in Judg 17–18. Manoah has no patronymic; his wife has no name; the messenger may also be nameless. **2–5.** This annunciation story has much in common with those in Gen 16:7–13; 17:15–21; 18:10–15; see also Matt 1:20–21; Luke 1:11–20 and 26–35, and compare v 5 with Matt 1:21. **4–5.** Unlike the children in all the other annunciations, Manoah's wife's child is consecrated from the womb (Jer 1:5; Isa 49:1) as a Nazirite. The pentateuchal rules require that a nāzîr not drink alcoholic beverages or any product of the vine, not be shaved, and not have contact with the dead; and the nazirate is a limited time of service (Num 6:1–21). In the Samson story the alcohol rule (and a rule about unclean food) is enforced on the nāzîr's mother and the shaving rule on the nāzîr; Samson is not explicitly required to abstain from alcohol or corpse contagion, though the stories of his violations seem to presuppose that he should have. There is no term to his service (v 7). Samuel is a nāzîr, but his service seems to start from birth (1 Sam 1:11; MT is garbled). **6.** As in the Gideon story, the terms for the divine messenger vary. The messenger does not tell Manoah's wife its name, though she does note that the appearance was "awesome" (nôrāʾ), a term often used of Yahweh (cf. Exod 15:11). **9.** Manoah's prayer is answered, as are Samson's prayers (15:19; 16:30). **12.** Manoah (cf. v 8) here inquires after the mišpāṭ of the boy; lit., "judgment" or "custom," the term refers to a set of instructions for the child's upbringing (→ 10 above). The angel again seems to place the burden of regulation on the nāzîr's mother. **15–20.** Cf. 6:19–22. At base these gifts are tokens of hospitality presented to those who have traveled a long way. Manoah asks to restrain the messenger and demands a name; cf. Gen 32:24–31. It seems that the angel refuses: "Why do you ask my name? It is wonderful (pelîʾ)!" It is possible that the angel's name is, actually, "Wonderful" (cf. D. Grimm, *Bib* 62 [1981] 92–102). **20.** Here the angel goes up in the offering's smoke. **22.** Manoah is afraid because he and his wife have seen God. The biblical tradition is divided about people seeing God (contrast Exod 33:11 and 20), and Manoah's wife quite reasonably dismisses her husband's fears. **24.** Hebr šimšôn is given in LXX as *Sampsōn,* the source of the Eng spelling with p, now largely archaic. The phrase šĕmô šimšôn, "his name Samson," is echoic. The name is derived from Hebr šamaš, "sun," and this fact, combined with the proximity of Zorah to Beth-shemesh, "House of the Sun" (cf. 1:33), and the prominence of certain motifs (fire, hair, sight), has led to Samson's being associated with a solar deity or myth. The account of Samson's maturity is similar to Luke 2:52. **25.** *Zorah and Eshtaol:* Cf. 16:31 and 18:2,

8,11. The Yahweh spirit here stirs Samson; later it will spring upon him (14:6). On Samson, see J. C. Exum, *JBL* 99 (1980) 43–59; Exum and J. W. Whedbee, *Semeia* 32 (1984) 5–40; J. L. Crenshaw, *Samson: A Secret Betrayed, A Vow Ignored* (Atlanta, 1978). On the annunciations, see E. W. Conrad, *CBQ* 47 (1985) 656–63; R. E. Brown, *BBM.*

43   (I) Samson's Marriage (14:1–15:8). The narrative of Samson's first Philistine liaison takes the form of a shaggy-dog story, a tale built around the quatrain given in vv 14 and 18a. The answer to Samson's riddle, never given in the text, is love, the proper subject of banter at wedding parties (P. Nel, *Bib* 66 [1985] 534–35); the tale is pieced together out of an improbable story about single combat with a lion whose corpse attracts bees. The third poetic fragment, in v 18b, provides in its vulgarity a counterpoint to the riddle proper. Samson's further reaction is a crude compounding of violence, first against men, then property; the Philistine threats to his wife also allude to unspeakable violence (14:15; 15:6; cf. 12:1). The various anomalous features of the Samson stories suggest that the saga as a whole is a riddle: "What appears to be Samson is the people Israel; what appears as the Naziriteship of Samson is the Israelite covenant" (E. L. Greenstein, "The Riddle of Samson," *Prooftexts* 1 [1981] 247).

14:2. The institution in view was some sort of arranged marriage, with Samson taking an apparently larger than usual role in the selection: this is illusory, since Yahweh is responsible for Samson's choice (cf. 16:20 for another case of Samson's ignorance) **3.** Samson says that "She's right (*yāšĕrâ*) in my eyes" (cf. v 7), anticipating the later refrain (17:6; 21:25). **6.** The Yahweh spirit rushes upon Samson here and in later passages (14:6,19; 15:14, cf. 1 Sam 10:6,10; 11:6; 18:10; 16:3). He presumably conceals his slaughter of the lion because it would involve corpse contagion (again in 14:8; 14:19; 15:15; 16:8). **8.** Samson finds a swarm of bees, called an *'ēdâ* (usually a civil or religious assembly; cf. 20:1). For Samson's oral needs, see on 15:18; "honey" is a high-energy food. **9.** After he twice goes down (*yārad*) in the first part of the story (cf. v 10), Samson here twice scrapes (*rādâ*) honey from the corpse; another word *rādâ* means "to rule over." There may be an implicit analogy; as Samson *scrapes* the honey from the bees' *assembly*, so he rules Israel's *assembly.* **10.** The force of the ethnographic note ("thus young men did") is unclear. Is this a peculiarity of Philistines or of men in the "olden days" (cf. Ruth 4:7)? **12–18.** The challenge posed by Samson to his feast-mates involves a *ḥîdâ*, a "puzzle" or "aphorism" as much as a "riddle"; it may be that they were to supply the second half of the *ḥîdâ* rather than the "answer." The little poem (two lines in v 14, two lines in v 18) surely has something to do with *'ărî*, "lion," and an unattested word *'ărî*, 'honey." **15–18.** The chronology is confusing. **15.** The Philistines order the woman to "deceive" or "make stupid" her husband; cf. 16:5. The threat of the burning building (cf. 15:6) harks back to Abimelech at Migdal-Shechem and Thebez (9:49,52). **19.** More corpse contagion. **20.** Samson's father-in-law has understood him to have abandoned the marriage.

15:1. The wheat harvest was an occasion for celebration, as was the contemporary sheepshearing (1 Sam 25:8; 2 Sam 13:23–29); the harvest festival was eventually canonized as the feast of Weeks or Pentecost (Exod 23:16; Deut 16:10), around mid-June. The kid would serve as a gift (cf. Gen 38:13). **2.** The interchangeability of women is implicit in 19:24, as well as in Laban's switching of his daughters (Gen 30:25). **3.** "Now," Samson claims, he is innocent, suggesting that he has surely been wronged this time, even if he had not

been earlier (14:18). **4.** As a textbook description of guerrilla tactics this verse is no more successful than 7:20, but the effect of the fire can be surmised. **7.** The root *nqm* refers to the use of force outside normal legal institutions; in some cases, as here, it is punitive (whence the standard translations, "revenge," " vengeance"). This incident is "a parade example of the futility of the escalation of wrongs, reprisals, and counterreprisals. It is told . . . with no obvious attempt to whitewash Samson or to make the Philistines appear in as evil a light as possible" (Mendenhall, *Tenth Generation* 92). On chaps. 14–16, see J. C. Exum, *JSOT* 19 (1981) 3–29,90.

44   (J) Samson's Rampage (15:9–20). Samson gives himself up to other Israelites but, with another guerrilla trick, refuses to submit to Philistines. As in 14:9, he touches flesh not ritually slaughtered (the fresh jawbone of an ass) and violates the restrictions of his Nazirite status. Only in this story is Samson simply the strong man of later legend, full of vain boasts like Lamech, whose taunt-song (Gen 4:23) is similar to his, and given to dim-witted exaggeration like Esau, who like him cries out for sustenance *in extremis* (Gen 25:32; contrast 1 Sam 28:23; 1 Kgs 19:7). The imagery is drawn from the animal world; in addition to the ass's bone, note the reference to the partridge (*haqqōrē'*), "the crier or caller," in En-hakkore (v 19).

14. The Philistines had done evil (*r''*) to Samson (15:3), had furnished him companions (vocabulary from the root *rā'â*), and now they greet him with shouts (*rûa'*). The Yahweh spirit again rushes upon him, and again the imagery of fire figures in describing his response. **16.** The two-line poem involves a pun on *ḥămôr*, "he-ass," and *ḥămôr*, "heap"; the second line in MT is "one heap, two heaps," like a children's counting song. **18.** In v 15 Samson found (*māṣā'*) the jawbone, and now he is thirsty (*ṣāmē'*). **19.** The demand for water and God's ready compliance is a parody of the Massah and Meriba trials during the wilderness wanderings (Exod 17:6; Num 20:11), a byword for lack of confidence in God (Ps 95:8).

45   (K) Samson's Loves (16:1–22). The leader's weakness for Philistine women appears again, first in the story of the anonymous Gazite and then in the Delilah tale. The Philistines try to capture Samson first by a simple ambush, and then, seeking the help of Samson's love, make an inside job of it. Even so, progress is slow. Eventually he describes the source of his strength, and having been deprived of his hair he is soon deprived also of his sight. The five attempts to capture Samson center on the three lies told to Delilah; the first ends with the hero dragging the city gates halfway across the country (16:4), and the last with the hero being dragged off.

3. Removal (lit., uprooting) of the city gates was a serious attack; above and beyond their defensive role, they had a symbolic value (cf. the curse in the Azatiwatas inscription; *ANET* 654). This story, like 15:8, does not mention divine assistance in providing strength. **7–15.** Samson treats the source of his strength as a riddle and gives Delilah three clues; instead of seeing them as clues, she acts on them as suggestions and fails. The clues to Samson's nazirate involve corpse contact (the moist tendon cords), work (a Nazirite works only for Yahweh), and hair; the third clue reveals the heart of Samson's status, but Delilah cannot figure out how to use it. The plaiting of the hair is in itself no threat, as long as the hair is attached. **13–14.** The MT has lost about sixteen words due to the repetitiousness of the text; they are easily restored from LXX (cf. *NAB, RSV*). The instrument, as in chap. 4, is a peg (*yātēd*), here a loom pin, and the verb, as often in chaps. 3–4, is *tāqa'*, here "to thrust." The act of uprooting (*nāsa'*) the loom pin is similar to that of removing the city gates (16:3).

15–16. Another round of whining, as in 14:7. Samson again loses his patience (cf. 15:18). **17.** Twice there is reference to Samson's strength turning from him (here and in v 19), but in the summary verse Yahweh is said to turn from him. **21.** Samson is taken to work "eyeless in Gaza," grinding grain (K. van der Toorn, *VT* 36 [1986] 248–53); the size of the mill is not specified, so the usual view that he is doing women's work is open to question. The handmill from which came the stone that killed Abimelech (19:53) was a woman's tool, but larger mills were in use.

46   **(L) Samson's Death (16:23–31).** The impression of Samson as an adolescent, present throughout the stories, is heightened in the story of his death. He is infantilized by his captors, who want him to entertain them (perhaps by dancing or fighting or playing ball in his chains, like a captive elephant or bear; the meaning of *śāḥaq*, "to sport," is not clear). He has only his guide boy to help him. He prays to God with the sort of single-mindedness that might be mistaken for purity of heart. The prayer is answered. The chronicle of twelve *šōpēṭ*-leaders ends with a bang, but the exploit is decidedly local and its effect on Israel's polity entirely uncertain.

23. Dagon, here the city-god of Gaza and elsewhere that of Ashdod/Azotus (1 Sam 5; 1 Macc 10:83), is a corn-god about whom little is known; he is West Semitic (as the Philistines were not originally) and is mentioned in both Amorite-influenced texts (the Code of Hammurabi, Prologue; *ANET* 165) and Ugaritic texts.

47   **(IV) Epilogues (17:1–21:25).** The last five chapters continue the narrative meditation on leadership. The refrain that unites them has two parts: "In those days there was no king in Israel; people did what was right in their own eyes" (see Boling, *Judges,* 294; W. J. Dumbrell, *JSOT* 25 [1983] 23–33). The full refrain occurs twice, once early (17:6) and again as the last verse of the book (21:25); the first half is used twice by itself (18:1, 19:1; the second half is used in Deut 12:8). See Mendenhall (*Tenth Generation* 131) for Amarna parallels to the refrain. The stories deal with tribes that have special statuses: the Levites are the unlanded "Yahwistic intellectuals" (Gottwald, "Two Models" [→ 8 above] 16; cf. Boling, *Judges* 32–33), while the Benjaminites are closely associated with Saul, the first monarch.

48   **(A) Dan and Micah (17:1–18:31).**

(a) MICAH'S SHRINE (17:1–13). Two short tales, both about a shrine, also have in common a decided vagueness. Micah stole his mother's money; she had cursed the thief, and now she follows the curse with a blessing. Is the silver used for the cult image a legitimate votive offering or another mistake, like Jephthah's vow? The Bethlehemite Levite has left the place of his sojourn, but why is he wandering around as a free-lance cult functionary? The Micah shrine, its fixtures and Levite transferred to Dan, will ultimately be condemned (1 Kgs 12:28–31), but this story of the shrine's private origins tells of misdirection rather than maleficence.

2. Cf. 16:5. **3–5.** The text refers to a *pesel* and *massēkâ*, usually taken as two separate images, one graven or sculptured and the other molten; but it may be that only one object is described by the phrase, which is simplified later to *pesel* (18:17,20,30). This image is of Yahweh, perhaps the only such image in the Bible; the ephod is an object associated with it (cf. 6:27); and teraphim are other idols (small in Gen 31; large in 1 Sam 19:13,16). At first a "son" (perhaps a relation or kinsman) serves as priest in this home shrine. **7.** The term *naʿar* may indicate that the Levite was young or that he was a dependent and thus here a runaway. "He was a Levite and

sojourned (*gār*) there (*šām*)"; the last phrase anticipates the mention of the name Gershom in 18:30. **10.** The Levite is to be "a father and a priest" to Micah (cf. 18:19), but the force of the phrase is unclear; in the next verse it seems Micah adopts the Levite. **13.** That the remark of Micah is self-satisfied is plain; why he is, in the narrator's view, wrong to feel that way is not so obvious.

49   (b) DAN'S MIGRATION (18:1–31). The vagueness of the actions in chap. 17 makes sense in terms of chap. 18. The improbably free-lance Levite is like the landless tribe of Dan, migrating from S to N near Sidon; the theft Micah perpetrated against his mother is like the Danites' theft of Micah's whole shrine. There are also threads of culpability: since Micah is a thief, his ill-gotten goods (despite his mother's efforts to spare him) are taken from him; since the Levite (apparently identified in 18:20 as Jonathan) settled with Micah in response to a good offer, he is willing to move on when a better one comes along. Jeroboam's cultic foundation at Dan (1 Kgs 13:20) is not mentioned, but the dubiousness of homemade gods is made plain.

1. Josh 19:40–47 puts the tribe of Dan in the S by tribal lot; after it lost the territory, it moved N and took Leshem (apparently the Laish of this story). Cf. Judg 1:34; Judg 13; 18. Judg 5:17 apparently refers to a northern Dan. **2.** Cf. Num 13. **3.** The Danites recognize the sound (*qôl*) of the Levite, i.e., his southern accent gives him away as a stranger to the Ephraimite hill country; along with 12:1–6, this verse is one of the few reminders of the linguistic diversity of early Israel. **16–18.** The order of events is confusing, as is the topography, in part because it is unclear whether "the house of Micah" is a building, a small compound, or a village (see Gottwald, *Tribes* 291). **25.** The Danites claim to have in their party uncontrollable elements whose attack might lead Micah to "gather" up his own soul. **31.** The reference here leads into 1 Sam 1, which concerns Shiloh. Note, too, the reference to the Babylonian Exile (lit., "the uncovering of the land"); an older view, associating this allusion with events of the late 8th cent. (cf. H. Cazelles, *DBSup* 4. 1406; Dumbrell, *JSOT* 25 [1985] 29), seems unlikely.

50   **(B) From Gibeah to Shiloh (19:1–21:25).**

(a) OUTRAGE AT GIBEAH (19:1–30). Another Levite, another study involving Bethlehem: the exploration of the plight of the landless Levites and of the home of the future king David continues. This Ephraimite Levite, having won back his concubine and met the demands of her father's hospitality, goes to the Israelite city of Gibeah (the home of the future king Saul) to stay overnight on his way home. He is welcomed by a non-Gibeaite and then threatened by the men of the city, who wish to rape him. They accept as a substitute his concubine and assault her until she is at death's door. The Levite spreads the news of this outrage perpetrated by Benjaminites. On the story, see Trible, *Texts of Terror* 65–91.

1. The principals are from both Ephraim (cf. 17:1) and Judah (cf. 17:7), but the scene of action for the first part of the chapter is the south. **2.** The LXX renders "She was angry at him" (so Boling, *Judges* 274), but the MT has "She was promiscuous with regard to him," whence "She deserted him" (*NJV*), "She was unfaithful to him" (*NAB*). **4–9.** The effusive hospitality of the Bethlehemite contrasts with the defective welcome of the Gibeaites. The woman does not speak, here or below. **10–12.** Jebus, later Jerusalem, is David's city, before his time unincorporated into Israel (contrast 1:7–8,21); the name Jebus was an alternative name of the city (cf. 1 Chr 11:4); Gibeah is Saul's city, associated with Benjamin (as is Jebus in 1:21). **15–27.** This story is similar to the rape story in Gen 19, and it may be more basic (S. Niditch,

CBQ 44 [1982] 365–78). **15–18.** There is no one "gathering them"; the term "gather" (v 15) is used apparently in innocent contrast to the murder sense in 18:25, though what happens later makes the contrast seem less innocent. **16.** The old man who helps the Levite's party is a foreigner as much as they are, though he has settled in Gibeah. **19.** The Danites travel with nothing but weapons of war and seize a land with nothing lacking (18:10), whereas this Levite travels fully equipped with nothing lacking. **22–23.** The attackers are "the men of the city, men of the sons of Belial," i.e., the entire male population was involved (cf. Gen 19:4). They surround the house and hurl themselves at the door; they demand that the Levite be sent out "so that we may know him" (cf. Gen 19:5), the crime in prospect rape (cf. 2 Sam 13:12–13) by homosexual anal intercourse (cf. Lev 18:22), an "outrage" or "infamy" (*NJB* for *nĕbālâ;* cf. 20:6–10; Mayes, *Judges* 71–72). **24.** Since rape is in view, the substitutes proposed (cf. Gen 19:8) can hardly be defended. "The lord of the house will himself give these women away. . . . The male protector becomes procurer" (Trible, *Texts of Terror* 74). The old man invites his compatriots to rape the women; he also begs them, "Do what is right in your eyes," quoting the refrain of 17:6, 21:25. **25.** The old man fails in his pacification attempt, and the Levite throws his concubine out. The men of the town "have intercourse with her and abuse her all night." **26–28.** The Levite does not investigate the scene of the crime. The MT does not specify when the woman died, though LXX does add "for she was dead" in v 28 (cf. Trible; Polzin, *Moses* 200–2). **29.** The gesture of "taking the knife" is also found in Gen 22:10. The victim is dismembered (cf. 1 Sam 11:7) (see R. Polzin, *HTR* 62 [1969] 227–40). **30.** The summons to take action is left implicit, and the story reflects on this lack of planning.

51   (b) ASSEMBLY AT MIZPAH (20:1–48). The Israelites foregather and listen to the Levite's story; Benjamin refuses to hand over the miscreants, and war is inevitable. As in Judg 1:2, the lot for first action falls to Judah (20:18). After two days of unsuccessful siege at the city, the Israelites enlarge the battlefield, drawing the Benjaminites away from the city and deploying ambush forces in the hill country. When the Benjaminites see the deceptive fire set back in the city, they lose the upper hand. One Israelite tribe is almost totally wiped out, at least in part because there were no mechanisms besides battle for adjudicating the Levite's grievance (or any grievance between the small federated groups of early Israel). A small number of Benjaminites escape.

1. The final two chapters use two terms for assembly, *ʿēdâ,* "an appointed group" (cf. 14:8), and *qāhāl,* "convocation," both referring to a leadership body representing the associated tribes, both Cisjordanian (from Dan in the N to Beer-sheba in the S; cf. 1 Sam 3:20; 2 Sam 3:10; 1 Kgs 5:5) and Gilead from Transjordan. **4.** The woman is for the first time said to have been "slain." The Levite's version of events is self-interestedly euphemistic. **6.** The crime is a *zimmâ,* "a plotted act of wickedness," as well as a *nĕbālâ* (19:23), i.e., "a premeditated infamy." **13.** The

assailants are here cited as if they may be only a subgroup of Gibeah's population. **14–48.** The battle story is complex, as is the similar account of the battle of Ai (Josh 7–8; cf. de Vaux, *EHI* 618–19). Many scholars seek to simplify the story (*NAB* rearranges parts of vv 15–16,22–23,31–35), but the account is in good order. **16.** Like Ehud (3:15), the 700 slingers are "bound as to the right hand," i.e., presumably left-handed. **18.** The relationship between the civil assembly at Mizpah and the religious meetings at Bethel (where the ark is, v 27) is unclear. **28.** Phinehas, Aaron's grandson, "lives" through a longer span of the Bible than anyone else: he is born in Exod 6:6 and nails the Midianite adulterers at Beth Peor (Num 25:7); this is his last appearance. **29–48.** "The complexity of the account is undoubtedly due, in part, to the need to present the activities of three different groups participating in the battle, a problem not often presented to the narrator, and difficult to solve within the linear conventions of Hebrew narrative" (Revell, "Hebrew Narrative Techniques" 432, cf. 427–33). **29.** The eventual Israelite victory is associated with a change in tactics; the simple siege is now supported by ambuscades and plans for rearguard action (v 38). **31.** The core of the strategy involves drawing away the men in the city (as in Josh 8:16, with the same verb; Hebrew idiom has it that the defenders are torn away, *nātaq;* cf. v 32). **38.** Smoke signals were used in various ways in ancient warfare (Mari: *ANET* 482; Lachish: *ANET* 322; cf. Jer 6:1).

52   (c) RAPE AT JABESH-GILEAD AND AT SHILOH (21:1–25). The Israelite leaders take an oath not to supply wives for the surviving Benjaminites, but their desire to preserve the tribe leads them to seek ways to circumvent their own oath (v 22). Their blatant hypocrisy leads to extreme measures. "What these men claim to abhor, they have reenacted with vengeance" (Trible, *Texts of Terror* 84). Two covert operations are undertaken: (1) Because Jabesh-gilead did not support the war against Benjamin, all people in that region are wiped out except for the unmarried women; this amounts to exterminating a region to save a tribe. (2) The Benjaminites abduct all unprotected Shilonite women. These two episodes of mass rape are meant to round off the consequences of the rape in chap. 19; the escalation has been overwhelming (cf. Hos 9:9; 10:9).

1. The oath of v 5 is made to solve the problem posed by the oath of v 1. **2.** The deliberative body is here called "the people" as well as the "convocation" and the "assembly" (20:1). **8.** The plot connects Gibeah and Jabesh-gilead, a link also found in 1 Sam 11. **10–11.** The orders do not contain a reference to unmarried women; the text may have been damaged. The *ḥērem* or "ban" invoked here also occurs in 1:17, one of the thematic links between the opening and closing of the book. **12–13.** The women are transported from Transjordan to Canaan proper, and the Benjaminites are called out of hiding; the numbers do not match. **19.** The feast is the fall harvest festival (probably also in 9:27) later known as the feast of Booths or Tabernacles (Deut 16:13). **25.** For the refrain, → 47 above.

9

1–2 SAMUEL

Antony F. Campbell, S.J.   *James W. Flanagan **

BIBLIOGRAPHY

1   Alter, R., *The Art of Biblical Narrative* (NY, 1981). Campbell, A. F., *Of Prophets and Kings* (CBQMS 17; Washington, 1986). Conroy, C., *Absalom Absalom!* (AnBib 81; Rome, 1978). Fokkelman, J. P., *Narrative Art and Poetry in the Books of Samuel* (2 vols. to date; SSN; Assen, 1981-). Gunn, D. M., *The Fate of King Saul* (JSOTSup 14; Sheffield, 1980). Hertzberg, H. W., *I & II Samuel* (OTL; Phl, 1964). Klein, R. W., *1 Samuel* (WBC 10; Waco, 1983). McCarter, P. K., Jr., *I–II Samuel* (AB 8, 9; GC, 1980, 1984). Mauchline, J., *1 and 2 Samuel* (NCB; London, 1971). Noth, M., *The Deuteronomistic History* (JSOTSup 15; Sheffield, 1981; Ger 1943). Peckham, J. B., *The Composition of the Deuteronomistic History* (HSM 35; Atlanta, 1985). Rost, L., *The Succession to the Throne of David* (HTIBS 1; Sheffield, 1982; Ger 1926). Sternberg, M., *The Poetics of Biblical Narrative* (Bloomington, 1985). Stoebe, H. J., *Das erste Buch Samuelis* (KAT 8/1; Gütersloh, 1973). Veijola, T., *Die ewige Dynastie* (AASF, B 193; Helsinki, 1975); *Das Königtum in der Beurteilung der deuteronomistischen Historiographie* (AASF, B 198; Helsinki, 1977). Würthwein, E., *Die Erzählung von der Thronfolge Davids— theologische oder politische Geschichtsschreibung?* (ThStud 115; Zurich, 1974).

INTRODUCTION

2   **(I) Topic.** The books of Samuel deal with the period in which two significant elements came into prominence in Israel: one is the figure of the prophet; the other, the institution of kingship. 1 Sam opens with the emergence of Samuel as a prophet to all Israel; 2 Sam closes on the eve of the first dynastic transfer of royal power, from David to Solomon. The traditions that form 1–2 Sam grapple with the interplay of these two forces and their implications for Israel's survival as a nation and its understanding of itself as people of God.

3   **(II) Text.** The problems of the text have inspired immense study and debate. The classic works are by J. Wellhausen (*Der Text der Bücher Samuelis* [Göttingen, 1871]) and S. R. Driver (*Notes on the Hebrew Text and the Topography of the Books of Samuel* [2d ed.; Oxford, 1913]). More recently, there are the extensive text-critical sections in McCarter's commentary and the work of D. Barthélemy (*Critique textuelle de l'Ancien Testament*, Vol. 1 [OBO 50/1; Fribourg, 1982]); also two monographs: E. C. Ulrich, *The Qumran Text of Samuel and Josephus* (HSM 19; Cambridge MA, 1978) and S. Pisano, *Additions or Omissions in the Books of Samuel* (OBO 57; Fribourg, 1984).

4   **(III) Composition.** The time of composition covers the centuries from the beginnings of the monarchy in Israel to the exile and the postexilic period.

Scholarly understanding of the growth processes that produced the books has moved through several phases. There are clear indications of duplication and discontinuity in the text. Influenced by the successes of pentateuchal source criticism, these phenomena were explained by the continuation of J and E, or equivalent sources, through Josh, Judg, Sam, and down into Kgs. In 1926, L. Rost proposed a different model, in which the emphasis shifted from continuous sources to originally independent narratives as the basic building blocks of 1–2 Sam (*Succession*). Rost focused on the succession narrative (2 Sam 9–20; 1 Kgs 1–2), together with the ark narrative (1 Sam 4–6; 2 Sam 6), the core of Nathan's prophecy (2 Sam 7), and the report of the Ammonite war (2 Sam 10:6–11:1; 12:26–31). When a story of David's rise to power is reckoned with (1 Sam 9 or 16–2 Sam 5), the bulk of 1–2 Sam has been accounted for. Before Rost's study, these had been discussed as blocks of tradition which had been taken up into the continuous sources; after Rost, the sources tended to fade from view and attention focused on the independent narratives themselves.

In 1943, M. Noth's hypothesis of a deuteronomistic history (Dtr), extending from Deut to 2 Kgs 25, integrated all of these components once again into a single continuous text, dated to the time of the exile (*Deuteronomistic History*). According to Noth, the Deuteronomist

---

*The introduction and comment on 1 Samuel are the work of A. F. Campbell; the comment on 2 Samuel is by J. W. Flanagan.

dealt extensively with the emergence of kingship in Israel (1 Sam 8–12), but otherwise added remarkably little to the traditions taken over. In 1975 and 1977, following on studies of redactional levels in Dtr, T. Veijola argued for a considerably more substantial contribution by the Deuteronomists to the text of Sam (*Ewige Dynastie; Königtum*). For an assessment of the discussion of editorial layers within Dtr, see A. D. H. Mayes, *The Story of Israel between Settlement and Exile* (GR, 1983). For a helpful evaluation of much of the central literature on 1–2 Sam, see R. P. Gordon, *1 & 2 Samuel* (Sheffield, 1984).

The present writer has argued for the identification of a late 9th-cent. prophetic document, extending from 1 Sam 1 to 2 Kgs 10 (*Of Prophets and Kings*). This text, dubbed the Prophetic Record, is claimed to lie behind both the present text of 1–2 Sam and the text of Dtr. It is attributed to northern prophetic circles, probably those associated with the figure of Elisha, and seen as composed to account for the prophetic legitimation of Jehu's *coup d'etat* and the subsequent attempt to eliminate Baal worship from Israel. At present, then, both concepts of independent narrative blocks and of continuous narrative documents play their role in explaining the phenomena of the text of 1–2 Sam.

5   **(IV) Outline.**

(I) Intimations of Change (1 Sam 1:1–7:17)
  (A) The Emergence of a Prophet (1:1–4:1a)
    (a) Birth of Samuel (1:1–2:11)
    (b) Emergence of Samuel among the Elides (2:12–3:18)
    (c) Recognition before All Israel (3:19–4:1a)
  (B) The Departure of the Ark (4:1b–7:1)
    (a) Departure from Israel (4:1b–22)
    (b) Peripeteia in the Land of the Philistines (5:1–12)
    (c) Return to Kiriath-jearim (6:1–7:1)
  (C) The Judgeship of Samuel (7:2–17)
(II) Introduction of a New Epoch in Israel (1 Sam 8:1–12:25)
  (A) Demand for a King (8:1–22)
  (B) Secret Anointing of Saul as King-to-Be (9:1–10:16)
  (C) Public Acclamation of Saul as King (10:17–27)
  (D) Demonstration of Saul's Kingly Charisma (11:1–15)
  (E) Instruction of Israel by Samuel on Ways of Kingship (12:1–25)
(III) The Beginnings of the Kingdom (1 Sam 13:1–2 Sam 5:10)
  (A) Rejection of Israel's First King (13:1–15:35)
    (a) First Account of Rejection (13:1–15a)
    (b) Battle at Michmash (13:15b–14:52)
    (c) Second Account of Rejection (15:1–35)
  (B) Rise to Power of Israel's Second King (1 Sam 16:1–2 Sam 5:10)
    (a) Secret Anointing of David (16:1–13)
    (b) Demonstration of David's Charisma (16:14–18:5)
    (c) Unfolding of David's Rise and Saul's Decline (18:6–31:13)
      (i) First intimations (18:6–16)
      (ii) Conflict at court (18:17–21:1 [*RSV* 20:42])
      (iii) Open rupture (21:2[1]–27:12)

    (iv) Ultimate failure of Saul (28:1–31:13)
  (D) Recognition of David's Leadership (2 Sam 1:1–5:10)
    (i) Report of Saul's and Jonathan's deaths (1:1–16)
    (ii) Elegy for Saul and Jonathan (1:17–27)
    (iii) David achieves paramountcy over Judah (2:1–7)
    (iv) Activity in the northern camp (2:8–11)
    (v) Hostilities erupt between David's and Saul's houses (2:12–3:1)
    (vi) Northern attempts at peace and leadership fail (3:2–4:12)
      (1) Hebron genealogy (3:2–5)
      (2) Abner's negotiations fail (3:6–39)
      (3) Ishbaal falls (4:1–12)
    (vii) David leads Israel (5:1–5)
    (viii) Zion is chosen as administrative center of the confederations (5:6–10)
(IV) David Centralizes Yahweh's Power in Jerusalem (2 Sam 5:11–12:31)
  (A) Relocating the Ark and Securing Allegiances (5:11–8:18)
    (a) David Secures His Position (5:11–16)
    (b) Philistine Battles (5:17–25)
    (c) Transfer of the Ark to Jerusalem (6:1–23)
    (d) Oracle of Nathan and Prayer of David (7:1–29)
    (e) David Subdues and Allies with Non-Yahwist Eastern Regions (8:1–14)
    (f) David's Administration (8:15–18)
  (B) Conflicts in David's Palace (9:1–12:31)
    (a) Meribaal's Protection and House Arrest (9:1–13)
    (b) David Is Tested by an Eastern Coalition (10:1–19 [+ 11:1 + 12:26–31])
    (c) The Bathsheba Affair, Nathan's Judgment, and Solomon's Birth (11:1–12:25)
    (d) David Assumes Direct Control of the Ammonites (12:26–31)
(V) David Loses and Regains Jerusalem (13:1–20:25)
  (A) Absalom Challenges his Father's Sovereignty (13:1–19:9a)
    (a) The Rape of Tamar and Absalom's Revenge (13:1–39)
    (b) Absalom's Exile and Reconciliation (14:1–33)
    (c) Absalom's Attempt at Succession (15:1–12)
    (d) David Abandons Jerusalem and the Ark (15:13–16:14)
    (e) Absalom's Foolishness (16:15–17:23)
    (f) David in Exile (17:24–19:9a)
  (B) David Processes to Jerusalem (19:9b–44)
  (C) Further Attempts to Topple David (20:1–25)
(VI) David Prepares for Israel's Future under Yahweh (21:1–24:25)
  (A) Suppression of the Saulides and Their Enemy, the Philistines (21:1–22)
    (a) David Allows the Massacre of Saul's House (21:1–14)
    (b) Philistine Unrest (21:15–22)
  (B) Praise and Thanksgiving (22:1–23:7)
    (a) The Psalm of David (22:1–51)
    (b) David's Last Words (23:1–7)
  (C) Submitting the Administration to Yahweh (23:8–24:25)
    (a) David's Warriors (23:8–39)
    (b) Census, Plague, and Preparations for Yahweh's House (24:1–25)

1 SAMUEL

COMMENTARY

6   **(I) Intimations of Change (1:1–7:17).** This first major section reflects the different understandings of the events concerned with the advent of kingship in

Israel. The first intimation of change is the emergence of a prophetic figure in Israel (1:1–4:1a). This derives from the Prophetic Record, with its emphasis on the role of the prophet in this formative period of Israel's national history. The second intimation of change is the departure of the ark from the mainstream of Israel's liturgical life (4:1b-7:1). Most probably an independent narrative originally, it owes its place in the present text to the compositional work of the deuteronomistic historians. The departure of the ark at this point and its absence from Israel's traditions until its coming to Jerusalem suited the Dtr interpretation of history. The judgeship of Samuel (7:2-17) combines the concerns of the Prophetic Record and Dtr: the aspects of the powerful prophetic figure come from the Prophetic Record; those of the deliverer judge are from Dtr.

7   (A) The Emergence of a Prophet (1:1-4:1a). This section is a carefully arranged composition, culminating in the statement of Samuel's recognition before all Israel (3:19-4:1a). Sandwiched between two major Samuel stories are alternating Samuel and Elide traditions, which set Samuel in a favorable light and the Elides in a most unfavorable one.

(a) BIRTH OF SAMUEL (1:1-2:11). The skillfully told story portrays the classic situation of the oppressed woman. Barren and childless, she is scorned by her rival within the household. No attentive listener could miss the echoes of Sarah's situation (cf. Gen 16:1-5). The overall impact of the story is clear: Samuel is the Lord's gift to an oppressed woman in Israel. His life is God's gift; in return, his life is given to God. To an oppressed Israel under Philistine threat, his can only be a figure heavy with significance for the future.

This is underlined by the song put on the lips of Hannah. With its reference to the king (2:10), it is clearly an anachronism; in the sentiments it expresses, it is an apt inclusion here. Hannah exults in the Lord and rejoices in her salvation; the Lord is the central figure of her song. None is holy like the Lord, none is protector like the Lord. Israel's foes will be broken; Israel's king will be exalted. This is the meaning of what Yahweh is to do in Israel through the ministry of Samuel, his prophet.

(b) EMERGENCE OF SAMUEL AMONG THE ELIDES (2:12-3:18). The compositional arrangement of the text, esp. in chap. 2, juxtaposes passages concerning the Elides with others concerning Samuel. The Elide material moves from the description of their sin, through the stubborn refusal to accept reproof, to the final, twofold announcement of judgment. The Samuel material, by contrast, begins with the family image of the growing child, then the growth of the lad in stature and favor before the Lord and Israel, to the point where he can receive and transmit the Lord's word of judgment. The two trajectories intersect in 3:1-18, where the final judgment is pronounced on the Elides in an encounter with God that is the beginning of Samuel's prophetic function. The origin of the material is far more complicated than this simple compositional pattern might suggest.

The Elide material is of disparate origin. In chap. 2, vv 12-17 concern sacrificial abuses and could be continuous with the admonition given by Eli in 2:22-25, although this now contains a clumsy reference to sexual abuses as well. Verses 27-36 direct their principal accusation against Eli himself rather than his sons. The sentence is that none of Eli's house will live to honorable old age (see M. Tsevat, *HUCA* 32 [1961] 191-216). The accusation of not rebuking his sons (3:13) directly contradicts 2:22-25. The Samuel material in chap. 2 is sparse in the extreme and stretched to the maximum to provide a contrasting alternation.

Chap. 3 moves to a new story. The reference to

Samuel's service in the sanctuary (3:1a) continues the contrast with the Elides, but it also prepares for the story to come, as does the note on the rarity of God's word in those days. This is a story about the reception of God's word; it contains a command to communicate that specific word — but no call to be prophet. In the Samuel traditions, it has to play the role of call narrative, but, as with the bare traditions in chap. 2, this can only be for lack of anything better. The message is disastrous for the Elides: all that Yahweh has said against them will be fulfilled. It implies familiarity with what precedes, but the language of the accusation is different.

(c) RECOGNITION BEFORE ALL ISRAEL (2:19-4:1a). At first sight, this may seem just one more counterbalance to the evil of the Elides. But on closer inspection, it is clear that it transcends the bounds of anything hinted at in the preceding traditions. The simple introductory "And Samuel grew" (v 19a) is a most inadequate bridge to a Samuel none of whose words Yahweh let fall to the ground (v 19b), and who was known to all Israel as a prophet of Yahweh (v 20), the vehicle of Yahweh's revelation at Shiloh (v 21), whose word went out to all Israel (4:1a). The passage portrays an image of Samuel as prophet to the nation which may have its foundations in the preceding traditions, but which has certainly gone beyond them.

8   (B) The Departure of the Ark (4:1b-7:1). Since Rost's study in 1926, these chapters have been seen as a unity, an ark narrative, often seen to have its conclusion in 2 Sam 6. Its precise extent and significance have been the subject of debate in recent years (see F. Schicklberger, *Die Ladeerzählungen des ersten Samuel-Buches* [FB 7; Würzburg, 1973]; A. F. Campbell, *The Ark Narrative (1 Sam 4-6; 2 Sam 6)* [SBLDS 16; Missoula, 1975]; and P. D. Miller, Jr., and J. J. M. Roberts, *The Hand of the Lord* [Baltimore, 1977]; also Campbell, *JBL* 98 [1979] 318-43; and Gordon, *1 & 2 Samuel* [→ 4 above] 30-39). Discussion of the differences cannot be undertaken here. The view maintained by the present writer is that the ark narrative puts forward one particular theological interpretation of history, current in the time of David and Solomon. This is that an epoch in Israel's history ended at Shiloh, with the departure of the ark, and that, with the coming of the ark to Jerusalem, a new epoch dawned. This theological interpretation, in its single-minded focus on the ark as the symbol of Yahweh's presence and purpose, leaves aside the very significant events that occurred while the ark was absent from the mainstream of Israel's cultic life. Although this is odd, it is not cause for objection; the same omission is made by Ps 78 (see Campbell, *CBQ* 41 [1979] 51-79). Whatever the interpretation given, it is important to take these seemingly strange stories seriously and search out a coherent horizon within which the various traditions fit into place and give sense to the whole.

(a) DEPARTURE FROM ISRAEL (4:1b-22). When the defeated Israelites returned to their camp, the narrator has the elders ask, "Why did Yahweh defeat us today before the Philistines?" (4:3a). It is a remarkable question, and the answer is provided only by the narrative as a whole — i.e., it was Yahweh's will to bring about a change of epochs. For the moment the question is left hanging. The ark is brought from Shiloh to the battlefield. The narrator, who knows full well what is to come, orchestrates a tumultuous reception for the ark, with both Israelite and Philistine camps sure that its coming means victory for the Israelites (vv 5-9). Then the second battle is reported, Israel is definitively defeated, and the ark is lost to the Philistines. Two anecdotes follow. Their significance: The loss of the ark is no passing moment in the fortunes of war; for the narrator, its meaning is deathly and definitive—"the glory has departed from Israel."

9   (b) PERIPETEIA IN THE LAND OF THE PHILISTINES (5:1-12). The point of the first story is clear: In his own temple, Dagon has been vanquished by Yahweh. It is a complete reversal of fortune. But its implications are ominous for Israel. In the light of the story's earlier question, "Why did Yahweh defeat us today?" (4:3), the conclusion seems inescapable: Yahweh, who was in control in the temple of Dagon, was also in control on the battlefield of Ebenezer-Aphek. Then Yahweh's departure was Yahweh's will.

The narrative continues with the Philistines afflicted by plagues on account of the ark (vv 6-12). First at Ashdod, then at Gath, and finally at Ekron—three of the five Philistine cities—wherever the ark goes, plagues, fear, and deathly panic result among the Philistines. From a narrative point of view, the message is the same: Yahweh is master in Philistine territory; therefore, Yahweh was master on the battlefield.

(c) RETURN TO KIRIATH-JEARIM (6:1-7:1). The narrative in this chapter is complicated. The Philistines consult their diviners about what to do with the ark of Yahweh. The response is twofold: What offerings to send back with the ark, and how to send it back in such a way as to know whether the plagues were in fact from Yahweh because of the ark. The divination is set up to force God to reveal his hand by doing the utterly unlikely—which is exactly what happened. The two cows headed straight for Israel with the ark; they went away from their home and their calves, toward the home of the ark. It should now be clear to all that Yahweh's power has been orchestrating the entire situation (cf. 6:9).

Naturally, the ark is received in triumph in Israel, at Beth-shemesh. But again the narrative has a surprise in store. Sudden death strikes among the people of Beth-shemesh. The ark may be back in Israel, but Israel is not back in favor. So the ark is lodged at Kiriath-jearim, a cultic backwater; and there it stays, far from the mainstream of Israel's life and worship. The narrative thread is here held in suspense until—either in the same narrative, or in a further reflection that is modeled on it—the ark, still under Yahweh's control, is brought to Jerusalem, now the city of David (2 Sam 6).

10   (C) The Judgeship of Samuel (7:2-17). After its exclusive focus on the ark, the text returns to the prophet Samuel. Samuel leads the people in a ceremony of repentance, described in vv 5-6; the reason is to be understood as Philistine oppression (cf. Judg 13:1 and what follows here). Verses 3-4 are almost certainly deuteronomistic, offering an interpretation of the sin responsible for the oppression.

Samuel is portrayed interceding for Israel, menaced by Philistine forces; Yahweh thunders, and the Philistines are defeated. It is possible that part of this text belonged in the Prophetic Record (→ 4 above), establishing the figure of the prophet Samuel. At the level of Dtr, Samuel is here seen as the last of the great deliverer judges, ending the epoch that began in Judg 2. Deliverance for Israel is provided by Yahweh, through the judge, and it lasts at least the lifetime of the judge (cf. 7:13). There is tension here between this lasting victory and the Philistine threat in 9:16; it is a clash of traditions.

11   (II) Introduction of a New Epoch in Israel (1 Sam 8:1-12:25). Up till this point in its history, Israel had apparently been largely devoid of political institutions on a national scale. At least, attempts to reconstruct premonarchical institutions, such as the amphictyony, have foundered on lack of evidence. With the emergence of the monarchy in Israel, a change of the greatest significance for national life took place; hardly a village in Israel escaped its effect, and hardly a theological aspect of Israel's self-understanding remained untouched by it. The present text of 1 Sam 8-12 explores differing views of the new institution. The precise analysis and attribution of the text in these chapters is greatly debated. Older views postulated two sources, one promonarchical and the other antimonarchical. Noth argued for an older presentation favorable to monarchy in 1 Sam 9:1-10:16; 11:1-15, with an exilic Deuteronomist expressing a more nuanced counterperspective in 1 Sam 8; 10:17-27; 12. The hypothesis of the Prophetic Record (→ 4 above) provides a literary setting for the favorable presentation. Proposals for more than one edition of Dtr have opened the way to further nuances in understanding the Dtr texts. A not unfavorable Josianic redaction, drawing on various traditions, may have been given increasingly negative coloring by exilic expansions (cf. Veijola, *Königtum;* and Mayes, *Story of Israel* [→ 4 above]; for the analysis adopted here, I am indebted to Fr. Mark O'Brien, O.P.).

12   (A) Demand for a King (8:1-22). This section begins with three little verses that serve as a reminder of how much we do not know of ancient Israel. Samuel is reported to have made his sons judges over Israel, based in Beer-sheba (8:1-3). We know nothing of the powers that might have enabled him to do so, nor of an institution of sufficient authority to have given rise to national discontent. In the present text, however, this serves as pretext for the demand for a king, based on the absence of social justice. The demand is acceded to by the Lord, after a warning has been issued (vv 11-17, probably an older polemic tradition). A unitary approach sees kingship originating from this popular demand, interpreted by Yahweh as rejection, with which Samuel is to comply, after issuing due warning. In a redactional approach, vv 6a,11-17,19-22 portray Samuel's indignation being overcome by Yahweh's order (v 22). The addition of vv 6b-7aα,9-10 changes the warning from Samuel into a warning from Yahweh. The addition of the rest of v 7 turns the demand into the people's rejection of Yahweh as their king; v 18 may express the consequences of this rejection. Verse 8 transforms this rejection into apostasy.

13   (B) Secret Anointing of Saul as King-to-Be (9:1-10:16). Evidently not a unitary text, 1 Sam 9:1-10:16 has been the subject of much controversy. In my judgment, the best analysis has been provided by L. Schmidt (*Menschlicher Erfolg und Jahwes Initiative* [WMANT 38; Neukirchen, 1970] 58-102; see my summary in *Of Prophets and Kings* 18-21). An old prophetic story, in which Saul was commissioned by an anonymous prophet to do whatever lay in his power on behalf of Israel (10:7), has been the subject of further prophetic redaction. The anonymous prophet is altered to Samuel, alerted to Saul's coming by Yahweh; Saul is to be anointed *nāgîd*, in order to deliver Israel from the Philistines (9:16). Samuel carries out this commission (10:1). A number of traditions about Saul have become attached to this significant passage: 10:5-6,10-13a incorporate one of the etiologies of the saying about Saul among the prophets; 10:8 prepares the way for Saul's rejection in 13:7b-15a; 9:2b and 9 are probably independent glosses.

The passage in its present form paints a picture of the origin of kingship in Israel as coming directly from the spontaneous and gracious initiative of Yahweh. Yahweh has seen Israel's affliction and heard their cry, so Saul is sent to receive the prophetic anointing as *nāgîd,* king-designate, the one who will save Yahweh's people.

Belonging in the Prophetic Record, it is part of the prophetic redaction of older traditions. The account of Saul's coronation (11:15) is not suppressed, so this anointing must be maintained as secret (10:14–16). The effect of this prophetic commission will be seen in the story of 1 Sam 11.

14   (C) Public Acclamation of Saul as King (10:17–27). The passage presents the second of three national assemblies, drawing on material of diverse origin. The people are summoned to Mizpah by Samuel and addressed by him (vv 17–19); the king is identified and acclaimed (vv 20–25); the subsequent reactions are categorized (vv 26–27).

This assembly can be seen as the implementation of Yahweh's order to hearken to the people, to which is prefaced a repeated warning by Samuel. Without Samuel's address (vv 18–19), the passage is basically favorable to kingship, with the king chosen by Yahweh. Those who rallied to Saul are described as "men of valor whose hearts God had touched," while those who cling to the former orthodoxy—"How can this man save us?"—are categorized as "worthless fellows." Epochs have changed. Verses 18–19 may well be a later exilic antimonarchical polemic (cf. 8:7,8).

The choice of the king is presented with two traditions blended. In one the choice was made between groups and then finally between individuals, apparently through the use of the lot (vv 20–21); in the other an oracular pronouncement, such as "He shall be king who stands head and shoulders above all the people," served to identify the man to be king (vv 22–24). The former technique may have seemed more revelatory of God's will than the latter, with its emphasis on physical stature and strength.

15   (D) Demonstration of Saul's Kingly Charisma (11:1–15). The preceding text speaks of the people's acclamation of Saul as king, but does not actually report his being made king. This subtle distinction allows the composer of the final text to juxtapose 10:17–27 with 11:1–15. The Jabesh-gilead episode demonstrates Saul's charismatic power to rally and deliver Israel, which leads to his being made king at the Gilgal sanctuary. The mention of Samuel in v 7 is unlikely to have been original; vv 12–13 correlate with 10:26–27—epochs have indeed changed; in v 14, "renew" the kingdom is probably the compiler's harmonization for an original "establish."

The story is told in such a way as to emphasize the powerlessness of Israel. Jabesh-gilead is about to yield to its besiegers, submitting to a harsh and most humiliating condition (v 2). So helpless is Israel that the besiegers are presented as willing to wait a week, while messengers from Jabesh-gilead scour Israel in search of deliverance. There is nothing in the story to suggest that Saul has already been chosen as king in Israel. The messengers come to the city which later bore Saul's name; they make their report to the people. There is no reference to Saul as already king. Instead, the spirit of God empowered Saul, he rallied Israel and delivered Jabesh-gilead. This can be correlated with the prophetic commission given him in 10:7. The result is Saul's establishment as king, at the sanctuary of Gilgal. Kingship has been portrayed as needed in view of Philistine affliction (9:16); it is portrayed as established as a result of deliverance from Ammonite oppression.

16   (E) Instruction of Israel by Samuel on Ways of Kingship (12:1–25). By linking directly with the festive gathering at Gilgal, the chapter portrays the third national assembly conducted by Samuel. Whether or not older traditions can be identified in the chapter (see D. J. McCarthy, *Treaty and Covenant* [AnBib 21A;

Rome, 1978] 206–13), its form and place here in the text are due either to the deuteronomistic historian (so Noth) or to a later deuteronomistic editor (so Veijola, *Königtum;* Mayes, *Story of Israel* [→ 4 above] 101). Although vv 1–5 pick up aspects of chap. 8, and vv 7–11 reflect aspects of Judg (cf. McCarter, *I Samuel* 211), there remains a largely unsolved puzzle: either this is a remarkably loose reading of the traditions, or there are selective criteria operating which so far escape us.

In a unitary understanding of the deuteronomistic contribution, chap. 12 is seen as bringing together the preceding traditions of popular demand and divine initiative (v 13) and validating the new institution. If it is a later exilic expansion, the negative tone may come to the fore: the demand for a king is viewed as disloyal and evil (vv 12,17,19–20; this is midway in tone between 8:9–10 and 8:7, but not as severe as 8:8). The primary evil is the failure to turn to Yahweh as in the time of the judges. In either case, the monarchy is accepted, without having ruptured Israel's relationship with Yahweh. The conditions are laid down: king and people must remain obedient to the Lord. Verse 14 should be understood in parallel with v 15: "*If* you will fear the Lord and serve him and hearken to his voice and do not rebel against the commandment of the Lord, *then* you and the king over you will truly be his followers" (see McCarthy, *Treaty and Covenant* 215; an alternative involving emendation is offered by McCarter, *I Samuel* 211–12).

If Israel remains within the parameters of its relationship with Yahweh, as understood in Dtr, then fidelity to Yahweh is possible, even under this new institution; on the other hand, if the monarchy engenders a confidence that inspires rebellion against Yahweh, it will spell disaster for Israel. Hence the possibility of forgiveness and the need for intercession (vv 19–25).

17   (III) The Beginnings of the Kingdom (1 Sam 13:1–2 Sam 5:10). The beginnings of kingship in Israel are decidedly shaky. No sooner is Saul in office than he is rejected. With David's emergence on the scene, conflict occurs between the two and rapidly expands. After Saul's death, it continues with Saul's heirs. Only in 2 Sam 5 is David undisputed king over both Judah and Israel and established in Jerusalem, a strategically placed and neutral capital city.

(A) Rejection of Israel's First King (13:1–15:35). While the story of Saul might be said to extend from 1 Sam 9 to 31, in the present text his fall from favor occurs promptly and David, his replacement, is very soon designated by Samuel. In this section of the text, two prophetic stories form a bracket around the traditions of the fighting at Michmash.

18   (a) FIRST ACCOUNT OF REJECTION (13:1–15a). Saul was anointed to deliver Israel from the Philistines, and now conflict with the Philistines looms up. It is presented as triggered by Jonathan's defeat of a Philistine garrison (13:3). The narrative sequence is interrupted by vv 7b–15a, an account that circulated in prophetic circles to explain Saul's rejection. It is prepared for by 10:8, also an insertion in its context (note the contrast with 10:7).

At one level, it might seem that Samuel is unreasonable: he had failed to meet his own deadline; Saul had waited the prescribed time and had only acted out of dire need. But in the view of the prophetic circles, obedience to the word of Yahweh is absolutely primary and outweighs all other considerations. While the formulation of vv 13–14 facilitates the insertion of this episode before chap. 15, the two accounts are doublets rather than a deliberate progression.

(b) BATTLE AT MICHMASH (13:15b–14:52). The narrative reverts to the conflict with the Philistines. While the Philistines were described in 13:5 as mobilizing in massive numbers, 13:17–18 suggests more limited skirmishing parties. The seriousness of even this level of Philistine threat is indicated by Israel's total dependence on the Philistines for metal-working skills and, therefore, for weapons (13:19–22).

14:1 begins the story of an episode of extraordinary bravado on Jonathan's part. Overall, it would seem that a story extolling a heroic feat of Jonathan has been built up, by traditions and embellishment, almost to the point of portraying a pitched battle against the Philistines. It is interesting that Saul comes out of it badly. Jonathan is clearly the hero: "Shall Jonathan die, who has wrought this great victory in Israel?" (14:45). Saul's behavior has been strange and unhelpful, and his encounter with the Philistines has been to some extent inconclusive (14:46). The narrative was probably preserved among circles which needed to keep Jonathan's memory alive. It gives an odd foretaste of Saul's later activity—strange, unhelpful, and inconclusive.

19   (c) SECOND ACCOUNT OF REJECTION (15:1–35). There is probably an old story behind this chapter in which Samuel rebuked Saul for disobedience in executing the ban or *ḥērem* against the Amalekites; it would have consisted of 15:1aα,2–9,13–15,17a,18–22,24–25, 31–35a (see Campbell, *Of Prophets and Kings* 132–36). The present text has been sharpened by prophetic redaction, transforming it from rebuke to rejection. Saul has failed in obedience to a specific divine command; he is therefore rejected from being king. The same language of the "tearing away" of the kingdom, used here, will later be used of Solomon's kingdom being torn away and given to Jeroboam (1 Kgs 11:31). The same understanding of the prophetic role is present in the prophetic dismissals of Jeroboam and Ahab, as well as in the prophetic designations of Saul, David, Jeroboam, and Jehu.

20   (B) Rise to Power of Israel's Second King (1 Sam 16:1–2 Sam 5:10). With the prophetic rejection of Saul, the focus of the narrative begins to shift toward David. In the present shape of the text, the secret anointing by Samuel brings David into the narrative as destined for kingship. This is finally achieved in 2 Sam 5:1–5. In between, there is a complex of stories reflecting the growing tension between Saul and David and usually referred to as the Story of David's Rise. Its exact extent and nature are still the subject of debate (see my *Of Prophets and Kings* 125–38). The story of David and Goliath (probably from 16:14–18:16, in the shorter LXX form) provided a microcosm of how David came to power. Empowered by Yahweh's spirit, he stepped into the leadership vacuum left by the dispirited Saul and acted to deliver Israel. The principals mentioned in the summary verses of 1 Sam 18:14–16 are the players in the drama of David's rise—David, Saul, and all Israel and Judah. The summary anticipates the conclusion in 2 Sam 5:1–3. The interplay of the story in 16:14–18:16* and the larger complex of stories suggests that this collection did form a story of David's rise, carefully arranged by a compiler to offer an interpretation of the events that brought David to power in Israel. It seeks to show that the trajectory which brought David to the throne was the will of God, that there was no justification for the charge of ruthless ambition, as later formulated by Shimei (2 Sam 16:7–8; see McCarter, *JBL* 99 [1980] 489–504). There are a number of doublets and other traditions that have since come into the narrative; in my judgment, these are 1 Sam 17:12–31,41,48b,50,55–18:6aα,10–11,12b,17–19,21b,29b–30; 19:3aα,18–20:1a, 14–23,37–39; 21:10–15; 23:6,19–24a; 24:1–23 (*RSV* 23:29–24:22); 25:1b; 2 Sam 4:2b–4; and from the Prophetic Record (→ 4 above), 1 Sam 16:1–13; 25:1a;

28:17–19a; 2 Sam 5:2bβ; and from Dtr, 2 Sam 2:10a,11; 3:2–5; 5:4–5,13–16.

(a) SECRET ANOINTING OF DAVID (16:1–13). This passage gives to David the legitimation that had been taken from Saul. There is no trace of it in the following Davidic traditions, until an oblique reference in 2 Sam 5:2. It is to be attributed to the prophetic redaction, bringing out in their particular theological language what is implicit in the stories of David's rise: David's success was due to the presence of Yahweh's spirit with him.

21   (b) DEMONSTRATION OF DAVID'S CHARISMA (16:14–18:5). The portrayal of David's emergence as the leader in Israel who possessed Yahweh's spirit probably extended originally from 16:14 to 18:16, in the text form now preserved only in the LXX; it concluded with the three summary verses in 18:14–16. The present text cannot be treated as a unity; despite the composer's skill, the discontinuity is insurmountable.

Two different stories have been combined. One, of folktale type, tells of the young shepherd who distinguished himself in battle in the hope of winning royal favor and the hand of the king's daughter in marriage (see 17:12–14,17–30*,41,48b,50,55–18:5; it is continued in 18:17–19,21b,29b–30, with the probability that a story has been suppressed between 18:21b and 29b–30). The other is a more sophisticated and theologically oriented story (see 16:14–23; 17:1–11, 32–40,42–48a,49,51–54; 18:6aβ–9,12a,13–16). It functions as a prelude to the collection of stories that portray David's rise to the throne of Israel (see A. F. Campbell, "From Philistine to Throne," *AusBR* 34 [1986] 35–41).

The interpretation of the story as a whole has frequently been bedeviled by the folktale's emphasis on the shepherd and the general conviction that David is portrayed as "small, apparently defenseless" (McCarter, *I Samuel* 297). Being the youngest son says nothing about size or age. The offer of his armor by Saul, who stood head and shoulders over Israel, would be incongruous if David were thought of as small; so too the exchange with Jonathan (18:4). Far from defenseless, the sling was an accurate specialist weapon (Judg 20:16), and David ideal to wield it (vv 34–37). Saul's objection relates to military experience (v 33).

The principal thrust of the second, more sophisticated and theological story is the comparison between Saul and David. Saul has been abandoned by Yahweh (16:14); Yahweh is with David. The story unfolds the contrast, presenting them side by side (v 11 juxtaposed with v 32), Saul dismayed by unkingly fear and David bearing himself in thoroughly spirited fashion. Saul is portrayed trusting in arms, while David trusts in God. Saul's objection portrays the dispirited despair of an abandoned king. Bereft of God's spirit, he is unable to deliver his people; instead, David demonstrates his leadership qualities, delivering Israel from this Philistine threat, and showing that God is with him. The victory over the Philistine is the beginning of David's move toward the throne. Even though this understanding has been diluted by the combination of the two stories, it can still be seen as the predominant thrust of the present text.

In the present text, after his victory and the demonstration of his charisma, David is taken into Saul's court and forms a friendship with Jonathan, elements that belong in the folktale version of the David and Goliath story. The episode is closed off by mention of David's success, implying the passage of time and emphasizing David's reputation with the people at large and even Saul's entourage.

22   (c) UNFOLDING OF DAVID'S RISE AND SAUL'S DECLINE (18:6–31:13). The stories assembled in the rest of 1 Sam point to the way in which David became king over Israel and Judah. Saul's fear and David's charisma were contrasted in the David and Goliath story. The stories that follow continue this picture of Saul's decline and David's rise. Originally this section began with the Michal story (in 18:20–21a,22–29a), following on the summary verses in 18:14–16. The combination of traditions in the present text takes its beginnings back to the first intimations of Saul's jealousy, starting with 18:6. The goal is intimated by 18:14–16. It will be accomplished when David has replaced Saul as king of Israel and Judah.

(i) *First intimations* (18:6–16). The text, in its present form, focuses on the first hint of the coming conflict. The women's song, echoing more the reality of the future than the facts of the past, celebrates David's triumph. The narrative draws attention to Saul's anger, his perception that David will take the kingdom, and his jealous observation of the man he sees as his rival. **10–16.** With a second episode (vv 10–11), the narrative moves from thought to action. It is a scene of terrible irony. The tormented king seeks to destroy the lyre player who can soothe him; the man who can save the people is threatened by this delirious onrush of evil from the king who can save no longer. Verses 14–16 provide a definite closure.

23   (ii) *Conflict at court* (18:17–21:1 [*RSV* 20:42]). The traditions that make up this section of the narrative portray David's survival despite Saul's enmity and place the responsibility for the rift between the two squarely on Saul's shoulders. **18:17–19.** A cruel portrayal of Saul's duplicity. First, he is made to offer the hand of his elder daughter to David, as the warrior who would fight "the Lord's battles" for him, and the motivation attributed to him is the hope that David will be killed fighting the Philistines. Then, when this stratagem fails, Saul also fails to keep his agreement. The passage belongs to the additional material in the MT, and probably continued the theme of 17:25. **20–29a.** The Michal story is more developed. Saul's thought is portrayed as the same: let David, this threat to his throne, be killed in battle by the Philistines. When this too failed, the narrator comments that Saul was able to read the events and recognize that the Lord was with David (vv 28–29a).

24   **19:1–7.** The next little story takes Saul's enmity a step further. Unsuccessful in having the Philistines kill David, he commands his own soldiers and his son to do so; a reconciliation is effected by Jonathan. The tradition could reflect a report of Saul's heightened hostility and Jonathan's eloquence in saving the life of his friend. But the reference to Jonathan standing by his father in the field where David is hiding (19:3) hints at the possibility of its use for a much more elaborate story, parallel to chap. 20. In the present text, it serves the dual purpose of presenting Saul's murderous attitude toward David and of emphasizing David's innocence of any disloyalty (vv 4–5). **8–10.** A combination of a short notice of David's continued successes against the Philistines with a repetition of the spear-throwing episode. It is more properly at home here than at 18:10–11. The irony is immense. David is successful against the Philistines; Saul fails against David. David goes out to battle Israel's foes; Saul sits at home seeking to spear David. The Philistines flee before David; David has to flee before Saul. After the reconciliation, the notice of David's success serves to motivate Saul's renewed jealousy; in turn, the spear throwing provides an appropriate context for the following anecdote.

25   **19:11–17.** The episode of the dummy-in-the-bed has all the ingredients for dramatic storytelling. The king plans murder; the wise wife counsels flight. She elaborates the stratagem which enables the escape to be effective; it gains time and lets David get clear away. It is rather a report of the story than an actual version of it. It provides the ingredients of the plot, without attempting their elaboration. So the dummy is given elaborate attention in v 13, yet is ignored at the appropriate time, when the soldiers needed to be convinced that David was indeed sick in bed; the reference in v 15b comes too late. The episode contributes to the basic tenor of the narrative at this stage: what drove David to his later role as a guerrilla leader was the unremittingly murderous enmity of Saul. **18–24.** The present text has David's flight take him to Samuel, and the story details the pursuit, ending with Saul's bout of naked prophecy. The story functions as an etiology for the saying "Is Saul also among the prophets?" (v 19). Another etiology for the same saying is given in 10:10–12. The story quite probably originated in prophetic circles; the three bands of messengers sent by Saul to Samuel find an echo in the three bands of soldiers sent by Ahaziah to Elijah (2 Kgs 1:2–16). It is in conflict with the comment of the prophetic redaction in 1 Sam 15:35 that Samuel did not see Saul until the day of his death. Although this story is probably a later addition to the text, it contributes to the general tenor by placing David under the protection of Samuel and the spirit of God (v 20), and by having the spirit of God explicitly immobilize Saul (vv 23–24).

26   **20:1–21:1** (*RSV* 20:1–42). The section on the conflict at court is concluded by this major story detailing David and Jonathan's attempts to ascertain Saul's real intentions. In the course of the story, Jonathan, who is reluctant to accept Saul's hostility to David, becomes convinced of it; the narrative intends to leave no doubt that David's guerrilla activities were forced upon him by Saul. Much of the story focuses on the clever stratagems devised to communicate with David without revealing his whereabouts. The need for this conveys the impression of just how actively Saul was now hunting David. The stratagems reveal a certain confusion in the narration (cf. vv 18–23 and 35–42). It is possible to see this as reflecting events, in which plans change in the heat of action and emotions can overwhelm earlier caution. Alternatively, the different stratagems or codes employed may be deliberate indications of different ways of telling the story.

Told as an independent story, this material—like so much in the story of David's rise—is open to a variety of emphases: the hostility of Saul, the loyalty of Jonathan, the foresight of David, or a rattling good story of the first experience of life under guerrilla conditions. In its present context, it has to relate to the final rupture between David and Saul. Saul emerges as determined to kill David (v 33); Jonathan, the crown prince (cf. v 31), emerges as David's firm ally. Jonathan is depicted legitimating the transfer of power: "May the Lord be with you, as he has been with my father" (v 13). It is in this context, probably, that vv 14–17 have been added to the story. They have the appearance of hindsight and belong with other traditions in 1–2 Sam concerned with placing Jonathan's descendants securely under David's protection.

27   (iii) *Open rupture* (21:2[1]–27:12). The next series of stories concerns David, the guerrilla leader, on the run from Saul. The bulk is about their conflict within Judah itself; at the end, David is driven out of his own country into an alliance with one of the Philistine lords. At the center of the section, two stories about Saul's pursuit of David's life, bracketing an assurance from Jonathan (chap. 23), are balanced by two stories about David's sparing Saul's life, bracketing a commendation from Abigail (chaps. 24–26).

The narrative has a very delicate task to perform. At

its original level, Saul is the established king and David is only an inordinately successful army commander. The preceding material has shown how David was hounded from the court by Saul's designs on his life. The text now portrays David as driven underground but still remarkably successful, as leader of a guerrilla force but respectful of the king, as relentlessly pursued but still blessed by the fact that the Lord is with him. In the present text, principally as shaped by the prophetic redaction, Saul has been rejected by Samuel and David has been anointed by Samuel. But at the level of events, nothing has happened to actualize this. The narrative is careful to make clear that David took no active initiative in this actualization; its unfolding was the Lord's doing alone.

28   21:2-10 (*RSV* 1-9). The first story details David's escape; it is a prelude to the horrifying episode of the slaughter of the priests at Nob. It is potentially damaging to David, since it could be considered that David's duplicity was responsible for triggering Saul's vengeance on the whole priestly population at Nob (cf. 22:22). On the other hand, David has been three days in hiding and he can assume that his home will be watched; he may be in dire need of food and weapons. His prevarication can then be understood as protecting Ahimelech from any involvement (cf. 22:15). Saul's folly is heightened by the depiction of his extraordinary reaction as totally groundless and unjustified. **11-16** (*RSV* 10-15). The anecdote about David at the court of Achish gives an example of David's quick-witted brilliance in the practice of the art of survival. In the hypothesis of a continuous narrative of the story of David's rise, it is in marked tension with the traditions now in chap. 27.

29   22:1-5. A collection of short notices prefaces the stories of David as guerrilla leader (see R. Rendtorff, in *Probleme biblischer Theologie* [Fest. G. von Rad; ed. H. W. Wolff; Munich, 1971] 428-39). David's first support comes from his family (v 1). The description of the rest of his followers is remarkable in its openness: the country's malcontents (v 2). The evacuation of his parents to Moab indicates a period of adversity and danger ahead. **6-23.** Several discrepancies serve as a reminder that many of these stories were independent before being combined into a sustained narrative. The picture of Saul's court is often contrasted unfavorably with the sophistication of David's; but one must remember that this tradition probably comes from Davidic circles. There is an indication of the immense economic changes involved in the institution of kingship (v 7). The brunt of the story is concerned with Saul's extraordinary aberration in wiping out a priestly house. The narrative portrays the deed as so repugnant that Saul's own soldiers would not do it; it is left to an Edomite to do it single-handedly, at Saul's explicit command. The picture is painted as darkly as possible (v 19), putting Saul in a very negative light. David benefits by the escape of Abiathar, a priest with the ephod, who is now numbered among David's adherents.

30   23:1-14. Two remarkable stories are used to sharpen the contrast between Saul and David. Using the ephod for divining Yahweh's will, David goes to the rescue of Keilah against all sound military sense (v 3), and he saves Keilah. "Save" is a strong word; the exploit recalls Saul's achievement at Jabesh-gilead. David is doing the delivering that Saul was anointed to do. The second story underlines the irony of this. Saul, who should be fighting against the Philistines, gathers his forces to fight against David—in vain. Forewarned by Yahweh, David and his men escape. **15-18.** The short notice of this last meeting between David and Jonathan has to have come from Davidic circles. Its purpose is to

claim legitimation for David's future leadership from Saul's crown prince; they are the final words of Jonathan in the narrative—almost his testament. **19-28.** Verses 19-24a are probably the introduction to the story of chap. 24; they do not cohere well with vv 24b-28. Verse 19b is intended to correlate with vv 18 and 24b (cf. 26:1-3). In their present position, they place maximum emphasis on Saul's pursuit, painting a picture of Saul in eager pursuit of David's life. The chase on either side of the mountain has the potential for gripping storytelling, where, irony of ironies, the Philistines are the cause of David's deliverance from Saul.

31   24:1-23 (*RSV* 23:19-24:22). The story is a doublet of chap. 26. There are a number of difficulties. The sequence in the cave episode is disjointed; vv 5b-6 (*RSV* 4b-5) appear to have been inserted between the soldiers' inciting David and his rejecting their proposal. The insertion allows the episode to be expanded along the lines of chap. 26. David's emergence from the cave, despite the presence of Saul's three thousand soldiers (v 3 [*RSV* 2]), and the motif of recognizing David's voice, as though it were night (v 17 [*RSV* 16]), all point to dependence on the version in chap. 26. The end of the story confirms this; Saul concedes more than in the later story, and David's oath sounds a stronger and more final note than the ending of chap. 26 (see also McCarter, *I Samuel* 385-87).

32   25:1-44. Samuel's death is noted, preparing the way for the story in chap. 28. Then follows the splendid story of David's encounter with Nabal and Abigail. At one level, it is a story of the guerrilla band living off the land. At another level, it is a model story for David's friends and foes; those who befriend him are richly rewarded, whereas those who oppose him are struck dead by God. At a third level, it is a story of Abigail's prudence and wisdom in preventing David from unnecessary bloodshed and in speaking with great foresight of his future.

As a story of the guerrilla band, it is careful to assert that David and his men did no harm and stole nothing (v 7) and to have this fully confirmed (vv 15-16). As a model story, it is colored in stark black and white: the villain is churlish and ill-behaved; the heroine is wise and lovely (v 3). It is Abigail's speech, eloquent in its appeasement and its discreet flattery, which has attracted most attention. Brilliantly she deflects the angry David from the possible bloodshed that would have wiped out her wealth and besmirched his reputation; prudently she speaks well of what the Lord will do for David and hints at a place for herself in that future felicity. Doubts have been raised about the originality of parts of the speech (e.g., Veijola, *Ewige Dynastie* 47-55; McCarter, *I Samuel* 401-2). The arguments are less attractive when the whole is viewed as a storyteller's creation, probably at David's court; there are no clear characteristics of Dtr language. The anticipation in v 26 is prudent rhetoric— the assumption that what the speaker desires will indeed become reality. The development in vv 28-31 is appropriate for courtly flattery of Abigail's perceptiveness without incautiously exaggerating her foresight (see Campbell, *Of Prophets and Kings* 58-60).

33   26:1-25. It is small wonder that this story was repeated in more than one version (cf. chap. 24). It has great potential for excitement and tension. Saul pursues David with 3,000 men; we know that David's band numbers 600 at this time. The narrator tells us that David sent out spies and then, with Abishai, penetrated Saul's camp. We are not told anything of David's intentions, until he declines to kill Saul and retires instead with Saul's spear and his water jar. In the dialogue in the night, David pleads his innocence and his right to stay in the land. In their exchange, Saul and David reach a certain level of reconciliation.

The irony of the story is that while here David pleads successfully not to be driven away from the land, in the next chapter he decides to escape to the Philistines. The concern of chap. 26 is less a reconciliation between Saul and David than a justification of David. The justification is most evident in David's speeches, over the sleeping body of Saul (vv 10-11) and in the dialogue with the wakened Saul (vv 18-20,23-24). It is confirmed in the speeches given to Saul (vv 21,25). David's fatalistic theology comes to the fore in vv 10 and 19; it will recur in 2 Sam 12:22-23; 15:25-26; 16:10-12 (cf. 1 Sam 22:3). Strangely, this theme is unparalleled elsewhere, and one wonders if it is a trait that does go back to David. Saul's blessing pronounced over David (v 25) is the last word spoken between the two. The story allows the narrator to achieve their parting on a relatively peaceful note, with David thoroughly vindicated by the very man who had sought so long to take his life. Yet they remain apart.

34   **27:1-12.**   The narrator renders the reconciliation extremely short-lived; David's expressed certainty that he will ultimately die at Saul's hands can only reflect negatively on the untrustworthiness of the troubled king. The reflection given to David (v 1) sets the tone for the traditions that follow. On their own, they could point to treachery; after v 1, they make it clear that the one man who might deliver Israel has been forced out of the country by the king who cannot deliver his country.

It is still to be made clear how David survived in this highly ambiguous situation. Nothing has been said explicitly of how David's men fended for themselves in Judah; the story of Nabal and Abigail both arouses suspicions and denies them. Will David's safety among the Philistines have been at the cost of his fellow Israelites? David is portrayed as playing a very cool double game. Based in an outlying town, he can raid Israel's foes and present the spoils to his Philistine master as having been plundered from the Israelites themselves. These traditions permit the narrator to bring this part of the narrative to closure: David is free of Saul and satisfactorily situated among the Philistines. But the situation cannot last.

35   (iv) *Ultimate failure of Saul* (28:1-31:13).   This section of the narrative, leading to the death of Saul and his sons on Mt. Gilboa, presents a very tricky task to a pro-Davidic narrator. The traditions are too important and probably too well known to be passed over (cf. McCarter, *I Samuel* 416), but they are capable of widely differing interpretations. In compiling the traditions, the narrator is careful to present them in such a way as to minimize any suspicion that might be cast on David.

There is a diversity in the traditions of chaps. 28-31, but they have been welded into a loose unity. The Philistine preparations for war are reported (v 1a) and also David's engagement to serve under Achish in this war (vv 1b-2). This is continued in 29:1-2, where the purpose of the war and the engagement of David are both presumed. But 28:3-25 presupposes a later stage in the preparations. The loose unity is evident in the reflection of chap. 29 in 30:1 and in the absence of the usual preparatory details in 31:1. Chaps. 28-29 are focused on the preparations for war: David is engaged by Achish (28:1-2); Saul is rejected by Yahweh (28:3-25); David is rejected by the Philistines (29:1-11). Chaps. 30-31 portray the contrasting destinies of David and Saul: David succeeds against the Amalekites (30:1-31); Saul fails against the Philistines (31:1-13). It is most likely that this is a deliberate compositional arrangement.

36   **28:1-2.**   The general notice on the Philistine preparations for war is followed by David's exchange with Achish. It highlights David's dilemma: acceptance would jeopardize David's integrity; refusal would jeopardize his safety. David's reply can be read as cleverly ambiguous. **3-25.** The story of the final encounter between Samuel and Saul, with the help of the medium of Endor, is prefaced by two necessary bits of information. Samuel has died, and Saul has banished the mediums and wizards. The gathering of the Philistine and Israelite forces is then reported, located in the Plain of Esdraelon. As he was afraid before Goliath (17:11), so Saul is once again portrayed as fearful before the Philistines; as Saul was then abandoned by the Lord (16:14), so now he is unable to reach the Lord. In desperation, he turns to a forbidden medium and the spirit of the dead Samuel. Samuel's words justify Saul's despair; the Lord has turned from him and become his enemy and the Philistines will be victorious. An addition by the prophetic redactors, generally identified as vv 17-19aα, links an older, more general saying explicitly with the prophetic redaction of the account of Saul's rejection and David's anointing (1 Sam 15; 16:1-13). The story concludes with emphasis on Saul's weakness from fear and lack of food; the woman can alleviate the hunger but not the terror.

For the narrator, the place of this story in the compositional arrangement of the narrative serves to make clear from the outset that Saul's death in this war is decreed by Yahweh. With David absolved from any responsibility, the narrative is free to explore what David will do or not do in the coming campaign.

37   **29:1-11.**   Verses 1-2 continue the preliminaries of a battle report from 28:1a. The stage of preparations is earlier than that implied by 28:4. The Philistines are gathering at Aphek, on the coastal plain, before marching north through the hills into the Plain of Esdraelon. For plausible storytelling, David's dismissal has to be set here, where the Philistines are envisaged as bringing their army together for the first time.

The tradition is two-edged, and the narrator must treat it with care. It redounds to David's credit: he has completely duped Achish, and he has a well-founded reputation among the Philistine commanders (vv 4-5). Their objection opens up the possibility that David is planning to enter the fight on the side of Saul; the ambiguity of David's own claim reinforces it (v 8b). But if David and his men could have struck such a blow on Israel's behalf, are they to blame, then, for their absence on the day of battle? Samuel's prophecy has revealed Saul's doom; there is nothing David could have done. The Philistine lords insist on David's departure; there is nothing he can contribute in the battle. He returns southward; the Philistines proceed to Esdraelon.

38   **30:1-31.**   This long story delays the narrative on the brink of Saul's final conflict with the Philistines. The overall effect is the human picture of David dispirited, turning to God for strength and guidance, and succeeding magnificently in battle, government, and diplomacy. Though it is not emphasized, the battle was against great odds; those who escaped equaled the number of David's troops (v 17). So Yahweh's favor has given David victory (vv 8,23). A battle with the Amalekites was the occasion of Saul's rejection. Here the narrative has David triumphant against the Amalekites, before relating the outcome of Saul's rejection—his death at the hands of the Philistines.

39   **31:1-13.**   The report of Saul's ultimate failure is briefly told. The preliminary information has already been given (28:1a,4). First the defeat is noted (v 1b), then the death of Saul's sons (v 2), and finally the focus is turned to the manner of Saul's own death (vv 3-6). The political consequences of the defeat are reported (v 7).

The two final notices portray the seriousness of Israel's plight. The Philistines despoil Saul's armor, dishonor his body, and spread the news of victory throughout the Philistine territory (vv 8–10). No one from central Israel rescued the body of their defeated king; the feat is achieved by the people of Jabesh-gilead, from across the Jordan (vv 11–13). It is an act of fidelity, honoring the man whose deliverance of their town had singled him out for kingship (chap. 11). Now Saul's reign is ended. The recognition of his successor as deliverer in Israel is yet to come.

2 SAMUEL

COMMENTARY

40   (d) RECOGNITION OF DAVID'S LEADERSHIP (2 SAM 1:1–5:10).

(i) *Report of Saul's and Jonathan's deaths* (1:1–16). David's story continues by exposing the paradox the Yahwists face: how to centralize and stabilize leadership and worship without becoming like other nations (1 Sam 8:20). The compilers of the predeuteronomistic books resolve the issue by superimposing three interlocking themes: (1) Tension between David and Saul results in David's gradual but reluctant acceptance of divinely authorized leadership (esp. chaps. 1–6). (2) The struggle for legitimacy sullies Saul's house and infects those in David's who would move too quickly (esp. chaps. 3–21). (3) The final legitimation of David and his family is reserved for a cosmic, ritualized plane where he contests the deity directly (esp. chaps. 21–24). The skillful work of later pro-Solomonic redactors attaches the dynasty question to a specific Davidic successor (esp. chaps. 11–12; 1 Kgs 1–2; see J. Flanagan, *JBL* 91 [1972] 172–81) and links it immediately to Jerusalem's legitimation (chap. 7).

An ethos of competing segmented tribal systems and rivalry among proponents of sedentary agrarianism and pastoral nomadism is envisaged. Separate but related northern and southern centralization processes are portrayed. Jerusalem is reached twice, first when the ark legitimates the new Yahwist center (chap. 6), and again when David's exile culminates in final displacement of his opponents and the ark itself. Then he subsumes its legitimacy in his role as seed for his own posterity. The nomadic shrine gives way to agrarian symbolism.

41   Readers are guided by a series of genealogical and officer lists that serve not as beginnings and conclusions of narrative units but as thematic centers, benchmarks, and a skeleton that is a road map and mnemonic device for charting the story's and David's course. The lists can be summarized as follows:

A. 2:2–3:   Ziklag to Hebron   : : 2 wives (named)
                                     : : [no sons]
                                     : : his men and their families

B. 3:2–5:   at Hebron   : : 6 wives (named)
                                     : : 6 sons (named)

C. 5:13–16:   Hebron to Jerusalem : : "more" concubines and wives (unnamed)
                                     : : "more" sons and daughters (11 sons named)

D. 8:15–18:   at Jerusalem   : : [no wives mentioned]
                                     : : [sons priests?] (unnamed)
                                     : : 6[+?] officers
                                     : : 5[6?] offices

E. 20:23–26:   return to Jerusalem : : [no wives mentioned]
                                     : : 8 officers
                                     : : 7 offices

Interests turn increasingly from the politics of marriage, reflected in the patronymics of wives, to concern for administration and succession, shown in records regarding filiation and officeholding. The lists indicate the compiler's proximity to narrators and oral culture where genealogists record shifting statuses, roles, and relationships and stories are crafted around genealogists' recollections (see J. Goody, *Domestication of the Savage Mind* [Cambridge, 1977] 74–111).

42   **1:1.** The book opens like Josh 1:1 and Judg 1:1. **1–12.** The Amalekites occupy S regions in the Negeb and Sinai (1 Sam 30:26–31). After gaining revenge among them (1 Sam 30:17–19), David learns of Saul's death from a fugitive seeking to ingratiate himself (v 10) and expecting patronage and protection in return (v 2). Both persons are taken with grief perhaps for different reasons (vv 2,11–12). **13–16.** The son of a *gēr*, translated "sojourner" or "resident alien," in the nomadic stateless society of the S is a "subjugated outsider and fugitive." The youth's act anticipates Abner and Israel (2 Sam 3:12; 5:1–5) by offering David Saul's regalia of authority. Subservience and assumptions of David's antipathy to Saul are implied. David is offended and orders the alien slain for dispatching the Lord's anointed. David's actions affirm his innocence by avenging the deaths and fulfilling his tribal duty to his former protector and wife's paternal kin.

43   (ii) *Elegy for Saul and Jonathan* (1:17–27). The poem is lifted from an ancient anthology, the Book of Jashar. Its inclusion reaffirms David's commitment to his familial responsibilities and to withstanding grudges against Saul's vengeance. **19.** *haṣṣĕbî yiśrā'ēl* is problematic: "gazelle of Israel?" It may refer to Saul, Jonathan, or poetically both. **20.** News of the death(s) would bring joy to enemies in the Philistine cities and signal Israel's vulnerability. **21.** The warrior's deteriorating shield signifies the peoples' defenselessness. **23–26.** The vacuum left by the deaths of ruler and most likely successor (vv 19,25,27; cf. 1 Sam 20:31) opens the way for another's ascent.

44   (iii) *David achieves paramountcy over Judah* (2:1–7). David takes advantage of dependencies and gratitude, gained earlier, by moving to Hebron, a city *ca.* 19 mi. S of Jerusalem that retained strong Yahwist allegiances. The Philistines apparently do not object. **1.** The decision to relocate is credited to the deity, although Israel's weakness enabled the advance. **2–3.** David's entourage had been with him in Gath and Ziklag (1 Sam 25:39b–44; 27:3; 30:5). A kinship list charts the course (→ 41 above). Abigail's former spouse's clan (the Calebites) may have controlled the Hebron area (J. Levenson, *CBQ* 40 [1978] 26–32), thereby facilitating David's advance. **4a.** David is anointed by the "men of Judah," the elders (cf. 1 Sam 30), a council of tribal heads who selects the paramount and has other continuing administrative functions. David is anointed *lĕmelek*, "as king" (vv 4,7). Many versions state correctly "anointed to rule." The assertion of kingship is consistent with the compiler's monarchical view and the vocabulary of contemporary ancient societies, but the semantic range of "king" in antiquity is broad. Here it implies only the permanence and stratification that a nomadic environment would tolerate (J. Flanagan, *JSOT* 20 [1981] 67-68). **4b-7.** *Jabesh-gilead:* In Transjordan where Saul vied with the Ammonites (1 Sam 11). David praises the inhabitants' loyalty (*ḥesed*) and proposes a similar bond with himself.

45 (iv) *Activity in the northern camp* (2:8-11). David's relationship to the N must be considered together with the report of Michal's childlessness (chap. 6), the house arrest of Jonathan's son and grandson (chap. 9), and the Gibeonite slaughter of Saul's male descendants (chap. 21), which effectively truncate Saul's line. Transferral of authority in Israel is characterized by uncertainty, intrigue, and violence. **8.** Abner's status rests on appointment, as Saul's commander, and on kinship, as son of Saul's father's brother (1 Sam 14:51). He is an eligible successor in a collateral line of descent. The variant Ishbosheth/Ishvi/Eshbaal (genealogical fluidity; cf. 1 Sam 14:49; 1 Chr 8:33; 9:39) is commonly corrected to Ishbaal. He appears as Abner's puppet, successor only because Jonathan is dead. *Mahanaim:* Probably Telul Dhahab, a double mound in the Zerqa valley in Transjordan *ca.* 5 mi. E of Deir 'Alla and the Jordan river. The setting provides defense, distance from the SSW regions of Philistia and Judah, and possibly control over the valuable iron mined nearby (cf. 1 Sam 13:19). **9.** The repeated *king over* + *N* suggests a paramount chieftaincy of segmented groups rather than full centralization. Israel resists integration into a single political entity. *Ashurites:* Problematical; others read "Geshurites," from whom David took a wife (2 Sam 3:3). The MT *yiśrā'ēl kullōh,* "Israel in its entirety," should be read "all Israel," a technical term for Israel + Benjamin at this time (see J. Flanagan, *NFL* 108). **10.** The verse is part of a pseudo-chronological frame imposed by redactors (see comment on 5:4-5; 1 Kgs 2:10-11; 11:41-43) who sought to contrast Ishbaal's rule as ineptly brief and David's as stable, longer (v 11), and therefore divinely favored. Synchronizing the reigns historically is not required for the story. David rules over the "house of Judah," an ancient name for the segmented southern peoples (vv 10,11).

46 (v) *Hostilities erupt between David's and Saul's houses* (2:12-3:1). Because segmented societies lack an overarching authority, competition for power is continuous. Its expansion is traced in four stages: (1) a ritual duel between designated representatives of David and the Benjaminites (vv 12-16); (2) conflict between David's followers and the men of Israel (vv 17-23); (3) an attempt at negotiated containment (vv 24-32); (4) a long war between the houses of Saul and David (3:1). **2:12-13.** *Servants:* Followers, i.e., personal allies. *Gibeon:* Sometimes confused with Gibeah, this is probably el-Jib, *ca.* 6 mi. NW of Jerusalem. Both are in the center of Benjaminite territory, nearly equidistant from Mahanaim and Hebron. The circumstances suggest that the allegiance of the Yahwist tribe of Benjamin rather than all Israel's or Ishbaal's sovereignty is at stake. David seeks only the first at this point. Joab's identification by his mother's name is unusual and suggests kinship with Nahash of the Ammonites (cf. 2 Sam 17:25; 1 Chr 2:16-17). Kinship between David and Amasa, son of Abigail, Nahash's daughter (2 Sam 19:15) is also hinted. The ties threaten Abner living in Mahanaim where Nahash rules nearby. **14-15.** Abner proposes trial by ordeal, a duel (*wîśaḥăqû,* "play" or "perform"), a practice common among tribal groups and in the ancient Near East a test of divine favor (cf. 1 Sam 17; 2 Sam 6:5,21).

Benjaminites: The religious core of all Israel, whose separate identity is maintained in 2 Sam (cf. 2:25; 3:17-19; chap. 20). **17.** Because the contest is inconclusive, the conflict widens. **22.** Abner's plea reflects his dilemma: contain the violence he began or precipitate a blood feud that will escalate to include non-Yahwist segments in the alliances. The compiler subtly hints that wider conflict would threaten Abner's already weakened position (cf. vv 30-31) and would also run counter to David's interests by engaging more than Yahwists in the struggle. **3:1.** Competition between Saul's and David's alliances is made explicit, and with it a major theme in 2 Sam is exposed.

47 (vi) *Northern attempts at peace and leadership fail* (3:2-4:12). (1) Hebron genealogy (3:2-5). **2-5.** David's sons born at Hebron are named and ranked according to mothers' statuses. The lineages of Abigail, wife of Nabal, and Maacah, daughter of the king of Geshur, indicate David's expanding web of political alliances.

(2) Abner's negotiations fail (3:6-39). Abner's and Ishbaal's mutual distrust deepens, and negotiations begin for bringing the northern alliance under David's paramountcy. **6.** Abner demonstrates increasing control: he, not Ishbaal, will negotiate. **8-9.** Claiming a woman from the leader's harem signals Abner's political ambitions (cf. 16:21). **10-11.** His pretense is voiced and Ishbaal's ineptness revealed. *Dan to Beer-sheba:* The limits of Israel and Judah under David. **12-14.** A treaty or pact (*běrît*) is offered and accepted by David. Abner proposes bringing "all Israel" to him. David's demand for his wife Michal is relayed directly to Ishbaal. Her return will enable David (see J. Flanagan, *JSOT* 20 [1981] 61) to govern in her stead as successor to Saul. David shows shrewdness; the wife's return (1) is a sign of the current peace treaty; (2) undoes the insult (cf. 1 Sam 25:44) of having Saul take her away without recompense for David's bride-price; (3) allows David to rule in her stead; (4) affords him a role in the destiny of Saul's house as spouse and potential father. **17-21.** Abner consults with the northern constituencies: the elders of Israel, the Benjaminites, and both, i.e., all Israel. **18.** A treaty ritual follows. **22-28.** Discord erupts within a lower segment of the alliance. **29-38.** As paramount, David avoids blame and resolves the conflict by accusing and cursing Joab's house (vv 28-29; cf. 1 Kgs 2:33), by participating in a burial and mourning rite (vv 31-37), and by contrasting his gentleness with the ruthlessness of Zeruiah's sons (v 39).

(3) Ishbaal falls (4:1-12). With strong man Abner dead, David is literally offered the head of the northern confederation. **1.** The news unsettles the entire alliance, but Ishbaal's lack of courage disqualifies him from leading alone. **2-3.** The verses show signs of editorial emendation. Men from Abner's ranks, one a Benjaminite, assassinate Ishbaal. **4.** The reference to Mephibosheth/Meribaal and his handicap is an editorial insertion. It explains why he is not offered leadership. **9-11.** David refuses to be implicated and assigns blame and a curse. **12.** Hands and feet, the instruments of death and the delivery of news, are cut from the assassins.

48 (vii) *David leads Israel* (5:1-5). David strikes a treaty directly with the elders of Israel making him the simultaneous head of northern and southern segmented coalitions. Seeking leaders among neighboring nomadic groups often resolves conflicts among agrarians when leadership crises arise. The literary tradition of this and the Jerusalem units that follow have been redacted by as many as three hands **1-2.** The verb *rāʿâ,* "to shepherd," and the title *nāgîd,* "chief" (J. Flanagan, *JSOT* 20 [1981] 67-68), correspond to 2 Sam 7:7-8 and indicate that both units were placed here by deuteronomistic redactors. A pastoral ruler using persuasion is depicted. **3.** The verse is original. *Běrît* recalls earlier treaty negotiations. **4–5.** Chronographers added the verses (→ 45 above). Judah is correctly distinguished from all Israel.

49 (viii) *Zion is chosen as the administrative center of the confederations* (5:6–10). David moves his residence to a personally held, non-Yahwist stronghold (see J. Flanagan, *JAAR* 47 [1979] 235–39). Jerusalem's neutrality and central location between Judah and Benjamin (and Israel) are gained. Access to E–W routes, highland regions, and desert zones is improved. Excavations have unearthed little of the earliest Yahwist occupation. Although obscured by redactions, the story line follows David's continuing expansion (vv 5,7,9,10). Theologically and socially, he is a centrist; he remains a tribal leader over discrete Yahwist confederations and disparate non-Yahwist peoples, but he also embodies overarching paramount authority. **10.** The tribes' deity is with him.

50 (IV) **David Centralizes Yahweh's Power in Jerusalem (2 Sam 5:11–12:31).**
(A) **Relocating the Ark and Securing Allegiances (5:11–8:18).**
(a) DAVID SECURES HIS POSITION (5:11–16) (= 1 Chr 11:1–9). **11.** Through an alliance, Phoenician construction materials and crafts are available to build David's house. The house theme is prominent in the remainder of the book. **12.** The verse is deuteronomistic. **13–16.** The genealogical list summarizes developments (→ 41 above) and marks the beginning of the ritual transfer of the ark to Jerusalem (J. Flanagan, in *WLSGF* 361–72; W. Brueggemann, *David's Truth* [Phl, 1985] 67–86, 124). Having many concubines and wives is an indicator of wealth and power.

(b) PHILISTINE BATTLES (5:17–25) (= 1 Chr 14:8–16). In contrast with 1 Chr, David reverses his vassal-suzerain relationship after relocating in Jerusalem. The sequence enhances the city's role in solving Israel's problems. Two battles commissioned by divine oracle thwart Philistine attempts to drive a wedge between Israel and Judah. By the end of the scene, David has access to the entire Mediterranean coast. **17–21.** Rephaim is a lowland area SW of Jerusalem. The exact location of Baal-perazim is uncertain. **23–25.** The battle site is also uncertain, perhaps by a grove, "balsam trees" (H. Hertzberg, *I & II Samuel* 273) or "Bachaim," a place name (K. McCarter, *II Samuel* 155). Gezer is Tel Jezer in the Shephelah *ca.* 15 mi. W of Jerusalem.

51 (c) TRANSFER OF THE ARK TO JERUSALEM (6:1–23) (= 1 Chr 13:1–16:43). **1–15.** Bringing the ark to the city ritually transfers legitimacy and power from Saul's house to David personally. The scene is now joined with the dynastic oracle in 2 Sam 7 which completes the transition to David's house, i.e., to dynasty (cf. Ps 89); but the arrangement appears to be a secondary effort by Solomonic or post-Solomonic editors to root their royal theology in the city's initial legitimation by making the dynasty theme part of the original relocation plans. Chap. 6 abounds with signs of ritual: cultic music and dance (vv 5,15–16,21), a procession (vv 3,12), blessings and sacrifices (vv 12,13,17–19), nudity and role reversals (vv 16,20–22), all indicators of a rite of passage remembered in the Jerusalemite cult (cf. Pss 89,132). **16–23.** The dialogue explicates the meaning of the ceremony. Michal's childlessness is a sign of David's control. It places Saul's line figuratively under house arrest and opens the possibility for Davidic, but non-Saulide, succession.

52 (d) ORACLE OF NATHAN AND PRAYER OF DAVID (7:1–29) (= 1 Chr 17:1–27). The chapter combines an oracle (vv 1–17) with David's prayer (vv 18–29). The unit is fundamental in Israelite, Jewish, and Christian royal messianism. A highly nuanced playing on house, dynasty, and temple themes connects it with narratives before and after. Deuteronomistic editors or earlier post-Davidic redactors may be responsible for the unit's present location (D. McCarthy, *JBL* 84 [1965] 131–38). **1–7.** The multivalent house theme connects with the story line in chap. 6. Nathan, who is mentioned elsewhere only where Bathsheba and Solomon appear (cf. chap. 12; 1 Kgs 1), is part of the dynasty theme. **10–17.** The prohibition against a temple, a sign of social stratification and political centralization, reflects tribal Yahwists' resistance to monarchy. **13.** The reference to a later builder is a feeble Solomonic or deuteronomistic attempt to transform the anti-temple tenor to pro-temple. **18–29.** A striking prayer affirms the deity's role in electing David and his house (vv 18,25). Perpetuity is stressed (vv 24,25,29).

53 (e) DAVID SUBDUES AND ALLIES WITH NON-YAHWIST EASTERN REGIONS (8:1–14) (= 1 Chr 18:1–13). The catalogue of David's successes seems exaggerated and stylized. It balances his pacification of the coastal zones (cf. 5:17–25) with winning access to all E regions, thereby forming an envelope of alliances surrounding Israel and Judah. In a segmented system, those not in an alliance are against it. All are portrayed as temporarily with David. **1.** Recent archaeological information reveals Philistine occupation in the Jordan Valley. The compiler may have the area in mind. **2.** Moab in Transjordan is David's ally elsewhere (cf. 1 Sam 22:3–5). **3–12.** Northern victories subdue regions stretching to the Euphrates. There is no archaeological information to confirm the reports. Precious and utilitarian metals are booty and signs of subservience (vv 8,10) that contrast with the foodstuffs and livestock collected and distributed during David's rise and exile (cf. 17:27–29; 1 Sam 30). They are worthy of the alliance's grandeur. **13–14.** The SE is secured by subduing the Edomites.

54 (f) DAVID'S ADMINISTRATION (8:15–18) (= 1 Chr 18:14–17). **15.** By now all Israel includes Judah. **16–18.** The list, part of the compilers' map (→ 41 above), balances with both the genealogical list in 5:13–16, marking the beginning of David's move toward Jerusalem, and the list of court officers in 20:23–26, ending the Court History (2 Sam 9–20). In keeping with tribal practice, patronymics are cited for all the named officers except Shawsha (1 Chr 18:16, an Egyptian name). **16.** Joab is commander; Jehoshaphat is *mazkîr*, i.e., a chancellor or recorder with duties as foreign minister and master of ceremonies. **17.** Two priests are named, representing either non-Yahwist and Yahwist or Aaronid and Mushite orders (see F. M. Cross, *CMHE* 212–14). The confusion of Ahimelech and Abiathar as name and patronymic is a case of genealogical amnesia (compare Mark 2:26). Shawsha is scribe (*sōpēr*). **18.** Benaiah is in charge of the mercenaries. The mention of David's sons as priests is disruptive and secondary (cf. 20:26; 1 Chr 18:17).

55 (B) **Conflicts in David's Palace (9:1–12:31).** L. Rost's (*Succession*) arguments for the literary unity and antiquity of the so-called succession narrative (2 Sam 9–20 + 1 Kgs 1–2) continue to influence biblical scholarship. However, assigning an exact date and marking a definite beginning for the unit are difficult (see D. Gunn, *The Story of King David* [JSOTSup 6; Sheffield, 1978]), and themes within it can be separated according to Davidic and Solomonic interests (J. Flanagan, *JBL* 91 [1972] 172–81). Accordingly, Solomon's succession is treated only in secondary material and in 1 Kgs, as the canonical division of the text and Rost's own study suggest. In the earlier story, the Court History (chaps. 9–20), and in 2 Sam 21–24, the compilers contrast David's conduct with that of others.

56 (a) MERIBAAL'S PROTECTION AND HOUSE ARREST (9:1–13). David's benevolence toward Saul's house contrasts with his subjugation of Israel's enemies (cf. chaps. 8, 9). His generosity exhibits kindness toward former opponents and their house. It brings potential contenders under his watchful eye, diffuses the family's independent power bases (cf. 1 Sam 20:28–31; 2 Sam 15:7–12), and incorporates opponents' allegiances into the patron's administration. **2.** Ziba, Saul's steward, is appointed to serve Meribaal and care for Saul's property (vv 7–12). The act accords Meribaal some independence and dignity. **3.** The motive is ḥesed, loyalty. **4.** Meribaal resides with a prominent family in the region of Mahanaim. **10.** The youth is honored by eating at David's table, where he can be observed daily.

57 (b) DAVID IS TESTED BY AN EASTERN COALITION (10:1–19 [+11:1+12:26–31]) (= 1 Chr 19:1–19 [+20:1–3]). Treatment of Yahwists and non-Yahwists is contrasted. Succession invites competition among contenders and with former allies and enemies. David presumes that his treaty relationship (ḥesed) will survive the transition in Ammonite office. **1–4.** Hadadezer's Aramean vassals become David's (chap. 10). David's loyalty contrasts with Hanun's distrust. **5.** Inflicting humiliation tests David's ability to hold his coalitions together. **8–14.** The new Ammonite leadership fails to steal away groups subjugated by David (8:1–14). **15–19.** David regains the allegiance of Aramean vassals and rules the Ammonites directly (cf. 11:1; 12:26–31).

58 (c) THE BATHSHEBA AFFAIR, NATHAN'S JUDGMENT, AND SOLOMON'S BIRTH (11:1–12:25). The unit is part of the Solomonic succession theme (→ 55 above) placed here to illustrate that a paternal weakness infects the family and enables Solomon to come to power (J. Blenkinsopp, in *Volume du Congrès: Genève, 1965* [VTSup 15; Leiden, 1965] 44–57). The episode also contrasts David's treatment of an ineligible sexual partner whom he marries with Amnon's incestuous rape of Tamar (chap. 13), and testifies that Solomon was conceived and born in wedlock. **1.** The Ammonite campaign provides the setting and heightens the sense of David's negligence. **2–5.** The adultery with a Hittite soldier's wife is told succinctly. **3.** Eliam and Uriah are both listed among David's warriors (23:34–39) hinting that Bathsheba was remembered as daughter of one and wife of the other. The dual references stress the injustice toward powerless subordinates. **6–13.** The first attempts to cover David's tracks would amuse ancient audiences. **8.** In order to maintain ritual purity during battle, Uriah disobeys the command to "wash your feet," i.e., to have intercourse. **14–24.** David's sin costs Uriah his life, and Bathsheba's sin costs her a husband! **20.** Joab veils his own failure behind news of Uriah's death. **25.** David absolves Joab of worry. **26–27.** Anxiety turns to relief. Bathsheba's honor is preserved in spite of the deity's displeasure with the affair. **12:1–4.** Nathan's parable, a māšāl, elicits David's self-judgment. **7–12.** The section has been redacted. It now predicts events that unfold in chaps. 13–24 and testifies that the illegitimately conceived child was not Solomon. **14.** Atonement for David's sin costs the child its life, and Bathsheba a son! **15–23.** David repents. **24–25.** An assertion of Solomon's legitimacy and favor is signified by his names.

59 (d) DAVID ASSUMES DIRECT CONTROL OF THE AMMONITES (12:26–31) (= 1 Chr 20:1–3). The battles begun in chap. 10 are completed. **26.** Rabbah and the royal citadel are in present-day Amman. **30.** The crown of Milcom, the state god of the Ammonites, symbolizes headship of the kingdom. Crowned Ammonite statues from the period have been found (S. Horn, *AUSS* 11 [1973] 170–80).

60 (V) **David Loses and Regains Jerusalem (13:1–20:25).**

(A) **Absalom Challenges His Father's Sovereignty (13:1–19:9a).** Tension outside David's house gives way to problems within, centering on changes that life in Jerusalem is forcing on tribal customs and norms — esp. evident in Amnon's treatment of Tamar and Absalom's attempt at *coup d'état.*

(a) THE RAPE OF TAMAR AND ABSALOM'S REVENGE (13:1–39). The differences between a passive, paternal leader (v 21) and a single-minded, filial pretender (vv 22,28) take precedence over Amnon's morality and David's obligations to Tamar (who could be his daughter?). The story is laced with sexual inferences and feeling for the castaway Tamar, which obscure the larger issues of social norms and rules addressed by the story. Absalom's greed shows through his subtle attempt, with Jonadab's complicity, to arrange Amnon's downfall by rendering him ineligible for succession — at the expense of his sister! **1–4.** All the actors are members of David's family. **12–13.** Tamar warns against breaching society's norms, bringing shame to her and rejection to Amnon. Her suggestion regarding an approved brother–sister marriage depicts rule changes occurring in the society (→ 61 below). Amnon and Absalom symbolize the uneasy merging of cultures. **16.** Violated, Tamar appeals again to custom for protection. **19.** Rejected and ruined, she mourns. **23–29.** Absalom schemes to kill the first-born brother during a pastoral festival. **32.** The "wise man" Jonadab continues his lackey's role by assigning a motive that preserves Absalom's standing. **37–39.** Absalom returns to the protection of his maternal kin to await another opportunity for power.

61 (b) ABSALOM'S EXILE AND RECONCILIATION (14:1–33). **2.** A second wisdom specialist, a woman from Tekoa, tries to sway David's views. **5–7.** The ploy appeals to tribal custom and practicality to prevent strife and blood feud amid the family. **10–18.** David decides for heirship and, prefiguring his exile, against vengeance, first by his own authority (v 10) and then by invoking the deity (v 11). **12–14.** The woman presses the case which, like a parable, points to someone else, Absalom. The woman's dilemma of guilt is complex (vv 13–14). The case alludes to the pressures of sedentarization and centralization: David has overruled a pastoral society's way of coping with violence; now how does it rid itself of guilt, i.e., restore justice, if the offender is restored to full life? **20.** A paradox is presented. The woman compares David's wisdom to that of an angel of God, but readers are told of Joab's role (vv 21–22). **23–33.** Absalom is allowed into the city only, and two years later with Joab's assistance, into the palace. David's kiss, the sign of forgiveness and reconciliation, resolves the woman's dilemma. He takes responsibility for the guilt.

62 (c) ABSALOM'S ATTEMPT AT SUCCESSION (15:1–12). The background issue in previous scenes bursts into the open. **1.** Horses and chariots are signs of increasing centralization. **2–6.** Absalom stirs discontent by accusing his father of failing to meet his tribal responsibilities as adjudicator and redistributor. Initial discontent is northern (vv 2,6,10), but once David's allegiances are ruptured, others join the opposition — David is becoming too much like a king. **8–12.** He ignores the obvious: Absalom is imitating him by going to loyalist Hebron where he weaves a broader web of opposition (vv 7–10) reaching into David's staff.

63 (d) DAVID ABANDONS JERUSALEM AND THE ARK (15:13–16:14). David tests divine will. **13–14.** Sensing his tenuous hold on northern Yahwists, he orders flight. **16–18a.** The exodus has the character of a ritual procession, but is made without the ark.

18b. David's foreign mercenaries are personal body-guards, loyal only to their employer. **23–29.** The ark and the concubines left to keep the house (v 16) offer a test for Yahweh (vv 25–26). David's return will confirm that Yahweh sanctions him because of his *laissez-faire* central leadership rather than because he possesses the ark. **31.** The "wise" Ahithophel's foolishness is exposed. **31–37.** David sends his own advisor to spy and confuse. **16:1–14.** Ziba and Shimei are met again during David's return. Ziba's explanation of Meribaal's absence (v 3) and Shimei's (a Benjaminite) curse (v 8) reflect continuing northern Saulide antipathy to David and a lingering hope for restoration.

64   (e) ABSALOM'S FOOLISHNESS (16:15–17:23). **16.** Hushai arrives in Jerusalem to set the stage with Ahithophel for the final test of Absalom's wisdom. Hushai's enigmatic reply affirms (v 18) that the test will reveal whom Yahweh has chosen (cf. 15:25–26). **20–23.** Losing control of the harem is a sign of inability to lead and a definitive indication that the former ruler is gone. Absalom's future and the narrative of the Court History hinge on the dialogue (J. Flanagan, *JBL* 91 [1972] 178). Ahithophel advises the symbolic gesture as well as a military tactic for catching David by surprise (17:2). **17:1–14.** Absalom foolishly submits again to hubris and accepts Hushai's urging to wait and lead the troops personally (vv 11–13; cf. 16:21; 17:11,13). **15–22.** David's messengers are protected by a clever woman whose response to interrogators is both accurate and deceptive. **23.** Ahithophel's suicide is portrayed as a premeditated act of despair. The ability to convince is a counselor's duty. His touch lost, his life ended, Ahithophel goes home to die. Hanging foreshadows Absalom's fate (18:9).

65   (f) DAVID IN EXILE (17:24–19:9a). **25.** Absalom retains the Jerusalemite bureaucracy, reappointing from within and respecting old alliances. **25–29.** David's support is with disparate and sundry coalitions. The scene depicts an old warrior, anxious for action (17:29–18:2). **18:1–5.** The troops are put under three commands, but David is persuaded to remain behind away from involvement with Absalom's fate. **6.** Absalom foolishly allows the encounter to occur in the thickets of the forest of Ephraim in Transjordan where David's men are more at home. **11–14.** Joab kills Absalom personally. **18.** The burial site is not the traditional "Absalom's Tomb" near Jerusalem. **19–32.** Joab prefers that a foreigner deliver both the good news of victory and the bad news of Absalom's death (v 21). Bearing bad news elicits no rewards (v 22). **19:1–9a** (Eng 1–8a). By mourning the fatality rather than honoring the victors David threatens allegiances. Joab speaks for the troops and for security; David responds with ceremony (vv 6–9a).

66   (B) David Processes to Jerusalem (19:9b–44 [RSV 8b–43]).   David's fate turns quickly (vv 9–10), and allies and enemies compete for the right to escort him (vv 11,14). He moves quickly to secure old alliances (v 12) and to make changes in his administration (v 13). **29–31.** Meribaal attempts to regain protection by disavowing his treason, but David refuses to adjudicate his and Ziba's contradictory claims. Meribaal rejects dual ownership of Saul's property for David's protection (v 31). **41.** The ritual conquest, which reverses David's exodus, is similar to the ark's entry in Josh 3–5 and goes first to Gilgal and then directly to Jerusalem (20:3).

67   (C) Further Attempts to Topple David (20:1–25).   The struggle for paramountcy continues unabated. Latent distrust between Israelites and Judahites, and the Benjaminites' uneasy commitment to either group, is exploited by Sheba (vv 1–2,4–7). Joab settles

a grudge with his rival, Amasa (vv 8–13), and the people of Abel Beth-Maacah are forced to choose sides (vv 14–22). **20:1–22.** Sheba's rebellion frames the other tests of allegiance. **3.** Three references to "house" in a single verse complete the story of Absalom's revolt and look ahead to dynasty. Yahweh has met David's challenge (cf. 15:25–26), but he returns to establish his house, not to view the ark. **6.** The Benjaminite's rebellion is likened to Absalom's. **14–22.** Sheba flees to Abel Beth-Maacah E of Dan, i.e., to the end of the territory where a wise woman's decision to surrender Sheba's life rather than risk destruction portrays the extent of David's support. **23–25.** The second list of court officers is part of the compilers' map (→ 41 above), and with the earlier list (8:15–18) it forms an *inclusio* for the Court History by demonstrating that conditions are restored to their original state. Now, however, military and tax officials are listed before others.

68   (VI) David Prepares for Israel's Future under Yahweh (21:1–24:25).   David allows the Gibeonites to take their revenge on the house of Saul (21:1–14), and he symbolically suppresses a Philistine stirring (21:15–22). House, dynasty, and temple themes reach their completion (21:1–23:7), and the final contest for Yahweh's favor is waged and celebrated (23:8–24:25). The pattern of the story, not the historical sequence of the maneuvers, concerns the compilers. The focus that has shifted from problems between ruling houses to tensions within David's own family now returns to the Philistines and the Benjaminites, Israelites, Saulides. David and his opponents are all ultimately placed under Yahweh's power.

(A) Suppression of the Saulides and Their Enemy, the Philistines (21:1–22).

        (a) DAVID ALLOWS THE MASSACRE OF SAUL'S HOUSE (21:1–14). Historically, the unit is misplaced, but it suits the compilers' purpose here by showing that David is no longer Saul-*in-absentia,* ruling in his stead. Although the portrayal contrasts sharply with earlier insistence on David's innocence, the ruler can now break away from old beliefs and set upon his own course which is to become ritually the sign of Yahweh's presence in Jerusalem. Saul's family is dispensable. **1.** The background is famine and bloodguilt. Neither is recorded earlier. Yahweh is credited with citing the latter as the cause of the former. **2.** David takes immediate action. **5–6.** The Gibeonites request a ritual slaughter of seven family members at the high place in Gibeon (cf. 1 Kgs 3). **6b–9.** David personally designates the victims. Virtually every known surviving male descendant in direct line of succession in Saul's family is accounted for. **10–14.** Rizpah, Saul's concubine and mother of two sons, fulfills her woman's role by protecting the decaying bodies for burial. Sometime later David buries them with Saul and Jonathan in Benjamin. Ending the episode with supplications gives it cultic overtones.

69   (b) PHILISTINE UNREST (21:15–22). David continues to secure his position by subjugating four Philistine leaders, the archetypal enemies of Saul and Israel. The arrangement of the anecdotes is artificial; their unity seems to be the warriors' membership in a cultic association, the Rephaim or giants (vv 16,18,20, 22) (cf. C. L'Heureux, *BASOR* 22 [1976] 83–85). **15–20.** The exaggerated size of weapons and warriors reflects the cultic character of the texts.

70   (B) Praise and Thanksgiving (22:1–23:7). The connection between Yahweh's power and David's security is emphasized in cultic expressions.

        (a) THE PSALM OF DAVID (22:1–51). This ancient poem, a doublet of Ps 18, asserts Yahweh's continual intervention in David's life. The deity protects the leader from enemies starting with Saul [*sic!*] (v 1), and will continue loyally with his descendants (v 51). **2–20.** The first of the poem's three parts depicts a cosmic and human struggle leading to the birth, as it were, of David's recognition and election (v 20). **21–28.** The poem's core states the reciters' perception of events. The presence of the doublet (vv 21,25) as well as imagery and vocabulary suggest that vv 21–25 is an insertion, possibly deuteronomistic. It expands vv 26–28 and offers an ancient interpretation of the poem's meaning: David is chosen because of his innocence. **26–28.** Implied are the reversals, again including David's displacing Saul, that are central to 1 Sam 29–31. The psalmist, i.e., David, is depicted as a victorious warrior whom the deity protects during campaigns to foreign lands (v 46). The warrior and the deity are partners in struggles that reach cosmic proportions.

(b) DAVID'S LAST WORDS (23:1–7). The ancient poetic oracle serves to extend the psalm above. **2.** Yahweh speaks through David not only in the leader's statements and actions, but also through the paradoxes in his life (vv 3–4). **5–6.** The house theme is introduced to express hope for the future. Enemies of the house will not sprout and grow as David, the seed for his house, has done.

71   (C) Submitting the Administration to Yahweh (23:8–24:25). The organizational list of David's soldiers makes the military prowess praised in the preceding poems concrete, creates the need for a census, the basis of conscription, and leads toward Yahweh's appearance as a warrior in chap. 24.

(a) DAVID'S WARRIORS (23:8–39). Ranking exemplifies the ancient penchant for organizing by means of genealogies and lists. Fluidity, as in genealogies, is evident (v 24). **8–11.** *the three:* Play a special role, perhaps as officers. **24–39.** *the thirty:* An official body comparable to the royal guard in other ancient Near Eastern societies.

(b) CENSUS, PLAGUE, AND PREPARATIONS FOR YAHWEH'S HOUSE (24:1–25). The delicate balance between centralizing and remaining subservient to divine will is first upset (vv 1–15) and then resolved by divine intervention (vv 16–17) and by David's purchasing a site for worship (vv 18–24), erecting an altar, and making offerings (vv 24–25). **1.** An enigmatic opening connects the census with the plague. David's ultimate struggle is with the deity (cf. 1 Chr 21:1)! **2–9.** Joab's route takes him through the territories surrounding Israel and Judah, the envelope constructed earlier (chaps. 5–12). Idealized, i.e., cultic, numbers are reported separately for Israel and Judah (v 9). **10–14.** The reason for David's remorse is not explicit. His apparent change of heart explains the connection between census and plague. **15.** The plague is Yahweh's *quid pro quo,* the divine defense in the cosmic struggle for legitimacy. **16–25.** The resolution legitimates David's actions, i.e., the centralizing that leads to the census and the purchase of a threshing floor, and it transfers the guilt to an altar where it is expiated through David's offerings.

10

1–2 KINGS

Jerome T. Walsh   Christopher T. Begg*

BIBLIOGRAPHY

1   Bright, J., *BHI.* Cross, F. M., *CMHE* 217–89. De Vries, S. J., *1 Kings* (WBC 12; Waco, 1985). Gray, J., *I & II Kings* (2d ed.; OTL; Phl, 1970). Hoffmann, H.-D., *Reform und Reformen* (ATANT 66; Zurich, 1980). Ishida, T. (ed.), *Studies in the Period of David and Solomon* (Winona Lake, 1982). Jones, G. H., *1 and 2 Kings* (NCB; GR, 1984). Long, B. O., *1 Kings* (FOTL 9; GR, 1984). Montgomery, J. A., *MGK.* Nelson, R. D.,

The Double Redaction of the Deuteronomic History (JSOTSup 18; Sheffield, 1981). Noth, M., *Könige* (BKAT 9/1; Neukirchen, 1968); *The Deuteronomistic History* (JSOTSup 15; Sheffield, 1981). Rehm, M., *Das erste Buch der Könige* (Würzburg, 1979). Würthwein, E., *Die Bücher der Könige* (ATD 11; Göttingen, 1977–84).

INTRODUCTION

2   **(I) Composition.**   The books of Kgs are the fourth part of what tradition calls the Former Prophets (Josh, Judg, 1–2 Sam, 1–2 Kgs). The division between Sam and Kgs is arbitrary and varies in ancient manuscripts. That between 1 and 2 Kgs is even more arbitrary, disrupting the account of the reign of Ahaziah of Israel. In fact, 1–2 Kgs form a continuous work.

Modern scholarship affirms the unitary character of the Former Prophets. Since the *Überlieferungsgeschichtliche Studien* of M. Noth (1943; Eng 1981), it has become standard to speak of this work as the "deuteronomistic history" (= Dtr) and to deem it the product of a single school, if not a single author. It is not a work of political or social history, however, but of theological history. It recounts, from a consistent theological point of view, Israel's life in its own land from the occupation under Joshua to the Babylonian Exile. It is less interested in accurately chronicling events, no matter how important they may seem to a modern historian, than in explaining the tragic fate of Yahweh's people. The Deuteronomist chooses sources, arranges and modifies them, expands and supplements them with this goal in mind, rather than with a view to reportorial accuracy, verifiability, or exhaustiveness. The sources used are many and varied, ranging from popular tales (1 Kgs 3:16–27) and miracle stories (2 Kgs 2) to archival records (1 Kgs 4:7–19). In Kgs, the Deuteronomist cites three sources by name and repeatedly refers the reader to them for further informa-

tion: The Acts of Solomon, The Chronicles of the Kings of Judah, and The Chronicles of the Kings of Israel. Unfortunately, all three are now lost. On sources used in Kgs, see Gray, *I & II Kings* 14–35.

It is not certain when the Deuteronomist compiled these sources into the theological narrative we have today. Surely the final version of Kgs dates from the exile: 2 Kgs 25:27 records the release of Jehoiachin from prison (*ca.* 560), but Dtr is unaware of the edict of Cyrus and the return from exile (538–537). Many scholars today, however, believe that the major work of shaping Dtr was done before the exile, perhaps in Josiah's reign (*ca.* 640–609), with a later, exilic redaction bringing the narrative up to date. (See Nelson, *Double Redaction;* and A. Mayes, *The Story of Israel between Settlement and Exile* [London, 1983] 1–21.)

The diversity of sources and the theological purpose to which even archival materials are submitted counsel caution in any attempt to extract historical data from Kgs. Certainly the main lines are historical—the names and the order of the kings, the separation of the kingdoms after Solomon's death, the overthrow of Israel, the exile of Judah. But, within those lines, historical reconstruction must proceed with care. For example, even the apparently objective data of chronology are problematic. Kgs regularly coordinates a king's accession with the regnal year of the other kingdom's ruler and also gives the length of each reign. In theory, it

*The introduction and comment on 1 Kgs are the work of J. T. Walsh; the comment on 2 Kgs is by C. T. Begg.

should be possible to date the whole line of kings in both kingdoms accurately. But it has not proven so. The figures cannot be made to agree without emendation or elaborate hypotheses. (See H. Jagersma, *A History of Israel in the Old Testament Period* [Phl, 1983] 124–26.)

3   (II) Purpose and Theology.   The purpose of Dtr — or at least of the exilic editor — is to explain how Yahweh's people came to be in exile. The explanation, essentially, is that both Israel and Judah, in the person of their respective kings, were guilty of cultic infidelities so numerous and so terrible that destruction was the only fit punishment. A number of subsidiary themes contribute to this explanation: the paradigmatic character of David and of Jeroboam I, the cult and the Temple, and the role of prophetism.

David is for Kgs the paragon for rulers of Judah. He was faithful and obedient to Yahweh (1 Kgs 3:14); therefore Yahweh promised him an unending dynasty (1 Kgs 8:25; cf. 2 Sam 7:4–16). But beginning with Solomon, most of the southern kings fail to follow David's ways (1 Kgs 9:4–9; 11:4,6; 15:3; 2 Kgs 16:2); even those who are faithful are praised with reservations (1 Kgs 15:11–14; 2 Kgs 14:3–4); only Hezekiah and Josiah receive unqualified approval (2 Kgs 18:3–5; 22:2; 23:25). The divine promise to David is what stays Yahweh's hand in the face of Judah's evils (1 Kgs 11:13; 15:4; 2 Kgs 8:19).

Jeroboam I, by contrast, is the paradigm of unfaithful Israel. Though chosen by Yahweh (1 Kgs 11:26–40), Jeroboam became guilty, in Dtr's view, of cultic heterodoxy (12:26–31). This the Deuteronomist calls the "sin of Jeroboam," and he considers it the foundational evil of the northern kingdom (→ 24). Israelite kings are condemned without exception, almost always for "holding to the sin of Jeroboam." Only Ahab is more roundly scored, for introducing the cult of Baal (1 Kgs 16:30–33). These cultic deviations led to Israel's destruction at the hands of Assyria, as the commentary on the fall of Samaria makes clear (2 Kgs 17).

Kings of both Judah and Israel are judged in terms of their cultic purity. In the north, the criterion for condemnation is the "sin of Jeroboam." In the south, the "high places" (sacrificial sites on hilltops used in the indigenous pagan cult and perhaps in the popular cult of Yahweh as well) are the commonest aberration for which the kings are condemned, while cultic reform is a basis for praise (1 Kgs 15:11–13; 22:46; 2 Kgs 18:3–5, 22–23).

The construction and dedication of the Temple are the centerpiece of the story of Solomon and that king's lasting glory, even though the judgment of Dtr on Solomon is ultimately negative (1 Kgs 11:9–13). The Temple remains a continuing topic of interest in Kgs; matters touching it, even matters not directly concerned with cultic deviations or reformations, are often recorded (1 Kgs 14:25–28; 15:15,18–19; 2 Kgs 11:3–16; 12:4–18; 14:14; 15:35; 16:8–18; 18:15–16; 24:13; 25:9,13–17).

Finally, the role of prophetism in the unfolding history of Israel is a central concern for Dtr. 1–2 Kgs in particular contain numerous prophetic narratives, including lengthy collections about Elijah and Elisha. Through the prophets Yahweh continually confronted the errant people to call them back to God's ways. The prophetic word could be an assurance of victory (1 Kgs 20:13) or a promise of peace (2 Kgs 7:1), a threat (1 Kgs 22:17) or a condemnation (2 Kgs 1:3–4). In every case it is Yahweh announcing in advance the plan of history — a plan that reaches fulfillment inexorably. Throughout 1–2 Kgs are very many notices of fulfilled prophecies; the point of Dtr is clear: Yahweh is in charge of history

and "reveals his counsels to his servants the prophets" (Amos 3:7).

4   (III) Outline.   The text of 1–2 Kgs contains well-crafted literary work. The author had a penchant for concentric organization of narrative materials. Some attempt has been made to reflect this structuring technique in the outline, especially in the large narrative units of 1 Kgs.

(I) The Reign of Solomon (1 Kgs 1:1–11:43)
  (A) Prophetic Intervention into the Royal Succession (1:1–2:11)
    (a) The King Is Cold (1:1–4)
    (b) Adonijah Exalts Himself (1:5–6)
    (c) Adonijah's Faction Gathers to Celebrate (1:7–10)
    (d) Nathan Plots to Make Solomon King (1:11–14)
    (e) David Decides for Solomon (1:15–37)
    (f) Solomon Is Made King (1:38–40)
    (g) Adonijah's Faction Flees in Fear (1:41–50)
    (h) Adonijah Abases Himself (1:51–53)
    (i) The King Is Dead (2:1–11)
  (B) The Security of Solomon's Throne (2:12–46)
    (a) Adonijah (2:13–25)
    (b) Adonijah's Supporters (2:26–35)
    (c) Shimei (2:36–46)
  (C) A Promising Beginning (3:1–15)
    (a) Narrator's Comments (3:1–3)
    (b) Yahweh Is Pleased with Solomon (3:4–15)
  (D) Yahweh's Gifts to Solomon (3:16–5:14)
    (a) "A Discerning Mind" — Solomon's Judgment (3:16–28)
    (b) "Riches" — Solomon's Administration (4:1–5:8)
      (i) Internal affairs (4:1–20)
      (ii) External affairs (5:1–5)
      (iii) Chariots and horses (5:6–8)
    (c) "Honor above Kings" — Solomon the Sage (5:9–14)
  (E) Solomon's Temple (5:15–9:25)
    (a) Before Beginning the Temple (5:15–32)
      (i) Solomon and Hiram (5:15–26)
      (ii) The corvée (5:27–32)
    (b) Construction of the Temple (6:1–7:51)
      (i) Building the Temple (6:1–38)
      (ii) The royal palace (7:1–12)
      (iii) Furnishing the Temple (7:13–51)
    (c) Dedication of the Temple (8:1–9:9)
      (i) Narrative prologue (8:1–13)
      (ii) Solomon's speech (8:14–61)
      (iii) Narrative epilogue (8:62–9:9)
    (d) After Finishing the Temple (9:10–25)
      (i) Solomon and Hiram (9:10–14)
      (ii) The corvée (9:15–25)
  (F) Yahweh's Gifts to Solomon (9:26–10:29)
    (a) "A Discerning Mind" — Solomon and the Queen (10:1–10,13)
    (b) "Riches" — Solomon's Trade (9:26–28; 10:11–12,14–22,26–29)
      (i) Maritime affairs (9:26–28; 10:11–12,22)
      (ii) Jerusalem's prosperity (10:14–21,27)
      (iii) Chariots and horses (10:26,28–29)
    (c) "Honor above Kings" — Solomon's Prestige (10:23–25)
  (G) A Tragic Ending (11:1–13)
    (a) Narrator's Comments (11:1–8)
    (b) Yahweh Is Angry with Solomon (11:9–13)
  (H) The Insecurity of Solomon's Throne (11:14–25)
    (a) Hadad of Edom (11:14–22)
    (b) Rezon of Damascus (11:23–25)
  (I) Prophetic Intervention into the Royal Succession (11:26–40)
  (J) Transition (11:41–43)
(II) Synchronic History of the Kingdoms of Israel and Judah (1 Kgs 12:1–2 Kgs 17:41)
  (A) Jeroboam I of Israel (12:1–14:20)
    (a) Ahijah Announces Jeroboam's Kingship (11:26–43)
    (b) Political Disunity (12:1–20)

COMMENTARY

5   (I) The Reign of Solomon (1 Kgs 1:1–11:43). The story of Solomon's reign is a coherent work of theological interpretation. It is less concerned with recounting the events of Solomon's kingship in chronological order than with evaluating the Solomonic era. The editor draws on a wide variety of materials, from archival data to popular legend, to weave a narrative tapestry of many panels. Central to the tapestry is a diptych—the building of the Temple (6:1–7:51) and its dedication (8:1–9:9). It is framed by pairs of panels, thematically parallel and concentrically arranged. Those that precede the account of the Temple tell of Solomon's accession and the rich promise of his reign; those that follow show the failure of that promise.

(A) Prophetic Intervention into the Royal Succession (1:1–2:11). The narrative's focus is the palace intrigue by which Nathan and Bathsheba thwart the royal pretensions of Adonijah, David's eldest surviving son, and insure the succession of Bathsheba's son

Solomon. The opening verses warn us that we are no longer dealing with the David of 2 Sam, potent and decisive, at the peak of his mastery. The king is aged, nearly senile; his physical deterioration prepares us for his mental helplessness before the plots of those he trusts. The story then moves in balanced fashion from Adonijah's self-exaltation through the conspiracy for Solomon and its success to Adonijah's abasement.

(a) THE KING IS COLD (1:1–4). The prologue paints a vivid picture of David's decline. He is bedridden and suffers from severe circulatory failure. The proposed therapy, contact with the warmth and health of a young virgin, is attested in Gk medical literature as well. The king's virility is also an issue: an impotent king would be deemed no longer fit to rule. The laconic remark that "the king had no relations with her" is not a comment about David's virtuous restraint, but a final proof of his infirmity.

(b) ADONIJAH EXALTS HIMSELF (1:5–6).

Adonijah was the heir presumptive, since his older brothers were dead (2 Sam 3:2–5; 13:23–29; 18:9–17). His bid for the throne begins, as did Absalom's before him (2 Sam 15:1; cf. 1 Sam 8:11), with the establishment of a personal military retinue—an ominous move that his father does not challenge.

(c) Adonijah's Faction Gathers to Celebrate (1:7–10). Rivalry for the throne divides the leading figures of the kingdom. Military leaders such as Joab and Benaiah are on different sides, as are religious figures such as Zadok and Abiathar (cf. 2 Sam 20:23–25). Adonijah's faction gathers at En Rogel to celebrate a religious sacrifice and meal (v 41). The name of Adonijah's chief rival for the throne first appears here, in a list of the uninvited: Solomon, son of Bathsheba and protégé of Nathan (2 Sam 12:24–25).

6 (d) Nathan Plots to Make Solomon King (1:11–14). Nathan enlists Bathsheba's aid in a plot to thwart Adonijah. Nathan's deftness at court intrigue contrasts sharply with his earlier straightforwardness and courage as David's court prophet (2 Sam 7; 12). He plays on Bathsheba's jealousy and fear as well as on her ambition. The story of the oath is his suggestion, not hers. Moreover, it is Nathan who interprets Adonijah's celebration as a coronation ceremony, thus pressuring Bathsheba to immediate action (cf. D. Gunn, *The Story of King David* [Sheffield, 1978] 105–6).

(e) David Decides for Solomon (1:15–37). In the king's inner chambers, the conspiracy to win David's support for Solomon proceeds in four stages: Bathsheba appeals to David (vv 15–21); Nathan seconds her appeal (vv 22–27); David swears to Bathsheba as she has prompted him (vv 28–31); David orders Nathan to see to Solomon's anointing (vv 32–37). **15–21.** Bathsheba's position at court is precarious. The king who committed murder to have her is near death. The sight of Abishag at David's side reminds Bathsheba that she herself is no longer young and beautiful and that she has been replaced in David's bed. Unless Solomon prevails, she will lose everything. She risks a bolder approach than Nathan counseled, rephrasing his words of appeal as a veiled rebuke to David. And she adds to those words arguments designed to touch David's pride and arouse his anger: the existence of a conspiracy for Adonijah, names of the chief conspirators, and the imminent danger to herself and her son. **22–27.** Nathan enters on cue. As befits a court official, he addresses the issue as a question of policy: Adonijah has claimed the throne. Has David approved this action? Since he knows David has not, Nathan's question serves to underscore what Bathsheba has already implied: Adonijah's action is a challenge to David's authority. He then sharpens the implications by contrasting Adonijah's rejection of himself, Zadok, Benaiah, and Solomon with their loyalty to David ("your servant[s]," vv 26–27). **28–31.** Presumably Bathsheba withdrew when Nathan appeared; the strength of their plan lay in the apparent independence of their carefully choreographed audiences with David. The king's oath is decisive and repeats exactly the words Bathsheba put in his mouth (v 17). His decision to act immediately means that Solomon will become coregent until David's death. **32–37.** David summons Solomon's partisans, whose names Nathan has conveniently supplied—Benaiah for armed protection, Zadok to perform the anointing, and Nathan himself for prophetic ratification of Solomon's kingship—and commands Solomon's immediate installation as king.

(f) Solomon Is Made King (1:38–40). The ceremony is carried out in strict conformity with David's directives. **38.** *Cherethites and Pelethites:* Mercenary

soldiers in the bodyguard under Benaiah's command (2 Sam 8:18).

7 (g) Adonijah's Faction Flees in Fear (1:41–50). At En Rogel, a half mi. S of Gihon in the Kidron Valley, it is Joab, the battle-wise veteran, whose ears pick out the distant trumpet. His wary question is answered by the sudden appearance of Abiathar's son Jonathan. Jonathan's speech is an ironic counterpart to Nathan's in vv 22–27 (cf. J. Fokkelman, *Narrative Art and Poetry in the Books of Samuel* [SSN; Assen, 1981] 1. 374–78). The two speeches epitomize the whole chapter. In v 22 Nathan (*nātān*) interrupts Bathsheba to announce to David Adonijah's alleged *coup d'état;* in v 42 Jonathan (*yô-nātān*) interrupts Joab to announce to Adonijah Solomon's successful rise to the throne. He recounts details of the ceremony and adds that Solomon has been enthroned and that the court has made its obeisance to the new king. **49–50.** Adonijah's guests disperse in panic, and Adonijah himself takes refuge at the altar of sacrifice (cf. Exod 21:13–14).

(h) Adonijah Abases Himself (1:51–53). Adonijah claims the asylum of the sanctuary until Solomon guarantees his safety. Solomon's conditional acquiescence, instead of the oath Adonijah hoped for, leaves the new king free to dispose of his rival when political expediency would permit. **53.** *he bowed down:* Adonijah's obeisance to the king reverses his earlier self-exaltation (v 5).

(i) The King Is Dead (2:1–11). David's final speech is framed by two announcements: that he is dying (v 1) and that he is dead (v 10), along with a summation of his reign (v 11). **2–4.** In its present form, the speech is an uneasy combination of religious platitudes and shrewd, unscrupulous political advice. Verses 2–4 reveal the hand of the deuteronomic editor, who often put deathbed valedictories into the mouths of major figures (Deut 31; Josh 23; 1 Sam 12). For official Davidic court theology, Yahweh's election of David's line was unconditional (2 Sam 7:14–15). Here the monarchy is subordinated to the demands of Mosaic law—a tenet central to the deuteronomic tradition (Deut 17:14–20). **5–6.** David's directive to kill Joab refers to two cold-blooded murders Joab committed (2 Sam 3:22–30; 20:4–13). David passes over in silence two incidents wherein Joab hurt him more personally, though with stronger justification: the death of Absalom (2 Sam 18) and Joab's rebuke of David (2 Sam 19:1–9). One can only suspect that David's motives include the settling of old grudges. (On Joab as the *éminence grise* of David's reign, see T. Ishida in *Studies in the Period of David and Solomon* [ed. T. Ishida] 181–85.) **7.** See 2 Sam 17:27–29; 19:32–41. **8–9.** *Shimei son of Gera:* Not to be confused with Solomon's supporter Shimei (1:8), who is probably the Shimei son of Ela of 4:18. For the events, see 2 Sam 16:5–14; 19:17–24. Here too David's motives may be complex. Shimei's death at Solomon's hand would relieve the dynasty of the continuing effects of Shimei's curse; it would also avenge David without his being forsworn. *a wise man:* The motif of Solomon's wisdom (*ḥokmâ*) first appears in v 6. It pervades chaps. 1–11 and continues to the very end of OT tradition (→ Wisdom Lit., 27:7–8). By and large it is an admirable quality in Solomon; but here we see that it can include a talent for ruthless political expediency. **10–11.** *slept with his fathers:* A common editorial formula to mark the end of a reign. It is, in fact, inappropriate for David, since he was buried not in his ancestral tomb in Bethlehem but in Jerusalem itself. For the two cities of David's reign, see 2 Sam 2:3–4; 5:1–9.

8 (B) The Security of Solomon's Throne (2:12–46). Solomon eliminates threats to his security in three steps: Adonijah; Adonijah's supporters, Abiathar and Joab; and Shimei. The whole account is framed by the repeated remark that Solomon's "kingdom was established" (vv 12,46b).

(a) ADONIJAH (2:13–25). Adonijah's request for Abishag is foolish and ill-fated. The royal harem was the property of the king; aspirations to it were tantamount to designs on the throne (2 Sam 16:20–22). Since Abishag is still a virgin (1:4), Adonijah's request is technically innocent. But it supplies Solomon with a convincing pretext to dispose of his rival. The drama unfolds in two scenes, Adonijah's interview with the queen mother, Bathsheba, and the latter's audience with Solomon. There is an ironic contrast between the scenes. In v 15 Adonijah recalls wistfully what might have been; when he then presents his request to Bathsheba, he seems to be asking for Abishag as a sort of consolation prize for his loss of the kingship. Bathsheba in turn conveys his request to Solomon, who interprets it quite differently; to him Adonijah's desire is proof that he has not given up his claim to the throne. The heat of Solomon's indignation and the fervor of his double oath (vv 23,24) betray his insecurity. Adonijah must die.

(b) ADONIJAH'S SUPPORTERS (2:26–35). Not content with his brother's death, Solomon determines to rid himself of Adonijah's most influential supporters. They are named in v 22, eliminated in vv 26–34, and replaced in v 35. **26.** Solomon exiles Abiathar to the nearby village of Anathoth since he has no sufficient pretext for executing the priest. Centuries later, the kings of Judah would hear the voice of prophecy spoken by "one of the priests of Anathoth," Jeremiah (Jer 1:1). **27.** Prophecy–fulfillment notices are frequent in 1–2 Kgs; the reference here is to the prophecies of 1 Sam 2–3. **28–34.** Joab knows that he cannot expect clemency. He takes refuge at the altar as Adonijah had done (1:50), where even Solomon's hatchet man, Benaiah, hesitates to do him harm. But David's earlier advice (v 5) supplies Solomon with an argument sufficient to annul Joab's claim of sanctuary: only involuntary manslaughter could find asylum at the altar; the willful murderer had no such recourse (Exod 21:12–14). Joab, like Adonijah, must die. **35.** Solomon replaces Adonijah's supporters with his own. Zadok, the new high priest, is of obscure origins, possibly even non-Israelite (→ Institutions, 76:20–21).

(c) SHIMEI (2:36–46). The narrative comprises two dialogues between Solomon and Shimei surrounding a narrative of Shimei's journey to Gath to retrieve his runaway slaves. Differences between the dialogues unmask Solomon's lack of scruples. In the first, Solomon forbids Shimei to leave Jerusalem (v 36), but imposes a death sentence only on crossing the Kidron valley to the E (v 37). Shimei is thus cut off from his home in Bahurim on the Mount of Olives (2 Sam 16:5; 19:17). In v 38, he accepts the king's command. His southward journey to Gath violates the king's first command, but it breaks neither the spirit nor the letter of v 37. In the second dialogue (vv 42–45), Solomon makes two false claims about the first dialogue: that the death sentence had been attached to *any* departure from Jerusalem, and that Shimei had bound himself by a solemn oath. Moreover, after asking Shimei a direct question (v 43), Solomon gives him no chance to speak. It is clear that Solomon intends Shimei's death by fair means or foul; the ever-ready Benaiah does the deed.

9   (C) A Promising Beginning (3:1–15). Having settled the uncertainties of the transfer of power, the narrator begins the account of Solomon's reign. The tone of these verses is optimistic. With a series of impersonal observations (vv 1–3) followed by a dramatic dialogue (vv 4–15), the narrator evokes the bright promise of the dawning Solomonic era. The key is Solomon's faithfulness to Yahweh, according to the example set by David his father (vv 3,6,7,14). Toward the end of the account of Solomon's reign (11:1–13), the narrator will return to the same structure and themes to highlight the tragic failure of that promise.

(a) NARRATOR'S COMMENTS (3:1–3). The information summarized in vv 1–3 is carefully organized to suggest an evaluation of Solomon at the beginning of his reign. The central affirmation is that "Solomon loved Yahweh, and followed the statutes of David his father." Three themes are used to support this verdict; the same three themes will lead to the opposite conclusion at the end of Solomon's reign (11:1–8).

(i) *Marriage to a foreign woman.* The text reads, literally, "Solomon became the son-in-law of Pharaoh, king of Egypt." The marriage is nothing more than a way of sealing an international alliance—a common political practice of the day. (The unnamed Pharaoh is probably one of the last of the weak 21st Dynasty rather than Shoshenq, the vigorous founder of the 22d.) Pharaoh's daughter is housed in Jerusalem more as an honored guest than as a wife. Solomon certainly has no emotional attachment to this foreigner; his "love" is for Yahweh alone (v 3).

(ii) *Building projects.* Solomon's reign will be characterized by extensive construction throughout the country. Three important and praiseworthy projects are foreseen here: the palace, Yahweh's Temple, and the wall around Jerusalem.

(iii) *High places.* Sacred sites, often on hilltops, for sacrificial worship. They were in common use in the Canaanite cult, and would later become the paradigm of all that was illegitimate in Israel's own worship. The narrator explains to the audience that worship of Yahweh at the high places, heterodox in their own times, was allowed before Solomon built the Temple.

(b) YAHWEH IS PLEASED WITH SOLOMON (3:4–15). Solomon's love for Yahweh (v 3) is dramatized in the account of Solomon's dream. The narrative framework, depicting his extravagant sacrifices at Gibeon (v 4) and Jerusalem (v 15), has a double effect: it attests to the king's generous devotion to Yahweh, and it presages his transfer of the center of worship from the high places to the temple. On the offering of sacrifices by kings, → Institutions, 76:13; de Vaux, *AI* 113–14. **6–9.** Solomon's prayer focuses in turn on (i) the past: his father David's fidelity and Yahweh's blessings; (ii) the present: Solomon's humble inadequacy to succeed David and to exercise leadership; and (iii) the future: Solomon's request for "a listening mind" (lit., "heart"; in Hebr *lēb* usually connotes mental rather than emotional faculties) and "discernment." **10–14.** Yahweh's response has four elements: (i) Solomon is praised for not requesting long life, riches, or domination over others; (ii) Solomon's request is granted: he is given "listening discernment" and "a wise and discerning mind"; (iii) he receives gifts corresponding to two of the three things he did not seek, riches and honor above other kings; (iv) he is promised the third, long life, on condition that he follow the faithful example of David. The entire dialogue contains a rich theology of kingship under Yahweh and of the duties of the Davidic monarch (cf. H. Kenik, *Design for Kingship* [SBLDS 69; Chico, 1983]).

10   (D) Yahweh's Gifts to Solomon (3:16–5:14). Eng versions follow different ancient traditions in numbering the verses of chaps. 4–5. Some follow the Hebr numbering (as we do), others follow the Vg: Hebr 5:1–14 = Vg 4:21–34; Hebr 5:15–32 = Vg 5:1–18. This section draws on a variety of earlier materials, from popular legend to official administrative lists. All of it is used to illustrate that the gifts promised by Yahweh to Solomon—"a discerning mind," "riches," and "honor above kings" (3:12–13)—did in fact characterize his reign.

(a) "A DISCERNING MIND"—SOLOMON'S JUDGMENT (3:16–28). (On this story, see Long, *1 Kings* 67–70.) The story betrays its roots in folk literature by the anonymity of its participants (even Solomon is simply "the king"); in fact over 20 similar tales have been identified from a wide variety of cultures (see *MGK* 108–9). **16–21.** The king's gift of insight is seen in his incisive handling of a complaint. The two women are not so-called sacred prostitutes (*qĕdēšôt*). They are apparently innkeepers (so the Tg), an occupation that could include prostitution (cf. Josh 2:1). The accessibility of the king to any citizen is a duty of office (cf. 2 Sam 14:1–11; 15:1–6). The tragedy occurs one night when there were no lodgers with them (v 18, *zār*, "stranger, foreigner"). **22–23.** Without witnesses, Solomon cannot decide between the women's competing claims. The balanced, repetitious language reflects the insolubility of the king's dilemma. **24–27.** Solomon must use guile to extract the truth. His stratagem reveals which of the two feels maternal compassion for the child; she will give it up rather than see it die. Her love shows too in her words: the "child" (*yeled*) becomes the "baby" (*yālûd*, v 26), a telling clue that the king hears and repeats in his decision (v 27). **28.** The narrator's language recalls both Solomon's prayer (v 9) and Yahweh's promise (vv 11–12).

11 (b) "RICHES"—SOLOMON'S ADMINISTRATION (4:1–5:8). Solomon inherited a widespread sphere of influence. Good government demanded practical, effective organization. The narrator has drawn on materials from the royal archives to illustrate Solomon's wise administration in internal and external affairs, and the benefits that accrued to Judah and Israel. The passage has two main sections; each begins with a reference to Solomon's dominion and ends with a reference to Judah and Israel (4:1–20; 5:1–5). There follows an addendum about the king's military forces.

(i) *Internal affairs* (4:1–20). Solomon's rule over all Israel (v 1) resulted in prosperity throughout Judah and Israel (v 20). Two documents are used to describe organization of that rule. **2–6.** The list of Solomon's cabinet officers (*śārîm*) is certainly based on an official record; similar lists of David's chief officials are found in 2 Sam 8:15–18; 20:23–26. On the duties of various officers, see de Vaux, *AI* 127–32; and Jones, *1 and 2 Kings* 1. 134–38. **7–19.** The list of Solomon's district commissioners or governors (*niṣṣābîm*) is also from an official document. The document describes the fiscal organization of the kingdom into twelve districts, each charged with upkeep of the royal household for one month per year. On the geography of the districts, see Gray, *I & II Kings* 136–40; and A. Alt, *KlS* 2. 76–89. **18.** *Shimei*: Perhaps Solomon's partisan named in 1:8. All districts listed lie N or E of Jerusalem. The dynastic homeland, Judah, is not mentioned. The last words of v 19 are obscure (lit., "and one commissioner [*nĕṣîb*] who was in the land"). If "the land" refers to Judah (as the LXX reads), reference may be to a thirteenth district, royal domains exempt from the monthly rotation. Others propose that Judah too was organized into twelve districts, perhaps already under David.

(ii) *External affairs* (5:1–5). (On the verse numbers, → 10 above.) Solomon's rule over "all kingdoms" (v 1) resulted in security for all throughout Judah and Israel (vv 4b–5). The narrator has vastly oversimplified the international political scene to illustrate Yahweh's gift to Solomon of unparalleled riches and

honor (3:13). Verses 1 and 4 portray Solomon as suzerain over the whole territory between Mesopotamia and Egypt. In fact, his hegemony was a complex mixture of political supremacy over some nations, international treaty with others, and economic influence upon still others (see *IJH* 349–56). Verses 2 and 3 have been transferred here from the list of commissioners (where they originally illustrated 4:7); in their present position they imply a daily tribute from Solomon's royal vassals rather than from his own kingdom. **2–3.** *thirty cors:* One cor was approximately 6.5 bushels. Estimates of the population supported by these provisions vary from 14,000 to 32,000 (see *MGK* 127–28). Similar documents from other ancient cultures make such figures plausible, but editorial exaggeration cannot be ruled out. **4.** *across the River:* The phrase is late, first appearing in 7th-cent. Assyrian documents; it refers to territory W of the Euphrates, as seen from a Mesopotamian viewpoint. Its presence here suggests the hand of an exilic editor in Babylon. **5.** *under his vine and under his fig tree:* A metaphor for peace and security; cf. Mic 4:4. *from Dan to Beer-sheba:* The conventional phrase for the whole land of Israel and Judah, from N to S; e.g., 2 Sam 3:10; 24:2,15.

(iii) *Chariots and horses* (5:6–8). (On the verse numbers, → 10 above.) These verses combine a remark about Solomon's chariotry (v 6) with material originally belonging to the document about his commissioners (vv 7–8; cf. 4:7–19; 5:2–3). **6.** *forty thousand stalls . . . twelve thousand horses:* The first figure is to be corrected to 4,000 (cf. 2 Chr 9:25; each stall would hold one team of three chariot horses—thus 12,000 horses (not "horsemen").

12 (c) "HONOR ABOVE KINGS"—SOLOMON THE SAGE (5:9–14). (On the verse numbers, → 10 above.) The narrator illustrates Solomon's unparalleled wisdom first by a series of comparisons (vv 10–11a), then by a list of his achievements (vv 12–13). Each illustration ends with a statement of Solomon's worldwide renown (vv 11b,14). **10–11.** Israel acknowledged and even drew upon the wisdom of non-Israelites (Prov 30:1; 31:1; Jer 49:7; Obad 8; Job 1:1; → Wisdom Lit., 27:18–32). **12–13.** Solomon's reputation for wisdom became a byword. Whole books were attributed to him (Prov, Cant, Wis; and, later, *Odes Sol., Pss. Sol.*), as well as parts of books (cf. Pss 72; 127; Prov 1:1; 10:1).

13 (E) Solomon's Temple (5:15–9:25). The centerpiece of chaps. 1–11 is the account of the establishment of the Temple. It is presented as the high point of Solomon's reign; but there are signs that it is a turning point as well. Hidden amid the glories of the occasion are the beginnings of Solomon's personal failure—the infidelity that would lead to Yahweh's repudiation of him and the disintegration of the Davidic empire (chaps. 11–12). The account of the Temple is carefully organized in four balanced units. The first (5:15–32) recounts Solomon's dealings with Hiram, king of Tyre, and the levying of a corvée preparatory to the building of the Temple. The second and third are longer (6:1–7:51; 8:1–9:9) and detail the construction and dedication of the Temple. The fourth (9:10–23) corresponds to the first and recounts Solomon's dealings with Hiram and the use of the corvée after the Temple's completion.

(a) BEFORE BEGINNING THE TEMPLE (5:15–32). (On the verse numbers, → 10 above.) Preparation for the building of the Temple entailed two projects: acquisition of materials and organization of labor. The first was accomplished through negotiations with Hiram, king of Tyre, and by local quarrying; the second by a corvée.

(i) *Solomon and Hiram* (5:15–26). **15.** Tyre, an island off the Phoenician coast about 25 mi. N of Acco, was the dominant port on the E Mediterranean littoral in Solomon's day. *loved David:* The phrase is a euphemism meaning that Hiram had reached a political understanding with David (2 Sam 5:11). His formal congratulation of Solomon constitutes an offer to continue the goodwill. **16–20.** Solomon seeks timber, for which the Lebanese mountains were a prime source; and he offers to send laborers to assist Hiram's skilled workers and to pay the wages of Hiram's workers as well as his own. **21–23.** Hiram's response is polite, but renegotiates the terms firmly. Israelite laborers are to remain on Israelite soil; and Solomon's payments are to go to Hiram, not directly to Hiram's workers. Solomon is to supply Hiram with agricultural products which the island kingdom could not grow for itself in abundance. **24–25.** *crushed oil:* Olive oil pressed by hand, rather than in large oil presses. It was the purest and finest available. The MT reads "twenty *cors*" (not "20,000"), or somewhere between 1,000 and 2,000 gallons (see de Vaux, *AI* 199–203)—an exorbitant but plausible yearly fee. **26.** Mention of Solomon's wisdom recalls the theme of the preceding section (3:16–5:14); but the prodigious annual drain on Solomon's resources will, in the end, reveal the irony of this remark. In order to pay his debts, Solomon will eventually be forced to sell territory to Hiram (9:10–14).

14   (ii) *The corvée* (5:27–32). (On the verse numbers, → 10 above.) The function of this passage is to depict the organization of Solomon's local labor force in preparation for building the Temple. It is clear that a system of conscription was used; but attempts to reconstruct the details of the system are plagued by insufficient and apparently contradictory information. These verses are probably a late composite of materials of diverse origin and varying historical worth (see Jones, *1 and 2 Kings* 1. 157–60); they are arranged according to timber work (vv 27–28), stone work (vv 29–31), and summary (v 32). **27–28.** *forced labor:* Various Hebr terms are used to describe Solomon's conscripted labor force: *mas* (vv 27,28), *mas 'ōbēd* (9:21), *sēbel* (11:28). Scholars debate whether the terms can serve to distinguish different forms of conscription (e.g., temporary for Israelite citizens, permanent for Canaanites or prisoners of war). See J. Soggin in T. Ishida (ed.), *Studies in the Period* 259–67. *all Israel:* This is to be understood as in 4:7—i.e., the northern tribes as differentiated from Judah. Such inequity was a prime reason for the separation of the kingdoms after Solomon's death (chap. 12). **29–30.** Stone was readily available in Solomon's territory; his "hewers" and "haulers" are those who quarried, then transported the cut stone. The numbers are unreasonably high and incompatible with estimates of the total population (see de Vaux, *AI* 65–67). The number of workers has led to a proportional inflation of the number of foremen; the figure 550 (9:23) is to be preferred. The foremen's title (*śārê hannissābîm*) suggests that they were subject to the commissioners of 4:7–19. **31.** *precious stones:* Not gemstones, but building blocks carefully cut and measured. The following phrase, "hewn stones," is a further description; cf. 7:9–11. Ashlars were often prepared with a flat, finely chiseled margin around the face; it was decorative and also facilitated laying the stones evenly.

15   (b) CONSTRUCTION OF THE TEMPLE (6:1–7:51). Chapters 6–7 report Solomon's construction of the Temple and of his own palace. The text has a long and complex history, and attempts to retrieve a clear image of the original Temple are blocked by insuperable difficulties: textual uncertainties reflected in divergent readings of the MT and the LXX; important structural or decorative elements left unmentioned; numerous architectural terms with obscure meanings; and the inevitable reworking of the text by later editors to

conform to the modified Temple of their own day (→ Institutions, 76:42–50; further references in *MGK* 140–42). The structure of the passage is: Temple building (6:1–38); royal palace (7:1–12); Temple furnishings (7:13–51).

(i) *Building the Temple* (6:1–38). The passage is framed by chronological notes (vv 1,37–38). The account itself is in two parts: basic structure (vv 2–10); paneling and decoration, esp. of the innermost holy place (vv 15–36). Central to the chapter is an oracle of Yahweh to Solomon (vv 11–14). **1,37–38.** *framework:* The figure 480 is not historically reliable. It leads to dating the exodus in the 15th cent., whereas other evidence makes a 13th-cent. date much more likely. The figure may simply be conventional (one generation of 40 years for each tribe); or it may be an attempt to reckon the founding of the First Temple as the midpoint between the exodus and the return from exile (537), or between the building of the Tent of Meeting (Exod 33:7–11) and the building of the Second Temple (520–515). *Ziv . . . Bul:* Month-names from the old Canaanite calendar, not the Babylonian system more commonly found in the OT. Ziv corresponds to April/May, Bul to October/November. **2–10.** The general structure of the Temple is most similar to Phoenician and Canaanite models: a tripartite building facing east, comprising an outer porch ('*ûlām*), a sanctuary or Holy Place (*hêkāl*), and an innermost holy place or Holy of Holies (*debîr*). **11–14.** The oracle is highlighted by its centered position in the chapter. Its conditional character is a cautionary reminder, amid the glories of Solomon's accomplishment, that his success as king depends not on the extravagance of the Temple but on his fidelity. Its wording recalls 3:14, and it will be balanced by another conditional oracle at the end of the Temple account (9:4–9).

(ii) *The royal palace* (7:1–12). The remarks in 6:37–7:1 and 9:10 portray Solomon as building the Temple first, in seven years, then spending the next thirteen years on the palace. The schema is probably artificial, but nevertheless sets the literary context for 7:1–12. By recounting the building of the royal house here, out of the chronological order implied by the text, and by inserting it within the description of the Temple, the narrator highlights these verses. The same techniques highlight the mention of the palace for Pharaoh's daughter (v 8b): it is inserted within vv 1–12 and taken out of chronological order. (The Hebrew reads, "He *was to make* a house for Pharaoh's daughter," a project whose completion is not reported until after the 20 years of construction; see 9:10,24.) In both cases the highlighting emphasizes Solomon's later failings. The position of vv 1–12 points up the contrast between 7 years spent on Yahweh's house (6:38b) and 13 years spent on Solomon's (7:1a). The imbalance in time reflects the much greater size of the palace, but it also raises suspicions about which house is more important to the king. In light of Hiram's costly annual demands (5:25), it is clear which house leads to Solomon's financial embarrassment (9:10–11). Verse 8 in turn foreshadows Solomon's fatal fascination with foreign women and his eventual willingness to build idolatrous places of worship for them (11:1–8).

(iii) *Furnishing the Temple* (7:13–51). On the organization of the passage, see Long, *1 Kings* 90–92. **13.** *Hiram:* A craftsman, not to be confused with the king of Tyre. **21.** On the columns, see Gray, *I & II Kings* 187–88.

16   (c) DEDICATION OF THE TEMPLE (8:1–9:9). The lengthy description of the building of the Temple (6:1–7:51) is balanced by a similarly lengthy account of its dedication. Vocabulary and style indicate a complex editorial process behind the text (see Jones, *1 and 2 Kings*

1. 191–210). But in the present text the material has been forged into a balanced, concentric unity: (a) narrative prologue (8:1–13); (b) Solomon's blessing of the assembly (8:14–21); (c) prayer of dedication (8:22–53); (b') Solomon's blessing of the assembly (8:54–61); (a') narrative epilogue (8:62–9:9).

(i) *Narrative prologue* (8:1–13). **1.** The Ark of the Covenant had been brought to Jerusalem by David after he conquered the city (2 Sam 6:1–19). **2.** *Ethanim:* A month-name from the old Canaanite calendar, corresponding to September/October (→ 15 above, on 6:1). The Temple seems to have been dedicated a few weeks before it was completed in the eighth month (6:38). The feast held during this period of the year is the feast of Tents (→ Institutions, 76:133–138). **4.** *Tent of Meeting:* → Institutions, 76:30–34; de Vaux, *AI* 294–97.

(ii) *Solomon's speech* (8:14–61). Solomon's speech at the dedication of the Temple is marked throughout by deuteronomic concerns: e.g., the attempt to combine Davidic dynastic theology with Sinai covenant traditions; the theme of a dwelling for "the name of Yahweh" (cf. Deut 12); the references to divine promises and their fulfillment. It comprises two short sections addressed to the assembly of Israel, surrounding the lengthy dedicatory prayer. **14–21.** Despite v 14, this is not a true blessing but a historical prologue preceding the dedicatory prayer. Its central theme is the dynastic promise to David (2 Sam 7) as the context for Solomon's succession and building of the Temple. **22–53.** The dedicatory prayer begins by recalling again the promises to David, but it adds a condition not found in Nathan's oracle (v 25; cf. 2 Sam 7:12–15). The conditional nature of the promise to Solomon is a recurrent theme (3:14; 6:12; 9:4–5) and prepares the way for his ultimate rejection by Yahweh (11:4,6,11). The major portion of Solomon's prayer asks for Yahweh's attention to supplications offered in or toward the Temple. Seven illustrative situations are described: the oath of innocence (de Vaux, *AI* 157–58), military defeat, drought, various plagues, a foreign pilgrim, military campaign, captivity. **54–61.** Solomon again addresses the assembly, blessing and exhorting them to obedience to Yahweh. The vocabulary is deuteronomic.

(iii) *Narrative epilogue* (8:62–9:9). This consists of two sections, each balancing an earlier introductory passage. **62–66.** The account of the dismissal of the assembly corresponds to the calling of the assembly in 8:1–13. In each case lavish sacrifices are mentioned, and the occasion is specified as "the feast" (i.e., of Tents; vv 2,65). **9:1–9.** The second part of the epilogue recounts a theophany and an oracle to Solomon, balancing the oracle that preceded the building of the Temple (6:11–13). In both, the conditional character of Yahweh's promise to Solomon is emphasized. **2.** As at Gibeon (3:4–15), Yahweh's oracle is delivered in the course of theophany.

17 (d) AFTER FINISHING THE TEMPLE (9:10–25). The report of Solomon's Temple closes as it opened — with a discussion of economic negotiations between Solomon and Hiram of Tyre and an account of the corvée (cf. 5:15–32).

(i) *Solomon and Hiram* (9:10–14). The arrangement of the text implies that Solomon was forced to cede cities to Hiram to pay for construction materials. This may be editorial embellishment of an archival notice about a straightforward sale of territory (vv 11b,14). In either case, Solomon's willingness to surrender land reveals his difficult fiscal situation; and the narrator uses the event to foreshadow the coming disintegration of the empire. **14.** *talent:* A unit of weight that varied through the centuries (see de Vaux, *AI* 203–6). A reasonable

approximation is 75 lbs., which means that Hiram sent four and a half tons of gold to Solomon — a clearly fantastic figure.

(ii) *The corvée* (9:15–25). In 5:27–32, the levying of the corvée prepared for the building of the Temple and the royal palace. That account permitted the inference that the corvée would be disbanded upon their completion. Here we learn that, on the contrary, Solomon's further construction projects require a permanent labor force. The list of projects may be drawn from an official document, with editorial expansions (vv 16, 19b–22). **15–19a.** *Millo:* The nature of this structure is uncertain (see Gray, *I & II Kings* 243–44); it seems to have formed part of the fortifications of Jerusalem. On the Solomonic remains at Hazor, Megiddo, and Gezer, see *EAEHL.* The parenthetical insertion about Pharaoh's capture of Gezer is of questionable historical reliability (Jones, *1 and 2 Kings* 1. 216). **19b–23.** The reference to building in Lebanon is scarcely credible in view of the parity treaty between Hiram and Solomon. The list of peoples is drawn from the traditional seven indigenous peoples of the land (e.g., Deut 7:1). On the Canaanites (v 16), Amorites, and Hittites, see *POTT.* Verse 22 is at odds with 5:27 and 11:28; see comment on 5:27. **24–25.** These verses, unrelated to each other or to their context, echo 3:1–3, where the same ideas appear in the same order. The last words of v 25 close the large unit that began in 5:15.

18 (F) Yahweh's Gifts to Solomon (9:26–10:29). This section draws on a variety of sources to illustrate that the king still possesses the gifts given him by Yahweh at the beginning of his reign. Both the editorial history and the principle of arrangement of the present text are obscure; but the same three gifts that organized 3:16–5:14 are leitmotifs here as well: discernment, riches, and honor above kings. There are, however, noteworthy differences. In the earlier passage, Solomon's gifts produced justice for the lowly (3:16–28), wise administration for the whole kingdom (4:1–19), peace and prosperity for Judah and Israel (4:20; 5:5), and a public outpouring of wise sayings and songs (5:9–14). Now, by contrast, his wisdom is privately displayed, redounding to his glory without public benefit (10:1–10); prosperity is centered in Jerusalem (10:27) and esp. in the royal palace (10:16–21); and mention of the duty of "justice" is found only on the lips of a foreigner (10:9). The contrast is clear: Yahweh remains faithful to the promises given at Gibeon (3:4–15). But the king has changed: his own glory and wealth have become more important than the good of Yahweh's people.

(a) "A DISCERNING MIND" — SOLOMON AND THE QUEEN (10:1–10,13). The story is a popular legend, but it may have a historical kernel in a visit by an Arab trade delegation. **1.** *riddles:* The queen measures Solomon's wisdom with riddles or "obscure questions" (*ḥîdôt*); such riddle tests are found elsewhere as part of Oriental diplomacy (see Gray, *I & II Kings* 257). **6–9.** The queen is impressed by both Solomon's prosperity and the wisdom upon which it is founded. But, ironically, it is she, not Solomon, who praises Yahweh and recalls the royal duties of justice and righteousness.

(b) "RICHES" — SOLOMON'S TRADE (9:26–28; 10:11–12,14–22,26–29).

(i) *Maritime affairs* (9:26–28; 10:11–12,22). Although each of these passages mentions Hiram, the three seem to refer to different fleets; but the texts all disclose the wealth and exotic luxuries that poured into Solomon's coffers from overseas. Maritime cooperation between Hiram and Solomon gave them collective control over trade between the Indian Ocean and the Mediterranean Sea. **9:26–28.** The fleet belongs to Solomon and is manned by Tyrian sailors. On the talent, see comment on 9:14; 420 talents (over 15 tons) seems exaggerated. **10:11–12.** The fleet belongs to Hiram, although Solomon also benefits from the trade. **10:22.** *ships of Tarshish:* A technical term for oceangoing ships. This fleet belongs to Solomon, but the term suggests that it is other than the fleet of 9:26.

(ii) *Jerusalem's prosperity* (10:14–21,27). **14–15.** Solomon's income is described in fabulous terms: the unrealistic figure 666 is probably based on the already exaggerated amounts in 9:14,28, and 10:10. For the size of the talent, see comment on 9:14. **16–17.** *six hundred shekels . . . three minas:* There were 50 or 60 shekels in a mina (both figures are attested in the OT), and 60 minas in a talent. The first figure, therefore, is around 12–15 lbs., the second just under 4 lbs. *house of the Forest of Lebanon:* See 7:2–5.

(iii) *Chariots and horses* (10:26,28–29). An isolated note about Solomon's military forces (v 26; cf. 5:6 and 9:19) precedes an obscure passage about Solomon's trade in chariots and horses.

(c) ''HONOR ABOVE KINGS''—SOLOMON'S PRESTIGE (10:23–25). Solomon's superiority in wealth and wisdom is greatly magnified. The offerings brought him are called a "present," a conventional euphemism for "tribute."

19   (G) A Tragic Ending (11:1–13). This section balances 3:1–15, the narrator's evaluation of the promising dawn of the Solomonic day. Like the earlier passage, this closing evaluation uses a series of impersonal observations (vv 1–8) followed by a divine word (vv 9–13); but here the conclusion is that Solomon failed to follow the example of David. What dawned in hope darkens to disaster (Long, *1 Kings* 62).

(a) NARRATOR'S COMMENTS (11:1–8). The central affirmation is that "Solomon did evil in Yahweh's sight, and did not follow Yahweh fully as David his father had" (v 6; cf. 3:3a). The same three themes used in 3:1–3 to support the verdict of Solomon's fidelity here testify to his failure. (i) *Marriage to foreign women.* In 3:1–3, the daughter of Pharaoh was a means of political alliance; Solomon's "love" was reserved for Yahweh. Now foreign wives have become an obsession far beyond their political usefulness, and he "loves" them—to the point of indulging their idolatrous ways and even joining in them. (ii) *Building projects.* Where one looked forward to the building of the Temple of Yahweh (3:1), one now finds Solomon constructing places of worship for foreign gods (v 7). (iii) *The high places.* Worship of Yahweh at the high places had been tolerated until the Temple was built (3:2); it is now, however, superseded by the Temple services. But the high places continue to be used; Solomon himself even establishes new sites to foreign gods within full view of the Temple of Yahweh! On the deities, see Gray, *I & II Kings* 275–79.

(b) YAHWEH IS ANGRY WITH SOLOMON (11:9–13). Yahweh's first word to Solomon (3:4–15) was a response to the king's pious devotion. God's last word, here, is a response to Solomon's idolatry. The conditional character of Yahweh's promise finally comes to term (3:14; 6:12; 9:4–5). Solomon has not been faithful to the way of David; his empire will not last, and his son will succeed him only by virtue of divine forbearance.

20   (H) The Insecurity of Solomon's Throne (11:14–25). We do not know when any of the reported events occurred. Their placement at the end of Solomon's reign is probably the narrator's way of illustrating the consequences of Yahweh's displeasure with Solomon. In Edom and Damascus, two countries over which Solomon claimed suzerainty, men hostile to the Davidic house come to power. Both had once fled their homelands to escape slaughter by Israelite forces.

(a) HADAD OF EDOM (11:14–22). The conquest of Edom is mentioned briefly in the OT, with the slaughter imputed variously to David (2 Sam 8:13), to Abishai (1 Chr 18:12), or to Joab (Ps 60:2).

(b) REZON OF DAMASCUS (11:23–25). Rezon's career offers a striking parallel to David's: a fugitive from the king, leader of an outlaw band, eventually acclaimed king in his own right. The rebellion of Rezon marks the rise of Damascus as Israel's chief rival in Syria–Palestine, a situation fated to continue until the Assyrian conquest.

21   (I) Prophetic Intervention into the Royal Succession (11:26–40). (On this passage, see Long, *1 Kings* 127–30; and R. Cohn, *ZAW* 97 [1985] 25–28. This passage at once closes the story of Solomon and begins that of Jeroboam; → 23 below.) Jeroboam, another adversary of Solomon, makes an abortive attempt at rebellion and is forced to flee the country (vv 26–28,40). The details of his uprising, however, have been supplanted in the present text by a prophetic story (vv 29–39). **27.** *this is the reason:* Lit., "this is the word" (*dābār*). In the original story of Jeroboam's rebellion, this would have been a typical narrative introduction: "this is the account of . . ." (cf. 9:15). With the replacement of that narrative by Ahijah's prophetic deed and speech, the narrower sense of *dābār* comes to the fore: "this is the [prophetic] *word* which raised rebellion against the king." *Millo:* See comment on 9:15. **29–39.** Ahijah of Shiloh is mentioned also in chap. 14, where he revokes the oracle given here. Prophets often preached by deed as well as word. Such a deed, called a "symbolic action" (→ Prophetic Lit., 11:23), was understood as unleashing an effective power just as inescapably as a divine word. Ahijah's action recalls Samuel's oracle repudiating Saul (1 Sam 15:27–28); the lengthy speech that follows is less a divine oracle than an exegesis of the action. It consists almost entirely of variations and embellishments of themes stated more simply in 11:11–13. **30.** *garment:* The word used for garment (*śalmâ*) plays on Solomon's name (*šelōmōh*). *twelve:* The 12 pieces represent the traditional 12 tribes of the whole people. The apparently faulty arithmetic (12 = 10 tribes for Jeroboam plus one tribe for Solomon's son) reflects political reality: the tribe of Levi no longer held territory (see further Jones, *1 and 2 Kings* 1. 244). **38.** Jeroboam is promised divine protection and a divinely appointed dynasty, in much the same language as David had been (cf. 2 Sam 7:11); like the promises to Solomon, this is contingent on Jeroboam's fidelity.

22   (J) Transition (11:41–43). The history of the kings uses standard formulaic material to mark regnal transition; → 27 below. **41.** *the Acts of Solomon:* → 2 above. **42.** *forty years:* A conventional figure (cf. 2:11), though in Solomon's case it may be approximately correct.

23   (II) Synchronic History of the Kingdoms of Israel and Judah (1 Kgs 12:1–2 Kgs 17:41).

(A) Jeroboam I of Israel (12:1–14:20). The story of Jeroboam is concentrically arranged and charts the course of his reign around the turning point of his religious policies. (a) His rise begins with an oracle of Ahijah of Shiloh (11:26–40; thematically and structurally, this oracle belongs to two literary units: it closes the account of Solomon's reign and opens that of Jeroboam's). (b) Political disruption follows with Israel's rejection of Rehoboam, and (c) a Judahite prophet, Shemaiah, announces Yahweh's approval of this state of affairs. (d) Jeroboam's cultic innovations are the center of the story (12:26–31). (c') The Bethel cult is condemned by an unnamed Judahite prophet, and (b') the religious unity of the kingdoms is seen to be seriously ruptured.

(a') Eventually Ahijah himself condemns Jeroboam, his house, and his kingdom.

(a) AHIJAH ANNOUNCES JEROBOAM'S KINGSHIP (11:26-43). → 21-22 above.

(b) POLITICAL DISUNITY (12:1-20). The disruption of political unity between Israel and Judah is shown in the story of Israel's refusal to accept Rehoboam, the son of Solomon, as king. The opening and closing verses reflect this theme: "all Israel came to make Rehoboam king" (v 1); "they made Jeroboam king over all Israel" (v 20). (i) *Narrative prologue* (12:1-3a). David's kingship had been dual—over Judah and over Israel; it had to be ratified by the elders of both regions (2 Sam 2:8-11; 5:1-5). Rehoboam has to journey from Jerusalem to Shechem to be accepted by Israel's elders. (ii) *First interview* (12:3b-5). The Israelites demand concessions; they will not acknowledge Rehoboam unless he reduces the burdens of taxation and corvée imposed by Solomon. (iii) *Rehoboam takes counsel* (12:6-11). The young king consults his father's advisers, but decides against their dissembling approach, preferring the hard line proposed by his own contemporaries. His words are boastful, threatening, and quite possibly obscene. (iv) *Second interview* (12:12-16). Rehoboam's heavy-handedness is portrayed as the immediate cause of the break between Israel and Judah; but the narrator discloses to the reader what the characters cannot know: the king's attitude is actually brought about by Yahweh in order to fulfill his word. **16.** The same cry of rebellion marked Sheba's revolt against David (2 Sam 20:1). (v) *Narrative epilogue* (12:17-20). Rehoboam's choice of Adoram, overseer of the hated corvée, to deal with the Israelites is singularly inept and only fuels the fires of insurrection.

(c) A JUDAHITE PROPHET'S APPROVAL (12:21-25). Rehoboam is dissuaded from war by a prophetic oracle announcing that the current state of political disruption is Yahweh's doing. Shemaiah may have been attached to the Jerusalem court (cf. 2 Chr 12:1-15). **25.** Jeroboam's preparations are defensive: he fortifies his capital, Shechem, and a site in Transjordan to counter Jerusalemite influence in Gilead.

24 (d) JEROBOAM'S CULTIC INNOVATIONS (12:26-31). The account of Jeroboam's reign, like that of Solomon's, turns on the king's cultic undertakings. Jeroboam's innovations are presented as the cause of his fall from grace: new sanctuaries, new images, a new priesthood—such things constitute the "sin of Jeroboam" condemned repeatedly in the deuteronomic tradition as the foundational evil of Israel (e.g., 13:34; 2 Kgs 17:21-23). The account, coming to us from a Judahite editor's perspective, puts the worst possible interpretation on Jeroboam's policies. **28-29.** *golden calves:* Like the cherubim atop the Ark of the Covenant, these figures were not intended to represent the deity. Despite the words put in Jeroboam's mouth, they were seats (or perhaps pedestals) for the invisible God enthroned upon them. Although the bull pedestal appears also in the cult of Baal, Jeroboam clearly intends to establish sanctuaries of Yahweh. (On the connection between Jeroboam's golden calves and Exod 32, see H. Tadmor in T. Ishida [ed.], *Studies in the Period* 255-56.) Bethel and Dan represent the southern and northern marches of Jeroboam's kingdom. **31.** *high places:* Jeroboam is charged with responsibility for the many Canaanite sanctuaries as well. *priests from throughout the people:* Judahite orthodoxy reserved the hereditary priesthood to Levites (de Vaux, *AI* 358-64; Jones, *1 and 2 Kings* 1. 260).

(e) A JUDAHITE PROPHET'S CONDEMNATION (12:32-13:10). Both Ahijah and Shemaiah, prophets of north and south, announced Yahweh's approval of the disruption of political unity. Jeroboam's cultic innovations, by contrast, draw prophetic condemnation first from an unnamed southern "man of God" and eventually from Ahijah as well (14:1-18). (On the parallels between Amos's ministry and that of the Judahite man of God, see J. L. Crenshaw, *Prophetic Conflict* [Berlin, 1971] 41-42.) **32-33.** A transitional passage sets the scene. Along with his other cultic innovations, Jeroboam establishes a new feast at Bethel, presumably to compete with the slightly earlier new year feast celebrated at Jerusalem (cf. 8:2). This feast is the occasion for the appearance of a prophetic figure from Judah, who denounces the altar upon which Jeroboam is offering incense. **13:3.** The words should be read as a parenthetical aside by the narrator: "(He also gave a sign the same day . . .)." **4-7.** Verse 5 is a further parenthetical remark averring that the preceding oracle had been fulfilled by the time of the narrator. It interrupts a sequence of statements by and about Jeroboam in the course of which the king's demeanor toward the man of God moves from wrath through entreaty to gratitude. **8-9.** The man of God's refusal of Jeroboam's hospitality is of a piece with his oracle: both are divine words, and both embody Yahweh's absolute, unconditional rejection of the northern kingdom. To share table fellowship with Jeroboam—indeed, to eat and drink with anyone in Bethel—would be to compromise with the unforgivable. The prophet's deed would gainsay his words. This sets the context for the following story.

25 (f) PROPHETIC DISUNITY; EVALUATION (13:11-34). The haunting story of the Bethel prophet and the Judahite man of God has received a number of sensitive readings (e.g., K. Barth, *Church Dogmatics* [Edinburgh, 1957] 2.2.393-409; U. Simon, "I Kings 13," *HUCA* 47 [1976] 81-117; Long, *1 Kings* 143-52; R. Cohn, *ZAW* 97 [1985] 32-35). As a self-contained narrative it is a compelling tragedy; as part of the Jeroboam story, it becomes an ominous portent for the two kingdoms' destinies.

The story unfolds in two closely parallel sequences, vv 11-24 and 25-32. The Bethel prophet hears news of the man of God (vv 11-12,25-26), has his sons saddle his donkey (vv 13,27), goes and finds the man of God (vv 14-17,28), brings him back and honors him (vv 18-19,29-30), and speaks or confirms a word of Yahweh (vv 20-22,31-32). The word is subsequently fulfilled (vv 23-24; cf. 2 Kgs 23:16-18, which many consider the original ending of the story).

As an independent story, vv 11-32 presuppose the man of God's oracle in vv 2-3, but not the surrounding narrative of Jeroboam. The Bethel prophet attempts to deceive the Judahite man of God out of loyalty to his own city: if the man of God can be led into disobedience, perhaps his oracle of condemnation will be nullified. The man of God moves tragically, from obedience through unwitting disobedience to death and alien burial. The Bethel prophet, whose lying prophecy deserves death (Deut 18:20), moves ironically, from patriotism through sacrilege to divine spokesman and witness against his own people. Behind this contrast stands the inexorable word of Yahweh, which, disserved by one bearer, casts him aside and seizes another, no matter how unworthy.

As part of the story of Jeroboam, vv 11-32 show the consequences of the king's religious innovations. The disunity decreed by Yahweh in the political sphere begins to infect the religious realm as well. Bethel is set against Jerusalem, cult against cult, feast against feast, prophet against man of God. Judah can still speak the word Israel needs to hear; but if Judah too compromises its worship (as history shows it will), then both are doomed to overcome their division only in death.

33–34. In evaluating Jeroboam's cultic policies, the Judahite editor uses the same terms found in 12:30–31, implying that the intervening prophetic events made no lasting impression on the king. The editor identifies this intransigence as the cause of the downfall of Jeroboam's dynasty.

26   (g) AHIJAH ANNOUNCES THE END OF JERO-BOAM'S KINGSHIP (14:1–20). Jeroboam's glory is toppled as it was raised—by a prophetic speech of Ahijah of Shiloh. As in chap. 11, Ahijah's words dominate, framed by minimal narrative. **1–6.** The king who once received 10 tribes from the prophet's hand now returns 10 loaves of bread. The narrative emphasizes Jeroboam's secrecy. In the context of chap. 13, this implies that Jeroboam fears Ahijah's rejection. Rather than go himself, he sends his wife to Ahijah in disguise and with a commoner's offering. Yet blind Ahijah, forewarned by Yahweh, recognizes her with undimmed inner sight. **7–16.** Ahijah's speech has two parts: a divine oracle against Jeroboam and his house (vv 7–11) and the prophet's own words about Jeroboam's son, dynasty, and nation (vv 12–16). **7–11.** The oracle alludes to Yahweh's earlier words through Ahijah (cf. 11:31,37–38) and accuses Jeroboam of violating the conditions contained in them. The punishment is extirpation of Jeroboam's whole house. Just as the "sin of Jeroboam" becomes paradigmatic for the northern kingdom (→ 24 above), so too his downfall sets a pattern for later Israelite dynasties (cf. 16:1–4; 21:21–24). The imagery is graphic, and promises not only death but disgraceful lack of burial to all Jeroboam's line. **10.** *bond or free:* The Hebrew is obscure (see Gray, *I & II Kings* 337–38). **12–16.** Ahijah's own words announce three dooms: the death and burial of Jeroboam's sick son, the overthrow of Jeroboam's dynasty, and punishment upon the whole nation. **17–18.** Jeroboam's wife leaves as she arrived, a silent and nameless pawn caught between God and king. She brings home with her not only a message of death, but the tragedy itself. The child's death and burial confirm Ahijah's words and assure us that his other predictions will be realized as well.

19–20. Like Ahijah's earlier oracle (11:26–40), this passage is followed by a formulaic account of the king's death and burial, and the accession of his son.

27   (B) Early Kings of Judah and Israel (14:21–16:34). Between the story of Jeroboam I and the lengthy narrative complexes set in Ahab's reign are found brief, summary notices about the reigns of the early kings of both kingdoms. The pattern established here will be followed through 1–2 Kgs: rulers are treated one by one, in chronological order of their accession, whether to Judah's throne or to Israel's. In this section three Judahite and six Israelite reigns are mentioned, covering approximately 60 years following Solomon's death. Each reign is treated according to a standard format, with variations in individual cases. (i) An *introduction* names the king, coordinates his reign with that of his counterpart in the other kingdom, and states length of reign and location of capital. The introductions to Judahite reigns add the king's age at accession and the name of the queen mother, who held the official post of Great Lady (*gĕbîrâ*) in the Jerusalem court. (ii) These data are followed by a *theological appraisal* of the king's reign. Israelite kings are all condemned, usually for following the "sin of Jeroboam" (→ 24). Judahite kings are variously evaluated, likewise according to cultic criteria. (iii) Next is a usually brief *account of some event* of the reign. Topics of frequent interest include conspiracies and assassinations and, in Judah, incidents touching the Temple and its cult. (iv) Finally a *conclusion* refers the reader to other sources of information and notes the

king's death and burial and the name of his successor (unless his death and his successor have already been mentioned, e.g., in recounting a *coup d'état*). See Long, *1 Kings* 158–65.

(a) EARLY KINGS OF JUDAH (14:21–15:24).

(i) *Rehoboam* (14:21–31). **22–24.** The whole kingdom of Judah, rather than Rehoboam alone, is condemned for engaging in Canaanite worship. The appurtenances of the indigenous cult included stone pillars and wooden poles (symbols of Baal and his consort Asherah); sacrificial sites on hills ("high places") and, perhaps, in association with sacred trees or groves; and male and female personnel (*qĕdēšîm, qĕdēšôt*—"consecrated ones") whose functions are generally supposed to have included ritual sexual intercourse (the so-called "sacred prostitutes"; for a contrary argument, see H. Barstad, *The Religious Polemics of Amos* [VTSup 34; Leiden, 1984] 22–34). **25–28.** Shoshenq (the Bible calls him Shishak) campaigned, according to his monumental inscription at Karnak in Egypt, against more than 150 cities in Israel and Judah. Jerusalem is not mentioned by Shishak and may have been spared in view of Rehoboam's tribute. The campaign is mentioned here because that tribute was taken from the Temple's treasuries. **29–31.** *Abijam:* The name of Rehoboam's son invokes the Canaanite sea-god: "Yamm is father." The author of 2 Chr 11–13 changes the name to the more orthodox "Abijah"—"Yahweh is father."

(ii) *Abijam* (15:1–8). The entire passage is composed of formulaic elements. Verse 6 is a misplaced copy of 14:30.

(iii) *Asa* (15:9–24). **9–10.** The queen mother's name is the same in v 2 and v 10, suggesting either a textual error (cf. 15:2 with 2 Chr 13:2) or Maacah's continued power after her son's brief reign. **11–15.** Unlike his predecessors, Asa is judged favorably for his cultic reform. The verdict is qualified, however: Asa did not remove the high places that had defiled Judah since the days of Solomon (cf. 3:2; 11:7–8). **16–22.** The historical note on Asa's reign, like that on Rehoboam's, recounts an escape from military conquest at the expense of the Temple's treasury (cf. v 18 with 14:26). Asa's reliance on foreign protection against Israel foreshadows the alliance of Ahaz and Tiglath-pileser, with its disastrous consequences for the Temple (2 Kgs 16).

28   (b) EARLY KINGS OF ISRAEL (15:25–16:34).

(i) *Nadab* (15:25–32). **27–28.** The first of a series of Israelite *coups d'état* is recounted according to a fixed pattern: the conspirator's name, the fact and location of assassination, and the accession of the conspirator (see also 16:9–10; 2 Kgs 15:10,14,25,30; with variations, 2 Kgs 21:23–24). **29–30.** Another conventional element in 1–2 Kgs is a notice of fulfillment of prophecy. Here the extermination of Jeroboam I's dynasty is referred back to the prophecy of Ahijah of Shiloh (14:7–11). **32.** A misplaced duplicate of 15:16.

(ii) *Baasha* (15:33–16:7). **16:1–4.** The second Israelite ruling house receives the same prophetic condemnation as the first (cf. 14:7–11). **7.** A late and somewhat awkward insertion into the catalogue of kings.

(iii) *Elah* (16:8–14). The account of Zimri's conspiracy against Elah closely parallels that of Baasha against Nadab. Thus, the first two Israelite dynasties share similar fates, in accord with similar prophetic oracles.

(iv) *Zimri; civil strife* (16:15–22). Omri's overthrow of Zimri's week-long regime is neither called a conspiracy nor recounted according to that pattern. Omri's rule is due to popular acclaim (although, in view of vv 21–22, the "all Israel" of vv 16–17 must be an exaggeration).

21–22. These verses are aptly placed between the conclusion to Zimri's reign and the introduction to Omri's. They recount a disruption in the line of kings where two rivals, each with a significant following, vied for the throne for four years.

(v) *Omri* (16:23–28). The extremely brief account of Omri's reign hardly does justice to the man. His dynasty lasted for over 40 years and so impressed other nations that, long after it had fallen, the Assyrians called Israel the "House of Omri." **24.** Omri's establishment of a new capital at Samaria compares with David's choice of Jerusalem (→ 1–2 Samuel, 9:49). The site was strategically placed, easily defended, and had no tribal ties.

(vi) *Ahab* (16:29–34). The account of Ahab's reign extends to 22:40, but it follows the standard format: introduction (v 29), theological appraisal (v 30, expanded by specifics in vv 31–33), historical note (v 34), conclusion (22:39–40). The historical note has been greatly expanded with stories of Elijah and other prophets and of Ahab's wars with Syria. **31–33.** Ahab's marriage to a foreign princess was doubtless a diplomatic maneuver like Solomon's (3:1). The narrator's interest, however, is less political than religious: Ahab's own participation in pagan cults outstrips even the "sin of Jeroboam" (→ 24 above). **34.** A prophecy–fulfillment notice illustrating a curse attributed to Joshua (Josh 6:26). On foundation sacrifices of children, see Jones, *1 and 2 Kings* 1. 300.

29   **(C) The Story of Elijah the Tishbite (17:1–19:21).** These stories about the prophetic ministry of Elijah the Tishbite, originally independent, now form a tightly organized literary unit. (Other stories of Elijah are found in 1 Kgs 21; 2 Kgs 1–2.) The overall framework is a concentric journey narrative: Elijah journeys to Transjordan (17:2–7), then outside Israel to the north (17:8–24). He reenters Israel (18:1–46), then goes outside Israel to the south (19:1–18). Finally he returns to Transjordan (19:19–21), bringing his journey full circle and affording the narrative a sense of closure. The unit develops two major themes: "opposition between Yahwism and Baalism" and "portrait of prophetic life" (R. Cohn, *JBL* 101 [1982] 333–50).

(a) ELIJAH DECREES A DROUGHT (17:1–24). **1.** The first theme sounds from the beginning. Baal was worshiped as the God of storms and fertility. A Yahwist claim to control rainfall constitutes a direct assault on Baalist religion. By proclaiming a drought, Elijah issues a challenge to the worshipers of Baal that will reach its climax in the contest on Mt. Carmel (18:21–40). The second theme begins here as well with the question of Elijah's authority. Elijah appears before us, as before Ahab, suddenly and unannounced. He is not called a prophet; and, although he claims to "stand before" (i.e., be a servant of) Yahweh, he decrees the drought on his own authority (lit., "the mouth of my word"). By what right does he claim and wield such power? The answer to this question, and a first portrait of the prophet, is revealed in the development of the motif of "word" throughout the chapter.

2–7. Elijah's claim to be Yahweh's servant is verified by his immediate and meticulous obedience to the divine word. Like Israel in the desert, Elijah is miraculously provisioned by Yahweh (cf. Exod 16:8,12).

8–16. Zarephath was a Sidonian town, i.e., territory acknowledged by all as Baal's, not Yahweh's. Yet the power of the God of Israel causes drought even there and protects those Yahweh favors with miraculous food similar to manna (cf. "cakes baked with oil," Num 11:8).

The theme of "word" reveals that the prophet does indeed speak a divine word of power, and that obedience to him wins Yahweh's favor: Elijah approves the widow's word (v 13) but adds his own qualification, which he claims to validate with a divine assurance (v 14). When the widow acts in conformity with Elijah's word (v 15), the divine assurance is fulfilled "according to the word of Yahweh which he spoke by Elijah" (v 16).

17–24. Yahweh's power in Baal's land extends even to life and death. Verse 18 is obscure but probably means that, having realized that Elijah is a "man of God," the woman feels her own unworthiness in his presence and understands her son's death as punishment. **20–22.** A new aspect of the prophet; he has the right to speak a human word to God, a word of powerful intercession. Yahweh's miraculous response is very like obedience (cf. Josh 10:14). The widow's final words bring both themes to a new stage: a Baalist woman confesses Yahweh's power, and acknowledges Elijah's authority in words that recall v 1: "truly Yahweh's *word* is in your *mouth!*"

30   (b) ELIJAH RETURNS THE RAIN (18:1–46). Opposition between Yahweh and Baal culminates in a contest between the two gods; in the wake of Yahweh's decisive victory, Elijah can announce the return of rain. The prophet's role throughout the contest parallels that of Moses in Exod 24 and 32. Elijah is a new Moses, and the events on Mt. Carmel are a new beginning for the Sinai covenant.

(i) *Entrance* (18:1–6). Two short scenes introduce the *dramatis personae* and set them en route toward one another. Famine is the inevitable result of drought in the Near East; when famine and drought are prolonged, livestock must be slaughtered both to provide food and to conserve water. This eventuality Ahab seeks to avoid. The text contrasts the king, whose concern is that the livestock not be "cut off," with his majordomo, who risks his life to keep prophets of Yahweh from being "cut off" by the king's wife.

(ii) *Elijah and the servant* (18:7–16). Elijah meets Ahab's majordomo, Obadiah (= "servant of Yahweh"), and sends him to fetch the king. Obadiah's lengthy protestation seems tinged with hysteria: three times he equates Elijah's command with a death sentence, and twice he repeats the command in full. Amid the flurry of words, he offers two clear indications of the danger both Elijah and he will incur if he does what the prophet asks. First, Ahab has been assiduously seeking to lay hands on Elijah, presumably to nullify the prophetic word and the drought it caused by killing the prophet. Second, Jezebel has been engaged in wholesale slaughter of prophets of Yahweh.

(iii) *Elijah and Ahab* (18:17–20). **17.** *troubler of Israel:* Ahab's accusation is not an acknowledgment of the prophet's (or Yahweh's) power to cause drought. More likely, Ahab attributes the drought to Baal's wrath, drawn down upon the people by Elijah's hostility to Baal. **19.** *eat at Jezebel's table:* The pagan prophets are subsidized from the royal treasury. (For the view that Jezebel was officially in charge of domestic and religious affairs in Ahab's kingdom, see A. Brenner, *The Israelite Woman* [Sheffield, 1985] 20–28.)

31   (iv) *Contest of the gods* (18:21–40). The pivotal issue in vv 21–40 is the religious loyalty of the people of Israel. Elijah addresses the people three times, gradually drawing them away from Baal toward Yahweh. Between his speeches to the people are the scenes of the Baalist prophets' futile offering and of Elijah's successful one. **21–24.** The first step of the people's journey back to Yahweh is taken by Elijah: he "draws near" the people and accuses them of being Baalists. Like the Baal prophets, they "hobble" (cf. v 26); like Baal himself they do not respond (cf. vv 26,29). Baal is indeed "their god" (v 24). The second step is the people's agreement to the contest; their acceptance of the Yahwist prophet's proposal presages—and in fact begins—their conversion (D. Jobling, *The Sense of Biblical Narrative* [JSOTSup 7; Sheffield, 1978] 73–76). **25–29.** Elijah has outmaneuvered the prophets of Baal by proposing the contest first to the people. By the time he addresses the prophets, the rules are already established. The prophets begin by invoking their deity throughout the morning, apparently chanting a single phrase hypnotically for hours. Their "hobbling" is probably some sort of ungainly cultic dance. Amid their exertions, Elijah sardonically urges them to greater efforts. His words are not entirely clear, but their intent is plain: Baal is so contemptible that his silence may be due to daydreaming, napping, or a need to answer a call of nature. Blind to Elijah's sarcasm, the prophets try harder, even shedding their own blood to attract Baal's attention. Ultimately they enter a prophetic trance, but all to no avail. **30–35.** At the center of the contest narrative, Elijah again addresses the people and calls them to take their next step: to "draw near" Elijah. When they comply, he begins preparations for his sacrifice. The altar he builds evokes traditions of Jacob/Israel, eponymous ancestor of the people (Gen 32:24–32; 35:9–15). The trench, both in purpose and in size, is a mystery (see N. Tromp, *Bib* 56 [1975] 487). Elijah then requires the people to drench bull, wood, altar, and earth with gallons upon gallons of water. In the third year of drought, this is a priceless libation, no less vital than the blood shed by the prophets of Baal. The entire passage recalls the covenant sacrifice on Sinai (Exod 24:4–8), where Moses builds a similar altar, involves the people in offering sacrifice, and pours precious liquid (the blood of the sacrificial animals) over altar and people. **36–38.** The people have "drawn near" Elijah (v 30); he in turn "draws near" Yahweh (cf. Exod 24:2). His prayer alludes to Moses' in Exod 32:13 ("Abraham, Isaac, and *Israel*"); both men ask Yahweh to forgive idolatrous Israel. In contrast to the Baalist prophets, Elijah prays soberly and succinctly; in contrast to Baal, Yahweh answers with incontrovertible power. **39–40.** Attention turns once more to the people. Their emphatic confession of Yahweh nullifies their silence (v 21) and enables Elijah to enlist their aid in executing the idolaters (cf. Exod 32:25–28). His single-handed slaughter of the multitudes of pagan prophets offsets his original complaint of isolation (v 22).

32 (v) *Elijah and Ahab* (18:41–42a). The people have declared themselves for Yahweh. It remains to recapture the loyalties of the royal house. In v 5, Ahab sought water at springs and in wadis (*nĕḥālîm*). In v 40, action arrived at the *naḥal* Kishon; but the Baalist blood that filled the wadi signaled the end of the Baalist king's hopes. Now, unexpectedly, he is told by Elijah that rain is near. Fire and blood have proved to the people Yahweh's sovereignty; rain will demonstrate it to the king. The meal atop Mt. Carmel parallels the covenant meal following the sacrifice on Sinai, where Moses and the elders of the people "saw God and ate and drank" (Exod 24:9–11). But v 42 is carefully worded: it says only that Ahab goes up "*to* eat and drink"— not whether he in fact does so. The king's response to Yahweh's theophanies is left unresolved.

(vi) *Elijah and the servant* (18:42b–45a). Elijah's servant, first mentioned here, keeps watch and carries messages while the prophet adopts a posture of profound prayer. His confidence that rain is imminent remains unshaken through a long delay, and he recognizes Yahweh's hand in an apparently insignificant wisp of cloud.

(vii) *Exeunt* (18:45b–46). From Carmel to Jezreel is about 17 miles. Elijah's exultation fills him with divine power (the "hand of Yahweh"), and he outruns Ahab's chariots through the downpour.

33 (c) ELIJAH RUNS FROM DANGER (19:1–21). Chapter 19 paints a vivid portrait of the prophet before his God, although the theme of opposition between Yahwism and Baalism is still present. Elijah undertakes a pilgrimage to Horeb, the mountain of Moses' theophanies (Exod 3–4; 33:18–34:8), to lay a complaint before Yahweh; there, in response, he experiences a revelation and receives a commission.

1–8. Chapter 18 left Ahab's loyalties unresolved. Here all comes clear: he remains attached to the Baalist cause of his queen. Indeed, Elijah's haste to flee and his later complaint against Israel suggest that even the people's conversion to Yahweh is unreliable. And so he flees into the southern desert to save his life. Yet, once there, he paradoxically prays to die. His ambivalence sets the tone for the narrative (R. Coote, "Yahweh Recalls Elijah," *Traditions in Transformation* [Fest. F. M. Cross; ed. B. Halpern and J. Levenson; Winona Lake, 1981] 115–20). His flight soon becomes a journey out of the ordinary world, symbolized by leaving behind companionship and food, and a pilgrimage to a sacred place.

9–19a. Elijah's encounter with Yahweh unfolds in two parallel sequences: (i) Yahweh's *question;* (ii) Elijah's *complaint;* (iii) Yahweh's *command;* (iv) Yahweh's further *response;* (v) Elijah's *compliance.* **9–13a.** Yahweh's question, "What are you doing *here*, Elijah?" implies that Elijah is expected to be somewhere else, viz., in Israel. Elijah does not answer directly, but lodges a triple complaint: he has been faithful while Israel has not; the people have used violence against Yahweh's cult and prophets; Elijah himself is isolated and in danger. His tone is peremptory and, in view of v 4, may well be a renunciation of his calling; cf. 18:22 with 19:10, where he no longer calls himself a "prophet"! Yahweh commands him to "stand . . . before me," i.e., to act once again as Yahweh's servant (cf. 17:1; 18:15). The command precedes an enigmatic theophany in which traditional manifestations of divine presence (wind, earthquake, fire—cf. Exod 19:16–19) are reduced to mere precursors of a mysterious "sound of fine silence." (On the importance of preserving the paradox in translation, see S. Prickett, *Theology* 80 [1977] 403–10; and R. Coote, "Yahweh Recalls Elijah," in *Traditions in Transformation* 118–19.) The whole scene, including Elijah's veiling his face, recalls the theophany promised to Moses in Exod 33:18–23. **13b–19a.** Elijah has obeyed Yahweh's command in part, but he stands in neither the place ("on the mountain") nor the posture ("before me") Yahweh has specified. Thus the question comes again, "What are you doing *here*, Elijah?" Unmoved by what he has witnessed, Elijah repeats his complaint. Yahweh's new command leads into a commission that answers the complaint point for point. To Elijah's desire to resign his mission in the face of Israel's infidelity Yahweh responds by naming his successor; to Israel's violence Yahweh responds with the swords of Hazael and Jehu; to Elijah's claim of isolation Yahweh retorts that there remain thousands of faithful in the land. Elijah will in fact fulfill only one of the three charges given him, the investiture of his successor; Elisha will be responsible for the other two.

19b–21. Elijah begins his return journey and soon encounters the successor Yahweh has chosen. Elijah's investiture of Elisha recalls Yahweh's treatment of Elijah: he "passes by" Elisha (v 19; cf. v 11) and he commands him, "Go, return . . ." (v 20; cf. v 15). Elijah's return to the ordinary world of food and companionship coincides with Elisha's abandonment of his family and previous life to follow Elijah. Elijah himself thus begins to function as a goal of pilgrimage, a locus of holy power to which Elisha is drawn and from which he will go forth, like Elijah from Horeb, a bearer of power and mission (2 Kgs 2).

34 (D) The Downfall of Ahab (20:1–22:38). Three stories focus on the death of Ahab. The materials are of diverse origin, and indeed the stories that recount battles between the kings of Israel and of Syria may not have been originally about Ahab at all (see J. Miller, *JBL* 85 [1966] 441–54). Their present context, however, identifies Israel's king as Ahab (though he is rarely named in chap. 20 and only once in chap. 22) and Syria's as Ben-hadad (though he is named only in chap. 20).

Each chapter combines a narrative about Ahab with a prophetic story. The latter depicts a progressively hostile prophetic community who announce Yahweh's negative judgment on the king's deeds and predict his punishment in ever clearer and more imminent fashion. The first prophetic narrative foretells Ahab's death and Israel's defeat in general terms; the second describes his death in lurid detail, adds condemnation of Ahab's queen and household, and foretells the end of his dynasty in the next generation; the third announces the arrival of Ahab's doom.

The first and third stories (chaps. 20 and 22) form a contrasting pair. (The LXX emphasizes the antithetic parallel by placing the two together and putting the intervening story of Naboth before them.) Both stories recount battles between Israel and Syria, separated by three years (22:1). In chap. 20 Ben-hadad clearly expects to win: he is the aggressor (20:1); he is allied with 32 "kings" (20:1); Ahab considers himself Ben-hadad's vassal (20:4); Ahab's troops are few (20:15,27), while Ben-hadad's are unimaginably many (20:29–30). Yet, with Yahweh on his side, Ahab emerges victorious. In chap. 22 Ahab is the aggressor (22:3); he is allied with the king of Judah, who considers himself Ahab's vassal (22:4); the Syrian's 32 allies are now mere chariot captains (22:31). Yet, abandoned by Yahweh, Ahab falls to a stray arrow and his army is dispersed (22:34–36). Both battle stories portray Ahab as noble and courageous. The attached prophetic narrative, however, transforms his conduct in each case into something blameworthy.

Between these two stories—set, then, during the three years of peace—is the account of Naboth's vineyard: the judicial murder of a righteous Israelite, the seizure of his property, and Yahweh's resultant condemnation of Ahab's house announced by Elijah.

35 (a) SYRIA ATTACKS ISRAEL (20:1–43). (On the structure, see Long, *1 Kings* 212–17.) The story of Ben-hadad's defeat by Ahab is chiastically arranged with scenes of negotiations surrounding two battle narratives. The picture of Ahab is quite positive: he welcomes Yahweh's word and acts on it. As a result, he is victorious. The following prophetic narrative (vv 35–43) has a very different tone. Ahab's lenient and politically expedient treatment of Ben-hadad is now interpreted as a serious offense against Yahweh.

(i) *Ben-hadad demands tribute* (20:1–11). **1–6.** Ahab understands Ben-hadad's first message as a formality, calling for a verbal surrender and declaration of vassalage. When Ahab answers in those terms, the Syrian requires more: free rein to plunder Ahab's capital city without hindrance. **7–8.** Ahab consults his advisers and, with their support, resolves to resist such demands. **9–11.** His refusal is polite but firm; Ben-hadad's response is a blustery threat. Ahab's last word is a laconic taunt (in Hebrew only four words): "Boast after battle, not before!"

(ii) *The battle of Samaria* (20:12–21). **12–19.** Ben-hadad's camp is in Sukkoth, across the Jordan, approximately 75 mi. from Samaria (Y. Yadin, *Bib* 36 [1955] 332–51). The text conveys the contrasting scenes in the two camps and the long march of the contending armies by a sort of split-screen technique: on one side we see Ben-hadad and his allies in camp, growing gradually drunker (vv 12,16); his orders are impulsive, given without consultation (vv 12,18). On the other side, Ahab receives an oracle of victory, consults Yahweh on strategy and follows the instructions received (vv 13–15); we see the Israelite forces marching, marching (vv 16a,17a,19). *the young men of the district commanders:* Probably handpicked commandos. **20–21.** The Syrians are routed and their military superiority undone.

(iii) *The battle of Aphek* (20:22–30). The account of the battle of Aphek follows the pattern of the preceding passage: a long description of preliminaries followed by a short account of the battle itself. **22–28.** The preliminaries are arranged in a series of contrasts: Ahab's consultation versus Ben-hadad's (vv 22–25), Syria's muster versus Israel's (vv 26–27a), and Israel's few versus Syria's multitudes (v 27b). As in the preceding passage, Ahab receives both strategic advice and assurance of victory from a prophet. **29–30.** The rout of the Syrians is even more definitive than at Samaria, with loss of infantry over and above the earlier loss of chariot troops.

(iv) *Ben-hadad pleads for his life* (20:31–34). The contrast with vv 1–11 is stark. Ben-hadad is now the suppliant, throwing himself on the mercy of the one he so recently contemned. Ahab, unlike his foe, shows himself magnanimous as well as politically astute—both praiseworthy qualities in a king. Ben-hadad formally offers vassalage ("your servant"; cf. Ahab's "my lord the king," vv 4,9); Ahab responds by offering to treat him as an equal ("my brother"). This is accepted, economic terms are negotiated, and a new treaty is established.

36 (v) *Prophetic narrative* (20:35–43). In a surprising twist, the preceding narrative, otherwise strongly favorable to Ahab, is used as the basis for a prophetic condemnation. A member of a prophetic group ("sons of the prophets," → Prophetic Lit., 11:7) makes elaborate preparations for confronting the king. **35–38.** The first incident, punishment for disobedience to the word of Yahweh, foreshadows Ahab's fate. The second disguises the prophet as a wounded soldier. **39–40.** A trap is set for the king, but not without warning. A talent of silver is sixty to one hundred times the price of an ordinary slave; the man who escaped his careless guardian must have been extraordinarily important. **41–43.** The trap is sprung. Ben-hadad, whom Ahab pardoned, was not his to set free; he belonged, according to the rules of holy war, to the God he had blasphemed.

37 (b) NABOTH'S VINEYARD (21:1–29). The second of the stories that trace Ahab's downfall differs from the surrounding narratives. It concerns an internal matter rather than Israel's wars with Syria, and it offers a strikingly different portrait of the king. Here Ahab appears petty and ineffectual, dominated by the forceful and unscrupulous Jezebel. The story unfolds in two balanced parts that contrast the destinies of Naboth and Ahab. In the first, Naboth owns a vineyard inherited from his fathers and safeguarded by the law of non-alienation of patrimony (on Lev 25:23–24, see R. Bohlen, *Der Fall Naboth* [Trier, 1978] 13–16, 320–50). Jezebel disrupts this situation and, by a hypocritical use of fasting and religious assembly, encompasses Naboth's death. The second part of the story is a prophetic narrative. Ahab is doomed to death because of Naboth's murder; the sentence is assured by the law of talion (v 19). Elijah's announcement of the sentence leads Ahab to repentance; and, by a sincere use of fasting and penitence, he is reprieved to life, bequeathing the death sentence to his sons.

(i) *Naboth's murder* (21:1–16). **1–7.** The opening dialogue between Ahab and Naboth is recalled repeatedly through the narrative, with subtle variations highlighting the characters' psychology. Addressing the landowner, Ahab first offers a land exchange; money is a second possibility, in the unlikely event that Naboth should prefer it to land. Naboth's reply reflects both religious horror ("Yahweh forbid!") and his legal basis for declining the king's offer ("the inheritance of my fathers"). The repetition of Naboth's words in v 4 should be read as Ahab's memory of the conversation; the king recalls the legal term accurately, but changes Naboth's religious feelings into a blunt refusal. When Ahab recounts the discussion to Jezebel, he mentions money as his first offer; unlike the Jezreelite farmer, the Tyrian princess would be more interested in money than in land. The king also ignores Naboth's religious and legal terms, and recounts only his refusal (v 6). Finally, when Jezebel refers to the offer after Naboth has been disposed of, she recalls only the money and the refusal (v 15). **8–14.** Verse 10 is likely a later insertion created by an editor out of v 13. Without it narrative tension is much higher. Jezebel issues a brief, enigmatic but innocent command which the elders obey sincerely. Suddenly the assembly is interrupted by two individuals, known to be good-for-nothings, who charge Naboth with *lèse majesté*. Their testimonies agree, and they lead the assembly in stoning him, according to the law (Deut 17:6–7). Only when the two send their report to Jezebel does all come clear to the reader: she must have engineered the entire operation. **15–16.** The murdered Naboth is named five times in vv 15–16. He haunts the narrative like a ghost that will not be laid to rest.

38   (ii) *Prophetic narrative* (21:17–29). **17–19.** Elijah is sent to announce Yahweh's condemnation of Ahab. The king's punishment corresponds to the crime even in gory details. **20–22.** The stereotyped condemnation (→ 26 above) foretells the same destiny for Israel's third dynasty as for its first two (14:7–11; 16:1–4). **23–26.** This series of comments is best read as a parenthetical interruption of the narrative. It includes an announcement of punishment for Jezebel (recalled at its fulfillment in 2 Kgs 9:36); another for Ahab's entire household (part of the stereotyped condemnation begun in vv 21–22); and an evaluative summary about Ahab and his idolatrous ways. (This last fits ill in this narrative context where the issue is Naboth's murder, not cultic infidelity.) **27–29.** The narrative resumes with an account of Ahab's repentance and Yahweh's decision to defer the end of his dynasty until the next generation. Thus, Ahab's children will wield royal power—his sons Ahaziah and Jehoram in Israel and his daughter Athaliah in Judah. But none will be succeeded by descendants.

39   (c) ISRAEL ATTACKS SYRIA (22:1–38). Chapter 22 is a companion piece to chap. 20 (→ 34 above). The death of Ahab and defeat of Israel foretold by the anonymous prophet (20:42) are here announced by Micaiah and realized in the course of a disastrous campaign against Ramoth-gilead. In chaps. 20 and 21 a prophetic narrative follows the story of Ahab and evaluates his actions after the fact. Here the prophetic narrative is inserted early into the battle story, disturbing the latter's symmetry and radically changing the context of Ahab's later actions. (On various interpretations of chap. 22, see W. Roth, in *The Biblical Mosaic* [ed. R. Polzin and E. Rothman; Phl, 1982] 105–37.)

(i) *Preparation for war* (22:1–4). Ramoth-gilead (lit., "Gilead Heights") is, presumably, one of the cities Ben-hadad promised to restore (20:34). Jehoshaphat's deference suggests Judah's status as lesser partner, perhaps even vassal, of Israel.

40   (ii) *Prophetic narrative* (22:5–28). **5–6.** At Jehoshaphat's request, Ahab solicits an oracle from his court prophets. Their advice appears favorable but is, in fact, ambivalent. It does not name the deity who will grant victory (cf. v 12), nor does it specify *which* king's hand will receive it (cf. the unambiguous "your hand" in 20:13,28). **7–9.** Jehoshaphat is unwilling to settle for such ambiguity and urges that a prophet be found who will speak in Yahweh's name. Ahab reluctantly sends for Micaiah, a confirmed doomsayer. **10–14.** While the messenger is fetching him, the narrative presents two brief scenes. First, the two kings in their regalia watch the court prophets expand and modify their original oracle. One of the prophets performs a symbolic action (→ Prophetic Lit., 11:23) that recalls Deut 33:17; the others rephrase their original words to include an explicit promise of success and to identify Yahweh as the victor's god. The second scene introduces Micaiah and establishes his credentials as a faithful prophet of Yahweh. **15–18.** Micaiah's first words to the king and the latter's response are puzzling—the faithful Yahwist prophet mouths the same placebo as the court prophets, and the doomed king devoutly demands the truth. The effect is to increase the bitterly ironic tenor of the whole narrative; ambiguity pervades all of life, even the behavior of otherwise faithful prophets and impious kings (see D. Robertson, in *The Biblical Mosaic* [→ 39 above] 139–46). Micaiah's second speech to Ahab foretells the king's death, using the common ancient metaphor of shepherd for the king. **19–23.** Micaiah's third speech is unsolicited; he recounts a scene he witnessed in Yahweh's heavenly court to explain the disagreement between his oracle and that of Ahab's court prophets. The prophets are truly inspired; but the spirit sent by Yahweh is a deceiver. It is Yahweh's purpose to mislead Ahab and so lure him to destruction. Yahweh's opening question to the heavenly court is already duplicitous: "Who will lure Ahab to fall upon [i.e., both "attack" and "die upon"] Gilead Heights?" The prophets' ambiguous oracle (v 6) is due to the "misleading spirit" whom Yahweh commissions to the deed. **24–25.** One of the court prophets accosts Micaiah with a sarcastic question about his own prophetic spirit: "If my spirit came from Yahweh's plan to deceive, where did yours come from?" Micaiah's response suggests that, in the end, only fulfillment can authenticate the prophetic word (cf. Jer 28:8–9). **26–28a.** *the king's son:* Probably an officer of the court, perhaps a prison warden (de Vaux, *AI* 119–20; but see J. Miller, *JBL* 85 [1966] 445). **28b.** The last words of v 28 are a gloss that has crept into the text. They erroneously identify Micaiah with Micah of Moresheth by citing the first words of the latter's prophecy (Mic 1:2).

41   (iii) *Ahab's strategy* (22:29–30). The battle story resumes. If it were not for the intervening prophetic narrative, Ahab's strategy would appear courageous. He hazards himself in battle without weakening his troops' morale by depriving them of a royal rallying point. But in the wake of Micaiah's words of doom Ahab's disguise is an act of cowardice: perhaps Jehoshaphat will draw the fatal blow Yahweh intends for Ahab.

(iv) *Battle* (22:31–34). At first Ahab's deviousness seems to work. But a single cry and a single arrow unravel his carefully woven strategy. Royal disguise cannot thwart a divine trap (Long, *1 Kings* 232–37).

(v) *Ahab's death* (22:35–37a). Unable to withdraw from battle because of the press of chariots, Ahab is propped up to appear unwounded, while his lifeblood drains away. Thus the theme of the king's disguise attains its morbid and ironic climax (S. De Vries, *Prophet Against Prophet* [GR, 1978] 27).

(vi) *Aftermath of war* (22:37b–38). Verse 38 is a prophecy–fulfillment notice recalling 21:19, to which, however, it does not fully correspond. The place is not the same (Samaria rather than Jezreel; cf. 2 Kgs 9:25–26), and 21:19 contains nothing about prostitutes.

42 (E) More Kings of Judah and Israel (1 Kgs 22:39–2 Kgs 1:18). Between the reigns of Ahab and Jehoram of Israel are brief treatments of Jehoshaphat of Judah and Ahaziah of Israel. Much of the material is formulaic (→ 27 above), with one substantial narrative about Ahaziah (2 Kgs 1:2–17a [MT 22:43–54 = Eng 22:43–53]). The division between 1 and 2 Kgs is wholly arbitrary and in no way corresponds to a significant division in the narrative.

(a) AHAB OF ISRAEL (22:39–40). Ahab's reign, begun in 16:29, concludes here with standard formulas. *ivory house:* Ahab's palace was decorated with finely carved ivory plaques; some have been unearthed by archaeologists. A century later Amos had harsh words for such ostentation (Amos 3:15).

(b) JEHOSHAPHAT OF JUDAH (22:41–51). The formulaic elements are strangely disordered: introduction (vv 41–42); evaluation (vv 43–44,47); historical notes (vv 45,48–50); conclusion (v 46,51). Jehoshaphat is evaluated in the same terms, and with the same reservation, as his father, Asa (15:11–14). **45.** Peace between Israel and Judah was sealed by marriage between Jehoshaphat's son Jehoram and Ahab's daughter Athaliah; the union was fraught with grave consequences for the southern kingdom (2 Kgs 11). **48–50.** Jehoshaphat's maritime activities at Ezion-geber suggest that Judah's control over Edom, lost after Solomon's death, had been regained.

(c) AHAZIAH OF ISRAEL (1 Kgs 22:52–2 Kgs 1:18). **52–54.** Ahaziah is condemned not only for continuing the "sin of Jeroboam" (→ 24 above), but for participating in the Baal worship introduced by his parents, Ahab and Jezebel. **2 Kgs 1:1–17a.** The historical note on Ahaziah's reign (v 1) has been expanded by a narrative about Elijah and the king.

2 Kgs 1:1. *Moab revolted:* This could be seen as a consequence of Ahaziah's sin mentioned in 1 Kgs 22:53–54. **2.** *dispatched messengers:* The following story consists of a series of sendings and involves a contest between Yahweh and the king as to which one can get his message delivered and his mission accomplished. The story likewise offers a gradually unfolding characterization of Yahweh's messenger, Elijah (see C. T. Begg, *JSOT* 32 [1985] 75–82). Finally, the narrative serves to concretize the Deuteronomist's previous general judgment on Ahaziah. *Baal-zebub:* The Hebr expression means literally "lord fly"; it is likely a deliberate deformation of the deity's actual title, i.e., Baal-zebul ("lord prince"), used in the NT as a proper name for the devil (cf. Mark 3:21). *Ekron:* This Philistine town was located some 40 mi. SE of Samaria. **8.** *hair:* Clothing made from hair appears as the prophetic uniform (cf. Zech 13:4; Mark 1:6). **9–14.** The overriding concern throughout this section is to inculcate due respect for a "man of God" as a matter of life and death for all approaching him. **10.** *fire:* Cf. 1 Kgs 18:38. **17.** Once again, in God's own time and despite human obstacles, a prophetic announcement reaches fulfillment.

43 (F) The Elisha Cycle (2:1–8:29). At this point commences a collection of stories (whose conclu-

sion stands now in 13:4–21) in which Elisha and his extraordinary power are the focus of attention. Dtr has incorporated this complex, among other reasons, because it exemplifies the conception of the prophet as dominant figure throughout Israel's history.

(a) ELISHA SUCCEEDS ELIJAH (2:1–25). **1–8.** This opening segment relates a testing of Elisha to determine the extent of his loyalty to his master. **1.** *Gilgal:* Several Israelite sites bore this name; most likely this is the one N (rather than SE) of Bethel. **3.** *sons of the prophets:* They figure prominently in the following stories as adherents and dependents of Elisha. **8.** *water:* Elijah's power recalls that of Moses (Exod 14) and of Joshua (Josh 3). **9.** *double portion:* Deut 21:17 stipulates such a portion for the oldest son. **11.** *fire:* Elijah is linked with fire right to the end. **12.** *saw:* This is the pivotal statement of the whole chapter; all that follows spells out its implications. *father . . . Israel's chariots:* The words are expressive of Elijah's role as Israel's guide and source of security; they will be addressed to Elisha himself at the end of his life (cf. 13:14). **13.** *cloak:* Clothes are an extension of the person; Elisha is thus assuming Elijah's identity here. **15.** *prostrated:* For the first time, Elisha receives the obeisance due him as Elijah's successor. **16–18.** This sequence serves to confirm that Elisha indeed "saw" what became of Elijah. **19–25.** Two short miracle accounts demonstrate both the new man of God's control over various natural phenomena and the diverse responses his appearance evokes. **20.** *new:* An object that will serve as a carrier of divine power must not have been put to "profane" purposes previously. **24.** The narrator is solely concerned with inculcating reverence toward a man of God; modern objections about extenuating circumstances and prophetic overreaction are beyond his purview. **25.** The two sites mentioned appear as the prophet's places of residence throughout the Elisha cycle (cf. 4:25; 5:3; 6:32).

44 (b) JEHORAM OF ISRAEL (849–842) AND THE MOABITE WAR (3:1–27). Dtr found the story of interest for its portrayal of another prophet–king encounter and for its cut at the reprobate Omrides (cf. 3:13). **1–3.** Jehoram of Israel, one of the main characters of the story, is introduced. His modest cultic reform involving the elimination of the Baal pillar will in no way mitigate the fate awaiting him (cf. 2 Kgs 9). **4.** *Mesha:* He is known to us also from the famous Moabite Stone discovered in 1868 at Dibon in Transjordania and now in the Louvre; on it Mesha recounts how he won back territory from Israel (see *ANET* 320–21; *ANEP* 209–10). **5.** *rebelled:* Mesha may have been emboldened to do this because he perceived Ahab's sons to be less dominant figures than their father. **7–8.** This exchange suggests that Judah was subordinate to Israel at this time (cf. 1 Kgs 22:4). *Edom:* The plan was to attack Moab from the S rather than from the N, from Israel itself. **11.** *inquire:* Jehoshaphat's suggestion recalls his proposal in a like situation in 1 Kgs 22:5. *poured water:* As Elijah's servant, Elisha assisted him with his ablutions. **15.** *musician:* Prophecy and playing of musical instruments are associated elsewhere (cf. 1 Sam 10:5; 1 Chr 25:3). *hand:* The term has the sense "power," this being understood as concentrated in a person's hand. **16–17.** Yahweh's characteristic prerogative of manipulating the earth's water supplies at will is affirmed. **19.** *tree:* With this injunction, contrast the prohibition of Deut 20:19. **22.** *red:* There is a play with the word "Edom" of 3:20. The waters receive their color from running over the reddish stone common in Edom. **25.** *Kir-hareseth:* The capital of Moab, it was located in the southern part of the country. **27.** *sacrificed:* Mesha hopes to incite divine favor by offering up what is most precious to him. *wrath:* The text leaves unspecified the source; perhaps in the original story it was Chemosh, god of Moab (cf. 1 Kgs 11:7), whereas for Dtr it was Yahweh who unleashed his anger against the wicked Jehoram. It is noteworthy that the prophetic announcement of 3:18 ends up—quite in contrast to the standard presentation—not completely fulfilled.

45   (c) A COMPLEX OF TEN LEGENDS (4:1–8:15). Each of the following stories evidences such hallmarks of the "legend" as the tendency to avoid naming characters (other than Elisha himself) and the intention of evoking wonderment at the hero's powers. Stories concerning the prophet's dealings with his own people alternate with those narrating his interactions with Gentiles.

(i) *The widow's plight* (4:1–7). **1.** *wife:* The narrative attests that at least some of the sons of the prophets were married. *seize:* Israel's law allowed a creditor's demands to be satisfied in this way (cf. Exod 21:7). **2–7.** Elisha's multiplication of oil here recalls Elijah's "oil miracle" in 1 Kgs 17:7–16, just as it looks ahead to his operation with the bread in 4:42–44.

(ii) *The Shunammite woman* (4:8–37). To be noted is the story's portrayal of the woman as initiator, resourceful and determined in her dealings with all the male characters. **8.** *Shunem:* The site lies *ca.* 30 mi. NE of Samaria. **9.** *know:* Only at the very end of the story will the woman fully realize Elisha's identity. **13.** *king:* Elisha's words point up his status as one with ready access to the highest authority. *my own people:* The woman is confident that her own clan can provide for all her needs. **14.** *childless:* This was regarded as a woman's greatest misfortune/failure (cf. Gen 16–18; 1 Sam 1). **16.** *deceive:* The woman's unconcealed skepticism serves to highlight the miracle that follows. **18–31.** The narrative's central section focuses on the woman's initiatives in response to her son's death. **21.** *bed:* Through its use by Elisha it has taken on some of the prophet's own powers, although not enough to effect a cure—only Elisha in person can do that. **23.** *new moon:* Like the Sabbath, this was a festive occasion (cf. Isa 1:13) and as such an expected time for the "pilgrimage" the woman speaks of. **25.** *Mount Carmel:* This promontory on the Mediterranean coast had previously been associated both with Elijah (1 Kgs 18) and with Elisha himself (2:25). **26.** Realizing that only Elisha himself can help her, the woman brushes aside his servant with a perfunctory response. **27.** *concealed:* Elisha's statement recalls that, even in the case of his chosen prophets, Yahweh always remains free to withhold his revelations. **29.** *my staff:* The object represents an extension of the prophet and his powers. *do not respond:* Cf. Luke 10:4; in both cases single-minded urgency in the mission at hand is being inculcated. **31.** Gehazi's failure underscores the extremity of the case and the magnitude of Elisha's ultimate success. **33–37.** With this third and climactic segment of the narrative compare 1 Kgs 17:17–24. **33.** For the motif of the privacy demanded for miracle working, see Mark 6:40. **34.** Elisha aligns his body with the corpse; in so doing he communicates the life-force present in each part of his body to the corresponding member of the boy's. **35.** *seven:* This is the number of completeness; mention of it signifies that the breath of life has fully returned to the boy. **37.** *prostrated:* The woman's gesture of recognition recalls that of the sons of the prophets in 2:15.

(iii) *Elisha counteracts food poisoning* (4:38–41). **38.** *Gilgal:* See comment on 2:1. *sitting:* Perhaps they had assembled to hear Elisha's teaching; he will also provide for their bodily needs. **41.** Compare Elisha's operation in 2:19–22.

(iv) *Elisha multiplies bread* (4:42–44). The text

is obviously the inspiration for NT multiplication miracles (cf. Mark 6:34–44; 8:1–10). **42.** *Baal-shalishah:* It lay *ca.* 10 mi. SW of Samaria. The man's gift bespeaks the esteem Elisha enjoyed among the people. **43.** Note the contrast between the servant's querulously doubting question and the prophet's calm self-assurance.

46   (v) *Elisha, master of leprosy* (5:1–27). The story links up with the preceding narratives in its emphasis on the role of "servants" and on Elisha's power over the lives of others. It widens the prespective of the "legend sequence" by depicting the prophet using his powers on behalf of a Gentile enemy (see R. L. Cohn, *VT* 33 [1984] 171–84). **1–9.** The introductory segment relates the process by which Naaman came to approach Elisha. **1.** *Yahweh:* Naaman's victories are attributed to Israel's own God; from the start the all-encompassing sovereignty of Yahweh is highlighted. *leper:* The reference is to some sort of skin disease. (cf. Lev 13–14). **2.** *little maid:* The contrast between this figure and mighty Naaman could not be greater, and yet without her and her speaking up he would never have been healed. **5.** *took:* Bringing of gifts when approaching a prophet was standard practice (cf. 1 Sam 9:6–10; 1 Kgs 14:2). *tore:* The customary gesture expressive of shock and dismay. **8.** *let him come:* Elisha's self-assurance contrasts with the king's agitation. The story revolves around people moving from ignorance and misconceptions to genuine knowledge. **10.** *sent:* Elisha maintains his superiority by dealing with Naaman only through an intermediary. *seven:* Naaman is directed to wash himself completely. **11.** Naaman's misconceptions about how a prophet ought to operate almost abort his healing. **12.** *rivers:* The Abana flows to the N of Damascus, the Pharpar to the S. **13.** *servants:* Once again, it is an intervention "from below" that moves Naaman toward healing. **14.** *small youth:* Mighty Naaman is assimilated to the "little maid" of 5:2. **15–27.** The story's final segment relates the sequels of the healing, first for Naaman and then for Gehazi, contrasting their dealings with its central figure, Elisha. **15.** *know:* Naaman has gone from enraged misconception (5:11) to full apprehension. **16.** *refused:* Acceptance would suggest that it was Elisha's own powers that had effected the cure. **17.** *earth:* Naaman articulates the common ancient conception that linked and limited a deity to some particular territory (cf. Ps 137:4); on these terms, if Naaman is to worship Yahweh in Damascus then he must take back some of Yahweh's domain with him. **18.** *Rimmon:* The deity's actual name was (Hadad) Ramman, "Hadad the thunderer." **19.** *peace:* Elisha expresses understanding for the compromises Naaman will have to make. **20.** Gehazi's misapprehension will bring him not the good he anticipates but lifelong affliction. **24.** *hill:* Presumably the reference is to the hill on which Samaria (cf. 5:3) was built (cf. 1 Kgs 16:29). **26.** *my heart traveled:* Elisha alludes to the clairvoyance for which he was famous (cf. 6:12). The money that Gehazi actually received would have enabled him to buy the objects mentioned here. **27.** In trying to get the goods of Naaman for himself, Gehazi ends up rather with his affliction. Once again, the point is made that no one can trifle with a prophet with impunity (cf. 2:23–25).

(vi) *An axhead recovered* (6:1–7). In its brevity and depiction of Elisha as one who provides for those approaching him in faith, the story recalls especially 2:19–22; 4:1–6,38–41. It is placed here because its use of master/servant terminology and its reference to the Jordan link it with the immediately preceding Naaman narrative. **6.** Cf. 2:21; 4:41.

47   (vii) *Elisha as military resource* (6:8–23). The story's master–servant interaction and depiction of

Elisha's activity on behalf of Gentiles prolong features of the preceding narratives. Throughout, Elisha's status as one who can dispose of the plans even of kings is underscored. **10.** Elisha's clairvoyant knowledge of events at a distance make him of great military intelligence value for Israel. **11.** The Syrian king surmises that one of his officers must be leaking his plans to Israel. **12.** *bedroom:* Even happenings in this most private locale are not hidden from Elisha. **13.** *Dothan:* About 10 mi. NE of Samaria. **17.** *see:* The term in various senses is a key word in the passage. *fire:* The expression recalls 2:12 and indicates that the fullness of Elijah's role has passed to Elisha. **18.** *blindness:* Through his prayer Elisha has total control over the sight of others. **21.** *my father:* Note the deference with which the king addresses Elisha. **22.** *kill:* Elisha argues a fortiori here: one is not justified in killing even those one has captured through one's exertions; far less is one allowed to kill those who come into one's power without such exertion. **23.** *banquet:* Such treatment of a foreign enemy is noteworthy; it recalls Elisha's dealings with Naaman in 2 Kgs 5. *no longer:* The problem with which the story began, i.e., Syrian raids against Israel, has been resolved because of the Syrians' experience of good treatment by the Israelites.

(viii) *Samaria delivered* (6:24-7:20). The lengthy narrative highlights the clairvoyant and predictive powers of Elisha as displayed in a crisis situation. **24-31.** This introductory segment cites several details pointing up the extremity of the city's plight; as such it serves to accentuate its eventual deliverance by Yahweh. **24.** *Ben-hadad:* The second Syrian ruler with this name, he ruled 870-842. **25.** *sold:* Samaria's situation is so desperate that food/cooking supplies that normally would be taken for granted suddenly command high prices. **26-31.** This exchange about a case of cannibalism further underscores the straits to which Samaria has been reduced. **27.** All sources of food have given out. **29.** *ate:* In Deut 28:53-57, as well as in extrabiblical texts, such eating of children by their own parents figures as a curse facing those who violate their treaty obligations. *concealed:* Cf. 1 Kgs 3:16-27 and contrast the responses of Solomon there with the unnamed Israelite king here. **30.** *sackcloth:* The king has donned penitential clothing (cf. Joel 3:5) in hopes of winning Yahweh's compassion. **31.** In invoking a curse upon himself, the king, in line with standard practice (cf. 1 Kgs 19:2), avoids mentioning what God is to do to him, thereby setting that in motion. It is not clear why the king's outburst should be directed against the prophet (contrast 6:21); perhaps he sees Elisha as the one whose activities have incited the Syrians to attack Samaria. **6:32-7:2.** This exchange between king and prophet constitutes the narrative's hinge, setting up its final conclusion. Noteworthy is the contrast between the hysteria and unbelief of those who approach Elisha and the prophet's calm assurance about the future. **32.** *his house:* As in 5:3 Elisha appears as a resident of Samaria. His question points up his clairvoyant powers (cf. 6:12). **7:2.** *heavenly windows:* Even if God were to open up the windowlike apertures of the sky through which the rain was thought to descend (cf. Gen 7:11; Isa 24:18; Mal 3:10) and pour down foodstuffs on the city, Elisha's announcement could not be fulfilled. **3-20.** The story culminates in the reversal of Samaria's initial situation and the vindication of Elisha's announcement. **3.** *lepers:* Because of their dreaded affliction, they had to sit out the siege in a no-man's-land between the city and the enemy camp—neither side will have them. **6.** *Yahweh:* The Syrian's flight is attributed to an action of Yahweh, manipulating their senses (cf. the blinding in 6:18). *Hittites:* Mentioned elsewhere as pre-Israelite inhabitants of Palestine (Gen 23). **8.** *hid:* The lepers' action

recalls that of the woman in 6:29. **12.** *king:* The lepers' report (7:9) is too good to be true; he suspects a Syrian ruse. **13.** *servant:* Once again, this is the one who points a master in the right direction (cf. 5:3,13). **15.** *Jordan:* The river lies *ca.* 25 mi. E of Samaria. **16-20.** The segment underscores the fulfillment of both parts of Elisha's announcement (cf. 7:1-2), just as it points up that wrongful stances toward a prophet will not go unpunished (cf. 2:23-25; 5:20-27).

48   (ix) *Property regained* (8:1-6). In content the story obviously coheres with 4:8-37; it has been placed at this point in the Elisha cycle because its references to famine (8:1), the prophet's clairvoyance, and the Israelite king all link it with 6:24-7:20. **1.** *famine:* The occurrence is attributed to Yahweh, acting for reasons left unspecified. **2.** *Philistines:* The woman's migration takes her from Shunem, SW of the Sea of Galilee, to the SW coast of Palestine. **3.** Property vacated for several years passed out of its owner's possession; this was the custom also, e.g., in Mesopotamia (see *ANET* 167). **4-5.** A happy coincidence brings the woman on the scene just when the (nameless) king was feeling a particular interest in her case. **6.** The woman not only gets back her property but is compensated for its output during her absence— those associated with Elisha prosper in every way.

(x) *Elisha and Hazael* (8:7-15). The story relates the approximate realization of the divine directive given Elijah in 1 Kgs 19:15. In content it goes with the material concerning Elisha and the Syrians in 2 Kgs 5; 6:8-20; and like 8:1-6 it associates Elisha with life and death. **7.** *Damascus:* No reason is given for the prophet's presence in the Syrian capital. *sick:* The contrast between the stricken pagan king who sends to the Lord and the injured Ahaziah's embassy to a foreign god in 2 Kgs 1 is striking. **8.** *Hazael:* His identity/position is not specified. *gift:* This is a routine feature in reports of visits to prophets (cf. 1 Sam 9:6-10; 1 Kgs 14:2; 2 Kgs 5:5). **9.** *son:* Note the deferential self-designation of the pagan king. **10.** *get well:* The king is to be told a reassuring word that will put him off guard. *revealed:* Once again, Elisha's famous clairvoyance (cf. 5:26; 6:26) is operative. **11.** *stared:* Elisha cannot keep his eyes off Israel's future oppressor. **13.** *dog:* In the OT it is a term of abuse (cf. 2 Sam 16:9). *great deed:* Contrast 8:4, which speaks of the "great deeds" done by Elisha in behalf of Israel. *king:* Elisha finally comes to the point. **15.** *covered:* Emboldened by the prophet's word, Hazael suffocates his master in whose stead he ruled *ca.* 842-806.

49   (d) JEHORAM OF JUDAH (849-842) (8:16-24). At this point the narrator pauses to bring us up to date concerning the two Judean kings whose reigns overlapped with that of Jehoram of Israel, i.e., Jehoram and Ahaziah. **16.** Contrast the dating indication in 1:17, which has Jehoram of Israel becoming king in the second year of Jehoram of Judah. **18.** *daughter:* Jehoram's wife is Athaliah (cf. 8:26; 11); Dtr insinuates that it was his foreign marriage that made Jehoram the bad king he was. **19.** *lamp:* The Hebr term might also mean "fief" (cf. 1 Kgs 11:36; 15:4). **20.** *rebelled:* Edom had been subjugated by David 250 years earlier (cf. 2 Sam 8:13-14). **21.** *Zair:* About 15 mi. SW of Jerusalem. **22.** *Libnah:* About 25 mi. SW of Jerusalem, close to the Philistine border.

(e) AHAZIAH OF JUDAH (842) (8:25-29). **26.** *Omri:* According to the Hebrew, Athaliah could be either the daughter or granddaughter of Omri, the father of Ahab; 8:18 points to the latter understanding. **27.** *son-in-law:* Ahaziah was actually either Ahab's grandson or grandnephew. **28-29.** These verses, which recur in 9:14-16, serve to make the transition to the account of 2 Kgs 9; their presentation is reminiscent in several respects of 1 Kgs 22 (Israelite and Judean king allied against Syria; Ramoth-gilead as scene of battle; Israelite king wounded by the Syrians). *Ramah:* The shorter name for the Transjordanian city of Ramoth-gilead.

50   (G) Synoptic History from Jehu to the Fall of Samaria (9:1–17:41). This segment relates the doings of the Israelite and Judean monarchs in the last 125 years of the two kingdoms' co-existence. As such, it is similar to the segment 1 Kgs 14:1–16:34, from which it is separated by the Elijah and Elisha cycles (1 Kgs 17–2 Kgs 8), where the focus is on prophetic rather than royal figures.

(a) JEHU OF ISRAEL (842–815) (9:1–10:36). This extended presentation is dominated by the concern to portray Jehu's bloody doings as the fulfillment of prophetic announcements and so as divinely sanctioned. Jehu is depicted on the famous Black Obelisk of the Assyrian king Shalmaneser III (see *ANEP* 122).

9:1–13. Jehu is designated king. **1.** *Elisha:* He, rather than the nameless "son of the prophets," is the true initiator of all that follows. **3.** *anoint:* Dtr makes mention of royal anointings only when a reign begins in somewhat exceptional circumstances, e.g., when a new dynasty comes to power (cf. 1 Sam 10:1; 16:13; 1 Kgs 1:39; 2 Kgs 11:12). *flee:* Elisha's representative is to vacate the scene immediately so as to avoid seizure for instigating rebellion. **6.** *anoint:* Here, indirectly, the directive given Elijah by Yahweh concerning Jehu (cf. 1 Kgs 19:16) is finally realized. **7–10a.** These words go beyond Elisha's instructions about what Jehu is to be told (cf. 9:3). In addition they are reminiscent of the prophetic speeches in 1 Kgs 16:2–4 and 21:21–24 and as such are generally seen as a deuteronomistic insertion making clear that Jehu's bloody elimination of the reigning house was divinely mandated (contrast Hos 1:4). **11.** *peace?:* The question will re-echo throughout 2 Kgs 9 (see vv 17–19,22; see also S. Olyan, *CBQ* 46 [1984] 652–68). *madman:* The same term is used of Jeremiah in Jer 29:26; it conveys a sense of how ambiguously the prophetic role was viewed in Israel. **12.** *lie:* Jehu is initially unwilling to reveal the treasonous truth. **13.** *clothing:* For a similar gesture of tribute, see Mark 11:8. Human acclamation ratifies the divine designation of Jehu (cf. 1 Kgs 1:39; 2 Kgs 11:12,14). **14–23.** Jehu eliminates the ruling powers in both Israel and Judah. **17–23.** A threefold sending to the advancing Jehu (cf. 2 Kgs 1:9–15) culminates in King Joram's coming face to face with his rival and recognizing—too late—his intentions. **17.** Joram supposes (or hopes) that the approaching group is bringing news of victory from the Syrian front. **20.** *Jehu:* The identity of the one advancing has now been ascertained; his intentions remain to be discovered. **21.** *Naboth:* The mention of the man murdered by Joram's father, Ahab (cf. 1 Kgs 21), sets up the following presentation. **22.** *whorings:* The term alludes to Jezebel's promotion of Baal as rival divinity to Yahweh (cf. 1 Kgs 16:31). The same terminology is used by Hosea (Hos 2:7) of Israel's worship of Baal; it presupposes an understanding of the relationship between Yahweh and Israel as that of husband and wife (Ezek 16). **23.** *treason:* Now, at last, Joram is fully enlightened concerning the identity of the one first glimpsed by the watchmen (cf. 9:17). **26.** Jehu cites an alternative version of the word attributed to Elijah in 1 Kgs 21:19, where there is no mention of Naboth's sons as here. Once again, Jehu's "treason" is presented as fulfilling a divinely announced doom. **27–28.** The hapless Ahaziah is likewise eliminated; his association with Ahab's house is reason enough. It is unclear why Ahaziah should suddenly proceed to Megiddo, NW of Jezreel, rather than continue S to Jerusalem as he had been doing. **29.** The notice duplicates

8:25 (which speaks rather of Joram's "twelfth year") and is out of place at this point. **51   30–37.** Jezebel, "the power behind the throne" in Israel, is eliminated in her turn, thereby ensuring Jehu a free hand. **31.** *Zimri:* With desperate fearlessness, Jezebel mocks Jehu with the name of an earlier Israelite regicide (cf. 1 Kgs 16:9–19) who himself quickly came to a bad end. **32.** *eunuchs:* The customary guardians of royal women's quarters (cf. Esth 1:10–12). **33.** Throughout 2 Kgs 9–10 Jehu appears as a dominant personality whose orders evoke immediate compliance by all. **34.** *ate:* Jehu's action emphasizes his contempt for Jezebel and studied unconcern for her fate. **36.** Jehu recalls the divine announcement of 1 Kgs 21:23. Jezebel's end is a particularly degrading one, given the low Israelite view of dogs (cf. 1 Kgs 22:38).

10:1–17. Jehu mops up survivors and supporters of the Israelite and Judean royal houses. **1.** *seventy:* As a multiple of seven, the number signifies the totality of Ahab's progeny. *Samaria:* The Israelite capital lies *ca.* 20 mi. SW of Jezreel. **2–3.** Jehu's message to the Samaritan worthies is a mocking challenge, daring them to resist and playing on the rivalries that certainly existed among them and their charges. It has the desired effect. **6.** Jehu aims to implicate the Samaritan leadership in his own treason; if they do as directed they irreversibly commit themselves to him. **7.** Compare the response of the Jezreel notables to Jezebel's letter in 1 Kgs 21:11–14. **8.** *piles:* Jehu manifests the same cold-bloodedness in the face of gruesome death he earlier evidenced in the case of Jezebel. **9–10.** Jehu intimates that the mysterious deaths of the Samaritan princes—neither he nor the Jezreelites are responsible—can only be attributed to an act of God foretold by Elijah. Once again, the writer is intent on legitimating Jehu's actions. **11.** *Jezreel:* Jehu solidifies his grasp over Israel by exterminating everyone associated with Ahab in the alternative royal residence. **12–17.** These verses are transitional, concluding the series of Jehu's political murders and leading into his cultic reform in Samaria. **12–14.** A group of Judean royalty, who like king Ahaziah have the misfortune to cross Jehu's path, are eliminated. *Beth-eked:* The site remains unidentified. **13.** The unsuspecting Judeans betray themselves as had Joram previously, with the same fatal results. **14.** The completeness of Jehu's exterminatory measures is emphasized (cf. 10:11); here too no one ventures to protest or resist Jehu's directives. **15.** *Jehonadab:* On this figure as the representative of old-time ("nomadic") Yahwism, see Jer 35. *hand:* The handshake serves to ratify an agreement (cf. Ezek 17:18). **16.** *zeal:* In his claim here Jehu is reminiscent of Elijah at Horeb (cf. 1 Kgs 19:14). **17.** *exterminated:* Jehu rounds out his campaign against supporters of the old regime in the capital city itself.

52   18–28. The Jehu narrative reaches its culmination. Jehu's political measures are a prelude to and a presupposition for his great religious reform. **19.** *Baal's prophets:* Baal has such figures just as Yahweh does (cf. 1 Kgs 18:22). *cunningly:* The writer wants to preclude any notion that Jehu was actually a Baal-worshiper. **20.** *hallow:* The term designates the preparations required for a cultic assembly, e.g., change of clothing and sexual abstinence (cf. Exod 19:14–15; Joel 1:15). **21.** *temple:* It has been built by Ahab (cf. 1 Kgs 16:32). **22.** *clothing:* For special garments used on cultic occasions, see 23:7. **23.** *seek:* Jehu wants to make sure that only guilty Baal-worshipers are punished. **24.** *he:* This is the original reading (so LXX; cf. 10:25); MT has "they," attempting to play down Jehu's role in the Baal sacrifice. *his life:* The talion principle will be applied if any Baal-worshiper gets away alive (cf. 1 Kgs 20:42). **25.** In v 25b MT has

Jehu's forces advancing into the "city of the Baal temple"; modern translators conjecture that the reference should be to the temple's inner sanctum where the image of Baal (cf. 10:26) was housed. **26.** *pillar:* It is unclear how this notice relates to 2 Kgs 3:2, where the object is already removed by Jehoram. **27.** *latrine:* The site is rendered permanently unfit for cultic purposes.

29–36. Various notices and comments conclude the Jehu narrative. **29.** *calves:* Dtr introduces a qualification concerning Jehu as cultic reformer: he failed to eliminate the images set up by Jeroboam I, a charge that is re-iterated in 10:31. **30.** *Yahweh:* The divine communication comes directly to Jehu, with no mention of a prophetic mediation; its fulfillment will be noted in 15:12. *right:* Contrast Hos 1:4. **32.** The juxtaposition with 10:31 suggests that Yahweh activates the Syrian king in punishment for Jehu's toleration of the calf cult.

53 (b) ATHALIAH OF JUDAH (842–837) (11:1–20). The chapter constitutes the Judean panel to the diptych concerning political-cultic turnarounds in both king-doms, 2 Kgs 9–11; numerous parallels with the presentation in 2 Kgs 9–10 may be noted. **1.** *annihilated:* Athaliah is the Judean Jezebel, equally cold-blooded and power-hungry. **2.** *Jehosheba:* Juxtaposed with Athaliah is another resolute and resourceful woman, her sister-in-law. **3.** *temple:* 2 Chr 22:11 clarifies how Jehosheba was able to hide Joash there, by making her the wife of the high priest Jehoiada. **4.** *Jehoiada:* According to 11:9 he was *the* (main) priest of the Temple; in 2 Kgs 11 he assumes the role of Jehu in 2 Kgs 9–10. *Carites:* Perhaps these are the same royal mercenaries called the Chere-thites elsewhere (cf. 1 Sam 30:14; 2 Sam 8:18; 1 Kgs 1:38). *agreement:* The terms are specified in 11:5–8: the forces are to guard the Temple and the person of Joash. **6.** *Sur:* A gate by this name is otherwise unknown; perhaps MT is a mistake for *sûs,* i.e., horse(-gate) (cf. 11:16). **10.** *David:* On the weapons presented by him to Yahweh, see 2 Sam 8:7,11,12. **12.** *crown:* For this royal insignia, see 2 Sam 1:10. *testimony:* The reference would be to a document similar to those presented to Egyptian kings on their accession containing their throne-names, titles, etc. Frequently, however, MT is emended in accordance with 1 Sam 1:10, which couples Saul's "crown" with his royal "bracelet." *anointed:* Compare 2 Kgs 9:6; MT's pl. vb. would make the troops of 11:11 the subject; perhaps they act through Jehoiada as their representative. **14.** *column:* The reference here and in 23:3 suggests that there was a special royal pillar in the Temple where the king used to stand on special occasions. *people of the land:* This is the first mention of this grouping in Judah's history; subsequently it will figure prominently when the continuity of the Davidic dynasty's rule is threatened (see 14:21; 21:24). The group seems to have consisted of the landed gentry of Judah. *trumpets:* Cf. 9:13. *conspiracy:* Too late Athaliah recognizes the trap; her cry re-echoes that of Jehoram in 9:23. **15.** *Temple:* Yahweh's house must not be defiled through bloodshed; contrast Jehu's desecration of the Baal temple by killing those gathered within it (10:25). **16.** *killed:* Nothing is said of burial for Athaliah such as even Jezebel was granted (cf. 9:35); the omission under-scores the narrator's abhorrence of Athaliah. **17.** *covenant:* Jehoiada now functions as the mediator of a double pact. A first covenant has people and king renew the nation's allegiance to Yahweh that Athaliah had disrupted. The other agreement regulates relations between people and ruler which had likewise been disturbed under Athaliah (for such a royal covenant, cf. 2 Sam 5:3). **18.** Just as in 2 Kgs 9–10, the account of 2 Kgs 11 climaxes in a cultic reform that eliminates all foreign religious forms. *Baal's temple:* This is the first mention of the existence of such

an institution in the south (cf. 2 Kgs 10:18–27). *Mattan:* Presumably he was a non-Judean Baalite whom Athaliah had brought with her from the north. **20.** *calm:* The story's finale contrasts with the preceding noise and violence. The omission of the usual concluding notices for Athaliah serves to underscore the illegitimacy of her rule in the view of the narrator.

54 (c) JEHOASH OF JUDAH (837–800) (12:1–21). **2.** Jehoiada remains the guiding force during Jehoash's reign. **4.** Dtr introduces the qualification concerning the persistence of the forbidden high places, which is applied to all Judah's "good kings" prior to Hezekiah.

5–16. This extended segment narrates a positive cultic counterpart to the destruction of the Baal temple described in 2 Kgs 11:18, i.e., the establishment of an arrangement for ensuring the upkeep of the Temple. At the same time, the story provides background for the subsequent presentation in 22:3–7. **5.** Jehoash, in his capacity as supreme authority over the Temple, promul-gates a regulation concerning the various monies com-ing into the Temple. **6.** *acquaintance:* Each priest would receive monies from his family and friends. **7–8.** The mildness of Jehoash's reaction to the priests' non-compliance with his regulation is surprising; perhaps he stood so much in awe of Jehoiada that he hesitated to confront them on the matter. **10.** From now on the priests are immediately to deposit the monies given them in a special chest; they lose their discretionary use of the sums contributed. **11.** *secretary:* This was an im-portant post whose incumbent was charged with impor-tant missions by the king (see 18:18; 22:3,12,14). *high priest:* In a preexilic context, the use of this postexilic title for the major priest is anachronistic. **11–15.** The uses for the money collected are specified. **16–17.** The account concludes on a positive note, emphasizing the trust-worthiness of the Temple repairmen and the fact that Jehoash's new regulation did not deprive the priests of all income since they continued to receive payment for their sacrificial activities. **18–19.** This brief incident links up with the preceding in that it too concerns the fate of the Temple under Jehoash, while as a "despoliation notice" it foreshadows the final loss of royal and Temple treasures in 587. **18.** *Gath:* Either the Philistine city or a site in the SW corner of Israel, also called Gittaim. In any event, the allusion indicates that Hazael was in a position to range far afield from his home base E of the Jordan. **19.** Note that no blame is pronounced against Jehoash for his initiative in buying off the Syrians in this way. **21.** *conspired:* The plotters' motives are left unspecified; perhaps they were angered by Jehoash's failure to resist the Syrians. *Millo:* See comment on 1 Kgs 9:15. **22.** The two regicides mentioned are otherwise unknown (cf. 14:5–6). *ruled:* The stereotyped brevity of the formula-tion leaves many questions concerning the situation after Jehoash's assassination unanswered: Did the assassins have a candidate of their own for the throne? If so, how was Jehoash's son able to secure power (perhaps through an intervention by the "people of the land")?

55 (d) JEHOAHAZ OF ISRAEL (815–801) (13:1–9). At this point, Dtr resumes the account of the Israelite kings which was broken off at 10:36 in order to relate the reign of Jehoash of Judah (2 Kgs 11–12). **2–7.** The presentation here is reminiscent of the cyclic sequence manifest in the Dtr view of the period of the judges: Israel's sin, divine abandonment to the enemy, appeal by Israel, and eventual intervention by Yahweh on Israel's behalf (cf., e.g., Judg 3:7–11). The application of this schema to the reprobate northern kingdom is remark-able—all the more so given the insistence (cf. 13:2,6) that Israel did not turn from the sin of Jeroboam at this time. **5.** *deliverer:* The same term is used of Othniel in Judg 3:9.

The identity of the nameless figure is uncertain—perhaps King Jeroboam II, through whom Yahweh is said to have "delivered" Israel (cf. 14:27).
56 (e) JEHOASH OF ISRAEL (801–786) AND THE DEATH OF ELISHA (13:10–25). The account of Jehoash's reign provides the framework for the conclusion (13:14–21) of the Elisha cycle, broken off at 8:14. **10.** *thirty-seventh:* The dating indication does not tally with 13:1. **12–13.** Duplicated in 14:15–16. **14–19.** The story has been placed here because of the mention of Joash (Jehoash), the Israelite king named in 13:10–13. **14.** The place of Elisha's final illness is not specified. *wept:* The king's action and accompanying words recall Elisha's own response to Elijah's departure in 2:12, and express his consternation at the prospect of losing Elisha's military intelligence capacities. **15–17.** In response to Joash's lament, Elisha initiates an act of "sympathetic magic" in which a desired result, i.e., military penetration into Syria, is symbolically enacted and anticipated. **17.** *Aphek:* In northern Transjordan, E of the Sea of Galilee in territory contested between Israel and Syria. **18–19.** A second procedure ordered by Elisha magically pre-enacts Syria's being struck by Israel's arrows. The king's failure to continue betrays his lack of confidence in the procedure and ultimately in the one prescribing it (compare Moses' striking the rock twice in Num 20:11; this evokes the prophet's anger and a diminution of the results the procedure might have had. **20–21.** Even in death, as so often in life, Elisha continues to be the conduit of Yahweh's life-giving powers (cf. 4:8–37). **22–23.** With its mention of Jehoahaz (cf. 13:1–9), this segment appears out of place in an account about his successor Jehoash. It prepares for the shift in Israel's situation to be related in 13:24–25. *covenant:* Remembrance of his ancient commitment to the patriarchs induces Yahweh to spare Israel; for a similar presentation, see Deut 4:31. *until now:* Apparently the exilic Deuteronomist simply lets stand an earlier formulation presupposing the continued existence of Israel. **24–25.** After the parenthetical material in 13:20–23, the fulfillment of Elisha's announcement in 13:17 is noted. *Ben-hadad:* He is the third Syrian ruler with this name to be mentioned in Kings (cf. 1 Kgs 20; 2 Kgs 6:24; 8:9).
57 (f) AMAZIAH OF JUDAH (800–783) (14:1–22). **3–4.** Dtr gives Amaziah a positive evaluation, but with a double restriction, i.e., he was not the equal of the exemplary David, and he tolerated worship at the high places. **5–6.** In dealing with his father's assassins (cf. 12:20–21), Amaziah acts in accordance with the law of Deut 24:16, limiting punishment to those actually guilty. Contrast the procedure of Jehu in 2 Kgs 10, and compare what is said concerning individualized divine retribution in Ezek 18. **7.** Amaziah campaigns against Edom, which had revolted under his great-grandfather Jotham (cf. 8:20–22). *the Valley of Salt:* The Arabah, the great depression in which stands the Dead Sea, also known as the Sea of Salt (cf. Gen 14:3); this configuration formed the western border of Edom. *Sela:* Generally localized due S of the Dead Sea, this city was the capital of Edom; its later name was Petra. **9–10.** Jehoash's fable reminds Amaziah that those puffed up with their own importance frequently end up being unexpectedly overthrown; compare Jotham's fable, also involving talking plants and citing the cedar(s) of Lebanon (Judg 9:8–15). At the same time, the terms of the fable serve to recall the discrepancy in strength between Israel and Judah which dooms Amaziah's challenge from the start. **13.** *wall:* Jehoash's action is a typical ancient military practice (cf. 25:10) intended to render a subjugated city permanently defenseless. The gates mentioned would have been part of the city's northern walls, as the reference to

"Ephraim," the Israelite territory N of Jerusalem, indicates. **14.** Jehoash likewise plunders the treasures of palace and Temple which had somehow been replenished following Joash's buying off of Hazael (cf. 12:13). **15–16.** These verses duplicate 13:12–13, thereby framing the sequence of events of Jehoash's reign (13:14–14:14). **19.** *plotted:* Unnamed malcontents bring Amaziah's reign to the same bloody end as that of his father, Joash (cf. 12:20). Here too the grounds for the conspiracy are not mentioned. Was it vengeance by relatives of Joash's assassins whom Amaziah executed? Popular discontent with the disgrace Amaziah had brought on Judah by his foolish challenge to Jehoash? *Lachish:* This important Judean fortified town lies SW of Jerusalem, close to the Philistine border. **21.** *people of Judah:* An alternative designation for the "people of the land"; see comment on 11:14. **22.** *Elath:* At the head of the Gulf of Aqabah. Also called Ezion-geber, it had earlier been the starting point for Judean trading ventures along the Red Sea (cf. 1 Kgs 22:48). The resubjugation of Edom by Amaziah (see 14:7) made it possible for his successor, Azariah, to reactivate the site as mentioned here.
58 (g) JEROBOAM II OF ISRAEL (786–746) (14:23–29). Dtr gives minimal attention to the long and successful reign of this last great northern king, under whom Amos functioned as a prophet (cf. Amos 1:1). On the other hand, as with his predecessors of the Jehu dynasty, his reign is described as a time of divine favor for Israel, notwithstanding the persistence of the reprobate calf cult. **25.** *entrance to Hamath:* The northern boundary of Solomon's empire (cf. 1 Kgs 8:65), lying between the Lebanon and Antilebanon mountain ranges in Syria. *Sea of the Arabah:* This OT name for the Dead Sea derives from its location in the hollow called the Arabah. *Jonah:* He is mentioned only here in Kings; subsequently he becomes the (anti-)hero of the book called after him. The name means "dove." **27.** *delivered:* See comment on 13:5. **28.** In this textually problematic closing notice, Jeroboam II is depicted as having subjugated the Syrian cities, Damascus and Hamath, both of which had been David's vassals (cf. 2 Sam 8:6,9). His successes were made possible by the temporary weakness of Assyria prior to the accession of Tiglath-pileser in 745.
(h) AZARIAH (UZZIAH) OF JUDAH (783–742) (15:1–7). The long reign of Jeroboam's Judean contemporary gets scant attention. **5.** The only particular cited is Yahweh's afflicting Azariah with some form of skin disease; when and why this happened are left unspecified. As a result, Azariah lives out his days in a kind of quarantine, with his son Jotham functioning as regent.
(i) ZECHARIAH AND SHALLUM OF ISRAEL (746–745) (15:8–16). **10.** After almost a century of rule, Jehu's line comes to an abrupt end with the speedy assassination of his great-grandson Zechariah. The background and motivations of the conspirator Shallum are not mentioned; moreover, the circumstances of the assassination are obscure because of the MT's corruption in this verse (the reference to "Ibleam" as the site of Zechariah's murder in the *RSV* and the *NAB* reflects the reading of some Gk mss.). **12.** Dtr calls attention to the exact fulfillment of Yahweh's announcement to Jehu in 10:30. **13.** *Uzziah:* An alternative name for Azariah, perhaps his regnal name. *Tirzah:* NE of Samaria; cf. 1 Kgs 16:18. After the briefest of reigns, Shallum suffers the same fate as his victim Zechariah. **16.** Menahem inaugurates his reign by an act of gruesome vengeance against those who had failed to support him (cf. 8:12).
59 (j) MENAHEM OF ISRAEL (745–738) (15:17–22). **19.** *Pul:* The throne-name of the great Assyrian ruler Tiglath-pileser III (745–727), who inaugurated the

Neo-Assyrian Empire (745–627). This is the first reference to Assyria; Assyrian records make clear, however, that Israelite–Assyrian interactions dated back more than a century before Menahem. *silver:* The Assyrian annals list Menahem among rulers paying tribute (*ANET* 283). **20.** Menahem obtains tribute money by an *ad hoc* tax on wealthy Israelites; the numbers cited suggest that Israel was still a rich nation at this point.

(k) PEKAHIAH AND PEKAH OF ISRAEL (738–732) (15:23–31). *plotted:* After the stability of Menahem's seven-year rule, anarchy resumes with the quick assassination of his son Pekahiah by an officer whose name is a shortened form of his own, Pekah. *Gileadites:* Pekah's supporters hail from the area across the Jordan; sectional animosities seem to have been operative in Pekah's revolt. **27.** *twenty:* The figure is certainly a mistake; Pekah reigned only about five years. **29.** *seized:* The reference is to Tiglath-pileser's campaign of 733–732, in which he stripped Israel of its N and E territories. The first five place-names cited are cities, all to the (N)E of the Sea of Galilee; the last three names designate regions in northern Israel, whether E (Gilead) or W (Galilee, Naphtali) of the Jordan. **30.** *plotted:* Israel's losses under Pekah spark yet another coup. Tiglath-pileser's annals claim that it was he who installed Hoshea as king in return for a heavy tribute (*ANET* 284).

(l) JOTHAM OF JUDAH (742–735) (15:32–38). **33.** *sixteen:* The figure includes the time spent by Jotham as regent for his father (cf. 14:7). **35.** *built:* The Deuteronomist again has little to relate concretely about the reign; he mentions this item because it concerns the Temple. **37.** *Yahweh:* The grounds for his unleashing this assault during the reign of a righteous ruler are not mentioned; in any event, the brunt of the attack falls under Jotham's successor, Ahaz (cf. 16:5).

60 (m) AHAZ OF JUDAH (735–715) (16:1–20). After the very summary presentation of the two preceding "good kings," Dtr becomes more expansive in the treatment of this "bad" monarch. Wicked Ahaz serves as a negative foil for his exemplary successor, Hezekiah (cf. 2 Kgs 18–20). **3.** *fire:* The Hebr formulation used (cf. Deut 18:10) leaves it unclear whether an actual burning up or simply a passing over the fire is being referred to. **4.** *he sacrificed:* For the first time, a post-Solomonic Judean king is charged with personal participation in the forbidden worship on the high places; previously the Deuteronomist spoke in general terms of the people as a whole doing this (cf., e.g., 15:35). **5.** *attack:* The two kings press their assault, which they had begun already under Jotham (cf. 15:37). Historians designate this conflict as the Syro-Ephraimite war. Isa 7 and Assyrian sources allow us to reconstruct the background of the event, i.e., the two kings were trying to overthrow Ahaz, who had refused to join in their anti-Assyrian revolt, and replace him with a more pliant figure. **6.** *Elath:* Judah's point of access to the Red Sea trade is lost once again (cf. 8:20–23; 14:7,22). **7.** *servant:* To save himself from the two kings, Ahaz submits his kingdom to Assyrian vassalship, under which it remains, with brief interruptions, until the end of the Neo-Assyrian Empire more than a century later. **9.** *Damascus:* Tiglath-pileser is happy to respond to Ahaz's request that he move against the rebel vassals; in 733–732 he wiped out Syria, Israel's long-time foe, and likewise greatly reduced the territory of Israel (cf. 15:29).

61 **10.** *altar:* The segment concerning Ahaz's altar in vv 10–16 leaves various points unclarified: Was the altar he saw in Damascus a Syrian or an Assyrian one? Did he intend it to be used for sacrifices to Yahweh, or (also) to Assyrian deities? Remarkable too is the absence of any explicit evaluation of the affair by the author. In any case, what does emerge is the total control over the Temple cult and its priests enjoyed by the king (cf. 12:5–7). *Uriah:* Probably this is the same as the priest cited in Isa 8:2 as a "trustworthy witness." *blood:* In the P legislation (Lev 3:13), disposal of the victim's blood in this way is reserved to the priest; Ahaz's action reflects earlier, less exclusivistic practice. **14.** Solomon's bronze altar (1 Kgs 8:64) is moved to a new site so as not to detract attention from Ahaz's new construction. **15.** Henceforth, the customary Temple sacrifices are to be offered at Ahaz's altar, whereas the older altar is to be put to some sort of divinatory use. **17–18.** An appendix to the preceding account relates Ahaz's measures regarding various objects and structures in the Temple; apparently these were inspired by his need to find the wherewithal to pay his Assyrian tribute. For the objects enumerated in v 17, see 1 Kgs 7:23–27.

62 (n) HOSHEA (732–724) AND THE FALL OF SAMARIA (722–721) (17:1–41). Dtr now reaches one of its key turning points with the definitive disappearance of the northern kingdom after an existence of two centuries. The chapter focuses not so much on the event of Samaria's fall as on the ultimate grounds for that happening and on subsequent religious developments in the former territory of Israel. **2.** The qualification introduced here concerning Hoshea's wickedness is puzzling in that no indication is given as to what may have prompted the Deuteronomist to make it. **3.** *Shalmaneser:* Tiglath-pileser's successor, Shalmaneser V, reigned 727–722. **4.** Hoshea commits a vassal's two cardinal sins: he makes overtures to a rival of his overlord, while also withholding tribute; it is not surprising that he ends up deposed and incarcerated. *So:* Possibly the reference should be to the N Egyptian city of Sais, which was the capital of Egypt at the time. **5.** The siege extended from sometime in 724 until late in 722. **5.** Samaria finally fell to Shalmaneser's successor, Sargon II (722–705), whose annals (*ANET* 284–285) speak of his deporting 27,290 Samaritans. Of the sites mentioned, Halah is unidentified, Gozan is on the river Habor at the W edge of Assyria, and the Medean cities lay E of Assyria in what is now Iran.

7. Dtr interrupts the chronicle of events in order to offer an extended theological reflection on why Israel ended as it did; the concern is to make clear that this was not due ultimately to political factors nor to impotence on Yahweh's part. In fact, it was he who used the Assyrians as his instrument in punishing Israel for its persistent sin. The segment consists of two parallel, though unequal, judgment-speech sequences, the first (vv 7–20) speaking of the sins of the people as a whole, the second (vv 21–23) focusing on the misdeeds of Jeroboam I. *feared:* A key term throughout the remainder of the chapter, it is equivalent to "worshiped." **10.** *Asherim:* Probably sacred poles; the word is the (masc.) pl. form of the divine female name "Asherah" used in v 16. **13.** Dtr articulates the understanding of the prophetic role as that of preacher of the (deuteronomic) law and of repentance. **15.** The Hebrew contains a wordplay with the term *hebel:* "they pursued vanity and became vain." **16.** *heavenly host:* The various bodies in the sky were understood as making up Yahweh's army (cf. Judg 5:20); worship of them, which seems to have arisen in Israel especially under Assyrian influence, is prohibited in Deut 17:2. **17.** *fire:* See comment on 16:3. The various mantic practices mentioned are prohibited in Deut 18:10–11. **19.** This parenthesis in the indictment of Israel foreshadows the following history of Judah and its ultimate outcome. **21.** At the end of the account of the northern kingdom's history, Dtr once again underscores the fatal role played by Israel's first king and his religious innovations in the whole course of that history.

63 **24.** The narrative, interrupted at v 6, resumes. The first two sites mentioned are on the middle Euphrates, the last three in NE Syria, on the Orontes River. Sargon's own annals (*ANET* 286) speak of his settling conquered Arab tribes in the territory of Samaria. **25.** *lions:* These were plentiful throughout the Near East, as royal Assyrian hunting inscriptions and reliefs attest. **26–28.** Such an involvement by the Assyrian king might seem implausible; it should be kept in mind, however, that the king did have an interest in maintaining a population that produced revenues for him. Note the alternation in the account between the narrator's own reference to "Yahweh" and the mention of the "god of the land" placed on the lips of the Assyrians. Underlying the latter formulation is the notion that a given deity has a specified territory as his sphere of power (cf. 5:17). *Bethel:* Given Dtr's overall presentation of this site (cf. 1 Kgs 13), the fact that the priest settles here sets up negative expectations about the future of religion in the former northern territory. **29.** The Yahwism adopted by the new population is not an exclusivistic one; the charge reflects the polemics between the Jews of Jerusalem and the "Samaritans," which intensified over the centuries. **30–31.** The divine names cited are the (often distorted) Hebr versions of the actual names of the Mesopotamian or Syrian deities. **32.** Even in their worship of Yahweh the foreigners fail to respect the requirement that priesthood be reserved to the Levites; the charge recalls 1 Kgs 12:31; 13:33, where Jeroboam I likewise disregards levitical prerogatives. Northern history is repeating itself. **33–34a.** The section closes with a reiteration of its opening charge of syncretism against the population of Samaria (cf. v 24). **34b.** The polemic against the Samaritans resumes on a still sharper note, denying that the Samaritans are worshipers of Yahweh at all. **35–39.** This statement of the terms of Yahweh's covenant represents a compendium of many passages of Deut (cf., e.g., 7:1–6; 8:19–20; 10:20; 10:26–28; 12:1–12,29–31). **41.** This verse shares with vv 29–34a a less unqualified negative view of the Samaritan religion than one finds in the intervening vv 34b–40.

64 **(III) Judah on Its Own (2 Kgs 18:1–25:30).** This last great segment of Dtr relates how, after surviving its sister kingdom by almost a century and a half, Judah came to the same end.

(A) Hezekiah (715–687) (18:1–20:21). The material may be divided up into the three segments 18:1–12; 18:13–19:37; 20:1–21 as follows:

(a) INTRODUCTION TO HEZEKIAH'S REIGN (18:1–12). This opening presentation underscores the differences between Hezekiah and his father Ahaz in both the cultic and political spheres. **1.** *third:* This would be 729/728. The chronological indication in 18:13, when coupled with the Assyrian material, suggests, however, a considerably later date for the start of Hezekiah's reign, i.e., 715. **3.** *David:* Hezekiah's actions make him another David, the standard against whom Dtr measures all Judean kings. **4.** *high places:* Hezekiah is the first Judean king ever to move against these centers of worship outside Jerusalem, which contravene the centralization requirement of Deut 12. *Asherah:* The existence of her cult in Judah is mentioned here for the first time since the reign of Asa (cf. 1 Kgs 15:16). *Nehushtan:* Hezekiah's iconoclastic zeal extends even to a serpent image attributed to Moses himself (for this tradition, see Num 21:6–9). **5.** *relied on:* The term points forward to the following Assyrian crisis and the stance displayed by Hezekiah there. *none like him:* Curiously, a very similar statement is used of Josiah in 23:25.

7. *succeeded:* In Hezekiah's case, obedience to the law brings prosperity, just as is promised so often in Deuteronomy (cf. Deut 28:1–14). A preeminent example of Hezekiah's "success" is his surviving a revolt against Assyria—something that did not often happen with disloyal Assyrian vassals. *Philistines:* According to Assyrian records (*ANET* 287) Hezekiah was implicated in a multination plot to depose the Philistine king of Ekron, a loyal Assyrian vassal; Hezekiah held him prisoner in Jerusalem but eventually handed him over to the Assyrians. *Gaza:* The southernmost of the five cities making up the Philistine confederation, the "Pentapolis." **9–12.** These verses are drawn from 2 Kgs 17, particularly vv 5–6. Their function here is to point up the difference between the religious stances of Samaria and Hezekiah's Judah (just depicted in vv 1–8) and their respective consequences.

65 (b) THE ASSYRIAN THREAT (18:13–19:37). The lengthy account of Hezekiah's Assyrian crisis is introduced by a summary narration concerning his submission in the face of an Assyrian advance against Judah (18:13–16). This section agrees essentially with the more extensive Assyrian documentation according to which the rebel Hezekiah, confronted with the Assyrian occupation of much of his territory and under tight siege in Jerusalem itself, responded by sending heavy tribute to the Assyrians (*ANET* 288). Its report differs so markedly from the following 18:17–19:37 (and the Assyrian records) that many see the latter as describing a distinct, later Assyrian campaign against Judah of *ca.* 688/687 (see *BHI* 298–309; W. H. Shea, *JBL* 104 [1985] 401–18). **13.** *fourteenth year:* The Assyrian documentation suggests that the reference is to the year 701, when the Assyrians undertook a campaign against Judah which ended with Hezekiah's buying them off. *Sennacherib:* Successor of Sargon II, he reigned 705–681. **14.** *Lachish:* Sennacherib's siege of this Judean town is depicted in a famous series of Assyrian palace reliefs (cf. *ANEP* 129–132).

17. Within 18:17–19:37 two parallel sequences can be distinguished, each consisting of Assyrian challenge, divine response, and notice of its realization: (1) 18:17–19:9a and 19:36–37; (2) 19:9b–35. The former sequence begins with an enumeration of three Assyrian officials who appear for negotiations at Jerusalem; only the second of these (Rabshakeh, or chief butler) has an active role in what follows. *conduit:* The meeting takes place adjacent to the tunnel carrying water from a reservoir at the N end of the old city of Jerusalem to another reservoir at the S end; it was the same site where Isaiah and Ahaz met, according to Isa 7:3. **18.** The first two Judean officials cited recur in a divine announcement concerning their respective fates in Isa 22:15–25. **19.** *rely:* This will be the key term throughout the officer's speech in vv 19–25. **22.** Yahweh will not help Hezekiah, who has curtailed worship of Yahweh with his centralization policy (cf. 18:4). **25.** The Assyrian's assertion here is based on the fact that the vassal treaty between Judah and Assyria (cf. 16:7) would have been solemnized by an oath invoking not only the Assyrian gods but also Yahweh, who thereby became enforcer of Judah's observance of its treaty obligations. **26.** *servants:* The Judean officials respond deferentially to one of whose superiority they are all too aware. *Aramaic:* From *ca.* 850 it increasingly became the language of international contacts throughout the Near East; here it is depicted as being known by important Judean officials, although not yet to the bulk of the people. *Judean:* Here and in Neh 13:24 this is the term for the language we call "Hebrew." The officials' concern is that the defenders of Jerusalem will become demoralized should they understand the Assyrian's speech. **27.** Realizing why the officials make their request, the Assyrian brushes it aside, announcing his intention of speaking directly to the defenders, who face the prospect of being reduced to starvation as the siege proceeds (cf. 6:24-30). **28.** The Assyrian's speech resumes, directed not to Hezekiah but to his troops and shifting from an affirmation of Yahweh's support for Assyria to a direct challenge to Yahweh (vv 28-35). **29-31a.** The defenders are warned not to let themselves be misled by Hezekiah and the Lord he invokes. **31b-32a.** Rather, they should give themselves up to the Assyrian king, who promises to provide them conditions similar to their present ones if they do so. **32b-35.** The Assyrian clinches his appeal with a series of rhetorical questions underscoring the inability of assorted deities to protect their worshipers against Assyrian attack. The gods mentioned are those of five cities in NE Syria and, most tellingly for the Judeans, the god of Samaria, who, of course, is Yahweh. Such an ending to the speech leaves one in suspense as to how Yahweh will respond to so direct a challenge to his ability to defend his people. **36-37.** The suspense is further accentuated by having the Assyrian challenge left unanswered by Hezekiah's officials. If answer is to be made, it will have to come from Yahweh himself. **19:1.** *heard:* A key word throughout the chapter. For the measures signifying distress and penitence mentioned, see comment on 6:30. **2.** The composition of the delegation underscores the status of the one to whom they go. *Isaiah:* He is the only "classical prophet" mentioned in Dtr. **3.** The Assyrian taunts have induced a kind of paralysis. **4.** The Assyrian king has indulged in hubris, a sin which in the OT invariably evokes a divine humbling (cf., e.g., Isa 2:6-22; 10:12-19). *intercession:* On this characteristic prophetic activity, see, e.g., 1 Kgs 13:6; Amos 7:2. *remnant:* A key term in Isa (10:21; 11:11,16). **6.** *fear not:* This exhortation recalls the address to Ahaz in Isa 7:4. **7.** *spirit:* For Yahweh's dispatching a spirit to lead someone to destruction, see 1 Kgs 22:22. **66   9.** *Tirhakah:* This Ethiopian general was successively regent and ruler of Egypt *ca.* 690-664. The reference to him as "king" is one of the arguments put forward by those who hold that 18:17-19:37 is describing a post-701 Assyrian assault on Judah, since in 701 Tirhakah was not yet king. *again:* This is a redactional insertion which makes what follows the continuation of the preceding rather than a parallel to it. **10-13.** These verses read like a condensed version of the Assyrian's speech in 18:29-35. The sites mentioned in v 10 are all in NE Mesopotamia, those in v 13 in NE Syria. **14.** *before Yahweh:* Hezekiah wants to be sure that Yahweh sees the insulting Assyrian message for himself. **15.** *prayed:* Here, in contrast to 19:4, Hezekiah appeals to Yahweh directly. His highly reflective prayer appears as an expanded version of his charge to the delegation in 19:4. **17-18.** Hezekiah concedes the truth of the Assyrian boast about the impotence of all the various national gods (cf. 19:12-13), and at the same time gives a specifically Israelite explanation for this, i.e., the unreality of the "gods" in question. **19.** Hezekiah concludes by imploring Yahweh to make clear that he is no impotent, unreal divinity like the others. *may know:* This "perception formula" is especially characteristic of Ezekiel (Ezek 35:15; 36:38). **20.** Yahweh's response to Hezekiah's intercession comes by way of Isaiah and consists of a lengthy poetic judgment speech directed against Assyria (19:21-28). **22.** The Assyrian mockery is directed ultimately against Yahweh himself as Israel's protector. *Israel's Holy One:* This title is typically Isaian (Isa 1:4; 43:14). **23.** The reference to Assyrian lumbering operations on Lebanon recalls many passages in the royal Assyrian annals which allude to this activity. **24.** *Egypt:*

Assyria conquered Egypt under Ashurbanipal in 663. **25-26.** It is Yahweh who has enabled Assyria to succeed, in accordance with his ancient plan; the conception recalls statements about the Assyrian and Persian empires in Isa 10:5-10; 44:24-45:3. **27.** The formulations underscore Yahweh's total knowledge of Assyria and its doings. **28.** The judgment speech ends with an announcement of punishment; the imagery used recalls that employed of Yahweh's mastering the sea monster Leviathan in Job 41:25. **29-31.** The address shifts from Assyria to Jerusalem. The Lord will provide for its sustenance during the two years of the Assyrian siege, after which normal agricultural activity will resume in the third year. **31.** *zeal:* Yahweh is concerned lest his reputation be called into question among the nations, should he allow his people to be annihilated (cf. Ezek 36:22). **32-34.** Once again Assyria is in focus, although not directly addressed as in 19:21-28; the announcement of Assyrian withdrawal is reiterated (cf. 19:28). Once more, remembrance of David leads Yahweh to uphold Judah in the face of threat (cf. 1 Kgs 15:4; 2 Kgs 8:19). **35.** For similar presentations of slaughters carried out by supernatural beings (Yahweh or his angel), see Exod 12:29; 2 Sam 24:6. **36.** *Nineveh:* The capital of Assyria was located in what is now Iraq. **37.** The names of Sennacherib's god and of Sennacherib's two assassins are undoubtedly deformed hebraized versions of their actual Mesopotamian designations. In the Assyrian and Babylonian documentation relating to the murder of Sennacherib (*ANET* 289-90, 302), the king's killers are unnamed. *Ararat:* This is the OT name for Armenia, N of Assyria. Sennacherib's murder took place a full two decades after his campaign of 701 against Judah; this argues in favor of the view that 18:17-19:37 describes a second, later attack nearer in time to the assassination of Sennacherib in 681.

67   (c) TWO APPENDED NARRATIVES AND CONCLUSION (20:1-21). **1.** The opening chronological indication vaguely dates the following incident at some point during the Assyrian crisis (cf. 20:6). **2.** *prayed:* Cf. 19:15; now Hezekiah's prayer is made in his own behalf; note that he does not ask Isaiah to intercede for him. **5.** The verse gives remarkable witness to Yahweh's capacity and readiness to modify and reverse previous announcements in light of the human response to them (cf. 2 Sam 12:13; 1 Kgs 21:27-29). *on the third day:* A standard indication for a short period after which something is to happen; cf. Hos 6:2. *Temple:* Hezekiah will offer public thanks for his cure there. **6.** *fifteen:* Reckoning from 701 as the year of Hezekiah's illness, this would make 687 the year of his death. In addition, Yahweh promises to intervene in behalf of besieged Jerusalem; cf. 19:34. **7.** Here, the prophet himself functions as a doctor, rather than leaving the cure to Yahweh (cf. 2 Kgs 5). **8.** *sign:* Hezekiah's initiative in requesting a confirmatory sign contrasts with Ahaz's refusal to take Isaiah up on his offer of a divine sign in Isa 7:9. Asking for signs need not then be a mark of disbelief, just as refusing to ask can be an expression of unbelief (cf. John 6:30). **9.** Far from being rebuked for lack of faith, Hezekiah is given a choice among possible signs. **10.** Making full use of his option, Hezekiah requests the more difficult of the possibilities. **11.** This is the only instance where a classical prophet is depicted as engaging in miracle-working activity in the style of Elijah and Elisha.

68   12. *Merodach-baladan:* Marduk-apal-iddina, who ruled in Babylon 720-709 and then again briefly in 703. As the Assyrian documentation makes clear, he was a serious threat to Assyrian hegemony in Mesopotamia.

His mission to Hezekiah was undoubtedly primarily an attempt to enlist Judah's support in an anti-Assyrian coalition; chronologically this must have occurred earlier than the events narrated in 18:13–20:11 since by 701 Merodach-baladan had been removed from the scene. **13.** Flattered by the Babylonian attention, Hezekiah wanted them to know that he had much to offer as an ally. **17.** Hezekiah's forgetfulness of Yahweh as the sole legitimate source of his security evokes a punishment in accordance with the talion principle: Everything he was so eager to display to the Babylonians will indeed go to them. This announcement serves to direct expectations toward the descriptions of the Babylonian despoliation of Jerusalem in 597 and 587. **18.** In addition, Hezekiah is to be punished personally in his offspring, who will end up as servants of the Babylonian court. **19.** Hezekiah admits the appropriateness of Yahweh's decrees. At the same time, he expresses relief that he will not live to see their execution. Noteworthy is the fact that here, in contrast to the previous narratives, Hezekiah neither in person nor through Isaiah appeals to Yahweh concerning the situation facing him but simply resigns himself to it. Such a depiction suggests the character of Judah's final years in the Dtr presentation, in which intercession will not even be attempted in the face of Yahweh's decision to destroy. **20.** *constructed:* An inscription commemorating Hezekiah's waterworks was discovered in situ in 1880 (*ANET* 321).

69   **(B) Manasseh (687–642) and Amon (642–640) (21:1–26).** **1.** Throughout Manasseh's extended reign Judah continued as an Assyrian vassal; the annals of Esarhaddon cite him as a tributary (*ANET* 291). The elaborate presentation of Manasseh's misdeeds in Dtr is designed to highlight by contrast the merits of both his predecessor, Hezekiah, and his successor, Josiah. The charges made against Manasseh are reminiscent of those leveled against Israel in 2 Kgs 17, the implication being that Judah awaits the same fate. **3–4.** Manasseh undoes his father's reforms (cf. 18:4) and defiles the Temple itself (cf. also vv 7–8). **9.** Manasseh is portrayed as the Jeroboam of Judah, who leads his people into the sin that eventually and inevitably will destroy them. **10–15.** Nameless prophets pronounce a judgment speech replete with Dtr formulations which provides the background for understanding the whole remaining course of Judah's history. With this announcement Judah's fate is fixed, even though the realization will take almost a century. **16.** In an afterthought Dtr depicts Manasseh as a bloodthirsty despot in the manner of Ahab. According to later Jewish traditions, one of his victims was the aged prophet Isaiah. **18.** *died:* Dtr omits the deportation of the wicked Manasseh to Assyria, his repentance, and his eventual restoration to Jerusalem, which are reported in 2 Chr 33. *Uzza:* A shortened form of Uzziah (Ahaziah), Manasseh's great great-grandfather, or the name of an Arab god whose cult Manasseh would have introduced. **19.** *Jotbah:* Amon's mother stems from a city in Galilee—an indication that even after 722 rather close contacts were maintained between S and N. **20–22.** Notwithstanding both his youth and the brevity of Amon's reign, Dtr does not fail to pronounce an elaborately negative judgment on him. **23.** Amon falls victim to the same sort of palace revolt as had his predecessors Joash (12:21) and Amaziah (14:19). **24.** Once again, the Judean gentry intervenes to restore the kingship to a Davidid (cf. 14:21).

70   **(C) Josiah (640–609) (22:1–23:30).** The extended account of Judah's last significant monarch centers on events of a single year of his reign related in 22:3–23:24, for which 22:1–2 and 23:25–30 constitute

the frame. **3.** *eighteenth year:* This would be 621, when Josiah was 26. *Shaphan:* He belongs to a family which, as Kgs and Jer attest, was to have a special prominence in the years down to 587 and after. **4–7.** For the background of Josiah's directive here, see 12:8–16. **8.** *book of the law:* Scholarship has long identified this with some form of Deut, which designates itself by the same expression (cf. Deut 29:20; 31:26). No further particulars concerning the circumstances of the discovery are forthcoming. **11.** The studied nonchalance of both Hilkiah and Shapan regarding the book serves to highlight the very different response of Josiah, who alone seems to appreciate the import of the find. **13.** *inquire:* This is the technical term (*dāraš*) for a consultation of Yahweh through a prophet (see, e.g., 1 Sam 9:9); Josiah desires prophetic guidance concerning the newly found book. **14.** *Huldah:* Her name means "weasel"; the first and last named prophets in Dtr are both women: Deborah (Judg 4:4) and Huldah. *Mishnah:* The newer section of OT Jerusalem, which developed to the NW of the old Davidic city. **16–17.** Huldah's response opens with a word of doom directed to the people as a whole, which recalls that of 21:10–15. **18–19.** The reference to Josiah's reaction and the divine mitigation of his personal fate recalls the presentation concerning Ahab in 1 Kgs 21:27–29. **20.** *in peace:* The expression need not mean that Josiah is to die a natural death, as in fact he does not (cf. 23:29). Even though he was killed in combat, Josiah can still be said to have died peacefully, since he was spared witnessing the annihilation of his nation. **23:1.** The account concerning the discovery climaxes in a description of the public reading and pledge of fidelity. **3.** *column:* See comment on 11:14.

71   **4.** Josiah systematically undoes Manasseh's cultic innovations, activating the various cultic laws of Deut. He begins by removing from the Temple the articles of foreign worship Manasseh had introduced (cf. 21:4,7). *Kidron:* This valley lay beneath Jerusalem to the SE. *Bethel:* The mention of this site serves to prepare for vv 15–17. **5.** Josiah deposes the functionaries of the foreign cults throughout Judah. **6.** Manasseh's image of Asherah (21:7) is thoroughly annihilated; even its pulverized remains are defiled by being brought into contact with the dead. **8.** The Temple rooms used by the male cultic prostitutes (cf. Deut 23:18), which had also been utilized by those making vestments for the Asherah cult (cf. 10:22), are destroyed. **8.** Also the Yahwistic priests (cf. 23:5) from places of worship outside Jerusalem are deposed. Of the cites mentioned, Geba lies just N of Jerusalem, Beer-sheba at the S boundary of Judah. Likewise destroyed is a worship site at one of the Jerusalem gates used by the city's governor. **9.** Presumably opposition on the part of the priests already installed in Jerusalem prevented Josiah from carrying out the directive of Deut 18:6–7, which gives priests from outside Jerusalem the right to function at the Temple; the deposed Yahwistic priests from the country are simply pensioned off. **10.** The Valley of Hinnom or Topheth (cf. Jer 24) lay SW of Jerusalem; the Gk form of the former term is Gehenna, which in the NT is used as a synonym for hell (e.g., Matt 5:29). *Molech:* See comment on 1 Kgs 11:7. **11.** Josiah eliminates from the Temple the chariots and horses which had been used in processions in honor of the divinized sun. **12.** Cf. 21:4–5. **13.** Cf. 1 Kgs 11:5–7. **14.** See comment on 17:12. The sites are forever defiled by being linked with the dead. **15–16.** After a lapse of two centuries, Josiah brings to fulfillment the prophecy of the Judean man of God in 1 Kgs 13:2. **17–18.** The prescience of the Bethel prophet who acted to ensure an undisturbed resting place for himself by being buried together with the Judean man of God

(1 Kgs 13:31–32) is now vindicated when Josiah spares their common tomb. **19–20.** The measures of Josiah recorded here in what was still technically Assyrian territory (the province of Samaria) were made possible by the rapid weakening of Assyrian power following the death of the last great Assyrian monarch, Ashurbanipal, in 627. **21–23.** Josiah's reform climaxes in a national celebration of Passover in Jerusalem, as prescribed by Deut 16:1–8. **24.** As an afterthought, Dtr notes Josiah's elimination of the various mantic functionaries prohibited by Deut 18:10–11.

25. Cf. 22:2. With the "incomparability" ascribed to Josiah here contrast the similar statement made about Hezekiah in 18:5. **26–27.** Dtr hastens to make clear that all Josiah's good deeds could in no way nullify the previous divine word against Judah evoked by Manasseh's misdeeds (cf. 21:10–15) and reiterated by Huldah (cf. 22:16–17). **29.** As Babylonian documentation indicates, Neco (610–594) was advancing to assist the Assyrians against the rising Babylonian power, which Neco feared as an eventual threat to Egypt. Josiah tried to block the Egyptian passage through the former territory of Israel, on which he had designs of his own. Once again, the Judean gentry intervene in the succession process, just as they had in the case of Josiah himself (21:24).

72   **(D) Jehoahaz (609) and Jehoiakim (609–598) (23:31–24:7).** **33.** Neco quickly disposes of Jehoahaz, probably because he was known to support the anti-Egyptian policies of his father. The heavy tribute is designed to weaken Judah's capacity for military operations. **34.** Neco installs another son of Josiah, presumably one regarded as more pliant to Egyptian interests. *name:* To name another signifies one's power over that other (cf. Gen 2:19–20); reception of a new name points to the new role or identity one is being invested with (cf. Matt 16:18). **35.** Like Menahem before him (cf. 15:20), Jehoiakim raises the tribute money by taxing his well-to-do subjects, the people of the land. **36.** *Rumah:* Like the mother of his grandfather, Amon (cf. 21:19), Jehoiakim's mother stems from a town in Galilee; Judean contacts with the North would have intensified following the breakdown of Assyrian power in the area after 627. **24:1.** *Nebuchadnezzar:* The king of Babylonia from 605 to 562. His triumph over the Egyptians at Carchemish in Syria in 605 (cf. Jer 46:2) led the Egyptian appointee Jehoiakim to briefly (605–602) switch his allegiance from Egypt to Babylon. **2.** *Chaldeans:* An alternative name for the (Neo-)Babylonians. Other problems kept Nebuchadnezzar from proceeding against Judah in force until late in the year 598; in the meantime he dispatched raiding parties made up largely of subject people from E of the Jordan. **3–4.** Dtr presents the preliminary Babylonian incursions as a first realization of Yahweh's announced resolve to destroy Judah for Manasseh's sins (cf. 22:16–17; 23:26–27). **7.** During the period 602–598 Jehoiakim received no support from Egypt, which had induced him to defect from Babylon; consistently during Judah's last years Egypt failed to deliver on promises of aid to those it had encouraged to rebel against Babylon (cf. Jer 2:36).

73   **(E) Jehoiachin (598–597) and Zedekiah (597–587) (24:8–25:30).** **10.** The actual Babylonian siege of Jerusalem began late in 598. During it Jehoiachin

opportunely died, leaving his son Jehoiachin to save the city from certain destruction by surrendering it to the Babylonians in March 597. Jehoiachin would remain in Babylonian prison for 37 years (cf. 25:27); Babylonian records concerning the rations distributed to him and his sons (cf. 1 Chr 3:17–18) have been discovered (*ANET* 308). **13.** In a final fulfillment notice Dtr represents the Babylonian despoliation of the Temple as a realization of Isaiah's word to Hezekiah in 20:18. **14–16.** The Babylonians aim to break Judah's capacity for further resistance by removing the leadership stratum. **17.** See comment on 23:34. Further details concerning Zedekiah's installation are found in Ezek 17:11–21 (which speaks of a vassal treaty concluded between him and the Babylonians) and in the Babylonian Chronicles (*ANET* 564). **18.** Zedekiah was a full brother of the deposed Jehoahaz (cf. 23:31). **20.** Dtr intimates the outcome of Zedekiah's reign. Like Jehoiakim, Zedekiah revolted at the urging of Egypt (cf. Ezek 17:15,17), which then failed to provide effective help against Babylonian retaliation. **25:1–2.** The second and final Babylonian siege of Jerusalem started early in 588 and continued to the summer of 587. **3–4.** In July 587 the advent of famine and a Babylonian penetration of the city walls provoked an attempted flight by the king and the army in the direction of the Jordan Valley. **5.** Zedekiah was overtaken in the low-lying area around Jericho NE of Jerusalem. **7.** The Babylonians eliminated any possibility that Zedekiah or his line might resume royal functions. **8.** During August 587 the local Babylonian commander proceeded to deal with the rebel city and its surviving inhabitants. **13–17.** The Babylonians plundered the remaining Temple treasures. For the items mentioned, cf. the account of Solomon's metalworks for the Temple in 1 Kgs 7:13–50. **18–21.** The Babylonians rounded up and executed the surviving religious and civil leadership of Jerusalem.

22. The Babylonians allowed Judah a native governor, Gedaliah, a grandson of Josiah's official Shaphan (22:12). The following story of his brief administration is drawn from the more expansive account in Jer 40:13–41:18 but omitting, curiously, any reference to the prophet Jeremiah. **23.** *Mizpah:* The site lies NW of Jerusalem; Gedaliah makes it his seat of government, Jerusalem being in too devastated a state. **24.** Gedaliah appears as an apologist for accommodation with the Babylonians. **25.** The Davidid Ishmael assassinates Gedaliah and his retinue. Jer 41:13–16 states that he had been dispatched by the king of Ammon and that Gedaliah had brushed aside warnings of his intentions. **26.** According to Jer 42:6 Jeremiah and his secretary, Baruch, were forced by the refugees to accompany them to Egypt. **27.** *thirty-seventh year:* Reckoning from 597, this would be 561. *Evil-merodach:* His actual name was Amel-Marduk ("man of Marduk"); he reigned 562–560. *released:* The significance of this report should not be exaggerated; basically Dtr relates it simply in order to bring readers up to date concerning the ultimate fate of one of the personages of the preceding history. The fact that Dtr concludes with this episode, while saying nothing about the rise of the Persian Cyrus, the future liberator of the Jews (cf. Isa 44:27–45:3), which was becoming clear by *ca.* 550, suggests that the final form of the work dates between 560 and 550.

11

INTRODUCTION TO PROPHETIC LITERATURE

Bruce Vawter, C.M. †

BIBLIOGRAPHY

1 Blenkinsopp, J., *A History of Prophecy in Israel* (Phl, 1983). Coggins, R., "An Alternative Prophetic Tradition?" *Israel's Prophetic Tradition* (Fest. P. R. Ackroyd; ed. R. Coggins, et al.; Cambridge, 1982) 77–94. Culley, R. C. and T. W. Overholt (eds.), *Anthropological Perspectives on Old Testament Prophecy* (Semeia 21; Chico CA, 1982). Eissfeldt, O., "The Prophetic Literature," *OTMS* 225–61. Fohrer, G., "Neuere Literatur zur alttestamentlichen Prophetie," *TRu* 45 (1980) 1–39, 109–32, 193–225; 47 (1982) 105–35, 205–18. Graham, W. C., *The Prophets and Israel's Culture* (Chicago, 1934). Gunkel, H., *Die Propheten* (Göttingen, 1917). Haran, M., "From Early Classical Prophecy: Continuity and Change," *VT* 27 (1977) 385–97. Heschel, A. J., *The Prophets* (NY, 1962). Kirkpatrick, A. F., *The Doctrine of the Prophets* (London, 1901). Koch, K., *The Prophets* (2 vols; Phl, 1982–84). Lang, B., *Wie wird man Prophet in Israel?* Düsseldorf, 1980). Limburg, J., "The Prophets in Recent Study

1967–1977," *Int* 32 (1978) 56–78. Lindblom, J., *Prophecy in Ancient Israel* (Oxford, 1962). Mowinckel, S., *Prophecy and Tradition* (Oslo, 1946). Rinaldi, G., *I Profeti Minori* (Turin, 1953). Ringgren, H., "Prophecy in the Ancient Near East," *Israel's Prophetic Tradition* 1–11. Robinson, T. H., *Prophecy and the Prophets* (London, 1923). Sawyer, J. F. A., "A Change of Emphasis in the Study of the Prophets," *Israel's Prophetic Tradition* 233–49. Scharbert, J., *Die Propheten Israels bis 700 v. Chr.* (Cologne, 1965). Skinner, J., *Prophecy and Religion* (Cambridge, 1922). Tucker, G., "Prophets and the Prophetic Literature," *HBMI* 325–68. Vawter, B., *The Conscience of Israel* (NY, 1961). Ward, J. M., *The Prophets* (Nash, 1982). Widengren, G., *Literary and Psychological Aspects of the Hebrew Prophets* (UUA 10; Uppsala, 1948). Wilson, R., *Prophecy and Society in Ancient Israel* (Phl, 1980).

OUTLINE

THE NATURE OF PROPHECY

3 Although our concern is with the OT prophets, specifically those whose names are attached to its prophetic books, we shall begin with some consideration of prophecy in general. The LXX did not *translate* the Hebr word *nābî'*, which it rendered consistently as *prophētēs;* rather, it used an equivalent term with a venerable Gk history that meant something in the non-

Jewish world of that time. Obviously, therefore, although the Jewish translators would have been among the first to insist that Israelite prophecy was something special, they recognized, and so must we, that it also stood in some kind of relation to the greater human culture of which Israel was but a part.

4 **(I) The Phenomenon of Prophecy.** Most

religions, if not all, have produced the phenomenon of prophecy either continuously or at some stage in their development. This observation holds good not only for the so-called primitive religions but also for highly sophisticated ones. By prophecy we understand not specifically or even principally the forecasting of the future—a fairly late conception of what is essential to prophecy—but rather the mediation and interpretation of the divine mind and will. It was in this sense that *prophētēs* (lit., "one who speaks for another" or "interpreter") was used, from about the 5th cent. BC, to designate those who interpreted the divine mind as made known in various ways to themselves or to others. The function of the *prophētēs* was considered to be preeminently one of public religion; other terms were used to refer to private soothsayers or diviners. The function was also customarily associated with rational speech and interpretation: the inspired person as such, the recipient of a revelation that might require interpretation, was known as a *mantis*. The *prophētēs* and the *mantis* could, of course, be one and the same person; however, the latter term came to be used especially in connection with revelations of the future (see H. Krämer, *TDNT* 6. 781–96).

The means of prophetic communication were, in general, the same that are presupposed in OT prophecy: dreams, visions, ecstatic or mystical experiences, and various divinatory practices. Our respect for the prophets of Israel does not require us to deny that many non-Israelite prophecies resulted from genuine religious experience. For centuries Christians felt no difficulty in recognizing genuine prophecies among the *Sibylline Oracles* (now acknowledged, however, to be Jewish and Christian interpolations), which have even found their way into the church's liturgy. Since prophecy is a charism that of itself says nothing about the orthodoxy or moral character of the prophet, there is no reason to restrict the prophetic spirit of God exclusively to the "normative" channels of *Heilsgeschichte*. The oracles of Balaam in Num 22–24 were regarded as true prophecies from Yahweh, although biblical tradition classified Balaam with the enemies of God and his people (Num 31:8,16; Josh 13:22; 2 Pet 2:15; Jude 11; Rev 2:14) As Aquinas explained, because prophecy is a transient motion rather than a habit, the same person might prophesy both truth and falsehood, depending on whether or not he had been touched by the Spirit of God (*Quodl.* 12, q.17, a.26).

True and false prophets abound not only in antiquity, in the OT and NT, within and without the people of God, but also in later times. Although the church has never officially applied the term "prophet" to anyone not so named in Scripture, it is nevertheless plain that God spoke to his people through such instruments as Francis of Assisi, Vincent Ferrer, Catherine of Siena, Bridget of Sweden, and others, often through experiences like those of the biblical prophets.

5   (II) Prophecy in the Near East. The most important analogies to OT prophecy are to be sought, of course, in the ancient Near East, of which Israel was a tiny part. A concomitant consideration that naturally arises here is the degree, if any, to which Israelite prophecy was dependent on the analogous institutions of culturally superior peoples, chiefly of Mesopotamia and Egypt, and also of the aboriginal civilization of Canaan.

From the earliest recorded time, a common pattern of seers and diviners existed throughout the Near East who were employed in ascertaining the mind of the protective divinity. "I lifted up my hand to Beʿelshamayn, and Beʿelshamayn heard me. Beʿelshamayn [spoke] to me through seers and through diviners. Beʿelshamayn [said to me]: Do not fear, for I made you king, and I shall

stand by you and deliver you . . ." (*ANET* 501). While Amos was prophesying in Israel, an Aramean king was having these words inscribed on a stone in Syria. The explicit reference to seers and diviners clarifies the statements of Mesha, the king of Moab, made on the 9th-cent. Moabite Stone: "Chemosh said to me, 'Go, take Nebo from Israel' . . . Chemosh said to me, 'Go down, fight against Hauronen' . . ." (*ANET* 320–21). The biblical parallel is in such passages as: "David inquired of Yahweh, 'Shall I go and attack these Philistines?' And Yahweh said to David, 'Go and attack the Philistines and save Keilah'" (1 Sam 23:2). David was accompanied by his prophet Gad (1 Sam 22:5), whose duty it was to make such inquiries of Yahweh. Even more explicitly 1 Sam 23:6–12 exemplifies the pattern: Abiathar, the priest of Nob who had joined David's band, brought with him the ephod, a divining instrument, by which David obtained yes-or-no answers to such questions as "Will Saul come down?" and "Will the men of Keilah surrender me to Saul?"

The existence of ecstatic prophecy in 11th-cent. Phoenicia is attested by the experiences of Wen-Amon, an Egyptian emissary at the port of Byblos (*ANET* 25–29). The harried Wen-Amon took the inconveniences caused him by the "possessed" boy fairly laconically: it was a routine occupational hazard to encounter the effects of ecstatic prophecy, just as they continued to be an embarrassment to Paul over a millennium later (Acts 16:16–18). The graphic story told in 1 Kgs 18:19–40 is witness to the character of ecstatic prophecy among the Canaanites in the time of Elijah. With few, if any, modifications, the external manifestations must have been hardly distinguishable from those of the bands of ecstatic Yahwistic prophets mentioned in 1 Sam 10:5–7,10–13; 19:18–24 in the time of Saul, and, certainly with no modifications at all, from those of a much later date spoken of in Zech 13:4–6 (this time with opprobrium).

We are even better informed about the Near Eastern pattern of prophecy from the Babylonian evidence. Prophecy was no exception to the rule of rigid organization in Babylonian society. In the Babylonian temples *bārū* priests delivered a *tērtu*, "message," to their clients chiefly through liver divination (one of the means of divination noted as characteristically Babylonian in Ezek 21:26). The word *tērtu* is probably cognate with the Hebr *tôrâ*, used to designate prophetic instruction in Isa 1:10 and elsewhere. Another type of Babylonian priest-prophet was the *maḫḫū*, "ecstatics"; their oracles were given in the throes of divine "possession," like those of the youth who plagued Wen-Amon. Neither must it be thought that these Babylonian prophets merely pandered to the magical conception of religion that characterized so much of Mesopotamian piety; the *maḫḫu* also served as judges and physicians. Their incantation formulas, although admittedly magical, nevertheless sometimes showed an awareness of that connection between religion and morality that is so much insisted on by the prophets of Israel.

The Near Eastern pattern, as we may already surmise, makes little or no distinction between prophet and priest. In Israel, the pattern seems to have been broken, for the difference between the two was well defined. The Israelite priesthood was hereditary and hierarchical, whereas prophecy was charismatic; prophets like Ezekiel and Jeremiah might also be priests, but there is no indication that such a man as Amos was a priest—indeed, many indications are against it. Still, the deviation is not as absolute as might first appear, at least as regards Israelite prophecy in the whole. It is difficult to separate the priestly from the prophetic functions of

Samuel in the story of 1 Sam 9:11–26. Throughout he is called "the seer," and in 1 Sam 19:18–24 we see that he heads a band of ecstatic prophets; yet some of his main duties are to bless the sacrifice on the "high place" and to preside at the sacrificial meal. Prophets are repeatedly encountered at the sanctuaries of Israel, at Shiloh (1 Kgs 14:1–2), at Bethel (2 Kgs 2:3), at Gilgal (2 Kgs 4:38), in the Temple of Jerusalem (Jer 23:11; 35:4), etc. Prophets and priests are frequently mentioned in the same breath and, often enough, they are both associated with the sanctuary (cf. Lam 2:20). The divinatory devices used by priests (cf. 1 Sam 14:3) are also used by prophets (cf. 1 Sam 28:6). Many psalms that evidently had their life situation in the Israelite cult also presuppose the presence of prophets performing some cultic function (e.g., Ps 95:7b–11). Among the Arabs, the inspired man, the prophet, is known as the *kāhin,* a word cognate with the Hebr *kōhēn,* "priest." In this respect, too, therefore, prophecy in Israel continues to have analogies with that of the remainder of the Near East.

It is important to see these similarities if we are to evaluate properly the prophets of Israel. There was, indeed, in the ancient Near East, of which Israel was a small and (politically speaking) insignificant part, a fairly consistent pattern of prophecy—of inspired men, who in various ways spoke the word of God to their coreligionists, whether of Babylonia, Canaan, or Israel. The recognition of this common pattern does not detract from, but instead enhances, the unique qualities of biblical prophecy.

(Guillaume, A., *Prophecy and Divination* [London, 1938]. Haldar, A., *Associations of Cult Prophets Among the Ancient Semites* [Uppsala, 1948]. Huffmon, H. B., "Priestly Divination in Israel," *WLSGF* 355–59. Porter, J. R., "The Origins of Prophecy in Israel," *Israel's Prophetic Tradition* [→ 1 above] 12–31. Weinfeld, M., "Ancient Near Eastern Patterns in Prophetic Literature," *VT* 27 [1977] 178–95. Wilson, R. R., "Early Israelite Prophecy," *Int* 32 [1978] 3–16; "Prophecy and Ecstasy: A Reexamination," *JBL* 98 [1979] 321–37.)

6   (III) Prophecy in Israel. The very prevalence of the prophetic pattern throughout the Near East both accounts for the origins of Israelite prophecy and underscores its distinctive character. To the extent that Israelite religion had traits in common with the religions of the other, mainly Semitic, peoples of the ancient Near East, it expressed itself in kindred institutions, one of which was prophetism. To the extent, however, that Israel's religion was something quite apart in this same Near Eastern world, its prophetism also became something unlike that of any other people.

(A) A History of Israelite Prophecy. What did the Hebrews think of when they spoke of a *nābî',* the word we translate, through the LXX, as "prophet"? This question, apparently so elementary, probably cannot be answered precisely on the basis of our present knowledge. No scholarly consensus has ever been achieved as to the origin of this word, which is probably a loanword in Hebrew. The Hebr verbal forms derived from the noun and translated "prophesy" merely mean, of course, "to act the part of a *nābî'.*" All that we can do to define the meaning of the term is to examine its use in OT literature as it is found in the history of prophecy. This examination will help to answer other questions, including one that arises from the paradoxical fact that the term seems to have been avoided by some of those who come first to mind when we think of the word "prophet."

7   (a) Early Prophecy. Biblical tradition traces the origins of Israelite prophecy to Moses, and, at least in the sense that this means prophecy began with Israel itself, there is no reason not to accept the tradition. The scene described in Num 11:24–30 (E) is doubtless modeled on assemblies of ecstatic prophets known from later times, but it is to this same kind of prophet that Amos 2:11 refers when ascribing the beginning of the *nĕbî'îm* to the Mosaic age. It was doubtless this kind of prophet that was first meant by the term *nābî'.* Admittedly, in later texts the term has become much broader in its signification, where it is applied to any kind of inspired person or, indeed, simply to anyone who was recognized as under special divine protection (as in the case of Abraham, Gen 20:7 [E]). Thus, Moses is commonly called a *nābî'* in the Pentateuch, as are Aaron (not only in Exod 7:1 [P] but also in Num 12:2–8 [E], where Moses is related to Aaron and Miriam as a prophet greater than they) and Miriam (also in Exod 15:20 [P]). In the deuteronomic Judg 4:4 (although not in the older parallel in Judg 5), Deborah is called a *nĕbî'â.* These texts do not tell us much about the early significance of the word; as 1 Sam 9:9 shows, *nābî'* was by this time no longer restricted to any single category of "holy man."

If there is no reason to question the tradition that traces the *nĕbî'îm* to Moses, we must admit that we do not hear much about them before the late period of the judges and the early monarchy, when they are mentioned in connection with the Philistine wars. This circumstance is not surprising, because a major function of these ecstatic prophets, as also of the Nazirites (→ Institutions, 76:111), seems to have been to stimulate patriotic and religious fervor. Usually these men prophesied in groups whose communal experiences are described in such passages as 1 Sam 10:6–8,10–13. Hence, they are often given the generic name "sons of the prophets" (*bĕnê hannĕbî'îm*), which has been variously interpreted "members of prophetic guilds," "professional prophets," and "prophetic disciples" (cf. 1 Kgs 20:35; 2 Kgs 2:3ff.; 5:22; 6:1; etc.). All of these interpretations may be justified. The ecstatic experience that served as the climate for prophecy was often induced by mutual contagion through dance and music. These prophets, too, are often seen to have served as disciples or apprentices under some noted prophet; however, they could also live apart as private individuals (cf. 2 Kgs 4:1). In either capacity, they can be found attached to the sanctuaries as "cult prophets" (cf. 1 Kgs 14:1ff.; 2 Kgs 22:14–17; Amos 7:10ff.) or serving the king as "court prophets" (cf. 2 Sam 7:1ff.; 12:1ff.; 24:11; 1 Kgs 1:8; 22:6ff.; 2 Kgs 3:11ff.; Neh 6:7). They wore a distinctive garb of haircloth (2 Kgs 1:8; Zech 13:4; cf. Matt 3:4 par.) and often bore other distinguishing marks (cf. 1 Kgs 20:38,41; Zech 13:6), possibly at times a tonsure (cf. 2 Kgs 2:23).

The ecstatic experience transformed the prophet, made him "another man" (1 Sam 10:6). In such a state, his antics could become grotesque, so that he could be called with rough familiarity "a madman" (2 Kgs 9:11), while his profession was regarded as hardly in keeping with responsible, respectable citizenship (1 Sam 10:11). In ancient times little distinction was made among psychic abnormalities, whether they originated in inspiration, frenzy, or insanity. Certainly this condition was the medium of genuine religious experience in which true contact was achieved with God. There is no doubt, too, that it could as easily be a source of delusion and superstition, as the later polemics of the classical prophets against the *nĕbî'îm* show.

Ecstaticism continued to some degree throughout the entire period of Israelite prophecy. Samuel is represented on one occasion as leading a band in ecstatic prophecy (1 Sam 19:20ff.). Both Elijah and Elisha are habitually associated with the "sons of the prophets" as masters and leaders, and in 2 Kgs 3:15 Elisha makes use of a customary device to induce ecstatic seizure. The extent to which ecstaticism played a part in later prophecy, specifically that of the classical literary prophets, continues to be the subject of considerable debate. In 1 Kgs 22:5-28, the false prophet Zedekiah points to the possession of "the spirit of Yahweh" by himself and his fellow ecstatics as proof against the prophecy of Micaiah, who apparently lacks this "spirit." Micaiah simply contents himself with ascribing his prophecy to his vision, by which he also knows Zedekiah's experience to be that of a "lying spirit." Similarly, Jer 29:26 shows that ecstatic prophecy was common in Jeremiah's time, but Jeremiah himself never appeals to any possession of a prophetic "spirit." On the other hand, however, Ezekiel certainly received many of his prophecies in ecstatic trance and testifies on any number of occasions to his having been seized by "spirit" and by "the hand of Yahweh."

The ancient relation of the "seer" (rō'eh or ḥōzeh) to the nābî' is uncertain. Etymologically, the seer would have been a visionary rather than an ecstatic, but it is not precluded that his visions would have been received as the result of ecstatic experience. Gad, a nābî', is also called David's ḥōzeh in 2 Sam 24:11; 1 Chr 21:9 (cf. also 1 Chr 25:5), which doubtless reflects the later identification of terms shown in 1 Sam 9:9 (so also 1 Chr 9:22; 26:28; 29:29). Although it is the seer's role to prophesy (i.e., "act the part of a nābî'," cf. Amos 7:12), still the seer is distinguished from the prophet in 2 Kgs 17:13; Isa 29:10; 30:10; Mic 3:6-7; etc. Deut 13:2-6 speaks of "prophets and dreamers of dreams," in which case it is doubtless with the latter that the seer is to be identified. In looking to dreams as a source of divine revelation, ancient Israel continued to share the Near Eastern pattern of inspired men. Divinatory usages may also have played a part in the seer's visions; in general, however, Israelitic religion tended to look on divination as superstition. The term "diviner" is never used in the Bible of an authentic spokesman for God.

With the sophistication, or simplification, of religious language, the words honored by non-Israelite religions ("diviners," "dreamers," etc.) became pejorative in connotation, and every kind of inspiration was subsumed in the concept of nābî'. This tendency in turn introduced a certain ambiguity, however, which was felt by Amos, who approved of the nebî'îm of the past but denied that he was a nābî' in the sense intended by Amaziah (7:12-15)—i.e., a cult prophet encroaching on the terrain of the prophet-priest of Bethel.

(Auld, A. G., "Prophets Through the Looking Glass: Between Writings and Moses," *JSOT* 27 [1983] 3-23. Johnson, A. R., *The Cultic Prophet in Ancient Israel* [Cardiff, 1962]. Mowinckel, S., "Ecstatic Experience and Rational Elaboration in Old Testament Prophecy," *ArOr* 13 [1935] 264-91. Vawter, B., "Were the Prophets Nābî's?" *Bib* 66 [1985] 206-20.)

8 (b) CLASSICAL PROPHECY. By "classical prophecy" we mean the prophecy of those whom the OT has taught us to regard as exemplifying what is distinctive about Israelite prophets—all that separates them from the Near Eastern pattern. These prophets are those whose teaching has been preserved in the OT and especially those whose names appear at the head of the prophetic books. The OT also called them nebî'îm, as part of the standardization of terminology, and, at least eventually, they doubtless referred to themselves in the same way. As a matter of fact, it is not impossible that some of the classical prophets were also nebî'îm in the sense of which we have been speaking. The professional prophet might also become a prophet through Yahweh's

special call, although such was not the normal event.

This consideration introduces a question that we may as well treat now—viz., that of the so-called false prophets. It is not a biblical term: the Hebr Bible knows only of nebî'îm (although they may be qualified as prophets who tell lies or who have a lying spirit), although the LXX translators have in a few places introduced the paraphrase pseudoprophētēs. Because of the ambiguity of the word nābî', the paradox arises that some of the most bitter denunciations to be found in the words of the literary prophets are addressed to, or concern, "the prophets." These literally countless passages accuse "the prophets," or, frequently enough, prophets and priests together, of every kind of moral and social crime against Yahweh and his people and of cooperating with the worst elements in Israelite rule and practice to frustrate Yahweh's will.

In the eyes of Israel and of the classical prophets themselves, of course, the false prophets were prophets indeed as much as were the classical prophets. Although among them may have been those who simply simulated prophecy, we must not think that first and foremost they were "false" in the sense that they willfully and knowingly pretended to be what they were not. They were, rather, prophets deluded by their own prophetic devices, erring in judgment, confusing their own hopes and aspirations with the authentic word of Yahweh (cf. Isa 28:7; Jer 23:5ff.). It was not precluded that the same prophet might alternately prophesy truth and falsehood, for a true prophetic word was in every case a distinct gift received from God (cf. Deut 13:2-6, restricting the somewhat unsophisticated criterion of true and false prophecy in Deut 18:21-22). In OT eyes, the activity of the false prophets was also willed by Yahweh as a means of testing his faithful followers (Jer 4:10; 1 Kgs 22:19-23; etc.).

The false prophets were often court prophets in whose interest it was to tell the king and his officials what they wanted to hear; just as often they were those who derived monetary benefits from favorable prophecies that assured their clients of divine blessings and troubled no consciences. Mainly, however, it is probably true that they were men caught up in the common tragedy of their people—i.e., those who had become so convinced that "the Israelite way of life" represented all that was godly that it had become second nature to measure Yahweh's will according to Israel's performance rather than the reverse. This oft-repeated tragedy has by no means been confined to ancient Israel. In an age when national pride spoke a religious language, it was inevitable that it should also speak in prophecy.

(De Vries, S. J., *Prophet Against Prophet* [GR, 1978]. Siegman, E. F., *The False Prophets in the Old Testament* [Washington, 1939]. Vogels, W., "Comment discerner le prophète authentique?" *NRT* 99 [1977] 681-701.)

It should be obvious that the distinction between false and true prophecy in the days of the classical prophets was not always clear. Possession of the ecstatic prophetic "spirit" was no sure criterion: prophets might be touched by the spirit and still prophesy falsehood, and most of the classical prophets give no signs of having been ecstatics. The fulfillment of prophecy, even if it had been always evident to the prophet's contemporaries, was not an infallible sign, as Deut 13:2ff. shows; moreover, true prophecy apparently often went unfulfilled, discouraging even the prophet himself (cf. Jer 20:7ff.). When the prophet Hananiah prophesied his own wishful thinking in predicting the end of the Babylonian exile in two years and the restoration of Jeconiah (Jer 28:1ff.), Jeremiah could offer little in rebuttal except his conviction of the truth of his own contrary prophecy. "Amen! Thus may Yahweh do! May he fulfill the things you have prophesied. . . ." Wistfully Jeremiah said this, for he would very much have preferred to prophesy as Hananiah did; however, he knew he could not, for such was not the word of Yahweh.

Jeremiah also justified his own prophecy in a way that at first seems strange to us: "From of old, the prophets who were before you and me prophesied war, woe, and pestilence against many lands and mighty kingdoms. But the prophet who prophesies peace is recognized as truly sent by Yahweh only when his prophetic prediction is fulfilled." Actually, Jeremiah is not saying simply that a prophet of doom is to be believed whereas a prophet who predicts peace is to be rejected. He is taking his stand on the prophetic tradition that had served authentic Yahwistic revelation, using essentially the same argument found in Deut 13:2ff. Anyone who really knows God will recognize his true prophet and discern him from the false, for the prophecy must conform to God's designs as he has revealed them. Jesus similarly argued his case before his generation according to John 5:37ff., etc. Anyone who recognizes Israel's situation in respect to the moral will of its God must also know that a prophecy of peace like Hananiah's could, in the circumstances, be no true word of God.

If the classical prophets could offer their contemporaries only the testimony of the prophetic word itself, they did nothing more or less than any true prophet could be expected to do: it is the word itself that must find a response in the heart attuned to the reception of God's word. Their own conviction of the truth of their prophecy rests on the same foundations; therefore, the narrative of the prophetic call, the experience of the divine presence, plays a prominent role in the records of the literary prophets. This testimony constitutes their credentials, both for themselves and for those to whom they have been sent.

9 Recognition of the unique purpose to which Yahweh had dedicated prophecy in its classical age is already found in the OT in the story of Samuel. Samuel was a *nābî*', at the head of a band of the *běnê hannĕbî'îm*, the existence of such bands on a wide scale being presupposed in the biblical chronicle; yet when Samuel is first introduced (1 Sam 3:1), we read that "the word of Yahweh was rare in those days—visions were not frequent." In other words, with Samuel, Israelite prophecy was to achieve a new dimension. What that new dimension was, at least in the eyes of the same biblical author, is made plain in Samuel's *apologia* (1 Sam 12:1-5), an anthology of the language of Amos, Micah, Hosea, and Malachi. The same may be said of the prophetic speech attributed to the *nābî*' Nathan in 2 Sam 12:1ff. The fearless revelation of the moral will of Yahweh, the God of Israel's covenant, that is to be the characteristic of classical prophecy setting it apart from all the other prophecy, both of Israel and its neighbors, has already begun with these representatives of the ancient *nābî*' class.

In like manner, Elijah denounces Ahab's sin in 1 Kgs 21:17-24, in language worthy of an Amos or a Jeremiah. 1 Kgs 19:4ff. describes, as a new call to prophecy and as the beginning of a new prophetic line (cf. v 14), Elijah's experience of the "gentle breeze," in which he heard the voice of Yahweh as he had not heard it before. Immediately afterward, Elisha was called to be Elijah's disciple and, ultimately, his successor as "father of Israel." While the author of the Elisha narrative has been mainly interested in this prophet as a wonder-worker, he still found time to represent his teaching, too, in terms that would find their echo in the later "social" prophets (cf. 2 Kgs 5:26).

Thus it is not hard to see why Amos, although he knew himself to be something other than a *nābî*' as this traditional institution continued into his days and beyond, did not repudiate the ancient institution. However, he attributed what was distinctive in his prophecy to his special vocation from Yahweh (Amos 7:15), as Elijah would have done and as so many of the other literary prophets do (cf. Hos 1-3; Isa 6; Jer 1; Ezek 1; etc.). In the same spirit, the classical prophets tend to give themselves names other than *nābî*'—names that more clearly define their significance as Yahweh's special designates. They are "messengers of Yahweh" (Isa 44:26; Hag 1:13; Mal 3:1), "servants of God" (Isa 20:3; Amos 3:7; Jer 7:25; 24:4), "shepherds" (Jer 17:16; Zech 11:4), "guardians" (Isa 62:6; Hab 2:1), "watchmen" (Amos 3:4; Isa 56:10; Jer 6:17; Ezek 3:17), etc.

10 The classical prophets best known to us are the so-called literary prophets of the 8th, 7th, and 6th cents. BC. In a roughly chronological order, these are Amos, Hosea, Isaiah, Micah, Nahum, Zephaniah, Habakkuk, Jeremiah, and Ezekiel. All, with the exception of Hosea, were apparently Judahites, although Amos is also, for all practical purposes, a prophet who continues the northern Israelite tradition of classical prophecy begun by Samuel and Elijah. Classical prophecy should not be limited to these great names, however; there are other literary prophets whose names we do not know. One of them, indeed one of the greatest, is the exilic prophet whom we call the Second Isaiah; in addition, numerous anonymous prophets are responsible for supplements to other of the prophetic books, for many of the psalms, and for other prophetic writings found elsewhere in the OT. Then, too, there were other prophets in the classical tradition whose actual words we have in small part or not at all. We do not even know the names of some. Jer 7:25; 11:7 simply speak of a continuous tradition of true prophecy from the time of Israel's origins. Of some we know the names only, such as the Uriah mentioned in Jer 26:20-23, whose prophecy was contemporary with Jeremiah's and in his spirit.

The special vocation of Yahweh that plays such an important part in the thoughts of the classical prophets is more than simply their title to prophecy. In the way it has been incorporated into their prophetic words, it is often the key—the leitmotif—of their prophecy, for the prophets are highly individualistic thinkers whose separate personalities were as many diverse instruments through which the word of the Lord was given. While it is true that there is a recognizably common prophetic doctrine on the essentials of Yahwistic religion and on many of its details as well, and that in the past there was a tendency to overemphasize the individual prophetic genius and originality, it is likewise true that no one who is at all familiar with the prophetic literature is in much danger of confusing one prophet with another. Their similarities derive from their devotion to common ideals and from their dependence on common traditions and institutions. Their mediation of the prophetic word, however, is quite personal. They rarely cite one another or even acknowledge one another's existence. The authority with which they spoke came, in other words, from their individual serene confidence of having the mind of Yahweh.

While preexilic classical prophecy, with variations, tends to be a prophecy of judgment against Israel and Judah, the prophecy of Nahum is apparently an exception. Nahum's prophecy is a paean of triumph over the dissolution of the Assyrian Empire, the end of which he foresaw as imminent. It does not necessarily mean that

Nahum was one of those "prophets of peace" whose nationalistic pride was so repugnant to Jeremiah. The humbling of the nations apart from Israel is also part of the message of other classical prophets who are far from being "prophets of peace." Another prophet who does not fall easily into the preexilic pattern is Habakkuk, not so much because of the content of his prophecy, the precise significance of which can still be debated, as because of its form. However, it would be a mistake to imagine that the prophets have to conform to a given list of uniform characteristics. Habakkuk was possibly a cult prophet, as presumably the prophetess Huldah was (2 Kgs 22:14). Those responsible for the royal Pss were also doubtless cult or court prophets, yet there is obviously some difference between the mind that produced Ps 2 and that which composed Ps 72. Given the nature of prophecy, by which the word of God has been voiced through every kind of chosen instrument, this result was only to be expected.

(Amsler, S., "La parole visionnaire des prophètes," *VT* 31 [1981] 359–63. Carroll, R. P., *When Prophecy Failed* [NY, 1979]. Causse, A., *Israël et la vision de l'humanité* [Strasbourg, 1924]. Davies, G. H., "The Yahwistic Tradition in the Eighth-Century Prophets," *Studies in Old Testament Prophecy* [Fest. T. H. Robinson; ed. H. H. Rowley; Edinburgh, 1950] 37–51. Hermisson, H. J., "Zeitbezug des prophetischen Wortes," *KD* 27 [1981] 96–110. Wolff, H. W., "Prophecy from the Eighth through the Fifth Century," *Int* 32 [1978] 17–30.)

11   (c) POSTEXILIC PROPHECY. Through the exile, Israel was granted a new vision of the divine economy—that of the great exilic prophets, Jeremiah, Ezekiel, and the Second Isaiah. The particulars of this new vision will be treated, of course, in the commentaries on these prophets. Here we wish only to note their influence on the final stage of Israelite prophetism—the period of Palestinian Judaism following the exile.

Postexilic prophecy lacks much of the vigor and spontaneity of preexilic prophecy; at all events, it forms a category apart that invites its separation from the age of classical prophecy. "To a great extent the prophets of this period lived on the ideas of the earlier prophets, and in particular those of the exilic prophets. Their special characteristics are seen less in original ideas of their own than in certain marked tendencies and in the ways in which they modified the ideas they borrowed" (Lindblom, *Prophecy in Ancient Israel* 404). The prophets who pertain to this category, listed in chronological order, are the prophet or prophets responsible for the final section of Isa (the so-called Trito-Isaiah), Haggai, Zechariah (chaps. 1–8), Malachi, Obadiah, Joel, and the anonymous prophets who produced Zech 9–11, 12–14, not to mention numerous prophetic hands that have intervened in the final production of various of the older prophetic books, esp. Isa, Jer, and Ezek.

The postexilic prophetic corpus is probably a more consistent unity than the preexilic. The postexilic Obadiah more or less corresponds to the preexilic Nahum in prophesying peace for Israel in the destruction of a hated enemy. However, the fact that the Book of Consolation of the Second Isaiah has preceded Obadiah's prophecy serves to set him in the postexilic tradition more firmly than Nahum's prophecy sets him in the preexilic tradition. In general, the postexilic prophets could take a more "optimistic" view of Israel's destiny than could the preexilic prophets, for the doom that the latter had foretold had now come and gone, and a new hope could be found in the figure of the Servant of the Lord revealed by the exilic Isaiah. Zechariah and Malachi show a concern for the Temple, the law, and matters of cult that cannot be discovered in a preexilic

prophet. This concern, however, is a continuation of Ezekiel's, an authentic prophet of Israelite doom who at the same time had seen the vision of a new covenant that Yahweh would effect on Palestinian soil when changed conditions would require new religious unities and stresses. Trito-Isaiah also has been greatly influenced by Ezekiel and the Second Isaiah. The bold apocalyptic imagery of Zechariah, Joel, and the Isaiah supplements (chaps. 24–27, 34–35) was foreshadowed in Ezekiel, whom many regard as the father of apocalyptic.

The diversity of postexilic prophecy, it seems, is mainly one of styles, which are often frankly derivative and lacking in the freshness of the earlier prophetic oracles. The themes are fairly common, proper to a people now living under Judaism, when Temple and Torah had become the enduring realities that would continue as Israel's unity after the voice of prophecy had been stilled. Prophecy itself helped in the transition to conditions under which the people of God could survive for many generations (although its lack would be continually felt, cf. 1 Macc 4:46; 14:41). It did so by responding to needs that Jeremiah and Ezekiel had already foreseen before the exile, by insisting on individual responsibility and fidelity to the law, speaking to an Israel with which God would no longer deal simply as a people good or bad, for better or for worse, but as a religion in which all members must follow the rule of life set before them until the dawn of an even better hope (cf. Ezek 3:16–21; 33:1–20). After a brief interest in a Davidic restoration (Zech 6:9–15), it reverted to other soteriological themes, the variety of which had already been enriched in exilic prophecy, and in this way continued the prophetic testimony to Yahweh's universal domination (cf. Mal 1:11; Isa 19:9–10; etc.). It finally promised that prophecy would return (cf. Mal 3:22–24) and that, in fact, in some fashion it would become the gift of all God's people (Joel 3:1–5).

The disappearance of prophecy in Israel was as unobtrusive as its beginning; it would be impossible to determine who was the last OT prophet. In the last 200 years BC, the wisdom writers consciously carried on the tradition inherited from prophecy (cf. Sir 24:31; Wis 7:27), without, however, claiming to possess the prophetic spirit.

(Andrew, M. E., "Post-exilic Prophets and the Ministry of Creating Community," *ExpTim* 93 [1982] 42–46. Chary, T., *Les prophètes et le culte à partir de l'Exil* [Tournai, 1958]. Fohrer, G., *Die Propheten seit dem 4. Jahrhundert* [Gütersloh, 1976]. Koch, K., *The Prophets* vol. 2. Mason, R., "The Prophets of the Restoration," *Israel's Prophetic Tradition* 137–54.)

12   (B) Its Distinctive Character.   From what we have already said, it should be easy to generalize about the distinctive character of Israelite prophecy, some of the particulars of which we shall treat in the following sections.

To the extent that Israel possessed cult and court prophets, or prophets whose gifts were at the disposal of the nation or of individual clients in public or private consultation, Israelite prophecy was part of the aforementioned Near Eastern pattern. Even in such cases, the conformity to the pattern was not exact, for the content of this prophecy was distinctively Israelite. It would be easy to find a non-Israelite parallel to the 400 prophets at the call of the king of Israel in 1 Kgs 22, but not to the prophet Micaiah, who was also at his call. It would be impossible to find a non-Israelite court prophet who would speak to his king as Nathan did to David, or even one who would speak of the king as the royal psalmists do. No true parallel to such literature has yet been found outside Israel, for it was the expression of a religion without true parallel in its contemporary world.

There is no non-Israelite parallel for classical prophecy, either in form or in content. There seems to be no valid reason to condition too much the judgment made some 80 years ago by a man who was never reluctant to minimize what was unique in Israel, that "the results of a search for genuine Babylonian prophecies are disappointing" and who thus ventured "to doubt [that Babylonia and Assyria] had any prophecies at all" (T. K. Cheyne, *The Two Religions of Israel* [London, 1911] 7–8). Neither has such a search proved to be productive elsewhere. The few scraps of "prophetic morality" that can be assembled from the hundreds of years of well-documented literary history of ancient Egypt certainly do not add up to anything remotely comparable to Israelite prophecy, let alone anything that could justify the fantastic theory once proposed by Egyptological enthusiasts—i.e., that the prophetic moral teaching of Israel was of Egyptian origin. The Egyptian material—wisdom literature of the Middle Kingdom or of the interregnum succeeding the Old Kingdom (cf. *ANET* 407–10)—is evidence that Egypt occasionally produced moral voices worthy of comparison with those of the OT but not that it ever possessed a prophetic tradition like Israel's. Israelite prophecy broke with the ancient pattern when it began to produce prophets who not only spoke from the Israelite institutions but also judged them and became their conscience. We thus have the distinctive literary forms that found no genuine echo in the other literature of antiquity.

PROPHECY AND ISRAEL'S INSTITUTIONS

As we have already mentioned, prophecy, at least in the classical sense of the word, was a charismatic phenomenon. Therefore, if we are to understand its historical significance in Israelite religion, it is relevant to see the relation of this phenomenon to the noncharismatic Israelite institutions.

13   (I) The Law and the Priesthood. Despite the fact that some prophets (e.g., Jeremiah, Ezekiel) were certainly priests, there was once a persuasion in critical circles that the prophetic and the priestly offices were somehow opposed, at least in the preexilic period. (It was always fairly obvious that exilic and postexilic prophecy had a concern for cult and priestly law, but this concern was explained by the emphasis laid on these institutions in postexilic Judaism.) Is it true to say that the preexilic prophetic tradition was a rival of the priestly tradition that became canonized in the written law of Moses in and after the exile?

The functions of priest and prophet were always carefully distinguished in Israel; however, these functions coincided in part. Jer 18:18 speaks of the "law" (*tôrâ*) of the priest, the "counsel" (*'ēṣâ*) of the wise man, and the "word" (*dābār*) of the prophet. While these three conveyed their teachings in different ways—the priest by an institutional tradition, the wise man by a professional tradition, the prophet by a charismatic prompting—they doubtless felt that they were contributing each in his own way to a common objective. When the prophets condemned the priesthood, as they often did, it was not for what the priests were teaching but rather for what they were not: they had rejected knowledge and had ignored the law (*tôrâ*) of God (Hos 4:6). In the same spirit, the "false" prophets were condemned, not to reject the idea of prophecy but rather a travesty of it.

The opposition between priesthood and prophecy was exaggerated because of several factors. One was the persuasion, now considerably corrected, that law was a relatively late development in Israel, representing the triumph of formal over spiritual religion. Another was the distorted perspective in which the religion of the prophets was viewed in respect to the "official" religion of Israel. It is quite true, of course, that some difference invariably existed between the attitudes and interests of priestly and prophetic religion, but they were attitudes and not different religions. At its best, the priesthood did the same work, or part of the same work, that prophecy did; i.e., it transmitted the revealed moral will of the God of Israel. The priesthood did so by the tradition of religious law preserved in the sanctuaries; prophecy accomplished the task by the communication of the living word. In principle, the latter was not intended to oppose the former.

Supposed citations of the law by preexilic prophets are often doubtful and, in any case, very few, which of course raises the question of the extent to which the law existed in preexilic times in written form, and in what form, a question into which we cannot enter here. These problems also point to the nature of prophecy, as we have discussed it, which is to depend for its authority on its own communication of the word and not on other prior, even prophetic authority. The teaching of prophecy is, in any case, always consistent with the law, even if it is expressed in its own way and with its own stresses.

Amos 3:2 expresses the idea of election with the thought, if not the precise words, of Deut 14:2; Amos's description of the exodus and desert wandering and their meaning (2:10; 3:1; 4:10; 5:25; 9:7) are of a piece with Exod 20:2, wherein Egypt is designated as "the house of slaves." This expression is also used by the prophets (cf. Mic 6:4; Jer 34:13), none of which proves that Amos depended on Deut or Exod as written texts, any more than his reference to a *tôrâ* in 2:4 is necessarily to a written priestly law. It does prove, however, that Amos taught a tradition contained in the law; and, although allusive and casual, his statements presuppose the account told in the Pentateuch, with which he agrees even in trivial details (cf. Amos 2:9; Num 13:32). Hos 8:1 explicitly connects the law of Yahweh with a covenant, which, of course, is precisely what the law professes to be; although Hosea does not say that the covenant is that of Sinai, he does connect it with the exodus (8:13; 9:3; 11:5; cf. Deut 28:68). Furthermore, the *tôrâ* that Hosea associates with the covenant in 8:1 is seen in 4:6 as a priestly *tôrâ* entailing social morality; from 8:12, there evidently existed some kind of written *tôrâ* or *tôrôt*. From the context, it appears that in the last instance Hosea was referring to cultic precepts.

The OT has been transmitted through various streams of tradition that have often mutually influenced one another without, however, becoming assimilated. The prophetic tradition requires no glorification at the expense of minimizing other traditions that served their own truths in their own way, supplementing without necessarily contradicting the truths of prophecy.

(Barton, J., "'The Law and the Prophets,'" *OTS* 23 [1984] 1–18. Gross, H., "Gab es ein prophetisches Amt in Israel?" *BK* 30 [1983] 134–39. Phillips, A., "Prophecy and Law," *Israel's Pro-*

phetic Tradition 217–32. Schmidt, K. W., "Prophetic Delegation: A Form-Critical Inquiry," *Bib* 63 [1982] 206–18. Vermeylen, J., "Les prophètes de la conversion face aux traditions sacrales de l'Israël ancien," *RTL* 9 [1978] 5–32. Whybray, R. N., "Prophecy and Wisdom," *Israel's Prophetic Tradition* 181–99.)

14   (II) The Cult. An extension of this problem is the relation of the prophets to the Israelite cult. Again, the problem arises with the preexilic prophets: No one will seriously question the deep involvement of an Ezekiel, a Zechariah, or a Malachi in the ritual of the postexilic community.

It might seem that there is little need to deal with this question today, when there has been a tendency to exaggerate in an opposite direction by assimilating even the classical prophets of Israel to the Near Eastern pattern of cult prophet with which we have just dealt. Nevertheless, the opinion is still shared by some biblical critics that the preexilic prophets were opposed to the cult religion of Israel on principle.

We have seen that there were cult prophets in Israel. Were the classical prophets also of this type? This question cannot be answered with a conclusive yes or no, simply from lack of evidence, but at least the great majority of them probably were not. There are some grounds to permit us to classify Nahum and Habakkuk of the preexilic prophets, and Joel and Zechariah of the postexilic prophets, as Temple prophets. Not even in these cases is the evidence necessarily peremptory (e.g., Zech 7:1ff.); in most other cases there is simply no probability in favor of the "cultic" hypothesis. Isaiah's call to prophecy almost certainly took place during a cultic celebration, but there is no proof that Isaiah was present in the Temple in any capacity other than as a pious Israelite. If mere interest in the cult would qualify a prophet as cultic, we should certainly have to make a cult prophet of Ezekiel. Yet it is simply impossible, for there was no Temple cult in the Babylonia where Ezekiel prophesied, and he apparently prophesied nowhere else.

If they were not cult prophets, however, the preexilic prophets were indeed involved with the cult. They were involved with it as Isaiah was, as those to whom it was the normal means of worshiping God, taken as much for granted by them as the Israelite traditions to which they appealed in identifying Yahweh with the moral God who had revealed himself to them. They took it for granted in this way, and yet, of course, they did not take it for granted at all, just as they took nothing for granted in the light of their prophetic vision. It was one of the institutions of Israel over which they had been appointed as judges, and judge it they did. In doing so, however, they no more excluded it than they excluded the priesthood, the covenant, the doctrine of election, or prophecy itself, all of which they also judged.

There are various assertions of the preexilic prophets that have been interpreted as expressing opposition to animal sacrifice in principle, as a less worthy or an unworthy way of worshiping Yahweh, possibly because it was imported from Canaan and certainly because it embodied an inferior conception of religion against the constant prophetic call for the spiritual sacrifice of service and personal integrity. Some of the chief passages involved are Amos 5:21–27; Hos 6:6; Jer 7:21–23; Isa 1:12–17; these are perhaps the strongest assertions of their kind, and they are typical of the rest.

When these passages are read in context and not as part of a preconceived theory of the origin of Israelite religion or of what the prophetic ideal of religion should have been, they make very good sense and are completely consistent with the rest of prophetic doctrine. The prophets are altogether existentialist in their approach to this aspect of Israelite life as to any other. They were not concerned with the issue of animal sacrifice or other forms of external sacrifice as an ideal or an abstraction. What was at issue were the sacrifices then being carried out in contemporary sanctuaries by men who were perpetrating a sacramentalism devoid of meaning. These sacrifices, say Amos and Jeremiah, Yahweh did not command. Love, not sacrifice, is the will of God, says Hosea; or, as we might rephrase it, there can be no true sacrifice without love. Absolutes of this kind are a commonplace of biblical language, in the NT as well as in the OT (cf. Luke 14:26 [note Matt 14:26]; 1 Cor 1:17 [note vv 14–16]; etc.); ordinarily they cause no trouble, as long as we are attentive to the context at hand. Isaiah's denunciation, perhaps the strongest of the lot, if interpreted out of its existential situation, would lead to the conclusion that Yahweh rejected prayer itself (cf. v 15) along with sacrifices, incense, festivals, and feast days.

One does well not to avoid an extreme by embracing another. We can frankly admit that, on their own reading, certain of the prophets would have had at best a minimal interest in the Israelite liturgy, which does not necessarily mean that they made a fetish of opposing rites the observance of which had become a fetish for others. Jeremiah frequented the Temple that he denounced, as did Isaiah before him. On the other hand, Ezekiel, who certainly left no doubt that for him the restoration of Jerusalem's Temple was a condition without which Yahweh could not be properly worshiped by the people he had made his own, nevertheless knew full well that Yahweh himself was the true sanctuary who alone could give any meaning to the Temple built with hands (cf. 11:16). The prophetic attitude to the cult was like the prophetic attitude to everything—one in which forms were always secondary to the realities they signified. It was only when forms no longer signified anything that they demanded condemnation.

(Hentschke, R., *Die Stellung der vorexilischen Schriftpropheten zum Kultus* [Berlin, 1957]. Murray, R., "Prophecy and the Cult," *Israel's Prophetic Tradition* 200–16.)

15   (III) The Monarchy. In respect to the monarchy, the prophetic attitude was characterized by a concern for spiritual realities and a lack of interest in forms as such. The relation of prophecy to the monarchy is important for many reasons, not the least of which was the influence that this institution exercised on prophetic messianic doctrine. Temporally, prophecy and the monarchy coincided almost exactly: the age of kingship in Israelite history was also the age of classical prophecy. In a history of salvation, the fact alone suggests even more intimate connections between the two.

The monarchy served partly as a stimulus to prophecy, for with it there entered into Israelite life a new conception of the relation of Israel to Yahweh, one that had to be under constant review by prophecy. That the popular call for a king was, in a sense, a repudiation of the covenant relationship (cf. 1 Sam 8:4ff.) was doubtless the preferred prophetic view in retrospect; but in any case, not only the tradition that reflects this antimonarchical view but also the older (?) tradition that saw in Saul the heaven-sent ruler to end Israel's woes (1 Sam 9:15ff.) are in agreement that prophecy presided over the transition to kingship. It was this, in fact, that alone could have made the monarchy acceptable to Israel—it provided the charismatic guarantees the lack of which had made Abimelech's ill-starred kingship such an aberration from Israelite tradition (Judg 9) and the transfer of which from Saul to David established the kingship with a permanency the like of which it could never have obtained under Saul (1 Sam 15:10-11). Paradoxically, therefore, prophecy was instrumental in establishing an institution for which its enthusiasm was always at best lukewarm and which it probably would have preferred never to have taken place.

Nevertheless, prophecy never headed any movement in Israel to replace the monarchy with another form of government that it might have been thought to prefer. That this is true is also singularly fortunate, for there is no indication that the prophetic tradition ever possessed either the taste or the talent for practical politics. Whenever prophecy intervened in these matters, it was as apt to be ill-advised as to succeed in its high purposes. Nathan's approval of Solomon over Adonijah (1 Kgs 1:8) was perhaps the blessing of legal processes and the indications of Yahweh's will (1 Chr 28:5) in opposition to an arrogant assumption that a man should rule simply because he was his father's son; however, from the standpoint of prophecy it could hardly be said that Solomon proved to be a wise choice. It is surely not by accident that nowhere in the biblical traditions is it recorded that Solomon either sought the advice of prophecy or received a prophetic oracle. The revolt of Jeroboam against the Davidic dynasty was similarly blessed by prophecy (1 Kgs 11:29-39), but Jeroboam later had to be repudiated by the same prophetic voice (1 Kgs 14:7-11). As in the case of the prophetic intervention that ended Omri's dynasty (2 Kgs 9:1ff.) by replacing it with another that became, if anything, something worse (Amos 7:9; Hos 1:4-5; 8:4), the prophetic record in political intrigue is one of failures rather than successes. It is just as well, then, that with certain exceptions the prophetic attitude, translated into terms of practical policy, was to try to make the best use of existing institutions.

Of course, this was as it should have been. The function of prophecy was to form the conscience of a people, not to dictate its politics. It did not necessarily desire the coming of the monarchy, but it assured that its coming would be in accordance with Yahweh's will. Once it had come, it played the role that destiny had now allotted it—to insist on obedience to the old covenant precepts relegated to the status of private law through the institution of the law of the king. It is in this role that Elijah is cast by 1 Kgs 21:17-24, where the prophet must denounce the crime that Ahab had committed against Israelite law and custom by submitting to the guidance of his Phoenician wife, who had tried to show him how to be a real king as the non-Israelite Near East understood kingship. In this episode, as in the action of the prophet Shemaiah against Rehoboam (2 Chr 12:5-7), Jehu against Baasha (1 Kgs 16:1-4), Isaiah against Ahaz (Isa 7:10ff.) or Hezekiah (2 Kgs 20:12ff.), and Jeremiah against the last kings of Judah (Jer 21:11ff.), the labor of prophecy was to make the kingship of Israel truly Israelite.

The effort was largely a failure. There were limited successes, as the historical books and some of the prophetic records testify. But the judgment of the deuteronomic author of Kgs on the history of the Israelite monarchy would doubtless have found agreement on the part of the majority of the classical prophets. Although based on more specific and somewhat different criteria from that which the prophets would always have used, his verdict is a prophetic one—that with extremely rare exceptions the kings had been failures from the standpoint of the issues that really mattered.

16 The messianic doctrine of the prophets (→ OT Thought, 77:155) fits consistently into the outline of their attitude to the monarchy. The royal messianism of the preexilic Judahite prophets, notably Isaiah, rests on the same religious premise that was held by the authors of the royal Pss—i.e., the prophetic oracle given to the house of David (2 Sam 7:4ff.; Ps 89:20-38). The classical prophets accepted this tradition as a revelation of Yahweh that had essentially conditioned their theology, even as the deuteronomic authors did, contrary to their instinctive dislike for monarchy (cf. G. von Rad, *Studies in Deuteronomy* [London, 1953] 88-91). But whereas the court or Temple prophets responsible for the royal Pss have, to a greater or less degree, entered wholeheartedly into the mystique that surrounded kingship in the Near East, adopting the *Hofstil* by which the kings were accorded divine titles and unending days, we find little or no trace of any such thing in the classical literary prophets. This is not to say that the royal Pss reflect a wholly uncritical acceptance of the Near Eastern kingly ideal; the ideal has been thoroughly Israelitized and made part of the Israelite eschatology of Yahweh's universality and the Davidic oracle (cf. H.-J. Kraus, *Psalmen* [rev. ed.; Neukirchen, 1978] 1. 147-48). Nevertheless, the psalmists can display an enthusiasm for kingship itself as represented in the anointed of Yahweh, and this has no counterpart in the oracles of the classical prophets. A more radical Israelitization has taken place in these oracles—a spiritualization that has deemphasized the king as king and stressed the king as the elect of Yahweh.

Isaiah perhaps comes closest to the language of the royal Pss in his prophecies regarding the Davidic kingship (cf. 7:13-17; 9:5-6; 11:1-5), yet only a brief reflection is necessary to show how much his thinking differs from theirs. For example, he never uses the royal title, even though it is beyond question that he is speaking of a Davidic king. Awesome titles are used, but they glorify the charismatic actions of Yahweh rather than their recipient. That we have here no mere circumstance but rather a studied policy seems to be borne out through the comparison of other prophetic passages of the same kind. Mic 5:1-4 (whether the work of Micah himself or of another Judahite prophet is not here important), also dependent on the ancient Nathan oracle, shows similar traits. All these prophecies predicate glorious things of the messianic ruler, but their entire stress is on the power of Yahweh acting through him. This prophetic peculiarity reaches some kind of culmination in the prophecy of Ezekiel. Ezekiel denies the title of king to the Davidic prince who will preside over the restored Israel (37:25), and, in view of the sharp restrictions that he places on the activity of this prince, we can hardly discern in his prophecy more than a faint reflection of the royal messianic idea (cf. 44:3; 45:7-8; 46:16-18; etc.).

If it is true that Jeremiah speaks of a Davidic scion who will reign as king with the justice of Yahweh (23:5-6), it is likewise true that it is probably the only reference made to him by the prophet in all the material that has come down to us (30:9; 33:14ff. are apparently later additions). Exilic prophecy in general placed no emphasis on royal messianism: the "messiah" (*māšîaḥ*, "anointed one") of Yahweh, according to the Second Isaiah (cf. 41:2; 44:28; 45:1), is no Davidic king, but Cyrus, the king of the Persians! For this prophet the only redeemer of Israel is Yahweh (41:14). In the postexilic period, Davidic messianism was again in prophetic vogue for a time. In the days of Zerubbabel, the prophets Haggai and Zechariah returned briefly to the old tradition, but their expectation was short, as the corrected text of Zechariah (cf. Zech 6:9-15) shows. It was doubtless in this same period that other prophetic hands interpolated earlier prophetic works with similar references to a Davidic ruler.

We must emphasize, of course, that none of the prophets ever denied the relevance of Davidic messianism to the divine economy. It is only that it was never one of their overriding ideas; they recognized that it had a proper place in Yahweh's salvific plan to the extent that they had been permitted to see it, but its place remained in the background of their thoughts. Amos and Hosea, who prophesied in northern Israel where there was a different, non-Davidic kingly tradition, characteristically prophesy nothing of royal messianism (although such prophecies were later inserted into their works). By disposition the prophets were not royalists, but they had to acknowledge that God had spoken through ancient prophecy regarding the destiny of the Davidic line. It was to honor this prophecy that they could await a king who would reverse the sad performance of most of the kings of Israel and Judah by being the true son of Yahweh that he was proclaimed to be. In all this the prophets anticipated to a marvelous degree the attitude that Jesus himself adopted toward royal messianism when he came to fulfill the expectations of the OT. For Jesus, too, royal messianism was a detail only in the divine economy of salvation. Without rejecting it as irrelevant to that economy, he nevertheless preferred to identify himself with other figures that more clearly defined the nature of the realization he gave to the hopes of Israel.

(García Cordero, M., "El messianismo dinastico-davidico y el concepto de realeza sacra en el antico Oriente," *De la Tôrah au Messie* [Fest. H. Cazelles; ed. M. Carrez, *et al.*; Tournai, 1981] 263–73. Harrelson, W., "Prophetical Eschatological Visions and the Kingdom of God," *The Quest for the Kingdom of God* [Fest. G. E. Mendenhall; ed. H. B. Huffmon, *et al.*; Winona Lake, 1983] 117–26. McKenzie, J. L., "Royal Messianism," *CBQ* 19 [1957] 25–52. O'Doherty, E., "The Organic Development of Messianic Revelation," *CBQ* 19 [1957] 16–24. Vawter, B., "Realized Messianism," *De la Tôrah au Messie* 275–80. Welch, A. C., *Kings and Prophets of Israel* [London, 1952].)

17   (IV) The Religion of Israel. Our final consideration in regard to prophecy's connections with Israelite institutions will be to sum up a few of the key concerns of prophetic teaching as viewed in the light of the popular religion of the times. From this point of view, we can more readily see both the prophetic originality, which is never to be minimized, and the conformity of the prophets to the traditional faith of their ancestors.

(A) Eschatology. Messianism is one aspect of eschatology; therefore, we have already noted one prophetic emphasis by which the prophets were both connected with, and separated from, other Israelites. By eschatology in this context we mean Israel's conviction that it was a people of election, that it had a part to play in the work of judgment and power exercised by God over the universe. As to whether this work was envisioned as a continuous one, extending into the historical future, or as a definitive one, pertaining to a time beyond history, is a secondary matter into which we need not enter. For all practical purposes, the eschatology of Israel's prophets was, in fact, historical, although the idea of a definitive judgment is proper to a later Judaism. However, this distinction probably could never have meant as much to the people of the OT as it does to us who have seen the passing away of the Israel known to the OT and have received the quite distinctive interpretation of eschatology contributed by NT revelation.

What is important, however, is recognition of the historical nature of prophetic eschatology in another sense—i.e., from the standpoint of the biblical conception of time, which has sometimes been called "linear" and opposed to the "cyclic" conception of time supposedly associated with other ways of thought. Perhaps too much has been made of the distinction, and there has doubtless been some exaggeration in the conclusions drawn from it. What seems to be a fact, however, apparent to anyone at all familiar with the Bible, is that with quite rare exceptions the biblical authors never conceived of time in the sense of a deterministic pattern but as a series of moments filled with distinctly willed events. To recognize this fact is to rule out the fanciful interpretations of prophecy that have ascribed to the prophet a photographic vision of a near or distant future that somehow had relevance for the people to whom he had been sent to reveal the word of God. "The prophet does not see history stretched out before him like a map, from which he need only pick out individual future events. Such foresight is not the prophet's gift. Rather he sees in which direction events are flowing. This is the scope of prophecy. The Hebrew conception of time excludes any other explanation of it" (C. Tresmontant, *A Study of Hebrew Thought* [NY, 1960] 27).

Whatever the explanation, it is a verifiable fact that it is not the nature of biblical prophecy to see the future as a photograph. Prediction was, indeed, often part of the prophetic message, but prediction was permitted to the prophet always in terms of the contingencies that he knew and that would be understood by his hearers. Isaiah's prophecy of Sennacherib's invasion (10:27–34) is a classical instance: the prophecy was fulfilled, but under circumstances not envisioned by the prophet. The same characteristics apply to the prophets' vision of Israel's eschatology (cf. J. van der Ploeg, *StudCath* 28 [1953] 81–93).

18   It might seem pointless to have to insist that the prophets shared Israel's conviction of its divine election. Nevertheless, it has been held at times that this was not so, and Amos 3:2, for example, has been called spurious because it contradicts Amos 9:7. Probably most everyone would agree that the once easy admission of such "contradictions" was in reality to miss much of the point of prophetic teaching. The prophets did believe in Israel's election; the vast majority of their utterances, as a matter of fact, would cease to make much sense if their life situation were not founded in such a belief. Election was part of the fundamental constitution of Israel, and the prophets were quite prepared, even if their contemporaries were not, to accept all the consequences of Israel's status as the chosen of God (cf. Amos 3:9–12).

The prophets spiritualized and moralized this belief. It would perhaps be more accurate to say that they remoralized it, for they did so without any claim to innovation. The very idea of election carries with it some obvious hazards, such as the temptation to complacency over its effects or haziness over its grounds. Many Israelites had fallen to these temptations. Israel had not been chosen for Israel's sake, the prophets had to insist, but for God's; Israel had not been chosen for its virtues, but because being drawn near God, it might find the way of virtue. When Amos agreed that Yahweh had chosen Israel, it was to remind Israel that in this fact lay his right to destroy it for its crimes: "Therefore I will punish you" (3:2).

Israelite tradition had expressed the conception of election in various metaphors and analogies, one of the most important of which was that of covenant. This conception, too, is to be found in the prophets, although again with their own proper reservations. The term never appears in Amos, who perhaps felt it impossible to rehabilitate it from its misuse. Most of the other prophets, however, show no reluctance to employ it, but they use it as Amos used the idea of election itself—

for them the covenant was a deed of Yahweh's grace and the foundation of moral obligation. The figure of Yahweh summoning his people before the bar of justice, which is so common in the prophets (cf. the technical term *rîb,* "litigation," in Hos 4:1; Mic 6:2; etc., and other equivalents elsewhere, was, we now recognize, borrowed from primitive covenant terminology. The prophets also usually insist on the tradition of the Mosaic covenant, which was conditioned, rather than on the patriarchal or Davidic covenants, which were unconditioned. In the Mosaic covenant, the moral character of election was most apparent. It is unusual for a preexilic prophet to dwell on the patriarchal traditions, although these are mentioned more frequently in exilic and postexilic prophecy (→ OT Thought, 77:83–85).

19   An idea that assisted the prophets in spiritualizing the conception of election was that of the "remnant." Associated most characteristically with Isaiah, this idea seems also to have been imbedded in Israel's best traditions older than the literary prophets. If Amos hardly considered it a viable possibility (5:15), and even scoffingly described a remnant that was not a remnant at all (3:12), he still seems to have honored the belief in his own fashion. Amos was far too convinced of Israel's perdition to waste time in speculating on the consequences of repentance, but other prophets were not so pessimistic. In the preaching of Hosea, Isaiah, and Jeremiah, the notion of a saved remnant that would survive Yahweh's judgment and become a restored Israel gave to the doctrine of election a theological depth in which the designs of a beneficent God could be envisioned better and laid the groundwork for postexilic prophecy.

Judgment itself was an eschatological idea profoundly spiritualized in prophetic teaching. The "day of Yahweh" to which Amos referred as something taken for granted by his contemporaries (5:18–20) is subject to various interpretations; in any case, he plainly had in mind some event that would celebrate Yahweh's triumph over his enemies. The significance of Amos's use of the expression was his identification of the enemies not as the unbelieving Gentiles but as Israel itself. Another preexilic prophet would take up this theme, agreeing with the popular notion that this day would mean the end of the peoples opposed to the people of God (cf. Zeph 2:1–15), but also agreeing with Amos that Israel was to be included among these peoples (Zeph 1:1–18). There seems to be no doubt that popular eschatology looked toward a future in which Yahweh would have a settling of accounts with his enemies, from which his people would emerge triumphant. Prophecy accepted the eschatology but made it clear, apart from all nationalistic considerations and in the light of moral law alone, just who this people would be. It would not be the Israel of the flesh, but the Israel of the spirit—the remnant, the truly chosen. This prophetic interpretation continues into the postexilic prophecy, where it becomes even plainer that Yahweh's judgment lies not between Israel and non-Israel but between the just and the wicked (cf. Mal 3:13–21; → OT Thought, 77:143).

(Huffmon, H. B., "The Covenant Lawsuit in the Prophets," *JBL* 78 [1959] 285–95. Jacob, E., "Prophètes et intercesseurs," *De la Tôrah au Messie* [→ 16 above] 205–17. Mendenhall, G., "Covenant Forms in Israelite Tradition," *BA* 17 [1954] 50–76. Rowley, H. H., *The Biblical Doctrine of Election* [London, 1952]. Vriezen, T. C., *Die Erwählung Israels nach dem Alten Testament* [Zurich, 1953].)

20   **(B) Prophetic Social and Moral Teaching.** The stress on social morality apparent among the preexilic classical prophets has sometimes earned for them the designation "social prophets." From what has already been said, it is evidently not precisely to the prophets' credit that we should single out this one aspect of their message as though they had given a disproportionate attention to it. The prophets certainly were not, as they were once called, "radical pamphleteers" (E. Renan, *Histoire du peuple d'Israël* [Paris, 1893] 2. 425) or "insurrectionists" (L. Wallis, *Sociological Study of the Bible* [Chicago, 1912] 168, etc.). The social message was admittedly a major emphasis, but its explanation is to be found in the function of an Israelite prophet—serving as a conscience for his people in precisely those matters where conscience was needed. Against the backdrop of Israelite history, prophetic social doctrine fits into its proper place and is not out of proportion. The prophets themselves could only have been puzzled by the designation "social." They were only insisting on the social virtues inherent in the doctrines of election and covenant, virtues which had been flagrantly violated in an Israel that had largely abandoned its ancient ideals, assimilating itself to Gentile ways. In presuming a social character to the religion of Yahweh, the prophets were proposing nothing new but recalling a known, although much ignored, morality.

From this prophetic emphasis, however, there emerges an OT theme that becomes a major assertion and extends into the NT doctrine of the kingdom of God (cf. Matt 5:3). This theme is that of Yahweh's poor ('*ănāwîm*)—i.e., of the socially oppressed whose redress could only come from Yahweh, and who, therefore, became virtually synonymous with the just, the faithful remnant with the right to call upon the Lord. In this theme, too, prophetic teaching maintained its accustomed balance. Poverty was never sentimentalized by the prophets of Israel; in keeping with the rest of the OT, they regarded it as an undesirable thing. The poor man was not just because he was poor, but the existential fact could not be ignored that poverty and unjust oppression were frequent companions. It was the evil of others that had created this situation, and the whole of prophetic effort was directed against the evil.

We do not mean to minimize the contribution made by prophecy when we assert that they inculcated a known morality, or at least one that should have been known. To the ancient traditions of Israel they also added the immediacy of the word of God in their own time drawn from their own experience of the God of Israel's history. Their preaching of the social and moral imperatives to be found in the events by which Yahweh had constituted Israel has given the OT its most authoritative basis for *Heilsgeschichte.*

21   **(C) Ethical Monotheism.** "Ethical monotheism" was the term once used to denote what was considered the most important of all the prophetic discoveries—i.e., that the God of Israel had a moral will, and that only by a moral life could he be worshiped according to that will. We have already pointed out that this "discovery" of the prophets was not new; it was, however, certainly the burden of their message to Israel. They discovered the principle where it was always available to all Israel—in its sacred traditions.

Theoretical monotheism appears relatively later in Israelite times (→ OT Thought, 77:17). The monotheism of the preexilic prophets has been called, for its part, a "practical" or a "dynamic" monotheism—i.e., it was an existential monotheism, the only form of monotheism to be reasonably expected in its historical context, and nevertheless a monotheism for not being theoretical. This monotheism is the same kind found in Israel's most ancient traditions, deriving even from the patriarchal narratives. In view of what we must conclude about the transmission of the words of the classical prophets, it would be simply incredible that the prophetic teaching could have been as much out of the mainstream of Israelite thinking as some critics once imagined. The transmission of the prophetic writings makes sense only when we recognize the obvious fact that they depended for their continued existence on their acceptance by a people who acknowledged in them the word of a God who was also the God of their faith, however reluctant they may have been to act on the word as delivered to them. The writings of the classical prophets are a heritage of the religion of Israel, that of Ahab as well as Elijah, of Zedekiah as well as Micaiah, of Hananiah as well as Jeremiah. Any other interpretation makes nonsense of history (→ OT Thought, 77:17–20).

Admittedly, the prophetic connection of religion with morality is something unique. If they found the basis for this connection in the common tradition they shared with their contemporaries, it is nevertheless true that it was owing to their ministry that the connection was cemented so that it could never again be sundered. This very fact has sometimes been held up to prophecy as a reproach, in that its answer to all social and moral problems was always religious rather than practical. As noted above, the prophets furthered no policy for the replacement of outworn institutions by better ones. If, on the one hand, they never proposed any reactionary reversion to the past like the Rechabites (cf. Jer 35), neither did they ever suggest any plan of action by which existing Israelite life could be harmonized with what they considered to be Israel's ancient ideals. To the harried politicians of Israel and Judah striving to give their tiny country a means of survival in a sea of power politics where neutralism was not tolerated, the prophets might have seemed to offer no hope in their reiterated condemnation of all political alliances as treason to the God of Israel's covenant. If Jeremiah could be misunderstood by the senseless partisans of a defeated land whose instincts were suicidal, he could also be misunderstood by honest patriots whose religion was as sincere, if not as informed, as his own. "Do good . . . perform justice . . . avoid evil . . ." are admirable injunctions, but they do not constitute an outline for state business or even for one's private professional life. Is it not a continuing objection against moralists that they content themselves with aphorisms and refuse to come to grips with the harsh realities of practical life?

It all must be faced, but not to denigrate the role of prophecy. The prophets were not moralists, statesmen, or politicians; they were prophets. Their function was to reveal the mind of God, which they had as others did not. In this function they had their *raison d'être,* and it was the function of others to translate the prophetic word into plans of action whether for personal or public life. The tragedy of Israel was not that it received from prophecy anything less than what prophecy was supposed to give, but that it had priests who would not know God and his law, rulers who made their laws apart from God, and a people who would not heed the prophetic word.

(Ballentine, S. E., "The Prophet as Intercessor: A Reappraisal," *JBL* 103 [1984] 161–73. Causse, A., "Les prophètes et la crise sociologique de la religion d'Israël," *RHPR* 12 [1932] 97–140. Gelin, A., *The Poor of Yahweh* [Collegeville, 1965]. Porteous, N. W., "The Basis of the Ethical Teaching of the Prophets," *Studies in Old Testament Prophecy* [→ 10 above] 143–56.)

THE PROPHETIC LITERATURE

22 The preceding is a necessary preliminary to our consideration of the prophetic literature of the OT. Only in its light can we understand what is meant by this literature, who produced it, and to what end. We are concerned, of course, with the prophetic literature as defined — i.e., that produced by the classical literary prophets. The Jewish canon (→ Canonicity, 66:21–31) is more inclusive in counting as "the early prophets" what we customarily regard as historical books (i.e., the deuteronomic corpus). Neither are we concerned with other kinds of literature, which, for various reasons, have often been grouped with the prophetical, represented by Lam, Bar, Dan, and Jonah. The literary categories of these works are considered in their respective commentaries.

(I) Literary and Nonliterary Prophets. In one sense, the distinction between literary and nonliterary prophets is based on a misconception of the history of literary prophecy, and, in any case, is incidental. Amos differs from Elijah, to the extent that we know of the latter at all, in little that is more significant than that we can read Amos's own words, whereas we can only read about Elijah's. The distinction, therefore, says less about the prophets concerned than it does about the subsequent fate of their prophecies. On the other hand, the distinction is not entirely accidental. As seems to be the case, it was the disciples of a great prophet to whom we are usually indebted for his prophetic writings — the same *běnê hanněbî'îm* who otherwise play such a mixed role in the history of prophetism. That a prophet attracted to himself such disciples as would guarantee the preservation of his prophecies can, at least sometimes, tell us something about the prophet himself.

The prophetic literature does not consist of books written by literary authors in the same way that the book of Ruth, say, is by a determined literary author, or even the Gospel of John. The names appearing at the heads of the prophetic books do, with some nuances, identify the substance of the words therein contained with distinct prophets. However, these prophetic words are, in the main, the collected and edited memorabilia of the prophets, not literary compositions of the prophets themselves. They are the result of the editorial joining of the smaller collections of prophecies that have been connected by catchwords, similarity of topic, literary forms, or some similar consideration.

Could not these collections have been made by the prophets themselves? It is not impossible, but it is unlikely, as an examination of the individual prophetic "books" tends to show. In many instances, the compilers of the prophecies evidently lacked information that would have been available to the authors. Another consideration is the biographical material in the third person that forms a substantial part of many of the prophetic books. It is, again, not impossible that the prophet wrote of himself in the third person; however, it is far more reasonable to think that this material is from the same sources responsible for the collections — the prophet's disciples. We are told explicitly of the existence of such disciples and of the role they played in preserving and transmitting their masters' words—e.g., Isa 8:16–20. Jer 36 is also a precious source of information, describing the first stage in the Jeremiah collection when some of Jeremiah's prophecies were first written at his dictation by his disciple Baruch. Many prophecies in other prophetic books likewise show signs of having been dictated. Even for Amos, whom we generally think of as an isolated figure, we have not only third-person material (7:10–17) but also first-person accounts that presuppose the presence of friendly auditors whose duty it was to remember and record (cf. 7:1,4,7; 8:1–2). It would have been in the circles of disciples, too, that originally private material such as the "confessions" of Jeremiah (12:1–6; 15:15–21; etc.) would have been preserved, made known by the master to his followers but not initially intended for the general public.

This possibility raises in some measure the question of the *ipsissima verba* of the prophet. To what extent do the prophecies of Amos, Hosea, Isaiah, and the rest appear precisely as they were originally uttered? The answer to this question is not simple, nor does a single answer suffice in every case.

In general, we probably have good reason to think that in the majority of the poetic texts primary to a given prophetic book we have a substantial transcription of the prophet's original words. It is not unthinkable that in some instances these had been actually written by the prophet himself, on ostraca or other familiar recording media. It was not really necessary, however, inasmuch as the poetic structure itself was of such a nature as to facilitate memory and precise transmission. As a matter of fact, from this poetic material distinct literary styles and constants frequently emerge, so that it is possible to speak of an Amosian or an Isaian characteristic, to separate easily the material of Jeremiah from that of Baruch, etc.

The prose material presents additional difficulties. A prophet could, of course, produce prose as well as poetry, and there is a great deal of prose in various of the prophetic books that surely has an authentic life situation in the ministry of the individual prophets. However, what we know of the ordinary processes of prophecy encourages us to think that its ordinary form was the utterance of relatively short poetic assertions. The prose sections of the prophetic literature frequently have the appearance of literary productions rather than of addresses to audiences, even when they record words of prophecy that were so spoken. Thus, they often seem to be paraphrases and summaries of prophecies rather than the actual prophecies themselves. These paraphrases could also have been the work of the prophet, just as John of the Cross wrote the prose commentaries on his poetical experiences, but it is usually more likely that they are recollections of the sense of the prophecies, sometimes preserving snatches of the original words as tradition had transmitted them. This hypothesis appears to be especially confirmed in the case of Jeremiah, many of whose prophecies have evidently been handed down in circles that were strongly influenced by deuteronomic style and vocabulary (→ Jeremiah, 18:7).

23   (II) Prophetic Literary Forms. The most characteristically prophetic of the material found in the prophetic books is the oracle—i.e., the revelation of Yahweh. As we have already pointed out, the oracle is ordinarily a brief poetic utterance, although in the prophetic literature oracles of a similar kind have often been joined into a larger unity, sometimes by the prophet himself but usually by an editor. To underline the divine origin of the oracle, the prophet has often prefaced, concluded, or interlarded it with appropriate reminders: "So says Yahweh"; "Yahweh speaks"; etc. However, the prophet may just as easily speak in his own name as the accredited spokesman for God.

Authors are accustomed to distinguishing various types of oracle, depending on the precise nature of the word of God being communicated. It may be distinguished as a woe or a weal prophecy, the revelation of a coming evil or a coming good. Preexilic prophecy is predominantly of the woe variety (cf. Jer 28:8), which does not necessarily mean that all or most of the weal prophecies in the books of the preexilic prophets result from subsequent supplementation from postexilic prophecy; even Amos, the most pessimistic of the preexilic prophets, could utter a qualified salvation prophecy (5:15). It is true, however, that salvation prophecy is characteristically postexilic, just as prophecy of doom is characteristically preexilic. Prophecies of doom for the Gentile peoples who oppose the reign of Yahweh are proper to pre- and postexilic prophecy alike.

Obscurity is frequently the characteristic of prophecy: the ambiguity of the Delphic oracle was proverbial in classical antiquity. Frequently, however, it is redactional activity that has obscured the meaning for us (however clear it may have been to the redactor's contemporaries), as when we try to sort out what is woe and what is weal in a text like Isa 7:13ff.

The word of God mediated through prophecy is not exclusively or even preeminently predictive. A prophetic oracle of woe may be, and far more frequently is, a divine denunciation of sin (cf. Isa 1:2–3; 3:12–15; etc.) or a summons to repentance (cf. Amos 5:4–5a; Zeph 2:3), which reductively may mean the same thing. It is in such prophecies as these that we find our chief source of the social and moral doctrine revealed through prophecy. As is evident, the oracle can often be at one and the same time a denunciation, an exhortation, and a prophecy of doom or salvation.

The exact circumstances under which the prophet uttered most of these oracles are not described for us, and we can only hypothesize. In some cases, however, the prophet has recounted his prophetic experience, recasting the oracle as part of the narrative; from such descriptions we gain a better idea of the prophetic process. Thus, Amos describes various visions in which the word of God was made known to him (7:1–9; 8:1–3; 9:1ff.), as do Jeremiah (13:1–11) and other prophets. In Ezek, these descriptions are often quite elaborate (e.g., 8:3ff.; 37:1–14) and, as such, become a model imitated in postexilic prophecy and apocalyptic, in which the vision itself is the substance rather than merely the occasion of the prophetic word. Some of Ezekiel's visions read like ecstatic experiences; however, the earlier prophetic descriptions seem to be of ordinary occurrences into which the prophet was given a special insight through his contact with God.

The recasting of the prophetic word by the prophet takes on many forms other than the vision narrative. Amos 1:3–2:8 makes use of an ancient poetic form also found in some of the sapiential literature (cf. Prov 30:15ff.). Ezek 19:2–14; 27:3–9; etc., and many other prophetic passages have been put into the form of a "dirge song" (*qînâ*), while Isa 5:1–7 begins as a love song like those sung by minstrels in the city streets. We have already mentioned the "covenant lawsuit," a form borrowed from ancient covenant ritual well known to the people. An extended form of this in Mic 6:1–8 looks very much as though it has been modeled on a Temple liturgy of which we have other examples in various Pss. Many other prophetic passages have been ascribed to liturgical influence with varying degrees of plausibility. Another form very common in the prophetic literature is the prophetic sermon (*tôrâ*), either in prose or poetry, an instruction corresponding to the priestly *tôrâ* of the sanctuaries. It is particularly from examples of *tôrâ* as found in the various prophetic books that we can extract typically prophetic doctrine and phraseology, for in time it built up its own literary tradition just as the priestly *tôrâ* did.

What are called the symbolic acts of the prophets may also be classed among the prophetic literary forms, for these acts were also prophecies. The symbolic act is found more frequently in Ezekiel than in any other prophet, but it is by no means confined to him. Hosea's marriage (Hos 1-3), Isaiah's nakedness (20:1-6), the name Shear-jashub that he gave to his son (7:3), Jeremiah's celibacy (16:1-4), and his purchase of Hanameel's field (32:6ff.) were all symbolic acts. We call them symbolic because we think of them as signs of some other reality. To the OT mind, however, they were realities in their own right, the prophetic word made visible. When Ezekiel drew the roads leading out of Babylon (21:23ff.), he was not merely figuring an event to follow; he was in a sense bringing the event into existence. The prophets' lives and deeds could be as filled with prophecy as their words, for the biblical mind made no real distinction between the two.

(Childs, B. S., "The Canonical Shape of the Prophetic Literature," *Int* 32 [1978] 46-55. Freedman, D. N., "Discourse on Prophetic Discourse," *The Quest for the Kingdom of God* [→ 16 above] 141-58. Tucker, G. M., "Prophetic Speech," *Int* 32 [1978] 31-45. Vawter, B., "Prophecy and the Redactional Question," *No Famine in the Land* [Fest. J. L. McKenzie; Claremont, 1975] 127-39. Westermann, C., *Basic Forms of Prophetic Speech* [Phl, 1967]. Wiklander, B., *Prophecy as Literature* [Stockholm, 1984].)

24   (III) Formation of the Prophetic Books. There is not space, nor is this the place, to enter into the history of composition of the individual prophetic books. This history is quite complicated and differs from book to book; the more important considerations for this or that book will be found in the respective commentaries. Here we shall note only those details of the history that apply to the formation of the prophetic literature in general into the books as we now have them.

The prophets' disciples are doubtless responsible for the initial work of gathering together and also, in large part, writing down their oracles, sermons, and other prose and poetic material, some of which was preserved in the prophets' own words and some of which the disciples remembered and paraphrased. To this material the disciples added biographical recollections and sometimes other related material (e.g., the creation hymn that has been used to form doxologies in Amos 4:13; 5:8-9; 9:5-6). The whole of the collections thus formed was put into some kind of order, on either topical or chronological considerations, or both. Sometimes original unities were preserved (e.g., probably Amos 1:3-2:8), but generally speaking the unities that emerged were the work of the disciples, for the prophetic material had usually been produced in bits and pieces during lengthy prophetic ministries. Thus, the biographical Amos 7:10-17 has been placed after Amos's own account of his vision in 7:7-9 because of the

reference there to the house of Jeroboam. Similarly, the biographical Hos 1, the oracles of Hos 2, and the autobiographical Hos 3 have been unified because of the identity of subject matter. It is in all likelihood a disciple-editor, too, who has put such a verse as Amos 1:2, from whatever period in the prophet's career, at the head of the book, where it now serves as an introduction to the prophetic collection.

The editorial work of the prophets' disciples doubtless entailed redactional retouching as well as collecting the prophets' words. Other retouching took place through the subsequent use made of these collections once they had left the disciples' hands. References to Judah in the present Hebr text of Amos 6:1; Hos 6:4 are probably, and certainly in the case of Hos 12:3, the result of change from an original "Israel." After the fall of the northern kingdom, the prophecies of Amos and Hosea circulated in the south, and such adaptations were made to show their continued applicability, Retouches of a similar kind have adapted other prophecies to a postexilic situation.

The present editions of the prophetic collections seem for the most part to have been postexilic. It was at this time that titles and chronological indications were attached to the beginnings of the books. The chronological indications are invariably Judahite, even for works like Amos and Hos, which were originally concerned exclusively with Israel. Furthermore, the indications do not always agree with the prophetic content.

The postexilic editors who had seen the fulfillment of the preexilic prophecy of doom, and who also had the continuing experience of exilic and postexilic prophecy, followed a fairly standard outline in distributing the prophetic collections. They tended to gather the woe oracles at the beginning of the book and the oracles of salvation at the end; in between, they placed the oracles against the Gentiles. The purpose of this arrangement was to express their faith in the restoration of a redeemed Israel through the defeat of the enemies of God and his people. At the same time they took advantage of the opportunity to supplement especially the second and third of these sections with other similar prophetic passages, updating the oracles against the nations (e.g., by the inclusion of the oracles against Babylon now in Isa 13:1-14:23) and including such new salvation themes as the reunification of Israel and Judah derived from Jeremiah and Ezekiel. All kinds of supplementary material have gone into this amplification of the prophetic books. Even such a thorough prophecy of doom as that of Amos has received a messianic epilogue (9:8b-15), and there are countless other additions of the same kind (cf. Hos 1:7; 3:5b; Mal 3:24b; etc.). For other reasons, other types of supplementation have been made, such as the extensive historical material that was available concerning important prophets like Isaiah (chaps. 36-39; cf. 2 Kgs 18:13-20:19) and Jeremiah (chap. 52; cf. 2 Kgs 24:18-25:30).

It is likely that the text of some of the prophetic literature at least remained fairly fluid until its inclusion in the canon (e.g., Jer). There are, of course, still further additions and alterations, the result of glosses or of deliberate interpolation, which are not scriptural.

THE PROPHETIC WORD

25   Our concern with the prophetic literature is not, it need hardly be said, merely the interest we have in an ancient religious phenomenon. Prophecy not only was, but still is, the word of God. If all Scripture is, in its own measure, the word of God, it is preeminently true of the prophecy in which God chose to speak directly with his people. It is, furthermore, not an archival record, but the living word of a living God.

This concept at least, is the biblical view. We have stated that the symbolic acts of the prophets were not signs only but efficacious works. The same is no less true of the prophetic utterances. Ahab's reproach of Elijah as the "troubler of Israel" (1 Kgs 18:17) and the king of Israel's complaint against Micaiah's failure to prophesy good for him (1 Kgs 22:8) are not the irrational petulance they might appear at first glance. They are, rather, a recognition that the prophetic word is power from God and that the prophet is the instrument through whom this power is transmitted. The prophetic word lives a life of its own once it has emanated from the prophet, and the prophet is very much identified with the word that he has uttered.

If we share this biblical view, we must recognize two things. First, the prophetic word is greater than the prophet, which the prophets themselves would have been the first to acknowledge. We know of this greatness from the NT fulfillment, which, in turn, is not an occurrence of the dead past but a continually living and growing reality. Second, the prophetic word is the word of Isaiah, or Amos, or Jeremiah, or perhaps a man whose name we do not know—a man, in any case, who was personally involved in the word, who lived for it and was prepared to die for it. If we are to take in this message as God has delivered it to us, we must take it in as it has come through the prophets of Israel. Anything less is not the prophetic word.

12

HEBREW POETRY

Aloysius Fitzgerald, F.S.C.

BIBLIOGRAPHY

1 Alonso Schökel, L., *Estudios de poética hebrea* (Barcelona, 1963). Alter, R., *The Art of Biblical Narrative* (NY, 1981); *The Art of Biblical Poetry* (NY, 1985). Baker, A., "Parallelism: England's Contribution to Biblical Studies," *CBQ* 35 (1973) 429–40. Berlin, A., *The Dynamics of Biblical Parallelism* (Bloomington, 1985). Budde, C., "Das hebräische Klagelied," *ZAW* 2 (1882) 1–52. Collins, T., *Line-Forms in Hebrew Poetry* (Studia Pohl, series maior 7; Rome, 1978). Cross, F. M., "Studies in the Structure of Hebrew Verse: The Prosody of Lamentations 1:1–22," *WLSGF* 129–55. Freedman, D. N., *Pottery, Poetry and Prophecy: Studies in Early Hebrew Poetry*

(Winona Lake, 1980); "Acrostic Poems in the Hebrew Bible: Alphabetic and Otherwise," *CBQ* 48 (1986) 408–31. Geller, S. A., *Parallelism in Early Biblical Poetry* (HSM 20; Missoula, 1979). Gray, G. B., *The Forms of Hebrew Poetry* (NY, 1915; the 1972 Ktav reprint has a useful introduction by D. N. Freedman). Hrushovski, B., "Prosody, Hebrew," *EncJud* 13 (1971) 1195–1240. Kugel, J. L., *The Idea of Biblical Poetry* (New Haven, 1981). O'Connor, M. P., *Hebrew Verse Structures* (Winona Lake, 1980). Stuart, D. K., *Studies in Hebrew Meter* (HSM 13; Missoula, 1976). Watson, W. G. E., *Classical Hebrew Poetry: A Guide to its Techniques* (JSOTSup 26; Sheffield, 1984).

OUTLINE

INTRODUCTION

3 Poetry for the purposes of this review is understood as speech organized in measured lines. The opposition presumed is verse as opposed to prose which is not so measured. The scope of the review is consonant with the thrust of similar reviews of Hebr poetry done by biblicists though other matters like genre, specific figures, and the like may receive more extensive treatment there. Such reviews generally pay comparatively little attention to another view of poetry ("speech framed for contemplation," G. M. Hopkins) which engenders another type of analysis and includes both verse and

prose. Here poetry is opposed to rhetoric (speech organized to persuade) and prose (speech organized to inform). There is, of course, the question of how rigorously this threefold distinction can be maintained with regard to most biblical texts (and many other texts too). The discussion by biblicists of Hebr poetry (verse and prose) from this perspective has traditionally not been conducted on a particularly sophisticated level. The monographs of the literary critic R. Alter are illustrative of the success with which the biblical text can be approached from this point of view.

HISTORY OF THE OT VERSE FORM

4   The OT verse form was not something invented by Hebr poets. It is rather a reflection of a traditional form widespread in the ancient Near East, the invention of which is lost in antiquity. There exists, e.g., considerably older material similarly cast from Egypt, Mesopotamia, and Ugarit on the Syro-Palestinian littoral. In early 12th-dynasty Egypt the sage Neferti encourages his heart to bewail the troubles in Egypt caused by the Asiatics during the first intermediate period:

> Stir, my heart!
> Bewail the land from which you have sprung!

In the Old Babylonian version of Gilgamesh, Siduri advises Gilgamesh:

> Gilgamesh, let your belly be full!
> Day and night rejoice!

In the Keret epic from Ugarit (destroyed *ca.* 1200 BC) the god El asks Keret:

> Does he desire the kingship of the Bull, his father;
> or authority like the father of mankind?

Measured lines involving balanced short sentences like those above (with ellipsis of the verb in the last instance) are typical of ancient Near Eastern poetry and are the characteristic of biblical poetry all through the 1st-millennium BC. The form with a certain loosening is typical of the collection of the Thanksgiving Hymns (1QH) from Qumran, which date probably from the Maccabean and Hasmonean periods. It is imitated in Greek in the NT, e.g., in the Magnificat:

> My being proclaims the greatness of the Lord,
> my spirit finds joy in God my savior.
> (Luke 1:46–47)

Sustained use of the form is evident as late as the early 2d cent. AD in *2 Apoc. Bar.*:

> O Lord, you summon the coming of the times,
> and they stand before you. (48:2)

5   The earliest subsequent witnesses to Hebr verse are the *piyyûṭîm* (poems composed for the liturgy; connected with *payṭan* = poet, from Gk *poiētēs*), where the form of the old verse line is abandoned—at a later stage for complicated and radically different forms.

There are here, nonetheless, certain reflections of the old form because of the pervasive influence of the OT itself.

Through the whole of the OT period the basic form of the line survived and it must be assumed that those who used it understood the form. Some poetry (Deut 32 and some psalms) is written in stichometric columns at Qumran. Most is not. That can be explained as due to the fact that parchment was an expensive item. I presume an understanding of the form in the period. But when we get the first attempts at a description of the form in both Jewish and Christian sources (Josephus, Origen, Jerome) what they have to say is not very enlightening and sometimes just plain wrong.

The masoretic tradition which has presented us with the *textus receptus* gives some signs of an awareness of the presence of verse. Job, Prov, and Pss are supplied with a special set of accents. These books are almost exclusively poetry, and the accents are known as the poetic accents (the terminology is relatively modern). For much OT verse, however, the regular prose accents are used. Deut 32 continued to be copied in two columns, each containing a half line of verse. The arrangement with some success marks out the half lines and lines. But that the tradition did not understand the system seems indicated. Starting with v 14 where the first tripartite line is met, the systematic layout collapses.

6   The rules governing OT versification had been forgotten and had to be relearned. The two important figures in the process were Rabbi Azariah dei Rossi in his *Mě'ôr 'ênayim* (1574) and Bishop Robert Lowth in his *Praelectiones de sacra poesi Hebraeorum* (1753; Eng trans. by G. Gregory, 1787) and more amply in the introduction to his *Isaiah, A New Translation with a Preliminary Dissertation* (1778). Lowth (still very much worth reading) knew dei Rossi's work, translated from and commented on it. He rediscovered parallelism for modern scholarship and on the basis of this discovery there was unleashed a torrent of literature, some of it misdirected, on the nature of OT verse. What follows is an attempt at a concise statement of the present state of the question. The still controverted question of how precisely the lines are measured (accents, syllables, not at all) will be treated apart in an effort to distinguish secure areas from controverted ones.

THE MAIN FEATURES OF THE OT VERSE FORM

7   **(I) The Line and Its Parts.** The entry into the understanding of the OT verse system is the recognition that the basic building blocks of Hebr verse are short sentences. This fact simplifies matters considerably. One needs only to think of the difficulties to be met by a metrician visiting from another planet in deciphering the prosody of late Shakespearean blank verse not laid out in lines but in prose paragraphs, without the services of a speaker experienced in the traditional articulation of English to perform Shakespeare for him. This blank verse freely allows sentences to run on from one line to the next (enjambment). Even if the visitor arrived at the point where he was able to translate Shakespeare with competence into his own language, he would still know little about its prosody. There are relatively rare instances of Hebrew verse sentences that run from one

line to the next, but even here the line is always end-stopped; i.e., there is a sense pause, the equivalent of a comma or semi-colon, marking the end of the line. There is in OT poetry no instance of enjambment like Katherine of Aragon to the lady, Patience—especially line five:

> When I am dead, good wench,
> Let me be us'd with honor. Strew me over
> With maiden flowers, that all the world may know
> I was a chaste wife to my grave. Embalm me,
> Then lay me forth. Although unqueen'd, yet like
> A queen, and daughter to a king, inter me.
> (*Henry VIII*, IV.2.167–72)

8   Roughly speaking, two types of shorter sentences appear in OT verse, short and extra-short; and the length of two extra-short sentences approximates that of the short sentence. "Sentence" here is used loosely, but what is intended will be clear from the discussion. Typical are the seven sentences of the initial lines (40:1–2) of the opening scene of Deutero-Isaiah (40:1–8):

1. *naḥămû naḥămû ʿammî*   2. *yōʾmar ʾĕlōhêkem*
3. *dabbĕrû ʿal lēb yĕrûšālayim*   4. *wĕqirʾû ʾēlêhā*
5. *kî mālĕʾâ ṣĕbāʾāh*   6. *kî nirṣâ ʿăwōnāh*
7. *kî lāqĕḥâ miyyad YHWH* | *kiplayim bĕkol ḥaṭṭōʾtêhā*

    1. Comfort, comfort my people,
      2. says your God.
    3. Speak to the heart of Jerusalem,
      4. and proclaim to her,
    5. That complete is her service,
      6. that expiated is her guilt.
    7. Indeed she has received from the hand of the Lord
       double for all her sins.

The sentences numbered 1–6 above for the purposes of this discussion are extra-short sentences. Sentence 1 has a doubled verb. Sentence 7 is a short sentence. It is to be noted that sentences 1–2, 3–4, 5–6 when combined approximate the length of 7. Further, 3–4 and 5–6 are bound very closely together. They say more or less the same thing. The same is not true of 1–2, but when attention is paid to v 4b the suspicion begins to arise that the combination of two extra-short sentences (1–2, 3–4, 5–6) and its rough equivalent, the short sentence (7), ought to be considered the OT line. Verse 4b, a two-sentence line with ellipsis of the verb in the second sentence, in view of the ellipsis simply must be read as a unit:

    The rugged land will become a plain;
      and the rough country, a broad valley.

Analyzed this way, the first three lines (1–2, 3–4, 5–6) of Isa 40:1–2 have a clear binary structure. They are divided into halves by a strong end-pause (sentence stop) and a mid-pause or caesura (sentence stop). In the case of the final one-sentence line (7), the end-pause is clear. Since it is a one-sentence line, it has no mid-stop marked by a sentence stop. But on the analogy of the preceding lines it is probable that it has one, induced in part by the rhythm of the lines that precede it. Following the masoretic division I have set it after "Lord." On the basis of analogy with contemporary English speech patterns, the line is certainly capable of being read this way.

    Most lines are of this bipartite type (half line, mid-stop; half line, end-stop). The system also allows a tripartite line. This is illustrated by vv 3 and 5, three-sentence lines:

A voice cried out:
    In the desert prepare the way of the Lord!
    Make straight in the wasteland a highway for our God!

                *

Then the glory of the Lord shall be revealed,
    and all mankind shall see it together;
    for the mouth of the Lord has spoken.

The other lines of 40:1–8 not treated to this point divide into two-sentence lines like those treated above. The slightly out-of-step lines are the opening line of v 6, where a sentence serves as the object of the main verb in each half line:

    A voice said, "Cry out!"
    and I said, "What shall I cry out?"

and the final two lines of the poem, vv 7–8:

    The grass is withered, the flower is wilted,
      for the breath of the Lord has blown upon it.
    The grass is withered, the flower is wilted,
      but the word of our God will stand forever.

As interpreted here, the opening colon (half line) of each line is a two-sentence colon. Such cola appear elsewhere, though it is not the norm. This is an example of Dt-Isa breaking out of the rigid confines of his inherited model. Both lines can be read as tricola (three-sentence lines). I have read them as bicola because this produces better length balance between the cola. The lines can be read this way, for it is clear the weighted sense pause is in each case after "wilted." The problem really does not amount to much for the articulation in performance will be the same in any case. The arrangement on paper is merely an attempt at an analysis of the performance. ("So then, the people is the grass" in v 7 is regarded as an interpretive gloss, a footnote set in the text in a period when the footnote had not yet been invented.)

9   The essential element of the discussion to this point is that the sentence analysis of an OT poem uncovers a series of extra-short sentences, occurring in pairs, roughly equivalent in length to other short sentences which, when divided by a sense pause less strong than a sentence stop, take on the appearance of the two-sentence lines. A variant of this is the three-sentence line. Laid out on the printed page in Hebrew or in translation as Isa 40:1–2 are laid out above, they clearly suggest measured lines, meter. This consistent use of measured building blocks, short sentences, is the criterion by which OT verse is distinguished from OT prose.

    A word needs to be said about terminology. There is no standard terminology. In discussions of OT line structure the terms line, verse, verset, stich, colon, and the like occur; sometimes they are used to refer to what has been called here the half line; sometimes, to the full line. This can at times give a false impression of divergent views. The terminology that will be used in the remainder of the discussion is as follows: line is a full line; the half line is the colon; the line with two parts (the two-sentence line and the one-sentence line divided by a caesura) is a bicolon. When a line has a third part added it is called a tricolon.

10   To this point the attempt has been made to isolate inductively the line and its components, the cola of the bicolon and tricolon. The conclusions reached are confirmed by certain OT poems where the text itself marks out the limits of the lines, notably the one-line proverbs, where the line is the poem, and the alphabetic acrostics, where the individual lines open with successive letters of the alphabet. This verse presents lines, clearly marked out, exactly like the ones dealt with to this point. Note the following examples from the one-line proverbs and Lam 3, where each line of the poem is marked off by the acrostic: (a) two-sentence lines, (b) two-sentence lines with ellipsis of verb in the second colon, (c) one-sentence lines with caesura:

(a) A wise son makes his father glad;
      but a foolish son is a grief to his mother.
                      (Prov 10:1)
    He has worn away my flesh and my skin;
      he has broken my bones.
                      (Lam 3:4)
(b) Truthful lips endure forever;
      the lying tongue, for only a moment.
                    (Prov 12:19)
    I have become a laughingstock for all nations;
      their taunt all the day long.
                    (Lam 3:14)
(c) As vinegar to the teeth and smoke to the eyes
      is the sluggard to those who use him as a
      messenger.
                    (Prov 10:26)
    I am a man who knows affliction
      from the rod of his anger.
                    (Lam 3:1)

Some alphabetic acrostics work the acrostic not on lines
but on individual cola. This proves that the ultimate
building block of OT verse is not the line but the colon.
The combination, acrostics that mark off cola and
acrostics that mark off lines, indicates that lines are built
out of combined cola. In Ps 111 individual cola are
marked off by the acrostic. Note the following one-
sentence line, two-sentence line, and the three-sentence
tricolon with which it closes:

> I will give thanks to the Lord with all my heart
>   in the company and assembly of the just.
> (Ps 111:1)
> Majesty and glory are his work,
>   and his justice endures forever.
> (Ps 111:3)
> The fear of the Lord is the beginning of wisdom;
>   prudent are all who live by it.
>   His praise endures forever.
> (Ps 111:10)

The binary and tripartite analysis of the OT line form
presented to this point is the barest possible surface
description of the line. Anyone who has read some OT
poetry in Hebrew or in translation knows that there is
a good deal more involved in the Hebr line, even if that
awareness has not reached the point where what is
perceived can be intelligibly articulated. The attempt
will now be made to articulate this good deal more. The
discussion will be conducted only in terms of the bicolon; it is equally applicable to the tricolon.

11   (II) The Balance of the Parts. The biblical
line consists of two balanced cola. The balance between
them can be metrical (the roughly equal length of the
cola), syntactic, morphological, phonic, semantic, and of
other types too disparate to catalogue here. Every line
has approximate metrical balance. In all of the other
areas the balance can run from nothing or next to
nothing, to moderate, to extreme. Some lines betray
significantly more balance of one type than another; and
the different types of balance can be combined in an in-
finitude of different ways. It is precisely here that the OT
poet has the opportunity to display virtuosity within the
confines of the basic line form. This balance between the
cola can be and is called parallelism. I avoid the term here
because it is too frequently employed in the restricted
sense of semantic balance, conceived of as the prime
characteristic of the OT line. That is a too limited interpretation of the data. For the same reason semantic
balance was presented well down on the list of the types
of balance characteristic of the Hebr line given above. It
is frequently present, comes across noticeably in translation, but is not essential, as is proved by the lines where
there is none.

12   Prov 15:32 will serve to illustrate the various
types of balance characteristic of the OT line as described
above. It illustrates every type of balance listed and is in
some ways a *tour de force*. Generally the line combines
more selectively various types of balance and in varying
degrees. This is always the case in longer poems and the
point will be illustrated by recourse to both Prov 15:32
and Isa 40:1–2.

> *pôrēaʿ mûsār môʾēs napšô   wĕšōmēaʿ tôkahat qôneh lēb*

> He who rejects admonition despises his own soul;
>   but he who heeds reproof gains an (understand-
>   ing) heart.
> (Prov 15:32)

The line has metrical balance. It is a two–sentence line
and each sentence (colon) has four words. The line has
syntactic balance; each sentence follows the pattern: participial subj. + obj. + participial predicate + obj., the only
variations being the "but" which opens the second colon

and the suffixed pron. "his own" on the end of "soul."
The line has morphological balance: the base-stem participial subj. and the base-stem participial predicate
repeat in each colon. Their nominal objects are of
different patterns. The line has phonic balance (the inevitable result of morphological balance but it goes
beyond that). For the sake of simplicity I note only the
repeating long /o/ vowels in each colon: ô, ô, ô / ô, ô, ô //.
The line has semantic balance: "he who rejects" balances
by contrast "he who heeds"; "admonition" is a synonym
for "reproof"; "despises" balances with a certain balance
of contrast "gains." "Soul" (= life breath, personality,
self) balances "(understanding) heart," perhaps as whole
to part. As a whole the cola are balanced by a balance of
contrast that describes the situation of the docile and
recalcitrant.

There is an additional balance here which I would include under the heading used above "of other types too
disparate to catalogue." Both cola use the figure oxymoron. The person who will never admit that his actions
are subject to criticism actually belittles and scorns
himself; the person who is willing to admit that he has
made a mistake, in turn becomes wise. The balance in
Prov 15:32 involves a good deal more than semantic
balance.

13   In the longer poems this balance necessarily
loosens up. That is made clear by Isa 40:1–2:

> *naḥămû naḥămû ʿammî   yōʾmar ʾĕlōhêkem*

> Comfort, comfort my people,
>   says your God.

The bicolon has metrical balance; there is also the phonic
balance of repeated /m/: m, m, m / m, m //. Overall the
balance is rather weak.

> *dabbĕrû ʿal lēb yĕrûšālayim   wĕqirʾû ʾēlêhā*

> Speak to the heart of Jerusalem,
>   and proclaim to her.

The line has metric balance; significant syntactic balance:
vb. + prep. + obj. + dependent gen.—vb. + prep. + pron.
obj.; some morphological balance, in that each colon
opens with an impv., though of different conjugations.
Phonic balance involves the repeating of long /u/ vowels
and the b, r, l, l, b, r, l alliterative pattern of the opening
colon which is picked up by the r, l of the second colon.
Semantically "speak" is balanced by "proclaim"; and "to
the heart of Jerusalem" in an abbreviated fashion, by
"to her."

> *kî mālĕʾâ ṣĕbāʾāh   kî nirṣâ ʿăwōnāh*

> That complete is her service,
>   that expiated is her guilt.

The line has metrical balance; three words balance three
words. It has syntactic balance; the two-sentence line
repeats the pattern: particle + vb. + subj. + affixed gen.
pron. Both cola open and close with morphological
balance: particle *kî* + 3d fem. sg. vb. (different conjugations) . . . + 3d fem. sg. pron. The noun subjects are of
different patterns. The phonic balance is heavy-handed.
The three words of each sentence rhyme with the
repeating pattern: î, â, āh. ("Service" is masc. and the
verb should be masc., *mālĕʾ*. The fem. *mālĕʾâ* was needed
for the rhyme and eased by the fem. pron. suffix, "her
service." Phonics can influence grammar.) The balanced
cola show end-rhyme; this occurs sporadically in OT
verse—rhyming cola and rhyming lines.

The semantic balance is close, but here there is an
important point to be made. It is difficult to see much of
a semantic difference in the balanced cola of the preceding line, though probably there is some heightening in

the sense that "proclaim" carries with it the nuance "in a loud voice" not present in "speak." In line 3 the semantic repetition is more typical. The second colon repeats but significantly modifies the first. The balancing terms for "complete is her service" are "expiated/accepted is her guilt/punishment." The second colon redefines the service of the exile as punishment for sin and explains why that service is ended. The Lord has accepted Jerusalem's suffering as punishment enough. Implicit here is the fact that the Lord alone controls Jerusalem's fate; the Babylonians in reality played no genuinely significant role in bringing about the exile or its end. Likewise implicit is the restoration of good relations between the Lord and his city (note "my people" in line one). It is always important to note the subtleties of this common type of off-balance semantic balance. It is a primary strategy by which the argument advances within the superficially repetitious line. It is clear that in this carefully crafted line the poet has all but exhausted the possibilities for balance in a line—much more noticeably so than in the two preceding lines. The line is also the climax of the argument to this point. The climax of argument and balance coincide and the latter serves to highlight the former.

Having reached a climax the balance recedes in the next line:

kî lāqĕhâ miyyad YHWH | kiplayim bĕkol hattō'têhā

Indeed she has received from the hand of the Lord double for all her sins.

This line, unlike the three two–sentence lines just treated, is a one-sentence line. There is the tendency for one-sentence lines to have considerably less internal balance than two-sentence lines. That is certainly true here, though it is to be remembered that the opening line (40:1), a two-sentence line, likewise had a similar limited balance. This fourth line has metric balance from the caesura after "Lord." It also has phonic balance, notably the repetition: k, l / k, l, k, l //. It is devoid of syntactic, morphological, and semantic balance.

14   (III) Balance between Lines.

The internal balance characteristic of the OT line does not exhaust the possibilities for balance in poetry. It is frequently extended to larger units (interlinear as distinguished from intralinear balance), several lines or quite commonly two lines. This latter situation produces many combinations of two lines that can extend through a whole poem. This combination of two lines I call a couplet (the term is sometimes used for what is called here a bicolon). This situation is well exemplified by the illustrative example used here, Isa 40:1–8. The poem contains 12 lines grouped into six couplets, all manifesting some balance like the balance studied to this point on the level of the line. This interlinear balance is best illustrated by the closing couplet of the piece, vv 7–8:

The grass is withered, the flower is wilted,
  for the breath of the Lord has blown upon it.
The grass is withered, the flower is wilted,
  but the word of our God will stand forever.

The most striking balance here is that between the opening cola of each line. The metrical, syntactic, morphological, phonic, and semantic balance involves exact repetition.

Interlinear balance is generally more restrained. I illustrate briefly, again from the first four lines (two couplets; 40:1–2). Since all lines have metrical balance and bicola repeat, this balance is not part of the discussion. Line 1 opens with a doubled imperative (comfort, comfort). Imperatives are repeated at the opening of the

first and second colon of the second line (speak . . . proclaim). This produces a certain syntactic, morphological, and phonic balance. There is some semantic balance between "people" in line 1 and "Jerusalem" in line 2. In Dt-Isa they are related as children to mother. More important, the semantic balance between "Comfort, comfort my people," "Speak to the heart of Jerusalem," and "Proclaim to her" in context is very close. The vbs. in fact work together as a kind of hendiadys, and each of these three cola ends up meaning "speak comforting words to my people—also to Jerusalem—also to her."

The syntactic arrangement of the cola of the opening line of the second couplet follows the pattern: particle *kî* + 3d fem. sg. vb. + subj. This pattern is partially imitated in the opening colon of the second line: particle *kî* + 3d fem. sg. vb. This inevitably involves some morphological and phonic balance. The final /-hā/ pron. suffix at the end of this fourth line probably rhymes with the /-āh/ pron. suffix that closes out the two cola of line 3. The /-hā/ suffix that ends the second couplet also rhymes with the /-hā/ suffix that ends the first couplet.

The semantic balance of the couplet revolves around the sharpening of the interpretation of the service of the exile. The opening colon of the first line of the couplet presents it as "complete/full/ended." The second colon of the line presents that "service" as "guilt/punishment" and says that it has been "expiated/accepted." That immediately implies the Lord as the explanation for the end of the exile and sin as the explanation of his hostile action that began it. The second line of the couplet builds on this. "Jerusalem has received . . . double for all her sins." That emphasizes the enormity of her punishment. In addition the "service" has come "from the hand of the Lord." That makes completely explicit the fact that not only the end but also its beginning is the Lord's doing—on the most meaningful level his doing alone. The semantic balance between the lines of the couplet is rather off center, but fraught with significance. The sense of balance the reader gets from the lines comes as much from the types of balance described above as from semantic balance.

15

Apart from repeating couplets the only standard OT verse form larger than the line (as, e.g., the Spencerian stanza or the sonnet) is the alphabetic-acrostic poem where in various ways the number of lines is determined by the number of the letters of the alphabet. Hebr poets can produce poems so measured even without the acrostic appearing; e.g., the 22-line poem, Lam 5. It is permissible to speak of sense paragraphs in poetry as in prose. These sense paragraphs can at times be of relatively equal length.

16   (IV) The Metrical Question.

I turn now to the question of OT meter and precisely the problem of how lines and their cola are measured. Discussion of the problem has been delayed for two reasons: (1) The problem at present cannot be resolved in a completely satisfactory way and probably never will be. (2) Experience trying to introduce students to the nature of the OT line has taught me that beginning students become so concerned with this problem that they fail to see the forest for the trees; i.e., a good deal that is solidly based in the text can be said about the OT line without even referring to the specifics of this problem.

The root of the difficulty is that the metrical question is ultimately a question of OT Hebr phonology, and books can be written about what is not known on the subject—as is true for other dead languages. The question is further complicated by the fact that when it was a living language OT Hebrew was written basically without vowels, though some consonants were eventually used in a secondary function to mark some vowels. The full vowel notation and accents of modern masoretic Bibles are ultimately the product of the work of scribes (masoretes) between the 6th and 10th cents. AD attempting to set guides for the proper cantillation of the text in the synagogue service. This had an undoubted leveling effect on the language, which explains the limited attempts to write grammars of Biblical Hebrew that distinguish, e.g., Old, Middle, and Late, as is done for other comparable languages of the ancient Near East spanning a millennium (or more). Only in a quite limited fashion can such distinctions be drawn. Biblical Hebrew is basically the dialect of the Tiberian masoretes. Though this dialect is undoubtedly a continuation and an approximation of more ancient pronunciations, it can be doubted that Dt-Isa would even understand Isa 40:1–8 read back to him by a 10th-cent. AD masorete or in any of the current pronunciations of the text. The problem here is not just individual words; it extends to sentence intonation, which is an important consideration in metrics. There is the further question to what extent original verse compositions have been transformed or modernized by scribes in the course of the long period of transmission.

17   There are three prominent views now current of how the Hebrew line was measured: (1) accents were counted; (2) syllables were counted; (3) there is no measure. This last view, nonetheless, recognizes that characteristic of the line are the short sentences dealt with above—implicitly, at least. The first point of view is the more widespread, though the second and third have received recent support in English-language treatments of the question.

The third view I regard as untenable. OT poets simply do not create bicola where the balanced cola contain 25 words each. When a series of bicola are laid out stichometrically on the printed page, they present an evenness that demands an explanation and that this nihilist view cannot explain—even if this evenness is a by-product of meter as articulated, not its essence.

The second point of view is essentially that of two prominent U.S. scholars, F. M. Cross and D. N. Freedman, and circles influenced by them. It should be noted that Cross's and Freedman's views are not the same. Freedman rigidly uses masoretic syllabication (a factor not always so clear as is sometimes assumed) to show that balanced cola and lines contain relatively equal syllable counts. This might well be expected in any case from such balanced cola and lines. He does not claim that syllable counting is the basis of the metrical system. Cross and others who follow him, with certain caveats and allowing room for accompanying controlled accent counts, do—at least, it is a basis for an OT verse system in the poetry they analyze this way. Essentially this form of the syllable-counting analysis claims that the balanced cola of the bicola have equal syllable counts (6 + 6; 8 + 8; 9 + 9; etc.). The system also recognizes the *qînâ* meter (→ 19 below) with the relatively consistent use of unbalanced cola (7 + 6; 7 + 5; etc.).

It is impossible to present or critique fairly in a few sentences this analysis of Hebr metrics, which is generally carried on with a good deal of philological and text-critical sophistication, but I do not think it will carry the field principally for the following reasons, all of which need to be spelled out in greater detail.

18   First of all, the syllable counters do not seriously pose the question: why are 9 + 9 syllables in the balanced cola permitted, but 35 + 35 syllables not permitted? Everyone admits that balanced bicola can contain a balanced syllable count. But is that the basis of the system or is it the fallout from the system? I think the first question suggests the latter possibility.

Second, it may be questioned whether the syllable counters can present an adequate text in which to count syllables. The analysis, though it modifies the vocalization of the Tiberian dialect in some respects, is essentially wedded to it. It notes that there are developments in Tiberian Hebrew which are properly late (e.g., *'ebed,* "servant," two syllables; but in earlier LXX transcriptions *'abd,* one syllable). Lists (hardly systematic—the evidence is not available) are drawn up of these late developments and a basically univocal Biblical Hebrew dialect is derived which is presumed to have spanned a millennium. The fundamental evenness of this dialect, for present purposes particularly in the area of syllabication, strains credibility.

I suppose it can be presumed that there existed in every period as many modifications in the area of syllabication of the postulated, basically proto-Canaanite, proto-Hebrew forms which become the basis for this constructed dialect as can be catalogued in the Tiberian dialect. The claim that syllables can be counted exactly in pre-Tiberian Hebrew rests on shaky grounds. It may well be granted that the counts are approximations. But that will not do. This analysis simply demands precise counts. This is the explanation for the lesser claims Freedman makes for his syllable counts.

It has been suggested that the syllable counters are asking questions that simply are too refined to permit serious answers based on real evidence. But simply correcting dialectal modernizations in the text still does not supply the syllable counters with the counts they need. Strategies must be developed to even off unbalanced cola. The syllable counters note that particles like *'et* (mark of accusative), the conjunction "and," the relative, the article, etc. are used more consistently in prose than poetry. That is true. These can be freely excised as prosaic pluses from any metrical text to balance the syllable count. Most of the time this does not make much difference, but sometimes it does, as when "and" is removed from in front of finite verb forms involving a change of tense. Another strategy is to isolate lines artificially when this helps discover syllabically balanced cola. Both strategies will be illustrated in the discussion below.

The possibility of adjusting syllable counts is further enlarged by serious text criticism. It is certain that there was an original text and that in the course of transmission, in the OT period and after, the text was modified in many ways, some major, some minor, catalogued in part in doublets in the Hebr Bible, the Qumran manuscripts, and the evidence of the versions. But I have serious doubts that picking and choosing among the various forms of a specific Hebr line guided by the hypothesis of balanced syllable counts in the cola of a bicolon will get us closer to the original. This is a new version of corrections *metri causa* of a previous age that has been discredited. Above it was argued that an understanding of the Hebr verse system ought to be presumed right into the beginnings of the Christian era. The old Hebr line was written; consequently it was understood. In this period we have manuscript evidence (Qumran) and the LXX witnessing to line types that the syllable counters correct to balance syllables. This suggests that a balanced syllable count was not a requirement for a Hebr line.

An example of the syllable-counting approach to a text will be helpful. The *textus receptus* of Exod 15:1 presents us with:

> I will sing to the Lord
>   for he is highly exalted;
> Horse and its rider
>   he has cast into the sea.

I would prefer to read this as a single bicolon instead of two lines or as a three-sentence tricolon. Either arrangement better reflects sentence structure and the sense stops. The bicolon is probably better. The weighted internal stop is after "exalted" and that produces cola of more clearly balanced length. For the sake of the argument I leave the arrangement, which is an obvious stratagem to ease the application of the syllable-balancing hypothesis. The syllable count is 6 + 5, 5 + 4. What can be done to get syllable balance? In the second line "its rider" is changed to "rider" with versional evidence to give 4 + 4 (I would prefer for reasons of sense "chariot," 3 + 4). In the first line "I will sing" is changed to "I shall sing" with "Sing (pl.)!" also allowed. This produces 5 + 5. There is versional evidence for "let us sing" (6 + 5). It should be noted that all these changes in the unvoweled texts are minuscule; and every one of these line variants makes sense. I would regard all of the forms of the Hebr lines involved as scannable and suppose that we get numerous slight variations like these in many lines precisely because they were equally scannable. If a rigid system of syllable counting were involved there would be far fewer variants. The scribes, who presumably understood the system at least up till the turn of the era, would have used it to control what they copied.

The hypothesis can, of course, be formed that there was an earlier line form, later forgotten, that used syllabically balanced cola as its basis. But the real evidence for that is a considerable number of bicola manufactured with considerable ingenuity by a variety of stratagems. That seems to me, at least, to undermine seriously this solution to the metrical problem presented by the Hebr line.

19   The third system for measuring Hebr lines is the counting of sentence accents. It is a system that can be and is used for measuring not only Hebr verse, with its vowels supplied by the Tiberian masoretes, but also Egyptian and Ugaritic verse, where the vowels are in general not indicated, and Akkadian poetry, where they are. Akkadian verse with the vowels indicated can at times produce syllabically balanced bicola, but that is certainly not the system. The accentual analysis presumes that the number of accents in a colon or line is controlled and the relation of the number of unaccented syllables to accented varies in accord with the normal speech patterns of the individual language. The system is similar to that in Coleridge's *Christabel:*

> 'Tis the middle of the night by the castle clock,
> And the owls have awakened the crowing cock,
> Tu-whit! — Tu-whoo!
> And hark again! the crowing cock.

The number of sentence accents in each line is carefully controlled, four. The number of syllables varies from twelve to four. The meter here is an imitation of the earliest English poetry and has analogues in "primitive" verse in numerous languages. In *Christabel,* of course, everyone is immediately aware of the meter, the repeated grouping of units of four prominent, accented syllables made obvious by stops.

That is because every speaker of English has learned from years of experience how to intone an English sentence. The problem in applying this system of analysis to dead languages is that we do not know how to intone the sentences and native informants do not and will never exist. Analysts just have to guess. Consequently, it comes as no surprise that accent counters can assign variant counts to the same line, e.g., 3 + 3 and 3 + 2. The rule of thumb is to regard as unaccented, small or relatively unimportant words. They form sentence-accent units with the accented, important words. For

example, the opening line of *Christabel:*

> 'Tis the middle / of the night / by the castle / clock.
> oo6o   / oo6   / oo6o   / 6

Some hint of this process of unaccented syllables grouping around accented ones in a sentence is given by the masoretic cantillation marks, though these cannot be followed blindly. They served the purpose of marking out the tune for synagogue chant. Deut 32:1, e.g., is read by both the masoretes and modern accent counters as 3 + 3:

> Give ear, O heavens, while I speak;
> let the earth hearken to the words of my mouth.

The English sentence accents here are 3 + 4.

Individual Hebr cola are generally thought to contain from two to four sentence accents and are combined in various ways. The 3 + 3 line is the most common. But mixed meter is also common. For example, my count of Isa 40:1–8 is: 3 + 2, 3 + 2, 2 + 2, 3 + 3, 2 + 3 + 4, 2 + 3, 3 + 2, 3 + 3 + 3, 3 + 3, 2 + 3, 4 + 4(+ 3), 4 + 3. Other poetry produces much more regular counts, e.g., Job, where 3 + 3 predominates. It is understood that all counts are educated guesses. That is unfortunate, but this view has stood the test of time and is still regarded as the more plausible interpretation of the data. It should be noted that in *Christabel* the metrical units are strongly end-stopped. That is a characteristic of this kind of meter that repeats units of balanced accent counts; it is the end-stopping that makes the units obvious. The same is true of OT verse units and ancient Near Eastern verse more generally. It is not difficult to infer from this that the stopping serves the same purpose there.

There is one line form, 3 + 2 in accentual notation, called *qînâ* (lamentation) because it characterizes with some consistency the first four chapters of Lam, though it is not limited to dirges.

20   The question may be asked, how much real difference is there between the three interpretations of the data presented to this point (→ 17 above). For example, Job 3:3:

> Perish the day on which I was born;
> and the night which said, "A boy has been conceived!"

The stichometry of the line is agreed upon by all. It is possible to conclude that the line is a two-sentence bicolon and let the matter rest. It is also possible to attempt to go beyond that and guess that the line has a 4 + 4 accent count (corresponding here to the masoretic accents). Between the first and the third view, the only real difference seems to be that the third refuses to speculate about what controls the shortness of the short sentences — a matter that in fact escapes adequate control.

The genuine differences between the first and the second view are of similar proportions. It is to be remembered that the syllable counters do not deny the possibility of line length measured by accent control. They simply add another control, syllable control. They do this in part because counting syllables is thought to produce more verifiable results. I have attempted to show that syllable counting is not without its perils either. Freedman, counting masoretic syllables, accepts relatively balanced syllable counts. Job 3:3 has a syllable count of 7 + 10 masoretic syllables (7 + 9 when adjusted into the postulated pre-Tiberian dialect). The count falls within the parameters worked out by Freedman for the OT line and cola. But this is no ultimate answer to the metrical question. Granted the regular numerical relation of unaccented syllables to accented ones in a language, accent control of the building blocks of verse will produce this kind of syllable control. In *Christabel* above the lines cited have 8 to 12 syllables, save for the unusual imitation of the hooting owl in line 3, which has 4. The accent counters have no disagreement with Freedman (nor he with them). They simply ask the further question about the ultimate control factor in the measuring of the line and colon. On the basis of verse like *Christabel* and Akkadian poetry, where the vowels are marked and the syllables can be counted rather accurately, they see the ultimate control as accent control.

Cross too allows for accent control; but he also insists on absolute syllabic balance between the cola of a line. The texts to prove this do not exist and various strategies must be developed to lengthen and shorten

cola to fit the hypothesis. This really is not difficult to do when the system works on already roughly balanced cola. It can be done to Job 3:3. The syllable count is $7 + 7$, if "and" and "the" are omitted as prosaic in the second colon (the "and" could also be explained as dittography and "day" in Hebrew lacks the article in the first colon). This approach to Job 3:3 I would regard as adjusting the evidence in defense of a doubtful hypothesis. The accent counters here have a genuine advantage. Their admittedly imprecise system of analysis can account for all the texts.

A kingdom for a tape of Second Isaiah reciting Isa 40:1–8!

13

AMOS

Michael L. Barré

BIBLIOGRAPHY

1 *Commentaries:* Amsler, S., *Amos* (CAT 11a; 2d ed.; Geneva, 1982) 159–247. Hammershaimb, E., *The Book of Amos* (NY, 1970). Mays, J. L., *Amos* (OTL; Phl, 1969). McKeating, H., *The Books of Amos, Hosea, and Joel* (CBC; Cambridge, 1971). Rudolph, W., *Joel—Amos—Obadja—Jona* (KAT 13/2; Gütersloh, 1971). Vawter, B., *Amos, Hosea, Micah* (OTM 7; Wilmington, 1981). Weiser, A., *Das Buch der zwölf Kleinen Propheten I* (ATD 24; Göttingen, 1967). Wolff, H. W., *Joel and Amos* (Herm; Phl, 1977).

Studies: Anderson, B. W., *The Eighth Century Prophets: Amos, Hosea, Isaiah, Micah* (Proclamation Commentaries; Phl, 1978). Coote, R. B., *Amos among the Prophets* (Phl, 1981). Craghan, J. F., "The Prophet Amos in Recent Literature," *BTB* 2 (1972) 242–61. Crenshaw, J. L., "The Influence of the Wise upon Amos," *ZAW* 79 (1967) 42–51. Grosch, H., *Der Prophet Amos* (Gütersloh, 1969). Kapelrud, A. S., *Central Ideas in Amos* (2d ed.;

Oslo, 1961). Koch, K., *Amos untersucht mit den Methoden einer strukturalen Formgeschichte* (AOAT 30; Kevalaer, 1976); *The Prophets I: The Assyrian Age* (Phl, 1982). Mays, J. L., "Words about the Words of Amos," *Int* 13 (1959) 259–72. Reventlow, H. G., *Das Amt des Propheten bei Amos* (FRLANT 80; Göttingen, 1962). Roberts, J. J. M., "Recent Trends in the Study of Amos," *ResQ* 13 (1970) 1–16. Schmidt, W. H., "Die deuteronomische Redaktion des Amosbuches," *ZAW* 76 (1965) 168–93. Smart, J. D., "Amos," *IDB* 1. 116–21. Terrien, S., "Amos and Wisdom," *Israel's Prophetic Heritage* (Fest. J. Muilenburg; ed. B. W. Anderson, et al.; London, 1962) 108–15. Van der Woude, A. S., "Three Classical Prophets: Amos, Hosea and Micah," *Israel's Prophetic Tradition* (Fest. P. R. Ackroyd; ed. R. Coggins, et al.; Cambridge, 1982). Ward, J. M., "Amos," *IDBSup* 21–23; *Amos and Isaiah* (Nash, 1969). Wolff, H. W., *Amos the Prophet* (Phl, 1973).

INTRODUCTION

2 **(I) Amos, the Man and His Times.** Amos is the first of the "classical prophets," the first whose oracles have come down to us in the form of a book. According to 1:1, he was a Judahite, from the small town of Tekoa in the hill country of Judah just S of the Israel-Judah border. The extent of his prophetic career is uncertain. He prophesied at Bethel, one of the main cult centers in the northern kingdom, near the Israel-Judah border (7:10–17), and perhaps elsewhere as well (Samaria? cf. 4:1–3). The superscription (1:1) dates his activity to the reigns of Uzziah of Judah (783–742) and Jeroboam II of Israel (786–746). By trade he was a breeder of livestock (Hebr *nōqēd* [1:1] suggests sheep, whereas *bōqēr* [7:14] suggests cattle). In addition to this he was a "tender of mulberry figs" (7:14), whose job was to puncture the immature fruit to make it turn sweet. This work must have taken him away from his native Tekoa, which is too high to support the growth of these trees. In recent years interest has centered on his connections with the cult and with the wisdom tradition. H. G. Reventlow (*Amt*) believes he was a cultic prophet and sees his ministry rooted in the covenant renewal festival. Though Amos undoubtedly prophesied at cult centers

(7:10–14) and was familiar with cultic language (4:4; 5:4–5,14), his precise relationship to the cult has not been established. S. Terrien ("Amos and Wisdom") pointed to the close relationship between the "wisdom tradition" and the prophet, a position carried further by H. W. Wolff (*Amos the Prophet*). Yet all one can safely conclude is that Amos was quite familiar with the folk wisdom of his day (see J. L. Crenshaw, "Influence"). Amos's career took place during a period of great material prosperity for Israel, but also a period of social and religious corruption. Politically, it was the calm before the storm—or rather, between the storms. During the second half of the 9th cent., Israel had felt the military might of Assyria. Shalmaneser III (859–825) exacted tribute from Jehu (see *ANEP* 355), as did Adad-nirari III (811–784) from Jehoash. After this, Assyrian power in the area weakened until the rise of Tiglath-pileser III (745–727). In 721 Samaria, the capital of the northern kingdom, fell to the Assyrians. Amos mentions Assyria only once (see comment on 3:9) and alludes to it in 5:27.

3 **(II) Message and Theology.** Four interrelated themes are of central importance in Amos.

(a) *Judgment.* Of all the classical prophets, Amos's message is the least hopeful. Israel's fate—destruction—is certain, inescapable, total. Although Amos never refers directly to the Sinai covenant, this concept lies at the heart of his message of judgment. Yahweh had acknowledged Israel as his covenant people (3:1–2), but they had abused this privilege. Therefore, Yahweh was dissolving the covenant (cf. Hos 1:9) and declaring war on Israel, who had now become his enemy. Like the messages of the other prophets, Amos's harsh words were directed in a particular way against the leadership—king (7:10–11), priests (7:16–17), and upper classes (4:1–3; 6:1). But the coming judgment would affect the entire people, for Israelite thought tends to perceive the nation as a unity, with a common destiny. (b) *Social justice.* A distinctive feature of Israelite religion was the interconnection between the relationship to one's neighbor and to God established by the covenant. The quality of one's relationship to God depended to some extent on how one related to fellow members of the covenant community. At the time of Amos many among Israel's powerful had chosen to ignore this aspect of Israelite religion and to treat the disadvantaged as they wished. Wealthy landowners oppressed the less fortunate, taking over the landholdings of many impoverished Israelites. The prophet expresses Yahweh's distress at the maltreatment of these people (2:7; 4:1; 5:7,11,24; 8:4–6). This indictment forms the ultimate reason for Yahweh's decision to execute judgment on his people. (c) *The cult.* There was no dearth of religious fervor in Israel during this time (5:21–24). Amos mentions major cult centers—Bethel (3:14; 4:4; 5:5,6; 7:10,13), Gilgal (4:4; 5:5), and Dan (8:4)—and at times imitates the language of the cult (4:4–5; 5:4–6,14). Those who disregarded the covenant and took advantage of the poor continued to go through the motions of worshiping the covenant God. Merchants were careful not to do business on days forbidden by divine law (8:4–8). Amos denounces this hypocrisy, at times with bitter irony (4:4–5). Unlike his near-contemporary Hosea, he has little to say on the question of worshiping other gods (see comment on 5:26; 8:14). In his view, the foremost sin involved in the cultic life of Israel was its separation from concern for the neighbor (5:21–24). (d) *The word.* Israel turned a deaf ear to the prophets who reproached them for their disloyalty and even tried to silence them (2:12; 7:12–13). In the eyes of the prophet, this was a particularly grave offense, since it amounted to a rejection of Yahweh himself. The fitting recompense would be a loss of the guiding word of Yahweh (8:11–12).

4   **(III) Outline.** In its present form chaps. 1 and 9 contain a number of parallels, forming an *inclusio* around what was probably an earlier form of the book. Note "(earth)quake" (1:1; 9:1,9); "the top of Carmel" (1:2; 9:3); *'ābal* ("wither" [1:2], "mourn" [9:5]); "Syria(ns) . . . Kir" (1:5; 9:7); "Philistia/Philistines" (1:8;

9:7); and the Temple setting presumed by 1:2 and 9:1ff. The book may be outlined as follows:

- (I) Editorial Introduction (1:1–2)
  - (A) Superscription (1:1)
  - (B) Opening Verse (1:2)
- (II) Oracles against the Nations (1:3–2:16)
  - (A) Damascus (1:3–5)
  - (B) Gaza (1:6–8)
  - (C) Tyre (1:9–10)
  - (D) Edom (1:11–12)
  - (E) Ammon (1:13–15)
  - (F) Moab (2:1–3)
  - (G) Judah (2:4–5)
  - (H) Israel (2:6–16)
- (III) Three Summonses to Hear Yahweh's Word (3:1–5:17)
  - (A) People of Israel (3:1–15)
    - (a) Israel as Yahweh's Covenant Partner (3:1–2)
    - (b) The Source of the Prophetic Word (3:3–8)
    - (c) Evil Samaria and Its Fate (3:9–11 + 12)
    - (d) The Houses of the Wicked (3:13–15)
  - (B) Cows of Bashan
    - (a) Oppression of the Poor (4:1–3)
    - (b) The Cult and Transgression (4:4–5)
    - (c) Litany of Unrepentance (4:6–12)
    - (d) Hymnic Fragment (4:13)
  - (C) House of Israel (5:1–17)
    - (a) Lamentation over Israel (5:2–3)
    - (b) Seeking Yahweh (5:4–6)
    - (c) Hymnic Fragment (5:8–9)
    - (d) Haters of Righteousness (5:7,10–13)
    - (e) Seeking Good (5:14–15)
    - (f) Lamentation over Israel (5:16–17)
- (IV) Three Warnings (5:18–6:14)
  - (A) Warning to Those Who Desire the Day of Yahweh (5:18–20)
  - (B) Israel's Corrupt Worship (5:21–27)
  - (C) Warning to Those Secure in Their Riches (6:1–3)
  - (D) Warning to the Idle Rich (6:4–7)
  - (E) Devastation and Aftermath (6:8–10)
  - (F) The Fruits of Israel's Depravity (6:11–14)
- (V) Five Visions (7:1–9:10)
  - (A) First Vision: Locusts (7:1–3)
  - (B) Second Vision: Fire (7:4–6)
  - (C) Third Vision: Plumb Line (7:7–9)
  - (D) Biographical Interlude (7:10–17)
  - (E) Fourth Vision: Summer Fruit (8:1–3)
  - (F) Pious Hypocrisy (8:4–8)
  - (G) The Day of Darkness (8:9–10)
  - (H) Famine for God's Word (8:11–12 + 13–14)
  - (I) Fifth Vision: Destruction (9:1–4)
  - (J) Hymnic Fragment (9:5–6)
  - (K) Israel and the Nations (9:7–8 + 9–10)
- (VI) Editorial Conclusion (9:11–15)
  - (A) Raising up the Booth of David (9:11–12)
  - (B) Restoration of Israel (9:13–15)

COMMENTARY

5   **(I) Editorial Introduction (1:1–2).**
(A) Superscription (1:1). The book begins with a historical notice, which provides valuable information on Amos's prophetic career. *shepherds:* Cf. 7:14, where a different Hebr word is used. *Tekoa:* A small town 10 mi. S of Jerusalem. *saw:* A standard way of referring to the fact that the prophet's words were revealed to him by God (cf. Isa 1:1; Hab 1:1). *two years before:* Does the time reference indicate that Amos's

ministry took place during the space of a single year? *the earthquake:* Earthquakes are common in this area. This one is referred to in Zech 14:5. Excavations at ancient Hazor have uncovered evidence of a major earthquake in the region datable to *ca.* 760.

(B) Opening Verse (1:2). Most likely, this does not come from Amos (v 2a appears in Joel 3:16; cf. Jer 25:30). It was placed here by the editors to serve as a keynote to the whole book, sounding the leitmotifs of

Yahweh's judgment and his word. *the top of Carmel withers:* Cf. 9:3; Nah 1:4. Carmel was a range of forested hills near modern Haifa, proverbial in ancient times for its lush vegetation (Cant 7:5; Isa 35:2; Jer 48:18). As Yahweh's "roaring" (cf. 3:8) produces catastrophic results in nature, so his prophetic word of judgment achieves its fateful purpose.

6 **(III) Oracles against the Nations (1:3-2:16).** This section consists of eight oracles, each with the same beginning; the body of the oracles is also generally uniform. Some scholars (e.g., Wolff, *Joel and Amos*) deny the authenticity of the oracles against Tyre, Edom, and Judah, which, unlike the others, do not end with "oracle of Yahweh." In the present arrangement the series is climactic, ending with the oracle against Israel (2:6-16). Presumably Amos's Israelite hearers would have listened with delight to the announcement of doom against neighboring nations and even more so to the words against Judah. However, the series does not end with the seventh (Judah), as would be expected. To the surprise of the hearers there is an eighth—the oracle against Israel. The six nations are seen here as members of the Davidic-Solomonic empire (see J. Mauchline, *VT* 20 [1970] 287-303). Yahweh is Lord of these nations (cf. 9:7) by reason of the fact that he is the God of the overlord state (Judah-Israel). As such, any affront to it by these "vassal" kingdoms was an affront to him as well. In this section Yahweh claims that he has had enough of the rebelliousness of these foreign states and intends to destroy them. But the same fate awaits rebellious Judah and Israel. Most likely the oracles against the six nations (and Judah) are merely introductory to the "punch line," which concerns Israel. On this section, see J. Barton, *Amos's Oracles against the Nations* (SOTSMS 6; Cambridge, 1980).

7 **(A) Damascus (1:3-5).** 3. *Damascus:* Capital of Syria (Aram), a kingdom NE of Israel. It had been subjugated by David (2 Sam 8:5-6) but regained its independence in Solomon's time. The city fell to the Assyrians in 732. *for three transgressions . . . four:* This expression refers to the "last straw," a rebellious act on the part of the nation that has exhausted Yahweh's patience. The "transgressions" mentioned here are not so many breaches of international ethics as treaty violations of one member of the ideal Davidic-Solomonic empire against another. *I will not take him back:* Probable translation of this recurrent phrase. Because of one sin too many Yahweh refuses to accept these nations back as "vassals" in good standing; they are now his enemies and he intends to destroy them like a king on a punitive campaign (see M. L. Barré, *JBL* 105 [1986] 611-31). 4. *the house of Hazael:* A short-lived dynasty in Damascus established by Hazael *ca.* 842 (cf. 2 Kgs 8:7-15). The Ben-hadad mentioned here was probably his son (2 Kgs 13:3). 5. *the valley of Aven:* Lit., "the valley of Sin"; it is not clear what geographical area is referred to here. *Betheden:* Lit., "house of pleasure." Probably equivalent to *Bīt-adini*, the Assyrian name of an Aramean city-state between the Euphrates and Balikh rivers, elsewhere simply called "Eden" (Ezek 27:23). There is no connection with the Eden of Gen 2-3. *exile:* The deportation of conquered peoples was practiced by a number of ancient Near Eastern powers, including Urartu, Assyria, and Babylon. This is the first mention of the ominous term in the book, the fate which the prophet foresees for Israel also (5:27; 7:17). *Kir:* 9:7 indicates that the Syrians (Arameans) had migrated from this area to Aram/Syria. Its precise location is unknown, though generally it is thought to be in Mesopotamia. The fate of returning to the place from which they emigrated represents a reversal of their "salvation history"; compare the prophetic

threat of Israel's returning to Egypt (Deut 28:68; Hos 9:3). According to 2 Kgs 16:9 the people of Syria were in fact deported to Kir by Tiglath-pileser.

8 **(B) Gaza (1:6-8).** 6. *Gaza:* The southernmost of five cities that made up the Philistine Pentapolis (Josh 13:3); the others were Ashdod (1:8; 3:9), Ashkelon (1:8), Ekron (1:8), and Gath (6:2). *a whole people:* Or "an ally." In this case the gravity of the crime does not stem from the number of people deported but from the fact that they were allies of Gaza (cf. v 9b). 8. *the remnant:* A term derived from the language of warfare, referring to the survivors after a military defeat (2 Kgs 19:30; 25:11). Cf. 5:3,15.

(C) Tyre (1:9-10). Tyre was a major Phoenician seaport, a city famed for its commerce and wealth (Ezek 28:5-6). The city enjoyed good relations with the united kingdom under David and Solomon, its artisans being employed in the building of Solomon's Temple (1 Kgs 7:13-47). 9b. *the covenant of brothers:* "Brother" was used as a technical term in the Near East for a "treaty/covenant partner" (see M. Weinfeld, *JAOS* 93 [1973] 193). For the treaty relationship between Tyre and the united kingdom, cf. 1 Kgs 5:12.

(D) Edom (1:11-12). 11. *Edom:* Located SE of the Dead Sea, immediately S of Moab, Edom was conquered by David (2 Sam 8:12-14) and periodically revolted against Judahite rule. *and destroyed his ally:* For the translation, see M. Fishbane, *JBL* 89 (1970) 313-18 (*RSV:* "and cast off all pity"). According to Gen 36:1,8 Edom is to be identified with Esau, the brother of Jacob (=Israel); cf. Num 20:14; Deut 2:4; 23:7. 12. *Teman . . . Bozrah:* Two principal cities of Edom, in S and N respectively; thus the two terms form a merism denoting the whole of Edomite territory.

9 **(E) Ammon (1:13-15).** 13. Ammon, E of the Jordan river (modern Jordan), was conquered by Saul (1 Sam 11) and by David (2 Sam 12:26-31). *ripped open pregnant women:* This kind of atrocity was not unknown in ancient Near Eastern warfare (cf. 2 Kgs 8:12; 15:16; Hos 13:16). Still, the "transgression" condemned here is most likely a breach of covenant, the attempt to usurp Israelite territory in Gilead (see M. Fishbane, *JBL* 89 [1970] 318). *Gilead:* An area in the Transjordan between Bashan and Moab, N of Ammon, which remained Israelite territory until the Assyrian conquest. 14. *Rabbah:* The capital city of Ammon, modern Amman.

(F) Moab (2:1-3). The territory of Moab lay S of Ammon, E of the Jordan. David subdued the Moabites, according to 2 Sam 14:47, but they proved to be a troublesome vassal. 1. *burned to lime:* This was an especially grievous act of desecration. In ancient Israel the bones of the deceased were treated with great respect (1 Sam 31:13). According to the canons of Near Eastern international diplomacy, vassal nations were not permitted to engage in aggressive acts toward fellow vassals; disputes were to be settled through the mediatorship of the overlord nation. Hence, though it does not involve Israel directly, even this act was an affront to Yahweh.

(G) Judah (2:4-5). A number of commentators doubt the authenticity of this oracle. The language and style are deuteronomic. 4. In contrast to the charges brought against the nations, Judah's crime is specifically against Yahweh's commandments (i.e., the Sinai covenant). This section leads into the similar set of charges against Israel.

10 **(H) Israel (2:6-16).** The climax of the series. Yahweh affirms that he will not take Israel back as his vassal, any more than he would the other rebellious nations. Israel's transgressions, like Judah's, are not "treaty violations" against other nations but violations of the covenant with Yahweh. The first charges listed concern the relationship to fellow Israelites, specifically the indigent. Like the six nations, Israel has broken the covenant/treaty relationship by actions against a "fellow vassal"—in the Israelite context, one's neighbor. **6.** Cf. 8:6. *sell the innocent:* Being sold into slavery to pay debts was not uncommon in the ancient Near East (cf. 2 Kgs 4:1). Impoverished Israelites fell deeper and deeper into debt to wealthy landowners and finally had to sell their land and even themselves. *for a pair of sandals:* This may mean (1) that to rich Israelites the poor are all but worthless or (2) that the poor are sold for being in debt for a trifling sum (B. Lang, *VT* 31 [1981] 482–88). **7.** *trample:* Cf. 8:4. *a man and his father:* Difficult. The action condemned here is usually considered sexual in nature (see N. M. Broznick, *VT* 35 [1985] 98–99). **8.** Amos skillfully combines the vocabulary of oppression with that of the cult (cf. 5:21–24). It was unlawful to keep overnight the cloak (of a poor person) which had been given as a pledge (Exod 22:26; Deut 24:17). The connection of these actions to cultic places ("altar," "house of their God") is not clear. **9–11.** This review of the saving actions Yahweh wrought for his people contrasts with the record of their ingratitude (vv 6–8,12). **12.** The climax of the charges against Israel is her attempt to obstruct the activities of Israel's sacred functionaries. *the Nazirites:* Holy men, specially dedicated to Yahweh by vow, characterized by an abstinence from alcohol and from cutting the hair (cf. Num 6). They seem to have been charismatic figures who, like prophets, originated in the premonarchical period. *the prophets:* Israel was also guilty of preventing the prophets from uttering Yahweh's word. This is seen as an especially perverse act. Cf. 1:2; 3:8; 7:12–13; 8:11–12. **13.** Difficult; the Hebr vb. occurs only here. **14–16.** The inescapability of Yahweh's judgment is a theme that concludes the book (9:1–4). **16.** *flee:* Forming an *inclusio* with "flight" in v 14, the word usually suggests escape (cf. 9:1); but the only flight for Israel will be from their cities into exile. *naked:* Possibly an allusion to exile; cf. Isa 20:3–4. *in that day:* A reference to "the day of Yahweh," a theme discussed at 5:18–20.

11   (III) Three Summonses to Hear Yahweh's Word (3:1–5:17).

(A) People of Israel (3:1–15).

(a) Israel as Yahweh's Covenant Partner (3:1–2). **2.** *you alone have I acknowledged:* This is probably modeled on "covenant" terminology (compare with Exod 20:2; Hos 13:4) or the language of international diplomacy (see H. B. Huffmon, *BASOR* 181 [1966] 31–37). Israel's relationship to Yahweh is special, though he controls the destinies of other nations as well (9:7). *therefore:* The conclusion is so abrupt that it takes one by surprise—probably purposely. What has to be supplied by the reader is the fact that Israel's unfaithfulness is the cause of Yahweh's judgment.

(b) The Source of the Prophetic Word (3:3–8). Amos poses a series of rhetorical questions dealing with cause and effect, culminating in v 8. The images move from the animal world (vv 4–5) to the human (vv 6–7) and alternate between the auditory and the visual. **7.** This line is in prose and probably represents an editorial expansion on v 6. *disclosing his counsel:* Cf. 4:13. Hebr *sôd* means both "confidential conversation" and "circle of confidants." The OT prophets saw themselves as participating in Yahweh's "council" (*sôd*), i.e., his heavenly court (1 Kgs 22:19–23; Jer 23:18, 22), where they were privy to the deliberations (*sôd*) that went on there. **8.** Note the repetition of "lion," forming an *inclusio* with v 4. The cause–effect series ends with the claim that the prophetic word has Yahweh as its source; it is the ineluctable response to Yahweh's action upon

the prophet (cf. Jer 20:9). On this passage, see S. M. Paul, *HAR* 7 [Fest. R. Gordis] (1983) 203–20.

12   (c) Evil Samaria and Its Fate (3:9–11 + 12). **9.** *Ashdod:* One of the cities of the Philistine Pentapolis (cf. 1:6). It is probably best to read "Assyria" here (cf. LXX), which in Hebrew appears similar to "Ashdod." This reading provides a better parallel to "Egypt" (cf. Hos 7:11; 9:3; 11:5[LXX],11; 12:1) and makes better sense in the context. The passage calls upon these great world powers, themselves not inept at "oppression," to come to Samaria and be shocked by the scale of oppression there. **12.** An independent oracle, perhaps joined to vv 9–11 by the catchword "Samaria" (vv 9,12). The point is that if there is any "rescue" of Israel from her divinely appointed fate it will be like the "rescue" of a half-eaten sheep from the predator's mouth—i.e., no rescue at all!

(d) The Houses of the Wicked (3:13–15). The key word here, "house," is repeated five times in this short passage ("Bethel" = "house of El"). The people as a whole ("house of Jacob"), the temples ("Bethel"), and the luxurious houses of the nobility will all fall under Yahweh's judgment. The theme of otiose luxury at the expense of the poor is continued in the next section. **14.** *the altars of Bethel:* The fulfillment of this prediction is found in the vision of 9:1. Bethel (cf. 4:4; 5:5,6; 7:10,13) was a sacred site a few miles from Judah's northern border associated with the patriarch Jacob (Gen 28:10–22); later it was one of the centers of the tribal league. After the split of the kingdom, Jeroboam I made it one of the two major sanctuaries and set up a golden calf there (1 Kgs 12:26–33). **15.** *winter house . . . summer house:* Royalty during this period had several residences, used according to variations in the climate. The wealthy of Israel followed their example. See S. M. Paul, *VT* 28 (1978) 397–400. *houses of ivory:* Archaeology has turned up elaborate ivory panels or screens used in the rich houses of Samaria (cf. *ANEP* 129–30). Cf. the "beds of ivory" in 6:4.

13   (B) Cows of Bashan (4:1–13).

(a) Oppression of the Poor (4:1–3). **1.** *cows of Bashan:* Bashan was a land E of the Sea of Galilee and N of Ammon. It was famous for its fine livestock, esp. cattle (Deut 32:14; Ps 22:12; Ezek 39:18). The women of Samaria are like them in their pampered contentment. They oppress the poor not by unjust practices (as their husbands do) but by their demand to be supported in a luxurious lifestyle of feasting and self-indulgence. **2.** Difficult. The verse refers to some means by which the people will be deported (*RSV:* "hooks . . . fishhooks"). Most likely the reference is to fisherman's baskets, which were used to pack and transport fish overland (S. M. Paul, *JBL* 97 [1978] 183–90). **3.** *every one straight ahead (of the other):* This pictures the women being led out of the conquered city single file, which corresponds to the Assyrian practice of deportation. The "breaches" are the gaps in the city wall made by the besieging army. *Harmon:* Difficult. D. N. Freedman and F. I. Andersen identify the site with modern Hermel (cf. Ugaritic *hrnm*), near Kadesh on the Orontes (*BASOR* 198 [1970] 41). Many commentators read "(Mt.) Hermon" here, a high peak in the Antilebanon range, in the territory of Bashan (cf. 4:1).

(b) The Cult and Transgression (4:4–5). Amos portrays Israelite worship as rife with "transgression" (cf. 2:6; 3:14; 5:12). **4.** In mocking tones, suggestive of the style of priestly exhortation, he invites the people to worship at the major shrines of Bethel and Gilgal. Their abundant offerings amount to so much "transgression," because they are substitutes for hearing and obeying the word of Yahweh. Cf. Mic 6:6–8, where the Judahite prophet similarly makes use of ritual language to mock the view that Yahweh can be bought off with sacrifices. *Gilgal:* Located near Jericho, this was the site where the Israelites first encamped after crossing the Jordan (Josh 4:19). **5.** *indeed, thus do you love:* Or "for so you love to do" (*RSV*). The people "love" Yahweh, i.e., show their covenant loyalty to him, by ritual actions; but as far as Amos is concerned, to love Yahweh means to "love good" and abhor what is wrong in his sight (5:14). On this passage, see W. Brueggemann, *VT* 19 (1969) 385–99.

14 (c) LITANY OF UNREPENTANCE (4:6–12). In the hope of turning them to repentance, Yahweh lists a climactic series of judgments wrought against Israel — but to no avail. At first only crops are directly affected (vv 6–9); then plague strikes humans and beasts (v 10); finally, the people are "overthrown." The refrain ("but you did not come back to me") contains the same vb. that is used in the refrain in chaps. 1–2 ("I will not take him back"). **6–7.** These first two judgments in the past involve famine (v 6) and thirst (v 7). Later Yahweh will threaten a different type of famine and thirst — the absence of his word in Israel (8:11–12). **11.** *I overthrew you:* The same verb is found in the traditional accounts of the destruction of Sodom and Gomorrah (Gen 19:21,25[J],29[P]). **12.** Difficult. The punishment is surprisingly vague and colorless ("such and such will I do to you") and is apparently based on the common curse formula, "May Yahweh do such and such to X and more if . . ." (Ruth 1:17; 2 Sam 3:9,35; 20:13; 1 Kgs 2:23). Possibly part of the text has been lost (Mays, *Amos* 81). *prepare to meet your God!:* Most likely this refers to "meeting" Yahweh on the battlefield (cf. 1 Sam 17:48); for Israel has now become Yahweh's enemy and must face him as a foe.

(d) HYMNIC FRAGMENT (4:13). The first of three hymnic segments (5:8–9; 9:5–6), probably derived from the cult. Some believe that they are all from the same hymn. The position of each is carefully related to Yahweh's word of judgment: (a) 4:13 comes at the conclusion of a rehearsal of past acts of judgment that went unheeded; (b) 5:8–9 occurs in the center of a section (5:1–17) bracketed by lamentations (vv 1–3,16–17) over doomed Israel; (c) 9:5–6 comes at the end of the climactic vision of Yahweh's destruction of the temple (Bethel?) in 9:1–14. The hymns speak of his majestic power at the creation. Since creation for the Israelites would bring to mind Yahweh's defeat of the powers of chaos, these sections serve to underscore the certainty of the defeat of his enemies — among whom Israel must now be listed. Note the vocabulary connections between these sections and the visions (cf. 7:1,4). **13.** *and declares his thought to humankind:* Cf. the similar connection between God's action in nature and the revelation of his will in Ps 147:15–19. An allusion to the role of the prophets may be intended here (cf. 3:7). *Yahweh, God of hosts:* This title (cf. 3:13; 5:14,16,27; 6:8,14; 9:5) refers on one level to the cosmic supremacy of Yahweh ("hosts" = "heavenly hosts" or stars) and on another to his power as the great warrior ("hosts" = "armies"). Yahweh, the creator of the cosmos, will turn his power against his sinful people to destroy them.

15 (C) House of Israel (5:1–17). A number of studies of this section have appeared in recent years, many arguing for its unity. It appears to have a chiastic structure (J. de Waard, *VT* 27 [1978] 170–77): note the sections on lamentation (vv 2–3,16–17) enclosing sections on "seeking" (vv 4–6,14–15).

(a) LAMENTATION OVER ISRAEL (5:2–3). The lament is cast in a metrical pattern called *qînâ*, which was apparently a standard type of "lamentation" (cf. v 1) in

Israel. **2.** *virgin Israel:* Or "Maiden Israel." Israel is likened to a young girl as yet unmarried; the image evokes her vulnerability and the tragedy of her untimely demise. Cf. "Virgin Daughter Zion" in the Judahite prophets.

(b) SEEKING YAHWEH (5:4–6). **4.** *seek me and live:* Cf. v 6. Again Amos imitates the language of the cult (cf. 4:4–5). Israelites believed that whoever "sought" Yahweh, i.e., visited and worshiped at his sanctuaries, would be blessed with long life. But Amos empties the expression of its normal meaning by forbidding the people to visit these holy places (v 5). See comment on vv 14–15. **5.** *Beer-sheba:* Located in the Negeb desert (thus in Judahite territory), this city was associated with the patriarch Abraham (Gen 21:25–33). The empire of David supposedly stretched from Dan to Beer-sheba (2 Sam 17:11; 24:2). In Amos's time it was an important religious center. *Gilgal:* Prophetic literature has many examples of wordplay (Isa 5:7b; 7:9b; Hos 8:9; Amos 6:13; 8:2). Although this literary device strikes readers in our culture as humorous (the "pun"), in Israel it may have served to keep the listeners' attention. Here Amos plays on the name "Gilgal": *haggilgāl gāloh yigleh*, "Gilgal will certainly go into exile."

(c) HYMNIC FRAGMENT (5:8–9). **8.** *who creates the waters:* Lit., "names the waters. . . ." Cf. 9:6b. **9.** Difficult. Some have suggested that more heavenly constellations are mentioned here, continuing the thought of v 8.

(d) HATERS OF RIGHTEOUSNESS (5:7,10–13). This unit was broken up by the insertion of the hymnic section. **7.** *you who turn justice to wormwood:* Cf. 6:12. This whole section is addressed to those in charge of administering justice in Israelite society. They have turned the judicial system into a bitter pill for the poor, whose wrongs they refuse to redress. **10.** Continues the thought of v 7. *who hate:* Lit., "they hate." Relative clauses in Hebrew are usually in the 3d pers. *in the gate:* Cf. vv 12b,15a. The city gate in ancient Palestine was the place where justice was administered. The sense of v 10 is that the unrighteous rich despise the established institutions of justice because these restrict their ability to defraud the poor. **11a.** A reference to the extortion of the poor man, turning him into a tenant farmer. **13.** *the prosperous will wail:* Probable translation; the Hebr word for "be silent" (*RSV*) can also mean "wail," "mourn." See J. J. Jackson, *ZAW* 98 (1986) 34–35.

16 (e) SEEKING GOOD (5:14–15). These lines may be Amos's "commentary" on the expression "Seek me [Yahweh] and live" in v 4 (see A. V. Hunter, *Seek the Lord!* [Baltimore, 1982] 79). They are the most hopeful lines in the book (but see comment on vv 16–17). **14.** For Amos, "seeking Yahweh" in the conventional cultic sense (cf. vv 4–6) was not enough. Israel had to seek (to do) good, i.e., to live righteously. Only in this way could God be "with" Israel, i.e., on Israel's side (cf. Ps 46:8,12). As things stand, Yahweh is "against" Israel (5:18–20; 9:4) and will come against Israel as an enemy. **15.** *love good:* This is the kind of "love" Yahweh desires from his people — contrast 4:4–5. *perhaps:* The OT recognizes God's freedom to forgive or not, even if sinners change their ways; cf. 1 Sam 6:5; 1 Kgs 20:31; Zeph 2:3. It is not something automatic, as "seek me and live" might suggest.

(f) LAMENTATION OVER ISRAEL (5:16–17). If vv 14–15 seem to sound a rare note of hope in Amos, the conclusion to this section nullifies it. By bracketing 5:1–17 with lamentations, the editors make judgment Yahweh's last word. **17.** *I will pass through your midst:* This could allude to Yahweh's passing through Egypt in the plague of the firstborn (Exod 12:12). M. J. Hauan (*HTR* 79 [1986] 337–48) takes it as a reference to a covenant ritual, meaning that God will cut Israel in half and pass between the two parts (cf. Jer 34:17–20). Cf. 7:8; 8:2, where Yahweh promises that he will never again "pass by" Israel.

17   (IV) Three Warnings (5:18–6:14). J. J. M. Roberts has recently demonstrated that the oracles in this section are not woe oracles as is frequently claimed; rather the particle *hôy* is used to get the hearer's attention (*Understanding the Word* [Fest. B. W. Anderson; ed. J. T. Butler, *et al.*; JSOTSup 37; Winona Lake, 1986] 155–56).

(A) Warning to Those Who Desire the Day of Yahweh (5:18–20). 18. *the day of Yahweh:* An unspecified date in the future when Yahweh would decisively defeat his enemies. The concept may derive from the language of "holy war." Israel assumed that because Yahweh's enemies were the same as Israel's that day would be one of rejoicing. But Israel too, by breaking the covenant, has become his enemy. The concept also appears in the phrase "on that day" (2:16; 8:3,9,13); cf. also "at that time" (5:13).

(B) Israel's Corrupt Worship (5:21–27). This section consists of two subsections (vv 21–24, 25–27); the common thread is the theme of sacrifices (vv 22,25). **21–24.** This strong language should not be taken as an outright rejection of the Israelite cult in principle. The prophet uses a literary device known as "dialectic negation" here, in which one aspect (here worship) is strongly negated in order to give emphasis to the other (here righteousness, v 24); cf. Hos 6:6. Israel's worship displeases Yahweh because it is offered as a substitute for the demands of the covenant. **25–27.** These verses may be a later addition, reflecting cultic practices after Amos's time. **25.** For the view that Israel did not offer sacrifices during the wilderness period, cf. Jer 7:22. **26.** *Kaiwan:* Probably the name of a deity, which scribes have distorted by changing the vowels (see comment on 8:14). It derives from an Akkadian name for the planet Saturn (Akk *kayyamānu,* "steady," "constant"). Many commentators also take Hebr *skwt* in this verse as another name for this god ("Sakkuth"); but this is more problematic. **27.** *beyond Damascus:* I.e., to Assyria or the Assyrian provinces north of Damascus.

18   (C) Warning to Those Secure in Their Riches (6:1–3). 1. *in Zion:* The reference to Zion (Jerusalem) has caused some commentators to see this as a later addition, since Amos' ministry was to Israel, not Judah. But the prophets held on to the ancient vision of a united kingdom. Hence, they did not feel that their words were necessarily restricted to Israel or Judah. **2.** *Calneh . . . Hamath:* Two city-states N of Israel (cf. Isa 10:9). The point of the oracle is that these once proud kingdoms have been overthrown or at least stripped of their independence. Will Israel's fate be any different? A historical problem here is that neither state seems to have been conquered (by Assyria) until 738, sometime after the traditional dating of Amos's prophecy. *Gath:* See comment on 1:6. Gath lies SW of Israel, in Judahite territory. It was captured by the Syrians late in the 9th cent.

(D) Warning to the Idle Rich (6:4–7). 4–6. The evil of the life of pleasure described here is not the self-indulgence itself so much as the refusal to notice or care about what has happened to Israel ("Joseph" in v 6). **6.** David became proverbial for his musical skill (2 Sam 23:1), but not for inventing musical instruments. Read with D. N. Freedman, "and like David improvise . . . on musical instruments" (*Bible Review* 1 [1985] 48–51). **7.** As the idle rich have been first in the receiving line of Israel's bounty, it is fitting that they be the first to experience deportation.

19   (E) Devastation and Aftermath (6:8–10). 8. *the pride of Jacob:* Although the Hebr word can mean "arrogance" (Jer 13:9), here it is part of a fixed expression that usually has a positive meaning (cf. 8:7; Ps 47:5).

It may be an epithet of the northern kingdom. **9–10.** This section contains a number of difficulties. In the present context it provides a striking illustration of Yahweh's threat to deliver up (for deportation) everyone in the city. The term "house" (v 9) connects it to the following section (cf. v 13). **9.** Cf. 5:13. **10.** Difficult. The scene appears to be one of terrible desolation, with hardly enough people left to remove the dead from the houses. The prohibition against mentioning (or possibly, "swear[ing] by") Yahweh's name is puzzling. Perhaps it comes from a fear that the name would evoke more devastation.

(F) The Fruits of Israel's Depravity (6:11–14). 12. The two questions are meant to point up the depravity of Israel's behavior, which has perverted justice and righteousness, the foundation of human society. *do they plow the sea with oxen?:* MT: "Do they plow with oxen?" The question makes no sense. Dividing one Hebr word gives "the sea with oxen." **13.** *Lodebar:* Cf. 2 Sam 9:4; 17:27. Apparently a variant of the place-name Debir, a Gadite city (Josh 13:26). The reference is to rejoicing over an Israelite victory against Syria. Amos mocks the emptiness of this boast by punning on the name of the city — Hebr *lōʾ dābār* means "nothing" (cf. 3:7). *Karnaim:* The name literally means "horns," a Hebr metaphor for strength. The warriors of Israel boast that by their own strength they have taken strength itself! **14.** The nation that Yahweh is raising against Israel (i.e., Assyria) will tyrannize Israel from one end to the other. Cf. 1 Kgs 8:65; 2 Kgs 14:25.

20   (V) Five Visions (7:1–9:10). The book concludes with a series of visions. The structure of the first part of visions 1 through 4 is identical: God shows the prophet something, asks what he sees, and then explains the significance of what is seen (cf. Jer 1:11–12). In the first two visions Yahweh relents because of the prophet's intercession. But in the third, fourth, and fifth, punishment is certain. The fifth vision forms a climax to the series and to the book itself (in its earlier form).

(A) First Vision: Locusts (7:1–3). 2. Intercession was thought to be an aspect of the prophetic office (Jer 15:1; 27:18); as the prophet was the mediator of God's words to the people, he also mediated their prayers to God.

(B) Second Vision: Fire (7:4–6). 4. *creating:* Lit., "naming," the same word used in the hymnic fragments (5:8; 9:6). *a rain of fire:* Difficult; lit., "a judgment by fire." By redividing the two Hebr words one can obtain the reading given above (D. R. Hillers, *CBQ* 26 [1964] 221–25).

(C) Third Vision: Plumb Line (7:7–9). 7. *standing beside a wall of lead:* Difficult. Note 9:1, where Yahweh is "standing beside/on" the altar. Some think the words "of lead" result from scribal error; others believe the Hebr word means "tin." **8.** *a plumb line:* Lit., "(a piece of) lead." Many commentators take this as an image of testing (cf. Isa 28:17). But plummet and line were also used in the demolition that preceded repairs (Lam 2:8; Isa 34:11; 2 Kgs 21:13); hence, it could be a symbol of destruction here.

21   (D) Biographical Interlude (7:10–17). This section was placed here by the editors probably because of the terms "Jeroboam" and the "sword" in v 9b (cf. vv 10,11a) and the reference to the "sanctuaries of Israel" (cf. "Bethel" in v 10). The priest's words to Amos are loaded with contempt. **12.** *seer:* An obsolete term for a prophet (1 Sam 9:9), which may have had insulting overtones. *eat your bread:* I.e., earn your living. The mention of Judah stresses Amos's status as a foreigner; as such he is interfering in Israelite political and religious affairs. **14.** → 2 above. *I am not a prophet:* Perhaps the most discussed verse in Amos. It is best understood as countering Amaziah's charge that Amos was nothing more than a prophet-for-hire. Note 3:8, which implies that Amos does "prophesy." *nor a son of a prophet:* One who belonged to "guilds" of prophets, known in Israel from the early days of the monarchy (1 Kgs 20:35; 2 Kgs 2:3,5,7,15; 4:1,38). Amos is thus denying any relationship to the "professional" prophets. His prophetic activity is not his choosing but is based on Yahweh's choosing him. **15.** Cf. 2 Sam 7:8; Ps 78:70–71 (in reference to Yahweh's choice of David). *go, prophesy:* The priest's command, "Go . . . do not prophesy" (vv 12–13), is a direct contradiction of Yahweh's words to the prophet. **17.** *an unclean land:* I.e., a foreign land. Dying in an "unclean" land would be a particularly distasteful fate to a priest, who is supposed to preserve ritual purity.

(E) Fourth Vision: Summer Fruit (8:1–3). The meaning of the vision depends on a play on words: Hebr *qais* means "end-of-the-season (summer) fruit" and *qēs* means "end." Cf. the wordplay in Jer 1:11–12.

(F) Pious Hypocrisy (8:4–8). 4–5. Cf. 2:6–7. **5.** *the new moon:* No work was permitted on this day (cf. Lev 23:24). *make the ephah large:* The excavation at Tirzah, the earlier capital of Israel, has brought to light the use of several sets of weights. The prophet condemns those who scrupulously observe holy days while practicing injustice against their neighbor. **8.** In the Hebr view, evil literally polluted the land. Here the land itself quakes (cf. 1:1) as a result of human sin (vv 4–6). The reference to the Nile is an odd simile for the quaking of the land, since its rise and fall are hardly sudden or violent. Cf. 9:5b.

22   **(G) The Day of Darkness (8:9–10). 9.** Amos had already characterized the Day of Yahweh as a day of "gloom without brightness" (5:20). Note the reference to Yahweh's power over light and darkness in the hymnic fragment in 5:8. **10.** *sackcloth . . . baldness:* Two common signs of mourning. The bereaved showed their grief by going about in rough garb (Gen 37:34; Lam 2:10) and even by shaving their heads (Isa 15:2; 22:12; Ezek 7:18).

(H) Famine for God's Word (8:11–12 + 13–14). 11–12. Because Israel has refused to heed Yahweh's word, spoken through his prophets, he threatens an appropriate punishment—the complete cessation of the divine word in Israel. This word was important to the nation not only in the religious realm but in the political as well. Without it—at least in theory—it would be impossible to select new leaders, to know when to wage war, etc. **12.** *wander:* Cf. 4:8. *from sea to sea:* I.e., from the Mediterranean (W) to the Red Sea (S), balancing "from north to east." **13–14.** This section may be a later addition, originally independent of vv 11–12, reflecting a period (after the Assyrian conquest?) when false gods were worshiped in the major cult centers of Israel. **13.** The word "thirst" provides a connection between the two sections. We hear an echo of 5:2 in "virgins . . . never rise again." **14.** To swear by a particular deity designated one as a worshiper of that god; cf. "those who swear by Yahweh" (Isa 48:1; Jer 12:16; Zeph 1:5–6). *Ashimah of Samaria:* The MT reads *'ašmat,* "the 'guilt' (of Samaria)," probably a deliberate corruption of "Ashimah" (*'ašimat*). This goddess was worshiped by the colonists from Hamath resettled in Samaria by the Assyrians after 721 (2 Kgs 17:30). *by the life of your god(s):* In the ancient Near East oaths were usually taken by the "life" of the god or king. *Dan:* After the split of the kingdom Jeroboam I made Dan and Bethel the two major sanctuaries (1 Kgs 12:26–33). A 3d/2d-cent. BC inscription, recently discovered at Tel Dan, mentions "the god who is in Dan" (J. C. H.

Laughlin, *BARev* 7 [1981] 34). *the "Way" of Beer-sheba:* Difficult. Possibly, "your pantheon, O Beer-Sheba" (F. J. Neuberg, *JNES* 9 [1950] 215–17). The word refers to a pagan god or gods worshiped in Beer-sheba (after 721?).

23   **(I) Fifth Vision: Destruction (9:1–4).** The series of five visions, and the book as a whole, climaxes with this final vision. **1.** *I saw the Lord:* This differs from the introduction to the other visions—"Thus (the Lord Yahweh) showed me"; the change signals the end of the series. In cultic contexts "to see Yahweh" usually had a positive meaning (Pss 42:3; 84:8; Isa 38:11)—to experience the presence of the deity in his Temple. In other contexts it could be life-threatening (Exod 33:20). When Isaiah sees Yahweh in the Temple he fears for his life (Isa 6:5). In the present verse the vision of Yahweh clearly bodes ill. *beside the altar:* Cf. 7:7. The destruction of the altar, a symbol of the Israelite cult itself, is foreshadowed in 3:14. **1b–2.** As in the conclusion to the first series of oracles (2:14–16), the theme is the inescapability of Yahweh's judgment. **3.** *the serpent:* The sea serpent was widely known in ancient Near Eastern mythology and was various called "Leviathan" (Ps 74:14; Isa 27:1), "Rahab" (Ps 89:11; Isa 51:9), "the Dragon" (Ps 74:14), etc. **4.** Even exile is not punishment enough for Israel. *I shall set my eyes upon them:* Ordinarily this expression has a positive meaning (Gen 44:21; Jer 24:6), but not here. The oracle which began with beholding Yahweh ends with Yahweh eyeing his people, likewise with disastrous consequences.

(J) Hymnic Fragment (9:5–6). The last and longest of the hymnic sections (4:13; 5:8–9), incorporating material that appears elsewhere in the book (v 5b = 8:8b; v 6b = 5:8b). **5.** *the Lord, Yahweh of Hosts:* In the other hymnic sections the divine name comes after the description of God's acts of creation. Most likely these words belong to the preceding oracle (vv 1–4); a word such as "says" has probably been lost (cf. 5:27).

(K) Israel and the Nations (9:7–8 + 9–10). Two independent oracles are juxtaposed here, connected by the word "sin-" (vv 8a,10a) and the theme of "the nations" (v 9a). **7.** An extraordinary statement of Yahweh's role in the history of nations other than Israel (cf. 1:3–2:3). Despite the fact that Yahweh has granted a special status to Israel (3:2), Israel is not the only people on earth that Yahweh cares for. Thus, Israel's status should not lead to complacency. *Caphtor:* Probably ancient Crete. The Philistines are associated with Caphtor in Jer 47:4. Known as the "Sea Peoples" in Egyptian records, they are thought to have come from somewhere in the Aegean area. **8a.** Cf. v 4b. **8b.** *except that I will not completely destroy the house of Jacob:* This is a prosaic editorial addition which contradicts v 8a. **9–10.** This oracle picks up the thought of v 4a ("I will command . . . sword"). **9b.** *not a pebble shall fall to the ground:* The purpose of sifting is to let the grain fall through the sieve and to retain what is undesirable (small stones, etc.). The point is that no one in Israel shall escape from this "shaking" (cf. v 1b). **10b.** *disaster shall never come near . . . us:* Following the LXX, with most commentators. Cf. Jer 5:12; Ps 91:10.

24   **(VI) Editorial Conclusion (9:11–15).** The majority of commentators agree that these verses are not part of Amos's message but were added by editors to form the conclusion of the book. The *inclusio* with chap. 1 (→ 4 above) is further evidence for this view. The perspective here seems to be that of the Babylonian Exile, in which the people long to return to their homes and rebuild their lives. Thus, the positive tone of these final verses serves to counterbalance the unrelieved fatalism of Amos's message. The conclusion consists of two sections (vv 11–12,13–15). The opening phrases, "on that day" (v 11) and "behold, days are coming" (v 13) repeat the beginnings of 8:13–14 and 11–12 respectively, where these expressions have an ominous significance. Thus, vv 11–15 may serve to undo these negative predictions of chap. 8, which had long since found fulfillment in the demise of the northern kingdom. This editorial appendix also serves to bring Amos's message into line with that of other classical prophets, for whom judgment was never Yahweh's final word (cf. v 8b).

(A) Raising up the Booth of David (9:11–12). Cited in Acts 15:16–17. **11.** *raise up:* This prophecy reverses Yahweh's statement that fallen Israel would never rise again (5:2; 8:14), since it too is included in the restoration envisioned here. *the fallen booth of David:* A "booth" was a temporary shelter. The reference is probably to the (united) kingdom of David, seen from the perspective of the exile. **12.** The restored kingdom will exercise dominion over its former vassals ("all the nations called by my name"). *remnant of Edom:* The LXX

(cited in Acts 15:17) has "men" instead of "Edom," reading Hebr *'dm* ("man") instead of MT *'dwm* ("Edom").

(B) Restoration of Israel (9:13–15). This section probably refers to the restoration of the entire people, including Judah. It describes what an Israelite would understand as "salvation." **13.** *the mountains shall drip sweet wine:* Cf. Joel 3:18. **14a.** *when I bring back my people Israel:* This idiom (lit., "cause the return to return") denotes primarily the reversal of exile (contrast *RSV:* "restore the fortunes"). Cf. a similar idiom in Ps 126:1. **14b.** Reverses the judgment of 5:11b; note the mention of "build . . . plant . . . vineyards . . . wine" in both passages. **15.** Yahweh promises a time when the people shall return, never to be deported from their land again. Cf. Jer 24:6. *the land I have given them:* Compare the stock expression in the deuteronomic writings, "the land which I am giving you." *says Yahweh your God:* The absence of the phrase "Yahweh your God" elsewhere in Amos supports the view that this section is an editorial addition.

14

HOSEA

Dennis J. McCarthy, S.J. †   *Roland E. Murphy, O.Carm.* *

BIBLIOGRAPHY

1   *Commentaries:* Andersen, F. I. and D. N. Freedman, *Hosea* (AB 24; GC, 1980). Lindblom, J., *Hosea literarisch untersucht* (Åbo, 1927). Mauchline, J., "Hosea," *IB* 6. 551–725. Mays, J. L., *Hosea* (OTL; Phl, 1969). Rinaldi, G., "Osea," *I profeti minori* (LSB 2; Turin, 1960). Robinson, T. H., "Hosea," *Die zwölf Kleinen Propheten* (HAT 1/14; 2d ed.; Tübingen, 1954) 1–54. Sellin, E., *Das Zwölfprophetenbuch* (KAT 12/1; Leipzig, 1929) 6–143. Van Hoonacker, A., *Les douze petits prophètes* (EBib; Paris, 1908). Ward, J. M., *Hosea* (NY, 1966). Weiser, A., "Hosea," *Das Buch der zwölf Kleinen Propheten* (ATD 24–25;

Göttingen, 1956). Wolff, H. W., *Hosea* (Herm; Phl, 1974).

    Studies: Buss, M. J., *The Prophetic Word of Hosea: A Morphological Study* (BZAW 111; Berlin, 1969). Craghan, J. F., "The Book of Hosea: A Survey of Recent Literature on the First of the Minor Prophets," *BTB* 1 (1961) 81–100, 145–70. Emmerson, G., *Hosea* (JSOTSup 28; Sheffield, 1984). Kinet, D., *Baal und Jahwe* (Frankfurt, 1977). Ostborn, G., *Yahweh and Baal* (LUA NF 1,51,6; Lund, 1956). Robinson, H. W., *The Cross of Hosea* (Phl, 1949). Utzschneider, H., *Hosea, Prophet vor dem Ende* (OBO 31; Freiburg, 1980).

INTRODUCTION

2   **(I) Historical Background.** We know nothing of Hosea, son of Beeri, except what we can glean from the book that collects his prophetic speeches. If it is a hazardous undertaking to try to reconstruct the personality of the man and the details of his life through inferences from the material contained in that book, we can at least learn something of his milieu, a factor indispensable for an understanding of his words. He spoke his oracles in the last days of the northern of the two kingdoms into which the Hebrews had divided themselves after the days of Solomon, Israel. We learn that his prophetic activity extended from the prosperous reign of Jeroboam II into the disastrous times that followed thereupon and saw the final disappearance of Israel from the political scene. All this is reflected in his oracles, which gives us the date of their origin, from *ca.* 750 until after 732.

Although Hosea was of Israel and not Judah, the compilers of the book of Hosea significantly ignore the miserable kinglets who followed Jeroboam in their superscription dating the prophet (1:1). They do list their contemporaries in the more stable kingdom of Judah, and well they might; the last days of Israel make a painful tale. The last century of the nation's existence was lived out under the sign of Assyria. After its first

serious thrust into the west in the 9th cent. BC, Assyria, confronted by enemies near to home and governed by a succession of weak kings, was quiescent during the first half of the 8th cent. In this breathing space the dynasty of Jehu was able to establish itself firmly in Israel, and under Jeroboam II (786–746) it expanded the kingdom to its greatest territorial extent and raised it to its greatest heights of material prosperity.

However, Jeroboam's death corresponded closely to the accession of a vigorous king in Assyria, Tiglath-pileser III (745–727). The renewed pressure which that monarch soon applied to the states of Syria and Palestine revealed the hollowness of Israel's power. The political life of the nation deteriorated to a succession of palace revolutions, assassinations, and dynastic changes. In the 20 years between Jeroboam's death and the end of the kingdom six kings reigned in Israel. Jeroboam's son and successor, Zechariah, was assassinated within six months. The murderer, Shallum, was himself slain after but a month by Menahem, who managed to survive from 745 to 738. He was the king who had to accept Assyrian overlordship and pay a heavy tribute (2 Kgs 15:19–20). Pekahiah, son of Menahem, survived two years; then Pekah, at the head of an anti-Assyrian party, murdered him and took over. To the folly of opposing

*R. E. Murphy has revised the *JBC* article of the late Dennis J. McCarthy.

the invincible Assyrian Pekah added the impiety of an alliance with Damascus against the brother kingdom of Judah in an effort to overthrow David's dynasty and impose a king ready to join the anti-Assyrian coalition. However, Ahaz of Judah rejected the advice of the prophet Isaiah and paid tribute to Assyria. Tiglath-pileser was happy to have an excuse to intervene in Palestine and he came to the rescue of his vassal (2 Kgs 16:5–9). Of course the Assyrian conqueror removed Pekah and replaced him by a certain Hoshea, who was to be a loyal vassal to Assyria. The kingdom of Israel itself was shorn of Galilee and Transjordan.

Despite everything, the lesson had not been learned. Eventually Hoshea joined Assyria's enemies after Tiglath-pileser's death. It was the end: he was taken captive, and, after a long siege, the capital, Samaria, was conquered in 722–721. Israel was led into exile and strangers were settled on the land.

3   (II) Doctrine. It is little wonder that the prophet favors the form of a judgment (*rîb*) for his oracles. This violent and ever-changing history is reflected on every page of his book. He condemns the empty pomp of Israel's purely external cult as well as the pride of the people in its wealth and military power. This denial can only reflect Hosea's reaction to the attitudes prevailing during the favored days of Jeroboam II. But he has equally harsh words for the self-seeking and irresponsibility of Israel's kings and leaders, their quarrels and plots, and the never-ending revolutions and changes of government. In fact, he has a fundamental quarrel with the monarchy in Israel, condemning the strong dynasty of Jehu and its weak successors, which many interpret as a rejection of kingship as such. However, the prophet's quarrel is not with the idea of monarchy among the Hebrews; it is with the monarchy of the northern kingdom, which separated the nation from Judah and the legitimate kingship of David, at the same time founding the paganizing sanctuaries of Dan and Bethel.

Hosea alludes to the impious war with Judah (5:8–15). Most of all, he holds up the threat of exile and final destruction, fulfilled to the letter in Israel's last days.

However, the political folly and the anarchy of Israel's last days were not Hosea's chief concern. He knew that they were only symptoms of the fundamental disorder: Israel had forsaken Yahweh, its true king and its salvation, to take up the cult of the fertility gods of Canaan, the Baals, so that it attributed its prosperity to this cult and not to Yahweh. This name "Baal" is actually an appellative meaning "lord" (in our Bible "Lord" is a surrogate for Yahweh that does not mean lord at all); used alone it stands for Hadad, the Canaanite fertility god par excellence, and proclaims the fact that each locality had its own Hadad who was lord of the territory.

The exact character of the Baalism that Hosea reproaches in Israel is complex. There was overt devotion to the pagan Baals—witness the reference to the sin with Baal-peor (9:10–14)—but the more pervasive sin was the contamination of the very cult of Yahweh with Baalism. Yahweh was considered a god of the same kind as the Baals, bound to the land and essentially a purveyor of agricultural plenty. His worship was performed with rites borrowed from the sanctuaries of the Baals—e.g., cultic prostitution—and the thought, the theology, behind it was pure Baalism: the ritual was thought to have the inevitable effect of constraining the divinity in a magical way to give what was desired, i.e., fertility. Such was the religion that Hosea saw around him masquerading as Yahwism, and against this he protested.

He understandably characterized this religion as harlotry (*zĕnûnîm, zĕnût*). Israel had forsaken its true lover to give itself to the Baals. The language is not merely figurative. It does, of course, refer to Israel's spiritual apostasy, but the Baalizing cults included the practice of the grossest sexual abuses, which were not forgotten in the characterization of Israel's attitude as harlotry. This statement, however, does not exhaust Hosea's thought in the matter. He was preoccupied with Israel's apostasy so that "lie" and "falsity" become characteristic words for sin in his vocabulary (cf. 7:1,3; 10:2,13; 11:12; 12:2,8,12). He repeatedly returns to the thought of an Israel that through its history has forgotten again and again the God who saved it from Egyptian slavery, devotedly strengthened it, and made it a nation. Even when the nation has seemed to return to Yahweh, Hosea sees it as lip service, insincere repentance filled with a proud confidence in its own deserts (e.g., 5:15–7:2).

Hosea draws a very clear conclusion: The people that has turned away from its true God, Yahweh, must suffer punishment. It is a juridical penalty announced in a judicial sentence, but it is no mere legal sanction, i.e., a chastisement imposed from without. It is the natural, inevitable outgrowth of the sin. This concept is implied in the nature of the punishments Hosea proclaims. Yahweh will forsake the people who forsook him. Selfish political schemes have as counterpart the destruction of the kingdom and exile, the loss of the national identity. The false cult, pompous and sensual, will give way to a deprivation of the cult altogether. The orgiastic rites aimed at producing plenty—rich crops and the material for feasts—and at fostering reproduction—animal and human—will actually produce famine and barrenness so that the people will die out.

However, these condign punishments are not the only nor even the principal reversal with which Hosea surprises us. Most striking of all and most basic is his transposition of the ideas of the fertility cult. Yahweh is the loving husband of Israel, an idea surely influenced by the *hieros gamos* of Baal. The vocabulary, such as the references to wine, wheat and oil, rain, (sacred) trees, seeking the divinity, etc., is often that of the fertility cult. It is Yahweh, not Baal, who brings rain and thus bread, wine, and oil. Taking over the enemy's strength is a bold and effective procedure (cf. E. Jacob, *RHPR* 43 [1963] 250–59).

4   So far we have seen Hosea's doctrine as negative. It rejects Israel's politics and denies and attacks the current popular form of religion. But it is much more. Again and again Hosea appeals to history, to the evidence that Yahweh has indeed been Israel's savior. The vehicle for this is a formula like "I am Yahweh who brought you out of Egypt," borrowed from the true Yahwist liturgy. Hosea is an eager proponent of Yahwism—one who, guided by the divinely given spirit, explains and develops the contents of Yahweh's revelation that was handed on to the people and kept fresh through its proclamation at the sanctuaries where the liturgy and the teachings of the priests, its custodians, still reflected the true traditions of Yahwism. He demanded a response in which the basic element is *hesed*, "faithful love" (usually "kindness" in *NAB*), i.e., fidelity to Yahweh in obedience to his demands. The word belongs to covenant making; it denotes the disposition which should characterize the true party to a contract. (On covenant in Hos, see D. J. McCarthy, *Bib* 53 [1972] 110–21; and J. Day, *VT* 36 [1986] 1–12.) To us it has a legalistic sound, but *hesed* is no mere matter of courts and rescripts. It does not mean mere justice, *quid pro quo*. True *hesed* is a matter of mind and heart, a true devotion to the covenant partner, an idea brought out by another typically Hosean formula. The true covenant partner has pity (*rhm*) for the other. Our translation is inadequate and misleading; it does not mean sorrowful compassion with its frequent overtone of condescension; rather it means love, a personal devotion eager to help and protect, for ultimately it derives from the attitude of a mother to her child (*reḥem*, "womb").

The richness of Hosea's idea of the true character of covenanted union is best evident in the image peculiarly his own, i.e., the presentation of Yahweh and Israel as husband and wife (chaps. 1–3). His own experience of the marriage union, characterized by a tender, understanding love and an unshakable fidelity despite a tragic mismatch, provides the insight through which he can understand and convey something of Yahweh's union with Israel. He knows beyond any doubt that Yahweh's love is unchanging no matter how the partner breaks faith.

With *ḥesed,* Hosea demands knowledge of Yahweh. We shall see that it has nothing to do with speculation but is an affective and effective relation implying complete readiness to hear and obey God's wish, i.e., attention to Yahweh's commandments (4:2). He is not concerned with cult and politics alone; he calls for a social conscience, right, order, respect for others.

Finally, Hosea holds out hope for the future. Warning and judgment are the heart of his message, but he also promises a future restoration that will finally bring Israel to Yahweh. The use of the word "finally" must not be taken to mean that Hosea presents an explicit and developed eschatology. He promises a restoration without claiming anything like the messianic kingdom of later eschatology. However, he does have the imagery and ideas which will be developed into the full eschatological system: a retributive reformation followed by paradisiac peace and a new, everlasting union (covenant) with God (cf. E. Maly, *CBQ* 19 [1957] 213–25).

5   **(III) Authenticity.** We know when Hosea spoke and what he said—if we have his own words or ideas. How much of the book is authentic? Around the turn of the century, drastic editing was fashionable, and large sections of the text were denied to the prophet. Especially the positive part of his teaching, the promises of restoration (chaps. 11, 14), could not, it was felt, be Hosea's work, for he was said to have preached unrelieved doom. Today scholars have abandoned such fancies. The style of the book of Hosea is homogeneous. Moreover, the prophet's passionate nature permeates the book, and the ideas are consistent. Even the much-attacked promises of restoration are now known to be Hosean. Hope was integral to his doctrine, for the promise of a new and better covenant is inseparably united to the most characteristic portion of the book, the analogy between Yahweh's love for Israel and human marriage. There are, of course, glosses in our text, but they are identified easily enough (e.g., several insertions of the name of Judah, the proverb-like conclusion). Aside from these, it is agreed that the substance of Hos comes from the prophet, which does not minimize the difficult problem of textual corruption; the book of Hosea has suffered more than almost any other OT book in this regard. However, a difficulty in reading a bit of text is no argument against its authenticity.

6   **(IV) The Book.** The circumstances in which the contents were produced are clear enough. Like almost all of the prophetic books it is a collection of the oracles which the prophet, speaking for God, delivered orally to warn, teach, and convert the people. The pro-

duction of the book as a book is another matter. We do not know when and how it was composed. We assume that the process was the same as that for the other prophetic books—the prophet's audience, esp. his close followers and perhaps he himself, noted down his sayings and groups of sayings more or less close upon delivery; the collection of these notes along with memorized sayings of the prophet into a book was a gradual process. Sayings about a common topic would be gathered into small collections (e.g., chaps. 11, 12) that would later be combined with other collections and individual sayings until the book emerged. For Hos, where and how long this process took place are matters for conjecture, although the occasional glosses referring to Judah indicate that part occurred there (see Andersen and Freedman, *Hosea* 52–76).

7   **(V) Outline.** The method of producing Hos indicates the problem with its organization. The whole is not a conscious, unified, literary production but is the result of more or less haphazard growth. Hence, we cannot expect an organization in the strict sense with logical subordination and real progression. From this point of view, all we can make is a list of topics, not an outline. The various divisions are based on the more or less frequent occurrence of something—a word, an idea, a literary form—that serves as a criterion for division. The individual sections, therefore, are a matter of convenience more than anything else. Usually they do not contain a single oracle that Hosea spoke as a unit at one time and in one place; they are collections of sayings more or less unified. On the other hand, this does not mean that they are merely arbitrary and that the individual sayings can only be interpreted in isolation. For one thing, passages that reveal the prophet's thought about a given theme are the best commentary on other passages where the theme occurs. Thus, collections of passages about a theme, as collections, are legitimate sources for Hosea's thought, even though he did not speak all the words together nor make the collection. Second, it is the inspired word of God that interests us, and it is the word as it appears fixed in a biblical context and not only the word as spoken by the prophet in isolation that is inspired.

(I)   Hosea's Marriage (1–3)
    (A) The Prophet's Children (1:2–2:3)
    (B) Indictment of the Faithless Wife (2:4–17)
    (C) Reconciliation (2:18–25)
    (D) The Prophet and His Wife (3:1–5)
(II) Condemnation of Hosea's Contemporaries (4:1–9:9)
    (A) Yahweh's Indictment of Israel (4:1–3)
    (B) Indictment of the Leaders of Israel (4:4–5:7)
    (C) Political Upheavals (5:8–14)
    (D) False Repentance (5:15–7:2)
    (E) Corruption of the Monarchy (7:3–12)
    (F) Lament over Israel (7:13–16)
    (G) Sins in Politics and Cult (8:1–14)
    (H) Exile without Worship (9:1–6)
    (I) Rejection of the Prophet (9:7–9)
(III) Sin and History (9:10–14:1)
    (A) Sin and Decline (9:10–17)
    (B) Punishment of Apostasy (10:1–8)
    (C) False Confidence (10:9–15)
    (D) Love Overcomes Ingratitude (11:1–11)
    (E) Israel's Perfidy (12:1–15)
    (F) Death Sentence (13:1–14:1)
(IV) Epilogue: Repentance and Salvation (14:2–9)

COMMENTARY

8   **(I) Hosea's Marriage (1–3).** This central experience of the prophet is a symbol revealing Yahweh's personal love of his people, faithful even in the face of

their gross failings. Less often noted is the marriage symbol's clear introduction of the idea of a contract, a union of wills, into the concept of the covenant with

Yahweh. The very importance of the matter, as well as the textual obscurities, makes it natural that the effort to define the exact nature of the marriage has raised many problems, some of which must be touched on briefly.

First, is it allegorical fiction? The allegorical view does not seem to do justice to the often brutal realism of the symbolic actions of the prophets (Isa 20:2-6; Jer 19; Ezek 5), nor to the intensity of Hosea's words. Moreover, we would expect details like the name Gomer and the sexes of the children to have meaning in an allegory, but they do not.

Second, do chaps. 1-3 recount a continuous story? If they do, we have a tale of marriage and children, divorce, and remarriage. A variant of the continuous-story interpretation of these chapters holds that chap. 3 does not tell of a remarriage with Gomer after divorce but of an entirely new marriage, which adds the complication that the new wife must be called adulteress proleptically. In any case, to get a good sequence we must rearrange the text (cf. *NAB*); even then the reconstruction is incomplete and problematic. For instance, the divorce in chap. 2 need not refer to the prophet's marriage at all but simply to Yahweh's relations with Israel. The account of the remarriage in chap. 3 is not integrated with chap. 1 as we would expect in a continuous narrative, for the vocabulary is different; it does not make a real sequel, and it is complete in itself. Furthermore, the MT presents three well-defined literary units—1:2-2:3; 2:4-25; 3—that move from accusation through chastisement to reconciliation. This arrangement of the text must surely be conscious, seeking to emphasize the theological meaning of the marriage symbol and not to tell a story. We can then consider chap. 3 to be parallel to chap. 1, not in telling the same tale but in treating the same experience from a different viewpoint.

Third, what is meant by "harlot wife" (1:2)? If it is adultery, then it is applied proleptically to the bride in 1:2. But why then say harlot and not adulteress? In view of this difficulty it is better to look for another explanation. Gomer might have been a sacred prostitute at a Baal shrine, or at least a devotee of a Baal whose worship involved orgiastic rites. Although such conduct certainly occurred in Israel, we can hardly say it was ordinary (Wolff, *Hosea* 13-15) in view of the value put on virginity (Deut 22:13-19). In fact, idolatry itself was called harlotry so that merely joining the worshipers of Baal would be enough to earn the title (see J. Coppens, in *Alttestamentliche Studien* [Fest. F. Nötscher; BBB 1; Bonn, 1950] 38-45).

9 **(A) The Prophet's Children (1:2-2:3).** This account of Hosea's marriage, with its symbolic meaning, is in the 3d pers. Chapter 1 is a series of parallel units, but the parallelism is flexible: the birth of each child is told in the same general fashion but with variation. Note the sequence of thought: Israel's idolatry (1:2b) and a specific sin (1:4) mean the loss of divine favor (1:6) and so the end of covenant (1:9).

2. *harlot wife:* Lit., "wife of harlotries." The pl. expresses a quality, "faithless" or the like, and need not refer to an actual harlot. So also "harlot's children" can be children of such a mother, not children born of adultery. The "harlotry" of the land is idolatry (cf. 5:4). **3.** *Gomer, daughter of Diblaim:* Neither name refers to Yahweh, as was usual in Israelite names. This may be a further hint at infidelity, i.e., service of the Baals. *bore him a son:* It is the prophet's own child, not the result of adultery. Yahweh gives the child a name, an action that always emphasizes the function of the person as a sign of divine intentions (cf. Gen 17:5, Abraham; 32:20, Jacob; esp. Matt 1:21, Jesus); hence, the names do not

represent Hosea's own attitude toward his children. **4.** *Jezreel:* The plain between Galilee, Samaria, and the Jordan. The bloodshed at Jezreel during the overthrow of the Omride dynasty is described in 2 Kgs 9-10, where it is commended by a prophet (2 Kgs 9:7). Hebrew thought ignored secondary causes; what was from one point of view a punishment deserved by the idolatrous Omrides was from another selfish murder. The punishment affects more than the house of Jehu; the kingdom— i.e., independence—will be removed. Verse 5 gives a new meaning for Jezreel by bringing in another, later saying of Hosea. *break the bow:* It indicates the destruction of Israelite power, probably in the Assyrian invasion of 733. The phrase itself belongs to the curses appended to ancient covenants and thus may imply the fulfillment of the curses that must follow covenant breaking (see Deut 28).

6. *Lo-ruhama:* "She is not pitied" or "she no longer holds the love of the parent," since the Hebr stem meaning "pity" carries overtones of parental love (→ 4 above; cf. chap. 11). "She" need not refer to the daughter; it may be the land (v 2), fem. in Hebrew, or perhaps we should translate it impersonally. The name of the first child emphasized Israel's sin; this name, the divine attitude: the long-suffering God will have to punish his people. **7.** A later addition in the interests of Judah, whose fate is contrasted with Israel's. Yahweh himself intervened to save Jerusalem from Sennacherib (2 Kgs 19:35-37); cf. Isa 31:1; Ps 20:7-9.

9. *Lo-ammi:* "Not my people" indicates that the covenant between Yahweh and Israel is ended, for the covenant made Israel the people of God (cf. Exod 6:6-7; Lev 26:12; Deut 26:18; Jer 31:33). *your God:* The Hebrew is "I am not Yahweh [lit., "not Ehyeh"] to you." The very name of God specially revealed to his people (Exod 3:14) is lost to Israel.

10 **2:1-3.** These lines, which are printed at the end of chap. 3 in the *NAB*, are a set of sayings reversing the meaning of the children's names. **1a.** A clear reference to the promissory covenant with the patriarchs (Gen 22:17; 32:13). Thus, these verses open and close (*'ammî*, "my people") with a reference to (a new) covenant; the emphasis is on the restored covenant relationship, not on a return from exile. **1b.** *children of the living God:* As his son (cf. 11:1), Israel owes Yahweh exclusive service (Deut 14:1). Yahweh is a "living God" in contrast to the dead Baals (Deut 32:17-21—"no-gods," "idols," i.e., nothings), or because he gives life (6:2). **2.** *other lands:* The Hebr phrase "the land," by referring to the exodus (cf. Exod 1:10), places the reunion of God's people, separated since Solomon's time (cf. Isa 7:17), in the context of salvation history. The idea of the new dispensation as a new exodus is developed in Isa 40-55 and is important in the NT. The exodus reference explains the neutral "head" instead of "king," which would be anachronistic in this context. Jezreel is no longer a threat but a promise. There is a play on the name's meaning, "God sows"; in the new dispensation, Yahweh will grant great plenty.

11 **(B) Indictment of the Faithless Wife (2:4-17). 4.** *protest:* The Hebr *rîb* indicates a formal juridical situation, reflected in the style of the whole section. There is an indictment (v 4a), warning (vv 4b-6), and then accusation plus judgment repeated three times (vv 7-9,10-14,15-17). It is the common object and situation that give unity to this collection of sayings, which, as inconsistencies and repetitions indicate, were originally separate units.

4a. Yahweh speaks in the 1st pers. as throughout this section. He summons the children to bear witness against their mother (on the procedure, see C. Gordon, *ZAW* 54 [1942] 277-80). In v 6, the children are themselves subject to judgment. The mother is faithless Israel; cf. v 7b referring to the service of the Baals (although they are named only in v 15), to whom are attributed in hymn tones the gifts of a fertile land. The children, of course, are the people of Israel; in the concrete, judgment of Israel must be judgment of the people, so that the image of the trial of the mother alone cannot be sustained. Behind the double role of the children may be the idea of diverse elements within the people—the faithful who are witnesses and the faithless who are judged. This would be an early adumbration of the doctrines of the remnant and of personal responsibility so important in later prophetic tradition.

4b. *her harlotry, her adultery:* Reference is to various insignia worn by devotees of the Baals. **8.** *therefore:* As in vv 11 and 16 (*NAB* "So"), it marks the change from accusation to sentence, which here looks beyond punishment to reformation. Faced by thorns instead of fruit and kept from the Baal rites ("runs after" and "looks for" are cultic terms), Israel will learn where her true good lies. The return of the divorcee must symbolize restoration of the relationship with Yahweh; according to the law, divorced partners might not actually remarry (Deut 24:1-4). **10.** A new accusation is made. Israel has turned Yahweh's gifts to the service of the Baals. The withdrawal of these gifts will show who is the true God. There is no hint of struggle; the Baals can do nothing to protect Israel from the results of her folly. Verse 13 indicates that Baalism was more than a competing cult; it had contaminated the very worship of Yahweh, even the specifically Israelite sabbath. Verse 14 sets forth the Baalist doctrine: Proper performance of rites must yield fertility, so that it is exact to speak of a half-magical earning of what Yahwism knew to be a grace (cf. Deut 9:1-6). After the renewed accusation in v 15, a new judgment appears in v 16: Israel must return to the desert. The point here, as in vv 8-9,11-14, is not that the prophet refers to some particular event, drought, or invasion, but to the need to reestablish contact with Yahweh. The desert is not a place for permanent withdrawal, but an ideal place to seek God (cf. 11:2; J. McKenzie, *The Way* 1 [1961] 27-39). It is a necessary discipline, an opportunity to find Yahweh again; the final promise is a return to the fertile land. **17.** *Achor:* On the border of Judah and Benjamin (Josh 15:7). It is a "door of hope" because the valley leads from the Jordan into the fertile land of central Palestine; therefore, the restoration follows the route of the conquest and is thus connected with the exodus.

12   (C) Reconciliation (2:18-25). A group of sayings unified by a common general theme and some points of style: Yahweh's speaking in the 1st pers., the repeated "on that day." The section is not juridical like 2:4-17, but it is a fitting development of the idea of a reconciliation following Israel's punishment.

18. *on that day:* The time of salvation when Yahweh saves his people, the expression can also refer to judgment (Amos 5:18). It retains both aspects as a technical term in Jewish and NT eschatology. In Hos it is not strictly eschatological but expresses confidence in the future restoration of Israel. However, the ideas of a new covenant and true peace here expressed will be much developed in eschatological thought. **19.** *invoked:* Hebr *zkr* refers to the liturgical invocation of a god; hence, v 19b means idolatry will cease. **20.** Yahweh restores by mediating a covenant between Israel and creation (cf. Gen 9:8-10). Even a right natural order depends on his free choice and covenant. Coupled with this order in nature is a promise that war will cease. Both are common

objects of hope (Isa 11:6-8; 65:25; 2:4; 9:4; Mic 4:3), but they are seldom joined as here (cf. Lev 26:6; Ezek 35:25-28). **21.** A continuation of the idea of covenant under the image of a marriage contract. *espouse in:* The preposition designates the bride-price, the gift the groom offers. The following words therefore describe Yahweh's dispositions, not his demands. *justice:* Lit., judgment, i.e., the concrete working out of "right." *love:* Hebr *ḥesed,* which means loyal adherence to the covenant partner. **22.** *know the Lord:* Not with speculative knowledge but with a religious recognition that brings devotion to his will (cf. 4:1-2,6, where "knowledge of God" is parallel to keeping his law); knowledge of the Lord [Yahweh] is religious knowledge in a comprehensive sense, and knowledge of God is especially knowledge of traditional Hebr morality (cf. J. McKenzie, *JBL* 74 [1955] 22-27). Despite Hosea's emphasis on the fact that God loves ('*hb*) Israel, when he speaks of Israel's response he demands knowledge (*yd'*), although we would expect that love should call for love. However, *yd'* has a strong affective color; the prophet probably shuns the direct '*hb* to avoid its erotic overtones. With its devotion to the fertility rites, Israel was all too ready to mistake the erotic for the religious (cf. W. Eichrodt, *Int* 17 [1963] 264). **23.** God answers the prayers of a drought-wasted land for crops. The abuses of the pagan cults had put nature into a condition contradicting its essence, which is to serve humanity and bring it to God. Hosea's personification pictures a restored nature fulfilling its true functions; the heavens link God to the earth, the earth gives its fruits, and humanity is brought to God. **24.** *Jezreel:* Israel. The uncommon usage comes from chap. 1, where it is one of the names of the children who symbolize Israel. **25.** *him:* Jezreel-Israel. If this is correct (MT has "her") the image changes. Israel does not receive the harvest but becomes the crop itself, and the divine promise that Israel will increase (Gen 15:5; 32:13) is fulfilled.

13   (D) The Prophet and His Wife (3:1-5). Hosea delivers his own account of his marriage; unlike chap. 1, it centers on the wife, not on the children.

1. *adulteress:* Need not be taken strictly; it can refer to unchastity or infidelity in general as in 2:4. However, actual adultery is a more meaningful symbol of Israel's conduct, for Israel fell away after it was chosen by Yahweh. The purchase price in v 2 is sometimes said to amount to 30 shekels, the price of a slave (Lev 27:4), but we know too little about the money values of the time to be sure. Hence, it is not clear whether there is here question of purchasing a slave or merely paying the usual bride-price. The new wife must live secluded for a time, which may be either punishment or a kind of training but more likely signifies that she is ritually unclean because she had joined in pagan rites. Only after a time of seclusion could a follower of Yahweh associate with her. The story of the marriage ends abruptly in v 4. Only enough has been given to serve as a symbol of Yahweh's relation with an Israel that must suffer the loss of its civil and religious organization, the latter symbolized by legitimate (sacrifice; ephod) and illegitimate (pillar, i.e., the *asherah,* a pagan symbol; idols) cult furniture. In the natural course of things it would mean loss of national identity in the circumstances of ancient Near Eastern culture. However, the deprivation is temporary, for Israel will return to Yahweh. The reference to David is usually considered an interpolation, but 2:2 shows that a reunion of all Israel under one leader was part of Hosea's vision. **5.** *come trembling:* With religious awe.

(The literature on Hosea's marriage is extensive. See the history of interpretation by S. Bitter, *Die Ehe des Propheten Hosea* [GTA

3; Göttingen, 1975]. Briefer treatment is provided by H. H. Rowley, "The Marriage of Hosea," *BJRL* 39 [1957–58] 200–33. See also J. Schreiner, "Hoseas Ehe, ein Zeichen des Gerichts, *BZ* 21 [1977] 163–83.)

(II) Condemnation of Hosea's Contemporaries (4:1-9:9). These chapters are a collection of diverse sayings of the prophet directed now at particular classes, now at the whole people. The theme of most of the sayings is the judgment that Yahweh passes on contemporary Israel for its sins, although occasional words of hope do appear.

14   (A) Yahweh's Indictment of Israel (4:1-3). The collection begins with a general introduction, a judgment on the whole people. The sons of Israel, sons of the promise who have received the land in fulfillment of the promise, have proved faithless. Fidelity (*'emet*) and mercy (*hesed*) are the virtues proper to covenant relationships; their concrete working out is "knowledge of God," i.e., action according to his moral will (cf. 2:22). The catalogue of Israel's sins in v 2 obviously recalls the Decalogue: precepts of the sort that were the condition for the continuance of the covenant have been violated and so the covenant is broken. **3.** *mourns:* The alternate meaning of *'bl*, "dries up," fits better with what follows. When the covenant is broken, the object of the covenant, the land, is turned to desert and Israel reverts to its primitive, uncovenanted, unredeemed condition.

15   (B) Indictment of the Leaders of Israel (4:4-5:7). These sayings unite around the themes of the infidelity of the ruling classes and of the abuses in the cult (cf. J. Lundbom, *VT* 36 [1986] 52–70). **4b.** *priests:* The MT has "priest"; perhaps the chief priest is addressed as head of the priestly guild, which itself becomes the center of attention in the following verses that use the pl. Once more (v 4) Yahweh uses legal language: Let no one take up the defense of the guilty priests. It is useless; the sentence has been passed; the priests shall "stumble," i.e., fall, come to ruin, and with them the prophets. These latter are not men of Hosea's stamp but rather the false prophets who troubled most of the true prophets of Yahweh. Here they are linked to the priests in a context concerned with cult, indicating their official place in cult and sanctuary (cf. A. R. Johnson, *The Cultic Prophet in Israel* [Cardiff, 1944] esp. 61). Priests and prophets are condemned for failing in their duty to teach Yahweh's ways, not for corrupting the cult. *in the day . . . at night:* Perhaps the priests sought oracles consciously, the prophets in dreams, but this phrase may mean simply "always." **5b.** *I will destroy your mother:* Perhaps a concretely expressed threat to wipe out the priestly house (the priesthood was hereditary in Israel); cf. the threat about the priests' sons in v 6b. **7–11a.** This passage was originally separate from the foregoing: instead of "you," "they" designates the priests. The people are not looked upon as victims but as subordinate partners in the priests' guilt; not only do the priests fail to teach as they ought, they foster idolatry. **7.** *glory:* The office of a true Yahwist priest. *shame:* The Baal cults involving sacrifices, called "sin" and "guilt" in v 8, on which the priests thrived. However, punishment must come, and it follows from the crime: Israel's idolatrous sacrificial meals will bring no divine favor, no plenty, and their fertility rites no fruit. This denial is inevitable, for they have abandoned the source of life, Yahweh. **11a.** *harlotry:* Idolatry, but alluding to the licentiousness that was part of the Baal cults.

11b. A new attack on idolatry begins with a proverb about the madness of the orgiastic fertility rites. "New wine" (*tîrôš*) can mean freshly pressed grape juice, not itself intoxicating but still the occasion for wild harvest festivals. However, *tîrôš* appears as wine at a Canaanite banquet for the gods (*UM* 2 Aqhat, VI:7), so we may reasonably assume that here it is an intoxicating element in the rites themselves. In any case, there is no need to reduce the madness of Israel to mere lust after good things as in 7:14. Another aspect of idolatry appears in v 12 — i.e., seeking oracles elsewhere than from Yahweh. **12.** *piece of wood:* Perhaps the *asherah,* a wooden pole and symbol of the mother goddess that was part of the furniture of the Baalist sanctuaries, or an oracle tree (cf. Judg 9:37, "diviners' oak"), while the wand may indicate some sort of divining rod. The "spirit of harlotry" brings on (Hebr "seduces to") these aberrations. The "spirit" is not personified; it is a force, an urge to act that comes upon one as though from outside; we might best say impulse. Harlotry is here explained as infidelity to Yahweh (v 12b), although the context gives it the overtones of licentiousness. **13–14.** High places and green groves were the typical locales for the Baalist sanctuaries (cf. 1 Kgs 14:23; Jer 2:20) where men sought pleasure and profit, not Yahweh. Because of the fertility cults, licentiousness flourishes among the people; however, the priests have the greater guilt because they lead the people to sin by consorting with hierodules as part of religious functions (v 14b). To get the full force here we must remember that unchastity was severely punished in women, not in men; Hosea reverses the received idea. **14b.** *a people without understanding:* The people lack instruction (v 6) and are given over to the frenzied cult (v 11). The sentence rounds out this unit of Hosea's words and v 15 begins a new set, where, in contrast to the foregoing, the nation as a whole is condemned without distinguishing degrees of guilt within it.

16   15–19. The text is very corrupt, and interpretation must often be hypothetical. **15.** *Judah:* Often treated as an interpolation but found in the ancient versions as well as in the MT, this serves as a rhetorical foil pointing up the northern kingdom's infidelity. *Gilgal . . . Beth-aven:* Famous Israelite sanctuaries that symbolize the infidelity and idolatry of the whole kingdom (cf. Amos 5:5). *as the Lord lives:* Or "that the Lord lives." This is a Baalist cult formula affirming the return of the god (cf. *UM* Text 49, III:8; F. Horst, *EvT* 17 [1957] 371), evidence of the syncretism that the prophet condemns. **17.** *associate:* Covenanted friend of idols rather than of Yahweh. *let him alone:* "There is nothing one can do to change him" rather than "do not join him." **18.** The nation, not only the priests as in v 7, is given over to shame — i.e., the licentious rites — for the "wind" (v 19) has captured them. Wind is the same word as spirit (v 12), the impulse to shameful acts, but "pinions" adds the idea of mighty physical force (cf. Pss 18:11; 104:3). The madness of idolatry is bringing material — i.e., political and economic — ruin on Israel.

5:1. A new charge against the leaders. *house of Israel:* The elders who served as judges in certain civil cases. Thus the three classes who held authority in Israel are named. *it is you who are called to judgment:* It should be taken to mean "you should exercise judgment." Judgment is not merely judicial decision; it means right order, civil, moral, and religious. This the leaders have failed to maintain; they have become a "snare" and a "net" (hunting gear) trapping Israel into sin. Mizpah and Tabor may have been centers of idolatry, although aside from the following context we have little real evidence for it. **2.** *they:* The change to the 3d pers. turns the charge against a new group, presumably the people. If the chiefs misled, the people were ready to follow. **3.** *Ephraim:* The largest tribe of the kingdom of Israel, it often represents the whole nation. *defiled:* Ritually unclean, unfit to approach God; but more than this uncleanness, Israel's sin keeps it from God. **4.** *spirit of harlotry:* An impulse toward idolatry (cf. 4:12) and from their lack of knowledge of God, i.e., devotion to his wishes. "Recognize" is the same Hebr root as "knowledge" in 4:1,6. **5.** *arrogance:* Ostentation. Jeroboam II's prosperous kingdom probably attributed its well-being to the splendor of its cult (v 6), so that this very splendor was a sign of its erroneous spirit. *stumbles in:* "Trips over his guilt," i.e., comes to ruin because of it; this is the sentence after the indictment. **6.** Verse 6 also has to do with punishment. The cult, the nation's pride and hope, is inefficacious. *seek . . . not find:* Terminology deriving from the cult of the dying and rising fertility god (cf. H. G. May, *AJSL* 48 [1931] 77), an allusion to the syncretism Hosea attacks. In any case, this splendid cult does not conciliate; it alienates Yahweh. **7.** *illegitimate children:* Lit., "strange children," i.e., whose birth is not attributed to Yahweh but to fertility rites foreign to him. Once more, error brings its own punishment, for idolatry, symbolized by the feast of the new moon, in itself legitimate but corrupted in Israel, will destroy Israel rather than bring it the desired plenty.

17 **(C) Political Upheavals (5:8-14).** **8.** *Gibeah . . . Ramah:* Benjaminite villages near Jerusalem on the frontier between Israel and Judah. Normally they belonged to Judah, but Jehoash may well have annexed them to Israel at the beginning of the 8th cent. (cf. 2 Kgs 14:8-14), so that they would be the first Israelite places to feel an attack from Judah. *look behind you:* In fear. The alarm is caused by an attack that probably came at the end of the Syro-Ephraimite war when Judah could attack Israel as its forces retreated N to face Assyria (cf. 2 Kgs 16; Isa 7:1-9). **9.** *day of chastisement:* Hebr *yôm tôkēḥâ* is an unusual expression for the day of judgment and may well connote remedial rather than vindictive punishment. Israel's punishment is deserved and inevitable; nevertheless, the instrument, Judah, is also culpable (v 10). The leaders of Judah have attacked their brother Israel. The implication that this action violated the covenant is carried by the image of the boundary movers, which recalls the deuteronomic law of the covenant (19:14), the violation of which brought the curse appropriate to the crime (Deut 27:17). **11.** *filth:* A common word for idols (but the text is uncertain). **12.** Verse 12 plays on the formulas of the cultic theophany (cf. W. Zimmerli in *Geschichte und Altes Testament* [Fest. A. Alt; Tübingen, 1953] 179-209): Yahweh is present not to save but to destroy. *maggots:* Lit., rottenness, corruption. Their difficulties led the Jews to seek help in political alliances; this was actually another sin because ancient pacts meant acceptance of the overlord's gods. Israel's seeking Assyria is usually referred to the reign of Menahem before the Syro-Ephraimite war (2 Kgs 15:19), but later King Hosea was Assyria's vassal too. In any case, such dealings were useless; natural aids could not help. **14.** The figure of illness changes to that of the raging lion to express the terror and inevitability of Yahweh's judgment.

18 **(D) False Repentance (5:15-7:2).** **15.** *my place:* Seems to attach this section to the preceding since it refers to the image of the lion who attacks and then withdraws to its lair.

6:1. *rend:* Continues the lion imagery. However, the theme begun here, false repentance, would fit after any prophetic warning or condemnation, and the sins alluded to in 6:6 are not those of chap. 5. The OT knows the idea of God's having a special place (cf. 1 Sam 26:19), and the comparison of Yahweh with a lion is not unique (cf. 13:7; Amos 3:8; Ps 50:22). It seems more likely that a separate saying on repentance has been attached adroitly to the preceding. **6:1.** Hosea puts insincere or at least

insufficient words of repentance in the people's mouth — such expressions as they, in their bad will, might use. They seem to realize that Yahweh has punished them and that he alone can save them. **2.** *revive:* Not "raise from the dead" but "restore to health," after wounds have brought them close to death. *two days . . . third day:* A short interval, not a precise time. The choice of "on the third day" may allude to the cult of the dying and rising fertility gods; at least in Babylonia the reawakening began on the third day (cf. "Ishtar's Descent," *ANET* 55). *to live in his presence:* Death was thought of as definitive separation from God (cf. Ps 6:6). **3.** Continues to exhort to repentance but in terms reminiscent of fertility rituals (rain, spring rain). **4.** Yahweh responds in oracle form. The rhetorical question reveals the struggle, characteristic of Hosea's thought, between Yahweh's will to save and his justice. Then the oracle exposes Israel's insincerity (v 4b) and failure to understand Yahweh, although he has disciplined it with chastisement interpreted by the prophets (v 5a). **5b.** Verse 5b (3b in *NAB,* "and his judgment" etc.) should read "and my judgment goes forth like the light" (LXX). Yahweh's unshakable judgment, figured by the never-failing light of the sun, is contrasted with Israel's inconstancy likened to the ephemeral dew.

6. An explanation of Yahweh's past actions, telling by implication — else it is inappropriate here — why Israel's repentance fails now; it has not learned its lesson and still counts on external cult without submission to Yahweh's commands. Hosea does not reject sacrifice entirely (cf. 9:4, where deprivation of sacrifice is a punishment, therefore the loss of a good thing). In Hebr fashion, he affirms now one aspect, now another, without troubling about nuances. In v 7, the tenor is less personal, and crimes of violence rather than false cult are condemned. This change could indicate a new beginning, but the list of infidelities fits here by broadening the illustration of Israel's unrepentant state of mind, the obstacle to true reunion with Yahweh. This theme is resumed expressly in 7:1-2, in view of which it seems that the present ordering was consciously constructed. **7.** *land:* Hebr *'ādām,* which can indeed mean "land" or "country" (M. Dahood, *Proverbs and North West Semitic Philology* [Rome, 1963] 57-58). However, the parallel with the place-names in vv 8-9 suggests the name Adam, a town in Transjordan. What particular covenant — the word refers to any sworn agreement — was violated there is unknown, just as we do not know the details of the crimes listed in vv 8-9. In the *NAB* version, the "covenant" could be Israel's special relation with Yahweh, destroyed when Israel joined in the Canaanite rites after the conquest. **8.** *Gilead:* An area in Transjordan. *tracked with blood:* Full of crimes of violence. **9.** *Shechem:* An ancient sanctuary (Gen 33:20; 35:1-4) and an important pilgrim resort (A. Alt, *KlS* 1. 79-88); the route thither was thus a good place for brigands, whose crimes were worse because they were degenerate priests. **11.** Apparently a gloss applying Hosea's words about Israel to the sister kingdom of Judah. *harvest:* Judgment (cf. Jer 51:33; Joel 4:13).

7:1. Sums up the ideas of chap. 6: Israel's wickedness impedes its salvation although Yahweh wills it. **2.** *remember:* Hebr *zkr,* "summon to testify" (cf. Isa 43:26). The "wickedness" and "crimes" of Israel are personified; they stand as witnesses against the people.

19 **(E) Corruption of the Monarchy (7:3-12).** Two aspects of Israel's political activity are condemned: the internal intrigues and disorders that followed the overthrow of the dynasty of Jehu (7:3-7); the search for foreign alliances as though these and not Yahweh were Israel's salvation (7:8-12). The monarchy as an institution is not condemned; it is rather the abuse of that institution—the bloody changes of dynasty, the intrigues, the luxury—that Hosea has in mind.

3. *princes:* Court functionaries charged with civil and military administration—the class from which Israel's frequent revolutions arose. **4.** *kindled to wrath:* The MT has "adulterers," and this, in the sense of deceivers, is possible in view of the accusation of deceit in v 3. The whole text of v 4 is badly corrupted and a number of interpretations are possible—e.g., the passions of the intriguers are like an oven that burns its contents; their mood is uncertain, like an oven whose fire burns down and does not bake the bread enough; like a baker who puts yeast in the dough and then banks the fire to keep the dough warm without baking it, they repress their passions until everything is ready and they can deliver the decisive blow. The extension of the oven image in vv 6–7a would seem to support the last interpretation. **5.** *on the day of our king:* Probably the celebration of the king's enthronement. The court is full of sensual corruption as well as intrigue. The Judahite Isaiah also reproves the drunkenness of Israel (28:1–4,7–8): the breakdown of responsibility in the kingdom must have been obvious to all. *he extends . . . :* The meaning is obscure; most likely it means the king consciously associates with dissemblers, i.e., becomes one himself. However, "dissemblers" is uncertain; it may mean "mockers" or "boasters." **7.** *none . . . calls on me:* Expresses the theological ground for the prophet's condemnation of the disorders. It is not merely that rebellion and assassination violate the law; the revolutions are not done for the sake of, and at the direction of, Yahweh. Traditionally, the Israelite dynasties assumed power with the help of prophets speaking for Yahweh (e.g., 1 Kgs 11:29–34; cf. A. Alt, *KlS* 2. 116–34).

20   Verses 8–12, like 5:13, condemn alliances with foreign powers. **8.** *mingles:* The vb. *bll* is often used of mixing oil in cooking (e.g., Exod 29:2b); hence, it belongs to the figure continued in the second half of the verse, and the transl. "is tossed about by the nations," which would support the idea that these verses refer to war and exile, is to be rejected. "Mingle" might still point to the exile Tiglath-pileser inflicted on Israel after 732. However, exile can hardly be reconciled with Israel's ignorance of its bad position (v 9) and its arrogance (v 10). Hence, v 8 must refer to seeking foreign alliances, conduct at once foolish and arrogant. **8b.** A warning that the policy of alliances is, lit., "half-baked," useless. Orientals bake their waferlike bread by placing it on heated stones or oven walls; if unturned, one side remains raw. **9.** *strangers:* The foreigners to whom Israel has turned do not strengthen but weaken the nation. *gray hairs:* Symbols of waning vigor. In its headlong rush to destruction Israel ignores the danger signals. **10.** This prophetic saying was already used in 5:5 with a different application. The Hebr *waw* ("yet") should probably be taken as explicative (GKC §484 n. 1, b); the arrogance of Israel is its self-sufficiency, its efforts to work out its salvation independently of Yahweh. **11.** A new image is introduced, indicating that it was originally a separate saying against alliances. *dove:* Defenseless in the world of great powers. *silly:* Easily led. In its folly and despite its impotence, Israel persists in meddling with the great powers. **12.** The condemnation follows the catalogue of Israel's failings. It continues the image of the dove: like a hunter Yahweh will capture it. The end of the verse in the MT is very obscure, seeming to say "I will chastise them according to their assemblies." If, with the LXX, we read "wickedness" for "assemblies," it simply affirms that the punishment will be fitting. The *NAB* makes it explicit that Israel deserted Yahweh to seek the aid of

strangers; it will be punished by exile.

21   **(F) Lament over Israel (7:13–16).** The prophet laments the ruin Israel has brought upon itself not, as we would expect after 7:3–12, by its disloyal politics, but by its use of Baalist cultic practices. The lamentation, a common enough form of discourse in prophetic literature, is rare and hence emphatic in Hosea.

13. *redeem:* Hebr *pdh* is a commercial term, used, e.g., of buying the freedom of slaves; perhaps we can paraphrase "ransom." *lies:* Probably refers to Israel's insincere repentance that frustrated Yahweh's desire to save (cf. 6:1–4). **14.** Verse 14 makes clear how false are Israel's religious dispositions; their very pleas for help are tainted with Baalist features. This, apparently, is not simple idolatry, for they "cry to" Yahweh, but not "from the heart" for they do it "upon their beds," which refers to sleeping in the "high places" of the fertility rites as part of a ritual (cf. Isa 57:7), and "they lacerate themselves," a pagan practice expressly forbidden in Israel (Lev 19:28). **15.** Yahweh was the God who led Israel in war and gave it victory, but it has deserted him, seeking help from others, or, if from him, in a manner he rejects. **16.** *become useless:* The MT is unintelligible and the *NAB* follows the LXX, linking v 16a to the following image. Another possible emendation attaches it rather to the foregoing: "They turn, but not to me." *they are like a treacherous bow:* A slack bow that will not shoot when needed (cf. G. R. Driver, *Alttestamentliche Studien* [→ 8 above] 38–45). The figure of the bow implies a telling reversal: Israel is or should be God's instrument, but it has adopted the pagan concept in which the divinity was to be used for human ends, compelled thereto by magical-religious rites. **16b.** The condemnation of the faithless nation. The sentence falls primarily on the leaders and through them on all the people. *insolence:* Hebr *za'am* means mocking speech with overtones of malediction and denunciation. Perhaps this reference is to a mocking rejection of the prophet's warnings by Israel's leaders. Punishment in any case cannot be avoided; eventually even the proverbial enemy, Egypt, will have the laugh on Israel.

22   **(G) Sins in Politics and Cult (8:1–14).** We have a new proclamation of Israel's inevitable punishment. First comes a warning (vv 1–3), then condemnation of the political and religious schism from Judah (vv 4–7), the policy of alliances (vv 8–10), and finally idolatry (vv 11–13). Although these units have been linked (e.g., v 4 explains v 3; "swallow" links vv 7 and 8), they must have had separate origins; note, e.g., the alternation between second and third persons.

1. *you who watch:* The MT and the LXX "like an eagle" can be retained: "A trumpet to your lips! Like an eagle (the enemy [v 3] falls upon) the house of the Lord!" The trumpet was an alarm signal, not a mark of the violation of the law; furthermore, the *NAB* leaves the explanatory clause in v 1b with nothing to explain; hence, another transl. is indicated. In his imagination, Hosea sees the enemy already falling upon a sinful Israel. *covenant . . . law:* The basic relationship with Yahweh formed at Sinai with its conditions. However, the link here with v 4 hints at the extension of this Sinai covenant in the covenant with David's line (2 Sam 7). **2.** The Hosean theme of insincerity is evident: Israel rejects the Lord and yet calls on him. Rejecting Yahweh means "throwing away" (the Hebrew is very strong: "treat as disgusting") all that is good (v 3), for all good is from Yahweh. Effectively, this is to choose chastisement at the hand of God's instrument, Israel's enemies. **4–6.** Kingmaking and idolatry are linked, specifically the setting up of the "golden calves," which points to Israel's original break with the Davidic kingdom, for Jeroboam I founded the shrines of the calves when he split with Judah (1 Kgs 12:26–31). The difficulty is that Jeroboam's rebellion, like many later dynastic changes in Israel, came at the behest of a prophet speaking on Yahweh's authority (1 Kgs 11:26–40). Hence, it might seem that Hosea condemns only the willful intrigues following Jeroboam II's death. However, Hosea felt free to condemn what other prophets had approved (cf. 9:4), so that it is perfectly possible that he is condemning the original foundation of the northern kingdom. If Yahweh permitted the selfishness of Jeroboam to run its course as punishment for Solomon's sins, it remained selfishness. Part of this self-will was expressed when official shrines were set up to rival Jerusalem. The original purpose was not idolatrous (cf. 1 Kgs 12:28, clearly based on a good Yahwist formula: Exod 20:2), but in fact the plurality of shrines led to idolatry.

23   5. *calf:* Not originally an idol. Calves were thought of as the mount on which Yahweh was invisibly present (cf. Albright, *FSAC* 299), but before Hosea's time they had come to be worshiped for themselves. *Samaria:* Jeroboam's shrines were at Dan and Bethel, but certainly Omri built some sort of shrine when he founded Samaria as his capital. In any case, the calf of Bethel was thought of as Samaria's own (cf. 10:5), so the reference to Samaria need not belong to the time after 732 when Dan had been lost to Assyria and replaced by a shrine at Samaria. **5b.** *how long:* The question and the reference to innocence belong to the lamentation style. **6.** The scorn of idols, mere human products, became a favorite theme in later OT literature (cf. Isa 44:6–20). **7.** A proverblike reflection on the results of Israel's idolatry; like the whirlwind destroying ripe grain, the false fertility cult brings only ruin. Again, it is like a barren stalk, useless. The figures teach the favorite Hosean idea that punishment is the natural product of sin, not an arbitrary, external judgment. **8.** A reference to the exile that began in 732, a fitting punishment for Israel's seeking help from foreign alliances instead of from Yahweh. **9.** *bargained for lovers:* It is doubly ironical: It is the prostitute (bargain is the same root as the technical "harlot's hire" of 2:14; 9:1) Israel who pays her lovers, and love is not to be bought anyway. Nevertheless, it as well as tribute was an element in alliances (cf. D. J. McCarthy, *Old Testament Covenant* [Oxford, 1972]). **10.** *an army:* Yahweh will bring an enemy force on Israel (but the transl. is conjectural). *burden:* The tribute paid to Assyria. **12.** *many:* It links vv 11–12. Israel has built many altars without following Yahweh's many directions. Since Hosea does not condemn the altars as such but rather their idolatrous misuse, the opposition, altar or law, is not absolute. The neglected law could well be the prescriptions for proper worship. Hosea's knowledge of a written law is important for the history of Israel's religion. **13.** The lawless sacrifices do not please but offend God. The verse thus concludes with the sentence, the common ending of prophetic accusations. **14.** *his maker:* It is unusual for Hosea to refer to God as creator, and the implied theme of ostentatious building at the expense of the poor reflects Amos (e.g., 3:9–15); hence, the verse is probably an addition. It condemns the Hebrews' self-sufficiency, their confidence in their mighty works.

24   (H) Exile without Worship (9:1–6). Here the prophet contrasts the festive cult gatherings and the gloomy assembly in the exile, an exile that punished the idolatry that had invaded Israel's cult. Regarding form, Hosea speaks about Yahweh, not in the person of Yahweh.

1. *rejoice not, exult not:* Reverses the customary call to rejoice in the cult. *like the nations:* They were not so

subject to condemnation as Israel because they were not specifically chosen by God. Israel's very election made it possible to "be unfaithful" (lit., "play the harlot") by imitating pagan fertility rites in search of rich harvests. **2.** In fact, Israel will be disappointed of the expected benefits, for the harvest will *"fail"* (lit., "deceive" or "betray") them. Inasmuch as this verb is drawn from the description of moral qualities, it may be better to translate the parallel "not nourish" by "hostile," a meaning demanding no change in the consonants of the MT. The switch to the 3d pers. results from a vivid style: the prophet is a prosecutor, now addressing the accused, now speaking of him to the judges (cf. Isa 10:3 for a similar change). The penalty here is not a bad harvest but the total loss of the land through exile, as v 3 shows. **3.** Unlike Assyria, there was no forced exile to Egypt, but it was a place of refuge. The return there reverses salvation history. In Assyria, Israel's food is unclean (ritually impure), because it is not produced by the Lord's land but by an unclean land (cf. Amos 7:17). **4.** Unclean food could not be offered to Yahweh; therefore, in exile the cult must cease. **5.** The rhetorical questions are ironic, emphasizing the impossibility of the exile situation. *festival day . . . Lord's day:* Synonymous general terms. Instead of assembling for Yahweh's feasts, Israel gathers in exile while the homeland is given over to desolation (v 6). **6b.** The Hebrew is very emphatic: "Precious was their silver—weeds will grow over it!"

25   (I) Rejection of the Prophet (9:7–9). This brief section resembles vv 1–6 in not using the prophetic "I" in the name of Yahweh, but it is marked off sharply because of the emphatic ending in v 6 and the different tenses used here. However, it is a fitting sequel: For the prophet, to attack the joyous cult was to invite rejection.

7. *they have come:* Probably a "prophetic perfect"; so sure is Israel's punishment that it is spoken of as a fact. *let Israel know it:* Read with v 7a. However, the LXX implies a Hebr consonantal text that can be read "Israel shouts: The prophet," etc. In any case, these last words quote Israel's scorn for a prophet. In 1 Sam 10:9–13; Jer 29:26, the prophet was evidently often thought mad. Hosea's words are general: Israel has rejected not one but the whole line of prophets, the natural, hostile response of the guilty to the reprover (v 7c). **8.** The image continues the last idea. The prophet is a watchman, one placed on a tower to see and warn of approaching danger. Although he is God's appointee, he meets opposition even on consecrated ground. **9b.** The usual concluding condemnation.

26   (III) Sin and History (9:10–14:1). This last group of Hosea's sayings is frequently concerned with Israel's sinful past, climaxing in the troubles of the prophet's own day, whereas up to this point there was only passing reference to historical events. The style is somewhat meditative; passion remains, but there is less direct address and more reflection.

27   (A) Sin and Decline (9:10–17). Two crimes from Israel's history are recalled, and it is made clear that their results continue; the nation that was to have been numberless as the sands of the seashore will waste away.

10. *grapes in the desert:* Unexpected and so all the more desirable. Like the "firstfruits" of the "prime fig," they would certainly be plucked. Hence, the image implies the divine election of Israel, although strangely the election takes place in the desert, not in Egypt (cf. 11:1, where it occurs in Egypt!). At Baal-peor, a shrine on the Moabite border, Israel first came in contact with the Canaanite fertility gods, and Israel fell as soon as the contact occurred. With dramatic speed the fall follows upon election. **11.** *glory:* The divinely promised fertility of Israel serves as a link to v 10 by contrasting with "shame." The Baal cult works in reverse: it brings not fertility but sterility. **11b.** Verse 11b in the *NAB* should be v 16b as in the MT, for here it disturbs the progression: sterility; then, worse, the loss of grown children; then, worst of all, the inaccessibility of God. **13a.** The text is difficult. With the MT, the *NAB* contrasts two stages of Ephraim's history: Once its prospects were as pleasant as Tyre's, the proverbially wealthy and strong Phoenician trading city, but the nation will fall and its people be slaughtered. The LXX offers a different reading, producing parallelism between vv 13a and 13b. **14.** Thus far the prophet has spoken in the person of Yahweh, the accuser; in v 14a he intercedes for his people. Then, confronted with Israel's guilt, he realizes punishment must come, so that in v 14b he pleads for the lesser evil (cf. David, 2 Sam 24:12–14). **15.** The history of Israel's sins is resumed in Yahweh's own words. Gilgal probably refers to the shrine near Jericho. The sequence Baal-peor, Gilgal would thus recall the tradition of the conquest, but negatively. Further contact with the promised land brings further corruption. *hatred:* The just will to chastise, explained in the rest of v 15. **16.** Israel's punishment is explained (depopulation as in vv 11–14). **17.** The prophet again speaks for himself. He cannot but agree to the justice of Yahweh's sentence because Israel has not heeded its God.

28   (B) Punishment of Apostasy (10:1–8). **1–2.** A prosperous Israel has multiplied its cult places, but its religion is "false," i.e., flattering and two-faced (Hebr *ḥlq*). *break down:* Lit., "break the neck of," a contemptuous expression. **3–4.** Two connective particles, lost in translation, link vv 3–4 to the foregoing as an explanation of Israel's falseness. Unexpectedly, the first concern is with social, not religious, faults, but unfortunately the exact interpretation is difficult. If we follow the emended text (*NAB* "they"; "them," for MT "we"; "us" in v 3b), v 3 seems to recall 1 Sam 8: the people complain that they lack a king like the nations, but the prophet reproves their seeking a king in place of Yahweh, and without Yahweh Israel is lost, king or no king. However, the MT can be kept, according to which the prophet identifies himself with his nation and expresses the hopelessness of the situation. Inasmuch as "fear of the Lord," the basis of all society, is gone, there is, in effect, no king. He cannot govern a group where all honor and fidelity are lost. Justice (v 4) and right order have given way to disorder like useful plants to weeds. **5–6.** These verses are added to include Israel's religious failure in the condemnation by mocking the cult Israel preferred to Yahweh's service. Instead of being joyful in the cult, Israel will mourn its idol, whose exile proves its worthlessness. **5.** *priests:* Hebr *kĕmārîm* is a contemptuous term used of pagans only; perhaps we could say priestlings. This oracle must date from a time well after 732, when new Assyrian attacks threatened the remaining fragment of Israel, which included Bethel. **6–8.** The picture of devastation is developed in three stages: people, leaders, and religion will all disappear. Indeed, no one will want to survive; they shall ask the land for burial (v 8b).

29   (C) False Confidence (10:9–15). This section differs from 10:1–8 in being a direct address to the guilty. The theme is the futility of self-confidence in place of trust in God.

9–10. They form a complete "judgment oracle" with accusation and sentence. The text is very corrupt, but the general idea of false confidence is clear. **10.** *two crimes:* The second cannot be identified, but certainly it is something recent—current guilt that continues Israel's history of sin and brings current punishment.

11–12. As often (2:17; 9:10; 11:1), Hosea turns to the

fair hopes of Israel's beginnings when Yahweh himself took a docile people and set it on the way to a good reward. *justice:* The Hebr word means more than the Eng word, implying total right order, and hence, in addition to moral order, order in nature with due rain, etc., so as to produce material plenty (cf. S. Mowinckel, *The Psalms in Israel's Worship* [NY, 1962] 1. 146). All the agricultural imagery surely implies a claim that Yahweh, not the Baals, governed fecundity. **13.** Israel turned to the wrong way, trusting in its Baalist rites and in its strength. **14–15.** As fitting punishment that strength will be crushed. **15.** *at dawn:* Enigmatic; a slight change in the MT allows "like dawn," i.e., swiftly.

30   (D) Love Overcomes Ingratitude (11:1–11). This passage, one of the high points of the OT revelation of God's nature, is also one of the most corrupt of OT texts. Even so, there is a clear enough flow of thought: Yahweh's fatherly love and Israel's ungrateful response (vv 1–4) are punished (vv 5–7), which calls forth God's love (vv 8–9) to produce Israel's redemption (vv 10–11). There is an abrupt change in style and content at v 8. Yahweh's reflections about Israel's unresponsiveness give way to an impassioned proclamation to Israel of his love. However, vv 8–11 presuppose some history like that in vv 1–7 to explain the pitying love they proclaim, the love that ultimately governs all history. The sequence is deliberate, and the chapter is to be interpreted as a whole.

1. *my son:* The ancient Near East often gave notables a divine ancestry, but this need not be the background here. A context treating of Yahweh's education of Israel with emphasis on the love with which it was carried out more likely reflects the common usage in which the wise man, the educator, was called the father of his protégés (e.g., Azitawadda, king of the Danunians, *ANET* 500; Prov 2:1; etc.). **2.** *I called:* From the LXX. If the MT "they called" should be correct, it alludes to the attractions of the Baal cult or of Canaan's superior culture. **4b.** *healer:* Savior from Egypt (MT v 3b). **5.** Because it has deserted Yahweh, Israel must be punished with exile. **6–7.** Too corrupt to permit any sure exegesis beyond this.

8. *How . . . ? How . . . ?:* Punishment is not Yahweh's last word. A startling anthropomorphism presents a Yahweh so moved that he addresses his people in the emotional terms of the lament. He cannot destroy his beloved people. **9.** As startling is the appeal to his "holiness"; God's total otherness, the *mysterium tremendum,* instead of producing awe and terror, explains his mercy! Unlike human love, God's love does not have that inevitable element of selfishness that renders it changeable and destructive, making the vengeance of disappointed love so terrible. Verse 9 can be made a question: "Shall I not give vent, etc."—i.e., a new threat after the moment of pity in v 8 (T. H. Robinson, "Hosea" 44–45). However, it conflicts with the lamentation style introduced by v 8 and the hope expressed in v 11; hence, v 9 must be kept as an expression of pity. Andersen and Freedman (*Hosea* 589–90) interpret *lʾ* as an asseverative (thus, "I will certainly . . ."). This view is guided by such texts as Deut 1:17; Num 23:19; etc.: "At best, v 9a, if negative, declares a reluctance, not a permanent decision." But their transl. does not represent the masoretic tradition. Moreover, it is very difficult to distinguish between what is permanent and what is temporary in the divine will. **10–11.** There is an evident reversal in Yahweh's attitude (note the difference from chaps. 2–3, where it was Israel that reversed itself), and this promise of salvation (vv 10–11) is expected. However, the use of the 3d pers. in v 10, in contrast to the divine "I" of vv 8–9 and 11, makes v 10 appear to be an insertion interpreting the "trembling" (in awe and respect rather than in mere fear) of v 11. Verse 10 introduces a return "from the west"; v 11 has only Egypt and Assyria, corresponding to 11:5.

31   (E) Israel's Perfidy (12:1-15). The chapter as a whole scarcely shows a complete logical plan. We are dealing with a collection of sayings about a common theme, Israel's perfidy illustrated in history and in Hosea's contemporaries who but continue the way of the past.

In Eng versions, 12:1-15 of the MT is often numbered 11:12-12:14. **1b.** The perfidy theme is introduced by a contrast between Israel's treachery and Judah's fidelity, for v 1b should probably be translated "but Judah still walks with God and is faithful to the holy one" (the meaning of *rād,* "walks with," is uncertain; the parallel "faithful" in v 1b indicates the general sense; cf. Vg). The pl. *qĕdôšîm,* "holy one," is also difficult. The transl. presumes it to be a pl. of majesty formed on analogy with *'ĕlōhîm* but it must be admitted that the parallel *'el* (v 1b) and *qĕdôšîm* is strange since the parallel is the sg. *'el,* and Hosea uses an *'el-qādôš* (sg.) parallelism in 11:9. The meaning "the holy ones," i.e., faithful followers of Yahweh, perhaps the prophets who were especially near to God, would unify the chapter by linking this verse to 11 and 14 (Wolff, *Hosea* 209-10). **2a.** A vivid image for fruitless activity, made specific in the last half of v 2: Israel's empty striving is its policy of alliances ("carries oil," i.e., makes covenants, for covenant by oil was familiar in the ancient Near East; cf. D. J. McCarthy, *VT* 14 [1954] 215-21). Whether with Assyria or Egypt, alliances are vain. Worse, they are betrayals of Yahweh, Israel's unique support. **3.** *grievance:* Once more the standard introduction for a juridical accusation is developed in the following verses. *Jacob:* The patriarch and the people, his heirs, up to the prophet's own contemporaries, face judgment. The people are one with their head, who concentrates in himself all their deceit. **4.** *as a man:* Treacherous as a child (Gen 25:24-26; 27:36), in maturity the patriarch presumed to contend with God himself (Gen 32:22-33). **5.** *angel:* Stands for God (cf. Gen 32, where Jacob's opponent changes from man [v 25] to God [vv 29, 31]). In the light of the foregoing, we may see Jacob's prayer ("tears" are a standard means of supplication; cf. P. R. Ackroyd, *VT* 13 [1953] 250-51) as a continuation of his trickery and presumption; i.e., it was insincere, a ruse, so that Jacob's great encounter with God at Bethel (Gen 28:10-22; Hosea reverses the order of the incidents in Gen) is reduced to some kind of trick. However, it is possible that v 5 presents Jacob's conversion: the tribal father on whom Israel prided itself was a sinner like the rest, needing God's grace, although, unlike the people thus far, he at least accepted grace and was converted. This interpretation gives a good introduction to the call to conversion in v 7 (probably Hosea's and directed to the people, although it might be Yahweh's answer to Jacob's prayer, a call to him to repent, and through him to the people). One way or the other Hosea reverses the view of the Patriarch expressed in Gen: rather than a special friend of God, he is the first sinner in Israel, the one in whom the people's history of infidelity begins. On Jacob, see F. Diedrich, *Anspielungen auf die Jakob-Tradition in Hosea 12:1-13:3* [FB 27; Würzburg, 1977).

32   6. An interpolated doxology. **7.** As Jacob returned (Gen 28:15,21), so Israel is exhorted to "return" (*šûb*). **8.** A return to the present condemning Israel's double-dealing and confidence in material wealth. Israel is the "merchant," in Hebr "Canaanite" (for the Hebr farmers, the old inhabitants of the land were the traders par excellence); thus, the very word implies Israel's religious infidelity too, for it has imitated all the ways of Canaan. **9.** Wealth, even though applied to the cult in rich sacrifices, cannot cover Israel's sin (5:6). In a typical contrast to the wealth acquired in Canaan comes the picture of Israel's beginnings, when Yahweh himself saved the people from Egypt. The picture is made more actual by Yahweh's speaking in the first person, a reminiscence of cultic theophanies. Yahweh tells Israel that it must return to the condition of those old days, not for reasons of asceticism but because it will thus rediscover its intimacy with God, for "appointed time" (perhaps we might translate "time of rendezvous") recalls the great meetings with Yahweh in the desert. **11-12.** The idea of God's nearness is continued in the reference to the prophets (v 11), for God spoke to his people through the line of prophets from Moses (Deut 18:15) on, but in vain, for Israel put its confidence in a cult contaminated with Baalism, a cult that works only ruin (v 12). **13.** The verse returns to Jacob. In the light of vv 3-6, the reference to his activity in Aram (cf. Gen 27:41-31) must be condemnatory, another instance of Israel's failings early as late in its history. Perhaps Jacob's willingness to undergo servitude to win a wife alludes obliquely to Israel's serving the Baals in the interests of fertility, or his going to Aram refers to the policy of foreign alliances. **14-15.** In contrast to Israel's continual infidelity is God's never-failing saving action. The abrupt change to the condemnation in v 15 points up the inevitability of the end: a just God must visit its sins upon Israel.

33   (F) Death Sentence (13:1-14:1). This collection of judgment sayings is made up of several units: typical judgment oracles (13:1-3; 13:4-8); a mocking condemnation of the monarchy (13:9-11); and a composite final sentence on the whole people (13:12-14:1). These are arranged to give mounting emphasis to the central theme, that Israel stands before the ultimate punishment, death, instead of mere defeat and exile. In Eng versions, 13:1-14:1 of the MT is often numbered 13:1-16.

13:1-3. The first oracle exposes the past sins of Israel's leader, the tribe of Ephraim. Admittedly, the past tense "died" seems to close off v 1 and separate it from the following. However, we can take the death to be moral decline, or sufferings, which the OT often likens to death, or, perhaps best of all, a "prophetic perfect"; i.e., the end is so certain that it is given as fact even though it is still to come. Hence, v 1 may be legitimately connected with the following: past sin continues in the present idolatry so contemptuously described. Israel's use of a superstitious cult designed to force the divine by magical rites ends in its degrading itself before mere creatures—kissing and adoring calves. The end can only be ruin (v 3; cf. 6:4 for the same imagery). **4-8.** In contrast to the ruin that idolatry brings, the familiar liturgical formula "I am Yahweh your God since Egypt" puts Israel's true salvation, Yahweh, before us. However, the sequel shows, in terms that will be favorites of the deuteronomic school (e.g., Deut 8:11-20), how Yahweh's very favors have swollen Israel's pride so that it has deserted him. This can only mean that Yahweh changes from a savior to an inexorable judge who is depicted as a ravening beast of prey (cf. 5:14), an image all the more vivid in that the predator is the classic enemy of the shepherd, the figure under which Yahweh has just been presented. **9-11.** This mocking of the kings points up the idea that without Yahweh Israel is helpless no matter to what institutions it turns. **10.** A seeming reference to the demand for Saul to be made king as it is reported in the antimonarchical tradition (1 Sam 8), but v 11 implies an ineffectual monarchy with frequent dynastic changes. This fits the unstable northern kingdom that broke away from the legitimate Jerusalem monarchy and cult (cf. 8:4–6). **12.** The final unit of this chapter is introduced as a legal document which is "wrapped" and "stored," alluding to the procedure in which a judicial sentence was recorded on papyrus that was folded and tied with string and then covered with a seal (cf. Isa 8:16); illustration in *AtBib* 98). **13.** *birth pangs:* A favorite image of the judgment in prophecy (e.g., Jer 6:24) and apocalyptic (Isa 26:17; cf. John 16:21), but it is used differently here. The focus is on the child's folly, not the mother's suffering; i.e., in casting Yahweh aside, Israel, the child, has cast aside its chance to live. **14.** Rather than save Israel, Yahweh will give the powers of death power over it (the verse, except the last sentence, may be taken as a cry of triumph [cf. 1 Cor 15:35], but the context demands that it be read as threatening questions, as in the *NAB*). **15.** A new image specifies the impending destruction after the general threat: as the sirocco comes out of the desert to wither the bloom of spring, so will Yahweh destroy Israel, whatever its seeming prosperity. **14:1.** The final sentence, on the other hand, is not figurative; it describes the common, terrible fate of the people of a conquered land, the punishment which Israel will in fact undergo.

34   (IV) Epilogue: Repentance and Salvation (14:2–9). Hosea's prophecy closes on a note of hope — hope based on the certainty that Yahweh loves his people. The proclamation of this love has two parts: the prophet's summons to the people to return to its God (vv 2–4) and God's answering promise of love spoken to the prophet about the people (vv 5–9). This structure is that of a penitential rite; first the people proclaim their repentance; then they receive God's assurance of forgiveness through a prophet. Hosea used the form in 6:1–3, but there it was ironical, for true repentance was lacking; here it is serious. In Eng versions, 14:2–9 is often numbered 14:1–8.

2. Israel has already "collapsed," suffered its definitive punishment, so the summons to "return" looks to a final repentance and union with Yahweh, an idea to which v 9 (in the *NAB* version) returns. The fact of collapse does not prove that the oracle is later than 722; the prophet

could have foreseen both ruin and restoration (which, in fact, he never experienced) much earlier. **3.** True return means more than mere external cult: sacrifices must represent true repentance expressed in sincere prayer ("words"). This is the good Yahweh will accept that makes the sacrifices ("bullocks") valuable because they symbolize true dedication. (Verse 3b is obscure: the *NAB* is one possible emendation of the MT, "that we may render bullocks, our lips." The LXX has "we will repay with [the] fruit of our lips," removing all explicit reference to sacrifice — although the implicit contrast with the empty, pompous sacrificial cult still cannot be overlooked — and making the verse a simple call to prayer and penance.) **4.** A sample of the words and attitude demanded: rejection of all Israel's fetishes, political schemes (such as the alliance with Assyria), military force (horses), as well as idols in the strict sense.

5. Israel is sick with a hopeless disease, infidelity, which only God can cure: hence, God's love is free, i.e., not earned in any sense. **6–8.** The results of Yahweh's love are described: Israel will flourish in beauty (vv 6–7) and plenty (v 8). The images taken from the plant world recall that Yahweh, not the Baals, gives increase. Moreover, the language reflects the strength and tenderness of God's love, for expressions like "fragrance of Lebanon," "blossom like the vine," "dwell in the shade," "wine," "lily" are taken from the love songs of Israel, such as are seen in Cant (cf. Wolff, *Hosea* 236). **9.** Probably a separate saying attached to the foregoing because of the cypress image. *I have humbled . . . :* As in v 2, a promise of final salvation after punishment. The transl., however, is uncertain; the verse may mean "I have answered him and watch over him," i.e., a simple promise that Yahweh will hear a repentant Israel. *because of me . . . :* Possibly, "on me fruit will be found for you." In either case, Yahweh is likened to the tree of life. This symbol was familiar from the fertility cults. Applied to Yahweh, it is one more assertion that he is the true master of life. **10.** An addition, in wisdom style, of the scribes who compiled the book of Hosea.

15

ISAIAH 1-39

Joseph Jensen, O.S.B.   *William H. Irwin, C.S.B.* *

BIBLIOGRAPHY

1   Blenkinsopp, J., *A History of Prophecy in Israel* (Phl, 1983) 106–18. Bright, J., *BHI* 269–93. Childs, B. S., *Isaiah and the Assyrian Crisis* (SBT 2/3; London, 1967). Clements, R., *Isaiah 1–39* (GR, 1980). Duhm, B., *Das Buch Jesaia* (HKAT; 4th ed.; Göttingen, 1922). Fey, R., *Amos und Jesaja* (WMANT 12; Neu-kirchen, 1963). Fohrer, G., *Das Buch Jesaja* (2 vols.; ZBK; 2d ed.; Zurich, 1966). Gottwald, N., *All the Kingdoms of the Earth* (NY, 1964) 147–208. Gray, G. B., *A Critical and Exegetical Commentary on the Book of Isaiah, I–XXXIX* (ICC; NY, 1912). Irwin, W. H., *Isaiah 28–33* (BibOr 30; Rome, 1977). Jensen, J., *The Use of tôrâ by Isaiah* (CBQMS 3; Washington, 1973). Kaiser, O., *Isaiah 1–12* (Phl, 1983); *Isaiah 13–23* (1974). McKane, W., *Prophets and Wise Men* (SBT 1/43; London, 1965). Rad, G. von, *OTT* 2. 147–75. Scott, R. B. Y., "The Literary Structure of Isaiah's Oracles," *Studies in Old Testament Prophecy* (Fest. T. H. Robinson; ed. H. H. Rowley; NY, 1950) 175–86. Watts, J., *Isaiah 1–33, 34–66* (WBC 24, 25; Waco, 1985–87). Whedbee, J. W., *Isaiah and Wisdom* (Nash, 1971). Wildberger, H., *Jesaja* (BKAT 10/1; 2d ed.; Neukirchen, 1980; 10/2, 1978; 10/3, 1982).

INTRODUCTION

2   **(I) The Prophet and His Times.** Isaiah was called "in the year King Uzziah died" (6:1), i.e., in 742 on the chronology here followed (see below). This was shortly after the accession in Assyria of Tiglath-pileser III (745–727), who was followed by other able and vigorous kings (Shalmaneser V, 726–722; Sargon II, 721–705; Sennacherib, 704–681); indeed, the period of Isaiah's prophetic ministry was overshadowed by the irresistible power of Assyria and its plans for world empire.

Isaiah's prophetic ministry was exercised in and around Jerusalem. Little is known of his personal life. His devotion to Jerusalem traditions, the literary quality of his compositions, and his contacts with the wisdom tradition suggest that he was from an upper-class family and was highly educated. He was married to a woman designated as prophetess (8:3) and had two sons with symbolic names (7:3; 8:3,18).

Some of Isaiah's oracles may have been given in the days of Jotham (750–735, coregent with Uzziah [Azariah] from 750 to 742), perhaps some of those that relate to social justice and pagan practices, though such materials are difficult to date. Oracles that can be dated securely relate mainly to political crises that occurred under Ahaz (735–715) and Hezekiah (715–687). In 735

Syria and Israel invaded Judah in an attempt to force it into the anti-Assyrian coalition, an attempt that ended with the Assyrian conquest of Israel (733) and Syria (732), with Judah becoming an Assyrian vassal in the process (2 Kgs 16:7–9); most of the materials in 7:1–8:18 relate to this time. There may have been a period of silence, but Isaiah spoke out again to protest Egypt's attempt to press Judah, along with Philistia, to revolt against Assyria in 714 and possibly earlier (20:1–6; 18:1–6 probably also dates from this period and possibly some of chap. 19). The temptation was renewed at the death of Sargon II in 705, but now Isaiah's fervent, sometimes bitter, words failed to move Hezekiah, who revolted in concert with other small states, with promise of help from Egypt. The revolt was crushed in 701 with great devastation in Judah; Hezekiah had to surrender and pay a huge indemnity (22:1–14; 2 Kgs 18:13–16; *ANET* 288). The account of a wonderful deliverance after this surrender raises questions that relate both to Isaiah's teaching and to matters of history; see comment on 2 Kgs 18:13–19:37. None of Isaiah's oracles can be securely dated after 701, and his ministry may have ended about that time.

3   The chronology followed above and in the commentary is that most commonly accepted. Assyrian

---

* The introduction and commentary on chaps. 1–23 are the work of J. Jensen; and the remaining commentary (24–39) is by W. H. Irwin.

records indicate that the Syro-Ephraimite revolt began in 735; since Ahaz was king at that time, he began to reign no later than this. Sennacherib's invasion of Judah, again according to Assyrian records, occurred in 701, which, according to 2 Kgs 18:13 (//Isa 36:1), was the 14th year of Hezekiah's reign, which must then have begun in 715. However, 2 Kgs 18:1 dates Hezekiah's accession to the 3d year of Hoshea, who, again on the basis of Assyrian records, must have begun to rule *ca.* 732. Thus, some propose an accession date for Hezekiah *ca.* 728 and find confirmation in 2 Kgs 18:9–10, where the beginning of the siege of Samaria (724) and its fall (722) are dated to the 4th and 6th years of Hezekiah respectively. No totally satisfactory solution to the problem of conflicting data has been found.

4   (II) Teachings. The controlling principle of much of what Isaiah taught was his conviction concerning the holiness and kingly power of the God of Israel, both of which he experienced in his inaugural vision (6:1–13); "the Holy One of Israel" was his favorite title for Yahweh, whose "glory" did not abide merely in Jerusalem but filled the whole earth (6:3). Oppression of weaker members of society offended Yahweh's holiness, and so Isaiah speaks vehemently concerning social justice (1:10–17,21–26; 3:13–15; 5:1–10,20–23; 10:1–4) and of the punishment incurred for rejecting Yahweh's instruction (5:24).

Yahweh's power is such that all lies under his control, including the destinies of the mightiest nations, who function only as instruments of his policy (5:26–29; 7:18–19,20; 10:5–6). Yahweh has a policy or plan which he carries out in history with supreme wisdom (28:23–29) and ineluctable power (14:26–27). All human plans to the contrary are doomed to futility (7:4–7; 8:9–10). Thus, Isaiah thought it folly for Judah to attempt to carve out its own destiny, esp. when this involved turning to Assyria (for help against Syria and Israel) or Egypt (for help in revolting against Assyria). To trust in Yahweh's help and protection is faith, whereas to fail to do so is lack of faith (7:9b; 8:17; 28:16–17; 30:1–5,15; 31:1–3). Because the royal advisers, acting on purely human wisdom, led Ahaz and Hezekiah into paths contrary to those advocated by Isaiah, he has a special polemic against these so-called wise (5:18–19; 6:9–10; 29:13–14,15–16). This same group was responsible for the administration of justice and are condemned for their failure to live up to the high ideals of the wisdom tradition in which they were trained.

Isaiah saw pride as the cardinal sin (J. Barton, *JTS* 32 [1981] 1–18); it is the antithesis of faith and brings judgment (2:11–12,17; 3:16; 5:15–16; 9:8–9; 10:7–16,33; 28:1–4,22; 29:5). Thus Isaiah sees Yahweh's intention to bring punishment on Israel and Judah (3:1–4:1; 5:25,26–29; 6:11–13; 9:7–20). Such punishment can, however, be medicinal and prepare the way for restoration (1:21–26). Thus, Isaiah opened a door for hope. His own followers exhibited the faith to be a remnant of sorts (→ 21 below), and the Jerusalem traditions which so influenced him (he makes no reference to Moses, Sinai, or covenant), i.e., the Zion tradition and the promises to David's dynasty, inspired him to leave some of the brightest promises for the future in the OT (2:2–4; 8:23–9:6; 11:1–9).

5   (III) The Book. The canonical book of Isaiah consists of 66 chapters, but it has long been recognized that chaps. 40–55 and 56–66 are collections that date from exilic and postexilic times; → Deutero-Isaiah, 21:3, 50. Chapters 1–39 consist of several smaller collections, some of which are products of complex development. The authentic words of Isaiah are found mainly in chaps. 1–11 (largely from the days of Ahaz) and 28–32

(largely from the days of Hezekiah). Authentic words of Isaiah are also found among the "Oracles against the Nations" (chaps. 13–23) and perhaps also in the historical appendix (chaps. 36–39, taken from 2 Kgs 18:13–20:19). The "Apocalypse of Isaiah" (chaps. 24–27) and the collection in chaps. 34–35 date wholly from later periods. For details, see introductions to these sections.

The MT of Isaiah, on the judgment of Cross and others, belongs to the Palestinian family of texts and is generally conflate and expansionistic. The LXX Isaiah is from a very similar *Vorlage* and manifests the same tendencies. The famous 1QIsaᵃ, often characterized as "proto-Masoretic," belongs generally to the text type from which the MT was derived, though it exhibits a *plene* style of orthography. Thus, although original readings can sometimes be recovered from 1QIsaᵃ or from the LXX or other ancient versions, important and striking variants are not frequent.

(Cross, F. M., *HTR* 57 [1964] 281–99; *IEJ* 16 [1966] 81–95. Ziegler, J., *Untersuchung zur Septuaginta des Buches Isaias* [Münster, 1934]; *JBL* 78 [1959] 34–59.)

6   (IV) Outline.

  (I) An Introductory Collection (1:1–31)
    (A) The Inscription (1:1)
    (B) Yahweh's Complaint against His Senseless Children (1:2–3)
    (C) Jerusalem Chastised (1:4–9)
    (D) Worship and Justice (1:10–17)
    (E) The Choice (1:18–20)
    (F) Purifying Judgment on Jerusalem (1:21–28)
    (G) Crime and Punishment (1:29–31)
  (II) Concerning Judah and Israel: Part I (2:1–5:30)
    (A) Zion, Focus of Future Peace (2:2–4)
    (B) The Day of the Lord's Judgment (2:6–22)
    (C) Disintegration of Leadership and Populace (3:1–12)
    (D) Yahweh Accuses the Leaders (3:13–15)
    (E) Fate of the Women of Jerusalem (3:16–4:1)
    (F) Jerusalem Purified and Protected (4:2–6)
    (G) Song of the Lord's Vineyard (5:1–7)
    (H) Series of Woes ([10:1–4] + 5:8–24)
    (I) Yahweh's Outstretched Hand (5:25–30)
  (III) Isaiah's Memoirs (6:1–8:18[9:6])
    (A) Isaiah's Call (6:1–13)
    (B) Encounter with Ahaz (7:1–9)
    (C) The Sign of Immanuel (7:10–17)
    (D) Some Fragments (7:18–25)
    (E) Maher-shalal-hash-baz (8:1–4)
    (F) The Waters of Shiloah (8:5–8)
    (G) Vain Plans of Nations (8:9–10)
    (H) Isaiah Conspires with Yahweh (8:11–15)
    (I) Waiting for the Lord (8:16–18)
    (J) Two Additions (8:19–22)
    (K) Prince of Peace (8:23–9:6)
  (IV) Concerning Judah and Israel: Part II (9:7–12:6)
    (A) Yahweh's Outstretched Hand (9:7–20 + 5:25–30)
    (B) Woe against Oppressive Rulers (10:1–4)
    (C) Woe against Assyria (10:5–15)
    (D) Some Completions (10:16–27a)
    (E) Enemy Advance (10:27b–34)
    (F) The Future King (11:1–9)
    (G) Later Additions (11:10–16)
    (H) A Concluding Song of Thanksgiving (12:1–6)
  (V) Oracles against the Nations (13:1–23:18)
    (A) Oracle against Babylon (13:1–22)
    (B) The Gentiles and Israel's Restoration (14:1–2)
    (C) Taunt-Song against the King of Babylon (14:3–23)
    (D) Yahweh's Plan for Assyria (14:24–27)
    (E) Warning to Philistia (14:28–32)
    (F) Concerning Moab (15:1–16:14)
    (G) Against Syria and Israel (17:1–11)
    (H) Attack and Deliverance (17:12–14)
    (I) Embassy from Egypt (18:1–7)
    (J) Concerning Egypt (19:1–25)

COMMENTARY

7   **(I) An Introductory Collection (1:1-31).** Chapter 1 is a collection of oracles from various times in Isaiah's ministry which have been compiled as an introduction to the rest of the book; it functions as an epitome of his most important teachings. Less convincing is the position that the chapter, or much of it, forms a unity (J. Roberts, *PSB* 3 [1982] 293-306).

(A) The Inscription (1:1). An editor identifies the prophet whose oracles follow and dates his ministry. "Isaiah" means something like "Yahweh is salvation" (derived from *yš'* + Yah). His father, Amoz, is not otherwise known.

(B) Yahweh's Complaint against His Senseless Children (1:2-3). Opening with an alliterative "call to attention" (*šimě'û šāmayim*), the prophet depicts Yahweh's relationship to his people as that of a father who has bestowed all diligent care upon his children (cf. 30:1,9) only to find them disobedient and rebellious. The address to the heavens and earth do not indicate a covenant lawsuit. When Yahweh speaks, all creation pays heed — a suggestion that condemns the heedlessness of his people. They are contrasted unfavorably with the ox and the ass, animals proverbial for stupidity and stubbornness; worse than these, Israel does not even recognize its master. Word order is used effectively for emphasis: *sons* I have raised . . . ; *knows* the ox. . . . The root of the problem is the failure to "know," to "understand." These vbs. are used without any object being specified or supposed, a usage reminiscent of the wisdom tradition. At home also in wisdom is the father-son relationship, the education context, the employment of proverb, and some of the vocabulary. Israel's failure to know/understand is given as the cause of disaster also in 5:13 and 6:9-10. (On Isaiah's contacts with the wisdom tradition, see further comments on 1:10-17; 2:3; 5:18-24; 11:2; 14:26-27; 29:9-16; cf. also 28:23-29; 30:9.) The precise nature of the rebellion is left unspecified; no punishment is threatened, but rebellious children are likely to come to grief.

(C) Jerusalem Chastised (1:4-9). Although some would join these verses to the preceding, it is likely that the catchword principle ("sons") has brought them

together. A different meter is found in vv 4-9 and *hôy* ("woe!"; → 15 below) normally marks a new section. The historical background for the piece is probably the devastation wrought by the Assyrians in 701 after Hezekiah's rebellion against Sennacherib, an action bitterly opposed by Isaiah (see chaps. 28-32, *passim*). Thus, the *hôy* relates not to a threat for the future but to the present condition. The passage can be divided into three parts (vv 4,5-6,7-9), with a different personification in each. In v 4 Judah is referred to by four terms that are progressively more intimate (nation, people, offspring, children — *gôy*, *'am*, *zera'*, *bānîm*); the effect is to heighten the culpability expressed in the qualifying words. Judah's sin is the rejection of trust in Yahweh through power politics (i.e., covenanting with Egypt in order to rebel against Assyria). **5-6.** Now Judah is depicted as a single individual covered from head to foot with bloody wounds. While this vividly describes the condition of the country after Sennacherib's invasion, the imagery also suggests a son who has been chastised with the rod in order to teach obedience; see Prov 10:13; 13:24; 20:30; 22:15; 23:13,14; 26:3; 29:15; cf. Isa 10:5-6. **7.** *desolate . . . burned:* Sennacherib claims to have destroyed 46 walled cities and their villages (*ANET* 288). The final phrase compares Jerusalem's lot to the overthrow of Sodom (read *sĕdōm* for *zārîm*) and is a later addition. **8.** Since daughter Jerusalem has escaped destruction, hope is not extinguished. **9.** Although Judah's sin is comparable to that of Sodom and Gomorrah, it has received the chastisement of sons and has not been wholly destroyed. The word that alludes to the few survivors (*śārîd*) is not elsewhere used by Isaiah and does not appear to relate to his remnant theme.

8   **(D) Worship and Justice (1:10-17).** A new section is linked to the preceding by its reference to Sodom and Gomorrah. *give ear to the instruction (tôrâ) of our God:* A new "call to attention" similar to that of a wisdom teacher begins this section. Tôrâ is to be taken here (as also in 2:3; 5:24; 8:16; 30:9) in the wisdom sense of generalized instruction rather than law (Jensen, *Use of tôrâ* 68-83). The contents show that the piece is directed to the rulers (even though the people are also addressed), those primarily responsible for just judgment. Like other prophets (see Amos 5:21–24; Jer 7:1–15), Isaiah says that God will not accept worship (not only sacrifice, but prayer itself!) from those who oppress and mistreat the poor and helpless, a teaching found also in wisdom (Prov 15:8; 21:3,27; *ANET* 417), where, as here, insincere actions are said to be an "abomination" to God (Prov 6:16–19; 12:22; 15:8; 21:27; *ANET* 423). In a series of nine imperatives, Yahweh says what is to be done. This concern for the helpless classes of society is rooted both in Israel's law and its wisdom (e.g., Exod 22:20–23; 23:6–9; Deut 24:17; Prov 14:31; 15:25; 19:17; 22:9,22–23; 23:10–11; 29:14).

(E) **The Choice (1:18–20).** In vv 4–9 past destruction is described, and in vv 10–17 a series of imperatives dictates future action, but here is issued an invitation to "reason together" and the alternatives of eating good things or being eaten by the sword are offered. *if your sins . . . they shall be as white as snow . . . as wool:* Many interpret these as rhetorical questions which expect the answer no, but this seems less probable. There are four "if" ('*im*) statements but only in the third and fourth is a choice offered. Upon that choice depends whether the sword or blessings shall be their lot and whether the sins referred to will find forgiveness.

(F) **Purifying Judgment on Jerusalem (1:21–28).** An *inclusio* ("faithful city") marks the beginning and the end of the original piece, with vv 27–28 being a later addition. The opening word ('*êkâ*), frequently used in contexts of grief and mourning, gives emotional impact to the accusation of vv 21–23; it is balanced by the *hôy* at the beginning of Yahweh's words of judgment (v 24). The personification implied in the transition from "faithful city" to "harlot" is probably that of "daughter Zion." The background is not Hosea, but rather the personification of a city as married to the patron deity (A. Fitzgerald, *CBQ* 37 [1975] 167–83). **23.** The crimes, as in 1:10–17, are mainly oppression of the helpless, here aggravated by bribery. **24–25.** Yahweh's response will be a judgment at once punitive and purifying. Read *bakkūr*, "in a furnace," in place of *kabbōr*, "as with lye." **26.** For Isaiah punishment could be medicinal and corrective, Yahweh's means of preparing for restoration (cf. 7:15). *judges . . . counselors:* Groups that relate to administration of justice and to national policy, two important poles of Isaiah's thought (→ 4 above). **27–28.** These verses are probably an editorial comment on the preceding. The *judgment* and *justice* (*mišpāṭ* and *ṣĕdāqâ*) can refer to the merciful qualities that lead Yahweh to redeem. Unlike v 26, which supposes a universal conversion for Zion, here a distinction is made between the lot of those who are converted and those who are not.

(G) **Crime and Punishment (1:29–31).** The Isaian authenticity of these verses is disputed, as is their interpretation. Although they are commonly understood to refer to the fertility cult, it can be argued that here the prophet condemns the rich for coveting the property of others (Fohrer, *Jesaja* 1. 45–46). The comparison of the wicked with vegetation that withers is common in wisdom (see Job 15:30–35; Ps 37:35–36).

(II) **Concerning Judah and Israel: Part I (2:1–5:30).** Organization of the materials becomes complicated at this point. The new inscription (2:1) shows that the collection of oracles "concerning Judah and Jerusalem" here introduced originally existed independently of 1:1–31. This collection perhaps originally included, without interruption, the authentic materials now in 9:7–11:9, but at some point the so-called "Memoirs of Isaiah" (→ 16 below) were inserted, thus disrupting the collection and occasioning other displacements (cf. 5:8–24,25–30). In the present state of the

book, the inscription serves for all the material up to 13:1.

9   (A) **Zion, Focus of Future Peace (2:2–4).** Although some deny this oracle to Isaiah, it coheres with his concept of Yahweh as universal king and with other aspects of his teaching. The oracle is found also at Mic 4:1–4, but the prophet who foretold the Temple's destruction (Mic 3:12) did not speak these words. **2.** *at the end of days:* This means hardly more than "in the future" (see E. Lipiński, *VT* 20 [1970] 445–50), sometimes with reference to a new order, and does not indicate an eschatology later than Isaiah. The choice of Zion as Yahweh's abode, the place of his special protection, and the goal of the pilgrimage of the nations, sometimes with motifs of peace and destruction of weapons, are themes found in the "Zion Psalms" (Pss 46; 48; 76; 87; → Psalms, 34:62) and others and express a faith that antedated Isaiah. **3.** The terminology is reminiscent of pilgrimage (one "goes up" to worship Yahweh). The emphasis is on seeking instruction (the proper meaning for *tôrâ* here; cf. 1:10) in moral deportment, and Yahweh's "ways" are recognized as the right ones. The difference between the present and the ideal future is that now Yahweh's *tôrâ* is rejected even by Judah (30:8–14), whereas then it will be accepted by all. **4.** The peace here described implies a renunciation of wars of conquest, as well as acceptance of Yahweh's general norms and specific judgments. Isaiah's love for peace is seen also in his descriptions of the ideal king of the future (9:5–6; 11:6–9). **5.** An exhortation by a later editor; the conclusion in Mic 4:4 is quite different.

10   (B) **The Day of the Lord's Judgment (2:6–22).** The "Day of the Lord," which first appears in Amos 5:18–20, becomes an important theme in Scripture, but only later does it relate to a final judgment and the end of the world. Isaiah here thinks of an event that is to take place within history. But he does not speak of foreign invasion; this judgment is Yahweh's act, and the language is reminiscent of storm theophany (see esp. Ps 29). The passage is badly preserved and, as it now stands, is probably pieced together from two or more incomplete poems. Wildberger postulates four original unities (vv 6,7–9,12–17, and 19) and thinks that vv 10–11 and 20–21 are secondary compositions from parts of other verses; others think that these repetitions form a deliberate refrain. Verses 9b and 22 are late additions.

The opening verses form a multifaceted indictment of Israel/Judah, but the description of Yahweh's day encompasses all humankind ('*ādām*, '*îš* '*ānāšîm*) and much of nature, so that it appears to be cosmic in scope. **6–8.** Here are listed various ways in which God's people place trust in things other than him (divination, foreign powers, wealth, military might, idols) and thus are guilty of pride, which for Isaiah is the capital sin, an obstacle to God's saving work and the object of Yahweh's special wrath (3:16; 5:15–16; 9:8–9; 10:7–15,33; 28:1–4, 22). **9–19.** The man-made objects against which Yahweh's wrath is directed are also indicative of human pride and self-sufficiency (on "Tarshish ships" see 23:1); even the lofty features of nature seem to be infected with human self-exaltation and therefore are the objects of Yahweh's wrath. Yet for all the violence and destruction supposed (though not described), the express purpose of Yahweh's action is the humbling of human pride (vv 9, 11,17,19). The abasing of human pride can be a positive thing in that it removes an obstacle to Yahweh's action in history. Wildberger uncovers in this composition extensive contacts with the wisdom tradition, where also it is a matter of the proud being humbled because they are proud (Prov 14:19; 25:7; 29:23). There are correspondences discernible between 2:2–4 and this piece (e.g., the parallel exaltation of Yahweh in both of them, and the antithetical abasement of everything else in this second piece—and cf. esp. v 2 with v 14), so that the editor who joined them may have intended to show how Yahweh would remove the obstacles that hindered the accomplishment of the vision in 2:2–4 (see further J. Jensen, *CBQ* 43 [1981] 181–86). **22.** The address is pl. and therefore not directed to the Lord.

11   (C) Disintegration of Leadership and Populace (3:1–12). There is a thematic unity to 3:1–4:1, but it is not a unified composition. The present passage describes a vacuum of leadership, near anarchy, which occasions many other evils. The removal of leadership and the resultant evils make this piece the antithesis of 1:26, where the restoration of leaders provides the circumstances for Jerusalem's restoration. Isaiah may here be anticipating deportation at the hands of the Assyrians, their practice being to remove the more influential classes, those who protect, govern, and advise. **1.** *support and prop:* Refers to the classes enumerated in vv 2–3. *bread and water:* A later, misleading addition. **2–3.** A similar listing is given of the Babylonian deportation of 597 in 2 Kgs 24:14–16. **5.** The want of leadership occasions general lawlessness and reversal of values. **6–7.** In these circumstances leadership would be thrust upon those with no more qualification than the possession of garments. **8–9.** The collapse is attributed to "their tongue and their deeds," but the precise nature of the sin is not specified. Rejection of Yahweh's word in, e.g., rebelling against Assyria, would explain deportation, but exile could also come as punishment for social crimes (10:1–4). **10–11.** A later expansion, in the wisdom mode, contrasting the lot of the just and the wicked. Possibly *'imrû* ("say") should be emended to *'ašrê* ("happy," "blessed") to give an antithetically parallel expression to the "woe" (*'ôy*). **12.** This cry of grief from Yahweh is a fragment by Isaiah from another context, here used as a transition to vv 13–15; it refers to a present situation rather than (as vv 1–7) to the future. *babe . . . women:* If the reading is correct, the historical reference is unclear. Some would emend to give "moneylenders . . . usurers."

(D) Yahweh Accuses the Leaders (3:13–15). The judgment is depicted as a legal trial, Yahweh acting as judge and accuser. While reference is made to "the people," the action is clearly directed against the "elders" and "princes." The elders were leaders who represented and spoke for those under them, but here they are among the oppressors. *devour:* The vb. (piel of *bā'ar*) normally means "to burn." *vineyard:* In sg., with def. art., could here refer to Israel (see 5:7). *plunder* (*gĕzēlâ*): Normally refers to that taken by violence, and the verbs also suggest violence, but this is probably Isaiah's way of condemning a social order which allowed the powerful to grow rich at the expense of the weak, even though this might be done by legal means (see on 10:1–4); all the more appropriate that Yahweh is here depicted as bringing the powerful to trial.

12   (E) Fate of the Women of Jerusalem (3:16–4:1). Although a thematic unity, the passage was not composed in one piece: 3:16–24 tells of the reversal to come upon the women of Jerusalem for their pride and luxury, while in vv 25–26 Jerusalem (in sg.) is personified, referred to first in 2d, then in 3d person. **16.** *daughters of Zion:* On Mt. Zion was located the ruling class, and the address is to women of this group. Isaiah sees them as vain and insouciant; the juxtaposition of this piece to vv 13–15 associates them with their men in despoiling the poor (see Amos 4:1), through whose impoverishment their luxuries are supported. **18–23.** A late listing of the items that might be worn by such

women supplements Isaiah's own modest enumeration in vv 16,24. **17,24.** A reversal of their fate is in store for them (see Amos 4:2–3). Verse 24 probably intends five reversals, though something has fallen out of the text; 1QIsa^a adds *bšt*, which would then give: "in place of beauty, disgrace." Isaiah could be thinking of enemy conquest, in which rich clothing would become plunder (cf. 3:14!), the wearers humiliated (Lam 5:11) and even carried off as slaves and concubines. **25–26.** Defeat in war was clearly in the mind of the editor who appended these verses. The personification is no doubt that of daughter Zion (1:8), a change from the "daughters of Zion" in v 16. **4:1.** The absence of men in the devastated city occasions the final reversal, as the rich women scramble to avoid what was considered a disgrace, to be unmarried and childless, even renouncing the support they ought to have claimed (Exod 21:10–11).

13   (F) Jerusalem Purified and Protected (4:2–6). Chapters 2–4 may have originally formed a short collection; it ends on a note of hope with this passage, which dates from considerably after Isaiah. It looks to a time when Jerusalem's suffering will have passed, leaving her purified and under the Lord's special protection. **2.** *growth* (*ṣemaḥ*): The parallelism with "fruit of the earth" shows that here, at least, *ṣemaḥ* is to be taken literally, not as a symbolic term for the messianic king (cf. Jer 23:5; 33:15; Zech 3:8; 6:12). *survivors* (*pĕlēṭâ*): A term used elsewhere for the escaped remnant who enjoy the Lord's favor (10:20; 37:31–32; Joel 3:5; Obad 17; see Blenkinsopp, *History of Prophecy* 259). **3.** Those who remain are not simply survivors but have been designated as holy (*qādôš*), as is the Lord himself (6:3). On the Lord's special book, see Exod 32:32–33; Dan 12:1; Ps 69:29. **4.** The very trials Jerusalem has undergone effect Yahweh's purifying action. The parallel here was probably originally "Zion's filth" and "Jerusalem's blood," but "daughters of" was added to relate the piece more explicitly to 3:16–4:1 and to mitigate the harshness of those verses. **5.** *cloud . . . fire:* Cf. Exod 13:21–22. **6.** *glory:* Cf. 6:3; but here it may be akin to the P tradition (→ Pentateuch, 1:7).

14   (G) Song of the Lord's Vineyard (5:1–7). Some see here the beginning of a new collection that accounts for the materials through chap. 12 (except for Isaiah's "memoirs" → 16 below). The "song" is a skillfully concocted parable which hints at unrequited love, contrasts the care lavished by Yahweh with his people's sinful response (social crimes), and speaks of judgment to come. **1.** Two terms for "friend" or "beloved" are used, *yādîd* and *dôd,* the second of which occurs frequently in Cant, where also we find vineyard used metaphorically of the beloved. By these devices Isaiah both conceals that he is speaking of Yahweh and gives a personal dimension to the betrayal. **2.** *bĕ'ušîm:* Not strictly wild grapes, but rotten ones (from a root that means "to stink"). **3.** A well-wrought parable leads the hearers to pass a judgment (cf. 2 Sam 12:5–6) which makes the point the speaker intends. **5–6.** Future devastation awaits the nation. **7.** Reveals that the "song" is a parable. The final half verse plays on words that sound alike but have radically different meanings: *mišpāṭ* and *ṣĕdāqâ* (judgment and justice) are what he looked for, *mišpāḥ* and *ṣĕ'āqâ* (violence and outcry) are what he found. The "judgment" desired is not a strict, impartial accounting, but rather a merciful vindication of the rights of the poor (see 1:17); *ṣĕdāqâ* suggests the behavior that regards circumstances, not an unconditioned norm. Yahweh's *ṣĕdāqâ* is seen esp. in his acts of deliverance (Judg 5:16; 1 Sam 12:7; Mic 6:5), and those in authority ought to imitate him. The "outcry" comes from the poor man, perhaps despoiled of his goods through unjust judgment, as he calls out for help or expresses bitter despair.

15   (H)   Series of Woes ([10:1–4] + 5:8–24).
The woe form (most commonly *hôy* + ptc.) may be a prophetic adaptation of the lament over the dead (see R. Clifford, *CBQ* 28 [1966] 458–64; W. Janzen, *Mourning Cry and Woe Oracle* [BZAW 125; Berlin, 1972]). It condemns the sort of behavior characterized in it and threatens those who practice it. The woe saying in 10:1–4 (minus the refrain in v 4b; see on 10:1–4) probably originally formed, along with the six in this chapter, a series of seven. All these woe sayings may be directed against more or less the same group as the preceding parable, viz., the court officials responsible for the administration of justice and for advising the king in matters of policy, men educated in and connected with the wisdom school that must have existed in Jerusalem (J. Olivier, *JNSL* 4 [1975] 49–60). These are "the wise" against whom Isaiah sometimes wages a polemic. **10:1–4.** *who enact iniquitous enactments:* They administer justice and have authority to establish its rules; they have enriched themselves at the expense of the poor (cf. 5:8). This perversion of legal process is described in terms normally used of the plunder taken in warfare (cf. 3:14; 8:3–4). *day of visitation:* Obviously Yahweh's, for the sake of punishment. *ruin from afar:* Suggests foreign invasion, probably by Assyria (cf. 5:26–29). **5:8–10.** Heavy sarcasm describes the luxurious isolation that the rich attain through the creeping latifundism of 8th-cent. Judah (and Israel), a process that, at the expense of the poor, changed an egalitarian society of small landowners into a highly stratified one. The process may have been made legal (10:1–4), but it was damnable, and the prophet attests to Yahweh's oath that the ill-gotten goods taken would never be enjoyed. *in my hearing:* The prophet is privy to God's intention (cf. 6:9–13; Jer 23:18). *bath . . . homer . . . ephah:* Cf. R. de Vaux, *AI* 199–203. **11–14.** The third woe condemns those guilty of a drunken luxury (cf. Amos 6:4–6) that makes them unable to perceive Yahweh's action in history (cf. v 19). These are the king's advisers, whose imperception leads to disastrous policies that result in destruction and exile (cf. 28:7–13). *the netherworld:* Depicted as a devouring monster. **15–16.** A later addition which takes much of its diction from 2:9, 11,17. **17.** *NAB* transfers this verse to after v 10 as appropriate to the context. **18–19.** Fourth woe. *cords . . . ropes:* Those addressed are constantly accompanied by sin as though harnessed to it (M. Dahood, *CBQ* 22 [1960] 74–75). They scoff at Isaiah's teaching on the "plan" or "purpose" (*'ēṣâ,* parallel with "work," *ma'áśēh;* cf. v 12) of Yahweh and taunt its nonfulfillment; i.e., these are "the wise," the king's policy makers; they seek to discredit Isaiah because his counsel is contrary to theirs. **20.** The reversals of truth reflected in the fifth woe refer both to perversion of right judgment and to advocacy of disastrous policies. **21.** Sixth woe. *in their own eyes:* But not in Yahweh's nor in reality; when Yahweh acts theirs will be seen to be the reverse of true wisdom (29:14,15–16). **22–23.** Seventh woe. Again a reproach for neglecting duties to the poor communicated in their schooling (Prov 14:31; 17:5; 21:13; 22:16, 22–23), in which they also learned of the evils of intemperate drinking (Prov 20:1; 21:17; 23:29–35; Sir 18:33; 19:2; 31:25–30), esp. as occasioning perversion of justice (Prov 31:4–5), and of taking bribes (Prov 15:27; 17:23). **24.** The first three woes had punishments given with them, and this verse is intended to supply punishment either for the last four (which are closely connected) or for the whole group. *instruction . . . word:* A summary of the crimes contained in the list of woes. The "instruction" (cf. 1:10) refers esp. to the ethical teaching of their

schooling which, because it is good and indispensable, is subsumed into Yahweh's teaching.

(I)   Yahweh's Outstretched Hand (5:25–30).
For the treatment of this section, → 23 below.

16   (III)   Isaiah's Memoirs (6:1–8:18 [9:6]).
We have in 7:1–8:18 materials pertaining to the crisis of 735–732, put together in a connected and chronological order, apparently to report Isaiah's words and actions during this period. These are introduced by the prophet's vocation narrative (6:1–13) and followed by 8:23–9:6. These materials may have been put together by Isaiah himself (note the use of the 1st pers. in chaps. 6 and 8); they have been called his *Denkschrift* (memoirs) by German scholars, with the term referring sometimes only to the central section, 7:1–8:18 (the rest functioning as framework), sometimes to the whole complex. Its insertion into the collection that begins at 5:1 and extends through 12:6 occasioned some dislocation of materials (see on 5:8–24 and 9:7–20).

17   (A)   Isaiah's Call (6:1–13). The call narrative stands at the beginning of the collection to which it pertains, though not at the book's beginning. An important function of a call narrative is to justify to his contemporaries the prophet's teaching, unpopular as it might be, irreverent or seditious as it might seem (see E. Jenni, *TZ* 15 [1959] 321–39; N. Habel, *ZAW* 77 [1965] 197–323: R. Knierim, *VT* 18 [1968] 47–68). **1.** Uzziah's death was in 742 (→ 3 above). Yahweh is depicted as king (cf. v 5), yet not as a nationalistic deity, since his sway extends through all the earth (v 3) and his hand falls heavily upon his own people (vv 11–13). **2.** *seraphim:* Adjective meaning fiery, here used substantively (or possibly with "cherubim" understood); depicts heavenly guardians of Yahweh's court, composite but not serpentiform (as is sometimes asserted because of the use of *śārāp* in Num 21:6; Deut 8:15; Isa 14:29; 30:6), for they have hands, faces, and sexual parts. *veiled their faces:* Out of reverence (Exod 3:6; 1 Kgs 19:13). *feet:* Euphemism for sexual parts (cf. 7:20). **3.** *holy:* The cry may reflect the liturgy of the Jerusalem Temple. Yahweh's holiness is his predominant attribute for Isaiah (→ 4 above). Moral perfection is included, but primarily it refers to his transcendence and otherness. The glory (*kābôd*) which fills the whole earth can hardly be the fiery splendor of P (cf. Exod 40:34–35). It probably includes Yahweh's kingly power over all nations, a point of some importance in the crisis of 735–732. **4.** *smoke:* Along with the earth tremor, an element of the theophany. **5.** *I am silenced:* Meaning uncertain; may mean that the vision calls to proclamation, whereas his "unclean lips" hinder this. *my eyes have seen:* Explains the "woe is me," on the conviction that no one can see God and live (Exod 33:20; Judg 13:22). In fact, Isaiah is now uniquely qualified to speak of God, and the cleansing of his lips (vv 6–7) prepares for the commission to do so (v 9). Both in terms of sinfulness and cleansing, "lips" are a *pars pro toto* way of designating the whole person under a particular aspect. **8.** *who will go for us?:* The context supposes that a session of Yahweh's council has just concluded (cf. 1 Kgs 22:19–23; E. C. Kingsbury, *JBL* 83 [1964] 279–86; H. W. Robinson, *JTS* 45 [1944] 151–57) and that a messenger is sought to carry news of the decision arrived at. **9–10.** *this people:* Implies reproach (see 8:6,11; 29:13). The Lord's desire is not to prevent that "they turn and be healed," nor did Isaiah attempt to prevent it. Failure to be converted results from the refusal to "hear" the word of the Lord through his prophet and to "see" what the Lord is about (cf. 5:12,19). The fault is primarily that of the leaders, ironically revealed in the command to harden (see also 30:11). **11.** *how long?:* A cry common in psalms of supplication, a prayer for pity and relief (Pss

13:2–3; 74:10; 79:5; 80:5; 89:47; 90:13; 94:3). *until:* The response mentions only devastation, but judgment does not preclude restoration and may even be the condition for it, as elsewhere in Isa (cf. 1:24–26). **12–13.** These may be a series of additions to adapt the saying to later circumstances, such as the Assyrian deportation of Israel in 721 and to threaten Judah (often taken as "a tenth" of the whole—cf. 1 Sam 11:8; 2 Sam 19:44; 1 Kgs 11:31), though the text and meaning of some parts of v 13 are disputed. *holy offspring:* Isaiah's teaching includes a remnant concept, but these words seem to be a later addition to mitigate an image that tells of destruction.

18 **(B) Encounter with Ahaz (7:1–9).** The attack of Syria (Aram) and Israel (Ephraim) on Judah, the so-called Syro-Ephraimite war, was an attempt to force it into the anti-Assyrian coalition. Ahaz resolved his difficulty, against the urging of Isaiah, by submitting as vassal to Assyria, whose king, Tiglath-pileser III, moved against Syria and Israel (2 Kgs 16:7–9). **2.** The insertion of v 1 (taken with small changes from 2 Kgs 16:5) gives the impression that the encounter between Isaiah and Ahaz took place after the siege had begun, but that may not be the case; v 2 speaks only of an alliance between Syria and Israel—if that is indeed the meaning of the Hebrew. (*NAB*'s "encamped in" rests on an emendation). *house of David:* I.e., Ahaz, as current embodiment of the Davidic dynasty and repository of the promises to it (cf. 2 Sam 7). **3.** *Shear-yashub:* "A remnant shall return" is not named again; but see on 8:18. *upper pool:* Water was brought from the spring Gihon to the upper pool (see on 8:6 and 22:9–11); Ahaz is inspecting the water supply that will be so important in case of siege. **4–5.** Yahweh's word is that Ahaz neither surrender to the threat nor submit to the Assyrians, though the latter course was apparently urged by his advisers; the present threat shall shortly come to nothing (see also 8:1–4). The formula "do not fear" comes from Israel's holy war tradition (cf. esp. Deut 20:3–4), but Isaiah thinks also of the special place of the Davidic dynasty and Jerusalem in God's plan. **6.** *son of Tabeel:* Assuredly someone who would be more amenable to anti-Assyrian policies than Ahaz, but otherwise the reference is uncertain (see W. F. Albright, *BASOR* 140 [1955] 34–35; A. Vanel, in *Studies on Prophecy* [VTSup 26; Leiden, 1974] 17–24). **7.** *this shall not stand:* The basis for this assertion is that the Syria-Israel stratagem is only human counsel (v 5—*yāʿaṣ*), which comes to nought (8:10), whereas Yahweh has his own purpose, which shall surely be carried out (5:12,19; 14:24; J. Jensen, *CBQ* 48 [1986] 443–55). **8.** Probably intended to suggest, in elliptical fashion, that Jerusalem, the city chosen by Yahweh, is head of Judah and that Yahweh (or Ahaz, embodiment of the Davidic dynasty) is the head of Jerusalem. **9.** *sixty-five years:* Verse 9a is a later addition and probably refers to the settlement of a foreign population in Samaria by Esarhaddon, seen as the *coup de grâce* to the northern kingdom. *unless you believe:* A play on words (different forms of *'āman*, "to be firm") which indicates that unless Ahaz manifests steadfast faith by looking only to Yahweh for help, he will no longer stand. This call for faith is characteristic of Isaiah, sometimes in other terminology (8:17; 22:11; 28:16; 30:15).

19 **(C) The Sign of Immanuel (7:10–17).** A new encounter with Ahaz, though in the same historical context. Ahaz may have been undecided, with the prophet urging one course, his advisers another, and this occasions Isaiah's offer of a sign. **11.** *sign:* The Hebr *'ôt* need not mean something miraculous (cf., e.g., 37:30), but here Ahaz is to ask for confirmation of the prophet's promise. **12.** Ahaz's refusal probably indicates that his mind is already closed. **14.** The sign now to be given is

no longer to persuade Ahaz but will, in the future, confirm the truth of what the prophet has spoken. *the young woman:* Hāʿalmâ is not the technical term for a virgin (*bĕtûlâ*). This is best understood as a wife of Ahaz; the child promised will guarantee the dynasty's future (note again "the house of David" in v 13; cf. v 2) and for this reason can be called Immanuel ("with us is God"). **15.** *curds and honey:* The only food available in a devastated land; see vv 17,21–25. *so that he may know:* Rather than "by the time. . . ." The discipline of hardship will teach Immanuel "to reject evil and choose good" and make him the antithesis of Ahaz. (Knowledge of good and evil in the OT means adult discernment and supposes a mature age; see J. Jensen, *CBQ* 41 [1979] 220–39.) **16.** Long before Immanuel comes to maturity, Israel and Syria will have been devastated, something Isaiah expected within a few years (see 8:1–4). **17.** *the king of Assyria:* This (correct) identification was added by a later editor. On 7:14, → Matthew, 42:11.

(D) Some Fragments (7:18–25). This section consists of shorter oracles (cf. "on that day" in vv 18,20,21,23) gathered here because they relate to the preceding material. **18–19.** Powerful nations are merely agents of Yahweh's policy (cf. 5:26–29; 10:5–15). *fly . . . Egypt:* Probably a later expansion. **20.** A similar teaching in different imagery. *the river:* The Euphrates. *king of Assyria:* Again a gloss. *feet:* See 6:2. The "shaving" may allude to denuding the country through tribute paid (see 2 Kgs 16:8) but also implies humiliating treatment (2 Sam 10:4). **21–22.** *keep alive:* Suggests difficult circumstances (cf. 1 Kgs 18:5), and therefore the "curds and honey" represent the food available in a land devastated, without agriculture. *abundant yield of milk:* Perhaps a later attempt to give "curds and honey" a favorable meaning. **23–25.** An expansion by a later hand.

20 **(E) Maher-shalal-hash-baz (8:1–4).** Isaiah's symbolic action proclaims the demise of Syria and Israel within a limited time, i.e., the two or three years from the conception of a child to its simplest words. By this Isaiah tells Ahaz (and the people—cf. v 5) that to seek help from Assyria is unnecessary. On Isaiah's use of symbolic names, see also 7:3,14; 8:18; 9:5). **1.** The kind of writing material employed is uncertain, but it must have been large enough for easy legibility. Maher-shalal-hash-baz means "quick spoils, speedy plunder." **2.** Uriah and Zechariah are perhaps those referred to in 2 Kgs 16:10–11 and 2 Kgs 18:2. **3.** *the prophetess:* Presumably Isaiah's wife; she is not otherwise mentioned.

(F) The Waters of Shiloah (8:5–8). Isaiah contrasts the quiet might of Yahweh ("the waters of Shiloah") with the power of Assyria ("the river," i.e., the Euphrates). By turning to Assyria for help (2 Kgs 16:7–8), Ahaz has substituted trust in human power for faith in Yahweh. The prophet foretells that Assyria will submerge Judah in its flood. **6.** *Shiloah:* Apparently a channel from the spring Gihon (see on 22:9–11), a perennial stream whose waters could enable Jerusalem to withstand a siege; this may have been where Isaiah encountered Ahaz in 7:3. *this people:* Not "my people." This expresses disapproval (see also 6:9; 8:11; 29:13) and suggests that Ahaz's policy enjoyed popular support. **7–8.** Ahaz has opened the land to Assyria and henceforth (until the late 7th cent.) Judah will be its vassal; Hezekiah's later revolt will bring Assyrian power in devastating force. *the spreading of his wings:* An abrupt change of imagery. Yahweh's wings are a symbol of protection (Deut 32:11; Pss 17:8; 36:8; 57:2; etc.), not threat. Though v 8b is often deleted, Isaiah saw Assyria's role as limited (10:5–15; 14:24–27) and could have expected final protection for Judah. Even the address to Immanuel, who grows to maturity in a devastated land (7:15–16), though often questioned, is not impossible here.

(G) Vain Plans of Nations (8:9–10). The might of the nations counts for nothing where Yahweh is involved; no plan (*'ēṣâ*) they form shall stand (cf. also 7:5–7), but only Yahweh's (14:24; see 5:19). The background for such assurance would be the Zion tradition, esp. as attested in Pss 46; 48; 76; in Ps 46:8,12 is found the equivalent of "Immanuel" ("the Lord of hosts is with us"). But this phrase also had its background in the Davidic tradition (cf. 7:10–17), and the present passage contains echoes of Ps 2. If the *peoples* addressed are Syria and Israel (cf. 7:3–9a), the piece has been displaced.

(H) Isaiah Conspires with Yahweh (8:11–15). 11. *this people:* See 8:6. **12.** *call not conspiracy:* The imperatives are pl. in form, so others along with Isaiah (cf. vv 16–18) are being addressed. Hebr *qešer* regularly means "conspiracy," "treason" (as, e.g., in 2 Kgs 11:14), and its use here indicates, with some irony, that Isaiah and his followers are considered seditious because they oppose the policy adopted by the state. **13.** *the Lord . . . you shall call holy:* Hebr *taqdîšû* should be emended to *taqšîrû* ("with the Lord . . . make your conspiracy"), parallel to the thought and terminology of v 12. **14–15.** *sanctuary:* Hebr *miqdāš* does not fit with "obstacle" and "stumbling stone"; it is usually emended to *môqēš*, "snare." The rejection of faith results in the stripping away of Yahweh's protection; he becomes, rather, a source of calamity to them.

21   (I) Waiting for the Lord (8:16–18). Here end Isaiah's "memoirs" proper. His message for the Syro-Ephraimite crisis, though rejected, has been given; now he and those with him, who form a remnant of faith, await the fulfillment of Yahweh's word (v 18). **16.** The folding and sealing, unless intended metaphorically, would apply to a written document (see also 29:11; 30:8, 18–26); it might have comprised substantially what are here called Isaiah's "memoirs." *disciples:* This is the only time that *limmuday* occurs in the OT; the same word is used of pupils in ancient scribal schools of the Levant (J. Olivier, *JNSL* 4 [1975] 56–57). **17.** *trust . . . wait for:* Expressions of faith, the characteristic religious quality in Isa (see 7:4–9); "waiting" relates to the concrete expectation of the fulfillment of Yahweh's word. *hiding his face:* Refusing to regard with favor, an expression frequent in the psalms (Pss 13:2; 27:9; 44:25; 88:15; etc.), where the petitioner expects Yahweh to relent; the people of Judah, however, have not shown the dispositions needed to sway the Lord. **18.** *children:* Two of Isaiah's sons have already been named, Shear-yashub (7:3) and Maher-shalal-hash-baz (8:1–4). While the latter is a "sign and portent" that Judah will be delivered from the threat posed by Syria and Israel, the former speaks of the conversion of a remnant, something fulfilled already in Isaiah's little group. Although *šûb* can mean "return" in the physical sense (as from battle or exile), here the reference is to conversion (as in 10:21–22, where the same phrase is used). *the Lord . . . who dwells on Mt. Zion:* The "memoirs" proper close as the vocation narrative opened, with reference to Yahweh's throning in Jerusalem.

(J) Two Additions (8:19–22). Verses 19–20 come from a later hand and build on v 16. The editor sees the "document" providing an antidote for the temptation to necromancy. Verses 21–22 may well be from Isaiah, transferred from elsewhere; in the present context, verbs and pronouns (in the sg.) have no subject/antecedent. The *NAB* transfers the fragment to after 14:25a.

22   (K) Prince of Peace (8:23–9:6). This passage is to be dated shortly after the Syro-Ephraimite crisis; for some it forms the concluding section of Isaiah's "memoirs." Isaiah's "Immanuel" oracle looked for a successor to Ahaz in whom the promise of the dynasty would be realized (7:14–15); here Isaiah describes him and the deliverance his coming would occasion. Although frequently contested, the piece accords well with the circumstances of Isaiah's ministry and his concerns. 9:1–6 has been variously identified as an accession hymn or a thanksgiving hymn. The advent of the new king is of special interest to Judah (cf. "to us" in v 5), but the concern of vv 1–4 is the deliverance of the northern territories. **8:23.** The opening line (transposed to the end of the verse in *NAB*), added by a later editor, forms a transition from the darkness of 8:22. *Zebulun and . . . Naphtali:* The northernmost tribes were the first subjugated by Assyria; other geographical references are to the three Assyrian provinces (Dor, Gilead, and Megiddo) fashioned from Israel's territory by Tiglath-pileser III after his conquest in 733. The subject of the verbs is Yahweh. **9:2.** *great joy:* An emendation. **3.** *yoke . . . staff . . . rod:* Symbols of Assyrian oppression. *day of Midian:* Alludes to the holy war tradition (7:4–5; Judg 7:15–25), in which victory comes from Yahweh (J. Olivier, *JNSL* 9 [1981] 143–49). **4.** *burned:* Holy war discipline often forbade the taking of booty. **5.** *a son is born to us:* Presumably the child would be Hezekiah (though there are chronological difficulties; → 3 above); he did not meet the expectations expressed here and in the Immanuel oracle (7:10–17), and Isaiah later projects his hopes into a remoter future (11:1–9). Alt believes this oracle deals with a coronation rather than a birth (*KlS* 2. 206–25; for arguments rejecting this position, see Wildberger, *Jesaja* 377). *wonder counselor:* The new king will have no need for advisers such as those who led Ahaz astray (see comment on 11:2). Linguistically this is very close to what is said of Yahweh in 28:29 (*hiplî' 'ēṣâ*). *God-warrior:* The same term (*'ēl gibbôr*) is used for Yahweh in 10:21; here *'ēl* is used in an attenuated sense (cf. 1 Sam 28:13; Ps 45:7). *Father everlasting:* "Father" describes the quality of his rule. (On Isaiah's use of symbolic names, see also 7:3,14; 8:1–4,18.) **6.** *peace:* Results from the qualities of the king (v 5), the promises to David (cf. 2 Sam 7:16), and the virtues of judgment and justice which sustain the Davidic throne.

(IV) Concerning Judah and Israel: Part II (9:7–12:6). The collection interrupted by insertion of the "memoirs" is here resumed.

23   (A) Yahweh's Outstretched Hand (9:7–20 + 5:25–30). This long oracle, directed against the northern kingdom, originally consisted of five strophes (9:7–11,12–16,17–20; 5:25[fragmentary],26–29), possibly of seven lines each. The parts are marked by a refrain repeated in 9:11b,16c,20b, 5:25c. The climactic fifth strophe threatens punishment through Assyrian invasion; since "from afar off" (5:26) suggests that the Assyrian presence will be something new, the composition must date from before 733. The vbs. in the first four strophes mix perf. and fut., so the temporal perspective is unclear and disputed. The position adopted here is that they refer to past trials sent to induce conversion; since this has failed to materialize, "his hand is stretched out still" (refrain) and a final, more severe judgment will be sent (fifth strophe). See Amos 4:6–12 for a similar pattern. The general theme of Yahweh's policy being carried out through acts in history, and human failure to perceive it, is characteristic of Isaiah. The events referred to in the first four strophes cannot be identified with any certainty. **7–11.** *word:* Decree of punishment. On the efficacy of Yahweh's word, → OT Thought, 77:40–46. The pride consists in failure to recognize and repent of the sin that had prompted Yahweh to send disaster. *Aram . . . Philistines:* Both were inveterate enemies of

Israel, but it is not clear whether specific incidents are envisioned. **12-16.** The reference to failure to repent (lit., "return," *šûb*) becomes explicit, with the clear implication that Yahweh's intention was that they should return to him. *head and tail:* Stand for rulers and people, as does the following pair, "palm branch and reed," images only partly understood by the glossator who supplied v 14. All members of society are involved in sin (cf. Jer 5:1-5; 7:17-18) so that even orphans and widows, normally the object of Yahweh's special concern, receive no mercy. **17-20.** Fire imagery expresses destructive and contagious aspects of wickedness, as well as Yahweh's punishment. The meaning of the vb. in v 18a (*ne'tam*) is uncertain; *NAB* reads *nā'at-mi,* with enclitic *mem,* and translates "quakes" (W. L. Moran, *CBQ* 12 [1950] 153-54). *each devours the flesh of his neighbor:* Read *rē'ô* for *zĕrō'ô. NAB* transfers this to the end of v 18 for the parallelism that was obviously intended. The violent imagery of cannibalism depicts the anarchic circumstances of Israel in its closing decades. *Manasseh . . . Ephraim:* Brother tribes, which makes their mutual destruction so much worse. **5:25.** *therefore:* Hebr *'al-kēn* introduces the punishment but supposes an explanation no longer found in this fragmentary strophe. The refrain at 9:20b suggests something still to come, which is one argument for inserting the present verse here. *mountains quake:* The language of theophany is used because Yahweh's judgment is a theophany (28:21; 64:1; Hab 3:4-7; Ps 18:8//2 Sam 22:8; Pss 77:17-19; 99:1); "earthquake" may be symbolic, but the unburied corpses point to a major calamity. *his hand is still outstretched:* The refrain occurs for the last time but points to further, ultimately conclusive action. **5:26-30.** *a nation from far off:* Assyria. *whistle:* That the nations are instruments of Yahweh's will is typically Isaian (7:18,20; 10:5-6,15). The description of Assyria's awesome military efficiency gives way to the terror-inspiring imagery of the lion (cf. Amos 3:8). Verse 30 is a gloss which replaces the lion's roar with that of the sea, perhaps with cosmological overtones.
    (B) Woe against Oppressive Rulers (10:1-4). → 15 above for treatment. Verse 4b is a later insertion occasioned by the use of the same refrain in 9:11b,16c,20b.
24   (C) Woe against Assyria (10:5-15). This important passage reveals Assyria as the agent of God's will but guilty of exceeding its commission and of pride. **5.** *rod . . . staff:* Assyria is an instrument of Yahweh's policy (cf. 5:26-29; 7:18-19,20), for the chastisement of Judah, but not its destruction. On the problems of the second half of the verse, see G. R. Driver, *JTS* 34 (1933) 383. **6.** *impious nation:* Judah. **7-9.** Assyria goes far beyond what Yahweh intended. The naming of Samaria suggests that Yahweh could not protect it and would not be able to protect Jerusalem. **10-12.** These verses are often taken as later glosses, the first (vv 10-11) to suggest that Samaria had fallen because of idolatry; the second (v 12) looks forward to the restoration of Jerusalem after its destruction and after retribution on Yahweh's enemies. **13-14.** The boast of vv 8-11 is resumed. **15.** Four expressions in the manner of wisdom sayings ridicule the pretensions of the creature that misunderstands its place in the order of things. No punishment is specified, though the "woe" of v 5 indicates dire things to come, and many believe that 14:24-27 was originally the ending of this oracle.
    (D) Some Completions (10:16-27a). Since the original oracle of 10:5-9,13-15 did not specify punishment, additions (vv 16-19,20-23,24-27a) have supplied the lack. Some may be new compositions, others by Isaiah from different contexts. **16-19.** Intended

as a continuation of the previous oracle ("therefore"), these verses take inspiration from some of Isaiah's genuine words (esp. 9:17-18 and 17:3-6); the imagery is somewhat mixed. **20-23.** A separate addition to deal with the outcome for Judah of Yahweh's judgment on Assyria; again the passage rests on genuine words of Isaiah but is far from unified. The "remnant" (*šĕ'ār, pĕlêtâ*) in vv 20-21 is not automatically identified as holy and saved (as in some later passages; cf. 4:2), but needs to exhibit the faith which rejects spurious sources of security (the identity of "him who struck them" is unclear). *Mighty God:* The name given to the future king in 9:5 is here applied to Yahweh, and "a remnant shall return" is taken from 7:3. Verses 22-23 emphasize the negative aspect of "remnant"; here it is a matter of God's justice (*ṣĕdāqâ*—a rare use of that term to refer to destructive judgment). **24-27a.** Some believe this to be the authentic continuation of vv 5-9,13-15, but it appears rather to be an addition that has utilized Isaian thought and vocabulary (as well as the exodus theme, not found in the genuine words of Isaiah). *rod . . . staff:* A shift from v 5, where Assyria itself is Yahweh's rod and staff. *Midian . . . Oreb:* Cf. Judg 7:25. The reference to Midian, as well as the terminology and content of v 27, comes from 9:3 (where also "rod" and "staff" are found).
25   (E) An Enemy Advance (10:27b-34). The present location of this piece shows that the editor understood the unnamed enemy to be Assyria. The dating of the event is uncertain (indeed, some believe the action is purely visionary, composed to warn Judah of likely consequences of rebellion). The Assyrian attack in 701, in response to Hezekiah's rebellion, came from the SW, whereas the route here depicted is from the N. Some suppose that on the occasion of the 714 rebellion of Ashdod (→ 38 below) the Assyrians made a feint toward Jerusalem as a warning to Hezekiah. **27b.** *he has come up:* Based on conjectural emendation; other conjectures supply Rimmon or Samaria. **29-31.** A vivid description of the terror such an invasion would inspire; cf. Jer 4:5-31; 6:1-5. **33-34.** Although sometimes taken as Yahweh's punishment of Assyria for its presumption (v 32), these verses more likely refer to the leaders responsible for Judah's dangerous policies, who would also be the first to suffer from Assyrian reprisal.
26   (F) The Future King (11:1-9). Some commentators think this passage connects to 10:33-34, where tree imagery to designate rulers is also used; there would thus be a deliberate contrast between the present rulers and the one to come. Although frequently denied to Isaiah, this oracle accords well with many elements of his thought, including his interest in David's dynasty, Jerusalem, and wisdom. Whereas 9:1-6 was related to the Syro-Ephraimite crisis and may have referred to Hezekiah, this passage seems to come from late in Isaiah's career and projects the expectation of an ideal king into the distant future. **1.** *Jesse:* David's father. In the tree imagery the branches would be historical kings, whom Isaiah had written off in favor of a return to the very source of the dynasty. Thus, the "stump" terminology does not require dating the oracle after the fall of the monarchy (cf. Mic 5:1 for a similar "return to origins"). **2.** *spirit of the Lord:* Yahweh's spirit was a divine force given to individuals to enable them to fulfill missions otherwise beyond them, as in the case of Moses (Num 11:17), the judges (Judg 3:10; 6:34; 11:29), prophets (Mic 3:8), David (1 Sam 16:13), and others; this king would represent a return to the charismatic tradition so long an ideal in Israel. The gifts named reflect Isaiah's experience with Ahaz and Hezekiah, esp. in that wisdom, understanding, and counsel would make the king independent of foolish advisers (see 5:21; 9:5;

29:14). *strength:* Makes good counsel effective. *fear of the Lord:* A favorite quality in the wisdom tradition (Prov 1:7). The LXX has seven terms instead of six (utilizing the repetition of "fear of the Lord" in v 3, a gloss), and from this come the "seven gifts of the Holy Spirit" of Catholic piety. **3–5.** A paragon of kingly virtues, he will administer justice in favor of the weak and lowly. Prophetic ideals have operated to transform expectations which sprang from the dynastic oracle (→ 18, 19 above), though such idealization has parallels in the royal psalms (Ps 72:1–4,12–14). Isaiah looked to the restoration of right judgment as a condition for an ideal future (1:26). **6–8.** Perfect justice leads to perfect peace, here depicted as a return to paradise. **9.** Ultimately all this is attributed to "knowledge of the Lord" (*dē'â 'et yhwh*), and we are reminded of the programmatic passages where failure to know/understand is the root cause of evil and the occasion for disaster (1:3; 5:12–13; 6:9–10).

(G) Later Additions (11:10–16). Verse 10 is built directly on the preceding, a hook on which to hang the originally independent vv 11–16; the term "signal" (*nēs*) provides the connecting link (cf. v 12). **10.** This verse is universalistic in seeing the "root of Jesse" (which now designates the individual rather than his origin) as a rallying point for the Gentile nations. There is obvious tension between this verse and the military action of v 14. **11–16.** These do not speak of the future king but only of Yahweh and what he will do for the remnant of Israel, dispersed through many lands (v 12). The reference is to the postexilic Diaspora rather than the Babylonian Exile; the allusion to jealousy between Ephraim and Judah thus has Jewish–Samaritan hostilities as its background (Ezra 4:1–3). The redemption envisioned is depicted as a new exodus, as Yahweh dries up the waters and leads forth his people (vv 15–16). The concept of a highway (*mĕsillâ*) comes from Dt-Isa (cf. 40:3), not from the old exodus tradition. Assyria no longer existed when this text was written, but Egypt and Assyria represent powers that oppress and enslave.

27 (H) A Concluding Song of Thanksgiving (12:1–6). This late composition concludes chaps. 2–12 on a fitting note. The language and form reflect the psalms, particularly the individual psalms of thanksgiving, rather than prophecy. Nevertheless, it presupposes the Isa collection, both its threats and promises; the threats have been (or are being — v 1) carried out and a time of salvation is at hand. **1.** *on that day:* The formula here alludes directly to "the day" referred to in 11:10–11 and elsewhere in the preceding chapters where it introduces promises of salvation. *you* (sg.) *will say:* Many see here the words that introduce instruction to a herald. *I give you thanks:* Characteristic opening of an individual psalm of thanksgiving (cf. Pss 9:2; 111:1; 138:1). **2.** *my salvation:* Hebr *yĕšû'â* occurs three times in this brief piece. **3–4.** *you will draw . . . will say:* The switch to the pl. possibly suggests a new source; the general tenor does not change. *his works* (*'ălîlōtāyw*): Isaiah spoke of Yahweh's "work" (see 5:12,19), but in more specific terms. *dweller of Zion:* A collective; the reference is to the redeemed community.

28 (V) Oracles against the Nations (13:1–23:18). The growth of this collection was complicated. The beginning of it appears to have been a collection of oracles against Babylon and other foreign nations from the late monarchic or early exilic period, before the fall of Babylon, but with other, later, pieces added to it. Each unit was introduced by the formula "an oracle (*maśśā'*) concerning. . . ." At some point this collection was inserted into the Isa book and provided with the inscription at 13:1. Probably at this time some of the genuine Isaianic oracles concerning foreign nations were

transferred here from the materials that now make up chaps. 2–11 and 28–32; some of these were provided with *maśśā'* introductions, but not all. Thus, some Isaianic materials are found here along with later materials. The *maśśā'* terminology is used to introduce individual units at 13:1; 15:1; 17:1; 19:1; 21:1, 11,13; 22:1; and 23:1. The word is from *nāśā'*, "to lift up" (i.e., the voice), and therefore means "oracle" (rather than "burden"), though it is regularly used to introduce a word of threat or judgment.

29 (A) Oracle against Babylon (13:1–22). This doom oracle divides into three parts: the call and mustering of Yahweh's troops (vv 2–5), description of the Day of the Lord, to which this attack is likened (vv 6–16), and the devastation of the city (vv 17–22). Although the assembling of Yahweh's attacking army is described in detail, it is not identified as the Medes until v 17. Similarly, the city under attack is not identified until v 19 (the inscription, v 1, comes from a later editor). Babylon came into prominence in the late 7th cent. and fell in 539; if this piece relates to Babylon, its composition would be within that period. Yet the Medes were at one time allies of Babylon, and the city fell not to them but to Cyrus the Persian. Thus it is often suggested that "Babylon" here functions as the type of any wicked nation under Yahweh's wrath, so that a date much later than 539 is not excluded. More likely, however, at some point before the rise of Cyrus the author expected the Medes to bring Babylon's downfall. **1.** *an oracle (maśśā'):* → 28 above. **2–5.** Yahweh himself (the "I" of v 3) takes the initiative in summoning an army. Since they are to carry out his will, they are his "consecrated ones" (v 3), suggesting that this is a holy war (cf. similar terminology in Jos 3:5; Jer 51:28; Joel 4:9). *gates of the volunteers:* Meaning uncertain; the reference is possibly to rallying points. *warriors of my wrath:* I.e., to carry it out; as in the genuine oracles of Isaiah, Yahweh uses pagan nations as agents of his policy (see 5:26–29; 7:18–19,20; 10:5–15). *from a distant land:* Cf. v 17. *all the land:* All of Babylonia. **6–13.** *the Day of the Lord:* A popular expectation which Amos (5:18–20) and Isaiah (2:6–22) turned against God's people; here, since it is directed against those who subjugated Judah, the concept has returned to its more favorable sense. Some of the elements of the description that refer to upheaval in nature, such as the shaking of the earth (v 13), are common in theophanies, while others, such as the dimming of heavenly luminaries, esp. as here employed (v 10), resemble later apocalyptic. Although, in the context, it is Babylon that experiences the terror and destruction, the language at places betrays a far broader scope (e.g., punishment visited upon "the world" [*tēbēl*, v 11]). Again, references to punishment of sinners (vv 9,11), humbling of pride (v 11; see 2:6–21), and annihilation of people (v 12), although they can be understood to refer only to Babylon, are consonant with descriptions of the Day of the Lord that see it as universal. **14–16.** These verses take up again the military attack in more conventional terms. The slaughtering of infants and the raping of women were among the cruel and shameful excesses visited upon the innocent and defenseless (2 Kgs 8:12; Hos 14:1; Amos 1:13; Ps 137:9; Lam 5:11; Zech 14:2). **17–22.** The suspense is ended as the attacker (v 17) and the city attacked (v 19) are finally named. *the Medes:* Sometime after the overthrow of Assyria through the combined Median and Babylonian forces, they had become Babylon's chief rival. *the bows of the young men:* Based on a repointing of the Hebrew; NAB transfers to end of v 15. *overthrown . . . :* Cf. 1:7,9; in fact, Babylon was not destroyed, but peacefully surrendered to Cyrus.

30   (B) The Gentiles and Israel's Restoration (14:1-2). These prose verses were probably intended as additions to the preceding piece; a correlative to Yahweh's judgment on Babylon is Israel's restoration. *again chooses:* The destruction of the nation and exile of the people suggested to some the end of their elect status (cf. 2 Kgs 23:27; Jer 31:31-34; Zech 1:17; 2:16). *resident aliens:* The restored Israel will be so esteemed that others will want to join them (cf. Zech 8:20-23). Israel's ancient laws had accorded the *gērîm* certain protections and privileges. Now the Jews themselves were resident aliens in the midst of others. *shall possess them as male and female slaves:* Another view is given from a less tolerant perspective; the peoples that the returnees will bring with them are their erstwhile captors, who are now, in their turn, subjected to servitude.

31   (C) Taunt-Song against the King of Babylon (14:3-23). It is only the prose introduction and conclusion (the taunt-song proper is found in vv 4b-21) that identify the tyrant as the king of Babylon, and Isaian authorship is sometimes defended by suggesting that the piece adapts a taunt by Isaiah over an Assyrian king. It is more probable that the identification in the prose sections is correct and that the king is Nebuchadnezzar, Jerusalem's destroyer, or possibly Nabonidus, the last king of Babylon. Or the unnamed king may stand simply as a type of the wicked world ruler. The poem is a magnificent composition, rich in imagination and allusive force, which skillfully utilizes elements of pagan myths (and has contacts with Ezek 28:11-19). It falls into four parts: the peace that prevails with the death of the tyrant (vv 4b-8), the netherworld's reaction to his coming (vv 9-11), the description of his (former) pretensions and fall (vv 12-15), reflections of the living over his body (vv 16-20). **3-4a.** *on the day the Lord gives you rest:* Deliberately ties to the resettlement in v 1 (cf. use of hiph. of *nāḥâ*. *taunt-song* (*māšāl*): → Wisdom Lit., 27:9. **4b-8.** *assault:* Reading *marhēbâ* for *madhēbâ* with 1QIsaᵃ and other witnesses. *Yahweh has broken:* The tyrant's death is God's action to deliver oppressed people. *staff . . . rod:* Cf. 10:24 (also 10:5,15). *cedars of Lebanon:* These were much in demand by those who built magnificent edifices (2 Sam 5:11; 1 Kgs 5:16-25; cf. Jer 22:15). **9-11.** *sheol:* → OT Thought, 77:170). This is here personified and more highly mythologized than is customary in the OT. *shades:* The residents of *sheol* take satisfaction in the fact that death has reduced the oppressor to the common lot of the dead, viz., weakness and corruption. The meaning of *rĕpā'îm*, as applied to the departed in sheol, is not clear; see C. L'Heureux, *HTR* 67 (1974) 265-74; and W. J. Horowitz, *JNSL* 7 (1979) 37-43. **12-15.** *How!:* Hebr *'êk* parallels the *'êk* that opens v 4b and probably intends to mark a major division. The poet applies to the king a non-Israelite myth of a god (the "shining star, son of the dawn" [v 12], conceals a proper name, Helel ben Shahar) who aspired to ascend the mountain of the gods and make himself equal to Elyon, for which presumption he was cast down to the netherworld. In the Latin Bible *hêlēl* was rendered *lucifer* ("light-bearer") and since some patristic writers saw in this piece an account of the fall of Satan, Lucifer came to be a name for the devil. *mount of the assembly in . . . the north:* Mt. Zaphon of pagan mythology, the mountain of the gods, identified with Mt. Casius. (In Ps 48:3 this terminology is applied to Mt. Zion; see R. Clifford, *The Cosmic Mountain in Canaan and the Old Testament* [Cambridge MA, 1972] 160-68.) *'Elyôn:* "Most High," an epithet frequently applied to Yahweh, but among the Canaanites it was a title of El, the one challenged in the myth here utilized. **16-20.** *those who look upon you:* It is now the living, on earth, who react. Again the contrast is between former might and

present helpless condition. *you are cast forth:* Proper burial was considered necessary to have peace in death; to be without burial was a sign of disgrace (Jer 22:18-19; 36:30). *because you have ruined your land:* The tyrant may have perished on the battlefield (v 19), but the real reason for disgrace in death was his unworthy conduct in life. **21.** A later addition to the original poem. The slaying of the tyrant's sons assures that none of his line shall succeed him, something done not infrequently in Israel (1 Kgs 15:29; 16:11; 2 Kgs 10:1-11). **22-23.** Another addition, which speaks of destruction of Babylon itself; its desolation will be complete (cf. 13:20-22).

(D) Yahweh's Plan for Assyria (14:24-27). This doom oracle is introduced by Yahweh's solemn oath concerning what he has purposed for Assyria. It accords with what Isaiah says elsewhere about Yahweh's "plan" and the punishment deserved by Assyria. Since no punishment is explicitly provided in the indictment of Assyria in 10:5-15, many have thought the present passage the completion of that one. It is at least likely that they both stem from around the same period in Isaiah's ministry. The solemn diction concerning Yahweh's plan (for all the earth—v 26) makes it unlikely that the piece is to be dated to 701 and represents a reversal of the prophet's conviction that revolt against Assyria would bring disaster for Judah. **24.** *I have proposed . . . it shall stand:* Elsewhere Isaiah used similar diction of the uselessness of human plans (8:10), and here the emphasis is both on Yahweh's resolution and on his power to carry it into effect. **25.** *in my land:* Supposes that the Assyrians are there for hostile purposes, but this does not necessarily point to 701 (much less to the Babylonians in 587, as some hold); the indictment of Assyria in 10:5-15 also supposes a hostile incursion, though it is difficult to fit it into any determined historical context. *then his yoke shall be removed:* Verse 25b is almost certainly a later insertion, taken from either 9:3 or 10:27. **26-27.** *the plan proposed for the whole earth:* Relates to Yahweh's broader design rather than a response to specific events of 701. Yahweh's control extends to all the earth and his plan is comprehensive; human planning must take it into account or end in disaster (5:12-13,19; 7:5-7; 8:9-10; 10:7,15; 29:15-16; 30:1-5; 31:1-3). *this is the hand stretched out over all the earth:* Previously it was said to be stretched out over Israel (5:25; 9:11,16,20). These verses are an example of the "summary appraisal" that occurs frequently in wisdom literature (Job 8:13; 18:21; 20:29; 27:13; Ps 49:14; Prov 1:19); see also Isa 17:14b; 28:29. *who can turn it back?:* Cf. Amos 1:3,6,9,11,13; 2:1,4,6.

32   (E) Warning to Philistia (14:28-32). Although this oracle is presented as having been delivered "in the year that King Ahaz died," its dating is problematical. It deals with the death of an Assyrian king; since it is almost certainly from Isaiah, the possibilities are Tiglath-pileser III (died 727), Shalmaneser V (died 722), and Sargon II (died 705), none of which correspond to 715, the date followed for Ahaz's death in the disputed Albright-Bright chronology (→ 3 above). For some this argues for a chronology which places the death of Ahaz ca. 727, for others that the introductory note is editorial and inaccurate. The general thrust is clear: the death of the Assyrian king occasions thoughts of revolt by subject peoples; Judah will receive overtures from Philistine envoys to join the revolt, but they are to be rebuffed. **29.** *the rod which smote you:* Since Philistine revolts were crushed by Assyria in 734, 720, and 711 (and 701), this "rod" could be Tiglath-pileser. But Shalmaneser V is favored (though he did not attack Philistia) because of the Philistine rebellion under Sargon II (see 20:1-6). *an adder shall come forth:* The dead king's successor shall be more deadly than he. *flying serpent:*

Legendary creatures referred to elsewhere (30:6; cf. Num 21:6,8; Deut 8:15). **30.** Verse 30a is out of place here and should be read after v 32. *I will kill your root:* A contrast between the fate of the Philistines and that of the Assyrian ruler; he will have a vigorous root (off-spring—v 29), whereas even their root (remnant) shall perish. Yahweh brings Philistia's downfall because the revolt would involve Judah in a foolish, sinful venture that rejects faith in him. **31.** *from the north:* The direction an Assyrian incursion into Palestine would take. *no straggler:* On Assyrian military efficiency, see 5:26–29. **32.** *what shall one answer?:* Consistent with the word of Yahweh that Isaiah proclaimed in 735 (7:4–5), 714 (20:1–6), and 705 (30:1–5), the response here implies that Judah's safety lies in the protection afforded by Yahweh. Isaiah's utilization of the Zion tradition always involves a renunciation of means which would betray lack of faith in Yahweh's power; it is esp. "the afflicted of his people" who are likely to have such faith. (On the Zion tradition, see 2:2–4; 7:8; 8:9–10; G. Tucker, in *HBMI* 332–35).

33   (F)   Concerning Moab (15:1–16:14). These two chapters, now a single redactional unit, consist of three originally distinct parts, plus editorial additions: 15:1–9 is a lament over a devastation of Moab; 16:1–5 concerns the fate of the fugitives; and 16:6–11 is a further lament (possibly based on chap. 15), with vv 12,13–14 later additions. There is little basis for either affirming or denying Isaian authorship. Parts of the poem appear, in altered form, in Jer 48:29–38. The events depicted have not been identified with any specific historical occasion; most aspects of the composition are disputed. The Hebrew is corrupt in spots; not all the places named can be identified. On Moab's relations with Israel, see comment on 25:10b. During Jehoiakim's revolt against Babylon (601) the Moabites (and others) raided Judah (2 Kgs 24:2), which helps explain the hostility against Moab in some OT texts. **1–8.** A lament, mostly in the *qinah* meter (3 + 2). *Ar-Moab . . . Kir-Moab:* While these may be specific cities, the former term might stand simply for the country of Moab in general (cf. Deut 2:18) and the latter (*qîr-mô'āb*) for all the cities of Moab or possibly the capital city. *Dibon, Nebo, Medeba . . . :* The cities named in vv 2–4, all north of the Arnon, are personified as lamenting, but it is not clear whether they lament the general devastation or have themselves fallen victim. Verse 2 should probably be emended to read "Daughter Dibon goes up . . . to weep," parallel to "Moab wails." Shaving, sackcloth, and wailing are all signs of mourning. *my heart cries out for Moab:* The poet's sympathy for the ravaged land, already implied, here comes to the surface. *her fugitives* (read *bārîhōh*) *reach Zoar:* Near the S end of the Dead Sea (cf. Gen 19:19–22). The place-names that can be identified in vv 5–8 are to the S, indicating that the flight was in that direction and perhaps suggesting that the attack was from the N. *Eglath-Shelishayah:* A gloss, under the influence of Jer 48:34. The fugitives carry all the possessions they can "across the Brook of the Poplars," probably the Wadi el-Hesi, near the S end of the Dead Sea. **9.** *the waters of Dimon are filled with blood:* Dimon is apparently to be identified with Dibon; the change would be for the sake of a play on the word for blood (*dām*). *I will bring still more:* The change from the sympathetic tone and to 1st-pers. address (words of Yahweh?) indicate a later addition. **16:1–5.** The Moabite refugees send an embassy to Jerusalem (v 1), asking for sanctuary for the fugitives (vv 3–4a), and receive response (vv 4b–5); v 2 was perhaps misplaced from chap. 15. **1.** *send a ram of the ruler of the land:* If the reading is correct, the Moabite leaders advise sending tribute, as in earlier days (cf. 2 Kgs 3:4); some

repoint the vb. and read "they have sent" (cf. *RSV*). In either case *kar* can be understood as a collective and translated as a pl., "rams." The LXX (followed by *NAB*) divides the consonants differently and arrives at a substantially different meaning. *Sela'*, "crag," refers to the rocky wilderness in which the fugitives are hiding. The same word also designates Sela, a city of Edom, but this would be far S of Moab and Judah. **3–4a.** The plea of Moab's ambassadors or their advocate in Jerusalem. **4b–5.** *a throne will be set up:* This future event can hardly be a response to the Moabite refugees in their need. Since the verse presupposes that the Davidic monarchy has been eclipsed, it is taken as an exilic or postexilic addition. *in the tent of David:* A still later, exegetical addition, identifying a future ideal Davidid as the enthroned judge. The qualities of his rule, fidelity, truth, judgment, and justice, correspond in large measure to those of Isaiah's ideal king (9:6; 11:1–5). **6–11.** While the previous sections treated Moab's plight with sympathy, v 6 appears to blame it on Moab's pride. Therefore, although vv 7–11 take up again the theme of lamentation, the piece may be but a thinly disguised taunt. Here mourning is almost exclusively over the destruction of viticulture and harvest. *raisin cakes:* Sometimes associated with cultic functions, whether legitimate or pagan (2 Sam 6:19; Hos 3:1). *the shout:* Hebr *hêdād* is normally used for the glad cries of those trampling grapes (Jer 25:30; 51:14), as in v 10 (and the parallel in Jer 48:33), whereas in v 9 the term expresses the cry of exultation of those despoiling Moab (some emend to *šōdēd*, "ravager"; cf. Jer 48:32). *is stilled:* Reading *hošbāt* for *hišbatî* with the LXX. **12.** A later hand denies that Moab's prayer (cf. 15:2) will be heard. **13–14.** This addition supposes a time when Moab's fortunes are restored; it takes the preceding compositions as prophecy to be fulfilled in three years. *like the years of a hireling:* A wearisome period (so also in 21:16); cf. Job 7:1. *remnant:* The writer allows a bare survival (see 17:3; cf. also 21:17).

34   (G)   Against Syria and Israel (17:1–11). Isaiah prophesied against Syria and Israel in the days of the Syro-Ephraimite crisis (7:4; 8:1–4), and both underwent terrible judgment. At least the nucleus of this oracle stems from Isaiah; since the blow had not yet fallen, it is to be dated before 733. Verses 7, 8, and possibly 9 are later expansions, and vv 10–11 come from a different context. **1–3.** Emphasis here is on the fate of Damascus. In fact, Damascus was not destroyed, but the Assyrians pillaged it, executed its king, and organized Syria's territory into four Assyrian provinces. Damascus survived to prosper (cf. Ezek 27:18). *given over to flocks:* Cf. 5:17. *glory:* See comment on v 4. **4–6.** Perhaps originally a separate composition. *glory:* The word *kābôd* designates wealth, power, and well-being. The reversal is expressed in two images: flesh wasting away and a harvest that yields only as much as a gleaner might expect. *Valley of Rephaim:* Located not in Israel but SW of Jerusalem and therefore familiar to those whom Isaiah was primarily addressing. *a scattering of grapes:* Does not relate to Isaiah's remnant teaching, for here he speaks only of the fewness of the survivors, not of any hope for the future. **7–8.** In the context of the Syro-Ephraimite crisis, the reason for Isaiah's pronouncement of doom would have been clear; this is not the case in its present literary context, so this later addition blames Israel's idolatry for her fall but also promises conversion. **9.** Sometimes taken as the conclusion to vv 4–6, this verse rather introduces vv 10–11; it warns that just as Yahweh had dispossessed the original dwellers in the land, so he can also dispossess Israel. The text of v 9a should be emended with the LXX (see *NAB*). **10–11.** These verses, in direct address, 2d pers. sg., do not resemble anything that precedes; they may be by Isaiah but from a different context. They were more likely addressed to Judah than Israel. They appear to relate to the pagan practice of setting out plants in small vessels so that they sprout rapidly and immediately wither away, symbolic of the death of Adonis, a vegetation deity. The section could have been attracted here by the reference to a scanty harvest in vv 5-6 and the desire to further implicate Israel in pagan practices. **35** **(H) Attack and Deliverance (17:12-14).** While this passage is to be attributed to Isaiah, there is little to specify the historical context; neither the attackers nor the attacked is named. Yet the pattern seems to be taken from the Zion psalms (→ 9 above), where many of the same elements are found. An assembling of the peoples against Zion is described, sometimes with roaring or roaring of waters (Ps 46:4), but Yahweh acts and the opposition is defeated (Ps 46:7,10; 48:6; 76:4,6-7) at his rebuke (cf. v 13 and Ps 76:7), before the morning (cf. v 14 and Ps 46:6). Isaiah follows the traditional diction, which spoke of the enemy in general terms, but this piece fits in with other oracles in which he spoke of Yahweh bringing an end to Assyria (see 10:5-15; 14:24-27). Isaiah opposed the rebellion of 705, so he is unlikely to have spoken of God's defense of Zion in unconditional terms in those circumstances. Some would relate it to the events of chap. 18. Another possible context would be the attack of Syria and Israel in 735, although the eloquence of this piece hardly agrees with the manner in which he dismisses them in 7:4. In any case, Isaiah here clearly uses a preexisting Zion tradition in a very positive manner to reassure Judah in concrete circumstances. **14b.** Summary appraisal; see 14:26-27.

36 **(I) Embassy from Egypt (18:1-7).** The passage is probably to be dated in the general period of the events of 714 (see 20:1-6), when Egypt was attempting to rally support against the Assyrians. After a period of internal weakness Egypt was subjugated, around 716, by the Ethiopian king Piankhi, who founded the 25th (Ethiopian) dynasty. Isaiah indicates that the response to the embassy here described should be a refusal. **1.** *woe:* Some translations take *hôy* as a simple exclamation ("Ah!"), but a case can be made for it introducing a true woe oracle (so Wildberger). *land of winged insects:* The meaning of *şilşal* is uncertain, and the expression may refer to swift boats (v 2) with their sails. *Ethiopia:* The biblical Cush, far S of Egypt, on the Upper Nile. **2.** *sea:* The Nile. *papyrus boats:* Made of bundles of the plant bound together (*BA* 47 [1984] 134-42). *go:* Return to those who sent you; see vv 4-6 for the response they are to give. **3.** An addition by a later editor which now addresses "all you who inhabit the earth." **4-6.** While ostensibly the response the Egyptian ambassadors are to take back, in reality this word is for Judah. The message, which accords with chap. 20 and other relevant passages, is that Judah is not to join Egypt in revolt against Assyria. Yahweh will not act at this time; later, however, there will be a "harvest" (destructive judgment). *they shall be left to the birds of prey:* An allusion to corpses of the slain rather than to vine cuttings. Since vv 4-6 contain the threat that goes with the opening "woe," the nation that is to be judged is Egypt/Ethiopia, not Assyria. **7.** A later editor uses phrases from v 2 to anticipate the conversion of Egypt to Yahweh (cf. also 19:18-22).

37 **(J) Concerning Egypt (19:1-25).** While this whole chapter concerns itself with Egypt, it is no unified composition. Verses 1-4,11-14 (with v 15 as a later expansion) belong together and are from Isaiah, while vv 5-10 are intrusive in their present context; vv

16-25 are a series of five later additions. The historical background for vv 1-4,11-14 seems to be slightly earlier than that of chap. 18, i.e., before Piankhi had unified Egypt, so probably the days of Osorkon IV (730-715), last king of the 23d dynasty. Yahweh is depicted as Lord of history, who can rouse the Egyptians to civil war and subject them to the ruler of his own choice; Egypt's fate is the result of the foolish plans of her leaders, probably plans of revolt against Assyria. All this agrees with what Isaiah has to say about Egypt. **1.** *the idols of Egypt . . . the heart of the Egyptians:* Both are equally without courage before the might of Yahweh. **2.** *Egypt against Egypt:* The period before the unification effected by Piankhi's takeover was one of much civil strife, with not only rival princelings but even rival dynasties: the 23d dynasty established itself while the 22d still claimed rule, and the 24th began before the 23d came to an end. **3.** *I will confuse their counsel:* In line with the Isaian theme that only Yahweh's counsel (*'ēṣâ*) can stand (7:7; 8:9-10; 14:24-27). *they shall consult:* The types of divination listed were forbidden in Israel (Lev 19:31; 20:6,27; Deut 18:11; cf. Isa 8:19), and Isaiah obviously considered them useless. **4.** *a hard master:* The reference is more likely to Sargon II of Assyria (721-705) than to Piankhi or another pharaoh—though in fact Assyria did not conquer Egypt until under Esarhaddon (680-670). **5-10.** These verses are intrusive. Whereas vv 1-4 deal with the political troubles of the country and vv 11-15 blame them on foolish policies, here we have a detailed description of the drying up of the Nile ("sea" [v 5], refers to the Nile, as in 18:2) and the consequences thereof. Egypt's cycle of (three) seasons was built around the annual inundation of the Nile, on which Egypt's agriculture and economy were dependent. Here is detailed the perishing of the marsh vegetation (v 6), sown fields (v 7), and industries dependent on what lives in the waters (fishermen, v 8) and what can be grown (materials for textiles, vv 9-10). **11-14.** What Isaiah here says of those in Egypt who should provide right counsel parallels what he said of the same class in Judah (5:13, 18-21; 29:14). Presumably the foolishness they demonstrate has to do, as in the case of Judah's sages, with advising a policy of resistance to Assyria, which has a specific role in Yahweh's plans (10:5-6). Opposition to this plan by Egypt would be just as foolish as resistance by Judah; moreover, Egypt usually attempted to draw Judah into its adventures against Assyria (see chap. 18). *let them make known:* Isaiah's polemic against "the wise" was provoked by their failure to take Yahweh's purpose into account; even those in Egypt were not exempted. *Zoan (Tanis) . . . Memphis:* Both cities of the Delta area, both closely connected with Osorkon IV; his 22d dynasty is called Tanite because his power was based there. **14.** Yahweh is the agent of Egypt's downfall, now acting through the foolishness of her leaders (cf. 29:9-10; also 6:9-10); on drunkenness as a contributing factor, see 5:11-13; 28:7-8. **16-17.** The first of the five additions, each of which begins "on that day." This one, written by a nationalistic spirit, picks up the "plan/purpose" (*'ēṣâ*) terminology of v 12. **18.** The reference here is probably to Jews in Egypt, rather than to Egyptian conversion. *five cities:* Specific places where the Jewish population is so large that "they will be speaking the language of Canaan," i.e., Hebrew. *city of the sun:* Heliopolis, but the reading is disputed. **19-22.** The outcome of the action is unambiguously given in v 22, but there are uncertainties in the previous lines. Commentators understand the "altar" and "sacred pillar" (v 19) to be already in existence; this text would both legitimize them (so that it must date to a time before the deuteronomic centralization of worship was universally accepted) and see in them a pledge of Egypt's future conversion. Themes of the exodus surface with the crying out to Yahweh and deliverance (Exod 8:8; 14:10,15; 17:4), only now it is the Egyptians rather than the Israelites. **21.** "To know the Lord" comprehends fidelity and true response (cf. Jer 22:15b–16; Hos 2:21–22; 6:6). **22.** The Egyptians will experience Yahweh's deliverance from oppression (v 20), just as Israel did. **23.** This new addition goes beyond the universalism of vv 19–22, broadening the perspective beyond Egypt and adding the note of international peace. *there shall be a highway:* A symbol of amicable commerce between the two inveterate enemies, Egypt and Assyria. Assyria had long disappeared from history and the author may have had in mind one of its successors (e.g., the Persian Empire), but because of the symbolic force of the names, the import would go far beyond that. *the Egyptians shall worship* (*'ābĕdû*) *with the Assyrians:* Reading *'t* as prep. **24–25.** These verses go even farther in that they put Egypt and Assyria on a par with Israel. *my people, the work of my hands:* Expressions elsewhere reserved for Israel (cf. 60:21; 64:7).

38   (K) Isaiah a Sign and Portent to Egypt (20:1–6). Symbolic acts dramatized prophetic words and made them more effective (cf. Jer 19:1–13; 27:2–8; Ezek 4:1–8,9–15; 5:1–4; 12:1–7; 37:15–22). The background of the one here performed is the Philistine revolt against Assyria in 714. Although the narrative concerns itself with Ashdod, Egypt, and Assyria, the act was directed to Judah and Hezekiah, who had been invited to join the conspiracy (see chap. 18). Isaiah's symbolic act warns of the consequences in order to persuade against it. In this case he was successful. **1.** This verse was formulated in 711 or later, after the symbolic act, since the capture of Ashdod is mentioned at the outset. This may have been in order to present its message anew when Isaiah attempted to counter a similar temptation to revolt in 705. **2.** *naked and barefoot:* May here mean simply semiclothed; the prophet was simulating the manner of a prisoner of war as a warning of the likely result of revolt (cf. v 4). **3.** *sign and portent:* The same terms as in 8:18. *against Egypt and Ethiopia:* I.e., Egypt under the Ethiopian dynasty (see chap. 18). **4.** *captives from Egypt:* The Assyrians did not enter Egypt, and it was the Philistines alone who suffered; thus, this explanation must have been formulated in 714, at the beginning of the revolt, even though v 1 was written later. **5–6.** *hope . . . help:* Egypt provided no help and even handed over the king of Ashdod who had sought asylum. Isaiah's objections rested not simply on the conviction that Egypt was an unreliable ally but on his teaching about Yahweh's purpose in history and sovereign control of events.

39   (L) On the Fall of Babylon (21:1–10). This *maśśā'* (→ 28 above) looks to the immediate fall of Babylon (not named until v 9) and therefore is probably to be dated shortly before 539. **1.** *wilderness of the sea:* Hebr *midbar yām* is doubtful as a designation for Babylon. Another term for Kaldu, the area in S Mesopotamia for which the Chaldeans (Neo-Babylonians) were named, *mat tamti,* "sealand," may possibly provide the explanation. **2.** *revealed to me:* The prophet is not identified, though v 6 describes his mission. *go up . . . besiege:* The speaker here presumably is Yahweh, who commands the forces that will bring Babylon's downfall. *Elam . . . Media:* If the attack described is that of Cyrus the Persian, these would have to be contingents of conquered peoples among his forces (see 22:5–8a); both had been allies of Babylon before Cyrus overcame them. **6–8.** The prophet is commanded to constitute a

watchman (*hamĕṣappeh* in v 6, read *hārō'eh* for *'aryēh* in v 8) or possibly to act as watchman (cf. v 11; Ezek 33:1–9; Hab 2:1) to give warning of the attack. **9.** The attack takes place, and word of the fall of the city goes out. *all the images of her gods:* Implies both that idolatry was part of Babylon's crime and that her idols could not save her. **10.** *my threshed and winnowed one:* Babylon's fall is consoling news to a Judah that had suffered much under her.

40   (M) Concerning Dumah, Dedan, and Kedar (21:11–17). These three short oracles (vv 11–12, 13–15,16–17) are placed together because all deal with locations in Arabia, SE of Judah; Dumah and Kedar are also linked as descended from Ishmael in Gen 25:13–14 (as is Tema, named in the oracle on Dedan). Since Arabia fell successively under Assyrian and Babylonian control, these oracles could fit into a wide time span, but Aramaisms suggest the later period. Nabonidus (556–539) took special interest in Arabia, living in Tema *ca.* 550–540, and this period has been suggested for vv 11–12 and 13–15. **11–12.** These verses take the form of a rather enigmatic dialogue. *Dumah:* (An oasis in Arabia) occurs in the inscription ("Edom" in *NAB*); the oracle itself mentions only Seir, a mountain in Edom, sometimes used as a metonym for it. Although the meaning is far from certain, it appears that to a "watchman" (i.e., a prophet) in Judah there comes from Dumah (therefore from the east, the direction of Seir) an interrogation concerning "the night," i.e., a period of trial, perhaps of the Babylonian domination. The response suggests a temporary relief only but does not close the door to future hope. **13–15.** Although usually rendered "oracle on Arabia," the inscription (missing in LXX) does not use the normal term for Arabia and has not been satisfactorily explained. The location is secure, however, because of the two places named, Dedan and Tema. Caravans of Dedanites have been ravaged and are advised to spend the night in the wilderness for safety's sake; the people of Tema are urged to aid them with food and drink. Again the period of Babylonian domination is possibly the background. **16–17.** This addition perhaps presupposes the preceding but takes the disaster as a prophecy soon to be fulfilled. *like those of a hireling:* See comment on 16:14. *glory:* Kedar was known for the wealth it had acquired through its flocks and caravan trade (60:7; Jer 49:28–29; Ezek 27:21).

41   (N) Oracle on the Valley of Vision (22:1–14). This announcement of doom can confidently be attributed to Isaiah; though of great importance, it offers many problems. It is not clear why it was placed among the oracles against the nations. The editor's inscription is taken from v 5. The oracle can be dated to 701, after Sennacherib's reprisal for Hezekiah's revolt of 705. Sennacherib destroyed 46 fortified cities of Judah, with their villages, and threatened Jerusalem; Hezekiah submitted, paid a huge indemnity (2 Kgs 18:13–16), and lost much of his territory. Isaiah had opposed and condemned as disastrous Hezekiah's attempt at power politics because it neglected to take Yahweh's "plan" into account and placed trust in human allies rather than in him (see 28:14–22; 29:15–16; 30:1–7,8–14,15–17; 31:1–3). Yet Sennacherib's withdrawal did not lead to reflection or repentance, but rather to wild rejoicing, and this is what occasions Isaiah's scathing denunciation of Jerusalem. **2a.** *presumptuous town:* The same term is applied to Tyre in 23:7 (and cf. 32:13). **2b–3.** The defenders had not even acquitted themselves with bravery, but had fled (cf. also Assyrian records, *ANET* 288). Verse 3aβ and 3bβ should be transposed, as in *NAB*. **4.** The prophet's pathos reveals itself in the term "daughter of my people" and in his refusal to be consoled, not least because the moral damage is seen to be irreparable. **5-8a.** Some deny these verses to Isaiah, esp. because of the identification of the attackers as Elam and Aram (both opposed Assyria in the 8th cent.). As in 21:2, this may be explained as contingents of conquered peoples being taken into the conquering army (as David did with the Philistines [2 Sam 15:18-22]). **6.** *Kir:* Mentioned in the OT only with reference to the Syrians (2 Kgs 16:9; Amos 1:5; 9:7). *valley of vision:* Not a known geographical designation. It was probably an assembly point for attacking forces, no doubt the Hinnom Valley, W of Jerusalem, now become the object of prophetic revelation or vision. *he has removed the cover:* Yahweh has denuded Judah of the protection of Jerusalem, often thought to be invincible. **8b-11.** Feverish preparations for the siege only highlight the neglect of Jerusalem's true source of security, Yahweh's will and power. This passage is sometimes taken as prose, but Wildberger and others scan it as poetry. Some believe that it reflects the preparations for the Babylonian siege of 588-587, but on inadequate grounds. *house of the forest:* Probably what is elsewhere called "the hall of the forest of Lebanon," which Solomon established, in part, as an armory (1 Kgs 10:16-17). *city of David:* The older part of Jerusalem, the Jebusite stronghold captured by David. *lower pool:* There is reference in 7:3 and 36:2 also to an "upper pool," but neither is located with certainty. *you made a reservoir between the two walls:* For the second wall, built by Hezekiah, cf. 2 Chr 32:5. The new reservoir would hold the water brought in by the famous tunnel Hezekiah had dug through rock (2 Kgs 20:20) and would now replace "the old pool" (probably "the upper pool" of 7:3 fed by the "waters of Shiloah"; see 8:6). *but you did not look to him who made it:* The antecedent of the (fem.) pronouns with "made" and "formed" must be conjectured (*NAB* supplies "the city"); probably it refers in a general sense to what is now happening and thus relates to Yahweh's work in history—a favorite theme with Isaiah. The people of Judah's failure to attend to Yahweh's purpose and to conform their actions to it necessarily leads to disaster (5:12-14; 30:1-5,8-14; 31:1-3).

42   (O) Shebna and Eliakim (22:15-25). The identification of Shebna as the official against whom vv 16-19 were spoken rests on what was originally an inscription (v 15b, *'al-šebnā' 'ašer 'al-habbāyit*) later taken into the text, and whose accuracy is sometimes questioned. However, there was an official named Shebna in Isaiah's day (36:3,22; 37:2//2 Kgs 18:18,26,37), and his position is given as *sōpēr*, "scribe," the equivalent of secretary of state (R. de Vaux, *AI* 129-32), a high official but inferior to master of the palace (*'al-habbāyit*), the title given him here. The texts cited above name Eliakim in that position, so they are consistent with the demotion of Shebna and elevation of Eliakim (but not with the exile of the former). Many contest the authenticity of vv 19-24, on the elevation of Eliakim; some take them as an investiture oracle by a contemporary of Isaiah, others as a much later piece describing an eschatological messianic figure. But, on the assumption that the inscription was correct, Shebna must have been demoted; and vv 20-24 are not addressed to Eliakim but to another whose authority is to be transferred to Eliakim (v 21). Verse 25 is a later addition. **15.** *steward:* Hebr *sōkēn* is not elsewhere found in the OT, though the fem. occurs in 1 Kgs 1:2,4; nonbiblical uses in cognate languages support its being here a synonym for "master of the palace." **16-18.** Although rock-hewn tomb and chariots may reveal blameworthy pride, they hardly explain the severe judgment. It is conjectured, therefore, that Shebna was a leading force in Hezekiah's Assyrian policy, which would also help explain the threat of exile.

The context (i.e., after 22:1-14) may suggest a connection with Hezekiah's Assyrian policy. **19-20.** The shift to Yahweh as the speaker and the "on that day" are indications of a new beginning. **21-22.** The things said of Eliakim and his office are intended to associate him closely with the royal house. On his being "father," see 9:5, but also Gen 45:8; Job 29:16; and Judg 5:7 (Deborah as "mother"). *the key of the house of David:* Symbolizes authority over all in the royal palace, but the placing of it "on his shoulder" may represent the actual investiture ceremony. **23.** *seat of glory:* A term that could be applied to the royal throne closely associates Eliakim with the royal line. *on him shall hang:* A family participates in the prerogatives of the high official, even future generations when the post is hereditary. **25.** A later addition, from a time when Eliakim's line had lost this post.

43   (P) Concerning Tyre (23:1-18). Although this poem possesses power and beauty and has some contact with Isaiah's thought, it is probably a later composition. The original unity is vv 1-14 ("Wail . . . laid waste" in v 1 and v 14 forms an inclusion), with vv 5 and 13a as interpolations and vv 15-18 composed of later additions. The inscription is probably correct in seeing Tyre as subject; "Sidon" in vv 4 and 12 and "Canaan" in v 11 should be taken as terms for Phoenicia generally. Although the commands to wail (vv 1,14) suggest lamentation, this is a sarcastic ploy; the overall message is that Tyre's downfall is the doing of Yahweh and that he has acted for good reason. There are no historical allusions that would date the piece directly, but, since the poem supposes that the blow came when Tyre was the center of a mercantile empire, a probable conjecture would be the expeditions of Esarhaddon against Tyre in 679 and 674 in punishment for revolt against Assyria (*ANET* 291, 292). The poem is developed in fine dramatic style, with ships, cities, the sea, and populations all personified. **1.** *wail:* The ships arrive to find no port, no buyers for the merchandise they have brought from afar. "Tarshish," according to Albright, means "refinery" (*BASOR* 83 [1941] 21-22) and came to designate a colony, or possibly several, where such activity was carried on; Tartessos on the coast of Spain is the best candidate. *Tarshish ships:* Originally so designated because of the port to and from which they sailed, but the term came to designate any large oceangoing vessel; it is used in that sense in 2:16; cf. also 1 Kgs 10:22; 22:49. *Kittim:* Designated different peoples at different times, usually distant and from the west; here it refers to Cyprus. **3.** *the grain of Shihor:* Parallel to harvest of the Nile; *šihōr* means "pond of Horus." **4.** *be ashamed:* Explained by the following words concerning childlessness (cf. Gen 30:1; 1 Sam 1:5-7), which, though spoken by the sea (by identification with its formerly illustrious city?), must refer to Phoenicia (Sidon). **6.** *pass over to Tarshish:* I.e., because the destroyer may return. **7.** *from of old:* A claim to have existed from antiquity would be part of Tyre's proud boast. *distant lands:* Tyre had a widespread network of colonies which contributed to her commercial success. **8-9.** The judgment on Tyre is explicitly attributed to Yahweh's planning in the same terminology Isaiah had used elsewhere (see 14:24-27); but here it does not relate to broader policy but is Yahweh's reaction to Tyre's pride. **10.** The Hebr text is in part corrupt. Emendation on the basis of the LXX and 1QIsa^a gives reasonable sense: "cultivate your own land" (i.e., turn to other means of livelihood) "because the Tarshish ships no longer have a port" (profit from trading has been cut off). **11-12.** Yahweh's initiative is again affirmed (cf. vv 8-9). *daughter Sidon:* Another personification (cf. vv 1,4,14). **13.** The verse is corrupt and in part, at least, a gloss. As it now stands it names the Chaldeans and may intend to accommodate the oracle to Nebuchadnezzar's long siege of Tyre (585–573). However, some read "Kittim" for "Chaldeans" and see an assertion that flight to Cyprus will be of no avail (cf. v 12). **15–18.** Glosses that acknowledge a possible future restoration of Tyre and lessen some of the hostility of the original oracle. Verse 16 is no doubt a secular song that mocks the condition of any overage harlot; v 15 simply introduces it, applies it to the situation of Tyre, and thereby offers a mitigation of the harsh sentiments of vv 1–14; originally it would not have included references to "seventy years" or to "the years of one king" (the latter remaining without satisfactory explanation). Verses 17–18 build on the preceding and are more positive, seeing Tyre again "at the end of seventy years" (a round figure for a time of punishment, as in Jer 29:10) dealing with all nations. It even speaks of Tyre's profit being consecrated to the Lord. Such flowing of the wealth of the nations to Jerusalem (supposing often also conversion to Yahweh) is frequent in exilic and post-exilic texts and is a fitting note upon which to end this collection of oracles on the nations.

44   (VI) The Apocalypse of Isaiah (24:1–27:13). After oracles against particular nations (chaps. 13–23), chaps. 24–27 announce the final end of the earth. This perspective and themes like the punishment of cosmic powers, the end of death, and the resurrection of the dead betray the late date of chaps. 24–27 and link them with apocalyptic writings—although characteristic features of the genre are missing; see P. D. Hanson, "Apocalyptic Literature," in *HBMI* 465–88.

(A) Earth's Final Downfall (24:1–20). Earth's destruction is announced (vv 1–3); earth reacts as though cursed (vv 4–13); the survivors are invited to praise Yahweh's name (vv 14–16a); the original announcement of destruction is amplified (vv 16b–20). **4.** *the earth mourns:* Hearing Yahweh speak, the earth goes into mourning, reacting as to a death sentence. E.g., Ahab puts on sackcloth when he hears Elijah's judgment on him for Naboth's murder (1 Kgs 21:27). Earth's "mourning" is manifested by a severe drought; cf. Amos 1:2 and, for the metaphor, D. R. Hillers, *Perspective* 1–2 (1971) 121–33. Verses 4–13 describe *not* the destruction by earthquake and flood announced in vv 1–3 but the reaction of earth and its inhabitants to the announcement of destruction. **5.** *eternal covenant:* Probably the covenant with Noah (Gen 9:16) because of the flood imagery unmistakable in vv 18b–20 below. But by that covenant God vowed never again to destroy the earth by water (Gen 9:11,14–16). To announce a new flood, the text must reinterpret Noah's covenant as conditional on human fidelity. Verse 5 mentions crimes in only general terms, but 26:21 refers to crimes of blood and recalls the stern warning against shedding human blood in Gen 9:6. **6.** *a curse:* The sentence of doom acts like a curse on the earth's fertility, and earth's inhabitants begin to perish in great numbers.

45   7. *the new wine mourns:* Hearing the sentence of doom affects vineyard (vv 7–9) and city (vv 10–12). Both are saddened by the failure of the wine, which had been a part of human life since Noah planted a vineyard and drank its wine (Gen 9:20–21). **10.** *city of chaos:* A succession of ancient cities might bear the epithet "of chaos" but none more suitably, in the same context with allusions to the flood and Noah, than Babel. The story of Babel, the city left unfinished as an eternal monument to confusion, concludes the epoch of the flood with the words: "and from there Yahweh scattered them over the face of the whole earth"; cf. Isa 24:1. **14.** *let them lift their voices:* The survivors of the curse are invited to praise the name of Yahweh, undoubtedly by those safely installed

under Yahweh's protection on Mt. Zion; see 24:23. **16.** *the Just One:* This title honors Yahweh as vindicator of the divine right and that of Israel through victory in battle. **17–18.** *the windows of heaven:* As in the flood, Gen 7:11.

46   (B) Yahweh's Triumph in Prophecy and Song (24:21–27:1). Prophecy and prayer alternate. The composition is framed by the announcement of divine vengeance on cosmic powers: the heavenly host in 24:21–22 and the monsters of the sea in 27:1. Notice the repetition in 24:21 and 27:1 of "on that day Yahweh will bring punishment on." After defeating the heavenly host, Yahweh is enthroned as king on Mt. Zion (24:22–23), and the image of the divine king making Jerusalem safe dominates what follows. A hymn to Yahweh, safe refuge of the poor (25:1–5), separates the enthronement from its sequel: a divine banquet on Mt. Zion for all the nations to feast the victory over death (25:6–10a). A much longer "song" in two parts (26:1–21) extols the protection of Yahweh's city (vv 1–6), then praises the power of Yahweh's commandments and prays for divine intervention against the people's enemies (vv 7–19). It is concluded by Yahweh's response (vv 20–21).

(a) YAHWEH'S KINGSHIP (24:21–23). 21. *the host of heaven:* The sun, moon, and stars; cf. Deut 4:29. **22.** The imprisonment and later punishment of Yahweh's enemies is a recurrent theme in apocalyptic; cf. Rev 20:1–3. **23.** *the moon will be abashed and the sun ashamed:* By the glory of the divine king. Creation is rolled back: after earth disappears beneath the waters, the heavenly host is imprisoned and the brilliance of sun and moon dimmed. Only the light from the divine king shines, as at the first moment of creation. *on Mt. Zion and in Jerusalem:* The image of Yahweh's mountain, succeeding that of the waters into which the earth has sunk, recalls the old tradition, perhaps going back to pre-Israelite Jerusalem, that Zion's God repels the raging waters which assault the city; see 17:12–14. In the flood the waters covered the highest mountains (Gen 7:19–20), and, according to Isa 30:25, the waters will again, "on the day of great slaughter." But Zion withstands the floodwaters (28:16). It will be higher than any other mountain in the future (2:2) and will be surrounded by water to protect it (33:21). *elders:* Since 25:6–8 will describe a banquet "on this mountain," the reference recalls the liturgical banquet of Exod 24:9–11 at which the elders of Israel feast the covenant before Yahweh on Mt. Sinai. See P. Welton, *TZ* 38 (1982) 129–46.

47   (b) HYMN TO YAHWEH, SAFE REFUGE (25:1–5). 1. *wonderful plans:* Cf. the wonder counselor in 9:5. **2.** The "ruined city" of 24:10–12 now has its ruin attributed to Yahweh. **3.** *fierce peoples:* May be an allusion to the conquest of Canaan; cf. Num 13:28.

(c) THE BANQUET ON MT. ZION (25:6–10a). The banquet is the sequel to the enthronement scene of 24:21–23; it celebrates the divine kingship. **7.** *the mourning veil:* Possibly the surface of the earth covering the dead; cf. 26:21. **8.** *he will swallow death:* Makes explicit the metaphors of "veil" and "cover." **9–10a.** A short hymn to Yahweh's power closes the scene of Yahweh's enthronement and banquet which begins with 24:23.

(d) ON MOAB (25:10b–12). Moab is the only enemy of Israel mentioned by name in chaps. 24–27, but this is probably not the unnamed enemy that appears elsewhere in chaps. 24–27; vv 10b–12 are a later addition. Moab, Israel's neighbor across the Dead Sea, was a son of Lot by his own daughter (Gen 19:37), and a longtime adversary, remembered for having summoned Balaam to curse Israel (Num 22–24) and for having oppressed Israel (Judg 3:12–30). Conquered by David, Moab regained its independence after Ahab's death.

Oracles against Moab are found in Amos 2:1–3 and Isa 15–16. See also Jer 48:26–27 and Ezek 25:8–11.

48   (e) PRAYER FOR DELIVERANCE (26:1–27:1). Verses 1b–6 extol the city of Yahweh and urge trust in the "Rock of Ages." A companion piece to the hymn of 25:1–5, it also has links with 24:14–16a. Verses 7–19, displaying some traits of a communal lament, pray for divine help against the people's enemies. Verses 1b–6 and vv 7–19 are identical in style, and they form two parts of one composition in the present state of the text. Verses 20–21 are the divine response to the people's prayer. **1.** *our city-stronghold is Salvation:* "Salvation" is a divine title, concretely "the Savior," as the following "he provides" shows. The common transl., "we have a city-stronghold," divides the verse wrongly and ignores a figure of speech characteristic of this chapter: the word that a colon ends with, or a like-sounding word, is the word that the next colon begins with (anadiplosis); see W. H. Irwin, *CBQ* 41 (1979) 244–45. **9b.** *when your commandments reach:* Reading *kĕ'aššēr,* piel infin. with *kĕ.* Verses 9b–10a contain a long chiasmus: each word or expression in v 9b has its parallel, in reverse order, in v 10a except for the vb. *yūḥan,* "pardon," on which the chiasmus pivots. The central position of "pardon" focuses attention on the treatment of the wicked: they should *not* be pardoned. **12.** *confer peace upon us:* Peace involves two things: destruction of the people's enemies (v 14) and the people's increase (v 15). **13.** *only your name do we invoke:* They appeal to their loyalty to the first commandment. **17–18.** The metaphor of false labor expresses the people's helplessness. *the inhabitants of the world do not drop:* The vb. "drop" may mean "give birth" or "fall in battle." To increase, they must defeat their enemies and give birth to new inhabitants of the world; both exceed their power.

49   **19.** *your dead will live:* Is this resurrection real or metaphorical, of individuals or of the nation whose oppression has been figuratively a "death"? Many take 26:19 as witnessing an emerging belief in individual resurrection. Neither the wording nor the immediate context is conclusive. Hos 6:2 uses similar language of a national revival, something Isa 26:15 prays for. But in the larger context of chaps. 24–27 with its announcement of the end of death, national revival seems to include individual resurrection. *dew of the east:* Lit., "dew of lights." A dew with divine properties, it both moistens the parched earth and inseminates it so that it may give birth to the dead; see J. Day, *ZAW* 90 (1978) 265–69. **20–21.** Yahweh responds by assuring the people that divine punishment for the iniquity of earth's inhabitants is imminent (v 21). During the "little while" of wrath, Yahweh's people must wait, hiding themselves in their "chambers" with the doors closed behind them (v 20); cf. Rev 6:9–11. These "chambers" undoubtedly refer to their literal or figurative entombment; cf. the *ḥdry mwt,* "chambers of death," in Prov 7:27 and the *ḥdr bt 'lm qbr,* "the chamber of the house of eternity, the grave," in *CIS* I 124, 1; and N. Tromp, *Primitive Conceptions of Death and the Netherworld in the Old Testament* (BibOr 21; Rome, 1969) 156–57. Their tombs will provide them with a hiding place. **27:1.** *on that day Yahweh will punish:* The wording is almost identical to the beginning of 24:21. The long composition is framed by these two announcements of punishment—there of the heavenly host, here of the monsters of the deep. *Leviathan:* A Ugaritic text similarly describes the mythical sea monster (*UT* 67:I:1) in announcing Baal's victory over it.

50   (C) Vineyard and City Revisited (27:2–13). This appendix to 24:1–27:1 centers on the future of Jacob-Israel within a more limited horizon.

(a) THE SECOND SONG OF THE VINEYARD (27:2–6).   So called by comparison with 5:1–7, the song begins with an invitation to sing of the precious vineyard watched over by its divine guardian (vv 2–3). **6.** The song's explanation (cf. 5:7) contains the first mention of Jacob-Israel in 24–27.

(b) THE FUTURE OF JACOB (27:7–13). After the mention of Jacob in v 6, three short passages (vv 7–9, 10–11,12–13) contrast Jacob's fate with that of his enemies. **10.** *the fortified city:* Is this Jerusalem? More probably it is the ruined city of 24:10–12; 25:2,12; 26:5–6,12–13. The "ingathering" of Israelites from their dispersion among the nations is a theme appearing in several late texts, e.g., Deut 30:3–5; Isa 56:8; 66:20; Jer 29:14.

51   (VII) Oracles in Hezekiah's Reign Reinterpreted by Promises of Future Salvation (28:1–33:24). Several Isaian oracles from the latter part (705–701) of Hezekiah's reign are preserved in this collection. Characteristically the prophet uses the form of a lament over the dead, the so-called "woe oracle" introduced by *hôy,* "woe to," "alas for," to express divine opposition to any alliance with Egypt against Assyria (→ 15 above). In addition, the collection includes post-Isaian salvation oracles. The whole is concluded by a long prayer (chap. 33; cf. Isa 12).

(A) Against Samaria (28:1–6). This woe (vv 1–4), which prefaces the entire collection, assumes that Samaria, destroyed in 721, is still capital of Israel. To preface a collection of oracles against Judah and Jerusalem with one against Samaria is implicitly to compare the fate of the two cities and lands. Verses 5–6 add a note of future hope to the old oracle. **1.** *proud crown:* King Omri built the city of Samaria at the head of a broad valley and made it his capital *ca.* 879; cf. 7:9; 1 Kgs 16:24; Amos 3:15. *fading garland:* The garland and the new fig in v 4 image the short-lived glory of the city. *the drunkards of Ephraim:* For Isaiah drunkenness is not just a social evil; it is a major symbol of the blind folly which according to 6:9–12, will lead the people to doom. **2.** *Keteb:* A companion deity to Reshep, "Plague" (Deut 32:24), or Deber, "Pestilence" (Ps 91:6), Keteb was one of Death's agents; see A. Caquot, *Sem* 6 (1956) 53–68. "Of Keteb" here is a superlative, e.g., "a devil of a storm."

52   **(B) Against the Ruling Classes in Jerusalem (28:7–22).** Priests and prophets (vv 7–13) and the "scoffers" ruling in Jerusalem (vv 14–22) are denounced for an arrogant self-confidence which blinds them to their folly and prepares the way for their downfall. **7.** *these by contrast:* Connects the following oracle to vv 5–6. The current ruling classes in Jerusalem compare badly with the inspired leadership of the future Israel promised in v 6. The drunken banquet of vv 7–8, where priests and prophets jest about the word of the Lord, is an emblem of the folly of the people's leaders; cf. 5:11–12. **9.** *knowledge:* A specific prophetic message // "report" ("our report," 53:1). **10.** *for it's sav le sav:* Mocking Isaiah's speech they babble nonsense syllables either to ape a child's first lessons or possibly a novice's attempts at prophetic oratory. Isaiah repeats the syllables with sinister meaning: Yahweh will speak an unintelligible language to them—another way to "make their ears hard of hearing" (6:10). **12.** *give rest to the weary:* The command is at the center of a chiasmus with "this is a place of rest" and "this is a place of repose" on either side. Yahweh had given the people a quiet place of their own after all their wanderings. Priests and prophets should have continued God's work in preserving the place of rest. Instead, they refuse to believe that "your safety will be in quietness and rest" (30:15) and urge an alliance with Egypt, thereby seeking someone other than Yahweh to secure their place of rest. **14.** *scoffers . . . rulers:* The prophet widens his perspective to include not only the priests and prophets but all the ruling classes. **15.** *a covenant with Death:* Death was the king of sheol, the underworld realm of the dead. But it was foolish to try to hide from Yahweh there; see Isa 2:6–22; 29:15; Amos 9:2; Ps 139:7–8; Job 14:13; → 49 above. The prophet mocks the proposed covenant with Egypt, famous for its preoccupation with the dead. **16.** Yahweh's foundation stone, not a covenant with Death, whose titles are "Lie" and "Deceit," gives the firmness required for Zion to stand against all dangers. According to Rom 9:33 and 1 Pet 2:6 the foundation stone is Christ. Originally Zion itself was probably meant, not a foundation stone "in Zion" but "consisting in Zion." For the connection between faith or "holding firm" and not acting hastily or falling away in time of trouble, see Sir 2:1–6. **17–18.** The scoffers' speech of v 15 is contradicted point by point, and the covenant with Death is undone. **19.** *understanding the message will be sheer terror:* Replies to v 9, the mocking "who understands the message?" **21.** The description in 2 Sam 5:17–25 of two of David's victories likens Yahweh to a "bursting flood" and the divine tread to the "sound of marching." **22.** *your bonds:* Ties bind them to Death in covenant, and fetters will chain them in Death's dungeon; cf. Ps 116:3. **23–29.** Yahweh, like a farmer wise in the ways of planting and harvesting, plans wisely and acts effectively; see 5:19; 31:2.

53   **(C) Ariel (29:1–8).** A woe announces a siege of Jerusalem by the following year (vv 1–4). Verses 5–8 announce deliverance from the siege. **1.** *ariel:* 1QIsaᵃ reads *'rw'l* (*'ûrû'el?*); cf. Amarna *urusalim* for Jerusalem. "Ariel" may mean either "altar hearth" (cf. Ezek 43:15 and the Mesha inscription, *KAI* 181:12, *'r'l dwdh*) or "netherworld" (cf. Akk *arallu*), the most generally accepted explanations. But a popular etymology, "lion of God," is also appropriate, since the image of a lion on Mt. Zion beset by shepherds occurs in 31:4, and hunting terminology is often used to describe a siege; see G. Gerleman, *Contributions to the Old Testament Terminology of the Chase* (Lund, 1946) 89. *add year upon year:* Either "keep on from year to year" or, more probably, "when next year comes." A similar phrase in 32:10 seems to refer to the next harvest. **4.** *from the earth:* From sheol, a variation on the "descent to the netherworld" theme of 28:15. In psalms of lament it is a commonplace expressing direst necessity. **5–8.** What began as a threat becomes assurance of salvation. Just as a rainstorm dissipates the dust storm over the city, Yahweh will relieve the siege. These verses, not part of the original oracle, strengthen the belief in Zion's inviolability, a belief that Jeremiah will try to shake in the next century.

(D) Two Speeches against the People's "Unknowing" (29:9–16). Two passages (vv 9–14 and 15–16) address a frequent theme of Isaiah's preaching: the people's inability to understand God's word or work. Verses 9–14 attribute the people's "unknowing" to a divinely induced trance. Their vision is impaired as by a drunken stupor, and the vision they should see is like a sealed scroll that neither the literate nor the illiterate can read. The passage has as its conclusion a judgment oracle (vv 13–14) with charge, verdict, and sentence of the people. This crime is their refusal to give their hearts to Yahweh; their punishment, loss of wisdom. Thus, the divinely induced "unknowing" has been preceded by the people's deliberate "unknowing" of Yahweh. The second passage (vv 15–16) is a woe upon those foolish enough to think that they can hide their thoughts from the Creator. **11.** The "sealed teaching" (*tôrâ*) figures prominently in 8:16. **13.** *their heart:* The seat of their thoughts as well as their

affections; hence, they are already unwise. *their fear of me:* Their worship of me, but also their faithfulness to the one God of Israel that worship should express. **14.** *the wisdom of its wise:* Their punishment is to have unwise leaders, in this case advisers urging the king to ally with Egypt; cf. 31:2. The passage is quoted in Matt 15:8–9; Mark 7:6–7; 1 Cor 1:19. **15.** *who hide their plan from Yahweh in the depths:* In sheol. Secret negotiations are in progress to seal the covenant with Death, i.e., with Egypt (28:15).

54   **Salvation as Reversal of the Present Situation (29:17–21).** Like vv 5–8 but on a larger scale, vv 17–21 describe a time of salvation beyond the condemnation of the preceding passages. The condition of the deaf, the blind, and the needy will be reversed, and the vicious, the scoffers, and the malicious will disappear. Deafness and blindness in Isa are often symbolic of the "unknowing" addressed in the preceding passages. The tenor of the oracle suggests a post-Isaian date.

(F) Jacob's Future (29:22–24). This salvation oracle is a later addition to vv 17–21 but has echoes of Isaian texts, e.g., 2:5–6; 8:12–13. **22.** *the God of Jacob's house:* Reading *'ēl* for *'el. who redeemed Abraham:* A unique reference to the "redemption" of Abraham in the OT. **23.** *they will hallow my name:* Cf. Ezek 36:23. As a result, "knowing" will be restored to Jacob.

(G) Woe to Rebellious Sons (30:1–5). This oracle and the next denounce negotiations to enlist Egypt's support in Hezekiah's rebellion against Assyria after the death of Sargon II in 705 and the accession of his son Sennacherib. **1.** To be a "rebellious son" was an offense punishable by death, according to Deut 21:18–21. **4.** *though his high officials are in Zoan, and his messengers reach Hanes:* Who "his" refers to is unclear. Since Judah is "going down to Egypt," "his" should mean "Judah's." But in 19:11,13 the "high officials of Zoan" are the "wise counselors of Pharaoh." Zoan was in the northernmost part of Lower Egypt, and Hanes (*Heracleopolis magna*) was just over its southern boundary in Upper Egypt. To go from one city to the other was to cross Lower Egypt, which the Pharaoh of the time, the Ethiopian Shabako, had only recently (712) conquered. The clause may mean: though Shabako now rules Lower Egypt too. **5.** *all have become odious:* The term "become odious" belongs to international affairs. The Ammonites "became odious" to David (2 Sam 10:6), and he declared war on them. If the officials are Shabako's, they have "become odious" to other nations because of Egypt's unreliability as an ally.

55   **(H) The Burden of the Beast(s) of the South (30:6–7).** Egypt's unreliability is denounced a second time. **6.** *burden:* Another name for "oracle" but also a "load" to be carried. The "burden" of tribute and of the prophet's word is carried by beasts to the great beast of the South, Egypt. **7.** *Rahab:* A mythical sea monster (Job 9:13; 26:12; Isa 51:9; Ps 89:11) and sometimes a symbol for Egypt (Ps 87:4). The other elements of the symbolic name are obscure but seem to characterize the monster as a raucous do-nothing; cf. the name for Egypt in Jer 46:17: "Bluster which lets the right moment pass."

(I) A Testimony to the Perils of Rejecting the Holy One of Israel (30:8–17). A command is issued to prepare a permanent record to witness against the people's rebellion. The speech has three parts linked by the title "the Holy One of Israel." The people order the prophets to rid them of "the Holy One of Israel" (vv 10–11), who answers their defiance with a judgment oracle accusing them of rejecting the divine word (vv 12–14), the command to stay quiet (vv 15–17). **11.** *who say to the seers "see not":* Cf. 6:9–10. The people themselves command the prophets to delude them. For details, see Irwin, *Isaiah 28–33* 81–82. **12a.** *you have rejected this word:* Referring to the "teaching of Yahweh" of v 9; see Jensen, *Use of tôrâ* 112–21. Verse 15 explains what that "teaching" is. **12b.** *perverse tyrant:* Lit., "tyranny and perversity," a hendiadys, of Egypt and its pharaoh. They rely on the great past oppressor of Israel. **15.** The rejected "word" was the command to remain quiet and trust.

56   (J) Those Who Wait for Yahweh (30:18–26).
This promise of relief from drought for the people of Jerusalem, usually assigned a late date, has links with the Isaian 8:1–4,16–18. There Isaiah and his children retire to "wait for" Yahweh, after preparing, sealing, and delivering a "testimony" and a "teaching" to his disciples as witness against the people. Here a witness against the people for rejecting a divine "teaching" is anonymously prepared, after which those who "wait for" Yahweh are addressed. 8:17 and 30:18 are the only references in Isa 1–39 to a group "waiting for" (*ḥākâ*) Yahweh. Jensen (*Use of tôrâ* 113) noted the similarity between 30:8–17 and 8:16–18, but not the connection between preparation of a "witness" and a group "waiting for" Yahweh. **20.** *bread of confinement:* Short rations as in prison; cf. 1 Kgs 22:27. *your teacher:* Lit., "your giver of Torah," but also "your raingiver"; see Hos 6:3; 10:12; Ps 84:7; Irwin, *Isaiah 28–33* 90–91. Yahweh gives rain when they abandon their idols; cf. the contest between Elijah and the prophets of Baal, esp. 1 Kgs 17:1; 18:1,39–45. **24–25.** These verses redirect an earlier oracle toward a vision of the last days. The simple promise of rain gives way to the vision of a flood covering all the mountains "on the day of great slaughter when towers fall"; cf. 2:12–16.

(K) The Defeat of Assyria (30:27–33). A divine theophany, the coming of the "name" of Yahweh to defeat Assyria, is announced. The Lord's people, assembled as for a feast, will watch and accompany the divine victory with music and song. The date is uncertain; Assyria still seems to be the major enemy of Israel.

(L) Woe against Reliance on Egypt (31:1–3). 1. *span horses:* Not "horsemen." There was no mounted cavalry at this time. **3.** "Flesh" contrasts with "spirit" as human with divine, weakness with strength.

(M) Against Assyria (31:4–9). Is the simile of the lion meant to threaten or reassure Zion? If a threat, then v 5 turns it into a promise of salvation. Verses 6–9 appeal for conversion and assure that in return Assyria will fall. The sequence is similar to that in 30:18–26. **4.** *on Mt. Zion:* Or "against Mt. Zion," depending on whether the preposition is connected with "come down" or "fight." The oracle, which is all simile, is ambiguous. **9.** *whose light is in Zion:* A play on the name Ariel.

57   (N) An Ideal Kingdom (32:1–8). This is either a wisdom instruction on the blessings of good rule, couched in hypothetical terms, or a prophetic oracle making use of the instruction form to announce a blessed future. Just rulers shelter the people (vv 1–2), who, if they saw and spoke clearly (vv 3–4), would not give princely titles like "noble" and "benefactor" to fools whose hearts and deeds are ignoble (vv 5–7). Noble is as noble does (v 8). **8.** *will stand:* Will prove innocent in a court of judgment; cf. Ps 1:5.

(O) The Complacent Women (32:9–14). Not as harsh as 3:16–4:1, 32:9–14 warns the complacent of the grief to come. **10.** *when next year comes:* The next fruit harvest is threatened. Thus, the obscure "days upon a year" probably means "when next year comes"; cf. 29:1. **12.** *gird sackcloth on the loins, on the breasts that mourn:* The vb. is strictly appropriate only to "loins" (zeugma). 2 Macc 3:19a describes a similar mourning scene: "The women, girded with sackcloth under their breasts, filled the streets."

(P) Reversal of Condition (32:15–20). The destruction of vv 9–14 will be followed by pastoral bliss. A judgment oracle is reinterpreted as an announcement of temporary chastisement before a time of salvation; cf. 28:5–6; 29:5–8,17–24; 30:18–26; 31:5–9. There will be a dramatic alteration in the vegetation of familiar geographical regions; cf. 29:17–24. Motifs such as "justice and righteousness" (28:17), the "spirit" Yahweh pours out (29:10), "quietness and security" (30:15) and Zion, "the place of rest" (28:12), used in speeches against the people, are resumed to describe the "peaceful meadows" of the people's future home. The passage concludes the Isaian collection, and the pronoun "us" (v 15) provides a transition to the "prayer" of chap. 33.

58   (Q) Prayer and Prophecy (33:1–24). Cálled a prophetic liturgy by H. Gunkel because of the alternation of prayer and prophecy, the passage supposes an assembly, a "we" who pray and hear the divine response. Verse 1 takes the form of the now-familiar woe oracle against an unnamed destroyer; vv 2–6 are a prayer for help; vv 7–9 describe a scene of human and nature's mourning; vv 10–12 are Yahweh's answer; vv 13–16 are a divine instruction in wisdom style on the qualifications for living on God's mountain; vv 17–24 conclude the section with the announcement of blessedness in the Jerusalem of the future.

(a) A PRAYER FOR SALVATION (33:2–9). *at the sound of your army:* By metonymy *hāmôn,* the noise made by a mob of people, signifies the mob itself; cf. 13:4. The military nuance derives from the context: Yahweh's army is on the move; cf. "and the Lord let the Syrian camp hear the sound of chariots, the sound of horses, the sound of a great army" (2 Kgs 7:6). By contrast, when the sounds of great armies mustering against Zion are heard, Yahweh's rebuke chases them away (Isa 17:12–14). *at the din of your troops:* Reading *mērôm mētēkā* with M. Dahood, in *Orient and Occident* (Fest. C. H. Gordon; ed. H. A. Hoffner, Jr., Neukirchen, 1973) 53–54. As in 3:25, *mētēkā,* "men," has a warlike connotation. **6.** *the mainstay of your times:* "Your" when "her" is expected (enallage). Yahweh's fidelity will support Zion through all the stages of its existence; cf. "in your hands are my times" (Ps 31:16). "Times" are the various stages in the life of a person or a city; cf. Qoh 3:1–8. *the treasures of Salvation:* "Salvation" is a divine title, concretely "the Savior," as the pronoun in parallel "his riches" shows (→ 48 above). *the fear of Yahweh:* Linked with "wisdom" and "knowledge" as in 29:13–14 and esp. in 11:1–5, the expression means fidelity to the God of Israel, which excludes allegiance to other gods. **7.** Who these "messengers of peace" may be is unknown. The form *'er'ellām,* the parallel, is unexplained but looks suspiciously like a variation of Ariel. **8.** *gods are rejected:* The correction of *'ārîm* to *'ēdîm* (cf. 1QIsa[a]), "witnesses, treaties," is unnecessary if Dahood (*Psalms I* [AB 16; GC, 1966] 56) is right in assigning *'ārîm* to the root *'yr,* "protect." The "protectors" are gods guaranteeing the covenants, and their rejection parallels the disregard for "humans" decried by the text.

(b) TO DWELL WITH YAHWEH (33:13–16). **14.** *the consuming fire:* Cf. Pss 5:5; 15:1–5; 61:5. The "consuming fire" burns on Yahweh's holy mountain; cf. Exod 24:17; Deut 4:11. **15.** *not to hear . . . not to see:* In certain contexts the Hebr. vbs. "hear" and "see" mean "hear willingly," "consent" and "look favorably," "approve." Pecksniff (Charles Dickens) misunderstood. **16.** The "heights" and the "rocky fastness" are at once Yahweh's home in heaven and on Mt. Zion.

(c) THE FUTURE JERUSALEM (33:17–24). Verses 13–16 and 17–24 are about living in Yahweh's presence. **17.** *let your eyes behold the king in his beauty:* An invitation to admire the Jerusalem of the future, which is the "city of the Great King" (Ps 48:3; this psalm has affinities with our passage). *a far-distant city:* Lit., "land of distances"; *'ereṣ,* depending on the context, may mean the "earth," a particular "land," or in this case a "city-state" like Jerusalem. The qualification "of distance(s)" always means "far distant" elsewhere, but here commentators usually avoid this meaning in favor of "spacious," "immense." Yet "far distant" is entirely appropriate to describe the Jerusalem seen in a vision of the future. So, e.g., Balaam says of Israel's future: "I see him but not now, I spy him but not near" (Num 24:17). Distant in time, the city may also be distant in space. It is at "the gathering of broad ocean streams no galley can cruise, no galleon can cross" (v 21); cf. the remoteness of El's dwelling at the edge of the earth where the heavenly and nether oceans flow together (*UT* 51:IV:21). Jer 31:3a says: "From afar Yahweh appeared to him." **18.** *let your heart contemplate a fearful thing:* See 60:5 for another example of a joyful vision inspiring fear. *where is one to count . . . to weigh?:* Rhetorical questions emphasize the greatness of Jerusalem; cf. Ps 48:13–14. But who "weighs" towers? Isa 40:12 asks a similar question: "Who has weighed the mountains in scales and the hills in a balance?" The answer is God. **20.** *behold Zion:* The city is only now identified, and the "king in his beauty" (Yahweh) only in v 21. The imperative confirms the volitive mood of the preceding vbs. *city of our assembly:* 1QIsaᵃ reads "assemblies," i.e., liturgical gatherings. But in Yahweh's heavenly city there is an assembly of heavenly beings. The divine mountain is described as "the mountain of assembly in the recesses of the north" (14:13). **21.** *a gathering of broad ocean streams:* Reading *miqwē-m nĕhārîm* with H. Hummel, *JBL* 76 (1957) 102; cf. Gen 1:9–10. Verse 21a is obscure, but according to 21b, the site of the new Zion is protected, like El's dwelling, by broad ocean streams. Metaphorically the "gathering" may be Yahweh; see Jer 17:13, which calls God *miqwēh yiśrā'ēl,* "the reservoir of Israel," and *mĕqôr mayim ḥayyîm,* "the fountain of fresh water."

59   (VIII) Judgment on Edom and Joy for the Redeemed (34:1–35:10). Chapters 34–35 are an appendix to 28–33. Often incorrectly called a "little apocalypse," they contain an oracle against Edom (chap. 34) and a salvation oracle featuring the flowering of the southern desert (chap. 35). Both are reminiscent of passages in 40–66.

(A) Judgment on Edom (34:1–17).   2–4. A general slaughter of all the nations together with an end to the heavens themselves and their armies of stars is announced but only to introduce a sentence of total destruction (v 5) on one of Judah's enemies, Edom, located across the Dead Sea to the SE. Oracles against Edom are frequent in the prophets and Obad is devoted entirely to Edom's doom. After Jerusalem's destruction in 587, Judah's principal reason for animosity toward Edom was the advantage the latter had taken of its neighbor's misfortune; see Obad 10–11; Ezek 35:3. For the connection of chaps. 34–35 with 40–66, see M. Pope, *JBL* 71 (1952) 235–43. The destruction and

desolation described in vv 9–17 suggest the fate of Sodom and Gomorrah; cf. Jer 49:17–18.

(B) The Flowering of the Southern Desert (35:1–10). A promise of salvation, which depicts the flowering of that same desert where Edom lay, has been fitted with an ending taken from 51:9–11.

60   (IX) Narratives about Isaiah and Hezekiah (36:1–39:8). This prose appendix is taken from 2 Kgs 18:13–20:19 with only two significant differences: 2 Kgs 18:14–16 is omitted and the psalm of Hezekiah in Isa 38:10–20 is added (→ 1–2 Kings, 10:64–68).

(A) Sennacherib in Judah (36:1–37:38). When Sennacherib came to the Assyrian throne in 705, he was faced with rebellion in his empire. One of the rebels was Hezekiah of Judah. In 701 the Assyrians invaded Palestine. Isa 36–37 copies its account of the campaign against Judah and the siege of Jerusalem from 2 Kgs 18:13–19:37, but fails to mention the heavy tribute Hezekiah paid to Sennacherib (2 Kgs 18:14–16). The record of Hezekiah's payment agrees with a contemporary Assyrian account which reports it as the conclusion of the incident; see *ANET* 287–88. By not mentioning the tribute, the Isa narrative focuses attention on the drama of the siege and rescue of Jerusalem. Two versions of the same story are combined. According to one, the threat of an attack on Jerusalem is lifted when Sennacherib hears a report that the Egyptian army of Pharaoh Tirhakah is in the field (36:1–37:9a,37–38). According to the other, the Assyrian army is destroyed by the angel of Yahweh (37:9b–36). That these two versions are legendary expansions of the events of 701 is defended by many scholars. New evidence in favor of a second campaign of Sennacherib to which these versions refer is offered by William H. Shea, *JBL* 104 (1985) 401–18. For a more detailed discussion, → 1–2 Kings, 10:65–66. **37:9.** *Tirhakah:* Became pharaoh in 690, but was active in Lower Egypt during the reign of his brother Shebteko (699/98–690). **25.** *the streams of Mazor:* Mazor is probably a mountain in Assyria whose streams Sennacherib diverted to the irrigation of Nineveh; see H. Tawil, *JNES* 41 (1982) 195–206.

61   (B) Hezekiah's Illness (38:1–22). Hezekiah's prayer (vv 10–22), a psalm of thanksgiving, is absent from 2 Kgs 20:1–11. **10.** *I said as I wept, "I have completed my days":* Reading *bĕdommî,* "as I wept," with Dahood, *CBQ* 22 (1960) 401–2. *the gates of sheol:* Sheol is often imagined as a prison where the dead are incarcerated; see Tromp, *Primitive Conceptions* 154–56 and *passim.* **12.** *my generation departs and leaves me:* Hezekiah watches from his prison in sheol as the living generation departs and leaves him behind. *like my shepherd's tent:* Elliptical for "as my shepherd pulls up his tent and goes." Hebr *nissa',* "depart," is lit., "pull up (tent-pegs)." **18.** A common motif; cf. Pss 6:6; 30:10; 88:11–13.

(C) The Embassy from Merodach-baladan (39:1–8). This account of the visit of envoys from the Babylonian king Marduk-apal-iddina (720–709; 702) is taken almost word for word from 2 Kgs 20:12–19; for details, → 1–2 Kings, 10:68. The event is probably to be dated between 713 and 711.

16

MICAH

Léo Laberge, O.M.I.

BIBLIOGRAPHY

1 Hillers, D. R., *Micah* (Herm; Phl, 1984). Jeppesen, K., "New Aspects of Micah Research," *JSOT* 8 (1978) 3–32. Mays, J. L., *Micah* (OTL; Phl, 1976); "The Theological Purpose of the Book of Micah," *Beiträge zur alttestamentlichen Theologie* (Fest. W. Zimmerli; ed. H. Donner, *et al.*; Göttingen, 1977) 276–87. Renaud, B., *La formation du livre de Michée* (Paris, 1977). Willis, J. T., "The Structure of the Book of Micah," *SEA* 34 (1969) 5–42. Wolff, H. W., *Micha* (Neukirchen, 1982); *Micah the Prophet* (Phl, 1981).

INTRODUCTION

2 **(I) Micah the Man.** Micah is the last of the four prophets of the 8th cent. BC (see the first verse of both Isa and Hos). The "days of Jotham, Ahaz, and Hezekiah" cover the years 740–687. As for Isa, Samaria's fall (721) is used in his preaching as an example for Jerusalem. Micah was from Moresheth-gath (1:1,14; Jer 26:18), a city from the lower country (the Shephelah) in SW Judah (most likely el-Judeideh, halfway between Beth-shemesh and Lachish, halfway between Hebron and Ashdod). His father's name is not given and Moresheth was definitely unimportant. His reputation as a prophet of doom was preserved (see Jer 26:18–19, a century later). His name may be compared to another prophet's name: Micaiah, son of Imlah, who lived more than a century earlier (see 1 Kgs 22:8). The name means "who [is] like [Yahweh]?" (possible allusion in 7:18: "Who [is] God like you: *mî 'ēl kāmôkā?*").

Nothing shows that Micah had a political role, and little is known of his personal life. His preaching is concerned with sin and punishment, not with political or cultic matters. He is preoccupied with social justice and does not fear princes, prophets, or priests. Not being a member of such groups, he affirms his independence through his message. The times were bad. The Assyrian armies of Tiglath-pileser III conquered Damascus in 732 (with a part of Israel), and Samaria in 722. Ashdod fell in 711. Sennacherib was occupying part of the coastal land, menacing Moresheth and the area; see 1:10–15. Jerusalem was besieged in 701. Danger was not only external. Prophets, priests, and judges accepted bribes; merchants cheated; Canaanite cults were used alongside the Yahwistic ones.

3 **(II) Structure and Composition.** The book shows a classical organization of prophetic literature: oracles of doom followed by oracles of promise (doom: 1:2 to 3:12; 6:1 to 7:6; promise: 2:12–13; chaps. 4–5). The concluding verses (7:8–20) seem to be a "liturgical text" from the days after the exile. Some other elements have been added to the message of the prophet. A minimal consensus considers 1:8–16; 2:1–11; and 3:1–12 as coming from Micah. However, 2:12–13 and at least part of chaps. 4–5 are later additions. Consideration must be given to 6:1–7:6 as being mainly from the prophet himself.

4 **(III) Text.** The Hebr text is difficult. The ancient copies (see, e.g., Qumran fragments 1Q*14*, 1Q*168*, and those from Murabba'at, Mur 88 xi–xiv) do not alleviate the situation. The ancient versions were already experiencing this problem.

5 **(IV) Message.** Micah is concerned with the people's rejection of God. Sin is the reason for the coming punishment. The Assyrian king is but an unconscious instrument of God's wrath. A false sense of security (3:11: "Is not the Lord in our midst?") has replaced an authentic allegiance to God. Jacob's rebellion is the reason why Samaria has fallen; Judah's sins are a menace for Jerusalem. The Lord must judge, and the prophet is the accuser in God's name. Like Hos, Amos, and Isa, Micah is preoccupied with social justice and with the astute wickedness of all leaders, political and spiritual. While princes and merchants cheat and rob the poor and humble, esp. women and children, priests and prophets adapt their words to please their audience. The leaders mistake evil for good and good for evil. Prophecy is rejected and sacrifices are emptied of their relation to God. The covenant is ignored and the Lord must turn his face away from the people and abandon them to their plight. In Mic, denunciation and accusation often take on the aspect of complaints.

6 However, a message of hope is inserted in the middle of the book. The Temple shall become once again the center of the land and of the world. People will come there in procession. A remnant will be at the origin of a new Israel, and its leader will be a true shepherd, a bringer of peace in the name of the Lord. Thus, Bethlehem and Jerusalem will be renewed and the sources of sin will be eliminated. The final verses of the book give us an example of the liturgy to be performed: having confessed their sin, the people no longer ask: "Where is Yahweh, your God?" A new exodus is taking place. God's wrath has abated and a new era is beginning. God's steadfast love, his *ḥesed,* will be shown to Jacob and Abraham, thus realizing the oath given to the fathers in the days of old.

7 **(V) Outline.** Based on the alternation of the oracles of doom and of promise and on literary indications (such as new beginnings and repetitions), the following outline is suggested:

(I) The Judgment of the Lord against His People (1:1–2:11)
  (A) Superscription (1:1)
  (B) Accusation against Samaria and Judah (1:2–7)
  (C) Lamentation (1:8–16)
    (a) The Dire Situation of Jerusalem (1:8–9)
    (b) The Fate of the Southern Cities (1:10–16)
  (D) Social Sins (2:1–11)
    (a) Woe-oracle against the Oppressors (2:1–5)
    (b) Rejection of Prophecy (2:6–11)
(II) A Remnant Will Return (2:12–13)

(III) Condemnation of the Leaders (3:1–12)
  (A) Against the Perverse Leaders (3:1–4)
  (B) Against the Prophets (3:5–7), with a Statement Concerning Micah's Mission (3:8)
  (C) Against the Leaders, Prophets and Priests Included (3:9–12)
(IV) A New Dwelling Place for God in a Renewed Israel (4:1–5:14)
  (A) All Nations Will Come to the Mount of the Lord's House (4:1–5)
  (B) The Lord as King of the Assembled Remnant (4:6–8)
  (C) Destruction and Exile (4:9–14)
  (D) A Messiah from Bethlehem (5:1–3)
  (E) Peace: Deliverance from Assyria (5:4–5)
  (F) The Remnant of Jacob in the Midst of Nations (5:6–8)
  (G) Destruction of the Causes of Sin (5:9–14)
(V) Accusation and Condemnation of Israel (6:1–7:7)
  (A) Yahweh's Lawsuit against Israel (6:1–8)
    (a) Address (6:1–2)
    (b) Lamentation Based on the Mighty Deeds of Yahweh (6:3–5)
    (c) True Religion (6:6–7)
    (d) The Answer (6:8)
  (B) Jerusalem Is Punished for Its Sin (6:9–16)
  (C) Lamentation (7:1–7)
    (a) Social Injustice and Consequent "Visitation" by God (7:1–6)
    (b) Attitude of the Prophet (7:7)
(VI) A Liturgy of Faith (7:8–20)
  (A) Confession of Sin and Address to the Enemy (7:8–10)
  (B) God's Answer: A New Jerusalem (7:11–13)
  (C) A Prayer to God for His People and Concerning the Other Nations (7:14–17)
  (D) A Hymn to God, Who Pardons and Who Is Faithful (7:18–20)

COMMENTARY

8 **(I) The Judgment of the Lord against His People (1:1–2:11).** As universal judge, Yahweh will condemn not only Samaria but also Jerusalem. The crimes of the people, and especially the social injustice of the leaders, show corruption everywhere (this first unit could include chap. 3).

9 **(A) Superscription (1:1).** An editorial account. This verse combines expressions found in the introductions to (1) Jer, Ezek; (2) Isa, Amos, Hab. For the names of the kings, see Isa (dates: 740–687). Micah's activity was probably during the last years of Ahaz and later (*ca.* 725–700). The mention of Samaria and Jerusalem comes from the first oracle of the book.

10 **(B) Accusation against Samaria and Judah (1:2–7).** This is an example of the oracles of doom, prominent in the book. Yahweh is accusing his people. Speaking from his heavenly abode (which refers also to the Jerusalem Temple), he shows that the impending destruction of Samaria is due to her sins. Political upheavals are seen as consequences of sin. The solemn address ("Listen") of 1:2 is also used to begin new sections in 3:1,9; 6:1,9b (cf. Isa 1:2; 7:13; 46:3; 48:1; Ezek 18:25). This is a lawsuit against the people of Samaria, the capital city of the northern kingdom (Jacob or Israel). In v 5, an application is made to Jerusalem, the capital city of Judah. Verses 2–4 describe a theophany (see Isa 40:3–5; Amos 4:13; Ps 97:5; Exod 19–20). Lord of the universe, Yahweh is also the universal judge. Verse 5b underlines the joint responsibility of both north and south (a later emphasis to ensure that the

message be understood?). Mic and also Isa, both preaching in the south, refer to Samaria's being besieged and conquered by the Assyrians as a lesson for Jerusalem. Compare v 6 to 3:12. Idolatry (v 7) is the main sin, the infidelity, which from the days of Hos and afterward is presented as prostitution. From the 8th to the 6th cent., this theme is frequently used (e.g., in Hos, Isa, but esp. in Jer and in the deuteronomistic literature). Idolatry will bring about the destruction of the idols and of their worshipers.

11 **(C) Lamentation (1:8–16).** The accusation now becomes a lamentation. An introduction (1:8–9) which gives us a cue for interpreting shows that even Jerusalem is endangered by the armies of Sennacherib (*ca.* 701). The fate of 12 southern cities (to the SW of Jerusalem) is alluded to in 1:10–16.

(a) THE DIRE SITUATION OF JERUSALEM (1:8–9). Jerusalem cannot escape punishment. Mourning, Micah suffers with his people. Jackals and ostriches utter their wailing sound; the city has become a place of destruction, even a desert place. The mention of Jerusalem in first place (before vv 10–16) stresses the fact that the capital city is the real "leader": the present menace against the 12 cities will not spare Jerusalem (v 9b refers to v 12b, and also to v 5).

12 (b) THE FATE OF THE SOUTHERN CITIES (1:10–16). These verses are the most difficult of the book. Plays on words are made, based on the names of the cities besieged by Sennacherib. Some are very well known: Gath, Lachish, Moresheth, Achzib, Maresha,

Adullam; others are less well known (or their names have suffered in the process of transmission): Shafir, Beth-le-aphrah, Zaanan, Beth-ezel, Maroth (see later), and most likely in v 10b Bakkon (or a similar name, based on "weeping"). Lament over destruction is certainly implied. All the puns bear that mark. All the cities, known and unknown, are from the territory of Judah. The nearness of these cities to the Philistine territory is evident from (1) the mention of Gath (one of the five cities of the Philistine confederation) and also from (2) the fact that "Beth-le-aphrah" (lit.: "house of dust") is asked to roll itself in the dust ("dust": pun on the name of the city; "roll yourself," in Hebrew: *hitpallaštî*): a pun on the name, which designates the Philistines). Moreover, 1:10a alludes to 2 Sam 1:20 (lament on the death of Saul and Jonathan). Another allusion to David's life may be found under the name Adullam, since this is the place where David took refuge from Saul (1 Sam 22:1–2). The "glory" of Israel (an allusion to its leaders) will not escape its fate, unlike the David of old.

A comparison with Josh 15 (and also with Josh 10 and 12) might unravel part of the mystery of the 12 southern cities. In Josh 15:35–44, among the towns of the lower country (= the Shephelah), we find Adullam, Zenan (compare Zaanan in Mic), Lachish, Achzib, Maresha, to which can possibly be added Yarmuth (see Josh 15:35; 10:3; 12:11; for Mic 1:12 Maroth), Cabbon (Josh 15:40, cf. Mic 1:10 "do not weep"). If Josh 15 is a source, other names could be alluded to, such as Bozqath (15:39; see Mic 1:11: *bšt* = shame), Sha'arayim (15:36: see the "gates" of Jerusalem in Mic 1:9b,12b), 'Adatayim (15:36: see the double *'ad* in Mic 1:9b). The pun is on the vb. *kzb*, "to deceive"; for Moresheth-gath on the vb. for "compensating" as a compensation gift when divorcing; and for Maresha on the vb. "inherit": instead of children inheriting, a "conqueror" is doing so. Verses 9b, 12b, and the end of 13 point to Jerusalem. In v 16, the imperatives are directed to a woman, i.e., Jerusalem, the capital city: mourning rites must be accomplished, since the children are sent into exile.

13   (D) Social Sins (2:1–11). Chapters 2, 3, and 6 are concerned with social justice.

(a) WOE-ORACLE AGAINST THE OPPRESSORS (2:1–5). With the introduction of monarchic rule, the 12 tribes gradually lost their sense of equality. More and more, a separation was worked out between the rich and the poor, between the leaders and the ordinary folk. Exploitation and oppression, and possessions acquired through illegal means became the objects of denunciation by the prophets. See vv 1–2 for examples of those who are "planning" iniquity: taking fields, houses, and even their owners with their inheritance. Their schemes work, because they have power to realize them. The night gives them time to finalize their plan. They monopolize properties and even sell as slaves persons who cannot repay their debts (see 1 Kgs 21:1–4: Ahab's unjust action against poor Naboth). Punishment is proclaimed in v 3, which uses the same vb., "to plan," but now it is the Lord who is planning against "this family," this people accepting such iniquities. At that time, no one will be able to withdraw his neck from the yoke (imprisonment and exile). Punishment is also part of the two comments found in vv 4–5; a satire and a lament are heard, concerning the complete ruin of the people, whose fields are divided among the captors (with reference to vv 2–3). But since the social injustice is measured against the standards of the covenant between God and the people, the sin consists in having been unfaithful to God, when robbing the poor. Hence, the expulsion from the religious assembly (*qāhāl*) of Yahweh (v 5).

14   (b) REJECTION OF PROPHECY (2:6–11). As in Amos 7:16, the prophet is rejected. The vb. usually rendered "to preach" means "to salivate," "to rant or rave." It is used three times in v 6 and twice in v 11. In v 6, the people object to the prophet's preaching. Nobody wants to hear such a message. Verse 7 retorts with two questions requiring an answer. God's spirit or his patience has not come to an end; Micah's words promise good to the righteous one. Then follows (vv 8–9) a description of the injustices performed against the poor, whose mantle is not given back (see Deut 24:10–13; Exod 22:25–26); women are driven out of their houses, and children are cheated of their inheritance (a possible allusion to the "land") or robbed of their freedom. The reason for it all is impurity, the sin that causes the coming destruction. Exploitation and injustice must be repaid: Up! there you go in exile! For the oppressors, the appropriate raving prophet is the one who is ready to say anything that pleases, provided they are ready to give the prophet strong drinks. See the accusation of falsehood (*šqr*) connected with wine and drinks (*škr*), e.g., in Isa 28:7–13; Amos 2:12. Note the expression "this people," taken in a negative sense, as also in similar contexts of Isa and Jer. The message was hard to listen to.

15   (II) A Remnant Will Return (2:12–13). The situation is now totally different. In order to smooth the harshness of the preceding verses, an allusion to the forthcoming liberation is introduced. These verses are usually considered additions composed during the exile, because they interrupt the flow of sentences which constitute a unity of thought between chaps. 2 and 3. We find here a promise of restoration, after the Babylonian Exile, in terms quite similar to the ones found especially in Dt-Isa (see Isa 45:1–2; 52:11; 62:10). The idea of assembling the people like a flock is found in Ezek 34 and 37, as well as in Jer 23. The people in exile will be led through the gate of the city where they live, and they will go back home, under the leadership of their king with God himself at their head. The future gathering of the exiles was the object of v 12; in v 13, it is considered done.

16   (III) Condemnation of the Leaders (3:1–12). A resumption of the themes of chap. 2, with the same imperative as in 1:2. A lawsuit is brought against the leaders (prophets included).

(A) Against the Perverse Leaders (3:1–4). Addressed are the "heads of states" and the "officials" of Jacob-Israel, the 12 tribes. They should know what is right (v 1) and apply it, giving each his due. What they do instead is tear down the people, cut them into pieces like a butcher (see again Ezek 34:10,18). As was the case for the people in 1:5 and 2:10, 3:4 states that because of the sinful conduct of the leaders, the Lord will not listen to them when they cry to him (see Jer 11:11; cf. Exod 2:23–24; Deut 26:7); he will turn his face away from them (see Deut 31:17; 32:20), thus rejecting them.

17   (B) Against the Prophets (3:5–7), with a Statement Concerning Micah's Mission (3:8). Rather than giving God's word to the people, the prophets lead them astray. As long as they receive food, they are ready to utter comforting and pleasing words. They do not act as authentic prophets but are like the prophets of 2:11. Well satiated with food, they proclaim peace (*šālôm*). If food is not provided any more, they announce war; they even proclaim a holy war! Prophets like Micah and Isaiah are sent to proclaim what they have seen without tampering with the message given by the Lord. Mercenary prophets have no vision. They just pretend to have seen one. Their punishment will consist in their being deprived of the sunlight. As a sign of distress and mourning, they will cover their faces. As was the case with the unfaithful leaders (v 4), no answer will be given them by the Lord (v 7). In contrast, 3:8 insists on the mission of the prophet sent by God: he is filled with the strength and the spirit of God (see Amos 3:3–8; Jer 20:9). He is given the courage to enounce the judicial decision (*mišpāṭ*) coming from God: he must denounce the sin of Jacob and the crime of Israel. Actually 3:8 alludes to the terms used in 1:5 for "sin and crime," and in 1:10 for the verb "to denounce." Further, 3:8 underlines the quality of Micah's role as an authentic prophet. Jacob and Israel refer to the 12 tribes in a Judean context, since Micah was preaching in the south. Once Samaria has disappeared as the capital of Israel (721 BC), Jerusalem is the direct object of consideration by both Isaiah and Micah.

18   (C) Against the Leaders, Prophets and Priests Included (3:9–12). "Listen" begins a new section, exactly as in 1:2; 3:1; 6:1; and 6:9. The reference to the heads of the house of Jacob and the chiefs of the house of Israel resumes the expressions found also in 3:1 and show that chap. 3 is composed of three sections. The leaders are accused of perverting (distorting) judicial decisions (*mišpāṭîm*) and what is right. Leaders (3:1–4), prophets (3:5–8), and now again leaders, among whom the prophets are counted (3:9–12), are addressed. *Mišpāṭ* was considered in vv 1 and 8; Jacob and Israel were mentioned in the same verses. These rulers lead the people astray (v 9) and hate *mišpāṭ* (the vbs. constitute marked assonances in Hebrew). Having rejected the right judicial decision, the leaders judge for bribes, the priests give their instruction for gifts, and the prophets divine for money (see v 6). The allusions to Jerusalem and to Zion in vv 10 and 12 (in chiastic order: Jerusalem–Zion–Zion–Jerusalem) insist on the punishment to come, in the terms used in chap. 1 for Samaria. Jerusalem will be ruined and the mountain of the Lord (v 12) will not escape its fate: it will become a "high place in the woods," i.e., a pagan place of worship or, rather, a hill covered by a forest, because of the sin of Jacob and the crime of Israel. This sin is shown to have materialized in the persons of the leaders ("because of you," v 12). The Temple will be destroyed because of the infidelity found in the leaders, who have become so arrogant as to say that they fear nothing, since Yahweh is there (cf. Deut 31:17). One century later, this text (3:12) will be quoted by Jer 26:18 and commented on in 26:19. The impact of the prophecy has not been lost. The call to conversion was still a necessary object of the message of prophets.

As in other prophetic books, these oracles of doom finally persuaded the people who meditated on them and acknowledged their responsibility before God. After the destruction of the city and during the exile, the people were ready to listen to a message of consolation. Note, however, that 6:1 to 7:7 will once again resume rhetorical and ideological considerations quite similar to the ones found in chaps. 1–3.

19   (IV) A New Dwelling Place for God in a Renewed Israel (4:1–5:14). Consolation and messianic hope are stressed. Part of the message of consolation may have come from Micah, but such a message was bound to be especially emphasized in the context of the return of the exiles to Jerusalem, after their "service" (Isa 40:2) in Babylon was ended. Expressions such as "on that day" (4:6; see 2:4) and "in days to come" (4:1) are typical of additions. Moreover, some words function as links between short oracles or as expansions of already existing texts. Note, for example, "and you" (sg., in 4:8; 5:1), "now" or "and now" (4:9,11,14), and the imperatives (fem. sg., in 4:10,13). Usually left untranslated, there is also the expression "and it will be/happen that" (*whyh*), which is an important initial feature in many a short section (4:1: 5:4,6,9). Thus, we obtain as units, with their subdivisions: 4:1–5; 4:6–8 (vv 6–7 and 8);

4:9–14 (vv 9,10,11–12,13, and 14); 5:1–3,4–5,6–8 (6, and 7–8),9–14.

20   (A) All Nations Will Come to the Mount of the Lord's House (4:1–5). This first section is explicitly linked with 3:10–12, thus reversing the oracle of doom. Note the resumption of the words "Zion" and "Jerusalem" (3:10,12; 4:2), and especially "Temple Mount" (3:12 and 4:1; see 4:2,7). This part of chap. 4 (vv 1–5) corresponds to Isa 2:2–5, except for the last verse. The unit is thus clearly identified. Well located in both Isa and Mic, it cannot be said to belong to one book as the source for the other. It is at home in both.

The internal structure is easy to show: the mountain of Yahweh is at the center of the world as its summit. Every nation will come to it, since from Zion comes the law (= instruction) of Yahweh and from Jerusalem the word of Yahweh. Consequently, a messianic peace will rule the universe (note the presence of "people" and "nation" in vv 2,3, and vv 3,5). Security and confidence will be given to everyone. The conclusion, proper to Mic, states that even if the nations come to this mountain in the name of their god, "we do come in the name of Yahweh our God for ever and ever." In Isa, the conclusion was showing all nations going in procession to the mountain of the Lord. Here the mention of the true God ("in the name of Yahweh our God") amounts to a profession of faith. A sense of security was borrowed from the agricultural background of the land (v 4). As a conclusion, v 5 becomes an example of a liturgical expression of faith. The expression at the end ("forever and ever") is found in Mic alone; it is alluded to at the end of v 7 and in 5:1.

21   (B) The Lord as King of the Assembled Remnant (4:6–8). Mount Zion (v 7) refers to the mountain of the Lord of 4:1,2 and to the Zion of v 2. Linked to this we find the expression "Daughter Zion" designating Jerusalem (vv 8,10,13; plus the "Daughter" of v 14). Verses 6 and 7 foretell the regrouping of the crippled and the persecuted. They will be assembled and will constitute a mighty nation (another link with v 3: "mighty nations"). This assembling of the remnant evokes 2:12–13, part of the same message of consolation. In v 7b, there is a development of vv 1–5: from Mount Zion (= the Temple), the Lord himself rules as a king (see 2:13 and the psalms of the kingship of Yahweh), "from now on and forever" (v 5). In v 8, with the double designation of the capital city as Daughter Zion and Daughter Jerusalem, plus the name Ophel, the predominance of the city of David is clearly stated. David was taken from the flock to become ruler in Jerusalem. The "pastoral" vocabulary recalls these elements (see Gen 35:21 for Eder).

22   (C) Destruction and Exile (4:9–14). Probably 4:9–14 already existed independently of 4:1–5 and 4:6–8. In vv 9–14 we hear of oppression, upcoming destruction, and exile. The message of consolation is partly lost, but literary links show that we must read first the message of consolation and not only this message of doom (note the sequence "Daughter Zion," "Zion," and "Daughter Zion" in vv 10,11,13 and "Daughter" alone in v 14; cf. 4:2,7,8 for "Zion"). Verses 9 and 14 ("now") with their allusion to the miseries concerning kingship ("there is no king," and "with a rod [= scepter] they strike the judge's [= the king's] cheek") show the distress of the people suffering from the presence of the invading armies. Was that in 587 or 701? ("Babylon" is mentioned; cf. vv 9,10,12 with Jer 8:19; 50:43,45). The woman suffering the pangs of childbirth is a classical image for the suffering of the people (see Jer and Isa). We seem to have in 4:9–14 the core around which were brought 4:1–8 and chap. 5 as a transformation of the message of doom. Oracles of doom and messages of consolation are combined. How the prophetic literature has come down to us is definitely a complex history, evidently difficult to restore.

The cry of the suffering person (v 9) is linked to the absence of the king, who was the counselor. The following unit (v 10) is an address in the 2d pers. fem. sg. (evidently Jerusalem as the mother who is enduring pain); she is leaving the city to go into exile in Babylon. A messsage of consolation has been inserted: "There shall you be redeemed" (a rare occurrence of that vb. in Mic; compare the last verses of the book). Verses 11–12 (at the center of this unit) show the "numerous nations" (see also v 13, and 4:2) assembling to fight the final combat (compare Ezek 38–39; Joel 4:9–17). The "assembling" of the remnant of Israel in both 2:12–13 and 4:6 contrasts with the belligerent assembly, eager to see the downfall of Zion. The same verb "gather" or "assemble" is found in vv 6 and 11, but what a strong contrast between these two sections! With its address to Jerusalem (2d pers. fem. sg.), v 13 refers to v 10, introducing the theme of revenge, which is immediately neutralized by v 14. In many Eng versions 4:14–5:15 = 5:1–15 (MT).

23   **(D) A Messiah from Bethlehem (5:1–3).** The somber words of 4:9,14 are now dispelled by the announcement of a new David coming to restore his kingship. Allusions are made globally to the messianic texts of Isa 7; 9; 11; 2 Sam 7; Ps 89. The Hebr text identifies this city of Ephrathah (see Josh 15:59; Ruth 4:11) as Bethlehem. It is the city of Jesse and of his son David, who was chosen to be king of the 12 tribes of Israel. Matt 2:5–6 shows how this text came to be interpreted. A link is established between 4:2 and 5:1 by the vb. "come forth," said of the law and of the messianic king. The Messiah will be a "ruler" and his origin is pronounced as "from ever" (an idealized king indeed; there is also an allusion to 4:5 and 7). He is linked to the promises of God and, because of the final context of the book, to the Temple (see 4:7). In v 2, the woman is giving birth (here she is the messianic king's mother). In the name of the Lord, the king shall shepherd his flock.

24   **(E) Peace: Deliverance from Assyria (5:4–5).** In v 4a a statement is given: The king shall bring (lit., "be") peace. The mention of "Assur," the arch-foe, is followed by a structure with two phrases starting in the same fashion, and then with four clauses beginning with the conjunction "and." This enumeration ends with the repetition of the double clause accompanying "Assur": this king would definitely save his people. We thus obtain a reversal of situation, as was the case in chap. 4.

25   **(F) The Remnant of Jacob in the Midst of Nations (5:6–8).** Verses 6 and 7–8 constitute a parallel construction, in which vv 6a and 7a are repeated, in order to stress the presence of the "remnant of Jacob" in the midst of "many nations" (cf. 4:13 and also 4:2,11; see also, for the remnant of Jacob, 2:12–13). Hope and confidence in the Lord are stressed by the image of dew and rain given by God. Once more a reversal of situation is hinted at in v 7. The vb. "to save" or "deliver" in vv 5 and 7 binds the two units together. The lion as a predator has now become the image of the "remnant" taking revenge on the enemy, an indication which v 8 emphasizes.

26   **(G) Destruction of the Causes of Sin (5:9–14).** The beginning of v 9 combines expressions present in vv 4,6,7 and esp. the first part of 4:6. It binds together chaps. 4 and 5. After the initial "and it will be that . . . ," we have a cascade of clauses all starting with "and" (nine times in vv 9b–12), followed by a clause without it, and then a series of three "and"-clauses, emphasizing the clauses without this conjunction at the end of both vv 12 and 14. The vbs. are predominantly

in the 1st pers. sg., stressing that the Lord himself is speaking. He is washing the land and the people of their sins. The word "covenant" is not used even once, but it is clear that we have a covenantal context. Abolishing idolatry, the sin that is directly against fidelity to the God of the covenant, is tantamount to abolishing the reason for the destruction of the city and the expulsion of the people from the land. This is a theme prevalent in Deut and in the deuteronomistic movement at large. Verses 11,12, and 14 contain the only three vbs. using another grammatical person. They show that idolatry is the main source of infidelity to the Lord (cf. 1:7). They bring home the message that fidelity to the covenant is a necessary condition for a new beginning. As with 4:13 and 5:7, the fate of the nations is brought to the fore in 5:14. It is worth noting that disobedience to God is implied, even for the nations.

27   **(V) Accusation and Condemnation of Israel (6:1–7:7).** With this section we find once again the context we had in chaps. 1–3.

    (A) Yahweh's Lawsuit against Israel (6:1–8). This section is delimited by the double "Listen" found in vv 1 and 9 (see also v 2); the same vb. was used as an important marker in 1:2 and also in 3:1 and 3:9. On the other hand, this lawsuit has important parallel texts in Isa 1 and 3, and also in Hos and Amos.

28   (a) ADDRESS (6:1–2). Three times the term "lawsuit" (*rîb*) is used where the cosmic dimensions of the trial are underlined ("mountains, hills, foundations of the earth"). Moreover, Yahweh is both judge and accuser, while Israel is the defendant ("my people"). This evokes the context of the covenant, even though the word is not used, as often in prophetic literature.

29   (b) LAMENTATION BASED ON THE MIGHTY DEEDS OF YAHWEH (6:3–5). Christian liturgies have used this text for Holy Week, esp. Good Friday. It is actually a resumption of the professions of faith of Israel, such as the one found in Josh 24:2–13, typical of deuteronomistic passages. The Lord is addressing his people ("my people" at the beginning of both vv 3 and 5 is a link with the address). The supplication can be compared to the lament found in the Psalms. Past events are recalled in order to bring the listener to repent and enter into proper consideration of the promised faithfulness. The mighty deeds of God are recounted from the exodus (liberation from bondage in Egypt) to the conquest and the entry into the land. What more could Yahweh have done? Note the vb. "to redeem" (*pdh*) (seldom in the Bible, though always in a technical sense), for God's initiative in saving his people (see Deut 9:26; 13:6; 21:8). The faith context is confirmed by the use of the technical term "remember" (*zkr*). Thus, the whole is part of the "memorial" of what God has done for his people.

30   (c) TRUE RELIGION (6:6–7). What is implied rather than stated is that confession of sins is presupposed as a background for the kind of questions asked here. The vb. "to come before" is used twice, emphasizing the proper attitude to adopt when presenting oneself to God. We read four questions: a general one ("With what . . ."), followed by three specific ones, dealing with three forms of cult ("Shall I come . . . ?" "Will Yahweh desire . . . ?" "Shall I give . . . ?"): (1) holocausts, using one-year-old calves; (2) two kinds of offerings—thousands of rams (repeated offerings) or myriads of streams of oil (thus alluding to the oil used for purifications, for anointing, and for other uses in the liturgy, e.g., lamps, etc.); (3) as a climax comes the last question ("Shall I offer my firstborn?"), alluding to the abominable practice of the Canaanites (see Lev 20:2–3; Deut 12:31; Ezek 20:26), a practice rejected by the Lord (see 1 Kgs 16:34; Jer 7:31; 19:5; compare Gen 22 and Exod 11 and 13). The last question is placed in a context of offerings for sins. The radical character of the offering is linked to the gravity of the sin it presupposes. The answer is definitely negative. Yahweh requires an internal conversion and a proper attitude of spirit, as the prophets proclaimed (cf. Isa 1:10–17; Amos 5:21–27; Hos 6:4–6; Jer 6:16–20; 7:21–24).

31 (d) THE ANSWER (6:8). The right answer is "to do justice" (making the right judicial decisions; cf. 3:1 and 3:8). What Yahweh asks is that they "love *ḥesed*," which implies fidelity, goodness, or kindness: an expression of love on their part in response to God's love. This is an important part of the message of the prophets (cf. Hos 2:21; Amos 5:24; Isa 1:17; cf. John 1:14). The whole is resumed in the image of the humble walking with one's God (an image used often in Deut and elsewhere, though in different words).

32 (B) Jerusalem Is Punished for Its Sin (6:9–16). This is one of the darkest oracles of the book. After the introduction mentioning the speaker and the addressee (God and the city), and before the solemn "Listen," the MT reads: "Success [= salvation?] your name shall see," which seems to be a reflection or a correction inserted to attenuate the harsh remarks which follow. The LXX reads: "He will save those who fear his name." Examples of injustice are given in vv 10–12 as the cause for the forthcoming destruction: fraudulent manipulations by merchants; the rich using violence to obtain what they want; the people in general using deceitful language and falsehood. Punishment shall come "because of your sins" (v 13; cf. 1:5). Three times a sentence starts with "you," emphasizing devastation, famine, and destruction; nature itself will refuse to give its yield. The worst days of a besieged Jerusalem are evoked (vv 14–15). God's answer began with a mention of sin as the cause of it all; it ends with an explicit reference to the sins of Samaria (v 16)—the unlawful conduct of Omri and Ahab, whose precepts the people observe (cf. 1 Kgs 16:23–34). As in 1:5–7, Samaria serves as an example of what Jerusalem is doing and also as an illustration of the form of punishment which is to come. For the last words of 6:16, compare Jer 18:16; 25:9,18; 29:18; 50:13,37).

33 (C) Lamentation (7:1–7).
(a) SOCIAL INJUSTICE AND CONSEQUENT "VISITATION" BY GOD (7:1–6). The prophet looks for righteousness and does not find it. He begins his speech with an expression of mourning (see 1:8; 2:1). He is like the one coming after everything has been harvested. Blood and violence are everywhere (see Jer 5:1; Isa 5:7). There is no "pious one" (or "loving/faithful one"); no one is right. Princes, judges, and leaders, all are perverse. The best among them (v 4a) are worth nothing. Hence (v 4b), "the day you were looking for has come: [a day of] visitation." It will be a "day for punishment" (see, e.g., Amos 3:14; Hos 12:3; Isa 13:11; 26:21; Jer 44:13). No one will trust anyone, since betrayal will be a common attitude in those days of distress (cf. Matt 10:35). This is evidently one of the most pungent oracles of doom in prophetic literature.

34 (b) ATTITUDE OF THE PROPHET (7:7). This verse may be a conclusion to vv 1–6, showing how the prophet, for his part, confides in God and reaffirms his trust in God alone. Actually, the beginning ("As for me") contrasts with the attitude of those he was speaking of in 7:1–6; moreover, the vb. ("I will look for") picks up the vb. (*sph*) of v 4b. It is a statement of confidence in God and a profession of faith. In this verse alone, God is mentioned three times by name; he is the savior, and he will listen to his messenger. This stands in stark contrast to the people who do not want to listen to the prophet's

message (see the important use of 'listen" in 1:2; 3:1; 6:1–2). Another way of reading v 7 would be to connect it with the following section as a transitional verse leading to the "liturgy" of penance found in vv 8–20.

35 (VI) A Liturgy of Faith (7:8–20). This section is probably a postexilic addition to the book. For a similar text, see Isa 33. Further, the similarity with the message of consolation found in Isa 40–55 is striking.

(A) Confession of Sin and Address to the Enemy (7:8–10). Jerusalem addresses its enemy ("my enemy": vv 8,10). The noun "light" (v 8) and the verb "to see" (vv 9 and 10) are elements responding to "my enemy"; the light and the sight will be given by God. At the center, in v 9, a reference is made to the "lawsuit" (see 6:1–2). A reversal of situation is called, based on the fact that an acknowledgment of guilt is presented: "I have sinned." For v 10, see 4:11.

36 (B) God's Answer: A New Jerusalem (7:11–13). We may consider v 13 as an oracle of doom, which was then corrected by the message of consolation found in vv 11–12. The destruction "because of its inhabitants" seems to point to 6:16 (note both "ruin" and "her inhabitants" used in common; there is also a possible allusion to the "misconduct" of 2:7). But the time has now come to see in the "day" of the Lord a day of renewal: three times in vv 11–12 is the word "day" used in a favorable sense. It is a day of rebuilding the walls, expanding the boundaries of the city. From all the lands the exiles are coming back.

37 (C) A Prayer to God for His People and Concerning the Other Nations (7:14–17). Verses 14–15 deal with God's people; vv 16–17 with the other "nations." The image of the shepherd herding his flock recalls 5:3. Forests and orchards (lit., Carmel), Bashan and Gilead, are used for the image of abundance they offer (see also the same ambivalent use of "orchard" or "Mt. Carmel" as an image of fertility in Isa 29:17; 32:15; 35:2; for a reversal of the image, see Jer 22:6). And "the days of old" are called to memory: they constitute a "memorial" of what the Lord has done for his people, a guarantee of what he is ready to accomplish once more, as in the days of the first exodus (see 6:3–5). A play on words between the first word of v 16 and the second to the last word of v 17 brings into focus a sharp contrast: "the nations shall see . . . / they shall be afraid of you." The unfriendly "nations" will be put to shame and reduced to nothing.

38 (D) A Hymn to God, Who Pardons and Who Is Faithful (7:18–20). This is likely the text which gives vv 8–20 its liturgical tone. It is a prayer addressed to God who forgives, who is compassionate. There is none like him. The Hebr text seems to allude to the name of the prophet in v 18 (*mî 'ēl kāmôkā = Mî . . . ka*: Micah; see, e.g., Isa 44:7; Pss 35:10; 71:19; 89:9; 113:5; cf. 77:14). For the vocabulary concerning the remission of sin, see Isa 33:24, which is a relevant parallel text, since both use this same theme at the end of a "liturgy." The main terms for sin are used in vv 18–19. It is a fitting conclusion to a book that was preaching against the sins of a people unfaithful to its God. By confessing their sin, the people are obtaining a total reversal of the situation. Blessing will follow penance. "Inheritance" (v 18) recalls 7:14 and 2:2. The "loving kindness" (*ḥesed*), mentioned in 6:8, is shown now to be given (vv 18 and 20), together with "stability" (*'ĕmet*). With the mention of "remnant" and "Jacob" in vv 18 and 20, an allusion is made to what were important terms in the whole book. The last verse (with the words "Abraham and the promise made by God to the patriarchs") is a further indication of some postexilic traits (see Isa 41:8; 51:2; 63:16; 29:22).

17

ZEPHANIAH NAHUM HABAKKUK

Thomas P. Wahl, O.S.B.   Irene Nowell, O.S.B.
Anthony R. Ceresko, O.S.F.S. *

ZEPHANIAH

BIBLIOGRAPHY

1   Boadt, L., *Jeremiah 26–52, Habakkuk, Zephaniah, Nahum* (OTM 10; Wilmington, 1982). Driver, S. R., *Zephaniah* (CBSC; Cambridge, 1906). Fensham, F. C., "Zephaniah, Book of," *IDBSup* 983–84. Hoonacker, Albin van, *Les douze petits prophètes* (EBib; Paris, 1908). Kapelrud, A. S., *The Message of the Prophet Zephaniah* (Oslo, 1975). Sabottka, L., *Zephanja: Versuch einer Neuübersetzung mit philologischem Kommentar* (Rome, 1972). Smith, G. A., *The Book of the Twelve Prophets* (NY, 1928). Smith, J. M. P., *Zephaniah* (ICC; NY, 1911).

INTRODUCTION

2   (I) Historical Background. The book stems largely from words of the prophet, possibly a descendant of King Hezekiah (tracing of an ancestry back four generations [1:1] is otherwise unparalleled in prophets). He prophesied in Josiah's reign (640–609), when there was an attempt, serious but of limited success and duration, to undo the apostasy of Josiah's predecessor Manasseh. Understanding Zephaniah's prophecy as an early part of this reform (2 Chr 34:3–7), we see why he does not include the king with the other orders of society that he condemns (1:8; 3:3–4). Judah had been a vassal of Assyria almost since Israel succumbed to that empire a century earlier. However, since the death of Ashurbanipal in 627, Assyria's power had been collapsing. Egypt, more ally than foe of Assyria since Ashurbanipal's father Esarhaddon had expelled the Cushites, was to attempt to extend its own power and to prop up the failing Assyrians against the rising Babylonian Empire.

3   (II) Message. In this world of political turmoil, Zephaniah sees the fates of nations in Yahweh's hands. The dominant theme is the Day of Yahweh (Amos 5:18; → OT Thought, 77:137), when Yahweh will devastate the old vassals (now rebellious), Philistia, Moab, and Ammon, and the foundering world power, Assyria. The same God will ravage his own people especially, but not exclusively (1:9), for their false worship. But because destruction is reserved for the rebellious and arrogant, its effect will be purification and formation of a people vastly smaller, but pleasing to Yahweh (2:3; 3:11–13). A later editor, who saw these prophecies fulfilled in Nebuchadnezzar's devastation of Judah, encouraged a dispirited people by magnifying the restoration (2:7; 3:9–20).

While most OT books are anonymous, in the case of the prophets like Zephaniah the tradition chose to identify author and time of pronouncement (by indicating the reigning king). The prophetic word is no perennial religious truth, but a message addressed to a specific moment in history. Additions and alterations by successive editors in antiquity reinterpreted the old message for their later days. But still the tradition wanted to associate even the new interpretation with the old message, much as the authors of Deut wanted to give Moses' authority to the speeches which they thought he should have made to Israel on entering the land of Canaan.

4   (III) Outline.

---

* Zephaniah is the work of T. P. Wahl; Nahum is the work of I. Nowell; and Habakkuk is by A. R. Ceresko.

COMMENTARY

(I) Title (1:1).
(II) Oracles of Doom (1:2–18).

5   **(A) Universal Destruction (1:2–3).** A threat against all the tilled earth introduces threats against Judah and Jerusalem and anticipates threats against the nations in chap. 2. It provides "a thundering fanfare which might serve to arouse the anxious interest of the prophet's audience" (Kapelrud, *Message* 16). Zeph reflects the theology behind Gen 1–3: all living creatures are meant for the use of *'ādām,* "humanity"; if Yahweh must destroy the latter, the former must go as well. The theme of universal and cosmic doom will later become central to apocalyptic thought. *I shall gather and destroy:* The intent of the Masoretic vocalization of these words is unclear, the grammar bizarre. However translated, the message is destruction. **3.** *and the stumbling blocks with the wicked:* "Stumbling blocks" is a doubtful transl., but the whole phrase, an editorial addition missing from the best LXX mss., provides a moral grounding for the destruction. *from the face of the ground ('ădāmâ):* A play on the word *'ādām* as in Gen 6:8 (J), where the threat of the flood uses several expressions found here.

6   **(B) Judah and Jerusalem (1:4–18).** Destruction will come upon Yahweh's people for their apostasy. It is difficult to distinguish where oracles of this chapter begin and end. While oracles beginning with phrases like "in that day" are often considered editorial additions, some may be original in a book like this, whose principal theme is the Day of Yahweh.

7   **(a) Canaanite Cult (1:4–6).** Zeph condemns a wide variety of cultic crimes. **4.** *remnant of Baal:* Most likely "Baal to his last vestige" rather than "the little that remains of Baalism." *names of the idol-priests with the priests:* The "name" is not just an identifying label, but the very identity of the person. Two Hebr terms for priest are used here: one, *kĕmārîm* serves to identify only non-Israelite or idolatrous priests. **5.** *army of heaven:* Typical Assyrian worship of sun, moon, and stars, done on the flat Israelite rooftops. For a hymn to the night gods, see *ANET* 390–91. Note the syncretism: They compromise their covenant oath *to* Yahweh by also swearing *by* another deity (MT *malkām,* "their king," if not the Ammonite deity Milkom, still refers to a non-Israelite royal god.)

8   **(b) Coming Day of Sacrifice (1:7–9).** Oracle of doom; an ironic call to sacrifice. **7.** *be still:* A direction derived from cult. *consecrated his guests:* They are to be ritually clean for cult (2 Chr 29:19). However, from what follows it is clear that the guests are the victims (cf. Jehu's guests in 2 Kgs 10:18–28) and that "consecrate" here has its sense of preparing a victim (Lev 27:26; Deut 15:19; Jer 12:3)! **8–9.** The sacrifice is defined as punishment for cultic offenses: wearing foreign clothes, presumably vestments for worship of foreign gods (2 Kgs 10:22). **9.** *leap over the threshold:* A practice found in the cult of Dagon (1 Sam 5:5). *violence and deceit:*

Condemning crimes against justice as well as cultic deviations.

9   **(c) Invasion of the City (1:10–13).** These threats abandon the image of sacrifice for battle within the city.

10   **(i) *Breakthrough* (1:10–11).** Zephaniah hears the troops storm various parts of Jerusalem. *Canaanites:* I.e., "merchants."

11   **(ii) *Looting of the scoffers* (1:12–13).** Looting follows immediately on invasion, with the rich having the most to lose. **12.** *search . . . with lamps:* In case anyone should escape punishment. *thickening on their lees:* An image derived from wine making. In Jer 48:11 the wine that is not disturbed on its lees is the best wine. Whatever the exact analogy here, these undisturbed people recognize no intervention of God in their affairs. **13.** Punishment corresponds to crime: Yahweh will indeed intervene forcefully and disastrously in their affairs.

12   **(d) Day of Yahweh (1:14–18).** The objects of destruction are nature (v 15), buildings (v 16), and finally the humans who are responsible for it all (v 17). **14.** As the day approaches rapidly, so do its sounds of devastation. **15.** *a day of wrath is that day:* First verse of Thomas of Celano's hymn "Dies Irae." *cloud and storm cloud:* Traditional elements of the epiphany, when God comes to intervene in battle (Ps 97:2–5). **16.** *trumpet:* These are typical sounds of war. **17.** *'āfār* means not only dust as it is usually translated, but mud as in Lev 14:42 (Sabottka, *Zephanja* 55–56). Although the text and transl. of v 17b are very problematic, the dreadful import is all too clear. **18.** They will be unable to avert destruction by paying tribute, whether to the antagonist (2 Kgs 18:13–15), or to a potential ally (1 Kgs 15:18–20).

(III) Exhortations Based on Threats against Nations (2:1–15).

13   **(A) Exhortations (2:1–3). 1–2.** The first appeal, notoriously difficult, must be some sort of ironical or sarcastic command addressed to the doomed. Although no suggested transl. is compelling, whatever is commanded is to be accomplished swiftly before the impending day of Yahweh's wrath. **3.** The righteous oppressed are now addressed. *seek Yahweh:* Often a cultic phrase, it is defined by what follows. *seek [to do] what is right and humble:* A summary of Zeph's general moral program against sin and arrogance. *perhaps:* The doubt is not about Yahweh's will and power to save but about the audience's will to heed the exhortation.

14   **(B) Reasons: Oracles against the Nations (2:4–15). 1.** As in Amos 1–2, the prophet backs up the warning to his own people by citing oracles against enemy nations. Philistia (W), Moab and Ammon (E), Cush (S), and Assyria (N) represent the four corners of the earth. Philistia, Moab, and Ammon (vv 4–11) had been vassals of Israel at the time of David and Solomon; prayers and oracles against such rebellious vassals were surely typical of Jerusalem's liturgy (Ps 2). Cush and

Assyria, on the other hand, are world powers (vv 12–15). Dating these oracles is difficult. The expression "remnant of the house of Judah/of my people" (vv 7,9) and the accusation that Moab and Ammon have taken pleasure in the downfall of God's people (vv 8,10) sound like exilic language (cf. Ezek 25:1–11). On the other hand, the oracle against Assyria (vv [12] 13–15) has to predate the collapse of Assyria in 605 and probably the fall of Nineveh in 612. Moreover, expectations of Judahite domination of Philistia fit well with Josiah's expansion of about the year 628 (D. L. Christensen, *CBQ* 46 [1984] 669–82). Most likely we have an authentic oracle against Philistia (vv 5–6 and part of 7) and Assyria (vv 12–15), supplemented in exilic times by an oracle against Moab-Ammon (vv 8–11) and additions to v 7.

15 (a) PHILISTINES (2:4–7). **4.** Four of the five great Philistine cities are named (Gath is no more at this time; see Amos 6:2), two with a play on words: Gaza depopulated, Ekron uprooted. [The people of] Ashdod are driven out at noon—the city will fall in only a half day (cf. Esarhaddon at Memphis [*ANET* 293], the Moabite Stone, lines 15–16 [ANET 320])—a rapid conquest in striking contrast to the 29-year siege by the Egyptians which, according to Herodotus, Ashdod was withstanding at that very moment (640–611; cf. J. Smith, *Zephaniah* 215–16). **5.** The Philistines on the seacoast seem originally partly Cretan (nation of Kerethites). *Canaan, land of the Philistines:* The only time Philistine territory alone is called "Canaan." **6.** Because of depopulation, the rich coastal plain will be treated as a wasteland to raise sheep rather than crops. *pastures: Kārôt* is a wordplay on "Crete." **7.** The allusion to the "remnant" of Judah suggests that we have an exilic redaction which expands Zeph's original message that through punishment Yahweh will purify Judah. The redactor found in the old message hope for his despondent community. The original would have omitted vv 7ab and 7ef, referring only to the shepherds of v 6, who pasture their flocks there. *in the houses:* As Arab shepherds today shelter flocks in abandoned Crusader fortresses.

16 (b) MOAB AND AMMON (2:8–11). Probably exilic. Geographic proximity and traditions of common origin (Gen 19:30–38) often bring oracles against Moab and Ammon together (Isa 11:14; Jer 27:3; 48–49; Ezek 25:1–11). **8.** Their crime here and in v 10 is that of rejoicing over the bad fortune of Yahweh's people, an accusation often renewed after 586 (Ezek 25:1–11). **9.** The threat: These nations will perish like neighboring Sodom and Gomorrah, become like the desolate salt flats of the Dead Sea. Like Philistia in Zeph's authentic oracle (v 7), Moab and Ammon will be plundered by the (redactor's) restored remnant of Judah. **11.** Probable transl.: "when he rules" (Sabottka, *Zephanja* 90) "all the gods of the earth, and each [god] will fall prostrate toward him." Probably an even later "updating" of the oracle, for here Yahweh's dominion extends far beyond Moab and Ammon to "all the islands of the nations."

17 (c) ASSYRIANS (2:[12] 13–15). **12.** The problematic allusion to the Cushites (lit., "You too are Cushites, who are dishonored by my sword") seems to say that the Assyrians are not better than the 25th Ethiopian dynasty of Egypt, destroyed a generation earlier by Ashurbanipal (who was only an instrument of Yahweh). **13–15.** Assyria, the old oppressor will be so devastated that its capital city Nineveh, like Philistia, will be good for nothing but pasture, and indeed its ruins will be infested by wild beasts. **15.** The sole and adequate reason given for its destruction is arrogance (cf. Isa 45:6,18,21; 46:9; 47:8,10).

18 **(IV) Salvation of Jerusalem and Judah (3:1–20).** In two ambiguous oracles (3:1–5,6–8)

accusations (vv 1–4,6–7) precede threats of justice (vv 5, 8), but these threats are then spelled out paradoxically (vv 9–20) as a promise of transformation and peace (vv 9–13). This is really no contradiction: although exilic redactors may have done some elaboration, Zephaniah himself had foreseen a purified nation, composed of the innocent poor and humble, who remained after the destruction of the sinful and arrogant (2:1–3).

19 **(A) Oracle I (3:1–5).** **1.** Only the nature of the accusations shows that Jerusalem rather than Nineveh is addressed. *polluted:* Ritually contaminated (v 4). **2.** Four descriptions of fundamental moral flaw, specified in vv 3–4, where the duty of each order of society defines its sins. Rulers and judges prey on their people; prophets are unfaithful to Yahweh; and priests fail to render the proper decisions. The words of v 5 would normally be understood as words of assurance, but the preceding accusation shows that it is the leaders of his people rather than their enemies who will be condemned by the righteous Yahweh. Various suggested emendations of the last clauses are no better than the MT: "By light [i.e., by dawn] he will not fail, but the unrighteous knows no shame."

20 **(B) Oracle II (3:6–8).** In vv 6–13 Yahweh speaks in the 1st person. This curious oracle begins with an accusation against Jerusalem (vv 6–7), but then issues into a threat against nations rather than against Jerusalem (v 8)! **6.** *their corners:* Synecdoche for battleworks (1:16). Yahweh destroyed other nations, but (v 7) Jerusalem ignores these warnings. **8.** The command to wait, addressed to Jerusalem, at first seems ironic ("Wait, while I rise up to destroy you," with God's people sharing in the universal destruction), but the oracle takes an unexpected turn.

21 **(C) Threat Becomes Promise (3:9–20).** (a) SERVICE OF YAHWEH FROM NATIONS (3:9–10). Unexpectedly reprieved, the nations become true servants of Yahweh—perhaps as a result of redactional activity (as in 2:7,8–11), indicated by "then," which often begins a later redactional addition. *I will give the peoples purified lips:* As in 2:3; 3:11–12, judgment brings salvation. While "the peoples" may originally have been "my people," the MT understands that the Gentiles will serve Yahweh by restoring the exiles to their homeland (Isa 66:20; cf. 60:9).

22 (b) MORAL RECOVERY OF JERUSALEM/JUDAH (3:11–13). **11.** *in that day:* Of Yahweh's rising. The 2d pers. fem. sg. expressions in vv 11–19 refer to Jerusalem. *you need not be shamed:* Not because you are shameless (v 5), but because you will be purged of the arrogant "in your midst" (cf. vv 12,15,17. *my holy mountain:* Temple Mount. **12.** As elsewhere, wickedness is identified with arrogance and wealth (1:11–13,16,18; 2:10,15; 3:1–3,5); only the "poor and afflicted" (cf. 2:3), who will put their confidence in Yahweh, will survive. The purified "remnant" will "graze and lie down" in peace (as in the additions 2:7,11).

23 (c) SUMMONS TO REJOICING (3:14–15). The jubilant remainder of the book consists of sayings about the coming day of vindication (vv 8,11). The summons to rejoicing has its setting in victory or escape from defeat, as at the raising of a siege. Here Yahweh has intervened (v 15a). The closest parallels are Isa 12:6–7; 52:9; Zech 2:14(10); 9:9; these are related to hymns of divine kingship (e.g., Pss 97; 99) and Zion songs. Also in the Zion Pss 46 and 48 Yahweh's presence "in the midst of" Jerusalem provides defensive rather than offensive help. Here the protective presence of Yahweh contrasts with the threatening presence in v 5.

24 (d) ORACLE OF REASSURANCE TO JERUSALEM (3:16–17). In other oracles (Isa 7:4; Jer 30:10–11; Isa

41:10; 54:4ff.; following summons to rejoicing and containing language about love as here) and in simple language of encouragement (2 Kgs 6:16; 1 Chr 22:13; 28:20), the expression "fear not," usually accompanies assurance of Yahweh's presence to save. **17.** *he shall be silent in his love:* Sabottka's claim that *ḥrš* (otherwise the work of skilled crafts like ploughing and engraving) represents any artistic activity including singing would give us three synonymous clauses about celebrating. Even if the current MT is hopelessly corrupt, the

imagery is charming: Yahweh in his love does not know whether to shout or be still. **25**   (e) ORACLE: CHANGE OF FORTUNES (3:18–20). At least v 20 is part of the exilic redaction (2:7,8–11). **18.** Irreparably corrupt. **19.** The words "lame" and "scattered," being fem. sg., represent Jerusalem. No longer reduced to shame by her afflictions, Jerusalem will be honored by all. **20.** Most of v 20 is an expansion of the last words of v 19. *when I change your fortune:* Cf. the promise of 2:7.

NAHUM

BIBLIOGRAPHY

26   Boadt, L., *Jeremiah 26–52, Habakkuk, Zephaniah, Nahum* (OTM 10; Wilmington, 1982). Cathcart, K., "More Philological Studies in Nahum," *JNSL* 7 (1979) 1–12; *Nahum in the Light of Northwest Semitic* (Rome, 1973); "Treaty Curses in the Book of Nahum," *CBQ* 35 (1973) 179–87. Christensen, D. L., "The Acrostic of Nahum Reconsidered," *ZAW* 87 (1975)

17–30. Keller, C.-A., *Michée, Nahoum, Habacuc, Sophonie* (Paris, 1971). Mihelic, J. L., "The Concept of God in the Book of Nahum," *Int* 2 (1948) 199–208. Rudolph, W., *Micha-Nahum-Habakuk-Zephanja* (KAT 13; Gütersloh, 1975). Schulz, R., *Das Buch Nahum* (Berlin, 1973). Van der Woude, A. S., "The Book of Nahum: A Letter Written in Exile," *OTS* 20 (1977) 108–26.

INTRODUCTION

27   **(I) Historical Background.** Very little is known about the prophet himself. A native of Elkosh (→ 31 below), he has been considered a cultic prophet, but there is no consensus that the sphere of his activity is limited to Jerusalem. The date of the prophecy is equally vague. The fall of Thebes (3:8) to Ashurbanipal in 663 provides the *terminus a quo;* the fall of Nineveh (612) is the *terminus ad quem.* Some scholars have placed the date closer to the fall of Thebes or around the time of the death of Ashurbanipal (626), because Assyria was still then at the height of its power (Rudolph, Keller). Others consider the time between Cyaxares' first attack on Nineveh in 614 and the city's fall to the combined armies of Babylonians, Medes, and Scythians to be a more likely date (Boadt). A. S. van der Woude proposes that Nahum, himself an exile in Nineveh, wrote the prophecy as a letter (cf. "book," 1:1) to sympathizers in Judah around 660–630. His theory, based on Assyrian loan words in the book, the absence of interest in Jerusalem, and a vivid ("eyewitness"?) description of Nineveh, has found few followers. It is likely that Nahum wrote in Judah close to 612 during the reform of Josiah (note the absence of castigation for Judah's sins), before the death of Josiah (609) and before the evidence of Babylonian imperial might quenched the spirit of optimism surrounding the fall of Assyria.
28   **(II) Poetic Style and Technique.** The prophecy of Nahum comes from a poet of great skill. The work is a combination of many forms. The whole prophecy is a "burden," *maśśā',* similar to other oracles against foreign nations. It contains a partial acrostic poem (1:2–8), a funeral lament ("woe," 3:1–7), and a taunt-song (3:8–19). Several images are drawn of Nineveh: pool (2:9), den of lions (2:12–14), prostitute (3:4–6), yielding fig trees (3:12), swarm of locusts (3:15–17). Most striking are the wordplay and use of sound. In 2:11, the final devastation of the city tolls like a bell (→ 36 below). The moaning and breast-beating of the servants is heard in the sounds of 2:8: *kĕqôl yônîm*

mĕtōpĕpōt 'al libbēhen. The ironic question in 3:7 plays with the roots *ndd,* "flee," *nwd,* "pity," "condole," and *šdd,* "destroy." The sound is echoed in 3:10 with *ydd,* "throw, cast." In 1:10, a notoriously difficult verse to translate, the hissing of the fire (?) or of the drunkards (?) can be heard: *sîrîm sĕbukîm ûkĕsob'ām sĕbû'îm.* Several other verses are alliterative, e.g., 1:2 (n), 2:3 (b, q), 2:6 (k), 2:9 (m), 3:4 (š, p).
29   **(III) Message.** There is one message: God will execute vengeance against Nineveh. The destruction of the oppressor will bring joy to God's people and to all who have suffered Assyria's cruelty. The fall of Nineveh, although once used as an instrument of God's wrath against the covenant people (cf. Isa 10:5–16), is an act of divine justice. Assyria has plundered the nations and torn them like prey for its voracious appetite; now Assyria in turn will be plundered and become the prey of another.

Nahum has been criticized for his unmitigated glee over the fall of the enemy and for the corresponding absence of any criticism of his own people (contrast his contemporary, Jeremiah). His prophecy, however, is only intended to make one statement: God who is faithful has not abandoned Judah. The enemy will not prevail forever; the punishment will come to an end. Just as once God delivered those enslaved by Egypt (and one looks in vain for expressions of sympathy for the Egyptians in Exod 1–15), so now God will deliver those oppressed by Assyria. The good news is already proclaimed; feasts of thanksgiving should be celebrated (2:1).
30   **(IV) Outline.**

(I) Title (1:1)
(II) Theophany of the Divine Avenger (1:2–8)
(III) Oracles of Hope (1:9–2:1)
(IV) The Fall of Nineveh (2:2–14)
   (A) Introduction (2:2–3)
   (B) Description of the Battle from Inside the City (2:4–10)
   (C) The Fate of the Lion (2:11–14)

(V) Final Destruction (3:1–19)
  (A) Funeral Lament for the Harlot City (3:1–7)
  (B) Taunt-Song (3:8–19)
     (a) Comparison to Thebes (3:8–11)

(b) Futility of Defense (3:12–15a)
(c) Comparison to Locust Swarm (3:15b–17)
(d) Final Destiny (3:18–19)

COMMENTARY

31   (I) Title (1:1). This short work is described
with three nouns: "burden" (oracle), "book," "vision."
burden: Often used with reference to oracles against
foreign nations (cf. Isa 13:1; 14:28). *book:* Nahum is the
only prophetic work to be called a book, although other
prophetic oracles were written (cf. Jer 36:2; Hab 2:2).
vision: A term often used for prophetic works (cf. Isa 1:1;
Obad 1; Hab 2:2). *Nineveh:* The capital of Assyria,
located near Mosul in modern Iraq. Nineveh stood as a
symbol for tyrannical cruelty and wickedness. *Nahum:*
"Consolation," "comfort" (compare the names Nehemiah, Menahem). His comforting message to Judah
concerns the fall of a hated enemy. *Elkosh:* A city yet
unidentified. Locations have been proposed in Galilee
(Elcesi), in Mesopotamia (Al Qush near Mosul in modern
Iraq), in the neighborhood of Jerusalem (Beit Jibrin). The
latter is most probable.
**32   (II) Theophany of the Divine Avenger
(1:2–8).** A hymn concerning the advance of the divine
warrior in the style of Deut 33:2–3; Judg 5:4–5; Pss
68:8–11; 77:14–21; Hab 3:3–15. The description of the
theophany begins with an apparent acrostic. The present
text, however, has only 10 (or possibly 11) letters in
order, and they are interrupted twice. Many attempts
have been made to restore the acrostic. (For a summary,
see D. L. Christensen, *ZAW* 87 [1975] 17–20.) **2.** *jealous
God:* Yahweh is described as jealous (cf. Exod 20:5;
34:14), avenging (cf. Deut 32:43), and wrathful. His
anger is directed toward his enemies. **3.** *slow to anger:* The
apparent contradiction is solved by the presumption that
God's patience is extended for the sake of his own people
(cf. Exod 34:6; Joel 2:13; Jonah 4:2). *whirlwind:* Yahweh
appears in the sirocco, the desert windstorm frequent
during the change of seasons. The sirocco imagery is
characteristic of hymns to Yahweh's kingship (cf. Pss
96–98) and descriptions of the great battle of nations on
the Day of the Lord (cf. Isa 13:1–22; 29:1–8; 30:27–33;
Hab 3:3–15). These seem designed for use at the feast of
Sukkoth in the fall, a new year celebration in much of
Israel's history. **4.** *sea:* The east wind of the sirocco, symbolizing Yahweh's rebuke, dries up everything before it.
The Ugaritic epic of Ba'al makes use of the same
imagery to describe the battle between Ba'al and Prince
Sea/Judge River at the time of creation (*ANET* 129–31;
cf. Pss 74:12–17; 104:6–9; also Ps 18:16; Isa 50:2).
Bashan . . . Carmel . . . Lebanon: Even these symbols of
luxuriant growth will be withered at Yahweh's advance.
5. The theophanic imagery continues with the earthquake (cf. Exod 19:18). *tiśśā',* "lifted up," should be read
tiśśā', "made desolate," with Syr and Vg. **7.** *good:* The
focus shifts from Yahweh's vengeance against his
enemies to his goodness toward those who hope in him
(cf. 1:2). *flood:* The similarity in spelling and meaning
between the names Nahum and Noah, "rest," suggest an
allusion here to Gen 6–9 (cf. Gen 5:29; Isa 55:9–10). **8.**
A difficult verse. D. T. Tsumura (*JBL* 102 [1983]
109–11) proposes that *mqwmh* should be read in Janus
fashion, meaning "her [the city's] place" when read with
v 8a ("When the flood passes over, he will make an end
of her place") and meaning "opponents" when read with

v 8c ("He will make an end of his opponents and his
enemies he will pursue with darkness").
33   (III) Oracles of Hope (1:9–2:1). A dialogue
addressed alternately to Nineveh (1:9–11,14) and to
Judah (1:12–13; 2:1). **9.** The transl. of the following
verses is difficult. If *ḥšb 'el* is understood as "plot
against," the accusation against Nineveh reads: "What
are you plotting against Yahweh? He indeed makes an
end. The enemy will not rise again." **10.** Jeppesen reads
kî 'ad at the beginning of the verse as *kî yā'ad,* "Indeed
he has set a destiny [for the entangled thorns]" (K.
Jeppesen, *Bib* 65 [1984] 571–74). The phrase "like
drunkards they are drunk" disrupts the meaning. It is
sometimes omitted as a gloss. **11.** *plotting:* The word is
repeated from v 9, forming an inclusion around the
decree of punishment in v 10. *Belial:* The king of Nineveh, possibly Sennacherib, who besieged Jerusalem in
701. The word is probably from the root *bl'* meaning "to
swallow" (cf. 2:1). The god of death was pictured as
swallowing his victims (cf. Prov 1:12; Isa 5:14; Hab 2:5).
The term becomes a name for Satan in the NT (2 Cor
6:15). **12–13.** An oracle against the pride of Nineveh,
promising Judah that Assyria will not be used to humiliate them again. **14.** A further oracle against Nineveh and
its idols. **2:1.** A great promise of joy to Judah. This
phrase is echoed in Isa 52:7, to describe the joy of return
from exile.
34   (IV) The Fall of Nineveh (2:2–14).
        (A) Introduction (2:2–3). 2. *scatterer:* Some-
times emended to read "hammer" (*mappēṣ*). Either image
aptly describes the enemy who comes up against the
city. The warning is followed by four staccato imperative phrases (infins. absol.) emphasizing the urgency of
the situation. **3.** A problematic verse that is sometimes
transposed before 2:2, since the promise of restoration
links more closely with 2:1. In the text, however,
restoration is interwoven as a direct consequence of the
fall of Nineveh. *height of Jacob:* Gk "pride." Sometimes
emended to "vine" to correspond to the image of
branches later in the verse. Jacob after 722 can signify
Judah (cf. Isa 43:1; 44:1). Thus Jacob/Israel would indicate the whole people. The phrase, "indeed the height of
Israel," often considered a gloss, is necessary to complete
the thought. Israel and Judah have both been stripped by
Assyria like fruit trees (722 and 701); now the plunderer
will in turn be plundered.
**35   (B) Description of the Battle from Inside
the City (2:4–10).** In vv 4–6 the attackers are portrayed with eschatological imagery of fire, lightning,
and frenzy. **4.** *red:* The soldiers and their weapons are
red, the red of blood or the scarlet of their dress. Herodotus reports that the Ethiopians in the army of Xerxes
painted their bodies red (*Hist.* 7.69). Ezekiel says the
Assyrian warriors dress in purple (23:5–6). *fire:* The
metal trappings of the chariots are like fire. *spears:* Lit.,
"cypresses," probably wooden spears (Boadt, *Jeremiah . . .
Nahum* 253; Cathcart, *Nahum* 27–30). **5–6.** The advance
is a vision of madness; the color and speed suggest fire
and lightning. **6.** *summoned:* Lit., "remember," probably
should be read as "are called." *covering:* As the soldiers

approach the walls they protect themselves with their upraised shields interlocked (*testudo*, tortoise shell) or by a wooden covering. **7–9.** The response of the inhabitants of Nineveh. Nineveh was situated on the Tigris and Khoser rivers. The gates of the canals are opened, probably to flood the city. Ancient commentators report that Nineveh was destroyed by flood (Diodorus, *Bibliotheca Historica* 2.26; Xenophon, *Anab.* 3.4.6–12). Whether or not this is in fact true, the image is an apt description of the overwhelming entrance of the enemy. **8.** Surrounded by the image of water (vv 7,9) is the portrayal of the mistress of the city, the goddess Ishtar, carried away captive while her votaries moan and beat their breasts. An alternate interpretation understands "mistress" to be the queen of the city. The verse is difficult to translate. The first word has been explained as "captive train," "wagon," "the Beauty" (i.e., Ishtar), "queen" (cf. Cathcart, *Nahum* 96–98; A. S. van der Woude, *OTS* 20 [1977] 114–15. The first word has also been emended to "be led out" and a later word to "lady" (*ba'ālâ*). In any case, the sense seems to be that the mistress (probably Ishtar) is carried away captive. **9.** *pool:* Nineveh itself becomes a pool with broken walls which cannot contain the escaping water, i.e., its people who flee from the onslaught in spite of the command to stop. The words *mîmê hî'* should be read as *mêmêhā*, "her waters" (cf. LXX). **10.** The final verse of this description returns to the perspective of the attackers and proclaims the great abundance of booty in the city.

36   (C) The Fate of the Lion (2:11–14). 11. A verse that looks both ways, pointing out the results of the conquest described in 2:4–10 and leading into the judgment oracle of 2:12–14. The sound of the opening carries the lament: *bûqâ ûmēbûqâ ûmēbullāqâ*, "empty, desolate, wasted." The three exclamations are followed by four phrases describing the physical results of human despair (3 + 4 = 7, i.e., completeness). **12–14.** Nineveh is portrayed as a lion (cf. Isa 5:29) whose complacent gathering of prey comes suddenly to an end in the judgment of Yahweh against it. **12.** There are three (or four) different terms for "lion." The fourth, *lābî'*, is often emended to *lābô'*, "to come" (cf. 4QpNah). **14.** The destruction, the good news announced to Judah in 2:1–3, has been accomplished. The final word, *mal'ākēkēh*, should be read as *mal'ākāyik*, "your messengers."

37   (V) Final Destruction (3:1–19).
(A) Funeral Lament for the Harlot City (3:1–7). The woe oracle is related to the funeral lament (see R. Clifford, *CBQ* 28 [1966] 458–64). Nineveh is falling; the funeral has already begun. C.-A. Keller (*Michée, Nahoum* 127) suggests that even the vivid sounds and sights of v 2 are those of a ghostly army. The only human images are images of death. **1.** *bloody city:* The extreme cruelty of Assyria to conquered nations is epic. Not only violence but deceitful diplomacy was part of Nineveh's stock-in-trade (Isa 36:16–17). **3.** *charging cavalry:* Lit., "ascending horse," sometimes seen as a gloss on the previous phrase or emended to "rider." *corpses:* The LXX mistranslates *laggēwîyyâ*, "corpse," as "nations." **4–7.** The reason for Nineveh's destruction is found in a judgment oracle of Yahweh (compare 2:12–14). The reason for judgment (v 4) precedes the statement of punishment (vv 5–7). **4.** Nineveh is portrayed as a woman who seduces with all the power at her command (compare the portrayal of Babylon in Isa 47; Rev 17–18). *enslaves nations:* Lit., "seller of nations," sometimes read as hophal of *nkr*, "known [by the nations for harlotry]" (M. Dahood, *Bib* 52 [1971] 395–96). **5.** *strip:* The punishment of the city is the punishment of the unfaithful woman. She is stripped naked, pelted with filth, and displayed for all to see (cf. Isa 47:3; Jer 13:22,26; Lam 1:8–9;

16:36–39; Hos 2:4–15; see also K. Cathcart, *CBQ* 35 [1973] 183–84; J. Huenergard, *CBQ* 74 [1985] 433–34). **7.** The prophet whose name means "consolation" proclaims the impossibility of consoling Nineveh (cf. Isa 51:19!).

38   (B) Taunt Song (3:8–19).
(a) COMPARISON TO THEBES (3:8–11). **8.** *No-Amon:* Nineveh is compared to Thebes, called No-Amon, "city of [the god] Amon." Thebes was the center of Egyptian power in the Middle Kingdom (2000–1750) and again for a short time during the 25th Dynasty (715–663). It was conquered by the Assyrian king Ashurbanipal in 663. *surrounded by waters:* Thebes is located on the Nile, but not surrounded by water. The phrase is sometimes considered a gloss. Nahum may simply be using a poetic image to describe the city's defenses. **9.** *Ethiopia:* The rulers of the 25th Dynasty, which was in power at the time of Thebes's collapse, were Ethiopian. *Put:* The territory of Libya. **10–11.** Just as Thebes's power did not save the city from Assyria, so Nineveh's power will not save it from the Babylonian-Median-Scythian coalition. **11.** The first phrase is problematic. The MT reads "be drunk." A common image in oracles of judgment is the city forced to drink the cup of Yahweh's wrath (cf. Isa 51:17–23; Jer 25:15–29; Lam 4:21; Ezek 23:31–35; Hab 2:15–16). Thus drunk, the city faints and seeks a resting place. Some emend *škr*, "be drunk," to *škr*, "hire yourself out" (Cathcart, *Nahum* 137) or *šbr*, "be broken" (*BHS*, KB). *faint:* Emend the MT *na'ălāmâ* to *ne'ēlāpâ*, "faint." Other suggestions include "be young," "be hidden."

39   (b) FUTILITY OF DEFENSE (3:12–15a). 12. *fig trees:* Nineveh is ripe for the fall, like figs that drop from the tree with no effort. **13.** *women:* The comparison of fighting men (*'am*, lit., "people") to women was a serious insult and reflects a curse (cf. Isa 19:16; Jer 50:37; 51:30; K. Cathcart, *CBQ* 35 [1973] 185). **14.** *gates:* Nineveh's fortifications are utterly useless. The gates might as well be opened to the invader. Historically, the siege of Nineveh lasted two years. Nahum reflects the ultimate futility of resisting the judgment of Yahweh. **14–15.** An ironic taunt instructing Nineveh to prepare for a siege, to draw water and prepare bricks to strengthen the wall. It is too late, however; the fire will catch the defenders before the preparations are finished. **14.** *draw water:* Nahum relies on the stock description of preparation for a siege in Palestine. Nineveh, situated on the Tigris and Khoser rivers, would seem to have no need to draw water.

40   (c) COMPARISON TO LOCUST SWARM (3:15b–17). Another image drawn from the animal world to describe the day of Nineveh's collapse. Even if Nineveh's people — the army who has defeated so many nations, the merchants and administrators who continue the oppression — should be multiplied like a locust swarm, yet they will vanish in defeat as the swarm, warmed by the sun, flies away.

41   (a) FINAL DESTINY (3:18–19). A final song of triumph over the king of Assyria. **18.** The image of a people scattered with no shepherd to lead them is common in prophetic literature (Ezek 34:5–6; Zech 13:7; cf. 1 Kgs 22:17). The mountains are not a reference to Assyrian geography but a part of the shepherd image. *slumber . . . rest:* The second verb, *škn*, ordinarily means "to dwell" or "to settle down." Paralleled to "slumber" (*nwm*), it is frequently emended to *yšn*, "rest." There is scholarly disagreement concerning the interpretation of "slumber/rest." Some consider it to mean the sleep of death (Rudolph, Keller). K. Cathcart points out that *škn* can also connote the repose of death. **19.** *no relief:*

Nineveh's destruction is complete (cf. 2:14; 3:7). Compare the description of Judah's incurable wound in Isa

1:5–6; Jer 14:17. *clap their hands:* All those conquered by Assyria rejoice at its defeat (see Tob 14:15).

HABAKKUK

BIBLIOGRAPHY

42   Albright, W. F., "The Psalm of Habakkuk," *Studies in Old Testament Prophecy* (Fest. T. H. Robinson; ed. H. H. Rowley; Edinburgh, 1950) 1–18. Alonso Schökel, L. and J. L. Sicre Diaz, *Profetas II* (NBE; Madrid, 1980). Boadt, L., *Jeremiah 26–52, Habakkuk, Zephaniah, Nahum* (OTM 10; Wilmington, 1982). Brownlee, W. H., *The Midrash Pesher of Habakkuk* (SBLMS 24; Missoula, 1979). Childs, B. S., *CIOTS.* Eaton, J. H., "The Origin and Meaning of Habakkuk 3," *ZAW* 76 (1964) 144–71. Emerton, J. H., "The Textual and Linguistic Problems of Habakkuk II. 4–5," *JTS* 28 (1977) 1–18. Fitzmyer,

J. A., "Habakkuk 2:3–4 and the NT," *TAG* 236–46. Gowan, D. E., *The Triumph of Faith in Habakkuk* (Atlanta, 1976). Hiebert, T., "The Use of Inclusion in Habakkuk 3," *Directions in Biblical Hebrew Poetry* (ed. E. R. Follis; JSOTSup 40; Sheffield, 1987) 119–40. Jeremias, J., *Kultprophetie und Gerichtsverkündigung in der späten Königszeit Israels* (WMANT 35; Neukirchen, 1970). Jöcken, J., *Das Buch Habakuk* (BBB 48; Bonn, 1977). Keller, C.-A., "Die Eigenart des Propheten Habakuks," *ZAW* 85 (1973) 156–67. Rudolph, W., *Micha-Nahum-Habakuk-Zephanja* (KAT 13; Gütersloh, 1975). Von Rad, G., *OTT* 2.

INTRODUCTION

43   **(I) Background.** The book itself tells us only the prophet's name and the fact that he was a *nabî'*, a "prophet." The main clue to the date of his prophecies comes from the mention in 1:6 of the Chaldeans, a people from S Mesopotamia who, with their center at Babylon, replaced the Assyrians as the masters of the ancient Near East in the late 7th–early 6th cent. BC. This plus the obvious turmoil both on the national and international scene which the concerns of the book reflect has led scholars to locate the prophecies themselves somewhere between the beginning of Assyria's decline after 626 and the fall of Jerusalem in 587. The question of more precise dates within this time period for the individual prophecies as well as their specific targets is a more contentious one and is linked to the question of the book's form. The liturgical character of the woes in 2:6–20 and the canticle in chap. 3 has led some scholars to characterize Habakkuk as a cult prophet and to describe the book as a "prophetic liturgy," i.e., a work composed for and used in the Temple worship. Others have noted links with Israel's wisdom tradition. Our commentary follows the lead both of B. S. Childs (*CIOTS*) and G. von Rad (*OTT*). Childs, on the one hand, stresses the literary unity of the book and argues that the author has purposely ignored the specific historical setting of the materials and has arranged them in such a way as to give priority to the theological message, i.e., the power of God over human history and the consequent call to trust and faithfulness (cf. 2:4). Von Rad, for his part, emphasizes the book's prophetic character. Thus the formal affinities to Israel's liturgical and/or wisdom traditions come from the fact that the author has appropriated and shaped them to express a specifically prophetic message.

Hab makes an important and original contribution to the sum of Israel's reflection on the nature of its God and of God's ways with Israel. The book begins with a question which the prophet dares to direct to God, raising doubts about divine justice and God's treatment of the wicked. The question represents a first step in an attempt to deal with a breakdown of order and justice, a situation to which God seems implicitly to assent by silence and apparent inaction. But despite the doubts the prophet expresses, there is an underlying attitude of faith and trust. This is especially due to the canticle in chap. 3,

which, with its ringing affirmation of God's absolute power over creation and history, places the disturbing events recounted in chaps. 1–2 in the wider context of God's saving design. Thus, the key sentence in 2:4 counsels confidence and trust in God's faithfulness, and the book repeatedly condemns all forms of oppression and exploitation as well as the pride and arrogance that stand opposed to the humble faith demanded by God. The history of the book's interpretation begins with the Qumran commentary on chaps. 1–2 (see Brownlee, *Midrash Pesher*). In addition, its ringing affirmation of the need for belief and trust (2:4) found a ready hearing among the early Christians. Indeed, Paul gives it a prominent place in his own teaching on faith in Rom 1:17 and Gal 3:11 (see also Heb 10:38).

44   **Outline.**

(I) Dialogue between the Prophet and God (1:1–2:5)
　　(A) The First Exchange (1:2–11)
　　　　(a) The Prophet's Complaint: There Is No Justice (1:2–4)
　　　　(b) The Lord's Response (1:5–11)
　　(B) The Second Exchange (1:12–2:5)
　　　　(a) The Prophet's Complaint (1:12–17)
　　　　(b) The Lord's Response (2:1–5)
(II) The Five Woes (2:6–20)
　　(A) Introduction (2:6a)
　　(B) The First Woe: Against Arrogant Greed (2:6b–8)
　　(C) The Second Woe: Against Presumption (2:9–11)
　　(D) The Third Woe: Against Vainglory and Violence (2:12–14)
　　(E) The Fourth Woe: Against the Degradation of Human Dignity (2:15–17)
　　(F) The Fifth Woe: Against Idolatry (2:18–20)
(III) The Canticle of Habakkuk (3:1–19)
　　(A) Title (3:1)
　　(B) Introduction: Fear and Salvation (3:2)
　　(C) The Theophany (3:3–15)
　　　　(a) Part I: God's Appearance and the Reaction of Creation (3:3–7)
　　　　(b) Part II: The Battle with the Forces of Chaos (3:8–15)
　　　　　　(i) Preparation for the battle (3:8–9a)
　　　　　　(ii) The reaction of nature (3:9b–11a)
　　　　　　(iii) The charge into battle (3:11b–13a)
　　　　　　(iv) The victory (3:13b–15)
　　(D) Conclusion: Fear and Salvation (3:16–19)
　　　　(a) Fear (3:16–17)
　　　　(b) Salvation (3:18–19)

COMMENTARY

45   (I) Dialogue between the Prophet and God (1:1–2:5). In both of the exchanges between the prophet (1:2–4,12–17) and God (1:5–11; 2:1–5), the prophet takes the initiative and questions God about the evil and suffering he sees in the world around him.

The problem of the identity of "the wicked" and "the just" is especially acute in this first section (e.g., 1:4b,13b; 2:4–5). Are "the wicked" a group within the Jewish community, or is the prophet referring to a foreign nation such as the Assyrians or Egyptians? No attempt to identify the protagonists or to set the oracles in a particular chronological sequence is without serious problems. Thus, Childs has proposed that the editor has purposely ignored the specific historical setting of the various oracles and has arranged them in such a way as to emphasize the power of God over human history: "In Habakkuk the historical sequence is replaced by a new theological pattern of redemptive history which blurs the original historical settings to make its theological point" (*CIOTS* 454).

This "new theological pattern" and the very style and spirit of the prophecies are in response to the burning theological issue of the time: Will God—indeed, can God—remain faithful to the promise and deal graciously with Israel, even in the face of the overwhelming power and arrogance of the great empires (von Rad, *OTT* 2. 266)? The author sharpens this latter question in Yahweh's surprising response (1:12–17) to Habakkuk's insistent questions. But this response of God, which describes an imminent catastrophe, implies that God already knows, indeed assents, to these developments. To this implicit acknowledgment of God's consistent purpose, despite the collapse and chaos of the international order, is added the call in 2:4 for faith and trust.

46   (A) The First Exchange (1:2–11). This reflects the traditional complaint psalm, in which the individual cries out to God for rescue and receives a divine response assuring help. Instead of a promise of rescue, however, we find a description of further troubles on the horizon.

(a) THE PROPHET'S COMPLAINT: THERE IS NO JUSTICE (1:2–4). **2.** *"Violence!"*: A key word in Hab (cf. also 1:3,9; 2:8,17 [twice]); and it refers to the violation of basic human rights which characterizes the confusion and anarchy of the times. **4.** A vivid description of the confusion and disorder that reign, whether "the wicked" were originally fellow Jews or foreigners. But the prophet is troubled not simply by the lawlessness that he sees around himself. A deeper source of agitation is the question of the willingness, even the ability, of Israel's God to restore some semblance of justice and order.

(b) THE LORD'S RESPONSE (1:5–11). Instead of the expected word of comfort or promise of rescue, God's response adds a further reason for dismay. The rise to power of the Chaldeans (Babylon) does not promise stability but, for the moment, further fear and suffering. **6.** *I am raising up:* The description begins with Yahweh's affirmation that it is at his instigation that their conquest takes place. *the Chaldeans:* A people from S Mesopotamia whose empire, centered at Babylon, replaced that of the Assyrians. They destroyed the Assyrian capital at Nineveh in 612 and assured their domination of the ancient Near East with their defeat of the Egyptian army at Carchemish in 605. **7.** In response to the prophet's complaint about perverted justice in v

4, God affirms that these new masters will impose justice, but a justice according to their own standards. **9.** *captives like sand:* This image of the hordes of captives taken prisoner by the advancing army recalls not only the fate of Israel at the hands of the Assyrians in 722; it also foreshadows the imminent ravaging of Jerusalem in 587 and the sufferings of the exile. **10.** *heaps up clay:* A reference to the earthworks constructed against a city's wall to bring forward engines of war (battering rams, etc.) during a siege. *their very god:* Whether explicitly through cult or implicitly simply by their attitude, they absolutize and divinize their own strength and will. The prophet underlines this people's arrogance and excessive pride.

47   (B) The Second Exchange (1:12–2:5). The unexpected nature of the first divine response elicits a second complaint from the prophet (1:12–17) followed by a climactic pronouncement from God (2:1–5).

(a) THE PROPHET'S COMPLAINT (1:12–17). The prophet raises the question of God's justice, the why of God's acting in the way he has (cf. 1:13). He continues with a chilling description of the Chaldean's barbarity and ruthlessness (vv 14–17). **12.** *we shall not die:* This phrase seems out of place here, and commentators often interpret it as affirming Yahweh's immortality rather than Israel's ("You [Yahweh] shall not die"); or the divine title Victor over Death). *for a judgment . . . for a punishment:* The prophet recognizes that this cruel and powerful people are but the instruments of Yahweh's designs, to serve as his chastising rod against the wicked. **13.** This is the real question that has been troubling the prophet. How can "the holy" and "pure" One allow this intolerable situation to continue; further, does not the use of "the wicked" to carry out the divine will contradict that holiness and purity which is the very essence of God? **14.** *he gathers:* Instead of an affirmation of God's sovereignty as creator ("You made human beings"), we take this verb as referring (collectively) to the Chaldeans ("He gathers men like the fish in the sea"). This fits better with the context, the rest of which has "the Chaldeans" as the subject (see H. J. van Dijk, *VT* 19 [1969] 446). *like fish:* This striking image, elaborated in vv 15–17, describes the cruelty and ruthlessness of the Chaldean conquerors, for whom human life has no more value than that of the mute creatures which swarm in the sea. **16.** *he sacrifices:* Whether some actual cultic act is being referred to here, or whether the reference is meant to be metaphorical, it reinforces the statement in 1:11b: the crimes perpetrated by this people flow from their excessive pride, which recognizes no source of meaning or authority apart from their own will and strength.

(b) THE LORD'S RESPONSE (2:1–5). The solemn introduction of vv 1–3 emphasizes the significance of the call for faithfulness and trust in v 4. The puzzling Hebrew of v 5a apparently elaborates the description of the wicked man's greed begun in v 4a and continued in v 5bc. **1.** The prophet readies himself for what he senses will be an important message from God in answer to his complaint. **4a.** Lit., "Behold, inflated, not straight (just), is his throat (soul) within him." The ambiguity of the word *nepeš*, which can mean "throat," "appetite," or "soul," allows the prophet to fashion a bizarre image: the wicked man's "throat" (*nepeš*), inflated and distended by greed, mirrors his "soul" (*nepeš*), which has been warped by pride. In v 5 the prophet associates this cupidity with the insatiable hunger of Death: "he opens his throat (*nepeš*) wide like Sheol." *the just by steadfast fidelity shall live:* The just, by contrast, trust in God and not in their own ability to accumulate power and riches (again, note v 5). They are characterized by their "faithfulness, steadfastness" to which they hold fast even in perilous and confusing times, and by which they "shall live." **5.** *like Sheol . . . like Death:* The prophet draws upon the tradition of Death's voracious appetite found in the Canaanite myths and alluded to frequently in the OT (cf. Isa 5:14; Ps 141:7; Prov 1:12; 30:15–16). He hints at the infernal nature of the wicked's pride and greed.

48 (II) The Five Woes (2:6–20). Although the woe (Hebr *hôy*) or lament originated as a song of grief over death or loss (e.g., 2 Sam 1), these five woes are adaptations of that form and, ironically, express great joy over the fate of an enemy. Here they are placed on the lips of the suffering peoples whom Babylon has oppressed and treated so cruelly, and the greed and arrogance of Babylon itself are the target. The woes represent a prophetic adaptation of a liturgical and/or wisdom form, and, although they are directed specifically at Babylon, they reveal God as the one who judges and condemns not a single empire but every form of oppression (see Alonso Schökel and Sicre Diaz, *Profetas II* 1094).

(A) Introduction (2:6a). This verse introduces the five woes and links these two sections of the book (1:1–2:5 and 2:6–20) by implying that it is the victim "nations" and "peoples" of 2:5 who are now celebrating the downfall and shame of their former oppressor, Babylon.

(B) The First Woe: Against Arrogant Greed (2:6b–8). **6b.** *goods taken in pledge:* The oppressor has acted as if the earth's inhabitants were his tenants and in his debt; thus they had to surrender security or "pledges" in return for their use of his property. Ironically, these exploited nations now consider these "pledges" (i.e., the booty and tribute payments he had exacted) as their loans to him, payment of which they now demand.

(C) The Second Woe: Against Presumption (2:9–11). 9–10. The passage plays on the two meanings of "house." In order to ensure the safety and impregnability of his "house" (= dwelling, palace, v 9) and the security and continuation of his "house" (= dynasty, v 10), no form of extortion or plunder was excluded. **11.** *the stones . . . the wood:* However, nature itself rebels against such presumption.

(D) The Third Woe: Against Vainglory and Violence (2:12–14). 12. *who builds a city with human bloodshed:* The tyrant seeks *de facto* legitimation of his rule by elaborate building programs (e.g., cities and palaces), but especially divine legitimation with the construction of temples (see 2:18–20). The products of such programs tend to justify any violence or bloodshed perpetrated in their accomplishment.

(E) The Fourth Woe: Against the Degradation of Human Dignity (2:15–17). 15. *drink:* A potent image for the violence with which the conqueror stuns subject peoples and for the shame and exploitation to which he exposes them. **16.** But the oppressor will be repaid in kind. The force of God's wrath will cause him to reel and stagger senselessly (compare Jer 25:15–29). **17.** *the violence of Lebanon:* An apparent allusion to the inevitable plundering of Phoenicia at the hands of successive invaders (cf. Isa 14:8; 37:24).

(F) The Fifth Woe: Against Idolatry (2:18–20). This final woe begins with two rhetorical questions which poke fun at the pretensions of idol worshipers. The impotence of idols contrasts with the

power of Yahweh about to be revealed (chap. 3). There is a clear link with the four preceding woes in that idolatry goes hand in hand with injustice. Since "idols" can be used to justify the conduct of their devotees, they can legitimate, even sanctify, the most blatant violations of human rights and dignity (see Alonso Schökel and Sicre Diaz, *Profetas II* 1104).

49 (III) The Canticle of Habakkuk (3:1–19). In celebrating Yahweh's unrivaled lordship in history and creation, this canticle sets the events of chaps. 1–2 in the larger context of his saving purpose. The effective use of Canaanite mythic traditions (cf. also Pss 18; 68; 74; 77) gives the poem unusual visionary breadth and imaginative power (cf., e.g., Exod 15; Judg 5). Although Israel's liturgical traditions provided the basic form (→ Psalms 34:5), in its present setting it belongs with Israelite prophecy, expressive as it is of a powerful visionary experience and exemplary of the prophet's role as intercessor. The canticle is linked structurally and thematically with chaps. 1–2, serving both as God's answer to the prophet's entreaties in 1:2,12 ("How long . . . ?") and offering the opportunity for the prophet to express that trust and confidence in God's rule (3:16–19) demanded by the oracle in 2:4.

T. Hiebert has provided a convincing description of the structure based on the poet's use of inclusion ("The Use of Inclusion in Habakkuk 3"). There are four parts: parts I (v 2) and IV (vv 16–19) develop the themes of fear and salvation; the central section has a two-part description of a theophany (vv 3–7 and 8–15).

(A) Title (3:1). This first verse provides the title and a liturgical notation which, along with 3:19d, indicates that the song may have occasionally been used separately in worship.

(B) Introduction: Fear and Salvation (3:2). This is linked with the conclusion (3:16–19) by common themes and by the literary device of *inclusio* (e.g., "Yahweh" [twice] in vv 2,19; "I have heard" in vv 2,16). *I am in awe . . . turmoil:* Fear and confusion fill the prophet at the report of the divinity's imminent appearance. *remember to have compassion:* Yet he trusts that God's coming will be an occasion of salvation and victory for his people.

50 (C) The Theophany (3:3–15). The two-part description of the theophany (vv 3–7 and 8–15) corresponds to the first two elements of a larger mythic pattern that describes the battle between the storm-god and the sea. For the poet's audience, the pattern was familiar enough so that mention of some of the elements was sufficient to evoke the pattern in its entirety. Verses 3–7 recount God's appearance and the reaction of creation; vv 8–15 narrate the battle between the divine warrior, Yahweh, and the powers of chaos represented by "Sea." The triumph of Yahweh in the cosmic battle mirrors and assures his triumph on behalf of his people Israel in the realm of history.

(a) PART I: GOD'S APPEARANCE AND THE REACTION OF CREATION (3:3–7). Although the two parts form a continuous narrative, each has its own structure and inner unity. Verses 3–7 are characterized especially by cyclic, inclusive structure. The description of nature's response (vv 6–7) matches, in reverse order, the description of God's approach (vv 3–5). God's coming "from Teman" and "from Mount Paran" in the S (v 3a) causes panic among the inhabitants of that region (Kushan and Midian, v 7). Further, in v 3b, the majesty and splendor of God's appearance "in the heavens" and "on earth" effect a tumultuous response among earth's "mountains" and "hills" and in the "eternal orbits" (i.e., of the sun, moon, and stars) in the heavens (v 6b). At the center (v

5) lies the description of God's entourage marching out before and behind him. *Pestilence . . . Plague:* Yahweh's companions are personifications of two of the inevitable attendants of war and turmoil. "Plague" (*rešep*) appears as a netherworld deity in Canaanite mythology.

51   (b) PART II: THE BATTLE WITH THE FORCES OF CHAOS (3:8–15). The second part draws on the imagery of the mythic battle of the divine warrior/creator against the forces of chaos, represented by the turbulent and uncontrollable waters ("River," "Sea," "Many-Waters"). Its narrative falls into four scenes:

(i) *Preparation for battle* (3:8–9a). *your victorious chariot:* The outcome of the struggle in vv 13b–15 is already foreshadowed.

(ii) *The reaction of nature* (3:9b–11). *earth . . . the Deep . . . the Sun, the Moon:* The whole universe — earth, the netherworld, heaven — panics at the approach of the divine warrior.

(iii) *The charge into battle* (3:11b–13a). *your lightning spear:* Yahweh is depicted in heroic terms as a

giant striding the earth (v 12) and using the very lightning as one of his weapons.

(iv) *The victory* (3:13b–15). *you trod Sea:* The final moment of triumph, as God's foes lie prostrate under his feet (cf. Isa 51:9–11; Ps 136:10–15).

52   **(D) Conclusion: Fear and Salvation (3:16–19).**

(a) FEAR (3:16–17). The prophet returns to and develops the account of his own fear at the display of God's awesome majesty and power (cf. 3:2). The turmoil in nature, described in terms of the collapse of the land's fertility (v 17) at the news of God's approach, complements the prophet's own panic.

(b) SALVATION (3:18–19). The canticle ends with a forthright expression of confidence and trust in Yahweh, even in the face of the upheavals and uncertainties of history. This echoes the trust in Yahweh's compassion voiced in 3:2; thus the prophet affirms his acceptance of the oracle uttered in 2:4, that "the just by steadfast fidelity shall live."

18

JEREMIAH

Guy P. Couturier, C.S.C

BIBLIOGRAPHY

1 *Commentaries:* Boadt, L., *Jeremiah 1-25/26-52* (OTM 9-10; Wilmington, 1982). Bright, J., *Jeremiah* (AB 21; GC, 1965). Carroll, R. P., *Jeremiah* (OTL; Phl, 1986). Haag, E., *Das Buch Jeremia* (GS 5/1-2; Düsseldorf, 1973-77). Holladay, W. L., *Jeremiah 1* (Herm; Phl, 1986). Hyatt, J. P., *The Book of Jeremiah* (IB 5; NY, 1956). McKane, W., *A Critical and Exegetical Commentary on Jeremiah: Jeremiah I-XXV* (Edinburgh, 1986). Nicholson, E. W., *Jeremiah 1-25/26-52* (CBC; Cambridge, 1973-75). Penna, A., *Geremia* (LSB; Rome, 1954). Rudolph, W., *Jeremia* (HAT 12; 3d ed.; Tübingen, 1968). Schreiner, J., *Jeremia 1-25,14* (Würzburg, 1981); *Jeremia II: 25,15-52,34* (Würzburg, 1984).

Thompson, J. A., *The Book of Jeremiah* (NICOT; GR, 1980). Volz, P., *Der Prophet Jeremia* (KAT 10; 2d ed.,; Leipzig, 1928). Weiser, A., *Der Prophet Jeremia* (ATD 20-21; 8th ed.; 1981-1982).

Other Literature: Le Livre de Jérémie (ed. P.-M. Bogaert, et al.; Leuven, 1981). A Prophet to the Nations (ed. L. G. Perdue, et al.; Winona Lake, 1984). Fohrer, G., *Die Propheten des Alten Testaments* (Gütersloh, 1974) 2. 50-173. Gelin, A., "Jérémie," DBSup 4. 857-89. Koch, K., *The Prophets* (Phl, 1984) 2. 13-80. Muilenburg, J., "Jeremiah the Prophet," IDB 2. 823-35.

INTRODUCTION

2 **(I) Jeremiah's Time.** Jeremiah lived through one of the most troubled periods of the ancient Near East. He witnessed the fall of a great empire and the rising of one even greater. In the midst of his turmoil, the kingdom of Judah, then in the hands of deplorable kings, came to its downfall by resisting this overwhelming force of history.

(A) The Near East. After the brilliant military campaigns of Ashurnasirpal (884-860) and Shalmaneser III (859-825), Assyria remained the leading power for about two centuries. The empire reached its zenith under Esarhaddon (681-670). Ashurbanipal (669-633) could maintain its prestige at the beginning of his reign, but toward the end, signs of the empire's decline were noticeable both within and without. Assyria would rapidly experience her eclipse from history, once Ashurbanipal had died (*ca.* 633).

If Herodotus's sole testimony is correct, at that time Scythian hordes from the Caucasus swept the whole of the Near East, not so much to occupy new regions as to plunder barbarously the already inhabited lands (I.1.103-6). Meanwhile, Babylon raised its head to see that the time had come for its turn to control the Fertile Crescent. Thus, the crown prince Nabopolassar (626-605) first revolted against Assyria. Once he had gained Babylon's full independence, he launched a series of attacks on Assyria with the help of Cyaxares, king of the Medes. Asshur fell in 614, and Nineveh, the capital, was totally destroyed in 612 (see Nah 3). Ashur-uballit II,

Assyria's last king, fled to Haran, where he resisted Nabopolassar for three years, with the help of Neco, pharaoh of Egypt. In 609, Nabopolassar took Haran and continued to spread his new empire southward until his death in August 605. At that time, his son and successor, Nebuchadnezzar, had just defeated the Egyptian armies at Carchemish; this victory yielded to Babylon the prevalence in politics. Nebuchadnezzar (605-561), a warrior by nature, spent most of his life outside Babylon at the head of his armies. Egypt was the only country that resisted his domination. In 601, the two armies met in an indecisive battle at the Egyptian frontier; apparently, the Babylonian king renewed his attempt at conquest only in 568, when he was successful. We now have ample information on this first part of the Neo-Babylonian Empire's history (see D. J. Wiseman, *Chronicles of Chaldaean Kings* [London, 1956]).

3 **(B) Judah.** During Manasseh's long reign (687-642), Judah remained Assyria's vassal; the political dependence brought a resurgence of idolatry in the form of a syncretist fusion of the Mesopotamian astral gods and the Canaanite fertility deities. This political and religious situation persisted during Josiah's (640-609) minority; but in 622-621, when the Book of the Law was discovered in the Temple, Josiah led a thorough reform in Judah, which he extended even to northern Israel, an Assyrian province since 721. The international political circumstances could permit such a move of independence; within Judah, we presume that a number of people had remained faithful to the Yahwistic covenant and really supported the king's new policy. In a solemn ceremony, the Mosaic covenant was renewed; there followed total destruction of all the high places where idolatrous practices were performed, leaving Jerusalem as the unique cult center. In 609, this glorious reign came to its tragic end with Josiah's death in Megiddo; the king had tried to stop Neco from joining Ashur-uballit in Haran to rescue him from an imminent downfall. Because Babylon had no control over Syria-Palestine, Neco acted as her suzerain. He deposed Jehoahaz, whom he sent as prisoner to Egypt, and replaced him with Jehoiakim (609–598). Under Jehoiakim the religious syncretism revived in Judah, and politically the country remained under Egyptian influence. Thus, to resist Babylon was the king's first preoccupation, which resulted in Jerusalem's first downfall and in Judah's first deportation in 597. Jehoiakim had died the year before and was succeeded by one of his sons, Jehoiachin. The young king was also exiled to Babylon, never to return, and Nabuchadnezzar replaced him with Zedekiah, his uncle (597–587). The new king did not bear the stamp of a ruler; he was caught between two parties and policies: the one urged submission to Babylon, for it recognized that no power could really oppose its strength; the second urged Zedekiah to join Egypt, and probably also the other minor neighboring states, to overthrow Nebuchadnezzar's domination in the west. This second party finally prevailed. In 587 Jerusalem was sacked and the Judean population experienced a new deportation. Zedekiah was blinded and sent in exile to Babylon; Judah was reduced to a Babylonian province. Then Nebuchadnezzar appointed Gedaliah, a Judean, as governor of the new province with Mizpah as the new administrative center. Gedaliah was assassinated two months later, at the instigation of the Ammonite king. Seized by fear, a number of Judeans fled to Egypt to escape Nebuchadnezzar's revenge, taking Jeremiah along with them.

4   (II) Jeremiah's Mission. Yahweh called Jeremiah to be a prophet to Judah and to the nations in the midst of these political convulsions. His ministry lasted about 40 years (cf. 1:1–3), and his book testifies that his interventions were numerous. In fact, the last decades of Judah's history required a continual flow of light from Yahweh's messengers; besides Jeremiah, Zephaniah, Habakkuk, Nahum, and Ezekiel delivered the word of God. In their work of bringing forth the authentic tradition of Yahwism, these prophets were assisted by the pious men responsible for the deuteronomic reform and literature. But of all these inspired men no one reached the stature of Jeremiah in his great sensitivity to Yahweh's love for his people and in his profound understanding of this very people's duty toward Yahweh through the covenant ties. Thus, Jeremiah's prophetic word is noted for its directness and acuity in stating the true nature of Yahwism and in denouncing the different religious deviations. The two predominant themes of his message are precisely to define true Yahwism and to proclaim the imminent wars as punishments of Judah's aberrations.

The first part of his ministry covers the years from his call (627–626) to the Josian reform (621); most of his early oracles now form chaps. 1–6. The religious atmosphere of Judah was very low: Josiah was a young king who could not yet eradicate Manasseh's apostasy. Jeremiah, under the influence of his predecessor, Hosea, recalls the covenant as basically a matter of love between Yahweh and Israel—a love symbolized by that which unites a man and a woman in marriage. If the chosen people does not convert itself from idolatry, a disastrous invasion from the north will be Yahweh's revenge against such an adulterous attitude. At this early date, Jeremiah probably had not seen clearly who this invader would be. Finally, with a number of exegetes, we believe that Jeremiah hoped then for the restoration of the northern kingdom (chaps. 30–31).

In 621, Josiah led a religious reform of his kingdom on the occasion of the discovery of the Law. Jeremiah certainly approved of the king (11:1–14), which is the reason we hear so little of him until his death in 609.

With Jehoiakim's accession to the throne, a new period opens in Jeremiah's life. The reformation was swiftly eclipsed by a universal return to idolatry; politically, the Egyptian party took power. Jeremiah then resumed his denunciations of idolatry and of the superficiality of the covenantal observances. The threat of war became more urgent. When Babylon defeated Egypt at Carchemish in 605, the prophet knew too well who the invader would be. That very year, he dictated all his previous oracles to Baruch, who wrote them on a scroll, as a solemn and last warning to both the people and its leaders (chap. 36) The prophetic words of this third period appear mostly in chaps. 7–20.

5   Even though Jeremiah's warnings had been explicit, Jehoiakim did not change any of his religious and political designs. We can assume that during the last phase of the king's reign (605–598), the prophet had to face opposition and persecution; he then experienced an interior crisis of his faith in his mission and in his God, which he described in lyric poems called his "confessions" (see 11:18ff.). These poems are now scattered in chaps. 11–20.

The last period of Jeremiah's life runs from the first downfall of Jerusalem (597) to his death in Egypt soon after the destruction of Judah (587). Zedekiah had been unable to handle the situation; in fact, the political parties were the real forces that led Judah to her final ruin. Jeremiah was never so active in the political field as during this last decade. The king had confidence in him and tried to save him from the hands of the officials who had a completely different policy. Most of his speeches and oracles were preserved by Baruch, who inserted them in narratives recording the circumstances and the effects of his interventions (chaps. 27–29, 32–45). Jeremiah then understood that a true conversion to Yahweh was humanly impossible; Yahweh himself had to change the very heart of a person, and only then could the new covenant bind forever the people to its God (31:31–34). This new order of things would unite again Judah and Israel, but only after the exile had purified their stubbornness in sin (for more details, see Bright, *Jeremiah* lxxxvi–cxi).

(III) The Book.

6   (A) Authenticity. In 1901, B. Duhm (*Das Buch Jeremia* [Tübingen 1901]) reduced the authentic passages to one fifth of the book. This radical position has been progressively put aside, and now critics recognize a much higher proportion of oracles to be authentic, even though some later additions and transformations can be detected clearly, as in all the prophetic books. We must study each passage to decide whether or not it belongs to Jeremiah. The passages that are still highly disputed are the biographical narratives and the so-called deuteronomic discourses.

S. Mowinckel published an important study on the different sources of the book, which is still influential in the present discussion (*Zur Komposition des Buches Jeremia* [Kristiania, 1914]). He distinguishes four literary sources: the poetic oracles (source A); the biographical narratives (source B); the deuteronomic discourses (source C); the oracles of salvation and the oracles against the nations (source D).

The authenticity of the poetic oracles (chaps. 1-25) is no longer suspect. Mowinckel, and several others after him, rejected the oracles of salvation (chaps. 30-31) and the oracles against the nations (chaps. 46-51) as a very late addition; however, a closer examination of these poems now proves that some of them are certainly Jeremiah's, and an authentic Jeremian nucleus is at the origin of the remaining ones. The long oracle against Babylon (chaps. 50-51) is clearly a late exilic composition.

The biographical narratives consist entirely of prose narratives and are generally attributed to Baruch (chaps. 26-45). Jeremiah's friend and secretary (chap. 36) had great confidence in, and devotion to, his master; he summarized the main lines of Jeremiah's message and set him in their historical context. Moreover, he wrote a detailed history of the prophet's sufferings during the last siege of Jerusalem (588-587) and the following months when Jeremiah lived at the side of Gedaliah in Mizpah. He was then forced to flee to Egypt, where he died as a witness of his people's deep-rooted idolatrous propensities (chaps. 37-44). These chapters, then, are considered to be of prime value for the reconstruction of Judah's history during these decisive years.

This current opinion has been questioned in the recent past. G. Wanke (Untersuchungen zur sogenannten Baruchschrift [Berlin, 1971]) still believes in a certain historical value of these narratives, but he doubts that they can be attributed to Baruch. He distinguishes three different levels of redaction, with their specific purposes; the main one (chaps. 37-44) should be attributed to an anonymous author who lived in the immediate circle of Gedaliah in Mizpah. The narrative of Baruch writing down the first oracles of Jeremiah (chap. 36), early in the reign of Jehoiakim, is fictitious and cannot be used to reconstruct the history of Jeremiah's book. K.-F. Pohlmann (Studien zum Jeremiabuch [Göttingen, 1978]) has proposed an even more radical theory for the origin of these narratives. He would isolate two different levels of redaction, both being strongly oriented toward the restoration of Judah after the fall of 587. The first one addresses the survivors left in Judah as a guarantee of the return of Yahweh to his people for a new common history. The present state of our texts reflects mainly this same hope of the restoration of the relationship between Yahweh and his people through the return of the Babylonian exiles, who are believed to be the sole beneficiaries of such attention by God. Such a redaction should be dated in the 5th cent., around the period of Nehemiah. We cannot rely on these narratives, therefore, for a reconstruction of the life of Jeremiah. Both studies have been criticized for overlooking a number of historical details recorded in these chapters that can be explained only in the time of Jeremiah; also, the style and the literary quality of these narratives are close to that of the deuteronomic discourses, whose authenticity, therefore, will bear on them.

7   The still most disputed section of the whole work is Mowinckel's third source (C)—i.e., the deuteronomic speeches of the prophet, which are usually introduced by the formula, "The message that came to Jeremiah from the Lord" (7:1-8:3; 11:1-14; 16:1-13; 17:19-27; 18:1-12; 19:1-20:6; 21:1-10; 22:1-5; 25:1-13b; 32:1-2,6-16,24-44; 34:1-35:19). Duhm had already established a special class for these passages, which he believed to be a postexilic rewriting of authentic Jeremian oracles in the style and the spirit of Deut. Mowinckel defended the same opinion in his 1914 study; some time later, however, he changed some details of this first view. He now would no longer speak of a

special "source," but rather of a "circle of traditions" within which certain of Jeremiah's sayings have been transmitted and transformed according to the ideas and the style that prevailed in the deuteronomic circle. In other words, a parallel oral tradition coexisted with that which preserved the poetic pieces, and it was responsible for these deuteronomic passages (Prophecy and Tradition [Oslo, 1946] 61-65). This deuteronomic revision or rewriting of Jeremiah's oracles is a view widely held by scholars who differ only in matters of dates and authors assigned to it (Rudolph, Jeremia xvi; Schreiner, Jeremia 6; Boadt, Jeremiah 1-25 xix-xx; etc.).

However, such a revision is highly questionable. Why should only Jeremiah's work have undergone this transformation? Also, if true similarities exist between the passages discussed and the deuteronomic literature, there also exist great differences that cannot be overlooked. Bright would even go so far as to affirm that these divergences are sufficient to give to the passages a style of their own that cannot be simply assimilated to the deuteronomic one. Would it not be, as W. O. E. Oesterley and T. H. Robinson first proposed, that we have to deal here with the Judean prose style of the end of the 7th and the beginning of the 6th cents.? Weiser accepts such a view and finds its Sitz im Leben in the liturgical exhortations for the edification of the people. Thus, Deut and deuteronomic discourses of Jer would be two different examples of this prose; even Baruch's memoirs (source B) would be another example, for the same style and language are also recognizable at times (cf. W. Oesterley and T. H. Robinson, Introduction to the Books of the Old Testament [London, 1958] 298-304; J. Bright, JBL 70 [1951] 15-35; Jeremiah lxxi-lxxiii; Weiser, Jeremia xxxvii, 60-61). This critical position has been very strongly sustained by H. Weippert (Die Prosareden des Jeremiabuches [Berlin, 1973]) through the detailed analysis of four of these discourses (7:1-15; 18:1-12; 21:1-7; 34:8-22). She has well demonstrated that even though a common list of expressions and formulas is found in both Jer and Deut, one should easily recognize that such a vocabulary has theological implications that are proper to Jer and is in full consonance with the theology found in the poetic oracles. She refuses therefore to attribute these discourses to some unknown deuteronomistic redactors. They are authentic Jeremian speeches; she thus urges us to recognize that the prophet used two different styles in his interventions: poetic oracles and "poetic prose" (Kunstprosa). W. L. Holladay (VT 25 [1975] 403) accepted this study as the definitive solution to this problem. One can see a clear confirmation of this conclusion in T. W. Overholt's studies of the notion of falsehood (The Threat of Falsehood [London, 1970]; JBL 91 [1972] 457-62) in Mowinckel's sources A,B,C, where no significant difference in meaning can be detected. Thus, one may question the existence of such a "deuteronomic" rewriting of Jeremiah's oracles. But we do recognize at the same time that the Deuteronomists have left sure signs of their work, as in other prophetic books; each case must be examined individually.

In the midst of this recent research on the redactional history of the book of Jeremiah a new thesis has been proposed: Mowinckel's sources B and C have one and the same origin, that is, the "deuteronomistic" circles of the exilic period. E. W. Nicholson (Preaching to the Exiles [Oxford, 1970]) was the first to see in both the narratives and the discourses the same attempt by these circles, acting in Babylonia, to explain to the exiles the reasons for the catastrophe of 587 and to provoke in their mind the hope of the restoration of the covenant between Yahweh and Israel; in this attempt, they reinterpret the acts and the words of Jeremiah in this new historical situation.

While J. A. Thompson (*Jeremiah* 47–50) and L. Boadt
(*Jeremiah 26–52* 3–5) are sympathetic to this explanation,
J. V. M. Sturdy ("The Authorship," *Prophecy* [Fest. G.
Fohrer; ed. J. A. Emerton; Berlin, 1980] 143–50), for
reasons of theological differences, would rather attribute
these "Prose Sermons" to disciples of Jeremiah. W. Thiel
has also published two important monographs on the
same subject (*Die deuteronomistische Redaktion von Jeremia
1–25/26–45* [Neukirchen, 1973 and 1981]), with very
similar results. He understands all these narratives and
prose sermons as small "editorial units" produced by the
Deuteronomists on the basis of authentic words of
Jeremiah in the new historical context of the exile; this
redactional activity is also present in the poetic parts of
the book and should be normally situated in Judah itself.
Obviously the author has not taken H. Weippert's work
into consideration. R. P. Carroll (*From Chaos to Covenant*
[London, 1981]) readily accepts Thiel's analysis of this
body of Jeremian literature, but he proposes a much
more complex history of its redaction. This history
develops between two poles: the catastrophic situation
of Judah after 597 (chaos) and the early postexilic period,
dominated by the "Jeremian" hope of the restoration
(covenant). If we do have to recognize a certain
"deuteronomistic" level of redaction, the great majority
of this prophetic book has to be attributed to many
different communities which reflected on these new
historical situations, relying on a very thin basis of
authentic words and deeds of Jeremiah. These communities would then have progressively created the
Jeremian tradition, leaving us very few clues about the
historical Jeremiah. This view governs Carroll's 1986
commentary.

In this commentary, because of all the literary
arguments well documented by Bright and others, and
the theological similarities between the poetic oracles
and the prose sermons, well demonstrated by Weippert,
we recognize a solid Jeremian nucleus in these much-
discussed parts of the book, not forgetting, though, that
true deuteronomic editorial notes have been also added.

8   (B) Composition. The history of the collection of Jeremiah's work into book form cannot be
retraced easily. At first glance, we are struck by the high
number of doublets which might have a redactional
purpose (A. Marx, "A propos des doublets," *Prophecy* [→
7 above] 106–20), the loose combination of poetic
oracles and biographical and autobiographical narratives, the frequent disorder in the chronological data,
etc. Explanations are numerous and varied. Most critics
begin with chap. 36. We are told how Jeremiah dictated
all his oracles in 605, to be reedited the following year
with additions. The attempts to reconstruct this scroll
have been in vain. We can only say that the oracles thus
written down were those directed against Judah and
Jerusalem before 605–604. In general, they are now
found in chaps. 1–25, but, again, each case must be considered separately.

E. Podechard (*RB* 37 [1928] 181–97) separated three
different collections, which have been simply joined to
one another. First is the scroll of 605; Podechard thinks
that it is now included, for the most part, in chaps. 1–17,
where the oracles are set in their chronological order, as
far as we know. Then chaps. 18–20 were joined, being
a separate collection of symbolic actions, and still later,
chaps. 21–23, the booklets on kings and prophets.
Finally, the book of the confessions was inserted at
different places in this first section.

The second collection, chaps. 26–35, is Baruch's
redactional work; the theme is the restoration of
Yahweh's people. Here also Podechard believes that the
compiler used already existing smaller units: chaps.

26–29 are a collection of Jeremiah's altercations with the
false prophets, which form a kind of apology of true
prophecy; chaps. 30–31 preserve the prophet's early
prophecies on the restoration of Israel; chaps. 32–33
unite the similar oracles under Zedekiah; chaps. 34–35
are an appendix on diverse matters.

The third and last section, chaps. 36–45, is easily
recognized as Jeremiah's biography by Baruch. The
latter prefaced his work with the story of the scroll of
605, which introduces him as Jeremiah's chief collaborator, and he closed it by the short oracle of hope, which
he deserved for his collaboration. Finally, Podechard
holds that the collection of oracles against the nations
(chaps. 46–51) has been set at two different places — after
25:13b and in chap. 45 — by very old traditions and that
we cannot know exactly the true reasons. The present
form of Jer can be dated at the end of the exile or soon
after.

9   (C) The Greek Version. The LXX of Jer,
according to K. Graf's calculation (1852), is one-eighth
shorter than the MT. Often only words or short sentences are omitted, but sometimes whole passages are
missing (see the list in Gelin, *DBSup* 4. 858). Another
characteristic of the LXX is the placing of the oracles
against the nations after chap. 25; moreover, a different
order is given to the nations (→ 109 below). The discussion of textual criticism has been recently stirred up by
the discovery of important fragments at Qumran; at
least two are in agreement with the MT, although a long
one represents clearly the LXX tradition. We should
recognize, then, that there were two different recensions. For both literary and theological reasons, the
LXX cannot be understood any longer as an abbreviated
form of the MT, and it certainly represents an older form
of the text (J. G. Janzen, *Studies in the Text of Jeremiah*
[Cambridge MA, 1973]; E. Tov, "Some Aspects," *Le
livre de Jérémie* 145–67; P.-M. Bogaert, "De Baruch à
Jérémie," ibid. 168–73).

10   (IV) Outline. The following outline has
been suggested for the Book of Jeremiah:

(I) Title (1:1–3)
(II) Oracles against Judah and Jerusalem (1:4–25:13b)
    (A) Call of Jeremiah (1:4–19)
        (a) The Dialogue (1:4–10,17–19)
        (b) The Visions (1:11–16)
    (B) Early Oracles under Josiah (2:1–6:30)
        (a) A Lawsuit against Israel (2:1–37)
        (b) The Return of the Apostate (3:1–4:2)
            (i) The poem on conversion
                (3:1–5,19–25;4:1–2)
            (ii) Two additions (3:6–18)
        (c) Evil of Judah and Evil of War (4:3–6:30)
            (i) The invasion (4:3–31)
            (ii) The moral corruption (5:1–31)
            (iii) The correction (6:1–30)
    (C) The Ministry under Jehoiakim (7:1–20:18)
        (a) The Mistaken Covenant (7:1–10:25)
            (i) The Temple discourse (7:1–8:3)
                (1) The Temple (7:2–15)
                (2) The Queen of Heaven (7:16–20)
                (3) Religion and sacrifice (7:21–28)
                (4) False cult and punishment
                    (7:29–8:3)
            (ii) *Nova et vetera* (8:4–10:25)
                (1) Universal estrangement (8:4–12)
                (2) The sacked vineyard (8:13–17)
                (3) The prophet's lament (8:18–23)
                (4) An attempt at evasion (9:1–8)
                (5) Dirge over the land (9:9–21)
                (6) True wisdom (9:22–23)
                (7) Circumcision is worthless (9:24–25)
                (8) A satire on idolatry (10:1–16)
                (9) In full flight! (10:17–22)
                (10) Jeremiah's prayer (10:23–25)

COMMENTARY

11   **(I) Title (1:1–3). 1.** *the words:* The Hebr pl. expression *dibrê* also means "actions" or "events," and therefore "history" (preferable here). *Jeremiah:* The prophet's name, *yirmĕyāhû*, is relatively frequent in the OT and is attested in the Lachish Letters (1.4). Some exegetes (e.g., Rudolph, Weiser), arguing from the Gk transcription, suppose that the first part of the name is from the vb. *rûm* and must be translated "Yahweh has exalted," but we prefer the verb *rāmâ* and translate, "Yahweh has established." *son of Hilkiah, of a priestly family:* This Hilkiah must not be identified with the high priest of Jerusalem at the time of Josiah, who cooperated in the discovery of the Book of the Law in the Temple (2 Kgs 22). *Anathoth:* The present village of Anata, over 3.5 mi. NE of Jerusalem, still preserves the ancient name of the prophet's native town; however, the precise site is to be situated on a nearby mound called Rās el-Kharrūbeh. The name is the pl. form of the goddess Anat, very popular among the Canaanites as Baal's sister (see A. S. Kapelrud, *The violent Goddess* [Oslo, 1969]).

2. *in the days of Josiah . . . in the thirteenth year:* Josiah reigned from 640 to 609; thus, Jeremiah's ministry began in 627–626. However, this date has been brought into question principally because no oracles can be dated during Josiah's reign; and the date has been referred to his birth (J. P. Hyatt, *ZAW* 78 [1966] 204–14; W. L. Holladay, *JBL* 83 [1964] 153–64; "A Coherent Chronology," *Le livre de Jérémie* 62ff.). There are no definite arguments to reject the date given here (see T. W. Overholt, *CBQ* 33 [1971] 165–84).

3. *Jehoiakim:* Jehoahaz succeeded first to Josiah, his father. After three months, he was deposed by Neco, who put him in chains and sent him to Egypt, where he died (2 Kgs 23:31–34). The pharaoh replaced Jehoahaz with Eliakim, another son of Josiah, changing his name to Jehoiakim as a sign of vassalage. These events all occurred in 609. Jehoiakim died three months before the first downfall of Jerusalem in 597 (2 Kgs 23:30–24:6). *until the end . . .:* The LXX omits this expression and the MT reads, "Until the end of the eleventh year of Zedekiah . . . until the exile of Jerusalem in the fifth month." According to 2 Kgs 24:18, Zedekiah did reign 11 years, and according to 2 Kgs 25:2–8, Jerusalem was destroyed the fifth month of the eleventh year of Zedekiah. Therefore, the redactor of the title gave here two synonymous expressions of the same date—i.e., August 587. Zedekiah became king of Judah in 597 by the will of Nebuchadnezzar, who had also changed his original name, Mattaniah, to Zedekiah as a sign of vassalage (2 Kgs 24:17–25).

This list of kings omits two names—Jehoahaz and Jehoiachin—because their short reigns of three months each were negligible. Thus, Jeremiah preached from 627 to 587, a dating that leaves out chaps. 40–44, which narrate his activity after the ruin of Jerusalem. To clarify the problem, we can retrace the history of the title as follows. Originally, v 2 was the introductory title of Jeremiah's call and must be joined to vv 4ff. Verse 3 was introduced when a longer collection of oracles was added, mainly chaps. 7–39. If vv 2–3 were from the same redactor, we would expect to find the preposition "*from* the thirteenth . . .," because the last part of the title mentions "until the exile. . . ." Finally, during the exile or soon after, Jer took its actual form, including Baruch's biographical notes on his master's ministry; then v 1 was set at the beginning of the whole work, connected awkwardly to v 2 by a relative pronoun. Thus, three redactional stages of the title could be registered.

12   (II) Oracles against Judah and Jerusalem (1:4–25:13b). This collection of Jeremiah's oracles of doom on Judah and Jerusalem covers the prophet's entire ministry. A certain attempt was made to respect their chronological order, although sometimes the affinity of subjects was regarded first.

(A) Call of Jeremiah (1:4–19). Two sections can be recognized easily: a dialogue between Yahweh and Jeremiah (vv 4–10,17–19) and two visions (vv 11–16). We do not know how these visions were inserted into the dialogue or when they occurred in Jeremiah's life, although it must have been early. The dialogue bears almost exclusively on the personal effects of this call, for the visions insist rather on the object of the prophet's mission. The detailed analysis of this narrative shows a long process of redaction, the strong influence of previous call narratives (Moses, Gideon), and Israel's election (B. Renaud, "Jér 1: structure et théologie," *Le livre de Jérémie* 177–96; J. Vermeylen, *ETL* 58 [1982] 252–78; F. Garcia Lopez, *VT* 35 [1985] 1–12)

13   (a) THE DIALOGUE (1:4–10,17–19). **5.** *I formed you:* The vb. *yāṣar* refers primarily to the modeling of pottery. Inasmuch as the J account of creation imagined God as a potter (Gen 2:7–8), the vb. took the technical meaning "to create" (Amos 4:13; Jer 51:19; Isa 45:18; 49:5; Ps 95:5). *in the womb:* After Jeremiah, it became an accepted idea that God himself forms the young child in its mother's womb; the significance is that God knows the human person and stands as unique master from the very first moment of a person's existence (Job 10:8–12; Ps 22:10–11; 71:6; 139:13ff.). *I knew you:* The vb. *yāda'* does not refer exclusively to an intellectual knowledge; it involves as well an action of the will and sensibility. *I dedicated you:* The vb. *qādaš* can also be translated "to sanctify" or "to consecrate." Its basic meaning refers to the separation of something or someone for a divine service. Jeremiah is set aside by God for his prophetic mission; the text does not refer to cleansing from original sin. *to the nations:* This extension of his mission, repeated in v 10, corresponds to reality. Former prophets were also concerned with the neighboring countries for two main reasons: the history of the chosen people was always closely mingled with the history of the entire Near East; the prophets had a keen sense of the ruling power of Yahweh over the universe—he was the God of all history. This represents, however, a later reflection on Jeremiah's mission.

6–9. Undoubtedly the word (*dābār*) is characteristic of the prophet, a witness of God's will for his people. Jeremiah is but a young man (*na'ar*)—i.e., in his early twenties; therefore, he has no authority (Isa 3:4; 1 Kgs 3:7). Moses had a similar reaction when Yahweh sent him as his messenger (Exod 4:10–15), but for a different reason: he had a speech defect, which is not the case here. Yahweh's answer (vv 7–8) shows the nature of both Jeremiah's fear and the prophetic mission quite clearly: Yahweh is the first one responsible for what has to be said; he provides the message and intimately sustains his messenger (see Ezek 2:6–7; Deut 18:18).

9. *touched my mouth:* This symbolic action realizes the promise just made, which is immediately explained: "I place my words in your mouth." In the prophetic calls of Isaiah (6:7), Ezekiel (2:8–3:3), and Daniel (10:16), a similar ritual is performed on their mouths. In each case, the same conviction of Yahweh delivering his message to the prophet is sensibly experienced. **10.** *to root up . . .:* Some exegetes suppress the middle stichos ("to destroy and to demolish"), which gives a verse in chiasmus of opposite vbs.; strong arguments for such a restitution have been proposed by W. L. Holladay (*JBL* 79 [1960] 363–64). The present assemblage of vbs. is a characteristic of Jeremiah's book (18:7–10; 24:6; 31:27–28; 42:9–10; 45:4–5). The antithesis defines the twofold aspect of a prophet's mission: to straighten what is crooked and to deepen the whole religious heritage, including occasionally new revelations.

17. *gird your loins:* This verse and those following are the logical sequence of v 10. They accentuate the attitude of the prophet during his ministry. The girding of loins points to the promptness in the accomplishment of an order (1 Kgs 18:46), as well as to the immediate preparation for combat (Job 38:3; 40:7). **18.** *a fortified city:* In Ezekiel's call (3:8–9), we find the same steadfast strength expressed in similar imagery. Those who will have to encounter such a firm man of God are the leaders of Judah, both political and religious, and their subjects, even the most humble ones (cf. 4:9; 32:32).

There is no doubt that Jeremiah is related to Moses in this call narrative, as his true successor in the delivery of the word of God (see W. L. Holladay, *JBL* 83 [1964] 153–64; 85 [1966] 17–27; L. Alonso Schökel, "Jeremias," *De la Tôrah au Messie* [Fest. H. Cazelles; ed. M. Carrez, et al.; Paris, 1981] 245–54). Furthermore, if we can compare Jeremiah's call with those of Isaiah (6:1–13) and Ezekiel (2:1–3:15), we are struck by three distinctive notes. The predestination of a prophet to his office is clearly underlined: Yahweh's plan for such a man originated from the first moment of his existence (cf. Judg 13:5; Isa 49:1–2; Luke 1:15; Gal 1:15–16). Second, this dialogue shows how intimate are the relations between Yahweh and his prophet; several other passages will prove that this intimacy never stopped growing. Jeremiah is the sole prophet who revealed to us the inner struggle that such a mission caused him. Finally, the inherent persecution following this mission is strongly stressed: The entire book is crisscrossed with such dark events.

14   (b) The visions (1:11–16). **11–12.** The first vision presents a pun. The sight of a branch from an almond tree (*šāqēd*) means that Yahweh is watching over (*šōqēd*) the fulfillment of his word. The oracle is comminatory, for in Jer, the vb. *šāqad* always foreshadows a calamity (5:6; 31:27–28; 44:27). **13–16.** The object of the second vision is obscure. The MT reads, "A boiling caldron whose face is from the North," and the versions do not help clarify its meaning. There are three main interpretations. The object of the vision is not the caldron itself but its support over the fire, the opening of which is on the N. Or, Jeremiah saw a caldron moving from N to S. Finally, some think that the caldron was leaning to the N, the most obvious solution (most commentators). The meaning of the vision is clarified by another pun, on the vb. *nāpaḥ*, "to boil" or "to blow." As a result of the idolatrous practices of Judah, a sweeping invasion from the north will lay waste the entire country. The historical problem of this invasion will be discussed after chap. 6.

Great similarities exist between these visions and those in Amos (7:1–9; 8:1–3; 9:1–4): we meet the same interrogations on the object of the vision, followed by the formulations of their meaning in plays on words.

15   (B) Early Oracles under Josiah (2:1–6:30). It has been recognized that chaps. 2–6 preserve the central themes of Jeremiah's preaching under Josiah — before the deuteronomic reform, for they give no sign of this renewal of the covenant (627–622) — and a good number of his oracles early in the reign of Jehoiakim (until 605). R. Albertz (*ZAW* 94 [1982] 20–47) has clearly demonstrated that this first section of the book should be divided into two main parts: 2:1–4:2 and 4:3–6:30. The first one addresses mainly Israel and Jacob (designations of the northern kingdom) and contains a series of accusations for its past infidelities, which are also occasions for a call to repentance. They can be easily dated during Josiah's attempt to unite Israel and Judah sometime after 627. The second part is addressed exclusively to Jerusalem and Judah, which are strongly condemned; there is no chance of salvation since the invasion is already at hand. If the enemy is identified as the Babylonians, the date would be *ca.* 605.

(a) A Lawsuit against Israel (2:1–37). The first

oracle stigmatizes Israel's religious desertion. The main fault is pagan cults, favored esp. by heathen alliances. The poem is cast in the "*rîb* (lawsuit) pattern," so characteristic of the prophetical discourse on the breaking of the covenant (see B. Gemser, in *Wisdom in Israel and in the Ancient Near East* [ed. M. Noth and D. W. Thomas; VTSup 3; Leiden, 1955] 120–37; H. B. Huffmon, *JBL* 78 [1959] 285–95; and esp. J. Harvey, *Le plaidoyer prophétique contre Israël* [Bruges, 1967]). Harvey has argued that the international law of the 2d millennium BC has given us the literary form of both the covenant and its rupture (cf. p. 36, Hos 4; Isa 1:2–3,10–20; Mic 6:1–8; Deut 32:1–25; Ps 50). The main elements of the pattern are the description of the tribunal calling attention to both the accused and the witnesses, a historical review of the accuser's favors, a list of charges often formulated in an interrogative manner, and, finally, the proposal of an ultimatum or the declaration of war. All these elements figure in this present chapter, although in a complex sequence. **1–3.** This first section of the poem is the redactor's introduction to the whole collection, which he has clearly dedicated to Jerusalem and Judah; the true lawsuit against Israel is introduced in v 4 only. The greatest proof of Yahweh's devotion to Israel, constantly repeated in the prophetic preaching, is the exodus, followed by the conquest of Canaan. **2.** *the devotion of your youth:* The word *ḥesed* defines the relationship between Yahweh and Israel at the time of exodus; the term refers to their mutual faithful and merciful love, made concrete in the covenant. This notion of love with the symbolism of marriage in history has been developed by Hosea (1–3; see A. Neher, *RHPR* 34 [1954] 30–49). Jeremiah was certainly influenced by his predecessor; both presented the idyllic desert period as an ideal in the history of Israel, not as a cultural way of life but as a period of high religious fidelity (M. DeRoche, *CBQ* 45 [1983] 364–76). **3.** *firstfruits:* They were Yahweh's portion (Exod 22:28; 23:19) and therefore sacred (*qōdeš*), i.e., "separated" or "reserved" to the divine world. Thus, an alien was forbidden to partake of them (Lev 22:10–15). Such was Israel by its covenantal bonds; being thus the "firstborn" of Yahweh (Exod 4:22), it was therefore "sacred," "untouchable" (*qādôš*; Exod 19:6). Here, the prophet evokes the period of the judges, when Yahweh repressed severely all attempts of the neighboring peoples to subdue his chosen one.

16   4–13. We can distinguish five different sayings in the lawsuit proper, according to the form of the vbs. Here Yahweh addresses his people using the 2d masc. pl. **5.** Idolatry is the central charge against Israel. Yahweh is the only God in Israel (Exod 20:3–5). The heathen gods have no right of existence in her midst; they are therefore "nothingness," "emptiness" (*hebel*); Jeremiah first applied the term to these idols. This step was the first taken toward the doctrine of monotheism, which is clearly found in Dt-Isa (Isa 43:8–12; 44:6–8; 45:5–6,14–15; etc.). **6–7.** We have here a fine definition of the nature of Israel's religion, as opposed to the heathen cults: it is the recognition of Yahweh's gifts to his people through his mighty acts in history. **8.** The accusations are now directed to all the leaders. The priests were not only responsible for the sacrifices, but they were also in charge of the divine oracle and gave short instructions (*tôrôt*) on particular matters, esp. those related to the sacrificial laws. Now that they are specialists of the law, their "knowledge" of Yahweh, or their entire religion, is reduced to nothing. Earlier, Hosea had addressed the same reproach to them (Hos 4:4–10). The "shepherds" must refer to all the official leaders. The "prophets" are the official ones, the spiritual heirs of the ancient diviners of the oriental courts. They are already distinct from the "vocational" prophets, whose oracles have been preserved in our biblical books. **9.** For such aberrations, Yahweh puts them all on trial; the technical word *rîb* (lawsuit) is repeated twice. **10.** *coasts of Cyprus:* The MT should be rather translated, "the isles of Kittim," the Hebrew name for Cyprus, derived from one of its seaports on the SE coast called Kition; but Jeremiah probably refers here to the islands of the Mediterranean coast, meaning the west. *Kedar:* This nomadic Transjordan tribe (Gen 25:13) represents the east. **11.** *their glory:* This attribute of Yahweh (Num 14:21; Isa 6:3) stands for Yahweh himself. **12.** *O heavens:* This invocation of "heavens," to which we may add "earth" and "mountains" as found in the previous examples of lawsuits, has been diversely interpreted: they are pure poetic auditors, or symbols of human and celestial powers, or simply the divine assembly. In the vassal treaties of the ancient Near East, these very elements appear with the rivers and lakes, and the gods of both parties, as witnesses of the mutual bonds just accepted (see *ANET* 201ff.). In the OT we meet them in the same context of covenantal ceremonies in Deut 4:26; 30:19; 31:29. Thus, it is quite natural that these elements must be mentioned in lawsuits following the rupture of such alliances. Therefore, the *rîb* pattern requires such an invocation. **13.** *cisterns:* The scarcity of water in Palestine prompted the device of digging underground cisterns to collect the winter rains. Jeremiah uses the beautiful image of "broken cisterns" to define the futility of foreign alliances, as it appears from v 18, the natural sequence of v 13. Forsaking thus Yahweh's covenant, Israel could expect only drought — i.e., severe punishment.

17   **14–19.** Yahweh now speaks to Israel as to a woman, since the vbs. are 2d fem. sg. She has been reduced to slavery by these political powers with whom she tried to conclude treaties. This is vividly pictured as a search of the waters of the Nile and the Euphrates, no better than broken cisterns in comparison to the source of living waters, which is Yahweh himself. We should not attempt to find the precise events referred to here, since many treaties were concluded in this period; however, alliances with Assyria should be dated before 612. Israel lost its freedom in 721, becoming a simple province in the Assyrian Empire. Egyptian incursions were quite frequent phenomena. **16.** *Memphis:* Noph is the Hebr form of the name (*mn-nfr*). Located about 13 mi. S of Cairo on the W bank of the Nile, Memphis was the chief city of Lower Egypt. *Tahpanhes:* A city on the E frontier of the Delta, it was called Daphne in the classical period and is now identified with the actual Tell Defneh. **20–28.** This is a new development in the lawsuit, even if the vbs. are still used in the 2d fem. sg. form. The subject is new — the idolatrous cult of Baal — and so the style, alternation of Israel's false creeds and their refutation by Yahweh (see S. Herrmann, "Jeremia," *Le livre de Jérémie* 203–14). **20.** *on every high hill:* The expression, traceable to Hosea (4:13), became a classical designation of the high places or sanctuaries of the Canaanites. The core of the cult there practiced was fertility rites, sacred prostitution being the most common. Hence, prostitution was often synonymous with idolatry in the prophets. **21.** *a choice vine:* Jeremiah recalls Isaiah's famous allegory of the vine as a description of Israel's religious history (Isa 5:1–7; cf. Hos 10:1; Ps 80:9). **23–25.** Israel's pursuit of fertility through the Baal cult is vividly described as a she-camel and a wild ass in heat; the sexual rites of such a cult suggested such an imagery (see K. E. Baily and W. L. Holladay, *VT* 18 [1968] 256–60). **23.** *valley:* The reference is to child sacrifice in the Hinnom Valley, S of Jerusalem (cf. 7:31). **27.** *wood . . . stone:* Jeremiah points clearly to the 'ăšērâ (an erect wooden post) and the

maṣṣēbâ (an erect stone), both cultic objects of the high places. In the Canaanite fertility cult, the first symbolizes the female principle, and the second, the male. He deliberately interchanges their symbolic significance to cover them with greater derision. This is also a dramatic negation of Yahweh's fatherhood toward Israel (Exod 4:22; Deut 14:1; Hos 11,1ff.). **29–32.** Here again Israel is addressed through vbs. in the 2d masc. pl. form. Israel cannot accuse Yahweh of being a deceitful husband to her, since she is the one who forgot her marriage vows. The different corrections of God's people through history have been useless. **33–37.** The vbs. are now in the 2d fem. sg. form. In this final accusation, Jeremiah evokes the two major breaches of the covenant: heathen cults and social violence, the basic counterparts of the Decalogue. The foreign alliances will never replace the Sinai covenant as Israel's personal strength; Israel's salvation rests exclusively in this context (chap. 3). **34.** The last sentence of the verse is obscure; cf. W. L. Holladay, *VT* 25 (1975) 223–24.

It has been maintained for some time that the prophets had little concern with the covenant. We now know that they had a most profound understanding of its religious meaning. Jeremiah seems to have been just as much concerned with the religious apostasy of his people, the rupture of the first stipulation of this covenant, as the former prophets were with the breaking of the other bonds, i.e., social justice and moral laws. We must recall that the covenant was not a purely material obligation but the care of Yahweh's plan of salvation. Therefore, Israel's history can only be a sacred one.

18   (b) The RETURN OF THE APOSTATE (3:1–4:2). Jeremiah's mission was twofold: "to root up and to tear down, to build and to plant" (1:10). The poem in 2:2–37 realized the first part of this task; the present poem is the second panel of the diptych. The gist of the whole section is the working out of the conditions required to bring about the reconciliation between Israel and Yahweh.

The pericope underwent at least two stages of redaction. We isolate an early poem on conversion (3:1–5,19–25; 4:1–2), which was later interrupted by two insertions (3:6–13 and 3:14–18). However, a profound unity of the entire composition was maintained through the constant use of the key word *šûb*. Basically, the root means "to return from one place to another." Transposed on the religious plane, the expression designates both an aversion from and a conversion to the right. Here Jeremiah plays on all these connotations (see W. L. Holladay, *The Root Sûbh in the Old Testament* [Leiden, 1958] esp. 1–2, 129–39, 152–53).

19   (i) *The poem on conversion* (3:1–5,19–25; 4:1–2). **1–5.** This first part of the poem shows that this conversion is impossible, according to the human viewpoint, through an analogous situation taken from the law. The symbol used here prohibits a renewed union of Yahweh and Israel, which is the opposite of a similar symbol used in Hos 2. **1.** All the commentators refer to Deut 24:1–4, which formulates a law on divorce that is very similar to the case specified here, but with differences (see T. R. Hobbs, *ZAW* 86 [1974] 23–29). The common situation is that of a man who has legally divorced his wife, who has then entered the house of another man; in such a situation, the first husband cannot remarry his estranged wife. Such is Israel's case: she had provoked a divorce from Yahweh by her worship of other gods. *land defiled:* It is a well-known idea in the OT that all kinds of sins against the laws of the covenant are attacks against the sacred character of the land itself, which is certainly a symbol of the nation that inhabits it (cf. Num 35:33–34; Deut 21:22–23; 24:4; Jer 2:7; 3:9; 16:18; etc.). **2.** *heights:*

Hebr šĕpāyîm means "bare heights," and is properly Jeremian. The prophet certainly took the image of the barren hills of Judah, so clearly seen from Anathoth, to designate the high places of idolatry, still called "harlotry." **3.** *showers:* The spring rains are of prime importance for the crops; the fertility cult aimed at their safe outcome. God certifies that these rites are vain, for he is the one who regulates the rains. If he retains them, the reason is precisely this grave religious error. **4.** *my father:* In 2:27, such an invocation was addressed to a Canaanite symbol in the fertility cult. Baal and Astarte were believed to cause the fertility of the fields, cattle, and even humanity; they were thus called "father" and "mother." The idea has been demythologized and applied to Yahweh by Hosea (11:1ff.), to serve, along with marriage, as a second covenant image. Jeremiah, here and in v 19, blends fatherly love and marital love as tangible expressions of this same covenant.

3:19–25; 4:1–2. Conversion is juridically impossible, but through sincere human repentance and by Yahweh's mercy, a new spirit will be created in the people. That these verses are the logical continuation of vv 1–5 is clear from vv 19–20, developing the idea of v 4. **21.** *heights:* The same word as in v 2, but with a different connotation; they are now the scene of lamentations for the evil suffered as the salary of the idolatry once practiced there. **22.** *return:* Jeremiah uses the same root šûb three times, giving the effect of a play on words. Yahweh is speaking; it is he who will achieve the return, if only Israel consents by penance and confession of her basic creed—Yahweh is her only God (Exod 20:2–6; Deut 5:6–10; 6:4). This acknowledgment meant a renewal of the covenant.

4:2 These expressions—'ĕmet (truth), mišpāṭ (judgment), and ṣĕdāqâ (justice)—to which we must add ḥesed (piety, love), define true religion in Israel and are frequently used in the entire prophetical tradition. *nations . . . in blessing:* Israel, authentic to her faith, will bring forth Yahweh's promises to the patriarchs (Gen 12:3; 18:18; 22:18; 26:4). The nations, at the sight of such a glory given by Yahweh to his people, will desire to serve him also. True conversion to the virtues of the covenant are thus Yahweh's answer to the question asked at the beginning of the poem (3:1).

20 (ii) *Two additions* (3:6–18). These verses were inserted in the poem on conversion; they are the first example of the prose discourses that may represent the second style of Jeremian speech. **6–13.** This first oracle is unanimously accepted as being a true reflection of a Jeremian discourse, but its composition date is controverted. However, we still hold that it must be dated between 627 and 622. Indeed, Jeremiah reproaches Judah with idolatry, and in the very same terms he used for Israel in 2:27 (cf. v 9). There is no allusion to this reform in our passage, and we have no proof that idolatry regained its popularity after Josiah had destroyed the high places. Jeremiah proposes an allegory of the divided kingdoms, figured as two sisters; Ezekiel will give ample proportions to the parable (Ezek 16; 23). Israel had been swept away by the Assyrians a century before for having fallen into idolatry without repentance, even though the prophets had heralded its necessity for salvation. Such a lesson should have profited Judah, but her "return" did not last longer than the "morning clouds or the dew" (Hos 6:4). Thus, her guilt is greater and does not deserve the forgiveness offered to her sister (vv 12–13).

14–18. This section is a small collection of four different sayings that should be situated at different moments in Jeremiah's mission. **14–15.** Israel is invited to return to Jerusalem and accept then the Davidic king,

defined as an ideal king (cf. 23:5–6). Yahweh himself is recognized as their sole God, active in history, a fact that makes him deserving of the title of *Baal,* or "master." **16–17.** Here Jeremiah rejects all religious value for the Ark of the Covenant, which was the sacred symbol giving to the Temple and Jerusalem the character of the residence of Yahweh himself, since it functioned as his royal throne (cf. R. de Vaux, *MUSJ* 37 [1960–61] 91–124). This function will now be fulfilled by Jerusalem itself, as the final word of Ezekiel's *tôrâ* proclaims (Ezek 48:35). Jerusalem, by its new splendor, will become the center where all nations gather (cf. Isa 2:2–3 = Mic 4:1–3; Isa 56:6–8; 60:11–14). **18.** Another significant theme of the passage is the reunion of the divided kingdoms, already foretold by the 8th-cent. prophets (Hos 2:2; Mic 2:12). But here this reunion is seen as possible only after both Judah and Israel have undergone exile (Ezek 37:15–28; Isa 11:10–16, which is postexilic). For all these reasons, critics would consider this oracle to be a postexilic work by a disciple of Jeremiah. However, both the vocabulary and the thought are Jeremian (cf. 23:1–8). In his early ministry Jeremiah hoped that with the end of her exile Israel would be restored to its ancient glory. The decline of the Assyrian power and the extension of Josiah's reform to Israel certainly increased this hope. The events did not permit its realization, but it continued to live in the prophet's mind; and when Judah suffered the same fate as Israel, he included Judah in this faith. Thus, the actual state of the oracle is quite understandable in the months following the destruction of Jerusalem in 587.

21 (c) EVIL OF JUDAH AND EVIL OF WAR (4:3–6:30). This long section must be considered a single poem for it deals with one subject matter: Judah must be punished for her sins, to be realized by a swift invasion. Thus, the descriptions of the war—with its effects on both the land and the minds of the people and the prophet—and the denunciations of moral depravity and exhortations to penance intermingle in vivid colors and pathetic accents throughout the entire poem. This unity is even noticeable on the literary level, esp. in chaps. 4 and 6: their exordia are extremely close and they both end with the anguish of a mother in childbirth as a symbol of great suffering (4:31; 6:24–26). Moreover, the same idea of a destructive fire opens and closes the poem in a manner of *inclusio* (4:4 and 6:29–30).

(i) *The invasion* (4:3–31). **3–4.** The poem is addressed to a new group of people who will remain in the foreground to the end of chap. 6—that is the Judeans and the Jerusalemites. The prophet invites them for a last time to repent, in order to avoid the final judgment already at work. This conversion is presented here as the circumcision of the heart which is proper to Jeremiah (9:25) and Deut (10:16; 30:6). A new step is taken in the religion of Israel by this proclamation of the primacy of the interior dispositions over the exterior ones, for the heart is the seat of intelligence and will. Thus, W. Rudolph could call this *logion* an "eternal word, the gospel" of the OT (cf. 31:31–34). The conversion that Jeremiah is asking of Israel is then much more than the restoration of neglected practices. Jeremiah follows in the whole tradition of deuteronomic circles that insisted on this necessity of conversion as one of their leading themes. **5–8.** Like a clap of thunder in a blue sky, a sudden alarm is heard all over the land: the invaders draw near. **5.** *proclaim it:* A similar outcry is repeated in 6:1; it echoes the same alarm of Hosea a century earlier on the occasion of the Syro-Ephraimite war (735–734); cf. 2 Kgs 16:5ff.; Hos 5:8. Later, another prophet will proclaim the coming of the eschatological Day of the Lord in analogous terms (Joel 2:1). Such an alarm is required, for in wartime all countrymen would flee behind the walls of fortified cities. **6.** *standard:* Hebr *nēs* also means "signal," i.e., a fire lighted on a height for the transmission of news (cf. Isa 13:2; 18:3; Lachish Letters 4.10–13). *evil from the north:* The same expression figures in the second vision (1:14), referring to the same event, which will be discussed at the end of the poem. **7.** *mauler of nations:* With Bright we translate thus *mašḥît*, meaning lit., "destroyer," to respect the symbol of the lion used here. The word evokes primarily the demonic force that attacked the Egyptians but spared the Israelites during the night of the Passover (Exod 12:23); but now there is no protection possible against it. **8.** *sackcloth:* This rough linen is frequently mentioned as a garment of mourning (6:26; 49:3; Isa 15:3; 22:12). **9–12.** Now Yahweh himself describes the profound consternation of the Judean leaders, both political and religious, before he announces his final judgment. **10.** *peace shall be yours:* This promise of welfare is said to be Yahweh's, and the present event shows that he lied; however, this allusion is clearly to the preaching of the false prophets (6:14; 14:13; 23:16–17). **11.** *daughter of my people:* Jerusalem is thus designated (cf. v 17). **13–18.** The impetuous march of the invader is compared to a swift disastrous storm from the desert (cf. Hos 13:15). **14.** *cleanse your heart:* The judgment was already given as final. Now it seems that true conversion would save the city; nevertheless, such a "return" is unthinkable. **15.** *Dan:* The town was situated at the sources of the Jordan, on the N border of the promised land, now identified with Tell el-Qadi. Inasmuch as the invasion was coming from the N, it would be the first town to suffer. *Mt. Ephraim:* The mountainous region from Shechem to Bethel. **19–22.** Jeremiah portrays here his inner emotions. By vocation he had to announce destruction and punishment, but by nature he was a man most devoted to his beloved people. His whole life will be spent in this painful paradox. **22.** This verse is now Yahweh's own lament. The knowledge of God is not an intellectual grasp of a sum of truths, but a conduct inspired by these truths. **23–28.** The prophet gives a new description of the invasion, which takes on the aspect of a cosmic conflagration. **23.** *waste and void:* The description of the primordial chaos (*tōhû wābōhû;* Gen 1:2) is used to give the impression of a perfect confusion. The entire universe is struck with horror at such a sight. This description is found, almost identical, in Joel in the same invasion context (Joel 2:1–11). Amos (8:9–10), Zephaniah (1:2–3,14–18), and Nahum (1:2–8) produced the same effects in their proclamations of the Day of the Lord, also on the occasion of wars. Finally, the scene will be purely apocalyptic in Isa 24, foreshadowing the eschatological discourse of the Synoptics. **27.** The MT *lō'*, "not," is certainly a later attenuation of *lāh*, "it." **29–31.** The end is irrevocable as Yahweh has just assured (v 28). Jerusalem is personified as a woman attiring herself to seduce the nearing enemy. This first section of the poem closes with the shrieks and the contortions of a woman in travail, symbolizing an extreme anguish (13:21; 22:23; etc.).

22   (ii) *The moral corruption* (5:1–31). In chap. 4, the certainty of the invasion had been so great that no chance of salvation could be expected. The prophet now gives the reason for such a disaster—the evil of the people. In chap. 2, this evil was exclusively religious, i.e., idolatry. Now the stress is on morals, both social and personal.

1–6. This first part is a dialogue between Yahweh and his prophet on the general corruption of the people, who did not convert after the harsh discipline of political hardships. **1.** Yahweh is scrutinizing the city for one just man, for he would spare it as he would have spared Sodom (Gen 18:22–32; see R. P. Carroll, *OTS* 23 [1984] 19–38 for a good study of this tradition). *uprightly . . . faithful:* Hebr *mišpāṭ* and *'ĕmûnâ* are covenantal realities ruling relations between men as well as between men and God. In the prophetic literature, they occur constantly with *ḥesed*, "love," and *ṣĕdāqâ*, "justice." **4–5.** The sinful state is universal; the low class could be excused for its ignorance, but not the leading one—i.e., kings, priests, and prophets (cf. 4:9)—for it is at the service of the word of God. **6.** These wild animals are none other than the invaders (cf. 2:15; 4:7; Hos 13:7–8; Zeph 3:3; Hab 1:8). **7–11.** The prophet now gives the catalogue of sins prevailing in Judah, particularly adultery, expressed in crude terms. **12–17.** Yahweh himself had formulated the previous reproaches (vv 7–11); Jeremiah now addresses the wicked people. **12.** *not he:* A theoretical atheism did not exist in the ancient Near East, but a practical one did: God was believed to be uninterested in human affairs; therefore, he could not intervene (cf. Amos 9:10; Zeph 1:12; see J. Schreiner, *TTZ* 90 [1981] 29–40). **13.** Such an attitude is substantiated by the word of "false" prophets, believed to be men of the *rûaḥ*, "spirit"; they are now called the "men of wind" ("windbags," says Bright), a play on the double meaning of *rûaḥ*. **14–17.** The results follow once more the accusations; Jeremiah will see the fulfillment of his mission (1:9–10), and the invasion will be a proof of its authenticity.

18–25. It is commonly accepted that this pericope consists of two additions to the original poem. **18–19.** This first addition is certainly inauthentic; it weakens the preceding threats, a device noticed twice already (4:27; 5:10). Both literary form and thought recall the speeches of Deut (e.g., 24:47–48; 29:23–27). The exilic period would be a good date for its composition. **20–25.** With W. Rudolph and A. Gelin, we hold this second oracle authentic; however, the general theme is no longer the "God of history" but the "God of creation" (cf. H. Weippert, *Schöpfer des Himmels* [Stuttgart, 1981] 17ff. On the occasion of a drought, Jeremiah warns the people that this calamity must be a divine punishment for their stubborn apostasy for Yahweh rules the universe.

26–31. The catalogue of sins continues. The stress now shifts to the social injustices and the oppression of the weak. The climax is reached with the denunciation of the religious leaders: the prophets consult Baal and the priests themselves decide the law. The whole section closes with a dreadful question mark.

23   (iii) *The correction* (6:1–30). The general theme of chap. 4 is resumed, but now the enemy is already devastating the country and besieging the fortified cities. However, conversion is still lacking. **1.** *Tekoa:* Amos's native country, about 5 mi. S of Bethlehem. *Beth-haccherem:* Recent excavations suggest Ramat Rahel, on the road from Jerusalem to Bethlehem, as the site (see Y. Aharoni, *BA* 24 [1961] 98–118). The signal, probably by fire, seems to indicate the route of the flight toward the south. **4.** *prepare for war:* Hebr *qaddĕšû* means, lit., "sanctify" for war; ritual purifications and sacrifices were performed before a battle because it was considered a religious act. **9–11.** As in 5:1, Jeremiah is asked to discover one just man; he cannot. No one listens, and his wrath breaks forth; the first part of his mission—"to root up and to tear down"—must be executed.

12–15. The same accusations are repeated. The evil is so anchored in everyone's heart that an absolute impenitence keeps them all impassive. **16–21.** This oracle has been diversely understood. For some commentators, it is a sign of Jeremiah's rejection of the deuteronomic reform, which led to an emphasis on cultic matters, at the expense of moral obligations. However, these lines can hardly be anything other than an appeal to the study of tradition so as to know the conduct pleasing to Yahweh, a theme well known from former prophets. It shows, moreover, that the prophets were not innovators but men solidly attached to tradition, which they kept alive by their new understanding of its old truths and by their addition of new truths through personal religious experiences and revelations. **20.** *incense:* Incense offerings, a luxury imported from South Arabia. This verse and many others (Amos 5:21-25; Hos 6:6; 8:11-13; Isa 1:10-15; Mic 6:6-8; etc.) constitute the so-called prophetic indictment against exterior cult. For a long while exegetes believed that the prophets rejected all exterior practices of religion to support only interior ones. Now a more balanced view prevails; the prophets teach that sacrifices and feasts are worth nothing if they are not accompanied with real interior dispositions. Indeed, a religion without a cult is unthinkable in the ancient Orient. **22-26.** The end of the poem is very similar to 4:29-31.

27-30. These verses do not belong to the original poem on the invasion; they are rather a kind of summary of Jeremiah's first ministry (chaps. 1-6). The result is rather deceiving! A number of obscurities makes the text difficult to understand; the prophet's work is compared to the work of a metallurgist. **29.** As silver could not be extracted from the slag, so is the new Israel through Jeremiah's efforts; therefore, she will be rejected.

24 The problem of the identification of the invader is a most disputed question. This enemy is said to come from the N, from afar (5:15), from the "ends of the earth" (6:22); they are horsemen, they also ride war chariots, they use the bow, and they know how to besiege a city by earthworks (4:7,13,19; 5:17; 6:4,6). Their origin is from "old" and their language is unintelligible to the Judeans (5:15). These are the only characteristics given.

A theory that had great influence identified this foe with the Scythians, who invaded Asia and the Palestinian coasts between 630 and 625 B.C., according to the testimony of Herodotus (1.103-6). Because the Scythian invasion of Palestine remains questionable historically, others prefer the Assyrians as this foe from the N (e.g., Penna, *Geremia* 35, 85; P. Dhorme, *BPl* 1. li). But the Assyrians were never a threat in Jeremiah's lifetime. Therefore, most commentaries think that this enemy has to be identified with the Babylonians, who dominated the whole political scene in the Near East with the accession of Nebuchadnezzar to the throne in 605; these oracles should be dated then under Jehoiakim, between 605 and 598.

All these identifications being so problematical, other exegetes have searched for a solution in a totally different direction. We have to deal here with a pure mythological question. In the Canaanite myths, the north is not only the residence of Baal but also the source of evil; Jeremiah then simply used these references in his proclamation of a correction to come. However, except for a short passage (4:23ff.), this enemy is not mythological but is clearly presented as a human agent. Finally, a group of exegetes reject all these explanations and hold rather that Jeremiah had no particular people in mind when he first wrote his poem; it was only later that he identified the invader with the Babylonians, after the year 605 (Volz, *Jeremia* 58ff.; Rudolph. *Jeremia* 43-45; Weiser, *Jeremia* 38ff.).

This last opinion is apparently the most satisfying. Indeed, apart from the alleged Scythian wars, no particular people was threatening Judah *ca.* 626. However, in the whole history of the chosen people, the rupture of the covenant through idolatry and injustice has never remained unpunished. Wars in the time of the judges, the Aramean wars of the 9th cent., and more recently the fall of Samaria (721) under the Assyrians were too well known not to confirm this prophetic faith in Yahweh's justice. Jeremiah had that same faith; at the sight of Judah's perversity, he was sure that a new war would cleanse her sins. Who would lead this war? He did not know and thus described the foe in very general terms. The northern origin was plausible because only Egypt could come from the south, and for centuries she had been no danger (see H. H. Rowley, *BJRL* 45 [1962-63] 198-234, for an excellent review of the exegetical problems in this first part of Jer).

(C) The Ministry under Jehoiakim (7:1-20:18). This section is commonly dated under the reign of Jehoiakim (609-598).

25 (a) THE MISTAKEN COVENANT (7:1-10:25). Another common assumption is that chaps. 7-10 form a collection of oracular fragments and short discourses; the identical titles at the beginning of chaps. 7 and 11 support this view. On the whole, they reflect the religious and moral state of Judah during the first years of Jehoiakim's rule, which is very similar to that described in chaps. 1-6. Josiah's reform seemed to have been dependent on his own personal action and not to have penetrated the people's spirit; in general, it was a failure.

(i) *The Temple discourse* (7:1-8:3). This first pericope is also a cluster of different sayings on related matters—the Temple and the cult.

(1) The Temple (7:2-15). This passage is the Temple discourse proper. Chapter 26 is a parallel narrative, where the message is reduced to its essentials, but the circumstances and the shock produced by this sharp criticism are fully covered. The prophet's intervention occurred in 609-608, shortly after Josiah's death at Megiddo (see H. Weippert, *Die Prosareden* [→ 7 above] 26-48). **4.** *Temple of Yahweh:* The triple repetition reflects the recognition of the inviolability of the Temple in the popular mind (J. Bright, *Covenant and Promise* [Phl, 1976] 49-77; M. Görg, *BN* 18 [1982] 7-14). As the shelter of the Ark of the Covenant, Yahweh's throne, it was sacred and could not fall to the enemy; for the same reason, the whole country would be preserved. **6-7.** This expected protection is conditional; the moral prescriptions of the covenant, which Jeremiah explicitly recalls (Exod 22:17-24), should be observed. **9.** *steal and murder:* The sins listed here are offenses against the Decalogue (Exod 20:1-17; Hos 4:2), the first stipulations of the covenant. **11.** *den of thieves:* Jesus stigmatized the sacrificial transactions in its midst (Matt 21:13), but Jeremiah meant that the Temple is now nothing but a hiding place for evildoers, for Yahweh has withdrawn his protection. **12-14.** Located at Khirbet Seilûn, 14 mi. S of Shechem, Shiloh had been the main religious center of the tribes during the last period of the judges (1 Sam 1-4). The city and the sanctuary of the Ark were most probably destroyed during the Philistine wars (see J. Day, in *Studies in the Historical Books of the Old Testament* VTSup 30; [Leiden, 1979] 87-94 for the evidence); its priesthood is later found at Nob (1 Sam 21:1; 22). Only Jeremiah recalls this destruction of Shiloh (see also Ps 78:60). He was from Anathoth, where the descendants of the Shiloh priesthood were exiled; understandably, the event was remembered there. In his reform, Josiah gave great importance to the Temple of Jerusalem, the only legitimate temple; however, this materialistic idea of the Temple's sanctity does not correspond to the king's intentions. In other words, Jeremiah does not condemn the Josian reform but recalls the very meaning of the covenant.

26   (2) The Queen of Heaven (7:16–20). This
short speech is the first of a series on cultic matters. It
deals with idolatry, esp. the fertility cult of Astarte,
a Mesopotamian goddess much honored in Canaan; she
was very popular in Judah under Manasseh, with many
other Mesopotamian gods (2 Kgs 21; 23:4–14). In
Mesopotamia she was also called the "Queen of Heaven"
(*šarrat šamê, belit šamê*), a name still attested in the Aram
papyri of the 5th cent. BC in Egypt. Inasmuch as she was
an astral divinity, her cult took place in the open on terraces (19:13; 32:29; 2 Kgs 23:12; Zeph 1:5); it consisted
in cake offerings (*kawwānîm*, a loanword from Akkadian
kamānu, kawānu), probably in the shape of a nude woman
(cf. M. Delcor, "Le culte de la Reine du ciel," *Von Kanaan
bis Kerala* [Fest. J. P. M. van der Ploeg; ed. W. C.
Delsman, *et al.*, Neukirchen, 1982] 101–22; W. E. Rast,
"Cakes for the Queen of Heaven," *Scripture in History and
Theology* [Fest. J. C. Rylaarsdam; ed. A. L. Merrill, *et al.*;
Pittsburgh, 1977] 167–80). Such a cult is another sign of
the reform's brevity.

27   (3) Religion and sacrifice (7:21–28). The
present oracle pertains to the "prophetic indictment" of
the sacrificial institutions (cf. 6:20). **22.** *no command:* This
verse and a similar one in Amos (5:25) seem to deny the
divine origin of the sacrifices. What Yahweh expects as
essential to religion is obedience of the heart to moral
laws, without need of sacrifices. However, these sacrifices in fact exist and are regulated in detail in the P tradition, under divine authority (Lev 1–7). Moreover, it is
impossible to admit that their origin is exilic, for they
were offered long before in Israel, although we recognize that they have only limited importance in the Covenant Code (Exod 20–23) and in Deut (12:1ff.). To bring
his listeners to a true evaluation of their religious duties,
Jeremiah went so far as to deny the divine origin of the
sacrificial cult, although he knew its remote past. Later,
in his definition of the new covenant (33:11), sacrifices
will still be included (see R. de Vaux, *AI* 454–56;
Rudolph, *Jeremia* 52–53). **24.** *hardness:* The word *šerîrût*
always used with the word "heart" is properly Jeremian
(9:13; 11:8; 13:10; 16:12; etc.; Deut 29:18; Ps 81:13).
Thus, Jeremiah, the prophet most sensitive to the problem of sin, goes so far as to speak of a kind of "sinful
state" of humanity, whereas the other prophets speak
only of sinful actions. **26.** *stiffened their necks:* This expression is another frequent one found in Jer and Deut. It is
synonymous with "hardness of the heart." External
practices and sacrifices have no value unless they are informed by a sincere devotion of the heart.

28   (4) False cult and punishment (7:29–8:3).
This last section of the discourse is a collection of
different sayings of Jeremiah: v 29 is a poetic exhortation
to mourning; v 30 is taken from another sermon (cf.
32:34), as are also vv 31–33 (cf. 19:5ff.); v 34 is also
borrowed from other oracles (cf. 16:9; 25:10). **8:1–3.**
This saying on violation of tombs and exposure of the
dead bodies was added here probably because question
of privation of sepulture exists in 7:33. Such a treatment
of the deceased is a terrible curse; they are exposed to the
heavenly bodies because they worshiped them.

(ii) *Nova et vetera* (8:4–10:25). The following
section is a compilation of several fragmentary sayings
on different subjects, old and new, that can be generally
dated to the early reign of Jehoiakim, *ca.* 605.

29   (1) Universal estrangement (8:4–12). **4–7.**
Jeremiah deplores the obstinate heart of his people, who
refuse conversion, through the same wordplay on the
different meanings of the verb *šûb*, "turn." The comparison used in v 7 has its parallel in Isa 1:3; in the very
nature of these animals there exists an instinct that brings
them back to their original place or to their masters; thus

should Israel turn toward her covenantal God! Sin
therefore is seen as a violence to nature (Weiser,
Rudolph). **8–9.** The passage has occasioned a long discussion that still continues. Since K. Marti (1889),
several authors have believed that the verses are a clear
condemnation of the deuteronomic reform. The scribes
would be the priests who created and fraudulently
imposed the deuteronomic law (J. Wellhausen), but the
origin of Deut as a pious fraud is now rejected and there
is no sign here of any opposition to a particular code of
law. Therefore, an increasing number of exegetes refuse
the idea of a Jeremian condemnation of Deut itself and
propose a condemnation rather of the spirit of the
reform following its discovery, or of the priests' false
interpretations of the law (Penna). Rudolph, Weiser, and
Bright, rejecting such a condemnation, would see here a
subtle distinction between the "law of the Lord" (v 8)
and the "word of the Lord" (v 9), i.e., the legalistic
religion and the teaching of the prophets. The possession
of the law has given a false security, rendering the priests
deaf to the word. **10–12.** This pericope, omitted in the
LXX, is a doublet of 6:12–15, which is in a better
context.

30   (2) The sacked vineyard (8:13–17). The
theme of this comminatory oracle reminds us of chaps.
4–6, the northern invasion. **13.** The image of the vine
reappears; it is now fruitless. The last stichos of the
verse, missing in the LXX, is obscure in the MT. **15.** The
verse interrupts the oracle and has been taken from
14:19b, where it was in better context. **16.** *from Dan:* The
invasion, as before (cf. 4:15), comes from the north.

31   (3) The prophet's lament (8:18–23). **19.** *her
king:* Because of the synonymous parallelism of the
verse, the king is Yahweh. *why do they provoke:* Yahweh
interrupts ironically the lament to explain his departure
from Jerusalem. **20–23.** This mourning over the sufferings of the people shows Jeremiah's sympathy and love
for them, even though his message had to foretell doom
constantly. The paradox will create a painful interior
conflict that his "confessions" will bring to light.

32   (4) An attempt at evasion (9:1–8). Jeremiah,
disgusted, is tempted to flee to the desert. Rudolph
would date the passage under Jehoiakim, when the
prophet was rejected by his fellow countrymen, family
(11:19; 12:6), and friends (20:10).

1. *in the desert:* We are reminded of Elijah's escape to
the desert to avoid Jezebel's wrath, but Jeremiah's motive
is somewhat different—i.e., his people's treachery by
false speech or calumny. **2.** *drawn bow:* The image of the
bow or the sword (Ps 64:4) suggests the lethal results of
the falsehood (v 7). **3.** *Jacob, the supplanter:* With Hosea
(12:3–4), Jeremiah evokes Jacob's cunning actions
against his brother (Gen 25:26; 27:35–36). In all these
texts, there is a wordplay on the different meanings of
the root of Jacob's name: *'āqab*, "to beguile" or "to sup-
plant," and *'āqēb*, "heel." **4–5.** Sin is so general and so
deeply rooted in man's heart that no conversion is possible. Such a sinful state of the people is called a refusal
to know Yahweh, which shows the dynamic aspect of
this notion (cf. 9:23).

33   (5) Dirge over the land (9:9–21). The original work was disrupted by a later prose insertion (vv
11–15), in the form of question and answer, as an
explanation of vv 9–10. The process has been already
noticed in 5:18–19. The poem supposes clearly that the
land has been sorely struck. According to the Babylonian Chronicles (Wiseman, *Chronicles* [→ 2 above] 73),
Nebuchadnezzar's first sweeping campaign in Judah
occurred in 597 (cf. 2 Kgs 23:10ff.), which would be the
suitable historical context of the present dirge. **9–10.**
This description of the country's desolation is extremely

frequent in Jer (2:15; 4:25; 34:22; 44:2–6). **14.** *worm-wood . . . poison:* These two poisonous herbs are often mentioned together in the Bible as a test of guilt or a final judgment (see W. McKane, *VT* 30 [1980] 478–87). **16–19.** In the Near East, even now, on the occasion of deaths or calamities, mourning is carried on by professionals, women uttering hoarse shrieks. **20–21.** This passage is at the origin of the classical imagery of "Death the Reaper." Following U. Cassuto, A. Pohl holds that the idea comes from the Ugaritic Baal myth. The god refuses to have windows cut in the walls of his newly built palace for fear that his enemy, the netherworld god Mot, could come through them and take away his daughters, Dew and Rain (cf. *ANET* 134; A. Pohl, *Bib* 22 [1941] 36–37). The explanation remains questionable; perhaps Jeremiah has simply personified death (cf. Hos 13:14; Isa 28:15–18; Hab 2:5; Ps 49:15; Job 28:22; etc.). **34** (6) True wisdom (9:22–23). This beautiful *logion* on true wisdom is in the purest sapiential tradition; basically it consists of a restyling and an expansion of a proverb (v 22) into a prophetic word (see E. Kutsch, *BZ* 25 [1981] 161–79). We cannot deny its Jeremian authenticity, for the theme of the true knowledge of God is often found on the prophet's lips (2:8; 4:22; 9:2,5; 22:16; 24:7; 31:34). This heritage is probably Hosean (Hos 4:1,6; 5:4; 6:4; 8:2). Both prophets believed strongly that true religion—i.e., an existential recognition of God—consists in merciful love (*ḥesed*), right (*mišpāṭ*), and justice (*ṣĕdāqâ*) (v 23; cf. Hos 2:21–22). The passage can be considered a high point in the religion of Israel. **35** (7) Circumcision is worthless (9:24–25). The external rite has no value if the heart does not inspire it. The list of people given here as practicing circumcision, the "shaved temples" being the Arabs (Herodotus, *Hist.* 2.8), is basically correct. **36** (8) A satire on idolatry (10:1–16). This satire is rejected by most scholars as inauthentic. For several reasons, we hold that the pericope is an exilic, or even a postexilic, addition. First, the order of the verses in the LXX is different, and some of them are missing (vv 6–8,10); the fact that v 11 is in Aramaic proves only that we have to deal with a simple gloss, probably a liturgical addition (see Bright, *Jeremia* 79–80, for the textual criticism; and M. E. Andrew, *ZAW* 94 [1982] 128–130). Most significant is the very theme of the poem; both the ideas and the literary expressions are extremely similar to certain sections of Dt-Isa (cf. Isa 40:19–22; 41:7–29; 44:9–20; 46:5–7) and to some psalms (115:9–16; 135:15–18; see also Bar 6 and Wis 13–15). A post-Jeremian date is therefore required. These compositions are not intended to correct a deviation of the Israelites, but to prevent them from falling into such a deviation, inasmuch as they are now living among the pagans. The existence of the gods is strongly denied; this strict monotheism is clearly attested for the first time in Dt-Isa. Finally, the theme is interwoven with that of the universality of Yahweh through his act of creation and his power over the elements. **12–16.** Repeated in 51:15–19, the passage is a development on the God of nature, in the style of wisdom literature (cf. Ps 104; Job 38; Prov 8:27–31; etc.). **37** (9) In full flight! (10:17–22). The panic described here is in the dreadful atmosphere of 9:9–21; there is certainly a close connection between the two poems, for the same vb., *'āsap,* "to gather," "to pick up," is used in 9:21 and 10:17. It seems that although the invasion has not yet occurred, the danger is imminent; we are probably close to the year 597. The form of the poem is a kind of dialogue between the prophet (vv 17–18,21–22) and Judah (vv 19–20). **17.** *lift your bundle:*

The command is an allusion to exile. **21.** The image of the "stupid shepherds" and the "scattered flock" refers to the kings and Judah, as Ezekiel's long allegory shows (Ezek 34). The kings, through their sacred anointing, were Yahweh's representatives for his people. Yahweh adopted them as his sons to continue the work of Moses and the charismatic judges, all of which is implied by the vb. *dāraš,* "to search," used here. The rejection of this sacred function is especially true of Manasseh and Jehoiakim, the actual king at the time of the oracle. **22.** The "foe from the north" is Babylon; even if Jeremiah still uses this indefinite expression, the identification is now clear to all auditors. The desolated land is also called a "haunt of jackals" in the other related poem (9:10). **38** (10) Jeremiah's prayer (10:23–25). Because of its overtones of wisdom literature, this prayer is sometimes eliminated as a late addition. This reason is insufficient, for a class of wise men existed in Jeremiah's time (cf. 18:18) that influenced the prophets both ideologically and literarily (see J. Lindblom, in *Wisdom in Israel and in the Ancient Near East* [→ 15 above] 192–204). **23.** *way . . . step:* These two key words (*derek* and *ṣa'ad*) are common and technical in the wisdom literature; some of its passages are even very close to the present one (cf. Prov 16:9; 20:24; Ps 37:23). For the wise man, the "way" is nothing other than the sum of rules leading to a happy and successful life, which is entirely in God's hands. He has a mastering power over all his creation of which humanity is a part. **24.** God's educational punishment (*yāsar*) is another current theme of the wise men (cf. Ps 6:2; 38:2). The prophet opposes here two types of justice: one punishes evil according to its objective gravity; the other proportions the correction according to human weakness. This latter is the justice for which Jeremiah prays to the Lord.

(b) THE BROKEN COVENANT (11:1–13:27). Chapters 11–13 can be considered to form a small unity; a new title is set at the beginning of chap. 14. Principal stress is placed on the rupture of the covenant. **39** (i) *Jeremiah and the covenant* (11:1–14). This prophetic speech presents a very complex and much-discussed problem: What relation exists between Jer, Deut, and the Josian reform? A definite solution is still wanted, although a good number of its elements seem accepted. On the literary level, this is the most "deuteronomic" of all Jeremiah's prose speeches (see Thiel, *Die deuteronomistische Redaktion* (→ 7 above] 139–57); most critics accept at least a Jeremian kernel for this stern critique. **3.** *cursed:* All covenantal ceremonies were concluded by blessings if the stipulations had been respected and by curses if they had not. *terms of this covenant:* The same expression reappears in vv 6 and 8. It is frequently used in Deut, in an analogical form, for the Sinai covenant. Thus, it would be rash to hold that Jeremiah must evoke here exclusively the Deuteronomic Code. Moreover, the context itself recalls Sinai, as does the rest of the prophetic tradition, and Josiah's covenant is basically nothing more than the renovation of the primitive one. **5.** The verse corresponds to the "blessings" of the covenantal treaties. *milk and honey:* This expression is found not only in Jer and Deut (6:3; 11:8) but also in the Pentateuch (Exod 3:8; 13:5; Num 13:27; 14:8; Lev 21:24; etc.). The particular blessing mentioned here is the one promised to the patriarchs—i.e., the gift of Canaan (Gen 12:7; 13:15; etc.)—and renewed with Moses (Exod 3:8ff.; 23:27ff.) and Joshua (Josh 24). **7–8.** Although these verses are missing in the LXX, there are good reasons to affirm their authenticity—e.g., the "hardness of the heart" is properly Jeremian (cf. 7:24). However, because the passage is very similar to 7:24–26, some scholars believe that we have to deal here with an interpolation. The end of the speech brings forth the main accusation against the covenantal people, which is still idolatry. The prophet directs an inquiring eye over the whole history of Israel and notices that this way of breaking the covenant even dates to the "forefathers," the very ones who first contracted it. Judgment is inevitable; a disaster will sweep away the chosen people, for its false gods are unable to save anyone (cf. 2:28), and the prophet is forbidden even to intercede in its favor (cf. 7:16; 14:11).

40   We now turn to the problem already mentioned: What was Jeremiah's attitude toward Josiah's reform? For a time, the common opinion held that Jeremiah was sternly opposed to this deuteronomic renovation of the covenant. Most exegetes today believe that Jeremiah did approve Josiah's action, although they would differ in more than one detail. It will suffice to indicate only the clearest signs of this positive attitude. Two main figures are connected with the discovery of the law and its new application: the priest Hilkiah and the scribe Shaphan (2 Kgs 22). In the difficult hours of the prophet's life, the families of these two supported him (26:22; 29:3; 39:14; 40:5). Also, if Jeremiah had condemned the reform, we could hardly understand his eulogy of Josiah (22:15–16). Moreover, Jeremiah refers directly to the Deuteronomic Code in some of his incriminations against transgressions (e.g., 3:1; cf. Deut 24:1–4; 34:8ff.; Deut 15:12–18), and his constant attack on idolatry, especially worship of the astral gods, corresponds quite evidently to both the letter of Deut and the spirit of the reform; the centralization of the cult had no other purpose. Finally, the interiorization of religion, so strongly stressed in Jer, was already at work in Deut (6:4ff.; 10:12; 11:13; etc.; see von Rad, *OTT* 1. 223–31).

We will probably never know what part Jeremiah played in this reform; to see him as its busy missionary is more the work of our imagination. His approval might explain why we have practically no oracles that can be dated between this reform and Josiah's death (622–609). However, when the reform faded away, he spoke out: the Temple discourse and the present speech could hardly have a better historical context.

41   (ii) *Misplaced logia* (11:15–17).   **15.** The verse, obscure in the MT, is better preserved in the LXX (see Rudolph, *Jeremia* 78, 81); a superficial cult has no salvific value. **16.** In this oracle of doom, Judah is seen as a magnificent olive tree (cf. Hos 14:7) that will be burnt down. **17.** This prosaic verse is a later commentary on v 16.

42   (iii) *The plot against Jeremiah* (11:18–12:6).   A plot against Jeremiah's life, instigated by his immediate family and acquaintances, is discovered through some divine intervention. Jeremiah then experienced a shock that urged him to reflect on his mission and on the meaning of human existence. The text has suffered a certain violence that has been corrected in different ways; the transposition of 12:6 after 11:18 seems sufficient to give a logical sequence to the entire narrative. **19.** *lamb led to slaughter:* A figure of complete innocence and simple confidence; see Isa 53:7). The end of the verse tells clearly enough that the plot is one of murder. **20.** *of mind and heart:* A more literal trans. would be "of loins and heart." The expression occurs again in similar contexts (17:10; 20:12); elsewhere it is found only in Pss 7:10; 26:2, which we assume to be Jeremian. The "loins" (*kělāyōt*) were understood to be the seat of inner reflections and affections (Pss 16:7; 73:21; 139:13; Prov 23:16; Job 16:13; etc.). What Jeremiah asks then is the death of these men, according to the law of retaliation.

12:1–5. These verses deal with the perennial and difficult problem, the suffering of the just (cf. Pss 37, 73;

Job). **4a–b.** With Rudolph, we would omit this first part of the verse; it refers to a drought and could come from chap. 14. **5.** God's answer to Jeremiah's question could be compared to the one given to Job (38–41); in fact, God refuses to give a solution. Jeremiah has to keep faith and courage in his actual sufferings, for they are negligible compared to the ones to come.

These reflections of Jeremiah on his life and mission are the first of a series, known since Skinner as his "confessions" (15:10–21; 17:14–18; 18:18–23; 20:7–18). They have no parallel in the whole prophetic literature; their interpretation has given rise to a wide variety of opinions. It has been customary to read these fragments of strong protest as both spiritual and psychological traits of Jeremiah's personality; but as most of the expressions and formulas used are also found in psalms of lament, the present tendency is to set aside such an interpretation. H. G. Reventlow has been a strong advocate of the collective interpretation of these texts: here Jeremiah is functioning as a cult prophet, expressing to God his people's anguish in order to bring forth a change in fate. Others (Gunneweg, Welten, Vermeylen) would rather see in these prayers late exilic or postexilic reinterpretations of Jeremiah's mission and experience in order to give to the contemporary suffering community a model to look at in the midst of its physical as well as its spiritual hardships. Since there are a good number of characteristic Jeremian expressions in these texts, along with specific circumstances in which these prayers were composed, we are still justified in accepting the basic authenticity of an actual Jeremian experience as the source of these utterances. Recently two major works have been published on the literary aspect of these prayers (Hubmann) and their theology (Ittmann); their main conclusions give good support for the position adopted here.

(Reventlow, H. G., *Liturgie und prophetisches Ich bei Jeremia* [Gütersloh, 1963]. Gunneweg, A. H. J., *ZTK* 67 [1970] 399–416. Welten, P., *ZTK* 74 [1977] 123–50. Vermeylen, J., "Essai," *Le livre de Jérémie* 239–70. Hubmann, F. D., *Untersuchungen zu den Konfessionen* [Würzburg, 1978]. Ittmann, N., *Die Konfessionen Jeremias* [Neukirchen, 1981]. Polk, T., *The Prophetic Persona* [Sheffield, 1984].)

43   (iv) *Yahweh's complaint* (12:7–13).   This poem, set on Yahweh's lips, is in the *qînâ* (lamentation) form. Apart from v 9, which is quite obscure in the MT (see Rudolph, *Jeremia* 84), the subject matter is clear and simple: the Lord's house, Judah (cf. Hos 8:1; 9:15), has been ruined by a recent war. The event is told with a host of Jeremian symbols and images. **13.** We notice that the invader is no longer the "foe from the north," but "vultures," "beasts of the field," and "shepherds." Thus, most exegetes suggest that this invasion is the work of a coalition of several nations; therefore, the raids of Chaldean hordes, Arameans, Moabites, and Ammonites would be the historical background of this lament (2 Kgs 24:2–4). In the new Babylonian Chronicles, Nebuchadnezzar failed to invade Egypt in 601; this loss obliged him to return to Babylon and reorganize his army the following year (Wiseman, *Chronicles* 71). The setback probably incited Jehoiakim to revolt once more (2 Kgs 24:1); Nebuchadnezzar would have commissioned these neighboring nations to check the rebellion until he could come to settle it himself (598–597).

44   (v) *Death or life for Judah's neighbors* (12:14–17). In this disputed passage, Judah's neighbors are condemned to exile and extermination for their evildoing to Yahweh's heritage; however, if they convert to Yahwism they will be saved. The pericope has therefore the clear colors of the universalism and proselytism of several other OT passages (Isa 2:1-4 = Mic 4:1-3; 19:16-25; 56:6-8; 60:11-14; etc.). Because these texts are exilic or even postexilic, the present one would fall into the same period. Its redactor seems to have had in mind the intention to reactivate the general goal of Jeremiah's mission, since he uses here the basic vocabulary of his call narrative (1:10ff.).

45 (vi) *Two parabolic discourses* (13:1-14). These two discourses were bound by the key word *šāḥat*, "to destroy" (vv 7-8,14).

(1) The rotten loincloth (13:1-11). The narrative has often been explained as a symbolic action, so frequent among the prophets. These actions were dramatizations of a mesage so as to strike the attention of the hearers (→ Prophetic Lit., 11:23). The main difficulty here stands in the identification of the river *Pĕrāt*. In the OT, it is the name of the Euphrates, and it was thus understood in the LXX. Jeremiah had to walk twice to the Euphrates, some 700 mi. from Palestine, which seems unlikely; furthermore, there would be no or few witnesses of the symbolic action, which is contrary to its very intention. To avoid the difficulty, some have proposed a vision, real or symbolic (Penna, Rudolph, Weiser). To this we object that nothing in the narrative has the characteristics of a vision. It seems much simpler to hold that the symbolic action is purely a literary device; therefore, the discourse is to be interpreted as a parable.

However, the meaning of the story is clear enough (vv 9-11). The loincloth represents the people of God; the prophet is Yahweh himself. Previously, Jeremiah had denounced the alliances with Mesopotamia as a betrayal of the covenant (2:18). Such alliances were necessarily the occasion of religious corruptions by the recognition of foreign gods, exactly the object of the prophet's reproaches here (v 10), symbolized by the deteriorating effect of the Euphrates' waters.

(2) The broken wineflasks (13:12-14). This simple comparison of the whole people of Judah to broken wine jars presents no problem. A forthcoming destructive war will level the entire land.

46 (vii) *Threatening words* (13:15-27). Three oracles of doom, of different periods, conclude this section of the book.

(1) The dark night (13:15-17). Jeremiah gives a last warning to his people before the final blow: a sincere service of Yahweh might withhold the calamity—i.e., light will still be shining over the land. Otherwise, this very land will be cast into darkness, which seems to have a double significance, symbolizing both the invasion and the flight it will occasion (Isa 8:21-23; Amos 8:9).

(2) The exile (13:18-19). **18.** *queen mother:* Apparently she had an official role to play at the court (cf. 1 Kgs 2:19; 15:13), corroborated by the fact that her name is almost always mentioned in the introductions to new reigns in Kgs. According to 2 Kgs 24:12-15, Jehoiachin was exiled in Babylon with the queen mother Nehushta in 597, and Jeremiah specified the fact twice (22:26; 29:2). The present oracle certainly has to be understood in the light of this first deportation (cf. 2 Kgs 24:10-17).

(3) Incurable sickness (13:20-27). Jerusalem is doomed once again! The Babylonian victory at Carchemish in 605 could have been an excellent occasion for the prophet to give this last warning. **20-21.** Most of the expressions used here occur in the early oracles (chaps. 2-6). Even if the "foe from the north" is not called by his name, everyone knew who it could be. **22.** *you are violated:* Lit., "Your heels suffer violence"; the word "heels" is a euphemism. The meaning of this threat is

clear from the end of the pericope: Judah is assimilated to a prostitute because of her idolatrous practices (vv 25-27); as a punishment, she will be exposed in the nude (cf. Hos 2:5; Isa 47:2-3). Inasmuch as prostitution is a symbol for idolatry, such must be also the stripping of a woman for God's vengeance against this evil. **23.** To this well-known interrogation, a negative answer must be given. The sinful state of Judah has now taken a "natural" character, so to speak; through her repeated downfalls into idolatry, she has set herself in a permanent state of rupture with Yahweh. However, this extremely pessimistic view will be mildly corrected at the end of v 27, where a slight hope for conversion is still expected.

(c) CRIME AND PUNISHMENT (14:1-17:27). Chapters 14-17 can also be considered as a unit, for chap. 18 opens with a new title. The general theme remains the sins of the people and the vengeance of Yahweh.

47 (i) *The great drought* (14:1-15:9). This long pericope is a kind of lament on the calamities of a drought and a war. Although several poems can be distinguished, they are related through a unity of style—i.e., their life setting is the penitential liturgies; such liturgies were performed on the occasion of a catastrophe brought on by natural or political disturbances (see Joel 1-2; Pss 74,79).

(1) Drought (14:1-16). These verses form the first lamentation; after a short description of the plague (vv, 2-6), three different reflections follow (vv 7-9,10-12,13-16). **2-6.** The drought has brought the whole nature to a standstill, as if struck by death. This situation has thrown the population into mourning, whose sign is the veiling of one's head (v 4; cf. 1 Sam 15:30). **9.** *your name we bear:* Yahweh protects them by his salvific presence; this is precisely what the last words of the prayer ask for—"Do not forsake us!" **10-12.** This passage and the one following are written in prose. Here we have Yahweh's answer. First he addresses the people (v 10): their iniquities are unforgettable and must be punished (cf. Hos 8:13; 9:9). This evil is called a restless wandering, probably an allusion to the multiple idolatrous sanctuaries or to the frequent attempts to enter foreign alliances. Then Yahweh turns to the prophet (vv 11-12): his intercession will be in vain (7:16; 11:14), and the people's sacrifices are void (6:20; 7:21ff.; 11:15). Therefore, the three classical plagues—war, famine, and pestilence (5:12; 14:13,15-16; 27:8; 29:18; cf. 2 Sam 24:13)—are inevitable. **13-16.** Jeremiah still pleads for his people. They have an excuse for their evildoings because they were misled by the false prophets who continually promised peace and prosperity, even though the covenantal relationship had been broken (cf. 4:10; 5:12; 6:14; 8:11; 27:11; esp. 23:9ff.). This excuse is rejected for lack of foundation: Yahweh did not send these prophets, so their message can be nothing else but a product of their own imagination.

48 (2) Lament (14:17-15:4). Following Weiser, we take this pericope as a new poem, built on the plan of the previous one—a description of the plague, a collective lament, and Yahweh's answer. **17-18.** Now a war is shattering Judah, personified as a young woman mortally wounded (cf. 8:21; 10:19). **19-22.** This collective lament presents again all the characteristics of its kind (cf. vv 7-9). **21.** *throne of your glory:* The name given to the Temple (17:22) is here applied to Jerusalem (v 19a; cf. 3:17). **22.** This verse presupposes a context of drought and might have been taken from the first poem. The Canaanite Baal cult included rites for the assurance of rains necessary for the fertility of the fields; these rites were adopted by the Israelites in their idolatrous practices. The actual drought is now a proof of their inanity and at the same time an appeal to attribute their power to Yahweh (cf. 5:24; Hos 2:7ff.). **15:1–4.** This new divine answer parallels the preceding one (cf. 14:10–12). **1.** Moses and Samuel have always been considered great intercessors for their people (Exod 32:11–14; Num 14:11–25; 1 Sam 7:5–9; 12:19–23; Ps 99:6). The refusal to hear their prayers any longer indicates how irrevocable Yahweh's decision can be. **49** (3) Tragedy (15:5–9). This gloomy oracle addressed to Jerusalem is similar to the preceding poem. Nebuchadnezzar's invasion of Judah and Jerusalem in 597 might be the historical context of these pathetic verses. **9.** *mother of seven:* Even such a great blessing (1 Sam 2:5; Ruth 4:15) is changed to as great a curse, for the lives of these sons ("her sun") are taken away in their full strength ("full day"). **50** (ii) *The renewal of the call* (15:10–21). This fragment of the "confessions" (cf. 11:18ff.) was probably inserted here because it opens with a lament on the prophet's mother, recalling the end of the preceding passage (15:9). This complaint is cast in extremely severe terms. Jeremiah describes an inner crisis. There are clear references to the narrative of his call (1:4ff.); thus, the present one can be considered a renewal of this vocation, once the crisis has been overcome (cf. J. Bright, *Int* 29 [1974] 59–74). The crisis probably occurred during the difficult years under Jehoiakim. The text is not absolutely clear and seems to have undergone several stages of redaction (cf. E. Gerstenberger, *JBL* 82 [1963] 393–408). It is our opinion that it consists basically of two complaints of Jeremiah (vv 10,15–18), to which Yahweh answers (vv 11,19–21). In this context, vv 13–14 have to be a later addition, since their subject matter can refer to Judah only and since they are found again almost word for word in 17:3–4; we can then explain the obscure short v 12 as a corrupt evocation of the "iron tool" of 17:1. We could explain this addition as a quotation within the lamentation to justify Jeremiah's complaint: as Judah is doomed, why should he keep on preaching (cf. G. V. Smith, *VT* 29 [1979] 229–31). **10.** This curse will take on greater proportions later (cf. 20:14–18). It also brings to mind a similar one in Job 3:3. We remember that his call dated from his mother's womb; cursing the day of his birth would then mean nothing else but a rejection of his very mission. *a man of strife:* It is what Yahweh intended him to be (1:10). What brings persecution to him is not his just conduct toward everyone, but precisely his message. **11.** *I have strengthened you:* This meaning for the first vb. is obtained by simply changing the vocalization (*šārôtîkā*), and it suits the context perfectly: Jeremiah has no reason to complain about his hardships as Yahweh has been faithful to his promise to sustain him firmly (1:18–19). **15.** Jeremiah is not satisfied with the answer, for the facts contradict it; he expresses a strong desire for vengeance against his persecutors (11:20; 17:18; 20:11–12); this is a characteristic of the imprecatory psalms. Such a desire has to be understood in the perspective of earthly retribution. **16.** *your words:* Yahweh had placed his own words in the prophet's mouth (1:9), and Ezekiel had to eat a scroll inscribed with Yahweh's words; this is a dramatic definition of the prophet's mission as the minister of God's word (*dābār;* cf. Jer 18:18). *I bore your name:* The expression reveals a protective presence of God on his messenger (cf. 14:9). **18.** *treacherous brook:* During the summer, most Palestinian brooks dry up. Here and in Job 6:16–21 they symbolize a profound deception. Thus, Jeremiah boldly accuses Yahweh of having forsaken him (cf. 20:7)—the climax of the present crisis. **19–21.** Yahweh now renews and confirms the prophet's

mission, in the very terms of the first call (1:18–19; cf. H. W. Jüngling, *Bib* 54 [1973] 1–24), but this time it is not a gratuitous gift; it will only be conferred once Jeremiah has converted himself—i.e., when he has regained confidence in that very mission by rejecting these rebellious thoughts.

51 (iii) *Jeremiah's celibacy* (16:1–13,16–18). The prophetic word is delivered not only through symbolic actions but also sometimes through events of the prophet's own lives (Hos 1–3; Ezek 24:15–27), and here, Jeremiah's celibacy. In the ancient Near East, and thus in Israel, a large family was a divine blessing (Gen 22:17; Ps 127:3–4); sterility, on the contrary, was a terrible curse (Gen 30:1; 1 Sam 1:6–8). Jeremiah's celibacy could not have been his personal choice, but an order received from his Lord. **3–4.** The prophetic meaning of this single state is here given. The existing families will disappear, and violently. The privation of sepulture, a typical oriental curse, is reaffirmed in the same terms as before (cf. 7:33; 8:2; 9:21; 14:12; 15:3). **5–7.** *house of mourning:* The technical word *marzēaḥ* is attested in Amos 6:7 as well as in Ugaritic and Aramaic; its fundamental meaning refers to a celebration, most often in a cultic context. Here, however, the gathering of the mourners seems to take place in a domestic context (see J. Fabry, "Marzeaḥ," *TWAT* 5. 11–16). This solitary attitude of Jeremiah symbolizes Yahweh's withdrawal of the covenantal blessings: peace, love, and piety, all virtues of an ideal married life, which Jeremiah was forbidden to experience. **6.** *gash . . . shave:* Incisions, shaved heads, and beards were signs of mourning (41:5; 47:5; 48:37). **7.** *break bread . . . cup of consolation:* These funeral meals have been diversely explained: either they were taken at the occasion of a death or they were offered to the dead person (cf. Hos 9:4; Ezek 24:17,22; Deut 26:14). Tobit speaks clearly of food offered to the deceased (Tob 4:17), and the excavations of tombs prove that such offerings were really made (see de Vaux, *AI* 56–61). **8–9.** Even the joyful gatherings have to be avoided. "The voice of the bridegroom and the voice of the bride" must allude to nuptial songs at the occasion of marriages (cf. 7:34; 25:10; 33:11). **13.** *serve strange gods:* A condemnation to exile. Before the idea of strict monotheism was acquired, Yahweh was believed to exist only in Palestine (cf. 1 Kgs 5:17); therefore, if his worshipers leave this land, they are bound to serve other gods—those of the new land in which they find themselves (1 Sam 26:19). Jeremiah still shared this belief. **16–18.** The means of the punishment will be an invasion, figured by hunters and fishermen. **52** (iv) *Disjecta membra* (16:14–15,19–21; 17:1–18). A number of short oracles or simply fragments of longer ones have been placed in this part of the book, without any clear reasons.

(1) Return from exile (16:14–15). The passage reproduces 23:7–8, with minor differences. It is probably inserted here to attenuate the threatenings of the preceding oracle.

(2) Conversion of the heathen (16:19–21). The pericope recalls the poem on the vanity of idolatry (10:1–16) and the oracle on the salvation of the foreign nations (12:14–17), which we regarded as later additions to the book. It is similar in thought and is close to Isa 40:20; 42:8; 45:14–25; etc. We meet with the same negation of the existence of the gods and the conversion of the nations.

(3) Judah's guilt (17:1–4). This short oracle is similar to 16:16–18, on idolatry. The passage is lacking in the LXX and vv 3–4 are repeated out of context in 15:13–14. **1.** *an iron stylus:* The expression is attested to in Job 19:24, indicating the indelible character of an inscription. *tablets of their hearts:* This image, borrowed

from the writing techniques, reappears in Prov 3:3; 7:3, and once again in Jer with a variant (31:33). Sin and virtue are much more than mere external rejection or conformity to rules; they are the expressions of the very heart. Through this new image, Jeremiah stigmatizes this profound and permanent reality of sin.

53 (4) *Sapiential sayings (17:5-11)*. The authenticity of this small collection of wisdom is still highly disputed; in fact, no definitive arguments can be given for or against it. **5-8.** This first saying on "true justice" uses the antithetical synonymity and the literary form of the blessings and curses. The idea of the just man being like a green tree is common (Ps 52:10; Prov 3:18; 11:13; Sir 24:13ff.), as is also the opposition between the trust in God and the trust in humans (Pss 39:5; 117:8-9; 145:3ff.). But the closest parallel is Ps 1, where this opposition is expressed with the very same comparisons, also attested to in the wisdom of the Egyptian sage, Amenemope (6:1-12; cf. *ANET* 422). The saying intends to put across the real heart of true religion: God is one's sole refuge. **9-10.** This new saying concerns the root of evil, the human heart. The expression "probe the heart and test the loins" is properly Jeremian (cf. 11:20; 20:12; Pss 7:10; 64:7) and shows how constantly he upheld the primacy of the interior sentiments in religious life. **11.** The proverb quoted refers to a partridge that lays eggs but does not hatch them, since its nest must be the prey to many dangers; so it is with a treasure acquired unjustly: a man will benefit nothing from it.

54 (5) *The source of life (17:12-13)*. **12.** The verse has been rejected by many as contradictory to the Temple discourse (7:1ff.), but it is nothing more than the simple affirmation of Israel's belief from old. **13.** *miqwēh:* The "hope" of Israel is Yahweh; the word also means "pool," and Jeremiah may be playing on the double meaning of the word here since he again calls the God of Israel a "source of living waters" as in 2:13.

55 (6) *A prayer for vengeance (17:14-18)*. This is a third fragment of the "confessions" (cf. 11:18ff.; 15:10ff.). **15.** *let it come to pass:* That his prophecies of wars and exile are late in coming is the reason why he is now an object of scorn. He must be a dreamer. This "confession" probably dates before 597. **16.** Jeremiah's message is not his but Yahweh's, for the misfortunes predicted are painful to his love for his own land (4:19; 8:21-23; 13:17; 14:17). The prayer closes with the same desire of vengeance common to the imprecatory psalms (cf. R. Brandscheidt, *TTZ* 92 [1983] 61-78).

56 (v) *Observance of the sabbath (17:19-27)*. The present passage is usually listed in the "deuteronomic" speeches of Jer, and its authenticity is most disputed. The institution of the Sabbath is extremely old in Israel, for it figures in all four Pentateuch traditions (Exod 32:12; 34:21; 31:12-17; 20:8-10 = Deut 5:12-14) and is also mentioned in the 8th-cent. prophets (Amos 8:5; Isa 1:13; see J. Morgenstern, *IDB* 4. 135-41; de Vaux, *AI* 475-83). In general, it is an accepted opinion that the sabbatical rest assumed great importance after the exile and that Nehemiah took all the measures necessary to have its observance strictly kept. He went so far as to close the gates of Jerusalem (Neh 13:15-22). With this last text in mind, we understand much better why there is such an insistence on the prohibition of carrying burdens (vv 21-22,24), which does not figure in the former traditions, and why the admonishment is proclaimed at all the city gates. Moreover, it is not in Jeremiah's mentality to defend a law without giving its religious meaning and motives. For all these reasons, the speech would seem to have been composed at the time of Nehemiah. Nevertheless, we still hold that an authentic oracle stands at its origin, as the following remark

indicates. **19.** *the gate of the sons of my people:* Because the kings are passing through it, it must be a gate between the royal palace and the Temple courts. The mention of the "kings" is rather difficult to explain if the whole passage is postexilic; but if an original sermon of Jeremiah had been reworked at that time, the difficulty vanishes. **26.** Sacrifices will be brought from all over the land (for this list of different sacrifices, see de Vaux, *AI* 415-23; G. Couturier, *EgTh* 13 [1982] 5-34).

(d) SYMBOLIC MEANING OF THE PROPHET'S LIFE (18:1-20:18). The new title (v 1) is a sign of another small unit; its main subject matter consists in the prophetic meaning of some experiences in the prophet's life with the insertion of two new fragments of his "confessions."

57 (i) *A visit to the potter's (18:1-12)*. The inspiration of this narrative and sermon comes from an ordinary experience of Jeremiah later interpreted as the Lord's command. See C. Brekelmans, "Jeremiah 18:1-12," *Le livre de Jérémie* 343-50). **3.** *wheel:* Its structure was simple: two stone disks were united by a vertical axis; the lower disk was activated by the feet, while the clay, resting on the upper one, was fashioned by the hands as the disk kept turning (cf. Sir 38:29-30). **4.** This verse states the essential point of comparison in the prophetical oracle. **6.** The symbolism emerging from this workmanship is now specified. First, Yahweh is the potter; the anthropomorphism is old in Israel (cf. Gen 2:7). Second, the clay represents humanity; the idea that human begins are made of clay is also a very common idea in the Near East, and its origin correlates to that of the potter. **7-10.** A reflection on the prophetic meaning of the image, which is set not on the level of creation but on that of God's decrees. As a bad vase can be reshaped into a new one, so a decree of God can be changed to a new one, provided that conversion has been achieved. **7-8.** A decree of doom, expressed in the terms of 1:10, can be suspended by conversion; therefore, God does not act arbitrarily but takes the human will into consideration — a proof of the effective value of penance (cf. 7:3ff.; 26:3; 36:3; Ezek 18:21-27; Jonah 3). **9-10.** The opposite is also true. A blessing, expressed again in the terms of 1:10, can be changed to a curse if one lapses into sin. In other words, the author teaches clearly that the free will has an important role to play in both salvation and damnation, even though he does not enter into the complexity of the relation between divine necessity and human freedom. **11-12.** The potter's symbol is applied to Judah, but the prophet has no hope for its salvation, because Judah's evil heart (šěrîrût; cf. comment on 7:24) obstructs the way of conversion.

(ii) *Israel forgets Yahweh (18:13-17)*. The present oracle of doom has been connected artificially (v 13a) to the preceding sermon. Undoubtedly there exists a relationship between this passage and chap. 2; both deal with a flagrant apostasy of the people and use the literary form of the lawsuit (*rîb*). **14-15.** The prophet borrows from nature some examples of constant faithfulness, in contrast to Judah's constant unfaithfulness through idolatry (cf. 2:32; 8:7). The purpose of these images is to show how unnatural is idolatry for God's people. **16.** *shake their heads:* This action, often joined to the one of "hissing," is a sign of derision and mockery (19:8; 48:27). **17.** *show my back:* By its apostasy, the people was said to have turned its back to Yahweh (2:27); therefore, Yahweh has rejected his people.

58 (iii) *Another prayer for vengeance (18:18-23)*. **18.** The motive of this new plot against Jeremiah is his message (11:19ff.). The three classes of spiritual leaders were characterized by the technical term attached to each function: the priestly instruction (*tôrâ*, "law"; cf. 2:18), the prophetic word (*dābār*), and the sapiental counsel ('*ēṣâ*). The full activity of all these functions will not be suspended by the suppression of Jeremiah. **19–23.** A new fragment of the "confessions" follows, presenting all the characteristics of these compositions (cf. 15:10–21; see F. D. Hubmann, "Jer 18:18–23," *Le livre de Jérémie* 271–96).

59   (iv) *The broken flask and Topheth* (19:1–20:6). This section of Jer lacks unity, as most scholars recognize today. The accepted opinion is that a narrative from Baruch's memoirs has been disrupted by interpolations of an oracle or oracles on Topheth.

(1) The broken flask (19:1,2bc,10–11a,14–20:6). We deal here with another symbolic action that shows the dynamic aspect of the prophetic word (cf. 13:1–14). The story is enacted in the presence of a small group of elders and priests at the entrance of the Potsherd Gate (v 2). This gate is mentioned only here; it must be located at the S end of the city, for a contemporary tradition specifies that it opens on the Valley of Ben-Hinnom (v 6). **10–11a.** The symbolic action proper consists in the smashing of a juglet, which recalls some magic rites often attested in the ancient Near East. In Egypt, one rite dating to the old kingdom consisted in writing the names of enemy people and cities on jars and figurines that would then be smashed to pieces; such an action was supposed to bring about the destruction of those whose names were written down on these objects (see J. A. Wilson, *The Culture of Ancient Egypt* [Chicago, 1951] 156–58). However, the magical value of such actions is out of place here. Yahweh alone will realize the curse, for the smashing of the juglet is but a dramatic illustration: "I smash this people . . . as one smashes a clay pot" (v 11a). **14.** *returned from Topheth:* The oracle first proclaimed at the gate is now repeated in the court of the Temple, thus provoking the anger of the Temple's chief officer. The word "Topheth" is probably not original; it replaced a similar one like "entrance" (*petah*) or "entrance of the gate" (v 2b), when the oracle on Topheth was later inserted (Rudolph, Volz, Bright). **20:1.** *Pashhur:* He must be different from the other Pashhur mentioned in 21:1 and 38:1ff. The prediction of his exile (v 6) probably occurred in 597, for in 594 another priest was holding his office, consisting mainly in the organization of the police guard to watch over the activities going on in the Temple courts (cf. 29:25–26). **3.** *terror on every side: Māgôr missābîb* is the *omen* of Pashhur's *nomen*. The expression certainly hides a pun that is still obscure, for the very meaning of *Pašḥûr* is uncertain; the word is probably of Egyptian origin (cf. M. Görg, *BN* 20 [1983] 29–33). "Terror on every side" is another Jeremian creation (6:25; 20:3,10; 46:5; 49:29), later used in Lam 2:22 and Ps 32:14. **4–6.** Jeremiah now renders more explicit the prophetic meaning of this new name: Judah and Pashhur's household will be exiled and Jerusalem will be plundered. For the first time, he calls the invader by name—Babylon. **60**   (2) Topheth (19:2a,3–9,11b–13). This discourse interrupts the story of the broken flask. **2a.** *Valley of Ben-Hinnom:* At times just called Valley of Hinnom (*gê' hinnōm*, our "Gehenna"), the valley is identified with the actual Wadi er-Rababi, running at first southward on the W side of Jerusalem and then turning sharply to the east on the S side. **3.** *kings of Judah and citizens of Jerusalem:* This vast audience, in full contrast to the small one mentioned in v 1, is a sign that two different events have been amalgamated. *ears tingle:* The expression is found elsewhere only in 1 Sam 3:11 and 2 Kgs 21:12, as the sign of a catastrophe unheard of before. **4.** *blood of the innocent:* A clear reference to child sacrifice (cf v 5; 7:31). Human sacrifices existed in the ancient Near East, esp.

in Phoenicia and Canaan (cf. A. R. W. Green, *The Role of Human Sacrifice* [Missoula, 1975]). In Israel, such a practice was condemned quite early. Child sacrifice is strictly prohibited (Lev 18:21; 20:2–5; Deut 12:31; 18:10). The law of the redemption of the firstborn child (Exod 34:20), for he belonged naturally to God (Exod 13:2; 22:28; 34:19; Num 3:13; 8:17), is another sign of this major cult correction. However, these sacrifices were revived under Ahaz (2 Kgs 16:3; cf. Mic 6:7) and Manasseh (2 Kgs 21:6). The sanctuary of the Hinnom Valley was then destroyed by Josiah, at the time of the reform (2 Kgs 23:10); the present text proves that Jehoiakim had reopened it. **6.** *Topheth:* The name derives probably from a root *tāpā'*, meaning originally "hearth" or "fireplace." According to the texts and extrabiblical sources, the victims were actually burnt. *Valley of Slaughter:* Here, again, a new name is given as a sign of doom. **9.** To the other evils often mentioned, Jeremiah adds a new one: the siege will be so long and so strict that the people will be forced to eat the flesh of their own children. This threat (Deut 28:53; Lev 26:29; Ezek 5:10) became real in Samaria during the Aramean wars (2 Kgs 6:26ff.) and also in Jerusalem during its last siege (Lam 2:20; 4:10). **11b–13.** Topheth and the whole city will become impure by the contact with dead bodies (cf. Lev 21:1ff.; Num 5:2; 19:11–22). *host of heaven:* The Mesopotamian astral divinities are thus designated (cf. 7:16–20).

61   (v) *Jeremiah's despair* (20:7–18). The redactor who inserted this last fragment of Jeremiah's "confessions" right after the prophet's altercation with Pashhur intended probably to give the event as the occasion of Jeremiah's most dramatic interior crisis. The text can be divided easily in three different parts: an individual lament (vv 7–10) and a self-curse (vv 14–18) encircle a prayer of confidence (vv 11–13; cf. D. J. A. Clines, *ZAW* 88 [1976] 390–409). **7.** *you duped me:* The vb. *pātâ* means "to seduce" and is used in the case of a virgin being seduced by a man (Exod 22:15). Quite often, it simply means "to deceive" and is applied to false prophets being duped by Yahweh (1 Kgs 22:19–23; Ezek 14:9; etc.). We see how daring Jeremiah's address to God could be! *you seized me:* The vb. *ḥāzaq*, "to seize," figures also in the context of sexual seduction (Deut 22:25; 2 Sam 13:11, 14; Prov 7:13); the imagery of the first part of the verse is maintained here. Jeremiah had already called his God "a treacherous brook" (15:18), but here the reproach is much bolder: Yahweh tricked his messenger! **8.** Jeremiah has been sent "to root up and to tear down, to build and to plant" (1:10); until now his message corresponded only to the first part of the program. Therefore, he had to face constant persecutions. He had been deceived, for if he could have built and planted, the situation would have been different. **9.** The verse is important for the study of the prophetic inspiration; its urge is irresistible. Yahweh is said to be a "consuming fire" (Exod 24:17; Deut 4:24; 9:3; Isa 33:14); only Jeremiah applied it directly to his word (cf. 5:14; 23:29). **10.** *terror on every side:* This Jeremian outcry (cf. 20:3) is now turned against the prophet in derision and mockery, a fact justifying the present lament. **11–13.** This authentic passage is often believed to be out of context, for its deep tone of confidence is a break in the prophet's depression. Rudolph's remark might be true: In a psychological and spiritual crisis like Jeremiah's, what we should expect is not logic but a real conflict of sentiments. **11.** This confidence has its foundation in Yahweh's promise (1:8,19), which the prophet often recalled (15:20). In the midst of strong contradictions he keeps his faith in Yahweh's loyalty. **13.** *the poor:* Hebr *'ebyôn* had already exceeded its sociological meaning to take on a religious tone; it refers to the pious man, the "client of Yahweh" (see A. Gelin, *The Poor of Yahweh* [Collegeville, 1953]). Again in several psalms of the "just sufferer," we have the same combination of themes: an appeal to glorify the Lord for he has taken care of the poor (cf. Pss 22:23ff.; 35:9–10,27–28; 109:30–31; 140:13–14). **14–18.** Jeremiah now gives full expression to his cursing of the day of his birth (cf. 15:10), for the crisis has reached its peak. The author of Job 3:3–12 uses the same language to express a similar distress; there is a real kinship between the two curses. **16.** *cities:* Sodom and Gomorrah (Gen 19); cf. Jer 23:14).

62 **(D) The Ministry under Zedekiah (21:1–24:10).** The forthcoming chapters have to be considered as a unit, dealing with two subjects: the kings and the prophets. Most of these oracles can be dated under Zedekiah (597–587); they were probably collected toward the end of his reign to reveal the main authors of the imminent final catastrophe. In chaps. 21–43 two basic positions on the future of God's people are laid out: life will continue in Judah through a small group around Gedaliah, and Jeremiah or the exiles of 597 will be the starting point of a renewed covenant. Both positions might have been proposed by Jeremiah under the fire of the present historical turmoil (see K.-F. Pohlmann, *Studien zum Jeremiabuch* [→ 6 above] and C. R. Seitz, "The Crisis of Interpretation," *VT* 35 [1985] 78–97).

(a) A CONSULTATION FROM ZEDEKIAH (21:1–10). This consultation took place during the siege of Jerusalem by Nebuchadnezzar, probably at its very beginning in 588. Similar consultations will be repeated (cf. chaps. 37–38). **1.** *Pashhur, son of Malchiah:* Different from the Pashhur in 20:1ff., as their fathers' names show; not too long after this consultation, Pashhur will be violently opposed to the prophet (38:1ff.). *Zephaniah:* A member of another delegation by Zedekiah (37:3); at the downfall of Jerusalem, he will be made prisoner (2 Kgs 25:18). **2.** Zedekiah expects Yahweh to repeat now what he did in 701, when Sennacherib besieged Jerusalem (2 Kgs 19:35–36 = Isa 37:36–37); the situations were too much alike not to ask for the same outcome, but Yahweh's answer ruins such hope. **5.** *I myself will fight against you:* Yahweh presents himself now as his own people's enemy, which is a very strong denial of all the covenantal ties. His enmity will be exercised by using the Chaldeans as his personal weapon. **8–10.** This answer to the whole people is repeated almost word for word in 38:2–3, not necessarily a doublet. *life and death:* This choice does not appear in 38:2–3. The proposal of surrender to the Chaldeans has occasioned all kinds of speculation on Jeremiah's political theory. We believe that his first principle is quite simple; Yahweh has abandoned his people because of their infidelities and Jerusalem's downfall is now inevitable. Slaughter can be avoided only by nonresistance and peaceful surrender. Such an attitude can hardly be called collaboration with the enemy.

63 (b) BOOKLET ON KINGS (21:11–23:8). The present section, as well as the following one on the prophets, probably existed in a separate form, as the titles seem to indicate (21:11a and 23:9a), before their insertion in Jer. We find references to all five kings under whom Jeremiah fulfilled his mission.

(i) *A general address to the royal house* (21:11–22:9). We note the double meaning of the Hebr word *bayit*, "dynasty" and "palace"; indeed, both realities are concerned in the following oracles, united as a general introduction to those on the individual kings. **12.** The collection opens with a general recommendation to the

king as guardian of justice, one of the main duties attached to the sacral kingship in the Near East. In Israel, this obligation was never lost; Solomon made it one of the elements of his prayer to Yahweh (1 Kgs 3:9; 8:32) and the royal psalms gave it a great importance (45:4–8; 72:1–4,12–14).

64 (1) Jerusalem (21:13–14; 22:6–7). These lines, joined to the preceding through the word "fire" (21:12–14; 22:7), deal with both Jerusalem and its palace. The inviolability of the city due to the presence of God in the Temple (cf. 7:1–15) is no longer a reality. **13.** *valley-site:* The word *'ēmeq* is probably an additional explanation of the word *mîšōr* (plain), for Jerusalem is surrounded only by deep valleys that could hardly be called "plains." On every side, except on the north, the city was naturally well defended. **14.** *I will punish . . . deserve:* This prosaic sentence is lacking in the LXX and is foreign to the oracle. *forest:* Because there is no forest in Jerusalem, it must designate the royal palace (cf. the "Hall of the Forest of Lebanon" 1 Kgs 7:2–4). If the "forest" is the palace, its "surroundings" is the city itself. **22:6.** *for thus says:* This title was added once the oracle had been separated by another. *Gilead, Lebanon:* These two regions were noted for their forests (2 Sam 18:6–9); the comparison is then natural. **7.** For the same reason, we understand why the Babylonians are called "woodcutters."

65 (2) Duty toward justice (22:1–5). This further development, in deuteronomic prose, is of the king's duty toward justice (21:12). As in the texts already quoted, the welfare and continuity of the dynasty depend on its fidelity to this duty (vv 4–5). What Jeremiah asks of the kings he has already asked of the people in his Temple discourse (cf. 7:1ff.). **3.** The protection that these three classes of the weak deserve is a firm covenant stipulation (Exod 22:20–26; 23:9; Lev 19:33–34; Deut 10:18–19; 24:17). If the king himself ought to fulfill it, it shows that the Mosaic and Davidic covenants were essentially the same. *innocent blood:* A clear allusion to child sacrifice at Topheth (cf. 19:2–3).

66 (3) Idolatry (22:8–9). This short pericope is an exilic addition (cf. 5:19) in the style of two deuteronomic passages (Deut 29:23–25; 1 Kgs 9:8–9). Idolatry is finally understood as being the basic rupture of the covenant (Exod 20:3; Deut 6:4).

67 (ii) *Jehoahaz* (22:10–12). According to 1 Chr 3:15, Jehoahaz was Josiah's fourth son and is also called Shallum. He was put on the throne by "the people of the land" (see J. A. Soggin, *VT* 13 [1963] 187–95) after his father's death at Megiddo in 609 (2 Kgs 23:30). Most historians hold that "Jehoahaz" is his coronation name and that his popular election manifested the will of the followers of Josiah's reform, i.e., the anti-Egyptian party. The prophet transfers the mourning from the "dead" Josiah to Jehoahaz, who is "going away." In fact, his reign lasted only three months, for he was deposed by Neco (2 Kgs 23:31ff.). **11–12.** A repetition in prose of the oracle of v 10.

68 (iii) *Jehoiakim* (22:13–19). Jeremiah's philippic against Jehoiakim is one of his sternest oracles. Jehoiakim was a typical oriental despot (Rudolph) who rejected his father's reform. Because he was chosen by Neco to succeed his brother (2 Kgs 23:34), he must have been a partisan of the Egyptian party. Jeremiah contrasts him with Josiah to show how far he is from fulfilling the idea of true kingship. **13–14.** The first attack is directed at the king's luxurious buildings, constructed at the expense of the people. The retention of salary was a direct offense against the law (Lev 19:13; Deut 24:14–15); the king, by office, had to secure its observance, and he himself is found guilty of its violation. **15–16.** In full contrast to

Jehoiakim, Josiah is given as the perfect model of the true covenantal king. **17.** Jehoiakim was attached to his "own gain" through his buildings; he favored idolatry by reactivating the sanctuary of Topheth (2 Kgs 24:3–4), and he committed "violence," as is illustrated later in his dealings with the true prophets (cf. 26:20ff.; 36). **18–19.** The divine judgment is pronounced over the impious king. In v 18 we are given formulas of lamentation (cf. 1 Kgs 13:30). The burial of an ass (v 19; cf. 36:30) remains a problem, because Jehoiakim seems to have had a normal burial (2 Kgs 24:6).

69   (iv) *Jehoiachin* (22:20–30). Jehoiakim's 18-year-old son succeeded him on the throne for a short reign of three months (2 Kgs 24:6–8). He was exiled to Babylon, with the queen mother and the Judean noblemen, when Nebuchadnezzar first took Jerusalem in March 597 (2 Kgs 24:10–16; Wiseman, *Chronicles* [→ 2 above] 73). The oracle is a little complex and can be divided into three parts: vv 20–23; vv 24–27; vv 28–30.

20–23. Grammatically (vbs. and suffixes are in the fem.) and ideologically, these verses refer to Jerusalem itself. If we remember that the siege and capture of the city covered Jehoiachin's entire reign, such an introduction has its place here. **20.** Jerusalem considers its ruin from all the surrounding heights: Lebanon, N; Bashan, NE of Transjordan; and on the wedge of N Moab overlooking the Jordan Valley, the mounts of Abarim, whose main peak is Mt. Nebo (Num 27:12; Deut 32:49). *lovers:* The term usually designates the idols or the foreign nations; here, it refers to Judah's own leaders (cf. v 22). **21.** The cause of the ruin is the people's refusal to obey ever since its origin (cf. 2:31; 3:24; 7:24ff.; 11:7ff.). **23.** Jerusalem is compared to a high cedar of Lebanon.

24–27. This first address to Jehoiachin, in prose, must have been uttered at the time of the events in 597, for what we read in Kgs is practically predicted in detail. **24.** *Coniah:* The abbreviated form of the king's name (37:1). *signet ring:* Rings bearing seals of important men were carefully kept, for they were used to stamp official documents (cf. Hag 2:24); thus Yahweh abandons the king to his own fate. **26.** *mother:* See comment on 13:18. *there you shall die:* Although Jehoiachin was released under Evil-merodach, he had to stay in Babylon where he did die (2 Kgs 25:27–30 = Jer 52:31–34).

28–30. This second oracle addresses the king as though he were already in exile. **29.** *land:* It is solemnly called to attention, probably as a witness of the final judgment pronounced on Jehoiachin (see chap. 2, the "*rîb*" pattern). **30.** *childless:* Contradicted by 1 Chr 3:17–18. However, Jeremiah specifies the meaning he attached to the adjective: none of Jehoiachin's descendants will ascend the throne. Zerubbabel, his grandson (1 Chr 3:19), returned to Jerusalem after the exile as high commissioner, not as king. Jeremiah knew well that the exiled king's history was over, not from speculations on political combinations but from insight into a different plan—i.e., Yahweh's plan (Rudolph).

70   (v) *The future king* (23:1–8). The oracles on the individual kings have followed a chronological order. Therefore, we would expect to read now an oracle on Zedekiah, but the prophet changes the perspective; the last king of Judah provides only his own name, transformed (v 6), in the proclamation of a new, messianic era. The present state of this description of the future also results from the combination of various short oracles.

1–4. This first oracle, in prose, concerns both the "shepherds" and the "flock." We can find a similar but longer oracle in Ezek 34 (cf. N. Mendecki, *Kairos* 25 [1983] 99–103). **1–2.** We may accept these oracles as authentic, since the bad shepherds, the kings, are still active; however, Yahweh is already at work to bring upon them his judgment. Indeed, all the last kings of Judah met tragic ends. **3–4.** Now Jeremiah turns to the people, in terms similar to the ones of another passage (cf. 3:14–18). Their perspective is that of the restoration of the people after the exile, with the full realization of the covenant's purposes, including true leaders.

5–6. The poetic oracle on the "Shoot of David" is certainly authentic. **5.** *days are coming:* Simply a way of calling attention to a very solemn proclamation (cf. 7:32). *righteous shoot:* The word *ṣemaḥ,* along with a synonymous expression in Isa 11:1, became a classic term for the Messiah (Zech 3:8; 6:12). The adjective *ṣaddîq* could refer to a "legitimate" heir of the Davidic dynasty (cf. J. Swetnam, *Bib* 46 [1965] 29–40). **6.** Both Israel and Judah will share this messianic salvation; Jeremiah never forgot his own homeland (cf. chaps. 30–31). *Yahweh our justice:* The future king's name is a wordplay on Zedekiah's own name; *Yhwh ṣidqēnû,* "Yahweh is our justice," compared to *ṣidqî-yāhû,* "my justice is Yahweh," presents only a change of the pronominal suffixes and of the position of itself (cf. J. J. Stamm, "Der Name Zedekia," *De la Tôrah au Messie* [→ 13 above] 227–35). The word "justice" here must be given its full meaning, which includes God's salvific presence and action (Judg 5:11; 1 Sam 12:7; Isa 45:24; Ps 103:6). The solemnity of the oracle certainly points to a new era. But just what is that era? The answer depends much on one's notion of messianism proper and of its relation to eschatology (→ OT Thought, 77:152–67). We believe that Jeremiah spoke of a royal messianism that is closely bound to history. The forthcoming bliss is not fixed at the end of time but at the end of a particular time that has turned bad. Moreover, the messianism here proposed is nothing more than the absolute fulfillment of sacred kingship as the means chosen by Yahweh to realize the blessings of the covenant—the peace and the justice of his people in the promised land. This ideal kingship has been defined in Nathan's prophecy (2 Sam 7) and repeated in the royal psalms (Pss 2,45,72,89,110). Prophets, in dark periods when the kings were unfaithful, recalled this very ideal and promised its realization in the future, using terms found in our present passage (see Isa 9:5–6; 11:1–9; Mic 5:1–5; Amos 9:11; Hos 3:5). Therefore, like his predecessors, Jeremiah predicts the restoration of David's dynasty, not so much on political grounds as on the level of the religious and moral obligations of the covenant. For further study see S. Mowinckel, *He That Cometh* [Oxford, 1956] 155–86; T. Mettinger, *King and Messiah* [Lund, 1976]; H. Cazelles, *Le Messie de la Bible* [Paris, 1978]; K. W. Whitelam, *The Just King* [Sheffield, 1979]; J. Becker, *Messianic Expectation in the Old Testament* [Phl, 1980]).

7–8. These lines are also read in 16:14–15, where they are out of context. They predict a return from exile of northern Israel in terms of a new exodus. We have no reason to suspect that they are not authentic, for Jeremiah had such a hope (cf. chaps. 30–31, esp. 31:7–14). However, their connection with the preceding oracle is rather loose; the fact that the LXX located them after 23:40 is a sign of a fluctuation in the tradition.

71   (c) BOOKLET ON THE PROPHETS (23:9–40). A second collection of oracles is relative to a class of leaders in Israel, the prophets, who have also done wrong; Jeremiah never stopped denouncing them (2:8; 4:9; 5:31; 6:13–15; 14:13–16). We can see in these different oracles the main criteria used by the Jeremian tradition to identify the authentic transmitter of the word of God. This catalogue and its subject matter have recently been the focus of major studies (H.-J. Kraus, *Prophetie in der Krisis* [Neukirchen, 1964] ; T. W. Overholt, *The Threat of*

Falsehood [→ 7 above]; F. L. Hossfeld and I. Meyer, *Prophet gegen Prophet* [Fribourg, 1973]; I. Meyer, *Jeremia und die falschen Propheten* [Fribourg, 1977]; the relative value of the various arguments listed here is also well assessed in the analysis of G. Münderlein (*Kriterien wahrer und falscher Prophetie* [Bern, 1979]). **9-12.** These introductory verses do not address the false prophets directly; they are Jeremiah's complaint, recalling his early preaching, on the universal corruption of Judah (cf. 5:1ff.; 9:1ff.). At such a sight, Jeremiah is taken with pain; these accents were heard once before (4:19). The adulterous state of the land has been caused by both idolatry and moral deprivation (cf. 5:7-8); the priests and prophets also have a share in these evildoings. The punishment to come is symbolized by a walk through the night on a slippery road (v 12; cf. Isa 18:21-23; Ps 35:6). **13-15.** The first characteristic of the false prophets is their moral conduct. Jeremiah establishes a comparison between those in Samaria and those in Jerusalem; both groups are found guilty. **16-22.** A second way to recognize false prophets is to look at the object of their message. They are but flatterers of the popular passions, always foretelling peace even if evil prevails; thus, they are liars, victims of their own imagination (cf. 6:14; 8:11; Mic 3:5). **19-20.** The verses are also read in 30:23-24 and are out of context in both places. They are usually considered inauthentic because of their strong apocalyptical trend. **21.** The verse is the logical sequence of 17. These prophets have not been sent; therefore, the divine mission is another sign of true prophecy (cf. 14:14; 27:15; 29:9). **22.** *council:* We translate thus the Hebr word *sôd,* "group of friends" (Ps 55:15; Job 19:19; Jer 6:11; etc.). It also designates the assembly of God and his "divine" councillors, well illustrated in 1 Kgs 22:19ff. and Job 1-2. This motif is attested in the Canaanite and Mesopotamian mythology. The purpose of such an assembly is to fix the "destinies" of the new year; in Israel, the creation of humanity and certain major events of history seem to have been its primary concern (cf. G. Couturier, "La vision du conseil divin," *ScEs* 36 [1984] 5-43). **23-32.** A final criterion is the form of communication; in itself, the dream has nothing in common with the word of God. Dreams served to reveal the call of the gods, but they were not very frequent in Israel (Num 12:6; 1 Sam 28:6; 1 Kgs 3:4ff.; Job 33:15-16). They are formally rejected as a means of revelation (27:9; Deut 13:1ff.; Zech 10:2; cf. E. L. Ehrlich, *Der Traum im AT* [Berlin, 1953]. **23-24.** These difficult verses could be explained as Jeremiah's own view on those dreams. The God of Israel is one who is very close to humankind, no one can pretend to be able to manipulate him for his own benefits, as these false prophets do; they should recognize and respect his transcendence, setting him on a level proper to his nature (cf. W. Lemke, *JBL* 100 [1981] 541-55). **33-40.** The end of the booklet is a development on one word. **33.** A technical term for oracle is *maśśā'*, derived from the vb. *nāśā',* "to lift up" (see W. McKane, "*Maśśā'* in Jer 23:33-40," *Prophecy* [→ 7 above] 35-54), but the same word also means "burden." The question was, *mâ-maśśā',* "What is the oracle?" And, following P. Wernberg-Møller's emendations (*VT* 6 [1956] 315-16), the answer given is, *'attēmâ maśśā',* "You are the burden." **34-40.** A very complicated justification of the avoidance of the term *maśśā':* Yahweh himself has forbidden its use, but we are not told why.

72 (d) THE TWO BASKETS OF FIGS (24:1-10). The closing chapter of this section brings us back to the opening one (21:1-10), with the same condemnation of Zedekiah and of those who survived the siege of 597. Chapter 24 narrates a prophet's vision similar to those in 1:11ff., and esp. to Amos's vision of the "basket of ripe

fruit" (Amos 8:1-3). In all these instances we meet with the same literary structure: the vision itself, a question from Yahweh, the prophetic meaning of the vision. We still hold here that we have to deal with the prophet's concrete experience expressed in this literary form. **1.** *placed before the Temple:* These words suggest that the figs were firstfruit offerings (Deut 26:2-11); but how is it possible to offer bad ones? Penna's hypothesis that the Temple has a simple symbolic meaning is enlightening; because the Temple is not inviolable (cf. 7:1ff.), it is therefore certain that those who will survive the downfall of 597 will be definitively rejected. *this was after:* This chronological datum is a short summary of 2 Kgs 24:14-16; the oracle occurred in 597, or soon after. **5-7.** The explanation of the vision begins. The good figs represent the exiles of 597. Surprisingly enough, they are now the choice portion of the people who will constitute the new Israel. **6.** *build . . . plant:* Jeremiah is now called to fulfill the second part of his mission (1:10). **7.** The new Israel will be faithful to the covenant because the Lord will change its heart. It is only when Israel will "know" Yahweh or observe his law wholeheartedly that the covenant really will be concluded. This change of heart will be at the center of the new covenant (cf. 31:33). For the Israelites, the heart (*lēb*) is not the seat of love and emotions, but of the mind and the will. **8-10.** The bad figs are all those who stayed in Palestine after 597, including the king and the noblemen. They considered themselves to be the choice portion of Yahweh, for they had escaped exile, whereas those who had been exiled were justly punished for their evil deeds. Jeremiah overturns such a belief, as Ezekiel does in a similar speech (Ezek 11:14-21). **8.** *settled in the land of Egypt:* The colony might have originated in 609 when Jehoahaz had been taken there (2 Kgs 23:34); it is also possible that partisans of the pro-Egyptian party had fled at the arrival of Nebuchadnezzar's armies in 598. **9-10.** The sentence pronounced on the "bad figs" uses a host of Jeremian expressions for doom (15:4; 21:7; 29:18; 34:17; see also Deut 28:37; Ps 44:14-15).

73 (E) A Foreword or Epilogue? (25:1-13b). Commentators agree in taking the present pericope as a summary of Jeremiah's ministry until the year 605-604, for it is dated exactly in the fourth year of Jehoiakim (v 1). Besides, a reference to a written book is given (v 13), and we know that in the same year Jeremiah dictated all his oracles to Baruch (chap. 36). There must be a relation between this passage and that book; we are inclined to take it as either its superscription or its epilogue. The many differences between the MT and the LXX are a sign of editorial amplifications (L. Laberge, *ScEs* 36 [1984] 45-66). In general, the critics agree to drop the following: all the references to Nebuchadnezzar and the Chaldeans, for in 605 the invader was still left in the shadow; the ending of vv 3-4, a gloss taken from 7:25-26; v 6, which interrupts the sequence of vv 5 and 7a; 7b, which is lacking in the LXX; "and against all these neighboring nations" in v 9, because the scroll contained only the oracles against Judah (cf. v 1); v 12, because the oracle against Babylon was also excluded. The text thus relieved of these glosses gives a logical and clear summary of Jeremiah's preaching. **5.** Jeremiah sums up his message in the necessity of conversion, for it is the basic condition for the fulfillment of the promises of the covenant (cf. 3:1-4:2). If it is not realized, punishment will follow (still expressed in the general terms of an invasion from the north; cf. v 8; 1:15; 4:6; 6:1ff.). **9.** *my servant:* Nebuchadnezzar is addressed as a "servant" (*'ebed*) of Yahweh; the title does not imply necessarily that he is a faithful follower of Yahwism, but simply that he plays the role of an instrument in God's hands for the punishment of Judah. *I will execrate them:* At the time of the conquest, the Israelites were to observe the law of *ḥērem,* which was essential to the holy war, consisting in the extermination of all living beings as a sacrifice to their God (Josh 2:10; 6:21; 8:26; 10:1,28). Now Judah must undergo the same fate since it turned itself into an enemy of its own God. **10.** There will be no more joy (7:34; 16:9). The halting of the millstone and the blowing out of the lamp are signs of the cessation of life (cf. Eccl 12:3–6). **11.** *seventy years:* This prediction (cf. 29:10), which is certainly at the origin of 2 Chr 36:31 and Dan 9:2, has been the subject of ample and frequent discussions. If we remember that 70 is often a symbol of "many" (cf. Judg 1:7; 8:14; 1 Sam 6:19; 2 Sam 24:15; Ps 90:10; etc.), then we would think that Jeremiah only intended a long period without any specification of time. The hypothesis has an extrabiblical confirmation, for an Assyrian text uses the same number to indicate simply an indefinite period (see E. Vogt, *Bib* 38 [1957] 236).

74   **(F) Judgment on the Nations (25:13c–38).** In this new section, Jeremiah acts as "a prophet to the nations" (1:5). The LXX presents these prophecies immediately (25:14–31:44) and sets the opening oracle at their end (32:13–38). On the contrary, the MT reads all these oracles at the end of the book and keeps here only the opening one. We shall discuss this problem later (→ 109 below).

Whatever be the original position of the oracles now placed in chaps. 46–51, the present discourse served as either a prologue or an epilogue to the whole collection. Considering its position in the LXX and the parallel problem of 25:1–13b in its relation to the first part of the book, we take it to be a closing summary of the prophet's new activity. **15–17,27–29.** The symbol of a cup of judgment has its probable origin in the ordeal procedures; the effect of the drink will be a confirmation of the guilt of the culprit (cf. Num 5:11–31; see W. McKane, *VT* 30 [1980] 474–92). The cup of wine symbolizes here the avenging wrath of the Lord (49:12; Hab 2:15–16; Ezek 32:32–34; Isa 51:17–23; Lam 4:21; Pss 60:5; 75:9). **18–26.** The list of nations breaks the logical sequence of the preceding passage; it was added once the oracles were put at the end of the book. The following four geographical names are missing in the LXX: Uz, a territory to be looked for probably in the Syrian desert; Zimri, unknown, unless it should be read "Zimki," which would give an *atbash* writing (substitution of Hebr letters in inverse order) for Elam; Sheshach, another *atbash* writing for Babel; and Arabia. These cryptograms are sure signs of late additions. The listing of Jerusalem, Judah, and their people is out of place here (v 18). **30–38.** This poem on the universal judgment of Yahweh, presented again as a lawsuit (*rîb,* v 31), is a kind of second summary of the oracles against the nations. **30.** *the Lord roars:* The anthropomorphism is inspired by the old theophanies in the midst of thunder (Exod 19:16). The present theophany also takes place in a storm (v 32; cf. 23:19; Amos 1:2; Joel 4:16), unless it is the roaring of a lion, to which Yahweh is also compared (Amos 3:8; Hos 10:11). **38.** *lion:* Symbolizes also Yahweh, and so the sword, his wrath (Ezek 22:1–22). The entire pericope shows well enough that Yahweh's action is not restricted only to Israel, but extends to all known nations.

75   **(III) The Restoration of Israel (26:1–35:19).** As in the other prophetic books, a section on the restoration of Israel (chaps. 30–33) follows the "oracles against the nations" (→ 74 above; 80 below). A small collection of narratives concerning Jeremiah and the false prophets has been added (chaps. 27–29), for these prophets were also promising such a restoration, but on false grounds.

Finally, Jeremiah's fight with the leaders of the people prefaces the whole section (chap. 26).

(A) Jeremiah Persecuted (26:1–24). The common opinion is that this chapter is Baruch's narrative on the circumstances and results of Jeremiah's Temple discourse (7:1–15). The original narrative has been amplified in the line of the Deuteronomists, in order to prove that a true prophet must be listened to (Deut 18:19–20; cf. F. L. Hossfeld and I. Meyer, *ZAW* 86 [1974] 30–49). **1.** *in the beginning of the reign:* If this chronological data (*bĕrēʾšît mamlĕkût*) corresponds to the similar Akk expression (*reš šarrûtim*), a technical term for the period between a king's accession and the following new year, then the incident occurred in 609, before the first regnal year in 608. **2–6.** The verses are a résumé of the Temple discourse: Yahweh will suspend his judgment if the people repent and observe the law. However, a new thought has been added: Yahweh reveals himself only through the ministry of the true prophets (cf. 7:25; 25:4)—a sort of introduction to the following chapters. The prophet's words provoked a general scandal and brought a charge against him (vv 7–9). **10–19.** The lawsuit is now described and should be compared to the parallel NT examples (Mark 14:55ff. and par.; Acts 6:11–14; 21:27–31). **10.** *princes of Judah:* Although the word *śārîm* could mean "princes," it often also refers to the high officials, closely associated to the "elders" (*zĕqēnîm,* v 17), who were the influential element of the people (see de Vaux, *AI* 69, 138). *New Gate:* Court sessions were customarily held at the gates (cf. Gen 23:10–20; Ruth 4:1; Prov 31:23; etc.). **11.** Jeremiah's sermon was interpreted as blasphemous, thus requiring a death penalty (Lev 24:10–16; 1 Kgs 21:13). **12–15.** Jeremiah presents his own defense: The words are not his but Yahweh's for he has been "sent"; this is a sign of true prophecy (cf. 23:21). **16–19.** The civil leaders, struck by the defense, stand against the religious authorities. They argue from a parallel case of a century before (Mic 3:12), thus proving that the oracles of the prophets were preserved and well known. The reaction to Micah's word was altogether different from the present case. Hezekiah did lead a religious reform (2 Kgs 18:4), and the evil avoided, alluded to here, might be Sennacherib's withdrawal in 701 (2 Kgs 19:35–36). **20–23.** Baruch now tells the story of the murder of a prophet, Uriah, who had preached in similar terms, but we do not know when it happened. The biographer's purpose is certainly to show the danger from which Jeremiah escaped. Elnathan will be present again in the scroll incident in 605–604 (36:12); he might be Jehoiakim's father-in-law (2 Kgs 24:8). The extradition of political refugees is a frequent clause of the treaties of the 2d millennium BC (see *ANET* 200–1, 203). The verse would be better situated after v 19. Shaphan is the royal scribe who participated in the Josian reform (2 Kgs 22:3ff.). If his son, Ahikam, protects the prophet, Jeremiah must have had good relations with this family. Such is confirmed by the fact that another son of Shaphan, Gemariah (36:10), will sympathize with him (36:25), and Ahikam's son, Gedaliah, will be greatly devoted to him (39:14; 40:5ff.).

76   **(B) Jeremiah's Controversy with the False Prophets (27:1–29:32).** The following three chapters once formed a separate collection, as proved by both their style and subject. Here the Babylonian king's name is written "Nebuchadnezzar" instead of "Nebuchadrezzar" as elsewhere, and Jeremiah's name is *Yirmĕyāh* instead of *Yirmĕyāhû.* We are told of Jeremiah's attempt, during the first years of Zedekiah, to bring the Judeans, both in Palestine and in exile, to complete submission under Nebuchadnezzar, instead of revolting against him as the false prophets urged. In this way, the discussion about the prophetic authority is fully illuminated (for bibliography, → 71 above and H.-J. Kraus, *Prophetie in der Krisis* [→ 71 above] 56-104). The MT is much longer than the LXX; the latter most likely represents the primitive text (cf. E. Tov, *ZAW* 91 [1979] 73-93); and esp. T. Seidl, *Texte und Einheiten in Jer 27-29* [St. Ottilien, 1977]; and *Formen und Formeln in Jer 27-29* [St. Ottilien, 1978] for a thorough literary and form-critical analysis).

(a) A COALITION OF THE WEST (27:1-22). The date given for the event is the beginning of Jehoiakim's reign; however, in the whole story, there is question of Zedekiah only. According to 28:1, the date is Zedekiah's fourth year (594-593). This chapter is the only source we have on the coalition of the small western states (v 3), but its historical context is somewhat illuminated by the Babylonian Chronicles published by Wiseman [→ 2 above]. In 596-595, Nebuchadnezzar was attacked at home by an unknown enemy (Elam?), and the following year (595-594) he had to muster a revolt within his own frontiers. In 594-593, he led a military campaign into Syria; the Chronicles stop there, leaving a gap from 594-593 to 557 (Wiseman, *Chronicles* 73-75). The Babylonian king being thus so busy in the east, these small states tried to join forces and overthrow his yoke, but in vain. According to Jer 51:59, Zedekiah sent a delegation to Babylon that same year; historians think its purpose was precisely to justify the king's conduct (cf. N. M. Sarna, ErIsr 47 [1978] 89-96).

2. *yoke:* The message is delivered in a prophetic action (cf. 13:1-11). 3-11. The prophet first addresses the ambassadors from the Transjordan states and the two city-states of Phoenicia. No doubt their intention was to win Zedekiah to their cause. Yahweh is the Lord not only of creation but also of history; he commissioned Nebuchadnezzar, his servant (v 6), to bring the people under his submission, symbolized by Jeremiah's yoke. Therefore, it is foolhardy to believe in the liberation predicted by their own prophets and diviners. Again, Jeremiah does not judge the situation politically but according to his faith in Yahweh's direction of world affairs. To resist Nebuchadnezzar is to resist Yahweh, which can only result in one's own destruction. 5-6. The prophet sees Yahweh's sovereign power over world history in his role of creator of the universe (see H. Weippert, *Schöpfer des Himmels* [→ 22 above] 65ff. 10. *falsehood:* The Hebr word *šeqer* is important in this collection of narratives opposing Jeremiah to the false prophets (cf. 27:14,16; 28:15; 29:9,21,23,31): it qualifies their activity, as the word *dābār* ("word") qualifies Jeremiah's; the "falsehood" basically consists of proclaiming as "word of God" one's own evaluation of events (see T. W. Overholt, *The Threat of Falsehood* [→ 7 above] 24-48).

12-15. The same message is now delivered to Zedekiah. 16-22. Finally, Jeremiah warns the priests and the people of the same false hope of these prophets. Their preaching is a provocation to rebellion, for they are confident that the end of the exile is near. But this rebellion is against Yahweh and therefore cannot be of his own inspiration. 21-22. The LXX has merely, "To Babylon they shall be brought"—a perfect conclusion for vv 19-20. The prediction of their return is out of place in this oracle of doom.

77   (b) PROPHECY AGAINST PROPHECY (28:1-17). The narrative is biographical and may go back to Baruch; the pers. pron. "me" (v 1) is usually corrected to "Jeremiah." The date of the event is given in a complicated text (v 1): if, with the LXX, we simply erase "in the beginning" (a probable harmonization with 27:1), then the incident happened in 594-593, about the time

that Jeremiah delivered his message to the ambassadors, for he still performs the symbolic action of the yoke. 1. *fifth month:* The precision is important (see v 17). Gibeon is identified with modern el-Jib, a few miles NW of Jerusalem. 2-4. Hananiah proclaims his oracle in the style of the true prophets. The core of his message is absolutely contrary to that of Jeremiah (chap. 27): Babylon's yoke will soon be broken and Jehoiachin will return to Jerusalem. 5-9. Jeremiah's answer is another attempt at establishing a clear distinction between the true and the false prophets. The constant message of the latter is one of peace (cf. 6:14; 23:17); thus, they are opposed to the true prophets who so often proclaimed oracles of doom. Jeremiah sets up another condition for authenticity: a prophecy has to be fulfilled (cf. Deut 18:21-22), if its object has been one of peace or a blessing. 10-11. Hananiah, with great confidence, performs a counter prophetic action in order to render powerless Jeremiah's prophetic action: the yoke, symbol of submission to Nebuchadnezzar, is broken, which means that victory and freedom will replace such a threat. Such a sudden reaction left Jeremiah completely dumbfounded and without an answer. 12-17. It is only after a certain length of time that the answer came; the true prophets were not dreamers or victims of autosuggestion, but depended entirely on Yahweh's inspiration. 13. We prefer the LXX: "You broke wooden yokes, now I will replace them with iron ones." Hananiah was calling for a revolt that would eventually lead to complete subjection to Nebuchadnezzar. 15-16. Hananiah now gets his own sentence, formulated in a play on the word *šālaḥ*, "to send." He was not "sent" by Yahweh to be a prophet, but he will be "dispatched." He deserves death, for he spoke without mandate (Deut 18:20). 17. Two months later (cf. v 1), Hananiah died. This fulfillment of Jeremiah's prediction is seen as an authentication of his mission (cf. vv 5-9).

78   (c) THE LETTER TO THE EXILES (29:1-32). The imminent and happy end of the Babylonian domination was announced not only in Palestine (chap. 28) but also in Babylon by the same type of prophet. The text, from Baruch's memoirs, has undergone some changes: A number of scholars read vv 8-9 after v 15 because they break the sequence of vv 7 and 10; again, vv 16-20 (lacking in the LXX) are a severe attack on Zedekiah, which is strange in a letter to the exiles in Babylon—they appear to be inspired by 24:8-10.

(i) *The letter* (29:1-23). 2-3. This letter is dated after the first captivity in 597, and it was sent through Zedekiah's delegation to Babylon. Even though some scholars think that its purpose was to pay the annual tribute, we hold that it was rather to justify Zedekiah (→ 120 below) after his attempt to join the coalition of the western states (chap. 27) in the year 594-593. *Elasah:* Son of Shaphan and most probably Ahikam's brother (cf. 26:24). *Gemariah:* Son of Hilkiah and must be also from the priestly family that played an important role in the Josian reform (cf. 2 Kgs 22). The two men must have agreed with Jeremiah's "pacifism"; they were an excellent choice to restore Zedekiah's relations with the Babylonian court. 4-7. The exiles have to settle in this foreign land and to collaborate for its welfare. 10-15. Jeremiah gives the reason for settling down in Babylon: the exile is going to last for an indefinite period (cf. 25:11; 28:3) and they must promote their new land's welfare (v 7). No doubt the recommendation was shocking. Yahweh could be worshiped in Babylon, for he protects his people even outside Palestine; Yahwism has finally burst through the enclosure of the holy land (cf. Ezek 10:18-22; 11:22-25). 21-23. The letter closes with the severe condemnation of two of these false prophets. They are to be turned over to Nebuchadnezzar to be burnt.

79   (ii) *An exile's reaction* (29:24–32). The letter caused great anger in Babylonia and one of the prophets sent a letter to Jerusalem to have Jeremiah arrested. **25.** *Zephaniah:* He consulted Jeremiah twice in Zedekiah's name (21:1; 37:3); he is now at the head of the Temple police (cf. 20:1). **31–32.** Jeremiah's answer to Shemaiah is similar to the one he gave to Hananiah (28:15ff.) — he has no mandate from Yahweh and deserves punishment; he will die in Babylon.

80   (C) **The Restoration of Israel (30:1–31:40).** All agree that this section of Jeremiah's book constitutes a climax, and some would even say the apogee of all prophecy (31:31–34). The work is not a unitary composition but a collection of poems on one basic theme: salvation after judgment. It is still the subject of very sharp disagreement between scholars on its authorship and its meaning. For a better understanding of the problem, we separate immediately two main blocks: 30:1–32:22 and 31:23–40.

One major problem discussed in conjunction with the study of these chapters is the place of the salvation oracles in the preexilic prophets. Indeed, the judgment of God on his people dominated prophecy at that period. The hope of a possible salvific intervention of God was thin and expressed in general terms only; exilic and even postexilic redactors of the prophetic books have expanded these oracles, adding new ones, under the strong influence of the deuteronomic school; Jer 30–31 is believed to be a good example of this process (see S. Herrmann, *Die prophetischen Heilserwartungen* [Stuttgart, 1965] 159–240; S. Böhmer, *Heimkehr und neuer Bund* [Göttingen, 1976]). We think that a saying of Jeremiah is at the root of most of the oracles in these chapters.

The next problem is the relationship between these oracles and Isa 40–55. There is no doubt that a similarity of view on the restoration exists between the two, but who is the primary cause? The answer to this question depends on the solution given to the first problem. And, finally, the most disputed question revolves around the identification of the "Israel" to whom these oracles are addressed. For some, it has to be the whole people, Israel and Judah, since these chapters are the work of an anonymous prophet who lived not long before Dt-Isa (see G. Fohrer, "Der Israel-Prophet," *Mélanges bibliques et orientaux* [Fest. H. Cazelles; ed. A. Caquot, *et al.;* Neukirchen, 1981] 135–48). Others think that the poems were written by Jeremiah at Mizpah, after the destruction of Jerusalem in 587, for the consolation of Judah (see esp. T. M. Raitt, *A Theology of Exile* [Phl, 1977]). However, there are good reasons to hold that they must date from Jeremiah's early ministry and concern northern Israel only, with a later edition extended to Judah also (e.g., 30:3–4,17; 31:27–28; etc.). The accumulation of geographical and personal names such as Samaria, Jacob, Ephraim, Ramah, etc., are better understood if Jeremiah had in mind the northern kingdom, experiencing exile since 721. Besides, both the expressions and the themes in the present section are very similar to those of the early poem on conversion (3:1–4:2): the "lovers" who prevent Israel from "turning" to her God; the laments on the heights; the healing of the wounds; the perversity since youth; etc. Moreover, the strong Hosean influence in that poem and these chapters is quite clear. The best historical context for such oracles directed to the exiled northern Israel would be the attempt of Josiah to extend his reform to the north, when the Assyrian yoke was practically inexistent (2 Kgs 23:15–20). Jeremiah thought that the chastisement was complete and the day had come to reunite the whole people under the sole rule of a Davidic king (Rudolph, Weiser, Bright; see esp. H. W. Hertzberg, *TLZ* 77 [1952] 595–602; N. Lohfink, "Der junge Jeremia als Propagandist," *Le livre de Jérémie* 351–86; U. Schröter, *VT* 35 [1985] 312–29). This return could not take place, since a new and overwhelming power — Babylonia — soon dominated the whole Near East. Jeremiah himself might have extended to Judah, at a later period and after 587, his earlier hope for northern Israel.

81   (a) NORTHERN ISRAEL WILL BE RESTORED (30:1–31:22). The following divisions are an attempt to separate the different poems of this first block.

(i) *Introduction (30:1–3).* These verses, in prose, serve as an introduction to the whole collection, with a close correspondence to its conclusion, which has a similar outlook (32:38–40). The leading message, written at Yahweh's command (cf. 36:1–2), is stated clearly: Yahweh will bring back Israel to her land. The technical expression for such a hope is a characteristic of this part of the book: *šûb šĕbût* (30:18; 31:23; 32:44; 33:7, 11). Its full meaning includes more than a simple reversal of God's judgment on Israel, but implies as well the return of the exiles and the entry into a new covenant, with all the gifts attached to such an event, culminating in the full prosperity of a people living free in its own land (see J. M. Bracke, *ZAW* 97 [1985] 233–44).

(ii) *Jacob's distress at an end* (30:4–11). The prophet describes in vivid hues, remembering the theme of the "Day of Yahweh" (Amos 5:18–20; Isa 2:12–21; Zeph 1:7–11; etc.), the sufferings of over 100 years of exile (vv 5–7). The pains of childbirth symbolize great distress (4:31; 6:24; 22:23); now men are experiencing them (cf. 50:43). The lament closes on the simple announcement of salvation (v 7). **8–9.** These prose lines are an addition, although they may be authentic. They deal with the whole people in the messianic times. Before, the new ideal king was said to be a descendant of David (23:5); here he is called simply David, as in Hos 3:5 (exilic) and Ezek 34:23–24; 37:24–25. A suitable date for the oracle would be after the destruction of Judah and its monarchy. **10–11.** The passage, not in the LXX, is reproduced almost literally in 46:27–28; it echoes themes in Isa 40–55.

(iii) *Healing of Israel's wounds* (30:12–17). This new poem is similar to the preceding one; Israel's miseries (wounds) are described and its restoration promised (v 17a is to be read after 17b [Rudolph]). Here, the "lovers" are no longer the idols, as before, but the foreign nations who have chastised them, to be themselves chastised in return.

82   (iv) *The restoration* (30:18–24). The restoration just announced (vv 7 and 17) is now fully described. The political community (*'ēdâ;* cf. 1 Kgs 12:20) will be reinstated with a new ruler (v 21) who will be the perfect intermediary between Yahweh and his people. Does Jeremiah here think in terms of the divided monarchy? The vagueness of the text does not allow a clear answer. Here he considers Jerusalem as the real center of worship for the northern kingdom; the Davidic king then would be also another bond of unity (Rudolph). Jeremiah seems to expect the return of the glorious era of David with its free and joyous life in the promised land. The spread of Josiah's reform into ancient Israel certainly encouraged him to have such a hope and to believe in its near realization.

83   (v) *Good news of return* (31:1–6). The following four poems have as their central theme the exuberant joy of the return. They are introduced by a new title in which "Israel" refers to the entire people. Throughout this section, we meet with parallel utterances of Dt-Isa, which we can explain by the similarity of subject — the return from exile seen as a new exodus. **2.** *favor in the desert:* Jer and Dt-Isa (41:17-20; 43:16-21; 48:20-22; etc.) describe the return as a new exodus, and in a much more glorious form; they are related as type and antitype. **3.** The covenantal love is said to be "age-old" or "eternal," for it originates from the desert period and it will never cease (cf. Deut 7:8; 10:15; Hos 2:21; 11:1-4; Isa 43:4; 54:8).

84 (vi) *The new exodus* (31:7-14). The triumphal march through the desert is the cause of great joy to both the repatriates and the foreign nations. **7.** The hymn opens with a solemn call to joy, for Yahweh has bestowed salvation on his people (see Isa 12:6; 40:9-10; 44:23; 55:11; Pss 47:2,9-10; 68:33-36; 95-99). These people are called the "remnant," i.e., the small number of those who have escaped the calamity of 721 and who have been purified through the exile to constitute the new Israel, faithful to her God. **8.** *ends of the world:* This expression is synonymous with the "north"—i.e., Assyria, where they have been kept captive (cf. Isa 43:5-6). The caravan is one composed of weak people, a sign of the miraculous nature of the event (see also Isa 35:5ff.; 42:16). **9.** *departed in tears:* The same opposition between sorrow and joy is the central theme of another hymn on the return from exile (Ps 126). *brooks of water:* An allusion to the "rock" incidents of the first exodus (Exod 17:1-7; Num 20:1-13); now it is not an occasional spring but constantly flowing brooks. *level road:* Accentuates the facility of the march, quite different from the one of the first exodus (cf. Isa 40:4). *father to Israel:* The notion of the fatherhood of Yahweh toward Israel, his firstborn, is sporadic in the OT. It first served to define their covenantal relationship (Exod 4:22; Deut 32:6). Israel is the firstborn not because it is superior to Judah, but because Yahweh will renew this same fatherly love for Israel. **10.** Nations and distant islands are invited to be witnesses of the marvelous event (cf. Isa 42:10; 49:1; see Jer 2:10ff.). The symbolism of the shepherd and his flock for Yahweh's salvific action is also a Jeremian theme (23:1ff.), at the origin of later developments (Ezek 34; John 10:1ff.). **11.** It is through Yahweh's help that Israel overcomes stronger enemies, as in the first exodus (Exod 15; Isa 49:24-25). **14.** *choice portions:* The Hebr word *dešen* means "fat." Jeremiah does not promise the priests an abundance of sacrificial portions, for the fat was reserved for the divinity. "Fat" is also the symbol of life and prosperity (Pss 36:9; 63:6; Isa 55:2; etc.); thus, the priests will share the same prosperity as the rest of the people, which is described in the enumeration of the Palestinian goods (v 12).

85 (vii) *End of Rachel's mourning* (31:15-20). The prophet now breaks into a profound lyricism on the afflictions of the northern kingdom, personified by Rachel, mother of Joseph (Manasseh and Ephraim) and Benjamin (Gen 30:24; 35:16ff.). He is influenced here mainly by Hosea (cf. B. Lindars, *JSOT* 12 [1979] 42-62). **15.** Ramah, in Benjamin (Jos 18:25; Judg 4:5), is located at er-Rām, about 5 mi. N of Jerusalem. The oldest tradition placed Rachel's tomb in the vicinity of Benjamin's territory, before a later one brought it close to Bethlehem (Gen 35:19; 48:7; 1 Sam 10:2-3; this was followed by Matt 2:18). **18.** *restore me:* The MT reads "Bring on my return, and I will return." The verb *šûb* has two main meanings: "to return from exile" and "to convert oneself" (see 3:1ff.). In the context (v 16), the return from exile is fundamental, but the prophet certainly superimposed the idea of conversion as well (v 19). **19.** *Yārēk* means "thigh" and to strike one's thigh is a gesture of pain and lament (Ezek 21:17), attested also in Mesopotamia (see "Descent of Ishtar" in *ANET* 108) and in Greece (*Iliad* 15.397-98; 16.125; *Odyssey* 13.198-99).

disgrace of my youth: The sin of the chosen people stems from its very origins; the prophets often recall this early ingratitude toward Yahweh's faithful love (see 3:25; 22:21; 32:30; Ezek 16; 23; Isa 48:8; 54:4; etc.).

86 (viii) *En route* (31:21-22). The collection of poems closes with a solemn command to start home. The only difficulty in the passage lies in the last sentence of v 22. The MT reads *nĕqēbâ tĕsôbēb gāber,* "female shall encompass a man"; the LXX has an entirely different text, i.e., "men will walk in salvation." A host of explanations have been proposed since Jerome's theory of a pure mariological and christological prophecy (PL 28.255; 24.880-81). We shall indicate only two explanations. The verb *sābab* would mean "to protect," as in Deut 32:10 and Ps 32:7,10; thus, woman protecting man is a sign of the great security to be experienced during the return and the new settlement in Palestine (Penna, Rudolph). But this seems to be foreign to the immediate context. We prefer to interpret the sentence in the context of symbolic language, where "woman" personifies Israel and "man," Yahweh. Indeed, Jeremiah still talks of Israel as an adulterous wife (Hos 1-3; Jer 2:20ff.) who had to be divorced by Yahweh, her husband (3:1). If she now adheres to her husband, certainly this is something new—something unheard of in her entire history (cf. v 19).

87 (b) ADDITIONAL FRAGMENTS (31:23-40). To this book of the consolation of Israel, a number of disconnected oracles on a similar subject, in which Judah is included, have been added.

(i) *The restoration of Judah* (31:23-26). This oracle and the one following are often denied to be Jeremian because they suppose the historical context of the exile. We believe that Jeremiah extended to Judah, at her downfall in 587, the hope he had for Israel. **23.** *the Lord bless you . . . abode of justice:* This liturgical blessing is on the assembly (cf. Num 6:24-26; Pss 128; 134:3). *holy mountain:* As in Isa (11:9), the whole of Judah is thus designated. **26.** The enigmatic saying seems to be a gloss by someone reflecting on the prophecy.

(ii) *Israel and Judah* (31:27-28). **28.** *watched:* A clear reference to 1:10-11. Yahweh's watchful (*šāqad*) eye was upon the prophet's first mission; now the time has come for the second one—the creation of a new people.

88 (iii) *Personal responsibility* (31:29-30). In Israel collective responsibility largely prevailed in the realm of morals and justice (Exod 20:5 = Deut 5:9; Num 14:18). Both Jeremiah and Ezekiel (18:2) quote the proverb (v 29) on the sons' miseries caused by the fathers' sins. They take the occasion of its rejection to propose a new truth, i.e., personal responsibility.

89 (iv) *The new covenant* (31:31-34). This short oracle has been justly called "one of the profoundest and most moving passages in the entire Bible" (Bright, *Jeremiah* 287). **31.** This is the only time "new covenant" is used in the OT. It is now attested to at Qumran, but it designates nothing more than the Mosaic covenant, with strong legalistic tendencies. Of course, it is reinterpreted in the NT (Luke 22:20; 1 Cor 11:25; esp. Heb 8:8-12, the longest OT quotation in the NT). *house of Judah:* This later addition, if we compare it with v 33, makes clear that the new covenant extends to the entire people. **32.** This verse makes it clear that the prophet compares this new covenant to the Sinaitic one (Exod 19:1-24:18). **33.** *after those days:* The expression is frequently used by Jeremiah (7:32; 9:24; 16:14; etc.) with an eschatological tone, for it indicates a kind of rupture in the course of Israel's history through a wonderful intervention of Yahweh. *write it upon their hearts:* The old covenant was written on stone tables (Exod 31:18;

34:28ff.; Deut 4:13; 5:22) or in a book (Exod 24:7; 2 Kgs 23:3). The heart as writing material is a Jeremian creation (cf. 17:1), even though it has a close parallel in Deut (6:6; 11:18; 30:14). *I will be their God:* This covenantal clause is widespread (Jer 7:23; 11:4; 24:7; 30:22; 31:1; 32:38; Ezek 11:20; 36:28; etc.; Zech 8:8; Lev 26:12). **34.** *teach:* In this new era, intermediaries such as Moses, priests, and prophets will be useless, for Yahweh will intervene directly (cf. Isa 54:13). *to know:* The practical recognition of God in every action and situation, a life attitude.

What is the exact nature of this covenant and what relations does it have with the former one? Although some scholars would see a complete rupture between the two, they are fundamentally the same: Yahweh concluded both on his own initiative; both are God-centered; the people are the same in both instances; the response is manifested in the same obedience to the law, which did not change. There is no question of the promulgation of a new law. Therefore, this newness is not found in the essentials of the covenant, but in the realm of its realization and of its means. It will not be broken, as the old one was repeatedly (v 33), for everyone will be faithful (v 34). The reason for such a drastic change is that the very inner nature of humanity is created anew: the prophet opposes the radical impossibility for Israel to respect the old covenant to its ability to fulfill the new one. Indeed, for Jeremiah sin has been the second nature of the people of God (13:23); the very absence of heart (*lēb*) explains why obedience to God is never realized (5:22; cf. 17:1). If we remember that for the Israelites the concept of "heart" (*lēb*) refers to human intelligence and will power (cf. H. W. Wolff, *Anthropology of the OT* [Phl, 1974] 46ff.), then the novelty of the new covenant has to be situated on the side of humankind itself, now created with the power to fulfill the plans God has for it. Some scholars still believe that this oracle should be attributed to a deuteronomic redactor ((Herrmann, Nicholson, Böhmer); however, the Deuteronomists do not expect a new heart to be put in the people, but rather that the old one will be transformed ("circumcised"), which means simply that conversion will become a reality (Deut 10:16; 30:6). Jeremiah himself, at a certain time, had the same hope (4:4; 9:24–25); but in 31:31–34, he goes far beyond this belief, since conversion has been proved to be impossible: Yahweh has to create a new people. There is continuity in the essentials of the former and the new covenant, but there is a profound discontinuity in the means given to Israel to fulfill the new one.

This extraordinary prophecy had a great influence and found a certain fulfillment at the hands of Ezek and Dt-Isa. They did not speak of a new covenant but of an eternal covenant, one that could not be broken (Ezek 16:60; 34:25; 37:26; Isa 55:3; 61:8). It is possible because a "new heart" is created in the people, a "new spirit" is given to them (Ezek 11:20; 18:31; 36:26; Isa 59:21).

(Apart from the commentaries, see Buis, P., *VT* 18 [1968] 1–15. Böhmer, S., *Heimkehr und neuer Bund* [Göttingen: 1976] 74–79. Coppens, J., *CBQ* 25 [1963] 12–21. Herrmann, S., *Die prophetischen Heilserwartungen im AT* [Stuttgart, 1965] 179–204. Potter, H. D., *VT* 33 [1983] 347–57. Schenker, A., *FZPhTh* 27 [1980] 93–106. Weinfeld, M., *ZAW* 88 [1976] 17–56. Weippert, H., *VT* 29 [1979] 336–51. Wolff, H. W., "What is new," *Confrontations with Prophets* [Phl, 1983] 49–62.)

90   (v) *The stability of Israel* (31:35–37). This new oracle evokes the stability of the laws of nature to prove the same stability of God's purposes in the history of Israel (cf. Gen 8:22; Ps 89:35–38).

(vi) *The rebuilding of Jerusalem* (31:38–40). The starting point is the Tower of Hananel, situated NE of the city (Neh 3:1; 12:39; Zech 14:10). The Corner

Gate is NW (2 Kgs 14:13; 2 Chr 26:9; Zech 14:10); hence, the measurements are taken counterclockwise. The hill of Gareb is mentioned only here, but the context asks for a western location; L. H. Vincent identified it with the long esplanade along the W wall of the city. Goah is also unknown; inasmuch as the following indication is at the south, the Valley of Ben-Hinnom, Goah must be at the southwest corner. The Horse Gate is E, in the vicinity of the royal palace (2 Kgs 11:16; Neh 3:28). The "newness" comes from the purification of the Ben-Hinnom Valley, with the abolition of the child sacrifice (cf. 19:1ff.). This brief description of Jerusalem is not apocalyptic but corresponds to the actual size of the city destroyed by the Chaldeans and rebuilt by Nehemiah (see Vincent, *Jérusalem de l'Ancien Testament* [vols. 2–3; Paris, 1956] 650–54). Even if Jeremiah could have spoken these words, it is preferable to see here a postexilic addition from the period of Nehemiah.

(D) The Restoration of Judah (32:1–33:26). To the preceding collection of poems dealing mainly with the restoration of northern Israel, a similar collection of sayings regarding Judah's future has been added, all developed around an event in Jeremiah's life, during the final siege of Jerusalem; the event has taken the form of an "acted prophecy" (E. W. Nicholson).

91   (a) A PLEDGE OF RESTORATION (32:1–44). This narrative, probably taken from Baruch's memoirs, underwent amplifications, especially in the last two sections.

(i) *The purchase of a field* (32:1–15). **1.** According to 39:1 and 52:4 (= 2 Kgs 25:1), the siege of the city began in January 588, to be interrupted during the summer because the Egyptian armies were marching against those of Babylon. Thus, Jeremiah's action took place after this interruption, in 587. **2–5.** A later redactor undoubtedly summarized the events recorded in chaps. 34,37–38 to show more fully the historical context of the situation (for a detailed analysis of the sequence of the events, see H. Migsch, *Gottes Wort über das Ende Jerusalems* [Klosterneuburg, 1981]). **7.** Sometime before, during the interruption of the siege, Jeremiah was already preoccupied with this affair (37:12). *first right of purchase:* Hanamel's transaction conforms with the law (cf. Lev 25:25–31; Ruth 4:1ff.). To keep the patrimony within the family, a brother must buy his brother's property; if there is no brother, the nearest relative is bound to do so. **10–12.** The contract is concluded in due form with the obligatory witnesses. The "sealed" and "open" copies are well known; one copy is sealed, and the second is left open for easy consultation. This is the first mention of Baruch in Jeremiah's book, and he appears as both secretary and friend to the prophet (cf. 36:4). **14–15.** Jeremiah now explains his action: if he bought a field in an occupied section of the country, one day, even in the distant future, he would be able to use its benefits, and others would also perform similar transactions. In a word, Judah will recover her freedom.

92   (ii) *Jeremiah's prayer* (32:16–25). Only v 17a ("Ah, Lord God") and vv 24–25 reproduce the original prayer, for it is the only part connected with the present event. The remaining verses are but a redundant complex of Jeremian and deuteronomic phrases and expressions (see Rudolph for the references). The same anthological style is used in a similar prayer in Neh 9:1ff.; they are postexilic compositions.

(iii) *The Lord's answer* (32:26–44). This answer has also been greatly expanded: only vv 27–29a and 42–44 are related to Jeremiah's prayer. Yahweh confirms the future restoration of Judah, geographically expressed in the terms of 17:26 and prophetically symbolized by the prophet's purchase of a field in Anathoth.

The long addition (vv 29b-41) is another free composition inspired mainly by a number of Jeremiah's prophecies. The sole differences are that the new covenant is called here "eternal" (v 40), and instead of the "knowledge of the Lord" there is question of the "fear of the Lord" (vv 39-40); both expressions are foreign to Jeremiah's vocabulary.

93 (b) MORE ON THE RESTORATION OF JERUSALEM AND JUDAH (33:1-26). The date of the present oracles is 587, as in 32:1. At the beginning of this century, critics rejected the entire chapter as unauthentic; we argue for an original nucleus behind its two sections.

(i) *Jerusalem and Judah restored* (33:1-13). The style of this hopeful passage is extremely repetitious and gives signs of the apocalyptic style (Rudolph; cf. v. 3: "revelation of mysteries"); if most of the ideas are Jeremiah's, their form is hardly his. Hence, we see here a disciple's reflections on the master's message. **4-5.** The MT is corrupt and unintelligible. **6-9.** The historical context is the period of the rebuilding of Jerusalem after the exile. **10.** A quotation from 32:43. **11.** *the cry of joy:* This enumeration of joyful manifestations is authentically Jeremiah (7:34; 16:9; 25:10), except that we have here the reversal of the divine judgment which had put an end to joy. The praise quoted here comes from the liturgical thanksgiving hymns (Pss 100:5; 106:1; 107:1; its last part is the refrain of Ps 136). **13.** This geography of the restoration comes from 17:26 (see also 32:44).

94 (ii) *An anthology on messianism* (33:14-26). This new section, missing in the LXX, is a small collection of Jeremiah's messianic oracles, mostly transformed. It is now accepted as being the work of a later redactor. **15-16.** The redactor reuses the prophet's oracle on the future king (cf. 23:5-6); Jerusalem replaces Israel and is called by this king's new name. **17-22.** The present prophecy is a solemn affirmation of the perennial permanence of the Davidic monarchy and the Levitical priesthood, which are closely connected; the phenomenon corresponds well to the postexilic institutional atmosphere (Zech 4:14; 6:13; etc.). This is the only place in Jer where the revival of the priesthood is an object of concern. **17.** The permanence of the dynasty is based on Nathan's prophecy (2 Sam 7:11-16; Ps 89:35ff.). **18.** *priests of Levi:* The Hebr expression says "priests-Levites," which is deuteronomic. **20-21.** Cf. 31:35-37. **22.** The promise of an innumerable posterity to the patriarchs is now applied to David and the priests (Gen 13:16; 15:5; 22:17). **23-26.** The atmosphere of these closing verses is one of disillusionment. The restoration was not realized exactly as foretold, and a kind of pessimism was trying the people's faith; the messianic hope had to be stirred up, which is what we find in Isa 56-66, Hag and Mal. The same apologetic intention is also present in this passage; the postexilic period of hardships under Zerubbabel or Nehemiah would be the right historical context.

(E) The Conditions for Salvation (34:1-35:19). Three incidents taken from Baruch's memoirs serve as a conclusion to the "book of the restoration." On the occasion of a gloomy situation in Judah, Jeremiah proclaims the conditions required for the salvation of the country with its people and king. The connection between these incidents is rather loose.

95 (a) ZEDEKIAH'S FATE (34:1-7). The first incident happened at a precise moment of the second siege of Jerusalem by Nebuchadnezzar (588-587). Besides Jerusalem, only Lachish and Azekah are still resisting the enemy (v 7). This phase of the war has been illustrated by the ostraca found at Tell ed-Duweir, identified with Lachish. On ostracon 4 we read: "Let [my Lord] know that we are watching for the signs of Lachish, . . . for we cannot see Azekah" (*ANET* 322); either Azekah had already fallen to the invader or an obstacle was hiding the city. Whatever the solution, this letter and the present text probably refer to the situation of the first phase of the war, sometime after January 588. **4-5.** The final condemnation of the city and Zedekiah is only conditional: a peaceful surrender will save both, as Jeremiah has constantly repeated (cf. chaps. 37-38).

96 (b) A DISHONEST DEAL (34:8-22). The second event is also dated from v 22 - "I will bring them back to the city" - which supposes that the siege has been interrupted. The pharaoh - i.e., Hophra (cf. 44:30) - marched into Palestine, surely to rescue Zedekiah; the Babylonians had to leave Jerusalem to stop this Egyptian advance (cf. 37:5). Ostracon 3 from Lachish (*ANET* 322) mentions a journey to Egypt of an army commander, Coniah son of Elnathan; its purpose must have been to seek such help from the pharaoh. The second event must therefore be during this interruption of the siege, sometime in the summer of 588. **9-11.** Under the king's initiative, a general manumission of slaves, both male and female, has been achieved in a religious ceremony before Yahweh (v 15). The reason for such a decision must come from the hardships of the siege; either the masters could no longer provide for their slaves, or the number of fighting men had to be increased. **14.** The law on the manumission of slaves to which Jeremiah is referring must be Deut 15:12-18 (cf. Exod 21:2-6). As soon as the danger disappeared, slavery was reimposed (v 16). **18.** *the calf . . . they passed:* This rite of covenant making is attested to in the OT only here and in Gen 15:9ff. Its meaning could only be an imprecation: the animal's fate will fall on the covenant makers if they break the agreement. The rite has its parallel in the covenantal ceremonies of the ancient Near East, in which a ram or a piglet is cut into pieces as a substitute for the vassal to serve as symbol of the fate that will befall him in the case of unfaithfulness (see E. Vogt, *Bib* 36 [1955] 566; H. Cazelles, *RB* 69 [1962] 345; D. J. McCarthy, *Treaty and Covenant* [AnBib 21A; Rome, 1978] 91ff. Jeremiah understood the rite as being imprecatory: "I will make them like the calf" (v 18) - they will find death at the hands of the Babylonians (vv 20-21). Thus, Jeremiah's message in all these circumstances is inflexible.

97 (c) THE EXAMPLE OF THE RECHABITES (35:1-19). The third incident occurred under Jehoiakim, when Chaldean and Aramean troops were marching against Judah (v 11). Our information from 2 Kgs 24:2-4 and the Babylonian Chronicles would indicate the year 601-600 for the invasion, the purpose of which was to crush Jehoiakim's revolt (cf. 12:7-13). **2.** *Rechabites:* According to 1 Chr 2:55, their origin was Kenite, a nomad tribe from the south. They cooperated with Jehu's radical extirpation of Baalism in Samaria, showing themselves to be fervent Yahwists (2 Kgs 10:15-17). **6-10.** From this description, the Rechabites appear to be reactionaries; their Yahwism is frozen in its nomadic phase, rejecting absolutely all sedentary culture. **13-17.** Jeremiah does not admire their nomadic reaction, but their sheer obedience to their forefathers' word; the Israelites should be as loyal to their own faith. This message (vv 15-17) is then proclaimed in the same style and thought as several previous ones (cf. 7:24ff.; 11:1ff.; 13:10; 25:4ff.; 26:2ff.; 29:17ff.). **18-19.** The promise of Yahweh to the Rechabites for their fidelity to their ideal takes the form of a covenant of grant, the reward given by a suzerain to a vassal for his good services (cf. J. D. Levenson, *CBQ* 38 [1976] 508-514).

98 (IV) **Martyrdom of Jeremiah (36:1-45:5).** The present section forms a homogeneous block, both in spirit and style, and is generally attributed to Baruch.

Chapter 36 is also the climax of a "tradition complex" starting in chap. 26. Even though Jeremiah's prophetic authority had once been recognized and vindicated, we see that his authority was progressively rejected afterward by the people and all levels of officials, including the king himself (cf. M. Kessler, *CBQ* 28 [1966] 389–401). Once his word had been eliminated from the religious life of Judah, we are informed about the different events that lead to the elimination of the bearer of the word himself (chaps. 37–45).

99   (A) The Scroll of 605–604 (36:1–32). This chapter is outstanding in Hebr narrative art; the number of vivid observations permits almost a photographic view of the scene. **1–4.** In 605, Nebuchadnezzar defeated the Egyptians in Carchemish and became king of Babylon. The "foe from the north" could now only be this leading power of the Near East; a policy of submission was the sole means of survival. **2.** *scroll:* This was a long strip of papyrus sheets or skins sewn together; the text was written in transverse columns (see R. L. Hicks, *VT* 33 [1983] 46–66). This was to contain all Jeremiah's oracles against Jerusalem (the LXX excepts Israel), Judah, and the nations since his call in 627–626. Several attempts have been made to reconstruct this scroll (cf. C. Rietzschel, *Das Problem der Urrolle* [Gütersloh, 1966]). W. L. Holladay has proposed the best hypothesis: the first scroll must have contained only the oracles calling for conversion (v 3); the second edition added all those that proclaimed that Yahweh's judgment was now inevitable, since his word had been rejected by both people and king (vv 29–31; cf. *VT* 30 [1980] 452–67). **4.** *Baruch son of Neriah:* This is his first appearance in Jeremiah's story. If he was Seraiah's brother (cf. 51:59), his family was influential and respected the prophet. A seal-impression has recently been found, which must be dated toward the end of the 7th cent.; it bears the name "To Berekyahu son of Neriah, the scribe" (cf. N. Avigad, *IEJ* 28 [1978] 53; *BA* 42 [1979] 115–16). All of this corresponds to Baruch as identified in our Jeremian text. **5–10.** The first reading of the scroll takes place in the Temple in the presence of the people. For the clarity of the narrative, v 9 must be transposed before v 5. **9.** *fifth year:* A year passed before the scroll could be read; the precise time is December, 604, for the weather is already cold (v 22). *fast:* It has to be a special fast on the occasion of some evil; would it not be to avert Nebuchadnezzar's armies? According to his Chronicles, that very month he conquered Ashkelon (see Wiseman, *Chronicles* 69). **5.** *I am prevented:* The obvious reason is the Temple sermon (7:1ff.) and the speech on Topheth (19:1–20:6), which aroused the Temple officials' anger. Jeremiah has to continue his mission through a secretary, keeping the oracles in a book as credential letters. **10.** Gemariah would certainly have supported both the prophet and the Josian reform (26:24). From his room Baruch was in a position overlooking the people gathered in the courtyards, where he could be seen and heard by every one. **11–19.** A second reading of the scroll is given to the heads of the administration, during a session for the state affairs. **12.** The scene takes place in the office of the secretary of state (see de Vaux, *AI* 131). Besides Gemariah, only Elnathan is known: he led the group sent by Jehoiakim to Egypt for Uriah's extradition (26:22). **19.** The attempt to protect the prophet and his secretary suggests that most of these dignitaries must represent Josiah's old administration. They knew what the king's reaction would be: Uriah's tragedy could not have been that long ago! **20–26.** The last dramatic reading of the scroll is in the king's presence. **23.** The scene of the king cutting the columns of writing to burn them in the brazier is in full contrast, by its cynicism, to

the one of his father at the reading of the Book of the Law; this contrast is even suggested in the following verse (see 2 Kgs 22:11–20; cf. C. D. Isbell, *JSOT* 8 [1978] 33–45). The prophet had already contrasted the two kings (22:13–17). Jehoiakim perhaps thought he would neutralize the dynamism of these prophecies by destroying them in a kind of execrative action. **26.** *Jerahmeel son of the king:* With the seal impression mentioned in the comment on v 4, another one was found bearing the inscription "To Jerahmeel son of the king," which also has to be dated toward the end of the 7th cent. (cf. N. Avigad, *IEJ* 28 [1978] 53–56; *BA* 42 [1979] 116–18); the title "Son of the King" (*ben hammelek*), attested elsewhere in the OT and on Hebr seals, is regularly interpreted as referring to a member of the royal family — therefore, a prince. **27–32.** Baruch writes a new edition of the scroll at Jeremiah's dictation, the occasion of a new oracle of doom against the king. **30.** The prophecy was only partly fulfilled, for Jehoiachin, his son, became king. However, his reign lasted only a short time, for he was deposed and died in exile (2 Kgs 24:8ff.). *his corpse:* This dishonorable death has been already announced: he will receive the "burial of an ass" (cf. 22:19). **32.** The second scroll was not just a copy of the first one but a new edition (see comment on v 2). A summary of Jeremiah's preaching may have been written that same year as a prologue or an epilogue to the entire work (cf. 25:1–13b).

100   (B) Zedekiah and the Prophet (37:1–38:28a). The encounters between Zedekiah and Jeremiah recorded here happened during the siege of Jerusalem (588–587). (a) ZEDEKIAH CONSULTS JEREMIAH (37:1–10). The consultation occurred during the interruption of the siege, in the summer of 588 (v 5), which occasioned the dishonest deal with the slaves (cf. 34:8ff.). **1–2.** To introduce these chapters, the redactor condensed the account of 2 Kgs 24:17–20 on Zedekiah. **3.** Zephaniah was a member of a similar delegation at the beginning of the siege (21:1–10). Jehucal replaced Pashhur; therefore, we have to deal with two different events. *pray to the Lord:* The object of the prayer must have been that Yahweh should renew the miracle of 701 (cf. 22:2). Zedekiah hoped beyond all hope: Jeremiah had already foretold his fate and that of the city at the beginning of the siege (cf. 34:1–7). **7–10.** The prophet's answer is as clear and stern as ever. His assurance about the outcome is even greater: even though Nebuchadnezzar was left only with wounded soldiers, he would still win a sweeping victory!

(b) JEREMIAH IS ARRESTED (37:11–16). The arrest took place during the same interruption of the siege (v 11), when there was a certain freedom of movement. **12.** The purpose of this trip to Anathoth is to be connected with the purchase of the field in chap. 32. **13.** The accusation of desertion had a foundation; some Judeans had already joined the enemy, probably more from fear than simply treason (38:19).

(c) A NEW CONSULTATION (37:17–21). Still later, Zedekiah consults Jeremiah directly and secretly, thus showing his full character. Even if he is sure of the prophet's policy of submission, his fear of the officials prevents him from taking a personal decision.

101   (d) JEREMIAH IN THE MIRY CISTERN (38:1–13). This new imprisonment of Jeremiah and Zedekiah's consultation closely resemble similar incidents narrated in 37:11–21; they may represent two accounts of the same events. Jehucal and Pashhur had consulted Jeremiah on Zedekiah's orders (21:1; 37:3). Gedaliah (not the future governor) may be the son of either this Pashhur or the prophet's persecutor (20:1–3). **2–3.** This message is exactly that delivered to the people at the beginning of the siege (cf. 21:8–10). Jeremiah's word never changed: Jerusalem's fate is irrevocable. **4.** *he demoralizes:* The full text is "For he weakens the hands of the warriors"—an expression attested in the Lachish Letters (6.6; cf. *ANET* 322). These Lachish texts have their historical importance; defeatism did not exist only in Jerusalem. **5.** The king states his own criticism! The true power is in the officials' hands. **6.** Their final intention was to bring about Jeremiah's death without bloodshed (cf. Gen 37:18ff.). **7–13.** Jeremiah is saved by the sympathy of an Ethiopian courtier (see de Vaux, *AI* 120–23).

102 (e) ZEDEKIAH'S LAST INTERVIEW WITH JEREMIAH (38:14–28a). This last encounter takes place at a vague spot in the Temple area. The king, eager as ever to hear a good word from Yahweh's messenger, appears in extreme anxiety, but he receives the same answer (vv 17–18; cf. 21:8–10; 38:2–3). The die was cast! **22.** *they betrayed you:* This quotation is probably from an ironic popular song. Jeremiah puts these words in their mouths and alludes to mud (in which he himself sank, 38:6). **24–28a.** Zedekiah's recommendation cannot find a better commentary than 38:5! These verses may belong after 37:21.

(C) **The Fall of Jerusalem (38:28b–39:18).** This pericope is a fine example of textual imbroglio. Many attempts have been made to restore the text to its primitive form; we will present here only the evident emendations (for further discussion, see Rudolph, *Jeremia,* 225–27). **38b.** *when Jerusalem was taken:* This protasis has been separated from its apodosis in 39:3 by the insertion of 39:1–2, a résumé of 2 Kgs 25:1–4a (= Jer 52:4–7a). The siege started *ca.* January 588, and Jerusalem fell in July 587.

39:4–13. The passage, missing in the LXX, comes from 2 Kgs 25:4b–12 (= Jer 52:7b–16). It was later introduced here. The logical sequence of v 3 is in v 14, but the role played by Nebuzaradan happened one month after Jerusalem's fall (cf. 2 Kgs 25:8 = Jer 52:12) so he could not have had the mission to free Jeremiah (vv 11–12). **14.** *Gedaliah:* The future governor's appearance here is also out of place, and contradicts the story of the next chapter; his name should be dropped. In a word, a short account of Jeremiah's fate at the downfall of Jerusalem (38:28b; 39:3,14) has been heavily interpolated with information borrowed from Kgs. **15–18.** This passage would be in a better context after 38:7–13. Although we are not told, Ebed-melech probably survived the catastrophe of 587; the redactor inserted the oracle here to show once more the fulfillment of Jeremiah's prophecies. The whole chapter shows the inevitable fate of all those who had attempted to suppress Yahweh's word and prophet.

103 (D) **A Tragedy in Mizpah (40:1–41:18).** 40:1 serves as a title for chaps. 40–44, the history of Jeremiah after the fall of Jerusalem. Some scholars would reject 40:7–41:18, since the prophet is not mentioned; but this section is the necessary historical background to Jeremiah's flight to Egypt. These chapters present many details concerning the period after the destruction of Jerusalem and throw much light on the short account of the same events in Kgs. An eyewitness is required for this precise record, and Baruch could be its primary source.

(a) JEREMIAH AT MIZPAH (40:1–6). Nebuzaradan came to Jerusalem one month after its fall (2 Kgs 25:8); his mission was to burn down the city and organize the caravans for exile. Moreover, he had Nebuchadnezzar's orders to treat the prophet humanely and to leave to him the choice of his fate (39:11–12). The Babylonian king must have been informed of the prophet's policy of submission. Released after the capitulation

of Jerusalem, it must have been by mistake that he was taken in the group of captives. **2–3.** Baruch puts his résumé of Jeremiah's preaching on the lips of the Babylonian captain. **5.** *Gedaliah:* This noble figure came from a family that strongly supported both the Josian reform and the prophet's mission (cf. 26:24). He must have been known by the Chaldeans to have opposed Zedekiah's policy. A seal impression found in Lachish, dating from the beginning of the 6th cent., bears the inscription "To Gedaliah, over the house," i.e., chief minister or intendant. If this seal is his, he had a high post in Zedekiah's cabinet (see R. de Vaux, *RB* 45 [1936] 96–102). **6.** Mizpah is usually located at Tell en-Nasbeh, some 8 mi. N of Jerusalem. It was once a political and religious center (Judg 20:1–3; 1 Sam 7:5–14; 10:17).

(b) THE COLONY AT MIZPAH (40:7–12). Gedaliah tried to organize the small colony of survivors; the future depended on a true submission to the Babylonians. Even if Judah were now simply a Babylonian province, it could keep its identity; no foreigners ever colonized its territory and it had a governor of its own, unlike northern Israel in 721 (2 Kgs 17:24ff). **10–12.** Life resumes its normal course. The invaders had respected the crops, for they were especially good; in fact, it was to their advantage. A wind of hope blows gently over the crushed country.

104 (c) THE ASSASSINATION OF GEDALIAH (40:13–41:3). **13–16.** Our only source of information on the plot; Baalis, the Ammonite king, is given as its chief instigator. In 594–593, the Transjordanian kings had tried to move Zedekiah into a coalition of the western states in order to overthrow the Babylonian domination (cf. 27:3). Thus, Baalis must have disliked Gedaliah's leadership. Gedaliah's refusal to believe that a plot was being fomented against him is another sign of his noble character. Recently the full name of the Ammonite king Baalis (*Ba'alyiša',* "Baal is salvation") has been attested for the first time on a seal impression to be dated *ca.* 600 BC (see L. G. Herr, *BA* 48 [1985] 169–72).

41:1–3. The assassination itself is recorded in much shorter form in 2 Kgs 25:25. Ishmael, of royal origin, may have been shocked to see that the Davidic dynasty had been supplanted, or he may have supported the anti-Babylonian party. Whatever his motives, Baalis saw in him an excellent tool. The brutal massacre produced deep consternation in the minds of the Judeans; they commemorated it by a fast, already attested to at the end of the exile on the third of Tishri—i.e., the end of September (Zech 7:5; 8:19).

(d) THE ASSASSINATION OF PILGRIMS (41:4–10). Two days later, Ishmael shed more blood, for some unknown reason. The pilgrims, in mourning attire (cf. 16:6; 48:37), were from the three cultic centers of northern Israel. Their pilgrimage to the ruined Temple, to present offerings, indicates that Jerusalem remained the main religious center for honoring Yahweh. Mourning rites continued during the whole exilic period in the ruins of the city and its Temple (Lam; Isa 63:7–64:12).

(e) FLIGHT AND PANIC (41:11–18). **12.** *great waters of Gibeon:* This landmark has to be connected to the "Great Pool" in 2 Sam 2.12ff. Gibeon is the present el-Jib; recent excavations there have brought to light an immense pool hewn in the rock (see J. B. Pritchard, *BA* 19 [1956] 68–70). Once Ishmael had escaped to Ammon, Johanan and the troop that the assassin had gathered by force took to flight. The crime could only be interpreted as a new revolt against Babylon; retaliation was to be expected (see 52:30). Egypt was the only neighboring country free from the Babylonian domination (cf. 2 Kgs 25:26). **17.** *lodging place of Chimham:* Chimham is only known as a personal name (2 Sam

19:38–41); the Hebr word *gērût,* "lodging place," corresponds to the Oriental *khan* (see A. Alt, *JTS* 11 [1960] 364–65).

105   (E) Sojourn in Egypt (42:1–44:30). These chapters present the last act of Jeremiah's martyrdom. The prophet closed his eyes forever on his mortally wounded country and on the undying idolatry of his people. His life had been a tragedy to the end.

(a) SEARCH FOR GUIDANCE (42:1–6). The group of fugitives, still in the lodging place near Bethlehem, hesitate regarding what should be done; an oracle from the Lord would cut short their perplexity. But Jeremiah's precaution to make sure that his answer would be accepted makes one suspect that the decision to go down to Egypt was already definitive.

(b) THE DIVINE ANSWER (42:7–18). The answer came to Jeremiah only 10 days later; the delay certainly aggravated the situation, for the fear of the Babylonians could only have increased. Also this delay proves well enough that true prophetical inspiration does not depend on human insight. **10.** The verse is a clear reminiscence of Jeremiah's call, which has been decisive for his entire life (1:10; 24:6; 31:4,28). The prophet affirms that they should not fear Nebuchadnezzar (vv 11ff.); in fact, we have no proof that the king avenged his governor's assassination (see 52:30). **16.** Jeremiah predicts an invasion of Egypt by Nebuchadnezzar; we shall discuss this historical problem later (cf. 43:8–13).

106   (c) THE REFUSAL TO STAY HOME (42:19–43:7). With a number of critics, we transpose 43:1–3 before 42:19–22 for a more logical sequence of the narrative. Azariah is afraid to attack Yahweh and his messenger directly, so he turns against a third party, the less dangerous Baruch. **43:5.** *whole remnant:* Only this small company now stationed near Bethlehem, among whom were some who had taken refuge in Transjordan and had recently returned to Judah (40:11–12). **7.** *Tahpanhes:* A frontier city of the eastern delta (cf. 2:16).

(d) NEBUCHADNEZZAR IN EGYPT (43:8–13). Once in Tahpanhes, Jeremiah reiterates his prediction of Nebuchadnezzar's invasion of Egypt, in a prophetic action. **9.** *brickyard:* The Hebr word *malbēn,* "brickmold," is hard to explain in this sentence. *royal building:* Lit., "the house of Pharaoh." Inasmuch as the king had no residence here, it must have been an administrative building, or the governor's palace. **10.** *my servant:* Jeremiah always believed that Nebuchadnezzar had been commissioned by Yahweh to rule over the entire Near East (cf. 25:9; 27:6; 42:7ff.).) **13.** *in the land of Egypt:* Better read with LXX, "That are in On." On is the Hebr form of the Egyptian name for Heliopolis, situated about 5 mi. NE of Cairo. The city was well known for its temple of Re (sun), whose entrance was preceded by two rows of obelisks, one of which still stands. According to a fragmentary tablet in the British Museum, Nebuchadnezzar did invade Egypt during Amasis's reign (570–526), in his 37th year (568–567), which corresponds roughly to the date given by Ezekiel for the same event (Ezek 29:17–20; cf. *ANET* 308).

107   (e) JEREMIAH'S LAST WORDS (44:1–30). The chapter presents the religious situation of the exiles in Egypt, soon after the fall of Jerusalem in 587. Jeremiah had to fight constantly against the recurring idolatry of his people, which, for him, had been the true cause of the kingdom's downfall; the punishment turned out to be meaningless for these Judeans.

1. *Migdol:* The name means simply "tower" or "fortress." Several places have this name; the present Migdol, as well as that in Ezek 29:10, seems to have been recently discovered (cf. E. D. Oren, *BASOR* 256 [1984]

7–44). For Noph and Tahpanhes, see 2:16. *Pathros:* The Hebr transcription of the Egyptian *p'-t'-rsy,* "Southern Land"—i.e., Upper Egypt. Jeremiah probably addressed only the refugees who had taken him down to Egypt, and who are now in the north. This title must come from a later redactor who extended the sermon to all Jewish colonies in Egypt. **2–14.** Jeremiah gives his explanation of the present miseries; idolatrous practices have broken the covenant. The original oracle is probably limited to vv 2 and 7–8 (Rudolph); the remaining part of the speech uses abundantly the former sermons of the prophet on related subjects (e.g., chap. 7). **15–19.** The people interpret the same history in an absolutely opposite way: these calamities have been caused precisely because idolatry has been eradicated by the Josian reform (see D. N. Freedman, *Int* 21 [1967] 32–49). When the "queen of heaven" (cf. 7:16–20) had her worshipers in Israel, great prosperity existed; thus, the future could be assured only by a return to that cult. **27.** *I am watching:* The threat is pronounced by the key word of the call narrative *šāqad,* "to watch" (see comment on 1:11–12; 31:28). **30.** The text merely compares the fate of Zedekiah with that of Hophra. From Herodotus (*Hist.* 2.161–63,169; 4.159) we learn that in 570 an Egyptian general, Amasis, proclaimed himself king and marched against Hophra, who was killed by the people.

108   (F) The Consolation of Baruch (45:1–5). This word of consolation is dated 605, the year of the writing of the scroll (chap. 36). **3.** Baruch uttered his own "confessions" (cf. 20:7–18). One of these sufferings must have been the obligation to hide, with his master, to escape Jehoiakim's persecution (36:26). **5.** *great things:* There is much speculation about what these "things" were. From the Lord's answer, he apparently asked Yahweh to suspend his sentence on Jerusalem and Judah. Such a prayer is hopeless; however, Baruch's life will be saved.

109   (V) Oracles against the Nations (46:1–51:64). In the LXX, these oracles are found immediately after the title in 25:13c and are concluded by the vision of the cup of judgment (25:15–38); in general, critics agree that the LXX represents the primitive order of the book. In other prophetic books (Isa, Ezek), the oracles against the nations are inserted between those against Israel and those promising the restoration of the chosen people. Within this section, the order of the nations is also different in both recensions. The MT follows a geographical pattern, moving from W to E, and the LXX adopts a logical pattern, the nations' political importance. Finally, the authenticity of this section has been the subject of long discussions. For a while, most exegetes rejected it totally as a later addition (Duhm, Volz, etc.). Now such a radical position is no longer accepted, and an authentic nucleus is acknowledged; in fact, each oracle has to be considered separately. Again, it would be strange if Jeremiah, like the other prophets, had not addressed the foreign nations! This was included in the very object of his whole mission (1:10) and had been a part of Baruch's scroll (36:2); Jeremiah even acknowledged that such oracles had been pronounced by his predecessors (28:8). However, these oracles underwent frequent expansions, much more so than any other section of Jer.

110   (A) Against Egypt (46:1–28) (LXX 26:2–28). Two different poems are directed against Egypt. The opening verse serves as title to the whole section (chaps. 46–51), which had to be repeated (cf. 25:13c) once these oracles had been displaced.

(a) THE BATTLE OF CARCHEMISH (46:2–12) (LXX 26:2–12). The first poem is dated the year Babylon and Egypt encountered each other in battle at

Carchemish (605). Nebuchadnezzar, then the general of the army, did defeat Neco at Carchemish in 605. Soon after, in August, his father, Nabopolassar, died; Nebuchadnezzar returned quickly to Babylon to be proclaimed king, leaving his victory limited to northern Syria. However, the event had been important enough to make Babylon the leading power of the Near East (see Wiseman, *Chronicles* 67–69). The poem is certainly authentic (compare v 5 and 6:25; 20:3,10; 49:29). **2.** *Carchemish:* The site of the ancient city is at the present Jerablus, on the upper course of the Euphrates. **9.** *Cush* is the ancient name for Ethiopia. The identification of Put is disputed; most likely it designates a part of Libya (see T. Lambdin, *IDB* 3. 971). *Lud:* Although the Bible mentions Lydians as a population related to Egypt and living in Africa (Gen 10:13), and some scholars would rather see here a reference to the remote Lydians of Asia Minor (which seems to be out of context), we prefer to read *lūbîm,* "Libyans," instead of *lūdîm* (Lydians); indeed they are associated with Put in Nah 3:9 as allies of Egypt. **11.** Gilead figures once more as an ideal place to search for balm (8:22; 51:8). Egypt's sole reaction is to cure her wounds.

(b) THE INVASION OF EGYPT (46:13–28) (LXX 26:13–28). We have seen that Jeremiah, soon after 587, had a similar prediction, which was realized only in 568–567, according to our present information (see 43:8–13). Some critics would still date the poem *ca.* 601–600, when Nebuchadnezzar and Neco met at the Egyptian frontier. We prefer to situate the oracle toward the end of Jeremiah's career. **14.** For the identification of the geographical names, see comment on 44:1. **15.** *Apis:* The sacred bull of the god Ptah, the protector of Memphis. **16.** *Up! let us return:* The reflection is from the mercenaries in the Egyptian army, mentioned in vv 9 and 21, who were quite numerous (Herodotus, *Hist.* 2.152–54). **17.** *the noise . . . go by:* Most exegetes find here a wordplay on Hophra's name *w'h-ib-r',* and the Hebr vb. *he'ĕbîr,* "go by"—as a sarcastic remark on the futility of the help Zedekiah expected from the Egyptian king during the final siege of Jerusalem (cf. 37:5–6). **25–26.** These verses, in prose and recalling the oracle against Hophra (44:30), extend the invasion to Upper Egypt, Thebes being its capital and Amon its main god; they are considered to be a later addition (cf. Ezek 29:13–19). The promise of restoration will be repeated for other nations (48:47; 49:6,39), which is clearly a reinterpretation of these prophecies (see P. Höffken, *VT* 27 [1977] 398–412).

111   (B) Against Philistia (47:1–7) (LXX 29:1–7). 1. The original title was only "Against the Philistines," as in the LXX. The date given, "Before Pharaoh attacked Gaza," is therefore irrelevant to the rest of the poem (cf. E. Kutsch, ". . . denn Jahwe vernichtet die Philister," *Die Botschaft und die Boten* [Fest. H.-W. Wolff; ed. J. Jeremias, *et al.;* Neukirchen, 1981] 253–67 for a good study of the history of this oracle). That event may have occurred *ca.* 609, when Neco had been victorious at Megiddo (see Herodotus, *Hist.* 2.159). The invasion "from the north," i.e. from Babylonia, is described in pure Jeremian style. The prophecy was fulfilled in 604–603; Nebuchadnezzar then appeared on the coastal plain and took Ashkelon after an arduous siege (see Wiseman, *Chronicles* 69). **4.** *Tyre and Sidon:* These two important Phoenician seaports are presented as allies of Philistia, which they no doubt were. *Caphtor:* Generally identified with Crete, where the Philistines originated (cf. Amos 9:7). However, the term might be generic, to designate the islands of the Aegean Sea, for the Philistines were not exclusively from Crete. **5.** *Gaza . . . Ashkelon . . . Ashdod:* Added from 25:20, they were the main Philistine cities along

the coast. *their valley:* We should read instead, with the LXX, the "Anaqim," a people of tall structure who terrified the Israelites on their arrival in Palestine (Num 13:22ff.; Deut 1:28). These cities are now left to their mourning (cf. 16:6).

112   (C) Against Moab (48:1–47) (LXX 31:1–40). The long oracle against Moab, the central state of Transjordan, appears as a complex mosaic of different poems and their expansions. For the identification of the large number of geographical names, we refer to Rudolph's *Jeremia* 263–65; cf. also Y. Aharoni, *LBib,* 305–9). Moab had been opposed to Israel from the time of the exodus (Num 22–24); in the 9th cent., her strong king, Mesha, succeeded in freeing himself from Israelite domination, which he celebrated in his famous inscription (*ANET* 320–21). In 601–600, Moabite groups were sent by Nebuchadnezzar to uproot Jehoiakim's revolt (cf. 2 Kgs 24:2; Jer 12:7–13), which may be the occasion of the present oracle. The prophecy came true in 582–581, when Nebuchadnezzar invaded Moab and Ammon, according to Josephus's testimony (*Ant.* 10.9.7 § 181).

1–10. The first poem describes the total destruction of Moab, personified as a woman; the invasion moves from N to S, obliging the Moabites to seek refuge in the desert (v 6). **5.** The verse is taken literally from Isa 15:5; the traditional Assyro-Babylonian policy of deportations will be applied also to Moab. **7.** *Chemosh:* This chief god of the Moabites is mentioned often in Mesha's inscription.

11–28. The following verses must be considered a new poem, for Moab is addressed as masc. The prophet proclaims the downfall of the whole land (vv 11–17) and applies then the same fate to the individual cities (vv 18–28). **11.** The Moabite wine, the central theme of Isaiah's oracle on Moab (Isa 16:6ff.), was reputed for its quality. Here it symbolizes the land's tranquillity; indeed, Moab was outside the normal route of invasions and was only rarely disturbed.

29–39. The present section is an awkward combination of texts borrowed from Isaiah's oracles against Moab (Isa 15–16). The interpolator's purpose is to give the reason for such a punishment—Moab's pride and loftiness of heart against Israel and its God; the same reason figures also in Zeph 2:8–11; Ezek 25:8–11.

40–47. This last part of the poem is another mosaic of biblical texts. Rudolph keeps only vv 40–42 as original. **43–44.** The verses are a quotation of Isa 24:17–18; doom is inevitable.

113   (D) Against Ammon (49:1–6) (LXX 30:17–21). This authentic oracle against Ammon can also be dated *ca.* 601–600 (cf. 48; 2 Kgs 24:2). Ammon was situated N of Moab, but her territorial limits were never clearly defined; her capital was Rabbah, modern Amman. The Ammonites rejoiced at the fall of Jerusalem (Ezek 25:1–7), and their king, Baalis, was the principal author of Gedaliah's murder (cf. 40:11ff.). For the fulfillment of the oracle, see the oracle against Moab. **1.** *Milcom:* The Ammonites' chief god. *disinherited Gad:* At the time of the conquest, Gad had received as his lot a part of the Ammonite territory (Num 32:33–37; Josh 13:24–28). But after Tiglath-pileser III had conquered this region in 734 (2 Kgs 15:29), the Ammonites probably kept it under their political influence, for they were themselves vassals of Assyria. In fact, at that time, Amos had already reproached them in the same manner (Amos 1:13). **3.** *Heshbon:* The city is located at modern Hesban, in the northern part of Moab; Heshbon had probably been an Ammonite possession in its early history (Judg 11:26). Now it lies down in mourning (cf. 47:5), and the Ammonite god and people are exiled, as happened to Moab

(48:7; Amos 1:15). **6.** For this promise of restoration, missing in the LXX, see 46:26 and 48:47.

114   (E) Against Edom (49:7–22) (LXX 30:1–16). Edom was the S Transjordan state, extending from the Wadi Zered to the Gulf of Aqabah. Her capital, Bozrah, is now situated at Buseirah, some 22 mi. SE of the Dead Sea. Although the Edomites had some relationship with the Israelites (Gen 25:19ff.; 36:1), their antagonism was ancestral. They rejoiced at Jerusalem's downfall and, apparently, they plundered the south (cf. Ezek 35:1–15; Obad 10–17; Lam 4:21; Ps 137:7). We have no record of a Babylonian invasion of Edom; she must have submitted as did her neighbors. The present state of the oracle shows a clear influence of Obadiah; we should probably keep as original only vv 7–8,10b–11, and 22. **7.** Edom was reputed for her wisdom traditions (Obad 8–9; Bar 3:22–23; Job 2:11; etc.). Teman is often identified with Tawilan, just below Jebel Heidan. In the present passage, Teman represents the whole of Edom. **8.** *Dedan:* Ordinarily it refers to a district in NW Arabia; there is a possibility that a clan of Dedanites had settled in Edom. *Esau:* The ancestor of Edom, as Jacob, his brother, was the ancestor of Israel (Gen 36).

115   (F) Against Damascus (49:23–27) (LXX 30:29–33). The true title should be "Against the Syrian Cities." These cities are not listed in the vision of the "cup of judgment" (25:15ff.). Inasmuch as all the Aramean city-states fell under Tiglath-pileser III in the 8th cent., the present oracle would have a more suitable context in that period. However, Jeremiah could have pronounced these words *ca.* 605, when Nebuchadnezzar crushed the Egyptians at Carchemish, or even more likely *ca.* 601–600, when Aramean groups were commissioned by the Babylonian king to settle Jehoiakim's revolt (2 Kgs 24:2–4; Jer 12:7–13).

116   (G) Against Arabia (49:28–33) (LXX 30:23–28). Jeremiah now turns to the Bedouin tribes of the Syrian desert, E of Transjordan, i.e., Kedar. In his chronicles, Nebuchadnezzar recorded the raid he led against these tribes in 599–598 (cf. Wiseman, *Chronicles* 71).

117   (H) Against Elam (49:34–39) (LXX 25:14–20). Finally, Jeremiah condemns Elam, NE of the Persian Gulf. The country fell under the Assyrian power when Ashurbanipal destroyed the capital, Susa, in 640. Thereafter, Elam came progressively under the control of the Medes; in 612, Cyaxares, the Median king, assisted Nabopolassar of Babylon in his final assault on Nineveh. For the following years, our information on Elam is scanty. **35.** *bow of Elam:* The Elamites were recognized as excellent archers (Isa 22:6). **36.** *four winds:* Probably Ezekiel's expression for "all directions" (Ezek 37:9). **39.** On this late promise of restoration, see 46:26 (cf. also 48:47; 49:6).

118   (I) Against Babylon (50:1–51:58) (LXX 27:1–28:58). Very few exegetes would still attribute this long poem or series of poems against Babylon to Jeremiah; we rather have to deal with the work of a disciple who wrote not long before 538, the year Babylon fell to the Persians. In fact, Jeremiah strongly believed that Babylon was Yahweh's instrument for vengeance; one should pray for Babylon and contribute to its welfare for the exile in its midst would be long (27:6ff.; 29). The present atmosphere is entirely different: Babylon is on the verge of downfall and the exiles will soon return home, the two constant themes of these chapters. Thus, we are in the context of the exile, and the poems are to be compared to Isa 13–14 (*ca.* 550) and Dt-Isa.

50:1–7. This first section presents the two leading themes: the fall of Babylon (vv 2–3) and the return from exile (vv 4–7). **2.** *Bel . . . Merodach:* Bel was the main god of Nippur, whose Sumerian name was EN-LIL, "the lord of wind." He was later identified with the main god of Babylon, Marduk (Merodach), who became the head of the Babylonian pantheon. Thus, the poet refers here to this one god. **3.** *a people from the north:* Jeremiah's common expression to designate the future invader in his early poems (cf. chaps. 2–6). The author does not use it properly here, for the Persians came from the east. **4–5.** The return from exile coincides with this last event; it is also the occasion to renew the covenant (cf. 31:31–34). **6–7.** The wandering of the sheep must be an allusion to Judah's idolatrous cult on high places (cf. 2:20; 3:2; 23:1ff.; Ezek 34; Isa 53:6).

8–20. The same themes are given further development. The catastrophe is so imminent that the foreigners— the exiled people—are asked to flee quickly. **17b–18.** The passage breaks the sequence of vv 17a and 19. Assyria had conquered northern Israel in 721 (2 Kgs 17:3ff.) and had been punished; the same fate is now befalling Babylon.

21–28. The destruction of the glorious city is proclaimed in Jerusalem. **21.** *Merathaim:* The dual form of the word *mārā*, "twice bitter"; the author proposes a wordplay on the name of the region N of the Persian Gulf where the Tigris and the Euphrates meet, called *nār marrūti*. *Pekod:* It means "visit" or "punishment," another wordplay on *Puqūdu*, a region E of Babylon (Ezek 23:23). **23.** *the hammer:* It symbolizes Babylon as the instrument of God's vengeance (51:20–23).

29–32. Babylon is destroyed for its insolence! Most of the expressions used here are already found in vv 14–16,21,26–27. **29.** *holy one of Israel:* This name of Yahweh is characteristic of Isa; it is found here only in chaps. 50–51. **33–40.** The second main theme, the restoration of Israel, is now evolved. Yahweh is called the redeemer of Israel (*gō'ēl;* cf. Lev 25:47ff.), a characteristic of Dt-Isa (e.g., Isa 41:14; 43:1,14; 44:6,22–24; etc.). **35–38.** The word "sword" is repeated emphatically in this frenetic judgment on both the people and the material civilization of Babylon; the enumeration has a close parallel in Dt-Isa (Isa 44:25,27; 45:3).

119   41–46. The present section is purely a collection of previous texts. **41–43.** The poem on the "foe from the north" is quoted, with the change of "Zion" for "Babylon" (cf. 6:22–24). **44–46.** The oracle against Edom is quoted, with the same required changes (cf. 49:19–21).

51:1–19. The combined themes of the destruction of Babylon and of the return of the exiles reappear. **1.** *Chaldea:* Instead of *kaśdîm* (Chaldeans), the MT has its cryptogram, in *atbash* (cf. 25:25–26), *leb qāmāy* (the heart of my adversaries). **7.** *golden cup:* We deal once more with an allusion to the "cup of judgment" (25:15ff.); it is now said to be of gold, for Babylon was fabulously rich. **11–14.** This assault against Babylon recalls the one against Egypt (46:3ff.). *Media's kings:* Previously the author used Jeremiah's expression, "the foe from the north" (50:3,9,41; 51:48); hence, this may be a gloss. Until the middle of the 6th cent., the Medes were the leading power of Iran; they then fell to Cyrus, the Persian king, who incorporated them into his empire. Because the Persians took Babylon in 538, it may well be that the Medes represent them, as in Isa 13:17. **15–19.** This passage is a doublet of 10:12–16.

20–26. The image of Babylon as the hammer of God's vengeance (50:23) is now developed in a frenzied war song (cf. 50:35–38). Now that its work is over, the hammer must be shattered, although its might is comparable to a lofty mountain.

27–33. Babylon is under the assault, being reduced to

a threshing floor. **27.** *Ararat, Minni, Ashkenaz:* These three geographical names are well known in the cuneiform texts (Urartu, Mannay, Ašguzaya). They are all regions of Armenia, in the neighborhood of Lake Van and Lake Urmia. They were successively conquered by the Medes and the Persians, and some of their contingents were part of the Persian army that conquered Babylon in 538.

44–48. The present section is a severe attack on Babylon's main god, Bel-Marduk (cf. 50:2), which is the occasion of a general joy for the remaining part of the universe.

49–57. The reasons for Babylon's downfall are now enumerated. The law of retaliation has to be applied; the heathens have profaned the Temple by their presence within its enclosure (cf. Lam 1:10).

58. A final verse proclaims the leveling of Babylon's mighty fortifications. But Cyrus did not destroy the city in 538, for it surrendered without a fight. It is only in 482 that it was totally laid waste by Xerxes I on the occasion of a revolt.

120   (J) The Oracle in the Euphrates (51:59–64) (LXX 28:59–64). It has been customary to consider this short narrative as fictitious to justify the presence of the long oracle against Babylon. Only a few would still doubt the historicity of this event, which occurred in 594–593, under Zedekiah. The ambassadors of the neighboring kings met in Jerusalem to form a coalition of the western states for overthrowing the Babylonian domination (cf. chap. 27). **59.** *Seraiah:* According to his genealogy, he was Baruch's brother (32:12). Zedekiah had to justify his conduct, which would have been the purpose of the present delegation. Through Baruch, he must have been friendly with Jeremiah. **61.** Seraiah has to read the content of the book; we presume that the reading has been done privately, for the divulgation of the oracle in Babylonia would have been quite imprudent. After all, Jeremiah has just assured the exiles that such a downfall of Babylon would be long coming, so that they would have to settle in their new land (cf. chap. 29) **62.** Probably another addition borrowed from the preceding poem (50:3; 51:26). We will never know what was written in the book, and the redactor of the present narrative did not know either. **63–64.** This action is prophetic (see comment on 13:1–14), dramatizing the word of doom on Babylon by the sinking of the book in the Euphrates. *weary themselves:* The last word of v 58 is *wĕyāʿēpû*, and the redactional note ("Thus far the words of Jeremiah")

probably followed it immediately. When the present pericope (vv 59–64) was introduced here, the note, wrongly separated from its primitive context, was put after it.

121   (VI) Historical Appendix (52:1–34). This last chapter, a later addition, as 51:64 testifies, reproduces 2 Kgs 24:18–25:30, with the exception of 25:22–26, which is Gedaliah's story, recorded in greater detail in Jer 40–41. In the present exposition, we shall limit ourselves to the main differences between the two texts; we refer to the commentary on Kgs for the remaining parts. **20.** *twelve oxen of bronze:* They are not mentioned in 2 Kgs 25:16, and with reason, for Ahaz gave them as a tribute to Tiglath-pileser III (2 Kgs 16:17–18). **28–30.** The verses are missing from both 2 Kgs and the LXX. A special source that follows the Babylonian chronology has been used; nothing can disprove its historical value. *seventh year:* According to the Babylonian practice of postdating, the accessional year is not counted; thus, Nebuchadnezzar's first regnal year was 604; the first deportation occurred, then, in 597. But the Hebr computation takes the accessional year as the first regnal; hence, 2 Kgs 24:12 dated it in the king's eighth year. *eighteenth year:* Both 2 Kgs 25:8 and Jer 52:12 have "nineteenth" for the same reason. *twenty-third year:* This third deportation, in the year 582–581, is known only from the present source. Some historians explain it as a reprisal for Gedaliah's murder, while others would rather believe that in the same year Judah joined in the Ammonite-Moabite revolt, which Nebuchadnezzar mastered (Josephus, *Ant.* 10.9.7 §181–82). A final solution has not yet been reached. Moreover, there is a great difference in the number of the deported people. The book of Kings gives only the number of the first deportation (2 Kgs 24:14,16): 10,000 and 8,000! These figures are certainly round numbers and much too high. Those given here, being so precise, must come from official lists of deportees; although we cannot suspect their authenticity, they still could represent only special categories of people and would not constitute the exact number.

This section of Kgs has been reproduced here probably to show how Jeremiah's prophecies were fulfilled. As he so constantly repeated, Jerusalem was to be destroyed and Judah sent into exile. With the liberation of Jehoiachin, his hope in the future was given a first sign of realization.

19

OLD TESTAMENT APOCALYPTICISM AND ESCHATOLOGY

John J. Collins

BIBLIOGRAPHY

1 Carroll, R. P., *When Prophecy Failed* (NY, 1979). Charlesworth, J. H., *OTP*. Collins, J. J., *The Apocalyptic Imagination* (NY, 1984); *Daniel, with an Introduction to Apocalyptic Literature* (GR, 1984); (ed.), *Apocalypse: The Morphology of a Genre* (Semeia 14; Chico, 1979). Gese, H., "Anfang und Ende der Apokalyptik, dargestellt am Sacharjabuch," *ZTK* 70 (1973) 20–49. Gruenwald, I., *Apocalyptic and Merkavah Mysticism* (Leiden, 1980). Hanson, P. D., "Apocalypse Genre;" "Apocalypticism," *IDBSup* 27–34; *The Dawn of Apocalyptic* (Phl, 1975); (ed.), *Visionaries and Their Apocalypses* (Phl, 1983). Hellholm, D. (ed.), *Apocalypticism in the Mediterranean World and the Near East* (Tübingen, 1983). Hengel, M., *Judaism and Hellenism* (Phl, 1974). Knibb, M. A., "Prophecy and the Emergence of the Jewish Apocalypses," *Israel's Prophetic Tradition* (Fest. P. R. Ackroyd; ed.

R. Coggins, *et al.;* Cambridge, 1982) 155–80. Koch, K., *The Rediscovery of Apocalyptic* (Naperville, 1972); *The Prophets*, vol. 2 (Phl, 1984); (ed.), *Apokalyptik* (Darmstadt, 1982). Plöger, O., *Theocracy and Eschatology* (Richmond, 1968). Rowland, C., *The Open Heaven: A Study of Apocalyptic in Judaism and Christianity* (NY, 1982). Rowley, H. H., *The Relevance of Apocalyptic* (Greenwood, 1980). Russell, D. S., *The Method and Message of Jewish Apocalyptic* (Phl, 1964). Schmithals, W., *The Apocalyptic Movement* (Nash, 1975). Sparks, H. F. D., ed., *AOT*. Stone, M. E., "Apocalyptic Literature," *Jewish Writings of the Second Temple Period* (CRINT 2; Phl, 1984) 383–441; *Scripture, Sects and Visions* (Phl, 1980). Wanke, G., "Prophecy and Psalms in the Persian Period," *CHJ* 1. 162–88.

2 OUTLINE

3 THE HISTORICAL DEVELOPMENT FROM PROPHECY TO APOCALYPTICISM

(I) Definitions. Eschatology and apocalypticism are ambiguous terms which scholars use with various connotations.

(A) Eschatology. *Eschatology* is literally the doctrine of the last things (→ OT Thought, 77:164). The term was introduced in systematic theology in the 19th cent. to refer to matters concerning the judgement after

death and the end of the world. In biblical studies it has a broader range and refers to the expectation of any decisive change in the course of history through the intervention of God. The prophets were primarily concerned with the fate of Israel and Judah. When Amos declared that "the end has come upon my people Israel" (8:2), he did not envisage the end of the world but only the end of Israel as a political entity. Nonetheless, it is important to note that the prophets often used cosmic imagery—i.e., they spoke of particular historical crises as if they involved the destruction or renewal of the world. So, e.g., Jer 4:23 expresses the impending Babylonian invasion in a vision of cosmic desolation: "I looked on the earth, and lo, it was waste and void," and Isaiah describes the reign of a future king in terms of a transformation of nature (Isa 11:1–9). In short, *national eschatology* (concern for the future of Israel) and *cosmic eschatology* (concern for the future of the world) cannot be cleanly separated, even in the preexilic prophets. The cosmic imagery probably derives from the language of the cult which addressed the God of Israel as the judge of all the earth (Ps 98:8–9). *Personal eschatology*, concern for the fate of the individual after death, does not become important until the end of the Old Testament period, in the apocalyptic literature, and then it is usually discussed in the context of national and cosmic expectation.

4   (B) Apocalypticism. *Apocalypticism* is a term derived from apocalypse, the Gk. word for revelation and the name of the last book of the Bible. There has been extensive debate about the terminology (see P. D. Hanson, *HBMI* 465–88). There is general agreement that the main corpus of Jewish apocalyptic literature was produced *ca. 200* BC–AD 100 and includes the canonical book of Daniel and such pseudepigrapha as *1 Enoch, 2 Enoch, 4 Ezra, 2 Baruch, 3 Baruch,* and *Apoc. Abraham* (see Koch, *Rediscovery* 23). Some scholars focus on the literary form of this material as the revelation of heavenly mysteries (e.g., Rowland, *Open Heaven;* H. Stegemann in D. Hellholm [ed.], *Apocalypticism* 495–530). From this perspective the visions in Zech 1–6 might be considered to constitute the earliest apocalypse (so H. Gese, *ZTK* [1973] 20–49). Others focus rather on the content of the literature and esp. on the eschatology involved (E. P. Sanders in Hellholm [ed.], *Apocalypticism* 447–59). Even here, differences arise. P. D. Hanson focuses primarily on cosmic eschatology, expressed in mythical language, and so he finds the "dawn of apocalyptic" in the early postexilic period in such documents as Third Isaiah. Others attach more importance to the introduction of personal eschatology in the writings of the Hellenistic period (so Collins, in Hanson [ed.], *Visionaries* 61–84; a good spectrum of opinion is represented in that volume). The position taken here is that an apocalypse is defined by both form and content: as a genre of revelatory literature, mediated by an angel or heavenly being, which is concerned with a transcendent world populated by angels and with transcendent eschatology which has a personal as well as a cosmic dimension (for elaboration, see Collins [ed.], *Semeia* 14, and *Apocalyptic Imagination,* chap. 1). On this definition, the earliest apocalypses are found in *1 Enoch* and Dan in the Hellenistic period, although these have important links with older traditions. Other material is called apocalyptic insofar as it resembles the apocalypses in some respect, but this usage is inevitably loose.

5   (II) Early Postexilic Prophecy.
(A) Second Isaiah. The postexilic period was inaugurated by the anonymous oracles in Isa 40–55. The opening verse, "Comfort, give comfort to my people, says your God" (Isa 40:1), is indicative of a major shift in emphasis in the history of prophecy. The preexilic prophets had sometimes prophesied salvation as well as destruction, but their dominant emphasis was on judgment. In Isa 40–55, however, the emphasis shifts to the expectation of final and lasting salvation.

Dt-Isa viewed the release of the Jewish captives from Babylon as a decisive event of cosmic significance.

According to Ezra 1:1–4 the exile was brought to an end by the decree of Cyrus, King of Persia. For the prophet, however, the crucial decree was issued in the heavenly council by the Lord (40:3,6). Israel was saved forever and would never be put to shame again (45:17). Henceforth the other nations too would recognize the sovereignty of the God of Israel (45:23–24; 49:22–26). The wealth of Egypt and Ethiopia would flow into Jerusalem (45:14). Kings would be astonished at the transformation of Israel, the servant of the Lord, who would be a light to the nations and would justify many by patiently enduring the sufferings of the exile and waiting for the manifestation of its God. The Persian king, Cyrus, was the instrument of Yahweh, or even his "Messiah" or anointed king (44:1).

6   Dt-Isa insisted (43:19; 48:6) that the liberation from Babylon was "a new thing." Yet it could only be comprehended by analogy with the great events of the past. The call to prepare in the desert the way of the Lord (40:3) was in effect announcing a new exodus (a theme already present in Hos 2:14–15). Isa 51:9–11 evokes an even more ancient model, asking God, "Was it not you who crushed Rahab, you who pierced the dragon? Was it not you who dried up the sea, the waters of the great deep?" The Bible does not tell the story of a battle between God and "the dragon," but it often alludes to it (e.g., Pss 74:12–17; 89:10–11; Job 26:12–13; see the comprehensive study of J. Day, *God's Conflict with the Dragon and the Sea* [Cambridge, 1985]). The story is now known from the Canaanite texts discovered at Ugarit in northern Syria in 1929, where the God Baal does battle with the Sea (Yamm) and monsters such as Lotan (Leviathan) (see *ANET* 129–42). In the cult of the Jerusalem Temple, Yahweh replaced Baal as the victorious god, and the story of his battle with the sea served as a metaphor for creation and, as in Isa 51, for the exodus. Second Isaiah tried to convey the significance of the restoration from Babylon by comparing it to this mythic battle. The imagery of the battle with the dragon would play an important part in postexilic eschatology (e.g., Isa 27:1; Dan 7).

The utopian prophecies of Isa 40–55 must surely have buoyed the spirits of the returning exiles. Before long, however, it became apparent that the actual future would not be as glorious as the prophet predicted. We can sense the emerging problem in Isa 62:6–7: watchmen are "to remind the Lord . . . until he reestablishes Jerusalem." The problem of the inadequate fulfillment of the prophecies of restoration can be seen more vividly, however, in the prophet Haggai.

7   (B) Haggai. Haggai 1:6 describes the extreme poverty of the postexilic community. According to Haggai there was a simple explanation for this great disappointment: "Because my house lies in ruins, while each of you hurries to his own house" (Hag 1:9). According to Ezra 6:14–15 the Temple was only rebuilt two decades after the return, at the urging of Haggai and his fellow prophet Zechariah. Yet the promised transformation did not follow. In the manner of prophets down to modern times, Haggai resolutely refused to admit that his prediction was mistaken (see Carroll, *When Prophecy Failed* 157–68). Instead he insisted that it would yet be fulfilled "in a little while."

We see here the basic strategy by which the time-bound oracles of the prophets were still regarded as valid after the time for their fulfillment had passed: they were projected into the future. Neither Dt-Isa nor Hag was discredited when the restoration did not turn out as they predicted. Instead they were understood to refer to a future eschatological time.

Haggai also introduces another aspect of postexilic

eschatology: messianic expectation. The concluding oracle (2:20–23) promises to overthrow kingdoms and set Zerubbabel (the governor) "as a signet ring." The clear implication is that Zerubbabel will become king on the throne of David (see D. Petersen, *Haggai and Zechariah 1–8* [Phl, 1984] 102–6). The oracle seems to predict the overthrow of Persia and restoration of Judean independence in the near future. Yet it does not call for rebellion or urge anyone to crown Zerubbabel king. Presumably Zerubbabel would restore the Davidic line. His reign would not entail the end of history but it would be part of the final and glorious restoration of Israel. The timing of this transformation, however, was in the hands of God.

8   (C) Zechariah. Messianic expectation is also reflected in Zech 1–8, contemporary with Hag. Unlike Dt-Isa and Hag, Zechariah reports visions which are highly symbolic in character and are reminiscent of Ezek. These visions are explained to the prophet by an angel, in the manner of later apocalyptic literature. Like the other prophets of the day, Zechariah predicted that "my cities shall again overflow with prosperity" (1:17) and that the Lord himself would dwell in their midst (2:14–15). In this scenario, however, he attaches special importance to two figures: Zerubbabel and the high priest, Joshua, who are described as two "sons of oil" or anointed ones (Messiahs), who stand before the Lord. In chap. 3 we learn that Joshua has his opponents, who are symbolized in the vision as Satan. Satan is rebuked by the angel of the Lord. Joshua is fully vindicated and his guilt is taken away. Then he is told that God will bring "my servant the Shoot," which is to say that he will restore the Davidic line, and remove the guilt of the land. Zechariah returns to these two figures in chap. 6. A crown is placed on the head of Joshua, who is then told that the "Shoot" or Davidic heir will be enthroned and that the priest will be at his right hand. Many scholars suspect that the crown was originally placed on the head of Zerubbabel (cf. *NAB*, *NEB*). In any case it is clear that priest and king share the leadership of the community.

Here, as in Hag, there is some question about the import of this messianic expectation. We are told that the "Shoot" will rebuild the Temple, but not that he would overthrow Persia. That must be left in the hands of God. Zechariah is no revolutionary. He is more interested in the purity of the land than in its independence. The Davidic shoot is overshadowed by the priest (at least if the crown is placed on Joshua's head, as the Hebr text of 6:11 has it). We should emphasize that these "Messiahs" are not transcendent savior figures in the Christian sense. They are functionaries who hold offices in the restored Jewish community. The model of two Messiahs rather than one appears again in the DSS (Collins, *Apocalyptic Imagination* 122–26; → Apocrypha, 67:117).

9   (D) Ezekiel 40–48. In Hag and Zech we see one strand of postexilic eschatology, which looked for the lasting and glorious restoration of Jerusalem and attached great importance to the Temple and the priesthood. A similar strand can be seen in Ezek 40–48 in the great vision of the restored Jerusalem, where the prophet is guided by a mediating angel (Hanson, *Dawn of Apocalyptic* 228–40). In Ezekiel's vision, however, the messianic figure is a "prince," apparently something less than a king in political power, and there is no mention of an individual high priest (J. D. Levenson, *Theology of the Program of Restoration* [Missoula, 1976] 55–107; see Petersen, *Haggai and Zechariah 1–8* [→ 7 above] 116–19, for further differences between Ezek 40–48 and Zech).

The Ezek passage may come from a slightly earlier period than Hag and Zech.

10   (E) Third Isaiah. A very different attitude to the Temple is found in Isa 56–66 (Third Isaiah), a loose collection of oracles which probably derives from the disciples of Second Isaiah. Isa 66:1–2 directly questions whether an adequate house can be built for God on earth (cf. 1 Kgs 8; Acts 7). It is clear enough that the prophet who uttered this oracle was opposed to the program of Hag and attached far less importance to the Temple; however, less clear are the nature, cause, and extent of the division within the Jewish community which these verses reveal.

In 1975 Paul D. Hanson published a sweeping reconstruction of the early postexilic situation under the title *The Dawn of Apocalyptic.* According to Hanson, two groups competed for the control of the Jerusalem cult after the return from Babylon. One was the "hierocratic party" of the Zadokite priests. Their viewpoint is represented in Ezek 40–48, Hag, and Zech. The other was the "visionary party" whose viewpoint is expressed in Isa 56–66. Hanson regarded the latter as "proto-apocalyptic" because of their appeal for supernatural intervention and their hope for cosmic transformation, which arose out of their alienation from the priestly cult.

Hanson's reconstruction is attractive in its comprehension of material which has always baffled scholars. He is undeniably right that there were sharp differences within the postexilic community (besides the dispute over the Temple, contrast Ezek 44:9, "no foreigners, uncircumcised in heart and flesh, shall ever enter my sanctuary . . . ," with Isa 56:1–8, "and the foreigners who join themselves to the Lord . . . them I will bring to my holy mountain and make joyful in my house of prayer"). Many scholars, however, feel that Hanson has oversimplified the situation. He reads Isa 56–66 as a sustained polemic against the Zadokite cult. So, when Isa 57:1–13 denounces various idolatrous practices, including human sacrifices, Hanson assumes that traditional rhetoric is being used to denigrate the official priesthood. Other scholars read the passage literally and assume that it describes actual abuses. The difficulty of interpretation can be seen in Isa 66:3. The Hebr text juxtaposes participial phrases: "slaughtering the ox, slaying a man, sacrificing the sheep, breaking a dog's neck." The *NAB* translates this as "merely slaughtering an ox is like slaying a man," etc. (so also *RSV*). On this interpretation, Third Isaiah was rejecting the sacrificial cult completely. It is possible, however, to read the passage as "one who slaughters an ox also slays a man." In that case the prophet is not attacking sacrifice as such, but the ethics of the worshipers, and the polemic is directed not against the priesthood but against another segment of the population which was reverting to old idolatrous practices (cf. J. Blenkinsopp, *A History of Prophecy in Israel* [Phl, 1983] 249).

At the least, however, Hanson has shown persuasively that the group which produced Isa 56–66 was a powerless group at the fringes of postexilic society. This much can be inferred from a passage like Isa 65:13: "Lo, my servants shall eat but you shall go hungry; my servants shall drink but you shall be thirsty . . ."—evidently in the present the "servants" are the ones who are hungry and thirsty. They react to their marginal situation by appealing to God to intervene: "Oh that you would rend the heavens and come down, with the mountains quaking before you." (63:19). God is portrayed as a warrior drenched in blood (Isa 63) marching out to save his people as he did at the time of the exodus. The appeal to the supernatural arises from the apparent helplessness of natural means of transforming this world.

11 Perhaps the most striking eschatological passage is Isa 65:17: "'Lo, I am about to create new heavens and a new earth." The phrase is repeated in Rev 21:1, and is a major reason why scholars such as Hanson have used the term "apocalyptic" with reference to Third Isaiah. The idea of a new creation initially appears more radical than anything in the preexilic prophets or in Hag and Zech. The nature of the new creation, however, is not as different from the old creation as we might expect. People will live longer lives — whoever falls short of a hundred years will be accursed (65:20). Also, "they shall live in the houses they build and eat the fruit of the vineyards they plant" (65:21). Yet this is still mortal life, as we know it, though longer and better. Isa 65:25 appropriately quotes Isa 11:6 on the wolf and the lamb lying down together. The idea of salvation in early postexilic prophecy is not greatly different from that of older Israelite tradition. By contrast, it is greatly different from what we find in the apocalypses of the second century BC, where the belief in the resurrection of the dead is introduced.

The significance of Isa 56-66 for the development of postexilic eschatology is that it shows one setting in which eschatological hopes arose. We should not conclude, however, that such hopes *only* arose at the fringes of Jewish society. Hag and Zech were no less eschatological, although their ideal of the restored society was different. Both groups were concerned with the immediate future of the land of Israel. It should, of course, be noted that while the "servants" of Isa 65:13 were powerless within Judah, Judah itself was powerless in the wider international context; and so, even in the case of Hag and Zech, eschatology was still an expression of the hopes of the powerless.

12   **(III) Oracles of Uncertain Date.** The anonymous oracles of Isa 56-66 can be placed with some confidence after the end of the exile, because of their affinities with Isa 40-55 and the controversy over the rebuilding of the Temple. In the case of other postexilic oracles we are less fortunate. With the exception of Joel, all the oracles after Hag and Zech are anonymous (Malachi is probably not a proper name; the word, which means "my messenger" is taken from Mal 3:1). In no case do we have an explicit indication of date (Mal may be placed around the time of Ezra, because of the prominence of the problem of mixed marriages, but even this is not certain). Many of these oracles are attached to older biblical books. We should include here editorial additions to prophetic books, such as Amos 9:8b-15, and many of the passages introduced by the phrase "on that day" throughout the prophetic corpus (Blenkinsopp, *History of Prophecy* 261-62; the phrase evokes the eschatological "Day of the Lord," Amos 5:18; Zeph 1:14; Joel 2:1; etc.). The more significant eschatological compositions include Mal, Joel, Ezek 38-39, Zech 9-14, and Isa 24-27.

13   **(A) Malachi.** In the case of Malachi we at least know the problems he was addressing: corrupt priesthood, mixed marriages, and divorce. The prophet's prediction, "suddenly there will come to the Temple the Lord whom you seek" (3:1), is reminiscent of the Day of the Lord in Amos (compare Amos 9:1: "I saw the Lord standing beside the altar . . ."). His main contribution to the development of postexilic eschatology is in the introduction of an angel or messenger who will prepare the way before the Lord (3:1). In an appendix (3:23-24), this messenger is identified with Elijah the prophet. This motif reappears later in the DSS and in the NT (→ Apocrypha, 68:116; NT Thought 81:3). The identification with Elijah rests on the tradition that Elijah had been taken up to heaven alive (2 Kgs 2:11) and so had not

completed his earthly career. Elijah shared with Enoch the distinction of having been taken up without suffering death. Such figures were later the focus of considerable interest in the apocalyptic literature.

14   **(B) Joel.** In chaps. 1-2 the eschatological language of the Day of the Lord is used to describe the effect of a plague of locusts. Chapters 3-4, however, refer to purely eschatological events, and many scholars think that they are the work of a different prophet (e.g., Plöger, *Theocracy and Eschatology* 96-105). Chapter 4 accuses the people of Tyre and Sidon of selling Jews to the Greeks. The prophet reacts to such abuse of the powerless Jewish people by fantasizing about a judgment of the nations in the valley of Jehoshaphat and about a utopian state of the Jews when God pours out his spirit (3:1; cf. Acts 2:16-21) and transforms Judah so that the mountains drip wine. These eschatological oracles echo other prophetic passages (for the gift of the spirit, see Ezek 36:27; for the transformation of the mountains, see Amos 9:13).

15   **(C) Ezekiel 38-39.** The famous prophecy against Gog in Ezek 38-39 is, like Joel 4, a fantasy of vengeance against the nations. To some extent it is modeled on the ancient theme of the "conflict with the nations" which we find in, e.g., Ps 2, and which may be regarded as an adaptation of the myth of divine combat with the sea and its monsters — this figuring so prominently in biblical poetry (see Day, *God's Conflict* [→ 6 above] 125-38). The details, however, are patched together from various sources and represented as a fulfillment of ancient prophecy (38:17). The name Gog may have been suggested by the famous king Gyges of Lydia, but the prophecy is not concerned with real history or geography. It is rather a fantasy in which the opposition of Israel and the nations comes to a definitive climax. Motifs from these chapters are used in a similar way in Rev 19:17-21 and 20:8-10. We find here the increasing tendency in the postexilic period to understand earlier prophecy as referring not to specific crises such as the Assyrian and Babylonian invasions, but to the end of all history.

16   **(D) Zechariah 9-14.** There is general agreement that Zech 9-14 is not the work of the same prophet as the one who authored Zech 1-8. There is no consensus, however, as to when these oracles were composed. The most popular view sees in Zech 9 a reflection of the conquests of Alexander the Great. Paul Hanson, by contrast, regards Zech 9 as a reworking of a mythic pattern, without specific historical reference; he tries to relate Zech 9-14 to the conflict in the postexilic community that is reflected in Isa 56-66. Some have even defended a preexilic date for Zech 9 (for summaries of scholarship, see Hanson, *Dawn of Apocalyptic* 287-92; and B. Childs, *CIOTS* 475-76). Chapters 9-11 seem to reflect quite specific historical events, but these events are now lost to us. The allegory of the shepherds in chap. 11 is critical of the Israelite and Jewish leaders for neglecting their flock, and chap. 9 expresses the hope for a just and humble king. At least these chapters would seem to arise from dissatisfaction within the Jewish community with the leadership of the day.

Chapters 12-14 are made up primarily of eschatological oracles, introduced by the formula "on that day." The dominant theme is "the destruction of all nations that come against Jerusalem" (12:9). As with Ezek 38-39, we do not know whether these oracles were inspired by specific events or simply reflect the resentment of a small and powerless people. The depth of the resentment is reflected in the plague with which the Lord shall strike the nations (14:12): their flesh shall rot while they stand on their feet. Yet, the remnant of the nations will come up to Jerusalem to celebrate the feast of Booths (14:16). These oracles still retained the same ideal of salvation as that which we found in Dt-Isa and Hag 2:7-9—the restoration of Jerusalem as a cultic center for the whole earth. The violence of the conflict with the nations and the confusion of the eschatological scenario reflect frustration at the discrepancy between the promised salvation and the actual historical circumstances.

17 **(E) Isaiah 24-27.** The most intriguing of all the eschatological oracles of the postexilic period are found in the so-called "Apocalypse of Isaiah" (→ Isaiah 1-39, 15:44-50). These chapters are not in the literary form of an apocalypse: they are oracles, not visions or heavenly journeys. Here again there is no consensus as to the date. Proposals have ranged from the 6th cent. to the 2d (see W. R. Millar, *Isaiah 24-27 and the Origins of Apocalyptic* [Missoula, 1976] 1-22). Debate has centered on the identification of the "fortified city" whose ruin is proclaimed (25:2; 27:10). Babylon, Samaria, and even Jerusalem have been proposed. In fact, it is not certain that the same city is intended throughout, as some of the oracles may be independent of the rest.

What makes this enigmatic composition intriguing for the study of Jewish eschatology is the way in which it uses mythological traditions. Chapter 24 paints a vivid, poetic picture of desolation in cosmic terms (24:18: "the windows on high will be opened and the foundations of the earth will shake"). Then, "on that day the Lord will punish the host of the heavens in heaven and the kings of the earth on the earth. They will be gathered together like prisoners into a pit; they will be shut up in a dungeon and after many days they will be punished" (24:21-22). This passage evidently presupposes a story about a rebellion by the host of heaven, which is never narrated in the Bible, although a few possible allusions are found in the Psalms (most notably Ps 82). The motif reappears in a noncanonical apocalypse, *1 Enoch* 18-19. The allusion in Isa 24 suggests the possibility that a far more extensive mythology was known to the Jews of the postexilic period than has been preserved in the biblical canon. Other mythological allusions can now be understood in the light of the Canaanite myths from Ugarit. In Isa 25:6-8 we read that "on this mountain" God will provide a great feast and will destroy death forever. Death (Mot) was a Canaanite god, the enemy of Baal, god of fertility (*ANET* 138-40). We have already seen an allusion to the myth of Leviathan in Isa 51:9-10 (→ 6 above), where it was associated with the exodus and again with the release from Babylon. Now in Isa 27:1 it is projected into the future. The decisive battle has yet to be fought. Moreover, it is not a battle with specific political powers, but involves the removal of "the veil that veils all peoples" (25:7), the destruction of the final enemy, death.

The destruction of death here is seen in the context of an earthly restoration of Jerusalem. The resurrection of the individual dead is not envisaged. In 26:19 the language of resurrection is used ("your dead shall live, their corpses shall rise") but this is most probably to be understood as a metaphor for the restoration and revival of the Jewish people, analogous to the vision of the valley of dry bones (Ezek 37). The destruction of death means the removal of every source of grief, at least for the Jewish people (25:8). The final goal is not essentially different from that of Dt-Isa or Hag: "The Lord of hosts will reign on Mt. Zion and in Jerusalem" (24:23).

18 **(F) The Setting of Eschatological Prophecy.** Some scholars have tried to attribute these eschatological prophecies to a particular party or group within postexilic Judaism. We have noted Paul Hanson's

thesis that much of this material derived from groups which were disaffected with the Jerusalem authorities in the 6th and 5th cents., and this is surely true in some cases. Otto Plöger dated many of the anonymous oracles to the Hellenistic period and suggested that they were the work of conventicles of the "pious" or Hasidim, who are mentioned in the books of Maccabees. Daniel and the other apocalypses would then have been composed in the same circles at a later point in their development. Although this proposal is attractive and is often accepted, it cannot be sustained in the light of the evidence. Neither the eschatological oracles nor the apocalypses of the 2d cent. BC can be ascribed to a single movement, and the earliest apocalypses, those of Enoch and Daniel, provide internal evidence about their own prehistory, which bears no clear relation to the eschatological prophecies or the conventicles posited by Plöger.

B. S. Childs (*CIOTS* 325-27) has pointed out that the addition of eschatological oracles to prophetic books played an important role in the "canonical shaping" of the biblical text. Oracles were preserved without reference to their original situation, because all prophecy was now referred to the end-time (this process can also be seen in the commentaries of the Dead Sea sect). Regardless of who initially composed these oracles, they were taken up and preserved by the scribes who fashioned the canon in an authoritative way. Eschatology cannot have been confined to sectarian conventicles but must have been more broadly accepted as an integral part of Jewish faith.

19 **(IV) Apocalypticism.**

(A) 1 Enoch. The apocalyptic literature of the 2d cent. was certainly indebted to the prophetic tradition, but was also characterized by significant new developments. Much of this literature lies outside the canon. Fragments of the book of *Enoch* in Aramaic from Qumran are dated to the first half of the 2d cent. BC (J. T. Milik, *The Books of Enoch* [Oxford, 1976]). Some parts of *1 Enoch* (chaps. 1-36, the Book of the Watchers, and chaps. 72-82, the Astronomical Book) are likely to have been composed in the early 2d or late 3d cent.—i.e., before the canonical apocalypse of Daniel (see Stone, *Scriptures, Sects and Visions* 27-47). Other parts (chaps. 85-90, the Animal Apocalypse, and chaps. 92-105, the Epistle of Enoch, which includes the Apocalypse of Weeks) were roughly contemporary with Daniel. The Enoch literature (→ Apocrypha, 68:8-15) then provides the earliest evidence for a Jewish apocalyptic movement in the strict sense (translations of *1 Enoch* can be found in Sparks, *AOT* 171-319; and Charlesworth, *OTP* 1. 5-89).

In contrast to the anonymous oracles of the postexilic period the apocalypses are pseudonymous—they are ascribed to ancient legendary heroes such as Enoch and Daniel. The choice of pseudonyms tells us something about the interests of the apocalyptic writers. Enoch is known from Gen, where he appears as the seventh antediluvian patriarch (Gen 5:18). We are told that he lived 365 years, walked with *'ĕlōhîm* (variously translated as God or angels) and that *'ĕlōhîm* took him. Enoch then could be expected to know about the heavenly world which was inaccessible to other mortals. The legend as it is developed in *1 Enoch* is influenced by Babylonian legends and may have been first developed in Babylonia (see further J. VanderKam, *Enoch and the Growth of an Apocalyptic Tradition* [CBQMS 16; Washington, 1984]). The earliest Enoch tradition is interested in such matters as the movements of the stars and the calculation of the calendar—interests which are quite different from those of the prophetic oracles.

The actual apocalypses of Enoch draw on a wide

range of traditions, including prophetic ideas of a final judgment (compare *1 Enoch* 27 and Joel 4). The worldview of Enoch, however, differs from that of the prophets in significant ways. Enoch is taken up into heaven and taken on a tour of the cosmos. His interest in cosmic geography is unparalleled in the prophets, and so is his interest in the angelic world. Most significant perhaps, he is allowed to see the places where the dead are kept until the judgment (*1 Enoch* 22). Insofar as we can now establish, the belief in the judgment of individuals after death is first attested in the Jewish tradition of *1 Enoch*. Chapter 104 assures the righteous that the gates of heaven will be opened to them and that they will be companions of the angels. This belief apparently developed before the persecution in the time of the Maccabees. Presumably, reflection on the assumption of Enoch to the angelic world played a part in this development.

20   (B) Daniel. Continuity with biblical prophecy is more obvious in the visions of Dan 7-12 (which resemble those of Zechariah in form), but here too other influences can be seen. There is evidence of a movement that is not related to the prophetic oracles. The first six chapters of the book are legends about Daniel and his friends at the Babylonian court. Chapters 7-12, on the contrary, are visions pertaining to the crisis of the Maccabean era. The visions were quite certainly composed in the years 168-164 BC. The tales, however, are older, as they contain no certain allusions to the persecution, and they are set in Babylon. Although they are fictional and in some cases have a long history of development, they may well reflect the context in which they were actually written. Daniel is distinguished by his ability to interpret dreams and mysterious signs (e.g., the writing on the wall) more successfully than the professional Babylonian diviners and wise men, because of the revelation he receives from his God. Here, as in *1 Enoch*, competition with Babylonian divination seems to have played a part in developing the apocalyptic idea of revelation (see further Collins, *Daniel*).

The continuity of apocalypticism with biblical prophecy is most readily evident in Dan 7, the central vision of the book, composed in the heat of the persecution of the Jews by Antiochus Epiphanes. There Daniel reports his famous vision of four beasts rising from the sea and one like a son of man riding on the clouds of heaven. This imagery is derived from the myth of God's battle with the sea monster (Isa 27:1; 51:9-11). In the Canaanite prototype of the myth, Baal, the god who overcomes the sea, is described as "rider of the clouds" (*ANET* 131-34). In the OT, this role was taken over by Yahweh (e.g., Ps 68:5). In Dan, however, the one who comes on the clouds is not Yahweh but a lesser heavenly being. Many scholars understand him as a collective symbol for the pious Jews (→ Daniel, 25:28), but this does not do full justice to the symbolism. In Dan 7:22 the "holy ones of the Most High" receive the kingdom which was also given to the "one like a son of man." Elsewhere in Dan (and usually, though not always, in Jewish literature) "holy ones" are angels (e.g., Dan 4:13, 23; 8:13), and angels are consistently represented as men in apocalyptic literature (e.g., Dan 8:15; 9:21; 10:18; 12:6-7). In Dan 10:21 and 12:1, the archangel Michael is singled out as the heavenly "prince" of Israel. The "one like a son of man" should also be understood as an angelic counterpart of the Jews, possibly identical with Michael. (See further J. Collins, *The Apocalyptic Vision of the Book of Daniel* [Missoula, 1977] 123-52; Day, *God's Conflict* 151-78.)

The prominence of an individual angel (and of angels in general) is one of the novel features of Dan over

against earlier prophecy, and thus was very important for later developments. While "Son of Man" was never an established title in Jewish circles, the language of Dan 7 is used in other apocalypses (*1 Enoch* 37-71, 4 Ezra 13) to describe a supernatural savior figure. Other texts (e.g., 1QM 17:7) look for an angelic deliverer. This apocalyptic belief in an "exalted angel" (Rowland, *Open Heaven* 94) forms the background against which the Christian belief in Jesus as the "Son of Man" must be understood.

21   Three other features, taken in combination, further distinguish Dan as "apocalyptic" over against earlier prophecy: (1) Daniel consistently receives his revelation from an angel, whether through interpretation of a vision (chaps. 7 and 8), interpretation of scripture (chap. 9) or direct speech (chaps. 10-12). We have noted above that an angelic interpreter is found already in Zech (→ 8 above), but the form is much more elaborate in Dan. (See S. Niditch, *The Symbolic Vision in Biblical Tradition* [Chico, 1983] chap. 3). (2) The revelations cover a wide sweep of history, most of which was already past by the time Dan was actually written. So Dan 11 gives an accurate account of Hellenistic history down to the time of Antiochus Epiphanes. It concludes, however, by predicting that the king would die in the land of Israel (Dan 11:45). Since this is not where he in fact died, we may infer that the passage was written before his death in late 164 BC. Such reviews of history after the fact are typical of the subgenre "historical apocalypses" (e.g., The Animal Apocalypse in *1 Enoch* 85-90, the Apocalypse of Weeks in *1 Enoch* 93, and 91:11-17). (3) The historical review in Dan 11 culminates in 12:1-3 with the resurrection of the dead. This is the first (and only) passage in the Hebrew Bible that speaks unambiguously of personal afterlife, although the idea was probably developed somewhat earlier in the Enoch tradition (→ 19 above). Dan does not envisage a general resurrection, but only the raising of the very good and the very bad. The "wise teachers" (*maśkîlîm*) will shine like the stars, which means that they will be elevated to join the angelic host (cf. *1 Enoch* 104:2-6). These wise teachers play a crucial role in the time of persecution (Dan 11:32-33). Their role is to "make many understand." They are not said to fight; but some of them are killed, and their death is a purification that prepares them for their final reward. Because of their belief in resurrection they could afford to lose their lives in this world, rather than succumb to the pressure of the persecution. It is highly probable that the author belonged to this circle.

22   (C) The Spread of Apocalyptic Ideas. In the years after the Maccabean revolt, many of the novel ideas of the *Enoch* and Dan apocalypses became widely diffused in Judaism. The production of apocalypses continued intermittently well into the Christian era. Notable examples from the 1st cent. AD are the Similitudes of Enoch (*1 Enoch* 37-71), 4 Ezra and *2 Bar* (cf. Charlesworth, *OTP* vol. 1; for discussion, see Collins, *Apocalyptic Imagination*). The discovery of the DSS has brought to light a community (probably a settlement of the Essene sect) whose way of life was heavily influenced by apocalyptic ideas (→ Apocrypha, 67:113-17). These ideas included interest in heavenly mysteries, a sense of participation in the angelic world, and expectation of a final battle between the Sons of Light and Sons of Darkness, led by their respective angels. Other ideas that were originally characteristic of the apocalypses came to be more widely accepted. Belief in resurrection was accepted by the Pharisees and others and gradually entered the mainstream of Jewish faith, although it was still rejected by the Sadducees in the 1st cent. AD.

23 **(D) Influence on Christianity.** The main historical importance of apocalypticism is that it set the stage for the origin of Christianity. Apocalypticism has been called "the mother of Christian theology" (E. Käsemann, "The Beginnings of Christian Theology," *JTC* 6 [1969] 40). The claim is exaggerated, but it is not without basis. Whether Jesus himself should be understood as an eschatological prophet or apocalyptic preacher is disputed. There is no doubt that his followers drew heavily on the understanding of history that had been developed in "historical" apocalypses of the Daniel type. For Paul, the resurrection of Jesus was the firstfruits of the general resurrection (1 Cor 15:20), which was therefore imminent. Indeed, the resurrection of Jesus was only credible in the context of an apocalyptic eschatological scenario: "If the dead are not raised, then Christ has not been raised" (1 Cor 15:16). The Synoptic tradition drew directly on Dan 7 and cast Jesus in the role of the Son of Man who would come on the clouds of heaven. The first generation of Christians did not use the literary form of the apocalypse, perhaps

because of their heightened sense of the immediate presence of the spirit. By the end of the 1st cent., however, the form appears in the book of Revelation, from which, in fact, the genre takes its name. Thereafter it flourished in Christian circles.

24 **(E) Theological Value.** Despite the historical importance of apocalypticism, Christian theologians have often viewed it with suspicion because of its obscure imagery and fanatical tendencies. The suspicions have sometimes been justified, esp. in the case of modern fundamentalist use of this material. The key to a proper appreciation of the apocalyptic tradition lies in the realization that apocalypses are more of the nature of poetry than of dogma. They are works of imagination, which cannot be regarded as sources of factual information. Their value lies in their ability to envision alternatives to the world of present experience and thereby to provide hope and consolation. As such they speak to enduring human needs and are a vital part of the Western religious heritage.

20

EZEKIEL

Lawrence Boadt, C.S.P.

BIBLIOGRAPHY

1 *Commentaries:* Carley, K., *The Book of the Prophet Ezekiel* (CBC; Cambridge, 1974). Cody, A., *Ezekiel* (OTM; Wilmington, 1984). Cooke, G., *The Book of Ezekiel* (ICC; NY, 1937). Craigie, P., *Ezekiel* (DSB; Phl, 1983). Eichrodt, W., *Ezekiel* (Phl, 1970). Fohrer, G., *Ezechiel* (HAT; Tübingen, 1955). Greenberg, M. *Ezekiel 1-20* (AB 22; GC, 1983). Stalker, D. M. G., *Ezekiel* (TBC; London, 1968). Tkacik, A., "Ezekiel," *JBC.* Wevers, J., *Ezekiel* (NCB; London, 1969). Zimmerli, W., *Ezekiel 1, 2* (Herm; Phl, 1979, 1983). Zurro, E. and Alonso Schökel, L., *Ezequiel* (Libros Sagrados; Madrid, 1971).

Other works: Carley, K., *Ezekiel among the Prophets* (SBT; Naperville, 1974). Fohrer, G., *Hauptprobleme des Buches Ezechiel* (Berlin, 1952). Hölscher, G., *Hesekiel, der Dichter und das Buch* (BZAW 39; Giessen, 1924). Hossfeld, F., *Untersuchungen zu Komposition und Theologie des Ezechielbuches* (FB 20; Stuttgart, 1977). Lang, B., *Ezechiel: Der Prophet und das Buch* (Darmstadt, 1981); *Kein Aufstand in Jerusalem* (SBB; Stuttgart, 1978). Lust, J. (ed.), *Ezekiel and His Book* (BETL 74; Leuven, 1986). Vogt, E., *Untersuchungen zum Buch Ezechiel* (AnBib 95; Rome, 1981). Zimmerli, W., *I Am Yahweh* (Atlanta, 1982).

INTRODUCTION

2 No prophetic book poses more of a question than does Ezek. It combines prophetic oracles with legal reflections, prose and poetry, extremely detailed historical descriptions with highly imaginative mythological allusions, sober judgment and wild vision, verbose sermonizing with vivid dramatic presentation. This leads to a wealth of material and a breadth of vision far greater than in other prophetic books. It also leads to a confusing array of scholarly opinions about almost every aspect of the book's composition and message. Strangely enough, this is not due to any uncertainty about the structure or order — the book is by far the most clearly organized book among the prophets. One thing is certain, no matter what we have learned so far about the man and his book, we have barely begun to understand the complexity and depth of this prophet, who preached at the worst of times and the most decisive of times in Israel's long history.

3 **The Place of Ezek in the Canon.** Ezek falls third among the great writing prophets in the current arrangement of the OT, right after Isa and Jer and before the book of the Twelve Minor Prophets. This order was decided relatively late so that the three great prophets would be placed in chronological order. But the Talmud (*b. B. Bat.* 14b) speaks of an earlier order in which Isa came last: "Jeremiah is all doom; Ezekiel begins with doom but ends with consolation; while Isaiah is all consolation." This early arrangement was built on moving from doom to hope with Ezek in the middle as a dividing

line between the two. Indeed, the book as it stands divides exactly into two halves: chaps. 1–24 contain oracles of judgment against Israel, and 25–48 propose a variety of words of support and hope.

Modern regard for the book also largely builds on this distinction between judgment and hope. Ezekiel is seen as a transitional prophet who breaks with older forms and ways of speaking to introduce new and non-prophetic elements from the priestly sphere into his preaching and writing. With one foot in the collapsing age of independence for Israel and Judah, and the other in a bleak time of exile without any of the traditional institutions of the faith to support the people, he openly seeks a program of reform and rebuilding that will survive such disaster. The book thus breaks with many oracular forms common in earlier prophets to shape a new language of prophecy that can call forth a major return to trust in God, revitalize the older traditions of God's acting in history and strengthen the practice of the faith through worship and observance of the law. In view of the subsequent development of Israelite faith toward study of the Book of the Law, i.e., the development of a canon of Scripture that stresses the Torah as central, it is no wonder that Ezekiel is often considered the "father of modern Judaism."

4 **The History of Criticism.** Up until 1900, most critics believed Ezek to be the most unified book in the OT. It had such clear indications of an overall plan and execution as the specific series of dates and visions that are found from beginning to end. But the first decade of the 20th cent. saw a great number of questions raised by German scholars such as A. Bertholet, R. Kraetzschmar, and J. Herrmann concerning the presence of doublets, editorial additions, and late insertions (for a full review, see Zimmerli, *Ezekiel 1* 3–9). In 1924, G. Hölscher (*Ezechiel, der Dichter und das Buch*) went further and attributed to an original Ezekiel only some 177 verses out of a total of 1,235 verses in the 48 chapters of the book. He considered Ezekiel to be an ecstatic prophet who delivered his oracles in poetic lines, and any apparently prosaic lines were to be attributed to a redactor or later commentator. In 1930, C. C. Torrey (*Pseudo-Ezekiel and the Original Prophecy* [New Haven, 1930]) proposed that the entire book was written in the 3d cent. as fiction. A year later, James Smith (*The Book of the Prophet Ezekiel: A New Interpretation* [London, 1931]) suggested that it was composed a century before the exile by a northern Israelite and then edited later in Judah by Ezekiel or his school. From being considered the most unified book in the prophetic canon, Ezek was suddenly the least agreed upon book among scholars. Scholarly work since 1950 has gradually moved back toward the position that the book is largely composed from Ezekiel's preaching. Yet recent scholars admit an extensive editing of Ezek by disciples working in the exile and shortly after. The most influential work of this period has been the massive two-volume commentary of W. Zimmerli completed in 1969 (Eng., Herm; Phl, 1979, 1983). He argues for a judicious process of "development" of the tradition, or an "updating of the text," or a "reworking" in the process of literary editing. He attributes this to a "school of the prophet" who applied the prophet's teachings to the changed situation of the exile and to hopes for a priestly reform. For a thorough review of his method, see L. Boadt, *CBQ* 43 (1981) 632–35. Subsequent work on the literary structures and style of the book has led M. Greenberg and other commentators to reaffirm the prophet's own contributions much more extensively than Zimmerli was willing to recognize.

5   The Historical Background of Ezekiel's Ministry. The prophetic ministry of Ezekiel must be understood against the turbulent background of the last days of Judah as an independent state. When King Josiah came of age to rule in 628, the Assyrian empire was weakened and tottering after the death of its last strong ruler, Ashurbanipal. Josiah began a major reform of Israel's religion along the lines of Deut's covenant (2 Kgs 22–24). But his untimely death fighting against Egypt in 609 ended any further reform. His son Jehoiakim was regularly accused by Jeremiah of rejecting the covenant (see Jer 7, 26, 36).

In 605 political events brought the Babylonians to power over Judah, and Jehoiakim eventually became embroiled in a scheme to fight for independence after Babylon seemed weakened by its near defeat by Egypt in 601. However, he had misjudged, and in 598, the Babylonian army sacked Jerusalem and exiled thousands of its leading citizens. Jehoiakim conveniently died, but they took the new king, Jehoiachin, off to Babylon as a prisoner. Nebuchadrezzar, the Babylonian king, appointed Zedekiah, a brother of Jehoiakim and uncle of the young king Jehoiachin, as king-regent. He, too, remained quiet for a number of years, and then planned rebellion. This time, the Babylonian siege lasted from 589 to 586 and wiped out all of Judah's cities before taking Jerusalem itself (see 2 Kgs 25; Jer 37–45, 52).

6   Ezekiel's Ministry. Ezekiel claims to have begun his ministry in 593 among the Judean exiles in the land of Babylon (1:2). His last dated prophecy falls in 571 (29:17). How old he was when he began to preach, or whether he lived on and wrote after 571, we do not know. Presumably he was among the 8,000 captives brought to Babylon after Jerusalem fell to Nebuchadrezzar in 598 (2 Kgs 24:16). From both the contents of his preaching and the series of dates that head many of his oracles, we can surmise that the bulk of his ministry took place between 593 and 586, during the reign of King Zedekiah and the period of devastation that followed the second and final fall of the city in 586. Like Jeremiah, Ezekiel seems to have opposed most of the thinking of Zedekiah and his advisors and to have resisted any attempts to overthrow Babylonian control. He engaged in a deeper struggle against the political ambitions of the ruling class in Jerusalem, proposing instead a strong theocentric concept of Israel as a community faithful in its religious observance and its obedience to Yahweh, whether politically independent or not.

7   Critical Problems in the Text. Several major questions arise because of the seeming inconsistencies between the historical claims for the prophet's ministry and the nature of the actual oracles in their edited form. How could he have known so intimately and clearly the situation in Jerusalem if he was in fact an exile in Babylon? How accurate are the dates in the book? Do the visionary transports from place to place and the strange symbolic actions reported in chaps. 4, 12, and 24 suggest a mentally unbalanced person or a wild ecstatic? Does the seemingly verbose and repetitive style of the text serve as a criterion for identifying the hand of glossators and editors who added to the original oracles? Does the distinction between prose and poetry help to identify the original core of Ezekiel's own words? Does the strong priestly coloring in his prophetic message exclude Ezek from traditional prophecy? Do the doublets of Ezekiel's call in chaps. 3 and 33 or of his words on individual responsibility in chaps. 14, 18, and 33 reflect two levels, one from the prophet and one from a redactor? Why is there no mention of Jeremiah? These questions have all been widely debated by scholars during the 20th cent., and disagreements still exist on many of the issues. Some contemporary directions may be discussed as positive developments in the following sections.

8   Time and Setting. 15 dates are spaced throughout the book according to a general chronological order:

EZEK	YEAR	MONTH	DAY	DATE
1:1	*30*	*4*	*5*	*July 593 (or 568)*
1:2	5	—	5	June–July 593
3:16	5	—	12	June–July 593
8:1	6	6	5	August–September 592
20:1	7	5	10	July–August 591
24:1	9	10	10	January 588
26:1	11	—	1	March 587–March 586
29:1	10	10	12	January 587
29:17	*27*	*1*	*1*	*March-April 571*
30:20	11	1	7	March–April 587
31:1	11	3	1	May–June 587
32:1	12	12	1	February–March 585
32:17	12	12	15	February–March 585
33:21	*12*	*10*	*5*	*December 586–January 585*
40:1	25	1	10	March–April 573

Only the italicized dates are out of order, all of them because of fitting special material closest to its proper thematic place. But the dated oracles and their specific contents can also be closely tied to known historical events of the period, thanks to numerous finds of records from Babylonian and Egyptian sites, including the chronicles of Nebuchadrezzar's reign! As a result, there can be little doubt that the substance of these particular oracles comes from the prophet himself.

Moreover, fewer commentators now worry about how Ezekiel could have known what was happening in Jerusalem while he was in Babylon. Jer 29 clearly shows that communication did take place between the homeland and the exiles in Babylon, and the visionary descriptions of the prophet can easily be explained by his earlier firsthand knowledge of the geography of Jerusalem and the Temple combined with reports of messengers arriving among the exiles.

(Freedy, K. and D. B. Redford, "The Dates in Ezekiel in Relation to Biblical, Babylonian and Egyptian Sources," *JAOS* 90 (1970) 462–85. Malamat, A., "The Twilight of Judah: In the Egyptian-Babylonian Maelstrom," *Congress Volume: Edinburgh, 1974* (VTSup 28; Leiden: Brill, 1975) 123–45. Wiseman, D. J., *Chronicles of Chaldean Kings (626–556 B.C.) in the British Museum* [London, 1956].)

9   Personality and Style of the Prophet. Earlier interest in a supposed abnormal personality behind the visions and symbolic acts has largely died as the result of the pioneering insight of W. Zimmerli that nearly all of the suggested aberrations are, on the contrary, conscious imitations or revivals of primitive forms used by the preclassical prophets. Thus, the use of the "hand of the Lord" or the "Spirit of the Lord" that seized the prophet is typical of the Elijah/Elisha cycles. The same is true of prophetic autodramatization, in which the prophet himself acts out the prophecy. In a similar fashion, many of Ezekiel's phrases and actions are not unique, but imitate the styles and expressions of the priestly sphere. The most striking aspect of the book is the consistent use of "I"; Yahweh himself speaks throughout. In choosing this device, the prophet emphasizes the power of the divine word that overwhelms him (see W. Zimmerli, *VT* 15 [1965] 515–27).

The book, however, is marked by certain formulas and expressions unique among the prophetic texts: "son of man," "so that you will know that I am Yahweh," "set your face against," "I the Lord have spoken." These and other expressions combine with the 1st-pers. narrative form to give a unified style to the whole. As already noted, the oracles seem much more verbose and repetitive than in earlier prophetic books. They also employ extensive allegories and imagery to introduce oracles, a use rarely found elsewhere (see L. Boadt, *Ezekiel's Oracles against Egypt* [Rome, 1980] 169–80). M. Greenberg (*Ezekiel 1–20*) has pointed out several more techniques of this book: the use of panels, in which parts are constructed parallel to one another; spiraling techniques, in which the oracle moves to a higher or more intense level; and "halving," in which an echoing oracle follows the main oracle as an afterwave. All of these observations have strengthened the case that the book maintains a definable style much more likely due to the prophet's own personality and intention than to a school of editors. Their contributions, although present and important, do not dominate the text.

Ezekiel's prophecy shows strong indications of its original oral form, not only in the use of dramatic gestures and its stress on both speaking *and* saying, but in the specific references within the oracles to individual moments of crisis that arose during the protracted siege of Jerusalem from 589–586. This in turn has been literarily reworked into larger and more elaborate oracles that differ from those of earlier writing prophets by their "baroque extravagance" and introduction of legal and priestly concerns (C. Westermann, *Basic Forms of Prophetic Speech* [Phl, 1967] 205–8). Much of this must be the work of Ezekiel himself since it is very difficult to distinguish a purpose or theology of the redactors

different from that of the core oracles or of the prose sections from the clearly poetic sections.

10   Ezekiel and Other Traditions. Ezekiel shows a strong affinity to Jer, esp. in the prose biographical and autobiographical passages that occur in Jer 21–45, where many phrases and expressions are repeated in Ezek. But even in Jer 1–20, themes such as Judah and Israel as sisters (3:6–11), the prophet called to withstand the people as a fortified wall (1:18), the concern with a false and lying spirit of prophecy (14:14), and the command not to mourn before the people (16:5), are found developed at greater length in Ezek 3:8; 12:24; 16:1–43; and 24:16. Above all, the two prophets share a common attitude to responsibility for guilt on the part of the individual (Jer 31:29–30 and Ezek 18:2 quote the same proverb) and to God's gracious will to restore the covenant in a new way (Jer 31:31–34; Ezek 36:26). Ezekiel probably was familiar with Jeremiah's prophecies, possibly even in a written form (J. W. Miller, *Das Verhältnis Jeremias und Hesekiels* [Assen, 1955]).

More striking, however, are the numerous affinities of Ezek with the Holiness Code in Lev 17–26. Scholars generally date it to the late preexilic period (4:35–54), since its language is very similar to that of Ezek. Many of the laws cited by Ezekiel occur in the code, and references to threats and blessings named in Lev 26 abound throughout Ezek. Extensive comparisons between Ezek and the code can be found in H. Reventlow, *Wächter über Israel* (BZAW 82; Berlin, 1962) and in Zimmerli, *Ezekiel 1* 46–52. Interestingly, the laws and religious demands of Ezek, while close to Lev, are not closely tied to the rest of the Priestly (P) source in the Pentateuch. For example, Ezekiel never ties the priesthood to the house of Aaron as P does. Certainly Ezek and Lev reflect a common concern with covenant demands, and both employ strongly cultic language to express those demands. Some critics even suggest that Lev 17–26 is tied to an autumn covenant renewal feast. They both represent an earlier stage than P's comprehensive creation theology, which developed as a result of the collapse of Israel's religious institutions in the exile.

Much less needs to be said about the so-called apocalyptic language in Ezek 38–39. It is usually treated as a later addition, but its picture of a great cosmic battle draws more on the older myths of a war for order in creation fought by the divine warrior (16:16) than on later hopes for a messianic age.

11   Later Traditions about Ezekiel. With very little historical support, legend has placed the tomb of the prophet Ezekiel near the town of Hilla in central Iraq. Far more interesting is the way that later reflection began to worry about Ezekiel's message. The first worry was over the mystical description of the divine appearance in chap. 1. A great number of highly suspect speculations developed, even among the early rabbis, so that a whole school of "Merkabah" ("Chariot") mysticism has persisted in Judaism through the ages. Chap. 1 was banned both from the reading of the prophet in the synagogue (b. *Meg.* 4:10) and from the study of the book by the schools (b. *Ḥag.* 2:1). Only later was it allowed in, against the opinions of the talmudic rabbis, as the prophetic reading for the first day of Pentecost.

The same passage in *Meg.* 4:10 records a second reservation about the book—it was too critical of Israel. Rabbi Eliezer forbade reading chap. 16 and its abominations because it might give ammunition to the Christians' claims (b. *Sanh.* 92b). The early rabbis also found grave difficulty in the fact that many of the Temple prescriptions in Ezek 40–48 contradicted those of the Pentateuch. The efforts to reconcile the two led to the decision to leave it to Elijah in the future (*b. Menaḥ.* 45a) or even to concede the contradictions (*b. Mak.* 24a).

12 The Theology of the Book. Ezek shares with earlier prophetic writings the conviction that God punishes disobedience and infidelity to the covenant by political disaster (Isa 10; Jer 4–6; Ezek 17); similarly, he treats violations of the covenant in the language of adultery and prostitution (Hos 2; Jer 2; Ezek 16; 23). He certainly agreed with Jeremiah that God willed an internal faithfulness to the covenant under Babylonian rule rather than a war for independence built on human pride and political motives alone; Babylon was an instrument of divine correction (Jer 29; Ezek 4; 21). What sets Ezek off from other prophetic books is the unique way the prophet develops certain traditional themes of (a) Yahweh's lordship over all nations and events, (b) his holiness (transcendence), (c) insistence on both moral and cultic integrity, (d) the responsibility of each generation for its own acts, and finally (e) a conviction that God intends to restore Israel out of a totally free gift of grace.

(a) THE DIVINE LORDSHIP. Ezek's doctrine of God is most clearly seen in the formula that ends nearly every oracle: "so that they (or, 'you') will know that I am Yahweh." God acts in events to manifest that he alone has the power to punish and restore. Divine activity reveals that Yahweh does indeed take seriously the punishment of sin while at the same time never forgetting his lasting promise of care and covenantal love toward Israel. Ezek rarely stresses the tender side of God (although it is present in 16:1–14; 34:1–31) when an oracle can emphasize the power of God to achieve his ends. Above all, the divine concern is seen in Yahweh's ability to give life when there appears to be only death (37:1–14; 47:1–12).

(b) GOD'S HOLINESS. Ezek stresses the distance between our human hopes and actions and the divine will. E.g., the prophet is regularly addressed as "son of man," to emphasize his mere mortality even as God's spokesperson. Similarly, in the great vision of the heavenly chariot, he sees only the "likeness" of the "appearance" of God (1:26). Finally, he does not use Isaiah's "Holy One" but speaks instead of the holiness of God's "Name" (20:39; 36:20; 43:7; etc.). Because Israel bears God's name, it must not profane that name by its disobedience, making God a victim of human whim (20:30).

(c) MORAL AND CULTIC DEMANDS. Ezek continues the traditions of vehement protest against the corruption of Israel in both injustice and in false worship (chaps. 5–6; 17–18; 20; 22). But the preponderance of specific offenses named are cultic, including profaning the sabbath (20:12,24), worshiping on high places (6:13; 20:28), and defiling the sanctuary (23:37–38). Ezekiel clearly understood that the root of Israel's turning from Yahweh was a loss of "knowing" God and his covenant statutes. Chap. 20, with its remarkable history of Israel's recalcitrance even from the time of the exodus, makes a sharp point—at no time did Israel follow Yahweh entirely from its heart—it was always rebellious! God gave his statutes and regulations to enable them to serve him faithfully, but it was not enough (20:40).

(d) INDIVIDUAL RESPONSIBILITY. Jer 31:29 and Ezek 18:2 both quote the same proverb about fathers eating sour grapes and the children suffering the consequences. Chap. 18 then develops the lesson by tracing the cases of a father, a son, and a grandson. It maintains the specific point that each *generation* will have to take responsibility for its own decisions. Now is the time to act in order to overcome the evil of both the past and the present and to stand before God in judgment and hope for a new future. The thematic passages on the prophet as watchman in chaps. 3 and 33 build upon this insight. Why should Ezekiel preach if no one will listen? The answer is in the twofold responsibility involved in warning. The prophet must be faithful to his charge to show God's justice and mercy in action whether anyone hears or not. The people can accept or reject the warning and the explanation of the prophet, but they must bear the burden. God will bring about punishment and salvation no matter what the response of the people is, but the prophet's words serve as a present sign to all of what is really happening and a lesson for all future generations.

(e) SIN AND GRACE. Ezekiel clearly takes sin seriously. Not only does he find the rebellious spirit deeply ingrained in the human heart, but he has high expectations of human conduct before the holiness of God. He also proclaims the possibility of repentance (see 16:54–63; 33:10–16). Yet God does not act as a result of people's repentance, but out of his own prior holiness and covenant love (16:53,60–61; 20:40–44; 34:11; 37:1–14). Chapter 36 especially underscores this divine promise: God will restore Israel because of his jealous wrath against the derision of other nations who mock his people's lowly fate (36:6); and he will act for the sake of his name in order to vindicate his holiness (36:22–23). Then he will give Israel a new heart and a new spirit so that they can obey and be faithful (36:26–28; cf. 11:17–20). Repentance *follows* God's initiative to save because Israel will recognize that God is still acting for them, and, as a result, they will be ashamed of their conduct (16:54; 36:32).

13 The Text of the Book. Generally speaking, the MT does not have an exceptionally large number of difficult readings if we exclude the so-called redundancies that are more a stylistic question than a problem of unintelligible words or grammar. Often scholars turn to the LXX for help. The LXX, however, is quite inconsistent, with different ways of handling common phrases and expressions in different sections; it is sometimes close to MT and sometimes quite free. Recent research indicates that the Gk text is not homogenous at all (L. McGregor, *The Greek Text of Ezekiel* [Atlanta, 1985]). The LXX almost certainly omitted lines it considered redundant or did not understand for the sake of conciseness and clarity. The more prolix text of the MT is also stylistically more consistent throughout the book and therefore is more likely to be close to the original.

14 Outline. The book of Ezek is divided into three stages of the prophet's ministry: oracles of judgment (chaps. 1–24), oracles against foreign nations (chaps. 25–32), and oracles of salvation (chaps. 33–48). This corresponds to a three-part program: divine punishment of Israel, a prelude to restoration by punishment of the foreign powers who oppress Israel, and a promise to Israel of restoration to a new order. This last section in turn has two parts: promise of a new exodus and conquest of the land, i.e., a return from exile (chaps. 33–39) and a new division of the land and rebuilding of the holy city (chaps. 40–48). The book may be outlined as follows:

COMMENTARY

15   **(I) Oracles of Judgment (1:1–24:27).** Fully one-half of Ezek is given over to warnings and judgments against the people of Judah and the city of Jerusalem. All belong to the period of Ezekiel's ministry between 593 and 586, during the reign of King Zede-

kiah, whom the Babylonians had placed on the throne in 598 as regent for his nephew, the rightful ruler, Jehoiachin, now held prisoner in Babylon. As the outline above shows, there is some order to these 24 chapters, although not perhaps what modern minds might expect.

Six groupings have been arranged artistically to alternate narratives or vision accounts with straight judgment oracles. Thus, the visions in chaps. 1–3 are followed by oracles in 4–7; the vision of chaps. 8–11 is followed by the oracles of 12–14; and the allegorical or metaphorical descriptions of chaps. 15–19 are followed by the strong condemnations of 20–24. Many themes touched in this first half of the book are taken up or echoed later in the oracles of restoration. The vision of the divine throne (chaps. 1 and 8) reappears in 43; the prophet as watchman (chap. 3) occurs again in 33; the mountains of Israel (chap. 6) are readdressed in 36. A close linkage between God's reluctant judgment on Israel and his eager desire to restore is established by this careful foreshadowing (L. Boadt, in J. Lust (ed.), *Ezekiel* 182–200).

16   (A) The Call to Prophecy (1:1–3:27). This introductory section sets the major themes of the book: the presence of the divine glory or majesty in the events of the exile, the call of the prophet to be a watchman on behalf of Israel, the accountability of each person for his or her actions, and the power of the word of God to act despite the people's rebellion and refusal to listen or obey. In the current religious crisis, Ezekiel sides with Jeremiah: Judah's defeat is due to God's punishment, and an even worse fate lies close at hand for those left in Jerusalem unless they repent. If, however, they do turn back to Yahweh, he will restore the people and the city after the time of punishment (R. Wilson, *Int* 38 [1984] 117–30).

Efforts to separate the divine throne vision in 1:4–28 from the commission of the prophet in chaps. 2 and 3 as two originally independent accounts never prove to be very helpful, since no real reasons for this double tradition can be found (Tkacik, *JBC* 21:13). Ezekiel was strongly influenced by the Isaian holiness tradition in his preaching, and the thematic connection between a vision of the divine glory and the prophetic call was established in the paradigm of Isaiah's call in Isa 6:1–13 (Zimmerli, *Ezekiel 1* 98–100).

17   (a) THE VISION OF GOD (1:1–28). This chapter consists of an opening superscription in 1:1–3, followed by an elaborate vision of the divine throne occupied by God. Much of the imagery is borrowed from typical Babylonian artistic descriptions of divine beings (*ANEP* 644–46), but also clearly shows connections to the priestly traditions of the ark of the covenant and its protective cherubim found in the Holy of Holies in the Temple (cf. Exod 25:10–22; 1 Kgs 6:23–28; R. Wilson, *Int* 38 [1984] 124–25). The close connection between the elaborate vision of what properly was to be experienced in the Temple in Jerusalem and the superscription that locates its time and place in a foreign land during an exile reveals a special emphasis: the exiles in Babylon share the same protective presence of God in their midst as did those in the homeland. When Jerusalem will be destroyed, Israel's hope will remain alive among the exilic community.

18   (i) *The superscription* (1:1–3). Two dates are given for Ezekiel's opening vision, and scholars have not agreed on whether they can be reconciled as referring to the same date or not (B. Lang, *Bib* 64 [1983] 225–30). **1.** *in the thirtieth year:* This is stated in the 1st pers. and continues in vv 4–28 as the account of the vision, so it is most natural to assume that "30" refers to Ezekiel's earliest prophetic experience and not to a time 30 years later when he or his editors wrote down the book of his prophecies. Verse 2 can be understood in this light to be an editor's clarification of the thirtieth year, since it is written in the 3rd pers. It specifies that the vision took place in 593, five years after Nebuchadrezzar captured Jerusalem. If this position can be maintained, then the

vision is dated by some event around 623–622, most probably the discovery of the law book in the Temple in Josiah's time, which led to his great reform movement based on the theology of Deut (2 Kgs 22–23). *river Kebar:* This is a well-known canal that left the Euphrates N of Babylon and flowed SE through the ancient Sumerian city of Nippur and rejoined the Euphrates. It was undoubtedly one of the locations where a colony of Jewish exiles was settled in 598. Excavations at Nippur have revealed commercial documents bearing Jewish family names from the 5th cent. (*DOTT* 95–96). **2.** *Jehoiachin:* Even though Zedekiah was ruling in Jerusalem, he must have been considered a regent for the true king, whom the Babylonians held in the hope that it would keep the vassal state of Judah from rebellion. **3.** *the hand of the Lord:* At crucial moments, God directly takes control of the senses and power of speech of the prophet (3:22; 8:1; 33:22; 37:1; 40:1). The prophet is here being described like Elijah, who was famed for being moved by the hand of the Lord (1 Kgs 18:46).

19   (ii) *The chariot vision* (1:4–28a). **4.** *a stormwind:* The vision is introduced in the language of a storm-god theophany, which has a long history in the Near East, associated with Baal and Hadad in Ugaritic and Babylonian mythology, and with Marduk in the *Enuma Elish* (*ANET* 60–71). Israel made use of the imagery and language of the God of the storm occasionally (cf. Pss 18 and 29). *from the North:* Summer storms in Babylon usually blew from the N, so that Ezekiel may well have experienced an actual summer thunderstorm with extensive lightning; but the north is also the mythical home of Yahweh (Isa 14:13; Ps 48:3), perhaps derived from apologetics against it as the mythical home of Baal. **5.** *four living creatures:* The use of *ḥay,* "living," suggests not just mere animals, but the quasi-divine beings well known in Assyrian art, the "cherubim," or guardian deities of gates and palaces, and thus of the king's person (→ 34 below). The following description mixes pl. and sg. terms so that grammatically it is nearly impossible to sort out whether each of the creatures had four faces, wings, hands, etc. or each had one set. The ambiguity may be purposeful to suggest the rapid motion, overwhelming the prophet with its visual awesomeness. **7.** *straight:* The legs were rigid like the front legs of Assyrian cherubim (*ANEP* 646, 647; W. B. Barrick, *CBQ* 44 [1982] 543–50). **8.** *the wings . . . touched:* As described in 1 Kgs 6:27, the two golden cherubim that stood over the ark of the covenant had wings that touched one to the other. **12.** The text distinguishes the creatures from the spirit that moves them, reinforcing the clear sense of the passage that it is the spirit or will of the one above them that directs their motion. **13.** Like the burning bush that signaled a divine presence to Moses (Exod 3:2–5), the fire and flame announce the divine character of this vision and emphasize the holiness of the scene. As with Moses, the prophet must not interfere but submit passively.

20   15–21. The wheels indicate not merely a throne, but a war chariot, suggesting the presence of the divine warrior in battle. The description of the wheels defy modern attempts to figure out how they moved. The Hebr text allows either wheels within wheels (concentric in design) or two sets at right angles to one another to indicate that they could move in any direction at will. The eyes on the rims are well known from Assyrian statues of the gods, which were depicted with eyes on their crowns (E. Vogt, *Bib* 59 [1978] 93–96). They reveal the all-seeing divine presence. Zimmerli sees these verses as a later addition (*Ezekiel 1* 54).

22. *firmament:* This divides the activity of the creatures and the wheels from the divine presence above.

It represents the vault of heaven as in Gen 1:6. God dwells above the heavens in Israelite cosmology (Pss 14:2; 33:13; 80:15; 102:20). **24.** Despite many modern commentators, "mighty waters" almost always carries a mythological overtone—these are the primeval deeps which symbolize the powers of chaos opposed to divine order (H. May, *JBL* 74 [1955] 9–21). **26–28.** *Likeness:* The vision appeared to be human but was wrapped in the numinous qualities of fire, brightness, and awesome holiness. The prophet identifies this figure with the "glory" of the Lord (*kābôd*), the manifestation of the divine majesty of Yahweh in Israel (Exod 16:7,10; Isa 6:3). In Exod 33:18 Moses sees not God's face but only the "glory" of his back—the only other example of the divine *kābôd* described in human form.

21   (b) THE CALL OF THE PROPHET (1:28b–3:11). The scene shifts from an overwhelming visual experience to an emphasis on hearing that in many ways resembles the auditory character of Jeremiah's call in Jer 1. It begins and ends in the description of Israel as obstinate and rebellious, but God's word shall prevail (2:4; 3:8–11). **1.** *son of man:* The term occurs over 90 times in Ezek to contrast the divine speaker with the mere mortal who is to transmit the message. It not only stresses that the message is God's not Ezekiel's, but that judgment and deliverance lie in God's hands not ours. **2.** *spirit:* The prophet could not endure a direct experience of God any more than Moses had (Exod 33), so that a divine empowering is necessary. Frequently, the "spirit of the Lord" gives a person extraordinary powers to act superhumanly (Judg 11:29; 14:6) or to become ecstatic (1 Sam 10:10). In most cases, Ezekiel experiences the latter. **3.** God charges Ezekiel with the mission to speak the divine word to a people so hardened in disobedience that they will not listen; rather, they will oppose him as a deadly enemy—he will sit on scorpions (v 6). But, as charged in both the call of Moses and Jeremiah, the prophet is to speak despite all opposition. **5.** *they shall know:* Ezekiel ends nearly all his oracles with the "recognition statement" (see Zimmerli, *I am Yahweh* 29–98), the formula that Yahweh has done something (→ 12 above).

2:8–3:4 adds a symbolic action to the first command, Ezekiel is told to eat whatever God gives. This description appears to echo the earlier words of Isaiah in Isa 30:8–10. **9.** *a written scroll:* This was made of papyrus and not parchment, which takes writing on only one side. The message was clear to Ezekiel before he swallowed it: his task would be totally taken up with preaching warning and woe. **3:2** He was to make it completely his own, by filling his stomach with the message. And it was accepted—it became sweet in his mouth. Jeremiah expresses a similar thought about his task at Jer 15:16 (cf. Ps 119:103).

3:5–11 returns to the theme of the hardhearted rebellion of the Israelites. **5.** *difficult speech:* The example highlights Israel's deaf ears to God's word.

22   (c) THE COMMISSION TO BE WATCHMAN (3:12–21). The tradition of the prophet being a watchman predates Ezekiel (see Hos 9:8; Hab 2:1; Isa 21:6) but is particularly effective in describing the prophetic role, which both sees ahead what God is about to do and stirs up the people to respond. The city watchman is pictured (2 Sam 18:24; 1 Kgs 9:17; Ps 127:1) as charged with the protection of the people from sudden attack. Ezekiel combines the imagery with his unique demand for individual responsibility (3:18–21). Both themes are repeated in chap. 33 for the second part of his ministry (→ 82 below). **12.** *spirit:* God's power drives the prophet away from the vision and back to the exilic community. **15.** *Tel-abib:* Babylonian *til abûbi* meant "the (ruined) mound of the flood," signifying a settlement area from

before the great flood of the Gilgamesh Epic. Modern Tel Aviv, named after the ancient settlement of Ezekiel's time, signifies "tell of the barley harvest" (i.e., of the fruit of the first month of the year). **18.** *you shall surely die:* This is a royal formula for giving the death penalty. It is delivered by kings in 1 Sam 14:44; 22:16; 1 Kgs 2:37,42 and by God in a cultic setting of law in Gen 2:17; 2 Kgs 1:4,6. Ezekiel is given a legal responsibility in a most solemn manner. **20.** *a stumbling block:* The *NAB* suggests that the virtuous person can fall when God puts some strong temptation in the way. The text may be clearer if we take the idea as sequential: the previously good person begins to consider evil, perhaps thinking he or she can always turn back, but then God's divine judgment intervenes and makes it impossible—to the ancient mind, evil deeds bear consequences which cannot be stopped, and divine justice brings it back on the heads of the evildoers (Pss 109:12; 137:8; 140:9).

23   (d) THE PROPHET CONSTRAINED (3:22–27). This is the fourth and last of the separate elements of the call narrative. It is resumed as a key to his preaching in 24:27 and 33:22 in which the fall of Jerusalem ends the enforced silence. **22.** *the hand of the Lord:* The last element in the chiastic use of "hand of the Lord" (1:4–28), "spirit" (1:28–3:11), "spirit" (3:12–21), "hand of the Lord" (3:22–27), which mark off each section of the call. The vision takes place in a plain, apparently different from the first vision but with the same effect on the prophet: the divine spirit makes possible the hearing of what follows. **24.** The prophet is commanded to stay at home, and from accounts of the elders coming to him (14:1; 20:1), it seems he did not go out to publicly preach, as, e.g., Jeremiah was wont to do (Jer 7; 26; 36), but spoke only on occasion from his own house (see C. Sherlock, *ExpTim* 94 [1983] 296–98). Apparently he had quite a reputation and drew people to ask him what God was doing (33:30–31). **25.** The bonds on the prophet were probably psychic rather than physical ropes. He is forbidden to speak his condemnations unless God explicitly gives him a message to deliver. J. Wevers (*Ezekiel* 57) sees 3:24–27 as a secondary addition to pave the way for mention of Ezekiel's temporary dumbness due to an ecstatic trance in 24:27. In any case, it is clear from the nature of the whole commissioning scene beginning with 1:28 that the dumbness was not an absolute silence but a restraint placed on the prophet to reinforce that his role was to speak only words commanded by God.

24   **(B) Symbolic Actions and Oracles (4:1–7:27).** This section is divided into three symbolic actions with elaborations of their meaning in 4:2–5:4, followed by three programmatic oracles of judgment in 5:5–7:27. Rather than a one-to one correspondence between the actions and the oracles, there is a complex interrelationship of themes and climactic buildup. The two parts are also interrelated in a legal formality: the symbolic acts serve as a literary indictment and accusation, while the oracles in chaps. 5–7 are short on accusation and long on the formal sentencing for Israel's crimes. The whole combination revolves around a basic charge against the people—idolatry, i.e., high treason against Yahweh, which will bring a death penalty (see Deut 13:8–17).

(a) THREE SYMBOLIC ACTIONS (4:1–5:4). It is not necessary to assume that Ezekiel acted out fully each symbolic gesture. Many of these may have been preached or described rhetorically more than performed.

(i) *The siege map and lying on the side* (4:1–8). **1.** Excellent examples of maps scratched on clay tablets exist from Sumeria and Babylon (see *ANEP* 260). This would be further confirmation that these passages did originate in a Mesopotamian and not a

Palestinian setting. **2.** *ramp . . . battering rams:* These all represent typical weapons employed in the siege of cities (see *ANEP* 368, 369, 373). **3.** *iron griddle:* An attacking army would build a wall around a city so that no help could reach the defenders nor survivors escape. **5.** *390 days:* The prophet is to act out this siege by lying on his left side tied up and staring at his model, i.e., attacking it with his eyes. How the total time was arrived at is not altogether certain. It could mean the time from the dedication of Solomon's Temple to its final destruction (approximately 975 to 585). Another plausible suggestion holds that it represents the time of the monarchy from Saul to Josiah's reform (1010 to 622). The analogy of a day of lying down for each year of sin reverses the punishment of the Israelites in the desert where 40 years were exacted for 40 days of rebellion (Num 14:33–34). **6.** *40 days:* Judah is to suffer a fate similar to the Israelites in their 40 years after the exodus (cf. Amos 2:10; 5:25). The 40 may be the period from Josiah's reforms to the fall of Jerusalem rounded out (622 to 585); or, better, it may be a prediction by the prophet that the exile to come will last 40 years as did the exodus wanderings.

25   (ii) *Eating unclean bread* (4:9–17). This scene represents the desperation brought on by famine. **9.** *lentils:* The combination of grains was considered inedible and represents a desperate attempt to scrape together enough to barely survive. **10.** *twenty shekels:* This is a weight equivalent to eight ounces. **11.** *one-sixth of a hin:* A hin is roughly a gallon, so one-sixth is two-thirds of a quart. **12.** Barley was considered inferior to wheat and so is identified with food for the poor or starving. According to Deut 23:12–14, human excrement was unclean and was to be kept outside of the military camp. Ezekiel insists on his priestly fidelity to the law which forbids priests to have contact with unclean animals and sacrifices (Lev 22:8; 7:18). Only the conditions of the siege make it necessary. God relents on the insistence that the symbolic act be performed literally, for Ezekiel's sake. **16.** *the staff of bread:* Bread was, and often still is, baked in the Near East with a hole in the middle so that the extra loaves may be strung on a pole which is then hung high to avoid mice and other predators.

(iii) *Cutting off the beard* (5:1–4). This symbolic action is inspired by a combination of Lev 26:33 and Isa 7:20. In the first case, God will draw his sword and bring Israel to ruin; in the second, he will use a foreign power to shave Israel. Ezekiel affirms both of these as coming and by joining them together enhances the threat of total degradation involved. **1.** By using a sword, which makes an unlikely razor, the prophet links the haircutting to killing in battle. Since hair was a sign of strength (Judg 16–17) and dignity (2 Sam 10:4–5), to be shaved bald was complete humiliation. It becomes a sign of the conditions of the exile. **2.** *a third part:* The three parts represent three evils of war: the burning city, death by sword, exile. **3.** The most probable meaning of the few hairs in the hem is that they represent those who will survive the destruction of Jerusalem; but even among these exiles, some will later die by violence.

26   (b) ORACLES OF JUDGMENT (5:5–7:27). Various groupings of three dominate the prophet's rhetoric in the symbolic actions. The succeeding three oracles in 5:5–17; 6:1–14; and 7:1–27 are similarly held closely bound together by triple repetitions. All three use the formula "plague, famine, and sword" (5:12; 6:11; 7:15); and all decisively state that the evil comes from God's wrath (5:13–15; 6:12; 7:3). The narration of the symbolic gestures in 4:1–5:4 served the purpose of making the listener or reader ask, "What is going to happen?" and "Why will these things happen?" The oracles in chaps. 5–7 answer these questions.

(i) *Oracle against Jerusalem* (5:5–17). **5.** The interpretation begins with the claim that Jerusalem is the navel of the earth (cf. 38:12), an image borrowed from ancient mythology of the exact place where earth was originally connected to heaven—hence, a special place for encountering the divine. **6.** *ordinances . . . statutes:* Include both case laws and apodictic laws (→ OT Thought, 77:87) arising from both secular and cultic areas of Israel's life. Israel's rebellion has been complete; no part of the covenantal bond has gone unscathed. **9.** *abominations:* Gross violations of the commandments against idolatry. This is a favorite charge of Deut and is specified in v 11 below: the placing of idols in the Temple sanctuary (cf. Deut 7:25; 13:15; 17:4; 32:16). **10.** *fathers shall eat sons:* The fate is particularly horrible because the crime is so horrible; cf. Lev 26:29. **11.** *no pity nor mercy:* This is an expression known only in Deut (13:9). The message of chap. 5 stays very close to the exilic theology shared by Deut, Jer, the Holiness Code, and Ezek. **12–17.** This vivid description of the horrors of the coming days borrows heavily from the language of the foregoing sources: v 12 is similar to Lev 26:25; v 14 echoes Lev 26:31; v 15 recalls many passages in Jeremiah (24:9; 29:18); v 16 has ties to Deut 32:23–24 and to Lev 26:25–26; v 17 resembles Lev 26:22,25 and also Deut 32:24–25.

27   (ii) *Oracle against the mountains* (6:1–14). The preceding oracle announced judgment against Jerusalem; the prophet now extends this to the mountain country of Palestine. This oracle foreshadows Ezekiel's concern with the restoration of the mountains of Israel in chap. 36. Although Jerusalem is implicitly connected to the mountains (20:40; 34:26), the prophet was disgusted with the abuses of the Zion theology, much as Jeremiah had been. In his vision of the purified mountains (33:28; 34:13,14; 35:12; 36:4,8), there is no mention of Zion. This is a powerful oracle full of repetition and alliteration. It can be divided into a series of stages, vv 3–7, 8–10,11–13a,13b–14. M. Greenberg (*Ezekiel 1–20* 137) has seen a balanced halving effect where the first oracle (vv 3–7) and its "afterwave" (vv 8–10) are matched by the second oracle and its afterwave (11–13a,13b–14).

The first oracle echoes Lev 26:30–31 and also has strong similarities to the vocabulary of David's lament over Saul and Jonathan in 2 Sam 1:18–20. **2.** *the mountains of Israel:* This phrase occurs only in Ezek, 14 times in all, mostly in the oracles of salvation in chaps. 33–39. The word "mountains" occurs three times in vv 2–3, a strong rhetorical opening. The formulaic character resembles royal herald announcements (2 Kgs 18:28) and is the same as the opening of 36:1. **3.** *high places:* A major feature of Canaanite worship, where sacrifice was carried out on large open platforms of stone (6 ft. high and 25 ft. or more wide). **4.** *incense stands:* These are well known in Canaanite worship. One of the titles of Baal was Baal Hammon, "Lord of Incense." *idols:* The Hebr term *gll* seems to mean a stele or pillar and is frequent in Deut, Jer, and Ezek—books closely associated with Josiah's cultic reform. A mocking pun is probably intended since *gillûlîm* can be translated "dungballs" as well as "idols." **5.** *bones:* Dead bones make a place unclean, and so Josiah, e.g., scattered them on the ground to defile pagan sanctuaries (2 Kgs 23:14).

9. *those who have escaped:* There is a remnant theology in these lines that foreshadows later more developed explanations in chaps. 12, 14, 16, 20, and 36. **12.** *pestilence, sword, and famine:* This threefold plague, a key to the unity of chaps. 5–7 (5:12; 6:12; 7:15), is borrowed from the Jeremiah tradition (Jer 14:12; 27:8,13; 28:8). **13.** *every high hill:* Verses 11–13a take up again the theme of vv 1–7, but now add the groves to the list of pagan cultic practices that are condemned. These shrines were particularly loathed by the prophets as threats to pure Yahwist devotion (see Deut 12:2; 1 Kg 14:23; Hos 4:13; Jer 2:20).

28 (iii) *Oracle against the whole land* (7:1–27). This is the third and climactic subject of the divine announcement of judgment in chaps. 5–7. The sequence has moved from Jerusalem to the mountain country, now to the whole land. The theme of the Day of the Lord is traditional among the prophets (Isa 2; Amos 5; Zeph 1). The chapter falls into two parts, vv 1–9 and 10–27. The first is a breathless poem that plays on the ideas of the "end" and the "day." The second is a long, rushing description of the disasters that will befall Israel when the day and the end do come. They should not be separated. Some scholars see a great deal of repetitive glossing in vv 1–9. Since most solutions have tried to make the poetry too logical, it is preferable to read the whole chapter as a literary unity. **2.** *four corners:* Literally, the four "wings" of the land, this emphasizes the divine judgment reaching the full breadth of Israel's claims (cf. 11:12; Job 37:3). **4.** *neither pity nor have mercy:* This is a favorite expression in Ezek; see 5:11; 7:4,9; 8:18; 9:5,10; again it may be borrowed from Jer 13:14. **7.** *near is the day:* A prophetic commonplace: Isa 13:6; Joel 1:15; 4:14; Obad 15; Zeph 1:7,14. The theme of consternation rather than rejoicing is taken directly from Amos 5:18–20, and the whole oracle may come under the influence of that prophet.

29 **11.** *nor shall it delay:* The imagery of vv 10–11 sharply contrasts the flowering of evil in wild abundance and the suddenness with which it is cut down (see a similar image in Isa 40:6–7). **12.** *the buyer rejoice:* The proverb quoted here summarizes ordinary times, when the buyer feels the purchase will last, whereas the seller regrets parting with a treasure. But when the Day of the Lord comes, no buyer will hold on to any purchase for long. It is a legal phrase borrowed from the laws on redeeming land during the jubilee year (Lev 25:23–24). **16.** *like doves:* Flight to rock cliffs like birds fluttering in terror is a common prophetic image for the horrors of war (Isa 16:2; Jer 48:9,28; cf. Ps 11:2). **17.** *run with water:* The warriors will be so frightened that they will lose control of their bladders. **18.** *baldness:* Shaving the head signified a state of mourning for a relative. **19.** *silver and gold:* A quote from Zeph 1:18. **20.** *refuse:* The literal meaning of *niddâh* is "an unclean thing," namely, the impurity of menstruation (Lev 15:19–24). Here it becomes a metaphor for the people's impurity and violation of the law. The image is made vividly concrete by vv 21–25. **24.** *worst of nations:* This is a common cipher for the Babylonians (see Jer 6:22–23; Hab 1:6). **26.** *prophetic vision shall fade:* Verses 26–27 list the common people ("people of the land") and four classes of leaders. The princes serve only in the political arena, but the other three function primarily as religious authorities: prophets, responsible for oracles and visions; priests, for instruction in the law; and elders, for wisdom (cf. Jer 8:8).

30 **(C) The Vision of the End of the Temple** (8:1–11:25). Chapters 8 to 11 form a unity that is determined by the *inclusio* of 8:1–3 and 11:22–25, in which the opening and close are made to match. Thus the prophet is with the elders (8:1a) when God's hand falls on him (8:1b) and the vision appears (8:2–3); it ends when the vision disappears (11:22–23), the spirit leaves him (11:24), and he returns among the elders (11:25). This is also chiastic in structure (A B C : C′ B′ A′), which signals the unity of all that is in between. But the dynamic forward movement of the action also indicates a unified conception. Chapter 8 is a vision of idolatry and sin with a formal judicial accusation of Israel, while

chap. 9 carries out the sentence. Together these form an elaborate and solemn oracle of judgment on Israel. Chapter 10 completes this with the divine rejection of the Temple and its worshipers, already foreshadowed in chap. 1. Finally, in a recapitulation, chap. 11 repeats the accusation but ends with an oracle of restoration, just before God's throne departs. That foreshadows the promise of a new heart in 36:26 (cf. Alonso Schökel, *Ezequiel* 55). The four chapters are further held together by the progressive stages of the divine departure: in 8:3 the glory of the Lord stands at the inner gate; in 9:3 the presence that resides in the Holy of Holies moves out to the threshold; in 10:3 the glory of the throne vision also moves to the threshold; and finally in 11:23 the glory leaves the city to the east (toward Babylon!). God rejects the claims of Jerusalem to special protection just because his glory dwells in the Temple. Contrary to the established "doctrine" that God would never desert his city and Temple (Jer 7; Pss 46:5; 48:8), Ezekiel proclaims that it is about to happen. He further alludes to the unthinkable, that God will go and dwell with the exiles in Babylon (the repetition of the throne vision of chap. 1 expresses this) and that the divine presence will return only when the exiles return (11:14–21).

31 (a) THE VISION OF THE TEMPLE ABOMINATIONS (8:1–18). Chapter 8 can be divided into two parts: vv 1–4 and 5–18, the first a setting for all of chaps. 8–11, the other the initial indictment. The *NAB* does extensive reordering of the verses but the attempts to improve the sense destroy the dramatic progression of the text.

The vision returns to Ezekiel in vv 1–4. The date is September 17–18, 592, soon after the completion of the 390 days on one side that Ezekiel was ordered to perform in 3:16 (dated to August 7, 593). There would not be time enough for the 40 days on the other side, however; but they may have been intended to be done separately in the future (→ 24 above). **2.** This verse repeats the description of 1:27 and identifies the visions as the same (see also v 4). **3.** *the form of a hand:* Ezekiel employs *tabnît* here and in 10:8 to describe the "likeness" of a hand, and in 8:10 for the "likeness" of creeping animals on a wall. The fact that nowhere else in the book does he use this word supports the basic unity of writing in chaps. 8–11. *seized me by the hair:* In Dan 14:36, the prophet Habakkuk is carried by an angel to Daniel in the lion's den by his hair. *the statue of jealousy:* This could be the same idol of Asherah erected by King Manasseh some 60 years earlier (2 Kgs 21:7; 2 Chr 33:7), although it seems unlikely that such a cult would have survived Josiah's reforms of 628–622 (2 Kgs 22–23). In any case, it was a statue of a divinity in total violation of the first commandment (Exod 20:4; Deut 5:8; cf. Deut 12:3), thus provoking "jealousy," a righteous anger or sense of outrage. **7.** *a hole in the wall:* The sequence of idolatrous scenes all take place in the two courtyards surrounding the Temple building proper: the outer and inner courts. **10.** *creeping things:* Hebrew has other words for wild and domesticated animals, birds and fish, so that these are usually understood to be insects and other unusual (and disgusting) creatures. What such a cult involved is unknown; animal totems or gods in animal form are known in various periods from both Babylon and Egypt. **11.** *seventy elders:* According to Exod 24:1, these represent the people of Israel at Mt. Sinai; in Num 11:16,24, the elders share the spirit of Moses in the community. Here they represent all Israel guilty of idolatry. *Jaazaniah, son of Shaphan:* Since the house of Shaphan is noted repeatedly in the reforms of Josiah and the life of Jeremiah as devoted to the true worship of Yahweh (2 Kgs 22:3; Jer 29:3; 36:12), it is a sign of the depth that sin has reached to find Jaazaniah in this group.

32   **14.** *Tammuz:* The cult of Tammuz (Sumerian Dumuzi) originated in Mesopotamia no later than the third millennium BC and commemorated the annual descent of the god into the underworld each year. This would be celebrated by lament rituals for the loss of the god, practiced especially by women. At least in later times, it became associated with dying and rising gods who represented the annual seasonal weather pattern, notably with the Greek Adonis. Further mention of this cult in Israel can be found in Isa 17:10 and Ezek 32:19, where Tammuz is called by his title "The Beautiful One." Traces of the Tammuz cult have been found throughout ancient Palestine (L. Boadt, *Ezekiel's Oracles against Egypt* 151–52). **16.** The number 25 is obviously significant to the prophet; it may represent the 24 courses of priests who were appointed to serve in the Temple in order, with the high priest at their head. *the sun:* Worship of the sun-god was known in both Egypt and Mesopotamia. It was practiced in Israel, at least in the time of Manasseh, since Josiah had to destroy the "horses and chariot of the sun" found at the Temple entrance itself (2 Kgs 23:11). Because this is the last in the series of abominations shown to the prophet, it is considered the worst—note that in order to worship the sun, the devotees had to turn their back on Yahweh! **17.** *the branch to my nose:* The MT actually reads "their noses," but even Jewish scribal tradition recognized that this was a deliberate change to avoid the blasphemous suggestion of doing something vile or obscene to God. It may be a deliberate snub (*b. Yoma* 77a) or an obscene phallic gesture. On the other hand, there are common Mesopotamian gestures of holding up a hand (often with a branch in it) before one's nose as a sign of humility before a god. The sin would be Israel's hypocrisy in committing idolatry while pretending devotion to Yahweh.

33   (b) THE ANGELS OF JUDGMENT (9:1–11).   Some commentators argue that chap. 9 should follow chap. 11 since it records the execution of the idolators, while chap. 11 continues to list more of them (→ 31 above). God now passes judgment on the sinners shown to the prophet in the preceding chapter. **2.** *man dressed in linen:* This is the typical costume of high officials in Egyptian art (*ANEP* 408, 409). In Israel, it was the required garment of the high priest (Lev 16:4) and the other priests (Exod 28:42). The scribe and the six destroyers together make seven, the symbolic number of completion; in this case, the time of total destruction. **3.** *the glory of God:* The *NAB* leaves out the notice that the divine glory moved from the Holy of Holies out to the door of the Temple at this point. But it is needed here (→ 30 above). **4.** *mark an X on the foreheads:* The scribe is commanded to mark the Hebr letter *tau* on those who are not guilty of idolatry. From Ezekiel's consistent proclamation that the whole city and people are to be destroyed, even those who manage to flee (7:16), we can presume that the number marked was small; and they in turn would be exiled (6:9). **7.** Dead bodies would defile and desecrate the Temple and make it unfit for divine worship or the divine presence. **9.** As in 7:23 and 8:17, the prophet suddenly introduces into the list of cultic sins and false worship the notion of violence and bloodshed. This reflects the language of the flood narrative in Gen 6–9 and stresses that this generation is as deserving of total destruction as was Noah's. 22:6–13 returns to this theme in more detail.

34   (c) THE CHERUBIM THRONE RETURNS (10:1–22).   This chapter has three parts, vv 1–7, 8–17, and 18–22. The first describes the fiery coals that come from God's throne to destroy the city; the second describes the throne chariot in the same general terms as chap. 1, but with more detail; and the third describes the chariot throne's leaving the Temple proper to stand over the east gate with the glory of the Lord upon it. **1.** *something like a throne:* This repeats 1:26. **2.** Isaiah's vision of the glory of God in the Temple involved burning coals also (Isa 6:6). The imagery is probably borrowed from the perpetually burning incense stand in the Holy Place of the Temple. The man in linen may have been instructed to get coals from the Temple not to destroy but to purify those marked with the X, as in Isa 6 (Cody, *Ezekiel* 55). *cherubim:* Eighteen times in this chapter alone the text mentions that the living creatures of chap. 1 are cherubim, a specification that now identifies them with the throne of Yahweh (the Ark) that stands in the Temple. **4.** *the glory of the Lord went up:* This key verse indicates that God's presence is abandoning the Temple itself to return on the chariot throne to the east. This scene resembles the description of the glory in the desert (Exod 16:10; Num 10:34). Verses 15 and 20 explicitly identify the two. **8.** *the form of a human hand:* A new element in the description of the throne vision. Possibly "hand" is merely idiomatic for a "spoke" on the wheels, but if taken as personal this makes the vision closer to that of Isa 6, where the angelic beings intervene directly with the prophet. **14.** *each had four faces:* M. Greenberg interprets the Hebrew to say that each of the four cherubim had four of the same face, so that one had four lion's faces, another four human faces, etc. (*Ezekiel 1–20* 182–83). The MT probably means that the faces toward the first side for each were cherubs, and those on the second (side) were human, etc. **18.** *the glory of the Lord left:* The throne above the firmament above the cherubim had been unoccupied (10:1) while the divine glory remained in the Temple. **20.** *the God of Israel:* The glory of the Lord from the Temple and the fiery form like a man in the visions of 1:26–28 and 8:2 are now fully identified.

35   (d) THE ORACLE OF DESTRUCTION FOR THE CITY (11:1–25).   Chapter 11 includes a word of judgment against Jerusalem similar to that in chap. 8 followed by the final scene of God's departure from the Temple and the city. The oracle of 11:1–13 is a far cry from the scenes of idolatry described in 8:3–18, each one worse than the one before. Here the political leaders plan social evil which will bring down God's wrath. Probably they were counseling an anti-Babylonian policy which sought military help from Egypt. Verses 14–21 condemn those left in Jerusalem who say that the exiles of 598 were the guilty ones and have no claim on the land anymore. On the contrary, says the prophet, God is with the exiles and in his good time will restore them to the land as an obedient and purified people totally loyal to God, whereas the Jerusalemites that are left will be destroyed for their idolatries. Jeremiah takes a similar position (Jer 24). **1.** *twenty-five men:* See comment on 8:16. Jaazaniah is a different person from the man mentioned in 8:11. **2.** *planning evil:* They probably represent the pro-Egyptian, anti-Babylonian political faction. **3.** *the city is the kettle and we are the meat:* A proverb, not otherwise known, but its meaning is clear from the context. A pot cooking with the best meat is a sign of prosperity. Ezekiel points out that the pot is filled with polluted meat, dead bodies, and that the so-called good meat of the Jerusalemites will be taken out and slain by the sword either in exile or while fleeing for their lives (11:9–10). **6.** *bloodshed:* A crime particularly charged against the political leaders; cf. 19:3,6; 22:6; Jer 2:30; 22:17; 26:20–24. **12.** *statutes and ordinances:* This repeats the charge made in 5:6–7. *Pelatiah:* The death is described graphically, but there is no certitude that Ezekiel had special powers to know this from his Babylonian Exile. It should not be taken as necessarily an actual happening but a visionary prophetic word (M. Fishbane, *Int* 38 [1984] 134-35).

Verses 14-21 represent perhaps the divine answer to Ezekiel's cry in v 13. **15.** *your kinsmen:* The triple naming of the exiles as kinsmen, fellow exiles, and the whole house of Israel is a dramatic means to shift the divine favor away from Jerusalem toward Babylon. It is a shocking claim: gods were supposed to remain loyal to the land they lived in, and devotion was difficult in a foreign land (cf. Ps 137). **19.** *a new heart:* This is better understood as a "single heart." The idea is that of Jer 32:29, that Israel will become single-hearted in its loyalty to Yahweh instead of having a heart seeking both Yahweh and the idols (cf. 36:26; Jer 24:7). **22-24.** → 30 above.

36 (D) Condemnation of All: People and Leaders (12:1-14:23). Following the vision of God's total rejection of Jerusalem, the editors have collected a series of oracles that elaborate on the unreality of the people's expectations. They cannot and will not believe that Ezekiel's dire prediction can come true. Chap. 12 depicts the flight and capture of the king; chap. 13 denounces the false prophets who reassure the people's hopes; chap. 14 rejects the argument that the people have been faithful to Yahweh and so cannot be held personally responsible and therefore subject to punishment.

(a) THE COMING EXILE (12:1-28). This section is a drama in three acts: Ezekiel acts out the siege and capture of Zedekiah (vv 1-16); he then acts out eating and drinking as a prisoner (vv 17-20); and finally he turns a common proverb of consolation into a word of imminent threat (vv 21-28).

(i) *Symbolic attempt to escape* (12:1-16). The oracle has two parts and three stages. The parts are (a) the acting out of the symbol (vv 1-7) and (b) the interpretation of its meaning (vv 8-16). The stages are dramatic: the command by God (vv 1-6), the performance (v 7), and the consequences or implications (vv 8-16). The theme of exile through the use of symbolic gestures recalls the acts of 4:1-5:4. **2.** *a rebellious house:* Israel refuses to see and hear. Ezekiel will detail the long history of rebellion that reaches back to the exodus (20:8,13,21). **3.** *in their sight:* Seven times this is repeated in vv 1-7. The prophet seeks for maximal visual impact, not on the citizens of Jerusalem but on the exiles in Babylon who pin their hopes for restoration on the continued safety and existence of Jerusalem. **4.** *baggage:* Ancient monuments show victims of Assyrian attacks going into exile with a small pack on their backs (*ANEP* 366, 373), obviously holding only the barest necessities. **5.** *dig a hole:* It was easy enough to burrow an opening through the mud-brick adobe of ancient houses. **6.** *cover the face:* A sign of shame (Jer 14:4) and of grief (2 Sam 15:30). **10.** The oracle is explicitly directed to Zedekiah *and* to all the people. Note that Ezekiel does not grant him the title of "King" but only a lesser role. In the vision of the restored Israel (chaps. 33-48) he never permits the leader to be a king. **13.** *the net over him:* The imagery has a long Near Eastern history. Marduk snares Tiamat in his net in the creation myth of Babylon (*ANET* 67). At Mari in the 18th cent. a prophecy promises King Zimri Lim that the god Dagon will snare Babylon in his net! (*ANET* 625). God hunts men with a net elsewhere in the Bible (Hos 7:12; Ezek 32:3; Lam 1:3).

37 (ii) *The food of exiles* (12:17-20). **19.** Hebr grammar does not make clear whether Ezekiel directly addresses the "people of the land" (*NAB*) or speaks about them (*RSV*). References from this period (2 Kgs 21:24; 25:19) suggest that they were the citizens from rural towns and villages — or at least people with no official government positions. They were strong supporters of

the Davidic dynasty. **20.** *waste and desolate:* Cf. Lev 26:43. The language of the Holiness Code continues to guide the words of Ezekiel.

(iii) *The proverb of the long day* (12:21-28). The prophet quotes two separate sayings of the people that ridicule the urgency with which Ezekiel preaches. Each in turn is contradicted by the prophetic word that God's timetable has been moved up even closer and there will be no delay. **23.** *an end to this proverb:* See 18:2-3, where another proverb is to be cancelled from use. **24.** *false vision:* In the following chapter and other passages on false prophets (e.g., Jer 23:9-40), the language of false vision refers to prophecies of deliverance or well-being that lull people into false confidence that their evil will not be punished; here the prophet is concerned lest people misjudge his words of threat and doom as mere rhetoric without real danger. God will not merely give Ezekiel words; he will perform them (vv 25,28). Many commentators overlook this and remove this verse as an added gloss (Cooke, *Ezekiel* 127).

38 (b) CONDEMNATION OF THE PROPHETS (13:1-23). The warnings in 12:21-28 lead into a more extended treatment of false prophecy. There are two major sections: vv 1-16 against the prophets who proclaim a deluded message of hope, and vv 17-23 against prophetesses who use divination and magic as though they were the word of God. In both cases the charge is the same, these so-called prophets speak not God's will but the empty promises and hopes that people want to hear so that they will not have to convert their ways and their thinking. In this, Ezekiel echoes passages such as 1 Kgs 22:13-28; Jer 23:16-32; 28:1-17; 29:20-28; Lam 2:14.

(i) *False prophets* (13:1-16). These verses contain two oracles back to back. The first (vv 1-10a) denounces empty visions that do not give people the truth by which they could defend themselves against Yahweh's just attack; the second (vv 10b-16) compares these prophets' words to defective plaster on a house wall, which fails to keep out the rain with the result that the house disintegrates. **3.** The oracle opens forcefully by mentioning the word "prophets" five times in vv 2-4. These prophets claim the divine spirit as much as does Ezekiel (2:2; 3:12; 8:3; 11:1,24), but instead their visions and insights come from their own wishful thinking or even intentionally false attempts to win popular favor; cf. Jer 23:16. **4.** *jackals among ruins:* The image is popular among the prophets, reflecting this shy scavenger's habits of marauding for food in ruined human habitations (Isa 13:22; 34:13; Jer 9:10; 10:22; 51:37; Ps 44:20). **5.** *built up a wall:* The wall imagery expresses the same truth as the command to Ezekiel to be a watchman for the people in 3:16-21. False prophets fail to discharge this responsibility. **7.** Worse even than deluded ideas of God's word, divination seeks to predict God's will by human manipulation of natural means such as the entrails of birds or the use of magical rituals. It is condemned under penalty of death (Lev 19:31; 20:6; Deut 18:10-11) although widely practiced (1 Sam 28:3-9; Isa 2:6; 2 Kgs 17:17; 23:24). **9.** *my people:* This phrase occurs seven times in this chapter, contrasting God's care for Israel with the callous disregard among the prophets for anything but their own way. Ezek 34 returns to this theme. *the book of the house of Israel:* This is God's census list of his people (see Exod 32:32; Pss 69:28; 87:6), the equivalent of the later idea of a book of life. **10.** *peace:* The prophets cry out that all is well, but there is a dangerous sickness in the land. **11.** *whitewash:* Houses in Palestine were made of adobe, a clay formed into bricks and dried in the sun. They hardened but needed waterproof plaster applied to keep them from disintegrating in the rainy season.

39 (ii) *False prophetesses* (13:17–23). The structure of this oracle matches the preceding one. Verses 17–19 detail the accusation; vv 20–23 hand down sentence against the evildoers. **17.** *daughters of your people:* Women who practiced divination and witchcraft are condemned in Exod 22:17 and Lev 20:27. The precise purpose of the following practices is not known any longer, they may have been borrowed from pagan rituals, or they may reflect attempts to discern Yahweh's will by actions associated with Israel's worship but forbidden by the law. **18.** *magic bands:* These may be cushions or rags wrapped around the arms and forehead as amulets or to mimic such official vestments of the priests as the ephod (Exod 28:6–14). *hunt down lives:* The misleading but alluring rituals of these women are like traps used to snare birds and animals. **19.** *handfuls of barley:* The cereal offering is part of the sacrifices approved for Israel's cult (Lev 2:1–16). This may imitate the proper sacrifices, or it may be part of a divination rite that interprets the divine will by analyzing the patterns of grain on a water surface.

40 (c) IDOLATRY AND UNFAITHFULNESS (14:1–23). Two oracles make up this chapter. The first (vv 1–11) centers on the key idea of idols as a stumbling block that will cause the people to fall to their own destruction. The second (vv 12–23) moves from the concept that both prophet and inquirer bear their own punishment (mentioned in v 10) to consideration of the question of personal responsibility.

(i) *Punishment of idolators* (14:1–11). The message seems to be that there are many in Israel, esp. among the exiles, who have given their loyalty to other gods or cults but think they can still call on Yahweh's word to give them prophetic guidance. In turn, those prophets who give them what they want are just as guilty. **3.** *stumbling block of iniquity:* See 7:19; 18:30; 44:12. The evil is the cause that makes a person stumble, and the evil is the loyalty to false gods, the idols. **8.** *a sign and a lesson:* Signs are evidence of God's power at work; thus, the exodus is accomplished in great "signs and wonders" (Deut 4:34; Ps 105:27). The word for lesson is *māšāl*, normally a proverb or parable (see 18:2). The sign and lesson will be the destruction of those who seek out a prophetic word while being idolators in their hearts. **11.** *that they may be my people and I their god:* This is the classical P formula for the covenant in Exod 6:7 and is used in the Holiness Code (Lev 26:12) and in Jer 7:23; 11:4; 30:21; 32:38. Ezekiel uses it here as a promise of the restored covenant, when the people shall return to be of "a single heart" (11:20) and of a "new heart" (36:28), and free from idol worship (37:23).

41 (ii) *Need for personal righteousness* (14:12–23). The heart of this oracle is that no one can be saved by the uprightness or goodness of another. More specifically, the message is that no past deeds or faithfulness in Israel will save this generation from God's punishment for the current infidelity and idolatry. The main body of the oracle is built on four acts of judgment: famine, wild beasts, sword, and pestilence (see v 21), which are enumerated in parallel paragraphs. It ends with a special reference to Jerusalem and the possibility that some survivors may actually bring out sons and daughters not in righteousness but through divine mercy. **14.** *Noah, Daniel, and Job:* These three "righteous" men represent figures of ancient times even to Ezekiel. Noah, of course, was from the period of the flood, and his just behavior led to the saving of the whole human race. Job is known to be a man "just and upright" from the East (Job 1:1), and the story implies that he lived long ago in a different type of age. Daniel is the hero of the biblical book, but he seems to be a late adaptation of a much more antique

figure of a king famed for his wisdom, right judgment, and closeness to the gods. The story of this "Dan'el" is known from Ugaritic literature before 1200 (*ANET* 150). Ezekiel even spells the name like the Ugaritic. So it seems that he too represents a legendary example of human uprightness before God. None of them is originally an Israelite figure.

42 (E) **Allegories and Metaphors of Judgment (15:1–19:14).** These chapters differ somewhat from the preceding in that all involve very elaborate use of metaphor, allegory, or a case study as the lead-in to an announcement of judgment. They are not all similar, but at the very least they represent a body of similarly constructed passages that reinforce the earlier oracles of judgment by the powerful use of story and allegory. The first, middle, and last units (15:1–8; 17:1–24; 19:10–14) all involve the image of the vine to make their point. From the context, it seems that the vine (*gepen*) symbolizes the contrast between Israel's lowly state and her hubris against God, a theme that links the five chapters as a whole together.

43 (a) THE ALLEGORY OF THE VINE WOOD (15:1–8). In order to understand the prophet's point here, a distinction must be made between the abundance of grapes and leaves that appear in the growing season and the woody, twisted vinestock itself, which must be regularly pruned. In contrast to the wonderful product of the grapes—wine—the product of the pruned wood is good for nothing but fuel for the fireplace. What makes the lesson more pointed is that Israel itself is often compared in biblical tradition to a vine that bears rich grapes (see Ps 80:8–15; Hos 10:1; Jer 2:21) or to a vineyard (Isa 5:1–7). Ezekiel reverses the image of Ps 80 by never mentioning the purpose for which God has cared so tenderly for this vine, viz., to bring forth good fruit. Instead, Israel is compared to the cut-off branches which have already been partially burned for fuel so that they are no longer much good even for that! **2.** *the vine branch:* Hebr *zĕmôrâ* refers to a branch that has been pruned rather than to a wild grape vine that has not been cultivated. **4.** *the middle is charred:* Some scholars want to make a complete allegory of this poem, so that the two burned ends are Israel and Judah, and the middle is Jerusalem. It is preferable to see vv 2–5 as an artistic metaphor in its own right and the application limited to what the interpretation in vv 6–8 explicitly suggests (thus J. Simian Yofre, in J. Lust (ed.)., *Ezekiel* 234–47).

44 (b) JERUSALEM AS THE UNFAITHFUL WIFE (16:1–63). This is the longest chapter in Ezek, but involves what are two distinct but related oracles: the allegory of the adulterous wife (vv 1–43) and the allegory of the three sisters (vv 44–58), followed by a word of hope that integrates the lesson of both allegories (vv 59–63). The subject remains Jerusalem throughout, and the purpose, to make known the city's guilt in rejecting obedience to Yahweh for other loyalties.

45 (i) *Jerusalem the harlot* (16:1–43). Jerusalem's past history of infidelity to Yahweh is told through a bold double allegory: the first part describes how a foster parent saves and brings up an orphan (vv 3–7), and the second relates the marriage of the two followed by the wife's infidelity. It is also a drama that unfolds in several acts, and the power of the narrative comes from the tragic sense involved. At any stage the turn for the worse could have been avoided; at every stage there was an opportunity for a different response. **2.** *make known:* What follows is a legal case with accusation and sentencing. **3–7.** Jerusalem was an important city of the Canaanites that was spared by the conquering Israelites. Like an unwanted girl baby, it was exposed to die; but God had plans for it and so preserved it alive. **4.** *rubbing* *with salt:* The customs named here are typical of Palestinian birth rituals even until recent times (Zimmerli, *Ezekiel 1* 338–39). Exposure of children was also frequently practiced in the Near East (Greenberg, *Ezekiel 1–20* 275). **6.** *I passed you by:* The text does not work out a careful analysis of every detail of Jerusalem's history. It is enough for the prophet to allude to God's care for Jerusalem during the early years of the judges. **8–14.** These verses describe the decision of the kind master to marry the girl. The imagery mixes the description of the bridal clothing with the garments of a queen, and the pledges of marriage with the language of covenant. The historical reference points are David's choice of the city for his capital (2 Sam 5), its fame and splendor under David and Solomon (2 Sam 5–8; 1 Kgs 3–11), and the special covenant made with David's dynasty by God (2 Sam 7). **23–34.** The charges move on to the political sphere. The prostitution involves making love to other nations (and their gods). Egypt, Assyria, and Babylon are all named. It is worse than ordinary prostitution because Jerusalem does not even want pay for her favors—she simply gives them away out of lust. Both v 26 and v 30 accent the sexual depravity involved. In calling the foreign nations "lovers" of Israel, Ezekiel is following the earlier language of Hosea (7:11–13; 8:9) and Jeremiah (22:20–22). **35–43.** The last act in the first allegory is the divine sentence of judgment, which will ironically make her very lovers and allies be the executioners of the death sentence for adultery that the law demands (Lev 20:10; Deut 22:23–24). **37.** *expose her nakedness:* See Nah 3:5; Jer 13:22; Hos 2:12. **43.** *remember:* The heart of Israel's faithful God is the act of "remembering" the divine mercy and goodness in the covenant (see Deut 1–11 and its commands to remember and not forget).

46   (ii) *Her sisters Sodom and Samaria* (16:44–58). The theme of lewdness leads into the second major oracle of the chapter, the comparison of Jerusalem with two other cities marked for punishment because of their crimes of lewd behavior: Sodom, infamous for the incident of Gen 18; and Samaria, which was destroyed for its idolatry (2 Kgs 17:7–18). The prophet uses a proverb to initiate the comparison. Verses 44–52 draw out the implications of this proverb for the shared likeness in sin, but vv 53–58 follow with a promise of restoration for all three, perhaps somewhat surprising after the total rejection in vv 1–43. **45.** *your mother was a Hittite:* Since Jerusalem was originally a Canaanite city, the maxim reminds us that it is only returning to the pagan ways of its parents. The echo here with 16:3 helps to link the two oracles together. **46.** *elder sister Samaria:* The northern kingdom, represented here by its capital city, was the larger of the two kingdoms, comprising ten of the twelve tribes; thus, it is the elder because of its size. The comparison between Samaria and Jerusalem is already found in Hos 5:5–15 and in 2 Kgs 17:17. **49.** *the guilt of Sodom:* The good life alluded to in this passage is built on a reference in Gen 13:10 that the Jordan Valley was as well-watered as the "garden of God." Her infamy for the sin of sodomy, however, is detailed later in Gen 18. **52.** See Jer 3:6–18 for a similar thought. **53.** *restore the fortunes:* The second half of the comparison is now made: God will restore all three sisters to their former positions of honor. The theme is probably borrowed from Jeremiah's oracles of hope (Jer 30:18; 31:23), which in turn have expressed the thought of Hosea (Hos 1–3).

47   (iii) *The covenant restored* (16:59–63). This small passage also speaks of restoration but can be separated from the preceding words of hope in vv 53–58 by its comprehensive theme of the covenant being renewed. **60.** Although everything said in vv 3–52

suggests that Israel has no grounds for hope in divine mercy, God promises the restoration based on the covenant that he gave at the exodus. If Israel has forgotten, God has not forgotten (see also Lev 26:42–44). **63.** This undeserved forgiveness will jar Jerusalem's own memory and bring up the shame for its sinful ways, which will make it realize what kind of God it worships. This final verse captures superbly the meaning of the recognition formula: "that they will know I am the Lord" (v 62).

48   (c) THE ALLEGORY OF THE EAGLES (17:1–24). This chapter presents a mixture of allegory and precise historical reference. It has a basic three-part structure that consists of an allegory (vv 1–10), its interpretation (vv 11–21), and a further allegory (vv 22–24), making an A B A "sandwich" pattern, in which vv 1–10 and 22–24 are both parts of a single artistic poem, but vv 11–21 are a prose explanation. However, Greenberg's suggestion that the section on interpretation in vv 11–21 can be divided further into a judgment on the human plane (vv 11–18) and one on the divine plane (vv 19–21) leads him to see a balanced spiraling effect of four sections: a nature fable on the earthly level (vv 1–10), followed by a human interpretation for Israel on the earthly level (vv 11–18), then by a second human interpretation but from God's level (vv 19–21), concluded by a second nature fable, this time from God's level (vv 22–24). The combination of fables from nature with explicit historical judgments allows the prophet to include the promise of future restoration in the real historical framework of Judah's experience and make it seem possible. The chapter forms a tight literary unity, and vv 22–24 should be considered integral to its structure.

1–10. Since the allegorical identifications are clear to us, the "riddle" is how God will bring about the promise in vv 22–24. The cast of characters is as follows: the first great "eagle" is Nebuchadrezzar, king of Babylon (v 3); "Lebanon" is an image for Israel and, more particularly, Jerusalem (Jer 22:6; Zech 11:1–3; Isa 10:34). The "topmost twig" (v 4) is Jehoiachin, taken into exile in 598 (2 Kgs 24:8–15). The "land of traders" is Babylon, and the "seed of the land" (v 5), Zedekiah, Jehoiachin's uncle, who was named king in his place (2 Kgs 24:17–18). It became a "vine" like a "willow" (vv 5–6) in that it grew extremely quickly and luxuriantly. The second "great eagle" (in v 7) is Psammetichus II of Egypt, with whom Zedekiah had made a treaty to help lift the Babylonian attack on Jerusalem in 588 (Jer 37:4–11). Finally, the "east wind" is the desert sirocco that blows during certain times of the year, withering up all in its searing heat and providing a metaphor for God's anger (Exod 10:13; 14:21; Ps 78:26). The instrument of this wrath will be Nebuchadrezzar.

49   **11–18.** The fable is interpreted almost point for point, but the passage emphasizes the reason why the prophet considers Zedekiah's rejection of Babylon so wrong: he had broken a solemn covenant treaty made with Nebuchadrezzar. He had violated his oath taken with God as a witness. **19–21.** The accusation continues but the 3d-pers. description becomes a 1st-pers. speech of God in which the covenant and the oath are no longer seen as primarily between Zedekiah and the Babylonian king but between Zedekiah and Yahweh. It is God who brings the judgment, even though he will use Babylon as an instrument of punishment. **20.** *net:* See the discussion at 21:36.

22–24. The imagery returns to the fable of vv 1–10. **22.** The new twig from the top of the cedar represents a future king from the house of David (2 Sam 7:13). **23.** *birds of every kind:* First used in the flood story to describe all the species on the ark, the image of the birds sheltered in the cedar is used again in Ezek 31:6 to describe Pharaoh as a great king. **24.** If the cedar is the king of Judah, then the trees are the kings of the surrounding nations. They will know that God humbles the mighty and raises up new power from nothing. The lesson is repeated in chap. 31, in which Pharaoh is humbled. Here God brings a new king of Israel to glory from the lowly state of punishment to which Judah has fallen in vv 1–21.

50   (d) A LAW CASE FOR INDIVIDUAL RESPONSIBILITY (18:1–32). The theme of individual responsibility plays an important role in Ezekiel's thought, with various aspects of the question treated in 3:16–21; 14:12–20; 33:10–20, and esp. in this chapter. The basic principle is already stated in Deut 24:16 and was known in Israel (Jer 31:29–30; 2 Kgs 14:6), although the prevailing theology stressed that guilt was often to be borne by the children and family of the guilty party (Exod 20:5; 34:7; Deut 5:9; Lev 26:39–40; 2 Kgs 10:1–11; 24:3–4; Jer 15:4; 18:21; Lam 5:9).

The chapter has two parts: vv 1–20 give three stages of individual responsibility: father, son, and grandson; vv 21–32 take up the case of the fate of those who repent from evil, a problem that is made urgent by the arguments in the first part. There are strong ties to both the law codes in Deut 12–26 and in Lev 17–26. It shows similarity to other lists of virtues that characterize the just person, such as Isa 33:14–16; Pss 15; 24; Mic 6:6–8, and to lists of crimes, such as Ezek 22:6–12 and Jer 22:1–5. Above all, however, the historical context for this message suggests that it is a summons to repentance with the hope that God will protect the exiles as a remnant. While ostensibly directed to evil done back in the homeland (v 2), its primary audience is the exiles, and its purpose is to initiate a reform that stresses personal appropriation of the Torah even when there is no land nor defined community that can be held collectively responsible for its practice.

51   (i) *A proverb for three generations* (18:1–20). **2.** *this proverb:* Since the saying is also known to Jeremiah (Jer 31:29), it must have been a common understanding of divine justice. **5–9.** The father follows the prescriptions of the law, here a combination of moral and ritual demands. For parallels, see Exod 22:20,24; Lev 18:19; 19:13,15,33,35; 25:14,37; Deut 23:17,20; 24:17; Prov 22:22; 28:8. **9.** *walk in my decrees:* A legal formulation closes the section; see Lev 18:4; 26:3. **10–13.** The son commits crimes that violate rather the social-justice obligations. **10.** *sheds blood:* See Exod 21:12; Num 35:16–21. **12.** *oppresses the poor:* See Deut 24:14; Pss 12:6; 35:10. **13.** *his blood be on him:* A legal sentence of death mentioned Lev 20:9,11,13,16. **14–18.** The grandson learns from his father's evil. **16.** Feeding the hungry and clothing the naked are known in both Mesopotamia and Egyptian lists of royal duties, as well as in the NT (Matt 25:35–36). **19.** *he shall surely live:* A key to Ezekiel's repetition throughout the chapter is the opportunity to affirm the possibility of life for those who would follow the Law.

52   (ii) *Conversion and mercy* (18:21–32). The previous case study dealt with people who chose to live either a good way or an evil way of life consistently. But what if one repents? Will past sins condemn such a person to death despite the change of heart? Ezekiel answers, "No! That one shall live" (vv 21–23). And then, what about the opposite case, when a good person turns to evil? That person shall be held accountable for the present evil attitude, and die (v 24). **25.** *the way of the Lord:* Is this also a proverb? Probably not. But it is worth noting that the entire chapter is in question-and-answer format, a lively rhetorical effect to imitate a real legal

trial. **31.** *a new heart:* Rhetorically the prophet urges the people to get a new heart and spirit, but in 11:19 and 36:36 it is more carefully stated that God gives it out of grace.

53   (e) TWO LAMENTS OVER ZEDEKIAH (19:1–14). The last two of the great metaphorical story illustrations in chaps. 15–19 are composed as funeral laments over King Zedekiah. Verses 1–19 picture the fate of a would-be lion; vv 10–14 the fate of a vine. Both laments share the common theme of a mother-and-son relationship. This chapter completes the catalogue of Israel's sins announced on the scroll the prophet was to eat, which had written on it laments and woe (2:10). The poetry is not totally regular, but it mostly maintains the 3:2 metrical beat of the typical lament style found in Lam 1–4.

(i) *The lioness and her cubs* (19:1–9). The first lament (vv 1–9) pictures a lioness with two cubs. The first cub seems to be Jehoahaz (609) because of the reference in v 4 that he was taken to Egypt (2 Kgs 23:34). The second cub is more difficult to identify. Some think that it represents Jehoiakim (609–598) because of the violent behavior listed in vv 6–7, but others argue for his son Jehoiachin (598) because he was taken prisoner to Babylon. Still another possibility is Zedekiah (598–586), who eventually was also brought to Babylon to die. This last gains strength from two factors. One is that both Jehoahaz and Zedekiah had the same mother, Hammutal. The second is that the second lament (vv 10–14) also speaks of Zedekiah. **2.** *your mother:* The lioness is not identified, so it may stand symbolically for Judah as well as Hamutal. **3.** *young lion:* The terms for lions are all different in this passage. The young lion was often a symbol for a warrior (Gen 49:9; Pss 10:9; 22:14,22; Ezek 32:2). God was sometimes pictured as a lion attacking Israel (Lam 3:10; Hos 5:14; Amos 1:2). A seal of a high official in the northern kingdom named Shema bore a lion on it (*ANEP* 276). **4.** *pit . . . hooks:* The Hebr words are sometimes interpreted to be rather a "snare" and "rings (in the nose)." Descriptions of prisoners with rings or hooks through the jaws are found in Ezek 29:4; 38:4; Job 40:26; and on a stele of Esarhaddon (*ANEP* #447).

(ii) *The scepter of vine wood* (19:10–14). The image and vocabulary have strong resemblances to both chap. 17 and chap. 31. The message of the passage also shares a theme common to both of those chapters: hubris of the ruler and its consequences, viz., to be uprooted and thrown out by God's anger. The majesty of the chosen branch is perhaps excessive for the hesitant and uncertain Zedekiah pictured in Jer 37–38, but that seems to be the best choice (see Alonso Schökel, *Ezequiel* 124), although some think that only Jehoiachin would fit (Tkacik, *JBC* 21:46). **11.** *the thick boughs:* A very close parallel to 31:3,10,14 is present here. **12.** *the east wind:* Cf. 17:9–10. **13.** *the desert:* A symbol for the exile in Babylon. **14.** *a fire:* This recalls the fable of Jotham where fire went from a bramble to destroy the cedars (Judg 9:8–15). The weakest and least significant often bring down mighty kingdoms. The entire passage ends with the label that this is a lamentation. It forms an *inclusio* with 2:10, encompassing all the oracles of judgment from chaps. 3–19.

54   (F) **Indictment and Condemnation** (20:1–24:27). The final five chapters of the first half of the book are a mixture of judgment oracles built around key themes: chap. 20 gives a historical overview for God's judgment; chap. 21 gathers a number of passages that use the sword image as a symbol of judgment; chap. 22 gives legal metaphors for judgment; chap. 23 returns to the allegories of Jerusalem's guilt first developed in chap.

16; and chap. 24 uses two metaphors for God's definitive rejection of the city. The section is set off from what comes before by the date given in 20:1 and by the address to the elders. The arrangement of chaps. 20-24 is thus somewhat loose. Like chaps. 15-19, it is a collection of unusual literary forms such as allegory and historical recital attached to words of judgment. Since it contains passages that duplicate earlier material (the two sisters in chap. 23 relate to chap. 16; the pot of meat in chap. 24 relates to chap. 11), it may have circulated independently before being joined to chaps. 1-19 by an editor (cf. Wevers, *Ezekiel* 6-7).

55   (a) ISRAEL'S HISTORY OF INFIDELITY (20:1-44). The very elaborate introduction in vv 1-3 is followed first by a lengthy recital of Israel's history of infidelity (vv 4-31) and then by an extended word of judgment which combines both destruction and restoration (vv 32-44). Many scholars think the differences between the two parts are so great that the word of judgment must be a secondary addition. However, as in the allegories of chaps. 16 and 23 and the legal case of chap. 18, the case study in the first part demands the word of direct application and interpretation that vv 32-44 provide. The whole is quite unified (so Fohrer, *Ezechiel;* Zimmerli, *Ezekiel 1;* Greenberg, *Ezekiel 1-20*).

(i) *Past history of rebellion* (20:1-31). The opening date and special mention of the elders in vv 1-3 underline the problem to be addressed: Israel wants to inquire formally of the prophet what God's will is. The prophet then recalls Israel's history of disobedience and infidelity in four stages: (1) the time in Egypt (vv 5-10); (2) the first generation in the desert (vv 11-17), (3) the children's generation in the desert (vv 18-26); (4) the time in the promised land (vv 27-29). It is a remarkable indictment that charges Israel with infidelity even from its days in Egypt and goes so far as to claim that God determined the Babylonian Exile and their punishment as early as the exodus period itself. God even provided the people with the laws and opportunities to sin! But this was done to bring them to punishment so that they would wake up. Ezek 20 closely resembles the P theology of Num 11-21 by stressing that God always punishes infidelity but also spares the people for the future. By this frightening recital of the past, the prophet hopes to teach the exiles that they cannot rely for their security or for the protection of Jerusalem on being God's chosen people. God's initiative has been at work all along preparing for punishment, and it will not be stopped.

56   **1.** *seventh year:* August 14, 591, a year after the date in 8:1. **5.** *I chose Israel:* The vb. *bāḥar,* "to choose," summarizes Israel's theology of special election (see Deut 7:6-10), but is found only here in Ezek. **7.** *idols of Egypt:* Nowhere does the Pentateuch suggest that Israel worshiped Egyptian gods. But the argument up through v 10 suggests that God resolved to save Israel from Egypt despite idolatry already practiced there. **9.** The reason for God's continual mercy was to protect the honor of his name and his holiness (vv 9,14,22,40,44), not for any obligations of the covenant. **12.** *sabbaths:* Ezekiel esp. stresses the sabbath (Ezek 22:8,26; 23:38). It is based on the P theology of Gen 17 and Exod 31:12-17 and ties proper cultic worship to the keeping of the covenant. Jer 17:19-27 may also influence Ezekiel's usage. **25.** *bad laws:* See 14:7 and Isa 6:9-11; 63:17; and the theme of God hardening Pharaoh's heart in Exod 7-10. Since vv 4-24 presuppose that Israel freely chose to reject God's laws, Ezekiel's meaning is best understood as that God abandoned them to their own worst evil inclinations. All things are under God's control in Hebr thinking—and even evil is for some purpose. The

next verse explains that God wished to make them aware of the horror of their crimes and return to acknowledging him. **29.** *high place:* A pun is involved: "What is the high place (*bāmâ*) to which you go (*bā'îm*)?" It expresses the final summary of Israel's crimes: idolatry.

57   (ii) *Divine judgment* (20:32-44). The natural response to the preceding recital of Israel's failure is to renew the exodus. Verses 32-38 describe a new deliverance, this time from exile, and a period of purification in the desert when rebels will be purged from the people. Verses 39-44 then present the plan for a new order in the land, when true worship and fidelity will be grounded in Israel's recognition that it is God who saved them out of exile. **32.** The statues of the pagan gods are merely "wood and stone" (Deut 4:28; 28:36). **33.** *mighty hand:* This phrase is also deuteronomic (Deut 4:34; 5:15; 7:19; 11:2). *wrath poured out:* Ezekiel's favorite term for divine judgment: 7:8; 9:18; 14:19; 20:8,13,21,33; 22:22. **39.** Once again the oracle singles out idol worship as the primary evil. It is possible that the elders came to ask about how to deal with pressures to set up a high place, altar, and possibly even a statue of Yahweh for the exiles since they could no longer worship at the Jerusalem Temple. Ezekiel is immediately reminded of the exodus experience of the golden calf (Exod 32) and subsequent violations of the first commandment (Exod 20:3-4). **40.** *holy mountain:* This phrase usually means the Temple Mount in Jerusalem: Isa 27:13; 56:7; 65:11; Joel 2:1; 4:17; Zeph 3:11; Dan 9:20. God will restore true worship according to the law. **43.** *remember:* See 16:60-63 for the importance of this theme. It is strong in Deut 5:15; 8:2-18; 11:15.

58   (b) ORACLES OF THE SWORD (20:45-21:32). Four oracles have been gathered together because they share the same image: God wielding the sword of judgment. (i) *A sword against the south* (20:45-49; 21:1-7). This oracle has two halves: a prophecy directed against the south using the metaphor of a forest fire in 20:45-49, followed by its allegorical interpretation against Jerusalem under the metaphor of a sword in 21:1-5. The two parts are made to match almost exactly. 21:6-7 rounds this out with a symbolic action that will provoke people's questions (as in 12:9; 24:19) and to which Ezekiel gives a gloomy conclusion similar to that of chap. 7. **46.** *the south:* The opening line uses three words for "south" plus three vbs. for "prophesy." The vbs. are repeated in 2:12 with three words for "Jerusalem," the real object of the oracle. All three words for the south are unusual and are found again only in the vision of the restored Temple in chaps. 40-48. **47.** *every green and dry tree:* A merism, in which the two extreme possibilities stand for all things in between—it means the whole forest (cf. 17:24; 21:26). **3.** *sword:* One of the three traditional images of divine destruction borrowed from the very real experience of invading enemy armies (famine, plague, and sword; cf. 5:12; 6:11; 7:15). The sword image often occurs by itself (6:3-7; Deut 32:41-42; Jer 50:35-38). **7.** *every spirit fail:* The entire verse is a description of the fear that comes over the recipient of bad news (cf. 7:17).

(ii) *The sword polished for slaughter* (21:8-17). This short oracle begins with a two-line poem on the glittering blade of a sword in vv 9-10. It is followed by an interpretation in vv 10-13 that builds on the proverbial wisdom that the rod trains a child to responsibility (Prov 13:24), but since Israel has spurned the rod's discipline, God has no choice but to send the sword. A second reflection in vv 14-17 returns to the poem's theme of bloodthirsty judgment to reinforce the coming terror.

59   (iii) *The sword of the king of Babylon* (21:18–27). The scene pictures Babylon's army marching across Syria and at some crossroad making the decision whether to cross over to Palestine or to continue down the E side of the Jordan to Rabbath Ammon, the capital of the Ammonite kingdom. The oracle has two parts: the description in vv 18–23 and the interpretive oracle in vv 24–27. **20.** *mark a way:* Nebuchadrezzar will attack both cities (see the continuation in 21:28–32), but he must choose one first. **21.** *divination:* Three forms are listed: (1) arrows that are marked with the names, shaken in a quiver, and then one pulled forth, a practice well known in pre-Islamic Arabia; (2) teraphim, which are usually understood to be small household images of gods that may be consulted through some means we do not presently understand; (3) livers of sheep, which are sacrificed and the configurations of nodes and blood vessels "read" by an expert to reveal God's will (see *ANEP* 594). **24.** *remembrance:* God remembers guilt and must punish because the sins are so public and so persistent. **25–27.** An addition applying the judgment to Zedekiah.

       (iv) *The sword against the Ammonites* (21:28–32). The words of the poem in vv 9–10 are now applied to the Ammonites, whom Nebuchadrezzar had temporarily spared to attack Jerusalem first (vv 20–21). Ammon was destroyed by the Babylonians in the years after Jerusalem's fall and lives on today only in the name of its major city, Amman, the capital of the modern nation of Jordan.

60   (c) LEGAL CHARGES AGAINST JERUSALEM (22:1–31). Three oracles are combined to make an impressive bill of indictment against Israel. Verses 1–16 accuse Jerusalem; vv 17–22 deliver a sentence against Jerusalem and the land together; and vv 23–31 charge the entire country with crimes. The listing has some similarity to 18:1–32, but stresses social and political evils rather than cultic offenses.

       (i) *A city of defilement and blood* (22:1–16). Jerusalem receives a triple accusation, each beginning with the shedding of blood: vv 6–8 list the violent crimes of the leaders; vv 9–11 list sins of defilement and lewdness; v 12 lists those who take bribes. In vv 13–16 the sentence is passed that they will be exiled in order to be purified. **4.** *shed blood:* This accents the violence committed against others by the powerful, which will lead to all the other offenses listed in the following verses. **7.** *parents:* See Exod 20:12; Lev 19:3; Deut 5:16. *the alien:* See Exod 22:21; 23:9; Lev 19:33,34. *the orphan:* See Exod 22:22–24. **9–11.** For the various sins of lewd behavior, see Lev 18:7–17 and 20:11–14. **12.** *bribes:* See Exod 23:8; Lev 19:35–36. **16.** *defiled:* Exile to a foreign land, which is unclean because it has not been blessed by the divine presence, will profane God's name.

       (ii) *Divine wrath in punishment* (22:17–22). The image of the divine smelter, in which Israel is pictured as ore that contains both good silver (or gold) and useless impurities, is common in the prophets: see Isa 48:10; Jer 9:7; Zech 13:9; Mal 3:2–3. **19.** *into the midst of Jerusalem:* The oracle was probably occasioned by the need for people in villages to flee to the protection of the walled capital when the Babylonian army appeared in 588.

       (iii) *All classes are guilty* (22:23–31). Four classes of leaders are named: leaders, priests, princes, and prophets. This is similar to the list in Zeph 3:1–4 and so may be a kind of typical prophetic catalogue. **25.** *leaders:* The MT reads "the conspiracy of her prophets," but the LXX has "leaders," which makes more sense and requires only one miscopied letter in the Hebr word. Zeph 3:3 also calls the leaders lions as here. Again, as in vv 1–16, the abuse of power by violence is stressed. **26.** *priests:*

These are charged with failing to treat God's law and cultic service as holy. They reduce God to the human level. **27.** *princes are wolves:* See Zeph 3:3, where the judges are wolves. **28.** *prophets who whitewash:* The charge is detailed in 13:10–16. **30.** *stand in the breach:* A reference to the role of the prophet or leader as intercessor with God. See Gen 18:23–33 and Ps 106:23.

61   (d) THE ALLEGORY OF THE TWO SISTERS (23:1–49). The allegory is presented in vv 1–35, followed by an application that lists the sins more fully in vv 36–49. The whole is similar to chap. 16, and the two accounts may have influenced one another in sharing details. But chap. 23 stresses the political infidelity of Samaria and Jerusalem in seeking out foreign alliances whereas chap. 16 focuses on the cultic. This chapter also uses some of the most graphic sexual imagery of the Bible, although other prophets share the taste for it (Jer 2:23–25; Hos 3:13–14).

       (i) *The allegory of Oholah and Oholibah* (23:1–35). The story proceeds in four steps. First, 23:1–4 sets up the allegory of daughters of one mother as Samaria and Jerusalem, which both stem from one people in Egypt. It expresses the same shocking charge as did 20:5–9 that Israel sinned from its time in Egypt. The meaning of the two names is not absolutely certain. Oholah might mean "her own tent," while Oholibah suggests "my tent (is) in her." This difference refers to the prophet's insistence that God chose to dwell only in the Temple in Jerusalem (Deut 12:5), whereas Jeroboam had established false shrines for Israel (1 Kgs 12:25–33).

       5–10. Israel came under Assyrian political domination by 850. The Black Obelisk shows King Jehu already offering submission to Shalmaneser III in 841 (*ANEP* #351, 355). There were constant efforts to break free, followed by intrigues on the other side. Finally the Assyrians destroyed Samaria in 722–721, providing the lesson that Ezekiel now uses.

       11–21. The third step is the conduct of Judah. Unlike her sister, who gave herself to only one other lover, Judah prostituted with three: Assyria (2 Kgs 16:7–8), Babylon (Isa 39; 2 Kgs 24–25), and Egypt (Jer 37:5). **14.** *painted figures:* Cf. Ezek 8:10–12; Jer 22:14. Ancient palaces were richly painted (*ANEP* #454). **20.** *members:* See 16:26. The sexual derision reflects Ezekiel's mockery of Egypt's claims to power, which are denounced more fully in chaps. 29–32.

       22–35. The fourth step is judgment and execution by the very lovers with whom the sisters had sinned. It is the same fate decreed in 16:35–41. **27.** *Egyptians:* The reference is to the aid sought by Zedekiah from Pharaoh Psammetichus II in 588. This reflects the allegory in chap. 17. **32.** The theme of drinking a cup of fate until intoxicated is a symbol of divine wrath; cf. Jer 25:15–25 and Isa 51:17–22.

62   (ii) *Interpretation for Jerusalem* (23:36–49). These verses are often considered a later reflection because they combine the various crimes of chaps. 16, 22, and 23. Verses 36–39 list cultic charges and idolatry; vv 40–45 repeat the description of political alliances as harlotry; and vv 46–49 return to the crimes of pollution or lewdness contained in 22:9–11. Verses 40–49 contain many echoes of chap. 16, so that 23:40–41 = 16:9–13; 23:45 = 16:38; 23:47 = 16:41; 23:49 = 16:52,54. The especially concrete description in vv 40–44 may reflect the particulars of Zedekiah's intrigues between 589–587.

63   (e) TWO SIGNS OF THE END (24:1–27). The allegory of a boiling pot (vv 1–14) and Ezekiel's actions upon the death of his wife (vv 15–27) bring the first half of the book to a close. Both convey a strong sense of finality about what is to happen. The chapter begins with a date, January 588, which marks the beginning of the Babylonians' siege of Jerusalem and signals that it is now too late to reverse Judah's fate. It ends with the mention of Ezekiel's name in v 24, the first time since 1:3; it is clearly an *inclusio* to mark the end of the 24 chapters of judgment.

(i) *The allegory of the boiling pot* (24:1–14). The allegory contains a mixed metaphor: a pot boiling meat until it is completely destroyed and a pot full of rust heated until all the impurity is burned off. Both convey the same message, the city has been so full of blood that it must be burned up to purify it. The first analogy is similar to Mic 3:3, where the inhabitants of Jerusalem are cooked as food for the conquerors. The prophet juxtaposes this with the metaphor of rust as bloodred. Only by burning off the rust completely will blood justice be accomplished. The two uses of blood and the two uses of cleaning a pot by fire work together as one oracle. **2.** *write down:* When the prophet's word has been rejected by his audience, he writes it for the future: see Isa 8:16; Jer 36:2,32. **7.** *bare rock:* Since blood was considered the substance of life, it must be treated as sacred and covered with earth (Lev 17:1–14; Deut 12:23–24; Gen 4:10–11; 9:4). **14.** *I the Lord have spoken:* The series of phrases makes a solemn statement of purpose. *I will judge you:* The judging resumes the question asked in 20:4, "Will you judge them?" and so links all five chapters in an *inclusio*.
64   (ii) *The death of Ezekiel's wife* (24:15–27). The prophet is forbidden to perform any sign of grief at the death of his wife. It is a very strong prophetic warning to the people. They are not to mourn for the loss of Jerusalem because it deserved the punishment it received (vv 20–24). The final statement in vv 25–27 links this moment back to the moment when he began his mission while speechless in 3:24–27. All the prophecies of chaps. 4–24 thus form one whole. **16.** *the delight of your eyes:* The expression occurs also in Lam 2:4 for the people of Jerusalem. The idea is so stunning that it is hardly likely that Ezekiel could simply have made up the metaphor of his wife dying. We do not know what personal drama of grieving he went through. As the speaker of God's word, however, the personal tragedy becomes a sign of the impending tragedy for thousands. **17.** *mourning:* For different Hebr rites of mourning, see 2 Sam 1:2; 3:31; 14:2; 15:30,32. **19.** *the people:* Here, as in 12:9, not the elders but the whole people seek the prophet's meaning. **26.** *on that day a fugitive will come:* No one could manage to get from Jerusalem to Babylon in a single day to bring the news. As a result many critics consider v 26 an insert between vv 25 and 27, which serves to establish a connection to 33:21 and permits the oracles against nations (chaps. 25–32) to be set in place more naturally. Originally, vv 25 and 27 were one and predicted that on the day Jerusalem fell, Ezekiel would be free to speak again. If we do not press the editors too exactly, v 26 may well have been added to clarify how Ezekiel got the news so that he would know when to speak again.
65   **(II) Oracles against Foreign Nations (25:1–32:32).** The major prophets all contain special collections of judgment oracles directed against foreign powers (see Jer 46–51; Isa 13–23). Occasionally these also occur in shorter prophetic books (Amos 1:3–2:3; Zeph 2:4–15). Almost without exception, the countries had been political enemies whose history was intertwined with that of Israel and Judah. As far as we know, the prophets themselves never uttered any of them before a foreign audience nor sent them out by messenger, so that presumably the real audience was Israel. These oracles served several purposes. One was to underscore that Yahweh, the God of Israel, was also Lord of all nations and held other nations accountable

for their deeds just as he did Israel. Another was to demolish foreign claims to divine authority by showing that they acted out of human pride, hubris, when they pitted their divinities (Marduk, Baal, or others) against Yahweh. Their pretensions would be demolished and brought to utter lowliness. A third purpose was to reassure the Israelites themselves that the attacks and oppression of these nations against God's chosen people would not go unpunished.

The editors carefully placed this body of oracles against seven nations (a symbolic number of fullness representing all nations; cf. Deut 7:2) between the oracles of judgment in chaps. 1–24 and the oracles of restoration in chaps. 33–48. This establishes a sequence: after Israel receives its judgment, God will begin the process of restoration by first punishing pagans who have profaned the holy people and their land, and then will restore the land and people of Israel themselves. Within the eight chapters of 25–32, there is a climactic order that moves from the small neighboring nations of Ammon, Moab, Edom, and Philistia (chap. 25), to the more significant opponents Tyre and Sidon (chaps. 26–28), to the most important symbolic foe, Egypt (chaps. 29–32). All were involved in anti-Babylonian intrigue in Ezekiel's day, esp. Tyre and Egypt.
66   **(A) Oracles against Israel's Small Neighbors (25:1–17).** Jer 27:3 lists Ammon, Moab, Edom, Tyre, and Sidon as conspiring with Judah to revolt against Nebuchadrezzar. More directly, the four nations named in this chapter, Ammon, Moab, Edom, and Philistia, later took advantage of Judah's defeat in 586 to ravage territory, perhaps even as sudden allies of Babylon! The oracles were probably all composed after Jerusalem's defeat as words of assurance for the future. (a) ORACLE AGAINST AMMON (25:1–7). 2 Kgs 24:2 reports that the Ammonites took part in the destruction of Judah in 586. The prophet denounces this and passes divine sentence: they will be conquered by foreigners from the east and their land become desolate. In fact, Ammon was destroyed near the end of Nebuchadrezzar's reign (about 570) and not settled again until Roman times. (b) ORACLE AGAINST MOAB (25:8–11). Moab too attacked Judah as an ally of Babylon (2 Kgs 24:2) and will receive the same fate meted out to the Ammonites. Moab's territory lay directly E of the N end of the Dead Sea, and the "shoulder" or "flank" of Moab with its cities, is the high, rounded plateau E of where the Jordan River enters the Dead Sea. (c) ORACLES AGAINST EDOM (25:12–14). Edom lay S of Moab stretching from the Dead Sea down to the Gulf of Aqabah. Israel's early traditions remembered the Hebrews and Edomites as brothers marked by hostility in the persons of Jacob and Esau (Gen 25:21–34). This hatred is reflected in many biblical passages: Obad 1:21; Isa 34; Jer 49:7–22; Amos 1:11–12; Mal 1:2–5; Ps 137; Lam 4:21–22. After the fall of Jerusalem in 586, Edom seized much of the Negev desert area of Judah. (d) ORACLE AGAINST THE PHILISTINES (25:15–17). Although the Babylonian army defeated the Philistine cities soundly in 605 and perhaps again in 601, they apparently had enough strength to take advantage of Judah's defeat in 586. Thus, they renewed the "never-ending hatred" begun in the time of the judges.
67   **(B) Oracles against Tyre (26:1–28:19).** Ezekiel vehemently opposed Tyre because it fought against Babylon with the help of Egypt. Situated on an island off the coast of southern Lebanon, it developed a powerful shipping trade, and with Egyptian naval help, held out against Nebuchadrezzar for 13 years after Jerusalem fell (585–572). Egypt and Tyre had long been

allied. An Assyrian carving of Esarhaddon about 672 (*ANEP* #447) shows the two kings of Egypt and Tyre tied together in defeat after an earlier alliance failed.

68 (a) TYRE DESTROYED BY BABYLON'S TIDAL WAVE (26:1–21). This oracle mixes siege imagery with that of a heavy sea sweeping the rocks bare. It progresses in four stages, each introduced by "thus says the Lord God." The first (vv 1–6) describes the geography of Tyre rather well, with its enemies pictured as waves battering it until it is washed bare. The second (vv 7–14) shifts gears and describes the same siege in the nearly breathless action of battle. Both of these stages end with the prediction that only fishermen will occupy Tyre again. The third (vv 15–18) and fourth (vv 19–21) are in the form of funeral laments, describing in turn the mourning rituals for the dead Tyre and then the descent of the corpse into the land of the dead. **1.** *eleventh year:* No month is named, but it would probably be near the end of the year, i.e., early 586. **2.** *gate of the peoples:* This is a reference to Judah, through whose territory the caravans had to pass to get to Tyre. Tyre would benefit from one less nation taxing the trade (1 Kgs 10:28–29). **6.** *daughters:* The mother city had suburbs and dependent villages on the mainland. **7.** *Nebuchadrezzar:* The details of battle are some of the most colorful in biblical literature. See also Nah 2 and the scene in *ANEP* 372–373. **11.** *the mighty pillars:* Many ancient buildings had pillars, but these may specifically refer to the famous temple of Melqart, the god of Tyre. **17.** *mighty on the sea:* The Phoenicians from Tyre and Sidon had established many colonies throughout North Africa, Sicily, and Spain during the preceding centuries. **20.** *the pit:* The underworld, properly called Sheol (→ OT Thought, 77:170), was often described as a pit into which the dead were dragged or fell. Verses 19–21 are highly mythological and parallel the language of Ezek 31:15–18 and 32:17–32.

69 (b) THE WRECK OF THE GREAT SHIP TYRE (27:1–36). This is an extended allegory that compares Tyre to a fully laden cargo ship, the pride of the fleet. It carries the cream of the navy and marine forces. But it is destroyed by a storm and sinks on the high seas. The oracle is cast in the form of a lament over the fall of the mighty, but with a biting, mocking tone. It has three parts: vv 1–11 describe in poetry the beauty of the ship and its crew; vv 12–25a lists the nations and their goods which the ship carried, apparently in prose; and vv 25b–36 describe in poetry again the sinking of the ship and the international lamentation at such a tragedy. Many scholars consider the central prose part to be a later addition. It is probably part of an older piece of literature inserted by the prophet or an editor. **3.** *I am perfect in beauty:* The sin of pride will be the cause of Tyre's downfall (cf. 28:11,17). The use of direct quotation to show overbearing hubris recurs in 28:9 and in 29:3 (referring to Egypt). **9.** *all the ships:* Suddenly the image changes to Tyre's harbor, crowded with ships and soldiers thronging its streets and fortifications. **12.** *Tarshish:* The farthest Phoenician outpost in Spain, Tartessos, opens the list of Mediterranean cities and states with which Tyre does business. For detailed treatment of each place-name in vv 12–25, see Zimmerli, *Ezekiel 2* 65–69. **26.** *the east wind:* God's anger is frequently described as the east wind (Ezek 17:10; 19:12). In Ps 48:8, God is said to shatter the ships of Tarshish with the east wind. **30.** *dust and ashes:* See Job 2:12; 42:6; Jer 6:26; 25:34. **35.** *fear:* The lesson for the nations is simple: Fear the same fate as Tyre received for its pride in resisting Yahweh's command to submit to Babylon.

70 (c) Tyre the Proud and Wise (28:1–10). This oracle addresses the king rather than the entire nation. In

this it resembles the oracle in 28:11–19 and those against Pharaoh in chaps. 29, 31, 32. Such oracles against rulers regularly employ strong mythical motifs. Although he is only human, the Tyrian monarch considers himself a god. This is the ultimate example of idolatry through pride. The king's description resembles that of the king of Babylon in Isa 14:12–14, and the casting down into Sheol of vv 8–9 matches the continuation in Isa 14:15–20. The conclusion in v 10 is close to Ezek 31:12,18. **7.** *strangers:* The Babylonians will be God's instrument. A later oracle of 29:17–20 (April 571) will note Babylon's failure to capture Tyre despite this earlier prediction.

71 (d) LAMENT OVER TYRE'S FALL (28:11–19). The poem is in the form of a lament like chap. 27. But it is built around a myth of creation that resembles Gen 2–3, where a first man is set in a paradisal garden with gemstones all around. Then he sins and is expelled by one of the cherubim. There are also major differences, such as the lack of a first woman, the setting on a mountain, and the wearing of precious stones, which are not part of the Gen tradition. Gen describes the sin of the first couple as disobedience to law, but Ezek sees pride and violence from commercial greed as the cause of Tyre's fall. Many creation story variants are known to us (cf. *ANET* 99–103); perhaps this is a local pagan form known in the area of Tyre and adapted by the prophet.

12. *signet ring:* A king or high official sealed state papers with his own ring; thus it beomes the symbol of God's personal favor to Tyre's king. He is to be God's ring; cf. Hag 2:23. **13.** *precious stone:* The list of stones as a garment is modeled after the high priest's breastplate in Exod 28:17–20. It is another sign of divine blessing. *Eden:* Cf. Ezek 31:8–9. **14.** *guardian cherub:* In Assyrian palaces, cherubim statues guarded the gates against all danger (cf. the comments above on Ezek 1:4–28 at 21:19). *holy mountain of God:* Canaanite myth saw the home of the god Baal on Mt. Saphon near Ugarit. Occasionally Yahweh is described as living on Mt. Saphon, rather than on Zion, to show his superiority to Baal (Ps 48:3).

72 (C) Oracles against Sidon (28:20–26). This single oracle against Sidon opens with the same formula as 25:1 and sets it apart from the series against Tyre. Sidon lies 25 mi. N of Tyre, and they are the two leading cities of the Phoenicians. It too conspired with Judah against Babylon (Jer 27:3). The oracle proper is very short, made up of vv 22–23, and is quite general, indicating that it was composed largely to fill out the series against Israel's neighbors. It lacks all the color and angry force of the words against Tyre. Verses 24–26 form a conclusion to chaps. 25–28. The summary in v 24 announces that those nations who have treated Judah with contempt will no longer be a source of trouble. This builds on the promise of Num 33:55. Verses 25–26 also reflect the promise in Ezek 37:25 and 34:25–28.

73 (D) Oracles against Egypt (29:1–32:32). There are seven oracles in this collection. All but one is dated, and the dates fall between 587 and 585, except for the date of 571 in 29:17. This suggests that the oracles were occasioned by specific historical circumstances. The most likely occasion was the attempted intervention of the new Pharaoh, Hophra, in the affairs of Judah. He not only incited Zedekiah to revolt but sent an army late in 588 or early in 587 to attack the Babylonian army. Unfortunately for Israel, the Egyptian forces were readily beaten back and never tried an attack again.

74 (a) CONDEMNATION OF PHARAOH'S HUBRIS (29:1–16). There are two halves to this oracle, vv 1–9a and 9b–16. Both major halves announce the same theme in their opening verse: "Because pharaoh declared himself the creator (god) of the Nile," he will be punished. *the tenth year:* January 587 is the date, shortly after Hophra's relief column had failed to free Jerusalem. **3.** *dragon:* The chaos monster *tannin* (Isa 27:1; Ezek 32:1–8). The crocodile was undoubtedly considered by people of Palestine to be some living form of this monster. **5.** *cast you forth:* God is the divine fisherman who brings chaos under control, in this case treating the fearsome monster no differently from an unwanted fish carcass. The clinging fish are probably Egypt's allies. **6.** *a reed staff:* The image of Egypt as an easily splintered reed on which Israel foolishly leans recurs in Isa 36:5 (2 Kgs 18:21). It is probably traditional. **10.** *Migdol to Syene:* The N and S boundaries of Egypt stand as a merism for the whole country. **12.** *forty years:* The symbolic use of 40 stands for an entire generation that will be wiped out. In 4:6, Judah was to be punished 40 years, as were the Israelites in the desert (Num 14:34). **14.** *Pathros:* The "Land of the South," the upper part of Egypt near modern Aswan. Ezekiel (as also Jer 44:1) calls this the original homeland of the Egyptians.

75 (b) NEBUCHADREZZAR'S COMPENSATION (29:17–21). See comment on 28:1–10. Ezekiel's predictions that Tyre would fall never came true; at a later date he transferred the judgment against Tyre to Egypt. **17.** *twenty-seventh year:* The latest date in Ezekiel, January 571, fell shortly after Nebuchadrezzar lifted his siege of Tyre. The new promise that Nebuchadrezzar would attack Egypt and take it did come true only a few years later, about 568 (*ANET* 308). **18.** *rubbed bare:* The image of head and shoulders rubbed raw hints that the siege of Tyre's island fortress involved trying to build up a rock causeway. The Babylonians failed, perhaps because of Egyptian naval harassment.

76 (c) THE DAY OF THE LORD FOR EGYPT (30:1–19). This chapter neither gives a date nor addresses the Pharaoh; it seems to be a loose collection of various words against Egypt. It has three parts: vv 1–9 on the Day of the Lord, vv 10–12 on Nebuchadrezzar's conquest of Egypt, and vv 13–19, a list of places that will suffer. **2.** See the similar woe on Israel in chap. 7. The theme of the Day of the Lord is found in Amos 5:18–20; Isa 2; Zeph 1. **4.** *a sword:* See chap. 21. **5.** *Cush:* The list of names contains mercenary units from Egyptian subject territories in North Africa. Cush is usually identified with Ethiopia. **9.** *swift messengers:* See Isa 18:2, from whom Ezekiel has borrowed. **13–19.** The list of placenames resembles similar lists in Mic 1:5–10; Isa 15:1–9; Jer 48:1–5; and Isa 19:5–15. Here the prophet mockingly imitates the great topographical conquest lists the Pharaohs would carve on the walls of their tomb shrines or the walls of the great temple at Karnak (*ANET* 328–29, 376–78). **18.** *the pride of its power:* This expression for the Pharaoh's hubris echoes v 6, linking both parts of the oracle together as a single sustained attack on Egypt.

77 (d) PHARAOH'S ARM (30:20–26). This is dated to April 587, when Nebuchadrezzar had returned to the siege of Jerusalem. Pharaoh's defeated army was one broken arm; if he tried to stop Nebuchadrezzar a second time, the other would be broken as well. The oracle is highly poetic, with a nice balance between vv 21–22 and 23–26: Egypt's broken arms versus the strong arms of Babylon. The wounded arm has not healed—that is, Judah had better not hope that Hophra can mount still a second assault on the Babylonians.

78 (e) THE ALLEGORY OF THE GREAT CEDAR (31:1–18). Although composed of three distinct parts (a poetic allegory in vv 1–9; and two judgment oracles in vv 10–14 and 15–18), this is a single unified chapter marked off by the *inclusio*, "this is pharaoh and his

horde," in vv 2 and 18. The whole has characteristics of a fable, metaphor, allegory, judgment speech, and lament and so is a complex literary masterpiece. Its unity comes from the theme of hubris, which dominates all the parts. The two judgment oracles point ahead to a fuller development in the two laments of chap. 32. Thus, vv 10–14 foreshadow 32:1–16, and vv 15–18 prepare for 32:17–32. But they also echo the fate given to Tyre in the underworld in 26:19–21. It is possible that 31:15–18 comes from the editors of the book who combined chaps. 25–32 together. The entire chapter is a biting satire on the divine claims of the pharaoh. In this it bears a close resemblance to the satire on the king of Babylon in Isa 14.

1. *to whom are you like?:* The derisive question introduces the satirical judgment. **3.** *a cypress (Assyria):* Hebr *'aššûr* usually means "Assyria," but that has no place in this oracle; most scholars agree that the word is a byform for a cypress. **5.** *boughs and branches:* These words are found also in chap. 17 together with several other terms not used elsewhere. The allegory in chap. 17 is paired with chap. 31 in numerous points; but the first judges Israel, the second Egypt. **8.** *no tree in the garden of God:* Eden was not only well watered but a place filled with divine blessing: the trees were not of ordinary height or size. **10.** *a proud heart:* The real point suddenly becomes clear: it was not God that made this tree seem so big; it was its own pride and self-importance. However, as in the story of the tower of Babel in Gen 11:1–9, it would be reduced to nothing. **15.** The second application describes the typical mourning rites for a dead leader who has been overthrown; cf. 27:28–32.

79 (f) LAMENT OVER PHARAOH'S DESTRUCTION (32:1–16). The structure of this lament falls into roughly two parts: vv 2–10, the cosmological judgment of Yahweh, and vv 11–15, the historical application of this to Egypt. Verses 2 and 16 form an *inclusio* by announcing the lament. **2.** *dragon:* Here the emphasis falls more squarely on the idea of the sea monster, whereas it fell on the river Nile in 29:3. But the fate of the dragon is the same in both cases. **5.** *your carcass:* The series of images describe the earth fed the body and blood of the monster. This plays on the Tiamat myth, where the earth is made from her carcass (*ANET* 67). **13.** *foot of a person:* The same imagery recurs in 29:11. **14.** *run with oil:* The image of a land running with oil is a sign of prosperity and blessing; cf. Gen 27:28; Job 29:6. Here the extermination of the pride of pharaoh and his hordes will be a blessing to the land of Egypt. **16.** *lament:* The nations are pictured as professional mourning women hired to wail for the dead (cf. 27:28–32 for the mourning nations; 32:18 for the professional women).

80 (g) LAMENT OVER EGYPT'S DESCENT TO SHEOL (32:17–32). This final oracle is cast as a lament over the death of a hero who must descend to Sheol (cf. Isa 14:15–20; Ezek 27:28–32; 31:15–18). It continues the basic theme that pharaoh's hubris has caused his downfall and that the mighty state he has achieved will be brought to total debasement. Its mournful tone is created by a massive repetition of stock phrases throughout its list of nations already buried in the underworld. While somewhat chaotic in consistency and full of grammatical difficulties, this poem remains a masterpiece of artistic effectiveness in prophetic preaching. **17.** This oracle now completely identifies the fate of pharaoh and the Egyptian people, although "hordes" might be more narrowly understood as the Egyptian army. *the twelfth year:* No date is given for which month is intended, so the most natural solution is to assume that the text means the same month as in the last date (32:1). **21.** *the mighty chiefs:* The kings of other military powers. **22.** *their graves around:* The twelfth tablet of Gilgamesh describes a Mesopotamian view of the underworld that allowed different quality graves for each individual depending on how honorable that person's life and death were (*ANET* 98–99). The lowest quality was for the unburied. **27.** *heroes of old:* A warrior fallen in combat but given full burial honors merited a special place in Sheol. Here the reference points to Gen 6:4, and the giants, who were the "heroes of old."

81   (III) Oracles of Restoration (33:1–39:29). With the fall of Jerusalem, Ezekiel turned from preaching warning and doom to words of hope. It developed in two stages. The second stage will be the great Temple vision of chaps. 40–48. But first the editors have gathered a series of oracles directed to the purification of the land and the people for the day of the renewed Israel. Chapters 33–39 can be divided into three parts: chap. 33 announces a new commission to the prophet, parallel to that of chaps. 1–3; chaps. 34–37 focus on the purification of the community in the land; and chaps. 38–39 picture a partly metaphorical, partly mythical war of purification that will scour the physical land of all foreign oppression and uncleanness and reveal the divine holiness in its glory and life-giving blessing.

82   (A) The Prophet Receives a Second Commission (33:1–33). This chapter serves as the turning point for Ezekiel's mission. The themes of the watchman (vv 1–9) and individual responsibility (vv 10–20) parallel and yet change the direction of the original commission in chap. 3. The final unit (33:21–33) sets the condition for the new message.

(a) THE PROPHET AS WATCHMAN (33:1–9). The prophet is again given the task to be watchman over Israel. This passage is parallel to 3:16–21, but there are two notable differences. (1) Verses 2–6 describe the general task of all watchmen in time of war; this is missing in 3:16–21. (2) Chapter 33 mentions only the warning to the wicked. Chapter 3 went on to speak of the righteous who turn away from God and must be warned. The reasons for the shift are in the nature of the conditions now faced: Babylon is about to destroy the city of Jerusalem, and the righteous will not be spared. The watchman's warning would have been the difference between life and death if heeded in time, but now it is too late.

(b) INDIVIDUAL RESPONSIBILITY (33:10–20). This section renews the message of chap. 18, with references also to 11:14–21 and 14:12–23. It is placed here to reemphasize that God wants conversion. The triple use of "turn back" in v 11 makes this clear. Thus, v 11 = 18:23; v 12 = 18:26–27; v 13 = 18:24; v 14 = 18:21–22; v 15 = 18:14–18; v 16 = 18:21–22; vv 17–20 = 18:25–27. The entire theme of repentance resembles Jer 3:12–23 — God wants Israel to live and not die (see Deut 30:15–20).

(c) CONDITIONS FOR THE NEW LAND (33:21–33). The third section also links to the first commission in 3:22–27. Ezekiel's silence is to be broken for good. Since the collection of oracles in chaps. 4–24 shows that he had not been silent but had freely spoken God's words, it must mean that he may now personally argue with the exiles about their hopes and ideas. This leads to countering their complaint in vv 23–29 that the people who were left behind are taking all the land, and to rejecting in vv 30–33 their interest in him because of his entertaining style. **21.** *twelfth year:* This would be January 585, 17 months after Jerusalem had fallen, according to Jer 52:6–12, far too long a time for word to reach Babylon. The usual explanation is that Ezekiel follows a calendar where the new year falls in the spring whereas Jeremiah used one where it fell in the autumn! This

would leave only a reasonable five months difference. **24.** *Abraham:* Mention of the patriarchal promises is rare in the prophets; cf. Isa 51:2. **27–28.** An echo of the warnings in 6:2,14; 7:24. **32.** *sings love songs:* This may indicate that prophets sang or played while they spoke. In any case, the people come only for the entertainment and pay no attention to the message.

83   (B) The Good Shepherd and the Sheep (34:1–31). Two themes stand out: vv 1–10 denounce the bad rulers who have shepherded Israel; vv 11–31 announce God's plan to shepherd the sheep himself and to appoint a new David over them.

(a) ISRAEL'S BAD SHEPHERDS (34:1–10). From Sumerian kings in the 3d millennium on, rulers of the ancient Near East referred to themselves as the shepherds of their people (*ANET* 159, 178); see also Jer 2:8; 10:21; 25:34–36; Zech 11:4–17. Ezekiel delivers a woe oracle (vv 2–6) followed by two divine sentences of judgment in vv 7–8 and 9–10. The imagery is natural, but it is also intended as a partial allegory: the lost, wounded, and strayed sheep are the Israelites defeated and exiled.

(b) GOD WILL BE THE GOOD SHEPHERD (34:11–31). A second biblical tradition sees God as Israel's shepherd (Ps 23; Isa 40:11; Jer 31:10; John 10:1–18). This is developed in three parts. In vv 11–16, God reverses the evil done by the bad human shepherds nearly point for point. A second part (vv 17–24) moves beyond the role of God as a good provider to God as defender of justice and upholder of the weak. Roles associated with human kings will be maintained by God. But the flock has both bad and good sheep and they must be separated. Jesus' parable of the sheep and goats may depend on this passage (Matt 25:31–46). The establishment of David as king over them (vv 23–24) looks ahead to 37:24–28. David will not be brought back from the dead, but a king from his dynasty will be chosen according to the divine promise (2 Sam 7). The third part (vv 25–31) reflects the vision of a covenant of prosperity in Lev 26:3–12 and Jer 33:14–33. All of Israel's blessings will be the fruit of faithful obedience to the covenant.

84   (C) The Mountains of Israel (35:1–36:15). After announcing the return to divine rule (chap. 34), the prophet proceeds to reverse the curse laid on the land in chaps. 5–7. First, a curse is laid against the mountains of Edom, who represent all of Israel's enemies. This reverses the condemnation of Israel's mountains in chap. 6. The second, a blessing is pronounced on Israel's mountain heights. Each requires a balanced 15 verses (35:1–15; 36:1–15).

(a) ORACLE AGAINST THE MOUNTAINS OF EDOM (35:1–15). Although Edom has already been condemned among the foreign nations in 25:12–14, it now serves as a special foil contrasted with the land of Israel. The name "Seir" here specifies the long ridge of mountains that stretch along the E side of the Arabah from the Dead Sea down to the Red Sea. Two charges are leveled in 35:5 (Edom assisted in destroying Israel) and 35:10 (it coveted Israel's land). Each accusation is followed by the appropriate sentencing: in vv 6–9, capital punishment is decreed for bloodguilt (Gen 4:10; 9:5–6; Exod 21:23; Job 16:18); in vv 11–15, those who craved others' land will lose their own. **6.** *blood will pursue you:* The image of the hunter suggests that the *gōʾēl* is meant here; i.e, the nearest male relative is charged with avenging the murder of someone in his clan (Num 35:16–22; Deut 19:6–12). **13.** *glorified yourself:* Edom's evil was rooted in the pride that opposed God's will.

85   (b) BLESSING FOR THE MOUNTAINS OF ISRAEL (36:1–15). Ezekiel now turns to the task of announcing God's word of blessing on Israel's mountains. This oracle reverses the doom pronounced against the mountains in chap. 6. Here, too, the mountains are personified as though they had committed the sins which made their land unclean and depopulated its cities and villages, but at the same time they are treated as the object of God's devoted love. The oracle is repetitious, and some commentators see a great deal of expansion beyond the core statement in vv 2,5, and 8-11 (Wevers, *Ezekiel* 267-68). Note, e.g., how every verse in vv 1-7 begins with a formula to open an oracle! **1.** *you mountains!:* This is the same opening formula as that of a royal decree in 6:1. **2.** *Aha!:* Cf. 25:3 and 26:2, where Ammon and Tyre also gloat over Israel's tragedy. **8.** *yield fruit to my people:* In contrast to Edom (35:3), Israel will not be desolate but fruitful again, not only in crops but in population growth (vv 10-12). **13.** *devour people:* Enemies ridicule the promised land as the killer of its own inhabitants. The prophet may mean famine or the sins of child sacrifice Israel has committed in the past (2 Kgs 16:3; 21:6).

86   (D) Divine Holiness and Israel's Restoration (36:16-38). The promise of blessing continues, this time reversing the charges of profanation leveled in chaps. 15-24. This section is profoundly covenantal in the P tradition. It understands the covenant to be a holy people in a cultically and morally pure land (cf. Lev 19; 26). A third section (vv 33-38) describes the recognition of Yahweh that will result from his blessing on the land. The whole unit is a summary of Ezekiel's theology, and its complexity may argue for numerous additions made by editorial hands. The promise of a new heart and new spirit in vv 26-27 resemble Jer 31:31-34 and are a high point of Ezekiel's theology of salvation and justification based solely on God's grace.

20. *they profaned my holy name:* What respect can be given to a god who cannot even protect his people on his own land! But God acts to prevent this ridicule of his name (v 21). The argument is similar to that of Moses with God in Num 14:13-19. **26.** *a new heart and a new spirit:* The heart is the seat of thinking and loving, so it will be a way of looking at life from God's point of view. The new spirit is the power to live as an entire nation, not just as individuals (see the development of this in 37:1-14). The covenant is not named explicitly here (but see 34:25 and 37:26). **28.** *you will be my people:* This is the P covenant formula found at Exod 6:7 and in the prophets at Jer 7:23; 11:4; 24:7; 31:33; Ezek 14:11; 37:23,27; Hos 2:23; Zech 8:8.

87   (E) Restoration of the People of Israel (37:1-28). The promise of covenantal blessing is followed by two dramatic realizations: a vision of a dead Israel restored to full life (vv 1-14) and the reunion of the twelve tribes as one as in the days of David and before (vv 15-28).

(a) THE VISION OF THE DRY BONES (37:1-14). The opening verses indicate that the prophet received a powerful visionary experience, but it did not require any physical bilocation. The vision was generated by the people's proverb in v 11: "Our bones are dried up!" The plain is probably intended to be the same as in 3:22. The action has two parts: a description of the vision in vv 2-10 and an interpretation in vv 11-14. The drama plays on the contrast between dry, dead bones and the *ruaḥ* (the wind, breath, spirit) of God. The shift in image to graves in vv 12b-13 may indicate a later addition to the text. The passage summarizes Ezekiel's mission to the exiles. He preaches the word of God to bring new life to a dead Israel. The bones, bleached, scattered on the ground and very, very dry (v 2), represent the total destruction of Israel by an attacking army, viz., Babylon. No reference to the resurrection of individuals

from death is intended. Especially important is the play on words involved in the oft-repeated "spirit" (vv 1,5,6, 8,9,10,14). Ezekiel begins with the notice that no "spirit" is present at all (vv 2-8). Suddenly, he is to summon *the* spirit in vv 9-10, and the passage finally climaxes in v 14 when God himself declares it *my* spirit. The divine initiative stands out clearly.

88   (b) THE TWO STICKS REJOINED AS ONE (37:15-28). The final symbolic action in the book has the prophet join two sticks together to form one staff. Since "Judah" is written on one and "Joseph" on the other, they represent the northern and southern kingdoms united as in the days of David and Solomon. Verses 15-22 provide the action and its basic interpretation. Verses 23-28 expand the implications in three areas: the people will be made ritually clean according to the P Torah (v 23); they will once again be under one king (vv 24-25); and the covenant will be reaffirmed as eternal (vv 26-28). **16.** *Joseph:* This stands for the northern kingdom. The two largest tribes, Ephraim and Manasseh, were sons of Joseph. The area left after Assyrian attacks in 732 was known simply as "Ephraim" and is used often by Hosea in the same way as in this verse. **25.** *Jacob:* References to the patriarchs occur very occasionally elsewhere: Hos 12:1-7; Ezek 33:24; 39:25. **26.** *an everlasting covenant:* See 16:60. This reflects the P theology of Gen 9:16 and 17:7, in which God made unconditional his covenants with Noah and Abraham. The "covenant of peace" reflects 34:25. **27-28.** *my sanctuary, my dwelling:* These two expressions prepare for chaps. 40-48, as does the final mention of God who sanctifies Israel.

89   (F) The Allegorical Vision of Gog (38:1-39:29). Since the final words of 37:26-28 prepare directly for chaps. 40-48, the oracles against Gog occupy a special place as a second finale that summarizes the restoration of Israel in eschatological terms and places a cosmic and mythological perspective on the historical promises of the preceding chapters. A series of four oracles make up the unit: 38:1-16 describe Gog's massive assault against the land of God's people; 38:17-23 tell of God's counterattack; 39:1-16 portray the divine victory; and 39:17-29 pull together the major themes of earlier chapters around the triumph of God's *kābôd*, his "glory." The language is certainly an early forerunner of the apocalyptic (20:21-24) found in Daniel and the NT (see P. D. Hanson, *The Dawn of Apocalyptic* [Phl, 1975]). Chaps. 38-39 and 40-48 together describe a final enemy attack on the mountain of God whose failure only lends further splendor to God's holy dwelling there.

90   (a) THE ATTACK OF GOG AGAINST ISRAEL (38:1-16). 2. *Gog:* This name is unknown. Some have proposed Gyges, king of Lydia, but more likely the name was invented to rhyme with Magog, a land mentioned in Gen 10:2 as far to the north. Gog symbolizes all of Israel's enemies, who traditionally come from "the north" (see Jer 4:6; 6:1). It may echo a divine myth that places God's dwelling in the north (Isa 14:13; Ps 48:2). **10.** *you will plan:* In vv 1-9 and v 16, the text implies that God will bring up Gog; here the evil is credited to the human agent alone to protect God from any charge of doing evil. **12.** *the center of the earth:* This is the mythical "navel of the world," where creation began and where contact with the divine is uniquely close. The restored Israel dwells here, i.e., in Jerusalem.

(b) GOD'S WAR AGAINST GOG (38:17-23). This oracle expands on v 3 in the preceding oracle. The language of violent storm and earthquake for a theophany appears throughout the Bible: Exod 19:16; 20:18; Ps 18:7-15; Isa 24:17-19; Hab 3:1-15. **22.** *plague and blood:*

God will punish Gog with the same evil as he brought against Israel in chaps. 5–7.

(c) GOD'S VICTORY OVER GOG (39:1–16). This begins the same way as 38:1–3, so that God's victory parallels the account of Gog's assault. **7.** *the Holy One of Israel:* This links Ezekiel to the Isaian tradition of using God's cultic title: "The Holy One of Israel" (Isa 1:4; 5:19,24; 10:17; 12:6, etc. **9.** *seven years:* This and the mention of seven months in v 12 symbolize the total and complete annihilation of the enemy in the battle. Thus, Gog's burial place would not be on the consecrated land of Israel. **16.** *city of Hamonah:* This is a fanciful etiology; *hāmôn* means "army" or "horde" as in vv 11 and 15.

(d) GOD'S GLORY KNOWN BY ALL (39:17–29). Verses 17–20 describe a great sacrificial feast in which the enemy is the victim and God's creatures the sacrificers who give glory to God by their banquet. It has apocalyptic and mythical overtones as in Isa 25, and a similar theme is also present in Isa 34:6; Jer 12:9. Verses 21–29 are a recapitulation of the major themes from chaps. 33–37. Everything proclaimed by the book up to this point, both judgment and restoration, serves one end: to reveal the glory and holiness of God that is seen as his spirit acts.

91 (IV) The New Temple and the New Cult (40:1–48:35). The common consensus of scholarly opinion has held that chaps. 40–48 are so different in style and content from what has preceded that they must represent a post-Ezekiel, and perhaps postexilic, program of priestly regulation for the Jerusalem community which may have been built around a small core of original words of Ezekiel still found in this section (cf. Eichrodt, *Ezekiel* 530–31; Cooke, *Ezekiel* 426–27). M. Greenberg, on the other hand, argues that the entire piece is a unity, consistent with all that has gone before and probably from Ezekiel himself (*Int* 38 [1984] 181–209). Several factors point in this direction. (1) Chapters 40–48 fulfill the promises of 20:40–44 and 37:23–28 that God's sanctuary will be restored. (2) 43:1–5 completes the vision series of chaps. 1 and 8–11, in which God's glory departs from Jerusalem to return only later. (3) Finally, chaps. 38–39 are tied to 40–48 after the design of Ps 48. Throughout the book, emphasis has fallen on Israel's cultic pollution and profanation as a cause for its destruction and exile. Naturally, the re-establishment of a proper cultic sanctity of land and people is called for by the plan of the book.

Ezekiel's extended vision is an integral conclusion to the book as a whole. It is a theological symbol of the ideal relationship of Israel to Yahweh for the future. It does not seem to have been a blueprint for building an actual Temple complex or for land distribution after the exile. In any case, it was never implemented as written. But this very fact argues that it must have been put together long before the return of 539 or else it would doubtless have reflected more closely the actual Temple of 520–516.

92 (A) The Description of the New Temple (40:1–43:27). The first stage of the vision is a guided tour of the new Temple and a description of the return of God's glory. The prophet must commit to memory every detail and bring them to the people for execution, just as he was their official witness and describer of the Temple's destruction in chaps. 8–11 (esp. 11:25). One role reverses the other.

(a) THE OUTER DIMENSIONS OF THE NEW TEMPLE (40:1–47). **1.** *twenty-fifth year:* This is one-half of the jubilee period (Lev 25), whose purpose was to give the land rest and renewed fertility once every 50 years. **2.** *high mountain:* Although carefully not named, the mountain is Zion, the place of the Temple just above

the city; cf. Isa 2:2; Zech 14:10. **6–16.** *the eastern outer gate:* The gate has a vestibule, 14 ft. by 35 ft.; three chambers on each side leading in from this, 10½ ft. square each; and seven steps leading up to it. The gate itself opened 22 ft. across. **17–19.** *the outer court:* This was a square of 100 cubits with chambers all around the walls for various unspecified uses of ordinary worshipers. **20–27.** *northern and southern outer gates:* These are identical in size to the east gate. **28–37.** *the inner gates:* These divided the outer court for lay worshipers from the inner priests' court around the Temple proper. They are exactly the same dimension as the outer gate. **44–47.** *the inner court:* This has two chambers, one for Zadokite priests in charge of sacrifices and the other for those who tend the Temple itself with its incense and showbread.

93 (b) THE DESCRIPTION OF THE TEMPLE PROPER (40:48–41:26). The Temple has three parts: a porch or vestibule (*'ûlām*); the sanctuary (*hêkāl*) with lampstands, table of showbread, and altar of incense; and the Holy of Holies (*dĕbîr*) that held the Ark of the Covenant. The dimensions were 35 ft. by 21 ft. for the porch; 35 ft. by 70 ft. for the sanctuary; and 35 ft. by 35 ft. for the Holy of Holies. 41:5–11 describes a series of chambers built around all but the E side (entrance) of the Temple. They are in three stories, with 30 on each story. **12–15.** *the building:* This stood behind the Temple to the W and was 175 ft. square. Its purpose is not stated. **15–26.** The author returns to a detailed description of the inner decoration of the Temple. Much of this is based on 1 Kgs 6:14–36. The panels seem to have been carved into the wood (see *BARev* 12 [July/Aug. 1986] 33 for how it might have looked). The palms and cherubim were mythical images of creation and life.

(c) THE PRIESTS' CHAMBERS (42:1–20). These chambers had three purposes, all for the priests' work in the Temple: (1) the priests' portions of the sacrificial offerings were stored in them; (2) there the priests ate the offerings; and (3) the special linen vestments of the priests were to be stored there, and in these chambers the priests vested and unvested. **15–20.** The angelic guide closes the grand tour with a final measurement of the entire outer complex. It comes to 875 ft. on a side (500 cubits). **20.** The reason for such careful measurements is now explained: the separation of the holy from the profane.

(d) GOD'S RETURN TO THE TEMPLE (43:1–12). Now that the sacred space is prepared, God returns with the same appearance as in chap. 1 and as he left in 11:23. **7.** *kings:* Royal hubris has been a major charge against both Zedekiah and foreign rulers throughout the book. Once again Ezekiel affirms that only God can be king over Israel.

94 (B) Regulations for the Cult (43:13–46:24). This section contains a wide mixture of regulations, most of which follow the Priestly legislation in Lev, although with some notable exceptions that caused the early rabbis grave doubts until they could reconcile them (*b. Sabb.* 13b; *b. Menaḥ.* 45a). Just as the vision has given in sharp detail the dimensions of the new Temple, so now the prophet must detail the proper boundaries of cultic action.

(a) THE ALTAR OF BURNT SACRIFICE (43:13–27). Verses 13–17 mark the physical size of the altar; vv 18–27 put forward the rules for its consecration. The dimensions of the altar resemble the shape of a Babylonian temple-tower, a ziggurat, on a miniature scale. It ascends in three levels or blocks from a base 18 cubits square. Each block is slightly smaller: from 16 cubits square to 14 to 12 for the top of the altar. On the altar top are four projecting corners that stand up one cubit high each. These are the "horns." **15.** *altar surface:* Hebr *har'ēl* literally means "mountain of God." The altar, like the ziggurat, is the place where God's presence visits. The description of the consecration generally follows Lev 8:14–15 and Exod 29:36–37 faithfully. **18.** *blood:* For the putting of blood on the altar, see Exod 29:16,20; Lev 1:5,11; 3:2. **24.** *salt:* See Lev 2:13 for salt on a cereal offering. **27.** *I will accept you:* Once the consecration and purification of the altar are completed, regular sacrifice on behalf of Israel can begin.

95 (b) THE OFFICIAL MINISTERS (44:1–31). The angelic guide takes up his task again, which was interrupted by the transitional description of the altar. He gives regulations concerned with holiness, i.e., the proper separation of the holy place from any profane use. They deal with priestly duties and limitation on others, esp. the ruler. Fittingly, then, chaps. 44–46 begin with the repeated insistence in 44:4–5 that God's glory was now present in the Temple. Chapter 44 deals with the priests, except for one item in v 3: the prince may take part in the communion sacrifice, commanded by Lev 2–3, in the vestibule of the east gate. This gate otherwise remained closed to symbolize that only God passed through it. **10.** The P tradition makes Levites subordinate helpers to the priests of Aaron's line (Num 3:5–10), whereas Deut 18:1–18 makes all Levites into priests. Here Ezekiel takes the P position. **15.** *the sons of Zadok:* Solomon appointed Zadok high priest (1 Kgs 2:26–27; 1 Chr 6:50–53). Apparently the Zadokites are the priests who served the Temple proper after that time.

The list of regulations in vv 17–31 covers priestly duties and benefits. Verses 17–19 deal with proper clothes, esp. the requirements for linen rather than wool garments; the linen garments are only to be worn while serving in the Temple. Verses 20–22 regulate the personal conduct of priests in accordance with Lev 10:9; 21:5; and 21:14. Verses 23–25 prescribe the two chief obligations of the priest: to teach what is holy and what is ritually clean to the people, and to serve as judges in all cases involving cultic matters (see Lev 10:10–11). Verses 25–27 repeat the restrictions of Lev 21:1–3 on a priest touching a dead body. The rites for purification after a priest has been defiled by touching the body of a blood relative are treated more fully in Num 19:11–19. Verses 28–31 set aside certain offerings for the support of the priests. This agrees with the similar legislation of Lev 6 and 7; Num 18:8–19. It will be further augmented by special grants of land in Ezek 45:1–5 and 48:8–14.

96 (c) DIVISION AND USE OF THE LAND (45:1–17). 45:1–8 sets aside special land for the use of Zadokite priests, Levites, the city of Jerusalem, and for the prince. Altogether, it is a strip 25,000 cubits from N to S, extending all across the land from the Mediterranean to the Jordan. At the center is a square, 25,000 cubits on a side, in which are three bands of territory: the N strip (25,000 cubits across by 10,000 deep) is for the Levites; the middle (25,000 by 10,000) is for the Zadokite priests and the Temple; and the S (25,000 by 5,000) is for the city of Jerusalem. The prince receives all the land both E and W of this square as his possession. **2.** The 500 cubits for the Temple agrees with 42:15–20, but the extra 50 cubits of space around it is new.

45:9–17 gives a series of commandments that specify further the role of the prince. He is to do justice and righteousness, the special obligation of kings (cf. Ps 72). This is applied particularly to just weights and measures in vv 10–11: a bath was about 5½ gal., an ephah about 5½ bu., so that a homer was either 55 gal. or 55 bu. The word homer comes from the Hebrew for an "ass." It is one ass-load. 45:9–17 coordinates the demands of justice with proper worship as one attitude before God.

97 (d) REGULATION OF FEASTS (45:18–46:24). The prophet turns to special regulations for certain feasts. The first occasion is new year's day according to the so-called spring calendar. The year began in March in Ezekiel's time; after the exile, it was reckoned from the month of Tishri in September. The new year's purification of the Temple in vv 18–20 is unknown to the Priestly law of the Pentateuch. The other two feasts, however, largely follow the P regulations: Passover treated in Num 28:16–25 and Exod 12:1–12; Tabernacles ("the feast" in v 25) in Num 29:12–38.

The further regulations in 46:1–24 control the goings and comings of the laity in offering sacrifice. The first case in 46:1–8 specifies both the offerings to be made by the prince and where he may place himself. Like the purification of the altar in 45:18–20, the list of sacrifices for the sabbath does not agree with the P legislation in Num 28:3–8. This caused many rabbis to deny canonical status to the book until they figured out ways to reconcile its laws with those of the Pentateuch (b. *Šabb.* 13b). Verses 9–10 limit the prince to worshiping at the same times that the ordinary people worshiped. Since these rules govern the great feasts required of all males (Passover, Weeks, and Tabernacles; Exod 23:17; 34:23; Deut 16:16), large processions would enter the outer court to pass by the open east gate to gaze on the Temple and "see the Lord" (Ps 42:3; Isa 1:12; Deut 31:11).

Limits on the prince's possession of land follow in vv 16–18. This protects both the royal territory, so that it does not become dispersed, and the people's lands, so that the ruler does not appropriate them. Land must be returned to the original ownership in the jubilee year (Lev 25:1–22). Finally, vv 19–24 describe the two cooking areas where the sacrifices that were eaten by priests and laity were to be prepared by boiling. In that way, the distinction between sacred and profane was maintained.

98 (C) **Vision of the Stream from the Temple (47:1–12).** Since all of chaps. 40–46 have dealt with the sacred precincts and ritual actions in the Temple, the climax comes in the vision of life-giving power pouring from the Temple. The prophet describes a river of fresh water that flows from the Temple out of the E side and slightly S through the Kidron Valley down to the Dead Sea. There it turns the lifeless salt waters into a place where fish abound and trees grow abundantly on the shores. It is a miracle that attests to the life-giving power of God dwelling in the sanctuary. While the geography is realistic, the themes are clearly mythical, calling on the paradisal language of Gen 2:10–14 that describes the streams in paradise which watered the Garden of Eden. Ezekiel in no way expected this vision to come about physically. It is symbolic of fertility and life-giving power. **3–6.** The drama of the ever-deepening river recalls the power of the vision of dead bones in chap. 37. Chapters 37 and 47 parallel each other in describing the renewed life God promises to the exiles. **7.** *trees:* Another detail from the Eden story of Gen 2. **10.** *En-gedi, En-eglaim:* En-gedi is an oasis halfway down the W shore of the Dead Sea. En-eglaim is unknown but probably is the only other oasis known along the W shore, at present day Ain Feshkha, 18 mi. N of En-gedi.

99 (D) **The Boundaries of the New Land (47:13–48:35).** This final section can be divided into three units: 47:13–23; 48:1–29; 48:30–35. The prophet is no longer addressed, nor does he speak in the 1st pers. For this reason, most commentators see this section as an added appendix. The "you" is consistently pl.; it is Israel as a whole. But if not by the prophet, it still maintains an important and intrinsic link to the program of the entire book. The distribution of the land is crucial to complete the new exodus from exile that chaps. 33–48 proclaim, just as Joshua completed the first exodus with land distribution in Josh 13–21.

(a) BOUNDARIES OF THE ENTIRE COUNTRY (47:13–23). The external borders are discussed first, listing key geographical points, esp. cities, on all four sides. The boundaries are largely traditional, with the Mediterranean on the W, the Jordan River on the E, and the "Brook of Egypt" (Wadi el-Arish, Josh 15:4) on the S. On the N, the borders are pushed up past Damascus toward Hamath, near ancient Riblah, and then in a line across to the Mediterranean. This is an ideal which partly reflects a memory of the conquests of David over the Arameans. That territory had been soon lost, however, and never became a part of the tribal possessions of Israel. **13.** *Joseph:* The tribe of Levi is excluded, and Joseph gets two portions divided among the tribes named after his sons, Ephraim and Manasseh (Gen 48). **22.** *aliens:* All foreigners who wished to become Israelites were to be counted in the tribe in whose territory they resided.

100 (b) PORTIONS FOR EACH TRIBE (48:1–29). Each tribe in turn is given a strip of land that reaches from the coast to the E border, so that all territories are equal in size. Seven are fitted N of the special section reserved for the Temple, priests, Levites, and prince. Five are fitted below this portion. **7.** Judah is placed closest to the special holy section on the N side, while Benjamin is placed closest on the S. These are the sons of the favorite wife of Jacob, Rachel. But their place in Ezekiel's scheme reverses their real geographical position, in which Judah was just below Benjamin.

Verses 8–22 treat of the dimensions and borders of

the portions reserved for the priests, Levites, and prince. See comment on 45:1–7. **17.** *open land:* With this common space, the total dimensions of the city come to 5,000 cubits on a side, precisely 10 times the Temple square.

101 (c) THE NEW JERUSALEM (48:30–35). The vision now turns back from the land as a whole to the sacred city. Just as each tribe received a share in the land, so it will have a place in the city. To symbolize this, the city will have 12 gates, each one named after a tribe. But the names of the gates follow a different division of the tribes from that found in 48:1–29. Ephraim and Manasseh disappear, while Joseph and Levi reappear, following the original list of sons in Gen 29–30. This shift in names between vv 1–29 and 30–34 hints that these last verses may be a separate tradition which has been attached to the tribal land distribution. The total of 12 gates reflects not only the 12 tribes but also perhaps a sacred tradition about sanctuaries. The temple-tower or ziggurat of Marduk in Babylon also seems to have had 12 gates.

35. *"The Lord is There":* The new name of the city is a pun in Hebrew on the name Jerusalem. They sound alike (*yahweh šammâ/yĕrûsālayim*). Ezekiel avoids mentioning Jerusalem by name right to the end. In the restored land and city, God will indeed be present, but no longer will his people act as did the citizens of the old Jerusalem before 586, who called Zion the home of God (Pss 46; 48; 76) but violated and profaned his presence by their sins. This final phrase forms a fitting close to the book. The glory of the Lord that had departed from Israel has now returned to stay.

21

DEUTERO-ISAIAH AND TRITO-ISAIAH

Carroll Stuhlmueller, C.P.

BIBLIOGRAPHY

1 Begrich, J., *Studien zu Deuterojesaja* (TBü 20; Munich, 1969). Bonnard, P.-E., *Le Second Isaïe* (EBib; Paris, 1972). Clifford, R. J., *Fair Spoken and Persuading* (NY, 1984). De Boer, P. A. H., *Second-Isaiah's Message* (OTS 11; Leiden, 1956). Duhm, B., *Das Buch Jesaja übersetzt und erklärt* (HKAT 3/1; Göttingen, 1902; 5th ed. 1968). Elliger, K., *Deuterojesaja 40,1–45,7* (BKAT 11/1; Neukirchen, 1978). Feuillet, A., "Isaïe (le livre d')," *DBSup* 4. 690–729. Hanson, P. E., *The Dawn of Apocalyptic* (2d ed.; Phl, 1979). Herbert, A. S., *Isaiah 40–66* (CBC; NY, 1975). Kissane, E. J., *The Book of Isaiah* 2 (Dublin, 1943). Knight, G. A. E., *Servant Theology: Isaiah 40–55* (ITC; GR, 1984); *The New Israel: Isaiah 56–66* (ITC; GR, 1985). Levy, R., *Deutero-Isaiah* (London, 1925). McKenzie, J. L., *Second Isaiah* (AB 20; GC, 1968).

Melugin, R. F., *The Formation of Isaiah 40–55* (BZAW 141; NY, 1976). Muilenburg, J., "The Book of Isaiah, Ch. 40–66," *IB* 5. 381–773. North, C. R., *The Second Isaiah* (Oxford, 1964). Orlinsky, H. M. and N. H. Snaith, *Studies on the Second Part of the Book of Isaiah* (VTSup 14; Leiden, 1967). Rignell, L. G., *A Study of Isaiah Ch. 40–55* (LUA; Lund, 1956). Schoors, A., *I Am God Your Saviour* (VTSup 24; Leiden, 1973). Scullion, J., *Isaiah 40–66* (OTM 12; Wilmington, 1982). Seitz, C. (ed.), *Reading and Preaching the Book of Isaiah* (Phl, 1988). Stuhlmueller, C., *Creative Redemption in Deutero-Isaiah* (AnBib 43; Rome, 1970). Torrey, C. C., *The Second Isaiah* (NY, 1928). Watts, J., *Isaiah 34–66* (WBC 25; Waco, 1987). Westermann, C., *Isaiah 40–66* (OTL; Phl, 1969). Whybray, R. N., *Isaiah 40–66* (NCB; GR, 1981).

INTRODUCTION

2 **(I) Author and Editor.** Until the 18th cent., it was presumed that Isaiah of Jerusalem (Isa) wrote all 66 chaps. of the book under his name. There is only a single superscription with the name and date of author (Isa 1:1); Isa 40 and 56 begin with no separate introductions. All 66 chaps., moreover, are edited under several unifying themes (see B. S. Childs, *CIOTS* 310–38; J. D. W. Watts, *Isaiah 1–33* (WBC 24; Waco, 1985) xxvii–xxxii). The tradition of single authorship was questioned by Ibn Ezra (*ca.* 1167; see Levy, *Deutero-Isaiah* 2), but the vigorous attack came from J. C. Döderlein (1775) and J. G. Eichhorn (1780–83). These scholars maintained that chaps. 40–66 were written by a different author, who lived some 150 years later during the Babylonian Exile. They named him Deutero- or Second Isaiah (Dt-Isa). In 1892, B. Duhm argued for a separate author of the Suffering Servant songs (see below) and of chaps. 56–66, whom he called Trito- or Third Isaiah (Tr-Isa). Protestant scholars were generally convinced by the soundness of the new arguments. Catholics, although with some hesitation, tended to agree (e.g., A. Condamin, *Le Livre d'Isaïe* [Paris, 1905]). A negative response of the Pontifical Biblical Commission, June 29, 1908, precipitated by fears of the Modernist movement, made Catholic scholars revert to an ultraconservative viewpoint of single authorship—*EB* 294; *RSS* 119.

Once the theological problems were solved, so that the inspiration of major parts of the Bible was not being questioned but only the literary and historical questions of an author's name and date, Catholics began to argue again for the split authorship of Isa; the opening came with the commentaries of F. Feldmann (Münster, 1926), J. Fischer (Bonn, 1939), and esp. E. J. Kissane. Most Catholic scholars now work with a Dt- and Tr-Isa thesis. (→ Church Pronouncements, 72:5, 27).

3 The reasons for separate authorship of chaps. 40–55 are, first of all, historical. The addressees are no longer inhabitants of Jerusalem but exiles in Babylon (43:14; 48:20). Jerusalem, in fact, has been destroyed and now awaits reconstruction (44:26–28; 49:14–23). Babylon is no longer an ally (2 Kgs 20:12–13), for she has destroyed Jerusalem and deported the Israelites. The former prophecies about Jerusalem's destruction have been carried out (Isa 1:21–31; Jer 7:1–15; Ezek 22,24), and Israel now awaits a new, more glorious future (41:21–23; 42:9–10; 54). Contrary to the author of chaps. 1–39, Dt-Isa mentions the Davidic dynasty, only once, and then to transfer its privileges to the entire nation (55:3–5). In Tr-Isa Israel is back again in her own land, and the problems are different from those pictured in Isa 1–39 (→ 50 below).

The literary arguments are just as impressive. The

tone has changed from threat and condemnation in Isa to consolation and sorrow in Dt-Isa, to sorrow and visions in Tr-Isa. Isa had been brief, cryptic, and imperious, brilliant in the use of contrast and paradox; his preaching is filled with autobiographical material. Dt- and Tr-Isa do not even reveal their names. The style of Dt-Isa is expansive, redundant, solemn, and lyrical; that of Tr-Isa lacks originality and fails to sustain images. Yet while plagued with melancholy and frustration, Tr-Isa sees new visions for the future. The prophetic mantle of Isa imparts authority to Dt- and Tr-Isa's preaching; they for their part enable Isa's original prophecy to keep in touch with later crises and new theological developments.

The doctrinal or pastoral themes of Dt- and Tr-Isa likewise manifest a shift in emphasis from Isa. Before the exile, Israel and especially the inhabitants of Jerusalem were relatively prosperous, overly self-confident, and material-minded; on the contrary, Dt-Isa saw a people discouraged, dazed, and destitute, severely tempted to apostasy. The people in exile must be consoled, not punished; their faith must be sustained, not further tried. In postexilic Jerusalem their faith must be open to the possibilities of Judaism's becoming a world religion. Isa looked upon foreign nations as scourges of divine anger (10:5), Dt-Isa as instruments for saving Israel (41:1–5; 45:1–7). Tr-Isa opens Temple services and priesthood to them (56:1–8; 66:21). Tr-Isa introduces us to the beginning of apocalyptic writing, so that not even death will mar the new heavens and new earth created by the Lord (66:17–20).

Even though the question of authenticity leads us to a succession of authors for chaps. 1–39, 40–55, 56–66, we still need to attend to the editor of the entire work. This person not only drew principally upon the oral and written traditions of three individuals but also included some of the reflections and teaching of their disciples (cf. 8:16; 30:8; 50:10; 54:17a; 52:6; 65:13). The editor centered the entire book on Jerusalem. Somehow the first Temple had to be destroyed and in the process the people purified of false hopes in externals. Yet even the new Temple of the postexilic age is itself tarnished by unworthy leaders. This sad, sinful situation leads to its final opening to the Gentiles. The editor has allowed all major sections to open with a sympathetic attitude toward the Gentiles: 11:10–16; 23:17–18; 27:12–13; 33:17–24; 35:5–6; 49:6; 56:1–8; 66:18–21.

4   (II) The Prophet. The poetry of Dt-Isa reveals someone pensive, earnest, optimistic, and sympathetic. So sturdy was his faith in the God of history that every episode contributed to the redemption of Israel (44:24–45:7).

The prophet places ancient traditions in a cosmic setting, so that the new exodus levels mountains or strikes flowing water in the heights (40:3–5; 41:17–20). The Mosaic covenant is expanded into a world covenant by mentioning the covenants with Noah (54:9) and with Abraham and Sarah (51:1–3), and in the latter case Dt-Isa sees the garden of paradise emerge before his eyes. The spirit of the liturgy breaks forth into new life through his hymns, laments, and proclamation of the word.

Dt- and Tr-Isa probably belonged to an Isaian school of religious thought (8:16). They carry forward several key phrases or motifs from Isa: e.g., the use of the word "sign" (7:11,14; 8:18; 19:20; 20:3; 37:30; 38:7; 55:13; 66:19) or the important title for Yahweh, "the Holy One of Israel" (17 times in Isa; 13 times in Dt-Isa; 4 times in Tr-Isa; see J. J. M. Roberts, *Int* 36 [1982] 130–43). Unlike Isa, however, they are also dependent on northern traditions: (a) Deut and Dtr (themes of election, word,

and obedience); (b) Hos (Yahweh spouse of Israel and the exodus theme); and (c) Jer (laments and prophetic commission). The Psalms certainly contribute to Dt- and Tr-Isa's form of preaching: universe as the arena of worship (Pss 8; 19; 29; 104); laments like Pss 22; 44; exodus in Pss 114; 136. Later Psalms will draw inspiration from the work of Dt- and Tr-Isa, (Yahweh as king, Pss 96–98; laments, Ps 51).

Dt-Isa preached during the latter part of the exilic period, around 550. Cyrus is already on the march (41:1; 45). Because there is a dramatic shift between chaps. 41–48 and 49–54, both in mood and in important themes, chaps. 49–54 represent the prophet's profound disappointment with those who dominated the first return to Palestine in 537 and his eventual rejection by them. The four major songs of the Suffering Servant derive from the repudiation of Dt-Isa by the returnees. Led by Hag and Zech, the high priest Joshua and the governor Zerubbabel, they preferred the theology of the other prophet of the exile, Ezek. Tr-Isa continues the same distancing from the returnees, a group much more narrow in their views, not at all open even to Israelites who remained behind in the land and never went into exile (Hanson).

5   (III) Religious Message.
(a) THE NEW EXODUS.   This is the controlling theme for Dt-Isa, sustained throughout his work (Snaith, *Studies* 147; Stuhlmueller, *Creative Redemption* chap. 4).

(b) FIRST AND LAST.   An entire series of poems is dedicated to first and last, mostly in the literary form of argument or trial speech (42:12–31; 41:1–5; 41:21–29 + 42:8–9; 43:8–13; 44:6–8; 45:18–22; 46:9–13; 48:1–11,12–19). These discuss the fulfillment of earlier prophecies, the first things, and therefore the necessary fulfillment of the final or last prophecy which ushers in an extraordinary age for Israel (see Stuhlmueller, *CBQ* 29 [1967] 495–511).

(c) YAHWEH CREATOR.   Dt-Isa does not introduce the theme of Yahweh Creator as a proof or reason but rather as an indication of the exceptionally new and expansive form of what is to happen for Israel. Dt-Isa's creation vocabulary is rich (*bārā'*, "to create," occurs 16 times).

(d) THE JUSTICE OF GOD.   Because every divine promise is on the point of fulfillment, Dt- and Tr-Isa extol the justice of God (41:2,16; 42:6; 61:3; 62:11–12); see Scullion, *Isaiah 40–66,* 138–40, 211–12.

(e) THE POWER OF THE DIVINE WORD.   From his opening statements (40:5,8) to his final summation (55:10–11), Dt-Isa dwells more than any other prophet upon the power of the divine word. This word does not consist so much in written or spoken messages as in wondrous deeds now.

(f) JERUSALEM.   Within Dt- and Tr-Isa, Jerusalem occupies a center role. At times the prophet sees Jerusalem as announcing Israel's return across the desert to its own land (40:9–10), at other times as a lonely widow who will become the happy mother of many children (54:1–10; 65:17–25). Only once, in a very disputed line (44:28b), does Dt-Isa mention the Temple. Dt-Isa transfers Temple imagery to the outside world (40:3–5; 53:4–6); Tr-Isa bitterly condemns the greedy Temple leaders of the postexilic age (56:9–57:13).

6   (IV) The Servant Poems. Duhm first isolated four songs. Their exact length has remained controversial; here we locate them as 42:1–7; 49:1–7; 50:4–9; 52:13–53:12. More and more scholars, like Muilenburg, Bonnard, Scullion, McKenzie, Clifford, and Melugin, are emphasizing the relation of the servant songs with the rest of Dt-Isa.

When the four major songs are studied within the context of other servant passages in 40–66, the personality and mission of the servant become more complex: (a) in a positive sense, the servant refers to a beloved and chosen one, redeemed by Yahweh, whether this be Israel (41:8,9; 43:10; 44:1,2,21), Israel under the name of Jacob (45:4; 48:20), or the prophet Dt-Isa and his disciples (42:1; 49:3,6), as contemplated by other Israelites or foreigners (50:10: 52:13, 53:11), or by the foreigner Cyrus (44:26); (b) in a negative sense, the servant is the people Israel—blind, deaf, and despoiled (42:19), the slave of kings (49:7)—burdened by its sins (43:23, here a vb. is used); or Yahweh as burdened by Israel's sins (again a vb. is used, 43:24); (c) in the pl., the word occurs once in Dt-Isa of all Israel (54:17) and consistently in Tr-Isa either of the few faithful Israelites (54:17; 63:17; 65:6,9,14,15; 66:14) or of foreigners who are called to minister in the Temple (56:6; as a vb., 60:12).

From these passages the servant appears ever more clearly with a mission: 43:10—Israel or Jacob are to be witnesses; 44:26; 45:4—Cyrus inaugurates Israel's new exodus; 42:1—the servant's silent mission distinguishes him from Cyrus; 49:1-7; 50:4-9—suffering unites the servant with all Israel, or 52:13-53:12—separates him from a sinful Israel. In 49:3 the servant is plainly called "Israel," yet in 49:6 the servant's mission reaches beyond Israel, to be a light to the nations. Within Tr-Isa the servants are the few good Israelites (62:1-3; 65:8-16) who are a source of conversion for sinful Israel (63:17).

While the servant songs blend into the larger development of thought within chaps. 40–66, nonetheless textually there are problems wherever the songs occur (see Stuhlmueller, *CBQ* 42 [1980] 21-27). Adjacent lines are misplaced from somewhere else (48:22; 57:21) or appear as editorial comments (50:10-11; 51:4-6). The four songs, moreover, if removed along with fragments around them, allow the text of Dt-Isa to read smoothly: the trial scene in 41:21-29 continues with 42:8-9; the new exodus in 48:21-22 with 49:9b-12; the image of cloth in 50:3 with 50:9b. When lifted out of the context, the four servant songs acquire their own unique theological development: 49:1-7—the servant, while abused and humiliated, is commissioned anew; 50:4-9—he is disciplined and strengthened by suffering; 52:13-53:12—even the Gentiles are seen to be in awesome contemplation before the suffering and rejected servant; 42:1-7—the servant's mission to the Gentiles is accomplished differently from the Gentile Cyrus; 61:1-3—the mission of the servant continues among his disciples back in the homeland.

The distinctiveness of the songs, therefore, allows us to move the collective interpretation to an individual servant of supreme holiness, greater than any single Israelite of the past. H. Hegermann has shown that pre-Christian Judaism gave a messianic interpretation to the servant songs, but it was Jesus who identified himself as the servant. Paul, however, continues the collective interpretation, for he regards himself as the servant (Acts 13:47; Gal 1:15; Rom 15:21). For the reinterpretation of the servant songs in Judaism and in early Christianity, see Grelot, *Les Poèmes* 77-260.

(DBT 531-33. Baltzer, K., "Zur formgeschichtlichen Bestimmung der Texte vom Gottes-Knecht," *Probleme biblischer Theologie* [Fest. G. von Rad; ed. H. W. Wolff; Munich, 1971] 27-43. Bonnard, *Second Isaïe* 37-56. Cazelles, H., *RSR* 43 [1955] 5-51. Dion, P.-E., *Bib* 51 [1970] 17-38 Grelot, P., *Les Poèmes du Serviteur* [LD 103; Paris, 1981]. Hegermann, H., *Jesaja 53 in Hexapla, Targum und Peschita* [Gütersloh, 1954]. North, C. R., *The Suffering Servant in Deutero-Isaiah* [2d ed.; London, 1956]. Scullion, *Isaiah 40-66* 133-37; → 16 and 44-46 below.)

Outsiders, under the rubric of nations, peoples, ends of the earth, or distant isles, are frequently addressed by Dt-Isa. According to D. E. Hollenberg (*VT* 19 [1969] 23-36), these words can embrace "crypto-Israelites," who apostatized and passed into the ranks of the Babylonians but are now being called to conversion (42:24-25; 43:22-28; 48:1-11; 50:1-2). In Dt-Isa the various words for "nations" can also refer to pagan Gentiles who are generally rejected (chap. 47; 49:26) or who come to Israel in humility and chains (45:14). In the fourth servant song (52:13-53:12) the nations stand stunned and aghast before the defeated yet triumphant servant, and in Tr-Isa they are called ever more closely and respectfully into the ranks of Israel.

7   (V) Style and Literary Form. Dt-Isa shows himself a master in using and at times blending traditional literary forms: (a) the oracle of salvation, well represented in the Bible (Gen 21:17; 26:24; Joel 2:21-22): Isa 41:8-13,14-16; 43:1-4,5-7; (b) a variation on the latter, identified by Westermann, the announcement of salvation: 41:17-20; 43:16-21; (c) the hymn, generally an embellishment within other forms, as an independent entity only in 42:10-13; 44:23; 48:20-21, to mark an important conclusion; (d) the judgment or trial speech (cf. Hos 4:1-3; Amos 4:1-3; Isa 1:2-3, 10-20), frequently employed by Dt-Isa in putting idolaters and their gods on trial: 41:1-5; 43:9-13; (e) disputation or argument, an informal variation on the latter: 40:18-24; 41:27-31; 44:24-28. See also Stuhlmueller, *Creative Redemption* 16-40.

No one has sensitized us to the rhetorical elegance of Dt-Isa better than J. Muilenburg: the use of alliteration (40:5; 47:1); onomatopoeia in which the Hebr sound suggests the meaning of the word (40:1a; 42:14); lines beginning and ending with the same sound (40:12ab; 45:9c,20e); strong contrasts (41:17-18); questions (43:19; 44:7); imperatives (43:11-12,25).

(VI) Text and Versions. The MT is very well preserved. Among the DSS 1QIsa[a] is remarkably similar to the MT and 1QIsa[b] is almost identical. The LXX is quite inferior. The Vg tends to sharpen messianic interpretations (42:8).

8   (VII) Outline. Dt- and Tr-Isa may be outlined as follows:

(I) Book of Comfort (40:1-55:13)
  (A) Overture (40:1-31)
    (a) Commissioning of the Prophet (40:1-11)
    (b) Disputations with Israel (40:12-31)
  (B) Prophetic Fulfillment in the New Exodus (41:1-47:15)
    (a) The Servant Hears and Is Saved (41:1-44:23)
      (i) Israel's salvation acclaimed and defended (41:1-42:13)
        (1) Champion of justice (41:1-20)
        (2) Military and peaceful ways of justice (41:21-42:13)
      (ii) Yahweh, Redeemer and Re-Creator (42:14-44:23)
        (1) The blind and deaf servant (42:14-43:21)
        (2) Yahweh alone saves (43:22-44:23)
    (b) Cyrus, Anointed Liberator (44:24-47:15)
      (i) Commissioning of Cyrus (44:24-45:13)
        (1) Disputation over world events (44:24-28)
        (2) Commissioning of Cyrus 45:1-8
        (3) Disputation with Israel (45:9-13)
      (ii) The Lord's decree (45:14-25)
      (iii) Trial against Israel (46:1-13)
      (iv) Taunt against Babylon (47:1-15)
    (c) Conclusion (48:1-22)
      (i) Yahweh, first and last (48:1-16)
      (ii) Message of promise (48:17-19)

COMMENTARY

9   **(I) Book of Comfort (40:1–55:13).**
(A) Overture (40:1–31).
(a) COMMISSIONING OF THE PROPHET (40:1–11). These opening lines combine: (a) the scene of God's heavenly council (1 Kgs 22:19–23; Isa 6; see F. M. Cross, Jr., *JNES* 12 [1953] 274–77); (b) the literary style of prophetic commissioning as in Isa 6 or Jer 1 (see N. Habel, *ZAW* 77 [1965] 296–323); (c) the religious motif of the new exodus; (d) preparations for the Babylonian new year with the paving of the *via sacra* and triumphant processions to the capital (see R. Largement, *DBSup* 6. 573–74; H. W. F. Saggs, *The Greatness That Was Babylon* [London, 1962] 384–89); (e) the messenger genre and the motif of God as shepherd in vv 9–11 (cf. Jer 31:10; Ezek 34; Ps 23).

1–2. God addresses the heavenly assembly in the pl.: "Comfort, comfort." Some scholars visualize God's addressing a group of prophets in whose ranks stands Dt-Isa (cf. Amos 3:7; Rignell, *Study* 9). A steady biblical tradition (see above) refers to heavenly beings who hear and ratify the divine decisions. *comfort, comfort:* This double imperative is the first of many (51:9,17; 52:1; 57:14; 62:10). A tone of mercy joined to a majestic style sets the pace for this entire ensemble of poems. *my people, your God:* The covenant bonding of Israel and Yahweh is expressed here (cf. Jer 31:1,33). **2.** *speak to the heart:* In Hebr anthropology the heart was considered the organ of reasoning; God is attempting to convince Israel of his concern (cf. Gen 34:3; 50:21; Hos 2:16; G. Fischer, *Bib* 65 [1984] 244–50). Jerusalem here is not a place but the chosen people in exile. To have "received . . . double for all her sins" does not so much imply an excess of divine anger as it proclaims a completion of the purifying process of sorrow (cf. Jer 16:18). The word of God begins and completes many of Dt-Isa's poems.

3. *a voice! It is crying out:* Someone speaks up from the celestial assembly that the Lord himself is about to lead a new exodus through the desert. Again the terms are more theological than geographical; the Mosaic days of covenant and deliverance are being actualized in the contemporary moment. *in the wilderness prepare the way of the Lord:* The LXX, Vg, and NT (Mark 1:3 par.) divide the phrases differently, so as to read, "a voice cries out in the wilderness." Dt-Isa introduces the theme of the way (see *TDOT* 3. 270–93): a manner of life for Israel (Gen 6:12;

Isa 55:7) and for God (Deut 32:4; Exod 18:25). John the Baptist is to announce "the way of the Lord" (Mark 1:3) and Jesus declares that he himself is that way (John 14:6; Heb 10:20). Christianity, therefore, is called simply "the way" (Acts 9:2; 19:9,23). The DSS saw a fulfillment of 40:3 in the community's retreat into the wilderness and in their "studying the Torah which He commanded through Moses" (1QS 8:14–15). **5.** *the glory of the Lord:* wondrous manifestation of God's redeeming presence (Exod 14:4,18; 16:7; Isa 58:8), particularly in the Temple (Exod 40:34–35; 1 Kgs 8:10–12). Ezek 43:1–2 sees this glory return to a new messianic temple, but Dt-Isa recognizes it in a worldwide theophany — cf. Pss 96:3, 7–8; 97:6; *EDB* 867–71; *DBT* 202–5. "All humankind" (Hebr "all flesh") denotes helplessness in contrast to the wonder of such an undeserved gift (*TDOT* 2. 317–32; *DBT* 185–88).

6. Following 1QIsaᵃ, LXX, and Vg, we translate in the 1st pers. sg., "I replied: 'What shall I cry out?'" For the first and perhaps only time (cf. 48:16c), the prophet speaks in his own name. The repetitious style lets the burden of human weakness fall upon the reader. Dt-Isa is following the pattern of a prophetic commissioning in which an objection always leads to further explanation from God. **8.** *the word of our God:* Cf. *EDB* 2598–2606; *DBT* 666–70. In the final strophe (vv 9–10) we sense the mounting crescendo: "Go up, cry out: fear not to cry out." Jerusalem here typifies the purified people of Israel on the way of the Lord. Dt-Isa never delays over the end of the journey but on the people Israel and their way toward redemption. *good news:* Not so much a message as the people whose glorious redemption manifests the divine redeemer.
10   (b) DISPUTATIONS WITH ISRAEL (40:12–31). While vv 1–11 focus on the glorious procession to Jerusalem, vv 12–31 shift attention back to exile and the weary people, faltering in their faith in Yahweh and tempted to apostasy. Whereas the tone of vv 1–11 resonated the exuberant hope of chaps. 41–48, that of vv 12–31 is overcast with the gloom of chaps. 49–54. Despite the complexity of this section, certain structural lines appear, esp. in vv 18–31. A strong hymnic note sustains the praise of Yahweh (vv 12–17,22–24,26,27–29), and catch phrases knit the section together: "who?" (vv 12,13,14,18,25); "do you not know" (vv 21,28); "create" (vv 26,28); "understand" (vv 14,21).

12–17. Without mediators as in vv 1–11, God's voice thunders upon earth in a series of questions. Dt-Isa, like Job (38:1–42:6), adopts the style of irony for the divine speech. This "is a delicate, even risky technique, especially when prolonged. . . . It may so easily become feeble, or else slip over into sarcasm" (MacKenzie, *Bib* 40 [1959] 441). Dt-Isa and Job succeed much better than Amos (3:3–8; 5:20; 6:2). Style in Dt-Isa is matched with a majestic theology of the Creator's careful planning, unlimited power, and parental concern. Dt-Isa blends aspects of wisdom literature into this prophetic disputation (R. F. Melugin, *VT* 21 [1971] 326–37). **12.** God demands an answer for what is happening now. Dt-Isa challenges fellow Israelites to measure God's works in the heavens or on earth with the hollow or span of one's hand, with a bushel measure, tongue of a delicate scale, or a balance scale (see B. Couroyer *RB* 63 [1966] 186–96). The obvious answer is: If you cannot do this, then why do you dare to question God's other works in history? This disputation presumes an intimate relationship between the cosmos, human history, and Israel's redemption from exile. In quoting this text, Paul associates the mystery of Christ crucified (1 Cor 2:16) and the mystery of Israel's temporary estrangement from salvation in Christ (Rom 11:34) with a new universal creation in Christ Jesus. **13.** Unlike other deities, Yahweh depends on no one else for knowledge. Angels approve and carry out the divine decisions, but they never form or challenge them. *spirit of the Lord:* The active, life-giving power of God (61:1; Gen 1:2; Ps 104:20). **14.** God's actions as creator closely follow a divine determination to secure human dignity. *justice:* This word (*mišpāṭ*) introduces another of Dt-Isa's favorite themes. Throughout the Bible, it indicates the authoritative declaration of what is just and the effective achievement of it. There are several other words for "justice," of different origin but practically synonymous in Dt-Isa. God will act in a way consonant with his own goodness and with the covenant between himself and Israel.

15–17. Structurally these lines balance the opening questions in v 12; each proceeds with a reference to water, clouds, and powder. **15.** *as clouds on the scales:* See Clifford, *Fair Spoken* 80. Not even the mightiest nation can stand in God's "way," neither the distant Gk colonies along the coast of modern Turkey (Ps 72:10; Isa 11:11; Jer 2:10) nor the neighboring giant powers, symbolized by the majestic cedars of Lebanon (1 Kgs 5:6; Isa 10:34; Ps 29:6). **17.** They can no more oppose God than the "void and nothing" of the black abyss in Gen 1:2 could block God's will to create (Isa 41:24–29).

11 **18–31.** In this second disputation there is a double movement, each introduced with an almost identical question about God, spoken either by the prophet (v 18) or by God (v 25), leading in each case to a hymnic interlude and then turning into another question about Israel (vv 21a,28a) and finally a response either about Yahweh's strength (vv 22–24) or human weakness (vv 29–31). **19–20.** Dt-Isa never tires of ridiculing the pseudo-deities of other nations, who posed such a severe temptation for many who felt that Yahweh had been defeated by these gods in the collapse of their own nation (see esp. 44:9–20). The Babylonians believed that the worship of the gods Bel and Marduk, Tiamat and Apsu, kept the process of creation from deteriorating into primeval chaos. Dt-Isa will argue that Yahweh announced Israel's destruction not out of weakness but out of concern for Israel's moral integrity. Yahweh, therefore, even controlled and made use of chaos (45:7). *NAB, NEB,* Schoors (*I Am* 246, 258), and others insert here 41:6–7.

21–24. Despite rapid questions and answers, time is suspended in a continuous present moment by the use of participles and similar-sounding words. **22.** *like grasshoppers:* Although the phrase can be demeaning (Num 13:34), it can also, as here, be a term of endearment (41:14). **23.** Dynasties were toppling and empires cracking up, even at the zenith of opulence and power (Isa 10:15–19; 13–14). **25–27.** *Holy One:* Isa popularized this proper name for God while developing his doctrine on faith (→ 5 above). **26.** The stars, prominent deities in Babylonian mythology, were created effortlessly by Yahweh, simply by calling out their name (Ps 147:4–5). A somewhat different view is taken in Deut 4:19; 29:25; 32:8–9, where these celestial bodies were deliberately left to other nations for worship. Dt-Isa represents a decided advance in Israel's dedication to monotheism. The technical term for creating (*bārā'*) occurs the first of 16 times. Seldom if ever used before Dt-Isa, it now assumes the special meaning of a mighty act of Yahweh (only the Lord is ever the subj.) that transforms chaos into a well-ordered universe. Creation of the material universe is not just the first of many creative-redemptive acts; it is a continuing quality of Yahweh's presence with Israel. See *TDOT* 2. 242–49; *DBT* 98–102; Stuhlmueller, *Creative Redemption* 209–13. **27.** *my way is hidden from the Lord:* Cf. 49:14; 63:15. By contrast, vv 3–5 spoke of a glorious way acclaimed by all humankind!

28. *an eternal God:* Recalls the way Abraham called upon the name of the Lord at Beer-sheba (Gen 21:33). This oblique reference to the patriarchal days, like 51:2–3, links Dt-Isa with an "eternity" that sweeps into the most distant past and across the distant parts of the world. *to faint and to grow weary:* Key words that reappear frequently and tie the servant songs with Dt- and Tr-Isa (40:29–31; 43:22–24; 44:12; 49:4; 50:4; 57:10; 62:8; 65:23). Throughout the ministry of both Dt- and Tr-Isa weariness seems to be a major obstacle. The servant turns this liability into a way of ministering to fellow Israelites! **31.** The prophet provides an excellent OT description of faith. Waiting upon God intensifies a sense of helplessness and an appreciation of God's redeeming power (Isa 8:16–18; Hab 2:3–4; Pss 25:3,22; 27:14). Another image of the new exodus (Schoors, *I Am* 257) is a link with the beginning of this chap.

12 **(B) Prophetic Fulfillment in the New Exodus 41:1–47:15).** These chaps. constitute the major work of Dt-Isa and form a systematized theology of creative redemption. Topics center on a new exodus, inaugurated by Cyrus, enabling the servant Israel to be a light to the nations. Dt-Isa argues his case against other gods in the hope of winning back the crypto-Israelites who had passed into the ranks of the pagan Babylonians (→ 5 above).

(a) THE SERVANT HEARS AND IS SAVED (41:1–44:23).

(i) *Israel's salvation, acclaimed and defended* (41:1–42:13). Through a series of trial speeches, Dt-Isa argues (a) that Yahweh alone is God on the grounds of announcing and already fulfilling the new prophecy about Cyrus as liberator of Israel (41:1–7,21–29; 42:8–9); (b) that the servant Israel, so silent and insignificant in comparison with Cyrus, is the object of the Lord's concern (41:8–16) and is commissioned as chosen leader (42:1–7). Two other sections add a joyful response, the announcement of the new glorious exodus (41:17–20) and the concluding hymn (42:10–13).

13 (1) Champion of justice (41:1–20). Cyrus was a Persian, of Indo-European stock, descended from a people who settled in the high plateau area SE of Babylon. In 559, he became king in Anshan, a vassal

within the larger domain of the Medes, but in 10 years he had already captured Ecbatana, the Median capital. In the winter of 546, he led his army over the frozen mountains of Lydia (in central Turkey) for a surprise attack on the "golden" capital of Croesus, and in 539 he was to become master of Babylon. Dt-Isa portrays Yahweh, summoning the world to his court of justice to witness the fulfillment of his eternal purposes (cf. Isa 1:2–3; Mic 6:1–2). The prophet draws on the legislative procedure of the ancient Near East (see C. Westermann, *Basic Forms of Prophetic Speech* [Phl, 1967]): v 1, the legal summons; vv 2–4a, the trial procedure; vv 4b–7, the verdict. **1.** *silence before me, coastlands:* With biblical precedence (Zeph 1:7; Hab 2:20) God's opening words lead to a solemn revelation to crypto-Israelites scattered throughout the empire and seemingly lost to their religious identification (see D. E. Hollenberg, *VT* 19 [1969] 23–36). **2–4a.** There is, perhaps, some allusion to Abraham (Torrey; Kissane; most Jewish authors), but Cyrus, though not named until 44:28, is the dominant figure here, coming so swiftly from the E that he hardly seems to touch the ground (cf. Ps 19:5c–7). Cyrus is the "champion of God's justice" (*NAB*), a transl. of *ṣedeq,* which denotes the Lord's fidelity to the promises to save Israel. Schoors (*I Am* 54) extends the scope of the Lord's *just* action in Dt-Isa by describing *ṣedeq* as "world order."
14 **4c–5.** God's verdict enunciates a theology of history. God is at the beginning of every event, no matter how cosmic and colossal (40:12–13), how familiar and insignificant (40:27–28); he is also at the conclusion, ensuring a perfect fulfillment of his designs (55:10–11). In Hebrew, "beginning" (v 4b) and "first" (v 4c) are almost identical words. From other poems we learn that "first" refers to prophecies already fulfilled and "last" to the great new one on the verge of fulfillment. Nonetheless, prophecy is seen not merely as words nor even as events but as a revelation of the person of Yahweh who is First and Last (44:6; 48:12). Dt-Isa twice emphasizes the divine "I" and frequently throughout his prophecy uses the sacred name Yahweh, revealed to Moses (Exod 3:14–15). This insight into world history strengthens the interpretation of the divine name that understands it to mean, "I am he who is always there [with you]" (see Eichrodt, *ETOT* 1. 187–92). **6–7.** These lines, transferred at times after 40:20, seem anticlimactic here, yet they harmonize well with the argumentation against idolaters in poems on "first and last" (41:21–29; 42:8–9).
8–16. Two oracles of salvation occur here, each telling servant Israel, "Do not fear," and then offering reasons and the final result of Yahweh's actions. For the first time God calls the exiles "my servant" (→ 6 above). *Abraham my friend:* Lit., "my beloved"; cf. 2 Chr 20:7; Jas 2:23. **10.** For this tense and solemn moment, Dt-Isa employs a phrase characteristic of worship and theophany, the trademark of an oracle of salvation: "Fear not" (Gen 15:1; Deut 20:1; Josh 8:1). **11–12.** The rhythm is retarded to the sorrowful *qînâ* meter of a 3–2 beat (cf. Lam), yet to Israel's consolation. There is tolled the death of every power opposing God's plans of salvation. **13–16.** A second oracle of salvation with "Fear not!" **14.** For the first of 14 times Dt-Isa introduces the title "Your Redeemer" (42:14; 44:6; etc.). Hebr *gō'ēl* always includes two ideas: (a) a close bond, usually of blood; (b) an obligation to come to the other's assistance. It can be translated "nearest of kin" (Lev 25:25). God established the *gō'ēl* relationship with Israel by the great redemptive acts of the exodus and the Sinaitic covenant (Exod 6:6–8; 15:13); God now lives up to this obligation (see Stuhlmueller, *Creative Redemption* 99–131).
15 **17–20.** A song of exquisite literary beauty. The opening line about the poor and needy searching for

water sustains an *im* (pronounced eem) sound, even in the phrase, "there is none." The next section, about parched tongues, carries a deep guttural sound, a gasping *ah.* God does not answer with words, but with actions of wondrous magnitude: rivers flowing atop mountains and in desert valleys and sacred trees of paradise (Isa 55:13; Ezek 31:8–9; Zech 1:8; Neh 8:15). **20.** God's redemptive acts bring a new creation.
16 (2) Military and peaceful ways of justice (41:21–42:13). Dt-Isa contrasts Cyrus's military advances (41:21–29 + 42:8–9) and the servant's peaceful means (42:1–7) and concludes on a happy note (42:10–13). The parts are stitched together with literary finesse: Only Yahweh declares the future (41:26,28; 42:9; 42:12); the gods are empty wind (*rûaḥ,* 41:29) and the spirit of Yahweh (*rûaḥ,* 42:1) anoints the servant; gods are chosen by their worshipers (41:24) but Yahweh chooses the servant (42:1); legal phrases abound in 41:21–29 and in 42:1–4; the Hebr word *ḥēn,* "favor," occurs at 41:24,27,29; 42:1,9 (Melugin, *Formation* 100–1; Muilenburg, *IB* 5. 447–64). **21–29.** A new trial scene begins, ridiculing the Babylonian idols and their worshipers. Would they ever have announced Cyrus's conquest of their own city Babylon, in order to set the Israelites free? Dt-Isa absolutely denies the existence of all gods except Yahweh. The trial concludes that the other gods are "wind and emptiness," the latter (*tōhû*) indicates in Gen 1:1 the dark, formless, and even chaotic mass before God's spirit began the process of creation. **27.** An extremely difficult text, probably a later gloss (Clifford, *Fair Spoken* 87), accentuating the role of Jerusalem.
17 Confirmation of the peaceful servant (42:1–7). Verses 1–4, spoken about the servant, represent one of the final songs by Dt-Isa—or, better, by his follower Tr-Isa, about the master (→ 6 above). There is textual disturbance, so that the trial against the idols has been interrupted and will continue in vv 8–9; vv 5–7 include fragments in the more exuberant style of the hymnic passages of Dt-Isa (E. Vogt, *EstBib* 34 [1960] 775–78). 1QIsaᵃ marks a distinction before and after vv 1–4. The servant is a "chosen one" like Moses (Ps 106:23), David (Ps 89:4), and all Israel (1 Chr 16:13; Isa 41:8); as servant, he fulfills the role of Davidic king (2 Sam 2:18) and messianic king (Ezek 34:23–24). Not only is he set in contrast to the military tactics of Cyrus, but he is commissioned to "bring forth justice" (*mišpāṭ,* 40:14), a legal decision ratifying and executing the divine will. Except in rare cases (Judg 4:5; 1 Sam 7:6; 3:20), this power was reserved to kings, priests, and local magistrates. Prophetic preaching is called judgment (*mišpāṭ*) only in Mic 3:8. The servant, however, has still other qualities, for he imparts teaching (*tôrâ*), a task never done by kings but only by prophets (Isa 8:16; Zech 7:12) and priests (Jer 2:8; Ezek 7:26); see North, *Suffering Servant* 139–42.
1. As God speaks, perhaps to the heavenly court (cf. 40:1–2), his words reach foreign nations (*gôyîm*) and distant isles. *my spirit:* This endowment, important for any extraordinary redemptive work, was promised the messianic king (Isa 11:1) and will later be given to the entire messianic community (Joel 3). While the LXX added the words "Jacob" and "Israel," the NT applied the words to Jesus at his baptism (Mark 1:11) and transfiguration (Matt 17:5). *my chosen one:* Only in Dt-Isa does *bāḥar,* "to choose," reach beyond Israel's national boundaries and in some fashion include other nations; see J. Scharbert, "Erwählung," *Dynamik im Wort* (Stuttgart, 1983) 13–33. **2–3.** The servant accomplishes his mission quietly. "To cry out" normally indicates a person in special need (Elliger, *Deuterojesaja* 209), so that the servant stands

quiet and strong. The descriptions of the servant as not breaking the bruised reed nor quenching the smoldering wick indicate a gentle respect for others, even a detection of strength in their weakness. The *NAB* omits the last part of v 3, "he will introduce justice effectively" and the first part of v 4, "he will never fail nor be discouraged." **4.** "Wait" (*yḥl*) indicates energetic striving for life (Job 6:11; 13:15). "Coastlands," apostate or crypto-Israelites, scattered throughout the Babylonian Empire and lost in the crowd (cf. 41:1), are being called to conversion.

5–7. These fragments of servant songs and pieces from the hymnic style of Dt-Isa insist on the power of God's word in recreating the universe (Elliger, *Deutero-jesaja* 224; cf. 40:25–27). A series of participles reveals the effects of God's word. What happened in the beginning continues at this moment, as Israel emerges from darkness to light. *light:* Not a new revelation but a source of warmth, life, and therefore liberation from slavery. Israel is the first to benefit from this creative-redemptive power of God. "People" ('*am*) ordinarily refers to Israel, so that the universal scope of salvation is not certain; see Š. Purúbčan, *Il Patto nuovo in Is 40–66* (AbBib 8; Rome, 1958). **6.** *for the victory of justice:* A single word in Hebrew (*ṣedeq*), with a rich nuance of meaning (41:8–10). *I have formed you:* Evokes the image of the creation of the first human being (Gen 2:7), like a potter carefully modeling clay. **7.** People must recognize their blindness and imprisonment before they can be cured and freed. These lines may help to explain Isa 6:9–10. **8–9.** A continuation of the trial scene interrupted by the servant song and its fragments.

18 **10–13.** The editor concludes an important section of Dt-Isa's preaching with one of the few independent hymns in the book. These lines are replete with phrases also found in the psalms (Pss 96:1; 98:7; Scullion, *Isaiah 40–66* 44). After announcing "new things" in v 9, the prophet intones a "new song" to Yahweh. God will claim subjects in Kedar in the Arabian peninsula (Isa 21:16; Jer 2:10) and Sela, S of the Dead Sea and capital of Edom (Isa 16:1; Obad). **13.** "Like a hero . . . warrior," God manifests his zeal for world salvation. Dt-Isa's language is reminiscent not only of Babylonian myths of primeval struggle (51:9–10) but also of Israel's early poetry (Exod 15:3; Ps 24:8).

19 (ii) *Yahweh, Redeemer and Re-Creator* (42:14–44:23). While servant Israel still holds a prominent place, Dt-Isa directs more attention to Yahweh, who achieves the new exodus and the new creation (42:14–43:21), announced and accomplished by himself (43:22–44:23).

(1) *The blind and deaf servant* (42:14–43:21). Dt-Isa contrasts helpless Israel (42:18–25) with a compassionate Lord (43:1–7). The opening lines, 42:14–17, remind us of 40:1. In an extraordinary use of feminine imagery, "God groans aloud like a woman in travail."

Trial of the blind servant Israel (42:18–25). Words like "blind" and "darkness," although with different nuances, link this poem with v 15 and 43:8. In putting Israel on trial Yahweh addresses the defendant (18), asks questions (19), sets forth the accusation (20–21) and the punishment (22), repeats the accusations (23–25). Underlying this trial is Israel's complaint that Yahweh deserted his people in the destruction of Jerusalem and their subsequent exile. **19b.** For Dt-Isa blindness amounted to the inability of Israel to accept the earlier prophecies of doom and to recognize a plan of God in the exile. "Covenanted one" translates *mešullām*, from the same root as *šālôm*, "peace," "well-being." **21.** *was pleased . . . for his justice:* These phrases connect these lines with two major servant songs (42:6; 53:10), to show that suffering purifies, strengthens, and enables one to share

salvation with many others. **25.** These lines have their own element of rhetoric; the conditions of the exile were not painful for everyone, nor were all the people so wicked (Jer 29).

20 New exodus, new creation (43:1–8). This poem, one of the finest of Dt-Isa, interprets the return from exile as a new creation, performed from the obligations of blood relationship. It is skillfully stitched into place and just as carefully structured: references to fire occur in 42:25 and 43:2; three key words form an *inclusio,* uniting vv 1,7 (create, form, name); blindness and deafness construct another *inclusio* between 42:18–19 and 43:8. Verse 1 begins with "now" and closes with "you," in Hebr almost identical in sound. A series of participles draws out the full effects of the phrase "Thus says Yahweh," creating you and forming you (42:5). The melodic sound of this line leads to the majestic tone of the next, where theophanic words are pronounced in the first of two oracles of salvation: "Fear not" (41:10). The reason not to fear is based on tradition and the people's faith: "For I am your kinsperson," (Hebr *gĕ'altîkā*), a variation on the word *gō'ēl* which before Dt-Isa was not a normal title for Yahweh but was used in secular life for the bonds of blood and its consequent obligations in an extended family (Stuhlmueller, *Creative Redemption* 100–4; *TDOT* 2. 350–55). The Lord acts out the *gō'ēl* relationship with Israel, bringing his children back from slavery, retrieving their family homestead in the promised land and raising up many children (54:1–10). **2.** *water . . . fire:* These symbolize danger and destruction (Isa 51:9–10; Gen 6–9 [deluge]; Exod 14:21–31; 15:8–13; Ps 89:10–11). **3.** Israel is preferred to all other countries, represented by Egypt and what lies beyond in Africa: Seba and Ethiopia. The word "ransom" is not to be taken literally; in saving his people, God never paid a price to the evil one. **5–6.** The great ingathering (Jer 31:1–22; Ezek 37:15–28) will exceed all expectations (Gal 3:26–29; Eph 2:13–16). **7.** So thoroughly do God's children share divine life that they are no longer addressed by their own name but by the Lord's.

9–13. This new trial against idols and their worshipers (41:21–29) adds a new element—Israelites are summoned as witnesses. **9.** Yahweh allows the nations (or does Dt-Isa have crypto-Israelites in mind? cf. 41:1; 42:10) one more chance to demonstrate whether or not Babylonian gods "foretold the earlier things" (42:9; 40:4). Because knowledge meant a total, experiential involvement, prediction implied a steady control of the flow of events. **10.** Israel, by her tenacious survival and by her still more wondrous resurgence, witnesses to the world that Yahweh alone is God and savior (cf. Acts 1:8). Three strong vbs., "know," "believe," and "understand," lead to the divine declaration, "I am he." **11.** *I, I, Yahweh:* This statement of strong personal divinity places God's full power at the service of Israel and the world—foretelling, saving, creating, and making known (44:6–8).

21 **43:14–21.** After a fragmentary oracle (vv 14–15, with v 14b "corrupt beyond restoration," Scullion, *Isaiah 40–66* 51–52), another masterpiece of poetry and theology occurs (vv 16–21). The prophet continues a favorite theme, the new exodus. **14.** Yahweh is to be known as the one at work "redeeming you," and as such is "the Holy One" (40:25). Nothing is so mysterious and distant about God—as the word "holy" connotes—as the extent of his redeeming love. **15–17.** A series of participles answers the question Who is Yahweh? by portraying the exodus out of Egypt, ending in the final scene in which the Egyptians lie defeated. **18.** The first exodus helped Israel to perceive what Yahweh was doing now, but it was also being eclipsed in a

fulfillment beyond all hopes (cf. von Rad, *OTT* 2. 248).
22 (2) Yahweh alone saves (43:22–44:22). While Yahweh appears forcefully as Israel's savior, nonetheless by contrast Israel shows up as a servant who has become a burden even to Yahweh, yet is chosen, forgiven, and redeemed, to the joy of the entire earth.

Trial speech against Israel bv servant Yahweh (43:22–28). Elements of a trial are incorporated here rather freely. Verses 23a and 24a closely parallel each other, as do vv 23b and 24b. Human ingratitude and divine mercy meet; God's invectives, delivered in courtroom style, are followed by forgiveness. The buildup is massive; each line in vv 22–24 begins with a negative. This section is difficult to interpret, precisely because the prophet shifts from preexilic days, when sacrifices were offered as though they were the essence of religion (Isa 1:11–15), into the exilic period, when sacrifices were impossible. **23a.** *you are making me your servant:* One of the most daring phrases about God in the entire OT, esp. so against the background of Dt-Isa's servant theology. One of the key words is "weary." Both Israel and God are weary, but for different reasons. **26.** "Remember" can be a technical juridical term; hence the rendering: "Bring a charge against me! Let us go to court" (Scullion, *Isaiah 40–66* 193–4). **27–28.** The strong "corporate personality" of Israel is here manifest. The future is seen to exist already in the forebears; ancient blessings and curses explain the present situation. *our first father:* Jacob (Gen 27; Hos 12:2–7; Jer 9:3). *your ancestors:* The unworthy prophets and priests (Mic 3:5–12; Isa 28:7).

44:1–5. This oracle of salvation begins in vv 1–2 with strong declarations: "Hear now," "Thus says Yahweh," "Fear not," each concluding with a theme of mercy. **1.** God speaks the word of divine election, and his people are formed in the womb of God's gentle care, a theme from Jer 1:5; 20:18, to be repeated in the servant song of 49:1 (cf. Ps 139:13–18; Job 10:10–11). **2.** God calls this child "darling" (*yĕšurûn*), a term of endearment, a diminutive probably from *yāšar* (to be upright) and here rhyming with Israel in v 1 (Deut 32:15; 33:5,26). **3.** As Israel receives the spirit, extending new life through her offspring, the land will be transformed into a new paradise. The symbol of water frequently accompanies the spirit of God (Ezek 36:25; Zech 12:10; 13:1; John 3:5; 7:37–38). **5.** Gentiles, at least individually, shall confess Yahweh as their only savior and shall even tattoo the name Yahweh on their hands (Exod 13:9; Ezek 9:4; Rev 7:3). Membership in the chosen people will not depend on blood descent but on faith imparted by the spirit of God (Rom 4:16–17; 8:14–17). **6–8.** In this trial speech Yahweh declares that he alone is Israel's king, redeeming his people. **6.** *Lord of hosts:* A title common with Isaiah of Jerusalem (6:3,5; 3:1; 5:14) and quite frequent in Dt-Isa (45:13; 47:4), extending Yahweh's domain over the sun, moon, and stars, imparting a sense of power and majesty (40:26; 45:12). In the present setting, however, Yahweh is discrediting the heavenly hosts, worshiped by the Babylonians, and thereby claiming for himself a cosmic sweep of power (*EDB* 1031–2). **7–8.** By his word God not only foretells but also accomplishes, and its glorious fulfillment in Israel will make that people his "witness" (43:10). Dt-Isa speaks of prophecy and revelation not as words whispered by God in the souls of ecstatic seers but rather as his mighty presence, directing human history for the redemption of Israel.
23 9–20. Some, like Muilenburg, *BHS,* and Scullion, recast all or part of these lines into poetic form. While there is no reason to deny this piece to Dt-Isa, still it differs stylistically from other poems that call the same defendants to trial (41:21–29 + 42:8–9; 43:9–13). This section is tied with the preceding trial against other gods and with the following poem, assuring Israel that all sins (especially of idolatry in the case of the crypto-Israelites?) are forgiven (44:21–22). The piece is dramatic in its momentum: workers with metal (v 12) and wood (v 13), and their procurement of material (v 14), deciding whether to burn the wood for cooking a meal or to make an idol (vv 15–16), then bowing in worship (v 17)—how absurd (v 18)! Similar to Jer 10:1–16 and Wis 13:11–13, the argument presumes that all images are idols and that all idols are gods and goddesses reduced to metal, stone, and wood. In the ancient Near East idolatry was not that simple, for at times the idol was the pedestal for the invisible deity, as the ark and its accompanying mercy-seat were for Yahweh in the Temple (Exod 25:17–22).
21–22. This prophetic exhortation shows many points of contact with other poems: "my servant," "I form you" (43:1; 44:2); "remember" (43:18,25–26); v 22 almost repeats 43:25 (Melugin, *Formation* 122). Yahweh carefully forms the character of his people, like a potter forming a vase (42:6; 43:1), and despite their complaints (40:27) he assures them: "You shall never be forgotten." IQIsa[a] expresses this divine promise in a slightly different way: "you shall not disappoint me." The instruction concludes: "Indeed, I am your kinsperson" (cf. 43:1–8). **23.** This finale, an independent hymn, intones a glad cry which echoes from every part of the earth. With Israel redeemed, the world is transformed (cf. Rom 8:18–22). The last two lines can be translated: "Indeed, the Lord is your kinsperson, Jacob, and in Israel he displays his masterpiece" (cf. *NEB*).
24 (b) CYRUS, ANOINTED LIBERATOR (44:24–47:15). This is the second major section of chaps. 41–48. While 41:1–44:23 centered on the role of the servant in fulfilling the prophecy of the new exodus, this series focuses on Cyrus, to be commissioned by name over the objections of Israel (44:24–45:13), according to the Lord's just decree (45:14–25), argued again with an obstinate Israel (chap. 46) and fulfilled with the collapse of Babylon (chap. 47). With alliteration, repetition, rhyme, and assonance, with the full orchestration of all his major themes of redemption, creation, word of God, and prophecy, Dt-Isa names Cyrus as the Lord's anointed. Dt-Isa clearly recognizes the Lord's positive direction of international politics and follows in the attitude of Isa. The Babylonian army was the Lord's instrument to fulfill earlier prophecies in the destruction of Jerusalem (what Dt-Isa consistently calls "first things"), and Cyrus is the chosen and anointed one for the fulfillment of the "last things." Later, in composing the servant songs, Dt-Isa distances himself from such an active role of political and military might and opts for a nonviolent solution (M. C. Lind, *CBQ* 46 [1984] 432–46). For this reason 42:1–7 was inserted into the first series of poems.
(i) *Commissioning of Cyrus* (44:24–45:13). This is a set of three independent pieces (44:24–28; 45:1–7[8]; 45:9–13) that are rather carefully stitched together, with an *inclusio* that unites 44:24 with 45:7, repeating three key words ("form," "make," "do these things"). The third poem responds to Israel's objections over the strong endorsement given to Cyrus in the first two poems.
(1) Disputation over world events (44:24–28). Dt-Isa quickly scans world history as it relates to Israel, from the devastation of their country to their imminent return to it. The prophet utilizes a series of 13 participles to impart the style of a hymn of praise: "redeeming you," "forming you from the womb [of history]," "making all things." **26.** *raising up the word of his servant:* God confirms

the hopes of his servant, Israel (41:8). The pl. "servants" in some translations (*NAB, NEB*) parallels the second line, "messengers," so that both words would refer to the earlier prophets, who announced the destruction of Jerusalem. **27.** Watery depths symbolized monstrous evil powers, releasing destruction upon the peaceful land (43:2; 51:9-10). **28.** For the first time, the prophet pronounces the name Cyrus; God declares him "my shepherd" (or king—40:10-11). The last two lines of this verse were probably added. They are introduced by an infinitive, clearly breaking the continuum of participles; the word "temple" is never used by this prophet, who is unsympathetic to Temple sacrifice.

25 (2) Commissioning of Cyrus (45:1-8). A divine decree (Pss 2; 110) announcing the royal enthronement of Cyrus. Only here in the OT is a foreigner called the Lord's "anointed"—Hebr *māšîaḥ* or "messiah"; Gk *christos*, hence "Christ"; see S. Mowinckel, *He That Cometh* (Oxford, 1956) 3-9. The OT never uses *māšîaḥ* as a title for the promised one to herald the final age of Israel. The title is reserved principally for kings (1 Sam 16:6; 2 Sam 19:22) but is shared also with prophets (Ps 105:15) and priests (Lev 4:3; Dan 9:25-26). **1.** *whose right hand I grasp:* At their coronation, Babylonian kings grasped the hand of the patron god, Bel-Marduk. Dt-Isa envisions Yahweh's grasping Cyrus as a legitimate king to preside over the restoration of Israel. How disappointed will the prophet be when later Cyrus grasps the hand of Bel-Marduk, as is declared in the Cyrus cylinder (*ANET* 315-16) and in the name of this god allows the Jews to return to their homeland. **2.** *level the mountains:* The phrase turns the march of Cyrus's army into another exodus (40:3-4). "Bronze gates" to the number of 100 are recorded by the Gk historian Herodotus (1.179; see Scullion, *Isaiah 40-66* 68). **3.** *treasures:* Those of such legendary figures as Croesus fell into Cyrus's hands. **4.** God was directing the steps of Cyrus, "even though you do not know me." Here is a practical expression of "God the first" (44:6). The Lord was making sure that world history converged upon his designs for a tiny captured group of people, Israel. Ancient historians like Herodotus and Xenophon would scorn such braggadocio. **7.** Although Yahweh is said to be the author of both good and evil, evil is no giant swaggering ruthlessly through the world; somehow, it accomplishes God's will for Israel (Amos 3:6; 4:13; Isa 10:5-20; Judg 2:6-3:6).

8. Because of the strong *inclusio,* uniting 44:24 and 45:7, this verse is evidently inserted here by the editor, a prayer in the style of a hymn, to conclude the anointing ceremony for Cyrus. It urgently beseeches God to bring salvation out of all these earthly events (Isa 11:1; 55:10-11). "Justice" (40:14) and "salvation" were translated by Jerome as proper names—the "just one" and the "savior," which in his commentary are interpreted of Cyrus. His Latin translation is well known in the Advent hymn *Rorate caeli desuper.*

(3) Disputation with Israel (45:9-13). Dt-Isa follows the earlier prophets in a strong invective against Israel (Amos 5:7,18; Isa 1:4,24), imitating a funeral lament to declare the deadly foolishness of acting against God; see R. J. Clifford, *CBQ* 28 (1966) 458-64; *TDOT* 3. 359-64. The lines are carefully interlocked by a series of key words ("work," vv 9,11; "children," vv 10,11; "hands," vv 9,11; "maker," vv 9,11). No one should be so foolish as to question God's wisdom. God's demand of absolute obedience is not based, however, on blind subservience, but rather on his delicate concern implied in the image of a potter and parent, with personal attention emphasized by the repetition of the pronoun "I." He refers to the creation account (Gen 2:7;

3:19; Jer 18:2-10; see C. F. Whitley, *VT* 11 [1961] 457-61). **12.** Both by reason of the images of forming pottery and begetting children and because of the world scene dominated by Cyrus, Dt-Isa is led to enunciate one of his clearest statements about the Lord's creating the universe and humankind.

26 (ii) *The Lord's decree* (45:14-25). These lines bring the preaching of Dt-Isa to some of its finest theological moments, but there are serious textual or literary problems. **14-17.** A concatenation of fragments united in the universal acclaim of Yahweh. Some of the textual problems are the following: in v 1, Zion is addressed in 2d pers. sg. fem., whereas in v 15 in 2d pers. sg. masc.; in v 17a Israel is spoken about in 3d pers. sg., but in v 17b in 2d pers. masc. pl. **14.** The wealth of all nations symbolized by the gifts of Egypt and other distant places in Africa (cf. 43:3), will flow into Israel (Isa 2:2-5; Ps 72:8-11). The ecumenical attitude is not exactly exemplary, as foreigners come "in chains." **15.** *truly you are a hidden God:* Some translators unnecessarily emend the Hebr to read "with you God is hidden." God's redemptive acts are concealed within human instruments, even within the pagan Cyrus.

27 **18-25.** This trial speech with Israel is held together by an *inclusio:* phrases of vv 18-19 are repeated in vv 21-23. In hymnic style it resounds with participles that are intercepted with victorious acclamations. **19.** Paradoxically "the hidden God" of v 15 never speaks in hiding! God's word is heard not by a few devotees acquainted with magical formulas but by every faithful Israelite. The God who creates empty waste and darkness (45:7) is not to be found in empty waste, for God is transforming the exile into a new creation. **20-21.** The trial of the crypto-Israelites gets seriously under way with the questioning of the defendant. The remnant of Israel is being summoned away from the false Babylonian gods who never anticipated the collapse of their own city (44:25). When Yahweh foretold the future through his prophets, he was setting in motion the means of its fulfillment. The "remnant" doctrine is implied in the phrase "survivors from among the Gentiles" (Isa 10:21-22). It is a difficult doctrine to define, for remnant is not to be decided numerically (prophets were not impressed by externals) nor by an interior state of lowliness (prophets were too realistic for that). Remnant at times implies destruction with only a few survivors (Amos 3:12; 5:15) who become the hope for the future (Zeph 3:12), out of whom God reconstitutes a new Israel (Zech 9:7). Remnant declares not only that God is the source of all life but also that God brings this life out of lowly origins and an attitude of faith (Joel 3-4); see G. F. Hasel, *The Remnant* (2d ed.; Berrien Springs, 1974); *DBT* 484-86. **22.** *ends of the earth:* Because of the *inclusio* formed by the phrase "descendants of Jacob/Israel" in vv 19 and 25, directing the poem to the chosen people, this reference must not be read as a call to universal salvation. Rather it refers to crypto-Israelites scattered through the Babylonian Empire and already succumbing to apostasy. The fulfillment of prophecy and of Israel's finest hopes is to be found "only in the Lord." **23.** These verses have inspired an early Christian hymn to Jesus (Phil 2:10-11; Rom 14:11).

28 (iii) *Trial against Israel* (46:1-13). While unmasking the ridiculous powerlessness of the Babylonian gods, Dt-Isa announces a proclamation of salvation (vv 1-4), follows with an impressive trial against crypto-Israelites, who are faltering and apostatizing (vv 5-11), and concludes with another speech for Israel's salvation (vv 12-13). Several key words act like yeast to leaven the mix: *nāśā',* "to carry," in vv 1b(twice),2a,3b,4b,7a; *sābal,* "to carry or to hold on one's lap," in vv 4a,4b,7a. The vb.

nāśā' frequently has a meaning of tender concern (Isa 40:11; Exod 19:4; Deut 32:11; Ps 91:2), and *sābal* conveys the legal idea of adoption, a ceremony enacted by placing the child upon one's lap near the genital organs (Gen 30:3; Ruth 4:16).

1–4. The poem begins with the humiliation of the gods. It is difficult to know if the prophet thinks of statues as carried in religious procession or as carted hastily out of the city for protection against Cyrus's advancing army (see *ANEP* 537–38). The short staccato phrases in vv 1–2 suggest the deities' quick downfall. The Hebr word "idol" resembles "toilsome work"! *Bel:* God of heaven and father of gods, merged with Marduk, the great god of Babylon (Jer 50:2; Bar 6:40; Dan 14:2–21). The elevation of Bel-Marduk was celebrated lavishly in the Babylonian ritual. As the great creation myth *Enuma Elish* was reenacted, the forces of chaos were thought to be withstood for another year (*ANET* 60–72; *DOTT* 3–16). *Nebo:* Marduk's son, "secretary-god," who possessed the tablets of destiny. His popularity can be judged from many Babylonian names: Nabopolassar, Nebuchadnezzar, Nabonidus. **2.** This prophecy was not literally fulfilled. Cyrus reversed the policy of conquerors, leaving the statues in their own temples and returning those that the Babylonians had stolen.

29 **3.** *the remnant of Israel:* Yahweh calls them his loving responsibility (45:20; Deut 1:31; Hos 11:3; Ps 21:10). Each line in v 3b ends with a Hebr word for womb. Israel always remains a child in need of Yahweh's care. **4b.** Rhetorically effective, not only by the repetition of the divine "I" but also by a reversal of tenses: "And I have done [this] and I will [always] do [this]; and I will carry [you] as I have [always] saved [you]." **5–11.** This trial scene has many points of similarity with 40:18–24: questions, sarcasm about Babylonian gods, a call to remember. **8.** The crypto-Israelites are called "rebels." A series of four imperatives demands immediate response. **10.** Yahweh acts effectively according to a personal plan of salvation. **11.** *the bird of prey from the east:* Cyrus (41:2; 45:1–7).

30 (iv) *Taunt against Babylon* (47:1–15). After the demise of the Babylonian gods, Dt-Isa chants this dirge in the 3 + 2 *qînâ* meter (→ Hebrew Poetry, 12:16–19). The sorrow is in mockery because the city before him is still wealthy, carefree, and independent; the prophet detects its corrupt interior. Its death sentence has already been formulated in the plans of Cyrus. God is soon to requite Babylon for the savage destruction of Jerusalem and the ruthless deportation of its people (v 6). Most of all the prophet condemns the city's pride (vv 7–8). This taunt-song corresponds to the oracles against the nations in many prophetic books (Amos 1:3–2:16; Isa 13–23; Jer 46–51; Ezek 25–32; see D. L. Christensen, *Transformation of the War Oracles in OT Prophecy* (HDR 3; Missoula, 1975). The prophet's virtuosity is displayed in a rich vocabulary; almost 40 words occur that are not found elsewhere in his writings. The poem possesses a compact strength through the interlocking of its various lines: vv 1a,5a; 5d,7b; 8d,10f; 9d,11a,11e. The Hebr text reveals striking onomatopoeia; v 2a reverberates with the crackling of a millstone grinding wheat. The sarcasm is sharpened by grandiose words of address: virgin daughter (v 1a), gentle and refined (v 1c), queen of the kingdoms (v 5), queen forever (v 7), voluptuous one (v 8). The latter term is from the same root as Eden, the name of the garden of paradise.

1. Babylon would like to consider herself a virgin, unravished and unconquered by any nation, but she is so only in her sterility. Babylon is called Chaldea, a Semitic

people who migrated *ca.* 1000 and founded the present dynasty. Chaldea later became the word for all Babylon (Dan 1:5). **3.** Babylon will exchange her pampered harem existence for the slave drudgery of grinding wheat and corn (Exod 11:5; Judg 16:21). She will be deprived of the veil worn by noble ladies to hide their faces from vulgar gazes; she will bare her legs, either to work more easily or to be treated more freely like a captured woman (Isa 20:4; Nah 3:5). **5–7.** Babylon's dark "silence" is full of despair. **8–11.** Babylon is pictured enthroned like a goddess accepting divine honors (Zeph 2:15), even the acclamation reserved for Yahweh (v 8d; cf. 45:5,18,21; 46:9). **12.** *keep up your spells:* The word Chaldean later became synonymous with sorcery and magic (Dan 2:2), emphatically condemned by Dt-Isa (44:25).

31 (c) CONCLUSION (48:1–22). Dt-Isa blends in every major theme, some for the last time, such as Cyrus, idols, first and last, and, with a slight exception, Babylon. He includes other familiar themes: creation, the power of the word, the new exodus. Characteristic features of style appear: imperatives, participles, questions, repetitions. At the same time this chap. is one of the most baffling of all. An unaccountable mixture of sg. and pl., of 2d and 3d pers., of stern cross-questioning and encouragement. Some scholars detect the hand of a later editor, inserting a severe censure against Israel within earlier passages of hope (Duhm, Elliger, Begrich, Westermann, Schoors).

(i) *Yahweh, first and last* (48:1–16). This first section reverts to the ancient prophetic style of threat and condemnation (45:9–13; 46:5–11). **2.** *naming themselves after the holy city:* Cf. Neh 11:1; Dan 9:24; Matt 4:5. Muslims still call Jerusalem *el-Quds,* "The Holy." Because this city symbolized the presence of God and the fulfillment of the covenantal promises, Isa had given it the symbolic name, "city of justice, faithful city" (Isa 1:26; Jer 3:17; Ezek 48:35). Israel, however, glories in a city of justice "without seeking justice" (i.e., salvation) in Yahweh (v 1). **3.** One of the most important verses of the entire Bible for interpreting prophecy. *first things:* Prophecies about Israel's exile. Even though the earlier prophecies were clearly enunciated by prophets like Isaiah and Jeremiah and certainly heard, their fulfillment came "suddenly," i.e., by surprise (47:11; Mal 3:1). Earlier prophecies prepare for the future, but one must still accept on faith what God is doing in the act of fulfillment. *announced ahead of time:* Not necessarily "long ago" (cf. Exod 4:10; 2 Sam 15:34). **4.** Israel has inflicted upon herself a spiritual exile from Yahweh (cf. Herbert, *Isaiah 40–66* 83). **6a.** A strange grammatical mix: "You have heard, behold a vision, all of it (dangling pronominal reference), have you not announced." **6b–7a.** This could not have been written a century before the exile. Dt-Isa declares now what is now happening, so immediately effective is the prophetic word. **9.** *I restrain my anger:* Cf. 40:2. The exile is another Egypt, which earlier tradition called "a furnace of affliction" (Deut 4:20; 1 Kgs 8:51; Jer 11:4), purifying and strengthening Israel's devoted love for Yahweh (Isa 1:25; Ps 12:7). **10b.** *I tested you:* Follows IQIsa[a] and the targum rather than the MT, bringing the text closer to passages in Jer about the disciplinary force of suffering (Jer 9:6; 12:3).

32 **12.** Typically Dt-Isa vintage: a combination of prophecy and fulfillment, "first" and "last," creation, and the ever-personal presence of Yahweh. **13.** Prophecy leads to a profound faith in Yahweh's personal direction of history, culminating in a new creation across the cosmos. The next step to universal salvation, dramatic though it be, will be a small one. **14.** Redemption is achieved through Cyrus, "the Lord's beloved." Like Abraham, he comes from the east to bring salvation to

the nations (41:8; Gen 12:1-3). **16.** As in earlier court scenes (41:1), God challenges all other gods whom the crypto-Israelites were tempted to trust. Yahweh alone foretells and accomplishes, and in doing so is ever present. **16c.** A difficult text: lit., "but now our lord Yahweh has sent me and his spirit." Individual words echo phrases in 61:1-3, sometimes considered a fifth servant song. Again, as in v 22, fragmentary pieces intrude upon us. Some emend to: "The lord Yahweh has sent me," making it one of the rare personal allusions of Dt-Isa to himself (cf. 40:6, again by textual correction).
33 (ii) *Message of promise* (48:17-19). This stanza opens in the solemn style of an oracle. Participles provide not only the spirit of a hymn of praise but also power and achievement to God's word: "acting as your kinsperson" (cf. 43:1), "teaching you," and "leading you." This word is "authoritative" (Clifford, *Fair Spoken* 145), so that obedience or disobedience has a lasting effect (Deut 27-28). If the word is obeyed, "prosperity" (*šālôm*) and "victorious vindication" (*ṣĕdāqâ*) will ensue. **19.** Dt-Isa echoes the promise to Abraham (Gen 12:2-3; 22:17).
(iii) *Concluding hymn* (48:20-22). With short, abrupt phrases Dt-Isa signals the start of the new exodus, "ringing with joyful shouts" (Isa 12:6; 44:23; Zeph 3:14). People (crypto-Israelites?) will be attracted to believe (again?) in Yahweh as they witness his redeeming power in "his servant Jacob" (cf. Isa 41:8-9). **21.** This description of the new exodus influenced the explanation of Num 21:17 in the Tg, so that the rock of Moses was thought to follow the Israelites through the desert as a ready source of water, hence Paul's application to Christ in 1 Cor 10:4 (see E. E. Ellis, *JBL* 76 [1957] 53-56). **22.** This verse belongs in 57:21, typical of isolated fragments that occur around the major servant songs, one of which follows immediately.
34 (C) **Comforting Zion (49:1-54:17).** Chapter 49 marks a serious shift in the preaching of Dt-Isa and in the organization of the book. Many familiar themes are no longer heard: Cyrus (41:8; 48:14), the foolishness of idols, and Yahweh as first and last in control of history (40:18; 41:23). Dt-Isa now addresses Zion/Jerusalem in place of Israel/Jacob. Songs of creation and of new exodus continue, but less enthusiastically. The cosmic panorama of chaps. 41-48 is concentrated now within a few lines of universal salvation. The servant Israel is less a rebellious group to be converted (42:18-25; 46:5-11) than a group of disciples persecuted, rejected, and suffering. The synthesis of important theological themes within chaps. 41-48, gives way to a narrower field of ideas, less integrated. The confidence modulates into a contemplative or somber attitude toward suffering and rejection.
Scholars explain the relation of chaps. 40-48 to chaps. 49-55 differently. In our position Dt-Isa writes from Babylon after Cyrus signed the edict allowing the Jews to return home (Ezra 1:1-4). Their new state is barely large enough to support the Jerusalem sanctuary, and in this poor tract of land, 20 by 25 mi., the people quickly succumb to discouragement, avarice, and cruelty (Hag; Neh 5; Ezra 9-10). Not till 515, upon the insistence of Haggai and Zechariah, did they complete the Jerusalem Temple, the foundation of which was laid in 536 (Ezra 3:7-4:5; 5:1). Some of this melancholy and sorrow echoes in these new poems. Yet the prophet's sorrow comes most of all from his failure to win back many of the crypto-Israelites and from his isolation by the group who controlled the return to the land, a group influenced by Ezek and the P tradition.
35 (a) FROM SORROW TO REDEMPTION (49:1-51:8). As Dt-Isa enters this new period of his life and

ministry, he experiences a new commissioning from the Lord (49:1-7) and a strong statement of peace in the midst of rejection and persecution (50:4-9). These two major servant songs lead to an announcement of a new exodus (49:8-13) and of salvation for Zion (49:14-26), disputations with Israel (50:1-3,10-11) and a concluding promise of salvation (51:1-8). Chapter 49 has much in common with chap. 40: the time of servitude has ended (40:2) and the time of grace has come (49:8); a way is prepared in the desert (40:3) and Yahweh's glory is manifest (40:5; 49:7). In each section we meet the shepherd image (40:11; 49:9), the leveling of mountains (40:3-4; 49:11), and consolation (40:1; 49:13). Chapter 49 opens with the second of the major servant songs (→ 5 and 17 above). We face again the literary problem of the song's length and the presence of fragments, as already in 48:16b,22. Like the other servant songs, vv 4-6 move in the style of Jeremiah's confessions (Jer 11:18-12:6; 15:10-21; 17:14-18; 18:18-23; 20:7-18)—the personal soliloquy of a sorrowing person of faith. With v 7 we are again back in the prophetic style of oracle, solemnly pronounced by Yahweh. Verses 5ab, 6,8,9a combine the style of servant songs and the Book of Consolation (E. Vogt, *EstBib* 34 [1960] 775-88). This song presumes that the servant has already been at work and is now discouraged by the fruitlessness of his ministry. God responds by widening even further the servant's apostolate with a message for the Gentiles.
(i) *Commissioning of servant prophet* (49:1-7). Dt-Isa speaks in his own name and addresses the crypto-Israelites. He presents himself as another Jeremiah: He is called from his mother's womb (v 1; Jer 1:5); he has a vocation to outsiders (v 6; Jer 1:10; 25:13-38); he reacts at times with heavy discouragement (v 4; Jer 14:17). **1.** *called from the womb:* Here we see in action the doctrine of God, first and last (41:4); God sets his chosen ones on the way of their vocation even before their birth (cf. Ps 139:13-15; Luke 1:15,31; Gal 1:15). **2.** *my mouth like a sharp sword:* An effective instrument in speaking the Lord's prophetic word (Jer 1:9; Heb 4:12; Rev 1:16). It is not clear, however, why God concealed the servant—perhaps to protect him (Pss 17:8; 27:5) or to provide time for appreciating Israel's mission (51:14-16; 52:13-15). **3.** The explicit designation of the servant as "Israel" is witnessed in all Hebr mss. except an insignificant one of the 14th cent. The servant comprises all faithful Israelites (a more restricted group than generally the case in chaps. 41-48), esp. the disciples of Dt-Isa and most particularly the prophet himself. Such a person or group within Israel can certainly have a mission to sinful members in Israel (see Rignell, *Study* 161). **3-4.** In strong contrast: "He [Yahweh] said to me . . . but then I myself said [to him]." Objections are commonly introduced in the literary genre of the commissioning of prophets (Isa 6:5; 40:6; Jer 1:6). The servant honestly expresses his dejection over what seems to him a wasted ministry, "for nothing" (*tōhû;* cf. Gen 1:2; Isa 41:29). The servant learns to seek his only "recompense (*mišpāṭ;* cf. 40:14) with Yahweh." This lesson is necessary, lest the servant gauge the extent of God's plans by human achievements or seek the glory for himself. **5.** This slightly damaged text provides a new introduction and repeats part of v 1. Throughout Dt-Isa the servant is not the one to lead the new exodus and to restore Israel; this is for Cyrus or God himself (40:1-11; 45:2-3,13). **6.** The mission to Jacob/Israel is contrasted with the mission to be "a light to the nations." The prophet declares openly what has been only inferred or intuited up till now. **7.** A fragment that reflects on v 4 and prepares for the fourth song. It combines ideas and aspects of style from chaps. 40-48 and the other major servant songs.

36 (ii) *Announcement of the new exodus* (49:8–13). In this poem (with its independent hymn at the end, v 13), the exile is over and Israelites are streaming out of the farthest dark corners back to their homeland. The poem is a filigree of ideas and phrases from elsewhere (cf. 40:1,11; 41:18; 43:5–6; 45:14; 49:4,6,21; 61:2). A disciple of Dt-Isa is meditating on the work of the master. **12.** The language moves energetically: "Behold some. . . . Behold others . . . and still others." **13.** This short hymn, like 42:10–13 and 44:23, concludes another section.

(iii) *Announcement of salvation for Zion* (49:14–26). Beautiful lines of consolation are sung to Zion-Jerusalem, so long bereft of her children. **14.** An effective contrast with the preceding hymn. **15.** One of the most touching expressions of divine love in the entire Bible. The feminine image for God is natural in the setting of a walled city which is pictured as a mother pregnant with life. **16.** Names written upon the palms of God's hand echo such texts as Deut 6:8, Jer 31:33. **18.** The seeming clash of images (Jerusalem as both child and spouse of God) is not unusual; cf. Hos 1–3. For the Yahweh-as-spouse tradition, see Isa 62:4–5; Hos 1–3; Jer 2:1–3. **19–21.** God fills Zion, once "bereaved and childless," with healthy children (cf. Rom 5:20). **22.** *my signal:* In contrast to Isa 5:26, God calls upon all nations to work together in the family of Israel. **23.** *lick the dust off your feet:* Ancient language for a vassal showing homage to a king (cf. Jehu in *ANEP* 355). **24–26.** Zion remains doubtful and an element of disputation dampens the enthusiasm. **26.** Cyrus took the city of Babylon without a battle and never leveled it to the ground. Either Dt-Isa spoke these lines before the fall of Babylon or else he is using stereotyped language. *the Mighty One of Jacob:* Cf. Gen 49:24. The final lines of v 26 may have come from 60:16.

37 (iv) *Confidence of the servant prophet* (50:1–11). It is difficult to detect the logical connections between vv 1–3,4–9a,9b,10,11 (Herbert, *Isaiah 40–66* 94). After the initial disputation with Israel (vv 1–3), the third major servant song occurs (vv 4–9a). Typical of the major songs, fragmentary pieces cluster nearby. Stylistically, however, the editor has adroitly knit the sections together: there is a series of questions (vv 1ab,2ab,8b, 10a) followed by answers each introduced by the Hebr particle *hēn* ("behold," vv 1c,2c,9a,9b,11). While the earlier chaps. frequently spoke of suffering, the words moved in a strong spirit of hope (40:2; 42:7). Dt-Isa now speaks with a spirit of resignation, even with a tone of reproach. **1–2b.** The exile could be interpreted as a temporary separation of Yahweh from his spouse Zion. Divorces were finalized by the husband (women did not divorce) when a written document was handed over (Deut 24:1–4). Yahweh never proceeded that far. **2c–3.** Dt-Isa recalls the ancient traditions of the plagues in Egypt (Exod 7:18,21; 8:10) and Yahweh's fierce struggles with sea monsters (51:9–10). Verses 2c and 3a are joined with an alliteration: "rot" (*tib'aš*) and "cloth" (*'albîš*).

38 **4–9.** Only in a fragmentary response in v 10 do we hear the word "servant." Within the song itself the author identifies himself with "disciples"; in Isa 8:16 and 30:8–14 this term refers to immediate followers who have the prophetic word sealed in their heart. Isa 30:8–14 and 50:4–11 have still other points of contact (Clifford, *Fair Spoken* 161–2). Through these disciples we detect a continuity from one section of Isa to another. "Disciple" is the passive form of the vb. "to teach" (*lāmad*); one must first experience what is to be transmitted to others. **4–5.** Textually disturbed and variously translated. We propose: "The Lord Yahweh has given me a disciple's tongue, that I may know how to sustain the weary. The word rouses me in the morning, in the

morning he rouses my ear to hear like a disciple" (cf. Scullion, *Isaiah 40–66* 106). "Weary" repeats a key word in Dt-Isa (40:29–31; 43:23–24). **6.** Like the prophets before him, the servant is ignored and even maltreated (cf. 49:4). **7.** *face like flint:* The phrase, frequent in prophetic preaching (Isa 48:4; Jer 1:8,18; Ezek 3:8–9; Luke 9–51), is all the more effective here in describing a face covered with spittle. **8.** The prophet reverts to court-room terminology (chap. 41). **9b.** The literary connection with v 3 serves to piece together the original form of chap. 50 before the servant song was inserted into it. It is also a fitting conclusion to the song. Clothing is frequently a substitute or metaphor for the person (1 Sam 24:5–7; Job 13:28; Mark 5:28); the servant's enemies will disappear like moth-eaten cloth. **10–11.** An editorial endorsement of the servant, followed by an obscure, dangling verse about the fate of apostate or crypto-Israelites.

39 (v) *Promise of salvation* (51:1–8). These poems reassure the followers of the servant in view of his personal humiliation and rejection. The patriarchal promises will be fulfilled (vv 1–3); a blend of various phrases from the major servant songs that Yahweh's victory will reach distant places, even against the dissolution of the cosmos (vv 4–6); an oracle of salvation against the scorn of apostate Israelites (vv 7–8). The sections have been carefully knit together: each begins with a call for attention; several key words recur: "listen," "instruction," and "victory" (*ṣedeq*). Such editing always imparts a new pastoral thrust (Melugin, *Formation* 159)—in this case a strong endorsement of the dispirited and rejected prophet and his disciples.

1–3. *you who are seeking the Lord:* A liturgical phrase in a nonliturgical context. Yahweh's just or complete fulfillment of ancient promises (*ṣedeq*) shall not be thwarted. Those who survive the exile and are regaining their promised land are proof supreme that the elderly and childless Abraham and Sarah did not believe in vain. Outside of Gen, Sarah is mentioned by name only here in the OT. **3.** Eden, "the garden of the Lord," is now a symbol of Israel's future (cf. Ezek 38:11–19). **4–6.** This promise of salvation draws on the major servant songs: judgment goes forth (42:1); light of nations (49:6); arm of Yahweh (53:1); islands wait (42:4). **5.** "The arm of the Lord" led the Israelites out of Egypt (Exod 6:6; 15:16) and created the world (Jer 27:5); it overcomes chaotic forces against creation to lead Israel now out of exile (Isa 51:9–11). **6.** The sun, stars, and moon, great deities in ancient religions, grow dark and vaporous like smoke. **7–8.** *people with my instruction at heart:* Recalls Dt-Isa's favorite sources, Deut 6:4–9 and Jer 31:31–34.

40 (b) COMFORTING THE MOURNERS (51:9–52:12). This poem is cast in the literary form of national mourning similar to Pss 44; 74; 79 (Clifford, *Fair Spoken* 169). Despite several serious textual problems, the individual poems follow with orderly momentum: 51:9–11, lament-appeal to Yahweh; 51:12–16, lament-response from the Lord; 51:17–23, lament-comfort for Zion; 52:1–2, comfort-exhortation for Zion; 52:3–6, exhortation to mourners; 52:7–10, the messenger of good news; and 52:11–12, the concluding hymn. A somber note is sustained by the almost continuous use of the *qînâ* meter (3 + 2). Several words and grammatical details knit the smaller sections together.

(i) *Lament and comfort* (51:9–52:6). **9–11.** A desperate spirit, plunged in darkness and yet firmly convinced of God's goodness and strength (cf. Pss 10:12; 44:26–27). God is implored to repeat the mighty, redemptive acts of the past. In this new struggle of creation God is warring against sea monsters as destructive as Rahab or the dragon worshiped by the Canaanites (cf.

Ps 89:11; Isa 30:7; Job 9:13; *ANET* 130–42). **10.** Dt-Isa moves to the exodus theme, where Yahweh battled mighty waters to make "a way" (40:3) for Israel (Stuhlmueller, *Creative Redemption* 82–91). **11.** Almost verbatim from Isa 35:10, the words break the anguish of lament.

12–16. Lines beset with textual problems. The point of reference slips from pl. to sg. in v 12. Verse 14 is variously translated in the ancient versions. Verse 15 is a quotation almost slavishly added by a later scribe from Jer 31:35, without adapting the Hebr text, as most Eng transls. do! Verse 16 gathers up phrases from the major servant songs (49:2; 50:10). Yet the thrust of a new creation within the new exodus or return from exile harmonizes well with the larger context.

41   **17–23.** In this and the next poem, many themes of Dt-Isa converge. The first part is addressed to Jerusalem, an abject widow, haunted by the memory of children whom she saw collapsing at every street corner (Lam 2:19). **17.** *cup of wrath:* The woes preached by many prophets (Jer 25:15–31; Hab 2:16; Lam 4:21). It was "drained to the dregs" when the Babylonians breached the walls of Jerusalem in July 587. **19a.** The question refers to the ritual of mourning. **19b.** Reflects Nah 3:7, where it is addressed sarcastically to the hated Nineveh; here it reads with a beautiful modulation, "Who? I will comfort you."

21–23. Stunned at so much grief, Jerusalem must be addressed repeatedly by God. The Lord will wrench the cup of wrath from the hand of Israel, the very cup forced upon her in v 17. **21.** *O afflicted one:* The spiritual movement of the *anawim,* inaugurated by Zeph 2:3; 3:12 and developed by Jer 15:10–21, reaches toward maturity in texts like this and 41:17. The psalms will keep this spirit vital and energetic in postexilic Israel (Pss 9:13; 22:25); the DSS will make it a way of life (1QS 8:1–9). See A. Gelin, *The Poor of Yahweh* (Collegeville, 1965); *TDNT* 6. 645–51; *IDBSup* 672–75; *DBT* 436–38.

42   **52:1–2.** Eight imperatives sustain a high pitch of excitement. Words addressed in a lament to Yahweh in 51:9 now call out encouragingly to Zion in this grand reversal. **3–6.** A reflection upon the words of Dt-Isa and the history of Israel. The meter is defective, so that *BHS* and many modern writers print the section in blocked prose. **3.** *redeemed, but without silver:* A different explanation from 43:3–4. The LXX has an interesting variation, "but without violence." At best Israel contributed nothing except a strong, humble obedience to God's will in its history. **5–6.** While admittedly obscure in details, the general message is clear enough: Yahweh will not tolerate Israel's enemies gloating over his people (cf. Pss 42:11; 79:10).

(ii) *Messenger of salvation* (52:7–10). Excitement rings out with staccato beats. *messenger of good news:* Cf. 40:9; 2 Sam 18:19–33. For a similar enthronement of Yahweh, see Pss 47; 93; 96–99. **8.** The joyful shout is now repeated by the watchmen guarding the ruined walls of Jerusalem, and people witness "the Lord restoring Zion" (cf. 62:6–7). **9–10.** A thanksgiving hymn in response to the messenger, resounding with OT texts (Zeph 3:13–18; Joel 2:21).

(iii) *Conclusion: A new exodus* (52:11–12). This hymn, in style like 52:1–2 and 7, reminds us also of 48:20–21. Six imperatives ring out, dealing with cultic purity; this concern is so rare in Dt-Isa that we suspect the hand of a later editor (cf. Isa 4:4–6). **12.** In contrast to the fearful haste of the first exodus (Exod 12:11; Deut 16:3), the army of God's people is moving peacefully and serenely with the Lord at the lead (Exod 13:21; Num 14:13; Deut 1:30–33; Isa 58:8; 1 Cor 10:1).

43   (c) THANKSGIVING FOR SERVANT PROPHET (52:13–53:12). In this fourth servant song, the servant remains one with all people in sorrow and yet distinct from them in innocence of life and total service of God. The doctrine of expiatory suffering finds supreme expression (vv 4,6,10). Style matches thought, for seldom does the Bible reach such extraordinary power of sound, balance, and contrast. Some 46 words occur, otherwise absent from Dt-Isa. North concludes that this occurrence of rare words does not point to a different author; chap. 40 included about 50 such words (*Suffering Servant* 168). Yet when joined to other stylistic flourishes, the fact suggests one who concentrates intensely and draws upon an extraordinary repertoire. The style is heavy, sobbing, and recurrent with a frequent intoning of *u* and *o* vowels, *h* and *l* consonants, the sounds of a dirge. Other rhetorical flourishes occur, yet so smoothly as hardly to be noticed. (a) Although the servant says and does nothing and is referred to simply as "he" or "him" in the main body of the poem (53:1–11a), he is the subject of 39 of the 61 vbs. and participles. (b) The dominant action is silent contemplation. A vb. oft repeated is *rā'â,* "to see" (54:14; 53:1,2,3,10,11). (c) Despite the intense emotion throughout the poem, little evidence is seen of *affective* terminology, at least as compared with chap. 54. Even words for pain and infirmity denote physical suffering. The ambiguity of the servant is heightened by this silence. It is a different kind of silence from that in 42:1–4. (d) Past, present, and future merge in the tenses of Hebr vbs. (Clines, *I, He, We, & They* [→ 46 below] 37–49).

The question of the servant's identity (→ 6 above). While the title of servant is given to all Israel, to the rebellious crypto-Israelites, to Cyrus and to the prophet himself, we have argued that the servant is Dt-Isa himself in the final stages of his career. Therefore, he speaks in his own name of a new prophetic call in 49:1–7, describes the poignancy of his rejection in 50:4–9, reflects back upon the silent period of his rejection in 52:13–53:12, and realizes that Yahweh's goals are not to be achieved by the military action of the anointed Cyrus but silently through the prophecy which he leaves to his disciples (42:1–7).

Another case of identity remains equally uncertain: who are the "we" who speak 53:1–11a? They are either the prophet himself, projecting his message into the persona of startled onlookers, or else his disciples, or the "kings" of 52:15 (cf. Whybray, *Isaiah 40–66* 172). Pre-Christian tradition among the Jews interpreted this song messianically. The DSS seldom if ever make use of this song (J. Carmignac, *RevQ* 2 [1960] 383–95), and the targums turned the one who suffers into an enemy of God (see J. F. Stenning, *The Targum of Isaiah* [Oxford, 1949] 178–81). Expiatory suffering does not seem to have been a part of official Judaism's messianic doctrine (O. Cullmann, *The Christology of the New Testament* [Phl, 1959] 52–60). Jesus uniquely combined the suffering servant theme with the messianic concept of the Son of Man (D. M. Stanley, *CBQ* 16 [1954] 385–425; J. Giblet, *LumVie* 7 [1958] 5–34). The NT identifies Jesus as the suffering servant at his baptism (Mark 1:11; John 1:34), in his miracles (Matt 8:17), and in his humility (Matt 12:16–21). John 12:37–43 sums up Jesus' public ministry in the words of the servant. This attribution of the servant theme to Jesus occurs in Acts (3:13,26; 4:27,30; 8:32) and in the hymns of the early church (Phil 2:7; 1 Pet 2:21–25). Paul, however, adapts it to himself (Acts 13:47; Gal 1:15; Rom 15:21).

This song is stitched carefully into the context with the repetition of "arm of the Lord" (51:3,9; 52:10; 53:1) and the vb. "to see" (49:7; 52:10,15). It is divided:

(1) 52:13-15, spoken by Yahweh about the amazement of the nations; (2) 53:1-11a, thanksgiving for sorrow, subdivided into: vv 1-3, narrative of sorrows; vv 4-6, sorrow as part of the servant's ministry; vv 7-9, sorrow, silently accepted; vv 10-11a, good results; (3) 53:11b-13, conclusion again spoken by Yahweh about the good effects of the servant's ministry. Against those who would separate 52:13-15 (Whybray, *Isaiah 40-66* 169), the unity of the poem is defended by the envelope effect of referring to the servant in 52:13-15 and 53:11b-13. For translations, see Clifford, *Fair Spoken* 173-75, and Scullion, *Isaiah 40-66* 117-18.

44   **52:13-15.** In these introductory lines God announces the triumph of the servant. **13.** *prosper:* The Hebr word implies prudence or insight, as though the servant's victory is a result of obeying God's wise plan of salvation (cf. Vg "intelligent"; Dan 12:3; Isa 50:4). **14.** *many:* This key word (52:11c,12a,14,15; 53:12) is not the opposite of "all" but implies "many beyond all count," like the sand on the seashore (Josh 11:4). *amazed:* This word is often used of vast desolate wastes (Gen 47:19; Lam 2:15; Isa 49:8,19); here, as in Ps 46:9, it carries the sense of being stunned into silence. *at him:* The MT, LXX, and 1QIsa^a read "at you," as though Yahweh turns for a moment toward the silent servant, then immediately resumes his words about him. 1QIsa^a has an interesting reading for v 14c: "I so *anointed* [his appearance] beyond everyone else." **15.** *startled:* So most translators, but *nāzâ* means "to sprinkle" or ritually cleanse for sacrifice. This liturgical allusion in a nonritual setting is typical of Dt-Isa (cf. 44:28).

53:1-3. We hardly notice the abrupt change in speakers from Yahweh to Dt-Isa or his disciples. While 52:13 denies that anything has been heard, 53:1 asks paradoxically: "Who would believe what we have just heard?" This effective intervention on God's "arm" does not imply military action (*TDOT* 4.136). **2.** These words have a generic sense of Yahweh's victory from hidden roots and tender sprouts (cf. Isa 11:1; Jer 23:5). **3.** The servant is rejected by his own people. The collective interpretation that considers the servant to be "Israel" (49:3) remains valid, here with a bitter sense of loneliness. The servant relives the persecuted role of Jer (15:17) and Job (19:13-19). **3.** *avoided:* Hebr *ḥādēl* can mean "fat" or "gross" and, in this context, "obtuse" and "foolish" (see P. J. Calderone, *CBQ* 24 [1962] 416-19). *hiding his face:* Like an outcast leper (cf. Lev 13:45-46).

45   **4-6.** Some Israelites, won over to the servant, repent of their persecution of him. The servant is said to bear the infirmity of others and even to become their sin-offering. The innocent servant is not a substitute before God for sinful Israelites, no more than the ritual killing of an animal automatically obtained grace for the offerer and reunion with the community and God. Num 5:5-10 clearly states the prerequisites of confessing one's guilt and restoring stolen goods plus 20 percent before performing the ritual acts at the sanctuary (see C. Stuhlmueller, *Communio* 1 [1974] 20-46). The ritual act externalized the interior attitude of the offerer and through this externalization the offerer began to participate in the full life of the community. The servant, therefore, is not freeing others of their responsibility for repentance but is suffusing within them his own spirit of sorrow and hope. **5.** *thrust through:* A strong word; in 43:28 it was translated "repudiated" or "profaned." *offenses:* A rebellion against God's personal concern. *chastisement:* Recalls the disciplinary or educative power of suffering. God teaches repentance through the calamity evoked by sin; cf. Jer 2:19,30; Ezek 5:15; Isa 3:2,7; J. A. Sanders, *Suffering as Divine Discipline* (Rochester, 1955). **6.** *sheep . . . way:* Cf. Isa 40:3,11; Jer 50:6; Ezek 34:5. *laid upon*

him: Soon a technical term, particularly in its ancient Gk transl. (*paradidōmi*), used in the Christian kerygma to designate God's handing over his Son to death (Matt 17:22; John 8:30,35; Acts 3:13; 1 Cor 11:23).

7-9. The servant's silence is most unusual, for people in agony usually cry aloud. *harshly treated:* Exod 3:7 uses the same word for the Egyptian oppression. **8.** A *crux interpretum,* variously emended and translated. The servant, after being seized, tried, and convicted, is taken away, psychologically into a loneliness almost to the point of despair. *destiny:* The word means a "state" or "change of fortune." H. Cazelles concludes to a "state" or "place" inaccessible and mysterious (*RSR* 43 [1955] 40). Is this passage implying that the servant was killed or at least died a natural death? Not necessarily, because identical language is used in Pss 31:23; 89:49; Lam 3:54; Jer 11:18-20, without the outcome of death (see J. A. Soggin, *ZAW* 87 [1975] 346-55). **8.** The MT reads "my people," thus strengthening the bonding between the servant and all Israel. Although innocent, the servant suffers with the sinful people and infuses his own heroic goodness into their attitudes.

46   **10-11a.** Victory, although never enjoyed by the servant during his lifetime, is proclaimed. These verses are textually very disturbed; v 10 is sometimes rejected. *pleased:* A key word in Dt-Isa (44:28; 46:10; 48:14). In the NT it expresses God's designs as fulfilled in Jesus (Matt 26:42; John 4:34; cf. Bonnard, *Second Isaïe* 282 n. 5). *offering for sin:* Dt-Isa advances beyond the ancient liturgical sacrifice for sins of inadvertence (Lev 4-5) to a heightened awareness of sacrifice for willful sins. Although Dt-Isa is transferring ritual language to a nonsanctuary sphere of life, nonetheless, passages such as this accentuated the heavy sin consciousness of Israel during the exile and so influenced the cult. From the exile, penitential liturgies commonly occur (Zech 7-8, Joel). The LXX *lytron,* "ransom," occurs in Mark 10:45.

11b-12. In this conclusion God is again the speaker. *through his suffering:* The Hebrew reads "by his knowledge," i.e., by a full experiential union with a suffering, sinful people. *justify many:* He will share his own goodness with them and thus fulfill all divine promises (cf. 40:14). Although the servant's innocence separates him from the rest of Israel, he is always slipping back into the collectivity.

(Clines, D. J. A., *I, He, We, & They: A Literary Approach to Isaiah 53* [JSOTSup, 1; Sheffield, 1976]. Whybray, R. N., *Thanksgiving for a Liberated Prophet* [JSOT 4; Sheffield, 1978] → 6 above).

47   (d) ZION, MOTHER AND SPOUSE (54:1-17). The silent anguish of the preceding poem modulates into tender emotion about Zion (cf. Clines, *I, He, We, & They* [→ 46 above] 44). Verses 1-3 are a blend of hymn and prophetic promise; vv 4-6, an oracle of salvation; vv 7-10, a disputation, changing the image from marriage and home to the world; vv 11-17, two announcements of salvation. These units are carefully stitched together: ever more emphatic conclusions at the end of vv 1,5, 7,10; sequence of mother (vv 1-3), wife (vv 4-6), loved one (vv 7-10), city (vv 11-17)—cf. W. A. M. Beuken, *OTS* 19 (1974) 29-70. Dt-Isa, different from Ezek, views the city not as turned inward upon the Temple but as turned outward toward the world. He reaches behind the Mosaic covenant which separated Israel from other nations, to the covenant with Noah (vv 7-10) which was worldwide in scope.

1-3. Strong imperatives and melodious paronomasia are sustained throughout. The Yahweh-spouse image (44:14; 50:1) combines with the familiar biblical situation of a sterile wife: Sarah (Gen 15:2; 16:1), Rachel (Gen

29:31), Manoah's wife (Judg 13:2), and Hannah (1 Sam 1:2). All bore children through God's special promise. Barren Jerusalem will also be peopled with children if she shares the faith of her ancestors. **3.** *the nations:* Those occupying the land promised to Israel (Ps 44:3). **4.** *fear not:* After this solemn introduction of an oracle of salvation (41:10,13–14; 43:1,5), Israel is assured that she can forget "the shame" of her youth, her preexilic apostasy (50:1). **5.** God's creative power exists for the sake of his redemptive love (Stuhlmueller, *Creative Redemption* 115–22). **7–8.** We meet the mysterious theology of Gen 6:6; 8:21–22, where God repented of what he had done, or of Hos 2:19–25; 11:1–12, where God could not cast off his beloved despite her repeated adulteries. **7.** The Hebrew contrasts the "small" moment of the exile with the "spacious" mercy of Yahweh (Clifford, *Fair Spoken* 183). **8.** The last line resounds with the everlasting *ḥesed* of Jer 31:3; cf. *TDOT* 5. 44–64. **9–10.** Calling upon the P tradition, Dt-Isa compares the exile to the flood; both were catastrophies of disobedience to the divine word. Even though God promised to Noah that such a horrendous destruction would not happen again (Gen 9:11–17), something comparable did in the exile! **10.** This "covenant of peace" (Num 26:12; Ezek 34:25; 37:26; Mal 2:5) will firmly unite the entire universe in harmony and happiness (44:28) according to the "fullness" implied by the word *šālôm*. Unlike Ezek 37:26, Dt-Isa does not join the phrase with the rebuilding of the Temple.

11–17. Two announcements of salvation complete this chapter (vv 11–15; 16–17). **11.** *storm-battered:* A literary link with Noah's deluge in v 10. God consoles the flood victims with a vision of the heavenly Jerusalem. Dt-Isa draws color and ideas from a mythological paradise and explains such luminous glory by the presence of Yahweh, thus basically differing from all mythologies. *afflicted one:* See 51:21. **12.** It is difficult to identify all the precious metal adorning the new Jerusalem. The foundations reflect the green and deep blue of the sky; the golden doors reflect the blazing fire of the sun (Zech 2:6–9; Rev 21:18–21). **13.** *your sons:* By a slight change of vowels, 1QIsaᵃ reads attractively "your builders." The word of God emanates from the splendor of the Lord's presence. Dt-Isa does not eliminate teachers—otherwise, why is he teaching!—but insists that all teachers are themselves obedient learners before God (50:4; Jer 31:34; John 6:45). **14.** *justice:* This one word recapitulates Yahweh's glorious victory in Zion (40:14). **15.** Textually difficult. This last great shout of hate against God and his people is powerless. **17b.** Very likely an editorial remark by Tr-Isa. "The servants" will receive full vindication (or victory).

48   (D) Conclusion to the Book of Comfort (55:1–13). Almost every major theme within chaps. 40–54 is blended into this glorious finale. Chapter 55 forms an *inclusio* with chap. 40, repeating many key words or themes: new exodus (40:1–11; 55:12–13); the way (40:3,27; 55:7–9); call to pasture or to eat (40:11; 55:1–2); word of the Lord (40:8; 55:11); king (Yahweh, 40:10,23; David, 55:3–5); heaven and earth (40:12; 55:8–11); disputation with Israel (40:12–31; 55:6–11); forgiveness (40:2; 55:6–7); participation of the nations (40:4; 55:12). Verses 1–5 follow a wisdom style of instruction; vv 6–7 imitate a priestly instruction, supported by statements in vv 8–9 and 10–11; vv 10–11 are a concluding announcement of salvation.

1–2. With a long series of imperatives, Dt-Isa invites poor people to a joyful banquet. The style is typical of wisdom literature (Prov 9:1–5; Sir 24:18–20; cf. Begrich, *Studien* 59–61; Melugin, *Formation* 26). The ritual meal is desacralized and extended into the daily lives of the people. The single condition is a thirst for

God (41:17; 51:21). The prophet is not insisting on a spiritual substitution for material bread but rather is inculcating a proper religious spirit or social attitude with which to share food. The Bible often evokes the banquet symbol to celebrate God's care for Israel: the Passover (Exod 12) and the Sinai covenant (Exod 24:5,11). The abundance of the new age is laid out by later prophecy as a banquet (Isa 25:6; 65:11–15; cf. *DBT* 342–44). **3–5.** After overlooking the Mosaic covenant and returning to more ancient agreements (51:2; 54:9–10), Dt-Isa proceeds to neutralize the covenant and special privileges of the royal Davidic family (2 Sam 7:8–16; 23:5; 1 Kgs 8:23–25; Ps 89:2–38). He has already transferred to the people Israel such royal titles as "my servant" and "my chosen one" (44:1; cf. Ps 89:4,21). *everlasting covenant:* Not a covenant beginning now and lasting forever, but one bringing the promises of the distant past to ever-present fulfillment (cf. Mic 5:1; 7:20). The phrase occurs in Isa 24:5; 59:21; 61:8; Ezek 37:26–28; Matt 26:28; Luke 22:20. Dt-Isa is not projecting a leaderless, nongovernmental society, but thinks along the lines of the former northern kingdom of Israel and opts for a less centralized system than that prevalent at Jerusalem (cf. 54:13), just as he moves away from the motif of a single sanctuary in favor of the multisanctuary practice in the former northern sector of the land; cf. O. Eissfeldt, "The Promises of Grace to David," *Israel's Prophetic Heritage* (Fest. J. Muilenburg; ed. B. W. Anderson, *et al.;* NY, 1962) 196–207.

49   6. *seek the Lord:* This phrase, which normally invited people to the sanctuary, exhorts them to find the Lord elsewhere. A literary dependence on Jer 29:10–14 (Clifford, *Fair Spoken* 193) accentuates this movement away from the sanctuary. **8–9.** God is transcendent and hidden (45:15), yet near enough to be burdened by human sin (43:24); we are but children (43:1–7) yet required to act energetically like adults! Divine paradoxes! **10–11.** The word comes gently from God, never intended to remain suspended like clouds in midair, but to soak the earth and to be drawn back toward God like plants and trees. God's spirit is infused within human beings where it brings forth divine fruits. Dt-Isa explains world history, particularly where Israel is involved, through the omnipotent presence of the word (cf. Wis 8:1; 2 Cor 9:10; John 6:32,35). Typical of other parts of Dt-Isa, God's word is less a message and more an event (41:17–20), or better an event perceived in the mystery of Israel's salvation (44:24–45:8). **12–13.** Recalls the constant exodus theme. All the world breaks into song as God brings Israel back wondrously. The course of thorns and sin is removed forever (Gen 3:18; Isa 7:23), and in their place grow the trees of paradise (41:19). The reestablishment of God's people constitutes "an everlasting sign" of divine love. All the world thus recognizes the name of Yahweh. Dt-Isa remains the "Great Unknown." He does not sign his own name at the end but the name of Israel's savior.

50   (II) Struggle for New Temple and New Leadership (56:1–66:24). This second and final major section, called Trito- or Third Isaiah (Tr-Isa), evinces a change in tone, vocabulary, and outlook (→ 3–6 above): (a) the *setting* is no longer Babylon but Palestine; (b) the *mood,* formerly a movement from exalted hopes to discouragement, now in chaps. 56–66 modulates from disappointment to a glorious future; (c) while *the object of promise* was all Israel, now it is the faithful few with an opening to Gentiles; (d) in chaps. 56–66 *Temple worship* emerges more prominently; (e) *God's dwelling* narrows from heaven and earth in 40–55 to the Jerusalem Temple in 56–66; (f) *idolatry* is no longer ridiculed but bitterly condemned; (g) the *editing* is not as well structured as in

40–55. This new emphasis on Temple, worship, sabbath, fasting, and law reflects a different spirituality. We meet a new phenomenon in biblical traditions, anthological composition with quotations from earlier inspired words. Dt-Isa no longer speaks; he is quoted or alluded to: 57:14–19; 58:5a,12b,14; 60:4–5,19; 66:12. We hear echoes of his doctrine: universal salvation; fulfillment of hopes for the sterile; true and false servants.

Because of this similarity and dissimilarity to Dt-Isa, the authorship of chaps. 56–66 is variously explained: by Dt-Isa (C. C. Torrey, E. König, E. J. Kissane); by a single author after the first return (B. Duhm, K. Elliger, E. Sellin); by a group in postexilic Judah (T. K. Cheyne, K. Budde, P. Volz, J. Steinmann, C. Westermann). "The extreme divergence of positions . . . shows that any unilateral solution risks being partially false" (T. Chary, *Les Prophètes et le Culte* [Paris, 1955] 94). This commentary opts for disciples of Dt-Isa, who integrated the message of their master with the changed situation of postexilic Israel. Because the Temple is rebuilt (an exception, 63:18), the time is after 515 BC (56:5–8; 60:7, 13), but the energetic reformers—Malachi, Nehemiah, and Ezra—have not yet purged idolatry and reformed Judaism. Already, however, the disciples of Ezekiel are in charge. This is the "day of small beginnnings" (Zech 4:10), reflected in the prophecies of Haggai and Zechariah, in the books of Ezra and Neh (see Hanson, *Dawn of Apocalyptic* 209–79; D. L. Petersen, *Late Israelite Prophecy* [SBLMS 23; Missoula, 1973] 23–27).

The careful editing of 56–66 is seen in an *inclusio* (56:1–8 and 66:17–24, Temple worship is open to non-Jews) and in an intricate chiastic arrangement, by which the steps forward are reversed, once the center is reached at 61:1–3 (see N. K. Gottwald, *The Hebrew Bible* ([Phl, 1985] 508; G. J. Polan, *In the Ways of Justice Toward Salvation* [Bern, 1986] 14–16). Three aspects show up clearly: (1) at the center are chaps. 60–62 with the anointing of the servant at its heart; (2) an outreach to the Gentiles frames the entire corpus; (3) a continuing struggle against false leaders is pictured.

51   (A) Oracle of Temple Worship for Outsiders (56:1–8). This poem opens with familiar themes from Dt-Isa: salvation, justice and the gathering of the dispersed. The spirit of Dt-Isa, however, is almost reversed with a preoccupation for cultic or purely religious matters: sabbath and [Mosaic] covenant (vv 2,4,6); holocausts, sacrifices, and altar (v 7). Whereas Dt-Isa and Ezek insist on circumcision, Tr-Isa is closer to Jer in relativizing it (Jer 4:4; Isa 52:1; Ezek 44:6–9). **2.** This summary of postexilic torah or instruction recalls Ps 1:1. Other similar passages, however, like Jer 17:7, Ps 8:5; Job 7:17; and 1QS 11:20–22 place less emphasis on human work. Tr-Isa finds relief in the faithful observance of the sabbath, a very ancient law (Exod 31:12–17; Amos 8:5) but rigidly set during or after the exile (Ezek 20; Neh 13:15–22); see N.-E. A. Andreasen, *The Old Testament Sabbath* (SBLDS 7; Cambridge, MA, 1972). **3–5.** Foreigners living within Palestine (*gērîm*) were granted limited rights and protection (Exod 22:20; Deut 10:19), but Tr-Isa extends full privileges even to the *nēkār*, those living outside the boundaries of the promised land. The disciples of Dt-Isa were thus aligning themselves with universalist tendencies as seen in Ruth and Jonah, rather than with the narrower stand as in Ezra 9–10 and Obad. Even Deut, a book within the theological and literary background of Dt- and Tr-Isa, did not go this far (Deut 23:2–9). Tr-Isa was reaching into Israel's early history to reintroduce the diverse kind of people whom God elected: Aramean (Deut 26:5); Amorite and Hittite (Ezek 16:3); mixed foreign elements (Exod 12:38; Num 11:4). *eunuchs:* Such were refused

admission "into the assembly of the Lord" (Lev 22:24; Deut 23:2), because it seemed improper for a person, deprived of the power of transmitting life, to associate with the God of life (*EDB* 702–3; *TDNT* 2. 765–68). Some Israelites were castrated for working within the harem of Israelite or foreign kings (1 Sam 8:15; 2 Kgs 9:32; Esth 2:3; 4:4–5). Tr-Isa urges their full readmission among God's people (Wis 3:14). Their contribution to Israel's vibrant religious life will be their "monument and name," lit., "hand and name." "Hand" is to be understood as a memorial monument (cf. 1 Sam 15:12). **7.** *house of prayer:* Cf. Matt 21:13.

52   (B) Struggle for True Leadership (56:9–59:21). A glimpse of the bleak, silent period between 500 and 428.

(a) FALSE LEADERS; SOME FAITHFUL PEOPLE (56:9–57:13). Composed around 515–510 (Hanson, *Dawn of Apocalyptic* 186–87, 194–95). After the wicked leaders are indicted (56:9–12), the innocent victims are lamented (57:1–2). Corrupt Temple worship is bitterly attacked (vv 3–11), apostates are threatened (vv 12–13a) and the faithful few are promised salvation (v 13b). The poem, rugged and bitterly blunt, revives an early prophetic form (Amos 2:6–16; 4:1; Isa 1:12–17). Some scholars (P. Volz, E. Dhorme, P. Auvray, J. Steinmann) look upon these lines as a preexilic composition because of the mention of the offensive fertility cult. Tr-Isa, we suggest, draws upon preexilic language to condemn sarcastically the worship of his own day. **9.** *beasts of the forest:* God summons foreign nations to devour his sinful flock (Amos 3:12; Jer 12:9). **10.** *dumb dogs:* A contemptuous reference to Israel's watchmen (1 Sam 17:43), "dreaming" or, according to LXX, "uttering incoherent sounds." **11.** *greedy:* Lit., "strong of life," with a voracious gullet, living off their sacred charge (Mic 3:1–5). **12.** From a drinking song (Isa 22:13; 28:7–10).

57:1–2. Only by faith (40:31) can we know that "the person of justice comes into peace" (44:28). Tr-Isa is not thinking of a happy immortality, as that doctrine is clarified only in the 2d cent. (Dan 12:1–3). **3–8.** The language is bitter. **5.** *in heat:* The Hebr word generally refers to animals at mating time, a crude expression for humans. It refers to the sensuous rites of the high places (Deut 12:2; 2 Kgs 17:10; Hos 4:11–19; Jer 2:23–27; 3:2). Child sacrifice is also introduced (2 Kgs 3:27; 16:3–4; Jer 7:31). **6.** *smooth stones, wadi, portion:* The Hebr alliteration bursts with pent-up anger. **8.** While the references to fertility are blatant enough, the exact sense of several words is unclear. One word means "remembrance" but it has the same Hebr consonants as "male." Another word, often translated "symbol," is the Hebr *yād,* "hand," the phallic symbol in Canaanite literature and in the Bible (cf. *TDOT* 6. 393–426). **9.** *king:* Refers to Melech, the god of the underworld to whom firstborn male children were sacrificed (v 5). **13.** *inherit:* Relates to wadi in v 6, to indicate ownership of the promised land. Word parallels of vv 1,6,13 with Ps 16 lead us to detect a note of hope within an otherwise dismal reflection on the state of religion.

53   (b) COMFORTING THE FAITHFUL (57:14–21). While vv 14–19 resonate the style and interests of Dt-Isa (repetition of first words, elaborate opening address, and a joyful message) the last two verses echo the more somber tones of Tr-Isa (Hanson, *Dawn of Apocalyptic* 78). **14.** As in Isa 40:3–4 a mysterious voice fills the air. While Dt-Isa envisages a glorious manifestation of Yahweh along the way, Tr-Isa is concerned lest the people stumble on their way. **15.** God is acclaimed as "Exalted," "Eternal," and "Holy," yet dwelling with the "oppressed" (cf. Isa 6 and Ps 113). The Hebr word for "dwelling" (*šākan*) recalls the early habitation of Yahweh in a desert tent and Yahweh's enthronement over the ark and mercy-seat (Exod 25:10-22; 40:34-38). **16.** Ends dramatically. Redemption reaches back into the responsibility of the creator. **17.** *hiding myself:* Nothing comes closer to eternal damnation than the silence of God. A different appreciation of the "hidden God" is given in 54:8; Tr-Isa did not simply copy from the master. **18.** *I give complete comfort:* The opening words of 40:1 are combined with a variation of the word *šālôm.* **21.** A floating fragment, more at home here than at 48:20.

54   (c) TRUE AND FALSE FASTING (58:1-14). This speech begins typically as a prophetic judgment (Amos 4:6-12; 5:21-27; Isa 1:2-3,10-17), but Tr-Isa does not conclude with a verdict of guilt; instead there is an announcement of salvation (vv 8-12). **1-7.** The judgment speech is carefully crafted: a formal summons (v 1), an indictment (vv 2-4a) and a verdict of probation (v 4b), another indictment (v 5) and a warning (vv 6-7). The speech centers on fasting, even though the purpose is much broader. Fasting reaches far back into Israelite history, enabling people to release their grief at times of bereavement (2 Sam 1:12; 3:35) and national tragedy (Josh 7:6; Judg 20:26). During and after the exile fasting days multiplied (Zech 7:1-5; 8:18-19; Joel). Eventually one great day of fasting was placed on *yôm kippur* (Lev 16; cf. de Vaux, *AI* 507-10). Fasting also occurred in the joyful moment of ecstatic prayer (Exod 34:28; 1 Kgs 19:8). Tr-Isa's legal speech is held together by two key words, each with double entendre: (1) *ḥāpēṣ* (vv 2a,2c,3c)—Israel's *desire* for external ritual and fasting contrasts with Yahweh's *desire* for compassion toward the poor; (2) *'ānâ*—intensely devout in *afflicting* oneself with fasting (v 3) yet neglecting *the afflicted* and needy in your midst (v 7)! See M. L. Barré, *BTB* 15 (1985) 94-97. **2-4.** *seek me:* A technical phrase for going to the sanctuary (Amos 5:4-6; Zeph 1:6; Isa 8:19), yet ironically the people's disposition turns them away from truly seeking the Lord. **3.** The Hebr words for "fast" (*sôm*) and "day" (*yôm*) sound almost alike. *drive all your workers:* In Exod 3:7 the expression refers to Egyptian slave masters. **5.** Tr-Isa lampoons the idea that cultic activity and fasting could turn this day into "a day pleasing to the Lord" (49:6; 61:2). Fasting enables comfortable people to share the lot of the hungry poor and from this hunger to look to God as the source of life and nourishment. To fast and yet neglect the poor perverts religion. **7.** In Matt 25:31-46 the eschatological judgment depends on the kindly acts mentioned here.

55   **8-14.** This announcement of salvation is tied into the preceding piece by key words: call out (vv 1,5,9); oppressed (vv 6,9); bread (vv 7,10); afflicted (vv 3,7,10); pleasure (vv 2,3,13); day (vv 3,5,13). At least stylistically this turn toward a new day has already begun within the sinful hearts. Again Tr-Isa manifests close ties with his master: light (vv 8,10 and 42:16; 51:4); Zion (the object of this announcement and 49:14-54:17); glory of the Lord (v 8 and 40:5); justice or vindication (v 8 and 40:14; 54:14,17). Verses 8b and 12a paraphrase 52:12b and 61:4a. When lowliness unites all men and women, God's glorious presence shall rest upon them. **10-11.** When fasting makes the wealthy poor in spirit and when the poor impart to the wealthy their attitude of humble waiting upon God, then God will answer with "glory," "light," and "springs of water." **12.** The poem was clearly composed before the reconstruction of the city walls in 445 (Neh 6:15), possibly before the rebuilding of the Temple in 515 (Ezra 6:16); for other symbolic names given Jerusalem, see Isa 1:26; 60:14; Ezek 48:35. **13-14.** Associating sabbath (Exod 20:8-11; Deut 5:12-15) with concern for the poor explains the addition of these verses. Verse 14 repeats liturgical

refrains found in Deut 32:13; Hab 3:10,19 and Amos 4:13; its final words repeat 40:5.

56   (d) INDICTMENT, LAMENT, AND VICTORY (59:1-21). A meditation on the meaning of the Lord's justice (cf. D. Kendall, *ZAW* 96 [1984] 391-405): indictment for abusing the Lord's justice (vv 1-8); the community laments its sins against this justice (vv 9-15a); victory for Yahweh the divine warrior who redresses this lack of justice (vv 15b-20). Verse 21 is a prose addition, collecting various biblical words of promise, esp. from 55:3 and 61:8. **1-8.** Tr-Isa defends God against false accusations (cf. 50:1-2). **3.** Israel is charged with total depravity, including the unjust use of the death penalty. **5.** They brood over designs as pernicious as adders' eggs, as flimsy as spiders' webs. **7-8.** With no qualm of conscience, they run in the way of sin. Dt-Isa's favorite word, "way" (40:3-5; 41:17-20), acquires strong ethical dimensions.

9-15a. A community confession of guilt admits that sin had put God's justice far from them (40:14). **12.** Parts of this verse are incorporated into Ps 51:5; both pieces reveal a rich vocabulary for sin. **13.** *rebellion:* Violations of charity, justice, and honesty amount to a denial of God. **15b-20.** Tr-Isa combines a very ancient cultic tradition, honoring Yahweh as warrior and king (51:9-10; Exod 15; Ps 24) with the prophetic demand for justice. **17.** The symbolic use of armor has widely influenced later biblical writing (Wis 5:17-23; 1 Thess 5:8; Eph 6:14-17). *glory:* Identical with God's redemptive presence (40:3). **20.** *God Redeemer:* Cf. 41:14; 43:1; 44:22. **21.** An endorsement by a later editor (cf. 50:10; 54:17b), a bridge to the following set of poems which include the spirit's anointing of Tr-Isa (61:1-3). "You" can apply to the entire community who receive the spirit (Ezek 37:1-14) or to a group of prophets (Deut 18:15; Isa 42:1).

57   (C) The Glorious New Zion (60:1-62:12). These songs are closest in spirit and vocabulary to Dt-Isa. Tr-Isa sees a restoration of all Israel (60:10b,15; 40:1-2; 54:7-8), gathered from distant places (60:4,9; 43:4-7) and receiving the wealth of the world (60:5-7,16; 45:14), so that even foreign kings serve Zion (60:13; 54:11-12). Israel in turn becomes a light to other nations (60:3; 49:6). Zion enjoys security from hostile invasions (60:12,14; 62:8; 41:11-13; 51:21-23), relieved of any shame of the past (62:4-5; 45:17; 54:4-8). Through Yahweh's eternal covenant (61:8; 54:10; 55:3), ancient promises are fulfilled (60:22; 49:19-22), for the glory of Yahweh (60:16,21; 48:11; 49:26b). See Hanson, *Dawn of Apocalyptic* 60-61. Yet there are also important differences from chaps. 40-55: all connection with world events disappears, like Dt-Isa's preoccupation with Cyrus and Babylon. Instead, Tr-Isa reverts to ancient names for countries in Gen. While Dt-Isa was indifferent to Temple and cult, Tr-Isa announces a new universal order of priests (61:6). This is a distinctive move away from Ezek, who restricted priesthood to the Zadokites (Ezek 40:46; 43:19; 44:10-31).

58   (a) GLORY OF THE NEW ZION (60:1-22). After a magnificent introduction (vv 1-3), all parts of the world process to Zion (vv 4-9) for rebuilding the city (vv 10-16) amid splendid prosperity (vv 17-22). **1-3.** Typical of Dt-Isa, the song opens with a double imperative: "arise! glow!" God is radiating a dazzling presence from within the city (Deut 33:2; Mal 3:19). Like the sunrise in this area, darkness immediately surrenders to brilliant light; there is neither dawn nor dusk. "Glory," repeated eight times as a noun or vb., pervades this chap. (cf. Exod 40:34; 1 Kgs 8:11; Ezek 43:1-9). These lines may be the source of Rev 12 (A. Feuillet, *RB* 66 [1959] 55-96) and of John 1:4-18 (Herbert, *Isaiah 40-66* 158).

4–9. Different from Isa 2:2–4 and Mic 4:1–3, the nations come to Jerusalem to rebuild the city, not simply to receive instruction from the Lord at the Temple. Nor is the focus future-oriented and centripetal as in Hag 2:6–9, a text composed very close to the time of Tr-Isa. This strophe opens by quoting almost verbatim 49:18,22. **6–7.** People from the Arabian peninsula associated with Abraham and the earliest ancestral days (Gen 25:1–4,13–15; 28:9; 36:3; Jer 6:20; Ezek 27:21; see also *ANET* 298–300) now participate in their ancient patrimony. One day all nations will become God's children through faith (Rom 4:17). Matt 2:1–12 weaves these and other themes into the infancy narrative. This passage thereby came into the ancient church liturgy for the feast of Epiphany. **9a.** A quotation of 51:5. *Tarshish:* Biblical references allude to a place in Africa (1 Kgs 22:49) or in southern Spain (1 Kgs 10:22; Jonah 1:3). Tarshish may connote here large stately ships ready for long journeys (Isa 2:16).

10–16. This strophe sings of peace and reconciliation (Rev 21:24–27), with a more kindly spirit than 1 Chr 22:2. It will be reversed by the hard line taken in Ezra 4:1–3. **12.** A prose addition, probably from Zech 14:16–19 (Kissane, *Book* 268), disturbing both the poetic style and the serene spirit of these lines. **15.** The charges of 49:14–15 or 54:6–7 are forgotten. **16b.** A quotation from 49:26. **17–22.** Justice is blended into an apocalyptic vision of the future (cf. Rev 21:23; 22:5).

59   (b) ANOINTING OF THE PROPHET (61:1–3). With these words Jesus announced that the messianic era had come (Luke 4:16–21). Originally they referred to one of the leaders of the early postexilic Isaian school; the targum, in fact, introduces this monologue with: "Thus says the prophet." There are many points of contact with the earlier major servant songs: soliloquy as in the second and third songs; spirit anointing (42:1); mission of mercy (42:2–3,6–7); year of favor (49:8). These contacts highlight the unique importance of the major servant songs.

1. Each phrase is rich in biblical tradition. *spirit:* Signals the special action of God (Judg 3:10; 11:19; 1 Sam 10:5–13). The spirit had been promised to the messianic king (Isa 11:1–2) and later was assured to all the messianic people (Joel 3; Zech 12:10). Ezek revived the important role of spirit and is also responsible for a dramatic priestly turn to prophecy. Tr-Isa perceives the spirit outside of priesthood and royalty, to anoint prophecy. Cf. *DBT* 569–76; H.-W. Wolff, *Anthropology of OT* (Phl, 1974) 32–39. *anointed:* This word is linked with preaching and hearing; it designates an interior enlightening to know God's word and a strengthening to follow it. *to bring glad tidings:* See 40:9; 41:27. *lowly:* See 51:21. *release to prisoners:* The first word can also be translated "light" (KB 775) as also in Luke 4:18. The meaning in both cases is the same: Prisoners are led out of dark dungeons to full daylight. Throughout the poem Tr-Isa looks to the total salvation of God's people—bodily and spiritually, individually and socially. **2.** *year of favor:* See 49:8. An extraordinary jubilee has arrived, and all the land reverts back to the Creator, who distributes it equally and bountifully (Lev 25:10; cf. R. North, *Sociology of the Biblical Jubilee* [Rome, 1954]). *vindication:* Almost always used of God, repairing the injured or weakened force of salvation (34:8; 59:17). Some transls. follow a Ugaritic root meaning "to rescue," which also explains the LXX and Luke 4:19. *comfort:* The opening word of Dt-Isa is repeated (40:1). **3.** *oaks of justice:* See 40:14.

60   (c) GLORY OF THE NEW ZION (61:4–62:9). Tr-Isa sings exaltedly of Zion emerging out of the ashes of destruction: a new Zion, a new priesthood (vv 4–9);

hymn (vv 10–11); new espousal (62:1–5); disciples of Tr-Isa (vv 6–9). **6a.** *priests of the Lord:* This text does not necessarily abolish a separate order of levitical priests, just as the priestly quality of all Israel left it intact (Exod 19:6; 1 Pet 2:9). Tr-Isa is opening the ranks of priesthood to non-Levites (Isa 56:6 and 66:21). This decision, though radical, has precedents. Very possibly the Zadokites, whose privileges were forcefully defended by Ezek (40:46; 44:10–16), were originally pagan, Jerusalem priests. When David conquered the city, he made their leader coequal with the high priest descended from Aaron (2 Sam 8:17). Kings, who were certainly not of the tribe of Levi, also functioned as priests on state occasions (2 Sam 6:11–19; 1 Kgs 3:4; Ps 110:4). See A. Cody, *A History of OT Priesthood* (AnBib 35; Rome, 1969) 88–93; *DBT* 459–64. **6b–7.** The Hebr text is disturbed, and the thought clashes with the otherwise mild spirit of this section. **8.** Again there occurs the covenantal acclamation of "I, the Lord" (41:4). *an eternal covenant:* See 54:10; 55:3; 59:21. **9.** The promises to Abraham are finally fulfilled (Gen 12:2). **10–11.** The targum correctly interprets the thought, adding: "Thus says Jerusalem." Jerusalem celebrates the fulfillment of love between herself and Yahweh (54:5–8; Jer 33:10–11; Rev 19:7,9; John 2:1–11). Justice springs from the earth, but "the Lord God" remains the source of all life (45:8; 53:2).

61   **62:1–5.** God breaks the silence of many years (42:14) in this song of "splendid impatience" (Herbert, *Isaiah 40–66* 166). **1.** Zion's "vindication" (cf. 61:2) "breaks forth" with the suddenness of the desert dawn (60:1). Never did this hope seem closer to fulfillment than on the feast of Tabernacles, when lights were kindled "at the place of the water-drawing" so bright that "there was not a courtyard in Jerusalem that was not illumined by the light of the place" (*m. Sukk.* 51a). **3.** Muilenburg (*IB* 5. 718) refers to the ancient practice of a god's wearing a crown patterned after the city walls. Yahweh holds such a crown in his hands. **4.** Names like "Forsaken" ('*āzûbâ*) and "My Delight in her" (*ḥepṣî-bâ*) are known in Israelite history (1 Kgs 22:42; 2 Kgs 21:1). "Espoused" (*bĕ'ûlâ*) as a name for Israel means that Hos 2:18 is forgotten and the association with fertility cults is no problem. **5.** The theme of Yahweh as spouse is not just repeated (49:14; 50:1), but adulterous Israel is restored to that joyful, innocent age of long ago when she was the virgin spouse of God.

6–9. The prophet is extending his ministry to a circle of followers. They are called "watchmen," sentinels on the walls of Jerusalem (cf. Isa 21:11–12; 40:9; 52:8), but their role is no longer to sound the alarm at the approach of invaders but to be "reminders" of the Lord's merciful promises and deeds. This office was an official one, functioning as professional or official recorders (2 Sam 8:16; Isa 36:3). **8.** *strong arm:* See Exod 6:6; Deut 4:34; Isa 51:5,9. The curses for disobedience will be removed (Deut 18:15–68) and protection will be assured against marauders. **9.** The harvesting especially of grapes may allude to a perpetual feast of Tabernacles (Deut 16:13–15).

(d) FINAL REFLECTION (62:10–12). **10.** The imperatives, sometimes doubled, echo the excitement of 40:1–11. This announcement of salvation concludes with a litany of titles for Zion in v 12. These final verses catch the spirit of Tabernacles and especially the joy of the glorious procession on the first day.

62   **(D) From Sorrow to a New Heaven and a New Earth (63:1–66:16).** The anthological style of chaps. 56–66 shows up strikingly. The movement is clearly toward the victory of Yahweh in a new heaven and new earth, to be reflected in a new Temple and new priesthood, but the somber tones of chaps. 56–59 are sustained.

(a) THE SOLITARY CONQUEROR (63:1–6). One of the strongest, most compact poems in all Isa. This violent portrayal of God's victory over Edom fits with other prophetic oracles against the nations (Amos 1:3–2:16; Isa 13–23; 47; Jer 46–51), yet it outdoes them in hatred. The fierce image of the Lord's garments splashed with enemy blood almost pushes the poem into apocalyptic literature (cf. 60:19–20). Yet there are clear enough ties with Tr-Isa or one of his disciples (cf. 59:15b–20). The enemies of God are identified as Edom (cf. *EDB* 620–24; *IDB* 2. 24–26). Descendants of Esau (Gen 36), they lived SSE of the Dead Sea. These people took advantage of the fall of Jerusalem in 587 to raid and loot Judah (Ezek 25:12–14). Hatred for them is expressed in Isa 34:1–17; Jer 49:7–22; Joel 4:19; Obad; Ps 137:7; Mal 1:2–5. Here Edom represents every foreign enemy of God's designs for Israel, a symbolic word like Huns or Nazis in the world today. An interchange of questions (vv 1ab,2) and answers (vv 1c,3–6) manifests careful structuring. **1.** A watchman or prophet (62:6) sees someone approaching from Bozrah, a major city of Edom (Amos 1:12; Jer 49:13). Bozrah means vintage time and intensifies the image here of winepressing. In answer to the question in v 1c (almost identical with 49:19c), the divine "I" rings out, "announcing vindication" and "salvation." **2.** *red:* In Hebrew the same consonants as Edom (Gen 25:25). **3.** In this apocalyptic struggle God single-handedly defeats the enemy. **4.** The poet contrasts the terrifying day of vengeance with the happy jubilee year (cf. 61:2). **5.** A variation on 59:16. **6b.** Cf. Jer 25:15–29; Zech 12:2.

63 (b) CONFESSION OF SIN (63:7–64:11). To pray in the devastated Jerusalem Temple (Jer 41:5–6) was at best a protestation against despair (Ps 79; Lam; cf. Hanson, *Dawn of Apocalyptic* 86–87; Herbert, *Isaiah 40–66* 172). Similar to other communal laments, this one includes a "creed" of Yahweh's great redemptive acts for Israel, imploring God to renew them (Ps 44; 74). The poem subdivides: 63:7–14, glorious deeds of Yahweh; 63:8–64:4a, lament; 64:4b–6, confession and appeal; 64:7–11, hope.

7–10. A strong faith in the Lord's glorious deeds stirs up questions at the same time as it sustains the questioner in God's presence. **7.** The opening verse begins and concludes with *ḥesed,* a dutiful love springing from a blood bond and leading to family obligations (43:1–7; chap. 54). Liturgical acts allowed Israelites to participate in God's remembrance of great redemptive acts (Exod 28:12; 30:11–16; Lev 2:3; Num 10:8–10; cf. B. S. Childs, *Memory and Tradition in Israel* [Naperville, 1963]). The memory of divine favors intensifies in strong crescendo; Israel is called (v 8), protected (v 9a), exalted (v 9b), delivered (vv 11–12), and safely led (vv 13–14). **8b–9.** God saves without mediators (Exod 33:14; cf. R. C. Dentan, *VT* 13 [1963] 34–51). If the passage is read without the negatives, according to another Hebr tradition, then the reference is to Exod 23:20–21; 33:41; Deut 4:37. **10.** *grieved his holy spirit:* God is affected by resistance to the prophets (43:24). In the OT "holy spirit" occurs elsewhere only in Ps 51:13 and Wis 1:5; 9:17.

11–14. Five participles cast this section in the style of a joyful hymn (40:28; 42:5), but that fact only sharpens the sense of frustration. **11.** *where is he?:* The question is not being asked as though spoken by foreigners through ridicule (Pss 42:4; 79:10). It lays bare the agony of an honest, humble person (Jer 2:8). *bringing up out of the sea:* An allusion to the naming of Moses in Exod 2:10 and to

the chaotic sea, whom God defeats in saving Israel (51:9–11; Exod 15:5,8). Heb 13:20 applies this text to Christ's resurrection.

64 **63:15–64:4a** [63:15–64:5a, *RSV*]. The style of lament becomes very pronounced. **15.** *look down from heaven:* As in another psalm of agony (Ps 80:15). **16.** *you are our father:* Twice the psalmist defends his status as an authentic Israelite and true child of God (cf. 64:7; Exod 4:22; Hos 11:1). *were Abraham not to recognize us:* A very different viewpoint from 51:1–2. **17.** *servants:* The faithful disciples of Dt- and Tr-Isa. **19b** [= 64:1, *RSV*]. The psalmist implores God's personal intervention, pleading for a theophany more wondrous than Sinai (Exod 19; Deut 4:32–36; cf. Mark 1:10). **64:1** [v 2, *RSV*]. *fire:* Symbol of God's wondrous presence in Exod 19:18 but here of divine anger (42:25). **3.** Cf. 1 Cor 1:9. **4a.** The customary prophetic insistence on justice (cf. chap. 59). **4b–6** [5b–7, *RSV*]. God has abandoned Israel to their guilt. **5.** *polluted rags:* Implies cultural shame and ceremonial uncleanness (Lev 15:19–24). **7–11** [8–12, *RSV*]. The rhetoric of this desperate appeal is emphatically, "Now, on the contrary, Yahweh, our father, You." The words "now" and "you" sound almost alike in Hebrew, so that one reinforces the other. A stubborn faith indeed (Ps 22:5–6)! **8c.** Equally insistent: "Behold! Look! We pray you! We your people, all of us!"

65 (c) TRUE AND FALSE SERVANTS (65:1–25). Editorially the final two chaps. fit neatly in place. (a) To the urgent petition of the preceding section to rend the heavens and come down, the Lord responds at once: "I am ready." The theme of call and answer occurs repeatedly: vv 1–2,10b,12,24. Many points of contact knit chap. 65 with the preceding section, evident by comparing 64:6 with 65:1b,24; or 64:11b with 65:6. (b) The condemnation of false worship resembles chap. 57, only this time true and false worshipers are clearly dividing the ranks of Israelites. (c) An *inclusio* or repetition of key words unites vv 1–2 and 10,12, and 24. Chap. 65 divides into a judgment oracle (vv 1–12) and a salvation oracle (vv 13–25). The section tends toward a protoapocalyptic composition as it sweeps beyond earthly politics and even Temple worship into a new heaven and new earth. It is different, therefore, from Hag 2:6–9 or even Zech 14. While the latter apocalyptic movement was located within loyalists to the Temple and its priests, that of Dt- and Tr-Isa perceived the Lord's presence extending beyond Jerusalem into the cosmos.

66 **1–12.** Despite some irregularities, the judgment oracle can be subdivided: indictment (vv 1–5), sentencing (vv 6–7), promise of salvation (vv 8–10), new indictment and sentencing (vv 11–12). **1–5.** Hebr grammar delicately nuances the thought. The niphal or passive conjugation expresses emotions which God allowed to react upon himself in appealing to Israel (cf. *GKC* §51c). **1.** *nation:* Hebr *gôy* is used often enough of the Israelite people (Isa 1:4; 26:15; 58:2; differently in Rom 10:20–21). **2.** *spread out my hands:* God stands in a gesture not of supplication but of welcome. This final appeal, when repudiated, evokes a terrible sentence of guilt (vv 5–7). **3.** *sacrifices in the groves:* Canaanite nature cults that contaminated preexilic Israel (Amos 2:7–8; Jer 2:8–3:5) were cropping up again (57:3–12). *burning incense:* See Jer 1:16; 7:9. *eating swine's flesh:* Condemned by Lev 11:7 and Deut 14:8. **6–7.** To target Temple priests and worshipers in this condemnation, Tr-Isa weaves in technical words for the cult. God cannot remain "quiet," lest mercy be confused with weakness and the triumph of good be delayed forever.

8–10. The prophet returns to the servant theme (seven times in vv 8–16); they will survive the sad ordeal of being crushed like grapes, to become the true descendants of Jacob and the receptors of the patriarchal promises (Gen 28:13). The promised land will again extend from the Valley of Achor in the SE corner where Joshua began his conquest (Josh 7:24; Hos 2:17), to the Plain of Sharon, then a swampy area on the NW coast beneath Mt. Carmel (Isa 35:2). **11–12.** The prophet points to "You!" who have committed all these crimes and who worship Gad and Meni. Gad means Fortune (*daimonion* in the LXX); it is the name of a Syrian god (Josh 11:17; 15:37) venerated in Phoenicia, Dura Europos, and Greece. Meni (Destiny) is the name of an Egyptian goddess of spring and fertility—(see *ANET* 250). **12.** God replies again to the charge of silent neglect (49:14; 64:6; 65:1).

67   **13–16.** The Temple personnel experience the reversal of the blessings of Gen 12:2–3 and turn into a curse symbol (Jer 29:22). The last line of v 15 and the beginning of v 16 are damaged in the MT; 1QIsaᵃ leaves a blank. They can be emended to read: "My servants will call out a new name. . . . God is the Amen." Hebr *'mn* means to be strong, reliable, and truthful. **17–25.** A panorama of joy extends before us. The verb *bārā'*, "to create," indicates that God is acting alone; by the active participle, Tr-Isa stresses that creation is happening *now*. *new heavens and a new earth:* God is completely transforming the cosmos. This phrase is familiar in apocryphal literature (2 Esdr 6:16). **22.** The LXX and the targum read: "according to the days of the tree of life," clearly referring to paradise (Gen 2:9; Rev 22:2,14). **24.** Unlike 58:3 and 64:12, Yahweh is neither silent nor indifferent to the cry of Israel. **25.** The Davidic Messiah, despite other contacts in this passage with Isa 11, is passed over in silence (cf. 11:1).

68   (d) CONTROVERSY OVER THE NEW TEMPLE (66:1–16). Verses 1–4, indictment and sentencing; v 5, salvation; v 6, judgment; vv 7–14, salvation; vv 15–16, judgment. Despite this oscillation, the parts are carefully stitched together. The final two judgment scenes enclose words of salvation. The mood and even the vocabulary of the preceding poem continue in this new section. The same eschatological war is being fought, but now the sides divide between the good and the evil in Israel. Tr-Isa argues against followers of Ezekiel, Haggai, and Zechariah, who rejected not only Gentiles but even those Jews who never went into exile; see Hanson, *Dawn of Apocalyptic* 170–86.

1–5. The prophetic crusade against formalism in worship is taken up again (Amos 5:21–25; Hos 6:6). While Tr-Isa is not totally rejecting the Temple, he is insisting according to a long tradition (Ps 29:10; 1 Kgs 8:27) that the Lord's first home is in the heavens. The Jerusalem Temple is only his footstool. Tr-Isa is clearly scaling down the central role of the Temple as heard in the preaching of Hag 2:6–9 (cf. Matt 5:34–35; Acts 7:48–50). **3.** Many translators, following the LXX, turn these lines into a series of comparisons (*NAB, RSV*) to become the fiercest condemnation of Temple worship in the Bible. Scholars like Muilenburg, Dhorme, and Scullion remain closer to the MT: "slaughtering an ox, killing a man; sacrificing a lamb, breaking a dog's neck"—it is all happening in the Temple. **4.** *living among the tombs:* To consult the dead (Isa 8:19). **5.** Encouragement for Tr-Isa and his servant-disciples.

69   **6.** *a sound:* Hebr *qôl* can refer to thunder (Pss 29; 42:8). Two short units (vv 6 and 15–16) elegantly surround the announcement of salvation (vv 7–14) with epiphanies of the warrior God (cf. 63:1–6). **7–9.** The wondrous birth of the messianic people continues a long biblical tradition (Mic 4:8–10; 5:1–2; Zeph 3:14–20; Isa 7:14; 54:1; 62:4) and, in turn, influences future writers

(2 Esdr 9–10; 1QH 3:9–10; Rev 12:3–5). God is always the unique source of life, most especially in the eschatological age. **10–14.** This stanza sings with the ecstatic joy of Dt-Isa; the poet is continually crying out "Rejoice!" to the new Jerusalem. Joy permeates many poems of Tr-Isa (56:7; 60:18; 61:3,7,10; 65:13–19), a fact easily overlooked in his strident opposition to false Temple worship. God's children nurse at the breast of Jerusalem—a lovely image of peace and contentment. For the motherhood of God see 42:14; 45:10; 49:15 (M. I. Gruber, *RB* 90 [1983] 351–59). **15–16.** Tr-Isa adapts Jer 4:13 to Yahweh's victory. "The Lord comes" with booming thunder and crackling fire (Isa 10:17–18; Ps 97:1–5), with chariots and clouds (Ps 18:10; Hab 3:8); people are "slain by the Lord" (Zeph 2:12; Jer 25:33). These symbols for the Lord's total victory for justice continue into the NT: 2 Thess 1:8; Rev 18:21–14; 19:17–21.

70   (E) **Foreigners at Home in God's House (66:17–24).** This section rounds out Tr-Isa and forms an *inclusio* with basic ideas in 56:1–6 (outsiders within the Temple) and 56:9–57:13 (idolatrous rites and false leaders in the Temple). **17.** Devotees follow a priest or priestess into a sacred grove for a secret idolatrous rite involving forbidden food (Lev 11:29). **18a.** *and I their deeds and their thoughts she [or it] comes:* The MT is unintelligible; cf. transls. **18b.** *glory:* As seen by Gentiles, the phrase is reminiscent of 40:5; as an object of pilgrimage in the Temple, the image is characteristic of Tr-Isa. **19.** *sign:* A link with the final verse of chaps. 40–55 and with 7:10; 8:18. The "sign" centers on the survival of Jerusalem, to become the object of the new exodus for Diaspora Jews and even for Gentiles. We glimpse a triumphal procession from all directions: "Tarshish" in southern Spain (Isa 60:9); "Put and Lud" in Africa (Ezek 27:10; 30:5; Gen 10:6,13); "Meshech and Rosh" (text here is uncertain; cf. Ezek 38:2; 39:1); "Tubal" near the Black Sea; and "Javan," Gk settlers in the Ionian Islands (Ezek 27:13,19). **21.** *some:* It is not clear if Tr-Isa understands these as Diaspora Jews or as Gentiles, as both are mentioned in the preceding verse. Because of the *inclusio* of this section with 56:1–8, "Gentiles" is the favored interpretation. The book ends then with a most radical announcement. Gentiles take their place in the priesthood. Just when Ezekiel, Haggai, and Zechariah were restricting priesthood to the Zadokites and dispossessing other Levites of important cultic functions (Ezek 40:46; 44:10–16), Tr-Isa extends priesthood.

22–24. This eschatological setting will become an eternal home or place of worship for "your offspring and name" (Rev 21:1–8). **23.** *all flesh shall come:* While in 40:5 humanity admires the glory of the Lord within Israel's new exodus, here they come to worship at the home of the Lord's glory in the Temple. **24.** The final verse is terrifying. "All flesh" (cf. v 23) "shall go out" of Jerusalem to the surrounding Hinnom Valley (Gehenna), to witness the burning corpses of rebellious people. Human sacrifice was once practiced here (Jer 7:31). It eventually became the city's refuse heap, so that even today the exit into this area is called "the dung gate." The proximity of the greatest joy and the greatest horror is typical of the eschatological battle, even as announced by Christ at the end of his ministry (Matt 25:31–46). Many texts are inspired by these lines (Jdt 16:17; Dan 12:2; Mark 9:48; see J. Chaine, *DBSup* 3. 572–73; A. Feuillet, *DBSup* 4. 719). The passage has strongly colored popular stories about hell, as Isa 14:12–20 inspired the account of Lucifer. The rabbis directed that when this chapter was read in the synagogue, part of v 23 be repeated after v 24 (cf. Mal 3:24). To hear the stern warning in good time prepares us well for the glory promised in the book of Isaiah.

22

HAGGAI
ZECHARIAH MALACHI

Aelred Cody, O.S.B.

BIBLIOGRAPHY

1 Ackroyd, P. R., *Exile and Restoration* (London, 1968). Chary, T., *Aggée-Zacharie-Malachie* (SB; Paris, 1969). Elliger, K., *Das Buch der zwölf kleinen Propheten 2* (ATD 25; 6th ed.; Göttingen, 1967). Galling, K., *Studien zur Geschichte Israels im persischen Zeitalter* (Tübingen, 1964). Mason, R., *The Books of Haggai, Zechariah and Malachi* (CBC; Cambridge, 1977); "The Prophets of the Restoration," *Israel's Prophetic Tradition* (Fest.

P. R. Ackroyd; ed. R. Coggins, *et al.*; Cambridge, 1982) 137–54. Mitchell, H. G., J. M. P. Smith and J. A. Bewer, *Haggai, Zechariah, Malachi, and Jonah* (ICC; NY, 1912). Robinson, T. H. and F. Horst, *Die zwölf kleinen Propheten* (HAT 1/14; 3d ed.; Tübingen, 1964). Rudolph, W., *Haggai, Sacharja 1–8, Sacharja 9–14, Maleachi* (KAT 13/4; Gütersloh, 1976). Stuhlmueller, C., "Haggai, Zechariah, Malachi," *JBC* 387–401.

HAGGAI

BIBLIOGRAPHY

2 (Also → 1 above.) Beuken, W. A. M., *Haggai-Sacharja 1–8* (SSN 10; Assen, 1967). Beyse, K.-M., *Serubbabel und die Königserwartungen der Propheten Haggai und Sacharja* (AzT 1/48; Stuttgart, 1972). Hesse, F., "Haggai," *Verbannung und Heimkehr* (Fest. W. Rudolph;

ed. A. Kuschke; Tübingen, 1961) 109–34. Petersen, D. L., *Haggai and Zechariah 1–8* (OTL Phl, 1984). Siebeneck, R. T., "The Messianism of Aggeus and Proto-Zacharias," *CBQ* 19 (1957) 312–28. Thomas, D. W., "The Book of Haggai," *IB* 6. 1035–49.

INTRODUCTION

3 **(I) The Prophet and His Situation.** The oracles were all delivered in the beginning of Darius I's long reign over the Persian Empire (521–486). Darius, more conciliatory than his predecessor, Cambyses II (529–522), renewed the policies, introduced by Cyrus II (538–530), which allowed persons deported by the Babylonians to return to their homelands, and which aimed at conciliating the loyalty of the empire's subject peoples by allowing them a certain amount of local government and by granting them freedom to practice their own religions. There is a fairly good consensus that not many Judeans returned from exile during Cyrus's reign and that the first large groups returned after Cambyses had finished his conquest of Egypt in 525. Not long afterward, when the oracles of Hag and of Zech 1–8 were being delivered, Judah already had its ethnically Judean civil leader, Zerubbabel, and hierarchical leader,

Joshua. The war between Persia and Egypt must have disturbed Judah socially and economically, for the Persian armies had to pass through Judah. The struggles for power in the Persian Empire itself continued after Cambyses' death in 522, even after Darius had consolidated his own fundamental position. They must have had an unsettling effect on Judeans—more, no doubt, on those in Babylonia but also on those in Judah. All this surely contributed to the tendency of the people in Judah to be more concerned with their own selfish interests than they were with work for the advancement of their society and its religious institutions (Hag 1:2–9).

4 It was in this situation that Haggai found himself around 520. It is generally assumed that he was one of the exiled Judeans who had recently returned to Judah, but we have no evidence confirming that. In Ezra 5:1–2; 6:14 we are told that he was successful in moving the Judeans to action in rebuilding the Temple. It has been suggested that he was a cultic prophet, but for him the Temple's importance lay not as much in its being a place of legitimate worship as in its being the place of Yahweh's presence on earth, and if he had any high interest in matters of worship it does not appear in the book. The civil governor, Zerubbabel, is given an imminent role as God's elect. In this respect Haggai might be thought to resemble a court prophet, like Nathan in 2 Sam 7. For Haggai, the future is the future of Judah, restored with a Davidic ruler and with God once again dwelling in his earthly Temple.

5   (II) Composition. Haggai's oracles are set into the editorial framework of 1:1,3,12,13a,14–15; 2:1–2,10,20, with 2:4 and the date in 2:18 probably also from the editor's hand, and with 2:5 as a secondary gloss which may be still later. The editorial framework is not likely to have been written by Haggai himself, but it was probably composed not long after his oracles. The editor has made no comment on the oracle to Zerubbabel

(2:21–23). The other oracles all seem to be addressed to the people of Judah, but in the framework the editor has enhanced the roles of Zerubbabel and of Joshua by having the oracles addressed primarily to them and by emphasizing the part they played in getting work on the Temple started (1:12–14). W. A. M. Beuken (*Haggai-Sacharja 1–8* 27–48, 80–83) sees the origin of the framework in the circle in which 1–2 Chr were compiled, but R. A. Mason (*VT* 27 [1977] 413–21) finds more significant kinship with deuteronomistic circles, with Ezek, and with the Pentateuchal P.

6   (III) Outline.

 (I) Hard Times from Neglect of the Temple (1:1–11)
 (II) Work on the Temple Is Started (1:12–15a)
 (III) A Good Future from Building the Temple
       (1:15b–2:23)
       (A) Glory in the Temple (1:15b–2:9)
       (B) A Priestly Decision (2:10–14)
       (C) Agricultural Prosperity (2:15–19)
       (D) Zerubbabel, God's Signet Ring (2:20–23)

COMMENTARY

7   (I) Hard Times from Neglect of the Temple (1:1–11). In v 2, editorially introduced (v 1) as a divine word to Zerubbabel and Joshua, the problematic occasion of Haggai's prophetic activity is announced. Another editorial introduction (v 3) leads to the first oracle (vv 4–11).
8   1. The date = 29 August 520. In the persons of the two leaders at this initial stage of the postexilic restoration continuity is established with leadership in preexilic Judean society. Zerubbabel is said to be the son of Shealtiel, who, according to 1 Chr 3:17, was the eldest son (and thus the crown prince) of the Davidic king Jehoiachin (Jeconiah), who had been taken with his family to Babylonia in 597 (2 Kgs 24:12). According to 1 Chr 3:18–19, however, Zerubbabel was the son of Pedaiah, a younger brother of Shealtiel; this is perhaps accurate. If Zerubbabel really was not the son of the crown prince, he would be less threatening in the eyes of the Persian administration on which his appointment in Judah depended. For him to be presented as the son of the former crown prince is more in keeping with the expectations centered on him in Hag 2:21–23. Joshua, according to 1 Chr 6:12–15 (5:38–41), was the grandson of Seraiah, the last preexilic chief priest in Jerusalem (2 Kgs 25:18–21). *governor of Judah:* The word translated "governor" is *peḥâ*. O. Leuze (*Die Satrapieneinteilung in Syrien und im Zweistromland von 520–330* [Halle, 1935] 18–19, 38–42) has shown that the Akkadian word *piḥat* or *paḥat* (which as a loanword is the Hebr *peḥâ*, con. st. *paḥat*) is a generic term for a civil administrative official at any level. A *peḥâ* could be a governor, a prefect, one of the Persian satraps, or simply a local administrator. A. Alt (*KlS* 2. 333–35) finds that a *peḥâ* could even be a delegate or commissioner with a specific mandate, limited in its object and perhaps also in the time of its validity, given by the central government; he suggests that it was in just this sense that Zerubbabel was *peḥâ* of Judah. The Persians may have chosen him to oversee Judah's reorganization because a member of the former royal house could command enough respect to settle conflicts arising within the community itself.
9   2. The problem addressed by Haggai is expressed as an excuse on the lips of the people: the rebuilding of the Temple has not advanced because the

time is not yet right. This excuse was surely based on economic conditions (1:5–6,9,10–11; 2:16–19). E. Janssen (*Juda in der Exilszeit* [FRLANT 69; Göttingen, 1956] 78) thinks that it may be based on a religious notion that the Temple should be rebuilt only when the final age has come, with its good conditions. In the oracle which follows, the economic argument is turned on its head: it is failure to build the Temple that has caused the economic difficulties themselves, and so the time for building is indeed now (see v 9). **8.** The climax and point of the oracle: God wants his house in which to dwell, and the people of Judah should get to work on it. They are neglecting what should be put above all else: the honor and glory of God. **9–11.** These verses remind us of an oracle of judgment, in which an account of previous behavior serving as accusation is followed by an announcement of judgment introduced by "therefore," but untypically the judgment here is not announced for the future but declared as an accomplished fact. These verses, coming after the climax in v 8 and repeating the essential elements of vv 4–6, may once have existed independently, but, granting that, the unity of vv 4–11 as they now stand is maintained by Beuken (*Haggai-Sacharja 1–8,* 184–208) and O. Steck (*ZAW* 83 [1971] 355–79). J. W. Whedbee (in *Biblical and Near Eastern Studies* [Fest. W. S. LaSor; ed. G. A. Tuttle; GR, 1978] 184–94) insists on the integral unity of vv 2–11.
10   (II) Work on the Temple Is Started (1:12–15a). 12. *the remnant of the people:* In Jer 23:3; 31:7 this phrase refers to those who were deported by the Babylonians, but in Hag it probably includes those who had remained in Judah, for most people old enough to have seen Solomon's Temple (2:3) would be too old to make the arduous trip back from Babylonia. **13–14.** Now that the people, by their change of heart, have met God's basic condition, the way is opened to a basic change of attitude on God's part too: from now on, he will be with them, and that will lead them from misfortune to blessings. **15a.** The date = 21 September 520. Work on the Temple began only three weeks after the initial oracle of rebuke and call. Since dates elsewhere in Hag introduce oracles, many have proposed 1:15a as originally the introduction to 2:15–19.

11   (III) A Good Future from Building the Temple (1:15b-2:23).

(A) Glory in the Temple (1:15b-2:9). 1:15b-2:1. The date = 17 October 520. The oracle (vv 3-9) is one of encouragement. The primacy of God and his house, already contrasted with the self-centered interests of the people in 1:2-9, is used here as a motive of encouragement to the builders. **3.** Apparently some discouraging sentiments are being broadcast by older Judeans, comparing the rising new building unfavorably with Solomon's splendid Temple, now destroyed, which they remember. The prophetic response is focused on the *kābôd* of the old Temple and of the new. *Kābôd* can mean "splendor" or even "riches" (Isa 10:3; 61:6; 66:11-12; Nah 2:10; Ps 49[48]:17-18). That is its primary sense here (vv 7-9). At the same time, *kābôd* means "glory," and in relation to the Temple it suggests that glory through which God in his transcendence dwells in the Temple, the glory which the visionary Ezekiel saw returning to the postexilic Temple (Ezek 43:1-4). **6.** A poetic expression of divine intervention in the functioning of the universe. **7.** *treasures of all nations:* Hebr *ḥemdâ* means "desire" or, as here, "the object of desire." In the Vg it is taken personally and given an implicitly messianic sense: *veniet desideratus cunctis gentibus*, but in Hebrew the pl. vb. shows that this noun too is pl., and so it is rendered in the LXX (*ta eklekta*). The context shows that the objects of desire are treasures. **8-9.** The Judeans can rest assured that the *kābôd* of the new Temple will be greater than that of Solomon's Temple. Because of it there will be well-being (*šālôm*) in Zion.

12   (B) A Priestly Decision (2:10-14). Questions, with or without answers, are an element of Haggai's oracular rhetoric (1:4,9; 2:19). In 2:11-13 he uses a particular type of question and answer: that of early priestly *tôrâ*, by which priests handed down decisions in answer to questions of distinction between the sacred and the profane, the holy and the impure. He then, in v 14, applies the answer to the situation of the people, thus using both the form and the conceptual categories of priestly *tôrâ* as the basis of his prophetic message. The questioning and answering here seems to take it for granted that sacrifice is already being offered on some altar in the ruins of the previous Temple. Clearly supposed is the Israelite concept of contagion by which the holy can contaminate the profane and vice versa. In the makeshift sacrificial arrangements current in the city, whatever there is that is ritually holy does not make anything else holy, but from the ritually impure objects or persons impurity does spread. **14.** *this people . . . this nation:* Judah. (On its alternative identification as Samaria, → 13 below.) The point of this prophetic conclusion drawn from the priestly *tôrâ* of vv 12-13 seems to be either that the people, metaphorically impure because of their behavior, render their agricultural offerings — and ultimately the altar — impure, or that the makeshift altar, impure because not yet properly hallowed, has its ritual impurity spread by contagion to the offerings — and ultimately to those bringing the offerings. (For the latter interpretation, which accounts well for the details in vv 10-19, see Petersen, *Haggai and Zechariah 1-8* 76-85.)

13   (C) Agricultural Prosperity (2:15-19). It was long the scholarly custom, following J. W. Rothstein (*Juden und Samaritaner* [BWANT 3; Leipzig, 1908] 5-41, 53-73) to separate 2:15-19 completely from 2:10-14 and to identify the people/nation of v 14 as that of the Samaritans, who, rejected in their bid for involvement in the rebuilding of the Temple, took steps which made the Judeans afraid to build until Darius's time (Ezra 4:1-5). More recently, the people/nation of 2:14 has been taken as Judah after all, and serious reasons of form criticism and of exegesis have been adduced for interpreting 2:11-19 as a single oracle in which the several parts are integrated. Thus, the ritual impurity of the people, of their agricultural offerings, and of the place of offering, which was the point of vv 11-14, becomes the reason for God's having permitted the agricultural misfortunes before the construction work began (vv 15b-17), but the event of the day of the oracle's delivery (given a date in v 10, restated in v 18 as the day on which the foundation was laid) has brought an end to the misfortunes (vv 15a,18-19). The situation of contagious ritual impurity (vv 11-13) which was the cause of the agricultural misfortunes must, then, also have been brought to an end, perhaps by the purifying elements of the ritual used in foundation laying.

(Koch, K., "Haggais unreines Volk," *ZAW* 79 [1967] 52-66. May, H. G., "'This People' and 'This Nation' in Haggai," *VT* 18 [1968] 190-97. Meyers, E. M., "The Use of *tôrâ* in Haggai 2:11 and the Role of the Prophet in the Restoration Community," in *WLSGF* 69-76. Townsend, T. N., "Additional Comments on Haggai II 10-19," *VT* 18 [1968] 559-60.)

14   (D) Zerubbabel, God's Signet Ring (2:20-23). This oracle is addressed directly to Zerubbabel. Both in this oracle and in that of 2:3-9 a glorious future is announced which will be introduced by God's shaking heaven and earth (vv 7,21). Both of these oracles are international or universalist in outlook. The view in both shows similarity to the view of the restored future which Ezekiel and his disciples held, with God's glory back in a rebuilt Temple (Ezek 20:40; 43:1-5), and with a new David as ruler (cf. Ezek 34:23-24; 37:24-28); but Haggai, quite unlike Ezekiel, sees the postexilic civil ruler as a particular person with a political importance radiating out from Zion into the wider world. **20.** The month is not given in this date formula, but since the formula introduces the word of God which came *again* on the 24th day, the date must be the same as that in 2:10,18: the day on which the reconstruction of the Temple was solemnly inaugurated. God has linked Zerubbabel's political future to the existence of God's house. **23.** *signet ring:* A symbol of authority. In Jer 22:24 it is used in an oracle of divine rejection of Jehoiachin; here it is used in an oracle of divine election of Jehoiachin's grandson. We do not know how Zerubbabel's career ended. As far as we know, he was the last member of the house of David to be involved in the reorganization of Judah. Haggai's royal expectation was not met in the reality of postexilic development. For Judah's future in the long run, it was the fulfillment of 2:6-9 which turned out to be significant: the finished Temple provided Judeans with a religious center, with Yahweh's glory dwelling in it and among them.

ZECHARIAH

BIBLIOGRAPHY

15   (Also → 1 and 2 above.) Gese, H., "Anfang und Ende der Apokalyptik, dargestellt am Sacharjabuch," *ZTK* 70 (1973) 20–49. Lamarche, P., *Zacharie IX–XIV* (EBib; Paris, 1961). Lipiński, E., "Recherches sur le livre de Zacharie," *VT* 20 (1970) 25–55. Otzen, B., *Studien über Deuterosacharja* (AThD 6; Copenhagen, 1964). Petersen, D. L., "Zechariah's Visions," *VT* 34

(1984) 185–206. Petitjean, A., *Les oracles du Proto-Zacharie* (EBib; Paris, 1969). Plöger, O., *Theocracy and Eschatology* (Phl, 1968). Saebø, M., *Sacharja 9–14* (WMANT 34; Neukirchen, 1969). Thomas, D. W. and R. C. Dentan, "The Book of Zechariah," *IB* 6. 1051–1114. Willi-Plein, I., *Prophetie am Ende* (BBB 42; Bonn, 1974).

INTRODUCTION

16   **(I) The Relation between Zech 1–8 and Zech 9–14.** The differences between Zech 1–8 and Zech 9–14 are great enough for most scholars to see them as two distinct and originally independent works and to refer to 9–14 as "Deutero-Zechariah." The lyric but simple style typical of the second part is different from the more pedestrian but complicated style typical of the first. Apocalyptic vision of a future time in which conflict will end with victory on the side of those who are faithful to God is characteristic only of the second part; it is particularly characteristic of chaps. 12–14, which are different enough from the rest of Zech for some to call them "Trito-Zechariah." A linguistic study of Zech, done with computers and with a program which, when applied to Isa, confirmed that the authors of Isa 1–39 and of Isa 40–66 were indeed different, led to the conclusion that neither the unity of Zech 1–11 nor a difference of authorship between 1–8 and 9–11 is demonstrable by statistical linguistics, but that the unity of 12–14 with the rest of Zech, while not impossible, is very improbable (Y. T. Radday and D. Wickmann, *ZAW* 87 [1975] 30–55).

17   Certain passages in both parts (in all three, if we will) do show some similarity of topic or of outlook. They share a view of Jerusalem at the center of the world's destiny, linked to a universalistic view of other nations turning towards Jerusalem in a coming age. They share a concern for purifying Judean society. There are frequent echos of earlier prophetic writings, mostly of Ezek 40–48 in Zech 1–8, while those in Zech 9–14 are more broadly derived. There is a common concern with the community's leadership, anonymous in chaps. 9–14, specific in 1–8. The final editor who put the parts together to form our present canonical book may have done so partly because of the topical similarities which he saw in them here and there. We should like to know more about his view of continuity in the prophetic tradition of postexilic Judah. Did he see in chaps. 9–14 a continuation of Zechariah's prophetic messages?

(Delcor, M., "Les sources de Deutéro-Zacharie et ses procédés d'emprunt," *RB* 59 [1952] 385–411. Mason, R. A., "The Relation of Zechariah 9–14 to Proto-Zecharie," *ZAW* 88 (1976) 227–39.)

(II) Chapters 1–8.

18   **(A) The Prophet and His Situation.** In Zech 1:1,7, Zechariah is said to be the son of Berechiah the son of Iddo. The name Iddo is included in a list of priests who returned from Babylonian Exile (Neh 12:4), but that list is probably not authentic (W. Rudolph, *Esra-Nehemia* [HAT 1/20; Tübingen, 1949] 191–93), and so we have no solid grounds for stating that Zechariah or

his immediate family had been in exile. Iddo is probably not his grandfather but the eponymous ancestor of a particular priestly family, the "sons of Iddo." In Ezra 5:1; 6:14, "Zechariah son of Iddo" is mentioned as one moving the people to build the Temple. In Neh 12:16, a Zechariah is named as the head of the priestly family of Iddo in the days of the high priest Joiakim (probably in the first decade or two of the 5th cent.). From this we may infer that our prophet was a responsible member of the postexilic Judean establishment, committed to priestly circles and to the establishment more generally. He was active at least as early as 520 (Zech 1:1) and at least as late as the beginning of the following century (Neh 12:16). The historical situation when Zechariah began to see his visions and hear the word of God was the same as that which provided the setting for Hag (→ 3–4 above). Both in Hag and in Zech we find emphasis on Jerusalem as the place of God's dwelling, on the importance of reconstructing the Temple, on the role of Joshua and Zerubbabel, but in Zech 1–8 Joshua has an importance that he does not have in Hag, and Zerubbabel's importance appears mainly in relation to the rebuilding of the Temple, probably because Zech 1–8 reflects a stage of political evolution at which Zerubbabel had already played his part out and had turned out to be of little real consequence in the historical destinies of Judah. In comparison with Hag, Zech 1–8 shows a greater sense of the importance of God's action and a correspondingly reduced sense of the importance of initiative taken by the people and their leaders. Zech 1–8 is less concrete than Hag, less static, more likely to entail movement, less fixed upon the phenomena of daily existence, more utopian. Whereas Haggai promotes immediate action and holds out a hope quickly to become reality, Zechariah promotes principles and outlooks that will assure right action when it is needed, and he holds out a hope for a coming age which seems less immediately imminent.

19   **(B) Composition.** The date formulas in 1:1; 1:7; 7:1 mark the division of the work into three sections: a prologue presenting the prophet and his fundamental approach (1:1–6); a collection of eight night visions, followed usually by an oracle in which the vision is interpreted, applied, or even modified (1:7–6:15); an inquiry addressed to Zechariah followed by a response which is actually a series of originally disparate oracles (7:1–8:23).

There is general critical agreement that the visionary and oracular passages narrated in the first person are the prophet Zechariah's. Some doubt may be raised about the disparate oracles strung together in 7:1–8:23, but there are no positive reasons for denying Zechariah their authorship. Since the oracular interpretations following the visions in 1:7–6:15 modify the content of the preceding visions at times, one may suspect their being added to the visions, and since the modifications which they introduce do not all reflect the same tendencies, one may also suspect that they do not all come from the same person. If that is so, then one may think of more than one editorial process involved in giving us Zech 1–8. Zechariah may himself have been an editor of his own prophetic words set down in writing in earlier years. The fourth night vision and its following oracular passage (3:1–10), as well as the fifth vision and its oracular interpretation (4:1–14), manifest some formal differences from the rest of 1:7–6:15, and 6:9–15 is not closely integrated with the vision which precedes it. 4:1–14 and 6:9–15 also show certain internal inconsistencies: there is room for differences of opinion on what is later and what is earlier in these passages, and on what, within them, should be attributed to Zechariah himself.

(III) Chapters 9–14.

20   (A) Situation. There have been vast differences of opinion among scholars trying to find the historical situations in which the oracles of chaps. 9–14 were uttered, so that we might understand the import of those oracles better. At first sight, the pursuit of historical situations seems to be one which might be crowned with success. One even finds places (other than Jerusalem and Judah) named in 9:1–17; 10:3b–11:17, but Ephraim (9:10,13; 10:17) and petty Aramean kingdoms (9:1) would hardly impinge on Judah's history after the fall of the northern kingdom in 722/721, and, on the other hand, the sons of *Yāwān* (Ionians, i.e., Greeks) could hardly be pitched against Zion (MT of 9:13) before the arrival of the armies of Alexander the Great in the Near East in 333. Assyria (10:10–11) was a political nonentity after 612, and so for all practical purposes was Egypt (10:11) after the Persians took it in 527. Oracles in Zech 9–14 have indeed been referred to the period before 721, or to the latter years of the kingdom of Judah, or, more commonly—since the now classical argumentation of B. Stade (esp. *ZAW* 2 [1882] 275–90)—to the early Hellenistic period (see Eissfeldt, EOTI 435–40, and the thorough survey by B. Otzen, *Studien* [→ 15 above] 11–34).

Reflection on the literary character of these chapters and on the rhetorical procedures used in them may suggest, for one thing, that mention of Ephraim and Damascus, Assyria and Egypt, is part of the tendency to draw ideas and images from the works of the earlier prophets, that mention of these places is meant not to allude to the present but to evoke the past in Judah's historical awareness. The purpose of these evocations of the past is one of exemplification: as God dealt with Judah and Ephraim and the foreign nations in the past, so will he continue to deal in the present and in the future. There are certainly allusions also to situations contemporary with the oracles themselves, and mention of Judah and Jerusalem may occur in connection with them, but such allusions are unspecified and veiled. We know too little of the historical vicissitudes of Judah in its first postexilic centuries to be able to match a detail or two which we do know with some veiled allusion in

Zech 9–14 which may be to something quite different of which we know nothing. Mention of the sons of *Yāwān* in the MT of 9:13 occurs in what many scholars consider a gloss inserted into an already existing text.

For another thing, the oracles in chaps. 9–14 manifest an eschatology that is increasingly apocalyptic—in chaps. 12–14 more than in 9–11. This means that they are less directly and concretely interested in contemporary historical reality than were those of earlier prophets, that they show more concern with a future lacking historical specificity and portrayed in colors which have a tone that becomes more mythological as the apocalyptic tendency is more fully developed.

(Childs, B. S., *CIOTS* 479–81. Hanson, P. D., *The Dawn of Apocalyptic* [Phl, 1975] 286–92. North, R., "Prophecy to Apocalyptic via Zechariah," *Congress Volume: Uppsala 1971* [VTSup 22; Leiden, 1972] 47–71.)

21   (B) Composition. Zech 9–14 comprises two collections of oracles (chaps. 9–11 and 12–14), each introduced by the phrase "Oracle (lit., "burden") of the word of Yahweh." The oracles of each collection are skillfully bound together editorially: in the case of chaps. 9–11 by catchwords and by bi-directional verbal pointers at the points of juncture; in the case of chaps. 12–14 by the repeated phrase "on that day," which introduces most of them. These two collections must have existed independently before they were joined and added to Zech 1–8. Possible reasons for their being joined to chaps. 1–8 have been suggested (→ 17 above).

22   (III) Outline.

COMMENTARY

(I) Zech 1–8.

23   (A) Prologue (1:1–6). The prologue manifests a significant characteristic of Zech: an appeal

to the past, to the "earlier prophets" (v 4), for examples to be pondered in the present. It also tells of a concern underlying all of Zech 1–8: that of the need for Judeans to turn/return (*šûb*). The vb. *šûb* is ambivalent, and its ambivalence appears here in the prologue. On the one hand, it has a spatial meaning of turning or returning, which in the situation addressed by Zechariah obviously applies to returning to Judah from the exile. On the other hand, it has a moral meaning of turning from wrong ways in order to return to God, which is also a concern underlying all of Zech 1–8. The latter meaning is that of the example drawn from the ancestors (v 4), who did not turn from their wrong ways (Jer 18:11; 25:5; 35:15; Ezek 33:11). It is also that of the imperative addressed to Zechariah's contemporaries in v 3, but in v 3 the ambivalence is fully operative; not only should they turn to God from their wrong ways, but they should also return to Judah from exile, rebuild God's house, and reestablish the society of God's people. If they rebuild God's dwelling and purify themselves from the things which cause God's displeasure, then God too will return (also *šûb*) to be present quasi-spatially in his earthly dwelling, in the city which he abandoned because of his displeasure with his people's moral attitudes. **1.** The date = 24 November 520. **6.** *they turned and said:* "Turned" is *šûb*. It is not clear whether "they" are the ancestors who learned their lesson in the past or Zechariah's contemporaries, learning their lesson from history. The point is the same: the lesson has been learned, and so hope is possible. (See A. S. van der Woude, "Seid nicht wie eure Väter!," *Prophecy* [Fest. G. Fohrer; ed. J. A. Emerton; BZAW 150; Berlin, 1980] 163–73.)

24   (B) Eight Night Visions and Their Oracles (1:7–6:15). Although the date in 1:7 is that of the first of these visions, the oracular introduction in which it is found serves as the heading under which all eight of the visions fall. There is a certain inner logic, a certain sequential progression, from vision to vision, esp. when the oracles following them are taken into account. In the first, God assures Zion's future, and in those that follow, God assures the conditions necessary for that future. A certain thematic unity is given to the whole when images and vocabulary of the first vision recur in the last one.

(Halpern, B., "The Ritual Background of Zechariah's Temple Song," *CBQ* 40 [1978] 167–90. Jeremias, C., *Die Nachtgesichte des Sacharja* [FRLANT 117; Göttingen, 1977]. Rignell, L. G., *Die Nachtgesichte des Sacharja* [Lund, 1950].)

25   (a) The Colored Horses and the Horsemen (1:7–17). The prophet sees a peaceful, restful scene in which messengers or inspectors return to announce that all the world is enjoying the peace and rest evident in the scene. A lamenting protest is raised (v 13), and God responds with an oracular promise of restoration for Jerusalem and Judah. **7.** The date = 16 February 519. **8.** *a man:* This is the figure called the "angel" in the following verses. In the vision, he has a human form. **9.** *the angel:* Hebr *malʾāk*, "messenger," addressed here with the honorific title "my lord." God's transcendence is safeguarded when his words are communicated through a supernatural messenger, seen in human form while God remains invisible. **12.** *seventy years:* The length of time, expressed in round numbers, from the destruction of Jerusalem in 587 to the time of the vision. The idea behind the protest here is that the peace prevailing throughout the world makes unlikely a liberation of Judah, which could naturally be expected only in conditions of political unrest and war. The protest is answered with an oracle of promise (vv 13–17) in which God reveals his real attitude: anger at the nations despite their peace, concern for Judah despite her misfortunes. **16.**

The theme of God's return to Jerusalem (1:3), to dwell in a new Temple, appears again. **26   (b)** The Four Horns and the Carvers (2:1–4) (LXX and Vg 1:18–21). The preceding vision closed with an oracular promise of a better future for Jerusalem and Judah, to confirm that side of the answer to the protest voiced in 1:12. In the oracle concluding this second vision there is assurance that God will also act to confirm the other side of his answer to the protest: the nations oppressing God's people will be discomfited after all, despite the peace and rest of the nations at the time of these visions. In this second vision the prophet sees four horns. The divine messenger interprets the horns as the oppressing nations, who have at different times scattered Judah and Israel, as an angry bull with his horns scatters all whom he charges. The horns are approached by four artisans; working with horn they would be carvers. Alternatively, *ḥārāš* in v 3(20) is not the word for "artisan" (Ugaritic *ḥrš*) but a word for "plowman" (Ugaritic *ḥrt*), and the image in v 4(21) is thus that of plowmen coming to frighten the horned animals and drive them off to their fold (*yādôt* instead of MT *yaddôt*; R. N. Good, *Bib* 63 [1982] 56–59. For a proposed secondary symbolism, see B. Halpern, *CBQ* 40 [1978] 177–78.) **27   (c)** The Surveyor (2:5–17) (LXX and Vg 2:1–13). From the removal of foreign power inhibiting the recovery of Judah and Jerusalem (in the preceding vision) we move to the first stage of actual recovery: the rebuilding of the city. The vision itself shows a false start: a human surveyor is ready to start measuring off the city's ground. The initiative behind the surveyor's project does not seem to come from God. Zechariah talks with the surveyor without any intermediacy of God's messenger or "angel," who is moving away from the scene. When an oracular message comes from God, through another messenger, it is corrective, but the correction does not quite seem to fit the vision. In the vision, the surface area of the city is about to be measured, but in the oracle it is a project of building walls around that area that is excluded. In any case, the essential elements of promise are an abundant and prosperous population (v 8[4]) and the protecting power of God (v 9[5]). **8(4).** *without walls:* Lit., "(as) unfortified villages" (*pěrāzôt*), a simile perhaps inspired by the idea of essentially agricultural prosperity expressed in the compound "human beings and animals." **9(5).** The imagery of fire, common in descriptions of theophany because it expresses the danger of approaching too near to God, and the imagery of glory which expresses his earthly presence in the Temple are used to show why the new Jerusalem will not need defending walls. God's own awesome presence in the city will suffice to ward off all earthly enemies. Similarities to Ezek 40–48 are obvious, but differences are also clear. In Ezek 40–42 the Temple is measured, and in Ezek 43:1–5 God's glory returns there. Here the whole city is about to be measured in the vision, and in the oracle God's glory is a numinous presence in the city as a whole.

In 2:10–17 (2:6–13) we have a collection of small oracles and small prophetic statements which are not a part of the preceding vision with its proper oracle, but which have to do with the return of the scattered exiles and with the future of Jerusalem as God's city. **28   (d)** Joshua the High Priest (3:1–10). The sequence of the night visions moves from the rebuilt city and the protecting presence of God to the city's sacral leadership. **1.** The visionary scene is set as a meeting of the divine council (cf. 1 Kgs 22:19–22; Job 1:6–12; 2:1–6; and see N. L. A. Tidwell, *JBL* 94 [1975] 343–55). As in all the night visions in Zech, God does not appear visibly. Here God's messenger or "angel," through whom he speaks, presides over the meeting. *the adversary:* Hebr *śāṭān* is an accuser. In a forensic context, a *śāṭān* functions as a prosecutor. The word connotes trouble-making. In this vision he has raised an accusation against Joshua the high priest, but the accusation itself is not expressed. It may be directed at some act known to Zechariah's contemporaries which those hostile to Joshua could use as a reason for claiming that he was unworthy of the high priest's office. It may simply be the fact that he had been in exile. **2.** God rebukes the accuser for advancing the accusation and points out that Joshua has been removed, damaged but basically intact, from whatever experience is at issue. **4-5.** Joshua's guilt, whether it comes from personal wrongdoing or from transference of collective sin or defilement to his own person, is symbolically removed. (For transference of collective guilt to one person, see Isa 53:6,11, and for transference of specifically cultic guilt to the one person of the high priest, see Exod 28:38; Num 18:1.) The clean, or ritually pure, turban placed on his head under the supervision of God's messenger (v 5) symbolizes his occupying the position of high priest under divine auspices. The divine oracle that follows (vv 6-10) definitely does not seem to be all of a piece. **7.** The administration of the Temple and the Temple courts is under the supreme jurisdiction of a high priest. Joshua's having that jurisdiction is made subject to his living in conformity with God's law, expressed in deuteronomistic language as walking in God's ways. **8.** While the vision and the oracle in 3:1-10 have to do with Joshua and the high priest's office, v 8 introduces the Branch, which in the symbolic language of the period can only be a scion of the Davidic lineage (cf. esp. Jer 23:5). If v 8 was introduced secondarily into the oracle after Zerubbabel had lost his place as a civil leader in Judah, then the reason for its introduction can have been that of reserving a place in the future for some other divinely mandated civil ruler. Since the Branch is not identified with Zerubbabel by name, v 8 may not be concerned with contemporary affairs, may be open to a messianic interpretation, even if the symbolic epithet "Branch" was originally applied to Zerubbabel. And yet there is nothing in this oracle about civil responsibility of the high priest (which the high priests acquired in postexilic Judah) or about the disappearance of a civilian governor from the postexilic scene. **9.** The meaning of the stone, both real and symbolic, remains a problem for exegetes.

29   (a) THE LAMPSTAND AND THE OLIVE TREES (4:1-14). The inherent obscurity of this vision's symbolism is not relieved by the oracular explanation that follows it. In times still close enough to the original situation for the intention of the vision and its explanation to be understood by those who had enough imagination to get the point, the text was interpolated with an oracle on Zerubbabel's role in building the Temple (vv 6b-10a). The rest of the text seems to have been tampered with too, as is generally the case with a text whose sense is obscure and whose programmatic intention is somehow disturbing to the person or persons who interpolate it or otherwise tamper with it. (For the philological and archaeological problems involved in the description of the lampstand, see R. North, *Bib* 51 [1970] 183-206; and for the different modern interpretations of the symbols and their possible backgrounds, see C. Jeremias, *Die Nachtgesichte* [→ 24 above] 176-88.) **6b.** The interpolation begins with an oracle of acclamation addressed to Zerubbabel by name. In the interpolated material Joshua is not named and not even mentioned, unless the "great mountain" (MT *har-haggādôl*) of v 7 is a symbol of the high priest (*hakkōhēn haggādôl*):

if that is so, the great mountain's reduction to a plain in comparison with Zerubbabel is significant. *capstone:* Perhaps by analogy with the brick removed from an earlier temple for incorporation into a new one in Mesopotamian ritual (E. Lipiński, *VT* 20 [1970] 30-33; A. Petitjean, *Les oracles* [→ 15 above] 216-38, 243-51). **8.** A second interpolated oracle emphasizing Zerubbabel's leading role in the building of the new Temple. **10a.** *tin stone:* A plummet (so the LXX) or a tin foundation deposit (D. L. Petersen, *CBQ* 36 [1974] 368-71; B. Halpern, *CBQ* 40 [1978] 171-73). **10b.** The visionary oracle is resumed after the interpolation. The septuple elements of the lampstand represent God's eyes roaming over the whole world, assuring his mastery over all events. This adds support to interpretation of the lampstand as a divine emblem. **12.** The obscurity of the text makes the question problematic. **14.** *sons of oil:* Commentators generally understand this as a symbolic reference to Joshua and Zerubbabel. Many take it as an allusion to their anointing as high priest and as king. Others wonder why an element of kingship would have been introduced in relation to the sacral emblem of the lampstand. The word for oil here, *yiṣhār*, is foreign to the vocabulary of anointing. Is the sense that the high priest and the civil administrator provide for the needs of the Temple, represented by oil for the divinely emblematic lampstand?

30   (f) THE FLYING SCROLL (5:1-4). The visionary sequence moves from the leaders of restored Judah to Judean society at large. There is in this society unpunished wrongdoing, against God (exemplified by swearing falsely) and against neighbor (exemplified by theft). The point of the vision and its oracular interpretation is that wrongdoing, which violates the covenant with God, makes one liable to the curses attached to violation of that covenant (Deut 29 *passim*). The curse is written on the scroll, as curses attached to violation of the stipulations of a treaty were written into ancient Near Eastern treaties. God will himself dispatch the scroll with the curse, which will fly around to ferret out the guilty and to bring about the punitive destruction of their worldly goods.

31   (g) THE WOMAN IN THE EPHAH (5:5-11). The visionary concern moves from the punishment of the guilty in Judean society to the removal of guilt and of evil behavior from Judah altogether. **6.** *ephah:* A unit of dry measure whose equivalent in modern systems has not yet been determined. Here the ephah is a container whose capacity is that of one unit of the measure. *their guilt:* (Joining the LXX and the Syr in reading the Hebr consonantal text as '*wnm* instead of the MT's '*ynm*.) That guilt whose removal is a concern more generally in Zech (cf. 3:4,9). **8.** *wickedness:* Hebr *riš'â*, anything which is offensive to God, contrary to his will. The object of the vision is not guilt alone but guilt with the offensive behavior which is at the core of guilt and which needs to be removed with the guilt. The reason for wickedness appearing as a woman in the vision is not necessarily an antifeminine reason. It may be determined by the fact that *riš'â* is grammatically of feminine gender, and it has been suggested that the Mesopotamian goddess Ishtar lies in the prophet's mind (K. Galling, *Studien zur Geschichte Israels* 120). **11.** *Shinar:* Lower Mesopotamia, Babylonia. Guilt, with its underlying cause in behavior offensive to God, is removed from Judah and carried off to Babylonia. Babylonia is thus repaid for its damage to Judah. The idea that the Babylonians will worship guilt and wickedness (= Ishtar?) is strongly suggested by the house to be built there for the ephah (cf. "house of Yahweh" for the Temple) and by the base or pedestal

pedestal on which it is to be set up there (see M. Delcor, *RHR* 187 [1974] 137–45).

32   (h) THE FOUR CHARIOTS; CROWNS AND LEADERS (6:1–15). The oracular material in vv 9–15 is not an integral part of the vision (vv 1–8), which shares some details with the first vision (1:7–17): colored horses (although not all the colors are the same) and divine missions sent out over all the earth (although in the first vision they have returned, while in the last they are setting out; and the first shows personal emissaries, while the last shows chariots). **1.** The two mountains made of copper, the chariots, and the winds in vv 5–6 give this vision a mythically cosmic tone. There is no dearth of parallels for each of these in the ancient Near East (see Jeremias, *Die Nachtgesichte* [→ 24 above] 110–13, 123–26), but no known parallel exists for their combination here. **2–3.** The number four is determined by the four winds (v 5). If the colors of the horses have any real value in the vision's symbolism, it is not readily apparent. **5.** The chariots are related to the winds (cf. Isa 66:15; Jer 4:13), and the winds are themselves God's messengers (Ps 104[103]:4), setting out in their four directions after presenting themselves before God as though to receive their mandate from him. There is nothing in the text that justifies the *RSV*'s having the chariots go forth "to the four winds" instead of being associated with the four winds. **6.** One may presume that the red horses setting off toward the East were inadvertently dropped from the text. The white horses go "beyond the sea" (to the W) instead of "after them" if the MT's '*hryhm* is emended to '*hr hym*. The point is that the cosmic messengers head off in all four directions, over all the earth (v 7). Given the symmetry between the first night vision and the last—with the first one showing the inspectors reporting all the earth at rest, to the dismay of those hoping for an unrest enabling Judah to rise in freedom (1:11–12)—the purpose of the cosmic emissaries in the last vision is probably that of stirring all the earth finally to unrest, making Judah's rise to freedom possible. **8.** Just as the peace on earth in the first vision met God's anger (1:15), so the unrest on earth imminent in this final vision will put God's spirit at rest. The mission to all the earth has a special target in the northland, for the route from Babylonia approached Judah from the N (cf. 2:6–7). Since guilt and wickedness have been removed from Judah to Babylonia (5:11), God's wrath has all the more reason to be aimed in that direction.

33   The night visions have come to an end with 6:8. To them the oracular section 6:9–15 has been appended. In it the contribution which well-to-do persons returning from exile are to make to the splendor of the future is indicated. **11.** A crown is to be made for Joshua the high priest. The MT in vv 11 and 14 has the pl. "crowns," which may reflect the idea that a crown should be made for the civil leader too. The LXX in both verses and some Hebr mss. in v 11 have the sg., and in the MT the vb. which must agree in number is sg. in v 14. **12–13.** Here, as in 3:8, we have an oracular fragment, in which the future civil leader—called Branch—is given high status in the future, in the midst of a passage having to do with the religious leader alone. In 4:6b–10a, in the midst of a passage having to do with both the religious leader and the anonymous civil leader, the civil leader is identified as Zerubbabel and is given a role in building the Temple, as Branch is here. In all three cases one discerns the purpose of emphasizing the place of the civil leader in the coming age. One may suspect a certain situational evolution, from clear identification of Zerubbabel as builder in 4:6b–10a, set into a passage already providing for both types of leader, to

Branch in 6:12–13 when the historical career of Zerubbabel had perhaps become uncertain but when the reconstruction of the Temple was not yet accomplished, to a Branch in 3:8 whose place in a coming age was less historically defined—more open, more messianic, if we will.

34   (C) **Various Oracles (7:1–8:23).** For the last time a date formula (7:1) marks the beginning of a new section, in which divers oracles, some of them quite brief, are strung together and presented as answers to the question put in 7:3. The oracles are marked off clearly, and literary devices are well used to give unity to the collection (see D. J. Clark, *BT* 36 [1985] 328–35). The moral language is often deuteronomistic.

35   (a) ASSESSMENT OF THE PAST (7:1–14). **1.** The date = 7 December 518. **2–3.** The model for the action portrayed is that of asking a priest for a *tôrâ* in the original sense, a priestly response to a question of correct procedure in a ritual or sacral matter (→ Institutions, 76:10). An element atypical of *tôrâ* is introduced here: the question is put not only to priests but to prophets as well. In Hag 2:10–14 a *tôrâ*, in authentically priestly form, is extended in prophetic form (2:14). Zechariah, a prophet but also a member of a priestly family (→ 18 above), could have responded to the question in 7:3 in the manner of a priest, but the oracles which follow are delivered in the manner of a prophet. The day of lamenting and fasting in the fifth month is generally taken as the anniversary of the destruction of the previous Temple with the rest of the city (2 Kgs 25:8–9). **4–7.** An oracle denouncing self-centered motivation. **5.** *fifth and seventh months:* For the fifth, see comment on v 3. In Jewish tradition a fast in the seventh month was observed in commemoration of the murder of Gedaliah (2 Kgs 25:25; Jer 41:1–3). *seventy years:* See comment on 1:12. An admonition to righteous behavior in vv 9–10 gives way to a review of the hearers'/ancestors' refusal to obey God as he manifested his will through instruction (*tôrâ*) and through the words of the prophets (v 12), ending in the exile inflicted upon the ancestors as a penalty for their refusal. Cf. 1:1–6.

36   (b) PROMISES FOR THE FUTURE (8:1–23). **2.** *jealous for Zion:* Repeated from 1:14. **3.** *come back to Zion:* Repeated from 1:16. Faithfulness or reliability in matters of ethical behavior and holiness in matters of religious practice will flow from the fact of God's presence in the city. **9.** The prosperity of the land results from the fact of work begun on the new Temple. **14–17.** The history of disobedience and punishment traced in 7:8–14 is reversed. Whereas God ended by punishing the ancestors, he now begins with a resolution to do good to Jerusalem and Judah. The ethical injunctions given at the beginning of 7:8–14 as a list of injunctions disobeyed in the past comes here at the end of 8:1–17 as a list of injunctions to be obeyed in the future.

18–19. The answer to the question in 7:3 is at last answered in a form closer to that of priestly *tôrâ*. To the question whether one shall continue to observe a fast in the fifth month, the answer is No; rather, that fast and three others will be changed into feasts of gladness. The fasts in the fourth and tenth months are not mentioned in 7:3,5. What they commemorated is not known. *love truth and peace:* Perhaps an addition to the answer, but a fitting conclusion to the answer, nevertheless. **20–23.** Although the presence of these verses at the end of the section may be due to editorial planning, there is a verbal connection to the beginning of the section: "to entreat the favor of the Lord" (7:2: 8:21,22). People will come from all the earth to Jerusalem because God is there. The Jews who are establishing a Jewish presence in the Diaspora have a special role to play in this. It is through them that other peoples will hear the good news of God's presence and will want to go along with them to Jerusalem.

(II) Zech 9-14.

37   (A) The First Collection (9:1-11:17). Both 9:1-11:17 and 12:1-14:21, as well as Mal, are headed by the word *maśśā᾿*, lit., "burden." In the prophetic parlance of the period, this word can be translated "oracle," although to do so is to veil some subtleties of usage (see M. Saebφ, *Sacharja 9-14* [→ 15 above] 137-44).

38   (a) GOD THE WARRIOR TAKES SIDES (9:1-8). In this section Judah is set on one side, Judah's neighbors on the other. God, whose power extends to all nations, takes Judah's side, and as a ruler who goes to war for his people he vanquishes Judah's neighbors. The neighbors named are those in Syria (Hadrach and Damascus), on the Phoenician coast (Tyre and Sidon) and in the enclave occupied by the Philistine city-states (Ashkelon, Gaza, Ekron, and Ashdod). What is said against them is largely an echo of earlier prophetic writings (cf. Amos 1:6-9, and Tyre in Ezek 28:2-6), but there are those who see allusions in this section to events as late as the days of Alexander the Great (K. Elliger, *ZAW* 62 [1949/1950] 63-115; M. Delcor, *VT* 1 [1951] 110-24). **1.** *eye of Adam:* Or "well of Adam" (E. Zolli, *VT* 5 [1955] 90-92), or "surface of the earth" (M. Dahood, *CBQ* 25 [1963] 123-24). Some emend Hebr *'ên 'ādām* to *'îrê 'ārām*, "cities of Aram" (Syria). **6b-7.** God will have the neighboring Philistines assimilated into Judean society, once they have been purged of cultic practices which are unacceptable: eating the blood of sacrificial victims (cf. Lev 17:10-14) and eating an "abomination," i.e., any food that is impure (cf. Lev 11:1-47; 17:15-16). **8.** The reason why no foreign neighbor will control Judah is that God's house is there.

39   (b) THE KING OF PEACE (9:9-10). The king here is an earthly king of the future, able to inaugurate his peaceful reign because of the divine victory announced in the preceding verses. **9.** There is no real distinction to be made between a "daughter" of Zion or of Jerusalem and the city itself. *just and saved:* Hebr *ṣaddîq* means both "just," in the sense of doing God's will, and "triumphant." The participle *nôšā'* is passive: the future king is not one who saves (although the LXX, VL, and Vg make him that) but one who has been saved, delivered, by God (cf. Ps 33[32]:16). *riding upon an ass:* Not a sign of meekness but of peacefulness, for in bellicose activity horses were ridden (de Vaux, *AI* 222-25). **10.** *I will cut off the chariot:* LXX and the Syr read "he will cut off," which harmonizes with "he will speak" later in the verse, but the 1st pers. form of the same vb. is used of cutting off the pride of Philistia in v 6b. From the point of view of literary form, the messenger formula of v 9 may be limited to that verse, with a return in v 10 to the formal characteristics of vv 6b-8. If that is so, then in v 10 God, speaking in the first person, says that he himself, the divine warrior, will vanquish the chariot and war horse, but that peace to the nations will be spoken by the earthly king. His peaceful rule will extend far beyond Judah into the rest of the inhabited world (cf. Ps 72[71]:8).

40   (c) THE DIVINE WARRIOR LEADS TO VICTORY (9:11-17). 11. *you:* Zion/Jerusalem of v 9, the direct address linking this section with what precedes. *the blood of your covenant with me:* The Sinaitic covenant was sealed with a blood rite (Exod 24:6-8), but it is hard to see what relevance this might have as a motive for God's freeing Zion's captives. **13.** *against your sons, O Javan:* Yāwān, originally Ionia, stands for Gk lands generally. This phrase breaks the thought and is probably a gloss. It is thus of little value for dating the original text. **14.** When God fights his battles, he does so with the cosmic com-ponents of theophany, like lightning and storm winds, but in the battle envisaged here the Israelites are also engaged (vv 13,15). **16-17.** The peaceful conditions following victory are described in bucolic, pastoral imagery which verbally, but not thematically, links this section with what follows (sheep and shepherds in 10:2-3).

41   (d) AGAINST ABUSERS OF CONFIDENCE (10:1-3a). 1. The divine warrior associated in the preceding section with the fearsome forces of nature becomes the divine provider of good things in nature. Implicitly there seems to be a condemnation of misplaced confidence in other gods in the false thought that they can give rain and fertility. **2.** *teraphim:* Household idols, perhaps a thing of the past, but the idea of using them in some procedure for seeking an oracle seems also to be present in Ezek 21:26. Those who do so and diviners who seek omens and interpret them are condemned as abusers of the people's religious confidence. **3a.** *shepherds:* Probably all those in positions of leadership and trust, condemned for failure to carry out their responsibility toward the people. *leaders:* lit., "he-goats" (cf. Ezek 34:17).

42   (e) GOD'S VICTORIOUS FOLLOWERS (10:3b-12). 3b. The catchwords "flock" and "visit" link this section with what precedes (v 3a), but the imagery returns to that of battle; the focus turns from untrustworthy leaders to the people led by God; the image of the people as sheep changes abruptly to that of the people as steeds of war, and God appears again as the Lord of hosts, the divine warrior. **6.** That both Judah and Israel should be restored is an example of the recollection of ancient days characteristic of these oracles directed toward the future. Verse 6b has a close parallel in Jer 33:26. **7-12.** The restoration which will take place after God has led his people to victory. Israel's ancient enemies, Egypt and Assyria, are mentioned, although they are no longer threats.

43   (f) DESTRUCTION IN LEBANON AND BASHAN (11:1-3). This short classical example of a mocking lament is linked to the preceding section by reference to Lebanon and to Bashan which is in Gilead (cf. 10:10); it is also linked both to what precedes and to what follows by the catchword "shepherds." The desolation of Judah's vanquished enemies is poetically described. It is somewhat curious that small neighbors to the north and northwest of Judah should be singled out for this. D. R. Jones (*VT* 12 [1962] 241-59) sees the oracles of Zech 9-11 coming from "prophetic activity and pastoral oversight in or near Damascus among Israelites of the northern dispersion of the fifth century" (p. 258). The hypothesis has few adherents.

44   (g) BAD SHEPHERDS, BAD FLOCKS (11:4-17). The oracular tone takes a negative turn, against both shepherds and flock. Jer 23:1-4 and Ezek 34:1-31; 37:15-28 stand in the background, but much that is said in those passages is contradicted by this one, which is the prophet's prose account of divine mandate to symbolic action (vv 4,13a,15) and of his own symbolic performance (vv 7-12,13b-14), with some interpretative reasons (vv 5-6,16). **4.** The basic mandate to the prophet. He is to play the shepherd of the flock, which is for killing. One suspects, without being sure, that the flock is all Judah. **6.** The motive for the basic mandate. It has to do with a negative judgment on rulers, without any clue to historical reasons. The reasons may have to do partly with the idea of the past repeating itself, typical of this part of Zech, partly with the prophet's own experiences (M. Rehm, "Die Hirtenallegorie Zach 11,4-14," *BZ* 4 [1960] 186-208). It is not clear whether the land or earth is the land of Judah or the earth broadly, or both but with Judah especially in mind. **7.** The prophet begins his symbolic action by taking two staffs, tagged "Favor" (properly: "delightfulness," which can be shown by favor; cf. Ps 90[89]:17) and "Ties," as he becomes the shepherd. **8.** *I undid the three shepherds:* Much ink has been expended in attempts to identify the three with historical persons and thus to date the oracle. Since the text provides no clue to their identity, the results are vastly divergent, and since this clause interrupts the flow of the text, it may be a later insertion anyway. The text continues with a statement of alienation between the symbolic shepherd and the flock. **10.** The breaking of the staff "Favor" is interpreted as a symbol of the breaking of a covenant "with all the peoples." We know of no such covenant, but Ezek 34:25 and esp. Ezek 37:26–28 may lie behind this. It is hard to see what the function of vv 11–13 is in their present context. **13.** *thirty shekels of silver:* It may be pertinent that this is the amount of indemnity to be paid for a slave gored by an ox (Exod 21:32). *treasury:* So the Syr. The MT's "potter," "one who forms" (*yôṣēr*) can be an error for "treasury" (*'ôṣār*). The LXX's "melting furnace" is attractive, but it is hard to justify textually. This symbolic action, with the sarcastic divine comment, may be a judgment against the priests of the Temple. (See M. Delcor, *VT* 3 [1953] 67–77; J. A. Hoftijzer, *VT* 3 [1953] 407–9.) **14.** The second staff, "Ties," is broken. The symbolism of a complete break between Judah and Israel is just the opposite of that in Ezek 37:15–19 of the two sticks joined. The symbolism is not explained here. **15–17.** The prophet receives a new mandate, to take up the trappings of an evil shepherd. This symbolic action is referred to a person described in v 16 and cursed in an oracle of woe in v 17. If he was a historical person, his identity escapes us. Cf. 13:7–9.

45   (B) The Second Collection (12:1–14:21).

(a) JERUSALEM VICTORIOUS (12:1–9). Again God promises Jerusalem victory over her enemies, but there is a certain rivalry between the inhabitants of Jerusalem and "the clans of Judah." This is especially clear in v 7, which also contains a remark which is not necessarily hostile to Davidic lineage but which expresses some reserve about that lineage's illustrious standing. Rivalry between the establishment and some other group may be suspected. **8.** *like God:* A phrase with a long history, to be taken not literally but as a mythic way of expressing heroic stature.

46   (b) MOURNING AND CLEANSING IN JERUSALEM (12:10–13:1). The topic changes, but there is again reference to the house of David and the inhabitants of Jerusalem, as in the preceding section. **10.** *a spirit of pleasantness and supplication:* That God will pour a spirit into people means that he will take the initiative in bringing about in them a new interior attitude. The tenor of this section indicates that the new attitude must be one flowing from repentance for some wrongdoing which sprang from an evil attitude. *Ḥēn* means "favor," "grace"; the context here suggests the word's sense of grace in the eyes of others, that quality which makes a person pleasant. *Taḥănûnîm* can only mean "supplication"; God will bring about an attitude in which they turn to him to implore favor of him. *they shall look to me/him:* The MT and all the ancient versions have "to me," which expresses the basic turning or converting toward God. If that reading is accepted, then what follows must be separated by a pause, to continue, after an initial *wāw* has been introduced: "and they shall mourn for him whom they have pierced." Many, by removing "to me," emend the text to read "they shall look on him whom they have pierced," which is the sense of the quotation of this in John 19:7 (cf. also Rev 1:7). *him whom they have pierced:* If "him" is taken as God,

to whom they shall look, then the vb. *dāqar* has to be taken in a metaphorical sense, "to offend," as in Prov 12:18, but to take the text that way entails taking the following mourning as a mourning for Yahweh, which seems improbable, but not impossible, given the allusion to a rite of mourning associated with a pagan god in v 11. *Dāqar* properly is used of piercing with a sword or lance. The allusion to a person whom the house of David and the Jerusalemites have caused to be pierced is too vague to permit his identification. Similarities to the Suffering Servant of Isa 53 have been pointed out. Some historical event or situation related also to the violent attitude toward the shepherds in 10:2–3a; 11:4–17, or to the milder expression of partisan spirit in 12:7, may have come immediately to the mind of contemporaries. **11.** *Hadad-rimmon:* The storm-god Hadad, with the epithet Rimmon added to his name, as in 2 Kgs 8:15. Rites of lamentation were associated not with Hadad but with Adonis/Tammuz. Perhaps the prophet simply confused gods as he used the pagan rite in the countryside as an analogy for what he envisaged in Jerusalem. **12–14.** Each of the major social classes in Jerusalem is involved in the mourning: the civil rulers (the house of David), the prophets (the house of Nathan), the Levites (the house of Levi), and the levitical priests (the Shimeites; cf. Exod 6:17). **13:1.** The fountain symbolizes the cleansing of the house of David and the Jerusalemites from their sin.

The parallel elements in this section and in Ezek 36:16–32 are striking: in both God will give or pour a spirit (Ezek 36:27; Zech 12:10), and in both water is used as a symbol of moral cleansing (Ezek 36:25; Zech 13:1) from sin tagged with the word for menstrual impurity (*niddâ:* Ezek 36:17; Zech 13:1).

(Delcor, M., *RB* 58 [1951] 189–99; *VT* 3 [1953] 67–77. Hoftijzer, J. A., *VT* 3 [1953] 407–9.)

47   (c) IDOLS AND PROPHETS REMOVED (13:2–6). The link with the preceding section is made with the catchwords "pierce" and "spirit" (12:10; 13:2,3). The prophet will be pierced because he has spoken falsely. This oracle is directed at all prophets without distinction, however. All will be removed, together with idols and defiling attitudes. **4.** *mantle of hair:* Cf. 2 Kgs 1:8. **5.** *I am no prophet:* Cf. Amos 7:14. **6.** *wounds:* The result of self-mutilation in moments of prophetic frenzy (cf. 1 Kgs 18:28–29).

48   (d) THE SORTING OF SHEPHERD AND FLOCK (13:7–9). **7.** *my shepherd:* Because the shepherd has some particular relation to God, he could be a civil ruler of Judah, or he could be a postexilic high priest. The person intended may be the worthless shepherd of 11:15–17. If, however, God's address to the sword expresses ironic bitterness toward the sword because of God's favor toward the shepherd whom the sword will strike, then other possible lines of interpretation are opened. Some think that this shepherd is the pierced person of 12:10. **8–9.** When the shepherd is struck, the people whom he shepherds will be struck too. The people will be sifted, and those remaining after that eschatological sifting will acknowledge God, as God will them. The final words are an echo of Hos 2:23.

49   (e) TRIAL AND EXALTATION OF JERUSALEM (14:1–21). In vv 1–5 the trial and suffering of Jerusalem on the eschatological "day" are described. Ancient ideas like that of God the divine warrior recur, but the scene is painted in apocalyptic style, with catastrophe and natural upheaval prominent. The trial will sift the people; half will be deported, but there will be a remnant (cf. 13:8). **5.** *reach the side of it:* MT *'ṣl* can be pointed as the word for "side," but the word was perhaps originally *yṣl* (cf. the question of *'ṣr/yṣr* in 11:13), as the LXX would indicate. If so, it may be the proper name of the short valley called Yaṣūl, which empties into the Kidron south of Jerusalem (F. M. Abel, *RB* 45 [1936] 385–400). *earthquake in the days of Uzziah:* Cf. Amos 1:1.

In vv 6–11 the scene changes. The eschatological trial is over, and the new age has been inaugurated. **6.** Cf. Gen 8:22. **7.** Cf. Ezek 47. **9.** In the eschatological age, Yahweh will be king of the universe, but it is also he (alone) who will be king in Jerusalem (cf. v 16). *the Lord will be one:* Cf. Deut 6:4. **10–11.** The spatial image of Jerusalem rising alone above a plain otherwise devoid of contours symbolizes the city's exalted position in the eschatological future. **12–15.** These verses describe the destruction preceding the victory already won; they interrupt the description of Jerusalem's happy position after the final victory, and yet they prepare v 16a.

50   16. As Jerusalem is sifted in the final battle, with a remnant left (13:8–9; 14:2), so will it be with the foreign nations. From that remnant of all the nations, pilgrims will come to Jerusalem to worship Yahweh there (cf. 9:7). It is significant that in the Jerusalem of the coming age envisaged in this passage there is no earthly king, no priest, no prophet. In 13:7–9 a sword was called to strike the shepherd (probably a symbol for king or civil ruler), without provision for a new shepherd to preside over the remnant. According to 13:2–6, prophets are to be eradicated from the future community

along with idols. Priests are completely ignored in all of Zech 9–14. Yahweh's presence is associated here with the city, not with the Temple. When the Temple is mentioned (14:20–21), its holiness is diffused so that it becomes a property of the entire city. The oracular sentiments of 10:3a; 11:4–17; 13:2–9; 14:20–21, and the oracular silences of 14:16–21 and of Zech 9–14 generally, manifest a disillusionment with all the key elements of establishment. This attitude stands in sharp contrast to the attitudes favorable to the establishment which we find in Zech 1–8. *feast of Booths:* The feast of Booths, or Tents, was the old autumnal agricultural feast (→ Institutions, 76:133–38). **17.** *there will be no rain upon them:* That there was a ritual action for obtaining rain, performed during the feast of Booths, has been proposed by M. Delcor (*RHR* 178 [1970] 117–32). Verses 16–19 have also been interpreted in the light of a hypothetically reconstructed feast of Yahweh's enthronement as king (→ Institutions, 76:141–46). **20–21.** The holiness proper to sacred spaces, sacred vessels, sacred persons attached to the Temple will cease to be proper to the Temple. Profane objects, represented by horses' bells and the most ordinary pots, will be just as holy as the holiest vessels of the temple. **21.** The sacrificial cooking reserved to priests and to Levites in Ezek 46:19–24 will be an activity open to anyone. A final sarcastic remark is directed at the conditions prevailing in the Temple: there will be no more venal activities there.

MALACHI

BIBLIOGRAPHY

51   (Also → 1 above.) Boecker, H. J., "Bemerkungen zur formgeschichtlichen Terminologie des Buches Maleachi," *ZAW* 78 (1966) 78–80. Dentan, R. C., "The Book of Malachi," *IB* 6. 1115–44. Fischer, J. A., "Notes on the Literary Form and Message of Malachi," *CBQ* 34 (1972) 315–20. Pfeiffer, E., "Die Disputationsworte im Buch Maleachi," *EvT* 19 (1959) 546–68. Von Bulmerincq, A., *Der Prophet Maleachi* (2 vols.; Dorpat [Tartu], 1926–1932). Wallis, G., "Wesen und Struktur der Botschaft Maleachis," *Das ferne und nahe Wort* (Fest. L. Rost; ed. F. Maass; BZAW 105; Berlin, 1967) 229–37.

INTRODUCTION

52   (I) The Prophet and His Situation. According to the superscription in 1:1, the book is the "word of God to Israel through Malachi (*bĕyad malʾākî*)." In the common opinion today, Malachi was not originally the proper name of the author but the appellative "my messenger" (*malʾākî*) of 3:1, taken later as an appellative referring to the author of the book, and editorially added to the end of 1:1, in the phrase which perhaps originally read "through his messenger" (*bĕyad malʾākô*), as the phrase in fact stands in the Gk of the LXX. To this, it has been objected that the messenger in 3:1 belongs to the eschatological future and that editorially (3:23[4:5]) he is identified with the returning prophet Elijah (B. S. Childs, *CIOTS* 492–94). For others, Malachi in 1:1 is the author's proper name. If that is so, and if the coincidence of the *malʾākî* in 3:1 is not fortuitous, the appellative in 3:1 may be a pun on the author's own name in 1:1.

We know nothing of the author's life, but from his small book we learn something of the kind of person he was. Despite his attacks on priests (1:6–2:4), he was favorable to the levitical priesthood (2:4–7), and he

insisted on the people's obligation to contribute to the expenses of the Temple and the support of the personnel (3:6–12). He had a humane concern for the wife who suffers rejection (2:14–16), for the people of Judah who wonder about God's love for them (1:2–5), and he was sure that those who wrong the defenseless would eventually receive their just deserts from God (3:5). He had a religious sense of God's honor (1:6–14) and of the transcendence which enables God to enforce his will wherever he wishes (1:5).

53   Although we have no way of dating Mal precisely, it is surely more recent than 515, because it presupposes the Temple already built, with its regular system of worship functioning. The regional administrator or governor of the Persian period, the *peḥâ* (→ 8 above), is mentioned in 1:8. Since some of the problems addressed in Mal are among those troubling Nehemia and reformed by Ezra—foreign wives (Mal 2:10–12; Neh 13:3,23–30; Ezra 9:1–15; 10:1–43) and inadequate Temple administration (Mal 1:6–2:9; 3:6–12; Neh 12:44–47; 13:10–14)—it might be easier to place Mal before the time of Ezra, but we are not quite obliged to

do so, for Ezra's reform may not have put a definitive end to the abuses. A study of grammatical usage undertaken in order to date Mal in relation to other postexilic OT works has at least shown that Mal's Hebr usage is fairly close to that of Hag and of Zech, with few of the late characteristics of Neh and Ezra and Chr (A. E. Hill, "Dating the Book of Malachi," *WLSGF,* 77–89). The enthusiastic expectations attached to the program of rebuilding the Temple, evident in Hag and in Zech 1–8, have in Mal given way to routine insouciance, and Zerubbabel (himself *peḥâ* at the time of Hag), instead of being God's signet ushering in a new age (Hag 2:20–23), has by Mal's time vanished from the stage of history. The new age, imminent in Hag and Zech, has not come, and one senses a certain morally stultifying disillusionment in what the people say in Mal 2:17–3:5; 3:13–15. In Mal, new hope is held out, but the coming age is no longer presented as something necessarily soon to be.
54   **(II) Composition.**   Mal, like Zech 9–11 and

Zech 12–14, is brought together under a heading beginning with the word *maśśā'*, "burden" or (with qualification) "oracle" (1:1). Each of Mal's six oracles has the same structure: An initial provocative statement by Yahweh or by the prophet is followed by a remark attributed to the people or to elements among them, which is in turn followed by a rebuttal in which the prophet provides the heart of his message. The book closes with two editorial appendixes.

55   **(III) Outline.**

(I) The Six Oracles (1:1–3:21)
    (A) God's Preferential Love for Israel (1:2–5)
    (B) Cultic Offenses (1:6–2:9)
    (C) Mixed Marriages and Divorce (2:10–16)
    (D) God Will Purify and Justly Judge (2:17–3:5)
    (E) Tithes for God, Blessings for the People (3:6–12)
    (F) Those Who Fear God Will Come Out Ahead (3:13–21) (LXX and Vg 3:13–4:3)
(II) The Two Appendixes (3:22–24) (LXX and Vg 4:4–6)

COMMENTARY

56   **(1) The Six Oracles (1:1–3:21). 1.** *oracle:* (→ 37 above).

(A) God's Preferential Love for Israel (1:2–5). The story of Jacob's supplanting his elder brother Esau and of Esau's ensuing enmity for Jacob (Gen 27:1–45) is used as the basis of an oracle assuring Israel (Jacob) of God's love, demonstrated by God's persevering repression of Israel's usually hostile neighbor Edom, represented by Esau (Gen 25:30; 36:1). **2–3.** *I love Jacob but I hate Esau:* Quoted in Rom 9:13. Here the context is one of God's freely preferring one group over another and of his steadfast perseverance in his original choice. **5.** *beyond the border:* The compound Hebr prepositions express being spatially above the border. Metaphorically God's might and power transcend spatial limitation. His power to determine events is not limited to his chosen land.

57   **(B) Cultic Offenses (1:6–2:9).** The issue is set up in the dialogue at the beginning. **7–8.** The priests have been offending God by offering him animals that are blind or lame, and thus unworthy and unacceptable (cf. Lev 1:3; 22:17–25; Deut 15:21). *governor:* The provincial administrator in the Persian imperial system (→ 8 above). The allusion here is to civil taxation in kind (Neh 5:14–15).

11. *from the rising of the sun to its setting:* Not temporally but spatially; everywhere on earth (cf. Ps 50[49]:1). *incense is offered:* Verbal and nominal forms based on the root *qṭr,* like *muqṭār* here, have to do with any kind of offering which gives off smoke, but in postexilic texts precise enough to let us see what is being offered they have to do with incense or other aromatic substances. The ptc. *muggāš* can be used of bringing any type of offering before God. *pure offering:* Hebr *ṭāhôr* in a cultic context means "pure" in the sense of being free from all that ritually defiles; the contrast with the blemished animals sacrificed by the priests of Jerusalem is thus clear. The word *minḥâ* as a technical cultic term designates a cereal offering (Lev 2); of itself, the word means a pleasant "gift" (and is so translated in the *NEB,* perhaps unfortunately). It will be noted that none of these cultic terms has to do with animal sacrifice, although the practice they describe is being compared with contemporary Israelite practice of animal sacrifice. This verse has received the most attention through the centuries. Many have taken it as referring specifically to the future

Christian eucharistic sacrifice, or to the sacrifice on the cross, or to the quality of sacrifice less specifically in the future messianic era. It is difficult to take the literal sense as having reference to the future. It is made up of nominal clauses, without any finite vb., and the ptc. *muggāš,* "offered," cannot by itself give these clauses future reference any more than do the ptcs. in v 12, whose time reference is clearly present. Many see here an allusion to Jewish worship in the Diaspora, although it can be objected that *baggôyîm* means among the pagan populations themselves, not just in their territory, and that "in every place" means more than just a few Jewish colonies in the Diaspora. It has also been suggested that the verse alludes to worship in the synagogues, in which it was said (in times much later than Mal) that prayer and study of the law took the place of sacrifice. Taken at face value, this verse contrasts the offensive sacrificial abuse (involving animals) in Jerusalem with pleasing oblatory practice (even without sacrificial animals) everywhere else in the world. Pagans at least show the right disposition; Judeans cheat Yahweh. To the objection that so favorable a view of worship among all nations is not consonant with Mal's particularism one may reply that the direct purpose of this verse is not that of praising pagan worship but rather that of shaming the priests of Judah by contrasting the quality of offerings to divinity everywhere else. That pagan offerings are everywhere ritually pure and that pagans everywhere give worship to the name of Yahweh are, in context, less statements of fact than they are rhetorical exaggerations meant to shame Judeans. They move a step further than the universal acknowledgment of Yahweh enunciated in v 14.

(Chary, T., *Les prophètes et le culte à partir de l'exil* [Bibliothèque de théologie 3; Tournai, 1955] 179–86. Rehm, M., "Das Opfer der Völker nach Mal 1,11," *Lex tua veritas* [Fest. H. Junker; ed. H. Gross and F. Mussner; Trier, 1961] 193–208. Swetnam, J., "Malachi 1,11: An Interpretation," *CBQ* 31 [1969] 200–9. Vriezen, T. C., "How to Understand Malachi 1:11," *Grace upon Grace* [Fest. L. J. Kuyper; ed. J. I. Cook; GR, 1975] 128–36.)

14. The blame for providing imperfect animals for sacrifice is now also put on the laypeople who bring the animals in the first place, as they pay a vow or provide a *zebaḥ*-offering. That Yahweh's name is held in fear among the nations is itself an exaggeration (cf. v 11), but it is based on the fact of his universal kingship, transcending the limits of Israel (1:5). In the background may lie the Persian idea that all peoples of the empire worshiped the same God of heaven, an idea from which Judeans in the Persian period reaped some practical benefits (see P. Frei and K. Koch, *Reichsidee und Reichsorganisation im Perserreich* [OBO 55; Fribourg, 1984]).

2:1–9. The priests are furthermore accused of abuse in giving instruction (*tôrâ*) and of disregarding God's ways more generally. Their comportment is now contrasted with the good behavior of the ideal eponymous priestly ancestor Levi and, in v 7, with the expectations which people have of a priest as one who communicates the mind and will of God. **4.** *covenant with Levi:* A covenant with levitical priests is mentioned in Jer 34:21–22, and in Num 25:10–13 a covenant is made with Aaron's grandson Phinehas in which God promises enduring priesthood for Phinehas's descendants.

58   (C) Mixed Marriages and Divorce (2:10–16). The objection to marriage with foreigners is made on religious grounds. **10.** Israelites are here reckoned as being an extended family, children of Yahweh, whereas foreigners are children of their own national gods (v 11). To marry outside the society of Israel is to be unfaithful both to Yahweh and to one's fellow Israelites. *covenant of our fathers:* This may be an allusion to the covenant of Sinai, violated by the danger of apostasy involved in foreign marriage, or it may be an allusion to the covenant with God to put away all foreign wives and their children, which Ezra required of the Judeans (Ezra 10:3). The objection to putting away one's own Israelite wife is made on humane grounds reinforced by God's kindly will. **14.** God himself will defend the wife's position, for he is the divine guarantor who is to punish violation of the stipulations of the marriage covenant (Gen 31:50; Prov 2:17).

59   (D) God Will Purify and Justly Judge (2:17–3:5). The problem addressed is the people's cynicism in the face of the prosperity of evildoers. It is met with a promise of future judgment in which justice will be meted out and elements of society will be purged and purified. **3:1.** *my messenger:* Hebr *mal'ākî* (→ 52 above). Some commentators, noting the change from first person to third person, believe him to be distinct from the messenger of the covenant of v 1b, while others identify them as the same. Some few see the person in v 1b as a human messenger, perhaps an anonymous priest, or Ezra, but the majority take him as an "angel" who is really to be identified with God himself, acting in the world through a visible form (see the survey in T. Chary, *Les prophètes et le culte* [→ 57 above] 176–78). Verse 1a, adapted slightly, is applied to John the Baptist in Matt 11:10 and Mark 1:2). *the lord:* Hebr *hā'ādôn* may be an epithet of God but is not necessarily so. The covenant intended may be the Sinaitic covenant, but it may also be the covenant with Levi (2:4–5), since the messenger of the covenant is to purify the ranks of the sons of Levi (3:3–4), thus ending the abuses that are the object of 1:6–2:9. **5.** God speaks again in the first person. It is he who will testify against all those who do wrong and commit injustice in violation of the laws of the covenant (see also 2:14).

60   (E) Tithes for God, Blessings for the People (3:6–12). In the initial dialogue the topic at issue is set as a matter of mutual return from the alienation that exists between the people and God. **10.** The practical way for the people to return to God lies in their providing for the upkeep of the Temple and of its personnel. This is somewhat unusual in comparison with the requirements for conversion in the prophetic books generally and in Deut, which have to do rather with turning from false swearing, false worship, and the oppression of the defenseless in violation of God's will. Here God's requirement, which the people must fill, lies in the economic necessities of the house of God. **10b–11.** The needs of the people which God will take care of if they return to him are also expressed as economic needs: those of abundant rain and of protection from agricultural misfortunes. Haggai earlier had proclaimed God's requirement of a rebuilt Temple as the condition for meeting the economic prosperity of the people (Hag 1:5–11; 2:15–19). This oracle in Mal has a similar proposal, but the Temple is already built, and the needs of God's house are now those of its upkeep. **12.** This announcement, universalist in its horizons but particularist in its reservation of beatitude to Israel alone, supplements the oracle on God's preferential love for Israel in 1:2–5.

61   (F) Those Who Fear God Will Come Out Ahead (3:13–21) (LXX and Vg 3:13–4:3). **13–15.** The problem addressed is much like that of 2:17–3:5: the murmuring of those who notice the empirical fact that those who prosper are not necessarily those who adhere to God's wishes. **16.** *a book of remembrance:* The image of a written record of the names of the just or of those who are destined for life is found in Exod 32:32–33; Ps 69(68):28; Isa 4:3; Dan 12:1; Rev 20:12,15. **17.** *special possession:* Hebr *sĕgullâ*, used of Israel in contexts in which God's election is expressed (Exod 19:5; Deut 7:6; 14:2; 26:18; Ps 135[134]:4). New here is the idea that God's special possession is the group of those who fear him—not all Israel distinguished from other peoples or nations but a group distinguished from the wicked within Israel itself. **19–21(4:1–3).** The image of the furnace recurs (cf. 3:2–3), but here only the wicked will be subject to the burning, while the group of those who fear the Lord will experience the healing warmth of the sun of justice. (For images of the winged solar disk, see *ANEP* nos. 281, 320, 321, 351, 447, 486, 534, 653, 706.)

62   (II) The Two Appendixes (3:22–24) (LXX and Vg 4:4–6). **22(4:4).** The first appendix is a call to be mindful of Moses and the law mediated through him. The striking thing in this short verse is its massively deuteronomic language: Horeb instead of Sinai, statutes and ordinances, the command to "remember."

23–24(4:5–6). The second appendix is a declaration of divine intention to send the prophet Elijah, that he may clear the way before the Day of the Lord. This seems to identify the anonymous messenger of 3:1 with Elijah, but here it is said that he will have a task of reconciliation to perform within the families of the community, without which God would destroy the land on the day of his coming. There is nothing in the account of Elijah's life in Kgs that explains why this task should be his. Since he departed this world not by death but by being taken up to heaven (2 Kgs 2:10–12), he might more easily return to earth for the mission of reconciliation before the day of the Lord's coming.

23

THE CHRONICLER: 1–2 CHRONICLES, EZRA, NEHEMIAH

Robert North, S.J.

BIBLIOGRAPHY

1 *Commentaries:* Ackroyd, P. R., *I–II Chronicles, Ezra, Nehemiah* (TBC; London, 1975). Becker, J., *1–2 Chronik* (NEchtB 14; Würzburg, 1988). Braun, R., *1 Chronicles* (WBC; Waco, 1986). Churgin, P., *The Targum to Hagiographa* (NY, 1945) 236–75. Coggins, R. J., *The First and Second Books of the Chronicles* (CBC; Cambridge, 1976). Dillard, R., *2 Chronicles* (WBC 15; Waco, 1987). Goldberg, A. M., *Könige I–II, Chronik I–II* (Freiburg, 1970). Le Déaut, R. and J. Robert, *Targum des Chroniques* (AnBib 51; Rome, 1971). McConville, J. G., *Chronicles* (DSB; Phl, 1984). Mangan, C., *1–2 Chronicles, Ezra, Nehemiah* (OTM 13; Wilmington, 1982). Michaeli, F., *Les livres des Chroniques, d'Esdras et de Néhémia* (CAT 16; Neuchâtel, 1967). Myers, J., *1 Chronicles, 2 Chronicles* (AB 12–13; GC, 1965). Roubos, K., *1/2 Kronieken* (Nijkerk, 1969/72). Rudolph, W., *Chronikbücher* (HAT; Tübingen, 1955). Saltman, A., ed., *Stephen Langton, Commentary on the Book of Chronicles* (Ramat-Gan, 1978). Slotki, I. W., *Chronicles* (London, 1978). Traylor, J. H., *1–2 Kings, 1 Chronicles* (Nash, 1981). Williamson, H. G. M., *1 & 2 Chronicles* (NCB; GR, 1982).

Studies: Ackroyd, P. R., IDBSup 156–58. Barthélemy, D., ed., *Critique textuelle de l'Ancien Testament* 1 (OBO 50; Fribourg, 1982). Ben-David, A., *Parallels in the Bible: Samuel–Chronicles* (Jerusalem, 1972). Childs, B., CIOTS 639–55. Graham, M. P., *The Utilization of I and II Chronicles in the Reconstruction of Israelite History in the Nineteenth Century* (diss. Emory; Atlanta, 1983). Japhet, S., "The Supposed Common Authorship of Chronicles and Ezra–Nehemiah Investigated Anew," *VT* 18 (1968) 330–71. Kaiser, O., *Einleitung in das Alte Testament* (Gütersloh, 1984) 178–94. Kegler, J. and M. Augustin, *Synopse zum chronistischen Geschichtswerk* (Frankfurt, 1984). McKenzie, S. L., *The Chronicler's Use of the Deuteronomistic History* (HSM 33; Atlanta, 1984). Mathias, D., *Die Geschichte der Chronikforschung im 19. Jahrhundert* (Leipzig, 1977). Mazar, B., *EncB* (Jerusalem, 1954) 2. 596–606. Micheel, R., *Die Seher- und Prophetenüberlieferungen in der Chronik* (BBET 18; Frankfurt, 1983). Mosis, R., *Untersuchungen zur Theologie des chronistischen Geschichtswerkes* (FTS 92; Freiburg, 1973). Noth, M., *The Chronicler's History* (JSOTSup 50; Sheffield, 1987). Saebo, M., TRE 8. 74–87. Soggin, J. A., *Introduction to the Old Testament* (Phl, 1982) 539–46. Welten, P., *Geschichte und Geschichtsdarstellung in den Chronikbüchern* (WMANT 42; Neukirchen, 1973). Willi, T., *Die Chronik als Auslegung* (FRLANT 106; Göttingen, 1972). Williamson, H. G. M., *Israel in the Books of Chronicles* (Cambridge, 1977).

INTRODUCTION

2 **(I) Genre.** The last books of the Hebr Bible are called "Annals" (*dibrê yāmîm*), i.e., Chronicles; in Greek "Leftovers" (from Kings-era: *paraleipomena*). Chronicles is by our standards a book of history. Partly it is a dull, dry listing of genealogies, partly a collection of lively sermons. Neither of these types exactly fits our definition of history, but then every history has its own ethos. Why was this *third* history written, after the deuteronomistic history (Josh–Kgs) and the final redaction of the Pentateuch? The answer must depend in part on whether Ezra is included in the Chronicler's work, and whether Ezra's law was the Pentateuch or part of it in the final form he gave it.

The principal block of Chr sets forth the achievement of David, chiefly the regulation of the Temple cult, narrated in 323 verses (as against only 77 in Samuel, and 73 in Chr on David's military or civil activities). Both David's rise to power in displacing Saul and the mel-ancholy saga of succession to David's throne are omitted. In exchange, the emergence of David is introduced chiefly by lengthy genealogies: his own Judah tribe in 100 verses (1 Chr 2–4); the Chronicler's Levite clan in 80 verses (chap. 6); a skeletal history of the human race from Adam to Saul (chaps. 1–9). Thus, from a surface look we may say that Chr was written to glorify and consolidate the ritual and dynastic authority of the Davidic covenant, almost wholly ignoring the covenant of Moses and Sinai so largely focused elsewhere in the Bible. Not only David but Solomon too is glorified, and these two along with two other "approved" kings (out of 21) occupy 480 of the 822 verses.

3 Since *JBC* there has arisen a forceful opposition to the notion of "a Chronicler including Ezra." Hence, in this *NJBC* we will no longer simply presume such a unity, which in 1968 was almost unanimously agreed. "The Chronicler's work *may* include Ezra, but to delineate 'his' theology [or his aim, or his sources] it is better to treat them apart" (M. Saebo, *TRE* 8. 83). Where we utilize below the word "Chronicler" it will be in reference to the hypothesis that his work included also the Ezra books. But wherever possible we will use the term "Chronicles" to refer to that work without presuppositions. Yet even the recent antagonists of such a "Chronicler" admit that we cannot evaluate the aim and authorship of *either* work without taking into account the arguments for and against the coalescence with Ezra.

S. Japhet in her 1973 Hebrew doctorate [partly available in *VT* 18 (1968) 330-71] may well be taken as spokesperson of the newer trend. Its advocates mostly follow and support her; its resisters reduce most later contributions to hers. Her notion of "common authorship" is rather monolithic, overlooking that the virtual 1920-1970 unanimity in favor of "a Chronicler" recognized fully (a) the peculiarities of the various Nehemiah as well as Ezra sections, foreign bodies not assimilated by "the Chronicler's" editing; and (b) even within the canonical Chronicles, *stages* of dual authorship or interpolation (*JBC* 24:6). Japhet takes for the pivotal point at issue the uniformity of *diction* between Chr and Ezra-Neh, which she rejects with methodological rigor. This aspect of her program was carried forward by H. Williamson (as mere preliminary to his original view of Israel in Chr). Others draw from Japhet's statistics only the conclusion that Chr is a different *work* of the same author (as already A. Fernández, *Comentario a los libros de Esdras y Nehemías* [Madrid, 1950] 20, which no one seems to notice). Validity of Japhet-style statistical disproofs has been largely relativized by lengthy reviews of Williamson by H. Cazelles (*VT* 29 [1979] 375-80) and S. Croft, *JST* 14 [1979] 68-72). The question must remain open.

4   (II) Historicity.   Confining ourselves therefore to canonical Chr and prescinding from Ezra, we find that the picture has changed notably since *JBC* 24:4. We there noted a growing trend to vindicate against Pfeiffer-style "debunking the fabrications of Chronicles" an insistence that it gives genuine historical details sometimes unknown from other sources, but now "confirmed by archeology." Against such glib "archeological proofs" we cautioned even there, and more searchingly in the Myers Festschrift (→ 75 below). Meantime there have been several researches into the question, Did the author of Chronicles really *intend* to write history, or what? (for a quick survey, see J. Newsome, *JBL* 94 [1975] 201-17).

"Chronicles is properly prophetic exegesis (of Kings); the 'other' sources which it names are simply in imitation of Kings" was the thesis of T. Willi (*Die Chronik* 233). R. Mosis in rejecting this "exegesis-aim" proposes that the differing Ezra-Nehemiah world was portrayed according to a David-Solomon era model, but leaving open still-remediable deficiencies. P. Welten (*Geschichte*), also rejecting "Chronicles as exegesis," claims to arrive at Willi's "essential" conclusion; we have here "the free creativity of a parable" and the structured literary work of a *single* Chronicles author; the building operations and standing armies described by 2 Chr (14:6; → 55 below) are for Welten "fictions" (p. 45) yet a true portrayal of history—of his own day.

This "flood of 1965-75 publications" inherits uncritically from the 19th cent. its denial of any *prophetic* aim in Chronicles, says D. Mathias (summarized by M. Graham, *JBL* 103 [1984] 442-44): he proposes instead that just as Samuel-Kings wrote "(Earlier) Prophets' history," so Chronicles wrote "Priest-Levite history," using prophetic figures but often turning them into Levites (*Geschichte* 309). (Chronicles' "prophets" are ser-

monizers *sans* professional uniqueness or power either to produce signs or to shape history in God's name: Y. Amit, *BM* 28 [1982] 113-33. But "it was by prophecy that the monarchy was founded [1 Chron 11:3], reproved [e.g. 2 Chron 24:20] and finally destroyed [2 Chron 36:15]," Mangan, *1-2 Chronicles* 6). Mathias (*Geschichte* 102) further warns against the 19th-cent. norm "nearer in time to the facts means historically more reliable" (implying perhaps also that a work using *documents* like Ezra gains credibility over earlier works which do not).

"Seer and Prophet Traditions in Chronicles," a fifth German doctoral dissertation by R. Micheel, specifies that the author uses for any prophet a designation which he finds in his *Vorlage,* but reserves *nābî'* for the chief among several and avoids giving the *same* title (*ḥōzeh, rō'eh,* "man of God") to several mentioned together. A similar focus of interest is shown by D. L. Petersen, *Late Israelite Prophecy* (SBLMS 25; Missoula, 1977).

We conclude: Chronicles adds rarely to whatever sources it used, chiefly canonical Kings, perhaps in an alternative *Vorlage* or from the composition cited as "Midrash on Kings" in 2 Chr 24:27. This could have included also the eleven separate prophets cited explicitly by name. In using this source, the author injects his own "clerical" or perhaps rather "prophetic" personality and convictions chiefly by omitting, suppressing, or slanting. But among the rare additions may be retained the six cases of impassioned pleading in 2 Chr and a seventh in 1 Chr, attributed to a preexisting volume of "Levitical Sermons" (G. von Rad, *PHOE* 267-80; see now M. Throntveit, *VT* 32 [1982] 201-16).

5   (III) Eschatology.   Presuming what is said above about Ezra, historicity, and sources, two factors still dominate. On the one hand, Chr seems clearly to accept the religious and political status quo, a levitical conservatism (O. Plöger, *Theocracy and Eschatology* [Oxford, 1968]; Rudolph). "The author assumes that the will of God has been made known through revelation. It does not need to be actualized or reinterpreted for a new era"; he did not *change* but "sought to explore the outer limits which the text allowed in order to reconcile the differences" between Kgs and legal traditions (Childs, *CIOTS* 644, 648). The alternative claim, naturally underlying recent proposals of a prophetic aim in the author of Chr, is that he is not fully satisfied with the status quo. The extreme messianism claimed by A. Noordtzij in *RB* 49 (1940) 168 was toned down by R. de Vaux in 64 (1957) 280 to what *JBC* accepted as a "middle way": Chr fosters a genuinely messianic hope—but in its preexilic dynastic form rather than with the eschatological stress it had come to take on in its time of composition—as an affirmation of the divinely willed definitiveness of the Davidic line, rather than as a remedy for its current deficiencies. A "middle way" meanwhile discovered in Cross and Newsome by Williamson (*TynBul* 28 [1977] 120, 149) is not really so different: Chr hoped for restoration of a Davidic-line ruler ("not properly 'messianic,'" p. 54).

6   (IV) Date.   As set forth in *JBC* 24:6, and practically also now in *TRE* 8. 83 and Welten (*Geschichte* 200), commentators have advocated for Chr (usually with Ezra) a spectrum of dates which seemed vast, but which upon closer look reduced to a cluster around 400, another around 200, apart from D. N. Freedman's 515. Moreover, most of these exegetes advocated (partially on account of the "genealogical vestibule" of 1 Chr 1-9) a "double edition," either by progressive accretions through all that time or in a clearly dated "First Chronicler" followed by a thoroughgoing "Second Chronicler" reedition (not excluding some few interpolations of even later date, e.g., 2 Chr 26:6 toponymy). To this picture must be added now chiefly favor shown for the *three* Chroniclers of F. Cross, all before 400: the first being Freedman's of 515 (the others — 450 without 1 Chr 1–4 or 2 Chr 35f., and 400 — relate to the light shed on "Sanballat" by the Daliyeh papyri; see below on Neh 4:1).

7   (V) Canon and Text. Chr is presumed to be the *last* book to be received into the Hebr canon, since it is put after Neh (2 Chr 36:22 having been then repeated in Ezra 1:1 "when they were detached"; but this conspicuous doublet is no real proof of unitary authorship). Not all Hebr mss. assign this last place to Chr; the "Palestine tradition" puts it immediately after the Psalms (whose organization it described) and puts Ezra-Neh at the end of the Writings (P. Ackroyd, *IDBSup* 157). The LXX preserves the natural order of Chr before Ezra, though with the embarrassing intrusion of 1 Esdras. This may prove that Alexandrian Jewry had a canon in that order or that the notion of "canonicity" was of Christian origin before Jewish readers felt its need.

Text study has been enriched by the discovery of Aleppo Codex 2 Chr 35:7–36:19 (M. Beit-Arié, *Tarbiz* 51 [1982] 171–73) and of the masorah of 1 Chr 4–9 (G. Weil, *Textus* 11 [1984] 70–87). The targum has been newly published, and its editorial observation is that the theologizing and clarifying aims of the targum continue those of Chr itself (R. Le Déaut, *Targum* 27). A special similarity of Chr with the Qumran Temple Scroll has been noted chiefly in the use of particles (T. Yohanan, *RevQ* 11 [1983] 423–26). The Chronicles' *matres lectionis* stem not from its author but from the Maccabee period when Jews were showing more interest in the study of Hebrew (conclusion from some statistics located in Willi, *Chronik* 82). The famed *Kaige* recension in "Reigns" begins to underlie the Chr parallels only after 2 Kgs 10:1; and the Gk translator used an existing Old Greek Reigns but modified it to bring it into conformity with the Hebr text of 1 Chr (J. Shenkel, *HTR* 62 [1969] 63–85).

Two volumes by L. C. Allen on *The Greek Chronicles* (VTSup 25, 27; Leiden, 1974) date the translation to 150 BC, and reject the attribution to Theodotion (AD 200), made by C. C. Torrey and E. L. Curtis; the translator varies in style between literalist and prudently free; in close proximity the article is sometimes used, sometimes omitted; conjunctions tend to be literal, prepositions more elegant; the Gk Pentateuch serves him as dictionary and commentary. With G. Gerleman, Allen (*Greek Chronicles* 25, 182) holds him likelier a "haphazard assimilator" than Shenkel's "ruthless redactor who works out a pattern of stock changes." For Allen, M. Rehm unduly claims that G (earliest Gk Chr form) used some Rg, rather than a Hebr text agreeing with Hebr Sam–Kgs; Rehm thus unduly ignores the psychological probability that Sam–Kgs even where corrupt carried authority because of their wider use: "often heard, it would creep into his mind and whisper its plausible message that here Chronicles needed 'correction' as from a master text" (*Greek Chronicles* 177).

8   (VI) Author's Personality and Theology. A fresh new outlook on his anthropology has been offered in several statistical researches of J. P. Weinberg. Chr never uses *ḥayyâ*, *nĕkēbâ*, *nĕšāmâ* or any other word applicable to both human and beast; and also his preference for other rare words shows how he sets human beings apart (*Klio* 63 [1981] 25–37); "forget," "weep" never occur, and there are more words for intellectual and less for emotional processes than in the OT overall (*VT* 33 (1983) 298–317; *OLP* 13 [1982] 71–89); ʿ*ēdâ* is never used, and *qāhāl* is "the orderly we" as contrasted with "the chaotic them," upon whom the judgment is milder than in Kgs, neither narrow-minded nor open-

hearted (*Klio* 66 [1984] 19–35; further 58 [1976] 5–20; 59 [1977] 27–29).

Observations in *JBC* on humanity's relation to God may now be amplified with information on theology of cult (T. Brzegowy, *Ateneum Kapłańskie* 99 [1982] 429–42) and on short range retribution (R. Dillard, *WTJ* 46 [1984] 164–72). Our claim that Chr was written to vindicate the definitiveness of David's covenant over Sinai seems unaffected by recent research, even by J. D. Levenson (*CBQ* 41 [1979] 205–19); it is supported by D. J. McCarthy, *Old Testament Covenant* (Richmond, 1972) 47; and Mangan can say (*1–2 Chronicles* 16), if we had only Chr we could question whether there ever was an exodus. R. Braun's view (*JBL* 92 [1973] 504) that our *JBC* downgrades Solomon has received tacit support in the several recent researches which make Solomon rather than David the key figure of Chr (→ 29 below). We may profess here an esteem for Solomon's (wisdom) achievements far above the exegetes' par; but every hero has the counterpart of his virtues, which may at times seem humorous even to the sympathetic observer. And we still "cannot escape the impression that the Chronicler himself would have preferred that David should build the Temple" (R. Mosis, *Untersuchungen* 96; so Williamson, *VT* 26 [1976] 357; Michaeli, *Livres des Chroniques* 27, 109; see now Im Tae-Soo, "Das Davidbild in den Chronikbüchern" [diss. Bonn, 1984]).

There is still general agreement that the author of Chr is a Levite cantor whose own genealogy is probably that given in 1 Chr 3:19–24; in general he mentions Levites 100 times (+ Ezra-Neh 60) as against once in Kgs and twice in Sam! The mention of the priesthood itself is by contrast uniformly belittling; cultic functionaries who do so little are better remunerated than the Levites and choir who do so much. This may be seen as a warning for the clergy today or, more broadly, as a social-justice norm: workers (even in the sanctuary) should receive realistic remuneration. More broadly still, the Chronicles' tender concern for a live ritual — aesthetic, vocal, and conservative — is perhaps its chief message for our century. Its rubricalism is not sterile but engulfs every zone of God's revealed word, wisdom and prophets no less than Torah and Psalms.

9   (VII) Outline [1–2 Chr].

(I) Threshold Genealogies (1 Chr 1:1–9:44)
  (A) The Semites in the Family of Nations (1:1–54)
  (B) The Twelve Tribes (2:1–7:40)
    (a) Judah's Line (2:1–4:23)
      (i)   Judah to Jesse (2:3–17)
      (ii) First Caleb saga (2:18–41)
      (iii) Two variant Caleb sagas (2:42–55)
      (iv) David's own line (3:1–24)
      (v)   Three more Caleb sagas (4:1–23)
    (b) Rest of the SE Amphictyony (4:24–5:26)
    (c) The Levites (6:1–81; MT 5:27–6:66)
      (i)   Moses and Samuel (6:1–30; MT 5:27–6:15)
      (ii) Lineage of the Levite choir (6:31–48)
      (iii) Zadokite legitimacy (6:49–53)
      (iv) The Levite settlements (6:54–81)
    (d) Pre-David Northern Elements (7:1–40)
  (C) Saul/Jerusalem Setting (8:1–9:44)
(II) David's Empire (10:1–29:30)
  (A) Legitimacy of the Succession (10:1–11:9)
  (B) David's Militia (11:10–12:40)
  (C) Theocratic Consolidation (13:1–17:27)
    (a) Recovery of the Ark (13:1–14)
    (b) Building Up the House of David (14:1–17)
    (c) Tabernacle Inauguration (15:1–16:43)
    (d) Temple Project Deferred (17:1–27)
  (D) Empire-Building Wars (18:1–21:7)
    (a) East-Jordan Campaigns (18:2–20:3)
    (b) Philistine Episodes (20:4–8)

COMMENTARY ON 1 CHRONICLES

10   Threshold Genealogies (1 Chr 1:1–9:44).
The Christian will value these chapters as a basis and
foreshadowing of Matt and Luke; cf. M. D. Johnson,
*The Purpose of the Biblical Genealogies with Special Reference
to the Setting of the Genealogies of Jesus* (SNTSMS 8; Cambridge, 1969). A title is furnished in 1 Chr 9:1: "genealogical records of all Israel from the book of the Kings
of Israel." From the basic genealogical core can be
distinguished added geographical data and minor notes.
Monotony and inconsistencies of this literary form must
not blind a modern reader to its indispensable role,
replaced nowadays by parish and civil record offices, in
vindicating legitimacy of both family and function.
Using Genesis (chap. 46, but telescoping the rest) and
Num 26, Chr also attains indirectly a more cherished
objective. By eliminating all narrative from the history
of humankind since Adam, it imposes the impression
that all was a rather unimportant preliminary to David.
The covenants of Noah, Abraham, Shechem, and esp.
Sinai are passed over. What is disapproved is not these
theophanies themselves, but a popular absorption in
them out of proportion to the now preeminent ascendancy of the David line. To this extent those covenants
are presumed in the hasty genealogies. To regard the
whole of chaps. 1–9 as a later addition would be to
misconceive the aim of the book: so now Coggins
(*Chronicles*) and Johnson (*Purpose* 55), after scrutiny of de
Vaux and others for whom chaps. 1–9 are a chief basis
for their hypothesis of a "Second Chronicler."

**11   (A) The Semites in the Family of Nations
(1:1–54). 5.** This classification, borrowed from some
compilation older than the P document of Gen 5:1, is
based on purely experiential appearances, as when we
say "the sun rises." The norm is not really geographical
adjacence. Sidon is made a descendant of Egypt, with
which it was linked commercially by sea. Canaan, too,
is identified with Egypt, doubtless because of the
hegemony Egypt had there. The assertion of such relationships via a common father is akin to the naming of
a town in 2:50 as parent of an individual or of another
town. **19.** The targum here begins to combine four
popular etymologies differing from *Gen. Rab.* (Le
Déaut). **32.** In so brief a "world history" is allotted considerable space to the off line of Abraham. The intention
seems to be to clarify for 3d-cent. readers the bonds of
proximity and enmity linking Arabs, Nabateans, Edom-
Seir, Midian, and Cain (see comment on 2:3,55; see also
Gen 25:4,13; 36:9).

12   (B) The Twelve Tribes (2:1–7:40).
(a) JUDAH'S LINE (2:1–4:23). **1.** Chr through-

out calls Jacob by his community name Israel, perhaps to
avoid recalling the lusty pranks of Gen 25:26 to 30:37.
See now Williamson, *Israel;* and "Sources and Redaction
in the Chronicler's Genealogy of Judah," *JBL* 98 (1979)
351–59. Jacob's sons are given as in Gen 35:23 but
without the intricacies of their four mothers amplified in
Gen 29–30. Dan should be with Naphtali; but 17
different sequences of the 12 sons are found in the Bible,
or 20 when we include *Jub.* and Philo.

(i) *Judah to Jesse* (2:3–17). **3.** Among the 12,
Judah is not singled out, but he is closely associated with
Levi (Temple and priesthood). Their descendants are
given at greater length: Judah, 102 verses; Levi, 81; all
the rest, 126. Within Judah, a chaotic sequence and
repetition result from preservation of every datum
regarding the presence of non-Israelite tribes, such as
Jerahmeel and even Cain among David's progenitors
(see 2:53). **4.** Perez is here father of Hezron; the other
four sons of Judah are Er, Onan (Gen 38:8!), Shelah, and
Zerah. In 4:1 the five sons of Judah are Perez, Hezron,
Hur, Shobal, and Carmi (Caleb). Thus is preserved not
only the real genealogy but also a variant in which some
disedifying ancestors are skipped, with the result that a
brother may appear as an uncle or even father. **5.** *Hamul:*
Also in Num 26:21; may be a variant for Mahol of 1 Kgs
4:31, linked via Heman (1 Chr 15:17) with the origins
of both wisdom and psalmody. **9.** *Chelubai:* Variant of
Caleb. **10.** Jerahmeel and Ram tribes (rather than the
shadowy Simeon and Reuben) formed part of M. Noth's
six-tribe southern "amphictyony," which we continue
here to regard as defensible and illuminating, despite
widespread recent rejection. **15.** *David the seventh:* In
1 Sam 17:12, Jesse has eight sons; David is the youngest;
since only the three oldest are there named, perhaps here
is omitted a fifth who had no descendants, possibly Elihu
of 1 Chr 27:18 unless this is a variant to Eliab. **17.** *Jether,
Ishmaelite:* Ithra in 2 Sam 17:25, where MT "Israelite" is
a copyist error; Jethro is a Midianite clan name for the
father-in-law of Moses (Exod 3:1).

13   (ii) *First Caleb saga* (2:18–41). The name
Caleb occurs here in seven separate settings, so interwoven that it is impossible to reduce them even to three
distinct individuals: those of Hezron, Jephunneh, and
Hur: cf. R. North, *BeO* 8 (1966) 167–71. (W. Beltz [*Die
Kaleb-Tradition im Alten Testament* (BWANT 98; Stuttgart, 1974)] focuses rather the relationships which he
finds with nomads, and with dogs.) **18.** *Azubah:* The
name of this first wife means "desert waste" in Isa 6:12.
Caleb's second wife is Jerioth, which means "tents." If
his third wife's name, Ephrath, stands for the town of

Bethlehem, we may have here the record of a progressive sedentarization (Wellhausen). Relevance of Judg 17–19 is noted by M. Nadav ("Ephraim, Ephrath and the Settlement in the Judean Hill Country," *Zion* 49 [1984] 325–31; Eng. XIII). **19.** On Hur, see Exod 31:1. Caleb's taking his father's wife is a way of indicating the legitimate inheritance of his possessions, as in 2 Sam 16:22. **21.** *Machir* in Josh 14:13 is the connecting link between the Joseph tribe Manasseh and the previous occupant of this NE Jordan area, Gilead. Linking of Caleb with Midian via Kenaz in Josh 14:6; Gen 36:15; 1 Chr 1:36; 4:13 (Judg 3:9) is confirmed by Caleb's late-in-life "espousal" or colonization of Gilead, the refuge of Midian in Judg 6. **22.** The cities of Jair here number 23; there are 30 in Judg 10:3, but 60 in Josh 13:30; 1 Chr 2:23. Geshur and Aram stand for Arabia (Neh 2:19) and Syria. **24.** *Ashhur,* also in 4:5, represents the Hur of 2:19. **25.** *Jerahmeel:* Here father of Ram, not his brother as in 2:9. **31.** Sheshan has a son Ahlai, but the assumption that he had no sons occasions in 2:34–41 the pedigree of Elishama, member of a known Egyptian border family, possibly the priest of 2 Chr 17:8, whose educational and reforming activities were congenial.

14 (iii) *Two variant Caleb sagas* (2:42–55). **42.** *Mareshah:* Twice, for the first of which MT (and *NAB* in brackets) reads Mesha, the name of the Moabite king (2 Kgs 3:4) whose monument was found at Dibon. Mareshah is the name of the town that in Greco-Roman times supplanted Beth-gubrin near Lachish. **45.** Beth-zur, N of Hebron, became important chiefly with 1 Macc 6:26. **50.** Reading "grandsons of Caleb: first, the sons of Hur," we pass farther N to the region of Bethlehem; perhaps there was pressure by invaders from the S, but the main concern is to explain how David of Judah is so intimately linked with the non-Israelite clans around Hebron (2 Sam 2:1; 5:5). **52.** *Kiriath-jearim* (= Baalah, 1 Sam 7:1) is 12 mi. W of Jerusalem; on the lowest slope W are Zorah and Eshtaol (Judg 13:25). **53.** These may be either personal names otherwise unattested, or descriptive terms, possibly connected with music and thus with David's cult reforms. **55.** *scribes:* Perhaps "inhabitants of scribe-city," Kiriath-sepher, called also "copper-city," and Debir, equated by W. F. Albright with the Mirsim mound excavated by him, but sought elsewhere by German experts. *Rechab:* See Jer 35:7.

15 (iv) *David's own line* (3:1–24). **1.** *sons of David:* Fits after 2:15. *Hebron:* Here is admitted what is cautiously suppressed after chap. 10: David's seven-year wait for the northern crown (2 Sam 5:5). The birth of Amnon, Absalom, and Adonijah in Hebron diminishes their claim to the succession, as rivals to Jerusalem-born Solomon. Bathshua is an alternative form for Bathsheba; no mention is made of the affair told in 2 Sam 11:4. **15.** Johanan did not reign. Zedekiah is given both as son (by blood) of Josiah and as legal son (successor) of his own nephew, Jeconiah. **18.** Shenazzar: See Ezra 1:8. **19.** None of these descendants of Zerubbabel occurs in the Matt/Luke genealogy (Coggins, *Chronicles* 26). **21.** The *RSV* prefers the LXX to the MT, making 11 instead of only 6 generations between Hananiah and Shecaniah. **22.** *six:* Thus MT and LXX, though both name only five.

16 (v) *Three more Caleb sagas* (4:1–23). **1.** Continues 2:55 or, rather, adds variants. Carmi, as probably also Chelub of v 11, is to be equated with Caleb of 2:18,19. **3.** The sporty maiden name Hazzelelponi borrows its *poni* from the following name (Penuel) by dittography. **8.** *Koz:* Contemporary of Ezra (2:61). **10.** A pun, by metathesis: "his mother called him 'hurts' (*'bṣ*) but God made it 'no-hurts'" (*'ṣb*); similarly Hos 2:23. **12.** *Recah,* for Rechab of 2:55, as LXX. **17.** *Miriam:* a strange addition to our knowledge of the heroine of

Exod 15:20, with no hint that she is Moses' sister (see 6:3 below). For the corrupt vv 17–19 has been proposed: "[Jether] fathered Miriam, Shammai, Ishbah. [Mered had two wives: one from Egypt and one from Judah.] His [Egyptian] wife bore him Jered . . . Jekuthiel. [17] These were the sons of Bithiah, the daughter of Pharaoh espoused by Mered. His other wife was [Hodiah, i.e., 'she of Judah'] the sister of Nacham; and her sons were fathers of [the towns] Keilah and Eshtemoa." **23.** Jerome's tendency to translate proper names may be in place here, because it suggests various guilds rather than localities, e.g., potters, gardeners, smelters.

17 (b) REST OF THE SE AMPHICTYONY (4:24–5:26). **24.** *Simeon:* With Num 26:13 is overlooked the Canaanite mother of Shaul (Gen 46:10). Mibsam is an Ishmaelite in 1 Chr 1:29–30. **33.** Simeon's prominence results from his adoption into Judah (Josh 15:26; Deut 33:6 omits), hinted by recording without a genealogical connection the cities they "occupied" from Josh 19:2, "they kept their own genealogies." **41.** *Meunim:* See comment on 2 Chr 20:1. We would expect Simeon's displacement to be SW (Ham, Gedor, Amalekites), but Seir points toward Ma'on near Petra in Edom.

5:2. *Reuben:* Apology for not putting the firstborn first is limited to the parenthesis that from Judah came the divine leader. Out of disdain for the schismatic north, the transfer of birthright to Joseph's sons (Gen 49:3; 48:5) is not made the occasion for inserting their lineage among the first children. **8.** *Aroer . . . Nebo:* The Reubenite homeland in Josh 13:16. **11.** *Gad:* Breaks the pattern of taking the sons' names from Gen 46:16 or Num 26:15. In both, the key figure is a Joel not sufficiently identified. **14.** *Gilead:* The tribe owning much of the territory taken over by Gad, euphemistically expressed as a marriage with Gad's daughter(s). **16.** *Bashan:* Gad's NE horizon, really occupied by E Manasseh (in the variants Josh 13:30; Num 21:13; 32:39, the E Jordan clan names are sometimes pushed farther S). *Mishor:* Here the Moab tableland, not Sharon near Jaffa. **18.** An expanded notice of a holy war common to the three E Jordan tribes against some descendants of Hagar (1:31). The 44,760 is a number symbolic of Yahweh's power. **23.** E Jordan possesses a natural unity; a portion is here assigned to a tribe not in the Judah (S) latitude. To fill out this fragmentary list, lacking even the pivotal Machir (7:17; Josh 13:31), is applied a moralizing summary of what befell N Israel in 2 Kgs 18:11f. *Senir:* Mt. Hermon (Deut 3:8) together with the rest of Antilebanon.

(c) THE LEVITES (6:1–81; MT 5:27–6:66).

18 (i) *Moses and Samuel* (6:1–30; MT 5:27–6:15). The disparity of the MT reflects the fact that vv 16–30 are a doublet of 1–15, which either add nonpriestly branches or take up in detail a preliminary affirmation of postexilic Jehozadak's legitimacy (see comment on Ezra 2:62). The author's own tribe is placed immediately after the Davidic line and its appendages.

The Levites were not segregated for priestly functions because of any peaceable unworldliness. On the contrary, Gen 49:7 sees in their "violent fury and cruel rage" the reason for their disbanding, "dispersed throughout Israel." They seem to have had liturgy thrust upon them because their murderousness emerged once when it was needed to stop the golden calf abuse (Exod 32:27). There is a modern flavor indeed in consigning to this roughest tribe the dice or oracular devices of Judg 18:20; Deut 33:9 (see comment on Ezra 2:63). Another factor prominent in the Levites' rise to theocratic functions seems to have been their willingness to roam from tribe to tribe (Judg 17:9), which only a reputation for ferocity could have made safe in those days. **3.** The children of Amram (from Exod 6:18; Num 3:19) are not enumerated in v 22, where a different Kohath genealogy is supposed. Because Miriam is called Aaron's sister while celebrating Moses' exploit (Exod 15:21), we may wonder whether this genealogy is juridical rather than biological for Moses just as for Zadok in v 53. At any rate, by suppression of any exploits at all with the name of Moses, or even of Aaron, is attained a main goal of the whole opus: to diminish the value of any vehicle of divine influence other than the Davidic covenant.

8. From Aaron to the Temple is exactly 12 generations, of just 40 years each: 480 years, as in 1 Kgs 6:1. Another 12 generations, 480 years, carry us to the Second Temple (Jeshua ben-Jozadak, Ezra 3:2). This stylized symmetry is obtained by omitting Jehoiada and Uriah (2 Kgs 16:11; 2 Chr 22:11; 26:20 on Azariah). **28.** Samuel and his father, Elkanah the fourth, were not from Levi but from Ephraim (1 Sam 1:1), which can scarcely be a geographic rather than an ethnic term. If Samuel had been born a Levite, there would have been no point in his mother's conspicuous surrender of him to the sanctuary. This Elkanah's connection with those of vv 23,25,35 is likewise disturbing. Samuel's sons are confused and unimportant (1 Sam 8:2f.). By a revelation God has transferred the "sonship" of the high priest Eli to the non-Levite Samuel.

19   (ii) *Lineage of the Levite choir* (6:31–48). **31.** The author's own family. The three pioneers are Heman, Asaph (Pss 73–83), and Ethan: second-son descendants of Levi's three sons Kohath, Gershom, and Merari. Despite the punishment Korah underwent for defying his uncle Aaron (Num 16:16), he merits in v 37 independant status as founder of the school that compiled Pss 42–49 and 84–88. The 20 generations between Heman and Izhar are really too numerous to span the 250 years from Moses to David; to equal them, five names for Gershom and eight for Merari were here supplied beyond those in vv 16–21. These 13 names are commonly alleged to be of postexilic type; possibly from the author's own generation but already used in his clan in those early days of which no records survived. Ethan is Jeduthun of 16:41; 25:1; see comment on 2:5.

20   (iii) *Zadokite legitimacy* (6:49–53). **53.** The NT name Sadducees means "sons of Zadok" (*CBQ* 17 [1955] 172), and already in Chronicles' time the whole legitimacy of the incumbent priests depended on their descent from Aaron via Zadok. The two sons of Aaron surviving the purge of Lev 10:6 were Ithamar (from whose line came Eli and Abiathar, 1 Chr 24:3,6) and Eleazar. Ahitub is given here and in v 8 as a descendant of Eleazar-Phinehas (Num 25:11) and as Zadok's father (also in 1 Chr 18:16; grandfather in 9:11). But the Ahitub of 2 Sam 8:17 should be rather father of Ahimelech (1 Sam 22:9), who is the father of Abiathar, the Elid priest supplanted by Zadok. If this (Wellhausen) emendation is admitted, Zadok is left without genealogy; and in fact an imposing convergence of modern experts sees in Zadok some pre-Israelite priest—most likely priest-king of Jebus. "*Melek*-Zadok" would be thus like his predecessor Melchizedek, priest-king of (Jeru-) Salem without genealogy (Heb 7:3), and worshiper of "God most high" acknowledged by Abraham (Gen 14:18). The enigmatic features of David's seizure of the Jebus crag (2 Sam 5:8) are best understood on the basis of a secret deal made with Zadok assuring to his descendants the high priesthood, second in rank in the theocracy after the king. Thus the lineage arranged for Eleazar is a legal adoption.

21   (iv) *The Levite settlements* (6:54–81). This is the longest of the few passages in Chr from Joshua (21:1–39); S. Japhet ("Conquest and Settlement in Chronicles," *JBL* 98 [1979] 205–18) holds that the view

of the people and the land in 1 Chr 6:50–81 = MT 6:35–66) is autochthonic and starts from when "Israel" was all the area occupied under David. **54.** No landed estate was assigned to the Levites in the distribution under Moses (Num 26:62); it was understood that they were to be supported by whatever people they were sanctifying. But the Levites' functions came to be viewed as having some natural relation to the cities of refuge. In fact Josh 21 includes in their allotment not only all the "sanctuary" cities, but every metropolis except Jerusalem; yet the Bible never shows them wielding any administration in those cities. **55.** *Hebron:* This coveted city had been the occasion for the complex insertion of Caleb into the line of Judah; note that though the city itself is allotted to the priests, the civilians retain control of all the villages subject to the city.

22   (d) PRE-DAVID NORTHERN ELEMENTS (7:1–40). With chap. 7 the MT verse numbering again coincides with the LXX (*RSV*, etc.), and the text no longer pursues the strictly genealogical links among David's relatives. Because the northern tribes meanwhile had rebelled, the only good to be said about them is what contributed to the success of David's dynasty. **1.** Issachar's four sons appear as in Gen 46:13; Num 26:23; but in Judg 10:1 "Tola son of Puah dwelt in Shamir" and no connections are indicated elsewhere. Tola's 22,600 armed descendants plus the 36,000 of Uzzi do not total 87,000; while Num 2:6; 26:27 give different figures still. **6.** *Benjamin:* See 8:1; here read "Zebulun," as in one Gk ms. **10.** *Tarshish:* An epithet of boats (see comment on 2 Chr 9:21) that suggests a coastal tribe, as Zebulun in Gen 49:13.

12. *Ir, Hushim, and Aher:* Read here "The sons of Dan: Hushim," as in Gen 46:23. Huppim from Num 26:39 may be the Akk *hipi* "so-and-so" (indicating a name that the scribe cannot read); Gen 46:21 has Muppim. **13.** The sons of Naphtali (from Gen 46:24) are as curtailed as Dan's. **14–19.** Studied in relation to Num 26 and Josh 17 by A. Demsky ("The Genealogies of Manasseh and the Location of the Territory of Milcah daughter of Zalphehad," *Harry M. Orlinsky Volume* [ErIsr 16; Jerusalem, 1982] 70–75; Eng. 254). Milcah is equated with Hammolecheth, and the genealogies are found to be re-expressed in favor of the West Jordan tribes. **20–23.** This corresponds to *one* of two conflicting traditions preserved in both prologue and epilogue of Job (42:11– 17); cf. R.-E. Hoffmann, *ZAW* 92 (1980) 120–32. **27.** Ephraim's most memorable descendant is Joshua, but involving 10 generations; but in 6:3 (= Exod 6:20) Moses is only three removes from Ephraim's peer Kohath. **30.** *Asher:* As farthest from Jerusalem, it is the tribe most nebulously portrayed, though outside the Bible best attested in occupancy of preexilic Canaan (Heber is perhaps an echo of the *Habiru;* the doublet Ishvi, not in Num 26:44, is kept from Gen 46:17).

23   (C) **Saul/Jerusalem Setting (8:1–9:44).** **1.** *Benjamin:* Saul's tribe; just as all David's connections are insistently put first, so Saul's are relegated to the last. **33.** The brother of Kish should be not Ner but Abner, Saul's uncle in 1 Sam 14:50. In 1 Sam 9:1, Ner is bypassed between Kish and Abiel, here called Abdon. **34.** Meribaal and Ishbaal were names no longer offensive; though during the struggle against Canaanite syncretism, the writers of 2 Sam 2:8; 4:4 changed their *baal,* "Lord," to *bosheth,* "abomination." 9:2–34 (not just vv 2–22 as *NEB* in Coggins, *Chronicles* 49) is comparable to Neh 11. In 1 Chr 8, Benjamin and Saul's lineage had been carefully located at the point most suited to leading into the narrative of David's heroism (colophon of 9:1 is title for what precedes: "Israel" twice meaning chiefly Judah), but now an interruption is required to correct a false impression left by 8:29. We must not imagine that the Holy City was properly Benjamin's inheritance. Those of his tribe who lived there really belonged to Gibeon (9:35). Of the tribe of Levi, the priest-choir-doorkeeper guilds loomed large in Jerusalem's population, as in Neh 11. Of the tribe of Judah, some clans are enumerated, halfway merged with some from Ephraim and Manasseh not in Neh. The Jebusite crag of Zion never fell within the distribution to the 12 tribes; it was first occupied by David (2 Sam 5:6) as an extraterritorial fief to serve as impartial center for governing the north and south. **9:11.** *Zadok:* Probably not the priest of David; Meraioth (see comment on 6:53) may be the Amariah of 6:11. **13.** The corresponding subtotals in Neh 11:12ff. total only 1,192, not 1,760. **22.** *Samuel:* Put here to represent pre-Temple days, when as a child he "opened the doors of Yahweh's house" (1 Sam 3:15). **27.** *watching:* Cf. J. R. Spencer, "The Tasks of the Levites," *ZAW* 96 (1984) 267–71. **35.** Saul's line is repeated from 8:33, not only to stress its link with Gibeon (only 5 mi. from Saul's Gibeah within Benjamin) but also to cue the account of Saul's doom.

(III) David's Empire (10:1–29:30).
24   (A) Legitimacy of the Succession (10:1–11:9). 2. *Saul:* Included because the restoration-era theme is "out of disaster comes good" (Ackroyd; though Willi [*Die Chronik* 12] implausibly extracts from the text much scene-setting for a postexilic renewal of Davidic kingship). Only Saul's crimes are mentioned, esp. the fact that Yahweh slew him—by Saul's own hand. **13.** Only by the word "unfaithfulness" is it implied that Saul indeed had a divine mission as founder of Israelite royalty; to show David's innocence of any guilt of usurpation is the burden of chap. 10; "David becomes the standard by which all future kings were to be measured" (J. Sailhamer, *First and Second Chronicles* [Everyman's Bible Comm.; Chicago, 1983] 32). Saul sealed his own doom by consulting a witch, despite his own prohibitions (1 Sam 28:9). He also defied Samuel, as is told ambiguously in 1 Sam 13:13; 15:10. All Saul's line died with him, despite the seven-year resistance of Ishbosheth and the threat of Mephibosheth. From 1 Sam 31:10ff. (about the dishonoring of Saul's headless trunk by his enemies and cremation by his friends) is taken over only the name of a god, Dagon—but not Astarte, because she was a sex symbol.
25   11:1–2. Taken over from 2 Sam 5:1, but in such a way as to imply an immediate gladsome acclaim by the elders of N Israel, instead of their capitulation after the seven Hebron years (1 Chr 12:39; 2 Sam 2:3). **3.** The manner in which David was brought into line for the succession to Saul involves Samuel here as in 1 Sam 16:1, but not the variants 16:18; 17:55: see R. North, *Bib* 63 (1982) 524–44. **5.** On Jebus as David's extraterritorial fief taken without a struggle, see 9:1; 6:53; 12:28. **6.** David's rash oath is stressed to explain how various defiances of Joab would be so long unpunished: 2 Sam 3:27–28; 14:19; 1 Kgs 1:7. **8.** "Joab repaired (MT: "left alive") the rest of the city" is not in 2 Sam 5:9.
26   (B) David's Militia (11:10–12:40). Here is officiously inserted what 2 Sam 23:8–39 tucks in among the "last words of David." **15.** *Adullam:* This adventure presumes some real facts about David's rise to power, ignored from 1 Sam 22:1. **19.** "Is the blood of the men who went 'along with' their lives?" of 2 Sam 23:17 is altered to "Will I drink the blood of these men along with their lives?" This recalls Gen 9:4; Lev 17:14, "life is blood." **22.** "Ariels" of the *RSV* are lions, or perhaps "heroes 'of God,'" a simple grammatical usage for "greatest ever," as 12:22. Lions are not now found in Palestine, but its climate is such that one could have

climbed up from Jordan jungle heat to hills high enough for sudden snows. **26.** *Asahel:* His slaying will cause the Abner-Joab feud, momentous for David's rise in 2 Sam 2:32. *Elhanan:* See comment on 20:5. **41b.** Adds 16 names not found in Samuel, perhaps to soften the tragic irony of Bathsheba's Uriah as "last of David's heroes." **12:1.** *Ziklag:* Presupposes unwelcome data from 1 Sam 27:5; instead we have here a soberly historical register of David's actual bodyguard in his self-defense against Saul. Into this roster (not a postexilic Jerusalem census) have been inserted also those feudal dignitaries who decided "soon enough" to make no last-ditch resistance to David's takeover. **18.** An example of Chronicles' constant stress on "all Israel" (Mangan, *1–2 Chronicles* 35); cf. H. Williamson, *OTS* 21 (1981) 164–76. **24.** The fact that so few are recorded from Judah is surprising and cannot be attributed to the prior rule of David in Judah alone. **29.** Zadok's 22 minions may reflect those of Neh 12:1. **33.** *the times:* Cultivated by Issachar, were likely astrological in origin, but are here explained in relation to opportunist politics. **40.** Commonsense portrayal of what feasting would have actually surrounded David's takeover after seven years of maneuvering, even if the wording serves as suitable symbol of an eschatological banquet in the Messiah's kingdom.
(C) Theocratic Consolidation (13:1–17:27).
27   (a) RECOVERY OF THE ARK (13:1–14). Two major differences from 2 Sam 6: (1) this exploit of piety is put ahead of every civil and military episode in David's administration; (2) there is dramatized a sort of democratic assembly (*qāhāl*, a favorite term) at which David adroitly proposes retrieving the Ark, although 1 Sam 14:18 had shown Saul already deploying it. For David, the Ark becomes the symbol and the impetus for a new style of political union for the 12 tribes (Michaeli). Our comment on chap. 9 stresses chiefly the Ark's conferring the status of extraterritorial capital on a Jerusalem which until then had been the center of a somewhat alien cult. **5.** This presumes from 2 Sam 8 the imperialistic conquests of David stretching far beyond the tribal terrain, as far NE as the Syrian desert and as far SW as Shihor, "the stream of Horus," a river of Egypt—really the Nile but here understood as Wadi el-Arish. **8.** *before God:* Yahweh of 2 Sam 6:5 is changed to *hā'ĕlōhîm* (as is frequent but capricious in Chronicles; cf. Rudolph, *Chronikbücher* xviii); further divergences from Samuel diction here are stylistic rather than ideological. **14.** Fetching the Ark results in disaster (2 Sam 6:7; 1 Sam 6:19, where the experience of Beth-shemesh is so similar as to suggest perhaps a literary convention); this is made the occasion for interrupting David's theocratic maneuvers for several months and inserting what had been skipped from 2 Sam 5:11–25.
28   (b) BUILDING UP THE HOUSE OF DAVID (14:1–17). Foreign affairs are the real issue in these apparently domestic scenes: Hiram's embassy and the multiplying of wives. **9.** To defend his new Jerusalem fief, David must take warlike measures against former allies; but as in 2 Sam 15:19, this activity is portrayed as a crusade, almost a ritual. **10.** *yhwh:* Twice in 2 Sam 5:19, changed once to *'ĕlōhîm* here. **17.** An addition to Samuel, softening by anticipation the bloody deeds to come in 18:5 and 22:8.
29   (c) TABERNACLE INAUGURATION (15:1–16:43). It had been suggested in 2 Sam 6:12 that David set about securing the Ark because it brought blessings to its holder; here instead we have an entirely original emphasis on the tent, set up by David in imitation and continuance of the desert situation (Num 1:50). Up to now the Mosaic ritual has not been prominent; see comment on 2:16. **11.** *Abiathar:* Reference to the two priests

is inopportune here and may be a gloss. **13.** Disaster befell the moving of the Ark because the bearers were not Levites (as the LXX wordily attempts to clarify the MT). **16.** Important for the history of the Second Temple cult singers. **20f.** Alamoth, "girls," may mean soprano; and Sheminith "octave" or bass, as in some psalm titles. **25.** From here to 16:3 the account of 2 Sam 6:12-19 is inserted almost verbatim, but the dramatizing of Michal's contempt in 2 Sam 6:20f. is replaced by the long levitical thanksgiving of 1 Chr 16, made up of Pss 96:1-13; 105:1-15; 106:1,47-48; cf. T. Butler (*VT* 28 [1978] 142-50), who indicates 45 textual differences (references to Temple and Diaspora are notably suppressed) and thinks Ps 106 added because the time of thanksgiving has not yet come.

16:3. *meat:* Date-cake. **8-36.** Literary source for Rev 14:6-7; cf. W. Altink, *AUSS* 22 (1984) 187-96; A. E. Hill, *VT* 33 (1983) 97-101. **37.** The Ark within its tent is attended by Obed-edom (now promoted to Levite status, as in 15:24) and Asaph. The tent of Gibeon, founded by Moses (21:29) will henceforth be attended by Zadok, Heman, and Jeduthun, and will still serve the royal cult after David's death.

30 (d) TEMPLE PROJECT DEFERRED (17:1-27). David is all-but-builder of the Temple with all its ritual. With art and skill is here inserted the momentous oracle which simultaneously predicts the stability of the messianic line and excludes David from executing the Temple project. Researches into the parallels of Ps 89 and 2 Sam 7 reveal that we may well possess here the primitive form of the oracle. **1.** David's proposal follows immediately his installation of the Ark in its provisional pavilion. The covenant name *yhwh* is used instead of Sam's *'ĕlōhîm;* the omitted "Yahweh had given him rest from all his enemies round about" is nevertheless implicit in v 8 and chaps. 18-20. **4b.** *you shall not built 'the'* ['a' in LXX, RSV, as 2 Sam 7:5] *house:* Implies that the essentials of the project are approved; in 21:18 Yahweh commands that David shall build an altar on the Temple site. **19.** Cited by Willi (*Die Chronik* 74) as a sample of Chronicles' *Vorlage,* less reliable than the MT (2 Sam 7:21). **23.** The humility of David's prayer now fits perfectly the acceptance of God's "minor" revisions for the Temple project.

(D) Empire-Building Wars (18:1-21:7).
31 (a) EAST-JORDAN CAMPAIGNS (18:2-20:3). Omitted from 2 Sam 8:2 are the savage and humiliating reprisals of David against Moab, his loyal ally in 1 Sam 22:3. **5.** The 22,000 slain Syrians may be a hyperbole, but its retention may vouch for its reliability. **9.** Because Hamath remains outside David's jurisdiction, the northern limit of his empire was at most near Emesa (modern Homs), including as far E as the Euphrates insofar as everything between was desert (except Palmyra; see comment on 2 Chr 8:4); but in *MUSJ* 46 (1971) 61-103, we gave lengthy proof for our view that *"entry* of Hama" could have been the southernmost point of the valley between Lebanon and Antilebanon, thus a northern boundary of Israel near Dan even under David. **12.** The death of 18,000 Edomites is charged to David only indirectly. **16.** On Zadok's parentage and Ahimelech (MT: Abimelech) see 6:53. **17.** David's sons also were priests in 2 Sam 8:18 MT, but in LXX and here "officials." The "Cherethites and Pelethites" may be the cognate Aegean Cretans and Philistines; but on the question of Crete, see now J. Strange, *Caphtor/Keftiu* (Leiden, 1980). The Meribbaal/Mephibosheth episode is omitted (2 Sam 9:7); though it shows David's kindness, it also stresses that there were survivors of Saul with a claim to the throne; see comment on 10:6; 2 Sam 16:3. Also suppressed are the dramatic story of Rizpah's non-

violent resistance to the revenge which David permitted to the Gibeonites; the weakness of aging David (2 Sam 21:1-17); and Ps 18 and a similar psalm in 2 Sam 22 emphasizing David's resistance to Saul; the rest of 2 Sam 23 was already in 1 Chr 11:10.

19:1. The people of (Rabbath-)Ammon, modern Amman, to whom David claims loyalty as in 2 Sam 10, in fact appear to be opposed to Saul's Jabesh-Gilead allies in 1 Sam 11:1; 31:11. **6.** *Aram-Naharaim:* So *NAB* with MT; others "Mesopotamia," but in 2 Sam 10:6 "(Aram-) Beth-rehob." **7.** *Medeba:* Not in 2 Sam 10:8; this may be for *mê-* "waters of" + *Rabbah* (= Ammon). **16.** Suppression of the Ammonites is now seen as essential to the completeness of David's Syrian campaign. Omission of the place of his meeting opposed to Saul's (Helam twice in 2 Sam 10:16f.) is taken by Willi (*Die Chronik* 96) as a sample of geographical omissions in Chr; another is Zair in 2 Chr 21:9. **18.** David kills nearly 50,000 Syrians helping Ammon.

20:1. *David remained in Jerusalem:* Followed by a massive silence about what happened there, the Bathsheba episode of 2 Sam 11:2-29. **2.** *their king: RSV* rather than *NAB* Milcom, the Ammonite god; David's bloodshed at least diverted treasures from pagan to Israelite cult.

32 (b) PHILISTINE EPISODES (20:4-8). The epic of the Amnon-Absalom threat to Solomon's succession (2 Sam 13:1-21:17) is skipped, doubtless because a part of the trouble there was aging David's indecisiveness. **5.** The exploit of the Bethlehemite Elhanan, son of Jair, was the slaying of the giant Goliath of Gath, according to 2 Sam 21:19. This historical kernel is amplified and credited to the Bethlehemite David in 1 Sam 17; just as in most histories even today is ascribed to the reigning authority any politically important decision or achievement of his subjects. Variants variously suggest the real facts: the LXX substitutes "Godoliah the Hittite" for Goliath of Gath; the Vg follows the targum in translating Elhanan and Jair as epithets of David, "God's (merciful) gift; son of the forest" (*yā'îr;* in Tg "waking up by night"). Chronicles here makes (Beth-)Lehemi(te) the object of Elhanan's slaying and then calls him the brother of Goliath, whom David slew; and Tg (Le Déaut, *Targum* 85) has David kill both Goliath and Goliath's brother-in-law Lahmi.

33 (c) THE FATEFUL CENSUS (21:1-7). This event at least in its outset appears as one of David's few secular activities with which Chr is concerned. In 2 Sam 24, it is set off as an isolated cultic episode between the long digression of 2 Sam 23 and David's end. **1.** *Satan:* Appears here as the instrument of what 2 Sam 24:1 calls Yahweh's own vexed incitement of David to a census (N. Émile, "Un cas de relecture," *Hokhma* 26 [1984] 47-55). What God permits can be attributed to intermediate causes. Satan in Job and Zech 3:1 is the name of an official of Yahweh's court charged with testing the virtue of the just. In Num 22:22, Satan is called a messenger, *mal'āk.* Only with Rev 12:9; 20:2 is the name given to "the slanderer," *diabolos,* who is then further identified with the serpent (Gen 3:15; Wis 2:24; John 8:44) and with the chief angel defeated in a battle (Luke 10:18) against Michael, according to apocryphal literature.

Why is a census seen to be against God's interests (though commanded by him in Exod 30:12)? Perhaps it represented a shift from reliance on the God of war to an efficient inventory of human resources; perhaps it seemed an effort to discover if God had been keeping his promise to multiply Abraham's seed; or "counting one's blessings arrests them." It is less likely that David intended an aggressive war against the northern tribes. **2.** *Israel from Beersheba to Dan:* In Chr usage it is needless to add "and Judah" as 2 Sam 24:1; but the inversion of traditional "Dan to Beersheba" perhaps implies that Joab would begin from where he is, in Judah. **3.** Joab incriminates David more outspokenly than in 2 Sam 24:3. **6.** Levi will in fact be numbered in 23:24; Benjamin is perhaps omitted because of Gibeon in v 29, rather than out of respect for Saul or for any special claim on Jebus-Jerusalem. On the implausible six million population, → *JBC* 24:33.

(E) Temple Under Way (21:8–29:30).
34   (a) RELIGIOUS IMPORT OF THE CENSUS (21:8–22:1). Nothing in Sam or Kgs links organically the hubris of David's census with the reopening and definitive localization of his Temple project. Stages of David's punishment are enumerated in terms so identical with 2 Sam 24 that we hardly notice the radical alteration of perspective effected by the six emendations. With a kind of unconscious art, what begins by heightening David's mad guilt with the intrusion of Satan and Joab's outburst gradually fades into making David the unresisting pawn of forces pushing him toward God's goal. **12.** Anticipates and dramatizes the "angel" appearing in only one passage of 2 Sam (24:16f.). This angel is not a "mode of divine presence" as in Gen 32:31 and elsewhere (R. North, *CBQ* 29 [1967] 419–49). Its interpretation as a term for "sickness" by Salomo Delmedigo in 1629 is called by Willi (*Die Chronik* 24) the earliest approach to a critical Chronicles commentary. But this angel is furnished with a drawn sword (proof of variant Samuel *Vorlage*? so P. Dion, *ZAW* 97 [1985] 114–17, with E. Ulrich, *Qumran Text of Samuel and Josephus* [HSM 19; Missoula, 1978]). The angel is seen by the Jebusite of v 20 as well as by David as an "executor" of God's will in preference to Yahweh's direct anthropomorphic action. **15.** *Ornan:* Ornah in 2 Sam 24:16, *kĕtîb* for Araunah, a Hurrian name (god Varuna? Jebusite king?); his "four sons" are only in 1 Chr 21:20, and unnamed. Tg (Le Déaut, *Targum* 86) surmises that Yahweh stopped the plague upon noticing the ashes of Isaac's interrupted sacrifice on Mt. Moriah (Gen 22:13; see comment on 2 Chr 3:1). **22.** Shows borrowings from Gen 23:9. The 50-silver-shekel price of 2 Sam 24:24, for what had become by that time one of the world's major real estate parcels, is interpreted as gold and 50 "per tribe"—a way of saying "priceless." **26.** The sacrifice ratified by fire from heaven as in 1 Kgs 18:38 is an addition to 2 Sam 24:25, giving the impression that overall God is well pleased with David.
   22:1: An echo of Gen 28:17: "not at Bethel [house of El] or anywhere in Samaria, but only here shall be the House of Yahweh." Continuation with the account of the Temple contracts opens out a horizon noticeably different from 2 Sam 24:25, where the aversion of the plague is followed by David's senility and peaceful death.
35   (b) DAVID'S BLUEPRINTS (22:2–19). David makes all the decisions regarding the building of the Temple. **2.** In 1 Kgs 5:1, these negotiations are handled by Solomon, and only after David's abdication; 1 Kgs 5:31f. specifies that although the stone quarrying was done by Canaanites (*gēr,* "resident minority"), still in order to keep the timber moving from the northern border there was required a levy of forced labor (cf. R. North on *mas* in *TDOT*). **5.** Solomon's age at his accession is unattested. Rashi guessed 12 and Josephus 14 (*Ant.* 8.7.8 § 211) but recent experts tend toward an age around 40. **7.** David's deathbed bequest to Solomon from 1 Kgs 2:3, expurgated of the vendettas by which it is there accompanied, is expanded by elements from 2 Sam 7:13f. into a status quo for authorship of the Temple. Here David dwells with a certain complacency on all the blood he shed for the Lord, incurring thereby

a technical irregularity (as in the pious burial of one's own father, Num 19:11; Lev 21:11). David is no less responsible for the Temple than is Moses for the takeover of the promised land: though in both cases the final step is left to a successor. **9.** Solomon, "the man of peace," did in fact wage one war—paradoxically attested only in 2 Chr 8:3. **14.** "With great pains" (*RSV*) is no word for it! The world's total annual production of gold in 1965 amounted to only one-sixth of the 5,000 tons here stipulated. In 1 Chr 29:4 only 3 percent of this amount is envisioned; and in Ezra 2:69; 8:26, only 1 percent. The meaning is simply "the Temple is an art treasure valued beyond any figure you could bid."
36   (c) THE LEVITE PERSONNEL (23:1–27:34). These chapters are regarded by de Vaux (*AI* 190f.) as later additions to the work of "the original Chronicler," for whom "the Levites were meant primarily for the service of the Ark" (1 Chr 15:2, from Deut 10:8, not any Priestly source). "The later additions to the book are meant to show the legitimacy of the institution of singers, and to give a more exact definition of their rights." They gradually encroached on the functions of the priests, such as teaching (2 Chr 17:8; 35:3; Neh 8:7–8); and Josephus, *Ant.* 20.9.6 § 216 tells us that as late as Agrippa II the singers secured the right to wear linen vestments as the priests did, and *all* the Levites serving in the Temple were promoted to the rank of singers. Though most experts would agree with de Vaux that these chapters largely contain the author's defense and promotion of his own cadre, still the basic outlook is original to "the Chronicler," and to a certain extent historical; cf. T. Polk, *Studies in Biblical Theology* 9 (1979) 3–22; B. Luria, *BM* 29 (1984) 193–207. **3.** *thirty:* The age of service also in Num 4:3; but in v 27 it is reduced to 20; cf. Num 8:24; 2 Chr 31:17; Ezra 3:8. A growing need (we might say "a decrease in unemployment") dictated progressively lowering the age (similarly 1QM 2:4; 7:1; *Bib* 39 [1958] 90). **5.** David's fashioning of musical instruments is attested doubtfully in Amos 6:5 but chiefly here and in 2 Chr 7:6; 29:26; Neh 12:36; cf. Josephus, *Ant.* 7.12.3 § 305–6; R. North, *JBL* 83 (1964) 373. **7.** *Ladan:* For Libni of 6:17 (also in 26:21), although Libni's sons seem to be those of Shimei here, possibly postexilic bearers of these patronyms. **14.** *Moses:* Though named "the man of God" as in Deut 33:1, he is less colorfully portrayed than Aaron; his sons are nonpriestly Levites (despite Judg 18:30).
37   **24:3.** Embarrassing mention of Abiathar is avoided, because it was Zadok who replaced him (see comment on 6:53; 15:11; 27:34); in his place, amiably paired with Zadok, is an Ahimelech who should be the father of Abiathar (1 Sam 23:6); but, following 2 Sam 8:17 (MT, not Pesh) he is made his son, called Abimelech in 1 Chr 18:16. **4.** The "courses of the Levites," in relation to Luke 1:8, are studied by R. Beckwith, *RevQ* 9 (1977) 77–91; 11 (1984) 507–11. This list has seven names in common with those of Neh 12:12f.; 10:3f.; of which only one appears also in the lists of Neh 12:1f.; 7:39f. (= Ezra 2:36f.), along with four other names from here.
   25:1–31. Here we have systematized a similar 24-turn calendar for the musicians, colleagues of the author already publicized in 15:16 and 16:4,37. The extra names found here may be either actual postexilic people or creative symbols. **4.** "The names of Heman's nine last sons, when put together, form a little poem, a fragment of a psalm" (de Vaux, *AI* 392): "Have mercy on me; my God [who says (Isa 1:2)] 'I have reared and raised'; helper of him who dwells in hardship, increase my eloquence (and) visions."

38   26:1. Gatekeepers, though with extended nobler functions in postexilic Judah, are shown in this chapter to be merely relatives of the real aristocracy, the singers. **8.** Obed-edom's descendants rely on their name (see comment on 13:14), after adoption into the clan of singers. **14.** Temple gates are described at the four cardinal points, doubtless as they were known to the writer a long time after David. **24.** The Hebronites are not here put in their customary relation to Caleb (see comment on 2:50). **25.** To a descendant of Moses falls the "treasure," perhaps an allusion to Num 31:54.

27:1. This final list contains officials of secular status but organized in relation to the clergy, or rather directly to King David for the building of the Temple. The names follow 11:10–25 closer than 2 Sam 23. **4.** *Dodai:* Rather, Dodo's son Eleazar, as in 2 Sam 23:9. **7.** Asahel in 2 Sam 2:23 had fallen in the Joel–Abner feud. **15–22.** See H. Reviv, "The list of the Officers of the Tribes of Israel," *Tarbiz* 53 (1983) 1–10. **17.** Zadok merits an extra place "for Aaron," but subordinate to the other Levites. **18.** *Elihu:* Unnamed among David's six brothers in 2:15; 1 Sam 17:12 supposes seven brothers. **23–24.** It is suggested that the evil of a census consists in numbering minors. **34.** This Abiathar is not mentioned as a priest; see comment on 24:3.

39   (d) DAVID'S ENTAILED ABDICATION (28:1–29:30). As in other known cases, it seems implied that the successful administrator should not leave too much to the personal initiative of his successor. Our view, retained from *JBC* 24:39, nevertheless acknowledges a strong recent trend to claim that Solomon is exalted in Chr even above David (or the Ark, or Zion) as the principal pivot in the whole structure of the book.

(Abramsky, S., "The Chronicler's View of King Solomon," *Harry M. Orlinsky Volume* [ErIsr 16; Jerusalem, 1982] 3–14; Eng. 252. Braun, R. L., "Solomonic Apologetic in Chronicles," *JBL* 92 [1973] 503–16; "Solomon, the Chosen Temple Builder," *JBL* 95 [1976] 581–90. Dillard, R. B., "The Chronicler's Solomon," *WTJ* 43 [1980] 289–300; "The Literary Structure of the Chronicler's Solomonic Narrative," *JSOT* 30 [1984] 85–99. Mosis, *Untersuchungen* 162. Peterca, V., *L'immagine di Salomone nella Bibbia ebraica e greca* [diss., Gregorian Univ., 1981; the published part treats the importance assigned to Solomon linked with the Temple; see *CBQ* 45 (1983) 294]. Welten, P., "Lade–Tempel–Jerusalem: Theologie der Chronikbücher," *Textgemäss* [Fest. E. Würthwein; Göttingen, 1979] 169–83. Williamson, H. G. M., "The Accession of Solomon in the Books of Chronicles," *VT* 26 [1976] 351–61 [p. 357: for successful Temple building Solomon depended on his father's preparations, but Solomon is esteemed not less than David; the David–Solomon transition is modeled on Moses–Joshua]. Zalewski, S., *'Aliyyat Šĕlōmōh* [Jerusalem, 1981]).

28:3. The most favorable possible impression of David's overall plan is created by putting into his own mouth a frank admission of how he effected it. **5.** David's inability to cope with the intrigues of his four principal heirs, which fills eight chapters from 2 Sam 13 to 1 Kgs 2, is reduced to the claim "God gave me many sons, but chose Solomon among them." **8–11.** Deuteronomic oratory; see D. J. McCarthy, "An Installation Genre," *JBL* 90 (1971) 31–41 (= AnBib 108 [Rome, 1985] 182–92). The blueprint or scale model is solemnly and publicly handed over; Solomon would hardly change it. **14.** Not only the building but also the details of its furnishings are regulated by David, rather than by Moses as in Exod 25:9–30. Indeed, we have here the inventory of materials already in hand, no longer mere contract specifications. **18.** *plan for the golden chariot of the cherubim that spread their wings and covered the ark* (RSV): It is debated whether these winged figures were

freestanding statues or incisions on the golden Ark lid, but the implication is that the throne of Yahweh's *shekinah* or presence is ready to bear him into battle. **19.** *by a writ from the hand of Yahweh:* Echoes Exod 31:18 and claims for David's work a divine origin equal to that of his rival Moses. **20.** From Deut 31:23, which continues however emphasizing the likelihood that the successors will fall short.

40   29:1. At no point does David admonish Solomon to take over responsibility with a firm hand. **5.** Perhaps an example of counterpart funds, as distinct from Exod 25:1; 35:4. **7.** *darics:* A major proof for the composition of Chr after Darius (400 BC); so flagrantly Persian a term could not have been plausibly inserted, even by an annotator. The invention of minted coins does not much antedate Croesus (550 BC); for lengthy documentation, see Williamson, *TynBul* 28 (1977) 124; and on the tardy interpolation of such wealth, see Mosis, *Untersuchungen* 105. **9.** One of the rare allusions to Solomon's backslidings (1 Kgs 11:4). **11.** This exquisite theologizing contains no reference to a future life, but neither does it reduce hope to earthly posterity, as 1 Kgs 8:25. **21.** This verse and 2 Chr 7:5 must come from records such as in R. Sigrist, *Les sattukku* (Malibu, 1984); cf. D. Wiseman, *BL* (1985) 123. **22.** Solomon is anointed as *nāgîd*, "charismatic leader," a role portrayed as coming to Saul from God, whereas he became *melek*, "king," by popular acclaim (1 Sam 9:16; 10:1; 11:25; de Vaux, *AI* 94). As in the Leviticus P tradition, the anointing is extended from king to high priest, a custom only after the exile when he held civil power (de Vaux, *AI* 347, 399). **26.** Mention of David's seven-year Hebron reign is so casual as to imply no delay in taking over the northern crown (see comment on 11:1). **27.** Hasty summation of the dubious 1 Kgs 1:4 (Abishag). **29.** On the "prophet"-sources explicitly cited here, see 24:5 above; H. Haag ("Gad and Nathan," *Archäologie und Alte Testament* [Fest. K. Galling; Tübingen, 1970] 135–42) notes that only Nathan is *nābî'* (Gad is *ḥōzēh* as in 2 Chr 29:25).

With due respect for the genuine greatness of Solomon and his importance for the overall structure of this book, we may neverthless repeat here (from *JBC* 24:41; Rudolph; now also Michaeli, *Livres des Chroniques* 141, despite p. 128) our summation of the portrayal of David. The sources, esp. canonical Samuel, are conscientiously followed in what is taken over from them, but everything tending to diminish David's greatness is systematically omitted. Even the narrative details are deftly heightened in David's favor, often by the insertion of plausible concretizations. The narration of David's strictly civil activities, omitting what concerns the succession to the crown, occupies roughly the same bulk (73 verses) as in Sam (45 verses, or 103 with the Bathsheba episode). But in what concerns liturgical piety, the Deuteronomist Sam gives only 77 verses for David, as against the colossal 323 in Chr. Like all empire building, David's cost heavily in blood, but the achievement was unique and stellar within the triangle of great powers surrounding him—the Jewish nation's finest hour, as political history goes. Yet all this is made to seem a trivial side issue in comparison with his massive dedication to the organization of liturgy. David so far outshines Moses that no Sinaitic or other covenant is any longer worth fostering as a vital force in the religious life of the people. The Temple was basically David's achievement, from cornerstone to parapet, although the details of its execution will suffice to dominate and galvanize the ensuing reign.

COMMENTARY ON 2 CHRONICLES

(III) Solomon's Reign (2 Chr 1:1-9:31).
41   (A) The Inauguration at Gibeon (1:1-17).
1. Although the awaited Temple did not yet exist, there would have to be for Solomon an inaugural ceremony at some suitably impressive religious center. There is no mention of the Gihon spring ceremonial of 1 Kgs 1:45, either because it conjured up specters of Moloch or of the rival anointing at En-rogel (2 Chr 28:3; 1 Kgs 1:9), or because both springs were at the bottom of a gorge, a far less impressive spot than the spacious heights of Gibeon. **3.** Solomon in fact went habitually and reprehensibly to solemn ceremonies at Gibeon's high place (1 Kgs 3:4). Here this is transformed into making a virtue of necessity on this single occasion. See now J. Blenkinsopp, *Gibeon and Israel* (SOTSMS 2; Cambridge, 1972) 100-4. **5.** At the Ark there was only chant, but David had expressly fostered continuing the sacrifices at Gibeon in veneration not of any high place but of the desert tabernacle (1 Chr 16:39) and its altar of Bezalel's making (Exod 38:1). But ms. variants, *šām*, "there," for *śām*, "[David] put," are traced to theological scruple in Barthélemy, *Critique textuelle* 474.
7. Emphasis on the divinatory dream in 1 Kgs 3:5,15 is expurgated; the name *yhwh* in that narrative is replaced by *'ĕlōhîm* somewhat more consistently than usual. Also omitted is the confirmatory episode which crystallizes for posterity the wisdom of Solomon; it seems repugnant that Solomon should have been sympathetic to the pleas of harlots, or should have even tentatively advocated child slaughter (but a doctor recently theorizes that "cutting up" the infant meant an operation capable of deciding its mother; cf. S. Levin, *Judaism* 32 (1983) 463-65). **14.** Solomon's gradual transformation of David's militaristic domain into an economic empire by skillful commerce is telescoped here as an echo of the divine promise of riches. It is not really said that any of this happened at the Gibeon inaugural or was even planned there.
(B) The Temple (2:1-7:22).
42   (a) CONTRACTS AND BUILDING (2:1-3:17). Verse 1 (MT 1:18) reduces to a fleeting phrase all the data of 1 Kgs 7:1-12 on the 13 years given to the building of Solomon's personal residence. **3.** *Huram*: Hiram of 1 Kgs 5:2; it seems implied that the Phoenician timber ordered and actually delivered during David's lifetime was for his private home rather than for the Temple as in 1 Chr 22:4. We may perhaps read between the lines that the canny businessman Huram felt it would be more diplomatic to make new bids to Solomon, whose free acceptance would lay a basis for more harmonious collaboration. **4.** The new structure will be a place for sacrificing to the deity, not a "dwelling" for some embodied form.
5. *our god is greater than all gods:* Written to a pagan from the paragon of wisdom among Israel's leaders. This is one of the neglected theological pronouncements of the Bible; it is surprising that O. Keel (*Monotheismus im alten Israel* [Fribourg, 1980]) does not cite *De diis gentilium* (Innsbruck, 1912) 68 and cognate outspoken booklets of F. Kortleitner. The name *'ĕlōhîm* is equivalently a plural of El, implying that Israel's one God is as much as the total of whatever is meant by that name among her neighbors. But the existential status of every other El was not so easy to formulate, esp. in treating diplomatically with the Great Powers who worshiped their own El (note the uncommitted tact of Huram's reply in

v 12). Basically, the devout Israelite felt that every other El had been degraded to the status of Yahweh's footstool (Ps 95:7); however, insofar as they were, if anything, supraearthly or heavenly beings, their status was thus imperceptibly merged with that of the angels, as the LXX sometimes renders *'ĕlōhîm* (Ps 8:6). The OT rarely or never (even in Pss 96:5; 135:6,15; 115:4) comes out and says that idols are not gods at all, that only Yahweh is God. Perhaps even today it is possible to attain an ecumenical Christian formulation of monotheism by reevaluating the OT caution about denying all reality or divinity to the content of the concept of God among primitive or non-Christian peoples.
10. Onto 1 Kgs 5:11 (MT 5:25) is grafted a growing awareness that good fences make good neighbors; if Solomon does not let Tyre dictate the price, this may mean that a businesslike advance understanding builds better friendships than capricious munificence. In v 15 Huram outdoes Solomon by stipulating payment in advance. **13.** Hiram-Abit, the craftsman sent by King Huram/Hiram, is "patterned on Bezalel of Exod 31:6 but less versatile"; his mother is displaced from Dan of 1 Kgs 7:14 to Naphtali "in order to echo Bezalel's helper Oholi-Ab of Exod 36:34," says Mosis (*Untersuchungen* 162); so also R. Dillard, *WTJ* 43 (1981) 297. The tribes of Dan and Naphtali shared rather vaguely the hinterland of Israel E and even N of coastal Tyre. **16-17.** On the log transfer at Joppa, see comment on 8:17. For the "ethnic minority work force," the figures are identical with those given in v 2 for the local work force, as in 1 Kgs 5:13 (MT 5:27). *Gēr*, "alien," does not mean "resident subject of a foreign land" but rather "non-Israelite dwelling permanently within Israel"; thus there is no difficulty in reconciling this verse with 2 Chr 8:8-9, or even with the slightly varied repetition in 1 Chr 22:2.
43   3:1. Moriah (elsewhere only in Gen 22:2) is equated with Jerusalem by both rabbinical tradition and L.-H. Vincent (*RB* 58 [1951] 360-71), but this is rejected by N. Glueck (*Rivers in the Desert* [NY, 1959] 63). Rudolph's commentary plausibly proposes to read, with Pesh, "the *Amorite* hill"—unless this link with Abraham was intended to suggest the bypassing of Moses. On Ornan, see 1 Chr 21:15. **2.** *fourth year:* This important date is bereft of any link with local or world chronology in 2 Chr 1:1 or in 1 Chr 29:27. To diminish whatever relates to Moses or exodus, the 480 years of 1 Kgs 6:1 is omitted, though favor is usually shown in Chr for numbers either concrete or mystical.
3. De Vaux writes that this description, shortened from 1 Kgs 6-7, with no notable insertion, "is very hard to interpret. The editor did not have the interests of an architect or an archaeologist, and he omitted details which would be essential for a reconstruction (e.g., the thickness of the walls, the layout of the facade, the way in which it was roofed). Moreover, the text is full of technical terms, and has been disfigured by scribes who understood it no better than we do; and it has been loaded with glosses meant to enhance the splendour of the building. . . . It is not surprising that the reconstructions which have been attempted differ considerably from each other" (*AI* 313; → 1-2 Kings, 10:17; L.-H. Vincent, *Jérusalem de l'Ancien Testament* [Paris, 1956] 377-590; and now T. Busink, *Der Tempel von Jerusalem* [Leiden, 1970]). *measurements:* So Pesh, *RSV*. This need not be preferred to MT "foundations" or ground plan (*NAB* "specifications"). The old standard is presumed

vaguely tantamount to a "royal cubit," some 10 percent larger than the standard 18 in. attested for Egypt and Mesopotamia (de Vaux, *AI* 197). **4.** *120 cubits high:* This results in a monstrosity, 180 ft. for a 30-by-90-ft. building; 1 Kgs 6:2 gives a height of only 45 ft. But since Chr here is speaking of the porch or structure *in front of* the Temple proper (for which Kgs assigns no special height), we may think rather of an entrance *pylon* as at Edfu, on whose proportions the reconstructions of Solomon's Temple are most warrantably based, as in P. Garber, *BA* 14 (1951) 2–24; *JBL* 77 (1958) 126–29. **6.** *Parvaim:* Possibly an alternative spelling for Ophir as gold source (see comment on 8:18). **8.** *600 talents:* At 80 lb. of 12 oz. each (Troy), at some 350 dollars per oz., amounts to 200 million dollars, only a fraction of the 20 billion or more in 1 Chr 22:14. **9.** The LXX understands this as meaning "each nail weighing one shekel supported 50 shekels of gold"; but Mosis (*Untersuchungen* 146), suggests that the "nail" not in 1 Kgs 6 was a Hebr letter *waw* (which has the form of a nail) for which some scribe wrote out *mismēr*.

10. *wood:* As LXX, for the MT "embossing," is perhaps borrowed from 1 Kgs 6:23. In that context, the description takes the cherubim for freestanding statues, a suggestion consciously pursued in 2 Chr 5:7. But in 1 Sam 4:4, when the Ark is brought into battle, it includes (presumably graven upon its golden lid) the cherubim upon which Yahweh is enthroned. De Vaux (*MUSJ* 37 [1961] 94) dates the freestanding cherubim earlier than the Ark lid relief portrayal in Exod 25:17; and he finds that the cherubs' function was to guard the tree of life and serve as Yahweh's throne. Even in the height (1 Kgs 6:23) and the wings reaching to the side walls of the Inner Sanctum may be the same kind of pious exaggeration that we have in the gold reckoning. The Ark lid itself is named *kapporet* "smearing," (J. M. de Tarragon, *RB* 88 [1981] 5–12), in reference to the ritual of Lev 16:14; from this comes its name of "propitiatory" or mercy-seat, put in relation to the cherubim by Heb 9:5 and regarded as the throne of Yahweh's *shekinah* or presence. **14.** The veil (Exod 36:35; Matt 27:51) is replaced by wood-carving decor as in 1 Kgs 6:29. **15.** Freestanding pillars, like Jachin and Boaz, are strangely lacking in Herod's reconstruction, but they stood also in front of the Hazor temple, as attested by the plinths unearthed there in 1958; the position of the great bird statuary before the Middle Sanctum of Edfu is similar.

44 (b) MINOR FURNISHINGS (4:1–22). This is taken with little variation from 1 Kgs 7:23–26,38–51. **1.** The bronze altar is not in 1 Kgs 7:23, but is presupposed there in 8:22,64. **3.** The bronze sea is supported on a cast base the ornament of which is called gourds in 1 Kgs 7:24, but here probably correctly equated with oxen. This verse, as also 22 and 21:7, is singled out as an example of how one variant *found* by "the Chronicler" led him to make further changes (Barthélemy [*Critique textuelle* 68*] seems to put Chronicles as a stage of *using* the formed biblical books rather than among the formed biblical books themselves). **5.** *measures:* Hebr *bat.* "Baths" in *RSV* seems unfortunately to refer to the fact that the sea was for the priests to wash in. The *bat* is a measure of capacity, perhaps 10 gal. or perhaps only half that. De Vaux (*AI* 202) focuses the hopelessness of determining it exactly: our clearest indication is here the 10-cubit diameter by 5-cubit depth, or 590 cu. ft., but the parallel 1 Kgs 7:26 to the same dimensions allots only 2,000 *bat.* C. Wylie (*BA* 12 [1949] 89) convincingly accounts for this difference by the fact that in Chr the receptacle is cylindrical and in Kgs it is hemispherical. **17.** Succoth is Deir 'Alla, excavated by H. Franken (*EAEHL* 1.

321–24). For Zeredah we have Zarethan in 1 Kgs 7:46, which may well be the conspicuous peak Sartabeh N of Jericho; though others claim it is Sa'idiyeh across the Jordan, where J. Pritchard's excavation had to be suspended.

45 (c) ENTHRONEMENT OF THE ARK (5:1–7:22). **3.** As in 3:2, the colorful month names of 1 Kgs 6:1; 8:2 are replaced with austere numerals, like the medieval *feria quinta* instead of Thor's Day. **4.** The Ark is carried not by priests, as in 1 Kgs 8:3, but by the Levites, as in 1 Chr 15:2. **5.** The priests are inserted as if by oversight, either with the Levites as in the LXX, or as in the MT by use of the enigmatic tag "levitical priests"; cf. Deut 17:9. **6.** *too many to be counted:* A hyperbole more acceptable to our occidental taste than Chronicles' customary use of a concrete number, exaggerated indeed, but less so than this sweeping generalization. **7.** The author may be envisioning unrealistically cherubim wings, which were part of the Ark lid (see comment on 3:10), just as in v 9 he says that the carrying poles for the Ark are there "unto this day," when they had long since been no longer needed. **10.** What was in the Ark? Heb 9:4 presumes it (always?) contained a specimen of the manna (Exod 16:32) and the flowering rod of Aaron (Num 17:25) beside the stone tablets of the law (Deut 10:2). Despite *EDB* 135, the stones in the Ark may have originally been the oracular Urim and Thummim (Deut 33:8; Num 27:21; 1 Sam 14:18,41). Indeed, the Ark itself may have been identical at some stage with the priests' encrusted and eventually freestanding breastplate. On the other hand, the Ark as a covered-in saddle very probably developed into the Arabic palanquin called *qubba, 'utfa,* or *mahmal* (insights of H. Lammens accepted in F. Cross, *BA* 10 [1947] 63). Perhaps by its very emptiness the Ark "contained" the *shekinah* or "glory of Yahweh" (*IDB* 1. 222–26); at any rate, its exposed surface functioned as a throne left empty for the invisible deity (see comment on 2 Chr 3:10).

14. As soon as a hymn had been intoned to the newly housed Ark, the Temple was filled with a blinding cloud, doubtless from the censers (1 Chr 28:17 = Exod 37:16). It gave occasion for Solomon to improvise a lengthy speech, beginning "Yahweh promised that he would dwell on a cloud," and continuing throughout chap. 6 (= 1 Kgs 8:12–50, almost word for word) in a vein of unusually rich theological and moral content. The admirable 1939 Bonner Bibel commentary of J. Goettsberger claims that the cloud was smoke caused by the "sacrificial fire from heaven," which our present text therefore misplaces in 7:1. But 1 Kgs 8:54 ignores this "fire from heaven," doubtless suggested by the Elijah episode of 1 Kgs 18:38. The "glory of the Lord filling the house" (2 Chr 7:1; *shekinah* in Pesh) recalls the inaugural vision of Isa 6:4, rather than astronomical or mythical phenomena.

46 **6:11.** *covenant with the sons of Israel:* Substituted for the Kgs reference to Moses' "covenant with the fathers he led out of Egypt." **13.** The only interruption in Solomon's long prayer is made occasion to correct any misapprehension that the king is usurping priestly functions in the sanctuary. A platform or balcony had been erected for him, like the emperor's loge in Saint Sophia of Istanbul. This long verse ends with the same conspicuous phrase as the preceding v 12; we may perhaps have here not an interpolation but an omission, caused by homoioteleuton of 1 Kgs 8:23. **18.** Heaven is the firmament; highest heaven the water reservoirs beyond it; and third heaven God's abode beyond that. **41.** Part of Ps 132:8–11, replacing the 1 Kgs 8:53 reference to Moses' leadership in Egypt. Strangely, we have here three times the pairing of the names Yahweh and Elohim, outside Chr almost exclusively in Gen 2–3. **42.** "The works of liturgical piety of David" (cf. M. Adinolfi, *BeO* 8 [1966] 31–36) are David's own, not God's.

7:1. *fire . . . from heaven:* See comment on 5:14; but the literary origin may be rather in Lev 9:24 than in 1 Kgs 18:28 or Judg 6:21 (Mosis, *Untersuchungen* 151). **5.** The sacrificial animals (as in Kings) had a cash value equivalent to at least two million dollars, a restrained symbol by comparison with 3:8 and 1 Chr 22:14. **6.** This addition to 1 Kgs 8:63 is hardly strong enough to counter the impression that Solomon has usurped priestly functions. **8.** It would seem that the solemn octave of the Temple dedication ended on the very day on which the feast of Tabernacles began with its octave (Lev 23:36); though for J. Goldingay (*BTB* 5 [1975] 117) this account of the Temple dedication has been modified to show it as Yom Kippur (Lev 16). The dedication service itself, though it furnished one of the rare OT borrowings formerly prominent in Catholic liturgy, does not seem to have become an annual commemoration until the "reconsecration" of 2 Macc 10:5 (John 10:22), perpetuated as the modern Jewish Hanukkah counterpart to our secularized Yuletide. **11–22.** The text is taken largely from 1 Kgs 9:1–9.

(C) Solomon's Civil Rule (8:1–9:31).

47   (a) COMMERCE AND URBAN RENEWAL (8:1–16). **2.** One of the most mysterious among all the discrepancies from the parallels is this acceptance *from* Hiram of the 20 cities in Galilee declared by 1 Kgs 9:11 ceded *to* Hiram in payment for Temple materials. The enigma is even greater within Kgs, where Hiram spurns as "worthless" (*kĕ-bûl?*) the cities [for which?] "he had sent 120 gold talents." A safe conclusion may be that to prime the pump of Solomon's trade, Hiram bought the Galilean cities, but returned them when he was dissatisfied (Josephus, *Ant.* 8.5.3 § 141–43). **3.** *Hamath-zobah:* In 1 Chr 18:3–8, in an area loosely bounded by Hamath and the Euphrates, David overcomes an expeditionary force of Arameans from Zobah, Damascus, and (2 Sam 10:6) Rehob. Zobah and Rehob are unknown, but the other names determine a Syrian desert triangle of which Palmyra is the center, though most of the city-states were doubtless concentrated along the W fringe, as today. **4.** *Tadmor:* The name Tamar in parallel 1 Kgs 9:18 really means what was expressed by the later Lat Palm(yra), a common enough name for desert oases. Palmyra itself was called Tadmor, which is claimed to have been substituted here because of the preceding context. Tamar in Judah is held to be more likely; there is one near Baalah and Gezer (1 Kgs 9:17, unless this is Gerar); but we cannot altogether exclude some prior phase of the romantic ruins of Palmyra from the commercial, if not military, conquests of David or Solomon. **48** **6.** *chariots . . . horsemen:* More graphic in 1:14 (= 9:25; cf. 1 Kgs 9:19; 4:26; 10:26). Certain structures excavated at Megiddo by P. Guy are imaginatively called "Solomon's stables," although identical structures at Hazor are called mere storehouses and dated after Solomon: see Y. Yadin, "Megiddo," *EAEHL* 3. 830. Solomon's activities at Megiddo and Hazor are mentioned, but not in connection with his stables or horse trade. **8.** Discrepancies in the corvée are explained in 2:18 (1 Kgs 5:13). **11.** *pharaoh's daughter:* In the targum (Le Déaut, *Targum* 49 and 121) called Bithyah = "(she shall not dominate in) the Lord's house." As implied in 1 Kgs 3:1; 7:8; 9:16, she plainly deserved a residence more palatial than Solomon's harems of lesser geopolitical importance. Commentators have added that she would defile the house of David not just because she was a pagan, but because all women were ritually less clean than men (Lev 15:19; 12:1). Only this verse is retained

from the long description of the residence that Solomon built for himself in 1 Kgs 7:1–12. **13.** *new moons:* They had really no official status in the liturgical calendar, despite 1 Chr 23:31; Neh 10:34; but we cannot exclude the influence of the moon on sabbath origins (cf. *NCE,* "Sabbath"; *Bib* 36 [1955] 193; against de Vaux, *AI* 477). This liturgical preoccupation of Solomon is continued through v 16 in expansion of 1 Kgs 9:25, where also Solomon is not kept outside the chancel; see on 6:13.

49   (b) FLEET AND FRINGE BENEFITS (8:17–9:31). **17.** Eloth or Eilat is present-day 'Aqabah on the NE coast of the Gulf of 'Aqabah. Ezion-geber is a variant name. In acknowledgment of further research by B. Rothenberg, N. Glueck abandoned his claim of Eilat copper refineries in the Tell Kheleifeh excavated by him (*EAEHL* 2. 713–16); see J. Muhly, *BO* 41 (1984) 275–92. **18.** *Ophir:* "Ophir gold for Beth-horon" is the remarkable content of a 589 BC ostracon (*IDB* 3. 606) discovered at the Tel Qasile excavation of B. Mazar, who claims that it was the then Jaffa, where Solomon's government offices supervised the transshipment of logs (2 Chr 2:16; Ezra 3:7; *IEJ* 1 [1950] 209). Ophir may be identical with Supara in India (3 Kgs 8:28 LXX; Josephus, *Ant.* 8.6.4 § 164; H. von Wissmann, PWSup 12. 969–80). More commonly, Ophir is situated along the S coast of Arabia, so near to Africa's apes and peacocks that its name can be extended to both shores of the gulf: like Sheba, or Cush for Midian as in Num 12:1 (Zimbabwe much farther south along the African coast has also been considered). Gold-bearing Parvaim of 3:6 could be simply a variant form of the word Ophir, rather than a Hyperborea/Hesperia; cf. R. North, in *Fourth World Congress of Jewish Studies* (Jerusalem, 1967) 1. 197–202.

9:1. *Sheba:* As in the Epiphany liturgy (Ps 72:10; Isa 60:6). This is the S Arabian port nearest Ethiopia (Josephus, *Ant.* 2.10.2 § 249; H. von Wissmann, *Die Geschichte von Saba* [2 vols.; Vienna, 1975, 1982]); Ethiopian royalty traced its origin to a romance between Solomon and this queen, who has received the name of Belqis (R. G. Stiegner, "Die Königin von Saba' in ihren Namen" [diss., Graz 44, 1979]). More prosaically, the queen's visit was a punitive expedition, to put a stop to interference with her lucrative India-to-Canaan spice monopoly. His "wisdom," which she so outspokenly admires in v 6, doubtless consisted in a canny merger guaranteeing increased profits to them both (v 12). The mysterious comparison of Solomon's wisdom with Edomite-Egyptian prototypes is omitted (1 Kgs 4:33; Alt, *KlS* 2. 90). **7.** Transls. differ: "Happy are your 'people'" (*BJ²*); 'men' (*NAB*, as MT and 1 Kgs 10:8); 'wives' (*RSV;* LXX in both places) seems harder to explain unless it was original. **10.** Algum is a Phoenician export in 2:8, perhaps better spelled *almug* as in 1 Kgs 10:11; an unknown tree, possibly sandalwood used for making lutes and harps. **13.** The gold glut is an old folk tale; the 666, as in 1 Kgs 10:14 (also the number of the beast in Rev 13:18), is 660 in LXX. **16.** 300 shekels for "three minas" (1 Kgs 10:17) could be *mē'ôt* for *mānîm.* The palace is called a "forest" merely because it utilizes so much cedarwood. **21.** *ships of Tarshish:* Now agreed to be the name of a special kind of ship suited to commerce between Lebanon and the Tartessus port in Spain; it is not likely that Solomon had a second fleet plying the Mediterranean in collaboration or rivalry with Hiram; or that Darius's anticipation of a Suez Canal (Herodotus 2.158) had made the Mediterranean available to the Gulf of 'Aqabah, even in the time long after Solomon when Chr was being written. **25.** Notable divergence from 1 Kgs 10:26ff.; on the horse mart, see comment on 8:6. **29.** Omits the severe judgment of 1 Kgs 11 on Solomon's sexual and cultic morality. That passage describes his failures and setbacks as signs of divine disapproval and suggests that the coming split of his realm was a result of his own ineptness. Instead of this condemnation, the farewell for Solomon (as for David in 1 Chr 29:29) emphasizes his good standing with the prophets. On the various names given to the sources called "Solomon's chronicle" in 1 Kgs 11:41, → 4 above.

(IV) The Kings of Judah-without-Israel (2 Chr 10:1–36:23).
(A) The First Israelite Dynasty (10:1–16:14).

50 (a) REHOBOAM CAUSES TROUBLE (10:1–12:16). Interplay of human motivation and weaknesses in the working out of God's salvation plan is discounted. The divinely established David had united N and S into one administrative unit, so it was to remain that way. Any departure from that norm was a sin, and its effecters played no positive role in God's plan. But we can discern even more of David's personal merit and of God's guiding hand if we recapture what has been left out: The division was a declaration of independence by the N kingdom, restoring a prior situation of the people of God. The materials of 1 Kgs 12 were also tailored to fit the Deuteronomist's message, but he was more concerned to show God's hand in history by the fulfillment of predictions and similar prophetic feats, esp. of Elijah and Elisha. Since these men worked mostly in the N, they fall wholly outside Chronicles' focus of interest. Kgs also shows disapproval of the northern kings, but by recurrently evaluating them, not by ignoring them. Chronicles does not *wholly* ignore them; mention of six of them can be taken to show a continuing interest in the separated brethren (R. L. Braun, "A Reconsideration of the Chronicler's Attitude toward the North," *JBL* 96 [1977] 59–62).

10:1. Rehoboam went to Shechem after he had begun to reign. He had been at once solemnly inaugurated in Jerusalem as head of the southern group to which his father and grandfather had belonged. The northerners did not object in principle to holding a similar ceremony. They were on the whole satisfied with the unification arrangement, but they did demand (as is evident in this expression borrowed from 1 Kgs 12:1) that a separate inauguration ceremony should make clear their underlying autonomy. **2.** Jeroboam as Solomon's laborer had been skillful and loyal (1 Kgs 11:28); when he became a boss, he turned against management (R. North, "Jeroboam's Tragic Social-Justice Epic," *Homenaje a J. Prado* [Madrid, 1975] 191–214). The northern civic leaders found in Jeroboam a suitable mouthpiece to present Rehoboam with a Magna Charta to sign before they would endorse his leadership.

5. The popular demand is received by Rehoboam with a moderation that may have been sincere. He asks for three days to think and even first seeks advice from the elder statesmen, on whom his father had relied for shaping policy; surprisingly, these were not inflexible, but recommended yielding a bit to the trend of the times. **8.** But Rehoboam then turns to his peers (chiefly the forty or more other sons of Solomon: A. Malamat, *JNES* 22 [1963] 247–53). Their hotheaded counsel prevails.

Though henceforth ignoring Jeroboam, Chr ascribes some of his activities to Rehoboam, or shows Rehoboam drawing advantage from Jeroboam's evils, says J. Goldingay (*BTB* 5 [1975] 103). The date of the separation of Israel from Judah is 922, according to Bright (*BHI*), defended also by the Freedman-Campbell chronology in *BANE* 265–99. However, this date is the latest of all those proposed by recent competent author-

ities; G. Ricciotti's *Storie d'Israele* (Turin, 1932–34) centers on a date 10 years earlier; de Vaux, 930; Noth, 926.

19. On "Jeroboam's Rise to Power," see M. Aberbach and L. Smolar, *JBL* 88 [1969] 69–72; *IDBSup* 473. Jeroboam's claims to legitimacy are bypassed, where 1 Kgs 12:20 adds, "There was none that followed the house of David but the tribe of Judah only." Bright defends this passage, but Noth emends it to "Benjamin only"; at any rate, 1 Kgs 12:21 (= 2 Chr 11:1) shows that it was meant as a hyperbole and did not exclude Benjamin. "Israel" is added in 2 Chr 11:3 to the citation of 1 Kgs 12:23, and this defiant claim that only Judah is the true Israel is reflected in the phrase "Israel in the cities of Judah" (2 Chr 10:17, taken from 1 Kgs 12:17). Although this snatch of archaic verse is from the mouths of hostile Ephraimites, it may well have been a taunt in which Judah and the house of David are told to go home: "To your tents, O Israel!" It does not seem plausible that at this tense moment Jeroboam would have demobilized. 2 Sam 2:9 is insufficient proof that the restriction of the name "Israel" to the north is archaic; there it may be a convenient anachronism, or it may refer to the still-pending unity with Hebron effected under Saul; cf. Williamson (*Israel* 103). He admits that at the time of Rehoboam, northern Israel was justified in withdrawing (p. 112), but by the time of Abijah the schism was no longer justified, and the low ebb at the end of northern independence shows that on the whole it was better for the N and S to be united; but his conclusion is that for Chr the Judah community should not be so turned in on itself as to exclude entitled outsiders (p. 140).

51 **11:1–4.** Exactly as in 1 Kgs 12:21–24. The implication is that Judah could easily have crushed the Samaria uprising, but preferred to obey God's prophetic word. **5.** Only Chr preserves this archival detail, but utterly without chronological link. Rehoboam's defense posts have been set forth as a sort of Maginot Line entrenchment; but really we have here every big village (at least of the strategic Shephelah foothills); the military measures of Rehoboam were more probably on the order of our civilian defense. Rehoboam's forts include two and only two names in common with the "surrounding belt" of Levite cities of 1 Chr 6:39–66 (= Josh 21:8–42): Aijalon and Hebron. The "Rehoboam list" may really thus be a certain number of the previously privileged cities which Josiah fortified in 620, after their Levites had been evacuated by his new cultic centralization (Deut 12:11; V. Fritz, in *Y. Aharoni Memorial* [ErIsr 15; Jerusalem, 1981] 46*–53*). Chr ignores any temporary transfer of Jeroboam's capital to Penuel (1 Kgs 12:25).

13. The Levites flock to Judah, not just because Jeroboam impiously opposes the legitimate worship of Yahweh but because he replaced security risks with loyalists. **15.** *the calves:* A scornful summary of 1 Kgs 12:26–33. Winged bullocks, called cherubim, were the legitimate symbol of the divine presence (see comment on 3:11). Jeroboam may have incurred some guilt by duplicating this essential of the Ark cultus; others see the evil rather in deceptive resemblance of these bullocks to symbols of Baal worship. At any rate, Jeroboam's efforts to retain within his own nation both his people's religious loyalties and the economic benefits attendant upon pilgrimages cannot be taken as idolatry or dissent from Yahweh worship, which continued to be strong in Israel (R. North, "Social Dynamics from Saul to Jehu," *BTB* 12 [1982] 114). It is even claimed that Chr begins to judge Rehoboam harshly *after* his resistance to the bull shrines (M. Augustin, "Beobachtungen zur Chronistischen Umgestaltung . . ." in *Das Alte Testament als geistliche Heimat* [Fest. H. W. Wolff; Frankfurt, 1982] 14). The real abuse was sex-crazed Baal syncretism; Elijah had to fight it in Israel, but it had been ravaging Judah ever since Solomon's time (1 Kgs 11:5; 16:32). The whole of 1 Kgs 13, against northern flouting of a prophet, is of no concern to Chr.

18. *Mahalath:* Dynastic legitimacy is reinforced by showing how (unknown to 1 Kgs) the blood of Rehoboam's wife was nearly as Davidic as his own. They not only shared one Davidic grandfather, but Mahalath's other grandfather was David's brother. **20.** *Maacah:* Rehoboam's second wife, known to 1 Kgs 15:2, was his first cousin; unless, as Rudolph maintains with Jerome (PL 23. 1457), her father was "a different Absalom." His 76 other espousals fall far short of Solomon's (1 Kgs 11:3); this detail can hardly have been recorded to account for Rehoboam's downfall in 12:1: he is still praised in subsequent verses, though he had already been depicted as a vicious character. **22.** *Abijah:* Maacah's son also in 1 Kgs 15:2; perhaps by textual corruption in 2 Chr 13:2 (MT, not LXX or Pesh), he is traced to Micaiah bath Uriel of Gibeah; but this latter reading is retained because it is not the kind of "plausible" change a copyist would have made.

52 **12:1.** Yahweh's crushing rejection of the northern dynasty in 1 Kgs 14:1–20 is omitted, and also the gruesome details of the moral collapse of Rehoboam and Judah, here called "Israel." But v 2 embellishes with a few further details the devastation of Jerusalem by Pharaoh Shishak: the Egyptian force includes Libyans, Ethiopians, and "Sukkiim" (called "cavemen" by the ancient translators but claimed to be "mercenaries" in Egyptian documents cited by W. F. Albright in *OTMS* 18). **5.** Shishak's invasion is made the occasion for an emphatic prophetic intervention, required to give sense to 2 Chr 11:2–4 and 1 Kgs 12:22f. (not in 1 Kgs 14:21–31); here the prophet is called a *nābîʾ* (important for the research of Micheel [*Seher und Prophetenüberlieferungen* 40; → 4 above]). There is no need to raise the question of whether the episode is historical, because it is certainly a theological interpretation of the invasion, whether composed as such by Shemaiah, by canonical Chr, or by an intermediate source. The Karnak wall record of Shishak's invasion reveals that Israel was damaged as much as Judah. This fact, passed over also in Kgs, makes us wonder how Jeroboam would have been harbored by Shishak in 1 Kgs 11:40. **10.** Rehoboam's replacement of the stolen Temple plaques earns him a softening of the disdain in which he is held. **14.** Harshness returns to dominate his epitaph.

53 (b) THE END OF JEROBOAM (13:1–22). **1.** The heir to the throne of Judah was given the same name as the son of Jeroboam—Abijah (1 Kgs 14:1). When he becomes king, however, he is called Abijam in most Hebr mss. of 1 Kgs 14:31; 15:1. This giving of an identical name to contemporary royalty in Israel and Judah is a constant source of confusion in later reigns. Perhaps the similar names were given deliberataly to cause this confusion, at least insofar as they represent ideological counterclaims, as in the names of recent "democratic republics." **2.** On Micaiah as the mother of Abijah, see 11:22. Abijah's three-year reign is passed over in 1 Kgs 15:1–7, where there are three verses about David and one about Rehoboam. The note on war between Abijah and Jeroboam is expanded by Chr into a tissue of descriptive clichés drawn from famous biblical battles (Judg 9:7; 20:29; 8:2; Num 10:9). **3.** Symbolic numbers compounded of 40 are used to show that Yahweh's mighty army in Judah met a bully twice its size (= 2 Sam 24:9). **4.** Abijah's long speech (his "Sermon on the Mount" according to Coggins [*Chronicles* 111]) is a reform program recalling Nathan of 1 Chr 17:14 and

David's taunt to Goliath in 1 Sam 17:8. It warrants dispensing Abijah from the tag of impiety which in 1 Kgs 15:3 he shares with most rulers. **5.** *covenant of salt:* As in Num 18:19 sealed by sharing a meal. **9.** We have here simultaneously a theology of history and a history of theology (Exod 29:1,38; 30:7; 25:30–31). Fabrication of a speech to express the genuine concrete situation is a device legitimate even in some strict historiographical traditions. **17.** This slaughter can be regarded as a theological conclusion; there must have been something stupendous to show that Yahweh favored Judah, or rather true worship as against apostates in all times. **19.** *Bethel:* Although only 10 mi. N of Jerusalem, this is not in fact a city of Judah a few years later (2 Chr 16:1; Amos 7:10); however, the border fluctuated over the years, and Abijah may well have gained control of Bethel as well as Ephron (4 mi. NE) and Jeshanah (near [Mt.?] Zemaraim). These geographical names are from Josh 18:21–24; the rest of this chapter is an embellishment of 1 Kgs 15:1–8; see R. Klein, *ZAW* 95 (1983) 210–17. Anti-Samaritanism here alleged by M. Delcor (*ZAW* 74 [1962] 281–89) must be considered in relation to claims of a Chronicler author of Ezra (→ 3 above). **20.** Part of Jeroboam's punishment was sudden death whereas Abijah continued to reign. But the synchronism of 1 Kgs 14:20; 15:9 puts the death of Abijah two years before that of Jeroboam; and Bright makes this *twelve* years by reading 7 instead of 17 years for Rehoboam's reign.

54 (c) ASA OUTLIVES JEROBOAM'S DYNASTY (14:1–16:14). The long reign of Asa in Judah (911–870, in *IDB* 243; 913–873 according to Bright, *BHI*) is presented with theological reserves complicating the few known historical facts. We should expect to find the greatest significance attached to Baasha's overthrow of the hated Israel dynasty after its second incumbent had reigned only two years (1 Kgs 15:25). But the presentation in Chr is ambivalent, perhaps because Asa for some 35 years relied on Yahweh and enjoyed success, but at the end relied on human help and became weak; see now R. E. Dillard, "The Reign of Asa: An Example of the Chronicler's Theological Method," *JETS* 23 (1980) 207–18; on Rudolph's complicated analysis, → *JBC* 24:54.

55 **14:1.** The 10 years of peace, contrary to 1 Kgs 15:16 ("war with Baasha all their days"), is the Chr idea of divine approval for the early piety of Asa (Rudolph). **2.** The approval of Asa is equally emphatic in 1 Kgs 15:11–14; but "like David" is suppressed in Chr. **3–5.** *Asherim . . . high places:* This negates 15:17 (= 1 Kgs 15:14), which states that the high places were not taken away (out of Israel). Asa's Spartan measures against the offenses of his own (grand)mother, Maacah (1 Kgs 15:13) are postponed to 2 Chr 15:16.

6. *fortified cities:* This verse is a pivotal example of the exciting and soberly demonstrated thesis of Welten's study (*Geschichte*), which draws "the Chronicler's" idea of historiography entirely from his description of military-building operations and standing armies. Building activity is attributed only to good kings in their "good years" (often with *ḥāzaq* as in 2 Chr 26:9); Asa's forts are not from a source but are an invented spinoff from 1 Kgs 15:21. Neither the fort-building nor the raising of armies is ever put into relation with any of the numerous actual war operations in Chr. **8.** The standing army was stronger than the wartime force of 13:3. According to Welten (*Geschichte* 73, 111) Judah was heavy-armed (lance), Benjamin light-armed (bow), and they also had different kinds of shields; but the only time such racial divisions (and catapults, 2 Chr 26:14) are found is in the *Greek* period; therefore to that late date he assigns "the Chronicler," who took from that *Sitz im*

Leben the factual basis for his fictional attribution of big armies to good kings.

9. *Ethiopian:* Hebr Cushite; applies not only to Nubia but also to the adjacent Arabian peninsula, including Sinai (Num 12:1). Since the Sinai Midianites roamed as far as Gilead (Judg 6:3), we may well have here a raid of Negeb Bedouin encamped at Gerar (v 14), not far from Mareshah in the SW foothills of Judah. Zerah is a Hebr name, and there is no basis for applying it to the Egyptian Pharaoh Osorkon or the Euphrates desert monarch Cushan-rishathaim, although in Judg 3:10 Cushan's undoing is ascribed to Mareshah's neighbors (A. Malamat, *JNES* 13 [1954] 231–42). Zerah's army is again just neatly double Judah's resistance. **14.** *fear:* Like the nameless dread causing chaos, called "panic" because it was supposedly sent by the god Pan.

56   **15:3.** The "prophecy" of Azariah is a masterpiece of historical theology. More factually, "God alone rules us" in the period of the judges (Judg 17:6; 21:25) meant unbridled selfishness. Micheel (*Seher- und Prophetenüberlieferungen* 46) claims that not only the prophecy but even the name of Azariah is a Chr invention; though on p. 55 Micheel more plausibly leaves open the use of some local oral tradition for Eliezer of 2 Chr 20:37. **8.** Asa's acceptance of the challenge is a doublet inconsistent with 14:5. **9.** *gērîm:* Local ethnic minorities; Simeon was part of Judah anyway and the Ephraimite refugees are probably (as in v 8) the type of border merchants who keep handy the flags of both nations disputing the border. **11.** The only "spoils" compatible with the narrative are those from the campaign against Zerah, which seems to have dragged on four years (14:12). **13.** This saber rattling is brutal if understood as a serious juridical punishment; but it was not applied in practice. **16.** *Maacah:* His grandmother, as in 11:21.

57   **16:1–6.** In 1 Kgs, Asa was 36 ten years after the death of Baasha. In Chr accuracy can be salvaged by supposing that he is here counting from the split of the kingdom (Albright, *BASOR* 100 [1945] 20). It is just as respectful of the sacred text to say that the author, knowing only that aging Asa suffered an illness in apparent connection with his mishandling of such men as Hanani (v 7) has taken from the record (1 Kgs 15:16–22, word for word) this specimen of Asa's reliance on human alliances rather than on Yahweh. **7.** This moral is pointed by the hindsight of Hanani, which naturally enrages Asa. **12.** Even consulting a doctor is blamed as seeking help from men rather than from Yahweh. "Healers" is exactly the Hebr word for physicians, even if its use here is intended to suggest rather medicine men or witch doctors.

58   **(B) The Century of Social Unrest (17:1–25:28).** This pivotal era in the history of Yahwism is characterized in Israel by the prophet Elisha's engineering the overthrow of Omri's profiteering dynasty. Judah's painful link with those disorders via its own murderous usurping queen Athaliah could not be overlooked in Chr. But the origin of all these woes in Judean Jehoshaphat's alliance with the northern king Ahab is transfigured into a lengthy "mystery play" incorporating an obscure prophet. Surprisingly ignored are Israel's more momentous earlier prophets or mantic guilds affiliated with Elijah and destined to be transformed into the writing prophets of Judah after 750.

59   (a) JEHOSHAPHAT (870–852?) (17:1–20:37). **17:1.** Jehoshaphat means "Yahweh judged," and it has been plausibly maintained that the entire presentation here is a cadenza on that theme. *grew strong over Israel:* May well mean "consolidated his power within Judah" (see comment on 10:16). Defense measures against Israel

or Ephraim, the nearest enemy, are indeed explicit. Such preparedness is not inconsistent with the jockeying and intrigues of diplomatic matrimonial alliance with the North (18:1; 20:35). The bride in such cases is ultimately a hostage, under cover of which each side might have been readying an attack.

3–6. Chronicles' own legitimate inference from the fact that no strife troubling Jehoshaphat's coregency is recorded (17:12). **7–9.** The concrete example of kingly good behavior, on the other hand, is inserted from a Levite instructional mission after 500, names and all (cf. Zech 6:10; Neh 2:10; 7:62). **11.** Exchange of gifts between neighboring heads of state is minimum protocol; by omitting mention of Judah's return gifts, the king of Judah is made out to be a sort of suzerain. **13.** The storage cities of Judah have been searchingly examined by Y. Yadin (*BASOR* 163 [1961] 6–12). **14.** The names of the colonels within Jerusalem are from some doubtless ancient list; the numbers presumably represent the total population on which each could draw, but with exaggeration even so. **19.** Here is omitted the whole of 1 Kgs 17–22, which describes the rise of Elijah, and specifically the hoarding of national resources fostered by Ahab's queen Jezebel.

60   **18:1.** The marriage alliance of Ahab's daughter Athaliah with Jehoshaphat's son Jehoram would seem to have been more interwoven with the ensuing diplomatic parleys than Chr indicates, but the event is not noted at all in 1 Kgs 22:1–35, otherwise transcribed here faithfully. **2.** It is by no means evident why the king of Judah should be paying a courtesy call to the ruler of his people's enemy. That Ahab has summoned Jehoshaphat is a fairly natural implication of 1 Kgs 22:2, even apart from the overtones of Ahab's servants around the conference table. Why should Judah's king, whom Chr has made out to be a terror to his Philistine and Arab neighbors, now answer meekly that his army is Ahab's to command, instead of asking rather "What advantages can I gain for my people by agreeing to cooperate with you on a partnership basis?" **4.** *inquire first:* But Jehoshaphat has already committed himself to the enterprise before he piously proposes to find out what the Lord thinks about it. **5.** As in Kgs, the clear implication is that the northern cultus is very bad. **22.** Yahweh inexorably makes clear his will to Samaria by the "weak and contemptible" (1 Cor 1:27) means he chooses; even his responsibility for the lying spirit of false prophets is taken over without demur (see comment on 1 Chr 21:1). **31.** Only by the insertion "God helped him," Chr transforms Jehoshaphat's cry of terror and identification of himself (1 Kgs 22:32) into a serene and noble prayer.

61   **19:2.** Echoes 1 Kgs 22:44, which seemingly puts Jehoshaphat's collaboration with Israel alongside his misdeeds of tolerating cultic high places. **3.** Here, however, Jehoshaphat is praised for having destroyed the Asherahs. **5.** His judicial reform need not be a doublet of 17:7 (see Albright in *Alexander Marx Jubilee Volume* [NY, 1950] 1. 61–82). It would seem that the civil or priestly judges, appointed by "Yahweh judged" (= Jehoshaphat) within the framework of an older spoils system, were arousing ominous dissatisfaction by their bribery and favoritism. To regain a good public image (as commended in Deut 16:18; 17:9), these political adventurers are replaced by plodding civil servants, levitical scribes who will know the law or be able to look it up, and who will apply it with unimaginative and unemotional objectivity. **11.** Moreover, for the execution of their writs and verdicts, they are provided with a corps of Levite bailiffs: *šōṭēr*, "policeman," is from Akk "writer" (de Vaux, *AI* 155).

62   Chapter 20 is entirely unparalleled in the Bible (M. Noth, *ZDPV* 67 [1945] 45–71), a "parable" (*OAB*) remotely like 2 Kgs 3:4–27. **20:1.** *Ammonites . . . Meunites:* The Hebrew has "the sons of Ammon (and with them some) Ammonites," often claimed to be a scribal echo of 2 Chr 26:7; but the (second) Ammonites is in the LXX Minaeans (a South Arabian tribe), which is their rendering in 26:7 and 1 Chr 4:41 for *mĕ'ûnîm*, possibly the adjectival form of Ma'on. There is one Ma'on S of Hebron and another near Petra, both part of the Edomite/Nabatean roaming area (Seir of v 10). **2.** Edom, in some Hebr mss Aram (= Syria), a frequent confusion of the letters *d/r*, especially likely here since the area E of the Dead Sea is meant. Barthélemy (*Critique textuelle* 1. 495) surmises the original Greek reading Edom survives in OL (and Alcalá Bible). The localization of Hazazon-tamar is (and probably was) not known; likely enough it was in the region south of Hebron where the best-known landmark is En-Gedi. **3.** To "seek the Lord" normally implies the use of some oracular devices (the contrary in 1 Chr 10:14). Here, only prayer and fasting are explicit. **5.** There is no reason to assume that this posturing of the king implies that no military operations are being begun; on the contrary, his prayer is typical of those who send armies into the field (cf. 14:11; 1 Sam 17:45). **14.** Yahweh's choice of a Levite cantor (see comment on 1 Chr 25:1; 15:16) rather than a priest or prophet for making known his will is significant; but A. Schmitt ("Das prophetische Sondergut in 2 Chr 20,14–17," in *Künder* [Fest. J. Schreiner; Würzburg, 1982] 273–85) compares Mari oracles rather than "levitical preaching." **17.** Victory was assured. **23.** Judah is unscathed because the surrounding enemy nations fight among themselves. **26.** An etiology: "There is a place called *bĕrākâ,* 'blessing,' because at one time a momentous blessing took place there." **36.** The short reign of an Ahaziah in Israel (some 12 years before a ruler of the same name in Judah) brings the commercialism of Ahab's dynasty near its end; his ill-fated "Taršiš ships at Ezion-geber" (see comment on 8:17; 9:21) enterprise was shared by Jehoshaphat, who thus has some responsibility for the oncoming social-justice revolution (see comment on 22:7). The insertion of the episode here is a postscript and anticlimax. For Eliezer, see comment on 15:3.

63   (b) ATHALIAH (841–835) (21:1–23:21). Racine's French classic *Athalie* has made prominent in world culture this sad low point in Judah's fortunes. She is presented as a symbol of the sin of Samaria from which she was born, (?grand-)daughter of Jezebel. She secured power by a trail of massacres comparable to medieval Marozia's enslavement of the papacy. Athaliah's crisis was apparently reached in the same year in which Jezebel was dominating Israel (2 Kgs 9:30, *ca.* 841). The rulers in Judah were Jehoram, then Ahaziah, while the same names in reverse order appear in the Samaria king list, and the dates of Jehoram of Israel are identical with (Bright) or begin slightly earlier than those of Jehoram of Judah. **4.** Jehoram's massacre of his own brothers seems to fit the *modus operandi* of his wife Athaliah, esp. since she is left unharmed. Verse 6 is taken from 2 Kgs 8:18, where Chr rejoins the deuteronomistic narrative after skipping seven entire chapters about Elisha. There is no mention of Jehoram's massacre in Kgs, but its historicity is agreed. Experts are hesitant about Noth's eruditely documented claim that names like Michael or Jehiel could not have been used so early. By "(princes of) Israel" is doubtless meant Judah. **5.** When Jehoram was 32, his youngest son and successor Ahaziah was already three years older, unless we correct Ahaziah's age 42 of 22:2 to 22 as in 2 Kgs 8:26. **7.** The

house of David, which Yahweh's fidelity bound him not to destroy, seems to mean his dynasty in Chr, but it is his *nation* in 2 Kgs 8:19. **8.** *Edom:* Because the portion of E Jordan opposite Judah was held by Omri, the only part left for Judah was S of the Dead Sea. The close ethnic and commercial relations between Petra and Hebron would eventually result in Judah's submission to Edom in the person of Herod the Great. **10.** Libnah is prominent in Joshua (10:29; 21:13); it is west of Lachish, at Safi mound (Abel; 5 mi. S at Borna for Albright). The Edom–Libnah troubles are taken from 2 Kgs 8:22, but a theological reflection is added.

12. This sudden burst of Elijah into the narrative, after sedulous suppression of his very name and of a dozen chapters dominated by him, is surprising. As far back as 2 Kgs 1:17 we see that Judah's Jehoram became king while Elijah was still functioning. It seems likely that Elijah, while roaming about Samaria, Gilead, Phoenicia, and Sinai (1 Kgs 19:8), knew what was going on in Judah and expressed himself about it. Whether these views were taken down by a disciple and sent as "Elijah's letter" during or after his lifetime or were first composed for insertion in Chr is no real problem of historicity. **16.** The Ethiopians (Hebr Cushites, as in 14:9) are the ever-raiding Midianite-Arab tribes of Sinai who shared a boundary with Judah and Philistia. **17.** *Jehoahaz:* "Yahweh-grasps," the youngest son of Jehoram as in 25:23, is the one we have been calling Ahaziah, "grasps-Yahweh," as in 22:1 and 2 Kgs 8:24. **19.** *bonfires for his fathers:* Attested only for Asa (16:14). **20.** *they buried him within the city:* So 2 Kgs 15:7; despite archaeological and exegetical assumptions of devout Jews' refusal to live in a city containing tombs, like Tiberias (*EDB* 2452; *IDB* 1. 475: despite warnings of J. Simons [*SJOT* 274, 309]; S. Yeivin, *JNES* 6 [1948] 30–45; S. Krauss, *PEQ* 79 [1947] 102–111).

64   **22:2.** Athaliah's name now occurs for the first time. Her influence doubtless became even more dominant over her son Ahaziah, esp. if we suppose he was only 22 when he inherited the crown (see comment on 21:5). **5.** For Ahaziah to share in Samaria's anti-Syria campaign (2 Kgs 8:28f.) meant merely supporting the policy of his grandfather; but the dramatic possibilities are here exploited. The often colorless pious editorializing blossoms with v 7 into a profound grasp of the significant politico-social movements of the time: in God's salvation plan, the quick eclipse of Ahaziah was interwoven with Samaria's momentous overthrow of the Omri dynasty. **8.** The name of Athaliah's mother (or close kinswoman) Jezebel is not mentioned in this account of the two kings' demise at Jezreel, but she dominates the scene in 2 Kgs 9:30. **10.** The savagery there shown to Jezebel, even more than the relatively routine execution of Ahaziah, accounts for the pathological cunning of Athaliah's reaction. **11.** This dramatic episode is taken from 2 Kgs 11:2. **12.** For a six-year reign of terror, Athaliah held all power in Judah.

65   **23:1.** *Centurions:* Hebr *śārê mē'ôt* as in 2 Kgs 11:4, but here provided with good Jewish names in place of the ethnic Carians (doubtless the Cretans of 2 Sam 8:18). Jehoiada is left strangely without an introduction. He would appear to be the chief of police, but turns out to be a high priest in v 8 (= 2 Kgs 11:9). **2.** To avoid the impression that a king of Judah is brought to power by foreigners invading the sanctuary, Levite cooperation is here invoked. Also, rather unrealistically, "all the houses of Israel" send delegates to the plot. **4.** Here we have no mention of the *rāṣîm,* "runners," of 2 Kgs 11:4 ("guards," *NAB RSV NJB;* see D. Frayne, "Šulgi, the Runner," *JAOS* 103 [1983] 739; J. Klein, "Šulgi and Išmedagan; Runners in the Service of the Gods," *Beer-Sheva* 2 [1985]

7*–38*). **7.** These orders are intended to protect the sanctuary (Rudolph) but also and chiefly the royal figurehead. **13.** *the people of the land:* They rejoice, as in 2 Kgs 11:14; on this disputed technical term, see on Ezra 4:4. *the singers with their musical instruments:* These are inserted, even at the cost of dramatic tension.

66   (c) Joash (835–797), Amaziah (797–792) (24:1–25:28). **24:2.** The boy king does a fine job as long as ("because" 2 Kgs 12:2) he lets the priest make the decisions. **3.** After 10 years, even a wife is chosen for the king by Jehoiada. **5.** The adolescent king's initiative in putting religious worship on a sound financial basis is somewhat coy, esp. when it involves reproaching the priests for not collecting the money fast enough. *from all Israel:* In 2 Kgs 12:5, the priests are expected rather to get the repairs paid for by their own contacts, but the "contact" (*makkār*, "acquaintance") seems rather to be the reason why the money is not going into Temple repairs in 2 Kgs 12:4, which contains several obscure technicalities about the source of funds. **6.** Our text does not report the fact that Joash allowed some 10 years to elapse before taking drastic action. **8.** The king gets credit for the collection box; in 2 Kgs 12:9 Jehoiada also gets the idea. **14.** A correction of 2 Kgs 12:13, curiously suppressing 12:15 (the priests kept no audit of the funds they passed to their paymasters, with whom they had an understanding; meanwhile the Temple repairs did not eat into the priests' stipends). Verses 5–14 are taken by B. Halpern ("Sacred History and Ideology: Chronicles, Thematic Structure—Indications of an Earlier Source," in *Creation of Sacred Literature* [ed. R. Freedman; Berkeley, 1981] 40) as a parade example of the fact that for Chr "more is better." The root *rbh* occurs 100 times (in Kgs, 30), and *lā-rōb* 35 (in Kgs 5); Kgs never, Chr often, speaks of rewarding a pious monarch with wealth.

18. After a life of virtue and helping the priesthood, why should Joash be punished by a Syrian invasion? And how could he buy off the invaders with consecrated funds? (2 Kgs 12:17f.). Chr answers with the theological reflection that after Jehoiada's death, Joash would have fallen from a good life into the sinful idolatry so typical of Judah's kings. **20.** This Zechariah-ben-Jehoiada is doubtless the one of Luke 11:51, called son of Barachiah in Matt 23:35 by assimilation to Isa 8:2. **23.** Even though Joash has now been classed among the evildoers, a king of Judah is not shown voluntarily opening the Temple treasury to pagan invaders; all responsibility falls to the Syrians. Their king Hazael is not named. **24.** Joash, instead of going free for his simony, is made out to have died of it. **25.** The conspiracy laconically condemned in 2 Kgs 12:20 appears here as an act of righteous moral retribution, and its punishing in 25:2–3. **26.** For M. Graham (*ZAW* 97 [1985] 256–58), comparison of this verse with Ezra 9–10 shows that Chr was written *after* Ezra.

67   **25:1.** Amaziah is a variant of *'Amoṣ*, "Yahweh has made strong." **4.** The singular prominence accorded this maxim (as in 2 Kgs 14:6) doubtless results from the fact that with Jer (31:30 = Ezek 18:20) and Deut (24:16), the new norm of individual responsibility had gained wide popular support as a reaction against primitive Mosaic morality (Exod 20:5; 34:7), though J. Scharbert (*Bib* 38 [1957] 149) holds that it was always implicit in the Mosaic legislation. **5.** Expanded to 12 verses is a brief etiological notice of 2 Kgs 14:7 without its point of departure (Joktheel = Sela). Since Sela may possibly be Petra, it is a pity that Hebr lexicography sheds no light on why Amaziah selected this new name. This campaign is presented in both Kgs and Chr as an unbridled aggression, neither defensive nor punitive. **7.** M. Johnson (*Purpose* [→ 10 above] 49) notes the Israel whom Yahweh

does not support is here Ephraim, exceptionally excluding Judah from "Israel." **9.** Amaziah doubtless decided that it is better to lose your investment than be strangled by it, a policy wise enough to be called divinely inspired; but the divine promise is hardly borne out by v 13. **14.** It was common in the ancient Near East, after successful wars of conquest, to foster the subjected people's religion, even by adding the statues of their gods to the conquerors' pantheon. Some gesture of this kind may well have been made by victorious Amaziah. **17.** This action is a manufactured link for the chain of theological argumentation needed to furnish the conclusion that Yahweh's Judah will be humiliated by godless Israel (= 2 Kgs 14:8–14). **24.** On the specially favored Obed-edom, see comment on 1 Chr 13:14; cf. 25:8. **25.** Strangely, Amaziah is granted 15 years of apparently prosperous reign after surviving his foe. **27.** Chr adds to Kgs only a hint that all this time a plot was simmering against Amaziah, who seems at any rate to have retained official good will, since after his fatal flight to Lachish he is restored to burial in Jerusalem.

(C) Rise of Book Prophecy (26:1–32:33).

68   (a) Uzziah's Architecture and Leprosy (26:1–23). Four details betoken special interest in this king. (a) He has a priestly mentor, Zechariah, like Jehoiada in 24:2. Relevance to Isa 8:2 being quite remote, this figure corresponds disconcertingly to Jehoiada's son of 24:20, perhaps by a dramatic license. (b) Chr alone furnishes information about Uzziah's military pursuits, both aggressive and defensive (on Welten's conclusions from the "lance" and [Gk-era] "catapult" of v 14, see comment on 2 Chr 14:6). One tower and cistern in the desert (v 10) have been recognized in the (pre-)Qumran building nucleus dated to the 8th cent. by its pottery, and called "Salt City" as in Josh 15:62 (M. Noth, *ZDPV* 71 [1955] 111–23). On the inroads into Philistine territory, see D. Freedman (*BA* 26 [1963] 134–39; for further progress of the Ashdod excavation, see M. Dothan, *'Atiqot* [1971] Eng. 9f.; *IDBSup* 71f.). Jabneh, matrix of post-Jerusalem Judaism, is mentioned only here in the Bible, unless it is Jabneel of Josh 15:11. Another exploit of Uzziah supposedly verified by excavation is his reconquest of the Red Sea port of Elath (v 2; N. Glueck, *BASOR* 72 [1938] 8; for reevaluations see comment on 8:17), but it is peculiar that this event is recorded in 2 Kgs 14:22 as part not of Uzziah's reign but of his father's. This anomaly is somewhat rectified in 2 Chr 26:2, "after the death of the king" (of Edom; not Amaziah: B. Alfrink, *OTS* 2 [1943] 112). On the "Carmel vineyards" of v 10, see A. Rainey, *Harry M. Orlinsky Volume* (ErIsr 16; Jerusalem, 1982) 177–81; Eng 258*. (c) Chr predictably expands the notice of 2 Kgs 15:5 regarding Uzziah's leprosy, making it a punishment dramatically inflicted at the very moment of his intrusion into the cult; it is even more dramatic, with earthquake and lightning, in Josephus (*Ant* 9.10.4 §225; J. Morgenstern, *HUCA* 12 [1938] 3). (d) Only Chr gives to this king the name Uzziah by which he is known to the prophets and modern scholars (2 Kgs 15:13,30 only in flashback). Strangely, this name is replaced by Azariah in 2 Kgs to describe both his accession and his entire reign (14:21f.; 15:1–8; also 1 Chr 3:12).

17. Azariah is also the otherwise unattested name of the high priest whose *lèse majesté* caused the king's leprosy (v 19). This priest thus seems to stand in the same relation of theocratic authority over Uzziah ascribed confusingly to Zechariah in v 5. Hence we have ventured to suggest that Azariah as a variant name for King Uzziah himself means really the priest-regent who issued official documents during a period between Uzziah's incapacitation by leprosy and the effective transfer of full powers to the boy Jotham (R. North, "The Qumran Reservoirs," *BCCT* 112 n. 27). Others conclude rather that Azariah (differing only by one letter in spelling, and hardly at all in meaning, from Uzziah in Hebrew) was the private name resumed after the abdication (*IDB* 4. 742; see 2 Kgs 14:21). **23.** Uzziah was buried in the royal cemetery "although" (not "because," as *RSV*) he died of leprosy. His remains are generally admitted to be those of a gravestone from 800 years later with the Aram inscription, "Hither were brought the bones of Uzziah, king of Judah; do not open." Neither Chr nor Kgs calls attention to the fact that during Uzziah's reign burst out that ferment of charismatic outspokenness which we call book prophecy—Isaiah's inaugural vision (6:1) around the time of the emergence of Amos (1:1).

69   (b) ISAIAH'S ROYAL ANTAGONISTS (27:1-28:27). The reign of Jotham is in 2 Kgs 15:33f. a bare transition, mildly approved and here expanded into the short chap. 27. Why should it be made into a glowing encomium by the rewording of adverse elements as in v 2? Perhaps it was a tendency to see everyhing in black and white: whoever is on the right side of the thin line of minimal submission to God is a hero, the rest are criminals. **3.** Jotham's Jerusalem wall may have been a trial run for the expansion of the city from SE to SW (J. Simons, *SJOT* 330), but the date of that event is one of the most fiercely contested in the whole of OT archaeology (→ 75 below). The indication of 2 Kgs 15:37 that the Rezin-Pekah threat prominent in Isa 7:1-17 was taking shape already in Jotham's time is here either suppressed or perhaps transformed into the successful war on Ammon, v 5.

70   **28:1.** Against the virtuous foil of Jotham, the evil of *Ahaz* is greatly intensified by Chronicles' rewriting in chap. 28. Intriguingly there is no mention either here or in the parallel 2 Kgs 16:7 of the lengthy history supplied in Isa 7:1-6. Here the description of the effects of the Assyrian alliance on the Temple altar is unaccountably euphemistic if, as seems probable, what is meant is either a diplomatic cultus of Assyria's god installed as partner to Yahweh, or at least a use of Temple funds for political entanglements. Verses 8-13 describe a remarkable boycott of the Samaria population in favor of Judah. The account betrays in many traits the oversimplified piety of the compiler; yet in essence it is so alien to his monolithic condemnation both of Samaria and of Ahaz that it cannot be a fabrication. Apart from these two episodes, we cannot readily summarize the alterations from Kgs under a few heads but must notice some special slanting in almost every verse.

3. *burned his sons:* Pl. instead of the sg. (2 Kgs 16:3) has no special force; vv 7 and 27 acknowledge the survival of other sons. In any case, there is no real proof that the odious rite reprobated here and in 2 Kgs 23:10 means "burning to death" instead of an ordeal or branding. **5.** Here, apparently from some objective record, is depicted the Aramean invasion of Judah as a thing independent of collusion with Samaria, and less gruesome. **9.** The antimilitarist flare-up in Samaria under the prophet Oded is remarkable for two reasons: it is a revolt against the authority of the military commanders and not of any king or civil ruler; and it contains no indication that the military maneuver being boycotted was itself under Samaritan leadership. Some would conclude that inserted here is the record of an event in which the Samaritan populace opposed a group which had invaded Judah, from Moab or Ammon ("kinsfolk," v 11) rather than from N Israel. **15.** Not only does the army release its spoils, both human and material, but the "good Samaritans" give clothes to the ragged and food and drink to all. P. Ackroyd, (*SEA* 33 [1968] 35) holds that this

episode, though improbable in itself, gives a whole new theological twist to what we learn from 2 Kgs 16, and may have influenced Luke 10:34; numerous lines of (indirect) influence upon Jesus himself are traced by F. S. Spencer (*WTJ* 46 [1984] 317-49). *Jericho:* The frontier where the captives are handed over to their Judean kinsfolk.

71   **16.** The appeal of Ahaz to Assyria for help is undoubtedly the result of the Syro-Ephraimite attack from the north in v 5 (as in 2 Kgs 16:7), although the connection is broken by insertion of a vivid side issue, as well as by stress on invasions from the southeast and west, Edom and Philistia, in vv 17-18. **20.** *Tiglath-pilneser:* As in 1 Chr 5:6, this is an unexplained variant of Tiglath-pileser (or Pul!) of 2 Kgs 15:19,29. There is no mention here of the emphatic intervention of Isaiah (7:14), although he is mentioned in 32:20. In 29:1 seem to be accepted the synchronisms of 2 Kgs 16:2, making Ahaz only 11 years old (and not yet king) at the birth of Hezekiah, a factor to be explained by the numerous experts who would consider Hezekiah to be Emmanuel. J. McHugh (*VT* 14 [1964] 452) puts Hezekiah's birth 10 years later, during Ahaz's lifetime. We cannot determine from the Isa narrative whether Ahaz persisted in his plan of inviting Pul, or whether the arrival of the Assyrian army did more harm than good to Judah. This does not seem to be the case in 2 Kgs 15:29; 16:9. The contrary indications of 2 Chr 28:21 ought perhaps to be regarded no less than v 23 as a theological inference rather than an item recorded in archives. By contrast, v 24 records details about the altar that are even more damaging in 2 Kgs 16:10-17; Chr may have exaggerated and inferred Ahaz's motivation. **27.** Burial of Ahaz outside the royal cemetery (MT: "inside Jerusalem city"; LXX adds "of David") does not exactly contradict 2 Kgs 16:20, but rather clarifies its stock phrase by a warranted theological warning: such a wicked king could not have received honorable burial.

72   (c) HEZEKIAH'S ECUMENICAL MOVE (29:1-32:33). Hezekiah appears chiefly as a weakling and antagonist in Isa 37:6; 38:1 and in 2 Kgs 20:19. But in Chr Hezekiah appears as one of the most noble reforming leaders. The ecumenical and national defense energies attributed to him, although not attested elsewhere, are altogether plausible and contribute indispensably toward our understanding of the deuteronomistic-Josian reforms. **1.** *twenty-five years old:* Only 15 according to McHugh (→ 71 above). In fact, a boy king is more apt to be a reformer, docile to the interests of his priests and elders (see 24:1 on Joash and 34:1 on Josiah; but in 20:31 the admired Jehoshaphat begins his reign at 35).

3. Hezekiah's first concern, in the ("postdated") first month of his first complete year, was to restore the cultus within Jerusalem. His acts and formulas set him in direct repudiation of the policies of Ahaz in 28:24. Out of 118 verses in Chr on the reform, 100 are not in Kgs (Myers). **4.** Nominally, priests are convoked for the task as well as Levites. **5.** The address is to the Levites, perhaps in tacit reproach for the priests' easy compliance with Ahaz in 2 Kgs 16:11. Priests were present where needed, to enter the restricted precincts as in v 16; however, they were too few, and the Levites more zealous (v 34; 30:3). **6.** The public confession is a favorite genre of the anguished reappraisal during the Babylonian situation (Neh 9:2). **12.** The nomenclature of the Levites, with special prominence of the choir directors, echoes 1 Chr 6:18,33; 15:5,17; 16:41; 25:1; "it has nothing to do with Hezekiah's time" (Rudolph). **17.** It is important to keep reminding ourselves that what is really meant by a term such as "holy" or "make holy" is far from easy to define. Here what is chiefly meant is to "sweep out" or "clean up": insofar as the "holy" place is being cleaned or repaired, the rendition "restore to its former and due state of holiness" is appropriate, but leaves holiness undefined. **20.** The "princes" (*NAB* as MT; *RSV:* "officials") bring the sacrificial animals, but the priests slaughter them (despite J. Hänel, *ZAW* 55 [1937] 46). **21.** The seven bulls etc. were originally intended for *each* of the beneficiaries named, but quickly changed to "all Israel," according to J. Milgrom ("Hezekiah's Sacrifices at the Dedication Services of the Purified Temple," *Biblical and Related Studies* [Fest. S. Iwry; ed. A. Kort; Winona Lake, 1985] 159-61). **23.** The laying on of hands is a ritual prescribed by Lev 4:24; the male goat is for the ruler (Lev 4:28 specifies a female goat for the civilians; for the priests and religious groups, bullocks are required in Lev 4:4,15). The common assumption is that the hand gesture here and in the context of Heb 10 signifies the passing of (unconscious) sin from the offerer to the victim. This notion of substitution would seem to derive from a telescoping of Lev 16:21, where only one of the two goats is loaded with the people's sins, but it is then sent away alive into the desert; the other goat is sacrificed, but without any hand-laying ritual or other suggestion of expiatory substitution. **24.** The verb for atone, *kippēr,* means really "to smear" (the blood); it is a gesture of obscuring rather than of removing (the guilt). **25.** The musical background and its Davidic origins are given with a complacency reinforcing the hypothesis that the author belonged to the choir guild. **34.** Very subtly it is implied here that the alleged intrusion of (postexilic) Levites into dignities above their station was no fault of their own at all, but of the priests' deficiencies noted as far back as Hezekiah's time. **36.** *suddenly:* Rather, "expeditiously"; there was joy that such a big job had been completed in only two weeks.

73   **30:1.** Hezekiah's ecumenical Passover is not hinted in the probably relevant Nehushtan episode of 2 Kgs 18:4; but it shares traits with the Passovers of 2 Chr 35 and Ezra 6:19 (H. Haag, *Vom alten zum neuen Pascha* [SBS 44; Stuttgart, 1971]). Some maintain that we have here a literary vesture for the prophetic hope of the return of the northern tribes to their Davidic loyalty, as in Ezek 37:19; others regard it as a way of saying that Hezekiah could not have fallen short of Josiah (35:18) in the splendor of his Passover. Doubtless the recorded facts of the case were relatively pedestrian. Somehow a small number of worshipers from various tribes of the northern kingdom were persuaded to come for a Passover in Jerusalem. Chr makes this event into the outcome of a grandiose plan. Hezekiah's wielding of influence in Samaria gains in plausibility if his inauguration (or this Passover) took place after Assyria's annexation of Samaria in 721, as Rudolph and other experts hold. Bright (*BHI*) dates Hezekiah's accession to 715. **2.** It is almost incredible that Passover would be postponed a whole month, even for so momentous a display of faith and unity; F. Moriarty ("The Chronicler's Account of Hezekiah's Reform," *CBQ* 27 [1965] 406) holds that the postponement is a fact but unexplainable. Admittedly there is precedent in Num 9:6 for an individual in a state of ritual impurity to defer his Passover by one month. But it is more plausible to interpret this date (also in v 13) as "the second Passover month" of Hezekiah's reign. **5.** Rudolph's commentary finds disproof of historicity in the fact that no prescription of united Passover celebration in Jerusalem existed before Josiah. This leaves unduly out of account the extent to which Josiah's reform itself may have been the expression of a religious conviction of the north, growing to a climax within Hezekiah's time, as many experts maintain. **7.** Those who maintain

an anti-Samaritan "Chronicler" author also of Ezra (see comment on Neh 4:1) find this eloquent appeal to the separated brethren to return to Davidic unity a formulation suited to the Samaritan estrangement of the Ezra books. It is less smug than the similar allocution of Abijah in 13:5.

74   **14.** The dismantled altars included doubtless some tokens of Assyrian divinities set beside the cult objects of Judah: the price Ahaz had had to pay for Pul's protection (2 Kgs 16:10) according to Middle Eastern traditions for signifying alliance between two nations. Thus Hezekiah's gesture of piety was also an effective step toward repudiating the political commitments of his predecessor. The crowd of pilgrims flooding the city may have been easier to rouse to violence against cultic irritants than the local population was too cautious to uproot. It may well be that the worshipers' indignation was vented also on purely Israelite superstitions and Canaanite syncretisms, the Nehushtan and Ashera of 2 Kgs 18:4, echoed in 2 Chr 31:1 (W. Maier, *'Ašerah* HSM 37; Atlanta, 1986). **18.** We have here an extraordinary trait of the ecumenical Passover; human values prevail over ritual technicalities (Lev 15:31), and this by decree of the king under pressure of political interests. Yet neither the Levites who were there nor the Chr author see anything insuperably reprehensible in this. **23.** According to J. Segal (*The Hebrew Passover* [London, 1963] 19, 226), chap. 30 was written after chap. 35, so as to outdo Josiah's Passover by adding seven days of festival, as a misunderstood application of 1 Kgs 8:66. But Segal's whole thesis, rendering the lamb sacrifice as well as the unleavened bread a sedentary Canaanite ritual, is rejected by de Vaux and is contrary to most expert opinion (→ Exodus, 3:22). **25.** *Aliens:* Northerners seeking refuge in Judah is a "Diaspora situation," described in terms of the writer's own later date (Mosis, *Untersuchungen*). To these refugees is due the extension of Jerusalem's southwest wall to the point discovered by N. Avigad's excavation, according to W. Meier (*BN* 15 [1981] 40-43); but see comment on Neh 3:13f.

31:1-21. Hezekiah's Passover had economic consequences which he foresaw or at least recognized as important for strengthening Judah's defenses and thereby its autonomy. The resumption of traffic to Jerusalem from the northern kingdom meant that free-spending tourists would be in the city, perhaps making excursion to points of interest farther south. **3.** The king contributes from his treasury, but expects the populace to be no less generous; with these details are concluded the 88 verses by which Chr expands the single verse of 1 Kgs 18:4 about the cult. **10.** The superabundance of offerings left a surplus even after the clergy had been abundantly taken care of. As at Delphi, the votive offerings to the shrine were both a symbol and a resource for national defense. Although our text does not say so, the crisis of Sennacherib's approach doubtless warranted defending the people of God out of funds that were surplus to the cult after all.

75   **32:1.** The fiercest scourge ever to befall Judah was Sennacherib's invasion in 701. Whether our Bible records two separate invasions of Sennacherib is controverted (→ 1-2 Kings, 10:65-66). Our text here is more compressed, omitting mention of the towns seized outside Jerusalem, and of Hezekiah's anxiety and capitulation (2 Kgs 18:14; 19:1,6). In place of any such defeatism, the whole episode is presented as a glorious reward for Hezekiah's cultic virtues. And indeed we must acknowledge that the survival of Judah's autonomy, even at heavy cost, brought immense and deserved prestige to Hezekiah in comparison with the ignominious obliteration of rival Israel and the disappearance of its royal line.

3. *they blocked the water-sources:* Our acceptance in *JBC* of this verse as "explicitly attested by archeology" was later examined more critically and retracted in "Does Archeology Prove Chronicles Sources?" (*Light unto My Path* [Fest. J. Myers; Phl, 1974] 375–80). Still utilized in Jerusalem today is a rock-cut tunnel from Gihon to Siloam, near the south issue of which was found in 1880 a Hebr inscription (*ANET* 321, now in Istanbul). But our research proves that there is *no* specific proof that this inscription was due to Hezekiah, nor even that 2 Chr 32:3,30 refers to the tunnel (so S. Victor, "The Siloam Tunnel Inscription," *PEQ* 114 [1982] 115). Archaeologists have traced some six other channels anciently deviating the Gihon outflow. For P. Ackroyd (*JSOT* 2 [1977] 12) the waters as repeated in v 30 are not natural but cosmic: Hezekiah is to Sennacherib as the people of God is to paganism. The two mammoth researches on OT Jerusalem by both H. Vincent and J. Simons maintain that this (Gihon-blocking) building activity of Hezekiah included extending the south wall of the city westward to include the whole of the west hill; but other experts put that extension as early as the Jebusites (G. Dalman), or as late as Nehemiah (K. Galling) or even the time of Christ (K. Kenyon; W. F. Albright, J. Germer-Durand) — an archaeologial uncertainty spanning 1,000 years! Now the 1971 excavations of N. Avigad (*IEJ* 22 [1972] 193–200; *Discovering Jerusalem* [Nash, 1983]) show a massive city wall of precisely this Hezekiah era on the east slope of the west hill, but this may imply that only a small portion of the west hill nearest to Tyropoeon valley had by then been included within Jerusalem's walls (*IDBSup* 475).

76   **18.** Emphasis of 2 Kgs 18:26 on the consternation of Hezekiah's curia at the fact that Assyria's envoy to Jerusalem speaks the local language to the populace is omitted. **19.** The speech is summarized as indicating to the people of Jerusalem that a test case is imminent to prove whether the God of Israel would be as effective in battle as the god of Assyria. This situation is fair enough; but we do not find here the indication of 2 Kgs 18:33 recalling Mic 4:5: it is precisely such a test of strength in which the God of Israel glories.

20. *Isaiah:* Only mention in Chr; he had in fact disapproved the lack of faith shown by Hezekiah's defense measures (Isa 22:11). The piteous comportment of Hezekiah is quickly passed over to stress the miraculous angel (2 Kgs 19:3,35). Why the author should omit the 185,000 slain in a single night is not clear. **24.** It is also perplexing why there is no mention of Isaiah's sundial shadow going backward (2 Kgs 10:11), nor of Isaiah at all in connection with Hezekiah's danger of death. **25.** In fact, more explicit here than in 2 Kgs 20:1 (20:17) is the view that this threatening death was a punishment for Hezekiah's pride and the sufferings it brought upon Judah. This alteration is alien in spirit to all the others made by Chr in copying the Kgs text; it can be explained only as dramatic heightening, in view of the splendid repentance of Hezekiah which quickly follows. **27–29.** These words are largely those which 2 Kgs 20:13 used to describe Hezekiah's friendliness toward the overtures of Babylon, bitterly reproved there by Isaiah as unconditioned cause of the coming exile. But Chr embodies this inventory of Hezekiah's wealth into its epilogue of the monarch's virtue. **32.** All Judah honored him at his death.

(D) Judah's Disillusionment (33:1–36:23).
77   (a) NOT-SO-WICKED MANASSEH (33:1–25). **7.** *statue:* Hebr *semel*, for C. Dohmen (*ZAW* 96 [1984] 263–66), means rather "function of accompanying," applicable to the worshiper — or even to a Yahweh consort allegedly now attested at 'Ajrud (J. Emerton, *JTS* 94

[1982] 1–20). **9.** The list of Manasseh's iniquities (as in 2 Kgs 21:2–9) so reflects Jer 7:31 as to mean "he violated every law in the book." His long reign (687–642, *IDB* and *BHI*) is unmitigated evil. For Chr this involves a contradiction; long life and power are a reward and blessing of God, and are not compatible with immorality. **11.** Some trace this insertion to records overlooked by Kgs, but published in Esarhaddon's Prism (*ANET* 291; cf. 294). Our research (in *Light unto My Path* [→ 75 above] 383–86) shows that Palestine-area kings *other* than Manasseh were in fact summoned to Babylon; Manasseh was forced to accompany Ashurbanipal to Egypt (and was possibly in the retinue with which he returned to Nineveh). Thus, even if the Chr formulation combines some factual data, its "captivity" of Manasseh remains a theorizing conclusion. **12.** Still more theorized are the consequent humility and prayer of the captive king. This verse is commonly held to have suggested the apocryphal Prayer of Manasseh, an official appendix to the Vg (→ Apocrypha, 67:37). But it is possible that the apocryphon already existed and was taken as historical evidence for the present narration, hinted also in some manuscripts of Tob 14:10. **15.** Some of the architectural and liturgical activities of the aging monarch may well have been such as the clergy might approve (on the Gihon wall, above v 3; L. H. Vincent, *Jérusalem de l'Ancien Testament* [→ 43 above] 328; J. Simons, "The Wall of Manasseh and the 'Mišneh' of Jerusalem," *OTS* 7 [1950] 191). Neither the events themselves nor their proof of short-range retribution is asserted, but simply the principle that good will somehow be rewarded and evil punished. **23.** Amon's reign is brief enough to be written off as a total loss. **25.** His assassination, despite its clearing the path for Josiah, is not condoned. But the anarchist violence by which so-called justice was done seems to have terrified the surviving officers of the curia into guiding the child ruler's steps along more God-fearing paths.

78   (b) JOSIAH (34:1–35:27). **3.** If eight year old Josiah came to power in 640 he would have been nearing manhood in 633. Perhaps his "beginning" then to seek God may refer to the fact that with Ashurbanipal's death in that year it was felt safe to evict Assyria's gods from Jerusalem, as had been done by Hezekiah (30:14). However, only Canaanite idolatries are mentioned by either Chr or 2 Kgs 23:13, which may confirm the Chr claim that Assyrian syncretism had already been outlawed by Manasseh. **6.** Gradually, as Ashurbanipal's successor turned out to be weak and short-lived, the chancery of Judah began taking over the administration of N Israel while the king was still in his late teens. **8.** By the time Josiah was 26, Assyria's weakness was irreparable, and he embarked on the celebrated reform that dominates 2 Chr 34–35 (= 2 Kgs 22–23), as well as Deut (12:11).

10. The finding of this Book of the Law, the pivotal event of Josiah's reform, occurred not during the actual repairs on the Temple but in a preliminary audit of the finances. In this, Chr agrees with 2 Kgs 22:3, but differs in seeing Josiah's religious reform already well under way when this event occurred (cf. A. Goldberg, *Chronik I–II* 283). Even the king's moral and ritual life up to that time is a kind of reform of the Manasseh-Amon tradition; the presentation need not be a theological postulate without historical basis. **12.** The author gives a detailed account of Levite-choir supervisors to replace the curious insistence of 2 Kgs 22:7 (= 12:15; see comment on 2 Chr 24:5) that the less known about financial transactions between curia and contractors the better. Rudolph cites excavated examples from Assyria and Egypt to show against von Rad that there is nothing implausible in having liturgical musicians set the tempo by a beat for masons at work. **19.** The young king's horrified dismay at hearing what the book contained (as in 2 Kgs 22:11) is difficult to reconcile with the assumption that the reform is already in progress. Today it is generally agreed that the content of Deut was fairly familiar from the preaching of Jeremiah, and probably (*pace* N. Lohfink, *Bib* 44 [1963] 492-94) stems from an origin in the northern kingdom around the time of Hezekiah's reform. It was essentially an updating of the Mosaic Torah. The king's violent reaction may indeed have been intended as a dramatic gesture to shake the resistance. **30.** The king reads aloud to the solemn assembly the "Book of the Covenant," not Exod 21-23 as is generally understood by that title, but (from) Deut, as is implied by the style of v 31. **33.** Except for what was anticipated above beginning with v 5, Chr strangely omits the picturesque and varied account of Josiah's implementation of his reform, esp. at Bethel (2 Kgs 23:4-20).

79 **35:3.** The presentation of the famed Passover celebrated by Josiah in the very year of his finding the book, greatly expanded from 2 Kgs 23:21-27, here shows chiefly that certain postexilic functions of the Levites were not an innovating usurpation. This Passover forms the point of departure for the apocryphon called in LXX Esdras A and in Vg 3 Esdras (→ 83 below). **3.** The Levites can hardly be envisioned as standing before Josiah with the Ark on their shoulders, since David in 1 Chr 16:37; 23:4 had already replaced this duty with others more suited to the Ark's fixed abode. Hence we may paraphrase thus: Your clan was by David's activities released from the carrying of the Ark and other traditional burdens; but do not exhaust your unflagging zeal; you may now lend a hand with the other sacristy jobs, which the priests are neglecting. From this verse and Neh 8:7 D. Mathias ("'Levitische Predigt' und Deuteronomismus," *ZAW* 96 [1984] 23-49) draws objections to von Rad's generally admitted "levitical homilies in Chronicles"; the counterview of R. Mason (*ZAW* 96 [1984] 221-35; *VT* 27 [1977] 413-21) is based on his belief in a "Haggai-Zechariah circle," similar but not identical with the milieu in which Chr itself arose. **5.** Laymen are prominent here, and the actual slaughter is not done by priests. This verse does not really say that the right of sacrificing belonged more primitively to the lay head of the family (which is true), but it perhaps hints this as a basis for transferring the preexilic prerogative from priests to Levites. **7.** From here to 36:19 we now have a lost leaf of the Aleppo Codex (M. Beit-Arié, *Tarbiz* 51 [1982] 171-73). **18.** Samuel emerges in this perspective with an altogether singular emphasis. The unexpected admission that not even peerless David had ever performed the Passover so fully in the primitive spirit is taken by commentators as a way of saying "What's so unusual about giving the primary role in sacrifice to others than priests when that is the way it was done in earliest times, and in fact even then the priests were recognized to be deficient?" **20.** Josiah's opposition to the pharaoh was not mere meddling, nor was it a firm stand regarding an administration of Galilee which he had recently and cautiously taken over. Instead, it was the necessary ground to defend himself against eventual fierce reprisals if the Egyptians should lose the impending battle. Omitted is the statement of 2 Kgs 23:29 that Neco was marching "against [rather than 'to (help)'] the King of Assyria"; it is from Nabopolassar (Gadd Chronicle, *ANET* 305) that we know Egypt was really helping Assyria to resist the

insurgence of Babylon. **21.** There is insufficient warrant for correcting "house (*bêt*) of my war" to "Babylon (*bābēl*) of my war." "What have I to do with you?" is interpreted by O. Bächli (*TZ* 33 [1977] 75) as "I never made trouble for you though I am stronger, so why make trouble?" **22.** A crux of exegetes is this reproach against Josiah for having refused to listen to the word of God from the mouth of pagan Neco. A largely Catholic controversy has flared over precisely what god Neco thought he was quoting—surely not Yahweh. B. Alfrink maintained (*Bib* 15 [1934] 173-84) that the king of Assyria was meant, honorifically called "a god" as when the Amarna pharaoh is addressed by Palestine kings as "all my gods." True, Egypt is no vassal of Assyria, but neither is "my god" as humble as "all my gods"; and in fact Egypt is helping Assyria. Nevertheless, B. Couroyer (*RB* 55 [1948] 388-96, following H. Bückers) insists that it is some Egyptian god, probably the one represented on the army standards. But according to 1 Esdr and R. Davidson (*VT* 9 [1959] 205) we have here Yahweh's own reproach to Josiah, echoed in Jer 17:5. We would rather explain the whole matter as Chronicles' theological postulate: Josiah could not have been cut off so early unless some sin had been involved, the only semblance of which is that he had done what "God" commanded him not to do. **24.** Perhaps here is preserved more factually than in 2 Kgs 23:29 the detail that Josiah did not actually expire until his royal person had been conveyed back to Jerusalem.

80 (c) THE BABYLONIAN PUPPETS (36:1-23). Only a dozen verses are allotted to sum up the last 58 verses of Kgs, but then are added 12 verses original to Chr. **1.** As in Kgs, it is the '*am hā-'areṣ*, "people of the land," as a sociological or perhaps religious technical term (see comment on Ezra 4:4) who promote Jehoahaz. The four monarchs of this chapter confuse us by their multiple and similar-sounding names. **3.** By the battle of Carchemish and simultaneous death of Nabopolassar, Nebuchadnezzar becomes warlord of Asia and finally reduces Judah to the subprovince status that had been threatening ever since a similar fate befell Samaria a century earlier. **4.** When Jehoahaz seeks asylum in Egypt, his brother Eliakim becomes king under the name of Jehoiakim. This event is seen as coinciding with the beginning of Jeremiah's prophetic mission by C. Whitley (*VT* 14 [1964] 467-83). **5.** Jehoiakim's son Jehoiachin succeeds him and after three years is allied to Babylon; honorably installed there, he outlives Nebuchadnezzar. **10.** The last king of Judah was a younger son of Josiah named Zedekiah or Mattaniah, here called Jehoiachin's "brother," a common Semitic term for "relative." **12.** Here is envisioned not any particular moment in Jeremiah's career, but the whole prophetic movement which he typified and which expressed divine judgment on a collapsing Judah, according to P. Ackroyd (*SEA* 33 [1968] 52); he notes that the story is told differently in Jer 52 and 37-44; also (remarkably without any mention of the prophet so clearly involved in the events) in 2 Kgs 24:18-25:2. **20.** Reflection on the evil of not listening to God's prophets culminates in a claim that the exile would last 70 years in fulfillment of Jer 25:12; moreover, it would be a homeopathic punishment for neglecting the sabbath-year law of Lev 25:4; Exod 23:10. **22-23.** These verses really belong to Ezra (1:1-3), but were repeated here when this portion of Chr was inserted into the canon after Ezra. Thus the narrative is rounded off into an optimistic ending for the whole Hebrew Bible.

EZRA AND NEHEMIAH

BIBLIOGRAPHY

81   *Commentaries:* Clines, D. J. A, *Ezra, Nehemiah, Esther*
(NCB; GR, 1984). Coggins, R. J., *The Books of Ezra and Nehe-
miah* (CBC; NY, 1976). Fensham, F. C., *The Books of Ezra and
Nehemiah* (NICOT; GR, 1982). Gunneweg, A., *Esra* (KAT 19/1;
Gütersloh, 1985). Holmgren, F., *Israel Alive Again* (ITC; GR,
1987). Kemner, H., *Glaube in Anfechtung: Das Buch Esra für unsere
Zeit* (Telos 67; Stuttgart, 1974). Kessler, W., *Gottes Mitarbeiter
am Wiederaufbau: Die Propheten Esra und Nehemia* (BAT 12; Stutt-
gart, 1971). Kidner, D., *Ezra and Nehemiah* (TBC; Downers
Grove, 1979). Myers, J. M., *Ezra-Nehemiah* (AB 14; GC, 1965).
Rudolph, W., *Esra und Nehemia* (HAT 20; Tübingen, 1949).
Slotki, J., *Daniel, Ezra, Nehemiah* (London, 1978). Williamson,
H. G. M., *Ezra, Nehemiah* (WBC 16; Waco, 1985); *Ezra and*

Nehemiah (OT Guides; Sheffield, 1987).
     Studies: Braun, R. L., "Chronicles, Ezra and Nehemiah:
Theology and Literary History," *Studies in the Historical Books of
the Old Testament* (VTSup 30; Leiden, 1979) 52–64. Davies,
W. D., ed., *The Persian Period* (CHJ, I; Cambridge, 1984).
McCullough, W. S., *History and Literature of the Palestinian Jews
from Cyrus to Herod* (Toronto, 1975). Sánchez Caro, J. M.,
"Esdras, Nehemías y los orígenes del Judaismo," *Salmanticensis*
32 (1985) 5–34. Smith, M., in *Fischer Weltgeschichte* 5 (Frankfurt,
1965) 356–79. Stern, E., *Material Culture of the Land of the Bible
in the Persian Period* (Warminster, 1983) Yamauchi, E. M.,
"Archaeological Background of Ezra/Nehemiah," *BSac* 137
(1980) 195–211, 291–309.

INTRODUCTION

82   (I) The Twofold Chronology Problem.
The first statement made about Ezra in the book which
bears his name is that he and some other latecomers
finally leave Babylon in the seventh regnal year of King
Artaxerxes (Ezra 7:7). Since no other historical reference
intervenes since Darius of 6:14, it is natural to suppose
that Artaxerxes I was meant (7th year, 458 BC), but the
biblical text does not affirm this. Nehemiah's position in
the canon seems to date him after Ezra, or (only in Neh
8:9; 10:1) contemporary. In *JBC* (as Eissfeldt *EOTI*, 553)
was outlined the history of A. van Hoonacker's pioneering claim that the "7th year" in Ezra 7:7 was of Artaxerxes not I but II in 398. Even more influential
throughout the mid-20th cent. has been Albright's adaptation of this view by correcting "7th year" of Ezra 7:7,8
to "37th year" of Artaxerxes (I: 428; others less helpfully
"27th," 438). This correction was accepted in Rudolph's
normative commentary; and in relation to "Nehemiah's
second ministry" after 430 by V. Pavlovský, "Chronologie der Tätigkeit Esdras," *Bib* 38 (1957) 275–305,
428–56.
     Since *JBC*, all three dates continue to be authorita-
tively defended, with chief emphasis on the two problems of whether the mixed-marriage reform of Ezra
(9:14) could have preceded that of Nehemiah (13:23);
and what relation existed between Eliashib of Ezra 10:6
and Neh 13:4. J. Emerton's pondered survey in *JTS* 17
(1966) 1–18, favors 398. But S. Talmon in *IDBSup* 320
hails a "widespread return" (supported by archaeological
finds) to Ezra-before-Nehemiah "as the Bible says."
Within the Albright school, Bright (*BHI* 402) rejects
Cross's return to the prior-Ezra sequence, which is
defended also in C. Tuland's survey (*AUSS* 12 [1974]
47–62, but only against van Hoonacker, rather than in
view of the Albright *via media*. E. Cortese (*BeO* 25
[1983] 11–19) prefers 398. U. Kellermann (*ZAW* 80
[1968] 54–87) puts only Ezra 7:12–26 (with 8:26f.)
before Neh and dismisses the rest of Ezra 8–10 and Neh
8–12 as a "Chronicler's Midrash." For A. H. J. Gunneweg (*Congress Volume: Vienna 1980* [VTSup 32; Leiden,
1980] 160) the (Chr) author probably had sound historical reasons for putting Ezra before Neh but his ordering
of the material was based on theological, not chronological, factors. *Extra chorum,* Coggins (*Chronicles* 7) finds
[Torrey's] Nehemiah date 384 the only alternative
worth considering.

Thus, our own position here will have to be even
more reserved than in *JBC.* We will still insist that the
change of 7th to 37th cannot be simply dismissed as
"conjectural tampering with the text," any more than all
the efforts to save 7th by expunging "Nehemiah" (8:9;
10:1). Otherwise (with O. Kaiser, *Einleitung* [1984] and
E. Jenni, *TRu* 45 [1980] 97–108) we will strive to set
forth the text in a way that leaves the option amid these
three chronological pivots wholly open, so that the
reader can and must supply at each stage his own decision as to whether Nehemiah worked before, after, or
along with Ezra.
     Apart from this chronology of the *events described,* we
have a second problem regarding the date of composition. This has perforce already been treated above under
the question of whether "the Chronicler" wrote (or
rather added to his compilation) also the materials on
Ezra and Nehemiah. As explained (→ 3), although we
still (and probably with the majority of exegetes) accept
this view, nevertheless in deference to a crescendo of
recent authorities who deny it, we have resolutely used
only the name "Chronicles" to refer to that part of the
text. Similarly now in explaining Ezra and Nehemiah,
"the Chronicler" will be used only in citation of, or
reference to, this *hypothesis,* leaving open to the reader
whether or not to attribute Ezra-Neh to the same author.
     The date of composition of Ezra-Neh, identical or
not with that of Chr, has been especially affected by
three controversies regarding "the Samaritans." First,
there is lively dispute as to whether in fact we find in
these books any real "anti-Samaritan bias." And if so,
there is a second debate amid much more spread-out
alternatives as to the *terminus post quem* which this factor
would imply for the composition of our books, ranging
from Sargon II's importation of pagans *ca.* 721 (2 Kgs
17:24) all the way to the Maccabean era as the outset date
of any real "Samaritan schism." We defer discussion of
these two problems to Neh 4:1, where they are most
acute. The third controversy regards the existence and
date of a "third Sanballat," in relation to the Daliyeh
papyri, on which also see Neh 4:1.

83   (II) Sequence of Chapters and Esdras A.
The other major phase of introduction is the vexed issue
of what historical sequence existed among the various
events described in the chapters which are now Ezra
7–10 and Neh 7–13 of our canonical Bible. It is

unmistakable that the sudden prominence of Ezra in Neh 8:1 bears no relation to Nehemiah's activity which precedes, but some relation to the other ministries of Ezra (chaps. 7–10). Really the name Ezra applied equally to *both* books, not only as in LXX-Vg but originally in the Hebr texts; separation of Nehemiah into a book bearing that name was a later "commentator" stage. Moreover, in the LXX there are *four* Esdras-books, of which the second and third correspond to Hebr Ezra and Neh respectively, while the fourth (published as 2 Esdras among the apocrypha in the *RSV*) is an altogether apocryphal apocalypse originating in the Christian era.

Much more relevant to our understanding of the canonical Ezra-books is the book called "Third Esdras" in the Vg and "Esdras A" (i.e., #1) in the LXX, but "1 Esdras" in the *RSV* and in this *NJBC* (see now Z. Talshir, "The Milieu of 1 Esdras in the light of its vocabulary," *De Septuaginta* [Fest. J. W. Wevers; Toronto, 1984] 129–47). Esdras A contains equivalently the whole of canonical Hebr Ezra (= Esdras B) plus only chaps. 7–8 (about Ezra) in Neh. But this core is preceded by a summary of 2 Chr 35–36, and interrupted by a vivid adventure of Zerubbabel at the Persian court (chaps. 3–4 of Esdras A, at a point corresponding to Hebr Ezra 4:24). In that "famous story [which] provides sufficient reason for the preservation of the book throughout the centuries" (W. Harrelson in *OAB*), the pages of King Darius propose to him four answers to "What is the strongest force in life?" Wine is one answer, "the king" a second; the third is Zerubbabel's "women; but Truth is strong(er still) and *prevails*" (not "will prevail" as Vg). Zerubbabel is invited to choose his own reward for his winning answer and eloquent discourse defending it; his choice is that the king fulfill some vow of his to rebuild Jerusalem and its Temple, and he himself receives a written commission to execute this project (Esdras A 4:48 similar to Hebr Ezra 6:7f.).

In Esdras A 8:6 ("Artaxerxes' 7th year" as in Ezra 7:7), Ezra returns to Jerusalem and makes his tearful confession (Ezra 7–10). But after the final verse of Ezra (10:44), Esdras A 9:37 gives the one verse of Neh 7:73, followed by 8:1–12. In the whole of Esdras A, Nehemiah himself and his work are not mentioned, though "Attharates" of 9:49 may represent *tiršātā'*, Nehemiah's title in Neh 8:9. Josephus (*Ant.* 11.5.5 §155), who closely follows Esdras A up to this point (including complacently the Zerubbabel riddle), nowhere mentions either Attharates or *tiršātā'* for Nehemiah, though beginning with 11 §159 he narrates in full the building project of Nehemiah (1:1 through 7:4). Josephus also (*Ant.* 11.5.8 §183, 11.5.3 §158) furnishes obituary notices of both Nehemiah and Ezra, on which Esdras A as well as canonical Ezra-Neh leaves us totally uninformed. Since the Gk Fathers as well as Josephus seem to cite Esdras A rather than Ezra, there have been several recent studies (as well as Torrey and Schneider in *JBC* 24:83) claiming that we learn from Esdras A the proper order of the events. Notably though, in Sirach 49:13 Nehemiah is exalted and Ezra wholly ignored.

The 1973 Bonn dissertation of W. T. In der Smitten (*Esra: Quellen, Überlieferung, Geschichte* [Assen, 1973]) concludes that the "memoir of Nehemiah" had a separate and independent existence and was included by "the Chronicler" virtually unchanged, though as an intentional anticlimax to Ezra; but all the information about Ezra is "the Chronicler's" own embroidering of the authentic firman of Artaxerxes, with the aim of favoring Ezra's work above Nehemiah's. In this the Chronicler had been anticipated by Esdras A, even more favorable to Ezra (omitting Nehemiah entirely; Josephus is held to be unfavorable to *both* leaders, but otherwise follows

Esdras A). The process of inventing glories for Ezra, begun by "the Chronicler," was continued by the rabbis, though not to the extent claimed in the Koran (9.30) "they make 'Uzair son of God'" (p. 88).

The research of In der Smitten appears largely as a refutation of K.-F. Pohlmann's Marburg dissertation (*Studien zum Dritten Esra* [FRLANT 104; Göttingen, 1970]; cf. his edition of 3 Esdras [JSHRZ 1.5; Gütersloh, 1980] and R. Hanhart's [Göttingen, 1974]). Pohlmann holds that Esdras A gives the primitive form of the Ezra narrative, without the "Nehemiah Memoir," but also without the riddle (added to an original Esdras A sometime before Josephus). Long after "the Chronicler's" editing, and even after Josephus, the Nehemiah Memoir was added (chaps. 1–6 + 8,13–18; Pohlmann's summary on p. 149 gives no help for determining the origin or sequence of Neh 9–13). Pohlmann is supported by R. Mosis (*Untersuchungen* 215), but *not* in claiming that the three pillars of Esdras A are Hezekiah = Solomon, Josiah = Samuel, and Ezra = Joshua. H. Williamson's *Israel in the Books of Chronicles* (p. 34) agrees with Pohlmann that the riddle was interpolated into 1 Esdras, not put there by its author, as In der Smitten claims; but against Pohlmann (and Mowinckel) he holds that Esdras A must have known Neh 7:72, and thus must not have been a compilation, nor intended as a simple translation of any Hebr Ezra. G. Widengren's clear and incisive presentation of the problem in *IJH* (p. 490) insists chiefly that the "Ezra-*memoirs*" (7:12–9:15; 1st pers. only after 8:15) are independent of the original "Ezra-*narrative*" (Ezra 10: 3d pers.; also Neh 8).

Before concluding, we must note that U. Kellermann (*Nehemiah: Quellen, Überlieferung und Geschichte* [BZAW 102; Berlin, 1967] 95, without particular focus on Esdras A) holds that Ezra 7–10 was written by "the Chronicler" in deliberate *imitation* of the "Nehemiah Memoir," in order to reduce Nehemiah to the status of a paltry reflection of Ezra: "everything he can do, Ezra can do better." And this same Chronicler took over Neh as is (except 6:10–13; 8:1–11:36; 12:27–13:3) because he found congenial its anti-Samaritanism and its opposition to certain eschatological currents within the Jerusalem community. But a "post-Chronicler Redactor" raises Nehemiah to a prominence alongside David and Ezra, *inserting* him not only with Ezra in Neh 8:9; 10:2 but also in 7:7f., and *inventing* 13:6f. about Nehemiah's absence in the Persian court during the evildoings in Jerusalem.

Our conclusion will have to be that Ezra 7–10 and Neh 7–13 can be reassembled in *various* ways; no single proposed sequence is decisive. Without allowing it to influence our commentary, we have doubtless reckoned with some such order as: Ezra 1–6; Neh 1–6 + 12 (cf. v 27, dedication of the wall) + 11 (bringing of a population to Jerusalem); Ezra 7–10; Neh 7:73–10:39 (Ezra's lawgiving with Nehemiah participation). We thus tentatively suppose that the prominence of Nehemiah *alongside* Ezra is historically plausible.

84 **(III) Outline.** The books of Ezra and Nehemiah can be outlined as follows:

COMMENTARY ON EZRA

85   (I) The Second Temple (Ezra 1:1–6:22).
Today's Jewish people rather tenderly favor the expression "Second Temple." It is a chronological term for an important period of their ethnic existence. That era after the return from exile and until the Diaspora is in a certain sense continuing today. But the century which culminated in the destruction of the Temple (AD 70) fostered the three most controversial phenomena of all Jewish history: the baptizing sectaries of Qumran and elsewhere; Hillel and Shammai; Jesus and Paul. Actually it was precisely Herod's Temple which during that century became a wonder of the world to replace the modest efforts of the returned exiles. Yet Jewish tradition never speaks of Herod's as a "Third Temple."
(A) Cyrus and the Return (1:1–11). 1.
Repetition of 2 Chr 36:22–23 here is usually invoked as a proof that the same author wrote both works. The contrary could also be inferred. Probably 2 Chr 36:23 continued directly into what is now Ezra 1:4. When the Ezra scroll was detached and put into the Jewish canon before there was felt to be any need for Chr, these two verses were borrowed to stand at the head. The first year of Cyrus's rule in Babylon began actually in October 539, but officially on the (March) New Year's Day of 538. This leaves us a "round" 70 years of exile as the meaning of Jer 25:11, without supposing that Judah's fall is to be dated from the outset of Jehoiakim's reign in 609 as in 2 Kgs 24:1. See H. Williamson, "The Composition of Ezra I–VI," *JTS* 33 (1983) 1–30; J. S. Wright, *The Building of the Second Temple* (London, 1958); and T. Busink, *Der Tempel von Jerusalem*, vol. 2 (Leiden, 1980) 776–903.
2. *thus says Cyrus:* A few explanatory interpolations do not suffice to deny that the decree is, on the whole, cited faithfully; cf. R. de Vaux in *BANE* 63–96. **3.** A basic Persian viewpoint is preserved even in "Yahweh, the God of Israel, is the God who is in Jerusalem." The fact that this unknown and foreign deity is acknowledged by Cyrus as his superior means merely that the king hereby gives to a cultus of his subjects the stamp of his official approval. It need not imply that Cyrus had taken the step of identifying Judah's Yahweh with Ahura-Mazda, whom his decree undoubtedly regards as "the god of heaven." See D. K. Andrews, *The Seed of Wisdom* (Fest. T. Meek; Toronto, 1964) 45–57. Even as cited, the words do not indicate that Cyrus had been converted to the Yahwist religion by reading his own name in Isa 45:1 (41:25) as in Josephus, *Ant.* 11.1.1 §4f. ("through the prophets" included in the decree, though prophets are not mentioned in Ezra or Esdras A). Any conqueror must count on securing the benevolence of the subject population by tolerating and even positively promoting their tenacious usages that do not interfere with his power. Indigenous religion especially, for a nonproselytizing power, is a vehicle of peace, order, and civil obedience. Cyrus boasts of having restored gods to their

sees (*ANET* 316). But P. Ackroyd (*Israel under Babylon and Persia* [Oxford 1970] 165) rightly warns that Persian "tolerance" was merely "flexibility," because in Egypt temples and opponents were ruthlessly destroyed; see also his "God and the People in the Chronicler's Presentation of Ezra," *La notion biblique de Dieu* (ed. J. Coppens; BETL 41; Leuven, 1976) 145–62. As to whether Zoroastrian ideas influenced the Ezra-Neh community, "we simply cannot know," though in general the repatriates were conservative and hence likely to be cool to religious views from outside (W. S. McCullough, "Israel's Eschatology from Amos to Daniel," *Studies on the Ancient Palestinian World* [Fest. F. Winnett; Toronto, 1972] 96). On the 14 Persian loanwords in Ezra-Neh see Fensham, *Books* 22 and *Nederduitse Geref. Tydskrif* 24 (1983) 5–14.
4. Cyrus has a special motive to favor the Jews as a minority oppressed by and hating his own Babylonian enemies. This need not mean that he took any initiative in suggesting or commanding that the Temple be rebuilt, or (despite 6:4,8) that he undertook to pay for the project, even by taxing non-Jewish neighbors. **6.** The return "laden with gifts" is seen as a reenactment of the exodus (11:2); it is also taken by modern Jewry and ecumenism as a prototype of (peaceful) Zionism. **7.** Restitution of the sacred vessels confiscated by Nebuchadnezzar (and misused, Dan 5:2) was undoubtedly a generous act, and because of it the name of Cyrus deservedly heads the list of contributors to the rebuilding.
8. *Sheshbazzar:* Senabassar in 1 Esdr 2:15. As prince of Judah and civil leader of the returning community, this is possibly a Persian surname for Zerubbabel (2:2). But in 1 Esdr 5:7 and Josephus, *Ant.* 11.4.6 §101, Sanabassaros is distinguished as a *prior* governor; and Zerubbabel is given no title or Davidic lineage in Ezra-Neh (*distinct* from Chr in accepting the Persian status quo, according to S. Japhet, *ZAW* 94 [1982] 66–98; 95 [1983] 218–29). Sheshbazzar is identified with Shenazzar of 1 Chr 3:18 by Albright-Cross and Avigad-Aharoni (Soggin, *HAI*, 267), but the claim of P. R. Berger (*ZAW* 83 [1971] 98–100) that they are distinct has now been supported by P. E. Dion (*ZAW* 95 [1983] 111f.) from the Faḥiriyya inscription.
11. No details of the return journey are given; the "joyous escort" of 1 Esdr 5:2 is asserted rather of Zerubbabel under Darius. The trip by the Fertile Crescent route probably took about 100 days, in the spring of 538. The number of repatriates in this first convoy may well have been only a few hundred. The Jews in Babylon had already prospered because of their facility in the Aram chancery language. Their usefulness as undercover agents in the chanceries was doubled when Persia conquered Babylon. Moreover, private concerns like "Murashu & Co." are shown by cuneiform records to have been tycoons of business. If even Ezra's Bible

editors (7:6) were loath to move, we may be sure that no eager torrent accepted the king's invitation to exchange comfort and security for the fulfillment of a religious urge, "Next year in Jerusalem."

86 (B) Zerubbabel and the List (2:1-70). Repeated word for word in Neh 7:6-73. The numbers amount to some 50,000. There is no cogent ground for presuming that the figure excludes women and children, thus amounting to some quarter million; but even so, the number better fits its place in Neh when a full century had allowed the idea of repatriation to gain popularity. Of the 153 numbers, 29 are given differently in Neh 7; and only a few can be clarified by word alteration, but many by cipher notation (H. Allrik, *BASOR* 136 [1954] 21; for R. Klein [*HTR* 62 (1969) 99-107], in 1 Esdr we may have a transl. of canonical Ezra 2, but from a time when it agreed better with Neh 7). The group here enumerated seems to have a flourishing cultus, as if the Temple had already been standing. On the other hand, Neh 7:5 asserts that the list as there given is old; and the stress on cultus is natural if the homesteaders' primary aim is to build the Temple. Archival and juridical parts of our Bible are now known to have been kept up-to-date by continuous accretion, so we may well conclude that the names stem mostly from the first return. But the numbers were progressively increased, and doubtless some important names were added as further caravans returned from Babylon and the population grew by natural increase within Judah. Rudolph finds confirmation in the alternation between clans and locality groups, but there is no reason for his limiting the accretion to the time before 515, even though Ezra 8:1 gives a separate list for his own convoy after 458. K. Galling (*JBL* 70 [1951] 199) holds that the list was a brief drawn up for the Persian court in 519; he refutes the view of G. Hölscher that it was a tax roll, and that of A. Alt that it was a register of land deeds. It seems tenable that a list utilized under Nehemiah after 445 was later copied into Ezra 2 because an authoritative scribe found it to be a warranted expansion of earlier data.

2. Zerubbabel, as civil leader of the repatriates with responsibility for the rebuilding of the Temple, is ambiguously equated with Sheshbazzar in Ezra 1:8,11; cf. 5:14,16. Like Sheshbazzar, he is called *pehâ* (also in Hag 1:1). The Nehemiah of this verse is doubtless distinct from the well-known Nehemiah (confused by 2 Macc 1:18; 2:13 as rebuilder of the Temple) and from a third Nehemiah of Neh 3:16. Zerubbabel represents the dynasty of David through Shealtiel in Matt 1:13, but (perhaps by levirate, Deut 25:5) through Pedaiah and Shenazzar in 1 Chr 3:18; see comment on Ezra 1:8. At the side of Zerubbabel stands Joshua, son of Jehozadak the highest-ranking priest (3:2). He is messianically paired with Zerubbabel in Hag 1:12; 2:23; and as a Qumran-style second or possibly *third* (priestly as opposed to "civil") Messiah in Zech 6:12; 4:11; 3:8; see now K.-M. Beyse, *Zerubbabel und die Königserwartungen der Propheten Haggai und Sacharja* (Stuttgart, 1972); "Zorobabel dans l'exégèse de Théodore de Mopsueste et de Théodoret de Cyr," *Aug* 24 (1984) 527-47; D. L. Petersen [on Zech 4:6-10], "Zerubbabel and Second Temple Reconstruction," *CBQ* 36 (1974) 366-72; F. I. Andersen, "Who Built the Second Temple?" *AusBR* 6 (1958) 1-35. *Bigvai:* A Persian name, appears also at Elephantine.

87 20. A shift from clan groups to localities, all close to Jerusalem, which is unmentioned. The geography is preexilic and thus somewhat idyllic. **31.** This intrusion of clan groups is followed by postexilic Sharon settlements in v 33. **36-55.** A list of priests and Levites, including "Oblates" (*netînîm*, v 43) and Canaanites (v 53)

with a minority status regularized under Solomon. **62.** A genealogy, juridical rather than biological, but extremely important. **63.** Governor (*tiršātā'*,) is here doubtless an appellation like "his honor"; Sheshbazzar is called "prince," *nāsî'*, in 1:8; see on Neh 5:14. *Urim:* It is remarkable that this rather primitive divinatory use should survive unexpurgated in so recent and priestly a document. The device is held to be unmistakably oracular here and is equated with the jewels of the breastplate (Exod 28:30), as in a Qumran comment on Isa 54:11f., according to K. Galling ("Serubbabel und der Wiederaufbau des Tempels in Jerusalem," *Verbannung und Heimkehr* [Fest. W. Rudolph; ed. A. Kuschke; Tübingen, 1961] 91), citing 4 QpIsa^d from J. Allegro, *JBL* 77 (1958) 221.

64. Census total is 49,897. Identical figures are given in Neh 7:66f., except for 45 additional singers. In the preceding subtotals, Neh has only 652 for 775 of v 5, 845 for 945 of v 8, and frequent smaller variations. The free citizens total only 29,818 in Ezra 2 (30,142 in 1 Esdr) and 31,039 in Neh, as against the total given as 42,360. The other 11,000 would make an unconvincingly scarce number of wives, not to speak of children; rather, some subtotals were just skipped. **68.** *daric:* An anachronism for the time preceding Darius. Moreover, Neh 7:70f. has only 41,000, audited according to donor groups. If the Attic coin then current in Persia is meant, some 300,000 dollars in gold may be involved and a roughly equal amount of silver, 5,000 *mna* (or 4,200, Neh 7:71) valued at about $50 each.

88 (C) Laying the Cornerstone (3:1-13). 1. *seventh month:* September; just one year after Cyrus took power would have allowed six months for the red tape in Babylon, plus three months after the arrival in Jerusalem—ample time for getting down to work, and corroborated by v 8. But the very reasonableness of this schedule, plus the choice of a month that was in fact crammed with liturgy, makes it legitimate to suspect that the compiler is here theorizing rather than drawing on any recorded data. Only by speculation can we claim that the year 520 is meant, 18 years after Sheshbazzar's group is supposed to have begun the Temple building.

2. *built the altar:* Experts differ as to whether this implies that those who had never been in exile had allowed the ruined altar to fall into disuse despite Jer 41:5, or whether the returning exiles disdained to utilize the cult paraphernalia of the inhabitants. **3.** *fear . . . peoples of the lands:* See comment on 4:4; 9:2. Although bracketed as a gloss by A. Vaccari and M. Noth, the reference here is doubtless to those Judeans who had not been kept pure in the crucible of persecution and had become absorbed in the province of Samaria. **4-5.** *daily . . . continual:* The two types of offerings. The holocaust ('*ôlâ*, Lev 1:13) is for the morning; for the evening, another holocaust is prescribed in Num 28:4 and at Warka (*ANET* 342); but in Ezra 9:4, the evening offering is called *minhâ*, identified as *tāmîd* in Num 4:16 and as grain plus libation in Lev 2:1 (*IDB* 4. 150). **6.** That so holy a work should not get under way without meticulous daily fulfillment of the very rites for which the Temple is being built seems reasonable, even if not based on any recorded facts.

7. *money:* This stress on an obvious prerequisite is in terms to indicate that religion keeps pace with technology: minted coinage was a recent invention. *Joppa:* More "reasoning" (rather than "falsification or fiction") based on Solomon's recorded moves in 2 Chr 2:16. **8.** *twenty years old:* The age limits were reduced because of the need; see on 1 Chr 23:3. **9.** Joshua is paired with Kadmiel as in 2:40; because his father's name is not given, it is not clear that he is regarded as a Levite distinct from the (high) priest just mentioned. The rather pagan name of Henadad (grace of Hadad/Apollo) is perhaps tidied up as Hodaviah (praise Yahweh) in 2:40. **11.** Cf. Ps 106:1. **12.** The old men wept chiefly because it was a moment of deep emotion. There may also have been anguish in recalling that the earlier Temple had been destroyed by enemies, as in the case of a Babylon cornerstone which reads "I started the work weeping and finished it rejoicing." The weeping may also have betrayed misgivings aroused by the already perceptible ground plan that the Temple would be inferior at its completion (Hag 2:3: which some earlier experts claim is anachronistically described in this verse).

89   (D) Interruption: The Samaritans (4:1–24). 1. *the adversaries of Judah and Benjamin:* Doubtless the bureaucrats (even if of Judean origin and part of the remnant), functioning for the Persian province of Samaria to which Judah was humiliatingly made subordinate. Prominence of such "Samaritan" hostility is one of the reasons (see v 6) for considering this chapter an episode misplaced from Neh 4 (or, in the variant of Michaeli [*Livres des Chroniques* 273, 312] a pre-Nehemiah effort to build the wall). Without either espousing or fully rejecting this possibility, we defer to Neh 4 the animated recent discussion of whether anti-Samaritanism already existed and was a primary motive for writing (Chr with) Ezra-Neh. **3.** Zerubbabel does not deny or question that these Samaritans and their Judah-born collaborators had really been worshiping Yahweh. Rather, he gives free rein to stubbornness and racial prejudice in ascribing to their mixed blood those imperfections which had doubtless crept into their observance of legal minutiae (Hag 2:12; Zech 7:2; John 8:48). His unacknowledged motivation was doubtless the reasonable one that a powerful entrenched group, offering to "help" as a unitary block instead of individual volunteers, would gradually snatch control of the enterprise right out of the returnees' hands.

4. *people of the land:* Not Alt's "foreign-born landowners" nor the former poor Judeans, enemies of the Deuteronomist movement, whom the Babylonians favored by furnishing with land, but the people who had remained in Judah during the exile and willy-nilly submitted themselves to the Samaria-based regime; see now J. Teixidor, "Contexto epigráfico y literario de Esdras y Daniel," in *Simposio Bíblico Español, Salamanca 1982* (ed. N. Fernández Marcos; Madrid, 1984) 129–40: "freedom of worship was understood in different ways by the Persian and Seleucid monarchs." Whatever the syncretistic guilt of these "people of the land," it can hardly be regarded as worse than that which the earlier prophets of Judah no less than Israel had constantly excoriated. The uncooperativeness of the repatriates, like every ghetto mentality, is the expression of a legitimate concern to preserve religious truth uncontaminated by contact with the imperfect. But this is not the only attitude religion requires toward outsiders, and a certain tension or apparent contradiction vis-à-vis dawning universalism and proselytizing tendencies must be taken in stride as part of the revealed datum and of God's salvation plan (R. North, "Centrifugal and Centripetal Tendencies in the Judaic Cradle of Christianity," *Populus Dei I* [Fest A. Ottaviani; Rome 1969] 615–51; and see comment on 9:29 below).

90   6. Ahasuerus is Xerxes I (485–465) who scourged the sea during his war with the Greeks in 481. There are three principal hypotheses to account for this insertion from 50 years later: (a) To a foreigner all names sound alike, and this exchange of letters fits the reign of Cambyses (between Cyrus in 530 and Darius I in 521) as supposed in v 24 and Josephus, *Ant.* 11.2.1 §21. (b) Some *later* episodes of underhanded maneuvers of the Samaritans at the Persian curia are here introduced as a

sample of the sort of thing that produced friction in 525. (c) The passage is simply misplaced, and because of building the wall (v 12), it belongs with Neh 4:8 (see comment on v 1 above).

91   7. *Artaxerxes* (I, 465–424): Unless this also is just a foreigner's garbling of names, we have to deal with an episode still later than that of v 6. However the presence of the Aramean named Tabeel as one of the signers has given great popularity to the view of H. H. Schaeder that this is no accusation sent to Artaxerxes, but a collation of existing accusations with the aim of defending the Judeans. *Aramaic:* At this point, and with this introduction, the language in which MT is written changes abruptly; we are told that a translation was made, not that it is given herewith—only that what comes after v 7 is (also) in Aramaic. The Aram parts of Ezra are seen as a Jewish attempt to establish the legality of *foreigners'* regulations, whereas the Hebr sections show rather how the Judean community tightened up against a hostile milieu, according to A. Gunneweg ("Die aramäische und hebräische Erzählung über die nachexilische Restauration—ein Vergleich," *ZAW* 94 [1982] 299–302).

92   8. Here begins really a third document. Its signatories are non-Israelites who emphasize their west-of-Euphrates origin and citizenship. *Bishlam:* Rather than a personal name, or "with the approval of" (A. Klostermann), this may mean "in Jerusalem('s regard)." *Rehum:* Also expunged by K. Galling (*ZAW* 63 [1951] 70), who makes the subject of the sentence "the chancery officials of Tripoli (Tarablus in Lebanon), Warka, and Susa, who judged on the matter." **10.** All Syria belonged to the one Persian province Abarnahara (Trans-Euphratene) along with Babili at first; Darius cut off Babylon, and Alexander separated it from Mesopotamia (the classic on these province divisions is O. Leuze, *Satrapieneinteilung* [Halle, 1935]; see there pp. 25 and 318). Osnappar may be intended as a rendition of Ashurbanipal (669–629), but might also be referred to Esarhaddon. **11.** There is no cogent reason for supposing either that the compiler identifies the three documents, the incipits of which he has already given, or that he distinguishes them. He records archival fragments available to him, taking over also or introducing narrative connectives to fit his aims.

14. *salt of the palace:* This expression for payroll is oddly paralleled in Lat *sal-arium,* "salt-allotment," Eng "salary." **15.** These warnings sound sincere and well-founded; they say nothing of any Temple or religious movement, even as disguising subversive intrigue. If truly addressed to Artaxerxes, this could be a loyal and salutary warning against letting his affection for Nehemiah overrule his common sense (Neh 2:2). **18.** The answer accords ill with what is narrated of Artaxerxes and would better fit the situation under Cambyses. **24.** *and ceased . . . Darius:* An insertion made in Hebrew, although what follows concerning the reign of Darius is in Aramaic. The claim that this whole Aram sequence forms a unit taken over integrally (Noth) is convincing. There is no real coherence of style between the preceding letter and the repatriates' (prophetic) activities; the "wall" of 5:3 is now plainly that of the Temple, "this house," the normal term; the events of 4:6–23 tie in no better after 6:18. We will conclude that with 5:1 we are fully in the time sequence of 3:13; we must leave as an insoluble enigma the date of chap. 4.

93   (E) Prophetic Nudge to Completion (5:1–6:22). 1. Whether or not because of complaints like Rehum's, progress on the Temple seems in fact to have been suspended during Cambyses' reign. Without denying "the law of the land" represented by Cyrus's decree, local authorities, abetted by the new curia, could hold up progress indefinitely. The Judeans themselves, however, were also dragging their feet because of poverty and misfortunes, until there arose among them an articulate leader. Haggai (1:4ff., 10) fearlessly blasts Zerubbabel and his coterie (not sparing the priest Joshua) for their self-indulgent inertia. **2.** The accession of a third monarch in 522 seemed an appropriate occasion to cut through barriers of bureaucratic red tape and confront the Persepolis regime with a *fait accompli.* **3.** But from Samaria comes the top man to size up the stature of those who defiantly build without having had their permit validated. Plainly it is no mere misdemeanor but a political hot potato—a test case engineered to establish the strength of the word of the Persian king. **5.** Tattenai cautiously notes the facts but tolerates no police intervention until he has sent Darius I a report of admirable objectivity. **9.** *structure:* For Aram "masonry," a derivative of "wall" but with no implication of Nehemiah's rampart. **12.** Both the Jews and the Samaritan governor sedulously avoid any mention of the blame attached to both sides for the unsatisfactory progress of the work since Cyrus. **16.** The letter does not say that Sheshbazzar is present or in command of the work. This is doubtless the implication of v 10, but perhaps the Judeans hoped to avoid more red tape by keeping the operations in the name of the original permit-holder even if he were no longer present. Undoubtedly it is strange that if Zerubbabel was meant, the text essays no harmonizing with v 2. The real enigma is that Zerubbabel flits so vaguely across these last pages (and Hag-Zech!) in the building of "his" Temple. H. Cazelles (*Histoire politique* [Paris, 1982] 211) suggests darkly that Zerubbabel may have been put to death, like the Aryandas (PW 2. 495] who had been entrusted with a similar temple rebuilding in Egypt, and thus Zerubbabel is put forward as a plausible candidate for the Servant of Isa 53.

94   **6:1.** *Babylonia:* The generic name for the whole empire is retained even after the Persians took it over. **2.** Although the official capital of the Achaemenids was in Persepolis, the empire outside Persia could be best administered from the more central chancery in Babylon, which contained also the records of the previous empire. Between the two lay Susa and Ecbatana, where in winter and summer respectively a large part of the Persian curia's work was done (R. North, *Guide to Biblical Iran* [Rome 1956] 31). **4.** Vertical rather than horizontal construction units are meant (P. Joüon, *Bib* 22 [1941] 39). *at the king's expense:* A mere grandiloquent gesture. Cyrus may have made a cash donation, but even the restoring of gold vessels from Babylon's storehouses sufficed to present the whole enterprise as "financed from public funds." No more than this is reaffirmed by Darius in v 8. If any actual drawing account had been budgeted, either from the Persian treasury or from taxes in Samaria, retards due to poverty and inertia would have been unthinkable. We are told plainly in 2:68 that the Jewish worshipers had to finance their project. **6.** The sense is "have no further anxiety"; there was no reason why this decree of Darius should reproach his loyal subordinates, *'ăparsĕkāyē',* "inspectors." **9.** Delivery of sacrificial animals means exemption from bureaucratic meat rationing rather than tax-supported cultus. **12.** Unmistakable echo of Deut 12:5; plainly also the measurements and some doxologies were taken over verbatim from some memorandum solicited from Jews in the chancery. **14.** Haggai seems to have been an aged man (perhaps knowing the earlier Temple, Ezra 2:9) and to have ended his career within three months of its dynamic start. His work was continued by (First) Zechariah. Artaxerxes is mentioned here only to take cognizance of 4:23, where

we saw that no alternative among the explanations imposes itself. **15.** The Second Temple was completed within five years. It was solemnly dedicated on a sabbath, March 12, 515. Or, to avoid the excitement on a sabbath, we may prefer the date given in 1 Esdr 7:5 and Josephus (*Ant.* 11.4.7 §107), April 1, a Friday, according to F. X. Kugler's chronology book. **16.** The joy was tempered by recognition that this hasty pioneering structure was a far cry from Solomon's. Yet it was destined to be honored by a longer life, even before the rebuilding by Herod. **19.** Although the dedication is described in the Aramaic of the chancery documents, the Passover in the following month is told in Hebrew, continuing into the remaining chapters. **20.** The lamb is killed "for their brothers the priests"—apparently implying that the Levites and not the priests did the immolating, as in 2 Chr 35:6 (also not lay heads of families as in Exod 12:6). **22.** The Lord "turned the heart" of the king (of "Assyria," perhaps for Syria, or to avoid saying "the Great [i.e. Persian] King"); this phraseology "sounds like a mild correction of the way divine and human causalities were set on an equal plane in verse 14" (Rudolph).

95   **(II) Ezra's Return and Torah (7:1–10:44).** See also on Neh 8–9. Insertion of this passage gives a strong initial impression that Ezra's ministry occurred between the Temple dedication of 515 and Nehemiah's arrival in 445; there is apparent continuity between "Artaxerxes . . . sixth year" of 6:14f. and "Artaxerxes' seventh year" of 7:7. Yet actually neither text affirms that Artaxerxes I is meant. The earliest traditions of Judaism recorded in the *Pirqe 'Abot* are often claimed to regard Ezra as "builder of the wall of the Torah" (Ezra 9:9) and thus predecessor of Nehemiah in the marriage reform and other isolating structures of the postexilic community. But Ezra's traditional editorship of the Torah must be seen in the light of its acceptance by the Samaritans. We are maintaining here that the segregationist trends were owing rather to Nehemiah and that Ezra is not "the Chronicler"; but our explanations will leave open the three possibilities that Ezra's activity was before, during, or after Nehemiah's.

The information about Ezra does not come from a document as compact and unified as the "Nehemiah memoir," and involves abrupt changes between 1st and 3d pers. (7:28; 10:1); but we cannot exclude that there was a similar existing Ezra source taken over by the compiler or "Chronicler" (K. Koch ["Ezra and the Origins of Judaism," *JSS* 19 (1974) 173–97], holds that Ezra's march from Babylon was "a cultic procession," and that his aim was neither to set up a theocracy nor to establish the absolute validity of the law, but to rebuild an Israel of the twelve tribes including Samaria). In *JBC* we noticed the prevailing opinion that Ezra was a kind of "sub-minister of cult" in the Persian regime; but after further research, we rejected any kind of Persian government post or "concordat" for Ezra (so in Neh 7:14; R. North, "Civil Authority in Ezra," *Studi in onore di Edoardo Volterra* (Milan, 1968] 6. 377–404).

1. *Artaxerxes:* II (398) for those who follow van Hoonacker; I (445) for those who maintain the view traditional for 20 centuries; I (428) for those who emend 7th to 37th rather than expunge Nehemiah in Neh 8:9; 10:1. **5.** Ezra means "(God's) help." The genealogy accentuates his priestly standing and importance, but it touches fewer than a third of his progenitors and omits Zadok (see on 1 Chr 6:53). In 1 Chr 6:14 (MT 5:41) Seraiah is father of the exiled priest Jehozadak; it is suggested that his son, Joshua of Ezra 3:8, before leaving Babylon fathered another Seraiah, who became Ezra's father.

6. *scribe:* Means interpreter, not just copyist; cf. F. Vattioni in *Studi Storici* (ed. C. Colafemmina; Molfetta, 1974) 11–26; N. Ararat, *BM* 17 (1972) 451–92. This can undoubtedly represent the highly technical term for "official" in Babylon (*šāpirum*), Egypt (Anastasi I Papyrus) and Gk Persia (Herodotus 3.128); but in Ezra's case we believe that its earlier implications of "scholarship" predominate. *skilled in the law of Moses:* Hence the view deeply rooted long before J. Wellhausen or J. Astruc that Ezra was the definitive "redactor" of the Pentateuch (see on Neh 8:1). Jerome wrote, in refuting Helvidius (P 23. 190), that we can call Moses the author or Ezra the editor indifferently; and Bellarmine wrote in *Controversies* (Milan, 1721) 1. 166: "It was Ezra who after the captivity edited a single corpus, adding to Deuteronomy the last chapter concerning the life of Moses, and various other transitional remarks" (see further R. North, *AER* 126 [1952] 249–54). While favoring this view, we admit that it gained plausibility from 4 Esdr 14:22, a book only slowly dismissed as noncanonical.

In the perspectives of modern research, we would say that the priests led to Babylonia found in the intensified study of their scattered "sacred oracles" a compensation for their inability to perform any longer the concrete ritual and other obligations linked with the soil of Palestine. Hence the "new Temple" of Ezek 40ff. and the similarity of his style to the Holiness Code (Lev 17–23). The school of priestly scribes in Neharda had doubtless just embarked on the mammoth project of publishing a critical edition of the Torah when Cyrus officially ended their exile. Although their whole life had been dedicated to convincing themselves and others that they must get back to Jerusalem as soon as possible, there were still obvious difficulties in abandoning or relocating such a project. Hence, it was agreed to defer the return to Jerusalem until the work was finished. The years dragged on to decades and almost a century. Meanwhile Ezra became head of the school (v 10) and, with the resoluteness his memoirs betray, brought both projects to a head; see comment on Neh 9:27.

It was altogether in accord with Persian policy to foster the compiling of local legislation, esp. ritual and moral codes likely to set public order and civil obedience into a loftier religious framework. (P. Frei, *Reichsidee* [OBO 55; Fribourg 1984] 7–43). Ezra was readily granted an exit visa (v 11; not "concordat" as K. Fruhstorfer, *Studia Anselmiana* 28 [1951] 178). Under Darius, to help the revolt of Inaros, Athens had taken Dor of coastal Palestine; so his successors had political motives for fostering Ezra's efforts to bring to unruly Jerusalem "law and order" (on Persia's side: F. M. Heichelheim, "Ezra's Palestine and Periclean Athens," *ZRGG* 3 [1951] 251–53; M. Smith in *Fischer Weltgeschichte* [→ 81 above] 5.361; In der Smitten, *Esra* (→ 83 above] 113; B. Jürgen, "Die Dependenz des Königs von Sidon vom persischen Grosskönig," *Beiträge zur Altertumskunde Kleinasiens* [Fest K. Bittel; Mainz, 1983] 105–20).

96   **7.** *seventh year:* 458 or 428 or 398, as in v 1. **8.** The hike to Jerusalem was to last 100 days; the end of the journey is awkwardly anticipated here: much is still to be told until 8:32, before Ezra's convoy ever leaves Babylonia. **14.** "Fact-finding mission" describes well the official relation of Ezra to the Persian chancery, although all too often bureaucrats who are sent to make "inquiries" wield an influence tantamount to punitive or even legislative authority. Hence, in v 25 Ezra is regarded as "appointing magistrates," but this is only "to judge those who acknowledge the law of Yahweh" and "according to the wisdom of his God which is in his hand." **23** *in detail:* ʾ*adrazdāʾ* (F. Rundgren, *Orientalia Suecana* 31–32 [1982–83] 143–46). **24.** Clergy exemption from taxation

was a plausible grant, as under Darius to the Apollo clergy of Magnesia; v 18 extends this explicitly to exemption from "hidden" sales or inheritance tax; but v 15 had emphasized that any funds given in cash for the project by the king or finance minister were (despite the customary flourish of v 20) purely personal donations, such as those of Jewish or Gentile contributors. **28.** Abrupt transition to the 1st pers. suggests that the compiler was in part using an "Ezra memoir" rather than just falling into inconsistency in a "fictional" (Noth; *JBC* on v 27) composition.

97   **(B) Rounding Up the Convoy (8:1–31).** **1.** Ezra counts here (mostly in round numbers, and only 15 by name) 1,511 men, plus doubtless as many dependents. The 12 families hint rather than represent the 12 tribes; 11 are families already named in the lengthier genealogy of Ezra 2. **2.** Ezra's own family stands first, thus reversing the order of 2:36, which relegates the priestly families to the end. Moreover, against Ezek 43:19, the Ithamar branch is put equal to the Zadokite, represented only by Phinehas (see comment on 7:5 and 1 Chr 6:53; and N. Ararat, *BM* 18 [1973] 387–417).

15. *Ahava:* Confluence of some unknown canal with the Euphrates. *no sons of Levi:* In the minimal technical sense of Levites; actually all the priests were sons of Levi, but something more—sons of Aaron. If this insertion is due to a "Chronicler," it is noteworthy that he tolerates this implication that the Levites were missing when needed; a meager 74 had been present in 2:40. Still, he may well have been gratified at how indispensably important the Levites are thus shown to be. **21.** Fasting and prayer, as a suitable replacement of normal "secondary causality" comes from a misapprehension regarding "faith in providence." **22.** It would be more defensible to assume that Ezra, having ascertained in a discreetly roundabout way that he would be unable to get a military escort, made a morale-building virtue of necessity. **24.** Ezra's human resourcefulness in guaranteeing the safe arrival of the funds leaves nothing to be desired. **28.** Holiness has its place, not as a mere tool to an economic end but as a pertinent factor of the existential situation. **30.** The value of the treasury deposits could be reckoned at some 10 million dollars. It would not contradict the practice of biblical writers or copyists to have added a few zeros to the recorded amounts, thus bringing home more vividly to a remote generation the essential theological truth of the mutual generosity between God and his people.

98   **(C) The Situation in Jerusalem (8:32–10:44).** **32.** Allowance is made for three days of rest and orientation after the 100-day trek. **22.** Ezra's doctrinal prestige, as well as his financial backing, must have engendered a certain obsequiousness in even the highest local hierarchs, but the formalities had to be punctiliously respected. **34.** Witnesses were in attendance, and a receipt was drawn up. **35.** Transition to the 3d pers. suggests use of other, less formulated sources here. Anyway, we must reckon with the possibility that Neh 8 is to be inserted at this point. It does in fact narrate Ezra's activities in the sequence that best fits here; and because it speaks of him in the 3d pers., a transition would be needed. But we leave open the possibility that the whole of Ezra's ministry was preceded by the work of Nehemiah, including his mixed-marriage reform in Neh 13: one of the main motives for dating Ezra after Nehemiah has been that Neh 13 seems to be coping with a new crisis, whereas Ezra 9 seems to take for granted an earlier effort at clarification of the juridical situation. In that case, we could assume that Ezra deferred the promulgation of his newly edited Torah until he had taken a firm position on scandalous violations of the Mosaic Law as already interpreted.

9:1. The 1st pers. merely introduces an extended citation, and could have been an adjustment made after Neh 8-9 was dropped from this point. *Canaanites . . . Perizzites:* This choice of "disapproved races" is not a concrete historical record of 5th-cent. conditions, but a citation from Deut 7:1. Nevertheless it is significant that the Samaritans are not included alongside Ammon and Moab (see also Neh 13:1,23). The major clash with Samaritans recorded in these books is concerned with the rampart building in Neh 4, esp. if Ezra 4 is taken as relevant to that episode. Even the Tattenai inquisition, during the building of the Temple a century before Ezra, ended with the Samaritan bureaucrats showing the Judeans exactly that measure of cooperation that was desired. Moreover, the ethnic segregation demanded in Ezra 10:5 is restricted to priests: not as in Neh 13:24, where marriages of the Judean populace are in question.

From these facts H. Cazelles (*VT* 4 [1954] 122-30) had drawn perceptive conclusions with which we are in substantial agreement. The reforms of Nehemiah are based simply on Deut, not on the law which Ezra edited in Babylon. In Judea Ezra was opposed neither by the higher Judean clergy nor by the Samaritans. Both classes were invited to the public mass meeting at which he promulgated his new Torah (Neh 8-9 to be inserted during the five months noted as elapsing between Ezra 7:9 and 10:7). The key contention of Cazelles is that Ezra was completely successful in bringing around the Samaritans no less than the Judeans to a wholehearted acceptance of his Pentateuch. This view accounts for the enigma that our Torah is identical with the Samaritan scroll which later became a symbol of their hostility to Judah. Nevertheless, Cazelles continues, Ezra was not successful in establishing a durable unity between Judeans and Samaritans, and his effort to do so backfired against him. The strongly anti-Samaritan party that inherited Nehemiah's ideology came to prevail in Jerusalem; its dominance during the 3d cent. dictates whatever animus against Samaria there is in Chr and in Sir 50:26 and 2 Macc 13. (Thus Ezra is rejected from inclusion beside Zerubbabel and Nehemiah in Sir 49:11: but singularly opposite conclusions are drawn by the five leading experts whom Rudolph follows: Sirach found it inopportune to praise the Ezra hostility to mixed marriages in a day when they had become frequent!) Now P. Höffken ("Warum schweig Jesus Sirach über Esra?" *ZAW* 87 [1975] 184-201), comparing the Ezra 9 prayer with Sir 36, finds that for Sirach the P strand of Ezra's Pentateuch had misrepresented the (properly Aaronid) priesthood and (like Chr) favored Levites.

99   **9:2.** *peoples of the lands:* Even with both words pl. as in 3:3, this is doubtless identical with the "ordinary people," as explained in 4:4. **3.** Ezra's reaction to the denunciation has been called histrionic or defended on the ground that distinction between genuine and theatrical emotion is an Occidental category. More fairly, it shows that a flair for the dramatic is not out of place in liturgy. **6.** Notably effective is his blaming of himself rather than others for what is, after all, a corporate guilt. The biblical theologian will not overlook here a certain

isolating protective religiosity. It soft-pedals that personal responsibility which appears in Jer 31:30 and Ezek 18:20 as a leadover to the universalism of Isa 60:3 and Mal 1:11.

8. *remnant:* Here and in v 13, *pĕlêṭâ* means "escapees," but in v 14 it is coupled with *šĕ'ērît*, a technical term for the portion of Judah not exiled (Jer 8:3; 41:10), the remnant of Isa is rather *šĕ'ār* (10:19-22), an eschatological penitence group more apt to be linked with the exiles themslves. Both BDB and KB find this latter nuance of a "spiritual elite" in this Ezra 9 passage; but if we accept Cazelles' imputation of a more ecumenical outlook to Ezra, we may see a humble and conciliating compliment to the "Samaritan *'am hā'āreṣ*" in his insistence on God's goodness in sparing a remnant while the elite Judeans were exiled. **11-12.** The only thing wrong with this splendidly apt quotation is that it is not in the Bible, although its spirit doubtless is in Deut 7:3; see comment on Neh 13:23.

10:3. Natural law obligations of justice and decency toward spouses in good faith and utterly innocent children seem never to have entered into the heads of these reformers, excited by a kind of mob psychosis for which Ezra cannot escape blame, esp. if Shecaniah's spontaneity is rigged, as seems to be the case since in v 26 he is not one of those involved in a mixed marriage. The dangerous and casual claim that "God's rights outweigh all human considerations" can only be called fanaticism. Still less does "maximum enforceableness for existing religious authorities" take precedence over profoundly human obligations of commutative justice. On the other hand, the need of safeguarding religious truth and duty is also a natural law obligation; but the fact that the conduct of those influenced by Ezra is presented in the Bible as praiseworthy and normative does not mean that it is impeccable or inerrant. **6.** Ezra's own demeanor is more moderate throughout the episode; he takes his religiosity out on himself rather than on others.

9. The assembly is graphically portrayed as "trembling because of the sin and the rain" (sin being here *dābār*, unimaginatively corrected to "hail" by P. Joüon, *Bib* 12 [1931] 85). **11.** Ultimately Ezra too requires that the guilty (priests only, as in 10:5?) should punish the innocent by renouncing their children as well as the wives who were either foreign or *'am hā'āreṣ* (nonexiled Judeans unwilling to conform to the full rigor of separatist "Judahism"). **29.** These verses are rich in corruptions. But Sheal is perhaps *Yiš'al*, as in the Oriental Hebr *kĕtîb*, and on a seal found in the 1963 Ophel excavation (J. Prignaud, *RB* 7 [1964] 378); all in all, it is not so clear that mixed marriages were prohibited before or even in Deut.

We must conclude that religion of its very nature is both protective and diffusive (see comment on 4:4) — simultaneously universalist, to bring all people to the benefits its votaries enjoy, and separatist, to protect them from the contamination and loss of their "treasure of great price." The proportions in which these two antithetical obligations are to be combined will call for human prudential judgments, which even among the maximally sincere and zealous will not always be objectively right.

COMMENTARY ON NEHEMIAH

100   The author of this memoir is one of the most genial personalities portrayed anywhere in the Bible. A volcanically emotional temperament (1:4; 5:6; 13:8,25) a bit of

vanity creeping into his designs (2:10,18; 5:15; 6:11) are the side views of a noble and leaderly character. *People* are important for him; he values contacts and spends himself for them (5:16). His eloquence is brief, and succeeds always in gaining the hearer's reaction (2:17; 5:7; 13:25). His optimism refuses to notice pockets of reserve or resistance in public opinion. He reckons with workableness. His attitude toward mixed marriages is more realistic than Ezra's; he has enough assurance to pass the first round and save his bet for the next (10:31; cf. 13:25ff.). He takes time out for reflection, as is indicated by the painstaking preparations at Susa for his mission, his inspection of the walls of Jerusalem all by himself, the cautious preliminaries to joining up communities, his waiting game in unmasking the blackmail of his foes. His recourse to prayer is based on the conviction that God directs events (2:8,18,20; 4:9; 5:13; 6:16) and that he prompts leaders (2:12; 7:5). This prayer is vibrant (3:36–37; 5:19; 6:14; 13:14,22,29,31) and is akin in spirit to Jer 3:36–37 (A. Gelin, *Esdras* [Paris, 1960] 23–24).

The memoir itself as composed by its protagonist was long taken to be a kind of ruler's self-glorification; but there is merit in G. von Rad's claim that it was a cult text deposited in a shrine (*ZAW* 76 [1964] 176–87). W. T. In der Smitten emphasizes the favoring comparison of Ezra (9:6–15) to Nehemiah in our present canonical books (*BZ* 16 [1972] 207–21) and supports U. Kellermann's claim that Nehemiah was of a lateral Davidic line (*JSJ* 5 [1974] 41–48; otherwise J. Emerton, *JTS* 23 [1972] 177–81).

(III) Rearmament of Jerusalem (1:1–7:5).
(A) Susa Report and Sequel (1:1–2:11).
Nehemiah was a bright young man at the Persian court. His official position as cupbearer (v 11) implies the ultimate both in confidence and in favor felt toward him by Artaxerxes I. The holder of this position was normally a eunuch, as is verified by traces in the youth's demeanor (Albright *BA* 9 [1946] 11; the best LXX mss. have *eunouchos* for *oinochoos*). But the eunuch hypothesis is not proved, e.g., by Persian art (E. M. Yamauchi, *ZAW* 92 [1980] 132–42; baffling is Fensham [*Books,* 157]—"he had been a eunuch"), and accords ill with Nehemiah's unusual energy and authoritativeness or with the requirements of Deut 23:2 for leadership in the community. Even if the title were officially "eunuch," it need imply no more than our "chamberlain" as in Acts 8:27. **1:1.** Both Hacaliah of the MT and Halakiah supposed by the LXX defy known Hebr name patterns. *twentieth year:* Of Artaxerxes I (445); Chislev is the month of December. *Susa:* See comment on Ezra 6:2. **2.** *Hanani:* As in Neh 7:2.

(a) THE JERUSALEM DISASTER (1:1–10). **3.** The sad news from Zion was that its rampart had been breached and its gates or courthouse destroyed in flames. Such a report is perplexing. The walls of Jerusalem had been destroyed by Nebuchadnezzar 150 years earlier. Surely Nehemiah knew all about that. Can it be that enough of the wall had been standing to be reutilized for a timber structure that caught fire? J. Morgenstern (*HUCA* 27 [1956] 173; 31 [1960] 16) draws sweeping conclusions from his claim that such a disaster occurred exactly in 485, but even this was before Nehemiah's birth. More plausible is some disaster of the year 448, in which an Egyptian revolt was put down (V. Pavlovský, *Bib* 38 [1957] 446: a group of Babylonian Jews including Hanani came to Jerusalem and tried to rebuild its wall between 448 and 445, and their failure is recorded in Ezra 4:21 as well as in Neh 1:3).

(b) NEHEMIAH'S PLEA GRANTED (2:1–11). **1.** The page, with prayerful shrewdness (like Daniel, 9:4; or Ezra, 9:5) waited four months before he showed the king signs of his distress (overlooked in Josephus, *Ant.* 11 §163, where also the king is named Xerxes). Nehemiah was doubtless spying out a moment when weariness and wine would have put the monarch into a maximally sympathetic mood. **5.** Artaxerxes is con-

fronted with a pampered youth's plea to be made rebuilder and virtual ruler of a historic and turbulent metropolis. The city wall was a true fortification (*bîrâ,* 7:2; 1 Macc 13:52, name of Antonia; cf. *Ant.* 13.11.2 §307), and the authorization of its building is a genuine rearmament. The king asks only how soon he would return. **8.** Politically, the king's concession is a dangerous caprice (see comment on Ezra 4:7). Even if that episode refers to Artaxerxes, there is no obligation to date it in the beginning of his reign (this is said in the preceding verse, but concerning Xerxes). More plausibly the letter of Rehum is a reaction to Nehemiah's coming. **9.** The governors whom Nehemiah finds in Palestine are doubtless Sanballat and Tobiah, and he is contemptuous of them. *Horonite:* Refers to the tiny village of Beth-horon on the NW slopes near Jerusalem. *Ammonite:* Means foreigner from across the E border (Deut 23:4). The Elephantine papyrus (30:29; *ANET* 492) records a Sanballat in Samaria some 37 years later; but other papyri discovered at Daliyeh have now forced searching reexamination of the Sanballat chronology; see comment on 4:1. Even later, the Tobiads of Ammon became paramount in Judean affairs (*ca.* 200 BC; Josephus, *Ant.* 12.4.2 §160); they are linked with the still-imposing castle at Araq el-Emir.

(B) Program of Reconstruction (2:12–3:32).
101 (a) WALL INSPECTION BY NIGHT (2:12–20). **13.** Nehemiah was not afraid of the yokels but did not want to bother with them. Apart from the supposition that there must have been a full moon, what this prowl leaves most in the dark is the burning question of whether at this date the SW wall of Jerusalem included also the W hill where a later Judeo-Christian tradition would locate the "Zion" (and tomb) of David (see on 2 Chr 32:3), or only the E hill, Jebusite crag or true Zion of David now commonly called Ophel, as maintained by Galling. Even if the maximum area were included, the number of gates is disproportionate for an era in which even big cities like Lachish and Megiddo had only one. Scholars have exercised their ingenuity in locating the gates at suitable points along today's wall (though this represents a rebuilding by Eudoxia around AD 400 several hundred yards farther N; cf. M. Burrows, *IDB* 2. 854; J. Simons, *SJOT* 441, 237; L.-H. Vincent, *Jérusalem* (→ 43 above) 1. 235–58. But really such names as "Valley" and "Fountain" gates afford not the slightest ground for affirming even in which direction Nehemiah was riding. "Dung" as the name of a gate has been equated implausibly with "potsherds" as Jer 19:2; or euphemized into "cheese" (*šĕpôt* for *'ašpôt*) = Tyropoeon ("cheesemakers," 3:1,13). The Kenyon Ophel excavation of 1961–68 is claimed to have shown that En-Tannim of Neh 2:13 was Siloam rather than Rogel spring; cf. J. Braslavi, in *Zalman Shazar Volume* (ErIsr 10; Jerusalem, 1971) 90–93; Eng xi; see on 3:8. The term for Nehemiah's "inspection" (*śbr,* only here, vv 13 and 15) is claimed to mean rather he "broke down" (*śbr* as LXX *syntribō*) the wall, i.e., cleansed it because it had been cultic (J. Heller, *Communio Viatorum* 11 [1968] 175–78). **16.** Whatever the details of his ride, it so encouraged Nehemiah that he summoned a meeting and stirred public interest. "Doers of the work" has been claimed to mean "the administration" rather than the doers of the work (H. Kaupel, *Bib* 21 [1940] 40). **19.** Another outsider now joins the local opposition: Geshem is doubtless one of the Arabs who had gradually been filtering northward as far as Nabatean Petra. **20.** Through this righteous reply glimmers a spiteful hint that the major guilt of Sanballat and colleagues (genuine "people of the land" and worshipers of Yahweh) was to have wanted to help in the project and thus share or dim Nehemiah's glory.

102 (b) THE LOCAL CHAPTER MASONS (3:1–32). The rebuilding of the wall was not an organically structured use of manpower. Complete autonomy was left to rival groups working on separate sections. It is hard to see how this policy could have been considered either more efficient or more expressive of that religious-ethnic solidarity by which alone the work could have been begun. The author of the memoir may have been imitating the historic wall building of Themistocles (Thucydides 1.89), so that the team rivalry was more or less a literary artifice.

The separatist groups of masons are not all ethnic. Five only represent clans from the list of Ezra 2. Five others are locality based, as indicated there. Five more are earlier districts as in Josh 15 (Jerusalem, Beth-kerem, Beth-zur, Keilah, and Mizpah). Important nearby towns like Bethlehem and Bethel are not mentioned; perhaps they staged a boycott better organized than that of Tekoa (v 5) out of sympathy with their Arab neighbors. Furthermore, doubtless in extension of the fact that the Zadok and Levi clans are more (priestly-) functional than ethnic, we have also some "guilds" represented, probably more than the goldsmiths, perfumers (= undertakers), and merchants, explicitly named in vv 8 and 32. Incompleteness of the listing may be inferred from several mentions of a "second half" to which no first half corresponds (vv 12,16,18–20). The work was not shared by a single fellow traveler of Ezra (8:1–24) — one of the indications that he came after Nehemiah.

3:1. A prestige name heads the list: Eliashib is Joshua's grandson of 12:10. His connections with disdained Tobiah (13:4–5,8; 2:10) must have made him a cool supporter of what a Flemish commentary calls Nehemiah's apartheid policy. *Sheep Gate:* It was customary within our present century to install periodically a sheep market inside the NE corner of Jerusalem's wall, where (without proof: neither the priests' nearness to the Temple, nor the "probatica" of John 5:2) commentators agree to put the outset of this allegedly counterclockwise circuit of the wall sections. *built:* Claimed to imply that this corner was more utterly razed than the later sections said to be "repaired"; but perhaps merely a style variant as in vv 13–14. *consecrated:* No need to emend to "renovated" (*ḥdš* for *qdš*; Rudolph) or "roofed"; what is more natural than that in their section, the priests should have given vent to a little extra rite? **6.** The "Old" or "Corner" Gate is conjecturally set in the NW corner. **7.** The Mizpah people were "for the throne" (of the province governor), probably a localization of some part of the wall. **8.** The "Broad Wall" is claimed to be the masonry excavated by N. Avigad on the slope west of Tyropoeon: thereupon left outside Nehemiah's rebuilding (P. Grafman, *IEJ* 24 [1974] 50; H. Williamson, "Nehemiah's Walls Revisited," *PEQ* 116 [1984] 81–88; in *ZAW* 97 [1985] 78, he claims there is no '*zb* II). C. G. Tuland in *AUSS* 5 [1967] 158–80) holds that the Nehemiah wall, though ampler than the minimalist view, was still confined to the E hill, involving the Kenyon excavation; and Fensham (*Books* 165, 171), though accepting as final Kenyon's declaration that "it is useless to try to correlate the Nehemiah description with Jerusalem topography," adds that on the *east* the biblical description corresponds to her discoveries. In vv 9–18, *pelek,* occurring 8 times and usually taken as "district," is held to be rather "labor levy" as Akk *pilku* (A. Demsky, *IEJ* 33 [1983] 242–44).

12. *daughters:* Perhaps suburbs. **13.** The Valley Gate is located farther S, in either Tyropoeon or Gehinnom, depending on whether one includes the SW hill (2:13), which the "thousand cubits" would seem to require, no matter how near Gihon the Dung Gate is placed. **15.** The fountain par excellence would be Gihon, but it must be

Rogel if we assume that the Shela-Siloam pool stood between it and the climb to the Jebusite-Davidic citadel; see comment on 2:13. **21.** We are brought finally to the priests' residences, appropriately located along the half-mile where the E wall of the city coincides with the retaining wall of the Temple esplanade above the Kedron-Jehoshaphat valley.

(C) Triumphalism (4:1–7:5).

103 (c) EMBATTLED PERSISTENCE (4:1–23). **1.** This verse is MT 3:33, and the discrepancy continues through 4:23 = MT 4:17. With the (Samaria) Sanballat of chap. 4 two major problems have become prominent. First is the chronological importance of the relation of this Sanballat-with-daughter-married-to-high-priest (Eliashib, Ezra 10:6; Neh 13:4) to *three* others, known from Josephus, Elephantine, and now Daliyeh. *Ant.* 11.8.2 §309 tells of an influential Sanballetes whose daughter Nikaso was married to a high-priest Manasses, for whom he built a temple on Gerizim (§324) in the time of Darius III and Alexander (335–330). But the Aram papyri dated around 407 at Elephantine include a letter written from there (*ANET* 492) mentioning two sons of Sanballat governor of Samaria and an apparently contemporary high priest Johanan (as Neh 12:22; = ?Jonathan, 12:11; cf. H. Rowley, *Servant of the Lord* [Oxford, 1965] 135–68; also *BJRL* 37 [1954–55] 528–61; 38 [1955–56] 166–98). Now the papyri found at Wadi Daliyeh in Samaria, insofar as their contents have been made known by F. Cross since 1963 (*BA* 26 [1963] 110), include a *bulla* seal with paleohebraic inscription "(Hanan)iah son of (San)ballat *peha(t)* of Samerina" and a fragment "? Jesus son of Sanballat (and) Hanan the prefect" amid 20 papyri, 20 fragments, and 128 *bullae.* Cross admits that it had seemed impossible that there should be a *second* such Sanballat a century after Nehemiah, but claims that with the Daliyeh evidence it is easier to admit that he was the *third.* His proof rests heavily on the claim that during those centuries "papponymy" prevailed: the grandson (often called "son" by genealogists) regularly received his grandfather's surname. On this basis Cross shows how two names could have fallen out of the relevant succession of high priests: an Eliashib in 545 apart from the one in 495; a Johanan in 520 apart from the attested one in 445; and a third one unattested in 395 ("A Reconstruction of the Judean Restoration," *JBL* 94 [1975] 4–18, which goes on to conclude to *three* editions of "the Chronicler," of which the second, dated around 450, had no Nehemiah memoir; this was then circulating separately, until incorporated in the "third edition" around 400; → 82 above). Thorough refutations of this view, presented in *BHI* 401f., and Widengren in *IJH* 506–9 leave more or less intact the assumption that the Sanballat of the Ezra books in 445 was still living in 407 (and is possibly the one mentioned by Josephus with a confusion of dates).

104 The second momentous problem raised by this Samaritan–Sanballat opposition is the date of the Samaritan schism and its relevance to the ("Chronicler's") purpose of compiling Ezra-Neh. A common view has been that the Samaritans (of Ezra 4:4 and after) were real inhabitants of Samaria but *pagans* descended from those imported from Assyria by Sargon II in 721 (2 Kgs 17:24; so Mosis, *Untersuchungen* 225). Anti-Samaritan intent in "the Chronicler" is denied by Welten (*Geschichte* 172; see on 2 Chr 14:6) with Willi, but with reserves about a further development. H. G. Kippenberg (*Garizim und Synagoge . . . zur samaritanischen Religion der aramäischen Periode* [Giessen, 1971] 39) and esp. J. D. Purvis (*The Samaritan Pentateuch and the Origin of the Samaritan Sect* [Cambridge, 1968]) hold that the crucial moment of division was not even as early as the building of the

Gerizim temple in Alexander's time, long after Nehemiah (as Josephus, *Ant.* 11.8.4 §324), but the editing of a distinctive Pentateuch contemporaneous with the *destruction* of that temple in the Hasmonean period. We get very little help from R. J. Coggins (1975); he is so intent on tracing a simon-pure "Samaritanism" of the Gospel era that he denies the name not merely to Ezra's "people of the land" (p. 67; and *JTS* 16 [1965] 124-27) but even to Sanballat, "not 'a Samaritan' in terms of this study" (p. 58); on p. 62 he opposes the view (attributed to A. Vink, not Cazelles; see on Ezra 9:1) that Ezra conciliated the Samaritans.

Our own position here as in *JBC* will continue to be that the "Samaritans" who opposed the construction of the wall (and perhaps Temple in Ezra 4) were "the people of the land," those Judeans who had not been in exile and who had lived under the administration of the Persian province Samerina; thus, we do not admit Kippenberg's key claim that at the time of Ezra 1f., Judah was made a *province* of Babylon. There had been a certain coolness between Judeans and Samaritans (as Purvis, Kippenberg, and Coggins admit) ever since the Assyrian deportation. It gained momentum with the return from exile, at which time we find Ezra trying to diminish it (Cazelles), but Nehemiah (as also the parties of Ezra 4:4) implacably opposing whatever local or northern "Samaritan" elements could diminish the prestige of the "true Judean" returnees from exile.

105   **4:2** (MT 3:3). The opposition's lively wit is recorded with surprisingly sympathetic flair. *Army:* Rather, "strength" (*ḥayil*) whether military or economic, a sociological term, controverted in relation to its antithesis *'am hā'āreṣ* (Ezra 4:4; 9:2). The LXX takes it as part of the taunt (Esdras B 14:2), "This is Samaria's strength, that the Judeans build a city," with what follows all attributed to Tobiah. **7** (MT 4:1). *Ashdod:* See comment on 13:23. With these Philistines to the west, the circle of the compass is complete: Samaria N, Ammon E, Arabs S (2:9,19). Israel is completely surrounded by its enemies. **10**. (MT 4:4). This snatch of verse, with its ballad introduction "Judah said" puts colorfully before us the Semite toiler's habit of singing lustily when the work is hardest, as in Arab excavations still—a monotonous refrain, howled by all, alternates with clever improvisations in the same rhythm. **11**. The opposition's reaction, though not in verse, is a kind of proverb put here artistically as an antiphon. **16**. "Half of them worked, half held weapons, and [the third half] supervised" is plainly an exaggeration for what follows, "those [few] who carried weapons also worked like the others." **18**. Nehemiah slyly admits that his own skin was the major defense objective, as indeed it was doubtless the enemy's prime target. But it was not so sharp of him to want everybody (including the enemy) to know exactly where he was. **23**. "They slept in their clothes, their weapons 'in hand'" is a conjectural correction of 'the water' (MT 4:17).

106   (b) SOCIAL JUSTICE REFORM (5:1-19). **1**. Another major hurdle confronts the masons. Now that the opposition has been neutralized, the workers find that their own fellow Judeans are causing them miseries. It is the wives who protest, because the household economy and children's welfare are involved. **2**. Some infer that concentration on the walls had led to economic crisis, or that the embargo on nightly return to outlying towns had cut off the continuing stream of fresh vegetables. But a realistic rereading shows that 4:22f. is an afterthought not chronologically prior to 4:15; all in all, it must have been a very brief crisis, convincing the opposition that their efforts were useless. The whole enterprise, building and defense alike, was completed in

only 52 days (6:15), not long enough to raise any problem of such annual harvests as would already be stored within the city. Nehemiah cannot have expected Judah's poor simply to starve while donating their services to a project financed (at least nominally, 2:8) by the imperial treasury, or even by the nobility that stood to gain most by the retrieval of Jerusalem's onetime metropolitan status. The workers must have been economically profited by some small but steady salary above their normal expectations. It is exactly a situation that lenders exploit, very much like the payday of excavation workers whose creditors are lurking at the fringe to grab most of what the workers have imprudently spent in advance.

3. This social evil can scarcely have resulted from a 20- to 40-day pinch of the work project. **4**. The king's tax also is a normal annual burden. The mortgaging must have occurred sometime previously, if only now the foreclosure is taking place, or even if the interest payments are now becoming intolerable. **5**. *our flesh is as the flesh of our brethren:* The real outcry results from the debtors' view of themselves as toiling and endangered side by side with (and for the benefit of) wealthier citizens who are presently going to turn on them, as in Matt 18:28. This temporary crisis merely dramatizes a situation that has lasted, and will last, as long as human nature itself: a free economy will result in debt, bankruptcy, and enslavement for the less energetic, talented, or sly. We shall therefore always have to seek new and better social legislation or enforcement (North, *Sociology of the Biblical Jubilee* [AnBib 4; Rome, 1954] 205; prominence there assigned to the priests as landholders is denied by Fensham, which makes our point all the stronger). The basic Hebr principle was inalienable distribution of private property among small family holders, although to debtors was allowed the genuine benefit of being allowed to entail their property or their (own or sons') persons for a period not to exceed 7, or maximally 49 years (Deut 15:1f.; Lev 25:10).

7. The grandiloquent oratory is suited to the patriotic crisis, but must not be pressed to unrealistic conclusions. First, to grant loans on interest even to victims of misfortune is not harmful to a sound economy; nor is it even a less desirable situation for the debtors themselves than simply to become beggars asking for a handout. Nehemiah does not regret that he has been granting such loans at interest (v 11; R. P. Maloney [*CBQ* 36 (1974) 1-20] concerns Nehemiah only indirectly). Second, what he proposes is simply to take cognizance of the reconstruction crisis by a grand act tempering justice with mercy (Prov 14:31). To write off all the loans as gifts is a tacit invocation of the *šĕmiṭṭâ* law of Deut 15:1,9. In a crisis this is fine, but it would be impractical and ultimately less charitable if the law required in advance that every loan would automatically be transformed into an outright gift after seven years without any benefit to the lender in the meantime. **11**. *hundred:* Nowhere else means "1 percent" (per *month* also is gratuitously assumed; hence we may approve the emendation to *maśśâ*, "interest (-rate)" (E. Neufeld, *JQR* 44 [1953] 199). **12**. *priests . . . from them:* Not "from the priests" (we may hope), but using the priestly office as a sort of law enforcement detail. Such a verse could have given rise to the judgment that in postexilic Judah "all powers without any exception belonged to the clergy" (J. Pirenne, *RIDA* 3/1 [1954] 208).

14. *governor 20th-32d year:* Although Nehemiah was doing all the work of a permanent officeholder, he made no complaint at receiving none of the perquisites. Virtually universal is the view that Nehemiah was truly "governor" of a "province" (W. In der Smitten "Der

Tirschātā' in Esra-Nehemiah," *VT* 21 [1971] 618–20; W. Vischer, "Nehemia der Sonderbeauftragte und Statthalter des Königs," *Probleme biblischer Theologie* [Fest. G. von Rad; ed. H. W. Wolff; Munich, 1971] 603–10). But our research into five different forms of "Civil Authority in Ezra" (→ 95 above; 6. 377–404) reaches the conclusion that *neither* had Ezra any "undersecretariate" or "concordat," *nor* was Nehemiah governor except in an honorific sense (which does not really retract the *JBC* on this verse; see R. Klein in *Magnalia Dei* [Fest G. E. Wright; ed. F. M. Cross, *et al.*; GC, 1976] 374; on p. 365 he finds our discounting of *peḥâ* "too radical"; as does J. Soggin [*History of Israel* (Phl, 1984) 273] who, however, notes [p. 270] that Nehemiah is not in the list of governors down to 375, in 1 Chr 3:19–24). **15.** Even the commentators who insist that Nehemiah had a true civil function within the Persian bureaucracy admit that he here puts himself in a series in which he had no predecessor, the only possibilities being his Samaritan rivals. But Nehemiah is plainly thinking rather of the prestige leaders who truly preceded him, such as Sheshbazzar (and) Zerubbabel. The claim of some few recent inquiries that Judah had been separated by Persia from Samaria into a true "province" (S. Japhet, *ZAW* 9 [1983] 86; see on Ezra 1:10) is denied by F. C. Fensham "Medînâ in Ezr-Neh," *VT* 25 [1975] 795–97). **18.** *one ox . . . six sheep:* Hardly to be called meager, even if Solomon had 10 or 30 oxen and 100 sheep (1 Kgs 4:23 [MT 5:3]). The opulence of Nehemiah as of wealthy bedouin sheikhs is shown not in their own standard of living but in the number of poor relations whom they let come to dinner.

107   (c) DRAMATIC COMPLETION OF THE MISSION (6:1–7:72). There is no doubt that Nehemiah is here describing what he firmly holds to have been deep dark plots against his life. But 6:17f. shows that many prudent and loyal Judeans felt that his judgment in the matter was warped. If Sanballat truly possessed some authority, either superior or at least equal to Nehemiah's within the Persian framework, what else could he do except try to come to an understanding that would avert complete breakdown in bureaucratic functioning and subsequent imperial displeasure?

6:2. Ono is held to be near Lydda (Alt, *KlS* 1. 344 claims proof from Sennacherib; *ANET* index refers only to Tutmoses III); at any rate the Lydda "plain" begins at Latrun, suspiciously near Sanballat's Beth-horon. **3.** *I am engaged on a great work and cannot come:* A noble reply to give to associates who try to break off one's idealistic plans and enterprises. **6.** Nehemiah's Gaullist grandeur and separatist assurance lend great plausibility to Sanballat's fear. **10.** *shut up:* The Hebr word *'āṣûr* for Shemaiah's confinement implies in Jer 36:5 "a state of ritual uncleanness," which, being of foreseen duration, need not have hindered Shemaiah from making plans to enter the Temple himself. But commentators prefer for *'ṣr* the sense of "performing a symbolic act of prophecy," or "seized by a prophetic spirit" as in 1 Kgs 22:11 (to which Isa 8:11 is similar). The word really means "imprisoned," and its detective-story overtones are doubtless intentional in this setting, even if in actual fact Nehemiah were merely visiting someone "confined" to his room with a cold. The prophet's statement is an oracle, whose strong hieratic rhythm is perceptible even in the English.

12. *hired:* Has the same connotation we would use today for someone who, whatever his motive, has espoused a course of action we disapprove. The plot seems flimsy at best—threats of assassination to induce a political figure to put himself in a position he himself calls ridiculous rather than compromising, with no allusion to any death penalty (Num 18:7 against 1 Macc

10:43?). **14.** Nehemiah takes a dim view of all "prophets," as indeed do several real prophets themselves (Amos 7:14; Jer 2:26). **15.** *52 days:* Pericles' wall at Athens was built in even less time: one month (Thucydides, 1.93); the 852 days of Josephus *Ant.* 11.5.8 §179 has been traced to a confusion likely in Gk numerals. "The walls which Zech 2:4–5 promised would be unnecessary and too restricting are built by Nehemiah"; so J. Goldingay, *BTB* 5 (1975) 125. **18.** Tobiah's marriage connections within Jerusalem are an afterthought and an unworthily personal motivation of opposition to the city's best interests. More objectively, we must say that there would be two ways of looking at Nehemiah's undoubtedly sincere but also self-glorifying whirlwind activity.

7:1. Mention of the Levite choir so casually in the passive suggests that Nehemiah took no interest in the matter, but "the Chronicler" here makes his voice heard. **2.** "Governor," or rather prince of the fortress, is an even nobler term than the *peḥâ* which Nehemiah claims for himself in 5:15. The only authority he really possessed to hand over was that conferred upon him by his personal prestige and favor with the king, and this he leaves to his brother to exercise (not too successfully, 13:7). According to In der Smitten ("Nehemias Parteigänger," *BO* 29 [1972] 155–57), he was a lone wolf; his few reliable supporters, called "God-fearing" here and perhaps "Judeans" in 6:6, did not continue his cause after his absence. **5.** At this point is to be inserted Nehemiah's fulfillment of his promise (2:6) to return as soon as possible to his royal patron's side (13:6). *gathering of the nobles:* May in fact refer to the "second ministry" of Nehemiah described in chap. 10, whether or not it is regarded as contemporaneous with Ezra. This was probably the original point of insertion of the list of returnees, which we now have at two places, as is explained under Ezra 2 above.

108   (IV) **Ezra's Torah Promulgated** (Neh 7:73–9:38). Ezra's assembly (a continuation from Ezra 8:35? or 10:44?) is here inserted as if his first ministry had been abruptly broken off and then his second begun after Nehemiah's first. Even in this assumption, there is no reason to suspect that he returned to Babylon as Nehemiah did; A. Fernández (*Bib* 2 [1961] 431) thinks he accompanied Nehemiah back from Babylon, but leaves unexplained why Ezra's presence is not mentioned in the convoy. The apparent continuity assured in such hypotheses is troubled by so many loose ends that most experts think that Neh 8:1 is a continuation of Ezra 10:44 even if it refers to his arrival (40 years) after Nehemiah's first. But if we once admit that Neh 8f. is notoriously displaced, there is no reason why its original situation must have been after Ezra 10:44 as in 1 Esdr 9:37. We here reckon with the possibility that Neh 8f. fits better after Ezra 8:35. Less plausible is the supposition that Ezra adopted *ad hoc* measures against abuses before promulgating his sweeping new codification of Mosaic law; more likely the abuses were attacked after his law was promulgated, and possibly long after the violent measures of Neh 13:23 to cope with similar abuses.

On the whole vexed question of the order of the chapters now given as Neh 7–13, see M. Saebo, *TRE* 10. 384. Childs (*CIOTS* 635) holds that Neh 8 was deliberately put here 12 years after Ezra's main work, and conjoined with Nehemiah's, as a declaration not of historical but of theological reality, "an extreme example of a canonical process which has disregarded a strictly literary or historical sequence."

We here continue to envision "Ezra's law (Neh 8:1) which was in his hands" (see on Ezra 7:14) as the final redaction of the whole Pentateuch. Hebr *tôrâ* is compared with Aram *dāt* by R. Rendtorff, ("Ezra und das 'Gesetz,'" *ZAW* 96 [1984] 165–84). C. Houtman (*OTS* 21 [1981] 91–115) notes that an 18-year-old boy named T. Aikenhaid was hanged in Edinburgh for claiming *inter alia* that Ezra was the author of the Pentateuch. We cannot exclude that the *portion* of the Pentateuch read aloud by Ezra was chiefly Lev (so Michaeli, *Livres des Chroniques* 337), nor that it was rather the chiefly deuteronomic non-P parts (as In der Smitten, *Esra* 127). D. McCarthy (*CBQ* 44 [1982] 26) finds the parallels to Neh 8–10 in Deut 26:17–19; R. Klein (in *Magnalia Dei* [→ 106 above] 361–76) agrees that there are still four possibilities open for "Ezra's law": (a) the whole Pentateuch; (b) some law code in it; (c) only P; (d) only Deut. We note as *extra chorum* M. Smith (*Fischer Weltgeschichte* [→ 81 above] 5. 369): The "law" of Neh 8:2 cannot be the Pentateuch because Yom Kippur of Lev 16 is ignored; Pentateuch tolerance of Judaizing foreigners shows that it was codified long after Ezra and Nehemiah; and the assimilationists managed to get *that* Pentateuch accepted by the Samaritans even at such a very late date.

109   8:1. To this verse most experts regard 7:73 or its last half as a preface. (We withdraw the alternative here in *JBC*.) *seventh month:* A sequence unknown to us; it is certainly not envisioned as the next after Elul of 6:15, which was in fact a sixth month by the Nisan-based calendar, but twelfth on the basis of the new year beginning in the "seventh" month, Tishri (October). There is a similar Jerusalem assembly in a "seventh month" immediately after the identical list of Ezra 2:70, so we must conclude that it is a colophon to the list. Rearrangement of the text could have resulted in part from overhasty identification among various seventh-month assemblies. See now M. Z. Solah, *BM* 29 (1984) 381–83. **9.** The pairing of the two otherwise unrelated leaders affords the chief ground for Albright-Rudolph-Pavlovský to date Ezra's ministry in 428 by altering the text of Ezra 7:7. Also without such alteration, the present verse can be upheld on the supposition that Nehemiah, in his twenties in 445, had become during an Ezra ministry in 398 an elder statesman in his seventies. "Governor" is here *tiršātā',* not *peḥâ* as in Nehemiah's own memoirs; we hold both to be prestige titles of popular acclaim, outlasting the occasion on which they were used; see comment on Neh 5:14. **10.** The clergy make a rather heavy-handed effort to cheer up a mob dismayed by the severity of Ezra's Pentateuch. **14.** (= Lev 23:42). **15.** The general sense of Lev 23:40 is loosely quoted here. **16.** Claimed to be one of "the Chronicler's" famed theological conclusions, like the Hezekiah Passover (imitation of Josiah's in 2 Chr 30:13; 35:1). This feast of Booths, which we know as the feast of Tabernacles from John 7:2, has the reading of the law as one of its characteristics, properly for the seventh year as prescribed in Deut 7:10, but suitably in any year after long desuetude. The Ezra activity of Neh 8–10 is in fact dated to the sabbath year 430 by F. Mezzacasa (*RevistB* 23 [1961] 94).

110   9:1. The Yom Kippur rite of Lev 16:29, or at least a ceremony in its spirit, may well be seen here as transferred from the 10th to the 24th day of the seventh month, because in Neh 8:9 either there had not yet been time to promulgate the Torah, or excessive melancholy had endangered its acceptance, though Rudolph following Torrey here inserts Ezra 9–10 between Neh 8 and 9, while Neh 9 is linked with Nehemiah's own reforms by E. Sellin and M. Rehm (*BZ* 1 [1957] 59). **2.** It is not really separatist to exclude others from our acknowledgment of faults whose guilt we do not wish to imply extends to them. F. Ahlemann (*ZAW* 59 [1942–43] 88) puts Neh

9:1–5 after Ezra 10:15 "upon this 'fast.'" **6.** On the long rhythmic prayer "of the Levites," see now M. Gilbert ("La place de la Loi dans la prière de Néhémie 9," *De la Tôrah au Messie* [Fest. H. Cazelles; ed. M. Carrez, *et al.;* Paris,1981] 307–16): the structure "sins–'and now'–plea" is also found in three individual prayers such as Num 22:34 and in five other texts like Exod 32:30 but always without "the law." Even in Neh 9 "the law" is not as central as it seems; often it relates to the sins not of the orant but of his ancestors, or to "the land"; despite the strongly deuteronomic flavor claimed by von Rad, Neh 9 distinguishes the Decalogue given by God from "laws" given through Moses; prophetic and P parallels suggest a composition date shortly before Nehemiah rather than 720–586. According to Fensham (*JNSL* 9 [1981] 35–51), this hymn of Nehemiah aimed "to instruct history"; curiously he asks "*Why* was there such an interest in history in that period?" Really we find here a certain type of preacher's unconcern for adapting sacrosanct formulas to current situations; the menace and slavery of Assyria (v 32) and Egypt seem to be more present realities than the freedom and revival fostered by the Persian regime. This prayer, although not preserved as such in the post-Ezra synagogue, influenced strongly the structure of its liturgy (J. Liebreich, *HUCA* 32 [1961] 228) and eventually the eucharist: see C. Giraudo on the *tôdâ* as forensic reaction of the guilty party (typical formulary Neh 9:6–37) in *La struttura letteraria della preghiera eucaristica* [AnBib 92; Rome, 1981] 81–125), comparing also Josh 24:2–15; Deut 26:5–10; 32:1–25; Ps 44 (p. 106) "leading to anaphora-anamnesis-epiklesis." **17.** *in their stubbornness:* MT: *běmiryām,* but underlying the LXX is *bě-miṣrayim,* "in Egypt." **38.** Nehemiah here (as 10:40) undertook the task which Malachi awaited from a Messiah: a reform of the priesthood which had got the upper hand, says A. Bentzen ("Priesterschaft und Laien in der jüdischen Gemeinde des fünften Jahrhunderts," *AfO* 6 [1930–31] 280–86; So Kellermann, *Nehemiah* [→ 83 above] 8).

(V)   Nehemiah's Reform (Neh 10:1–13:20).
111   (A)   The Pledge (10:1–39). This is a bloodless archive fragment which could fit equally loosely any of the several Ezra-books assemblies or reforms. Verse 1 undoubtedly dovetails with 9:38, numbered 10:1 in the MT. But this leaves open whether 9:38 was part of the present archive record or whether 10:1/2 was inserted or modified to connect Neh 9 with a list originally unrelated to it. Some join Neh 10:1f. to Ezra 10:44 or to Neh 13 (Neh 10:30f. echoes 13:23,21, but also 5:11 and Deut 15:1); but it is equally possible that Neh 10 belongs with 8–9–where it is, whatever the chronological position of 8–10. **29.** *people (of the land):* Only from the time of this verse did the term take on the Hillel sense of "impious," according to A. H. J. Gunneweg ("'Am ha-areṣ–a Semantic Revolution," *ZAW* 95 [1983] 437–40); see comment on Ezra 4:4. **32–35.** The devaluation of the half-shekel (Exod 30:13; Matt 17:24) is ingeniously linked with the observation that a Persian shekel weighed 21 gr. and a Phoenician shekel 14 gr. The wood offering is unusual, but sufficiently virtual in Lev 6:12 (Josephus, *J.W.* 2.17.6 §425). On the lottery, see 1 Chr 25:8.

(B)   Repopulating Jerusalem (11:1–12:26). Chapter 11 really fits better after Neh 7:7a than the repetition of (Nehemiah-era) Ezra 2 inserted there. **1.** "The holy (city)" has become the name of Jerusalem in Arabic, *al-Quds.* **3–19.** A Chronicles-style genealogy; perhaps the original from which 1 Chr 9:2–17 was copied. **23.** Interest in the economic well-being of the Levite choir, of which "the Chronicler" was a member.

112   **12:1.** A further genealogical appendix to 7:39. It could fit equally well with what precedes or what follows. **7.** *chief among the priests:* Cannot mean technically here high priests, for they are too numerous; but that term began to be used about this time; and in v 10 (also 13:28) we seem to have a sequence of high priests continuing 1 Chr 5:41. Hence, Book of the Chronicles (v 23), not that of our canonical Bible. **13.** The Ezra named in this verse is held to be different from the (principal) one of v 1, and both are different from the Ezra of v 33 (M. Smith in *Ex Orbe Religionum* [Fest. G. Widengren; NumenSup 21; Leiden, 1972] 141). **26.** Nehemiah (445) was not contemporary with Joshua (520); even if the verse is a gloss, the presence of an Ezra after Nehemiah may be a chronological clue.

113   **(C) Solemn Dedication of the Wall (12:27–13:14).** The abrupt return to 1st pers. between vv 31 and 39 might be equally applicable to Ezra or to Nehemiah of v 26. The reading of the law in 13:1 suggests Ezra, but the continuation in v 6 is surely Nehemiah. It is his wall which is being inaugurated, and in view of all the other quirks of chronological sequence, we might well attach 12:27 to 7:1, where it normally would belong. Singers are stressed there too, as in 12:27–30, 44–47, but these are 3d-pers. additions flanking the relevant Nehemiah memoir. But it is perhaps more common among commentators to treat Neh 11–13 as continuous, dealing with the hero's maneuvers after his journey to and back from the Persian capital. **27.** Dedication (*ḥanukkâ*, "inauguration") is also the name of modern Jewry's yuletide festival commemorating the cleansing rite after Seleucid desecration of the Temple (1 Macc 4:54; John 10:22). Its date also comes coincidentally close to the 25 Kisleu (December) assigned by 2 Macc 1:18 to the rededication and also to a (? dedication) sacrifice of Nehemiah in the Temple; this date can scarcely be put in relation to the 25 Elul (September) assigned by Neh 6:15; see comment on 8:1. **38.** *to the left:* Emended to "opposite" by those who locate the Water Gate of Neh 8:3 near Rogel Spring, and the "probatica" Sheep-Gate of Neh 3:32 just north of the Temple esplanade where the procession would presumably end (M. Burrows, *JBL* 54 [1935] 29–40 on Neh 12 as distinct from the night ride of 3:1).

13:1. *on that day:* Shows that the compiler considered at least some earlier verses of chap. 13 to belong to the dedication of the wall, which he thus sees as pertaining to Nehemiah's second ministry. Although v 1 undoubtedly recalls Ezra (and Deut 23:4f.), actually everything before v 14 is sufficiently relevant to a ceremony culminating in the Temple. The wall itself, in the course of the quarter mile where it serves to bound the Temple area, would have contained chambers for both storage and lodging, according to usages attested by excavation. Even if the penthouse of Nehemiah's political enemies were none of these, the convergence of the processions on the Temple area gave him occasion for ostentatiously "exorcising" or reconsecrating the sacristies occupied by "the foreigner" (vv 3 and 28): rooms in part identical with the "stations" assigned within the Temple as lodging for the Levites. **7.** *Eliashib:* He let Tobiah occupy the tithe room, and was the high priest according to some commentators (denied by Rudolph). Presumably the octogenarian priest may not have noticed what tenants were receiving his nominal approval; but the compiler's report is from 100 years later.

114   **(D) Nehemiah as Defender of the Faith (13:15–30).** Glowing with the success of those religious purges occasioned by his architectural and political interests, Nehemiah now frankly busies himself with cult. His opposition to mixed marriages was doubtless due also to outsiders' using them to strengthen a political position (W. Vischer, "Nehemia" [→ 106 above] 604, following Alt; Ackroyd [*JSOT* 2 (1977) 14] notes that "non-Ezra traditions of the foreign-marriage theme" are here incorporated wih unrelated materials). Like many amateurs, Nehemiah as marriage reformer seems unaware of the profound values of human freedom enshrined in the odd-sounding *odiosa sunt restringenda* ("laws must be applied in favor of the one whose freedom they impede"). Loopholes in good laws will always be misused by evil people, but the effort to close them results progressively in an iron juridicalism (v 24). **23.** Massive silence about the enthusiastic public measures taken under Ezra (10:10) to cope with mixed marriages is taken by defenders of the traditional 458 (or even 428) dating of Ezra as a sign that those efforts had been a fiasco. For this there is no evidence, and it is equally possible to suppose that the reform of Ezra had simply not yet happened. The argument cuts both ways: in Ezra's reform too there is no mention of that of Nehemiah. But Ezra as a priest and scribe possessed the competent authority in this matter, and Nehemiah did not. As noted on Ezra 9:2, it is not clear that he extended the ban beyond priests' marriages. The passages in Exod 34:16; Deut 7:3 which seem to prohibit *any* mixed marriages are in a setting and motivation excluding only those marriages which involve anti-Yahwist political entanglements. And Deut 21:13 explicitly approves marriage with enemy foreigners devoid of influence or religious rights. We should not forget that Joseph, Moses, and David had foreign wives, and from the less-tolerated examples of Solomon and Ahab we might conclude that the forbidden mixed marriages were only those which furnished proximate occasion of idolatry. The self-protecting or centripetal character of any religious covenant is as such hostile to seeking a marriage partner in an out-group; but the centrifugal or diffusive character of religious conviction finds in marriage alliances a most potent vehicle. In any given situation, the existing authority may and must decide to what extent ghetto restrictions are called for.

24. *Ashdodite:* "Half-breed" in Zech 9:6 may be a synonym of "bastard" (*mamzēr*, Deut 23:3; S. Feigin, *AJSL* 43 [1926] 59). **25.** Nehemiah's mere guarded threat of physical violence in v 21 proved so effective that he here resorts to the real thing. **28.** His zeal and the picturesque extroversion of his manhandling are partly due to resentment against Tobiah's political support within what is after all the undying achievement of Nehemiah—the wall of Jerusalem.

115   **(E) A Spirituality of the Exilic Histories.** Since Williamson's 1985 commentary in WBC though denying Ezra to the Chronicles author emphasizes that their spiritual atmosphere is the same, we may fittingly conclude by integrating into his survey our own proposals. He rightly rejects subsuming chance references of these books into an existing systematized religiosity; but against the prevailing trend (and our own) to gather up the relevant themes into categories of the books themselves, he prefers emphasizing "the narrative approach." This means partly that with Childs he favors taking the message of the books as they stand rather than assigning them to the presumed background of their sources; at any rate "events are now judged [not with a view to their chronology or cause-and-effect, but] by their theological significance; it is at this level, the level of divine causality, that continuity is to be perceived" (p. xlix).

Nehemiah's frequent "God remember me for good" (5:19; 13:14; W. Schottroff, *Gedenken* [WMANT 15; Neukirchen, 1967] 218) may be seen as a personalized application of the basically correct Chronicles' view that a good clean dutiful life normally brings health and thus prosperity; there are many exceptions or delays, as in Job, so that we must regard as poetic or ideal some Chronicles' "examples" of a very short-range retribution. God's will comes to us normally through those fellow humans who have some special competence or authority; and this is legitimated in all our books by frequent *lists*, in part genealogical; some such justification of authority is very needful, even though in our time it is supplied by democratic procedures which sometimes alas seem just as chaotic. Authority embodied in titanic figures of the past like David and Solomon (and to some extent continuing from them down into the present) is seen in the Ezra books as transferred in part to the Persian and other overlords; no authority is perfect, but the one which *exists* must be taken as starting point of our striving to fulfill God's plan for us; though not in such a closed way as to exclude eschatologically or even politically messianic action when the need becomes so great.

Noble projects of religion or defense require a tightly united community, but in this ideal can often be glimpsed the danger of undue severity in excluding others suitably qualified for sharing in our religious or community

benefits. The community has especially a just concern that its marriages be with partners who share appropriate cultural backgrounds, above all the religion which is accepted as sovereign; but here again the praiseworthy intentions of the Ezra books reveal also the danger of unfairness to partners in good faith. Curiously Williamson finds that resistance to out-groups was not so strong in the Nehemiah-style returnees as in the Judah "people of the land."

Prominent in these books is the leadership of human beings, whether the lofty remote David and Solomon of Chr or the next-door-neighbor type we see in Ezra and Nehemiah, who gave of themselves and their talents for the needs of God's people, even while recognizing "the defects of their virtues" which would arouse opposition or leave an example not to be imitated. It remains a mystery why Ezra was never admitted at the side of Nehemiah in Sir 49:13. The piety shown in the "levitical sermons of Chronicles" becomes a spirit of constant prayer esp. in Nehemiah ("God remember me for good"); the more public prayer of Ezra (9:6–15) and (? also) of Neh 9:6–37 shows many insights into the community's sense of liturgy and of law. All in all, these last two books afford a helpful spiritual reading for "times of change" not unlike theirs.

24

JOEL
OBADIAH

Elias D. Mallon

JOEL

BIBLIOGRAPHY

1 Allen, L. D., *The Books of Joel, Obadiah and Micah* (NICOT; GR, 1976). Ahlström, G. W., *Joel and the Temple Cult* (VTSup 21; Leiden, 1971). Bourke, J., "Le jour de Yahvé dans Joël," *RB* 66 (1959) 191–212. Deissler, A., *Zwölf Propheten Hosea, Joël, Amos* (NEchtB; Würzburg, 1981). Myers, J. M., "Some Considerations Bearing on the Date of Joel," *ZAW* 74 (1962) 177–95. Prinsloo, W. S., *The Theology of the Book of Joel* (BZAW 163; Berlin, 1985). Rudolph, W., *Joel, Amos, Obadja, Jona* (KAT 13/2; Gütersloh, 1971). Thompson, J. A., "The Date of Joel," *Old Testament Studies* (Fest. J. M. Myers; ed. H. N. Bream, *et al.;* Phl, 1974); "Joel's Locusts in the Light of Near Eastern Parallels," *JNES* 14 (1955) 52–55. Weiser, A., *Die Propheten Hosea, Joel, Amos, Obadja, Micha* (ATD 24; Göttingen, 1979). Wolff, H. W., *Joel and Amos* (Herm; Phl, 1977).

INTRODUCTION

2 **(I) Author.** The superscription attributes the book to a man named Joel ben Pethuel. The name *yô'ēl* means "Yô (a shortened form of Yahweh) is God." Although one of David's sons is named Joel (1 Sam 8:2), the name appears most often in the later book of Chronicles. A dialectal form of Joel's patronym may appear in Gen 22:23; 24:15,24,47; 1 Chr 4:30. However, the author of the book is not mentioned elsewhere in the OT. Unlike the case with names such as Malachi and Qoheleth, there is no need to see the name as anything other than a genuine personal name.

As is typical for most biblical books, no biographical information is given about the author. The text makes it clear, however, that Joel had a deep appreciation for the worship conducted in the Temple (1:8–9; 2:27; 4:16–17). The book contains cultic terms such as vegetable offering and libation (*minḥâ, nesek*), fast and solemn assembly (1:14; 2:12,15). Temple personnel such as priests (1:9,13; 2:17), ministers of Yahweh (1:9; 2:17), ministers of the altar (1:13), and "ministers of my God" (1:13) appear. The appreciation for the cult and the use of cultic terms have led some to believe that Joel was a cultic prophet (see A. R. Johnson, *The Cultic Prophet* [Cardiff, 1962] 74–75; J. Lindblom, *Prophecy in Ancient Israel* [Phl, 1962] 277; and J. Chary, *Les prophètes et le culte* [Paris, 1955] 211 n. 4). This may be deducing more than the text can bear. It is not at all certain that cultic prophets existed (see de Vaux, *AI* 384–85), and appreciation for the cult does not necessarily make one a cultic functionary.

3 **(II) Date.** Joel is one of the six books within the "Twelve Prophets" (Minor Prophets) which does not have a synchronology in its superscription. The date of the book must be deduced from criteria within the text itself. There is probably a greater scholarly divergence concerning the date of Joel than there is concerning the date of any other biblical book. A minority position would situate Joel in the reign of Joash (837–800) (see M. Bič, *Das Buch Joel* [Berlin, 1960]). The majority of scholars places the book in the postexilic period, although there is considerable divergence as to whether an early or a late context best fits the book. The reasons for a postexilic date are compelling. Nowhere in Joel is mention made of a king or a royal court. This despite the fact that all classes of people from priests to elders, from infants to brides are invited to the lament in 2:16–17. In times of emergency it was the king who represented the people before God (2 Sam 21:1; 2 Kgs 6:30). Joel must have been written during a time when the monarchy no longer existed. The people and rulers of the Neo-Babylonian Empire are also never mentioned, although it was they who brought the kingdom of David to an end and destroyed the Temple in 587. We assume, therefore, that they had already been conquered by the Persians (539) at the time Joel was written. Since the Temple plays an important role in the book, Joel must have been written after 515 when the Temple was rebuilt. With the year 515 we have a *terminus post quem* for Joel. Since Tyre and Sidon are still in existence as cities to be punished (4:4), we are able to set a *terminus ante quem* in the latter half of the 4th cent. Tyre was destroyed by Alexander the Great in 332 and Sidon by Artaxerxes III Ochus in 343. Greater precision involves more conjecture. Wolff sees a reference to the walls of Jerusalem in 2:7,9. Since these were rebuilt by Nehemiah in 445, Wolff sees this date as a *terminus post quem* for the book. While a date after the time of Nehemiah is likely, it cannot be deduced from Joel 2:7,9 for two reasons: first, it is likely that there was already at least a partial wall around Jerusalem before the time of Nehemiah (Ahlström, *Joel* 115); and, second, there is no indication that 2:7,9 are intended as literal references to the city walls of Jerusalem. If the book is to be dated after the times of Nehemiah, it is because the cultic reforms of Ezra-Neh seem already to have taken place at the time Joel was written. This is indicated by the fact that Joel does not mention any cultic abuses. In addition to Joel's cultic concerns, his anti-foreign tone is reminiscent of the period of Ezra-Neh and later.

There are also points of contact between Joel and postexilic prophetic works. Joel 2:11 is similar to Mal 3:2, although the similarity is not striking. Joel 3:4b is identical to Mal 3:23b and Joel 3:5bα is very likely a citation of Obad 17aα (*pace* Rudolph, *Joel* 73 n. 16). One can also compare Joel 4:2–3 with Obad 11 and Joel 4:19 with Obad 10. All of this indicates that Joel would have been written after Obad and Mal (5th cent.). In summation we may say that it is clear that the book was written after the rebuilding of the Temple in 515 and before the destruction of Sidon in 343, and after the time of Obad and Mal. A date between the last half of the 5th and the first half of the 4th cent. seems best to fit the context.

4   (III) Unity, Structure, and Purpose. As almost every commentary has noticed, the book easily falls into two large sections. The first (chaps. 1–2), differently divided by scholars, deals with the locust plague and drought. The second (chaps. 3–4) is often termed "eschatological." Several scholars are of the opinion that the differences between the two sections are such as to require more than one author (B. Duhm, *ZAW* 31 [1911] 1–43, 184–88; J. A. Bewer, *Obadiah and Joel* [ICC; Edinburgh, 1911] 56). Other scholars question the relationship between the different parts of the book. Wolff (*Joel* 6) holds that the locust plague does not form the theme of chap. 2, although both form a prophecy rooted in its own time. Chapters 3–4 are a "purely eschatological message" (p. 7). J. Lindblom (*Prophecy* 277) sees chaps. 3–4 as purely eschatological prophecies "which have no direct connection with the foregoing" but were nonetheless written by Joel.

A closer examination of the text obviates the need for such radical division. Although 4:4–8 is generally accepted as an addition, the book develops its theme in such a way as to indicate that it is a theological and artistic unit. Wolff (*Joel* 8) has shown that many of the catchwords and word groups of chaps. 1–2 are repeated in chaps. 3–4 and has thereby indicated a strong semantic unity in the text.

It is, however, in terms of the style and theme that the book is most clearly seen to be a unity. Starting with a locust plague and drought, Joel develops a theme of reversal of fortunes. Chapters 1–2 deal with the immediate crisis of the locusts and drought; chap. 1 presents the effects which the locusts have on the countryside and the crops. This has a direct effect on the worship in the Temple. The people who are immediately effected—harvesters, farmers, and cultic personnel—are called to lament. In chap. 2 Joel uses the metaphor of an army to describe the effects of the locusts on the city. Using the

merism of city-countryside Joel underlines the totality of the destruction. Now everyone is called to lament. Using metaphor and hyperbole of the Day of Yahweh, Joel dramatizes the extent of the catastrophe.

Most commentators see 2:18 as a pivotal point in the book. Israel has reached the nadir of its misery; all the population is lamenting. Yahweh, however, has mercy and the plague and drought are lifted. Yahweh's gracious act has a double effect. Israel recognizes that Yahweh is in its midst (2:27). The relief from the specific plague initiates a far broader "reversal of fortune" (4:1). Chapter 3 describes the immediate effects of Yahweh's presence in Israel. The cosmic imagery of the Day of Yahweh is once again employed. This day can operate as an image for the destruction or the vindication of Israel. In Joel it does both, using often the same vocabulary. In chaps. 1–2 the devastation was so great as to be described as a destructive day with darkening of sun, moon, etc. (2:10). However, with the recognition of Yahweh's presence and the reversal of fortune, there is a reversal of imagery. Now the day is one of vindication for Israel and judgment of the nations, also with concomitant astronomical phenomena (3:4). Relief from the drought and locusts results in Israel recognizing that Yahweh is in its midst (2:27). The complete reversal of fortune in which Israel is restored and the nations are judged also results in Israel recognizing Yahweh's saving presence (4:17).

Theologically the message is one of hope built on experience. The devastation visited upon Israel by the locusts and drought was immense. However, if Yahweh responded to Israel's heartfelt lament and removed this particular disaster, it was a sign that Yahweh had not abandoned his people; God was still in their midst. Armed with that conviction, there was every reason for them to hope that the reversal of fortune brought about by the end of the locust plague and drought would continue and bring the final vindication of Israel. While it is clear that Joel has used a great deal of previously existing material, it has been thoroughly reworked, and the book presents a stylistic and theological unity.

5   (IV) Outline. The work may be outlined thus:

COMMENTARY

6 **(I) The Locust Plague (1:1–2:17).** The devastating plague of locusts, together with a drought, provide the occasion for Joel's oracle. The movement is from description of the actual plague, to the hyperbolic metaphor of an attacking army, to the Day of Yahweh and its consequences for Israel and Israel's neighbors. A liturgical setting cannot be excluded as the *Sitz im Leben* of the book.

7 **(A) The Attack on the Countryside (1:1–20).** (a) IMMEDIATE EFFECTS (1:1–4). **1.** The LXX, Vg, and Pesh have the patronym Bethuel, a name that occurs also in Gen 22:23; 24:15,24,47; 1 Chr 4:30. Shifts between the voiced labial /b/ and the unvoiced labial /p/ are not unheard-of in Northwest Semitic languages. In any case, the name Joel ben Pethuel does not appear elsewhere. **2.** The oracle opens with a traditional call for attention (see Hos 5:1; Amos 3:1; Deut 32:1). **3.** The first of Joel's literary reversals. In underlining the unprecedented devastation by the locusts, Joel uses the expression "recount it to your children." The "recounting" of fathers to their children or to later generations is relatively common in the OT. However, in the vast majority of instances what is being recounted is positive: Yahweh's praise, his wonderful acts, etc. (Judg 6:13; Exod 10:2; Ps 44:2; and esp. Ps 78:3,6). What is recounted here is unheard-of devastation. **4.** The locusts are described as "cutter" (*gāzām*), "locust" (*'arbeh*), "hopper" (*yeleq*), and "stripper" (*ḥāsîl*). For the etymology of the different terms and their relationship to the different growth stages of the insect, see O. R. Sellers, *AJSL* 52 (1936) 81–85. The order of the words in v 4 probably does not follow the natural order of appearance, since the generic word "locust" appears in the second place. A more natural order may be found in 2:25. A locust plague which afflicted Palestine beginning in late February 1915 is vividly described with photographs by J. D. Whiting (*NatGeog* 28 [1915] 511–50). Three stages are described: wingless larva, pupa with developing wings, and the flying adult. The destruction wreaked by a locust plague was total and proverbial (Judg 6:5; 7:12; Ps 105:34–35).

8 (b) CALLS TO LAMENT (1:5–14). (i) *"Wake up, drunkards!"* (1:5–7). **5.** Drunkards and winebibbers form an odd opening in a list that will include priests, ministers of the altar, farmers, and viticulturists. Although drunkards are treated very negatively as symbols of loss of control or as recipients of Yahweh's wrath (Isa 19:14; 24:20 [the earth]; 28:1,3; Jer 23:9), there does not seem to be any opprobrium here. Perhaps the plague took place during or just before Sukkoth, the festival of the harvesting and pressing of the grapes and a time of high-spirited revelry (see de Vaux, *AI* 496; Deut 16:13–16; *m. Sukk.* 5:4). The destruction brought by the locusts would certainly have eliminated the grapes. Instead of the normal joy and revelry of the harvest, there will be weeping and wailing. There has been some attempt (A. Kapelrud) to connect the mourning with Canaanite cults of Baal. In these cults the worshipers lamented the death/absence of the god Baal, who was responsible for fertility. The mourning may have been accompanied by orgiastic rites. There is no indication, however, that Joel is referring to such practices here. **6.** The insects are compared to a people (*gôy*), a metaphor that will be intensified in 2:4–9, where the people becomes an army. The locusts are without number (*mispār*), echoing the command to "recount"

(*sappēr*) the event in v 3. With ability to eat even tree shoots, the locusts have the teeth of lions and molars like lionesses. In the plague of 1915 the locusts ate the bark from the tender shoots of the fig trees. These denuded tips blanched in the sun (Whiting, *NatGeog* 28 [1915] 544). Joel gives a realistic description of similar damage.

9 (ii) *"Wail!"* (1:8–10). **8.** The call to lament is repeated. The mourning is to have all the poignancy of a young bride who has lost her husband. The use of the word *ba'al* for husband indicates the lack of the normal polemic, in which *bōšet*, "stink," is substituted for the word *ba'al* (contrast 2 Sam 11:21 with Judg 6:32; 2 Sam 2:8 with 1 Chr 8:33). It is the priests who are to mourn like young widows. The extravagance of the simile underlines the extent of the tragedy. The *minḥâ* and the *nesek* are no longer possible because of lack of provisions. The *minḥâ* was a grain or vegetable offering which is described in detail in Lev 2. Consisting of flour, baked and unbaked, first fruits and grain, it was often accompanied by a *nesek* or wine libation. Joel stresses the agricultural offerings since it is these which are most immediately effected by the locusts. The interruption of the cult is a major tragedy for the people; a main point of contact with God has been eliminated. Appropriately the priests and ministers of the Temple mourn the national tragedy. As if in sympathy, the earth itself mourns (*'ābēlâ 'ădāmâ*) with the priests (*'ābēlû hakkōhănîm*). Three agricultural products, often used in the context of blessing (Deut 7:13; 28:51; etc.), are destroyed: grain, new wine, oil. The lines are characterized by chiastic sound patterns (*hôbîš tîrôš*), assonance (*'āṣê haśśādeh yābēšû*) and alliteration (*šuddad śādeh 'ābēlâ 'ădāmâ*). The artistry with which the lines were composed heightens the sense of tragedy by giving a sonorous note to the poem.

10 (iii) *"Be ashamed, farmers!"* (1:11–12). The call to lament moves from the priests and the cult to the people most immediately effected by the locust plague—the farmers. The poet artfully connects the two occupations (see also Isa 61:5; 2 Chr 26:10) by the repetition of the letters *kaph*, *resh*, and *mem* (*'ikkārîm*, "farmers;" *kōrĕmîm*, "viticulturists"). The products proper to both occupations are then listed as objects of lament. Grain and the harvest of the field are mourned by the farmer; the vine, fruit trees, and their produce are mourned by the viticulturist. **12.** Not only do the locusts cause the vegetation to wither and the land (*'ădāmâ*) to mourn; they cause joy itself to wither from among the "children of man (*'ādām*).

11 (iv) *"Gird yourselves, priests!"* (1:13–14). The prophet returns to the priests who were mentioned in v 9. The traditional mourning rites—wearing sackcloth, fasting (see Jonah 3:7–8; etc.), holding a solemn assembly—are to be initiated at the Temple.

12 (c) LAMENT FOR "THE DAY" (1:15–18). **15.** In traditional fashion the lament begins with an exclamation of grief (Josh 7:7; Jer 4:10; etc.). The expression is used to convey dismay, confusion, and grief. For the first time in the book we come upon the expression "the Day of Yahweh." Although this may have had joyful connotations at one time in Israel's history (Amos 5:18), by the time of Joel it had taken on ominous overtones of cosmic upheaval. For Joel the day means "destruction from Shadday" (*šod miššaday;* cf. also Isa 13:6), echoing the phrase of v 10 *šuddad śādeh*, "devastated is the field."

The extent of the destruction is recited in the lament. Not only the agricultural products (with the effect of their loss upon the cult), but food has now been cut off. By finally referring to food the prophet underlines the human dimension of the disaster. Not only is the cult curtailed; people will starve. And not only people; the animals upon which humans depend will also die of starvation (v 18).

13   (d) PRAYER TO YAHWEH (1:19–20).   Not strictly separate from the foregoing section, the prayer of lament turns very personal. After listing the reasons for the lament, the priest turns directly to the source of help: "To you, Yahweh, I cry out." Here for the first time a drought is also mentioned and aptly described as a fire devouring the fields. All sentient creation, human and animal, looks to Yahweh for relief. The expression "fire has devoured the pastures of the steppes" serves as an *inclusio,* or envelope structure, which opens and closes the section (vv 19–20).

14   **(B) The Attack on the City (2:1–17).**   The scene changes from the open country to the city. This is accomplished through a military metaphor. The focus had been on the attack of the locusts on the open fields outside the city. This is certainly natural in that a locust plague would first manifest itself in open country and not in the city. The city, however, could not be spared the onslaught of the overwhelming mass of insects.

15   (a) NARRATIVIZING THE MILITARY METAPHOR (2:1–11).   There is absolutely no reason to see in vv 1–11 a reference to a historical military attack on the city. The expressions used for the "army" are certainly appropriate for locusts. More to the point, the locusts are called "my great army" in 2:25. Although the direction of the metaphor is different, the Ugaritic poem *Keret* compares King Keret's army to locusts in *Krt* 103–4, 192–3. **1.** *blow the shofar in Zion!:* The shofar or ram's horn was used for summoning troops into battle and for warning of approaching attackers. The summons to blow the shofar is often used in the prophets as a prelude for an account of an attack (Jer 4:5; 6:1; 51:27; Hos 5:8). **2.** *a day of darkness and gloom:* The prophet has just mentioned the Day of Yahweh and now uses four words for darkness which often appear in cosmic contexts (Zeph 1:15b). Witnesses, however, speak of locust clouds literally blocking out the light of the sun. Here, as often in the book, a realistic description supports a hyperbolic metaphor. **2b.** *like dawn spread out on the mountains is this great and powerful horde:* The word for dawn, *šaḥar,* is very similar to the word for black, *šāḥōr.* Perhaps the poet intended that. As dawn spreads on the hills, so too the insects spread out over the landscape. But unlike the red of dawn, the insect horde is dark and black. **3b.** *before them it was like Eden; after them it is a desolate waste:* Joel reverses the imagery of Isa 51:3. Reversal of imagery, which is important for Joel, also occurs in 4:10 where Isa 2:4 and Mic 4:3 are reversed. **4–5.** Job 39:20 compares a horse to locusts in that both leap. Whiting writes of the very ground seeming to quiver with the seething mass of insects. The sound of the locusts is compared to the roar of chariots or the sound of burning stubble; v 5aβ provides an onomatopoeic representation of the crackling sound of the fire. **7–9.** The attack on the city intensifies; there is no stopping the attackers. Photographs of the plague of 1915 show the locusts covering the walls of the Tower of David and of the American Consulate. The imagery is once again both realistic and metaphoric. To use the reference to the insect soldiers scaling the walls as a means of dating the book simply does not take the artistry of Joel into account. **10.** Once again a realistic representation is intensified. The earth seems to

be moving under the mass of the insects; when they take to the air, the sun, moon, and stars cannot be seen. However, the prophet is more than reporting since his imagery moves toward the cosmic description of the Day of Yahweh (see Isa 13:10).

16   (b) CALLS TO REPENT (2:12–17). **12–13.** When the situation is literally darkest, Yahweh calls the people to repentance. They are to fast (see 1:14), with weeping and mourning (see 1:5,13). Nowhere does Joel indicate disapproval of the cult. Hence, the call for interiority — "rend your hearts and not (just) your garments" — must be seen as an intensification of what Joel has already called for in chap. 1. The litany of God's qualities in v 13b appears in slightly different formulations in Exod 34:6; Num 14:18; Nah 1:3; Pss 86:15; 103:8; 145:8; and Neh 9:17. The same formula appears in Jonah 4:2. **14.** The hoped-for result of the repentance is that perhaps Yahweh will act according to the characteristics listed. The prophet underscores the sovereign freedom of Yahweh (see Amos 5:15; Jonah 3:9; Zeph 2:3). There is a play on the word *šûb,* "turn," "repent." Twice the people are called to "repent" (vv 12, 13). Then Yahweh may "turn" and have mercy. Although Yahweh is free and cannot be manipulated by the cult, his response is not disconnected from the actions of the people. The people hope for a blessing. Deut 7:13–14 describes Yahweh's blessing in terms of the agricultural, pastoral, and personal fertility which was so important in ancient Israel. With the restored fertility, the *minḥâ* and the *nesek,* tragically interrupted (1:9,13), will be reinstated. **15–17.** *blow the shofar:* The shofar was used not only in military settings (2:1) but also in the cult (Lev 25:9; Pss 81:4; 150:3; etc.; *m. Pesaḥ.* 5:5; *m. Sukk.* 4:5; etc.). The shofar blast now heralds the cultic observance which will bring Yahweh's relief. The calls to fast and to hold an assembly are identical to those of 1:14. However, the earlier call was to summon the priests and inhabitants of the land. In this summons the participants are listed in detail. There is a merism connecting the elders with the infants, nursing at the breast. Even the bride and bridegroom are called to join the penance ceremony. **17.** Often in laments the sufferer complains that his adversaries ask him where God is (Pss 42:4,11; 79:10; Mic 7:10; Mal 2:17).

17   **(II) The Plague Interpreted (2:18–4:21).** The locust plague and drought and their end are interpreted for Israel's future.

         (A) The End of the Plague and the Restoration (2:18–26). 18. A pivotal point in the book has been reached. Yahweh answers the prayer of his people. The "grain, new wine, and oil" which the locusts destroyed (1:10) will be restored. **20.** *I will remove the "Northerner" far from you:* The north is the direction from which trouble traditionally and historically came to Israel (Jer 1:13–16; 4:6; etc.). In his description of the locust plague of 1915 Whiting notes that the insects moved NE to SW. A realistic description, however, does not exclude the use of the traditional motif of the invader from the north. **20.** *the eastern sea . . . the western sea:* The Dead Sea and the Mediterranean; the expression occurs only here and Zech 14:8. *stink . . . stench:* Whiting mentions the unpleasant smell arising from the mass of dead locusts. **23.** *and he will give you a "teacher" for righteousness and he will cause the rain to fall on you:* The word for teacher here is *môreh.* The meaning of the text is quite problematic. The difficulties have been compounded by the presence of a "Teacher of Righteousness" in the so-called Dead Sea Scrolls (CD 1:5–12; 1QpHab 1:13; 5:10; etc.). However, the expressions here and at Qumran are not exactly the same. In addition, there is the homograph *môreh,* which means "early rain" and would fit the present context. Nonetheless, note the connection between rain, justice, and teaching in Isa 30:19-26; 1 Kgs 8:35-36; 2 Chr 6:26-27.

18   (B) The Purpose of the Plague (2:27). The removal of the locusts and the alleviation of the drought are not merely inevitable phenomena in the rhythm of nature. They are saving acts of Yahweh and "proof" that Yahweh is in the midst of Israel as a savior.

19   (C) The Effects of Yahweh's Presence in the Midst of Israel (3:1-4:21). The implications of the salvation from the plague and drought and the implications of the recognition that Yahweh is in the midst of Israel are profound for Israel's present and future.

20   (a) COSMIC, "PNEUMATIC" EFFECTS ON ISRAEL (3:1-5 [= 2:28-32 in many Eng versions]). **1.** The presence of Yahweh brings with it a charismatic outpouring of the spirit of God. The universal outpouring is reminiscent of Num 11:24-30 where Moses prayed that Yahweh give everyone the spirit. As such God's spirit brings life (Ps 104:29-30) and ecstatic experience (Num 11:24-30; 1 Sam 10:10; etc.). An outpouring of Yahweh's spirit is also found in Isa 32:15 and 44:3-5. **4.** Not only are the insects removed; there are also signs in the heavens. The astronomical effects of the locusts are now taken over by Yahweh in his power. The ominous Day of Yahweh has become a day of vindication for Israel.

21   (b) REVERSAL OF FORTUNE (4:1-21 [= 3:1-21 in many Eng versions]). Israel's situation is now reversed. The locusts are gone; the drought has ended; now Yahweh will perform even greater wonders.

          (i) *Judgment of the nations in the Valley of Jehoshaphat* (4:1-3). **2.** *Valley of Jehoshaphat:* A play on the name Jehoshaphat, which means "Yahweh has judged." Ahlström (*Joel* 80) believes that Joel is referring here to the Kidron Valley, where idols were ritually destroyed (2 Chr 29:16). It is, however, possible that Joel had no specific place in mind. **3.** In the trial Yahweh, as judge and prosecutor, will avenge the sufferings which the nations have inflicted upon Israel.

22   (ii) *Additional oracle against Tyre, Sidon, and Philistia* (4:4-8). The section is somewhat alien to the whole in that it lists specific people who will be punished. Yahweh has identified himself with the sufferings of Israel and is now going to punish the nations of the Levant. Tyre and Sidon were coastal cities and engaged in trade. An important commodity of trade was slaves, and the Phoenicians traded enslaved Israelites to the Greeks to the northwest. Once again Yahweh will bring a reversal. The slaves will return and their sellers will be sold to the Sabeans, a people to the southeast.

23   (iii) *War against the nations* (4:9-11). The theme of vv 1-3 is taken up again. **10.** *beat your ploughshares into swords, your pruning knives into spears:* As

he has done before, Joel reverses an image here. The peaceful citations of Isa 2:4 and Mic 4:3 are turned into a call for war. It is a total war in which even the weakling fights, believing himself to be a warrior. **11.** *bring down your warrior, Yahweh:* All indications are that this is a later addition to the text. Perhaps it was a pious marginal note which has become incorporated into the text.

24   (iv) *Judgment of nations in the Valley of Jehoshaphat* (4:12-17). This is a continuation of the call to war. The final encounter is to take place in the Valley of Jehoshaphat. **13.** Joel uses agricultural imagery (sickle) to describe Yahweh's punishment of the nations. The winepress, as a metaphor for punishment, is found in Isa 63:1-6. **14.** The agricultural imagery allows Joel to speak of the valley of *ḥārûṣ,* "decision." The word *ḥārûṣ* refers to a threshing sled (Amos 1:3) and continues the agricultural imagery, but it can also mean judgment (1 Kgs 20:40). Clearly the prophet intends both meanings. For Joel the Day of Yahweh has meant punishment but ultimate salvation for Israel; now with a reverse of fortunes it means the total destruction of the nations. It is accompanied by the traditional cosmic, astronomical phenomena (2:10; 3:4). **16.** Yahweh's roaring is an image of power (Jer 25:30; Amos 1:2) which shakes the very heavens and earth. **17.** The purpose of the locust plague was to convince Israel that Yahweh was in its midst as savior (2:27). That recognition opened the way for Yahweh to wreak vengeance on the nations, which has the same purpose: Israel will recognize that Yahweh is God in its midst. Jerusalem recovers its former inviolability (Ps 125:1; Isa 2:2-5). The aftermath of the events of 587 is undone, and foreigners will no longer enter Jerusalem, much less rule it.

25   (v) *Judah and Jerusalem compared with Edom and Egypt* (4:18-21). The theme of Israel's vindication is further developed in what may have been a later addition. Egypt, as archetype of the oppressor, and Edom, as archetype of the treacherous brother (Obad; Amos 1:11-12), are compared to Israel. **18.** The agricultural fertility of the land, so dependent on water, will be excessive. The springs will never dry up (Job 6:15-20; Jer 15:18). A stream will flow out of the Temple (see Ezek 47:1-12; Zech 14:8) as rivers flowed out of Eden (Gen 2:10-14). **19.** The waters of the Nile, Egypt's source of water and fertility, will dry up. Edom will become uninhabited steppes. **21.** *Yahweh is dwelling in Zion:* The theme of Yahweh's presence closes the book. Throughout the locust plague, drought, and lament, Joel has firmly held that Yahweh is in the midst of Israel. With relief from the plague and the drought, Israel recognized Yahweh's presence. Joel then further developed the full import of that presence, namely, a complete reversal of fortune. At the end of the dramatic description of that reversal, Joel closes with a reaffirmation that Yahweh, the savior, dwells in Zion.

OBADIAH

BIBLIOGRAPHY

26   Allen, L. D., *The Books of Joel, Obadiah and Micah* (NICOT; GR, 1976). Deissler, A., *Zwölf Propheten II Obadja, Jona, Micha, Nahum, Habakuk* (NEchtB; Würzburg, 1984). Fohrer, G., "Die Sprüche Obadjas," *Studien zu alttestamentlichen Texten und Themen (1966-1972)* (BZAW 155; Giessen, 1981) 69-81. McCarter, P. K., "Obadiah 7 and the Fall of Edom,"

BASOR 221 (1977) 484-87. Myers, J. M., "Edom and Judah in the Sixth-Fifth Centuries B.C.," *Near Eastern Studies* (Fest. Albright; Baltimore, 1971) 377-92. Rudolph, W., *Joel, Amos, Obadja, Jona* (KAT 13/2; Gütersloh, 1971). Watts, J. D. W., *Obadiah* (GR, 1969). Weiser, A., *Die Propheten Hosea, Joel, Amos, Obadja, Jona, Micha* (ATD 24; Göttingen, 1979).

INTRODUCTION

27   (I) Background and Date. The Hebrew Bible recognizes bonds of kinship between Edom and Judah, tracing the bloodlines to Esau and Jacob (Gen 25:19-26). The relationship between the two peoples—as the oracle in Gen 25:23 suggests—was hardly fraternal. During the exodus Edom refused passage to the Israelites (Num 20:14-21). Although Israel was explicitly instructed not to attack Edom or annex Edomite land in Deut 2:2-8, David made Edom a part of his empire (2 Sam 8:13 [with LXX] and 1 Chr 18:12-13). Joab, David's general, engaged in a campaign of genocide against Edom (1 Kgs 11:15-16) but Hadad, a member of the Edomite royal family, escaped to return later and to rebel against Solomon's rule (1 Kgs 11:25b [with LXX]). During the period of the monarchy, Judah and Edom seem to have been in constant conflict, with Edom sometimes free, sometimes under the hegemony of Judah. Jehoshaphat seems to have been in control of Edom and the port city on the Gulf of Aqabah (1 Kgs 22:49). This control was lost in the next generation when Edom revolted against Jehoram (2 Kgs 8:20-22). During the 8th cent. Edom was under the control of Amaziah (2 Kgs 14:7) and Uzziah (2 Kgs 14:22).

During the last days of Judah, Edom was involved in a plot against the Neo-Babylonian Empire. Jer 27 reflects an attempted coalition between Judah, Edom,

Moab, Ammon, Tyre, and Sidon against Babylon. The outcome was disastrous. Jerusalem and Judah were destroyed. Josephus mentions the subjugation of Ammon and Moab (*Ant.* 10.9.7 §*181-82*) but does not mention an attack against Edom. Lam 4:21-22 singles out Edom for its sins and crimes while 1 Esdr 4:45 accuses Edom of burning the Temple. While it is not certain that Edom actively took part in the destruction of Jerusalem, its treachery in the aftermath embittered Judah and is the memory behind Obadiah's oracle and Ps 137:7.

The destruction of Jerusalem in 587 can be taken as the *terminus post quem* for the book. The conquest of Edomite territory by the Nabateans, which was completed by at least 312 (see Diodorus Siculus 2.48; 19:94-98; Mal 1:2-5; Neh 2:19; 6:1ff.), is the *terminus ante quem*. However, as early as the 5th cent. Edom had been expelled from its lands across the Jordan. It is during this period that the main oracle of Obad was most likely written. A slightly later period is reflected in vv 15a,16-21.

28   (IV) Outline. The work may be outlined thus:

(I) Oracle against Edom (1-14,15b)
    (A) Edom Is Doomed (1-9)
    (B) Reasons for Edom's Destruction (10-14,15b)
(II) Day of Yahweh, Punishment of Nations (15a,16-21)

COMMENTARY

29   (I) Oracle against Edom (1-14,15b). Obadiah's oracle against Edom stands within a long tradition of oracles against foreign nations in general and against Edom in particular. Edom's treachery had evoked oracles of intense bitterness throughout Israel's history (Amos 1:11-12; Isa 34:5-17; 63:1-6; Jer 49:7-22; Ezek 25:12-14; 35; Mal 1:2-4). Obadiah's oracle against Edom is very similar—in some places identical—to that found in Jer 49. The points of contact are: Obad 1b-4 and Jer 49:14-16; Obad 5 and Jer 49:9; Obad 6 is similar, though not identical, to Jer 49:10a. It is probably that both Obad and Jer used and adapted an already existing oracle. Rudolph (*Joel* 297) and Watts (*Obadiah* 33) hold that the form of the oracle in Obad is earlier but disagree on whether a common source can be posited for both.
30   (A) Edom is Doomed (1-9). 1. *the vision of Obadiah:* In its present context "vision" is to be understood in a broader sense such as "revelation." The word *ḥāzôn* is used also in Isa 1:13; Nah 1:1. Since the subject of "we have heard" cannot be Yahweh, transpose "thus says the Lord Yahweh concerning Edom" to immediately before "Arise! Let us march. . . ." **3.** *you dweller of the rocky crags:* The phrase, which appears also with slight alteration in Jer 49:16b, is an apt one for Edom, which was located in the highlands on the E side of the Dead Sea. The reddish (Hebr *'ĕdôm,* "Edom"; *'ādom,* "red") mountains of Edom, rising higher than 3,500 ft., provided significant military security for the Edomites. The capital of Edom was Sela (Judg 1:36; etc.), a name which means "rock" and which provides a nice instance of paronomasia (the "rock" is both the mountains of Edom and its capital), and of synecdoche (the part, Sela, is used for the whole, Edom; see Albright, *AP* 160-61). **4.** *should you go high as an eagle . . . :* The geological

heights of Edom have encouraged hubris. Images of height are often used to convey a sense of arrogance and false security as is the image of placing one's nest in the heavens or on high (Isa 14:13-14; Jer 49:16; Amos 9:2; Hab 2:9; Ps 139:8). Obadiah stresses that such trust is overweening when confronted with the power of Yahweh. **5.** The imagery of thieves and vintagers is complicated. Both thieves and vintagers leave something behind—vintagers because the law demands it (Lev 19:10; 23:22; Deut 24:21); thieves because they are limited by what they can haul away. If for different reasons thieves and vintagers leave something behind, that will not be the case with Edom. It will be thoroughly plundered. **7.** Historically Edom was driven out of its land by bedouin tribes invading from the E desert, until it finally disappeared from the stage of history (see J. Starcky, *BA* 18 [1955] 84-106; N. Glueck, *HUCA* 11 [1936] 111-57). The punishment is an example of poetic justice. Edom was unfaithful to its ally Judah during the war of 587. Now its allies are unfaithful to Edom, bringing about its destruction. *those who eat your bread . . . :* Although the meaning of these lines is uncertain (cf. G. I. Davies, *VT* 27 [1977] 484-87), the context demands some sense of an ally or friend being treacherous. *there is no understanding in it/him:* A marginal gloss referring to the difficulty in understanding the preceding phrase? **8.** Traditionally Edom was renowned for its wisdom (Job 2:11; Jer 49:7). Neither its geographical position nor its intellectual gifts will be able to save Edom from the destruction to come. **9.** *Teman:* A region of Edom; another example of synecdoche.
31   (B) Reasons for Edom's Destruction (10-14,15b). 10. *[because of the killing] because of the violence against your brother Jacob, shame covers you:* Beginning with

the last word of v 9 the crimes of Edom are listed with a staccato intensity. In quick succession the phrase "on the day" sets the historical context of Edom's crime—the fall of Jerusalem. Eight times the accusations are hurled against Edom. Each one begins with "you should not have. . . ." Seven times the poignancy of Edom's crime is underlined by stressing the miserable and helpless condition of Judah, expressed by the phrase "on the day of Judah's anguish, etc." The impression created is one of an almost breathless anger which contrasts the cruelty of Edom with the misery of Judah in a rapid-fire fashion. **15b.** *just as you did, it will be done to you:* The punishment of Edom will take the form of poetic justice. The evil it has done will recoil on it. It will suffer the same fate as Judah with one difference: Edom will never rise again.

32   (II) Day of Yahweh, Punishment of the Nations (15a,16–21). The cup of Yahweh's wrath is now passed to all the nations. The cup of Yahweh which brings judgment, drunkenness, and disgrace is given to Edom and the other nations also in Jer 25:15–29; 49:12–13; Hab 2:16; and Lam 4:21. With the inclusion of the nations the horizons of the oracle have broadened. The Day of Yahweh is a day of destruction. In the monarchic period the Day of Yahweh was often a threat to Israel (Amos 5:18–20; Isa 2:10–12; Zeph 1:15); in the postexilic period it is a promise of hope and vindication (Isa 63:4; Joel 3:4–4:1). **17.** *but on Mt. Zion there will be*

escape: This also appears in Joel 3:5, where the majority of commentators see it as a citation. Mt. Zion provides security and refuge, whereas there is no such security for Edom, the House/Mt. of Esau (vv 18–19). *it will be holy:* It is difficult to know what will be holy here. Grammatically it appears to be Mt. Zion, which is certainly not impossible. A similar passage in Isa 4:2–3, however, speaks of the refugees, the remnant, being holy. **18.** As in v 10, the house of Jacob refers to Judah, the house of Joseph to Israel (Amos 5:6; 6:6; Zech 10:6; Ezek 37:16, 19; etc.). A reunited kingdom is part of the final victory of Yahweh (Ezek 37:15–28). The imagery of stubble being suddenly and completely consumed by fire is frequent (Exod 15:7; Isa 5:24; 33:11; 47:14; Joel 2:5; Mal 3:19). **19.** Lands which have over the years been lost to conquerors are returned to Israel. The points of the compass are indicated: the Negeb (S), Ephraim (N), Philistia (W), Gilead (E). **20.** The exiled people of Israel were settled in Halah (2 Kgs 17:6; 18:11) by the Assyrians. This district may be mentioned in the difficult phrase at the beginning of v 20 (Rudolph, *Joel* 315). If that is the case, the exiles of both kingdoms will inherit the land from which they have been driven—and more land still. **21.** Mt. Zion, a place of victory, is contrasted with Mt. Esau, a place where Edom will be judged and condemned. Israel's vindication is ultimately the vindication of Yahweh's sovereignty over all (Pss 22:28–29; 103:19).

25

DANIEL

Louis F. Hartman, C.SS.R. †   *Alexander A. Di Lella, O.F.M.* *

BIBLIOGRAPHY

1   *Commentaries:* Anderson, R. A., *Signs and Wonders: A Commentary on the Book of Daniel* (GR, 1984). Bentzen, A., *Daniel* (HAT 1/19; 2d ed.; Tübingen, 1952). Charles, R. H., *The Book of Daniel* (Oxford, 1929). Delcor, M., *Le livre de Daniel* (SB; Paris, 1971). Dennefeld, L., *Les grands prophètes: Daniel* (Paris, 1946). Driver, S. R., *The Book of Daniel* (CBSC; Cambridge, 1900). Engel, H., *Die Susanna-Erzählung* (OBO 61; Freiburg, 1985). Gammie, J. G., *Daniel* (Atlanta, 1983). Goettsberger, J., *Das Buch Daniel* (HSAT 8/2; Bonn, 1928). Hammer, R., *The Book of Daniel* (CBC; Cambridge, 1976). Hartman, L. F. and A. A. Di Lella, *The Book of Daniel* (AB 23; GC, 1978). Heaton, E. W., *The Book of Daniel* (London, 1956). Jeffrey, A., "The Book of Daniel," *IB* (Nash, 1956). Lacocque, A., *The Book of Daniel* (Atlanta, 1979). Montgomery, J. A., *The Book of Daniel* (ICC; NY, 1927). Nötscher, F., *Daniel* (2d ed.; Würzburg, 1958). Plöger, O., *Das Buch Daniel* (KAT 18; Gütersloh, 1965). Porteous, N., *Daniel* (OTL; Phl, 1965). Rinaldi, G., *Daniele* (4th rev. ed.; Turin, 1962). Russell, D. S., *Daniel* (Phl, 1981). Steinmann, J., *Daniel* (Bruges, 1961). Towner, W. S., *Daniel* (IBC; Atlanta, 1984).
    Studies: Baumgartner, W., "Ein Vierteljahrhundert Danielforschung," *TRu* 11 (1939) 59–83, 125–44, 201–28. Casey, M.,

Son of Man: The Interpretation and Influence of Daniel (London, 1979). Collins, J. J., *The Apocalyptic Vision of the Book of Daniel* (HSM 16; Missoula, 1977); "The Court-Tales in Daniel and the Development of Apocalyptic," *JBL* 94 (1975) 218–34; *Daniel, with an Introduction to Apocalyptic Literature* (FOTL 20; GR, 1984). Coppens, J., "Le livre de Daniel et ses problèmes," *ETL* 56 (1980) 1–9. Davies, P. R., "Eschatology in the Book of Daniel," *JSOT* 17 (1980) 33–53. Dexinger, F., *Das Buch Daniel und seine Probleme* (SBS 36; Stuttgart, 1969). Driver, G. R., "The Aramaic of the Book of Daniel," *JBL* 45 (1926) 110–19. Gammie, J. G., "On the Intention and Sources of Daniel i–vi," *VT* 31 (1981) 282–92. Ginsberg, H. L., *Studies in Daniel* (NY, 1948); "The Composition of the Book of Daniel," *VT* 4 (1954) 246–75. Good, E. M., "Apocalyptic as Comedy: The Book of Daniel," *Semeia* 32 (1984) 41–70. Koch, K., "Is Daniel Also among the Prophets?" *Int* 39 (1985) 117–30; with Till Niewisch and J. Tubach, *Das Buch Daniel* (ErF 144; Darmstadt, 1980). Mertens, A., *Das Buch Daniel im Lichte der Texte vom Toten Meer* (SBM 12; Stuttgart, 1971). Milik, J. T., "Daniel et Susanne à Qumrân?" *De la Tôrah au Messie* (Fest. H. Cazelles; ed. M. Carrez, *et al.;* Paris, 1981) 337–59. Trever, J. C., "The Book of Daniel and the Origin of the Qumran Community," *BA* 48 (1985) 89–102.

INTRODUCTION

2   **(I) Title.** The title is named not after its author but after its protagonist, who is presented here as living in Babylonia during the reign of the last kings of the Neo-Babylonian Empire and their first successors, the early kings of the Medes and the Persians—i.e., during most of the 6th cent. BC. The name Daniel, "my judge is God" or "God (or El) has judged," in Hebrew, was also borne, according to the Chronicler, by one of David's sons (1 Chr 3:1 = Chileab of 2 Sam 3:3) and by one of the Jews who returned from the Babylonian Exile at the time of Ezra and Nehemiah (Ezra 8:2; Neh 10:7) in the second half of the 5th cent. Obviously neither can be identified with the Daniel of this book. The prophet Ezekiel speaks of a certain Daniel (or, more exactly,

Dan'el, according to the Hebr consonantal text) who was renowned for his piety (Ezek 14:14,20) and wisdom (28:3). Inasmuch as this Daniel, however, is presented as living long before Ezekiel at the time of Noah and Job (14:14,20), he could scarcely have been regarded as living in the 6th cent., either by the author of Dan or by his first readers, who knew their Bible too well to make such a mistake. The Daniel of Ezek should probably be connected in some way with the *dn'l* (God judges) who plays an important role in the Ugaritic Tale of Aqhat, which dates from about the middle of the 14th cent. (see *ANET* 149–55). A distant echo of this wise and pious Daniel of the Ugaritic epic, who "judges the cause of the widow and decides the case of the fatherless" (2 Aqhat

* Alexander A. Di Lella has revised the *JBC* article of Louis F. Hartman.

5.7–8), is found in the wise young judge of the Susanna story (Dan 13).

(II) Contents. As preserved in the MT, Dan lends itself to a natural division of two roughly equal parts. The first part (chaps. 1–6) contains six edifying stories about Daniel and his three companions at the royal court in Babylonia; the second part (chaps. 7–12) is made up of four visions in which Daniel beholds, under symbolic images, the succession of the four "kingdoms" that God's people, the Jews, occupied from the time of the Babylonian conquest of Judea until God's establishment of his own kingdom for them. As the book has come down to us in its Gk version, it also contains two additions in chap. 3 and three stories of Daniel's exploits with Susanna, the priests of Bel, and the Dragon (chaps. 13–14).

3   (III) Historical Background. To understand the literary nature of this book, we must have some idea of the pertinent historical circumstances. In the 8th cent. BC, the Assyrians had turned the kingdom of Israel into a province of their vast empire and reduced the southern kingdom to a vassal state. Toward the end of the 7th cent., Cyaxares, king of the Medes, with the assistance of the Babylonians, captured Nineveh and utterly destroyed the Assyrian Empire. Although Nebuchadnezzar of Babylon soon took over most of the former realm of the Assyrians and even extended it by his conquest of Judah in 587, his successors allowed the Babylonian power to deteriorate until the Persian king, Cyrus the Great, who had already conquered Media and made himself master of both the Medes and the Persians, captured Babylon in 539 from its last king, Nabonidus, and his son, Belshazzar. Thereafter the ancient Near East was ruled by the Persian successors of Cyrus the Great, among whom the only outstanding king was Darius I

the Great, until Alexander the Great placed it under Gk dominion in 331. In the 3d cent., Palestine was governed by the Gk dynasty of the Ptolemies, whose capital was at Alexandria in Egypt. In the 2d cent., it was under the dominion of the Gk dynasty of the Seleucids, whose capital was at Antioch in Syria.

Useful for an understanding of Dan is a conspectus (see below) of the rulers of these dynasties that controlled the Near East from the 6th to the 2d cent. BC (→ History, 75:117–39).

Most of the people who survived Nebuchadnezzar's conquest of Judah were deported to Babylonia between 598 and 582. But after 539, when Cyrus permitted the exiles to return to their homeland, there was a slow but steady growth in the number of Jews living in Palestine. Under their Persian and Ptolemaic rulers they enjoyed limited political autonomy and complete religious liberty. But the Seleucid ruler Antiochus IV Epiphanes, in his endeavor, both for political and for cultural reasons, to hellenize the Jews of Palestine, tried to force them to abandon their ancient religion and to practice the common pagan worship of his realm. The ultimate outcome of this bloody persecution was armed revolt among the Jews, as told in 1–2 Macc. This conflict between the religion of the Jews and the paganism of their foreign rulers is also the basic theme of Dan. However, in Dan it is regarded from God's viewpoint as long foreseen and tolerated by him, both to show the vast superiority of Israel's wisdom over all pagan philosophy and to demonstrate the truth that the God of Israel is the master of history, who "deposes kings and sets up kings" (2:21), until he ultimately establishes his universal kingdom on earth.

4   (IV) Literary Genre. In developing such a thesis the author makes use of two literary genres that

KINGS OF THE NEO-BABYLONIAN EMPIRE	KINGS OF THE PERSIAN EMPIRE	
Nebuchadnezzar (605–562)	Cyrus (550–530)	Darius II (423–404)
Evil-merodach (562–560)	Cambyses (530–522)	Artaxerxes II (404–358)
Neriglissar (560–556)	Darius I (522–486)	Artaxerxes III (358–338)
Labashi-marduk (556)	Xerxes I (486–465)	Arses (338–336)
Nabonidus (556–539)	Artaxerxes I (465–424)	Darius III (335–331)
	Xerxes II (423)	

GREEK RULERS

Alexander the Great (336–323)
|
Philip Arrhidaeus (323–316)
|
Alexander IV (316–309)

PTOLEMAIC DYNASTY		SELEUCID DYNASTY
Ptolemy I Soter (323–285)		Seleucus I Nicator (312–280)
Ptolemy II Philadelphus (285–246)		Antiochus I Soter (280–261)
Ptolemy III Euergetes (246–221)	Bernice ————— Antiochus II Theos (261–246) —— Laodice	
		Seleucus II Callinicus (246–226)
Ptolemy IV Philopator (221–203)		Seleucus III Soter (226–223) Antiochus III the Great (223–187)
Ptolemy V Epiphanes—— Cleopatra (203–181)	Seleucus IV Philopator (187–175) Antiochus IV Epiphanes (175–164)	
Ptolemy VI Philometor (181–146)		

may seem strange to modern readers: the haggadic genre and the apocalyptic genre. The latter, employed in chaps. 7–12, consists in a certain mysterious "revelation," received in fantastic visions or transmitted by angels, both about past and present history and about the eschatological establishment of God's messianic kingdom. Inasmuch as this literary device makes use of some famous character of the distant past as the recipient of this revelation, events that are past history to the writer are presented as prophecies of future happenings. In a broad sense, however, this form of writing can rightly be regarded as a kind of prophecy, because it gives an interpretation of history in God's name, as seen by him.

The haggadic genre, used in chaps. 1–6 and 13–14, gets its name from the mishnaic Hebr word *haggādâ*, lit., a "setting forth," a "narrative," but often used in the sense of a "story" having little or no basis in actual history but told for the sake of inculcating a moral lesson. If such a story is a free elaboration of some true event of actual history, it is more exactly called an "haggadic midrash." But the story may also be a pure "haggada," i.e., a free composition throughout with no historical basis at all. Often it is impossible to say how far, if at all, a haggadic story is based on actual history.

Stories about Daniel are clearly haggadic; in their entirety, they cannot be taken as strict history. Inasmuch as their author does not intend them as historical, he cannot be accused of error if he makes inaccurate statements about history. We have no way of knowing whether the Daniel of these stories was really a historical character, about whom popular legends gradually clustered, or whether he was simply a creation of Jewish folklore. A similar case is that of Ahiqar of the Aram Ahiqar legend, who, as a wise counselor of the Assyrian kings (see *ANET* 427–30), is not too different from Daniel. For the inspired author of our book this question was unimportant. He stressed the spiritual message that he wished to convey by these haggadic stories. (→ Apocrypha, 67:133).

5   (V) Date and Authorship. Having lost sight of these ancient modes of writing, until relatively recent years Jews and Christians considered Dan to be true history, containing genuine prophecy. Inasmuch as chaps. 7–12 are written in the 1st pers., it was natural to assume that the Daniel in chaps. 1–6 was a truly historical character and that he was the author of the whole book. Few modern biblical scholars, however, would now seriously defend such an opinion. The arguments for a date shortly before the death of Antiochus IV Epiphanes in 164 are overwhelming. An author living in the 6th cent. could hardly have written the late Hebrew used in Dan, and its Aramaic is certainly later than the Aramaic of the Elephantine papyri, which date from the end of the 5th cent. The theological outlook of the author, with his interest in angelology, his apocalyptic rather prophetic vision, and esp. his belief in the resurrection of the dead, points inescapably to a period long after the Babylonian Exile. His historical perspective, often hazy for events in the time of the Babylonian and Persian kings but much clearer for the events during the Seleucid dynasty, indicates the Hellenistic age. Finally, his detailed description of the profanation of the Temple of Jerusalem by Antiochus IV Epiphanes in 167 and the following persecution (9:27; 11:30–35) contrasted with his merely general reference to the evil end that would surely come to such a wicked man (11:45), indicates a composition date shortly before the death of this king in 164, therefore probably in 165.

6   (VI) Unity of Authorship. Until now we have spoken of the "author" as if Dan were entirely the

work of one person. It is possible, for there is surely a singleness of religious outlook, spirit, and purpose throughout. If several authors wrote it (a more probable view), they all at least shared the same school of thought. Unity of authorship would not, of course, exclude the possibility that the author used older, even written sources for the stories in the first part of the book; indeed, such does seem to be the case. Some exegetes (e.g., Ginsberg, Hartman and Di Lella) consider the visions in chaps. 7–12 to have been written by two, three, or even four different men; but the arguments for such a hypothesis have not convinced all scholars. It seems, however, that the book, even as it is preserved in the MT, received certain secondary additions after its original composition; such a supposition helps to explain some apparent inconsistencies in the text. The prayer in 9:4–20, which is not entirely appropriate for the context and is written in much better Hebrew than is found in the rest of the book, may be an older composition that was later inserted into the original work.

7   (VII) Language. A still unsolved problem is Dan's strange mixture of Hebrew and Aramaic. The difference in language corresponds only partially to the division of the book into its haggadic and apocalyptic sections. The latter is written in Hebrew, except the first vision (chap. 7), which is in Aramaic; the former is in Aramaic, except 1:1–2:4a, which is in Hebrew. Probably the whole book (except the Hebr prayer of 9:4–20) was originally composed in Aramaic, and later on (to ensure it a place in the Jewish canon of Scripture, or for nationalistic reasons?) its beginning and end were translated into Hebrew, a theory that explains certain difficult Hebr passages as representing faulty translations. Or perhaps the author of the Hebr visions of chaps. 8–12 prefixed to his work an older Aram collection of four stories (chaps. 2–6) and one vision (chap. 7), then rounded out the whole by composing or translating in Hebrew the introductory story of chap. 1 and, for a smoother nexus, the opening verses of the second story (2:1–4a).

8   (VIII) Canonicity and the Deuterocanonical Sections. There has never been any difficulty regarding the inspired character of Dan as such, although whereas the MT places it in the Hagiographa, the third part of its canon (after Esth and before Ezra), the LXX and Vg put it with the prophets (after Ezek). The difficulty is that the canonical Dan as given in the LXX and the Vg is considerably longer than the canonical Dan of the MT. Actually, there is some reason to think that this book circulated at first in more than two forms. We now know from the manuscripts found at Qumran that there were at that time more stories about Daniel in circulation than are contained in any modern Bible (→ 20 below). In any case, the Gk version is much longer than the Aram text of the MT in chap. 3, where the Greek gives, over and above the Aramaic, the Prayer of Azariah (3:24–45) and the Hymn of the Three Jewish Men (3:46–90). These sections were not deleted from the MT; they never formed part of the edition represented by the MT. Moreover, the Gk version contains, under separate headings and in varying positions in the manuscripts (hence, originally as distinct little books), the three stories of Susanna, Bel, and the Dragon, which are placed in the Vg and in Catholic vernacular versions at the end of Dan as 13:1–64; 14:1–22; 14:23–42, respectively. These additional sections of the Gk text come from Hebr or Aram originals, including most likely the story of Susanna, despite the play on words in the Gk text of 13:55–59 (→ 36 below). The Gk text of Dan has come down to us in two forms. The first is that found in almost all the manuscripts, designated (for want of a better name) "Theodotion-Daniel" (see Hartman and Di

Lella, *Daniel* 76–84). The second is that of the LXX, which until recently was known from only one Gk manuscript, although the newly published Papyrus 967 also has most of Dan according to this form of the text. Inasmuch as the early church accepted as its canon of the Bible the Scriptures according to the Gk text, Catholics have always held the additional (or so-called deutero-canonical) sections of Dan as divinely inspired on a par with the rest of the book.

9 (IX) Message of the Author. The work was written primarily for the purpose of encouraging the Jews to remain faithful to their ancestral religion at a time when they not only felt the allurement of the higher worldly culture of Hellenism, which was intimately connected with Hellenistic paganism, but also were suffering a bloody persecution to make them abandon the law of Moses and accept the religion of Antiochus IV Epiphanes. The author of Dan, therefore, is particularly concerned with demonstrating the superiority of the wisdom of Israel's God over the merely human wisdom of the pagans, and with showing his immense power, which can and will rescue his faithful ones from their persecutors. Yet not only for believers of his own age and place, but for believers of all times the author of Dan has a message of enduring worth: God is the master of history, who uses the rise and fall of nations as preparatory steps in the establishment of his universal reign over all people.

(X) Theological Significance. In several respects, the ideas expressed in Dan are of prime importance in the history of religious thought. Even in its literary form, this work presents in chaps. 7–12 the first clear example that we have of the apocalyptic style of writing in its fullest development, a literary genre destined to have tremendous influence during the next few centuries. Then too, in the significant role that Dan gives to the angels as the ministers of God, who reveals through them his will to humans, this book goes con-

siderably further than previous books and points the way to the highly developed angelology of the rabbinic and early Christian literature. Likewise, a theological contribution of immense significance is the clear teaching on the resurrection of the dead (12:2), which is something unique in the Hebr OT and is much more meaningful to the Semitic mentality than the doctrine of the immortality of the soul. Finally, the messianism of Dan brings Israel's hope of salvation to the final stage before its full realization in the NT. Although the "son of man coming with the clouds of heaven" (7:13) does not refer directly to an individual Messiah (→ 26 below), before long this term was destined to acquire such a connotation and to become the favorite expression by which Jesus of Nazareth would refer to himself.

10 (XI) Outline. The book of Daniel can easily be divided into the following main divisions:

(I) Exploits of Daniel and His Companions at the Babylonian Court (1:1–6:29)
   (A) The Food Test (1:1–21)
   (B) Nebuchadnezzar's Dream of the Composite Statue (2:1–49)
   (C) Daniel's Companions in the Fiery Furnace (3:1–97)
   (D) Nebuchadnezzar's Dream of the Great Tree (3:98[31]–4:34)
   (E) The Writing on the Wall at Belshazzar's Feast (5:1–6:1)
   (F) Daniel in the Lion's Den (6:2–29)
(II) Daniel's Apocalyptic Visions (7:1–12:13)
   (A) The Four Beasts (7:1–28)
   (B) The Ram and the He-Goat (8:1–27)
   (C) The Interpretation of the 70 Weeks (9:1–27)
   (D) The Revelation of the Hellenistic Wars (10:1–12:13)
(III) Other Exploits of Daniel (13:1–14:42)
   (A) Daniel's Rescue of the Chaste Susanna (13:1–64)
   (B) Daniel and the Priests of Bel (14:1–22)
   (C) Daniel's Destruction of the Dragon (14:23–42)

COMMENTARY

11 (I) Exploits of Daniel and His Companions at the Babylonian Court (1:1–6:29). The six stories in this collection are loosely strung together, and most of them probably circulated originally as independent tales. They reveal a fairly good knowledge of the customs in Mesopotamia at the time of the Persian Empire, indicating that these stories go back, at least in part, to this period. However, the many Persian loanwords in the Hebrew and Aramaic in which they are told show that in their present form these stories cannot antedate the Persian period. The Gk names of the musical instruments in 3:4,7,10,15 suggest that at least the story in chap. 3, as we now have it, cannot have been written before the Hellenistic age, even though a considerable amount of Gk culture had invaded the Near East before Alexander the Great. Certain allusions to historical events of the Hellenistic period allow a more precise dating within this period. When the author prefixed these stories to the account of his visions, he may have edited them to some extent. But since they already illustrated sufficiently well the lessons that he wished to inculcate—Israel's religion is superior to pagan wisdom and Israel's God is able to rescue his faithful ones from mortal danger—the compiler left the tales substantially as he found them. He did not even try to make Nebuchadnezzar into a symbol of Antiochus IV Epiphanes, the archvillain of the book.

12 (A) The Food Test (1:1–21). This story, told in Hebrew and not in Aramaic like the other stories, was probably composed by the author to serve as an introduction to the whole collection, even though he may have used older material in its composition. Here he sets the stage and introduces the heroes for the following scenes. The three companions are clearly secondary in the rest of the book. Only the story of the fiery furnace (chap. 3), in which Daniel himself does not appear, is truly concerned with them. In chap. 2 they play a merely minor role, and in the rest of the book they are not even mentioned. In chap. 1, however, because they must be introduced, they are put practically on a par with Daniel. The lesson of this story must have been clear to the Jews, whom Antiochus IV Epiphanes tried to force to eat pork (1 Macc 1:62–63; 2 Macc 6:18; 17:1)—i.e., their God, who did not allow the young men of the Babylonian Exile to suffer harm when they refused to partake of the pagans' food and drink, would also in the present persecution come to the aid of those who refused to violate the Mosaic law.

1. *the third year:* This year would be 606 BC, but Nebuchadnezzar became king only in 605, and his first siege of Jerusalem was in 597, shortly after Jehoiakim's death (cf. 2 Kgs 24:8–12). The author of Dan, who perhaps combined 2 Kgs 24:1 (Jehoiakim's three-year vassalage to Nebuchadnezzar) with 2 Chr 36:5–7

(Jehoiakim's imprisonment in Babylon), was not concerned with such historical details that meant nothing for his spiritual message; thus, this inaccuracy is not contrary to the inerrancy of inspired Scripture. 2. The ancient Hebr name for Babylonia (Gen 10:10; 11:2; Isa 11:11; Zech 5:11) is Shinar—used here as an intentional archaism. *his god:* Marduk, also called Bel (lit., "lord"; see comment on 1:7).

3. Ashpenaz (MT *'ašpĕnaz*) is apparently a Persian, rather than Akkadian, name, although its etymology is uncertain. *nobility:* In the MT, *partĕmîm*, derived from a Persian term. Daniel and his companions, who belonged to this group (v 6), are thus presented as members of the Jewish aristocracy. 4. *the language and literature of the Chaldeans:* Not the cuneiform writing of the Babylonians as such, but the well-known omen literature of ancient Mesopotamia. The term Chaldean designated originally the Aramaic-speaking people who invaded Babylonia in the early centuries of the 1st millennium and to whom the kings of the Neo-Babylonian Empire belonged; it is used in this sense in 5:30; Ezra 5:12. But at a later period, this term was applied to the professional astrologers and fortune-tellers who were skilled in Babylonian omen literature; such is the common meaning of the word in Dan. 5. *three years of training:* According to the common Persian practice, as prescribed in the Avesta (*Sacred Books of the East*, 2d ed., 4. 311ff.). *(royal) menu:* The MT reads *patbag*, from the old Persian word *patibaga;* perhaps the author uses this foreign word for alluding to the exotic nature of the food. 6. The Hebr names are *ḥănanyâ*, "Yahweh is gracious," *mîšā'ēl*, "Who belongs to God?," and *'ăzaryâ*, "Yahweh has helped."

13   7. Daniel's name in the MT, *bēlṭĕša'ṣṣar*, is a word that the author apparently thought contained the name of the Babylonian god Bel (cf. 4:5); actually it represents the shortened Babylonian name *balāṭšu-uṣur*, "Guard his life!," the full form of which would begin with the name of one of the Babylonian gods—e.g., Marduk, Nabu, or Bel. The words *šadrak . . . mêšak* are of uncertain derivation; the MT reads *'ăbēd-nĕgô* for *'ebed-nĕbô*, "servant of [the god] Nabu."

8. *resolved not to defile himself with the royal menu or wine:* The author presupposes that this food and drink would be forbidden by Mosaic law, but the only pertinent legislation would be Lev 11:1–47, part of the Priestly Code, which was probably not promulgated till the end of the 5th cent. The older dietary laws in the Book of the Covenant (Exod 21–23), in Deut, and in the Holiness Code (Lev 17–26), known to the Jews of the 6th cent., were much more liberal. The author of 2 Kgs 25:29–30 saw nothing wrong in the fact that the exiled Jehoiachin "received a regular allotment of food from the king" of Babylon—a passage that served as a literary source for the present passage in Dan. But here the viewpoint is that of a Jew of the 2d cent., when abstinence from any "Gentile" food became the touchstone of orthodox Judaism. 12. A spiritual trial of 10 days duration is a common motif in the apocalyptic literature (cf. Rev 2:10; *Jub.* 19:8; *T. Joseph* 2:7; *Pirqe 'Abot* 5:4). 15. *they looked healthier:* Lit., "their appearance seemed better"; also, according to the roughly contemporaneous Jdt 8:6–7, fasting improved a person's health and looks.

17. *God gave knowledge:* Although the author may have been influenced by the widespread idea of his time that fasting was a necessary preliminary for receiving heavenly revelations, he regards the extraordinary wisdom of the young men not as the automatic result of their ascetic life but as a gift of God. 19–20. This general statement regarding the superior wisdom of the young men serves as an introduction to the following stories that give examples of Daniel's superior ability to interpret dreams

and ominous signs. 21. *the first year of King Cyrus:* It is 539–538. The author is concerned with neither Daniel's age—he would then have been almost 90 if he were a young man of 20 in 606 (v 1)—nor the apparent inconsistency with the date of the third year of Cyrus in 10:1, which may be from another source (but see comment on 10:1). The purpose of the present date is probably to imply that Daniel was released from service at the royal court in the year when Cyrus issued his edict in favor of the Jews (Ezra 1:1–4).

14   **(B) Nebuchadnezzar's Dream of the Composite Statue (2:1–49).** This narrative contains an apocalypse within a story. The purpose of the story is to demonstrate the superiority of Israel's God-given wisdom over the highly vaunted worldly wisdom of the pagans, as exemplified by Daniel's ability, with God's help, to divine and interpret Nebuchadnezzar's dream when the pagan soothsayers were unable to do so. (Note the parallel with the Joseph story in Gen 40–41.) The lesson that the author wished his contemporaries, in their conflict with Hellenistic paganism, to learn from this story is stated in v 47: Israel's God "is the God of gods and Lord of kings and a revealer of mysteries."

Yet this story is really only of secondary importance here. It serves primarily as a frame in which is set the king's apocalyptic vision of the multimetal statue. This vision of the four different metals, representing the four pagan kingdoms that successively ruled the then known world but would eventually be supplanted by the kingdom of God's chosen people, is essentially the same in meaning as the apocalyptic vision of the four beasts in chap. 7—a fact that points to the essential bond binding the first and the last of the Aram sections of the book into a distinct literary unit. The purpose of these two visions, as also of the other apocalyptic visions in chaps. 8–12, is to strengthen the faith of the author's contemporaries in the ultimate establishment of God's eschatological kingdom.

Although the story of chap. 2, with its vision of the composite statue, may have received its present form only in the reign of Antiochus IV Epiphanes, it is apparently based on older materials—literary accounts as well as oral traditions of a folkloristic nature. It would be hard to say how far our author found them already combined into a single narrative, or to what extent he himself fused them, but their presence is unmistakably revealed in the inconsistencies and unevenness of the narrative.

1. *the second year:* The date is inconsistent with 1:1,5,18, according to which Nebuchadnezzar was king for at least three years before he met Daniel for the first time. The author does not try to bring the older source that he uses here into harmony with his introductory story (chap. 1). 2. *Chaldeans:* Here, as almost always in Dan, "astrologers," "soothsayers" (see comment on 1:4). This term and the preceding ones have the same general sense in Dan (cf. 1:20; 2:10,27; 4:4; 5:7,11,15). 4. *Aramaic:* A gloss telling the reader that what follows from here to 7:28 is in Aramaic and not in Hebrew (→ 7 above). *live forever!:* A greeting, derived from the Akkadian, which was used until the Muslim period in addressing the kings of Persia; for similar greetings, see 1 Kgs 1:31; Neh 2:3. 5. *this is what I have decided:* Lit., "The thing is decreed [Persian *'azdā'*] by me"; therefore, this decree of the king is immutable and irrevocable under the Mede and Persian law (6:9). The wise men must not only interpret his dream, they must tell him the dream itself! Nebuchadnezzar had not forgotten the dream, as Josephus thought (*Ant.* 10.10.3 § 195); he was rather using this device to see how reliable the soothsayers' interpretation would be (v 9).

15   **13–23.** This section is apparently a later insertion into an earlier form of the story. Verse 24 would flow smoothly immediately after v 12; on the other hand, vv 25–26 (the king's lack of acquaintance with Daniel) seem inconsistent with v 16 (Daniel's bold entry into the royal court and the obtaining of his request from the king). Verse 16 presupposes 1:18–20 and thus seems to come from the author of the book, who wrote chap. 1 as an introduction to the older stories of chaps. 2–6. **14.** *Daniel prudently took counsel:* He acts like the wise scribe of Sir 39:1–11. **17–18.** Daniel's three companions are not mentioned elsewhere in chap. 2, another indication that vv 1–23 were inserted into the older story by the author of chap. 1. **19.** *the mystery:* In Aramaic, *rāzâ,* derived from the Persian word *rāz,* "secret"; on the pre-Christian Semitic concept of "mystery," see R. E. Brown (*CBQ* 20 [1958] 417–43) and J. A. Fitzmyer (*Genesis Apocryphon* [2d ed.; Rome, 1971] 78).

20–23. In this hymn of praise, Daniel thanks God for having revealed to him the king's dream. The keynote of the whole book is struck in the statement that Israel's God "causes the changes of the times and seasons"—i.e., that he is the master of human history, "who deposes kings and sets up kings"; therefore, he can and will lead human history to its climax, the establishment of his universal eschatological reign on earth. For a poetic analysis of this hymn, see A. A. Di Lella (*Studia Hierosolymitana* 3 [1982] 91–93). The same idea is essentially the theme of Rev.

28. *in the last days:* Lit., "at the end of days," i.e., in the final period of history when God establishes his kingdom on earth. *this was the dream . . . in bed:* We would expect the account of the dream to follow immediately. Besides, v 29 seems to be merely a variant form of v 28. Perhaps the author inserted vv 29–30 from another source to record the statement of v 30 that this revelation of God's plan in human history is really made by God, with Daniel simply acting as his agent.

31. The image that the king saw in his dream was like the well-known colossal statues of Memphis, Rhodes, Athens, and Rome, except more terrifying. **32.** The ancient concept of world history as divided into four decreasingly happy ages characterized by the four metals of decreasing value—gold, silver, bronze, and iron—was made famous by Hesiod (*Works and Days* 109–80). The Persian variety of this four-age concept—the ages of gold, silver, steel, and iron mixed with clay—is also reflected here. **33.** *its feet partly of iron and partly of terra-cotta:* It is not clear how this combination of iron and terra-cotta is conceived: perhaps it is either an iron framework filled in with baked clay or a core of baked clay with an iron coating, similar to the clay and bronze statue of Bel in 14:7.

16   **36–45.** Formerly the four kingdoms of Dan were commonly understood as being the Babylonian, the Medo-Persian, the Greco-Seleucid, and the Roman empires. Although this theory, defended by Jerome, was once regarded as the "traditional" Catholic interpretation (in connection with the attempt to explain the "seventy weeks of years" in 9:24–27 as culminating in the death of Jesus Christ), it would now find few modern Catholic exegetes to support it. Daniel's interpretation of the dream and the description and interpretation of the vision of the four beasts representing the same four kingdoms, as given in chap. 7, make it unmistakably clear that the kingdoms are those of the Babylonians, the Medes, the Persians, and the Greeks. The inscriptions of the old Persian Empire speak of three successive empires: the Assyrians, the Medes, and the Persians. After the time of Alexander the Great, the Gk historians added a fourth empire to this traditional

series—the Greek Empire. The Jews of the Hellenistic age, taking all the Assyro-Babylonian dynasties as a single unit, substituted Babylonia (with which they were more familar) for Assyria in their reckoning of the four world empires. Besides, because Cyrus, the conqueror of Babylon, and his successors called themselves "the kings of the Medes and the Persians," it was natural for the Jews to place the Medes chronologically between the Babylonians and the Persians. Although this situation resulted in the historical inaccuracy of having Babylon captured by the Medes (see 6:1), whereas it was really captured by the Persians, who had previously conquered the Medes, our author followed this popular Jewish idea of world history. **38.** *you are the head of gold:* Nebuchadnezzar, with his Neo-Babylonian Empire, is thus identified with the first of the four kingdoms. **39.** *another kingdom . . . inferior to yours:* The kingdom of the Medes was hardly inferior to the Babylonian Empire. *a third kingdom . . . shall rule over the whole earth:* At the height of its power, the Persian Empire was master of almost the whole civilized world. **40.** *the fourth kingdom . . . will crush and break all these others:* The empire of the world-conquering Alexander. **41–45.** *toes:* Not mentioned in the dream and therefore perhaps the author's insertion into the older story. *a divided kingdom:* The Greek Empire after Alexander's death was divided among his generals, particularly (as far as the Jews in Palestine were concerned) into the Ptolemaic kingdom of Egypt and the Seleucid kingdom of Syria. *they will be mingled by intermarriage, but they will not hold together:* The reference is probably to the marriage of Antiochus II to Bernice, the daughter of Ptolemy II Philadelphus, in *ca.* 250, which ended not in peace but in war between the two kingdoms (see comment on 11:6). But cf. 11:17. *in the days of those kings:* Ginsberg renders this as, "In the days of those kingdoms" (reading *molkayyā'* for *malkayyā'*), and understands this to mean, "while the first three kingdoms are still in existence" (the fourth, Gk kingdom being smashed by the "stone"). He concludes that for the Hellenistic period, such would be true only in 292–261, when there existed a nominal kingdom of Babylon and residual kingdoms of the Medes (Atropatene) and and of the Persians (Persis). The original form of this chapter would therefore have been written at this time. Ginsberg regards 2:41b–43 as a somewhat later addition, written between 246 and 220. *the stone . . . cut from the mountain without a hand being put to it:* Daniel interprets it as the kingdom that the God of heaven will establish; it will end all of these pagan kingdoms and will itself last forever. The symbolism of the "stone" as representing the holy people of God occurs elsewhere in the OT (Ps 118:22; Isa 51:1; cf. also Isa 18:14; 28:16). In the NT (Mark 12:10–11; Matt 21:42; Luke 20:17–18; Rom 9:32–33; 1 Pet 2:6–8), the sense of these passages is transferred from the theocratic kingdom to the King, Jesus Christ.

(Flusser, D., "The Four Empires in the Fourth Sibyl and in the Book of Daniel," *Israel Oriental Studies* 2 [1972] 148–75. Siegman, E. F., "The Stone Hewn from the Mountain," *CBQ* 18 [1956] 364–79.)

46–49. Just as Joseph was raised to a high position in the government by Pharaoh as a reward for interpreting his dream (Gen 41), so Daniel is similarly made a sort of prime minister by Nebuchadnezzar, while his three companions (again appearing as secondary elements in the story) are appointed local governors. It is rather surprising that Daniel apparently accepts without demur the sacrifice and worship offered to him as a god (cf. Acts 14:11–17). Probably the author regarded this divine honor as paid not so much to Daniel as to Daniel's God (thus Jerome). For a different view, see B. A. Mastin,

ZAW 85 (1973) 80–93. This older story, which portrays the pagan king as practically converted to Judaism, was not changed here by the author of the book to make Nebuchadnezzar a type of Antiochus IV Epiphanes.

17   (C) Daniel's Companions in the Fiery Furnace (3:1–97). From a literary viewpoint, this haggadic story is only loosely connected with the other narratives in the book; in fact, Daniel is not even mentioned here. On the contrary, this account is concerned with the three Jewish men who, in its original form, are identified only by their "Babylonian" names. The purpose is to show that the God of Israel protects his people from harm so long as they remain faithful to him (see v 95). Although the story as such probably antedated the 3d cent., its lesson was pertinent for the Jews in Palestine at the time of Antiochus IV Epiphanes, who set up a pagan idol in the Temple of Jerusalem and ordered the Jews, under pain of death, to take part in pagan worship (1 Macc 1:43–62; 2 Macc 6:1–11), even as Nebuchadnezzar ordered the three companions to worship his pagan idol. Yet the compiler who incorporated this story into the Dan cycle that he edited at the time of the Maccabees did not rewrite it in an attempt to make Nebuchadnezzar into a type of Epiphanes. On the contrary, he let the old story end as it had previously ended, with the pagan king passing a law in defense of the Jewish religion—an ideal situation that would have contented most Jews.

A peculiar literary device in this story is the frequent repetition of certain groups of words, such as the names of musical instruments (vv 5,7,10,15), the titles of government officials (vv 2–3,94), and "nations and peoples of all languages" (lit., "all nations and peoples and tongues" [vv 4,7,96]; but the same phrase is also in 3:98; 5:19; 6:26; 7:14). Likewise, certain set phrases occur over and over again—e.g., "the statue which King Nebuchadnezzar had set up" (vv 3,5,7; cf. 12,14,18).

1. *a golden statue:* Not of the king himself, but of his pagan god; to worship the statue was to serve the god it represented (vv 12,14,18, etc.). *sixty cubits high and six cubits wide:* About 90 ft. high and 9 ft. wide. The great height is seemingly out of all proportion to the narrow width, the monument resembling more an obelisk than a statue, but the use here of the Babylonian sexagesimal system of numerals should be noted. *Dura:* Many place-names in ancient Mesopotamia began with this word, meaning "fortress" in Akkadian; perhaps no actual place in particular is intended in the story. **2.** *satraps . . . magistrates:* The exact meaning of some of these terms in the original is uncertain, but there seems to be a correct order in their descending importance. Of these seven terms, two (*signayyā'*, "prefects"; *paḥăwātā'*, "governors") are of Akkadian origin and the other five are of Persian origin, which would seem to indicate that the original story told in this chapter arose during the Persian period. **5.** Of these six musical instruments, three have Gk names: *kîtārôs* (so the *kĕtīb*), "lyre"; *pěsantē-rîn*, "psaltery," a sort of harp; and *sûmpōnyâ* (for the Gk word from which the word "symphony" is derived), "bagpipe" (?). These terms could hardly have been introduced into the story before the Hellenistic period. **6.** The execution of criminals by fire, although rare in ancient times, was not unknown either in Israel (Gen 38:24; Lev 20:14; 21:9) or in Babylonia (Code of Hammurabi, paragraphs 110 and 157; Jer 29:22). Jewish martyrs in the persecution under Antiochus IV Epiphanes were sometimes burned to death (2 Macc 6:11; 7:5). The white-hot furnace seems to be pictured here (cf. vv 20–23) in the form of a limekiln, although there may also be an echo here of the Canaanite-Phoenician custom of throwing human victims into a burning furnace in

honor of Molech; therefore, the furnace might be thought of here as a sort of altar of holocaust in front of the statue (thus Steinmann).

18   8–12. This story, like that in chap. 6, also contains the motif of professional jealousy among court officials, as in the Ahiqar and the Mordecai (Esth 3) stories; the three Jews had been "made administrators of the province of Babylon," and apparently out of envy they were accused by the Chaldeans (i.e., the professional soothsayers), who, as courtiers, had free access to the king. **17–18.** The exact translation of these two verses is somewhat disputed, but their general sense is clear enough: the three Jews do not question God's ability to save them; rather, they affirm it, but at the same time they assert that even if God decides not to rescue them they will still refuse to worship an idol. See P. W. Coxon, *VT* 26 (1976) 400–9. **21.** *coats, hats, shoes:* The meaning of these terms in the original is uncertain; all three words refer to Persian articles of dress, and when compared with similar Persian words, should perhaps be rendered as "trousers," "shirts," and "hats." The items of clothing are mentioned for the sake of stressing the remarkable nature of the miracle—i.e., the fire consumed the bonds of the three Jews, but not their clothing (vv 92,94).

24–90. This part of the chapter, embracing the Prayer of Azariah (vv 26–45) and the Hymn of the Three Men (vv 52–90a), with the prose introduction (vv 24–25), interlude (vv 46–51), and conclusion (v 90b), is preserved only in the Gk version and the ancient transls. made from it. The original was in either Hebrew or Aramaic. Although not present in the MT, this so-called "deutero-canonical fragment" has always been regarded as part of the canonical, inspired Scriptures. However, it is not part of the original story, but rather an addition made by an inspired author who took existing liturgical prayers, adapted them slightly, and inserted them here, with a few sentences of his own to make a smoother nexus.

26–45. The prayer that is here put in the mouth of Azariah is a "supplication of the community," including a confession of national guilt, similar to the older prayer in 9:4–19 and the prayers in Ezra 9:6–15 and Bar 1:15–3:8. **32.** *an unjust king, the worst in all the world:* Antiochus IV Epiphanes is surely meant. **46–51.** Some exegetes regard this prose interlude as part of the original story, because it prepares the reader for the king's surprise at seeing an angel with the three men in the furnace (vv 91–92). Yet the secondary nature of this insertion is evident from the inconsistency between v 46 ("The king's men who had thrown them in continued to stoke the furnace") and v 22 ("So huge a fire . . . that the flames devoured the men who threw Shadrach, Meshach, and Abednego into it"), and the dramatic effect is better without this previous explanation of the angel's presence. **52–90.** This hymn of praise, apart from the addition at the end (vv 88–90), consists of two litanies, similar to the litany of Ps 136, in which each half verse, sung by a soloist or a choir, is followed by the repetition of the same refrain, sung by the people. The first litany (vv 52–56) is a doxology. The second (vv 57–87) is an invitation to all of God's creatures to praise him, similar to, but longer than, the call to praise in Ps 148 (cf. also the litany in the Hebr text after Sir 51:12). **88–90.** These verses were added to the older hymn when it was inserted into the story of Dan 3. The writer overlooked the fact that the three men (here called by their Hebr names!) were themselves pictured as singing this hymn, and so should not be inviting themselves here to sing it. However, in answer to the invitation they respond with the next four lines, "He has delivered us . . . from the fire," which words are here meant to be understood literally, although originally such expressions were mere figures of speech for deliverance from any mortal danger (cf. e.g., the hymn in Sir 51:1–12, which is itself a cento of older Ps passages).

(Christie, E. G., "The Strophic Arrangement of the Benedicite," *JBL* 47 [1928] 188–93.)

91–97. (Verses 24–30 in the MT.) The king acknowledges the miracle. **92.** *a son of God:* A supernatural being, an "angel" (v 95) (the same term, but in the pl., appears in Job 1:6; 2:1; 38:7; Pss 29:1; 89:7). **93.** *the most high God:* Although used by the Israelites, esp. in Pss, in speaking of Yahweh, this term, which had a long history in NW Semitic religion, is considered by the OT writers as the name by which their God was known to non-Israelites — e.g., Melchizedek (Gen 14:18), Balaam (Num 24:15), and the king of Babylon (Isa 14:14). **95–96.** The king is not presented as a convert to Judaism, but as passing a law making it a legitimate religion of his realm, protected by the civil authority. He is, therefore, the antithesis of Antiochus IV Epiphanes, who proscribed the practice of Judaism. **97.** The conclusion of the story goes back to the motif of the jealous courtiers; the good men are triumphant in the end and are rewarded with political promotion.

19   (D) Nebuchadnezzar's Dream of the Great Tree (3:98[31]–4:34). For a poetic analysis of 3:98[31]–100[33], see A. A. Di Lella (*Studia Hierosolymitana* 3 [1982] 93–94). This story is written in the form of an encyclical letter or proclamation published by Nebuchadnezzar in the 1st pers., in which he tells of a strange vision that he had and of his subsequent madness. In the middle of the story, however, the narrative speaks of the king in the 3d pers. (vv 16–30, or at least 25–30), although there is a return to the 1st-pers. narrative at the end. If the writer made this shift intentionally, perhaps his purpose was to imply that the king himself could not give a rational account of what happened to him during the period of his insanity.

In general, this story is similar to the one in chap. 2; in both stories, Nebuchadnezzar has a dream that no one but Daniel can interpret. However, this dream concerns not the distant future as in chap. 2, but the king's own fate: he will become insane and live for seven years like a beast, exiled from human society. It happens, but after this period, he is restored to sanity and returns to his throne, where he thanks God for his cure. The moral of the story is pointed out in its concluding words: God humbles the proud, and to him alone belongs all glory (v 34). On the possibility of a historical basis for the king's insanity, see comment on 4:25–34.

4. *I related the dream:* The king does not make his soothsayers guess what the dream itself was, or threaten them with punishment for their failure, as in chap. 2. **5.** See comment on 1:7. **6.** *the holy God:* In Aramaic, this term ('*ĕlāhîn qaddîsîn* is pl. and is, therefore, sometimes translated "holy gods" (Vg); Nebuchadnezzar would thus be speaking as a polytheist (thus Jerome). More likely, the term is to be understood, like the corresponding Hebr word '*ĕlōhîm*, as sg.; the full Hebr equivalent, '*ĕlōhîm qĕdōsîm*, is, in fact, used of Yahweh in Josh 24:19.

7–14. For an analysis of these verses as poetry, see A. A. Di Lella in *Mélanges bibliques et orientaux en l'honneur de M. Henri Cazelles* (ed. A. Caquot and M. Delcor; AOAT 212; Neukirchen-Vluyn, 1981) 247–58. This account of the symbolic tree that is cut down seems to be borrowed from Ezek 31, where the great tree of Lebanon, symbolizing the king of Egypt, is also "cut down" (31:12), "because it became lofty in stature, raising its crest among the clouds, and because it became proud in heart at its height" (31:10). **8.** *its top touching the*

heavens: Cf. the tower of Babel "with its top in the heavens" (Gen 11:4) and the king of Babylon in Isa 14:14 who boasts that he "will scale the heavens"; in all these cases, the biblical writers had in mind the insolent pride that would raise humans above God. **9.** As in Ezek 31:8–9, here also is an echo of the paradise theme; Nebuchadnezzar would take God's place in sustaining human life. On the great fruit tree with birds of all kind in its branches, see also Ezek 17:22–24. **10.** *a holy sentinel:* Lit., "a vigilant and holy one" ('*îr wĕqaddîš;* cf. v 14). This chapter is the only place in the OT where the word '*îr,* "watchman," is used in reference to an angel, although it is commonly used in this sense in the Jewish Apocrypha and the QL. Although the concept of the angels as "watchmen" may have been influenced by the pagan (esp. Persian) notions, it is not foreign even to older books of the OT (e.g., Zech 4:10; Isa 62:6). **12.** *its stump and roots:* Cf. Isa 11:1; 6:13. *let him . . . his lot:* The shift from the symbol to the one who is symbolized by it also occurs in Ezek 31:14–18. **14.** For the concept of angels as forming God's council, cf. 1 Kgs 22:19–23; Job 1:6–12; 2:1–6; Ps 89:7–8. *the Most High rules over the kingdom of humans:* This theme is basic in Dan; the kingdom of God will ultimately triumph over the kingdoms of this world (cf. Rev 11:15). **20.** *fettered with iron and bronze:* Hardly to be understood in the sense of a metal band around the trunk of a tree to keep it from splitting, more probably it refers to the chains by which a madman was held in check (Jerome). **22.** The king is afflicted with zoanthropy (a form of insanity whereby a person imagines himself changed into an animal); the victim acts like an animal, in the present case like an ox. **24.** These words clearly indicate the efficacy of good deeds, esp. acts of charity, in obtaining divine forgiveness of sin (see also Tob 12:9; 14:11).

20   25. *all this happened to King Nebuchadnezzar:* There is no historical evidence that this famous king of Babylon was ever afflicted with any form of insanity. However, it seems probable that there were folktales about the last king of Babylon, Nabu-na'id (better known as Nabonidus), being crazy. Although this king was actually a capable ruler, many of his subjects may have thought that his mind was somewhat unbalanced; he acted strangely by staying for long periods in his desert retreat at the oasis of Tema in Arabia. The Babylonian priests, whom he had alienated by his favoring of the worship of the moon-god, Sin, of Haran, certainly spread calumnies about him after his dethronement. The story of Nebuchadnezzar's madness in Dan 4 was therefore probably told originally of this later king of Babylon. This supposition has now been made all the more plausible by the discovery of a fragment of a "prayer of Nabonidus" (J. T. Milik, *RB* 63 [1956] 407–11; see also D. N. Freedman, *BASOR* 145 [1957] 31–32). In this prayer, Nabonidus writes, in the 1st pers., that he was once afflicted by God with a bad skin disease, which forced him to live away from other men for seven years, until God sent him a Jewish soothsayer who taught him to confess his sins and give honor and glory to the true God and not trust in idols of silver and gold, bronze and iron, wood, or stone and clay. Some common source probably exists for both this prayer and the story of Nebuchadnezzar's seven-year madness as told in Dan 4. In any case, this and other smaller fragments found at Qumran show that there was a sort of "Daniel cycle" of popular tales in circulation among the Jews in the last few pre-Christian centuries, several of which were used by the inspired author of Dan.

(Coxon, P. W., "The Great Tree of Daniel 4," *A Word in Season* [JSOTSup 42; Sheffield, 1986] 91–111. Hartman, L. F., "The

Great Tree and Nabuchodonosor's Madness," *BCCT* 75–82. McNamara, M., "Nabonidus and the Book of Daniel," *ITQ* 37 [1970] 131–49. Reed, W. L., "Nabonidus, Babylonian Reformer or Renegade?" *LTQ* 12 [1977] 21–30.)

21   (E) The Writing on the Wall at Belshazzar's Feast (5:1–6:1). Although the framework of this story—a puzzle that only Daniel can solve and his reward for doing so—is essentially the same as that of the stories in chaps. 2 and 4, its substance is quite different. Here the riddle to be solved is not a vision given by God in a dream, but the writing by God of mysterious words on the wall of the royal palace. The king in this story is not the same either in person or in character as the king of the preceding stories. This king does not repent and his doom is absolute. Finally, the moral here is different: God punishes those who, instead of glorifying him in whose hands lies the fate of their lives, worship idols and profane his sacred vessels at a sacrilegious feast. Yet this story is closely connected, from a literary viewpoint, with the preceding one. Its king is not only presented as the son of the king of the tale that was just told, but he also hears the account of what happened to his father related in almost the same words as in the former story.

The absence of any allusion to the king's persecution of the Jews shows that this story must antedate the time of Antiochus IV Epiphanes; in fact, its conundrum—the meaning of the cryptic words Mene, Tekel, Peres—had perhaps even an older, independent history. But its moral was very pertinent for the time of Antiochus IV Epiphanes. Like Belshazzar, this Syrian king had also desecrated the Lord's sacred vessels (2 Macc 5:16; 1 Macc 4:49). Therefore, the persecuted Jews could receive comfort from this story that a fate like that of Belshazzar would also befall Antiochus IV Epiphanes.

1. Belshazzar's name is given as *bēlša'ṣṣar* in the MT. In the LXX, Vg, and Douay his name appears with the same spelling as that of Daniel's Babylonian name, "Baltas(s)ar." What is unquestionably meant is the Akkadian name, *Bēl-šarra-uṣur*, "O Bel, protect the king!" and the Belshazzar of Dan (also mentioned in 7:1; 8:1) is undoubtedly meant to be the *Bēl-šarra-uṣur* of history. Although the latter was the son of the last Chaldean king of Babylon, Nabonidus, and as crown prince assisted him in the government of the country, he himself did not bear the title "king," nor did he hold the new year's festival at Babylon, which was the right of the king alone, in the years when Nabonidus was absent from the capital at the time of this feast (see R. P. Dougherty, *Nabonidus and Belshazzar* [New Haven, 1929]). **2.** Also in Bar 1:11 is Belshazzar called Nebuchadnezzar's son. Although it is possible to argue that Belshazzar's mother may have been the daughter of Nebuchadnezzar, who could thus be called his "father" in the sense of "grandfather" (thus M. J. Gruenthaner, *CBQ* 11 [1949] 421–27), it seems much more reasonable to suppose that Jewish tradition abridged the history of the Neo-Babylonian Empire by confusing Nabonidus with Nebuchadnezzar, as was evidently also done in Dan 4. Neither the author of Bar 1 nor the author of Dan intended to teach history. *concubines:* The Aram word is fem., *lĕḥēnāt,* and the sense here is "harem women." Compared with the "wives" (Aram *šēglāt,* "queenly consorts"; cf. Ps 45:10; Neh 2:6), they were the women of lower rank in the royal harem (on the two classes of women in the royal harem, cf. 1 Kgs 11:3; Cant 6:8). **4.** *they praised their gods:* The reference is probably to hymns of thanksgiving sung at the banquet; there may have been libations of wine to the gods, but Steinmann goes too far in seeing in this "a sacrificial banquet, a religious rite."

22   5. *lampstand:* Probably mentioned merely for the sake of stressing that the writing appeared on a well-illuminated part of the wall; the author possibly meant that the seven-branched lampstand of Solomon's Temple (cf. Jer 52:19) was included in "the gold and silver vessels taken from the house of God in Jerusalem" (v 3) and was now used at this profane banquet. *the wrist and the hand:* Lit., "the palm of the hand" (*pas yĕdā*) the king saw not only the fingers but the whole hand as far as the wrist. **7.** *collar:* The Aram word used here, **hamyānkâ* (for the *kĕtîb, hmwnk'*) is really a Persian word designating a typically Persian ornament of rank, a gold "torque." While there is a clear echo here of the honor that Pharaoh bestowed on Joseph when "he dressed him in linen robes and put a chain of gold around his neck" (Gen 41:42), the royal "purple" and the gold "torque" that Belshazzar offers are more in keeping with later customs. *third in the government:* The Aram term *taltā'* (here "third") is a loanword from Akk *šalšu,* originally meaning "triumvir" but later used as the title of various kinds of high officials; hence, there is no need to speculate on who the "second" in the kingdom was. **10.** *the queen:* Not the wife, but the mother of Belshazzar is meant; as the wife of Nebuchadnezzar, she is able to recount the story of her royal husband's madness. *she entered the banquet hall:* Like Queen Vashti of Esth 1, she would ordinarily not be present at the king's banquets.

25–28. Daniel must first say what words were written on the wall; evidently no one else could even decipher the script. His interpretation involves a play on words that is possible only in a purely consonantal script, such as Hebrew or Aramaic. The three words that were written in the consonantal script would be *mn', tql,* and *prs,* which could be read, as Daniel apparently first read them, *mĕnē', tĕqēl,* and *pĕrēs*—i.e., as three monetary values, the mina (equivalent at different times to 50 or 60 shekels, and mentioned in Luke 19:12–25), the shekel (the basic unit of weight), and the half mina. Daniel, however, "interpreted" the writing by reading the three words as verbs, *mĕnâ,* "he counted," *tĕqal,* "he weighed," and *pĕras,* "he divided," with God understood as the subject and Belshazzar or his kingdom understood as the object. Thus, God has "numbered" the days of Belshazzar's reign. (Things that can be counted are few in number.) God has "weighed" the king in the balance of justice and found him lacking in moral goodness. (The idea of the "scales" of justice, which goes back to an old Egyptian concept, is met with elsewhere in the OT: Job 31:6; Ps 62:10; Prov 16:11; etc.) God has "divided" Belshazzar's kingdom among the Medes and the Persians. For good measure, there is an additional pun on the last of the three words, *prs,* which is also read as *pāras,* "Persia," "Persians." An older form of the conundrum may also have connected the word *māday,* "Media," "Medes," with the root *mdd,* "measure." The conundrum seems to have existed in an older form, independently of its present context. The statement that Belshazzar's "kingdom has been divided and given to the Medes and Persians" does not fit well with the statement at the end of the story, according to which Belshazzar's whole kingdom was handed over to the Medes, with no mention of the Persians. Ginsberg even opines that the conundrum was originally applied to the only three Babylonian kings who were known to the Jews of the Hellenistic period: the mina would stand for the great Nebuchadnezzar, the shekel for the insignificant Evil-merodach, and the half mina for Belshazzar.

23   6:1. *Darius the Mede:* On the idea common among the Jews of the Hellenistic age that the Medes conquered Babylon, see comment on 2:34–35. The "Darius the Mede" of Dan is not a historical character.

His name is borrowed from the Persian king, Darius I the Great, who recaptured Babylon in 521 after it had fallen into the hands of the rebel, Nebuchadnezzar IV. According to history, Belshazzar was not slain in Babylon, but he fell on the field of battle N of the city while resisting the Persian army; Babylon was treacherously handed over to the Persians without a struggle, and Nabonidus was taken prisoner as he sought to return from Tema to his capital.

(Alfrink, B., "Der letzte König von Babylon," *Bib* 4 [1928] 187–205. Alt, A., "Zur Menetekel-Inschrift," *VT* 4 [1954] 303–5. Kraeling, E. G., "The Handwriting on the Wall," *JBL* 63 [1944] 11–18. Rowley, H. H., *Darius the Mede and the Four World Empires in the Book of Daniel* [2d ed.; Cardiff, 1959].)

24   (F) Daniel in the Lions' Den (6:2–29). This last of the haggadic stories in Dan is very similar to the story in chap. 2. The essence of both lies in the readiness of the faithful Jew to suffer martyrdom, if need be, rather than give up the practice of religion. In both stories, examples of witness literature, God comes to the rescue of his faithful servants and saves them miraculously from certain death, which instead is inflicted on those who would harm them. Both stories end with the pagan king acknowledging the power of Israel's God; however, in the present case, the pagan king is much more favorably inclined to his loyal Jewish official than is the monarch in Dan 2. Here, the motif of the "jealous courtiers" is much clearer than elsewhere in Dan.

Although nothing suggests a date of composition after the late Persian or early Hellenistic period, the Jews at the time of Antiochus IV Epiphanes could find in chap. 6 solace and encouragement in their own religious trials: God would protect them even by miraculous means, as he had protected Daniel in the lions' den. Like Daniel, they too felt the effects of a pagan king's edict that made the public worship of their God a crime punishable by death. Like him, they too would give the age-old answer of the martyrs: God, rather than humans, must be obeyed. If it is his will, he will rescue them from death, for "He is a deliverer and savior, working signs and wonders in heaven and on earth" (v 28). **2.** *one hundred and twenty satraps:* The Persian king, Darius I, did indeed institute a good reorganization of his vast empire, but the number of satraps (large provinces) that he established was never higher than 30. The writer is using the term "satrap" in a broad sense to include various lesser officials who governed the subdivisions of the satrapies (cf. Esth 1:1; 8:9). **3.** *three supervisors:* Nothing is known from history of any such "supersatraps." Perhaps the author has in mind Daniel's appointment as one of the triumvirate (see comment on 5:7). **4.** The king planned to make Daniel a sort of grand vizier, such as Pharaoh made Joseph in Egypt (Gen 41:39–41). **5–6.** The hostility of Daniel's colleagues is not primarily a matter of religious bigotry; they merely use his religion as a means of satisfying their political jealousy. **8.** *no one is to address any petition to god or human for thirty days, except to you, O king:* Such a prohibition would be entirely foreign to the religious toleration of the Persian kings, but it would be quite in keeping with the attitude of the Hellenistic monarchs, who regarded themselves as divine and who, on special occasions, suspended the public cult of other gods for a month while all official worship was paid solely to themselves. **9.** *immutable and irrevocable under the Mede and Persian law:* That the Persian kings could not change a law that they had made may have been true for the last kings of the Achaemenian dynasty (cf. Esth 1:19; 8:8), but not for Darius I, who was a strong-minded ruler and was not at all subservient to his courtiers like the Darius of Dan 6.

25   11. *to kneel in prayer:* Although the Jews ordinarily stood at public prayer, in the postexilic period they began the custom of kneeling during private prayer (cf. 2 Chr 6:13; Ezra 9:5; Luke 22:41; Acts 9:40; 20:36). *in the upper chamber:* Either in an upper-story room in a two-story house, or on the roof of any house; such a place of quiet retirement (cf. 1 Kgs 17:19; 2 Kgs 1:2; 4:10–11) was regarded as very suitable for prayer (Acts 1:13; 10:9; 20:8). *with the windows open toward Jerusalem:* Daniel prayed in that part of the house where, through openings that were left in the wall for light and ventilation, he could face Jerusalem (cf. Tob 3:11). In speaking to God in prayer, a Jew naturally faced God's house, the Jerusalem Temple (1 Kgs 8:35; Ps 28:2). *three times a day:* "In the evening, and at dawn, and at noon" (Ps 55:18; see also Dan 9:21). The early church continued the Jewish custom of praying three times a day (*Didache* 8). **17.** *the lions' den:* Both in Assyria (as known from the inscriptions and the sculpture) and in Babylonia (cf. Ezek 19:2, 8–10), lions were kept in captivity to be released for a royal hunting party. Their den is pictured here as a deep pit with an opening that could be closed by a large stone (v 18). **19.** *entertainers:* The Aram word used here, *daḥāwān*, means "portable table" (so F. Rosenthal, *Aramaic Handbook* 1/2 [Wiesbaden, 1967] 21), hence, "food." The *NAB* (without textual note) apparently corrects the text to read *lĕḥēnān*, the word that is used in 5:2 (see comment on 5:2). **23–24.** Daniel's rescue by God's angel who "closed the lions' mouths" is referred to in 1 Macc 2:60 and probably also in Heb 11:33. In the early church, the representation of Daniel standing unharmed among the lions was frequently used as a symbol of the resurrection of the body. **25.** *the men . . . along with their wives and children:* The punishment of a whole family for the crime of one of its members was based on the ancient concept of group solidarity and collective responsibility (cf. Num 16:25–33; Josh 7:24; 2 Sam 21:6,9; Esth 9:13–14). **26b–28.** On the poetic analysis of these verses, see A. A. Di Lella (*Studia Hierosolymitana* 3 [1982] 94–96). **29.** That "the reign of Darius" ("the Mede") is followed here by "the reign of Cyrus the Persian" is in keeping with the chronology of the whole book, in which the kingdom of the Medes is succeeded by the kingdom of the Persians.

26   (II) Daniel's Apocalyptic Visions (7:1–12:13). The second half of the protocanonical book of Daniel consists of four apocalypses (→ OT Apocalyptic, 19:20–21): chaps. 7, 8, 9, and 10–12. Although one apocalypse is usually connected in some way to another one in the collection, each one forms a distinct unit. All four were written between 168 and 164, but all were not necessarily written at the same time or even by the same author. In fact, there is some reason to believe that each was written at a slightly different time, although not necessarily in their present sequence in Dan. Moreover, it seems probable that the earlier apocalypses received certain minor additions when the later ones were joined to the collection.

From a literary viewpoint, the Aram apocalypse of chap. 7 is superior to the three following Hebr ones. Strictly speaking, only the first two of the four consist primarily of symbolic visions, which are explained to the seer by an angel. The other two are, rather, direct revelations made to the writer by an angel without the intermediary means of symbolic visions. All four apocalypses use the same device of presenting past events as if these were still to happen. Thus, they instill confidence in the genuine prediction that the pagan kingdom now so hostile to Israel shall soon be overthrown as its pagan predecessors had been overthrown in the past, and that the eschatological reign of God and his holy people shall soon be established.

(A) The Four Beasts (7:1–28). All exegetes now agree that the four beasts of this apocalyptic vision stand for the four successive pagan empires of the Babylonians, the Medes, the Persians, and the Greeks, as the same four empires are represented by the four different metals of the colossal statue in chap. 2. But to understand more fully the symbolism and its application in this chapter, it seems necessary to distinguish, with Ginsberg (*Studies in Daniel*), between a primary stratum (the original vision and its interpretation in this chapter) and a secondary stratum (later additions). The key to the primary stratum is to be found in the use of symbolic numbers to distinguish the four beasts. Concerning the fourth beast, which all agree represents the Gk kingdom, it is expressly stated in v 24 that its 10 horns represent 10 kings. Two suppositions follow: each of the three preceding beasts has symbolic numbers representing respectively the number of kings in each of these dynasties, although it is somewhat obscured in the present state of the text; inasmuch as the tenth horn of the fourth beast in the primary vision stands for Antiochus IV Epiphanes, the sections concerning the "little horn" springing up among the 10 other horns, which also represents Antiochus IV Epiphanes, must be later insertions. The message of the whole chapter, however, is perfectly clear: When the last horn of the fourth beast is broken—i.e., when the reign of the persecutor, Antiochus IV Epiphanes, comes to an end—"then the kingship and dominion and majesty of all the kingdoms under the heavens shall be given to the holy people of the Most High, whose kingdom shall be everlasting" (v 27).

27 **1.** *the first year:* This date may have been added by a later editor who prefixed successive dates to each of the four apocalypses; in any case, it goes back beyond the last date in the haggadic stories (6:29). *the account began:* A more likely rendering of the Aram *rē'š millîn* *'āmar* than "he gave a summary of the matters"; cf. v 28: "The report concluded." **2.** *the four winds:* The four cardinal points of the compass, to show the universality of the cosmic tempest. *the great sea:* The primeval abyss of Gen 1:2, which, according to ancient concepts, was the abode of horrendous monsters hostile to God (Job 7:12; 26:11–12; Ps 74:13–14; Isa 27:1; 51:9–10). **4–7.** Although some of the elements in the description of the beasts may ultimately derive from the widespread mythological images in the ancient Near East, the author drew most of his imagery from the older books of the Bible, particularly from the prophets. In Rev 13:1–2, where the imagery of Dan 7 is applied to the pagan Roman Empire as hostile to God's people of the new covenant, a composite beast is made from the chief characteristics of the four beasts of Dan 7. The bear's feet and the lion's mouth are stressed. It would seem, therefore, that John had a text of Dan 7:4–5 differing from the current MT in that certain words now in the middle of v 4 were transposed with words now at the end of v 5. Restoring, therefore, these words to what seems to have been their original position, we may translate vv 4–5 literally as follows: (4a) The first was like a lion, but with eagle's wings, (5b) and among the teeth in its mouth there were three fangs. It was given the order: "Up, devour much flesh!" (4b) While I watched its wings were plucked, and it was lifted up from the earth. (5a) And behold, there was another beast, a second one, resembling a bear; it raised up one side, (4c) and it was made to stand on its feet like a human, and it was given a human heart.

In this restored text, each beast has its own symbolic number representing all the kings of each dynasty that were known from the Bible to the Jews of the Hellenistic period. The first beast, the lion, representing the Baby-

lonian Empire, has in its mouth three tusks or fangs (lit., "ribs," but see R. Frank, *CBQ* 21 [1959] 505–7) to symbolize the only three Babylonian kings known from the Bible—Nebuchadnezzar, Evil-merodach (2 Kgs 25:27 = Jer 53:31), and Belshazzar. Its wings were plucked and it was taken from the earth when "Darius the Mede" captured Babylon (Dan 5:30–6:1). The second beast, the bear that takes the natural upright stance of a bear, representing the kingdom of the Medes, lifts up one side (one paw?) to symbolize the only one king of the Medes known from the Bible, "Darius the Mede" (Dan 6:1). Its "human heart" points to its humane character in benefiting the Jews by destroying the hated Babylonian Empire. The third beast, the leopard, representing the Persian Empire, has four heads (and also four wings, if this is part of the original text) to symbolize the only four kings of Persia (cf. 11:2) known from the Bible—Cyrus, Ahasuerus (or Xerxes), Artaxerxes, and "Darius the Persian" (Neh 12:22). The fourth beast, representing the kingdom of the Greeks, which is too horrible to be likened to any animal of the earth, differs from the first three beasts (Oriental dynasties) in its Western origin and has 10 horns (explicitly stated at the end of v 7, but omitted in *NAB*), symbolizing the 10 rulers of this dynasty up to the time of the writer. According to Berossus, Seleucus I Nicator was reckoned as the third Gk ruler in the Near East (Alexander the Great being the first, and either Alexander Aegus or Philip Arrhidaeus being the second), so that the tenth horn (ruler) must be Antiochus IV Epiphanes. **8.** This whole verse belongs to the secondary stratum. *a little horn:* This new symbolism for Antiochus IV Epiphanes is taken from 8:9. *three of the previous horns were torn away to make room for it:* This translation is based on the interpretation supposing that three of Antiochus IV Epiphanes' predecessors died violent deaths so that he could succeed to the throne. Even if this is true, he was responsible for none of these deaths. But in v 20, also part of the secondary stratum, it is stated that "three of the horns fell before him"—i.e., were defeated by him in battle. Therefore, for the writer of the insertions, the 10 horns do not represent 10 successive Gk kings, but 10 kings of various countries contemporaneous with Antiochus IV Epiphanes—the "little horn" that "sprang up among them" (*silqāt bênêhēn,* v 8). Actually, as Porphyry first noted (quoted by Jerome, PL 25. 531), Antiochus IV Epiphanes "laid low three kings" (*ûtĕlātâ malkîn yĕhašpil,* v 24) in defeating Ptolemy VI Philometor in 169, Ptolemy VII Euergetes II in 168, and King Artaxias of Armenia in 166. *this horn had eyes like human eyes and a mouth that spoke arrogantly:* The word "human" is here used in a derogatory sense to contrast with God; the whole sentence is based on Isa 37:23, which is addressed to the king of Babylon.

28 **9–14.** The description of the celestial court scene at which the fourth beast is condemned and destroyed is all from the primary stratum, except v 11a. **12.** *the other beasts:* The second and the third; the first had already been taken from the earth (v 4). Although they lost their "dominion," i.e., empires, Media and Persia still remained petty kingdoms. *they were granted prolongation of life for a time and a season:* They were allowed to linger on for a short indeterminate period. **13.** *one like a son of man:* Or "one in human form." An image appeared in the vision resembling a human being, just as the first four images resembled different beasts. These came from the great abyss below, i.e., from the powers of evil; he comes from above, "with the clouds of heaven," i.e., from God. Just as the beasts are figures of the pagan kingdoms, so also the one in human form symbolizes "the holy ones of the Most High" (v 18). In the context, therefore, the one in human form is not a real individual but a symbol. However, because in Dan the thought of "kingdom" often shifts imperceptibly into that of "king," the concept of the "son of man" eventually shifted from a figure of speech for the theocratic kingdom into a term for the messianic king himself. This change appears in *Enoch*, written a century or two before the time of Christ (on Jesus' application of this term to himself, → Jesus, 78:38-41; → Apocrypha, 67:8-15).

15-27. The explanation of the vision is all from the primary stratum, except v 20 (apart from the first few words) and vv 24b-25. Verses 21-22 were probably added still later, combining as they do words from both strata. **16.** *one of those present:* One of the angels attending the divine court. **25.** *thinking to change the feast days and the law:* On Antiochus IV Epiphanes' efforts to do away with the Jewish feasts, the sabbath, and the whole Mosaic law, see 1 Macc 1:41-64. *a year, two years, and a half year:* Three and one-half years, i.e., half the perfect number, seven, and thus symbolizing a period of evil (cf. 8:14; 9:27; 12:7). **28.** *I kept the matter to myself:* Daniel understands the meaning of the vision, but he keeps the revelation a secret (so also in 8:26; 12:4,9; but cf. with 8:27). The primary stratum in Dan 7 was written in the reign of Antiochus IV Epiphanes, but before he began his active persecution of the Jews toward the end of 167; the secondary stratum was added after his victory over Artaxias in the second half of 165, but before the end of his persecution in December 164.

(Beasley-Murray, G. R., "The Interpretation of Daniel 7," *CBQ* 45 [1983] 44-58. Di Lella, A. A., "The One in Human Likeness and the Holy Ones of the Most High in Daniel 7," *CBQ* 39 [1977] 1-19. Feuillet, A., "Le Fils de l'homme de Daniel et la tradition biblique," *RB* 60 [1953] 170-202, 321-46. Manson, T. W., "The Son of Man in Daniel, Henoch, and the Gospels," *BJRL* 32 [1949] 171-93.)

29   (B) The Ram and the He-Goat (8:1-27). There is no difficulty at all in interpreting the symbolism of chap. 8, for it is clearly explained to Daniel by his angelic interpreter. It was probably written by a different author from the one who wrote chap. 7, apparently composed soon after the desecration of the Temple. It is written in Hebrew, although Aramaic may have been its original language. Like chap. 7, it also seems to have suffered some later insertions.

1-2. *Susa in the province of Elam:* Daniel would hardly have been at this capital of the Persian Empire during the reign of Belshazzar (see comment on 7:1). *the river Ulai:* Susa was indeed on this river, but it is not certain that the Hebr word *'ûbal* should be translated "river"; perhaps it should be read as *'ābûl* and translated "city gate" (from Akk *abullu*, "city gate"). Daniel would then have had his vision near the Ulai Gate at Susa. **3-4.** Interpreted in v 20 as representing the kingdom of the Medes and Persians (here regarded as a single kingdom!). **5.** *the he-goat:* The kingdom of the Greeks (v 21). *a prominent horn:* Alexander the Great (v 21). **8.** *four others:* The Gk kingdoms into which Alexander's empire was divided after his death: W, Macedonia, under Cassander; N, Thrace and Asia Minor, under Lysimachus; E, Syria, Mesopotamia, and Persia, under Seleucus; S, Egypt, under Ptolemy. **9.** *a little horn:* Antiochus IV Epiphanes of the Seleucid dynasty; he began his reign as a "little horn" because he inherited a weakened realm, but he soon strengthened his kingdom and extended its sway. *the glorious country:* Palestine. **10.** *the host of heaven . . . the stars:* God's holy people (cf. 12:3). *the prince of the host:* Israel's God.

13-14. Probably an insertion, added by the author of chap. 9, to whom vv 16, 26a, and 27b are attributed; this writer was especially interested in calculating the length of the persecution. *a holy one:* Here an angel, although "the holy ones" are the Jews in v 24. *the desolating sin:* In Hebrew, *peša' šōmēm*, like *šiqqûṣ (mĕ)šōmēm* (the appalling abomination of 9:27; 11:31; 12:11), is an intentional deformation of the Phoenician name *Ba'al šāmēm*, "the Lord of Heaven," for the Gk god Zeus Olympios, whose statue Antiochus IV Epiphanes erected in the Temple of Jerusalem (1 Macc 1:54; cf. Matt 24:15). **14.** The number is equivalent to 1,150 days, or three and one-half years (see comment on 7:25). **16.** This verse seems to introduce Gabriel unnecessarily from chap. 9 into this chapter. Originally, this vision was probably explained to Daniel by the unnamed "humanlike figure" (angel) of v 15. **23-25.** A description of Antiochus IV Epiphanes and his persecution. **27b.** *the vision, which I could not understand:* Inconsistent with the words of the angel in v 17 — "Understand . . . the vision" — and therefore this whole sentence apparently belongs to the later insertions.

30   (C) The Interpretation of the 70 Weeks (9:1-27). This chapter consists not of a symbolic vision, as in chaps. 7-8, but of a revelation made directly by an angel. In answer to Daniel's prayer for a solution to the problem of why Jeremiah's prophecy of a restoration of Israel after 70 years has not been fulfilled, the angel Gabriel explains to him that the prophecy means 70 weeks of years—i.e., 7 times 70 years. Moreover, Gabriel divides these 490 years into three very unequal periods of 49, 434, and 7 years, respectively. Because the writer's calculations are only approximate and his historical references not always clear, there is still some difference of opinion in interpreting certain details in Gabriel's explanation. But practically all exegetes now agree that the 490 years terminate in the end of Antiochus IV Epiphanes' persecution; the once-common opinion that saw in vv 26-27 a reference to the death of Jesus Christ is now abandoned by almost all exegetes. If, as claimed by some, there are later insertions from the author of this chapter in chaps. 7-8 and 10-12, this would be the last chapter of the book to be written (shortly before the end of this persecution), and its author was probably the editor of the whole book.

1. The date has no chronological value (see comment on 7:1). Among the Persian kings, Darius I was the father, not the son, of Xerxes. But "Darius the Mede" is the imaginary character (6:1), and any imaginary name can be given to his father. **2.** On two different occasions, Jeremiah spoke of a 70-year period before the restoration of Zion (25:11-12; 29:10). In both cases, the prophet used the round number 70 to signify a full lifetime (cf. Ps 90:10). His prediction found fairly accurate fulfillment in the return of the first Jewish exiles to Jerusalem soon after Cyrus's conquest of Babylon in 539. But the author of Dan 9 is not satisfied with this fulfillment, which appears to him too incomplete a restoration of Zion. **3.** Therefore, he prays for further enlightenment.

4-20. This whole section is a later addition to the chapter, which originally read: (v 3) "I turned to the Lord God, pleading in earnest prayer, with fasting, sackcloth, and ashes; (v 21) and while I was still occupied in prayer, Gabriel, in human form, whom I had seen before in vision, came to me," etc. This mention of Daniel praying, although no prayer is given, suggested to a later scribe the possibility of inserting a prayer here. The older, inspired prayer that he inserted is written in much better Hebrew than that of the rest of the book. It is not a prayer of an individual but of the community, and it is not a plea for enlightenment on the meaning of Jeremiah's prophecy, as the context would demand, but an acknowledgment of public guilt and a supplication for the restoration of Zion. To the later scribe are also attributed the connecting links of vv 4a and 20. **13.** *as it is written:* The earliest biblical occurrence of this formula for citing Scripture. The sanctions referred to in v 11 are from Lev 26:14-39; Deut 28:15-68.

(Gilbert, M., "La prière de Daniel, Dan 9, 4-19," *RTL* 3 [1972] 284-310. Jones, B. W., "The Prayer in Daniel IX," *VT* 18 [1968] 488-93. Lacocque, A., "The Liturgical Prayer in Daniel 9," *HUCA* 47 [1976] 119-42.)

31   24. *seventy weeks:* Or "seventy sabbatical periods." The change from the 70 years of Jeremiah to 7 times 70 years is based not only on the fact that Israel's lack of complete repentance merited this sevenfold punishment (Lev 26:18) but also on 2 Chr 36:21, where Jeremiah's prophecy is connected with the sabbatical years spoken of in Lev 26:34-35. **24.** A brief summary of the whole period of the 490 years. If reckoned at its longest, from the time that Jeremiah first spoke his prophecy (605) to the end of Antiochus IV Epiphanes' persecution (164), this period would be only 441 years. But the writer, who no doubt knew little of the chronology of the early postexilic period, would not be disturbed by this discrepancy between his symbolic numbers and the historical facts. *a most holy will be anointed:* Almost certainly refers to the consecration by Judas Maccabeus of the restored Holy of Holies in the Jerusalem Temple, but the Church Fathers often applied it to Jesus, "the Anointed One."

25-27. The three main periods of the 490 years. **25.** *an anointed leader:* Cyrus the Great (cf. Isa 45:1) or Zerubbabel or the high priest Joshua ben Jozadak. Only if one reckons from the second utterance of Jeremiah's prophecy (*ca.* 595) to the anointing of Cyrus as king of Persia (558—a date the writer of Dan 9 would hardly know!) could the required 49 years be approximately obtained. But the following words imply that the first period extends to the beginning of the rebuilding of Jerusalem, which would embrace much more than seven weeks of years. *sixty-two weeks:* The 62 weeks of years, or 434 years, allowed for the rebuilding of Jerusalem are too many by far; from 538 to 171 (the next date) is only 367 years. **26.** *an anointed shall be cut down:* The reference is certainly to the murder of the deposed high priest, Onias III, in 171, in Antioch; hence, "when he does not possess the city of Jerusalem" (cf. 2 Macc 4:5,33-36). *the soldiers of a leader:* The Syrian army of Antiochus IV Epiphanes, which plundered the Jerusalem Temple in 169 and 167. **27.** *for one week:* If counted from the murder of Onias in 171, this period would last from 170 to 163. The writer's hopes that the persecution would not last beyond 163 were fully realized. He probably wrote a few months before the persecution ended in December 164. *a firm pact with many:* An alliance made by Antiochus IV Epiphanes with renegade Jews who favored the hellenization of their culture (cf. 1 Macc 1:11-14). *half a week:* The second half of the seven-year period beginning in 170. (On the symbolic value of three and one-half years, see comment on 7:25.) The desecration of the Temple actually lasted only three years—from December 167 to December 164 (1 Macc 1:54; 4:52). See R. T. Beckwith, "Daniel 9 and the Date of Messiah's Coming in Essene, Hellenistic, Pharisaic, Zealot and Early Christian Computation," *RevQ* 10 (1981) 521-42.

32   (D) The Revelation of the Hellenistic Wars (10:1-12:13). This last apocalypse is also the longest and the most elaborate in the book. After a lengthy introduction that gives the setting of the revelation (10:1-11:1), an unnamed angel offers Daniel a brief account of the history of the Persian Empire and of Alexander the Great (11:2-4), and then a very long account of the history of the Seleucid dynasty, which becomes more and more detailed as the writer approaches his own times, the reign of Antiochus IV Epiphanes (11:5-45). The apocalypse ends with poetic solemnity (12:1-3) and the customary warning to keep the revelation a secret (12:4). What follows (12:5-13) are later additions. This apocalypse has the usual purpose of guaranteeing the truth of the prediction of ultimate salvation by recounting in the form of prophecies what are actually past events. The author's style is considerably different from the style in the other apocalypses in Dan, which would seem to indicate a distinct author for this section. The Hebrew of this apocalypse is quite poor, and there are good grounds for thinking that it is based on an Aram original. The author must have composed his apocalypse before the campaign of Antiochus IV Epiphanes in the east in the summer of 165, for instead of predicting this, he foretold a successful campaign of the Syrian king in Egypt for this year—a campaign that never actually took place.

1. *the third year of King Cyrus:* 536; since Daniel's mission began in 606, this vision took place in the 70th, or "perfect," year of his ministry. *a great war:* If this rendering is correct, the reference would be to the Hellenistic wars (11:5-45) rather than to the struggles of individual angels (10:13,20-21). But the transl. and significance of the Hebr expression ṣābāʾ gādôl, are uncertain; it would ordinarily be translated as "a great army" or "a great service," but the sense of such phrases in the context would be obscure. **3.** Daniel's fasting is not in penance for sin, but a preparation for mystical knowledge (v 12). **4-9.** In the description of his angelic visitor, the author borrows heavily from Ezek (esp. from chaps. 1, 9, and 11), while his description in turn serves as a model for the NT Rev (particularly Rev 1-2). **12-13.** The angel explains why Daniel had to wait three weeks (vv 2-3) for the revelation: The angelic messenger was prevented for this length of time by the "prince of the kingdom of Persia" from delivering to Daniel this revelation that is partly concerned with announcing the destruction of the Persian Empire. He was finally free to deliver the message only when Michael, Israel's "prince" (v 21), came to his aid. The idea was common in Judaism that every nation had its guardian angel, but this concept was very old in Israel (cf. Deut 32:8 [corrected according to the LXX]). Inasmuch as Michael is Israel's guardian angel, he is "one of the chief princes" or archangels.

10:20-11:2a. The text seems to be confused. The *NAB* omits the first half of 11:1. However, by assuming that the order of the clauses has been disturbed in the MT, it can be preserved (with a few slight corrections) to read as follows: (20a) "Do you know," he asked, "why I have come to you? (21a) I will tell you what is written in the Book of Truth. (20b) Soon I must fight with the prince of Persia again; when he [!] leaves, the prince of Greece will come. (21b) No one supports me against all these except Michael, your prince (11:1), and since the first year of Darius the Mede he has been standing as a reinforcement and bulwark for me." The confusion in the text was probably caused by the author of Dan 9, who inserted here the mention of Darius the Mede (11:1) to identify this unnamed angel with Gabriel, for it was Gabriel who brought Daniel the revelation in the first year of Darius the Mede (9:1).

33   11:2-4. Only four kings of Persia were known to the 2d-cent. Jews (see comment on 7:6). These rich Persian kings (that the last of them was the richest is purely imaginary) are to be conquered by "a powerful king," Alexander the Great, whose empire shall be divided among four of his generals (see comment on 8:8).

5. *the king of the south:* The first ruler of Egypt after the division of Alexander's empire—i.e., Ptolemy I Soter

(323–285). *one of his princes:* Seleucus I Nicator (312–280), who at first was a petty vassal of Ptolemy I Soter, but later won a vast kingdom for himself, making Antioch on the Orontes its capital. **6.** In *ca.* 250, Ptolemy II Philadelphus (285–246) gave his daughter Bernice in marriage to Antiochus II Theos (261–246). But the latter's divorced wife, Laodice, eventually had not only Antiochus II Theos, but also Bernice and her infant son, with their Egyptian entourage, put to death. **7–8.** In revenge for these crimes, Bernice's brother, Ptolemy III Euergetes (246–221), invaded Syria, put Laodice to death, defeated Laodice's son, Seleucus II Callinicus (246–226), devasted the land, and carried off enormous booty to Egypt. **9.** In 242–240, Seleucus II undertook a counteroffensive against Egypt but failed miserably.
10. *his sons:* Seleucus III Soter (226–223) and Antiochus III the Great (223–187) were the sons of Seleucus II Callinicus. The figure of the surging flood is from Isa 8:8. **11–12.** The victory of Ptolemy IV Philopator (221–203) over Antiochus III in the battle of Raphia (S of Gaza) in 217. **13–16.** The victories of Antiochus III the Great over Ptolemy V Epiphanes (203–181) in Palestine (202–198), including his successful siege of Sidon. **17.** The marriage of Cleopatra, daughter of Antiochus III, to Ptolemy V at Raphia in 193. **18.** The invasion of Antiochus III into western Asia Minor ("the coastland"), which was checked at Magnesia in 190 by "a leader," the Roman consul L. Cornelius Scipio. **19–20.** After the assassination of Antiochus III in 187, while he was plundering a temple in Elymais, he was succeeded by his older son, Seleucus IV Philopator (187–175), who sent his minister of finance ("tax collector") to seize the treasury of the Jerusalem Temple, and who was later murdered at the instigation of Heliodorus.
21–24. *a despicable person:* Antiochus IV Epiphanes (175–164), who usurped the throne, supplanting Demetrius, the young son of Seleucus IV Philpator. *the prince of the covenant:* The Jewish high priest, Onias III, who was murdered at the court of Antiochus in 170 (cf. 2 Macc 4:33–35). **25–27.** The first campaign of Antiochus against Egypt. Ptolemy VI Philometor, betrayed by his friends and defeated by Antiochus IV Epiphanes in 169, pretended to become a vassal of the king of Syria. **28–30a.** The second campaign of Antiochus IV Epiphanes against Egypt. In 168 he defeated Ptolemy VII Euergetes II, but was forced by Roman legate C. Popilius Laenas to leave Egypt. The Hebr term *kittîm* originally designated the inhabitants of Cyprus; it was later used for other peoples of the eastern Mediterranean, here for the Romans. **30b–31.** On his return from Egypt, Antiochus IV Epiphanes plundered the Temple and began his active persecution of the Jews. *the appalling abomination:* See comment on 8:13–14. **37.** *the one desired by women:* The god Tammuz-Adonis (cf. Ezek 8:14). **38.** *the god of strongholds:* Probably the Roman god Jupiter Capitolinus, equated with the Gk god Zeus Olympios. **40–45.** Prediction of a successful campaign of Antiochus IV Epiphanes in Egypt, which actually did not take place. **45.** *between the sea and the beautiful holy mountain:* Between the Mediterranean and Jerusalem. Although the author is inexact regarding the place of Antiochus IV Epiphanes' death (who actually died in 164 in Persia), he is essentially correct, for the death would be miserable.
34 **12:1–3.** Magnificent poetic conclusion of the revelation given in chaps. 10–11. Despite the terrible sufferings in the eschatological crisis, the elect of God, whose names are "found written in the book" of life (cf. Exod 32:32–33; Ps 69:29), will be saved. *sleep:* A euphemism for "are dead" (cf. John 11:11–13; Acts 7:60; 1 Thess 4:13). *shall awake:* Shall come back to life. This passage is remarkable as the earliest clear enunciation of

belief in the resurrection of the dead (see B. Alfrink, *Bib* 40 [1959] 355–71). *some shall live forever:* lit., "some unto life everlasting" (*lĕḥayyê ʿôlām*) — the first occurrence of this term in the Bible (See M. S. Moore, *TZ* 39 [1983] 17–34.) **4.** Prose ending of this revelation and the original ending of this section. *keep the message secret and seal the book:* Essentially the same expression as in 8:26b. By a literary device common to several apocalyptic writers, an ancient seer is pictured as receiving a revelation that is not to be made public until the proper time, which is, of course, the time of the apocalyptic writer. **5–10.** Evidently an addition to the apocalypse of 10:1–12:4, it is probably by the same writer who composed the apocalypse of the 70 weeks of years (9:1–3, 21–27) and who inserted 8:13–14,16,26a,27b into the apocalypse of the ram and the he-goat. Daniel overhears a conversation of two heavenly beings as in 8:13–14. *Gabriel:* As in chap. 9. *a year, two years, a half year:* Three and one-half years (see 7:25; 8:14). **11–12.** Two distinct later additions. The time of distress was to last three and one-half years (7:25; 12:7) or 1,150 days (8:14). In v 11, however, a glossator who saw that the period of persecution had not yet ended after so many days increased the number to 1,290, and for the same reason a still later glossator lengthened the time to 1,335 days. **13.** Perhaps from the same hand that wrote 12:5–10, although it expresses the same belief in the resurrection of the dead as does v 2.
35 **(III) Other Exploits of Daniel (13:1–14:42).** At the end of Jerome's Lat transl. of the Hebr-Aram book of Daniel, the Vg has three other stories about Daniel that have been translated into Latin from the Gk text called "Theodotion-Daniel" (→ 8 above). The type of Greek used in these stories shows that their original language was Semitic, either Hebrew or Aramaic. The Gk transl., however, was made with considerable liberty, as can be seen in its frequent use of participial constructions. Besides "Theodotion-Daniel," the Greek has also come down to us in another form, commonly called the LXX, which is quite different in many places.
All these stories are haggadic folktales, like the stories in the first half of the book (chaps. 1–6). Fragments of a "Daniel Cycle" found at Qumran indicate that all these stories are but a small part of numerous folktales about a legendary Daniel that circulated among the Jews of the last pre-Christian centuries.
36 **(A) Daniel's Rescue of the Chaste Susanna (13:1–64).** The Theodotion form of this story, on which the *NAB* is based, is told in a more dramatic form than in the shorter LXX version. Although the latter seems to be, in general, an abridged recension, it has perhaps preserved a few passages that seem closer to the original than the corresponding passages in the other form. One of these is Daniel's question to the false witnesses, which, according to the LXX, reads: "Under what tree and in what part of the garden did you see them together?" It seems to imply that the original Semitic story involved a question not only about trees but also about the locality of the supposed crime. The Gk pun on the names of the trees (see comments on vv 55,59) could then be considered a new element added in the Gk form of the story and thus no argument against the presumed Semitic language of the original.
Superficially, at least, the primary purpose of the story is to show that virtue (here in the form of conjugal chastity) triumphs, with God's help over vice (here in the form of lust and deceit). Inasmuch as this story belongs to the "Daniel Cycle," it also offers another example of this hero's God-given wisdom. Exegetes, however, have seen deeper meanings in the tale. For some exegetes it is a sort of parable. The two wicked elders ("offspring of

Canaan," i.e., idolators) would symbolize the pagans and the apostate Jews, esp. at the time of Antiochus IV Epiphanes, who tried to make the Jews, here symbolized by Susanna, fall into the sin of apostasy from Yahweh — the sin that the prophets often called fornication and adultery. The "daughters of Israel" — i.e., the Samaritans — might indeed be seduced by the alluring pagan Hellenism, but not the "daughter of Judah" (v 57) — i.e., the good Jews. Susanna's heroic statement, "It is better for me to fall into your power without guilt than to sin before the Lord" (v 23), would then be a fine expression of the sentiments of the Maccabean martyrs when offered the choice between apostasy and death. Still other exegetes would see in this story an indictment by some writer of the Pharisees against the worldly minded Sadducees who acted as "elders" or leaders of the people. In this case the story would be a midrash on the pseudo-biblical quotation of v 5 (cf. R. A. F. MacKenzie, "The Meaning of the Susanna Story," *CJT* 3 [1957] 211–18).

2. *Susanna:* The corresponding Hebr word *šôšannâ* is the name of a flower that is traditionally translated as "lily." **5.** *two elders:* An ancient Jewish opinion, witnessed to by Jerome, identifies them with the two false prophets spoken of in Jer 29:21–23; the author of this story may indeed have borrowed the picture of his two wicked elders from that passage. *the Lord said:* Although introduced like a quotation from Scripture, the words attributed here to the Lord are not found in any biblical or apocryphal book. But the reference may be to Jer 23:15 or 29:21–23. **7–14.** The story as told in the LXX is somewhat different. After seeing Susanna and becoming enamored of her as she walked one afternoon in her garden, each of the elders secretly decided to return there alone early the next day. Scarcely had one of them come there on the following day when the other also arrived and said, "Why did you come here so early and not wait for me?" Thereupon they admitted to each other their common passion. **15–24.** For these 10 verses of "Theodotion-Daniel" the LXX has only three verses; omitting the bathing scene, it simply relates the elders' resolve to violate Susanna and her refusal to submit to them (vv 22b–23). Strangely, she is here called "the Jewish (woman)." **30.** According to the LXX, Susanna is accompanied by not only her father and mother but also "her 500 male and female servants and her four children." **34.** *laid their hands on her head:* As prescribed in the law for witnesses (Lev 24:14; cf. Deut 13:9–10; 17:5,7). **45.** *God stirred up . . . a young boy named Daniel:* In the LXX it is "the angel of the Lord" who acts. Inasmuch as Daniel is presented here as "a young boy" (Theodotion, *paidarion neōteron*) or "a youth" (LXX *neōteros*) in most Gk mss. this story is put at the very beginning of Dan. **50.** No doubt

the elders say this in sarcasm. **52–59.** By divine inspiration Daniel was sure of the elders' guilt; therefore, there is no need to quibble that the inconsistency of their testimony on a relatively minor circumstance would not necessarily, at least in a modern court of law, prove that their main contention was false. The Gk play on words cannot be accurately reproduced in English: "Under a mastic tree (*hypo schinon*). . . . The angel shall . . . split (*schisei*) you in two. . . . Under an oak (*hypo prinon*). . . . The angel shall cut (*prisai*) you in two." **56.** The LXX reads "Why was your offspring corrupted like Sidon, and not like Judah?" although "offspring" (Gk *sperma*) should probably be taken here as "seed." **61.** *according to the law of Moses:* As prescribed in Deut 19:18–19.

37   **(B) Daniel and the Priests of Bel (14:1–22).** This little "detective story" is another folktale of the "Daniel Cycle." It is a Jewish satire on the crudities of idolatry, although actually it is a caricature of pagan worship. The offering of food and drink in sacrifice to pagan gods did not differ substantially from similar offerings made to Yahweh in the Temple. In both cases, a certain amount of the sacrificial offerings went quite legitimately to the priests and their families. However, the Jews of the last pre-Christian centuries were so convinced of the folly of idolatry (cf. Wis 13:1–15:17) that this unfair ridicule of pagan worship is understandable.

1. This story is correct in these facts of secular history; Astyages, the last king of the Medes, was in fact defeated and succeeded by Cyrus the Persian in 550. **2.** The LXX, which in general does not differ much in this story from Theodotion, is different here: "A certain priest, whose name was Daniel, son of Abal, was the companion of the king of Babylon." **3.** *Bel:* The Babylonian title (meaning "lord") of the god Marduk (Merodach; cf. Isa 46:1; Jer 50:2; 51:44; see also comment on Dan 1:7). **21.** *they showed him the secret door:* According to the LXX, Daniel showed it to the king.

38   **(C) Daniel's Destruction of the Dragon (14:23–42).** Another short story of the "Daniel Cycle," it is basically a variant of the story told in Dan 6 (Daniel in the lions' den). Here is included another satire on pagan worship — Daniel's blowing up of the Babylonians' divine serpent. Although once an independent story, in its present form it is edited to follow the preceding narrative (cf. v 28); in all the Gk manuscripts, the two stories are together, and the LXX even prefixes to the former the title "From the prophecy of Habakkuk, son of Jesus, of the tribe of Levi." **33.** The canonical prophet Habakkuk (of *ca.* 600) is no doubt meant, although most implausibly at the time of Cyrus. **38.** *O God, you have not forsaken those who love you:* This moral is valid for all time.

26

1-2 MACCABEES

Neil J. McEleney, C.S.P.

BIBLIOGRAPHY

1 Abel, F. M., *Les livres des Maccabées* (EBib; 2d ed.; Paris, 1949). Abel, F. M. and J. Starcky, *Les livres des Maccabées* (3d ed.; Paris, 1961). Bartlett, J. R., *The First and Second Books of the Maccabees* (London, 1973). Bickermann, E., *The God of the Maccabees* (Leiden, 1979). Bringmann, K., *Hellenistische Reform und Religionsverfolgung in Judäa* (Göttingen, 1983). Collins, J. J., *Daniel, First Maccabees, Second Maccabees* (OTM; Wilmington, 1981). Corbishley, T., "1 and 2 Maccabees," *NCCHS* (NY, 1969). Dancy, J. C., *1 Maccabees: A Commentary* (Oxford, 1954). Doran, R., *Temple Propaganda: The Purpose and Character of 2 Maccabees* (CBQMS 12; Washington, 1981). Farmer, W. R., *Maccabees, Zealots, and Josephus* (NY, 1956). Fischer, T., *Seleukiden und Makkabäer* (Bochum, 1980). Goldstein, J., *I Maccabees* (AB

41; NY, 1976); *II Maccabees* (AB 41A; NY, 1983). Hanhart, R., *Maccabaeorum Liber II* (Göttingen, 1959). Kappler, W., *Maccabaeorum Liber I* (2d ed.; Göttingen, 1967). Lefevre, A., "Maccabées, les livres des," *DBSup* 5. 597–612. Moffatt, J., "2 Maccabees," *APOT* 1. 125–54. Oesterley, W. O. E., "1 Maccabees," *APOT* 1. 59–124. Osty, E. and J. Trinquet, *La Bible: Premier et Deuxième Livres des Maccabées* (Paris, 1971). Penna, A., *Libri dei Maccabei* (Roma, 1953). Schaumberger, J., "Die Neue Seleukiden-Liste BM 35603," *Bib* 36 (1955) 423–35. Sisti, A., *I Maccabei: Libro Primo* (Roma, 1968); *I Maccabei: Libro Secundo* (Roma, 1969). Tedesche, S. and S. Zeitlin, *The First Book of Maccabees* (NY, 1950); *The Second Book of Maccabees* (NY, 1954).

INTRODUCTION

2 **(I) Title.** There are four books known by the title "Maccabees." All four owe their name to Judas Maccabeus, the third son of the priest Mattathias, who began the Jewish revolt against the Seleucids in 167 BC. The name *Makkabaios,* Judas's surname (1 Macc 2:4), probably derives from a Hebrew form, *maqqabyāhū,* meaning "designated by God," although some interpreters have understood it to mean the "hammer" (striking the enemy) or "hammer-headed" (with reference to a physical defect). Each interpretation has defenders, but most likely the first is correct, since Judas's position of leadership (1 Macc 2:66) and of honor among the people (1 Macc 5:63–64) call rather for the meaning "designated by God" (see Isa 62:2) than for the more warlike or physical interpretations.

The earliest designation for 1 Macc, which originated in Hebrew, seems to be that preserved by Origen's commentary on Ps 1 (cited in Eusebius, *HE* 6.25.2) in the textually corrupt phrase *sarbēthsabanaiel.* When this Hebr phrase is corrected, it yields the title *sēper bēt śar bĕnê 'ēl,* "the book of the house of the leader of the sons of God." There is a corresponding title in the description of Simon (1 Macc 14:27) as "leader of the people of God."

Early Jewish literature, ignoring this title, uses instead the designation "Hasmonean," when referring to Judas

and his family. Most scholars take this to be an ancestral name. Thus Josephus, the earliest witness to it, speaks of *Asamōnaios,* who is the father (*J.W.* 1.1.3 §36) or grandfather (*Ant.* 12.6.1 §265) or even the great-grandfather (not reading *Asamōnaiou* in apposition with *Symeōnos*) of Mattathias, the father of Judas and his brothers (1 Macc 2:1–5). Zeitlin, however, thinks the term "Hasmonean" is not a personal name but an honorific title equivalent to "prince" (*First Maccabees* 248).

The earliest explicit Christian reference to these books—in Clement of Alexandria, near the beginning of the 3d cent. AD (*Strom.* 1.21.123)—cites *to (biblion) tōn Makkabaikōn,* "the (book) of things Maccabean." This early title, *ta makkabaika,* was perhaps affixed to the beginning of 2 Macc by the epitomist, when he abridged the work of Jason of Cyrene (2 Macc 2:19–32). From there it passed into use as a title for the first book of things "maccabean," when that came to be translated into Greek. After Clement's time, both Gk and Lat authors shifted the term slightly to speak of the books "of the Maccabees."

3 **(II) Canonicity.** Disillusionment with the politics of the later Hasmoneans explains, in part, why the Qumran community and the Pharisees, both successors to the Hasideans (1 Macc 2:42), had so little regard for these books of the Maccabees. As yet, no copy

421

of either book has been found at Qumran, nor, as we might have expected, has the rabbinic tradition, which stems from Pharisaic Judaism, preserved the Hebr text of 1 Macc. Josephus, himself a Pharisee, reflects the prevailing view of 1st-cent. and subsequent Judaism when he omits these books from those he holds sacred (*Ag. Ap.* 1.8 §38–41).

Within the Christian community, however, 1 and 2 Macc have had a better fate. The Roman Church places these works in its canon of the Scriptures, pointing to an ancient tradition. First to cite them in antiquity is Clement of Alexandria. He is followed by Hippolytus, Tertullian, Origen, Cyprian, Eusebius, Aphraates, Jerome, Augustine, and Theodoret. The provincial councils of Hippo (393) and Carthage (397 and 419) recognized the sacred character of 1 and 2 Macc, and the general councils of Florence (1441), Trent (1546), and Vatican I (1870) declared them to be inspired by God.

Protestant Christianity, however, does not consider 1 and 2 Macc to be canonical literature, although it accords these works a special place and esteem among the apocrypha.

4   (III) Text and Ancient Versions.   The prime witnesses to the text are the Gk uncials and the OL version. The Hebr original of 1 Macc has been lost. The canonical Gk text is to be found in the uncial codices S (Sinaiticus, 4th cent.), A (Alexandrinus, 5th cent.), and V (Venetus, 8th cent.). The last two also contain the text of 2 Macc.

The OL is represented by three 9th-cent. codices—L (Lyon), X (Madrid), and G (Sangermanensis, which lacks 1 Macc 14ff. and 2 Macc)—and by two 11th–12th cent. codices, B (Bologna) and M (Milan, for 2 Macc).

The Vg derives from the OL and the Lucianic recension of the Greek. It can be found in several manuscripts and in two codices P (Milan, 9th–10th cents.) and in M (Milan, 11th–12th cents. for 1 Macc).

5   (IV) Sources.   The author of 1 Macc relied, at least in part, on the personal recollections of eyewitnesses for his account of Judas's exploits. To what extent this and the earlier part of his work also had written sources is not at all clear. The ambiguous text of 1 Macc 9:22 (see 1 Kgs 11:41) has been variously interpreted as pointing to a larger Judas chronicle, to written notes, or to no written sources at all. Whatever his sources for the deeds of Judas (and his father), the author of 1 Macc certainly had the Temple treasury at his disposal for his narrative of Jonathan and Simon. In the Temple archives (1 Macc 14:49), which were probably begun by Nehemiah (see 2 Macc 2:13), he could draw upon the annals of the high-priesthood (1 Macc 16:24; 10:21; 14:41) and the following official documents with dates:

LETTER	DATE	1 MACC
Roman Senate to Judas	161	8:23–32
Demetrius I to Jonathan	152	10:3–6
Alexander Balas to Jonathan	152	10:18–20
Demetrius I to Jonathan	152	10:25–45
Demetrius II to Jonathan	145	11:30–37
Antiochus VI to Jonathan	145	11:57
Jonathan to the Spartans	144	12:6–18
Arius to Onias	ca. 300	12:20–23
Demetrius II to Simon	142	13:36–40
the Spartans to Simon	142	14:20–23
the Jews honoring Simon	140	14:27–45
Antiochus VII to Simon	139	15:2–9
Consul Lucius to Ptolemy VIII	142	15:16–21

Other letters are mentioned in 1 Macc 1:41–51 and 5:10–13. In addition to these documents and other sources from which he drew his material, the author made particular use of a Seleucid source, which, in detailing the history of that empire, gave him chronological checkpoints for his own narrative.

2 Macc is the work of an epitomist who abbreviated the five-volume work of Jason of Cyrene (2 Macc 2:23). It begins, however, with two letters which the epitomist translated into Greek and prefixed to his own work. Both letters are addressed to the Egyptian Jews by their Palestinian brethren, and both urge the observance of the feast celebrating the Temple's rededication (in 164).

The first letter, 2 Macc 1:1–10a, dated to 124, contains reference to another (vv 7–8) written in 143. The second letter, 2 Macc 1:10b–2:18, which is undated, is considered by Abel and Starcky (*Maccabées* 27–30) to be substantially authentic and a literary unity; they assign it to a contemporary of Judas writing in 164. See also B. Z. Wacholder, *HUCA* 49 (1978) 89–133. Other authors (W. Brownlee, *IDB* 3. 208; Dancy, *1 Maccabees* 15–16; Eissfeldt, *OTI* 580–81; Goldstein, *II Maccabees* 154–88), consider it spurious, and even a composite, because 2 Macc 1:19–2:15—a later addition—seems to interrupt the flow of the letter.

The major source of 2 Macc, however, is the work of Jason of Cyrene, whose five volumes were abbreviated by the epitomist for his own theological purposes. Jason's sources are similar to those of 1 Macc, namely, a Judas tradition, a Seleucid chronicle, and the Temple archives for the following documents:

LETTER	DATE	2 MACC
Antiochus IV to the Jews	164	9:19–27
Lysias to the Jews	164	11:16–21
Antiochus V to Lysias	163	11:22–26
Antiochus IV to the Jews	164	11:27–33
the Roman embassy to the Jews	164	11:34–38

Various other sources, biblical and nonbiblical, alleged for 1–2 Macc by Goldstein (e.g., *I Maccabees* 72, the hypothetical *DMP*), W. Mölleken, K.-D. Schunck, and others are quite speculative and have been severely criticized by, among others, N. J. McEleney (*CBQ* 40 [1978] 92) and S. Kochavi (*BM* 28 [1982] 278–90).

6   (V) Unity and Authenticity.   The authenticity of the final chapters of 1 Macc has been questioned by J. von Destinon (*Die Quellen des Flavius Josephus* [Kiel, 1882]) on the grounds that Josephus discontinued use of 1 Macc as his historical source after the selection of Simon as high priest (Josephus, *Ant.* 13.6.7 §214; 1 Macc 13:42). But this discontinuity can be explained by Josephus's adherence to his own earlier work, *J.W.,* in which he leaned heavily on Nicolas of Damascus, the court historian of Herod the Great, and was apparently unaware of 1 Macc. Another, simpler explanation offered is that Josephus' copy of 1 Macc lacked its final roll. In another matter, Oesterley (*APOT* 1. 61–62) has questioned the authenticity of some documents cited in 1 Macc.

These theories, although taken up again by some (e.g., Tedesche and Zeitlin, *First Maccabees* 29–32; see 38–48), have lost ground since the study of H. W. Ettleston (*The Integrity of 1 Maccabees* [New Haven, 1925]). Dancy's judgment expresses the more recent view: "Stylistically and dramatically the book is a unity, and on those grounds alone it is no longer credible that the work as we have it contains considerable later interpolations, neither documents . . . nor the whole of the last three and a half chapters . . ." (*1 Maccabees* 6).

Against the unity of 2 Macc, some authors have alleged the later insertion of the prefatory letters and the disarrangement of the text's sequence, when compared with 1 Macc. But the arrangement of 2 Macc has adequate explanation in the epitomist's use of Jason's work and in his own activity of prefixing the prefatory letters to what he had composed.

7   (VI) Literary Genre and Characteristics.
1 Macc describes the rescue of Judaism and the rise of the
Hasmonean dynasty. It is a work of history. In writing
it the author made little attempt at literary artifice. This
is most evident from the way his sentences are strung
together by the Hebr conjunction *waw* (Gk *kai*).
Although translators generally minimize this repetitious
"and," it occasionally shines through; see *NAB,* 1 Macc
1:41-50. Nevertheless, direct and simple as his style is,
the author of 1 Macc was capable of vivid description
(6:39), and even of enthusiasm (2:48; 4:24; 5:63). At
times, his intense feeling led him to include poetry
(1:26-28; 1:36-40; 2:7-13; 3:3-9; 3:45; 14:6-15), but,
for the most part, his narrative reflects the sober historian of the events described.

Written in the genre of pathetic or rhetorical history,
2 Macc is characterized by exaggerated numbers (as is
1 Macc), the invention of dialogue, and the introduction
of miracles. Jason's work thus represents the best of this
genre, and it can rank well with the similar works of
earlier writers in the school of pathetic history:
Theopompus of Chios, Clitarchus, and Phylarchus of
Naucratis. In this genre, truth alone is not the writer's
aim; he also seeks to give pleasure by stimulating the
reader's emotions. Nevertheless, once allowance is made
for the literary genre in which he writes, Jason's work
has considerable historical value and merit.

To edify is also the epitomist's aim. He tells the
reader that he is not concerned with exact detail (2:28),
leaving that to Jason (2:30); instead, he aims to please
(2:25). This he does by simplification of Jason's work,
excerpting some sections, abbreviating others. Throughout his work, there breathes the spirit of piety, in the
Pharisaic strain. For the view that 2 Macc narrates the
defense of Jerusalem and its Temple by God and so is
"Temple propaganda," see Doran, *Temple Propaganda.*

8   (VII) Authorship and Date. What little is
known about the author of 1 Macc must be gathered
from the book itself. He is a Jew, an ardent nationalist,
and apparently an enthusiastic supporter of the Hasmoneans (5:61-62). Both his intimate knowledge of Palestinian topography—which marks him out as resident
there, probably in Jerusalem—and the vivid detail with
which he describes the events he narrates show that he
had access to the participants in the struggle for
liberation.

These characteristics help also to date his work. No
nationalist author could have praised the Romans in the
manner of 1 Macc 8 once Pompey had captured Jerusalem, and so 63 BC is the latest possible date for the
composition of 1 Macc. The early chronological limit of
1 Macc lies in the author's reference to the Hasmonean
family monument, which was built at Modin in 143 and
remained standing "to this day" (13:27-30). This
sepulchral reference places the book near the end of the
2d cent. BC, and the note on John Hyrcanus (134-104)
in 16:23-24 specifies this date further, since it presupposes that a considerable part, or all, of John's reign had
passed. For these reasons, scholars generally agree that
1 Macc was composed (in Hebrew) near the beginning
of the 1st cent. BC. At what time it made the further step
into Greek—its canonical language—is not known.

2 Macc is earlier and was written in Egypt (Doran
[*Temple Propaganda* 112-13] says Jerusalem). Jason of
Cyrene was its primary source and first author, a man
steeped in orthodox Judaism and skilled in the Hellenistic art of rhetorical narration. He appears more clearly
in his work than the canonical author, the unnamed
abbreviator. The epitomist appears to have been a man
of Pharisaic tendencies, though these are sometimes
ascribed to Jason, sometimes to both.

The bulk of Jason's report spans 180-160. He must
have written shortly thereafter, because the epitomist
who reduced Jason's five volumes to one seemingly
completed the task in 124, at least if we are to judge by
the date found in the first of the festal letters (1:9). Since
these letters are authentic and were translated into Greek
by the epitomist, there is no need to postulate another
author, the later revisor advanced by Eissfeldt and
Dancy or the forger alleged by Goldstein for the second
letter.

9   (VIII) Purpose and Addressees. Although
1 Macc is a historical work, it is meant to convey a
lesson. Probably intended to show God at work in
Jewish history in the Seleucid Empire as he was earlier
in Jewish history, it depicts his salvific action in the
Maccabean struggle against paganism. The lesson of
Mattathias and his sons is there for every true Israelite
to learn. Fidelity to the law and faith in God achieved
more than the size of one's army or the strength of one's
arm (2:61-64). Through Judas and his brothers, the
agents of a merciful providence, relief from pagan oppression came to Judaism (2:48; 4:24-25; 9:21; 9:73;
14:26; 14:29). Their efforts won independence and a
kingdom, and prepared the way for God's future intervention (4:46; 14:41). All Israel should look to their
example.

Similarly, 2 Macc is intended to instruct and to edify.
It is perhaps less openly partisan than 1 Macc and lays
more emphasis on the importance of the Temple and
religious themes. It too shows the success of Palestinian
Jews against their pagan masters and seeks to strengthen
Jewish faith everywhere by the heroic example of persecuted brethren (6:31). 2 Macc tends also to propagate
the doctrines dear to the Pharisaic heart, for instance, the
resurrection of the just (7:9; 14:46), but how consciously
the author pursues this aim is difficult to say.

10   (IX) Historical Value. Several complaints
have been lodged against the historical reliability of
1 Macc. The nationalism of its author and the exaggerated
importance he gives Judean events (1:41-43; 3:27-31;
6:5-13) are said to make his objectivity suspect. He is
anti-Seleucid (1:9-10), and, moreover, he shows ignorance of the history, geography, and political organization of foreign peoples. His Jewish nationalism leads him
to inflate the numbers of the enemy, so as to have a more
striking divine intervention on behalf of the Hasmoneans. And he has erred in placing the death of
Antiochus IV after the dedication of the Temple. These
and other historical shortcomings are thought to discredit him as a reliable reporter of the period.

Nevertheless, one cannot dismiss him so easily.
Within the context of his culture and the canons of
historiography then in force, he is a trustworthy witness
of men and events. His care, for example, in matters of
topography (7:19; 9:2,4,33) and Jewish chronology
(1:54; 4:52; etc.) illustrate his genuine concern to report
matters accurately within the limits of his capabilities
and aims. His placing of Antiochus's death is wrong, but
his description of it corresponds to that of an independent witness, the secular historian Polybius of Mega-
lopolis (*Histories* 31.9). Despite his limitations, then,
1 Macc's author has, as Dancy notes, "such large stretches
of honest and sober narrative that 1 Macc deserves to be
regarded as equal if not superior in historical worth, not
only to any book of the Old Testament but also to most
surviving Hellenistic history" (Dancy, *1 Maccabees* 8).

With greater allowances for the rhetorical nature of
2 Macc's historiography, its author, too, may be considered reliable. Without him, we would not be nearly so
well informed about the struggles for the high priesthood involving Onias III, his brother Jason, and the

impious Menelaus, nor about the other events preceding the accession of Antiochus IV (2 Macc 3–4). At times, 2 Macc is supported by the secular historian even in details—e.g., the dedication to Zeus of the temple on Mt. Gerizim (2 Macc 6:2; Josephus, *Ant.* 12.5.5 §261). In short, he too has historical competence, although this judgment must not be magnified into one of his absolute historicity. His descriptions and his redistribution of events are to be evaluated in the light of his theological aims.

11   (X) Relationships between First and Second Maccabees. It is in the area of relating these two books to each other that the most serious historical difficulties occur. A full description of the problems involved lies outside the scope of this work (see Abel and Starcky, *Maccabées* 35–49), but the establishment of the correct sequence of Lysias's first campaign and the letters that followed, the death of Antiochus IV Epiphanes, the purification and dedication of the Temple, and Judas's wars with neighboring peoples is a matter of sufficient importance to merit mention here.

The principal block of material that stands out of historical sequence is 2 Macc 11, which describes the first campaign of Lysias against Judas while Antiochus IV Epiphanes was still in Persia. Three letters note the outcome of the campaign—the Jews were to be given their religious freedom. To have its proper spot in history, 2 Macc 11 should be moved to follow chap. 8. As it now stands, chap. 11 errs in attributing this campaign of Lysias to the reign of the next king, Antiochus V Eupator (who succeeds Epiphanes in 2 Macc 10:10–11). The mistake occurred because the epitomist associated Lysias's campaign and the three letters from Epiphanes' reign (11:16–21,27–33,34–38) with the letter of his son Eupator (11:22–26). Assigning all the material to Eupator, the epitomist made this first campaign of Lysias follow the death of Antiochus IV, whereas in reality it had preceded it.

Judaism in the Maccabean period followed a calendar basically similar to that of the Seleucid monarchy. The Seleucid year had this oddity, however, that its inception was sometimes counted from spring (from 1 Nisan—our March-April—in Babylon and in Jewish liturgical reckoning) and sometimes from autumn (from 1 Dios—corresponding to the Hebr Tishri, our September-October—in the official Seleucid reckoning).

Earlier exegetes thought that 1 Macc counted the inception of years in its chronology from the spring and that 2 Macc (except for 2 Macc 1:1–2:18) counted the year's beginning from autumn. But the discovery of British Museum Tablet 35603 (A. Sachs and J. Wiseman, *Iraq* 16 [1954] 202–12, plate 52) led to the reevaluation of the chronology of both books by Schaumberger (*Bib* 36 [1955] 423–35), whose study has contributed much to the clarification of the Maccabean chronology. In actual fact, 1 Macc follows an autumn computation for the beginning of the year (except where the Temple is concerned), and 2 Macc begins its years counting from the spring, according to the more ancient, Babylonian reckoning.

This reformed chronology demands a revised sequence of the events in 1–2 Macc. The latter is correct in placing the death of Antiochus IV Epiphanes before the Temple's dedication (2 Macc 9:1–29; 10:1–9), and 1 Macc has the wrong order (1 Macc 4:36–61; 6:1–17). Antiochus died toward October of 164 BC (in the Seleucid year 148, if one begins the year in the spring, as B. M. Tablet 35603 does; in the Seleucid year 149, if one counts from autumn as 1 Macc 6:16 does), and the Temple was dedicated on December 14, 164 BC (1 Macc 4:52; 25 Kislev, year 148 of the Seleucids, counted this

time as beginning in the spring). Correct placement of Antiochus's death in 1 Macc requires the moving of 1 Macc 6:1–17 to precede 4:36–61.

This change then gives an accurate historical perspective to the battles of Judas narrated in 1 Macc 5, which occurred after Epiphanes had died, as 2 Macc 10 and 12, the parallels to 1 Macc 5, suppose.

These events are properly aligned in the following synopsis:

1 Macc		2 Macc
4:1–27	The battle at Emmaus (165 BC)	8:8–29, 34–36
4:28–35	Lysias's first campaign and its sequel (164)	11:1–21; 11:27–12:1
6:1–16	The death of Antiochus IV Epiphanes (164)	9:1–29
6:17	The accession of Antiochus V Eupator (164)	10:10–11
4:36–61	The Temple's recovery and dedication (164)	10:1–8
5:1–68	Judas's battles with neighboring peoples (163)	10:14–38; 12:2–45

12   (XI) Theological Teaching. Reflective of a period in Jewish history that is little known, 1–2 Macc have special significance in the development of revelation. Their absolute monotheism is unquestionable. 1 Macc even carries its respect for the transcendent deity to the point of not mentioning the name at all. So ineffable is God that the author of 1 Macc can do no more than allude to the deity by the appellation "Heaven" (3:18,50; 4:10; etc.)—scaled down from the earlier "God of Heaven" of the Persian period (Ezra 1:2; Neh 1:4)—or even by the mere personal pronoun "Him" (2:61) or "You" (7:37,41). Although distant, God can be found in prayer (3:50–53; 4:30–33) and in the law (3:48), where his voice is heard now as clearly as it was in the words of the prophets (Jer 1:9), who have disappeared for the time being (4:46; 14:41). The law continues the covenant of the Fathers (2:20–21,50), the holy covenant (1:15), and observance of the law brings honor (2:49,64; 3:3; 9:10) and the realization of the ancient promises (Jer 31:31; see Bar 2:35). Infidelity to the law results in death and punishment (3:21–11; 3:49). Judas and his brethren have acted as savior (9:21; 14:29) and judge (9:72), delivering Israel and restoring its ancient inheritance (15:33–34). Zealous for the law, the bond between God and his people, they do battle with the pagan oppressors and their allies, the renegade Jews (2:44–48).

Developed as the theology of 1 Macc is, that of 2 Macc is richer. In Semitic fashion, Jonathan describes the majesty of God by detailing the divine attributes in 1:24–25. God alone is king and kind, provident, just, omnipotent, and eternal. So great is the divine power, that creatures were not made from things that existed (7:28), but *ex nihilo.* He has been provident in choosing his people and watching over them (1:25). He dwells among them in the Temple (13:35–36), the greatest, holiest, and most famous Temple on earth (2:19,22; 5:15; 14:31; 15:41).

The Jews have the law, and if they are observant of it, particularly of the sabbath (8:27; 15:1–4), God will be merciful to them (8:27). But toward the ungodly, he is a righteous judge (12:6), and when calamities befall, Israel has only itself to blame (4:10–17; 6:12–16; 7:18; 10:4; 12:40–41). Penance, however, can restore the bond of friendship and harmony with the divine (7:32–33,37–38; 8:5; 12:42–45).

God does not leave his just ones without aid. He is their defender (7:6; 8:36; 12:11), whose help can be sought in prayer and sacrifice (3:22). He even sends heavenly hosts to do battle on behalf of the people (3:23–30; 10:29–31; 11:6–10). Whoever falls in righteous battle (12:45) or in persecution as martyrs (chaps. 6, 7) can hope to be raised again (7:9,23; 14:46) in full health (7:11; 14:46), while the impious will be punished and remain in torment (5:9–10; 7:13–14,17,19,35; 9:18; 13:7–8). Intercessory prayer increases the commerce between heaven and earth, as not only the angels (as formerly, Job 5:1; 33:23) but also the saints of the past implore God for Israel (15:12–16). There is intercessory prayer on earth, too, by means of which the people can help their departed with prayer and sacrifices (12:44–45).

In his doctrinal positions, 2 Macc belongs to the Pharisaic school, while the thought of 1 Macc is closer to that of the Sadducees.

13   (XII) Outline. The books of 1–2 Maccabees may be outlined as follows:

1 MACCABEES
- (I) Preamble (1:1–64)
  - (A) Alexander and the Diadochi (1:1–10)
  - (B) Hellenizers (1:11–15)
  - (C) Antiochus's First Campaign in Egypt (1:16–19)
  - (D) Antiochus Despoils the Temple (1:20–24a)
  - (E) Dirge (1:24b–28)
  - (F) Apollonius Attacks Jerusalem (1:29–35)
  - (G) Dirge (1:36–40)
  - (H) Antiochus Proscribes Judaism and Imposes Pagan Practices (1:41–51a)
  - (I) The Execution of Antiochus's Edict (1:51b–64)
- (II) Mattathias Begins Active Resistance (2:1–70)
  - (A) Mattathias's Lament (2:1–14)
  - (B) Resistance Flares (2:15–28)
  - (C) The Slaughter on the Sabbath and Its Sequel (2:29–41)
  - (D) The Hasideans (2:42–48)
  - (E) Mattathias's Testament (2:49–70)
- (III) Judas Maccabeus Takes Command of the Struggle (3:1–9:22)
  - (A) Praise of Judas (3:1–9)
  - (B) Judas Defeats Apollonius and Seron (3:10–26)
  - (C) Antiochus Goes East (3:27–37)
  - (D) Judas Defeats Gorgias and Nicanor (3:38–4:27)
  - (E) Judas Defeats Lysias at Beth-zur (4:28–35)
  - (F) The Purification and Dedication of the Temple (4:36–61)
  - (G) Judas Battles with Neighboring Peoples (5:1–68)
    - (a) Idumea (5:3–5; 2 Macc 20:14–23)
    - (b) Ammon (5:6–8; 2 Macc 8:30–33?)
    - (c) Gilead (5:9–13,24–54; 2 Macc 12:10–31)
    - (d) Galilee (5:14–23)
    - (e) The Land of the Philistines (5:55–68; 2 Macc 12:3–9,32–45)
  - (H) The Death of Antiochus IV Epiphanes (6:1–17)
  - (I) Siege of the Citadel (6:18–27)
  - (J) Lysias's Second Campaign in Judah (6:28–63; 2 Macc 13:1–26)
  - (K) The Expedition of Bacchides and Alcimus (7:1–25)
  - (L) The Defeat of Nicanor (7:26–50)
  - (M) Judas's Treaty with the Romans (8:1–32)
  - (N) The Defeat and Death of Judas (9:1–22)
- (IV) Jonathan Continues the Struggle (9:23–12:53)
  - (A) Jonathan Succeeds Judas as Leader (9:23–34)
  - (B) Jonathan Avenges His Brother John (9:35–42)
  - (C) Bacchides Ambushes Jonathan (9:43–49)
  - (D) Bacchides Fortifies Judea; Alcimus Dies (9:50–57)
  - (E) Jonathan Escapes and Frustrates Bacchides (9:58–73)
  - (F) Alexander Balas (150–145) Claims Demetrius's Throne (10:1–14)
  - (G) Jonathan Supports Alexander Balas and Becomes High Priest (10:15–50)
  - (H) At Alexander's Marriage, Jonathan is Promoted (10:51–66)
  - (I) Jonathan Defeats Apollonius, the General of Demetrius II (10:67–89)
  - (J) The Alliance between Demetrius II and Ptolemy (11:1–13)
  - (K) The Deaths of Alexander and Ptolemy (11:14–19)

- (L) Jonathan's Pact with Demetrius (11:20–37)
- (M) Trypho's Intrigue against Demetrius (11:38–40)
- (N) Jonathan Aids Demetrius (11:41–53)
- (O) Jonathan's Alliance with Trypho (11:54–62)
- (P) War between Jonathan and Demetrius (11:63–74)
- (Q) Treaties of Friendship with the Romans and Spartans (12:1–23)
- (R) Military Activities of Jonathan and Simon (12:24–38)
- (S) The Capture of Jonathan (12:39–53)
- (V) Simon as Leader of the Jews (13:1–16:24)
  - (A) Simon Becomes Leader of the Jews (13:1–11)
  - (B) Simon Blocks Trypho (13:12–24)
  - (C) Simon Constructs a Family Monument at Modin (13:25–30)
  - (D) Simon Joins Demetrius II (13:31–42)
  - (E) The Capture of Gazara and the Citadel (13:43–53)
  - (F) Demetrius II Is Captured by the Parthians (14:1–3)
  - (G) The Glory of Simon (14:4–15)
  - (H) Renewal of the Alliances with Rome and Sparta (14:16–24)
  - (I) Decree of the Jews Honoring Simon (14:25–49)
  - (J) Antiochus VII Grants Privileges to Simon and Besieges Trypho (15:1–14)
  - (K) The Return of the Embassy Sent to Rome (15:15–24)
  - (L) Antiochus Breaks His Alliance with Simon (15:25–36)
  - (M) John Hyrcanus and Judas Defeat Cendebaeus (15:37–16:10)
  - (N) The Murder of Simon and His Two Sons (16:11–22)
  - (O) Conclusion to 1 Macc (16:23–24)

2 MACCABEES
- (I) Letters to the Jews of Egypt (1:1–2:18)
  - (A) The First Letter (1:1–10a)
  - (B) The Second Letter (1:10b–2:18)
- (II) The Epitomist's Preface (2:19–32)
- (III) The Decline of the High Priesthood (3:1–4:50)
  - (A) The Episode of Heliodorus (3:1–40)
  - (B) Simon's Plot against Onias (4:1–6)
  - (C) Jason the High Priest Introduces Hellenism (4:7–20)
  - (D) Antiochus Is Received by Jason in Jerusalem (4:21–22)
  - (E) Menelaus as High Priest (4:23–50)
- (IV) Antiochus Epiphanes and the Imposition of Hellenism (5:1–7:42)
  - (A) Antiochus Ravages Jerusalem (5:1–14)
  - (B) Antiochus Despoils the Temple (5:15–23a)
  - (C) Apollonius Attacks Jerusalem (5:23b–26)
  - (D) Judas Maccabeus in the Desert (5:27)
  - (E) Antiochus Imposes Hellenism (6:1–11)
  - (F) The Epitomist's Evaluation (6:12–17)
  - (G) The Martyrdom of Eleazar (6:18–31)
  - (H) The Martyrdom of the Mother and Her Seven Sons (7:1–42)
- (V) The Triumph of Judaism Under Judas Maccabeus (8:1–10:9)
  - (A) Judas Organizes Resistance to the Persecution (8:1–7)
  - (B) Judas Defeats Nicanor and Gorgias (8:8–29,34–36)
  - (C) Judas's Other Victories (8:30–33)
  - (D) The Death of the Persecutor (9:1–29; 10:9)
  - (E) Judas Purifies the Temple (10:1–8)
- (VI) The Subsequent Struggles of Judas (10:10–15:39)
  - (A) The Suicide of Ptolemy Macron (10:10–13)
  - (B) Judas Fights in Idumea (10:14–23)
  - (C) Judas Defeats Timothy (10:24–38)
  - (D) Victory over Lysias at Beth-zur (11:1–15; 12:1)
  - (E) The Letters (11:16–38)
  - (F) The Battles with Neighboring Peoples (12:2–45)
  - (G) Lysias's Second Campaign in Judah (13:1–26)
  - (H) The Accession of Demetrius I Soter (161–150) (14:1–2)
  - (I) The Hostility of Alcimus (14:3–11)
  - (J) Judas and Nicanor (14:12–36)
  - (K) The Death of Razis (14:37–46)
  - (L) The Defeat of Nicanor (15:1–37a)
  - (M) Epilogue of the Epitomist (15:37b–39)

COMMENTARY ON 1 MACCABEES

14   **(I) Preamble (1:1–64).** This preamble sets the stage for the Maccabean struggles. Antiochus IV Epiphanes appears and begins his forcible repression of Judaism, thus inducing the resistance of Jews faithful to the Law.

(A) Alexander and the Diadochi (1:1–10). Alexander the Great (356–323) began his victorious march from Kittim (Cyprus in Gen 10:4; 1 Chr 1:7; here and in 8:5, Macedonia) in 334. After defeating Darius III Codomannus (336–331) at the Granicus River (334), at Issus (333), and Gaugamela (331), he pushed on to "the ends of the earth," actually in the E to the Hyphasis (modern Beas) River in the Punjab. The rise of his kingdom is noted in the visions of Dan 2:33,40 (statue's iron feet), 7:23 (fourth beast), 8:5–8,21 (he-goat), and 11:3 (mighty king). **3.** *he became proud:* Alexander accepted divine honors (see, similarly, Ezek 28:2,5).

1 Macc's author repeats the erroneous story of Alexander's deathbed division of his kingdom among "his servants," his officers who had been educated with him. Josephus (*Ant.* 11.8.7 §346) contradicts this story, and the slow breakup of the empire—Seleucus occupied Babylon in 311; he and four others became "kings" in 306—confirms his statement. Eventually, Alexander's successors (Diadochi), esp. the Ptolemies and Seleucids, claimed direct inheritance from the Macedonian. Alexander died at Babylon in June 323, at the age of 32, having ruled several months longer than the round number of "twelve years" (v 7).

10. *Antiochus Epiphanes:* 1 Macc skips to September 175, when Antiochus IV Epiphanes (175–164) succeeded his brother Seleucus IV (187–175) on the Seleucid throne (see 2 Macc 4:7). Antiochus III, their father, had suffered defeat by the Romans at Magnesia in 190, and under the treaty of Apamea (188), the younger Antiochus was taken to Rome as hostage. He returned after his brother's murder to assume joint regency with his nephew (another Antiochus, who ruled with Epiphanes until he died in 168), effectively deposing the latter. About 169, the elder Antiochus took as his title *theos epiphanēs,* meaning "God manifest," but his subjects soon nicknamed him *epimanēs,* "madman."

2 Macc 3:1–4:6 may be read here. It narrates events in the reign of Seleucus IV which provide background for Antiochus's robbery of the Temple.

15   **(B) Hellenizers (1:11–15).** This section is expanded in 2 Macc 4:7–20. Chief among the Hellenizers is Jason (actually, Joshua), the brother of the high priest Onias (III). Jason bought the high priesthood and introduced Gk ways. He gave up the religious concessions won for the Jews from Antiochus III (Josephus, *Ant.* 12.3.3–4 §129–53; 2 Macc 4:11) to adopt the "practices of the Gentiles." This Grecian way of life included the establishment of a *gymnasion* (a place of exercise, philosophical lectures, and even worship) and an *ephebeion* (an organization for training youth in cultural, physical, and premilitary affairs; 2 Macc 4:9–10). Since the mark of circumcision (1 Macc 1:15)—the sign of their covenant with Yahweh (Gen 17:10–14)—was all too evident in the nudity of the gymnasium, Hellenizing Jews attempted to resume their natural appearance by an operation.

Some authors (e.g., Abel and Starcky, *Maccabées* 54–56) say the most drastic innovation at this time was the change in the city's status. At Jason's request, Jerusalem became a Gk *polis* and as such was called to participate in the feasts and sacrifices of the gods (2 Macc 4:9,18–20). Such a change in the city's constitution amounted to apostasy from Yahwism. E. Bickermann (*Der Gott der Makkabäer* [Berlin, 1937] 59–65) says that at this time Jason established only a *politeuma,* a corporation of hellenized Jews with certain rights and privileges. Goldstein (*I Maccabees* 117–119) plausibly contends that Antiochus (once hostage at Rome) copied the Romans and established an Antiochene citizenship analogous to the Roman. Jason now sought this for Hellenizing Jews (2 Macc 4:9).

In all this process of hellenization, Jews themselves provided the initiative. Abandoning the covenant with Yahweh for a covenant with pagans, "they sold themselves to do evil" (see 1 Kgs 21:20,25; 2 Kgs 17:17; Sir 47:24). (The events of 2 Macc 4:21–50 belong here.)

(C) Antiochus's First Campaign in Egypt (1:16–19). Although forbidden by the treaty of Apamea to attack Rome's friends, Antiochus invaded Egypt on a pretext, to establish his control there. This campaign (169) resulted in victory for his forces, although Alexandria was not taken. Tiring of the war, Antiochus left its conduct to his unwilling puppet, his nephew Ptolemy VI Philometor (180–145), who continued to besiege Ptolemy VIII Euergetes II (145–116) in Alexandria.

(D) Antiochus Despoils the Temple (1:20–24a). Although 2 Macc 5:15–21 places this event after Antiochus's second campaign in Egypt, Dan 11:25–30 (esp. 28) shows that it belongs after the first. **23.** *hidden treasures:* 2 Macc 5:21 says 1,800 talents. Antiochus was supported in this theft by the impious high priest Menelaus who had supplanted Jason (2 Macc 4:23–26; 5:15). **20.** The 143d year of the Seleucid kingdom began in autumn 169 BC.

16   **(E) Dirge (1:24b–28).** This lament portrays the universal sorrow in Israel over the sacrilege; even the land is depicted as trembling. **24b.** *deeds of murder:* The allusion is obscure. Abel and Starcky (*Maccabées* 87) say it recalls the events of 2 Macc 5:12–14. These events are not otherwise noted in 1 Macc. *arrogance:* Antiochus's pretensions to divinity—he identified himself with Zeus Olympios officially—were well known (see Dan 11:36). (Here 2 Macc 5:1–14 fills in. Antiochus invaded Egypt in 168 for the second time, having himself crowned king at Memphis. Forced by Rome to retire, he turned his wrath on Judah, which he thought to be in revolt.)

(F) Apollonius Attacks Jerusalem (1:29–35). This has a parallel in 2 Macc 5:23b–26. **29.** *two years later:* Than his first Egyptian campaign, and so in 167. *chief tribute collector:* The text's *archonta phorologias,* "chief tribute collector" is the Gk translator's misreading of *śar hammissîm,* "master of levies" (in Exod 1:11, of workers) for *śar hammusîm,* "chief of the Mysians," as Apollonius is designated in 2 Macc 5:24. This is most likely the Apollonius of 3:10. **30.** *suddenly fell:* The ruse is in 2 Macc 5:25–26. **31.** *tore down . . . walls:* A typical punishment for a city in revolt; see 2 Kgs 25:8–10. **33.** *fortified the City of David:* In 2 Sam 5:7,9, this is the southern part of the hill between the Tyropoeon and Kidron valleys, the easternmost of Jerusalem's two principal hills. Here J. Simons locates the new citadel (Simons, *SJOT* 144ff.). Goldstein places the citadel (*Akra*) on the northern end of this hill (*I Maccabées* 213–20). By Maccabean times, however, the city built on the westernmost hill was known by David's name. Consequently, Abel (*Histoire de la Palestine* [Paris, 1952]

1. 122) locates the fortress here. Whatever its exact location, the Seleucid troops and their Jewish allies (v 34) built and provisioned the citadel, or Akra, that overlooked the Temple area. For one view of this garrison, see B. Bar-kochba, *Zion* 38 (1973) 32-47. **35.** *great snare:* A source of danger to the city and Temple. Whether this fortress now became Jerusalem the Gk city, with unwalled Jerusalem looked upon as a surrounding village, is uncertain; see 1 Macc 15:28. The Seleucid garrison occupied the fortress until 141, when Simon drove them out (1 Macc 13:49-50). **(G) Dirge (1:36-40).** In a style reminiscent of Ps 79, the author deplores the actions of the Akra's inhabitants and their effect on Jerusalem, esp. on its religious life.

17   (H) Antiochus Proscribes Judaism and Imposes Pagan Practices (1:41-51a). To unite a kingdom so diverse in ethnic and linguistic groupings, politically unstable and geographically diffuse, Antiochus thought it necessary to foster the process of cultural and religious syncretism that had received such impetus under Alexander. Since Hellenism and the cult of a supreme, syncretistic deity—known officially as Zeus Olympios (2 Macc 6:2), but also as Ba'al, or Hadad—offered the best prospect for achieving the desired cultural and religious unity, he favored their establishment everywhere in his realm. Judah was especially troublesome, however, because there religion and the surge toward national independence were inseparable and coterminous—the law cried out for autonomy and theocracy. Antiochus felt that the assimilation of this province into the common social order demanded first the suppression of the local religion. He initiated repressive measures in 167, as soon as the Akra in Jerusalem was sufficiently strong.

The decree of vv 41-42 is not found elsewhere in ancient historians, and some modern authors question its existence, while conceding that as v 43 notes, it may echo Antiochus's general policy. As v 43 notes, many welcomed the change and gladly adopted the king's religion.

The letters sent to Judah (vv 44-50) were specific and severe, calling for the proscription of Judaism and the imposition of pagan worship under pain of death. They abolished the last of the religious concessions granted by Antiochus III (Josephus, *Ant.* 12.3.3-4 §129-53). **46.** *the holy ones:* Obscure. It may mean all the faithful (see Dan 7:17-21); the context specifies it to "priests." **47.** *shrines for idols:* Holding statues and incense altars.

(I) The Execution of Antiochus's Edict (1:51b-64). 2 Macc 6-7 vividly exemplifies the manner of executing the king's edict. **51.** *overseers: Episkopoi.* The chief overseer, the *geronta* of 2 Macc 6:1, has been variously identified as "Geron" (BJ), "senator" (*RSV*), "an old man" (Dancy, *1 Maccabees* 76). He is an Athenian, probably from Athens itself, and not, as Dancy suggests, from a certain section of Antioch's citizens. **52.** *many:* The "reforms" were accepted gladly by some (v 43), under compulsion by others (2 Macc 6-7). **53.** *hiding:* Some were discovered and died (2 Macc 6:11).

On December 7, 167, the 15th of Kisleu in the 145th year of the Seleucid kingdom, Antiochus reached the zenith of his evil in the eyes of the faithful; he erected an altar to Zeus in the Temple of Yahweh! **54.** *desolating abomination:* The phrase *bdelygma erēmōseōs* parallels that in Dan 11:31. It translates the Hebr *šiqquṣ mĕšōmēm,* which conveys the idea of a detestable idol, a horrendous sight to the pious beholder. The *šiqquṣ,* "abomination," substitutes for *ba'al,* the Semitic deity and with *mĕšōmēm,* "desolating" (or simply *šōmēm* in Dan 12:11) plays upon *ba'al šāmēm* (earlier *šāmayim*), "lord of heaven," by this time a title for the Syrian divinity, which Antiochus

identified with Zeus Olympios and hoped to make the religious focal point of his kingdom. (For identification of this god with *'El,* see R. A. Oden, *CBQ* 39 [1977] 457-473.) It was the *ba'al šāmēm,* now Zeus Olympios, after whom the Temple was newly called (2 Macc 6:2). The way in which this deity was established in the Temple was by the erection of an altar upon the altar of holocausts (see v 59). This now replaced the Holy of Holies as the center of worship in the Temple. The altar erected in the marketplace of Jerusalem (2 Macc 10:2) and the altars built in the *surrounding cities of Judah* further decentralized Jewish worship, against the prescriptions of Deut 12:5-18. **55.** *burned incense . . . doors:* Apparently the Jews adopted Grecian shrines in their streets and in the porches of their houses. **56.** *books of the law:* The Pentateuch. **58.** *each month:* Those not joining the monthly celebration of the divinized king's birthday were caught and punished (2 Macc 6:7). **59.** *twenty-fifth day of the month:* The 25 of Kisleu in that year (December 17, 167) was most likely Antiochus's birthday, and this event was now celebrated monthly throughout Judea.

Some Jews accepted the king's new ordinances gladly; some obeyed under duress. But there were faithful Jews who resisted to death. Eleazar and the seven brothers with their courageous mother, all exemplified this.

18   (II) Mattathias Begins Active Resistance (2:1-70). The revolt which began as resistance to the proscription of Judaism escalated into political rebellion. Mattathias and his early followers concentrated on removing the sacrilegious altars, forcing observance of the law, and striking down apostates from the Jewish religion. But their struggle soon assumed the proportions of a movement for independence.

(A) Mattathias's Lament (2:1-14). 1. *Mattathias:* In Hebrew, *mattityāhû,* "gift of God." Josephus makes him the "son" (*J.W.* 1.1.3 §36)—i.e., the "grandson" (*Ant.* 12.6.1 §265)—of Asamonaios, from whom the designation "Hasmonean," which is applied to the Maccabee dynasty, is traced. *Joarib:* This is the Jehoiarib of 1 Chr 24:7, who heads the first of the 24 classes of the priesthood. *Modin:* Modern *el-Midyah,* seven miles E of Lod (Lydda). **2.** The surnames of Mattathias's sons are said to mean respectively: "Fortunate," "Burning," "Designated by Yahweh" (or "the Hammerer" or "Hammerheaded"), "Awake," "Favorite" (see Abel, *Maccabées* 31-32. All died violently.

Mattathias's lament over the Temple is constructed in earlier OT phraseology (see v 9 and Lam 2:11,21), with allusions to current evils (see v 9 and 1:23,61; 2 Macc 5:24). **10.** *what nation . . . ?* Judah is so weak anyone could despoil it. This is Semitic hyperbole.

(B) Resistance Flares (2:15-28). The enforced sacrifice recalls the monthly celebration honoring the king's birthday (2 Macc 6:7). Mattathias had moved from Jerusalem (2:1), perhaps to avoid such sacrifices, since those left in Jerusalem complied (2:18). It was not likely that he would now sacrifice. **18.** *friends of the king:* The lowest of the four ranks in the order of "friends of the king" (friends, honored friends, first friends, first and preferred friends). There is mention of first friends in 10:65; 11:27; 2 Macc 8:9. **19.** *relinquish the worship of his fathers:* Mattathias projects the Jewish view that worship of other gods would be apostasy from one's own religion; the Gentiles would have less difficulty with the king's syncretism, as practice showed. **24.** *righteous anger:* Mattathias acted according to the law; see Deut 13:7-10; Exod 34:13. **25.** *king's man:* Josephus calls him Bacchides (*J.W.* 1.1.3 §36) and Apelles (*Ant.* 12.6.2 §270). **26.** *Phinehas:* Phinehas's action in Num 25:6-15 is recalled in Ps 106:28-31; Sir 45:23.

Mattathias led a group of disaffected into the wild hill

country, probably the area E of Modin. 2 Macc 5:27 notes the group's escape.

19   (C) The Slaughter on the Sabbath and Its Sequel (2:29–41). Refusal to worship according to the king's edict meant death or flight. 1 Macc now narrates the fate of dissenters. **29.** *righteousness:* According to the law; see Isa 56:1; Ps 106:3. *wilderness:* the traditional home of the political outcast; see 1:53; 1 Sam 23:14. **31.** Philip and his men ordered these Jews out of the caves (2 Macc 6:11) on the sabbath (v 32) to fulfill the king's edict. **38.** *they died:* By suffocation caused by heaping brush against the caves' entrances and burning it (Josephus, *Ant.* 12.6.2 §274–75). The rigors of their piety prevented them from defensive measures, because these actions would violate the sabbath rest. L. Rabinowitz considers these Jews the first Essenes; cf. *JSS* 4 (1959) 358– 61. Mattathias and his men made the more practical decision to fight in a similar situation. See further A. Johns, *VT* 13 (1963) 482–86.

(D) The Hasideans (2:42–48). The *Asidaioi* of the text represents an Aram *ḥāsīdayyāʾ*, Hebr *ḥăsîdîm*, the "faithful" or "loyal" men. The name fits them well, since their principal interest lay in the law and its observance. They now appear as a group for the first time in history. Although 2 Macc 14:6 seems to identify them with all the followers of Judas, this equation may be too general (2:42). Later some of the Hasideans sued for peace (7:13), beginning the drift away from the Hasmoneans. The Hasideans are often thought to be the forerunners of the Pharisees (the Separated) and the Essenes (the Pure), two of the three Jewish "philosophical" schools described by Josephus (*J.W.* 2.8.2–14 §119–66), the third being the Sadducees (sons of Zadok). But P. Davies questions this; cf. *JJS* 28 (1977) 127–40. **43.** *joined them:* 2 Macc 8:1 speaks of the force now actively recruited as though it were led by Judas (as later it was) and not by Mattathias. It came to number 6,000. **44.** *organized an army:* What was done with this army is told in the verses which follow and in 2 Macc 8:5–7. *sinners . . . lawless men:* The sinners are the pagans (1:34; 2:48,62), and the lawless men, apostate Jews (1:11). **47.** *arrogant:* The Seleucid agents (see 1:21). **48.** *rescued the law:* By their militant action, they prevented the submersion of Judaism in a syncretistic cult and thus did not permit the "horn" (power) of the *sinner* (Antiochus v 62) to abolish their Mosaic law and Yahweh's covenant.

(E) Mattathias's Testament (2:49–70). The deathbed scene recalls Jacob's farewell admonitions (Gen 49) and Moses' departure (Deut 33). The content of the passage, however, is closer to Sir 44–50, the "Praise of the Fathers." Mattathias recalls the faith of Abraham (Gen 22), Joseph (Gen 39), Phinehas "our father" (v 26; Num 25), Joshua (Josh 1), Caleb (Num 13), David (2 Sam 7), Elijah (1 Kgs 18; 2 Kgs 2), Hananiah, Azariah, Mishael (Dan 1:6), and Daniel (Dan 6). Mattathias urges his sons to emulate these heroes. The author of 1 Macc shows his acquaintance with the material and aims of the book of Daniel. **49.** *furious anger:* The Lord's anger against his sinful people (see 2 Macc 6:12–16). **51.** *great honor:* As heroes of the people, which, by the time 1 Macc was written, they were. **62.** *filth and worms:* An allusion to the death of Antiochus, described in detail by 2 Macc 9. **65.** Although older than Judas and Jonathan, Simon succeeded to the leadership only after their deaths. His wisdom, however, is evident in his career. **70.** The 146th Seleucid year places this event in the spring of 166. *Modin:* See comment on 13:25–30.

20   (III) Judas Maccabeus Takes Command of the Struggle (3:1–9:22).

(A) Praise of Judas (3:3–9). The author praises Judas' accomplishments in this poetic passage. **5.**

burned: See 5:5,35,44; 2 Macc 8:33. **7.** *kings:* Antiochus IV Epiphanes (3:27), Antiochus V Eupator (6:28), Demetrius I Soter (8:31; 9:1). **8.** *wrath:* God's punishment of his sinful people ended; see 2 Macc 6:12–16. **9.** *ends of the earth:* At least to Rome (8:20); see also 3:26.

(B) Judas Defeats Apollonius and Seron (3:10–26). This section has no parallel in 2 Macc. Since 1 Macc only summarizes Judas's victory over the hated Apollonius (1:29–35; 2 Macc 5:23b–26), it is odd that he should recount the detail that Judas took Apollonius's sword (see, similarly, 1 Sam 21: 9–10). **10.** *Samaria:* Josephus says Apollonius was *stratēgos,* "military commander," and *meridarchēs,* "governor," of Samaria (*Ant.* 12.5.5 §261, 264; 12.7.1 §287). He could, then, have recruited much of his force locally.

Next to suffer defeat was Seron, the Syrian commander (3:13–26). Josephus calls him *stratēgos* of Coele-Syria, but it is not likely that he was so important an officer in the kingdom; otherwise he would not be so anxious to make a name for himself against such a force as Judas's. 1 Macc 5:55–60 notes a similar ambition, similarly thwarted, of lesser military commanders. **15.** *ungodly men:* Renegade Jews, whom Judas had antagonized; see 2:44. **16.** *the ascent of Beth-horon:* There were two towns named Beth-horon, about two mi. apart— Upper Beth-horon and Lower Beth-horon. They lay at the beginning and end of the pass connecting the coastal plains with the highlands just N of Jerusalem. Catching his foe in the narrow and steep ascent, Judas could, even with a small contingent weak from fasting (v 17), defeat Seron's much larger force. Judas also gives credit where it is due, to God (3:18–22). Routed, Seron's men tumbled down to the plain and out toward the sea coast, called anachronistically land of the "Philistines." **18–19.** *heaven:* A circumlocution for God; the author of 1 Macc never uses the names "God" or "Lord" but contents himself with "heaven" or simply the personal pronoun (2:21; 3:22,53; 16:3). Judas's victories win him renown, bringing him to the king's attention (see 2 Macc 8:7).

(C) Antiochus Goes East (3:27–37). Although 1 Macc seems to make Judas's success the reason for the gathering of Antiochus's forces, other considerations were perhaps more important, such as the necessity to subjugate the Armenian satrap Artaxias, who had declared himself independent since the death of Antiochus III, and the need to recover other eastern provinces while protecting those threatened by growing Parthian power. **28.** *year's pay:* See 1 Macc 10:36. Seleucid kings paid their mercenaries in advance, and probably their own troops as well. **29.** *money . . . was exhausted:* Due to his own extravagance and Jewish refusal to cooperate with his regime. **31.** *Persia:* This means all the area E of the Tigris (see 2 Macc 1:19).

32. Lysias, the king's "kinsman," i.e., one belonging to the highest court order of the realm (1 Macc 10:89; 2 Macc 11:1), is left in charge of the west (v 32) and of the younger Antiochus (V Eupator, 164–161), who was only seven at this time. **34.** *half of his troops:* Josephus says "part" of his force, which seems more likely; Judas was not that serious a threat to Antiochus, else he would not have begun other campaigns.

Other monarchs had deported Israelites (2 Kgs 17:6) and colonized their territory (Ezra 4:2,10; 2 Kgs 17:24), but Antiochus went further, in his plan to eradicate the Jews. **37.** *147th year:* 165 BC. By Hellenistic times, the "upper provinces" included those of the Tigris and Euphrates valley; in the Persian period, only the provinces on the Iranian plateau were meant.

21   (D) Judas Defeats Gorgias and Nicanor (3:38–4:27). The parallel account in 2 Macc 8:8–29 gives the preponderant role to Nicanor, one of the "first friends" of the king, associating Gorgias with him as an experienced general or *stratēgos*. But 1 Macc features Georgias, the commander of the separate contingent in the battle. **38.** *Ptolemy:* 2 Macc 8:8 makes him governor (*stratēgos*) of Coele-Syria and Phoenicia (Coele-Syria designated in Hellenistic times first the region between the Lebanon and the Antilebanon mountains and then also Palestine generally); see 2 Macc 4:45. *Nicanor:* See 1 Macc 7:26ff.; 2 Macc 8:9; 14; 15. *Gorgias:* See 1 Macc 5:58; 2 Macc 8:9; 10:14; 12:32ff. *friends:* See comment on 2:18. **39.** *infantry . . . cavalry:* The numbers conflict with the 20,000 of 2 Macc 8:9, which is another "round number." For a possible source of the figures involved, see 1 Chr 18:4; 19:18. The comparison of Judas and David is subtle but intended. **40.** *Emmaus:* In the Shephelah, the foothills of Judah, about 20 mi. WNW of Jerusalem. **41.** *traders:* Invited by Nicanor (2 Macc 8:10–11) to make up a sum of 2,000 talents, owed to the Romans as tribute (the indemnity mentioned in the treaty of Apamea?). The price—90 slaves per talent—was half the current price for slaves in Greece.

Unable to go to Jerusalem, because the enemy garrisoned the Akra, Judas assembled his followers at Mizpah, the ancient sanctuary, 8 mi. N of Jerusalem, which was associated with the judges (Judg 20) and Samuel (1 Sam 7:5; 10:17), and—after a similar profanation of the Temple (2 Kgs 25:8)—with Jeremiah and the remnant of the people (Jer 40:6). There they made ready for battle and prayed for help. For the similarity to an ancient holy war rite, see P. Davies, *JTS* 23 (1972) 117–21. The dirge of v 45 explains why they chose Mizpah for assembly and prayer: no true Israelite remained in Jerusalem; its sanctuary was unclean. After the exile, the priests did not possess the sacred lots Urim and Thummim (Ezra 2:63; Neh 7:65), so Judas and his band consulted the book of the law to discover a sign of the future in it. The watchword, "God's help" (2 Macc 8:23), could be inspired by such passages as Gen 49:25; Exod 18:4. It was customary in classical times to inscribe standards with such slogans (see 2 Macc 13:15; 1QM 4:13; etc.). The slogan is also the answer sought. See further P. Davies, *JTS* 23 (1972) 117–21; and A. Gelson, *VT* 34 (1984) 82–87. The groups sent home are those weeded out of the army in Deut 20:5–8. 2 Macc 8:13 speaks simply of cowardice and lack of faith. 2 Macc 8:22 names the divisional commanders of Judas's forces: his brothers Simon and Jonathan, and also Joseph, son of Zechariah (1 Macc 5:18,56). The organization of the army units is that given in Exod 18:21.

22 **4:1–9.** Jewish renegades (Josephus, *Ant.* 12.7.4 §305) from the citadel (v 2) guided Gorgias to Judas's camp. Judas appeared on the plain S of Emmaus with half his force (v 6; 2 Macc 8:16,23) and delivered an exhortation (vv 8–11) that is paralleled in 2 Macc 8:16–20, although the incidents mentioned are different. Here the reference is to Exod 14. **10.** *Heaven:* God; see comment on 3:18–19. **15.** The survivors of Nicanor's army flee to refuge in Gazara (Gezer), Azotus (Ashdod), and Jamnia (Jabneh), three cities in Philistine territory. The "plains of Idumea" (v 15) apparently stretched farther N at this time, at least N of Beth-zur (4:29). Judas returned to frighten off Gorgias's detachment, which had searched vainly for him in the hills. The imminence of the sabbath forbade further pursuit (2 Macc 8:25–26). **23.** *great riches:* Including the money that the slave traders could not now use (2 Macc 8:25). **24.** Judas's army gave thanks in the manner of Pss 118–36. After the sabbath, they gave some of the spoils to the needy (2 Macc 8:28–30). The survivors of Nicanor's forces (v 26) and Nicanor himself (2 Macc 8:34–36) reported the results of the fight to Lysias.

23 **(E) Judas Defeats Lysias at Beth-zur (4:28–35).** There is a parallel account of this battle and its sequel in 2 Macc 11:1–15. Lysias was unable to defeat Judas at Beth-zur, retired to Antioch, and negotiated peace with the Jews. **28.** *the following year:* The Seleucid year 148 (3:37; 2 Macc 11:21) or 164 BC. Lysias came with 60,000 infantry and 5,000 cavalry to invade Judea. In a fishhook maneuver, he descended the coastal plain to come up again on Beth-zur, (Khirbet et-Ṭubeiqah), about 20 mi. S of Jerusalem. The stronghold was garrisoned by Jews whom Lysias besieged. Judas rushed to arms to relieve the siege, hastily gathering a force of 10,000 men to meet Lysias (4:29; 2 Macc 11:5–7). Seeing the tremendous odds against him (which 2 Macc 11:2,4 inflates further), Judas prayed for divine assistance before joining battle. His prayer (vv 30–33) recalled the exploits of David (1 Sam 17) and Jonathan (1 Sam 14), who also faced superior might and were victorious with divine help. (1QM 11:1–3 contains a similar allusion to David and the Philistines in the prayer of the high priest before battle.) Judas was heard—the heavenly horseman of 2 Macc 11:8 appeared, to signify that the battle was the Lord's (1 Sam 17:47). **34.** Lysias's ranks, weakened by Judas's imprecatory prayer, began to give way before Judas (4:35), and so Lysias broke off hostilities and retired to Antioch, with every intention of returning later (as he does in 6:31). 2 Macc 11:11–15 gives a more impressive recital of Judas's victory, noting also that Lysias sued for peace after the battle. Although 1 Macc narrates the Temple's dedication following the early victories of Judas, the death of Antiochus IV Epiphanes (6:1–16) and accession of Antiochus V Eupator (6:17) preceded this event. 2 Macc has the right sequence; → 12.

24 **(F) The Purification and Dedication of the Temple (4:36–61).** (The parallel account is in 2 Macc 10:1–8.) Judas set out to cleanse (vv 36–51) and dedicate (vv 52–61) the sanctuary, thus providing the name for the annual celebration commemorating this event. Over the years, the feast has had many titles: (1) Dedication (*enkainismos*, 1 Macc 4:59; 2 Macc 2:9.19—in John 10:22, *enkainia*); (2) Purification (*katharismos*, 2 Macc 2:16,18; 10:3,5); (3) the feast of Tabernacles (*skenopēgia*) in Kisleu (2 Macc 1:9,18), because it was celebrated for eight days in imitation of the feast of Tabernacles (Lev 23:33–36); (4) the feast of Lights (*phōta*, Josephus, *Ant.* 12.7.7 §325; *m. B. Qam.* 6:6); and (5) more commonly, it is known by its Jewish title, Hanukkah ("Dedication").

Judas and his army ascended Mt. Zion (now inclusive of the Temple area; Isa 18:7; Ps 75:2). **41.** *Judas appointed men:* To harass the inhabitants of the Akra, while the Temple was under repair. The citadel overlooked the Temple area (1:33–35) and proved a source of constant annoyance until Simon took it in 141. **42.** Priests now began the work of cleansing the Temple, as Hilkiah and his priests had done before them (2 Kgs 23; 2 Chr 29). **43.** The stones of the defilement, the altar to Zeus Olympios (1:54,59), were now taken to an unclean place (the Kidron Valley? see 2 Kgs 23:4,6,12). **44.** *the altar of holocausts which had been desecrated:* Because the altar to Zeus had been built on it, the desecrated altar was itself a problem. Fearful lest the use of any profaned object in divine cult incur retribution (see Mal 1:6–14), Judas was reluctant to chance using the altar. He longed for a prophet. Prophets had been associated with the rebuilding of the Temple (Haggai and Zechariah) and were the sources from which to draw God's word (Jer 1:9). But prophets had disappeared (4:46; 9:27; 14:41), so Judas set the stones carefully aside "until a prophet should come" who could settle the matter. (The Qumran sectaries also expected a prophet; 1QS 9:10–11;

4QTest.) The altars mentioned in 2 Macc 10:2 were also destroyed at this time.

The new altar was built of "uncut stones" according to the law (Exod 20:25; Deut 27:5–6); the Temple was repaired in various places; and the furnishings were placed in it. **50.** It was the practice of lighting homes during this feast that earned it the name "feast of Lights" and not the fact that the lights were symbolic of religious liberty, as Josephus (*Ant.* 12.7.7 §325) thought.

52. Finally, the work of repair was done. Judas and his men dedicated the restored Temple on 25 Kislev in the Seleucid year 148 (Dec. 14, 164; 2 Macc 1:10; Josephus, *Ant.* 12.7.6 §319). **53–54.** *according to the law:* E.g., Exod 29:38–41; Num 7:10–88. They offered sacrifices in their renewed liturgy "on the anniversary of the day" on which the Gentiles had defiled the Temple.

This day, 25 Kislev, 145 (Dec. 17, 167) was exactly three years prior to the Dedication (1:54,59). The date is confirmed by Josephus (*Ant.* 12.7.6 §319) and is checked there by cross-reference to the Gk Olympiads. The two years of 2 Macc 10:3 are a mistake, one based on the author's incorrect dating of the death of Antiochus IV, which he knew preceded the Dedication, to 165.

56. The people celebrated the feast for "eight days," like the feast of Tabernacles (Lev 15:33–36) and the reconsecration of the Temple under Hezekiah (2 Chr 29:17). **60.** To prevent further trouble from those in the citadel, Judas fortified the Temple area itself, and at the same time strengthened the fortifications of Beth-zur to the south, which guarded the approaches from Idumea.

25   (G) Judas Battles with Neighboring Peoples (5:1–68). (The parallels are found in 2 Macc 8:30–33; 10:14–23; 12:2–45.) The shaky peace established after Lysias's first campaign (4:28–35; 2 Macc 11) was not to last beyond the death of Antiochus IV (6:1–16). According to its provisions, the Jews were to remain subject to the king, but they would be left free to follow their own "food and laws," i.e., to have their own religious freedom (2 Macc 11:27–33; see 10:12). In effect, the king's edict (1:41–50) was revoked insofar as it applied to the Jews. Gorgias, however, smarting under his earlier humiliation (4:1,19–22; 2 Macc 8:9), could not leave the Jews alone (2 Macc 10:14). Other governors shared his hostility (2 Macc 12:2), and soon a wave of anti-Jewish incidents broke out (5:1–3,9,15), so that the Jews were persecuted even to their deaths (2 Macc 12:3–9). The Jews under Judas fought back, taking up arms against the "Gentiles round about" the circle of Idumea (5:3–5; 2 Macc 10:14–23), Ammon (5:6–8; 2 Macc 8:30–33?), Gilead (5:9–13,24–54; 2 Macc 12:10–31; 10:24–38), Galilee (5:14–23), and the "land of the Philistines" (5:55–68; 2 Macc 12:3–9,32–45). For the moment, these were punitive and defensive measures and not attempts to throw off the Seleucid yoke, but the battles soon turned the struggle into a war for full independence.

In the description of these battles, archaic titles appear. "The sons of Jacob" (5:2), "Israel" (5:3), contend with the "sons of Esau" (5:3,65), with "Ammon" (5:6) and in the "land of the Philistines" (5:68). The biblical author wants his readers to know that Judas and his brothers are really engaged in a conquest similar to that of David (see 2 Sam 5–8), to establish their rights to an ancient heritage (15:33).

Another cause of anti-Jewish hostility at this time was the Temple's reconstruction and fortification (4:36–61), which the surrounding governors and peoples took badly. For them, it was the monument to Jewish nonconformity and contrariness, in which the Jews flaunted their opposition to the stated policies of the empire. This, added to their smoldering hatred for

Judaism (2 Macc 10:14; 12:2), led them to persecute the Jewish minorities among them.

It is not possible to establish a perfect sequence of the battles in 1 Macc 5 and its parallels, nor to construct a harmony between 1–2 Macc, because the conflicts were not fully chronicled (5:7,14; 2 Macc 10:19), and there has been transposition of the material by the biblical authors (→ 11 above). The events, however, may be assigned to the year 163.

An immediate effect of these battles was to secure the safety of those Jews who could not adequately be protected at a distance, by removing them to Judea (5:23, 45). Another sequel, brought on by the siege of the citadel (6:18–27), was the second campaign of Lysias, this time acting for Antiochus V Eupator (6:28–54).

26   (a) IDUMEA (5:3–5; 2 Macc 10:14–23). After fortifying Beth-zur, Judas began defensive measures, by moving against the sons of Esau "in Idumea" (the better reading; A has "in Judea") at Akrabattene (5:3). The precise location of Akrabattene is uncertain. Several scholars propose the region about "the ascent of scorpions" (*'aqrabbîm:* Num 34:4; Josh 15:3; Judg 1:36), SW of the Dead Sea. But this seems too far S. Others locate Akrabattene in Samaria SE of Shechem. Apparently Idumeans besieged Akrabattene, and Judas rescued it. Then he moved eastward, eventually crossing the Jordan into "Ammon." **4.** The "sons of Baean" are also difficult to identify. They were probably nomads, the mercenaries of 2 Macc 10;14. Abel locates them W of the Jordan near the "stone of Bohan" and so astride the trade route from Jerusalem to Jericho (Josh 15:6; 18:17; Luke 10:30). Judas invoked the *herem* upon them and accomplished their total destruction (see Josh 6:17).

(b) AMMON (5:6–8; 2 Macc 8:30–33?). Triumphant over those who infested the trade route, Judas now crossed the Jordan to encounter Timothy and his forces and defeat them. The particular reasons for this expedition are not given. **8.** *Jazer:* Probably the town of Num 21:32, modern Khirbet Jazzer near es-Salt. The displaced fragment in 2 Macc 8:30–33 may describe the same series of conflicts.

(c) GILEAD (5:9–13,24–54; 2 Macc 12:10–31). The Jews in Gilead (in Hellenistic times Gilead included the district N of the Yarmuk River) were forced to flee for their lives into the stronghold of Dathema, whose location is unknown beyond the fact that it lay within a night's march of Bozrah (5:29). Appeal was made to Judas. If he does not intervene, there will be another massacre like that of the Jews in the land of the Tobiads (in reprisal for Timothy's defeats in Ammon?), because Timothy is preparing to take Dathema. Judas set out to relieve the siege, taking his brother Jonathan with him. As Dancy suggests (*1 Maccabees* 105), Judas probably accompanied Simon (5:21) as far N as Beth-shan before crossing the Jordan (5:52) to enter the desert for a three-days' journey of about 60 miles (5:24). Although the sequence of Judas's campaign in Gilead is not at all clear, the next few paragraphs will attempt to correlate the events narrated in 1 Macc 5:24–54 and 2 Macc 12:10–31.

Judas and his followers met a Nabatean caravan and learned more about the plight of the Jews in Gilead (5:25–27). Since Bozrah was closer, Judas turned to relieve it (5:28). Then he continued on to Dathema (OT Edrei?, Num 21:33), routing Timothy's forces (5:34). Judas then took Alema (5:35), Caspho (5:36; Caspin in 2 Macc 12:13–16), Maked, Bosor, and other cities.

Judas's main opponent, however, eluded him. Timothy assembled another army, hired Arab mercenaries, and encamped near a tributary of the Yarmuk, opposite Raphon (5:37). Not finding Timothy (and the captives of 5:13?) at the fortress (*charax*) where he thought him to be (2 Macc 12:17), Judas moved on. He detailed some men to take one of Timothy's strongholds (2 Macc 12:18–19) and continued searching.

Eventually, he found Timothy's camp (5:38–39). Timothy's Arab mercenaries attacked Judas, who defeated them, then made peace with them (2 Macc 12:10–12). As Judas approached, Timothy sent women, children, and baggage (of 1 Macc 5:13?) into the stronghold of Carnaim. He then waited to see if Judas were too tired from his pursuit, or too fearful, to enter battle immediately (5:40). Timothy's orders to his officers also smack of the superstitious hope that a divine sign will be given. He had his answer in the orders of Judas to his officers ("scribes," see Deut 20:5–9). Again Judas was victorious in battle; Timothy's army fled to refuge at the sanctuary of the *Atergation,* the temple of the horned Astarte at Carnaim. Timothy himself fell into the hands of Dositheus and Sosipater, Tobiad Jews, who had been left behind to besiege the fortress of 2 Macc 12:19 and who were now coming up to join Judas. Timothy persuaded them to let him go, since he had their relatives in his power (2 Macc 12:24–26). Then Judas attacked Timothy's men in Carnaim, took and destroyed the town and its temple (5:44; 2 Macc 12:26).

Finally, Judas removed the Jews of Gilead to Judea. Along the way home, he encountered opposition at Ephron (et-Tayibeh) and crushed it (5:46–51; 2 Macc 12:27–28); the people of Beth-shan (Scythopolis of 2 Macc 12:29) were more friendly (5:52; 2 Macc 12:29–31). Judas arrived in Jerusalem in time to celebrate the feast of Pentecost (2 Macc 12:31). (For another view of Judas's Gilead campaign, see J. Simons, *Geographical and Topographical Texts of the OT* [Leiden, 1959] 422–25).

27   (d) GALILEE (5:14–23). At the same time that appeal was made to Jerusalem from Gilead, the Jews of Galilee made a similar plea. The same assembly that sent Judas to Gilead commissioned Simon to relieve the distress of the Galilean Jews. **15.** *Galilee of the foreigners:* The "land of the foreigners" in 1 Macc is ancient Philistia (4:22; 5:66,68), and so the Galilee spoken of here is along the seacoast. The names of the cities mentioned provide confirmation. This region is somewhat distinct from the Galilee of the Gentiles, the region further inland; see Isa 8:23. Simon also was victorious, crushing the enemy. He brought back to Judea the Jews of Galilee and Arbatta (read: Narbatta). Narbatta was in the toparchy of Narbattene, near what was later Caesarea Maritima on the seacoast; it was probably then in Samaria (Josephus, *J.W.* 2.14.5. §291–292; 2.18.10 §509).

(e) THE LAND OF THE PHILISTINES (5:55–68; 2 Macc 12:3–9,32–45). The punitive raids of 2 Macc 12:3–9 apparently occurred before Judas's campaign in Gilead, but this is not certain. The treacherous citizens of Joppa invited the Jews on an outing—at public expense (12:3)—then drowned them. In reprisal, Judas burned the city's port. When he learned of similar plans in Jamnia, he gave it the same treatment.

The accounts of 1 Macc 5:55–68 and 2 Macc 12:32–45 are interrelated. While Judas was returning from Gilead (Simon was nearly finished with his campaign; compare 5:22; 5:55), the two commanders he had left in Jerusalem (5:18) disobeyed orders and engaged Gorgias near Jamnia in hope of glory. Joseph (see 2 Macc 8:23) and Azariah (also Eleazar in 2 Macc 8:23 and Esdris in 2 Macc 12:36) were defeated and sent flying homeward, with Gorgias in pursuit. Possibly they were besieged in Beth-zur (4:61), where they had found refuge. If so, this explains the locale of the subsequent battles.

Judas rested his men briefly during Pentecost (2 Macc 12:32), then took to the field in support of the besieged

Azariah (Esdris, 2 Macc 12:36). He met Gorgias, who came out to him (2 Macc 12:32–35), and defeated him near Hebron, which he destroyed (1 Macc 5:65; this destruction need not have been completed at once). Gorgias escaped to Marisa (Mareshah of Josh 15:44). Judas fell upon those besieging Esdris and routed them (2 Macc 12:36–37). Then he bypassed Marisa (5:66; correct "Samaria" of S, A, with the OL and Josephus, *Ant.* 12.8.6 §353), and regrouped at Adullam, where he spent the sabbath (2 Macc 12:38). Judas then collected the decaying bodies of those who had fallen before Gorgias at Jamnia and returned them for burial. He also sent money to Jerusalem for an expiatory sacrifice (2 Macc 12:39–45). 1 Macc 5:67 may be another reference to the defeat of Joseph and Azariah. Next, Judas struck at Azotus (OT Ashdod) and unnamed cities. He then returned to Judea with his men (1 Macc 5:68).

28   **(H) The Death of Antiochus IV Epiphanes (6:1–17).** There is a parallel in 2 Macc 9:1–29; 10:9; and possibly in 2 Macc 1:13–17, which does speak of Antiochus but with a story that differs from the present accounts. The author of 1 Macc assumes that Antiochus died late in the Seleucid year 149 (which 1 Macc 6:16 counts as beginning in autumn) and so after the Temple's dedication and the campaigns of 1 Macc 5. In fact, Antiochus died early in that year (accepting 1 Macc 6:16), and so the order of 2 Macc is better (→ 12 above). **1.** *Elymais:* Ancient Elam (Gen 10:22). There is no city by this name, which designates rather the country around Susa, particularly to the N and E. The city and temple(s) that Antiochus tried to pillage are in Persia (1 Macc 6:1), but the city was not Persepolis (2 Macc 9:2), about which the king would not need to be told. Both 1–2 Macc mislocate the city. Except for this, their accounts match fairly well. Polybius (*Histories* 31.9) narrates Antiochus's death in much the same way. **2.** *temple:* If 2 Macc 1:13 is to be trusted here, this was the temple of the Sumerian goddess Nanaea or Anaitis, worshiped by the Elamites and in Hellenistic times identified with Artemis. *first king of the Greeks:* Alexander (1:1). **4.** Antiochus planned to reach Babylon, but got only as far as Ecbatana (2 Macc 9:3) in Persia (1 Macc 6:5) where he learned of Judas's activities. Ecbatana is often identified with Aspadana (Isfahan) because Polybius says that Antiochus died at Tabae (corrected to Gai or Gagai), S of Isfahan. **7.** *pulled down the abomination:* See 1:54 and 4:43. According to the peace terms of 2 Macc 11:15, which resulted from Lysias's first campaign and which Antiochus had approved, the Jews had gained religious liberty. Consequently, they purified the Temple and fortified Mt. Zion and Beth-zur. The dedication of the Temple, however, came after Antiochus's death, so his anger would have to be posthumous. 1 Macc has simply added to the mention of Lysias's defeat (6:5–6) a summary of the contents of 1 Macc 3–5. **8.** *ill with grief:* Antiochus now fits the nickname some of his subjects have given him—*epimanēs,* "madman." **10.** *friends:* See comment on 2:18. **11.** When Antiochus said that he was "kindly and beloved," he overrated himself, at least where his Jewish subjects were concerned. **12–13.** The biblical author sees the king's death as punishment for his crimes against Judah and not for any faults committed in a "strange land." **14.** As he lay dying, the king committed to Philip the tutelage of his son. Earlier this task was given to Lysias (3:33), who was faithful to the charge, declaring Antiochus V Eupator to be the new king (6:17). Apparently, Philip became ambitious later on (6:55–56,63; 2 Macc 13:23), was defeated, and fled (2 Macc 9:29). Josephus says Antiochus captured and killed him (*Ant.* 12.9.7 §386). **16.** The 149th Seleucid year is counted here as beginning in autumn. Antiochus

IV died about October 164. **17.** *Eupator:* The new king's nickname means "of a good father."

29   (I) Siege of the Citadel (6:18–27). This passage has no parallel in 2 Macc. Since the citadel, garrisoned by Gentiles and renegade Jews (1:33–34) proved continuously troublesome, Judas besieged it. By this time, the fighting which began with defensive measures and punitive raids had assumed its true appearance of a war for liberation from Seleucid power. Unfortunately for Judas, a few of the besieged escaped and reported to Eupator what had happened, Menelaus among them (2 Macc 13:3). **20.** In the official Seleucid calculation, the 150th year began Oct. 11, 163 and ended Sept. 29, 162. Judas besieged the citadel near the beginning of this year, after the expedition that carried him through Idumea to the "land of the Philistines" in the summer of 163 (5:55–68).

30   (J) Lysias's Second Campaign in Judah (6:28–63; 2 Macc 13:1–26). Judas's revolt now assumed great importance in the empire, and the king determined to crush it. He, or rather Lysias, almost did so, but the threat of Philip taking over the whole empire drew the Seleucid army out of Judah. Again Lysias made peace with the Jews.

Upon hearing Menelaus's report, the king conferred with his officers. Actually, since the king was so young, it was Lysias who made the decisions (6:57; 2 Macc 13:2). The importance of the struggle is evident in the force Lysias gathered, which was supplemented by mercenaries, elephants, and chariots (6:29; 2 Macc 13:2), and in the presence of the king himself. The numbers, however, are exaggerated. At the earlier, more important battle of Magnesia (190) and in the parade at Daphne (166), the Seleucid army totaled only 52,200 and 50,500 men respectively.

Because of the elephants and chariotry, Lysias kept to the coastal plains until he was ready to come up again through Idumea to besiege Beth-zur. The Jewish garrison defended the stronghold with courage (6:31; 2 Macc 13:18–19). Meanwhile, Judas struck at the king's forces near Modin in a nightly foray (2 Macc 13:14–17), then made the mistake of taking his troops down to Beth-zechariah to save Judea and "the city" (Jerusalem? Beth-zur?; see 2 Macc 13:13). The king turned to meet this challenge with the main body of his forces. Both sides prepared for battle, the king's men intoxicated the elephants with the "juice of grapes and mulberries" (6:33–39). See P. Maxwell-Stuart, *VT* 25 (1975) 230–32; and J. Kipper, *PerspT* 9 (1977) 143–71, 261–65. Once on lower ground, Judas and his army were no match for the superior armament and the professionalism of the king's soldiers. Despite heroic courage—Judas's brother Eleazar Avaran stands out—Judas was beaten back (6:40–47).

Beth-zur now capitulated for lack of food (6:49; 2 Macc 13:22) because it was a sabbatical year, in which the land had to lie fallow (6:49; Exod 23:11; Lev 25:3–7). Lack of supplies also kept the fortress on Mt. Zion undermanned (6:53–54). All seemed desperate, until Lysias received news that Philip was attempting to seize control of the government (2 Macc 13:23). Lysias made peace with the Jews (6:57–59; 2 Macc 13:23) and went home, leaving them again with religious, but not civil, liberty. Menelaus was executed, a victim of political expediency (2 Macc 13:4–8). Before he left to defeat Philip (6:63), the king razed the Jewish fortifications on Mt. Zion (6:62). News of the peace treaty nearly provoked a riot at Ptolemais (2 Macc 13:25–26; see 1 Macc 5:22). 2 Macc sees the whole campaign as a series of Jewish victories in the light of its final outcome. The letter of 2 Macc 11:22–26 belongs here; it describes the

terms of the peace. The Jews were to be left in possession of the Temple and of their religious liberty. The year was 163.

31   (K) The Expedition of Bacchides and Alcimus (7:1–25). Demetrius I Soter (161–150), the oldest surviving son of Seleucus IV (187–175), had been frustrated earlier by the Roman Senate in his bid to succeed Epiphanes (175–164) whom he considered the usurper of a throne rightly his. The Romans had recognized Antiochus V Eupator (164–161) instead, feeling that they could better serve their own purposes with a youth on the Seleucid throne. With the connivance of his friend the historian Polybius, Demetrius finally escaped Rome and went to Tripolis, where he set himself up as rightful king (Polybius, *Histories* 31.2, 11–15). The populace and army at Antioch came over to him, and he finally went there to take possession of the royal palace of his ancestors in 161. Eupator and his minister Lysias were quickly executed (7:2–4). This opened the way for a new policy toward the Jews; it was one of repression.

Most of 7:1–25 has no parallel in 2 Macc (see 2 Macc 14:1–11, however). In 7:1, the 151st Seleucid year is counted as beginning in autumn. When correlated with 2 Macc 14:1,4, this verse dates the visit of Alcimus to the spring of 161. The "city by the sea" is Tripolis (2 Macc 14:1).

5. With Alcimus, a new priestly line appears. Onias III, who belonged to the traditional family of high priests—who were descended from Zadok (2 Sam 8:17) by way of Joshua (1 Chr 6:8–15; Hag 1:1; Neh 12:10–11) and Jaddua (Ezra 2:36)—had been replaced by his brother Jason (2 Macc 4:7), then by Menelaus (2 Macc 4:23–26). Menelaus was a priest, but of the family of Bilgah (2 Macc 3:4). Josephus (*Ant.* 12.5.1 §237) makes him the "brother" of Onias, which is incorrect if blood brother is meant. Now, in Alcimus, still another priestly family appears (1 Macc 7:14), perhaps that of Jakim (1 Chr 24:12). It seems that under the peace terms of 163, Alcimus became the high priest when Menelaus was deposed and executed (2 Macc 13:4–8; Josephus, *Ant.* 12.9.7 §385). Alcimus, whose Gk name, which means "brave," shows his disposition toward hellenization, is known also in some mss. and Josephus (*Ant.* 12.9.7 §385) as Jakeimos. His full name in Hebrew may have been Eliakim or Jehoiakim (Joakim).

Alcimus's earlier defilement (2 Macc 14:3) is not specified, but the time of "separation" (*amixias*) from the Gentiles (2 Macc 14:3,38) seems to be that of the persecution under Epiphanes, when even priests defiled the Temple (2 Macc 4:14; 6:3–6) and when those Jews who refused to be defiled died (2 Macc 6:25). If Alcimus were so defiled, Judas would definitely not have wanted him in the high priesthood, even though circumstances in 163 might have forced Judas to accept Alcimus for a while, until he could prevent Alcimus from exercising the high priesthood (2 Macc 14:3) and drive him out (7:6).

The events which follow are best understood if Judas was once again in possession of Jerusalem. Perhaps the change of regime in Antioch was the signal for Judas to take Jerusalem and drive out Alcimus, who then went to Demetrius to complain. Since Alcimus was obviously hostile to Judas and in sympathy with Seleucid interests, the king listened willingly to his complaint (7:5–7); see also 2 Macc 14:6–10) and then decided to act ruthlessly in establishing Alcimus at Jerusalem. Bacchides' commission was to take vengeance on Judas's followers and to put down any opposition to the high priest.

8. Bacchides was one of the "king's friends" (7:8; see comment on 2:18) and governor of "the province beyond the river," i.e., the area between the Euphrates (the "river") and Egypt. His task was to subdue Judea while

Demetrius went E—as Epiphanes did (3:27-37)—to meet the challenge to the empire there, this time from Timarchus, the satrap of Media, who had proclaimed himself independent. Eventually, Demetrius defeated Timarchus and killed him. **13.** Although Judas was wary of Bacchides' peace feelers, some of his followers from the ḥǎsîdîm (see comment on 2:42) led by scribes believed Bacchides' promises and relied too much on the fact that Alcimus was a priest (7:14). Their confidence cost them their lives. No reason is given why these ḥǎsîdîm should now have deserted Judas and sued for peace. At any rate, Bacchides soon broke his oath. 1 Macc 7:16-17 applies Ps 79:2-3 to the situation. Goldstein thinks the text says Alcimus wrote the words cited (and Ps 79), but "he wrote" refers to divine authorship of the psalm.

Bacchides withdrew from Jerusalem to Bethzaith. Again he slaughtered without compunction those who had deserted to him from Judas, thus fulfilling his commission (7:9). Then leaving a force with Alcimus, whom he reestablished in Jerusalem and placed in charge of the province, Bacchides returned to the king at Antioch (7:20). His mission had not been completely successful; Judas was still at liberty and too strong to take by force with the men at hand.

21. Alcimus fought to maintain his high priesthood, taking out his animosity on any opposition (7:21-22). Judas realized that he had to act to prevent further damage to his supporters. He made raids against Alcimus's men and those who had gone over to him. So successful were Judas's reprisals, that Alcimus and his partisans could not travel freely in the countryside. Realizing that time was favoring Judas, Alcimus returned to the king to beg a larger force.

32 (L) The Defeat of Nicanor (7:26-50). The parallel passage is 2 Macc 14:1-15:36. Demetrius sent Nicanor, who had ample reason (3:38-4:25; 2 Macc 8:8-29) to be an enemy of Israel (7:26). Nicanor had escaped Rome with Demetrius (Josephus, *Ant.* 12.10.4 §402) and was, at the time of his appointment as governor (*stratēgos*) of Judea, in charge of the elephants of Demetrius's army. **9.** Once again orders went out to destroy Judas and supporters. Those pagans whom Judas had terrorized joined Nicanor (2 Macc 14:14). Judas (the "leader" of 2 Macc 14:16) moved his camp to Adasa. Earlier Simon had skirmished with Nicanor at Dessau (Adasa?); alarmed at the sudden appearance of Nicanor's men he backed off (2 Macc 14:16-17).

Nicanor decided on diplomacy and offered acceptable terms, apparently promising that Judas would succeed Alcimus in the high priesthood (2 Macc 14:18-22, 26). For a time, life continued normally (2 Macc 14:25), then Alcimus, fearful of the growing friendship of Nicanor and Judas, complained to the king, with the result that the king ordered Judas sent to Antioch as a prisoner (2 Macc 14:26-27). Nicanor waited to catch Judas by a ruse (presumably because Judas was well defended at all times) because he did not want to stir up trouble, but Judas sensed a change in Nicanor's attitude, assessed it correctly and took to the field with his forces, leaving Nicanor in possession of Jerusalem (2 Macc 14:28-30). All these events are capsulized in 1 Macc 7:27-30.

Nicanor suspected the priests of complicity in Judas's escape and blasphemed the Temple, promising to raze it and build a temple to Dionysius if Judas were not handed over to him (2 Macc 14:31-33). Nicanor then left Jerusalem to fight Judas at Capharsalama (location uncertain) where he was beaten (7:31-32). The episode of Razis (2 Macc 14:37-46) may narrate the taking of one of Judas's strongholds nearby.

Returning to Jerusalem, Nicanor regrouped, threatened the Temple again (7:33-35), and went out once more to meet Judas. The priests, in tears, prayed for divine aid to save the Temple (7:36-38; 2 Macc 15-19). Their prayer ironically comments on Isa 56:6-8. Nicanor encamped at Beth-horon, being joined there by Syrian reinforcements. Judas, meanwhile, was at Adasa encouraging his men before battle (7:40; 2 Macc 15:7-19). Nicanor's plan was to attack Judas on the sabbath, but this drew opposition from the Jews with him, and the plan ended in frustration (2 Macc 15:1-5). In contrast, Judas relied on God to help him and his men and to punish the blasphemer as once he had punished Sennacherib's army (2 Kgs 19:35; 2 Macc 15:20-24).

On 13 Adar (March, 160), Judas was victorious in battle. Nicanor was struck down, and his forces fled toward Gazara (Gezer) but were cut off by partisans of Judas, driven back toward their pursuers and destroyed (7:43-46; 2 Macc 15:25-27). Nicanor's head and arm, with which he had blasphemed the Temple, were brought to Jerusalem. There Judas displayed them before the pagans, hanging them from the Jewish citadel on Mt. Zion (7:47; 2 Macc 15:31,35). The feast of Nicanor on the 13th Adar fell out of the Jewish calendar after the destruction of the Temple in AD 70 (7:49; 2 Macc 15:36; Josephus, *Ant.* 12.10.5 §412).

33 (M) Judas's Treaty with the Romans (8:1-32). By the middle of the 2d cent. BC, Rome had extended her power throughout the Mediterranean world. 1 Macc now recounts a series of Roman victories to explain her presence and power in the Middle East. **2.** *the Gauls:* Most likely the Cisalpine Gauls, whose conquest was complete in the first decade of the 2d cent. BC. **3-4.** *in the region of Spain:* The Romans came to power after winning the country from the Carthaginians, at the end of the 3d cent. BC. They then exploited Spain's mining in their own interests. *the kings:* Unspecified, unless this is a reference to what follows in vv 5-8. **5.** Philip V of Macedon was defeated by Titus Quintius Flamininus at Cynoscephalae (in Thessaly) in 197. Philip's son, Perseus, lost to the Roman general Aemilius Paulus at Pydna (in Macedon) in 168.

6-8. Antiochus III, "the Great, king of Asia,"—i.e., of the lands bordering on the eastern end of the Mediterranean—lost at Magnesia to Lucius Scipio, despite having the superior force. The 120 elephants really numbered 54, according to Polybius and Livy. Nor was Antiochus "taken alive"; he escaped. Under the treaty of Apamea (188), he was forced to pay the costs of the war, some 15,000 Euboic talents, a "heavy tribute," and to give hostages (notably the future Antiochus Epiphanes). Antiochus was also forced to retire from Asia Minor, but hardly from India, which he never occupied, nor from Media, which he did. Some authors suggest India, Media, and Lydia (v 8) should be read as Ionia, Mysia, and Lydia, territories in Asia Minor which were given to Eumenes II, the king of Pergamum, who had been the ally of Rome at Magnesia.

9-10. 1 Macc notes the defeat of the Achaean League in 146 by the Roman consul Lucius Mummius, who devastated Corinth once he had taken it. The reference to 146 is anachronistic at this point in 1 Macc's story. **10.** *even to this day:* See the similar phrase in 13:30. **13.** *became kings:* The Romans liked to make kings; some they helped were Masinissa of Numidia, Eumenes I and Eumenes II of Pergamum, Prusias and Nicomedes II of Bithynia, Alexander Balas of Syria (10:1), Ariarathes V of Cappadocia, and all the later Egyptian kings. **15.** *every day:* The Roman Senate did not meet daily; it met on the calends, nones, and ides of the month, and on festivals. Nor were there 320 senators; there were 300. **16.** *one man every year:*

The consul—one of two—with whom the Jews came in contact (see 15:16). The whole description of Rome in this chapter fits the adage, "too good to be true."

To keep Demetrius off balance politically and to scare him, Judas concluded a treaty with the Romans. The exact moment when the envoys were sent can only be conjectured, but perhaps it was as soon as Demetrius appeared in the east and Judas had driven Alcimus from the high priesthood, for then Demetrius was *persona non grata* at Rome. This estimate is borne out by the letter cited in Josephus (*Ant.* 14.10.15 §233), in which the consul C. Fannius Strabo (consul, 161) asked for safe passage through Cos for a Jewish embassy. **17.** Judas sent Eupolemus—whose father John had won concessions for the Jews from Antiochus III (2 Macc 4:11) and who was from the priestly line of Hakkoz (1 Chr 24:10; Ezra 2:61)—and with him Jason, son of Eleazar. They were to establish a treaty of amity (*philia, amicitia*) and alliance (*symmachia, societas*) with the Romans, a treaty which in effect was often the first step toward Roman domination of a country. **18.** The Gk yoke had not yet been broken to the extent of defeating Nicanor. **22.** The bronze tablets recording the treaty remained in Rome's Capitol (Josephus, *Ant.* 12.10.6 §416); a copy was sent in a letter to Judas.

The treaty (8:23–30) is similar in form to other Roman treaties. In v 26, the phrase translated as "without receiving anything" was, in the original Latin of the treaty exactly the same phrase as in v 28: "without deception." The original *sine dolo* (*ou meta dolou* of v 28) was misread as *sine dote* (and so *outhen labontes* in v 26). **31–32.** The senate sent a threatening letter to Demetrius at the same time. Its contents are summarized here from the point of view of 1 Macc's author. See further T. Fischer, *ZAW* 86 (1974) 90–93.

34   (N) The Defeat and Death of Judas (9:1–22). Demetrius avenged the death of Nicanor (7:43) by sending a larger force to meet and overcome Judas, killing him in the battle at Elasa.

An enemy force—from the Jewish standpoint the "right wing" of the descending Seleucid army (9:1)—entered Galilee (the Gk text mistakenly reads *Galgala;* Hebr *gilgal*) and encamped along the highways (Gk *maisaloth* transcribes the Hebr *mĕsillôt,* "highways") at Arbela, taking and killing many there. **3.** The main body of the Syrian army moved against Jerusalem (again in Jewish hands) in May 160. Not finding Judas there, the Seleucid generals moved the army to Berea, 10 mi. N of Jerusalem, opposite Judas's camp at Elasa.

At the sight of so strong an opponent, the Jewish army dwindled through desertion to 800 men. Discouraged, Judas was still determined to do battle, going against the sound advice of his loyal followers, because he was reluctant to stain his glory (2:51,64; 3:3; etc.).

In battle, the Seleucid army closed itself pincerlike around Judas's small band. He chose to fight against the stronger wing, where Bacchides was, and beat it back toward Mt. Hazor (reading *azorou orous;* the *azōtou orous* [Mt. Azotus] of v 15, and also the *aza orous* of Josephus, *Ant.* 12.11.2 §429 are the result of scribal errors). Hazor is mentioned in 2 Sam 13:23; Neh 11:33; 1 QapGen 21:8).

The left wing of Bacchides' army swung in behind Judas, and before the day was done Judas was dead. The remnants of his followers fled. Josephus says (*Ant.* 12.11.2 §432) that Judas's brothers obtained his body under a truce. Perhaps they did, for with Judas gone and the Jews defeated, Bacchides could afford to be more lenient. On the family memorial at Modin, see 13:25–30. **21.** This cry combines the plaint over Saul (2 Sam 1:19) with the notion that Judas was a "savior" or "judge" (Judg 3:9; 2 Kgs 13:5). **22.** *but the rest:* An echo of the

stock phrase used of the kings (1 Kgs 11:41; etc.).

35   (IV) Jonathan Continues the Struggle (9:23–12:53). With Judas gone, the revolt collapsed for a while, but soon Jonathan took command and, although he was pursued for a while, was eventually victorious over Bacchides. Then, aided by Seleucid intrigue for power, Jonathan achieved positions of importance—high priest, governor—under Alexander Balas and succeeding kings. In time, however, he fell victim to the treachery of the ambitious Trypho.

(A) Jonathan Succeeds Judas as Leader (9:23–34). After Judas's death, the "transgressors of the law" came to power again. Famine sped the collapse of resistance in the countryside, because whatever stores were on hand were controlled by the government. Bacchides and Alcimus used their power to follow up their advantage, rooting out and destroying those sympathetic to Judas. **27.** *a prophet no longer appeared:* Judea's anguish was similar to that experienced in the disappearance of prophecy immediately after the exile.

The reprisals stirred up Jewish antipathy once more. Passing over Simon, the elder brother, for a reason unknown to us, the resistance elected Jonathan as its leader. He accepted and led his newly assembled followers into hiding at the pool of Asphar, now thought to be about 3 mi. SW of Tekoa. **34.** This may be a misplaced doublet for v 43.

36   (B) Jonathan Avenges His Brother John (9:35–42). For mobility, Jonathan decided to store much of his equipment with the Nabateans across the Jordan, a move made necessary by Bacchides' search for him (9:32–34). **35.** His brother John (Gaddi, 2:2) was detached as leader or officer in charge of bringing the baggage train (and presumably families) to the Nabateans for safety. Along the way, John was ambushed by "the sons of Jambri," who had their center of operations at Medaba, near the NE tip of the Dead Sea. John's company was killed (9:42) and the spoil taken away.

In revenge, Jonathan and Simon turned the wedding of a Canaanite (or rather "trader"; the Nabateans were skillful merchants) nobleman's daughter into a massacre. **37.** *Nadabath:* To be read with Josephus, *Ant.* 13.1.4 §18 as Nabatha, the Aram form of Nebo (Num 32:3). **41.** An allusion to Amos 8:10.

(C) Bacchides Ambushes Jonathan (9:43–49). News was brought to Bacchides of Jonathan's attack on the wedding party, and he went to the Jordan (9:32,43) to ambush Jonathan on the sabbath. The Jordan marshes (9:42) mentioned here refer to the thickly wooded area at the Jordan's bed, particularly large and swampy in its southernmost extremity, near the entrance to the Dead Sea.

45. Before Jonathan reached safety, perhaps in a loop of the river, the trap was sprung. *before and behind us:* Bacchides blocked the path from the Jordan. **46.** *heaven:* The reference is to God. Jonathan fought, then plunged into the Jordan and crossed it. Bacchides neglected to pursue, perhaps to pick up the spoils of the wedding party (9:40) that Jonathan had to abandon. **49.** Bacchides' losses seem exaggerated.

(D) Bacchides Fortifies Judea; Alcimus Dies (9:50–57). Bacchides strengthened his grip on the land by establishing strongholds and fortifying cities throughout Judea. Fortresses were built at Jericho, at Emmaus, Beth-horon (see comment on 3:15), Bethel, Timnath-serah (see Josh 19:50), Pirathon (see Judg 12:13,15), and Tappuah (see Josh 12:17). The last three were in the province of Samaria and are called Judea (9:50) because Jews lived there. Bacchides added to the defenses of Beth-zur, Gazara, and the citadel of Jerusalem, also holding hostages in the latter.

54. In the second month (Iyyar) of the 153d Seleucid year (about May 159), Alcimus began renovations in the Temple. He ordered the removal of the wall separating "the inner court of the sanctuary," to which the Israelites had access, from the outer court, where Gentiles had access. Thus "the work of the prophets," Haggai and Zachariah, who brought about the reconstruction of the Temple, was destroyed. The author views the stroke Alcimus suffered as punishment for this nefarious act. **57.** Bacchides' work effectively curbed the resistance movement for two years. H. Stegemann identifies Alcimus's (unnamed) successor as high priest with the Teacher of Righteousness of the Essenes; see *Die Entstehung der Qumrangemeinde* (Bonn, 1971) 213-20.

(E) Jonathan Escapes and Frustrates Bacchides (9:58-73). Two years later (157), Jonathan's enemies plotted his capture but the plot failed, and he in turn avenged himself on its ringleaders. Then Jonathan withdrew to Beth-basi (S of Bethlehem), which he fortified. Bacchides besieged Beth-basi, but Jonathan slipped out and created a diversionary nighttime attack on "Odomera and his kinsmen and the sons of Phasiron," presumably allies of Bacchides. While the latter was distracted by this, Simon sallied forth and burned his siege machines.

68. Frustrated, Bacchides decided to go home. He took out his anger on Jonathan's enemies, whom he accused of treachery (Josephus, *Ant.* 13.1.5 §31), made a pact with Jonathan, and departed. Bacchides did not, however, release the hostages in the citadel (9:53; 10:6). What military necessity or other reason drew him elsewhere, leaving Jonathan still unpunished, is not known, but his going left Jonathan in peace at Michmash for five years, during which time he pursued his policy of punishing the ungodly whenever possible. Verse 73 likens him to the judges of old, a warrior fighting the battles of the King of Heaven.

37   (F) Alexander Balas (150-145) Claims Demetrius's Throne (10:1-14). In the 160th Seleucid year (152), a rival for the Seleucid throne appeared and occupied Ptolemais—Josephus says by treason (*Ant.* 13.2.1 §35). Alexander, surnamed Balas (for *ba'al*) and also Epiphanes (supposedly after his father), claimed to be the son of Antiochus IV. In this claim he had the support of the kings of Cappadocia, Pergamum, and Egypt; he also won the friendship of Rome. Ancient historians, notably Polybius, the friend of Demetrius, rejected his claim and called him an imposter from Smyrna. But the chief factor in antiquity for the acceptance or rejection of the new king as legitimate seems to have been the ancients' attitude toward Demetrius. 1 Macc and Josephus accepted Alexander at face value, because they opposed the reigning monarch.

Demetrius put in the first bid for Jonathan's loyalty, allowing him to recruit and equip troops and ordering that the hostages in the citadel (10:6; 9:53) be released to him. Jonathan immediately began restoration of the defenses of the city and of the fortress on Mt. Zion, which earlier Apollonius and Eupator had pulled down (1:31; 4:60; 7:62). Since Jonathan was once again in a position of power, the Gentiles fled the strongholds built by Bacchides (9:50); presumably some went to the aid of Demetrius in the battle against Alexander. Only the renegade Jews remained, safe in the defenses of Beth-zur (and, Josephus adds, in the citadel at Jerusalem; *Ant.* 13.2.1 §42). It seems they retained Gazara also (11:41; 13:43).

38   (G) Jonathan Supports Alexander Balas and Becomes High Priest (10:15-50). Alexander also appealed to his "brother" Jonathan for support. In return, he offered the high priesthood and a position as the king's "friend" (see comment on 2:18). **20.** *a purple robe and a crown of gold:* The first is symbolic of the rank of king's friend; both are symbolic of the high priesthood. Although the legitimate heir to the high priesthood was Onias IV, who had fled to Egypt when Alcimus was appointed high priest (Josephus, *Ant.* 12.9.7 §387), neither 1 Macc nor Josephus seems to question the validity of Jonathan's appointment. For them, if Alexander were king, then by oriental custom long established, he had the right to appoint his choice as high priest. Jonathan was, in fact, a member of a priestly family (2:1).

Abel and Starcky (*Maccabées* 57-58) give this moment as that in which those *ḥăsîdîm* later to be known as the Essenes withdrew their support from the Maccabees. The bulk of the Hasideans continued to favor the Hasmoneans until the time of John Hyrcanus (134-104). The Essenes' disappointment lay in Jonathan's assumption of the high priesthood. Consequently, the sectaries followed their Teacher of Righteousness into the desert in protest. (The date of the Teacher of Righteousness, however, is much disputed.) Perhaps, say Abel and Starcky, this is the moment when Onias IV chose to build the rival temple at Leontopolis near Cairo.

Jonathan put on the "sacred vestments" (10:21; see Exod 28) and began functioning as high priest at the feast of Tabernacles, which was celebrated from the 15th to the 23rd day of the seventh month (Lev 23:33- 36) in the Seleucid year 160 (October 152).

22-25. Demetrius, not to be outdone by Alexander, appealed once more to Jerusalem, not only to Jonathan but also to the Jews as a whole. **26.** Either he did not know, or he pretended not to know, that Jonathan had gone over to Alexander. The prizes he offered included: exemption from tribute, i.e., various taxes, including that on salt (taken from the Dead Sea?); remission of monies paid to the crown (10:29); release of Demetrius's share of the grain and fruit (10:30; see Lev 27:30, where tithes from the land are paid to God); tax exemption for Jerusalem and environs, which as "holy" have now to pay their former taxes to God (10:31); cession of the citadel to the "high priest" (here Demetrius seems implicitly to recognize Jonathan's new status, which was granted him by Alexander!); the return of captives (and the restoration of their cattle without payment of back taxes?); freedom for Jews throughout the empire from performance of civic duties on holy days (10:34-35); service in the king's army (10:36-37; at the king's expense, not Judea's, as was customary—with this would go positions of status and trust in the military service, and also religious freedom [presumably not to fight on the sabbath; see 2 Macc 15:1-5]); annexation of three "nomes" (i.e., three toparchies [11:28] or districts) from Samaria and Galilee (10:30; Galilee here is an administrative division otherwise unknown; the three districts are actually in Samaria [10:38]); the gift of Ptolemais and environs (which Alexander now controlled!) with their revenue to be used for support of the Temple (10:39); further revenue for the Temple, to be gathered from taxes elsewhere (10:40), unpaid official contributions (10:41), and release of funds formerly appropriated by royal officials (10:42); remission of debt and return of property for those who fled to sanctuary in the Temple (10:43); reconstruction of the Temple at the king's expense (10:44); defensive construction at the king's expense (10:45). Dancy (*1 Maccabees* 146-47) hesitates on the authenticity of this letter's contents. For J. Bunge's view that Demetrius wrote only one letter, which preceded Alexander's, see *JSJ* 6 (1975) 27-43. J. Murphy-O'Connor holds that the letter is authentic but composed of a letter and an official list of grants; see *RB* 83 (1976) 400-20.

Jonathan, who is slighted in the letter, and the people reject Demetrius's friendship, preferring Alexander. **47.** *first to address them:* Actually, Demetrius was first (10:3–4). The idea here is that Alexander's friendship was preferable. **48–50.** Fortunately for Jonathan, he chose the right side. Demetrius died bravely in battle against Alexander (Jospehus, *Ant.* 13.2.4 §60), and possession of the monarchy was settled. The year was 150.

39   (H) At Alexander's Marriage, Jonathan Is Promoted (10:51–66). In the Seleucid year 162 (150 BC), Alexander arranged for his marriage with Cleopatra Thea, daughter of the same Ptolemy VI Philometor for whose sake ostensibly Antiochus IV Epiphanes had invaded Egypt in 169 (1:18). Jonathan was called to the wedding and met the two kings at Ptolemais. There, he was honored by Alexander, who refused to hear complaints against Jonathan and instead promoted him to the rank of first friend (see comment on 2:18), making him also a general (*stratēgos*) and provincial governor (*meridarch*), presumably of the enlarged Judea (10:30).

    (I) Jonathan Defeats Apollonius, the General of Demetrius II (10:67–89). Three years later, a new claimant to the throne appeared, Demetrius II (145–139, 129–125), son of the slain Demetrius I. Setting out from Crete with mercenaries led by Lasthenes (11:31), Demetrius landed in Cilicia and soon proved a serious threat to Alexander, who hurried home to secure Antioch (Josephus, *Ant.* 13.4.3 §87). Demetrius appointed Apollonius over Coele-Syria (see comment on 3:38) — the same Apollonius who had helped Demetrius I to escape from Rome (Polybius, *Histories* 31.11–15). Apollonius descended on Jamnia and camped there. His challenge to Jonathan (10:70–73) brought the angry response of battle. **72.** *your fathers:* Probably alludes to the two defeats of Judas (6:47; 9:18). **73.** *in the plain:* Wherever superior armament — cavalry, chariots, elephants — could be brought to bear, i.e., on the lower lands along the coast, the Israelites throughout history were generally no match for their technologically more advanced adversaries (note the slow conquest of the Philistines). **74–86.** Jonathan got behind Apollonius, taking Joppa and cutting off his line of communications. Apollonius countered by pretending to withdraw toward Azotus, meanwhile edging farther into the plain. He left a large detachment of cavalry behind to swing in behind the pursuing Jonathan. Jonathan fell into the trap but then stood his ground, and when the enemy cavalry was tired, Simon's men (held in a sort of reserve?) moved up to attack the weary enemy phalanx. This counterattack succeeded, and the enemy was routed. Jonathan chased them to Azotus, burned that city and its surrounding towns, and then destroyed those who had taken refuge in the temple of Dagon (a stronghold of sorts?). Ashkelon capitulated without a fight.

87–89. Jonathan returned with his plunder to Jerusalem. The overjoyed Alexander rewarded him by giving him Ekron and its territories and making him a "kinsman" of the king. The insignia of this highest court order in the empire was a gold buckle fastening the purple cloak at the recipient's shoulder.

40   (J) The Alliance Between Demetrius II and Ptolemy (11:1–13). Ptolemy VI Philometor now tried to add part of Alexander's domains to his own. Josephus says that he was alienated from Alexander by an assassination attempt at Ptolemais, but 1 Macc calls this camouflage (11:11; *Ant.* 13.4.6 §106). Apparently Ptolemy fooled Jonathan as the latter accompanied him to the river Eleutherus (*nahr el-kebir*, 19 mi. N of Tripolis). Ptolemy certainly made his intentions clear when he reached Antioch: "he put on the crown of Asia." Meanwhile he took control of the coast northward to

"Seleucia-by-the-sea" (slightly N of the Orontes). He also gave his daughter, Alexander's wife, to Demetrius. Diodorus says (*Hist.* 32.9) that Ptolemy was not ambitious for the whole of Asia but only for Coele-Syria, being content to leave the rest of the Seleucid Empire to Demetrius, partly, at least, because he feared the Romans. Josephus (*Ant.* 13.4.7 §114–15) supports some of this.

    (K) The Deaths of Alexander and Ptolemy (11:14–19). To the north, Alexander was busy with revolt in Cilicia, but he returned to do battle with Ptolemy at the river Oenoparas, near Antioch (Strabo, *Geogr.* 751). Defeated, he fled for refuge to the Arab Zabdiel (called Diocles by Diodorus [*Hist.* 32.9]), who murdered him immediately, cutting off his head. Ptolemy also died, of wounds inflicted in battle, but not before he saw the head of Alexander that Zabdiel had sent him. Demetrius now had a clear path to the throne of the whole Seleucid Empire, which is what Josephus says (incorrectly) Ptolemy had in mind for him anyway (*Ant.* 13.4.7 §114–15). With Ptolemy dead, the coastal cities in his power rose against their Egyptian garrisons to kill them. The rest of the Ptolemaic army returned to Egypt. It is at this point that Demetrius became *de facto* ruler of the empire, in the 167th Seleucid year, 145 BC. He had begun his bid for power two years earlier. Now also, he began to call himself Nicator, "conqueror," because of his double victory over Alexander and Ptolemy.

41   (L) Jonathan's Pact with Demetrius (11:20–37). Jonathan felt that it was time to rid the citadel in Jerusalem of its pagans and renegade Jews. When report was made to Demetrius of Jonathan's siege, the king summoned him to Ptolemais. Jonathan went at the risk of his life, but he also disregarded the king's command and left orders that the siege was to continue. Once at Ptolemais, Jonathan won Demetrius over, as earlier he had won over Alexander (10:59–66). Many of the privileges granted by Demetrius I (10:25–45) were confirmed by his son. What reasons, apart from Jonathan's personality, impelled the king to generosity with a former adversary (10:67–85) are matter for conjecture. Perhaps he needed allies, for he was becoming increasingly unpopular at home. **30.** *his brother:* Jonathan was "kinsman" to Demetrius, as he was to Alexander (10:89). *Lasthenes:* Chief minister to Demetrius (Diodorus, *Hist.* 33.4), and so he received the original letter for his files. **34.** *all those who offer sacrifice:* They could now pay certain royal taxes to the Temple instead. **37.** The royal rescript granting these privileges was to be posted publicly on Mt. Zion.

    (M) Trypho's Intrigue Against Demetrius (11:38–40). Once in undisputed possession of the throne, Demetrius's next objective was to make his reign secure. On the advice of Lasthenes, presumably, who dominated the 16-year-old king, Demetrius dismissed the bulk of his army, asked them to give up their arms, and did not pay them peacetime wages, as previous kings had to assure their loyalty in times of stress. He retained only the mercenaries from Crete and the islands (Josephus, *Ant.* 13.4.9 §129). Naturally, the king became more unpopular, and Trypho, one of Alexander's generals, took advantage of it. This man, Diodotus Trypho (he adopted his surname "self-indulgent" after his victory over Demetrius II), was a native of Apamea and had served in the army of Demetrius I. He had gone over to Alexander, then to Ptolemy. Now he went to Imalkue and promised to set up Alexander's son Antiochus (VI) as king.

    (N) Jonathan Aids Demetrius (11:41–53). While Trypho was with Imalkue, Jonathan helped

Demetrius put down a revolt in Antioch. **41.** The king offered his troubles with his army as his excuse for not now removing the troops from the citadel in Jerusalem and from the fortresses (Beth-zur and Gazara; 10:14; 13:43). He appealed to Jonathan for help and got it. 1 Macc says that the Jews—and Diodorus says (*Hist.* 33:4) that the Cretan mercenaries—put down the uprising of the populace at Antioch. No doubt both were responsible (as Josephus implies: *Ant.* 13.5.3 §137), the Jews turning the tide of battle for the mercenaries loyal to Demetrius. Their victory did not help the Jews, however, except for the booty gained, because Demetrius reneged on his word and rewarded Jonathan by afflicting him greatly. Josephus says the king threatened invasion to collect tribute (*Ant.* 13.5.3 §143).

42   (O) Jonathan's Alliance with Trypho (11:54-62). As Diodorus notes (*Hist.* 33.4), their subjects were beginning to find the descendants of Antiochus IV Epiphanes a more pleasant lot of masters than the offspring of his brother Seleucus IV. Consequently, when Trypho proclaimed Antiochus VI the new king at Chalcis (SW of Aleppo), he soon had the backing of the dismissed troops of Demetrius, the city of Apamea (NW of Hamath), and the elephants captured from Ptolemy. The young king began his reign in the Seleucid year 167 (145 BC), with Trypho as the real power directing affairs.

Disappointment with Demetrius now put Jonathan in Trypho's camp, and he began to serve the new Antiochus VI Theos Epiphanes Dionysius as faithfully as he had served his father Alexander (10:47). **57.** In turn, when Antiochus gained control of Antioch, he confirmed Jonathan in the high priesthood and in his former ranks of "friend" and "kinsman" (the gifts signify the latter; 10:89). He also reappointed him as governor (*meridarch;* 10:65) over the four districts or nomes. Three of these are probably those in 10:34,38; 11:34—Aphairema (Ephraim), Lydda, and Ramathaim (Arimathea of Matt 27:57). The fourth is uncertain, but possibly is Akrabattene rather than Ekron of 10:89. **59.** At the same time, Simon was made general (*stratēgos*) for the area along the *paralia* or seacoast, from the Ladder of Tyre (N of Ptolemais; Josephus, *J.W.* 2.10.2 §188) to the frontier of Egypt at Rhinocolura or Raphia.

Jonathan traveled throughout the country "beyond the river," i.e., W of the Euphrates, gathering troops for the coming struggle on behalf of Trypho, encountering only temporary resistance at Gaza.

(P) War Between Jonathan and Demetrius (11:63-74). After the battle in which he was defeated by Antiochus's army (11:55), Demetrius established himself at Seleucia-by-the-sea, where he retained control of Cilicia, Mesopotamia, and the coastal cities of Tyre, Sidon, and Gaza (until Jonathan's visit to Gaza in 11:61-62) (see Livy, *Periochae* 52). In the summer of 144, Demetrius sent a force against Jonathan to Kadesh in Galilee with the intention of destroying Jonathan's power. Jonathan went northward to meet this army, leaving Simon to recapture and garrison Beth-zur (11:65-66). Jonathan encamped near the waters of Gennesareth (the plain on the NW shore of the Sea of Galilee, which is also called in the NT the Sea of Tiberias; John 6:1). Then he moved to do battle in the plain of Hazor.

Demetrius's generals, Sarpedon and Palamedes (Diodorus, *Hist.* 33.28) had apparently set another ambush for Jonathan, who had a penchant for falling into them. His soldiers panicked, and Jonathan, seeing this, made the traditional signs of distress (11:71) and prayed. However, Mattathias, the son of Absalom (of 2 Macc 11:17), and Judas, son of Calphi, stood firm. Josephus says that about 50 men also stood their ground (*Ant.* 13.5.7 §161). Once again, as in 10:79-82, deter-

mination turned defeat into victory.

43   (Q) Treaties of Friendship with the Romans and Spartans (12:1-23). After the defeat of the Achaean League by Lucius Mummius in 146, Sparta, which had not associated with the league, attained new prominence in Hellas. Jonathan now (144) decided that it was time to make a new friend for his people and to renew friendship with the Romans. His envoys were received favorably in Rome, where the official policy was still to foment division as a means of conquering the Syrian empire. In Sparta, equal acceptance was given the Jewish ambassadors Numenius and Antipater (Is his father the Jason of 8:17?). **6.** *council:* The technical term (*gerousia*) for what was later to be the sanhedrin. Here it is equivalent to the "elders" of 7:33; 13:36; 14:20,28.

7. The letter of Areus to Onias cited by Jonathan in his letter to the Spartans is accepted by Josephus at face value in *Ant.* 13.5.8 §167, and he cites a variant of it in *Ant.* 12.4.10 §225-27, where he identifies the letter's Onias with Onias III (died 170 BC). Since, however, Onias III would be too late for the Spartan king Areus I (309-265) and also for Areus II, who died as a child of eight in 254, Josephus must be wrong. The proper correlation of sender and recipient exists if they are Areus I and Onias I (high priest about 300). Goldstein prefers Onias II, grandson of Onias I, as recipient of the letter. "Areus" is a correction for "Darius," based on Josephus and 1 Macc 12:20.

Opinion on the letter itself is divided. Dancy (*1 Maccabees* 167-68) thinks it fictitious. The practice of constructing a common ancestry for originally distinct peoples or tribes was not unknown in the OT (Gen 10; 35:22-26). It extended into the Hellenistic world too; there is inscriptional evidence from 126 for a similar diplomatic fiction of a common origin for the Tyrians and the inhabitants of Delphi. Goldstein, however, holds the letter to be genuine (*I Maccabees* 444-62). This is less likely. Whether a nation honored such "common origin" or not depended on its foreign policy at the moment. The Spartans saw no reason to deny Jonathan's allegation (see 14:20).

In vv 9 and 14-15, Jonathan somewhat undiplomatically reminded the Spartans that the Jews made no demands on them, since Jewish reliance was on "Heaven" (God) and the "holy books" (the Scriptures); the latter are not further specified. On the supposed common ancestry of the Jews and Spartans, see S. Schüller, *JSS* 1 (1956) 257-68. For an economic interpretation of Areus's letter (vv 19-23), see W. Wirgin, *PEQ* 101 (1969) 15-20.

44   (R) Military Activities of Jonathan and Simon (12:24-38). Demetrius's generals, anxious to avenge themselves (11:63-74), marched against Jonathan with a larger army. Again Jonathan went to meet them, this time warily (12:26; see 11:68). He found them in the "region of Hamath." This cannot be the region immediately adjacent to ancient Hamath, which is too far N. More likely it is the area at the "entrance to Hamath," the great plain between the Lebanon and Antilebanon mountains. Once Jonathan's adversaries were aware that he could not be taken by surprise—he apparently had superior strength—they slipped away by night and retired beyond the Eleutherus, which was apparently the northernmost limit of Jonathan's military command (11:7,60). Jonathan then continued his march to establish his military power throughout his area. He suppressed the Zabadeans, Arab nomads, who presumably had opposed him.

Simon, meanwhile, established himself along the coast, in his own military district (11:59). He learned of a projected coup in Joppa and placed a trustworthy garrison there.

Jonathan called the Jewish elders together, no doubt in the winter of 144, to plan further defensive structures in Judea. He was particularly concerned with strengthening Jerusalem's defenses, which had been torn down by Antiochus IV (1:31) and Antiochus V (6:62) and were now only partially rebuilt (10:10). He also planned to starve out the men in the citadel (12:36). **37.** Work was begun and completed on Chaphenatha, whose location, though uncertain, is thought to be that of the "Second Quarter" in NW Jerusalem (2 Kgs 22:14). Simon built a headquarters (13:13) and fortress at Adida in the Shephelah, the foothills or low country between the hill country of Judea and the coastal plain.

45   (S) The Capture of Jonathan (12:39–53). Trypho's ambition aroused him to plot against Antiochus VI. For his intended coup to be effective, however, he realized that he must curb the growing power of the Jewish leaders. He decided to neutralize Jewish resistance to his plan by seizing their leader. Jonathan, unsuspecting, met Trypho at Beth-shan and was persuaded to dismiss the army he had brought with him. Trypho lured him to Ptolemais, killed his followers, and made him prisoner there. **49–52.** The forces of Jonathan remaining in "Galilee and the great plain" (of Esdraelon) made a strategic retreat to Judea. **52.** *they mourned:* Because they naturally assumed that Jonathan had been killed along with his men (13:23 shows that it was not yet true). **53.** News of Jonathan's capture signaled an upsurge of anti-Jewish feeling.

46   (V) Simon as Leader of the Jews (13:1–16:24). The last of Mattathias's sons (2:1), Simon did not become the leader of his people until after the deaths of his younger brothers Judas and Jonathan. As leader, however, he was more successful against the deteriorating Seleucid Empire. He fortified Jerusalem and Judea, held off Trypho, allied himself successfully with Demetrius II and for a while with Antiochus VII, built a family tomb at Modin, renewed friendship with Rome and Sparta, and in general showed constructive leadership of the Jews until he, too, was murdered, a victim to the treachery of Ptolemy, son of Abubus.

(A) Simon Becomes Leader of the Jews (13:1–11). With Trypho about to attack Judea, Simon acted quickly to assure leadership for the Jewish defense. He reminded the Jerusalem assembly (presumably the leaders or elders of 12:6; 13:46, etc.) that the house of Mattathias had acted out of zeal for the law and the Temple to the extent that Judas (9:18), Jonathan (see comment on 12:52), Eleazar (6:46), and John (9:36–42) had all perished in the struggle. Only Simon was left to fight for his people, and he was now willing to assume leadership and give himself for their cause. His speech rekindled their enthusiasm, and they elected him their leader.

Simon's first defensive measures were to speed construction of Jerusalem's walls and to strengthen the garrison at Joppa (12:33–34), driving out the native populace there, because he feared that they would hand over the city to Trypho (Josephus, *Ant.* 13.6.4 §202).

(B) Simon Blocks Trypho (13:12–24). On the pretext that Jonathan owed the government money, Trypho bargained with Simon for ransom and hostages. Simon, at Adida (see 12:38), knew that Trypho was lying, but he had to meet Trypho's demand lest he be thought to allow the death of Jonathan through ambition. Trypho, of course, broke his word.

20–24. With Simon's fortress at Adida blocking the direct route to Jerusalem from the coast, Trypho tried the same fishhook maneuver that Lysias had attempted earlier (4:29; 6:31), so as to come up on Jerusalem from the south. Again Simon was in the way, blocking Trypho at Adora (about 5 mi. SW of Hebron), always staying between Trypho and his objectives. **21.** The men in the citadel begged Trypho to relieve the siege which Jonathan began (12:36) and to try another approach by way of the desert. This desert is not identified. Possibly Trypho tried to approach Jerusalem from the Transjordan; v 22 places him in Gilead later, and Abel locates Baskama (13:23) NE of the Sea of Galilee. More recently, however, some authors have identified Baskama with the Sycaminum of Strabo's *Geography* (16.2.27; Tell es-Samak, W of Haifa). In that case, Gilead must be changed to Galilee in 13:22. Trypho then went home the way he came. Frustrated, Trypho executed Jonathan (and his sons? v 16) before reaching Baskama.

(C) Simon Constructs a Family Monument at Modin (13:25–30). Amid great lamentation, Simon brought the remains of Jonathan home to Modin, where the last of the Maccabean brothers now began construction of a family monument. The memorial tomb now built was covered with polished white marble (Josephus, *Ant.* 13.6.6 §211–12) and topped by seven pyramids, one each for Simon's parents, his four brothers, and, presumably, himself. In the base of the monument, supporting the pyramidal superstructure, columns were set in half relief, and at the top of the base a decorative frieze of panoplies and ships alternately encircled the structure. Possibly the ships commemorated the only "naval" victories of the Maccabees, the burning of the harbors at Joppa and Jamnia (2 Macc 12:6,9); if so, the frieze memorialized victories on land and on sea. The tomb, which could be seen by sailors, was extant, at least in part, as late as the 4th cent. AD, according to Eusebius (*Onomasticon*, "Modeim").

47   (D) Simon Joins Demetrius II (13:31–42). 31. At this point in the Maccabean history, there is some confusion over the order of events. 1 Macc 13:31–32 tells of the murder of Antiochus VI by Trypho, who succeeded the young king in 170 (142 BC). This account is followed in 1 Macc 14:1–2 by the Median expedition of Demetrius II in 172 (140) and the subsequent capture of Demetrius by the Parthians in 173 (139).

Diodorus (*Hist.* 33.28), Livy (*Periochae* 55), and Josephus (*Ant.* 13.7.1 §218) say, however, that Trypho killed Antiochus VI (at the age of 10, and so in 173 or 139 BC [Livy, *Periochae* 55]) only after Demetrius had been captured by the Parthians.

The correct sequence is probably the deposition of Antiochus VI (142), the Median expedition of Demetrius (140), and his capture (139), and the murder of Antiochus VI (139), with the subsequent proclamation of Trypho as king, although he had been reigning effectively for four years. Quite possibly, 1 Macc anticipates the young king's murder at the time that it speaks of Trypho's open seizure of power. Josephus and Livy tell the mode of Antiochus's death: Trypho bribed the kings' doctors to operate on their young patient for a bladder stone and to kill him in the process.

32. Trypho now "put on the crown of Asia," i.e., of the Seleucid Empire (1 Macc 8:6). **33.** Meanwhile, Simon took defensive measures in preparation for a change in allegiance. Because Trypho's taxes amounted to pillage of Judea, and because he was moreover the murderer of Jonathan, Simon went over to Demetrius. The first step was to send an embassy to the king.

35. The hard-pressed Demetrius was glad to welcome Simon as an ally and to grant him whatever favors would assure his friendship, although Demetrius may not have intended to keep his word (see 11:53). The king's letter repeats many of the concessions of 1 Macc 11:33–36 (see 10:25–45), but of special importance is the remission of the annual tribute from Jerusalem, an act equivalent to removal of the "yoke of the Gentiles" (v 41). **36.** The title "friend of kings" was probably added by the author of 1 Macc on the basis of 14:39. **37.** The "gold crown and palm branch" were peace offerings, not the crown of annual tribute (v 39), which was now remitted. **38.** All the tax remissions of 145 BC (11:33–36) remained in effect, and Simon was left in peaceful possession of the fortresses he had built (e.g., Adida, 12:38). **39.** The "oversights and offenses," i.e., Jewish support of Trypho, were forgiven, and Jewish troops, of fierce memory (11:41–51), were invited to join Demetrius's soldiery.

41. The remission of the crown tax brought about the removal of "the yoke of the Gentiles" from Israel, and a new era began—that of Simon the great high priest. This new period did not replace the Seleucid era; it simply coincided with the first year of Simon's authority. Simon was also called *stratēgos* (governor) and *hēgoumenos* (leader) of the Jews, titles presumably conferred on him by the king, showing that Jewish independence was not yet complete and that the Jews remained within the framework of the Seleucid Empire. The "170th year" was 142 BC. (Here Josephus ends his paraphrase of 1 Macc as the main source of his *Ant.; see Ant.* 13.6.7 §217.)

48   (E) The Capture of Gazara and the Citadel (13:43–53). Simon evidently decided that while Demetrius and Trypho were occupied with each other's ambitions and could not afford to invade Judea, the time had come for purging unwanted elements from the midst of Israel. Bacchides had fortified various places in and about Judea (9:50–52), but most of these had since come into Jewish hands (10:12–14; 11:65–66). Only Gazara and the citadel at Jerusalem remained to be taken, and this Simon now proposed to do. **43.** Gazara was taken by storm, with the aid of a siege machine. (Despite ms. evidence to the contrary, Gazara and not Gaza is to be read as the city here. See 14:7,34; 15:28,35; Josephus, *Ant.* 13.6.7 §215; *J.W.* 1.2.2 §50). **47–48.** The renegade Jews and pagans who garrisoned Gazara and who had provided refuge for Judas's enemies (4:15; 7:45) were expelled, and men who observed the law replaced them; see R. Reich, *Qad* 15 (1982) 74–76.

Siege (lasting for three years? see 12:36; 13:21) reduced the citadel in Jerusalem to submission. Again Simon purifies his conquest of its "impurities" (Gk *miasmata;* see comment on 4:43), particularly of the idols of the pagan garrison. **51.** The date given corresponds to June 4, 141 BC. **52.** This day was made a festival (for similar decrees, see 4:59; 7:49). The citadel had been a thorn embedded in Israel's flesh since Antiochus IV Epiphanes had it constructed in 167. **53.** Simon's son, John Hyrcanus (134–104), was appointed military commander of the forces resident in Gazara.

49   (F) Demetrius II Is Captured by the Parthians (14:1–3). For the correct order of events, see comment on 13:31–42. The Parthian king Mithridates I (also known by the dynastic name of Arsaces VI [171–138 BC]) had extended his rule over the whole of the Iranian plateau; in July 141, he had defeated Dionysius, Demetrius's satrap, and had taken away Babylonia also. Demetrius began his campaign to dislodge Mithridates from the Tigris-Euphrates valley, and ultimately from the Iranian plateau, in the 172nd year of the Seleucids, 140 BC. **2.** Initially successful, Demetrius was taken prisoner by the Parthians, who violated an armistice to capture him. Arsaces, "the king of Persia and Media"—i.e., the Parthian conqueror of these territories that Demetrius was trying to win back—treated his captive kindly and even married him to the Parthian princess Rhodogune (Appian, *Syriaca* 67). Demetrius was freed in 129. For a time he recovered his throne, but

he was assassinated in 125.

50   (G) The Glory of Simon (14:4–15). The praise of Simon covers his activities in 1 Macc. **4.** *the land was in peace:* Because no Seleucid army invaded it while Simon ruled. **5.** *he took Joppa:* See 12:33; 13:11. Joppa became "a gateway to the islands of the sea," presumably Cyprus, Rhodes, and Crete. **6.** *he enlarged the boundaries of his nation:* By capturing Joppa, Gazara, and Beth-zur; Josephus adds Jamnia (*Ant.* 13.6.7 §215). **7.** *he recovered . . . captives:* In Galilee (see 5:23). For the captured Seleucid strongholds, see 13:43–48; 11:65–66; 13:49–52. **8.** The benefits promised for observance of the law in Lev 26:3–4 are now realized. **9.** See Zech 8:4. **10.** See 1 Macc 12:34; 12:38; 13:33; 14:33. **12.** See Mic 4:4; Zech 3:10. **14.** The "lowly" among the people (see 2 Sam 22:28; Ps 17:28 LXX; Zeph 3:12) are the true keepers of the law, in contrast to the lawbreakers and the wicked. It was for the law that the whole struggle had begun (13:3; 14:29). "He was zealous for the law": This sentence may be a later insertion to explain the "lowly" of 14:14a. For the place of 14:4–15 in the development of levitical messianism, see T. Donaldson, *JETS* 24 (1981) 193–207.

51   (H) Renewal of the Alliances with Rome and Sparta (14:16–24). It was customary in Hellenistic diplomacy to renew treaties of friendship whenever one of the governments party to the treaty changed hands. Upon Simon's accession to the high priesthood and leadership of the Jews (in 142; 13:41), he would have sent an embassy to Rome and Sparta to renew the pledges given by Judas (to Rome in 161; 8:1–32) and Jonathan (to Rome and Sparta in 144; 12:1–23). The present position of the materials in 14:16–24 and 15:15–24 gives the impression that the treaty renewals took place after the capture of Demetrius II in 139 (14:1–3). But 14:40 and 15:22 presuppose that Demetrius had not yet fallen into the power of the Parthians. A more precise dating for the treaty renewal is derived from the Roman reply in 15:16—Lucius Caecilius Metullus Calvus was Consul in 142. Thus the embassy from Simon visited Sparta and Rome in 142 and returned in the same year.

Verses 17–19 refer only to the Romans, because Judas did not make a treaty with Sparta. He is referred to in v 18. The Roman letter is not preserved, and only a summary of its contents is found here. An accompanying letter, to surrounding kings and countries is quoted in 15:15–24. **18.** *they wrote:* In reply to Simon's embassy (14:21–22,24). *bronze tablets:* These are at Rome. See comment on 8:22. **22.** Numenius and Antipater were also the envoys of Jonathan (12:16). Josephus (*Ant.* 14.8.5 §146) mentions this embassy, but he places it much later, in the reign of Hyrcanus II (63–41). He also adds Alexander, son of Dorotheus, to the envoys (see 1 Macc 15:15 "companions"). **24.** *after this:* Although the results of the more important mission, that to Rome, have already been given in 14:17–19, in the order of accomplishment, the trip to Rome must have been subsequent to, and a continuation of, the trip to Sparta. The gold shield Numenius brought with him was "worth" (not "weighed") 1,000 (silver) minas. Its weight was about 100 lb. and its size comparable to decorative shields found at Pompeii.

52   (I) Decree of the Jews Honoring Simon (14:25–49). The decree now recorded on Mt. Zion is similar in form to that found praising public benefactors in many Gk cities of the period. It details the merits of the recipient and the honors decreed to him. **26.** *bronze tablets:* For similar important documents so inscribed, see 8:22; 14:18. The tablets were presumably affixed to pillars of the porticoes surrounding the Temple. **27.** This date, 18 Elul (the sixth month of the vernal year), 172 of the Seleucid era, the third year of Simon's rule, is approximately September 14, 140 BC. *in Asaramel:* The translator of 1 Macc apparently took this as a place-name, reading an original *beth* before the phrase as the Hebr preposition "in." Following him, several authors (among them, Simons and Starcky) reconstruct Asaramel in Hebr as *ḥăṣar ʿam ʾēl,* "the court of the people of God." But the *beth* should rather be read as introducing a description, the *beth essentiae,* and the phrase reconstructed as *śar ʿam ʾēl.* Thus, the transl. would read, ". . . the third year of Simon the high priest as ruler (lit., "prince") of the people of God." The title is then the equivalent of the Gk title "ethnarch."

In the body of the decree, the deeds of Simon are largely those mentioned in 1 Macc 13; even the language is similar. **29.** *Joarib:* See comment on 2:1. Verses 29–30 summarize the bulk of 1 Macc and lead up to Simon's accomplishments, particularly as noted in 1 Macc 13. **31.** *enemies desired to invade:* Trypho (13:1). **32.** *spent much of his own money:* An allusion to 13:15–19? Simon also out-fitted the army at his own expense, a fact that shows him not only as a benefactor of his nation but an independent prince as well. Earlier, Jewish soldiers were paid out of the royal treasury. **33.** *fortified:* See 13:33. *Beth-zur:* See 11:65–66. **34.** *Joppa:* See 13:11. *Gazara on the borders of Azotus:* Ashdod; see comment on 5:68. The borders of the province of Ashdod now reached to within 5 mi. of Gazara (Gezer). **35.** See 13:7–8; 13:42. **36–37.** See 13:49–52.

Not so much because he wanted to but because he had to recognize Simon's achievements, Demetrius made Simon the high priest and his "friend" (13:36). The king also made him *stratēgos* (governor); see 13:41. **41–43.** The honors decreed for Simon by the Jews. The Gk cities began the recital of honors by saying, "it seems good to the people . . ." This formula is paralleled here in v 41, "and the Jews . . . were pleased to make Simon. . . ." Simon (and his family—note the "forever") was estab-lished as Jewish high priest and leader until the coming of a "true prophet." The Jews of this time believed that prophecy had ceased; see 4:46; 9:27. When a prophet worthy of belief should arise, he would decide—i.e., God would tell him—whether it was legitimate for Simon's descendants to hold the high priesthood. Apparently, some contested the right of the sons of Joarib to the office of high priest; see comment on 10:20. For the (implausible) suggestion that the true or "faithful prophet" really refers back to Samuel, see W. Wirgin, *PEQ* 103 (1971) 35–41. **43.** *contracts . . . dated by his name:* See comment on 13:41f. The purple robe and golden buckle (see v 44) are now restricted to Simon; cf. 10:20. **47.** Simon accepted the roles of high priest, *stratēgos,* and ethnarch (see v 28). **49.** Because these offices were to be hereditary, Simon and his sons were entitled to copies of the decree.

53   (J) Antiochus VII Grants Privileges to Simon and Besieges Trypho (15:1–14). Antiochus VII (139–129) was the son of the slain Demetrius I (see 10:50) and the brother of Demetrius II. Sent by his father to a place of safety, Antiochus VII had grown up at Side in Pamphylia. Hence he was popularly known as Sidetes. Officially his surname was Euergetes (Benefactor) Josephus (*Ant.* 13.7.1 §222 and 13.8.2 §244) gives addi-tional surnames: Soter (Savior) and Eusebes (Pious). Hearing of his brother's capture by the Parthians, he accepted the invitation of Demetrius's wife, Cleopatra, to come to Seleucia and marry her (for her earlier mar-riages, see 10:57–58; 11:12), thus establishing a claim to the Seleucid Empire. **1.** *from the islands:* Antiochus was at Rhodes at the

time (Appian, *Syriaca* 68). **3.** *wretches:* Notably Trypho. **4.** Antiochus proposed to land his army, probably at Seleucia, where Cleopatra waited. **5–6.** Antiochus, adding to the previous tax exemptions (see 10:25–45; 13:36–40), granted Simon the right to mint coinage. Actually, Simon minted no coins, and the privilege was soon revoked by Antiochus anyway (15:27). **7.** Jeru-salem and the Temple area were declared free (see 10:31; 10:43), but in fact all of Judea was effectively in Jewish hands and beyond Antiochus's control. See 15:25–36. **10.** The 174th Seleucid year was 139 BC. The soldiers of Trypho first went over to Cleopatra (Josephus, *Ant.* 13.7.1 §221), and she, in turn, put them under Antio-chus's command. Antiochus then defeated Trypho in battle (Josephus, *Ant.* 13.7.2 §223) and pursued him to Dor, S of Mt. Carmel. There Trypho was tightly besieged. On Dor, see E. Stern, *BAIAS* (1982) 17–20.

54   (K) The Return of the Embassy Sent to Rome (15:15–24). See comment on 14:16–24. This letter of Lucius Caecilius Metullus Calvus was addressed to Egypt, to Ptolemy VIII Euergetes II Physcon (145–116), who was asked to hand over any rebels to Simon. **22–24.** A copy of this letter was sent to Simon. The letter was circulated to five kings in all: Ptolemy, Demetrius II (see comment on 14:2), Attalus II of Pergamum (159–138), Ariarathes V of Cappadocia (162–131), and Arsaces of Parthia (i.e., Mithridates I [171–138]). The letter was also sent to various free states, particularly the cities in Greece, the Gk islands, and various places and leagues in Asia Minor.

55   (L) Antiochus Breaks His Alliance with Simon (15:25–36). Antiochus finally succeeded in shutting up Trypho in Dor (15:10–14). In support of this undertaking, Simon sent Antiochus a considerable amount of men and materiel, which Josephus (*Ant.* 13.7.2 §224) says that Antiochus accepted, although 1 Macc notes the contrary. In reply, the king sent Athenobius to demand the return of places seized by Simon, or at least indemnification for them. **30.** *places . . . outside the territory of Judea:* Most likely, the four districts of 11:57.

Simon's reply to Athenobius justifies possession of these territories named on the grounds that they were Israelite lands unjustly taken from his people by their enemies. Despite the practical exigencies of Seleucid politics, the Maccabees, as all true Yahwists, had never conceded ownership of the holy land to a foreign people. Simon was willing, however, to pay an indemnity for Joppa and Gazara. The king became furious when his envoy returned with this message.

56   (M) John Hyrcanus and Judas Defeat Cendebaeus (15:37–16:10). Once Trypho had suc-cessfully escaped to Orthosia (N of Tripolis), Antiochus must pursue. Eventually he captured Trypho at Apamea and had him killed (Josephus, *Ant.* 13.7.2. §224). Mean-while, Antiochus appointed Cendebaeus as *epistratēgos,* "governor-general," placing him over the seacoast (*paralia;* see 11:59) and giving him special powers to deal with the Jews. From Jamnia, the capital of the *paralia,* Cendebaeus built up a forward base of operations at Kedron (about 3 mi. SE of Jamnia), from which he harassed Judea.

When John Hyrcanus, whose fortress Gazara (13:53) lay nearest Cendebaeus's activity, reported to his father what was happening, Simon, now about 60 years old, sent John and Judas, another son, to remove the threat posed by Cendebaeus. **4.** *cavalry:* First mention of Maccabean cavalry. **6.** John's crossing without fear is reminiscent of the action of Judas in 5:40–43. **7.** John's tactic was to place his cavalry so that the infantry pro-tected their flanks; in this way he could offset the

numerical superiority of the Seleucid cavalry. **8-10.** Defeated in battle, Cendebaeus and his forces fell back to Kedron and to strongholds near Azotus that John then destroyed before returning to Judea.
57 (N) The Murder of Simon and His Two Sons (16:11-22). Ptolemy, Simon's son-in-law was now driven by ambition to plot against his in-laws. As governor of the fertile region just N of the Dead Sea, he invited Simon and his sons Judas and Mattathias to a banquet at Dok, and there he slew Simon and his sons. **14.** The 177th Seleucid year was 134 BC; the month Shebat roughly corresponded to February in that year, with the year beginning in the spring. **15.** *Dok:* A hill fortress 5 mi. NW of Jericho; see H. Burgmann, *Judaica* 36 (1980) 152-74.

Ptolemy wrote to Antiochus VII and to the Jewish troop commanders (*chiliarchs*) to seek support. Mean-

while he sent other men to Gazara to kill John, who, warned in advance, turned the tables on his would-be assassins and killed them. Josephus notes that John's brothers were not killed with their father but were held captive in Dok, which John besieged. When a sabbatical year caused John to end the siege, Ptolemy killed Judas and Mattathias and their mother, and fled (*Ant.* 13.7.4 §228-9; 13.8.1 §230-35).

(O) Conclusion to 1 Macc (16:23-24). With the escape of John from Ptolemy's assassins, 1 Macc ends the story of the Hasmoneans. The formula of 16:23-24 is similar in style to the summations of 1-2 Kgs (1 Kgs 14:19,29; etc.). The walls alluded to in v 23 are presumably those built by John after the death of Antiochus VII, who had destroyed the walls of Jerusalem (Josephus, *Ant.* 13.8.3 §247).

COMMENTARY ON 2 MACCABEES

Since much of 2 Macc traverses the same ground as 1 Macc, it should not be necessary to repeat much of the commentary on events treated in both books. The reader will find amplification of remarks pertinent to 2 Macc in the earlier part of this commentary.
58 (I) Letters to the Jews of Egypt (1:1-2:18). For the authenticity and date of these letters, → 5 above.
(A) The First Letter (1:1-10a). This letter, urging the observance of the "feast of Tabernacles in the [ninth] month of Kisleu," i.e., Hanukkah, was written in the Seleucid year 188 (124 BC). It refers to another letter (vv 7-8), which was probably written to inform the Jews in Egypt of the loss of Jonathan (1 Macc 12:48; 13:23). This earlier letter, dated to 169 (143 BC), contained an account of the apostasy of Jason and its aftermath up to the dedication of the Temple (174-164) and presumably urged the Jews in Egypt to observe this feast which commemorated the cause for which Judas and Jonathan had struggled. The present letter is a continued reminder to observe the feast. Its incorporation and date (124 BC) probably mark the completion of the epitomist's work.
1. *greetings:* The customary Hellenistic salutation (put in by the translator of the letter?). *peace:* The Palestinian, Hebr greeting; the wish here expressed is for a "good," an enduring peace. **2.** *may he remember his covenant:* See Lev 26:40-46; God will not forsake his faithful in strange lands. **4.** *may he open your heart to his law:* To keep you from the false worship of Onias IV's temple at Leontopolis? **6.** *we are praying here:* Worship at Jerusalem and in the Temple there was considered particularly efficacious. **7.** *the critical distress:* The loss of Jonathan and its sequel. *Jason:* See 2 Macc 4:7-5:10. *holy land:* Zech 2:16; Wis 12:3. **8.** *we offered:* See 1 Macc 4:36-51.
(B) The Second Letter (1:10b-2:18). This letter, written in 164 (→ 5 above), asks the Jews of Egypt to join with their Judean brethren in celebrating the new feast of the Temple's purification (1 Macc 4:36-59; 2 Macc 10:1-8). It is to be celebrated in the manner of the feast of Tabernacles (10:6), which coincided with Solomon's dedication of his Temple (1 Kgs 8:2,65) and Joshua and Zerubbabel's establishment of their new altar (Ezra 3:3-4). The added reference in this new feast to "fire" — since commemorated in the special lighting of Hanukkah — recalls 2 Chr 7:1 and is explained in the letter by appeal to the memoirs of Nehemiah (1:19-2:13). For a description of the feasts of Tabernacles and Hanukkah and of the relationship between them, see de

Vaux, *AI* 495-502, 510-14.
10. *senate:* The *gerousia* or elders of 1 Macc 12:6,35. *Aristobulus:* A Jewish "philosopher" of Alexandria, who "taught" Ptolemy VI Philometor (180-145) by dedicating a book to him which purported to show that the Greeks derived their wisdom and philosophy from the Law and the Prophets (Clement of Alexandria, *Stromateis* 1.22). **11.** The "king" is Antiochus IV Epiphanes (175-164). **12.** *drove out:* Eventually, see 10:1. **13-17.** See comment on 1 Macc 6:1-17. **14.** *intending to marry her:* Antiochus hoped by such "marriages" to appropriate temple treasuries and thus to pay the cost of his wars and indemnities (9:2; 1 Macc 6:1-4). **16.** *secret door:* Similarly Dan 14:12,21. *leader:* The Gk text leaves the impression that (only) Antiochus was trapped and slain in this way. Actually, he was driven off and died later (9:2-3,28-29; 1 Macc 6:4-16). The information available to the author of this letter may have confused the death of Antiochus IV with that of his father, Antiochus III, who was killed while attempting to rob the temple of Bel in Elam.
59 1:19-2:13 derives from the (lost) memoirs of Nehemiah, which included the "records" mentioned in 2:1,4. For the day of the feast to be held, 25th Kisleu, see 1 Macc 1:59; 2 Macc 6:7; 10:5. The "fire" (v 18) probably alludes to the fire from heaven of 2 Macc 2:9-10. Nehemiah (v 18) did not rebuild the Temple or its altar; Ezra 3:2; 6:14. Ezra 2:2, however, associates him with the first returnees from exile. Goldstein (*II Maccabees* 174) suggests Nehemiah was Zerubbabel's Hebr name. **19.** *Persia:* Then, Babylonia. The pious priests were given the sacred fire by Jeremiah, according to 2:1. **20.** *thick liquid:* A pool of petroleum; see 1:34. This liquid's "fire" was thought to have fallen from heaven. Thus, the flame that consumed Nehemiah's sacrifices (1:22-23) was successor to that of Moses (Lev 9:24) and Solomon (2 Chr 7:1), though its miraculous element is muted by the appeal to natural elements, such as heat and the sun. See also Judg 6:21; 1 Kgs 18:38; 1 Chr 21:26. **23.** *Jonathan:* Unknown. Goldstein identifies him with Mattaniah of Neh 11:17 (*II Maccabees* 178). **24-29.** This prayer stresses Israel's monotheism and its special place as God's chosen people. **29.** *plant:* See Exod 15:17; Deut 30:5. **31-32.** The fire-containing properties of the liquid are now seen clearly in the fact that it flares up when poured out upon presumably heated stones. **34.** The Persians as Zoroastrians considered fire holy. **35.** The verse should be understood to say that the king gave the newly founded temple many gifts. **36.** The Persian word

for this petroleum substance is *neft,* and the common name *naphtha* reflects this word. Nehemiah and his associates, playing upon the Hebr root *thr,* "to purify," called the substance *nephthar.*

60   **2:1–3.** When Jeremiah entrusted the sacred fire to the priests (1:19), he also exhorted them to keep the law and to avoid idolatry (see Bar 6:3).

4–12. Jeremiah's hiding of the Ark of the Covenant on Mt. Nebo is taken up again by the 1st-cent. apocryphal book *Lives of the Prophets.* Here he also hides the tabernacle and the altar of incense. The whole story is improbable in the light of Jer 3:16. **4.** *mountain:* Nebo (Deut 32:49). **8.** God, says Jeremiah, will manifest himself so as to disclose the hiding place of the Ark. The manifestation will be like that which took place at the exodus (Exod 16:10; 40:35) and at the dedication of the Temple (1 Kgs 8:10–11). The mention of the Temple's dedication recalls the fire from heaven upon the sacrifices of Moses (Lev 9:24) and Solomon (2 Chr 7:1), the latter at the Temple's dedication. Verse 11 is obscure; see Lev 10:16–20. **12.** See 1 Kgs 8:65–66; 2 Chr 7:9.

13–15. The memoirs of Nehemiah also record his gathering of books considered important to the community. **13.** *kings:* The MT's Sam-Kgs. *David:* The Pss. "The letters of kings concerning votive offerings" are the documents of Persian kings; their inclusion shows that Nehemiah's collection is not a canon of inspired books. Judas similarly made a collection of "scattered" books, which were then available to the Egyptian Jews. For long-distance library lending at this time, see M. Kellermann, *ZDPV* 98 (1982) 104–9.

The remaining vv 16–18 urge the Egyptian community to participate in the new feast of the Temple's purification. **17.** An allusion to Exod 19:3–6 (see 1 Pet 2:9). **18.** See Deut 30:1–5.

61   **(II) The Epitomist's Preface (2:19–32).** Jason of Cyrene's five-volume work will be abbreviated to one, says the epitomist, but Jason must take responsibility for the accuracy of details in the story (2:28–31). The epitomist will concern himself with the arduous task of abbreviating so as to produce a result that is readable, memorable, pleasurable, and profitable (2:25). **21.** The miraculous element is characteristic of the genre of Jason's work—pathetic or rhetorical history. *Judaism:* The earliest known occurrence of this term (see also 8:1; 14:38; Gal 1:14) to describe the way of life in contrast to Hellenism (4:13). The epithet "barbarian" is not only an allusion to savagery (4:25; 5:22) but also a studied insult to the civilized status that Seleucid Hellenism arrogated to itself. **23.** Jason of Cyrene is otherwise unknown. Culturally, Cyrene was one with Egypt, and the Jews there were religiously dependent on their Alexandrian brethren. As Jason's book proved, the influence was mutual.

62   **(III) The Decline of the High Priesthood (3:1–4:50).** The author now traces the rapid decline of the office of high priest. Perfect observance of the law marked the term of Onias III (3:1); a corrosive hellenization, that of the usurper Jason (4:13); theft and murder, that of Menelaus (4:25,32–34).

(A) The Episode of Heliodorus (3:1–40). After the treaty of Apamea (188), the Seleucid monarchs were badly in need of money for indemnities. When Simon alleged that the Temple treasury was full of money (with the implication of irregularities?), Seleucus was delighted and immediately moved to confiscate the treasure. God, however, protected the Temple's deposits from the king's agent, Heliodorus. (In 4 Macc 4:1–14, the episode happens to Apollonius, not to Heliodorus.) **1.** *Onias:* Onias III, son of Simon II, whom Sir 50:1–21 praises, and grandson of another Onias

(Josephus, *Ant.* 12.4.10 §225), whose Gk name appears (from the Hebr text of Sir) to be a contraction based on the Hebr *Yohanan,* "God is gracious." The family of Onias were descendants, through Jaddua (Ezra 2:36; 1 Chr 24:7; Josephus, *Ant.* 11.8.7 §347), of Joshua, the high priest of the postexilic community (Neh 12:10–11). **2.** *place:* Throughout 2 Macc, the Temple is often referred to in this way. **3.** *Seleucus:* Seleucus IV Philopator (187–175). *king of Asia:* See comment on 1 Macc 8:6. **4.** Simon is of the priestly class of Bilgah (1 Chr 24:14), as the readings of the Lat codices L, B, and P reflect. The Gk text has him descend from "Benjamin." Simon's office as administrator (*prostatēs*) of the Temple led him into conflict with Onias, who presumably overruled him in some matter relating to administration of the city market. Simon's next step was to go over the high priest's head to the governor of Coele-Syria and Phoenicia with a story calculated to bring about Onias's embarrassment, if not his dismissal on charges of corruption. **5.** *Apollonius of Tarsus:* The son of Menestheus (4:4,21); he is identified here as being "of Tarsus" (the Cilician city) and not as "son of Tharseus," as the Gk text might otherwise be read. Apollonius later left office when Antiochus Epiphanes became king, going to Miletus (Polybius, *Histories* 31.13). For Coele-Syria and Phoenicia, see comment on 1 Macc 3:38. **7.** *Heliodorus:* The son of Aeschylus and a native of Antioch. Later, he killed Seleucus in an unsuccessful attempt to seize the throne (Appian, *Syriaca* 45). His present expedition is mentioned in Dan 11:20. **11.** Hyrcanus is really the grandson of Tobias, his father being Joseph. The Tobiad family was sympathetic to Ptolemaic interests; and later, when Hyrcanus committed suicide for fear of Epiphanes, his property was confiscated by the Seleucid crown. (Josephus, *Ant.* 12.4.11 §236). **12.** Onias pleaded a form of "sanctuary" for the funds but to no avail. The amount of the deposits seems exaggerated—their value today would be in the millions. **15.** *law of deposits:* See Exod 22:6–14.

22–30. God answered the populace's prayers. Some authors (e.g., Tedesche and Zeitlin, *Second Maccabees* 128) suggest that Heliodorus made some arrangement with Onias, since Heliodorus was shortly to assassinate the king. But 4:1 leaves the impression that some physical evil had befallen Heliodorus. The dressed-up story supplied by Jason of Cyrene (2:21), for whom the Temple's deposits were saved by a miraculous intervention, is typical of the literary form in which Jason writes. In the epiphany, Heliodorus is incapacitated (see a similar story in 3 Macc 2:21–23). **31–34.** Not wishing to be charged with the murder of Heliodorus, the Jews prayed for his recovery, and once again the divine element is introduced. Verse 33b recalls Job 42:7–8. **35–40.** Heliodorus acknowledged the supreme might of Israel's God and the protection he afforded his sanctuary.

63   **(B) Simon's Plot against Onias (4:1–6).** Frustrated, Simon continued to plot the removal of Onias. **1.** Onias's fear in 3:32 was justified. **2.** *laws:* Of the Seleucid kingdom, not the Torah (see B. Renaud, *RB* 68 [1961] 39–67, esp. 64). **5–6.** Onias reached the king too late; Heliodorus had already assassinated Seleucus. After some difficulty, Antiochus IV Epiphanes, the dead king's brother, succeeded him (Appian, *Syriaca* 45).

64   **(C) Jason the High Priest Introduces Hellenism (4:7–20).** For the important changes now taking place in Judaism, see comment on 1 Macc 1:11–15. **8.** Jason promised an increased tribute. The usual amount seems to have been 300 talents (1 Macc 11:28). **11.** *Eupolemus:* See comment on 1 Macc 8:17. *law:* Here the law of Moses. **12.** *the Greek hat:* The *petasos* was a wide-brimmed hat worn by Hermes, the god of

gymnastic skill. To "wear the *petasos*" was to take part in gymnastic exercises. **13.** *no high priest:* Josephus (*Ant.* 12.5.1 §237) says that Antiochus gave Jason the high priesthood when Onias III died, because the latter's son, Onias IV, was still an infant. But 2 Macc says Jason was no high priest, because he obtained the office by bribery. **14.** The priests neglected their own ministry to take part in the "liturgy" (*chorēgia* – the author is being sarcastic) of the wrestling school when the gong summoned them. **18.** Games were held at Tyre as early as Alexander's time. **19–20.** *Antiocheans of Jerusalem:* For the importance of this designation, see comment on 1 Macc 1:11–15. *Heracles:* The Syrian god Melkart was, in Hellenistic fashion, assimilated to Heracles (the Roman Hercules). Even the envoys saw the impropriety of Jewish money going for pagan sacrifices, and so they applied it to a less compromising purpose, the construction of ships.
65   (D) Antiochus Is Received by Jason in Jerusalem (4:21-22). Earlier, Epiphanes had recalled Apollonius from Miletus (see comment on 3:5) and had sent him to Rome (Livy, *Periochae* 42.6). Now, in 172, he sent him to Egypt to attend the coronation of Ptolemy VI Philometor (180–145). Ptolemy's mother, Cleopatra I (the sister of Antiochus Epiphanes), had governed Egypt for her son in his minority, until her death in 176. Subsequently, the king's ministers Eulaeus and Lenaeus made plans to regain Coele-Syria for Egypt (Diodorus, *Hist* 30.16). Antiochus wisely sent an experienced diplomat to assess Egyptian intentions, and Apollonius learned that the newly enthroned king, who had now come of age, was hostile to his Seleucid uncle. Antiochus then prepared for the impending invasion by stationing troops in Joppa and other Phoenician ports. At this time, too, Antiochus visited Jerusalem, where Jason welcomed him warmly with torches and acclamations.
66   (E) Menelaus as High Priest (4:23-50). The low state to which the high priesthood had sunk is evident in Menelaus's theft of the Temple vessels to advance his own career. More successful than his brother Simon, he managed to have Onias murdered. **23.** *three years:* These are counted from the beginning of Jason's pontificate in 174, so the year was 171. **24-26.** By the usual route of bribery (the sum seems excessive; 4:27 bears this out), to which he added flattery, Menelaus won the office of high priest for himself. On his ancestry, see comment on 3:4. Ousted, Jason fled to Ammon, probably to the southern part of Transjordan, held by the Nabataeans (5:8). **27-38.** Menelaus and Sostratus, the latter the king's agent and commander of the Cypriot mercenaries at Jerusalem, were summoned to Antioch to explain their delay in forwarding the king's revenue. Coincidentally, Antiochus was called away to suppress a revolt by the Cilician cities Tarsus and Mallus (the latter on the Pyramos River near the Gulf of Issos), whose citizens objected to transfer of their revenue to the king's concubine Antiochis. Menelaus then bribed Andronicus, the king's deputy in the matter, using vessels stolen from the Temple to obtain a favorable verdict. Onias denounced Menelaus for these thefts, first fleeing to sanctuary in the temple of Apollo at Daphne, about 5 mi. from Antioch. Andronicus's murder of Onias, at Menelaus's urging, shocked even the Greeks, for it violated a solemn pledge and showed contempt for the right of sanctuary. Antiochus promptly executed Andronicus in reprisal, first degrading him. **39-42.** Apparently Lysimachus, Menelaus' brother and deputy (v 29), had also been his agent in the theft of the Temple's vessels. When the crowds at Jerusalem grew riotous over this, Lysimachus sent a force against them which was beaten back. **42.** *the Temple robber:* Lysimachus. **43-50.** The Jewish elders (*gerousia;* see

1 Macc 12:6,35) brought charges against Menelaus, but when all seemed lost, bribery again won Menelaus success. Later, as *stratēgos* of Coele-Syria and Phoenicia, Ptolemy opposed the Maccabean revolt (8:8; 1 Macc 3:38). The Scythians lived N of the Black Sea, in what is now the Soviet Union; they were proverbially cruel.
67   (IV) Antiochus Epiphanes and the Imposition of Hellenism (5:1-7:42). The author now turns to the troubles unleashed by the "Greeks" whom the Jews emulated (4:16). Antiochus despoiled the Temple, ravaged the city, and proscribed Judaism, with dire results for those who remained faithful to the law.
(A) Antiochus Ravages Jerusalem (5:1-14). Antiochus's second campaign in Egypt, during which he was crowned king of Egypt at Memphis but then was forced to retire by the Romans, led to the events which culminated in his slaughter of Jerusalem's citizenry. Looking back, Jason of Cyrene described an ominous foreboding of these events by painting the scene of celestial cavalry in combat over Jerusalem. Josephus describes a similar omen presaging the Temple's destruction in AD 70 (*J.W.* 6.5.3 §296-299). **5-7.** Jason, hearing the news of Antiochus's check by the Romans in Egypt, was led to believe that the king was dead. With the support of Jerusalem's populace, he unsuccessfully attempted to capture Jerusalem and drive out Menelaus, who was backed by the pro-Seleucid Tobiad faction (Josephus, *Ant.* 12.5.1 §239). **8-10.** Driven from his place of refuge with Aretas (Harith I, king of the Nabataeans), Jason set out to seek refuge, first in Egypt, then with the Lacedaemonians (Spartans; see comment on 1 Macc 12:1-23). He died in exile. **11-14.** Antiochus, frustrated by events in Egypt, interpreted Jason's attack as a Jewish revolt and ruthlessly vented his anger upon his Jewish subjects. In keeping with the rhetorical nature of Jason's account, the number of those killed or sold is exaggerated.
(B) Antiochus Despoils the Temple (5:15-23a). See comment on 1 Macc 1:20-24a. Theological reasons now explain the Temple's spoliation. Had not the people sinned by following Gk ways, Antiochus would have been beaten back as Heliodorus earlier (3:1-40). Puffed up by his own pretensions, which reached even to divinity, so that he thought himself in control of nature (v 21), Antiochus cannot perceive that it is the power of a God temporarily angry, and not his own, which has allowed the sacrilege. **16.** *other kings:* Seleucus IV (3:3), for example. **21.** *1,800 talents:* Another inflated number. **22.** *administrators: Epistatai;* see 1 Macc 1:51. Philip appears again in 6:11; 8:8. This is not the Philip of 9:29 and 1 Macc 6:14,55. **23.** Andronicus is not the murderer of 4:31,34,38.
68   (C) Apollonius Attacks Jerusalem (5:23b-26). See comment on 1 Macc 1:29-35. Josephus (*Ant.* 23.5.5. §261) notes that Apollonius was *meridarchēs* (governor) of Samaria. Later, Judas defeated and killed him (1 Macc 3:10-12).
69   (D) Judas Maccabeus in the Desert (5:27). Mention of Apollonius leads the epitomist to introduce Judas, Apollonius's nemesis, thus skipping the story of Mattathias in his sources (see 1 Macc 2). But because this does not suffice to explain his own narrative, the epitomist immediately breaks off to introduce Antiochus's forced hellenization of Judea, adding stories which elaborate 1 Macc 1:62-63. This done, he returns to Judas in 8:1ff.
70   (E) Antiochus Imposes Hellenism (6:1-11). See comment on 1 Macc 1:41-64. To unify his kingdom (1 Macc 1:41), the king commanded the adoption of Hellenism and the establishment at Jerusalem's Temple of the syncretistic cult of Zeus Olympios. What had

been voluntary (4:7–20) now became obligatory. The year was 167 BC.

1. *Geron:* See comment on 1 Macc 1:51. **2.** *Olympian Zeus:* See comment on 1 Macc 1:54. *Gerizim:* The rival Samaritan temple was built on Mt. Gerizim. *Zeus the Hospitable: Dios Xenios,* the protector of strangers. Josephus *Ant.* 12.5.5 §261) says that the Samaritans petitioned Antiochus to name their Temple *Dios Hellenios,* dissociating themselves from the Jews, whom they knew to be under the king's wrath. **5–9.** While illicit sacrifices (6:18,21; Lev 11:7; 1 Macc 1:47) were offered, a man could not follow Jewish religious law. Instead, thanks to the citizens of Ptolemais, Jews throughout Coele-Syria and Phoenicia were forced to partake of swine on the king's birthday (1 Macc 1:58) and to join in the popular cult of Dionysius, god of wine and the grape harvest (a Hellenistic feast of Booths!). See J. G. Bunge, *JSJ* 10 (1979) 155–65. **10.** See 1 Macc 1:60–61. **11.** See comment on 1 Macc 2:29–41.

71 (F) The Epitomist's Evaluation (6:12–17). See comment on 5:15–20. The epitomist reminds his readers that the Jewish affliction is medicinal (7:33). God punishes his people now lest they become more wayward through lack of discipline and suffer the effects of a greater divine wrath in a later visitation. This is the paternal discipline of Prov 13:24; 20:30; 23:13–14; Tob 13:5. With regard to the Gentiles, however, he waits until the measure of their sins is full and then punishes them; see Dan 8:23; 9:24. A complementary biblical view holds that God withholds punishment from men in view of their salvation. He allows them time for a change of heart and so delays the day of reckoning (Wis 11:23; 12:20; Rom 2:4–5). This is also why he delays the Parousia (2 Pet 3:9).

72 (G) The Martyrdom of Eleazar (6:18–31). The story of Eleazar is elaborated in 4 Macc 5–7 (see also 3 Macc 6:1ff.; Heb 11:35b). By refusing the unclean food (Lev 11:7–8), Eleazar spurned the unlawful sacrifice and remained faithful to the law, becoming a witness (*martyr*) to its importance and to its claims upon Jewish obedience. His refusal of the deception urged by his pagan(ized?) friends shows a conscience alert to the possibility of scandal. **23.** *Hadēs:* The abode of the dead. **26.** Eleazar seems aware of punishment after death for the sinner, a development over earlier OT ideas (see also Dan 12:2; Hen 22:10–11). **29.** *madness:* See Wis 5:3.

73 (H) The Martyrdom of the Mother and Her Seven Sons (7:1–42). Eleazar's example to the young (6:28) was not wasted. The author now shows that women and children are also willing to die for the law. In this narrative, the author's artifice is more apparent. (For a fuller development of the story, see 4 Macc 8–18.)

There is an evident progression in the words the brothers address to the king before dying: (1) The just die rather than sin (7:2); God will vindicate them (7:6; Deut 32; 36). (2) God will raise them up (7:9). (3) They will rise with bodies fully restored (7:11). (4) But for the wicked, there will be no resurrection to life (7:14). (5) Instead, God will punish them (7:17). (6) The just suffer because of their sins, as will the wicked (7:18–19). (7) The death of the saints has impetratory and even expiatory value (7:37–38). Thus the author states the theology of martyrdom and the resurrection of the just. See Dan 12:2.

1. *the king:* Since the story is contrived, the chief persecutor himself is addressed. **6.** *Moses . . . canticle:* Deut 32:36. **8.** *language of his fathers:* Hebrew; see vv 21,27; 12:37; 15:29. **17.** *descendants:* See 2 Macc 9 (Epiphanes); 2 Macc 14:2; 1 Macc 7:2–4 (Eupator); 1 Macc 11:17 (Alexander Balas); 1 Macc 13:31 (Antio-

chus VI). **22–23.** See Ps 139:13–16; Wis 7:1–2; Qoh 11:5. **24.** Antiochus suspected insult, because the mother spoke in Hebrew; 7:21,27. **28.** The first biblical mention of creation *ex nihilo.* See also Heb 11:3. **29.** *I may get you back:* He will be restored to life with his family in the resurrection of the just, if he perseveres. **33.** See 5:17. **37.** See 9:12. **38.** See vicarious suffering in Isa 52:13–53:12. See also U. Kellermann, *BN* 13 (1980) 63–83.

74 (V) The Triumph of Judaism under Judas Maccabeus (8:1–10:9). In this section, the epitomist follows Jewish resistance to Antiochus's edicts up to the point where the wicked persecutor dies and the victorious Judas purifies the Temple and rededicates it.

(A) Judas Organizes Resistance to the Persecution (8:1–7). See comment on 1 Macc 2:42–48. The epitomist now continues the narrative he had interrupted in 5:27. **2–3.** The guerrilla band prayed, then fought. Similar descriptions of the woes faced are in 1 Macc 1:24–28,36–40; 2:7–12; 3:45,50–53. Destruction either visited or threatened the city in 1 Macc 1:31 (see 2 Macc 5:23b–26); 1 Macc 3:35; 2 Macc 9:4,14. (For the historical order of events at this point, → 11).

(B) Judas Defeats Nicanor and Gorgias (8:8–29,34–36). See comment on 1 Macc 3:38–4:27. **8.** *Philip:* See comment on 5:22. *Ptolemy:* See 4:45 and comment on 1 Macc 3:38. **9.** Nicanor looms larger as the adversary in 2 Macc than in 1 Macc. **14.** *sold their property:* Lest it fall to Nicanor anyway. These men apparently joined Judas. Note the continual emphasis on prayer. **18.** See Ps 20:7–8. **19.** *Sennacherib:* See 2 Kgs 19:35. **20.** *the battle with the Galatians:* This incident of Jewish mercenaries in support of Macedonian troops is otherwise unknown. J. Goldstein (*II Maccabees* 332–33) plausibly suggests that the Galatians were mercenaries serving Antiochus Hierax in his war against Seleucus II in the late 3d cent. BC. **23.** *Eleazar:* Abel and Starcky suggest Esdris, as in 12:36; see also 1 Macc 5:18,56, where he is called Azariah (which basically has the same meaning, "God— 'El or Yāhû—has helped"). This Eleazar is not Judas's brother (1 Macc 2:5; 6:43). **28.** For division of spoils, see Num 31:25–47; 1 Sam 20:21–25. **36.** Here the author gives the theological reason for victory: God defends those who keep his law and makes them invincible.

(C) Judas's Other Victories (8:30–33). See comment on 1 Macc 5:6–8,9–13,24–25. The parts of this fragmentary passage are difficult to locate. See 9:3; 10:24–38; 12:10–31. **30.** *Bacchides:* See comment on 1 Macc 7:1–25. **33.** *Callisthenes:* Otherwise unknown. For the gate-burning, see 1 Macc 1:31. (The events of 2 Macc 11 should be placed here; → 11 above.)

75 (D) The Death of the Persecutor (9:1–29; 10:9). See comment on 1 Macc 6:1–17. Antiochus had agreed to peace terms after the defeat of Lysias at Bethzur (1 Macc 4:28–35; 2 Macc 11 [except vv 22–26] but still was not disposed kindly toward the Jews. Frustrated in his Temple-robbing expedition, he now resolved to wreak vengeance on the Jews. Perhaps the immediate cause of the death now described was injury resulting from the fall mentioned in 9:7. What caused this fall, however, is not clear (heart trouble? v 5). **8.** See 5:21; 9:12. The false god, Epiphanes "(Zeus) manifest," falls by the manifest power of the true God.

The vivid account in 9:9–12 of the king's last moments seems more theological than descriptive of events. It echoes Isa 66:24; 14:11; Sir 7:17; 19:3; Jdt 16:17. For similar description in the deaths of God's enemies, see Josephus, *Ant.* 17.6.5 §168–69 (on Herod the Great); Acts 12:12 (on Herod Agrippa).

Antiochus's vow (vv 13–18) is equally unlikely, or at least it is the measure of a desperate man and not a true change of heart (see, particularly, v 17). See the fall and conversion of Nebuchadnezzar in Dan 4. 2 Macc does not allow God to hear Epiphanes' prayer. See comment on 6:12–17. See D. Mendels, *IEJ* 31 (1981) 53–56.

The letter in 9:19–27, if addressed to the Antiocheans and to the hellenized Jews, is credible. Placed here, it seems to have other recipients, the Jews faithful to the law, to whom the converted king commends his son. But remembrance of the king's beneficence (v 26) would not likely endear his son to these subjects. **23.** Antiochus III had appointed Seleucus IV his successor. **29.** *Philip:* See comment on 1 Macc 6:14.

76   (E) Judas Purifies the Temple (10:1–8). See comment on 1 Macc 4:36–61. Unable to celebrate the feast of Booths earlier (6:6; 5:27), Judas and his men now celebrate the purification of the Temple in the manner of the feast of Booths (10:6). **3.** *flint:* Starting a new fire; see 1:19–2:1. **4.** Again, the note of prayer and penitence.

77   (VI) The Subsequent Struggles of Judas (10:10–15:39). The remaining chapters of 2 Macc detail Judas's various struggles against neighboring peoples and lead up to his victory over Nicanor and the subsequent establishment of a feast commemorating it.

(A) The Suicide of Ptolemy Makron (10:10–13). Again the author introduces a fragment somewhat cryptically. The epitomist notes the accession of Antiochus V Eupator (164–161) and his appointment of Lysias as chief governor, over Coele-Syria and Phoenicia (previously, Lysias was Epiphanes' regent in the west; 1 Macc 3:32–33). Then, by contrast to the death of Epiphanes, the author narrates the death of an official friendly to the Jews. Ptolemy Makron (the nickname means "large-[headed]") governed Cyprus for the Egyptian king Ptolemy VI Philomotor (180–145). When Epiphanes' fleet approached Cyprus for an invasion, he switched to the Seleucids rather than fight. Branded as a traitor even by his new allies, who despised his moderate Jewish policies, he was accused before the king (for another change of allegiance, to Jewish interests?) and, unable to bear another disgrace, killed himself.

78   (B) Judas Fights in Idumea (10:14–23). See comment on 1 Macc 5:3–5. Gorgias was governor (*stratēgos*) of Idumea (12:32) and the "land of the Philistines," the maritime zone (1 Macc 5:68; see 1 Macc 11:59). **16.** Prayer again preceded battle; the author never loses sight of the source of victory. **17.** *20,000:* This number, like the 9,000 of v 18 and the 70,000 of v 20, seems to be inflated to make the victories all the more striking. **19.** Judas left Simon his brother and Joseph (1 Macc 5:18) to besiege the towers.

79   (C) Judas Defeats Timothy (10:24–38). This passage, for which there is no parallel in 1 Macc, belongs chronologically sometime after 1 Macc 5:9–13, 24–54; 2 Macc 12:10–31.

After earlier defeats (8:30ff.), Timothy mounted a more powerful expedition against the Jews. Again penitential prayer (10:25–26) preceded Judas's army into battle (10:27–28), and again divine aid—graphically represented by Judas's angelic bodyguard—assured a Jewish victory (10:29–30). Timothy was defeated, pursued, besieged, and killed (10:32–37). The victors gave God thanks (10:38). **26.** See Exod 23:22. **32.** *Gazara:* Because it was Simon who took Gazara (1 Macc 13:43) and not Judas, it is better to correct the text to read Jazer, as in 1 Macc 5:8.

80   (D) Victory over Lysias at Beth-zur (11:1–15; 12:1). See comment on 1 Macc 4:28–35. This narrative chronologically precedes the death of Antiochus Epiphanes (→ 11 above). Lysias (see comment on 1 Macc 3:32ff.) was angry over the defeat of Nicanor

and Gorgias and set out to accomplish the king's directives (1 Macc 3:34–36). But he was beaten at Beth-zur. **1.** *king's guardian:* Of Eupator, not Epiphanes (1 Macc 3:33; 2 Macc 10:10). **3.** *high priesthood for sale:* See 4:7–8,24. This was to be the high priesthood of a hellenized community, once the troublesome Jews were eliminated (1 Macc 3:34–36). **5.** *five leagues:* Beth-zur was about 20 mi. S of Jerusalem. **6–12.** Again there is the familiar pattern of penitential prayer, angelic assistance, victory, and flight of the opponent. **6.** *good angel:* Cf. 15:23; Tob 5:21. **11.** For different numbers, see 1 Macc 4:34. **13–15.** The sequel to the battle was an agreed-upon peace, in which the Jews were given their religious liberty. See the letters following. 1 Macc 4:35 anticipates the later invasion under Eupator (1 Macc 6:28–63).

81   (E) The Letters (11:16–38). The three letters in vv 16–21,27–33,34–38 belong to the peace negotiations following Lysias's campaign described above. The letter in vv 22–26 belongs to Eupator's reign.

16–21. Lysias addresses the people, not their leader Judas. The letter alludes to the agreements of v 15, although Lysias still notes some reservations (11:18). **17.** *John:* May be Mattathias's son (1 Macc 2:2). Absalom's son is also active in the struggle; see 1 Macc 11:70; 13:11. **21.** The 24th Dioscorinthius (the month is equivalent to the month Xanthicus; see vv 30,33,38) of the 148th Seleucid year would occur in March 164.

27–33. The letter of Antiochus Epiphanes to the *gerousia,* i.e., elders, of the Jews, offers an amnesty and religious freedom. **29.** *Menelaus:* Was probably sent by Lysias to the king in Persia. Antiochus sent him back with the idea of restoring everything to the status quo preceding the imposition of Hellenism (4:50). Apparently Judas had already rejected Menelaus; see the reservations in Lysias's letter when he forwarded the king's decision. Note also the disposal of Menelaus in 13:3–8 and Judas's further reluctance to accept Alcimus as high priest (1 Macc 7). Eventually, the Hasmoneans themselves (Jonathan being the first) assumed the high priesthood (1 Macc 10:21). **33.** The 15th Xanthicus, in the 148th Seleucid year would be sometime in late March 164. (For the problems connected with this impossible dating [and the dates of vv 21,30,38], see Abel and Starcky, *Maccabées* 39–43.)

34–38. The letter of the Roman legates confirms Lysias's arrangements and asks that they be informed about the Jewish reaction before the king's disposition of the matters still unsettled (v 36). **34.** Abel and Starcky correct the text to give three legates: (1) Quintus Memmius, about whom nothing else is known; (2) Titus Manilius (Torquatus), who was Roman consul in 165 BC and on a diplomatic mission in the east in 164; (3) Manius Sergius, also a well-known diplomat, who had been sent to Antiochus IV Epiphanes in 164 (Polybius, *Histories* 31.1,6f.).

22–26. This letter, belonging to Antiochus V Eupator, and so to the peace negotiations after the second campaign of Lysias (1 Macc 6:28–63; 2 Macc 13:1–26), reconfirms the religious freedom of the Jews and restores the Temple to them (which they possessed anyway; 1 Macc 4:36–61; 2 Macc 10:1–8). These terms were forced on Antiochus and Lysias by necessity.

82   (F) The Battles with Neighboring Peoples (12:2–45). See comment on 1 Macc 5:1–68. Because of harassment by surrounding peoples, whose governors provoked hostility, the Jews took up arms in a series of punitive raids and defensive measures. **2.** *Timothy:* See 8:30–33; 10:24–38; 12:10–31; 1 Macc 5:24–54. *Apollonius:* Not the mysarch of 5:24–26; 1 Macc 29–35; nor the Apollonius of 2 Macc 4:21. *Nicanor:* Not the son of Patroclus in 8:9.

3–9. For the atrocity at Joppa, see comment on 1 Macc 5:55–68. **9.** *240 stadia:* Approximately 30 mi.; the distance seems excessive. **10–31.** See comment on 1 Macc 5:9–13,24–54. **15.** See Josh 6:1–21. **27.** *Lysias:* Not the governor of 10:11.

32–45. See comment on 1 Macc 5:55–68. **35.** *Dositheus:* See 12:19,24. **40.** The hidden objects were apparently amulets, etc., taken from the enemy dead in the attack on Jamnia (1 Macc 5:58). Deut 7:25–26 ordered these materials burned, but cupidity had led the soldiers to conceal them. The author makes this act the cause of the soldiers' deaths, but 1 Macc 5:19,61–62 and Josephus (*Ant.* 12.8.6 §352) attribute the casualties to disobeyed orders. **42–45.** These verses contain clear reference to belief in the resurrection of the just (see 7:11; 14:46), a belief which the author attributes to Judas (v 43), although Judas may have wanted simply to ward off punishment from the living, lest they be found guilty by association with the fallen sinners (see Josh 7). The author believes that those who died piously will rise again (v 45; 7:9), and who can die more piously than in a battle for God's law? (see 14:46). Thus, he says, Judas prayed that these men might be delivered from their sin, for which God was angry with them a little while (7:32–33). The author, then, does not share the view expressed in *1 Enoch* 22:12–13 that sinned-against sinners are kept in a division of Sheol from which they do not rise, although they are free of the suffering inflicted on other sinners. Instead, he sees Judas's action as evidence that those who die piously can be delivered from unexpiated sins that impede their attainment of a joyful resurrection. This doctrine, thus vaguely formulated, contains the essence of what would become (with further precisions) the Christian theologian's teaching on purgatory. See J. Alonso Diaz, *ByF* 3 (1977) 259–75; T. Long, *BTB* 20 (1982) 347–53.

83   (G) Lysias's Second Campaign in Judah (13:1–26). See comment on 1 Macc 6:28–63. **1.** The 149th Seleucid year was 163 BC. **2.** The figures differ from those in 1 Macc 6:30; both sets seem inflated.

3–9. This execution fits more logically after Lysias's frustration in Judea (see v 4 and Josephus, *Ant.* 12.9.7 §385). But perhaps another cause led to Menelaus's execution; see 4:27,43–47. The method of execution was Persian. **4.** *king of kings:* See Ezra 7:7 (Artaxerxes). *Beroea:* The name given to Aleppo by Seleucus I Nicator (305–281). **5.** *fifty cubits:* About 75 feet.

The battles in chap. 13 appear to be a series of victories for the Jews, but 1 Macc gives a better perspective. The Jews were on the point of complete disaster until news arrived of Philip's coup in Antioch (v 23). Then the king made peace with the Jews so he would be free to face the greater threat at home. The letter of 2 Macc 11:22–26 belongs here chronologically. It confirms Jewish religious freedom and possession of the Temple (as in v 23). **24.** *Gerar:* This is S of Gaza and on the seacoast near Pelusium. The administrative district now formed, the *paralia*, seems later not to have extended so far. See comment on 1 Macc 11:59.

84   (H) The Accession of Demetrius I Soter (161–150) (14:1–2). See comment on 1 Macc 7:1–4 and the paragraphs preceding it. **1.** *Tripolis:* So called because the merchants of Sidon, Tyre, and Arados once possessed separately walled city-quarters; hence the name of the city (Diodorus, *Hist.* 16, 41).

85   (I) The Hostility of Alcimus (14:3–11). See comment on 1 Macc 7:1–25. 2 Macc omits the expedition of Bacchides (1 Macc 7:8–25). The charges subsequently brought against Judas, mentioned in 1 Macc 7:25, are detailed here (see also 1 Macc 7:5–7). **4.** The year was 161. **6.** *Hasideans:* See comment on 1 Macc 2:42–48; 7:12–18.

86   (J) Judas and Nicanor (14:12–36). See comment on 1 Macc 7:26–38. 1 Macc 7:27–30 speaks of Nicanor's treachery, because it capsulizes 2 Macc 14:18–30 and presents the result. But 2 Macc speaks of friendship between the two for a time. Eventually, however, Alcimus succeeded in restoring the old enmity.

87   (K) The Death of Razis (14:37–46). This story, unparalleled in 1 Macc, resembles the martyrdoms of 6:28–7:42. Perhaps also it is related to the defeat of Nicanor at Capharsalama, narrated in 1 Macc 7:31–32. **46.** Razis, too, believed in the resurrection of those who died piously. He had ample precedent for his suicide to avoid enemy hands in the death of Saul (1 Sam 31:4, from which 2 Macc 14:41–42 may have drawn).

88   (L) The Defeat of Nicanor (15:1–37a). See comment on 1 Macc 7:33–50. The impending struggle is seen by the author as one between rival majesties— Yahweh (v 4) and Nicanor (v 5)—for possession of the Holy City and its Temple. Nicanor's reliance on himself and his army (15:5–6) is in contrast to Judas's reliance on God (15:7–8). Again, 2 Macc gives assurance of God's help through presentation of a heavenly vision, this time of Onias and Jeremiah.

1–5. Nicanor seemingly did not know, nor did the Jews with him, that Judas's followers had determined to fight on the sabbath when necessary (1 Macc 2:41). **3.** *thrice accursed:* See 8:34. **4–5.** See Exod 20:8–11. **6–11.** The confident Nicanor, relying on his army's strength, was already contemplating the post-battle memorial of his triumph (v 6), while Judas, who relied on God, encouraged his men for battle. **10.** *perfidy:* In violating pledges given to the *ḥǎsîdîm* (1 Macc 7:12–18). Judas told his soldiers what they could expect if they surrendered. See also 4:34; 5:25; 12:3; 1 Macc 6:62.

12–16. The vision of Onias III and Jeremiah, representing the law (embodied in the priesthood of the Temple) and the Prophets (v 9), is the author's way of portraying divine support for Judas and the gift of victory (symbolized in the golden sword). The vision also illustrates the author's belief in the intercessory power of the saints. **12.** *Onias:* The description recalls 3:1,31–34; 4:2,37; see 6:18–31. *Jeremiah:* See 2:1–8.

17–27. The Jews decided to carry the battle to Nicanor (v 17). **21.** *savagery of the elephants:* See comment on 1 Macc 6:34. **22.** Judas prayed for a victory such as that over Sennacherib (Isa 37:36; 2 Kgs 19:35), and was heard.

28–37. Instead of having a "trophy" or monument to his enemy's defeat (15:6), Nicanor became one (15:35). **29.** *language:* Hebrew. **36.** *Adar:* This month was the Seleucid Xanthicus (11:30,33,38). *Syrian language:* Aramaic. *Mordecai's day:* See Esth 3:7; 9:20–23; 10:3.

89   (M) Epilogue of the Epitomist (15:37b–39). *the city:* Jerusalem. The epitomist has attempted to please his readers (2:25). Picking up the imagery of the tempered wine at a banquet (see 2:27), he says that he has mixed the recitation of history with a pleasing style of narration. He commends his best efforts to his readers.

27

INTRODUCTION TO WISDOM LITERATURE

Roland E. Murphy, O.Carm.

BIBLIOGRAPHY

1 *Studies:* Crenshaw, J. L., *Old Testament Wisdom* (Atlanta, 1981). Dubarle, A.-M., *Les sages d'Israël* (Paris, 1946). Küchler, M., *Frühjüdische Weisheitstraditionen* (OBO 26; Fribourg, 1979). Murphy, R. E., *Wisdom Literature* (FOTL 13; GR, 1981). Preuss, H. D., *Einführung in die alttestamentliche Weisheitsliteratur* (Stuttgart, 1987). Schmid, H. H., *Wesen und Geschichte der Weisheit* (BZAW 101; Berlin, 1966). Von Rad, G., *WI.*
    Extrabiblical wisdom texts: ANET; AEL; LAEg; BWL.
    Bibliographies: R. E. Murphy, R. J. Williams, G. Buccellati in *JAOS* 101.1 (1981) 21–34 (OT); 1–19 (Egypt); 35–47 (Mesopotamia); J. Crenshaw in *SAIW* 46–60, and *HBMI* 369–407.

OUTLINE

2

(I) Extent and Characteristics (§ 3–6)
(II) Origins, Setting, and Forms (§ 7–10)
(III) Theological Aspects (§ 11–17)
    (A) Retribution (§ 12–13)
    (B) Creation (§ 14)

(C) The Personification of Wisdom (§ 15–17)
(IV) Extrabiblical "Wisdom" Literature (§ 18–37)
    (A) Egypt (§ 19–26)
    (B) Mesopotamia (§ 27–32)
    (C) Hellenistic Literature (§ 33–36)

3 **(I) Extent and Characteristics.** Five books are usually classified as "wisdom literature": Proverbs, Job, Ecclesiastes, Sirach, and Wisdom. In addition, the counsels in Tob 4:3–21; 12:6–13, and the poem in Bar 3:9–4:4 should be mentioned. There has been considerable discussion of wisdom influence on other books, such as the Joseph story (Gen 37–51), Deut, Amos, Esth, etc. See the critique and bibliography in J. Crenshaw, *SAIW* 481–94, and in D. Morgan, *Wisdom in the Old Testament Traditions* (Atlanta, 1981). The question remains moot. Wisdom (Hebr *ḥokmâ*; Gk *sophia*) is a wide-ranging term, designating the skill of an artisan (Exod 36:8), royal judgment (1 Kgs 3:28), cleverness (Prov 30:24–28), proper rules of conduct (Prov 2:1–22), piety (Prov 9:10; Job 1:1), a way of coping with life (cf. G. Fohrer in *SAIW* 63–83). About three-fourths of the approximately 400 occurrences of the word (vb., noun, or adj.) in the OT appear in these five books.
4 Certain features are characteristic of this literature: (1) An absence of any reference to the sacred traditions, such as the patriarchal promises, exodus, Sinai, covenant, etc. The exceptions in Sir 44–50 and Wis 10–19 only prove the rule. (2) A certain international flair. This is shown by the appearance of non-Israelites,

such as Agur and Lemuel in Prov 30–31 and Job with his three friends, by the explicit comparison of Solomon's wisdom to that of the people of the East and of Egypt (1 Kgs 4:29–34 [5:9–14]), and by the obvious influence of extrabiblical wisdom (e.g., Amenemope; → Proverbs, 28:51–53).
5 Wisdom is both content and style. The content can be summed up in one word: life (cf. R. E. Murphy, *Int* 20 [1966] 3–14). The goal of wisdom is the good life, here and now, which is marked by length of days, prosperity, and prestige, as recalled in Job 30:2–20. A necessary ingredient is a proper relationship to God; indeed, fear of the Lord leads to wisdom (Prov 9:10; 1:7; Job 28:28; Ps 111:10; Sir 1:16).
    The content can also be described according to kinds: (1) judicial, as when Solomon prayed for and received a "listening heart" (1 Kgs 3:9,12) – this would have been part of the training of royal counselors (Ahithophel in 2 Sam 15:34); (2) nature, a knowledge of which is attributed to Solomon (1 Kgs 4:33 [5:13]) and which is illustrated in Prov 30:15–33 and Job 38–41; (3) theological wisdom, in which the sages reflected more intensely on the nature of wisdom (Prov 8; Sir 24); (4) experiential wisdom, the broadest and most common category.

Experiential wisdom is a human response to environment, an attempt to understand and cope with it. Successful insights are captured in pithy sayings. Pride goes before a fall (Prov 16:18; 18:12)—has this not been borne out many times in practice? What view should be taken about harlotry (Prov 23:26–28)? A quarrel should be checked at once (Prov 17:12). Laziness leads to poverty (Prov 10:4). The sages reflect on a wide area of life in order to provide insights into the way things are and the way they should be. Their lessons consist of simple observations as well as moral exhortation. Compared to the commandments of the Torah, their teaching deals with the grey area of life which has to do with formation of character. Control of the tongue and of all the appetites is the ideal.

6   More should be said about the style if the content is to be properly understood. The style offsets what might be judged as a simplistic view of life. The sages were also aware of the ambiguities of experience, the paradoxes of life. Victory comes from the Lord (Prov 21:31), but neither can one do without counselors (24:6). At times even the bitter is sweet (Prov 27:7). Poverty is not necessarily the result of laziness, and the poor deserve consideration (Prov 14:31; 17:5). Naturally, the sages aimed at transmitting sure and tried lessons, but uncertainties were recognized. Wisdom had limits, and the most severe limitation was the Lord. No wisdom or counsel could stand against God (Prov 21:30). Human beings can plan, but "what the tongue utters is from the Lord" (Prov 16:1; cf. 16:2,9; 19:14,21; 20:24).

The most severe judge of traditional wisdom was himself a sage, Qoheleth (Eccl 12:9). He was well schooled in the sayings that were handed down, and he was at pains to refute them (e.g., 7:23; 8:17). The modern reader must learn to evaluate the style of the sages and the ambiguity of a proverb (contrast "Look before you leap" with "The one who hesitates is lost"). On the unpredictability of experience, see J. J. Collins in *Gnomic Wisdom* (ed. J. D. Crossan; Semeia 17; Chico, 1980) 1–18.

7   **(II) Origins, Setting, and Forms.** The Psalms are usually considered to have their origins in Temple worship. What are the origins of wisdom literature? Each book has its own particular history, but how did the wisdom movement originate? At the present time it seems best to recognize two sources: (1) the clan or tribe within which lessons would have been transmitted in the home; (2) the court school(s), in which more technical instruction was available. For neither view is there any direct evidence. The first solution has been ably defended by J.-P. Audet (in *25th International Congress of Orientalists* [Moscow, 1960] 1. 352–57) and by E. Gerstenberger, (*Wesen und Herkunft des "apodiktischen Rechts"* [WMANT 20; Neukirchen, 1966]). The teachings would probably have been transmitted orally at first, and have formed the legacy about life and living that parents communicate to children; the elder Tobit provides an example (Tob 4:1–19). The home must have served as a focal point for the training of youth, as suggested by the "my son" phraseology frequent in Proverbs. Examples of popular wisdom are scattered throughout the Bible: Judg 8:2,21; 1 Sam 16:7; 24:14; 1 Kgs 20:11 (on these see C. Fontaine, *Traditional Sayings in the Old Testament* [BLS 5; Sheffield, 1982]).

On the other hand, the majority of scholars have emphasized the role of the school, probably attached to the Jerusalem court. Again, the evidence is only indirect (cf. J. Crenshaw, *JBL* 104 [1985] 601–15). (1) Wisdom has a long association with royalty and the court, as can be inferred from the role of Solomon, the mention of King Hezekiah (Prov 25:1), and the many "king" sayings

in Prov. (2) An analogy can be drawn between Israel and the countries of Mesopotamia and Egypt, where schools certainly existed. (3) One may infer from the reign of Solomon (characterized by von Rad as the "enlightenment") that court schools would have been necessary for the training of courtiers in the new bureaucracy. These arguments find support in A. Lemaire, *Les écoles et la formation de la Bible dans l'ancien Israel* (OBO 39; Fribourg, 1981); H.-J. Hermisson, *Studien zur israelitischen Spruchweisheit* (WMANT 28; Neukirchen, 1968); B. Lang, *Die weisheitliche Lehrrede* (SBS 54; Stuttgart, 1972). On the other hand strong criticism has been registered by F. Golka in *VT* 33 (1983) 157–270, but see 34 (1984) 270–81. It can be said that while teaching may have been more vigorously cultivated in a court school, there is still no reason to eliminate the family as another source; both are likely. Moreover, the wisdom literature, in its present form, was edited and written in the postexilic period when there would have been no court schools. Unfortunately, we know practically nothing about scribal schools in this period. One can only speculate about the style of Qoheleth's activity (Eccl 12:9) or about the "school" (lit., "house of instruction") mentioned in Sir 51:23.

8   There is wide scholarly consensus that the setting of wisdom is not to be placed in Solomon's personal life. His great reputation for wisdom doubtless is the reason for his "authorship" of three wisdom books, but none of them can rightfully claim him as author. Prov is basically a gathering of collections from various historical periods. Eccl (cf. 1:1) was certainly written in the postexilic period. Neither could Solomon have composed Wis in the 1st cent. BC in Greek. Doubtless the attribution to him was a means of enhancing these books.

It is possible to speak of a setting within a particular book. Thus, the corpus of sayings in Prov 10ff. has received a certain orientation from the introductory chapters and esp. from 1:1–7, which proposes a way of reading what follows. Similarly, one should read Job against the background of the optimism of Prov. Qoheleth is better understood when his views are seen in tension with traditional wisdom.

9   The literary forms of wisdom literature are varied, according to a given book. However, the saying, command, and prohibition are certainly basic. "Proverb" is the usual translation of Hebr *māšāl,* but *māšāl* is used too broadly to be of much help. "Saying" is a more neutral term, designating a sentence, usually in the indicative mood, drawn from experience. Usually the saying is expressed in a short pithy form, and when it gains currency among a community it can be viewed as a "proverb." The wisdom sayings are normally two lines, characterized by the usual Hebraic features of parallelism (→ Hebrew Poetry, 12:6–12). Some can be purely observational, such as the paradox in Prov 11:24. But usually the saying is clearly didactic, characterizing a particular act or attitude as wise or foolish. A certain value is inculcated (Prov 14:31; 19:17). The sages also had an eye to literary expression (Prov 25:11), as shown by the frequent paronomasia, alliteration, etc. Sometimes the "numerical saying" occurs (Prov 30:15–23; cf. Amos 1–2). It may be related to the riddle: What item is common to the things enumerated?

The saying can also be put in the form of a command (compare Prov 16:3 with 16:20), or a prohibition. Sometimes a command is in parallelism with a prohibition (Prov 8:33). Frequently a motive clause is added to strengthen a prohibition (Prov 3:1–2; 22:22–23).

10   The literary genre of the book of Job is unique; it partakes of various forms derived from law (litigation), from Psalms (complaint and hymn forms), as well as from wisdom (sayings). These are, as it were, sub-genres exploited in this unusual work.

Qoheleth employs many forms, but the reflection based on experience ("I have seen" and "I know" occur very often) is characteristic. The style of his reflection is clear from such phrases as "I said in my heart" (1:16–17; 2:1,15; 3:17). His use of sayings demands careful reading; often he cites them only to modify them (chap. 7). He also makes use of an example story (9:13–16; cf. also Prov 7:6–23; 24:30–34).

Ben Sira has composed a *vade mecum* of various literary genres: sayings, admonitions, hymns, etc. (→ Sirach, 32:4). The Wisdom of Solomon is difficult to classify (→ Wisdom, 33:4), but there clearly seems to be an example of midrash in chaps. 11–19. Within it are to be found sayings, admonitions, and even prayers (Wis 9:1–18). For more details see Murphy, *Wisdom Literature*.

11   (III) Theological Aspects. The role of wisdom in OT theology becomes problematical when theology is limited to salvation history, and concerns about right living are judged as profane or secular. It has even been considered a foreign import, not really reconcilable with "Yahwism," however that is to be defined. See R. E. Murphy, "Wisdom and Yahwism," *NFL*, 117–26.

Perhaps the best reply to these considerations is to deny the major premise. Wisdom is not, by Israel's standards, profane, even if moderns might consider it so. "Yahwism" is a scholarly reconstruction of Israel's pure and primitive response to *yhwh*, but the fact is that the worshipers of *yhwh* did not limit their talk about God to salvation and were able to canonize the wisdom literature without betraying their faith. The ostracizing of wisdom seems to be the result of operating with a "canon within the canon" (→ Canonicity 66:92–97). Some key theological contributions merit discussion here: retribution, creation, and the personification of wisdom.

12   (A) Retribution. Wisdom and folly are practical, not theoretical, virtues, as can be seen by their equivalence with justice and wickedness in Prov. The attitude and actions of the wise begot prosperity; folly led to disaster. This optimistic doctrine of the sages was not presented without reservations (→ 6) but it was the dominant view, and it shared in the general biblical belief in divine retribution (Deut 28, 30; the prophets, etc.). The manner in which the connection between wisdom/folly and their results has been described has led some to find here a mechanical correspondence. Thus the good or evil deed produces of itself a good or evil consequence (Prov 26:27; Ps 7:16). This is supposedly a "deed–consequence" order of things (*Tat-Ergehen Zusammenhang*), established in creation and watched over by God (K. Koch, *ZTK* 52 [1955] 1–42 [reprinted in *Theodicy in the Old Testament* (ed. J. L. Crenshaw; IRT 4; Phl, 1983) 57–87]). Such a reconstruction of an Israelite world view may have some validity, but it is overshadowed by the more frequent portrayal of the Lord as intervening directly in human existence, punishing or rewarding (Prov 10:3,22; Jer 18:1–11, where the Lord "repents" of the evil he intended to inflict). This "deed–consequence" mentality is interpreted by some as a dead end of wisdom, precipitating a crisis, which Job and Qoheleth solved by their rejection of it. But the Lord is not the "God of order," nor is there any buffer zone of mechanical correspondence which separated God from direct action. In general one may question the adequacy of the concept of "order" that is current in the explanation of Israelite wisdom. The wisdom enterprise is more than a "search for order," an idea which seems to have derived from Egyptian understanding of *ma'at* (→ 19).

**13   ** Retribution came to be conceived rigidly by some sages, in the name of divine honor. This is particularly clear in the speeches of Job's three friends. There could be a token recognition of corrective chastisement (Job 5:17; 33:14–30; cf. Prov 3:11–12; Ps 94:12), but the basic explanation of adversity was wrongdoing, at least on someone's part (cf. John 9:1–2). Only thus, many thought, could divine justice be defended. However, the dynamism of wisdom thinking broke through this cul-de-sac with the books of Job and Eccl. As Robert Frost put it in his "Masque of Reason," the Deuteronomist was stultified, and the Lord set free to reign by Job's words. It is not that Job or Qoheleth provides any "answers" to the problem of retribution, but they do contribute to living with the mystery of suffering portrayed in the OT (see also Isa 53).

Ben Sira comes down more or less on the side of the traditional theory of retribution, although he is aware of problems (Sir 2:1–6). It is with the book of Wisdom that a breakthrough occurs, and in a manner consonant with wisdom dynamic. The great promise of traditional wisdom was life, but it was limited to this side of sheol. The vision of the author of Wisdom is that "justice is undying" (Wis 1:15). In other words, wisdom, or justice, does lead to life even beyond death. He does not argue from the nature of the soul, although he may have believed it to be immortal in the Gk style. Instead, he understands immortality from the point of view of one's relationship to God; righteousness (or wisdom) is the key to a future life with the Lord.

14   (B) Creation. Wisdom theology has rightly been characterized as "creation theology" (W. Zimmerli in *SAIW* 314–26). That is to say, the created world is the source of wisdom's insights. G. von Rad has expressed this aspect well: "the most characteristic feature of her [Israel's] understanding of reality lay, in the first instance, in the fact that she believed man to stand in a quite specific, highly dynamic existential relationship with his environment" (*WI* 301). The "environment" ranges through the entire realm of creation from humans to ants to trees. Job admonishes his friends to go to the beasts and birds, to reptiles and fish, to learn the activity of God in all that happens (12:7–9). The series of comparisons in Prov 30:15–31 draws on the observation of humans and animals. Human experience, the way in which humans interact with one another, becomes the basis for the sages' comments: the relationship of parent to child, master to servant, equal to equal. But experience cannot be left unbridled. One must learn from it how to live and thus ensure development of character.

Creation not only offers the raw material for human development. It also serves as a line of communication for God, as Ps 19 indicates. The language of creation may not be verbal, but it is continuous, and it is heard (19:2). The glory of God which it proclaims is paralleled in 19:8 by the Torah, which "gives wisdom to the simple." The message of creation is further exemplified in Job 38–41, where it becomes the defense of the Lord's government of the world. Many theologians are uncomfortable with this language of wisdom/creation, and it is often categorized as "natural theology." However justified such a category may be, it is not applicable to Israel. As von Rad has remarked, "The experiences of the world were for her [Israel] always divine experiences as well, and the experiences of God were for her experiences of the world" (*WI* 62). Faith and reason were not separated in the Bible as in later scholastic theology. The fact that creation has a language also emerges from the role of Lady Wisdom. See R. E. Murphy, "Wisdom and Creation," *JBL* 103 (1985) 3–11; O. H. Steck, *World and Environment* (Nash, 1978).

15   (C) The Personification of Wisdom. We are dealing with a personification, not a person or hypostasis within the divinity. Literary personification is not rare in the Bible (cf. Prov 20:1), but the case of Lady Wisdom is unique in its intensity and scope. The principal texts are Job 28; Prov 1,8,9; Sir 24; Wis 7-9; Bar 3:9-4:4.

The personification in Job 28 does not emphasize the female characteristics of wisdom. The question is: Where is wisdom to be found? (28:12,20). The answer: Wisdom is inaccessible; only God knows where it is, because God saw it, "appraised it, gave it its setting, knew it through and through" (28:27 NAB). This obscure statement supports the claim that God alone knows the location of wisdom, but one may still ask what he did with it, or where he placed it. Wherever wisdom is, the only approach to it available for humans is fear of the Lord (28:28).

16   The figure of Lady Wisdom emerges more clearly in Prov 1,8,9. In chap. 1 (cf. R. E. Murphy, CBQ 48 [1986] 456-60), she speaks in the style of an OT prophet, threatening her audience, should they not heed her; she will laugh at their doom, just as the Lord laughs at his enemies (1:26). But she also offers peace and security to those who obey her. In Prov 9 there is a change of tone, as she invites the "simple" to the banquet she has prepared (9:1-6). This is in stark antithesis to the meal prepared by Dame Folly (9:13-18), who offers bread and water, and stolen, at that! — an invitation to Sheol.

The lengthiest personification occurs in 8:3-36, where again Lady Wisdom speaks in public, and in an encouraging vein. The truth she proclaims is more valuable than silver or gold, and she loves those who love her (8:17). No fewer than six times does she affirm her existence before creation (8:22-26). She is described as 'āmôn (8:30), a word of uncertain meaning: either crafts(wo)man or nursling. Wis 7:22 (cf. 8:6; 14:2) understood her to be actively engaged in creation as technitis (craftsman). The common interpretation of Prov 3:19 ("The Lord by wisdom founded the earth") makes her a divine attribute. Her precise role in the act of creation remains unclear. However, she does have a role in the created world, for her delight is to be with human beings (8:31). The nature of her dealings with human beings can be inferred from her preaching and teaching in chaps. 1, 8, 9, and esp. from her promise of life in 8:32: "the one who finds me finds life."

Who is Lady Wisdom? G. von Rad identified her as "the self-revelation of creation" (WI 148-76). It is the mysterious "order" in the world which addresses humanity. She is distinct from the works of creation, yet somehow present. This aspect is well described in Sir 1:9-10, "He has poured her (wisdom) forth upon all his works . . . he has lavished her upon his friends" (Sir 1:9-10). But one may question whether the lyrical description of Lady Wisdom is adequately captured by the concept of order. She certainly cannot be viewed apart from the Lord from whom she originates. Her authority also suggests that she is the voice of the Lord, the revelation of God, not merely the self-revelation of creation. She is the divine summons issued in and through creation, who finds her delight among the humans God has created (8:31). Lady Wisdom, then, is a communication of God, through creation, to human beings.

17   The description of her in Sir 24 is also elaborate. She speaks in the presence of the heavenly court, and her message is for all who desire her (24:2,19). After journeying through the heavens and the abyss, she obeys the wish of the creator to take up her dwelling in Jacob (24:8-10). This residence makes possible the explicit identification of Lady Wisdom with the Torah (24:23; this was already prepared for by Ps 19; cf. also Deut 4:6-8).

The identification with Torah is not taken up in Wis 7-9. Instead, her intrinsic qualities are developed. She "reaches from end to end mightily" (8:1); she is a spirit who fills the world (1:6-7; cf. 7:7,22). Her relationship to the Lord is most intimate: she is an effusion of divine glory, the refulgence of eternal light (7:25-26), sharing the divine throne (9:4). At the same time she is intensely involved with human beings, "passing into holy souls from age to age" (7:27) and showing herself a savior (chap. 10).

The interpretation of wisdom as a communication of God is continued in the Christian tradition: Christ is called the wisdom of God in 1 Cor 1:24; and Heb 1:3 seems to reflect Wis 7:25-26. The role of Lady Wisdom in the development of Christology is an important chapter in the history of theology.

(For a full bibliography, see Lang, B., Frau Weisheit [Düsseldorf, 1975]; Wisdom and the Book of Proverbs [NY, 1986]. See also Camp, C., Wisdom and the Feminine in the Book of Proverbs [BLS 11; Sheffield, 1986]. Gese, H., "Wisdom, Son of Man, and the Origins of Christology," HBT [1981] 23-57. Terrien, S., "The Play of Wisdom," HBT 3 [1981] 125-53.)

18   (IV) Extrabiblical "Wisdom" Literature. A broad corpus of writings in ancient Egypt and Mesopotamia is commonly, if somewhat inexactly, categorized as "wisdom" literature. It is clear that they have exercised some influence upon biblical wisdom. In this brief sketch emphasis will be placed on the texts themselves, and some similarities will be pointed out. English translations of the pertinent texts have been noted in the bibliography (→ 1). For convenience references will be to ANET, but some texts are to be found only in other works (AEL, etc.).

19   (A) Egypt. The Egyptian Sebayit ("instruction") is of primary importance. The term designates the purpose (teaching) rather than the literary form. The instructions span about 25 centuries of Egyptian life, from that of "prince" Hardjedef of the 5th Dynasty down to the Demotic instruction of Ankhsheshonq and the Papyrus Insinger of the Ptolemaic period. For the most part they are school copies which served as text books for scribal instruction (cf. R. Williams in JAOS 92 [1972] 214-21). The pattern is regular: a teacher transmits rules of conduct to his "son" (student): "the beginning of the instruction which X made for his son Y." The writings bear the names of authors who are usually high officials or kings, whether genuine or pseudepigraphic. Hence, Egyptian wisdom, in contrast to the biblical books, evinces a kind of civil-service or class ethic. The teaching is expressed in imperative commands, prohibitions, and sometimes by means of gnomic sayings. As in biblical verse, parallelism is frequent. The object is to ensure human conduct that is in line with ma'at ("justice," or "order," but it is almost untranslatable; cf. H. Frankfort, Ancient Egyptian Religion [NY, 1961] 43-87). Ma'at designates the right order of things established by God (netjer) in creation, and with which human conduct must agree. This central concept was also deified as a goddess. Ptahhotep proclaimed that ma'at is great and lasting, undisturbed since the time of its creator (ANET 412). The teachings were designed to place human beings in harmonious agreement with ma'at, and from this arose the ideal of the "silent" one (patient, calm, and in control of oneself), who will achieve prosperity. The opposite is the "passionate" or "hotheaded" one, who lacks the necessary discipline, and hence comes to ruin. Frankfort (*Ancient Egyptian Religion* 54–56) denies that this teaching is pragmatism; rather, it is deeply religious, since human actions are to be integrated into the divine order of things. The advice handed down to the student was intended to preserve him in justice, and the student's task was to memorize and observe these rules. The knowledge was practical, not theoretical; he must *hear,* i.e., obey, as Ptahhotep repeatedly emphasizes in his epilogue (*AEL* 1. 73–75). Attention is called to the following *Sebayit:*

20   The *Instruction of Ptahhotep* (vizier, *ca.* 2400 BC) has 37 stanzas covering various aspects of human conduct: kindness, justice, etc. He counsels against pride and urges listening to the unschooled as well as to the wise: "Good speech is more hidden than the emerald but it may be found with maidservants at the grindstones" (*ANET* 412; cf. Prov 2:4). "No one is born wise!" Conduct at the table of an important host is to be very circumspect (Prov 23:1ff.; Sir 31:12ff.). A messenger must be reliable (Prov 25:13); friends are to be tested (Sir 6:7ff.). Evil women are to be avoided (Prov 6:24ff.; Sir 9:1ff.). For modern limericks based on Ptahhotep, see C. Fontaine in *BA* 44 (1981) 155–60.

21   The *Instruction for Merikare* is in fact a royal testament in which a king admonishes his son about wise rule and relates some of his problems. Reminiscent of 1 Sam 15:22 is "More acceptable is the character of one upright of heart than the ox of the evildoer" (*ANET* 417). Explicit reference is made to judgment in the next life. Another royal testament is the *Instruction of King Amenemhet I* (20th cent.; cf. *ANET* 418–19).

22   The *Instruction of Ani* (18th Dynasty) is less aristocratic than the others, for Ani was a minor official. The ideal of the "just, silent" man is upheld, but the son in the epilogue objects to the pressure his father is putting on him, only to be told that he must obey! (*AEL* 2. 144–45).

23   The *Sebayit* best known to biblical students is the *Instruction of Amenemope* (*ca.* 1200), which bears remarkable similarity to Prov 22:17–24:22 (→ Proverbs, 28:51–53). The 30 (Prov 22:20) "houses" or chapters delineate the typical ideals of the silent man (as opposed to the hotheaded man), and manifest a strong religious tone.

24   According to the accompanying narrative, the *Instruction of Ankhsheshonq* (text in *AEL* 3. 159–84) was written by this priest while in prison. The style is characterized by many commands and prohibitions and especially aphorisms.

25   Another Demotic writing, also dating from the Ptolemaic period, is the Papyrus Insinger, of which 20 out of 25 instructions are extant (text in *AEL* 3. 184–217). Each unit usually deals with a single topic and concludes with paradoxical observations and a refrain about fate and fortune. For an analysis of the Demotic compositions see M. Lichtheim, *Late Egyptian Wisdom Literature in the International Context* (OBO 52; Fribourg, 1983).

26   In addition to the instructions, there are more speculative works that deserve mention. *The Dispute between a Man and His Ba* (*AEL* 1. 163–69), known also as *A Dispute over Suicide* (*ANET* 405–7), dates from at least the 12th Dynasty. It presents a dialogue between a man and his "soul" about the miseries of life and the desirability of death. It is not clear that suicide is an issue here (cf. *AEL* 1. 163). *The Eloquent Peasant* (*ANET* 407–10) dates from about 2000 BC, and contains nine speeches which develop notions about justice, set in a narrative framework of a peasant's successful plea for justice. *A Satire on Trades,* written perhaps by a certain Kheti, son of Duauf, contrasts in exaggerated and derisive fashion the other professions in order to exalt

that of the scribe (*ANET* 431–34). It is in contrast to (not similar to, as some have claimed) Sir 38:24–39:11. Although Ben Sira finds the role of the scribe the most honorable, he treats the various professions with enthusiasm and respect.

27   **(B) Mesopotamia.** The pertinent texts from this area have been written in Sumerian and Akkadian, and some of the latter are transls. of the former (bilingual proverbs; *ANET* 593–94). E. Gordon distinguished several genres within the Sumerian corpus: precepts, maxims taunts, etc. (*Sumerian Proverbs* [Phl, 1959]; *BO* 17 [1960] 122–52). The transl. of Sumerian leaves room for uncertainty, and one does not find much comparative material here. The sayings were probably original compositions of the scribes in the Edubba ("house of tablets") or schools of ancient Sumer, although some may have been popular. But it is clear that scribal schools functioned here, as well as in Egypt.

28   In 1975 B. Alster published *The Instructions of Suruppak* (Mesopotamia 2; Copenhagen), a collection of Sumerian sayings given by a certain Šuruppak to his son, Ziusudra, the hero of the Sumerian flood story. It dates from before 2500, and was also translated into Akkadian (*ANET* 594–95). Similar in style and subject is the Akk *Counsels of Wisdom* (*ANET* 595–96), which deals proper speech, with avoidance of bad companions, etc.

29   The problem of the "righteous sufferer"—the theme of Job—is well represented in ancient Mesopotamia. A Sumerian text "Man and His God" (*ANET* 589–91) and the Akk *Ludlul bēl nēmeqi* ("I will praise the lord of wisdom," *ANET* 596–600) are two examples. It has even been maintained that the latter work provides the literary form of Job, a paradigm of an answered complaint. But this misconstrues the book of Job, which provides no "answer" in the style of the *Ludlul.* What the two works have in common is to blame the divinity for failure to act in favor of a suffering devotee. The poignancy of the problem is not explored in the Babylonian poem; the "answer" is given by a convenient divine intervention that brings about the cure. That is not the function of chap. 42 in Job.

30   Another poem, dating from about 1000 BC, is called "The Dialogue about Human Misery" or "The Babylonian Theodicy" (*ANET* 601–4), and it has been compared to Job and Eccl. The work is an acrostic of 27 stanzas with 11 lines each. Like Job it is a dialogue, but the characters are a suffering person and a sympathetic friend. The former develops the point that suffering and evil conflict with the justice of the gods, and he illustrates this with many examples. Thus, he complains that he was born to parents already advanced in age and that he was soon left an orphan. Why do not the gods defend such helpless creatures? His friend reminds him that all must die—even one's parents—and that prosperity is the result of piety, etc. The dialogue passes on to other items: Why should the firstborn be favored ahead of later children? Why does crime pay? The friend answers sympathetically—never, like the "friends" of Job, accusing him of sin and saying that he deserved his suffering. But the consolation of the friend is dubious; he continues to mouth the old belief that piety will be rewarded, until finally he makes the astounding admission that the gods have made human beings evil, for they "gave twisted speech to the human race. With lies, and not truth, they endowed them forever" (*ANET* 604). As W. Lambert (*BWL* 65) has remarked, this conclusion undoes the premises of the discussion; when one admits that the gods are responsible for human proclivities to evil, the argument is finished, and without a real conclusion.

31   Another dialogue is called "The Dialogue of
Pessimism" (*ANET* 600-1), and it is deserving of comparison with Eccl. This is a relatively late composition,
perhaps after 1200 BC. It is a lively conversation between
a master and his slave about a variety of topics, including
love of woman, piety toward the gods, and loans. When
the master proposes a particular course of action, the
slave agrees and supplies more reasons. When the master
then proposes the opposite, the slave reverses his stand,
even pointing out adverse effects that could have followed. At the end death is the topic, and perhaps by
suicide. The interpretation of the poem has varied. W.
Lambert (*BWL* 139-41) argues that the work is to be
taken seriously, and not as a farce.

The resemblance to Eccl lies in the fact that Qoheleth
took extreme positions, somewhat in the fashion of both
master and servant. The readiness to search out contradictions, to portray two sides of a question, and to seek
out every possible disadvantage is characteristic of both
writings.

32   Finally, there is the work of Ahiqar, a narrative with collections of sayings, fables, riddles, and
proverbs (*ANET* 427-30; cf. J. Lindenberger, *The
Aramaic Proverbs of Ahiqar* [Baltimore, 1983]). The work
is phenomenal in the ancient world in that it became part
of many literatures and has been transmitted in about a
dozen languages (Lindenberger, *Aramaic Proverbs* 4-7). It
was written perhaps as early as the 7th cent. BC, and
many claim Aramaic rather than Akkadian as the original language. The most ancient recension is the Aramaic,
found among the famous 5th-cent. BC papyri that were
discovered at the beginning of the 20th cent. on
Elephantine Island in the Nile. The work consists of narrative and "proverbs." The narrative tells the story of the
betrayal of Ahiqar, an upright official under Sennacherib
of Assyria (704-681) by his relative (Nadin), and also his
eventual restoration. The sayings presumably form part
of his statements to Nadin. They were perhaps inserted
later, since only lines 139-40 (*ANET* 429) show close
relationship to the story line.

There are some clear similarities to the Bible. Line
207 (*ANET* 430: "Let not the rich man say, 'In my riches
I am glorious' ") is reminiscent of Jer 9:22[23]. The
words about discipline in line 81 (*ANET* 428) are comparable to Prov 26:3 and 23:13-14. The figure of a soft
tongue breaking a bone (Prov 25:15; Sir 28:17) is reflected
in lines 105-6 (*ANET* 428). On the basis of restorations,
lines 94-95 have been interpreted as referring to the
divine origin (?) of wisdom and her (eternal?) reign. But

the text is very fragmentary; (cf. *ANET* 428; and
Lindenberger, *Aramaic Proverbs* 68-70).

33   **(C) Hellenistic Literature.** "Wisdom literature" is not used as a tag to designate a given corpus of
Hellenistic writings, in contrast to what we have seen
for ancient Egypt and Mesopotamia. However, it is clear
that schools existed and teaching was imparted. Modern
scholarship has been satisfied to point out the broad
Hellenistic influence on the Bible, rather than analyze a
narrow vein of what might be termed "wisdom." The
sources of this influence embrace an area of literature too
vast to be considered here. Instead a brief orientation to
the scholarly discussion concerning three of the biblical
works written in the Hellenistic period will be given.

34   *Ecclesiastes.* The measure of the indebtedness
of Qoheleth to the Gk world is a matter of debate. The
discussion has moved beyond the alleged Grecisms
which were advanced decades ago. O. Loretz has argued
vigorously in favor of Mesopotamian influence as
opposed to Egyptian and Greek (*Qohelet und der Alte
Orient* [Freiburg, 1964]). R. Braun has proposed
numerous parallels between the thought of Eccl and
early Hellenistic popular philosophy (*Kohelet und die
frühhellenistische Popularphilosophie* (BZAW 130; NY,
1973). The evidence is still out on the precise relationship of Qoheleth's relationship to Hellenism.

35   *Sirach.* Ben Sira was very much a man of the
Hebrew Bible, as proved by the echoes of the text in his
work. Since he wrote just before the outbreak of the
Maccabean revolt, one expects to see reflected in his
work an attitude to Hellenism, pro or con. Instead, any
dialogue that he has with current Gk thought is rather
subdued. For a different point of view, see M. Hengel,
Judaism and Hellenism (2 vols.; Phl, 1974) 1. 131-75; and
B. Mack, *Wisdom and the Hebrew Epic* (Chicago, 1985).

36   *Wisdom of Solomon.* The author utilized the
LXX in his original Gk composition, and biblical influence is very great. On the other hand there are present
clear Gk elements both in thought and vocabulary, as
shown by the studies of C. Larcher, *Etudes sur le livre de
la Sagesse* (EBib; Paris, 1969); J. Reese, *Hellenistic Influence
on the Book of Wisdom and Its Consequences* (AnBib 41;
Rome, 1970); and D. Winston, *The Wisdom of Solomon*
(AB 43; GC, 1982) 14-63.

37   Wisdom literature is clearly an international
phenomenon in the ancient world. The biblical books fit
into this development and were influenced by it in varying degrees. However, biblical wisdom retains its own
peculiar stamp.

28

PROVERBS

Thomas P. McCreesh, O.P.

BIBLIOGRAPHY

1 *Commentaries:* Barucq, A., *Le Livre des Proverbes* (SB; Paris, 1964). Gemser, B., *Sprüche Salomos* (HAT 16; 2d ed.; Tübingen, 1963). McKane, W., *Proverbs* (OTL; Phl, 1970). Plöger, O., *Sprüche Salomos (Proverbia)* (BKAT 17; Neukirchen, 1984). Ringgren, H., *Sprüche* (ATD 16/1; Göttingen, 1962). Scott, R. B. Y., *Proverbs* (AB 18; GC, 1965). Toy, C. H., *Proverbs* (ICC; Edinburgh, 1899).

Studies: Aletti, J. N., "Séduction et parole en Proverbes I–IX," *VT* 27 (1977) 129–43. Barucq, A., "Proverbs (livre des)," *DBSup* 8. 1395–1476. Boström, G., *Proverbiastudien: Die Weisheit und das fremde Weib in Sprüche 1–9* (LUA 30,3; Lund, 1935). Camp, C. V., *Wisdom and the Feminine in the Book of Proverbs* (Sheffield, 1985). Hermisson, H.-J., *Studien zur Israelitischen*

Spruchweisheit (WMANT 28; Neukirchen, 1968). Kayatz, C., *Studien zu Proverbien 1–9* (WMANT 22; Neukirchen, 1966). Lang, B., *Wisdom and the Book of Proverbs* (NY, 1986). Murphy, R. E., *Wisdom Literature* (FOTL 13; GR, 1981). Robert, A., "Les attaches littéraires bibliques de Prov. I–IX," *RB* 43 (1934) 42–68, 172–204, 374–84; 44 (1935) 344–65, 502–25. Skehan, P. W., *SIPW.* Skladny, U., *Die ältesten Spruchsammlungen in Israel* (Göttingen, 1962). Whybray, R. N., *Wisdom in Proverbs* (SBT 45; London, 1965).

Bibliographies: Camp, *Wisdom* 325–44; Murphy, *Wisdom Literature* 48; Plöger; F. Vattioni, "Studi sul libro dei Proverbi," *Aug* 12 (1972) 121–68.

INTRODUCTION

2 **(I) Survey of Modern Criticism.** Prov is an anthology of short, two-line sayings (chaps. 10–29), prefaced by long poetic instructions (chaps. 1–9) and concluded by a section of longer sayings and short poems (chaps. 30–31). The tenor of the contents is didactic and moralizing. In the past, the description of wisdom in chap. 8 attracted interest; otherwise, the book was regarded simply as a "manual of conduct" (Toy, *Proverbs* x).

3 The 1923 publication of the Egyptian *Instruction of Amenemope* (→ Wisdom Lit., 27:23) and the analysis of its relationship to Prov 22:17–24:22 by A. Erman in the following year, ended isolation of the book as the only extant example of ancient Near Eastern aphoristic literature. It could now be compared with the material provided by the Egyptian "instructions," the Mesopotamian wisdom texts, and the Aram proverbs of Ahiqar (→ Wisdom, Lit., 27:20–32). At the same time, its value came to lie in what it shared about human experience with other literatures, and any theological dimension in the work was attributed to later editorial activity which gave it a "Yahwistic reinterpretation." The sayings were classified as secular or religious in outlook and concern, then dated accordingly (McKane, *Proverbs* 10–22; R. Whybray in *La Sagesse de l'Ancien Testament* [BETL 51; Leuven, 1979] 153–65).

4 Other research assumed that short, one-line sayings evolved into longer, literary compositions with the addition of motive clauses and literary embellishment (O. Eissfeldt, *Der Maschal im Alten Testament* [BZAW 24; Giessen, 1913]). Thus, the sayings of chaps. 10–29, being short, were presumed to be part of earlier collections. But artistic style and fullness are not necessarily late and can be part of early, "folk" sayings. The longer essays of chaps. 1–9 were treated as postexilic additions which gave the book its final form. However, the similarities between the Egyptian instructions and chaps. 1–9 (C. Kayatz) has challenged this dating as well. The study of imagery to determine the settings of the proverbs is also inconclusive. Agricultural imagery, for instance, can be employed in royal circles, and early clan wisdom can refer to kings.

5 **(II) Formation of Book; Date.** A date for the present book is hard to determine. Two stages can be inferred. First was the family or clan collections of proverbs. Then, under Solomon and other kings (25:1), the collecting and editing of the traditional wisdom was fostered. The book itself represents a special redaction of some of these earlier materials. Not only was the introduction (chaps. 1–9, some of which may represent early materials) prepared by an author/editor, but Skehan (*SIPW* 15–26) has shown that the proverbs, too, were edited by this same hand. A probable date for the book is the late 6th or early 5th cent. Personified Wisdom in chap. 8 is certainly behind the portrait of wisdom in Sir 24. Proverbs also fails to develop the concept of Torah as Sirach does, and shares terminology and insights with Deuteronomy, Second Isaiah and Jeremiah (A. Robert, *RB* [1934–35]). The proverbs dealing with the king would also seem to indicate a time not far removed from the monarchy.

6   (III) Literary Forms.   The two main genres are the instruction and the proverb.

(A) Instructions.   The instructions, probably modeled on Egyptian parallels (→ Wisdom Lit., 27:19–25), are addressed by a teacher/sage to a student ("son") and appear in chaps. 1–9; 22:17–24:22; and 31:1–9. The divisions between the instructions in chaps. 1–9 are not clear in every case. All are exhortations to follow the path to wisdom and to be mindful of the consequences of one's actions, using graphic examples and dramatic language.

7   Three texts (1:20–33; 8:1–36; 9:1–6) are called "Wisdom speeches," wherein personified Wisdom speaks in a highly personalized style, unique in the OT. It imitates the Egyptian portrayals of the deity *Ma'at* ("justice, order"), but also recalls prophetic literature. There are also "alphabetizing" poems, as suggested by Skehan (*SIPW* 9–10), which have as many verses as there are letters in the Hebr alphabet (22). Chapter 2 is an excellent example (→ 21–22 below). But not all the poems can be analyzed in this way without rearranging verses in order to accommodate the presumed 22 lines.

8   (B) Proverbs.   A proverb is a pithy statement expressing some truth in a striking and memorable way (→ Wisdom Lit., 27:9). The biblical proverb is usually a couplet, with some form of parallelism, and appears in chaps. 10–29, although individual proverbs are found in the instructions (3:32–35). Their power lies in the use of various figures of sound and sense. An effective device for characterizing people or behavior is synecdoche, which specifies a part (e.g., the ear) but implies the whole person, as in 25:12b, ". . . a wise reprover to an attentive ear." Metonymy, too, substitutes the name of one thing for another. So, the mouth, the tongue, and the lips symbolize the person's speech, as in 10:31a, "A just man's mouth bears wisdom. . . ." Different parts of the body are used in similar fashion: eyes, nostrils, ear, hand, foot, bones, belly, kidney, and the heart. Some other figures used are hyperbole (22:13) and oxymoron (25:15b). There are also numerous examples of alliteration, assonance, and wordplay.

9   Among the various types of proverbs are simple observations about life. They may use juxtaposition (Hermisson, *Studien* 144–52), in which the thought is expressed by the simple placement of various phrases together, as in 13:24, "One who spares his rod—one who hates his son, but one who loves him—one who eagerly seeks discipline for him." The priamel lists things, the last item of which evokes surprise, even humor (26:3). The numerical proverb numbers things having something in common (chap. 30). Other proverbs make their point with simple but striking pictures (19:24). Comparisons abound. Some are implicit through the use of juxtaposition (25:23); others indicate the comparison by such particles as "like" or "so" (10:26). Sometimes a value judgment is expressed in the comparison, as in the "better" proverb (27:5). Other sayings contrast types of people and behavior, appearing especially in chaps. 10–15, and to a lesser degree in chaps. 28–29.

10   (IV) Structure of the Book.   No clear, unifying structure manifests itself. The proverbs are discrete entities gathered into seemingly random collections (→ 14 below). Links between them and chaps. 1–9 have been sought through the use of imagery. These would include the "house" (*bayit*), described for Wisdom (9:1), for Folly (2:18; 7:8,27; 9:14), and for the *'ēšet ḥayil,* "woman of worth," in chap. 31; the "way," which abounds in the book and emphasizes a journey motif; and the various images of wives and mothers (e.g., 19:13–14), which foreshadow the portrayal of the wife and mother in chap. 31 (Camp, *Wisdom and the Feminine* 183–208). Certain catchwords can also link a series of sayings (Murphy, *Wisdom Literature* 68–80). Another artificial structure has been based on the numerical value of the names in the titles to the proverb collections (Skehan, *SIPW* 43–45). An aspect of this problem is whether the proverbs create a context within which they can be interpreted (Hermisson, *Studien* 171–83). It seems, however, that although one saying can relativize the meaning of another, each one retains its own meaning, undetermined by the context.

11   (V) Interpretation of the Book.   The work seems easy to understand, but actually conceals deep and profound insights.

(A) The Nature of Wisdom.   Wisdom is not an esoteric knowledge reserved for a few, but can be sought by all. It is found through the difficult process of making well-informed choices in life. The need to inform, train, and persuade the young about the right choices is the book's rationale. Wisdom is also at the service of others. The emphasis on the effects that attitudes and actions have on others and the stress placed on the power of speech to build up or destroy make this clear. This wisdom recognizes limits, ambiguities, and uncertainties (→ Wisdom Lit., 27:6). For example, the statement of one proverb is often qualified, even denied, by the advice of another (26:4–5). And the ultimate qualification of wisdom is the Lord, against whom no wisdom or counsel can stand (21:30).

12   (B) Wisdom as Symbolized.   The instructions (chaps. 1–9) describe Wisdom as a woman who is courted. This is an apt symbol since wisdom must be sought out and cherished with dedication and devotion. Her call must be discerned amid myriad appeals of pleasure and easy success, which are the ways of folly. Once attained, though, she will be faithful to her followers, building up their houses with peace and prosperity, like the good wife in 31:10–31 (T. McCreesh, *RB* 92 [1985] 25–46). Wisdom has divine attributes as well. She is to be loved above all else; from her comes wealth and sound government; rejection of her means death. Her identity is obscured by this paradox (8:30b–31): she is with God and yet at home in this world. The mystery can be resolved to this extent: Wisdom is a gift from God meant to be the goal for all human searching (Murphy, *Wisdom Literature* 62; *JBL* 104 [1985] 3–11).

13   (C) Theological Interpretation.   Wisdom mediates between God and the world. Immanent in creation, she is the source of all meaning about this world. Coming from God, she is also a revelation of God and a call from him to the world (→ Wisdom Lit., 27:16). Consequently, human experience and study of the created world can be the matrix for religious experience and can be revelatory of the divine. By the same token, the heart of this wisdom is "the fear of the Lord" which opens us to heed what God reveals and respond to him. But this divine communication comes not only in terms of knowledge but also in terms of love. It is a divine appeal through creation which seduces, draws, and eventually embraces us. Thus, Christian theology has applied the figure of Wisdom to Jesus who, as the Incarnate Word of God, is the mediator par excellence between God and this world (1 Cor 1:24).

14   **(VI) Outline.**

COMMENTARY

15   **(I) Prologue (1:1–9:18).** These chapters introduce the entire book with a series of instructions. They encourage the pursuit of wisdom as a faithful guide for life and warn against other influences which can lead to a self-destructive life. Four women figure prominently in developing these themes. (1) Personified Wisdom is gradually defined more clearly. (2) The "bad woman," actually at times an individual, at times several, with various names — "stranger" (2:16a; 5:3a,10,17; 7:5a), "adulteress" (2:16b; 5:20b; 6:24b; 7:5b), "harlot" (6:26a; 7:10b), "another's wife" (6:26b; 6:29a) — speaks for herself in 7:14–20. (3) The "wife of your youth" is briefly described in 5:15–19. (4) The "woman of folly," Wisdom's rival, is introduced in 9:13–18.

16   After stating the purpose and theme of the book (vv 1–7), chap. 1 presents the first instruction (vv 8–19) and concludes with the first speech of personified Wisdom (vv 20–33). Chapter 2 summarizes the benefits of wisdom and warns against the "bad woman," ideas developed in chaps. 3–7. Wisdom then presents a magnificent summary of all her benefits in chap. 8. The whole section closes with Wisdom and Folly extending rival invitations to their own banquets in chap. 9. Thus, the prologue ends on the question of an ultimate choice between them.

17   **(A) Introduction (1:1–33).**

(a) TITLE AND PURPOSE (1:1–7). The title for the whole book (v 1) and a concluding independent saying (v 7) frame vv 2–6, which state the purpose and intention of the book and even suggest its contents. **1.** *the proverbs of Solomon:* Describes the book as a whole, but more especially the Solomonic collections (10:1–22:16; 25:1–29:27). The use of Solomon's name lends authority to the whole collection (cf. 1 Kgs 4:32–33). *the son of David, king of Israel:* The full title is used only here and not at 10:1 and 25:1. Skehan (*SIPW* 25–26) has pointed out that the numerical value of the three names in the title (Solomon, 375 + David, 14 + Israel, 541 = 930) represents the number of lines in the book. **2.** *wisdom:* Originally designated any particular skill or ability, and such meaning is not excluded here. *discipline:* A prerequisite for wisdom, this can mean training, correction, and self-control. *words of intelligence:* A mark of the wise man is perceptive and illuminating discourse. **3.** Wisdom requires respect for the demands of right living (*sedeq*), what is the just thing to do (*mišpāt*), and whatever is proper and true (*mêšārîm*). **4.** The book is especially concerned with the "simple," who are naïve and inexperienced, and the young, who are susceptible to harmful influences. **7.** A statement of the theme for the entire book. *fear of the Lord:* A recurring phrase that indicates a reverential and loving obedience to the will of God. *fools:* The contrast between wisdom and folly, a major theme of the book, is stated here at the beginning.

18   (b) FIRST INSTRUCTION: WARNING ABOUT SINNERS (1:8–19). **8.** *hear:* The imperative, followed by a motive clause (v 9), is a mark of the instruction. Parental teaching is the first "school" of wisdom (cf. Ptahhotep, *ANET* 414). **10–19.** A warning against those who appeal to youth and inexperience with promises of easy companionship, power, and quick wealth through violence and injustice. **11.** *unprovoked:* Hebr *ḥinnām* is repeated again in v 17 so that the senseless attack of the wicked on the innocent (cf. Jer 2:34, 19:4; Ps 10:8–10) is joined in ironic contrast with the trap that will eventually catch the wicked themselves "unawares" (v 18). **12.** *sheol, the pit:* The realm of the dead is pictured beneath the earth. Sheol is an insatiable mouth swallowing the dead (cf. Isa 5:14; Hab 2:5). A premature death was considered punishment for sin. **15.** *way, paths:* The two ways of life are a fundamental theme (cf. 2:12–22; Ps 1). **17.** This obscure fowling image illustrates v 18; just as with birds, warning bandits about the trap they are falling into has no effect. **19.** The warning concludes with the principle of retribution (cf. 15:27; 28:16).

19   (c) FIRST SPEECH OF PERSONIFIED WISDOM (1:20–33). In response to the warning of vv 11–14, Wisdom, personified as a woman, makes her first appearance and delivers warnings of her own. **20–21.** *wisdom:* Hebr *ḥokmôt*, a fem. pl. form, also used in 9:1, may designate an abstract noun or emphasize the comprehensive and superior stature of wisdom (Gemser, *Sprüche Salomos* 22). Since the vbs. are sg., it has also been described as an archaic (Canaanite) sg. form. Wisdom's stance in the most public places is reminiscent of the prophets (cf. Jer 7:2; 17:19–20; 19:1–2). Her message reaches the ordinary person in the "street" and "open squares," as well as the officials and professionals who work at the "city gates." **22.** Wisdom calls to the simple (*pětāyim*), who don't know better: the scorners (*lēṣîm*), who relish their cynicism, and the fools (*kěsîlîm*), who despise knowledge. **23.** Wisdom's promise of "my spirit" (= "my words" on the basis of parallelism) is a promise of the destruction to come. It is a threat, not a promise of blessing (R. E. Murphy, *CBQ* 48 [1986] 456–60). **20   24–25.** Wisdom echoes the prophets' condemnation of Israel (cf. Isa 65:12; 66:4; Jer 7:23–27). **26–28.** Reproach becomes threat. Wisdom's mocking laughter will repay their disdain (cf. Pss 2:4; 59:9), her refusal to heed them (cf. Mic 3:4; Isa 1:15; Jer 11:11; Hos 5:6) will repay their stubbornness. These threats frame an image of the coming disaster as a sudden and violent storm. **31–32.** The seeds of punishment are contained in the evil deeds themselves. **33.** Security and freedom from evil are promised only for those who heed Wisdom's call.

21   (B) The Benefits of Wisdom (2:1–7:27).
(a) SECOND INSTRUCTION: WISDOM'S BENEFITS (2:1–22). Six stanzas (vv 1–4,5–8,9–11,12–15,16–19, 20–22) summarize themes to be developed in 3–7. Skehan (*SIPW* 9–10) analyzes this as an "alphabetizing" poem (→ 7 above), which also introduces some of the stanzas with word repetition. **1–4.** The first stanza names the conditions for acquiring wisdom: docility, earnest seeking, and untiring zeal. **2.** *heart:* The seat of intellectual and moral life. **4.** Wisdom is like a precious metal or valuable treasure that is found only in difficult and remote places (cf. Job 28). **5–8.** The first result of acquiring wisdom is God-given knowledge and protection. This theme is developed in 3:1–12. **7.** Seeking wisdom has moral implications: justice, honesty, and integrity. **8.** *paths, way:* Stanzas 2 and 3 of this poem delineate the "good way"; stanzas 4 and 5, the "evil way." **9–11.** The third stanza presents another benefit of wisdom: discernment and understanding for a prudent and upright life, ideas elaborated in 3:27–35. **10.** The indwelling of wisdom is reminiscent of Jeremiah's new covenant (Jer 31:33).
22   12–15. Wisdom is protection from evil people, such as have been described in 1:10–19, a theme to be developed in 4:10–27. **16–19.** The fifth stanza asserts that Wisdom is also protection from the "strange woman" (*'iššâ zārâ*) and the "adulteress" (*nokriyyâ*); see also the admonitions of Ptahhotep and Ani (*ANET* 413b; 420a). This theme encompasses chaps. 5 and 7, and 6:20–35. **16.** *the strange woman:* Boström (*Proverbiastudien*) interprets this woman as a cultic fertility figure, tempting to idolatry as well as adultery. Others give the sense "wife of another," a woman already married who is acting promiscuously. *the adulteress:* Lit., "foreign woman/wife," but the parallelism with "strange woman" indicates an adulteress. **17.** *companion of her youth:* On the basis of v 16b, this refers to the woman's first husband, suggesting an elevated conception of marriage fidelity (Exod 20:14,17; Mal 2:14). *the pact with her God:* Marital infidelity breaks the covenant with Israel's God as well. **18.** *her house: NAB* has "her path" for the sake of parallelism with v 18b; but the symbol of this house as the path to Sheol is found at 7:27, and affirmed of Folly's house at 9:13–18. **20–22.** The ultimate purpose of wisdom is goodness and justice; the reward is continued life in the land.
23   (b) THIRD INSTRUCTION: FIDELITY TOWARD THE LORD (3:1–12). **3.** *loyalty and fidelity:* Adornment for the wise person (cf. Exod 13:9,16; Deut 6:8; 11:18); they characterize the Lord (Exod 34:6) and are meant to characterize the people as well (Hos 4:1). **5.** *with all your heart:* The understanding of "heart" in v 1 as memory and understanding is complemented here by an emphasis on its powers of commitment and trust. *intelligence:* Has a

pejorative sense here (cf. 26:12; 28:11), best understood as conceit. **8.** *flesh . . . bones:* The whole person is referred to by the mention of two physical parts (merismus). **8b.** Dried-up bones were a metaphor for suffering and distress (cf. 17:22; Ps 22:15–16; Job 30:30). Note the connection between physical health and interior dispositions in 15:13,30; 16:24; 17:22. Ill health was often considered punishment for sin. **9.** The only instance of a cultic command in Prov (cf. Exod 34:26; Lev 27:30; Deut 26:1–2). **11–12.** Adversity is interpreted as discipline administered by a loving God (cf. Job 5:17; 33:14–30; Heb 12:5–6).
24   (c) FOURTH INSTRUCTION: THE VALUE OF WISDOM (3:13–26). Verses 13–18 are a hymn in praise of wisdom, and vv 21–26 are an admonition to keep wisdom. They are linked by the middle couplet which praises wisdom's role in creation. **13–18.** The hymn opens with a beatitude, whose first word, "happy" (*'ašrê*), forms an *inclusio* with the last word, "happy" (*mě'uššār*), in v 18. **18.** *a tree of life:* A common image in ancient mythology and a recurring metaphor in Prov (cf. 11:30; 13:12; 15:4). It recalls the tree of Gen 2:9, which symbolized the human yearning for immortality; here it represents sustenance and healing for a happy life (cf. Ezek 47:12; Rev 22:2). **19–20.** Wisdom's role in creation is praised; an anticipation of chap. 8 (cf. Pss 102:26; 104:5; Isa 48:13; 51:13). **23–24.** The mention of "the way" is illustrated by images of "walking" and "resting," which are meant to embrace all activities of life (cf. Deut 6:7; Ps 91:11–12).
25   (d) FIFTH INSTRUCTION: RIGHT CONDUCT (3:27–35). Five prohibitions express concern for relationships with others (vv 27–31), and these find motivation in four antithetic sayings (vv 32–35), which emphasize that both the "good way" and the "evil way" are judged by the Lord. **27–28.** A generous and prompt response to need is best. **31.** The seeming prosperity of the wicked is a constant source of temptation (cf. Ps 37). **32.** *abomination:* Expresses the radical separation between God and the sinner. **34.** Quoted in Jas 4:6 and 1 Pet 5:5. *the humble:* The *'ānāwîm* of the psalms and the prophets; the "poor in spirit" of Matt 5:3.
26   (e) SIXTH INSTRUCTION: EXHORTATION TO GET WISDOM (4:1–9). **1–3.** The search for wisdom is portrayed as a parent's loving guidance and the child's affectionate response. **6–9.** The personal tone is enhanced by the portrayal of personified Wisdom herself. **6.** Wisdom appears as a faithful friend, even lover, who requires the same love and devotion in her followers. **8–9.** The imagery is that of wisdom as a wife (cf. Sir 14:20–27; 51:13–22; Wis 8:2) or as an influential patron who bestows favors on her protégé.
27   (f) SEVENTH INSTRUCTION: THE TWO WAYS (4:10–27). The theme of 2:12–15, the two ways of life, is developed, reinforced by the use of similar images: way, road, track, step, feet, go, walk, advance, run, stumble. **14–15.** The cluster of imperatives (three negative, three positive) underline the urgency in the warning about "the way of the wicked." **16–17.** The wicked not only live *by* their wickedness but also live *for* it. **20–27.** These warnings invoke various organs of the body as sources of either good or evil, life or death. **24.** The mouth and lips betray what is in the heart. These organs and the power of speech are an important theme in the sayings of Ahiqar (cf. *ANET* 428b). **25.** The eyes can communicate without words. The way, also, can only be walked with one's gaze fixed straight ahead.
28   (g) EIGHTH INSTRUCTION: WARNING AGAINST ADULTERY (5:1–23). The elaboration of the theme in 2:16–19 begins here and ends with chap. 7, the longest such treatment in the prologue. The concern, however,

is not only to warn susceptible youths but also to contrast a life of promiscuous infidelity, represented by the adulteress, with the promise of life held out by the attractive fidelity of Wisdom. **2-3.** The reserved "lips" (speech) of the student are contrasted with the flattering "lips" of the woman. By her deceitful speech, the woman subverts language itself, on which education in wisdom depends (J. N. Aletti, *VT* 27 [1977] 129-44). **7-14.** The results of not heeding the teacher are realistically drawn. **9-11.** Reputation, health, vitality, and wealth can all be forfeit for entering the temptress's house. The words used are ambiguous: the "merciless" one (v 9b) can be the woman (who turns "bitter as wormwood," v 4) or the angry husband. The "strangers" and "aliens" (v 10) can be the seductive women or those to whom the youth is in debt for his extravagances. **11.** *your end:* An allusion to the same word used of the woman in v 4.

29   **15-20.** The joy and fulfillment of sexual union in marriage are portrayed under the metaphor of refreshing and life-giving water. Water, being scarce, is valued and cherished; hence the aptness of the symbol. **18-19.** The language recalls the Song of Songs and its extolling of the pleasures and joy of love. **21-23.** The theme of the two ways returns. The judgment on infidelity is accomplished as the guilty person falls prey to his own devices.

30   (h) INTERLUDE: FOUR WARNINGS (6:1-19). Four small pieces with no obvious connection to what precedes or follows. They resemble 22:17-24:34 and 30:15-33 in style and content. **1-5.** A warning against pledging to cover another's possible business losses (cf. 11:15; 17:18; 20:16; 22:26-27). **6-11.** A warning against sloth using the lesson of the ant (cf. 30:25); cf. a similar sketch in 24:30-34. **12-15.** A portrait, an almost exact antithesis of 4:24-27, describing the devious person whose every movement mocks truth. **16-19.** A numerical proverb listing parts of the body whose proper use has been perverted.

31   (i) NINTH INSTRUCTION: WARNING AGAINST ADULTERY (6:20-35). The warning against adultery is resumed from chap. 5. **30-31.** The adulterer, unlike the thief, cannot pay off the husband from whom he stole (v 35).

32   (j) TENTH INSTRUCTION: WARNING AGAINST ADULTERY (7:1-27). This section illustrates the ways of the adulteress. **3-4.** This intimacy with Wisdom is in stark contrast to the phony intimacy now to be described. **6-23.** The lavish and long description of the seduction (vv 10-20) contrasts vividly with the short and violent "death scene" (vv 21-23). **8-9.** The naïveté of the youth is suggested and a somber tone is evoked by the repetition of words for night and darkness. **22-23.** The youth, oblivious to his fate, is compared to dumb animals who rush into the trap unawares. **24-27.** The imagery of "the way" and the "house" becomes, in the context of this woman, metaphors for death (cf. 2:18-19; 9:18).

33   (C) **Second Speech of Personified Wisdom** (8:1-36). The climax of the prologue. Wisdom recommends herself and her teaching. The poem can be divided into seven stanzas of five couplets (except the second, which has six couplets): vv 1-5 (Wisdom's universal call), vv 6-11 (her truth, integrity, and inestimable value), vv 12-16 (her intellectual gifts), vv 17-21 (her favors), vv 22-26 (her priority to all things), vv 27-31 (her presence at the creation), and vv 32-36 (her appeal to be heeded).

2-3. Wisdom's stance here is the same as that in 1:20-21. **4-5.** But her call here is to all people without distinction. **7-8.** A pair of antitheses emphasizing her opposition to anything dishonest and insincere. **12-16.** Wisdom is the source of a political wisdom and power

that are just. The same attributes belong to the messianic king (Isa 1-5) and to God (Job 12:13,16). **17.** The love and zeal with which Wisdom is pursued will be reciprocated. **20-21.** The material prosperity promised does not upset the claims of justice and equity.

34   **22-31.** Wisdom's superiority over all things is due to her origin before them. **22.** *qānānî:* LXX, Syr, and Tg translate "(The Lord) created me." Variations are "begot," "brought forth," or "formed," paralleling the vbs. in vv 24-25. This means Wisdom would be the first product of creation. Hebr *qnh* ordinarily means "get," "possess" (cf. B. Vawter, *JBL* 99 [1980] 205-16), and is so rendered by Aq, Sym, Theod, and Vg. Then the Lord *utilizes* Wisdom in creation, and no indication of her exact origins is given. *rē'šît darkô* means "first fruit," "firstborn," "at the beginning of his way," or "principle," "model," depending on the verbal sense of *qnh* (cf. W. Irwin, *JBL* 80 [1961] 140; G. Yee, *ZAW* 94 [1982] 58-66). **23.** *I was poured forth:* As an image of birth, cf. Job 10:10. **27-30.** Wisdom witnessed the creation and came to know its secrets. **30.** *'āmôn:* Either "craftsperson" (reading *'ommān*), or "little child," "ward" (*'āmûn*). The latter fits the birth imagery of vv 24-25. The sense of artisan is found in the principal ancient versions and in Wis 7:22-8:1. **32-36.** Final exhortation, including two beatitudes, vv 32b and 34a.

35   (D) **Invitations to the Banquets** (9:1-18). Wisdom and Folly each invite the "simple" to a banquet. Thus, the prologue is open-ended and leads into chaps. 10ff., which illustrate what each choice represents. The two invitations (vv 1-6 and 13-18) bracket a section of miscellaneous sayings (vv 7-12).

(a) INVITATION TO THE BANQUET OF WISDOM (9:1-6). **1.** The house symbolizes the school over which Wisdom presides, the banquet her teaching (Lang, *Wisdom* 90-96). The house is also the world with its pillars (cf. Job 26:11), at whose construction Wisdom was present (8:27-30) and within which she delights to live (8:31).

36   (b) INTERLUDE: SIX PROVERBS (9:7-12). **7-9.** These verses contrast the scoffer with the wise on the basis of teachability. The scoffer was addressed by Wisdom in 1:22b; but now, instead of being threatened and warned, he is left to his folly. **10.** The opening theme (1:7) is recalled. **11.** Wisdom speaks for herself; this verse is placed after 9:6 in *NAB*. **12.** In the choice between Wisdom and Folly, one is responsible for one's own fate.

37   (c) INVITATION TO THE BANQUET OF FOLLY (9:13-18). **13.** *woman of foolishness:* Folly is explicitly personified here. The phrase contrasts with the "woman of worth" of 31:10. **14-15.** Folly also takes her stance in public places, appealing to all. *high places:* Cf. 8:2; 9:3. **16.** Folly uses Wisdom's words (v 4), mocking her; but this also underscores the need for discernment to distinguish the very similar and enticing calls. Folly can appear to be good—at first! **17.** Folly's food is only bread and water—and stolen as well! The enticement to fast riches and an easy life (cf. 1:10-19) is a tempting contrast to the long discipline of Wisdom. **18.** The choice between Wisdom and Folly is a choice between life (v 6) and death (cf. Deut 30:15).

38   (II) **The Major Collections of Proverbs** (10:1-29:27). The collections are distinguished by the titles that appear at the head of each (10:1; 22:17; 24:23; 25:1; 30:1; 31:1).

(A) **First Solomonic Collection of Proverbs** (10:1-22:16). This is the longest collection in the book: 375 proverbs. Chapters 10-15 are marked almost exclusively by the presence of antithetic parallelism. With 16:1ff., however, the format becomes largely synonymous and synthetic parallelism. **10:1.** The antithesis between the wise and foolish son echoes major themes of the prologue. **6.** The word "blessing" links this saying with the following. How v 6b (identical to 11b) parallels v 6a is problematic; the *NAB* substitutes v 13b here. **10b.** The MT repeats v 8b here, possibly in a comparative sense: a sly wink can be less destructive than foolish speech (cf. v 18). The *NAB* and others follow the LXX, which is antithetic. **12.** Linked to v 11 by the verb *ksh,* "conceal," "cover" (cf. 1 Pet 4:8; Jas 5:20). **13.** The exact connection between the cola is not clear. The *NAB* puts v 13b (nearly identical with 26:3b) with v 6a, and reads v 11b here. **18–21.** About the proper and improper use of speech. "Lips" appear in each saying except v 20, which uses "tongue." **18.** Not antithetic; possibly comparative: spreading slander is worse than concealing hatred. **27–32.** Sayings highlighting the contrast between the "just" and the "wicked" (v 29, the "blameless" and "evildoers").

39   **11:1.** Justice in business dealings (cf. 11:15,26; 16:11; 17:18; 20:10) is a common theme. **3–11.** Variations on the antithesis between the righteous and the wicked. **3,5–6.** A similar theme is in all these sayings: Virtue is its own reward; vice its own punishment. **4.** *day of wrath:* Any kind of adversity, such as premature death. **7.** The MT can be synonymous, associating the wicked with their presumptuous reliance on riches. The LXX translates antithetically, reading "just one" in the first colon and "wicked" in the second. **10–11.** The city powerfully dramatizes the power that personal malice or good will can have on a community. **16.** It is uncertain whether the proverb is antithetic. **17–31.** Generally concerned with the theme of retribution. **24–25.** The paradox inherent in generosity. **31.** The certainty of divine retribution; quoted according to the LXX in 1 Pet 4:18.

40   **12:4.** *a woman of worth:* Described fully in 31:10–31. *rot in his bones:* Cf. 3:8b. **6.** *words . . . lie in wait:* A forceful use of metonymy dramatizing the awesome potential of human speech for destroying others. **12a.** The MT is uncertain and the versions offer various interpretations. **13–23.** Sayings generally concerned with the effects of speech. **23.** *conceals knowledge:* Not a question of deception, but of prudence and reserve in speech (cf. 10:19; 11:12–13; 21:23). **26a.** The MT is uncertain; the versions offer differing solutions. **27.** The meaning of the vb. in v 27a is uncertain, as is the exact sense of v 27b. The antithesis seems to be between examples of industry and sloth.

41   **13:2.** *nepeš:* Links this and the next two verses, with the meanings "appetite," "desire" (vv 2 and 4) and "life" (v 3). **8.** The poor, with no resources to be extorted, cannot be threatened. **13–14.** Docility to authoritative instruction is urged. **19.** The precise relationship between the two cola is obscure. **22.** Wealth (and the power to dispose of it) is a sign of blessing; sinners lose both (cf. 28:8; Job 27:16–17; Sir 14:4). **24.** The saying urges its point through paradox: leniency is hatred, whereas discipline is love.

42   **14:1.** The antithesis between Wisdom and Folly, the house-building motif, and the feminine imagery evoke chap. 9. The blurring of Wisdom's identity in the unusual phrase *ḥakmôt nāšîm,* "the wisest women," or "the wisdom of women," if textually correct, may hint at the woman in 31:10–31, who also builds her house (cf. 24:3–4; C. Camp, *Wisdom and the Feminine* 192). **3.** *branch of pride:* So MT. The fool's words issue from an arrogance that will hurt him. **5.** Verse 5b appears in 6:19a; other phrases of this saying appear in 12:17; 14:25; and 19:5,9, suggesting the artificial nature of some of these proverbs. **7b.** The MT is difficult. It either refers to the fool directly or it contrasts in some way with v 7a. **15–17.** Examples of the contrast between

rash behavior and caution, restraint. **19.** An optimistic view of the doctrine of retribution. **26–27.** Two sayings about fear of the Lord. Synonymous parallelism is relatively more frequent from this point on and there is evidence for editorial work from here to 16:15 (cf. Skehan, *SPIW* 18–20). **31.** Respect for the creator is indicated by our treatment of fellow creatures (cf. Mal 2:10; Job 31:13–15).

43   **15:1–2,4.** The quality and manner of one's speech are part of its power and can have profound effects. **5,31–32.** The need for discipline and correction on the path to wisdom. Oxymoron highlights this (esp. in vv 5 and 32). **8–9.** Two sayings, linked by the key phrase "abomination to the Lord." Interior dispositions can determine the acceptability of worship and life-style. **11.** Cf. 1:12 (→ 18 above); Ps 139:8; Job 26:6. **13.** Cf. 3:8b (→ 23 above); but also 14:13. **16–17.** A telling comment on the price often paid for riches; parallel in *Amenemope* (6.9.5–8; *ANET* 422b). **19.** The contrast of the "lazy person" with the "upright" (rather than with the "diligent," as might be expected) suggests something about the very nature of this sloth. A fuller picture is drawn in 24:30–34. **22.** Cf. 11:14. **23.** Knowing what and when to speak is an important part of wisdom. **24.** *upward, below:* These alternatives, evoking the theme of the "two ways" (with affinity to Deut 28:13–14), are in relation to sheol alone and do not express a belief in the afterlife. **25.** The prophetic view is less sanguine (cf. Amos 2:6–7; Mic 2:2; Isa 1:16–17). **33.** "Fear of the Lord," elsewhere "the beginning of wisdom" (1:7; 9:10), is now the "discipline" or "instruction" (*mûsār*) for wisdom.

44   Chapter 16 opens with a series of sayings about the Lord (vv 1–7,9,11) and the king (vv 10,12–15), the longest successive grouping of such themes so far. It is the central section of this Solomonic collection (10:1–22:16) and gives evidence of heavy editing (see Skehan, *SIPW* 17–20). **16:1,9.** Human wisdom is limited in scope and must ultimately submit to God, who alone can bring successful and even unimagined results. Similar sentiments are found in *Amenemope* (18.19.16–17; 20.5–6; *ANET* 423b–424a) and Ahiqar (8.115; *ANET* 429a). **2.** Only God can plumb the depths of the human heart (cf. 21:2). **3.** The first clear example of a command among the sayings. The successful outcome of plans depends on trust in God. **4.** *day of evil:* Cf. 11:4. This is the middle proverb of the 375 in the Solomonic collection. **8.** Cf. 15:16. Wealth itself is not condemned, but wealth achieved at the price of injustice. **10,12–15.** The character of an ideal king is sketched. The king's decisions share divine authority (v 10), but his rule is secure only when justice is upheld throughout the kingdom (v 12). **13–15.** Practical advice about winning the king's favor. **16–33.** The remaining proverbs in chap. 16 are about wise conduct for all. **17.** A good example of the use of juxtaposition (→ 9 above) and sound patterns; v 17b recalls 13:3a. **21,23–24.** Only wise and prudent speech is effective and even salubrious (v 24). **25.** Identical to 14:12. **27–30.** In contrast to vv 21–24, evil speech brings discord, disunity, and violence. **30.** Cf. 6:13–14. **32.** Anger and passion are the enemies of wisdom; self-control is essential for ruling others. **33.** The casting of lots is under divine control.

45   **17:1.** See comment on 15:16–17. **2.** The domestic order established by blood rights can be reversed by intelligence and industry. The proper family relationships are illustrated in v 6, but vv 21 and 25 repeat the theme of the shameful son who destroys the family harmony. **3.** A tightly constructed comparison (→ 9 above). The two metaphors, repeated in 27:21a, express the exacting nature of the Lord's testing. **4,5,**

11,27. Descriptive of those who threaten the social order, esp. by the power of speech. Verse 27 portrays the opposite type of personality whose careful use of speech manifests wisdom. A variant of v 5 is found at 14:31. **7,15,26.** The political order is threatened by those who are unfit for their roles (v 7), or act improperly (v 26), and by flagrant injustice (v 15). **8,23.** Practical wisdom recognizes that a bribe can be useful for effecting results (v 8), but its potential for perverting justice brings condemnation (v 23). **12.** Ironic hyperbole dramatizes this comparison. The fool is prominent in several sayings of this chap. (vv 10,16,21,24,25). **17.** If the parallelism is synonymous, v 17b is a particular instance of v 17a; if the cola are antithetic, the saying is distinguishing a blood relationship from friendship. **19b.** The meaning of the image is unclear. **22.** See comment on 3:8. **28.** The ambiguity of silence (cf. v 27).

46 Concern for the proper use of speech is a major theme in chap. 18 (cf. vv 4,6-8,13,20-21). **2.** The fool simply wants to hear himself talk. **4.** If the cola are synonymous, "deep waters" imply profundity and wisdom in speech; if they are antithetic, the image refers to words that are obscure and difficult to comprehend. **8.** Gossip, like food, is eagerly devoured and becomes part of the person who receives it. **10-11.** The very juxtaposition of the otherwise neutral statement in v 11 with v 10 suggests a contrast between the righteous and the rich, whose sources of protection are quite different. **16.** The same pragmatic attitude as in 17:8. **19.** The MT is difficult; the general sense is that quarrels create impenetrable barriers.

47 **19:1.** The contrast here is between the upright but poor individual and the lying fool (cf. v 22); see 28:6. **2.** *zeal:* The *nepeš* goes astray without the knowledge to guide it, as the example in v 2b illustrates. **4,6-7.** Wealth breeds greed, and poverty disloyalty. **5,9.** These sayings differ only in the verbal phrase used in the second colon of each. See comment on 14:5. **7c.** The MT is unintelligible. **12a.** Cf. 20:2a. **13-14.** Scattered throughout the sayings are references to domestic problems. The "foolish son" is one recurrent theme (10:1; 15:20; 17:25; 19:26; 20:20; 23:22; 28:24; 29:15). Another is the "worthy" (12:4a; 18:22) or "contentious" (12:4b; 21:9,19; 25:24; 27:15) wife. These themes, which echo the invitation to Wisdom's house (9:1-6), are all drawn together in the final, summarizing scene of domestic tranquillity (31:10-31). **15.** The slothful person, often caricatured (19:24; 22:13; 24:30-34; 26:13-15), is the direct antithesis of the diligence required by wisdom and exemplified by the wife of chap. 31. **16.** *commandment, word:* Authoritative instruction of a wisdom teacher (not the Mosaic law; cf. 13:13). **18b.** Indulging the child with no discipline could lead to disaster; cf. 13:24. **22.** The MT is uncertain.

48 **20:1.** The point is emphasized by the personification of "wine" and "strong drink." **5.** On "deep waters," see comment on 18:4. **6.** Virtue is tested by its fidelity. **8,26.** *winnows:* Metaphor for the king's role as judge, carefully scrutinizing all claims. *wheel:* Most likely an instrument for threshing that symbolizes the king's powers of judgment. **9.** The limits of human wisdom apply even to judgments about personal moral probity; cf. 16:2. **12.** The moral is that the Lord who made eye and ear is wiser and more perceptive than his own creatures. **14.** Reflects bargaining rituals where the buyer pretends he is losing on the deal. **16.** Advice (repeated at 27:13) reflecting a dim view of giving security for a loan. **19.** Lack of restraint in speech can destroy trust and confidentiality. **20.** *his lamp will go out:* A full and prosperous life will be denied him. **22,24.** Encourage trust in God. **25.** Another example of rash

speech; cf. v 19. **27.** The power to know oneself and articulate it is to share in the Lord's spirit.

49 **21:1.** The themes of 16:1,9 are applied to the king. **3.** Not a rejection of sacrifice, but an assertion of its proper relationship to morality; cf. v 27; 15:8. **7.** The wicked are ultimately caught in their own snares; cf. 1:18-19; 12:13a. **9,19.** Cf. 25:24 and comment on 19:13-14. **11.** Cf. 19:25. **12a.** *just one:* May refer to God, who would bring on the ruin (v 12b). **13b.** The consequences of a merciless attitude (see v 7 and Sir 4:1-6; Jas 2:13). **14.** The pragmatism of 17:8 and 18:16 again. **16.** The "wanderer's" ways lead to death, possibly premature death; see comment on 15:24. **18.** May simply mean that the wicked, and not the just, bear the brunt of this world's evils. **22.** Wisdom is mightier than brute strength; cf. 16:32; 24:5. **28.** The liar contrasted with the thoughtful listener, who will always be heeded; cf. 19:5,9.

50 **22:1.** Good name and reputation alone assure one of remembrance after death; cf. 10:7. **2.** Our common bond as creatures of God supersedes all distinctions. **5-6.** The two ways; training in wisdom helps one stay on the right way. **7.** Warnings about the power of money; cf. vv 26-27 and 6:1-5. **8-9.** One reaps what one sows. **11.** Translation uncertain; probably lists qualities ("pure heart," "gracious speech") which attract the king's attention. **12.** *the eyes of the Lord:* God's providence vindicates truth and destroys lies; cf. 15:3. **14.** Once ensnared by seductive speech ("mouth"), it is almost impossible to escape the woman's grasp ("deep pit," a possible allusion to sheol); cf. 5:3-6; 7:10-23. **16.** The MT is ambiguous; possibly an oxymoron: the amassing of wealth leads to poverty; cf. 11:24; 28:8.

51 **(B) Sayings of the Wise (22:17-24:22).** The beginning of a second collection of proverbs. It is unique because of its affinity to the Egyptian *Instruction of Amenemope,* generally dated to the Ramesside period (→ 3 above; Wisdom Lit., 27:23; *ANET* 421-25). The latter's division into 30 chapters is presumably imitated by Proverbs (22:20), but efforts to delimit 30 units therein have not been consistent. Ties to the Egyptian work are readily seen on the level of thematic correspondence between individual sayings. Although a dependence upon Amenemope is generally accepted, 22:17-24:22 is independent in its choice, editing, and organization of material. It is formally constructed as a series of commands, prohibitions, and sayings of varying lengths, with the frequent addition of motive clauses. The setting is that of chaps. 1-9: a teacher/sage tells a student how to live wisely.

52 **22:17-21.** Characteristic introductory exhortation; cf. *Amenemope* 1.3.9-11 (*ANET* 421b). The MT has the presumed title for this section, "The words of the wise," in the middle of v 17. **19.** The purpose is given here and in v 21. Verse 19b is uncertain; the NAB reads "the words of Amenemope." **20.** Cf. *Amenemope* 30.27.7-8 (*ANET* 424b). **22-23.** Cf. *Amenemope* 2.4.4-5 (*ANET* 422a). *at the gate:* See comment on 1:20-21. A legal move to cheat the poor is presumed. **24-25.** Cf. *Amenemope* 9.11.13-14; 13.8-9 (*ANET* 423a). An allusion to the theme of the "ways." **26-27.** No parallel in *Amenemope.* **28.** Cf. 23:10; *Amenemope* 6.7.12-13 (*ANET* 422b). **29.** The courtier, described in *Amenemope* 30.27.16-17 (*ANET* 424b).

53 **23:1-3.** Diplomatic etiquette—another practical aspect of wisdom. Cf. *Amenemope* 23.23.13-18 (*ANET* 424a); also Ptahhotep (*ANET* 412b). **4-5.** Wording close to *Amenemope* 7.9.10,14; 10.4-5. **6-8.** The meal of the "stingy person" (lit., a person "of evil eye") is a metaphor for evil plans carried out under the guise of friendship; cf. *Amenemope* 11.14.5-10,17-18 (*ANET* 423a). **9.** Concerned about the fool, while the supposed parallel in *Amenemope* (21.22.11-12 [*ANET* 424a]) is really about the garrulous person. **10.** Cf. 22:28. **11.** A distinctly Israelite assertion. Parallels to *Amenemope* end here; some sayings still echo Ahiqar (→ 3 above; Wisdom Lit., 27:32). **12.** Standard introduction for an instruction—does a new section begin here? **13-14.** Cf. 19:18; Ahiqar 81-82 (*ANET* 428b). **19-21.** Gluttony, drunkenness, and sloth prevent one from functioning properly in society and so are opposed to wisdom. **22.** The topics from here to 24:2 echo chaps. 1-9 and 31: warnings against the harlot (vv 26-28), strong drink (vv 29- 35) and violent men (24:1-2). The house-building imagery in 24:3-4 also recalls Wisdom's invitation in 9:1-6, and foreshadows the wife's house in 31:10-31. The section may be a "bridge" linking themes developed at the beginning and end of the book (cf. Camp, *Wisdom and the Feminine* 198-202). **29-35.** This portrayal begins with riddlelike questions that serve as motives for the central prohibition (v 31); the vividly described consequences of drink (vv 32-35) are further motivation.

54   **24:5-6.** Cf. 11:14, 21:22. **10.** Meaning uncertain. **11-12.** Presumably describes an innocent person condemned to death. Such a situation is ignored by the wise person to his own peril. **15-16.** The righteous always recover from the evils they endure; the wicked are destroyed by the evils they create. **17-18.** This unusual prohibition may be a way of recognizing that victory and judgment belong to God alone.

55   **(C) Other Sayings of the Wise (24:23-34).** Possibly an appendix to the previous collection; consists only of sayings. Two themes prevail: honesty in speech (vv 23b-26,28-29) and the value of work (vv 27,30-34). The LXX inserts 30:1-14 between this collection and the previous. **24:23a.** The title reads literally, "These also belong to the wise," alluding probably to the title in 22:17. **23b-25.** Verses 24-25, which deal with judges, serve as illustration for v 23b (repeated in 28:21a; cf. also 18:5). **26.** Candor and honesty are signs of real friendship. **27.** Prudence in saving resources for building a house or raising a family is urged. **29.** Cf. 20:22. **30-34.** This comically drawn example of the slothful person concludes with the same two lines as the warning in 6:6-11.

56   **(D) Second Solomonic Collection of Proverbs (25:1-29:27).** The title's reference (v 1) to Hezekiah is historically questionable if the king's name is used only for its numerical value (Skehan, *SIPW* 44). The literary form is the individual saying. Chapters 25-27, rather distinct from the last two chapters, have a mixture of commands, prohibitions, and comparisons (about two-thirds of the sayings). Some sayings are several lines long (25:6-7,9-10,21-22; 26:18-19; 27:15-16,23-27). Images from nature abound; considerable attention is paid to the fool and the proper use of speech. In chaps. 28-29, the couplet format prevails again, along with antithetic parallelism; religious and moral concerns are more pronounced. U. Skladny (*Spruchsammlungen* 58-62) and B. Malchow (*CBQ* 47 [1985] 238- 45) describe chaps. 28-29 as part of a collection for training future kings. In the LXX this section comes after 30:15-31:9.

57   **25:2-27.** G. E. Bryce (*JBL* 91 [1972] 145-57) describes this as a literary unit modeled on Egyptian instructions for king and subject. **2-3.** The superior wisdom necessary for kings is placed in proper relationship to God's wisdom and human knowledge. **4-5.** An implicit comparison. **6-7.** Cf. Luke 14:7-11. **8-10.** Against rash and hasty words. **11-14.** Illustrations of the proper and improper use of words. **16-17,21-22,27-28.** About moderation and self-control; vv 16 and 27, both

about eating honey, may form an *inclusio*. **20.** The MT is difficult. **24.** See comment on 21:9. **27b.** The MT is uncertain.

58   Chapter 26 has three topics: the fool (vv 1,3-12), the lazy person (vv 13-16), and the misuse of speech (vv 17-26,28). **26:3.** A priamel (→ 9 above). **4-5.** Antinomy (juxtaposition of contraries) indicates that each verse contains an aspect of the truth. **7,9.** Wisdom is useless to the fool. **10.** The MT is uncertain; transls. are conjectures. **13.** Cf. 22:13. **15.** Cf. 19:24. **17-19.** The meddler. **20-22.** The talebearer. **23-26,28.** The liar and deceiver.

59   **27:1.** Cf. Sir 11:18-19; Luke 12:16-21; Jas 4:13-16. **3.** Cf. Ahiqar 8.111 (*ANET* 429a). **5-6.** The value of sincere correction. **7.** Cf. Ahiqar 12.188 (*ANET* 430). **9b.** Uncertain. **10.** Three examples giving advice on friendship; a friend can be more loyal than a blood relative. **12.** Cf. 22:3. **13.** Cf. 20:16. **14.** An oxymoron. The greeting is really a curse; and the very length of this saying seems to mock the pretentious greeting. **19.** As water reflects the face, so the mind reflects the person. **20.** A riddlelike saying characterizing insatiable human appetite; cf. 30:15-16. **21.** Another version in 17:3. **23-27.** Similar to 24:30-34 or Isa 28:23-29; about the prudent use of resources.

60   **28:4,7,9.** "Law" here is "instruction" (v 7), with a deep religious sense (v 9), not exclusively the Mosaic law. **5.** To "seek the Lord" is to learn his will as the basis for justice and morality. **6.** Poverty is not commended, but it is better than loss of integrity; cf. 16:8; 19:1. **8.** The greed and injustice associated with wealth are condemned; cf. vv 20,22. **10.** The evil results of his deed will overtake the perpetrator; cf. v 18; 26:27. Verse 10c may be a gloss. **12,28.** The societal effects of evil or good; cf. 29:2,16. **13.** Cf. Ps 32:3-5. **19.** The verb repetition is ironic: poverty fills nothing! A variant at 12:11. **25-26.** True wisdom is not total self-reliance.

61   Many of the themes of chaps. 1-9,10-22 reappear in chap. 29. **29:7.** The practice of justice and mercy is constitutive of wisdom. **8.** See comment on 11:10-11. **11,22.** Cf. 14:17. **12.** There will always be those willing to serve the base instincts of superiors. **13,26.** All are equal before the Lord. "Light to the eyes" is a symbol for life; cf. Ps 13:4. **14.** See comment on 16:10,12. **15,17,19,21.** The need for discipline, even of the physical kind, is wise training. **25.** The only proper fear is fear of the Lord.

62   **(III) Smaller Collections of Proverbs (30:1-31:9).** These two chapters have varied material which recall major themes.

(A) Sayings of Agur (30:1-14). It is uncertain where Agur's words end. Verses 1-4 appear to be a riddle (v 4). **30:1a.** The title indicates a non-Israelite provenance (Massa is a north Arabian place-name; Agur and Jakeh are otherwise unknown). However, literary artifice may be operative: Agur ("I am a sojourner") could mean Jacob/Israel (Gen 47:9), while Jakeh could be an acronym for "Yahweh, blessed is he"; Massa can also mean "oracle" (Skehan, *SIPW* 15, 42-43). **1b.** *lĕ'îtî'ēl . . . wĕ'ukāl:* The interpretation is problematic. The first word is a palindrome (possibly Aramaic) with meanings, "There is no God," or "I am not God" (C. C. Torrey, *JBL* 73 [1954] 95-96). A contrast between human knowledge and the hidden wisdom of God seems intended; cf. vv 2-4. **2-3.** Ironic: The speaker has not the same assurance about divine knowledge that others appear to have. **4.** Questions reminiscent of Job (26:8; 38:4ff.) and Isa (40:12-18), emphasizing God's transcendence. Verse 4c poses the riddle; "his name" = Yahweh, and "his son's name" = Israel (Exod 4:22; Deut 32:19; cf. Skehan, *SIPW* 42-43). **5-6.** Cf. Ps 18:31

(2 Sam 22:31); Deut 4:2; 13:1. As opposed to mere human knowledge about God (vv 1–4), only the knowledge that comes from God can be relied on. **7–9.** A prayer in the form of a numerical saying. The wise seek only truth and a sufficiency for livelihood. **11–14.** In antithesis to vv 7–9, these verses give four examples of wicked people. This, too, could be a numerical saying whose opening line has dropped out.

63   (B) Numerical Proverbs (30:15–33). The first clear examples of this genre begin here. **15–16.** A saying (v 15a) followed by a numerical proverb (v 15b); about insatiable desire. **17.** Recalls v 11. The ultimate disgrace is to be left unburied. **18–19.** Three natural phenomena highlight the mystery of human love. **20.** The matter-of-fact and nonchalant manner of the adulteress contrasts with the sense of wonder in v 19. **21–23.** Intolerable people presented in comic satire (v 21, hyperbole). **24–28.** Insignificant but clever creatures; a contrast to the arrogance of 21–23? **29–31.** Four regal figures. The MT of v 31 is difficult, containing several obscure words. **32–33.** A final warning about misconduct.

64   (C) Sayings of Lemuel (31:1–9). An instruction, unusual in being attributed to a king's mother (cf. 1:8b = 6:20b). The preparation of future rulers for their duties was often a concern of wisdom literature (cf. *Merikare* and *Amenemhet, ANET* 414–19). **1.** The name "Lemuel, king of Massa" indicates a non-Israelite origin for the instruction (cf. 30:1a); but possibly the name is fictitious. **2.** The repetition of "what" may be equivalent to "Listen!" **3–7.** Warnings against loose women and drink, reminiscent of chaps. 1–9. **8–9.** Asserts the royal duty to implement justice; cf. 16:10–15.

65   (IV) Acrostic Poem on the Good Wife (31:10–31). An alphabetic acrostic (each verse begins with a successive letter of the Hebr alphabet) echoes major themes of the book. This portrait completes the feminine imagery found throughout the book, possibly forming an interpretative framework for the whole (→ 10 above; see comment on 19:13–14; Camp, *Wisdom and the Feminine* 186–208; T. McCreesh, *RB* 92 [1985] 25–46). The wife is an everyday, practical, and domestic counterpart to the exalted, didactic, and public figure of Wisdom presented in chaps. 1–9. Indeed, she may represent Wisdom finally settled down in her house and serving those who have accepted her invitation. **10.** A rhetorical question which emphasizes the incomparable value of this woman. Wisdom is compared to jewels in 3:15; 8:11,19; 16:16; 20:15. **11–12.** The woman's value to her husband is reminiscent of Wisdom's value to her followers (cf. 3:13–18; 4:6,8–9). **13–27.** The poem focuses on the woman's extraordinary and ceaseless activity. **14,16,24.** Emphasize her commercial dealings. **15.** Cf. 9:1–3. **21–23.** Allusions to wealth and nobility. **25b.** Cf. 1:26. **27.** *she looks to:* Hebr ṣôpiyyâ is a hymnic participle and a play on the Gk word for wisdom, *sophia* (A. Wolters, *JBL* 104 [1985] 577–87). **28.** Cf. 27:2. **30b.** This could be interpreted, "The woman, the fear of the Lord, she is to be praised." The book ends on the same theme with which it began (1:7): the fear of the Lord.

29

CANTICLE OF CANTICLES

Roland E. Murphy, O.Carm.

BIBLIOGRAPHY

1   Bea, A., *Canticum Canticorum* (Rome, 1953). Buzy, D., *Le Cantique des Cantiques* (Paris, 1949). Gerleman, G., *Das Hohe Lied* (BKAT 18; Neukirchen, 1963). Gordis, R., *The Song of Songs* (NY, 1954). Joüon, P., *Le Cantique des Cantiques* (Paris, 1909). Keel, O., *Das Hohelied* (ZBK AT 18; Zurich, 1986). Krinetzki, L., *Das Hohe Lied* (Düsseldorf, 1964). Krinetzki, G. (= L.), *Hoheslied* (NEchtB; Würzburg, 1980). Loretz, O., *Das althebräische Liebeslied* (AOAT 14/1; Neukirchen, 1971). Lys, D., *Le plus beau chant de la creation* (LD 51; Paris, 1968). Meek, T., *The Song of Songs* (IB; NY, 1956). Murphy, R. E., *Song of Songs* (Herm; Phl, forthcoming). Pope, M., *Song of Songs* (AB 7C; GC, 1977). Robert, A., *Le Cantique de Cantiques* (EBib; Paris, 1963). Rudolph, W., *Das Hohe Lied* (KAT; Gütersloh, 1962). Würthwein, E., *Das Hohelied* (HAT 18; Tübingen, 1969).

Extrabiblical parallels: Egypt: Texts in *LAEg* 296–325; *AEL* 2. 181–93. Fox, M., *The Song of Songs and the Ancient Egyptian Love Songs* (Madison, 1985). Schott, S., *Altägyptische Liebeslieder* (Zurich, 1950). White, J. B., *A Study of the Language of Love in the Song of Songs and Ancient Egyptian Poetry* (SBLDS 38; Missoula, 1978). Mesopotamia: Texts in *ANET* 637–45; Kramer, S. N., *The Sacred Marriage Rite* (Bloomington, 1969). See also the commentary of M. Pope, *passim;* and that of A. Robert with the excursus by R. Tournay, pp. 339–426.

History of Interpretation: Ohly, F., *Hohelied Studien* (Wiesbaden, 1938). Scheper, G. L., "The Spiritual Marriage" (diss., Princeton, 1971). See also the summaries in C. D. Ginsburg, *The Song of Songs* (Ktav reprint; NY, 1970) 20–102; and M. Pope, *Song* 89–288.

INTRODUCTION

2   **(I) Title and Date.**   The title in 1:1 ("Song of Songs"; Vg, "Canticle of Canticles") is the Hebr idiom for the superlative, "the greatest song." It imposes a unity on a collection of songs or poems. The unity is further indicated by the ascription to Solomon as author, perhaps because of the appearance of his name in 3:7ff. and 8:11ff. There are no convincing arguments for the date (see Pope, *Song* 22–33). Although common opinion gives a postexilic date, individual poems might have been composed much earlier. Despite some opposition, Cant was acknowledged early on as canonical by both Jews and Christians. It became one of the five Megilloth, or scrolls, chosen for public reading at the Passover.

3   **(II) Structure, Unity, and Forms.**   There is no agreement concerning the structure or even the number of poetic units within Cant. It has been portrayed as a drama with two main characters (Solomon and the Shulammite), or even three (Solomon attempts to woo the Shulammite from her rustic lover), but this view has been largely rejected as arbitrary. The work is dramatic in the sense that there is dialogue between the following speakers: a woman, a man, and the Daughters of Jerusalem. The gender differences are clearly indicated in the Hebr text, and some modern translations (*NAB, NEB*) offer marginal identifications with a fair amount

of certainty. The main speaker is the woman; the man appears as both shepherd (1:7) and king (1:4,12), by a fiction common in literature.

4   Cant has the appearance of a collection of love poems, but these are not without some signs of unity. There are several refrains (e.g., 2:7; 3:5; 8:4; 2:6; 8:3); very many words and phrases are repeated, and the same themes consistently appear. On the other hand, there are sudden shifts in dialogue (2:13–15; 3:5–6) and scene (5:1–2) that are hard to explain. This commentary will adopt a dialogical structure, associating the poems by means of dialogue as a thread of unity (R. E. Murphy in *CBQ* 39 [1977] 482–96; for a contrast, see the structural analysis of J. C. Exum in *ZAW* 85 [1973] 47–79).

5   Several literary forms appear: poems of yearning (1:2–4; 2:14–15), teasing (1:7–8; 2:15), admiration (1:15–2:3; 4:9–5:1; 6:4–7), reminiscence (2:8–13), boast (6:8–10), and description of physical charms (the so-called *wasf*, 4:1–7; 5:10–16; 7:1–6). Similar forms appear in the love songs of ancient Egypt. Although these poems are monologue and not dialogue, they have many parallels to Cant, such as the use of the term "sister" to designate the woman (Cant 4:9–12). They also contain several themes common to Cant and to all love literature: lovesickness, the name, obstacles to love, uniqueness, etc.

6 (III) Interpretation. Remarkably, both synagogue and church agree on a religious interpretation: Cant refers to the love of the Lord for his people or, for Christians, to the love of Christ for the church (or the individual soul). This view was supported by the theme of the marriage between the Lord and Israel (Hos 1–3; Isa 62:5, etc.). Hence the targum treated the song as an allegory on the history of Israel, from the exodus on. For Christians, Origen set the pattern for allegory in his works (see R. E. Murphy in *CBQ* 43 [1981] 505–16).

The basic insight of the traditional interpretation has much to recommend it. Human love is not to be viewed apart from divine love, as the biblical symbolism of marriage indicates. But the allegorical method, whereby the details in the poem are each given a transferred meaning, cannot be recommended. Cant was not written as an allegory. In the literal historical sense it refers to love between humans. When the details are transposed to another level, the door is open to fanciful interpretations which disfigure the original insight. The language of love, whether human or divine, is too delicate for that.

7 In modern times a cultic theory has been proposed. Literary and thematic contacts between Cant and the sacred marriage songs of the Tammuz-Ishtar ritual (cf. S. N. Kramer; T. Meek) have led to the claim that the poems were originally used in pagan cult, and then later passed into Israel's tradition. Such a reconstruction calls for more evidence than similar language and themes shared by Cant and cultic poems. The language of love cuts both ways; the marriages of the gods must ultimately be described in terms of the human experience of love, and vice versa the imagery of the cult can influence human expression. The cultic theory does not really interpret Cant; instead it reconstructs a prehistory.

8 Current scholarly opinion holds that the literal sense of Cant is the expression of human sexual love. Whatever be the differences of opinion concerning the number of characters, or the structure, or dramatic nature of the work, there is a wide consensus on this point. It seems to be the obvious meaning of the language. However, one would not want to argue that the literal historical sense exhausts the meaning of Cant. Modern hermeneutical theory recognizes that any text has an afterlife, that it acquires meaning as it lives on in the community that treasures it. This does not mean a revival of the allegorical approach. Rather, it recognizes another dimension to human love—it shares somehow in divine love. As Cant 8:6 puts it, human love is "the flame of Yah(weh)."

9 (IV) Literary Style. Cant manifests unusual literary qualities. One easily recognizes the pleasant profusion of images drawn from the atmosphere of the fields: gazelles and hinds, doves and foxes, sheep and goats. The gifts of nature abound: wine and vineyard, cedars and cypresses, figs and pomegranates. The imagery is drawn from many worlds. Not only places but also persons become transfigured. There is a "make-believe" character about love, an idealization that knows no bounds when lovers speak about each other. Hence, one hears of a "tower of ivory" (7:5) and of lips that drip choice myrrh (5:13). The modern reader has to adjust somewhat to the imagery because it is both representative and evocative, as the comparison of the woman's hair to a flock of goats streaming down Mt. Gilead. The poetry and images are present not for the sake of analysis, but for the enjoyment of imagination. Love has created a world of its own (cf. M. Fox, *JBL* 102 [1983] 219–28; O. Keel, *Deine Blicke sind Tauben: Zur Metaphorik des Hohen Liedes* [SBS 114/115; Stuttgart, 1984]).

10 (V) Theological Importance. The traditional Christian interpretation of Cant arose from a christocentric understanding of the OT. However valid, it is not the only approach to the OT, and it needs also to be broadened by hearing the text on its historical level. Israel resisted the divinization of sexuality characteristic of the ancient Near East. The Lord had no female consort. Human sexual love was seen as intrinsically good; it could even be a symbol of divine love. Cant presents us with a biblical model of human intimacy (see R. E. Murphy, *Concilium* 121/141 [1979] 61–65). The mutuality and fidelity between lovers, the sensuousness of their relationship, their devotion to each other, clearly emerge from Cant. It is widely held that the sages of Israel are responsible for its preservation and transmission (cf. B. Childs, *CIOTS* 574–79) because they recognized a sound expression of the values of human love (cf. Prov 5:18; 18:22). Christianity can be grateful for this insight, esp. in the light of some early gnostic doctrines. The traditional interpretation provides another level of meaning, but not a halo, to a work that is a true commentary on Gen 1–2 (cf. O. Loretz, *BZ* 10 [1966] 29–43).

11 (VI) Outline. Since there is no discernible structure (→ 3), the course of the dialogue serves as the basis of this outline.

(I) Superscription (1:1)
(II) Introduction (1:2–6)
(III) Dialogue between Lovers (1:7–2:7)
(IV) Reminiscence (2:8–17)
(V) Loss and Discovery (3:1–5)
(VI) Solomon's Wedding Procession (3:6–11)
(VII) Dialogue between Lovers (4:1–5:1)
(VIII) Dialogue between the Woman and the Daughters (5:2–6:3)
(IX) Dialogue between Lovers (6:4–12)
(X) A Dialogue (7:1–8:4)
(XI) Appendixes (8:5–14)

COMMENTARY

12 (I) Superscription (1:1). → 2 above.

(II) Introduction (1:2–6). 2. The woman expresses her yearning for the kisses of her beloved, who is addressed in both 3d and 2d pers., although he may be present only in desire. The intoxicating effect of love (1:2,4; 4:10) and the power of the name (v 3) are common themes in love poetry. **4.** The idealization of the man as king is a literary fiction, exalting him in the "make-believe" world of love. The pl. pronouns associate the "maidens" (v 3) in her praise of the man. **6.** *Daughters of Jerusalem:* These serve as a foil throughout the work so that the woman can develop the theme of love (cf. 2:7; 5:8,16; 8:4). Here she attributes her swarthiness to laboring in the vineyard, a task imposed by her brothers (cf. 8:10). The vineyard motif (1:5; 6:11; 7:13; 8:11–12) suggests that she is alluding to herself; she is the true vineyard, given to her lover.

13 (III) Dialogue between Lovers (1:7–2:7). 7. The woman asks for a noon ("midday") rendezvous with the lover, who is now (cf. 1:4) in the role of the shepherd. **8.** His indirect reply teases her: "follow the tracks." **9–11.** His true feelings are expressed in his admiration of her beauty, set off by finery comparable to Pharaoh's chariotry. **12–14.** She responds by praising the intimacy and charm which his presence (symbolized by "henna" and "myrrh") brings to her. **18–19.** When he admires her beauty, she returns the compliment. **2:1–2.** The duet of mutual admiration continues as he turns her comparison of herself to ordinary flowers (narcissus, lotus) of the Sharon plain into a compliment. **3.** She returns his compliment, with a comparison in his favor, addressing him in the 3d pers. She develops the metaphor of the apple tree, in order to show the delights of his love ("shadow," "fruit"). **4–5.** The meaning of "house of wine" and "emblem" (Hebr *dgl*) is uncertain, but she is led to proclaim her lovesickness, another common theme (cf. *LAEg* 320–21). The paradox is that what causes her sickness is also its cure.

6–7. The dialogue closes with a sudden turn to the Daughters in what seems to be a refrain (5:8; 8:3–4). She describes her lover's embrace and issues an adjuration to them not to arouse love "until it please." This is not a prohibition against waking the loved one from sleep. The point is that love is not artificial or calculated; it has its own time. The oath "by the gazelles and hinds of the field" is unique, and possibly a reference to the deity (gazelles = *şebā'ôt* = [Lord of] hosts), as R. Gordis claims.

14   **(IV) Reminiscence (2:8–17).** The woman recalls a scene in which her lover pays a springtime visit, ending with an *inclusio* (mountains, gazelle, stag, vv 8–9 and 17). **8.** *springing . . . leaping:* The speed of the lover's approach is continued by the comparison to the animals in v 9. **10.** *arise . . . come:* These words are repeated at the end (v 13 *inclusio*). **11–13.** The description of spring is "the most beautiful song to nature in the OT" (W. Rudolph). There is a heightening effect in the picturesque succession: season, blossoms, singing, figs, and vines in bloom. **14.** The reminiscence continues: He finds her inaccessible, "in the clefts of the rock," and wants to see and hear her. **15.** She answers his request with a saucy reply, a tease. She reminds him that this is the season when the "little foxes" invade the vineyards that are in bloom. The vineyard is a symbol for woman (cf. 1:6), and the foxes are ardent suitors. She is not as inaccessible as he thinks (v 14). **16.** The words are almost a formula to express mutual possession; cf. 6:3; 7:11. **17.** *until . . . :* The Hebr text can be interpreted to mean either all day or all night. In any case, she invites him to be as a gazelle (v 9) on the Bether mountains (i.e., herself).

15   **(V) Loss and Discovery (3:1–5).** This unit obviously marks a new beginning and forms a kind of doublet to 5:2–6, where the loss and search are repeated (but not the finding!). The entire unit is marked by repetitions: "seek," "find," "whom my soul loves," four times each. **3:1.** *on my bed at night:* Many interpret what follows as a dream (cf. 5:2), but it could be a daytime fantasy. The theme of presence/absence of the beloved recurs constantly in love poetry. **3.** *have you seen:* In the vivid style of vv 1–3 she questions the watchmen or city guardians, who "find" her, although she cannot "find" him. **4.** There is a triumphant return to the house of the girl's mother, who is mentioned frequently (1:6; 3:4; 6:9; 8:2,5). **5.** The scene suddenly closes with the adjuration refrain (cf. 2:7) to the Daughters (→ 12 above).

16   **(VI) Solomon's Wedding Procession (3:6–11).** This poem stands out because the speaker cannot be identified, and there is no dialogue. Two descriptions are given: a procession of Solomon's "bed" coming from the desert (vv 6–8), and his ornate "carriage" (vv 9–10). The Daughters of Zion are called upon to witness King Solomon on his wedding day. This is the only explicit reference to a marriage setting in the entire work. **6.** This question is also found in 8:5, where it refers to the woman, but in this context (v 7) it refers to Solomon's

bed and bodyguard. **10.** The MT has the carriage "inlaid with love," whatever that might mean.

17   **(VII) Dialogue between Lovers (4:1–5:1).** There is a sudden break from the wedding procession in 3:6–11, as the lovers engage in dialogue. **1.** The man opens with a description of the physical charms of the woman. This genre (the *waṣf*) is well known in love literature (see W. Herrmann, *ZAW* 73 [1963] 176–97). In vv 1–5 he singles out the various parts of the body that call for praise. The comparisons evoke a picture more than give an actual description. Her black "hair" suggests the goats in Gilead in the northern Transjordan plain. **2.** Her teeth are white and full. **3.** The pomegranate resembles an orange, deep red in color. **4.** The reference is obscure; perhaps the ornaments on her neck are compared to the trophies (?) on the city walls (cf. 1:9–11). **5.** The breasts of the woman are compared to twin fawns, for beauty and grace; cf. 2:16 and 7:4. **6.** There is a play on 2:17 where the woman invited him to the mountains (herself). Now he expresses his acceptance of the invitation.

18   **8.** The summons to depart from the mountain wilderness of Lebanon is another sudden change of scene, esp. when he has just called her a mountain of incense. Mt. Hermon is a dominant summit in the Antilebanon range N of Palestine, also called by its Amorite name, Senir (Deut 3:9). The Amana is probably the mountain range where the rivers of Damascus (2 Kgs 5:12) originate. The mention of two such disparate locations indicates that geography is not the issue here; these places symbolize her inaccessibility (2:14), which is further emphasized by the mention of wild animals which bar access to her (a task performed in Egyptian love poems by the crocodile; cf. *LAEg* 310). Behind this verse may be an allusion to the myth of the sacred marriage (see Pope, *Song* 474–77).

9. The man continues speaking down to v 16 in a song of admiration for her person. She is repeatedly called "my sister" (a term of endearment also in Egyptian love poetry) and "bride." He describes the effect her eyes have on him, a common motif in love poetry. **10–11.** He returns the compliment she paid him in 1:2 (love and wine) and presumably refers to her kisses (lips that drip honey). **12–15.** The mention of her fragrance leads into the description of the woman as an exotic garden of sweet-scented plants (vv 13–14). She is a garden "sealed," i.e., reserved for him alone, and not only a garden, but a sealed fountain (vv 12,15). The wide variety of precious and fragrant growth cannot be found in any one place. Botany yields to an imagination that strives to capture female charms. **16.** The man (rather than the woman; cf. *NEB*) calls upon the winds to rustle through "my garden" (the woman) and scatter the scent. At this point, (v 16ef), she interrupts and invites him to "come to the garden" (5:1; 6:2,11). In 5:1 he replies that he has indeed come, and he possesses her (symbols of spices, honey, wine). The ending of 5:1 is obscure and transls. vary. Apparently, unidentified speaker(s) address "friends" (the man and the woman?) to drink deeply (of love?).

19   **(VIII) Dialogue between the Woman and the Daughters (5:2–6:3).** It is possible that disparate poems have been united by the Daughters' questions in 5:9 and 6:1. **5:2–6.** This unit is clearly parallel to 3:1–5 (→ 15 above), despite the obvious differences. The knocking on the door and the lover's request could have awakened the woman from sleep, but she may be recounting a fantasy as in 3:1–5. **3.** Her reply to him has to be a tease, since she rises to let him in. **4–5.** The episode at the lock of the door is a highly charged scene leaving many questions unanswered. Does he leave the myrrh on the lock as a sign of his presence? **6.** His departure signals the search motif, but now the guardians beat her, and he is not to be found, in contrast to 3:3–4. **8.** Her words are modeled on 2:7; 3:5, but the message is different: lovesickness (cf. 2:5). **9.** The function of the Daughters is exemplified once more. If they are to look for him, they must first know how to identify him; this is a cue for the *wasf* that follows.

9–16. The description of his physical charms is reminiscent of the Jerusalem Temple, and proceeds from head to toe. **11.** The head of "pure gold" is precious; the "palm fronds" symbolize his thick hair. **12.** The metaphor of doves washing in milk is obscure. **13.** The comparison of the cheeks to "spice" suggests the usual perfuming of the beard. She continues with the rest of the body and returns to the mouth (vv 13,16) because of the kisses and words of love that she has received. **6:1.** The question is modeled on 5:19. The Daughters now desire to seek this handsome man. **2–3.** In effect, the woman replies that he is not really lost, or in any way available to anyone else; see 4:16; 5:1 for the garden motif, and 2:16 for mutual possession.

20   (IX) Dialogue between Lovers (6:4–12). As if to confirm the words of 6:1–3, the absent lover now appears and delivers another *wasf*. **6:4.** Tirzah was once the capital of Israel (1 Kgs 16:23), but it may be chosen here because the root meaning of the word is "pleasant." "Bannered troops" (*nidgālôt*) is an uncertain, if traditional, transl. (cf. v 10). **5–7.** See 4:1–3. **8–9.** He describes how the royal harem praises her radiance.

11–12. Because v 12 is not really translatable, these verses remain a puzzle (cf. commentaries). The identity of the speaker (perhaps the woman) is not clear. There seems to be a reference to some event which transpired in the nut garden (v 11; cf. 7:13).

21   (X) A Dialogue (7:1–8:4). An exchange between the woman and bystanders (v 1) leads to another *wasf*, perhaps uttered by the man, who is certainly the speaker of the passionate avowal in vv 7–10, to which she replies in 7:10–8:4. **1.** Unidentified bystanders command the Shulammite to "turn" that they may gaze upon her. Shulammite is variously interpreted: (1) as a reference to *Šulmānîtu*, a Mesopotamian goddess; (2) as a Shunammite, a woman from Shunem (cf. 1 Kgs 1:1–4); (3) as deriving from Solomon and *šālôm* (peace)—hence, "the Solomoness" or the "peaceful one." In the context, she has to be the heroine of Cant. "Turn" is usually interpreted to mean "dance"; then the description in vv 2–6 supposedly accompanies the dancing maiden. This is far from certain. The Shulammite replies: "Why do you look at me as upon the *mahănaim* dance?" She seems to refuse to be a spectacle for the bystanders. The *mahănaim* dance (the dance of the two camps) is otherwise unknown. **2.** The *wasf*, more sensuous than previous ones, begins with her feet and ends with her head. **3.** Hebr *šōr* means "navel-cord" in Ezek 16:4, but seems to be a euphemism here, mentioned between the thighs and the belly. **4.** See 4:5. **5.** The "ivory tower" to which her neck is compared is otherwise unknown. Heshbon is the old Amorite capital in Transjordan; the "pools" may suggest sparkling eyes. Bath-rabbim is unknown, as is the Lebanon tower to which her stately neck is compared. **6.** The Carmel promontory is a natural comparison for a proud, noble carriage. The lover is again referred to as a "king" (cf. 1:4,12).

22   7–10. In a passionate outburst the man expresses his desire for physical possession of the woman, who is symbolized by the "palm tree." When he compares her mouth to wine (v 10a), she adroitly continues the metaphor of wine flowing over lips and teeth (instead of the MT "lips of sleepers" in v 10b). **11.** She

continues with the formula of mutual possession (cf. 2:16; 6:3), and deliberately turns around the "yearning" of Gen 3:16; now the yearning is for her! **12–14.** She invites him to the fields for a tryst. The awakening of nature (2:11–13; 6:11) is a recurring motif. **14.** The "new with the old" is perhaps an idiom for all (kinds of fruits). **8:1–2.** She expresses the wish that he were her brother, since public signs of affection would be more easily accepted. The lessons she would learn from him in her mother's home would be lessons of love, here symbolized by "wine" and "juice." A neat play on the words for kiss and drink occurs (*'šqk*). **3–4.** A reprise of 2:6–7.

23   (XI) Appendixes (8:5–14). These verses support the claim that Cant is a collection of disparate poems. Although they echo previous lines there is no connection between these scenes: 5; 6–7; 8–10; 11–12; 13–14. **5.** This appears to be a homecoming scene. *who is this:* A repetition of 3:6 (where it hailed Solomon's carriage); now unidentified speaker(s) hail the approach of the woman. *I awakened you:* These words are attributed the woman in the MT, but they make better sense if the man speaks them; nowhere else is his mother mentioned.

24   6. These beautiful and touching lines about love are spoken by the woman. The image of the "seal" conveys her desire for constant presence with him. Since a seal was used for signatures, etc., it would be regularly kept on one's person. She compares the power of love to that of death and sheol. For the Hebrew, these were often personified as unrelenting powers since no one escapes them. True love (*'ahăbâ*) and devotion (*qin'â* means ardor here rather than passion or jealousy) will prevail just as surely. The fiery quality of love is said to be *šalhebetyâ*, "a flame of yah." This is usually explained as a superlative: "a Yahweh flame" of high burning intensity. However, it could mean that the fire of love is a fire of Yahweh, a participation in the Lord's white-hot love. **7.** *deep waters:* This phrase conjures up the powers of the Sea and the Abyss (Isa 43:2; 51:10). The metaphor shifts from fire to water, but the point remains the same: the power of love, which is beyond any price.

25   8–10. One must infer that the woman quotes her brothers' words of long ago in vv 8–9 and then replies to them in v 10. **8.** The metaphors of "wall" and "door" have been variously interpreted. The idea seems to be that if she is a wall (virtuous) they will adorn her, but if she is a door (yielding), they will curtail her freedom. To this autocratic program she responds (from a later vantage point, not as a "little sister") that she is mature ("breasts") and also independent ("wall"). For she has found *šālôm* ("peace" or well-being) "in his eyes" (presumably of her lover).

26   11–12. These enigmatic verses have been variously interpreted, according to the identity of the speaker. If it is the man, then he seems to be comparing his vineyard (the woman) to Solomon's (the royal harem) in a favorable light (cf. 6:8–9). If the woman addresses an imaginary Solomon, she seems to be saying that his vineyard has merely monetary value. But she is making a free disposal of her vineyard (herself) to her lover—an attitude in keeping with 8:7b, which disdains the bride-price. **11.** *Baal-hamon:* This unidentified place has a royal vineyard valued at 1,000 silver pieces (very precious; cf. Isa 7:23) **12.** *my own vineyard:* The woman; cf. 1:6. It is contrasted with the precious vineyard of Solomon (v 11). In what appears to be a satirical ending, 200 pieces of silver are allotted to the vineyard keepers.

27   13–14. As in 2:14, the lover asks for a word or song, and she replies with an invitation similar to that found in 2:17. Cant opened with her yearning for his kisses (1:2); now she invites him to herself ("mountains").

30

JOB

R. A. F. MacKenzie, S.J.   Roland E. Murphy, O.Carm. *

BIBLIOGRAPHY

1   *Commentaries:* Alonso Schökel, L., *Job* (Madrid, 1981). Anderson, F. I., *Job* (TynOTC; Leicester, 1976). Davidson, A. B., *The Book of Job* (CBSC; rev. ed., Cambridge, 1918). Dhorme, P., *A Commentary on the Book of Job* (London, 1967). Driver, S. R., and Gray, G. B., *A Critical and Exegetical Commentary on the Book of Job* (ICC; Edinburgh, 1921). Fedrizzi, P., *Giobbe* (Rome, 1972). Fohrer, G., *Das Buch Hiob* (KAT 16; Gütersloh, 1963). Gordis, R., *The Book of God and Man* (Chicago, 1965). Habel, N., *The Book of Job* (OTL; Phl, 1985). Horst, F., *Hiob* (BKAT 16/1; Neukirchen, 1960). Janzen, G. J., *Job* (IBC; Atlanta, 1985). Kissane, E., *The Book of Job* (Dublin, 1939). Pope, M., *Job* (AB 15; 3d ed.; 1973). Rowley, H. H., *Job* (CentB; Nash, 1970). Terrien, S., *Job* (CAT; Neuchâtel, 1963). Weiser, A., *Das Buch Hiob* (ATD; 2d ed.; Göttingen, 1956).

Studies: Cox, D. *The Triumph of Impotence* (AnGreg 212; Rome, 1978). Crossan, J. D. (ed.), *The Book of Job and Ricoeur's Hermeneutics* (Semeia 19; Chico, 1981). Duquoc, C. (ed.), *Job and the Silence of God* (Concilium 169; Edinburgh, 1983). Fohrer, G., *SBH.* Gese, H., *Lehre und Wirklichkeit in der alten Weisheit*

(Tübingen, 1958). Gray, J. "The Book of Job in the Context of Near Eastern Literature," *ZAW* 82 (1970) 251–69. Greenberg, M., *et al., The Book of Job* (Phl, 1980). Kuhl, C., "Neuere Literarkritik des Buches Hiob," *TRu* 21 (1953) 163–205, 257–317; "Vom Hiobbuche und seinen Problemen," *TRu* 22 (1954) 261–316. Lévêque, J., *Job et son Dieu* (Paris, 1970). Maag, V., *Hiob* (Göttingen, 1982). Müller, H., *Das Hiobproblem* (Darmstadt, 1978). Murphy, R. E., "Job," *Wisdom Literature* (FOTL 13; GR, 1981) 14–45. Polzin, R., & D. Robertson (eds.), *Studies in the Book of Job* (Semeia 7; Missoula, 1977). Richter, H., *Studien zu Hiob* (TA 11; Berlin, 1959). Rowley, H. H., "The Book of Job and Its Meaning," *BJRL* 41 (1958) 167–207. Skehan, P., *SIPW.* Tsevat, M., "The Meaning of the Book of Job," *HUCA* 37 (1966) 73–106. Van der Ploeg, J., and A. van der Woude, *Le Targum de Job de la grotte XI de Qumran* (Leiden, 1972). Vawter, B., *Job and Jonah* (NY, 1983). Vermeylen, J., *Job, ses amis et son Dieu* (StudB 2; Leiden, 1986). Westermann, C., *The Structure of the Book of Job* (Phl, 1970).

INTRODUCTION

2   **(I) Preliminary Remarks.** The proverbial phrase "the patience of Job" seems to derive from the Epistle of James (*KJV*). It is both a nuisance (Job is not patient) and inexact (*hypomonē* means steadfastness or perseverance). Job does persevere, despite the highs and lows of his experience. The structure of the book is essential for understanding it. Job was known in Hebr tradition as a holy man (→ 5), and the story of his trial and restoration is found in the prologue (chaps. 1–2) and epilogue (42:7–17) that form the framework. The poetic dialogue (chaps. 3–31) deals with the profound theological problem of the meaning of suffering in the life of a just man. It is a literary creation, not a report of a literal debate. In a series of disputation speeches Job defends his integrity against the charges of the three friends who think they are defending God. In chaps. 29–31 he closes out the debate with a formal protestation of his inno-

cence and issues a challenge to God. At this point Elihu intervenes to speak against Job (chaps. 32–37). Finally, the Lord appears in a theophany to deliver two speeches (chaps. 38–41), and Job gives his final reaction (42:1–6). The author, perhaps more than modern readers, knew that suffering is a mystery, but he comes to it with all the wisdom available for his time.

3   **(II) Language and Date.** The book of Job is the most difficult work in the OT to translate. This judgment is borne out by the differences existing in both modern and ancient versions. Already the original version of the LXX reflected a form of the text about 100 verses shorter than the MT. The book has many *hapax legomena* (about 100) and rare words, and many verses appear to be hopelessly corrupt. Hence, translators are often forced to make educated guesses. The language has been analyzed from at least two viewpoints: the presence

---

* Roland E. Murphy has revised the *JBC* article of R. A. F. MacKenzie.

of Canaanisms (esp. Ugaritic influence; cf. A. Blommerde, *Northwest Semitic Grammar and Job* [BibOr 22; Rome, 1969]) and Aramaisms (esp. in the Elihu speeches), but the issue is far from settled.

The date of the book is unknown, despite a general tendency to regard it as postexilic. The question is complicated by the claims of some scholars that portions of the work are later additions (the poem on wisdom in chap. 28; the Elihu speeches, etc.). There are no historical allusions within the book (J. Roberts, *ZAW* 89 [1977] 107–14). Neither do the parallels to Job in ancient Near Eastern literature (→ Wisdom Lit., 27:29– 31) shed light on the dating. Some have argued that Job 3 depends on Jer 20:4–18, or have detected the influence of Dt-Isa, or have judged that the exile has had an impact on the book, but all such literary and theological arguments are quite frail. As M. Pope (who regards the 7th cent. as the "best guess") remarks, the date remains an "open question."

4 (III) Justice in Job. That Yahweh was just and the source of justice had always been an axiom. But this justice could be conceived of in two very different ways. From the viewpoint of the helpless and oppressed, justice is liberation, salvation; the early "judges" are heroes and champions, deliverers of Yahweh's people from oppression. In the experience of the exodus from Egypt, Yahweh's was a saving justice; his intervention produced justice, the state in which all have what they ought to have. His covenant partners, naturally, ought to have security and well-being (→ OT Thought, 77:93, 136).

But if these covenant partners were disloyal and became his enemies, then they ought to experience the other side of justice, which is destruction. And that, according to the perspective of the Deuteronomist and the prophets, is what befell Judah in the exile. Hence, in the postexilic period, there was increasing insistence on loyalty to Yahweh, which found concrete expression in the ritual and social observance of a detailed external law.

At the same time, the wisdom teachers stressed the efficacy of righteous living. In their effort to understand human existence, they aimed at reducing the arbitrary and unpredicted elements in life. They held that there are moral laws that govern life, of which God is the custodian and the guarantor. These can be known, and, by prudent choice and blameless behavior, one can live in harmony with them and be assured of happiness and success.

Ezekiel's extreme individualism (e.g., 18:1–32) was a pastoral necessity in his effort to deliver the remnant of Judah from the dead hand of the past. But it heightened the difficulty of squaring real-life experience with "what ought to be." The emphasis of the authors of Prov on their infallible equation—wisdom = virtuous living = "success"—no doubt helped people to form virtuous habits. But for the thinker it aggravated the problem of "justice" in human life (→ Wisdom Lit., 27:12–13).

5 (IV) The Author's Purpose. The author undertook to show, in the light of a more adequate concept of the relationship of humanity to its loving creator, that the problem was wrongly posed: i.e., God may have other purposes than merely the exercise of retributive justice. As his medium he chose an old story that was no doubt familiar to his contemporaries. Ezek 14:14,20 refers to three legendary figures of the past, Noah, Danel (not Daniel, but Danel of Ugaritic legend) and Job, as proverbial for their righteousness. The story of Ezekiel's Job would be roughly that which is represented in the prologue and epilogue. The dialogue between the Lord and Satan has been interpreted as a crude representation of a divinity who cruelly permits the torture of his

creation (C. Jung). This fails to see the deep issues that lie in the text. The Satan's question is one of the most important in the Bible: Do humans serve God for themselves and their own profit (or, put abstractly, is disinterested piety possible)? J. Janzen sees this as an existential question for God: Can God create one who worships freely? "In other words, what sort of covenant is possible between God and humankind?" (*Job* 41).

The author makes the three friends, Eliphaz, Bildad, and Zophar, eloquent defenders of the "traditional" view of divine retribution. In keeping with the international character of the wisdom tradition, they are non-Jews, like Job himself. The writer's purpose is not to ridicule the traditional doctrine, but to show that it is simply inadequate. Insofar as this doctrine is positive, it is sound and helpful (cf. Ps 37, simple to the point of naïveté, yet beautiful and consoling). It contains much moral and religious truth but they spoil it by exaggeration. They are not willing to leave a margin of uncertainty, to admit limits to their understanding, to write after each of their theses, "If God so wills." All the workings of divine providence must be clear to them, explicit, mathematical. They have fallen victims to the occupational hazard of theologians: they forget they are dealing with mystery. They have "studied" God as a subject to be analyzed, predicted, and understood. And in forcing facts to agree with their understanding, they become willfully dishonest (Job 13:6–11). Meantime, the reader of the book knows what the friends (and Job) do not know.

As the author has carefully constructed it, Job's is the extreme case; here, consequently, they are extremely wrong. But their simplified retribution doctrine has had a long life. In John 9:1–3, Jesus' disciples take it for granted; they are intrigued by the man's blindness, only because he was born so. They do not ask: "Is this because of sins?" (of course it is!). Their problem is: "Were they his own sins in a previous existence or those of his parents before his birth?" Jesus corrects them very explicitly, and what he says would apply equally to Job: he suffers, not because of any sins but "that the works of God may be shown forth in him."

6 The correction of the friends' distortion is comparatively simple and can be accomplished by Job himself. His own error is more subtle, and his correction must come from God. In the prologue, he makes no connection between his suffering and divine justice. But that loyal simplicity is not sufficient to refute the friends' accusations, and in maintaining his innocence as though God were denying it, he overvalues it. It is not a bargaining counter; it is not a token he can hold up to God, saying, "For this, you owe me happiness." He is in the right, against the friends; he is not in the right, against God. He can make no claim on him. Job has to insist on his integrity, but he cannot say "God must" (cf., von Rad, *WI* 219–22). Christ was to warn us in that profound text, Luke 17:10, "When you have done all things that you have been commanded, say, 'We are unprofitable servants; we have done what we were obliged to do.'"

The book is full of irony (see J. G. Janzen's commentary) and paradoxes, for it attempts to approach divine truth, which is beyond human reach (chap. 28), from various viewpoints. It is essential that Job should be a lover of God, a saint. Otherwise, his affliction would inevitably contain some proportion of just punishment. Job has to affirm his sinlessness if he is to remain a person of integrity. Furthermore, only such a person could support the test. This observation should temper the scandal some readers feel at what they call the callousness of God in chaps. 1–2. The Lord is put in a "no-win" situation by the author. If God were to refuse the test which the Satan proposes, would it be a sign of fear that human beings serve him only for themselves (and then the Satan is right)? On the other hand, the acceptance of the Satan's wager makes God almost "demonic," but we are meant to understand that the Lord trusts those who serve him, and this is Job's opportunity.

7   (V) God in Job. The variety of divine names in Job is worth noting. In the prologue and epilogue, the narrator refers in normal Israelite fashion to "Yahweh" (the Lord), the one true God and supreme Lord. But the speakers in the prologue, including Yahweh (1:8b; 2:3a), employ the generic word *'elōhîm* (God). The one exception is in 1:21b, where Job three times uses "Yahweh"; but here, the second stich is a quotation. In the dialogue, on the other hand, "Yahweh" is named only once (12:9b), and that again is in a quotation. "Elohim" also is used once (5:8b). Otherwise, three archaic poetic names are consistently adopted: *'ēl, 'ĕlōah,* and *šadday* (the Almighty). Of these, the first and second never parallel each other, but each may parallel *šadday.* This elaborate convention establishes monotheism—the five names all apply to the one and only God; and it maintains the non-Israelite situation—Job and his friends are "true believers," but they are outside the ambit of the covenant with Israel. They speak for humankind in general, in the face of a God known indeed by revelation to Israel, but to whom these men are related only by the fundamental fact that they are his creatures. They expect no salvation from God other than individual well-being in this life. Only Job is groping for a more intimate and permanent relationship, based not on the mere exchange of gifts or services but on a communion of love. They never talk to God; only Job does.

8   (VI) Style. (On Hebr metrics and parallelism, → Hebrew Poetry, 12:7-10; 16-20). In the following pages, "stich" is used to denote a phrase in parallelism with another phrase; a "line" includes two parallel stichs (a "distich"—rhymes with "mystic"), or occasionally three (a "tristich"; e.g., 3:9 is one line, a tristich). In citing poetic passages, "a," "b," etc., added to a verse number indicate the successive stichs in that verse. Grouping of lines into stanzas or "strophes" is regular throughout the poem (see the convincing demonstration by P. W. Skehan, in *SIPW,* 96-113). The strophic analysis adopted in chaps. 3-23 mainly follows that of Skehan, with occasional variations, as in chaps. 16-17,19,21,22.

It is impossible to classify the book in terms of a literary genre. As M. Pope has remarked (*Job* xxxi), it is *sui generis* in this respect. C. Westermann characterized it as a dramatization of a lament. H. Richter saw in it a judicial process. H. Gese termed it a "paradigm of an answered lament" (in the style of the Babylonian poem, "I will praise the Lord of Wisdom," *ANET* 434-37). J. W. Whedbee (in *Studies* [ed. R. Polzin and D. Robertson] 1-39) deemed it a comedy in line with the claim of Northrop Frye. Perhaps G. Fohrer has pointed the way out of this wilderness. He emphasizes the three dominant features: lament, law, and wisdom. The book is a mixture of all these (see Murphy, *Wisdom Literature,* 16-20).

Modern scholarship has devoted much attention to the text of Job, not only to its integrity but also to possible glosses, displacement of verses, and corrupt verses. Whatever displacement (e.g., chaps. 25-27) or insertions may have occurred, these had to have happened early on. The Targum of Job (11QtgJob), discovered in cave 11 of Qumran and dated from the 1st cent. BC, provides no support to modern scholarly reconstructions of the sequence of the text. It supports the MT, but also some LXX readings. At the same time, it must be admitted that the LXX transl. of the book often provides an uncertain basis for textual emendation (cf. J. Ziegler, "Der textkritische Wert der Septuaginta des Buches Hiob," *Miscellanea Biblica* [Rome, 1934] 2. 277-96).

9   (VII) Outline. The Book of Job may be outlined as follows:

COMMENTARY

10 (I) The Prologue (1:1–2:13). This prose narrative is divided into six scenes that sketch vividly the course of the events giving occasion for the dialogue. The style is deliberately archaizing, reminiscent of the patriarchal narratives in Gen—i.e, dramatic, picturesque, schematized, rhythmically constructed, with set phrases and much verbal repetition. The characters are few and sharply defined; their psychology is realized with a minimum of words. Each dialogue is between two persons only, and the speeches are as economical and pointed as possible.

(Fohrer, G. *SBH,* 19–36, 37–59. Sarna, N. M. "Epic Substratum in the Prose of Job," *JBL* 76 [1957] 13–25.)

11 (A) Job's Character and Prosperity (1:1–5). "Once upon a time . . ." gives the flavor of this opening. The period is that of the seminomadic patriarchs; the area is the land of Uz, part of the territory of Edom (Gen 36:28; Lam 4:21), S and E of Palestine (but cf. Fohrer, *Hiob* 72–73, for arguments in favor of NE Transjordan). Job is pictured as a great potentate (not an old man, but comparatively young; cf. 15:10), outstanding for his goodness and blessed with great possessions. His virtue is analyzed in four expressions. "Blameless" (*tām*) is like the Lat *integer* (perfect), a whole man with no defect or inconsistency in his character. "Upright" or "righteous" (*yāšār*) means that his life and actions were right, in accordance with a standard. "Fearing" God means realizing one's relationship to him by showing him reverence and obedience. "Avoiding evil" affirms a good conscience deliberately and constantly choosing the good. **5b.** *blasphemed God:* The MT and versions have "blessed" (so also in 1:11; 2:5,9), but it is presumably a euphemism.

12 (B) The First Scene in Heaven (1:6–12). Cf. 1 Kgs 22:19ff. (H. W. Robinson, *JTS* 45 [1944]

151–57). Yahweh is anthropomorphically represented as an Oriental monarch seated on his throne receiving the reports of his servants and issuing his commands. These servants, the agents through whom he governs, are the "sons of Elohim," originally conceived of as lesser divinities but in Israelite theology reduced to the rank of Yahweh's ministers. Among them is the Adversary ("the Satan"; not to be treated as a proper name), the prosecutor who spies on men's wrongdoing and reports it to his master (cf. Zech 3:1ff.). He is not yet the "devil" of later Jewish and Christian theology; to identify him as such distorts the understanding of the book. Still, he is an unpleasant figure, and his cynical attitude toward human possibilities of good contradicts the optimistic estimate of Yahweh himself. When the latter, with evident pleasure and even a kind of pride, draws his attention to "my servant Job" (a title of high honor) as an example of perfect human loyalty to himself, the Satan skeptically interprets Job's virtue as mere self-interest. **9.** This penetrating question is one of the fundamental themes of the book. Hebr *ḥinnām,* "for nothing," means gratis, without looking to payment or reward—therefore, out of love. Does Job serve God thus? And we might ask, does any man? Can he? And should he? The Adversary does not think so and neither do Job's three friends. **12.** Yahweh accepts the challenge and permits the test to be made. The withholding of his gifts from Job will demonstrate whether Job's affections center on them or on the giver.

13   (C) The Loss of Job's Possessions (1:13–22). In four rapid stages these are all destroyed in a single day. The items of vv 2–3 are all accounted for, and in four "moments" Job finds he has passed from wealth to utter destitution. **20–21.** The first effect naturally is that he "goes into mourning" according to the customs of the time. The second is that he proves the Adversary wrong: he blesses Yahweh instead of cursing him. To sharpen the contrast, the narrator has him pronounce, three times, the name Yahweh, which otherwise he avoids; the last phrase in v 21 is a standard liturgical formula (cf. Ps 113:2); therefore, it is natural to use the same name in the preceding stich.

14   (D) The Second Scene in Heaven (2:1–7a). Verses 1–3a repeat 1:6–8 almost word for word. In v 3b, "without cause" is the same adverb as in 1:9, "for nothing"; but with almost grim humor the meaning is inverted: Not Job's loyalty goes for nothing, but the Adversary's cynicism. However, he does not admit defeat. There is a new stress on individualism (as against the older idea of solidarity of the individual with family and tribe) in his answer: Goods and even children are not a man's self. Let Job be stripped of honor and health—of all but bare existence. When he has absolutely nothing left to thank God for, will he still "fear him"?

15   (E) The Affliction of Job's Person (2:7b–10). Job is smitten with some unnamed and disfiguring disease, which causes continual pain and sleeplessness and makes him a disgusting sight (its symptoms are frequently alluded to in his later speeches). **8.** *among the ashes:* Seems to imply his exclusion from human society; his place of refuge is a community dump such as may be seen today outside an Eastern village. **9.** Not Job but his wife reacts as the Adversary had expected. She interprets the situation somewhat as the friends will do; but she takes her husband's side. God has now shown himself to be Job's enemy; the latter should express that fact before he dies. **10.** Job's second speech is a parallel to 1:21. His rebuke is kindly but firm (and the pl. shows that he is sensitive to his wife's distress; she has, after all, suffered the losses with him). It excludes any obligation on God's part toward his creatures. One can never say to God,

"You ought not to treat me thus." Thus, Job is now very literally fearing God "for nothing." Yahweh's trust in his servant is vindicated, and the Adversary's skepticism is disproved (he is not mentioned again in the book). For a possible ambiguity in Job's response, see Janzen, *Job* 51–55.

The original story probably went on from this point (or even from 1:22) to tell of Job's consolation and restoration, as in 42:11ff. (A. Alt, *ZAW* 55 [1937] 265–68). But the inspired author chose this point to insert his long and profound analysis of what a man like Job might experience, while this desperate situation lasted.

16   (F) The Coming of Job's Friends (2:11–13). This passage prepares for the following dialogue. A certain interval of weeks or even months is supposed to have elapsed before the friends' arrival, so that Job has time to meditate on his condition and to experience its full effects. The three are professional wise men from different localities. Their friendship is genuine, and their intention is truly charitable. Their sympathy with him in his deplorable state—evidently even worse than they had expected—is expressed in the ritual gestures of mourning for the dead and in a week-long silence. (Cf. N. Lohfink, *VT* 12 [1962] 260–77.) They wait for Job to speak before venturing to try to comfort him.

17   (II) The Dialogue (3:1–31:40). Apart from brief introductory rubrics (e.g., 3:1–2), this section is entirely in poetic form. Between Job's initial (chap. 3) and concluding (chaps. 29–31) soliloquies, we find a series of alternate speeches by the friends, in succession, and by Job. Because of the textual disorder of chaps. 25–27, we cannot be sure of the last few speeches, but inasmuch as Eliphaz speaks first (chaps. 4–5), after chap. 3, Zophar should speak last, before chaps. 29–31. Thus there would be nine addresses by the friends alternating with eight responses from Job. (The conventional grouping of the speeches into three "cycles" obscures this point; it also imposes a modern category of style, which was not the author's, and is better avoided.) In these "disputation speeches" the form of lament is prominent in Job's case (→ 8). The function of the friends is to console, by joining in the lamentation and the petition. But, because of their doctrine on retribution, they come prepared to take part in a psalm of penitence, whereas Job is uttering a psalm of innocence. This clash of views means that to Job they become enemies, unjustly oppressing him and increasing his suffering. Hence, two subordinate themes become prominent in Job's lament: denunciation of enemies and the oath of exculpation. Worse than that, the friends persist in claiming that their are pronouncing God's judgment, that what they profess is divinely guaranteed wisdom; thus, Job is led to include God among his enemies, i.e, God as presented to him by the friends. This is his real trial: Against human authority and outward appearances, he is fighting to maintain and affirm his faith that God loves him.

(Barthélemy, D., "A Wrong View of God: Job," *God and His Image* [NY, 1966] 1–15. Feuillet, A., "L'énigme de la souffrance et la réponse de Dieu," *Dieu vivant* 17 [1950] 77–91. Robinson, T. H., *Job and His Friends* [London, 1954].)

18   (A) Job's First Soliloquy (3:2–26). It corresponds to the "complaint" theme of the psalms of lament; i.e., it is mere lamentation, a description and expression of pain. It does not include direct petition for relief, and its invocation of God is implicit only, when the sufferer asks the reason for his affliction. Job begins with the most radical possible declaration of his misery, uttering a rejection of life itself (cf. the parallel in Jer 20:14–18; also 1 Kgs 19:4; Jonah 4:3,8; Sir 23:14). By cursing the day of his birth, he implies that the life God has given him is not good, and he would prefer never to have received it. The passage contains a skillfully graded transition from the patient Job of the prologue to the impatient Job of the dialogue. The complaint of vv 3–10 can well be uttered by the speaker of 1:21; 2:10, turning his attention from God to himself; but a crucial development comes with the query "Why?" in vv 11–12, and again in v 20. (For the question element in the lament, compare Pss 13:2–4; 22:2; 42:10; 44:24–25; 74:1,10–11; 77:8–10; 88:15.) In the prologue, Job had not asked why. The first two questions are still rhetorical, but they lead to the third in v 20, which expresses a real inquiry; it formulates a problem concerning God's treatment of humanity. There is as yet no reference to divine justice (the friends will introduce that theme), but there is bewilderment about God's goodness: How is it shown in a gift that is no gift—i.e., a miserable life? Job is beginning to wonder about the meaning of his experience, which is just what the friends are ready to explain to him. This repeated "Why?" launches the following debate, much as the Adversary's question in 1:9 had initiated the experience.

The speech contains seven strophes of 4, 4; 3, 3, 3; 4, 3, lines. Verse 16 should follow v 11 (or possibly 12).

(Freedman, D. N., "The Structure of Job 3," *Bib* 49 [1968] 503–8. Moore, R., "The Integrity of Job," *CBQ* 45 [1983] 17–31. Skehan, P. W., *SIPW*, 97–100.)

19   (a) The Curse of Job's Anniversary Day and Night (3:3–6,7–10). Job never does curse God, but these imprecations (like Jeremiah's) are directed against something God has created. Verse 3 joins day of birth with night of conception; then vv 4–6 (reading *yôm*, "day," in 6a) treats of the former, vv 7–10 of the latter. They are personified as sentient beings not only conscious of but also responsible for the events they witnessed (cf. Ps 19:3–4); Job wishes that God may blot them out of the calendar, may "uncreate" them (v 4a is, lit., "That day—let there be darkness!" reversing the "Let there be light!" of Gen 1:3). **7–10.** The night, time of conception and fertility—therefore of joy—is to be barren and mournful. **8.** The reference is to magicians who claimed to be able to control the abyss and the monsters that inhabited it. *Leviathan:* "A personification of the evil forces of the primeval chaos which Yahweh overcame when He created the world" (*EDB* 1330; cf. Pope, *Job* 276–78). **9.** Not eyes or eyelids but "the eyelashes of the dawn," i.e, the rays fanning out from the still-hidden sun.

20   (b) Better an Early Death (3:11,16,12). **11.** *at birth:* Read "[while still] in the womb" (M. Dahood, *Bib* 44 [1963] 205). **12.** *the knees:* Rather than to mother or nurse, this may refer to the father acknowledging his child; if such acknowledgment were refused, the child might be cast out to die.

21   (c) Reasons for the Curse (3:13–15,17–19). Consigned to the underworld at birth, Job would at least have "enjoyed" an untroubled nonexistence, preferable to his present anguish. He would be in the company of the ghosts of the great ones of the earth (vv 14–15) but also (vv 18–19) of the ghosts of the wretched, whose release from suffering he would share. **17.** *troubling:* The word means distress caused to others; equivalently, "there one is no longer oppressed by cruel tyrants." Notable is the poet's sensitive feeling for the hopeless misery of prisoners and slaves (cf. 7:1; 31:13–15); Job's feelings are similar—and hence, implicitly, slave driver and harsh master are images, in his present experience, of God (supporting the MT reading in v 20: "Why does He give light . . . ?").

22   (d) Renewed Lament (3:20–23,24–26). Why make a gift that is a painful burden to the recipient? **22a.** "They would rejoice on [arriving at] the tomb," reading *gal*, "tumulus." **23b.** Cf. Lam 3:7. Verse 26 makes an *inclusio* with v 13, repeating "ease" (same word as "tranquil") and "rest"; it also echoes the "trouble" and "rest" of v 17.

23   **(B) Eliphaz's First Speech (4:1–5:27).** Eliphaz is presumably the oldest of the three and therefore the wisest; he is certainly the most courteous and the most eloquent. He has a genuine esteem for Job and is deeply sorry for him. He knows the advice to give him, the wisdom that lays down what he must do to receive relief from his sufferings. But Eliphaz has been mildly shocked by Job's lament, in which he had merely wished for death and had uttered no prayer for recovery of prosperity and happiness. He had even implied unbecoming criticism of God and seemed to consider his misfortune as an unaccountable mystery. For Eliphaz there is no mystery; he has diagnosed Job's case at a glance. Obviously, these calamities have been sent to punish Job for some transgression or culpable negligence, perhaps unnoticed. Eliphaz intends to help him examine his conscience, to repent of his sins, and so to regain God's favor. Ps 32 would fit Job's case exactly, esp. vv 3–5.

The structure of the speech is elaborate, consisting mainly of eight five-line strophes; a two-line conclusion (5:1–2) ends the first section; the second is interrupted by a three-line strophe (5:14–16) and is ended by the one-line conclusion (5:27).

24   (a) The Doctrine of Retribution (4:2–6,7–11). The friends' speeches regularly start with a question and reference to Job's words. Eliphaz first begins with the utmost gentleness, appealing to Job's own good advice to others in the past. Unfortunately, this approach is already beside the point; Job had accepted the standard retribution doctrine (cf. 29:18–20) unthinkingly, but now he is beginning to question it precisely because it does not explain his present situation. Next (v 6), Eliphaz bids him take confidence from his past faithful service of God; he acknowledges Job's piety and integrity (corresponding to "God-fearing" and "blameless" of 1:1,8). (Later on, he will deny both: 15:4; 22:4–5.) **7–9.** Eliphaz sums up the orthodox teaching and innocently asks Job if he doesn't remember it. He claims to base it first on experience: he has seen divine justice working infallibly in the world (cf. Ps 37:25). A man who makes this claim must have shut his eyes to many facts, as Job will trenchantly point out (9:22–24; 21:7–17); in particular, Eliphaz is not considering the case before him; he has not investigated Job's position. In short, he has a closed mind and is completely satisfied with his tidy comprehensible doctrine, which he applies complacently and rather unfeelingly to Job. **7.** *perishes:* The word recurs in vv 9a, 11a, and 20b. **8.** As a general principle, this is sound; but Eliphaz makes it so absolute that he can turn it around and say infallibly, "Those who reap trouble must have sowed it by their wickedness." **10–11.** The author's rich vocabulary finds five different terms for lions.

25   (b) Eliphaz's Revelation (4:12–16,17–21; 5:1–2). Besides experience ("seen," 4:8 and 5:3) Eliphaz can bring a proof from a private revelation ("heard," 4:16). He describes—with great evocative power and mystery—a ghostly audition; but the source of the message remains undetermined. It is called (v 12) *dābār* (a word) and *šemeṣ* (a whisper), which produced preternatural dread. The speaker seems to be hinting at something he cannot affirm; the passage may be a deliberate parody of attempts to claim a quasi-supernatural authority for wisdom teachings, on a par with that claimed by oracle givers and prophets. The aptness of the message to Eliphaz's argument makes it rather suspect. **17.** The meaning may be general—"Can man be [considered] just and pure, in comparison with the transcendent justice and purity of God?"—or specific— "In a given case, can a man, by proving himself to be in the right and innocent, prove God wrong and blameworthy?" In either case, Eliphaz's point is that Job should accept God's clear verdict that he is a sinner, whether he understands his sinfulness or not.

5:1–2. A warning against mere unprofitable lament. None of the "holy ones" (the servants and messengers of 4:18) can save from God's displeasure and just resentment (*NAB* "impatience" and "indignation") a sinner who refuses to acknowledge his offense or to ask God's forgiveness.

26   (c) RECOMMENDATION (5:3–7,8–13,14–16). **3–5.** Eliphaz illustrates the point made in 5:2. Verse 4 refers, callously enough, to the fate of Job's children. Verse 6 refers to 4:8. **7b.** *sparks:* Lit., "sons of Resep," an underworld god of fire and pestilence. **8.** *in your place:* Not expressed in the Hebrew; the MT has "But I, I would seek God." "Seeking God" (*dāraš*) is a favorite theme with the prophets (e.g., Amos 5:4,6). It implies that one (in this case Job) has for a time abandoned God and must now penitently return to him. **9.** Omit v 9, transferred in error from 9:10. **10–13.** A doxology in hymnal style (*EDB* 589, 1044). Verses 11, 15–16 are echoed in the Magnificat (Lk 1:51–53).

27   (d) ENCOURAGEMENT (5:17–21,22–26,27). Eliphaz ends with a flourish, with two carefully matched strophes in elaborate sapiential style. **17.** The first begins with a beatitude (cf. Ps 94:12). Verse 19 introduces a numerical "proverb" (cf. Prov 6:16–19; 30:15ff.; Sir 25:7–10; A. Bea, *Bib* 21 [1940] 196–98; W. M. W. Roth, *VT* 12 [1962] 300–11). In vv 20–21, six calamities are mentioned, which God will avert: famine, death, war, sword, calumny, and ruin. Verse 22a continues with "ruin [same word] and hunger" (repeating the sixth and first calamities), and these add up to the seventh, wild beasts. **23–26.** Next are listed seven blessings God will bestow; six of these each occupy a stich (the calamities were mentioned more briefly, 20–21), and the seventh occupies v 26 with its picturesque simile. **27.** Eliphaz sums up. Experience and revelation ("searched . . . heard") make his teaching certain. The last phrase ("You, apply it to yourself") expresses his calm assurance that it only remains for Job to put it into practice.

This speech is eloquent, and its content is orthodox; yet in the context it is a parody. The reader knows from the prologue that Eliphaz's analysis of Job's situation is wrong; in fact, with his stress on the "profit motive," his outlook is indistinguishable from the Adversary's. He takes for granted that Job will be encouraged by all sorts of rewards held out to him, whereas the latter (in chap. 3) had desired only the quietude of death. When he does call for something more positive, he will not call for renewed prosperity but for an explanation of God's acts (10:2ff.).

28   (C) **Job's First Response (6:1–7:21).** Job does not answer like a debater, point for point, but develops his own analysis of the situation, quite different from that formed by the friends. Here he first complains of Eliphaz's prejudgment of his case. This would-be consoler has not properly considered the monumental scale of Job's disaster, nor the fundamental problem it has raised in Job's mind. He and his companions are bound to Job by a covenant of friendship and should exercise *ḥesed,* "covenant love," toward him (v 14). That would mean expressing compassion (which they did, at first, by their silent mourning) and then sympathetically

entering into his view of the case. They should take into account his own testimony as to his sinlessness; or, if they disagree, they should testify in turn (6:24). They should not take his wickedness as proved merely by the fact of his suffering. After this vehement protest, Job reaffirms his innocence, describes his pain, and then makes a pathetic appeal to God, mingled with bitter reproaches for this unkind treatment.

The speech contains 16 strophes, of which every fourth has four lines, and the rest have three lines each.

29   (a) JOB'S MISERY (6:2–4,5–7,8–10). Job continues in the vein of his lament in chap. 3, but with more express reference to God. **2a.** *anguish:* Hebr *ka'as,* translated "impatience" in 5:2 (and "displeasure" in 10:17). Not God's "indignation" at the foolish sinner, but Job's, at his undeserved suffering, is the theme to be considered. **2–3.** Anguish and calamity correspond in parallelism; either of them would outweigh the sands. **4.** A Homeric image: the divine archer, shooting poisoned arrows at his victim. The title *šadday* (the Almighty) was used by Eliphaz, 5:17; what he referred to as discipline is felt by Job as torture. Verse 5 justifies Job's "roaring" (3:24b; 4:10); he is deprived of the necessities of life—i.e, what is needed for normal human existence. **6–7.** Eliphaz's advice has been no help to him. "White of an egg" is a traditional but uncertain rendering; something nauseating is meant. **8–10.** Job is not allured by the happiness Eliphaz had augured for him; his affliction does not result from any act of his and it cannot be removed by any facile "repentance." All he desires (as in chap. 3) is a speedy death. **10.** His one consolation will be that he has not, as his wife had proposed, failed in loyalty, even when so severely treated (cf. 23:12). Job here seems to have an inkling of the aspect of his trial that is presented in the prologue.

30   (b) A TRANSITION STROPHE (6:11–14). With great pathos Job bursts into protests against the increase of his suffering by failure of the expected comfort from his friends. **12.** "Stones" and "bronze" imply reference to statues; men of marble or metal feel nothing, but Job is living flesh and blood. **14.** An obscure verse. "Kindness" is *ḥesed,* owed to a friend. Read, possibly, "He who withholds kindness from his friend forsakes. . . ."

31   (c) JOB'S DISILLUSIONMENT WITH THE FRIENDS (6:15–17,18–20,21–23,24–27). Without (as yet) going into any arguments, Job expresses his profound disappointment. Instead of bringing him comfort, they are acting as his enemies. His reaction is illustrated by a Homeric simile, the most elaborate in the book. The streams that flow down wadis, in Arabia and Syria, are mostly not perennial; they run furiously in the rainy season but sooner or later dry up completely when the rains cease. (A few may flow all summer one year and run dry the year following.) Desert travelers who counted on finding water in a particular wadi might be exposed to death by thirst, if that stream had ceased to flow. Their disappointment and despair are the images of Job's reaction to his friends' attitude, as revealed in the speech of Eliphaz (21a). **22–23.** He has not asked much of his "brothers" (15a)—not to pay out money nor to risk their lives (their covenant of friendship would oblige them even to that); he has only asked them to show him sympathy by adopting his point of view and by helping him, if they can, to make sense of this waking nightmare. **26–27.** In effect, Eliphaz's complacent lecturing is inhumane. He is more interested in the disease than in the patient.

32   (d) TRANSITION STROPHE (6:28–30). Job makes a formal challenge, appealing to the bond of friendship and affirming his own truthfulness. **29a–30a.** The same word is used, *'awlâ* (translated "falsehood" in

13:7 and 27:4): There is no dishonesty in him; let there be none in them.
33   (e) Soliloquy (7:1–3,4–6,7–10). Presumably the friends show their rejection of the appeal, and Job ceases to address them. He returns to the theme of his lament. He compares human life in general to forced military service, to the work of a day laborer, and to simple slavery—three proverbially wretched states of life. (Cf. M. David, *Revue philosophique* 147 [1957] 341–49.) It is his retort to Eliphaz's easy optimism in 5:17ff. Each man has a life span and work allotted to him; Job's life span and work are full of misery. Verse 4 is a tristich; therefore, vv 4–6 form a three-line strophe. **7.** *remember:* Eliphaz's word to Job in 4:7; but now, suddenly, Job is addressing God. From "my eye will not again see . . ." (so, lit., v 7b), he passes to "the eye of my beholder" (v 8a), and then to "your eye" (v 8b, lit., "your eye upon me—but I am gone"). The tone of this first address to God is revealing. It is not the penitential plea that Eliphaz had recommended (5:8); Job, accustomed to an untroubled relationship with his divine benefactor, appeals implicitly to the love God has for him. His human friends have failed him, but he takes for granted that his divine friend will come looking for him—only it may then be too late. **9–10.** This statement of the finality of death is important and will recur several times (cf. 7:21; 10:21; 14:10,12,18–22; 17:13–16). The whole program would be different if Job knew anything of a judgment and possible happiness after death, but he has no evidence or basis for such a belief (cf. 14:13–17; and see comment on 19:25–27).
34   (f) Complaint to God (7:11,20cd,12; 13–15; 16–18; 19–20ab,21). Job's first formal prayer. Eliphaz must be shocked at hearing it. Job has not conceived his relationship to God as one of retributive justice, whereby a man observes certain rules, does certain things and avoids others, and the just judge rewards him in due proportion (Eliphaz's concept, and also that of the Adversary). Job has known God as a person adored and loved, whom he can address intimately; the relationship is a personal one, whose possible categories are friendship and enmity, love and hatred. This dearly loved friend has now turned on Job, maltreating and tormenting him. There is no question of justice or its opposite; the problem is: Why is a friend suddenly acting like a vicious enemy? Verse 20cd, placed in *NAB* after v 11, provides an emphatic beginning, with its *lāmâ,* "Why?" as in 3:11,20: "Why have you set me up as your target? . . ." (cf. 6:4). **12.** *yām* and *tannîn* are sea and sea monster, mythological symbols of the powers of chaos, vanquished by the creator in a cosmic battle but still requiring surveillance as potential threats to God's power (cf. comment on 3:8). **13–14.** God is persecuting him night and day. **15.** Read, "My soul prefers choking, my bones prefer death" (N. M. Sarna, *JJS* 6 [1955] 109). **16–18.** A somber analysis of the presence of God, when that presence, as with Job now, is not benignant, fatherly, and loving, but hostile and oppressive. **17.** Ps 8:5 is an exclamation of wonder and gratitude at God's care for insignificant humanity; with bitter irony Job quotes it and applies it to the sort of surveillance God is now applying to him (J. Hempel, *Forschungen und Fortschritte* [vol. 35; Berlin, 1961] 123). Surely it is unworthy of the Almighty thus to occupy himself in tormenting so unimportant a creature. **19b.** An idiom still used in Arabic, to request a moment's respite. **20b.** Perhaps read (with LXX), "You Inspector of the hearts of men!" **21a.** This verse follows v 20b immediately: Even if Job has sinned, he cannot have done any harm to God, and the latter's greatness would be better shown by his function of forgiveness. **21cd.** Job ends by making more explicit the

idea in v 8. God cannot really mean to treat him like this; but when he realizes what he is doing, Job will be dead and it will be too late to put things right.
35   (D) **Bildad's First Speech (8:1–22).** Bildad is younger, more narrow-minded, and less tactful than Eliphaz. He is scandalized at Job's freedom, or irreverent familiarity, in speaking about (and to) God. These protests and complaints seem to him to undermine a main principle of religion, that God can do no injustice. Like Eliphaz, he considers that strict retributive justice is the only principle underlying God's dealings with humanity. In fact, he implies that God's functions are automatic: Humans have freedom to choose this or that, but no allowance is made for liberty or love in the judgments of God. The latter can only react to human conduct. Hence, Bildad's crude representation: Humankind is divided into two groups, the wicked and the righteous; the former, perhaps after brief prosperity, God utterly destroys; the latter God blesses. Bildad argues, not from personal experience but from the tradition of former generations, the unquestionable source of wisdom.
The speech consists of seven three-line strophes.

(Habel, N., "Appeal to Ancient Tradition as a Literary Form," *ZAW* 88 [1976] 253–71. Irwin, W. A., "The First Speech of Bildad," *ZAW* 51 [1953] 205–16. Löhr, M., "Die drei Bildad-Reden im Buche Hiob," [Fest. K. Budde; BZAW 34; Giessen, 1920] 107–12.)

36   (a) Introduction (8:2–4,5–7). Beginning as usual with a rhetorical question and with a reference to Job's words, Bildad firmly concentrates on the question of divine justice—which Job had not raised at all. **4.** He does not shrink from the obvious conclusion: Job's sons and daughters must have been very sinful, and they have received what they deserved. (Eliphaz had only hinted at this, 5:4). **5–7.** Having made that clear, Bildad proceeds, according to his original intention (2:11b), to comfort Job and to encourage him (ineptly) by promising renewed prosperity if he accepts his friends' advice. Verse 5a corrects Job's last words, 7:21d, using the same verb, *šihar:* Job should seek God, not expect God to seek him. **5b.** *make supplication:* For forgiveness of his sins. **6.** Omit first stich as a gloss.
37   (b) Doctrine (8:8–10,11–13,14–16,17–19). After citing his authorities, Bildad develops his doctrine in similes, which have an Egyptian coloring. **11–13.** Papyrus and reed promptly wither if their marsh bed dries up; thus do the wicked when God withdraws his favor. **14–19.** The text is corrupt and may be disordered; read, perhaps, 14–15,18,16–17,19. Like a garden plant, the wicked can be uprooted and destroyed in a moment. Others (Gordis, Habel) find in vv 12–19 a parable of two plants.
38   (c) Conclusion (8:20–22). Bildad ends on an optimistic, even complacent, note. He has surely convinced Job and so "consoled" him. **21.** An adaptation of Ps 126:2ab. **22b.** The last word, *'ênennû,* "is no more" echoes Job's last word, 7:21d, *'ênennî,* "am no more"; i.e., if Job talks like that, he is setting himself among the wicked.
In this strophe, the author's irony is very clear; Bildad's promises will be verified, but not as he intends. **20.** Job has already been declared perfect (*tām;* not "upright") by God (1:8; 2:3), and Bildad uses the sg.: ". . . not cast away the perfect man" (=Job). But "the wicked" is pl. (= the friends)! Verse 21 is to come true without Job's following Bildad's advice, and v 22a is spoken by Bildad against himself (cf. 42:7–8).
39   (E) **Job's Second Response (9:1–10:22).** Has the same general structure as chaps. 6–7: a section answering the friends (9:2–24); a briefer soliloquy

(9:25–10:1a); and a direct address to God (10:1b–22). It is less personal than the previous speech; in fact, the friends are addressed only indirectly. Bildad's speech is mostly ignored, but Job picks up Eliphaz's remark about the justice of man before God (4:17). God's justice is really his power; he can do what he chooses; none can withstand him; and if he declares a man to be guilty, then it is so. No appeal can be made, and no other standard of justice can be invoked. Yet if one's conscience is clear, what he suffers is not felt as justice but as divine anger; thus it is with Job. The third section is another impassioned argument and appeal to God, which subsides into a mournful plea that God leave him alone (K. Fullerton, "On Job, Chapters 9 and 10," *JBL* 53 [1934] 321–49; "Job, Chapters 9 and 10," *AJSL* 55 [1938] 225–69).

The first section is in seven three-line strophes interrupted by a transition couplet, 9:11–12. The soliloquy has three strophes, of four, three, and four lines. The address to God has a couplet (10:1b–2), followed by four five-line strophes. Verses 9:24,33–34a; 10:3,15,17 are tristichs (cf. Skehan, *SIPW* 103–4).

40 (a) GOD IS IRRESISTIBLE IN POWER, THEREFORE IN JUDGMENT (9:2–4,5–7,8–10,11–12). **2.** Job changes Eliphaz's dictum (4:17) slightly to emphasize the lawsuit imagery. If God is one party in such a suit he must necessarily win it, not because he will not pervert justice but because justice is whatever he decides. **4a.** The MT does not say "God is . . ."; the line may mean "What man, however wise. . . ." **5.** Job begins a doxology, more magnificent than that of Eliphaz (5:10–16), but significantly limited to works of power, not of justice or salvation. **9.** Cf. G. R. Driver, *JTS* 7 (1956) 1–11. **11–12.** The divine cosmic activity is beyond human understanding or control; it is strictly a mystery. For Job, the same is true of God's interventions in human life. But the friends insist that they can explain the latter, infallibly, as retributive justice.

41 (b) GOD IS ARBITRARY (9:13–15,16–18,19–21, 22–24). Job passes from the general to the particular; it is impossible for him to "sue" God or to establish his innocence if God condemns him. Nevertheless, that does not mean that he must have given cause for this ill-treatment—i.e., have rebelled against God. **13.** *Rahab:* "A mythological sea monster personifying the forces of chaos" (*EDB* 1977; see comment on 3:8). **22.** *innocent:* Hebr *tām,* "perfect," as in 8:20; Job contradicts Bildad. Verses 22–24 must have sounded "blasphemous" to the friends. The verisimilitude with which the author describes the reactions of Job (and of anyone who suffers) is striking. It sets up the pathos of his questions and charges in 10:3–12.

42 (c) JOB'S HELPLESSNESS (9:25–28,29–31,32–10:1a). Soliloquy, but with asides to God (vv 28b,31). If suffering is an infallible sign of guilt, then Job has already been condemned by God and there is nothing he can do about it. Guilt is conceived of as a state of damnation produced by the judge's sentence; it is objective and independent of one's conscience. **30.** On handwashing, see R. Press, *ZAW* 51 (1933) 246–47. **32–33.** If only there were a court of appeal, a super-god to hold the scales even between Job and his oppressor! This daring concept illustrates another grave defect of the friends' theology (according to which Job is arguing): Their idea of a sort of commutative justice between God and humanity destroys God's transcendence and tends in this respect to bring God to the human level. Hence this *reductio ad absurdum* suggested by Job. In a lawcourt the function of an arbiter or umpire (*môkîaḥ* in v 32; cf. *'ēd* in 16:19; *mēlîṣ* in 33:23) is to create a common ground between disputants (Job and God). But this is simply

impossible because, as Job says, "he is not a man like myself" (v 32; cf. Janzen, *Job* 94–97).

43 (d) SPECULATION AND APPEAL (10:1b–2,3–7, 8–12). Job addresses himself to the "real" God. The friends' understanding of his case is false; Job must try to find a truer one. Desperately he speculates on possible motives for this persecution, proposing (and rejecting) wild theories, trying to provoke an answer. **3.** Is God sadistic or (v 4) making a mistake or (v 5) jealous of human happiness because his own is limited in time? **8–12.** "Hand" in v 7 leads to "hands" in v 8 and to this most interesting strophe, which outlines the embryology of the ancient world (cf. Ps 139:13–15). Job recalls with awe the process of his formation in the womb, by the hands of God, and the gifts then made and continued. **12a.** *grace and favor:* The MT has "life and *ḥesed,*" a special love (cf. Ps 63:4a). For all this solicitude, Job could never be sufficiently grateful.

44 (e) THE MOURNFUL CONTRAST (10:13–17,18–22). **13.** But now, that gratitude is poisoned, if all along God was only preparing a victim to be tortured. **15.** Here is the denial of the friends' idea of the strict moral causality of human acts. Whether Job acts rightly or wrongly makes no difference; God has chosen to torment him for reasons of his own. **17b.** *displeasure:* Hebr *ka'as,* as in 5:2a; God's "impatience" is not reserved for the foolish; it also afflicts the just. **18.** The last strophe returns to the theme of chap. 3 and begins with an emphatic *lāmâ,* "Why?" echoing 3:11,20. Verse 20 repeats the theme of God's unwelcome presence, as in 7:16,19; Job can desire only that God withdraw from him. Verses 20b–21a quote, with slight modification, Ps 39:14.

45 (F) Zophar's First Speech (11:1–20). Zophar of Naamah shows himself the least original and the most vehement. He does not appeal (like Eliphaz) to his personal experience nor (like Bildad) to the tradition of the ancients. His authority is wisdom itself, a self-authenticating knowledge possessed by him and identical (at least in its application to human life) with the wisdom of God. This doctrine is not only clear and certain in itself, but its exemplification in Job's case is equally so. In form, the speech is a well-developed parallel to Bildad's first two strophes; 11:2–6 to 8:2; 11:7–12 to 8:3–4; 11:13–19a to 8:5–7. But where Bildad undertook to defend divine justice, Zophar is glorifying divine wisdom, which he feels must equally be vindicated against Job's scandalous and ignorant criticisms. Finally, like the other two speakers, Zophar encourages Job with the prospect of restored happiness. Instead of foolishly claiming to be innocent (his condition is clear proof of the contrary), let him repent of his iniquity and ask God's pardon; thus he will enjoy renewed prosperity.

The speech consists of three six-line strophes and a concluding couplet.

46 (a) JOB'S FOOLISHNESS (11:2–6,7–12). **2.** *be right:* A juridical sense: "Be judged to be right, and acquitted." Job's words are mere words, without substance. **4.** Not an exact quotation, but summing up what Zophar finds objectionable in Job's attitude (cf. 9:21; 10:7,15b). **6a.** Read: "And declare to you the secrets of wisdom, which are marvelous to our understanding"; the fifth line of the strophe. **8–9.** A fine poetic statement of God's transcendence with regard to all human understanding. **12.** A proverb cited as conclusion, whose meaning is obscure.

47 (b) COUNSEL AND ENCOURAGEMENT (11:13–19a,19b–20). Zophar sincerely desires Job's amendment and recovery. He leaves the latter's sins to his own conscience (v 14) and glowingly (and naïvely) pictures the rewards of repentance. **15.** *surely then:* Emphatic, contradicting what Job has said in 10:15. **19b-20.** The brief concluding strophe is an implicit warning; the last phrase indicates that the death wish, which Job has repeatedly expressed, is itself a mark of the wicked man; cf. a similar "sting in the tail" of Bildad's speech, 8:22b.

48 **(G) Job's Third Response (12:1-14:22).** This speech is Job's longest apart from his final soliloquy. Each of the three friends has spoken now, and, as he realizes their unanimous and blunt refusal to accept the testimony of his own clear conscience, he turns on them all with withering sarcasm. Much of what they have said is true, but it is the merest commonplace; it needs no great wisdom to declare that God governs the world and can do all things. Job underlines this with another doxology, this time describing the divine government of human affairs, and how God, for his own mysterious reasons, brings about the rise or fall of peoples and kingdoms. But of these principles, in which Job is as well grounded as they, they are making a false application to his case. God's ways, in the concrete, are not so easy to interpret and understand; they are extremely mysterious to men. The friends will not admit the mystery. In the teeth of the evidence, they are defending God in human terms and are even telling lies on his behalf. This outrageous perversion is denounced by Job in strong terms. He, on the other hand, holds that reverence for God demands respect for truth in the first place. He will testify to that truth and will proclaim his clear conscience, if need be, before God himself. For a moment, he proposes the friends' conclusion: If he is a guilty man, let God make clear his guilt. But he knows God cannot do that—he is only treating Job as though he were guilty. Is this then a temporary aberration on God's part? Job seizes on this idea: He could endure this estrangement if assured that there would be a future reconciliation—if, for instance, there would be a happy reunion with God after this unhappy life. But this is wishful thinking: Death is the end; no restoration or recovery of happiness is possible. The speech ends on the same mournful note as chaps. 7 and 10.

Strophic division is somewhat uncertain because of textual obscurities; see Skehan, *SIPW* 105-8.

49 **(a) Job's Wisdom Matches Theirs (12:2-6, 7-12,13-19,20-25). 2.** The MT reads "you are people" (no "the"), so a word is certainly missing, probably "of discernment" or something similar. In any case, the sarcasm is clear from the parallel stich. **3b.** The *NAB* translation rightly omits "I am not inferior to you," inserted here from 13:2b. **4-5.** Text is obscure, probably corrupt. Suggested emendations (Terrien, Horst) would give ". . . neighbors, as one who calls on God, but he oppresses him; For misfortune there is mockery, for weakness contempt, for one staggering, an extra push. . . ." The point is (as Job is going to develop in the following strophes) that calamities, whether of nations or individuals, demonstrate God's supremacy and mystery, but not necessarily wickedness in the sufferers; therefore, the friends are being unjust to him. **7-9.** *you:* Singular pronoun, so one of the friends is being addressed; presumably the last speaker, Zophar, is being ridiculed for his remarks in 11:7-9. In v 9b, the MT reads "the hand of Yahweh," the only occurrence of this name within the dialogue. The phrase is a quotation from Isa 41:20, which accounts for the anomaly (cf. the quotation in 1:21). **12.** Possibly a sarcastic phrase at Eliphaz's expense. **13-19,20-25.** These two strophes, praising God's "wisdom and might . . . counsel and understanding . . . strength and prudence," surpass what Zophar had to say on the subject, 11:7-10; but he had jumped to a conclusion about "iniquity" (11:11), which Job denies.

50 **(b) Summary and Warning against "Defending" God Dishonestly (13:1-5,6-11). 1.** Job opposes his experience to that of Eliphaz (cf. 4:8,12; 5:3,27); he, too, has seen, heard, and understood. **3.** Eliphaz had said (5:8), "But I would seek God . . ."; Job repeats the first words, "But I would speak. . . ." Job can say this because he has been accustomed to speaking thus. Throughout the dialogue he alone utters prayers to God. The friends praise him, but they do not address him. They have no need of such personal reference. Their God works retribution in strict accord with human deserts, and they need only act correctly. There is nothing they need or wish to say to him, and there is no place for a relationship of love. They do not "reason with God," only about him—and, in part, wrongly. **5.** A pointed rebuke to wisdom teachers!—cf. Prov 17:28. **6-11.** After the emphatic "Hear!" the remaining lines of this strophe begin each with the same letter. This famous passage is a powerful warning against a temptation that may come to all controversialists and apologists, in theological as in other contexts. **7a.** The Vg version is still more forceful: Numquid Deus indiget vestro mendacio? "Does God need your lies?"

51 **(c) Job Reasons with God (13:12-16,17-22, 23-27).** This protest and plea for explanation are genuinely religious, inspired by Job's past experience of God's love and by his intense concern over his personal standing with him. Yet the imagery adopted is inevitably forensic; i.e., according to the conventions of the psalm of lament, enemies are thought of as opponents in a lawsuit, against whom the sufferer must defend and establish his innocence. The friends have shown themselves to be such enemies, and such an enemy, according to outward appearances and the general estimation of human beings, is God himself. Thus, Job pictures him as his adversary at law (cf. 9:32ff.), which leads him to conceive an illusory equality between himself and God and thereby to conceive a relation of justice, one to the other. It is for this misrepresentation that Job must repent at the end of the book. But it does not, happily, corrupt his intense faith in God's love. **12b.** Hebr *gabbîm* can be interpreted as "answers": "Your answers crumble like clay" (lit., "are answers of clay"). **14-15.** Job is risking his life in thus approaching God, but he no longer cares for it. **15a.** *I will wait for him:* The reading of the MT and versions; but the consonantal text has "I have no hope," which better fits the context. Thus, "He may (or will) slay me—I hope for nothing else—yet I will defend . . ." **16.** Paradoxically, Job sees his readiness to face God as the best guarantee of his innocence, of his truthfulness, and therefore of God's admitting he is right ("salvation"). He has complete faith that God, if he speaks, will speak in Job's favor. **17.** The strophe begins with another emphatic "Hear!" (pl., addressed to the friends), parallel to 13:6. **18b.** *in the right:* More technically, "I shall be found innocent, acquitted." **19.** Job promises to abide by the judgment of the court. **20-22.** Job begs (sg., addressed to God) that God will meet his arguments and not use his infinite superiority to crush him. He is willing to be either defendant (v 22a) or plaintiff (v 22b). **23.** Receiving no answer, Job speaks first. He repeats the challenge he has uttered to the friends: He is confident he has committed no such misdeeds as would be reason for his suffering. **24.** God remains silent. He neither declares Job's guilt nor confirms his innocence. And Job resumes his reproaches. **26b.** *faults of my youth:* These are mentioned as something inconsiderable, for which the grown man should not be held responsible. **28.** Replace after 14:2. There is a disconcerting switch from 2d to 3d pers. for which no antecedent is given. The verse deals with the ephemerality of human existence and fits better in 14:2–3.

52   (d) Lament over Human Life (14:1–2, 13:28, 14:3; 4–6; 7–9; 10–12). Job generalizes his lament, returning in v 3 to the theme of 7:17. **4.** A quite obscure verse; possibly some words are missing. The *NAB* version (like most translations) paraphrases. Some Church Fathers, relying on the OL or Vg versions, saw here a reference to original sin, but it is not justified by the Hebrew. Verses 7–9 and 10–12 are parallel strophes, emphasizing human mortality by a striking poetic contrast between the fate of a tree (it blooms again) and humans.

53   (e) A Dream and Reality (14:13–17,18–22). Two parallel five-line strophes. In the first, Job contemplates, with eagerness and even passionate longing, the possibility of a restoration to God's intimacy after death, a reconciliation in which God would show himself again the loving benefactor that he really is. **13a.** *netherworld: Šĕ'ôl,* the abode of the dead (cf. 3:17ff). Job here supposes a remarkable duality in God: He would hide Job—from his own wrath. Verse 15b echoes 10:8 (rather than 10:3, where the Hebr words are different). Similarly, v 16b refers to 10:6; God would resume the old relationship of gracious kindness. **17.** Another obscure text; in any case, not a confession of guilt (cf. 13:23). **18–20.** In the second strophe, Job returns to sad reality. **21–22.** He rejects even the traditional consolation of leaving a prosperous family. Anyway, Job now has no children to leave.

54   (H) Eliphaz's Second Speech (15:1–35). Eliphaz's tone is notably different here from what it was in chaps. 4–5. At first, he had looked on Job as a fundamentally wise and God-fearing man (4:3–6) who had happened to incur God's sudden and just anger by some particular fault. But now he has heard him, in three successive speeches, deny any such guilt, reject the sacrosanct principle that suffering is always, and only, punishment for wrongdoing, and challenge God to give some other explanation of his affliction. Eliphaz is not only offended at Job's blunt rejection of the traditional doctrine of the sages; he is profoundly shocked at such fundamental questioning, by which he feels his own religious security threatened. His faith in God is bound up with his narrow retribution doctrine, which he must defend at all costs. Hence, the vigor and the angry tone of his attack. Instead of the encouraging subject—reward of the righteous—stressed in his first speech, he now develops the negative and menacing one—punishment of the wicked.

The speech contains six five-line strophes, an intermediate three-line strophe (vv 17–19), and one one-line conclusion.

55   (a) Job Has Spoken Impiously and Presumptuously (15:2–6,7–11,12–16). **2.** *wise:* Emphatic—"a truly wise man" (cf. v 8b). **4.** Eliphaz had acknowledged Job's piety (cf. 4:6), but now he claims that his attitude is destructive of piety and prayer; his words are "offensive to pious ears." **6.** Eliphaz no doubt has in mind such passages as 9:20,24; 10:3; etc. **7–8.** Here, there is reference to the myth of the *Urmensch,* the first man, who enjoyed equality with the sons of God, and, in particular, had access to divine wisdom. The theme is reflected in Ezek 28:11–19 and in Prov 8:22–26, where it is transferred to divine Wisdom personified. Verse 7b here is practically identical with Prov 8:25b. Eliphaz conveniently forgets that he himself had claimed superhuman wisdom, at least, through the audition of 4:12–21; but then, his revelation was soundly orthodox, in fact, conventional. **10.** Presumably, the speaker is referring to himself. **11.** *consolations . . . speech:* The latter is *dābār,*

more properly "word"; both refer to the "word" of 4:12 in Eliphaz's first speech (the only one to "deal gently" with Job), and both attribute to it an authority belonging to the words of a prophet—another ironic touch by the author, in view of the ending of the story. **14–16.** Eliphaz repeats in substance his "word" of 4:17–21 (also quoting Job's phrase, 14:1), but with harsher expressions in v 16; in v 16b, read "a man," not the genus but an individual, whom Eliphaz need not name.

56   (b) Punishment for the Impious and Presumptuous (15:17–19,20–24,25–29a,29b–34,35). **18–19.** Eliphaz stresses the antiquity and purity—and hence the authority—of the sapiential tradition, which Eliphaz represents. **20–24.** The first of three strophes describing the frightful calamities that are sure to come upon "the abominable, the corrupt" one. First he is shown as tormented by his evil conscience and in constant apprehension of disaster. **25–28.** Two examples are given (vv 25,27) of his impiety, which provokes the disasters of vv 26,28. Verse 25 especially is Eliphaz's interpretation of Job's attitude. In vv 27–30, the text is corrupted and uncertain in detail. **29b–34.** The third strophe uses botanical comparisons to illustrate the wretch's downfall. **35.** Summary: "the fruit of evil is evil" (Habel).

57   (I) Job's Fourth Response (16:1–17:16). This passage continues the lamentation form and especially develops the motif of denunciation of enemies. These are, in turn, Eliphaz, the three together, and God himself. But in the middle comes the unexpected appeal to a "witness in heaven," who is taking up, or will take up, Job's defense. The speech ends as before with consideration of Job's approaching death and final descent to the underworld.

Twelve strophes can be distinguished in the speech, of which the fourth, seventh, and twelfth have four lines each; the rest have three lines.

58   (a) Afflicted by Men and by God (16:2–4b, 4c–6,7–9b,9c–11,17,12–13,14–16). Job starts with a statement of weariness: He has heard all this, and it is unprofitable. He knows these words and gestures; they do not deal realistically with his case. **2b.** In 15:11, Eliphaz had offered "divine consolations." Using a cognate word, Job calls the friends "wearisome consolers." **3b.** The vb. is sg., addressed to Eliphaz; in vv 4–5 the pronouns are pl., referring to all three. Similarly v 8 (sg.) followed by vv 9c–10 (pl.). **8b.** A corrupt text, it is omitted in the *NAB;* emended, it may be read "and utters calumnies to my face." **9c–11.** The friends are called impious and wicked according to the conventions of the psalm of lament. Job is affirming his innocence; therefore, the opposing party in the suit must be "guilty." **17.** This verse should probably follow v 11. Job reiterates what Zophar had quoted in 11:4, using the same word, *zak,* "pure." **12–16.** But behind the friends is God, and it is his actions that have given occasion for their abuse. In drastic terms Job describes how God has attacked him. Verses 12c–13a repeat the St. Sebastian image (cf. 6:4; 7:20c); Job is God's target, shot full of his arrows.

59   (b) The Witness in Heaven (16:18–21). Abruptly, from the depth of his despair, Job utters a cry of hope. It is first an adjuration to the earth, which will "receive his blood" unjustly shed (cf. Gen 4:10; Isa 26:21; Ezek 24:8); according to the old idea, innocent blood cries to God for vengeance on the one who shed it (who in this case is God himself!). Let the earth not stifle this cry. **19.** But for the cry to be effective, there must be someone to hear it; Job envisages that someone as his "witness" and defender in heaven, who on hearing of his fate will intervene to vindicate him. Many attempts have been made to identify this witness as a heavenly being, angel or intercessor (cf. 5:1; and Elihu,

33:23–24; S. Mowinckel, in *Vom Alten Testament* [Fest. K. Marti; BZAW 41; 207–12); but more probably it is God himself. He seems to be Job's adversary at law, but is really on his side (the same duality as in 14:13); cf. the following verses. **20b.** *drop tears:* Read instead, from Akk *dalāpu,* "stay awake" (Horst): "My eyes strain sleeplessly toward God."

60   (c) COMPLAINT CONTINUED (16:22–17:2,3–5, 6–8,10–12,13–16). Job seems to envisage his vindication taking place in heaven rather than on earth, where his situation is hopeless. He is resigned to dying but not to being estranged from God. **3.** Inasmuch as the friends will not "witness" for him, Job begs God himself to find a guarantor who will "go bail" for Job in his presence. **5.** This obscure verse (half-omitted in *NAB*) may be understood as a proverb applicable to the friends: "A man invites his neighbors to share [food], while the eyes of his children are failing [from hunger]"; i.e., the friends are "consoling" the prosperous, while leaving Job in his misery. **5–9.** These verses are obscure; Job seems to describe his misery again, with reference to the scandal that it causes. If v 9 is not a gloss, it must be understood ironically. **10.** A sardonic invitation to the friends. **12.** The verse is obscure, and lacking in the LXX; perhaps Job mocks their easy optimism, e.g., Zophar in 11:17. **13–16.** The speech ends with an ironic and decisive rejection of the prospects of happiness they had earlier held out to him, as part of their "consolation." Job does not believe in them, nor does he particularly desire them; he merely wants to know his standing with God. Meanwhile, he would rather face the grim truth, which he describes with unflinching vividness.

61   (J) **Bildad's Second Speech (18:1–21).** Bildad's answer is comparatively restrained and all the more unfeeling. He rebukes Job for his abusive language and his contempt for ancient wisdom, and he insinuates that suffering as punishment for sin is a universal law from which Job cannot claim exemption. The bulk of his speech is a lurid description of the fate awaiting the man "who knows not God." Like Eliphaz, Bildad this time has no word of consolation for Job, only warning and implicit threats.

The speech contains six three-line strophes and a one-line conclusion.

62   (a) REBUKE TO JOB (18:2–4). **2.** Bildad begins as in 8;2, with, "How long [will you not put an end . . .]?" The vbs. are pl. (also the pronoun "your" in 3), which makes a difficulty. Most commentators make them sg., as referring only to Job. **3.** *beasts:* May refer esp. to 16:9–10. **4.** Bildad coldly remarks that Job is the cause of his own torment because he will not take the right means to remove it. He would like the laws of the universe changed to suit himself. The last phrase echoes 16:9a and 14:18b.

63   (b) FATE OF THE WICKED (18:5–7,8–10,11–14, 15–17,18–20,21). **5–7.** This strophe develops the image of the failing light. **8–10.** Here the image of the snare that entangles the wicked. **11–14.** Text is corrupted; there should be three distichs. After ". . . at his side" in the *NAB,* read "Pestilence consumes his skin, the firstborn of death consumes his limbs. He is plucked from the security of his tent, he is conducted before the king of terrors." This last striking phrase is a personification of death, as the "firstborn" is of disease. **15.** Begin, "In his tent no trace of him remains, over his abode. . . ." **20.** *after . . . before:* Better understood as points of the compass (reckoned by facing E); translate, "At his fate men of the West are appalled, and men of the East are struck. . . ."

64   (K) **Job's Fifth Response (19:1–29).** In contrast with the friends' rigid adherence to their predetermined positions, Job's successive speeches show a certain development. The friends' criticisms have compelled him to analyze his situation in order to seek an alternative to their unacceptable verdict. In this, his central discourse, he achieves an insight and a profession of faith, which supply at least a provisional solution and enable him to triumph over his worst temptation. Even the style reaches a certain climax of power and pathos. Job here draws together themes touched on in his earlier speeches: the validity of his clear conscience (6:30; 9:29; 10:7; 16:17), which the judge—if only he will hear the case—must certainly ratify (10:2,7; 13:23; 16:21); his intuition that God must yearn for him, even as he does for God (7:8,21; 10:8–9; 14:15); his longing and hope that God will finally remember and vindicate him (14:13–15; 16:19–20).

65   The problem is the apparent change in God's attitude to him: he was Job's friend; he seems now to be his enemy. Job's solution is an affirmation of faith. The change is only apparent; the abandonment is only temporary. The friends are uncharitable and unjust in their conviction that God is declaring him to be a sinner. His sufferings, which must speedily lead to his death, have been decreed by God in spite of his innocence, and for the moment, for some unexplained reason, he will not receive Job's pleas and protests. Nevertheless, he will eventually, in his own good time, remember him and pronounce his vindication. And Job—even though he has died in the meantime—will be present at this, and will see God as he truly is, his friend.

Between introductory and closing two-line strophes, the chapter contains four three-line strophes, one four-line, another three-line, one five-line, i.e., 2; 3, 3, 3; 3, 4, 3; 5; 2.

66   (a) GOD'S DOING, NOT A HUMAN'S (19:2–3, 4–6,7–9,10–12). **2.** Job begins by throwing Bildad's exordium back at him (using the same expressions, "How long . . . ?" and "words," as 18:2). That he has to bear God's mysterious displeasure is bad enough; need they make things worse by their inhumanity? **4.** If Job is wrong, he will only harm himself; why must they be so bitter and so intolerant? (The reason is that he threatens their religious existence; he must not be right, otherwise their whole faith would be undermined. It is their insecurity that makes them cruel.) **6.** They persist in seeking "the root of the matter" in him, whereas it is really to be looked for in God; and whatever else it is, it is not God's justice. Job here contradicts Bildad, 18:4a; cf. 18:8. Verses 7–9 and 10–12 picture in highly pathetic terms what Job is experiencing. **7.** To "cry 'Injustice!' " is the technical phrase for a public act, by which a man suffering personal injury could demand that the community (and eventually God) take action to vindicate him and put right his wrong (cf. Hab 1:2). Job's sufferings (vv 8–12) are not felt by him as the automatic and impersonal effects of wrongdoing (cf. the images used by Bildad in 18:5–7,8–10); they are inflicted by deliberate and personal acts of God. Note esp. v 11.

67   (b) ISOLATION AND LONELINESS (19:13–15,16–19,20–22). The apparent hostility of God produces hostility of human beings. A certain climax is probably intended in the sequence of relationships; i.e., they proceed, broadly, from less to greater intimacy. **13a.** *my brethren:* Probably refers to his three interlocutors (cf. 6:15). **17b.** *men of my family:* Lit., "sons of my womb," i.e., of his mother: full brothers. **19.** The inner circle of intimates, of whom even greater loyalty was expected than of wife or brothers. *my intimate friends:* Lit., "men of my secret council." The network of human relationships that constitute a person's life has been ripped apart. Job is ostracized, isolated, on the verge of nonexistence.

20. The translation is uncertain, but the meaning is something like, "I am nothing, and have nothing, but my skin and bones." He is reduced to bare survival, physical existence, but nothing more. **21.** At least the three are still present to him; communication is still possible, and Job utters his famous cry to the only audience he has. *hand of God:* This echoes 1:11 and esp. 2:5 (cf. also 6:9; 12:9; 13:21). God's hand is the instrument of creation and salvation, but it also works destruction (cf. 5:18). **22b.** *insatiably prey:* Lit., "and are not sated with my flesh?"; this idiom means, "and will not stop calumniating me?"

68 (c) HOPE OF THE VISION OF GOD (19:23–27). Even the foregoing appeal has been in vain, as we see by the speeches that follow. At this climax, Job is utterly alone, abandoned by family, friends, men, and apparently God. Yet from this depth (as in 16:18) he achieves a "leap of faith." If God will not speak now, then he must in the future. It is to the future that Job appeals. Because he will soon die, he wants his testimony recorded, against the day when his case will come to judgment. The record must be an inscription, as permanent and indestructible as possible. **23.** *inscribed in a record:* Hebr *sēper* is usually understood as a scroll of leather or papyrus, but it can mean anything written, an inscription; "inscribed" here is lit. "chiseled" or "incised." Thus, vv 23 and 24 refer to the same process (H. S. Gehman, *JBL* 63 [1944] 303–7). **24.** *lead:* This word can be explained from Persian practice, as in Darius I's Behistun inscription: "The wedges . . . cut into the rock were themselves filled in with lead" (G. G. Cameron, *NatGeog* 98 [1950] 844; K. Galling, *WO* 2 [1954] 3–6). **25–27.** These are the words (v 23a) to be solemnly recorded. Unfortunately they have suffered textual corruption, esp. in v 26a, and the translation is much debated (see H. H. Rowley, *BJRL* 91 [1958] 203–5 for a survey, and also N. Habel for recent attempts). *vindicator:* Hebr *gōʾēl* means the next of kin whose obligation it was to rescue from poverty, redeem from slavery, or avenge a death (A. R. Johnson, in *Congress Volume: Copenhagen 1953* [VTSup 1; Leiden, 1953] 67–77). Presumably it must be God, but commentators differ (cf. 16:19). Does Job hope for the act of vindication before or after his death? And if the latter, how does he conceive of his own state at the time? The former solution seems very unlikely, given his constant expectation of an unhappy death, also the preceding "inscription" passage. If the latter is correct, then Job apparently expects to have, in (or from) the underworld, a vision of God pronouncing his vindication "on the dust," i.e., on earth (?). This is admittedly strange, yet consistent with what he has said earlier and, on the whole, the most likely interpretation. *lives:* Or "is living." A much-discussed Ugaritic religious text has "I know that [he is] living, mighty Baʿal!" (*ANET* 140; cf. E. G. Kraeling, *The Book of the Ways of God* [NY, 1939] 89), but the parallel may be fortuitous. More relevant is the belief of Israel; it stressed that Yahweh was "the living God," and this dynamism seems to provide a connection of thought with Job's "survival of consciousness" after death. The divine vitality is such that it will cause Job, even in the underworld, to have at least momentary knowledge, or rather vision, of what occurs on earth. (A similar line of thought is carried much further in Christ's argument for the resurrection of the patriarchs, from the nature of "the God of the living"; Matt 22:32.) But we must not (as did Jerome in the Vg) read into the text any idea of an actual "resurrection of the body," even if limited to Job's unique case. *at last:* Hebr *ʾaḥărôn* can be construed as a noun, "the Last" (applied to the Lord in Isa 44:6).

Verses 26–27 have five stichs, but only these phrases are fairly sure: ". . . from my flesh I shall behold God . . .

my eyes shall see—no stranger! My emotions are consumed within me." "Behold" is *ḥāzâ,* the vb. used of seeing visions. This sight of God, emphasized three times, is what Job really craves (cf. 42:5).

(Dhorme, E., "L'idée de l'au-delà dans la religion hébraïque," *RHR* 123 [1941] 113–42, esp. 140. Irwin, W. A., "Job's Redeemer," *JBL* 81 [1962] 217–29. Larcher, C., *Le livre de Job* [BJ; Paris, 1957] 27–31. Lindblom, J., " 'Ich weiss, dass mein Erlöser lebt,' " *ST* 2 [1940] 65–77. Martin-Achard, R., *De la mort à la résurrection d'après l'Ancien Testament* [Neuchâtel, 1956] 133–44. Meek, T. J., "Job XIX,25–27," *VT* 6 [1956] 100–3. Mowinckel, S., "Hiobs gōʾēl und Zeuge im Himmel," [→ 59 above] 207–12. North, C. R., "The Redeemer God," *Int* 2 [1948] 3–16. Tournay, R., "Relectures bibliques concernant la vie future et l'angélologie," *RB* 69 [1962] 481–505, esp. 489ff.)

69 (d) WARNING TO THE FRIENDS (19:28–29). *persecute:* The same word (*rādap*) as "hound" in v 22. **28b.** This verse puts in a nutshell the error of the friends. They insist that this reversal of fortune must be explicable by Job's acts; to attribute it to a mysterious action of God would invalidate their claim to understand the workings of divine retribution. **29.** The last word, *šaddîn* (or *šaddûn*), is unknown and hard to explain. It is tempting to understand it as a variant of *šadday,* "that [so] you may come to know the Almighty" (L. R. Fisher, *VT* 11 [1961] 342–43).

70 (L) Zophar's Second Speech (20:1–29). This speech closely parallels Bildad's speech in chap. 18; both deal with the same subject—the destruction of the wicked. Together they frame and set off Job's great credo in chap. 19. In contrast to his living and developing faith, they present the unchanging rigidity of the "traditional" retribution doctrine. Zophar's distinguishing marks are greater vehemence and some rather crude images (vv 7,15). The probable strophic division is a two-line introduction, four six-line strophes, and a one-line finale. (B. H. Kelley, "Truth in Contradiction: A Study of Job 20 and 21," *Int* 15 [1961] 147–56.)

71 (a) THE TRIUMPH OF THE WICKED IS BRIEF (20:2–3,4–9). **2.** The MT begins with *lākēn,* "therefore," which suggests that a preceding distich is missing. The *NAB* version interchanges the first stichs of vv 2 and 3, which is also possible, but we miss the usual rhetorical question and the reference to Job's words. However, for the first and only time, one of the friends admits to being impressed by Job's utterance; his "reproach" (19:21? or 29?) has momentarily shaken Zophar. But the latter recovers and reacts all the more violently to reassure himself. Prompt disaster falling on the wicked: this is, always has been, and always must be a fact of universal experience. He wants to hear Job acknowledge this principle and confess that it has been verified in his case. **7.** The wicked is said to perish in his dung (*NAB:* "fuel of his fire").

72 (b) HE MUST GIVE UP ILL-GOTTEN GAINS (20:11–16,17–22,23–28,29). The text is obscure and overloaded, but the main image is clear: the riches of the impious are like food that turns to poison in his stomach. He has to vomit them up. **10.** "His sons must make compensation to the poor, his [or their] hands give back his wealth." The line is out of place and may be a gloss. In the *NAB,* v 10b is joined to 21a. **23.** Although the word "God" does not appear in the Hebrew, it must be the subject. In general, the friends avoid speaking of God's actions in crudely physical terms. **29.** A conclusion very like Bildad's (18:21) and ending with the same divine name "El."

73 (M) Job's Sixth Response (21:1–34). Job has emerged victorious from his personal struggle; he has overcome the temptation presented to him by his friends, as earlier he overcame that of his wife. He has stated his faith that God knows his innocence and will one day (although after Job's death) testify to it. Thereby, though his present misery is not lessened, his belief in God's goodness is preserved and he has a firm basis for his rejection of the friends' accusations. Now he passes from mere defensiveness to the attack. They have condemned him on the ground of a fixed principle. Job undertakes to show that their condemnation is unjustified because the principle is false. In human experience generally, God does not send sure retribution in this life; the wicked and godless are not destroyed in a moment. The gravity of this statement, which to the sages must sound like blasphemy, is brought out in vv 5-6. Job himself is horrified by it, but it is the truth: not that the impious always prosper, but that they often do (cf. Jer 12:1ff.; Ps 73; Eccl 7:15).

This speech is the only one of Job's orations that is exclusively polemical; it contains no soliloquy or prayer. For the moment his own case is "solved," and he is dealing simply with the doctrine of the friends.

The strophic division is uncertain. Verse 16 (and perhaps 18) appears to be a gloss; v 22 belongs to the following speech; vv 30-33 are obscure. Probably there are eight strophes, of 5; 3, 4, 4 (or 3); 3, 4; 3, and 5 lines. **74** (a) INTRODUCTION (21:2-6). Job warns them that what he has to say will shock them more than anything they have heard so far. **2.** Cf. 13:5; 16:3. **3b.** *you:* Sg.; the other 2d pers. vbs. in the context are pl.; therefore this address may be directed to Eliphaz. If so, he responds with something worse than mockery (chap. 22). **5.** Laying hand on mouth is a gesture of voluntary silence (cf. 29:9; 40:4), here signifying horror and amazement. **6.** The facts were always there; Job had not adverted to them until his calamities (and his friends' arguments) forced him to look anew at human life and to ask himself whether the principle of retribution works universally and infallibly. Honesty compels him to a flat denial. He himself is appalled to realize how experience contradicts a fixed (and exaggerated) religious doctrine. **75** (b) THE HAPPINESS OF PEOPLE WITHOUT GOD (21:7-9,10-13,14-18). It is evidence of the author's subtlety and insight that he does not propose the trite example of the successful tyrant who breaks divine and human laws and sows misery and disaster on all sides. It is too easy to argue (cf. Eliphaz, 15:20; Zophar, 20:12-14,18; and Plato's *Republic*) that such a man finds no real happiness and is the worst sufferer from his own vices. Instead, Job describes "the good pagan," the good-living, moral atheist, who by any external tests that can be applied enjoys a naturally happy life, filled with all the blessings that can be granted by God alone. Such a person, possessing the good things of life independently of any religious belief or practice, feels no need of God. On the other hand, since *ex hypothesi* this happiness really is God's gift, is he not, by such indiscriminate bestowal of his bounty, encouraging atheism? (In Matt 5:45, Christ cites this very fact as evidence of the heavenly father's love for humanity: He "sends rain upon the just and the unjust alike." This is intelligible in terms of love, but not in terms of retributive justice.) Again are shown the limits and insufficiency of the friends' commercial morality. Throughout the dialogue they have advanced no motive for serving God apart from fear of punishment and hope of reward. Anything higher—the possibility of serving God "for love" (as Job did)—is utterly beyond them. **7.** Contrary to 20:5, the prosperity of the "wicked," i.e., the irreligious, does sometimes endure and increase. Job does not bother to give instances; he asks: How do you explain it? Verses 8-13 are to be compared with Eliphaz's description in 5:20-26. All that was

there pictured as reward of repentance is here enjoyed without reference to God. **10.** The homely detail of animal fertility is significant; this was regarded as a mysterious and important divine blessing. So, likewise, were numerous and healthy children (v 11). **14-15.** "What does it profit . . . ?" These happy people have no motive of self-interest or necessity to induce them to acknowledge or worship God. The friends could suggest nothing else. Only Job could say they have an "obligation" of gratitude and love. **16.** Omit as gloss. **17.** Job refers scornfully to Bildad's glib claim in 18:5-6 ("lamp . . . put out"), 18:12 ("destruction"), and 18:10 ("noose," same word as "portion"). **76** (c) NO EVIDENT CONNECTION BETWEEN VIRTUE AND HAPPINESS (21:19-21,23-26). **19-21.** A facile answer could be given to the "difficulty" that an irreligious man had apparently prospered all his life. The sages would appeal to the principle of solidarity and insist that his children would suffer the penalty of his impiety. Job objects that in such a case justice would not be satisfied; the guilty party would know nothing and feel nothing of such "punishment." **23-26.** A blunt and factual summary of human life (cf. Eccl 8:14; 9:2,11). The friends simply will not face this truth (cf. v 34b). **77** (d) PEACEFUL DEATH AND POSTHUMOUS FAME OF THE GODLESS (21:27-29,30-34). **28.** Not a verbatim quotation, but cf. 18:15,21; 20:9. **34a.** *comfort:* Makes an *inclusio* with "consolation" (a cognate word) in v 2. **34b.** *perfidy:* Hebr *ma'al,* meaning usually a sacrilegious offense against God; the friends are "lying on behalf of God" (cf. 13:7). **78** (N) Eliphaz's Third Speech (22:1-30). Eliphaz, of sterner stuff than Zophar, is not in the least shaken by Job's argument. He is horrified, although hardly surprised. From the beginning he has found Job obstinately perverse. His denial of the very foundations of morality (as it seems to Eliphaz) in the speech just heard is the last straw. Eliphaz drops all attempt at gentleness and forbearance and speaks his mind. In his first speech (chaps. 4-5) he has been all encouragement; in his second (chap. 15) he has spoken severely of Job's present irreverence; now he declares openly that Job must have been, all along, a hypocrite and a secret sinner, and he cites by way of examples some of the crimes he must have committed. The inspired author here give a chilling but all-too-credible portrayal of the intellectual and moral corruption of a devoutly religious man who has confused his own simple reasonings with divine revelation. The theistic principle from which Eliphaz starts is true (that God is just), but it is not the whole truth (God is also loving); and by treating it in isolation and drawing conclusions from it as though it were the whole truth he distorts humanity's whole relationship to God. Moreover, he himself commits grave sins of injustice and uncharity by uttering lies and calumnies against his neighbor.

The speech contains six strophes, but the lengths of the first four are uncertain. Probably vv 8 and 18 should be omitted as glosses, and 21:22 should be replaced before 22:12. Thus, the strophes consist of 4, 5; 4, 5; 5, 5 lines, but cf. Skehan, *SIPW* 110-11. **79** (a) EXORDIUM (22:2-5). Eliphaz still cannot imagine serving God "for nothing." Somebody must gain by it; if—according to Job—religion brings no profit to one, then it must bring profit to God! **2-4.** Eliphaz puts a series of rhetorical questions, meant to show the absurdity of Job's position. Here again the irony of the author is at work, for the questions can, in all seriousness, be answered in the affirmative. Job's love and loyalty are, indeed, a "gain" to the Almighty, who in 1:8 and 2:3 expressed his pleasure in his servant's perfection; he seemed almost to be proud of Job. In a sense, it is precisely because of Job's piety that he is being "reproved"; that was what had prompted the Adversary's attack. But to Eliphaz, confined in his narrow doctrine of retributive justice, these are fantasies. The only possible alternative to admitting God to be unjust is declaring Job to be wicked, which he proceeds to do on no better evidence than the logical requirements of his dogmatic system. **80** (b) Job's Sins (22:6–11). Eliphaz takes almost at random the standard list of social crimes that could be committed with impunity by the wealthy and powerful in the ancient world. **6.** Cf. Exod 22:25–26; Deut 24:6, 12–13,17. **7.** Cf. Ezek 18:7; Isa 58:7. **9.** Cf. Deut 24:17–22. **10.** *therefore:* An emphatic word, which makes the fallacy the more obvious. Eliphaz's real reasoning has been just the opposite: Because Job is suffering "snares . . . terror . . . darkness . . . deluge," "therefore" he must have done the deeds of vv 6–9. **81** (c) Rebuttal of Job's Argument (21:22; 22:12–14,15–20). **12–14.** Eliphaz suggests that Job thinks God is too far away to see him, whereas it is his own sight that is dim; cf. "he cannot see" (v 14a) with "you cannot see" (v 11a). The apparent quotation is hard to connect with statements made by Job so far (cf. later, 23:8). **17.** Eliphaz picks up the sayings Job had attributed to the "good pagans" (21:14–15), insinuating (v 15) that this is Job's own outlook. In fact, he claims (v 16), it was the "way" of the ancient sinners destroyed by the flood; i.e., there were people such as Job describes, but, far from living out their lives in peace, they suffered the most dreadful of disasters. Verse 20b may be intended to link the destruction of Sodom with the flood, considering its citizens to be successors of the antediluvian sinners (Gen 6:11ff.; 19:24ff.). **82** (d) Recommendation to Be Reconciled with God (22:21–25,26–30). Despite his denunciations, Eliphaz has not given up hope of his friend's conversion. His admonitions are sincere (and beautifully expressed); but to him "conversion" is making a bargain with God (v 21) that will be profitable to Job (v 28). **22.** Betrays Eliphaz's arrogant assurance that he is God's mouthpiece and bearer of his words.

83 (O) Job's Seventh Response (23:1–24:25). It is not sure if this speech is complete. Chapters 24–27 are in obvious disorder, and in some places the text is so corrupted it makes no sense.

As chap. 21 was entirely polemical, chap. 23 is entirely devoted to Job's personal reflections and his search for God. There is no reference to the friends or their doctrine, except for the indirect rejection of Eliphaz' calumnies in vv 11–12. Compared with Job's earlier speeches, this lament is notably less passionate, although it is profoundly mournful. His profession of faith (chap. 19) has resolved his doubts but has not lightened his desolation. He now dwells on God's inaccessibility and remoteness, which make it impossible for Job to "get through" to him. In terms of mystical theology, Job here describes a dark night of the soul, in which the real absence of God is the keenest of all torments to the one who loves him and used to experience him (see *VSpir* 95 [1956] 372–91).

There are five strophes of 3,3,3,4,3 lines.

84 (a) Yearning for the Encounter with God (23:2–4,5–7). **2–3a.** The MT reads, "Still today my complaint is rebellious, my hand is heavy upon my groaning. Oh, that I knew how to reach him. . . ." Apart from "his hand," the *NAB*'s other corrections seem unnecessary. **3b–7.** Job once more evokes the courtroom scene of 9:13–21; 13:14–27, but in a more peaceful vein. He is no longer afraid that God would crush him or

refuse to hear him. Rather, he would listen and respond with words of consolation. **7.** An echo of 13:16. *preserve my rights:* "Secure my acquittal, vindication." **85** (b) God Is Inaccessible and Unpredictable (23:8–10,11–14,15–17). **8–9.** Cf. just the opposite in Ps 139:8–10. **11.** A denial of 22:6–9. **12.** A reference to 22:22. Job has always done this; he does not need to receive God's words from Eliphaz. **14b.** Cf. 10:13. **17.** Corrupt and obscure text. Perhaps a statement; "Because from him I am hidden by darkness, and my face is veiled in thick gloom" (imitating Hebr word order). This is Job's spiritual state—the dark night. **86** (c) Misery of the Oppressed Poor (24:1–12). As in chap. 21, Job passes from his particular experience to the general. In moving terms, he describes the oppression practiced by unscrupulous rulers and the misery of the poor and unprotected. The passage is a negative parallel to 21:7–17. There, God did not intervene to punish the impious; here he does not rescue the oppressed. These, according to all orthodox Israelite theology, were two of his chief functions. **1.** *times . . . days:* Namely, of judgment. **9.** "They plunder the field of the orphan, they take pledges from the poor." This is omitted in *NAB,* as a duplicate of v 3. **87** (d) Enemies of the Light (24:13–17). A short wisdom essay. Murderers, adulterers, and thieves have this in common: they hate the light (cf. John 3:19–20). The connection with Job's speech is doubtful. **88** (e) Obscure Section (24:18–24). At some early stage in the ms. transmission of the book, this section must have become nearly illegible. The next copyist did his best but could not make much sense of it; the same is true for us. It may not even be in its right place. **89** (f) The Conclusion of Job's Speech (24:25). *this:* May refer esp. to 24:2–12. **90** (P) Obscure Chapters 25–27 (25:1–27:23). These chapters, one would expect, should contain Bildad's third speech, Job's eighth response, and Zophar's third speech. Whether through mutilation or partial destruction of a manuscript at some early stage of the book's history—or possibly by deliberate editorial rearrangement—the text has become disordered and probably incomplete as well; some of the original may have been lost altogether. Many reconstructions of the original sequence have been proposed by commentators, but none has gained an accepted consensus. For one proposal, see MacKenzie in *JBC* 31:90. The sequence of the MT will be followed here.

(Barton, G., "The Composition of Job 24–30" *JBL* 30 [1911] 66–77. Dhorme, P., "Les chapitres XXV–XXVIII du Livre de Job," *RB* 33 [1924] 343–56. Kuhl, C., *TRu* 21 [1953] 277–81. Régnier, A., "La disposition des chapitres 25–28 du livre de Job," *RB* 33 [1924] 186–200. Tournay, R., "L'ordre primitif des chapitres XXIV–XXVIII du livre de Job," *RB* 64 [1957] 321–34.)

91 (a) Bildad's Third Speech (25:1–6). **2–3.** Without the customary sharp words (cf. 8:2; 18:2–3), this speech begins in the style of a hymn (cf. 12:13,16) in praise of God's sovereign power. God establishes "peace" in the heavens by means of countless "armies." **4–6.** An a fortiori argument; if there is impurity in the heavens, how can a mortal, like a "worm" or a "maggot" and destined for decay, be innocent? This echoes the thoughts of Eliphaz in 4:17–19 and 15:14–16. **92** (b) Job's Eighth Response (26:1–4). **2–4.** Job usually addresses the friends as pl., but here "you" is sg., hence, these lines are a sarcastic response to Bildad. Who is Bildad, lacking in both strength and wisdom, to offer counsel? Job seems to imply that the "breath" that animates Bildad's speech is not from God (cf. 33:4).

93 The magnificent passage in 26:5-14, sometimes attributed to Bildad or Zophar, is the finest cosmological section in the dialogue for scope of imagination and force of language. In vv 5-11 the vbs. are ptcs. or in the impf. (to be translated as pres.) describing God's continued cosmic action; in vv 12-13 they are in the perf., narrating deeds accomplished at the creation (read "stirred . . . crushed . . . ," etc.). **5.** The "shades" (rĕpā'îm) are the inhabitants of sheol, which is below the watery deeps, and they tremble before God. **6.** The point is that these powers of chaos (see comment on 28:22) are impotent. **7.** God is said to have stretched out ṣāpôn (north) over tōhû (the void; Gen 1:2); i.e., he stretched out the heavens, or the pole star and the constellations. Elsewhere ṣāpôn refers to Mt. Saphon, the dwelling of the Canaanite gods (Ps 48:3; Isa 14:13). The suspension of the earth over emptiness is remarkable: the earth is pictured as hanging in empty space, not supported by pillars (contrast 9:6; 38:4,6). **8.** The clouds which contain the waters above (Gen 1:7) still do not burst under that weight. **9.** God seems to have a personal cloud which cuts off a view of the heavenly throne. It is no wonder that Job cannot find God's dwelling (23:3). **10-11.** God contains the waters of chaos by a circle at the horizon (i.e., "where light and darkness meet"). Heaven is supported by "pillars," apparently the mountains that are visible on the horizon (2 Sam 22:9; Ps 18:8). These were produced by the divine rebuke addressed to the primeval waters (Ps 18:16). **12-13.** The divine creativity is portrayed in images derived from Ugaritic mythology: the battle with Yam ("Sea"), paralleled here with Rahab, the mythological monster. The serpent (Isa 27:1) is described as bāriaḥ (fleeing, or primeval, or perhaps evil) and is another symbol of chaos. The NAB inserts 27:22 into v 13. **14.** The poem concludes in an atmosphere of wonder at God's creative activity. The previous lines are a mere "whisper" of his power. NAB omits the final line of the MT, "Who can understand the thunder of his power?"

94 (c) JOB'S MĀŠĀL (27:1-23). This chapter is separated from the previous response by a new formula (27:1 = 29:1): Job takes up his mašal, or theme. This introduction may be a sign of the disarray which commentators find in the sequence of the text. Among those who attempt to interpret the MT in its present form, F. I. Andersen regards this chapter as a "closing statement balancing chapter 3," but it must be admitted that the balance seems contrived. The chapter is surely problematical.

95 2-6. Job's integrity is at stake, and he affirms it to the friends under solemn oath. In his stark honesty never is he more admirable (as the reader knows from the prologue). Were he to admit that the friends were right, he would be denying his own conscience. **2.** The oath is "by the life of God"—even that very God who does not seem disposed to recognize him. Job is appealing to the God he ultimately believes is his "vindicator" (19:25). **3.** "Life" is equated with the "breath of Eloah in my nostrils"; cf. Ps 104:29-30; Gen 2:7. **5.** "Far be it from me" or "may I become profane" reiterates the oath. With this self-imprecation Job affirms the integrity (tummâ) which the Lord had acknowledged in 1:8; 2:3,9. Job's conscience is clear.

96 7-23. Most of these verses are commonly assigned to Bildad (MacKenzie, JBC 31:95-96) or to Zophar. But they can be understood as an imprecation against the friends (vv 11-12, "you" is pl.). Verses 13-23 seem inappropriate on the lips of Job since they describe in conventional terms the lot of the wicked. The wicked are struck in their families and survivors; all their wealth is lost. Their house is "like a moth" (v 18; perhaps

"cobwebs" [NAB]), and finally the "east wind" devastates them (vv 21-23). On the other hand, these lines can be taken as Job's description of what will happen to the friends (who were addressed directly in vv 11-12), or even as a parody of Zophar's words in 11:13-20 and 20:4-29 (so Janzen).

97 (Q) The Search for Wisdom (28:1-28). This beautiful poem is hard to situate in the dialogue or, for that matter, in the book as a whole. It lacks the personal references of the speeches and is only distantly connected with the problems treated by the speakers. Besides, the transl. and sequence of many verses are uncertain, as differences between the NAB, RSV, NEB, etc., demonstrate. For one reconstruction, see MacKenzie in JBC 31:97. However faulty it may be, the sequence of the MT is adopted here. Scholars describe the poem in different ways: as an interlude (MacKenzie, Andersen), a bridge (Lévêque, Job 600), or simply as a later insertion (Dhorme). It can be seen as another contribution to the issue raised by the book: humans do not know the answer to the problem; the best they can do is fear the Lord.

98 The theme is the transcendence of divine wisdom and its inaccessibility (see the refrain in vv 12,20). Humans can explore and find treasures, but wisdom, most precious of all, is beyond their reach. Wisdom is located with God and (somehow?) in his creation (vv 23-27). The final verse associates wisdom with fear of the Lord ('dny, not yhwh). Four main ideas are developed: (a) humans explore the interior of the earth but find no "vein" of wisdom; (b) the most farsighted or distant creatures cannot tell where to look for it; (c) the most precious treasures cannot purchase it; but (d) God alone knows and possesses it. For the correlation of this poem with personified wisdom, → Wisdom Lit., 27:15-17.

99 (a) THE FINDING OF PRECIOUS METALS (28:1-11). The assumption is that human activity is referred to, even in vv 9-11, which lack an explicit subject. **1.** The poem plays on the words môṣā' (place of going forth; cf. yōṣī' in v 11, and then the key word, timmāṣē' in v 12) and māqôm (place). The following verses (2-6), although tantalizingly obscure, may provide a glimpse of ancient mining techniques. **7-8.** Neither birds nor beasts know the path to "it" (the place, māqôm, of wisdom, mentioned in v 6). **9-11.** The subject of the vbs. is presumably human beings; others (NAB) refer these verses to the activity of God.

100 (b) WISDOM CANNOT BE FOUND OR BARTERED FOR (28:12-19). **12.** The key question (cf. v 20). Though precious metals can be found, wisdom cannot. **13.** The MT has 'erek, "price," "value," but the LXX apparently read derek, "way," a reading that suits the context of vv 12-14; the way to wisdom is unknown. **15-19.** A series of negative statements proclaims that wisdom cannot be bought, even with the most valuable and exotic metals and stones. The incomparable value of wisdom is a frequent topic in Prov (3:13-15; 16:16; 31:10).

101 (c) WISDOM BELONGS TO GOD ALONE (28:20-27). **20-22.** After the refrain (cf. v 12), wisdom is said to be hidden from the eyes of humans and beasts. Death and Abaddon: Destruction; cf. 20:6. These are personifications of elemental powers, like Sea and Deep (v 14), which represent chaos. None of these knows where wisdom is. **23-24.** Only God knows the way to wisdom's place, and the reason given is the divine farseeing vision. Interestingly, wisdom seems to be somewhere in the world (in a "place"), and not to be a divine attribute. **25-27.** The relationship of God to wisdom is tied in with the act of creation (wind, waters, rain, and lightning). The four vbs. in v 27 underline the divine intimacy with wisdom, without indicating where wisdom is. It is somehow connected with creation; cf. Sir 1:9.

102   (d) ANNOTATION (28:28). The final verse is widely considered to be a later addition. In any case it gives a certain twist to the poem on wisdom. Wisdom is inaccessible (vv 1– 27), and the only way for humans to reach it is through "fear of the Lord" (a reprise of 1:8 and 2:3); then wisdom means piety and service.

(Hulsbosch, A. *Sagesse créatrice et éducatrice* [Rome, 1963]. Niccaci, A., "Giobbe 28," *SBFLA* 31 [1981] 29–58. Von Rad, G. *WI* 144–49. Zerafa, P. *The Wisdom of God in the Book of Job* [Rome, 1978] 126–83.)

103   (R) Job's Final Soliloquy (29:1–31:40). With its 95 verses, this is the longest of Job's speeches. Technically, it is outside the dialogue, to which it furnishes a conclusion (chap. 3 gave the introduction). It is formally soliloquy, although it supposes listeners who can testify to the oath, if need be. Here is summed up all that Job wishes to affirm regarding his situation and the question of his own responsibility for it. This renewal of the psalm of lament develops three themes: past happiness (chap. 29), contrasted with present misery (chap. 30), followed by the oath (chap. 31) that he is an innocent man. The other important elements of such a psalm—denunciation of enemies and direct plea to God for salvation—are merely touched on—the former in 30:9–14, the latter in 30:20–26 and 31:35–37, where it takes the form of complaint that his prayer has not been heard and assurance of acquittal if it were.

104   (a) PAST HAPPINESS (29:1–25). Job describes in terms of the patriarchal way of life the ideal existence of the great sheikh, rich in material goods, in his family, and in universal esteem and honor. The way of life pictured is not properly nomadic (although the livestock would have to be moved from one pasturage to another), for Job had the place of authority in a sedentary community, a city. There he distinguished himself by his wisdom, his beneficence, and his generous protection of the poor and helpless.

Many translations and commentaries rearrange the sequence of verses in order to achieve a "logical" order, e.g., reading vv 21–25 after v 10. For the sequence in the *NAB*, see the comment by MacKenzie in *JBC* 31:104. The order of the MT will be followed here, without imposing an outline.

1. The formula of 27:1 introduces chaps. 29–31. **2–6.** There is much pathos in Job's definition of his happy time as "when God watched over me," and when "my children were round about me." **6.** This is a vivid poetic expression for idyllic abundance. **7–11.** In the administration of public business (at the "city gates") Job was the acknowledged leader to whom all deferred. **12–17.** The reasons for his preeminence and prestige were charity and kindness—esp. in the protection of the weak and the needy—even to those who were not his kin or neighbors (v 16). **18–20.** In his reminiscence Job wryly recalls the confidence and hope he enjoyed that such blessings would continue. In v 18 *ḥôl* has been interpreted as sand and also as the phoenix (the legend is that the phoenix died after a long life, and from its ashes a new bird arose; cf. the discussion in Pope). Job's prosperity is further described in terms of a tree (v 19) and a bow (i.e., his natural vigor, v 20). **21–25.** These verses return to the theme of vv 7–10, the esteem that Job enjoyed among his contemporaries. The transl. of v 24 is uncertain, but the general idea is his beneficence to all.

105   (b) PRESENT MISERY (30:1–31). This is felt all the more keenly because of the contrasts introduced by the repeated "but now" in vv 1,9,16. The description naturally corresponds to that of chap. 29, only reversing the order of 29:2–7 and 29:8–11,21–25.

(i) *Public contempt* (30:1–15). Elders, chiefs, and princes had revered Job (29:8– 10); now the meanest and most wretched of human beings despise him. The description of the latter is surprisingly elaborate (vv 3–8); they are outcasts living on bitter roots and leaves (v 4), but Job is even worse off than these unfortunate people. Similar detailed presentations of enemies are found in psalms of lament (Pss 59; 64; 73; etc.). **11a.** In the MT the vb. is sg., and God seems to be the subject (cf. vv 18–19).

(ii) *The hostile presence of God* (30:16–22). Worse than this abuse is God's persecution. **16.** The *NAB* omits v 16, which can be translated: "But now, my soul is dissolved within me, days of affliction have seized me." This verse introduces the affliction by God. **19.** "Dust and ashes" is a metaphor for human frailty (both origin and destiny are indicated); cf. 42:6. **20.** Since his fourth response (17:3), Job has not directly addressed a prayer to God. Now, after the 3d-pers. reference in vv 18–19 (cf. 16:12), he resumes the style of petition; but is God listening to him? **22.** The metaphor is that of being driven by the wind; cf. 13:25.

(iii) *Reasons against this abuse* (30:23–26). Verses 24 (admittedly difficult to translate) and 25 present an intensely poignant passage. In 6:13–30 Job had felt most keenly the lack of sympathy from his friends (cf. also 19:21). Now he ventures to recall the sympathy that he, a mere mortal, had shown to the suffering and sorrowful (29:12–17). Will not God show as much toward him? (Cf. the praise of sympathy as a Christian virtue in Rom 12:15; 1 Pet 3:8). Verse 26 contrasts with 29:18–20.

(iv) *Job's misery* (30:27–31). Verses 27 and 30 refer to his disease; v 29 to his loneliness. **30b.** *heat:* Presumably means fever. **31.** The only music Job knows is mournful; contrast 21:12.

106   (c) OATH OF EXCULPATION (31:1–40). In the legal procedures of ancient Israel, the "oath of innocence" denying an accusation was important. It supplemented testimony or could supply for it. In default of clear evidence, it was accepted as settling a case; i.e., it transferred the decision to God himself, who, if the defendant had sworn falsely, would bring down on his head the curses he had expressly invited in the oath. Thus, the swearing was a solemn religious act, submitting the case to a divine verdict. Furthermore, if the question at issue was not a mere conflict of human rights but involved an accusation of impiety or blasphemy, one's religious "existence" might depend on it, one's right to take part in the worship of God and receive his blessing. Cf. Ps 139, which seems to be an oath denying worship of other gods (E. Würthwein, *VT* 7 [1957] 165–82). Job now swears that he is innocent of the crimes imputed to him by the friends—crimes, which, according to them, are also imputed to him by God. He challenges the divine judge to give his verdict, i.e., to acknowledge Job's innocence.

This oath is no mere formality. Job examines his conscience and spells out exactly what crimes he, in his time and situation, might have been tempted to commit. The code of ethics here implied is that proper to the ancient Oriental aristocrat, the head of a patriarchal family who need fear no constraint from government or other power. Only religious motivation and, to a lesser degree, public opinion will impel such a man to virtuous action and self-restraint. Job's motive was simply the desire to please God. His moral standards are, in fact, the highest to be found in the OT; cf. a somewhat similar code in Ezek 18:5–9. Notable are the sensitive respect shown for the dignity of fellow men (even slaves) and the stress on interior attitudes toward God. Eliphaz's accusations in chap. 22 are incidentally refuted (as already in 23:11; 29:11ff.): 31:16–18, cf. 22:7,9; 31:19–20, cf. 22:6.

The form is the standard one for Hebr oaths: "If I have done so-and-so, may this happen to me!" (e.g., 31:9–10,21–22). By dropping off the apodosis, the phrase "If I have . . ." by itself comes to mean "I swear I haven't . . ." (e.g., 31:5,16). The exact list of Job's disclaimers is hard to determine (some authors find 12, others 14, others 16); the question is complicated by textual uncertainties and possible glosses. For the same reason strophic division is uncertain.

107 (i) *No deceit or injustice* (31:1–12,38–40ab). Verses 1–4 are omitted altogether by the LXX, and in the MT they pose a problem. The *NAB* transposes and corrects: the MT has no "if" before v 1, and nothing corresponding to "man's" and "his" in v 2—which is almost a repetition, in question form, of 20:29 and 27:13. Verse 3 implies the opposite of what Job maintains, and v 4b conflicts with v 37a ("account" is, lit., "numbering"). Thus, vv 2–4 are most probably early annotations to the text. Verse 6 makes a likely beginning (after 30:31), and the *NAB* is probably right in displacing vv 1 and 5. The sequence of the *NAB* will be followed here: see the commentary of F. I. Andersen for a defense and explanation of the MT sequence.
5. The first disclaimer. By parallelism, one crime is here presented: deceit, with all it implies (cf. 27:4). **7.** Second denial; any deviation or corruption. **8.** The self-condemnation completing the oath formula.
38–40ab. Original position is uncertain; its closest similarity is with vv 13–15. It denies cruel exploitation of peasants or sharecroppers. Note the personification of land in v 38. **1.** In the MT, a simple statement (no "if"). The two stichs are not parallel and may belong to different verses. In the *NAB*, "made an agreement" (lit., "covenant") has to denote a vicious intention, which is questionable. **9–10.** Denial of adultery. The penalty contemplated is according to the law of talion; "grind" can mean slave labor or sexual subjection. **11–12.** Probably a gloss.
(ii) *No failure in equity or charity* (31:13–23). A list of specifically social crimes, showing a remarkably evolved conscience. They are arranged in chiastic order: vv 13–15 parallels 21–22; vv 16–17 parallels 19–20. **13–15.** Denies unjust treatment of slaves, who in the ancient world generally were not regarded as subjects of justice at all, any more than were animals. But Job bases their claim to it on the common creation of all human beings by God. **16–20.** Job insists that he has shared his goods with the poor, whose rights are based on the common fatherhood of God (if v 18 is rightly interpreted). **21–22.** Job has not exploited his standing in the community to win legal but unjust victories over weaker men. *supporters at the gate:* Friends in court; the local community, sitting in judgment, would have been too much in awe of Job ever to give a verdict against him. The imprecation in v 22 invokes the talion law against Job's raised hand (v 21). **23.** An adaptation of 13:11, perhaps a gloss.
(iii) *No false worship* (31:24–28). Two kinds of idolatry: the first (vv 24–25) is what the NT calls "worshiping Mammon." "Trust" and "rejoiced" are emphatic—in his money, rather than in God. The second (vv 26–28) is the secret infidelity of invoking as divinities the sun and the moon; v 27 seems to refer to throwing kisses with the hand.
(iv) *No vindictiveness or hypocrisy* (31:29–34).

29–30. This concern is considerably above the level of most of the OT. The only parallel is Sir 28:3–7 (cf. Prov 24:17—and its following verse). **31–32.** Similar to vv 16–20, these verses affirm Job's constant practice of the virtue of hospitality—sacred and all-important in that society. **33–34.** He denies hypocrisy, any mere pretense of virtue inspired by human respect.
(v) *Summary* (31:35–37,40c). Job has come a long way from the unquestioning acceptance of 1:21; 2:10, and even from the longing for nonexistence in chap. 3. The vindication of his truthfulness and integrity, which in chap. 19 he had looked forward to in faith, he now demands in challenging terms. The scroll of indictment would be a badge of honor; it could contain nothing to his discredit.
35b. "Here is my *taw;* let the Almighty answer me!"; placed by the *NAB* after v 37 (*taw* is the last letter of the Hebr alphabet). However, it is possible that v 35a should read "Oh that God would listen to me!" and v 35b follow in parallelism. Then vv 35c–36 will be a tristich: "If my accuser has written out his indictment, I swear I will carry it on my shoulder, I will wear it as a crown!" **37.** *a prince:* A dramatic affirmation of the proud assurance of innocence with which Job defends his conduct before God (cf. 13:14–16). **40c.** Janzen comments: "'The words of Job are ended (*tammu*)'—completed, finished, and—like himself—blameless (*tam*)."
108 Thus, Job has delivered his final answer to his friends and his challenge to God. For the former, there is nothing more to be said. The oath must prevail (in default of evidence); therefore, Job has won his case against them. But Job has not won any case against God. The image of a judicial hearing, of plea and argument, simply cannot represent the situation of a person before the creator; it only falsifies it. Insofar as Job has fallen in with his friends' analysis of his situation, thinking of God as his adversary in a lawsuit, he has put himself in a false position. His unblemished record gives him no claim in justice upon God; from it and from his suffering he has no right to draw any conclusion about what God ought to do. To think otherwise is to forget the divine transcendence and the infinite difference between creator and creature.

However, Job has here proclaimed his "right" (cf. 9:20; 13:18; 19:7; 23:7; 27:2,6), his truthful unanswerable demonstration that he has been what God pronounced him to be (1:8; 2:3): God-fearing and morally perfect. And inevitably there is an element of presumption here, of what the Greeks called hubris. The just man's precious integrity has become a barrier between him and God, a condition that God must accept. Job has overshot the mark (Weiser, *Das Buch Hiob* 212–16).

(Ceresko, A., *Job 29–31 in the Light of Northwest Semitic* [BibOr 36; Rome, 1980]. Cox, D., "Structure and Function of the Final Challenge: Job 29–31," *PIBA* 5 [1981] 55– 71. Dick, M. B., "The Legal Metaphor in Job 31," *CBQ* 41 [1979] 37–50. Fohrer, G., "The Righteous Man in Job 31," *SBH* 78–93.)

109 (III) The Elihu Speeches (32:1–37:24). This section is generally (not universally) admitted to be a supplement inserted into the book by another writer (here, for convenience' sake, called the "critic," as distinct from the author of the book). If so, it was not an independent piece (as was perhaps chap. 28), but was composed expressly for this purpose. The critic presumably was dissatisfied with the original conclusion of the book (chaps. 38–42) and wished to provide a more explicit corrective to some of Job's outbursts. He also felt that the friends' speeches had not done justice to the traditional wisdom teaching and that a better case could be made for it. His work, then, is an interesting specimen of early doctrinal and literary criticism and is almost contemporary with the original composition. He had the initiative—we might also say the courage—to dramatize his criticism in speech form, to create another character as his spokesman, and to integrate his own contribution, quite skillfully, into the great masterwork he had studied so closely. (Needless to say, the section is to be regarded as an integral part of the canonical book, and its author, whoever he was, as having had the grace of inspiration.)

Several kinds of arguments have been advanced in favor of a later insertion of Elihu: (1) linguistic, e.g., presence of Aramaisms; (2) structural, e.g., Elihu is not mentioned in the epilogue; (3) theological, e.g., Elihu merely repeats, in turgid fashion, the doctrine of Job's friends. Such arguments are somewhat delicate and scholars are often divided in their assessment. Thus, it is difficult to show that the Elihu speeches must be a later insertion by the same author. Could not the writer have envisioned his role from the beginning? J. G. Janzen rightly points out that much depends on "how one construes the book as a whole" (*Job* 218). He regards the Elihu material as integral to the whole and makes a strong case for an ironic (some statements mean something else than what they seem to say) interpretation. Thus, the bombastic style of Elihu's introduction of himself in chap. 32 may be a tipoff to the ironic edges of the poem (e.g., Elihu's pompous claims to speak out of a divine revelation; cf. 32:8,15–22; 33:4). See also the commentaries of N. Habel and F. I. Andersen.

From the literary point of view, the Elihu speeches are wisdom writings on a high level, comparable with the best parts of Prov. But they are much inferior to the brilliance of the original dialogue; their style is severely didactic, argumentative, and somewhat repetitious. The language is much less picturesque and also shows a higher proportion of Aramaisms. Doctrinally, the critic disapproves Job's self-assertion before God and his insistence on his own integrity and blamelessness. But he also disavows the exclusively retributory function ascribed to suffering by the friends. Affliction, according to him, may be a warning, a paternal admonition from God against the human tendency to hubris. If the man promptly humbles himself, God restores him to his favor; if he is obstinate, God will further punish him for that obstinacy, but with the purpose of leading him to repentance. Thus, Elihu disagrees with the friends on the grounds of suffering, stressing its medicinal purpose; but in practice, his advice to Job is the same as theirs. On the other hand, he forcibly reminds Job of God's infinite superiority to human beings (which Job had seemed in danger of ignoring), and he anticipates the divine speeches of chaps. 38ff. by insisting on God's sublimity and the mystery of the divine plans.

The section begins with a prose introduction and continues with a poetic composition of nearly 150 lines (compare the total of roughly 220 lines allotted to all three friends in the dialogue). This is broken into four unequal sections by the rubrics in 34:1; 35:1; 36:1. However, the last of these (worded differently from the others and from 32:6) is probably an erroneous insertion. In reality, 33:1–36:25 constitute only three discourses, composed in an identical pattern. Each begins with a summons to Job (twice) or the friends, to listen. Then some of Job's sayings are quoted and contradicted. Elihu lays down a first thesis and then a second, developed at slightly greater length. A conclusion admonishes Job and praises the divine goodness and mercy. (This structural analysis is taken, with slight modifications, from Fohrer [*Hiob*]. The strophic analysis is independent but often agrees with the divisions indicated in the *NAB*.) In

Elihu's oration as a whole, therefore, we distinguish: an introductory address (32:6–22); the three discourses (33:1–30; 34:1–37; 33:31–33 + 35:2–36:25); a hymn (36:26–37:13); and a concluding address (37:14–24).

(Dennefeld, L., "Les discours d'Elihou," *RB* 48 [1939] 163–80. Fohrer, G., *SBH* 94–113. Freedman, D. N., "The Elihu Speeches in the Book of Job," *HTR* 61 [1968] 51–59. Habel, N., "The Role of Elihu in the Design of the Book of Job," *In the Shelter of Elyon* [Fest. G. A. Ahlström; ed. W. B. Barrick, *et al.;* JSOTSup 31; Sheffield, 1984]. Irwin, W. A., "The Elihu Speeches in the Criticism of the Book of Job," *JR* 17 [1937] 37–47. Kroeze, J. H., "Die Elihu-Reden im Buche Hiob," *OTS* 2 [1943] 156–70. Staples, W. E., *The Speeches of Elihu* [Toronto, 1924].)

110   (A) Introductory Narrative (32:1–5). If 38:1 followed immediately upon 31:40, no one would ever suspect a lacuna. The critic, wishing to make room for his own contribution, had to indicate an occasion and a reason why a new character hitherto unmentioned should suddenly break into the discussion. This he does plausibly enough by explaining that the friends have ceased to argue (on the reason, see comment on v 1); thus, the field is clear for another speaker. He is Elihu, son of Barachel (unlike Job [1:1] and the other three [2:11], he is given a patronymic). Elihu is the original "angry young man"; both attributes are insisted on (anger, vv 2a–3,5; youth, 4,6b,9–10). He is also, at least to modern sensibilities, amazingly self-satisfied, pompous, and naïve. He takes 24 verses (32:6–33:7) to say, in effect, "Look out! I'm going to speak," and outdoes Eliphaz (from whom he borrows some of his material) in his self-confidence and complacency. There is such an odd contrast between the ludicrous self-importance of the character and the serious religious value of the doctrine he imparts (after 33:7), that one wonders if the critic was parodying some particular "younger school" of wisdom teachers.

1. *his own eyes:* The LXX and Pesh read "in their eyes," probably correctly. It is not necessarily the intention of the author of the dialogue, but it gives a logical reason for their ceasing to argue, the critic seems to suppose it by making Elihu distribute blame impartially to Job and to the friends, and it fits better with v 3. **3.** MT reads "they condemned Job." This is one of the 18 emendations of the scribes (*tiqqunê sōpĕrîm*) of Jewish tradition. The original "condemning God" was felt to be offensive, and "Job" was substituted.

111   (B) Introductory Address (32:6–22). A remarkably elaborate and verbose exordium. There are four strophes: The third has three lines, the others have five each.

(a) REBUKE TO THE FRIENDS (32:6–10,11–14). **8.** *it is a spirit:* The phrase is strange; perhaps read according to the parallelism, "the spirit of God," and omit "that." Elihu claims something like prophetic inspiration. **13.** Brings out the critic's idea that the friends have been forced to agree with Job.

(b) SOLILOQUY (32:15–17,18–22). Dramatically, Elihu describes the discomfiture of the friends and his own compulsion to speak. **21–22.** Cf. Job in 13:8,10. Elihu, in his hyperbolic style, envisages the extreme penalty.

112   (C) Elihu's First Discourse (33:1–30). There are nine strophes, of 3, 4, 4; 3, 4, 4,3; 4, 2 lines, respectively.

(a) SUMMONS TO JOB (33:1–3,5–6,4,7). **4.** Probably to be read after v 6 (omit initial "for"; not in the MT). Elihu refers (sarcastically?) to Job's complaint that he could not speak freely in God's terrifying presence (9:17,34; etc.).

(b) QUOTATIONS (33:8–11). Elihu cites two of Job's claims: that he is innocent (cf. 9:21; 10:7; 16:17; 23:10–12; 27:5; 31) and that God is his enemy (cf. 10:17; 13:24,27; 19:11).

(c) CORRECTION AND FIRST THESIS (33:12–14, 15–18). Elihu deals with the second claim (the other comes in the next speech). **12b.** *greater than a human person:* "Enemy" implies a certain equality; God is too far above humanity for this to be apt. (Job's keen awareness of God's personality easily leads him to this too human way of thinking of him.) **13–14.** In 19:7 and 30:20 Job complained that God did not answer. Now Elihu retorts that God was already speaking to Job, who was refusing to listen. The first way was by the terrifying dreams Job had referred to (7:14); they were meant to warn him against pride and were the effect of God's kindness.

(d) SECOND THESIS (33:19–22,23–24). God's second way of speaking is by affliction itself. Job's sufferings therefore had a medicinal purpose; they were meant to keep him humble, but by his rebellious reaction he has revealed his pride. Note that Elihu avoids the crude simplification of the friends' doctrine; he does not claim that Job's calamities are sure evidence of previous sin or that divine rewards are an automatic consequence of human repentance. **23–24.** A beautiful and much-discussed text (F. Stier, *Das Buch Iyyob* [Munich, 1954] 333–34). Elihu does not share Eliphaz's skepticism (5:1). A heavenly messenger may be mediator, lit., "interpreter"; i.e., make the man understand the meaning of his affliction, show him his faults, and intercede for him with God. Thus, people need grace and instruction even to repent as they should.

(e) CONCLUSION (33:25–28,29–30). Verses 25 and 26 should perhaps change places. **27–28.** A typical thanksgiving psalm (cf. Pss 30; 41; 116). Verse 29 makes an *inclusio* with v 14, and v 30 echoes v 22 (vv 31–33 introduce 35:2).

113 (D) Elihu's Second Discourse (34:1–37). Eight strophes, of 5, 5; 4, 5, 5, 5(?); 4, 4 lines, respectively.

(a) SUMMONS TO THE FRIENDS AND QUOTATION (34:2–6). Elihu now returns to deal with the first point he had cited, in 33:9. **3.** Cf. 12:11. **5.** Cf. 27:2.

(b) QUOTATION AND CORRECTION (34:7–11). To Job's statement of innocence, Elihu joins (v 9) the saying of the "good pagans" that had so shocked Eliphaz (22:15–17). Elihu prefixes it with his own expression of horror (v 7) and says (v 8) that Job agrees with these atheists—which is true, on this one point (cf. 9:22). "Fearing God" is not an infallible recipe for temporal prosperity, as Job has discovered. But Elihu understands Job's words as an attack on the justice of God's providence and denies them accordingly.

(c) FIRST THESIS (34:12–15). God is the supreme Lord, subject to none. If he were unjust, the universe simply could not function. **14–15.** Cf. Ps 104:29.

(d) SECOND THESIS (34:16–20a,20b–24,25–30). Elihu applies the same argument to the divine direction of human life. **17.** If God were unjust, he would not be supreme (there would be a standard of justice higher than God). But, in fact, all other justice derives from him; all creatures are equally subject to him, and partiality in him is unthinkable. In him might and right are one. **23.** Perhaps an answer to 24:1; God needs to hold no inquiries, no "hearings." (If v 25 is placed after 22, with the *NAB*, the strophe ends with v 23.) **26.** (Omitted by the *NAB*.) "On account of their wickedness he blasts them, he binds them in the place of the damned" (the MT, emended). **29.** If God's actions cannot be perceived, one still has no right to say he is not acting. **30.** With the *NAB*, omit as doublet.

(e) CONCLUSION (34:31–33,34–37). Elihu produces an *argumentum ad hominem:* Job disapproves of all God's work—therefore he must disapprove of his customary loving forgiveness! If he denies God freedom to act "arbitrarily" for his own good reasons, then he must (like the friends) want him to exercise merely automatic retribution. Undoubtedly, Elihu here scores a point. Job's criticisms, prompted by his own unhappy experience, are subjective. **33c.** *you who must choose:* Whether to admit that God may temper justice with mercy. **36.** Job has experienced God's warning: because he rejects it, he deserves extreme punishment.

114 (E) Elihu's Third Discourse (33:31–33; 35:2–36:25). The missing introduction has been misplaced at the end of chap. 33. There are eleven strophes of 3, 3; 4, 4, 4; 3, 3, 5, 3; 5, 5 lines.

(a) SUMMONS TO JOB (33:31–33). **32.** Not, as one might think, an invitation to disagree and put forward his point of view. Elihu is not arguing with Job, he is teaching him. Here he invites him to express contrition, which will show that he is "justified."

(b) QUOTATIONS (35:2–4). **2b.** Job had not said this, but he is very sure about his own justice, while holding God's to be quite mysterious (cf. 13:18; 19:6–7; 27:2–6). **3b.** *what advantage have I more:* Because of the following strophe, we should read with the LXX, "what harm can I do you by sinning?" and keep "profit you" (so MT) in v 3a.

(c) CORRECTION AND FIRST THESIS (35:5–8, 9–12,13–16). Cf. 7:20; 22:2–3. Elihu agrees with both: human beings' evil actions cannot harm God (so Job), nor can their good ones benefit him (so Eliphaz), although they have real effects on fellow humans. **13.** But simply because he is just, God does impose sanctions. **36:1.** Omit, as mistaken editorial insertion.

(d) SECOND THESIS (36:2–4,5–7,8–12,13–15). But more than the effects on fellow humans are the results of one's behavior on oneself. When God does intervene, he treats persons according to their deserts— although always first encouraging the wicked to repent (8–10). **13.** They do not accept the warning to repent, implicit in their affliction. This is the second and graver stage of impiety.

(e) CONCLUSION (36:16–20,21–25). The text of the first strophe is hopelessly corrupted. **21b.** The consonantal text can be read "for this is why you are being tried by affliction." **24.** Instead of criticizing, Job should join in the hymns of praise, which are human beings' fitting response to God. **25b.** *from afar:* Cf. 26:14.

115 (F) Hymn (36:26–29,30–33; 37:1–4,5–8,9–13). Appropriately, Elihu himself intones a hymn in praise of God, who manifests himself in the winter rains. In these storms are experienced both God's mighty power and—because they give fertility to the soil— God's solicitude for his creatures (cf. Pss 8; 19:2–7; 29; 104; 147). The text is somewhat uncertain, but there seem to be five four-line strophes.

116 (G) Concluding Address (37:14–18,19–21, 22–24). Elihu resumes his address to Job. This section seems to be expressly formulated so as to lead up to the speech of Yahweh that is to follow. Elihu describes an increase in darkness but also a splendor coming "from the north," traditional source of the theophany (Isa 14:13; Ezek 1:4). **15–16.** The questions anticipate the style of the following speech. **17–18.** Perhaps, in sequence to the preceding hymn, this reference is to the dry season following the rainy one. Verses 22–23 are the description of God's advent; both power and justice are emphasized. **24b.** In the MT, "He does not see all the wise of heart." The *NAB* correction is possible, but the following is perhaps better: "to him reverence is given by all the wise of heart," a conclusion similar to 36:25.

With these words, Elihu disappears from the book as abruptly as he appeared. The critic has had his say and has felt no need to introduce his spokesman also into prologue or epilogue.

117   (IV) God's Speech and Job's Answer (38:1–42:6). The key section of the book. Although its originality and connection with the dialogue have often been questioned, the majority of modern commentators accept it in principle as an integral part of the original author's work. Doubts are still commonly expressed on certain passages, e.g., 39:13–18; 40:15–32; 41:1–26 (but cf. Skehan, *SIPW* 114–23).

After the naïve story of the prologue in heaven and the sophisticated debate in the dialogue on earth, a word is spoken from heaven to earth by God himself. He is the Yahweh of the prologue, and he addresses the Job of the dialogue, the tormented, devout, rebellious man who has raged against the human situation and demanded that God "justify his ways to humans." The author, with the audacity of genius, tackles the problem of putting in God's mouth words that will not be an anticlimax after the tempestuous eloquence of his hero. He brilliantly succeeds. The divine speech sweeps away all the irrelevancies and false problems in which the argument with the friends had entangled Job. It puts Job's problem in a new perspective and opens up a vista in which, although still without an answer, it ceases to require one. Throughout this long speech Yahweh does not (apart from mere description) make a single statement; he only puts to Job, majestically, patiently, ironically, a series of unanswerable questions. A critic should know whereof he speaks; and he who would "correct God" must himself have divine knowledge. Yahweh pretends to believe this of Job and cross-examines him on the divine activity in the universe. If Job is incapable of the simplest answer, how can he and Yahweh hold debate? How can Yahweh even explain to him the deeper mystery of his providence over humanity and his treatment of those who are dear to him? The questions cover the most familiar phenomena of nature: the stars, the weather, land and sea, a selection of beasts and birds. Everywhere are marvels, everywhere is mystery. (And be it said parenthetically, the mystery is not less for us today. We know far more than did the ancient poet about the mechanics of these things; but their inner secrets remain as elusive as ever.) Two points clearly emerge: One is the loving concern of Yahweh for his innumerable creatures, even, or especially, those most independent and far removed from humanity; the other is the infinite variety and richness of creation, extending to beings that to humans seem grotesque or monstrous. In the divine wisdom they have their place, and God finds pleasure in them. The analogy holds in the moral order, where also his ways are not human ways.

But the foregoing is only the superficial meaning of this passage. Its content, after all, adds nothing essential to what has been already affirmed by other speakers, in hymnal praises of God (cf. 5:10–16; 9:4–10; 12:13–25; 22:12–14; 26:5–14). More striking still, Job's personal problem is completely ignored: Yahweh says not a word about his guilt or innocence, his suffering or its meaning. In his acknowledgement (42:5), Job does not say "I understand your teaching"; he says "I have seen you." This speech is a revelation of the speaker. It is God's Word, in which God is known. The theophany, the encounter with God, is Job's real experience, and this sublime poetry gives back a pale reflection of it for the reader's benefit.

The book of Job has never lost its attraction for poets and artists. Among modern poems, "A Masque of Reason" by Robert Frost presents an acute interpretation. In a short skit Frost portrays the Lord in a gracious mood. Some thousand years later (!) God thanks Job for the role he played in setting him free—God is no longer boxed into the situation of having to reward good and punish evil (Frost sees this as stultifying the Deuteronomist), but free to reign, as God.

(Couroyer, B., "Qui est Béhémoth?" *RB* 82 [1975] 418–43. Fohrer, G., *SBH*, 114–34. Fox, M. V., "Job 38 and God's Rhetoric," *Book of Job* [ed. J. D. Crossan; → 1 above] 53–61. Gammie, J. G., "Behemoth and Leviathan," *IW* 217–31. Keel, O., *Jahwes Entgegnung an Ijob* [FRLANT 121; Göttingen, 1972]. Kubina, V., *Die Gottesreden im Buch Hiob* [FTS 151; Freiburg, 1979]. MacKenzie, R. A. F., "The Purpose of the Yahweh Speeches in the Book of Job," *Bib* 40 [1959] 435–45; "The Transformation of Job," *BTB* 9 [1979] 51–57. Richter, H., "Die Naturweisheit des Alten Testaments im Buche Hiob," *ZAW* 70 [1958] 1–20. Skehan, P. W., *SIPW* 114–23. Von Rad., G., *PHOE* 281–91. Wilson, J. V. K., "A Return to the Problem of Behemoth and Leviathan," *VT* 25 [1975] 1–14.)

118   (A) Yahweh Speaks (38:1). From 3:2 to 26:1, and again in 32:6; 34:1; 35:1, an invariable formula has been used to introduce each speech (*NAB* varies, for no evident reason): "Then X spoke, and said. . . ." Now, with simplicity, but also with dramatic effect, the formula includes the divine name and two extra phrases: "Then Yahweh spoke—to Job—out of the storm—and said. . . ." The first indicates the fulfillment of Job's longing (cf. 13:22; 23:5; 30:20; 31:35b). The second suffices to evoke the traditional setting of the theophany (cf., e.g., Ps 18:8–14).

119   (B) Does Job Understand Yahweh's "Counsel"? (38:2–38). This first part of the speech deals with (what we call) "inanimate" nature—lively enough to the poet. The division, roughly, is by past, present, and future, relative to Job. Does he know the history, how it all started? Was he present at creation? Does he now know "where to find everything" (i.e., all the distant corners of the universe and what they contain)? Does he know the procedure? Could he, from now on, run things, give the necessary orders?

The strophic structure is carefully symmetrical: 11 strophes of 2; 4, 4, 4; 3, 3, 3; 3, 3, 3; 4 lines. There seems no need to rearrange the text; only v 36 is intrusive.

120   (a) "Who Is This?" (38:2–3). The tremendous interrogatory begins with this pointed reminder. Who and what, after all, is Job? Another God, rival to Yahweh? **2a.** All he has done is to "darken counsel." The last word, *'ēṣâ,* means the sum total of God's plans and works. **3b.** Job had rashly invited this, in 13:22a.

(b) Was Job Present at Creation? (38:4–7, 8–11, 12–15). The origins of earth, sea, and light are described in succession (cf. the reverse order in Gen 1:3–10). The earth is pictured as a building: an architect planned it (v 5a), a surveyor mapped out the site (v 5b), foundations were laid (v 6a), then the cornerstone (v 6b), to the accompaniment of songs and shouts of rejoicing (v 7). Cf. the ceremonies described in Ezra 3:10–13. The sea, on the other hand—that tumultuous and threatening element—is pictured at first as a baby, which needed and received Yahweh's tender care. **13–14.** The imagery is obscure to us. Perhaps v 14 indicates first the gray outlines of things seen before dawn, then their full color when the sun rises.

(c) Does Job Know His Way about the Cosmos? (38:16–18, 19–21, 22–24). It is all familiar to Yahweh: the abyss, leading to the underworld (v 17); the "places" where light and darkness are kept when they are "not in use" (light during the night, darkness during the day!); the treasuries from which he produces snow, hail, and winds.

(d) Would Job Know How to Operate It? (38:25-27,28-30,31-33). For all of this, Yahweh has his own supreme "counsel," and it is not exclusively for human benefit (vv 26-27). **31-32.** Stars and constellations were regarded as having an effect on the weather, which explains their position here.

(e) Has Job the Needed Authority and Power? (38:34-38). Even if he gave the right orders, would they be carried out? **36a.** *heart:* Hebr *ṭuḥôt,* of unknown meaning, but by parallelism it should be the name of a bird. This verse is out of place, perhaps an addition to the text (cf. its position in the *NAB* before v 41).

121   (C) Is Job Capable of Providing for the Animals and Birds? (38:39-39:30). Eight creatures are described, in increasing detail (two lines to the first, two strophes to the last); lion; raven, hawk, eagle; mountain goat, wild ass, wild ox; war horse. The first seven are free and independent of human beings, yet all are wonderfully nourished and cared for by their creator. The horse, in a different way, is the most amazing of all. **39:26-30.** Should be restored to its place after 38:41; note the common theme of "their young ones" in 38:39, 41; 39:3-4; 39:30. The three birds go together, symmetrically with the three beasts that follow. **39:13-18.** An insertion that breaks the symmetry. There are seven strophes, of 3, 4; 4, 4, 4; 4, 3, lines.

(a) Can Job Feed the Little Ones? (38:39-41; 39:26-30). Even the strongest and fiercest beasts and birds depend on God for food for their offspring. **39:27b-28.** The *NAB* omits two variants and combines to get two stichs instead of three, probably correctly.

(b) Are the Wildest Animals under His Control? (39:1-4,5-8,9-12). The mountain goats need no human help in giving birth, but Yahweh knows even the dates of their pregnancies. He sees to it that the wild ass finds the pasture it needs. And the wild ox serves him, although it is comic to think of it as serving Job (vv 9-12), like its domesticated cousin. The animal is the *rîmu,* a sort of buffalo (now extinct), powerful and dangerous to humans.

(c) The Ostrich (39:13-18). This wisdom essay is a comparatively recent addition to the text (it is not contained in the LXX). It lacks the interrogative introduction common to all the other items (38:39,41; 39:26,27,1,5,9,19); unlike them, it does not make the specific point, essential in this context, of Job's incapacity. It merely stresses the curious contrast between the ostrich's (apparent) callousness (which was proverbial; cf. Lam 4:3) and its remarkable speed. The reference to the horse in v 18b explains the passage's insertion here.

(d) Is Job Responsible for the Fiery Nature of the Horse? (39:19-22,23-25). This famous passage is the climax. In the ancient East the donkey was the beast of burden; the ox did the plowing, and donkeys or mules were riding animals. The horse was reserved for warfare or hunting, at first (in pairs) to draw a chariot, then, after about the 8th cent. BC, as a cavalry mount. It is the latter, the war horse, that the poet admires and marvels at. The animal's excitement and eagerness for the battle, its reaction to the trumpet call, its disregard of danger, have deeply impressed him.

122   (D) Summary and Job's First Response (40:1-5). In chaps. 40-41, the chapter divisions (established in the 13th cent. AD) and the verse numeration (16th cent.) are unhappily varied and may cause confusion in references. Our commentary uses the numeration of the Hebr text, as followed by the *NAB.* The table that follows illustrates the three different systems in use and will help readers with other texts to make their own adjustments.

Hebr Printed Bibles LXX, BJ, NAB		Non-Catholic Eng Versions: AV, RSV, etc.		Vg, Douay-Challoner, Knox
40:1	=	40:1	=	39:31
40:6	=	40:6	=	40:1
40:25	=	41:1	=	40:20
41:1	=	41:9	=	40:28
41:2	=	41:10	=	41:1
41:26	=	41:34	=	41:25

The introduction (40:1), which interrupts Yahweh's speech, creates a difficulty. Like similar anomalies in 27:1 (omitted by *NAB*) and 29:1, and the repetition in 40:6-7, it may be a sign of textual disorder. Various interpretations have been offered for the text as it stands. Habel regards 40:1-5 as the end of the Lord's first speech, and Job is in a submissive mood. Janzen regards 40:1-2 as the end of the speech and interprets Job's reply in vv 3-5 as evasive. In any case, the Lord begins again in a second speech (40:6-41:34).

(a) Challenge (40:2). Note that this conclusion returns to the solemn use of the third person, as in 38:2 (K. Fullerton, *AJSL* 49 [1933] 197-211).

(b) Job's Response (40:3-5). Job had insisted that the explanation of his problem must be sought in God, not in himself (cf. 19:28). Now his attention has been forcibly transferred to God, and his complete incapacity to understand God's ways has been demonstrated. What can he do but acknowledge the mystery, and the vanity of his efforts? But at least, the presence of God from which he had prayed to escape, a presence manifested only by successive blows of calamity and suffering, has changed to a speaking presence, in which Job knows God as addressing him personally and concerned with him as his servant.

123   (E) Yahweh Speaks Again (40:6-41:26). Here we have two very different sections. The speech in 40:8-14 is in the same style as the first speech: ironic questions and invitations addressed to Job, which make evident to the point of absurdity his human inability to "be like God." The subject matter is different, but related: Instead of divine providence at work in the cosmic order and the animal kingdom, it is shown in the moral order and in the world of human beings. Job's incompetence in this field is also exposed. The section following, 40:15-41:26, differs in style, and its theme is harder to relate to the preceding. Two strange beasts are described, the second in much detail. Only in 40:15, 25-32 is the style of address and questioning maintained, but even here (and more so in the rest) the tone is didactic and objective; the urgency and challenge of chaps. 38-39 are missing. Therefore, many critics have denied the originality of this second passage. But its defenders (several recent writers) maintain that it is an essential part of the divine proclamation. Behemoth and Leviathan are symbols of chaotic powers, monstrous, menacing, and incomprehensible; yet they, too, are of God's creation; in them God takes pleasure; through them aspects of the divinity are manifested.

124   (a) Can Job Administer Divine Justice? (40:6-14). Verse 6-7 are virtually identical with 38:1,3. **8.** Now, at last, Yahweh makes a reference to Job's situation: he retorts on him his accusation of "twisting justice" (9:24; 19:6; 27:2). Is Job so convinced of his righteousness that he is ready to believe, of the two, that God is unjust? The divine guilt would follow from the concept (which Job had accepted) of a lawsuit, in which one party must be found right, the other wrong. Job is in error because no such relationship can exist between creature and creator. **9-14.** The essence of the situation (anticipated in Elihu's speech, 34:10ff.): only the omnipotent and all-seeing governor of the world can lay claim to perfect justice. **14.** *save you:* An emphatic word: "bring you justice and salvation."

125   (b) LOOK AT BEHEMOTH! (40:15-24). The word is the pl. of "animal," but one creature is certainly meant, and the description suggests the hippopotamus. The hugeness of the beast, its strength, its sexual potency, are specially marvelous. **17.** Read probably "he stiffens his penis like a cedar-beam, the sinews of his testicles are closely knit." **19a.** The same phrase is used of this creature as is applied to Wisdom in Prov 8:22: He is the masterpiece (first and greatest effect) of God's power (not "ways"). Verse 19b is an uncertain text. **24.** "Can one seize him by his eyes [in traps]? Can one pierce his nostrils?" The brackets must be a gloss, and the whole verse is doubtful.

126   (c) LOOK AT LEVIATHAN! (40:25-41:26). The name belongs to a mythological sea monster (cf. 3:8) and might refer to the same creature as "Behemoth." But the description dwells rather on ferocity and invulnerability; probably a mythical dragon is meant, pictured as a giant crocodile. On Lotan, see the commentary of M. Pope.
   (i) *Can you make a pet of him?* (40:25-32). The same idea as in 39:9-12, and the same direct address. The idea is merely ridiculous; yet (it is implied) Yahweh can play with Leviathan as he wishes. **25a.** This verse may mean "draw up Leviathan with a hook," i.e., land him with rod and line like an ordinary fish.
   (ii) *Can anything overcome him?* (41:1-26). The belligerence of the crocodile is described, and his hide, which is proof against any weapons (vv 4-9; cf. 18-21). His fearsomeness is conveyed in mythological terms, as of a fire-breathing dragon (vv 10-13); even the ocean is in dread of him (v 17). **25-26.** This terrifying monster, supreme over all beasts, is beyond human control. Yet he too is one of Yahweh's creatures, whom he cares for and with whom he is pleased.

127   (F) **Job's Final Response** (42:1-6). In the MT three phrases are interjected (vv 3a and 4), two of which are quotations from 38:2,3b; the third is "Listen now, while I speak." The *NAB* omits these phrases, with most commentators (Dhorme), as marginal annotations.
   2-3. Job acknowledges the lesson. Verse 2b echoes the phrase applied by Yahweh to the builders of the tower of Babel (Gen 11:6). **3.** Job renounces the hubris into which he had fallen and confesses that God's ways and plans are infinitely beyond his understanding. **5.** The great contrast. Job's model service had been based on faith. That faith had been strong enough to withstand the assault of the friends' argument, but at what a cost in struggle and pain! Far different is the experience of the face-to-face meeting. The words of Yahweh may have been very different from what Job expected, but that is unimportant. The dark night is over; God has deigned to let himself be found by Job. **6.** The meaning is elusive. What Job rejects (*m's*) is not stated. He repents '*al* (concerning? in?) dust and ashes. See further discussion in Habel and Janzen. The *NJV* translates, "being but dust and ashes." Job can *not* be saying that he is sorry for his sins (a move that his friends had unsuccessfully tried to persuade him to adopt); the whole tenor of the book is against such a view. Neither is it clear that he "repents" of his more outrageous statements in the debate. The verdict of the Lord in 42:7 is that Job spoke "rightly."

128   (A) **Expiation of Job's Three Friends** (42:7-10a). Without further mention of the storm, Yahweh is presented as speaking to Eliphaz, as he did to Job; but (in spite of repetitions) the speech is a brief one.

It declares God's anger against the three, to appease which they must offer a holocaust in Job's presence, with Job uttering prayers for them. (The holocaust appears to be the same as Job had formerly offered weekly for his seven sons, 1:5, and the implication may be that the friends' speeches amounted to blasphemy.) They comply, and Job's intercession is effective. This apparently artless narrative has the following important implications:
   (1) It establishes—what the speech to Job himself had completely passed over—the truth of Job's vehement affirmations against the friends, during the dialogue: he is the perfect and blameless man, and his prayers are acceptable to God. Their doctrine, the conclusions they drew, and their accusations against him were false; their bigotry and uncharity (by which they thought they were defending God and his justice) were culpable and have provoked God's anger. Job's warning in 13:7ff. is verified.
   (2) Yahweh treats them with mercy and indulgence; his forgiveness is easily obtained—but by means of the man whom they had condemned as obstinately wicked. Four times (vv 7b-8) he contrasts them with "my servant Job" (cf 1:8; 2:3). If the question of justice is still to be raised, they must admit, by their humble request, that Job is more just than they. This gentle, ironical, decisive turning of the tables fits with the author's taste for irony; he prepared for it in the dialogue by letting the friends condemn themselves in advance (e.g., Bildad in 8:20-22).
   (3) If the friends must humble themselves, Job also must forgive them. They have added immeasurably to his suffering; nevertheless, he must be reconciled to them and become their "redeemer," acting out what he had claimed in 31:29. Verse 10a carefully stresses this concept: Yahweh restored Job's fortunes "when he interceded for his neighbor" (MT has sg.).
   (4) There is here an approach to the idea of vicarious atonement, developed further in the fourth Servant Song (Isa 52:13-53:12). If Job is such an effective intercessor, it is partly because of the sufferings he has borne. Even while the friends were abusing him, he was actually being "qualified" to obtain for them the forgiveness they would need.

129   (B) **God's Blessing of Job Restored and Increased** (42:10b-17).   Nothing is said of the removal of Job's physical affliction, the effect of the Adversary's second attack; only the remedying of the loss of children and property is described. **11.** This seems a rather awkward insertion; probably it is quoted by the author from a preexisting form of the Job story, in which, after the deprivations of chap. 1, this consolation from his family was narrated. The author had replaced it by the visit of the three friends, as a setting for the dialogue; but here he chose to preserve this notation from the older version. **12-17.** The careful doubling of Job's possessions is a similar archaism; it is a way of saying "Job was twice as dear to God from then on." Many readers feel a scruple over this crude emphasis on material possessions, as though it contradicted Job's insistence in the dialogue on the separability of virtue and prosperity. But Job never questioned that material goods are a natural effect of God's love for human beings; what he denied was that they are always, and only, withdrawn from the wicked. Also, this state is "normal" for such as Job, as we see at the beginning of the book. No reason, other than God's goodness, is required for his bestowing gifts; it is their absence or withdrawal that requires explanation—which may be human sin or, as with Job, human virtue.

31

ECCLESIASTES (QOHELETH)

Addison G. Wright, S.S.

BIBLIOGRAPHY

1 Barton, G. A., *The Book of Ecclesiastes* (ICC; Edinburgh, 1908). Barucq, A., "Qohéleth," DBSup 9. 609–74. Braun, R., *Koheleth und die frühhellenistische Popularphilosophie* (BZAW 130; Berlin, 1973). Crenshaw, J. L., *Ecclesiastes* (OTL; Phl, 1987). Fuerst, W. J., *Ecclesiastes* (CBC; Cambridge, 1975). Galling, K., *Der Prediger* (HAT; 2d ed.; Tübingen, 1969). Ginsburg, C. D., *Coheleth* (London, 1861; repr. NY, 1970). Gordis, R., *Koheleth—The Man and His World* (3d ed.; NY, 1968). Hertzberg, H. W., *Der Prediger* (KAT; Gütersloh, 1963).

Lauha, A., *Kohelet* (BKAT; Neukirchen, 1979). Loretz, O., *Qohelet und der alte Orient* (Freiburg, 1964). Lys, D., *L'Ecclésiaste ou Que vaut la vie?* I (Paris, 1977). Murphy, R. E., *Ecclesiastes* (Herm; Phl, forthcoming). Podechard, E., *L'Ecclésiaste* (EBib; Paris, 1912). Scott, R. B. Y., *Proverbs. Ecclesiastes* (AB 18; GC, 1965). Whitley, C. F., *Koheleth: His Language and Thought* (BZAW 148; Berlin, 1979). Williams, A. L., *Ecclesiastes* (CBSC; Cambridge, 1922). Zimmerli, W., *Prediger* (ATD; Göttingen, 1962).

INTRODUCTION

2 **(I) Date, Author, Title.** The book is the work of an unknown Jewish sage of the postexilic era. A copy of the book was in circulation about 150 BC (cf. Hebr fragments found at Qumran); the language of the book is late and similar to Mishnaic Hebrew; consequently most scholars date the work in the 3d cent. BC. The author is stated to be Solomon (1:1,12) but the language of the book precludes this, as well as the fact that the royal posture disappears after the experiment with luxury in chap. 2, and the author speaks as one without power to correct oppression. All indications are that the Solomonic attribution is a literary convention typical of the wisdom tradition (→ Wisdom Lit., 27:8). The author calls himself "Qoheleth," a term that remains a mystery. The word is from *qhl* ("assemble") and probably designates one who has some relationship to an assembly or congregation (e.g., a teacher) or one who assembles wisdom teaching. One author is responsible for the work (1:1–12:8), and an editor/disciple has added an epilogue (12:9–14). Although Gk influence upon the author has been alleged, the evidence for this is weak. Rather, he is in the mainstream of the ancient Near Eastern wisdom movement. The Eng title "Ecclesiastes" is derived from the Gk transl. of "Qoheleth" (*ekklēsiastēs*); the "Preacher" derives from Luther (*Prediger*) and ultimately from Jerome (*concionator*).

3 **(II) Structure.** In this book structure is not a secondary or aesthetic matter, but is of the utmost importance for exegesis. The book can be made to say

many different things depending upon how one divides it into units, as the history of its interpretation illustrates. The structure that the author intended to give to this enigmatic book has finally been recovered. Fortunately the author has marked the ends of sections with refrains ("vanity and a chase after wind" in chaps. 1–6; "find" in chaps. 7–8; "not know" in chaps. 9–11). That this simple structural device is indeed the key to the book's units is amply proved by the extensive numerical design discoverable in the verse count of the resulting major and minor sections. Thus, the refrains indicate that the whole book is to be divided into two parts (1:1–6:9; 6:10–12:14); each part contains 111 verses. The refrains indicate that the body of the book is in two parts (2:1–6:9 and 6:10–11:6); each part contains 93 verses. These 186 verses are flanked by an 18-verse introduction (1:1–18) and an 18-verse conclusion (11:7–12:14). The numbers 18, 93, 111, 186, 222 are all related to the number 37 (the numerical value of *hebel*, "vanity," which itself occurs 37 times in the book). In addition, and most important, the assorted and varying verse quantities of the smaller units as indicated by the refrains are not random numbers but are in a fixed pattern, for the numbers have been systematically derived from additive series and have been systematically assigned to each of those units. Finally, Qoheleth's book (1:1–12:8, minus the epilogue) contains 216 verses, corresponding to the numerical value of the book's *inclusio* (cf. comment on 1:2), a further indication if any is needed that the author is engaged in numerical composition. No alterations of the text are necessary to achieve the verse count. For the details, see A. G. Wright, *CBQ* 30 (1968) 313-34 (= SAIW 245-66); *CBQ* 42 (1980) 38-51; *CBQ* 45 (1983) 32-43.

4   The literary and numerical analysis indicates the following structure:

(I) Qoheleth's Investigation of Life and His Advice (1:1-6:9)
    (A) Introduction (1:1-18)
        (a) Opening Poem (1:1-11)
        (b) Preface (1:12-18)
    (B) A Report of His Investigation and Advice (2:1-6:9)
        (a) An Experiment with Luxurious Living (2:1-11)
        (b) An Evaluation of Wisdom and Folly (2:12-17)
        (c) The Problem of Inheritance (2:18-26)
        (d) Toil Is Chancy (3:1-4:6)
        (e) The Problem of a "Second One" (4:7-16)
        (f) Loss of Enjoyment (4:17-6:9)
(II) The Inadequacy of Other Advice and of Our Knowledge of the Future (6:10-12:14)
    (A) Introduction (6:10-12)
    (B) The Development of the Two Topics (7:1-11:6)
        (a) No One Can Find Out What Is Good to Do (7:1-8:17)
            (i) Critique of advice to seek sorrow and adversity (7:1-14)
            (ii) Critique of advice to avoid ethical extremes (7:15-24)
            (iii) Critique of advice on women (7:25-29)
            (iv) Critique of advice to heed authority (8:1-17)
        (b) No One Knows the Future (9:1-11:6)
            (i) The time of misfortune is not known (9:1-12)
            (ii) Events in general are unpredictable (9:13-10:15)
            (iii) You know not what evil may happen (10:16-11:2)
            (iv) You know not what good may happen (11:3-6)
    (C) Conclusion (11:7-12:14)
        (a) Closing Poem on Enjoyment, Youth, and Old Age (11:7-12:8)
        (b) Epilogue (12:9-14)

5   **(III) Thought of the Book.** Qoheleth represents the skeptical side of Israelite wisdom. He does not reject the wisdom movement, but he does challenge some of its cherished beliefs. That he shares many ideas with the more conventional sages is clear. Qoheleth believes in God and in the fear of God (3:14; 5:6) and in an ethical code and in God's judgment on human behavior (11:9); and, like his contemporaries, he does not believe in an afterlife (9:10). Although he points out that wisdom has its limitations, he never recommends folly. He shares with the sages some secondary beliefs: God has given everything its appropriate time (3:1-11); God gives the ability to enjoy (2:25-26, etc.); what God has decreed one cannot change (1:13; 3:14-15; 6:10; 7:13; 11:3); the folly of many words (4:17-5:6; 6:11; 10:12-15); and, if they are not his creations, he endorses a number of traditional proverbs (1:18; 4:5-6,9-12; 5:7-11; 6:9; 7:7-12; 9:17-10:1; 10:8-11:4; 11:7).

6   Qoheleth's quarrel is with any theology that ignores experience and thereby tends to become unreal. Thus he attacks the simplistic statements of the traditional theology of retribution (3:16-18; 7:15; 8:12-14;

9:1-3) because they do not square with experience; God judges, but how that works is very much a mystery. He attacks the glib statements about the advantages of wisdom, because experience shows that one fate comes to the wise and the foolish (2:13-16; 9:1-3,11), because the wise cannot predict the future (3:22; 6:12; 8:7; 9:1-11:6) esp. the time of misfortune (9:12), and because wisdom is vulnerable to a small amount of folly (9:13-10:1). Nor is he optimistic about the success of the human quest for wisdom (1:13-18; 3:11; 7:13; 8:17; 11:5). He rejects advice that recommends focusing on death and adversity (7:1-14), avoiding ethical extremes (7:15-24), identifying folly with women (7:25-29), and advice that recommends simplistic obedience to authority (8:1-14), because experience indicates that they are not worthwhile postures. Above all he rejects the wisdom tradition's emphasis on industriousness if it means total absorption in work, because such feverish labor robs one of enjoyment (2:22-23; 4:7-8; 5:11,16), because the prospects of labor's success are chancy (3:1-11), because the fate of accumulated wealth is uncertain (2:18-21; 4:7-8; 5:12-16), and because toil brings neither profit, progress, novelty, nor remembrance (1:3-11). Qoheleth does not believe in laziness, but he believes that one hand full of toil and one hand full of rest are better than two hands full of toil (4:5-6).

7   Tremendously impressed by the transitory nature (vanity) of all things, he believes that enjoyment is the thing to be focused on in life, not a pursuit of luxury because it is not worth the labor involved (2:1-11), but an acceptance of the ordinary joys which God sees fit to give us (affirmed seven times in the book: 2:24; 3:12,22; 5:17; 8:15; 9:7-9; 11:9-10). Enjoy the good day and accept the evil day as God giving variety so we cannot find fault with him (7:14). Enjoy what is at hand and do not long for the unattainable (6:9). Enter into life with zest (9:10); provide for the future (11:1); keep one's options multiple in the face of uncertainty (11:2); be not overcautious (11:4); and enjoy while one can, because old age and death are coming (11:7-12:8).

(Crenshaw, J. L., "The Shadow of Death in Qoheleth," *IW* 205-16. Good, E. M., *Irony in the Old Testament* [Phl, 1965] 168-95. Johnston, R. K., "'Confessions of a Workaholic': A Reappraisal of Qoheleth," *CBQ* 38 [1976] 14-28. Mitchell, H. G., "'Work' in Ecclesiastes," *JBL* 32 [1913] 123-38. Murphy, R. E., "Qohelet's 'Quarrel' with the Fathers," *From Faith to Faith* [Fest. G. Miller; ed. D. Y. Hadidian; Pittsburgh, 1979] 235-45. Von Rad, G., *WI* [Nashville, 1978] 226-39. Whybray, R. N., "Qoheleth, Preacher of Joy," *JSOT* 23 [1982] 87-98. Williams, J. G., "What Does It Profit a Man?: The Wisdom of Koheleth," *Judaism* 20 [1971] 179-98 [= *SAIW* 375-89]. On the history of the book's interpretation, see R. E. Murphy, *VT* 32 [1982] 331-36.)

8   **(IV) Religious Value.** The presence of the book in the canon validates in every age the same kind of critical assessment of theology, conventional wisdom, and piety as Qoheleth practiced, and validates it not as an optional activity but as one constantly necessary to keep religion honest and in touch with reality. The book's insistence on enjoyment is an important voice to be heard by anyone who locates the message of biblical religion more in asceticism than in love and social concern, and who feels that biblical religion in some way militates against enjoyment. Qoheleth's negative assessment of the workaholic should be constructively provocative for those who believe that posture to have value or to be synonymous with religious dedication. Finally, in no way can Qoheleth be said to have had a close personal relationship with God. Not infrequently the rhetoric of the believing community creates the impression that all the faithful should be experiencing such a relationship and that they are in some way at fault if they do not. Clearly, countless thousands of devout people travel in the dark as did Qoheleth, and they can find dignity in the believing community because

Qoheleth was deemed worthy to have a place among the biblical writings. Surely the book needs to be complemented by the other voices of Scripture, but its voice is of considerable importance.

COMMENTARY

9 (I) **Qoheleth's Investigation of Life and His Advice (1:1–6:9).** The book begins (→ 3 above) with 18 verses of introduction (1:1–18) followed by 93 verses which contain the actual report of Qoheleth's investigation (2:1–6:9). These features will be balanced in the second half of the book by another 93-verse discussion of two related topics (6:10–11:6) and an 18-verse conclusion including the editor's epilogue (11:7–12:14). **10** (A) **Introduction (1:1–18).** The introduction consists of an opening poem (vv 1–11) and a preface summarizing the activities that led to the writing of the book (vv 12–18). **11** (a) OPENING POEM (1:1–11). After the title (v 1) and a statement of the negative aspect of the book's thought (v 2), Qoheleth poses a question in v 3 (What profit is there from all the labor?), which provides the context in which vv 4–11 are to be read. There follows a poem on the endless round of events (vv 4–6) and on the lack of progress in nature and human activity (vv 7–8). The prose (or poetic?) conclusion states that there is nothing new, and, if something seems to be new, it is because one does not remember the previous occurrence; the same lack of remembrance will obtain in the future (vv 9–11). Thus, there is no profit in toil because nothing is gained, neither progress, novelty, nor remembrance. **1.** *David's son, Qoheleth:* → 2 above. **2.** This motto is repeated at the end of the book and thus serves as the overall *inclusio* (see comment on 12:8). The numerical value of its consonants (*hbl hblym hkl hbl*) is 216, and there are 216 verses in 1:1–12:8. Clearly Qoheleth has counted his verses (→ 3 above). *vanity:* A favorite word, having a numerical value of 37 and used 37 times in the book. Hebr *hebel* literally means "breath" or "vapor" and designates what is transient and lacking in substance. **3.** This negative assessment of toil anticipates a substantial negative theme of the first part of the book. **8.** *there is nothing one can say:* With adequacy, achievement, or novelty. On the poem, see E. M. Good, "The Unfilled Sea," *IW* 59–73. **12** (b) PREFACE (1:12–18). Qoheleth introduces his book with a general statement that he has studied all aspects of life and that it is all an unpleasant subject to deal with because it is all vanity (vv 12–14). This is followed by a proverb to the effect that what is is and there is nothing one can do to change it (v 15). Qoheleth has become fully acquainted with the traditional learning of the sages (v 16), but when he attempted to relate theory to actual life experiences he discovered that the quest for wisdom was very elusive (v 17). As the proverb says: the pursuit of wisdom brings trouble and pain, in the enterprise itself and in its findings (v 18). **13.** *wisdom:* Here, a guiding principle. For Qoheleth it is a principle of questioning, and not a source of assured insights. **16.** *wisdom:* Here, the accumulated observations of the sages. **17.** *know wisdom:* In practice. He has found that what is theoretically wise is often in practice foolish and vice versa. **13** (B) **A Report of His Investigation and Advice (2:1–6:9).** This part of the book states in detail those aspects of Qoheleth's study of life which he

chooses to report on, and it offers his recommendations in the face of that study. This part consists of six sections each concluding with the refrain "vanity and a chase after wind." Each section offers a separate consideration. **14** (a) AN EXPERIMENT WITH LUXURIOUS LIVING (2:1–11). In v 3 the author specifically states for the first time the purpose of his quest: to "understand what is best for people to do" in life. His first experiment was a total dedication to luxury. He describes his efforts and affirms that he indeed found pleasure in the fruit of his toil (vv 4–10). However when he reflected on all that he had done and the labor involved in doing it, he judged that it was vanity and lacking in profit (v 11). **2.** An anticipatory statement of his final judgment on the experiment. **3.** *wisdom:* It was not an inebriated experiment. *folly:* Ways of living which seem reasonable but which turn out to be unwise; or ways of living which are widely seen as folly, but which should be examined anyway. *what is best:* A controlling stance to life. He is not testing whether to be religious or not; he is testing various postures to life available to the believer. **9.** *wisdom stayed with me:* The experiment did not degenerate into a mindless dissipation. **11.** The pleasure was fleeting and transitory and was not commensurate with the effort that went into it. Hence, it could not be classified as profit. For Qoheleth, however, pleasure is one's *ḥeleq* ("portion" or "share" or "lot") in life, whether derived from luxury (2:10) or from a simpler life style (3:22; 5:18; 9:9). Qoheleth will subsequently recommend less toil (4:5–6) and recommend enjoyment on a more modest scale (2:24). See J. G. Williams, *Judaism* 20 (1971) 179–98 (= *SAIW* 375–89). **15** (b) AN EVALUATION OF WISDOM AND FOLLY (2:12–17). Qoheleth next examines the merits of wisdom. He recalls the traditional teaching on the superiority of wisdom over folly (vv 13–14a), but severely qualifies it with his own observation that the same things happen to the wise and to the fool. Where is the profit then in wisdom? (vv 14b–15). Moreover, sage and fool die alike in that they both alike are forgotten (v 16). **12.** *what will the man do . . . :* The second half of v 12 is obscure and probably corrupt. The *NAB* places it before v 12a as a conclusion to vv 1–11. **13.** *I saw:* He saw the traditional teaching of vv 13–14a, but he "knew" (v 14) otherwise from experience. **14.** *one lot* (*miqreh*): The way things turn out in life (as in 9:1–3, 11–12) or one's final lot, death (as in 3:19). The former is probably meant here, the idea of death being introduced in v 16. **15.** *why should I be wise:* Qoheleth values wisdom (1:13; 2:3,9; etc.), and folly is never an option for him, but he does feel obliged to attack the inflated statements of the sages on its advantages. **16.** *remembrance:* With no hope in future life (cf. 9:5,6,10) immortality of name was important, and it was promised to the just by the sages. *wise man dies . . . fool:* How alike they are in death. **17.** *I loathed life:* Basically Qoheleth loves life (cf. 11:7), but he despises the patterns in which it unfolds. **16** (c) THE PROBLEM OF INHERITANCE (2:18–26). The author turns to the subject of toil and the fruits of toil, the topic of the remaining four sections. Qoheleth at first enjoyed the fruits of his toil (2:10), but now he finds reason to detest them, beause they must be left to an heir who may play the fool with them (vv 18–19) and who certainly will not have labored for them (vv 20–21) with all the sorrows and trials which accompany toil (vv 22–23). Since work is arduous, and long-range planning for one's possessions is impossible, he concludes that what is good is to find present enjoyment in the modest fruits of modest toil. Unfortunately the ability to enjoy is a gift of God which some do not receive, and that is another vanity in life (vv 24–26). **18.** *fruits of toil:* A reference to the experiment in 2:1–11, but the discussion henceforth is stated increasingly in terms typical of everyone's life. **24.** This is the first positive statement in the book, and it will be repeated with increasing emphasis and greater prominence (3:13,22; 5:17; 8:15; 9:7–11; 11:9–10). It is the basic posture to life which he recommends and around which he will cluster other pieces of advice. The enjoyment is not the striving after luxury rejected in 2:1–11, but is that enjoyment which God chooses to give in the ordinary course of life and which compensates for the inevitable toil. *eat and drink:* An expression that connotes well-being, prosperity, happiness, the full range of life's blessings, the table being the place of fellowship as well as refreshment and relaxation (cf. the simple description of the well-being of Solomon's reign: "they ate and drank and enjoyed," 1 Kgs 4:20). **26.** In view of 9:1–3 etc., the "one seen fit" and the "sinner" probably have no moral connotation, but mean simply "lucky/unlucky."

17   (d) TOIL IS CHANCY (3:1–4:6). Qoheleth begins this section by quoting a poem which states that everything has an appointed time (vv 1–8). He immediately applies the poem to the ongoing topic of toil (v 9). There is no profit in toil because God has appointed a time for everything, but he has not equipped humans with the ability to determine the proper times so as to synchronize with them. Toil then is chancy, for it may not succeed (vv 10–11). He concludes again in favor of enjoyment, recalling once more that it is a gift (vv 12–13) and that what is is and there is nothing one can do to change it (vv 14–15).

18   Qoheleth then digresses apropos of the poem. Wickedness prevails even in courts of justice (v 16). Since everything has its time (as the poem states), it is widely said that this wickedness will at some time not escape God's judgment (v 17). But Qoheleth does not see that judgment taking place, and, if God is to be said to be doing anything, he is showing people that they are but beasts (v 18), for humans and beasts die alike (vv 19–21). Consequently, one should enjoy now because one cannot predict what the future holds in store (v 22). In a second reflection on injustice he notes that no one helps the oppressed because the oppressors are too powerful (4:1). Thus, death is preferable to life, and the unborn state is better yet (vv 2–3). Not only is there covetous oppression in life, but envy permeates all human aspiration and endeavor (v 4). The section ends with a threefold comparison which recommends a midcourse (v 6a) between idleness, which will ruin one (v 5) and total involvement in toil (v 6b). Better to have less and time for leisure than to have more with no leisure at all.

19   **2–8.** The poem is to be read as seven couplets in two stanzas (vv 2–4,5–7). Both stanzas end with a couplet on mourning (vv 4 and 7) and each stanza expresses a separate idea: constructive/destructive actions (vv 2–3) and union/separation (vv 5–6). The final couplet (v 8) is an "umbrella" for the whole poem. The meaning of the poem as a self-contained unit appears to

be that the joys and sorrows of life come from constructive/destructive actions and from separations and unions caused by love and hate on the individual and larger social levels. (See A. G. Wright, in *De la Tôrah au Messie* [Fest. H. Cazelles; ed. M. Carrez, *et al.*; Paris, 1981] 321–28.) If written by Qoheleth, the poem does not seem to have been composed for this book. **5.** *scatter stones:* A euphemism for sexual intercourse (cf. *Midr. Qoh.*). **7.** *rend . . . be silent:* Expressions of grief. **11.** *the timeless* (*hā'ōlām*): However the word is to be understood ("eternity," "duration," etc.), it impedes our discovery of "the work which God has done," i.e., the arrangement of the times. On the verse see J. L. Crenshaw, in *Essays on Old Testament Ethics* (Fest. J. P. Hyatt; ed. J. L. Crenshaw, *et al.*; NY, 1974) 23–55. **12–13.** See comment on 2:24. **19.** An echo of 2:14b–15, where the wise and the fool were compared; the only comparison left is that of humans and beasts. **21.** Whatever speculation is referred to, it yields no evidence of a difference between humans and beasts. **22.** See comment on 2:24. Here enjoyment is commended because God's judgment does not seem to be operative and because the future is unknown. *lot:* See comment on 2:11. *what is to come after:* Not a remote future after death, but the proximate future in which one must live (the topic of 9:1–11:6). **4:4.** *rivalry (qn'):* Or "envy." For Qoheleth it belongs to a basic triad of human activity (love, hatred, rivalry, cf. 9:6) and represents a substantial segment of life. Verse 4 may be connected with the oppression in 4:1 in that the coveting, which lies at the root of oppression (cf. Mic 2:2), finds its noncriminal expression in envious toil. If *comfort* (*nhm*) in 4:1 and *tranquillity* (*nḥt*) in v 6 are related roots for the author, then 4:1–6 would possess another unifying thread: two groups deprived of rest, one at the hand of oppressors, one by filling both their hands with toil (*inclusio: hand[s],* vv 1 and 5).

20   (e) THE PROBLEM OF A "SECOND ONE" (4:7–16). Qoheleth examines another vanity of toil: the case of the solitary worker who has no "second one," either son or brother, who will benefit from the riches gained (vv 7–8). There follows a series of examples which extol the value of a "second" or companion (vv 9–12). The concluding story (vv 13–16) relates how an old and foolish king loses popularity to a poor but wise youth (to a "second"; cf. *šny*, v 15). The story relativizes vv 9–12: a second is an advantage—but not always. **8.** It is not clear whether the man's avarice is the cause of his solitary state or the result. In 2:18–23 Qoheleth was resentful of others enjoying after his death the fruit of his labors; here he recognizes the futility of toiling for merely personal gain.

21   (f) LOSS OF ENJOYMENT (4:17–6:9). The final section begins with an assemblage of proverbs which (like 3:1ff.) set up the ideas to be discussed in this section: acquisition of goods, greed, loss of enjoyment (5:7–11). Qoheleth then states his final observation on toil. Sometimes one will anxiously accumulate riches and then lose them in a bad venture and have nothing to show for all the toil and experience no enjoyment (vv 12–16). He repeats for the fourth time his advice to enjoyment (vv 17–19). Enjoyment, however, is a gift of God (v 18) and unfortunately some do not have the ability or opportunity to enjoy; in their case it would be better not to have lived (6:1–6). He then offers a concluding observation on enjoyment. Human appetite is never satisfied (v 7), and no one has an advantage in this regard (v 8). Therefore, to find true enjoyment one is to be content with what is at hand; longing for the unattainable is vanity (v 9). **4:17–5:6.** The common denominator of all the proverbs is the folly of many words. Here, as he approaches the end of the first half of the book, he signals that he will not foolishly babble on and on. A similar unit with the same function occurs in 10:12–15 near the end of the second part of the book. **7–8.** Obscure. Perhaps a picture of a hierarchy of greedy acquisition of wealth (to be developed in 5:12–16). **9.** The more one gets the more one wants (addressed in 6:7–9). **10.** One acquires but another enjoys (an aspect of the case in 5:12–16 reflected on in 6:1–6). **11.** Loss of enjoyment due to anxiety (an aspect of the case in 5:12–16). **12–16.** The man is involved in a double loss of enjoyment. He anxiously watches over his wealth (*šmr*, v 12) to his own hurt and lives in the state described in v 16; in addition he loses his wealth to others. **17.** See comment on 2:24. *lot:* See comment on 2:11. **6:3.** *deprived of a burial:* In the Hebrew these words can and should be construed with the stillborn (cf. *NJV*). **6.** *same place:* The grave and sheol. **3–6.** For Qoheleth the traditional blessings of many children and old age mean nothing if one does not enjoy.

22   (II) The Inadequacy of Other Advice and of Our Knowledge of the Future (6:10–12:14).   In the first half of the book Qoheleth wrestled with the question of what one's controlling posture toward life should be, and he recounted his own experience and offered his own advice. In the second half of the book he turns to the only other sources for a solution to the problem: other people's advice (chaps. 7–8) and a knowledge of the future (9:1–11:6).

23   (A) Introduction (6:10–12).   The author repeats two ideas from the first half: what is is, and nothing can be done about it (v 10) and the folly of many words (v 11). He then asks two questions which announce the two topics of the second half of the book: Who knows what is good for people? And who knows the future? The answer to both questions, of course, is "no one," and Qoheleth will develop the first topic in four sections in chaps. 7–8 and the second topic in four sections in 9:1–11:6. **10.** *named:* I.e., created. *one stronger than he:* God. **12.** *who knows what is good:* The same question that governed the quest in the first part of the book (cf. 2:3). *who knows what will come after:* Not future life but how things will turn out on earth from the present moment on. Such knowledge, if it were available, would be an immense help in knowing what is good to do.

24   (B) The Development of the Two Topics (7:1–11:6).

(a) No One Can Find Out What Is Good to Do (7:1–8:17).   This part of the book consists of four sections each concluding with the refrain "(not) find." Each section contains a proposed stance toward life and is followed by Qoheleth's critique and/or rejection of it.

25   (i) *Critique of advice to seek sorrow and adversity* (7:1–14).   Qoheleth cites an assemblage of proverbs (vv 1–6) that recommend preoccupation with death, mourning, and sorrow and with the unpleasantness of rebuke. This grim view of life, evidently proposed by some of his contemporaries, he dismisses as vanity (v 6b) and then assembles a group of proverbs (vv 7–12) that challenge the validity of vv 1–6 as a way of life. At the end he offers his own advice (vv 13–14): Enjoy the good day and, when the evil day comes, view it as God giving variety so that one cannot find fault with him. **1.** The treasure of a good reputation (cf. Prov 10:7; 22:1) is vulnerable during life and only becomes fixed at death (cf. Sir 11:28); hence the value placed on the day of death. Ointment was probably chosen for the play on words (*šem*, "name"; *šemen*, "ointment") and stands for costly possessions. **3.** Sadness better matches the realities of life. **6.** *this also is vanity:* Consistently used as a divider within sections, this here divides the proverbs into two groups: the advice under examination (vv 1–6) and its

critique (vv 7–12). The sentence is also a judgment on vv 1–6. As one might suspect from Qoheleth's "enjoyment" passages, vv 1–6 do not accord with Qoheleth's thought. **7.** *oppression:* Perhaps here the root (*'šq*) conveys the general sense of distress as in Isa 38:14. In citing this proverb Qoheleth makes the point that there is more to be said about adversity than the advantages noted in vv 2–5; here is a proverb which points out the liabilities of adversity. *and a bribe corrupts the heart:* With different vowels the Hebr text can also be rendered "and (oppression) takes away his vigor." **8.** *better is the end of speech* (or "thing" [*dbr*]) *than its beginning:* This proverb states the idea of v 1, but it recognizes a liability in the advice and hastens to add that one needs to be patient if one is to live on that principle. **9.** *discontent* (*ka'as*): This is the same Hebr word as is found in v 3 ("sorrow"). In v 3 *ka'as* is recommended. Here Qoheleth recalls another proverb which very definitely does not recommend *ka'as*. **10.** One should not live in a frame of mind which sees the past as good and the present grim. A grim present is precisely what is recommended in vv 2–5, and this proverb challenges that advice. **11–12.** The operative word in this proverb is "life." As his final critique on vv 1–6, Qoheleth quotes a proverb which affirms that wisdom is for life and is not to be focused on "death" (v 1) and on an anticipation of death (vv 2–4). **14.** *find fault with him in anything:* The Hebrew is literally "so that man cannot find after him anything." The *NAB* and others recognize here an idiom corresponding to Syriac: find after = find fault.

26   (ii) *Critique of advice to avoid ethical extremes* (7:15–24).   Qoheleth turns to another opinion on what is good to do. This advice would have it that, in view of the fact that the traditional theology of retribution does not work out in practice (v 15), one should not attempt to be perfect because that is impossible (v 16); one should not be excessively wicked either, because God's retribution of death upon the wicked may indeed function in extreme cases (v 17). The God-fearing person who heeds both these admonitions will come through successfully (v 18). Supporting observations for the advice are given in vv 19–22. In conclusion Qoheleth states that he probed these ideas but did not find wisdom in them (vv 23–24). **16.** *lest you be ruined* (*šmm*): Possibly a state of confused silence or bewilderment. The cause is given in v 20; the effort to be totally just is doomed to failure. **16–17.** How much and what kind of wickedness this advice tolerates are not clear. In any event the practitioner of it is to "fear God" (v 18). **19.** An affirmation of the value of wisdom as a basis for what is said in vv 16–18. **20.** The basis for the statement in v 16 and a qualification of v 19. **21–22.** An illustration of the truth in v 20. **23–24.** No reason is given for the negative evaluation of the advice in vv 16–22.

27   (iii) *Critique of advice on women* (7:25–29). Qoheleth states again his search for wisdom (v 25) and quotes some traditional advice which he has found which warns against women (v 26). He then reacts unfavorably to another saying which he has found: "One man in a thousand (is good) but no woman" (vv 27–28). In conclusion he states that the only thing of value which he has been able to find is that God made all (male and female) upright, but they have all sought out many devices. **26.** Probably a seductress, but possibly a possessive and harmful woman; or the line may be a general statement that one cannot trust women. **29.** Wisdom and folly are not to be located in the simplistic categories of male/female; both sexes are equally devious.

28   (iv) *Critique of advice to heed authority* (8:1–17). Qoheleth cites traditional material (vv 1–6a) which recommends listening to the expert/sage (vv 1 and 5b) and obedience to the king (vv 2–5a). Qoheleth's critique of that advice follows in vv 6b–14. The great human affliction is ignorance of the future, and no one, including the sage, is an authority in that area (vv 6b–7); nor does anyone, including the king, have authority over death (v 8). In fact, the exercise of authority is often downright hurtful to people (v 9). Thus the wicked retain respectability in society (v 10), and the fact that justice is not executed speedily actually promotes evil-doing (v 11). Traditional theology says that the good will prosper and the wicked will not (vv 12–13), but reality does not square with that belief (v 14). Having rejected four pieces of others' advice in chaps. 7–8, Qoheleth concludes by repeating his own advice to enjoyment for the fifth time (v 15) and by a triple acknowledgment that the work of God is beyond human discovery (vv 16–17). **6b–7.** In all our attempts to understand life's mysteries and gain wisdom, it is our ignorance of the future that undermines the desired effect of such activity. This subject will be the topic of 9:1–11:6. **8.** Death terminates and dissolves all attempts to control life, and the inability to ward it off is the crowning proof of human incapacity. *struggle:* The battle between life and death. *nor are the wicked saved:* Nor does wickedness give life. **11.** *sentence executed:* By the civil judiciary. **12.** *I know:* He is aware of the traditional belief, even though he does not share it. **15.** See comment on 2:24.

29   (b) No One Knows the Future (9:1–11:6). This part of the book develops the second question in 6:12: "Who can tell what will come after?" It has four sections, each ending with the refrain "not know" and each developing the theme of human ignorance of the future.

30   (i) *The time of misfortune is not known* (9:1–12). *People do not know* whether God loves them or hates them, because things *happen* in the same way for the just and wicked alike, and then they both alike die (vv 1–3). The living have one advantage over the dead in that the living know how they will die, whereas the *dead know nothing* and have no *portion* in life here (vv 4–6). One should *enjoy* while still alive and live life to the full. That is one's *portion* in life here, and joy and activity will be impossible after death because the *dead know nothing* and do nothing (vv 7–10). The reason why things turn out the same for all is that misfortune *happens* to all alike, and, since *people do not know* in advance the time of misfortune, they cannot ward it off (vv 11–12). (The section is arranged concentrically; see the italics above.) **1.** *in the hand of God:* Not benign protection, but a position of helplessness. *love . . . hatred:* God's love and hatred. **4–5.** From the point of view of oppression, he felt in 4:2 that the dead were more fortunate than the living; here, from the point of view of knowledge, he states ironically that the living have an advantage—they know that they will die. **5–6.** He does not believe in a future life, but believes in sheol, an abode of the dead, as described here and in v 10. **7–10.** The sixth commendation of enjoyment; see comment on 2:24. **12.** *time:* Of misfortune as well as death.

31   (ii) *Events in general are unpredictable* (9:13–10:15). The unifying theme of this section is found in the conclusion: "No one knows what is to be" (10:14). Qoheleth here assembles a story and a number of proverbs that variously illustrate inability to predict the future. The section is divided into four paragraphs. (1) One Cannot Control the Future with Wisdom (9:13–10:1). The story (vv 13–15) gives a typical example of a wise man who was not heeded. Wisdom has value, but it is vulnerable to even a small amount of folly (9:16–10:1). (2) Of Roads and High Places (vv 2–7).

Proverbial material on what to expect on the road (vv 2–3) and how to keep good people in high places (v 4) is of little help in predicting and controlling the future. In Qoheleth's experience folly is set in many high places (vv 5–6) and one will meet the most unexpected things on the road (v 7). (3) Of Accidents and Surprises (vv 8–11). Four proverbs which in the present context depict the unexpected and unintended in life. (4) The Folly of Many Words (vv 12–15). As in 4:17–5:6 Qoheleth signals again that it would be foolish to belabor further the point he is trying to make.

32   **14–15.** The poverty of the wise man was probably the reason that he was not heeded (cf. 10:6). **15.** *he delivered the city . . . no one remembered:* These words can also be translated: "he could have delivered the city . . . no one had any thought for him," and this seems preferable since v 16 states that the man's words were not heeded. **10:2.** *right . . . left:* The right side is the side of success and good fortune; the left is that of failure and bad luck. **3.** *that he is a fool:* That he himself is a fool, or that everyone else is. **4.** *do not leave your place:* Lest a fool take your place. **10.** Probably a picture of a sharpened tool accidentally blunted (cf. *NAB*). **15.** His walk and talk avail nothing; he merely tires from it all.

33   (iii) *You know not what evil may happen* (10:16–11:2). The concluding line (11:2b) provides the title for the section. As in the preceding section proverbs are assembled for their picture dimension and provide four examples of ever-possible evils (10:16–20). The concluding proverbs (11:1–2a) offer advice in the face of such uncertainty. **16–17.** A reminder of the possibility of incompetent government. **18.** One may lose the industrious spirit and suffer ruin (cf. Prov 6:10–11; 24:33–34). **19.** That money is needed for the joys of life is a sober reminder of the uncertainties of financial security. **20.** The most guarded utterance may be divulged. **11:1.** Whatever the precise reference may be, the saying advises one to provide for the future. **2.** One should not put all the eggs in one basket.

34   (iv) *You know not what good may happen* (11:3–6). The title of the section is again provided by the concluding line (v 6). Qoheleth recalls once again that what is to be, is to be, and nothing can be done about it (v 3). He adds a proverb to the effect that over-caution can lead to inaction (v 4). He concludes the section in vv 5–6 by recommending an optimistic diligence and by a triple acknowledgment that the "work of God" is beyond human discovery (to match a similar threefold acknowledgment in 8:16–17). **5.** *work of God:* The mystery of divine governance which has preoccupied the author and which is mentioned at the beginning, midpoint, and end of the second half of the book (7:13; 8:17; 11:6) is compared to the origin of life. **6.** Probably envisions two sowings, morning and evening. One does not know which time is right and profitable (cf. 3:1–11), and indeed both may turn out successfully.

35   (C) Conclusion (11:7–12:14).
             (a) Closing Poem on Enjoyment, Youth, and Old Age (11:7–12:8).   In a unit which balances the opening poem (1:2–11) Qoheleth singles out his advice to enjoyment and gives it a seventh and final expression: Life is sweet and one should rejoice in it all while one is young and able, and (as an incentive to enjoyment) one should remember that old age and death lie ahead (vv 7–8). The theme of enjoyment is developed in vv 9–10 and that of old age and death is developed in 12:1–8 (in three parts marked by the word "before" in vv 1,3,6). **7–8.** This perhaps unexpected approval of life (cf. 2:17; 4:2; 9:4) indicates that the author himself appreciated life deeply. **9.** *ways of your heart . . . vision of your eyes:* Not an

invitation to hedonism; see comment on 2:24. Nor is it
an invitation to selfish immorality, as the remainder of
the verse indicates. *judgment:* He believes in divine judgment; he simply is unable to see it in its manifestations.
12:1–7. In 7:1–14 he rejects preoccupation with death,
but here he is not above remembering death as an incentive for enjoying the present. **1.** *creator:* The word ill fits
the context (one is after all to remember the darkness; cf.
11:8). One should probably read "grave" (*bwrk*) instead
of "creator" (*bwr'yk*). **2.** The Palestinian winter; here a
metaphor: the winter of life. **3–4a.** A house and its
inhabitants in winter and in deterioration; again a
metaphor for old age. Here the poem becomes allegorical
of the declining human faculties: "guardians" (arms/
hands), "strong men" (legs), "grinders" (teeth), "lookers
through the windows" (eyes), "doors" (ears or lips).
4b–5. These verses are less clear. The fear of heights and
streets is a direct description of an elderly person as well
as the caper berry (a stimulant) failing to have effect, as
well perhaps as the waiting for the sound of a bird
(sleeplessness?). The almond blooming is the last event
of winter and is white (gray hair?) and the locust of
winter is sluggish (the feeble human gait?). **6.** Four
images of death. **7.** *life breath:* Death is described in terms
of Gen 2:7; the breath returns to God. This is not the
soul and there is no statement of immortality here (cf.
9:10). In 3:21 he questioned whether there was any
difference between the breath in humans and animals.
Here he is simply affirming that God is the owner of that
breath. **8.** The overall inclusion for the book (see comment on 1:2). The line is an appropriate summary of the
negative aspects of Qoheleth's thought, but it does not
express the positive advice which he has offered.
36   (b) EPILOGUE (12:9–14). In adding these six
verses the editor makes the 105 verses of 6:10–12:8
balance the 111 verses of 1:1–6:9. In the epilogue the
editor speaks approvingly about Qoheleth (vv 9–11) and
offers a perspective from which the book can be read (vv
12–14). **10.** *pleasing:* Elegant in form. How much pleasure
they gave may be a matter of dispute. **11.** *goads:* To stimulate thought. *spikes:* Centers around which to organize
one's thinking. *collector:* Lit., "shepherd"—God or perhaps
Qoheleth. **12.** *beyond these:* Seemingly a reference to the
"words/sayings" in vv 10 and 11 and a statement that
now, with the addition of the work of Qoheleth, there
is no need to add to whatever collection of wisdom
writings then existed. **13–14.** The editor chooses to
emphasize fear, commandments, and judgment for a
conclusion. Qoheleth himself recommended the fear of
God (5:6) and expressed belief in judgment (11:9). He
does not speak of the commandments of God but he
surely promoted them, for he never recommends folly
or iniquity. It would seem that the ideas of fear, commandments, and judgment are really presuppositions for
Qoheleth as he discusses the concrete problem of how
specifically one is to conduct one's life within that
religious context; hence, those ideas are not prominent
in the book. What the editor does is to give those presuppositions a greater prominence lest anyone misunderstand. From the concluding sentence, one might surmise
that God's judgment is less mysterious for the editor
than it was for Qoheleth.

32

SIRACH

Alexander A. Di Lella, O.F.M.

BIBLIOGRAPHY

1 *Texts and Versions: Biblia Sacra iuxta latinam vulgatam versionem* 12 (Rome, 1964). *The Book of Ben Sira* (Jerusalem, 1973). Di Lella, A. A., "The Recently Identified Leaves of Sirach in Hebrew," *Bib* 45 (1964) 153-67; "The Newly Discovered Sixth Manuscript of Ben Sira from the Cairo Geniza," *Bib* 69 (1988) 226-38. Sanders, J. A., *The Psalms Scroll from Qumrân Cave 11 (11QPsª)* (DJD 4; Oxford, 1965). Vattioni, F., *Ecclesiastico: Testo ebraico con apparato critico e versioni greca, latina e siriaca* (Naples, 1968). Yadin, Y., *The Ben Sira Scroll from Masada* (Jerusalem, 1965). Ziegler, J., *Sapientia Iesu Filii Sirach* (Septuaginta 12/2; Göttingen, 1965).

Commentaries and Special Studies: Box, G. H. and W. O. E. Oesterley, "The Book of Sirach" *APOT.* Crenshaw, J. L., "The Problem of Theodicy in Sirach: On Human Bondage," *JBL* 94 (1975) 47-64. Di Lella, A. A., "Conservative and Progressive Theology: Sirach and Wisdom," *CBQ* 28 (1966) 139-54; *The Hebrew Text of Sirach* (The Hague, 1966); "The Poetry of Ben

Sira," *Harry M. Orlinsky Volume* (ErIsr 16; Jerusalem, 1982) 26*-33*. Duesberg, H. and I. Fransen, *Ecclesiastico* (LSB; Turin, 1966). Haspecker, J., *Gottesfurcht bei Jesus Sirach* (AnBib 30; Rome, 1967). Kearns, C., *Ecclesiasticus* (NCCHS; London 1969). Lévi, I., *L'Ecclésiastique* (Paris, 1898-1901). MacKenzie, R. A. F., *Sirach* (OTM 19; Wilmington, 1983). Middendorp, T., *Die Stellung Jesus ben Siras zwischen Judentum und Hellenismus* (Leiden, 1973). Peters, N., *Das Buch Jesus Sirach oder Ecclesiasticus* (EHAT 25; Münster, 1913). Prato, G. L., *Il problema della teodicea in Ben Sira* (AnBib 65; Rome 1975). Rickenbacher, O. *Weisheitsperikopen bei Ben Sira* (OBO 1; Freiburg, 1973). Rüger, H. P., *Text und Textform im hebräischen Sirach* (BZAW 112; Berlin, 1970). Skehan, P. W. and A. A. Di Lella, *The Wisdom of Ben Sira* (AB 39; GC, 1987). Smend, R., *Die Weisheit des Jesus Sirach erklärt* (Berlin, 1906). Snaith, J. G., *Ecclesiasticus* (CBC; Cambridge, 1974). Spicq, C., *L'Ecclésiastique* (Sainte Bible 6; Paris, 1951).

INTRODUCTION

2 **(I) Title, Author, and Purpose.** Among the earliest of the deuterocanonical OT books, Sirach is one of the rare biblical works that was actually composed by the author to whom it is ascribed. One of the longest books of the Bible, Sir contains the most extensive portion of Israelite wisdom literature to come down to us. The original title in Hebrew, according to the subscription of Cairo ms. B, was "The Wisdom of Yeshua [Jesus] ben [son of] Eleazar ben Sira." The title "Sirach" is a transliteration of the name found in the Gk mss. The title "Ecclesiasticus," which probably means the ecclesiastical (or Church) [book], is found in many Lat mss. and can still be seen in the *NJB, NEB,* and *RSV.*

Note that all chapter and verse numbers in Sir are those found in Ziegler's critical edition, a numbering followed in *The Wisdom of Ben Sira* (AB 39) and the *New RSV* (1990). Unfortunately, most transls. (e.g., *NAB, RSV, NEB*) have enumerations that correspond to neither the Gk nor the Lat numbering; the result has been confusion.

There is little doubt that the entire book was composed by one author, Ben Sira, who lived during the 3d

and early 2d cents. BC. A native of Jerusalem (50:27 Gk), he devoted his life to the study of the Law, Prophets, and Writings (cf. foreword) and became a highly respected scribe and teacher, who ran an academy for young Jewish men (51:23-30). In his extensive travels (34:12-13) he came in contact with other cultures and wisdom traditions and acquired "much cleverness" (34:11); and he did not hesitate to utilize what he had learned as long as he could make it conformable to his Jewish heritage and tradition (39:1-11).

Ben Sira wrote his book not for personal gain (51:25) but "for all who seek instruction" (33:18). He did not intend to write a systematic polemic against Hellenism, which had made its impact felt throughout the Near East. Rather, his purpose was to demonstrate that the Jewish way of life was superior to Hellenistic culture and its blandishments and that true wisdom was to be found primarily in Jerusalem, and not in Athens. Hence, the good Jew should not give in to the temptation to follow the Gk way of life.

3 **(II) Date of Composition.** Ben Sira's grandson states in the foreword to his Gk transl. that he arrived in Egypt in the 38th year of the reign of King Euergetes, who can only be Ptolemy VII Physcon (146–117). Hence the year would be 132 BC. The grandson made the Gk transl. in the following years and published it after the death of Euergetes in 117. Going back two generations (40 to 50 years) from 132, we come to a date *ca.* 180 for the composition of the book. This date is confirmed by the panegyric, in 50:1–21, on Simeon II, high priest from 219 to 196; Ben Sira writes in such a way as to suggest that Simeon had been dead for some time.

4   (III) Literary Genres and Manner of Composition. Taking Prov as his model, Ben Sira employed the following literary genres: *māšāl* (proverb, aphorism, maxim; comparison; paradigm, model; word play), hymn of praise, prayer of petition, autobiographical narrative, lists or onomastica, and didactic narrative. In his poetry he skillfully employs the devices of *inclusio*, chiasm, alliteration, assonance, and rhyme (see Di Lella, "The Poetry of Ben Sira" [→ 1 above]). He often composed units of 22 lines (the number of letters in the Hebr alphabet—or by way of variation 23 lines) to signal the opening or closing of a part of the book, to show the unity of a section, or simply to add elegance; see, e.g., 1:11–30, the opening poem; 5:1–6:4; 6:18–37, the opening of part III; 22:1–21; 49:1–16, the final unit on Israel's ancestors; 51:13–30, an alphabetic acrostic to close the book. Ben Sira learned this technique from such texts as Prov 2; 31:10–31; Pss 9–10; 25; 33; 34; 119; Lam 1–5.

5   (IV) Text and Versions. The book was composed originally in Hebrew, as the grandson states in the foreword. But the Hebr text, except for a few quotations in rabbinic literature, had been lost for centuries. Between 1896 and 1900 four Hebr mss. (A, B, C, D), from the 10th to 12th cents., were recovered from the Geniza of the Qaraite synagogue in Cairo. Ms. E was discovered in 1931 and more of mss. B and C in 1958 and 1960. Another fragment was discovered in 1982 by A. Scheiber. It is in fact a sixth ms., F (cf. Di Lella, *Bib* 69 [1988] 226–38). Some questioned whether this Geniza text was authentic, but the general consensus favored authenticity even though the text contained some retroversions from Syriac and possibly from Greek (see Di Lella, *Hebrew Text of Sirach*, 23–105). Fragments from Qumran (2Q18 [1st cent. BC] and 11QPs^a [1st cent. AD]) and Masada (1st cent. BC) have corroborated the substantial authenticity of the Geniza Hebr text (see Yadin, *The Ben Sira Scroll* 7, 10). About 68 percent of the Hebrew is now extant. Two recensions of the Hebr text are found in these fragments.

The Gk version is preserved in two different forms, called GI (found in the Uncials A, B, C, S, and dependent cursives) and GII (in the Origenistic and Lucianic mss.). In Ziegler's critical edition, GII is printed in smaller type. GI is generally based on the earlier Hebr recension, and GII on the later recension. The Syriac was translated from a Hebr *Vorlage* that had fused the two Hebr recensions.

The *NAB* and *The Wisdom of Ben Sira* (AB 39) offer a critical transl. based on the Hebr text as well as the Gk and Syr texts. The *New RSV* (1990), though translated primarily from Greek, utilizes the Hebrew and Syriac far more extensively than the *RSV* (1957).

6   (V) Canonicity. A deuterocanonical book, Sirach, though written in Hebrew and published in Jerusalem before Daniel (*ca.* 165 BC), was not included in the Jewish canon probably because the Pharisees who defined that canon near the end of the 1st cent. AD frowned on some of Ben Sira's theology (e.g., his denial of retribution in the hereafter). Nonetheless, Sir was often quoted, even as Sacred Scripture, by many of the later rabbis.

The early church (e.g., *Didache,* Clement of Rome, Irenaeus, Tertullian) considered Sir canonical. There are many allusions to the book in the NT, esp. in James. The fathers of the church attest more frequently to the canonicity of Sir than to several protocanonical books.

7   (VI) Outline. It is virtually impossible to outline the book because, except for chaps. 44–50 ("Praise of the ancestors of old"), Ben Sira seems to have had no clear plan for arranging the various subjects about which he wrote his thoughts and exhortations. He dealt with some of the same topics in different parts of the book; e.g., children in 7:23–25; 16:1–4; 22:3–4; 25:7; 30:1–13; 41:5–10; and parents in 3:1–16; 7:27–28; 23:14; 41:17. Since the book is basically a compilation of class notes that Ben Sira accumulated over many years of teaching, it is not surprising that there is little order in the presentation of topics. The following outline, which is adapted from *The Wisdom of Ben Sira* (AB 39), is little more than a description of the contents of the book.

(I) Foreword or Prologue
(II) Part I (1:1–4:10)
   (A) Introduction: The Origin of Wisdom (1:1–10)
   (B) Fear of the Lord as Wisdom for Humans (1:11–30)
   (C) Trust in God (2:1–18)
   (D) Honor Due to One's Parents (3:1–16)
   (E) Humility (3:17–24)
   (F) Docility, Almsgiving, Social Conduct (3:25–4:10)
(III) Part II (4:11–6:17)
   (A) Rewards and Warning of Wisdom (4:11–19)
   (B) Cowardice (4:20–31)
   (C) Presumption, Duplicity, Unruly Passions (5:1–6:4)
   (D) True and False Friendship (6:5–17)
(IV) Part III (6:18–14:19)
   (A) Exhortation to Strive for Wisdom (6:18–37)
   (B) Conduct toward God and Neighbor (7:1–17)
   (C) Family Life, Religion, and Charity (7:18–36)
   (D) Prudence in One's Affairs (8:1–19)
   (E) About Women and the Choice of Friends (9:1–16)
   (F) About Rulers and Pride (9:17–10:18)
   (G) The Believer's True Glory (10:19–11:6)
   (H) Providence and Trust in God (11:7–28)
   (I) Care in Choosing One's Friends (11:29–12:18)
   (J) Rich and Poor (13:1–14:2)
   (K) The Use of Wealth (14:3–19)
(V) Part IV (14:20–23:27)
   (A) Wisdom and Her Blessings (14:20–15:10)
   (B) Free Will and Responsibility (15:11–16:23)
   (C) God's Wisdom as Seen in Humans (16:24–18:14)
   (D) Prudential Warnings (18:15–19:17)
   (E) Wisdom and Folly in Word and Deed (19:18–20:32)
   (F) Various Kinds of Sin and Folly (21:1–22:18)
   (G) Preserving Friendship (22:19–26)
   (H) Against Destructive Sins (22:27–23:27)
(VI) Part V (24:1–33:18)
   (A) Praise of Wisdom (24:1–33)
   (B) Gifts That Bring Joy (25:1–12)
   (C) Wicked and Virtuous Women (25:13–26:18[27])
   (D) Dangers to Integrity and Friendship (26:28–27:21)
   (E) Malice, Anger, Vengeance, Evil Tongue (27:22–28:26)
   (F) Loans, Alms, Surety (29:1–20)
   (G) Frugality and Training of Children (29:21–30:13)
   (H) Health, Cheerfulness, Riches (30:14–31:11)
   (I) Food, Wine, Banquets (31:12–32:13)
   (J) Providence of God (32:14–33:18)
(VII) Part VI (33:19–38:23)
   (A) Property and Servants (33:19–33)
   (B) Trust in the Lord and Not in Dreams (34:1–20)
   (C) True Worship of God and His Response (34:21–36:22)
   (D) Choice of Associates (36:23–37:15)

COMMENTARY

8   (I) Foreword or Prologue. Like the classical historical prefaces composed by Herodotus, Thucydides, and Polybius, this may also be compared with the prologue to Luke (1:1–4). The foreword, found in most Gk mss., contains valuable information about Ben Sira and the translator himself. Thus, it is usually included with the text even though it is not canonical. In translation, the foreword has 6 (*RSV*) to 10 (AB 39) sentences. But the Greek has only three elegant periodic sentences, which correspond to the three paragraphs usually found in English; references here are to those paragraphs.
9   1. *the Law . . . later authors:* The first mention of the threefold division of the OT; the third was later called "the Writings," Hebr *kĕtûbîm.* Cf. Luke 24:44. Ben Sira had spent a lifetime in "the study" (lit., reading) of Israel's Scriptures; hence he felt constrained to write a book himself for the benefit of those who wanted to live "in conformity with the divine law." Cf. 33:18; 51:23–30. **2.** *you:* The Jews of the Greek-speaking Diaspora. The grandson asks his readers to be indulgent for any failures on his part to render "particular passages" of the Hebr original faithfully. He articulates the grief of all translators: how to render a text accurately into another language. He criticizes not only his own attempt but also the LXX, most of which already existed (→ Texts, 68:00–00). **3.** *thirty-eighth year . . . Euergetes:* 132 BC (→ 3 above). *many sleepless hours . . . publication:* The grandson refers to his trials as a translator. The expression "the interval" refers to the years 132–117. The grandson worked hard "for the benefit of those . . . abroad," i.e., in the Diaspora, so that they might "acquire wisdom" by living "according to the . . . law." The law is mentioned at the beginning and at the end, thus forming an *inclusio* for the purpose of emphasis.
10   Part I (1:1–4:10). The explicit theme of Part I is wisdom, which consists essentially in the fear of the Lord as a day-to-day religious commitment in the life of the faithful Jew. Wisdom as fear of the Lord is also the principal thesis of the whole book; in the *RSV* Sir, "wisdom" occurs 60 times.
11   (A) Introduction: The Origin of Wisdom (1:1–10). This poem serves as introduction to the whole book. In GI, it has two stanzas of equal length, 4 + 4 bicola (or lines). GII and Lat have three extra bicola, all glosses, vv 5, 7, 10cd. The theme is: All wisdom comes from God (v 1), who alone can know all "her subtleties (or secrets)" (v 6); he gives her as a gift to "those who love him" (v 10); cf. Prov 8:22–31; Wis 7:27–27; 9:4,6. **3.** *depth(s) of the abyss:* With Lat; most Gk mss. have "the abyss and wisdom." **4.** *before all things:wisdom::prudent understanding:from eternity:* Note the *a:b::b':a'* chiasm. Cf. J. Marböck, *Weisheit im Wandel* (BBB 37; Bonn, 1971) 17–34.

12   (B) Fear of the Lord as Wisdom for Humans (1:11–30). This opening poem contains 22 bicola, the number of letters in the Hebr alphabet; the closing poem (51:13–30) is an alphabetic acrostic of 23 bicola (→ 4 above), thus forming an *inclusio.* This poem has two sections, each with 11 bicola (vv 11–21 and 22–30); there are five stanzas in the first section and four in the second (see Skehan and Di Lella, *Wisdom*). The purpose is to identify "wisdom" with "the fear of the Lord," two concepts interwoven throughout the poem, esp. in vv 25–27. In vv 11–13 "fear of the Lord" occurs in each bicolon. The expression also appears in vv 14a, 16a,18a,20a; thus, in the first colon, respectively, of each of the following four stanzas, each composed of two bicola. At the beginning of these cola occur four words, each followed by "of wisdom," arranged in an *a:b::b':a'* pattern: *beginning:fullness::garland:root.* The second part (vv 22–30) offers maxims and exhortations to the faithful so that they may do what is necessary to practice "fear of the Lord" and thus become wise. The poem begins (v 11) and ends (v 30) with "fear of the Lord," thus forming an *inclusio.*
13   11–13. *fear of the Lord:* The essential component of biblical faith; cf., e.g., Deut 4:9–10; 8:5–6; 2 Chr 19:7; Prov 1:7; Job 28:28. Fear of the Lord brings to believers all they could hope for: glory, splendor, gladness, festive crown, joy of heart, length of days, a happy death, all these during their earthly life, for retribution in the afterlife was not yet a generally accepted Jewish doctrine. All people, good and bad, go to sheol where they have a dark, listless existence without God or any semblance of real life; cf. 14:16. A person "will be blessed" on the day of death (v 13) because a good life brings the favor of God; cf. 1 Chr 29:28. But the wicked, even though they may seem to prosper and to be successful during life, will die miserably; cf. 11:25–28. **14–15.** *the beginning:* Gk *archē,* which also means "most important part", (cf. 29:21; 39:26) and "essence of a thing" (cf. 11:3); here all three meanings are meant. Wisdom, like life itself, is a gift bestowed on "the faithful" (cf. 1:9–10) and "their descendants." **16–17.** *fullness:* See also 2:16; in Prov 8:19, wisdom's fruits are better than "pure gold." *her fruits:* Cf. Prov 9:1–6. **18–19.** *garland:* Or "crown," a word occurring also in other wisdom passages: 25:6; Prov 12:4 (crown of a husband); 16:31 (crown of glory); 17:6 (crown of the elderly). *peace:* Hebr *šālôm* also means well-being, prosperity, serenity, safety, contentment, all that a person desires for the good life. *knowledge . . . understanding:* The blessings of wisdom as fear of the Lord, more fully spelled out in Lev 26:3–13 and Deut 28:1–14. **20–21.** *root . . . her branches:* For the tree imagery, see 24:13–14,16–17. *length of days:* As in v 12. Though found

primarily in GII, v 21 must be authentic because each stanza from v 14 to v 21 is composed of two bicola; see above regarding the structure. *all wrath:* This expression serves as a catch phrase leading into the next section, which begins with a bicolon on human anger.

14 **22-24.** *unjust anger:* Mentioned often in the wisdom literature; cf., e.g., 27:30; 28:3-11; Prov 10:18; 15:1,18; 29:11. *the patient person:* In contrast to the short-tempered, the patient do not lose their composure; the result is that they are considered wise; cf. 39:9. **25-27.** Ben Sira gives his great equation: fear of the Lord = wisdom = gift of the Lord = discipline = keeping the commandments. Because sinners lack wisdom, they do not fear the Lord. *faith and humility:* Gk *pistis* and *praütēs,* also mentioned in 45:4; *pistis* is a lead-in to the next stanza. **28-30ab.** *be not faithless:* Gk *mē apeithēsēs;* the vb. is related to *pistis* (v 27). *duplicity of heart:* Lit., "double heart," an idea taken from Ps 12:3. In OT thought the heart was considered to be the seat of a person's intelligence and will. Self-exaltation was widely condemned; cf., e.g., 10:15; Ezek 17:24; Dan 4:34; Prov 11:2; Matt 23:12; Luke 1:52-53. **30c-f.** The poem concludes with the warning that those who do not practice fear of the Lord and have hearts "full of guile" will be disgraced publicly; cf. Prov 5:12-14.

15 **(C) Trust in God (2:1-18).** Fearing the Lord by loving and serving him faithfully is difficult. But the true believer will remain steadfast in the face of trials and distress. **1-3.** *my son:* The usual form of address for one's disciples; cf. 3:12,17; 4:1; Prov 2:1; 3:1. Sometimes "my children" is used; cf. 3:1; 23:7; Prov 4:1. *testing . . . affliction:* The faithful must be prepared for adversity even though they "serve the Lord." The deuteronomic theory of retribution allowed for probationary suffering as a test of fidelity; see A. A. Di Lella, *CBQ* 28 (1966) 143-46. **5.** The key passage that legitimates trials for the virtuous; cf. Zech 13:9; Prov 17:3; Wis 3:6; Jas 1:12. **6.** *trust God . . . hope in him:* Essentials of biblical faith. **7-9.** *you who fear the Lord:* This phrase occurs in each verse, indicating the unity of the stanza; an imperative follows each occurrence. The catchwords "trust" and "hope" (vv 8,9) connect this stanza with the preceding one. **9.** *lasting joy:* Not the bliss of an afterlife (cf. 1:12) but happiness in this life; cf. Isa 35:10; 51:11; 61:7. **10.** The rhetorical questions require the answer No. The experience of Israel's past generations proves that the Lord is "compassionate and merciful" (v 11). **12-14.** The "Woe" at the head of each verse indicates the unity of the stanza. **12.** *woe . . . double path:* Ben Sira excoriates the weakhearted and the compromisers, i.e., those who temporize with Hellenism; cf. 1:28. **15-16.** *those who fear the Lord:* The truly faithful, who obey the Lord and please him and are humble before him. Cf. 3:18; 7:17. **18.** A couplet in praise of God's mercy; cf. 2 Sam 24:14.

16 **(D) Honor Due to One's Parents (3:1-16).** True religion, i.e., fear of the Lord in all its implications (1:11-30), also involves duties to others, first of all to parents. **1-6.** Honoring father and mother, the cornerstone of biblical ethics (Exod 20:12; Deut 5:16), will bring a person long life (cf. 1:12), forgiveness of sins, and other blessings; cf. Exod 21:17; Tob 4:3-4; Prov 1:8; Matt 15:3-6. **9.** Parents will bless their child who reveres and serves them; the result is that the child will have "firm roots." But the child who shows parents no respect will be uprooted; cf. Prov 20:20. **16.** One must cherish aged, feeble, and senile parents too; one who fails to do so is "a blasphemer" who "provokes God" himself; cf. Lev 20:9; Prov 20:20.

17 **(E) Humility (3:17-24).** Cf. 1:27; 4:8; 7:16-17; 10:26-28; humility is emphasized also in Prov

(11:2; 15:33; 18:12; 22:4) and the Qumran Manual of Discipline (1QS 2:23-25; 3:8-9; 4:3; 5:3,24-25). **18.** The high and mighty have a greater need to be humble than the lowly and weak. **21-24.** The pious Jew should have no concern for "what is too sublime" or for "what is hidden" (i.e., the pretensions of Gk learning), for he has enough to attend to in the law (vv 21-22). Ben Sira also warns against the dangers of intellectual pride and the futility of Hellenistic philosophy and science (v 24).

18 **(F) Docility, Almsgiving, Social Conduct (3:25-4:10).** There is little connection between the three poems here; Ben Sira tends to place together unrelated topics (→ 7 above). **3:25-29.** The first poem contrasts "the heavy [hence, stubborn] heart" (vv 26-27; Hebr *lēb kābēd,* as in Exod 7:14 to describe Pharaoh) with "the wise heart" (v 29; Hebr *lēb ḥākām,* as in Prov 10:8 and 16:21 to describe the wise person). Hebr *lēb,* "heart" = "mind" in western thought. The stubborn "fare badly" because they lack wisdom, whereas the wise find joy in wisdom; cf. Prov 23:15. **3:30-4:6.** This poem extols the value of almsgiving, an important part of Ben Sira's ethics (7:10; 12:3; 16:14; 29:8,12; 40:24); cf. Deut 24:13; Prov 16:6; Tob 4:7-11; Dan 4:24. **4:1-6.** You should never mock the poor (cf. Prov 17:5) or aggrieve the hungry (cf. Tob 1:17) or delay in giving them alms (cf. 29:8) or reject their plea (cf. Ps 22:25); otherwise they may curse you, and God will hear their prayer. **7-10.** This poem gives selected maxims on how to behave toward people in various social classes. **7.** *the assembly:* Hebr *'ēdâ,* Gk *synagōgē,* the community of the Jews; cf. 7:7; 42:11. **8-10.** Here are featured the poor, the oppressed, the orphan, and the widow, who are entitled to special consideration; cf. 35:15-22; Deut 24:17-22; Job 29:11-16; Jas 1:27. **9.** Social injustice (cf. also 34:21-27) was severely condemned by the prophets (Amos 1:6-8; 5:7,10-15,21-24; Isa 1:15-17). **10.** Note the images of God as father and mother.

19 **(III) Part II (4:11-6:17).** This part contains four sections on the theme of applied wisdom in day-to-day living. As is the case elsewhere, there is little logical connection between the sections (→ 7 above).

20 **(A) Rewards and Warnings of Wisdom (4:11-19).** In this poem, divided into three stanzas, Wisdom is personified as a concerned mother who "teaches her children and admonishes" them (v 11). **11-14.** Those who love and seek and serve Wisdom serve "the Holy One" (a favorite title of God in Dt-Isa [e.g., 41:14,16,20]), who will love them in return. Again Ben Sira equates Wisdom with fear of the Lord; cf. 1:11-30. **15-16.** Here and in the next stanza Wisdom herself is the speaker. Those who obey her "will judge the nations" (v 15); cf. Wis 3:8; 1 Cor 6:2. **17-19.** Wisdom tests the virtuous (as does God in Gen 22:1; Exod 15:25; Deut 8:2) with her discipline: if they are faithful, she will reveal to them "her secrets" (cf. 39:3,7; 51:19; Job 11:6); if they fail her, she will abandon them. One can never attain her without the pain of discipline and trials.

21 **(B) Cowardice (4:20-31).** The first two stanzas of this section offer advice on true and false shame; the third stanza contains three unrelated maxims. **20-24.** Many Jews of that day were tempted to give up their faith for the Gk way of life; hence the warnings given here. **20.** *evil:* Probably the devastating compromise with Hellenism. *to be yourself:* Be proud to be a Jew; cf. 1 Macc 1:11-15. **23.** Do not hesitate to speak of your glorious heritage of wisdom. **25-28.** Speaking the truth is paramount in every ethical system. **27.** *a fool:* An apostate from Judaism (see W. M. W. Roth, *VT* 10 [1960] 408). *favoritism:* Cf. Jas 2:1-4.

22   (C) Presumption, Duplicity, Unruly Passions (5:1–6:4). The unity of this section is suggested by its 22-line structure (→ 4 above). **1–8.** Presumption, whether based on wealth or social, physical, or mental power, is condemned (cf. Ps 62:11–12); and to presume on God's mercy is to invite disaster (cf. Isa 1:18–20). **5:9–6:1.** Duplicity in speech and other sins of the tongue must be avoided. **11.** *swift to hear . . . slow to answer:* A maxim found also in Jas 1:19; cf. Prov 18:13. **14.** *double-tongued:* So Hebrew (cf. 28:13; Greek reads "whisperer," "slanderer"); such people will be utterly disgraced (6:1). **2–4.** Note the colorful images Ben Sira uses to deplore unruly passions.

23   (D) True and False Friendship (6:5–17). Ben Sira deals with friendship also in 7:17; 9:10–16; 11:29–12:18; 22:19–26; and 37:1–6; he has more to say on the subject than any other biblical author. **5.** As abuse of speech brings disaster (5:9–6:1), so "a kind mouth," or pleasant speech, brings one many friends; cf. Prov 16:21. **7–12.** One must be cautious and test friends to see if they are sincere, for there are many types of fair-weather friends who would turn away if one should suffer adversity. **13–17.** Various images are used to describe the value of a true friend. But only the one who fears the Lord, Ben Sira insists, will be blessed with such friends.

24   (IV) Part III (6:18–14:19). The opening poem (6:18–37) is a 22-line (nonalphabetic) poem, which is one of the means used to indicate the beginning of a new unit; → 4 above. Again we have here a loose collection of poems on the search for Wisdom and the behavior of the wise who find her.

25   (A) Exhortation to Strive for Wisdom (6:18–37). This 22-line poem is divided into three sections, each of which begins with "my son" (vv 18,23, 32). **18–19.** In the wisdom literature, the young were not considered to be as wise as the elderly (cf. 32:3,7–8); hence the need to start early if one wishes to become wise. Biblical authors often use agricultural images (cf. Isa 5:1–7; John 15:1–8; 1 Cor 3:6–9). **20–21.** The fool, finding Wisdom a burden, casts her aside. **22.** *discipline is like her name:* A play on the Hebr noun *mûsār,* "discipline," and the hophal participle *mûsār,* "withdrawn," "turned aside." Discipline is indeed withdrawn from the person who refuses to be subjected to it. **23–31.** The one who would be wise must have determination and zeal. The graphic imagery of hunting (vv 24,29) and the yoking of animals (vv 25,30) adds emphasis to the admonitions. In Matt 11:29–30, Jesus uses the images of burden (v 21) and yoke to describe Christian discipleship. **29–31.** The splendid apparel described here suggests the garments of the high priest (cf. Exod 28:28, 37); hence, one who achieves wisdom will share in the splendor of royalty and in the glory of the high priesthood. **31.** *crown:* Cf. 1:11. **32–37.** One becomes wise only if one applies oneself; wishful thinking will not do. The steps to wisdom are listening, seeking out the wise and their discourse, and associating with the prudent. **37.** Wisdom, virtually identified with the law (cf. 1:25–27; 24:23), again is described as a gift of God; cf. 1:10,26.

26   (B) Conduct toward God and Neighbor (7:1–17). Having described how one should pursue Wisdom, Ben Sira now offers detailed ethical maxims on the behavior of the wise. **1–2.** The topic sentence: avoiding evil is paramount if one wishes to live in peace and contentment. **3.** *sevenfold:* Those guilty of injustice will be punished many times over (cf. 20:12; Prov 6:31; Matt 18:22). **4–6.** Seeking honors in society is dangerous: a warning for those Jews who served as functionaries in the courts of the Seleucids and Ptolemies (cf. 2 Macc 3:4–13). **7.** The evils one can commit in court are many:

false witness, accepting a bribe, showing partiality to the rich or the poor, unjust accusation. **8–9.** God cannot be bribed by our offerings. **10–12.** One must show kindness and compassion to those in need. **15.** In Gen 2:15, work is meant by God to be a pleasant and fulfilling experience. **16–17.** Again the need for humility is stressed; cf. 3:17–24. *worms:* So Hebrew; Greek has "fire and worms" because in the grandson's day the Jews believed in retribution in the afterlife; cf. 11:26; 14:11–19.

27   (C) Family Life, Religion, and Charity (7:18–36). Maxims concerned primarily with personal life. **18–21.** Advice about the significant people in a man's life: friend, true brother, sensible wife, wise servant. **23–25.** Children are always a concern, esp. daughters in a patriarchal society. **26.** Ben Sira's views about women as daughter, wife, seductress, etc., are for the most part deplorable and chauvinistic but nonetheless typical for that day; see H. McKeating, *ExpTim* 85 (1973–74) 85–87; Di Lella, *Wisdom* (AB 39) 27–28. Cf. 3:1–16. **29–31.** Ben Sira, unlike other sages, has much to say about priests and the liturgy; cf. 45:6–22; 50:1–21. **32–35.** Cf. comment on 3:30–4:10.

28   (D) Prudence in One's Affairs (8:1–19). Practical advice on how one should relate to the following: the great and rich, the loudmouth, the senseless, the repentant sinner, the elderly, the dead, the wise, the scoundrel, the borrower, the judge, the ruthless, the quick-tempered, the simpleton, the stranger. Generally, the motivation given is pragmatic: one's conduct should be to one's advantage. **8–9.** Even the pursuit of wisdom has its earthly rewards. *tradition of the elders:* The wisdom that was handed down from one generation to the next.

29   (E) About Women and the Choice of Friends (9:1–16). **1–9.** Ben Sira has more to say about women than any other biblical author, and much of what he says is unacceptable to most contemporary readers in the West (see comment on 7:26). Here as elsewhere he urges an ethics of caution; see J. T. Sanders, *HUCA* 50 (1979) 73–106. **1.** Jealousy may actually bring on the evil feared. **3.** *strange woman:* A prostitute or an adulteress, as in Prov (e.g., 2:16; 5:3,20; 7:5). **4.** *singing girl:* Cf. 2 Sam 19:36; Isa 23:15–16. **5.** *virgin . . . damages:* Cf. Exod 22:15–16; Deut 22:29. **6–7.** The sages constantly warn against consorting with prostitutes (e.g., Prov 5:3–14; 7:10). **8–9.** Cf. 18:30–31. **10–16.** One must exercise extreme care in the choice of friends; cf. 6:5–17 with comment. **13.** Court intrigue is dangerous; cf. 2 Macc 4:43–50. **14–16.** The wise make the best friends because they fear the Lord.

30   (F) About Rulers and Pride (9:17–10:18). This section, which may be considered a tract on government (so Prato, *Il problema*), deals with rulers, good and bad, and with arrogance and pride, esp. in rulers. **9:17–10:3.** The wise make not only the best friends but also the best rulers. **4–5.** Sovereignty belongs to God alone, who delegates it to the ruler; cf. Dan 2:21; 4:14,31–34; 7:11–12; Luke 1:52. **6–11.** Arrogance is hateful to God and humans. **8.** Probably a reference to the transfer of Palestine from Egyptian to Syrian control after the battle of Panium (198 BC). **9–11.** Probably an allusion to the horrible death of Ptolemy IV (203 BC) after a lifetime of licentiousness. **12–18.** In this essay, with no maxims given, Ben Sira condemns pride not only in the Egyptian and Syrian kings of his time (vv 6–11) but also in ordinary mortals (v 18).

31   (G) The Believer's True Glory (10:19–11:6). A splendid poem in five symmetrical stanzas; see A. A. Di Lella, "Sir 10:19–11:6," *WLSGF* 157–64. **19.** The topic sentence. *the commandment:* Deut 6:45. **20,22.** Fear of the Lord is the glory of people in all social classes, including the disadvantaged. **24.** Whoever fears God is greater than those who have power. **28-29.** This stanza, the center of the poem, emphasizes the value of accurate and humble self-esteem; self-depreciation is wrong and wrongheaded. **10:30-11:2.** This stanza extols the poor who are wise. **3-6.** The final stanza is a reminder that God can reverse the fortunes of the oppressed and of the exalted.

32 (H) Providence and Trust in God (11:7-28). This section contains six mini-poems. **7-9.** Six wise and practical warnings against rash judgment and useless arguments; cf. 5:11-12; Prov 18:13. **10-13.** A short essay on the futility of pursuing wealth; cf. Prov 11:18, 28; 15:27; 28:20, 22; Eccl 5:9-11. Ultimately, it is the Lord alone who grants success. Verses 14,17-19 (15-16 are from GII) are a discourse on success as a gift from the Lord and on the stupidity of the miser's life. **14.** *good and evil . . . riches:* The contraries of life come from God; cf. Isa 45:7; Job 1:21. **20-21.** Remain faithful, says Ben Sira, and do not marvel at the prosperity of sinners, for it will not last; cf. Prov 3:31-34; 23:17-18. **22-24,26.** Note the (correct) order of verses here and in the next poem. These are admonitions against presumption. The deuteronomic theory of retribution, which Ben Sira maintained, held that God repays each person, but only during the present life — the righteous with blessings, the sinner with disaster; cf. 7:17. **25,27-28.** More on how God sets things right during the lifetime of the virtuous and the wicked; cf. Eccl 12:13-14.

33 (I) Care in Choosing One's Friends (11:29-12:18). This is a favorite topic with Ben Sira; cf. 6:5-17 with comment. **29-34.** The wicked, who have many guises, will never be true friends; they will only cause ruin; cf. Prov 11:13. **12:1-18.** A 22-line non-alphabetic poem (→ 4 above). **1-6.** This pragmatic advice is typical of Ben Sira and the later rabbis, but it is at variance with the teaching of Jesus (cf. Matt 5:43-47; Luke 19:5-7). **8-12.** One must be cautious with both friends and enemies. **9.** Cf. 6:10-12; 13:21-23; Prov 19:4. **10.** Cf. Luke 6:27. **13-18.** Keen observations about the conduct of the proud who feign friendship but seek to cause harm. **16.** Cf. Prov 26:24; Jer 41:4-7. **18.** Cf. Lam 2:15.

34 (J) Rich and Poor (13:1-14:2). At that time there were only two classes, rich and poor. Ben Sira advises against associating with a person not of one's class. **1a.** A popular proverb twice quoted in Shakespeare. **1b.** *scoundrel:* Hebr *lēṣ,* a person to avoid at all costs; cf. 3:28; 8:11; 15:8. **3.** A common occurrence; cf. Prov 18:23. **4-7.** An accurate description of how the rich often manipulate the poor for selfish gain. **9-13.** Precautions to be taken when approaching the powerful. **9-10.** Cf. Prov 25:6-7; Luke 14:7-11. **13.** *men of violence:* Probably a reference to the pagan nobility in Palestine; cf. Prov 1:10-15. **15-23.** An essay on how like associates with like, and on how rich and poor are treated so differently. **15-16.** Variants on the classic proverb: *Similis simili gaudet,* "Like rejoices in like." **17-19.** Again Ben Sira describes the exploitation of the poor by the rich. **20-23.** The rich, unlike the poor, receive quick support and a ready audience. Even when the poor speak wisely, they are not taken seriously. **24.** An important principle: justly acquired wealth is not evil. **25-26.** A keen insight that modern psychology has verified. **14:1-2.** Two beatitudes on persons with a clear conscience; cf. Ps 1:1-3. **1.** Regarding sins of the mouth, see 25:8; Jas 3:2-10.

35 (K) The Use of Wealth (14:3-19). A poem in two stanzas: vv 3-10 (note "the miser" in 3 and 10, an *inclusio*), and vv 11-19. **3.** *the mean person:* Lit., "the small heart," the opposite of "the bighearted." *the miser:* Lit.,

"the man evil of eye," a graphic image taken from Prov 28:22. **5-10.** Because the miser has no proper self-love, he deprives not only others (cf. 4:4-5) but even himself of his wealth (cf. 11:18-19; Eccl 5:9-12). **11-12,14-19.** Since all must die and there is no retribution or any real life in the hereafter (16; cf. 7:17; 11:16; 41:1-4), one should enjoy what one has now; cf. Eccl 5:17-19. **13.** One should also share one's wealth; cf. Prov 3:27-28.

36 (V) Part IV (14:20-23:27). This part opens, just as the first three, with a poem on the value of wisdom. Again there is no clear connection between the various sections (→ 7 above).

37 (A) Wisdom and Her Blessings (14:20-15:10). A poem in two stanzas (14:20-27; 15:1-10) that describe the happy state of the one who seeks Wisdom and her ways. **20-27.** Colorful images that depict the determination, persistence, and eagerness of the person who searches for Wisdom, which is again personified. **20.** Cf. Prov 3:13. **22-25.** Regarding Wisdom's house, see Prov 8:34; 9:1. **24-25.** *tent:* Means either one's place of residence or, metaphorically, one's moral life or existence (cf. Job 8:22; 22:23); both senses are meant here. **15:1.** Only those who fear the Lord by obeying the law will attain Wisdom; cf. 1:11- 30; 6:32-37. **2.** *motherlike:* Cf. Isa 49:15; 66:13. *bride:* Cf. Prov 5:18. **3.** Cf. Prov 9:5; Isa 55:1; John 4:10-15. **7-8.** The wicked can never attain Wisdom, for they do not fear the Lord; cf. 1. **9-10.** Only the wise can and should offer praise to God; cf. Ps 33:1-5.

38 (B) Free Will and Responsibility (15:11-16:23). **11-20.** One of the clearest statements in the Bible on freedom of the will. **11-12.** In no way can God be held responsible for sin or its occasion (cf. Wis 11:24; Jas 1:13); Ben Sira flatly contradicts earlier statements (e.g., Exod 11:10; 2 Sam 24:1) that seem to imply that God was the cause of a person's sin. **14-17.** The heart of the argument: each individual has the radical freedom to choose "life" by obeying the law or "death" by refusing to obey; cf. Deut 30:15-10. **14.** *free choice:* Hebr *yēṣer,* Gk *diaboulion;* see Prato, *Il problema* 237- 46. **18-20.** It is a lie to say that because God is omniscient (Prov 15:3; Job 34:21-22) he causes sin. Verse 20 forms an *inclusio* with the thought of v 11. **16:1-4.** Only children who fear God are a blessing (cf. Gen 12:2; Deut 28:4; Prov 17:16). Children who do not fear God are "worthless" (v 1) and no cause for joy since they will come to an untimely end (cf. Deut 28:18; Ps 55:24); it is better to "die childless" (v 3) — an astounding statement, for to be childless was considered a reproach (cf. Luke 1:25). **5-14.** God punishes the wicked, for they alone are responsible for their sins (cf. 15:11-10). **6a.** Cf. Num 16:1-35. **6b.** Cf. Num 11:1-3. **7.** Cf. Isa 14:4-21. **8.** Cf. Gen 19:4-25. **9.** *doomed people:* The Canaanites; cf. Exod 23:33; Deut 7:1-2. **10.** Cf. 46:8; Exod 12:37. **11.** No "stiff-necked person" is spared God's wrath; cf. 32:9; Exod 33:3,5. **12-14.** God judges justly each person's works; cf. 3:14-16,30-31; 17:22-23. **15-16.** Found in Hebrew, GII, and Syriac, but not in GI and Latin; these verses are probably not original. **17-23.** The words of the foolish who think that God gives no thought to their sins. **17,20-22.** The knave's skeptical questions; cf. Pss 14:1; 139:7-18.

39 (C) God's Wisdom as Seen in Humans (16:24-18:14). This long section, divided into four poems, deals with the Lord as Creator and with humans as creatures made in the image of God. **24-30.** A poem extolling God's wisdom as seen in the order and providence of creation. **24-25.** A wisdom teacher's typical opening; cf. 23:7; Prov 1:8. **26-30.** God's wisdom in ordering creation in so marvelous a way. God has given every creature a proper place and function (cf. Wis

11:20) so that it may exist in harmony and equilibrium with the rest of creation. **26–28.** Reference is to the heavenly bodies; cf. Gen 1:14–18; Ps 104:19. **29.** Cf. Gen 1:20–31; Ps 104:24,28. **30.** All life comes from God (cf. Ps 104:24–30) and must eventually return to the earth (cf. 40:11). **17:1–24.** Verses 5,16,18,21 are glosses found in GII. This is the longest poem of the section; it speaks of the creation of humans, the gifts they receive from God, and God's knowledge of their deeds and his recompense of their virtue and vice. **1.** Cf. Gen 2:7; 3:19; Ps 146:4. **2a.** Cf. 18:9–10; Ps 90:10. **2b–4.** Humans, made in God's image (Gen 1:26–27), share in the divine dominion over all other creatures; cf. Gen 1:28; 9:2; Ps 8:6–9. **6–10.** God has gifted humans with splendid intellectual and moral endowments, including fear of the Lord (v 8a), so that they may marvel at his works (cf. 18:4) and "praise his holy name" (cf. 51:17,22,29), two essential activities of Israelite life and religion (cf. vv 27–28). **11.** Israel's "knowledge" is the "law" that gives "life" (cf. 1:11–30; Deut 30:11–20). **12–13.** The Sinai experiences; cf. Exod 19:2–20:17; 24:15–17. **14.** The great commandments of the law; cf. Deut 6:5; Lev 19:18. **15,19–20.** God's omniscience; cf. 16:17,20–23; Ps 94:11. **17.** Cf. Deut 32:8–9; Dan 10:13–21. **22–23.** The value of almsgiving and kindness (Gk *charis*); cf. 3:14–15, 30–31; Tob 12:12. **24.** There is always hope for the sinner who repents. **25–31.** This poem opens with a prophetic call to repent, i.e., to "turn back" to God by giving up sin; cf. Mal 3:7. **27–28.** Because in sheol the dead cannot praise God, they have no real life (cf. Ps 88:11–13); only the living can glorify him (cf. Isa 38:18–19; Ps 115:17–18). See A. A. Di Lella, *CBQ* 28 (1966) 143–46. **29.** Cf. Pss 86:5,15; 145:7–9; Joel 2:13. **30.** Humans, being mortal, are not as merciful as the Lord. **31.** Cf. Job 15:14–16; 25:4–6. **32.** *hosts . . . heaven:* The sun, moon, stars, and angels (cf. 42:16–17; Deut 4:19), which are accountable because pagans and reprobate Israelites worshiped them (cf. Isa 24:21; Jer 8:2); how much more will humans come under divine judgment (cf. Job 4:17–21). **18:1–14.** Verses 2b,3 are glosses found in GII. The final poem (18:1–14) is a hymn in praise of God as righteous and merciful judge. **1–2.** In contrast to humans, who are "dust and ashes" (17:32), the Lord "lives forever" (cf. Dan 4:31; 6:27) and alone is "just" (cf. Ps 51:6). **4–7.** Humans are incapable of appreciating the divine majesty and glory manifested in creation; cf. 1:3,6; Ps 145:3. **8.** Cf. Pss 8:5; 144:3; Job 7:17. **9–10.** Cf. Ps 90:3–6,10; Isa 40:15. **11–12.** Humans are so short-lived that God is all the more merciful to them; cf. Ps 36:6–10. **13–14.** Human mercy is limited; God's mercy extends to all. The imagery of God as shepherd derives from Isa 40:11; Ezek 34:11–16; Ps 23; cf. John 10:11–18.

40   (D) Prudential Warnings (18:15–19:17). A series of loosely connected mini-poems containing maxims and comments about various aspects of life. **15–18.** God's benevolence and compassion, the subject of the previous poem, occasions these astute and sensitive observations on the art of gift giving. The words accompanying a gift can either enhance it or spoil it. The gracious person realizes that how one gives a gift is often more significant than the gift itself. But the fool spoils the excitement of a gift by giving it grudgingly; cf. 20:14–15. **19–21.** A series of practical exhortations occasioned by the thought of God's generosity in forgiving (18:1–14). **19–20.** As one should be informed before speaking or be prepared before becoming ill, so should one examine oneself before God's judgment in order to obtain mercy. **21a.** On the need for humility, see 1:27; 3:17–24; 7:16–17. **21c-f.** Found only in Syriac but apparently original (see Skehan and Di Lella, *Wisdom*).

One must not delay in forsaking sin, for sin (according to deuteronomic doctrine) brings on an untimely death. **22–23.** The need for circumspection in making vows. If one has made a vow, one should fulfill it promptly; cf. Deut 23:22–24; Eccl 5:3. **24–26.** The thought of God's wrath, which can reverse one's fortunes (Deut 8:10–20), should help one avoid sin. **27–29.** The wise (i.e., those who heed the previous injunctions) stay away from sin. They make known their wisdom (= fear of the Lord; cf. 1:11–30) and "declare her praise" to encourage others to become wise. **18:30–19:12.** This poem, entitled in Gk and Lat mss. "On Self-Control of the Soul," contains warnings against inordinate, hence unlawful, sensuality. **30.** The topic sentence; one can hardly be considered wise unless one keeps one's "desires in check." **31.** *laughingstock . . . enemies:* The result of unbridled lust; cf. 6:4; 42:11. **32.** Giving in to carnal pleasures brings financial ruin; cf. 9:6; Prov 5:10. **33.** Gluttony and drunkenness are condemned also in Deut 21:20; Prov 23:20. **19:1.** The results of overindulgence in food and drink; see Prov 21:17; 23:21. **2–4.** Only the fool drinks wine to excess and consorts with prostitutes (cf. 31:25–30; Prov 31:3–5; Hos 4:10–11); his unrestrained appetite and lust bring him prematurely to "rottenness and worms" (cf. Gal 6:8). **5–12.** On control of the tongue and the evils of gossip. Carnal desires and sins of the tongue are major vices that the sages deplore and the wise avoid; cf. 22:27–23:27; 28:13–26. **6.** The fool alone repeats gossip. **7.** The gossipmonger is trusted by no one and reviled by all; cf. Prov 17:9; 25:9–10. **10.** *burst:* Like a new wineskin; imagery taken from Job 32:18–19. **11–12.** Colorful metaphors to describe the fool's uncontrolled urge to get out gossip once it lodges in him. **13–17.** This last poem deals with the charitable concern one owes a friend after hearing gossip about him. Though often gossip is simply slander (v 15), one should admonish a friend in case he did do or say what was reported; thus he may avoid the mistake in future. **17.** Cf. Lev 19:17–18.

41   (E) Wisdom and Folly in Word and Deed (19:18–20:32). Several loosely connected poems on wisdom and folly. **18–19,20c–21.** Glosses found in GII. **20ab,22–24.** A poem on wisdom as fear of the Lord. **20b.** *law:* Also in v 17b, it serves as a *mot crochet* or catchword that links this section to the preceding one. Again Ben Sira insists that wisdom = fear of the Lord = keeping the law; cf. 1:11–30; 6:32–37; 15:1; 21:6. **22.** Not all knowledge is wisdom, as the Greeks thought. **23.** It is better to be thought a fool who is "free from sin" (so Syriac; Greek, "who lacks wisdom") than to be a clever person who is detested by God. **24.** It is better to be less intelligent and to fear God as a pious Jew than to be very intelligent and to break the law as a hellenizer. For Ben Sira, true wisdom is a practical matter of fearing God by keeping the law, and not a speculative matter involving intelligence and schooling alone. **25–30.** A poem on the attitudes and behavior of the wicked who are clever; it is connected to the previous one by the *mot crochet*, Gk *panourgia*, "shrewdness, cleverness," in vv 23 and 25. **25.** Winning a judgment in court by shrewd but unjust means was severely condemned in the OT; cf. Exod 23:6–8; Ps 18:27–28. **26–28.** One should be on guard against the wicked who pretend grief to gain an advantage (cf. 12:11); they cannot be trusted, for they will do harm when they find "the opportunity." **29–30.** A person may be known by his appearance: his attire, his laughter, his gait; cf. 13:25–26; 2 Macc 6:18–28; 15:12–13. **20:1–8.** On the value of silence and of speech at the right moment. **1.** Admonitions are called for in many circumstances (cf. 19:13–17); but there are occasions when it is wise to keep silent. **2–3.** A timely admonition can help another avoid disgrace; cf. 19:13–14. **4.** Just as a eunuch cannot have sexual intercourse, so a sinner cannot be compelled to do what is right. **5a.** A maxim with many echoes: "Silence is golden." "Let a fool hold his tongue and he will pass for a sage" (Publilius Syrus, 1st cent. BC). **5b,8a.** Nobody likes a babbler; cf. 22:6. **6–7.** The wise know the right moment to speak (cf. Prov 15:23; 25:11), but the boasting fool just keeps on talking (cf. 20:20; Eccl 3:7). **8b.** *authority:* Of the wise who should speak. Presumably the boasting fool is meant here; cf. Ps 12:4–5. **9–17.** An essay on the appearances of things. **9.** A keen observation that rings true in the experience of most people: What seemed to be a disaster turns out to be a success; and, conversely, what seemed to be a profit turns out to be a loss. **11.** Cf. 1 Sam 2:4–9; Pss 75:8; 113:7–9. **12.** *seven times:* Many times; cf. 7:3; Gen 4:15,24. **14.** *seven:* So Latin and Syriac; Greek has "many," a good interpretation of the symbolic number. The rogue expects much in return for his one gift. **16–17.** The fool has no friends because he expects to be repaid many times over for the gift he gives (cf. 10,14). Even those who share his hospitality mock him for his attitude about gift giving. **18–20.** A mini-poem deploring slips of the tongue and other forms of inappropriate speech. **19.** It is only the "uneducated" or "undisciplined" (Gk *apaideutoi*) who tell "the untimely tale." **20.** Spoken by a fool, the proverb itself (a prized literary form in the ancient Near East) is "unwelcome," for it is uttered out of place; cf. 15:9; Prov 26:7,9. **21.** Poverty may help one avoid occasions of sin (cf. 19:28). **22.** Shame may lead to ruin: probably a reference to those Jews who compromised their faith for the advantages Hellenism had to offer; cf. 4:20–22; 41:14–42:8. **24–26.** On the evils of lying, also discussed in 7:13; 25:2; cf. Prov 6:6–19; Ps 5:7. **24.** The "uneducated" (cf. v 19), because they lack wisdom, constantly lie and, like the thief, are in disgrace. **27–31.** The wise and prudent, in contrast with the "uneducated" of vv 19 and 24, get ahead: a reference to the Jewish sages at the gentile courts of Palestine; cf. Gen 37–41; Dan 1–6. **28.** Cf. Dan 1:5–20; 6:5–29. **29.** Bribes were severely condemned in the OT; cf. Prov 15:27; 17:23. **30–31.** Wisdom must be shared with others; otherwise it becomes futile; cf. Matt 25:14–30. **32.** A gloss in Codex 248.

42   **(F) Various Kinds of Sin and Folly (21:1–22:18).** This section opens with two 11-line poems for a total of 22 lines; → 4 above. **1–10.** An exhortation to avoid sin in general (vv 1–3) and an essay on various types of sin (vv 4,6–10; 5, the central bicolon, deals with the efficacy of the prayer of the poor, often the victims of injustice). **1.** Since even the wise sin, one must pray for forgiveness; cf. 17:25. **2–3.** *serpent:* Cf. Gen 3:1–5. *lion's teeth:* Alluded to in 1 Pet 5:8. *two-edged sword:* Proverbial for its destructive power; cf. Prov 5:4; Rev 1:16. Note the strong images Ben Sira uses to evoke a horror of sin. **4.** Pride causes ruin; cf. Prov 15:25. **5.** On justice being granted to the poor, cf. Ps 17:1–2. **6.** *correction:* Or "discipline"; Hebr *mûsār*. Without it, one cannot be wise (cf. 6:18–22). **8.** To amass wealth (cf. Ps 49:17) by injustice will bring on premature death; cf. 7:17. **9.** Graphic images to suggest the impermanence of the criminal's life. **10.** *sinners . . . netherworld:* Since saint and sinner alike went to sheol, the reference is not to retribution in the afterlife but to the sinner's untimely death in disgrace; cf. 14:16; 17:28; 22:11; Eccl 9:9–10. **11–21.** A poem that contrasts the conduct of the wise and the foolish. **11.** Again Ben Sira's formula: wisdom = keeping the law = fearing the Lord; cf. 1:11–30. **12.** One must be "shrewd" (Gk *panourgos*), to be taught; but there is a "shrewdness," *panourgia*, that causes grief; cf. 19:23,25. **13–14.** Striking images to contrast the abundant knowledge of the wise and the fool's total ignorance. **15.**

The wise add to the store of wisdom; but "the fool" (so Syriac; Greek has "the wanton") has no taste for Wisdom, discarding her altogether (cf. 1 Kgs 14:9). **16.** The words of the wise are charming (Ps 45:3), but "a fool's chatter" is burdensome (Eccl 10:12). **17.** *the assembly:* The religious place of honor; cf. 15:5; Job 29:7–23. **18–19,21.** Read v 20 before 25. *a house in ruins:* So Greek; Syriac has "a prison," perhaps a better reading. The stupid and undisciplined fool looks upon wisdom as something that hampers his style. In stark contrast, the wise cherish and display their learning with pride. **22–24.** The fool is boorish and rude, lacking in basic civilities and good manners. The cultured person is tactful and well mannered. **20,25–26.** The speech of the wise and that of the fool are compared. Lacking restraint, the fool talks loud and laughs inappropriately; he speaks of things not his concern (so GII), for he cannot mind his own business. But the prudent person, considerate of others, weighs his words carefully; cf. 28:25; Prov 16:23. **26.** An *a:b:c::c:b':a* chiasm: "In the *mouth:of fools:*[is] their *heart* [= seat of intelligence]::in the *heart:of the wise:*[is] their *mouth.*" "They never taste who always drink; / They always talk who never think" (Matthew Prior). **27–28.** A couplet on the evil effects of cursing and slander. The slanderer dirties himself, and not his victim. **22:1–2.** *filthy stone:* Used for wiping oneself after a bowel movement. *dung:* Another strong metaphor for the sluggard. **3–5.** On good and bad children. **3a.** Cf. 16:1–5; Prov 17:21. **3b.** Ben Sira is misogynistic, reflecting his typically Jewish bias against women. **4–5.** A woman's value derived primarily from the benefit she brought her father or her husband and children; she was not considered an autonomous human being; see Skehan and Di Lella, *Wisdom.* Cf. 26:1–4,13–18; 42:9–14; Prov 12:4; 31:10–12. **6.** Words often are not enough; the rod must also be used in disciplining a child; cf. Prov 22:15; 23:13–14; 29:15. **7–8.** Glosses in GII. **9–10.** Trying to teach a fool is a waste of time; cf. Prov 1:7; 27:22. **11–12.** On the two great tragedies in life: death and folly. The fool should be mourned for a "lifetime" because, lacking intelligence, he is as good as dead. In fact, he is worse off than the dead, who are "at rest," for he lacks wisdom that alone makes life worthwhile. *seven days:* The "Shibah" (from Hebr *šib'â*, "seven"), the customary mourning period for the dead even for orthodox Jews today. **13.** More on the fool, who is now compared, caustically and harshly, to the "brute" (lit., unintelligent being; Syriac has "pig," a reading preferred by Smend and others), which the wise should stay clear of; cf. 21:16. **15.** The fool is more burdensome than "sand, salt, and an iron lump," elements traditionally viewed as difficult to carry; cf. Prov 27:3; Deut 28:48; Syriac Ahiqar 45–46. **16.** In contrast to the fool, the wise make their plans only after "careful deliberation." For the construction imagery, cf. 1 Kgs 7:12. **17.** Cf. 1 Kgs 6:29. **18.** *small stones:* These were placed on walls around a vineyard and garden so that when animals jumped onto the wall to enter the area, the stones would make noise, thus alerting the custodian.

43   **(G) Preserving Friendship (22:19–26).** A poem in two stanzas: vv 19–22,24 and 23,25–26 (note the correct order of verses). The first stanza gives comments and advice on how to refrain from hurting a friend; the second details the responsibilities one has toward a friend. **19.** The eye and the heart are the body's most delicate and sensitive organs: the heart is seat of intelligence and higher emotions; the eye is the organ that reveals what is inside the heart. Mention of these two organs suggests the sensitivity one should cultivate in friendship. **20.** Cf. 20:15. **21–22.** Friends will at times disagree, even sharply; but they can be reconciled.

Insults, broken confidences, and personal attacks, however, destroy friendship; cf. 27:16–21; 42:1; Prov 11:13. **24.** A variant of the proverb "Where there's smoke, there's fire." **23–25.** Being faithful to a friend, even when he is poor or in trouble or in need of help, is the hallmark of true friendship; and it has its practical rewards too. Cf. 6:10–17; 19:13–17. Ben Sira's attitudes are hardly disinterested; compare the teaching of Jesus in Luke 6:27–38.

44   (H) Against Destructive Sins (22:27–23:27). This section, the conclusion of Part IV (14:20–23:27) opens with a prayer in two stanzas: the first (22:27–23:1) is the theme of 23:7–15; the second (23:2–6), of 23:16–26. The first four parts of the book are summarized in the phrases "the fear of the Lord" and "obeying the commandments" (23:27cd), which are prepared for by "the lash to my thoughts" and "the rod of discipline" (23:2ab). See P. C. Beentjes, *Bijdr* 39 (1978) 144–51. **22:27–23:1.** The opening stanza asks the Lord for protection against sins of the tongue. **27.** Cf. 28:24–26; Ps 141:3. For the dangers of the lips and tongue, see also Prov 13:3, 18:7,21; Jas 3:5–12. **23:1a,c.** Verse 1b follows 4a; God is our Father (cf. v 4; 23:1,4 in Syriac; 51:1,10) and Master; hence, we can pray to him with utter confidence, for he alone can help us avoid sins of speech. **2–6.** This stanza of the prayer asks God for help in avoiding sins of the flesh, which have their origin in one's thoughts and heart. **2.** *lash . . . rod of discipline:* So Syriac (cf. Prov 22:15); Greek has "whips . . .discipline of wisdom," which spoils the parallelism. Only the rod of strict discipline can keep one from multiplying sensual sins. **3.** Punishment for sins takes place in this life; cf. 14:16. GII has a gloss after v 3d. **4–6.** The wise pray to be freed from the tyranny of impure desires and the lustful eye; cf. 26:9; Gen 39:7; Prov 6:25; Matt 5:28. **7–15.** Many Gk mss. entitle this section *paideia stomatos* (the first two words of v 7), "instruction concerning the mouth." There are two stanzas (vv 7–11, 12–15); each deals with sins of the tongue, a topic introduced in the first stanza of the opening prayer (22:27–23:1). **8.** *lips:* Often the instrument for sins of pride; cf. 20:18; Prov 6:2. **9.** Against swearing without adequate reason; cf. Matt 5:34–37; Jas 5:12. *Holy One:* A favorite title of God, esp. in Isa (e.g., 1:4; 5:19,24; 41:14,16,20). **10–11.** Swearing without good cause is to be avoided, for one may swear rashly and thereby incur guilt (cf. Lev 5:4). Swearing falsely was severely condemned in the law (Exod 20:7; Lev 19:12; Deut 5:11). **12–15.** Against blasphemy (punishable by death: Lev 24:11–16), coarse talk, and abusive language. **16–26.** Three stanzas that resume the theme of unholy passion, the topic of the second stanza of the opening prayer (vv 2–6). **16–17.** The first stanza opens with a numerical proverb, a common literary form (cf., e.g., 25:1–2,7–11; 26:5–6,28; Prov 6:16–19). The three vices are unrestrained sexual desires, incest (the various forms of which are condemned in Lev 18:6–18; 20:11–21), and adultery. The adulterer never stops looking for new liaisons; cf. Prov 9:13–18. **18–21.** This stanza excoriates the adulterer even more. **18–19a.** Keen observations on the psychology of the adulterer and the rationalizations he uses to dull his conscience, his principal concern being to avoid detection and punishment by the courts (cf. 21). **19b–20.** The Lord sees all things (cf. 17:19–20; Prov 15:3,11) and knows everything, past as well as future (cf. 42:18; Ps 139:1–16). **21.** Since capital punishment is not mentioned, it seems that the death penalty decreed in Lev 20:10 and Deut 22:22–24 was mitigated in Ben Sira's day, perhaps to scourging (cf. Prov 5:11–14; 6:32–33), as also in talmudic law. **22–27.** A stanza on the evils the adulteress commits. **23.** The reasons given why the

adulteress will be punished number three, probably to balance the numerical proverb in v 16. **24–26.** Not only is the adulteress disgraced "before the assembly," perhaps publicly scourged like the adulterer, but also her children suffer in her disgrace, for the issue of adulterous unions could not belong to the community (cf. *b. Qidd.* 78b). Under talmudic law (*m. Soṭa* 6:1), the husband of the adulteress had to divorce her, and she lost all property rights under her marriage contract. Typically, Ben Sira says nothing about the injustice an adulterer does to his wife or about the children of his adultery. **27.** Conclusion of the section and elegant summary of the first major division of the book (1:1–23:27); cf. 50:28–29. **28.** A gloss on v 27cd in GII; cf. Ps 73:24 LXX.

45   (VI) Part V (24:1–33:18). Here begins the second major division of the book (chaps. 24 to 51), which has four parts, as does the first division. As an introduction to this division, there is a major poem in praise of wisdom, as was also the case at the opening of the first division (1:11–30).

46   (A) Praise of Wisdom (24:1–33). This magnificent poem has seven stanzas: 2, 5, 6, 5, 6, 6, 5 poetic lines (see Skehan and Di Lella, *Wisdom*). After a two-line introduction (vv 1–2), personified Wisdom delivers a 22-line speech (vv 3–17,19–22; v 18 is a gloss in GII), in four stanzas (→ 4 above). A six-line stanza (vv 23,25–29; v 24 is a GII gloss) equates Wisdom with the Law. The final stanza (vv 30–33) is Ben Sira's account of himself as a wisdom teacher. The poem has 35 lines, precisely the number in Prov 8, which served as model. See P. W. Skehan, *CBQ* 41 (1979) 365–79. **1–2.** *her own people:* The Israelites, "the people of God," as Syriac reads. *assembly . . . host:* The angelic attendants at God's throne (cf. Ps 82:1), where Wisdom resides. **3–7.** Wisdom describes her divine origin and her activity in heaven and on earth. Ben Sira derived the idea of personified Wisdom from Prov 1:20–33; 8:4–36; 9:1–6,11. **3.** *mouth . . . Most High:* Wisdom, like everything else, was created by the word of God; cf. Gen 1:3–31. *mistlike:* Because Wisdom is a spirit that covers the earth. In Gen 1:2, the spirit of God hovers over the waters of chaos prior to his uttering the creative word. **4.** *heights:* Cf. Prov 8:2,12. *pillar of cloud:* The means God used to manifest his presence during the desert wanderings (Exod 13:21–22). Thus Wisdom dwells with God. **5–6.** Imagery and ideas from Prov 8:15–16,24,27–30. Wisdom was present and active throughout history. **8–12.** Jacob/Israel, by God's command, is Wisdom's special dwelling place. **9.** Cf. 1:1,4,9,15; Prov 8:22–23. **10.** A reference to Wisdom (= the Law) giving the rules for the proper worship of God. **11.** *city he loves:* Zion/Jerusalem; cf. Ps 50:2. **12.** *glorious people:* Jacob/Israel (v 8), "the Lord's portion." **13–15.** The formal unity of this stanza is indicated by the word "like" in each colon. The plant imagery may seem bombastic to Western readers, but in the ancient Jew these images would evoke a feeling of pleasure and a desire for Wisdom. **16–22.** Verses 16–17 contain more flora imagery; see A. Fournier-Bidoz, *VT* 34 (1984) 1–10. **19–22.** Wisdom formally invites her disciples to come to her to be filled with her fruits; cf. 6:18–38; Prov 8:4–10,32–36; 9:4–6,11. **23,25–29.** Ben Sira, again the speaker, now explicitly and emphatically identifies Wisdom with the Law or Torah of Moses; cf. 1:11–30; 6:32–37. **23bc.** A direct quotation of Deut 33:4 LXX. **25–27.** Since the Law (like Wisdom) is viewed as a spirit, Ben Sira uses the imagery of flooding rivers to describe its abundance. **28.** A merism: Wisdom is beyond the grasp of any and all human beings, from the first to the last person on earth. **30–33.** In this final stanza, Ben Sira speaks of himself as a student of wisdom and as teacher. **30–31.** Ben Sira now applies the water images (cf. vv

25–27) to himself. **33.** He is aware of his own divine inspiration, as were the prophets of theirs; cf. Jer 1:7,9. Cf. M. Gilbert, *RTL* 5 (1974) 326–48.

47　　**(B) Gifts That Bring Joy (25:1–12).** A brief section with three loosely connected poems. **1–2.** Two numerical proverbs; cf. 23:16–17. *proud:* Cf. 10:7–18. *dissembler:* Cf. 20:24–26. *old:* The elderly, who were supposed to be wise (vv 3–6), are fools when they commit adultery; cf. Dan 13:5–27. **3–6.** To acquire wisdom one must begin early; cf. 6:18–37. **4–6.** Probably autobiographical. Fear of the Lord (= wisdom) is the old man's glory; cf. 1:11. **7–12.** A numerical proverb, which contains Ben Sira's ten beatitudes; cf. Matt 5:3–11; Luke 6:20–22. **8b.** From Syriac; Greek omits. Reference is to Deut 22:10, but the context suggests that what is meant is a marriage to two incompatible wives. **8d.** Compare Luke 22:27; John 13:13–16. **10–11.** The ninth and tenth beatitudes. Since wisdom = fear of the Lord (cf. 6:32–37; 24:23–29), the one who finds wisdom also fears the Lord. **12.** A GII gloss; cf. 1:10cd.

48　　**(C) Wicked and Virtuous Women (25:13–26:18[27]).** Ben Sira has more to say, as usual, about the evil woman or wife (23:13–26; 26:5–12,22–27) than about the good one (26:1– 4,13–18). His (mostly deplorable) comments should not be explained away or exaggerated; he simply reflects the kind of instruction the young Jewish male received at that time. **13.** The topic sentence that sets the tone for the unflattering observations to follow. **14–15.** The evils of polygamy, still practiced then: rival wives become "foes" and "enemies" of each other and of their husband; the "venom" from their feuding is worse than a serpent's (cf. Gen 29:31–30:24). **16.** Typically Semitic (but nonetheless preposterous) hyperbole; cf. Prov 21:19; 25:24. **19–26.** The dismal litany of (supposed) woes continues. **19.** Another cruel exaggeration. In Israel's history, men caused far more evil than women. **21.** Don't marry for beauty alone or wealth. **24.** In Gen 3:6, the woman sinned before the man; cf. 2 Cor 11:3; 1 Tim 2:14. *on account of her:* St. Paul (Rom 5:12–19; 1 Cor 15:22) attributes the entrance of sin and death to Adam, not to Eve. Cf. T. R. Tennant, *JTS* 2 (1900–1) 207–23; H. Cazelles, *VT* 9 (1959) 212–15. **26.** *cut her away:* Strong language for divorce. **26:1–4.** Ben Sira finally speaks, briefly, of the good wife (a gift to the one who fears God), but only in terms of the good she can bring to her husband; cf. 36:26–31. **5–12.** More on the troublesome wife. **5–6.** A numerical proverb in which the fourth and final element, the jealous wife with "scourging tongue," is the worst. **9.** Cf. v 11; 23:4; Prov 6:25. **12.** *drinks . . . water:* A metaphor for adultery; cf. Prov 9:17. *peg . . . quiver:* Euphemisms for penis and vagina, respectively. **13–18.** A concluding poem in high praise of the gracious wife; cf. Prov 31:10–31. **19–27.** Found only in GII and Syriac, these verses are an integral part of the book (so Peters).

49　　**(D) Dangers to Integrity and Friendship (26:28–27:21).** **28.** A numerical proverb as in 23:16–17 and elsewhere. **26:29–27:2.** The moral hazards of commerce; cf. Amos 8:4–6; Lev 19:35–36. **3.** Fear of the Lord will keep one honest in business. **4–7.** Speech is the principal criterion for evaluating a person. **8–9.** General observations on attaining righteousness. **9.** Variant of "birds of a feather flock together." **11–15.** The theme of speech again. **12.** Cf. 22:13–15. **16–21.** On the evils of revealing a confidence. Cf. 22:22; Prov 20:19; 25:8–10.

50　　**(E) Malice, Anger, Vengeance, Evil Tongue (27:22–28:26).** **22–27.** The effects of malice coupled with insincerity and treachery. **22.** *winks the eye:* A sign of duplicity and mischief; cf. Prov 16:30; Ps 35:19. **24.** The double-dealer is detestable to God and humans; cf. Prov 6:16–19. **27:28–28:1.** A poem the

limits of which are marked by the *inclusio* "vengeance" in the opening and closing bicola. It probably refers to Haman's plot to kill Mordecai and the other Jews (Esth 3:2,5) and to the results of that treachery. **29.** Cf. Esth 5:14. **27:30–28:1.** Haman became the victim of his own "wrath" and "vengeance" (Esth 5:9; 7:9–10). **2–7.** The duty to forgive others and not to hold grudges or to hate one's neighbor is also a Christian imperative; cf. Matt 6:12,14–15; 18:32–35; 19:19; Mark 11:25; Jas 2:13. **8–11.** A poem on the need to avoid quarreling. Gk *machē*, "strife," "quarrel," occurs in the opening and closing lines, thus forming an *inclusio*. Cf. Prov 15:18; Matt 5:21–26. **12–16.** The evils of the "double-tongued" (cf. 5:14–6:1) and "the third tongue" (so called because it butts in between two others as a third and sows discord), i.e., the slanderer. **17–23.** More on the evils of the tongue; cf. 19:5–12; 20:18–20,25–26; 23:7–15. **17.** Cf. Prov 25:15. **18.** Like the Japanese proverb "The tongue is more to be feared than the sword." **22–23.** For the image of the tongue as a flame, see Jas 3:5–6.

51　　**(F) Loans, Alms, Surety (29:1–20).** This section, containing three poems about the person in need of help, has 23 lines (→ 4 above). **1–7.** Though one should be quick to lend to a needy person, one should also be cautious in order to avoid loss. **1.** The Law enjoined generosity in lending; cf. Deut 15:7–11. Charging interest was forbidden (cf. Exod 22:24; Lev 25:36–37). **2–6.** The borrower should repay a loan promptly and graciously (cf. Ps 37:21); otherwise he gains an enemy "at no extra charge" (Gk *dōrean*, lit., as a free gift; note the irony). **8–13.** The duty to give alms to the poor promptly and generously; cf. 3:14–15; 3:30–4:6; Prov 14:21,31; 25:21–22. **9.** *precept:* Deut 15:7–11. **11–13.** The efficacy of almsgiving; cf. 12:2; Tob 4:7–11; 14:9,10–11. **14–20.** Providing surety or collateral for a neighbor (a bad practice according to Prov [e.g., 6:1–5; 11:15; 17:18; 22:26–27]) may be virtuous, but one must be cautious lest one be ruined.

52　　**(G) Frugality and Training of Children (29:21–30:13).** These three poems have exactly 22 lines; → 4 above. **21–28.** A poem on the blessings and satisfactions of the simple life compared with the misery and pain of living off others as a "freeloader." **30:1–6.** The need for strict discipline in rearing a son of whom a father could be proud (vv 2–3). **4–6.** Children provided surrogate immortality for parents. **7–13.** A final poem on the value of physical punishment, if necessary, in disciplining a son. **9.** The sad experience of many a parent.

53　　**(H) Health, Cheerfulness, Riches (30:14–31:11).** Four loosely connected poems: the blessing of good health (vv 14–20); the advantages of cheerfulness (30:21–[27]); the anxieties of the wealthy (31:1–7); the happy state of the blameless rich (vv 8–11). **14.** A truism. "The first wealth is health" (Emerson). **16.** Before this verse some Gk mss. have the title "On Foods." **17.** Cf. Job 3:11; Tob 3:6,10,13. **18.** *food . . . tomb:* A custom probably alluded to in Tob 4:17; cf. 7:33. **19.** Idols were often ridiculed (cf. Deut 4:28; Ps 115:4–7; Isa 44:9–11). **21–27.** Advice conducive to good mental and physical health. **21.** Cf. Eccl 11:10; Matt 6:34. **22.** Cf. Prov 17:22; Eccl 11:9. **23.** Resentment and grief can be fatal. **(27).** Ziegler's verse number (→ 2 above), is from the Latin, which, like the Hebrew and Syriac, has the proper sequence of chapters and verses. All the Gk mss. place 30:25–33:13a after 33:13b–36:16a. **31:1–3.** The anxieties of the sinful rich to pile up wealth give them little rest; cf. 40:5–8; Eccl 5:11; Wis 17:11–15. **5–7.** Greed for gold and profit trips up the fool; cf. Prov 11:4. "Riches serve a wise man but command a fool" (English proverb). **8–11.** On the rich who are wise, i.e., "without fault." **9.** The question implies that virtuous rich people are rare, hence worthy of praise.

54   (I) Food, Wine, Banquets (31:12–32:13). Three related poems on good manners and moderation in eating and drinking. **12–13.** The evils of gluttony (Hebr *'ayin rā'â*, lit., "evil eye"); cf. 14:10; Prov 23:1–3. **14–18.** Maxims on courtesy and etiquette at table. **19–20.** The person with understanding eats moderately, so he sleeps well and awakes refreshed; but the glutton gets indigestion and tosses all night (cf. 37:29–31). **21.** Overeating can happen unintentionally. There is no point in getting sick; hence, vomiting is a practical measure. Ben Sira does not urge the disgusting practice of wealthy Romans who induced vomiting so that they could eat some more. **22–23.** One should be moderate in eating but generous in providing food for others; cf. Prov 22:9. **25–31.** Wine, one of God's good creations (cf. Ps 104:15), is a joy when taken in moderation (cf. 40:20); when drunk to excess, it can cause ruin (cf. Prov 20:1; 23:29–35; Amos 6:6). See A. A. Wieder, *JQR* 61 (1970–71) 155–66. **32:1–2.** Reference is to the Gk custom of choosing a banquet master (*architriklinos*; cf. John 2:8–10), who had the responsibility of seating the guests, preparing the menu, selecting the wines, etc. (cf. 2 Macc 2:27). **3–4.** The elderly have the right to speak but they should also know when to listen. **7–10.** The young may speak (briefly and modestly), but only when asked; cf. Job 32:6–7. **11.** Overstaying a welcome is a gross infraction of good manners. **13.** The duty to say grace at meals; cf. Deut 8:10.

55   (J) Providence of God (32:14–33:18). Hebr *mûsār*, "discipline," "guidance," occurs in the opening and closing colon of this section, thus forming an *inclusio*. Except for this indication of unity, the section contains miscellaneous maxims and comments on the behavior of the pious (= wise) Jew and the sinful (= foolish) one. **14–24.** Discipline (*mûsār*), a key concept of the book (cf. 6:22; 21:19,21; 42:5,8; 50:27), is essential if one is to fear the Lord by keeping the law, which like a beacon will provide sure guidance in life (cf. Prov 6:23). **17.** The sinner uses the law when it suits his purposes but ignores it otherwise. **21.** *bandits:* Mugging was common in Ben Sira's day too; cf. 34:12–13; Luke 10:30–35. **33:2.** Because sinners hate the law they have no wisdom. **3.** The law is as dependable a guide as the Urim and Thummim of Exod 28:30. **5–6.** The fool and unscrupulous friend, both devoid of wisdom, act impulsively, for they lack discipline. **7–15.** An important poem on the polarities or opposites in creation; see Prato, *Il problema* 13–61; P. Winter, *VT* 5 (1955) 315–18. Ben Sira attributes the differences between the opposites in creation and between the pious/wise and impious/foolish to God's ordering of the universe in general and of humans in particular. But he does not deny freedom of the will, a doctrine he teaches explicitly (15:11–20). Those God blesses and curses (v 12) are the Israelites and the Gentiles, respectively. The point of the poem is that the Jewish hellenizers were wrong to question Israel's divine election. **16–18.** An autobiographical note (cf. 24:30–34; 51:13–28).

56   (VII) Part VI (33:19–38:23). The call to listen introduces this part. It contains, like the others, a loose collection of poems on various aspects and concerns of Jewish life.

57   (A) Property and Servants (33:19–33). Various aphorisms on personal independence and treatment of slaves, important subjects for the prosperous Jewish male. **19–24.** *listen to me:* Ben Sira appeals to his own authority as wisdom teacher. The rest of the poem, in effect, urges against imitating the sad example of King Lear. **25–33.** Harsh maxims, tempered only in vv

30cd–33 (cf. Exod 21:1–11; Deut 23:16–17), on how to treat slaves. Slavery was at the time a socially and religiously legitimated institution.

58   (B) Trust in the Lord and Not in Dreams (34:1–20). **1–8.** A poem deploring reliance on dreams, divination, and omens, which are called unreal or foolish (v 5). Belief in dreams was widespread even in the OT (cf. Gen 40:8–19; 41:1–32; Dan 2:1–19,27–45); but Ben Sira was ahead of his time in saying that only the fool trusts in dreams (unless they are sent by God [v 6]). **9–20.** A poem in praise of the person who through discipline and observance of the law gains wide experience. **11–13.** On the value of travel and its dangers; cf. 32:21. **14–20.** On the virtues and blessings of the wise.

59   (C) True Worship of God and His Response (34:21–36:22). **21–24.** Ben Sira excoriates the tainted sacrifices of the wicked (cf. Amos 5:21–24; Isa 1:11–15), esp. when they offer goods stolen from the poor, who are very dear to God (cf. Ps 68:6). **25–27.** Depriving the poor of charity or the worker of his wages is like slaying them; cf. 4:1–6; Lev 19:13; Deut 24:14–15. **28–31.** On the futility of prayer and fasting for sins without genuine conversion; cf. Isa 58:3–7; Jer 14:12. **35:1–5.** Keeping the law, giving alms, and avoiding injustice are true worship and meaningful sacrifice; cf. 1:28; Hos 6:6. **6–13.** One should be generous (cf. Exod 23:14–17), cheerful (cf. 2 Cor 9:7), and just when making an offering to the Lord, for he will repay "seven times over" (v 13). **14–22a.** Warnings against exploiting the poor and powerless, who enjoy the special love and concern of the Lord. One cannot bribe God by sacrifices; cf. Deut 10:17–18. God hears the cry of the poor, the orphan, the widow—privileged characters in the Bible; cf. Exod 22:21–23; Deut 24:17–18; Prov 23:10–11. **22b–26.** This poem, which serves as a lead into the following prayer for deliverance, declares Ben Sira's faith that God will save his people who are now under foreign domination. **36:1–22.** A lament, in which Ben Sira begs God to rescue his chosen people; cf. Ps 44:2–9; 2 Macc 1:24–29. **1–5.** Avowal of faith and confidence in God's power to save the nation. **1.** *God of all:* Of Jews, Gentiles, the cosmos; cf. Ps 151:4 (11QPsa 28:7–8). **6–12.** Plea to punish, as God has done in the past (cf. Exod 15:6–8), the Seleucid oppressors. **12.** The hubris of the pagan rulers will not go unnoticed; cf. Isa 47:8–10. **13–19.** Request that God bring back to Palestine all the Jews who never returned after the exile.

60   (D) Choice of Associates (36:23–37:15). The text here is difficult; see Skehan and Di Lella, *Wisdom.* The poems are related only in terms of the types of persons one associates with. The advice given is pragmatic. **26–31.** On the value of a good wife; cf. Prov 31:10–31. **26.** A chauvinistic comment. **29.** *richest treasure:* Hebr *rē'šît qinyān*, a phrase which, deriving from Prov 8:22, suggests that the wife may be compared to Lady Wisdom (high praise indeed). **37:1–6.** On true and false friends, see also 6:5–17; 22:19–26. **7–11.** Caution is to be exercised in seeking counsel; disinterest and objectivity are essential for good advice. **12–15.** The godly person is the best associate and gives the soundest counsel. **14.** *watchers:* Allusion to astrologers.

61   (E) Wisdom and Temperance (37:16–31). **16–26.** Observations on how the wise behave and often benefit themselves and society; cf. Prov 12:14; 18:20. **19.** At times, however, a person may be judged wise because he helps others but is unable to manage his own affairs. **20.** Cf. 20:20; 21:16–17. **22–24.** Self-interest is compatible with true wisdom. **26.** Cf. 39:9–11; 41:11–13. **27–31.** Hygienic reasons for practicing temperance, the lack of which can lead to death; cf. 31:19–31; Prov 25:16. "Intemperance is the physician's provider" (Publilius Syrus, 1st cent. BC). This poem serves as a transition to the next one on the physician.

62 (F) Sickness and Death (38:1–23). 1–15. Though one may have observed moderation, the point of the previous poem, one may still become ill; hence, the physician is essential (v 1). Many refused, on religious grounds, to see a physician; others were skeptical of doctors. **2.** The physician's wisdom, also from God (cf. 1:1), should not be ignored. **4.** The prudent will not hesitate to take medicine, another of God's gifts. **5.** Cf. Exod 15:23–25. **9–11.** Granting the necessity of the physician, one should, when ill, pray and perform other religious exercises, for it is God who heals. Wicked King Asa, in his illness, "did not seek Yahweh but only the physicians" (2 Chr 16:12). **16–17.** Weeping and wailing were normal at funerals (cf. Jer 9:16–19) but only for "a day, two days"; the customary mourning period (even for orthodox Jews today) was seven days (22:12). **18–23.** Excessive grief does no good for the deceased or for oneself; cf. 2 Sam 12:23.

63 (VIII) Part VII (38:24–43:33). This part, like several of the others, opens with a poem on wisdom (the practical wisdom of the skilled worker) in 22 lines; → 4 above.

64 (A) Vocations of Skilled Worker and Scribe (38:24–39:11). Two poems: the skilled worker and the scribe. **24–34.** Though concerned with manual labor, this poem opens (v 24) and closes (v 34cd) with a couplet in praise of the scribe. The poem is roughly parallel to the Egyptian work "The Satire on the Trades" (*ANET* 432–34). But Ben Sira, unlike the Egyptian author, does not ridicule manual workers but expresses appreciation for the essential contributions they make to society (v 32). **39:1–11.** Nonetheless, the scribe has the highest vocation of all, for he has the leisure to devote himself to "the fear of God" (so Syriac) and to the study of the law, the wisdom of the ancients, and the prophecies (38:34d–39:1); note the threefold division of the OT also alluded to in the prologue (→ 9 above). The poem is autobiographical; cf. 51:13–30. **5.** Prayer, and not just diligent study, is needed if the scribe is to be truly wise. **6–8.** Wisdom, God's gift (1:6,8–10), enables the scribe to compose his own wise sayings. **9–11.** The scribe, because of his labors for others, earns the respect and praise of the community. Cf. J. Marböck, in *La Sagesse de l'Ancien Testament* (ed. M. Gilbert; BETL 51; Leuven, 1979) 293–316.

65 (B) Praise of God the Creator (39:12–35). The theme of this long poem, in five stanzas, is the goodness and purposefulness of creation and of God's providence. In its intent to provide a theodicy it can be compared to Job and Eccl; see Prato, *Il problema* 62–115. **12–15.** An invitatory calling the wise to sing the praises of the Lord "for all his works." **16–31.** The song may be summarized: All God's works are good (cf. Gen 1), and God provides for every need in due time (v 16). **17–18.** Creation by God's word; cf. Gen 1:9–10. **19–20.** God's omniscience; cf. 15:19; 17:15,19. **21.** God has a purpose for everything (cf. Eccl 3:11) though we may not always be aware of it (cf. 42:17). **23.** Cf. Gen 19:24–28. **24–31.** The doctrine of equilibrium in creation: persons, things, and events ultimately fulfill God's will and plan (cf. Prov 16:4). **26–27.** *water . . . cloth:* The 10 essentials for life in Palestine; these are used properly by the virtuous but abused by the wicked. **28–31.** Nine destructive forces, to counterbalance the 10 good things (vv 26–27); God uses these obedient creatures to punish sinners, who are disobedient. **32–35.** The epilogue. All God's works are good, even those that destroy (vv 28–31), for each serves the purpose for which it was created; hence we have no right to say, "This is not as good as that" (v 34).

66 (C) Miseries and Joys of Life (40:1–41:13). Five poems: the first two (vv 1–10 and 11–17) have a pessimistic tone in sharp contrast to the optimistic outlook of the previous poem; the third (vv 18–27) relieves the somberness by a series of "better than" proverbs about life's blessings available to those who fear the Lord; the last two (40:28–41:4 and 41:5–13) return to the melancholy strains of the first two. The arrangement is deliberate: the third poem with its optimistic mood is at the center of the section, thus indicating its importance. For a Babylonian analogue on pessimism, cf. *ANET* 438–40. **1–10.** The miseries of human life, from which no one is spared, are, according to the Church Fathers, the results of original sin. **1d.** *mother:* The earth from which humans were created (Gen 2:7) and to which they must return (Gen 3:19); cf. 16:29–30; 51:5. **11–17.** The retribution that comes, in this life, to each person: disaster for the wicked, but long life for the righteous. Cf. 10:7–17; 41:5–10. **18–27.** Ten "better than" proverbs, culminating in fear of the Lord, "a paradise of blessings" (v 27; cf. Isa 51:3); cf. 1:11–30. **40:28–41:4.** On the demeaning life of the beggar and on death, which is bitter when one is prosperous but is welcome when one is old and feeble. **5–13.** The cursed fate of the wicked and their children, and the lasting value of a good name (cf. Prov 10:7; Eccl 7:1).

67 (D) True and False Shame; Care of Daughters (41:14–42:14). 41:14–42:1d. A list of things (immortality, lying, disloyalty, theft, etc.) one should be rightly ashamed of. **1e–8.** A list of things (the law, justice, honesty in business, training children, etc.) one should never be ashamed of. **6a.** *seal:* Cf. 22:27b; Dan 14:11,17. The comment may not be chauvinistic; cf. 23:22–26. **9–14.** On care of daughters. Ben Sira's misogynistic male bias reaches its climax here. **9d.** It was thought that childlessness was always due to the wife's sterility, never the husband's. **13.** A cynical remark that disallows the part men play in the sins of women; cf. 25:24. **14a.** The meanest and grossest statement of all.

68 (E) The Works of God in Nature (42:15–43:33). A lengthy lyric poem (in four stanzas) similar to Job 38–41 and Prov 30:15–31; it resembles the onomasticon from Egypt, a literary form that uses a list of names of places, occupations, flora, fauna, etc., to make its point. The theme is praise of God, Lord of creation. **17.** *holy ones:* Angels; cf. Job 5:1; Ps 89:8. **18–21.** God's omniscience; cf. Isa 41:21–23. **22–25.** The beauty and harmony of creation; cf. 39:33–34. **24.** *in twos:* Light and darkness, hot and cold, etc. **43:1–12.** Praise of individual creatures and their beauty and purpose. **6–10.** The moon gets more space than the sun because it marks the religious festivals dear to Ben Sira. **13–26.** The elements of nature (snow, rain, clouds, hail, etc.) do God's will unfailingly; cf. Ps 29. **27–33.** Invitation to praise the Lord for his awesome and marvelous power in creation; cf. Ps 104.

69 (IX) Part VIII (44:1–50:24). These chapters form the most unified division of the book, having in Cairo ms. B the title "Praise of the Ancestors of Old." This part, which celebrates the heroes of Israel where Wisdom resides (24:8–12), flows naturally from the preceding section, which extols God's wisdom and might in creation. Similar historical surveys are found in Pss 78; 105; 106; 135; 136. See T. Maertens, *L'Éloge des Pères* (Bruges, 1956); R. T. Siebeneck, *CBQ* 21 (1959) 411–28; J. L. Duhaime, *EstBib* 35 (1976) 223–29; B. L. Mack, *Wisdom and Hebrew Epic* (Chicago, 1985); T. R. Lee, *Studies in the Form of Sirach 44–50* (SBLDS 75; Atlanta, 1986).

70 (A) Praise of Israel's Great Ancestors (44:1–15). In this introductory poem, Ben Sira lists the

12 categories of "godly people" (in the 12 cola of vv 3–6) he will describe in detail. The number 12 is sacred: 12 tribes of Israel, 12 months in the year, etc.; cf. Rev 21:12–14. The purpose of this survey is to encourage the Jews, who may be tempted to compromise with Hellenism, to remain loyal to the traditions of Israel and to take pride in the glorious heroes of their past. **9.** *others:* A class of the pious who were not remembered, but whose praises Ben Sira sings in vv 10–15.

71   (B) The Early Patriarchs (44:16–23a). 16. Enoch is the first mentioned of Israel's glorious ancestors and appears again in the conclusion (49:14) of this part, thus forming an *inclusio;* cf. Gen 5:24. **17–18.** Noah, "the righteous" (cf. Gen 6:9), was the second founder of the human race. God made the first covenant with Noah; cf. Gen 9:9–17. Now Ben Sira praises the other persons with whom God made a covenant: Abraham, Isaac, Jacob/Israel, Moses, Aaron, Phinehas, and David (44:19–47:11). **19.** *Abraham . . . peoples:* Cf. Gen 17:4–5. *without stain:* Cf. Gen 12:10–20; 20:1–18. **20.** The covenant with Abraham (Gen 17:9–14). *tested:* The ordeal on Mt. Moriah (Gen 22:1–14). **22.** God renewed the covenant with Isaac; cf. Gen 17:19; 26:3–5,24. **23.** On Jacob/Israel see Gen 27:1–29; 28:13–15.

72   (C) Moses, Aaron, Phinehas (44:23f–45:26). 44:23g–45:1. Moses was dear to God and "all the living," to his own people of course and to Pharaoh's daughter (Exod 2:5–10), Reuel and his daughters (Exod 2:16–22), Pharaoh's servants (Exod 11:3). **3–5.** Moses' greatest claim to fame is that God gave him the commandments, "the law of life and understanding" (cf. 17:11; Deut 30:15–16), the essence of wisdom; cf. 24:23–29. **6–22.** In giving Aaron the lion's share of attention (32 bicola), Ben Sira shows his love of the cult and levitical priesthood. He describes in minute detail the high priest's vestments and liturgical functions; cf. Exod 28; Lev 6–8. **18–19.** Cf. Num 16:1–17:15. **23–25d.** Ben Sira is intent on proving that Phinehas, Aaron's grandson, was the legitimate successor to the high priesthood; cf. 4 Macc 18:12. **23.** *crisis:* Cf. Num 25:1–15. **25e–26.** Prayer for the current high priest and his successors.

73   (D) Joshua, Caleb, the Judges, Samuel (46:1–20). 1–7a. Joshua succeeded Moses as leader of the people (Num 27:18–23). **1.** *name implies:* Joshua (Gk Jesus) means "Yahweh is salvation." For his exploits, cf. Josh 10. **2.** Cf. Josh 8:18–26. **3.** Cf. Josh 8:14. **4–10.** On Caleb; cf. Josh 10:7–14; Num 14. **11–12.** The judges in general are treated. **13–20.** Samuel was the last and greatest of the judges. **13.** *pledged:* As a Nazirite; cf. 1 Sam 1. Samuel was also a prophet who offered sacrifice; cf. 1 Sam 7:7–9. He established the monarchy by anointing Saul as king (1 Sam 9:15–17). **15.** Cf. 1 Sam 3:20; 9:9. **19.** Cf. 1 Sam 12:1–5. See P. C. Beentjes, *Bib* 63 (1982) 506–23. **20.** Cf. 1 Sam 28:8–19.

74   (E) Nathan, David, Solomon (47:1–22). 1. Nathan was the principal prophet in David's time (2 Sam 7:2–17; 12:1–15). **2–11.** David was lifted up from Israel as the choice fat was lifted up from the holy offering so that it could then be burnt on the altar (v 2; cf. Lev 4:8,10,19)—high praise indeed. **3–7.** David's exploits became legendary; cf. 1 Sam 17:17–58; 18:7. **8–10.** In biblical tradition the Law is attributed to Moses, Psalms to David, and Wisdom to Solomon. Cf. 1 Chr 15:16; 16:4–6; 23:5,31–32. **11.** David's sins and God's forgiveness; cf. 2 Sam 11; 12:13. **12–22.** Solomon, David's wise son and successor, built the Jerusalem Temple (1 Kgs 6) but ultimately became disloyal to the covenant and was rejected. **14–17.** Solomon's proverbial wisdom; cf. 1 Kgs 5:9–14; 10:1–13. **18.** *name:* Jedidiah (2 Sam 12:25), i.e., "beloved of Yahweh." **19–20.**

Foreign women were the cause of Solomon's downfall; cf. 1 Kgs 11:1–10. **21.** Because of his sins, the kingdom was split in two, Judah and Ephraim/Israel; cf. 1 Kgs 12:16–25. **22.** But the Davidic dynasty will last; cf. 2 Sam 7:14–16; 1 Kgs 11:13,39; Ps 89:29–38. Cf. P. C. Beentjes, *Bijdr* 45 (1984) 6–14.

75   (F) Elijah and Elisha (47:23–48:15d). 23–24. Rehoboam, Solomon's son who ruled in Judah, and Jeroboam, first king of Israel, were, in Ben Sira's eyes, so despicable that he does not even mention their names. Jeroboam made the golden calves in Bethel and Dan (1 Kgs 12:26–32), thus causing the ruin of Israel in 722 (2 Kgs 17:20–23). **47:25–48:11.** The awesome exploits and holy zeal of Elijah (= "Yah[weh] is my God"); cf. 1 Kgs 17–19. **8.** Cf. 1 Kgs 19:16. **9.** Cf. 2 Kgs 2:1,11. **12.** Elisha (= "God has saved") was famous for the "signs" and "marvels" he wrought—"twice as many" as Elijah; cf. 2 Kgs 2–6,8. **13–14.** Cf. 2 Kgs 13:21. **15.** Because the people of Israel did not repent, they were led away captive by Assyria in 722.

76   (G) Hezekiah and Isaiah (48:15e–25). Ben Sira now turns to the southern kingdom, Judah, and to one of its great kings, Hezekiah, and the famous prophet of his reign, Isaiah. Though a tiny nation, Judah had a successor of David as king (v 15e) whereas Israel had only usurpers on its throne. **17.** Cf. 2 Kgs 20:20. **18–21.** Sennacherib's invasion; cf. 2 Kgs 18:13–37; Isa 36. Isaiah assured Hezekiah that Sennacherib would not capture Jerusalem but instead would be punished (2 Kgs 19:20–35; Isa 37:21–36). **22.** Isaiah was noted for his visions; cf., e.g., Isa 1:1; 2:1; 6:1–13. **23.** Cf. 2 Kgs 20:8–11; Isa 38:7–8. **24–25.** Cf. Isa 40:1–11; 42:9; 49:8–13; 61:1–3; Ben Sira attributes to Isaiah himself the whole book bearing his name.

77   (H) Josiah and the Prophets; Various Heroes (49:1–16). This final section has 22 bicola, thus signaling the conclusion of this part of the book (→ 4 above). **1–3.** The greatness of Josiah; cf. 2 Kgs 22:10–13; 23:4–25. **4.** Of Judah's kings only David, Hezekiah, and Josiah were good; the rest were wicked. **5–6.** The Babylonians destroyed the southern kingdom in 587; cf. 2 Kgs 25:1–15. **7.** Jeremiah: cf. Jer 1:5,10; 20:7–10; 37:13–16; 38:4–6. **8.** Cf. Ezek 1:4–28. Cf. J. Marböck, *BZ* 25 (1981) 103–11. **9.** Cf. Ezek 14:14,20. **10.** Ben Sira places the Twelve Prophets as a single book after Ezekiel, as in the MT. **11–13.** Zerubbabel, Jeshua, and Nehemiah are praised because they rebuilt the Temple and the walls of Jerusalem (Ezra 3–6; Neh 2:17–7:3); cf. P. Höffken, *ZAW* 87 (1975) 184–201. **14–16.** The most famous of Israel's ancestors: Enoch (Gen 5:24; 2 Enoch 18:2); Joseph (Gen 50:25–26); Shem, son of Noah and father of the Semites (Gen 11:10–26); Seth, son of Adam (Gen 4:25; 5:3); Enosh, son of Seth (Gen 4:26); Adam, the first human being, created directly by God (Gen 2:7).

78   (I) Simeon, Son of Jochanan (50:1–24). This lengthy panegyric serves as an appendix to the "Praise of the Ancestors." Given the graphic depiction of the high priest's liturgical vestments (cf. Exod 28) and actions, it is probable that Ben Sira knew Simeon personally. **1–4.** *Simeon:* Simeon II, high priest from 219 to 196; he renovated the Temple, fortifying its precincts (cf. Josephus, *Ant.* 12.3.3 §138–144). **5–21.** A lyrical description of the ceremonies of the daily whole offering, and not of the Day of Atonement (Yom Kippur), as most commentators have thought; see F. O. Fearghail, *Bib* 59 (1978) 301–16. **20–21.** Cf. Lev 9:22–23; Num 6:22–27.

79   (X) Conclusion (50:25–51:30). A concluding couplet on three groups Ben Sira despises and the epilogue or subscription to the book. Two appendixes follow: a psalm of praise and an autobiographical poem.

80   (A) Judah's Neighbors; Epilogue (50:25–29).   25–26. A numerical proverb. *in Seir:* The Edomites or Idumaeans, bitter enemies of the Jews; cf. Obad 2–14. *in Shechem:* The Samaritans, the most hated group (cf. Ezra 4:1–24); see J. D. Purvis, *JNES* 24 (1965) 88–94. **27–29.** The epilogue, in which the author gives his full name: Yeshua [Jesus] ben Eleazar ben Sira.

81   (B) Ben Sira's Psalm (51:1–12).   This psalm and the autobiographical poem (vv 13–30) are two appendixes; cf. 50:27–29. Some scholars have questioned the authenticity of these pieces: but the language, form, and contents prove that Ben Sira wrote them. The skillfully crafted psalm has six stanzas in two groups: 3, 3, 3 and 4, 4, 3 bicola. See A. A. Di Lella, *CBQ* 48 (1986) 395–407. **10.** *Father:* A frequent title of Yahweh; cf., e.g., 23:1,4; Deut 32:6; Isa 63:16.

82   (C) Hymn of Praise (51:12 i–xvi).   Found only in ms. B from the Cairo Geniza, the hymn is probably inauthentic but old, prior to 152 BC; see Di Lella, *Hebrew Text of Sirach* 101–5. Patterned on Ps 136, it is completely biblical in orientation; see T. Vargha, *Antonianum* 10 (1935) 3–10.

83   (D) Autobiographical Poem on Wisdom (51:13–30).   An elegant alphabetic acrostic, like the conclusion of Prov (31:10–31), in 23 lines; see P. W. Skehan, *CBQ* 23 (1961) 127; *HTR* 64 (1971) 387–400; M. Delcor, *Textus* 6 (1968) 27–47; I. Rabinowitz, *HUCA* 42 (1971) 173–84; C. Deutsch, *ZAW* 94 (1982) 400–9. This final poem forms an *inclusio* with the opening poem on wisdom (1:11–30) in 22 lines; → 4 above). The first half is found in 11QPs a, 1st cent. AD. **16.** Cf. 6:19. **17.** *teacher:* God, the author of wisdom; cf. 1:1–10,26. **20.** Cf. 1QH 16:10. **22.** Because God made him a great teacher, Ben Sira offers him praise. **23–26.** The invitation to acquire wisdom by submitting to her yoke; cf. 6:23–31; Prov 9:1–6. **23.** *house of instruction:* With Greek and Syriac; ms. B, "my house of instruction," is interpretive, not original; see Skehan and Di Lella, *Wisdom.* **27–28.** A little labor produces much wisdom and profit. **29.** Praise of God is the appropriate response to God's gifts.

33

WISDOM

Addison G. Wright, S.S.

BIBLIOGRAPHY

1 Clark, E. G., *The Wisdom of Solomon* (CBC, Cambridge, 1973). Feldmann, F., *Das Buch der Weisheit* (Bonn, 1926). Fichtner, J., *Weisheit Salomos* (HAT; Tübingen, 1938). Fischer, J. *Das Buch der Weisheit* (Würzburg, 1950). Geyer, J., *The Wisdom of Solomon* (TBC; London, 1963). Goodrick, A. T. S., *The Book of Wisdom* (London, 1913). Gregg, J. A. F., *The Wisdom of Solomon* (CBSC; Cambridge, 1909). Heinisch, P., *Das Buch der Weisheit* (EHAT; Münster, 1912). Larcher, C., *Études sur le Livre de la Sagesse* (EBib; Paris, 1969); *Le Livre de la Sagesse ou la Sagesse de Salomon* (EBib; 3 vols.; Paris, 1983–85). Reese, J. M., *Hellenistic Influence on the Book of Wisdom and Its Consequences* (AnBib 41; Rome, 1970); *The Book of Wisdom, Song of Songs* (OTM 20; Wilmington, 1983). Reider, J., *The Book of Wisdom* (NY, 1957). Weber, J., *Le Livre de la Sagesse* (Paris, 1946). Winston, D., *The Wisdom of Solomon* (AB 43; GC, 1979). Ziener, G., *Die theologische Begriffssprache im Buche der Weisheit* (BBB 11; Bonn, 1956).

The critical edition of the text is J. Ziegler (ed.), *Sapientia Salomonis* (Göttingen, 1962).

INTRODUCTION

2 (I) Title, Language, Date, Origin. "The Book of Wisdom" is the title of the work in the Vg; LXX mss. entitle it "The Wisdom of Solomon," and it is today referred to under either name.

The book is not in the Hebrew Bible and is known to us only in the Greek. Although it has been argued that some or all of the book was originally written in Hebrew, it is generally held today, because of various linguistic features, that Greek was the original language. In addition, it is clear that the author frequently utilized the OT in the LXX transl., and that LXX readings influenced the thought of Wis in the formative stages of its composition.

Clearly, then, despite the claim for Solomonic authorship, Wis was written many centuries after the time of Solomon. It was certainly written after the completion of the LXX of the Prophets and the Writings (*ca.* middle of the 2d cent. BC), and, while it appears to be unacquainted with the writings of Philo (20 BC–AD 54), it seems to belong to the same milieu of thought (see Larcher, *Études* 151–78). If we assign to it a date in the last half of the 1st cent. BC, we shall not be far from wrong. Wis, then, is the last of the OT books.

The place of composition is apparently Egypt, probably Alexandria, the great intellectual and scientific center of the Mediterranean world and one of the largest centers of the Jewish Diaspora. The thought of Wis closely resembles that of other Jewish-Alexandrian works of the same period. Other indications are the emphasis on Egypt and its relationship to Israel in chaps. 11–19 and the polemic against animal worship (chaps. 13–15), so prevalent then in Egypt.

The author of the book claims to be Solomon. The claim was questioned by Origen, Eusebius, Augustine, and Jerome, and it is clear from the preceding data that the claim is simply a literary device, conventional in OT wisdom literature (→ Wisdom Lit., 27:8). The author of the book remains anonymous, and the most we can say is that he was a learned Greek-speaking Jew and probably a teacher, and that he was familiar with Hellenistic philosophy, rhetoric, and culture.

3 (II) Unity of the Book. Many scholars have proposed that Wis is the work of more than one author, and they distinguish two independent sections (1:1–11:1; 11:2–19:22 or 1–5; 6–19); some point out even three or four sections. Arguments in favor of composite authorship are the following: the difference in style and tone between the first and last parts of the book; the absence of references in chaps. 11–19 to wisdom (save for 14:2,5) and immortality; a number of striking linguistic differences (see S. Holmes, *APOT* 1. 522–23). However, the majority of critics defend the unity of authorship, finding that the factors mentioned are far outweighed by the homogeneity of vocabulary and of outlook throughout, as well as by the allusions in chaps. 11–19 to passages in the first part of the book (→ 8 below) and the numerical patterns (→ 10 below). The differences between the sections can be accounted for by postulating that the book was written over an extended period of time. (On the unity of Wis, see Reese, *Hellenistic Influence* 122–45).

4 **(III) Genre.** The genre of the whole book is that of the protreptic discourse or didactic exhortation known from Hellenistic literature. A blend of philosophy and rhetoric, it is not an abstract treatise but a practical appeal that one's learning should have an impact on one's moral life. This type of discourse readily lent itself to the incorporation of other genres — in the case of Wis, the diatribe (1:1–6:9; 13–15), the philosophical inquiry (6:10–9:18), the proof from example (chap. 10) and the *synkrisis* or comparison (chaps. 11–19) (see Reese, *Hellenistic Influence* 90–121). The poetry of the book (well sustained in chaps. 1–5 and 9; sporadic elsewhere, although more prevalent in chaps. 6–8 and 10–12 than in 13–19) is a blend of Hebr parallelism and Gk prosody; at times it is truly impressive.

5 **(IV) Occasion, Purpose, Content.** From the book itself we can conclude that the author's purpose was to strengthen the faith of his fellow Jews in Alexandria. Living in the midst of pagans, the Jewish community was in frequent contact with all the elements of the new society that was the Hellenistic world. Conquests in science were opening up to people the beauty and mystery of the world around them (7:17–20). A variety of religions and philosophical systems offered wisdom or salvation or a view on the real meaning of life. There existed the new cosmopolitan and individualistic mentality, skepticism, and dissatisfaction with traditional ideas. It was a time of crisis for faith, which some Jews had abandoned (2:12), replacing it with pagan religions, secular philosophies, or their own superficial versions of these (2:1–20); other Jews were in danger of following their example. The problems created for the Jews by the intellectual atmosphere were compounded by an age-old problem that afflictions and anti-Semitism had evoked once again — retribution. How is it that the wicked and godless prosper and the just suffer? How and where does God mete out justice?

It was to these issues that our author addressed himself, and for solutions he searched the Scriptures. The 19 chapters of Wis contain not many lines and few connected passages that have not been derived in large part from fruitful meditation on the earlier sacred books. (See P. W. Skehan, *SIPW* 149–236; Larcher, *Études* 85–103). In fact, if we are to seek a principle of unity in Wis, it is this feature that provides it. To say it is a book about wisdom or immortality or providence will not define Wis. Rather, it is the expression of the fullness of all that one man in Egypt, with what must have been years of devoted study, could draw from the entire sacred literature of his people to give hope and consolation to his contemporaries. In addition, throughout the book he expressed himself in a vocabulary highly influenced by contemporary Hellenistic philosophy, religion, and science. About 20 percent of the vocabulary appears nowhere else in the LXX, and this creative effort to communicate in the language of his culture must have been judged impressive by any who admired the syncretistic spirit of his day. (See A. A. Di Lella, *CBQ* 28 [1966] 139–54 = *SAIW* 401–16; T. Finan, *ITQ* 27 [1960] 30–48; Larcher, *Études* 181–236; Reese, *Hellenistic Influence* 1–89. The Hellenistic dimensions of the book are conveniently presented in the commentaries of Reese and Winston). The book, then, seems to have been addressed to Jewish students and intellectuals who shared the author's wide background. Only they would have been able to grasp the allusions, and only they would have been disposed to follow the presentation.

6 Wis is one of the witnesses to a trend in late postexilic Jewish thought that looked forward to life after death (→ OT Thought, 77:168–74), and in the opening chapters the author situates the problem of retribution in that context. According to the traditional view, the lot of all beyond the grave was to be the same, a weak and pale existence in sheol separated from God; reward and retribution were to be in this world, with long life, a large family, riches and prestige for the just, and misfortune in all of these areas for the wicked. This theory was not borne out by the hard facts of experience, and there had been advanced various solutions to the problem in its national (Dt-Isa) and individual aspects (Job, Eccl). Some psalms had expressed a hope of a life with God beyond the grave for the individual (Pss 49:16; 73:23–24), and Isa 26:19; Dan 12:2; 2 Macc 7 witness to an indeterminate form of resurrection belief. Wis synthesizes and builds on these and other texts, states the reward of life with God with an emphatic assurance, reassesses the problem of the suffering of the just and the value of children and old age in the light of his beliefs, and presents the most extensive discussion on the subject in the OT.

The author may have been aided in his thinking on future life by the Gk concepts of body and soul (→ 12 below). However, his reasoning process is Jewish, for he does not conclude to immortality from the nature of the soul but from one's relationship to God, for immortality in Wis is a gift of God to the righteous (→ 13 below). Moreover, his picturing of the reward of the just in terms of a sharing in the angelic life (5:5) could have been formulated within the framework of the developing aspirations of OT piety without the aid of philosophical beliefs on the immaterial nature of the human soul. It seems to have been so formulated at Qumran (cf. 1QS 11:7–8; 1QH 3:21–23). (For a discussion of similarities and differences between Wis and the QL and the anthropology of Wis, see Larcher, *Études* 112–32, 263–79).

There is no mention of a resurrection of the body in Wis as there is in so many other writings of the period. Some critics have maintained that the silence on this point is out of deference to the Greeks and that the doctrine is implied in chaps. 3–5 and in 16:13 and 19:6–21. The arguments are unconvincing, and it would seem that Wis (like QL thus far) does not envision a resurrection of the body.

In discussing the events of the afterlife, the author is understandably (and perhaps deliberately) vague. (a) The book presumes a separation of the just and the wicked at death; the just are in the hand of God and at peace (3:1–3) and the wicked go to sheol, which is understood as a place of torment (4:19). (b) Several texts speak of a judgment (3:7,13,18; 4:6,20) which includes a definitive exaltation of the just (3:7–9). Does this judgment take place immediately after death, or is it seen as another event at the end of time and connected with the apocalyptic scene in 5:17–23? (c) If (b) is at the end of time, what is the intermediate state of the just who have died? Are they with God or in another place? (d) If (b) is immediately after death, what is the nature of the apocalyptic scene in 5:17–23? Those are the ambiguities. The present commentary sees (b) as taking place immediately after death, and understands 5:17–23 simply as the final devastation of the earth — there being envisioned no messianic age, renewed creation, or resurrection, for the "kingdom of God" (10:10) is extraterrestrial (as also in *As. Mos.* 10).

(For other views and the eschatology of Wis in general: Beauchamp, P., *Bib* 45 [1964] 491–526. Delcor, M., *NRT* 77 [1955] 614–30. Grelot, P., *À la rencontre de Dieu* [Fest. A. Gelin; ed. A.

Barucq, *et al.;* Le Puy, 1961] 165-78. Larcher, *Études* 237-327. Nickelsburg, G., *Resurrection, Immortality and Eternal Life in Intertestamental Judaism* [Cambridge, MA, 1972] 48-90. Taylor, R., *ETL* 42 [1966] 72-137. Weisengoff, J. P., *CBQ* 3 [1941] 104-33.)

7   Since it is Wisdom who instructs in the righteousness that leads to immortality, the second part of the book (6:22–11:1) sets forth Solomon's quest for Wisdom as a model for the reader and describes who Wisdom is and how she came to be. It is in this section especially that the author addresses himself to the problem of the allurements of Hellenism and attempts to show his Jewish audience that they are not barbarians, as has been alleged, and that they have no reason to envy the wisdom of the pagans inasmuch as they possess true wisdom. He does not reject Gk culture but attempts something of a synthesis. He begins with the personification of God's Wisdom in Prov 1; 8–9; Job 28; Bar 3:9–4:4; Sir 24 (→ Wisdom Lit., 27:15–17) and identifies it with the Spirit of the Lord (→ 12 below; OT Thought, 77:32–39) and with the Word of God (9:1–2,17; → OT Thought, 77:40–46). He states that it is really Wisdom who possesses the qualities of the pagan goddess of wisdom, Isis, and of the world soul of the Greeks (7:22–8:1). It is she who is the true initiator into the divine mysteries (8:4) and who teaches the four cardinal virtues of Plato (8:7). He attempts a synthesis between anthropocentric Gk humanism and theocentric Hebr humanism by broadening the purely ethical connotations of wisdom to include the profane learning of Hellenism (7:17–20). However, in typically Hebr manner he reminds us that Wisdom teaches above all the righteousness that is God's pleasure (chaps. 9–10). In addition, by identifying Wisdom with the Spirit of the Lord, the author bestowed upon Wisdom the contemporaneity and nearness of action that were associated with the Spirit. Whereas Prov and Sir identified Wisdom with the law, Wis imparts a dynamic vitality to her.

(On the figure of Wisdom in the book: Bonnard, P. E., *La sagesse en personne* [LD 44; Paris, 1966] 89–112. Larcher, *Études* 329–414. Mack, B. L., *Logos und Sophia* [SUNT 10; Göttingen, 1973]. Reese, *Hellenistic Influence* 34– 50. Rylaarsdam, J., *Revelation in Jewish Wisdom Literature* [Chicago, 1946] 99–118. Winston, *Wisdom* 33–40, 178–83.)

8   In the second half (11:2–19:22), the author recalls the precision with which God saved Israel and punished the Egyptians at the exodus and how God "stands by his people in every time and circumstance" (19:22). These chapters are not only an exhortation for Jews suffering once again in Egypt, but they also and especially provide the historical basis for the eschatological statements about the just and the wicked in chaps. 1–6. Whatever other factors may be involved in the avoidance of proper names in the book (flattery of the audience, riddling, etc.), the use of the simple terms "the just," "the wicked," etc. to designate Israel and Egypt in chaps. 11–19 serves above all to make the exodus events an image or type of God's dealings with the just and the wicked at death. This use of persons as types is characteristic of the protreptic genre, and the idea is explicit in 17:21. In addition, there are a number of allusions in chaps. 11–19 to chaps. 1–6 (e.g., 11:8–10, 15; 13:10; 14:12–14; 15:3; 18:1– 4,13,15–16; 19:8), and these also link the discussion of the exodus with the eschatology of chaps. 1–6 (see Reese, *Hellenistic Influence* 123–40). Also of interest is the author's explanation of miracles in terms of Gk philosophy (19:18–21), his viewing of the exodus as a new creation (19:6– 13), his discussion of the possibility of a knowledge of God through creation (13:1–9), and the digressions on God's

mercy (11:17–12:22) and on false worship (chaps. 13–15).

9   The book is a remarkable example of the fusing of the wisdom tradition with a number of other elements: the study of sacred texts, salvation history, apocalyptic, as well as Hellenistic culture. In addition, the author was not one to preserve unchanged the responses of the past as the only adequate solutions for present problems. In taking the cultural developments of his day seriously and being willing to rethink and recast his traditions in new and relevant ways, he has left a model of religious thinking for later generations.

10   **(V) Outline.**   A wide variety of outlines of the book has been offered in the past by the critics. However, the author of Wis, like the author of Heb, has used various techniques to structure his work, and with the discovery of these it has become possible to provide an outline of the book that can confidently be proposed as being the one the author intended (see A. G. Wright, *Bib* 48 [1967] 165–84).

First, the author has marked the limits of each paragraph with *inclusios* — i.e., the repetition, at the end of a section, of a word or phrase used at its beginning. The *inclusios* for each section are indicated in the commentary. The manner in which these paragraphs are to be grouped has been indicated by the author in two ways; some are arranged in a concentric symmetry (chaps. 1–6; 7–8; 9; and the digression of 13–15), others in a linear fashion to develop an announced theme by repetition (chap. 10, and the homily of chaps. 11–19, in which there is not a sevenfold division, as is often stated, but a fivefold one; → 53 and 57 below).

In addition, throughout the book the author has counted his verses (not biblical verses, of course, but poetic verses; monostichs, distichs, and tristichs). In the symmetrical sections there is a quantitative symmetry in the number of verses as well as the qualitative symmetry already mentioned. Moreover, in all parts of the book, except in the two digressions in 11:17–12:22 and 13:1–15:17, the number of verses in each smaller section stands to the number of verses in its neighboring larger one in the same ratio as the larger stands to the sum of the two (m/M = M/m + M) — i.e., in the neighborhood of 0.618. The major sections (1:1–6:21; 6:22–9:18; 11–19) also stand to each other in that ratio. This ratio is the well-known golden mean or divine proportion, famous in mathematics, art, architecture, and aesthetic theory and utilized by Vergil, Catullus, Lucretius, Horace, Ennius, Lucan, and Aratus in proportioning sections of their literary works (cf. G. E. Duckworth, *Structural Patterns and Proportions in Vergil's Aeneid* [Ann Arbor, 1962]). Finally, with the addition of chap. 10 and the two digressions of 11:17–12:22 and 13:1–15:17, the book consists of two halves (1:1–11:1; 11:2–19:22) of 251 verses each (for the details, see A. G. Wright, *CBQ* 29 [1967] 524–38). As with the *inclusios,* so also with the numerical patterns the rationale is to be sought in the artistic sense of the author. He had a sense of, and a desire for, completion; therefore, he repeated at the end of a section a key word from the beginning. He also had a sense of proportion and thus constructed his book on the basis of the golden mean.

The literary and numerical analysis indicates the following structure:

(I) The Praises of Wisdom (1:1–11:1)
   (A) Immortality Is the Reward of Wisdom (1:1–6:21)
      (a) Exhortation to Justice (1:1–15)
      (b) The Wicked Invite Death (Speech of the
         Wicked) (1:16–2:24)
      (c) The Hidden Counsels of God (3:1–4:19)
         (i) Suffering (3:1–12)

The commentary below is based on the *NAB* transl. The *inclusios* spoken of above are indicated for each section.

COMMENTARY

11 **(I) The Praises of Wisdom (1:1–11:1).** The first half of the book is divided into two sections. The first section, sometimes called the Book of Eschatology, deals with the problem of retribution for good and evil and with the immortality that Wisdom offers; it concludes with an appeal to the reader to seek Wisdom (1:1–6:21). The second section describes Wisdom and her operations in the world and explains how she is to be found (6:22–11:1).

 (A) Immortality Is the Reward of Wisdom (1:1–6:21). The section is divided into five parts arranged concentrically. The central part (3:1–4:19) contains the author's teaching on retribution.
12 (a) EXHORTATION TO JUSTICE (1:1–15). *Inclusio: justice*, 1:1,15. The author begins with an exhortation, which the rest of the book will reinforce: Live a virtuous life and trust in God because these qualities make possible union with God and with wisdom (vv 1–5; *inclusio: justice/injustice*, 1 and 5; *counsels; rebuke*, 3 and 5). Grumblings against God's providence do not go unnoticed, and God, who is jealous of his honor, punishes such transgressions by not granting immortality (vv 6–11; *inclusio: tongue[s]*, 6 and 11). The author then introduces the theme of this part of the book; humans are made for immortality; death comes from sin and from our free choice; God is not responsible for it (vv 12–15; *inclusio: destruction/destructive*, 12 and 14; *death/undying*, 12 and 15).

 1. *justice:* Righteousness, virtuous thought and action. *you who judge:* Rulers. Such an address was a Gk literary device of the day and here quite in keeping with the fiction of Solomonic authorship (Solomon speaks to his fellow kings). There may also be an allusion to collective human dominion over the earth (Gen 1:26; Ps 8; Wis 9:2–3) and the eschatological rule of the just (3:8; 6:20–21). *in goodness:* Have good thoughts about the Lord and do not grumble against his providence. **3–11.** Cf. 2:1–20 for an example of the perverse counsels and evil utterances that lead to death. **4.** *Wisdom:* Wisdom is personified in Prov 1:20–23; 8:1–36; 9:1–6; Job 28; Bar 3:9–4:4; Sir 24:1–21, as well as by our author. It is not

a person separate from Yahweh but a personification of functions of Yahweh. Such personification is common in the OT (e.g., Spirit, Word, Justice). In the earlier wisdom literature, wisdom was an effect of the Spirit of God; in Wis (here in vv 5–7 and in 7:22–23; 9:17) Wisdom is identified with the Spirit of the Lord and becomes an immanent cosmological principle and the internal principle of physical and moral life (→ 7 above). *soul, body:* The Hebrews did not conceive of humans as constituted of a material body and a spiritual soul (→ OT Thought, 77:64–66). Under the influence of Hellenism, these concepts appear in the OT clearly for the first time in Wis 8:19– 20; 9:15; 15:8, and less clearly here where the terms are in parallelism. However, Wis has not adopted the Platonic idea that the body is evil, nor the tripartite division of body, soul, and spirit. In Wis, soul (8:19; etc.) and spirit (15:16; etc.) are used interchangeably for the vital principle and are put in synonymous parallelism in 15:11 and 16:14. *body under debt of sin:* The phrase is parallel and synonymous with the "soul that plots evil" in v 4a. The body is not seen as the source of sin in opposition to the soul. **5.** *discipline:* In the wisdom literature, the term means religious instruction, training, and correction. **12–13.** *death:* It becomes clear in 2:24 that the author is not speaking of physical death but of spiritual death, the eternal separation from God. Our author seems to be indifferent regarding the fate of the body (→ 6 above). **14.** *destructive drug:* The physical world around us does not have the capacity to cause spiritual death. *netherworld:* Sheol, the abode of the dead, here equated with personified Death. **15.** *justice is undying:* It leads to immortality. As chap. 3 makes clear, the term "immortality" for the author is neither fame with posterity, as in the OT, nor the philosophical notion of the native immortality of the soul, but the freely granted divine gift of unending life with God.
13 (b) THE WICKED INVITE DEATH (SPEECH OF THE WICKED) (1:16–2:24). *Inclusio: in its [his] possession,* 1:16 and 2:24. The author next explains that it is the wicked who invite death by their evil deeds, and he sets

forth their erroneous philosophy of life in the form of a speech. Some have suggested that the wicked depicted by the author are Epicureans or Sadducees, or even that the section is a polemic against the views set forth in Eccl. Actually, the philosophy of life pictured here differs essentially from the doctrine of all those mentioned and is really an eclectic assemblage of ideas. The wicked the author has in mind are apostate Jews, probably seen as a type of the wicked in general. On the speech, see P. W. Skehan, *SIPW* 213–36; J. P. Weisengoff, *CBQ* 11 [1949] 40–65; Winston, *Wisdom* 114–20.

In their view of life and death, the wicked espouse a practical atheism and attribute human origins to chance. Their concept of life is completely this-worldly, and they deny survival after death (vv 1–5; *inclusio: dying,* 1 and 5). Consequently, they resolve to pursue a hedonistic existence and to make might the norm of right (vv 6–11; *inclusio: use/useless,* 6 and 11). They resolve to persecute the just because their lives and words are a reproach (vv 12–16; *inclusio: God,* 13 and 16), and they determine to test the claims of the just (vv 17–20; *inclusio: his words,* 17 and 20). The author concludes the section with his judgment on these thoughts of the wicked and announces the subject of the next section (vv 21–24).

16. *friend:* Irony. *covenant:* the terminology is from Isa 28:15,18. **2:1.** *dying:* The word "death" on the lips of the wicked means, of course, physical death. **2.** *haphazard:* The allusion is probably to the Epicurean doctrine that objects were formed by a chance combination of atoms. **2–3.** *smoke, spark, ashes:* An allusion to a Gk theory that the soul is a fiery principle. **4.** *name will be forgotten:* The wicked reject even the OT hope of remembrance by posterity. Ironically, the statement is true on the lips of the wicked (cf. 4:19). **7–8.** The emphasis on flowers is Greek. **11.** *weakness proves itself useless:* Therefore, it has no right to exist. **12.** Cf. Isa 3:10 LXX. From 2:12 to 5:23, the author draws heavily on Isa 52–66. His teaching on retribution is the fruit of meditation on these chapters in their LXX form, and he sets forth that teaching in a series of characters or types taken from Isa, presented in their Isaian sequence and embellished with additional details from elsewhere. See P. W. Skehan, *CBQ* 2 (1940) 289–99 (=*SIPW* 163–71); M. J. Suggs, *JBL* 76 (1957) 26–33; Nickelsburg, *Resurrection* 48–92.

13. The picture of the just here and in 3:1–9 is based on the fourth Servant song (Isa 52:13–53:12), as well as on Isa 42:1 and Ps 22:8. **16.** *destiny of the just:* Immortality. **22.** Announces the subject of the next section. **23.** *image:* The author connects the "image of God" of Gen 1:26 with the immortality to which humans are destined but which can be lost by sin. Wis never says that we are by nature immortal, but rather that we receive immortality as a divine gift (3:4; 4:1; 8:13; 15:3). *nature:* Gk *idiotētos.* Read with some mss. *aïdiotētos,* "eternity." **24.** Here it is clear that "death" in 1:11–14 and in this verse does not mean physical death but rather spiritual death because it is experienced only by the wicked. Likewise, *aphtharsia* (*NAB:* "imperishable"), here and in its other occurrences in Wis (6:18,19), means the gift of life with God and not an innate immortality. The author apparently views physical death as the result of our earthly origins (cf. 7:1), and this would explain his disinterest in physical death and the lack of mention of bodily resurrection. (On the notions of life and death in Wis, see J. P. Weisengoff, *CBQ* 3 [1941] 104–33; Larcher, *Études* 280–300.) *envy of the devil:* One of the rare OT texts which refer to the fall in Gen 3 (cf. also 10:1 and Sir 25:23) and the first biblical text to equate the serpent with the devil (see later John 8:44; Rev 12:9; 20:2). The author apparently interprets the threat of death in Gen 3 as referring to spiritual death. *envy:* Because Adam was

in the image of God (*Life of Adam and Eve* 12–17 in *OTP* 262–64) or because Adam had control of all creation (*2 Enoch* 31:3–6). On the text, see S. Lyonnet, *Bib* 39 (1958) 27–36; A.-M. Dubarle, *Fest. E. Tisserant* (Vatican, 1964) 1. 187–95.

14 (c) THE HIDDEN COUNSELS OF GOD (3:1–4:19). In this section, the author begins by stating that immortality is the reward of the just. Then, in the light of that belief, he comments in three paragraphs of 14 verses each on three points of the traditional discussion of the problem of retribution (the suffering of the just, childlessness, early death), and in each paragraph he contrasts the fate of the just and of the wicked.

15 (i) *Suffering* (3:1–12). *Inclusio: foolish,* 2 and 12; *thought(s),* 2 and 10; *hope,* 4 and 11. The just seem to have died, but they are really alive with God. Their sufferings in this life appear to be punishments (a frequent OT assumption), but their sufferings are not punishments at all but a discipline, correction, and testing of fidelity in which God recognizes those worthy of him. The just are full of hope for immortality, and at the judgment the just shall enjoy the kingdom of God. The wicked, however, have no hope for the future and their sufferings are punishments and they begin even in this life.

1. *in the hand of God:* Under his protection (cf. Deut 33:3; Isa 62:3). *torment:* After death (cf. 4:19). **2.** *affliction:* Cf. Isa 53:4. **3.** *peace:* See Isa 57:1–2. The author is vague on the state of the souls of the just immediately after death (→ 6 above). They probably are thought to be with God and the angelic court (5:5). **4.** *punished:* Their sufferings in life appear to many to be punishments, but they are really education (cf. vv 5–6). *hope:* During their earthly life. *immortality:* Again, eternal life with God; the first occurrence of this noun in the OT. **5–6.** *chastised, proved:* The author takes up the lead of Deut 8:2–5; Prov 3:11–12; Sir 2:1–6; 4:17–19. **6.** *sacrificial offerings:* The idea was suggested by Isa 53:7–10. **7.** *visitation:* A biblical term (cf. Isa 10:3, etc.) meaning a divine intervention, here referring to divine judgment probably immediately after death (→ 6 above). *shine, sparks:* Images of triumph (Obad 8; Dan 12:3). **8.** *judge:* Synonymous with "rule"; for the allusion, cf. Dan 7:18–27. *nations, peoples:* The author does not identify them. Many Jews hoped for the rule of Israel over the rest of the nations in the messianic age. Perhaps this image is used here to express the triumph of the just over the wicked. **9.** *truth:* Probably the knowledge of God and of heavenly wisdom (cf. 1QS 4:22). **10.** *punishment to match their thoughts:* Compare their punishment in v 11 with their thoughts in 2:1–5. **11a.** Cf. Prov 1:7. **11b–12.** The ideas of offspring, length of days, and fruit seem to be from Isa 53:10–11 (cf. Isa 65:23) and are applied to the wicked in accordance with the traditional thought (cf. Prov 10–11; Sir 41:5–10; etc.). **12.** *foolish:* Folly is the equivalent of wickedness in the sapiential books (cf. 1:3). *children wicked:* Because of the example of their parents.

16 (ii) *Childlessness* (3:13–4:6). *Inclusio: wicked-(ness),* 3:14 and 4:6; *fruit,* 3:13 and 4:5. The traditional view was that children are a sign of God's favor and sterility a curse, esp. inasmuch as one's hopes for immortality dwelled above all in the memory of one's children. The author, taking up Isa 54:1ff.; 56:2–5 and Sir 16:1–3, submits that the true and lasting fruit of life is virtue and not children, and that the numerous progeny of the wicked, seemingly a blessing, will in fact be a disappointing fruit and good for nothing. The thought is developed in four paragraphs arranged in a chiasm. (a) The barren, if virtuous, are not a dry tree, but their virtue will bear fruit and have an unfailing root (3:13–15). (b) Children of the wicked will not be honored and have no hope of immortality (3:16-19). (b') Better to be childless with virtue, for virtue is honored by all and is rewarded with immortality (4:1-2). (a') The children of the wicked are trees which lack deep root and which bear useless fruit (4:3-6).

13. A transfer to the individual order of the promises made to Jerusalem in Isa 54:1ff. *childless:* Not celibacy but sterility. *transgression:* The adultery theme throughout this passage seems to refer to all sinfulness (as frequently in OT) and is here inspired by Isa 57:3. *visitation of souls:* The judgment at death (→ 6 above). **14.** The author sees Isa 56:2-5 (the eunuch is not a dry tree) as being fulfilled in the spiritual order at the judgment. *more gratifying:* Than sons and daughters (cf. Isa 56:5). **15.** *root of understanding:* The root that is understanding (wisdom). The image of the tree for the just and wicked here and in 4:3-5 is common in OT and here is based on Prov 11:30; 12:12. **16.** *remain without issue:* Better: "will not reach maturity." **18.** *day of scrutiny:* The judgment at death (→ 6 above). **4:1.** *immortal:* In two senses — fame with posterity and life with God. **3-5.** Cf. Sir 23:25; Isa 40:24. **6.** The verse is unclear. The children's misfortunes of vv 3-5 will suggest a parental sin (according to a popular view of things; cf. Sir 41:5-7; John 9:2) when the children (and the parents?) are scrutinized by people at the time of the misfortunes (and by God at the judgment?).

17 (iii) *Early death* (4:7-19). *Inclusio: honorable/dishonored,* 4:8,19. The traditional view of retribution was that the wicked die young and the just are blessed with an honorable old age. The author, however, observes that an early death is no evil for the just because the true "old age" that is honorable is really virtue, and, as in the case of Enoch, God may snatch the just from the world before their time to preserve them from contamination. But the old age and death of the wicked will not be honorable.

7. The author has moved on to Isa 57:1-2 LXX; cf. also Isa 65:20-23. **9.** Cf. Prov 16:31. *understanding:* Wisdom. **10.** Enoch (Gen 5:21-24), young by patriarchal standards. **14.** Cf. Isa 57:1. *people:* The wicked. **15.** For the omission of v 15 in the *NAB,* see A. G. Wright, *CBQ* 29 (1967) 221. **16.** *condemns:* Will provide a standard of comparison, which will end with the condemnation of the wicked. There may be an allusion to 2:20. **19.** A description of the fate of the wicked after death in imagery from Isa 14:16-19; 19:10; 66:24.

18 (b') THE JUDGMENT (SPEECH OF THE WICKED) (4:20-5:23). *Inclusio: lawless(ness),* 4:20 and 5:23; *confront,* 5:1 and 23. When they die (→ 6 above) the wicked will behold the salvation of the just (4:20-5:3a). In a speech that parallels that of chap. 2, they acknowledge the error of their evaluation of the just as well as the error of their way of life, which has left them with nothing, esp. with no sign of virtue (5:3b-13; *inclusio: held,* 3 and 13). The author this time concurs with the statements of the wicked and describes the reward of the just in a picture that develops into an apocalyptic description of God's destruction of evil (vv 14-23; *inclusio: tempest,* 14 and 23).

4:20-5:7. The author has moved on to Isa 59:6-14. **5:5** *sons of God, saints:* The angels (cf. 1QS 11:7-8; 1QH 3:19-23). Wis pictures the reward of the just in terms of an association with, or assimilation to, the angels. **6-7.** Cf. Isa 59:8-9. *impassable:* Better "trackless"; they went their own way and not the way of the Lord. **10-11.** *ship . . . bird:* Cf. Job 9:25-26 LXX. **15-16.** For the imagery, cf. Isa 62:3,11; similarly 1QS 4:6-8. **17-23.** Cf. Isa 59:16-19; 60:12; 13:5-9. The divine warrior lays waste the earth, a standard apocalyptic theme. There is, however, no mention here of the rest of the usual

scenario, the renewal of creation (→ 6 above). **17** *foes:* The last generation of the wicked. **23.** *thrones:* A transition to the next section.

19 (a') EXHORTATION TO SEEK WISDOM (6:1-21). *Inclusio: kings,* 6:1,21. The author resumes the direct address of 1:1 and concludes this section of the book with a warning of impending judgment (vv 1-8; *inclusio: power,* 2 and 8; *scrutinize/scrutiny,* 3 and 8), an exhortation to hear his words (vv 9-11; *inclusio: my words,* 9 and 11), a statement on the accessibility of wisdom (vv 12-16; *inclusio: seek[ing],* 12 and 16), and a sorites, which shows how the search for wisdom leads to immortality and an eternal reign (vv 17-21; *inclusio: desire,* 17 and 20).

1. *kings:* See comment on 1:1. **4.** *ministers of his kingdom:* In that their dominion is from God. *judged:* Ruled. *Law:* Of Moses (cf. v 10). **5-6.** Cf. Moses (Num 20:12) and David (2 Sam 24:10-17). **10.** *learned:* Not a mere intellectual knowledge but also a vital inner correspondence. *response:* A defense at the scrutiny. **12.** Cf. Prov 3:15 LXX; 8:17. *resplendent:* Because of her divine origin (cf. 7:26). *Wisdom:* For the personification of Wisdom, see comment on 1:4. **13-16.** Cf. Prov 1:20-21; 8:1-36. **15.** *free from care:* Like Wisdom herself (7:23). **20.** One step in the sorites is to be supplied from 3:7-8: To be close to God is to reign. Here, again, Wis transposes the traditional teaching of the sages. For them, wisdom and justice assured the stability of an earthly throne (Prov 16:12; 20:28; etc.), but the reign of which our author speaks is eschatological.

20 (B) **The Nature of Wisdom and Solomon's Quest for Her (6:22-11:1).** In this section, the author, identifying himself with Solomon, praises the beauty of Wisdom and describes how he sought her out. After a brief introduction (6:22-25), Solomon's speech (7:1-8:21) is presented in seven paragraphs arranged concentrically with the description of Wisdom in the central paragraph (7:22b-8:1). At the end, and standing outside of this structure, are Solomon's prayer (chap. 9) and a transitional section (10:1-11:1), which leads into the second half of the book. In these chapters the relationship between Solomon and Wisdom is set forth as a model for all the wise, so that the readers of the book will take the proper steps to become the true rulers of the earth (1:1). On the figure of Solomon in these chapters, see M. Gilbert, *Études sur le judaïsme hellénistique* (ed. R. Kuntzmann, *et al.;* LD 119; Paris, 1984) 225-49; Reese, *Hellenistic Influence* 71-87.

21 (a) INTRODUCTION (6:22-25). The author announces the subject matter of chaps. 7-10 and his desire to share with others the mysteries of Wisdom. **22.** *how she came to be:* The author probably has in mind 7:25-26 (cf. the similar brief treatment of Wisdom's origin in Prov and Job), but the bulk of his attention will be on the effects of Wisdom, esp. in Solomon's life. *secrets:* The origin of Wisdom (cf. Job 28:20ff.), the knowledge of which has been given to the heavenly assembly (Sir 24:1ff.); also the teachings and blessings that she imparts. *beginning:* Gk *archē geneseōs,* either the beginning of Wisdom (7:25-26), or of creation (chap. 10), or of Solomon's life (the same two words occur in this sense in 7:5). **23.** *jealousy:* Possibly a gibe at the pagan mystery religions and philosophers that kept their teachings for the select few. **24.** Cf. Prov 11:14; Sir 10:1-3; Wis 10, where Wisdom saves her own.

22 (b) SOLOMON'S SPEECH (7:1-8:21). (i) *Solomon is like other men* (7:1-6). *Inclusio: all; same,* 7:1,6. Solomon was not especially disposed by birth toward wisdom but had the same origin as all others. **1.** *mortal:* In sharp contrast to the divine origin claimed by rulers. **2.** *ten months:* Lunar months. **3.** *kindred:*

Not that Solomon and the earth were related, but rather Solomon and other mortals.

23 (ii) *Solomon prayed and Wisdom and riches came to him (7:7– 12). Inclusio: came to me, 7:7,11; riches, 7:8,11.* Solomon preferred Wisdom over power, riches, health, comeliness, and light. He prayed for her and Wisdom came to him with all these good things besides, much to Solomon's joy. **7.** *prayed:* Cf. 1 Kgs 3:6–9; 2 Chr 1:8–10. The author's version of the prayer is given in Wis 9. *prudence:* Understanding; the spirit of wisdom of the following stich (synonymous parallelism). **10.** *never yields to sleep:* Wisdom never ceases to exist. Cf. 7:29–30.

24 (iii) *Solomon prays for help to speak of wisdom (7:13–22a). Inclusio: hide/hidden,* 13 and 21. Once again, Solomon expresses his desire to share what he has learned about Wisdom for the benefit of humanity, but, before beginning his description of her, he asks for help from God who gave him his encyclopedic knowledge. **14.** *discipline:* Wisdom is the spirit of discipline (1:5). **17–20.** Embellishing on the Solomonic material in 1 Kgs 4:32–34, the author attributes to Solomon a knowledge of those sciences that were the special pursuit of the Hellenistic world. **17.** *elements:* The four constitutive elements of the world, according to the Greeks, were fire, water, air, and earth. **18.** *beginning, end, and midpoint of times:* The line is so indefinite that it is impossible to be sure of its meaning. Perhaps it is a poetic expression for the knowledge requisite for constructing an astronomical calendar. **19.** *cycles of years:* Perhaps an allusion to the 19-year lunar cycle of Meton of Athens. **20.** *natures of animals and tempers of beasts:* Solomon is supposed to have known the ways and habits of animals and to have spoken parables about all sorts of living creatures (cf. 1 Kgs 4:32–34) *human thoughts:* Not the thoughts of human hearts, which are known only to God, but the way the human mind works—its reasonings, plottings, and tricks. **22.** *Wisdom taught:* Wisdom is identical with God (v 17; see comment on 1:4).

25 (iv) *The nature of Wisdom (7:22b–8:1).* This central of the seven paragraphs begins with an enumeration of 21 (7 [perfection] × 3 [the divine number] = 21 [absolute perfection]) characteristics of Wisdom (7:22b–23; *inclusio: spirit, intelligent, subtle,* 7:22,23). The author then singles out two of these characteristics for further comment. Wisdom is mobile because of her purity and divine origin. She is omnipotent in producing holiness because she is fairer than the sun and wickedness cannot prevail over her (7:24–8:1; *inclusio: all,* 7:24 and 8:1; note the use of the stem *[pas]* seven times in these verses). **22–23.** For the personification of Wisdom, see comment on 1:4. Much of the terminology here and in the rest of the paragraph is borrowed from Gk philosophy and religion, where these qualities are attributed to Isis, the pagan goddess of wisdom, and to a world soul or Logos (→ 7 above for bibliography). In using this vocabulary, the author wishes to show that it is really the divine Wisdom that possesses these attributes. It is not always easy to define precisely the meaning of each attribute, esp. inasmuch as the author has sometimes repeated himself to arrive at the number 21. *there is in her a spirit:* The mode of expression results from the author's personification of Wisdom. The attributes of this "spirit" are the attributes of Wisdom. *holy:* Because of Wisdom's origin (7:25–26), her avoidance of evil (1:5), and the holiness she produces (7:27). *manifold:* In her manifestations and activity, even though she is one (unique). *subtle:* Spiritual, immaterial. *clear:* In utterance (cf. the same word in 10:21). *unstained:* Despite her contact with the beings she pervades. *certain:* As a moral guide. *keen, unhampered:* In penetrating. *firm, secure, tranquil:* Because she is unchanging in her plans, unerring, and unable to

be hindered. **24.** *by reason of her purity:* Metaphysical rather than moral purity; there is in her nothing gross or of the earth as the following lines show. **25–26.** The author, enlarging on Prov 8 and Sir 24, seeks the most immaterial images possible to describe the origin and divinity of Wisdom. **27.** *renews:* Apparently one generation after another. Cf. Pss 104:30; 102:26–27. **29.** *fairer:* A moral purity. *she takes precedence:* The text should be emended to, "she is found more brilliant" (Ziegler). **8:1.** *end to end:* Of the universe. *governs well:* Because of her goodness.

26 (iii) *Solomon sought Wisdom, the source of knowledge (8:2–8). Inclusio: understand(ing),* 8:4,8. Solomon returns to the subject of his quest for Wisdom. He sought her as his bride, for she instructs in knowledge. She is God's friend and collaborator; she gives wealth and skill; she teaches the four cardinal virtues of Plato (*Laws* 631) and the Stoics, the knowledge of past and future, the understanding of the utterances of the sages. **3.** *nobility:* Wisdom's nobility of origin. *companionship:* The term (*symbiosis*) is normally used of marriage; it is found in this sense in vv 9 and 16 to describe the marriage with Wisdom that Solomon sought. Unless each element of the symbolism is to be taken separately, the term here must refer simply to Wisdom's association with God (cf. 9:9). **4.** *for:* Refers to "sought" in v 2. *understanding of god:* The knowledge that God possesses. *selector of his works:* The author conceives of God as giving Wisdom a voice in choosing what his works should be. **5.** *produces:* The Gk vb. *ergazesthai* also means to make money from something; apparently both meanings are intended here (cf. 7:11; 14:2; Prov 8:18). **6.** *prudence:* Practical intelligence. **7.** *justice:* In the first stich, it designates the ensemble of all the virtues; in the fourth, the cardinal virtue. *works:* Labors. **8.** *turns of phrases . . . solution of riddles:* The wisdom of the ancients found in maxims and stories (cf. Prov 1:6; Sir 39:2–3). *signs and wonders:* Eclipses, storms, and earthquakes. *outcome of times and ages:* The course of history.

27 (ii') *Solomon sought Wisdom as his counselor and comfort (8:9–16). Inclusio: life/living with,* 8:9,16. Through Wisdom's counsel, Solomon would have glory in life and be remembered in death, for he would be wise and would be a noble and brave king; his private life would be serene. **12.** *hands upon their mouths:* A gesture of respectful silence (cf. Job 29:9). **13.** *immortality:* In the memory of posterity, as in the previous OT books.

28 (i') *Solomon realizes that Wisdom is a gift of God (8:17–21). Inclusio: my heart,* 8:17,21. In view of all the blessings that come from Wisdom's company, Solomon went about seeking her for his own. He was of noble birth, but he knew that Wisdom came not with nobility but was a gift of God; therefore, he went to the Lord and besought him. **17.** *heart:* The seat of the intellect for the Hebrews. *immortality:* Apparently in the sense of v 13, for these lines recapitulate 8:2–16. **20.** Some have proposed that the author here espouses the Gk doctrine of the preexistence of the human soul. Taken in itself, the verse could appear to reflect such an idea, but it should be read in the context of the whole book. According to the Gk doctrine, the preexistent soul is sullied by its contact with the body and seeks deliverance through death. Our author's remarks on created things (1:14) and on the possibility of an "unsullied body" (7:20) and a "soul that plots evil" (1:4) show how foreign these ideas are to him. Moreover, in the present context the author is not concerned with the preexistence of the soul but rather with the preeminence of the soul (correcting v 19, which appears to give priority to the body). *unsullied:* Matching his noble nature. The question of original sin lies outside the author's view.

29 (c) SOLOMON'S PRAYER FOR WISDOM (9:1–18). *Inclusio: wisdom; human being/beings,* 2 and 18.) The author presents his version of Solomon's prayer (cf. 1 Kgs 3:6–9; 2 Chr 1:8–10). The prayer is divided into three strophes arranged concentrically: (a) vv 1–6; (b) vv 7–12; (a′) vv 13–18, and each strophe is itself constructed concentrically (see the paraphrases which follow). In the first strophe, God, who has created human beings to rule over creation, is asked to give Solomon Wisdom because he is a human being and therefore weak and lacking in understanding (*inclusio: wisdom; human being/beings,* 2 and 6). In the second strophe, God, who has chosen Solomon to rule over his people and who has with him Wisdom who knows what is pleasing to God, is asked to send Wisdom, so that she may be with Solomon and disclose what is pleasing to God, so that Solomon may rule over god's people justly (*inclusio: your people,* 7 and 12). In the third strophe, Solomon reflects that no human knows God's counsel because our understanding is feeble. We are subject to physical weakness. With difficulty we understand what is on earth let alone what is in heaven. Unless God gives Wisdom, we will not know God's counsel, as history shows (*inclusio: know counsel,* 13 and 17; *human being/beings,* 13 and 18). For a detailed discussion of the prayer, see M. Gilbert, *Bib* 51 (1970) 301–31.

1. *God of my fathers:* An appeal to God's fidelity to the promises made to the patriarchs and to David. *word:* The creative Word of God (cf. Gen 1; Ps 33:6) is here identified with Wisdom. **2.** *to rule:* Cf. Gen 1:26–28. **4.** *attendant at your throne:* Cf. Prov 8:27–30. *reject:* Solomon deprecates a fate that he knows must befall him if he thinks to dispense with Wisdom. The terminology is reminiscent of Ps 89:38. **8.** *copy:* The Chronicler represents David as having received from God a detailed account of the Temple, which he passed on to Solomon (1 Chr 28:11–19). The holy tabernacle that Solomon was meant to copy is not the tabernacle of Moses but an ideal archetype, which the writer pictures as existing in heaven (for the same concept, cf. Heb 8:2,5; 9:23). **9.** Cf. Prov 3:19–20; 8:22–30. **11.** *by her glory:* By her power. The divine glory is the manifestation of God's power and attributes. **14.** *timid:* Uncertain. **15.** This verse, reminiscent of Plato (*Phaedo* 81c), has caused the author to be falsely accused of a dualism, which pronounces matter evil. In fact he simply states that our deliberations are weak (v 14) and earthbound (v 16) because of the body and its concerns. **17.** *counsel:* Gk *boulē* here and in v 13 is probably not the plan of God, but what God wishes people to do. See M. Gilbert, *NRT* 93 (1971) 145–66. *holy spirit: Inclusio* with 1:5. See comment on 1:4. **18.** An announcement of the next section.

30 (d) TRANSITIONAL SECTION: WISDOM SAVES HER OWN (10:1–11:1). In this transitional section which leads into the second half of the book, the author expands on 9:18 and shows how Wisdom has saved people throughout history: the whole race in Adam and Noah (10:1– 4); Abraham (v 5); Lot (vv 6–9); Jacob (vv 10–12); Joseph (vv 13–14); and the people of Israel (10:15–11:1). The paragraphs are not marked off with *inclusios* as elsewhere but with the emphatic pronoun *autē* (she) at the beginning of each paragraph (10:1,5,6,10,13, 15). Following his usual custom (→ 8 above), the author does not name the individuals discussed but merely refers to each as "the just" (10:4,5,6,10,13,20). Throughout this section, as well as in the second part of the book (chaps. 11–19), we find the sacred history embellished with imaginative details and with popular traditions, which we find elsewhere in Philo, Josephus, and the targums. On the chapter, see A. Schmitt, *BZ* 21 (1977) 1–22.

1. *father:* Adam. *he alone:* Before the creation of Eve. *raised him up:* Vague; perhaps by giving him repentance or by giving him the power spoken of in v 2. *his fall:* In the Greek, "his own fall"; neither Wisdom nor Eve was to blame. **2.** *power to rule:* To carry on the mandate received before the fall (Gen 1:26,28) in the face of a hostile environment (Gen 3:14–15,17– 19) and rebellious animals (cf. *Apoc. Mos.* 11; 24). **3.** *unjust man:* Cain (Gen 4:8–13). *perished:* Perhaps the legend that his house fell upon him and he was killed by a stone, in return for having killed Abel with a stone (cf. *Jub.* 4:31). **4.** *on his account:* The wickedness that brought the flood is attributed to Cain instead of to the "sons of God" (Gen 6:4–6). The wickedness of Cain's descendants is a Jewish tradition (Josephus, *Ant.* 1.2.2 §66) not found in the Bible. *again:* She saved the race the first time by preserving Adam (v 1). *just man:* Noah. **5.** *universal wickedness:* The allusion is to the tower of Babel (Gen 11:1–9). *just man:* Abraham. *pity for his child:* When God commanded him to sacrifice Isaac (Gen 22:1–19). **6.** *just man:* Lot (Gen 19). *Pentapolis:* The five cities of the plain: Sodom, Gomorrah, Admah, Zeboiim, and Bela (or Zoar; Gen 14:2). **7.** *smoking desert:* A legendary exaggeration prompted perhaps by mists rising from the Dead Sea basin or smoke from the bituminous soil. *fruit:* Apparently the "apples of Sodom" referred to by Josephus (*J.W.* 4.8.4 §483–485)—a fruit of the area seemingly fit to be eaten, but with a black, powdery interior. *pillar of salt:* Cf. Gen 19:26. **8–9.** These verses divide the poem into two parts: the rare just men in a wicked world (vv 1–7); Jacob, Joseph, and Israel in a new age (10:10–11:1). The pls. here very likely refer to all that has gone before by way of summary, and not just to the Sodom affair. **8.** *those who forsook:* Adam, Cain, the nations, and the Sodomites. *memorial:* Death, the flood, the tower of Babel, the ruins of Sodom. **9.** *those who served:* Adam, Noah, Abraham, and Lot. **10.** *just man:* Jacob, who fled from his brother Esau (Gen 27:41–28:10). *showed him:* In the dream at Bethel (Gen 28:10–17). *kingdom of God:* Although found in the intertestamental literature, this important NT phrase occurs only here in the OT. Here it is localized in heaven, an unusual usage (→ 6 above; see D. S. Russell, *The Method and Message of Jewish Apocalyptic* [OTL; Phl 1964] 285–91; N. Perrin, *The Kingdom of God in the Teaching of Jesus* [NTL; Phl, 1963] 160–81). *holy things:* Perhaps heavenly realities in general; or perhaps the heavenly sanctuary (9:8; see E. Burrows, *Bib* 20 [1939] 405–7). **11.** *defrauders, enriched:* The allusion is to Jacob's stay with Laban (Gen 29:1–31:21). **12** *foes:* Perhaps Laban and his brothers (Gen 31:23–29) or Esau (*Jub.* 37–38). *struggle:* At the Jabbok (Gen 32:22–32). **13.** *just man:* Joseph (Gen 37–41). **14.** *glory:* Undying fame. **15.** *blameless:* Holy insofar as they were chosen and set apart by God. The author overlooks Israel's infidelities to her vocation. **16.** *Lord's servant:* Moses. *kings:* The pl. is puzzling if the reference is to Pharaoh, but cf. Ps 105:30, where the pl. is likewise used. However, perhaps the kings outside Egypt are included. **17.** *recompense:* The precious objects of the Egyptians (Exod 3:21–22; 11:2–3; 12:35–36) and liberation from slavery were Israel's recompense for its slave labor. *shelter:* The cloud was thought of not only as a guide but also as a protection from the heat (cf. Ps 105:39; Isa 4:5–6). **20.** *despoiled:* The despoiling of dead Egyptians at the Red Sea is not in the Exod account but is a tradition found in Josephus (*Ant.* 2.16.6 §349; 3.1.4 §17–18). *sang:* The allusion is to the Song of Miriam (Exod 15). **21.** *opened the mouths of the dumb . . . speech to infants:* A targumic legend (see P. Grelot, *Bib* 42 [1961] 49–60). **11:1.** *prophet:* Moses.

31 (II) **God's Fidelity to His People in the Exodus (11:2–19:22).** The second half of Wis is a homily on the exodus, done in the form of an apostrophe to God. The homily recalls for the Alexandrian Jews that once before the Jews had suffered in Egypt and the Lord came to their rescue; it thus provides an historical basis for trust in God. Because the homily has a theme in common with chaps. 1–6 (retribution for the just and the wicked), and because it has been deliberately paralleled with chaps. 1–6 by the author (→ 8 above), it also has an eschatological dimension: The exodus events are recounted as an image of God's final intervention on behalf of the just. The idea is explicit in 17:21.

The work takes its departure from a short summary of the biblical narrative of Israel's desert wanderings (11:2–4), after which one is perhaps expected to supply mentally an *et reliqua.* The author next states a pattern that he detects in the exodus events: the Israelites were benefited by the very things that punished the Egyptians (11:5), and then, in a *synkrisis* or comparison (on this Gk figure, see F. Focke, *Hermes* 58 [1923] 327–68), he illustrates this observation in five antithetical diptychs (11:6–19:22). In the homily there is, on the one hand, a careful attention to the details of the biblical account and a desire to explain the reasons for happenings (11:8; 16:3–4,6–8) and to draw out applications for the present (e.g., 16:26,28; 19:22); on the other hand, the biblical material is handled creatively: details are altered to fit the purposes of the author and events are idealized and even embellished upon with legendary and imaginative material to make them more ample, vivid, and edifying (cf. esp. the description of the plague of darkness in chap. 17).

(On chaps. 11–19: Camps, G. M., in *Miscellanea biblica B. Ubach* [Montserrat, 1953] 97–113. Heinemann, I., *TZ* 4 [1948] 241–52. Kuhn, G., *ZNW* 28 [1929] 334–41. Siebeneck, R. T., *CBQ* 22 [1960] 176–82. Stein, E., *MGWJ* 78 [1934] 558–75. Wright, A. G., *Bib* 48 [1967] 176–84.)

32   (A) Introductory Narrative (11:2–4). The homily begins with a brief account of Israel's desert wanderings, which is partly dependent, as are several features of the homily, on Ps 107, apparently understood by the writer as referring to the exodus. **2.** *they:* Throughout the composition the author avoids proper names (→ 8 above). **3.** *enemies:* The biblical account mentions the Amalekites (Exod 17:8–16), Arad, Sihon, and Og (Num 21) and the Midianites (Num 31:1–12). **4.** *thirsted:* Cf. Exod 17:1–17; Num 20:2–13. *they called upon you:* The writer ignores Israel's murmurings and presents an idealized version suggested by Ps 107:6.

33   (B) Theme: Israel Is Benefited by the Very Things That Punish Egypt (11:5). Apropos of the mention of the water from the rock, the author makes an observation on the exodus events that will be the theme of the homily: the Israelites were benefited by the very things that punished the Egyptians. The idea also appears in Philo (*De vita Mos.* 1.143).

34   (C) Illustration of the Theme in Five Antithetical Diptychs (11:6–19:22). Immediately after the statement of the theme, the author proceeds not with a continuation of the narrative of 11:2–4 but with the first of his contrasts. The preposition *anti,* "instead of," serves as the "hinge" of the first four diptychs (11:6; 16:2; 16:20; 18:3).

35   (a) FIRST DIPTYCH: WATER FROM THE ROCK INSTEAD OF THE PLAGUE OF THE NILE (11:6–14). *Inclusio: thirst,* 11:8,14. Water punishes the Egyptians (cf. Exod 7:17–24) and benefits Israel (cf. Exod 17:5–7; Num 20:8–11) in the desert (vv 6–7). The Israelites thirsted in the desert as did the Egyptians during the plague, but for Israel it was only a test and to show them how their enemies were punished (vv 8–11). For the Egyptians, the news of Israel's good fortune added to their grief (vv 12–14). **6.** *instead of a spring:* The *NAB* envisions the wells

the Egyptians dug to get water when the Nile was turned into blood (Exod 7:24) and contrasts this meager source with the abundance of water granted to Israel. It is also possible to translate "instead of a river's perennial source troubled with impure blood," in which case the contrast is punishment by water vs. blessing by water. **7.** *decree:* According to Exod 7:14–24, the purpose of this plague was to induce Pharaoh to let Israel go; Wis sees the plague as a punishment for Pharaoh's decree of Exod 1:16,22. *gave them:* The Israelites. **8–9.** In Deut 8:2–5, Israel's sufferings in the desert are interpreted as a testing, and so also below in v 10, but here Wis gives an additional reason for the thirst. *punish, chastise:* A repetition of the theme of 3:4–10 (cf. also 12:22). **9.** *being tormented:* The author envisions some of the plagues in Egypt as continuing during Israel's desert journey (cf. 16:4,22). **11–10.** For the transposition of verses in the *NAB,* see P. W. Skehan, *SIPW* 132–33. **11.** *those afar off and those close by:* From the point of view of Israel in the desert. **12.** *twofold grief:* Perhaps the memory of their suffering is doubled by their recognition that Yahweh had triumphed over the gods of Egypt; or perhaps the twofold grief is the recognition of Yahweh (v 13) and of the success of Moses (v 14). **13.** The writer assumes that the Egyptians are being informed of the desert events, as also in 16:8; (cf. Exod 32:12; Num 14:13; Deut 9:28). **14.** *proved unlike:* The Egyptians had no relief for their thirst (or cf. v 10).

36   (b) SECOND DIPTYCH: QUAIL INSTEAD OF THE PLAGUE OF LITTLE ANIMALS (11:15–16:15). The diptych is presented in three passages (11:15–16; 12:23–27; 15:18–16:4), each of which is followed by a digression (→ 10 above).

(i) (11:15–16) *plus digression on God's power and mercy (11:17– 12:22).* The diptych begins by recalling the plagues of little animals, which were sent upon the Egyptians, according to the author, as a punishment for worship of animals (11:15–16). **15.** *serpents:* The crocodile, serpent, lizard, and frog were worshiped in Egypt. *insects:* Beetles, scarabs. *dumb creatures:* Frogs (Exod 8:1–15), gnats (Exod 8:16–19), flies (Exod 8:20–24), and locusts (Exod 10:3–15). The verse is an echo of 1:5. **16.** The idea, familiar from Pss 7:15–16; 57:6; Prov 26:27; 2 Macc 9:6; *Jub.* 4:32, is a truth of experience but not an absolute principle.

37 The digression on God's power and mercy, prompted by the mention of punishment for sin in 11:6, is divided in two parts: (1) God is merciful because he loves (11:17–12:8); (2) God is just and lenient because he is master of his might (12:9–22). The three strophes of the first part are matched by three closely paralleled strophes in the second part (see the paraphrases that follow).

38   (1) God is merciful because he loves (11:17–12:8). (a) God did not lack the means to kill the Egyptians with terrible beasts, for God is all-powerful and none can oppose him (11:17–22; *inclusio: universe,* 17 and 22). (b) But he has mercy because he loves his creatures and gives them a chance to repent (11:23–12:2; *inclusio: sins,* 11:23 and 12:2). (c) When he gave the holy land to his children, he even offered the Canaanites a chance to repent because they too were his creatures (12:3–8; *inclusio: land,* 3 and 7).

39   (2) God is just and lenient because he is master of his might (12:9–22). (a) God did not lack the means to kill the Canaanites immediately with terrible beasts; nor was he ignorant of their inborn wickedness; nor was he afraid of anyone, for there is no god or king to oppose him (12:9–14; *inclusio: condemn,* 10 and 13). (b) But he governs with justice and lenience because he is master of his might (12:15–18; *inclusio: master*[y]; *lenient/lenience;*

might, 16 and 18). (c) By the way he treats their enemies God teaches his children to temper justice with mercy and to hope for mercy from him (12:19–22; *inclusio: your sons,* 19 and 21; *enemies,* 20 and 22).

40   **11:17.** *formless matter:* An allusion to the primeval chaos of Gen 1:2 in Aristotelian categories of matter and form. **20.** *measure, number, and weight:* God will not unnecessarily interfere with the regular course of nature (cf. 4 Ezra 4:36–37). **21.** *for:* Refers to vv 17–20. *great strength abides:* Even though he did not use it. (On 11:21–12:2, see M. Gilbert, *Mélanges bibliques et orientaux* [Fest. H. Cazelles; ed. A. Caquot, *et al.*; AOAT 212; Neukirchen, 1981] 149–62.) **22.** *grain:* A tiny particle used for weighing in scales. **23.** *you can do all things:* He can be merciful too. **24–26.** God would not have created and preserved what he did not love, and since all things are his and he loves them, he pardons and is patient. **12:1.** *imperishable spirit:* Either Wisdom as the agent of God's immanence (1:7; 7:24; 8:1) or the breath of life put in creatures by God (Gen 2:7; Wis 15:11). *hated:* Manifestly in a different sense than in 11:24; the word here expresses God's antagonism toward sin. **4–5.** *works of witchcraft, etc.:* Cf. Deut 18:9–12. **5.** For a discussion of the damaged text and the rearrangement of stichs in the *NAB,* see P. W. Skehan, *SIPW* 133–34. **6.** *willed to destroy:* Cf. Num 33:52. **8.** *wasps:* Cf. Exod 23:28; Deut 7:20; Josh 24:12. **10.** *for repentance:* Other opinions for God's gradual condemnation of the Canaanites are offered in Exod 23:29 (cf. Deut 7:22); Judg 2:22; 3:1–2. *accursed:* Probably an allusion to Gen 9:25. **16.** *might is the source of justice:* Cf. 2:11, where the wicked say that their might is the norm of justice. Unlike the wicked, whose weakness and insecurity prompt them to use unjustly what strength they have, God, being all-powerful and unchallenged, experiences no disturbed moral equilibrium and is therefore just and even merciful. **17.** *disbelieved . . . those who know you:* Reminiscent of Pharaoh (cf. 12:27; Exod 5:2; 10:16; 14:4,18) but true of anyone. **18.** *power:* God's might as well as his ability to control it. **19.** *these deeds:* Cf. vv 18 and 20. **20.** *enemies . . . doomed to death:* In the Greek, two groups: "enemies" (the Egyptians) and "those doomed to death" (the Canaanites). **21.** *exactitude:* Of leniency, not severity. *fathers:* The patriarchs. **22.** *thousand blows* (*myriotēti*): The idea fits the context poorly; the text should probably be emended to *metriotēti,* "with moderation"; and "you chastise" (*paideuōn*) should probably be translated "you instruct" (see A. Vanhoye, *RSR* 50 [1962] 530–37; M. Gilbert, *Bib* 57 [1976] 550–53).

41   (ii) (*12:23–27*) *plus digression on false worship* (13:1–15:17). Having concluded the first digression, the author returns to the Egyptian "panel" of the second diptych. **25.** The Egyptians were treated as if they were children. If children worshiped animals, their animals should make sport of them. *mockery:* Not a mock punishment but a real one that made both gods and people ridiculous. **26–27.** The Egyptians took no heed of the plagues of animals (the child's play). They did, however, come to recognize the true God (Exod 10:16), but, continuing to oppose him, they experienced the final condemnation: the death of their firstborn and the destruction of their army in the Red Sea.

42   Apropos of the Egyptians' failure and success in recognizing the true God, the author digresses once again, this time on false worship. He divides such worshipers into two groups: those who worship nature and those who worship idols. The digression is structured as follows:

(1) Nature worship (13:1–9)
(2) Idolatry (13:10–15:17)

(a) Introduction (13:10)
(b) The carpenter and wooden images (13:11–14:2)
(c) Apostrophe (14:3–6) and transition (14:7–11)
(d) The origin and evils of idolatry (14:12–31)
(c') Apostrophe (15:1–3) and transition (15:4–6)
(b') The potter and clay images (15:7–13)
(a') Conclusion (15:14–17)

(On the digression, see M. Gilbert, *La critique des dieux dans le livre de la Sagesse* [AnBib 53; Rome, 1973]).

43   (1) *Nature worship* (13:1–9). *Inclusio: succeed in knowing,* 13:1,9. Foolish were all who failed to know God from studying his works and who considered the works themselves as gods. The works are great and mighty, but he who made them is exceedingly so and he can be known through these works. Such nature worshipers are well intentioned and look in the right direction; therefore, they are less blameworthy than others. But, because of their superficial use of their intelligence, they are not to be excused entirely. The writer is not presenting an argument for the existence of God. As a Hebrew, he does not even conceive of the pure atheist. That God exists is a fact; it is identifying him that poses a problem. The section is unique in the OT. Israel's knowledge of God was derived not from rational arguments but from the experience of God's saving acts on Israel's behalf. The Greeks, on the other hand, strove to know God in a philosophical manner, and here our author acknowledges this approach, too, as a valid way to know the true God of Israel. The idea is taken up again by Paul in Rom 1:19–25. **1.** *by nature:* Either "not illuminated by wisdom," or, as we say, "born foolish." *him who is:* An allusion to the Hebr name of God in Exod 3:14, but perhaps, under Platonic influence, it also expresses here the idea of God as absolute being and pure existence, something not contained in the Exod text. **2.** *governors of the world:* Cf. Gen 1:16. (On this section, see C. Larcher, *LumVie* 14 [1954] 197–206).

44   (2) *Idolatry* (13:10–15:17). *Inclusio: dead things; hands; made/makes,* 13:10 and 15:17. Our author next launches into a satire on idols inspired by Isa, Deut, Hos, Jer, and Pss. The central section of the digression attacks idolatry as being of human origin and the source of all evil (14:12–31); it is bracketed by a satirical depiction of a carpenter and wooden idols (13:11–14:2) and of a potter and clay idols (15:7–13).

45   (a) *Introduction* (13:10). *Inclusio: work(s); hand(s).* Much more miserable than nature worshipers are those who put their hope in lifeless, handmade idols. *useless stone, the work of an ancient hand:* Probably a sacred meteorite with some regularity of shape, either accidental or the result of human workmanship (cf. Acts 19:35). The verse is an echo of 3:11.

46   (b) *The carpenter and wooden images* (13:11–14:2). *Inclusio: produce(d); art/artificer,* 13:11 and 14:2. A carpenter produces useful things from wood, uses the scraps to cook his food, and from the worthless wood that is left makes an image in his spare time. Then he prays to the helpless thing. The ultimate in this absurdity is the case of someone in a wooden ship none too strong who seeks help from a wooden idol inferior to the ship. (The section is based on Isa 44:9–20; 40:18–20; 41:6–7; 46:7). **14.** *red:* Ancient authors speak of idols being painted red. **14:2.** The ship has two advantages over the idol: it was made out of decent motives (not in idleness; cf. 13:13) and under the guidance of Wisdom.

47   (c) *Apostrophe* (14:3–6) *and transition* (14:7–11). The mention of the ship develops into an apostrophe to God who is the real guide of every ship that puts to sea (v 3). He has demonstrated his ability to save by making navigation safe (v 5) and by guiding Noah (v 6; *inclusio: guides/guidance,* 3 and 6). **3.** The words of Isa

(43:16) are associated with the exodus but are here reapplied to navigation, for the results of the action in v 3 are stated in v 4 and the meaning of v 4 is given in vv 5–6. **4a.** This is developed by v 5 (cf. *save* in v 4 and *safe* in v 5). **4b.** The reference to Noah ("one without skill") is developed in v 6. **5.** *works of your wisdom:* Ships (cf. 14:2). **6.** *giants:* Cf. Gen 6:4. *hope:* Noah.

In 14:7–11, the author begins with the idea of "wood" (the topic since 13:11) and returns the thought to 13:10 (application of "god" to handmade images), and, by way of transition to the next section he adds the idea that the idols themselves will undergo judgment because they ensnare people in evil (*inclusio: comes/become,* 7 and 11). **7–8.** Blessed is the right and honorable use of wood in general, but accursed is idol making.

48   (d) The origin and evils of idolatry (14:12–31). *Inclusio: idols,* 14:12,30. The initial verses introduce the topics of this central section: idols are of human origin, and they lead to countless evils (vv 12–14; *inclusio: devising/devised,* 12 and 14). The author proposes two examples of how idolatry originated. A father grieving for a child makes an image of the child; soon it is honored as a god with its own rites; in time, its worship is even prescribed by law. Again, an image of a king soon becomes an object of worship (vv 15–20; *inclusio: honored; man,* 15 and 20). Idolatry, evil as it is in itself, also leads to other evils in the immoral rites connected with it (vv 21–27; *inclusio: evil,* 22 and 27). Idolatry also gives rise to false oaths, and those who practice both idolatry and perjury will be punished (vv 28–31; *inclusio: sworn,* 29 and 31).

12–14. An echo of 2:23–24. **14.** *vanity:* Empty imagining, foolish fancy. **15ff.** The more natural process would be for children to venerate their deceased ancestors (cf. 2 Macc 11:23), but instances of the worship of deceased children in ancient Egypt and elsewhere are known. **20.** The theory that pagan gods were originally deified rulers had been popularized by Euhemerus about 290 BC. **21.** *grief:* As described in vv 15–16. *tyranny:* Cf. vv 17–20. *incommunicable Name:* The name "God," which cannot be shared with creatures (cf. Isa 42:8). **22.** *war:* Disturbance of passions within and violence without (cf. 14:23ff.) caused by ignorance of the true God. *peace:* For a Jew, spiritual and temporal well-being. **28.** *go mad . . . prophesy:* Mantic frenzy. **30.** *thought ill of God:* Thought wrongly.

49   (c′) Apostrophe (15:1–3) and transition (15:4–6). The discussion of the punishment of the wicked develops into an apostrophe to God (*inclusio: know your might,* 15:2,3), who is merciful and who, unlike the idols, has might. Even if we sin with idols we still belong to God, and this we know because we have experienced his mighty deeds on our behalf. But if we know that we belong to him, then we will not sin, for true knowledge of God (i.e., total dedication) is complete justice (and justice is immortal; cf. 1:15). Hence, the first step to immortality is to experience God's might. **3.** *might:* May also mean God's death-destroying power. The verse is difficult (for a survey of opinions and fuller discussion, see R. E. Murphy, *CBQ* 25 [1963] 88–93).

The following verses (15:4–6; *inclusio: form; long[s],* 5 and 6; *evil,* 4 and 6), with vocabulary reminiscent of 14:9–11 ("senseless"; "make") and 13:10 ("dead"; "hopes"), sum up the thought to this point and provide a transition into the final section. **6.** *hopes:* Futile trust in idols, or the idols themselves.

50   (b′) The potter and clay images (15:7–13). *Inclusio: vessels: earth(en),* 15:7,13. The potter, like the carpenter, produces useful vessels for our service (cf. 13:12), but out of the same clay from which he himself and his vessels were made he forms an idol. His whole

existence is worthless because he did not recognize his creator but saw life as a time to make profit (cf. 13:19; 14:2). Indeed, the potter who makes idols is more guilty than any other because he knows well the brittleness of those images. **7.** Cf. Isa 45. **9.** *vies:* Clay idols were glazed and gilded. *counterfeits:* On two counts: because they are imitations of valuable images and because they represent nonexistent gods. **11.** *soul, spirit:* See comment on 1:4. **12.** *evil:* Unlike the carpenter, this idolmaker has no belief in the idols he produces.

51   (a′) Conclusion (15:14–17). The thought returns to the Egyptians (v 14) and to the dead, handmade idols of 15:5 and 13:10. **15.** Cf. Pss 115:4ff. and 135:15ff. *idols of the nations:* The author projects back upon the past the religious syncretism of the Hellenistic period. **16.** *spirit:* See comment on 1:4. *has been lent:* Cf. 15:8. **17.** *mortal:* Because one is doomed to die one can only make dead things. "Death" in the second half of Wis means simply physical death (12:20; 16:13; 18:12–20; 19:5).

52   (iii) (15:18–16:4) *plus digression on the serpents in the desert* (16:5–15). *Inclusio: tormented,* 16:1,4; *came/come,* 16:5,14. The author returns to the Egyptian "panel" of the second diptych. Worse even than the religious syncretism of the Egyptians (cf. 15:15) is their worship of animals and, indeed, animals that have neither intelligence nor beauty to recommend them; therefore, they were punished by the plagues of little animals. But whereas animals plagued the Egyptians, they became a blessing to Israel in the desert, for God gave them quail (Exod 16:2–13; Num 11:10–32). Loathsome creatures were sent upon the Egyptians so that they might loathe the sight of food and not be able to satisfy their hunger, whereas Israel received quail to satisfy its hunger. For hunger had to come upon Egypt as punishment for its tyranny, but on Israel only to show it once again (cf. 11:8) how its enemies were being afflicted. **15:18.** *compared as to folly:* From the point of view of the animals' lack of intelligence. *rest:* Of the animals. **19.** *escaped:* the line is obscure. Perhaps the curse of the serpent is thought of (Gen 3:14–15) or perhaps a legend that reptiles were exempted from God's blessing and approval in Gen 1. **16:2.** The author again gives us a glorified account and fails to mention Israel's murmuring in the desert (Exod 16:2–8) and the wrath of Yahweh (Num 11:33–34). **3.** *turned from craving:* The allusion is apparently to the frogs in the ovens and kneading troughs (Exod 8:3). **4.** *being tormented:* The author implies that Israel's hunger was contemporaneous with Egypt's.

53   Digression (16:5–15). This section is often stated to be one of the diptychs or comparisons, but it does not illustrate 11:5 as do the other comparisons, for the events narrated are not a blessing for Israel but an admonition. The section is simply a concluding digression. It anticipates the objection that Israel endured a plague of animals (the serpents of Num 21:6–9) just as did the Egyptians, and it shows that this parallel is only apparent. (a) The serpents sent against Israel were not a punishment unto death but only a brief admonition (vv 5–7). (b) God thereby showed the Egyptians that it is he who saves (vv 8–10). (a′) The serpents sent against Israel were not a punishment unto death but only a brief admonition (vv 11–12). (b′) God has dominion over life and death (vv 13–15). **6.** *they had:* The author seems to suppose that the sign of salvation (the bronze serpent) already existed when the plague of serpents appeared (yet cf. Num 21:9). *to remind:* The whole episode (not just the bronze serpent) reminds. Cf. v 11 for the full thought. **8.** He once again (cf. 11:13) assumes that the Egyptians are being informed of the desert events (cf. Exod 32:12; Num 14:13; Deut 9:28. **9.** *locusts and flies:*

The plague of little animals. *slew:* Hyperbolic; perhaps it is based on Exod 10:17 or on the legend recorded by Josephus (*Ant.* 2.14.3 §300–303). *deserved:* Cf. 15:18–16:1. **11.** It was the murmuring of Israel against God and his beneficence in the desert that brought on the attack of the serpents (cf. Num 21:5). **13.** *lead back:* Means not an eschatological resurrection but that God can restore to life or save from death (cf. Deut 32:39; 1 Sam 2:6; 1 Kgs 17:17–23; etc.). **14.** *spirit, soul:* See comment on 1:4. *confined:* By the "gates of death" (Pss 9:13; 107:18). **15.** The verse goes with the digression and not with the following diptych (cf. Deut 32:39; Tob 13:2).

54   (c) THIRD DIPTYCH: THE ELEMENTS BRING FAVOR TO ISRAEL INSTEAD OF PUNISHMENT (16:16–29). *Inclusio:* water, 17, 29. The diptych proper is set forth in 16:16–22 (*inclusio: rains, hail, fire,* 16:16,22) and is followed by a digression on creation (16:23–29), a theme that will be taken up again at the conclusion of the work (19:6–21). Whereas the Egyptians were punished by wondrous downpours of rain and hail and their crops were destroyed by thunderbolts (fire), passing unquenched through the showers and sparing the animals sent to plague the Egyptians (cf. Exod 9:22–26), God rained down manna—food of angels (Ps 78:25), bread from heaven (Ps 105:40)—upon the Israelites in the desert. The manna assumed every conceivable flavor, and, although similar to hoarfrost and ice, fire did not melt it when it was cooked (Exod 16:23; Num 11:8) so that Israel, seeing this alteration in nature, might know that fire was destroying Egypt's crops even in the midst of rain. **17.** Cf. 5:17. **18.** *beasts:* Despite Exod 8:13,31, the author presumes that the plagues of animals lasted until the plague of rain and hail. **20.** This is the hinge of the diptych. The contrast is between unquenchable fire from heaven that destroys food and food from heaven that fire will not destroy. It is difficult to determine the primary comparison. *conforming:* A legend found also in the rabbinic literature. **22.** *snow and ice:* The manna was "like hoarfrost" (Exod 16:14) and had "the appearance of ice" (Num 11:7 LXX).

The author then takes up the idea of v 17 in a digression on creation (16:23–29). God works through creation when he punishes and blesses, and he thereby teaches moral lessons. For the nourishment of Israel, creation was transformed in many ways to teach Israel that it is not food but God's Word that saves (vv 23–26; *inclusio: nourish,* 23 and 26). Moreover, the manna, which was not destroyed by fire in the oven, could nevertheless be melted by the sun (Exod 16:21). Therefore, one must thank God before the sunrise, for the melting manna is an image of the hopes of anyone who is ungrateful (vv 27–29; *inclusio: melt,* 27 and 29).

55   (d) FOURTH DIPTYCH: THE PILLAR OF FIRE INSTEAD OF THE PLAGUE OF DARKNESS (17:1–18:4). *Inclusio: darkness; confined,* 17:2 and 18:4. Whereas the Egyptians were imprisoned in the total darkness (Exod 10:21–23), haunted by frightening apparitions, terrified by sounds, and seized by a panic induced by their bad conscience, the Israelites, who had enjoyed great light in Egypt (Exod 10:23), were guided in the desert by the pillar of fire (Exod 13:21–22; 14:24; etc.), for they were the future bearers of the light of the law. In the magnificent description of the plague of darkness, the biblical account is embellished with legends, Hellenistic psychology, and the author's imagination to make the account more vivid.

1. For the thought, see Ps 92:6–7; Wis 5:3ff. **2.** *exiles:* The darkness screens them even from God. **3.** *secret sins:* Cf. perhaps 14:23. The author sees in this plague another instance of the law of talion (11:16); moral darkness is punished by physical darkness. *apparitions:* A legendary

embellishment on the biblical account, as are many of the other details. **6.** *fires:* Probably lightning. *these, that sight:* The fires; they were more fearful than the darkness. **7.** A reference to the magicians (Exod 7:11,22; 8:7; 9:11), who were powerless against the plague. **9–10.** During the protracted darkness, when there was nothing really terrible near the magicians, the memory (or continuation) of the previous plagues caused them to people the darkness with terrors to the extent that they feared even the air. **11.** *cowardly, testifies:* The wicked are fearful as a result of their wrongdoing, and thus bear witness to their guilt. Verses 12–13 develop the thought. *conscience:* The first appearance of *syneidēsis* in this meaning in biblical Greek. **12–15.** Perhaps intended to be a digression (*inclusio: fear; surrender; expectation/unexpected,* 17:12, 15). **13.** *expectation:* Fear is uncertain expectation. **14.** *powerless:* The night was powerless to hurt; the netherworld is the place whose inhabitants have no strength. *sleep:* Rhetorical; to describe the rest imposed by the darkness the author resorts to terms of night. **15.** *surrender:* Of reason (cf. v 12). **16.** The subject is no longer the magicians but the Egyptians generally. **18–19.** Seven natural sounds, which became terrifying in the darkness. **21.** *next should come:* In the netherworld. *burdensome:* Their bad conscience. **18:2.** *thanked:* Not in the biblical account. *for the sake of the difference:* They pleaded with Israel to leave so that the plague that only Egypt suffered might cease. **3.** *mild:* They were sheltered from its heat by the cloud (cf. 10:17). **4.** An echo of 5:6–7.

56   (e) FIFTH DIPTYCH: THE TENTH PLAGUE AND THE EXODUS BY WHICH GOD PUNISHED THE EGYPTIANS AND GLORIFIED ISRAEL (18:5–19:22). *Inclusio: your people,* 18:7 and 19:22; *glorified,* 18:8 and 19:22. The section begins with a general summary: when the Egyptians resolved to destroy the Israelite children, God killed the Egyptian firstborn and later drowned their army in the Red Sea; while thus punishing the Egyptians, God also in the same events glorified his people (18:5–8). Then follows a detailed description of the events. As Israel was celebrating the Passover, the Word of God brought death to the Egyptian firstborn (18:9–19)—an episode quite different from the brief plague which Israel later endured in the desert (18:20–25). The Egyptians then foolishly resolved to pursue the Israelites; thus they experienced the completion of the punishments begun in the tenth plague, and Israel experienced a wondrous journey (19:1–5). For in marvelous fashion the exodus was in fact a new creation, paralleling that of Gen 1 event by event, to the benefit of Israel and the punishment of Egypt (19:6–13a)—a punishment that was just, for the Egyptians were more inhospitable than the Sodomites of old (19:13b–17). Indeed in this new creation the elements rearranged themselves in the same way that a rearrangement of notes produces a new melody (19:18–21). (In 19:6–21, as a finale, the author recalls the second [vv 10–12], third [vv 20–21] and fourth [v 17] diptychs.)

5. *boy:* Moses. *reproof:* Exod does not assign any relation between the killing of Israel's sons and the tenth plague; but for Wis the events furnish another example of the law of talion (11:16). The Egyptians who had killed the male children of Israel lost their firstborn, and those who had used the Nile to drown Israel's children were themselves drowned in the Red Sea. **6.** *fathers:* Either the Israelites at the time of the exodus (Exod 11:4–7) or, better, the patriarchs (Gen 15:13–14; 46:3–4; etc.), to whom God swore he would deliver their descendants. **8.** *summoned:* Chosen, out of all the peoples of the earth. **9.** *sacrifice:* The Passover, which created a religious unity. *institution:* Refers either to the law commanding the Passover or to the idea expressed in the next line. *praises* of the fathers: The author pictures the Israelites singing the praises of the patriarchs just as later Israel sang the Hallel (Pss 113–118) at the Passover. **10.** cry: Cf. Exod 12:30. **12.** not sufficient: An embellishment on Num 33:3–4. **13.** sorceries: Cf. Exod 7:11; 8:7. God's son: An amplification of Exod 4:22–23; 12:31. Also an echo of Wis 5:5. **14–19.** The description is inspired by Exod 12:23; Job 4:13–15; 1 Chr 21:15–27. It is also an echo of Wis 5:18–21. **15.** word: In the OT, Yahweh's Word was regarded as the executor of divine judgments (Hos 6:5; Jer 23:29; etc.). **17.** them: The firstborn. dreams: The detail is from Job 4:13–15, rather than from the Exod account. Not only were the survivors to recognize God's hand but also the victims.

57   **20–25.** Digression. Inclusio: trial; anger, 20 and 25. These verses are often understood as the Israelite blessing corresponding to the death of Egypt's firstborn and as the completion of the diptych begun in 18:5. (In this view, 19:1–22 is interpreted as another separate diptych on the exodus.) However, the events of these verses (20–25) are presented as a "trial of anger" (cf. vv 20 and 25) and not as a blessing, and thus they do not illustrate 11:5 as do the other comparisons. Moreover, 18:5–19:22 is all one dipych, for the author views the tenth plague and the exodus as a unit (cf. 18:5), the exodus being the perfect completion of the tenth plague (cf. 19:1,4). These verses (20–25) are simply a brief digression anticipating the objection that Israel also experienced a plague of death (Num 16:44–50) and pointing out that the parallel is only apparent: the plague was speedily overcome by Aaron. This digression, then, is similar to the one in 16:5–15. **22.** smiter: Called an angel in 4 Macc 7:11. **23.** cut off the way: Blocking the smiter. **24.** whole world: Aaron's garments were symbolic. Jewish tradition had it that the long blue robe denoted the sky; the girdle, the ocean; the buttons on the shoulders, the sun and moon; etc. (cf. Philo and Josephus). four rows: The four rows of precious stones in the high priest's breastplate, upon which were engraved the names of the 12 patriarchs or tribes of Israel (cf. Exod 28:15–21). grandeur: On the high priest's miter were engraved the words "Holy to the Lord" (Exod 28:36). **25.** destroyer: The term is introduced from Exod 12:23. enough: To warn Israel; they were not like the Egyptians, who needed to drain the cup to the dregs.

58   **19:1.** he knew: God (cf. Exod 14:3–4). **5.** wondrous . . . extraordinary: Unprecedented and characterized by miracles and wonders. **6–13a.** Creation, in cooperating in the exodus events, was made over anew, for the miracles were like a repetition of the first creation. The cloud covered the camp (Exod 14:19–20), just as the darkness covered the waters (Gen 1:2); dry land appeared out of the Red Sea (Exod 14:21–22) as it had from the primeval waters (Gen 1:9–10), and from the

land came vegetation ("grass," v 7; Gen 1:11–13); the land brought forth gnats (Exod 8:16–19) instead of animals (Gen 1:24); the waters swarmed with frogs (Exod 8:2) instead of fish (Gen 1:20); a new bird appeared from the sea (Exod 11:13; Num 11:31), as at the first creation birds had appeared (Gen 1:20 LXX); and thunder accompanied the exodus (Ps 77:17–18) as it had the creation (Ps 104:7). **6.** kinds: Reminiscent of Gen 1:21,24,25. its natural laws: Read "your commandments" with many LXX mss. and Latin; cf. a similar sentence in 16:24. **7.** grassy: Another embellishment on the biblical account. **8.** sheltered by your hand: An echo of 5:16. **13b–17.** Perhaps the mention of the thunderbolts led to the thought of the Sodomites, who were overwhelmed with a tempest of fire (Gen 19:24), and provided the author an opportunity to present one final comparison. **13.** they suffered: The Egyptians. guests: Hospitality was the supreme law of the ancient Near East. more grievous: Than the Sodomites. **14.** those others: The Sodomites, who were inhospitable to the angels (Gen 19:1–11). these: The Egyptians. beneficent: Because of the services rendered by Joseph (Gen 39–47). guests: Israel had been invited to come into Egypt (Gen 45:17–18). **15.** Refers to the Sodomites. **16.** "These" (the Egyptians) "oppressed those" (the Israelites). same rights: The author supposes that the Israelites already possessed the civil privileges enjoyed by the Jews at this time under the Ptolemies. There may well be allusions in these verses to conditions in Egypt contemporaneous with the author. **17.** they were stricken with blindness: The Egyptians, with the plague of darkness. the just: Lot. **18.** The author explains the biblical wonders in the light of the Gk idea of the harmony of the cosmos; see J. P. M. Sweet, Miracles [ed. C. F. D. Moule; London, 1965] 113–26). **19.** land creatures: Apparently the reference is to the Israelites and their cattle going through the sea. those that swam: The frogs. **20–21.** Cf. 16:17–22. **21.** ambrosial: Heavenly. (On chap. 19, see P. Beauchamp, Bib 45 [1964] 491–526.)

59   Conclusion (19:22). The author draws a conclusion from his discussion for the encouragement of his fellow Jews and provides an inclusio with 18:7–8. The tedious verbosity of the concluding chapters and the abruptness of the ending have been remarked by most of the commentators, and it has been suggested that some verses have been lost or that the author having finally exhausted himself, "has no more to say, and it is a pity that he did not recognize this before" (Goodrick). The numerical patterns (→ 10 above), however, indicate that the text is intact. These final chapters are wordy simply because, having adopted mathematical composition, the author needed sections with larger and larger verse counts in order to maintain the numerical proportions within chaps. 11–19 and to establish an overall proportion with chaps. 1–9.

34

PSALMS

John S. Kselman, S.S.

Michael L. Barré, S.S.

BIBLIOGRAPHY

1 *Bibliographical information and summary of modern trends:* Eaton, J. H., "The Psalms and Israelite Worship," *Tradition and Interpretation* (ed. G. W. Anderson; Oxford, 1979) 238–73. Gerstenberger, E., "Psalms," *Old Testament Form Criticism* (ed. J. H. Hayes; San Antonio, 1974) 179–223; "The Lyrical Literature," *HBMI* 409–44; *Psalms, Part I* (FOTL 14; GR, 1988).

Commentaries: Allen, L. C., *Psalms 101–150* (WBC 21; Waco, 1983). Anderson, A. A., *Psalms 1–2* (NCB; London, 1972). Beaucamp, E., *Le Psautier* (SB 7; Paris, 1976–79). Buttenwieser, M., *The Psalms* (Chicago, 1938; repr. 1969). Craigie, P. C., *Psalms 1–50* (WBC 19; Waco, 1983). Dahood, M., *Psalms I–III* (AB 16, 17, 17A; GC, 1966–70). Kraus, H.-J., *Psalmen I–II* (BKAT 15/1–2; 5th ed.; Neukirchen, 1978); *Psalms 1–59* (Minneapolis, 1988). Stuhlmueller, C., *Psalms 1–2* (OTM; Wilmington, 1983). Weiser, A., *The Psalms* (OTL; Phl, 1962). Westermann, C., *The Living Psalms* (GR, 1989).

Studies: Anderson, B. W., *Out of the Depths: The Psalms Speak for Us Today* (Phl, 1983). Brueggemann, W., *The Message of the Psalms* (Minneapolis, 1984). Craghan, J. F., *The Psalms* (Wilmington, 1981). Eaton, J. H., *Kingship and the Psalms* (SBT 2/32; London, 1976). Gunkel, H., *Einleitung in die Psalmen* (Göttingen, 1933; repr. 1966); *The Psalms* (Phl, 1967 [from *RGG*]). Johnson, A. R., *The Cultic Prophet and Israel's Psalmody* (Cardiff, 1979). Keel, O., *The Symbolism of the Biblical World* (NY, 1978). Kraus, H.-J., *Theology of the Psalms* (Minneapolis, 1986). Miller, P. D., *Interpreting the Psalms* (Phl, 1986). Mowinckel, S., *Psalmenstudien I–VI* (repr. Amsterdam, 1966); *The Psalms in Israel's Worship* (NY, 1962). Sabourin, L., *The Psalms* (Staten Island, 1969). Westermann, C., *Praise and Lament in the Psalms* (Atlanta, 1981). Wilson, G. H., *The Editing of the Hebrew Psalter* (SBLDS 76; Chico, CA, 1981).

INTRODUCTION

2 **(I) Texts and Versions.** The standard Hebr text of the OT (the "Masoretic Text" [MT]) dates in its present form from about the 10th cent. AD. Despite its shortcomings, there is a greater respect for the basic integrity of the received text of the pss among commentators today. Nevertheless, the Hebr text shows evidence of a good deal of textual corruption, as would be expected in the case of a book so widely used throughout antiquity. The corruption can be seen by comparing parallel pss (e.g., 40:13–17 = 70) or pss with parallels in other books (e.g., Ps 18 = 2 Sam 22). Individual words, phrases, or verses have suffered in transmission, making interpretation difficult.

Direct witness to the Hebr text near the beginning of the Christian era is now possible through the discovery of the DSS (→ Texts, 68:31), among which are about 30 mss. of pss. The text of these does not depart appreciably from that of the MT, though the sequence often differs.

The Gk transl. known as the Septuagint (LXX) is the most important ancient version. Dating from the 3d to 2d cent., it appears to be based on a Hebr text somewhat different from the MT. The great majority of citations from the pss in the NT (85 percent) are taken from the LXX. A critical edition of the LXX Psalter has been available for some years. Beginning in the 2d cent. AD several other transls. were made into Greek, notably those of Aquila, Theodotion, and Symmachus.

The ancient Aram transl. (Targum) of the Psalter also survives. It involves not simply straightforward transl. but a good deal of interpretation as well. Mss. of this version do not date earlier than the 5th cent. AD, and no critical edition of this version has appeared to date.

Latin transls. date from the 2d cent. AD (*Vetus Itala*, a transl. of the LXX). Several important transls. into Latin were made by Jerome. His revision of the *Vetus Itala* in the late 4th cent. was known as the *Roman Psalter*. Somewhat later he revised this translation, working from the Greek of Origen's *Hexapla* (→ Texts, 68:83, 135). This was the *Gallican Psalter* and was used in the Divine Office and incorporated in the Vg. His still later transl. from the Hebrew (*Psalterium juxta Hebraeos*) did not meet with popular acceptance.

3 **(II) The Formation of the Psalter.** The most obvious division of the Psalter is its arrangement into five "books" (Pss 1–41; 42–72; 73–89; 90–106; and 107–150). This sectioning into a five-part "Torah" in imitation of the Pentateuch is an ancient Jewish tradition.

The first four books each end with an appended doxology, not part of the ps to which it is attached (41:14;
72:18–20; 89:53; 106:48). Pss 146–150, each beginning
with *hallĕlû yāh* ("Praise Yahweh"), form together the
extended doxology that concludes not only the fifth
book but indeed the whole psalter.

Smaller collections of pss, some of which cut across
the traditional five-book division, include Pss 3–41, the
first book of the psalter without prefatory Pss 1–2.
These pss share the heading "psalm of David" and (with
three exceptions—Pss 19; 24; and 33) their character as
pss for individuals. Pss 42–83 are designated as the
"Elohistic" section because of the prominence of *'ĕlōhîm*
as the name by which God is addressed; some have associated this collection with the Pentateuchal "E" tradition.
Pss 93–99 (except Ps 94) are a collection grouped by a
common topic (God's kingship) and are followed by Ps
100, a thanksgiving ps that serves as a conclusion to this
sequence of pss. Pss 120–134, each of which is prefaced
by the formula "song of ascents," seem to be a collection
of pilgrimage songs sung by pilgrims to Jerusalem. Like
Ps 100, Ps 134 serves as a concluding doxology to this
collection.

There are other indications of editorial arrangement.
The psalter is prefaced by a wisdom poem (Ps 1) describing the joy of the righteous in the study of the Torah.
Ps 1 is paired with Ps 119, the great Torah psalm, to
form a frame around what may have been an earlier version of the Psalter, before the addition of the pilgrimage
songs (Pss 120–134) and the subsequent material.
Finally, a noticeable feature is the tendency of laments to
cluster in the first half with psalms of praise predomi-
nating in the second half. This movement from lament
to praise in the final canonical psalter mirrors the same
shift from complaint to praise that is the basic structure
of the commonest type of poem in the collection, the
lament psalm.

4   (III) Psalm Headings. The superscriptions
or ps headings are of three types: (a) technical musical
terms and instructions for performance; (b) personal
names with which the ps is associated; (c) historical
headings. The first superscription (Ps 3:1) has all of these
elements: "(a) a *mizmōr* (b) of David (c) when he fled from
Absalom his son." Found both in the LXX and in the pss
preserved at Qumran, these superscriptions are additions to the text by pre-Christian Jewish-rabbinic
tradition.

The technical musical terms include the general terms
šîr and *šîrâ* (song) and more specific terms like *mizmōr*
(psalm), a term applied to compositions with an especially religious tone, *tĕhillâ* (hymn of praise), *tĕpillâ* (plea,
lament). The meaning of several other terms (*miktām,
maśkîl, šiggāyôn*) is unclear. Performance instructions
begin with the general note "to the director" and continue with instructions for accompaniment.

Of the personal names prefaced to the pss, the most
common is David. Solomon appears in the heading of
Pss 72 and 127, Moses in Ps 90, and Jeremiah in Ps 136
LXX (= MT Ps 137). Other names include Asaph, the
sons of Korah, Heman, and Ethan. The attribution of 74
pss in the MT to David led to the Jewish tradition of
David as the author of the whole psalter (as Moses was
the author of the Pentateuch and Solomon of the wisdom
literature). Although David is indeed portrayed as a
musician and poet in 1–2 Sam, such features may come
from royal ideology rather than from authentic historical
memory.

5   The historical headings are early exegetical
traditions. In these traditions a historical locus for a ps
was sought in the narratives about David in 1–2 Sam;
generally the connection of a ps to a historical incident

was the result of a perceived verbal link (e.g., compare
Ps 51:6 and 2 Sam 12:13). In the MT 14 pss have such
historical headings (3; 7; 18; 30; 34; 51; 52; 54; 56; 57;
59; 60; 63; 142). Of modern English translations, *RSV*
does not number the headings (resulting in a different
versification from that of the MT), and *NEB* does not
include them. The practice of the *NAB* (including the
heading in the enumeration of vv as in MT) will be
followed in the commentary.

6   (IV) Literary Types. Pss study in the 20th
cent. rests upon the contributions of two significant
figures, H. Gunkel and S. Mowinckel. Since their contributions have been reviewed elsewhere (→ OT
Criticism, 69:39,46), here we need only note the chief
characteristics of their work. Gunkel's commentary
(1926) and his posthumous *Einleitung in die Psalmen*
(1933) demonstrated the importance of form-critical
study; the types discussed below were developed by
Gunkel and refined by such scholars as H.-J. Kraus and
C. Westermann.

Like Gunkel, Mowinckel had the advantage of an
increasing amount of comparative ancient Near Eastern
literature. His study of the background supplied by
Babylonian cultic and mythic material led him to propose a new year's festival celebrated in Sept.-Oct.
(Tabernacles; cf. Exod 23:16; 32:22), a feast of thanksgiving for the harvest. The controversial element in his
reconstruction of this feast (chiefly from the pss) was the
ceremony described as the cultic enthronement of
Yahweh, in which Yahweh's dominion over the world
was proclaimed and cultically renewed. Mowinckel's
emphasis on the cultic origin and use of the pss marks an
advance over Gunkel's view that many of the pss are
private prayers modeled on older cultic forms.

In his *Psalmenstudien* Mowinckel suggested that
Babylonian ideas might have been mediated to Israel via
Canaan. The subsequent discovery and decipherment of
Canaanite religious and mythic material from Ugarit (→
Biblical Archaeology, 74:72) proved him to have been
prescient. Since then, the Canaanite material has been
employed by many OT scholars (C. H. Gordon, M.
Pope, F. M. Cross, D. N. Freedman), but none has used
the material so consistently and controversially as M.
Dahood, in his commentary (1966–70). Like Mowinckel,
he has argued for the royal character of many more pss
than is accepted by more traditional commentators.
Another controverted claim is the presence of allusions
and references to eternal life that Dahood finds in the
pss. Despite its limitations, his commentary is a significant contribution, and its basic methodological principle
(the importance of ancient Near Eastern and particularly
Canaanite material for OT interpretation) is sound.

7   Modern understanding has been considerably
enriched in recent years by the study of ancient Near
Eastern literature. (a) *Vocabulary:* Poetry tends to make
use of words uncommon in the day-to-day language.
Thus the meaning of a number of terms was forgotten
even in antiquity. Their transl. has been aided by
investigating cognate terms in related languages. The
identification of parallel word pairs common to Hebrew
and other ancient Near Eastern literatures has also proved
helpful in clarifying obscure terms. (b) *Literary level:*
Recent studies have shown a tendency to eschew large-
scale alterations of the Hebr text. Rather the emphasis
has been on analysis of the individual pss as they have
come down to us. Particular attention has been given to
the structure and literary devices (chiasm, merism, *inclusio,* etc.). Since these devices are encountered in the
poetry of other areas of the ancient Near East, the study
of their function there has shed light on their use in Hebr
poetry. Moreover, certain literary categories have close

structural parallels in other ancient Near Eastern prayers, (e.g., the lament and Babylonian *šu-ila* prayers). In particular, the poetry recovered from ancient Ugarit has advanced scholars' understanding of Hebr poetry and (according to some) its meter. (c) *Imagery:* Students of Hebr poetry have long noted the use of "stock" images and concepts that reappear in a number of compositions. In a good many cases these images are part of the wider conceptual world of the ancient Near East. The view of the universe (see O. Keel), of humanity's relation to the divine world, of death and life, etc. remained remarkably consistent throughout this area for millennia.

8   (a) HYMNS OF PRAISE. In Hebr the Psalter is called *tĕhillîm.* Properly the term refers to a specific type of ps, the "hymn." To this literary category belong Pss 8; 19; 29; 33; 65-66[:1-12]; 100; 104-5; 111; 113-14; 117; 135-36; 145-46; 148-50; some would also include here the "Songs of Zion" (Pss 46; 48; 76; 84; 87) and the "Enthronement Psalms" (Pss 47; 93; 95-99). Examples are also found outside the psalter. The typical hymn consists basically of three parts. (a) The introduction sets the characteristic tone of praise. It usually mentions the intention of praising or blessing Yahweh or invites others to do so. (b) The body flows from the introduction and gives the reasons for praising God. In some pss the connection is made explicitly by the word "for" (Pss 33; 100; 117; 135-36; 147-49) as is often found in the thanksgiving psalms. Others use a participial construction (translated as a relative clause in English) to achieve the same result (e.g., Ps 103:1-3). (c) Many pss in this category have a recognizable conclusion, though its content varies. It may reiterate the language or thought of the introduction (Pss 8; 103-4; 135-36) or contain a wish or blessing (Pss 29; 33; 146; 148).

9   (b) LAMENTS. These comprise the largest category, including about 40 individual laments and at least a dozen national or communal laments. The standard format of these pss includes the following elements: (a) the invocation of God's name; (b) a description of present need; (c) prayer for help and deliverance, frequently with an imperative ("hear," etc.); (d) reasons why God should help the one praying; (e) vow to offer praise or sacrifice when the petition is heard; (f) grateful praise to God.

A prominent feature of the lament is the abrupt shift from the lament proper—elements (a) to (e)—to the concluding confession of praise for divine aid (f). The language of praise is usually in the past tense, with the psalmist praising God for help that seems already to have been given. Two explanations are given for this phenomenon. (a) The whole ps is written from the perspective of past distress overcome with divine assistance, and so it ends with thanksgiving and praise for the divine aid already experienced in answer to prayer. (b) Between the uttering of the lament and the thanksgiving, the psalmist heard (from a cultic prophet or priest) an oracle of salvation, in which God promises to deliver him (Pss 12:6; 35:3; 60:8-10; 91:14-16); and so certain is the assured deliverance that God can be praised as if it were already accomplished. The chief difficulty with this theory is the relative infrequency of such salvation oracles in the laments. However, this difficulty is mitigated if one views the laments as exemplars of the worshiper's part of a dialogue with a cultic official.

Two subtypes are related to and perhaps developed from the lament: *psalms of trust* and *thanksgiving psalms.* Expressions of trust occur regularly in laments (Pss 3:5-7; 5:12; 22:5; 28:7; 44:7-8). When the emphasis in the poem falls on such expressions of confidence or trust, it is classified as a *psalm of trust.* Like the laments from which they originated, psalms of trust can be individual

(Pss 4; 11; 16; 23; 62; 91; 121; 131) or communal (Pss 115; 125; 129).

Similarly, the thanksgiving that concludes many of the laments can so predominate that the poem is classified as a *psalm of thanksgiving.* Although thanksgiving can be expressed in very general terms (Ps 34), the psalmist can give thanks for such specific benefits as recovery from serious illness (Pss 30; 116) or forgiveness of sins (Pss 32; 103). There are both individual (Pss 9-10; 30; 32; 34; 41; 92; 103; 116; 118; 138) and communal thanksgiving psalms (Pss 65-68; 124). It is not always easy to distinguish a psalm of trust from a lament, or a thanksgiving psalm from a hymn of praise. However, if employed without rigidity, the classification of psalms of trust and of thanksgiving can be helpful.

10   (c) ROYAL PSALMS. This is a broad designation covering a number of types. There are royal laments (144:1-11), royal thanksgiving songs (Pss 18; 21; 118), etc. Royal psalms are those in which the king is the speaker (e.g., Pss 18; 101) or in which he is the focus of attention (e.g., Pss 2; 21; 45; 110). The royal character of a number of pss is generally recognized. But the issue of how many are "royal" is debated. An earlier generation of critics ascribed a large percentage of the pss to the Maccabean period (2d cent.), which means that few would be datable to the monarchical period (*ca.* 1000-600). But study of the poetry of Ugarit on the one hand and Qumran hymns on the other indicates that the Hebr pss point more in the direction of Ugaritic poetry than of poetry from the Maccabean period; hence they are likely to be earlier than the time of the Maccabees. A higher percentage may be datable to the monarchical period than had been previously supposed, which opens the possibility that a greater percentage of them may be royal. Although the number of royal psalms is still rather small according to the majority of commentators (Pss 2; 18; 21; 45; 72; 101; 110; 144:1-11), several scholars (e.g., Mowinckel, Eaton, Dahood) have argued that a larger number should be included in this category than has generally been recognized. It is possible that some royal psalms, or parts of them, were "reread" or "democratized" by later generations in such a way as to lose their originally royal character (e.g., Ps 23).

11   (d) WISDOM PSALMS. By their form and content these show connections with OT wisdom literature. At the same time, there is wide divergence among scholars about the three central issues: the problem of what pss are to be so designated and classified, their *Sitz im Leben* (the institutional setting in life in which they took on their characteristic shape), and the characteristics of form by which they can be recognized.

Many scholars would agree that at least the following are wisdom psalms: 1; 34; 37; 49; 112; 128. Others would add 32; 73; 111; and 127. On the issue of their cultic or noncultic origins, Mowinckel argued that the wisdom psalms were private, noncultic compositions of the sages for instruction and edification. Finally, as to the features and style, the following formal characteristics (found as well in the wisdom literature) can be noted: the '*ašrê* ("Happy the one who . . .") formula (Pss 1:1; 32:1-2; 127:5; 128:1-2); the "better" saying (Ps 37:16); the address of a teacher to a pupil or "son" (Ps 34:12-15); the occurrence of proverbs (Ps 37:9,22,28b-29a,34b = Prov 2:21-22; Ps 111:10 = Prov 1:7; and note the proverbial character of Ps 127:1-2,3-5; and the acrostic form (Pss 34; 37; 111; 112; 119).

In addition to these formal characteristics, content plays an important part in determining what pss are wisdom compositions. Several major themes of the wisdom literature occur: the polarity of the righteous (*saddîq*) and the wicked (*rāšāʿ*), and the two ways set before human beings; practical advice on the conduct of ordinary life; "fear of Yahweh"; veneration and observance of Torah; concern with the problem of retribution. The wisdom teachers were concerned with discovering and affirming the order of the created world, and a central characteristic of this order was a theology of just retribution. But when the righteous suffered and the wicked prospered, voices of protest like that of Job were raised. The same Joban perspective and problem of theodicy are present in Pss 49 and 73.

12   (e) LITURGICAL PSALMS. The liturgical setting of the pss in general is widely recognized today. Individual pss may allude to some aspect of the cultic life of Israel; but only several whole pss are generally recognized as deriving from the cult, such as entrance liturgies (Pss 15; 24:3–6; Isa 33:14b–16; [cf. Jer 7:2–15; Mic 6:6–8]). This group was probably part of a rite of entrance to the Temple. Would-be worshipers stood at the gate of the Temple seeking admittance. The question was asked by those seeking admittance, who was worthy to enter the Temple? (Pss 15:1; 24:3). The fixed response by cultic personnel in the Temple described the behavior of the morally upright person, focusing on the relationship to neighbor (Pss 15:2–5a; 24:4) and concluding with the assurance that such a person would be permitted access to God (Pss 15:5b; 24:5–6). The rest of Ps 24 (vv 7–10) may also reflect a liturgical sequence—namely, a procession into the Temple. According to some, Ps 134 is to be considered a liturgical ps. This brief ps, the last of the "Songs of Ascent" (→ 3 above), consists of an exhortation to bless Yahweh (vv 1–2) and a concluding (priestly) blessing (v 3).

13   (f) HISTORICAL PSALMS. A number of pss contain narratives recounting God's great works throughout the history of Israel. Under this heading may be listed Pss 78; 105–6; 135–36. Since this classification is based on content rather than structure, pss of this type may belong formally to other categories (Ps 78 = wisdom; Pss 105; 135–36 = hymns). The various pss in this category narrate different segments of "salvation history" and for different purposes. Pss 78 and 106 contrast the history of Israel's rebellion with God's graciousness; Ps 105 praises Yahweh for his faithfulness to the covenant.

14   **(V) The Theology of the Psalter.** The picture of the God of Israel presented in the Psalter is not radically different from what we find elsewhere in the OT. Basically his activities fall into two categories: savior and creator. He alone is the savior of Israel, the people whom he "created" at the time he brought them out of Egypt (Exod 15:16). This activity entails his deliverance in the Exodus, preserving the people in the wilderness, and bringing them safely to the promised land. In terms of the individual, God's salvation is seen in rescuing from sickness, death, and enemies and providing health, happiness, and long life.

A number of pss emphasize God's role as creator. Several contain brief "creation accounts" (Pss 74:12–17; 89:10–13; 104:3–10; 136:5–9) describing Yahweh's victory over the powers of chaos, the ordering of the cosmos, and occasionally his consequent kingship over the created world. The pss emphasize the aspects of power and providence visible in God's role as the creator (33:6–7; 36:6–10; 65:10–14; 95:3–4; 96:10–13; 104). Several make a direct connection between the creation and the election of Israel, as the Pentateuch does (135:6–12; 136:5–9).

15   The pss share with other Hebr literature, esp. poetry, a number of epithets for the God of Israel. The

ordinary word for God is *'ĕlōhîm* (a pl. with a sg. meaning). Some of Yahweh's titles and epithets are drawn from the larger world of Canaanite religion and mythology. For example, he bears the title "El," the proper name of the supreme god of the Canaanite pantheon. El was the father of the gods and humankind as well. This title underscores Yahweh's supreme status among the gods and his fatherly kindness and compassion (Ps 86:15). Yahweh is also "Lord," a title that eventually replaced the sacred name in Judaism (Pss 2:4; 16:2; 30:9; 35:17,22; 37:13; 38:16,23; etc.), and "king" (Pss 5:3; 10:16; 24:7–10; 29:10; 47:7–8; 68:25; 84:4; etc.), both of which emphasize his supremacy in the divine and human worlds. A number of titles highlight his role as savior, esp. titles that describe him as a place of safety. Thus, he is a "Rock," an inaccessible crag similar to the Rock of Gibraltar (Pss 28:1; 31:3; 42:10; 62:3,7; 71:3; 78:35; etc.) and a "(place of) refuge" (Pss 14:6; 46:2; 48:4; 57:2; 59:17; 62:8; etc.).

16   The psalter has been called the songbook of the Temple. It is not surprising, then, to note the importance of the Temple in the theology of the pss. The Temple was the deity's palace. Just as every human king had a palace from which to rule, so did God. From this "palace" (*hêkāl*) God reigned on earth, bestowing salvation and blessing (Pss 18:7; 20:2,7; 36:10) and judging humankind (9:8–9; 11:4–6; 33:13–15). The Israelite went to the Temple, where he hoped to "see" God (i.e., be granted an "audience" with him) as subjects of a king went to the palace. The notion of God as a "refuge" shades into that of the Temple as the place of safety par excellence (Pss 17:8; 36:7–8; 57:2; 61:5; 63:8; 91:4).

As a palace, the Temple had its courts. Thus, the Temple is called "the courts of Yahweh" (Pss 65:4; 92:14; 100:4; 116:19; 135:2). Since in the ancient Near East the gods were thought to dwell on mountains, the Temple site is occasionally called "the mountain of Yahweh" or his "holy mountain" (Pss 15:1; 24:3). The pss also refer to the Temple by the archaic term "tent," which properly denoted the Tent of Meeting (Pss 15:1; 27:5,6; 61:5).

At other times references to the Temple are indirect: "the shadow/shelter of [Yahweh's] wings" (Pss 36:8; 57:2; 61:5; 63:8); "the land of life" or "the land of the living" (27:13; 52:7; 56:14 [= 116:9]); "in the presence of Yahweh" (56:14 [= 116:9]; 61:8; 68:3; 96:6). Because supplicants hope to obtain a hearing from God in the Temple, the idiom to "see/seek (the face of) God" (27:4, 8,13; 42:4; 63:2; 84:7) points to the Temple. But those who seek Yahweh's face may find that he has "hidden" it or "turned [it] away" from them (10:11; 30:8; 44:25; 88:14; 89:47; 143:7).

17   Israelites had no clear belief in an afterlife until the end of the OT period; yet they believed in a shadowy existence after death—in "sheol" or "the netherworld." The OT does not give us a detailed picture but presents it as a pale reflection of life on earth (cf. Isa 14:9). It was a forbidding place, a land of darkness (Pss 74:20; 88:7, 13,18; 143:3).

The netherworld was carefully distinguished from "life," which connoted vivacity and good health. From this results the common ancient Near Eastern view that not only the dead but also the seriously ill were in the realm of death. Hence psalmists suffering from some illness occasionally refer to themselves as "going down" to the netherworld (22:30; 28:1; 115:17; 143:7). Entering the netherworld meant not only the end of life but of all experience of God's presence. In the early Israelite view earthly existence was the only sphere of God's saving activity for humans (Pss 6:6; 88:11–13). Therefore, the dread of sheol was more than a fear of death or illness;

it was the fear of separation from the power of Yahweh's love (contrast Rom 8:38-39).

18 The "enemies" of the psalmists receive a good deal of attention. The identification of these figures is controversial. To a certain extent the problem is connected with the identity of the psalmist. If the majority of pss are compositions by private individuals, the enemies may simply be personal foes. If, however, a larger percentage are royal compositions than is commonly supposed, these enemies would take on a more "cosmic" coloration. Egyptian and Mesopotamian kings identify those who oppose their rule with the cosmic forces of chaos. Ridding the land of such evil influences was one of the first tasks of the ancient Near Eastern king; for as representative of the divine rule he continued in the world of human society the primordial battle with the forces of chaos and disorder. In the Israelite view the evil were to be "purged" from the nation lest they corrupt the land (Deut 13:5).

19 Several attributes of God or the psalmist are highlighted. "Justice" or "righteousness" (Hebr *ṣedeq*, *ṣĕdāqâ*) in the Israelite view is essentially a relational concept. One is righteous when acting in accordance with the obligations that flow from certain relationships. Thus, Yahweh—creator, savior of his people, covenant God of Israel—manifests his righteousness by maintaining the world in order and saving his people from harm. He also does this when he punishes the wicked and defeats Israel's enemies. Similarly, the psalmist is "righteous" when he is faithful to the covenant God by keeping the divine commands and dealing uprightly with his neighbor. The psalmists show no self-consciousness about asserting their righteousness when praying to God, hoping that this would dispose Yahweh to grant their petition.

An important dimension of Yahweh's righteousness was his fidelity to his role as covenant God. Thus, the pss speak often of his faithful love for the people or for the psalmist, rooted in the covenant, a concept expressed by *ḥesed* (commonly translated "steadfast love"). This word stresses the permanent aspects of a relationship (cf. Hos 6:4). The adjectival form (*ḥāsîd*) occurs frequently and often describes the psalmist. Variously translated "faithful (one)," "pious," etc., it designates one who is loyal to the covenant with Yahweh. Because *ḥesed* carries the nuance of permanence, it is often paired with *'ĕmet*, *'ĕmûnâ* (usually translated "fidelity" or "truth"). Derived from a root meaning "to be firm," it emphasizes the enduring reliability of Yahweh as savior or that of the psalmist as his servant.

COMMENTARY

20 **Ps 1.** A wisdom psalm, serving as a preface to the Psalter. Structure: two parts chiastically arranged: vv 1-2 (A): the righteous person diligent in the study of the Torah; v 3 (B): simile of a tree; v 4 (B): simile of chaff; vv 5-6 (A): the wicked and their fate. **1.** *happy:* Typical of wisdom (Prov 3:13; 8:32-33; Pss 32:1; 34:9). **2.** The identification of wisdom with Torah is characteristic of late postexilic wisdom (Sir 24). **3-4.** The righteous person and the wicked are depicted in two contrasting similes: the righteous as a productive tree rooted near abundant water (Jer 17:7-8; Ps 92:13-15); the wicked as chaff—dry, lifeless (Zeph 2:2; Job 21:18; Isa 17:13). **6.** The theme of the "two ways" is frequent (Deut 30:15-20). The "way of the wicked" in v 6 forms an *inclusio* with the "way of sinners" in v 1.

21 **Ps 2.** A royal psalm, placed at the beginning of the psalter to announce the messianic theme, it has a number of verbal links to Ps 1. Perhaps originally a coronation hymn for a king of Judah, its language contains the hyperbole of "court style." Structure: vv 1-3 (rebellious disorder on earth); vv 4-6 (God's reaction in heaven); vv 7-9 (the king recites the divine oracle); 10-11 (the divine decree applied to the rebellious vassals). **1-3.** The vassal nations and their rulers plot rebellion (cf. Jer 27:1-11). While such a historical situation existed for Israel only in the era of David and Solomon (10th cent.), its use beyond this period is part of court style. *against Yahweh and his anointed one:* Political rebellion against Yahweh's royal representative was tantamount to rebellion against Yahweh. **4-5.** The scene changes to the heavenly court, where Yahweh responds with derision and anger (Ps 59:9). **6.** God's choice of the Davidic monarch and of Zion for his sanctuary (Ps 132:11-14). **7.** At this point we hear the voice of the monarch, who responds with the words of the divine adoption formula: "You are my son. . . ." **10-11.** With the revolt quelled, the Judahite monarch addresses the subdued kings. Verse 11 is difficult; many proposals have been offered for the awkward phrase (lit., "kiss the son"). The ps ends with two echoes of Ps 1: the "perishing" of the rebel kings and the concluding congratulatory formula "happy."

22 **Ps 3.** An individual lament uttered by someone (perhaps the king) beset by enemies. Structure: vv 2-3; vv 4-7; 8-9. **1.** The heading associates the ps with Absalom's rebellion and David's flight from Jerusalem (→ 5 above; 2 Sam 15-16). **4.** The second strophe begins like the first with an appeal to Yahweh, addressed as a shield protecting the psalmist. *my glory:* May be a divine title here (cf. "glorious king" in Ps 24:8, 10). **6.** Although some have seen an incubation rite here (cf. Gen 28:10-17; 1 Kgs 3:4-14), this is more likely an expression of confidence in God's protective power. **7.** The many enemies of vv 2-3 reappear, arrayed against the now-fearless psalmist. In v 3 the sin of the psalmist's enemies involved speech; here the organ of speech ("jaw . . . teeth") is marked for divine punishment. **9.** Continues the theme of v 7, where the enemies' denial of divine help for the psalmist is countered by "to Yahweh belongs salvation." *may your blessing be upon your people:* This concluding prayer may point to a royal speaker for the ps.

23 **Ps 4.** An individual lament with several links to Ps 3 (compare 3:4 with 4:8; 3:8 with 4:7; 3:6 with 4:9); the note of trust is prominent. Structure: v 2 (appeal to God); vv 3-6 (the psalmist's trust in Yahweh unlike the idol worshipers); vv 7-9 (prayer for Yahweh's blessing and the psalmist's security). **2.** *my just God:* May point to a legal setting in which the lament is a prayer of the unjustly accused. *you who save me in distress:* The words for "salvation" and "distress" here include notions of "spaciousness" and "narrowness" (to be "in distress" is to be "in a tight spot"; cf. Pss 18:7,20; 118:5). **3.** *sons of men:* Either influential people (*NAB:* "men of rank") or simply "mortals" (*NEB*). The "empty thing" or "lie" that they love may refer to idols (Dahood; cf. Deut 4:28-29; 11:13-17). **5.** *be silent:* Or "weep copiously," addressed to the idolatrous people of v 3. **7.** *lift up the light of your*

face upon us: Cf. Num 6:23–27; Ps 67:2. The image suggests God's smiling face bestowing favor (Pss 44:4; 89:16). **9.** Cf. Deut 33:28.
24   Ps 5. An individual lament with similarities to pss concerned with access to the Temple (→ 16 above); Pss 15; 24:3–6; 26; 101). Structure: vv 2–4 (appeal for divine hearing); vv 5–7 (Yahweh's abhorrence of evildoers); vv 8–9 (the psalmist's worship of Yahweh in the Temple); vv 10–11 (evildoers' sins of speech and prayer for their divine punishment); vv 12–13 (Yahweh's protection and blessing of the just one). **4.** Appeal to God for help "in the morning," a common motif (Pss 46:6; 59:17; 90:14; 143:8; Lam 3:22–23). **5–7.** Cf. Pss 26:4–5; 101:3–5 for similar descriptions of those denied entrance to the Temple. **8.** Unlike the evildoers, the psalmist is permitted access to the Temple. **10.** The sins of speech recall the "speakers of lies" and "deceitful people" of v 3. **11.** *because of their abundant rebellions:* Contrasted with "because of your [Yahweh's] abundant kindness" in v 8.
25   Ps 6. An individual lament, the first of the seven "penitential psalms" (6; 32; 38; 51; 102; 130; 143); a prayer for healing from mortal illness. Structure: vv 2–4 (lament); vv 5–6 (prayer for healing); vv 7–8 (lament); vv 9–11 (thanksgiving). **3–4.** "My bones" and "my soul" = "I" (cf. "I" in v 3). **4.** *how long?:* A phrase common in laments (Pss 74:10; 80:5; 90:13). **6.** The absence of knowledge and praise of God in the netherworld (→ 17 above) is a motif found in other laments (30:10; 88:11–13; 115:17; Isa 38:18). **7–8.** The "dimming of the eyes" is vision blurred by tears (cf. Ps 31:10–12). **9–11.** On the sudden change of tone from petition to praise, → 9 above. **11.** *let them turn and be suddenly ashamed:* Or "let them again be ashamed" (as in v 5).
26   Ps 7. An individual lament, a "psalm of innocence" or "prayer of one unjustly accused." Structure: vv 2–3 (appeal to Yahweh for deliverance); vv 4–6 (oath of innocence); vv 7–10 (prayer for divine intervention to obtain justice); vv 11–14 (confidence in God's protection); vv 15–18 ("poetic justice" for the evildoer; thanksgiving to Yahweh for justice). **3.** *lest he rend my life:* Cf. Ps 50:22. The image might be of a lion tearing out one's throat (Pss 17:10; 22:14). **5.** *if I have ever repaid my ally with treachery, and rescued his enemy:* The language may be drawn from ancient Near Eastern treaties, where a vassal swears to treat the suzerain's enemies as his own. **8.** *assembly of the peoples:* I.e., all humankind. **10.** *searcher of mind and heart:* Cf. Jer 11:20. **16–17.** Such "poetic justice" is common in ancient Near Eastern and biblical literature (Pss 9:16; 35:8; 57:7; Prov 26:27; 28:10).
27   Ps 8. A hymn of praise to Yahweh as creator with several connections with Gen 1. Structure: vv 2–3 (Yahweh's glory); vv 4–9 (humanity as ruler of creation). **2a.** The hymn is framed by an *inclusio* (v 10). The "name" of God is the sacramental bearer of the divine reality. **2b–3.** Scholars' efforts to elucidate these difficult lines have not met with success. **5.** The poet contrasts the divine majesty and human insignificance (Ps 90:1–3). *what is man . . . ?:* Cf. Ps 144:3 and Job 7:17, where the question is used in a different sense. **6.** *little less than the gods:* A reference to the divine council; cf. Gen 1:26. *glory and splendor:* These two terms recall God's splendor and majesty in vv 2–3. Their association here with a human being who is "crowned" with them may point to the king; blessed with these divine attributes, he is almost a god. Heb 2:5–9 applies this passage to Jesus. **7–9.** Human dominion over creation follows immediately the reference to the divine council, just as in Gen 1:26.
28   Pss 9–10. A thanksgiving psalm (9) followed by an individual lament (10). Pss 9–10 form an acrostic, in which successive lines of poetry begin with the letters

of the alphabet in their normal sequence. The (incomplete) acrostic arrangement marks Pss 9–10 as an original unity. The sequence of thanksgiving followed by lament is unusual; but cf. Pss 44; 89. **9:4–5.** Introduction of two major themes: (a) the defeat and destruction of the psalmist's enemies, (b) by the divine king and judge. **6.** The "names" of the wicked may refer to their progeny (Deut 25:6–7; Ruth 4:10; 1 Sam 24:21). **8–11.** Yahweh enthroned, governing with justice, is a stronghold for the powerless. **12–15.** An echo of the opening words of praise, introducing another prominent theme of the poem: God has not forgotten "the cry of the afflicted" (9:19; 10:11,12). **10:1,2–6.** The description of the activity of the wicked is obscure. The charges seem to include their pursuit of the afflicted and holding God in contempt. **7.** Cf. Ps 41:7–9. **8–10.** Cf. Ps 59:4; Prov 1:11; 24:15; Lam 4:19. In 9:4 it was the psalmist's enemies who stumbled and fell into destruction; in 10:10 it is the oppressed who fall to the ambush of the wicked. **11.** The motif of God hiding his face is common in the pss (→ 16 above; 13:2; 22:25; 27:9; etc.). **14.** Countering the statement in v 11 that God hides his face is the statement "You *do* see!" **15.** The broken power (lit., "arm") of the evildoer (Ps 37:17; Job 38:15) is contrasted with the effective, controlling hand of God in vv 12 and 14.
29   Ps 11. A song of trust. Structure: vv 1–3 (description of bad times, when the wicked prevail); vv 4–7 (God sees all and knows the righteous from the wicked). The theme is similar to that of Ps 12: Though the wicked wreak havoc, God is a sure refuge for the righteous. **1.** *"flee like a bird . . .":* Probably the demand of the wicked that the psalmist get out of their way. "How can you say?" almost always carried an accusatory tone (Jer 2:23; 8:8; 48:14). The quote ends with v 1. **7.** *behold his face:* I.e., experience God's presence in the Temple (Pss 24:6; 42:3; 84:8; 104:14); in theory only the upright could be admitted into the divine presence (Pss 15:1–2; 17:15; 24:3–4; cf. Matt 5:8). God "beholds" all human beings (v 4) but only the righteous may "behold" him.
30   Ps 12. A community lament. Structure: vv 2–3 (traditional description of bad times); vv 4–5 (curse against the wicked); vv 6–7 (God's reliable promise to save the "poor"); vv 8–9 (prayer for divine protection from the present evil society). As in Ps 11, the main idea is that God will not let the wicked prevail. **2–3.** Cf. Mic 7:1–7; for Egyptian parallels, cf. *ANET* 441–46. **6.** A response to the prayer of vv 4–5, perhaps an oracle pronounced by a priest or prophet. **8.** *protect us:* An expression of confidence ("You will protect us") or more likely a prayer: "May you protect us. . . ." *this generation:* A particular group of people rather than an age; the phrase often has a negative connotation (Gen 7:1; Deut 1:35; Ps 95:10; Matt 11:16).
31   Ps 13. An individual lament. Structure: vv 2–3 (the lament); vv 4–6 (the request). Each line of the lament begins with "How long?" (cf. Ps 6:4). **2.** *forget me?:* I.e., stop caring about me, cease providing protection, etc. (cf. Pss 31:13; 77:10). **4.** *my eyes:* Eyes that are enlightened ("bright eyes") denote vitality, life, happiness (cf. Ps 4:7; 19:9); for the opposite image, see Ps 38:11.
32   Ps 14. An individual lament. Another version of this ps (Ps 53) occurs in the "Elohistic" Psalter (→ 3 above). Structure: vv 1–3 (description of the "fool"); vv 4–6 (the recompense of such people); v 7 (prayer for the deliverance of Israel). **1.** The type of person described as a "fool" (note the actions mentioned in v 1) is one who ignores the sovereignty of God. **3.** In Rom 3:10–12 Paul refers to this verse as in his argument that all people (Jews and Gentiles) are sinners. But the ps simply emphasizes the present breakdown of moral order (cf. Ps

12:2–3). **7.** *when Yahweh brings his people back:* If this is a reference to the exile (cf. Ps 126:1), it may be a later addition.

33   Ps 15. An "entrance liturgy" (→ 12 above). Structure: v 1 (question by worshipers); vv 2–5a (answer by a cultic official); v 5b (assurance). **1.** *who may dwell:* I.e., what sort of person is worthy to worship God? *in your tent:* The Temple; → 16 above. *your holy mountain:* I.e., Zion, so called because of the view that gods dwelt on mountains. **2–5.** The person worthy to enter God's presence is one who does no wrong to the neighbor (cf. Rom 13:10). **2.** The just person is one who is righteous in word (speaking) and deed (walking, doing). **4.** *he swears to his neighbor:* Following the reading of the LXX rather than the MT ("to his [own] hurt"). **5.** Charging interest on a loan was strictly forbidden (Exod 22:25; Lev 25:36–37; Deut 23:19–20; Neh 5:7) because it was seen as extortion. *will never stumble:* Walking unhindered by obstacles is an OT image of happiness; stumbling or falling is an image of ruin (Prov 3:23; 4:12; Isa 40:31; 63:13; Jer 31:9).

34   Ps 16. A song of trust. Structure: vv 1–6 (confession of faith in Yahweh alone); vv 7–11 (expression of confidence). Each part ends with a description of God's providence, present (vv 5–6) and future (vv 10–11). **1–2.** An overview of the whole ps. *guard me:* Points to vv 7–11; "you are my Lord" fits well with vv 3–6. **3.** *the holy ones:* Notoriously difficult; probably refers to pagan gods, not pious Israelites. The psalmist vows to have nothing to do with pagan gods. **5.** *my allotted portion and my cup:* Cf. Ps 142:6. **6.** A reference to dividing up the promised land among the Israelites (cf. Josh 18:8,10; Ps 78:55). The Levites' "portion" was not any particular territory but God himself (Num 18:20). **8.** *I shall not stagger:* Cf. Ps 15:5. **10.** *the grave:* Hebr *šahat* means "pit" (i.e., grave or netherworld). The LXX (cited in Acts 2:25–31; 13:35) translates by a word meaning "corruption." **11.** Most likely an expression of the common motif of experiencing God's presence in the Temple (cf. Pss 36:9; 63:6). *the path to life:* In OT wisdom literature this refers to the proper way of living (Prov 2:19; 5:6; 6:23; 15:24). But here it may allude to the fullness of "life" experienced in God's presence in the Temple (→ 16 above).

35   Ps 17. An individual lament. The view that this is a "psalm of vigil," prayed by one who spends the night in the Temple, is based on slender evidence. The setting of the ps is difficult to reconstruct, whether it was prayed by someone wrongfully accused or by the king threatened by rebels and foreign enemies (see Ps 18). Structure: vv 1–5 (the psalmist prays for God's help, confident because of his righteousness); vv 6–12 (petition for deliverance from enemies); vv 13–15 (final petition: destruction of foes and the blessedness of the divine presence for the psalmist). **1.** *a righteous cause:* This word (lit., "righteousness") appears in the last verse, forming an *inclusio.* **3–5.** This seemingful boastful language was an accepted way of reminding God of the petitioner's fidelity to him (Pss 7:8–11; 18:21–24; 26:2; → 19 above). **7–10.** The Hebr text is difficult. **14.** Difficult; probable transl.: "Destroy them with your power, O Yahweh, destroy them from the world! Make them perish from among the living!" (Dahood). **15.** *may I be sated when I awake with your form:* Or perhaps "May I be sated with beholding your form" (cf. LXX), reading a rare vb. meaning to "gaze on" (*hāṣîṣ;* Cant 2:9) rather than "awake." The expression probably refers to seeing God in the Temple in contrast to the fate of the psalmist's enemies in vv 13–14.

36   Ps 18. A royal hymn of thanksgiving. Another version is preserved in 2 Sam 22:2–51.

Structure: Part I (vv 2–31): vv 2–4 (praise to God the savior); vv 5–7 (the psalmist's distress); vv 8–20 (deliverance as a theophany); vv 21–31 (God saves the just); Part II (vv 32–51): vv 32–46 (God empowers the psalmist to defeat his enemies); vv 47–51 (praise to God, who saves the king). **2–4.** A heading to the whole ps which sounds its major theme: When the just call upon God he delivers them from their foes. **5–7.** Mythological language; Death and sheol are trying to ensnare the psalmist and drag him down. **8–16.** The description of God the warrior coming to the rescue is typical of the language of theophany (cf. Exod 19:16–20a), which often stresses phenomena like storm and earthquake. **20.** *to a wide space:* See comment on Ps 4:2. **26.** Hebr *tāmîm,* "wholehearted," is a key term (cf. vv 26b,31,33). God "goes all the way" for those who do the same in their devotion to him. **32–46.** Part I described God's intervention to save the king from his foes. In Part II God equips him with strength to be victorious over them. **44–46.** Difficult; the gist seems to be the acknowledgment of the king's rule by his enemies after their defeat. **45.** A reference to the vanquished foes' acknowledgment of the victor's overlordship. **47–51.** The poem ends with a section praising God as one who saves the psalmist from his enemies.

37   Ps 19. The ps falls into two distinct parts: vv 2–7 (a creation hymn) and vv 8–15 (a wisdom hymn). The second part can be further subdivided into vv 8–11 (Torah hymn) and vv 11–15 (confession of sin and prayer for forgiveness). Although many commentators have argued that Ps 19 is composed of two originally distinct poems, the thematic connections speak against this view. The connection between creation and wisdom theology is well known. **2.** For the attribution of glory to El ("God"), see Pss 24:7,10 ("king of glory") and 29:3 ("El the glorious"). "Glory" suggests both the nimbus of light enveloping the deity and the storm cloud (Exod 40:34; Ps 18:12–13). **3.** A possible transl.: "Day after day, they [the heavens] pour forth his word; night after night it [the firmament] declares his knowledge." **5–7.** The focus now narrows to the sun, the god of law and justice, here demythologized to one of God's works. **8.** The perspective of the poem shifts from God's work of creation to Yahweh's gift of the law (the Torah) to Israel (reflected in the change in divine names). For wisdom and Torah, cf. Ps 1:2. **9.** *giving light to the eye:* Cf. Ps 4:7. **14.** There is an *inclusio* here with the beginning of the Torah hymn in v 8. The perfection or blamelessness of the law is mirrored in the prayer of the psalmist that he be blameless.

38   Ps 20. A royal psalm, a prayer of the people that God grant the king victory in battle. Structure: vv 2–6 (petition by the people); vv 7–10 (prayer of confidence). **2–4.** The people pray for the king not simply as an individual but as the person through whom God bestows blessing on the nation and protects it from enemies. **2.** *answer:* Equivalent to "save" in v 7 (also Ps 118:21). **5.** *may he grant your heart's desire:* Probably refers to standard royal petitions that have a bearing on the life of the nation (see 1 Kgs 3:10–11; Ps 21:2–12). **7.** Cf. Ps 60:7b and the comment on Ps 71:16,18. **8.** *some swear by horses:* Exact meaning disputed; cf. Ps 33:17. "Boast of" or "be strong (through)" are also possible. **10.** The vb. means either "answer us" (*NAB*) or preferably "answer him" (i.e., the king).

39   Ps 21. A royal hymn of thanksgiving; some have suggested that the context is a victory in battle. Structure: vv 2–7 (Yahweh's blessing of the king); v 8 (midpoint and transition); vv 9–14 (prayer for destruction of the king's enemies by Yahweh). **2.** *O Yahweh, in your strength:* The recurrence of this phrase in v 14 creates an *inclusio* that frames the poem. **5–6.** On the divine blessing of "glory . . . majesty and splendor," cf. Ps 8:6. **8.** This "hinge verse" is connected with both parts of the poem: to v 2 by "the king" and to both v 2 and v 14 by "Yahweh." **9–11.** Yahweh's steadfast love for the king involves the destruction of the king's enemies and their descendants by the divine wrath (Gen 19:24; Lev 10:2; Num 11:1). For Yahweh's "devouring fire" cf. Exod 24:17; Deut 9:3.

40   Ps 22. An individual lament, whose opening words occur on the lips of the crucified Jesus (Matt 27:46; Mark 15:34). Structure: vv 2–12 (present distress contrasted with God's mercy in the past); vv 13–22 (the enemies of the psalmist); vv 23–27 (invitation to join in praise of God); vv 28–32 (universal chorus of praise). The thematic unity of all parts of the ps make a composite origin highly unlikely. **2.** *far from saving me:* Frequently emended to "far from my cry." Cf. Pss 18:42; 27:10. **3.** *by day . . . by night:* To the psalmist's experience of God's distance in space (v 2) is added his absence in time. **4.** Perhaps "You sit enthroned among the holy ones [the divine council]" or "in the holy place [the heavenly sanctuary]." **9.** *he relied on Yahweh:* In place of the expected oracle of salvation (cf. Ps 6:9–10) the psalmist hears the mockery of his enemies. **10–11.** The psalmist recalls God's maternal care experienced in infancy. **17.** Very difficult: lit., "Like a lion my hands and feet." Suggested transls. include: "They have pierced [lit., "dug"] my hands and my feet"; "they have picked clean my hands and my feet"; "my hands and my feet are shriveled up (by illness)." **23–24.** The psalmist's isolation from God (vv 2–3) and the community (vv 7–9) has been overcome as he is reunited with his "brothers." **28–29.** The psalmist's call to all Israelites to join him in praising God now widens to include all humankind. Space, experienced in v 2 as empty of God, now resounds with his praise. **30–32.** The dimension of time also recurs at the end of the poem (cf. v 3). Present (v 30: "the living of the earth"), past ("those who go down into the dust"), and future (vv 31–32: "the generation to come") join the chorus of praise. **32.** *salvation:* The last words recall the opening words of the lament ("from saving me") and frame Ps 22 with an *inclusio.*

41   Ps 23. A song of trust, probably a royal prayer reinterpreted after the exile. Structure: vv 1–4 (Yahweh as the good shepherd); vv 5–6 (Yahweh as the divine host). The poem is a unity, since the images of shepherd and host are closely related in ancient Near Eastern thought. **1.** *shepherd:* A universal image of the king in the ancient world, emphasizing leadership and providence for his subjects. *he lets me lie down:* This vb. is used predominantly of sheep and small cattle. Rev 7:17 applies these words about "the good shepherd" to the Lamb (Christ). **4.** *the valley of deep darkness:* "The shadow of death" is also possible. **5.** *a banquet:* Ancient Near Eastern kings would give lavish banquets on special occasions (cf. 1 Kgs 8:65–66); hence, this image continues the theme of the provident shepherd-king. **6.** *may only (your) goodness and steadfast love pursue me:* The psalmist prays that only the good effects of the covenant now "pursue" him throughout life. **7.** *may I dwell:* Cf. Ps 27:4. The vb. could mean "return" or "dwell"; the ambivalence is probably deliberate, alluding to the exiles' hope of returning home. *the house of Yahweh:* While this generally refers to the Temple, the term can also mean the land of Israel in general.

42   Ps 24. A hymn of praise to Yahweh the victorious creator, including an entrance liturgy (→ 12 above). Structure: vv 1–2 (Yahweh the creator); vv 3–6 (entrance liturgy); vv 7–10 (return of the victorious Yahweh to his dwelling). **1–2.** The establishment of the earth on the "seas and rivers" recalls the creation myth

(→ 14 above), which told of the divine conquest of the unruly forces of chaos ("Sea"/"River" in Canaanite mythology). **7–10.** Parallel to the entrance of the worshipers into the Temple is the entrance of Yahweh returning victorious to his dwelling. Like vv 3–4, this section involves the question and answer style. **7.** *lift up your heads, O gates!:* In one Canaanite myth, the gods with heads bowed cower at the challenge of the powers of chaos. When the creator god returns from battling these forces the assembled gods hear his triumphant cry ("Lift up your heads!") and acclaim him king. In this demythologized version, the gods are replaced by the gates of Jerusalem.

43   Ps 25. An individual lament in acrostic form. **4.** The "way" of Yahweh is a major theme (cf. vv 4–5, 8–10,12), alternating with sections about the psalmist's need for the forgiveness of his sins (vv 6–7,11). **6–7.** The psalmist's sins are enclosed by words denoting God's mercy. **13.** Cf. Deut 1:35–36; 6:18. **17.** On "spaciousness" and "narrowness," cf. Ps 4:2. **19.** *how numerous are my foes:* Cf. Ps 3:2–3.

44   Ps 26. An individual lament (Gunkel), a communal protective psalm (Mowinckel), or a protestation of innocence by one falsely accused (Kraus). The references to altar and Temple in vv 6–8 and the similarity to Exod 30:17–21 point to a priest as speaker. Structure: five sections chiastically positioned around a central panel: vv 1–3 (A), 4–5, (B) 6–8 (C), 9–10 (B), 11–12 (A). **1.** Note the *inclusio* between v 1b ("in my integrity . . . walked") and v 11a ("in my integrity . . . walk"). **2.** Cf. Pss 7:10; 11:4; 17:3. **4–5.** The psalmist's negative confession (cf. Ps 101:3–4; Job 31). For his nonassociation with the wicked, cf. Ps 1:1. **6–8.** In the center of the chiasm the focus shifts from persons (the wicked) to place (the Temple). **10.** The hands of the evildoers, filled with evil schemes and bribes, are contrasted with those of the psalmist, washed in innocence (v 6; cf. Pss 24:4; 73:13). **11–12.** A further link between the outer sections is the echo of v 1 ("I shall not stumble") in v 12a ("my foot stands firm on level ground").

45   Ps 27. A poem consisting of a psalm of trust (vv 1–6), an individual lament (vv 7–12), and a conclusion (vv 13–14). It has a number of parallels with Ps 23. **1.** In the biblical tradition, "light" has associations with "life" (see v 1b) and "happiness" etc. (cf. Ps 13:4). **3.** *confident:* A major theme in this ps (cf. "trust" in v 13). **4–6.** The wish to dwell in God's house is closely related to the preceding subsection about enemies. The Temple was the place of refuge par excellence. **4.** *may I behold the beauty of Yahweh:* Cf. v 13; perhaps an emphatic expression for "seeing" God. *may I draw near his Temple:* Difficult; transl. conjectural. **8.** *"come," says my heart:* See Dahood and Ps 11:7. **12.** *witnesses:* A rare word identified on the basis of Ugaritic documents; cf. also Prov 14:5. **13.** *O that I might maintain my trust! That I might see . . . :* Difficult. See M. Barré, *Bib* 64 (1983) 417–20. *land of the living:* Or "the land of life"; in a number of poetic texts this expression seems to refer to the Temple (Pss 52:7; 56:14; 116:9; Isa 38:11). Thus the poem ends with a reference to the Temple, a dominant motif of vv 1–6. **14.** Perhaps a later addition to the poem.

46   Ps 28. An individual lament, with lament proper (vv 1–5) followed by a thanksgiving hymn (vv 8–9). **1.** *O my rock:* Cf. Ps 19:15. *going down into the pit:* Cf. Ps 16:10. **2.** *when I lift up my hands:* A gesture of supplication (cf. Ps 141:2). **3–4.** *who speak peace . . . with evil in their hearts:* Cf. Ps 41:7,10. The evil "work of their hands" contrasts with the psalmist's lifting up his hands (v 2) and the work of Yahweh's hands (v 5). **7.** The trusting, joyful heart of the psalmist contrasts with the treacherous hearts of his enemies (v 3). **8.** *his anointed:*

This may be a royal lament, uttered by the king. **9.** Cf.
Pss 3:9; 29:11. The reference to the divine shepherd
would be particularly appropriate in a royal psalm.
47   Ps 29. Widely thought to have originated as
a hymn to the Canaanite god Baal, the ps is a powerful
expression of God's supremacy and universal rule.
Structure: vv 1-2 (address to the heavenly court); vv
3-9a (description of God's "glory"); vv 9b-10 (acclamation in the Temple by the heavenly court); v 11 (prayer
for blessing for God's people). **1.** *O divine beings:* Lit.,
"sons of El." In Israel explicit monotheism is probably to
be dated to the 6th cent. The Psalter contains several
references to gods other than Yahweh (Pss 8:6; 58:2;
82:1,6). On "El," → 15 above. To "attribute glory and
might" to Yahweh here may mean to acknowledge his
royal supremacy among the gods. **2.** Difficult. Probably
either "worship Yahweh in his holy place" (the Temple)
or "worship Yahweh when the Holy One appears" (a
theophany of Yahweh). **3-9a.** The phenomena pictured
here are appropriate to the storm-god as the divine
warrior, passing from the (Mediterranean) sea to land;
nothing in his way can resist his power. **3.** *the voice of
Yahweh:* This expression (*qôl Yahweh*), repeated seven
times, is meant to suggest peals of thunder crashing in
rapid succession. *over the waters:* Or "against the waters."
For the motif of God battling the watery elements, cf.
Pss 24:1-2; 74:13-15; 89:10-11; 93:3-4. **5.** *the cedars of
Lebanon:* Proverbial symbols of grandeur and might (cf.
Pss 104:16; Isa 2:13). **9b.** *and in his temple let all cry
"Glory!":* Difficult. Probably a command to the gods to
acknowledge Yahweh's supremacy by crying "Glory!"
—i.e., "Glory (be) to Yahweh!" (cf. Luke 2:14). **10.** In the
mythology, the victorious god ascends his throne after
defeating the powers of chaos and is acclaimed in his
(new) temple by the lesser gods. **11.** Perhaps a later addition to the ps, most likely to be understood as a prayer
("May Yahweh give . . .").
48   Ps 30. An individual psalm of thanksgiving
for deliverance from mortal illness. Structure: v 2
(hymnic introduction); vv 3-4 (the deliverance of the
psalmist from death); vv 5-6 (invitation to others to join
in praise); vv 7-11 (lament by one threatened with
death); vv 12-13 (restoration of psalmist and praise and
thanksgiving to God). **2.** *extol you:* Lit., "raise up." This
term is particularly appropriate here, where the psalmist
"raises up" praise to Yahweh who "raised him up" from
sheol. **5.** The joyful reintegration into the community of
one who had been at the point of death (Ps 22:23-24).
9-11. In the "silent" netherworld (→ 17 above) the
psalmist could no longer give thanks to Yahweh (Ps
115:17).
49   Ps 31. An individual lament. Structure: Part
I (vv 2-19): vv 2-5 (prayer); vv 6-9 (expression of trust);
vv 10-14 (lament); v 15 (expression of trust); vv 16-19
(prayer); Part II (vv 20-25): vv 20-23 (the psalmist's
praise of God); vv 24-25 (address to the faithful). Note
the chiastic structure of Part I: prayer, trust, lament,
trust, prayer (Craigie). A major theme is the safety one
finds in the "hand" of God (vv 6,16), when he delivers
from the "hand" of the foe (vv 9,16); cf. Ps 28:2-5. **2.**
The concepts of honor and disgrace played an important
role in Israelite consciousness. The latter may be compared to "losing face." **5.** *get me out of the net:* A common
motif (Pss 9:16; 10:9; 25:15). **6.** *in your care I entrust my
life:* In Luke 23:46 Jesus utters this expression of serene
confidence just before he dies. **7.** *I hate:* The psalmist sees
himself as deserving of God's protection because of his
loyalty (see 17:3-5). **14.** *"terror on every side":* Cf. Jer
20:10. **15-17.** These verses echo vv 6-8. **16.** *my times are
in your hand:* In the ancient Near Eastern view the events
in life (esp. birth and death) are fixed by the gods. **20-25.**

For the sudden change from lament to praise, see comment on Ps 6:9-11. **23.** To be banished from God's presence most likely refers to being excluded from his
life-giving presence in the Temple (cf. Jonah 2:4).
50   Ps 32. A wisdom psalm, cast in the form of
a psalm of thanksgiving. The wisdom features (vv 1-2,
8-10) envelop the thanksgiving elements, which are
themselves largely didactic. Structure: vv 1-2 (introductory beatitudes); vv 3-5 (teaching on acknowledging
one's sin); vv 6-7 (God hears those who confess their
sins); vv 8-10 (divine oracle); v 11 (concluding exhortation). Because of its emphasis on the confession of sin,
this poem is counted among the "penitential psalms" (see
Ps 6). **1.** *covered:* When God is the subject, to "cover" sins
means to take them away (Prov 17:9; Neh 4:5; 1 Pet 4:8);
cf. 2 Sam 19:19. **3-5.** In antiquity, the admission of sin
usually took the form of a recounting one's sins in
general terms (Ezra 9:6-15; 10:1; Neh 1:6-11). Not to
confess one's sins meant to persist in iniquity. **4.** *your
hand was heavy upon me:* An expression denoting serious
illness. **8-10.** The speaker changes. Although some see
here an admonition from a wisdom teacher, more probably it is a divine oracle. In response to the psalmist's
confession of his sin, God promises to lead him in the
way of righteousness. **11.** As in Ps 31:24-25, the conclusion directs attention to the congregation, calling them
to praise God.
51   Ps 33. A hymn. Structure: vv 1-3 (introductory exhortation to praise God); vv 4-9 (God's creative
word); vv 10-15 (God is supreme over the nations of the
earth); vv 16-19 (God alone is savior); vv 20-22 (conclusion). **1.** The beginning echoes Ps 32:11. **3.** *a new song:*
Certain rituals specify that "new" objects be used (cf.
1 Sam 6:7; 2 Sam 6:3); analogously it was proper to offer
God a "new song" of praise (cf. Pss 96:1; 98:1; Rev 14:3).
13-19. The insignificance of human beings when viewed
from God's vantage point in heaven (cf. Isa 40:22). God
alone is the proper object of human trust. **17.** *the horse:*
Not the ordinary means of transportation, but used
primarily in warfare. **18.** Cf. 34:16. The theme of the all-
seeing God was introduced in vv 13-15. The same God
who "has his eye on" all people as their supreme judge
also "eyes" his faithful with compassion.
52   Ps 34. An individual song of thanksgiving.
The ps is an acrostic addressing the just and encouraging
them to join with the psalmist in praising the God who
delivers those who trust in him. The teaching is typical
of traditional wisdom doctrine, viz., that all goes well
for the righteous (cf. Ps 37), who will never lack "any
good thing" (v 11). **8.** *the angel of Yahweh:* Cf. Exod
14:19; 23:20. Contrast the role of "the angel of Yahweh"
in the next ps (35:5-6). **10.** *fear Yahweh:* The first half of
the ps concludes on the note of "fear" of God, just as the
second half begins with this theme (v 12). This basic
theme of wisdom literature means recognizing the
supremacy of God over one's life and expressing this
recognition by obeying his commandments and worshiping him. **12.** *children:* Lit., "sons." One of the origins
of OT wisdom traditions is certainly the home, where
parents would instruct their children in right conduct.
The address to "son(s)" is common in ancient Near
Eastern wisdom literature (cf. Prov 4:1; 5:7; 7:24; 8:32;
Sir 2:1; 3:1). **20.** The sentence is best taken as concessive:
"Though the trials of the righteous person be many . . ."
(*NJV, NEB, NIV*).
53   Ps 35. This ps does not fit any of the standard
literary categories. In some respects it resembles the individual lament. Several commentators (Eaton, Craigie)
see it as a type of royal psalm, in which the king is
accused of treaty violation by his allies. Structure: Part
I (vv 1-10): vv 1-3 (appeal to God for deliverance); vv

4–8 (seven petitions against the foe); vv 9–10 (vow [?] to praise God for his deliverance); Part II: vv 11–16 (unjust treatment of the psalmist by his enemies); Part III (vv 17–28): vv 17–18 (appeal to God and vow [?] to praise him); vv 19–26 (seven petitions against the enemy); vv 27–28 (appeal to the righteous to join the psalmist in praising God). **2.** The petition for God to "arise" against the enemy counters the false witnesses' "arising" against the psalmist at the beginning of Part II (v 11). **4–8.** Seven curses against the enemy (vv 4–6,8) matched by seven similar petitions in Part III. **6.** *and may the angel of Yahweh be their pursuer!:* A reversal of the situation in v 3, where the psalmist's enemies are his "pursuers." **11–16.** This section contains the key to understanding the setting of the ps. If the background is an international treaty, these verses relate how the king is accused of violation by his treaty partners (the "hostile witnesses" of v 11), who repay him evil for "good" (= good relationship with allies). **13.** Difficult; lit., "My prayer returned upon [or "to"] my breast." This could refer to unanswered prayer or to praying from the heart. **17–26.** This section balances Part I with another seven petitions against the foe. The enemies' evil use of speech (vv 20–21) is countered by the petition that Yahweh not be "silent" (v 22) and that the psalmist's supporters "shout for joy" at his vindication (v 27). **27.** To the seven petitions against the psalmist's foes is added this eighth, which invites his supporters to rejoice and praise God with him.

54   Ps 36. This ps defies simple classification, consisting of elements of wisdom (vv 2–5), the hymn (vv 6–10), and the lament (vv 11–13). Structure: vv 2–5 (description of the wicked ruled by sin); vv 6–13 (contrasting description of Yahweh's steadfast love). "Wicked" (vv 2,12) envelops the ps with an *inclusio*. **2.** *sin speaks to the wicked:* Lit., "An oracle of sin to the wicked person . . . ," probably a parody of an oracle from Yahweh (cf. Ps 110:1). The wicked person heeds the voice of evil rather than the voice of God in his life. **4.** *he has ceased to act wisely:* In OT wisdom the "wise" are the morally good. **6–7.** The grandeur of God's faithful love (*ḥesed*) is contrasted with the pettiness of human evil, with images of height and depth. **8–10.** To know God's life-giving presence in the Temple, described here in the language of a banquet, is the supreme experience of his love (cf. Ps 63:3–6). **8.** *gods and humankind:* A merism meaning "all rational beings" (cf. Judg 9:13), which balances "human and beast" in v 7 (Dahood). *the shade of your wings:* An image of God's protection (Pss 17:8; 63:8). **10.** To "see (the) light" means to live; cf. Job 3:16; 33:28; Ps 49:20.

55   Ps 37. A wisdom psalm in acrostic form composed of three sections of eight stanzas (vv 2–15), six stanzas (vv 16–26), and eight stanzas (vv 27–40). The major theme is that the just shall be blessed, esp. by coming to "possess the land" (vv 3,9,11,22,29,34), whereas the wicked will be "cut off" (vv 9,22,28,34,38). **2.** The wicked are described with plant imagery. They will quickly dry up like green grass (v 2), will fade "like the splendor of the pasture [?]" (v 20), and—unlike the mighty tree—will not last (vv 35–36). **3.** *dwell in the land:* Introduces the key word "land" (vv 9,11,22,29,34). According to the OT the land belongs to Yahweh (Lev 25:23) and is his to allot to whom he will. **11.** *the meek:* The traditional transl., based on the LXX and Matt 5:5. Hebr *'ănāwîm* originally meant "overwhelmed by want" but became part of the religious vocabulary, denoting those aware of their dependence on God. **25–26.** A classic statement of what is sometimes called the "traditional" view of retribution (→ Wisdom Lit., 27:12–13): the wicked will be punished and the just will be rewarded (in this life).

56   Ps 38. An individual lament, the third penitential psalm (see Ps 6). Structure: Part I (vv 2–9): v 2 (cry to God); vv 4–5 (suffering as the result of the psalmist's sins); vv 6–9 (catalogue of ailments); Part II (vv 10–15): vv 10–13 (reaction of others to the psalmist's suffering); vv 14–15 (the psalmist's reaction to his enemies' treachery); Part III (vv 16–23) (reprise of themes [enemies, ailments, sin] enveloped by cry to God). **4–6.** The interconnection between sin and physical affliction is also attested in the NT (John 9:2). **6.** In wisdom literature "folly" is roughly equivalent to "immorality" (cf. Pss 36:4; 69:6; Prov 24:9). **12.** The psalmist's sin has not only resulted in bodily pain but also has alienated him from his friends (Pss 22:7–8; 31:12). **14–15.** A picture of the psalmist either as silent in reaction to the plotting and slander of his foes (cf. Ps 39:2–3) or as ignorant of their doings; Jer 11:19–20 might suggest the latter interpretation. **21.** *those who repay me evil for good, who accuse me rather than seek (my) welfare:* Most transls. imply that the psalmist's foes hate him because he "pursues good."

57   Ps 39. An individual lament, with wisdom overtones (vv 2,5–6,9,12). Structure: vv 2–4 (the psalmist is resolute and silent); vv 5–7 (the psalmist speaks to God); vv 8–12 (reprise; petition for deliverance); vv 13–14 (prayer that God let the psalmist live in peace). The poem is unusual in some respects, with a "Joban" conclusion (v 14). Though many have tried to reconstruct its setting, consensus still eludes the commentators. **2–3.** The psalmist tries to maintain silence in the presence of "(the) wicked" but eventually has to speak out. The reason for his silence is unclear (cf. Prov 10:19; 11:12; 12:16; Sir 8:1–3; 14:1). **4.** *my heart grew hot:* In Egyptian wisdom literature the "cool" person is commonly contrasted to the "hot" one, someone unable to control the temper. **5–7.** Rather than speaking out to the wicked, the psalmist addresses God. He is not meditating on the brevity of life but is trying to evoke God's pity and so ease his suffering. **6.** The last colon might be translated: "Surely (each) one must dwell in darkness," referring to the common fate to enter the netherworld (Job 10:21; 38:17). **10.** The poet does not speak out in his adverse circumstances (cf. vv 2–3) but appeals to God. Cf. the silence of the Suffering Servant in Isa 53:7 and of Jesus during his passion (Acts 8:32). **13.** *look away from me:* God's gaze can have either positive or negative results (cf. Ps 34:16–17). Here the psalmist, like Job (7:19), prays that God will let him be in peace for the remainder of his brief life. Cf. also Job 10:20; 14:6.

58   Ps 40. The ps is composed of two parts: a thanksgiving hymn of an individual (vv 2–11) followed by an individual lament (vv 12–18). As to the reversal of the usual order (lament followed by thanksgiving), note that Ps 27 similarly begins with a psalm of confidence (vv 1–6) and concludes with a lament. Cf. also Pss 44 and 89. **3.** The psalmist uses the image of the river ordeal, known from Mesopotamian literature. A person accused of wrongdoing is cast into a river for judgment; survival is an indication of innocence. Here the image describes his affliction by his enemies (cf. Pss 18:1–20; 69:2–5; 88:7–9; 144:5–8; Jonah 2:3–10). **6.** God's wonders for the psalmist are too many to count. The same language appears in v 13 referring to the calamities that overwhelm him. **7–9.** For the superiority of obedience to sacrifice, cf. 1 Sam 15:22–23; Mark 12:33. **10.** The psalmist's claim that he has not restrained (lit., "withheld") his lips from announcing Yahweh's justice leads to his prayer that Yahweh not withhold his compassion in v 12. **14–18.** For comment, cf. the doublet in Ps 70. **15–17.** Contrasted to the enemies who "seek [his] life" (v 15) and who speak mocking words to him (v 16) are those who "seek Yahweh" and whose words are always "Great is Yahweh!"

59   Ps 41. The ps begins with a didactic section (vv 1–4) in the style of the wisdom literature (cf. Prov 14:21; 19:17; 22:9), followed by a lament of a sick person abandoned by his friends (vv 5–11) and concluding with a statement of confidence (vv 12–13). **4.** *Yahweh will support him on his sickbed . . . :* The meaning of the rest of the verse is uncertain. **9.** The first two words (lit., "a thing of *bĕlîya'al*") have been variously understood: "a malignant disease" (*NAB*), "an evil spell" (*NEB*), "a lethal substance" (Dahood). Hebr *bĕlîya'al* probably means "(the place from which there is) no coming back up," i.e., the netherworld. **10.** Quoted in John 13:18, where it refers to Judas. **11.** The psalmist's prayer "Raise us up!" takes up the last word of his enemies in v 9 ("He will not get up again"). **13.** *you let me stand in your presence forever:* Probably refers to access to the Temple, permitted the psalmist because of his "integrity" (lit., "wholeness," which would include his renewed health). Cf. Ps 61:8. This parallel may suggest that the speaker in Ps 41 is also the king. **14.** A doxology which concludes Book 1 (→ 3 above).

60   Pss 42–43. An individual lament. The refrain (42:6,12; 43:5) and other connections (e.g., 42:10; 43:2) lead to the conclusion that Pss 42–43 form a single poem (wrongly divided like Pss 9–10). **42:2–3.** *my soul thirsts:* Cf. a similar sequence of ideas in Ps 63:2–3. The prominent image of water is introduced in vv 2–3 and taken up in the psalmist's tears (v 4) and in the life-threatening sea (v 8). *see the face of God:* I.e., enter the Temple. In the Hebr text the vb. has been changed to the passive: "when can I be seen/appear before the face of God?" **4.** *by day and night:* The continuing lament of the psalmist is complemented by his continual experience of Yahweh's covenant love (*hesed*) in v 9. **5.** The psalmist's memory of his joyful participation in Temple rites in the past. This memory corresponds to the prayer that he might know such participation in the future. **6.** *why are you cast down, my soul?:* Or "Why do you lament, my soul?" *my savior:* Lit., "the salvation of my face," meaning something like "my personal savior." 42:6 is the first occurrence of the refrain. **11.** The meaning of the first two words is uncertain. **43:3.** "Light and Truth" are personified as two of Yahweh's attendants, sent from the divine council as "guardian angels" to guide the psalmist to the Temple.

61   Ps 44. A communal lament, composed of a confession of faith (vv 2–9) and the lament proper, which includes the complaint (vv 10–23), and the appeal for divine aid (vv 24–27). For the sequence of confession followed by lament, cf. Ps 89. **2.** An appeal to the days of the conquest era. The connection with the lament is this question: If we have the same trusting attitude as did our ancestors, why does God not deal favorably with us as he did with them? Compare v 8 and v 11. **4–8.** The language of holy war, wherein the divine warrior alone does the fighting; Israel is merely to look on with faith. The reference to God's powerful arm and right hand recall the reference to his hand in v 3. **4.** *the light of your face:* God's favor and good will toward his people. It may also suggest the nimbus of fearful splendor that envelops the divine warrior, terrifying the enemies (Exod 14:24). **10.** Cf. Ps 60:12 (= 108:12). **12.** *you make us like sheep:* Or "you sell us." Note the *inclusio* with the end of the complaint in v 23 ("like sheep for slaughter"). **24.** *do not reject us forever:* This recalls v 10, using the same vb. *why do you sleep?:* Cf. Pss 7:7; 35:23; 59:5–6; 121:4. *why do you forget:* Since Israel has not forgotten God (v 21), why then does

God forget them? **27.** Cf. Ps 3:8 for a similar prayer at the end of a lament.

62   Ps 45. A royal wedding song—very old and with a number of obscurities. Structure: v 2 (introduction of the psalmist); vv 3–9 (praise of the groom); vv 10–16 (praise of the bride); vv 17–18 (concluding words to the king). **2.** *my heart is astir:* The vb., which occurs only here, probably refers to poetic inspiration. **4–5.** Only the first line is clear, speaking of the king's military prowess. *in your splendor and majesty:* Cf. Ps 8:6. **7.** The most controverted verse of the ps. "Your throne, O God [addressed to the king], is eternal." If correct, this interpretation would suggest the entrance of the Near Eastern concept of divine kingship into the royal court. The king has already been described as endowed with the divine attributes of "splendor and majesty" (v 4); cf. also Pss 2:7; 89:28; 2 Sam 7:14. However, other transls. are possible (see the commentaries). **13.** Obscure: the first two words can mean "daughter [princess] of Tyre," "Lady Tyre" (a personification of the city), or even "Tyrian linen." If the following phrase means "among the gifts," that might suggest the last of these possibilities. **14–15.** The bride's wedding garments and the procession to the royal palace are described. **17–18.** The psalmist speaks of the dynasty, from the king's predecessors to the sons who will succeed him. The reference in v 18 to the king's "name" may connote his descendants.

63   Ps 46. The first of the Zion hymns, hymns of praise to the Temple (also Pss 48; 76; 84; 87; 122), an identification made likely by the presence of several motifs of the Zion tradition (the river of paradise, Yahweh's battle with and victory over the chaotic powers of the sea, the defeat of the foreign nations). Structure: vv 2–4 (outbreak of chaos); vv 5–8 (the peaceful city of God amid political turmoil); vv 9–12 (end of warfare and exaltation of God). Note the refrain in vv 8 and 12. **2–4.** The outbreak of chaos is described as earth quaking, mountains collapsing, seas roaring. **5.** The peaceful "city of God"; the unruly waters have been transformed into the river that brings joy to the city. **6.** Though mountains quake, the city where God dwells is immovable. For the theme of God's help in the morning cf. Ps 5:3. **7.** Parallel to the outbreak of chaos is political turmoil (cf. "roaring" in v 4, "quaking" in v 3). **9–10.** Just as the picture of unruly chaos shifted to the peaceful city, so the description of political turmoil concludes with a reference to the cessation of war and the destruction of weapons (Ps 76:4; Hos 2:20; Zech 9:10).

64   Ps 47. One of the enthronement psalms (including also 93; 96–99) celebrating God's kingship. The cultic setting of these pss, according to Mowinckel (→ 6 above), is the new year celebration. A date in the Davidic-Solomonic era (10th cent.) is likely. Structure: vv 2–5 (praise of Yahweh as Elyon); vv 6–8 (enthronement of Yahweh in heaven); vv 9–10 (tribute to Yahweh on earth). **2.** Cf. 2 Kgs 11:12. Compare "Yahweh has become king" from the enthronement hymns (Pss 93:1; 96:10; 97:1; 99:1). **3.** *Yahweh is awesome Elyon:* "Most High" (*'elyôn,* an epithet of Yahweh drawn from Canaanite polytheism) was the overlord of the divine world as well as the human (Ps 97:9). **4–5.** These verses recall the events of the conquest as well as the more recent imperial expansion under David. **6–9.** The enthronement of Yahweh is accomplished amid praise from the heavenly court (Ps 22:4). Not only are "all peoples" (v 2), vassal nations of the Davidic-Solomonic empire, called upon to praise the imperial god; Yahweh Elyon is to be praised by the gods of these vassal states as well (Pss 96:4–5; 97:9). **10.** *gathered to the God of Abraham:* Probably a reference to the annual trips by vassal rulers to the imperial center to pay tribute (2 Sam

8:2,6,10–12; Isa 2:2–3). The claim that shields belong to God may be related to the destruction of weapons motif found in the Zion hymns (Ps 46:10).

65   Ps 48. Like Ps 46, a Zion hymn, focusing on the motifs of the divine mountain and the defeat of the nations gathered against Israel (Ps 2:2–3). Another Zion motif, the pilgrimage to the sanctuary, may be present in vv 9–15. Structure: vv 2–4 (praise of Yahweh in Zion); vv 5–8 (defeat of political foes); vv 9–12 (praise of God in the Temple); vv 13–15 (journey through Zion). **2–3.** *in the city of our God: NAB, RSV,* and *NEB* all link this with what precedes. Dahood and Craigie connect it to what follows. **4.** *God is in its citadels:* Cf. Pss 46:6; 76:2–3; Mic 3:11; Zeph 3:15,17. **5–8.** The attacks of the nations on Zion and their flight and destruction (Pss 2:4–9; 46:7–8; 76:5–7). The fear that grips the kings is the characteristic language of holy war (Exod 15:14–16; Josh 2:9–11). **9.** The vision of the impregnable city protected by God that brought terror to the hostile kings brings joy to the pilgrims. **10.** *within your Temple:* The goal of the pilgrimage is participation in the Temple cult. **11.** *as your name, O God:* The "name" and "praise" of God may denote his manifestation in luminous splendor. Note the shift from descriptive praise (words about God) in v 1 to prayer (words addressed to God) in vv 10–11. **13–14.** The worshipers join a procession around the holy city. "Its towers" forms an *inclusio* with the same word (translated "citadels") in v 4. **15.** *this is God:* Consideration of the impregnable city leads the pilgrims to a consideration of the divine source of the city's strength.

66   Ps 49. A wisdom psalm. The themes of the success and prosperity of the wicked, the psalmist's enemies, and the fate of death awaiting wise and fool alike, give the ps a Joban cast. Like Job, Ps 49 is concerned with theodicy. The text is frequently obscure, and the meaning consequently uncertain. Structure: vv 2–5 (address of wisdom teacher); vv 6–13 (death, the common fate of all); vv 14–16 (redemption from sheol by God); vv 17–21 ("you can't take it with you"). **2.** The invitation perhaps recalls the universalistic perspective of the wisdom teachers. **4–5.** The wisdom language of these verses includes "wisdom," "insight," and "proverb," or "wise instruction" (Hebr *māšāl*). **8–9.** Extremely difficult. A suggested transl.: "Surely a person of high degree cannot redeem himself or pay to God his ransom; the redemption of one's life is so costly that (since one cannot pay it) he ceases forever." **10–11.** Death is the common fate of all — the wise, the foolish, and the brute animals. **13.** A kind of refrain (repeated with variations in v 21), reflecting on the transitoriness of life. **15.** *with Death shepherding them:* The language calls to mind the Canaanite god Mot ("Death"). **16.** *from the clutches of sheol he will certainly take me:* Some interpreters see here an implication of future life with God (cf. Ps 73:23–26). "Take" is used for the assumptions of Enoch (Gen 5:24) and Elijah (2 Kgs 2:10). **21.** *for all his wealth, man does not understand:* Cf. the similar statement in v 13. These two refrain-like verses take up the themes of knowledge and mortality significant in the Yahwist creation story (Gen 2–3), a text whose wisdom associations have been noted.

67   Ps 50. This ps appears to be a part of a covenant-renewal liturgy and may have close ties to prophetic circles. God, the overlord, raises charges against his vassal, Israel, for violating the covenant. Structure: Part I: vv 1–6 (call to judgment); Part II: vv 7–15 (the issue of sacrifices); Part III: vv 16–23 (rebuke of those who do not obey God): vv 16–17 (general indictment); vv 18–21 (specific indictment); vv 22–23 (summarizing conclusion). **1–6.** Yahweh as divine judge summons earth (v 1) and heaven (v 4) as witnesses in a "covenant lawsuit" against his people (cf. Jer 2:9–13). **5.** Introduction of the theme of sacrifice, developed at length in Part II (cf. also v 23). For sacrifice in a covenant context, cf. Gen 31:51–54; Exod 24:22. **7–21.** The two sections deal with what kinds of actions are pleasing to the covenant God. The first (ending with vv 14–15) reminds the people that sacrifice is not enough; obedience to God's will must accompany it (cf. Ps 40:7,9). This is the subject of vv 16–21. **14.** Sacrifice as a response to God's saving deeds. The "thank offering" and the "vow" were two types of "communion sacrifice," which established union between God and the offerer. **15.** Calling upon God's name often accompanied sacrifice (cf. 1 Kgs 18:26; 1 Chr 21:26). **16–21.** The heart of the "case" Yahweh brings against the people — failure to keep the laws of the covenant; compare the "entrance liturgy" (Pss 15; 24:3–6). **16.** Many commentators make a sharp separation between vv 7–15 and 16–21, understanding the latter to be addressed to a different group. But more likely "the wicked" means "the accused (Israel)." **23.** Conclusion, summarizing the ps and reiterating its major themes: the importance of the thank offering (Part II) and of walking in God's way — i.e., keeping his covenant law (Part III).

68   Ps 51. An individual lament, one of the penitential psalms. The historical heading relates the ps to the incident of David's adultery with Bathsheba (2 Sam 11–12). Structure: vv 3–9 (lament: prayer for pardon and confession of sin); vv 10–14 (prayer for restoration); vv 15–19 (praise of God before the community and the sacrifice of a humble heart); vv 20–21 (prayer for the rebuilding of Jerusalem and the restoration of the Temple cult). **3.** *have mercy on me:* Pss 56 and 57 also begin with this expression; cf. 2 Sam 12:22. *your steadfast love and the abundance of your compassion:* Cf. Pss 69:14,17; 106:45–46; Isa 63:7; Lam 3:32; Neh 13:22. *blot out my rebellions:* Cf. Isa 43:25; 44:22. **4.** Cf. Jer 2:22. **6.** Cf. 2 Sam 12:9,13. **7.** Being "born in sin" is poetic hyperbole meaning "thoroughly sinful" (cf. Ps 58:4; Isa 48:8). **10.** *let me hear:* The psalmist prays here for an oracle of salvation. **11.** The single instance in the pss where God's "hiding his face" is understood positively. Here it is not a sign of divine displeasure (Pss 27:9; 69:18; 88:15; etc.) but of grace and forgiveness. **12.** For the theme of a new heart and spirit, cf. Ezek 11:19; 36:28. **16.** *bloodguilt:* The psalmist prays not to be held responsible for the death of sinners in their sin (Ezek 3:18–21; 33:7–9). **17–19.** God's supposed disinterest in animal sacrifice may be an indication that Temple worship is now no longer possible; all that can now be offered is "a broken spirit. . . ." Cf. 1 Sam 15:22; Ps 40:7. **20–21.** The psalmist concludes by looking forward to the rebuilding of the Temple and the reinauguration of its cult. These verses are clearly late. Given the allusion in vv 17–19 to a destroyed Temple and an interrupted cult, they are probably not an addition to the ps (as many commentators believe); rather the whole poem is exilic or postexilic.

69   Ps 52. This ps is difficult to fit into the standard categories, though it is usually classified as an individual lament. Structure: Part I (vv 2–7): vv 2–6 (activity of the wicked); 7 (curse and fate of the wicked); Part II (vv 8–11): vv 8–9 (the reaction of the righteous); vv 10–11 (the happy fate of the psalmist). This poem echoes the wisdom theme of the doom of the wicked contrasted with the happy lot of the righteous (cf. Ps 37). **2–6.** The psalmist addresses a "mighty man" — perhaps a particular individual or someone representing a larger group of the unrighteous. His wicked activity consists of plotting (v 4) and slanderous speech (vv 4–6). **3.** *O champion!:* The exact meaning in this context is unclear.

4. The evil actions of the wicked have to do mainly with speech. Note how they are framed by "tongue" (vv 4,6). **6.** *every (sort of) hellish deed:* Originally a name for the netherworld (see comment on Ps 41:9), *bĕlîya'al* (emended text) was used to form epithets to designate the vilest type of person or thing (cf. Deut 13:13; Judg 19:22). **7.** A curse, with parallels in other ancient Near Eastern curses. In the overall context of the ps (cf. v 10) the poet may be asking that God refuse the wicked person access to the Temple, called "tent" here (Ps 15:1; → 16 above) and in parallelism with "land of life" (cf. Ps 27:13). **8-11.** The subject of the second part of the ps is the righteous contrasted with the wicked. **8.** A continuation of v 7. "Fear" here means "fear God" for his just judgments (cf. Pss 40:4; 64:9-10). **10-11.** Whereas the wicked one is excluded from God's tent (v 7), the psalmist will be rooted in the Temple (v 10a); whereas he trusts in his riches (v 9), the psalmist trusts in God's steadfast love (v 10b); whereas he uses speech to evil purpose (vv 4-6), the poet uses it to praise God (v 11).

70   Ps 53. The "Elohistic" version of Ps 14 (→ 3,32 above). The differences between the two pss are slight, except for one verse (14:5-6 = 53:6). **6.** Corresponds to 14:5-6. The two pss are similar enough to suggest some kind of literary dependence. A number of phrases in v 6 are obscure.

71   Ps 54. An individual lament. Structure: vv 3-5 (petition to God with description of affliction); vv 6-7 (confession of trust); vv 8-9 (vow). **5.** If "foreigners" (*zārîm*) is the correct reading here (rather than "insolent men" [*zēdîm*], as in Ps 86:14), Dahood's identification of the psalmist with the king is strengthened. *who do not keep God in mind:* Lit., "in front of them." Not to keep God "in front of" oneself (cf. Ps 16:8) means to ignore him and his statutes; cf. Ps 50:17. **7.** An example of talion; the bad fate his foes planned for the psalmist should be theirs (cf. Pss 37:14-15; 64:5). **8-9.** The psalmist vows an offering to God in thanksgiving for deliverance from enemies. **9.** *because you have delivered me:* Or "O that you would deliver me!" (cf. Ps 3:8).

72   Ps 55. An individual lament, whose structure is difficult to discern. Probably: vv 2-3a (petition to God); vv 3b-6 (description of the psalmist's suffering); vv 7-9 (wish to flee distress); vv 10-16 (curse against enemies; confession of trust); vv 17-19 (confidence in a saving God); vv 20-24 (curse against enemies; confession of trust [v 24d]). **8.** Tranquillity "in the wilderness" contrasts with violence "in the city" (v 10). **10-12.** Some have theorized that the psalmist dwells in a pagan city (Gunkel). But the prophets use similar language to refer to Jerusalem (Jer 6:6-7; Ezek 7:23). **13-15.** The identity of the psalmist's former companion remains problematic —perhaps a personal friend or (vv 21-22) a political ally. **24.** *cast them down, O God:* Most likely a curse like vv 10,16, and possibly 20. The psalmist's last word, however, is one of trust, echoing vv 17-19.

73   Ps 56. An individual lament. Structure: vv 2-5 (petition to God); vv 6-8 (persecution by enemies); vv 9-12 (confession of trust); vv 13-14 (concluding vow); a refrain (vv 5,11-12) concludes the first and third sections. **7-8.** Somewhat unclear. The reference to the psalmist's foes as "peoples" may point to the king as speaker. **9.** Tentatively, "Keep a record of my lament; enter my tears on your parchment, yes, in your ledger" (cf. Dahood). **14.** Cf. Ps 116:8-9. Note the chiasm "death . . . feet . . . walk . . . life." *in the land of life:* Preferable to "light of life" (cf. John 8:12) as Dahood has shown; cf. Ps 116:9. This may be a reference to the Temple (cf. Ps 27:13).

74   Ps 57. An individual lament. Structure: vv 2-4 (petition); vv 5-7 (complaint); vv 8-12 (vow). A

refrain (vv 6,12) focuses on Yahweh's loftiness. **4.** *steadfast love and fidelity:* Two "guardian angels" sent by God to protect the psalmist (cf. Ps 43:3). **5-6.** God's lofty state is contrasted with that of the psalmist, who lies down among lions. **6.** *your loftiness is above the heavens, O God:* See Dahood. Preferable to "Be exalted above the heavens . . ." (*RSV*). In the ancient Near East the gods were pictured as being of gigantic stature (cf. Isa 6:1). The refrain thus uses images of height and breadth. **11-12.** Yahweh's steadfast love and fidelity to his faithful are on a scale comparable to his own grandeur and glory, which are likewise "as high as the sky."

75   Ps 58. The form of this ps is difficult to define and depends to some extent on the interpretation of v 2. It appears to be a lament bemoaning the evil wrought by the wicked. If in fact the gods are addressed in v 2, it may be considered a polemic against pagan deities, similar in some respects to Ps 82. Structure: vv 2-3 (address to pagan gods); vv 4-6 (description of the ruinous ways of the wicked); vv 7-10 (appeal to God to set things right; [sevenfold?] curse against the wicked); vv 11-12 (wish that the righteous may celebrate God's victory over the wicked). **2-3.** In the ancient Near Eastern view the human world was ruled by the supreme deity in concert with the lesser gods (cf. Deut 32:8 [LXX]). According to the ps they were not doing their duty, so the wicked (lit., "the guilty") had power to do harm in the world (cf. Ps 82:2-4). **2.** *do you pronounce sentence justly, O gods?:* The key word (*'lm*) could mean "gods" or "powerful men" (lit., "rams"). "Gods" is the more likely reading. **4-6.** The wicked and their venomous character (v 5). The analogy of the "deaf adder" could refer to their obduracy. **7-10.** Some have seen here a sevenfold curse against the wicked (cf. the sevenfold curses in Ps 35:4-8, 19-26). **10.** Transl. and meaning uncertain. **11.** *let the righteous bathe his feet in the blood of the wicked:* A vivid expression denoting complete victory over a foe, common in the ancient Near East. **12.** An *inclusio* with vv 2-3 by repeating "gods/God," "humanity," and "on the earth."

76   Ps 59. An individual (probably royal) lament. The king, besieged by his enemies, cries to God for deliverance. The ps divides into two almost equal parts, vv 2-11a and 11b-18, each ending with a refrain—vv 10-11a,18) and containing another refrainlike verse (7,15). **2-4.** The context indicates that the description of the psalmist's foes is more than poetic imagery: they are foreigners intent upon killing him. **7-8.** Perhaps a picture of enemies besieging a fortified town, using the cover of darkness to penetrate the city's defenses. **9.** *but you laugh at them, Yahweh:* A motif of the Zion tradition: Because of God's impregnable defenses the enemies' schemes are in vain (cf. Pss 2:4-5; 48:6). **12.** *slay them, O God:* The MT has "Do not slay them," which contradicts the context. Read Hebr *'l* as *'ēl*, "O God" (cf. *NAB*), rather than as *'al*, "do not." Unless Yahweh shows himself as the divine judge, punishing the wicked (in this case, the attacking foe), the people may well "forget" God.

77   Ps 60. A communal lament, probably following a military defeat. The specific enemy in mind would seem to be Edom (see below on v 11). The ps might be dated to the monarchic period (so Dahood), though the concern with Edom (cf. Ps 137:7; Lam 4:21-22) could point to the exile. Structure: vv 3-7 (description of affliction and prayer for deliverance); vv 8-11 (God's response); vv 12-14 (reprise of the themes of 3-7). **3-7.** The pattern of distress (vv 3-6) followed by prayer (v 7) is repeated in the concluding section (vv 12-14). **3b.** Most likely Dahood is correct in taking this verse as a continuation of the negative theme: "You turned away from us" (contrast *RSV, NAB*). **7–14.** These verses are also found in Ps 108:7–14. **8–11.** The central part of the ps, which forms a direct response to "answer us!" in v 7. Probably an oracle of salvation; God asserts his supremacy over Judah-Israel (vv 8–9) and her traditional enemies (vv 10–11). **11.** Most likely part the divine oracle: "Who will bring me [God] the Rock City [as tribute]? Who will set me on Edom's throne?" (Dahood). **12–14.** Note the repetition of "God, you have rejected" (v 3) and the resumption of 1st pers. pl. pronouns ("us," "our"). Though reflecting the pattern of vv 3–7, the weight of this section is less lament (v 12) than petition (vv 13–14). **14.** Either a continuation of the petition or a statement of confidence in God's power in light of the oracle of vv 8–11.

78   Ps 61. Without the prayer for the king in vv 7–8 this ps could be classified as a fairly typical individual lament. Mowinckel, Dahood, and Eaton make these verses central to the ps and so classify it as a royal psalm. Structure: vv 2–3 (prayer of a suppliant near death); vv 4–6 (trust in God who hears the prayer); vv 7–8 (prayer for a long life and reign for the king); v 9 (concluding note of praise). **3.** *from the brink of the netherworld:* So (correctly) Dahood. *when my heart fails:* Cf. Ps 143:3–4 and Jonah 2:7–8 for descent to the netherworld joined with the psalmist's fainting heart. *lead me to a high mountain:* The psalmist moves from the brink of the depths to a towering mountain. **4.** *the enemy:* The netherworld context of v 3 makes likely Dahood's suggestion that this is "the last Enemy," Death personified (Ps 49:15; 1 Cor 15:26). **5.** Cf. Ps 15:1; the king prays that he always have access to the Temple. **8.** *may he dwell forever in the presence of God:* Note the movement from the presence of the enemy to the presence of God. The similarity to v 5 shows "dwell" to be the correct transl. (so *NEB*). Cf. Ps 23:6.

79   Ps 62. A psalm of trust, despite a number of obscurities (esp. in vv 2–4 and 10), which contains some of the most powerful language of trust in God in the Psalter. Structure: vv 2–5 (the psalmist's trust in God despite harassment by enemies); vv 6–9 (invitation to the community to follow the psalmist's example and trust in God); vv 10–12 (human insignificance and warning against ill-gotten wealth); vv 12–13 (concluding divine oracle). **2.** The first part of this verse is obscure; the equally obscure parallel phrase in v 6 does not elucidate it. **4.** *like a sagging fence, a wall knocked down:* Could refer either to the psalmist or to his foes (so Dahood). **8.** *my glorious savior:* Lit., "my glory and my salvation." **10.** *only a breath is humankind:* Cf. Ps 144:4. Ps 39:6–7,12 also joins the motif of human transitoriness with the futility of amassing wealth (cf. Ps 49:7–11). **12–13.** Appropriately after a passage on human insignificance, the divine oracle speaks of the might and steadfast love (*ḥesed*) of God. **13.** *you repay:* Or "O that you would repay. . . ." Cf. 2 Sam 3:39.

80   Ps 63. Usually considered a psalm of trust, though difficult to classify. The psalmist (perhaps the king) longs for the reviving presence of God in the Temple. Perhaps no other ps so vividly expresses the intimate relationship of love between God and his faithful one. Structure: v 2 (setting: the psalmist far from God); vv 3–4 (prayer to see Yahweh in the Temple); vv 5–6 (prayer that the psalmist may be able to go on blessing and praising God); vv 7–9 (expression of intimacy with God); vv 10–12 (curse against enemies [vv 10–11] and blessing for the righteous [v 12]). **2.** The imagery here is spatial: the psalmist finds himself distant from God and longs to be near him. **3–6.** Two matching sections (vv 3–4,5–6), each beginning with *kēn*, "thus"(?), and each with *śpty*, "[my] lips," in the last line. Both parts

are probably to be construed as a prayer or wish ("May I gaze . . . May I bless"). **3.** For Israelites, life was the supreme good; only here in the OT is anything prized above it—God's love. Insights like this eventually led to the belief that God's love extended even beyond death (cf. Rom 8:38–39). **9.** *my soul clings to you:* The vb. "cling," often used to denote the proper relationship with God in the deuteronomistic literature (Josh 23:8; Deut 10:20; 11:22; etc.), expresses great intimacy (Gen 2:24; Ruth 1:14). **10–12.** The serene picture of the poet's relationship with God is overshadowed by the thought of those intent upon his death. Hence he asks God to destroy them. In vv 10 and 11 the first part of the verse describes evil the enemies want to do to the psalmist, and the second is a curse against them.

81   Ps 64. An individual lament, or a psalm of trust (Mowinckel). Structure: vv 2–7 (prayer for divine aid against the enemy); vv 8–11 (overcoming of enemies by God and thanksgiving of the psalmist). **4.** Difficult; perhaps "They string (their bows); their arrows (are) bitter words." Cf. Ps 120:2–4; Jer 9:7. **5.** *from ambush:* Lit., "from hiding places," which recalls the psalmist's plea "Hide me!" in v 3. **8.** By the principle of talion, those who were shooting arrows at the innocent become themselves targets for God's arrows. *shake their heads:* A gesture of contempt; cf. Pss 22:8 and 109:25. **10.** *all humankind will fear:* Possibly to be emended to "all humankind will *see* and proclaim the work of God." Cf. Ps 66:5.

82   Ps 65. A prayer for rain. The psalmist looks to God's past benefits to Israel (esp. the sending of rain) and prays that God show the same benevolence at the beginning of a new agricultural year. Structure: vv 2–5 (praise of God who hears prayers and forgives sins, filling the people with the goodness of his Temple); vv 6–9 (hymnic celebration of God the creator); vv 10–14 (the life-giving effects of the winter rains). Cf. Jer 5:22–25. **2.** *in Zion:* The reference here and the mention of the Temple in v 5 may indicate that the cultic setting is the fall pilgrimage feast of Tabernacles. **3–4.** The confession and forgiveness of sins are necessary since sin can prevent the coming of the rain (1 Kgs 8:35–36; Amos 4:7–8). **5.** *the goodness of your house:* Primarily the presence of God, "goodness" also alludes to God's benefits, abundant rain and food. **6.** *with awesome deeds:* A reference to creation (cf. Ps 139:14). **8.** *the uproar of the peoples:* Successful agriculture in Israel depended not only on the rains but on security from military attack. **10.** *you prepared for the grain:* An elliptical phrase, meaning "you prepared (the earth for the planting of) grain (with the coming of the winter rains)." **12.** *your tracks dripped lush growth:* As in v 10, an elliptical expression for "your tracks (left by your rain-cloud chariot) dripped (the rain that produced) lush growth." **13.** *the pastures of the steppe dripped:* I.e., the untilled grazing land overflowed with water. *the hills were clothed with joy:* Another ellipsis for "the hills were clothed with (the vines that produce the wine that brings) joy" (Judg 9:12–13; Ps 102:13–15). **14.** *they shout for joy:* "They" includes the people blessed with God's bounty and all nature as well (Pss 96:11–12; 98:7–8; Isa 42:11–12; 44:23).

83   Ps 66. This ps is made up of a hymnic section of divine praise (vv 1–7), a communal thanksgiving for deliverance (vv 8–12), and an individual thanksgiving (vv 13–20). Mowinckel has argued that it is a unity, a national thanksgiving spoken by the king (as representative of the people). **5.** *come and see the works of God:* Cf. Pss 46:9; 64:10. **6.** An instance of merism, whereby the whole history of salvation is suggested by the mention of the first event (crossing of the Reed Sea) and the last (crossing of the Jordan). **7.** *he is ruler . . . forever:* Just as the hymn of Exod 15 moves from the crossing of the sea (vv 4–10) to the crossing of the Jordan (vv 16–17) and concludes with an affirmation of Yahweh's eternal kingship (v 18), so in summary fashion do vv 6–7 at the conclusion of the hymnic section of Ps 66. **12b.** *through fire and water:* A merism meaning "every possible kind of difficulty"; cf. Isa 43:2; Sir 15:16. **13.** *I will go with holocausts to your house:* Cf. Ps 5:8 for similar reference to access to the Temple (often a royal motif; cf. 2 Kgs 20:5–6; Ps 61:7–8). **19–20.** An *inclusio* with the beginning of the communal thanksgiving in v 8: "God has heard . . . the sound of my prayer" (cf. "Make heard the sound of his praise" in v 8), "blessed be God" (cf. "bless our God, O peoples").

84   Ps 67. Most commentators consider this ps to be a communal thanksgiving for a good agricultural year, perhaps composed for use at the feast of Tabernacles. Dahood understands it rather as a prayer for a good harvest, by the reading he proposes for the first vb. in v 7. Structure: the refrain divides the ps into vv 2–4, 5–6,7–8. **2.** The opening verse alludes to the Aaronic blessing (Num 6:24–26); cf. Pss 4:7–8; 31:17. **5.** *NAB,* on the basis of Ps 96:10, translates: "May the nations be glad and exult, because you rule the peoples in equity; the nations on earth you guide." **7.** *the earth has given its produce:* Or "May the earth yield her produce" (Dahood). This transl. fits well with the petitionary prayer in vv 2, 4,6,8, and in the refrain. Cf. Lev 26:4 and Ps 85:13.

85   Ps 68. Probably the most obscure and difficult of the pss. The difficulties include not only many individual words and lines but the nature of the whole poem itself. Is it a coherent whole or an ancient catalogue of lyric poems (as proposed by W. F. Albright [*HUCA* 23 (1950–51) 1–39])? For Albright Ps 68 is composed of 30 "incipits" (first lines or strophes) of a series of ancient hymns. Such catalogues are found in Mesopotamian literature. Recent attempts to understand Ps 68 in more unitary fashion include the work of Dahood, who considers it a triumphal hymn. **2.** Cf. Num 10:35 where the same language is used of the movement of the ark. **3.** *like the melting of wax before the fire:* The language of theophany, as in Ps 97:5 and Mic 1:4. **5.** *the rider of the clouds:* In the Ugaritic literature, a standard appellation of the storm-god Baal, now transferred to Israel's God (cf. Deut 33:26; Ps 18:10; Isa 19:1; and v 34 below). **6.** Similar descriptions of the concern for the fatherless and the widow (cf. Deut 10:18; 27:19; Pss 82:2–3; 146:9) are found in Ugaritic literature. **7.** *God causes the unmarried to set up a house:* I.e., to have a family—Albright's interpretation, preferable to the *NAB*'s "God gives a home to the forsaken." Cf. Ps 113:9. **8–9.** The close parallel with the theophany described in Judg 5:4–5. **13–15.** One of the most obscure passages in the Psalter; no proposed transl. has won assent. **16–17.** The rivalry of the mountains and the choice of Zion as the divine dwelling (cf. Ps 132:13). If the ps is a unitary composition, this reference to the Temple would point to a 10th-cent. *terminus a quo.* The theme of the mountains vying to be the divine abode may point to a time before the choice of Zion was an accepted fact. **18b.** The *NAB* is probably correct: "The Lord has come from Sinai to the sanctuary [Zion]" (cf. Isa 2:2–4). **19.** The enthronement of the victorious God in the sanctuary, applied in Eph 4:8–9 to the heavenly enthronement of the ascended Christ. **23.** In the context of vv 20–24 (the triumph of God), Albright sees here a reference to the battle of creation between Baal and Sea (as do Dahood and the *NEB*) and translates the (emended) text, "Yahweh said, 'From smiting the serpent I return, I return from destroying Sea!'" **30.** For kings bringing gifts to the Jerusalem Temple, cf. Isa 60:6–7,11–14. **33–34.** Cf. v 5 for similar language and

motifs. The reference to the storm-god leads naturally to a reference to thunder, the storm-god's voice. **36b.** Cf. Ps 29:11.

86   Ps 69. An individual lament, in which the psalmist, unjustly accused of theft, appeals to God for justice. Structure: vv 2–5 (prayer for salvation from injustice and perjury of enemies); vv 6–13 (alienation of psalmist from the family and community); vv 14–19 (renewal of appeal for salvation from enemies); vv 23–30 (the psalmist's curse of his enemies); vv 31–37 (thanksgiving). If vv 36–37 are original to the ps (see below), then Ps 69 should be dated to the exilic or postexilic period. **2.** *the waters have risen up to my neck:* So *RSV,* correctly. The imagery of vv 2–3 is that of the river ordeal; cf. Ps 40:3 for discussion. **4.** The hot, parched throat and the eyes dimmed (by tears) are a poetic description of weeping; the same imagery reappears in vv 20–22. Cf. Pss 31:10–11; 38:9–11; Lam 2:18–19. **10.** The first line is quoted in Rom 15:13; the second, in John 2:17. **13.** *those who sit at the gate:* The elders who administered justice; cf. Deut 21:19; 22:15; Amos 5:12,15, etc. This phrase is paired with "wine drinkers" to form a merism in which the psalmist claims to be mocked by everyone, from the most respected to the scorned. **16.** Poetic language referring to the netherworld, from whose raging waters the psalmist prays to be delivered. **19b.** Difficult. Dahood plausibly renders Hebr *lm'n 'yby,* "because of my enemies," as "from the abode of my Foe," i.e., the netherworld presided over by Death. **22.** Alluded to in Matt 27:34; Mark 15:23; Luke 23:36; John 19:29. **25–26.** The imagery derives from the language of the sirocco, spoken of as God's "fury" and his "burning anger." **30.** The final line of the lament ends with the psalmist's appeal ("May your salvation, O God, protect me"), recalling the opening words in v 2. **31–32.** The claim that songs of thanksgiving are better than sacrifice may indicate that the Temple cult is no longer possible. This would point to an exilic or early postexilic setting for all of Ps 69, not just vv 36–37, which would be the original conclusion of the ps and not a late addition. Cf. Ps 51:17–19 for a similar judgment. **33–34.** Cf. Ps 22:25–27. **35.** The sea that threatened to engulf the psalmist now joins heaven and earth in praising God. The reference to the sea forms an *inclusio* with the threatening watery depths in v 3.

87   Ps 70. An individual lament, a doublet of Ps 40:14–18; the two texts vary in minor details. In 70:2,5–6 the divine title used is *'ĕlōhîm,* "God," while it is *Yahweh* in the parallel passages in 40:14,17–18 (if *'ădōnāy* in 40:18 represents an original *Yahweh*). The situation is reversed in the final line of Ps 70, where *Yahweh* is used where Ps 40:18b has *'ĕlōhāy,* "my God." **2.** *O God, rescue me:* Ps 40:18 has "Be gracious, Yahweh, rescue me." **3.** *who seek my life:* 40:15 adds "to snatch it away." **4.** *let them turn back:* 40:16 has "let them be stunned." **6.** *O God, hasten to me:* 40:18 has "May my Lord (*'ădōnāy*) take thought of me." 70:6 forms with 70:2 an *inclusio* that is not present in 40:18.

88   Ps 71. An individual lament. Structure: Part I (vv 1–15): vv 1–6 (appeal to God for deliverance); vv 7–11 (complaint); vv 12–15 (curse against enemies; praise of God); Part II (vv 16–24): vv 16–19a (praise of God's righteousness); vv 19b–21 (confidence in God's future saving acts); vv 22–24 (concluding praise; defeat of enemies). The dominant motifs are: (a) the psalmist's determination to go on praising God despite present distress (vv 8,15,24); (b) the reliance on God as the source of strength (vv 3,5,18); (c) the psalmist's confidence in God's saving righteousness/righteous deeds, which forms an envelope around the ps (vv 2,24; cf. also vv 15–16,18). **5.** God's protection of the psalmist throughout life is underscored by the double reference to his youth (vv 5,17) and his old age (vv 9,18). **7.** *a portent to many:* An evil portent was dangerous and to be avoided. The expression here is perhaps best taken to mean that the psalmist has become something to be "avoided like the plague." Cf. Isa 8:18. **12–13.** Cf. v 24 and Ps 70:2–3. The similarity to Ps 70 may account for placing Pss 70 and 71 together. **18b.** Difficult; perhaps "until I announce your might to the throng [in the Temple], Your righteousness to all who enter your holy place." **24b.** A repetition of v 13 in slightly different form, which Dahood takes as a wish ("O that they would be shamed . . .").

89   Ps 72. A royal psalm. The heading "Of Solomon" (only here and in Ps 127) is appropriate in this dynastic prayer for the royal family. Structure: vv 1–4 (the king as provider of justice); vv 5–8 (prayer for a long reign for the king, provider of fertility); vv 9–11 (the tribute brought by foreign nations); vv 12–15 (recapitulation of the first three sections); vv 16–17 (prayer for fertility and for the king's progeny). An early, even a 10th-cent. date, is possible. **1.** The endowment of the king and his son (the heir) with justice by God is a common motif in ancient Near Eastern royal theology, as is the king's special responsibility for justice to the poor. The motif reappears in vv 12–14. Cf. Ps 82:2–4; Prov 29:14. **5.** On the basis of the LXX, the first word of the MT ("may they fear you") should be emended to "may he endure." Cf. Deut 17:20 and Ps 61:7. **6–7.** The king as provider of cosmic order and the fertility of the earth is a motif found in Egyptian royal theology. **8.** *from sea to sea:* Probably a reference to the Mediterranean in the W and the Persian Gulf in the E; "the river" is the Euphrates. The language of sea and river also recalls the Canaanite mythology discussed in Ps 24. **9.** In the context of vv 9–11 the desert dwellers (v 9) would be one of the foreign peoples subject to the king. **16.** Obscure and very difficult. The concern seems to be fertility, as in vv 6–7. **17.** The king's "name" here probably includes the notion of his offspring, "the king's son" of v 1. The prayer for the king and his progeny in vv 15–17 forms an *inclusio* with the prayer in v 1 for the king and the crown prince. *in him shall all the tribes of the earth be blessed:* An echo of the promise to the ancestors (Gen 12:3; 22:18; 26:4; 28:14; 48:20). It may allude to the covenant of royal grant which served as a pattern for God's covenant with both the patriarchs and the kings of Judah.

90   Ps 73. This ps begins Book III of the Psalter, largely a collection of levitical pss. It begins with the "Psalms of Asaph" (Pss 73–83 [also 50]; Ezra 2:41 lists Asaph as the ancestor of the Temple musicians. Like Ps 49 this wisdom psalm deals with the well-being of the wicked as a scandal to the righteous. The text is frequently obscure. Structure: Part I: the wicked (vv 1–12): vv 1–3 (introduction); vv 4–12 (description of the wicked); Part II: the psalmist (vv 13–28): vv 13–20 (his trial of faith; the recompense of the wicked); vv 21–26 (the psalmist's reward); vv 27–28 (conclusion). **1–3.** An introduction that states the psalmist's final conclusion about God's goodness and his personal trial. **1.** *to the virtuous:* The MT reads *lyśr'l,* "to Israel" (*TEV*); many commentators emend to *lyśr 'l,* "to the virtuous" (*NAB, RSV*). *the pure of heart:* Upright in intentions as well as actions (cf. Ps 24:4; Matt 5:8). **4–12.** The well-being of the wicked is a scandal to the psalmist. As creator and judge of the world, God is supposed to punish such people, not reward them with a happy life (Pss 37:1–2; 58; 75). **9.** *they set their mouths in heaven:* Or perhaps "against heaven" (i.e., against God). **10.** Extremely difficult. Most likely the verse describes the prosperity of the wicked. **14.** *afflictions:* Unlike the wicked (v 4) the

psalmist suffers much; here his woes are described in physical terms. **15.** The wicked "proclaim" not Yahweh's deeds (Pss 9:2,15; 78:4; 96:3; etc.) but their own imagined greatness (v 9). The psalmist refuses to imitate them but vows to recount the mighty deeds of God (v 28). **16–20.** The psalmist finds the "answer" to his dilemma in the presence of God—in the Temple. He comes to realize—perhaps through an oracle or a theophany—that in the end the wicked will perish (cf. Ps 37:1–2). **23–26.** The psalmist's happy fate is somehow to be with God. This may refer not to afterlife but to the experience of God's presence in the Temple. **28.** *drawing near to God:* Contrast v 27a. To "draw near" is a technical term for access to the holy place, usually reserved to priests. *I have made Yahweh my refuge:* Cf. Ps 91:9. The same vb. occurs in v 9. Whereas the wicked have "set" their mouths in heaven (v 9) the psalmist "sets" Yahweh as his refuge.

91   Ps 74. A communal lament. References to the destruction of the Temple (vv 4–7) may indicate that this ps is to be dated to the exilic period. Structure: vv 1–11 (first invocation of God to remember and save his people); vv 12–17 (recollection of God's power in creation); vv 18–23 (second invocation of God). The first and third sections, framing a creation hymn, contain the key term "remember" (vv 2,18,22). **4.** *standards:* The invading army has placed its military standards (cf. Num 2:2) in the Temple area. **9.** Prophets would reveal how long a tragedy was supposed to last (cf. Jer 25:11–12). The "signs" here are probably indications by divine revelation of the duration of the crisis. The lack of such signs contrasts with the many standards (lit., "signs") that the enemy has set up (v 4). **12–17.** A segment of a creation poem, reminding God of his mighty act at creation, when he defeated the powers of chaos. If he could annihilate them then and create the ordered cosmos (vv 16–17) could he not do the same now—i.e., destroy Judah's foes and restore her? **18–23.** This section echoes the theme "remember" (vv 18,22) from the beginning of the poem (v 2), adding "do not forget" (vv 19,23).

92   Ps 75. This ps contains elements of several literary types: communal thanksgiving, divine oracle. Some (Gunkel) would classify it as a prophetic liturgy, wherein a prophetic or cultic official delivers God's words of judgment. Structure: v 2 (opening statement of communal thanksgiving); vv 3–9 (divine oracle of judgment); vv 11–12 (concluding statement of praise). **2.** God is praised or thanked specifically for his "wondrous deeds," which would include judging the wicked (vv 3–9). **3–4.** God speaks (perhaps through a prophet), announcing judgment upon the wicked. In so doing he continues the process of creation (v 4), defeating the powers of chaos and asserting his absolute sovereignty (→ 18 above). **3.** *assembly:* Hebr *mô'ēd* can mean an appointed time or place. Here it is best taken as a reference to the divine assembly, the setting for God's judgment (Ps 82:1). **5–6.** "Horn" is a symbol for power (cf. v 11). The boasting of the wicked entails their self-exaltation (cf. vv 7–8) and failure to acknowledge Yahweh's universal rule. **9.** The "cup" is a metaphor for one's lot or fate from God's hand. The image of Yahweh's wrath as a cup (cf. Job 21:20; Isa 51:17; Hab 2:16; Rev 14:10) contrasts with the "cup of salvation" from God (Ps 116:13). **10.** *but I will exalt . . . :* The vb. is problematic. "I" may stand for the community. **11.** Divine judgment entails not only putting the wicked in their place but rewarding the righteous.

93   Ps 76. Probably to be classified as a Song of Zion (cf. Ps 46), celebrating God's abode in Jerusalem (vv 2–3) and his defeat of her attackers (vv 4–7). The ps is structured around three epithets of Yahweh: vv 2–4 (Yahweh the "renowned" one, dwelling on Zion); vv

5–7 (Yahweh the "resplendent" one, whose brightness overwhelms the foe); vv 8–13 (Yahweh the "awesome" one, to be feared and worshiped by all). **3.** *Salem:* Jerusalem (cf. Gen 14:18; Jdt 4:4). **4.** God's shattering the weapons of war does not speak of pacifism but rather echoes the "divine warrior" theme: It is God alone who defeats the enemies of Jerusalem (cf. Ps 46:10). **5–7.** The epithet "resplendent" is appropriate here, since it is Yahweh's "glory" that brings about the defeat of the enemy (Ps 44:4). **6.** Probably a description of the enemy's fainting and paralysis from the panic inspired by God's splendor. **8–13.** This section is marked off by the title "awesome one" (Hebr *nôrāʾ*) in vv 8 and 13. Verses 11–13 in particular are difficult but deal with acknowledging the sovereignty of the divine warrior. Most likely the nations are addressed. **10.** *the lowly ones of the land:* Most likely Israel, elsewhere designated Yahweh's "lowly ones" (cf. Pss 22:27; 69:33; 149:4). **11.** Edom was an often rebellious subject of Judah (cf. Ps 60:10–11). Hamath, on the Orontes River, marked the N limit of the promised land (Num 34:8; Ezek 47:15). **94** **Ps 77.** An individual lament (vv 2–11) followed by a hymn recalling the events of the exodus (vv 12–21). Each of these major divisions has three subsections: the lament divides into vv 2–3,4–7,8–11; the hymn, into vv 12–13,14–16,17–21. According to Kraus the "I" of the ps speaks for the community. **3.** The hand of the psalmist outstretched to God is the first appearance of a major unifying theme of the ps; cf. vv 11,16,21. **4–7.** The memories of the past give no comfort; the question of v 8 is the first of a series of questions central to the ps. **9–10.** These questions about God's care for his people allude to the famous creedal statement of Exod 34:6. The psalmist questions whether this confession of a merciful God is still credible, given the distress experienced. **11.** *the right hand of the Most High has changed:* I.e., Yahweh no longer seems interested in saving the psalmist (contrast Exod 15:6). **12–13.** Now the memories of God's acts of salvation in the Exodus bring hope (contrast vv 4–7). **14–16.** Cf. Exod 15:11. **15.** Redemption by the "arm" of God is the answer to the psalmist's fear that God's right hand had "changed" (v 11). **17.** *the waters saw you:* The terrifying theophany of the divine warrior. Cf. Exod 15:14–15, where it is the human enemies of Israel that tremble in fear. **18–19.** The twice-repeated "voice" of the psalmist in v 2 is matched by the two occurrences of the divine "voice." **21.** The hand of the psalmist in v 3 is balanced by the guiding hand of Moses and Aaron in v 21. **95** **Ps 78.** A historical psalm, narrating the story of Israel from the exodus to the early monarchy. Its purpose is to teach fidelity and to justify God's rejection of worship in the northern kingdom (v 67) and his choice of Judah as his dwelling place (vv 68–69). Structure: the ps consists of a didactic introduction (vv 1–11) followed by two parallel recitals of salvation history: vv 12–32 and 40–64, each with a sequel (vv 33–39 and 65–72). **1–8.** The didactic beginning is reminiscent of the wisdom psalms (cf. Ps 49:2–5). This section introduces the major themes of the ps: remembering/not forgetting (vv 7,11,35,39,42), God's saving deeds (vv 4,7,11–12, 32,43), keeping God's commandments/law (vv 7,10,56). **2.** Hebr *māšāl* has a wider range of meanings than "parable": here it means "wise instruction." Cf. Jesus' citation of this verse in reference to his teaching (Matt 13:35). **8.** *whose spirit was not faithful:* Cf. the similar v 37 and the etymologically related "believe" in vv 22,32. **13–14.** The terms "sin," "rebel," "test" recur as a kind of refrain of unfaithfulness in the ps: vv 32,40–41,56. **25.** *the food:* A reference to the manna (cf. Exod 16:21). **27–31.** Cf. Num 11:16–34. Yahweh became angry with the people because their demand for meat was an expression of their lack of trust. **43–51.** The plagues against Egypt. Though the number is 10 as in Exod 7–12, the sequence varies from one account to another and not all contain the same plagues (cf. Ps 105:28–36). **59–66.** A reference to the capture of the Ark and its aftermath (1 Sam 4–5), seen here as a foreshadowing of Yahweh's rejection of the northern kingdom as his dwelling place (vv 59,67). **67–72.** Yahweh chooses Judah, not "Ephraim" (the northern kingdom), as the site of his dwelling with humankind. **72.** *he shepherded them:* The subject is David (vv 70–71), not Yahweh. The poet may intend a contrast here between David with his upright heart and those earlier generations whose "heart was not steadfast" to God (v 8). **96** **Ps 79.** A communal lament. Like Ps 74 it refers to the sack of the Temple—thus probably to the siege by Babylon in the 6th cent. Throughout the poem, requests that God hear the psalmist alternate with requests for punishment of the pagan conquerors. Structure: vv 1–4 (the sacrilege and havoc wrought by the enemy); vv 5–10 (plea for God to act on his people's behalf); vv 11–13 (final petition). **3.** The blood of God's faithful poured out around Jerusalem may allude to the practice of pouring out the blood of a sacrificial victim at the base of the altar (Lev 18:7,18,etc.). **4.** *a laughingstock to our neighbors:* Cf. Ps 44:14; in v 12 we see that this mockery of Judah is tantamount to mockery of Yahweh. **6.** *pour out your wrath on the nations . . . :* By so doing God avenges the blood of his people that was "poured out" by the attackers (vv 3,10). **9.** Because this people is Yahweh's, his reputation is at stake; if he does not come to their aid God will be scorned as an ineffective "saving God" and will suffer a diminution of his "glory"—or honor—among the peoples. **11.** The common request that the words (or, as here, the sighs) of those who pray may come into Yahweh's presence—i.e., that he would pay attention to them. Cf. Pss 18:7; 88:3; 102:2; 119:170. **13.** Cf. Pss 23; 95:7; 100:3. **97** **Ps 80.** A communal lament. Its mention of areas in the N (v 3) as well as of "Israel" and "Joseph" (v 2) may indicate an origin in the northern kingdom. A refrain (vv 4,8,20—cf. also v 15) divides the poem into its various sections. Structure: vv 2–4 (introduction and appeal for help); vv 5–8 (description of the nation's woe); vv 9–14 (God has spurned the "vine" he has planted); vv 15–20 (plea that God save his people; repentance). **2.** *seated on the cherubim:* This epithet of Yahweh derives from the early period of Israel's history, when he moved about with the people in the Tent of Meeting (2 Sam 7:6), seated on the figures of the cherubim on the Ark (1 Sam 4:4; 2 Sam 6:2; Isa 37:16). **4.** *take us back, O God!:* Cf. Jer 15:19. Israel asks that Yahweh receive her back in the covenant relationship. Prophets in the northern kingdom did not hesitate to declare the covenant nullified because of Israel's infidelity (Amos 1:3–2:6; Hos 1:9). **9–14.** The psalmist reminds God of his solicitude for Israel in olden times, bringing this "vine" (Isa 5:1–7; 27:2–6) out of Egypt. **13–14.** Cf. Ps 89:41–42, where the vine stands for the king. **17.** The plea that Israel's enemies perish at the rebuke of his face (his frowning countenance) is the opposite of the prayer in the refrain: that God—i.e., his face—"shine" (smile) on his people again. **19.** *we will never be disloyal to you again!:* Israel confesses to being a disloyal subject and repents. **98** **Ps 81.** A prophetic liturgy (cf. Ps 50), probably associated with the feast of Tabernacles and of northern provenance. The presence in the hymn of a divine oracle uttered by a cultic official is a noteworthy feature. Other such oracles occur in Pss 2:7; 12:6; 32:8–9; 101:6–7. Structure: vv 2–6a (hymn); vv 6b–17

(divine oracle). Structurally Ps 81 is similar to Ps 95.
3–4. Cf. parallels in Pss 31:27; 149:3; 150:3–4; etc. **6.** *he made it [the feast] an ordinance for Joseph:* Difficult; this can also be translated "He [God] made a pact with Joseph." The second phrase can be rendered either "In his [God's] going forth over/against Egypt" (*RSV*) or "In his [Israel's] going forth from Egypt" (*NAB;* cf. Ps 114:1). **8.** *I tested you:* Cf. Exod 16:4; 20:20; Deut 8:2,16; 13:4. **10–11.** Cf. Exod 20:2–3. **16.** *those who hate Yahweh would cringe before him:* Cf. Deut 33:29; Ps 18:45. The sense of the vbs. may be optative: "May they cringe . . . may their fates be fixed." *finest wheat . . . honey from the rock:* Cf. Deut 32:13–14.

99   **Ps 82.** A prophetic vision report whose closest parallel is Isa 6. While the date of the poem is uncertain, its ideology points to the preexilic period. The ps is the theological midpoint between Israel's early faith, in which the "other gods" were real but subordinate to Yahweh (Deut 4:19), and Israel's later monotheism. Cf. also Ps 58. Structure: v 1 (God as judge of the gods); vv 2–7 (address of God to other divine beings: vv 2–5 [the gods' failure to provide justice]; vv 6–7 [the divine sentence]); v 8 (prayer of the psalmist). **1.** *God takes his stand:* Cf. Isa 3:13–14; Ps 76:10. For the idea of a legal proceeding instituted by Yahweh against the other gods, cf. Isa 41:21–24. *in the divine council:* The assembly of the gods, presided over by Yahweh (Deut 4:19; Ps 95:3); cf. 1 Kgs 22:19–22; Isa 6; Job 1–2. **3–4.** The gods are guilty of not upholding justice for the powerless in the domains assigned to them by the supreme God (Deut 32:8–10). **5.** For "darkness" as ignorance, cf. Job 12:24–25; 37:19; Eccl 2:14. Also suggested by the context is the darkness of the netherworld (1 Sam 2:9; Job 10:21–22; Ps 88:13; Prov 20:20), to which the dead gods are consigned. *the foundations of the world are shaken:* The failure of the gods to provide justice destabilizes the physical world (Ps 46:3,7; 60:4). **6.** *you are gods:* Cf. Isa 41:23; John 10:34. **7.** *die like humankind:* Immortality was a jealously guarded privilege of the gods (cf. Gen 3:22); cf. *ANET* 90 (the Gilgamesh Epic) and 150 (the Tale of Aqhat). **8.** A prayer of the psalmist that forms an *inclusio* with v 1, both by the parallelism of "stand" in v 1 with "rise" in v 8 (Exod 33:8; Ps 94:16) and by the balancing of the judgment passed in the heavens (v 1) with the judging of the earth (v 8).

100   **Ps 83.** A national lament provoked by a threat of invasion by Israel's surrounding enemies. While its date is debated, the reference to Assyria in v 9 probably points to the era of Assyrian ascendancy (9th–7th cent.). Structure: vv 2–9 (appeal and lament); vv 10–19 (prayer of imprecation against enemies). **2.** *O God, be not still!:* The vb. can refer to both speech (= "be not silent") and motion (= "be not inactive"—cf. *NAB*). **3.** Normally a posture of joy, the lifting up of the head here suggests arrogance (Judg 8:28; Zech 2:4; Job 10:15). **6.** The description of the conspiracy of Israel's enemies resembles Ps 2:1–2. **7–9.** Ten nations form the coalition against Israel. **10–12.** These verses call to mind the complex of stories in Judg 4–8. **13.** *the abode of God:* The land of Canaan; cf. Exod 15:13; Jer 31:23. **14–16.** The language of chaff, fire, and storm refers to the sirocco, the east wind as the weapon with which God destroys Israel's enemies. Cf. Hos 13:15; Isa 29:5–6. **19.** For Yahweh as Elyon ("Most High"), cf. Pss 47:3; 97:9.

101   **Ps 84.** A Song of Zion (cf. Ps 46) and a song of pilgrimage to Jerusalem (Pss 120–134). Structure: vv 2–4 (longing for the Temple); vv 5–8 (the happiness of the pilgrim); vv 9–10 (prayer for the king); vv 11–13 (God and his Temple as the source of blessing). **2.** *lovely:* Hebr *yĕdîdôt* may contain an allusion to Solomon the

Temple builder, whose name at birth was *Yĕdîdyāh* = Jedidiah, "beloved of Yahweh" (2 Sam 12:25). **5.** *happy they who dwell in your house:* Verses 5,6,13 all begin with "Happy!" "House" refers both to the Temple, the goal of the pilgrimage, and to the land of Israel; cf. Pss 23:6; 27:4; 61:8. **6b.** Obscure. Dahood suggests, "From their heart are your extolments"—i.e., "They praise you from their hearts." **7–8.** These verses may envision the pilgrimage to Zion as a sort of "new exodus" whose goal is Zion; cf. Isa 35:6–10; 41:18; 43:19–20. **10.** For the close association of king and Temple, cf. 2 Sam 7:1–13; Ps 132. **12.** For God as "sun," cf. Isa 60:19–20; Mal 4:2; Rev 21:23; 22:5.

102   **Ps 85.** The classification of this ps is controverted. Generally considered as a national lament, a communal liturgy of supplication, it is viewed by Mowinckel and Dahood as associated with a harvest festival (perhaps Tabernacles), a prayer for rain (Pss 65, 67). Structure: vv 2–4 (hymn of praise for Yahweh's past blessings); vv 5–8 (lament); vv 9–14 (oracle of salvation pronounced by some cultic official). **2–4.** The six past tense vbs. in these verses suggest to most commentators that they form a hymn praising Yahweh for his past benefits. Dahood understands them rather as imperatives that begin the prayer which extends through v 7. **5.** *restore us:* This recalls the "restoration of fortunes" mentioned in v 2. **6.** Cf. Ps 77:8. **7–8.** The benefits prayed for include restoration to life (cf. Ps 104:29–30) and salvation (= a good agricultural year). **9.** *let me declare:* Dahood's transl. is preferred to "I will hear" (*NAB*) or "let me hear" (*RSV*). **9–10.** Cf. Pss 25:12–13; 145:18–19. **11.** Yahweh's "kindness" (*ḥesed*) prayed for in v 8 is now granted to his "devoted people" (i.e., the people bound to God by *ḥesed*). **13.** According to Dahood the "good" granted by Yahweh is the autumn rains (Lev 26:4; Deut 11:14–17; Ezek 34:25–27; Zech 8:12).

103   **Ps 86.** An individual lament. Dahood and Eaton identify the speaker as the king, under attack by enemies (v 14). Structure: vv 1–7 (supplication for divine aid); vv 8–11 (expression of confidence); vv 12–13 (response of thanksgiving to an oracle of salvation); vv 14–17 (lament [vv 14,16] alternating with expressions of confidence [vv 15,17]). **1.** *humble and poor:* The presence of equivalent expressions in royal inscriptions from the ancient Near East supports the royal interpretation of Ps 86. **5.** *forgiving:* This adjective occurs only here in the OT; the related vb. (always with God as subject) occurs in Pss 25:11; 103:3; 130:4. **8.** The incomparability formula, expressed either as a negation ("there is none like") or a rhetorical question ("who is like?"); cf. Exod 8:6; Pss 35:10; 71:9; 77:14; etc. **13–14.** The Lord's great kindness "toward me" (*'ālāy*) is balanced by the hostility of those who rise "against me" (*'ālay*). **15.** The confession of faith (Exod 34:6) quoted here occurs in Pss 103:8; 111:4; 145:8 and is alluded to in Ps 77:9–10. **17.** *show me a sign of your favor:* I.e., a sign of the continued good relations between the speaker (the king?) and the divine suzerain. The alternation of lament and confidence in vv 14–17 shows these verses to be a microcosm of the ps in its movement from lament (vv 1–7) to confidence (vv 8–11).

104   **Ps 87.** A Zion hymn; its type and general tenor are clear, despite many obscurities. Structure: vv 1–3 (Yahweh's choice of Zion as his dwelling); vv 4–7 (Zion, the mother of all peoples). **1–2.** The belief that the gods founded major cities, esp. religious centers, was common in the ancient Near East. **3.** *glorious things are said of you:* Or, more likely, "He [Yahweh] speaks glorious things about you." **4–6.** Obscure. The thrice-repeated "This one/each one was born there/in her" seems to refer to non-Israelites who acknowledge Yahweh and can therefore claim Zion as their home. **5.** *the Most High will firmly establish her:* A regular theme of the Zion theology (cf. Ps 46:9). **6.** *in the register of the peoples:* The same image of divine record keeping that Dahood and others see in v 4. **7.** Obscure; *NAB* amends and translates, "All shall sing, in their festive dance."

105   Ps 88. An individual lament of a person near death. Two notable features are the number of terms for the abode of the dead and the absence of the characteristic change of tone from lament to praise and thanksgiving. Structure: vv 2-9 (appeal of a person near death to an apparently uncaring God); vv 10-13 (the inability of the dead to praise God as a reason for sparing the psalmist); vv 14-19 (why has God rejected me?). Each of the three sections has a similar sequence of ideas: appeal to God (vv 2-3,10,14) for rescue from the realm of death (vv 4-8,11-13,15-18). **4-7.** The terms associated with the netherworld in these verses include sheol, the pit, the dead, the slain, the grave, darkness, and the depths. **6.** *they are cut off:* An idiom for dying; cf. Isa 53:8; Ezek 37:11; Lam 3:54-55. **7-8.** *in the depths . . . all your breakers:* Both terms related to the sea, a common symbol for chaos and death (Pss 18:5-6; 40:3). **9.** The alienation from the community experienced by the mortally ill psalmist (cf. 19). **11-13.** The realm of the dead is described by such terms as the grave, Abaddon ("[the place of] perishing"), darkness, land of forgetfulness (cf. v 6). Cf. Pss 6:6; 30:10. **14.** *in the morning:* Cf. Ps 5:4. **16.** The obscurity of most of this verse is reflected in the divergent transls. (compare the *NAB* and the *NEB*). **17-18.** Note again the use of sea imagery for death. **19.** The ps ends with the word "darkness," a motif that occurs in vv 7 and 13.

106   Ps 89. In its present form this complex ps is a royal lament, uttered by the king after some military defeat. Since the king acts as representative of the people, Ps 89 can also be classified as a communal or national lament. Hymn (2-19), oracle (20-38), and lament (39-52) share common vocabulary and motifs. **2.** *the favors of Yahweh:* His acts of mercy and kindness, including creation (v 12) and the establishment of the Davidic dynasty as part of the created order. **4-5.** Cf. 2 Sam 7:16; Ps 132:11. **6-19.** The focus of the hymn now shifts from the establishment of the dynasty to cosmogony. It begins and ends with praise: in vv 6-9, praise of Yahweh by the members of the heavenly court; in vv 16-19, praise from his people on earth. This chorus of praise from heaven and earth frames a cosmogony which reflects the ancient Near Eastern myth of the battle with and triumph over the chaotic forces (the sea in vv 10-11) by the god who creates the habitable world (vv 12-13). **6-8.** *the assembly of the holy ones:* The heavenly court is the Israelite equivalent of the ancient Near Eastern pantheon; Israelite monotheism "demoted" these divine beings to members of Yahweh's royal entourage. Cf. Ps 29:1. **19.** Translate, "Indeed Yahweh is truly our shield, the Holy One of Israel is truly our king." **20-38.** An oracle of the deity upon returning from his triumph, appointing David (and his descendants) as his earthly vice-regent. Cf. 2 Sam 7:11-17. **20.** *your faithful ones:* Read "your faithful one" (= David). **27-28.** For the divine adoption formula, cf. Ps 2:7; 2 Sam 7:14. **27.** Yahweh, who triumphed over the sea with his powerful arm (vv 10-11), now places the right hand and arm of the king upon the subdued sea and rivers. **29-38.** Violations of the divine law by the kings will be punished (vv 31-32) but will never mean the end of the dynasty. **37-38.** A throne established forever "in heaven" means a dynasty exercising supreme dominion, unaffected by earthly adversities. **39-52.** The concluding royal-communal lament. The promise of the eternal dynasty and the covenant with David (2 Sam 7) have been

put into question by some unspecified historical disaster, probably a military defeat. **45.** "Splendor" is the brilliant radiance characteristic of divinities and persons or things (kings, temples) closely associated with them (Pss 8:6; 21:6). **53.** The benediction that closes Book III of the Psalter.

107   Ps 90. Although Gunkel designated this meditation on human mortality as a "mixed form" (hymn and lament), Mowinckel's description of it as a national lament has been accepted by many commentators. Wisdom language and characteristics are also present. Structure: vv 1-2 (hymn); vv 3-6 (lament on human mortality); vv 7-11 (lament on human misery); vv 12-17 (concluding petitions for wisdom and for respite from the divine wrath). **1.** *a prayer of Moses, man of God:* The only ps so designated; cf. Exod 32:12; Deut 33:1. **1-2.** The language of birth at the center of this chiastic hymn on the eternity of God points up the maternal character of God (Deut 32:18). **3.** The lament on the brevity of human life begins with a reference to another biblical consideration of human mortality — Gen 2-3, the Yahwist story of the creation and fall (cf. Ps 103:14; Job 10:9). **4-6.** Between the origin of humanity as dust (v 3) and its end as withering grass (vv 5-6) we find the first reference to the major theme of "days" and "years" (v 4), continued by the references to morning and evening in vv 5-6. Cf. vv 9-10 and 12-15. **6.** Cf. Pss 92:8-9; 102:12-13; Isa 51:12-13. **7-11.** The lament now changes focus from human mortality to human misery, with a powerful presentation of the sinner under God's wrath. For the association of divine anger with the withering of vegetation, cf. Isa 34:2-4; Ezek 19:12; Nah 1:2-4. **13-14.** The appeal "Return, Yahweh!" is the positive counterpart of humanity's "turning" to dust in v 3. In the same way, "your kindness in the morning" corresponds to the withering in the morning in vv 5-6, and rejoicing "all our days" to God's fury "all our days" in v 9. **15.** The prayer that began in v 12, that God would teach us to number our days correctly, concludes with a request that our days and years of happiness at least equal those of misfortune. **16.** The reference to "children" recalls the language of birth in v 2 and brings the discussion of human ephemerality to a conclusion by speaking of continuance in one's children.

108   Ps 91. A psalm of trust, possibly royal (Dahood), concluding with an oracle of salvation (vv 14-16). The speaker may be a cultic official (a priest or prophet). The ps is unusual in that it speaks of God's protection not against enemies but "pestilence" (vv 3[?],6) and "plague" (v 10). Structure: vv 1-2 (address to a worshiper in the Temple); vv 3-6 (deliverance from evils); vv 7-10 (the psalmist's security); vv 11-13 (protection through angels); vv 14-16 (oracle of salvation). **4.** *he will cover you with his wings:* A figurative reference to God's motherly protection of his faithful (cf. Pss 17:8; 36:8; 57:2; 61:5; 63:8); some deities in the ancient East were pictured as winged. **9.** *Most high . . . Lord . . . refuge:* The repetition of these divine titles from vv 1-2 summarizes the thrust of the ps thus far: The one who dwells in God's presence will suffer no harm. **11.** The idea that Yahweh provided his devotees with guardian spirits was not common in Israelite religion until late OT times (Tob 5-12; Bar 6:6); but cf. Exod 23:20; Ps 34:8. This verse is cited by Satan in the temptation of Jesus (Matt 4:6; Luke 4:10-11). **13.** Protected by angels, the feet of the righteous are not only safe from accidents (v 12b) but can trample down fierce beasts. Thus the ps moves from God's protecting his faithful one to his equipping him to battle evil (cf. Ps 18). **14-16.** The promise of divine protection by the cultic official is confirmed by a direct communication from Yahweh — an oracle of salvation.

The vocabulary ("glorify . . . length of days") points to the king as the addressee (cf. Ps 21:5–6).

109   Ps 92. A thanksgiving psalm of the individual, comparing the fate of those who find joy in God with that of evildoers. Structure: vv 2–5 (the psalmist rejoices over Yahweh's works); vv 6–12 (the recompense of the wicked and of the psalmist); vv 13–16 (the reward of the righteous). **5.** This verse, the end of the first section, leads into the central section with the term "works" (cf. v 6) and "deeds" contrasted with "evildoers" (cf. vv 8,10). **9a.** *you thrust them down forever, O Yahweh!:* Reading *mwrm,* "thrust down," for MT *mrwm,* "on high" (cf. Job 30:19). **11–12.** The wicked are contrasted with the psalmist on several points: (a) they are dull-witted (v 7), he is perceptive (v 12); (b) they sprout like plants—but die (v 8), he is invigorated with plant oil (v 11); (c) they are thrust down (v 8b), God raises him up (v 11). **11.** *fresh oil:* Olive oil, widely used throughout the ancient Near East. Cf. "fresh" in v 15, in reference to the righteous. **13–15.** The wicked, who "flourish" but wither (v 8a), are contrasted with the righteous, who "flourish" forever in the Temple.

110   Ps 93. This ps begins a series of "enthronement psalms" (→ 6, 8 above) celebrating Yahweh as victorious king of creation. Mowinckel has argued that these reflect a new year feast of the enthronement of Yahweh, though evidence for this is slender. Ps 93 echoes the ancient myth of the creator god's victory over the powers of chaos, after which he is proclaimed king by his heavenly court (Ps 89:6–19). Structure: vv 1–2 (Yahweh as king of the world); vv 3–4 (Yahweh's victory over chaos); vv 5 (Yahweh's decrees are eternal). **1.** *Yahweh is king!:* I.e., he has won the battle for world kingship against the forces of chaos. *majesty . . . glory:* Aspects of the nimbus of light that surround Yahweh, marking him as supreme god. *yes, the world has been firmly established:* In the Near Eastern myth the creation of the world follows upon the god's victory over chaos. **3–4.** Yahweh's battle with chaos, described here as "rivers . . . mighty waters . . . sea." **5.** *your decrees are exceedingly firm:* Since God is king of the world, his "decrees" are now fixed like the earth itself (v 1). The statement about Yahweh's "house" (= Temple) is difficult. Perhaps "In your Temple the holy ones [= the gods] will laud you" (Dahood).

111   Ps 94. Probably to be classified as a communal lament, although the second part of the ps is in the 1st pers. sg. This ps creates a counterpoint to the surrounding enthronement hymns by asking in effect that Yahweh exercise his rule by judging the wicked. The poem contains a number of wisdom motifs (esp. in vv 8–13). Structure: vv 1–15 (request that Yahweh intervene to save his people and punish the wicked); vv 16–23 (prayer of confidence that Yahweh will destroy the wicked). **1.** *God of vengeance:* Appeal was made to Yahweh as avenger in the sense that he was the last court of appeal, righting the wrongs that human justice could not. **2.** *render to the proud what they deserve!:* Cf. Ps 28:4. The Hebr. vb. translated "render" (lit., "return") is a key term and occurs at three important junctures: here and in v 15 with reference to the righteous and in v 23 with reference to the wicked. **7.** Cf. Ps 73:11. **12–15.** This subsection creates a chiasm with vv 4–11: A: "all the evildoers" (v 4), B: "your people . . . your inheritance" (v 5), C: "train . . . teach" (v 10); C: "train . . . teach" (v 12), B: "his people . . . his inheritance" (v 14), A: "all the upright of heart" (v 15). The effect is a contrast: The wicked seem to gain the upper hand in vv 4–11, but Yahweh's will triumphs in vv 12–15. **16–23.** The poem switches to the 1st pers. sg. Perhaps the speaker represents the community. **16.** *who will stand up for me . . .?:*

The terms are probably drawn from language of the lawcourt, to "stand up for" meaning to "testify in behalf of." **20.** Difficult. The basic meaning is probably that evil rule ("the throne of destruction[?]") is incompatible with Yahweh's rule. Cf. Pss 5:5; 125:3.

112   Ps 95. Often classified as an enthronement hymn, this ps has also been listed as a prophetic liturgy. It relates to the neighboring enthronement psalms with its emphasis on entering Yahweh's presence with praise and song and his supremacy over the other gods. It has a number of parallels to Pss 81; 100. Structure: vv 1–7a (invitation to worship Yahweh as supreme deity and as shepherd); vv 7b–11 (admonition to be faithful to Yahweh). **1–7.** The themes of Yahweh as savior and creator are interwoven here: A: savior (v 1), B: creator (vv 4–5); B: creator (v 6), A: savior (v 7a). **3.** *for he is El the Great, the Great King over all gods:* El was the head of the Canaanite pantheon and thus the name of the supreme deity (→ 15 above); "Great King" was a title borne by emperors in the ancient Near East (Pss 47:3; 48:3). **7a.** Translate: "For he is our God, and we are his people, the sheep of his pasture" (cf. Pss 79:13; 100:3). **7b–11.** The tone of the ps shifts abruptly here to a warning about infidelity to Yahweh drawn from the wandering tradition. Cf. Ps 81, where the same shift takes place. **8.** *Meribah . . . Massah:* According to Ps 81:8 it is God who tested the people at Meribah. Cf. Exod 17:1–7. The place names mean "strife" and "testing" respectively. **11.** Especially in the deuteronomic literature the promised land is the place where God's people may "rest" from their wanderings and wars and enjoy a permanent dwelling place (Deut 12:10; 25:19; Josh 22:4). Since this land belongs to Yahweh he refers to it here as "my rest."

113   Ps 96. An enthronement hymn. The ps has a number of parallels to Ps 98 and a doublet in 1 Chr 26:23–33. An unusual feature of this ps is its "missionary" character, commanding God's people to make his glory known throughout the world (vv 2,10). Structure: vv 1–6 (call to Yahweh's people to make known his glory); vv 7–9 (call to the nations to worship Yahweh); vv 10–13 (call to all creation to acknowledge Yahweh's rule). **1.** *a new song:* See comment and references at Ps 33:3. **5.** *all the gods of the nations are nothings!:* Though this need not be taken literally here, the statement marks a step toward absolute monotheism. **7–9.** Taken from Ps 29:1–2. But here the "families of nations," not the gods, are commanded to glorify Yahweh in the Temple (cf. vv 6 and 8). Is this another indication of incipient monotheism in this ps? **7–8.** Ascribing "glory and might" to God means recognizing him as the supreme God. **8.** *bring tribute and enter his courts!:* Subject kings in the ancient Near East were obliged to present themselves before the suzerain ("enter his courts") on a regular basis. **10.** Cf. Ps 93:1. The cry of the enthronement psalms, "Yahweh is king!" (cf. Pss 93:1; 97:1; 99:1), is now proclaimed to the world. **11–13.** Not only the nations but all creation is called to join in joyfully receiving the good news of Yahweh's universal reign. **12.** A theophany (Ps 50:3) or the cultic rite when the Ark is carried in procession (cf. 2 Sam 6:5,9) and "enters" the Temple (Ps 24:7,9). Such a cultic event would dramatize the ancient myth of the divine warrior entering his palace and beginning his world reign after defeating the powers of chaos.

114   Ps 97. An enthronement hymn, emphasizing the supremacy of Yahweh as "Lord of all the earth" and the joy his reign brings. Structure: vv 1–5 (theophany: Yahweh's supremacy over the earth); vv 6–9 (Yahweh's supremacy in heaven); vv 10–12 (Yahweh's reign brings joy to the righteous). **1–5.** Framed by the term "earth" (vv 1,5), this section describes the awesome theophany of Yahweh as he comes from heaven to earth (cf. Ps

18:7–16), asserting his claim to universal rule. **1.** *Yahweh is king!:* See comment on Ps 93:1. **6–9.** In this central section Yahweh asserts his supremacy in the "heavens" (v 6), esp. over the other deities (vv 7,9). His supremacy is underscored by the fivefold repetition of "all." **9.** *Elyon over all the earth:* On "Elyon," see comment on Ps 47:3. **10–12.** These verses describe the kind of "rule" exercised by the good king Yahweh. In his kingdom those who hate evil are faithful to him; righteous and upright may live in joy, praising his name.

115   Ps 98. An enthronement hymn, similar to Ps 96 (see comment). Structure: vv 1–3 (call to God's people to praise Yahweh for his saving deeds to Israel); vv 4–6 (call to all humanity to join in the joyful worship of King Yahweh in the Temple); vv 7–9 (call to all creation to acknowledge Yahweh's rule). **1–3.** The key term in this section is "salvation" (*RSV:* "victory") in vv 1b,2a, 3b. The focus is the saving acts he has performed for "the house of Israel" (v 3). Only then does attention shift to the nations ("all the earth" in v 4). **3.** *steadfast love and fidelity:* Hebr *ḥesed* and *'ĕmûnâ* refer to Yahweh's covenant commitment; "remember" has a concrete meaning (cf. Exod 2:24): God has taken action to save Israel. **4–6.** The reference to musical instruments and song indicate a setting in the Temple (note "in the presence of Yahweh" in v 6b). Israel's "missionary" outlook, though never a major motif in the OT, saw the nations coming to Zion to worship Yahweh (Isa 2:1–4). **7–9.** Cf. Ps 96:11–13. The alternation of words denoting watery places ("sea" in v 7, "floods" in v 8) and dry land ("world" in v 7, "hills" in v 8) is a kind of merism, emphasizing that all creation should join in the chorus of joy.

116   Ps 99. The last of the enthronement hymns. The two main sections are marked off by a refrain (vv 5,9). Structure: vv 1–5 (call for the nations to worship Yahweh); vv 6–7 (Yahweh's actions in salvation history); vv 8–9 (appeal to Yahweh as a God of mercy and justice; final exhortation to worship Yahweh). **2.** *great is Yahweh of Zion:* Lit., "Yahweh-in-Zion," a common type of Near Eastern divine epithet (cf. Ps 65:2; Acts 19:28,34). **3–4.** *"holy is he, and mighty!":* So *NEB;* perhaps the cry of the worshipers when they extolled Yahweh; cf. Ps 22:4; Isa 6:3; Rev 4:8. **6–9.** The second part of the ps develops a thought in v 4c: "You exercise judgment and righteousness in Jacob [= in Israel]." Yahweh shows these qualities by answering the people in need (vv 6,8), giving them just laws (v 7), and forgiving or punishing them when necessary (v 8). **6.** *Moses . . . Samuel:* Mentioned here for their renown as great intercessors with God (cf. Jer 15:1). **8.** *El the forgiving:* The supreme Canaanite god El—identified with Yahweh in Israel—was pictured as a kindly, fatherly god; cf. Exod 34:6–7.

117   Ps 100. A hymn of praise. In its present position this ps serves to conclude and climax a series of enthronement hymns (93; 95–99), a number of which (95; 96; 98; 99) explicitly call upon Israel and the nations to join in the worship of Yahweh and the acknowledgment of his divine rule. Ps 100 consists of two sections (vv 1–3,4–5), each of which is a full-fledged hymn. **1.** *shout to Yahweh, all the earth:* Cf. Ps 98:4a. **3.** *acknowledge that Yahweh is God:* The whole world is called upon to recognize that Yahweh (alone) is God; cf. the "missionary" tone of Ps 96. *he made us, we are his:* A transl. achieved by a slight emendation of the MT, which reads, "He made us and not we ourselves." Cf. Pss 79:13; 95:5a. **5.** The concluding "for"-clause is based on a common refrain (cf. Pss 118:1; 136:1–26). In this context "good" refers to Yahweh's concrete acts of covenant love (*ḥesed*) shown to Israel. Thus, while the first section of the ps exalts Yahweh because he alone is God, the second

praises him because of his faithful beneficence toward his people.

118   Ps 101. Generally considered a royal psalm, whose speaker is the king. However, since there is a change of speaker from vv 1–5 (the king) to vv 6–7 (Yahweh), the ps is not a royal monologue but a dialogue between king and deity. Structure: vv 1–2 (introduction); vv 3–5 (king's negative confession); vv 6–7 (divine oracle); v 8 (conclusion of the divine oracle or response to it by the king). **2.** *in the way of integrity . . . in the integrity of my heart:* Wisdom parallels to the first phrase (which also occurs in v 6) include Prov 2:7; 10:9; 13:6; 19:1; etc. For the second, cf. Ps 78:72 (David) and 1 Kgs 9:5 (Solomon). *in my house:* The royal palace; the same phrase in v 7 refers to the Temple. **3–5.** The king's protestation of innocence. This section is similar to the entrance liturgies of Pss 15 and 24, which also include a negative confession. **6–7.** The divine oracle (which may include v 8 as well). Ps 32 (a ps with wisdom associations) is a significant parallel, including both a confession of sin (vv 3–5) and a divine oracle (vv 8–9). Cf. also 1 Kgs 9:3–7. *my eyes:* Cf. Ps 17:2; 33:18; 34:16–17; Jer 5:2–3; 16:17 for parallels to the motif of the "eyes of Yahweh." Note the similarity to the structure of Ps 32: vv 1–2 (introduction); vv 3–7 (confession of sin and expression of confidence); vv 8–9 (divine oracle); vv 10–11 (response of the psalmist).

119   Ps 102. Fifth of the penitential pss. An individual lament of someone seriously sick; its communal characteristics (vv 14–23, 29) have led some to assume the presence of two originally independent pss; others (Mowinckel) argue for an originally individual lament adapted with additions for community use. Structure: vv 1–3 (appeal); vv 4–12 (lament); vv 13–23 (confession of trust); vv 24–29 (renewal of lament and hymnic conclusion). **1–3.** The opening appeal uses traditional language (cf. Pss 18:7; 31:2–3; 71:2; 143:1). **3.** *do not hide your face from me:* For parallels cf. Pss 13:2; 27:9; 69:18; 88:15; 143:7. **4–6.** Cf. Ps 107:17 and Job 33:20–21 for the association of sickness and disinterest in food. **7–8.** The images of birds are probably meant to underscore the isolation of the sick person. Cf. Ps 31:10–12. **12.** *my days . . . I wither like grass:* The lament section ends with an *inclusio* that looks back to vv 4–5. For the shadow as a symbol for the transitoriness of human life cf. Pss 109:23; 144:4; Job 8:9; 14:2; Eccl 6:12; 8:13. **13–23.** As Allen points out, this confession of trust is dominated by the sevenfold occurrence of the divine name ("Yahweh" six times, "Yah" once); "name" occurs in vv 13,15, and 22. **14–15.** The reference to destroyed Jerusalem points to an exilic (or later) date for the ps. Cf. Pss 51:20; 69:36. **17.** For the rebuilding of Zion by Yahweh and the appearance of his glory, cf. Ezek 40:2; 43:2–4. **24–25.** The same theme of the brevity of life and death before one's time occur in Job 14:1. Verses 25–27 are quoted in Heb 1:10–12. **26–28.** The eternity of God the Creator and the brevity of human life are also contrasted in Ps 90:2–6; cf. Isa 51:6. **29.** If the psalmist's life is transitory and brief, at least he has the conviction that the children of God's servants will continue (Isa 53:10).

120   Ps 103. An individual thanksgiving, perhaps for recovery from illness (v 3), whose hymnic features have been noted by Gunkel and subsequent form critics. Structure: vv 1–5,6–18 (subdivided into 6–14 and 15–18),19–22. **3.** The association of the forgiveness of sin and the healing of physical illness is a motif present in the NT (Mark 2:10–11); the association of sin and sickness is found in both the OT (Job; Pss 32:3–5; 107:17) and NT (John 9; James 5:14–16). **4.** The redemption of the psalmist's life "from the pit" (sheol) continues the theme of mortal illness. **5.** *he fills your lifetime with* *good:* The "good" may refer to God's benefits in general, or it may refer more specifically to the divine presence, as it does in Exod 33:19. **7.** *he made known his ways to Moses:* In addition to the explicit quotation of Exod 33:13 here and of Exod 34:6 in v 8, note also the allusions to Exod 34:9 in v 3. **9–13.** The verses immediately following the quotation of Exod 34:6 provide a commentary on it: v 9 discusses the anger of God, v 10 his grace, v 11 his covenant love (*hesed*), and v 13 his mercy. **15–16.** Either an allusion to Isa 40:6–8 or the independent appearance of a common motif. Cf. Ps 90:5–6; Job 14:2; Isa 51:12. The "wind" that desiccates the vegetation is the sirocco, the east wind. **17–18.** Contrasted to human transitoriness is the eternal love of Yahweh to those who keep his covenant. **20–21.** The psalmist invites all the members of the divine council, the whole army of heaven, to join in the praise of Yahweh enthroned in heaven. **22.** The whole of creation joins in the chorus of praise, and the ps ends by repeating its opening words. **121   Ps 104.** A hymn of praise of Yahweh who created and providentially maintains the habitable world. As the first of a trilogy of poems (Pss 104–6), its initial position in this sequence is appropriate for a hymn to the creator, followed by two pss that focus on salvation history. Structure: vv 1–9 (creation of the world); vv 10–18 (the provision of water); vv 19–26 (creation of moon and sun, acquisition of food by night and day); vv 27–35 (prayer for rain). **1.** *bless Yahweh, O my soul!:* Note the *inclusio* with v 35. **1b–2a.** *splendor . . . majesty . . . light:* The nimbus of radiance that is characteristic of gods in the ancient Near East. **2b–3a.** The poet describes God's creation of his heavenly dwelling, built on the chaotic waters (Ps 29:10). **3b–4.** *the clouds . . . on the wings of the wind:* Rain clouds, borne by the west wind from the sea. *the winds . . . flaming fire:* A poetic description of the sirocco, the hot east wind. **6.** *above the mountains the waters stood:* Even the tops of the mountains are submerged (Gen 7:19–20). **9.** This section of the ps, which mentions the deep covering the earth (v 6), ends with a divine prohibition of this happening again (Jer 5:27; Prov 8:29). **13–14.** The winter rain and its effects. The first effect is the growth of the winter grasses that provide fodder for the domesticated work animals (Ps 147:8–9). **14c–15.** *grain from the earth . . . wine . . . oil:* A compressed description of a complete agricultural year. **19–23.** The creation of moon and sun and their role in bringing night (when predatory animals hunt their food) and day (for human work directed to the acquisition of food). **27–35.** This final section describes what happens when Yahweh maintains his providential care for his creation (vv 27–28,30) and what happens when he does not (v 29). **29.** Without the agriculture and food production that rain makes possible, human beings would die (here Hebr *rûah* means "breath"). **30.** *when you send forth your word:* The west wind bringing the rain that will recreate or "renew" the earth with vegetation. With the coming of the fall and winter rains (Isa 32:15–20; 44:2–4) we are back to the beginning of the agricultural cycle that began in v 13 (cf. Gen 8:22). **31.** "Glory" (Hebr *kābôd*) here probably refers to the magnificence of the created world, the visible manifestation of Yahweh's glory (Ps 19:2). Yahweh's "joy" in his creation is expressed in his regular and repeated sending of the rains, which bring joy to the Israelite dependent on those rains for agriculture. **32.** There is the possibility that the rains will not come and that the hot, dry east wind will continue to blow. **35.** Because the presence of sinners could cause God to refrain from sending the fall rains as a punishment, the ps concludes with a prayer for their annihilation. **122   Ps 105.** A hymnic recital of Israel's history from the ancestors to the Exodus and conquest. The

presence of the patriarchs and Joseph in the historical recital (e.g., Josh 24:2–4) is unique in the psalter. The structure of the poem has been debated, but the most natural division is: vv 1–6 (call to worship); vv 7–11 (announcement of the theme of the gift of the land); vv 12–15 (the people in Canaan); vv 16–22 (Joseph); vv 23–24 (Israel in Egypt); vv 28–34 (the plagues and the exodus); vv 39–41 (the desert); vv 42–44 (Israel in the land). Verses 1–15 are cited in 1 Chr 16:8–22, in a composite of material from Pss 105; 96; and 106. **1.** *call upon his name:* Or "proclaim his name" (Allen). **4.** *seek his face continually:* The "face" of Yahweh means his presence. **12.** *sojourners:* More accurately, "immigrants," people no longer directly related to their original social setting, who have entered into dependent relationships with groups in a new social setting. The "kings" are Pharaoh in Gen 12:17 and Abimelech in Gen 20:3. **18.** *his feet with shackles and his neck . . . through irons:* A merism meaning "completely bound," like the English equivalent "bound hand and foot." **20.** *the king sent and released him:* I.e., Joseph (Gen 41), according to Dahood. Cf. God's "sending" of Joseph in v 17, of Moses and Aaron in v 26, and of darkness in v 28; all of these "sendings" stress that God is the providential actor in salvation history. **23.** A "hinge verse" placed between the two halves of Ps 105, each with 22 verses, in imitation of the 22 letters of the alphabet (like Lam 5). **28.** The plague of darkness is particularly appropriate in the context of Egyptian solar worship; Yahweh's sending darkness upon Egypt suggests his supremacy over the high gods of Egypt (cf. Exod 12:12). **37.** The tradition of the "despoiling of the Egyptians" (Exod 12:35–36). **38.** *fear of them had fallen upon it:* The language of holy war (Exod 15:16; 1 Sam 11:7). **41.** *he opened the rock:* This description of God's power to provide water recalls the use of the same vb. in v 20 ("open" = "release"). If the subject of the vb. in v 20 is Pharaoh (see above), then vv 21 and 41 effectively contrast Pharaoh, who "releases" Joseph, and Yahweh, who "releases" a stream of water from the rock. This interpretation recalls the motif of the superiority of Yahweh over the gods of Egypt in v 28. **44–45.** The association of the gift of the land and obedience to the stipulations of the covenant repeats a theme that appeared in vv 8–11 (Ps 25:12–14). **123   Ps 106.** A historical recital like Pss 78 and 105. Unlike Ps 105, it is not a hymn but a communal lament, with hymnic characteristics esp. at the beginning. The historical review that constitutes vv 13–43 is the story of Israel's rebellion against God, framed by hymnic celebrations of Yahweh's salvation (vv 8–12,44–46). Like Ps 105, this ps shows evidence of dependence on the Pentateuch in its final canonical form and can therefore probably be dated to the postexilic period. Verses 47–48 are quoted in 1 Chr 16:35–36; the ps is also used in Rom 1:23–28. Structure: vv 1–12 (hymnic call to praise Yahweh for his saving action at the sea; confession of sin); vv 13–43 (history of Israel's sinful rebellion and faithlessness [vv 13–39]; Yahweh's consequent anger [vv 40– 43]); vv 44–47 (God's compassion; final prayer for salvation). **3.** A blessing on those who are characterized by righteousness, contrasting sharply with the picture of Israel's conduct in the historical review. **6–7.** A confession of sin by the generation of the exile experiencing God's judgment on their sin, as did their ancestors in the exodus/wilderness period. **8–12.** The paradigmatic act of salvation by Yahweh at the sea. **13.** The tradition of the rebellion in the wilderness begins here. Cf. Ps 78:14–31. **16–18.** Cf. Num 16 for the incident referred to. **19–23.** Cf. Exod 32. **24–27.** A reference to the report of the spies and the people's refusal to enter the land (Num 13–14; Deut 1:19–28). **28.** *sacrifices* offered to the dead: "The dead" are the Moabite gods (Num 25:2)—ineffective, as good as dead—in contrast to the living God (Lev 26:30; Jer 10:1–6). **32.** *the waters of Meribah:* Cf. Exod 17:1–7; Num 20:13; Pss 81:7; 95:8. **35–37.** Not learning from the Baal Peor incident, the people once again associated with the other nations. This led to idolatry and even human sacrifice (Jer 19:4–5) and provoked God's anger (vv 29,40). **41.** God's handing the people over to the nations as punishment (= the exile?) contrasts effectively with his handing them over to mercy in v 46. **45.** *he relented, in his abundant love:* Cf. Joel 2:13; Jonah 4:2. **47.** *gather us from among the nations:* This concluding appeal is an indication of exilic provenance.

124   Ps 107. A communal thanksgiving hymn which is marked by a kind of alternating double refrain: "They cried to Yahweh in their trouble, and from their distress he rescued them" (vv 6,13,19,28); "Let them give thanks to Yahweh for his love, for his wonders to human beings" (vv 8,15,21,31). Structure: The poem can be divided into two large sections, vv 1–32 and 33–43. The possibility that vv 33–43 are not part of the original composition but a later supplement is reinforced by the absence of the twofold refrain that occurs eight times in the first section and not at all in the second. Allen argues that the addition of vv 2–3 and 33–43 transformed an older individual thanksgiving into a postexilic communal thanksgiving. **2–3.** The redemption in v 2 and the gathering of the redeemed from the four corners of the earth in v 3 suggest to many commentators a postexilic date. **4–9.** The people who had been wandering in the desert are led by God, who satisfies their hunger and thirst. **10–16.** Wandering is replaced by imprisonment because of their rebellion against the commands of God, until he leads them out, in answer to their cry. **23–27.** Matching the danger of the desert (vv 4–9) is the danger of the sea. Both these places of danger have roots in Canaanite mythology, where Baal's opponents are not only Sea but Death, who rules over the arid, lifeless desert. Cf. the threatening, chaotic sea in Gen 1:2–3 and the lifeless desert in Gen 2:4–5, both overcome by Yahweh. **28–29.** Since it is God's power that subdues the stormy sea, this motif in the sea-calming miracles of Jesus (Mark 4:35–41) is an expression of the divine authority of Jesus. **33–36.** If God transforms river into desert because of the wicked, his reverse action of turning desert into well-watered land (Isa 41:18–19; 43:19–20) is done for the "hungry." **37–38.** These verses may portray the division of labor in ancient Israel: ploughing and harvesting grain (along with warfare) were men's work, while caring for vineyards was work that was done by women as well as men; reproduction was the most important female role, to build up the large family pictured in v 41. **41.** Cf. 1 Sam 2:5; Ps 113:7,9. **42–43.** These concluding verses have a strong wisdom flavor and are very similar to the wisdom conclusion of Hos 14:10. Their originality can be questioned, since without them Ps 107 would end, like Pss 77 and 78, with the simile of the people like a flock of sheep (77:21; 78:71–72).

125   Ps 108. A lament, which appears to be partly individual and partly communal. The ps is probably postexilic and is made up of Pss 57:8–12 (an individual lament) and 60:7–14 (a communal lament) with few variations from the earlier pss. Yet it is not simply a compilation of these two. By skillful reuse of these earlier poems the psalmist creates a ps that speaks to the postexilic community. Structure: vv 2–5 (petition); vv 6–7 (prayer for deliverance; divine oracle); vv 8–14 (prayer for deliverance and expression of trust). **4.** *among the peoples . . . among the nations:* In this context (contrast Ps 57) a reference to the poet's dwelling in exile. **6.** *be*

exalted above the heavens, O God!: In the present context the prayer is a request for a theophany in which God would shatter the might of his people's enemies ("the nations" in v 4). **8–14.** By citing this ancient divine oracle of deliverance, the psalmist recalls Yahweh's power over the nations (cf. v 4), implying his ability to deliver his people from exile. **10–11.** *Edom:* Relations between Judah and her vassal state Edom were seldom peaceful (1 Kgs 11:15; 2 Kgs 8:20; 2 Chr 28:17). At the time of the exile Edom took delight in aiding Babylon against her former master and earned the undying hatred of Judahites (cf. Ps 137:7; Lam 4:21–22; Obad).

126   Ps 109. An individual lament uttered by a person falsely accused in a legal proceeding. Structure: Part I (vv 1–19): vv 1–5 (introductory petition and description of distress); vv 6–19 (either a quotation of the charges and imprecations leveled against the psalmist or the psalmist's prayer for the destruction of his enemies); Part II (vv 20–31): vv 20–25 (prayer and repeated description of the psalmist's distress); vv 26–31 (prayer for divine aid against the adversaries and praise of the saving God). **1.** *do not be silent:* Cf. Pss 35:22; 39:13; 50:3; 83:2. **2–3.** Over against the silence of God are the words of lying, deceit, and hatred directed against the psalmist. *they accused me without cause:* Legal terminology; cf. Ps 69:5. **6–19.** Difficult. Some hold that these are the psalmist's words (his prayer against his enemies); others understand them as those of his adversaries quoted by him. The latter is more likely (cf. Allen). **6.** *let the accuser stand at his right hand:* Cf. Zech 3:1. "Accuser" (*śāṭān*) is a legal term ("prosecuting attorney"). In the final verse of the ps it is God, not the "accuser," who stands at the right of the poor person. **8.** Quoted in Acts 1:20 (along with Ps 69:26) as scriptural warrant for the election of Matthias to replace Judas in the Twelve. **9–11.** After a wish for the psalmist's early death, his enemies pray as well that his widow and children be homeless beggars and that all his property go to creditors and strangers. It is such cruel situations that call for God's special care for the widow and fatherless (Exod 22:21; Pss 68:6; 146:9). **13–15.** The enemies hope that the psalmist's progeny will be destroyed and their names blotted out. Cf. Pss 9:6; 34:17; 37:38. **17–19.** By the talion principle, the psalmist's enemies pray that his curse rebound to him. **20.** Here begin the words of the psalmist, last heard in v 5. "My accusers" in vv 20 and 29 recalls "the accuser" in v 6; "those who speak evil against me" in v 20 recalls vv 2–3. **28.** The psalmist rejoices in Yahweh's blessing, far more powerful than the curses of his enemies. **31.** The confidence of the psalmist that God will "stand at the right hand of the poor" to save him from those who would bring him to trial recalls the opening words of the psalmist's foes in vv 6–7.

127   Ps 110. The ps consists of two divine oracles to the Davidic king through a prophet, perhaps at the coronation or its anniversary. The structure is determined by the oracular introductions in vv 1 and 4: 1–3,4–7. It is probably to be dated to the early monarchic period; Mowinckel considers it Solomonic. For the NT use of v 1, the OT text most frequently quoted in the NT, see D. M. Hay, *Glory at the Right Hand: Psalm 110 in Early Christianity* (SBLMS 18; Nash, 1973). **1.** *oracle of Yahweh to my lord:* the speaker is the prophet announcing a divine word to his lord, the Davidic king. *sit at my right hand:* Cf. 2 Kgs 2:19. In the royal context of this ps the vb. probably means "sit enthroned" (1 Kgs 1:46; Ps 132:12). *a stool for your feet:* Cf. Josh 10:24. **3.** Perhaps the most difficult and obscure verse in the entire psalter, as a review of the transls. and commentaries will attest. **4.** *you are a priest forever, after the model of Melchizedek:*

Although the text is clear, the meaning is debated. The point seems to be the succession of the Davidic monarch to the status (including priesthood) of the former Jebusite kings of Zion (Gen 14:18-24). **5-6.** The focus changes from the king as priest to the king as victorious warrior. **5.** The vb. "judge" in Hebrew means more than administering justice; the meaning of the phrase is close to "he will govern among the nations." **7.** The meaning is unclear. Some have suggested that it describes a coronation ceremony, since the acclamation as king of both Adonijah and Solomon took place near water sources (1 Kgs 1:9,33,39).

128   Ps 111. An acrostic hymn of praise concluding with a wisdom saying (v 10a; cf. Prov 9:10). Although the speaker in v 1 is an individual, the emphasis on the salvation of the people in the exodus and Sinai experiences probably marks this as a communal hymn. A postexilic date is accepted by many (although Weiser and Dahood demur). **2.** *great are the works of Yahweh:* Yahweh's deeds are a major theme of the poem; forms of the Hebr root *'āśâ,* "to do, make," occur six times (vv 2,4,6,7[twice],10) and its synonym *pā'al* once (v 3) for a total of seven references to the deeds of Yahweh. **3.** *splendor and majesty:* Cf. Ps 104:1. **4.** *he has gained renown for his wondrous deeds:* Given the explicit reference to Exod 34:6 in v 4b, v 4a probably refers to Exod 34:10: "In the sight of all the people I will do wonders." **5.** In the Exodus context this verse refers to the provision of food for the people in the wilderness (Exod 16; Num 9); cf. Pss 105:40; 106:14. **7-8.** The giving of the law seen as one of Yahweh's great works. **10.** In the present form of the poem the introductory "Halleluyah" forms an *inclusio* with "his praise" in v 10.

129   Ps 112. An acrostic poem; like the similar Ps 1, its first word is "happy" and its last, "perish." More striking is its similarity to the preceding acrostic Ps 111, with which it shares common vocabulary and themes (cf. 111:3 and 112:3,9; 111:4 and 112:4; 111:8 and 112:8), including the application to the wise person of language describing God in Ps 111 (compare Ps 111:3 with Ps 112:3; 111:4 with 112:4). **1.** *happy:* This opening beatitude is characteristic of wisdom (cf. Pss 1:1; 119:1-2). In Ps 111:2 it was Yahweh's works that were the source of delight; here it is his commands. **8.** *until he looks with triumph at his foes:* For this idiom, cf. Pss 54:9; 118:7. Contrasted with the psalmist's looking on in triumph is the anger of the wicked who sees the psalmist's exaltation in v 10. **10.** *the desire of the wicked will perish:* Cf. Prov 10:28; 11:23.

130   Ps 113. A hymn with both the imperatival and participial forms characteristic of the hymn (→ 8 above). Structure: vv 1-3 (praise of Yahweh's name); vv 4-6 (exaltation of Yahweh); vv 7-9 (Yahweh's reversal of the situation of the poor and childless). **2b-3a.** *from now and to eternity; from the rising of the sun to its setting:* A merism, stating that Yahweh's name is to be praised always and everywhere. **4.** Note the connection of Yahweh's elevation with his elevation of the poor in v 7. Yahweh's activity flows from his character. **5-9.** For a passage similar in form and in content cf. Ps 35:10. The connections of vv 5-9 with the Song of Hannah in 1 Sam 2:1-10 suggest literary dependence, although the direction of that dependence is not clear.

131   Ps 114. A hymn celebrating Israel's sacred history from the Exodus to the crossing of the Jordan. The poem's structure is chiastic: A (vv 1-2, the exodus from Egypt and the settlement in Canaan); B (vv 3-4, the transformation of nature at the anticipated appearance of God); B (vv 5-6, why this transformation?); A (vv 7-8, the theophany). **1-2.** The opening verses compress the sacred history into its initial (departure from

Egypt) and final (arrival at Canaan) events. The intervening events are referred to in v 8. **3.** *Sea . . . Jordan:* This parallelism in vv 3 and 5 recalls not only the passage through the Reed Sea and the crossing of the Jordan (Josh 4:23) but more distantly the ancient Near Eastern myth of the conquest of Sea by the creator god (Ps 24:1-2). Clearer in v 5, where the personified sea and river are addressed, the theme has been demythologized by its connection to the sacred history. **4.** The inclusion of mountains and hills here and in v 6 is probably a reference to the tremors accompanying the Sinai theophany (Exod 19:18; Judg 5:5; Ps 68:9). **8.** The provision of water for Israel recalls the events at Kadesh (Exod 17:1-7; Num 20:8-13; Deut 8:15).

132   Ps 115. The form and structure of this ps (in some Hebr mss. and versions joined to the preceding Ps 114) are unclear and controverted; vv 1-3 look like the beginning of a communal lament, followed by a hymn-like section in vv 4-8, a call to trust and an assurance of divine blessing in vv 9-15. Many commentators have seen in the poem's shifts in tone an antiphonal liturgy composed perhaps of words of the congregation (vv 1-8) answered by a cultic official (v 15) to which the community responds in vv 16-18. **2.** Cf. Pss 42:4,11; 79:10; Joel 2:17. **4-8.** This section, reminiscent of similar material in Dt-Isa (40:18-20; 44:9-20), may be an indication of the lateness of Ps 115. **9-11.** *Israel . . . house of Aaron . . . fearers of God:* Repeated in the blessings of vv 12-13; such repetitions, and the responsorial "their savior and shield is he," are evidence for the antiphonal character of the ps. **15.** *maker of heaven and earth:* Yahweh the creator of the universe is contrasted with the created and lifeless idols (vv 4-8). **17.** *who go down into silence:* For the netherworld as a place of silence where no praise of God is uttered, cf. Pss 88:11-13; 94:17.

133   Ps 116. An individual psalm of thanksgiving. A number of Aram features in the ps (vv 7,12,16) point to a late date. The LXX divides it into two pss (vv 1-9 = LXX Ps 114; vv 10-19 = LXX Ps 115), which correspond to its major parts. Structure: Part I (vv 1-9): vv 1-4 (the psalmist's distress); vv 5-9 (Yahweh's deliverance); Part II (vv 10-19): vv 10-14 (the psalmist's faith and his vow); vv 15-19 (his loyalty and his vow). **1-4.** This section resembles Ps 18:2-7a. **1.** *I love (Yahweh):* Cf. Ps 18:2. Lit., "I love because [kî] Yahweh has heard." Another vb. with implied object begins Part II (v 10): "I trusted (in Yahweh) because [kî]. . . ." **7.** *return, my soul:* When someone was faint (from hunger or fright) it was thought that the soul/spirit had "gone forth" from him. When that person revived, the soul "returned." The psalmist is reassuring his soul that it is safe to return after his terrifying experience (vv 3-4). Cf. Gen 35:18; 1 Sam 30:12; Ps 23:3; Dan 10:17. **13.** *and call on Yahweh's name:* In v 2 the psalmist calls on Yahweh's name out of fear; in vv 13 and 17, the same phrase denotes praising him in the Temple. **15.** *precious in Yahweh's sight is the death of his faithful ones:* Difficult. Just why their death should be "precious" to Yahweh is not easy to see. **19.** As the ending of Part I (v 9) speaks of "the land of life" (i.e., the Temple), the last verse of Part II explicitly mentions "the house [Temple] of Yahweh."

134   Ps 117. A textbook example of the hymn and the shortest ps in the Psalter. The thought is consistent with the standard OT position on the "salvation" of the gentiles. The nations are called upon to praise Yahweh (v 1)—i.e., to acknowledge him as God—when they realize the great deeds he has done for his people (v 2), esp. his steadfast love for them.

135   Ps 118. An individual song of thanksgiving. The ps contains a number of 1st-pl. vbs. and pronouns in vv 23-24,26-27, which are somewhat puzzling.

Perhaps it was originally an individual song that was later "democratized"; if the king is the speaker, it is easier to understand the vacillation between sg. (the king) and pl. (the people). Structure: The ps appears to consist of six stanzas: vv 1-4 (call to all Israel to praise Yahweh); vv 5-9 (the psalmist's trust in Yahweh); vv 10-14 (the battle with the nations); vv 15-19 (victory shout; petition to enter Temple); vv 20-25,26-28 (praise in the Temple); v 29 (*inclusio*). **1.** Cf. Pss 106:1; 107:1; 136:1. Note the envelope formed around the ps by the repetition of this phrase in v 29. **2-4.** On the sequence "Israel . . . Aaron . . . those who fear Yahweh," cf. Pss 115:9-11; 135:19-20. **14.** A citation of Exod 15:2a, part of Israel's classic victory song. Exod 15:2b is paraphrased at the end of the 6th stanza (v 28). **15.** This appears to begin a new section, after victory has been won through Yahweh's "acting" to save king and people (vv 15,16, 24). **19.** The king comes from the battle to give thanks to Yahweh in the Temple. The "gates of righteousness" may have been an actual name of a Temple gate or a figurative way of alluding to the fact that only the "righteous" may enter Yahweh's dwelling (cf. v 20). **22.** *"the stone which the builders rejected . . .":* Probably an ancient proverb. A piece of stone judged unworthy of a position of prominence in the structure by the "experts" has become the most prominent. In the present context this may refer to the king's rise to power or to his recent victory. This text was very important in the early church's attempt to understand the rejection and execution of Jesus by his people (cf. Matt 21:42; Acts 4:11; 1 Cor 3:11; Eph 2:20; 1 Pet 2:7-8). **24.** *this is the day Yahweh has acted:* Cf. "acted" in vv 15-16. Traditionally, "This is the day Yahweh has made" (cf. *RSV*). The reference is to some act by Yahweh to save his people or to punish the wicked (cf. Ps 119:126). **25.** *please save us!:* The Hebr vb. is *hôšî'a-nnā'*; from the shortened form, *hôša'-nnā'*, comes "Hosanna." **26.** Probably spoken by the priests, welcoming the righteous (cf. v 20) into the Temple. "In the name of Yahweh" recalls the battle context of vv 10-14. The verse is applied to Jesus by the crowds in Mark 11:9. **27.** *Yahweh . . . has shed his light on us:* Or possibly "O Yahweh . . . shed your light upon us!"—an allusion to the priestly blessing of Num 6:22-27. The mention of the procession and branches brings to mind the feast of Tabernacles, in which olive branches were used.

136 **Ps 119.** The sheer size of this, the longest of the pss (176 verses), makes it too unwieldy to fit into the standard ps categories. It is often described as a wisdom psalm, though it contains elements of various ps types. It is an alphabetical *tour de force* consisting of 22 sections, each containing eight poetic lines and each beginning with a successive letter of the Hebr alphabet. Most of these contain one of approximately eight terms for Yahweh's "law" or "Torah," the theme celebrated in the ps. Westermann believes that Ps 119 concluded an earlier edition of the Psalter, forming an envelope around the collection together with Ps 1, which likewise emphasizes Yahweh's "Torah." This enveloping by the theme of Torah may indicate that even at a relatively early stage the Psalter was the subject of study and meditation. **2.** *with all their heart:* Cf. vv 10,34,58,69,145. Devotion to God with one's "whole heart" is demanded in Deut 6:4; the idiom is probably derived from covenant or treaty language. **26.** *I recounted your ways:* MT: "my ways." Since "recount" is almost always used in the sense of telling God's deeds, the LXX reading is probably correct here (see Dahood). **28.** *raise me up according to your word:* I.e., cause me to stand up straight after my depressing experience. The idiom is from the language of healing; cf. "Give me life according to your word" in

vv 25,107. **34.** *give me understanding:* Cf. vv 73,125,144, 169. The psalmist prays for wisdom in the biblical sense—not intellectual acumen, but the ability to see how all things in God's creation work together, and specifically to see how his commandments bring "life," the goal of all human striving. Cf. v 93. **38.** *make your promise come true:* Lit., "make your word stand"—i.e., come to pass (cf. Isa 40:8). **58.** It is probably best to read "Give me life [rather than the MT's "Have mercy on me"] according to your promise" with the Syriac. Cf. vv 25,107. **96.** *I have seen the end of all perfection:* Difficult. The Hebr word translated "perfection" occurs only here and its precise meaning is uncertain. All that is called perfect in our experience has its limitations, but not God's commandment, which is "exceedingly broad." **98-100.** True wisdom is not a matter of age, education, or social status but of adhering to the divine commandments. **120.** "Fear" is not the dread of a hostile being but the supreme "awe" that one is expected to feel before God and his decrees. **169-76.** These verses should probably be construed as petitions (cf. Allen).

137 **Ps 120.** The first of a collection of pss (120-34), each of which is headed by a phrase traditionally rendered "song of ascents." They are probably a collection of pilgrimage hymns to be sung on the journey up to Jerusalem (→ 3 above). The irregular parallelism and the language (archaizing rather than genuinely archaic) point to a late date of composition for the collection (i.e., sometime between the late 7th cent. and the postexilic period). In form, Ps 120 is closest to the individual lament. Structure: vv 1-2 (prayer); vv 3-4 (formula of self-curse); vv 5-7 (lament). **1.** The psalmist bases his prayer for aid on past experiences of answered prayer. **2.** As in so many individual laments the psalmist complains of malicious speech directed against him (cf. Pss 3:3; 5:7,10; 10:7; 12:3, etc.). **3.** The formula "what will he [Yahweh] give . . . and add" is based on earlier self-curse formulas (2 Sam 3:9; 1 Kgs 2:23). **4.** For weapons as metaphors for evil speech, cf. Pss 52:4; 57:5; 64:4. **5-6.** *Meshech . . . Kedar:* Two distant peoples. The sense of the verse is generally understood as "Woe is me that I dwell among enemies warring against me like hostile foreigners."

138 **Ps 121.** A psalm of confidence. The change from 1st pers. (vv 1-2) to 2d (vv 3-8) has suggested to some commentators a dialogue between a worshiper and a priest, who pronounces a blessing reminiscent of Num 6:24-26 on the pilgrim. Structure: vv 1-2 (Yahweh the creator); vv 3-8 (Yahweh the protector). **1.** *to the mountains:* The dwelling place of God (Pss 48:2-3; 87:1-2); both the heavenly mountain and Zion are implied. Cf. Pss 123:1; 134:3. **1-2.** *my help:* In Pss 124:8 and 146:5-6 as here, divine "help" is almost equivalent to "salvation." **3-4.** The constant wakeful protection of Yahweh contrasts with the sentiments of Ps 44:24 and with Elijah's mockery of Baal in 1 Kgs 18:27 ("Maybe he's asleep!"). **5-6.** *by day the sun will not harm you:* Cf. 2 Kgs 4:19 for an instance of sunstroke; also Isa 49:10. **7-8.** These verses form an *inclusio* with vv 1-2 by the repetition of the vb. "come" (Allen).

139 **Ps 122.** Best classified as a Zion hymn (cf. comments on Ps 46) sung by pilgrims rejoicing at their arrival at the Temple. Characteristic of Zion hymns are the motifs of the pilgrimage to Zion (Ps 48:13), its impregnability (cf. Pss 46:5-8; 48:4), and the sort of imperatives found in vv 6-7 (cf. Pss 46:9,11; 48:13-14; 76:12). Structure: vv 1-2 (pilgrimage and arrival); vv 3-5 (praise of Zion); vv 6-9 (prayer for Jerusalem and those who worship there). **1.** *I rejoiced with those who said to me:* This would seem to be the sense of the ptc. rather than the traditional ". . . when [or "because"] they said to me."

3. If the meaning is that Jerusalem is "joined together in unity" (compact, ordered), it may be an allusion to the inviolability of the city; note the references to gates (v 2), walls, and battlements (v 7). **6–7.** The prayer for peace that follows the description of the royal administration of justice in v 5 reminds one of the same sequence of ideas in Isa 2:4. **8–9.** An *inclusio* with vv 1–2 by the reference to the "house of Yahweh" and by the recurrence of 1st pers. sg. vbs. and of 1st pers. pl. pronominal suffixes.

140   Ps 123. A psalm of confidence, in two sections (vv 1–2,3–4). **1.** Cf. Pss 121:1; 141:8. *enthroned in heaven:* Equivalent to the heavenly mountain where God dwells in Ps 121:1. **2.** The hand is here seen as the source of blessings, particularly abundant food; cf. Ps 104:28. **4.** The same Aramaizing idiom occurs in Ps 120:6.

141   Ps 124. A thanksgiving psalm. The pl. references throughout (and "Israel" in v 1) suggest a national or communal thanksgiving. Structure: vv 1–5 (situation of past danger); vv 6–8 (thanksgiving for divine act of deliverance). **1.** *if Yahweh were not for us:* Cf. Ps 94:17. **3.** *they would have swallowed us alive:* Prov 1:10–12 describes "sinners" swallowing the innocent alive like sheol; cf. Num 16:30–33. **4–5.** The image of the chaotic waters engulfing the psalmist occurs also in Jonah 2:4 and in Ps 69:2–3,15–16. **6–8.** After a description of the dangers facing the community and their fate without divine aid, the mood changes to the community's thanksgiving for Yahweh's salvific activity. **6.** *prey for their teeth:* Associated with lions (Amos 3–4; Job 4:10–11; Ps 104:21) and wolves (Gen 1:9–10,24–25). **7.** *like a bird:* Shifts attention from the carnivores on earth to the heavens, the domain of the birds (Gen 1:20,22,etc.). **8.** *maker of heaven and earth:* This concluding formula of the ps recapitulates in inverted order the sequence of land animals and birds in vv 6–7.

142   Ps 125. This has been classified both as a communal psalm of trust and as a national lament. Structure: vv 1–3 (expression of trust); vv 4–5 (complaint). **1.** The stability of Mt. Zion is a central theme of the Zion psalms (cf. Ps 46:6). The motifs of trusting in Yahweh (v 1) and possessing the land (v 3) occur together in Ps 37:3. **3.** *the allotted portions of the righteous:* I.e., the land apportioned to them by lot (Josh 15:1; 17:1; 21:38). For the possession of the land by the righteous, cf. Pss 25:12–14; 37:29. *peace be upon Israel!:* Possibly an addition to the ps; however, it occurs at the end of another ascent psalm (128:6) and is echoed in 122:6–8.

143   Ps 126. A communal lament recalling God's past intervention on behalf of the people, who pray that such aid in the past may serve as motivation for help in the present (cf. Ps 44). Structure: vv 1–3,4–6. Like other ascent psalms, Ps 126 has a high degree of repetition. **1.** *when Yahweh restored the captives of Zion:* The idiom (or a similar phrase) occurs again in v 4 (also Pss 14:7; 53:7; 85:2). *like dreamers:* Variously rendered by the versions and modern commentators. "Like those healed" (*NEB*, supported by the versions) is also possible. **4.** Prayer for divine aid, in language like that of v 1. Supporting the synonymity of vv 1 and 4 is the fact that both are followed by a simile ("like dreamers . . . like torrents"). **5–6.** Verse 5 may be a proverb amplified in v 6. The language of planting and growth in these verses suggests a reversal of situation, with tears turned into joy, in language drawn from agriculture.

144   Ps 127. A wisdom psalm, with close links to the following Ps 128. As in Ps 72, "concerning Solomon" is added to the heading common to the ascent psalms. The reasons for this specification probably include Solomon's role as patron of the wisdom tradition and

Temple builder. Structure: vv 1–2 (the futility of human activity apart from Yahweh's active involvement); vv 3–5 (the blessing of a large family with many sons). Although the unity of the ps has been questioned, it displays such strong thematic links between the two parts that its origin as a single composition is more likely. **1.** The word "house" is intentionally polyvalent, including the nuances of Temple, royal palace, and dynasty (Ps 122). The house that Yahweh builds includes the sons who are the subject of vv 3–5. *if Yahweh does not guard the city:* Cf. Ps 121:4 for Yahweh as "guardian of Israel." Because of the canonical context of Ps 127 as a "song of ascent," "house" and "city" take on the specific meaning of Jerusalem and the Temple. **2.** *you who eat the bread of labors:* The food produced by long hours of hard, grueling work (cf. Gen 3:17–19). *his beloved ones:* "Beloved" is to be read as a pl.; the sg. entered the text because of the association of the ps with Solomon, whose birth name was Jedidiah, "Beloved of Yahweh" (2 Sam 12:25). *sleep:* Probably to be rendered "honor" (J. A. Emerton, *VT* 24 [1974] 15–31) or "prosperity" (Dahood). **5.** Beatitudes are characteristic of wisdom language (Pss 1:1; 32:1; 34:8; Prov 3:13).

145   Ps 128. A wisdom psalm and a companion piece to Ps 127, sharing with it common vocabulary and wisdom themes: the formula "happy" (127:5; 128:1–2), the blessing of many sons (127:3–5; 128:3,6), the "house" (127:2; 128:3), reflections on human effort (127:2; 128:2), and the similes in both pss (127:4; 128:3). Wisdom themes in Ps 128 include the fear of Yahweh and his way. Structure: vv 1–3 (the fear of Yahweh and the reward of sons); vv 4–6 (divine blessings on the one who fears Yahweh). **2.** The human effort necessary to produce food is viewed here in a more positive light than in 127:2. In 127 the theme of work is introduced by "in vain," while here it is framed by "happy." **5.** Cf. the parallel in Ps 134:3. **6.** *peace be upon Israel!:* This benediction concludes Ps 125 as well. For a similar concluding prayer, cf. Ps 29:11.

146   Ps 129. The classification and division of this ps are disputed. On the basis of vv 1–4 some designate it a communal thanksgiving (cf. Ps 124), concluding with a prayer of imprecation against Israel's enemies (vv 5–8). Dahood classifies it rather as a national lament and divides it into two sections: vv 1–3 (oppression of Israel by enemies); vv 4–8 (prayer for overthrow of enemies). **1–2.** *much have they afflicted me:* See comment on Ps 123:4. **3.** For "plowing" as language of destruction or devastation, cf. Mic 3:12. **4.** If the vb. "cut" is interpreted as a past tense (so most commentators), v 4 concludes the first section of Ps 129. However, if Dahood is correct in taking the vb. in an optative sense ("May Yahweh cut"), v 4 begins the series of optative vbs. in vv 5–6. Understood thus, the ps concludes with a prayer for divine aid, not with an expression of confidence in the certain punishment of the foe (so Allen). **6.** More likely is the transl.: "like grass . . . which the east wind blasts so that it withers." Cf. Gen 41:6,23,27; Ezek 17:10; 19:12. **8.** *nor will those who pass by say:* An *inclusio* with "let Israel say" in v 1.

147   Ps 130. One of the seven penitential pss, Ps 130 is an individual lament that divides into three sections: vv 1–3 (lament); vv 4–6 (trust in Yahweh's forgiveness); vv 7–8 (address to the community after an oracle of salvation). **1.** *from the depths:* "Depths" occurs in only four other OT texts: Isa 51:10; Ezek 27:34; Ps 69:3,15. Here the psalmist pleads for release from distress, which he compares to the chaotic waters (cf. Jonah 2:2). **3.** *Yah, Lord, who can stand?:* Cf. Amos 7:2. The Hebrew for "who can stand?" is connected with the first word ("from the depths") by similarity in sound. **4.** *forgiveness, that you may be revered:* Cf. 1 Kgs 8:39-40. **5.** *for his word I wait:* Cf. Ps 119:74,81,114,147. The expected divine word is probably an oracle of salvation. **7-8.** If original to the ps, these vv may function as the address of the psalmist to the community after the reception of an oracle of salvation, as in Ps 22:23-27. **7.** *let Israel wait for Yahweh:* The same phrase occurs at the end of the following ps (131:3). **8.** This verse has been considered by some (e.g., Westermann) an addition to Ps 130, a communal interpretation of what was originally an individual lament. However, the turn to the community in Ps 22 (mentioned above) may argue against this view. Finally, the structure of vv 7-8 also argues for its retention: "Let Israel wait for Yahweh" (v 7) and "He will redeem Israel" (v 8) are linked by a grammatical chiasm.

148   **Ps 131.** One of the most beautiful psalms of trust in the Psalter. The first part (v 1) resembles the "negative confession" (cf. Pss 15; 24:4-5; 101:3-4) and contrasts with the positive cast of the second (v 2). **1.** The sin implied by a heart "lifted up" (Prov 18:12) and "haughty" eyes (Ps 18:28) may be more than vanity: an arrogant self-reliance that defies God (cf. Ps 73:6-9). **2.** The verse contains some difficulties but intends a contrast with v 1; the psalmist trusts in Yahweh like a weaned child in its mother's bosom (cf. Matt 18:3-4). Perhaps the poet means to say that as a weaned child no longer cries fitfully for its mother's milk, but is quiet and content upon her lap, so the psalmist reposes in Yahweh's love. **3.** The original ps probably ended with v 2, v 3 being a later "liturgical" conclusion (v 3a = 130:7a).

149   **Ps 132.** A royal psalm celebrating the themes of the "Zion tradition" (Yahweh's election of Zion as his dwelling place and of David's royal line). It is similar in many respects to Ps 89:20-38, except that in the latter Yahweh's promise to David is unconditional (cf. 89:31-34), whereas the promise in Ps 132 is based on obedience to the covenant (v 12). Structure: The ps divides into two sections of 10 lines each (vv 1-10, 11-18). The two sections show a number of matching phrases and terms. "David" occurs at the beginning and end of each section. **1.** *and all his piety:* "Piety" is to be preferred to the common transl., "hardships" (*RSV, JB, TEV*). Near Eastern kings often proclaimed their piety by building temples for their gods, as David does here by his (unfulfilled) desire to build a Temple for Yahweh. **8-10.** Cf. 2 Chr 6:41-42. **8.** *arise, Yahweh, to your resting-place!:* Perhaps part of an ancient prayer associated with the Ark (cf. Num 10:35). In the present context the verse looks ahead to the "resting-place" in v 14 (i.e., Zion). *your glorious Ark:* Lit., "the Ark of your might." Yahweh's "might," synonymous with his "glory" (cf. Ps 63:3), was experienced in the Temple. **11.** For Yahweh's oath/ covenant with David, cf. 2 Sam 7. **12.** David's successors sitting "forever" on his throne is paralleled in v 14 by Yahweh's dwelling (lit., "sitting") "forever" in Zion; Yahweh's eternal presence in Zion makes the eternity of David's dynasty possible. **15.** In Near Eastern thought, blessing was possible because of the presence of the temple, where the divine and human realms met. **18.** *but upon him his crown will shine:* The king's crown was the focus of the "glory" that was his as a reflection of the divine refulgence (cf. Ps 8:6); here it is contrasted with the "disgrace" that covers his enemies.

150   **Ps 133.** Difficult to classify, this ps fits well with the other songs of pilgrimage (Ps 120-34). It also has connections to the wisdom psalms, though it is probably not to be classified among them. The ps is too brief to be divided into sub-sections. **1.** What is "good and pleasant" is most likely not so much the comradeship

of the worshipers as the place where they are gathered (for festival), viz., Zion. "Where" in v 1 is picked up by "there" in v 3b. **2-3.** "Oil" and "dew" were symbolic of refreshment in the hot climate of Palestine. **3.** *the dew of Hermon:* Mt. Hermon (9,100 ft.) lay far to the N of Jerusalem in the Antilebanon range. Its "dew" may have been proverbial for cool refreshment. The "dew" that comes from Zion is more refreshing than that of Hermon, for its dew is life itself (cf. v 3 below; Isa 26:19). *the mountains of Zion:* Read "Mt. Zion" with several ancient mss. **3.** *life eternal:* In the mentality of the ancient East the Temple was the place from which the gods' benefits flowed into human life (cf. Ps 132:14-15), the chief of these benefits being "life." It was "eternal" in the sense that it flowed from the inexhaustible source of life, Yahweh himself.

151   **Ps 134.** The last of the "songs of ascent," concluding with a blessing upon the pilgrim to Zion (v 3). It may be part of a liturgy. **1.** According to some, the priests are addressed here. However, the words may be spoken to the worshipers in general. **3.** *Yahweh of Zion:* A common type of divine epithet, formed with the name of the deity's major cult center (cf. "Ishtar of Nineveh"); cf. Pss 128:5; 135:21. *bless you:* The psalmist prays that Yahweh now reciprocate, blessing those who "bless" (praise) him (vv 1,2).

152   **Ps 135.** A hymn of praise, containing some elements of the historical psalm. In this it is like Ps 136 (see also vv 8-12); this resemblance probably accounts for its present position in the Psalter. Ps 135 also parallels Ps 115 in several places. Structure: vv 1-4 (summons to praise); vv 5-18 (Yahweh the supreme God); vv 19-21 (concluding blessing). Verses 5-18 further breaks down into vv 5-7 (Yahweh's great deeds as creator); vv 8-12 (his great deeds in Israel's history); vv 13-18 (contrast with pagan gods). **1-3.** The triple "Praise Yahweh!" is echoed at the end by a fourfold "Bless Yahweh!" (vv 19-20). **5.** *indeed, I acknowledge that Yahweh is great:* The use of "acknowledge" here may be based on the language of international relations, in which a minor king recognized the supremacy of the "Great King." **6.** Cf. Ps 115:3. This verse introduces vv 7-12. Hebr *'āśâ,* "do," also means "make." Verse 7 is concerned with Yahweh as "maker" or creator; vv 8-12 deal with what he as "done" in Israel's history. **8-12.** Cf. Ps 136:10,17-22. **11.** *Sihon:* Cf. Num 21:21-24; Deut 2:30-33. *Og:* Cf. Num 21:33-35; Deut 3:1-6. **13-18.** Cf. Ps 115:4-8. This section contrasts the pagan gods with Yahweh. Whereas he "made/did" wonders (vv 5-12), they are "man-made" and hence not even as powerful as their creators. **21.** *blessed be Yahweh of Zion:* See comment on Ps 134:3.

153   **Ps 136.** A hymn of praise, which may also be classified as a historical psalm. It is unique in its antiphonal pattern, with a refrain following each colon (cf. Ps 118:1-4). Like the Pentateuch, it combines the traditions of Yahweh as creator with his saving deeds for Israel (cf. also Ps 135:6-12). Structure: vv 1-3 (general praise of Yahweh); vv 4-9 (praise of Yahweh as creator); vv 10-22 (praise of Yahweh for his deeds for Israel); vv 23-26 (summary and *inclusio*). **1.** The ps begins with the same words as Pss 106; 107; 118. *for his steadfast love lasts forever:* The psalmist views everything that Yahweh has done as evidence of the enduring nature of his love for his people. **4.** Cf. Ps 72:18. Yahweh's "great wonders" refer both to the section on creation (vv 5-9) and on Yahweh's deeds for Israel (vv 10-22). Hebr *'āśâ,* "make," "do," likewise refers to both. **10-22.** Cf. Ps 135:8-12. "Struck" (i.e., "struck dead") opens each subsection of vv 10-22 (vv 10,17). **23-25.** These verses form a kind of summary of the preceding: vv 23-24 look back to the section on Yahweh's saving deeds (vv 10-22), while v 25 takes up the theme of Yahweh as creator and sustainer of all. The reference to "us" in vv 23–24 links the present generation, who sing this ps, with the experience of Israel's past; cf. Deut 26:5–10.

154   Ps 137. A communal lament, clearly exilic or postexilic, as the references to Babylon (vv 1,8) indicate. Despite the poignant beauty of the opening verses, it contains some of the most vengeful language in all the Psalter (v 9). Structure: vv 1–3 (suffering in Babylon); vv 4–6 (remembering Daughter Zion); vv 7–9 (imprecation against Edom and Daughter Babylon). **1.** *beside the streams of Babylon:* A reference to the canals of ancient Babylon. *there we sat down:* Or "there we settled," referring perhaps to the practice of settling deportees in Babylonian territory. **3.** *"the 'songs of Zion'!":* A mocking reference to songs glorifying Zion, now in ruins. **5.** *let my right hand wither:* A possible translation of the vb., which is identical in form to the vb. "forget" in the same verse. Because "wither" is not a well-attested meaning of this vb., some prefer "let my right hand be forgotten"—i.e., cease to function. **6.** *let my tongue cleave to my palate:* If Jerusalem is not remembered, the curses the psalmist has invoked upon himself will both prevent him from playing a stringed instrument (with a withered right hand) and from singing (with a tongue clinging to his palate). Cf. Ps 33:2–3. **7.** *the Edomites:* Cf. Ps 108:10–11. **9.** Such atrocities occurred in ancient Near Eastern warfare (Isa 13:16; Hos 13:16; Nah 3:10) and were no doubt committed by the conquering Babylonians. In an extreme example of the law of talion (Pss 54:7; 64:8; 109:17–19; 140:12, 141:9–10), the psalmist hopes that his people have the opportunity to "pay them back" in kind for what they have done.

155   Ps 138. An individual psalm of thanksgiving. Structure: vv 1–3 (thanksgiving for deliverance); vv 4–6 (prayer that all nations acknowledge Yahweh); vv 7–8 (statement of confidence). **2a.** Yahweh's steadfast love forms an envelope around the ps (cf. v 8). **3.** With a slight change of the Hebr vb., read: "You widened my throat by (your) power." The idiom may suggest God's deliverance of the psalmist from distress, pictured as an inability to breathe freely. It may also suggest the opening or "widening" of the psalmist's throat for praise in vv 1 and 2, and for prayer in v 3. Cf. Ps 51:17. **4–5a.** These verses are best taken as wishes: "Let all the kings. . . ." The psalmist "praises" Yahweh and "gives thanks" to him in v 1; here all rulers are called upon to do the same. *let them obey the words of your mouth:* Preferable to the translation, "for they have heard. . . ." (*RSV*). **6.** God's "glory" is sometimes associated with his surpassing height (Pss 57:6,12; 113:4; 148:13). From his lofty vantage point Yahweh can see all things, high and low. Translate: "How exalted is Yahweh—he can see the depths (below)! He perceives the heights far (below him)!" Cf. Ps 113:5–6. **7.** Cf. Ps 23:4.

156   Ps 139. The classification of this ps has been debated. While it exhibits features of the individual lament (vv 19–24), the earlier sections seem to have features in common with the hymn. Structure: vv 1–6 (Yahweh is all-knowing); vv 7–12 (Yahweh is all-present); vv 13–18 (Yahweh's knowledge of the psalmist); vv 19–24 (prayer against enemies). **1–4.** The theme of Yahweh's "searching" and "knowing" the psalmist's "thoughts" and "ways" is repeated at the end of the ps (vv 23–24). **7–12.** Often regarded as some of the most exquisite poetry in the Psalter, perhaps unsurpassed as a description of the inescapability of God's presence (cf. Amos 9:2). **13–18.** A second reason for Yahweh's intimate knowledge of the psalmist is based on the fact that Yahweh created him. **14.** The poet praises the wonder of God's works, in particular the

mystery surrounding the creation of human beings. **16.** *in your book they were written down:* This verse probably goes with what follows, referring to the number of days Yahweh assigned to the psalmist's life. **24.** *any idolatrous way:* Cf. Allen. The psalmist disassociates himself from the wicked of vv 19–22 by implicitly claiming that he is not an idolater.

157   Ps 140. An individual lament of one unjustly accused. Structure: vv 2–6 (Yahweh called upon for help against enemies); vv 7–8 (confession of trust); vv 9–12 (renewed petitions against enemies); vv 13–14 (assurance of divine help resulting in thanksgiving). In this structure there is a correspondence between the first and the third sections in length and topic, and between the shorter second and fourth sections in their expressions of confidence introduced by "I say" and "I know." **4.** The violence directed against the psalmist is verbal (cf. also vv 10 and 12). Such verbal attack is described by the simile of a venomous snake, which also harms with its tongue. **6.** The psalmist now uses a hunting metaphor: Violent enemies attempt to trip up and entrap him. **12.** *as for the violent, let evil hunt them down:* A good example of the law of talion: the psalmist prays that the enemies who hunted him with net and trap (v 6) may themselves be hunted down. Cf. Ps 140:9–10. *the man of tongue:* A slanderer or informer. **14.** *the righteous shall dwell in your presence:* Cf. Pss 11:7b; 101:7. Note the antithesis between this verse and "May the slanderer not be established in the land" in v 12.

158   Ps 141. An individual lament containing wisdom motifs. Structure: vv 1–2 (introductory appeal to God); vv 3–6 (petitions); vv 7–10 (expression of confidence). **2.** *may my prayer be accepted as incense before you:* Some have interpreted this as a replacement of cult and sacrifice by prayer (Pss 51:17–19; 69:31–32); but such "spiritualizing" is probably anachronistic. **3–4.** The concern with sins of speech is a wisdom theme, as is the refusal to associate with evildoers. **4.** *to evil deeds:* Rather than "to evil deeds" (so *NAB*). *to practice deeds of wickedness . . . evildoers:* Here the psalmist turns his attention from sinful speech to sinful deeds. **5–7.** Very difficult. Verse 7 seems to include a reference to agriculture and a mythological reference to the Canaanite god Death pictured as a devouring monster. **8.** *do not expose my neck:* I.e., to the sword. **9–10.** The law of talion is operative as the wicked are themselves caught in the traps they set for the psalmist.

159   Ps 142. An individual lament pleading for divine help against persecutions by enemies. Structure: vv 2–5,6–8. **2.** Note the similar opening of Ps 77:2. **3.** *I pour out before him my complaint:* Cf. Ps 102:1 (title). The repeated "before him" may point to a cultic setting for Ps 142 (cf. 1 Sam 1:15). **4.** Cf. Ps 77:4. **5.** *I look to the right:* The right is the position of the defense witness in a legal proceeding (Ps 109:31); it is also the place from which divine help comes (Ps 121:5). **8.** *prison:* Perhaps a reference to the realm of death. Cf. Lam 3:6–9. *the righteous shall gather around me:* His isolation overcome, the psalmist is rejoined to the community (cf. Ps 22:23–27).

160   Ps 143. An individual lament, the last of the seven penitential psalms (see Ps 6). There is a high degree of repetition and stereotypical lament language. Structure: vv 1–6,7–12. Gunkel, followed by Dahood, considered these two sections to be independent compositions. **3.** Note the parallels in Ps 7:6; Lam 3:6. For the motif of dwelling in darkness like the dead, cf. Job 10:21–22; Ps 88:7. **4–5.** Cf. Ps 77:4,12–13. The psalmist's fainting spirit is balanced by God's good spirit in v 10. **7.** *going down into the pit:* For "pit" as the netherworld, cf. Isa 38:18; Ezek 26:20. **8.** Note the contrast of "in the morning" with "in darkness" in v 3. For the motif of divine help in the morning, cf. Ps 5:3. *show me the way I should go:* Cf. Ps 25:4. **10.** *for you are my God:* Note the corresponding "For I am your servant" in v 12. **10-11.** *your good spirit . . . your name:* Two "hypostases" of Yahweh; cf. God's "light and truth" in Ps 42:3.

161   Ps 144. The difficulties of this ps affect both its form and its meaning. Verses 1-11 can probably be best described as a royal lament: Attacked by former allies, the king prays for divine aid and concludes his prayer with a song of thanksgiving. The meaning of vv 12-15 and their relation to vv 1-11 are obscure; the 1st pers. pl. suffixes suggest a communal form. The similarity of vv 1-10 to Ps 18 has often been noted. **1.** *my hands for war, my fingers for battle:* The king's role as commander in chief. The motif occurs again in v 7 (God's hand), and in vv 7,8,11 (the hands of the enemy). **3.** The psalmist contrasts the catalogue of epithets suggesting God's power to protect and save with human frailty and transience. Cf. the same contrast in Ps 90:1-3. **3-4.** For the human being pictured as a shadow, cf. Job 8:9; 14:2; as a breath, Job 7:16. **5-7.** Cf. Ps 18:8-15. Compare the prayer for deliverance in v 7 with Ps 18:17-18. **8-9.** The psalmist contrasts the lying mouths of the enemies with the king's mouth filled with a new song to God, and the enemies' treacherous right hand to the king's hand playing the lyre to praise Yahweh. **10.** *kings . . . David your servant:* The reference to the dynasty and to David its founder is appropriate. **12-14.** Difficult; meaning unclear. The blessings of fertility seem to be in view: sons and daughters (v 12), abundant stores of food (v 13a) great flocks and herds of cattle (vv 13b-14) undisturbed by disease, loss of young, or drought. It may be connected with what precedes in that the king's pacification of hostile enemies is what makes agriculture and prosperity possible. **15.** Cf. Ps 33:12.

162   Ps 145. An acrostic hymn with a number of links to acrostic Ps 111; compare 111:2-4 and 145:5-8, 111:12 and 145:21. Structure: vv 1-10 (praise of God's greatness and might); vv 11-13 (God's eternal kingship); vv 14-21 (God's universal beneficence). Verses 1-10 are dominated by vbs. of speaking by the psalmist, joined by others; vv 14-21 focus rather on Yahweh's deeds. The beginning and end of the poem are linked by a number of *inclusios* in vv 1-2 and 21. Some late language has suggested a postexilic date to a number of commentators. **8.** An allusion to Exod 34:6 as in Pss 86:15; 103:8. **11-13.** At the center of the poem is its central affirmation, adumbrated in v 1 ("O king!"): the kingship of God. The line beginning with the letter *nun*, missing from the Hebr text, can be supplied from versional and Qumran evidence ("Faithful is Yahweh in all his words, and loyal in all his works") and is adopted by most modern transls. (*RSV, NEB, NAB*). Cf. also v 17. **20.** For a similar concluding sentiment, cf. Ps 1:6.

163   Ps 146. An individual hymn, the first of the five pss that provide a doxological conclusion not only to Book V but to the psalter as a whole. Each of these is framed by *hallĕlû yāh.* Structure: vv 1-6a (praise of God the creator); vv 6b-10 (praise of God the redeemer of the oppressed and helpless). On linguistic grounds a number of commentators have dated Ps 146 to the postexilic period. **1-2.** Invitation to praise God. **3-6a.** These lines have a sapiential character, with their contrast of human mortality and God the creator; cf. Ps 90:2-3 for the same themes. Wisdom language reappears in vv 8-9. **5-6.** Cf. Ps 121:2-3 for the same sequence describing God as the source of help, maker of heaven and earth, and "keeper." **6-7.** *the maker of heaven and earth . . . the doer [*"maker"*] of justice:* The same creative power upholds the physical universe and moral order. Cf. the reverse in Ps 82:2-5, where the absence of justice is responsible for

the shaking of the very foundations of the earth. **7b.** The provision of food for the starving and the release of prisoners recall the events of the exodus, as do vv 9-10 below. **8a.** *Yahweh gives sight to the blind:* An idiom for the freeing of captives (cf. Isa 42:7; 61:1). **8-9.** *Yahweh loves the righteous . . . the way of the wicked he subverts:* Cf. the same wisdom thought in Ps 1:6. **9.** *strangers . . . fatherless and widow:* Cf. Exod 22:20-21. Deut 10:18. **10.** *Yahweh is king forever:* Cf. Exod 15:18. For the royal responsibility to protect the alien, fatherless, and widow, cf. Jer 22:1-4. *O Zion!:* Note the *inclusio* with vocative "O my soul!" in v 1, and the move from the individual psalmist to the community.

164   Ps 147. A communal hymn, generally dated to the postexilic era; support for this dating is provided esp. by vv 2-3, containing such late themes as the rebuilding of Jerusalem by Yahweh (Ezek 40-48) and the gathering of the exiles (Isa 56:8; Neh 1:9). Structure: the three parts of Ps 147 share common themes—an argument for the unity of the ps: vv 1-6 (invitation to praise God, the creator who cares for the afflicted); vv 7-11 (invitation to praise God, who renews each year his act of creation with the gift of rain); vv 12-20 (invitation to praise God, whose creative word is visible in the natural world and whose revelatory word is given to Israel). **1.** *how good . . . how pleasant:* The two clauses that begin Ps 147 are understood as exclamatory, as in Ps 133:1. **2.** *Yahweh is (re)building Jerusalem:* Cf. Pss 102:17 (which the majority of commentators see as exilic or postexilic); 51:20-21; 69:31-32. **4-5.** The one who rebuilds and heals is also the creator. There are echoes of Isa 40:26-28 in this passage; cf. also Ps 136:5; Prov 3:19-20; 8:22-31. **8.** God the creator also provides for the needs of his creatures, esp. with the winter rains that make food production possible. **13-14.** The themes here are also found in Pss 127-28: the security of the city protected by Yahweh (127:1), the provision of food (127:2; 128:2), the blessing of children (127:3-5; 128:3-4,6), and the prosperity and peace of Jerusalem (128:5-6). **15-18.** The creative word of God active in the phenomena of nature, from the cold of winter to the spring thaw. Cf. Ps 33:6. **17.** *before his cold the waters stand frozen:* This transl. is suggested by the context and produced by a slight textual emendation. **19.** Parallel to the creative word in the natural world (vv 15,18) is God's word to Israel. **20.** *he has not done thus to any other nation:* Cf. Deut 4:8; 7:6-7; 2 Sam 7:23. *his ordinances he has not made known to them:* Transl. based on a slight emendation of the MT as suggested by versional evidence.

165   Ps 148. A late communal hymn of praise to the Creator. Its literary antecedents are not the learned traditions of the Egyptian onomastica (so von Rad, *PHOE* 281-91) but a tradition of hymnody common to Israel and Mesopotamia (Isa 44:23; Ps 103:20-22). Structure: vv 1-6 (praise to Yahweh from heaven); vv 7-12 (praise to Yahweh from earth); vv 13-14 (conclusion). **1.** *praise Yahweh from the heavens . . . in the heights:* Cf. Ps 102:20; Job 16:19. This opening line is paralleled by "Praise Yahweh from the earth" in v 7 (the beginning of the second part of the ps). **5.** *let them praise the name of Yahweh:* Here and in v 13 this jussive expression closes the series of creatures called upon to praise God. **9-10.** *fruit trees and all cedars, wild beasts and domesticated animals:* Two examples of merism: cultivated and uncultivated trees, wild and domesticated animals. **13.** *his majesty is over the earth and the heavens:* Another instance of merism (earth and heavens = everything) that resumes chiastically the two parts of the hymn, the praise from the heavens (vv 1-6) and from the earth (vv 7-13). Cf. Gen 1:1; 2:4.

166   Ps 149. A communal hymn of praise in two parts: vv 1-4 (praise of the divine creator and king with music); vv 5-9 (praise of God who leads his people to victory over their foes). The hymn is considered late by many commentators; however, its many parallels with Pss 96-98, pss which may be preexilic, counsel caution in assigning a postexilic date. **1.** *a new song:* Cf. the comment and references at Ps 33:3. *in the congregation of the devout:* The loyal or devout (*ḥāsîdîm*) appear twice more, at the beginning and end of the second part of the ps. **4.** The reason for praise is Yahweh's delight in his people and his deliverance of the poor. For the same parallelism of "people" and "poor," cf. Ps 72:2; Isa 49:13. **5.** *let the devout exult in the Glorious One:* Understanding "glory" (*kābôd*) here as a divine title (Dahood), as in Ps 62:8; cf. Pss 29:2; 24:7,10. *upon their beds:* I.e., "in private"; the expression forms a merism with "in the assembly of the devout" (= in public) in v 1. Cf. Mic 2:1,5. **6.** *a two-edged sword:* Two further instruments of punishment ("chains . . . iron shackles") are mentioned in v 8, neatly balancing the three means of rejoicing in v 3 ("dancing, tambourine, lyre"). **9.** *the written decree:* What God has

decreed as the fate of the enemies mentioned in vv 7-8; the idea probably recalls the setting of the fates by Mesopotamian divinities.

167   Ps 150. The doxology for Book V of the Psalter, and the last of the sequence of Pss 146-50 that conclude the whole collection. Structure: vv 1-2 (invitation to praise and the grounds for it); vv 3-5 (praise of God with music); v 6 (conclusion). Verses 1-5 repeat the imperative "praise God/him" 10 times. **1.** *praise God:* An *inclusio* is formed with v 6, which contains the only other occurrence of a divine name (*Yāh*). *in his sanctuary . . . in his mighty firmament:* The parallelism shows that the heavenly sanctuary is meant; the ps calls upon the members of God's heavenly council to join in the universal chorus of praise. **2.** The grounds for praise are God's mighty acts of creation and redemption. **6.** *let everything that breathes praise Yah!:* The change of grammatical form from the 10 imperatives to a jussive marks the end of the ps.

35

RUTH

Alice L. Laffey

BIBLIOGRAPHY

1 Beattie, D. R. G., *Jewish Exegesis of the Book of Ruth* (JSOTSup 2; Sheffield, 1977). Bertholet, A., "Das Buch Ruth," in *Die Fünf Megilloth* (KHAT 17; Freiburg, 1898). Bertman, S., "Symmetrical Design in the Book of Ruth," *JBL* 84 (1965) 165–68. Boecker, H. J., *Law and the Administration of Justice in the Old Testament and the Ancient East* (Minneapolis, 1980). Campbell, E. F., Jr., *Ruth* (AB 7; GC, 1975). Craghan, J., *Esther, Judith, Tobit, Jonah, Ruth* (OTM 16; Wilmington, 1982) 197–226. Eissfeldt, *EOTI* 477–83. Fisch, H., "Ruth and the Structure of Covenant History," *VT* 32 (1982) 425–37. Gerleman, G., *Ruth* (BKAT 18/1; Neukirchen, 1960). Glanzman, G. S., "The Origin and Date of the Book of Ruth," *CBQ* 21 (1959) 201–7. Gordis, A., "Love, Marriage, and Business in the Book of Ruth," in *A Light Unto My Path* (Fest. J. M. Myers; ed. H. N. Bream, *et al.*, Phl, 1974) 241–64. Gray, J., *Joshua, Judges, and Ruth* (NCB; London, 1967). Green, B., "The Plot of the Biblical Story of Ruth," *JSOT* 23 (1982) 55–68. Gunkel, H., "Ruth," in *Reden und Aufsätze* (Göttingen, 1913) 65–92. Haag, H., "Ruth," *DBSup*

10. 1108–18. Hals, R., *The Theology of the Book of Ruth* (FBBS 23; Phl, 1969). Hertzberg, H. W., *Die Bücher Josua, Richter, Ruth* (ATD 9; 2d ed.; Göttingen, 1959) 255–81. Humbert, P., "Art et leçon de l'histoire de Ruth," *RTP* 26 (1939) 257–86. Hunter, A., "How Many Gods Had Ruth?" *SJT* 34 (1981) 427–36. Joüon, P., *Ruth* (Rome, 1924). Keil, C. F., and Delitzsch, F., *Joshua, Judges, Ruth, I & II Samuel* (GR, 1978) 465– 94. Loretz, O., "The Theme of the Ruth Story," *CBQ* 22 (1960) 391–99. Murphy, R. E., *Wisdom Literature* (FOTL 13; GR, 1981) 84–95. Myers, J., *The Linguistic and Literary Form of the Book of Ruth* (Leiden, 1955). Petrus Cellensis, *Commentaria in Ruth* (CC 54; Turnholt, 1983). Rauber, F. D., "Literary Values in the Bible: The Book of Ruth," *JBL* 89 (1970) 27–37. Rudolph, W., *Das Buch Ruth* (KAT 17/1; Gütersloh, 1962) 23–72. Sasson, J., *Ruth* (Baltimore, 1979). Smith, L. P., "Ruth," *IB* 2. 829–56. Trible, P., "A Human Comedy," in *God and the Rhetoric of Sexuality* (OBT 2; Phl, 1978) 166–99.

INTRODUCTION

2 **(I) Genre, Purpose, and Date.** Most scholars (e.g., Campbell, Craghan, Eissfeldt, Murphy) agree that the book of Ruth is fiction, a short story set in history. Although the narrative is historically plausible—for centuries its literal truth went unchallenged—scholars have come to believe that the book is a literary creation which accomplishes several goals. It succeeds in entertaining its audience—with plot complications, with suspense, and with a satisfying denouement—and also holds up to its readers Hebr models—heroines and a hero. Further, it affirms the possibility of a non-Israelite becoming a faithful Yahwist. Finally, it exalts levirate marriage tracing King David back to two levirate unions.

The author(s) may have composed the book of Ruth for any one of the above stated reasons or for a combination of them. Efforts to determine why the book was written are closely related to hypotheses regarding the date of its composition. The fact that Ruth appears in the Hebr Scriptures among the *kĕtûbîm*, the writings, suggests a later period in Israel's history for its composition. Postexilic dating allows scholars to posit that Ruth, in

the spirit of Dt-Isa and consistent with the thrust of Jonah, was written to strengthen the theological position that non-Jews, provided they were faithful to Yahweh, were acceptable to Yahweh, and as such, should also be acceptable to the Jews. At a time when intermarriage was convenient and most likely common, many deemed it wrong (e.g., Ezra and Nehemiah). In such a period the book of Ruth would stand as strong testimony that non-Jewish people were not to be condemned out of hand. After all, a Moabite woman was King David's great grandmother.

Scholars who believe the book to be the product of the exile or even later (e.g., Bertholet, Eissfeldt, G. Fohrer, Gordis, Gray, O. Pfeiffer, A. Weiser) also point to what they consider Chaldean influences in the text; they likewise note the presence of certain vocabulary which occurs only rarely in attested early literature.

In the LXX Ruth is placed between Judg and 1 Sam. Though contemporary scholars would see this as an interruption of Dtr (Josh-2 Kgs), not composed by the deuteronomistic editor nor controlled by Dtr's theology, such a position fits the story line. Ruth begins with a notice that the events recorded therein took place "in the days when the judges were judging" (1:1) and ends with the notice that Ruth is an ancestor of King David (4:17, 22). Since the book of Judg deals with the period "when the judges were judging" and since David arrives on the scene in 1 Sam 16, it is reasonable to assume that anyone presuming the text's literal historical accuracy would rearrange the books to give Ruth its logical place in the sequence. If one accepts the rearrangement, one is more likely to date the book to the early monarchy, perhaps even to the reign of Solomon.

Support for dating the book of Ruth in the period of the monarchy may also be found in the hypothesis that the book's author intended the work to establish David's lineage (Joüon, Loretz). The emphasis then shifts from the fact that Ruth was a Moabite to the exemplary God-fearing people (Myers) who compose David's ancestry. (The fact that David's marriage to a non-Israelite in 1 Sam 25:43 is not problematic—i.e., that it did not lead to idolatry or other unfaithfulness to Yahweh—further substantiates this position.) Moreover, the text's language and especially its affirmation of levirate marriage do not necessarily relegate Ruth to the exile or later (e.g., Campbell, Craghan, Delitzsch, Hertzberg, Rudolph).

A dating compromise has been achieved by scholars who posit an early *and* later authorship for the book of Ruth (e.g., Glanzman, Sasson, Smith). It is quite possible that the basic story line circulated orally centuries prior to its final editing and embellishment.

3   **(II) Message.** One theme that permeates the story is that of fidelity (*hesed*), loyalty born of covenant bonding (Gordis). Naomi prays that the Lord will act according to covenant faithfulness with her daughters-in-law, Orpah and Ruth, who have so acted toward the dead and toward her (1:8). Naomi later praises God, who, through Boaz's concern for Ruth, has shown covenant fidelity both to the dead and to the living (2:20). Finally, Boaz asks God's blessings on Ruth because of the depth of her covenant fidelity: she has not only cared for her widowed mother-in-law; she has also sought out Boaz, her dead husband's close relative, for her own future spouse (3:10).

Covenant fidelity in the book of Ruth echoes Israel's covenant with Yahweh. They are God's people, and Yahweh is their God. Naomi asks God to provide for the well-being of her daughters-in-law; her words to Ruth about Boaz are a prayer that God will bless him. Likewise, Boaz's words to Ruth are a prayer that God will bless her.

The characters' relationships with one another evidence a fidelity which is grounded in the firm conviction that Yahweh will be faithful to his covenant people. Orpah and Ruth remain faithful to their widowed mother-in-law. Even though Orpah eventually returns home to Moab, she had been willing to accompany Naomi to Judah. Such loyalty Naomi lauds. Boaz expresses his commitment to covenant fidelity by allowing

a widow to gather the remnants of his harvest (Deut 24:19-21) and by protecting the widows of his dead relatives' family. Ruth, who comes to accept Israel's God, will seek a levirate marriage.

4   The practice of levirate marriage made possible the perpetuation of a patriarchal line in those families where the husband died before his wife had conceived any offspring (Boecker, Gordis). Because the ancient Israelites did not believe in life after death, the only way to continue one's existence after death was through one's children. Absence of children, therefore, meant that one would cease to exist in Israel. In order to prevent such a tragedy, the levirate law provided that the deceased man's brother (or closest male relative) was to take and marry the deceased's widow so that she could bear a child who would, in fact, be considered the dead man's. Such a practice made possible the continuation of the dead man's name and line in Israel as well as the retention of his property within the family (Fisch, Gordis, Loretz). Deut 25:5-10 may indicate that the practice became restricted, whereas Lev 18:16 and 20:21 suggest that levirate marriage eventually became unacceptable.

Feminist scholars (e.g., Trible) point to the levirate law as an egregious example of patriarchy. The woman's purpose as wife is herein portrayed as the partner to produce a man's children; if he dies before she has fulfilled her motherhood mission, she must make herself—for the sake of her husband—available to his close relative. Though a male should willingly become his sister-in-law's new husband (but see Gen 38:9), the faithful woman—in patriarchal terms—is one who is conscientious about procuring a descendant for her dead husband (e.g., Tamar in Gen 38; cf. Ruth 4:12). Perez is the son Tamar conceives through Judah in fulfillment of the levirate obligation to Er (Gen 38:29). Similarly, Obed is the son Ruth conceives through Boaz in fulfillment of her levirate obligation to Mahlon (Ruth 4:17).

5   **(III) Outline.** The structure of the book of Ruth may be understood in the following way:

(I) Act I: Famine, Moab, and Death (1:1-22)
    (A) Introduction: Three Widowed Women (1:1-7)
    (B) The Action: Relationship and Return (1:8-21)
    (C) Narrative Transition (1:22)
(II) Act II: Ruth Encounters Boaz (2:1-23)
    (A) Introduction (2:1)
    (B) Scene One: Ruth and Boaz (2:2-16)
    (C) Narrative Transition (2:17-18)
    (D) Scene Two: Naomi and Ruth (2:19-22)
    (E) Narrative Transition (2:23)
(III) Act III: Boaz Encounters Ruth (3:1-18)
    (A) Scene One: Naomi and Ruth (3:1-5)
    (B) Narrative Transition (3:6-8)
    (C) Scene Two: Ruth and Boaz (3:9-13)
    (D) Narrative Transition (3:14-15)
    (E) Scene Three: Naomi and Ruth (3:16-18)
(IV) Act IV: The Resolution (4:1-22)
    (A) The Closer Kinsman-redeemer (4:1-12)
    (B) Climax (4:13)
    (C) Conclusion (4:14-17)
(V) Appendix (4:18-22)

COMMENTARY

6   **(I) Act I: Famine, Moab, and Death (1:1-22).** The first chapter introduces the three female characters—Naomi, Orpah, and Ruth—and a situation of profound loss for Naomi—loss of food, for which reason she had been forced to leave her homeland and live in Moab; loss of husband; and, finally, loss of sons.

7   **(A) Introduction: Three Widowed Women (1:1-7). 1.** This situates the story in the period of the judges and establishes its setting among Bethlehemites of Judah living in Moab. Dating a work is commonly the function of the first verse(s), e.g., Amos 1:1; Isa 1:1; Hag 1:1, and serves to lend historical credibility to what follows.

Though leaving one's land to escape famine is not uncommon in the biblical literature (Joseph and his family move to Goshen [Gen 47:27] and a widow follows Elisha's advice and moves to the land of the Philistines [2 Kgs 8]), going to Moab and settling among the people there is unexpected in light of the prohibition in Deut 23:4. Perhaps Deut 23:4 reflects later problems with the Moabites legitimized by reference to Israel's past and their historical entrance into the land, whereas Ruth represents an earlier period when the Moabites were merely Israel's neighbors (Gerleman).

2. Naming the four persons who comprise the family—the husband and father Elimelech ("my God is king"), the wife and mother Naomi (*n ʿm* means "pleasant"), and their two sons Mahlon (perhaps meaning "sickness") and Kilion (perhaps meaning "wasting")—is significant. Names provide an identity, and, perhaps for the author, they lend a certain historical probability. Elimelech's name foreshadows Ruth's eventual commitment to Yahweh, and Naomi's name contrasts with the name she suggests for herself when she perceives that her destiny has changed. The names of their two sons may be symbolic, in which case they allude to the future: both die. Elimelech's name, "my God is king," is perhaps meant to echo such texts as 1 Sam 8:7, where Yahweh tells Samuel that the Israelites have not rejected him but that in asking for a king they have rejected Yahweh who is their true king, and Zeph 3:15, which describes the time of exile when Yahweh himself will again be the people's king. The name may form an *inclusio* with David (Ruth 4:17), who became Israel's first dynastic king.

3–5. The story's opening leaves us with three widows. First Naomi's husband dies. She then turns to her two sons to provide for her well-being. Though they each subsequently take a wife, we may nevertheless presume that they continued to care for their widowed mother. Unfortunately, however, in time they both die also. Then all that remains is an old woman—who lacks the protection of father or husband or son, an old woman who lacks even the protection of her own land and her own people, a truly powerless person—and two young women, both attached through marriage to Naomi but both now widowed and childless. The OT literature is replete with examples of the widow as symbol of powerlessness within Israel's patriarchal culture (e.g., Exod 22:21; Deut 24:19–21; Isa 1:17; Jer 7:6; 22:3; Zech 7:10). **6–7.** Moab had provided a family from Judah with food during famine, but Bethlehem—"house of bread"—is Naomi's homeland and she desires to return there. The stage is set for the action.

8   (B) The Action: Relationship and Return (1:8–21). Naomi is first to speak, out of her longing for her own land. How can she deprive these already suffering women of the small consolation that their own homeland would provide them? She who desires to return to her home cannot take others from theirs. There is a play on the vb. *šûb,* "to turn (to)," "to turn (back from)," "to return" (vv 6–8,10–12,15–16,21–22; 2:7; 4:3,15). At one point it is Naomi who wishes to return to Judah; Orpah and Ruth are returning with her. Then Naomi tells Orpah and Ruth to return, this time to Moab. For their part, Orpah and Ruth are willing to return with Naomi to Judah; Naomi, however, insists that they turn back to their own land. Orpah returns and Naomi tries to persuade Ruth to do likewise. Ruth, however, does not wish to turn back from Naomi. Finally, the Lord causes Naomi to return empty (v 21).

8–10. Naomi tells Ruth and Orpah to return to their mothers' houses. Such a reference is unusual in the OT (but see Gen 24:38 and Cant 3:4); a house is usually designated as one's father's. Here, however, the phrase reinforces the absence of men in the women's lives. Naomi blesses her daughters-in-law for their past and for their future, for what they have done on behalf of her sons and herself, and for the future husbands which she hopes they will have. These are the first of many blessings which occur throughout the book of Ruth (cf. 2:4, 12,20; 3:10; 4:11–12,14). In reply to Naomi's blessing, Orpah and Ruth express their love and loyalty for their mother-in-law by wanting to return with her.

11–13. Naomi, however, continues the dialogue with questions, a literary technique the author frequently uses to further the plot (cf. 1:19,21; 2:5,10,19; 3:1–2,9,16). Here Naomi's questions are rhetorical, affirming quite plainly that any hope that Orpah and Ruth might have for another husband and children lies not with Naomi but with their own people. It is impossible for Ruth and Orpah to wait until Naomi has borne more offspring. One notes the move from "daughters-in-law" (vv 6–8) to the more intimate "daughters" (vv 11–13; cf. 3:1,16,18); their loyalty justifies the intimacy, and foreshadows Boaz's patriarchal address to Ruth (2:8; 3:10–11). Naomi's comment to Orpah and Ruth that it is "more bitter" for her than for the women because "the Lord's hand has gone out against me" foreshadows the name she later appropriates to herself (v 20) and affirms her recognition of who is Lord. Her Lord is their Lord, whether they know it or not, and that Lord, who has allowed her to become a childless widow, is somehow the source of her suffering. **14.** The author places Orpah's decision to return to Moab on the narrator's lips. She who had "kissed" her mother-in-law and "wept" and decided to go back with her to Judah (v 9) now again "weeps" and "kisses" her mother-in-law. This time, however, she heeds Naomi's advice and bids her farewell; she will return to her own people. The contrast of Orpah and Ruth is drawn in quick strokes. Choice separates the two young daughters-in-law. One goes back (*šûb*); the other holds on (*dbq*). **15–18.** Naomi has succeeded in persuading Orpah to return to her people. She now offers additional encouragement to Ruth: Be like your sister-in-law. Ruth, however, does not submit. She who "clung to" Naomi (v 14) cannot "turn back" (*šûb*) from her (v 16). Ruth pledges covenant fidelity. Ruth claims as her own Naomi's location and Naomi's people and Naomi's God. They had become so through Ruth's marriage, but without the male, the bonds might be severed (Hunter). Ruth, however, clings not to a past but to a present, not to a male, through whom she may achieve power and access, but to a female, one who needs her, one for whom she will provide protection and access. Naomi had sought God's blessings for her daughters-in-law (vv 8–9). Now Ruth swears by God, seeking curses for herself (v 17) if she fails to remain faithful to Naomi till death. **18.** Naomi, who had urged first both Orpah and Ruth and then just Ruth, now ceases her efforts. It is decided. Ruth will remain with her. **19–21.** The two together return to Bethlehem, where their arrival is greeted by town women who ask, "Is this Naomi?" Perhaps their question is prompted by her changed appearance—years had passed since her departure to Moab—or by her changed bearing. Is this the woman whose name—and one's identity is associated with one's name (cf. Gen 17:5,19; 35:18)—signifies "pleasant?" Hearing their question, Naomi's response is to name her changed situation with a change of name. No longer "Pleasant," she is "Mara," because the Lord has made her life "bitter" (cf. v 13). In contrast to barren women whom God blesses with children, Naomi had been "full" (husband and sons) and is now "empty." She testifies that the name "Naomi" is no longer appropriate. God has afflicted her.

9   **(C) The Narrative Transition (1:22).** The narrator concludes this act with a transitional comment, summarizing the previous development and suggesting what is to come in Act II. Ruth has returned (*šûb*) from Moab to Bethlehem with Naomi. "The house of bread" will not desert them. The city whose famine had forced Naomi's departure now provides a harvest at her return.

10   **(II) Act II: Ruth Encounters Boaz (2:1–23).** The chapter introduces a new character, a male, Boaz, and narrates his first meeting with Ruth. It is his fields which provide food for the widowed women.

11   **(A) Introduction (2:1).** The fact that Boaz is a "covenant-brother" (*md‘*) of Elimelech (Fisch) sets the stage for marital possibility for Ruth. Accompanying Naomi back to Judah had effectively eliminated the possibility that Ruth would find a husband from among her own people. Moreover, though being a Moabite may or may not have meant a problematic union at this time in Israel's history (e.g., Num 25:1; Deut 23:4; Neh 13:1, 23), she nevertheless would not have been the most desirable candidate for a Hebr male— unless, of course, that Hebr male were a kinsman-redeemer for her deceased husband.

12   **(B) Scene One: Ruth and Boaz (2:2–16).** **2–3.** In Judah the dialogue begins again. Ruth asks Naomi for permission to go to gather grain remnants in accordance with the provisions of Lev 19:9–10. Naomi consents. By a fortunate coincidence of circumstances, Ruth gathers in Boaz's fields. The narrator reminds the reader (cf. v 1) of what is yet unknown to Ruth: Boaz is from the family of Elimelech. **4–7.** Boaz's greeting to his harvesters and their reply is one indication of the covenant context in which these Israelites live. One concludes, from the ownership of fields, that Boaz is a man of some means. He notices Ruth and asks his foreman about her. Verse 5 provides another example of patriarchy. Boaz does not ask who the woman is, as though she had an identity, but whose she is, indicating that she is possessed by someone else, a man. The foreman's reply is in keeping with the question. Ruth is not named; rather, her place of origin and her family connection with Israel define her. The foreman does, however, comment favorably on her industry. **8–9.** The reader can presume that Boaz now knows what Ruth does not know: she is "connected" to his dead relative. He addresses her not by name but in a manner which is either relational or diminutive, "daughter." His instruction to her indicates that he is willing to assume some responsibility for her: stay here; gather here; be protected here; be refreshed here.

10. Ruth's response to Boaz recalls v 2. She had wished to go where she would find favor; she has found favor. Ruth has been noticed (*nkr;* cf. v 19; 3:14). Her response, in the form of a question, projects the reader forward: Why? **11–12.** Boaz's reply does not refer to any relationship. Rather, he says that Ruth has earned his concern solely on her own merits. Her sacrificing and risk taking on behalf of her mother-in-law deserve reward. Just as Naomi had asked God to bless her daughters-in-law (1:8–9), so now Boaz asks the Lord's blessings for Ruth, who has taken refuge under the protective wings (*knp;* cf. 4:9) of the God of Israel. **13–14.** Ruth's answer to Boaz emphasizes her need: may she continue to find favor (*mṣ' ḥn;* cf. vv 2,10). With self-abnegation she admits that she is an outsider. Yet Boaz responds by inviting her to eat and drink, a foreshadowing of 3:3,7. He provides for her generously. **15–16.** Boaz directs his workers to act in accordance with Israel's covenant obligations to the poor and to widows. They are to allow Ruth a place to glean and to leave grain for her to gather.

13   **(C) Narrative Transition (2:17–18).** A comment by the narrator ends Ruth's working day. Having gleaned and gathered, she threshed the grain. Then she carried it, the measure of an ephah (*'ph*), and the surplus from the food Boaz had provided her and returned home to Naomi.

14   **(D) Scene Two: Naomi and Ruth (2:19–22).** This scene takes place in the city. Naomi greets Ruth with questions about her day. Where (*'ph*) has she gleaned? One notes the play on the Hebrew word "ephah" (v 17) and "where" (v 19). Before Ruth has time to respond, Naomi utters a blessing on behalf of "the man" who took notice of Ruth. Ruth replies to her mother-in-law with a description of the man culminating in an assertion of his identity. **19–20.** The greeting/blessing which Boaz had offered his workers we now find on Naomi's lips, this time in reference to Boaz. Naomi further remarks that through Boaz the Lord is continuing his covenant faithfulness to both the living and the dead, implying also in her comment both herself and Elimelech. The verse recalls 1:8 and Ruth's own posture. Naomi than tells Ruth what the reader (2:1,3) and perhaps Boaz (2:6) already knew. Boaz is their close relative, a kinsman-redeemer (*gō'ēl*). He therefore has the right to redeem all the possessions of Elimelech, including both land and women. **21.** Ruth continues the dialogue seemingly failing to grasp the import of the relationship and its potential effect on her future. Yet her next comment emphasizes a future. Boaz had told her to remain with his workers through the harvest. **22.** The final comment of the act is Naomi's. She does not carry forward prematurely the potential union of Ruth and Boaz; rather, she returns to another comment Boaz had made to Ruth (v 8), and emphasizes it, perhaps with double entendre. Remaining in Boaz's fields with Boaz's servant girls will result in food and safety but also, it is hoped, in a spouse.

15   **(E) Narrative Transition (2:23).** The narrator allows time to pass, the time of the grain harvest. Ruth lives with Naomi and works in Boaz's fields.

16   **(III) Act III: Boaz Encounters Ruth (3:1–18).** In Act II Ruth had met the owner of the fields in which she gleaned and secured both her own and Naomi's food. Now, in Act III, Boaz will discover Ruth at his feet, seeking to secure not sustenance but a spouse.

17   **(A) Scene One: Naomi and Ruth (3:1–5).** We know only that a period of time has elapsed, a fair portion of the harvest season. Ruth and Naomi are again together. **1–2.** The scene opens with a dialogue between the two women. Naomi questions Ruth about her future. She wishes to help Ruth find another husband (cf. 1:9) and, quite specifically, Boaz.

18   **(B) Narrative Transition (3:6–8). 6.** The scene moves to Boaz's threshing floor. Ruth arrives— washed, perfumed, and well clad. **7.** The narrator advises us that she patiently waits until Boaz has eaten and drunk and lain down. Then she uncovers his feet and lies down. The description excites its reader's imagination. The reference here to "feet" or "legs" is provocative— its cognate a euphemism for the penis— yet the term is deliberately ambiguous (Campbell). Ruth, who has sought food in the manner appropriate to widows, now, by this obvious but discreet gesture (Humbert), seeks a husband. **8.** The narrator builds to a highpoint of suspense. In the middle of the night "the man" (cf. 2:19) awakes to find "a woman" at his feet.

19   **(C) Scene Two: Ruth and Boaz (3:9–13). 9.** No longer does Boaz ask "whose" she is (2:5) but rather, "who" she is. The change in form is no literary accident. On the contrary, the new phrase gives to Ruth an identity she previously lacked. Perhaps the question as here stated implies that she belongs to no one. It would thus imply that Boaz can take her and, in the patriarchal culture in which they live, make her "his own." Ruth identifies herself vis-à-vis Boaz. She is his servant. But Ruth goes further. Because (*kî*) Boaz is a kinsman-redeemer vis-à-vis the family of Elimelech, Ruth asks that he spread a corner of his garment over her. (Garments are often symbolic as, e.g., 1 Sam 18:4 and 1 Kgs 11:29–31 testify.) Many commentators (e.g., Craghan, Murphy, Rauber) believe the author is pointing back to Yahweh's wings (*knp;* 2:12), in which case Yahweh's protective wings are being symbolically transferred to Boaz's skirt (*knp*). Ruth asks to be put intimately under Boaz's protection and even into his possession. **10–11.** Boaz's response to Ruth is to ask God to bless her. Just as Boaz had shown the Lord's covenant faithfulness to Elimelech and his family (2:20), so Boaz remarks Ruth's covenant fidelity. This last act of loyalty (*hesed*) is greater (*tb;* cf. 4:15) than her first. She is not seeking for herself a young husband; rather, she is here seeking an appropriate one. Just as Ruth had done all that Naomi asked her, so now Boaz will do all that Ruth asks. **12–13.** Boaz will see to it that Ruth is able to fulfill the levirate marriage, if not with her family's nearest of kin—for there is one nearer than himself—then with him. Boaz tells Ruth to lie at his feet until morning.

20 (D) The Narrative Transition (3:14–15). The narrator reports what followed, including additional dialogue which took place between Ruth and Boaz. Ruth obeyed Boaz's admonition to stay at his feet until morning. He instructed her to keep secret the fact that "a woman" had come to the threshing floor. He also gave her barley to bring back to her mother-in-law.

21 (E) Scene Three: Naomi and Ruth (3:16–18). 16. When Ruth returns from the threshing floor, Naomi greets her with the very same question Boaz had asked: Who are you (*mî-'at;* cf. v 9); the phrase is most frequently translated, "How did you fare?" **17.** The narrator summarizes that Ruth told her everything but then quotes (for the first time) Boaz's words to Ruth about not returning to her mother-in-law "empty" (*rêqām*). Surely the literary artist wants us to know that Boaz, in spite of the complication and retardation of action which the kinsman-redeemer presents, will cooperate with Ruth so that Naomi will no longer be empty (cf. 1:21). **18.** Naomi responds to Ruth with a comment about the future. "The man" (cf. v 8; 2:29) will not rest (*šqt* but cf. 1:9; 3:1; 4:14) until Ruth's situation is resolved. Heightened suspense is promised a speedy resolution.

22 (IV) Act IV: The Resolution (4:1–22). Food has been restored, a potential spouse is in sight, and implicit with him is the hope of descendants. Only through a son can Naomi's emptiness be made full.

23 (A) The Closer Kinsman-redeemer (4:1–12). 1–3. When the unnamed kinsman-redeemer (*gō'ēl*) arrives the next morning at the city gate, Boaz is waiting for him. The dialogue is brief. Boaz brings together the kinsman-redeemer and 10 elders. In typical patriarchal fashion the subject matter is not the women—Naomi and Ruth—but rather the dead man Elimelech's land. Boaz tells the kinsman-redeemer that Naomi is selling it and he is first in line to acquire it (Gordis). **4.** The kinsman-redeemer agrees to redeem Elimelech's land. Boaz, however, counters that the Moabite Ruth is part of Elimelech's property. Since Elimelech's daughter-in-law is still able to provide an heir for her dead husband's name and land, the kinsman-redeemer is, in effect, committing himself to providing that heir by buying the land. **5–6.** This new information changes things. It is one thing to buy land—and convenient that being a close

relative to the deceased gives one the first option to do so. It is quite another thing to realize that the land will ultimately belong to the son whom one will raise up for the deceased. The kinsman-redeemer understands the purchase of Elimelech's land to entail risk to his own inheritance and so declines the opportunity to purchase it. He then passes on to Boaz the right to redeem the land. **7–8.** A narrative parenthesis explains the significance of what happens next (perhaps betraying that although the story is set in early Israel, it was written at a later time when its readers would need the explanation). Transfer of right of ownership of property was solemnized not by a handshake nor by a written contract as it is today but by each party's removing his sandal and giving it to the other.

9–10. Boaz then announces to the elders their function as witnesses to what has occurred. He publicly proclaims that he has thereby acquired all the property of Elimelech's family including the Moabite Ruth. Boaz also indicates his intention to fulfill levirate law and thereby keep alive Mahlon's name. The name of Ruth's husband has not been designated before 4:10—and there only to specify whose name Boaz's marriage to Ruth will perpetuate. **11–12.** The elders publicly testify that they are witnesses to the contract (cf. Josh 24:22). They also bless Ruth (cf. 1:8–9; 2:12,19; 3:10), wishing her many offspring (this is the only place in the entire OT where one is blessed with a wish to be like other women!), and they bless Boaz, wishing him renown (cf. 2 Sam 7:9). Their third and final blessing refers to Boaz's offspring through Ruth; they compare them to Perez's family, that is, to the family of the offspring whom Tamar bore to Judah. The text alludes to another levirate marriage, and to another outstandingly "just" woman (cf. Gen 38:26).

24 (B) Climax (4:13). The narrator brings full circle the emptiness of chap. 1. The famine has been replaced by an abundant harvest; the foreign land, by homeland. Now the Lord who had testified against Naomi (1:21) gives Ruth conception. Now, through this new life the dead will live.

25 (C) Conclusion (4:14–17). 14. The elders' blessings are fulfilled and echo in the women's words to Naomi. No longer is Naomi deserving of pity (cf. 1:19–21) but rather women celebrate her blessings. A kinsman-redeemer renews the aged woman. **15.** Just as Tamar was more righteous than Judah, so Naomi's daughter-in-law Ruth is better (*tb;* cf. 3:10) to her than seven sons. **16–17.** Just as Boaz provides Mahlon with a son, Ruth provides Naomi with a son. This son, whose name, Obed, evokes servanthood, is the ancestor of David. Just as Naomi is Obed's grandmother, Obed is David's grandfather. Though restricted by patriarchal expectations, these women—Naomi and Ruth—emerge as models of covenant fidelity for Israel.

26 (V) Appendix (4:18–22). Most scholars (e.g., Bertman, Campbell, Eissfeldt, Murphy) believe these verses to be a priestly addition. They add no new information to the story line and are, in fact, anticlimactic. Nevertheless, they do specify the genealogy which brings together Perez and David. **27.** The story has been developed with three major characters—Naomi, Ruth, and Boaz—with Orpah and the closer kinsman-redeemer as foils for Ruth and Boaz, and with three choruses of minor characters—the women of Bethlehem, Boaz's workers, and the elders. Whether one seeks the text's purpose in its dating and setting, or whether one allows for the several hypotheses regarding the book's origin and approaches the text primarily as literature, one is here presented with a masterful testimony to the literary genius of ancient Israel.

36

LAMENTATIONS

Michael D. Guinan, O.F.M.

BIBLIOGRAPHY

1 *Commentaries/Studies:* Albrektson, A. B., *Studies in the Text and Theology of Lamentations* (Lund, 1963). Fuerst, W. J., *The Five Scrolls* (CBC; Cambridge, 1975). Gordis, R., *Lamentations* (NY, 1974). Gottlieb, H., *A Study on the Text of Lamentations* (Arhus, 1978). Gottwald, N., *Studies in the Book of Lamentations* (Chicago, 1954). Harrison, R. K., *Lamentations* (Downers Grove, 1973). Hillers, D. H., *Lamentations* (AB 7A; GC, 1972). Kaiser, O., *Klagelieder* (ATD; Göttingen, 1981). Meek, T. J., "Lamentations," *IB* 6. 3–38.

Articles: Barré, M. and J. Kselman, "New Exodus, Cove-

nant and Restoration in Psalm 23," *WLSGF* 97–127. Cross, F. M., "Studies in the Structure of Hebrew Verse: The Prosody of Lamentations 1:1–22," *WLSGF* 129–55. Gelin, A., "Lamentations (Livre des)," *DBSup* 5. 237–51. Johnson, B., "Form and and Message in Lamentations," *ZAW* 97 (1985) 58–73. Lanahan, W. F., "The Speaking Voice in the Book of Lamentations," *JBL* 93 (1974) 41–49. McDaniel, T. F., "Philological Studies in Lamentations," *Bib* 49 (1968) 27–53. Mintz, A., "The Rhetoric of Lamentations," *Prooftexts* 2 (1982) 1–17. Tigay, J. H., "Lamentations, Book of," *EncJud* 10. 1368–75.

INTRODUCTION

2 **(I) Title, Text, and Canon.** In the MT this book takes its name from its opening word *'êkâ*, "Oh how," a characteristic beginning of a lament (1:1; 2:1; 4:1; see 2 Sam 1:25; Isa 1:21; Jer 48:17). The Talmud (*b. B. Bat* 15a) and rabbinic tradition call it *qînôt*, a title reflected in the LXX *threnoi*, the Vg *Threni* or *Lamentationes*, and the Lamentations of modern transls. The received Hebr text is in relatively good condition, but there are still places where the exact transl., syntax, and meaning are obscure. The LXX is not always helpful because its transl. adheres rather closely to the MT (Albrektson, *Studies* 208–13; Hillers, *Lamentations* xxxix–xl).

The canonicity of Lam has never been in dispute, but its place within the canon varies in the two major text traditions. In the Hebrew tradition, it is located in the third part, the Writings, in varying places, finally settling as part of the *mĕgillôt*, the five "Scrolls," read on various Jewish feast days. The Gk and Lat tradition places it in the second part, the Prophets, attached to the name of Jeremiah, and often preceded by the notice, "And it came to pass, after Israel was taken captive and Jerusalem was laid waste, that Jeremiah sat weeping and lamented with this lamentation over Jerusalem and said . . ."

3 **(II) Historical Setting and Authorship.** In the year 587, on either the 7th (2 Kgs 25:8–9) or the 10th (Jer 52:12) of the 5th month, Ab (July–Aug.), the Babylonians destroyed Jerusalem and its Temple and

deported a large segment of the population, leaving only the poorest and the weakest (2 Kgs 24:8–25:30, Jer 39; 52). The five poems corresponding to the five chapters of Lam were almost certainly composed in Palestine in response to this crisis in the political, social, and religious life of ancient Israel. Since some kind of ritual mourning continued to be carried out at the site of the Temple after its destruction (Jer 41:4–5; Zech 7:1–5; 8:18–19), it is possible that these laments were used in such a setting.

The poems themselves are anonymous. Although it is possible that more than one author is involved, the overall style, content, and vocabulary point rather to one. Since they contain almost no historical information (D. Hillers, *CurTM* 10 (1983) 155–61), attempts to relate these poems more concretely to specific situations or factions within Israel are highly speculative.

As already noted, a very old tradition ascribes the authorship of these poems to Jeremiah. This seems based on the notice in 2 Chr 35:25 that he composed laments over the death of Josiah and that these were passed on and preserved in "the lamentations." The erroneous belief that Lam 4:20 referred to Josiah would have led to connecting Lam with Jeremiah, who became the patron of lamentations, as did Moses of law, David of psalms, and Solomon of wisdom. Beginning in the 18th cent., modern scholarship has challenged this tradition and almost unanimously rejected it. Arguments from style and vocabulary are more indecisive, but questions of content carry more weight. Contrast, e.g., 1:10 with Jer 7:7,14; 2:9 with Jer 42:4; 4:17 with Jer 2:18; 37:5–10; 4:20 with Jer 24:8–10; 37:17. Further, it is easier to explain how the name of Jeremiah was attached to an originally anonymous composition than how an authentic Jeremian authorship would be completely lost in the Hebr text tradition (Gelin, *DBSup* 5. 248–50; Hillers, *Lamentations* xix–xxiii; Gordis, *Lamentations* 124–26).

4 (III) Poetic Composition. In terms of the two basic elements of the Hebr poetic line, parallelism and meter, Lam shows peculiarities. With the exception of chap. 5, over 40 percent of the poetic lines show no real parallelism (or, in traditional terminology, synthetic parallelism), making it difficult at times to determine where the pause in the line occurs. The meter has been described as the *qînâ* (lament) meter, 3 stresses followed by 2 stresses. At best, the 3 + 2 meter is dominant in the book, but other patterns (e.g., 3 + 3, 2 + 2) occur randomly. It has been questioned further if this is well described as a *qînâ* meter since, on the one hand, it does not occur in all laments (e.g., 2 Sam 1:17–27) and, on the other, it is used in nonlament contexts (e.g., Isa 1:10–12; Cant 1:9–11; see Hillers, *Lamentations* xxx–xxxv; Gordis, *Lamentations* 117–24).

On the next level of organization, the lines are arranged into stanzas based on the 22-letter Hebr alphabet. Similar acrostics occur elsewhere in the OT (→ Sirach, 32:4) as well as in nonbiblical ancient Near Eastern literature (*ANET* 438). The exact purpose of the acrostic device is unclear; various suggestions have been offered. It served to aid the memory in public recitation, to help teach the alphabet, to demonstrate the skill of the author, to express fullness or completeness (A. Ceresko, *VT* 35 (1985) 99–104; Gottwald, *Studies* 23–32).

The poems show individual variation in their use of the acrostic. The first three contain 66 lines divided into 22 stanzas, each beginning with a successive letter of the alphabet. In chaps. 1 and 2 only the first line of each stanza begins with the respective letter, whereas in chap. 3 each line of the stanza begins with it. Chap. 4 is shorter, having 44 lines, 22 stanzas of 2 lines each; chap. 5 is the shortest with only 22 lines; in addition, it lacks the acrostic form. For no apparent reason, chaps. 2, 3, 4 reverse the 16th (*'ayin*) and 17th (*pē*) letters.

On the highest level of organization, does the book as a whole show any overarching structure or unity? Two patterns appear. (1) The five laments present a chiastic (A + B + C + B′ + A′) arrangement. Chapters 1 and 5 are more generalized descriptions of the disaster; chaps. 2 and 4 describe more explicitly the details of death and destruction. Chapter 3 stands in the center, because of both its form (the fuller acrostic) and its content (confession of sin and trust in the goodness of God) (Gottwald, *IDB* 3. 62). (2) In contrast to this more static structure, a more dynamic one has been proposed (W. Shea, *Bib* 60 [1979] 103–7). As noted above, the dominant meter is the 3 + 2 *qînâ* meter. The book as a whole is organized likewise on the rhythmic 3 + 2 pattern. The first 3 chaps. form the first unit, which rises to its fullest expression in chap. 3. Then, after a pause, come the two decreasingly shorter chapters, 4 and 5. The book forms one grand lament which rises and then gradually fades away.

5 (IV) Literary Genre. The poems employ literary forms known elsewhere in the OT. Chapters 1, 2, 4 reflect the funeral dirge (Jer 22:18; 2 Sam 1:19–27) applied to the people as a whole (Amos 5:1–2). Chapter 3 is basically an individual lament (e.g., Pss 5; 6; 7; 22), and chap. 5, a communal lament (Pss 73; 79). None of these represents a pure form; all are mixed to some

degree with other elements (Hillers, *Lamentations* xxvii–xxviii; Gelin, *DBSup* 5. 239–43). The form "lament over a fallen city" is known from Mesopotamian literature (*ANET* 455–63); recognizing similarities and dissimilarities, scholars dispute whether any direct influence on Lam can be detected (no: Hillers, *Lamentations* xxviii–xxx; T. J. McDaniel, *VT* 18 (1968) 198–209; yes: W. C. Gwaltney, Jr., *Scriptures in Context II* [ed. W. H. Hallo, *et al.*; Winona Lake, 1983] 191–211).

Lamentation is not simply petition; it is rather a spontaneous response to the presence of chaos, brokenness, suffering, and death in life. When we hurt physically, we cry out in pain; when we hurt religiously, we lament. *God* is addressed directly with heartfelt questions: "Why?" (I do not understand) and "How long?" (I am at my limit; what happens next?). The afflictions of the *speaker(s)* are described in stereotyped ways with which all sufferers can identify: sickness, loneliness, shame, mistreatment by others, the danger of death. The role of *enemies* is often presented with feelings of anger and frustration. As a form, lament has as its medium dramatized speech: who speaks to whom about whom? God, Israel (or Israelite), and adversary play out the drama of covenant. Suffering, grief, and anger are experiences that can also lead to chaos; lamentation, both individual and communal, provides a structure (accentuated in Lam by the tight acrostic) which enables one to face and express these feelings as well as to work through them to a fuller, healthier situation (W. Brueggemann, *Int* 28 (1974) 3–19; *Int* 31 (1977) 263–75; R. Davidson, *The Courage to Doubt* (Phl, 1983) 155–60; Mintz, "Rhetoric"; C. Westermann, *Praise and Lament in the Psalms* [Atlanta, 1981]).

6 (V) Theology. How was Israel to understand religiously the trauma of its recent history? Several options were open: return to a more wholehearted devotion to the gods of Canaan (Jer 44:15–19); worship the obviously stronger gods of Babylon (see Isa 40:18–20; 41:21–24); remain within Yahwism and seek there some understanding of the present suffering (P. Ackroyd, *Exile and Restoration* [OTL; Phl, 1968]; R. Klein, *Israel in Exile* [Phl, 1979]). Lam was probably one of the earliest attempts to do the latter.

Lam begins by taking a good hard look at the *present*. The reality must be faced in all of its starkness. The poet is overwhelmed by the magnitude of suffering (2:11). There has been death, and grief is the only appropriate response.

It looks then to the *past*. Yahweh was the God who had led them from Egypt, covenanted with them at Sinai, and led them into their inheritance in Canaan. If they remained faithful to this covenant they could expect blessing; if not, covenant curse would follow disobedience (Deut 28). Yahweh had further chosen David and promised that his descendants would always occupy the throne (2 Sam 7:8–17) in Jerusalem, which would stand firm forever (Pss 46; 48; 76) because Yahweh was enthroned in Zion (Pss 91; 96–99). Lam recognizes that its present suffering is not the sign of Yahweh's weakness, but just the opposite. It is Yahweh's power which punishes them. Israel's enemies are mentioned on occasion (1:21–22; 3:52–66; 4:21–22), but more often they fade from sight. Yahweh has become Israel's main enemy (2:1–9), destroying both people and Temple.

Israel has become enemy to Yahweh because of its sin; this is the real cause of the destruction. While all have sinned, the religious leaders are held esp. accountable (e.g., 2:14; 4:13). Words of confession come from Zion (1:18,20,22) and the people (3:42; 5:7,16). The nature of the sin remains vague; specific details are not given. They are all part of the one major sin: breach of covenant. Violation of the covenant has brought on covenant curse. Compare 1:15,18 with Deut 28:41; 1:9 with 28:43; 2:20 with 28:53. There is no hint that this is unjust; in fact, "Yahweh is righteous, I have disobeyed his command" (1:18).

Israel laments and confesses; these are acts of faith. But what of the *future*? Is there any basis for a continuing faith? The poet prays for Yahweh to "be near and redeem my life" (3:57–58) and tells Zion, "Your punishment is complete . . . he will not exile you again" (4:22). In chap. 3 these hopes are more fully expressed. Yahweh's mercy and graciousness never come to an end (3:22); Yahweh "does not cast off forever" (3:31). In 3:56–61, the poet is sure that Yahweh has heard his prayers. Yahweh still sits enthroned forever (5:19). In spite of the great trauma of recent events, the door to Yahweh's renewed mercy is still open.

7   (VI) Later Usage. The traditional ascription of Lam to Jeremiah gave rise to the literary term "jeremiad" in the sense of a long, mournful lament about one's troubles. In art, perhaps best known is Michelangelo's painting of a sorrowing Jeremiah on the Sistine Chapel ceiling. In music, Lam has proven more popular; the major composers of the 16th cent. set them to music. After a decline of interest, some 20th-cent. composers (e.g., Leonard Bernstein, Igor Stravinsky) have returned to these texts for inspiration (L. E. Cuyler, *NCE* 8. 350; B. Bayer, *EncJud* 10. 1375–76).

Within the Jewish community one of the earliest midrashim (4th–5th cent.) was *Lam. Rab* (M. D. Herr, *EncJud* 10. 1376–78). Later Judaism assigned Lam to be read on the 9th of Ab. The First Temple was destroyed

by Babylon on either the 7th or 10th of Ab; the Second Temple, by Titus and the Romans on the 10th of Ab, AD 70, and the last stronghold of Bar Cochba at Beth-Ter, by the Romans on the 9th of Ab, 135. The Talmud settles on the 9th of Ab as the day on which great disasters occurred, thus making it one of the saddest days of the Jewish calendar (M. Ydit, *EncJud* 3. 936–40).

Among early Christian writers, 4:20 was a very popular text interpreted in reference to Jesus. Most of the commentators writing on Jeremiah usually included Lam also. Lam made its way too into the Christian liturgy, being read in the Office for the last three days of Holy Week. It was for these especially that many of the musical settings were composed. Thus the expression of sorrow, the confession of sins, and the hope in God's continuing mercy found in Lam were transferred by both religious communities to traumatic events in their respective histories.

8   (VII) Outline.

(I) The Desolation of Zion (1:1–22)
   (A) Lament *over* Zion (1:1–11)
   (B) Lament *of* Zion (1:12–22)
(II) The Day of Yahweh's Wrath (2:1–22)
   (A) The Lord's Day of Wrath (2:1–10)
   (B) The Poet and Zion Respond (2:11–22)
(III) Out of the Depths I Cry (3:1–66)
   (A) Loneliness (3:1–20)
   (B) Memory and Reflection (3:21–39)
   (C) Experience of Reconnection (3:40–66)
(IV) The City Revisited (4:1–22)
   (A) The Distress of the City (4:1–16)
   (B) Our Futile Hope (4:17–22)
(V) The Prayer of the People (5:1–22)

COMMENTARY

9   (I) The Desolation of Zion (1:1–22). The tragic reversal experienced by Zion is described first by one who comments on the contrast between her former glory and present disgrace (1:1–11). The perspective then shifts (1:12–22) as Zion speaks in her own voice, jolting us to share her internal experience in a more personal way.

(A) Lament *over* Zion (1:1–11). 1. Once full of people, Zion now sits alone. *widow:* Her social status is open to mistreatment because she lacks legal protection. **2.** The absence of consolation is a recurring refrain (vv 2,9,16,17,21). *friends and lovers:* Political allies (v 19; Jer 27:3; 30:14) now become enemies, a theme common in laments (Pss 38:12; 88:19). **3.** *rest:* An important part of God's promises to Israel (e.g., 2 Sam 7:11); no rest suggests withdrawal of that promise (Ps 95:11). **4.** *the roads to Zion mourn:* This image may derive ultimately from Canaanite myth (D. Hillers, *Perspective* 12 [1971] 121–33) **5.** For the first time, Israel's covenant disobedience is mentioned, along with Yahweh's punishment. Verse 5a reverses the covenant blessing of Deut 28:13, and 5c echoes the curse of Deut 28:41. **6.** *all her glory:* Refers to Zion's rulers and nobility. **7.** This verse is too long; various emendations have been proposed (see Cross, "Prosody" 140–41). In the honor–shame culture of the ancient world, to be mocked by one's enemies was particularly painful (Job 30:1–19; Pss 22:7–9; 44:14). **8–9.** Zion's nakedness and the pollution of her skirts (probably menstruation, see Lev 15:19–24) are the direct result of her sin. In v 9c, the mute figure begins to speak. **10.** The Temple was the seat and symbol of God's presence and protection in Israel; heathens were forbidden to enter (Deut 23:4). Now they enter

and plunder with impunity. **11.** The ravishing specter of famine first appears; it will recur often. *their treasures:* May refer either to possessions or to their precious children (Hillers, *Lamentations* 25). Unable to restrain herself any longer, Zion pours out her lament.

10   (B) Lament *of* Zion (1:12–22). Zion begins by speaking *about* God (1:12–19) and ends by speaking *to* God (1:20–22). **12.** The text is difficult. "Come, all you who pass by the way," is a simple emendation. **13–15.** Yahweh's actions are described in a series of images: fire, a net, sickness, a heavy yoke braided of sin. Instead of leading Israel's warriors to victory as before, Yahweh has summoned an army against them. The poet interrupts in v 17, but then Zion continues (vv 18–19), reaffirming Yahweh's righteousness and her sinfulness. She had called to her "lovers" for help (see v 2), but they had failed her. She now turns and cries to the only one who can help. **20–22.** In very concrete terms, Zion describes her condition. *my intestines . . .:* In the ancient anthropology, when one was in distress, the intestines pressured the liver and the heart, which broke down, turning to liquid which left a bitter taste in the throat before exiting the eyes as tears (T. Collins, *CBQ* 33 [1971] 18–38., C. L. Seow, *CBQ* 47 [1985] 416–19). The prayer against enemies is a standard element in laments (e.g., Pss 6:11; 10:15; 109:6–19) and reflects Israel's belief that God's justice is universal and that all come under its sway.

11   (II) The Day of Yahweh's Wrath (2:1–22). The theme of chap. 2 is clearly set out at the beginning (v 1) and the end (v 22): the day of Jerusalem's destruction was the day of the wrath of the Lord. The first part (2:1–10) describes this event from the outside, and in the second part, the poet and Zion respond (2:11–22).

(A) The Lord's Day of Wrath (2:1–10). This theme, prominent in the prophets, describes particularly Yahweh's victory over forces of chaos, destruction, and sin, often represented by the enemies of Yahweh's people. Amos (5:18–20) strongly points out that this is too simple; the important distinction is not social or political but moral (→ OT Thought, 77:137). The Day of Yahweh was a powerful concept available to interpret historical events, past, imminent, or future (A. J. Everson, *JBL* 93 [1974] 329–37). Here the poet looks back to the recent past. **1–10.** Yahweh is depicted as a marauding warrior who strips, smashes, razes, cuts down, burns out, lays waste, and, like the devouring Death of Canaanite mythology, swallows down (*blʿ*, vv 2,5,8). Jerusalem (the "glory of Israel," v 1) is destroyed along with its gates (v 9), walls (vv 7–8) and fortifications (vv 2,5). Yahweh personally tore down the Temple ("his footstool," v 1; "his tent," v 4; "his dwelling," v 6) with its altar and sanctuary (v 7). The only festive sounds to be heard are the victory shouts of the enemy (v 7). Israel is cast down (v 1; Ezek 28:17; Isa 14:12), her strength ("horn," v 3; Ps 75:11; Jer 48:25) smashed to pieces. Political leadership is gone, king and princes disgraced and scattered among the nations (vv 2,9). Also helpless are the three circles of religious leadership, the priests with their instruction (*tôrâ*), the prophets with their vision and word, and the wise elders with their counsel (Jer 18:18; Ezek 7:26). The elders can only sit in wise silence (Job 13:5), engaging in traditional signs of mourning (v 10; Job 2:12; Ezek 26:16; 2 Sam 13:31).

12   (B) The Poet and Zion Respond (2:11–22). **11–12.** The poet is overwhelmed and cannot continue. *my intestines . . .:* Words very like those of Zion in 1:20–22. This is brought on not by the vision of magnificent Jerusalem destroyed but by the sight of small children dying in the streets from hunger, "pouring out" their lives into their mothers' bosoms. **13.** The poet turns to address Zion (2:13–19). *to what can I compare you?:* Israel's suffering is so vast that the poet's ministry through healing language comes to a standstill; no metaphors are adequate for consolation (Mintz, "Rhetoric" 6–7). **14.** For a brief moment the poet glances backward. The prophets, supposed to be spiritual leaders, had failed, whitewashing the sin of the people (Ezek 22:28; Jer 23:9–40). **15–16.** Jerusalem had once exulted in her beauty and joy (Ps 48:3); now passersby are shocked, and enemies rejoice. *we devoured her:* The same vb. (*blʿ*) is used of Yahweh in vv 2,5,8. **17.** Let there be no mistake; it was not the enemies' doing but God's. **18–19.** The poet urges Zion to take up the lament. *pour out her heart like water:* See 1:20–22. **20–22.** First described (vv 1–10), then addressed (vv 13–19), Zion now begins to speak for herself, and attempts to move Yahweh to pity. **22.** The day of God's wrath is like a victory banquet, but Israel is the slaughtered food (Isa 34). There is no prayer against enemies here (as in 1:21–22; 3:60–66; 4:21–22), for Yahweh is the enemy (v 5). Zion can only bewail the loss of her children.

13   (III) Out of the Depths I Cry (3:1–66). Forming the center of the book, chap. 3 has the fullest acrostic and the most consistent use of the 3 + 2 meter (→ 4 above). In contrast to the bereft woman of chaps. 1–2, the speaker now is a man (vv 1,39) who expresses his individual lament and prayer of trust and thanksgiving in a language filled with familiar words and phrases (see Hillers, *Lamentations* 65–74). Late in the poem, "we" appears (vv 40–47) in a way suggestive of communal laments. Through the language of traditional faith, the whole people is called to share the experience

of the individual; the speaker is a model for the city (B. Childs, *CIOTS* 594–95).

Overconcern with historicizing and identifying the speaker probably misses the point. More important is the movement, which progresses through three stages in vv 1–20,21–39,40–66 (see Mintz, "Rhetoric" 10–16).

(A) Loneliness (3:1–20). 1. The first word, "I," sets the tone; the poet focuses on himself and his pain. The enemy is an unnamed "he." The first part moves between these two, "I" and "he." **4–9.** The poet ("I") is beset, hemmed in, encircled, abandoned. **10–13.** The enemy ("he") is like a marauding bear or lion; he is an archer shooting arrows into the victim's body (Job 16:12–13). **15–18.** The enemy is an ungracious host who torments his guest and feeds him gall and wormwood. It is only near the end of this section that the enemy is finally named (v 18): it is Yahweh! The basis for hope would seem to be gone. Many of these images occur in the psalms, but especially interesting is Ps 23, whose language the poet seems to be deliberately reversing; compare vv 1–2 with 23:4; v 6 with 23:6; v 9 with 23:3; v 15 with 23:5 and v 17 with 23:16 (see Barré and Kselman, "New Exodus" 101–3).

14   (B) Memory and Reflection (3:21–39). **21.** Contrary to v 18, there is a basis for hope: memory of Yahweh's ways and justice. **22–30.** The covenant fidelity (*ḥesed*) and mercy (*rāḥămîm*) of Yahweh do not end but are renewed each day. *Yahweh is my portion:* See Pss 16:5; 73:26; 142:6. **25–27.** Each line begins with "good" (*ṭôb*). Confident of Yahweh's goodness, the sufferer can hope in silence for deliverance and bear up under the yoke, which can have an educational value. These ideas reflect the wisdom tradition (e.g., Prov 13:24; 23:13–14). **31–39.** The poet reflects, in a more theological way, on God's justice. Punishment is transitory; what lasts is God's fidelity and mercy (the same words as in v 22). The syntax of vv 34–36 is difficult; the sense seems to be that nothing happens without God's knowledge. **37–39.** In words similar to Gen 1, God is seen as the creator of all, evil as well as good (Amos 3:6; Isa 45:7). Like section 1, which postpones naming the enemy until v 18, section 2 postpones naming the cause of the suffering to the final word of v 39 ("sin").

15   (C) Experience of Reconnection (3:40–66). **40–47.** Up to this point, the speaker has been isolated. Now, having recovered a sense of sin and turned back to God, the "I" becomes "we." Reintegrated into the community, the "I/we" can address its covenant partner. Likewise, God, up till now a "he," becomes a "you." Complaint and reflection about God become prayer spoken to God in faith. **48–51.** Instead of bewailing personal pain, the poet is moved by the plight of the people and intercedes on their behalf. **52–55.** From isolated loneliness, the poet has come through memory and reflection on God's mercy to a sense of sin and a merging with the community. (A very similar movement can be seen in Ps 77). He has just spoken on behalf of the people; now he prays as the people. The "I" is a communal voice calling from the pit (Ps 130). **56–66.** Addressed in faith as "you," God is no longer the enemy but a protector and defender. Mentioned first in v 52, the enemies are separate from God, existing in history as the agents of affliction. The poet prays that God's justice be manifested in their regard as well.

16   (IV) The City Revisited (4:1–22). This poem is similar in theme and content to chap. 2. Save for three occurrences in the stock phrase, "daughter of my people," the "I" does not appear again (nor in chap. 5). Yahweh's ultimate responsibility is still faced (vv 11,16), but the guilt of Zion's leaders (vv 12–16) and that of her enemy (vv 21–22) are stressed.

(A) The Distress of the City (4:1-16).   1-2.
The traditional *'êkâ*, "Oh how," recurs; also recurring is
the theme of tragic reversal. Gold and jewels, once held
precious, are now spurned; so it is with the people of
Zion. **3-10.** The poet returns to the theme that had moved
him so deeply in 2:11-12,19-20, the famine and its
effects on the children. The ostrich was known for its
cruel treatment of its young (Job 39:13-18). The suffering of hunger is so severe that a quick death, like that of
Sodom (v 6) or by the sword (v 9), would be more
merciful. Cannibalism is one of the covenant curses (Deut
28:53-57). **11-12.** In the official Jerusalem theology, it
was believed that Yahweh had made Zion safe from
attack because it was "the dwelling place of the Most
High" (Ps 46:5) before which enemies trembled (Ps
48:4-7; S. Talmon, *JES* 8 [1971] 300-16). Yahweh has
now personally brought it down. **13-16.** The blame for
this is laid at the door of the religious leadership: priest
and prophet have shed innocent blood (2 Kgs 21:16; Jer
22:17); a slightly different reason is given in 2:14. Those
once respected for standing especially close to God are
now shunned as unclean lepers (Lev 13:45). The third
group of leaders, the elders, fare no better (2:9-10).
17   (B) Our Futile Hope (4:17-22).   17. The
poet admits what the prophets had stressed: no foreign
alliance could avert Yahweh's judgment. Such a hope
was futile (Jer 2:18-37; 37:5-10). **20.** The Jerusalem
theology also believed that the king, God's anointed one
(*māšîaḥ*), was invincible (2 Sam 7:13-16; Ps 2; → OT
Thought, 77:152-63). "The breath of our nostrils" and
"the shadow" of the people were common expressions
for the king (Hillers, *Lamentations* 92; W. Wifall, *CBQ* 36
[1974] 237-40). **21-22.** Edom, Israel's neighbor, had
apparently taken advantage of Jerusalem after the fall
and comes in for much castigation (Obad; Ps 132:7; Jer
49:7-22). **22.** The hope expressed here is echoed by Isa
40:2.
18   (V) The Prayer of the People (5:1-22).
Chapter 5 stands apart in several important respects: It
shows more regular parallelism; its meter is more

consistently 3 + 3; though it has 22 lines, it is not an
acrostic. The suggestion that the initial letters of each
line spell "The apostate people I despise, punishing with
contempt, as your God complains," is ingenious but
depends on some textual rearrangement (S. Bergler, *VT*
27 [1977] 304-20). The poem, in the form of a communal
lament, is called "The Prayer of Jeremiah" in the Vg.
   1. Earlier, personified Zion had called on Yahweh to
"see and consider" (1:9c,11c,20a; 2:20); the community
prays the same now, but in its own name. When God
sees and remembers, there is deliverance (Exod 2:24;
3:7). **2-4.** The *naḥălâ*, the land which God gave in fulfillment of the promise (Deut 4:21), has been turned over
to strangers (also vv 6,8). The Israelites have become like
the most helpless in society (1:1). **5a.** Uncertain; read
"yoke is on our necks, we are pursued." "Rest" is a gift
of God and an important theological idea (1:3; Matt
11:29-30; W. Brueggemann, *CBQ* 34 [1975] 19-38). **7.**
The situation here is not the same as in Jer 31:29 or Ezek
18:2 because the speakers recognize their solidarity in
guilt with their ancestors (see v 16). **11-14.** Social chaos
is described which respects neither sex nor rank nor age.
17. The same vocabulary of extreme weeping as in
1:20-22 and 2:11-12. **18.** The collapse of order is complete; Zion, the abode of God, has suffered the fate of
wicked cities (Isa 13:19-22; 34:11-17). Does this mean
that Yahweh is powerless too? **19.** No! "Yahweh is
enthroned forever," and as long as that is the case, hope
remains. **20.** Why? is a common question in laments (Ps
10:1,13), but here the focus is on length of time: How
long? (Ps 13:2-4). They know the reason why (vv 7,16).
21. *lead us back to you, O Lord:* In the sense of "help us to
repent." **22.** *you have indeed rejected us; you have been
exceedingly angry:* A statement of fact, not a question. And
so the great lamentation fades away not with a cry for
revenge nor with cheap optimism but with a prayer for
repentance and a sober recognition of the facts. The
Jewish tradition repeats v 21 so the book will not end on
such a bleak note.

37

BARUCH

Aloysius Fitzgerald, F.S.C.

BIBLIOGRAPHY

1 Ball, C. J., *APOT* 1. 596–611. Eissfeldt, *EOTI* 592–95. Saydon, P. P. and T. Hanlon, *NCCHS* 628–31. Tov, E., *The Book of Baruch* (SBLTT 8; Missoula, 1975). Whitehouse, O. C., *APOT* 1. 569–95.

INTRODUCTION

2 (I) Divisions. Bar is a collection of several distinct pieces, grouped together because all are too short to stand alone and all are set against the background of the fall of Jerusalem in 587 and the exile. The LXX mss. generally arrange Jer, Bar, Lam, and finally the Letter of Jeremiah (Ep Jer) as a distinct work. The Vg, reflecting another Jewish tradition, reorders to Jer, Lam, Bar, and makes the Ep Jer the concluding part of Bar (6:1–72).

3 (II) Original Language. The earliest extant text of Bar is the Greek. Jerome knew no Hebr text (*PL* 24. 680), but it cannot be doubted on the basis of evidence too technical for discussion here that at least in part Bar was originally composed in Hebrew. That is certain for the opening prose section (1:1–3:8), and the case can be made with varying degrees of probability for the rest of the book.

4 (III) Date of Composition. Superficially the approximate dates of composition of the parts of the book seem simple to determine. The introduction to the confession and prayer of Baruch indicates that he composed it five years after the destruction of Jerusalem by Nebuchadnezzar, i.e., in 582 (1:2). The introduction to Ep Jer indicates that it was sent to the exiles on their way to Babylon in 597 or 587 (6:1). The prophetic address presumes the conditions of the exile, and thus dates from before 538. In this context 3:10–11 of the wisdom poem refers to the exile as a present reality.

Generally the various parts are dated much later. Certain things indicate that the history Bar presents is not even history in the sense that the narratives of these events in Kgs are history. The historical books know nothing of the return of the Temple vessels (1:8–9) or of the presence of Baruch in Babylon (1:1). There is something of a contradiction between the prayer itself, which presumes that the Temple is in ruins (2:26), and

the introduction, which presumes that the Temple is standing and that normal worship is carried on there (1:10,14). Belshazzar is not the son of Nebuchadnezzar (604–562; 1:11–12), but of Nabonidus (555–539), the last Chaldean king. This confusion, although witnessed to in later Jewish tradition (Dan 5:1–2), could not have existed at the time when the prayer is said to have been written. Ep Jer is rather clearly postexilic. The Babylon described in it is not the great city of Nebuchadnezzar (6:14,48). In any case, if the letter were really written by Jeremiah to the Jews going to Babylon, why was it not included in the definitive edition of Jer, which dates from the postexilic period? Perhaps a more precise indication of date is contained in 6:2, where Jeremiah's prediction of a 70-year exile (Jer 25:12; 29:10) has become a prediction of seven generations of exile, roughly 280 years (Num 32:13). A writer of the Gk period would, then, be holding out to the Diaspora of that period the promise of speedy assistance from God.

5 Some older exegetes saw in Nebuchadnezzar and Belshazzar pseudonyms for Vespasian and his son, Titus, and they regarded the destruction of Jerusalem described in 1:2 as the destruction of AD 70. But it is impossible to imagine a pious Israelite urging his fellow Jews to pray for Vespasian and Titus (1:11), though on the basis of Jer 29:7 prayers for Nebuchadnezzar are understandable. In addition Bar is laced with allusions to and citations from the OT and, more significant, late books like Dan. These facts combined with the fact that the book gives no indication of an awareness of the events of AD 70, suggest a date for the individual pieces of Bar somewhere before AD 70 and after 300 BC.

6 (IV) Authorship. In the introduction (1:1–14) to the confession and prayer (1:15–3:8) the narrator attributes them to Baruch. It may be assumed that the editor intends to attribute the following wisdom poem

(3:9–4:4) and prophetic address (4:5–5:9) to Baruch. Ep Jer (6:1–72) is expressly attributed to the prophet (6:1). The authors are in fact unknown. The dating of the materials indicates that the attribution to Baruch and Jeremiah involves literary pseudepigraphy as in Cant, Eccl, and Wis.

7   (V) Outline of Book:

COMMENTARY

8   **(I) Confession and Prayer of Baruch (1:1–3:8).** The confession and prayer are prefaced by a brief introduction (1:1–14). It presents the most difficult exegetical problems in the text. As 1:1b–2 stand, they indicate that the confession and prayer were composed "in Babylon, in the fifth year, on the seventh day of the month at the time when the Chaldeans took Jerusalem and burnt it with fire." The absence of a number before "month" is strange, but it is generally agreed that the fifth month is intended; the date of composition is just prior to Ab 7, 582, the fifth anniversary of the burning of Jerusalem on Aug. 25, 587 (2 Kgs 25:8). That is the occasion for the assembly of 1:3 at which the confession and prayer were first read. But this understanding of the passage presents serious difficulties. First, the introduction (1:10–14) presumes that the Temple is standing and that the services are being conducted in the normal manner; 1:2 itself and what is known from other sources (2 Kgs 25:8–10; Ezra 3:1–13) indicate that such was not the case in 582. This is not contradicted by Jer 41:4–5. Second, if the occasion for the composition of the prayer was an assembly held on Ab 7, the chronology of the introduction becomes difficult: assembly, Ab 7 (month 5, day 7); Baruch's arrival in Jerusalem, Sivan 10 (month 3, day 10; 1:8); the reading of the confession and prayer on Tabernacles (month 7, day 15; "the feast," 1:14). "The feast" here, as in 1 Kgs 8:2,65; etc., is frequently understood as Tabernacles, the most important of the three pilgrim festivals.
9   The problem with the chronology is that the text seems to suggest that Baruch leaves Babylon right after Ab 7 and takes 10 months to arrive in Jerusalem on Sivan 10. That is too long a time for the journey. The route presumably followed the Euphrates north to Syria, then turned west and down the Beqaʿ to Jerusalem, some 1,050 mi. If we can presume a march averaging about 19 mi. a day, the journey should take about two months (M. Noth, *ZDPV* 74 [1958] 137). For example, Ezra and his large party with women and children in tow take three and a half months for the journey (Ezra 8:31; 7:8–9).
        The solution that seems best to solve the problems of 1:1–14 is to regard "on the seventh day of the month at the time when the Chaldeans took Jerusalem and burnt it with fire" (1:2b) as a gloss that misinterprets the text. The "fifth year" (1:2a) then becomes the fifth year of Jeconiah (1:3; also the fifth year of Zedekiah) 593/592. This immediately explains why the text presumes the normal functioning of the cult in the Temple. Another "fifth year" with no month given is found in Ezek 1:2. Here clearly 593/592, the fifth year of Jeconiah (Zedekiah), is the date indicated. That date suggests the source of the incident recounted in 1:8–9 (see comment on 1:8–9). It is not hard to uncover a reason for this concern

with the situation in 593 rather than that of 582. The situation in 593 with the Temple standing and functioning and Israel in exile was more parallel to that of the audience for whom the tale was intended (→ 4–5 above).
10   This reading of 1:2 makes perfect sense of the chronology of the introduction. The clear date is that of Baruch's arrival in Jerusalem on Sivan 10 (month 3, day 10; 1:8) which is five days before the feast of Weeks (month 3, day 15). This suggests that the assembly and collection of funds of 1:3–6 are events connected with Passover (month 1, day 15). That provides for the two months' travel time between Babylon and Jerusalem by Baruch's small caravan. The feast day upon which Baruch's confession and prayer are to be read in the Temple is possibly Weeks, but more probably Tabernacles (month 7, day 15). It was noted (→ 8 above) that "the feast" in Hebrew can denote "Tabernacles." In addition Weeks has no octave whereas Tabernacles does. See 1:14: "the day of the feast and during the days of the solemn assembly." Finally, in 1:14 Baruch asks a "you" (pl.; presumably the priests and people of 1:7) to present his prayer on the feast day. Why does he not present it himself? This would have been no problem for as eminent a person as Baruch clearly present in Jerusalem for Weeks. The answer seems to be that the feast of 1:14 is Tabernacles and Baruch could not wait for that feast if he was to return to Babylon before the onset of the rains. Distant travel during the rainy season was regularly avoided because of its difficulties. This also explains the departure at Passover (like Ezra's, Ezra 8:31) after the close of the rains. Weeks, presumably, was always the feast best attended by the distant Diaspora (Acts 2:5–11; 20:16).
11   **(A) Narrator's Introduction (1:1–14). 1.** *scroll:* Here and in 1:3,14, the confession of 1:15–2:10 and the prayer of 2:11–3:8. For the genealogy of Baruch see Jer 32:12; there is no parallel for the longer genealogy given here. No OT evidence places Baruch in Babylon. Later Jewish legend does (L. Ginzberg, *The Legends of the Jews* [7 vols.; Phl, 1909–38] 6. 399). **3.** Jeconiah (Jehoiachin) was brought to Babylon by Nebuchadnezzar in 597 after a reign of only three months (2 Kgs 24:6–12; M. Noth, *ZDPV* 74 [1958] 133–57). **4.** *the kings' sons:* Male members of the royal family not in direct line of succession. Note "kings'" (pl.) and see Jer 36:26; Dan 1:3. *the river Sud:* An unidentified Babylonian canal. **5–6.** For fixed days of mourning and fasting during and after the exile, see Zech 7:1–5; Ezra 8:21; Neh 1:4; 9:1; Dan 9:3. The obligation to contribute to the support of the Temple was incumbent on all Jews (Exod 30:13; 2 Chr 24:6; Matt 17:24) including the Diaspora (Ezra 8:25; Tob 1:6). From the late Hellenistic period and abundantly in the Roman period there is evidence for a systematic tax collected in the Diaspora

and sent to Jerusalem each year. After the destruction of the Temple in AD 70, Vespasian appropriated the tax (*fiscus iudaicus*) for the temple of Jupiter Capitolinus in Rome. These contributions to Jerusalem and the holy land among Jews, and from Paul's time (Rom 15:25–27; etc.) among Christians, have continued till the present day (J. Juster, *Les Juïfs dans l'empire romain* [2 vols.; Paris, 1914] 1. 357–88; 2. 282–86). **7.** *Jehoiakim:* He may have been a member of the family of the high priest (1 Chr 5:39–41), but is otherwise unknown. It is not clear why the funds are sent to him while the high priest Seraiah was still in Jerusalem (2 Kgs 25:18–21). **8–9.** These verses may be a secondary expansion; v 7 reads directly into v 10. They presume the following chronology: the surrender of Jerusalem in 597 and the seizing of the Temple vessels (2 Kgs 24:13); Zedekiah's making new silver vessels; the handing over of these silver vessels to Nebuchadnezzar as tribute; the return of Zedekiah's vessels in 593. The historical books know only of the return of vessels under Cyrus (Ezra 1:7–11). The basis for the legendary account seems to be Jer 28:1–6, where a false prophet in the fifth month of the fourth year of Zedekiah (594/593) announces the return of the vessels removed in 597 within two years and is told by Jeremiah: Would that it were so! Only an atomistic reading of Jer 28:1–3 by a writer little concerned with historical fact can allow such an interpretation. The Lord's word, even one uttered by a false prophet and never fulfilled, must be fulfilled. **11.** Jeremiah had always advocated submission to Babylon. **12.** *light to our eyes:* The force within the eye that enables a person to see (Ps 6:8; 38:11; Job 3:20).

12   **(B) The Confession (1:15–2:10).** Both the confession and the prayer (2:11–3:8) that follows bear marked resemblances to the prayers of Ezra 9:6–15; Neh 1:5–11; 9:6–37, but esp. to Dan 9:4–19. The confession (1:15–2:10) is distinguished from the prayer proper (2:11–3:8) by address. In the prayer the Lord is directly addressed; in the confession the exiles address their fellow Jews in Jerusalem. Throughout the confession and prayer (and the rest of the book) is the view of Deut and the Deuteronomists that God's great gift to chosen Israel is the law; that obedience to the law brings prosperity; and disobedience brings disaster and exile; that repentance and renewed obedience are the conditions of restoration (e.g., Deut 28; 1 Kgs 8:22–53). **20.** *the evils and the curse:* See Lev 26:3–39; Deut 28.

2:2–3. See Deut 28:53; Lam 2:20; 4:10. The reference seems to be to the siege of 587, not 597. Jerusalem rapidly surrendered in 597 with a minimum of destruction or loss of life (2 Kgs 24:10–12; M. Noth, *ZDPV* 74 [1958] 137–39). It was argued above that Bar 1:1–3:8 is concerned with the siege and exile of 598/597. But the author, writing in a period after the restoration of Jerusalem destroyed in 587, telescopes history allowing his knowledge of the events of 587 to color his presentation of those of 597. See comment on 2:26.

13   **(C) The Prayer (2:11–3:8). 14–18.** The Lord is asked to save Israel for his own sake. The argument is: Israel renders him praise; Israel is the Lord's people; the demise of Israel will be a source of embarrassment for the Lord. **15.** *you are . . . our God and Israel and his descendants . . . bear your name:* The two sentences say similar things. To bear the name of someone in contexts similar to the present one means to be possessed and protected by that person.

17. If Israel perishes, God's nation will not be able to praise him. For the idea that the dead do not praise God see Ps 6:6; 88:11; 115:17–18; Isa 38:18–19. Reflected here is the typical OT view of the human composite, death and the afterlife. Dust plus the breath of life (Gen 2:7) or flesh plus God's "spirit" (Gen 6:3) makes one a living *nepeš*, "being," "person." Death occurs when the two are separated. The dust returns to the earth; the life breath returns to God who gave it (Eccl 12:7). This would seem to leave nothing of the human being, but an undefinable something does remain (Gen 37:35; 1 Sam 28:11–19). A live man is a living *nepeš*; a dead man is a dead *nepeš* (Num 6:6; Lev 21:11). This undefinable something sinks to the netherworld, sheol, located in the depths of the earth (Deut 32:22; Isa 14:9), where it endures a shadowy and sorrowful existence (Job 26:5–6; Isa 14:9–11; Ezek 32:17–32; Eccl 9:4–10). The doctrine of a true afterlife and of reward and punishment after death is a late development in OT history (Wis 3:1–9; 2 Macc 12:38–46). **18.** The subject of this sentence ("He") is Israel, the personified nation. The sense follows: The dead do not praise the Lord (v 17), but Israel, though struck a mortal blow, declares his glory and justice. That is done in what follows, where it is shown that the present condition of Israel, far from being a manifestation of God's impotence, is a just manifestation of God's power. The argument is: If the Lord does not save Israel, there will be no one to praise him. **21.** The particular refusal to serve the Lord referred to (vv 19–21) was the refusal to heed Jeremiah's pro-Babylonian policy (Jer 27:12–13). **23.** Citation of Jer 7:34. **24–25.** See Jer 8:1–2; 14:12; 22:19; 36:30. The historical books present no account of such a desecration of the tombs at the hands of the Babylonians in either 597 or 587. Honorable burial was an important consideration because death was not a complete annihilation (see comment on 2:17). The dead *nepeš* in sheol still in some way experienced what was done to the body. Hence, for a corpse to be left unburied, the prey of birds and beasts, was a terrible fate (1 Kgs 14:11; Isa 14:18–20; Jer 16:4; Ezek 29:5; Eccl 6:3).

14   **26.** *the house which bears your name:* The Jerusalem Temple. The text here and in vv 24–25 presumes the destruction of the Temple and the events of 587. See comment on 2:2–3. **27.** The nature of the divine clemency and mercy is made clear by vv 30–35. God's punishment is not for revenge but to bring about a change of heart, which is the occasion for restoration. **29–35.** The quotation here put in the mouth of the Lord is based on Deut 30:1–10; 31:24–27. **31.** *hearts and heedful ears:* The capacity to understand the truth and the willingness to act in accord with it.

3:3. *sit enthroned forever:* God, the king of all that is, has the power to effect Israel's restoration. **5.** *hand and name:* God is called upon to remember his might and his reputation, i.e., what he must do to have his name glorified. This is the equivalent of asking God to save Israel for his own sake. See comment on 2:14–18. **7.** The Lord's chastisement is not vindictive but purifying (Deut 30:1–10; 1 Kgs 8:46–51; Jer 31:33).

15   **(II) A Wisdom Poem (3:9–4:4).** The whole import of the confession and prayer of 1:15–3:8 is this: Obedience to the Lord's commands offers the possibility of unbounded prosperity; "stiff-necked" (stubborn and stupid, 2:30) Israel disobeyed these commands and received a just punishment. These commands are identified with the written law of Moses (2:28), and the possibility of restoration is presented on the basis of obedience to that law (2:28–35). This suggested to an editor the joining of the wisdom poem (3:9–4:4) to Baruch's confession and prayer (1:1–3:8). The poem celebrates the Mosaic law as wisdom (Deut 4:6; Pss 19:8; 119:97–98), a connection which becomes increasingly more pronounced in postexilic Judaism (Ezra 7:6,14,25; Sir 24:1–31; 39:1–11). In the poem, as elsewhere in the OT

(Prov 8:1–36; Sir 24:1–22), wisdom is personified and endowed with quasi-divine attributes.

Wisdom is the most prized possession, for it is the source of prosperity for all who possess it. Without it one experiences only disaster. No one can achieve wisdom by his own efforts; God alone can bestow it. He has chosen to bestow it on the Jewish people, to whom was given the law, the source of deliverance from present difficulties. The speaker in the poem is a wisdom teacher who addresses the Jewish nation, particularly the Diaspora (3:10).

16   (A) The Importance of Wisdom (3:9–14). 9. *commandments of life:* Commandments that give life (prosperity of every kind) when they are observed (Deut 30:15–20). *commandments . . . prudence:* The parallelism here in the opening line identifies wisdom as the law. See 4:1. 10. *defiled with the dead:* The Diaspora is defiled by association with pagans, who are all but dead and ready to depart for the netherworld because they do not know and observe the law, the source of life. For the idea that contact with a corpse defiles a person, see Lev 21:1–4; 22:4; Num 19:11–16. 12. *fountain of wisdom:* God who gives wisdom (Jer 2:13; John 4:13–14). 14. *light of the eyes:* See comment on 1:12.

17   (B) No Man Can Find Wisdom (3:15–31). 16. For the notion that the dominion of kings extends even to beasts and birds see Jdt 11:7; Jer 27:6; Dan 2:37–38. 17. *they who heaped up silver:* The kings of v 16. 20. To come to see the light is to be born; to see the light is to be alive (Job 3:16; 33:30; Ps 49:20). 22. Both Canaan (here, Phoenicia) and Edom, of which Teman is a part were renowned for human wisdom (Jer 49:7; Ezek 28:12; Obad 8–9; Zech 9:2). 23. *sons of Hagar:* Ishmaelites (Gen 16; 21). Ishmael was the traditional ancestor of 12 tribes (Gen 25:12–16). Gen 25:18, at least, identifies them as nomads on the borders of Palestine from the Sinai to Syria. Midian is the region S of Edom and E of the Gulf of Aqabah. For the Midianites as traders, see Gen 37:25–28. 24. *house of God:* Here, the created universe. 26. *giants:* See Gen 6:4; Num 13:33; Wis 14:6. 29–31. A summary of vv 15–31: no one is capable of discovering wisdom.

18   (C) Wisdom Is the Law (3:32–4:4). 33. *the light:* The sun. Sunset and sunrise are presented as the personified sun obeying God's commands. 34. *at their posts:* The stars are presented as sentries keeping watch during the night. 37. *way of knowledge:* The way to wisdom. 4:2. *her light:* Wisdom is presented as the sun. 4:3. The idea seems to be that if Israel fails to observe the law, God will abandon Israel and give the law to another nation (Exod 32:10; Num 14:12; Deut 9:14). Israel's glory and privileges are the gift of the Mosaic law.

19   (III) A Prophetic Address (4:5–5:9). This piece was brought into the collection because, like the two pieces that precede it (2:28–30; 3:10–12), it speaks of exile as the result of not obeying the law of Moses (4:12). The first (2:28–35) and second (4:1–4) pieces both assume that, if Israel returns to the observance of the law, the exiles will return. The confession and prayer of Baruch indicate that the needed conversion has in fact taken place. The prophetic address gives divine recognition to this fact. It presents both Jerusalem (here a prophetic figure) assuring the Diaspora that after repentance it will certainly return (4:17–29) and the prophet-speaker of the poem assuring Jerusalem that the exiles are already on the way home (4:30–5:9). That is rhetoric for "will soon return." In the collection both speeches are intended as the Lord's answer to Baruch's confession and prayer.

The speaker in the poem is a prophet who addresses the Diaspora (4:5–9a). But after the mention of grieving Jerusalem in v 8 the development of the argument becomes dramatic. Jerusalem, personified as the mother of the nation, addresses her neighbors (4:9b–16) and the Diaspora (4:17–29). The prophet addresses Jerusalem (4:30–5:9). The setting for this drama is the mourning ceremony in which Jerusalem, dressed in sackcloth (4:20), laments the loss of her children. The speaker of the poem in his address to Jerusalem (4:30–5:9) becomes a figure like Job's comforters (Job 2:11–13; 16:2).

20   (A) The Prophet Addresses the Diaspora (4:5–9a). 6. *you were sold:* The exile is presented as the Lord "selling" his people, his "slaves" acquired in Moses' time out of bondage in Egypt, as slaves to Babylon. But the figure is not completely parallel. The Lord received no payment (Isa 52:3). The exiles remain his people, and that is the basis for hope. *not for your destruction:* The Lord's chastisement aims rather at purification (2:28–35).

(B) Jerusalem Addresses her Neighbors (4:9b–16). 12. *widow . . . desolate:* The condition of Jerusalem is like that of a woman who has lost not only her husband but also her children and is thus without means of support (see Lam 1:1–2).

21   (C) Jerusalem Addresses the Diaspora (4:17–29). 17. The rhetorical question implies a negative response. 19. Note the telescoping of temporal perspective. Jerusalem bids farewell to the departing exiles of 597 or 587, but the whole of her speech (4:17–29) presents them as already in Babylon. The answer to her speech (4:30–5:9) speaks of their imminent return in 538. As was indicated (→ 4 above), the poem in fact looks forward to the ingathering of the Diaspora in a much later period. 20. *garment of peace:* The royal raiment has been exchanged for sackcloth worn during the rites of mourning (Gen 37:34; see comment on 5:1). 24. This is the theophany described in 5:5–9. The Lord comes to Babylon to lead home captive Israel. The "great glory and splendor" are in the first place the visible light that signals the divine presence. Ultimately behind this language lies the picture of the shining sun (once considered divine) rising in the east and moving west toward Jerusalem. In the second place, the glory and splendor belong to the returning Diaspora, which reflects the light of the divine presence. The poet here uses the language of nature myth to emphasize that no matter how in fact the return of the diaspora may seem to work out in the course of human history, God alone is the real explanation of the promised return. Only God controls the sun, can appear in it (from an older point of view) for the exiles, and can lead them home basking in its light. There is a similar use of imagery in Isa 60:1–3; see Isa 40:5,10–11; 58:8–9. 25. *trample upon their necks:* A gesture symbolizing the defeat of an enemy (Josh 10:24; Isa 51:23).

22   (D) The Prophet Addresses Jerusalem (4:30–5:9). The prophet answers the speech of Jerusalem (4:9b–29). He assumes the role of Jerusalem's comforter at the mourning ceremony and tells her to remove her mourning garment (5:1; see 4:20), for her children are on their way home (4:36–37; 5:5–9). She is to clothe herself with splendid garments (5:1–2). The crown Jerusalem places on her head is "the miter of the glory of the eternal (name)" (5:2). This is Aaron's miter (Greek *mitra* = Hebr *miṣnepet* = Aaron's miter) upon which is written "sacred to Yahweh" (Exod 28:36–37; 39:30–31; Wis 18:24). Lady Jerusalem, the city of the worship of the true God, becomes a priest, Aaron's successor. She receives forever from God the symbolic titles "the peace of justice" and "the glory of God's worship" (5:4). Jerusalem will be forever (5:4) a place where peace and justice prevail and she will receive eternal glory from the fact that worship of the true God is conducted there. Under these circumstances the procession of the Diaspora to Jerusalem (4:36–37; 5:5–9) becomes a pilgrimage. The text of 5:5–9 is clearly modeled on Dt-Isa (e.g., Isa 40:3–5,9–11; 41:18–19; 49:22–23). The case can be made there for the journey to Jerusalem being a pilgrimage to the feast of Tabernacles (see comment on 5:8). Baruch comes to Jerusalem with offerings for the Temple, but must return to Babylon before Tabernacles (→ 10 above). Here in the prophetic address (4:36–37; 5:5–9) the Diaspora returns to Jerusalem for Tabernacles to begin a new age of divine favor. The poet, for whom the words of Dt-Isa had not been fulfilled in 538, adapts them for his own age. See Isa 40:8.

23 **30.** *your name:* Not "Jerusalem," but "city of the Lord" and the like (Isa 60:14; Ps 46:5; see comment on 2:15). **32.** *the city that took your sons:* Babylon, but here a code name for the powers that prevent the return of the Diaspora. **35.** *fire:* See Isa 34:8–11. Again the poet has recourse to the language of myth to interpret the expected historical return of the Diaspora to make perfectly clear that the punishment of Jerusalem's enemies, like the return of the Diaspora (see comment on 4:24), will be ultimately God's work. *demons:* Demons and wild animals were thought to inhabit deserts and desolate places. Compare "ghost town" and Isa 34:11,14; Isa 13:20–22; Tob 8:3; Matt 4:1; 12:43. **36.** *east:* Babylon is due east of Jerusalem. **37.** The worldwide Diaspora is apparently thought to be first joined to the group in Babylon before beginning the procession home from there. *the glory of God:* See comment on 4:24. **5:1–2.** *the splendor of the glory from God:* Jerusalem removes her mourning garment (4:20) and clothes herself in the garment of light that emanates from her Lord, who is presented as the sun rising in the east. This garment is "the cloak of justice from God," the guarantee of the sum of harmony, security, and prosperity that come from the divine presence. **6.** *borne aloft:* See Isa 49:22. The other nations now subject to Israel carry the Diaspora home on portable thrones (*ANEP* 538). **7.** *lofty mountain:* As in Isa 40:3–4 a road is leveled through Arabia Deserta for the most direct march to Jerusalem. *glory of God:* See comment on 4:24. **8.** *forests:* As in Isa 41:18–19 Arabia Deserta by a miracle receives abundant rain, and the road home is adorned with miraculously fast-growing trees that require such rain. The fact that dry ground is rained on for the first time makes these rains the first fall rains. This suggests that the feast for which the Diaspora returns is Tabernacles, though in fact the first rains normally come immediately after Tabernacles. **9.** *light of his glory:* See comment on 4:24. *mercy and justice:* Divine attributes, here thought of as personified attendants of the Lord's epiphany, angels.

24 **(IV) The Letter of Jeremiah (6:1–72).** There is an evident strategy in the compilation of the three preceding pieces and a clear climax is reached in the speech of 4:30–5:9. There is some tension between what precedes and chap. 6. Chapter 6 has for its setting the beginning of the exile (6:1), and it looks forward to a lengthy stay (6:2); the speech of 4:30–5:9 speaks of an imminent return. This seems to indicate that chap. 6 was secondarily added to Bar and that the original collection ended with 5:9 as in the LXX (→ 2 above). The letter is said to have been written by Jeremiah to those being led into exile to Babylon (6:1)—either in 597 or 587.

25 **2.** The change here from Jeremiah's 70 years of exile (Jer 25:12; 29:10) suggests a date of composition in the Gk period (→ 4 above). **3.** The idols throughout this chapter are wood (consequently portable) plated with gold and silver. See *ANEP* 537–38. Processions in which statues of the gods were carried were a regular feature of Babylonian cult (S. A. Pallis, *The Babylonian Akitu Festival* [Copenhagen, 1926] 131–39). **6.** *my angel:* A guardian angel (Exod 23:20–21; Tob 5:4–5). The pronoun is in 1st pers. because Jeremiah regards his message as God's own. **10.** *harlots:* Temple prostitutes. **12.** *house:* Here and throughout the letter, a temple. **17.** The comparison indicates the manner in which these gods are locked in their temples, but the fact that they are compared to criminals in jail adds to the satire. **19.** *eaten away:* The wood cores are consumed by termites or the like. **26.** *gifts . . . as for the dead:* The significant part of the comparison equates idols with the impotent dead. Behind "gifts" may lie the practice of providing food offerings in tombs for the dead. See Deut 26:14; Sir 30:18.

26 **27–30.** The practices described here were all forbidden by the law of Jewish cult. See Deut 14:28–29; Lev 12:2; 15:19–20. Women did not hold priestly office in Israel. Priests were forbidden to shave their heads or beards, lacerate their bodies or rend their garments (Lev 21:5–6,10–11), a sign of mourning (Job 1:20; Jer 16:6; 41:5; 48:37). The text may be reflecting here and in v 31 mourning for the descent to the underworld of the Mesopotamian god, Dumuzi (OT Tammuz, Ezek 8:14). **31.** *funeral banquet:* A wake. When death occurred in a house, the house was unclean and food could not be prepared there. Relatives and friends brought food to the house and stayed to console the bereaved (Jer 16:7; Ezek 24:17,22). **40.** The Chaldeans (Babylonians) do not ask their gods to speak to those who can hear. They thereby acknowledge that their gods cannot speak. The precise divination practices that are the basis for the ridicule here are unknown. **42–44.** The issue is cult prostitution. The "chaff" is apparently an aphrodisiac. The "unbroken cords" are a sign that the rite has not been performed. Herodotus (1.199) describes similar rites in honor of a goddess Mulitta (Babylonian: she who causes to give birth; probably Ishtar) who is equated with Aphrodite. **50.** *God's work:* The capacity to do what the God of Israel does. **54.** *crows:* These gods have as much power as a crow. The precise sense of the figure is unclear. **59–64.** The elements of nature, once thought of as independent gods and still powers to be reckoned with, all obey the one true God.

38

TOBIT JUDITH ESTHER

Irene Nowell, O.S.B. **Toni Craven**

Demetrius Dumm, O.S.B. *

TOBIT

BIBLIOGRAPHY

1 Alonso Schökel, L., *Tobias* (Libros Sagrados; Madrid, 1973). Craghan, J., *Esther, Judith, Tobit, Jonah, Ruth* (OTM; Wilmington, 1982). Deselaers, P., *Das Buch Tobit* (OBO 43; Fribourg, 1982). Dommershausen, W., *Der Engel, die Frauen, das Heil: Tobias, Ester, Judit* (SKK; Stuttgart, 1970). Gerould, G. H., *The Grateful Dead* (Publications of the Folklore Society 60; London, 1908; repr. Folcroft PA, 1973). Ruppert, L., "Das Buch Tobias," *Wort, Lied, und Gottesspruch* (Fest. J. Ziegler; ed. J. Schreiner; Würzburg, 1972) 109–19. Thomas, J. D., "The Greek Text of Tobit," *JBL* 91 (1972) 463–71. Thompson, S., *The Folktale* (NY, 1946). Zimmermann, F., *The Book of Tobit* (JAL; NY, 1958).

INTRODUCTION

2 **(I) Text and Language.** There are three separate Gk recensions of the book of Tobit. The longest recension (R-S), which has a strong Semitic flavor, is represented by Sinaiticus (S) and VL and is supported by the Qumran fragments held by J. T. Milik. A second, shorter recension (R-V) with fewer narrative details is represented by Vaticanus (B) and Alexandrinus (A). A third, fragmentary recension (R-C), dependent on the other two, is represented in mss. d, p, and 44 and supported by some Syriac mss. Considerable scholarly debate has centered on the priority of the recensions. Verbal similarity between R-S and R-V indicates a borrowing from Greek to Greek, and the Semitic flavor of R-S suggests that R-V is a simplification of R-S into more idiomatic Greek. A few scholars, however, consider R-V to be prior (Dommershausen, Deselaers).

The priority of the recensions has a bearing on the question of original language. If R-S is prior, the original language is Semitic. Internal characteristics in the Gk recension such as spelling and grammar and the discovery of four Aram fragments of Tobit at Qumran indicate an Aram original. Alonso Schökel posits a Hebr original and Deselaers, a Gk original.

3 **(II) Date and Place.** The most probable date for the writing of the book of Tobit is between 200–180 BC. A late date is indicated by confusion concerning 7th-cent. Assyrian history, the reflection of postexilic customs of tithing, and the acceptance of the prophets as canonical. There is no evidence of either the turmoil or the apocalyptic ideas surrounding the Maccabean revolt. There is no conclusive evidence regarding the place of composition, whether Palestine, Egypt, or Mesopotamia.

4 **(III) Genre and Literary Form.** This is best described as a Hebr romance. Its fictional character is demonstrated by several characteristics such as historical inaccuracy and literary manipulation of time and character. Two folktales, "The Grateful Dead" and "The Monster in the Bridal Chamber," provide the structure of the plot (Gerould, Thompson). The form of the successful quest in the central part of the book puts it in the genre of romance.

5 **(IV) Canonicity.** The book of Tobit is deuterocanonical, i.e., it is not included in the Hebr canon and therefore is not in the Protestant canon. Jerome did not consider it canonical, but, as a favor to his friends, translated it from Aramaic into Latin in one day with the help of an Aram interpreter. Augustine and Ambrose upheld its canonicity. It was accepted by the Council of Hippo (393) and, because of its presence in the Vg, was declared canonical by the Council of Trent.

6 **(V) Message.** The purpose of the book is didactic. The tale of the two families joined by marriage is told both to edify and to entertain. The message of the book, illustrated through ordinary faithful lives, is that God is indeed both just and free. Suffering is not a

---

*Tobit is the work of I. Nowell; Judith is the work of T. Craven; and Esther is by D. Dumm.

punishment but a test. God does, in the long run, reward the just and punish the wicked. The believer is called upon to trust God and to mirror in daily life the justice, mercy, and freedom of God.

7   (VI) Outline.

(I) Distress in Ecbatana and Nineveh (1:1–3:17)
    (A) Title (1:1–2)
    (B) Tobit's Background (1:3–22)
    (C) Tobit's Distress and Prayer (2:1–3:6)
    (D) Sarah's Distress and Prayer (3:7–15)
    (E) Raphael's Commission (3:16–17)

(II) Preparation for the Journey (4:1–6:1)
    (A) Tobit's Speech (4:1–21)
    (B) Hiring of Raphael (5:1–6:1)
(III) Journey (6:2–18)
(IV) Resolution (7:1–11:18)
    (A) Sarah's Healing (7:1–8:21)
    (B) Recovery of Money (9:1–6)
    (C) Tobit's Healing (10:1–11:18)
(V) Conclusion (12:1–14:15)
    (A) Revelation of Raphael (12:1–20)
    (B) Tobit's Prayer (13:1–18)
    (C) Epilogue (14:1–15)

COMMENTARY

8   (I) Distress in Ecbatana and Nineveh (1:1–3:17).

(A) Title (1:1–2). 1. *Tobit:* The Gk form of *ṭwby,* which abbreviates *ṭwbyh,* "Yahweh is my good." The names in the book are clues to character, most are theophoric. **2.** *Shalmaneser:* Shalmaneser V (726–722). The Assyrian king responsible for the deportation of Naphtali from Galilee was Tiglath-pileser III (745–727; cf. 2 Kgs 15:29), not Shalmaneser V, who was in power at the time of the fall of Samaria in 722. An example of the many historical inaccuracies in the book.

9   (B) Tobit's Background (1:3–22). 3. *truth and righteousness . . . works of mercy:* These three virtues, which are a key to Tobit's character (cf. 2:14; 7:7; 9:6; 14:2),form an *inclusio* which closes in 14:9. God is also described as true, righteous, and merciful (3:2,5; 13:6). *Nineveh:* Capital of Assyria, on the E bank of the Tigris across from modern Mosul. **5.** *young bull:* After the kingdom divided in 922, Jeroboam I, king of Israel, established shrines at Bethel and Dan to replace Jerusalem as the center of worship for his subjects. Corresponding to the Ark, throne of Yahweh in Jerusalem, he set up golden calves (cf. 1 Kgs 12:26–33). **6.** *alone to Jerusalem:* Tobit's fidelity is measured according to deuteronomic principles, such as worship in the one sanctuary in Jerusalem (cf. Deut 12:1–28). **6–8.** Tobit is apparently following rigorously the postexilic interpretation of the pentateuchal texts on tithing (Lev 27:30–33; Num 18:21–32; Deut 14:22–29) in which the law is taken to prescribe three tithes rather than three distributions of the one yearly tithe. In this interpretation, firstfruits and firstlings went to the priests (Lev 27:26–27,30–33), the first tithe to the Levites (Num 18:21–24), the second tithe to the banquet (Deut 14:22–26), and the third tithe to the poor (Deut 14:28–29). Josephus (*Ant.* 4.8.22 §240) also considers the tithe for the poor to be a third tithe. **8.** *Deborah:* Tobit mentions his grandmother as a primary source of his religious instruction. Women are highly regarded in this book as persons capable of prayer (3:11–15), wage earning (2:11–12), and religious education. **10.** *food of Gentiles:* Another example of Tobit's fidelity is his keeping of the dietary laws (cf. Lev 11:1–47; Deut 14:3–21). **12.** Tobit's success is seen as a result of his fidelity, an expression of the deuteronomic theory of retribution in which the righteous are blessed and the wicked punished (cf. Deut 28). Retribution is a major theological theme of the book. **14.** *Media:* Kingdom in northwestern part of modern Iran, subject to Assyria from *ca.* 750–650. *ten silver talents:* Approximately 3,000 shekels of silver or the price of 1,500 rams. The money deposited with Gabael in Rages performs a major function in the plot. It is the initial reason for Tobiah's journey which results in Sarah's healing and ultimately

in the healing of Tobit. **15.** *Sennacherib:* Shalmaneser V was succeeded by Sargon (721–705). Sennacherib, Sargon's son, succeeded his father in 704. The author may have obtained his list of Assyrian kings from 2 Kgs 17:1–6; 18:9–13. In that account Sargon is not mentioned by name.

10   16. Tobit's charitable works are corporal works of mercy—feeding the hungry, clothing the naked, and burying the dead—performed even at risk of his life. **18.** *fugitive from Judea:* The unsuccessful invasion of Judea by Sennacherib in 701 (cf. 2 Kgs 18:13–19:37). **21.** *Esarhaddon:* Assyrian ruler from 680–669. *Ahiqar:* The hero of an Assyrian folktale who is saved from death because of his righteousness. His story is another example that the theory of retribution holds. Aram fragments of the story found at Elephantine are dated to the 5th cent. BC (*ANET* 427–30). A synopsis of the story is in Tob 14:10–11. Tobit is made a relative of Ahiqar, ostensibly to add to Tobit's importance.

11   (C) Tobit's Distress and Prayer (2:1–3:6). 2:1. *Pentecost:* The feast of Weeks, celebration of the wheat harvest (cf. Deut 16:9–12). Festival meals are to be shared with "alien, orphan, and widow" (Deut 16:14), a prescription Tobit follows by sending Tobiah to find a poor kinsman. **5.** *washed:* Contact with a corpse rendered one ritually unclean (Num 19:11–22). There are several problems regarding Tobit's uncleanness. Lustral water for purification was probably not available in Nineveh. The need for purification was less urgent, since ritual worship at the Temple was impossible. **9.** *courtyard:* Apparently also because of ritual uncleanness, Tobit sleeps outside. Thus, his observance of the law sets up the circumstances which lead to his suffering. **10.** *Elymais:* Modern Elam. **14.** Anna's sharp words attack his most vulnerable point, his righteousness. She poses a major question of the book: Does God indeed reward the righteous? **3:2.** *righteous . . . :* These are the same virtues by which Tobit is characterized in 1:3. **5.** *according to my sins:* Theory of retribution: Sin deserves punishment. **6.** *everlasting abode:* Sheol, place of darkness inhabited by the dead. No belief in fullness of life after death is expressed in this book.

12   (D) Sarah's Distress and Prayer (3:7–15). 7. The story is narrated in 3d pers. from this point on. *same day:* Simultaneity is a deliberate literary technique to indicate the parallel between Tobit and Sarah and to foreshadow the binding of their respective families (cf. 3:10,11,16,17; 4:1). The day which begins with the payment of Anna's wages (2:12) does not end until the night when the travelers encamp by the Tigris (6:2). *Ecbatana:* Hamadan in modern Iran, ancient capital of Media. *Raguel:* "Friend of God," also the name of Moses' father-in-law (Exod 2:18; Num 10:29) and of an archangel in

1 Enoch 20:4 (*APOT* 2. 201, 204). **8.** *Asmodeus:* As in the folktale "The Monster in the Bridal Chamber," the author attributes Sarah's affliction to a demon. The name seems to be derived from the Persian *aeshma daeva,* "the demon of wrath." **10.** *to hang herself:* Suicide is not specifically prohibited in the OT although the prohibition is implied (cf. Gen 9:4–6; Exod 20:13). Examples of suicide are usually connected with military defeat, e.g., Saul (1 Sam 31:4–5), Zimri (1 Kgs 16:18), Razis (2 Macc 14:41–46), cf. Ahithophel (2 Sam 17:23). **11.** *toward the window:* It was customary to face Jerusalem when praying (cf. Dan 6:11). **15.** The custom of marrying within the family (cf. 1:9; 4:12–13; 6:12–13,16; 7:10) seems to be derived from the case of the daughters of Zelophehad in which there was no male heir to guarantee the retention of ancestral property (Num 27:5–11; 36:2–12). This custom died out by the 1st cent. BC.

13   (E) Raphael's Commission (3:16–17). 16. The prayer of both is heard and answered at the same time, another example of simultaneity (cf. 3:7). **17.** *Raphael:* "God heals." *God's sunlight:* The imagery of light and darkness carry the story of Tobit's life (cf. 5:10; 10:5; 11:8,14; 13:11; 14:10).

14   (II) Preparation for the Journey (4:1–6:1).
(A) Tobit's Speech (4:1–21). This is in the form of a farewell discourse (cf. A. A. Di Lella, *CBQ* 41 [1979] 380–89). In a "wisdom" exhortation he encourages his son to practice the virtues he himself practices: charity, esp. almsgiving and burying the dead; faithfulness to the law, esp. regarding marriage; and trust in God. **6.** A statement of the theory of retribution. **7.** From 4:7–19 there is a lacuna in S. The text must be supplemented from BA (→ 2 above). **8.** Tobit states the principle that almsgiving should be in proportion to one's possessions, a theory advocated in the same century by Sirach (Sir 35:9–10) and later by Paul (2 Cor 8:12–15). **10–11.** Alms free one from death (cf. Sir 29:10–13; 40:17,24) and are a worthy offering to God (cf. Sir 34:18–35:4). **12–13.** See comment on 3:15. **15.** *what you hate, do to no one:* An OT statement of the golden rule. **17.** This exhortation, borrowed from *The Wisdom of Ahiqar* (Syr 2:9–10A; *APOT* 2. 730), probably refers to the giving of alms in honor of the dead. It was also customary for friends to bring food to the family on the occasion of death (cf. Jer 16:7; Ezek 24:17,22). **19.** *if the Lord chooses:* God is free to do what he wills in the lives of his creatures. Tobit, while he consistently affirms the freedom of God, also consistently expresses his trust in God.

15   (B) Hiring of Raphael (5:1–6:1). The hiring of Raphael is a prime example of the irony in the story. The reader and author know that Raphael is an angel, that Raphael is his name, and that his purpose is to bring healing in answer to the prayers of Tobit and Sarah (3:16–17). Tobit and Tobiah, however, see only a kinsman named Azariah, who is skilled as a guide. **3.** A document was signed by both parties; then it was divided and one part given to each party. The authenticity of a claim could be verified by possession of the matching half of the document. **4.** The narrator always refers to Raphael as "the angel," "the angel Raphael," or simply "Raphael." The characters in the story call him "Azariah." **6.** Perhaps for an angel it is a two-day trip, but Alexander's army took eleven days to cover the 185 miles (see Arrian, *Anabasis Alexandri* 3.20). Ecbatana is on a hill rather than a plain. **10.** Raphael claims extensive knowledge of Media: all the routes, all its plains and mountains, every road. **12.** Messengers from God are often reluctant to reveal their identity (cf. Gen 32:30). **13.** Raphael claims to be Azariah, "Yahweh has helped," son of Hananiah, "Yahweh is merciful." That he is "son of"

Yahweh's help and mercy is true, but not in the way that Tobit understands it. **14.** *Nathaniah:* "Yahweh gives." *Shemaiah:* "Yahweh hears." **16.** *in good health:* Healing is a major theme of this story and the word *hygiainō,* "to be healthy," which occurs 26 times in the book, is found 8 times in 5:16–22. **17.** *his angel:* A further irony, since Tobit does not suspect the truth of his words (cf. 5:22). **18.** The possessive pronouns used by Anna to refer to Tobiah reveal the working of a mother's mind. When she is concerned about his travels she refers to him as "my child" (5:18; 10:4,7). When she sees him returning, she informs the blind Tobit with sensitivity, "Your son is coming" (11:6).

16   (III) Journey (6:2–18). 3. The story of Tobiah's journey has much in common with the form of the romantic quest. One typical motif is the struggle between the hero and a dragon or sea monster. Frequently, when the monster which threatens death is conquered, it becomes a source of life and healing (cf. 6:5). **8–9.** The author hints at the forthcoming healings. A woman is afflicted by a demon; a man has cataracts. The ritual for the deliverance of Sarah resembles an exorcism, whereas the application of the gall to cataracts reflects a medicinal treatment common at the time (cf. R. Pautrel and M. Lefebvre, *RSR* 39 [1951] 118–20). **12–13.** *right to marry her:* See note on 3:15. Nowhere, however, is there evidence of the death penalty attached to this custom. **14–15.** Although Raguel's family does not seem to know that Tobit has a son (7:2), Tobiah knows of Sarah's affliction and understandably fears marriage with her. **16.** *your father's command:* Tobiah and Sarah marry in obedience. Tobiah risks his life to obey his father. Sarah, in spite of affliction, obeys her father Raguel (cf. 7:12). Raguel obeys the custom which interprets the law of Moses. **17–18.** The instructions for the deliverance of Sarah include two elements: the ceremony of exorcism and prayer. **18.** *set apart for you:* The theology of marriage in this book portrays the bond between husband and wife as fashioned by God from all eternity (cf. 7:11). **19.** Tobiah falls in love with Sarah before he has seen her.

17   (IV) Resolution (7:1–11:18).
(A) Sarah's Healing (7:1–8:21). 3–5. The arrival scene is modeled directly on the arrival of Jacob at Haran when he is sent by his father to find a proper bride (Gen 29:4–6). Tobiah's betrothal is thus set in the context of patriarchal betrothals (cf. also Gen 24). **7.** Tobit's character is again extolled in an echo of 1:3. **9.** *welcomed them graciously:* Raguel, "friend of God," is reminiscent of Abraham, who entertained angels unawares (Gen 18:1–15). **10–11.** The wedding scene is surrounded by eating and drinking (cf. 7:14; 8:1). Raguel begins and ends his warning to Tobiah with the encouragement to eat and drink before a decision is made. Tobiah refuses until the matter is settled (cf. Gen 24:33). **11.** *you are her brother, and she is your sister:* Common terms for spouses (cf. Cant 4:9–10,12; 5:1–2, cf. *TDOT* 1. 191). The marriage formula is similar to that of Mibtahiah in the Elephantine papyri: "She is my wife and I am her husband from this day forever" (*ANET* 222). **12.** *a scroll:* The marriage is sealed by a written contract (cf. 5:3). **17.** Gk *tharsei,* "be brave," is connected to each healing (5:10 bis; 7:17 bis; 11:11; cf. 8:21 bis).

18   8:3. After Tobiah has followed Raphael's instructions and expelled the demon, Raphael pursues and binds him in Upper Egypt, the desert which is presumed to be the haunt of demons. **4–8.** *let us pray . . . Amen:* Tobiah and Sarah follow the second of Raphael's instructions and pray to God for mercy and blessing. Their prayer recalls the Yahwist creation account (Gen 2:18–23) and recognizes marriage and its joys as part of God's creative design. Sarah's "Amen" is the only word she speaks in the presence of another human being. **9.** *went to bed:* It should be presumed that the marriage is consummated on the wedding night. The tradition of three nights of continence is derived from the Vg, but is found in none of the Gk recensions. **9-14.** Raguel's grave digging is one of the delightful ironies of the book. He has not been able to refuse the marriage, but he is so fearful of its outcome that he prepares for the worst. He cannot even bear to check on the couple, but sends his wife's maid to see if Tobiah is alive or dead. **15-17.** Every major turning point in the story is punctuated by a prayer. Raguel prays in gratitude that God's mercy is greater than his expectation. **19.** Again Raguel prepares a feast. His major role is that of gracious host. **20.** *fourteen days:* The wedding celebration is twice the normal length. There will be yet another seven-day feast in Nineveh. **21.** *father . . . mother:* The marriage has established a family bond between the family of Tobit and that of Raguel.

19   (B) Recovery of the Money (9:1-6). The ostensible purpose for the journey (cf. 4:1-2) was the recovery of the money deposited with Gabael. God's purpose, the healing and marriage of Sarah and the preparation for the healing of Tobit, has taken over primary interest. The task of recovering the money, now secondary, is delegated to Raphael. The author's misinformation concerning the distance between Ecbatana and Rages (see comment on 5:6) makes Raphael's round trip, which is accomplished before the 14-day wedding feast is over, seem unusually swift. **6.** Gabael repeats the evaluation of Tobit's character (cf. 1:3; 7:7) and applies it also to his son Tobiah.

20   (C) Tobit's Healing (10:1-11:18). 1-7. The double wedding feast has delayed Tobiah beyond the expected time. Both his parents worry in characteristic fashion. Tobit, who has counted the days, fears that Gabael is dead. Anna, although she declares her certainty that Tobiah is dead, watches every day at the road by which he will return. Tobit, in reassuring her, belies his own worry. **7.** *ever see me again:* Tobiah understands his parents and accurately portrays their worry. **11-13.** The farewell in Ecbatana points out the expectations of the marriage. The two families have been joined; father and mother are shared by each spouse. Children are desired and joy is expected. **14.** Tobiah departs in prayer, in keeping with the spirit which permeates the book.

21   11:2-4. Raphael, who was not mentioned in the farewell, emerges to give Tobiah instructions for the healing of Tobit. **5-6.** Anna, still watching the road (cf. 10:7), announces the good news to Tobit. **7-8.** Raphael repeats for the third time (cf. 6:9; 11:4) the instructions for the healing. **9.** Anna, who was so sure her son was dead (10:7) is now ready to die herself for joy at seeing him. **11.** *courage:* The key word *tharsei* (cf. 7:17) marks the second healing. **14-15.** Tobit responds to the healing with the fifth formal prayer of the book. **15.** Affliction and healing are both attributed to God (cf. 1 Sam 2:6). Suffering is not seen as a punishment for sin, but rather as a part of the mysterious working of God's plan. *told his father:* In one sentence the progress of the plot thus far is summarized (cf. 3:17; 12:3,14). **16.** *rejoicing and praising God:* The healings and all the joy of the latter part of the book are attributed to the blessing of God. **17-18.** The arrival at Nineveh reiterates the joining of families brought about by the marriage of Tobiah and Sarah. In this short speech Tobit refers to Sarah four times as "daughter." **18.** *Ahiqar:* See comment on 1:21. *seven days:* The second wedding celebration.

22   (V) Conclusion (12:1-14:15).
**   (A) Revelation of Raphael (12:1-20). 1.** Tobit practices what he preaches with regard to prompt

payment of a just wage (cf. 4:14). **2.** *half:* A motif from the folktale "The Grateful Dead" (→ 4 above), in which the wonderful guide is promised half of all the hero acquires. **6.** Raphael points out that all their blessing is due to God. Tobiah was the instrument of God's providence, Raphael the messenger. It is God who heals, to whom praise is due. **7.** *a king's secret it is good to keep:* Cf. Prov 25:2. Raphael's instructions continue with the exhortation to proclaim the goodness of God to others. **8.** A major theme of the book is the importance of almsgiving, i.e., good deeds done for another. Along with the contemporaneous Sir, Tob is largely responsible for the development of this notion of almsgiving (cf. Sir 3:30-31; 12:1-7; 18:15-18; 29:10-13; 34:18-35:10; Tob 4:8-11, 16-17; 12:8-10; 14:10). Almsgiving saves from sin and delivers from death. The blessing expected by the righteous according to the theory of retribution is connected in this book to the giving of alms. **11-15.** Raphael reveals his identity as one of the seven angels who stand before the "glory of the Lord" (cf. Rev 8:2). Others have been named in biblical literature (Michael, Dan 10:13,21; 12:1; Gabriel, Dan 8:16; 9:21) and in apocryphal writings (Raguel, *1 Enoch* 20:4; Uriel, *1 Enoch* 9:1; 19:1; 20:2). In addition to his primary functions in the book as guide and messenger, Raphael reveals his tasks of mediating prayer and testing. The development of angelology, which became a subject of interest after the Babylonian Exile, is a major contribution of this book. **19.** The understanding of angels as spirits precludes the possibility of Raphael's eating or drinking.

23   (B) Tobit's Prayer (13:1-18). Heeding the command of Raphael to praise God, Tobit proclaims the sixth formal prayer of the book. This hymn can be divided into two sections: (1) 13:1-8, a proclamation of God's mercy and freedom; (2) 13:9-18, a hymn to Jerusalem. Three levels are paralleled: Tobit's own experience of suffering and deliverance, the suffering and deliverance of the exiles, and the suffering and restoration of Jerusalem. The hymn echoes the prophetic descriptions of the new Jerusalem (Isa 54:11-12; 60:1-14; 66:10-14; Mic 4:2; Zech 8:22; cf. Rev 21). There is a lacuna in S from 13:6-10; the text must be supplemented by BA (→ 2 above). **2.** God's power does all things. **3-5.** *scattered:* The deuteronomic theme of the dispersal of the people in the exile and the regathering in Jerusalem (cf. Deut 4:25-40). **5.** Suffering and exile as punishment for sin according to the deuteronomic theory of retribution (cf. Deut 28). **6.** *turn:* A favorite prophetic theme (cf. Jer 3:13-16,22-4:2; Zech 1:3). **10.** *tent:* The Temple. *joy:* A consistent theme in this hymn (13:7,10,11,13,14,18). **14.** *happy:* Beatitude for all who love the city of God.

24   (C) Epilogue (14:1-15). 1. Old age was a sign of God's blessing of the righteous (cf. Prov 3:2; 4:10; 8:35-36; 10:27). **3.** Tobit declares his belief in the power of the prophetic word of Nahum. In the BA recension, the prophet Jonah (→ Jonah, 39:2-3) appears instead of Nahum. **4-5.** *desolate . . . rebuilt:* The movement of Tobit's life, from desolation to restoration, is echoed here in the description of the people's fate, from exile to return. The repetition of the words "desolate" (three times) and "rebuild" (four times) emphasizes the point. **6-7.** These verses describe the author's picture of true believers and their reward. **9.** This verse closes the *inclusio* opened in 1:3. **10-11.** A short story of Ahiqar (*ANET* 427-30), to illustrate a major principle of the book: Almsgiving gives life. **12-13.** Tobiah obeys his father's instructions given in 4:3-4. **14.** *a hundred and seventeen:* See comment on 14:1. **15.** The fall of Nineveh (612 BC) illustrates the other half of the theory of retribution: The wicked are punished.

JUDITH

BIBLIOGRAPHY

25   *Bibliographical Surveys:* Review of 1970s research: Craghan, J. F., "Judith Revisited," *BTB* 12 (1982) 50–53. Complete bibliography: Moore, C. A., *Judith* (AB 40; GC, 1985) 109–17.

Commentaries: Alonso Schökel, L., *Rut, Tobias, Judit, Esther* (Libros Sagrados 8; Madrid, 1973) 99–163. Craghan, J., *Esther, Judith, Tobit, Jonah, Ruth* (→ 1 above) 63–126. Dancy, J. C., *The Shorter Books of the Apocrypha* (CBC; Cambridge, 1972) 67–131. Enslin, M. S. and S. Zeitlin, *The Book of Judith* (JAL 7; Leiden, 1972).

Studies: Craven, T., "Artistry and Faith in the Book of Judith," *Semeia* 8 (1977) 75–101; *Artistry and Faith in the Book of Judith* (SBLDS 70; Chico, 1983); "Tradition and Convention in the Book of Judith," *Semeia* 28 (1983) 49–61. Delcor, M., "Le Livre de Judith et l'époque grecque," *Klio* 49 (1967) 151–79. Dubarle, A. M., *Judith* (AnBib 24; Rome, 1966); "L'authenticité des textes hébreux de Judith," *Bib* 50 (1969) 187–211; "Les textes hébreux de Judith," *Bib* 56 (1975) 503–11. Haag E., *Studien zum Buche Judith* (TTS 16; Trier, 1963). Hanhart, R. (ed.), *Iudith* (Septuaginta 8/4; Göttingen, 1979); *Text und Textgeschichte des Buches Judith* (MSU 14; Göttingen, 1979). Priebatsch, H. J., "Das Buch Judith und seine hellenistischen Quellen," *ZDPV* 90 (1974) 50–60. Skehan, P., "The Hand of Judith," *CBQ* 25 (1963) 94–110. Steinmann, J., *Lecture de Judith* (Paris, 1953). Zenger, E., "Der Juditroman als Traditionsmodell des Jahweglaubens," *TTZ* 83 (1974) 65–80.

INTRODUCTION

26   (I) Text and Canonicity. The text comes from the Gk mss. of the LXX, supported and sometimes corrected by other versions such as OL and Syr (for details about the four major recensions and the characteristics of individual texts, see Hanhart, *Iudith* and *Textgeschichte*). Despite Jerome's claim in the Vg to have translated an Aram text, no original Aram or Hebr mss. have ever been found (on the medieval Hebr texts, see Dubarle, *Judith*). Jdt is not mentioned in the QL or in the writings of Philo or Josephus.

A Gk book found only in the LXX, Jdt was excluded from the Hebr canon as an "outside book." Jdt received a mixed reception in the early Christian church (→ Apocrypha, 67:4–6). The Western church generally accorded Jdt canonical status, while the Eastern church did not (see Moore, *Judith* 86–90). Jdt was authorized as part of the Roman Catholic canon by the Council of Trent in 1546, and it was designated one of the deuterocanonical books by Sixtus of Sienna in 1566. Adapting the practice of Martin Luther's transl. of 1534, which grouped the deuterocanonical books at the end of the canonical OT under the heading: "Apocrypha: these are the books which are not held equal to the Sacred Scriptures and yet are useful and good for reading," Protestants came to regard Jdt as noncanonical Jewish religious literature (→ Canonicity, 66:44).

27   (II) Contents and Compositional Outline. Jdt is a dramatic fictional narrative composed of two balanced, proportional parts. A threefold chiastic pattern marked by thematic repetitions structures each half of the story (see Craven, *Artistry* 47–64).

In Part I, chaps. 1–7, "fear" or its denial influences every group or character. The western nations refuse to join Nebuchadnezzar in battle against the Medes because they do not "fear him" (1:11). These nations later experience "fear and terror" (2:28) of Holofernes, who executes Nebuchadnezzar's revenge. The Israelites are "greatly terrified" (4:2) by Assyria's actions. The Assyrians boast that they "do not fear" the people of Israel (5:23). And the Bethulians are described as "greatly terrified" (7:4) by the approaching Assyrian army.

Closely intertwined with these sentiments about fear are convictions about the identity of the true God. Holofernes is instructed to require political submission from the nations (see Nebuchadnezzar's only words in

the story, 2:5–13), yet he also demands that they worship his king (3:8). When Achior suggests that the God of Israel might defeat the Assyrian army (5:21), Holofernes flares, "Who is God except Nebuchadnezzar?" (6:2). After 34 days without water, the people of Bethulia lose faith and declare, "We have no helper, for God has sold us into their hands" (7:25). In crisis they judge apostasy and slavery their only salvation (7:27).

False guilt confuses the people of Bethulia. They ask their leaders to surrender to Holofernes, saying that God is punishing them according to their sins and the sins of their ancestors (7:28). The officials make no attempt to dissuade the people from this faulty understanding of reality. The leaders, too, are disoriented by crisis. Their faith, as well as that of the people, is found wanting when tested. As Part I ends, only a compromise to give God five days to deliver them stands between the Israelites and the worship of Nebuchadnezzar.

The contents of Jdt 1–7 can be schematized as follows:

(I) Nebuchadnezzar's Eastern Campaign and Revenge against the Disobedient Western Vassal Nations (1:1–7:32)
   (A) Introduction to Nebuchadnezzar and His Campaign against Arphaxad (1:1–16)
   (B) Nebuchadnezzar Commissions Holofernes to Take Vengeance on the Disobedient Vassal Nations (2:1–13)
   (C) Holofernes Attacks the Western Nations (2:14–7:32)
      (a) The Campaign against the Disobedient Nations; The People Surrender (2:14–3:10)
      (b) Israel Hears and Is "Greatly Terrified"; Joakim Orders War Preparations (4:1–15)
      (c) Holofernes Talks with Achior; Achior Is Expelled from the Assyrian Camp (5:1–6:11)
      (c′) Achior Is Received into Bethulia; He Talks with the People of Israel (6:12–21)
      (b′) Holofernes Orders War Preparations; Israel Sees and Is "Greatly Terrified" (7:1–5)
      (a′) The Campaign against Bethulia; The People Want to Surrender (7:6–32)

28   In Part II, chaps. 8–16, "beauty" counters fear. Judith, the "beautiful" widow of Manasseh (8:7), lays aside the sackcloth which she has worn for the three years and four months of her widowhood to make herself "very beautiful, to entice the eyes of all men who might see her" (10:4). The leaders of Bethulia (10:7), the Assyrian patrol (10:14), the entire Assyrian camp (10:19), and, most important, Holofernes (10:23) marvel at her "beauty." Holofernes and his servants acclaim her not only "beautiful in appearance" but also "wise in speech" (11:21,23). "This beautiful womanservant" so arouses Holofernes that he instructs his eunuch, Bagoas, to persuade Judith to eat and drink with them so that he might have an opportunity for sexual intercourse with her (12:13). Judith, who "fears God exceedingly" (8:8) proves more than equal to his seduction and to the theological confusion which has brought her own community to within five days of surrendering to the enemy.

Judith reprimands the leaders of Bethulia for "putting God to the test" (8:12). She defends God's freedom to protect or to destroy (8:15) and argues that faith means "waiting for deliverance" (8:17), not coercing God. Judith reminds the officials that since their generation has not sinned by knowing other gods, they have every reason to hope that God will not disdain them (8:18-20). She argues that they are being tested (8:25), just as Abraham, Isaac, and Jacob were tested (8:26). She exhorts them to serve as examples of confidence in God, reminding them that the safety of the sanctuary, Temple, and altar rest upon their and her actions. She herself promises to deliver Israel within the allotted five days by a secret plan (8:32-34).

After praying that God give her the strength to crush the arrogance of the Assyrians by the deceit of her lips (9:10), dressing alluringly, and preparing a bag of ritually pure food, Judith and her maid go to the enemy camp. She explains to Holofernes that she has come to reveal the moment when he can successfully capture Jerusalem itself (11:5-19).

For three days, Judith follows a routine of praying, bathing nightly outside the camp, and eating her own food. On the fourth night, she is invited to the tent of Holofernes for a party (12:13). When the two are alone, Holofernes falls into a drunken torpor (13:2). Judith seizes the opportunity of the moment, prays, takes his sword, prays a second time (13:7), and with two mighty strikes, cuts off his head (13:8). She puts his head into her food bag; then she and her maid walk out of the camp and return to Bethulia.

The townspeople and officials praise Judith's great deed (13:17-20). She outlines a plan of attack for the next morning and asks that Achior, whom Holofernes had condemned to share the fate of the Bethulians, be brought to her (14:1-5). Achior is overwhelmed at the sight of the head of the enemy general, converts, and is circumcised that very night (14:6-10). The next day, the Israelites successfully rout the Assyrians (14:11-15:7).

Joakim, the high priest of Jerusalem, comes to praise Judith's great victory for God (15:8-10). And after plundering the enemy camp for 30 days, the Israelites triumphantly process behind Judith to Jerusalem for a three-month celebration (15:11-16:20).

When they return home, Judith's fame spreads and many men desire to marry her (16:22). Judith chooses to live alone for the remainder of her long 105-year life. Before she dies, she frees her maid and distributes her property. She is buried with Manasseh and mourned by Israel for seven days (16:24). The book closes with the note that for a long time after her death no one spread terror among the people of Israel (16:25).

The threefold chiastic pattern which organizes Jdt 8-16 can be schematized as follows:

(II) Judith Executes Yahweh's Triumph over Assyria (8:1-16:25)
    (A) Introduction to Judith (8:1-8)
    (B) Judith Plans to Save Israel (8:9-10:9a)

    (C) Judith and Her Maid Leave Bethulia (10:9b-10)
    (D) Judith Overcomes Holofernes (10:11-13:10a)
    (C′) Judith and Her Maid Return to Bethulia (13:10b-11)
    (B′) Judith Plans the Destruction of Israel's Enemy (13:12-16:20)
    (A′) Conclusion about Judith (16:21-25)

29   **(III) Author, Provenance, and Date.** Jdt was written by an anonymous author about whom virtually nothing is known. Often scholars reconstruct a social/historical context for the author from clues in the text. Using data like the facts that the central events of the story are set in Palestine; that the Greek reflects Hebr idiom and syntax; and that the kind of lifestyle described with its pietistic emphases on prayer, devotion, ritual, veneration of the Temple, and orthodox adherence to Mosaic law suggest a Pharisaic orientation, the majority of scholars posit that the author of Jdt was a Pharisaic Palestinian Jew.

Because Jdt is fiction replete with historical and geographical inaccuracies, it is difficult to date its composition (on the range of scholarly proposals from the 5th cent. BC to the 2d cent. AD, see Zeitlin, *Judith* 26-31). The *terminus ad quem* is easily set at no later than the 1st cent. AD by a reference to Jdt in the first epistle of Clement of Rome. The *terminus a quo* is more difficult to establish because events in the narrative can be identified with five centuries of real history (on the references assigned Assyrian, Babylonian, Persian, and Gk antecedents, see R. H. Pfeiffer, *History of New Testament Times* [Westport, 1976] 293-96). Most likely Jdt was composed early in the 1st cent. BC during the late Hasmonean period, perhaps during the reign of John Hyrcanus (135-104) for historical and theological rationale, see Moore, *Judith* 67-70).

30   **(IV) Literary Genre.** Critics are virtually agreed that Jdt is a didactic fictional narrative. Most identify it as a short story or novel. Others have proposed special genre designations that include folktale of the example type (Moore, *Judith* 86); theological *roman* (E. Zenger, "Juditroman" 75); haggada for Passover (P. W. Skehan, *CBQ* 28 [1966] 349); haggada and apocalyptic vision (Steinmann, *Judith* 129); part apocalypse and part midrash (Delcor, "Judith" 178); and free parabolic presentation of history (Haag, *Judith* 125).

31   **(V) Significant Theological Conceptions.** God in Jdt is portrayed as the one true transcendent God of heaven and earth (5:8; 6:19), the unfathomable (8:14) ruler and creator of the universe (9:12; 13:18). God of the ancestors (7:28; 9:2) and champion of the weak (9:11), the Lord shows mercy to the faithful (16:15) and crushes enemies through the agency of a female (9:10; 13:15; 16:5).

Concern for physical survival and the continuance of the Jerusalem cultus in the face of fear and the existence of evil misinterpreted as punishment for sin result in a prophetic call for noncoercive trust in the God of tradition. Though the high priest, Joakim, is accorded religious and military authority (4:6-8), Judith, the widow, leads the people to triumph. She models right relationship with God in ways that shatter narrow orthodoxy. It is unconventional in ancient Israel that a woman chops off a man's head (13:8), lies for the sake of her people and the sanctuary of their God (11:8), upbraids the theology of the male leaders of her community (8:9-34), delegates the management of her household to another woman (8:10), and refuses to marry (16:22). Jdt conserves traditions as old as Exod (see Skehan, *CBQ* 25 [1963] 94-110) and serves as a paradigm for human liberation (see Craghan, *Esther, Judith* 66-67). Jdt upholds the fundamental truths that faith does not depend on visible results (8:17) and that God's "might is not in numbers" (9:11).

32   Outline. For details, → 27–28 above, the compositional outline.

(I) Nebuchadnezzar's Eastern Campaign and Revenge against the Disobedient Western Vassal Nations (1:1–7:32)

(II) Judith Executes Yahweh's Triumph over Assyria (8:1–16:25)

COMMENTARY

33   (I) Nebuchadnezzar's Eastern Campaign and Revenge against the Disobedient Western Vassal Nations (1:1–7:32). Part I tells the story of a military and religious struggle contesting Nebuchadnezzar's political sovereignty over the nations and Yahweh's divine sovereignty over Israel. Historical and geographical details are at the service of the storyteller's theological concerns.

1:1. *in the twelfth year of the reign of Nebuchadnezzar who ruled over the Assyrians in Nineveh:* A pseudo-historical preexilic date of 593 and a fictitious identification open the story. Nebuchadnezzar was the most famous of the Neo-Babylonian kings and ruled from 605–562. His father, Nabopolassar, together with Cyaxares, the king of the Medes, destroyed Nineveh in 612. **2.** *Arphaxad:* An invented character. *Ecbatana:* Modern Hamadan, 300 mi. NE of Babylon and 325 mi. SE of Nineveh, built by Deioces (Herodotus, *Hist.* 1.96), favorite summer palace of Cyrus. **5.** *Rages:* Median city commonly identified as Rai, 200 mi. NE of Ecbatana, later mentioned as the place where Arphaxad is slain (1:15). The narrative does not record the details of the military confrontation between Arphaxad and Nebuchadnezzar, but rather tallies those nations which joined Nebuchadnezzar and those which did not. **11.** The nations of the west refused to ally with Nebuchadnezzar because they "regarded him as an ordinary man." Most versions read *hōs anēr heis,* "as one man." B reads *hōs anēr isos,* "as an equal." **13.** *the seventeenth year:* In 588 Nebuchadnezzar defeated Arphaxad. **16.** *then he returned:* Presumably to Nineveh, where he and his army rested and banqueted for 120 days.

34   2:1. *eighteenth year:* This reference to the catastrophic year 587, when Jerusalem actually fell to Nebuchadnezzar, is the only factual detail in Jdt 1:1–2:13. **2.** *secret plan:* Nebuchadnezzar's detailed plan for retaliation. **4.** *Holofernes:* An anglicized form of the Persian name Orophernes. This general is instructed to marshal a huge army in order to require political submission of the nations of the west according to the king's instruction (see 2:5–13).

35   3:2. *lie prostrate:* The seacoast people, witnessing the destruction of their neighbors, humbly surrender. **6.** *hilltop cities:* Holofernes stations garrisons. **8.** *boundaries:* The LXX has *oria,* "boundaries" or "borders" (as elsewhere in 1:10,12; 2:25; 15:5; 16:5). Most modern transls. follow the Syriac's "sanctuaries." "Boundaries" may echo Nebuchadnezzar's order that Holofernes capture all the *orion* of the rebellious nations (2:10). It is specifically in 3:8 that Holofernes exceeds the instruction of his king by requiring that "all should worship Nebuchadnezzar." Moore (*Judith* 143) notes that the Egyptian king Ptolemy V (203–181) was the first king to present himself as "God Manifest." No Assyrian, Babylonian, or Persian king is known to have claimed divinity.

36   4:2. *great alarm for Jerusalem:* Concern for the holy city and the Temple motivate the terrified Israelites to cry out to God. **3.** *recently returned from captivity:* This postexilic reference to 538 is inconsistent with 2:1 and is further complicated by mention of the rededication of

the Temple, referring either to sometime after 515 or perhaps even 165. **4.** Of the eight cities listed only Samaria, Beth-horon, and Jericho can be located. **6.** *Joakim the high priest:* See also 4:8,14; 15:8. Joakim exercises both religious and military authority suggestive of the responsibilities held by Jonathan (1 Macc 10:18–21). *Bethulia:* Important site; geographic location unknown (see Moore, *Judith* 150–51). **8.** *council:* Unknown until Maccabean times (2 Macc 11:27). Delcor ("Judith" 161) maintains that the use of *gerousia* here and in 11:14; 15:8 indicates that Jdt was composed prior to the time of John Hyrcanus II (67) when the term *synedrion* was employed to designate the Jerusalem senate. **10.** *sackcloth:* The penitential use of sackcloth in vv 10–12 is extreme. It is put on the men, women, and children of Israel; on their cattle, every resident alien, hired laborer, and purchased slave; and even on the altar itself. More regularly, only Israelites would wear sackcloth (but cf. Jonah 3:8). **13.** *heard their cry:* God listens but does not act as the Israelites desire. On Jdt 1–7 as a lament gone awry, see Craven, "Tradition and Convention" 52–55.

37   5:2. *he was greatly enraged:* Holofernes seeks the identity of the resisters. **3.** *Achior:* "Brother of light," an Ammonite. **23.** *we shall not fear:* The angry response of those who want to go to battle with the Israelites.

38   6:2. *who are you?:* See also 8:12 and 12:14. *who is god except Nebuchadnezzar?:* Jdt addresses the question as to who is the more powerful God, Nebuchadnezzar or Yahweh. Holofernes posits his king as divine. **5.** *you shall not again see my face:* Ironically, Achior will again see the general's face, but his body will not be with him (14:6). **13.** The Assyrians deposit Achior at the foot of the hill below Bethulia, and the townspeople take him in. **15.** *Uzziah:* The chief elder of Bethulia, who, like Judith, is of the tribe of Simeon (see 9:2). Uzziah (or Ozias), Chabris, Charmis, and the people assemble to hear from Achior what was decided in the Assyrian council. **21.** *made a feast:* Gk *potos,* lit. "a drinking party."

39   7:2. Holofernes moves against Bethulia with an army swelled by 50,000 additional foot soldiers (see 2:5,15). **12.** Surprising, in light of v 7, where the springs below Bethulia were already taken. **13.** *thirst will slay them:* A plan whereby the Bethulians will die, while the Assyrians will suffer no casualty. **20.** *for 34 days:* The duration of the siege of Bethulia; later paralleled by the four days Judith spends in the Assyrian camp (12:10) and the 30 days the Israelites plunder the enemy camp (15:11). **25.** *we have no helper for God has sold us:* Israel declares God the doer of a terrible thing (in 9:11 Judith identifies God as "helper of the oppressed"). **26.** The desperate Bethulians beseech Uzziah to surrender, judging slavery better than death (cf. Exod 14:10–12). **28.** Like the three friends of Job, the Bethulians believe suffering is proof of sin. **30.** *hold out for five more days:* Uzziah strikes a compromise, hoping for rain, which would require a miracle, inasmuch as it was well over a month since harvest and the almost rainless summer months were at hand (cf. 4:5; 7:20).

40   (II) Judith Executes Yahweh's Triumph over Assyria (8:1–16:25). Part II tells how a widow counters the arrogance, cowardice, and faulty understanding of those who would bind the purposes of God.

8:1. *Judith:* "Jewess" is the daughter of a man descended from Israel himself. **4.** *a widow:* No longer a wife and apparently never a mother, Judith is described as exceedingly pious, beautiful, and wealthy. **10.** *the woman who was over all her possessions:* This unnamed woman is designated *abra,* "favorite slave" or "graceful one" (8:10, 33; 10:2,5; 13:9; 16:23); "maid" (10:10); and "servant" (12:19; 13:3). Judith's first action is to send this woman to summon the town officials. Judith upbraids the leaders of Bethulia for putting God to the test (vv 11–27), listens to Uzziah defend his compromise and ask her to pray for rain (vv 28–31), responds with a plan to deliver Israel by her own hand (vv 32–34), and receives the blessing of the officials, who depart from her house (vv 35–56). J. C. Dancy claims that the treatment of faith and suffering in this passage allows the author of Judith to "stand comparison with the author of Job" (*Shorter Books* 99).

41   **9:1.** Alone, Judith asks three things of the Lord: (1) that God hear her widow's prayer (9:4), (2) that God break the strength of the Assyrians (9:8), and (3) that God grant her the strength to defeat the Assyrians by the deceit of her lips (9:10). **10.** *a female:* Gk *theleia,* rather than *gynē,* emphasizes the disgrace of such a demise (Judg 9:52–54).

42   **10:2.** *she arose from her prostrate position:* Her prayer finished, Judith dresses beguilingly (vv 3–4), prepares a bag of ritually pure food (v 5), and goes out to the town gate with her maid to meet the officials, who marvel at her transformation and pray that God grant her success (vv 6–9). **12.** *arrested her:* Judith is met by an outpost of Assyrians, who take her to Holofernes. **14.** Judith's beauty arouses the interest of the patrol, the people in the Assyrians camp (v 19), and Holofernes and his attendants (v 23).

43   **11:1.** *I am not one to harm anyone who serves Nebuchadnezzar:* Holofernes lies to Judith, forgetting his actions in 3:1–8. **5.** *I will say nothing false to my lord:* Judith "deceives" the enemy as she prayed she might (9:10,13). In this instance, her words have a double meaning, depending on whether *kyrios* refers to God or to Holofernes. She speaks truth in v 10 when she urges Holofernes to heed Achior's counsel. She lies in v 8 as she flatters Holofernes into believing that she has come to hand over Jerusalem. See Craven, *Artistry* 95.

44   **12:7.** *three days:* With Holofernes' permission, Judith goes outside the camp nightly to bathe and to pray. **11.** *on the fourth day:* Holofernes instructs his eunuch, Bagoas, to invite Judith to a party. **12.** *we will be put to shame if we let such a woman go without having intercourse with her:* Seduction and forced relations are suggested by the Gk verbs *homileō* (cf. Dan 13:37) and *epispaō.* **16.** Holofernes and Judith are each desirous of "deceiving" the other (cf. 9:10,13; 10:4). **20.** Inebriated, Holofernes renders himself powerless.

45   **13:2.** The guests leave and Holofernes falls asleep. **6.** *his sword:* Judith uses Holofernes' own weapon. **8.** With the courage of two blows, Judith decapitates Holofernes. She gives his head and the canopy from his bed to her female attendant. **10.** As was their nightly custom, the two women went out of the camp, this time to return to Bethulia. **11.** *God, our God, is with us:* Judith credits God with the triumph. **16.** Judith remained un-

violated; her face "deceived" Holofernes. **18.** Uzziah blesses Judith. Moore (*Judith* 233) comments that this blessing is closely modeled after Gen 14:19–20 LXX; he cites an article by B. McNeil (*DRev* 96 [1978] 199–207), which summarizes the usage of Jdt in the liturgy of the Roman Catholic church.

46   **14:1.** *listen to me:* Judith instructs the people to display the head of Holofernes on the town wall and to rush the Assyrian camp as morning dawns. (In 8:11,32, she used this same imperative to chastise the leaders of Bethulia.) **6.** *he fell on his face:* Achior's fainting and Judith's actions as assassin and military strategist reverse stereotyped sex roles (so Moore, *Judith* 235). **10.** *he was circumcised:* Achior's admission into the assembly contradicts the Pentateuchal prohibition: "No Ammonite or Moabite shall enter the assembly of the Lord" (Deut 23:3). On baptism and the admission of proselytes, the legal interpretation that allowed the canonical acceptance of Ruth, and the reasons Jdt was excluded from the canon, see Zeitlin, *Judith* 235.

47   **15:2.** *fear and trembling:* This phrase appears twice in Jdt. Here the Assyrians experience what they caused in 2:28. Moore notes that probably the oldest extant text of Jdt is a 3d-cent. AD ostracon on which 15:1–7 are preserved (*Judith* 93). **8.** *Joakim:* See 4:6. *council:* See 4:8; 11:14; and Enslin, *Judith* 81–82. God's accomplishment is celebrated, then Judith's agency is praised. **11.** The Israelites loot the enemy camp for 30 days and give a sizable portion of their spoils to Judith. **13.** *with olive:* The women and Judith garland themselves in a fashion suggestive of Gk, not Hebr, custom. *in dance:* See Exod 15:20. **14.** *thanksgiving:* Judith's hymn of "confession" (lit.) is taken up by the people as they triumphantly process behind her to Jerusalem.

48   **16:1–17** is a liturgical poem (see Craven, *Artistry* 105–12) which opens with a hymnic introduction (vv 1–2) in which Judith calls the people to worship and proclaims Yahweh victor and deliverer. Verses 3–12 are a narration of the epic event in which Judith describes the Assyrian threat (vv 3–5), and the voice of another tells of her triumph (Dancy points out that only vv 6–10 refer specifically to Judith and suggests that though these verses may once have been the "original core" of the poem, they can no longer convincingly be dissected from their poetic context [*Shorter Books* 124–25]). Verses 13–17 are a hymnic conclusion in which Judith praises God with a new song (v 13) and summons all creation to join her song of praise. Right "fear" of Yahweh is entitlement to mercy and true greatness (vv 15–16). Ruin is the fate of those who arise against God's people (v 17).

21–25. An epilogue tells that Judith lived in Bethulia (16:21), remained a widow even though many desired to marry her (v 22), and reached the age of 105 years (Enslin [*Judith* 181] notes that the Maccabean period was exactly 105 years long). Judith's last act is to free her favorite female attendant (v 23; cf. 8:10). **24.** *seven days:* See Sir 22:12. **25.** *no longer any who spread fear:* Judith modeled transformative freedom and courage. The Vg adds a final verse: "But the day of the festivity of this victory is received by the Hebrews in the number of holy days, and is religiously observed by the Jews from that time until this day." Cf. Esth 9:27–28. Zeitlin (*Judith* 37) notes that it is probable that Jdt was read in the synagogue during Hanukkah.

ESTHER

BIBLIOGRAPHY

49   Anderson, B., "Esther," *IB.* Bardtke, H., *Das Buch Esther* (KAT 17/5; Gütersloh, 1963). Berg, S., *The Book of Esther* (Missoula, 1979). Clines, D., *The Esther Scroll* (Sheffield, 1984). Moore, C. A., *Esther* (AB 7B; GC, 1971); *Daniel, Esther, and*

Jeremiah: The Additions (AB 44; GC, 1977). Murphy, R. E., "Esther," *Wisdom Literature* (FOTL 13; GR, 1981) 152–70. Paton, L., *The Book of Esther* (ICC; Edinburgh, 1908).

INTRODUCTION

50   **(I) Text.** The work has been preserved in a shorter Hebr version which is assumed by most scholars to be the original text. But it exists also in a substantially longer Gk version which freely translates the Hebr text and then intersperses six sizable additions. This Gk text exists in two significantly different forms: (1) the LXX or B-text, which is relatively faithful to the Hebrew, and (2) the A-text, once thought to be Lucian's recension of the LXX, but now recognized as a separate Gk transl., probably of a distinct Hebr prototype. Jerome noted the Gk additions in the Vg but lumped them all together at the end. They are here restored to their proper places and designated by capital letters (as is now commonly done) with the Vg references in brackets.

(II) Canonicity. Only the Hebr story has been accepted by Judaism and that only after considerable hesitation, probably because of the lack of religious elements in the story. This may also account for the absence of any evidence of Esth at Qumran. The Gk additions were declared canonical by the Council of Trent but are listed among the Apocrypha in Protestant Bibles.

51   **(III) Author, Place, and Date of Composition.** The nucleus of the Hebr story may go back to the 5th cent. BC, with subsequent editing in the Gk period. The Gk additions were probably composed in the 2d cent BC in Egypt and/or Palestine. See comment on F:11 [11:1].

52   **(IV) Literary Form.** Scarcely any scholar would now argue for the historical character of the work. It may reflect remembrances of a real or threatened pogrom against the Jews in the Persian Empire or even a historical Mordecai and Esther with influence at the Persian court. Moreover, the description of Persian customs is generally faithful to what is known about that culture. However, the story as it now exists is a fictional narrative, told for more or less religious purposes and expressing well-known themes of OT wisdom literature (S. Talmon, *VT* 13 [1963] 419–55). Mordecai and Esther are classic examples of the righteous wise who seem naïve and helpless but who eventually turn the tables on clever schemers like Haman. The story of the patriarch Joseph (Gen 37ff.) appears to have exercised considerable influence on the author. Like Joseph, Mordecai and Esther acquire high positions in a foreign land and use that power to save their people.

The Gk additions are universally acknowledged to be religious and devotional commentary composed out of the religious convictions and fertile imaginations of later translators/authors. They change radically the focus of the original story by giving the heroic role to God rather than to Mordecai and Esther. They also greatly expand the horizons of the story by giving it an apocalyptic perspective through the dream of Mordecai that intro-

duces the story and the interpretation of that dream at the end; the story thus takes on cosmic proportions.

53   **(V) Message.**
(A) The Hebr Version. This underscores the dramatic deliverance of the Jews from the power of a great empire that found them guilty of nonconformity. This is presented as the cost of fidelity to Jewish claims of uniqueness. The author carefully avoids any reference to the divine election that was the basis for this uniqueness. The total absence of references to God or to the primary religious institutions of Israel is striking. The conventional wisdom notes the profane nature of the Purim festivities and concludes that religious references were eliminated to separate God from such behavior. This explanation merits consideration but does not appear to be altogether satisfactory.

Like most writings of the postexilic period, Esth is concerned with the painful and urgent problem of how to be a faithful Jew in a foreign environment. One common solution to this problem was the creation of Jewish enclaves where the faithful could be insulated against the pagan world and fervently nourish a very explicit piety. Esth has a different emphasis: The Jews must participate in the affairs of state; they must appreciate the good elements in non-Jewish society and cooperate wherever possible; they must assume responsibility and not wait for God to provide some miraculous solution. To highlight this theme of personal responsibility, God is represented as a hidden deity while the personal courage and resourcefulness of Mordecai and Esther are given full play. In fact, one notes a preference for the attitude of Esther, who goes beyond the hurt pride and stubbornness of Mordecai to rely on personal talent, diplomacy, and a trust in the basic fairness of life. The relatively slow pace of the story (e.g., 11 months between edict and execution [3:13], two banquets for the king and Haman [5:4,8]) may very well be, in this perspective, a reminder to the Jews to be patient and persistent as they strive to be true to their calling in difficult circumstances.

It appears doubtful that the book was originally written to provide a basis for the observance of Purim. It seems more likely that this was a later adaptation to give a Jewish justification for a festivity that was probably borrowed from the Babylonians.

(B) The Gk Additions. The sections added by the Gk translator/author change the focus of the book and affect its teaching. Where the emphasis had been on the courage and resourcefulness of Mordecai and Esther it is now shifted to the intervention of God. Indeed, not only is the subtlety of the Hebr story lost but the religious emphasis is so overdone as to be somewhat tedious. The introduction of an apocalyptic perspective further emphasizes the helplessness of the human participants and, because everything is painted in black and white, the subtle colorings of the original are overwhelmed. Finally, the Gk sections move away from the broad-mindedness of the original by suggesting narrow ethnic perspectives and by adopting anti-Gentile attitudes (e.g., A:6, C:26, F:5).

54 **(VI) Outline.** The book may be outlined as follows:

(I) Prologue: Mordecai's Dream (A:1-17 [11:2-12:6])
(II) Esther Replaces Queen Vashti (1:1-2:23)

(III) Haman Plots to Destroy the Jews (3:1-15; B:1-7 [13:1-7])
(IV) Esther and Mordecai Plead for Help (4:1-16; C:1-30 [13:8-14:19])
(V) Deliverance Is Prepared (D:1-16 [15:1-16]; 5:1-14)
(VI) A Dramatic Reversal of Fortunes (6:1-8:12 E:1-24 [16:1-24]; 8:13-9:19)
(VII) The Feast of Purim (9:20-10:3)
(VIII) Epilogue: Interpretation of Mordcai's Dream (F:1-11 [10:4-11:1])

COMMENTARY

55 **(I) Prologue: Mordecai's dream (A:1-17 [11:2-12:6]).** **1.** *Ahasuerus:* The Gk reads Artaxerxes, almost certainly a mistranslation of the Hebr Ahasuerus (see 1:1), who would be Xerxes I (485-465). *first day of Nisan:* About March 15. *Mordecai:* A name derived from the Babylonian god, Marduk; he may have had a Jewish name also. Mordecai is described as a descendant of Saul (1 Sam 9:1-2). **2.** *Susa:* In Elam, winter residence of Persian kings. **3.** *one of the captives:* The deportation of Jeconiah (Jehoiachin of 2 Kgs 24:8,15) occurred in 598. Mordecai could not have been alive at that time if he is still living during the reign of Xerxes I (485-465)! The important point is that he is a Jew living in exile.

5-11. The imagery is apocalyptic. Israel, at the mercy of powerful oppressors and drained of all human hope, looks for a divine intervention that will dramatically turn the tables and establish her in peace and glory. This divine visitation is depicted as a convulsion of nature, followed by the sudden repose of total victory. The Gk redactor adapted the story of Esther to illustrate this eventual cosmic victory of God's people over the apparently invincible powers of this world. The dream itself is interpreted in the Epilogue (F:1-11 [10:4-12]). The dream of Mordecai, much like that of the patriarch Joseph (Gen 35:5f.), presages the unexpected success of a faithful Jew in a foreign land.

16. *rewarded him:* This contradicts the Hebr text (6:3). **17.** *Haman . . . the Agagite:* Haman is the villain of the story. The Gk author here calls him a "Bougaion" but most versions follow the Hebrew (3:1), where he is called an Agagite. The Gk A-text reads "Macedonian" here as does the LXX in 9:24 and E:10. The best explanation is that all three designations were derogatory. The meaning of "Bougaion" is unknown. Agagite makes Haman an Amalekite, whose king was Agag and a bitter enemy of Saul, slaughterer of the Amalekites (1 Sam 15:7). Mordecai is in turn a descendant of Saul (A:1). Thus, there is a kind of blood feud btween Haman and Mordecai. "Macedonian" would be an updating for the benefit of Jews who knew how much the Persians despised the Macedonians, their eventual conquerors. Such flexibility suggests that Haman is a symbolic figure who represents all the irrational hatred experienced by the Jewish people as they strove to maintain their identity in a foreign environment.

56 **(II) Esther Replaces Queen Vashti (1:1-2:23).** **1.** *Ahasuerus:* Xerxes I (485-465) is called Ahasuerus here and in Ezra 4:6; cf. Dan 9:1. *provinces:* Probably subdivisions of the well-known Persian satrapies. **2.** *citadel:* The royal acropolis which was separated from the city. *Susa:* See A:2. **4.** *a hundred and eighty days:* Probably entertainment of successive groups rather than a continuous banquet. **9.** *Queen Vashti:* No other source knows of a Persian queen of this name. Moreover,

Herodotus names Amestris as Xerxes' wife (*Hist.* 9.108-13). **11.** *display her beauty:* Perhaps an obscene display, but in any case highly offensive to her. **13.** *he conferred:* It is inconceivable that the matter would have been handled in this way. In vv 13-22, the author is making fun of the clumsiness of the Persian bureaucracy. **19.** *to one more worthy:* The purpose of this exercise is not to record history but to make room for Esther.

2:2. *beautiful young virgins:* It would be naïve to take this literally. Such a search is a standard feature of harem stories. **5.** See A:1, where the Gk author has already introduced Mordecai. **7.** Hadassah, meaning "myrtle," is a Hebr name; Esther is derived from the Babylonian goddess, Ishtar. Jews in exile frequently bore a Jewish and a foreign name. The relationship between Mordecai and Esther is tender and trusting. He is the wise, cool head; she is the warm heart. But later she will develop her own wisdom. **9.** Esther combined a winsome, natural beauty and subtle personal qualities of tact, thoughtfulness, and sensitivity. **10.** *her nationality:* Premature disclosure would spoil the story. **12.** *beauty treatment:* A period of massages with oils and perfumes. The year of such treatment has more to do with building suspense than enhancing beauty. **15.** Esther has the good sense to follow the suggestions of Hegai, who knows the king's preferences. **16.** *tenth month:* Mid-December to mid-January. *seventh year:* This would be three full years after Vashti's deposition. The pace is very deliberate. **17.** Esther is now in a position to help her people.

19-22. *to resume:* The MT is corrupt here; whatever the exact meaning of the passage, it is clear that the author wishes to remind the reader (after the harem distractions) of the main elements of the story to this point, viz., Mordecai's position, Esther's hidden nationality, Mordecai's unrewarded service, and the record of this in the royal annals.

57 **(III) Haman Plots to Destroy the Jews (3:1-15; B:1-7 [13:1-7]).** **1.** *Haman . . . the Agagite:* See A:17. Haman is moved into a position where he can do grave harm to Mordecai. **2.** *did not bow down:* There is no reason to believe that this was more than a conventional gesture of courtesy and respect. Mordecai seems to want to provoke a crisis. **4.** *a Jew:* Mordecai represents all the Jews who tried to maintain their religious and ethnic distinctiveness in a foreign environment. **6.** *all the Jews:* The author wishes to extend Haman's resentment so that Esther can be a heroine for all her people and not just for Mordecai. **7.** *the twelfth year:* This would be five years after Esther was made queen. *Pur,* "lot," is a Babylonian word that the author is careful to translate. The ancients commonly resorted to casting lots to determine the propitious time for some important action. "Pur" provides the name for the feast of Purim, which probably originated with the Babylonians (note the Hebr pl. ending).

in Haman's presence: Some authorized person would cast the lots (perhaps marked pebbles) before Haman so that he could see the results. *Adar:* Mid-February to mid-March. This whole verse may be an interpolation to connect the story with the Purim feast.

8. The Jews are indicted because they are perceived as unassimilable and disobedient. This must have presented a painful dilemma to postexilic Judaism. Is it possible or desirable to cling to one's distinctive heritage against such odds? This is the real issue of the story. **9.** *ten thousand talents of silver:* 650 tons—an astronomical sum that cannot be taken literally. **10.** *signet ring:* The king's ring seals the decree and implies permission. The Xerxes of history bears no resemblance to this naïve and easily manipulated monarch. **11.** The king seems to be refusing the bribe; perhaps it is merely a diplomatic way of accepting it, or the author may wish to safeguard the innocence of the king to put all the blame on Haman. **13.** Eleven full months must pass before the edict is executed. Such harsh and merciless measures would not be typical of the Persian rulers. The story may be based on a historical pogrom in the Persian Empire, but it is unlikely to have been officially sanctioned. The Gk text (B:1–7 [13:1–7]) provides a copy of the letter.

58   B:1 (13:1). *the letter:* This florid and pompous letter, composed by the Gk author, dwells on the alleged faults of the Jews. No doubt the Jews had experienced this kind of misunderstanding. **3.** This unstinting praise of Haman was of course Haman's own composition. **5.** Unfortunately, it is very easy to imagine the worst things about people who perform unconventional rites and are guided by unfamiliar principles. **6.** *fourteenth day:* This must be a scribal error since the thirteenth day is given elsewhere (3:12; 8:12; 9:1; E:20) in both Hebr and Gk versions.

3:14. *a copy of the decree:* The more sober Hebr account continues with a mere mention of the decree's promulgation. **15.** *in haste:* With 11 months remaining before the fateful day there does not appear to be need for haste. The author seems to admire all things Persian, including the postal system. **16.** The author delights in ironic contrasts. The populace is in consternation while the king and Haman relax.

59   (IV) Esther and Mordecai Plead for Help (4:1–16; C:1–30 [13:8–14:19]). **1.** *sackcloth and ashes:* A rough camel's-hair garment and disheveled hair sprinkled with ashes effectively publicized a tormented spirit. Elsewhere in the Bible such behavior usually had a religious motivation (e.g., 2 Sam 12:16) but the Hebr text of Esther is careful to avoid all religious references (→ 53 above). **4.** *he refused:* This will tell Esther that the situation is desperate. **8.** *for her people:* Esther is reminded that high station brings heavy responsibility. One of the purposes of the story is to illustrate how more fortunate Jews should care for their less favored compatriots. **11.** *without being summoned:* There is no historical evidence of such drastic penalties. The story, however, requires that the heroine be put at great risk. Esther may no longer be the king's favorite. **13.** *do not imagine:* This warning is intended for all Jews in high places lest they forget their roots. **14.** *from another source:* One can scarcely avoid concluding that this is a divine source. The MT avoids any explicit reference to God (→ 53 above). For Esther, as for the Jews of the Diaspora, standing together will ultimately bring far quicker salvation than standing alone. *for just such a time:* The author believes in a providential design in human affairs. **16.** *fast for me:* This is an act of solidarity with implicit religious motivation. *I perish:* Esther has made the generous and unselfish decision; she is a true model of concern for others.

60   C:1–30 [13:8–14:19]. The Gk author, ever

intent on supplying religious motifs, inserts two prayers meant to etch clearly the spiritual physiognomy of the two favored actors. **2–4.** Mordecai reminds the Lord of his power to save and recalls how he used that power in the past to deliver Israel. **5–7.** The Gk author provides a noble religious motivation for Mordecai's disrespectful behavior. **8–9.** The customary themes of a national lament appear: "your people," "your inheritance," "your portion which you redeemed"; cf. Pss 74; 79. **10.** *to sing praise:* A familiar motif in the lament: God must spare his people so that they may declare his praises (Ps 79:13). **11.** *death staring them in the face:* No slightest doubt must linger about the definitive nature of the threat; it is an apocalyptic scenario.

12 [14:1]. Esther's prayer highlights first of all her own desperate situation. **13.** *dirt:* Probably a euphemism for dung. **14.** The prayer combines elements of individual and national lament: she is "alone"; the nation has "sinned" (v 17); God's fidelity to the promises is at stake (v 20). **22.** The Lord is reminded that failure to intervene would give credence to idolatry which puts confidence in "non-beings." Actually, Esther is making an act of faith reflecting Israel's conviction about the reality and goodness of her God. **24.** *the lion:* The king, who is duped but never evil in this story. The author has great respect for civil authorities. **26–29.** The Gk author has scruples that are not evident in the Hebr text.

61   (V) Deliverance Is Prepared (D:1–16 [15:1–16]; 5:1–14). The Esther who now emerges is no longer the child-woman who must look to Mordecai for directions; she is fully in charge and makes the most of her considerable talents. The Gk version turns the sober Hebr account (5:1–3) into a vivid, dramatic scene which highlights Esther's peril and courage. **5–7.** The pathos in this scene prepares for the climax in v 8. **8.** *God changed:* The suspense is broken as the king's fierce anger melts into smiling benevolence. The Gk author attributes the change to God whereas the Hebr account (5:1–3) credits the resourcefulness of Esther. **10.** The text is obscure but it appears that the king is aware of Esther's nationality in spite of 2:10. The Gk author occasionally seems to ignore the Hebr text. **5:3.** *half my kingdom:* An exaggeration equivalent to "almost anything." **4.** *come today with Haman:* Esther's strange request is intended to set Haman up rather than to entertain the king. **8.** *come with Haman tomorrow:* This delay contributes to the suspense of the narrative and leads Haman to the height of pride and self-satisfaction. **9–14.** Attention now shifts to Mordecai, who continues to defy Haman. As Haman contemplates this fly in his ointment, he is filled with chagrin. Like Ahab with Jezebel (1 Kgs 21:5–7), he must rely on his wife to suggest a solution. The extraordinary height of the gibbet (*ca.* 75 ft.) is meant to advertise his victory.

62   (VI) A Dramatic Reversal of Fortunes (6:1–8:12; E:1–24 [16:1–24]; 8:13–9:19). **1.** Royal sleeplessness is a fairly common theme (cf. Dan 6:19). The reading of the annals, though possibly dull, was meant to occupy the time rather than to be a soporific. **3.** *nothing was done:* This clearly contradicts A:16. The discrepancy probably must be laid to the carelessness of the Gk author. **4.** Haman's arrival on the scene is hardly coincidental; the author delights in such ironic developments. **7.** The proud and selfish Haman, seeing only his own interests, is trapped into providing glory for the very one for whom he had planned death! This is delightful poetic justice. **8.** Cf. Gen 41:42–43 for a similar account. **10.** The trap is sprung and the lots of Mordecai and Haman are dramatically reversed. The fact that no sensible king would ask his prime minister to do such a thing is beside the point in fictional narrative.

12. *his head covered:* The exact meaning is uncertain, but it is a sign of grief and humiliation. **13.** Haman's wife senses that the triumph of the Jewish Mordecai (and of his race) is fated. Here again, the Hebr author implies divine providence (see 4:14).

7:3. *the lives of my people:* The king does not yet know the nationality of Esther, at least in the Hebr version (cf. 2:10 and D:10). **5.** *who and where:* Making use of the very effective thou-art-the-man technique (cf. 2 Sam 12:7), the author prepares for the identification of the despicable culprit who would dare attack the loyal Mordecai or the incomparable Queen Esther. In real life, the king's ignorance would be incomprehensible (cf. 3:11–15); in the story, it serves to highlight Haman's culpability. **6.** He who just yesterday was the self-satisfied companion of king and queen is today an isolated and shunned man, darkened by the shadow of death. The same dread that Haman had so lightly cast upon the Jews now falls heavily upon himself. **8.** *violate the queen:* Such was certainly not Haman's intention, but now he is a doomed man and everything he touches turns to ashes. *was covered:* Probably a preparation for execution. **9–10.** The wheel has turned full circle. The biblical warning that he who digs a pit shall himself fall into it (Ps 7:16) is proved valid.

8:1–3. Mordecai's elevation does not end the crisis; the decree against the Jews is still in effect. **8.** *what you see fit:* In effect, the king declares his inability to deal with the problem of revoking an irrevocable decree. **9.** *Sivan:* About May 15–June 15. **11.** This decree responds to every point of the previous decree against the Jews (3:13), thereby cancelling its provisions and resolving the crisis—a historically unbelievable development. **63** A copy of the decree is provided in the Gk addition, E:1–24 (16:1–24). **E:4–6.** The Gk author makes King Xerxes a believer who, rather implausibly, has been duped by his prime minister. But fortunately the plot has been discovered before irreparable harm can be done. **7.** *ancient stories:* A general reference to the common problem of court intrigues. **10.** *Macedonian:* See A:17. **12.** Haman's persecution of the Jews, whom he misrepresented as disloyal subjects, was a treasonous act contrary to the king's best interests. **14.** *Macedonians:* The Greeks, under Alexander of Macedon, would eventually conquer Persia. **16.** Just as the Hebr version ignores God completely, so does the Gk author overstate the matter. **17–18.** For the Gk author, the royal decree simply lapses because its chief executor is dead. **20.** *help them:* The permission (or polite command) may be intended to explain how a Jewish minority could defend itself successfully. **22–23.** The author wishes to underscore the importance of the Purim feast by the unlikely proposal that even the Persians should celebrate it. **64** **8:15–17.** The MT records the celebrations in Susa and the provinces. **17.** *embraced Judaism:* This is probably the author's wishful thinking reflecting his conviction that all honest persons must eventually recognize the validity of Jewish revelation. D. Clines (*Esther Scroll* chap. 3) argues persuasively that the original Hebr story ended here and that 9:1–10:3, with its Persian anti-Semitism and concern for Purim, is secondary. **9:1.** *the situation was reversed:* An unexpected change of fortunes is characteristic of apocalyptic litera-

ture. For Israelites in exile this seemed the only way to vindicate their trust in God's promises. **2.** The fear of Jewish violence here seems to be quite different from the reverential fear of 8:17. **10.** *plundering:* Failure to take booty indicates that their motives were unselfish; this is retribution, not pillage. **13.** *again tomorrow:* The extra day of vengeance in Susa is probably intended to explain a discrepancy in the date of the Purim celebration (cf. vv 18–19). The real reason for the difference is unknown. **65** **(VII) The Feast of Purim (9:20–10:3). 21.** *celebrate every year:* In the opinion of most commentators, the Hebr story, at least in its present form, was written to provide a basis for the celebration of the feast of Purim. This feast would originally have been borrowed from the Babylonians and later given a "historical" basis by adapting an existing popular story for that purpose. **23–28.** The story of Purim is summarized. **24.** *foe of all the Jews:* Haman represents Israel's enemies in all ages. For the *pur* or lot, see comment on 3:7. **27.** *inviolable obligation:* Such strong language suggests contemporary Jewish indifference to the feast (cf. v 28). **29.** Esther is Mordecai's adopted daughter (cf. 2:7). *second letter:* Probably not Mordecai's letter (cf. vv 20 and 23) but a distinct letter from Esther. **30–31.** The tedious repetition of "data" about this feast strongly suggests a later date for vv 20–32. *fasting and supplication:* A reflection of a later practice of fasting and prayer the day before Purim in imitation of Queen Esther and the Jews prior to her crucial appeal to the king (cf. 4:16).

10:1. *tribute:* This rather irrelevant statement seems to be intended to show that the king prospered after the elevation of Mordecai. *islands:* The Grecian isles. **2.** *in the chronicles:* A formula borrowed almost verbatim from Kgs (e.g., 1 Kgs 16:14,20,27). **3.** The Hebr text ends by evoking the figure of Mordecai as a symbol of the inevitable triumph of God's people. **66** **(VIII) Epilogue: Interpretation of Mordecai's Dream F:1–11 [10:4–11:1]). F:1.** *the work of God:* In contrast to the Hebr text, the Gk additions focus on the overt action of God. **2.** Mordecai's strange dream (A:5–11 [11:5–11]) is now interpreted as a foreshadowing of his fate. **3.** *the river:* Esther represents the unpromising agent that God delights to employ for the dramatic accomplishment of his purposes. Note the similar role for Judith. **5.** Mordecai and Haman, the "dragons," symbolize the two protagonists in the continuous struggle between good and evil. **6.** *signs and great wonders:* From exodus to Armageddon, the salvation of the just is due to divine interventions (the *magnalia Dei*).

7. *two lots:* Unlike the Purim lots (3:7), these lots show that God controls many apparently fortuitous happenings in human history. **10.** *celebrate these days:* For the Gk author, divine providence is the theme of the Purim feast. **11 [11:1].** *Ptolemy:* Three Ptolemys had a Cleopatra as wife: the fourth year of Ptolemy VIII would be 114 BC, of Ptolemy XII, 77, and of Ptolemy XIV, 48. Most commentators opt for Ptolemy VIII or XII. *letter of Purim:* The Book of Esther itself. The Gk transl. and augmentation no doubt immediately preceded the introduction of this feast into the Jewish community in Egypt. *Lysimachus:* Allegedly the person who translated Esth into Greek.

39

JONAH

Anthony R. Ceresko, O.S.F.S.

BIBLIOGRAPHY

1 Allen, L. C., *The Books of Joel, Obadiah, Jonah and Micah* (NICOT; GR, 1976). Alonso Schökel, L. and J. L. Sicre Diaz, *Profetas II* (NBE; Madrid, 1980). Burrows, M., "The Literary Category of the Book of Jonah," *Translating and Understanding the Old Testament* (Fest. H. G. May; ed. H. T. Frank, *et al.;* Nash, 1970) 80–107. Childs, B. S., *CIOTS* 417–27. Clements, R., "The Purpose of the Book of Jonah," *Congress Volume: Edinburgh, 1974* (VTSup 28; Leiden, 1975) 16–28. Cohn, G. H., *Das Buch Jonah* (Assen, 1969). Cross, F. M., "Studies in the Structure of Hebrew Verse," *The Quest for the Kingdom of God* (Fest. G. E. Mendenhall; ed. H. B. Huffmon, *et al.;* Winona Lake, 1983) 159–67. Duval, Y. M., *Le livre de Jonah dans la littérature chrétienne grecque et latine* (Paris, 1973). Feuillet, A., *Études d'exégèse et de théologie bibliques* (Paris, 1975) 395–433. Fretheim, T. E., *The Message of Jonah* (Minneapolis, 1977). Good, E. M., *Irony in the Old Testament* (BLS; Sheffield, 1981).

Hauser, A. J., "Jonah: In Pursuit of the Dove," *JBL* 104 (1985) 21–37. Landes, G. M., "The Kerygma of the Book of Jonah," *Int* 21 (1967) 3–31; "Linguistic Criteria and the Date of the Book of Jonah," *Harry M. Orlinsky Volume* (ErIsr 16; Jerusalem, 1982) 147–70. Lohfink, N., "Jonah ging zur Stadt hinaus," *BZ* 5 (1961) 185–203. Magonet, J., *Form and Meaning* (BLS; Sheffield, 1983). Pesch, R., "Zur konzentrischen Struktur von Jonah 1," *Bib* 47 (1966) 577–81. Rudolph, W., *Joel, Amos, Obadja, Jona* (KAT 13/2; Gütersloh, 1971). Vawter, B. M., *Job and Jonah* (NY, 1983). Von Rad, G., *OTT* 2. 289–92. Walsh, J. T., "Jonah 2,3–10: A Rhetorical Critical Study," *Bib* 63 (1982) 219–29. Weimar, P., "Jonapsalm und Jonaerzählung," *BZ* 28 (1984) 43–68. Wolff, H. W., *Studien zum Jonabuch* (2d ed.; Neukirchen, 1975); *Dodekapropheton 3: Obadja und Jona* (Neukirchen, 1977).

INTRODUCTION

2 **(I) Literary Form.** From the standpoint of the author, Jonah belongs to a period that had already become the stuff of legend. 2 Kgs 14:25 indeed reports briefly on the activity of a certain "Jonah ben Amittai" during the reign of Jeroboam II of Israel (786–746). But the author is clearly not intent on presenting us with a historical account. The issues with which he deals— primarily the mercy and justice of God—as well as the obvious exaggerations the book contains indicate that he has another purpose in mind. Thus, critical scholarship has rightly abandoned the attempt to treat the book as history. Nor have attempts to see the book as an allegory of Israel's exile experience, in which the "great fish" represents Babylon and the "three days and three nights" the period of captivity, won many followers. Recognition of the book's literary qualities has turned the attention of interpreters to the work's character and function as story (or *Novelle;* cf. Wolff, *Dodekapropheton 3* 60). It is a story, however, that has not been written simply to entertain. The central role given to God indicates that a primary motivation is theological. Also, the description of the relationships between God and Jonah, and between God and the pagan sailors and Ninevites serves to elaborate and reinforce a particular world view. In other words, the work has a didactic function as well. It thus may accurately be described as a *māšāl* or parable: a "comparison" in brilliant story form that seeks to illuminate an issue, and in the process touches a number of other issues. Although the book has contacts with wisdom (note also its attention to "creation theology," which characterizes the wisdom writings; see 1:4 [→ Wisdom Lit., 27:14]), yet it is found among "the Prophets," and rightly so. Its story form is reminiscent of the so-called prophetic legends, tales such as those told of Elijah and Elisha in 1–2 Kgs. It also embodies to an extraordinary degree prophecy's self-critical spirit (→ 4 below). In Jonah, one of the last representations of a prophetic figure, we find not someone of heroic stature but a caricature of a prophet. There is certainly irony in this, and even satire, which may reflect something of the disillusionment with and disappearance of prophecy that marked this period. But it also reflects a profound humility. The author turns the audience's gaze away from the prophetic messengers themselves to the One whose messengers they were, the One who is able to achieve his ends sometimes even in spite of envoys like Jonah.

3 **(II) Date.** Once the historical links to Jonah ben Amittai of 2 Kgs 14:25 and thus to the 8th cent. had been severed, the "universalism" implicit in the outlook of the book led scholars to date it to the late 5th cent. and to read it as a reaction to the separatist and exclusivist tendencies of the period of Ezra and Nehemiah. Recent scholarship has been reluctant to restrict the book's intent so narrowly, and arguments for a postexilic dating based on linguistic considerations (e.g., the number of "Aramaisms" in the text) have been critiqued by G. M. Landes ("Linguistic Criteria" 147–70). Nevertheless, the work's concern with the question of God's justice and the need for and possibility of repentance coincides well with Israel's historical experience of the exilic and postexilic periods.

Proposals for more specific dates include the 6th cent. (contemporary with Jer [cf. 18:7–8], Joel [cf. 2:13], Ezek [cf. 33:11]), the mid-5th cent. (note, e.g., Mal 2:17; 3:14–15), and the early Hellenistic period (late 4th–early 3d cent.). The *terminus ad quem* is 200, by which time it had been included in the "Book of the Twelve" (cf. Sir 49:10).

4 **(III) Interpretation.** Contrary to popular opinion, the importance of the work lies neither in the "miracle" of the 72-hour sojourn in the belly of a fish nor in Jesus' reference to the "sign of Jonah" in his preaching (Matt 12:38–42; 16:4; Luke 11:29–32; Matt and Luke differ on exactly what kind of "sign" Jonah was). Responding to the particular situation of the Israel of his day, the author (A) gives us insight into developments in the role that prophecy came to have after the monarchical period and (B) dares to deal with the very mystery of God.

(A) Prophecy. Although the only oracle that Jonah delivers is a brief and blunt announcement of imminent destruction (3:4), the book as a whole emphasizes the possibility and desirability of repentance as well as the merciful and forgiving nature of God. Some have seen these emphases as evidence of a shift in the role that prophecy began to play from the 6th cent. on, a shift from simply the announcement of what God was about to do, usually judgment and punishment, to the call to repentance (Clements, "Purpose" 16–28). The theme of repentance is also prominent in other literature of this period, e.g., Dtr, Jer, and Ezek.

Others have seen in this caricature of a prophet (Jonah at first flees from his mission and then sees his prophecy proved inaccurate) "a mild parody of prophecy," written not only to counter a rigid deuteronomistic doctrine of retribution but also to give voice to "doubt, perplexity, and unease over simple solutions and glib orthodoxy" (Vawter, *Job and Jonah* 23). Note, e.g., the satire implicit in the inconsistency between Jonah's confessions of faith in 1:9 and 4:2 and his accompanying actions. But this critique comes not from outside but from within the prophetic tradition and thus represents that "prophetic proclivity for self-questioning" which, as von Rad notes, is "one of the best aspects of its spirit" (*OTT* 2. 292; → 2 above).

(B) Theodicy. In Jonah, the central human character in the book, the author draws not a stick figure nor a cardboard character but a real human being who, despite his obvious failings, manages to evoke a certain sympathy in his struggle to understand the God in whose service he finds himself. At the root of Jonah's sometimes inexplicable actions and acerbic disposition, one can begin to recognize a sincere striving to reconcile the concept of a just God with the reality of God's mercy. In inviting us to view the problem through the eyes of this reluctant prophet, the author brings us close to the mystery of God.

Not only is it the mercy of God which the author highlights in his parable story; it is a particular quality of that mercy. That mercy is free and unmerited, and, above all, God is free to bestow it on such as the Ninevites. During this postmonarchic period, Israel had been the victim of the oppression of Babylon, Persia, and the Hellenistic kingdoms, successively. The legendary city of Nineveh represents all that is hateful, repugnant, and cruel in such oppressors, and the notion of a God who is willing to show compassion to such as these must have been a challenging one indeed, but no less challenging than the God whom Jesus preached (cf. Matt 5:45, and the story of Zacchaeus in Luke 19:1–10).

5 **(IV) Structure, Literary Devices, Outline.** The parallel between the two accounts of God's commands to Jonah first in 1:1–3 and again in 3:1–4 indicates the book's overall division into two parts. The story itself is told in four "scenes" or episodes which deal alternately with a group of pagans and then with Jonah and God. In chaps. 1 and 3, the sailors and their captain and the people of Nineveh with their king are led to belief in God through their encounter with Jonah. Chapters 2 and 4 focus on Jonah, and the theme of "death" assumes a prominence: Jonah praises God for rescuing him from death by means of the "great fish" in chap. 2 and Jonah wishes for death out of obstinacy and frustration in chap. 4. The author's artistry is evident not only in the obvious symmetry and balance that characterize the book's structure. A number of literary devices serve to knit the episodes in the book more closely together and to enhance the work's subtlety and complexity. These include the use of key words such as "great" (*gdl*), "evil" (*r‘h*), "appoint" (*mnh*), "fear" (*yr'*), "descend" (*yrd*); not without significance is the way in which the author plays on and exploits the various nuances of these words (see Magonet, *Form and Meaning* 85–112; D. L. Christensen, *RB* 90 [1983] 261–63). Irony, which according to some interpreters, borders on satire, is also a key interest of the author. Note, e.g., the contrast between the piety and responsiveness to God's word of the pagan sailors and Ninevites and the narrow-mindedness and obstinacy of the Israelite Jonah (and a prophet no less!). Allied to irony is the author's almost comic use of exaggeration (the word "great" is repeated fourteen times) and of what Wolff calls "the grotesque" (*Dodekapropheton 3* 62), e.g., the episode with the "great fish" (chap. 2) and the image of the animals of Nineveh in sackcloth (3:8).

The book may be outlined as follows:

(I) First Mission (1:1–2:11)
   (A) Jonah and the Sailors (1:1–16)
      (a) Jonah's Flight (1:1–3)
      (b) The Storm (1:4–16)
   (B) Jonah and the Great Fish (2:1–11)
(II) Second Mission (3:1–4:11)
   (A) The Conversion of Nineveh (3:1–10)
      (a) The Action of the Prophet (3:1–4)
      (b) The Reaction of the City (3:5–10)
   (B) God's Attempt to Convert Jonah (4:1–11)

COMMENTARY

6 **(I) First Mission (1:1–2:11).**
(A) Jonah and the Sailors (1:1–16).
(a) JONAH'S FLIGHT (1:1–3). In these densely packed opening verses, the author introduces the persons and places significant for the story, engages the reader's attention by the unrelenting forward movement of the

action, and immediately raises a number of questions: Why did Jonah disobey? How will God respond? Why a mission to pagan Nineveh?

7   **1.** *Jonah, son of Amittai:* → 2 above. Jonah's name, which means "dove," suggests the notions of "flight" and "passivity," both of which characterize the prophet, at least in the first two chapters (see A. J. Hauser, *JBL* 104 [1985] 21–37). Also, the patronym "son of Amittai" (= trustworthy) provides the first hint of the irony that pervades the narrative: the prophet forthwith demonstrates his untrustworthiness by blatantly shirking his responsibility as a prophet. **2.** *Nineveh:* Assyria's capital during the latter days of its empire, the city assumes a symbolic function as evidenced later in the story by the exaggeration both in the description of its size (3:3) and the suddenness of its conversion (3:5). The city represents the epitome of inhumanity in the ancient world (cf. Nah 2:12–14; 3:1–4,19; Zeph 2:13–15; Jdt 1:1; Tob 14:4,15). The report of Nineveh's "wickedness" which has reached God (compare Gen 18:20–21) is later (3:8) specified as "violence, lawlessness" (*ḥāmās*), a term used frequently by the prophets in denouncing oppression and the arbitrary disregard of justice and the rights of others. **3.** The repetition of "Tarshish" at the beginning, middle, and end of this verse emphasizes Jonah's flight in the opposite direction from Nineveh (see N. Lohfink, *BZ* 5 [1961] 200). While Nineveh lay E, Tarshish (most likely in Spain) represents the farthest known point to the W. The author further engages the reader by implicitly posing the question, Why did Jonah flee? The answer will not be forthcoming until 4:2: Jonah could not bear the possibility that God's mercy might be extended to this wicked and hateful people, the Ninevites (see Landes, *Int* 21 [1967] 13–15). *he went down to Joppa:* As Jonah flees, he begins, ironically, not a journey W as he intends, but a descent (Hebr *yrd*), first to Joppa (modern Jaffa), down into a ship (v 3), into its hold (v 5), and finally to the bottom of the sea (v 15).

8   (b) THE STORM (1:4–16). God intervenes to ensure that Jonah's ill-fated flight continues in a figuratively downward direction (rather than westward and away from Nineveh). R. Pesch (*Bib* 47 [1966] 577–81) first noted the concentric structure of this scene. It begins and ends with the sailors, whose "fear" of the storm (v 5) becomes a "great fear" (v 10) when they learn the storm's source, and finally turns into religious "fear" (awe) when, delivered from danger, they acknowledge the God of Israel (v 16). Jonah, the cause of all the trouble, appears only after the narrative is under way (v 5) and disappears beneath the waves before it concludes (v 15). His affirmation of belief in the God "who made the sea and the dry land" stands at the center of the whole scene (v 9). The irony of the situation is unmistakable: in his very flight from God's service, Jonah unwittingly serves God as the one through whom the pagan sailors come to know and fear Yahweh.

9   **4.** *Yahweh hurled a great wind:* The story emphasizes again and again God's absolute power as creator in the way he makes use of creatures to effect his designs: the wind (1:4; 4:8), the great fish (2:1,11), the castor-oil plant (4:6). This stress on God's creative power serves to sharpen the question of his justice and his mercy in dealing with his creatures. **5.** *each cried to his god:* The author implies the variety of the crew's nationalities and religions; all the more striking will be their unanimity in their "fear of Yahweh" (v 16). **6.** *perhaps God will take notice of us:* The captain's words here and the crew's prayer in v 14 express not only their piety but a theological insight as well. As in the case of the king of Nineveh later in the story (3:9), they acknowledge God's

sovereign freedom to respond to their prayers and penitence as he in his wisdom sees fit. **7.** God controls even the roll of the dice which designates Jonah as the one who can provide the explanation for their unhappy situation. In supplying the answer, Jonah unwittingly becomes the means for these pagans' knowledge of and subsequent submission to Yahweh.

10   **9.** *I fear:* Jonah's confession of faith stands at the center of the entire episode. In the straitened circumstances of the moment, the formulaic terms in which Jonah's creed is framed (cf. Pss 95:5; 136:26) give it a somewhat stilted and hollow ring, underlining his apparent lack of enthusiasm in the service of this God. Note also the inconsistency between Jonah's words of belief in the God "who made the sea" and his action of flight from that same God by means of the sea. The irony in this contrast between word and deed becomes even sharper in 4:2 where Jonah acknowledges that God is merciful, yet the prophet is vexed because God shows mercy to the Ninevites. **10.** The sailors are obviously smitten by Jonah's words. Their almost miraculous conversion, even at Jonah's laconic confession of faith, foreshadows and parallels in miniature the reaction of the pagan Ninevites in chap. 3, whose vast city will be "turned upside down" before five words are out of Jonah's mouth (3:4). *for they knew:* The author does not always follow strict chronological order but sometimes reports an event or conversation at a moment where it would have greater impact (see also 3:5; 4:25). Jonah imparted this piece of information either when he first hired the ship (v 3) or during the conversation given in abbreviated form in v 9. **13.** Not only out of fear of incurring guilt for shedding innocent blood (see v 14) but perhaps out of real compassion for their fellow passenger, the sailors make one last attempt to reach safety before resorting to the drastic measures suggested by Jonah. **16.** Jonah has disappeared beneath the waves and once more, as at the beginning of the scene, the focus is on the sailors. Their simple "fear" in the face of the storm (v 5) has evolved into "fear of Yahweh."

11   **(B) Jonah and the Great Fish (2:1–11). 1.** *Yahweh ordered:* As undisputed master of his creation, God intervenes a second time, making use of a creature to carry out his will (see 1:4). Contrary to popular interpretation, which has often seen it as a means of punishment for Jonah, the "great fish" acts in fact as God's agent to save him. As Jonah descends into the heart of the sea (v 4), God appoints this creature to snatch him from "the belly of Sheol" (v 3). Nevertheless, it must be granted that the whole episode has a grotesque and comic air to it; the bizarre image of the prophet spending "three days and three nights" in the belly of this huge fish accords with the other extraordinary and incongruous aspects of the narrative such as the sudden appearance and disappearance of both the storm in chap. 1 and the castor-oil plant in chap. 4. *three days and three nights:* Presumably the period of time it took the fish to return Jonah from the ocean depths/Sheol. In both biblical and extrabiblical usage "three days" represents a standard period of time for a journey; in particular, the goddess Innana required three days to reach the abode of the dead in the Sumerian myth "The Descent of Innana into the Nether World" (*ANET* 52–57; cf. G. M. Landes, *JBL* 86 [1967] 446–50).

12   Verses 3–10 form a classic example of a song of thanksgiving (→ Psalms, 34:9, 47), in which the worshiper recounts the great distress he was in (vv 4–7a), his cry to God for help (vv 3,8), and God's response (v 7b). Jonah, realizing that God has intervened to save him, intones this song presumably from the interior of the great fish. Some have argued that the author of the book borrowed the psalm from another source or that a later editor inserted it. Recent studies, however, have focused on its poetic qualities (Cross, "Studies in the Structure of Hebrew Verse" 159-67; J. T. Walsh, *Bib* 63 [1982] 219-29) and its appropriateness at this point in the story (G. M. Landes, *Int* 21 [1967] 3-31). The poem draws on Semitic mythological lore in picturing death, or the approach to death, alternately as entrance into the underworld (vv 3,7) or as submersion in the cosmic waters (vv 4,6). The latter imagery is particularly appropriate to Jonah's situation as one whom "the waters" were encompassing and "the deep" surrounding (v 6). **6.** *seaweed:* See B. Batto (*JBL* 102 [1983] 32-34) who argues that *swp* should be translated "extinction" here. **7.** This verse is central not only to the psalm but to the entire book. Jonah's "descent," begun with his flight from Yahweh in 1:3, has been dramatically reversed. By deferring the account of the cry to God for help to v 8, the author of the psalm stresses the gratuitousness of Yahweh's intervention (J. T. Walsh, *Bib* 63 [1982] 228). Against the background of this expression of thanksgiving from the disobedient but now forgiven prophet, Jonah's complaint against God's mercy to Nineveh in chap. 4 appears inconsistent and even foolhardy coming as it does from one who has himself experienced the divine compassion. **9.** *Mercy:* Yahweh's *ḥesed,* the mysterious motivating force behind all his acts of kindness toward his creatures. **11.** This verse forms an *inclusio* with 2:1, bringing to a close the account of God's rescue of Jonah. The episode ends on a comic note: the prophet is spewed out onto the dry land, presumably where he had begun his hapless flight.

13   (II) Second Mission (3:1-4:11).
(A) The Conversion of Nineveh (3:1-10).
This third episode of the story roughly parallels the structure of the first episode in chap. 1. The reader notices this immediately with the repetition in 3:1-3 of God's command to Jonah in 1:1-3. In each of these chapters Jonah's encounter with a group of pagans results in their conversion, and in both cases the group's leader (ship's captain, king) plays a prominent role. The use of exaggeration continues, e.g., with the description of Nineveh's extraordinary size (v 3), in the almost incredible suddenness and totality of the city's conversion, and in the quaint and humorous picture of the animals donning sackcloth and crying out for God's mercy (vv 7-8).
14   (a) The Action of the Prophet (3:1-4). 3. *Jonah sets out:* There are a few moments of suspense before it becomes clear that this time Jonah will obey. He apparently realizes the futility of flight after his experience with the storm and the great fish; there may also be a lingering hope that the Ninevites will reject his message and thus receive their just reward from God's wrath (see 4:5b). The author describes Nineveh, drawing on legendary reports of its size (and wickedness), which had grown in the popular imagination after its demise in 612. **4.** *one day's journey:* The bare beginning of a minimal effort by an unenthusiastic prophet in this city known in legend not only for the enormity of its size but for the enormity of its violence and cruelty heightens the enormity of the miracle of its sudden and total conversion. The actual oracle of Jonah which effects this astounding change of heart consists of scarcely five words in Hebrew. The use of the word *hpk,* "to destroy," "overturn" (cf. Gen 19:25) and other parallels (cf. Jonah 1:2 and Gen 18:21; 19:13) call to mind the story of Sodom and Gomorrah in Gen 18-19. Note also Abraham's dialogue with God about divine justice on that occasion (Gen 18:22-33).

15   (b) The Reaction of the City (3:5-10). The author's ignoring of a strict chronology in the sequence of events in this section gives us insight into his narrative skill. He begins with a summary statement in v 5 describing the totality of the city's conversion in response to Jonah's message. This heightens and underlines the enormity of the change that swept over the city in contrast to the half-hearted efforts of the reluctant prophet. Then the author backtracks in vv 6-9 to rehearse in more detail the various stages in which this conversion took place. **5.** *believed in God:* It was not just a matter of believing Jonah's words of warning. The Hebrew word describing the reaction of the Ninevites ('*mn,* "to believe," "trust") occurs in such key texts as Gen 15:6 and Exod 14:31, where Abraham and the people of Israel respectively respond with true faith in God.
16   7. *a decree of the king and his nobles:* The wording of the decree that follows in vv 7-9 demonstrates concretely their "belief in God" and presents a model of true repentance in three stages. The first stage consists in the acknowledgment of guilt by means of outward actions: the fasting, the sackcloth, the incessant prayers (vv 7b-8a). The second stage focuses on the interior, the change in attitude toward one's fellow human beings in turning away (*šwb*) from "evil" and "violence" (*ḥāmās;* cf. 1:2) toward them (v 8b). The third stage involves the acknowledgment of God's freedom in how he will respond to their repentance (v 9). **8.** *man and beast:* The incongruous picture of the animals in the city joining their masters in putting on sackcloth and crying out to God lends a comic note and underlines the totality of the city's response. **9.** *perhaps:* Lit., "Who knows . . . ?" Like the ship's captain and the sailors in chap. 1 (1:6,14), the king does not expect God to react automatically and inevitably to their repentance (cf. Jer 18:7-10). "It is the heathen rather than Jonah who have such extraordinary insight into the sovereign freedom of God. They, in fact, articulate what Jonah refuses to allow in his God: God acts as it pleases him, which may or may not conform to human expectations" (Fretheim, *Message of Jonah* 112-13). **10.** *God repented:* Augustine notes that Nineveh was indeed "overthrown": ". . . overthrown in evil, but rebuilt in goodness" (*En. in Ps.* [PL 36. 592]).
17   (B) God's Attempt to Convert Jonah (4:1-11). The author's constant use of questions (cf. 1:6,8,10,11; 3:9) by which he draws the reader into the story here reaches a peak as God himself becomes the questioner, and the reader, at the end, is left with a question. **2.** We now discover the reason why Jonah fled toward Tarshish in 1:3: he feared that his preaching would have the positive effect that it did in fact have (3:5), and he wanted nothing to do with the possible extension of divine mercy to these hateful people. On the author's liberty with the chronology of events and conversation, see 1:9; 3:5; 4:5. *for I know:* The phrases that follow occur in the same or similar form in a number of places (e.g., Exod 34:6-7; Num 14:18; Neh 9:17; Pss 86:15; 103:8; 145:8). They function almost as a creed and most likely have their origin in a cultic context. Only here and in Joel 2:13 are the words "and repents of evil" added. Important is the affirmation of the priority of God's mercy and love in dealing with his creatures. His mercy and love may, in the end, override every other consideration. On the inconsistency between Jonah's words and actions here, see 1:9. **3.** *take my life:* Jonah wants totally to dissociate himself from a God who presumes to act in such a manner. His bewilderment in the face of such a display of divine "justice" drives him to doubt the meaning of his own service to

such a God; he can no longer bear to live under the burden of his frustration. The author most likely intends a parallel with Elijah's request for death in 1 Kgs 19:4. The contrast between the two situations is not lacking in irony: Elijah asks for death because his preaching has failed to effect conversion, while Jonah makes the same request because his preaching has been an overwhelming success. **5.** *Jonah had gone out:* Again the author has delayed reporting an occurrence which chronologically follows immediately after 3:4; see also 1:9; 3:5; 4:2.

18 **6.** *castor-oil plant:* Jonah has apparently refused to answer God's query on whether or not Jonah's anger is justified. God responds to his sullen silence by an act of kindness; a large-leafed plant miraculously springs up overnight and provides refreshing shade for Jonah from the sun's heat. Jonah's exaggerated joy over the little bit of extra comfort provided by the plant contrasts with his callous anger at God's mercy to the Ninevites. **8.** *an east wind:* The sirocco, an almost unbearably hot, dry wind that blows in off the desert. *he prayed for death:* Jonah's physical suffering as a result of the disappearance of the plant with its shade is not the principal reason in his request for death. A deeper source of discontent is God's apparent unfairness. God had lavished his mercy on the hateful Ninevites yet cannot allow more than a few moments' shade for Jonah. **9.** *Do you do well to be angry. . . ?:* God's question backs Jonah into a corner. If Jonah answers No, he admits he is wrong to question

God's sovereignty as creator and God's freedom to deal with Nineveh as he chooses. If Jonah answers Yes (as he in fact does), he admits the validity of pity as a motive for sparing a creature from destruction.

19 **11.** *May I not have pity. . . ?:* God seizes upon Jonah's response and drives home the lesson. As sovereign Lord of creation he asserts his freedom to spare even Nineveh from destruction. God's question here focuses on the issue of divine freedom, not in a theoretical sense but in a concrete case of the experience of one man faced with the reality of God's mercy bestowed on a people who, by any definition of justice, seem totally unworthy of such mercy. Other issues are touched on as well: the universal, indeed cosmic, scope of God's saving purposes; indirectly, God's dealings with Israel; and the very mystery of God himself, who ultimately eludes and transcends any attempt to define or limit him. Commentators have noted connections with NT parables. Jerome quotes from the story of the Prodigal Son (Luke 15:11–32, note vv 25–32; *Commentariorum in Jonam Liber* [PL 25. 1151]), and Luther mentions the parallel with the parable of the Workers in the Vineyard (Matt 20:1–16, note 15; "Lectures on the Minor Prophets" [*Luther's Works* 19; St. Louis, 1974] 51–52, 93–94). *and also much cattle:* The inclusion of the innocent children and the city's animal population here gives added reason to God's pity on Nineveh and underlines the wider, cosmic scope of his saving purpose for all of his creation.

PART TWO

THE
NEW TESTAMENT
AND
TOPICAL ARTICLES

Edited by

JOSEPH A. FITZMYER, S.J.
RAYMOND E. BROWN, S.S.

PART TWO

THE
NEW TESTAMENT
AND
TOPICAL ARTICLES

EDITED BY

JOSEPH A. FITZMYER, S.J.

RAYMOND E. BROWN, S.S.

40

SYNOPTIC PROBLEM

Frans Neirynck

BIBLIOGRAPHY

1   General. Bellinzoni, A. J. (ed.), *The Two-Source Hypothesis* (Macon, 1985). Farmer, W. R., *The Synoptic Problem* (2d ed.; Macon, 1976). Kümmel, W. G., *INT* 38–80. Neirynck, F., *The Minor Agreements of Matthew and Luke against Mark* (BETL 37; Louvain, 1974); *Evangelica* (BETL 60; Louvain, 1982). Schmid, J., *Matthäus und Lukas* (Freiburg, 1930). Schmithals, W., *Einleitung in die drei ersten Evangelien* (Berlin, 1985). Streeter, B. H., *The Four Gospels* (London, 1924). Tuckett, C. M., *The Revival of the Griesbach Hypothesis* (SNTSMS 44; Cambridge, 1983). Vaganay, L., *Le problème synoptique* (Tournai, 1954). Wik-Schm, *ENT* 272–89.
2   Synopses. In Greek: Aland, K., *Synopsis quattuor evangeliorum* (13th ed.; Stuttgart, 1985). Huck, A. and H. Greeven, *Synopsis of the First Three Gospels* (Tübingen, 1981). Orchard, J. B., *A Synopsis of the Four Gospels in Greek* (Macon, 1983). Swanson, R. J., *The Horizontal Line Synopsis of the Gospels.*

Greek Edition. I. Matthew (Dillsboro, 1982). In English: Aland K., *Synopsis of the Four Gospels* (Gk-Eng, 7th ed.; Stuttgart, 1984). Funk, R. W., *New Gospel Parallels* (Phl, 1985). Orchard J. B., *A Synopsis of the Four Gospels in a New Translation* (Macon, 1982). Swanson, R. J., *The Horizontal Line Synopsis of the Gospels* (Dillsboro, 1975). Throckmorton, B. H., *Gospel Parallels* (4th ed.; Nash, 1979; based on 9th ed. of the Huck-Lietzmann Gk Synopsis [1936]).
3   Tools. Gaston, L., *Horae Synopticae Electronicae* (SBLSBS 3; Missoula, 1973). Hawkins, J. C., *Horae Synopticae* (2d ed.; Oxford, 1909). Neirynck, F. and F. Van Segbroeck, *New Testament Vocabulary* (BETL 65; Louvain, 1984; Part II: "Synoptic Parallels and Synonyms").
(→ 37 below. Note: in this article a slash / used in a pattern like 8:56/9:1 means "between" those two verses.)

OUTLINE

5   The first three Gospels in the canon (called "Synoptic"), Matt, Mark, and Luke, have much in common and are significantly different from John. Similarities and dissimilarities among the Synoptics give rise to the question of interrelationship, the so-called Synoptic problem. The "Augustinian" hypothesis assumed the order of composition to be Matt, Mark, Luke. For a period this was replaced as the leading theory by the Griesbach hypothesis (Matt, Luke, Mark). The priority of Mark was first suggested at the end of the 18th cent. as an alternative to the traditional view of Matthean priority, leading to decisive debate in the 1830s to 1860s. As a result, the Marcan hypothesis became the predominant scholarly opinion.

Mark contains 661 verses, of which some 80 percent are reproduced in Matt and about 65 percent in Luke. Only a few pericopes have no parallel in at least one of the other Gospels. The Marcan material that is found in the three Synoptic Gospels is called the Triple Tradition. The non-Marcan material that Matt and Luke have in common (about 220 verses) is called the Double Tradition. The Two-Source theory, or Two-Document hypothesis, would have Matt and Luke depend on Mark for the Triple Tradition and derive the Double Tradition from a Gk written source, a hypothetical *logia* or sayings source dubbed Q (the abbreviation of the Ger word *Quelle*, i.e. *Logien-, Spruch-,* or *Redenquelle*). Matt and Luke are much longer than Mark (total 1,068 and 1,149 verses respectively) and include a large amount of special material, which partly derives from the creative activity of the evangelists.

6   (I) The Synoptic Gospel Order. A study of Marcan order compared with that of Matt and Luke has influentially supported the priority of Mark.

(A) Order of Episodes in the Triple Tradition. The Marcan material appears to a large extent in the same order in the three Synoptic Gospels. The general outline of Mark can be recognized in Matt and Luke:

	Matt	Mark	Luke
Preliminaries	3:1–4:11	1:1–13	3:1–4:13
Galilean ministry	4:12–18:35	1:14–9:50	4:14–9:50
Journey to Jerusalem	19–20	10	9:51–19:28
Ministry in Jerusalem	21–25	11–13	19:29–21:38
Passion	26–27	14–15	22–23
Resurrection	28	16	24

As for the differences in order, the main literary-critical solutions to the Synoptic problem (Marcan priority, Augustinian hypothesis, Griesbach hypothesis) agree about this: wherever Matt departs from Mark's order, Luke supports Mark, and whenever Luke departs from Mark, Matt agrees with Mark. This absence of Matt-Luke agreement against Mark in terms of order can be interpreted in more than one way. It can be explained by Marcan priority, but also by any other hypothesis that proposes Mark as the middle term:

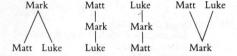

The idea that there was a primitive gospel (sometimes called Proto-Mark) that influenced the canonical Gospels remains a possibility, but this phenomenon of order is not satisfactorily explained by positing dependence only on gospel fragments or oral tradition. On the assumption of Marcan priority, the absence of agreement of Matt and Luke against Mark becomes an indication for the independence of Matt and Luke in their use of Mark. But the real argument from order for Marcan priority is that the differences in Matt and Luke can be plausibly explained as changes of Mark made according to the general redactional tendencies and the compositional purposes of each Gospel.

7   (B) Marcan Order in Matt. We should distinguish between Matt 4:23–13:58, where there are notable changes from the Marcan order of pericopes, and the rest of Matt, where the Marcan pericope order is unchanged. We begin in (a) and (b) below with the latter

phenomenon, and then in (c) treat the former phenomenon at greater length.

(a) MATT 3:1–4:22 (par. MARK 1:1–20). No change of pericope order:

	Matt	Mark
John the Baptist	3:1–12	1:1–8
Baptism of Jesus	3:13–17	1:9–11
Temptation	4:1–11	1:12–13
Preaching in Galilee	4:12–17	1:14–15
Call of first disciples	4:18–22	1:16–20

(b) MATT 14:1 TO END (par. MARK 6:14–16:8). No changes of pericope order, but a few changes of order within pericopes (by way of anticipation):

	Matt	Mark
Tradition of the elders	15:3–6	
	15:7–9	7:6–8
		7:9–13
Question about divorce	19:4–6	
	19:7–8	10:3–5
		10:6–9
Cleansing of the Temple	21:12–13 (14–17)	
	21:18–19	11:12–14
		11:15–17 (18–19)

8   (c) MATT 4:23–13:58 (par. MARK 1:21–6:13). An anticipating movement can be observed also in Matt 4:23–13:58. All the transpositions of Marcan pericopes are found in Matt 8–9 and 10. Those chapters contain, in the relative order of Mark, the parallels to Mark 4:35–5:20 (Matt 8:18–34); Mark 5:21–43 (Matt 9:18–26); Mark 6:6b (Matt 9:35); Mark 6:7–11 combined with 3:16–19 (Matt 10:1–16). The remaining Marcan pericopes in Matt 12–13 follow strictly the order of Mark:

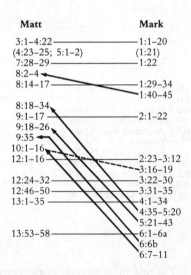

The preceding synopsis of parallel material in Matt 3:1–13:58 (par. Mark 1:1–6:13) indicates that the Sermon on the Mount (Matt 5–7) is placed in the Marcan order at the first mention of Jesus' teaching in Mark 1:21. Matt 4:23–25; 5:1–2 is a complex Matthean composition in which Mark 1:39 and several other passages

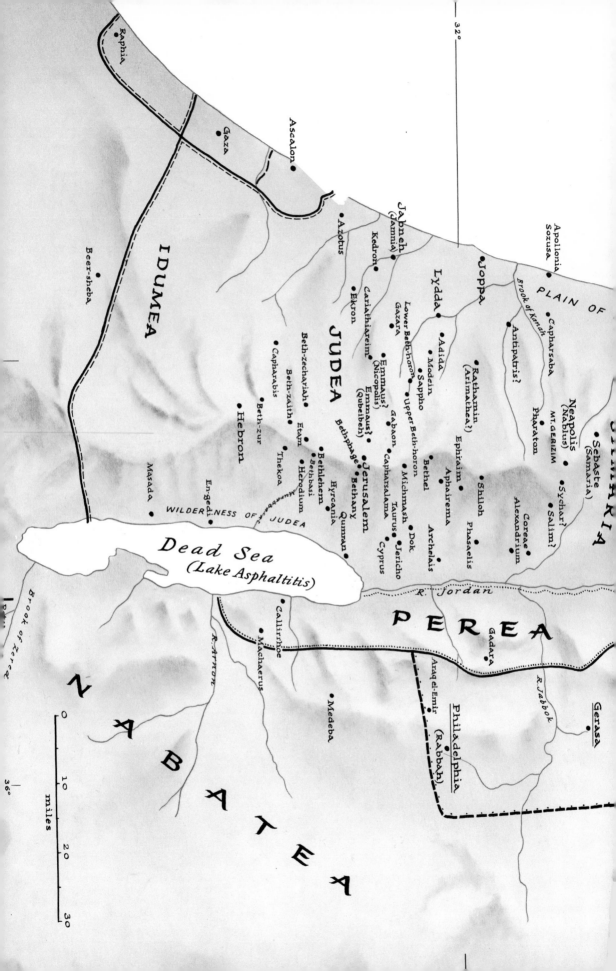

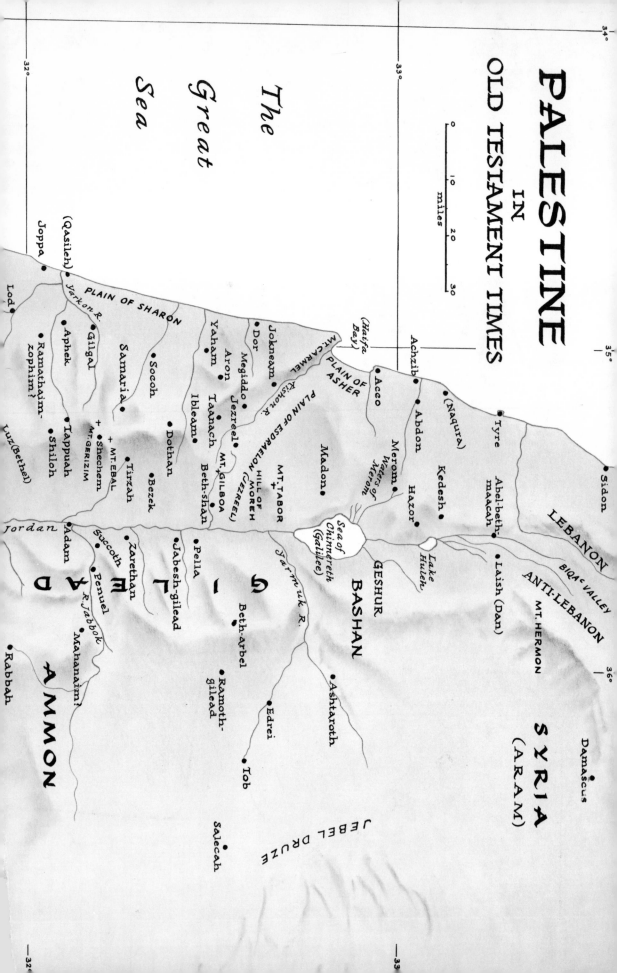

PALESTINE

IN
OLD TESTAMENT TIMES

0   10   20   30
miles

The Great Sea

PLAIN OF SHARON

(Qasileh)
Joppa
Lod
Aphek
Gilgal
Ramathaim-zophim?
Luz (Bethel)
Tappuah
Shiloh
Shechem
MT. GERIZIM
+ MT. EBAL
Samaria
Socoh
Dothan
Bezek
Tirzah
Ibleam
Beth-shan
Taanach
MT. GILBOA
Megiddo
Jezreel
Aron
Yaham
Dor
Jokneam
Kishon R.
PLAIN OF ESDRAELON (JEZREEL)
HILL OF MOREH
MT. TABOR
Madon
PLAIN OF MT. CARMEL
PLAIN OF ASHER
(Haifa Bay)
Aceo
Achzib
(Naqura)
Tyre
Abel-beth-maacah
Sidon
Abdon
Kedesh
Merom
Waters of Merom
Hazor
Lake Huleh
Laish (Dan)
MT. HERMON
LEBANON
BIQAʿ VALLEY
ANTI-LEBANON
SYRIA
(ARAM)
Damascus

Sea of Chinnereth
(Galilee)
GESHUR
BASHAN
Ashtaroth
Edrei
JEBEL DRUZE
Salecah

Yarmuk R.
Pella
Jabesh-gilead
Beth-arbel
Ramoth-gilead
Tob

Jordan
Adam
Succoth
Zarethan
Penuel
R. Jabbok
Mahanaim?
GILEAD

AMMON
Rabbah

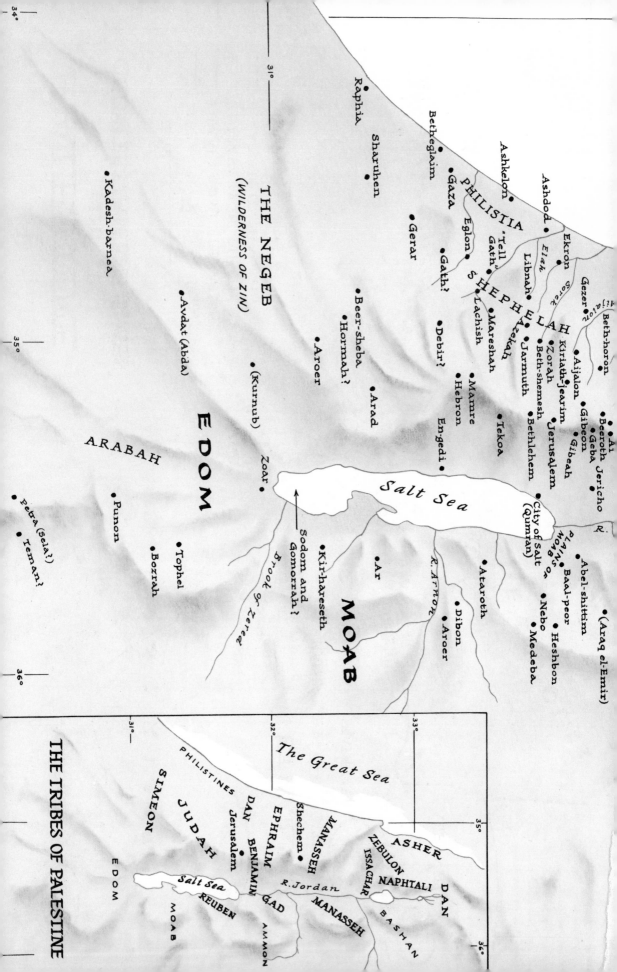

34°

31°

Raphia

Sharuhen

Bethgluim

Kadesh-barnea

THE NEGEB
(WILDERNESS OF ZIN)

35°

Avdat (Abda)

(Kurnub)

ARABAH

EDOM

Petra (Sela?)

Teman?

Punon

Bozrah

Tophel

Zoar

Brook of Zered

Sodom and
Gomorrah?

36°

PHILISTIA

Ashkelon

Ashdod

Gaza

Eglon

Gath?
"Tell Gath"

Gerar

Beer-sheba

Hormah?

Debir?

Aroer

Arad

Lachish

Mareshah

Mamre

Hebron

Engedi

SHEPHELAH

Ekron

Libnah?

Elah

Zorah
Beth-shemesh

Jarmuth

Azekah

Tekoa

Bethlehem

Kiriath-jearim

Aijalon

Gibeon

Jerusalem

Gibeah

Sorek

Gezer

Geba

Beeroth

Jericho

Ai

Beth-horon

Ajjalon

Salt Sea

City of Salt
(Qumran)

Kir-hareseth

Ar

MOAB

R. Arnon

Aroer

Dibon

Ataroth

Nebo

Medeba

Heshbon

Baal-peor

Abel-shittim

PLAINS OF MOAB

(Araq el-Emir)

R.

THE TRIBES OF PALESTINE

31°

32°

33°

35°

36°

The Great Sea

PHILISTINES

SIMEON

JUDAH

DAN

EPHRAIM

Shechem

MANASSEH

BENJAMIN

Jerusalem

Salt Sea

GAD

REUBEN

EDOM

MOAB

AMMON

R. Jordan

MANASSEH

ZEBULON

ISSACHAR

NAPHTALI

ASHER

DAN

BASHAN

The Great Sea

PALESTINE
IN
NEW TESTAMENT TIMES

.... TETRARCHY OF HEROD ANTIPAS
– – – – ROMAN ADMINISTRATION
————— TETRARCHY OF PHILIP
–·–·– DECAPOLIS (Cities underlined)

33°

35°

36°

Mediterranean Sea

SHARON

Caesarea Maritima

Socoh

Narbata

Dor

MT. CARMEL

PLAIN OF ESDRAELON

R. Kishon

Ptolemais (Haifa Bay)

Achzib

Ladder of Tyre

PHOENICIA

Tyre

Sarepta

Sidon

R. Leontes

MT. LEBANON

ITURAEA

BIQA'

Ba'albek

ABILENE

Damascus

MT. HERMON

SYRIA

Caesarea Philippi (Baniyas)

Danos
Daphne

Seleucia

L. Semechonitis (Lake Huleh)

GALILEE

Gischala

Sepphoris
Beth-shearim
Nazareth
Jotapata
Cana? (Kh.Qana)
Cana? (Kefr Kenna)
Arbela
Tiberias
Gennesaret
Capernaum
Chorazin
Safed

Sea of Galilee

Bethsaida Julias

GAULANITIS

BATANAEA

TETRARCHY OF PHILIP

TRACHONITIS

Raphana

AURANITIS

Canatha

MT. GILBOA
HILL OF MOREH
Nain
Tabor

Aenon
Salim? (Beth-shan)
Scythopolis
Pella
Brook Cherith

DECAPOLIS

Gadara
Abila
Arbela

Hammat
Gader
Hippos
Gergesa?
R. Yarmuk

Dion

of Mark have been anticipated and combined into a solemn summary-introduction:

Matt	Mark
4:23	1:39 (1:15); 6:6b
4:24a	1:28
4:24b	1:32,34
4:25	3:7-8
5:1	3:13
5:2	1:21

The inversion of Matt 8:2-4 (Mark 1:40-45) and Matt 8:14-16 (Mark 1:29-34) shows the dismantling of Mark's "day of Jesus" in Capernaum (1:21-39). The cleansing of the leper is brought forward as the opening section of Matt 8-9 (with the use of Mark 1:43-45 in Matt 9:30-31 by way of inclusion).

From Matt 8:18 on, the theme of discipleship appears and prepares for the discourse of Matt 10. Jesus' healing activity (4:23; 9:35) will be transmitted to the disciples (10:1). Matt has combined the Marcan material with Q passages; and here too there is a similar movement of anticipation before Matt 11:2 ("When John heard about the deeds of the Christ"), as we can see by comparing Matt and Luke (the two witnesses for Q).

Matt	Luke	
5-7 ———————	6:20-49	
8:5-13 ———————	7:1-10	
8:19-22 ◄		
9:37-10:16,40 ◥		
11:2-19 ———————	7:18-35	Answer to JBap
	9:57-60	Call of disciples
	10:2-12,16	Mission of disciples
11:21-24 ———————	10:13-15	
11:25-27 (28-30) ——	10:21-22	

Matt 4:23-11:1 concentrates on the teaching and healing of Jesus and on discipleship. It is a typical Matthean composition, unique in the Gospel, and all dislocations of Marcan pericopes are found in this editorial construct and nowhere else.

9   (C) Marcan Order in Luke. None of the transpositions in Matt 4:23-11:1 corresponds to a similar Lucan change of the Marcan order. Luke follows the order of Mark throughout the Gospel. The blocks of Marcan material are interrupted by the interpolation of non-Marcan material:

Mark	Luke	Lucan Interpolation
1:1-15	3:1-4:15	4:16-30
		Nazareth (cf. Mark 6:1-6a)
1:21-39	4:31-44	5:1-11
		Simon (cf. Mark 1:16-20)
1:40-3:19	5:12-6:19	6:20-8:3
		Little Interpolation
3:31-9:40	8:4-9:50	9:51-18:14
		Big Interpolation
10:13-52	18:15-43	19:1-28
		Zacchaeus, Parable
11:1-13:37	19:29-21:38	
14:1-16:8	22:1-24:12	

The visit to Nazareth, Mark 6:1-6a (comparable context at Luke 8:56/9:1), is placed by Luke at the beginning of Jesus' ministry. The call of the first disciples, Mark 1:16-20 (before the "day of Capernaum"), has its parallel in Luke 5:1-11, after the "day of Capernaum." Transpositions of individual pericopes are explicable on the basis of Mark. For instance, the inversion of Mark 3:7-12, 13-19 in Luke 6:12-16,17-19 comes before the Sermon

on the Plain. Mark 3:31-35 (before the parable section) is transferred to the conclusion of the parable section in Luke 8:19-21. See also the changes of order in the passion narrative (Luke 22:18,21-23,24-27,33-34; 22:56-62,63-65,66-71; 23:26-49 passim—Neirynck, Evangelica, 757-69).

10   The absence of an episode in the Marcan sequence is not always an omission in the strict sense. The episode can be lacking because of Lucan transferal to another context (transposition) or because of Lucan substitution giving preference to a parallel text from a different source (Luke's avoidance of doublets). In this last case, verbal reminiscences can betray Luke's knowledge of the Marcan text, and sometimes it will be difficult to distinguish between Luke's use of a special tradition and Lucan rewriting and expansion of Mark. In the list of Lucan omissions of Marcan pericopes (see the chart on the following page), minor omissions (cf. Mark 1:1,5,6,33,43; 2:13b,19b,27b, etc.) are not included. For some of them, also, an echo can be found in a distant context (cf. Mark 13:10 and Luke 24:47).

11   The most famous omission in Luke (at 9:17/18) is that of Mark 6:45-8:26 (the so-called Great Omission). Some have suggested that this section (74 verses) was missing in the form of Mark used by Luke (a truncated copy [a thesis now generally abandoned] or Proto-Mark). It should be observed, however, that the omissions by Matt of the individual passages in Mark 7:3-4; 7:31-37; and 8:22-26, and the omission by Luke of the entire section can hardly be cited as a negative agreement of the two Gospels against Mark. Nor can a source-critical conclusion be drawn from the resemblance between Luke 9:10-17,18-21 and John 6:1-15,66-69 (the feeding of the five thousand followed by Peter's confession); for John 6:16-21 recounts the walking on the water (par. Mark 6:45-52), which Luke omits. It is difficult to find a convincing reason for Luke's Great Omission, but there is probably more than one reason. Avoidance of doublets can be at least part of the explanation. The double feeding miracle in Mark 6:30-44 and 8:1-9 (underscored in the saying of 8:19-20) is absolutely unique in Mark; and the omission of 8:1-9 would involve also the omission of 8:14-21. More important, we note possible reminiscences of the omitted Mark 6:45-8:26, both in the immediate Lucan context of the omission (cf. Mark 6:45; 8:22 with Luke 9:10 as to Bethsaida; and Mark 6:46 with Luke 9:18 as to Jesus' praying alone), and elsewhere in Luke (cf. Mark 6:49-50 with Luke 24:36-40; Mark 6:55-56 with Luke 9:11c and Acts 5:15-16; Mark 7:1-5 with Luke 11:37-38; Mark 7:30 with Luke 7:10; Mark 8:11 with Luke 11:16,53-54; Mark 8:15 with Luke 12:1). Such reminiscences suggest that Luke knew the material in the omitted section of Mark and that there is no need to posit a Proto-Mark (Urmarkus) without Mark 6:45-8:26.

12   (D) Argument from Order. We have discussed the common order of the Triple Tradition pericopes and have explained differences from the Marcan order as editorial divergences by Matt and Luke. The argument from order, as understood since K. Lachmann (1835), constitutes the main reason for positing Marcan priority. The objection that the argument from order explains Matt in relationship to Mark on the one hand and then Luke in relationship to Mark on the other, but that the relationship among all three remains unexplained (W. R. Farmer, NTS 23 [1976-77] 294) is hardly convincing. Mark need not be explained "in relationship to both Matthew and Luke taken together," for it cannot be decided a priori that all three Synoptic Gospels should be interrelated. A solution of independence between Matt and Luke is possible.

OMISSION AND TRANSPOSITION OF MARCAN PERICOPES IN LUKE

Luke	Mark		Luke
(at vv below an *omission* of what is in Marcan column)			(at vv below a *transposition* and/or doublet of what is in Marcan column)
4:15 (4:16–30)	1:16–20		5:1–11
6:19 (6:20–8:3)	3:20–35	22–26	11:15,17–18
		27	11:21–22
		28–29	12:10
		31–35	8:19–21
8:18 (8:19–21)	4:26–34	30–32	13:18–19
8:56/9:1	6:1–6		4:16–30
9:9/10	6:17–29	17–18	3:19–20
9:17/18	6:45–8:26		(→ 11 above)
9:22/23	8:32–33		
9:36/37	9:11–13		
9:43a/b	9:28–29		
9:50 (9:51–18:14)	9:41–10:12	42	17:2
		50a	14:34
		10:11	16:18
		38	12:50
18:34/35	10:35–45	42–45	22:25–27
19:40 (19:41–44)	11:12–14		(13:6–9)
19:48/20:1	11:20–25	22–23	17:6
		24	(11:10)
		25	(11:4)
20:39/40	12:28–34		10:25–28
21:24/25	13:21–23		17:23
21:2/3	14:3–9		7:36–50
22:53/54	14:51–52		
22:66/67	14:56–61a		(Acts 6:13–14)
23:25/26	15:16–20		23:11

13   **(II) The Q Source.** Our treatment of order (→ 6–12 above) suggesting the priority of Mark as a solution to the Synoptic problem is incomplete, for the non-Marcan material shared by Matt and Luke is still to be considered.

(A) Existence of Q. The presence in Matt and Luke of similar non-Marcan passages (the Double Tradition), some of them with a high degree of verbal agreement, is explicable only if there was interdependence between Matt and Luke, or if (independently) each drew on a common source. We speak of source in the singular because a certain coincidence of order in the Double Tradition militates against positing a plurality of sources. The fact that some of the Double-Tradition material duplicates material in the Triple Tradition (and thus material that appears in Mark) suggests a second source, separate from Mark. Two further reasons can be given for positing Matthean and Lucan independence in the use of the source. (1) The more original tradition can be recognized sometimes in Matt and sometimes in Luke. (2) In the Triple Tradition Matt and Luke never agree in their divergences from the Marcan order of episodes (→ 6 above) and a similar observation can be made with regard to the Double Tradition. With the exception of the first two pericopes (JBap's preaching and Jesus' temptations, par. Mark 1:7–8 and 12–13) Matt and Luke have never inserted the Double-Tradition passages into the same Marcan context.

Recent studies tend to confine Q material to (all the) passages attested in *both* Matt and Luke. Too uncertain for consideration is the possibility that only Matt or only Luke preserved a passage from Q (although some scholars assign to Q Matt 10:5b–6; 10:23; Luke 6:24–26; 9:61–62; 12:32,35–38,49–50(54–56); 15:8–10; 17:28–29).

On the other hand, the Q origin of some Matt-Luke parallels is disputed because of insufficient verbal agreement (Luke 14:16–24; 19:12–27; 22:28–30) and because some short proverbial sayings might have come from oral tradition.

The original order of Q is probably best preserved in Luke. The different arrangement of the Q material in Matt can be explained by Matt's editorial compilation of great discourses and the insertion of the Q passages in Marcan contexts.

14   **(B) Synoptic Table of the Double Tradition** (in the Lucan order)

Matt	Luke	
3:7b–10 ———— 3:7–9		A
3:11–12 ———— 3:16b–17		
4:2b–11a ———— 4:2–13		B
5:3,6,4 ———— 6:20b–21		C
5:11–12 ———— 6:22–23		
5:39b–40,42 ⤬ 6:27–28		
5:44 ⤬ 6:29–30		
7:12 ———— 6:31		
5:46–47 ———— 6:32–33		
5:45,48 ———— 6:35b–36		
7:1–2 ———— 6:37a,38c		
15:14 ———— 6:39		
10:24–25a ———— 6:40		
7:3–5 ———— 6:41–42		
7:16–20 ———— 6:43–45		
7:21 ———— 6:46		
(12:33–35)		
7:24–27 ———— 6:46–49		
8:5–10,13 ———— 7:1–2,6b–10		D

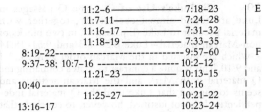

		11:2-6 ————————	7:18-23	E
		11:7-11 ———————	7:24-28	
		11:16-17 ——————	7:31-32	
		11:18-19 ——————	7:33-35	
8:19-22 --------------------------------			9:57-60	F
9:37-38; 10:7-16 ---------------------			10:2-12	
		11:21-23 ——————	10:13-15	
10:40 -----------------------------------			10:16	
		11:25-27 ——————	10:21-22	
		13:16-17	10:23-24	

Matt 5-7	Matt 10	Matt	Luke	
6:9-13			11:2-4	
7:7-11			11:9-13	
	(9:32-33)	12:22-30 ————————	11:14-15,17-23	G
		12:38-42	11:24-26	
		12:43-45	11:29-32	
5:15			11:33	
6:22-23			11:34-35	
		23:25-26,32 ————————	11:39-41,42	H
		6-7,27 ———————	43-44	
		4,29-30,13 ———————	46,47-48,52	
		23:34-36 ———————	11:49-51	
	10:26-33		12:2-9	
		12:32	12:10	
	10:19-20		12:11-12	
6:25-33			12:22-31	
6:19-21			12:32-34	
		24:43-44,45-51	12:39-40,42b-46	
	10:34-36		12:51-53	
5:25-26			12:58-59	
		13:31-32	13:18-19	
		33	20-21	
7:13-14			13:23-24	
7:22-23			13:25-27	
8:11-12			13:28-29	
		23:37-39 ———————	13:34-35	
		22:1-10	14:16-24	
	10:37-38		14:26-27	
5:13			14:34-35	
		18:12-14	15:4-7	
6:24			16:13	
		11:12-13	16:16	
5:18			16:17	
5:32			16:18	
		18:7	17:1	
		18:15,21-22	17:3b-4	
		17:20	17:6	
		24:26-27,28 ————————	17:23-24,37	I
		37-38 ———————	26-27,30	
	(10:39)		(17:33)	
		24:40-41	17:34-35	
		25:14-30 ————————	19:12-27	
		19:28	22:28,30	

15   **(C) Matt's Use of Q.** In the first part of the accompanying Double-Tradition table (sections A, B, C, D, E, F in Luke 3–10), the original order of the Q material is clearly detectable in Matt if we take into account the redactional anticipation of the mission discourse in Matt 10 before Jesus' answer to JBap in Matt 11:2-19 (→ 8 above). The Marcan contexts in Matt are worth noting: Mark 1:7-8 for A; 1:12-13 for B; 1:21/22 for C; 1:40-45/1:29-34 for D; 4:35/36; 6:7-11 for F. The first Q section in Matt that has not been inserted into a Marcan context is Matt 11:2-6. This, together with the inversion of the Q order of sections E and F, confirms that Jesus' answer to JBap has been prepared for by the editorial composition of Matt 4:23–11:1.

The material of the Q sermon in Luke 6:20-49, with the exception of the sayings in 6:39,40, has its counterpart in Matt 5–7. Differences in order are minimal: the use of Matt 7:12 at the conclusion of the central section is redactional. Matt has combined the Q sermon with the other Q material: Matt 5:13,15,18,25-26,32;

6:9-13,19-21,22-23,24,25-33; 7:7-11,13-14,22-23. Compare also the expansion of the mission discourse in Matt 10:(19-20?),26-33,34-36,37-38,(39?). The presentation of these passages in the order of the parallels in Luke 11-17 (in the table above) reveals some coincidence with individual sequences of Q sayings in Luke. The best illustration is Matt 7:13-14,22-23; 8:11-12; and if we leave aside these passages of Matt 5-7 and 10 (presumably Matt's first and second discourse compilations), the order of the remaining Q parallels agrees to a large extent with the Lucan order (sections G, H, I). The convergence with our conclusions regarding the Marcan order in Matt (→ 8 above) is impressive: first there is anticipation and concentration of the source material in Matt 5-10, and then (from Matt 12 on) no more changes of order.

16   Inversions of order in smaller units such as Luke 4:5-8,9-12; 6:21a,21b; 6:27-28,29-30; 10:5-7, 8-9; 11:31,32; and 11:24-26,29-32 can be explained by Matthean or Lucan rearrangement of the common source. Some sayings have a more elaborate form in Matt. The expansion of the Beatitudes in Matt 5:5,7-10 is the classic example. Verse 10 can be assigned to Matthean redaction, but some scholars consider 5:5,7-9 as a pre-Matthean addition to the common source: Q came to Matthew in an expanded form. Other sayings occasionally attributed to QMatt are: Matt 5:14b,19,41; 6:34; 7:6; 10:5b-6,23; 11:28-30; 18:16-17,18; the pre-Matthean form of the Q parables 22:1-14 and 25:14-30; and a pre-Matthean wording of some Q sayings. This QMatt as an intermediate stage between Q and Matt tends to reduce Matthew to a "conservative" redactor. Other scholars, however, emphasize more correctly Matthew's editorial revision of and additions to the traditional Q source material.

17   The Q influence can be seen in Matt's repetition of phrases and in its use of some Q expressions as redactional formulas. The phrase *gennēmata echidnōn,* "brood of vipers," in Matt 3:7 (Q) occurs again in 12:34 and 23:33; Matt 3:10b (Q) is repeated in 7:19; and Matt 3:12b (Q) is echoed in 13:30. The word *oligopistoi,* "of little faith," in Matt 6:30 (Q) becomes a favorite Matthean expression: 8:26; 16:8; 14:30; 17:20 (substantive). The phrase "there shall be weeping and gnashing of teeth" in Matt 8:12 (Q) appears again in 13:42,50; 22:13; 24:51; 25:30. The influence of the Q material in Matt 11:12-13; Luke 16:16 is traceable in Matt's use of "the law and the prophets" (5:17; 7:12; 22:40) and in the phrase *apo tote,* "from that time," in 4:17. The phrase "blind guides" in Matt 23:16,24 echoes 15:14 (Luke 6:39). Matt 10:15 (Luke 10:12) is used again in 11:24, and Matt 7:16-20 (Luke 6:43-44) in 12:33. Matt 12:22-23 (Luke 11:14) is used already at the conclusion of the miracles in chaps. 8-9; thus:

9:27-31	cf. 20:29-34	Mark 10:46-52
9:32-33	cf. 12:22-23	Luke 11:14 (Q)

But not all "doublets" in Matt are redactional doublets, explicable by editorial repetition of the traditional passages.

18   **(D) Doublets from the Source(s).** Passages occur twice in Matt or Luke, once in the Triple-Tradition material shared with Mark, and once in the Double-Tradition material of the same Gospel. For those who hold the priority of Mark "the proof from doublets" is part of the argument for the existence of a second source.

The accompanying list includes 14 instances of doublets in Matt (#5, 10, 11, 12), in Luke (#1, 2, 4, 8, 13, 14), or in both (#3, 6, 7, 9). The references are given in the order of Mark, with the non-Marcan parallels on the second line of the corresponding entry under Matt and Luke. Conflations in Matt ("condensed" doublets) are marked with an asterisk (#4, 13, 14).

#	Mark	Matt	Luke
1	4:21	–	8:16
		5:15	11:38
2	4:22	–	8:17
		10:26	12:2
3	4:25	13:12	8:18
		25:29	19:26
4	6:8-11	*10:7-14	9:3-5
			10:4-11
5	8:12	16:4	–
		12:39	11:29
6	8:34	16:24	9:23
		10:38	14:27
7	8:35	16:25	9:24
		10:39	17:33
8	8:38	(16:27)	9:26
		10:33	12:9
9	9:37	18:5	9:48
		10:40	10:16
10	10:11	19:9	–
		5:32	16:18
11	10:31	19:30	–
		20:16	13:30
12	11:22-23	21:21	–
		17:20	17:6
13	12:38-39	*23:6-7	20:46
			11:43
14	13:11	*10:19-20	21:14-15
			12:11-12

The Q origin of some of these sayings is not certain. Luke 17:33 (#7) can be a Lucan rewriting of Mark 8:35, one of the "Marcan" insertions in the Q discourse (17:25,31,33). The proverbial saying in Matt 20:16 (#11) can be a repetition of 19:30 (before the parable); and although the same inverted order of last/first is found in Luke 13:30, the non-Marcan common origin is only a possibility. But on the whole, the list of source doublets is impressive. Less convincing examples of overlapping (such as the parallels in Mark 4:8c; 9:35; 11:24; and 13:12) are not included.

19   Besides #4, 13, and 14 there are other instances of Matthean conflation and combination of Mark and Q where the Marcan passage is omitted in Luke (in the following list, #19 and 25 are dubious). Omissions of Mark both in Matt and Luke (#15, 21) are added in the list in order to include all instances of overlapping (Mark and Q).

#	Mark	Matt	Luke (Q)	
(15)	1:2	11:10 Q	7:27	
16	1:7-8	3:11-12	3:16-17	+ Mark
17	1:12-13	4:1-11	4:1-13	+ Mark
18	3:22-26	12:24-26	11:15,17-18	
(19)	3:27	12:29 (?)	11:21-22 (?)	Mark
20	3:28-29	12:31-32	12:10	
(21)	4:24	7:2 (Q)	6:38	
22	4:30-32	13:31-32	13:18-19	
23	9:42	18:6-7	17:1-2	+ Mark
24	9:49-50a	5:13	14:34-35	
(25)	12:21-34	22:34-40 (?)	10:25-28 (?)	Mark
26	13:21(-23)	24:23(-25),26	17:23	

20   **(E) Luke's Use of Q.** The Q passages in Luke are found almost exclusively, together with material peculiar to Luke (L passages), in two blocks of non-Marcan material—Luke 6:20-8:3 and 9:51-18:14 —which are inserted in the Marcan order at Mark 3/4 and 9/10. This is quite a contrast to Matt's conflating the Q material with Mark and the Marcan settings and seems to suggest that Luke used the Q material independently. It is not justified, however, to conclude that the juxtaposition of Q and L has its origin in a pre-Lucan gospel (Proto-Luke) into which the blocks of Marcan material were inserted by Luke. And it is a gratuitous assumption that the Q text in Luke 9:51-18:14 is wholly uninfluenced by Mark. Reminiscences of Mark can be shown in the doublets #7, 10, 14, 18, (19), 22, 23, 24 (Luke 10:25-28 comes from Mark 12:28-34).

The Lucan journey to Jerusalem had its basis in Mark (10:1,32), but Q provided the materials. The mission, at the beginning of the journey, and the day of the Son of Man, at the end (doublets of Luke 9:1-6 and 21:5-36), produce the effect of a duplication of the Marcan story line. This may be due to the insertion of the second source in the outline of Mark. Luke's division of the Q material into two separate interpolations corresponds to the division in Q itself: first the JBap sections surrounding the great sermon (from Luke 3:7-9 to 7:31-35), and then the central part beginning with the mission (Luke 9:57-10:16).

(Bibliography pertinent to Q: Edwards, R. A., *A Concordance to Q* [SBLSBS 7; Missoula, 1975]; *A Theology of Q* [Phl, 1976]. Havener, I., *Q: The Sayings of Jesus* [Wilmington, 1986]. Hoffmann, P., *Studien zur Theologie der Logienquelle* [NTAbh 8; Münster, 1972]. Kloppenborg, J. S., "Bibliography on Q," SBLASP 24 [1985] 103-26; *The Formation of Q* [Phl, 1987]. Lührmann, D., *Die Redaktion der Logienquelle* [WMANT 33; Neukirchen, 1969]. Neirynck, F., "Recent Developments in the Study of Q," in *Logia: Les paroles de Jésus—The Sayings of Jesus* [ed. J. Delobel; BETL 59; Louvain, 1982] 29-75. Neirynck, F. and F. Van Segbroeck, "Q Bibliography," ibid., 561-86; ETL 62 [1986] 157-65. Polag, A., *Die Christologie der Logienquelle* [WMANT 45; Neukirchen, 1977]; *Fragmenta Q* [Neukirchen, 1979]. Schenk, W., *Synopse zur Redenquelle der Evangelien* [Düsseldorf, 1981]. Schulz, S., *Q—Die Spruchquelle der Evangelisten* [Zurich, 1972]. Stoldt, H.-H., *History and Criticism of the Marcan Hypothesis* [Macon, 1980; also Ger orig., 2d ed. 1986]— against Q. Vassiliadis, P., *The Q-Document Hypothesis* [Athens, 1977]. Zeller, D., *Kommentar zur Logienquelle* [Stuttgart, 1984].)

21   **(III) The Originality of Mark.** If the arguments given above favor the priority of Mark, some points invoked against that priority need discussion.

     (A) Source-Critical Methodology. Scholars have offered general criteria for deciding which is the more ancient among parallel traditions. Sanders (*Tendencies*) has examined these criteria: increasing length and detail, diminishing semitism, and the use of direct discourse and conflation, as they occur both in the Synoptic Gospels and in postcanonical material. His conclusion is that "the tradition developed in opposite directions" and therefore "dogmatic statements" on the basis of these criteria are never justified (272). Since Sanders's book the criterion of increasingly becoming more specific has been withdrawn by Farmer (*Synoptic Problem* 228) from the list of canons he had originally proposed. In response to Farmer's canon of Palestinian or Jewish provenance as a sign of the more ancient, Tyson (450) reckons with the possibility of re-Judaization. The message of Sanders's *Tendencies* can be understood as a warning against generalization rather than an invitation to Synoptic skepticism. More important than his negative conclusion is the recommendation to be alert to "the editorial tendencies of each particular writer" (272).

22   Tyson's view accepts the classic principles of

literary criticism (e.g., as proposed by Burton) but finds application of these principles difficult: "The identification of glosses, redactional material, and interrupting insertions is a hazardous occupation." Stressing a diversity of viewpoints, Tyson sees some hope for a solution to the Synoptic problem in "a kind of literary criticism that brackets the source question" (451). But a mere synchronic approach, in structural analysis or rhetorical criticism (→ Hermeneutics, 71:55–70), can hardly become an appropriate method for solving problems of sources. On the other hand, the Synoptic problem is only one aspect of the source issue; for if Mark and Q are judged to be sources of Matt and Luke, then the traditions or sources behind Mark and Q deserve further study—as does also the origin of the material peculiar to Matt or to Luke. Among the upholders of the Two-Source hypothesis there is a great diversity of opinion concerning the history of all pre-Synoptic tradition. Synoptic source criticism and redaction criticism are inseparable for determining the interrelationship of the Synoptic Gospels.

The appearance of one Gospel's redactional material in another Gospel is probably the most useful criterion for determining interrelationship. It has been formulated by Farmer as the "inadvertent" criterion: "The presence, *in a fragmentary form*, in the work of one synoptic author, of the favorite expressions or redactional characteristics of one or both the other synoptic authors . . . constitutes *prima facie* evidence for literary dependence" ("Certain Results" 106). But the possibility that a phrase found in the source becomes a favorite expression in a later Gospel is also to be taken into consideration.

23   Streeter offered five arguments for accepting the priority of Mark, the fourth of which is the primitive character of Mark "shown by (*a*) the use of phrases likely to cause offence, which are omitted or toned down in the other Gospels, (*b*) roughness of style and grammar, and the preservation of Aramaic words." More simply we can distinguish two dimensions in a single argument for Marcan priority: *taxis* or order, which we have studied above (→ 6–12), and *lexis* or style. Arguing from order involves the macrostudy of contents and arrangement; arguing from style involves the microstudy of similarities and differences among the evangelists. (See, e.g., *FGL* 1. 107–27; U. Luz, *Das Evangelium nach Matthäus* [EKKNT 1/1; Zurich, 1985] 31–59.) The two main objections against the priority of Mark, now to be discussed, are drawn from such a microstudy.

(Farmer, W. R., "Certain Results . . . if Luke knew Matthew, and Mark knew Matthew and Luke," in *Synoptic Studies* [ed. C. M. Tuckett; Sheffield, 1984] 75–98. Sanders, E. P., *The Tendencies of the Synoptic Tradition* [SNTSMS 7; Cambridge, 1969]. Tyson, J. B., "The Two-Source Hypothesis. A Critical Appraisal," in Bellinzoni [ed.], *Two-Source Hypothesis* [→ 1 above] 437–52.)

24   **(B) Minor Agreements.** As old as the Marcan hypothesis itself is the problem of short passages where Matt and Luke agree with each other over against Mark (e.g., both Matt 8:2 and Luke 5:12 have the *kai idou* and *kyrie* missing in Mark 1:40). If both Matt and Luke depend on Mark in the Triple Tradition, how can they agree with each other and differ from Mark? The following suggestions have been made:

(a) *Proto-Mark* (or *Urmarkus*). Matt and Luke used the same earlier version of Mark, shorter than our Mark (hence the negative agreements or common "omissions") and different in wording (hence the coincidences in content, vocabulary, style, and grammar).

(b) *Deutero-Mark.* The Marcan text used by Matt and Luke is slightly different from our Mark, because of textual corruption, revision, or edition. That Mark was already combined

with Q in a Deutero-Marcan redaction has been suggested by Fuchs.

(c) *Common source.* Both Matt and Luke depend on another source besides Mark: a primitive Gospel, Proto-Matthew (Vaganay, Boismard; → 30–31 below), or depend on Gospel fragments or oral tradition.

(d) *Luke's dependence on Matt.* Luke, who follows Mark as his basic source in the Triple Tradition, is also acquainted with and influenced by Matt. See R. H. Gundry, *Matthew* (GR, 1982) 4 and *passim*.

25   The writings of Vaganay, Farmer, and Boismard have given new prestige to the minor-agreement issue. The problem is centered not so much on the difficulty of some individual cases (Goulder), but on the high number of agreements, the concentration in particular passages, and the conjunction of negative and positive agreements. Although they are cited as objection number one against the priority of Mark, it can be argued that often these agreements are in fact not so striking and that for most of the "significant" agreements a satisfactory redactional explanation can be given.

The minor agreements are, first of all, agreements against Mark and the primary cause of the common change that appears in Matt and Luke is the text of Mark. Mark's overuse of *kai*, of historic presents, pleonasms, etc.; Mark's having Jesus ask questions and the disciples remain unintelligent; and many other motifs in Mark are "corrected" in Matt and Luke. A priori it is not unlikely that two independent redactions on the basis of Mark show some coincidences. "If Matt omits something, it is unattractive to him for some reason; and what is unattractive to one Christian author has by that very fact an increased chance of being unattractive to another" (McLoughlin, *DRev* 90 [1972] 202).

26   The word "atomization" has been used pejoratively with reference to the variety of explanations of the agreements. But there is also the atomization of the evidence by concentrating on one passage, collecting all sorts of agreements without studying each type of agreement, together with similar changes of Mark elsewhere in Matt or Luke. The minor agreement works like a signal by drawing our attention to Matthean or Lucan noncoincidental parallels. Cf. Neirynck, *Minor Agreements* 197–288, for material from the Triple Tradition.

It is, of course, not a reasonable expectation that in every instance a redactional explanation can be made acceptable to all proponents of Marcan priority. Some will be inclined to ascribe one or another agreement to the influence of Q. Others will reckon with oral tradition and the possibility of tradition variants. Others will give more importance to textual factors such as corruption and harmonization. But these various explanations given to residual "difficult cases" do not at all modify the general Synoptic hypothesis. M. Goulder's contention that some agreements are Matthean in style but characteristically un-Lucan (*NTS* 24 [1977–78] 218–34) has been answered by Tuckett (*NTS* 30 [1984] 130–42). M.-É. Boismard's similar observation with regard to Luke 9:10–11 (*NTS* 26 [1979–80] 1–17) has been answered by Neirynck (*ETL* 60 [1984] 25–44). On Matt 26:68, see *ETL* 63 (1987) 5–47.

(Fuchs, A., *Die Entwicklung der Beelzebulkontroverse bei den Synoptikern* [Linz, 1980]. McLoughlin, S., "Les accords mineurs Mt-Lc contre Mc et le problème synoptique," in *De Jésus aux Évangiles* [ed. I. de la Potterie; BETL 25; Louvain, 1967] 17–40. Neirynck, *Minor Agreements; Evangelica* 769–810.)

27   **(C) Duality in Mark.** Sometimes when there is a redundant or duplicate expression in Mark (1:32: "It being evening, when the sun had set"), Matt has a parallel to one part of the Marcan expression (Matt

8:16: "It being evening") while Luke has a parallel to the other part (Luke 4:41: "the sun having set"). In the Griesbach or "Two-Gospel" hypothesis, such duplicates are explained in terms of Mark's using and combining Matt and Luke, or, in Rolland's adaptation of the Griesbach hypothesis, as combinations of a (Proto-) Matthean source and a (Proto-) Lucan source. On the thesis of Marcan priority, this phenomenon is explained through Matt's and Luke's independent use of Mark. Three observations: (1) The Griesbach approach whereby Mark has combined Matt and Luke would explain only some of Mark's many dual expressions; duality is a frequent feature of Marcan style. (2) The dual expression in Mark is not a mechanical combination of two parts but an original stylistic unit with a progression to greater precision in the second half of the expression. (3) The parallel to half the expression in Matt and to half in Luke is not a selection made at random or by chance. In many instances the choice of each evangelist can be explained in the light of the redactional context and the general tendencies of the respective Gospel.

(Neirynck, F., *Duality in Mark: Contributions to the Study of the Markan Redaction* [BETL 31; Louvain, 1972]; "Les expressions doubles chez Marc et le problème synoptique," *ETL* 59 [1983] 303–30. Rolland, P., *Les premiers évangiles: Un nouveau regard sur le problème synoptique* [Paris, 1984]; articles in *RB* 89 [1982] 370–405; 90 [1983] 23–79, 161–201. Tuckett, *Revival* 16–21.)

28   (D) Mark and Q. The Two-Source theory as a solution to the Synoptic problem has obvious limitations. The assumption of Marcan priority does not preclude a variety of opinions regarding many aspects of Mark. Some scholars recognize (rightly) characteristics of Marcan usage throughout the Gospel (Dschulnigg), whereas for others "no redactional style exists in Mark" (Trocmé). There is no consensus about the sources of Mark or about the existence of pre-Marcan collections, especially of a traditional passion narrative (see proposal of R. Pesch, *Das Markusevangelium 2* [HTKNT 2; Freiburg, 1977], and analysis by Neirynck, *Evangelica* 491–515).

(Dschulnigg, P., *Sprache, Redaktion und Intention des Markus-Evangeliums* [SBB 11; Stuttgart, 1984]. Pryke, E. J., *Redactional Style in the Markan Gospel* [SNTSMS 33; Cambridge, 1978]. Reiser, M., *Syntax und Stil des Markusevangeliums* [WUNT 2/11; Tübingen, 1984]. Trocmé, E., *The Passion as Liturgy* [London, 1983].)

29 Opinions diverge concerning Mark's knowledge and use of Q. The overlapping sections of Mark and Q are listed above (→ 18). It is common practice to give a tentative description of Mark's redactional activity by comparing the saying in Mark with the Q version. But Mark's dependence on Q (Lambrecht) and not on individual traditional sayings or on some pre-Q collections of sayings will remain a mere supposition as long as no demonstration is given of Marcan dependence on what is proper to Q *redaction*. Research on the hypothetical Q source is still in progress, especially in regard to the growth of the sayings tradition and stages of composition and redaction.

(On Mark and Q: Devisch, M., in *L'évangile selon Marc* [ed. M. Sabbe; BETL 34; Louvain, 1974] 59–91. Lambrecht, J., *Bib* 47 [1966] 321–60; also in *Logia* [→ 20 above] 277–304. Laufen, R., *Die Doppelüberlieferungen des Logienquelle und des Markusevangeliums* [BBB 54; Bonn, 1980]. Neirynck, in *Logia* [→ 20 above] 41–53.)

30   (IV) Alternative Solutions. The priority of Mark has often been advocated simply as more plausible than other proposed theories.
    (A) Modified Two-Source Theory. The

claim of Papias (in Eusebius, *HE* 3.39.16) that Matthew collected the *logia* (sayings) of the Lord in the Hebr (= Aram) language has left its mark on Synoptic-problem discussion, even though such a collection has never been discovered (→ Church Pronouncements, 72:28). In the mid-1900s objections were raised against the Two-Source theory, mainly by Catholic scholars pleading for Matthean priority in the form of a Proto-Matthew (L. Cerfaux, L. Vaganay) or of canonical Matt, according to the pure Augustinian tradition (J. Chapman, B. C. Butler). Vaganay's theory is in fact a primitive gospel theory (Mg or the Gk translation of Aram Matt as the common source of Matt, Mark, and Luke), combined with the Two-Source theory. Purportedly, Mark is used as a source by both canonical Matt and Luke, while the Double-Tradition sayings material in the central section of Luke is derived from a supplementary source S. One can schematize Vaganay (whose theory was most influential in the 1950s) in this manner:

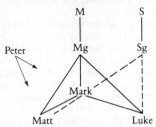

31 The complex theory of M.-É. Boismard constitutes a continuation and further development of Vaganay's hypothesis. Here too the Two-Source theory is still recognizable in the diagram (Q and Intermediary Mark). More attention is given to the pre-Synoptic sources: the primitive gospels A, B, and C, and the document Q at the first level, three Proto-Gospels at the intermediary level (Multiple-Stage hypothesis). One can schematize Boismard thus:

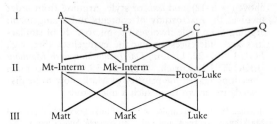

The combination of sources in Mark (cf. Griesbach, who had Mark combining Matt and Luke) takes place both in Intermediary Mark and in final Mark.

    X. Léon-Dufour and A. Gaboury (1970) proposed a fragmentation of sources, at least with regard to Mark 1:14–6:13 and parallels (Multiple-Document theory).

(Boismard, M.-É., *Synopse des quatre évangiles*, 2–3 [Paris, 1972–77]. Neirynck, F., *Jean et les Synoptiques* [BETL 49; Louvain, 1979]; *Evangelica* 691–723 [on Gaboury]. Vaganay, *Le problème*.)

32   (B) Luke's Dependence on Matt. B. C. Butler's more radical defense of Matthean priority (*The Originality of St Matthew* [Cambridge, 1951]; "St. Luke's Debt to St. Matthew," *HTR* 32 [1939] 237–308) is at the origin of an anti-Streeter reaction in British and American Gospel studies, with A. Farrer's "On Dispensing with Q," in *Studies in the Gospels* (Fest. R. H. Lightfoot; ed. D. E. Nineham; Oxford, 1955) 55–88, and W. R. Farmer's *Synoptic Problem* (1964).

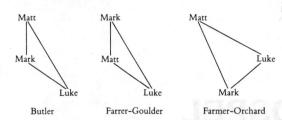

Butler   Farrer-Goulder   Farmer-Orchard

In all three hypotheses Luke borrowed the Double-Tradition material from Matt and there is no need for a hypothetical sayings source. With regard to Mark, conflicting views are defended: absolute priority of Mark (Farrer), Mark's dependence on Matt (Butler), Mark as a secondary combination of Matt and Luke (Farmer).

Luke's use of Matt is not without serious difficulties, and the main reasons for denying such use are summed up by J. A. Fitzmyer: Luke is apparently reluctant to reproduce typically Matthean "additions" within the Triple Tradition; it is difficult to explain adequately why Luke would want to break up Matt's sermons, esp. the Sermon on the Mount; with the exceptions noted above (→ 13) Luke has never inserted the Double-Tradition material into the same Marcan context as Matt; in the Double-Tradition material sometimes Matt, sometimes Luke has preserved the more original setting; finally, if Luke depends on Matt, why has he almost constantly omitted Matthean material in episodes where there is no Marcan parallel?

33 To explain the minor agreements between Matt and Luke over against Mark in the Triple Tradition, R. H. Gundry (→ 24d above) and R. Morgenthaler (see Neirynck, *Evangelica* 752–57) would allow a subsidiary influence of Matt upon Luke. Elsewhere, however, in the Triple Tradition Luke would have been using Mark despite his knowledge of Matt. This observation refutes the thesis of M. Goulder (*NTS* 24 [1977–78] 218–34), who rejects the existence of Q because of 12 instances of non-Lucan style where Luke agrees with Matt against Mark. If Luke can be eclectic in using Matt and Mark when he knows both, he can be eclectic in using Matt and Q if he knows both.

For a critical examination of E. P. Sanders's much-quoted list of exceptions to the claim that Matt and Luke never agree in arrangement against Mark (*NTS* 15 [1968–69] 249–61), see Neirynck, *Evangelica* 738–43; *FGL* 1. 67–69.

34 **(C) Griesbach or Two-Gospel Hypothesis.** The essential thesis of J. J. Griesbach (1789) that Mark conflated and alternatively depended on Matt and Luke remains the same in the neo-Griesbachian Two-Gospel hypothesis (W. R. Farmer, B. Orchard, D. L. Dungan). A Griesbach-approach commentary has been written by C. S. Mann, *Mark* (AB 27; GC, 1986). A description and critical evaluation of the theory are supplied by Tuckett (*Revival*) and Neirynck (*ETL* 59 [1982] 111–22).

The neo-Griesbachians differ from Griesbach in two ways. (1) Luke's dependence on Matt is explicitly affirmed and studied. (See B. Orchard, *Matthew, Luke and Mark* [Manchester, 1976].) (2) The relevance of patristic evidence is emphasized, esp. Clement of Alexandria's reference to "the gospels with genealogies which are written first" (in Eusebius, *HE* 6.14.5; see H. Merkel,

ETL 60 [1984] 382–85). Both aspects, together with the traditional view of Matthean originality, are studied more particularly by B. Orchard, who is also the author of a synopsis (in the "chronological" order: Matt, Luke, Mark; see Neirynck, *ETL* 61 [1985] 161–66).

Since Farmer's book (1964), the Griesbach hypothesis has been discussed in numerous Gospel conferences, from Pittsburgh (1970) to Jerusalem (1984), with a great variety of published papers; but new developments in the theory can scarcely be noted.

35 **(D) John and the Synoptics.** Perhaps most Johannine scholars hold that John is not dependent in a major way on the canonical, final form of the Synoptic Gospels (see D. M. Smith, *Johannine Christianity* [Columbia, 1984] 95–172); for the contrary view, see Neirynck, *Jean* (→ 31 above). There is virtually no support for the dependence of the Synoptic evangelists on the final form of John. Thus, John can tell us little about the composition of the Synoptic Gospels, which is the core of the Synoptic problem. Nor do possible contacts between pre-Synoptic and pre-Johannine sources have much direct bearing on the issue. Highly problematic is the use of John as a witness to a hypothetical Q source or, in Boismard's theory (→ 31 above), to a hypothetical C gospel (composed in Aramaic in Palestine about 50), supposed to be a Synoptic source as well.

36 **(E) Apocryphal Gospels.** Most apocryphal gospels were composed in the 2d cent. or later, with only a few possibly datable to AD 100–150. There is no convincing evidence that in the form known to us they were written as early as the canonical Gospels. The Jewish-Christian gospels (known through fragmentary patristic citations; → Apocrypha, 67:59–61) played a role in discussions of Aramaic Matt (→ 30 above).

The current debate concerns the primitiveness of the traditions transmitted in apocrypha such as Papyrus Egerton 2, *SGM,* and *Gos. Pet.* (→ Apocrypha, 67:62,63, 72). The more probable hypothesis involves dependence (oral or written) of the apocryphal gospels on the canonical Gospels (see Neirynck, *ETL* 44 [1968] 301–6; 55 [1979] 223–24; 61 [1985] 153–60; R. E. Brown, *NTS* 33 [1987] 321–43). From different viewpoints, however, Boismard, Cameron, Koester, and M. Smith have argued to the contrary (see J. D. Crossan, *Four Other Gospels* [Minneapolis, 1985]). The genre of the Synoptic sayings source Q has a representative in *Gos. Thom.* (→ Apocrypha, 67:67); but dubious are Koester's claim of "the absence of any influence of the canonical gospels" and his dating to the 1st cent. AD (*Introduction to the NT* [Phl, 1982] 2. 152). For comparing noncanonical and canonical sayings, see J. D. Crossan, *Sayings Parallels* (Phl, 1986).

37 **(F) Ongoing Study.** Literature on the Synoptic problem continues to appear, supplementing 1, 2, 3, 20, and 23 above respectively: R. H. Stein, *The Synoptic Problem* (GR, 1987). M.-E. Boismard and A. Lamouille, *Synopsis graeca quattuor evangeliorum* (Louvain, 1986; see *ETL* 63 [1987] 119–35). R. L. Lindsey and E. C. dos Santos, *A Comparative Greek Concordance of the Synoptic Gospels* (vol. 1; Jerusalem, 1985; see *ETL* 63 [1987] 375–83). J. S. Kloppenborg, *Q Parallels: Synopsis, Critical Notes and Concordance* (Sonoma, 1988). W. Schenk, *Die Sprache des Matthäus* (Göttingen, 1987; see *ETL* 63 [1987] 413–19).

41

THE GOSPEL ACCORDING TO MARK

Daniel J. Harrington, S.J.

BIBLIOGRAPHY

1 Best, E., *Mark: The Gospel as Story* (Edinburgh, 1983). Blevins, J. L., *The Messianic Secret in Markan Research 1901–1976* (Washington, 1981). Ernst, J., *Das Evangelium nach Markus* (RNT; Regensburg, 1981). Gnilka, J., *Das Evangelium nach Markus* (EKKNT 2/1-2; Zurich, 1978–79). Harrington, W., *Mark* (NTM 4; Wilmington, 1979). Hultgren, A., *Jesus and His Adversaries* (Minneapolis, 1979). Humphrey, H. M., *A Bibliography for the Gospel of Mark 1954–1980* (NY, 1981). Kealy, S. P., *Mark's Gospel: A History of Its Interpretation* (NY, 1982). Kee, H. C., *Community of the New Age* (Phl, 1977). Kelber, W. H., *The Kingdom in Mark: A New Place and a New Time* (Phl, 1974); *The Oral and the Written Gospel* (Phl, 1983). Kermode, F., *The Genesis of Secrecy* (Cambridge MA, 1979). Kingsbury, J. D.,

The Christology of Mark's Gospel (Phl, 1983). Marxsen, W., *Mark the Evangelist* (Nash, 1969). Nineham, D. E., *Saint Mark* (Phl, 1978). Pesch, R., *Das Markusevangelium* (HTKNT 2/1-2; Freiburg, 1976–77). Quesnell, Q., *The Mind of Mark* (AnBib 38; Rome, 1969). Rhoads, D. and D. Michie, *Mark as Story* (Phl, 1982). Robbins, V. K., *Jesus the Teacher* (Phl, 1984). Robinson, J. M., *The Problem of History in Mark and Other Marcan Studies* (Phl, 1982). Schweizer, E., *The Good News According to Mark* (London, 1970). Taylor, V., *The Gospel According to St. Mark* (London, 1966). Tuckett, C. (ed.), *The Messianic Secret* (Phl, 1983). Wrede, W., *The Messianic Secret* (Cambridge, 1971).

DBSup 6. 835–62. *IDBSup* 571–73. Kümmel, *INT* 80–101. Wik-Schm, *ENT* 207–24.

INTRODUCTION

2 (I) Authorship; Date and Place of Composition. Nothing in the Gospel identifies its author by name, since the label "according to Mark" was added later. That label probably reflects the identification made in patristic times between the author of this Gospel and John Mark (Acts 12:12,25; 13:5-13; 15:37-39; Col 4:10; Phlm 24; 2 Tim 4:11). Although Mark is usually portrayed as Paul's companion, 1 Pet 5:13 describes him as Peter's coworker ("my son Mark"). The earliest explicit statement about Mark as the author of a Gospel came from Papias of Hierapolis (early 2d cent., quoted in Eusebius, *HE* 3.39.15): "Mark, having become Peter's interpreter, wrote down accurately whatever he remembered of what was said or done by the Lord, however not in order." On the strength of Papias's statement and the affirmation of it by other early Christian writers, the Gospel is traditionally ascribed to Mark the "interpreter of Peter" and placed in Rome after Peter's death *ca.* AD 64–67.

Although the patristic tradition is unanimous in asserting that Mark wrote this Gospel, some problems with Papias's witness suggest caution in regarding Mark as the "Gospel of Peter." What does "interpreter" (*herme-*

neutēs) mean? Is the comment about the order of material an apology for differences among the Gospels? Why did Papias go on to insist on the accuracy and veracity of the Gospel? Although such questions do not warrant cavalier dismissal of the Papias tradition about Mark, they warn against naïve reliance upon it. Peter appears in many incidents in the Gospel and could have been a source of information about sayings and deeds of Jesus. Nevertheless, as an interpretative principle, it is better not to lean too heavily on the assumption that Peter was Mark's sole or even primary conduit to Jesus' public ministry.

That Mark wrote in Rome is suggested not only by Papias but also by Latin loanwords in the Gk text and by the atmosphere of impending persecution that pervades the Gospel. Since Mark 13 does not presuppose the destruction of the Jerusalem Temple, the Gospel was most likely composed before AD 70. A setting in the 60s at Rome seems best, for then the Christian community lived under the threat (or reality) of persecution and looked upon incipient revolt in Palestine as a source of potential trouble for the Jewish (and even Gentile) Christians at Rome.

3   (II) Literary Structure and Content. As the outline proposed below indicates, the Gospel displays a tight geographical-theological structure. The geographical aspect features the movement from Galilee to Jerusalem. After the prologue (1:1–15), the first half of the Gospel describes Jesus' activity in Galilee and beyond (1:16–8:21). The second half focuses on Jerusalem: the journey from Galilee to Jerusalem (8:22–10:52), the symbolic actions and teachings during the first part of passion week in Jerusalem (11:1–13:37), and the passion and death there (14:1–16:8). There may be some narrative opposition between Galilee and Jerusalem (acceptance vs. rejection, order vs. chaos), though this insight should not be applied too mechanically.

The theological aspect of the outline highlights the authority (*exousia*) of Jesus. Once we know who Jesus is (1:1–15), we see his authority revealed in work and word (1:16–3:6), his rejection by his own people (3:7–6:6a), and the misunderstanding of him even by his disciples (6:6b–8:21). On the way up to Jerusalem (8:22–10:52), Jesus clarifies the nature of his authority and spells out its consequences for his followers. At Jerusalem he encounters resistance to his teaching (11:1–13:37) and meets a cruel and tragic death at the hands of those who reject his authority (14:1–16:8).

With the imposition of this geographical-theological outline on his sources, Mark created the literary genre of Gospel. Paul and other early Christians used the term *euangelion,* "gospel," as the "good news" about God's action in Jesus Christ. As the first one to write an account of Jesus' ministry in an orderly fashion, Mark appears to have created a model followed and developed by other evangelists.

Mark had various kinds of traditions at his disposal: sayings, parables, controversies, healing stories and other miracles, and probably a passion narrative. Some of these traditions may also have been grouped: controversies (2:1–3:6), seed parables (4:1–34), miracles (4:35–5:43), etc. Mark gave an order and a plot to these sayings and incidents, connected them with bridge passages, and added parenthetical comments for the sake of his readers.

Mark wrote his Gospel to deepen the faith of the members of his community. By showing them how the traditions about Jesus related to their belief in the saving significance of the cross and resurrection, the evangelist equipped them to face persecution and resist the temptations of their world. Other theories about Mark's purpose are more speculative: to preserve the reminiscences of Peter and other eyewitnesses, to combat a false christology or some other heresy, to provide a lectionary for Christian worship, or to provide material for Christian baptismal or Easter liturgies.

(Kuhn, H.-W. *Ältere Sammlungen im Markusevangelium* [SUNT 8; Göttingen, 1971]. Maloney, E. C., *Semitic Interference in Marcan Syntax* [SBLDS 51; Chico, 1981]. Neirynck, F., *Duality in Mark: Contributions to the Study of Markan Redaction* [BETL 31; Leuven, 1972]. Pryke, E. J., *Redactional Style in the Markan Gospel* [SNTSMS 33; Cambridge, 1978]. Reiser, M., *Syntax und Stil des Markusevangeliums im Licht der hellenistischen Volksliteratur* [WUNT 2/11; Tübingen, 1984]. Robbins, *Jesus the Teacher.* Standaert, B., *L'Evangile selon Marc: Composition et genre littéraire* [Bruges, 1978]. Stock, A., *Call to Discipleship: A Literary Study of Mark's Gospel* [GNS 1; Wilmington, 1982]. Weeden, T. J., *Mark — Traditions in Conflict* [Phl, 1971].)

4   (III) Marcan Theology. The focus of Mark's theology is the focus of Jesus' theology — the kingdom of God. What is taught about christology (who Jesus is) and discipleship (response to Jesus) takes its framework from the kingdom of God. The prologue of the Gospel (1:1–15) climaxes in a sample of Jesus' preaching: "The time is fulfilled, and the kingdom of God has drawn near. Repent and believe in the good news." In Judaism of Jesus' time the "kingdom of God" referred to the definitive display of God's lordship at the end of history and its acknowledgment by all creation. Much of Jesus' teaching (esp. the parables) aimed at deepening the people's understanding of the coming kingdom and preparing for it. Even his healings appear as anticipations of what life in God's kingdom will be like. That kingdom is now largely hidden, though in Jesus it is inaugurated and anticipated.

While Jesus taught about the kingdom of God in parables, his life was really the parable par excellence of the kingdom. Mark's message is that whoever wishes to understand the kingdom must look at Jesus the healer, the teacher, and the crucified-and-risen one. The large amount of space devoted to healings and exorcisms proves that Mark knew and revered Jesus as a wonderworker. The miracles are balanced by teaching in both word and deed. But the way in which Mark has outlined the story of Jesus suggests that the passion and death constituted its climax. Without the cross, the portrayals of Jesus as wonder-worker and teacher are unbalanced and without a directing principle. Within this framework, Mark made ample use of the common stock of christological titles available: Messiah, Son of God, Son of Man, Lord, Son of David, Suffering Servant, and Suffering Just One.

A peculiar feature of Marcan christology is often called "the messianic secret." The idea took its rise from the several instances in which Jesus commands people to be silent about his action or identity (see 1:34,44; 3:12; 5:43; 7:36; 8:26,30; 9:9). W. Wrede explained this phenomenon as Mark's way of accounting for the fact that Jesus in his public ministry neither claimed to be the Messiah nor was recognized as such. Jesus, indeed, does not take to himself the title of Messiah without serious qualification (see 8:27–38). Moreover, the whole thrust of Mark shows that the real meaning of Jesus' messiahship became clear only with his death and resurrection. Also, since in some Jewish circles (*Pss. Sol.* 17) the longed-for Messiah had political and military functions, the Marcan ambivalence in this matter may reflect an unwillingness to provoke the Roman authorities. However, the commands to silence and the development of Jesus' messiahship in Mark are more complex than Wrede's theory allowed.

The response to Jesus' person is discipleship. Mark's presentation of the earliest disciples was based on the parallelism between them and the members of his community. The passages relating the call of the first disciples (1:16–20; 2:13–14; 3:13–19; 6:6b–13) are among the most positive stories in the Gospel. The Marcan ideal of discipleship is "being with" Jesus, sharing his mission of preaching and healing (3:14–15). As the narrative proceeds, the disciples repeatedly fail to understand Jesus (6:52; 8:14–21). On the way to Jerusalem Jesus predicts his passion and resurrection three times (8:31; 9:31; 10:33–34); each prediction is followed by disciples' misunderstanding (8:32–33; 9:32–37; 10:35–45). The passion narrative pivots on the betrayal of Jesus by Judas (14:17–21; 14:43–52) and the denial of Jesus by Peter (14:26–31; 14:54,66–72). In the first half of the Gospel the disciples are portrayed as examples to be imitated; in the second half, they are examples to be avoided. The effect of this shift is to highlight the person of Jesus as the only one who deserves imitation. But the idea that Mark waged a polemic against the disciples seems farfetched.

(Achtemeier, P. J. "'He Taught Them Many Things': Reflections on Marcan Christology," *CBQ* 42 [1980] 465–81. Ambrozic, A., *The Hidden Kingdom* [CBQMS 2; Washington, 1972]. Blevins, *Messianic Secret*. Kertelge, K., *Die Wunder Jesu im Markusevangelium* [SANT 23; Munich, 1970]. Kingsbury, *The Christology of Mark's Gospel*. Räisänen, H., *Das "Messiasgeheimnis" im Markusevangelium* [Helsinki, 1976]. Steichele, H.-J., *Der leidende Sohn Gottes* [Regensburg, 1980]. Tuckett [ed.], *Messianic Secret*.)

5   (IV) Outline. The Gospel according to Mark is outlined as follows:

(I) Prologue (1:1–15)
(II) Jesus' Authority Is Revealed in Galilee (1:16–3:6)
  (A) Call of the First Disciples (1:16–20)
  (B) The Eventful Day in Capernaum (1:21–45)
    (a) Teaching and Healing at Capernaum (1:21–28)
    (b) Healing of Peter's Mother-in-Law (1:29–31)
    (c) Evening Healings (1:32–34)
    (d) Jesus' Temporary Withdrawal (1:35–39)
    (e) Healing of the Leper (1:40–45)
  (C) Five Conflict Stories (2:1–3:6)
    (a) Healing of a Paralytic and Forgiveness of Sin (2:1–12)
    (b) Call of Levi (2:13–17)
    (c) Question about Fasting (2:18–22)
    (d) Work on the Sabbath (2:23–28)
    (e) Healing on the Sabbath (3:1–6)
(III) Jesus Is Rejected in Galilee (3:7–6:6a)
  (A) Positive Responses (3:7–19a)
    (a) People Come to Jesus (3:7–12)
    (b) Appointment of the Twelve (3:13–19a)
  (B) Negative Responses (3:19b–35)
  (C) Parables and Explanations (4:1–34)
    (a) Setting (4:1–2)
    (b) Parable of the Seeds (4:3–9)
    (c) Parables' Purpose (4:10–12)
    (d) Explanation (4:13–20)
    (e) Parabolic Sayings (4:21–25)
    (f) Parable of the Growing Seed (4:26–29)
    (g) Parable of the Mustard Seed (4:30–32)
    (h) Summary (4:33–34)
  (D) Three Miraculous Actions (4:35–5:43)
    (a) Stilling the Storm (4:35–41)
    (b) Exorcising a Demon (5:1–20)
    (c) Healing the Sick (5:21–43)
  (E) Rejection of Jesus by His Own People 6:1–6a)
(IV) Jesus Misunderstood by Disciples in Galilee and Beyond (6:6b–8:21)
  (A) The Disciples' Mission and John's Death (6:6b–34)
    (a) The Disciples' Mission (6:6b–13)
    (b) John's Death (6:14–29)
    (c) The Disciples' Return (6:30–34)
  (B) Acts of Power and a Controversy (6:35–7:23)
    (a) Feeding the Five Thousand (6:35–44)
    (b) Walking on the Waters (6:45–52)
    (c) Healing the Sick (6:53–56)
    (d) Controversy about Ritual Purity (7:1–23)
  (C) More Acts of Power and a Controversy (7:24–8:21)
    (a) Healing a Gentile Woman's Daughter (7:24–30)
    (b) Healing a Man Incapable of Hearing and Speaking Properly (7:31–37)
    (c) Feeding the Four Thousand (8:1–10)
    (d) Controversy about Signs (8:11–21)
(V) Jesus Instructs His Disciples on the Way to Jerusalem (8:22–10:52)

  (A) Healing a Blind Man (8:22–26)
  (B) Jesus the Christ (8:27–30)
  (C) First Instruction on Christology and Discipleship (8:31–9:29)
    (a) First Passion Prediction and Its Consequences for Discipleship (8:31–38)
    (b) Jesus' Transfiguration and the Elijah Question (9:1–13)
    (c) Healing a Possessed Boy (9:14–29)
  (D) Second Instruction on Christology and Discipleship (9:30–10:31)
    (a) Second Passion Prediction and Its Consequences for Discipleship (9:30–50)
    (b) Jesus' Teaching on Marriage and Divorce (10:1–12)
    (c) Jesus' Blessing of the Children (10:13–16)
    (d) Jesus' Teachings about Riches (10:17–31)
  (E) Third Instruction on Christology and Discipleship (10:32–45)
    (a) Third Passion Prediction (10:32–34)
    (b) Its Consequences for Discipleship (10:35–45)
  (F) Healing Blind Bartimaeus (10:46–52)
(VI) The First Part of Passion Week in Jerusalem (11:1–13:37)
  (A) Entrance on the First Day (11:1–11)
  (B) Prophetic Teachings on the Second Day (11:12–19)
  (C) More Teachings on the Third Day (11:20–13:37)
    (a) Explanations (11:20–26)
    (b) Controversies (11:27–12:37)
      (i) Jesus' authority (11:27–33)
      (ii) Parable of the vineyard (12:1–12)
      (iii) Taxes to Caesar (12:13–17)
      (iv) Resurrection (12:18–27)
      (v) The great commandment (12:28–34)
      (vi) David's Son (12:35–37)
    (c) Scribes and a Widow (12:38–44)
    (d) Jesus' Final Discourse (13:1–37)
      (i) Introduction (13:1–4)
      (ii) Beginning of the sufferings (13:5–13)
      (iii) The great tribulation (13:14–23)
      (iv) Triumph of the Son of Man (13:24–27)
      (v) Exhortation to confidence and vigilance (13:28–37)
(VII) Jesus' Death in Jerusalem (14:1–16:20)
  (A) The Anointing and the Last Supper (14:1–31)
    (a) Plotting and Anointing (14:1–11)
    (b) Arrangements for the Passover Meal (14:12–16)
    (c) The Last Supper (14:17–31)
      (i) Prediction of Judas's treachery (14:17–21)
      (ii) The supper (14:22–25)
      (iii) Prediction of Peter's denial (14:26–31)
  (B) Jesus' Prayer and Arrest (14:32–52)
    (a) Gethsemane (14:32–42)
    (b) Arrest (14:43–52)
  (C) The Trials (14:53–15:15)
    (a) Trial before the High Priest; Peter's Denial (14:53–72)
    (b) The Trial before Pilate (15:1–15)
  (D) The Crucifixion and Death (15:16–47)
    (a) The Mockery (15:16–20)
    (b) The Crucifixion (15:21–32)
    (c) The Death of Jesus (15:33–39)
    (d) The Burial (15:40–47)
  (E) The Empty Tomb (16:1–8)
  (F) Later Endings (16:9–20)

COMMENTARY

6   (I) Prologue (1:1–15). The prologue relates the promise of OT prophets (1:1–3) to JBap as the one who prepares the way (1:4–8) and to Jesus the Lord as

the "coming one" (1:9–15). It introduces Jesus as God's Son and Servant. As preparation for his ministry, Jesus undergoes baptism (1:9–11) and is tested by Satan in the wilderness (1:12-13). The summary of his preaching of God's kingdom (1:14-15) is the climax of the prologue and the bridge to the revelation of Jesus' power in Galilee (1:16-3:6). **1.** *beginning:* The first verse both launches the story ("the starting point") and introduces the foundation for the good news proclaimed by the early Christians—the story of Jesus. *good news of Jesus Christ: Euangelion* is not the literary genre of gospel but rather the message about salvation in Jesus, as in Paul's letters (→ Pauline Theology, 82:31-36). This usage was the basis for the later use of the word for the "genre" of the story about Jesus. *Son of God:* Though absent from a few mss., this phrase is well attested from the 2d cent. on. It prepares for the important Marcan theme of Jesus as the Son of God, which reaches its climax in the centurion's confession (15:39). **2.** *Isaiah the prophet:* A variant reading "the prophets" can be explained because the quotation in 1:2b is not from Isa. Mark may have used a collection of OT quotations and so attributed it to Isaiah. *behold I send . . . :* The quotation is a combination of Exod 23:20 and Mal 3:1. In Exod 23:20 (LXX), God promises to send his messenger before Israel and guide it to the promised land. Using phrases from Exod 23:20, Mal 3:1 (MT) placed God's promise in an eschatological context and prepared for the identification of the precursor as Elijah (3:23). **3.** *prepare the way . . . :* Isa 40:1-5, which describes Israel's way back from exile in Babylon, became in Jewish circles a classic expression of God's comfort and salvation. Mark 1:3 quotes the LXX text of Isa 40:3 except at the very end, where "his" (Jesus') appears instead of "our God's." In the Christian context, JBap was the voice in the wilderness and Jesus was the Lord whose ways JBap prepared and made straight. **4.** *was baptizing:* Participation in John's ritual of baptism expressed the person's willingness to change and God's willingness to forgive sins before the coming of God's kingdom. **5.** *all the Judean country and all the people of Jerusalem:* Josephus (*Ant.* 18.5.2 § 116-19) also describes John as a preacher of repentance who used baptism and attracted large crowds. Comparison with Josephus's political-military perspective on JBap brings out Mark's major interests: JBap was a prophetic figure after the pattern of Elijah, and his preaching prepared the way for the "stronger one" who would baptize with the Holy Spirit. **6.** *camel's hair and a leather belt:* JBap's clothing was reminiscent of Elijah's (2 Kgs 1:8). What point was he trying to make? Was it merely that he stood in the line of the prophets? Or was he presenting himself as the new Elijah (see Mal 3:1; 4:5)? *locusts and wild honey:* JBap's motivation for his unusual diet may have been ritual purity rather than asceticism (S. L. Davies, *NTS* 29 [1983] 569-71). **7.** *the stronger one:* In JBap's preaching this epithet could have referred to God's arrival in power at the coming of the kingdom, but in the Marcan context it undoubtedly refers to Jesus; John prepared the way of the Lord Jesus. *to loosen the strap of his sandals:* With respect to Jesus, JBap confesses his unworthiness even to perform the service customarily done by a slave. **8.** *the Holy Spirit:* The Synoptic parallels (Matt 3:11; Luke 3:16) read "the Holy Spirit and fire." Perhaps an earlier form of the saying simply read "wind and fire," which described the coming of God's eschatological kingdom (see J. D. G. Dunn, *NovT* 14 [1972] 81-92). **9.** *was baptized by John:* The event is described without any embarrassment about a "baptism of repentance for the forgiveness of sins" (cf. Matt 3:13-17). Mark does not tell us why Jesus received John's baptism; his chief interest was the revelation of Jesus' identity. **10.** *he saw:* The modern explanation of these events as a private vision experienced only by Jesus is probably not what Mark had in mind. That the story originated in connection with early Christian

baptismal practices is even less likely. *the heavens rent:* The opening of the heavens symbolizes the end of separation from God and the beginning of communication between heaven and earth (see Isa 64:1; *2 Apoc. Bar.* 22:1). *the Spirit descending dovelike:* This motif also develops the idea of communication from God; the Spirit comes with a "dovelike" (adverbial) descent, possibly an allusion to its hovering over the waters at creation (Gen 1:2). **11.** *a voice from heaven:* Rabbinic literature often mentions a *bat qôl,* "daughter of voice," as a description of a communication from God. All three motifs—the rending of the heavens, the Spirit's dovelike descent, the voice from heaven—prepare for the identification of Jesus that follows. *You are my beloved son:* The most obvious OT text is Ps 2:7 ("You are my son; this day I have begotten you"); the adj. "beloved" echoes Gen 22:2; Isa 44:2. It is doubtful that Mark understood Jesus' sonship as one of adoption, beginning at the baptism. Rather, the evangelist probably interpreted the heavenly voice as confirmation of the already existing relationship between God and Jesus. *in you I am pleased:* The second part of the heavenly communication echoes Isa 42:1, suggesting a connection between the Son of God and the Servant of God. **12.** *immediately:* The adverbial phrase *kai euthys* occurs often in the early incidents in the Gospel, thus heightening the dramatic sense and the tension. The brevity and simplicity of this Marcan account contrasts with the elaborate scriptural debate between the devil and Jesus in Matt 4:1-13; Luke 4:1-11. The fundamental idea in both versions is the same: the Son of God overcame testing by Satan before he began his public ministry. *wilderness:* Although no details are given, this wilderness is probably meant to be the Judean desert where JBap had been active (see 1:4). **13.** *forty days:* Rather than recalling Israel's wandering in the wilderness for 40 years, the number was an echo of the 40-day testing undergone by Moses (Exod 34:28) and Elijah (1 Kgs 19:8). *Satan:* In the late books of the OT Satan functions as a kind of prosecuting attorney (Job 1-2; Zech 3:1-2) and even the cause of disaster for Israel (1 Chr 21:1; cf. 2 Sam 24:1). In Jewish apocalyptic writings he serves as the leader of opposition to God's people. Here he puts Jesus to some kind of test whose precise nature is not stated. *with beasts:* The Judean wilderness is the habitat of various wild animals; the connection drawn between ministering angels and protection from dangerous animals suggests a background in Ps 91:11-13. **14.** *after John was handed over:* The verb *paradothēnai,* "was handed over," is prominent in Marcan references to Jesus' passion and death. Its occurrence here makes JBap's fate foreshadow Jesus' fate. *Galilee:* Jesus had been at the Jordan River with JBap and in the Judean wilderness. Now he returns to the place of his ministry—Galilee, which is generally more favorable to Jesus than Judea will be (though Jesus is rejected by the people of Nazareth [6:1-6], and John is killed by order of Herod Antipas of Galilee (6:14-29]). *preaching the good news of God: Euangelion* echoes the Gk terminology of Dt-Isa (see 40:9; 41:27; 52:7; 60:6; 61:1-2). The good news came from God (subjective gen.) and had God's action as its content (objective gen.). **15.** *and saying:* As an eschatological warning, the summary of Jesus' preaching will frame all that he says and does in the rest of the Gospel. *the time is fulfilled:* Dividing human history into periods was a common practice among Jewish apocalyptists (see *1 Enoch* 93:1-10; 91:12-17; *As. Mos.* 10). When the timetable reached its goal, then God's kingdom was to appear. The thrust of Jesus' warning was that this moment was now occurring. *the kingdom of God has drawn near:* In Judaism of Jesus' time, the "kingdom of God" referred primarily to God's future display of power and judgment, to the future establishment of God's rule over all creation. Here it is said to "have drawn near" (*ēngiken*). *repent and believe in the good news:* God's kingdom will demand a reorientation of life, as John had already made clear (1:4). The call to "believe in the good news" relates Jesus' preaching to post-Easter faith as expressed in the terms *pistis*, "faith," and *euangelion*, "good news," so prominent elsewhere in the NT.

(Guelich, R. A. "The Beginning of the Gospel'–Mark 1:1–15," *BR* 27 [1982] 5–15.)

7   **(II) Jesus' Authority Is Revealed in Galilee (1:16–3:6).** Having set Jesus on stage, Mark describes the beginning of his public activity in Galilee. After summoning his first disciples (1:16–20) in an authoritative way ("come, follow me"), Jesus reveals himself in Capernaum as a healer and a teacher (1:21–45) and enters into debate with various opponents (2:1–3:6). Everything contributes to the picture of Jesus as the authoritative teacher and healer. Although the initial reactions to him are positive and even enthusiastic, by the end of the debate his opponents are plotting against his life (3:6).

8   **(A) Call of the First Disciples (1:16–20).** Besides introducing the two sets of brothers (1:16–20), who figure in 1:29–31, the account of Jesus' calling his first four disciples provides a model of response to Jesus. Their lack of preparation and the absence of interest in their psychological development serve to underline the point of the story: So compelling were Jesus and his call that no preparation or getting used to the idea was necessary; the first disciples required little or no deliberation to make an enthusiastic commitment. It was customary for Jewish students to approach a distinguished teacher and attach themselves to him (see John 1:35–42); here Jesus summons the students. Cf. Matt 4:18–22; Luke 5:1–11. **16.** *passing by the Sea of Galilee:* Jesus encounters his first disciples at their place of work on the shore of the Sea of Galilee. Except here and in 7:31, Mark describes it simply as "the sea" (2:13; 3:7; 4:1; 5:1,13,21). *Simon and Andrew:* The first disciple to be called is variously named "Simon" and "Peter," the latter being a nickname connected with his character. Andrew is a shadowy figure in the Gospel (see 1:29; 3:18; 13:3). *fishermen:* The first disciples were engaged in fishing—a major industry in Galilee. They owned nets (1:16) and had employees (1:20). Thus they left behind a thriving and secure business to follow Jesus. There is every reason to think that they could read and write and perhaps had good familiarity with the Bible. The idea that they were uneducated arises from a too literal reading of Acts 4:13. **17.** *fishers of human beings:* The metaphor is best interpreted against the background of their occupation rather than in the light of Jer 16:16 or early Christian tradition (W. Wuellner, *The Meaning of "Fishers of Men"* [Phl, 1967]). **18.** *they followed him:* The response is described by means of the technical term for discipleship (*akoloutheō*, "follow") in the NT, thereby endowing this story with exemplary value. **19.** *James the son of Zebedee and John his brother:* Along with Peter, the sons of Zebedee form a kind of inner circle among the Twelve (see 1:29–31; 3:16–17; 5:35–43; 9:2–13; 10:35–45; 13:3; 14:32–42). **20.** *with the hired men:* The expression is best understood as a reminiscence rather than as symbolic language. The story emphasizes the costliness of discipleship with its demands to leave behind family and financial security.

9   **(B) The Eventful Day in Capernaum (1:21–45).** The incidents narrated in the remainder of Mark 1 are placed in the framework of an "eventful" day

consisting mainly of healings done at Capernaum.

(a) TEACHING AND HEALING AT CAPERNAUM (1:21–28). In his first action on the "eventful day," Jesus heals a man with an unclean spirit. The exorcism story follows this outline: the encounter between Jesus and the possessed man, the exorcism, the departure of the demon, and the impression made on the bystanders. Mark has interwoven into the exorcism story references to Jesus as an authoritative teacher (see vv 22,27), thus portraying Jesus as powerful in both deed and word. **21.** *Capernaum:* This city on the NW shore of the Sea of Galilee was the center of Jesus' activities in Galilee. *going into the synagogue, he taught:* On the sabbath, the service in the synagogue would feature prayers, Scripture readings, and teaching. Anyone of sufficient learning could be invited to teach; there was no need for rabbinic "ordination" in Jesus' day. **22.** *they were amazed at his teaching:* Mark's reference to Jesus' teaching places the miracle that follows in a wider context than wonderworking. *as one having authority and not as the scribes:* In the Gospels the scribes are the interpreters and teachers of the OT law, not simply secretaries or clerks. Their mode of teaching involved appeals to Scripture and to the words and deeds of Jewish teachers. Jesus' mode of teaching was apparently direct and confident of its own authority. **23.** *in an unclean spirit:* The man was possessed by an evil force; it was not a matter of ritual impurity. The idea was that the man's behavior was due to an outside force under the direction of Satan (see 1:12–13). Jesus' exorcisms were viewed as victorious moments in the ongoing struggle with Satan. **24.** *what have you to do with us:* The man (and the demon speaking through him) objects to Jesus' meddling in the domain of evil. *Nazarene:* The term derives from Jesus' hometown of Nazareth; efforts to connect it with *nēṣer*, "branch," "shoot," or *nāzîr*, "consecrated," seem forced, though the latter interpretation is rendered more attractive by the address to Jesus as "the holy one of God." *you have come to destroy us:* The sentence is better taken as declarative than as interrogative. The coming of God's kingdom would spell the end of the demons' power. The demon recognizes Jesus' identity and his significance for the coming kingdom. **25.** *be silent and go forth from him:* The fact that Jesus cures the possessed man by word alone and without ritual or magical display heightens the supernatural character of the healing. The power of his healing word reinforces the authority of his teaching (vv 22,27). **27.** *all were astonished:* The amazement of the crowd is a standard feature in the Gospel miracle stories, serving to confirm the miracle and to end the story on a numinous note. *a new teaching with authority:* "With authority" may go with what follows, as in the *RSV:* "With authority he commands. . . ." But in the light of v 22 it seems best to take it as modifying "a new teaching." **28.** *the report of him went forth immediately everywhere:* The Marcan tag to the story introduces a theme prominent in the early parts of the Gospel: Jesus' fame spreads, sometimes even against his will. Here it spreads to the areas of Galilee that surrounded Capernaum.

10   **(b)** HEALING OF PETER'S MOTHER-IN-LAW (1:29–31). The story is told simply, with some details suggesting a basis in an eyewitness recollection. The woman's condition is described; Jesus heals her; and her serving proves the completeness of the cure. Two terms—*ēgeiren*, "he lifted her up," and *diēkonei*, "she served"—may suggest some symbolic-theological currents in the story; but did Mark intend them as such? **29.** *going forth, they came:* Some mss. put these vbs. in the sg., thus focusing attention on Jesus. *the house of Simon and Andrew, with James and John:* Archaeologists may have discovered this house S of the synagogue at Capernaum (see J. F. Strange and H. Shanks, *BARev* 8 [6, 1982] 26-37). The four disciples are those called in 1:16-20. The Synoptic parallels (Matt 8:14-15; Luke 4:38-39) mention only Peter/Simon. **30.** *Simon's mother-in-law:* The assumption is that Peter was married at the time of his call. 1 Cor 9:5 may suggest that his wife accompanied him on his apostolic journeys. **31.** *she served them:* The primary function of this detail is to demonstrate the suddenness and completeness of the cure; it is proof of the miraculous nature of Jesus' healing action.

11 (c) EVENING HEALINGS (1:32-34). After healing one possessed man (1:21-28) and one sick woman (1:29-31), Jesus heals large numbers of possessed and sick persons in the evening. **32.** *that evening, when the sun set:* This account is still part of the eventful day at Capernaum. The use of double temporal expressions, in which the second member ("when the sun set") specifies the first ("that evening"), is common in Mark. *all the sick and the possessed:* The two general categories of people healed by Jesus (see 1:34) have already been exemplified by Peter's mother-in-law and the man in the synagogue. **33.** *the door:* The house of Peter and Andrew (see 1:29) functions as the center for Jesus' activity. **34.** *he healed many:* Mark probably intended no distinction between "all" in 1:32 and "many" here, though Matt 8:16 and Luke 4:40 do clear up the ambiguity. *he did not let the demons speak:* As in Mark 1:24, the demons recognize Jesus' true identity. Jesus' refusal to allow them to speak is usually taken as part of the so-called messianic secret in Mark. While the preternatural opponents of Jesus know who he is, human beings (represented by the disciples) need to get a fuller picture of Jesus before they can know him as the dying and rising Messiah.

12 (d) JESUS' TEMPORARY WITHDRAWAL (1:35-39). The report about Jesus' withdrawal to pray puts the healing activities narrated thus far into perspective. His motive for withdrawing appears to have been communion with God. **35.** *very early while it was still night:* This complicated description of time consists of three Gk advs. (*prōi ennycha lian*); see comment on 1:32. *into a deserted place:* Since there are no deserts around Capernaum, the idea must be that Jesus went to a lonely place, away from other people. **36.** *Simon and those with him:* Their pursuit of Jesus apparently stemmed from the conviction that Jesus was missing a great opportunity in Capernaum (see 1:37). **38.** *the neighboring towns:* The decision to broaden the mission of preaching to "the whole of Galilee" (1:39) does not necessarily demand the rejection of Capernaum. *for this I came out:* Jesus undertook his mission in order to proclaim the kingdom of God (1:14-15). The verb *exēlthon* need not be taken as a rejection of Capernaum ("I went away") or as a theological statement about the divine origin of Jesus' mission ("I came forth"). **39.** *preaching . . . and casting out demons:* The terms summarize what we have learned of Jesus so far; now his field of activity embraces "the whole of Galilee."

13 (e) HEALING OF THE LEPER (1:40-45). The first part of the story (1:40-42) follows the usual outline of healing accounts: the disease is described; Jesus heals; and the healing is clearly complete. Then it is complicated by Jesus' command that the man should show himself to the priest (1:43-44). But the most complicating feature comes in the final verse: Does this verse belong with 1:40-44? If so, did the man disobey Jesus? How does the result fit in with Jesus' desire to keep his true identity a secret? **40.** *a leper:* Biblical leprosy (*sāra'at* in the OT, *lepra* in the NT) was not the disease now known as leprosy. It was a general term for any "repulsive scaly skin disease" such as psoriasis, favus, and seborrheic dermatitis (see E. V. Hulse, *PEQ* 107 [1975] 87-105). Lev 13 describes the various kinds of afflictions and their detection by the priests. *make me clean:* The Gk vb. *katharisai* could mean "declare clean." Thus the leper would be asking the Galilean lay teacher Jesus rather than the Jerusalem priests to declare him ritually pure. But everything in the present form of the story indicates that the leper was seeking a cure. **41.** *moved with pity:* Some mss. read "being angry." The argument is often made that a scrupulous copyist deleted the reference to Jesus' anger, but Mark provides other references to Jesus' anger (1:43; 3:5; 10:14) that were not deleted. In either case—pity or anger—we are dealing with Jesus' deep emotions. *touched him:* The healing takes place by touch and word. For Jesus to touch the man required great compassion—another argument in favor of reading "moved with pity" in the first part of the verse. **43.** *moved by deep feeling:* The Gk ptc. *embrimēsamenos* denotes strong emotions that boil over and find expression in groaning. There is no need to suppose that Jesus was angry at the man. *he dispatched him immediately:* When the phrase is taken with what follows in 1:44, the motive for Jesus' action is to have the man fulfill the rulings in Lev 14 as soon as possible. **44.** *say nothing to anyone:* Though often taken as part of Mark's messianic-secret device, the instruction can be interpreted merely as an indication of Jesus' desire that the man proceed to the priest-inspectors as soon as possible. *show yourself to the priest:* The regulations for proving that one had been cleansed from leprosy and the accompanying sacrifices are detailed in Lev 14. **45.** *but he going out began to preach:* If "he" is Jesus, the verse begins a new paragraph, summarizing Jesus' activity between 1:40-44 and 2:1-12 in terms already used in 1:38 ("preach," "come out"). When "he" is identified as Jesus, the problem of the healed man's alleged disobedience disappears and the connection with the "messianic secret" vanishes.

14 (C) Five Conflict Stories (2:1-3:6). The five stories in this series introduce various opponents of Jesus and of the early Christians (scribes, scribes of the Pharisees, JBap's disciples and Pharisees, Pharisees, Pharisees and Herodians). These opponents move from admiration (2:12) to active hostility (3:6). Early Christians would have used these stories in the defense of their claims about and/or practices involving forgiveness of sins, eating with notorious characters, fasting, and sabbath observance. Most of the stories reflect a setting in Palestine, though Mark (or the pre-Marcan tradition) has reworked them into a tight package (J. Dewey, *Markan Public Debate* [SBLDS 48; Chico, 1980]).

15 (a) HEALING OF A PARALYTIC AND FORGIVENESS OF SIN (2:1-12). The first of the controversies combines a healing (2:1-5a,10b-12) and a debate with the scribes (2:5b-10a). The point of the combination here (as in 1:21-28) is to show that Jesus is powerful in both word and deed: his power to forgive sins is confirmed by his power to heal the paralyzed man. Early Christians could point to this passage as proof for their claims about forgiveness of sins through Jesus. **1.** *at home:* Mark's assumption seems to be that Jesus used Peter's house in Capernaum (see 1:29,33) as his base. **2.** *there was no longer room, even at the door:* The picture is similar to that of 1:33. *he was speaking the word to them:* The use of *logos* here as "word" confirms that "he" in 1:45 was Jesus, for one of his tasks there was to spread "the word" (*diaphēmizein ton logon*). **3.** *carried by four:* Since the paralytic could not walk, he needed help in order to get to Jesus. In fact, "their faith" (2:5) suggests that the four men took the initiative. Were the "four" Peter, Andrew, James, and John (see 1:16-20,29,36)? **4.** *they took off the roof:* The four got to the roof by the outside staircase customary in Palestinian houses (see 13:15). The roof itself was made of wooden beams covered with thatching and mud; it would not have been difficult to open up a hole in it. **5.** *their faith:* The most obvious reference is to the four men who had gone to such trouble to bring the paralyzed man to Jesus, though "their" could also include the paralyzed man. *he said to the paralytic:* The same phrase occurs in 2:10b, where the content of the subsequent saying is more coherent with 2:1–4. *Child, your sins are forgiven:* The address "child" is affectionate. The authoritative declaration of the forgiveness of sins may not have been what he and his friends wanted to hear (see 2:10b–12). The combination of the healing (2:1–5a, 10b–12) and the controversy (2:5b–10a) has the effect of linking in a causal relationship illness and sin—a linking elsewhere rejected by Jesus (see Luke 13:1–5; John 9:2–3). **6.** *some of the scribes:* These scribes (see 1:22, where Jesus is contrasted with the scribes) are the first of five groups of opponents introduced in 2:1–3:6. **7.** *he blasphemes:* According to several OT passages (Exod 34:6–7; Isa 43:25; 44:22), the one who forgives sins is God. According to the reasoning of the scribes (they do not say it directly; see 2:6,8), Jesus' claim to forgive sins would thus qualify as blasphemy. Indeed, it does constitute an implicit claim to divine authority—something perfectly acceptable to early Christians who read Mark's Gospel. **9.** *which is easier:* It is surely easier to say that the man's sins are forgiven (for which there is no empirical test) than to say that the paralytic should get up and walk (for which there would be an immediate empirical test). In the composite account of 2:1–12, the healing functions as the sign for the validity of Jesus' declaration about forgiveness. **10.** *the Son of Man:* This phrase is used often in Mark (2:28; 8:31,38; 9:9,12,31; 10:33,45; 13:26; 14:21,41,62), but each occurrence must be taken separately since *ho huios tou anthrōpou,* "Son of Man," functions in various ways. Here it must refer to the earthly Jesus as God's representative (see 2:7), not to humanity in general or to an eschatological figure (→ Jesus, 78:38–41). *he said to the paralytic:* The same phrase as in 2:5a, thus resuming the healing story begun in 2:1–4. **11.** *rise, take up your mat:* Jesus heals by word alone—a fact that confirms the authority of his words about forgiveness in 2:5b–10a. **12.** *all were amazed:* The standard conclusion to a miracle story is a description of the crowd's reaction. Here "all" would include the scribes (2:6)—another indication of the composite nature of 2:1–5a, 10b–12 and 2:5b–10a. In the Marcan context, the object of the crowd's amazement included both Jesus' healing power and his claim to forgive sins.

16   (b) CALL OF LEVI (2:13–17). The first part of the passage (2:13–14) features the call of a toll collector to discipleship, and the second part (2:15–17) is a controversy story that explains how Jesus could allow such persons to follow him. The two parts may have once been separate in the pre-Marcan tradition. Early Christians would have used the passage to explain the presence among them of persons whose religious and moral backgrounds were suspect. **13.** *the sea:* See comment on 1:16. The call of Levi not only occurs in the same place but also has Jesus passing by (*paragōn*) and summoning Levi to follow (*akolouthei*) him—two key words in 1:16–20. **14.** *Levi the son of Alphaeus:* The parallels with 1:16–20 suggest that Levi was one of the Twelve, but there is no one named Levi in the list of the Twelve in 3:16–19. Some mss. solved the problem by reading James the son of Alphaeus here (cf. 3:18). Matt 9:9 names him Matthew (see Mark 3:18). *toll house:* Levi was a toll collector in the service of Herod Antipas. Such persons were suspected of financial dishonesty and disloyalty to the Jewish cause (J. R. Donahue, *CBQ* 33 [1971] 39–61). **15.** *in his house:* The banquet is usually envisioned as taking place in Levi's house, though he has

just been portrayed as "following" Jesus. Perhaps Peter's house is meant (see 1:29,33; 2:2). *many toll collectors and sinners:* The sinners (*hamartōloi*) were persons whose occupation or life-style prevented them from full observance of the Jewish law. Though some of them may have been notoriously immoral, the designation of them as "sinners" was more a social characterization than a moral judgment. Jesus' willingness to share meals with such persons was an enactment of his preaching about preparing for the coming of God's kingdom (see 1:14–15). *for they were many and they followed him:* This parenthetical comment probably refers to "his disciples," not to "toll collectors and sinners." Mark has told about the call of only five men but assumes that many more had been called to follow Jesus. **16.** *the scribes of the Pharisees:* Being a scribe meant having an occupation (see 2:6); being a Pharisee meant belonging to a fraternity of pious persons. This group did both. Some mss. represent the scribes of the Pharisees as following Jesus. Commentators often ask what scribes were doing in Galilee at a sinner's (= Levi's) house. **17.** *those who are well:* The first saying is a philosophical commonplace; it is so natural that there is no need to consider it as a direct borrowing of any sort. *I have come not to call the righteous but sinners:* The call is to repentance in preparation for God's kingdom (see 1:14–15; cf. Luke 5:32). Thus the designation of these scribes as "righteous" is ironic; i.e., they considered themselves righteous but really were not since they failed to acknowledge God as the source of genuine righteousness.

17   (c) QUESTION ABOUT FASTING (2:18–22). This time the opponents are JBap's disciples and the Pharisees, and the controversy concerns fasting. Their question (2:18) leads to Jesus' identification of himself as the messianic "bridegroom" and the claim that his public ministry is a unique time (2:19a). This is followed by the first hint about his death (2:19b–20) and the consequent permission for Christians to fast. Whatever the original context of the sayings about the cloth and the wine may have been (2:21–22), now they appear to contrast the new and the old forms of religious practice. The real focus of the passage as it now stands is not so much religious practice as Jesus the messianic bridegroom; his public ministry is a special time in which the old forms of religious practice were not appropriate. **18.** *the disciples of John and the Pharisees were fasting:* The only fast stipulated in the OT was the Day of Atonement (Lev 16:29), but additional fasts were observed by the Pharisees (see Luke 18:12) and presumably by JBap's disciples. *but your disciples do not fast:* The assumption of the debate is that Jesus' disciples did not fast during his public ministry, though Matt 6:16–18 assumes that they did. **19.** *the bridegroom:* The application of this term to Jesus probably had messianic overtones (see John 3:29; 2 Cor 11:2; Eph 5:32; Rev 19:7; 21:2), under the influence of the OT depiction of Yahweh as Israel's husband (Hos 2:19; Isa 54:4–8; 62:4–5; Ezek 16:7–63). *as long as the bridegroom is with them:* The rationale for Jesus' disciples not fasting is the unique character of the time of his earthly ministry. **20.** *when the bridegroom is taken away from them:* The thinly veiled allegory of Jesus' death and the saying's power to justify the early church's practice of fasting (see *Did.* 8:1) have led many commentators to take 2:19b–20 as the product of the early church. At any rate, the allusion to the crucifixion of Jesus stands at the midpoint in this series of five controversies. **21.** *a patch of unshrunk cloth:* No one does this because the undressed patch will shrink and make the tear even greater. There is no certainty about the original context of this (or the following) saying. **22.** *new wine into old skins:* No one does this because when the wine ferments and expands, it bursts the old, brittle skins. The structure and dynamic of the two sayings in 2:21-22 are the same; in both cases the goal is to preserve both the patch and garment and the wine and skins.

18 (d) WORK ON THE SABBATH (2:23-28). The Pharisees object to what they interpret as the disciples' infringement of the law about doing work on the sabbath (2:23-24). Jesus' response consists of an OT analogy (2:25-26) and direct statements about the sabbath (2:27-28). The passage would have served as a defense of the early church's free attitude toward sabbath observance in their debates with more observant Jews like the Pharisees. The juxtaposition of the man/Son of Man sayings in 2:27-28 gives the pericope a christological climax and bases Christian sabbath practice on the authority of Jesus. **23.** *his disciples began to pluck heads of grain:* The Pharisees criticized the disciples, not Jesus directly. Their offense was not simply exceeding the distance that one was allowed to walk on the sabbath; it had to do with an action that was construed as working on the sabbath. **24.** *the Pharisees:* Why pious Pharisees should spend a sabbath shadowing Jesus and his disciples in a Galilean cornfield is not explained. Attempts at such explanations miss the point of the literary form of the controversy anyhow. *not allowed on the Sabbath:* The commandment broken by the disciples involved harvesting on the sabbath: "Six days you shall work; on the seventh day you shall rest; in time of plowing and in harvest you shall rest" (Exod 34:21). Everything about their action except its timing is allowed by Deut 23:25. **25.** *what David did:* The story of David and his companions eating the bread of presence (see 1 Sam 21:1-6) has the following features in common with the action of Jesus and his disciples: Both broke a commandment; the forbidden food satisfied hunger; and the incidents involved a great leader who gave permission to help out his followers. But the chief point at issue—breaking the sabbath—is not explicitly covered by the OT analogy. **26.** *when Abiathar was high priest:* According to 1 Sam 21:1-2, the high priest was Ahimelech, Abiathar's father. Some mss. omit the phrase, thus harmonizing the Marcan account with Matt 12:4 and Luke 6:4. There is little doubt, however, about the originality of the reading "Abiathar" (see C. S. Morgan, *JBL* 98 [1979] 409-10). *the bread of presence:* According to Lev 24:5-9, 12 cakes were set out in two rows before God in the tent and later consumed by the priests. In 1 Sam 21:1-6, the priest gave the sacred bread to David because there was no other bread there. David did not take it by force or even on his own initiative. **27.** *the sabbath was made for man:* This extraordinarily radical saying has the effect of subordinating sabbath observance to human needs (see 1:21-28; 3:1-6). Both Matt 12:1-8 and Luke 6:1-5 omit the saying, perhaps because it went too far. **28.** *the Son of Man is lord of the sabbath:* The radical character of 2:27 is tempered by suggesting that the "man" for whom the sabbath was made was the Son of Man, who in Mark is Jesus (see comment on 2:10).

19 (e) HEALING ON THE SABBATH (3:1-6). The fifth controversy, like the first (2:1-12), interweaves a miracle and a debate, showing that Jesus is powerful in deed and word. The general point at issue is sabbath observance; like 2:23-28, this story would have served as a defense of the early church's free attitude toward the sabbath. The reactions of the opponents have hardened considerably from the first to the last story in the series. **1.** *the synagogue:* That this was the synagogue at Capernaum (1:21-28) is confirmed by the adv. *palin*, "again." *a withered hand:* The nature of the man's affliction or when it began (at birth? or later?) cannot be determined by the generic Gk terminology. **2.** *if he would heal him on*

the sabbath: The problem is the timing (the sabbath) and the nature of the illness (not life-threatening). Rabbis allowed healing actions on the sabbath when the sufferer was in severe danger (see *m. Šabb.* 18:3). A passage from *m. Yoma* 8:6 is pertinent here: "Every risk of (losing) lives supersedes the sabbath (law)." The controversy revolves around whether Jesus will go beyond this limitation in order to heal someone not in danger of death. **4.** *is it lawful on the Sabbath to do good or to do harm:* Jesus' question has the effect of transcending the parameters of rabbinic debate (see 3:2) and making the issue one of doing good or harm on the sabbath. The story carries the implicit claim that Jesus, the Son of Man (see 2:27-28), has authority over the sabbath. **5.** *with anger:* For other Marcan references to Jesus' emotions, see 1:41,43; 7:34; 8:12; 10:14,21. **6.** *The Herodians:* These people were friends and supporters of Herod Antipas, tetrarch of Galilee; they did not constitute a sect or party like the Pharisees, Sadducees, or JBap's disciples. W. J. Bennett (*NovT* 17 [1975] 9-14) suggests that they may even have been a Marcan redactional creation, part of Mark's parallelism between JBap and Jesus (see 6:14-29). *how to destroy him:* In the course of the five controversies in 2:1-3:6, the opponents' reaction has gone from amazement (2:12) to overt hostility here. Even during the revelation of God's power in Galilee, there is beginning the kind of opposition that will result in Jesus' death on the cross.

20 (III) **Jesus Is Rejected in Galilee (3:7-6:6).** The negative note on which the preceding section ended is developed here. First Mark gives examples of positive response to Jesus on the part of the people in general (3:7-12) and the Twelve (3:13-19a). These are balanced by the negative response on the part of Jesus' family and the scribes (3:19b-35). Then Mark presents some parables and explanations regarding Jesus' teaching (4:1-34), which result in mounting opposition from "those outside." A cycle of miracle stories (4:35-5:43) shows Jesus' power over nature, possession, disease, and death. The final story (6:1-6) explains how Jesus was rejected by the people of his own hometown.

21 (A) **Positive Responses (3:7-19a).**
(a) PEOPLE COME TO JESUS (3:7-12). This passage is often described as a transitional Marcan summary. It is transitional in that it tells of the enthusiastic reception accorded to Jesus the healer and points forward to his teaching in parables (4:1-34) and his exorcism (5:1-20). It is Marcan in that almost all the words have occurred before and the whole piece seems to come from his pen. It is a summary in that it shows a generalizing tendency rather than narrating specific events. But the passage's character as a transitional Marcan summary should not distract from its important contributions to this evangelist's story of Jesus: the description of people from many areas converging on Jesus (3:7-8), and Jesus' command to the unclean spirits to be quiet about his identity (3:11-12). **7.** *withdrew:* The Gk vb. *anechōrēsen* does not necessarily imply flight on Jesus' part; it means that he turned aside from Capernaum to some site by the Sea of Galilee. *from Judea . . . Tyre and Sidon:* These people are coming to Jesus from all directions. Only Samaria is not mentioned; the cities of the Decapolis are deferred until 5:20. Areas outside the land of Israel (Idumea, beyond the Jordan, Tyre and Sidon) had Jewish populations. **8.** *came to him:* Whereas Jesus came to his first disciples (1:16-20), now people are converging on him as the center of attraction. The description of the crowds points forward to the audience for the teaching in parables (4:1-2). **9.** *a boat:* For Jesus' use of a boat as a refuge from the pressure of the crowd, see 4:1-2. **10.** *he healed many:* As in 1:34, many (*pollous*) need not be taken as

"some, but not all." Nevertheless, Matt 12:15 does change *pollous* to *pantas* ("all"). **11.** *unclean spirits:* As in 1:23-24, demons recognize Jesus' true identity. This description also points forward to 5:1-20 (especially v 5). *the Son of God:* The preternatural beings recognize Jesus as a supernatural figure; his power over them is part of his ultimate victory over evil. For Jesus as Son of God in Mark, see 1:1; 5:7; 15:39; cf. 1:11; 9:7; 14:61 for related titles. **12.** *not to make him known:* As in 1:25,34, Jesus forbids the demons to make known his identity.

22   (b) APPOINTMENT OF THE TWELVE (3:13-19a). Although Jesus has already called several people to follow him (1:16-20; 2:14) and many others are following him, his appointment of the Twelve has great significance as the first symbolic step in Jesus' constitution of the people of God. The Twelve alludes to the tribes of Israel and points to the eschatological people of God's kingdom. Mark's list of the Twelve (3:16-19) agrees in most cases with the other NT lists (Matt 10:2-4; Luke 6:14-16; Acts 1:13); for minor discrepancies, → NT Thought, 81:135-46. The Marcan ideal of discipleship — being with Jesus and sharing his ministry — is the chief theological feature of the passage (3:14-15). **14.** *twelve:* Mark often uses the expression "the Twelve" (see 4:10; 6:7; 9:35; 10:32; 11:11; 14:10,17,20,43). Some mss. add the clause "whom he also named apostles" (but cf. Luke 6:13). *that they might be with him:* The idea of being with Jesus is the basis of discipleship according to Mark. This fellowship allows the Twelve then to share in Jesus' ministries of preaching (3:14) and exorcism (3:15); they fulfill the commission only in 6:7-13. **16.** *Simon to whom he gave the name Peter:* Mark does not tell us why Jesus called Simon the "Rock"; in Matt 16:18 the name is connected with the foundation of the church; in John 1:42 it may imply something about Simon's character (see *PNT* 58-59, 89-91). **17.** *Boanerges:* The nickname *Boanērges* and its explanation, "sons of thunder," have occasioned many theories but no definitive explanation (see H. Balz, *EWNT* 1. 535). **18.** *Andrew:* Nothing is known from Mark about the calling of the eight in the list after Andrew; note that the second James is called "son of Alphaeus" (see 2:14). *Simon the Zealot:* The Gk adj. *kananaios* probably does not derive from Canaan or Cana, but rather from the Aram word *qan'ānā'*, "zealot." Even though this term referred to a group of Jewish revolutionaries against Rome *ca.* AD 66-70, it need not have had political connotations in Jesus' time. At least Luke showed no embarrassment in translating the term into the Gk *zēlōtēs* (Luke 6:15; Acts 1:13). Simon may simply have been "zealous" in the religious sense. **19.** *Judas Iscariot:* The surname *Iskariōth* probably has a geographical reference, "man of Kerioth" (see Josh 15:25; Jer 48:24). The inclusion of Judas in the list of the Twelve and the early Jerusalem community's haste to fill his place (see Acts 1:15-26) speaks for the origin of the Twelve in Jesus' ministry and the recognition of the group's symbolic significance.

23   (B) **Negative Responses (3:19b-35).** The pericope follows this outline: (A) the charge made by Jesus' family (3:19b-21); (B) the charge made by the scribes (3:22); (C) Jesus' defense (3:23-27); (B′) Jesus' judgment on the scribes (3:28-30); (A′) Jesus' judgment on his relatives (3:31-35). From an apologetic standpoint, the text refutes charges made against Jesus during his ministry and even after his death: (1) he was out of his mind; (2) he was possessed by a demon; (3) he was an agent of Satan. It also contains positive theological teachings about the forgiveness of sins (3:28) and Christians as the family of God (3:35). **19.** *home:* The Gk expression *eis oikon*, "to a house," refers to Nazareth, where Jesus' relatives still lived. **21.** *those about him:* The

Gk phrase *hoi par' autou* is used apparently to describe the relatives of Jesus (*RSV*, "his family"; *NJB*, "his relations"); see 3:31-35. They aim to take control of Jesus lest he embarrass the family. A few mss. altered the expression to read "the scribes and the others" — obviously to tone down the shocking nature of the incident in which Jesus is opposed by his own relations (including Mary, 3:31). *they said that he is out of his mind:* Some commentators take "they said" in an impersonal sense "people say," making the relatives into reporters of a popular opinion about Jesus. Others see *exestē* as a comment about the behavior of the crowd, i.e., as being out of control (see *MNT* 51-59). **22.** *the scribes who were from Jerusalem:* This new set of opponents raises a new charge; for Jesus' comment on them, see 3:28-30. Matt 12:24 identifies the opponents as Pharisees, and Luke 11:15 reads "some of them." *possessed by Beelzebul:* The first charge is that Jesus is possessed by a particular demon. *Beelzebub* is the name found in some ancient versions, but not in Gk mss.; that form is based on 2 Kgs 1:2, "the lord of the flies." *Beelzeboul* is variously explained: "the lord of dung," or "the lord of the height or dwelling." None of these is certain. *by the chief of demons:* The second charge is that Jesus' exorcisms took place through the mediation of Satan. Although the two charges — possession and being the instrument of Satan — are related and are answered together in 3:23-27, they are not making precisely the same point. **23.** *in parables:* The expression here refers to the way in which Jesus answers the charges, and it prepares for the teaching in parables in 4:1-34. *how can Satan cast out Satan:* The charges made by the scribes assume that Jesus' power was so remarkable that it could not be explained on natural grounds alone. Jesus' reply assumes that Satan is the lord of the forces of evil (H. Kruse, *Bib* 58 [1977] 29-61). Since Jesus' exorcisms are defeats for Satan, they could hardly be performed through Satan. **24.** *if a kingdom is divided against itself:* The basic point is illustrated in three ways, each having the same structure: If a kingdom/a household/Satan is divided against itself, it cannot stand. The unexpressed conclusion is that Jesus in no way belongs to the realm of Satan. **25.** *house:* Gk *oikia* can refer to both the building (house) and the people inhabiting it (household). **26.** *Satan:* The initial two members of the series (vv 24-25) were analogies. The third member is plain speech: If Satan really were responsible for Jesus' activity, he would be setting one of his subjects against his other subjects, thus destroying himself and his kingdom. **27.** *the house of the strong man:* Jesus the "stronger one" (see 1:7) has entered Satan's house and tied him up; otherwise, Jesus could not have done the exorcisms. Not only was Jesus not on Satan's side; he was his enemy. **28.** *sins and blasphemies:* The saying has the solemn "Amen" introduction. The extraordinary scope of the claim that all sins (including murder, unchastity, and apostasy) can be forgiven should not be overlooked by excessive concentration on the exception made in the following verse. **29.** *blasphemes against the Holy Spirit:* In the Marcan context, the unforgivable sin is attributing the work of the Holy Spirit in Jesus' healings to the power of Satan. "Blasphemy" here describes irreverent behavior vis-à-vis the Holy Spirit — the failure to discern the Spirit's presence in Jesus' ministry. **30.** *they said, "He has an unclean spirit":* Thus far Jesus' response has been directed to the second charge made by the scribes. This explanatory comment added by the evangelist comes back to the first charge of possession by a demon. But in fact, it has been answered implicitly in the course of the preceding argument by affirming that the Holy Spirit rather than Satan was the source of Jesus' power. **31.** *his mother and his brothers:* This group is the same as (or at least part of) the *hoi par' autou* mentioned in 3:21. On Jesus' "brothers," see 6:3 (cf. *MNT* 59–67, 253–82). **32.** *crowd:* The crowd shows no hostility to Jesus; it passes the word about his family outside. *your brothers:* Some mss. add "and your sisters." Its originality is suggested by (1) its absence in 3:31,33,34, and (2) the ease with which it could be omitted by scribes. **33.** *who are my mother and my brothers:* This central saying contains at least a harsh note about Jesus' natural family. They are contrasted with his real (spiritual) relatives, all those who do God's will. **35.** *whoever does the will of God is my brother:* In a society in which family relationships were extraordinarily important, the idea of a spiritual family had the effect of relativizing other relationships and making Jesus' followers judge them in the light of the criterion of God's will.

24   (C) Parables and Explanations (4:1–34). The passage consists of parables comparing the kingdom of God with the marvelous growth of seeds and the abundant harvest coming at the end of this process (4:3–9; 4:26–29; 4:30–32), as well as parabolic sayings (4:21–25), an interpretation of one of the seed parables (4:13–20), explanations related to Jesus' teaching in parables (4:10–12,33–34), and a picturesque setting (4:1–2). **25   (a) Setting (4:1–2).** Mark places Jesus in a boat, teaching the crowds on the shore. **1.** *by the sea:* From Nazareth, Jesus has returned to the Sea of Galilee (3:7–12). **2.** *in parables:* The Gk term *parabolē* signifies a comparison or analogy, but its Hebr equivalent *māšāl* has a much wider range of meaning, including sayings, stories, and even riddles (→ NT Thought, 81:59–60). There is no doubt that Jesus used parables as teaching devices, though their original meaning in some cases may have been lost in transmission in the early church. Thus parables can be interpreted at three different levels: Jesus, the early church, and the Gospel. C. H. Dodd's definition of a parable has become classic: "a metaphor or simile drawn from nature or common life, arresting the hearer by its vividness or strangeness, and leaving the mind in sufficient doubt about its precise application to tease it into active thought" (*The Parables of the Kingdom* [NY, 1961] 5). **26   (b) Parable of the Seeds (4:3–9).** The parable follows the rules of good storytelling: concision, repetition so as to set up a pattern, and surprise or contrasting ending. Since the focus is the seeds and what happens to them, the best title is "the seeds." The different kinds of soil are also prominent, and thus the title "the fourfold field." The least likely is the traditional title "the sower," for he does not appear to be the center of attention (cf. Matt 13:18). The parable illustrates God's lavish offer of the kingdom in Jesus' preaching and the mixed response given to it. Nevertheless, the results will be amazingly rich (see 4:8). Jesus (or the early church) could have used the parable as an explanation for the mixed reception accorded to Jesus' preaching and a source of encouragement in the face of opposition: God's kingdom will come with marvelous abundance. The seeds planted in the good land anticipate the future kingdom. **4.** *some fell by the way:* Why did the sower toss seed on the path (4:4), the rocky ground (4:5), and among the thorns (4:7)? One explanation: In Palestine sowing often preceded planting, and the sower would have returned to cultivate where he had sown (see J. Jeremias, *NTS* 13 [1966–67] 48–53; P. B. Payne, *NTS* 25 [1978–79] 123–29). Thus the parable would give evidence of an original setting in Palestine. But nothing is said about cultivating after sowing in the parable. Another approach: The sower's action illustrates the lavishness of God in extending the invitation to the kingdom. **8.** *the good land:* This soil stands in contrast to

the other three kinds of soil. The fate of the seeds sown in it also contrasts with the fate of those sown elsewhere. The point of the parable lies in these contrasts. *thirtyfold and sixtyfold and a hundredfold:* The Gk numeral *hen*, "one," preceding each number reflects the Aram idiomatic use of *ḥad*, "one," for "—fold." See Matt 13:8 where the sequence of numbers is reversed. **9.** *he who has ears to hear, let him hear:* This formula (see 4:23; 7:16; also Matt 11:15; 13:9,43; Luke 8:8; 14:35; Rev 2:7,11,17,29; 3:6, 13,22; 13:9) balances the introductory summons and suggests that the parable demands close scrutiny. **27   (c) Parables' Purpose (4:10–12).** The parable of the seeds occasions an explanation of why Jesus taught in parables. The explanation is that Jesus deliberately concealed the mystery of the kingdom by means of the parables (here taken as "riddles"). Although the text may well contain material going back to Jesus, its present form is Marcan. The evangelist probably took it as a reflection on the partial failure of Jesus' ministry among his own people (see 4:4–7). **10.** *alone:* The scene so carefully drawn in 4:1–2 is left behind; Jesus is now either on his way or at home. *those around him with the Twelve:* In contrast to 3:21, those "around" Jesus here are disciples in addition to the Twelve. *the parables:* But only one parable (4:3–9) has been told. The pl. suggests that 4:10–12 may have once been a unit separate from what it now follows. **11.** *to you has been given the mystery of the kingdom of God:* The background is the OT (esp. Dan 2) where the mystery (*rāz*) is unveiled by God to the seer. Jesus' teaching (and action) has the effect of unveiling the mystery of God's kingdom; the disciples' task is to transmit this teaching. *in parables:* Here the term "parables" appears to have the sense of "riddles" designed to mystify "those outside." But Jesus used parables to instruct people, though the element of mystery is part of the parable form. **12.** *in order that seeing . . . :* The quotation is from Isa 6:9–10, which describes the predicted result of the prophet's ministry rather than its purpose. But Mark's use of *hina*, "in order that," suggests that the purpose of Jesus' use of parables was to conceal the mystery from "outsiders" and thus prevent their repentance and forgiveness. *lest they should then turn and it be forgiven them:* The use of the 3d pers. pl., "they," and the presence of "it be forgiven them" are paralleled in *Tg. Isaiah* 6:9–10 (B. D. Chilton, *A Galilean Rabbi and His Bible* [Wilmington, 1984] 90–98). Various attempts have been made to resolve the problem posed by the phrase: (1) The Gk conj. *mēpote*, "lest," may be a mistranslation of the Aram *dilmā'*, "unless"; thus the original saying held out the possibility of repentance and forgiveness. (2) The saying reflects a time when the original meanings of Jesus' parables were lost and therefore seemed to be riddles to outsiders. (3) The irony contained in Isa 6:9–10 is continued in Mark 4:12 (". . . because the last thing they want is to turn and have their sins forgiven!"). **28   (d) Explanation (4:13–20).** The interpretation is commonly taken as a sermon outline on obstacles to belief developed in early Christian circles, since the interpretation focuses not on the amazing harvest (4:8) but on the fates of the seeds in the different kinds of soils. Other reasons for taking 4:13–20 as an early Christian adaptation of 4:3–9 are its use of Gk terms found in the epistles, its assumption that the details have a symbolic meaning, and the kinds of experiences that it presupposes. The interpretation outlines various obstacles to belief— Satan (4:15), persecutions (4:16–17), and worldly concerns (4:18–19); it concludes by sketching the characteristics of the ideal disciple (4:20). **14.** *the sower:* The term *speirōn* is to be taken as a reference to Jesus, or perhaps God. *the word:* For use of *ho logos* to describe the Christian message, see 1 Thess 2:13; 1 Cor 14:36; 2 Cor

2:17; 4:2; Col 1:25. **15.** *those by the way:* The seeds sown in the first kind of soil are identified with people who initially hear the gospel but then fall prey to Satan. **16.** *those on rocky ground:* The second group receives the gospel with joyous enthusiasm; but when persecution comes, their shallowness leads them to fall away. The interpreter speaks from the perspective of bitter experience in the early church. **18.** *those among thorns:* The third group is choked off by worldly concerns, the deceit of wealth, and desires for other things. Again the voice of sad experience speaks, as other NT books illustrate. **20.** *those upon the good land:* Because this group is given equal space with the preceding three groups, some of the contrast that characterized 4:3-9 is lost. The ideal disciple hears the word, accepts it, and bears fruit (i.e., acts accordingly).
29   (e) PARABOLIC SAYINGS (4:21-25). The sayings about the lampstand (4:21-22) and the measure (4:24-25) continue the discussion about the purpose of Jesus' parables begun in 4:10-12. They are joined by a common structure: introduction ("he said to them"), similitude, and explanation ("for . . ."). They also may have been put together by the catchword "measure" (*modios* and *metron*). They are sandwiched around a summons to hear (4:23). In the Marcan context, the first saying affirms that ultimately Jesus' mysterious teaching will be made manifest to all; the second saying reiterates the teaching of 4:10-12 on the analogy of the rich getting richer and the poor getting poorer. **21.** *the lamp:* An oil lamp made of pottery in a dishlike shape. A lamp is lit not to be hidden away, but rather to be placed where it can give the most light. *beneath the bushel:* The Gk term *modios* is based on the Lat *modius*, a dry measure consisting of almost two gallons. **22.** *for there is nothing hidden . . . secret:* The explanatory section ("for . . .") indicates that concealment was not the ultimate purpose of Jesus' teaching in parables. The kingdom proclaimed in that teaching will one day be made manifest to all creation. **24.** *in what measure you measure it will be measured to you:* Whoever has some spiritual insight already will have it increased by exposure to Jesus' parables, whereas whoever does not will end up in greater spiritual ignorance. The Marcan message parallels that of 4:10-12. The original context may have been a proverb commenting on socioeconomic matters: The rich get richer, and the poor get poorer.
30   (f) PARABLE OF THE GROWING SEED (4:26-29). Like other seed parables, this one emphasizes the contrast between the smallness of the seed and the greatness of the final harvest. Its focus is the eschatological kingdom of God, but the kingdom is enough of a present reality to be described in terms of a seed and its growth. God guides the growth of the kingdom toward its future fullness. It is coming as certainly and mysteriously as the harvest follows sowing; meanwhile, do not give in to discouragement or impatience regarding it. **26.** *the kingdom of God is like . . . :* The kingdom is being compared with the whole picture sketched in 4:26-29, not only with the man who sowed the seed. There is no need to identify the sower with Christ. **27.** *how he knows not:* The process by which the seed grows takes care of itself; the sower does not analyze it, nor does it help for him to be anxious about it. **28.** *without visible cause:* The word *automatē*, "of its own accord," "of itself," introduces a description of the gradual growth of the seed prior to the harvest. In the context of comparison with the kingdom, the emphasis is on God's hidden and gradual action in bringing it about ("without visible cause"). **29.** *he puts in the sickle, for the harvest has come:* The parable concludes with an allusion to Joel 4:13 (cf. Rev 14:15), underscoring the eschatological nature of the kingdom.

31   (g) PARABLE OF THE MUSTARD SEED (4:30-32). The kingdom is compared to a small seed that grows into a great shrub. The coming of God's kingdom is inevitable; therefore, there is no need for discouragement or impatience regarding its coming. Again the kingdom is enough of a present reality to be described in terms of a growing seed, though God is clearly the one who makes it grow. **31.** *mustard seed:* The point is the smallness of the seed (4:31) and the greatness of the shrub produced by it (4:32), again illustrating the small beginnings of the kingdom and the great result of its arrival in fullness. **32.** *greater than all shrubs:* Just as the mustard seed is not exactly the smallest of all seeds, so the shrub of 8-10 ft. produced by it is not the greatest of all. Concern for literalism should not obscure the basic point of contrast. *beneath its shade the birds of the heaven settle:* The imagery is reminiscent of that in Dan 4:12 and Ezek 17:23; 31:6. That it suggests the gathering of the Gentiles into the kingdom is not certain.
32   (h) SUMMARY (4:33-34). Some interpreters take 4:33 as a traditional statement about Jesus' use of parables as a teaching device and 4:34 as Mark's comment based on his understanding of the parables as "riddles." **33.** *with many such parables:* The metaphorical language of parables allowed Jesus to speak about God and the coming kingdom and to involve his hearers more than plain speech could do. **34.** *in private to his own disciples he explained everything:* That Jesus used parables for all his hearers but provided explanations or expositions for "his own" coincides with 4:1-20.
33   **(D) Three Miraculous Actions (4:35-5:43).** Jesus' teaching in parables is followed by three (or four) miracle stories in which he reveals his power over Satan in nature (4:35-41), possession (5:1-20), disease (5:25-34), and death (5:21-24,35-43).
34   (a) STILLING THE STORM (4:35-41). The first in the series of miracles follows the usual pattern: an obstacle to overcome (a squall at sea), Jesus' mighty action (a command to be silent), and the confirmation (the great calm and the disciples' fear). The background for this story was possibly the ancient Near Eastern idea of the sea as symbolizing the powers of chaos and evil that struggle against God. By controlling the storm at sea, Jesus does what God does and defeats the forces of evil. How much of this symbolism was grasped by Mark's first readers is hard to know. Thus the disciples' question at the end ("who is this . . . ?") expresses the Marcan emphasis on Jesus' identity and constitutes an implicit christological claim regarding the divine character of Jesus, for Jesus does what God does. **35.** *on that day, when it was evening:* On the double time expression, see comment on 1:32,35. *to the other side:* I.e., to the eastern shore of the Sea of Galilee. Why he wished to go there—to escape opposition? to find a new field for teaching?—is not clear. **36.** *as he was in the boat:* This phrase refers to the setting for the teaching in parables (4:1-2) in which Jesus was seated in a boat with the crowds on the shore. *other boats:* As the story progresses, the other boats disappear from the scene. Some commentators find an allusion to Ps 107:23-32, which portrays God as stilling a storm. **37.** *a great windstorm:* Squalls are common occurrences on the Sea of Galilee. **38.** *sleeping:* Jesus' ability to sleep in the back of the boat in the midst of the raging storm shows his complete confidence in God (see Ps 4:9; Prov 3:24-26). *Teacher, do you not care that we are perishing?:* The disciples' question to Jesus is softened considerably in Matt 8:25 ("Lord, save us, we are perishing") and Luke 8:24 ("Teacher, Teacher, we are perishing"). **39.** *commanded the sea:* Jesus' ability to control the sea is an implicit statement about

his divine power, for God alone can rule the sea (see Ps 74:13–14; 89:10–12). *be quiet, be still!:* Jesus addresses the sea, not the disciples. A similar formula in 1:25 (where Jesus performs an exorcism) suggests that here Jesus is manifesting his control over the powers of evil. *great calm:* This feature indicates the completeness and effectiveness of Jesus' action in controlling the sea. **40.** *have you no faith?:* This rebuke is the strongest yet directed to the disciples (see 8:14–21). Did they lack faith in God or in Jesus? If the former, then they were rebuked for not following Jesus' example of trust in God (4:38). If the latter, then the rebuke focuses on the power of Jesus the wonder-worker. **41.** *who is this . . . ?:* Since only God could control the wind and sea, the disciples' question carries an implicit confession of Jesus' divinity, at least to the extent that he does works customarily predicated of God in the OT.

35 (b) Exorcising a Demon (5:1–20). Just as the stilling of the storm showed Jesus' power over Satan in nature, so his exorcism of the demon shows his power over Satan in a case of possession. The story shifts its focus from the possessed man (5:1–10), to the herd (5:11–13), to the people of the area (5:14–17), and back to the man (5:18–20). Some commentators explain it as a simple exorcism story enlarged by means of colorful and legendary details. Others point to the wealth of details and the comparative length of the account as indications of eyewitness testimony. **1.** *Gerasenes:* Gerasa was 30 mi. SE of the Sea of Galilee; 5:2 (see also 5:13) suggests that it was by the shore. Perhaps Mark intended to describe a general area between Gerasa and the Sea. Some mss. read "Gadarenes" (see Matt 8:28), but Gadara was 6 mi. SE of the Sea. Still others read "Gergesenes," following the conjecture made by Origen. The most probable Marcan reading is "Gerasenes" (see *TCGNT* 23–24, 84). It can explained either as a general term for the area or as proof that Mark did not possess precise knowledge of the geography of Palestine. **2.** *from the tombs a man with an unclean spirit:* Tombs were considered favorite dwelling places for demons. Thus a connection is made between death and demonic possession. **4.** *no one was able to subdue him:* The description of the man's violent behavior features several words that occur only here in Mark (*halysis, damazō, diaspaō, katoikēsis, pedē*). **6.** *he worshiped him:* The action is sometimes interpreted as a genuine acknowledgment of Jesus' power and sometimes as a ruse designed to get power over Jesus. **7.** *what have you to do with me Jesus, Son of God Most High?:* The possessed man's address to Jesus is similar to that of the possessed man in 1:24 (see 3:11). Again demons recognize the true identity of Jesus. Some commentators view the use of Jesus' name as part of the demon's strategy to gain control over Jesus (see 5:9). *do not torment me:* The request may reflect the demon's recognition that with Jesus' coming the kingdom of God is breaking in—an event that spells disaster for the demons and other evil powers. **8.** *go forth, unclean spirit:* Jesus correctly perceives that the demon possessing the man, rather than the man himself, was addressing him. **9.** *what is your name?:* Jesus' inquiry here strengthens the approach to 5:7 as part of the demon's strategy to gain power over Jesus by saying his name. Here Jesus is turning the tables, thus gaining power over the demon possessing the man. *Legion, for we are many:* Whether the Lat name *legio* hints at a verbal attack on the Roman legions occupying Palestine is not certain. It could simply be a way of saying that many demons possessed the man, or even a device whereby the demon avoided giving his precise name. Attempts to connect the name with multiple personality or schizophrenia are even more speculative. **10.** *they begged him:* The idea that demons had to find a dwell-

ing place is common (see Luke 11:24), lest they reach their eternal place of punishment (Rev 9:1; 20:10). Here the demons ask the favor of being allowed to stay in the same general area. **11.** *a great herd of pigs:* The presence of pigs indicates that the incident took place in non-Jewish territory, since swine were unclean to Jews and presumably not raised for food (see Lev 11:7–8). **13.** *the herd rushed down the bank into the sea:* Jesus permitted the demons to leave the man and enter the swine; they entered the swine, and the swine fell into the Sea of Galilee. The event has been interpreted in various ways: Jesus' exorcism caused a stampede in the herd; the story illustrates the motif of the deceived demon; a story told about a Jewish exorcist was transferred to Jesus. The problem is that the story attributes destructiveness to Jesus (see 5:17). It apparently assumes that the destruction of the animals brings about the destruction of the demons. **15.** *they saw the man who had been possessed:* After the herdsmen's witness (5:14), more proof of the completeness of the cure is provided by the picture of the demoniac—seated, clothed, and in his right mind. The first response to this scene by the people of the area is awe ("they were afraid"). **17.** *request him to go away:* The mood of reverential awe yields to the conviction that Jesus presents a public danger, presumably because his exorcism led to the destruction of the herd. Only here and in the story of the withered fig tree (see Mark 11:12–14,20–21) is Jesus' power used for destructive purposes. **18.** *that he might be with him:* The way in which the formerly possessed man's request is presented suggests that he was asking to become part of the Twelve (see 3:14) and join in their Galilean mission. **19.** *what the Lord has done for you:* The title "Lord" may simply refer to God, but the parallelism with the following verse ("what Jesus did for him") suggests that Jesus is meant. **20.** *began to preach in the Decapolis:* The man's action is portrayed as the obedient fulfillment of Jesus' command. The Decapolis was the area in N Transjordan, consisting of "ten cities" of heavily Hellenistic character (→ Biblical Geography, 73:52, 55); the area was outside the traditional boundaries of the land of Israel.

36 (c) Healing the Sick (5:21–43). This passage combines two healing stories—the healing of Jairus's daughter (5:21–24,35–43) and the healing of the woman with the flow of blood (5:25–34), thus providing another instance of the "sandwich" device in Mark (see 1:21–28; 2:1–12; 6:7–30; 11:12–21). The two stories have several points in common: female sufferers, the number 12 (5:25,42), and vocabulary ("faith," "fear," "sane," "daughter," etc.). Nevertheless, the style in which they are told points to a separate origin. The story of Jairus's daughter (5:21–24,35–43) is told in short sentences, with few ptcs. and in the so-called historical pres. tense; the story of the woman with the flow of blood (5:25–34) is narrated in longer sentences using many ptcs. and in the aor. and impf. tenses. **21.** *to the other side:* Jesus returns to the W shore of the Sea of Galilee from which he and his disciples set out in 4:35. **22.** *one of the synagogue leaders:* Jairus was at least a prominent member of the Jewish synagogue, most likely one of the board of elders who exercised oversight for the community's religious and social affairs. The Hebr name *Yāʾîr* (see Num 32:41; Judg 10:3–5) means "may he (= God) enlighten," but there is no need to search for a symbolic significance. Some mss. omit the phrase "Jairus by name" (see Matt 9:18), but the evidence favoring its inclusion is very strong. **23.** *begged him:* Jairus's position (5:22) and request (5:23) make him a suppliant, showing how in an extreme case a Jewish official sought out Jesus' help. *my little daughter is nearing the end:* Mark says that she was at the point of dying, whereas the other evangelists say that she was already dead (Matt 9:18; Luke 8:42). *may lay hands on her that she may be healed and live:* The imposition of hands on the sick was a common feature in ancient healing rituals, based on the idea of the healer as a powerful person (see 5:27–30 for the reverse procedure). The terms used in the expression of Jairus's hope ("be healed," "live") were the technical terms in early Christian circles for salvation and resurrected life, suggesting that early Christians may have taken the restoration to life of Jairus's daughter as a preview or anticipation of the resurrected life of Jesus and those who believe in him. **24.** *they thronged about him:* This phrase prepares for the story of the woman with the flow of blood (5:25–34) where the milling about of the crowd is an important feature. **25.** *a woman with a flow of blood:* The description of the woman's malady and her action appears in a single long sentence connected by several ptcs. Her condition is diagnosed as menorrhagia or perhaps vaginal bleeding from fibroids (see J. D. M. Derrett, *Bib* 63 [1982] 474–505). **27.** *she touched his garment:* Her action is based on the belief that contact with Jesus the powerful person could heal her. The indirectness of her approach was motivated by the fact that someone in her condition was ritually unclean and conveyed this uncleanness to whatever she touched (see Lev 15:25–30). **28.** *I will be healed:* The Gk vb. *sōthēsomai* is also the technical term for "salvation" in early Christian circles (see 5:23). **29.** *suddenly the flow of her blood was dried up:* The cure is instantaneous and complete; Jesus has spoken no word, nor has he imposed his hands (see 5:23). Jesus is in full control of the situation and of the divine power that he bears. **31.** *his disciples said to him:* Jesus' question ("Who touched my garments?") seeks an answer. The disciples' intervention points out the difficulty of finding an answer. **33.** *the woman fearing and trembling:* Her fear may have been due to involving Jesus in ritual uncleanness (see Lev 15:25–30). Or perhaps it was due to the miraculous effect that had been worked in her. *told him the whole truth:* The woman told Jesus everything that happened—her touching his garments and the result. **34.** *your faith has healed you:* The same formula appears at the end of the story of Bartimaeus (10:52). Her faith was directed toward Jesus as the vehicle of God's power. The verb "has healed" (*sesōken*) can also be translated "has saved" (see 5:23,28). *go in peace, and be healed:* The OT farewell formula is accompanied with the promise of a permanent cure. **35.** *your daughter is dead:* The message conveyed to Jairus about the girl's death dashed his hope in Jesus the healer. The rough question put to him ("Why are you bothering the teacher?") increases the mood of hopelessness and prepares for the girl's restoration to life. **37.** *except Peter and James and John:* These three disciples form an inner circle among the Twelve; they alone are present with Jesus on the Mount of Transfiguration (9:2) and in Gethsemane (14:33). **38.** *confusion and people weeping and wailing loudly:* The description of the commotion about the girl confirms that she had really died; it indicates a ritual of mourning. **39.** *not dead but asleep:* Although the story seems to involve the resuscitation of a dead person, the possibility of Jesus' superior insight into the girl's condition (she was in a coma or simply unconscious) cannot be ruled out; thus the story would be another healing against all odds and against the wisdom of all the bystanders (see 5:43). **40.** *they ridiculed him:* This strong expression of the crowd's reaction to Jesus heightens the extraordinary character of what Jesus is about to do. The parents serve as witnesses along with Peter, James, and John. All apparently shared the opinion that the girl was dead. **41.** *Talitha koum:* The phrase is Aram *tĕlîtā' qûm;* for other Aram words and phrases in Mark, see 3:17; 7:11,

34; 11:9–10; 14:36; 15:22,34. The occurrence of Aram expressions is usually interpreted as indicating the antiquity of Mark's Gospel, though in the case of a healing story some have argued that *Talitha koum* functions as a kind of magical word (see 7:34). *arise:* The vb. *egeirein* is used often in the NT for Jesus' resurrection, thus suggesting that the story is about resuscitation and has symbolic significance. **42.** *suddenly the little girl arose and walked about:* The girl's action and the crowd's reaction of amazement confirm the reality of the miracle. The vb. used in describing her action (*anestē*) is part of the NT vocabulary of resurrection. The note about her age, "for she was 12 years old," links this story with the preceding one (5:25). **43.** *that no one should know this:* This injunction to silence could be taken as indicating that the girl was only sleeping and the common opinion about her death was wrong; thus Jesus would be commanding silence in order to avoid giving a false impression. But such a rationalistic approach was probably not what Mark had in mind, and the injunction is best viewed as part of the Marcan concern for a correct understanding of Jesus' identity as including the cross. *to give her something to eat:* This detail confirms the fact of the healing while indicating Jesus' compassion.

37   (E) Rejection of Jesus by His Own People (6:1–6a). This section of the Gospel ends with a story of the rejection of Jesus by his own people. It summarizes some of the themes developed thus far: discipleship and faith, Jesus as teacher and miracle worker, and the misunderstanding and rejection of Jesus. The Lucan version of this incident (Luke 4:16–30) occurs at the outset of Jesus' public ministry, whereas in Mark we are now prepared for the rejection of Jesus in the light of all we have read so far. **1.** *he went forth from there:* The preceding incidents (5:21–43) had taken place near the W shore of the Sea of Galilee (5:21). Now Jesus moves inland toward Nazareth. *to his native place:* The Gk *patris* can have a broad meaning, "fatherland," but attempts at interpreting 6:1–6 as all Israel's rejection of Jesus go too far. The idea here is that people from Jesus' hometown rejected him, whereas some from Capernaum and elsewhere had accepted him to the extent of following him back to Nazareth. **2.** *began to teach in the synagogue:* The description of Jesus as teacher and healer is reminiscent of 1:21–28. The initial reaction to his wisdom and mighty works is astonishment. Their question about the origin of both, "Where did this one get these things?," is ironic: Whereas the townspeople seek the name of his teacher, the origin of Jesus' powers is God. **3.** *is not this the craftsman, the son of Mary and brother of James and Joses and Judas and Simon?:* The irony is compounded by the harsher and more negative comments in this verse. The description of Jesus as the "son of Mary" may be an insult, since Jews were customarily known by their father's name, "son of Joseph." The explanations of "son of Mary" as indicating that Joseph was dead or as alluding to the virginal conception of Jesus are unlikely here. For the meaning of "brothers" and "sisters," see *MNT* 65–72; cf. Mark 15:40. *scandalized at him:* The root idea of *skandalon* is "stumbling block." The positive or perhaps neutral reaction to Jesus has turned to negativity. **4.** *no prophet without honor except in his hometown . . . :* This proverb provided an apt commentary on the rejection of Jesus by the people of Nazareth. **5.** *he could not do any mighty work there:* Matt 13:58 softens the phrase ("He did not do many mighty works there"); Luke 4:16–30 omits it entirely. The second clause ("except that . . .") modifies and softens the first clause. Mark's attention was directed more to the lack of faith displayed by the people than to what the earthly Jesus could do or to the psychological aspects of faith healing. **6.** *he marveled at* *their lack of faith:* The previous part of the Gospel ended with the ominous report of opposition to Jesus from the Pharisees and Herodians (3:6).

38   (IV) Jesus Misunderstood by Disciples in Galilee and Beyond (6:6b-8:21). The first part (6:6b-34) focuses on Jesus' disciples, portraying them in a favorable light. But by the end of the third part (7:24-8:21) their failure to understand Jesus is exposed by a series of brutal questions. The last two parts (6:35-7:23; 7:24-8:21) have a similar structure (three miracle stories and a controversy); both feature a miraculous feeding of the crowd.

39   (A) The Disciples' Mission and John's Death (6:6b-34). The initial part of this major section uses the "sandwich" device. It begins with Jesus sending his disciples out on a mission (6:6b-13), tells the story about the death of JBap (6:14-29), and then describes the disciples' return from their mission (6:30-34). Discipleship may involve suffering and death, and JBap's fate foreshadows that of Jesus and his disciples.

40   (a) THE DISCIPLES' MISSION (6:6b-13). Mark has constructed an editorial framework (6:6b-7,12-13) for sayings on provisions for ministry (6:8-9) and dealing with hospitality and rejection (6:10-11). The disciples' activities are an extension of Jesus' ministry of proclaiming God's kingdom in word and deed. In the days before mass media, religious and philosophical ideas were propagated mainly by traveling missionaries. Thus in the early church the instructions given in 6:8-11 would have served as a checklist for missionaries and for those whose hospitality they sought. The thrust of these sayings is the subordination of material and physical concerns to the task of preaching God's kingdom. The details reflect the conditions of 1st-cent. Palestine. **6.** *he went around the villages nearby, teaching:* If 6:6b is read with 6:6a, it appears that the consequence of Jesus' rejection at Nazareth was his decision to teach elsewhere. If 6:6b is read with 6:7-13, it marks a new period in Jesus' Galilean ministry when he shared his preaching and healing with the Twelve. **7.** *power over unclean spirits:* Mark presents the mission of the Twelve as the extension of Jesus' own ministry of teaching and healing (chiefly exorcism). See 9:18, where the disciples are not able to cast out a demon. **8.** *that they take nothing for the journey:* The lack of concern for material comforts on the journey reflects the urgency of the disciples' task and the trust in God that it demands. *except a staff:* Matt 10:10 and Luke 9:3 prohibit the disciples from taking a staff. The Marcan singularity can be explained either as a moderating tendency or as a misreading of Aram '*l*', "except," for the original *l*', "not." *neither bag nor copper money in the belt:* A bag or pouch would hold a substantial sum of money, whereas the money in a belt would be a relatively small amount. All sources of financial security are forbidden. **9.** *wearing sandals:* Matt 10:10 and Luke 10:4 prohibit the disciples from taking along shoes; perhaps an extra pair is meant, since walking barefoot in rocky Palestine would be difficult. *two shirts:* The Gk word *chitōn* refers to the inner garment worn close to the skin. **10.** *whenever you enter a house, stay there:* Traveling missionaries depended on local hospitality. This command was intended to prevent "social climbing," i.e., spending undue time and energy in searching for better accommodations. Traveling missionaries presented problems for the local communities, as *Did.* 11:4-5 indicates with its counsel that an apostle is to be welcomed for a day or two, but after that further stay suggests that he is a false prophet. **11.** *shake the dust from beneath your feet:* When local hospitality is not offered, the disciples are directed to take symbolic action only, not violent reprisal; that action had the function of provoking thought among the local people. There may be some connection with shaking dust from one's feet on returning to Palestine; the idea would be that the inhospitable town does not belong to the true Israel. **12.** *they preached that people might repent:* Mark's summary of the disciples' preaching echoes the summary of Jesus' preaching in 1:14-15, thus underscoring the theme of the disciples' sharing in Jesus' mission. **13.** *they cast out many demons and anointed with oil many sick people:* Apart from the reference to anointing with oil (see Luke 10:34; Jas 5:4), the description echoes the activities of Jesus already narrated in the Gospel. The use of oil in connection with healing was common in antiquity.

41   (b) JOHN'S DEATH (6:14-29). Between Jesus' sending forth his disciples (6:6b-13) and their return (6:30-34), Mark inserts an account about Herod Antipas's interest in Jesus and popular opinions about Jesus (6:14-16), which leads into a flashback narrative about the death of JBap (6:17-29). By sandwiching these stories in between the material about the disciples, Mark has indicated what discipleship may finally cost. Mark's chief concern in his account of JBap's death is to develop a parallel between it and Jesus' fate (and the disciples' fate). **14.** *King Herod:* This is Herod Antipas, one of the sons of Herod the Great. His proper designation was "tetrarch" (see Matt 14:1; Luke 9:7; → History, 75:165). Herod's concern about Jesus does not seem to have been based on the possible political threat posed by him. *they said:* Although the sg. *elegen,* "he [i.e., Herod] said," appears in most mss., the pl. *elegon,* "they were saying," fits better with 6:15. People were identifying Jesus with JBap, Elijah, or one of the prophets (see 8:28 for the same list). *John the Baptizer has been raised from the dead:* The idea that JBap had been raised from the dead points forward to the resurrection of Jesus. John 10:41 states that "John did not do any sign," which is not inconsistent with Herod's idea that John *redivivus* could do miracles. **15.** *It is Elijah:* Elijah's return is based on his having been taken up into heaven (2 Kgs 2:11). For his expected return in an eschatological setting, see Mal 3:1,23. *a prophet like one of the prophets:* The phrase may refer to some prophetic figure, or to the prophet like Moses promised by Deut 18:15. **16.** *Herod said: "John whom I beheaded has been raised":* Mark presents Herod's opinion as a sigh of exasperation ("It's JBap all over again"). The reference to him in this context serves as the occasion for Mark to tell the story of how Herod was responsible for JBap's death. **17.** *Herodias the wife of Philip his brother:* Herodias was the niece of Herod Antipas. She had been married not to Philip but to another brother of Herod Antipas, who also bore the name Herod (Josephus, *Ant.* 18.5.4 § 136; → History, 75:165). Either the tradition or Mark got the relationship wrong. Philip was married to Salome (see *Ant.* 18.5.4 § 137). **18.** *not lawful to have the wife of your brother:* JBap's accusation was based on Lev 18:16; 20:21, which forbade a man from marrying the wife of his own brother. **19.** *she wanted to kill him:* Mark attributes JBap's death to the rage of Herodias on account of his prophetic accusation against her marriage with Herod Antipas, whereas Josephus (*Ant.* 18.5.2 § 118) traces it to the political threat posed by JBap's growing popularity. Jezebel in 1 Kgs 21 may have been the literary model for Mark's portrait of Herodias. **20.** *Herod feared John:* Herodias's inability to get JBap killed is traced to Herod Antipas's peculiar fascination with him. **21.** *his courtiers, officers, and leading men of Galilee:* The presence of such persons at Herod's birthday feast suggests that it took place in Herod's capital city of Tiberias in Galilee. But Josephus (*Ant.* 18.5.2 § 119) says that JBap was killed at the fortress of Machaerus on the E shore of the Dead Sea. Herod may have invited his aides down for a vacation period to Machaerus, where JBap had been imprisoned for safekeeping (i.e., to get him out of the public eye). **23.** *up to half my kingdom:* Herod's words are the same as those of the Persian king Ahasuerus to Esther (see Esth 5:3). That the girl pleased the king echoes Esth 2:9, and the setting at the royal banquet reminds one immediately of the banquet scene in Esth 1:1–22. But to interpret this gospel story as a midrash on the OT Esther story goes far beyond these few parallels. **24.** *the head of John the Baptizer:* Herodias's immediate response to Salome's request for advice has the effect of suggesting that Herodias had the whole scenario planned out beforehand. It places the blame chiefly on her, making Herod Antipas into the victim of his own foolish promise. **25.** *on a platter:* The Gk *pinax,* which originally described a "board," "plank," later was used to refer to a wide, flat dish. The girl's quickness to make the request ("immediately") and the gruesome idea of displaying JBap's head on a platter at the banquet fill the reader with revulsion. **26.** *the king became sad on account of his oaths:* The OT model of the foolish vow is Jephthah (Judg 11:29–40). Mark presents Herod Antipas as caught between his public boast that he would give whatever Salome asked and the concrete reality of her request. The fact that his word and reputation were more important to him than the life of JBap adds to the squalor of the story. **28.** *gave it to the girl:* The passing of JBap's head from the soldier to Salome and finally to Herodias is yet another horrifying detail. **29.** *his disciples came and took his corpse and laid it in a tomb:* The description will be echoed with regard to Jesus' corpse in 15:45–46; the parallelism between the fates of JBap and Jesus seems to have been Mark's major concern in this passage.

42   (c) THE DISCIPLES' RETURN (6:30–34). It can be argued that these verses constitute the beginning of the story of the feeding of the 5,000 (6:35–44). However, their obvious verbal relationships with the missionary charge (6:6b–13) and the sandwich that those two passages form with 6:14–29 indicate that in the overall structure it belongs with 6:6b–29. Nevertheless, several elements in 6:30–34 set the stage for the multiplication of the loaves and fishes. The pericope underscores the disciples' participation in Jesus' ministry, the popular enthusiasm for Jesus, and the compassion displayed by Jesus. **30.** *the apostles:* Perhaps the reason for "apostles" here is the fact that Mark had used the term "disciples" with reference to the followers of JBap in 6:29. *everything that they did and that they taught:* This somewhat vague summary of the disciples' mission ties the account to the Marcan redactional parts of the missionary charge (6:7,12–13), suggesting that it too was supplied by Mark. **31.** *come by yourselves into a lonely place:* This and the remaining verses in the pericope point forward to the multiplication of the loaves (6:35–44). That Jesus and his apostles are in a lonely place and have taken only enough food for their own needs sets the remote situation for the miraculous feeding of the 5,000. **33.** *they got there ahead of them:* The idea is that the crowds on foot beat Jesus and his disciples with their boat. Their unexpected presence provides the proximate situation for the multiplication. **34.** *like sheep not having a shepherd:* The phrase is based on Num 27:17; 1 Kgs 22:17; and Ezek 34:5–6.

43   **(B) Acts of Power and a Controversy (6:35–7:23).** This and the following section (7:24–8:13) have a similar structure of miraculous actions followed by a controversy. All the episodes put the spotlight on Jesus, the wonder-worker, healer, and teacher. Most important are the implicit christological claims made about him as the Messiah (6:35–44), the Son of God (6:45–52), and the authoritative interpreter of the OT law (7:1–23).

44   (a) FEEDING THE FIVE THOUSAND (6:35–44). The miraculous feeding points back to God's feeding of his people in the wilderness and to Elisha's feeding of 100 men (2 Kgs 4:42–44). It points forward to the idea of life in God's kingdom as a banquet at which the Messiah will preside. Thus Jesus is teaching about the nature of God's coming kingdom. Some obvious connections are made with the Last Supper (see 6:41; 14:22), suggesting a eucharistic aspect to the account. Mark and his readers saw this incident as an anticipation of the Last Supper and the messianic banquet, both of which were celebrated in the community's eucharists. The story of Jesus' feeding of 5,000 is told in all four Gospels (see Matt 14:15–21; Luke 9:12–17; John 6:1–15); a parallel story of his feeding of 4,000 appears in Mark 8:1–10; Matt 15:32–39. **35.** *his disciples:* Mark has gone back to his more usual term for Jesus' followers. In the first part of this story (6:35–38), the disciples engage in dialogue with Jesus and fail to perceive his purposes. The theme of their misunderstanding of Jesus will be further developed. *it is a lonely place, and the hour is now late:* The disciples' first statement makes clear the problems involved in feeding the crowd. They suggest in 6:36 that Jesus let the people go buy food for themselves. The description of the place as *erēmos,* "lonely," may have some connection with the OT manna motif, though this place with towns around it hardly qualifies as a desert. The traditional location of the multiplication is the region of et-Tabgha (E. Bagatti, *Salmanticensis* 28 [1981] 293–98). **37.** *you give them to eat:* Jesus' answer to their "reasonable" suggestion takes them off guard; their second statement about buying 200 denarii worth of bread is close to hostile in tone. One denarius was a day's wage for a laborer (Matt 20:2). **38.** *two fish:* The references to fish (6:41,43) throughout the story seem like afterthoughts. Their role in the story is interpreted in various ways: as an indication that fish was used in some early Christian eucharists, as sea creatures for food like the quails on which Israel fed in the wilderness (Num 11:31; Wis 19:12), or as anticipating the sea creatures that would be part of the messianic banquet (4 Ezra 6:52; 2 Apoc. Bar. 29:4). The third interpretation is the most likely. **40.** *in groups:* Gk *prasia* means "a bed for leeks," which are planted in straight rows. The vivid portrayal of the crowd in 6:39–40 gives a sense of order and decorum, thus contributing to the idea of the messianic banquet. **41.** *looking up into heaven he blessed and broke the breads:* The similarity in phraseology between 6:41 and 14:22 (at the Last Supper) indicates that this meal in the wilderness was understood as an anticipation of the eucharist (which in turn anticipates the messianic banquet). The blessing would have been the traditional Jewish blessing before meals. *gave them to the disciples so that they might place them before the people:* The description of the disciples' activity is sometimes viewed as part of the eucharistic anticipation, for they function as distributors of the bread. **42.** *all ate and were satisfied:* Another element of the story's background may have been Elisha's miraculous feeding of 100 men (2 Kgs 4:42–44), in which all eat and even have some leftovers. **43.** *twelve baskets full of fragments:* Gk *klasmata,* "fragments," appears in a eucharistic context in *Did.* 9. The number 12 may have some symbolic reference to Israel; cf. seven (= Gentiles?) in 8:8. **44.** *five thousand men:* The greatness of the number of persons fed means that Jesus' miraculous feeding far outstrips the one performed by Elisha.

(Fowler, R. M., *Loaves and Fishes* [SBLDS 54; Chico, 1981]. van Cangh, J.-M., *La multiplication des pains et l'Eucharistie* [LD 86; Paris, 1975].)

45 (b) WALKING ON THE WATERS (6:45–52). The approach to this story as an epiphany/theophany is most consistent with Mark's presentation. The twin focus is Jesus and the disciples: (1) The divine identity of Jesus is suggested by his walking on the waters, his passing by them, and his words, "It is I." (2) The disciples run a gamut of emotions, ending in their astonishment and Mark's comment about their failure to understand the true identity of Jesus. **45.** *to the other side, to Bethsaida:* Bethsaida Julias was on the NE side of the Sea of Galilee. But according to 6:53 they land at Gennesaret on the NW side, below Capernaum. **46.** *to pray:* That Jesus prayed after his miracle of the loaves and before his walking on the water makes clear that the Father was the source of his power. **47.** *the boat was in the middle of the sea:* The latter phrase describes not the geographical center of the Sea of Galilee but rather the fact that the disciples were far out from the shore on which Jesus stood. *he was alone on the land:* The prep. *epi,* "on," locates Jesus on the land; its occurrence here makes it difficult to interpret *epi tēs thalassēs* (6:48) as "by the sea." **48.** *for the wind was against them:* The wind (see 6:51), while a factor in the story, does not play the same kind of role as it did in the stilling of the storm (4:35–41). *about the fourth watch of the night:* The fourth watch according to the Roman reckoning was between 3 A.M. and 6 A.M. *walking on the water:* Mark meant "on the water," not simply "by the shore"; a naturalistic explanation cannot be built on the preposition *epi* here (see 6:47). The OT portrays walking on water as a divine function (see Job 9:8; 38:16). The representation of Jesus as walking on water thus carries an implicit claim about his divinity. *he wanted to pass by them:* The implicit christological claim is strengthened by the use of the vb. *parelthein,* which was linked with the theophany tradition in the LXX (see Exod 33:19,22; 34:6; 1 Kgs 19:11). Its appearance in the LXX of Amos 7:8; 8:2 also suggests that Jesus desired to help his disciples in their difficulty (H. Fleddermann, *CBQ* 45 [1983] 389–95). **50.** *I am he:* In the context of self-disclosure and theophany, this phrase must allude to the OT revelation formula (Exod 3:14; Deut 32:39; Isa 41:4; 43:10) applied to Yahweh, thus contributing to the implicit christological message of the whole text. The formula *egō eimi* is prominent in John. **52.** *they had not understood about the breads:* Mark's comment on the disciples' astonishment focuses on their hardness of heart (see 8:14–21, where this theme is much stronger). Perhaps the problem was that, according to Mark, the disciples needed to pass beyond the interpretation of Jesus the Messiah presiding at the messianic banquet (see 6:35–44) to an understanding of him as the Son of God (see 1:1; 15:39); i.e., as a divine being.

46 (c) HEALING THE SICK (6:53–56). The vocabulary of the passage indicates that Mark composed it, possibly on the basis of some traditions. Although it is anticlimactic after the multiplication of the loaves and the walking on the water, it brings back into focus a key theme of the Gospel, Jesus the healer. The enthusiastic reception given to him by the general populace contrasts with the carping attitude of the opponents in the following controversy (7:1–23). **53.** *at Gennesaret:* The journey that set out for Bethsaida Julias ends at Gennesaret — well off course (see comment on 6:45). The detour is attributed to the wind (6:48) or (more likely) to the joining of originally independent pieces of tradition. **56.** *that they might touch the fringe of his garment:* This idea appears in the story of Jesus' healing of the woman in 5:25–34; it is generalized here. *they were made well:* Gk *esōzonto* can also mean "saved." The literal sense of healing is surely primary here, but the choice of this vb. does set the healing in the context of the Christian kerygma.

47 (d) CONTROVERSY ABOUT RITUAL PURITY (7:1–23). The controversy that climaxes this section (see 8:11–21) begins with a challenge from the Pharisees and scribes regarding the disciples' failure to perform ritual washings before eating (7:1–8). Jesus' criticism that his opponents are substituting their human traditions for divine commandments leads to the example of the practice of *korban* (7:9–13). Finally Jesus gives a public statement and a private explanation about the invalidity of the Jewish food laws (7:14–23). Thus the pericopes are loosely connected by subject matter (ritual washings, *korban,* food laws). The theological focus is the OT law in relation to Jesus. He rejects the Pharisaic tradition surrounding the law's observance, warns against substituting human teachings for divine commandments and using the law as a way to escape from one's obligation, and abrogates the OT food laws. The implicit christological claim is that Jesus is the authoritative interpreter of the OT law. **1.** *the Pharisees and some of the scribes:* These opponents are already familiar from the series of controversies in 2:1–3:6. That the scribes came from Jerusalem indicates that the incident occurred in Galilee, though nothing specific is said about time or place. **2.** *with common hands, that is, unwashed:* The complaint was that Jesus' disciples failed to follow the traditional Jewish practices of ritual purification; the issue was not hygiene. The explanation added by Mark ("that is, unwashed") indicates that he wrote for an audience unfamiliar with such practices. **3.** *the Pharisees and all the Jews . . . :* The parenthetical explanation in 7:3–4 is directed clearly to a non-Jewish audience, thus giving evidence about the Gospel's audience and purpose. *unless they wash their hands:* The *RSV* leaves untranslated the difficult Gk word *pygmē,* which may be a Latinism based on *pugnus/ pugillus,* "handful," i.e., with a handful. Mark was describing the amount of water used in the Jewish ritual washing (see *m. Yad.* 1:1; see H. Balz, *EWNT* 3. 473). *the tradition of the elders:* The rabbis developed a notion of traditions in which great teachers of Israel formed a chain reaching back to Moses on Sinai (see *m. 'Abot* 1:1–12). The Pharisees wished to extend the laws of ritual purity applied to priests in the OT to all Israelites, thus making actual the vision of a priestly people. **4.** *washings of cups and pots and bronze vessels:* Some commentators find an ironic, impatient tone in the list. Several mss. add "and beds" to the list (see Lev 15); it may have been omitted accidentally or because of the incongruity of washing beds. **6.** *well did Isaiah prophesy about you hypocrites:* The quotation is applied to the religious life-style of the Pharisees and scribes. The Gk term *hypokritēs* describes an actor whose face was hidden behind a mask; here it carries the tone of "phony." *This people honors me with their lips . . . :* The quotation of Isa 29:13 is from the LXX, not the Hebr text, though there are some differences from the LXX. Perhaps Mark (or his tradition) used a variant Gk transl., which may have been part of an anthology of OT quotations. **7.** *in vain do they worship me, teaching as doctrines the commandments of humans:* The LXX reads ". . . teaching commandments of men and doctrines" (cf. Col 2:22). The Pharisees and scribes pay only "lip service" to God and present their human teachings as divine commandments. The context of this debate in Jesus' time may have been the Pharisaic program of extending the obligation of ritual purity to all Israel. For the early church, the incident gave an explanation of why Jesus' followers did not observe the Jewish traditions. **8.** *Leaving behind the commandment of God, you hold fast to human tradition:* The sentence makes explicit what was implicit in the quotation from Isa 29:13. The Pharisees and scribes would have vigorously denied this charge, for they perceived themselves as making practical and concrete the teachings that were not clear from the law itself. **9.** *you reject the commandment of God in order to establish your tradition:* This charge recapitulates the thrust of 7:1-8 and prepares for the *korban* illustration in 7:10-13. **10.** *Moses said:* The divine commandment (see Matt 15:4, "For God said") involves honoring one's parents (Exod 20:12; Deut 5:16) and not speaking evil of/cursing them (Exod 21:17; Lev 20:9). **11.** *but you say:* The verse draws a sharp contrast between the divine commandment and the teaching of the scribes and Pharisees on *korban*. Gk *korban* is a transliteration of Aram *qorbān,* "offering," "gift." The recipient of the gift is God. By declaring property or money a gift to God, a son could remove any claim on it that his aging parents might have. The term appears on an ossuary inscription found near Jerusalem: "Everything that a man will find to his profit in this ossuary is an offering to God from the one within it." This was intended to keep tomb-robbers from stealing valuable objects in the ossuary (J. A. Fitzmyer, *ESBNT* 93–100). **12.** *to do anything for father or mother:* Jesus claims that the result of the *korban* practice is to deprive parents of benefit from their son's property, thus constituting an infringement of the commandment (see 7:10). What looks like pious behavior is actually a way of circumventing religious obligation. Some later Jewish teachers agreed with Jesus (see *m. Ned.* 9:1-2). **13.** *annulling the word of God by your tradition:* The concluding comment returns to the general principle (7:8-9) illustrated by the practice of *korban.* The *korban* is not an isolated example but rather a general direction among the scribes and Pharisees. **14.** *summoning the crowd again:* Mark has given a narrative framework to a series of sayings loosely connected with the preceding material by the clean/unclean theme. **15.** *nothing outside a man that by going into him can defile him:* Jesus appears to abrogate the OT laws dealing with ritual impurity and food (see Lev 11; Deut 14), which not only occupied large sections of the Pentateuch but also must have directly concerned Jews in their everyday lives. The radical nature of Jesus' statement and its sharp break with Jewish tradition have led many scholars to attribute it to the earthly Jesus without hesitation (N. J. McEleney, *CBQ* 34 [1972] 431–60; J. Lambrecht, *ETL* 53 [1977] 24–82). But if the saying were so clearly Jesus' teaching on the Jewish food laws, why did no one use it in the debate about the obligation of Gentile Christians to observe the food laws (H. Räisänen, *JSNT* 16 [1982] 79–100)? **16.** *if anyone has ears to hear, let him hear:* The verse is the sequel to the summons to hear (7:14; see 4:3), and may derive from 4:9 and/or 4:23. The *RSV* follows several important mss. in omitting it. **17.** *the parable:* Mark has constructed a scene for the explanation that recalls 4:10 (when Jesus explained the purpose of parables and the parable of the seeds). *Parabolē* here has the sense of "obscure saying" or even "riddle," though 7:15 seems remarkably clear. **19.** *it does not enter his heart:* The preceding part of the sentence (7:18b) merely repeats the teaching of 7:15. This part explains that, since food does not enter the heart (the Hebr seat of both learning and feeling) but only the stomach, therefore unclean food does not defile the inner core of the person. The explanation suggests a distinction between the inner person (religion and morality) and the outer person (ritualism) unusual in the Jewish tradition. *(making all foods clean):* Again the problem: If Jesus had been so explicit about the observance of Jewish food laws, why were there so many debates on this matter in the early church (see Gal 2:11-14; Rom 14:14-20; Col 2:20-23; Acts 10:14-15; etc.)? **20.** *whatever comes out of a man:* Whereas the first part of the explanation (7:18b-19) focused on "whatever comes in," the second part attributes real defilement to

the things that come out of a man. The idea is that evil deeds and vices proceed from evil persons. **21–22.** *evil thoughts, fornication . . . :* The catalogue of sins features both evil actions and vices. Other such lists appear in Gal 5:19-21; Rom 1:29-31; 1 Pet 4:3; many of the terms are common in the Pauline letters. The catalogue device was common in the Greco-Roman world and was known also in Judaism (see 1QS 4:9-11). **23.** *all these evil things come from within:* The final sentence summarizes the message of the second part of the explanation (7:20-23).

48   (c) More Acts of Power and a Controversy (7:24–8:21). This section has the same general structure—three miracles and a controversy—as 6:35-7:23. Again the spotlight is on Jesus and the implicit christological claims made about him. The major development here concerns the disciples' failure to understand Jesus and his care for them (see 8:14-21).

49   (a) HEALING A GENTILE WOMAN'S DAUGHTER (7:24-30). Although this incident has the features of a healing story (an unclean spirit, Jesus' healing power, proof of the healing), its real focus is the dialogue between Jesus and the Gentile woman. It takes place on Gentile soil. In reply to the woman's request of healing for her daughter, Jesus utters a saying that appears to exclude non-Jews as recipients of his power. The woman's reply criticizes such exclusivity and shows how there can be a place for non-Jews in God's plan. Mark's Gentile-Christian readers would have taken this story as an explanation of their presence in the people of God. **24.** *Tyre:* This region bordered on NW Galilee and was Gentile in character. How far Jesus penetrated into the region is not known. He apparently went there for rest and reflection. For the enthusiasm regarding Jesus among people of that area, see 3:8. **25.** *she fell at his feet:* The woman's posture is one of supplication (see 3:11; 5:23) on behalf of her daughter who is possessed by an unclean spirit. Her request is described in 7:26. **26.** *a Greek, a Syrophoenician by birth:* The first adj. describes the woman's religion ("a Gentile"; cf. Matt 15:22 "a Canaan-ite"), and the second adj. specifies her nationality. She was not part of the Jewish population of the region of Tyre. **27.** *let the children be fed first:* The children surely are the Jews. The saying embodies the Pauline idea of the order of salvation history ("to the Jew first and then to the Greek," see Rom 1:16). *not good to take the children's bread and throw it to puppies:* Jewish writers sometimes described Gentiles as "dogs." There may be some softening through the diminutive "puppies." **28.** *even puppies beneath the table eat from the children's crumbs:* The woman's witty reply builds on Jesus' pronouncement by turning it to her advantage. Without denying the salvation-historical precedence of Israel and the focus of Jesus' ministry, she rejects the idea of exclusivity for Jesus' power. For an OT use of the image of eating scraps beneath a table, see Judg 1:7. **29.** *on account of this word, go:* Jesus takes the woman's reply as a sign of faith in God's plan and in his power. The assumption seems to be that the girl was healed by Jesus at a distance, though it is conceivable that the miracle consisted in Jesus' knowing that she had already been healed. **30.** *she found the child lying on the bed and the demon gone:* These details serve to prove the completeness of the cure.

50   (b) HEALING A MAN INCAPABLE OF HEARING AND SPEAKING PROPERLY (7:31-37). After a geographical introduction, the passage follows the usual outline of healing stories. Jesus' command that the crowd be silent about the healing (7:36) and its subsequent violation bring up the theme of his identity, suggesting that healing is not the whole story about him. The words that express the crowd's enthusiasm for Jesus (7:37) are taken from an apocalyptic section of Isa, suggesting that in

Jesus' activities the kingdom of God is present. **31.** *went through Sidon:* The roundabout route taken by Jesus has intrigued commentators: "According to the reading supported by the best representatives of the Alexandrian and the Western texts, as well as by noteworthy Caesarean witnesses, Jesus took a circuitous route, passing north from Tyre through Sidon and thence southeast across the Leontes, continuing south past Caesarea Philippi to the east of the Jordan and thus approached the lake of Galilee on its east side, within the territory of the Decapolis" (*TCGNT* 95–96). This journey through largely Gentile territory may have been intended by Mark as an anticipation of the church's mission to the Gentiles. **32.** *who was deaf and had a speech impediment:* Gk *kōphos,* used in reference to hearing, means "deaf," but Gk *mogilalos,* "speaking with difficulty," describes a speech impediment (see 7:35, "he spoke properly"). *lay a hand on him:* The sg. "hand" is unusual in Mark in the context of imposition of hands (see 5:23; 6:5; 8:23). **33.** *put his fingers into his ears, and spat and touched his tongue:* Taking the man apart from the crowd, Jesus performs a ritual of healing. For the use of spittle in Jesus' healings, see Mark 8:23; John 9:6. **34.** *looking up to heaven, he groaned:* The straightforward meaning of these actions is that Jesus prayed to God and was moved with compassion for the man. They need not be considered part of a magical rite. *"Ephphatha," that is, "Be opened":* The gloss "be opened" explains the meaning of the Semitic word, usually understood as Aram *'eppattaḥ* (= *'etpattaḥ;* see S. Morag, *JSS* 17 [1972] 198–202). **35.** *his ears were opened, and the bond of his tongue was released:* The completeness of the cure is underscored. Some mss. include the adv. *eutheōs,* "immediately." *he spoke properly:* The best transl. of the adv. *orthōs* is "properly," which is more idiomatic than "rightly" and less rigid than "correctly." **36.** *he commanded them to tell no one:* Jesus' prohibition of talking about the cure is probably part of Mark's insistence that Jesus is more than a healer and that his full identity will be revealed only in the cross and resurrection. The prohibition has the opposite effect. The reaction of the crowd gives witness to the reality of the cure, while underlining the theme of Jesus' identity. **37.** *makes the deaf hear and the mute speak:* The crowd's statement alludes to Isa 35:5–6, which is part of a vision of Israel's glorious future (Isa 34–35), related to Isa 40–66. The use of this OT text here indicates that Israel's glorious future is already present in Jesus' ministry.

51   (c) FEEDING THE FOUR THOUSAND (8:1–10). There are some clear differences in the feeding of the 4,000 (8:1–10) from that of the 5,000 (6:35–44). The crowd has been with Jesus for three days; the disciples know what supplies are available; there are two blessings; seven baskets of fragments remain; and 4,000 are fed. Despite these differences, there are so many similarities that the feeding stories are usually taken as two accounts of the same incident. The theological motifs of 8:1–10 are the same as those of 6:35–44: God's feeding his people in the wilderness, the messianic banquet, and anticipation of the eucharist. The distinctive theological element is found in the number of loaves and the baskets of leftovers—seven, often taken as a reference to the Gentile mission of the early church. **2.** *I have pity on the crowd:* The reason for Jesus' compassion is that the crowd has been without food for three days. In 6:34, they were like sheep without a shepherd. The first incident seems to take place all on one day, whereas this one is spread over three days. **3.** *if I send them away fasting:* In 6:35–36, the disciples suggest that Jesus dismiss the crowd. **4.** *with bread in the wilderness:* The combination of "bread" and "wilderness" calls to mind the OT manna motif. Nothing is said about the fish here (see 8:7). The

disciples' failure to comprehend what Jesus was going to do in the light of the first multiplication (6:35–44) is taken as a strong indication that the second story is a doublet. **5.** *seven:* In 6:38, the number of loaves was five. Many interpreters find in the number "seven" a reference to the Gentile mission, i.e., to the 70 nations of the world, undertaken by the seven "deacons" of Acts 6:1–7. The disciples know how much food is available without making an inquiry (cf. 6:38). **6.** *to recline on the ground:* The arrangement of the crowd is far less colorful and elaborate than in 6:39–40, though the result is the same. *he blessed and broke and gave to his disciples:* As in 6:41, the description of Jesus' action is an anticipation of what he will do at the Last Supper (see 14:22), which in turn anticipates the messianic banquet and the church's eucharist. The disciples again function as distributors of the food. **7.** *they had a few small fish:* As in 6:38,41,43, the reference to the fish seems to be an afterthought. But the eucharistic interpretation of the action would tend to drive out the reference to the fish, and so its bare survival may be evidence of its originality. **8.** *seven baskets full of fragments:* There were twelve baskets full of leftovers at the first multiplication (6:43). Many commentators find a numerical symbolism in the amounts of leftovers: twelve = Israel, seven = Gentiles. **10.** *into the region of Dalmanutha:* The first part of the verse is very close in wording to 6:45. The location of Dalmanutha is uncertain and has generated many scholarly conjectures. Some mss. equated it with Magdala or Magadan (see Matt 15:39). The site was most likely on the W shore of the Sea of Galilee.

52   (d) CONTROVERSY ABOUT SIGNS (8:11–21). The controversy that climaxes this section (see 7:1–23) begins with the Pharisees' request for a sign from heaven regarding Jesus (8:11–13) and goes on to recount Jesus' rather brutal questioning of the disciples (8:14–21). He refuses to give the Pharisees a spectacular public display (*sēmeion*) of his messiahship and exposes his own disciples' failure to understand him and his care for them. **11.** *the Pharisees:* As in 7:1, the opponents in the climactic controversy are the Pharisees (though in the previous controversy there were scribes also). The way in which their action is described ("testing him") suggests bad will and even some connection with Satan's testing of Jesus (see 1:13). *a sign from heaven:* The usual Marcan word for Jesus' miracles is *dynamis,* not *sēmeion.* Perhaps the request for a *sēmeion* here has some relation to the promise of the Jewish pseudomessiah Theudas that he would divide the Jordan River and give his followers easy passage over it (see Josephus, *Ant.* 20.5.1 § 97–98). In other words, the Pharisees are asking for a spectacular public display that will confirm Jesus' messiahship. Of course, they expect that Jesus will fail the test and thus lose popular support. Their demand that the sign be "from heaven" is another way of saying that it must come from God. **12.** *why does this generation seek a sign?:* Jesus refuses to give "this generation" (see Mark 8:38; 9:19; 13:30) such a sign. Compare Matt 16:4, where only the sign of Jonah is promised; see also Matt 12:39; Luke 11:29. **13.** *getting into the boat again:* This geographical notice prepares for the second part of the controversy, in which Jesus' own disciples are the opponents. **14.** *they had only one loaf:* The presence of the one loaf will serve as the point of misunderstanding between Jesus and the disciples. He will teach on a spiritual plane, but the disciples remain on a material plane. **15.** *the leaven of the Pharisees and (the leaven) of Herod:* "Leaven" symbolizes something with an inward, vigorous vitality; here it refers to an evil influence that can spread like an infection. The saying is a comment on the Pharisees' demand for a sign (8:12). **16.** *we have no bread:*

The disciples' comment on Jesus' warning in 8:15 underscores their obtuseness and sets the stage for the series of questions that follow. After all the Twelve's witnessing of Jesus' activity and teaching, their understanding of him gets worse. **18.** *having eyes, do you not see . . . having ears, do you not hear?:* Jesus applies to the disciples the language applied to "those outside," who failed to understand the parables (see 4:11-12). Thus the disciples join "those outside" in their lack of understanding about him. **19.** *I broke the five loaves:* This verse and the following one recapitulate 6:35-44 and 8:1-10, respectively. The disciples should have recognized Jesus' ability to care for their physical needs from those two incidents. **21.** *do you not yet understand?:* His final question summarizes the entire series and points forward to the next part of the Gospel, in which the disciples will have to struggle with the mystery of the cross as an essential aspect of Jesus' identity.

53 **(V) Jesus Instructs His Disciples on the Way to Jerusalem (8:22-10:52).** At this point in the Gospel, the Galilean ministry is put aside; Jesus and his disciples journey from Caesarea Philippi in N Galilee to Jerusalem. The focus is instructing the disciples about the identity of Jesus (christology) and what it means to follow Jesus (discipleship). The segment begins and ends with a healing of a blind man (8:22-26; 10:46-52); the symbolic significance is obvious. After Peter's confession of Jesus as the Messiah (8:27-30), there are three sections, each of which has a passion prediction (8:31; 9:31; 10:33-34) and a misunderstanding by the disciples (8:32-33; 9:32-37; 10:35-45), followed in the first two cases by teachings on the demands of discipleship.

54 **(A) Healing a Blind Man (8:22-26).** If any story in Mark has a symbolic function, it is the healing of the blind man at Bethsaida (8:22-26) (and the healing of Bartimaeus [10:46-52]). On the way, Jesus will impress upon the disciples the necessity of his death and resurrection. Nevertheless, the disciples are slow to understand Jesus. In the case of the blind man of Bethsaida, the coming to sight is gradual and imperfect; he does not follow Jesus. Bartimaeus is healed immediately and follows Jesus on the way. Describing these stories as "symbolic" does not deny their basis in history, nor does it mean that they were intended purely as allegorical statements. **22.** *Bethsaida:* Finally the destination announced in 6:45 is reached. There some people bring a blind man to Jesus and ask that he lay hands on him (see 7:32). **23.** *spitting in his eyes:* For the use of spittle in a cure, see 7:33. This story differs from 7:31-37 in that the healing takes place here in two stages. Implicit in 8:23 is that Jesus placed his hands on the man's eyes (8:25) and removed his hands before asking the question. **24.** *I see men . . . :* The syntax ("I see men that like trees I see them walking") is difficult, suggesting to many commentators that the Aram particle *dĕ,* "who," "that," etc. has been mistranslated. The point is that the man's return to sight is gradual, at first not completely perfect. **25.** *and he looked, and was restored, and saw all things clearly:* Three verbs serve to underline the completeness of the man's cure after the first, only partial healing. **26.** *do not enter the village:* Some mss. either substitute or add in some form the words "speak to no one (in the village)," which seems like an attempt at clarifying why the newly healed man should not enter his village. It is another command to silence after a miraculous action on Jesus' part (see 1:44; 5:43; 7:36).

55 **(B) Jesus the Christ (8:27-30).** Peter's confession of Jesus as the Messiah/Christ is pivotal in Mark. The passage suggests that this identification is correct (as opposed to JBap, Elijah, or one of the prophets), but it needs explanation in the following three instructions,

with particular attention to the meaning of Messiah/Christ as applied to Jesus. What the disciples (and Mark's readers) need to learn is how the passion and death of Jesus fit in with his identity as the Jewish Messiah. **27.** *the villages of Caesarea Philippi:* The city was built by Philip and named Caesarea Philippi to distinguish it from Caesarea Maritima; → Biblical Geography, 73:57. The "villages" refer to the settlements around the city. *who do people say that I am?:* Jesus' general question prepares for his more concrete query to the disciples in 8:29. It also gives the theme for the teachings along the way—christology (and its implications for discipleship). **28.** *John the Baptist, and others Elijah, and still others one of the prophets:* The same guesses appeared with reference to Herod Antipas's execution of JBap in 6:14-16. Messiah is not among the popular identifications of Jesus. **29.** *you are the Christ:* To Jesus' concrete query to the disciples, Peter as spokesman acknowledges Jesus to be the Messiah. Hebr *māšîah* is translated as Gk *christos;* both words mean "anointed" (→ Jesus, 78:34; OT Thought, 77:152-54). Though various figures in ancient Israel were anointed, the term came to be applied most distinctively to kings. Some writings in Jesus' time (esp. *Pss. Sol.* 17) used it to describe Israel's future leader in the period before the *eschaton* and during it; he would fulfill Israel's hopes based on God's promises. See *PNT* 64-69. **30.** *not to tell anyone about him:* By counseling his disciples to be silent, Jesus avoids false interpretations of his messiahship and prepares for the three instructions that follow.

56 **(C) First Instruction on Christology and Discipleship (8:31-9:29).** Having presented a transitional miracle story about coming to see (8:22-26) and having identified Jesus as the Christ (8:27-30), the Marcan narrative explains what it means to call Jesus the Christ and what its implications are for disciples.

57 (a) FIRST PASSION PREDICTION AND ITS CONSEQUENCES FOR DISCIPLESHIP (8:31-38). In 8:31-33, Jesus clarifies the nature of his identity as the Messiah/Christ by means of the first passion prediction. Peter's impetuous rejection of the prediction serves as a foil for Jesus' insistence on his suffering, death, and resurrection. 8:34-38 is a collection of sayings about discipleship in which the theme of suffering predominates: the need for self-denial (8:34), losing one's life for the gospel (8:35), the value of the true self (8:36-37), and not being ashamed of the Son of Man (8:38). The combination of the two incidents shows that the christology expressed in the first incident has implications for the discipleship sketched by the four sayings in the second incident: As the master goes, so must the disciple go. **31.** *the Son of Man must suffer many things:* Instead of Messiah/Christ, Jesus uses Son of Man (see 2:10,28) in referring to himself. The vb. for "must" (*dei*) has the sense of compulsion in accordance with God's plan. The extent to which the wording of the three passion predictions (8:31; 9:31; 10:33-34) has been influenced by the events that took place (*vaticinia ex eventu*) is difficult to assess. Surely there is some verbal influence (esp. in 10:33-34), but this fact does not mean that Jesus had no intimation of the fate that awaited him in Jerusalem. *by the elders and chief priests and scribes:* There is no reference to the Pharisees; in the Marcan passion narrative the Pharisees play no explicit role in Jesus' condemnation and death. *after three days rise again:* For the third day as marking a decisive turning point, see Hos 6:2; Jonah 1:17; 2:10. This OT background makes it plausible that Jesus spoke about his future exaltation, though it probably was not as explicit as the present form of the text. **32.** *he spoke the word boldly:* Prior to this, Jesus met speculations about his identity with commands to silence. **33.** *he rebuked Peter* *and said, "Get behind me, Satan":* Peter's impetuous action fits in with the portrayal of his character in the gospel tradition; it is also hard to imagine early Christians creating a story in which Peter is addressed as "Satan." Peter expresses the incorrect understanding of Jesus' messiahship that Mark wished to rectify. Anyone who denies the passion, death, and resurrection of Jesus stands on the side of Satan (see Matt 4:10). By calling Peter "Satan," Jesus indicates that the false view of his messiahship is a temptation (see Job 1–2; Zech 3:1–2). **34.** *the crowd with his disciples:* Mark's editorial framework for the sayings on discipleship presents them as public teachings that allude to sufferings of Jesus made explicit to the inner circle of disciples in 8:31–33. *carry his cross:* Crucifixion was well known to Jews as the ultimate Roman punishment. The condemned man carried the upper part of the cross (the crossbeam; see Mark 15:21). The image (see Matt 10:38; 16:24; Luke 9:23; 14:27) may express submission to divine authority on the analogy of the condemned criminal's submission to Roman authority. Whether the earthly Jesus used this specific image to refer to his own fate cannot be determined with certainty, though the early Christians surely read it with Jesus' death in mind. **35.** *whoever loses his life for my sake and the gospel's will save it:* What is distinctive in Mark is the phrase "and the gospel's" (cf. Matt 16:25; Luke 9:24); "gospel" refers not to a book or a literary genre but to the good news about Jesus or Jesus himself. **37.** *for what can a man give in return for his life?:* "Life" (Gk *psychē*, Hebr *nepeš*) is used in the sense of "the true self." In following Jesus, the disciples can find their true selves, and nothing is more important. **38.** *the Son of Man will be ashamed of him:* Some commentators find a distinction between Jesus ("me and my words") and the future Son of Man (see Dan 7:13–14). But it is doubtful that the early Christians perceived such a distinction. The earthly Jesus may have envisioned his role at the last judgment as advocate or accuser before God in relation to the response to his teaching.

58 (b) JESUS' TRANSFIGURATION AND THE ELIJAH QUESTION (9:1–13). The first incident (9:1–8) establishes Jesus' glorious identity as the beloved Son of God, and the second incident (9:9–13) places his divine sonship in the context of Jewish expectations about the kingdom and resurrection. The discussion about Elijah's coming (9:9–13) is linked to the transfiguration story through their common reference to Elijah. This external link enables Mark to balance the glorious aspects of Jesus seen in the transfiguration with references to his death and resurrection, esp. when Jesus' fate is taken in connection with the fate of JBap. Once more the implication for disciples is that, as the master goes, so the disciples must go. **1.** *until they have seen the kingdom come with power:* The most obvious meaning of Jesus' promise is that it refers to the full flowering of God's kingdom at the end of human history. The kingdom will come before some of the bystanders die. In the present context the saying may refer to the anticipation of the kingdom in Jesus' death and resurrection (see 8:31), the judgment (see 8:38), or the transfiguration (see 9:2–8). The most convincing explanation is that Mark presents the transfiguration as a preview or anticipation of the final coming of God's kingdom, and thus as a commentary on 9:1 (M. Künzi, *Das Naherwartungslogion Markus 9,1 par* [BGBE 21; Tübingen, 1977]). **2.** *after six days:* The temporal reference may have been part of the traditional story. Or there may be some connection to Israel's preparation and purification at Sinai (see Exod 24:15–16). Or since the seventh day occurs after six days, there may be an anticipation of passion week in Jerusalem. *Peter, James, and John:* See comment on 5:37. Luke 9:28 says that Jesus

went up the mountain to pray; Mark does not tell us why he went up. *a high mountain:* Among the traditional identifications of the mountain are Tabor and Hermon. Mountains are the usual settings for supernatural revelations and theophanies. *was transformed before them:* The term *metamorphōthē* indicates that the form of Jesus was changed. The disciples are granted a glimpse of him in his glorious state, which is to be his eternal state after the death and resurrection (see 2 Cor 3:18). There may be a connection with the glorification of Moses (see Exod 34:29). **4.** *Elijah with Moses:* If the two OT figures represent the Law and the Prophets, the order is strange (cf. Matt 17:3). There may be some reference to their having been taken up into heaven (see 2 Kgs 2:11; Deut 34:6) or their expected roles in the coming of the kingdom (see Mal 3:23–24; Deut 18:15,18). **5.** *Rabbi, it is good for us to be here:* The address of Jesus as "Rabbi" is strange; Matt 17:4 has "Lord," and Luke 9:33 has "Master." The reason why it was good was the unique and glorious nature of the experience. Peter's suggestion to construct three booths aims at prolonging the experience; there is probably a reference to the feast of Tabernacles (see Lev 23:39–43). **7.** *a cloud was overshadowing them:* Given the allusions to Exod in this account, it is best to take the cloud as the vehicle for God's presence as in Exod 16:10; 19:9; 24:15–16; 33:9. The voice from the cloud is a divine voice. *this is my beloved Son:* The heavenly voice corrects Peter's confession (see 8:29) and alludes to the identification of Jesus at the baptism (see 1:11). The command to hear Jesus may point to his passion predictions (8:31; 9:31; 10:33–34). **8.** *Jesus alone with them:* The experience ends abruptly. Its visionary character establishes it as a preview of Jesus' eternal glory. But before that state can begin, he must make his way to Jerusalem. **9.** *as they were coming down from the mountain:* This phrase ties the conversation about Elijah's coming to the transfiguration story, thus giving the latter a more obvious connection with Jesus' passion. *until the Son of Man arise from the dead:* Unlike the other commands to silence, this one has a good chance of being obeyed (because only three disciples are involved) and has a definite time limit. **10.** *questioning what it is to be raised from the dead:* The disciples' problem was how Jesus could be raised from the dead before and apart from the general resurrection, which was to occur at the coming of God's kingdom. **11.** *the scribes say that Elijah must come first:* According to Mal 3:23–24, Elijah's return will precede the coming of the great and awesome day of the Lord. The disciples' puzzlement was how Jesus could be raised from the dead unless Elijah came first. **12.** *should suffer many things and be treated with contempt:* While conceding that Elijah must come first, Jesus also insists that his own passion and death will precede his resurrection. **13.** *Elijah has already come:* The statement indirectly identifies Elijah as JBap. The fate that JBap met (see 6:14–29) foreshadows that of Jesus, the Son of Man.

(Nardoni, E., *La transfiguración de Jesús y el diálogo sobre Elías . . .* [Buenos Aires, 1977]. Nützel, J. M., *Die Verklärungserzählung im Markusevangelium* [FB 6; Würzburg, 1973].)

59 (c) HEALING A POSSESSED BOY (9:14–29). This healing story is remarkable for its length and vivid details (cf. Matt 17:14–21 and Luke 9:37–43a). It begins (9:14–19) and ends (9:28–29) with the focus on the disciples' inability to heal the boy; in the middle (9:20–27) the father and the boy are central characters. The core of the account is the dialogue between the father and Jesus (9:21–24), which is only in Mark. The father's profession of faith emerges as a necessary element in the healing process. The disciples' inability to perform the healing is finally explained with reference to reliance on God's power alone (9:29). **14.** *when they came to the disciples, they saw:* The pl. vbs. do not flow well from the preceding story; several important mss. have changed them into sg. forms. *a great crowd:* Whereas the presence of the crowd is assumed from the beginning of the story (see 9:15,17), in the middle of the story (see 9:25) the crowd is beginning to form or is at least coming together. *scribes arguing with them:* In the present context we are to imagine the nine disciples (apart from Peter, James, and John) engaged in dispute with the scribes. Thus the scene is set for Jesus' powerful action, one that can be done by him alone. **18.** *it throws him down, and he foams, grinds his teeth, and becomes rigid:* The description of what happens when the "speechless spirit" (*pneuma alalon*) seizes the boy is usually explained as an epileptic seizure. The disciples' inability to deal with this case is somewhat surprising in the light of their earlier success (see 6:7,13,30). **19.** *O faithless generation:* Jesus' comment has the tone of one worn out by the inappropriate responses to his teaching and activity; it sets him over against his whole age, not simply the crowd, the scribes, and the disciples. There may also be an intimation of death in the comment. **20.** *the spirit saw him and immediately convulsed him:* On seeing Jesus, the spirit convulsed the boy, thus illustrating the symptoms described in 9:18. Note that the story assumes the fact of demonic possession, not merely a medical problem. **23.** *If you can! All things are possible to one who believes:* The first part of Jesus' statement repeats the father's words from 9:22 in order to challenge them. The second part assumes that faith on the father's part is integral to the healing action to be done by Jesus. **24.** *I believe; help my unbelief:* The father's eloquent prayer affirms his faith in Jesus' healing power and admits that as yet his faith is still mixed with doubts. As the story proceeds, it is clear that this protestation of faith was sufficient for the healing to occur. **25.** *O speechless and deaf spirit:* Before this address, the spirit is also described as "unclean," whereas in 9:17 it is called simply a "speechless" spirit. **26.** *he was like a dead man:* The state of repose induced in the boy by the exorcism leads the crowd to assume that he was dead. This guess prepares for the resurrection terminology in the next verse. No reaction of wonder or amazement is attributed to the crowd. **27.** *he raised him up, and he arose:* The two Gk vbs. *ēgeiren* and *anestē* are technical terms in the NT used in connection with resurrection. Thus the healing is perhaps presented as a preview of Jesus' resurrection, at least as having the resurrection as its background. **28.** *his disciples asked him privately:* The focus of attention shifts back to the disciples as in 9:14-19. In the Marcan framework, their puzzlement about their inability to heal the boy arose from their earlier commission (6:7) and success (6:13,30). **29.** *except by prayer:* Jesus' explanation suggests that the disciples must rely on God's power symbolized by prayer. The phrase "and by fasting" in some mss. is a later addition.

60   (D) Second Instruction on Christology and Discipleship (9:30-10:31). What holds these very different teachings together is the theme of the kingdom of God and what entering it might demand. Many of the demands are quite radical, seeming to have their basis in Jesus' experience with his first disciples and the early church's effort at continuing this life-style of renunciation as a way of contributing to the proclamation of God's kingdom.

61   (a) SECOND PASSION PREDICTION AND ITS CONSEQUENCES FOR DISCIPLESHIP (9:30-50). The second explanation of Jesus' messiahship begins with a passion prediction (9:30-32), corrects another misunderstanding about discipleship (9:33-37), tells the story about the strange exorcist (9:38-40), and concludes with various sayings (9:41-50). The true disciple of Jesus must be the last and the servant of all (9:35). The artificial catchword-links ("in my name," "scandalize," and "fire") suggest that the sayings were put together at the pre-Marcan stage for purposes of memorization and catechesis. **30.** *they passed through Galilee, and he did not wish anyone to know it:* The reason for the secrecy about the journey through Galilee seems to be Jesus' desire to instruct his disciples about his passion and resurrection (9:31). The public ministry in Galilee is over (see 10:1). **31.** *the Son of Man is to be delivered into the hands of men:* The vb. *paradidotai,* "to be delivered," will become increasingly prominent as the passion story proceeds (see 14:21,41; 15:1,10,15). Although there may be some allusion to Jesus' betrayal by Judas, the more basic meaning concerns the divine plan of salvation in which Jesus' death is pivotal. *having been killed:* In none of the passion predictions (8:31; 9:31; 10:33-34) is the precise mode of Jesus' death made clear. **32.** *but they did not understand the saying:* In the light of the first passion prediction (8:31) and the explanations surrounding it, one would think that the disciples could hardly fail to understand. Mark's insistence on the point suggests that he was developing an increasingly negative portrait of the disciples. **33.** *they came to Capernaum, and when he was in the house:* As part of the journey from Caesarea Philippi (8:27) to Jerusalem, Jesus and the disciples stop at Capernaum (see 1:21; 2:1), presumably at Peter's house (1:29). **34.** *who is the greatest?:* Matt 18:1 adds "in the kingdom of heaven," and the same perspective is suggested by Mark 10:37. But here the emphasis may be the present group of disciples. At least nothing in the rest of the story demands an eschatological setting. **35.** *if anyone wishes to be first, he shall be the last of all and the servant of all:* For a similar teaching, see 10:43-44. The ideal of leadership as service will be exemplified by Jesus as the Gospel story continues. **36.** *taking a child:* The child is not so much a symbol of innocence or humility as someone without legal status and therefore helpless. The child can do nothing for the disciple; to receive a child is to perform a good act for an insignificant person, without hope of earthly reward. Since Aram *talyā'* can mean both "servant" and "child," the demonstration in 9:36 may be a better proof of the teaching in 9:35 than an Eng. transl. can convey. **37.** *whoever receives one such child in my name:* The idea behind the saying is that whoever receives someone's emissary receives the man himself. So whoever receives a child receives Jesus, and whoever receives Jesus receives God who sent Jesus. The key word in the saying is "in my name," which attracts the following episode (see 9:38-39) about exorcism in Jesus' name (see also 9:41). **38.** *we forbade him because he was not following us:* An OT parallel to the story of the strange exorcist is the account about Eldad and Medad, who prophesy without being registered (Num 11:26-30; see Acts 8:18; 19:13-14); Moses' attitude toward them is tolerance. The exorcist was using Jesus' name as a powerful tool (see Mark 1:24; 5:7). **39.** *do not stop him:* Jesus' tolerant attitude is grounded in the idea that anyone who exorcized in his name would be slow to speak ill of him. The example of tolerance may have been used to criticize tendencies toward exclusivism and cliquishness in the early church, though this use hardly explains the creation of the story. The saying in 9:40 is a generalization in proverb form of the more concrete teaching in 9:39. **41.** *because you have the name of Christ:* The connection of this saying with the preceding material is based on the "name" (see 9:37,38-39) rather than content. The situation is the opposite of that in 9:37, for here someone does a kindness to the disciples in Jesus' name. **42.** *whoever scandalizes one of these little ones:* The vb. "scandalize" ("cause to sin," "put an obstacle in front of") is the catchword for the whole group of sayings in 9:42–48 (see 9:42,43,45,47). The little ones in this saying may well be members of the community of the disciples (cf. Mark 9:37). **43.** *if your hand scandalizes you:* The structure of the sayings in 9:43,45,47 is the same: If one part of the body causes you to sin, cut it off in order that you may enter life/kingdom and avoid Gehenna. That these sayings had a communal dimension and served to exclude members of the church who gave offense is plausible in view of ancient Greco-Roman uses of the body as a communal metaphor. *Gehenna:* According to 2 Kgs 23:10, the Valley of Hinnom (Hebr *gē' hinnôm*) had been used as a place for child sacrifice (see Jer 7:31; 19:5–6). Although the term Gehenna originally described the valley to the W and S of Jerusalem, it came to be used as the name for the place of eternal punishment (see *1 Enoch* 27:2; *4 Ezra* 7:36). *the unquenchable fire:* This added description of Gehenna is probably based on Isa 66:24 (see 9:44,46,48). **44.** *where their worm does not die . . . :* In some mss., 9:44,46,48 all give a quotation from Isa 66:24. Whereas the textual evidence for its presence in 9:48 is good, the earliest and best mss. omit it in 9:44,46. **47.** *to enter the kingdom of God:* In the structure of the three scandal sayings, to enter the kingdom (see 10:15,23–25) is the same as to enter life. **48.** *where their worm does not die . . . :* This description of Gehenna is taken from Isa 66:24. Its final clause about unquenchable fire attracted the sayings in 9:49–50 on the basis of the catchword "fire." **49.** *for everyone will be salted with fire:* The images of salt and fire probably had something to do with purification during the period of suffering (the "woes of the Messiah") before the final coming of God's kingdom. **50.** *but if the salt becomes tasteless:* Here salt is a seasoning rather than a purifying agent; the salt metaphor probably refers to the disciples' function as "salt of the earth" (Matt 5:13) and agents of spiritual wisdom (Col 4:16). *have salt in yourselves:* The third salt saying alludes to hospitality and friendship among Jesus' followers.

62   (b) JESUS' TEACHING ON MARRIAGE AND DIVORCE (10:1–12). Jesus' teaching about marriage and divorce appears as a further challenge to those who wish to follow him. The radical teaching in Mark 10:1–12 (see Luke 16:18) most likely reflects the view of Jesus himself. Its positive thrust is that the married couple constitutes "one flesh" and therefore their relationship cannot be dissolved. The reverse side is the prohibition of divorce and remarriage. Other NT passages (Matt 5:32; 19:9; 1 Cor 7:10–16) introduce some exceptions into the absolute teaching of Jesus. **2.** *Pharisees came up:* Some mss. have an impersonal introduction ("people asked him") without any mention of the Pharisees (see Matt 19:3). But the idea that they were testing Jesus later in the verse suggests that some mention of the Pharisees was original. Note that Jesus has moved his teaching ministry from Galilee to Judea. *if it is lawful for a husband to divorce a wife:* The question concerns the legality of divorce, not the grounds for divorce (see Matt 19:3). The question is expressed in such a way as to indicate that the questioners knew that Jesus' prohibition of divorce conflicted with the assumption behind Deut 24:1–4. The question may have been designed to draw Jesus into conflict with the much-divorced Herod family. **3.** *what did Moses command you?:* Deut 24:1–4 takes the institution of divorce for granted; it concerns only the procedure to be followed when the husband has decided to divorce his wife, and the prohibition of remarriage after her second marriage has ended. The grounds for divorce are stated vaguely as "some indecency in her" (*bāh 'erwat dābār*). This vagueness led to a rabbinic debate

about specifying the meaning of this phrase (see *m. Giṭṭ.* 9:10); in this context the so-called Matthean exceptive clauses (Matt 5:32; 19:9) are to be read. But in Mark the issue is more basic: Is divorce lawful? **4.** *Moses allowed a man to write and divorce:* To Jesus' question, the Pharisees respond on the basis of Deut 24:1–4. Divorce in ancient Judaism was not a public legal action in a court. The husband simply wrote out a decree ("I release and divorce my wife this day") and presented it to his wife. **5.** *on account of your hardness of heart:* Jesus regards the teaching of Deut 24:1–4 as a concession to human weakness and a dispensation from the original plan of God for marriage. As the story proceeds, Jesus will play one OT passage against another. **6.** *from the beginning of creation:* As proof that his prohibition of divorce was biblical, Jesus quotes Gen 1:27; 2:24. The effect of the quotation is to assert that God's original plan was that married persons constitute "one flesh" and so divorce is forbidden. Deut 24:1–4 allowed divorce as a concession to human weakness. Jesus' teaching is a restoration of God's plan for creation, not something in opposition to Scripture. No exceptions are foreseen (cf. Matt 5:32; 19:9; 1 Cor 7:10–16). **8.** *they are no longer two but one flesh:* This ideal of marriage is a deduction based on Gen 2:24; it supplies the reason why divorce is impossible. **9.** *let not man put asunder:* The "man" is the husband, not some third party like a judge. Since according to Deut 24:1–4 the husband could initiate and carry out the procedure, there was no need for a third party. Here Jesus abrogates the OT procedure. **10.** *in the house the disciples asked him again:* The house could not be the one in Capernaum (see 1:29; 9:33), since Jesus and the disciples have already left Galilee. The framework of private instruction is the occasion for plain teaching about divorce and remarriage. **11.** *whoever divorces his wife and marries another, commits adultery against her:* This same absolute teaching appears in Luke 16:18a. CD 4:19–5:2 seems to forbid polygamy rather than remarriage after divorce, though 11QTemple 57:17–19 forbids remarriage after divorce (J. A. Fitzmyer, *TAG* 79–111). **12.** *if she divorces her husband:* It is usually said that according to Jewish law only the husband could institute divorce proceedings (see Deut 24:1–4; Josephus, *Ant.* 15.7.10 § 259). The teaching in Mark 10:12 is frequently taken as an adaptation of Jesus' teaching to conditions in which Roman law (which allowed women to initiate divorce proceedings) prevailed. There are, however, some examples of Jewish women who divorced their husbands (E. Bammel, *ZNW* 61 [1970] 95–101).

63   (c) JESUS' BLESSING OF THE CHILDREN (10:13–16). After a passage about marriage, one about children is appropriate. But this text is really about the kingdom of God and what kind of people can expect to be part of it. Only those who recognize and receive it as a gift (as a child receives gifts) can expect to be part of God's kingdom; the kingdom is for those who make no claims to power or status, for the kingdom transcends all human power and status. **13.** *that he might touch them:* As the conclusion of the story makes clear (10:16), those who brought the children were seeking a blessing from Jesus in the form of the imposition of hands. The children could have been of any age from infancy up to 12. **14.** *Jesus grew indignant:* This further reference to Jesus' emotions (see 1:43; 3:5; 8:12; 14:33–34) is directed at the disciples' failure to understand Jesus and the nature of the kingdom that he preached. The disciples once more serve as a foil for Jesus' positive teaching. *of such is the kingdom of God:* The chief characteristic of children is receptivity. Without physical power and legal status, children know best how to receive. The kingdom must be received as a gift, for no human power or status can create it or force it. **15.** *whoever does receive the kingdom of God like a child:* This saying clarifies the latter part of 10:14, showing that only those who accept the kingdom as a gift can expect to enter it. **16.** *he blessed them, laying hands on them:* In writings of the time, children are presented as either examples of unreasonable behavior or objects to be trained. In this passage (see also 9:33-37) they are taken seriously as persons and enjoy a relationship with Jesus and the kingdom.

64   (d) JESUS' TEACHINGS ABOUT RICHES (10:17-31). The final part of this section consists of three units on wealth and the kingdom: the story of the rich man (10:17-22), Jesus' instruction to the disciples (10:23-27), and his teaching about rewards for giving up riches (10:28-31). The chief theological teachings are that wealth can be an obstacle to discipleship and that the rewards of discipleship are infinitely greater than the sacrifices. **17.** *a certain one ran up and knelt before him:* Only at the end of the story do we learn that he was rich (10:22); no mention is made of his age (cf. Matt 19:20). *Good master, what shall I do to inherit eternal life:* The address "good master" is unusual; perhaps it was taken as too effusive and obsequious, thus prompting the testy reaction in 10:18. The phrase "eternal life" is a synonym for the kingdom of God (see 9:43-47). **18.** *no one is good except God alone:* A gulf between Jesus and God is contrary to much of the gospel tradition. It is explicable as either a testy reaction on Jesus' part or a pedagogical device on Mark's part regarding the identity of the Son of God. **19.** *you know the commandments:* The list that follows is taken mainly from the second part of the Decalogue (Exod 20:12-17; Deut 5:16-21), which deals with human relationships. *do not defraud:* This may be a restatement of "do not steal," or a way of summarizing the ninth and tenth commandments, or a reference to the *korban* controversy (7:9-13). **21.** *Jesus looking on him loved him:* The love was based on the man's genuine efforts and success at observing the commandments (see 10:20). This love issues in the call to discipleship (10:22). *go, sell what you have and give to the poor:* Jesus' challenge to the man is better taken as related to his particular case than as a general principle of Christian life or even as the basis of a superior religious state. In Judaism wealth was often taken as a sign of divine favor with an obligation to give alms to the poor. What was so hard in this man's case was the invitation to forgo even the privilege of almsgiving for the sake of sharing in Jesus' life-style of dependence on God while proclaiming the coming of his kingdom. **22.** *for he had many possessions:* These possessions probably had to do with the ownership of property and the financial benefits accruing from it. The first part of the verse paints a poignant picture of the difficult choice made by the rich man: he asked the question, but Jesus' answer was too hard for him. **23.** *Jesus said to his disciples:* Once again the private instruction of the disciples follows a public teaching (see 4:10-20,34; 9:28-29; 10:10-12). The saying is a general comment on the preceding story of the rich man who failed to accept Jesus' invitation to discipleship. **24.** *the disciples were amazed:* The amazement stems from Jesus' reversal of the idea that riches are a sign of divine favor. **25.** *easier for a camel to pass through the eye of a needle:* The grotesque image drives home the point that it is practically impossible for a rich person to enter the kingdom. The substitution of *kamilon*, "rope," for *kamēlon*, "camel," in some mss. and the fanciful idea that there was a gate in Jerusalem through which a camel could squeeze are attempts at blunting the hyperbole. **27.** *all things are possible to God:* To the disciples' astonished question, "Who can be saved?" (10:26), Jesus' reply emphasizes the power of God and the reliance on him as the only ways to salvation. Thus mere renunciation of

wealth (see 10:17-22) by itself is not even enough to guarantee salvation. **28.** *we have left all things and followed you:* Peter as spokesman for the disciples juxtaposes their actions to the missed opportunity of the rich man (10:17-22). Behind the statement is the question, What is the reward for accepting the challenge of discipleship? **30.** *now in this age . . . and in the age to come eternal life:* Jesus promises rewards not only in the *eschaton* but also in the present, when a disciple can enjoy a rich social and religious fellowship. The phrase "with persecutions" appears to be a Marcan editorial twist, suggesting that discipleship necessarily involves persecution and suffering. **31.** *the last will be first:* In its present Marcan context (cf. Matt 19:30; 20:16; Luke 13:30), the saying is encouragement to disciples about the reality of the "great reversal." The rewards of discipleship surpass its sacrifices now and in the future.

65   **(E) Third Instruction on Christology and Discipleship (10:32-45).** This segment consists of the third passion prediction (10:32-34), which is more detailed than the preceding ones (8:31; 9:31), and an incident (10:35-45) in which the disciples show that they still have not grasped the meaning of Jesus' teaching and example.

66   (a) THIRD PASSION PREDICTION (10:32-34). The third prediction foretells the handing over of Jesus to the chief priests (= Mark 14:53); his condemnation by the priests (14:64); the handing over to the Romans (15:1); the mocking, spitting, and scourging (14:65; 15:15-20); the execution (15:24,37); and the resurrection (16:1-8). The only omission is any reference to crucifixion as the mode of Jesus' death. **32.** *was going ahead of them:* There is something of the same tone as in Luke 9:51, where "Jesus sets his face to go to Jerusalem" despite his awareness of what awaits him there. The passage indicates Jesus' conscious acceptance of his destiny. **33.** *the Son of Man will be handed over . . . and they will hand him over:* On the Gk vb. *paradidōmi*, see comment on 9:31. **34.** *after three days:* This typically Marcan formula (see 8:31; 9:31) has been changed in some mss. to the more common NT expression "on the third day."

67   (b) ITS CONSEQUENCES FOR DISCIPLESHIP (10:35-45). An incident highlights the obtuseness of the disciples. To the request made by James and John (10:37), Jesus gives three answers: a place in the kingdom demands suffering (10:38-39); it is not Jesus' prerogative to determine status in the coming kingdom (10:40); and leadership in Jesus' community means service (10:41-45). **35.** *James and John:* They, along with Peter, have formed an inner circle among the disciples (see comment on 5:37); they should have known better than to make the request they made. *we want you:* In Matt 20:20 their mother makes the request—probably part of Matthew's attempt to tone down Mark's negative portrait of the disciples. **37.** *grant us to sit, one at your right and one at your left, in your glory:* The request concerns status in the coming kingdom. Perhaps the image is Jesus enthroned as eschatological judge, or (more likely) as the Messiah presiding at the messianic banquet. **38.** *to drink the cup that I drink, or to be baptized:* The images of the cup and the bath concern suffering and death in this context (see Isa 51:17-22; Ps 69:2-3,15). Whatever eucharistic and baptismal significance may be in these images is derived from their primary message of identification with Jesus' passion and death. For the "cup" image in the passion story, see Mark 14:23; 14:36. **39.** *we can:* The disciples' confident protestation is full of irony in the light of their cowardice during the passion. Jesus' response to them is a promise of martyrdom, intense suffering related to his own suffering. **40.** *not for me to grant:* Matt 20:23 assigns this prerogative to the Father.

The saying implies some subordination of Jesus to the Father; for this reason it was exploited by the Arians in the early christological debates. For whom these places are prepared is not at all clear. **41.** *the ten began to be indignant:* This note serves to attach teachings about Christian leadership as service to the preceding story and makes them into part of Jesus' response to James and John's request. **42.** *those who are supposed to rule over the Gentiles:* Irony marks the beginning of the statement; the vbs. "lord it over" (*katekyrieuousin*) and "exercise power over" (*katexousiazousin*) are vivid ways of describing leadership as raw power. **43.** *whoever wishes to be great among you shall be the servant of all:* See 9:35. The key term in both passages is *diakonos* (lit., "one who waits on tables"); it contrasts sharply with the power terminology of the preceding verse. **44.** *the slave of all:* Here the key term is *doulos*—an even humbler word than *diakonos*. **45.** *the Son of Man came not to be served but to serve:* This part of the verse is a fitting conclusion to the teachings contained in 10:42-44; it grounds them in the example of Jesus. *to give his life as a ransom for many:* "To give one's life" refers to martyrdom in 1 Macc 2:50; 6:44. *Lytron,* "ransom," conveys the idea of deliverance by purchase on behalf of a captive, a slave, or a criminal. The "for many" echoes Isa 53:11-12. The whole clause presents Jesus' death as effecting a deliverance that could not be brought about by the "many" through their own power.

68   **(F) Healing Blind Bartimaeus (10:46-52).** In 8:22-26 an unnamed blind man is brought to Jesus, has his sight restored gradually, and is told to keep his healing a secret; in 10:46-52 Bartimaeus actively seeks out Jesus, is healed immediately, and becomes a disciple on the way. The second story not only rounds off the unit but also illustrates some progress in faith. It is as much a call story as a healing story. Bartimaeus's reaction to Jesus and his willingness to follow him on the way of discipleship contrast with the disciples' misunderstanding and blindness displayed during the journey. **46.** *Jericho:* The place is 15 mi NE of Jerusalem and 5 mi. W of the Jordan River (→ Biblical Geography, 73:66). Thus the journey that began in Caesarea Philippi is reaching its destination in Jerusalem. *the son of Timaeus, Bar Timaeus, a blind beggar:* It is unusual for Mark to supply the name of a person to be healed (see 5:22); it appears first in its Gk transl. and then in its Aram form. **47.** *Son of David, have mercy on me:* This is the first public application of the messianic title "Son of David" to Jesus. It is also a first recognition (apart from Peter) of Jesus' true identity by a human being rather than a demon. **50.** *throwing off his garment:* The "garment" may have been clothing, but more likely the cloth that Bartimaeus spread out to receive his offerings. The many references to garments in Mark (2:21; 5:25-30; 6:56; 9:3; 11:7-8; 13:16; 15:20,24) suggest that Bartimaeus was leaving behind the "old order." **51.** *what do you wish that I should do:* The question provides the occasion for a profession of faith about Jesus' power to heal. **52.** *your faith has saved you:* See comments on 5:23,28,34; the faith of the person has been essential to the healing. *he followed him on the way:* On *ēkolouthei,* "followed," see comment on 1:18. In the light of the journey begun at 8:22 and leading up to Jerusalem, the description suggests that Bartimaeus joined in Jesus' passion experience.

69   **(VI) The First Part of Passion Week in Jerusalem (11:1-13:37).** Jesus' activity in Jerusalem prior to the passion is described in the framework of three days (11:1,12,20), in which the third day features sayings, controversies, parables, and an eschatological discourse. The section as a whole prepares for the passion by means of symbolic actions, shows who Jesus' Jerusalem opponents are and what gets them so angry,

and places Jesus' death and resurrection in the context of events leading up to the *eschaton.*

70   **(A) Entrance on the First Day (11:1-11).** Jesus' entrance into Jerusalem is best understood in line with symbolic actions done by the OT prophets. The heart of the symbolic action is Jesus riding into Jerusalem from the Mt. of Olives. According to Zech 9:9, the Lord as a divine warrior would ride into Jerusalem, seated on the foal of an ass. According to Zech 14:4, the great eschatological battle would occur at the Mt. of Olives. The demonstration suggests that with Jesus the eschatological events are happening and that he is a key figure within them. **1.** *to Jerusalem, to Bethphage and Bethany, at the Mount of Olives:* The journey described in 8:22-10:52 has reached its goal—Jerusalem. The Mt. of Olives runs parallel to the E side of the city of Jerusalem. Josephus (*Ant.* 20.7.6 § 167-72) tells the story of a messianic pretender who claimed to be able to bring down Jerusalem's walls while standing on the Mt. of Olives. Bethphage and Bethany are small villages near Jerusalem (→ Biblical Geography, 73:95). **2.** *you will find a colt: Pōlos* can refer to a young horse, but here in view of the obvious allusion to Zech 9:9 ("your king comes to you; triumphant and victorious is he, humble and riding on an ass, on a colt the foal of an ass") it refers to a young donkey. There is some ambiguity about whether Jesus' instructions were predictions reflecting supernatural knowledge on his part or simply the reflection of an arrangement that he had made beforehand with the owner. **3.** *The Lord has need of it, and he will send it back here soon again: Kyrios,* "Lord," is most likely Jesus rather than "the owner," though its meaning would be something like "the master" or "the gentleman" (but later Christians would read into it a more developed christology of Jesus' lordship). The second part of the sentence belongs to Jesus' instruction, conveying a promise that he would return the animal as soon as he completed his entrance into Jerusalem. **6.** *told them what Jesus said:* This expression gives the impression of a fulfillment of Jesus' prediction based on his supernatural knowledge. At least, everything is proceeding according to his instructions. **7.** *he sat upon it:* Thus Jesus' entry into Jerusalem fulfills Zech 9:9. There the victorious king seems to be Yahweh understood as the divine warrior. **8.** *others having cut leafy branches:* Unlike John 12:13, the Marcan account does not specify the nature of the branches as palms. In fact, palm branches would be better suited for the feast of Tabernacles (see Lev 23:39-43) or Hanukkah (see 2 Macc 10:7; 1 Macc 13:51) than for Passover. **9.** *Hosanna! Blessed is he who comes in the name of the Lord:* The crowd greets Jesus with words from Ps 118:25-26. *Hōsanna* is the Gk transliteration of *hôšaʿ-nāʾ,* "save, please," though here it functions as a greeting of homage rather than a cry for help. **10.** *blessed is the coming kingdom of our father David:* Not part of the OT quotation, this comment by the crowd gives the event a messianic direction in line with the hopes expressed in *Pss. Sol.* 17 for a glorious Davidic ruler who will restore and perfect Israel's fortunes on earth. *in the highest:* The "highest" refers to the heights of heaven where God dwells (see Ps 148:1; Job 16:19). **11.** *entered Jerusalem and went into the Temple:* For Jesus and his Galilean companions it was natural to visit the Temple immediately after the entry was over. In contrast to Matt 21:12 and Luke 19:45, Mark has a night intervene between Jesus' entrance and his cleansing of the Temple.

71   **(B) Prophetic Teachings on the Second Day (11:12-19).** The cursing of the fig tree (11:12-14) is curious on several counts: it is the only miracle in the environs of Jerusalem; it destroys property (see 5:1-20); and Jesus' behavior seems irrational and destructive.

Mark understood the cursing and its fulfillment (11:20–21) as an act of power done by Jesus, but perhaps the pre-Marcan tradition had transformed a parable told by Jesus (see Luke 13:6–9) into a story about Jesus. The symbolic level of the story focuses on Israel's lack of readiness to accept Jesus (or more likely, his message of the kingdom). The OT background is a series of passages about plants and their fruits (see Isa 1:30; Ezek 17; Joel 1; Amos 2:9; Hos 9:10,15–16; Jer 8:13; Mic 7:1; Job 18:16; see G. Münderlein, *NTS* 10 [1963–64] 89–104; H. Giesen, *BZ* 20 [1976] 95–111). The cleansing of the Temple (11:15–19) has an even more obvious symbolic value, though it surely qualifies as having historical foundations. John 2:14–22 places the event at the beginning of Jesus' public ministry and gives quite a different account. The Marcan version makes it the third in a series of prophetic actions: the Davidic Messiah purifies the house of God. By placing this incident between the two parts of the fig tree incident (11:12–14 and 11:20–21), Mark has created another "sandwich" in which the symbolic significance of both stories is enriched. **13.** *it was not the season for figs:* This explanation was added by Mark. Figs in Palestine are not ripe before June. The way the story is told suggests that Jesus really expected to find fruit on the tree and destroyed it out of disappointment. The Marcan explanation makes his action seem even more irrational, for he should have known better than to expect to find such fruit at Passover. **14.** *may no one ever eat fruit from you:* The effect of Jesus' curse is described at the beginning of the third day (11:20–21), although the punishment of withering goes beyond the terms of the curse. **15.** *those selling and buying in the Temple:* Those people traded in sacrificial victims and other cultic necessities in the Court of the Gentiles in the Temple area. The money changers gave out Jewish or Tyrian coins (see Exod 30:11–16) in return for the pilgrims' Gk or Roman money. The dove sellers provided the proper sacrifices for women (Lev 12:6–8; Luke 2:22–24), lepers (Lev 14:22), and others (Lev 15:14,29). **16.** *to carry a vessel through the Temple:* Again the general area of the Temple is meant. The vessel may have been the "moneybags" of the buyers and sellers; or perhaps the prohibition was more general (as in *m. Ber.* 9:5) against carrying baggage or making the Temple area into a shortcut. **17.** *a house of prayer for all the nations:* The statement is a quotation of Isa 56:7 LXX. The "house" is the Jerusalem Temple. Although "for all the nations" would have struck a responsive cord in Mark's readers, it is not the real focus of the OT quotation in this context. *a den of thieves:* The phrase is taken from Jer 7:11. For the Davidic Messiah's role in purifying the Temple, see *Pss. Sol.* 17:30. **18.** *the high priests and the scribes:* As in the passion predictions (8:31; 9:31; 10:33–34), there is no reference to the Pharisees. Mark states that the high priests and scribes sought to destroy Jesus but feared to do so on account of his popularity. At a pilgrimage feast like Passover, their fears would be especially strong.

72   **(C) More Teachings on the Third Day (11:20–13:37).** After an explanation of the withered fig tree (11:20–26), Mark presents five controversies plus a parable (11:27–12:37), contrasts two characters (12:38–44), and gives the eschatological discourse (13:1–37). The aim is to show who Jesus' opponents were and what issues got him into trouble with the Jerusalem authorities (W. R. Telford, *The Barren Temple and the Withered Tree* [JSNTSup 1; Sheffield, 1980]).

73   **(a)** EXPLANATIONS (11:20–26). The third day begins with the sequel to the cursing of the fig tree (11:20–21). Since Mark understood the withering of the fig tree as an act of power on Jesus' part, he has appended by way of explanation three sayings on faith and prayer

(11:23,24,25). These sayings are joined artificially on the basis of key words, and in the pre-Marcan tradition they constituted a catechesis on prayer. The insistence on the certainty that prayers will be answered seems to have been part of Jesus' distinctive teaching (see Matt 7:7–11; Luke 11:9–13). **20.** *the fig tree withered away from its roots:* The withering of the fig tree went beyond the curse of fruitlessness uttered in 11:14. **21.** *Peter remembered:* Peter acts as spokesman for the disciples, who had heard the curse uttered by Jesus (see 11:14). **22.** *Jesus answered:* The sayings in 11:22–25 are presented as an explanation of the fig tree incident. Mark's point in joining them to this incident was to draw attention to God as the source of Jesus' power. *have faith in God:* The phrase *pistin theou,* lit., "faith of God," must be an objective gen., "in God." The sentence as a whole may have functioned as the heading for the sayings that follow. It could also be taken as a question, "Do you have faith in God?" with the following sayings taken as illustrations of the ideal kind of faith. **23.** *whoever says to this mountain: Be taken up:* For parallel versions of the saying, see Matt 17:20; Luke 17:6; 1 Cor 13:2. In the present context "this mountain" could be Jerusalem as a whole or the Mt. of Olives, but there is no certainty that Jesus uttered the saying in those places. The withering of the fig tree was only a minor display of Jesus' power based on his relationship with God in prayer—a relationship that he wishes to share with his followers. **24.** *everything that you pray and ask for, believe that you will receive it:* The second saying on prayer is linked to the first by the word "believe" and to the third saying by "pray." **25.** *forgive if you have anything against anyone:* The third saying is really about forgiveness (see Matt 6:14) and was attached to the other two sayings through its introduction "whenever you stand praying." The traditional Mark 11:26 ("but if you do not forgive, neither will your Father who is in heaven forgive your trespasses") is absent from many important mss. of Mark (see Matt 6:15).

74   **(b)** CONTROVERSIES (11:27–12:37). As in 2:1–3:6, this section gives five stories about Jesus' controversies with his opponents (plus one parable). The five stories differ in form and tone; whether they formed a pre-Marcan collection is debatable.

75   **(i)** *Jesus' authority* (11:27–33). The opponents' question was designed to trap Jesus into a public claim that his authority was from God, thus laying the groundwork for a charge of blasphemy (see 14:64). Jesus avoids such a public claim by asking a counterquestion about the origin of JBap's authority. The strategy has the effect of reducing the opponents to silence while making clear the divine origin of Jesus' authority. **27.** *the chief priests, the scribes, and the elders:* These three groups were mentioned in the first prediction (8:31) and will appear again in the passion narrative (14:43,53; 15:1) as the prime movers of the plot against Jesus. Here we are to imagine a small representative body rather than the whole sanhedrin. The occasion for their interrogation may have been Jesus' cleansing of the Temple (11:15–19). **28.** *by what authority do you do these things?:* The most likely referent of "these things" is the cleansing of the Temple, though perhaps the entrance into Jerusalem and even Jesus' entire ministry of teaching and healing are included. **30.** *was John's baptism from heaven or from men?:* Behind Jesus' question was the implicit claim that JBap's authority came "from God." In the light of the parallelism between John and Jesus developed throughout the Gospel, the question also indicates the divine origin of Jesus' teaching and healing. **31.** *if we say "from heaven":* If the opponents admitted the divine origin of JBap's authority, they would have to explain why they did not welcome him; they would also have to admit the divine origin of Jesus' authority. If they denied the divine origin of JBap's authority, they would run the risk of opposition from the general populace, who held him to be a prophet from God. Recognition of their dilemma reduces them to silence. **33.** *neither will I tell you:* Although the conversation seems to end in a stalemate, in fact it is clear that Jesus' authority is from God. The opponents, who sought to trap Jesus, have themselves been trapped by him; their silence makes Jesus' victory in the controversy all the more delicious.

76 (ii) *Parable of the vineyard* (12:1-12). The parable comments on the hostility of the Jewish leaders toward Jesus and places the harsh treatment given to Jesus in the tradition of the harsh treatment given to God's earlier messengers. There are some obvious allegorical identifications in the parable as it stands: the vineyard = Israel; the owner = God; the tenant farmers = Israel's leaders; the beloved son = Jesus. Whether the servants = the prophets and the others = Gentiles is more problematic. Other features in the story (the hedge, the winepress, the tower) have no allegorical significance. That Jesus uttered this parable in its present form has been denied on several grounds: the quotations from the LXX (12:1,10-11), the foreknowledge of his death and his openly messianic claim (12:6), the possible allusions to the fall of Jerusalem and the Gentile mission (12:9), and the allegorism. But efforts to reconstruct the primitive form of Jesus' parable or to explain it entirely as an early Christian creation are necessarily speculative. **1.** *began to speak to them in parables:* Though different in form from the surrounding stories, the content is the relationship between Jesus and his opponents. Despite the pl. "parables," there is only one parable here. *planted a vineyard:* The vocabulary of the description is taken from Isa 5:1-2 LXX, leaving no doubt that the vineyard symbolizes Israel. The hedge was designed to keep animals out; the winepress was used for pressing the grapes into wine; and the tower was a place for watchmen and a shelter. *let it out to tenant farmers:* The practice of leasing vineyards and other farms to tenant farmers was common in Palestine in Jesus' day. In fact, absentee landlords were a common feature of the Greco-Roman economic system. **2.** *sent to the tenant farmers a servant at the proper time:* The proper time may have been the fifth year (see Lev 19:23-25). The three servants (12:2-3,4,5) receive progressively more severe treatments from the farmers: beating, wounding and shameful treatment, and death. Although it is tempting to identify these servants as OT prophets, it is better to take a wider view of them as God's messengers to Israel (Moses, Joshua, David, etc., as well as the prophets). **5.** *some whom they beat and some whom they killed:* After the series of three individual servants, this concluding description generalizes the fate of God's messengers to Israel. **6.** *a beloved son:* The master's assumption was that the farmers would treat his son with respect even if they had not done so to his servants. Since the expression "beloved son" (*ho huios mou ho agapētos*) was used by the voice from heaven to identify Jesus at his baptism (1:11) and transfiguration (9:7), there can be no doubt that Mark and his readers identify Jesus as the son. **7.** *this is the heir:* The tenants' expectation was not based on legal practice but on the hope that in the ensuing confusion they would gain possession of the property. **8.** *killed him and cast him outside the vineyard:* There is no mention of crucifixion, nor the slightest hint of resurrection. The idea of casting the son outside the vineyard may be connected with Heb 13:12 ("Jesus suffered outside the gate") and with the location of the place of Jesus' crucifixion as being outside the city limits of Jerusalem. **9.** *he will come and destroy the tenant farmers and give the vineyard to others:* Matt 21:41,43 reflects the Christian claim that the identity of God's people and its place in God's kingdom were transferred from Israel to the church. Mark, however, seems more concerned with Israel's leaders in Mark 11-12, and so his vision of the parable's significance is more narrow. The description does not necessarily reflect the events of AD 70, though Matt 21:41,43 and Luke 20:18 seem to have taken it as such. It is not clear that Mark understood the "others" as Gentiles. **10.** *the stone that the builders rejected:* The quotation in 12:10-11 is from Ps 118:22-23 LXX. The rejected stone (= Christ) becomes the cornerstone (which holds the walls of the building together) or the capstone (which crowns and holds up an arch or gateway). The same quotation is applied to Jesus in Acts 4:11 and 1 Pet 2:7; for other "stone" quotations attached to Jesus, see Rom 9:33 and 1 Pet 2:6,8. Perhaps the similarity between the Hebr words *ben*, "son," and *'eben*, "stone," generated this identification. The quotation of Ps 118:22-23 in Mark 12:10-11 makes the same point as the parable in 12:1-9 made: the rejection of God's Son by Israel's leaders was a tragic error on their part. **12.** *he spoke the parable against them:* The fact that the opponents understood the parable is unusual in Mark (see 4:10-12, 33-34). This ending is typical of the controversy stories in which Jesus' enemies perceive that they have been outsmarted.

(Snodgrass, K., *The Parable of the Wicked Tenants* [WUNT 27; Tübingen, 1983].)

77 (iii) *Taxes to Caesar* (12:13-17). The issue is payment by Jews of the poll tax to Caesar. Even though the opponents carefully set Jesus up for defeat and discredit, he manages to elude their trap and takes their query as an occasion for teaching about relationship to God. The text probably should not be pressed into a metaphysical doctrine of church and state (see Rev 17-18 for a very hostile description of the Roman Empire). We must not forget the particularities of the situation: Jews are asking Jesus, their fellow Jew, about paying a tax to the Roman ruler. Jesus allows them to pay the tax (cf. Matt 17:24-27; Rom 13:1-7; 1 Pet 2:13-17), but goes on to challenge his audience to be as exact in serving God as they are in serving Caesar. **13.** *some of the Pharisees and the Herodians:* The presence of Herodians in a Jerusalem story is somewhat odd. For an earlier reference to an alliance between Pharisees and Herodians, see comment on 3:6. Since Herod Antipas owed his political power to the Roman Empire, a negative answer to the question posed in 12:14 would have got Jesus in trouble with the Romans. The Pharisees were not ardent nationalists like the Zealots and managed to coexist with the Roman officials. **14.** *we know that you are true:* The compliments with which Jesus is greeted are designed to elicit from him a direct answer and to put him on the spot (cf. 11:27-33, where Jesus avoids giving a direct answer). Mark makes it clear that the motives of the opponents are base ("to entrap him" in 12:13, and "knowing their hypocrisy" and "why do you test me?" in 12:15). *is it lawful to pay the tax to Caesar, or not?:* The Gk term *kēnsos* is the transliteration of the Lat *census;* this tax was a reminder of the Jews' subjection to Rome and had to be paid in Roman coinage. If Jesus answers positively, he will be discredited among Jewish nationalists for collaboration with Rome. If he answers in the negative, he will be shown to be a revolutionary and a danger to the Roman Empire. **16.** *whose image and inscription is it?:* The denarius brought to Jesus would have borne the image of the emperor Tiberius (AD 14-37); the inscription probably read *Tiberius Caesar divi Augusti filius Augustus.* **17.** *give back Caesar's things to Caesar, and God's* *things to God:* Jesus answers the question put to him in 12:14 in a positive way: it is lawful to pay the poll tax to Caesar. But his reasoning allows him to avoid the trap set for him: since the coins in which the tax is to be paid are Roman coins and belong to the emperor, paying the tax is simply a matter of giving back to the emperor what already belonged to him. By adding "God's things to God," Jesus turns his pronouncement on paying taxes into a spiritual challenge to meet one's obligations to God as conscientiously as one meets obligations to the state. *they were amazed:* Commentators usually say that the crowd was amazed at Jesus' ability to get away without giving too much offense (though his answer would have offended Jewish nationalists). Perhaps their amazement was at his success in transposing the issue from the political level to the spiritual level.

78   (iv) *Resurrection* (12:18–27). The Sadducees based their rejection of the resurrection on the silence of the Pentateuch about it. They cite a passage from Deut 25:5–10 that they think will be irrefutable proof for their position and attach to it an application designed to reduce to absurdity those who favor belief in the resurrection. Their trap serves as an occasion for Jesus to teach about the nature of resurrected life (it is very different from earthly life) and to show that resurrection is implied at least in what the Pentateuch says about God in Exod 3:6,15–16 as the God of the living. The theological message of the text is that hope in a resurrected life is based on the character of God, who can overcome death and give life, not on human nature or human efforts. **18.** *Sadducees who say that there is no resurrection:* The Sadducees accepted only the Pentateuch as authoritative and rejected the idea of an oral law in addition (see Josephus, *Ant.* 18.1.4 § 16–17). The few OT passages that talk about the resurrection of the dead (see Isa 25:8; 26:19; Ps 73:24–25; Dan 12:1–3) were not part of the Pentateuch and so were not given authoritative status by the Sadducees (see Acts 23:8). The burden of the controversy here is for Jesus to show that the doctrine of the resurrection is present even in the Pentateuch (see 12:26). The Sadducees' question assumes that Jesus shared the Pharisees' belief in the resurrection. **19.** *Moses wrote:* The content of what "Moses wrote" in Mark 12:19 is a free version of Deut 25:5–10, which enjoins the obligation of levirate marriage (see Gen 38; Ruth). The motive of the OT practice was to keep property within the male's family. **20.** *There were seven brothers:* The story told in 12:20–23 takes Deut 25:5–10 as its starting point and tries to reduce belief in the resurrection to absurdity and to prove its incompatibility with the Pentateuch. Seven brothers had the same wife; whose wife will she be in the resurrection? **24.** *knowing neither the Scriptures nor the power of God:* In the subsequent explanation, Jesus answers the Sadducees first with reference to the power of God (12:25) and then with reference to the Scriptures (12:26–27). God's power can overcome death and give life; the resurrection is implied in Scripture. **25.** *when they rise from the dead, they will neither marry nor be given in marriage:* The Sadducees' reduction to absurdity in 12:20–23 is based on a misunderstanding of the resurrected life; for the angelic character of the resurrected, see 1 Cor 15:35–50; *1 Enoch* 15:6–7; 104:4; *2 Apoc. Bar.* 51:10; *b. Ber.* 17a. The manner of resurrected life will be so different from earthly life that the Sadducees' example really has no logical force, for it prescinds from God's power to conquer death and bring life out of death. **26.** *about the bush:* This was a customary Jewish way of referring to the passage about the burning bush in Exod 3 before the introduction of chapter-and-verse indicators. *the God of Abraham and the God of Isaac and the God of Jacob:* Exod 3:6,15–16, where Yahweh is identified as the God

of the fathers of Israel, is from the Pentateuch and so must be taken seriously by the Sadducees. **27.** *not God of the dead but of the living:* Jesus takes Exod 3:6,15–16 as implying that Abraham, Isaac, and Jacob were still alive and continued their relationship with God. Therefore the resurrection is part of the pentateuchal teaching. The use of an OT text in this artificial way is compatible with Jewish methods of interpretation at the time.

79   (v) *The great commandment* (12:28–34). The fourth controversy concerns the greatest among the 613 precepts of the OT law, a topic commonly proposed to distinguished Jewish teachers. Jesus' answer combines two OT quotations (Deut 6:4–5 and Lev 19:18), thus underlining his orthodoxy as a Jewish teacher and illustrating his fondness for going to the root of things. The passage is important not so much for its originality as for its emphasis on inner and basic dispositions. See Matt 5:21–48 for an even more radical emphasis on inwardness, leading to the abrogation of some OT precepts. **28.** *one of the scribes:* This interrogator differs in his lack of hostility and in the approval he receives from Jesus (cf. Matt 22:35; Luke 10:25). His attitude and sincere desire to learn make the incident into a learning exercise rather than a true controversy. *what commandment is the first of all?:* The question was frequently put to Jewish teachers. Hillel's famous answer according to *b. Šabb.* 31a was this: "What you hate for yourself, do not do to your neighbor. This is the whole law; the rest is commentary. Go and learn." This answer was in response to a request from a proselyte who wished instruction while he was standing on one leg. Hillel's assumption was that this saying would summarize the whole law and give its 613 commandments some coherent principle. The early Christians understood Jesus' summary of the law as a permission to disregard its ritual commandments; whether this was Jesus' intent here is not clear. **29.** *the first is "Hear, O Israel: The Lord our God, the Lord is one":* Jesus' response is a quotation of Deut 6:4–5, the first of the three texts recited twice daily (Deut 6:4–9; 11:13–21; Num 15:37–41) by pious Jews. The command to love God flows from his nature as the only God. The four nouns in 12:30 (heart, soul, mind, strength) refer not to the various parts of the person but are a way of stressing that the whole person should love God with all available resources. **31.** *the second is, "You shall love your neighbor as yourself":* Although only asked for one commandment, Jesus adds a second. There is no attempt at equating the two commandments or joining them (cf. Luke 10:27). The second commandment is a quotation of Lev 19:18 (cf. Rom 13:9; Gal 5:14; Jas 2:8). The two commandments are connected by the word "love," and their juxtaposition by Jesus was an original theological move. Neither Lev 19:18 nor its NT developments show any consciousness of the modern psychological discovery of low self-esteem and the need to love oneself before one can love another. **32.** *well said, teacher:* The scribe expresses agreement with Jesus by paraphrasing his statement without any hint of hostility or irony. **33.** *more than all holocausts and sacrifices:* The scribe's comparison merely echoes Hos 6:6 and 1 Sam 15:22 and need not be construed as a condemnation of the sacrificial system. In his framework, love of God and love of neighbor were the great principles underlying the sacrificial system. **34.** *not far from the kingdom of God:* Rather than being future, here the kingdom of God is accessible and seems to have a spatial dimension. The scribe's correct understanding of what is important in the OT Law places him close to the coming kingdom and prepares him to receive it properly (see 10:13–16). **80**   (vi) *David's Son* (12:35–37). The aim behind the complicated exegesis of Ps 110:1 is to show that Son

of David is not a totally adequate and exhaustive definition of the Messiah. Something more lofty like *Kyrios,*
"Lord," is needed to capture the character of Jesus' messiahship. **36.** *David himself declared in the Holy Spirit:* It is
essential to the argument based on Ps 110:1 that David
be understood as the author of the psalm. For other NT
quotations of Ps 110:1, see Acts 2:34-35; 1 Cor 15:25;
Heb 1:13. Allusions to it appear in Mark 14:62 par.;
16:19; Rom 8:34; Eph 1:20; Col 3:1; Heb 1:3; 8:1; 10:12.
Its multiple uses in the NT writings suggest that it was
part of an anthology of OT quotations thought to be
particularly applicable to Jesus. **37.** *David himself calls him
Lord; and how is he son?:* Assuming that David is the
speaker of Ps 110:1, he must be talking about someone
other than himself. The first "Lord" is God; the second
"my lord" must be someone different from and superior
to David. Therefore the Messiah is not adequately and
exhaustively described as Son of David.

81   (c) SCRIBES AND A WIDOW (12:38-44). The
two incidents in this section (12:38-40; 12:41-44) form
a diptych in which characters are contrasted. The ostentatious and hypocritical scribes criticized in this passage
are the opposite of what Jesus wants his disciples to be.
Jesus warns against the scribes' search for honor and
prestige (12:38b-39) and their draining the resources of
widows while keeping up the pretense of piety (12:40).
While not nearly so strong as Matt 23, this passage has
been used in the service of anti-Jewish sentiments in the
past; but it does not criticize all scribes, only a certain
kind (cf. 12:28-34), and still less all Jews. **38.** *the scribes
wishing to walk about in robes:* The scribes were the interpreters of the OT law, the ancient Jewish version of
lawyers. The kind of scribes criticized here were putting
themselves on public display, esp. in religious contexts.
Their robes (*stolai*) probably were garments designed to
enhance their prestige and honor, not necessarily prayer
shawls as in Matt 23:5. **40.** *who devour the houses of widows
and for pretense make long prayers:* Lawyers in antiquity
could serve as trustees of a widow's estate. A common
way of receiving their fee was to get a share of the estate.
Lawyers with a reputation for piety had a good chance
of improving their prospects of participating in this
process (J. D. M. Derrett, *NovT* 14 [1972] 1-9). As a
result of their greed and hypocrisy, these lawyers will
receive a stiff condemnation at the last judgment, the
highest court of all.

82   The story of the poor widow is connected
with the preceding incident by the term "widow" and
provides a contrast to the conduct of the scribes. The
woman's inner dedication and generosity also serve to
introduce the passion narrative in which Jesus will
display those same qualities. **42.** *two copper coins, which
make a penny:* The two copper coins (*lepta*) were the
smallest coins in circulation. The explanatory clause *ho
estin kodrantēs* features the Lat loanword *quadrans*—
another feature suggesting the Roman provenience of
Mark. **43.** *this poor widow put in more than all:* Jesus' initial
comment states a paradox that demands an explanation
(12:44). The explanation is that the widow made a real
sacrifice to support the Temple, whereas the rich simply
gave out of their surplus.

83   (d) JESUS' FINAL DISCOURSE (13:1-37). After
Jesus' prediction of the Temple's destruction (13:2), he
tells about events that are future from the perspective of
Jesus but at least in part present realities for the Marcan
community (13:5-13). Then he describes the "great
tribulation" (13:14-23) and the triumph of the Son of
Man (13:24-27), and concludes with exhortations to
confidence and vigilance (13:28-37). Since the 1860s
scholars have assumed that underlying Mark 13 was a
small Jewish or Jewish-Christian apocalypse edited and

expanded by Mark or one of his predecessors and put
into the mouth of Jesus (though it may contain some
sayings of Jesus too). In the light of the conflicting
assessments of the text's origin and development, it is
best to take it as it stands and see what it may have said
to the Marcan community. By this discourse, Mark
sought to cool down eschatological fears and to inculcate patient endurance. He warns about the necessity of
persecution and suffering, while encouraging the community to face whatever horrors the future may bring in
the firm conviction that the climax of human history is
the coming of the Son of Man and the kingdom of God.

(Hartman, L., *Prophecy Interpreted* [ConBNT 1; Lund, 1966].
Lambrecht, J. L., *Die Redaktion der Markus-Apokalypse* [AnBib 28;
Rome, 1967]. Pesch, R., *Naherwartungen* [Düsseldorf, 1968]).

84   (i) *Introduction* (13:1-4). There is some tension between Jesus' prediction about the Temple's
destruction (13:2) and the rest of the discourse, which
concerns the end of the world as we know it. **1.** *one of
his disciples said to him:* The disciple's amazement at the
size and the splendor of the Temple buildings serves as
the occasion for Jesus' pronouncement in 13:2. The
disciple's reaction fits in with Mark's chronology of one
visit to Jerusalem by Jesus and his disciples, for the impression is given that they were seeing Jerusalem for the
first time. **2.** *there will not be left here one stone:* That Jesus
predicted the destruction of the Jerusalem Temple is
asserted in many NT texts (Mark 14:57-58; 15:29; John
2:19; Matt 26:61; Acts 6:14). In prophesying the
Temple's destruction, Jesus stood in the tradition of OT
prophets (see Mic 3:12; Jer 26:18). There is no need to
assume that this prediction reflects the events of AD 70,
though early Christians saw in those events the fulfillment of Jesus' prediction. **3.** *the Mount of Olives opposite the
Temple:* The scene for the eschatological discourse is
most appropriate, given the eschatological connotations
of the Mt. of Olives in Zech 14:4 (see Mark 11:1). The
audience consists of the first four disciples (see 1:16-20),
three of whom formed an inner circle (see comment on
5:37). **4.** *when will these things be:* The disciples' question
logically points back to Jesus' prediction about the
Temple in 13:2, but in the present context also points
forward to the whole discourse that follows.

85   (ii) *Beginning of the sufferings* (13:5-13). The
first stage in Jesus' presentation of the future concerns
events on the grand scale (13:5-8) and the fate of the
disciples (13:9-13). The overall message is one of patient
endurance in the face of cosmic upheavals and persecutions. The way in which the disciples' persecutions are
described (esp. with the vb. *paradidōmi,* "hand over")
points forward to Jesus' own sufferings in the passion
account and places the sufferings of the followers in line
with those of the master. **5.** *beware lest anyone deceive you:*
The opening sentence of the discourse expresses its aim
at cooling off eschatological enthusiasm and instilling a
cautious wait-and-see attitude toward the coming of
God's kingdom. **6.** *many will come in my name saying that
I am he:* More seems to be involved than a reference to
Jewish messianic pretenders (see Acts 5:36-37), since the
many will come "in my name." For *egō eimi,* see comment
on 6:50. Early Christian healers and teachers may have
claimed to be reincarnations of Jesus. The present context indicates that they claimed to be Jesus come back
from the right hand of God (see 14:62). See 13:21-23,
for predictions of false Christs. **8.** *the beginning of the birth
pangs:* Predictions of wars and rumors of wars, uprisings, earthquakes, and famines are presented as part of
the divine plan for the coming kingdom. These tribulations are described by analogy with the first stages of

giving birth (see *m. Soṭ.* 9:15). However serious they may be, they are not the *eschaton.* **9.** *will hand you over to councils:* The focus shifts from world events to the fate of the disciples, who are promised persecution and suffering. The "councils" (*synedria*) were local Jewish courts (see 2 Cor 11:24), which could punish Jewish offenders. The reference to "rulers and kings" does not demand a situation outside Palestine; Pilate and Herod Antipas would be good examples. Jesus' disciples will encounter opposition from Jews and Gentiles alike. **10.** *first the gospel must be preached to all the nations:* The Marcan vocabulary of the saying suggests that it has been inserted between 13:9 and 11 by the evangelist. This hypothesis is confirmed by the logical flow between 13:9 and 11 and by the fact that if the earthly Jesus had been so explicit on this matter, there would have been no debate in early Christianity about the Gentile mission (see Gal 2; Acts 15). Its insertion here has the effect of slowing down the eschatological timetable dramatically, since a grand detour outside of Palestine is to be taken. **11.** *not you who speak but the Holy Spirit:* What is prohibited is anxious care (*mē promerimnate*), not thought or preparation. **12.** *brother will hand over brother:* The idea of the *eschaton* as a time of personal divisions was a commonplace in Jewish apocalyptic writings (see 4 Ezra 5:9; 6:24; *Jub.* 23:19; *2 Apoc. Bar.* 70:3; cf. *m. Soṭ.* 9:15). **13.** *he who endures to the end will be saved:* This concluding saying captures Mark's message of patient endurance during the "birth pangs of the Messiah" and the ultimate reward of salvation.

86   (iii) *The great tribulation* (13:14-23). The second stage in Jesus' presentation of the future moves beyond the present experience of Mark and his first readers into events that are in the future from their perspective. Those events are summarized by the term "tribulation" (*thlipsis*). Even though some of the imagery reflects wartime conditions, it has been placed in a wholly new context. By foretelling these events, Jesus prepares his followers for them and makes possible their patient endurance. **14.** *the abomination of desolation:* The expression is taken over from Dan 9:27; 11:31; 12:11, where it refers to the pagan altar (see 1 Macc 1:59) erected by Antiochus IV Epiphanes upon the altar of holocausts in the Jerusalem Temple in 168 BC. The masc. sg. ptc. *hestēkota,* "standing," suggests the transformation of a thing into a person, i.e., the reader is expected perhaps to identify it with a person. *let the reader understand:* The comment may refer to the events leading up to the destruction of the Temple in AD 70. Perhaps the vagueness of the expression was designed to avoid Roman hostility by means of a code. If the comment was part of a pre-Marcan source, it may allude to the emperor Caligula's abortive plan to have a statue of himself set up in the Jerusalem Temple in AD 40 (see Josephus, *Ant.* 18.8.2 § 261; Philo *De legat.* 188, 207-8; Tacitus, *Hist.* 5.9; → History, 75:173-74). In other words, the Caligula incident is presented as a repetition of the Antiochus incident. *let those who are in Judea flee to the mountains:* According to 13:15-16 the tribulation will come so fast that there will be no point in trying to salvage anything from one's house; likewise pregnant women and nursing mothers will be sorely tried according to 13:17. **18.** *that it not happen during winter:* Winters in Palestine are cold and rainy, making the wadis impassable. Nor would there be crops available then from which refugees might be fed. **19.** *such tribulation as there has not been from the beginning of creation:* The effect of this expression is to show that the subject is not warfare but something far more serious. The description alludes to Dan 12:1: "There shall be a time of trouble, such as never has been since there was a nation till that time" (cf. Rev

1:9; 7:14). **20.** *unless the Lord shortened the days:* The assumption is that God has established a time schedule for the coming of the kingdom (see Dan 12:7). For the idea of shortening the time, see *1 Enoch* 80:2; *2 Apoc. Bar.* 20:1-2; 83:1,6. **21.** *here is the Christ:* Although 13:21-23 has much in common with 13:5-6, this passage is more obviously concerned with messianic pretenders and false prophets (see 13:22) than with those who claim to be Jesus returned at the parousia. The appearance of these false messiahs and false prophets is taken as the climax of the great tribulation (see 13:24). **23.** *I have foretold to you all these things:* The discourse returns to the four disciples who constitute its audience. They should practice patient endurance in the midst of these events, for they have been forewarned about their sequence and they know that patient endurance will result in their salvation (see 13:13).

87   (iv) *Triumph of the Son of Man* (13:24-27). The OT language of cosmic signs, the Son of Man, and ingathering has been blended together in a new context in which the eschatological coming of Jesus as the Son of Man is the key event. His glorious arrival at the *eschaton* will be the final proof of God's victory; expectation of it serves as the basis for the patient endurance recommended throughout the discourse. **24.** *the sun will be darkened:* The cosmic portents preceding the coming of the Son of Man echo certain OT texts: Isa 13:10; Ezek 32:7; Amos 8:9; Joel 2:10,31; 3:15; Isa 34:4; Hag 2:6,21. Nowhere in the OT, however, do they precede the coming of the Son of Man. The list of portents is a way of saying that all creation will signal his coming. **26.** *they will see the Son of Man coming in clouds:* The description is taken from Dan 7:13. The Son of Man in Mark, however, is clearly Jesus, not the angelic figure "in human form" of Dan 7:13. Whether Jesus spoke in such terms of himself is a matter of debate (→ Jesus, 78:38-41); but see 14:61-62. **27.** *he will gather his elect from the four winds:* The Son of Man's action is the reversal of Zech 2:10. God's gathering of elect people is found in Deut 30:4; Isa 11:11,16; 27:12; Ezek 39:27; and other OT and Jewish writings; but nowhere in the OT does the Son of Man perform this ingathering.

88   (v) *Exhortation to confidence and vigilance* (13:28-37). The exhortation consists of a parable (13:28-29), a saying about the time of the *eschaton* (13:30), a saying about Jesus' authority (13:31), another saying about the time (13:32), and a second parable (13:33-37). The material has been put together by catchwords: "these things," "pass away," "watch," and "gate." The saying about "these things" happening in "this generation" (13:30) is balanced by the admission that only God knows the exact time (13:32). The parable about the clear signs of the end (13:28-29) is balanced by the parable of constant vigilance (13:33-37). **28.** *from the fig tree learn a parable:* The fig tree's natural process of growth in spring and summer is compared with the sequence of events leading up to the coming of the Son of Man. When you see these events happening, know that the Son of Man will come soon. **30.** *this generation will not pass away until all these things happen:* The phrase "all these things" must refer to the events leading up to the Son of Man's coming (see 13:29), though it may have been taken by early Christians as referring to Jesus' death and resurrection or to the destruction of Jerusalem (see Mark 9:1). The definiteness of the saying is blunted by 13:32. **31.** *heaven and earth will pass away:* Jesus speaks the language of Isa 51:6 and 40:8 to underscore the divine authority of his teaching. This saying is linked to the preceding by the catchword "pass away." **32.** *no one knows:* That only God should know the exact time is understandable, but the inclusion of the Son with the angels and human beings as not knowing is surprising. In patristic debates about the divinity of Jesus, this saying was used as an opposing argument. **34.** *like a man going on a journey:* The second parable compares watchfulness with regard to the kingdom to the watchfulness required of a doorkeeper when the master has gone on a journey: You do not know when the master of the house will come! Since the exact time is not known, constant vigilance is required.

89   (VII) Jesus' Death in Jerusalem (14:1–16:20). The Gospel of Mark has been described as a passion narrative with a long introduction. This observation throws into relief how important the final part of the Gospel is to the whole. Jesus knows beforehand what awaits him. Throughout, he behaves as the Suffering Servant and shows himself to be the king of the Jews despite the mocking and blindness of his opponents. The disciples, however, reach the bottom of their descent in Judas's betrayal and Peter's denial.

(Dormeyer, D., *Die Passion Jesu als Verhaltensmodel* [NTAbh 11; Münster, 1974]. Kelber, W. H. (ed.), *The Passion in Mark* [Phl, 1976]. Schenk, W., *Der Passionsbericht* [Gütersloh, 1974].)

90   (A) The Anointing and the Last Supper (14:1–31). The initial section of the Marcan passion narrative identifies Jesus as the Messiah (14:1–11), places his death in the context of the Jewish Passover (14:12–16), and highlights Jesus' self-sacrifice (14:17–31). Jesus knows what is happening to him and compares well with the characters who are contrasted with him.

91   (a) PLOTTING AND ANOINTING (14:1–11). The center of this introduction to the passion story is the account of how an unnamed woman anoints Jesus (14:3–9), thereby pointing to his dignity as Messiah, "the anointed one," and forward to his burial. Her spiritual insight and generosity are contrasted with the spiritual blindness of the high priests and scribes (14:1–2) and Judas (14:10–11). At the heart of the story is the christological saying in 14:7 that marks Jesus' time as special. **1.** *Passover and Unleavened Bread:* The spring agricultural festival of Unleavened Bread had been combined with the celebration of ancient Israel's release from bondage in Egypt (see Exod 12:15–20; 34:18–20). It began on the 15th of Nisan (March–April) and lasted for eight days. *the chief priests and the scribes:* Some of these may have been Sadducees, since they were represented among those in charge of the Temple. The plot by the chief priests and scribes was already under way in 11:18 and 12:12. **2.** *not during the feast:* Since Passover was a pilgrimage feast drawing large crowds to Jerusalem, the public execution of Jesus might spark a riot. The question remains, Did the priests hope to arrest Jesus before or after the feast? The latter seems more likely. Judas's willingness to betray Jesus led them to execute him during the feast (according to Mark) or before it (as seems more likely on the historical level). **3.** *in Bethany in the house of Simon the leper:* So unusual is such precision about places and names in Mark that the details must have been part of the original story. The alabaster vessel was a round perfume flask containing unguent made from a rare Indian plant. The estimate of its worth in 14:5 at 300 denarii makes it very expensive indeed (see Matt 20:2). *poured it over his head:* Cf. Luke 7:38 and John 12:3, where the woman anoints the feet of Jesus. Anointing Jesus' head was an acknowledgment of his messianic dignity (see 2 Kgs 9:6). **7.** *you do not always have me:* The saying explains Jesus' tolerant attitude of 14:6 and his description of the woman's act as a good deed. The focus is the presence of Jesus, not the assertion that poverty is a permanent social problem. The woman's anointing of Jesus' head has marked him as the Messiah; she alone in

contrast to the chief priest and scribes and even Judas has correctly perceived his identity and the special significance that his physical presence had. It is a christological saying like the bridegroom saying in Mark 2:19, not a social commentary. **8.** *she has anointed beforehand my body for burial:* A secondary interpretation placed on the woman's action relates it directly to his death and burial: the Messiah is anointed for burial at the very beginning of the passion story. The verse is sometimes explained as an addition to the story that aimed at covering the disciples' embarrassment over not having anointed Jesus' body before burial (see 16:1). **9.** *it will be told in memory of her:* The story of her deed will be part of the story of Jesus' passion, death, and resurrection. The woman remains nameless (cf. John 12:3, where she is Mary, the sister of Martha and Lazarus). **10.** *Judas Iscariot:* His betrayal is contrasted with the fidelity of the woman. His initiative allowed the chief priests and scribes to carry out their plot. **11.** *they promised to give him money:* The other evangelists make Judas's motives explicit: greed (Matt 26:15), Satan (Luke 22:3), and Satan plus a habit of stealing (John 13:2; 12:6).

92   (b) ARRANGEMENTS FOR THE PASSOVER MEAL (14:12–16). This passage identifies the Last Supper as a Passover meal in the strict sense that it took place on the 15th of Nisan; the other Synoptic evangelists followed Mark's chronology. John 19:14, however, places Jesus' death on the afternoon of the 14th of Nisan and thus makes the Last Supper a pre-Passover meal. John's chronology is more likely correct, since it is dubious that the chief priests and scribes would have acted as they did on the first day of Passover. The effect of Mark's making the Last Supper a Passover meal was to draw Jesus' death more closely into the great Passover themes of sacrifice and liberation. **12.** *on the first day of Unleavened Bread, when they sacrificed the Passover lamb:* The sacrifice took place on the afternoon of the 14th of Nisan before the first day began at sunset. Thus the disciples were sent out to make preparations for the Passover meal celebrated at the beginning of the 15th of Nisan. For the double time expression, see comment on 1:32. **13.** *a man carrying a jar of water:* Is this an example of Jesus' extraordinary foreknowledge, or was it the result of prearrangement? See 11:1–6 for a similar problem. **15.** *an upper room, furnished and ready:* Jesus and the Twelve are going to use a guest room in an upper story of a house in Jerusalem. The lack of amazement on the disciples' part in 14:16 is an indication of prearrangement between Jesus and the man carrying the jar of water.

93   (c) THE LAST SUPPER (14:17–31). The account as a whole sandwiches Jesus' words and deeds at the Last Supper (14:22–25) between the predictions of Judas's treachery (14:17–21) and Peter's betrayal (14:26–31). The technique highlights Jesus' self-sacrifice in contrast to the behavior of Judas and Peter.

94   (i) Prediction of Judas's treachery (14:17–21). The first incident in the Last Supper account stresses Jesus' foreknowledge regarding Judas's plot to betray him and Jesus' willing submission to God's will in his suffering and death. **17.** *when it was evening he came with the twelve:* In the light of 14:12–16, it is the beginning of the 15th of Nisan (since Jewish days were reckoned to begin at sunset). The two disciples are already at the appointed site according to 14:12–16, but here they are in the party coming to it. **18.** *one of you will betray me, he who eats with me:* The second part of the prediction may allude to Ps 41:10 (cf. John 13:18). The prediction shows that Judas's betrayal did not catch Jesus by surprise; the detail about eating together (see 14:20) highlights the enormity of the treachery. **21.** *the Son of Man goes as it is written about him:* Although fulfillment of the OT is a major theme in the Marcan passion story, there is no OT passage that speaks of the sufferings of the Son of Man. The second part of the verse emphasizes that just because God's plan is at work in Jesus' death, it does not mean that Judas had no responsibility. **95** (ii) *The supper* (14:22–25). The Marcan version of the Last Supper (see Matt 26:26–29; cf. 1 Cor 11:23–25; Luke 22:15–20) connects the bread and wine of Jesus' final meal with his disciples with his imminent death, and interprets them in the light of OT sacrificial traditions (see Exod 24:8; Isa 53:12) and the hope for the messianic banquet in God's kingdom. **22.** *take, this is my body:* The disciples are invited to share in Jesus' sacrificial death. Transls. such as "represents" or "symbolizes" fail to do justice to the realism of the words. **23.** *taking the cup:* At a Passover meal the bread would be shared toward the beginning and the cup (actually three cups) in the course of it. Here the cup follows after the bread (cf. 1 Cor 11:25; Luke 22:20), which suggests that it was not an official Passover meal. **24.** *this is my blood of the covenant, poured out for many:* The "blood of the covenant" alludes to Exod 24:8, where Moses seals the covenant by sprinkling the blood of sacrificial animals on Israel. The "poured out for many" alludes to Isa 53:12 (one of the Suffering Servant passages) and gives the action a sacrificial dimension. The two OT allusions serve to characterize the death of Jesus as a sacrifice for others. The phrase *hyper pollōn,* "for many," is based on the Hebr of Isa 53:12; it means for all, not just for one or a few. **25.** *until I drink it again in the kingdom of God:* The concluding saying places the Last Supper in the context of the messianic banquet (see 6:35–44; 8:1–10). Rather than seeing the Last Supper (and the eucharist) as an isolated event, it is important to connect it with Jesus' earlier meals with tax collectors and sinners (see 2:16) and to the future eschatological banquet.

96 (iii) *Prediction of Peter's denial* (14:26–31). The third incident goes back to the first in the series (14:17–21). It is hard to imagine early Christians inventing so damning a story as that about Peter's denial. **26.** *when they sang a hymn:* The hymn is usually identified as Pss 113–18. **27.** *I will strike the shepherd:* For this identification of Jesus, see 6:34. Zech 13:7 predicts both the death of Jesus and the flight of the disciples. **28.** *I will go before you into Galilee:* This saying points forward to Mark 16:7, where it seems to assume the occurrence of resurrection appearances in Galilee. Some interpreters take it as an unfulfilled plan made by the earthly Jesus or as a prediction of the parousia (see 13:24–27). **30.** *before the cock crows twice, you will deny me three times:* The prediction points forward to Peter's triple denial in 14:66–72, in the face of his claim that he will be the exception among the flock (14:29) and his protestation (14:31).

97 (B) Jesus' Prayer and Arrest (14:32–52). The two incidents move Jesus closer to the cross, showing how he faced death alone, apart from his friends. What sustains him is his unique relationship to God and his conviction that God's will revealed in the Scriptures is being fulfilled. **98** (a) GETHSEMANE (14:32–42). The Marcan version of the agony in the garden presents Jesus as the obedient Son of God who struggles to accept God's will in his passion. It portrays the disciples as hopelessly unaware of what is going on, thus as an example to be avoided. **32.** *Gethsemane:* The place was a small garden outside the E wall of the city of Jerusalem on the Mt. of Olives. The name means "oil press." **33.** *began to be greatly disturbed and troubled:* The Gk vbs. *ekthambeisthai* and *adēmonein* vividly express the agitation that Jesus experiences. The text expresses his deep emotional plight in the face of his impending death. This emphasis does not

necessarily contradict the stress on Jesus' foreknowledge and acceptance of God's will in the preceding passages, since one can be terrified of what awaits one (e.g., a cancer patient). **34.** *my soul is sorrowful, even unto death:* In his address to the three disciples, Jesus uses the language of Ps 42:6,12. **36.** *Abba, Father . . . remove the cup from me:* This prayer and the instruction that follows in 14:38 ("lest you enter into temptation") bear some relationship to the Lord's Prayer (Matt 6:9–13; Luke 11:2–4). The cup is the "cup of suffering" (10:39), a theme that also has a eucharistic dimension (14:24). *not what I will but what you will:* The statement indicates that Jesus had to school himself to accept his sufferings (see Matt 6:10). **38.** *the temptation:* As in Matt 6:13, the temptation is preeminently the period of eschatological testing that will precede the coming of God's kingdom (see 13:9–13). This kind of language underlines the eschatological significance of Jesus' own passion. **41.** *the hour has come; behold the Son of Man is handed over:* Jesus had come to the disciples three times and found them sleeping (14:37, 40,41). Even Peter, who claimed that he would die with Jesus (14:31), is asleep. The "hour" of Jesus' betrayal by Judas is to be the climax of his ministry. The three passion predictions are being fulfilled (see 8:31; 9:31; 10:33–34).

99 (b) ARREST (14:43–52). This passage consists of several short episodes: the capture (14:43–46), the cutting off of an ear or earlobe (14:47), Jesus' assessment (14:48–49), and the disciples' flight (14:50–52). It develops several familiar themes: the treachery of Judas, Jesus' foreknowledge, the fulfillment of the Scriptures, and the disciples' faithlessness to Jesus. **43.** *a crowd:* The arrest is carried out by a kind of mob, rather than the Temple police (see Luke 22:52) or the Roman soldiers (see John 18:3,12). For the groups responsible for the arrest, see 14:1,53. **44.** *the one I shall kiss:* During the pilgrimage festival of Passover, Jerusalem would be crowded. Moreover, those sent to arrest Jesus would not have known him by sight. Judas' signal to them used the traditional greeting given to the teacher—a device that increases the horror of Judas's action. **47.** *a certain one of the bystanders drew his sword:* According to John 18:10, Peter cut off the ear of a slave named Malchus. According to Luke 22:50–51, Jesus healed the man's ear. The diminutive *ōtarion* suggests that perhaps only part of the ear or just the lobe was struck. **48.** *as against a brigand:* By describing the manner of Jesus' arrest in this way and emphasizing its inappropriateness, the saying makes clear that in fact Jesus was no brigand (*lēstēs*)—a term that may also have carried the connotation of revolutionary against the Roman government. **49.** *day after day:* This statement about Jesus' teaching in the Temple appears to conflict with Mark's chronology, according to which Jesus had only been in the city for three days (unless this is what Mark understood by *kath' hēmeran*). *let the Scriptures be fulfilled:* The saying apparently refers to 14:27 (where Zech 13:7 had been quoted), though it may have been meant in a more general sense as in 14:21 ("the Son of Man goes as it is written about him"). **51.** *a certain young man followed him:* The identity of the young disciple who flees away naked has attracted many guesses through the centuries. Whoever or whatever he was, in the present context he is the individuation of 14:50, "And all left him and fled."

100 (C) The Trials (14:53–15:15). Mark presents two trials—one before the Jewish leaders, the other before Pilate. He regarded the Jewish trial as the more decisive one, though from a legal perspective the Roman trial was more important. Throughout the trials, Jesus the innocent sufferer remains almost entirely silent (see Isa 53:7).

101 (a) TRIAL BEFORE THE HIGH PRIEST; PETER'S DENIAL (14:53–72). Mark again uses the sandwich technique to place side-by-side the faithfulness of Jesus and the cowardice of Peter. He presents the hearing at the high priest's house on the first evening of Passover as a full-scale trial (though there are serious historical problems connected with this portrayal). The two charges raised during the trial are that Jesus threatened to destroy the Jerusalem Temple and that he committed blasphemy. **53.** *they led Jesus to the high priest:* The Jewish trial is situated at the house of the high priest. Could the whole Sanhedrin meet there (see 14:64)? Would they have met there on the first night of Passover? These problems suggest that Jesus underwent a preliminary hearing at the house of the high priest on the evening before the first evening of Passover (see 14:12–16). The preliminary hearing was conducted by a small group or committee of Jewish leaders. **54.** *Peter:* The reference to Peter at this point makes the story into a "sandwich" contrasting the noble silence of Jesus with the cowardly denials of Peter (see 14:66–72). **55.** *the chief priests and all the Sanhedrin:* Mark is intent on presenting the hearing as a full-scale trial before the whole Sanhedrin. This tendency was probably part of the general Christian effort to play down Roman involvement and to play up Jewish involvement in Jesus' death. **56.** *their testimonies were not in agreement:* For the Jewish legal principle regarding the need for at least two witnesses to a crime, see Deut 19:15 — a principle dramatized in the Susanna story, which is part of the Gk version of Dan. **58.** *we heard him saying that I will destroy this Temple:* Jesus may have contrasted Temple worship in the present with the kind of worship that will prevail when God's kingdom comes. The "I" may have been God, or perhaps even Jesus speaking in God's name. The saying probably had some relation to the cleansing of the Temple (see 11:15–19). Later NT writers tended to spiritualize it (see Matt 26:61; John 2:21; Acts 6:14) in the light of the fact that the Romans rather than Jesus destroyed the Jerusalem Temple in AD 70. **61.** *he was silent and answered nothing:* The silence of Jesus (see also 15:5) fulfilled Isa 53:7 and Ps 38:13–15. The high priest's question whether Jesus was the Christ the Son of the Blessed One combines identifications already made in 8:29 and 1:11; 9:7. **62.** *I am, and you will see the Son of Man:* For the connotation of "I am," see comment on 6:50. For expectations about the glorious Son of Man, see comment on 13:24–27. **64.** *you have heard the blasphemy:* The charge of blasphemy is used loosely, for according to Lev 24:10–23 blasphemy involved the divine name and was punished by stoning. *all condemned him to be deserving of death:* Jesus was probably viewed as a Jewish political-religious agitator (see Josephus, *Ant.* 17.10.4–88 § 269–85; 18.4.1 § 85–87; 20.8.6 § 167–72) who threatened the power of both the Romans and the Jewish leaders. Mark presents the condemnation as the legal decision of the whole sanhedrin. Does the "all" include Joseph of Arimathea (see 15:43)? See Matt 27:57; Luke 23:50–51 for alternative solutions to the problem. **65.** *prophesy:* The request accompanying the cruel treatment of Jesus carries the irony that the treatment fulfills the OT prophecies about the Suffering Servant (see Isa 50:4–6; 53:3–5). It may also allude to popular perceptions about Jesus as a prophet (see Mark 6:15; 8:28). **66.** *as Peter was below in the courtyard:* The story begun in 14:54 is resumed so as to contrast Jesus' faithfulness and Peter's faithlessness. Peter's denial appears in all four Gospels (see Matt 26:69–75; Luke 22:56–62; John 18:17,25–27). Note the progression in the audiences for Peter's denials: one maid (14:66), the maid plus some bystanders (14:69), and the bystanders (14:70). **68.** *but he denied it:* There seems to be an inverse relationship between the three charges ("You were with Jesus the Nazarene" in 14:67; "He is one of them" in 14:69; "Certainly you are one of them, for you are a Galilean" in 14:70) and the vehemence of Peter's denials (failure to understand in 14:68; simple denial in 14:70; an oath in 14:71). **72.** *a second time a cock crowed:* With Peter's third denial of Jesus, the prediction made in Mark 14:30 comes to fulfillment.

(Donahue, J. R., *Are You the Christ? The Trial Narrative in the Gospel of Mark* [SBLDS 10; Missoula, 1973]. Juel, D., *Messiah and Temple: The Trial of Jesus in the Gospel of Mark* [SBLDS 31; Missoula, 1977].)

102 (b) THE TRIAL BEFORE PILATE (15:1–15). The Roman governor Pontius Pilate was legally responsible for Jesus' death by crucifixion. The charge that led to the crucifixion was the claim that Jesus was "king of the Jews" — a title that carried revolutionary overtones for the Romans. Mark and the other evangelists present the Jewish authorities as the prime movers and Pilate as merely acceding to their pressure tactics; this portrayal probably reflects the early Christian tendency to play down Roman involvement and to play up Jewish responsibility in Jesus' death. The Marcan account of the trial before Pilate actually passes over the verdict. Jesus acts as the silent Suffering Servant of Isa 53:7. **1.** *as soon as it was morning:* This verse seems to assume the occurrence of a second official meeting of the sanhedrin in the morning (cf. Matt 26:66; 27:1). The result is the handing over of Jesus to the Roman authorities (see 9:31; 10:33). **2.** *Pilate:* Pontius Pilate was the prefect of Judea from AD 26 to 36 (→ History, 75:168). The Gospels' portrayals of Pilate as indecisive and concerned for justice contradict other ancient descriptions of his cruelty and obstinacy. Pilate's headquarters were at Caesarea Maritima; he came to Jerusalem to oversee the Passover pilgrimage, lest trouble break out. *are you the king of the Jews?:* Pilate's question is a political translation of the titles Messiah and Son of God. It shows that the strategy against Jesus was to connect him with political-messianic movements of the time and to condemn him as a revolutionary. *you have said so:* Jesus' answer to Pilate is noncommittal, not denying the ultimate truth of the title "King of the Jews" as applied to him but not accepting the political framework implied in Pilate's use of it (F. J. Matera, *The Kingship of Jesus* [SBLDS 66; Chico, 1982]). **3.** *the chief priests accused him of many things:* Mark presents the Jewish officials as the prime movers in raising charges against Jesus, while assuming that these men must convince Pilate to have Jesus crucified. Their repeated accusations contrast with the silence of Jesus (see Isa 53:7; Ps 38:13–15). **6.** *he used to release to them a single prisoner:* There is no extrabiblical evidence for the annual custom of releasing a prisoner at Passover. Perhaps the occasional practice of amnesty has been made into a custom by the evangelists or their sources. **7.** *Barabbas:* The name is a transliteration of the Aram *bar 'abbā',* "son of the father." The prisoner was a revolutionary and a murderer, just the kind of person that the Romans should fear most. **9.** *to release to you the king of the Jews?:* The account passes over the fact that there must already have been a trial before Pilate in which Jesus had been declared guilty. Pilate is now presenting the crowd with a choice between two condemned prisoners. **13.** *crucify him:* Crucifixion was a Roman punishment to be administered by Roman soldiers. The account indicates that Pilate had Jesus crucified not because he was guilty but because the high priests through the crowd put pressure on him ("wishing to satisfy the crowd," according to 15:15). **15.** *having scourged Jesus:* The scourging inflicted as preparation for crucifixion was done with leather whips containing pieces of bone or metal applied to the victim bound to a pillar.

103   (D) The Crucifixion and Death (15:16–47).
The four incidents in this climactic part of the passion story and of the entire Gospel tell of Jesus' death as king of the Jews in accordance with the OT.

104   (a) THE MOCKERY (15:16–20).   Before the actual crucifixion, a group of soldiers mocks Jesus on the basis of the title "king of the Jews." The irony is that the soldiers are correct in identifying Jesus as the king of the Jews. **16.** *the soldiers:* These men were natives of Palestine and Syria, recruited by the Romans. The phrase "the whole battalion" is probably used in a loose way, since a *speira* consisted of anywhere from 200 to 600 soldiers. *the praetorium:* Praetorium was originally the general's tent in a camp and came to designate his headquarters. There is a debate over whether this praetorium was at Herod's palace or the Fortress Antonia in the city of Jerusalem (→ Biblical Archaeology, 74:151). **17.** *plaiting a thorny crown:* The crown of thorns is part of the mockery. **18.** *hail, king of the Jews:* The soldiers' greeting is based on the charge on which Jesus was condemned (see 15:2,9,12) and parodies the greeting to the Roman emperor *Ave Caesar, victor, imperator.*

105   (b) THE CRUCIFIXION (15:21–32).   The story of the crucifixion is told simply and without dwelling on the physical details of Jesus' suffering (though these are certainly part of the passage). The account emphasizes that Jesus' death took place in accordance with the OT, without playing down the implacable hatred displayed by Jesus' adversaries (see 14:21). **21.** *Simon the Cyrenian:* Simon was a Jew born in Cyrene (in north Africa); whether he was in Jerusalem as a pilgrim or as a permanent resident is unclear. The reference to his sons Alexander and Rufus (see Rom 16:13) suggests that they were known to the early Christians. Simon was forced to carry the crossbeam for Jesus. The description of him as "coming from the field" could refer to his working on a farm or simply his visiting there. **22.** *Golgotha:* The Gk place-name is the transliteration of the Aram *gulgultā'*, "skull," which refers either to its shape or use. In Jesus' time this place was outside the city walls of Jerusalem. The traditional name "Calvary" comes from the Lat word for "skull" (*calvaria*). **23.** *wine mingled with myrrh:* On the basis of Prov 31:6–7, the phrase is usually interpreted as a narcotic to ease the pain of the dying person. **24.** *they crucified him:* The crucifixion is described in the briefest and starkest terms possible. The garments of Jesus became the property of the soldiers who carried out the execution. In the light of the prominence of Ps 22 in the Marcan passion narrative, their action must also have been viewed as the fulfillment of Ps 22:19. **25.** *the third hour:* The third hour was 9:00 A.M. The Marcan chronology conflicts with John 19:14, according to which Jesus was condemned "about the sixth hour" (i.e., noon). **26.** *the King of the Jews:* This official charge had already been raised in the trial before Pilate (see 15:2, 9,13) in contrast to the two charges raised in the trial before the high priest (see 14:58,61). The official charge very likely reflects the historical situation that Jesus was executed by the Romans on the charge of claiming kingship. As in 15:16–20, the irony is that from Mark's perspective Jesus is the king of the Jews. **27.** *two brigands:* These men may have been social revolutionaries like Barabbas, and as Jesus was supposed by the Romans to have been. **29.** *the passers-by:* The first group of mockers repeats the charge raised in 14:58 about threatening to destroy the Temple. **31.** *the high priests:* The second group of mockers echoes the charge in 14:61 that Jesus claimed to be the Messiah. **32.** *those crucified along with him:* The third group that also mocked Jesus. Cf. Luke 23:39–43, where one of the criminals acknowledges Jesus' inno-

cence and asks to be remembered when he comes into his kingdom.

106   (c) THE DEATH OF JESUS (15:33–39).   Jesus' death took place according to God's will made known in the OT. The tearing of the Temple veil and the centurion's confession give to Jesus' death a depth dimension with respect to the old Israel and the Gentile mission. **33.** *darkness over the whole land:* The "land" is most likely Judea. The darkness from the sixth hour (noon) to the ninth hour (3:00 P.M.) has been variously interpreted as a sandstorm, an eclipse of the sun (see Luke 23:45), or the fulfillment of Amos 8:9. **34.** *Elōi, Elōi, lema sabach-thani:* Jesus' cry is an Aram version of the opening words of Ps 22, the prayer of the righteous sufferer that ends with an act of trust in God. The use of Ps 22 does not rule out an emotional experience of abandonment on Jesus' part (see 14:32–42). **35.** *behold he is calling Elijah:* The call to God (*Elōi, Elōi*) is mistaken (perhaps with malice) as a call to Elijah. For Elijah as forerunner of the kingdom, see Mark 1:6; 9:11–13. **36.** *a sponge full of vinegar:* Perhaps the intention was to ease Jesus' pain (see 15:23). At any rate, the action fulfilled Ps 69:22, "for my thirst they gave me vinegar to drink." **37.** *Jesus uttered a loud cry and breathed his last:* A sudden, violent death is indicated; there is no dwelling on its details. We are not told what the content of Jesus' final cry was (cf. Luke 23:46; John 19:30). **38.** *the curtain of the Temple was torn:* The curtain divided the holy place from the holy of holies (see Exod 26:33). Its rending at Jesus' death suggests the end of the old covenant with Israel. **39.** *truly this man was the Son of God:* The centurion's confession echoes the opening words of the Gospel (1:1). The juxtaposition of this Gentile's confession with the torn veil in 15:38 imbues it with symbolic significance for the Gentile mission.

107   (d) THE BURIAL (15:40–47).   The burial is the necessary preparation for the empty tomb story. **40.** *Mary Magdalene:* Mary Magdalene is the principle of continuity insofar as she saw Jesus die (15:40), knew where he was buried (15:47), and went to the tomb on Easter (16:1). The other Mary (not the mother of Jesus; see 6:3) appears again in 15:47, and Salome is mentioned in 16:1 only. There has been no preparation in Mark (cf. Luke 8:1–3) for the description of the women's service to Jesus and their role as disciples. **42.** *the day before the sabbath:* The sabbath would begin at sunset on Friday afternoon, thus demanding that the burial take place before the day of rest began. **43.** *Joseph of Arimathea:* Arimathea is probably derived from Ramathaim-zophim (1 Sam 1:1). Mark does not specify that he was a follower of Jesus (cf. Matt 27:57) and assumes that he was part of the sanhedrin that condemned Jesus (cf. Luke 23:50–51). **45.** *learning from the centurion:* Pilate's investigation provides official confirmation that Jesus was really dead; there can be no question of a coma or shock. **46.** *laid him in a tomb:* The area around Jerusalem in Jesus' time has been described as a gigantic cemetery. The tomb of Joseph was a cavelike structure cut out of limestone and sealed with a large, circular rock. The corpse would be laid out on a shelf cut out of the rock and allowed to decompose for a year. Then the bones would be gathered and placed in a bone-box ("ossuary").

108   (E) The Empty Tomb (16:1–8).   The emptiness of the tomb was not a proof of Jesus' resurrection, but it was a necessary condition for the disciples to proclaim that Jesus had risen (see Matt 28:11–15 for the Jewish charge that the disciples had stolen the body). Other NT writings stress the importance of the appearances of the risen Jesus (see 1 Cor 15:3–8; Matt 28; Luke 24; John 20–21). Mark probably assumed some familiarity among his readers with the appearance traditions, and so he chose to end the Gospel subtly and dramatically by leaving the readers acknowledging the resurrection and looking forward to the parousia. **1.** *Mary Magdalene:* Mary had seen Jesus die (15:40) and the tomb in which he was buried (15:47). The designations of the other Mary in 15:47 (Mary the mother of Joses) and 16:1 (Mary the mother of James) have led some to suppose that there were two distinct persons (see 15:40; cf. 6:3). *anoint him:* According to John 19:40, Jesus' corpse had already been prepared for burial, but Mark 14:8 and 16:1 assume that the preparations had not been completed. According to Matt 28:1, the women went simply to see the tomb. **2.** *on the first day of the week:* According to the Jewish calendar, Sunday was the first day of the week. The "after three days" of the passion predictions (8:31; 9:31; 10:34) is equated with "on the third day" counting from late Friday (Nisan 15) to early Sunday (Nisan 17). **3.** *who will roll away the stone:* The stone was a large round slab fitted into a groove at the entrance of the tomb. Why the women did not consider this problem before setting out is not explained. Neither is there an explanation of how the stone was rolled away. **5.** *a young man:* According to Matt 28:5, the herald was an angel. The Marcan term *neaniskos*, "young man," was used previously in reference to the young man who fled naked at Jesus' arrest (14:51-52). **6.** *he has been raised; he is not here:* The emptiness of the shelf or niche on which Jesus' corpse had been laid (see 15:46) is explained in terms of resurrection. The pass. *ēgerthē*, "he has been raised," assumes that God raised up Jesus. **7.** *going before you into Galilee:* The message points back to Jesus' prophecy in 14:28 ("I will go before you to Galilee") and forward to appearances of the risen Jesus in Galilee after the disciples returned there from Jerusalem (see Matt 28:9-10). Luke 24:13-49 and John 20 recount appearances in Jerusalem. **8.** *for they were afraid:* The women's reaction to the messenger is trembling and silence, which Mark explains as due to fear (*ephobounto gar*). Did Mark intend to end his Gospel here? If he did, it was

probably because he assumed a knowledge of the appearances of the risen Jesus (14:28; 16:7). A book could end with *gar*, "for," (P. W. van der Horst, *JTS* 23 [1972] 121-24). Mark ended stories by explanatory comments with *gar* (6:52; 14:2) and by descriptions of the characters' emotions (6:52; 9:32; 12:17).

109   (F) Later Endings (16:9-20). The longer ending, traditionally designated Mark 16:9-20, differs in vocabulary and style from the rest of the Gospel, is absent from the best and earliest mss. now available, and was absent from mss. in patristic times. It is most likely a 2d-cent. compendium of appearance stories based primarily on Luke 24, with some influence from John 20; it consists of appearances to Mary Magdalene in 16:9-11 (see Matt 28:9-10; Luke 24:10-11; John 20:14-18), to two travelers in 16:12-13 (see Luke 24:13-35), and to the 11 disciples in 16:14-18 (see Luke 24:36-43; John 20:19-23,26-29; Matt 28:16-20), and ends with the ascension of Jesus in 16:19-20 (see Luke 24:50-51; Acts 1:9-11) → Canonicity, 66:91.

The so-called shorter ending consists of the women's report to Peter and Jesus' commissioning of the disciples to preach the gospel. Here too the non-Marcan language and the weak ms. evidence indicate that this passage did not close the Gospel.

The so-called Freer Logion in Codex W at 16:14 of the longer ending is a late gloss aimed at softening the condemnation of the disciples in 16:14. All the endings attached to Mark in the ms. tradition were added because scribes considered 16:1-8 inadequate as an ending. Establishing that none of the extant endings was written by Mark is not the same as proving that Mark ended the Gospel at 16:8. After all, an ending consisting of appearance stories could have been lost. Or Mark could have been prevented from finishing his Gospel. Yet there are good literary and theological reasons for holding that the Gospel ended at 16:8 (J. Hug, *La finale de l'évangile de Marc (Mc 16, 9-20)* [EBib; Paris, 1978]).

42

THE GOSPEL ACCORDING TO MATTHEW

Benedict T. Viviano, O.P.

BIBLIOGRAPHY

1   Beare. F. W., *The Gospel according to Matthew* (SF, 1981). Benoit, P., *L'Evangile selon Saint Matthieu* (Paris, 1972). Bornkamm, G., G. Barth, and M. J. Held, *Tradition and Interpretation in Matthew* (Phl, 1963). Cope, L., *Matthew* (CBQMS 5; Washington, 1976). Davies, W. D., *The Setting of the Sermon on the Mount* (Cambridge, 1966). Didier, M. (ed.), *L'Evangile selon Matthieu* (BETL 29; Gembloux, 1972). Dupont, J., *Etudes sur les évangiles synoptiques* (BETL 70A-B; Leuven, 1985). Ellis, P. F., *Matthew* (Collegeville, 1974). Frankemölle, H., *Jahwebund und Kirche Christi* (NTAbh 10; Münster, 1974); *Biblische Handlungsanweisungen* (Mainz, 1983). Giesen, H., *Christliches Handeln* (Frankfurt, 1982). Grundmann, W., *Das Evangelium nach Matthäus* (Berlin, 1972). Gundry, R. H., *Matthew* (GR, 1982). Hare, D. R. A., *The Theme of Jewish Persecution of Christians in the Gospel according to St. Matthew* (SNTSMS 6; Cambridge, 1967). Hummel, R., *Die Auseinandersetzung zwischen Kirche und Judentum im Matthäus-Evangelium* (BEvT 33; Munich, 1966). Kilpatrick, G. D., *The Origins of the Gospel according to St. Matthew* (Oxford, 1946). Kingsbury, J. D., *Matthew* (Phl, 1976). Kretzer, A., *Die Herrschaft der Himmel und die Söhne des Reiches* (SBM 10; Stuttgart, 1971). Künzel, G., *Studien zum Gemeindeverständnis des*

Matthäus-Evangeliums (Stuttgart, 1978). Lagrange, M.-J., *Evangile selon Saint Matthieu* (EBib; Paris, 1927). Luz, U., *Das Evangelium nach Matthäus* (EKKNT 1/1; Zurich, 1985). Marguerat, D., *Le jugement dans l'évangile de Matthieu* (Geneva, 1981). Meier, J. P., *Matthew* (NTM 3; Wilmington, 1981). Mohrlang, R., *Matthew and Paul* (SNTSMS 48; Cambridge, 1985). Pregeant, R., *Christology beyond Dogma* (Phl, 1978). Przybylski, B., *Righteousness in Matthew* (SNTSMS 41; Cambridge, 1980). Sand, A., *Das Gesetz und die Propheten* (Regensburg, 1974). Schweizer, E., *The Good News according to Matthew* (Atlanta, 1975). Senior, D., *What Are They Saying About Matthew?* (NY, 1983). Shuler, P. I., *A Genre for the Gospels* (Phl, 1982). Stanton, G., *The Interpretation of Matthew* (Phl, 1983). Stendahl, K., *The School of St. Matthew* (Phl, 1968). Strecker, G., *Der Weg der Gerechtigkeit* (FRLANT 82; Göttingen, 1971). Trilling, W., *Das wahre Israel* (SANT 10; Munich 1964). Viviano, B. T., *Study as Worship* (SJLA 26; Leiden, 1978). Walker, R., *Die Heilsgeschichte im ersten Evangelium* (FRLANT 91; Göttingen, 1967). Zumstein, J., *La condition du croyant dans l'évangile selon Matthieu* (OBO 16; Fribourg, 1977).
    DBSup 5. 940–56. *IDBSup* 580–83. Kümmel, *INT* 101–21. Wik-Schm, *ENT* 224–47.

INTRODUCTION

2   **(I) Authorship: Date and Place of Composition.** This Gospel early acquired prestige not only because of its intrinsic merits (e.g., the Sermon on the Mount, chaps. 5–7) but because it bore the name of an apostle (mentioned 9:9; 10:3). But, since the author of the final Gk text seems to have copied with modifications the whole Gospel according to Mark, it is now commonly thought that it is improbable that in its present form it is the work of an eyewitness apostle. Why would an eyewitness need to copy from someone who was not? The Gospel as we have it is best understood as a work of mature synthesis, combining the earliest Gospel, Mark, with an early collection of sayings of Jesus (the so-called *Logien-Quelle* or Q), which it shares with the Gospel according to Luke. The apostle Matthew may, however, have been at the start of the gospel tradition if he gathered the sayings of Jesus together in a collection like Q. This is what our earliest (*ca.* AD 125) patristic

source of information, Papias of Hierapolis, suggests: "Matthew compiled the *Sayings* in the Aramaic language, and everyone translated them as well as he could" (Eusebius, *HE* 3.39.16). Granted the truth of this, it still leaves unresolved the question of who wrote the full Gospel in Greek as it has come down to us. On this anonymous evangelist our patristic sources are silent. We must look to the Gospel itself for information. To begin with, it is evident that the evangelist was an early Christian teacher and church leader. It has further been proposed that he was a converted rabbi and catechist. Such a formula employs the term rabbi in a loose and careless way. The Gospel itself offers the less partisan, more biblical model of a scribe. The verse "Every scribe who has been made a disciple of the kingdom of the heavens is like a householder who brings forth from his treasure new things and old" (13:52) has often been taken as a description of the evangelist and his working methods. The verse is more informative surely than the story of the call of the tax collector (9:9–13). Nor does it exclude the possibility of a collaborative effort, in which the Gospel is the product of an early school of higher biblical studies (Stendahl), backed and accepted by a major local church. The Gospel contains some internal contradictions or puzzles, e.g., on the Gentile mission (cf. 15:24; 10:6 with 28:19), which could be explained as representing different currents of opinion within the same community. Other explanations are possible, e.g., a distinction between earlier traditions and final redaction. Some interpreters lay emphasis on the Gospel as a work of literary art from the hand of a single author (Frankemölle), so that any team effort would have been firmly controlled by the final decisions of the evangelist.

3   The character of the Gospel is a difficult question. Traditionally the Gospel has been understood as Jewish-Christian in outlook. Recently claims have been made that the final stage of the Gospel is Gentile-Christian and that the contact with Judaism has been broken. Although this view is not quite correct as stated, it has helped to clarify matters. Does Matthew stand inside or outside of Judaism? This question seems straightforward but conceals an ambiguity. Supposing, as now seems likely, that Matthew's community had recently been placed outside of Judaism by the rabbis of Jamnia through a ban called the *birkat hammînîm* (*ca.* AD 80), it is still possible that many leading members of the community felt themselves to be Jewish. This feeling of belonging, and indeed of being the true Israel, would explain the harsh polemics against the rabbis of Jamnia in chap. 23. It is a bitter family feud. Thus, the Gospel represents a predominantly Jewish-Christian outlook, though open to the Gentile mission—outside the confines of Jamnian Judaism yet still defining itself over against rival forms of Judaism. See comment on 5:17–20 and G. N. Stanton, "The Origin and Purpose of Matthew's Gospel: Matthew Scholarship from 1945 to 1980," *ANRW* II/25.3, 1890–1951.

4   As to the date and place of composition, Matt must have been composed after Mark (AD 64–69) and before AD 110, since it seems to be known to Ignatius of Antioch. If it be granted that the evangelist was in dialogue with the rabbinic academy of Jamnia/Yavneh, which sat from about 75 to 90, it would be reasonable to date the Gospel between 80 and 90, and later rather than earlier within that decade. The place of composition is in itself not of great importance except insofar as it would provide a setting for the characteristic features of the Gospel. The earliest tradition speaks of Judea as the locale for the Aram gospel. A number of other locales have been suggested in modern times for the Gk gospel: Antioch, the Phoenician cities Tyre or Sidon, southern Syria, even Alexandria and Edessa. The southern Syrian suggestion is plausible but needs greater precision. South Syria could embrace the Phoenician cities, which included also at one time Caesarea Maritima, or the Decapolis, e.g., Damascus or Pella. The choice between these alternatives depends on the weight one gives to certain maritime references (8:32; 14:28–29; see G. D. Kilpatrick, *Origins* 132) or to the east-of-Jordan hints some have seen in 4:15 and 19:1. I have given reasons for preferring Caesarea Maritima (*CBQ* 41 [1979] 533–46).

5   **(II) Literary Structure and Content.** The evangelist is both a faithful transmitter of traditions he has received from the early church about Jesus and the Christian life and, at the same time, a creative shaper of those traditions into new combinations with new emphases. He has a number of purposes in writing: to instruct and exhort members of his community; perhaps to provide liturgical reading and sermon material; but also to offer a missionary address to outsiders of good will, as well as apologetics and polemics directed to hostile critics and rivals. He has employed two broad categories of material, narrative and discourse, to achieve these various ends. It is little wonder, given the rich combinations of goals and means in the Gospel, that interpreters have laid emphasis on one aspect or another, as though it were the whole or chief goal or means of the evangelist. Thus, some have seen the Gospel as a liturgical lectionary, others as a handbook for church leaders, others as primarily a story. Still others try to combine these goals in formulas such as a book for the service of God in worship and teaching-preaching (Strecker), or as an interpretation of history modeled on the deuteronomistic historian's and Chronicler's works in the OT (Frankemölle), or as a fusion of lectionary and homiletic midrash (Goulder). Noticing the effort of the evangelist to define his community over against the rival efforts of the rabbis at Jamnia to codify and thus salvage Pharisaic Judaism, some have stressed the polemical side of the Gospel, either toward Jamnia (Davies) or even toward the Pauline churches (Weiss).

If we take seriously the combination of discourse and narrative in the Gospel and understand this as at least in part owing to the insertion of the Q sayings into the Marcan narrative framework, we must admire the delicate balance the evangelist has attained. But if we note the five great discourses into which Matthew has gathered so much teaching material, viz., the Sermon on the Mount (chaps. 5–7), the Missionary Discourse (10), the Parable Discourse (13), the Community Discourse (18), and the Apocalyptic Judgment Discourses (23–25), and the obvious care and mastery with which he has put them together, we discern the center of Matthew's positive interest and creativity. (The apologetic and polemic material tends to be inserted in narrative material, with the obvious exception of chap. 23.) Certainly later Christians have been quick to find in the discourses the masterpieces of the Gospel. Thus, we should conclude that Matthew's primary intent was to write a handbook for church leaders to assist them in preaching, teaching, worship, mission, and polemic. But he has inserted this handbook into the story of a living person, Jesus Christ, to keep it from becoming merely an academic or a gnostic doctrine and to keep it focused on Christ and his kingdom as the good news of salvation.

6   **(III) Matthean Theology.** This Gospel has two focuses, Jesus as the Christ and the near approach of the Kingdom of God which Jesus proclaims. These focuses should not be separated, whereas the entire Gospel could be read with either focus in view. The two themes are closest together at the beginning of the Gospel, where Jesus is set forth as royal Son of God and Immanuel, God with us, and at the end, where Jesus is given all (divine) authority as Son of Man over the kingdom of God, in heaven and on earth. Recent studies have discerned the title Son of God as especially important, occurring at crucial moments in the story: the baptism (3:17), Peter's confession (16:16, representing the confession or faith of the church), the transfiguration (17:5), and the trial and the cross (26:63; 27:40,43,54). Fitting in with this role is the title Son of David (10 times in Matt, e.g., 9:27). With this title Jesus is seen as a new Solomon, with connotations as healer and wise man. Jesus speaks as wisdom incarnate in 11:25–30 and in 23:37–39 (→ 136 below). Equally, if not more, important is the nonconfessional but public title of Jesus as the Son of Man, which runs through the Gospel, culminating in the grand finale in 28:18–20. This title is based on the mysterious figure of Dan 7:13–14, where it is also connected with the kingdom theme. The identification of the earthly Jesus with this heavenly figure had probably already been made in Q (not by Jesus himself); but, if so, Matt has carried the link much further.

The kingdom of God is the great object of hope, prayer (6:10), and proclamation (3:2; 4:17), which unifies the entire Gospel, esp. the five great discourses, and provides its eschatological horizon and goal. It contains God's definitive and ultimate promise of salvation to redeemed humanity, on earth as in heaven, in time and eternity, socially and politically as well as personally. It entails justice (6:33), peace (5:9), and joy (13:44). Because of its moral content it leads naturally to two other themes in Matthew's Gospel: justice or righteousness and the law. Justice is a special Matthean emphasis (3:15; 5:6,10,20; 6:1,33; 21:32) and refers for the most part to the human response of obedience to the Father's will rather than, as in Paul, to the gift of pardon. The law or Mosaic Torah is affirmed as a whole as of abiding significance (5:17–20), but, although some ceremonial precepts are maintained (sabbath observance, 12:1–8), or even encouraged (23:23), the Pharisaic development of Torah is firmly rejected in favor of Jesus' interpretation of the Torah. In fact, Jesus speaks mainly about ethical precepts, the Ten Commandments and the great commandments of the love of God and neighbor, and about other matters (e.g., divorce, 5:31–32; 19:1–10) insofar as they have an ethical aspect.

7   Two other characteristic features of Matthew are his explicit concern for the church (mentioned in 16:18; 18:18 [twice] and nowhere else in the four Gospels) and his special use of the OT. As a representative of second- or third-generation Christians, "Matthew" presupposes faith in Christ and tries to provide the community of believers with guidelines and authoritative leaders. The guidelines are contained in the great discourses, esp. in chap. 18, where authorization for decision making and procedure for conflict resolution are provided. Concern for the straying sheep, for the little ones, for forgiveness and humility are other central guidelines therein. Matthew does not have the threefold ministry (or hierarchy) of bishop, priest, deacon, but he does mention educated leaders or scribes. There are apostles with Peter at their head (10:2), who share the authority of Christ himself (10:40; 9:8). After them come prophets, scribes, and sages (10:41; 13:52; 23:34). As a court of final appeal there is Peter (16:19). Since power is dangerous, though necessary, the leaders need humility (18:1–9). Matthew has no illusions about the church. Anyone can fall (even Peter, 26:69–75); prophets can be false (7:15); and the church is a mixture of saint and sinner until the final sorting out (13:36–43; 22:11–14; 25). Nevertheless, the church is called to worldwide mission (28:18–20). The style of apostolic or missionary life is described in 9:36–11:1. The whole Gospel, finally, is framed by a covenant formulary in which God is united with his people through Jesus Christ (1:23 and 28:18–20). The outcasts of old Israel (21:31–32), together with the Gentile converts, become the new people of God (21:43).

The covenant framework leads naturally to a consideration of Matthew's use of the OT. Besides this OT framework and many allusions to and quotations of the OT which the evangelist derives from his sources, he has added a series of 10 (some count 11 or 12) OT quotations introduced by a formula like "This happened to fulfill what was spoken by the Lord through the prophet." Because of this formula, the series has been called "fulfillment citations": 1:23; 2:[6],15,18,23; 4:15–16; 8:17; 12:18–21; 13:35; 21:5; [25:56]; 27:9–10.

Almost half occur in the infancy story; the others relate to Jesus' public ministry, entry into Jerusalem, passion and death. They act as meditations by the evangelist on the events he records. The text of the quotations indicates a careful use of both Hebr and Gk forms of the OT. As a whole, the series reflects Matthew's conviction that Jesus came "not to destroy but to fulfill" (5:17) the promises made of old. Thus, there is continuity within the discontinuity under the plan of God. The series also suggests Matthew's conviction that one could find explanations of the puzzling or scandalous aspects of Jesus' story, esp. his death on the cross and the rejection of his mission by Jewish leaders and their followers, through consulting the OT.

Some recent authors seek to find a scheme of salvation history in the Gospel as a way of resolving some of its tensions. There is a threefold scheme: (1) a period of Israel stretching from Abraham to JBap; (2) the time of Jesus' own life; (3) the time of the church, from the resurrection of Jesus until the end of the world (so Walker, Strecker, and Meier, summarized here without nuances). Kingsbury has offered a two-part scheme: (1) Israel; (2) Jesus and the church. Others reject the category of salvation history altogether as an artificial construction foreign to Matthew and prefer a covenant theology (Frankemölle). Some take as the starting point for their understanding of the Gospel its last verses (28:18–20). By this can be meant that the verses cancel out everything in the Gospel that represents a Jewish-Christian perspective, e.g., 5:18; 10:5–6; 15:24; and, implicitly, circumcision. But, since Jesus here tells the disciples to "carry out everything I have commanded you"—and this could include even the embarrassing verses—it is wisest to assume that Matthew meant to affirm all of Jesus' commandments precisely in their dialectical tension. We should not impose on the early church a harmony it did not possess or read into the Gospel later syntheses. Only the ongoing life of the church would resolve some of the tensions, but some tensions would remain "until the close of the age."

8   **(IV) Outline.** In recent years a number of outlines of the Gospel have been proposed. One is a simple three-part structure based on the words "from then on Jesus began to," which occur in 4:17 and 16:21 (cf. 26:16). Thus, 1:1–4:16 would introduce the person of Jesus Christ, 4:17–16:20 would present the proclamation of Jesus Christ, and 16:21–28:20, the suffering, death, and resurrection of Jesus Christ (so Kingsbury). This plan is so general and vague and follows Mark's structure so closely that it fails to make visible the specifically Matthean features of the first Gospel. Another simple scheme would note that it is in chaps. 1–9 that Matthew's redactional creativity is at its height; there he presents Jesus as the Messiah of word and deed. In chaps. 10–18 he follows the Marcan order more closely but keeps introducing themes connected with the church. In chaps. 19–28 there are the journey to Jerusalem and the Jerusalem ministry of conflict and warning, culminating in the death, resurrection, and Galilean farewell. Here Matthew follows Mark even more closely, while continuing to supplement Mark from his own special sources and redactional art.

The most unified and more detailed outline is provided by C. H. Lohr (*CBQ* 23 [1961] 427). It is based on the symmetry of ancient compositions and employs the concepts of *inclusio* or bracketing, chiasmus or criss-crossing of literary elements, and ring composition technique. In the case of Matt there are alternating rings of narrative and sermon or discourse, built up around a central section consisting of seven parables about the kingdom of God. It will be noted that this outline retains earlier discernments of five great discourses in Matt but includes them in a larger, more integrated whole. It does not accept the idea of a Matthean Pentateuch, five books each consisting of narrative and discourse, since this would leave the passion-resurrection narrative outside the structure. (A recent proposal by W. Wilkens in *NTS* 31 [1985] 24–38 offers a six-part division which is rather church-centered and tends to break down after 22:1). Lohr's division runs thus:

1–4	Narrative:	Birth and Beginnings
5–7	Sermon:	Blessings, Entering the Kingdom
8–9	Narrative:	Authority and Invitation
10	Sermon:	Mission Discourse
11–12	Narrative:	Rejection by This Generation
13	Sermon:	Parables of the Kingdom
14–17	Narrative:	Acknowledgment by Disciples
18	Sermon:	Community Discourse
19–22	Narrative:	Authority and Invitation
23–25	Sermon:	Woes, Coming of the Kingdom
26–28	Narrative:	Death and Rebirth

Note the balancing of the first and last sermons and of the second and fourth. Some symmetry is apparent in the narrative sections, though it is not so consistent as in the sermons. The titles of some sections could be more concrete, as in chaps. 8 and 9 one could speak of 10 miracle stories that show the authority of Jesus and invite to discipleship. The Gospel could also be unified around the theme of king and kingdom in every chapter.

In the commentary the Gospel according to Matthew is outlined thus:

(I) Birth and Beginnings (1:1–4:22)
  (A) The Genealogy of Jesus (1:1–17)
  (B) The Birth of Jesus (1:18–25)
  (C) The Visit of the Wise Men (2:1–12)
  (D) The Flight to Egypt (2:13–15)
  (E) The Slaughter of the Innocents (2:16–18)
  (F) The Return from Egypt (2:19–23)
  (G) The Preaching of John the Baptist (3:1–12)
  (H) The Baptism of Jesus (3:13–17)
  (I) The Temptation of Jesus (4:1–11)
  (J) The Beginning of the Galilean Ministry (4:12–17)
  (K) The Call of the Disciples (4:18–22)

(II) The Sermon on the Mount (4:23–7:29)
  (A) Introduction (4:23–5:2)
  (B) The Exordium (5:3–16)
    (a) Beatitudes (5:3–12)
    (b) Salt and Light (5:13–16)
  (C) The New Ethic: Its Basic Legal Principles and Six Hypertheses (5:17–48)
    (a) The Higher Righteousness (5:17–20)
    (b) Anger (5:21–26)
    (c) Adultery (5:27–30)
    (d) Divorce (5:31–32)
    (e) Oaths (5:33–37)
    (f) Retaliation (5:38–42)
    (g) Love of Enemies (5:43–48)
  (D) Reformation of Works of Piety (6:1–18)
    (a) Almsgiving (6:1–4)
    (b) Prayer (6:5–15)
    (c) Fasting (6:16–18)
  (E) Further Instructions (6:19–7:12)
    (a) Treasure in Heaven (6:19–21)
    (b) The Single Eye (6:22–23)
    (c) God and Mammon (6:24)
    (d) On Care and Anxiety (6:25–34)
    (e) Judging Others (7:1–6)
    (f) Ask, Seek, Knock (7:7–12)
  (F) Conclusion of the Sermon (7:13–27)
    (a) The Narrow Gate (7:13–14)
    (b) Bearing Fruit (7:15–20)
    (c) An Episode in the Last Judgment Described (7:21–23)
    (d) Houses Built on Rock and Sand (7:24–29)

(III) Authority and Invitation (8:1–9:38)
  (A) The Cleansing of a Leper (8:1–4)
  (B) The Cure of the Centurion's Servant (8:5–13)
  (C) The Healing of Peter's Mother-in-law (8:14–15)
  (D) The Sick Healed at Evening (8:16–17)
  (E) On Following Jesus (8:18–22)
  (F) Stilling the Storm (8:23–27)
  (G) The Cure of the Gadarene Demoniacs (8:28–34)
  (H) The Healing of the Paralytic (9:1–8)
  (I) The Call of Matthew the Tax Collector (9:9–13)
  (J) The Question about Fasting (9:14–17)
  (K) The Healing of a Ruler's Daughter (9:18–26)
  (L) The Healing of Two Blind Men (9:27–31)
  (M) The Healing of a Dumb Demoniac (9:32–34)
  (N) The Compassion of Jesus (9:35–38)

(IV) Mission Discourse (10:1–42)
  (A) The Mission of the Twelve Apostles (10:1–4)
  (B) The Commissioning of the Twelve (10:5–16)
  (C) How to Face Future Persecutions (10:17–25)
  (D) Appropriate and Inappropriate Fear (10:26–31)
  (E) Confessing Jesus before People (10:32–39)
  (F) Rewards of Discipleship (10:40–42)

(V) Rejection by This Generation (11:1–12:50)
  (A) John the Baptist and Jesus (11:1–19)
  (B) Woes on the Cities (11:20–24)
  (C) Cry of Jubilee and Savior's Call (11:25–30)
  (D) Plucking Ears of Grain on the Sabbath (12:1–8)
  (E) Healing the Man with the Withered Hand (12:9–14)
  (F) The Chosen Servant (12:15–21)
  (G) Jesus and Beelzebul (12:22–32)
  (H) A Tree and Its Fruits (12:33–37)
  (I) The Sign of Jonah (12:38–42)
  (J) The Return of the Evil Spirit (12:43–45)
  (K) Jesus' Family (12:46–50)

(VI) Parables of the Kingdom (13:1–52)
  (A) The Parable of the Sower (13:1–9)
  (B) The Purpose of the Parables (13:10–17)
  (C) The Parable of the Sower Explained (13:18–23)
  (D) The Parable of the Weeds among the Wheat (13:24–30)
  (E) The Parables of the Mustard Seed and the Leaven (13:31–33)
  (F) Jesus' Use of Parables (13:34–35)
  (G) The Interpretation of the Parable of the Weeds (13:36–43)
  (H) The Parables of the Treasure, the Pearl, and the Dragnet (13:44–50)
  (I) Old and New (13:51–52)

(VII) Acknowledgment by Disciples (13:53–17:27)
  (A) The Rejection of Jesus in His Own Country (13:53–58)
  (B) The Death of John the Baptist (14:1–12)
  (C) The Feeding of the Five Thousand (14:13–21)
  (D) Walking on the Water (14:22–23)
  (E) The Healing of the Sick in Gennesaret (14:34–36)
  (F) Jesus and Pharisaic Tradition on Purity and Vows (15:1–20)
  (G) The Canaanite Woman's Faith (15:21–28)
  (H) The Healing of Many People (15:29–31)
  (I) The Feeding of the Four Thousand (15:32–39)
  (J) The Demand for a Sign (16:1–4)
  (K) The Leaven of the Pharisees and Sadducees (16:5–12)
  (L) Peter's Confession (16:13–20)
  (M) First Prediction of the Passion and Sayings on Discipleship (16:21–28)
  (N) The Transfiguration (17:1–13)
  (O) The Healing of the Moonstruck Boy (17:14–20)
  (P) Second Passion Prediction (17:22–23)
  (Q) The Stater in the Fish's Mouth (17:24–27)

(VIII) Community Discourse (18:1–35)
  (A) True Greatness (18:1–5)
  (B) Leaders Who Cause Little Ones to Sin (18:6–9)
  (C) The Parable of the Lost Sheep (18:10–14)
  (D) Trial Procedures (18:15–20)
  (E) The Parable of the Unforgiving Servant (18:21–35)

COMMENTARY

9   **(I) Birth and Beginnings (1:1–4:22).**
    (A) The Genealogy of Jesus (1:1–17) **1.**
book: By calling his work a book, Matthew may be suggesting that his writing is a textbook or manual for church leaders (with a narrative framework). Contrast Mark's calling his writing a "gospel" (a form of preaching), and Luke's calling his a "narrative" (in their opening verses). The closest NT parallel to Matt is John 20:30, *biblion. genealogy:* The Gk word *genesis* could be translated "birth," "beginning," "genealogy," besides a possible allusion to the OT book of creation. It is hard to decide where the emphasis lies. The word recurs once, in v 18, meaning "birth"; here it leads into the genealogy in vv 2–16. *Jesus Christ:* The central figure of the book is introduced: Jesus, the Gk form of Joshua, in popular etymology means "savior" or "God saves" (originally and more correctly it means "Yahweh, help!"). Christ, the Gk form of messiah, means "the anointed." Several anointed savior figures were expected in Jesus' day in Israel— royal, priestly, and prophetic (1QS 9:10–11). In Greek it also has the connotation "kindly," because it sounds like another word with that meaning. *the Son of David:* Here the term means the end-time successor of King David as the restorer of Israel as God's people, free and sovereign. Matt alone emphasizes Jesus as the royal Christ, even though Jesus is called the son of David in all major writings of the NT except Hebrews. The title could well go back to a family tradition. It is a restrictive term, quickly qualified by the "Son of Abraham," a much more inclusive title, since Abraham was the "father of all who believe" (Rom 4:11), including Gentiles (Gal 3:7–9). This verse compresses two important elements. It forms a bracket with v 17 around the genealogy. This bracket or *inclusio* contains a chiasm or ring composition and the structure of vv 2–16 in reverse order: Christ, David, Abraham, whereas in v 17 the order runs

Abraham, David, Christ. But the verse also forms a bracket (implicitly) with 28:19 around the entire book in which faith in Christ is offered first to Israel (10:6; 15:24) and then to the Gentiles or nations (28:19).
10   **2–16.** The Genealogy of Jesus, from Abraham to Joseph (cf. Luke 3:23–38). Seldom has such an important book begun in such a repellent way. It is a Near Eastern way of beginning a book (see Num, Josh, Chr, or the memoirs of King Abdullah of Jordan, who begins by tracing his ancestry back to Muhammad). Though difficult for the modern reader, the genealogy teaches an important lesson. It briefly incorporates the whole of OT history and thought into the Gospel as the proximate background of Jesus. It says, in effect, if you want to know and understand Jesus, then read the OT (and the intertestamental literature). This explains its extreme density.

    The genealogy is divided into three parts, and each part is supposed to have 14 generations (v 17). This arrangement suggests that it is schematic and not absolutely historical, at least in this sense, that five names have been omitted from the second part in order to arrive at 14. The sources for the first part are Ruth 4:18–22 and 1 Chr 1:34–2:15, to which the names of two women have been added, Rahab and Ruth (Tamar is in 1 Chr); for the second part the source is 1 Chr 3:1–16; for the phrase about the exile (vv 11–12; see 2 Kgs 24:14; Jer 27:20); and for the first three names in the third part, Ezra 3:2; Hag 2:2; 1 Chr 3:16–19. The names that follow may come from oral tradition. All are biblical but not otherwise genealogically related. The monotony of the genealogy is broken up by the mention of David's title, by the reference to the exile, and esp. by the mention of five women: Tamar (see Gen 38), Rahab (see Josh 2), Ruth, Bathsheba the wife of Uriah (see 2 Sam 11:1–27), Mary. Why are these women mentioned? Earlier answers were that, aside from Mary, all were sinners (but does Ruth fit?), or that all were Gentiles or proselytes (so Luther, but this remains unclear). Today it is thought that (a) there was something extraordinary or irregular in their marital union; (b) they showed initiative and played an important role in God's plan. Since Matthew is not esp. partial to women, the presence of these women is all the more striking (see further *MNT* 77–83). **16.** This verse is carefully constructed to avoid saying that Jesus was the son of Joseph. There is a paradox in presenting a genealogy through Joseph only to have the pattern broken at the end. But broken patterns are a feature of the Gospel throughout. **17.** The numerical pattern imposed on the material reflects a rabbinical technique called *gematria* (a corruption of "geometry"). The number symbolism here could involve the numerical value of the consonants in the Hebrew of David's name *dwd* ($d = 4$, $w = 6$; $4 + 6 + 4 = 14$). Thus the whole list would be Davidic. There are also 14 names in the rabbinic chain of tradition in *m. 'Abot* and *'Abot R. Nat.*, but from Moses to Hillel. This is not a list of descent by blood but of succession in teaching and was perhaps modeled on the lists of heads of the Gk philosophical schools. Another problem concerns the third series of names, which gives only 13 instead of the stated 14. Various solutions to this puzzle have been proposed: Is Christ the fourteenth? Or is the fourteenth place reserved for the coming Son of Man? Or does Matt imply a generation between the second and third sections: Jehoiakim was the father of Jechoniah. The puzzle remains.

11   (B) The Birth of Jesus (1:18–25). The joining of the genealogy to this section, the combination of two episodes (angelic dream appearance; annunciation of birth) that may have had separate origins, and the incorporation of a fulfillment citation make this the most complicated section in the infancy narrative. It shows structural similarities to 21:1–7. **18.** *the birth of Jesus Christ:* In Judea betrothal included the right of cohabitation, and *m. Yebam.* 6:4; *m. Nid.* 5:6,7 give the normal age of girls at betrothal as twelve and a half but these rules may not have held in Galilee. The text teaches the virginal conception of Jesus but remains silent on the perpetual virginity of Mary, although not excluding it. Divine intervention in the birth of God's chosen was a tradition in Israel's faith (Isaac, Gen 18:11–14; Jacob, 25:21; Samuel, 1 Sam 1:4–20), but Matt goes further, replacing the male role. *the Holy Spirit:* This is a late OT formula for what is more commonly referred to as "the spirit of God." It occurs only three times in the MT (Ps 61:13; Isa 63:10–11). The spirit of God is the cause of human life in Ezek 37:1–14; Job 27:3; Isa 42:5 and active in creation in Gen 1:2. Here there is a particular, concrete, and special case of that creative activity. (Extrabiblical parallels are often cited: Plutarch, *Life of Numa Pompilius* 4.4; Philo, *De cher.* 40–52; *2 Enoch* 23 [71], but they are not close.) The virginal conception may be regarded as an outward physical sign of an invisible, inner reality, the birth of the Son of God. **19.** *a just man:* Joseph's justice consists in obedience to the law (Deut 22:20,21), but this is tempered by his compassion, which prevents him from wanting to exact the full penalty of the law, stoning. *secretly:* In contrast to the trial by ordeal through the waters of the red heifer (Num 5:11–31). **20.** *behold:* This is a favorite introductory particle in Matt. *dream:* The Gk term *onar* is found only in Matt in the Bible and only in chaps. 1 and 2 and in 27:19. *angel of the Lord:* He explains to Joseph why Mary is not an adulteress, something the reader knows from v 18. **21.** *from their sins:* The evangelist exploits the popular etymology of Jesus' name (see comment on v 1). Salvation from "sins" is used, since oppression, exile, and foreign

domination often were regarded as punishment for sins; oppression also involved separation from God, the essence of sin, since it hindered obedience to the commandments. Jesus will achieve this "salvation" through his death (26:28), but also through his proclamation of the kingdom of God (4:17). The conflict with a cruel king in chap. 2 supports this interpretation. **22.** This verse contains a formula that introduces an OT quotation. The fulfillment formula occurs 10 times in Matt (→ 7 above). The formula shows an interest in the fulfillment of Scripture, in fullness generally, and the two passives, "fulfilled" and "spoken," presuppose God as the agent and thus stress the divine initiative. The quotations function as a reflection by the evangelist on the meaning of events in the life of Jesus and act as a vehicle of continuity in the midst of the discontinuity entailed in God's new act in Christ. **23.** *a virgin shall conceive:* It is thought that the text type used for the 10 formula citations is usually a conflation by the evangelist on the basis of his study of the OT in Hebrew and in Gk and Aram versions. Since this could not be done without a library, it has been conjectured that the Gospel is the product of an early Christian school of higher biblical studies. Here the quotation is from Isa 7:14, which has Hebr '*almâ*, "young woman," where the Greek reads *parthenos*, "virgin." Matt very likely knew both readings and consciously chose the latter here. The son is a royal child. *Emmanuel . . . God with us:* This represents a strong christological outlook, even though it is expressed more in biblical functional than in Hellenistic ontological terms. Two OT themes lie behind it. The covenant formulary runs in its most classical form: "I will be your God and you will be my people." Here it occurs in a shorter form: God with us. This formula is echoed in 18:20 and recurs powerfully in 28:20, the close of the Gospel. 1:23 forms a great covenantal bracket with this verse. The second theme is that of the glory or presence (*šĕkînâ*) of God, usually conceived of as a shimmering luminosity hovering over individuals and groups. Before the NT, questions of the materiality, carnality, corporeality, much less personality, of the *shekinah* as distinct from God, were simply not discussed or analyzed. The NT authors, Matt in particular, seem to be the first to identify the *shekinah* with a person. But the identity found a toehold already in Isa 8:8,10. Solomon's question in 1 Kgs 8:27 is answered in a new way. **24.** *he did:* Like the patriarchs in Gen, Joseph is obedient to the divine instruction. **25.** *until:* The idiom in itself neither affirms nor denies the perpetual virginity of Mary. In naming the child, Joseph acts as legal father. But it is paradoxical that he names him Jesus rather than Emmanuel. The context suggests that Jesus is the fulfillment of the Emmanuel prophecy.

12   (C) The Visit of the Wise Men (2:1–12). **1.** *when Jesus was born:* The birth is related in a participle and immediately put in relationship to wider political and social events. *Herod:* Herod the Great was a vassal king (*rex socius*) under the Roman emperor; he reigned from 37 to 4 BC, an extraordinary, dominant personality (→ History, 75:156–59). See Luke 1:5. The events here recorded of him are not otherwise known but are in character. *magi:* These were a caste of wise men, variously associated with interpretation of dreams, Zorastrianism, astrology, and magic. In later Christian tradition they became kings under the influence of Ps 72:10; Isa 49:7; 60:10. Their number settled at three, deduced from the three gifts (v 11). Eventually they were named: Caspar, Balthasar, and Melchior in the Western church, and Caspar became a black. They were understood as representatives of the Gentile world in all its racial diversity who come to Christ. *from the East:* This could be Persia, East Syria, or Arabia. **2.** *king of the Jews:* Jesus is designated a royal messiah. *his star:* The star that leads to Christ is probably a midrashic element derived from Num 22–24, the Balaam narrative, esp. 24:17, the fourth oracle; the star there is identified with the Messiah in *Tg. Onq.* and *Tg. Yer. I.* If historical, it could be a supernova, a comet (see Virgil, *Aeneid* 2.694: "a star leading a meteor flew with much light"), or a planetary conjunction. **5.** *Bethlehem:* The town of the humble David is contrasted with Herod's Jerusalem. Bethlehem was the city of David's ancestor Ruth (Ruth 1:1–4) and of his immediate family (1 Sam 16; 17:12), yet, despite Mic 5:2, there does not seem to have been a dominant belief at this time that the Messiah would be born there (see John 7:42). **6.** The quotation is from Mic 5:2, but Matthew changes "clans of Judah" to "rulers of Judah" to bring out the messianic point and adds "who will shepherd my people Israel" from 2 Sam 5:2; 1 Chr 11:2. **8.** Classical political duplicity. **11.** *the child with Mary, his mother:* The magi offer a model of sound mariology as worshipers of Christ in a Marian context. *gold, frankincense, myrrh:* The list of gifts may be inspired by Isa 60:6,11,13, which along with Ps 72:10–11 is implicitly cited. In later tradition gold came to signify the kingship of Christ, incense his divinity, myrrh his redemptive suffering—or virtue, prayer, and suffering. Some early Christians were scandalized at this narrative because of the role of the star. Did this feature favor astrology? Ancient people, experiencing social chaos, felt attracted to astral religion because of the cold regularity of the stars. But this religion became oppressive, making people feel helpless under the tyranny of *heimarmenē,* "fate." Matthew shows no interest in this problem. But because the star here serves God's purpose and leads the magi to Jesus, we can say that the power of astral determinism is broken.

13   (D) The Flight to Egypt (2:13-15). 15. *out of Egypt:* The quotation is from Hos 11:1; the reference is to the basic experience of salvation, the exodus from Egyptian bondage. The "son" in the prophecy is Israel, the people of God. Matthew here applies the exodus typology to an individual, Jesus, who represents the beginning of the restoration of all Israel (19:28; 21:43). This double meaning of son of God as both individual and collective will recur in 4:1–11. In Jesus, the history, the people, and the institutions of Israel are concentrated and condensed for an assault on the next epoch of salvation. The flight is a new exodus with a new and greater Moses. Matthew has used Moses traditions as reshaped in Josephus, *Ant.* 2.9.2–6 § 205–31.

14   (E) The Slaughter of the Innocents (2:16-18). 16. *Herod . . . had all the male children killed:* Herod acts in character; the story may not be historical but possesses verisimilitude and is reminiscent of Pharaoh's command to kill the male offspring of the Israelites (Exod 1:16), a classic example of genocidal abuse of power. If the incident is historical, the number of children killed need not have exceeded 20. **18.** Matthew introduces a deeply moving quotation from Jer 31:15. A mother's loss of her own children is a unique grief. In Gen 35:16–20 Rachel grieves not because her son dies but because she dies in birthing him. In Jer she weeps for the exile of her sons Joseph and Benjamin. It may be that in citing Jer, Matthew wishes to associate Jesus with Jeremiah as the suffering prophet of the new covenant (Jer 31:31–34; Matt 26:28). Jeremiah lived on in Jewish end-time hopes (2 Macc 2:1–12; 15:13–16).

15   (F) The Return from Egypt (2:19-23). Verses 19–22 explain why Joseph settled his family in Galilee rather than in Judea. Verse 20 echoes Exod 4:19 closely. **23.** *he dwelt in a city called Nazareth:* Joseph, involved in the building trade, probably settled in Nazareth because he could find abundant work in neighboring Sepphoris, which Herod Antipas was rebuilding as his capital at that time. The reference to a prophecy here poses a classic problem of interpretation since there is no exact correspondence to any known OT text. Perhaps Matthew inserted it here to provoke the reader to consider a number of elements: (1) a reference to a little town not mentioned in the OT; (2) a reference to the messiah as a branch (*nēṣer*) in Isa 11:1 and elsewhere; and, most interesting, (3) a reference to Jesus as a *nāzîr,* "consecrated person," in the line of Samson and Samuel. In Num 6:1–21 we find the conditions for being a *nāzîr;* in Judg 13–16 we find the story of a lifelong *nāzîr,* Samson, a heroic savior figure. Other references are Amos 2:11–12, Josephus, *Ant.* 19.6.1 § 294; Acts 21:24; 4QSam[b] (= 1 Sam 1:22): *m. Nazir;* Eusebius, *HE* 2.23.4–5. If Matthew intended this third reference, it would say that Jesus is strong to save his people (not that he led an ascetic life, which rather points to JBap in the next verse).

16   Looking back over chaps. 1–2 we can see that Matt has introduced Jesus to the reader as Son of Abraham in the genealogy, Son of God and Emmanuel in 1:18–25, Son of David in 2:1–12, a new Moses in 2:13–15, a new Jeremiah in 2:16–18, and a new Samson in 2:19–23. He is the all-around savior figure.

The literary genre of these two chapters has been much discussed. For centuries they have been regarded as a family history, though hard to reconcile with Luke 1–2 in many details. In recent decades it has become common to regard them as a Jewish-Christian midrash. A midrash is a homiletic interpretation of the OT, often employing storytelling. Since Matt 1–2 is not primarily an interpretation of OT texts but of a person, Jesus, it is not a midrash in the strict sense. But it doubtless employs midrashic techniques of exposition. This means that in addition to some historical information there are also some legendary elements in the chapters. R. E. Brown has proposed as the appropriate genre "infancy narratives of famous men," which allows us to embrace these different aspects (*BBM* 561).

A close comparison of the narratives in Matt and Luke would yield 11 points in common (*BBM* 34–35). The three most important are that Jesus is said to be a son of David (i.e., of the tribe of Judah), born in Bethlehem and raised in Nazareth, and that he was conceived virginally. It would be convenient to make these points the historical kernel of the narratives, but they are in fact at differing levels of historical probability. The first has the highest chance of being historical. Both the Bethlehem birth and the virginal conception are potentially so highly influenced by the authors' reading of OT prophecy that the historian hesitates where the believer need not. Yet it is more probable that the stories existed first without the formula citations than that the stories were created to encase them. The five citations are Matthew's contribution to the received tradition, a contribution he continues to make in 4:14–16; 8:17; 12:17–21; 13:35; 21:4–5; 27:9–10. The early Christians recognized Jesus as Son of God first at his resurrection (Paul), then at his baptism (Mark), then at his conception (Matt/Luke). In its story of rejection and divine triumph the prologue contains the gospel story in miniature. It foreshadows a union of Jew and Gentile in a new universal kingdom and shows that God can make the barren fruitful, that in weakness his strength is hidden, his plan at work.

(Brown, R. E., *The Birth of the Messiah* [GC, 1977]. Nolan, B. M., *The Royal Son of God* [OBO 23; Fribourg, 1979]. Soares Prabhu, G. M., *The Formula Quotations in the Infancy Narrative of Matthew* [AnBib 63; Rome, 1976]. Vögtle, A., *Messias und Gottessohn* [Düsseldorf, 1971].)

17   (G) The Preaching of John the Baptist (3:1–12). Matthew rather abruptly moves from Jesus' infancy to the beginning of his public ministry. At this point Matt joins the narrative of Mark, to which phrases and sayings from Q are added (here vv 7–12, part of 11, all of 12); this complicates the literary situation. Matt begins with the activity of JBap. **1.** *in those days:* Ca. AD 26. *John the Baptist:* A Jewish preacher of repentance, John comes out of a priestly Essene milieu and is known outside of biblical sources from Josephus, *Ant.* 18.5.2 § 116–19. Matthew introduces him here because of his traditions and because, although there were differences between them, John and Jesus were felt by early Christians to be related by their prophetic preaching, religious seriousness, practice of baptism, and expectation of the end-time in the near future. Some of the JBap's disciples developed his movement as a rival to Christianity (Matt 11:2); yet, because of his martyrdom and because of Jesus' respect for him, Christians began to regard him as a forerunner of Jesus. Matthew goes further than other evangelists by making John a "little Jesus," putting Jesus' own central message in his mouth (cf. v 2 with 4:17), and identifying JBap with Elijah (11:14; 17:10–13). **2.** *repent:* Gk *metanoein* connotes a "change of mind"; the Hebr term *šûb* means "to (re)turn" (away from sin and toward God), a major theme of OT prophets (see *m. Yoma* 8:8–9; G. F. Moore, *Judaism* [Cambridge MA, 1927] 1. 507–34; E. E. Urbach, *The Sages* [2 vols.; Jerusalem, 1975] 462–71; J. Behm, *TDNT* 4. 975–1008, for rabbinic ideas of repentance; for classical analogues to JBap's preaching in the Cynic-Stoic diatribe, see S. K. Stowers, *The Diatribe* [SBLDS 57; Chico, 1981]). *the kingdom of heaven is near:* See comment on 4:17. Unlike the other Synoptics, Matt postpones the forgiveness of sins till 26:28. **3.** Isa 40:3 is quoted in the LXX form, and references to Yahweh are transferred to Jesus. This is the first quotation from Dt-Isa, the prophet of consoling good news of deliverance and return from exile. Dt-Isa is very important for the NT as a kind of proto-gospel, but the NT denationalizes it and removes the note of vengeance. This passage was important also to the Essenes (1QS 8:14). **4.** *camel's hair:* The clothing is that of a prophet (1 Kgs 1:8; Zech 13:4), esp. Elijah. *locusts and wild honey:* His diet suggests wild food. In later tradition JBap became a model for monks, who were not to eat meat; since locusts were a form of meat, they were reinterpreted to be carob pods. **5.** *the country bordering the Jordan:* This could include not only Galilee but also Transjordan and the pools of Aenon (John 1:28; 3:23), a wide area. **6.** *baptized:* Gk *baptizein* means to "dip" or "immerse," ceremonially perhaps also to "pour." Here baptism is a religious rite of cleansing or purification, with analogues in OT priestly, Pharisaic, and Qumranite washings; here they are done not by the penitent alone, but by John. *confessing their sins:* A sense of moral guilt is widespread, as is the need to confess, but the forms this need takes vary greatly. It is not clear how it was done here, but perhaps we should think of the Day of Atonement, when general laments of broken promises occur. **7.** The Q source begins here. Matt narrows the addresses to Pharisees and Sadducees (cf. Luke 3:7). Why this severity to these two groups? According to Josephus (*J.W.* 2.8.2–14 § 119–66), there were three major sects within religious Judaism at this time: Pharisees, Sadducees, Essenes; a fourth group was often associated with the later Zealots. Although Pharisees were not always unfriendly to Jesus (Luke 13:31) and, in Mark, take no part in his death, Jesus felt obliged to criticize them severely (e.g., chap. 23 par) precisely because their religious leadership was so serious. Though the movement in its origins (the Maccabean period) had helped to save Judaism, it had now become dangerously rigid and exclusivistic. By Matthew's time, its heirs, the rabbis, had become the chief Jewish opponents of Christianity, and Matthew is determined to show that Christianity represents the true Israel. Sadducees were the priestly party connected closely with the Temple and thus more directly implicated in the death of Jesus (26:3–4). *brood of vipers:* This phrase is repeated in 12:34; see Rev 12:9; John 8:44. *wrath to come:* Though the basic idea is as old as the prophets (→ OT Thought, 77:99–102), there is a new note of eschatological urgency in the call to repentance; the judgment of God is close. **8.** *fruit:* Good works that go beyond the good intentions of repentance are the "follow-through." **9.** *children to Abraham:* Salvation is not hereditary. This hints at a basic Matthean theme: Gentiles can be saved. Cf. Amos 3:2. God does not show ethnic or social partiality (Deut 1:17; 16:19; 2 Chr 19:17; Acts 10:34; Rom 2:11; Gal 2:6; Eph 6:4; Col 3:25). **10.** *even now:* The situation is politically and spiritually tense and urgent. *ax:* Isa 10:34; Jer 46:22. *tree:* Matt 7:19. **11.** *sandals I am not worthy to carry:* Matt differs from the other Gospels and Acts 13:25 by reading "carry" instead of "untie." This may reflect a later rabbinic refinement, which teaches that a disciple should do for his teacher anything a slave would do except take off his shoes (*b. Ketub.* 96a). *with fire:* Here we must distinguish what JBap probably said from later Christian additions. If the words "the Holy Spirit and" are dropped as a later addition, then JBap points to the judgment of God himself. **12.** *wheat ... chaff:* Harvesting provides images of the separation at the judgment. *fire:* See Isa 48:10; 6:24; Jer 7:20; etc.

18   (H) The Baptism of Jesus (3:13–17). The baptism of Jesus by JBap in the Jordan is so important theologically that it is treated by all four evangelists, each in his own way. Mark has a straightforward account (1:9–11), theologically naïve and unembarrassed. But, after he had written it down, the story quickly became an embarrassment to the early church, because it was thought unsuitable that the sinless Jesus should be baptized for his sins. Matthew therefore omits the reference in Mark 1:4 to the forgiveness of sins and adds vv 14 and 15. **15.** *let it be so for now:* This verse expresses a temporal limitation, implying a change, after the cross and resurrection, or after the death of JBap. *justice:* "Justice" and "righteousness" are two transls. of the same Gk word *dikaiosynē*. Justice is the second great theological theme of Matt, after the kingdom of God, to which it is closely related (6:33). Here as elsewhere in the Gospel it refers to ethical justice or righteousness of life. *to fulfill all justice:* I.e., to do perfectly whatever is just and makes just, because one is obedient to the will of God. Fulfillment or fullness is also a Matthean emphasis. (Here as elsewhere Jesus identifies himself with the people, as in the meals with sinners he shows his solidarity with them.) Luke 3:21–22 displaces the baptism into a subordinate clause, adds his characteristic praying, and puts the descent of the Holy Spirit in the center; the event becomes a little Pentecost. John 1:29–34 feels the embarrassment of the baptism so acutely that he fails to mention it at all. Instead JBap hails Jesus as the Lamb of God. The obvious conclusion from this tradition history is that Jesus was indeed baptized by JBap in the Jordan. The early church preserved the incident even though it was troubled by it. But the next part of the text, vv 16 and 17, represents a more supernatural element, which early form critics classified as a myth. It now seems more accurate, however, to see it as an interpretative vision (*Deutevision*), as in the targums of Gen 22:10; 28:12 (so Lentzen-Deis), which comments on the event itself. **16.** *Jesus having been baptized:* Matt mentions the baptism in a participle and relates the opening of the heavens and the message of the heavenly voice in a public, objective manner, though the descent of the Spirit of God (OT phraseology) is still described as a private experience of Jesus himself ("he saw"), as in Mark (cf. Luke). *dove:* See Gen 1:2. That the Spirit descended on him means that Jesus has been anointed as Messiah (Acts 10:37–38), i.e., that he has received the power, wisdom, and holiness for that role. **17.** *a voice:* This is what the rabbis called a *bat-qôl* (lit., "the daughter of a voice," i.e., a little voice or whisper), an agent of revelation for some, yet usually rejected as invalid in matters of law by the later rabbinate (*b. Pesaḥ.* 1114a; *b. Yebam.* 102a). Cf. Matt 17:5. *This is my beloved son:* The words are an allusion to Isa 42:1 but with some reference to Gen 22:2 and Ps 2:7. They signify that Jesus is to be the Suffering Servant of God and only in this humble sense Messiah. The servant is a mysterious figure who though innocent suffers for his people. He is the subject of four songs in Dt-Isa (42:1–4; 49:1–7; 50:4–11; 52:13–53:12). The Hebrew reads "servant," not "son." Philologically the shift was made possible by the Gk word *pais,* sometimes used in the LXX to translate *'ebed,* "servant," but also meaning "boy," "child." From that sense to son is a small step. Nevertheless, the change could have been made deliberately, owing to the realization of the unique sonship of Jesus as his servanthood. The objection of M. D. Hooker that at that time the servant was not understood to be a particular person is not decisive because there is a continuous reinterpretation, fusion, and transformation of OT and Jewish messianic ideas going on in the NT. Jesus becomes a magnet of salvific titles. In later Christian tradition the baptism is regarded as the first NT revelation of the Trinity, economically, because Father, Son, and Spirit are here together (Jerome), and Jesus' baptism becomes a model for Christian baptism.

(Cullmann, O., *Baptism in the New Testament* [Naperville, 1950]. Hooker, M. D., *Jesus and the Servant* [London, 1959]. Lentzen-Deis, F., *Die Taufe Jesu* [Frankfurt, 1970]. Wink, W., *John the Baptist in the Gospel Tradition* [Cambridge, 1969].)

19   (I) The Temptation of Jesus (4:1–11). Mark relates this event in a mere two verses (1:12–13). He tells the fact of the temptation but not the details. This is important because it probably accurately reflects the situation of the disciples regarding this event: they knew that Jesus had been tempted (the historicity of the event need not be doubted), but since temptation is essentially a personal, inner experience they did not know exactly what had gone on in Jesus' consciousness. The Q version in Matt and Luke thus represents a narrative midrash or interpretation of the event in such a way as to make it pastorally useful for believers. This is done by connecting the 40-day fast with Moses and Elijah in the desert and with the great temptation or trial of God's patience by the people in the exodus who rebelled against the divine nourishment (the manna) and worshiped the golden calf; and by identifying Jesus as the Son of God (v 3), meaning Israel, the people of God (see 2:15), not the Messiah. All of Jesus' answers to the tempter are quotations from Deut 6–8. The individual temptations in Matt are not as bizarre as they appear at first glance; they are all based on various ways of sinning against the great commandment to love God "with all your heart, and with all your soul, and with all your might" (Deut 6:5) as the command was understood by the early rabbis: "heart" refers to the two affective impulses or drives, good and evil; "soul" means life, even martyrdom; "might" means wealth, property, and other external possessions (*m. Ber.* 9:5). This basic theme of love of God unites the whole narrative. **3.** *Son of God:* So

the tempter calls Jesus, i.e., the representative of Israel. *stones:* Turning stones into bread would involve the sin of rebellion against the divine will. **4.** *by bread alone:* Jesus' reply comes from Deut 8:3. To grasp its full significance one must read the entire context in Deut 6–8. The word of God is made the chief nourishment. **5.** Only the first temptation takes place in the desert. *the holy city:* Jerusalem. **6.** *the Son of God:* Again Jesus is addressed as the representative of the people and invited to test God's providential care by unnecessarily risking his life, a mockery of real martyrdom and the future passion. *angels:* The devil quotes Scripture, in this case Ps 91:11–12 in the Gk form. **7.** *not tempt the Lord:* Jesus' reply comes from Deut 6:16 (see 1 Cor 10:9). One must serve the Lord with all one's life but not lightly. **8.** *all the kingdoms of the world and their glory:* Glory is the biblical term for outer or manifest splendor or wealth, fullness of being. Here it represents the temptation to prefer power and wealth to the love of God understood as fidelity to the covenant with him. **10.** *him only shall you serve:* Jesus' reply comes from Deut 6:13, which summarizes the great OT message of ethical monotheism. Only God is worthy of our worship. The temptation of Jesus has universal significance: (a) Jesus stands for Israel because he is the beginning of the new people of God, the founder of a new humanity; (b) the basic temptation is not to love God with a unified heart, at the risk of life, at the cost of wealth. Jesus is here shown to be the perfect lover of God (Heb 4:15).

(Dupont, J., *La tentation de Jésus* [Tournai, 1967]. Gerhardsson, B., *The Testing of God's Son* [Lund, 1966].)

20   (J) The Beginning of the Galilean Ministry (4:12–17). 12. Jesus' move to Galilee after JBap has been "handed over" to prison and execution has been understood both as a courageous taking up of his mission and as a move to greater safety. **13.** *Nazareth:* Here spelled Nazara (cf. Luke 4:16), it was too centrally located for safety, near the government center of Sepphoris. *settled down:* The vb. *katoikein* implies the acquiring of a house in Capernaum (→ Biblical Geography, 73:61) on the NW bank of the Sea of Galilee. Escape to the Decapolis or some other political jurisdiction would be easy; one slips away by boat at night. Matthew uses the old Israelite tribal names (Capernaum is in Naphtali), even though they had fallen out of use in his day, because he wishes to defend the activity of the Messiah in this unexpected place rather than in the religious capital Jerusalem or the desert. **14.** The sixth formula quotation comes from Isa 8:23–9:1 (→ 7 above). **15–16.** The citation is based on the MT, but the first half is condensed so that only the geographic references are retained. These five references point to northern Galilee and Transjordan, which had fallen to the Assyrians in 734 BC (→ History, 75:102–4). Isaiah's promise of their liberation Matthew sees fulfilled by Jesus' arrival. *the way of the sea:* This could be the highway from Damascus to the sea (the probable route of the Assyrian invasion, 2 Kgs 15:29), or, as often, the coast road. In any case, "the sea" referred originally to the Mediterranean, not to the Sea of Galilee. *Galilee of the Gentiles:* Originally meaning "the circle of the Gentiles," i.e., encircled by Gentiles, Galilee was by Matthew's day at least half Gentile in population, half pagan in cult (cf. the Venus of Dan), and bilingual (using Greek and Aramaic). These facts may have had some influence on Jesus and earliest Christianity, opening it to the Gentile mission, often expressing itself in Greek, shaping its message, set in a Jewish matrix, in such a way as to be readily intelligible to Gentiles of good will. The atmosphere was different from Judean Judaism. The gospel arises in a specific time and place. *the people who sat in darkness:* Originally this referred to the oppressed Israelites, but perhaps here "the people" includes also Gentiles. Light-darkness symbolism is not so frequent in Matt as in John, 1QM, or the gnostic writings, but it is present here: Jesus' preaching the kingdom is the light of consolation to the suffering people (cf. Luke 1:79). **17.** *from then Jesus began:* This introductory formula (used again only in 16:21) solemnly inaugurates Jesus' ministry. *repent:* See comment on 3:2. *the kingdom of the heavens is at hand:* The proclamation of the near arrival of God's kingdom is the central message of Jesus and, along with the resurrection, the basis and object of Christian hope. Derived from the night vision of Daniel (7:13-14), it represents the future, final salvation of all humanity socially, politically, and spiritually through an exercise of the sovereignty of God, establishing justice and peace on earth as well as in heaven (6:33; Rom 14:17). In Dan 7:13-14 it is given to "one like a son of man," and Q and Matt identify this mysterious figure with Jesus coming again in glory. Thus, for Christians the kingdom hope includes faith in Christ as end-time savior. Since Christ has already come (in humility and suffering) we have a foretaste of the kingdom (12:28), esp. in his ministry of healing and feeding the multitude, though the fullness is not yet. Matthew avoids the direct mention of God out of reverence. He does this by reverent circumlocution, as in the phrase "kingdom of the heavens," though he is not consistent in this and 4 times writes "kingdom of God" (12:28; 19:24; 21:31,43), as do the other Synoptics. The circumlocution is unfortunate because it misleads people into thinking that the kingdom is only in heaven and not to be on earth (6:10). The kingdom was also to be the content of the disciples' preaching (10:7).

(Fitzmyer, J. A., "The Languages of Palestine in the First Century A.D.," *WA* 29-56. Freyne, S., *Galilee from Alexander the Great to Hadrian, 323 B.C. to 135 A.D.* [Wilmington, 1980]. Perrin, N., *The Kingdom of God in the Teaching of Jesus* [Phl, 1963]. Schnackenburg, R., *God's Rule and Kingdom* [NY, 1963]. Weiss, J., *Jesus' Proclamation of the Kingdom of God* [Phl, 1971].)

21   (K) The Call of the Disciples (4:18-22). Matt here follows Mark (1:16-20) closely. **18.** *Peter:* Matt anticipates Jesus' later renaming of Simon as *Petros* (16:18), Greek for Aram *kêpā'*, "rock" (whence Cephas, cf. John 1:42; → NT Thought, 81:138). The Galilean fishing industry was quite prosperous and exported its products a considerable distance. **19.** *come after me:* This is technical language of a teacher to disciples. Yet Jesus goes beyond the ordinary learner-teacher relationship by taking the initiative. Gathering disciples is the closest Jesus comes to founding a church before the crucifixion (see 16:17-19). *fishers of men:* This figure may be proverbial, derived from their trade, or literary (Jer 16:16). It is one of the two main images for ministry in the NT; the other, shepherd, is less missionary in direct connotation. **20.** *leaving their nets immediately:* That Jesus expected a radical, prompt obedience from his followers may be seen from 8:21,22. Yet here the story may have undergone extreme compression; in reality there may have been some chance for a psychological growth in attraction, which would make such an important decision more understandable (cf. John 1:35-51). In later tradition the nets could be understood as a symbol of worldly entanglements. **21.** With the sons of Zebedee the circle of intimates is complete (cf. 17:1-8). Matthew emphasizes brothers here and in v 18, because he is interested in this as a theme of community life. **22.** *followed him:* Following Jesus sometimes means rupturing family ties,

yet Jesus opposes neglect of parents in their old age (15:4-6).

(Wuellner, W., *The Meaning of "Fishers of Men"* [Phl, 1967].)

22   (II) The Sermon on the Mount (4:23-7:29). **(A) Introduction (4:23-5:2). 23.** This important verse gives a summary report of Jesus' ministry. It consists of a main clause followed by three participial clauses which together form a triplet. The triplet itself has a ring structure ABA' in which the B element, "preaching the gospel of the kingdom," is the kernel, the center of importance. It is framed by "teaching in their synagogues" and "healing." The relationship of the three elements is this: the gospel of the kingdom is preached and incipiently realized by the ministries of word and deed. Verse 23 forms a bracket with 9:35. Matthew depicts Jesus as minister of the word in chaps. 5-7 and of the deed in chaps. 8-9. *their synagogues:* As opposed to our Jewish-Christian ones (Jas 2:2). *gospel of the kingdom:* This phrase is unique to Matt (three times: here, 9:35; 24:14). That the message of the kingdom of God precedes the Sermon on the Mount, which speaks of our duties to God, means that God has the primacy of initiative; we place our ultimate trust in him, not in ourselves. *healing every illness and every weakness:* That Jesus was a healer was an embarrassment to later Christians; therefore, it is certainly historical. He was among other things an itinerant Galilean wonder-working prophet in the pattern of Elijah. The repetition of "every" reflects Matt's striving for fullness. **24.** *all Syria:* The Roman province of Syria included four parts (Strabo, *Geogr.* 16.2.2): Commagene (Samosata), Seleucia (Antioch), Coele-Syria (Damascus), Phoenicia-Palestine. In Josephus Syria seems to include Galilee and the coast down to Gaza, but not Judea. It embraces Tyre, Sidon, and Idumea (cf. Mark). The "all" is plerophoric. *demoniacs, lunatics, paralytics:* The three types of illness are all nervous disorders, psychosomatic, sometimes curable by a strong personality. **25.** *Galilee:* See comment on v 15. *Decapolis:* This is a loose geographic term to describe 10 Hellenistic towns in southern Syria; the list is not fixed, but according to Pliny (*Nat. Hist.* 5.16.74) it includes Damascus, Philadelphia-Amman, Raphana, Scythopolis-Bethshan, Gadara, Hippo-Susita, Dion, Pella, Gerasa, Canatha. *Jerusalem and Judea:* They are in penultimate place, though in Jewish expectations they would be primary—a shift of emphasis from Pharisaic Judaism. All told, a wide field of influence is depicted (see S. T. Parker, *JBL* 94 [1975] 437-41; I. Browning, *Jerash and the Decapolis* [London, 1982]). **5:1.** On the basis of this verse one might think that the sermon was addressed to the disciples alone, but in 7:28 the "crowds" have heard and react. So the disciples form the *corona fratrum* (cf. Neh 8:4), and the crowds the second concentric ring. *the mountain:* It is not named, but functionally it is a mount of revelation (as frequently in the Bible and in Matt), a symbolic Sinai. There is no need to harmonize it with Luke 6:17, "a level place." *sitting:* This is a posture of Oriental teachers. Outdoor teaching was a hallmark of Jesus' ministry. **2.** A solemn introduction. The sermon is a Matthean construction, pieced together from material scattered in Q (cf. Luke 6:20-49), Mark, and other material. There is no reason to doubt that most of this material derives from Jesus himself; but each case must be weighed on its own merits, and the sayings have undergone revision. It has been proposed that Matthew does not really accept the sermon as still applicable to his readers or as fitting into the rest of his Gospel; but this view is hardly tenable in the light of the inclusions between 4:23 and 9:35 and between 5:1-2 and 28:19-20.

23 The Sermon on the Mount is the first of five major discourses in the Gospel (→ 8 above). It is Matthew's masterpiece and was early the most frequently cited section. Its literary genre remains disputed. G. Bornkamm (*NTS* 24 [1977–78] 419–32) holds that it is without real analogy. H. D. Betz (*Essays*) compares it with a philosopher's epitome. G. A. Kennedy (*New Testament Interpretation through Rhetorical Criticism* [Chapel Hill, 1984] 39–72) analyzes it as a piece of deliberative rhetoric that persuades us to take action in the future and that serves as the proposition or thesis of the whole Gospel, giving intellectual satisfaction and security. Biblically, one can consider it to be eschatological, ethical, legal wisdom, or law as instruction (Torah) in view of the kingdom, not coercively but eschatologically enforced, a fusion of several OT genres. The dominant themes of the sermon are the kingdom of God and justice. Its structure can be seen from the outline of the Gospel (→ 8 above): an exordium (5:3–16) with beatitudes and sayings about salt and light (that state the missionary meaning of disciples' life); the new ethic (5:17–7:12): its basic legal principles (5:17–20); its six hypertheses (5:21–48); its reformation of works of piety (6:1–18); and its further instructions (6:19–7:12) — how to love God with one's whole heart, love, and strength (instructions loosely arranged around the necessities of life and culminating in the golden rule); a conclusion (7:13–27), a teaching on the two ways, the covenant formulary that makes Matt an extension of the deuteronomic theology of history in the NT; and a concluding parable.

The sermon is fairly systematic, covering the main areas of ethical and religious life as understood in Israel. It is neither purely arbitrary nor exhaustive, but a series of pointers illustrated by "focal instances." The sermon has been criticized as setting too high a standard, which remains unfulfillable ("you cannot govern with the sermon" [Bismarck]); but, understood against its Jewish background, it becomes a possible but still high standard of moral wisdom about life.

24 **(B) The Exordium (5:3–16).**

(a) Beatitudes (5:3–12). Cf. Luke 6:20b–23. A comparison of the two versions shows that Luke has four (3 + 1) beatitudes and Matt eight (7 + 1). Probably only Luke's first three are authentic; his fourth comes from the early church; Matthew's additional beatitudes are his own expansion from the Psalms. The common source is Q, and beyond that Jesus' use of Isa 61:1–4. In form, a beatitude is an exclamation of congratulations that recognizes an existing state of happiness, beginning with the Hebr noun *'ašrê* or the Gk adj. *makarios*. Here the gospel begins with a cry of joy, based on the nearness of the kingdom of God. The original beatitudes about the "poor," the "mourners," and the "hungry" express Jesus' mission to the needy in Israel and the dawn of a new era of salvation history. All three refer to the same people. The poor, etc. are happy not because they are morally better than others but because of God's special care for them. God was conceived of as an Oriental king, and a king's duty was to protect the weak. The long, last beatitude about the persecuted reflects the experience of martyrdom in the early church and is explicitly christological (vv 1–12). Matthew's editorial additions may be seen in several places. First he adds "justice" in vv 6 and 10, both as a formal divider and as one of the great themes of his Gospel. To "blessed are the poor" he adds "in spirit." The poor are the needy ones of Israel, the *'ănāwîm* or *'am hā-'āreṣ*, who prefer the divine service to financial advantage. Their poverty is real and economic, but with a spiritual dimension. In Matt the addition of "in spirit" changes the emphasis from social-economic to personal-moral: humility, detachment from wealth, voluntary poverty. In the Bible economic destitution is an evil to be corrected (Deut 15:11), and wealth is not an evil in itself; indeed, it is a necessity for the well-being of the kingdom, but it risks neglect of God and of the poor. God's first priority is the care of the poor. *the meek:* This term, derived from Ps 37:11, means "slow to anger," "gentle with others," connoting a form of charity. *mourners:* They mourn to see evil reign on earth (originally, over Israel). *merciful:* This refers to the pardoning of one's neighbor (Matt 6:12,14–15; 18:35), to love (9:13; 12:7; 23:23), esp. of the needy (Matt 25:31–46), and even of one's enemies (5:44–47). All vengeance is excluded. *the pure in heart:* In the OT this refers to ritual and moral impurity being cleansed (Ps 24:4; 51; Isa 1:10–20). In Matt "purity of heart" stands close to justice and includes covenant fidelity, loyalty to God's commands, sincere worship. *peacemakers:* This term is based on OT *šālôm*, a many-sided concept involving total well-being. The rabbis had democratized the royal ideology of the king as peacemaker and enjoined it on everyone. In Matt peacemaking is closely related to the love of neighbor and hence to the beatitude of the merciful. Matthew thus transforms a short messianic manifesto into a program of life, a list of desirable qualities or virtues. Each beatitude is composed through synthetic parallelism. All of the rewards will find their realization in the kingdom of God. The pass. voice of the vb. in many of the reward clauses is a theological pass.: God will comfort, fill, have mercy, call them (*ZBG* § 236). All of the reward vbs. are in the fut. tense, except the first and last; future eschatology predominates throughout.

(Broer, I., *Die Seligpreisungen der Bergpredigt* [BBB 61; Bonn, 1986]. Dupont, J., *Les Béatitudes* [3 vols; Paris, 1954–73].)

25 (b) Salt and Light (5:13–16). Matthew has taken early sayings from the Jesus tradition (Mark 9:50; 4:21; Luke 8:16; 11:33; 14:34–35), using the metaphors of salt and light, and applied them to the hearers of the sermon. Cf. Pliny, *Nat. Hist.* 31.102: "nothing is more useful than salt or sunshine." Matthew emphasizes the personal address by his repeated "you" and "your." He says to the disciples in effect: though persecuted, you have a vocation for the world. **13.** *if salt be insipid:* I.e., useless. Strictly speaking, salt cannot lose its flavor and remain salt, but in Judaism it can become unclean and need to be thrown out. Salt is both a spice and a preservative. So is a good teacher. The description of the fate of the salt uses imagery for the divine judgment. **14.** *light:* Light imagery is applied to God, to Israel (Rom 2:19). In the NT it is applied to Jesus (Matt 4:16; Luke 1:79; 2:32; Phil 2:15; Eph 5:8). *a city set on a mountain:* See Isa 2:2–5. If a specific Galilean hilltop city is meant, a good candidate would be Hippos; otherwise, Jerusalem. With the confidence of faith, the disciples are not to shrink from their world mission. **15.** The imagery presupposes a Palestinian one-room house, a common clay oil lamp, and a meal shovel. The disciple lives not only for self but for others; cf. 25:26; 2 Cor 4:7. **16.** *let your light so shine:* Matthew draws his conclusion from the elements he received from tradition. The verse contains a delicate balancing act between doing good works and not being proud or taking the credit. The life of discipleship described in the rest of the sermon should not lead to arrogance but to the conversion of many to "your father who is in the heavens." It is characteristic of Jesus to address God as Father; it is characteristic of Matthew to surround "Father" with "my/your . . . in the heavens" (or "heavenly"). See 5:45,48; 6:1,9,14,26,32; 7:11, etc.

26   (C) The New Ethic: Its Basic Legal Principles and Six Hypertheses (5:17-48).
(a) THE HIGHER RIGHTEOUSNESS (5:17-20).
These verses give the basic legal principles of the sermon. They are the most controversial verses in Matt, and there is no consensus on their interpretation. The interpreter must try to state the problem clearly and to provide a historically honest judgment, even at the price of theological tidiness. The problem arises because the plain sense of the words is that Jesus affirms the abiding validity of the Torah; but this contradicts Paul (e.g., Gal 2:15,16; Rom 3:21-31). Moreover, no major Christian church requires observance of all 613 precepts of the OT law, ethical and ceremonial, but only the ethical commands such as the Decalogue and the commands to love God and neighbor. Thus, there is a gap between the teaching here and the teaching and practice of the churches. The position adopted here is the following: (a) There are contradictions within the NT on penultimate matters; this is not necessarily a disadvantage, since it should widen Christian tolerance of variety within the church and help ecumenism (see E. Käsemann, "The Canon of the New Testament and the Unity of the Church," *ENTT* 95-107; H. Küng, "The Canon of the New Testament as an Ecumenical Problem," *The Council in Action* [NY, 1964]). (b) Historically Matt (and James) inclined more to the Jewish-Christian side of early Christian polemic, though Matt is clearly open to the Gentile mission (28:19-20). Yet he never mentions circumcision, the most divisive issue between Paul and James, though he may presuppose it as desirable even if not absolutely necessary. Moreover, Matt 5:21-48 does not discuss ceremonial precepts in detail, but concentrates on the ethical. There are two common exegetical strategies for evading the plain meaning: (a) reinterpretation, esp. through v 18d; but cf. 23:23; (b) denial of authenticity. This latter approach contains much truth. Apart from v 18, the verses are probably postpaschal and reflect the outlook of Jewish Christianity, which, as a separate movement, was eventually defeated by Paulinism and died out (perhaps to be reborn in a different form as Islam; see H.-J. Schoeps, *Jewish Christianity* [Phl, 1969]; J. Daniélou, *The Theology of Jewish Christianity* [London, 1964]). But denial of the authenticity of vv 17,19,20 does not make Jesus hold the same view as Paul.
27   Law in Matt. *Jesus* probably did not break in principle with Torah but only with Pharisaic halaka. Yet he was a free spirit who directly confronted and resolved life situations in his healings and parables without carefully citing texts. *Matthew* remains in the same line of basic fidelity to Torah but with a concentration on the more important values (23:23) and with a lawyerly concern to provide textual support for innovations. *Paul* prefers an ethics of values like faith, hope, love, and walking in the Spirit to a legal ethics, but he does cite the Decalogue as applicable to Christians (Rom 13:8-10) even though the ceremonial laws do not bind Gentile converts according to his gospel. As far as most modern Christians are concerned, Paul won this fight and they follow him. But Matthew, by exerting a powerful influence on church life, has acted as a moderating influence on radical Paulinism, which can easily become libertinism and antinomianism. Both Paul and Matthew cherish the Decalogue and center it on love.
28   17. *do not think:* This introductory phrase supposes an erroneous view that needs to be corrected. *the law and the prophets:* A formula frequent in Matt (7:12; 11:13; 22:40); it refers to the whole of God's revelation in the OT. *destroy . . . fulfill:* This contrast teaches that Jesus' basic attitude toward the Jewish inheritance was fundamentally positive and sympathetic, even though it

included criticism of some developments he judged harmful (see chaps. 15 and 23) and the start of a new era. In the background lies a pair of rabbinic expressions, *qwm* and *bṭl. Qwm* means to "confirm" or "establish" the law by putting it on a better exegetical footing (see Rom 3:31); *bṭl* means to "void, abolish, suspend, neglect, cancel" a law. But Matthew's wording replaces "establish" with "fulfill," which goes beyond a purely legal discussion to a broader christological perspective. **18.** *till heaven and earth pass:* This is the fundamental verse of the unit because it is rooted in a word of Jesus (Q: Luke 16:17). It asserts the permanence of the law while the physical universe lasts. Matt provides the saying with a solemn introduction "Amen . . ." and frames the central part of it ("not one jot . . .") with two temporal clauses in strict parallelism (until . . . until), which mean exactly the same thing, the end of the world. When commentators find this meaning unacceptable, they often interpret the second until-clause as referring to the crucifixion of Jesus, but there is little to support this; see 24:34f. The meaning of the verse is twofold: (1) The whole of the OT has religious value for the followers of Jesus and should continue to be preserved, prayed, studied, and preached in the movement he began. (2) The prescriptions of the law still bind the immediate (Jewish-Palestinian) followers of Jesus; see Isa 40:8. *jot or tittle:* "Jot" refers to *yôd*, the smallest letter of the Hebr alphabet; "tittle" is a slight serif on a Hebr letter that distinguishes it from another, similarly formed letter. **19.** *whoever relaxes:* This verse stems from Jewish-Christian polemic against the hellenizing Christians, particularly Paul and his followers. It teaches that even the small matters of the law are important (see *m. 'Abot* 2:1; 3:18; 4:21; Matt 23:23). Yet the verse is careful not to exclude the laxists from the kingdom; they are simply called "least." This reflects a delicate, ecumenical way of fighting: you make your point but do not damn your opponent. *do and teach:* This characteristic order reflects Matthew's horror of hypocrisy, teaching one thing and doing another. Jesus later will grant church leaders the authority to bind and to loose (16:19; 18:18). **20.** *your righteousness:* This verse almost certainly comes from Matthew's redaction and provides the thematic heading for the rest of the chapter, a "more abundant righteousness/justice." A sense of abundance (*perisseuein*) is characteristic of every level of early Christianity. For Matthew the essence of what Jesus brought is a superior ethic, a higher justice. His is a moral piety. His great opponents are the rabbinic heirs of the Pharisees at Jamnia. Note that he does not explicitly say that the Pharisees will not enter the kingdom. The verse is a warning to Christians.
29   (b) ANGER (5:21-26). The first of six hypertheses. They are usually called antitheses, because interpreters were impressed by Jesus' sovereign authority over the OT Torah and by the cases where his teaching seems to contradict the OT or be opposed to it, e.g., on divorce, which the OT presupposes and which Jesus prohibits (or restricts). The present interpretation emphasizes rather that Jesus seems to go beyond OT teaching by deepening and radicalizing it, by returning to the original will of God, but that he never moves in a lax direction, whence hyperthesis (P. Lapide). Also to be noted is that the formula "It was said . . . , but I say" is close to an exegetical formula common in the rabbinic schools: first a Bible quotation, then "You might think this means . . . but I say to you. . . ." As a matter of fact, here in the sermon an OT text is followed by a false interpretation, which Jesus then corrects; see on 5:43. Yet the hypertheses, although exegetical in form, are materially revelation for Matthew. **21.** *you have heard:* This

presupposes an audience which has been taught the Jewish law. *that it was said:* The vb. is a theological pass.; God said (see *ZBG* § 236). *to the ancients:* This refers to the generation of Sinai which first heard the law from Moses. *thou shalt not murder:* Exod 20:13; Deut 5:17. Biblical law comes in two forms: apodictic and casuistic. Apodictic takes the "Thou shalt not" form familiar from the Decalogue; casuistic takes the forms, "If anyone . . ." or "Whoever . . ." or "In the case that. . . ." Here we have an apodictic command followed by case law: "Whoever commits murder shall be liable to judgment." This is a traditional interpretation of the commandment. **22.** *but I say:* Jesus regards the traditional interpretation as inadequate, though not false. He shifts the ground from the act of murder to the emotional prelude to murder, anger. He thus effects an interiorization that gets at the roots of moral activity. Since murder is a relatively rare temptation but anger is a common experience, we can see a tendency to bring the clan-leader law of the Decalogue down to the level of the ordinary Israelite in daily life, a tendency toward democratization of Torah. (The Pharisees too moved in this direction but differed in their preference for complexity over simplicity.) A problem arises today in that modern psychology teaches that neurotically repressed anger is the source of much mental illness. We must be careful, therefore, not to think that Jesus is advocating neurotic repression. We should acknowledge our emotions but not act them out in rage or killing or other violence. *fool: Raka* may be the Gk transl. of Aram *rêqā'*, "empty-headed" (*EWNT* 3. 497). There may be an escalation in the penalties, from small synedrium to large synedrium to *Gehenna* (the Hinnom Valley outside Jerusalem, which because of the industrial slag, blast furnaces, and the burning bodies of plague victims became a symbol for hellfire). These three cases are all expressed in casuistic form. The same is true of the next case. **23-24.** This case presupposes the Temple standing and must stem from before AD 70. It also presupposes that Jesus approves of the Temple and the sacrificial system. After the crucifixion some Christians would regard the Temple system (or administration) as spiritually bankrupt, as did the Qumran community, although others would continue to worship there. *first . . . then:* This priority of ethics over cult reflects OT prophetic teaching: there can be no true worship of God without justice, a doctrine called ethical monotheism for short and often considered the center of the OT. Since perfect justice eludes us until the kingdom comes, we must worship imperfectly, trusting in God's mercy. *be reconciled:* Reconciliation is primarily a Pauline theme in the NT. Cf. Mark 11:25. **25-26.** The advice of these two verses is to settle out of court, still good advice. *make friends:* This verse employs a very Gk concept, *eunoia*, "well-mindedness," "good will," "affection." There is an escalation in the penalties: judge, servant-guard, prison. **30**   (c) ADULTERY (5:27-30). **27.** After a shorter introductory formula, Exod 20:14; Deut 5:18 are quoted. By analogy with v 21 we could insert after the citation the inadequate interpretation: "Whoever commits adultery shall be liable to judgment." Jesus will correct and deepen this view now. **28.** *everyone looking at a woman to desire her:* Jesus moves from the level of action to the level of lustful intention. Since this verse has troubled many consciences, sometimes unhealthily, it is important to try to grasp its point as exactly as possible. Since adultery is a serious matter, a wrong of injustice as well as of unchastity, acts that lead to it can also be morally seriously wrong, e.g., alienation of affection. Jesus' words here are to be taken strictly in connection with adultery. They do not condemn any thinking about sexual matters such as would be involved in the study of

medicine or simple velleities. *has already committed adultery with her in his heart:* This teaches the truth of experience that when a person has seriously decided to commit a wrong the moral evil is already present, even though it can be increased by further action. **29-30.** *if your right eye causes you to sin:* These verses parallel Mark 9:43-47 but are omitted by Luke, probably because they are liable to be misunderstood because of the Oriental hyperbolic mode in which they are expressed. The point is that Jesus calls for a radical ordering of priorities. The logic of one's decisions and moral choices is important. It is better to sacrifice a part of one's moral freedom than to lose the whole.

31   (d) DIVORCE (5:31-32). This unit contains only two verses; it is extremely brief on a subject of immense human significance and delicacy: marriage, family, and separation (see the fuller treatments in Matt 19:1-12; Mark 10:1-12; Luke 16:18). The foundations of human society are involved, a grave matter: "Divorce is to family life what civil war is to the state" (Aristotle). The interpretive task must be to uncover the presuppositions, to retrieve the original problematic and deep intentions of the text. There is an enormous literature on the subject but the main positions are represented by J. Bonsirven, *Le divorce dans le Nouveau Testament* (Paris, 1948); J. Dupont, *Mariage et divorce dans l'Evangile* (Bruges, 1959); but esp. C. Marucci, *Parole di Gesù sul divorzio* (Brescia, 1982).

The abbreviated introductory formula suggests a subordination to or at least a close connection of subject matter with the preceding section on adultery. Source-critically we have here a Marcan-Q overlap; this early multiple attestation is a strong indication of early, authentic Jesus material, reinforced by a parallel in 1 Cor 7:10-16. There is in fact no historical doubt that Jesus held to a very high doctrine on marriage, viz., its indissolubility, a position probably without parallel in the Judaism contemporary with him, though not without some prophetic precedent (Mal 2:13-16). Formally, this unit represents a brief halakic decision in the form of a comment on a cited biblical text; the fuller version 19:1-12 is a classic scholastic dialogue. **31.** Deut 24:1-4 is cited in compressed form. The full text is a complicated and odd fragment of old law that directly concerns only the particular case of a second marriage to a wife one has divorced and who herself has since been divorced. Neither this text nor any other in the Hebr OT explicitly declares divorce licit or regulates it juridically. Indirectly Deut 24:1-4 describes divorce and therefore implicitly ratifies it. (Sir 25:26 counsels separation from a disobedient wife.) The prophet Malachi (2:13-16) denounces easy divorce in moving terms and stresses the covenant relationship in marriage. At Qumran, CD 4:19-5:11; 13:15-17; 11QTemple 57:17-19 seem to prohibit polygamy and incest but not divorce itself (at least explicitly). To understand Matt it is important to realize that in Israelite law an adulterous woman is in principle punished by death (Lev 18:20; 20:10; Deut 22:20-21; John 8:1-11). A text from the rabbis is also strictly relevant: "The School of Shammai says: A man may not divorce his wife unless he has found in her *indecency* in anything. . . . And the School of Hillel says: He may divorce her even if she spoiled a dish for him, for it is written, 'Because he hath found in her indecency in *anything*.' R. Akiba says: Even if he found another fairer than she, for it is written, 'And it shall be if she find no favor in his eyes'" (*m. Git.* 9:10). **32**   Summary of the evolution of the institution of marriage in Israel. At first there was no contract, polygamy was common, divorce was easy and informal. Then, with the spread of writing, a juridification took place. There was a written marital contract (*kĕtubbâ*, see Tob 7:12-14), and also at times a written bill of divorcement (*gēṭ*), as a protection for the woman to assure another man of her freedom to remarry. Third, a movement toward monogamy appears in the LXX; its version of Gen 2:27 adds "two" to the phrase "They shall become one flesh." Fourth, there was a prophetic reaction against easy divorce. Jesus then rules out divorce for a man (the woman was not considered). Finally, Mark 10:12 ruled out divorce also for a woman, an application of Jesus' teaching to Gentile circumstances. The tendency is toward the refinement and stabilization of manners and the protection of the needs of all parties, but it started from a position of male superiority with no rights for the woman except what her family could and would enforce. Jesus aims for the ideal, the paradisiacal will of God (see 19:8 and the analogy of kingship in 1 Sam 8:7-9), not a minimalist view. This background prepares us for Matthew's contribution in the next verse (D. Daube, "Concessions to Sinfulness in Jewish Law," *JJS* 10 [1959] 1-13). **32.** *except for reason of unchastity:* Unlike the parallels (1 Cor 7:11; Mark 10:11; Luke 16:18) Matthew has here and in 19:9 this famous exceptive clause. It is commonly assumed that this is his own redactional addition or that of his tradition. *Porneia,* translated here as "unchastity," means unlawful sexual conduct, which could include adultery but is not the technical word for it (*moicheia*). Three main solutions to the difficult problem are proposed for this clause. (1) The so-called Greek Orthodox solution holds that the clause contains a real exception to the absolute prohibition of divorce and second marriage. In this case Matthew's position would be the same as that of the Shammaites and different from Jesus'. A difficulty is that in this view the text should read *moicheia,* not *porneia.* This view has recently been defended at length by Marucci, who argues that the clause was intended to safeguard Christians who were Roman citizens from the Augustan *Lex Iulia de adulteriis coercendis,* under which a husband was compelled to accuse an adulterous wife under pain of being charged with the capital offense of *lenocinium.* This argument remains very uncertain. (2) The classic "Catholic" solution (Dupont) holds that the clause does not contain a real exception since it does not refer to divorce but to separation without remarriage in the case of an adulterous wife (who in Israelite law would be stoned). Again, the text does not use the word for adultery. (3) In the "rabbinic" solution also the clause does not contain a real exception to the prohibition of divorce because the key term *porneia* is understood as translating the Hebr *zĕnût,* "prostitution," understood in the sense of an incestuous union due to marriage within forbidden degrees of kinship (Lev 18:6-18). Such a union would not be true marriage at all and would not require a divorce but a decree of nullity or an annulment. *Porneia,* as used in Acts 15:23-29, stands close to this; as does *zĕnût* in the Qumran documents (e.g., CD 4:20-21). This solution fits the text best; it represents Matthew's legal finesse and his loyalty to Jesus (see Bonsirven, *Le divorce;* H. Baltensweiler, *Die Ehe im NT* [Zurich, 1967] 87-102; J. A. Fitzmyer, *TAG* 79-111).

Since the matter of divorce is often painful, it is useful to remember that Jesus' deep intent was not to cause pain but to set out a clear and high ideal of human relations, a vision of marriage as a covenant of personal love between spouses which reflects the covenant relationship of God and his people. Unfortunately this vision does not always fit the vagaries of the human heart (Jer 17:9). **33.** (e) OATHS (5:33-37). **33.** *again:* This is a resumptive hint that a new section is starting, that we have reached the halfway point. After the introductory

formula in full, there is a composite OT citation: Lev 19:12 (rather than or as a summary of Exod 20:7); Num 30:3. There seems to be a logical tension between the first part, "you shall not swear," and the second, "you shall perform what you swear" (which implies that you do swear). It is possible that the second part could be understood as a common corrupt exegesis of the first part that Jesus then corrects in v 34a with his eschatological radicalness. **34.** *do not swear at all:* Formulated as a command in the negative. The examples that follow in vv 34b,35,36 (citing Isa 66:1 and Ps 48:2) are oath formulas, which contain subterfuges for the divine name, which the devout tried to avoid pronouncing. But in employing subterfuges an element of untruthfulness was introduced which had as its intention the assurance of truth. Jesus implies (v 36) that there is nothing in creation that is not from God and dependent on him, reflecting his glory as creator. **37.** *yes, yes, no, no:* This is the crucial verse in the unit because it gives a positive command about the character of speech (*logos*), to balance the negative command in v 34, followed by a terse reason. The only NT parallels to this unit are Matt 23:16-22 and Jas 5:12 (which may reflect the original Jesus tradition more closely than Matthew's developed forms); cf. 2 Cor 1:17-19 (which confesses that Jesus is the permanent yes of God to us). The problem they all address is that of language (cf. the Mishnaic tractates *Šebuʿot, Nedarim,* and *Nazir,* which all deal with vows and oaths; Diog. Laertius 8.22; *2 Enoch* 49:1; Pseudo-Phocylides 1.16). Jesus is here opposing the hypocrisy, sophistry, and academic trivialization of life and replacing them with an ideal of simplicity and directness of speech. This ideal need not be opposed to poetry or metaphor (see his parables) or oath formulas as such so long as they are truthful. (According to *b. Sanh.* 36a yes and no become oaths when they are repeated, as Jesus does here.) Jesus is here taking the line of the Decalogue. The Decalogue says nothing about swearing, oaths, or vows, but it says that "you shall not take the name of God in vain," and "you shall not bear false witness," i.e., you shall speak the truth in important matters. Jesus combines the two commandments by saying that you shall not swear by God's name or any substitute for it and you shall speak the truth simply. Greek philosophical tradition from the Delphic oracle and the Pythagoreans to the Stoics of Jesus' day moved in the same direction (*TDNT* 5. 176-85, 457-67).

34 (f) RETALIATION (5:38-42). This and the next hyperthesis, on love of enemies, are closely related in subject matter, and their relationship to each other and to earlier tradition will be treated after v 48. This unit expands the Q saying (see Luke 6:29-30). **38.** *an eye for an eye:* This quotes a legal rule (talion) regulating revenge and retaliation for damages (Exod 21:22-25; Lev 24:20; Deut 19:21). The same rule is found in the Code of Hammurabi, the Roman Law of 12 Tables 8, and Aeschylus, *Coeph.* 309-10. Though the rule sounds barbarous today, its original intention was humanitarian, to limit revenge (only *one* eye for one eye, not two or three) to an exact reciprocity. When first introduced, it constituted genuine moral progress. By the time of Jesus the rabbis already felt it too harsh and began the process of commuting the penalty to fines, but the principle of corresponding restitution remained dominant in legal thinking. (The etymology of *talion* is the Lat *talis,* "such, the same.") **39.** *do not resist evil:* Jesus teaches non-resistance to evil in the sense of avoiding physical violence or damages. This leaves open the possibility of psychological or moral resistance, "media fighting," exemplified by Mahatma Gandhi or Martin Luther

King. The parallel in Rom 12:19–21, based on Prov 25:21–22, is important in showing that Jesus' teaching is a strategy for winning, not for passive resignation or indifference to evil. The goal is to shame the opponent into a change of heart. This presupposes the requisite dispositions in the opponent, which are not always present. In such difficult cases recourse to other biblical principles may be necessary (see comment on v 48). *turn to him also the other cheek:* Striking the right cheek with the back of the hand is considered particularly dishonoring in *m. B. Qam.* 8:6; cf. John 18:22–23; Isa 50:6; Lam 3:30. **40.** *would sue you:* One should avoid litigation; see v 25. There is a noteworthy parallel in a judicial plea written in Hebrew on a 7th–6th cent. BC ostracon found at Meṣad Hashavyahu in 1960 (see D. Pardee, *Maarav* 1 [1978] 33–66). **41.** *compels you to go one mile:* The Gk word *angareuein,* "compel," is a Persian loanword, reflecting the imperial messenger service, taking horses in a courier relay, like the old Pony Express, but not paying for the horse. **42.** *give:* The theme of giving to beggars and borrowers goes beyond the scope of nonresistance to evil to advocate general kindness, forbearance, generosity, and an open attitude toward people.

35 (g) LOVE OF ENEMIES (5:43–48). **43.** *love your neighbor:* The unit begins with an incomplete quotation from Lev 19:18, leaving out the important "as yourself." This is followed by the nonbiblical words "you shall hate your enemy," a negative view that would confine our love in a narrow ethnocentric framework. It is regrettable that some transls. include these words in the same quotation marks with the biblical citation. Jesus is attacking a false interpretation of the OT. This view is not found verbatim in the OT but it may be in 1QS 1:9–10: "And that they (the saints) may love all the sons of light each according to his lot (*gôrāl*) in the Council of God; and that they may hate all the sons of darkness, each according to his fault in the vengeance of God." It is also hinted at in the OT (e.g., Deut 7:2). **44.** *love your enemies and pray for those who persecute you:* This is not hopeless idealism but a wise strategy for overcoming the persecutor. The heroic stance of the martyr gives the persecutor a bad image and is hard for governments to control. Early Christian martyrs gave late antiquity a bad conscience. Christianity is not introverted aggression, but aggression transmuted into a strategy for winning through the wisdom of love. **45.** *sons of your Father:* Adoptive sonship is also a Pauline theme (Rom 8). There is a chiastic arrangement of "evil, good, just, unjust." **46.** Cf. Luke 14:12–14. *reward:* Jesus here distinguishes implicitly between earthly human rewards and rewards from God. If you love those who love you, your reward is an increase in their love. If you love those who hate you, your reward is an increase in God's love. Some theologies regard all talk of ethical motivation in terms of reward as sub-Christian but this is foreign to the Gospels. Nevertheless, one must not think that God can be forced by strict claims of justice rather than by humble supplication. The reward is variously described as the kingdom or the vision of God (5:3,8). *tax collectors:* They are here a symbol of low morality because they were often extortioners and collaborators with the Roman occupier. Jesus befriends them but never approves of their sins (cf. Luke 19:1–10). **47.** *if you greet:* In the Near East a greeting is a prayer of blessing upon the one greeted (*m. 'Abot* 4:15). *Gentiles:* This term is a hint that the text was addressed primarily to Jewish Christians. **48.** *be perfect:* This verse comprises a complex fusion of two OT texts and Matthean redaction. Deut 18:13 reads *tāmîm,* "blameless," instead of "perfect"; Lev 19:2 has *qĕdōšîm,* "holy," but Luke (6:36) reads "merciful." *Teleios,* "perfect," is a rare word in the Gospels (found

only here and 19:21), though used by Paul and James. It is common in Gk thought, where it can mean conformity to the divine ideal. In QL the perfect man is the one who observes the whole law. Luke's version emphasizes covenant fidelity and steadfast love. These various accents could all be present in Matt, making the text rich and suggestive. Here it also forms an *inclusio* with 5:20. **36** General conclusion on retaliation and love of enemies. We can trace a five-stage evolution in biblical thinking on this topic: (1) unlimited revenge (Gen 4:15, 24); (2) talion or limited revenge (Deut 19:16–21); (3) the silver rule, "Do not do unto others what you would not have them do unto you" (Tob 4:15; Hillel, *b. Šabb.* 31a); (4) the golden rule (Matt 7:12, more positive than the silver, reaching out to do good, taking the initiative to create an atmosphere of good will); (5) loving one's enemies, an invitation to moral heroism and sanctity. This last is the loftiest level. Is it lacking in ethical sobriety, as its critics have suggested? It can be quite effective (Gandhi). It need be no more unsober than a general strike is. The question that remains is: Is it the only legitimate rule of conduct for Christians in conflict situations? Are the earlier stages of biblical teaching simply cancelled out? No. Rather, the earlier stages represent a permanent resource for believers when appropriate. It depends on the moral level of the opponent which level of biblical ethics should be employed. Given this range of options, you can govern with the Sermon on the Mount, despite Bismarck's skepticism, provided you also include the earlier moral stages which it presupposes. The sermon is not the whole of biblical revelation but does represent a summit of moral wisdom whose validity proves itself in daily life when wisely applied.

37 (D) Reformation of Works of Piety (6:1–18). (a) ALMSGIVING (6:1–4). Verses 1–18 treat of three works of piety—almsgiving, prayer, and fasting. They concern our relationship to God and constitute a reformation of conventional attitudes. It is a Jewish list, though there is nothing about the Temple, and it may be based on Deut 6:5. After the introductory verse, there follow three units of very similar structure 2–4,5–6, 16–18, which are without Synoptic parallel. This pattern is broken by the insertion of older material in vv 7–15, including the Lord's Prayer. Formally it resembles a catechism. **1.** *take care not to perform your righteousness before people: Dikaiosynē,* "righteousness," "justice," both represents a thematic word in the Gospel and leads cleverly into the theme of almsgiving, since its Aram equivalent, *ṣĕdāqâ,* came to mean "almsgiving," as charity did in English. *reward:* See comment on 5:46. Cf. *m. 'Abot* 1:13; Seneca, *Ep.* 19.4.32: "Whoever wants to publicize his virtue labors not for virtue but for glory." The text is concerned throughout that our relationship with God be a living, personal one. **2.** *almsgiving:* It was well organized in ancient Judaism (see Moore, *Judaism* 2. 162–79) and was accorded a high value; in *m. 'Abot* 1:2 it is one of the three pillars of the world; cf. *m. 'Abot* 2:7; *m. Pe'a* 1:1. *hypocrites:* This is a Matthean emphasis among the Gospels, thematic here in 6:1–18 and in chap. 23, where it is associated with the scribes and Pharisees. Originally, Gk *hypokritēs* was a theatrical term, meaning "actor"; it comes to refer in Matt 23 to false interpreters of Scripture, religious teachers who fail in their responsibility. **38** (b) PRAYER (6:5–15). In vv 5–8 the positive teaching is that prayer should be sincere personal communion with God and that it should be brief because it is for our good, not God's, since he already knows what we need. It is the food of faith. This teaching does not disparage public worship as such, since Jesus participated in the synagogue service (Mark 1:21) and builds upon it in the Lord's Prayer, though he also prayed privately.

39 **9-13.** These verses give an example of a short prayer, similar to the 18 Benedictions and the Qaddish of the synagogue liturgy, to which are added the address to God as Father (characteristic of Jesus) and the note of forgiveness (see Sir 28:2). Matthew probably adds to the earliest form found in Luke 11:2-4 the words "our . . . who art in heaven," since he is troubled by the intimate familiarity of *Abba.* He explains that the kingdom means the will of God on earth, and he completes the last petition with a positive request for salvation. **9.** *Our Father in heaven:* See comment on 5:16. This address replaces the OT Yahweh as the characteristic NT mode of address to God, suggesting childlike trust, intimacy, and readiness of access; see Rom 5:2; Eph 2:18; 3:12; Heb 10:17-20. **10.** *thy kingdom come:* This request stands in strict parallelism with "thy will be done." God's will is for peace and justice (Rom 14:17). The prayer presupposes that the kingdom is not yet here in its fullness and thus expects a future eschatology. *as in heaven so on earth:* The prayer expects an earthly, this-worldly realization of God's will. It presupposes a certain analogy between heaven and earth, which is found both in Gk philosophy (Plato's myth of the cave) and in the ancient Near East (Babylonian ideas of the temple and ziggurat; Exod 25:9,40). Since the kingdom is brought by the Son of Man there is an implicit christology. *kingdom:* See comment on 4:17. **11.** *bread:* This can refer to daily needs, the messianic banquet, or, as in early Christian interpretation, the eucharist as a foretaste of the messianic banquet. *daily: Epiousion* is a rare Gk word whose exact meaning and etymology remain disputed. The four main possible transls. are: "tomorrow's," "daily," "needful," or "future." These four can be combined: "the bread then is earthly bread, the bread of the poor and needy, and, at the same time, because of the eschatological hour in which it is prayed for and eaten, it is the future bread in this today, the bread of the elect and the blessed" (Lohmeyer). **12.** *forgive us our debts:* See Mark 11:25. Debts is an Aram euphemism for sins. *as we forgive:* This clause presupposes mutuality and asserts some connection between our treatment of one another and God's treatment of us, but it does not affirm an exact proportionality. God is more merciful and generous than we are; cf. 18:21-35; 20:1-16. We have a responsibility to imitate God, to follow his lead in forgiving. Forgiveness is a social necessity if society is not to be paralyzed by an accumulation of grievances of one against another. Traditionally it is achieved through sacrifice, but the sixth of the 18 Benedictions is a prayer for forgiveness. **13.** *lead us not:* This probably means "do not let us succumb to the end-time trial" or "do not let us fall when we are tempted." *evil:* This almost certainly refers to the Evil One, the devil, evil personified. The Our Father is the basis for all patristic treatises on prayer. Thus, prayer is not something difficult since everyone can say this prayer. Tertullian calls it the summary of the whole Gospel.

(Jeremias, J., *The Prayers of Jesus* [London, 1967]. Lohmeyer, E., *Our Father* [NY, 1966]. Petuchowski, J. and M. Brocke, *The Lord's Prayer and Jewish Liturgy* [NY, 1979].)

40 (c) FASTING (6:16-18). Fasting is a common religious practice and can be both public and private. The sermon presupposes its legitimacy. In Mark 2:18-20 (= Matt 9:14-15) the disciples are told not to fast in Jesus' lifetime, but its subsequent legitimacy is affirmed. Jews do not have a season of fasting like Lent but have a few days of communal fasting, esp. *Yôm Kippûr,* the Day of Atonement; and the 9th of Ab. According to *Did.* 8:1

Jews kept private fasts on Mondays and Thursdays, whereas Christians chose Wednesdays and Fridays (the latter in memory of Jesus' suffering). Fasting was understood as humbling oneself before God (Isa 58:3-9), as strengthening prayer (Tob 12:8; 2 Chr 20:3), as related to almsgiving ("The merit of a fast is in proportion to the charity dispensed," *b. Ber.* 6b), as an expression of mourning (Matt 9:14-15). **16.** *cover their faces:* There is a wordplay in Greek between the words *aphanizousin,* "cover," and *phanōsin,* "be seen." **17.** *wash your face:* This verse is chiastically constructed and seems to contradict *m. Yoma* 8:1, which says that you should not wash or anoint yourself on the Day of Atonement. **18.** *not be seen:* The details are not important so long as the essential point is held, that a fast is really directed toward God, not toward human beings. It requires faith (see Moore, *Judaism* 2. 55-69, 257-66; *TDNT* 4. 924-35).

41 **(E) Further Instructions (6:19-7:12).** This section of the sermon contains further instructions on how to love God with one's whole heart (v 21), one's two *yĕṣārîm* (v 24), soul (i.e., life, v 25) and strength (wealth, throughout vv 19-34); cf. Deut 6:5. It has also been understood as a list of deeds of loving-kindness (*m. 'Abot* 1:2), or as a commentary on the second part of the Lord's Prayer: bread (6:19-34), forgiveness (7:1-12), temptation (7:13-20), deliverance from evil (7:21-27) (so Grundmann, Bornkamm, Lambrecht). The first two smaller units, vv 19-21 and vv 22-23, contain wise teaching on true values expressed by means of two images.

42 (a) TREASURE IN HEAVEN (6:19-21). A Q saying considerably reworked from the form preserved in Luke 12:33-34. Formally the unit consists of a negative and a positive command, followed by a proverb that justifies the commands. The whole is chiastically arranged in Matt. **19.** *treasure:* A Matthean interest; cf. 13:44. In vv 19-20 the contrast is between corruptible and incorruptible treasures. This teaching should not be overly spiritualized in a Platonic, exclusively other-worldly, fashion. It is better to understand the text as referring to treasures that are already experienced in this life but continue to be valuable for eternity. Cf. *m. Pe'a* 1:1: "These are things whose fruit one enjoys in this world, while the capital is laid up for one in the world to come: honoring father and mother, deeds of loving-kindness, making peace between a man and his fellow; and the study of the law leads to them all." Cf. Sir 20:30 and 41:14.

43 (b) THE SINGLE EYE (6:22-23). Derived from Q, this form is shorter and perhaps more original than Luke 11:34-36. There is a four-part structure: a definition, followed by two conditional sentences in contrasting antithetical parallelism, and then a final conditional sentence which ends with an ominous, open-ended question. For the OT background, see Prov 22:3; Sir 13:25f.; 14:8,10; also *T. Benj.* 4; *m. 'Abot* 2:8-9 runs: "R. Yohanan ben Zakkai said to his five disciples, 'Go forth and see which is the good way to which a man should cleave.' R. Eliezer said, 'A good eye. . . .' R. Eleazar said, 'A good heart.'" Eleazar wins. Matthew and the *'Abot* saying, though using different terminology, agree on the main point: the ground of one's personal being must be sound. If the basic orientation of your life, your fundamental option, is sound, the overall results will be positive. This teaching can be abused, but used in an upright manner it can spare the believer false or unnecessary scruples. *if your eye be simple:* The Greek for "simple" could also be translated "single," "sound," "undivided," "perfect" (see 5:48). The term points toward singleness of purpose, purity of heart (5:8), undivided loyalty. But often we are two-souled (Jas 1:7-8). We must receive this wholeness and harmony of soul as a gift. (For the Hellenistic background, see H. D. Betz, *Essays on the Sermon on the Mount* [Phl, 1985] 71–87).

44   (c) GOD AND MAMMON (6:24). This is another Q saying (see Luke 16:13). It teaches again the impossibility of serving God with a divided heart, or, positively, the need to make a basic decision to love God above all things and all other things only insofar as they fit into that basic love. The rival "lord" can be anything or anyone, but at the end of the verse one example is given, "mammon," a Semitic word for money or wealth. This verse offers a commentary on Deut 6:5; cf. Matt 19:22,23; *m. Giṭ.* 4:5.

45   (d) ON CARE AND ANXIETY (6:25–34). This section consists of Q material except for v 34 and a few redactional touches. This teaching presupposes Galilean prosperity and would be insensitive in places or situations of destitution. It perhaps reflects a young person's interest in discovering the limits of human existence, the real necessities and true values of life. It comments on basic human needs, eating, drinking, clothing (no shelter, which was not so urgent in the Near East) insofar as they can become idols or fetishes. (Calvin defined an idol as anything that stands between us and God; in this sense the human mind is a factory of idols). A key term throughout is *merimnaō*, "be anxious." According to N. Baumert (*Ehelosigkeit und Ehe im Herrn* [FB 47; Würzburg, 1984] 479–504), this term does not mean "be anxious," but "consider," "think about," in the sense here of "be preoccupied with" or "absorbed by." Verses 25 and 34 form an *inclusio*. H. D. Betz believes that the whole passage is an apology for divine providence in the face of a crisis of faith in providence. The passage is a combination of wisdom theology and eschatology. The natural order is good, but this view is not based on Gen 1 so much as on daily experience. Nature is not romanticized; there are dangers such as rain, flood, storm. But the fatherhood of God makes the world endure and gives the possibility for conversion from human folly and sin. Faith in providence is rooted in a special relationship to God, being sons (and daughters) of the heavenly Father. Ethical behavior consists in learning the way and manner in which God loves and preserves his creation. **28.** *neither toil nor spin:* Perhaps here the two vbs. reflect field labor for men and housework for women. Although it is not obvious that this distinction was observed in the Near East, the text treats both kinds of work equally. **33.** *seek first the kingdom and his justice:* This is the climactic verse of the whole chapter. The ultimate goal of all our activity must be the highest value, the kingdom of God, which is here defined as justice (cf. Rom 14:17 and Matt 6:10). The literary function of the verse is to solder vv 19–34 into the rest of the sermon, a function similar to that served by 5:20 and 6:1. "In Matt seeking the kingdom and seeking justice are not two distinct quests; he wants to say that there is no authentic search for the kingdom except in a quest whose immediate goal is justice" (Dupont, *Béatitudes* 3. 297). The justice envisaged is not a justice in God alone but one that we are to produce on earth ourselves.

46   (e) JUDGING OTHERS (7:1–6). **1.** Cf. Luke 6:37–40; Matthew abbreviates and transforms the original Semitic parataxis "judge not and . . ." into the better Greek and clearer logic of "judge not that you may not be judged." This verse liberates us from the need to be everyone's conscience or censor, but it does not free us from all need for judgment. Every simple sentence such as "This cow is brown" is a judgment, and in adult life we cannot escape the obligation to make some judgments even on the moral character of others. Parents, fiancés, employers, civil judges, church administrators,

etc. all have this duty. Jesus' teaching warns against usurping the definitive judgment of God, who alone sees the heart. By contrast, our judging must be tentative, partial, and inadequate (see 1 Sam 16:7; Jer 17:10). But wherever possible, we should try to mind our own business and not meddle in others'. **2.** *you shall be judged . . . it shall be measured:* The vbs. are theological passives; God is the agent (see *ZBG* § 236). Cf. *m. Soṭa* 1:7–9. The measure formula can be traced back to commercial papyri in Egyptian Demotic and Gk texts from the first millennium BC (B. Couroyer, *RB* 77 [1970] 366–70). **3–5.** These verses contain a warning against hypocritical judges, which, however, presupposes some judging of others as necessary. Cf. John 8:1–11. **6.** The sense of this verse is uncertain. *the holy:* In the OT this refers to sacrificial meat (Exod 29:33); here it means the message of the kingdom of God; later it will mean the eucharist (*Did.* 9:5; 10:6). *pearls:* In this context pearls could mean the message of the kingdom or the sermon itself. *cast pearls:* The Hebrew for "cast," "throw," is *yārâ.* From a homonym (*yārâ* III) is derived *tôrâ,* "instruction" (possibly from the shepherd throwing a pebble in the direction the traveler asks for); thus, a pun on Torah-teaching may be involved. *dogs . . . swine:* Unclean animals in the OT; figures for unlearned men in rabbinic literature (cf. Ps 22:17,21); also for Gentiles ('*Abot R. Nat.* 34:2; Matt 15:26); and heretics (2 Pet 2:20–22). Here perhaps for unsympathetic listeners.

47   (f) ASK, SEEK, KNOCK (7:7–12). **7.** *Seek:* In this context all the vbs. refer to prayer; as in 6:33, one should above all seek the kingdom of God and justice also in prayer. In Hebrew "seek" would be *dāraš,* whence the term *midrash,* the "study" or investigation of Scripture. Perhaps aware of this more intellectualist usage, early Christian gnostics took this phrase "seek and you shall find" out of its context and used it to justify their theological speculations. At first the Church Fathers resisted this application of the text, but by the time of Augustine it was used also by the orthodox to ground their theological reflection. Questioning is the piety of thought. **7–11.** God's answering of prayer. **11.** *you who are evil:* This phrase suggests an unreflective assumption of the doctrine of original sin or sinfulness on the part of adults. *good things:* Luke reads instead "holy Spirit," which could be a spiritualization of an originally material expectation. **12.** The golden rule (→ 36 above). From a literary point of view this is the end of the sermon, a summary of its content, before the concluding covenant curses and blessings. It is related to other structuring verses, 5:17,20; 6:1,33, but also to 22:34–40, where the formula "this is the law and the prophets" recurs. The rule has a long prehistory. Something like it is implied in Deut 15:13; Tob 4:15; *Ep. Arist.* 207; Sir 31:15; Obad 15. Later in *b. Šabb.* 31a Hillel gives the inquiring proselyte the rule in the negative "silver" form and then says, "The rest is commentary, now go and study." The rule also has a Hellenic prehistory, emerging in 5th-cent. BC popular ethics as promoted by the Sophists (see Aristotle, *Rhet.* 2.6.19 [1384b]). This ethics is based on retribution and on morals as a balance of obligations. It needs to be controlled by a notion of the good. A masochist would wreak havoc with the rule (see *IDBSup* 369–70).

48   (F) Conclusion of the Sermon (7:13–27).
    (a) THE NARROW GATE (7:13–14). These verses express the covenant theology of the two ways, one leading to life, the other to death (Deut 28; 30:15; *Did.* 1:1; *Barn.* 18:1; 1QS 3:18–25); see K. Baltzer, *The Covenant Formulary* (Phl, 1971); and, for Matt, Frankemölle, *Jahwebund* (→ 1 above).
49   (b) BEARING FRUIT (7:15–20). Cf. Luke 6:43–44; this and the following unit (vv 21–23) have a

complex relationship to the Q source, since they have been considerably reworked by the redactor, who introduces the new theme of false prophecy. *you will know them by their fruits:* This bracket in vv 16,20 identifies the theme of this unit. "Fruits" are lived faith or ethical conduct, the test of a good person. **15.** *false prophets:* Prophecy is a spirit-related or charismatic activity. Some think Matthew was anticharismatic and played down the role of the Spirit in his Gospel. Others point out that he added the mention of prophecy and prophets when it was not in his source; this shows that he was interested in the theme and leads to the conclusion that there were prophets in his community. Matthew was probably more concerned with regulating prophecy and with restraining abuses by keeping prophecy within moral bounds than with suppressing it outright. There is, no doubt, a sober, moral tone in Matt and a centering of attention on the teaching of Jesus. But Matthew was too much a teacher and too interested in creativity (see comment on 13:52) to oppose prophecy or the work of the Spirit altogether. He remains the able, concerned pastor, not an inquisitor.

50   (c) An Episode in the Last Judgment Described (7:21–23).   God is the judge, Jesus the advocate (in contrast to Matt 25:31–46). Verse 22 is influenced by Jer 14:14 and 27:15 (34:15 LXX). **23.** *depart from me, you workers of lawlessness:* This derives from Ps 6:9. The only Synoptic source is Q (see Luke 6:46). Parallels include Matt 10:32–33; 25:1–13,31–46; Luke 13:23–30; Mark 8:38; Rev 3:5; *2 Clem.* 3–4; Justin, *Apol.* 1.16.9–11; *Dial.* 76.5.

The dominant point from v 13 to v 23 is that no one will emerge triumphant from the last judgment on the basis of right words or spectacular deeds of spiritual power alone. Only a life of love and justice will avail. This point reflects Matthew's characteristic link of ethics with eschatology and his related view of the church as a mixed body of saints and sinners until the final sorting out by God (in contrast to a doctrine of the church as an invisible communion of saints). Matt's view challenges Christian complacency and arrogant assurance of salvation. This view may seem opposed to Paul's, but Paul too strove to prevent his followers from drawing immoral or amoral conclusions from his gospel and warned Christians that they too would be judged (e.g., 1 Cor 3:13–15). Still there can be different pastoral emphases, one for the excessively scrupulous, one for the lax.

51   (d) Houses Built on Rock and Sand (7:24–29).   Cf. Luke 6:47–49. This parable, which Matthew shapes into a parable of the wise man and the fool, concludes the sermon by returning to the two ways theme of covenant theology (see comment on 7:13–14). It is customary in the Mishna to end a legal tractate with a bit of story or parable. The contrast here, developed in strict antithetic parallelism, is between "hearing" and "doing" and "hearing" and "not doing," whereas in vv 21–23 the contrast was between "saying" and "doing" or "not doing." **24.** *these words of mine:* This phrase points back to the sermon itself as a kind of Torah. For Matthew following the word of Jesus is wisdom about life. (This sapiential emphasis is absent from Luke). **25.** *the rain fell:* The natural situation envisages the kind of flash floods common in the holy land in the winter rainy season. **28–29.** The effect of the sermon. **28a.** *and it happened when Jesus finished these discourses:* This is a Matthean formula (repeated in 11:1; 13:53; 19:1; 26:1), which occurs at the end of each of the five great blocks of teaching material that help to structure this Gospel. **28b–29.** Matt here rejoins his Marcan source (1:21,22). He adds the word "their" to "scribes" because in his church there were scribes (13:52; 23:34), an office hallowed in Israel since

the days of Ezra, as well as prophets, sages, apostles, and righteous ones (persons who had suffered for the faith, 10:41). *authority:* Authority in antiquity derived from fidelity to the tradition. Both Jesus and the Jewish scribes taught with a certain authority (*rĕšût*) based on the tradition. But the scribes did not present themselves at this time as revealer figures with a direct access to the will of the Father (7:21). To the crowds, to the early Christians, to Matthew Jesus was such a figure, with a more immediate access both to the Father and to lived reality and to a wider range of the biblical tradition than the primarily halakic scribes. It is from this unique combination that Jesus' authority derived.

(Betz, H. D., *Essays* [→ 43 above]. Davies, W. D., *The Setting of the Sermon on the Mount* [→ 1 above]. Lambrecht, J., *The Sermon on the Mount* [Wilmington, 1985]. Lapide, P., *The Sermon on the Mount* [Maryknoll, 1986].)

52   **(III) Authority and Invitation (8:1–9:38).** Having just shown Jesus as the Messiah of the word, Matthew now presents him as the Messiah of the deed (Matt 11:2). Matthew here rejoins the Marcan narrative framework (1:40–2:22), which he expands with miracles drawn from elsewhere. There are nine miracle pericopes, but ten individual miracles (the raising of the dead girl is sandwiched into the story of the woman with a hemorrhage). The series of 10 miracles is often thought to correspond to the series of 10 plagues which Moses and Aaron caused in Egypt as the precondition of liberation from bondage (Exod 7:8–11:10). Matthew breaks up the monotony of the series with buffer pericopes (8:18–22; 9:9–17). He differs from Mark in his handling of the miracles. He shortens them, strips away novelistic detail, and, being a cerebral type, drains away strong emotion. Positively, he shapes them into paradigmatic conversations that stress four themes: christology (or the authority of Jesus), faith, discipleship, and soteriology.

Ever since the Enlightenment, miracles have been a controversial element in the gospel story. Thomas Jefferson edited a version of the Gospels that eliminated the miraculous and kept the teaching. Historically speaking, there can be no doubt that Jesus went about healing and working marvels that astonished the beholders, even though it may not be clear what exactly happened in every case. In this he followed the pattern of the earlier Galilean itinerant wonder-working prophets, Elijah and Elisha. Our earliest sources, Christian and Talmudic, agree in transmitting this aspect of Jesus' activity. Philosophers like Hume distinguish between healing miracles (credible but not strictly miraculous) and nature miracles (stilling the storm, walking on the water, multiplying the loaves and fishes, raising the dead to life). The latter are regarded as incredible unless explained away rationalistically. This distinction is not biblical. The Bible is rather concerned that miracles not become a substitute for faith (John 2:23–25; 6:25–29) and love (1 Cor 13:2). Miracle-faith is regarded as an inadequate, but often necessary, starting point to be transcended as quickly as possible. In his ministry as healer-savior we may say that Jesus used his miracles as an attention-getting device as well as an expression of God's love, compassion, and power to save his people. The feedings of the multitude, esp. in Matt, involve such large numbers as to take on social significance and to become a foretaste of the kingdom (see comment on 14:13–21; 15:32–39). Just as in Bible times, so today some are interested in charismatic healing and healing shrines like Lourdes, and others are not. To all, miracle stories are useful in showing that reality is not statically fixed and irreformable but open to the transforming power of God and faith; Jesus in these stories also crosses the boundaries of social reality to allow access to salvation even to the outcasts.

(Gerhardsson, B., *The Mighty Acts of Jesus according to Matthew* [Lund, 1979]. Heil, J. P., "Significant Aspects of the Healing Miracles in Matthew" *CBQ* 41 [1979] 274–87. Held, H. J., "Matthew as Interpreter of the Miracle Stories," in G. Bornkamm, *et al., Tradition and Interpretation in Matthew* [Phl, 1963] 165–299. Kingsbury, J. D., "Observations on the 'Miracle Chapters' of Matthew 8–9," *CBQ* 40 [1978] 559–73. Theissen, G., *The Miracle Stories of the Early Christian Tradition* [Phl, 1983]. Thompson, W. G., "Reflections on the Composition of Mt 8:1–9:34," *CBQ* 33 [1971] 365–88.)

53   (A) The Cleansing of a Leper (8:1–4). See Mark 1:40–45. 1. *many crowds followed:* This suggests that people in some measure became his discples. 2. *a leper:* Leprosy could here mean Hansen's disease or other skin diseases (see *IDB* 3. 111–13; cf. Lev 13). *Lord:* Matthew strengthens the religious force of the text by having the leper so address Jesus and worship him. 3. *touched him:* Jesus' love reached even to the unlovable and did not fear sense contact with them. 4. *show yourself to the priest:* See Lev 13:49; 14:2–32. This command shows Jesus observant of Torah (5:18) and respectful of the Temple priests, who will later conspire to arrest him. *as a witness to them:* This phrase is ambiguous; it could refer to the priests or to the people.

54   (B) The Cure of the Centurion's Servant (8:5–13). This episode represents a remarkable counterpart to the preceding cure of an Israelite according to Torah norms. It is a foretaste of the Gentile mission (28:19f.). The story is not found in Mark but is in Luke 7:1–10 and, in a rather different form, in John 4:46–54. Matthew expands the basic story with vv 11 and 12 (cf. Luke 13:28–29). We thus probably have a Matthean composition from early traditions found in Q and oral sources. 5. *centurion:* A commander of a hundred men; here a Gentile, likely in the service of Herod Antipas in this garrison town. 6. *servant:* The Gk *pais* could mean "boy," and thus "son" (John 4:46). 8. *only say a word:* The centurion's words show his politeness, his humility, and his sensitivity to the reluctance of observant Jews to enter the home of a Gentile, lest they encounter ritual defilement (*m. Ohol.* 18:7; John 18:28; Acts 10:1–11:18). These words have been found so remarkable that they have entered the eucharistic liturgy of the Latin rite as a confession of unworthiness to receive the Lord. 9. *under authority:* The theme of authority is characteristically of interest to Roman officials. 10. *such faith:* The scandal that troubled Matthew's community was the lack of faith (in Jesus as Messiah), which the majority of Israelites showed. This scandal becomes a dominant theme in the latter part of the Gospel. 11. The phraseology comes from Ps 107:3; Isa 49:12; 59:19; Mal 1:11. 12. *sons of the kingdom:* Here Jews, but elsewhere in Matt Christians (13:42,50; 22:13; 24:51; 25:30). Matthew warns against religious complacency of every sort. 13. *at that hour:* The healing takes place at a distance, as it does in the case of another Gentile believer (15:21–28).

55   (C) The Healing of Peter's Mother-in-law (8:14–15). See Mark 1:29–31. Matthew streamlines the homely story to heighten the authority of Jesus as lord. 14. *saw:* Jesus does not have to be told the woman is sick. He sees it at once. 15. *touched:* His healing touch suffices for the fever to leave her. No undignified heavy lifting is needed on his part. She is restored to health and to the dignity of active service of Christ ("him," not Mark's "them").

56   (D) The Sick Healed at Evening (8:16–17). See Mark 1:32–34. Matthew may here have arranged the summary description to parallel the OT quotation with which he rounds it off. Thus, expulsion of demons cor-

responds to weaknesses, and healing the sick to diseases. The citation, introduced by a fulfillment formula (→ 7 above) comes directly from the Hebrew of Isa 53:4, i.e., from the fourth Suffering Servant song, crucial to the Gospel's understanding of Jesus' death. The LXX spiritualizes the sickness and pains into griefs and sorrows. The song speaks of the servant's taking the sickness upon himself personally, whereas the Gospel here suggests that Jesus took it away. The point of the quotation is to show that Jesus' healing ministry is endorsed by prophecy. Matthew notes that the expulsions occur at the word of Jesus but does not go into details of healing.

57   (E) On Following Jesus (8:18–22). See the Q parallel in Luke 9:57–62. There is an OT parallel in 1 Kgs 19:19–21, where Elijah calls Elisha to be a prophet; this is alluded to in proverbial form in Luke 9:62. The case of Elisha appears less radical than that of the disciple because Elijah allows him to say good-bye, but it is also quite radical since Elisha burns his yokes, his secular means of livelihood. 19. *scribe:* Matthew adds the professional terms "scribe" and "teacher" to his source. *I will follow you:* This amounts to saying, "I will be your disciple." Scribes were educated leaders in communities and religious parties. Matthew was probably one himself. See comment on 6:28b–29 above. The terminology of teacher (*môreh, mělammēd, rab, rabbônî, rabbî*) and "disciple" (*talmîd*), rare in the OT, acquired increased importance among religious Jews as they tried to develop their own schools to compete with the culturally prestigious Hellenistic gymnasia (2 Macc 4:9,10). The terms reflect an academic, scholastic background; but, since the object of study was how to live a life pleasing to God, the terms have a broader, more existential connotation. 20. *foxes have holes:* Jesus answers with a figurative saying which teaches that since he leads a risky, unsettled, itinerant way of life, the disciple can expect no better. *The Son of Man:* The first occurrence of this peculiar phrase in Matt. Save possibly for Mark 2:10 and pars., it is found only on the lips of Jesus in the Gospels, a fact which probably reflects an authentic tradition that Jesus did refer to himself in this way (→ Jesus, 78:38–41). 21. *let me first go:* This and the following verse contain a powerful teaching on the radical, eschatological, and charismatic character of discipleship to Jesus, which far exceeds the demands of discipleship to a Pharisaic master. The key term here is "first." For the Christian, discipleship to Jesus must be the number one priority. 22. *let the dead bury their own dead:* Jesus' harsh reply must have sounded shocking to an audience used to *m. Ber.* 3:1: "He whose dead lies unburied before him is exempt from reciting the *šěma'*, from saying the Tepillah, and from wearing phylacteries" (*l.v.,* "from all duties enjoined by the law"). The full, complex Matthean understanding of discipleship only unfolds gradually throughout the Gospel (see M. Hengel, *The Charismatic Leader and His Followers* [NY, 1981]).

58   (F) Stilling the Storm (8:23–27). See Mark 4:35–41 for the interpretation of the miracle story. There may be some influence from Ps 107:23–32; 104:5–9, but this is uncertain. Matthew reshapes the story so that it can be used for instruction on the life of the church after the resurrection. (Matt has been called the great Gospel of the church because of its interest in this theme.) Throughout, Jesus is central and treated with respect, in contrast to Mark; only the brief human moment of sleep is retained. Matthew moves the dialogue with the disciples to a position ahead of the miracle proper and thereby reveals his didactic priorities. 24. *great storm:* In Matt it becomes actually an "earthquake" (*seismos*, in place of the Marcan *lailaps*); see also 24:7; 27:54; 28:2, where *seismos* is often used to suggest the horrors of the last days. 25. *Lord save us, we are perishing:*

This has become the prayer of the threatened church of all ages, often depicted in art as a fragile, storm-tossed barque. **26.** *O you of little faith:* Matthew's change is from Marcan "no faith" to "little faith" (a mostly Matthean term, 6:30; 14:31; 16:8; cf. Luke 12:28). Little faith presupposes some faith and thus conversion, but suggests a faith grown too weak or paralyzed to act. It is the problem of a second or third generation of Christians (cf. 24:12). **27.** *the people:* This may refer to the members of the later church (see G. Bornkamm, *Tradition and Interpretation* 52-57).

59   (G) The Cure of the Gadarene Demoniacs (8:28-34). For the full version of this story of demon expulsion, a study of Mark 5:1-20 is indispensable. This is the closest the Gospels come to comic storytelling. To the Israelites, pigs were not only unclean but also funny; to the Gentiles, the Jews' horror of swine was a subject for laughter and teasing (cf. 2 Macc 6:18; 7:1; Josephus, *Ant.* 12.5.4 § 253; 13.8.2 § 243; Juvenal, *Sat.* 6.159). Matthew abbreviates drastically, but the main Marcan points are made: Jesus has power to expel demons; he is Son of God (v 29); the demons enter a herd of swine; the herd stampedes over a cliff and drowns. Since the story clearly takes place in Gentile territory (Mark 5:20, the Decapolis), there may lurk beneath the surface some kind of comment on Gentile uncleanness and consequent unreadiness to receive Jesus, but this is not obvious. **28.** *Gadarenes:* For Mark's "Jerash," 30 mi. from the sea, Matthew substitutes Gadara, 6 mi. from the sea. He also raises the number of demoniacs to two. **29.** *before the right time:* This Matthean gloss reflects the intertestamental idea that the demons were free to trouble humanity until the end-time (*1 Enoch* 15-16; *Jub.* 10:8-9; *T. Levi* 18:12). **30.** *at some distance:* This phrase covers the miles between the town and the sea. **34.** The flat ending, the townspeople begging Jesus to leave, need not mean an ultimate rejection of Jesus but confusion and fear at the series of astonishing incidents — not to mention resentment at the destruction of a herd of animals valuable to them, but which they knew Jews reviled and taunted them for keeping. For, in the story, the demons have made a double confession, directly that Jesus is the Son of God, indirectly that the swine are as unclean as they themselves are (Luke 15:20; Matt 7:6; 2 Pet 2:22).

60   (H) The Healing of the Paralytic (9:1-8). See Mark 2:1-12. Mark tells a double story, still easily separated, of a healing miracle (vv 1-5a,11-12) and an act of forgiveness (vv 5b-10), perhaps reflecting his sandwich technique or the growth of oral tradition. Matthew has melted the two parts more tightly together and eliminated the colorful detail of letting the sick man down through the roof, while providing in the last verse a powerful double theological point. Note that in this and the following two stories (9:1-17) there are three groups of opponents: scribes (v 3), Pharisees (v 11), and disciples of JBap (v 14). This reflects Matt's care to produce a neat, systematic coverage of the situation. **3.** *blaspheming:* The scribes correctly recognize that the forgiveness of sins, which entail an offense against God, belongs to divine activity. Whoever controls the channels of forgiveness in a society controls that society (H. Arendt); thus the stakes are high. It is the charge of blaspheming that will, in Matt, eventually get Jesus crucified (26:65). **4.** *which is easier:* This is a confusing question. It is easier to *say* "Your sins are forgiven," since there is no visible control; it is harder to *do*, since only God can do it. It is harder to *say* "Rise and walk," because your words can be checked for their effectiveness by the result or lack of result (unless you are Jesus). **8.** *such authority to human beings:* This is Matthew's crucial change from Mark. He shifts attention away from astonishment

at the miracle to the theological theme that Jesus as the Son of Man (v 6) has the authority to forgive sins (already in Mark) and then extends that authority to members of the church. This is a hint of Matthew's interest in the church (16:18; 18:17). It reflects his concern that Christ's authority be available in and through the church, a second- or third-generation problem, which presupposes faith in Christ.

61   (I) The Call of Matthew the Tax Collector (9:9-13). See Mark 2:13-17 and Luke 5:27-32. The story is told in two parts: the call of Matthew is related very abruptly in v 9 and the sequel of a dinner with sinners follows in vv 10-13. Together with vv 14-17 this unit constitutes the second break in the series of 10 miracles. Formally, v 14 is a call narrative (cf. 4:18-22), and vv 10-13 are an apophthegm in which the accent falls on the final three logia. This is the only description in Matt of Jesus actually sharing a meal with sinners (but cf. 8:11,12; 21:31,32; Luke 19:1-10). This seems to have been a genuine practice of the historical Jesus and helps us to see an important aspect of the originality and specificity of his ministry. Here he clearly breaks with the model of the Pharisaic sage, not to destroy Judaism but precisely to save its increasingly marginalized members (10:6; 15:24). His goal is the same as that of (early) Pharisaism, but his strategy is different. (On the meals of Jesus, see E. Schillebeeckx, *Jesus* [NY, 1979] 200-18.) **9.** *Matthew:* Why is he so named, when the other Synoptics call him Levi? Perhaps by the time this Gospel was written Levi was no longer important, but Matthew, as an apostle, remained constitutive. In 10:3 he is called a tax collector. Thus this pericope is drawn into the circle of main characters in the narrative. It is not impossible that a literate apostle (a tax collector would need to know how to write) stands at the base of the gospel tradition, perhaps as a collector of sayings of Jesus. But he is not the author of the final Gk form of Matt. For a description of that author, 13:52 is the better place to look. *he rose and followed him:* The immediate obedience to the call is psychologically implausible. Such a response presupposes normally some prior knowledge of Jesus and his mission and some reflection on one's possible place in that mission. This extreme concision is explainable by the demands of oral transmission and antique book production and can be overcome by the imagination of the reader. **10.** *tax collectors and sinners:* The text presupposes that these people are social outcasts. Why? Tax collectors were collaborators with the Roman imperial authorities and hence were considered disloyal and suspected of treason. Since they made their margin of profit by extortion of more than was legally due, they were also viewed as exploitative. *sinners:* A technical term for members of despised trades thought susceptible of ritual uncleanness and other blemishes (one list [*m. Qidd.* 4:14] gives ass-driver, camel-driver, sailor, caster, herdsman, shopkeeper, physician (= blood letter?), butcher; others add tanner, bath-attendant, tax collector). For nuances, see J. Jeremias, *Jerusalem* (Phl, 1969) 303-12; J. R. Donahue, *CBQ* 33 (1971) 39-61. **12.** *those who are well have no need of a physician:* Jesus answers with a commonsense proverb, found in Stobaeus, Plutarch, and Diogenes Laertius; Gk thinkers thought of the philosopher as a physician of the soul. The physician must expose himself to the danger of contagious diseases (here, legal impurities) to heal them. **13.** Matthew adds, here and in 12:7, a citation from Hos 6:6. This text had become important to rabbis like Yohanan ben Zakkai (after AD 70) to help to compensate for the loss of Temple sacrifices as a means of attaining forgiveness of sins. Study of Torah and deeds of loving-kindness were deemed substitutes (*'Abot R.*

Nat. 4). *I came not to call the just:* Whether a doctrinal expansion or an authentic saying of Jesus, this sentence accurately describes the social orientation of Jesus' ministry.

62   (J) The Question about Fasting (9:14–17). The novelty of Jesus. A composite section, containing a controversy dialogue (vv 14–15, punch line 15a) and two little parables (vv 16,17); the unifying link is the difference the presence of Jesus makes. The unit parallels Mark 2:18–22. **14.** *fasting:* See comment on 6:16–18. *your disciples:* Notice the courtesy of the questioners, who do not ask about Jesus' own practice. **15.** *mourn:* Matthew understands fasting as a sign of mourning sorrow by changing Mark's vb. "fast" to "mourn." *sons of the bridegroom:* A Semitic idiom. Jesus compares the disciples to wedding guests, i.e., to participants in an event of joy. In rabbinic interpretations of Cant, the bridegroom is regularly interpreted as God himself. *days are coming:* This is a formula of prophetic character suggesting a salvation-historical perspective. There are the times of Jesus and then the time after Jesus, but the end is not yet. In this in-between time there will be tribulations and thus occasions for fasting. **16.** Matthew does not use the word "new" in this parable, unlike Mark. But two words have double meanings: "patch" is *plērōma* (lit., "fullness"); "tear" is *schisma,* "schism." Matthew thus understands the schism or separation between Christians and the disciples of the Pharisees as the difference between the old (and good) and the fullness of the good. **17.** Matthew modifies the next parable in the same vein by an addition. *both are preserved.* The old is good and is to be preserved in and with the *novum* in Jesus. See J. A. Ziesler, *NTS* 19 (1972–73) 190–94.

63   (K) The Healing of a Ruler's Daughter (9:18–26). For the full version, see Mark 5:21–43. Matthew abbreviates drastically. Another healing narrative (a woman with a hemorrhage) is sandwiched between the two parts of the other. Two women are healed. In one story the woman takes the initiative in looking for help from Jesus. In the other the woman is under age, so her father approaches Jesus for her. **18.** *my daughter has just died:* Matthew heightens the ruler's faith by having him say that his daughter is already dead when he makes the request. In the other Synoptics this is known only through a later messenger. **20.** *hemorrhage:* Such a woman was regarded as a perpetual menstruant in Jewish law and hence as permanently unclean (*m. Nid.*). Thus, like the earlier leper and centurion's slave, she is socially marginal, a pariah. In the *Acts of Pilate,* the woman's name is Bernice. Eusebius records a story (*HE* 7.18.1–3) that she was a Gentile from Caesarea Philippi. *fringe:* This was part of the prayer shawl worn by the devout Jew (Num 15:38–41; Deut 22:12). The woman's grasping it is a gesture of request known from 1 Sam 15:27 and Zech 8:23 as well as Akkadian prayers (M. Hutter, *ZNW* 75 [1984] 133–36). **22.** *from that hour the woman was saved:* Matthew stresses the prompt effectiveness of Jesus' healing word. **23.** *flute players:* These were hired to accompany mourning dirges (Josephus, *J.W.* 3.9.5 § 437), but were also used in revels (Rev 18:22). **25.** OT parallels to this kind of healing are 1 Kgs 17:17–24; 2 Kgs 4:17–37.

64   (L) The Healing of Two Blind Men (9:27–31). This unit has affinities with 20:29–34 and Mark 10:46–52. Here the accent falls on faith. Each of the 10 miracles in chaps. 8 and 9 addresses a different problem: leprosy, slavery, fever, natural disasters (storm), demon-possession, paralysis, death, hemorrhage, blindness, muteness. One sees an effort to cover all the bases systematically. Jesus is presented as a healer-of-all, a new and greater Asclepius, in fulfillment of Isa 35:4–6

(the program of Matt 4:23; 9:35; 11:5). The early church was not slow to use physical blindness as a symbol for spiritual obtuseness; cf. John 9, a universal theme. **27.** *Son of David:* See 1:1; 15:22; 20:30; 21:9,15. The problem is: Why call a healer Son of David, since David did not heal? There is now some evidence that Solomon, a son and the successor of David, was regarded as a healer in Judaism contemporary with the NT (see D. C. Duling, *HTR* 68 [1975] 235–52).

65   (M) The Healing of a Dumb Demoniac (9:32–34). As in the previous unit, we have here a doublet, this time with Matt 12:22–24. The story is quickly told; the cure itself is mentioned only in a subordinate clause. The reaction of the crowd in v 33 suggests that Jesus' wonder-working activity has significance for Israel as such. **34.** *by the ruler of demons:* The Pharisees cannot let this evaluation pass unresisted. The shadow of conflict and of the cross falls over Jesus here. He is no harmless magician. His healings have religious implications. On the importance of speech and its abuses, see comment on 5:33–37.

66   (N) The Compassion of Jesus (9:35–38). These four verses are clearly transitional; they close off the section 4:23–9:34, which shows Jesus as Messiah in word and deed, and they open the way to the mission of the disciples and the mission discourse in chap. 10. The use of sources reflects this complexity, weaving together bits from Mark and Q. **35.** See comment on 4:23. **36.** *he felt compassion:* The Gk *splanchnizein* derives from the noun for "entrails," "bowels," "guts," as the seat of emotions. *crowds:* Jesus' love and mercy extend to them; i.e., they are social. The genesis of his commitment to pastoral work is an experience of the people's need for spiritual leadership. *as sheep without a shepherd:* Shepherd imagery is common throughout the Bible for political and religious leadership (Num 27:17; Ezek 34:5; 1 Kgs 22:17; 2 Chr 18:16; Zech 10:2; 13:7). It will recur in Matt 10:6; 15:24; 18:12; 26:31. **37.** *the harvest is abundant:* Jesus turns the problem into an opportunity. *laborers are few:* This is so necessarily and permanently, because pastoral work is psychically straining even when it is not physically demanding. **38.** *therefore pray:* Only a community that nourishes its faith through powerful prayer is apt to receive and to generate more pastoral workers. Cf. *m.* '*Abot* 2:15, "R. Tarfon said, 'The day is short; the task is great; the laborers are idle; the wage is abundant, and the master of the house is urgent.'"

67   (IV) Mission Discourse (10:1–42).
    (A) The Mission of the Twelve Apostles (10:1–4). This pericope serves, along with 9:36–38, to introduce the second great discourse of the Gospel, the missionary discourse to the twelve apostles. S. Brown prefers to call it the "central section" because it also includes narrative (9:36; 10:1–5a) and is not missionary in the modern sense. As with the Sermon on the Mount, the section is compiled from parts of Mark and Q, much of it heavily reworked by Matthew himself. Peculiar to Matt are vv 5a–8,16b,41. The boldest stroke is transferring vv 17–25 from the apocalyptic discourse in chap. 24 (= Mark 13). In Matthew's editing, the whole addresses the disciples of old, but also his own community. **1.** *the twelve disciples:* Normally the disciples are a broader group but here and elsewhere (chap. 18?) Matthew narrows them to the Twelve. This usage both keeps the Twelve together with the other disciples and yet singles them out as special disciples. *gave them authority:* All the Synoptic evangelists stress the importance of Jesus' emissaries having real power and authority from him. In calling them, Jesus takes the initiative. The number 12 comes from the number of the tribes of Israel (Matt 19:28) and is symbolic of the restoration of all Israel.

Matthew presupposes that they have all been called earlier, though he has only described the call of four (4:18–22). **2.** *the names of the twelve apostles:* The word apostle occurs only here in Matt. On the origin and meaning of *apostolos,* → NT Thought, 81:149–52. The religious character of this sometimes secular emissary function derives in the Gospel from the nature of the commissioner (Jesus) and the content of the message (v 7). Both the rabbis and the NT know emissaries of the congregation (2 Cor 8:23) and of individuals (1 Cor 1:1). The very simple functional view of Matthew and Mark 6:30 receives more complex and full development in Luke and Paul. The list of apostles with slight variations occurs also in Mark 3:16–19; Luke 6:12–16; Acts 1:13. *first Simon:* For this primacy, see 16:17–19. Matthew also puts Andrew with his brother. **3.** *Matthew:* Labeled a "tax collector"; cf. 9:9. **4.** *Judas Iscariot:* The surname may mean "man of Kerioth" or "liar."

68   (B) The Commissioning of the Twelve (10:5–16). See Mark 6:7–13; Luke 9:1–6. **5.** *do not go to the road of the Gentiles:* This command to avoid evangelizing the Gentiles and Samaritans follows Jesus' own practice, as given in 15:24. The great difficulty is how to reconcile these verses with the great commission in 28:19. There is no easy answer, but an opening to the Gentiles is perceptible elsewhere in Matt (10:18; 3:9; 8:11f.; 21:43; 22:1–14; 23:38–39). Perhaps Matthew included this command here because it was important to members of his community and expressed the strongly Jewish consciousness of his own special tradition. Yet v 18 implies the existence of a Gentile mission of others, the stage of Gal 2:9. 28:19 remains a surprising *deus ex machina* despite the subtle preparations for it earlier. For bibliography, → 72 below. **6.** *the lost sheep of the house of Israel:* This phrase (Ezek 34:2–6) refers first of all to Israel as a whole including the "lost tribes." But it refers also to a group within Israel, the *'am hā'āreṣ,* lit., "people of the land," people who for whatever reason (need to make a living, disreputable trade, lack of interest or education) were marginalized, alienated from the main circles of religious leadership and zeal. For these, Jesus had a particular, but not exclusive, concern. His goal was not to weaken the people of God but to bind it together. These "lost sheep" responded to his care. **7.** *the kingdom of heaven is near:* The message of the apostles is to be the same as JBap's and Jesus' (see 3:2; 4:17). **8.** *freely have you received:* A surprisingly Pauline phrase (Rom 3:24; 2 Cor 11:7), the point of which is that the divine truths of salvation are so important for everyone that they must be taught without regard for the listeners' ability to pay. This ideal is shared by the rabbis, e.g., Hillel said, "He that makes worldly use of the crown shall perish" (*m. 'Abot* 1:13; 2:20; 3:18; 4:5). This ideal is tempered by reality in v 10b: the laborer is worthy of his food (Num 18:31). The missionary must live. The tension between these two principles is not absolute, but the balance is delicate. **9.** *take no gold:* The list consists of travel gear. In *m. Ber.* 9:5 one is forbidden to enter the Temple court in this gear. The Marcan parallel (6:8–11) allows sandals and a staff (to ward off wild animals and robbers). The harsher rule stresses the sacred urgency of the mission. **11.** *whatever town:* The missionaries are to depend on local hospitality, to share the life of the people to whom they are sent — with all the risks and inconveniences this entails. **16.** *wise as serpents:* This is a teaching peculiar to Matt (cf. Rom 16:19; 1 Cor 14:20; *Midr. Cant.* 2:14: "God says of the Israelites, Towards me they are as sincere as doves, but towards the Gentiles they are prudent as serpents," a late text which may show that Matt was known or that the saying is proverbial). The

saying is important in distinguishing innocence from naïve gullibility. Cf. Luke 16:8.

69   (C) How to Face Future Persecutions (10:17–25). On this subject, see D. R. A. Hare, *The Theme of Jewish Persecution.* Much of this section is taken from Mark 13:9–13 and is repeated with variations in Matt 24:9–14. **17.** *their synagogues:* Perhaps in contrast with Jewish-Christian synagogues (Jas 2:2), but perhaps suggesting that Matthew's community had already been banned from the synagogue. On the procedures of the sanhedrin, see *m. Sanh.;* on flogging, see *m. Mak.* **18.** *dragged before prefects and kings:* "Prefects" are Roman provincial governors; "kings" would be vassal rulers like Herod Agrippa I (Acts 12:2) under the emperor, or the emperors themselves. *a witness . . . to the Gentiles:* Not necessarily missionary preaching (cf. v 5) but the making of a statement by endurance of persecution (28:19). **19.** *it will be given you . . . what to say:* This verse is sometimes used to excuse not preparing sermons, but the context points only to emergency situations. **20.** *the spirit of your father:* In contrast to the Lucan parallel, Matt stresses that the holy Spirit is the spirit of God the Father. **21b.** See Mic 7:6. **22.** *who endures to the end:* This persistent patience in the face of eschatological suffering (the end) is saving faith for Matthew. **23.** *the cities of Israel:* Strecker (*Weg* 41–42) thinks this refers to wherever Jews live in the whole world, but this forces the text. This verse, along with Mark 9:1; 13:30, led A. Schweitzer to think that Jesus predicted the coming of the Son of Man within the lifetime of the apostles and that he erred in this (see further M. Künzi, *Das Naherwartungslogion Matt 10:23* [2 vols.; BGBE 9, 21; Tübingen, 1970, 1977]). On the knowledge of Jesus, see R. E. Brown, *Jesus God and Man* (NY, 1967) 39–102. The simplest solution is that Jesus expected the coming after an interval which he left undetermined in detail (Mark 13:32). Historically, Jewish Christians did flee to Pella in the Decapolis (Eusebius, *HE* 3.5.3). **24.** *the disciple is not above his teacher:* This and the following verse are important for understanding discipleship in the Gospels (see Viviano, *Study* 158–71). "Disciple" means learner or student. The follower of Jesus is to be a life-long student of Jesus, because what he teaches is wisdom about life itself. In the background stands the Jewish school relationship of that time, but precisely that poses a danger. In the normal school relationship, once the disciple has learned what the master has to teach, he moves on to another master or becomes a teacher himself. This is what the gnostics did — make Jesus only one among many teachers. It was to block the possibility of twisting Jesus' original simple statement (as it can still be found in Luke 6:40) in a gnostic direction that Matthew reshaped it to include the words "nor a slave above his lord." This means that for the believer Jesus is not only a teacher but also an abiding lord. (For the gnostic view, see *Gos. Thom.* 13.)

70   (D) Appropriate and Inappropriate Fear (10:26–31). See the Q parallel Luke 12:2–7. Matthew has carefully shaped his source so that it not only ends with fear but also begins with it; he thus unifies the material by creating an *inclusio.* He has also changed his source so that there is a contrast between the hidden ministry of Jesus and the (more) public ministry of the disciples in v 27. Compare Luke's theological passives (*ZBG* § 236), which look to a future divine exposé. Matthew retains the passives in v 26 as the basis for bold proclamation in v 27. **26.** *so have no fear of them:* The ministry of preaching is intrinsically frightening. Only faith in a revealing and judging God can overcome that fear. **28.** *fear him who can destroy both soul and body:* The psychology presupposed seems Hellenistic, viz., that the soul is intrinsically immortal (cf. 1 Tim 6:16). The force of the verb "destroy" is uncertain. Does it mean that God will annihilate both body and soul and that thus hell means annihilation? Or does it mean "to trouble," "to torment"? **29.** *two sparrows:* The cheapest life in the market is cited; yet God's providential care extends to it. **30.** *worth much more than sparrows:* A rabbinic argument (*qal wā-ḥōmer,* comparing a light matter to a heavy) is used to overcome fear and to encourage the disciples to trust God.

71   (E) Confessing Jesus before People (10:32–39). Cf. Luke 12:8–9. Two parallel verses that speak of confessing or denying Jesus before human beings and the respective results before God; cf. Mark 8:38; Luke 9:26. These verses may represent a Marcan-Q overlap and are thus of great antiquity and significance; in their original form they are perhaps best represented by Mark 8:38. There a distinction is presupposed between Jesus and the future coming Son of Man. Yet this distinction is only implicit in order to be limited by the main assertion: How you react to Jesus will determine your future destiny regarding salvation. Matthew's form presupposes that Jesus is identified as the Son of Man, a link already made in Q. Similarly, though Matthew often refers to angels, he prefers here to concentrate on the heavenly Father. The pattern of these two verses is first found in 1 Sam 2:30, where it is God who speaks (see R. Pesch, "Über die Autorität Jesu," *Die Kirche des Anfangs* [Fest. H. Schürmann; ed. R. Schnackenburg, *et al.;* Leipzig, 1977] 25–55). Here it concerns the anguish of discipleship (10:34–39). See Luke 12:51–53; 14:25–27; 17:33; these are sayings from Q. Note also the Lucan introduction (12:49,50). In Matthew's arrangement we have first the paradoxical results of obedience to the divine will in the life of Jesus, then in that of his disciples. **34.** *I have come:* This important formula (3 times here and in v 35) emphasizes the mission of Jesus (see E. Arens, *The ēlthon-Sayings in the Synoptic Tradition* [OBO 10; Fribourg, 1976] 64–89). *not peace but a sword:* The sword is not to be understood as implying a zealotic uprising but as a regrettable side effect of tension and division resulting from the uncompromising proclamation of the kingdom. Elsewhere Jesus declares peacemakers blessed (5:9). **35.** *a man against his father:* Matthew makes the quotation from Mic 7:6 more exact and complete than in Luke, only omitting "son." **36.** *those of his own household:* Though part of the OT allusion, these words express well the painful fraternal struggle between the members of Matthew's community and their fellow Jews in the rival movement for the OT inheritance. The struggle is not a goal in itself but an inevitable consequence of the absolute allegiance Jesus claims from his disciples. **37.** *who loves father and mother more than me:* See the internal parallels in 16:24–25; 19:29; cf. Mark 8:34–35; 10:29–30. We may have here another case of Marcan-Q overlap, two early independent sources for the Jesus tradition. Thus, the historical probability is high that Jesus said something like this and that he called some to radical discipleship. But the precise wording in the details is harder to determine. Matthew seems to have simplified and clarified v 37 in comparison with the Lucan form, replacing the easily misunderstood but authentic Semitic idiom "hate" with the quite correct phrase "love more," and less wisely substituting "not worthy" for "is not able to be my disciple." It is more difficult to decide which evangelist is more faithful when it comes to the list of family members. Luke includes wife, brothers, and sisters. This would imply celibacy as an element in radical discipleship. According to E. Schüssler Fiorenza (*In Memory of Her* [NY, 1983] 145) it excludes women from such discipleship; but, in fact, the text speaks of "wife." Because Luke has altered Mark

10:29 by the addition of "wife" in 18:29, most authors speak of the word as a Lucan redactional gloss, but we have seen how Matthew softens radical sayings from Q on poverty and divorce. Perhaps, therefore, Q had the more difficult form and Luke faithfully reproduced it and then made his transmission of Mark conform to the Q text. Jesus' radical demands may seem to make him antifamily, but 15:4–6 shows this is not so. Rather, his radical demands are necessitated by the urgent priority of the kingdom of God, and, in his social context (the Jewish family of that day), he could safely presuppose that most family life would go on undisturbed. Some cultures have such an extreme family loyalty that sociologists speak of them as suffering from amoral familism. **38–39.** See comment on 16:24–25.

72   (F) Rewards of Discipleship (10:40–42). In this present form these verses show careful Matthean crafting. But at least vv 40 and 42 must go back to early tradition; see Luke 10:16; John 13:20; Mark 9:37,41; Matt 18:5. Verse 41 may be a Matthean development from the preceding. **40.** *who receives you receives me:* This verse is important because it explains the nature of the apostolic office on the legal principle governing a Jewish emissary: "A man's agent is like himself" (*m. Ber* 5:5). It deepens the religious basis of the apostolate by deriving it ultimately from God himself in a cascading succession mediated by Jesus, who is himself the apostle of the Father. The dignity of the Christian ministers standing in this line is great indeed, but all depends on their being received freely. **41.** *who receives a prophet:* Matthew's community seems to have had prophets (7:15–16; 23:34; *Did.* 11:3–6). *who receives a just person:* Various identifications have been proposed: the faithful Christian, the teacher, the one who has suffered persecution for the faith and remains in the community as an honored witness. **42.** *these little ones:* "Little one" could refer to the apostles/disciples, but more likely it refers to the uneducated members of the community (see 18:6,10,14). In that case we would have in vv 40–42 an outline of the structure of the Matthean community (see 23:34). It has been observed that if God will reward one who gives a cup of cold water to a disciple, how much more will he reward one who installs an entire city water system.

(On chap. 10: Beare, F. W., "The Mission of the Disciples and the Mission Charge: Matthew 10 and Parallels," *JBL* 89 [1970] 1–13. Brown, S., "The Mission to Israel in Matthew's Central Section (Mt 9:35–11:1)," *ZNW* 69 [1978] 73–90; "The Twofold Representation of the Mission in Matthew's Gospel," *ST* 31 [1977] 21–32; "The Matthean Community and the Gentile Mission," *NovT* 22 [1980] 193–221. Hengel, M., *Between Jesus and Paul* [Phl, 1983] 48–64. Jeremias, J., *Jesus' Promise to the Nations* [SBT 24; London, 1967]. Meyer, P. D., "The Gentile Mission in Q," *JBL* 89 [1970] 405–17.)

73   (V) Rejection by This Generation (11:1–12:50).

(A) John the Baptist and Jesus (11:1–19). This and the following section come almost entirely from Q; cf. Luke 7:18–35; 10:12–15. Verses 1 and 20 are purely editorial seams; vv 14–15 may be editorial or may come from oral tradition. **1.** *when Jesus had finished:* See comment on 7:28a. **2–6.** These verses contain a school debate, probably of postresurrection origin, over the nature of Jesus' mission, held between disciples of JBap and Christians. **2.** *the works of the Messiah:* This striking phrase created by Matthew turns the debate into one on the nature of Jesus' messiahship, but originally it may have been over whether he was a divine messenger like Elijah (see B. V. Malchow, "The Messenger of the Covenant in Mal 3:1," *JBL* 103 [1984] 252–55; and the modern debate of M. M. Faierstein, D. C. Allison, and J. A. Fitzmyer, *JBL* 100 [1981] 75–86; 103 [1984]

256–58; 104 [1985] 295–96). **5.** *the blind receive their sight:* This summarizes Jesus' answer in vv 4–6, the main thrust of the passage. Jesus defines his role not as one of sovereignty or judgment, as expected, but as one of blessing on the needy. Verse 5 is built in part on Isa 28:18–19; 35:5–6; 42:18; 61:1; but these passages do not mention the lepers or the dead. Since this is a new model of the savior figure, v 6 offers a blessing on one who is not disappointed by the new model. **7.** *what did you go out into the desert to behold?* Verses 7–10 give Jesus' testimony to JBap, first in a series of six rhetorical questions, then in three positive assertions about him. He is a prophet and more, the messenger of God (Mal 3:1; Exod 23:20), and the greatest human (not explained). Verse 11b may be an early Christian gloss. As messenger, JBap is implicitly identified with Elijah; verse 14 will make this identification explicit. **12.** *violent ones take it by force:* A puzzling saying, it perhaps means that the Romans occupy Israel by force and mistreat JBap, who preaches the kingdom. **13.** *prophesied until John:* This contains a statement of the periods of salvation history. Up till JBap was a time of prophetic promise; now the time of fulfillment has begun. **14.** See Mal 3:23 (= Eng 4:5). **16–19.** Jesus' judgment on his generation comprises a little parable (vv 16–17), an explanation of the parable (vv 18,19a), and a wisdom saying (v 19b), which was probably added later. The parable is difficult to interpret. The most probable explanation runs thus: The children are John and Jesus; the call is to play wedding, then funeral; the "others" are their Palestinian contemporaries, who reject both the severe way of John and the light yoke of Jesus. **19.** *wisdom is justified:* In the Lucan form "by her children" is probably original; thus John and Jesus are children of wisdom. Matthew's change to "by her works" forms an *inclusio* with v 2.

(Linton, O., "The Parable of the Children's Game," *NTS* 22 [1975–76] 159–79. Meier, J. P., "John the Baptist in Matt's Gospel," *JBL* 99 [1980] 383–405. Schönle, V., *Johannes, Jesus und die Juden* [Frankfurt, 1982]. Suggs, M. J., *Wisdom, Christology, and Law in Matthew's Gospel* [Cambridge MA, 1970] 33–61.)

74   (B) Woes on the Cities (11:20–24). See Luke 10:13–15. **20.** *then he began to reproach the cities:* Matthew creates a title for vv 21–24, which come to him from Q, stressing "mighty deeds" and "repentance." **21.** *woe to you, Chorazin:* This is the first of a series of two units that are structured: doom, explanation, comparison. The cities are addressed in apostrophe, as if they were persons. The two towns are near the Sea of Galilee and today lie in ruins; the synagogue of Chorazin is visible. Tyre and Sidon were Gentile cities in Phoenicia doomed by the prophets (Isa 23:1–18; Ezek 26–28). **23.** *and you, Capernaum:* The structure resembles that in vv 21,22, but the emotion is heightened. Capernaum is Jesus' own residence (4:13); he addresses it directly, alluding to Isa 14:13–15 and Ezek 26:20. The fate of Sodom is told in Gen 19:24–28. The point of the miracles was to provoke national conversion. In this they have failed, and ground for tragedy is laid (see J. A. Comber, *CBQ* 39 [1977] 497–504).

75   (C) Cry of Jubilee and Savior's Call (11:25–30). See Luke 10:21–22 for the Q parallel to vv 25–27. The passage consists of a revelation discourse in which Jesus appears as revealer of divine wisdom. Structurally the unit may be broken down into three parts: (a) vv 25, 26, thanksgiving for revelation; (b) v 27, content of the revelation; (c) vv 28–30, invitation to revelation. This is similar to Sir 51:1–12,13–22,23–30, but only 51:23–30 is really close to vv 28–30. The question of authenticity is often discussed in terms of source. Were vv 28–30 in Q? It could be argued yes, since they are necessary for

the structure; Luke's omission of them could be explained on the grounds of their Jewish symbolism, which might be unintelligible to Gentile readers. But it is more probable that they are a Matthean addition, even though the vocabulary is not typical. If the crucial v 27 is authentic, as it may well be, it would give us a most important clue to Jesus' self-understanding as absolute Son of the absolute Father. There is a Marcan-Q overlap of idiom here; cf. Mark 13:32. **25.** *I praise you, Father:* This is a typical Jewish blessing formula, but with Jesus' intimate *Abba*-Father address added (5 times in three verses). *babes:* Lit., "simple," "the uneducated." *revealed:* Divine communication is a powerful irreducible religious mystery. **26.** *good pleasure:* I.e., God's decision to elect some to salvation. **27.** *all things have been handed over:* Jesus is the personal tradition of God. *no one knows:* In this verse a claim to unique access of knowledge and love of the Father is asserted, as well as a reciprocity of knowledge and love. Jesus is the exclusive revelation of the Father (cf. 1:23; 28:18; John 3:35; 10:15; 13:3). Harnack saw this verse as the historical germ of all later christology. **28.** *come to me:* Here Jesus speaks as Wisdom personified (Prov 8), with feminine characteristics as the giver of rest and comfort, extending the great invitation. *all who labor:* Originally, both the people excluded by the Pharisees (the '*am hā-'āreṣ*) and also the Pharisees themselves were probably meant. **29.** *take my yoke:* The rabbis spoke of the yoke of Torah and the yoke of the kingdom. Here it refers to Jesus' interpretation of the law. *learn from me:* The disciple is to be a life-long learner. Jesus as humble is both the model teacher and the ideal subject matter since he is Torah personified (see comment on 18:20). *rest:* The sabbath rest is a symbol for the kingdom of God (Jer 6:16). **30.** *my yoke is easy:* In comparison with the halaka of the Pharisees, Jesus' teaching is quantitatively easier because shorter and centered on the essential. But in view of the exceeding righteousness demanded in 5:20, it is qualitatively more difficult, because the demands of love of God and neighbor are inexhaustible (see Suggs, *Wisdom* [→ 73 above] 71–97; Viviano, *Study* 183–192).

76   (D) Plucking Ears of Grain on the Sabbath (12:1–8). See Mark 2:23–28; Luke 6:1–5. Matthew now returns to the Marcan outline, which he had left in 9:18. In this chapter he shows Jesus in mounting conflict with his contemporaries. In two controversy stories (vv 1–8 and 9–14) the tendency of the Matthean editing is to tighten the legal force of the debate so that it becomes clear that Jesus is not anti-Torah or anti-sabbath, but against the Pharisaic overdevelopment of sabbath legislation to the point where it becomes, in their own words, "mountains hanging by a hair, for they are very little Bible and a great many rules" (*m. Ḥag.* 1:8). In fact the OT gives a simple command to keep the sabbath holy (Exod 20:8–11; Deut 5:12–15), but the rabbis went on to classify 39 kinds of work as forbidden (*m. Šabb.* 7:2), including reaping. **1.** *his disciples were hungry:* The disciples "transgress," and not Jesus himself. Matthew adds the hunger factor on humanitarian grounds (the rabbis allowed the saving of life to take precedence over observance) and to tie the disciples' behavior more closely to the case of David in v 3. **3–4.** See 1 Sam 21:1–7, with Lev 24:8, which shows that the incident happened on the sabbath. **5.** *the priests:* Matt here offers an even better legal argument based on Num 28:9–10. Moreover, the reaping of the *omer* (Lev 23:10–14) overrides the sabbath in rabbinic but not Sadducean law (*m. Menaḥ.* 10:1,3,9). **6.** *something greater:* What is this? Either the Messiah, or the corporate Son of Man (Dan 7:13 and 18), or the kingdom of God. **7.** Hos 6:6, cited already in Matt 9:13. Since at the time the final form of the Gospel was composed the Temple was no more, substitutes had to be found for it. Here deeds of loving-kindness replace it. **8.** *lord of the sabbath:* The christological conclusion, hinted at in v 6, becomes explicit.

(Daube, D., *The New Testament and Rabbinic Judaism* [London, 1956] 67–71. Levine, E., "The Sabbath Controversy according to Matthew," *NTS* 22 [1975–76] 480–83.)

77   (E) Healing the Man with the Withered Hand (12:9–14). See Mark 3:1–6; Luke 6:6–11. The scene moves indoors from the fields, and a sabbath dispute is combined with a healing, which reinforces with divine approval Jesus' humanitarian interpretation of the sabbath. Matthew strips away all emotion from the Marcan version and adds a legal argument in vv 11,12. **11.** *what one of you:* This counterquestion offers a bit of case law (a *ma'ăśeh*) argument recognized by the later Talmud (*b. Šabb.* 128b; *b. B. Meṣ.* 32b) and concludes (v 12) with a *qal wā-ḥōmer* argument (→ 70 above). The summary follows that it is legal to do good on the sabbath. Jesus stands within the law yet works a legal revolution. This earns him only resentment. Matthew reduces the opponents to Pharisees, but in the oldest source, Mark, they are not mentioned during the Passion.

78   (F) The Chosen Servant (12:15–21). See Mark 3:7–12. Matthew summarizes Jesus' healing activity and then interprets it through one of his fulfillment citations (→ 7 above). This time it is from Isa 42:1–4, from the first song of the Suffering Servant (→ Deutero-Isaiah, 21:17). The prophecy speaks of God's love for the Servant; the Servant is Spirit-filled. The images reflect his gentle, quiet care for the weak, the discouraged, the hurt. But the repeated terms are "judgment" for the "Gentiles." The finale brightens with a promise of hope and victory. The text form of the quotation differs from both the MT and the LXX; it shows careful reflection upon and interpretation of the OT.

79   (G) Jesus and Beelzebul (12:22–32). See Matt 9:32–34; Mark 3:20–30; Luke 11:14–23; 12:10. This rather complex unit begins with Jesus healing a blind and dumb demoniac. The miracle leads people to think that Jesus may be the Messiah, Son of David (see Matt 9:27; 15:22). **24.** *only by Beelzebul:* The growing admiration of the people provokes the opposition of the religious leaders. In Matt the villains are usually Pharisees, because only they survived the debacle of AD 70 in sufficient strength to make trouble for Matthew's church (in Mark they are scribes). Miracles are by nature ambiguous; they can be worked for good or ill, and one must test the spirit behind them. The Pharisees come to a negative conclusion, in character with their later rejection of heavenly voices in determining the law (*b. Pesaḥ.* 114a). Since miracles really do remain ambiguous, the later church largely lost interest in them as a means of theological proof. Yet their popular appeal has usually remained powerful. Verses 25–27 give Jesus' reply to the accusation. **25.** *every kingdom divided against itself:* The saying about the kingdom divided teaches a basic lesson of political science: in unity there is strength. Satan's realm is described as a kingdom (which is at war with God's). Life is a struggle, in which God wins only at a terrible price. Since Jesus' specific form of miracle working is expulsion of demons—and this would be counterproductive if he were himself demonic—the argument is valid, but only for that kind of miracle. **27.** *by whom do your sons cast them out?:* This verse perhaps contains a taunt that the Pharisees do not practice this form of healing. When they do (Acts 19:13–19), the results are not impressive (see Justin, *Dial.* 1.2.85; cf. Urbach, *The Sages* 115 [→ 17 above]). **28.** *if I by the Spirit of God:* Matthew

has changed "finger" into the more theological "Spirit"; it reminds us of 12:18 and points forward to vv 31,32. *kingdom of God:* Only here and in 19:24; 21:31,43 is this phrase used instead of "kingdom of Heaven." *has come upon you:* The vb. *phthanō*, "come before," "precede," is used only here in Matt and means that the kingdom has actually arrived, by anticipation, in the ministry of Jesus (*BAGD* 856). This is the legitimate basis for realized eschatology, but it does not exclude a future coming of the kingdom in its fullness (6:10). Bultmann's judgment deserves to be quoted: [This verse] "can, in my view, claim the highest degree of authenticity which we can make for any saying of Jesus: it is full of that feeling of eschatological power which must have characterized the activity of Jesus" (*HST* 162; see further B. Chilton (ed.), *The Kingdom of God in the Teaching of Jesus* [Phl, 1984] 52–71). **29.** *binds the strong man:* The little parable of the duel portrays Jesus as Satan's vanquisher, perhaps an allusion to his temptation (4:1–11 par). **30.** *who is not with me:* This unecumenical attitude contrasts with the lenient view of Mark 9:40; Luke 9:50 and perhaps reflects the experience of the early church (7:21–23). **31.** *blasphemy against the Spirit:* This difficult saying has been transmitted in both Marcan and Q forms. Matthew attempts to combine them here. Characteristic of the Q form is the two-step structure: sin against the Son of Man, forgivable; sin against the holy Spirit, unforgivable. Historically, this sin has been understood in various ways: presuming to attain salvation without faith and love, despair of salvation, obstinacy in sin or error, final impenitence, apostasy. Exegetically, the likeliest view is "persistence in consummate and obdurate opposition to the influence of the Spirit" (*FGL* 964). Theologically, the last interpretation may offer hope for the salvation of people who lack an explicit faith in Jesus Christ yet who are implicitly open to his saving power through their trust in the Spirit, who is less sharply defined historically. This view conflicts with v 30 above, but perhaps the dialectic is intentional (see R. Scroggs, *JBL* 84 [1965] 359–73).

80   (H) A Tree and Its Fruits (12:33–37). Matthew takes Q material (cf. Luke 6:43–45), part of which he has already used in 7:16–20, and adds the introduction (v 34a) and the conclusion (vv 36,37) from a stock of biblical commonplaces (Prov 12:6; Matt 15:18; Luke 19:22; Jas 3:6; Jude 15; Rom 4:12). This he shapes to express his characteristic emphasis on judgment. As in 5:33–37; 23:22, he is concerned with problems of language and abusive speech. At its worst, this concern may reflect a merely intellectualist and verbal bias; at its best, a moral and religious sensitivity that one can kill with words, one can sin against the Spirit.

81   (I) The Sign of Jonah (12:38–42). See Mark 8:11–12; Luke 11:29–32. This passage contains a striking example of the growth of the gospel tradition through the combination of originally separate sayings and interpretative glosses. Matthew reproduces the Marcan form in 16:1–4, and the Q form here. To the latter he adds his OT quotation (Jonah 2:1) and its application in v 40. As it stands the passage teaches several lessons: (a) the uselessness of looking for spectacular signs (v 39); (b) Jonah's fate as a type of Jesus' resurrection (v 40), a spectacular sign to believers after all; (c) the importance of preaching and repentance (v 41); (d) that Gentiles are sometimes more receptive than Jews to God's messengers (vv 41–42); (e) the importance of the quest for divine wisdom, in which women also share and sometimes excel (v 42); (f) that Jesus is greater than previous prophets and wise men (vv 41,42), because he is the absolute revelation of the Father (11:27). The text is rich and multivalent to the point of internal contradiction (see further *FGL* 929-38; R. A. Edwards, *The Sign of Jonah* [SBT 2/18; Naperville, 1971]; E. H. Merrill, *JETS* 23 [1980] 23-30). **38.** *to see some sign from you: Sēmeion,* "sign," often used in the Johannine Gospel for Jesus' miracles, refers rather to a flamboyant sign perceptible to the senses that would vindicate Jesus' authority. **39.** *bad, adulterous generation:* See 16:4; cf. Mark 8:38. *sign of Jonah the prophet:* It proves to be double in this Gospel: Jonah in the fish's belly (v 40—an interpretative gloss editorially added to the Q form) and "Jonah's preaching" (v 41). **40.** *in the whale's belly:* See Jonah 2:1. *three:* Counting both ends, one arrives at three. *in the earth's heart:* So the early church reckoned with the burial of Jesus—in the Johannine reckoning, from the day of preparation for the Passover/sabbath, the feast itself, and the first day of the week. **41.** *Ninevites:* See Jonah 3:5. *greater than Jonah:* Matthew continues his comparison of Jesus with figures or objects dear to Judaism; see 11:11b; 12:6; cf. 18:1,4. **42.** *queen of the south:* The queen of Sheba does not figure in the OT Jonah story; she appears in 1 Kgs 10:1-13 and was mentioned in the Q form of this episode. There she was introduced as a foil to wise Solomon. But here she is used as a foil to Jesus himself, who is even "greater than Solomon." Yet even she, along with the Ninevites, will judge the sign-seekers "at the judgment." Like Jonah and like Jesus, she came from "the bounds of the earth."

82 **(J) The Return of the Evil Spirit (12:43-45).** See Luke 11:24-26. At first this seems a puzzling story. We must remember that Jesus was an exorcist, and, in this sense, a healer of troubled people. Here he reflects on the results of his ministry, astonishingly, from the viewpoint of the demon expelled. The results are not necessarily permanent. Trouble can return if one does not fill the empty place left by the departed demon with faith, hope, love, new life. **43.** *waterless places:* See Lev 16:10; cf. Isa 34:13-14. **45c.** *so shall it be also with this evil generation:* Matthew adds this phrase (not in Luke) to give the intimate insight a polemical social application to his own time and place and to tie it in with v 39.

83 **(K) Jesus' Family (12:46-50).** See Mark 3:31-35; Luke 8:19-21. Matthew shapes this pronouncement story so that the high point, Jesus' answer in vv 48-50, is well coordinated and its different elements mutually illumine one another. If v 47 was not in the text as Matthew wrote it (it is missing in a few of our best mss.), then the narrative introduction has been pared to the bare minimum. **49.** *stretching his hand over his disciples:* Matthew defines Jesus' true family as the disciples and accompanies it with a gesture that is almost an ordination (cf. 17:7). The point of the saying is not to deny natural family ties, but to assert the primacy of intentional ties in the new community which Jesus had begun to gather. **50.** *whoever does the will of my father:* This defines true disciples as those who obey God and act out their faith. In its Marcan form this verse may have originally circulated separately (see W. Trilling, *Das wahre Israel* 29-32).

84 **(VI) Parables of the Kingdom (13:1-52).** The third great discourse (13:1-52) consists of seven parables and some explanations of them. Structurally this is the center and high point of the entire Gospel. Everything is concentrated on the kingdom, which, however, remains mysterious (13:11). All the material up to v 35 has a parallel in Mark or Luke. But from v 36 on Matthew goes his own way. This shift is indicated by a move from public speaking to a more intimate discourse to the disciples in the house. Two of the three parables in the latter section (vv 44-46) envisage the reaction of an individual person to the kingdom, whereas the others envisage a group. Parables as a teaching form, while characteristic of Jesus, are also found in the OT

(2 Sam 12:1-14; 14:1-11; 1 Kgs 20:35-40; → NT Thought, 81:59-88). The evangelists themselves probably composed parables to illustrate aspects of Jesus' teaching as well as reshaped his parables to fit new circumstances. On the definition of a parable, see comment on Mark 4:2. Although chap. 13 is a discourse, it is a discourse that consists of narratives. So it is a blend of both constitutive formal elements of the Gospel, discourse and narratives, a higher synthesis. Thus, the chapter is a climax formally as well as structurally and in content (the kingdom).

(Carlston, C. E., "Parable and Allegory Revisited," *CBQ* 43 [1981] 228-42. Dupont, J., "Le point de vue de Matthieu dans le chapitre des paraboles," *L'Evangile selon Matthieu* [ed. M. Didier; BETL 29; Gembloux, 1972] 221-59. Gerhardsson, B., "The Parable of the Sower and Its Interpretation," *NTS* 14 [1967-68] 165-93; "The Seven Parables in Matthew XIII," *NTS* 19 [1972-73] 16-37. Kingsbury, J. D., *The Parables of Jesus in Matthew 13* [Richmond, 1969].)

85 **(A) The Parable of the Sower (13:1-9).** See Mark 4:1-9; Luke 8:4-8. **1.** *he sat by the sea:* Jesus prefers outdoor teaching to the academic hothouse. **2.** *great crowds:* The press of the crowd must have been great indeed to justify such an unprecedented and odd posture of teaching from a boat. **3.** *sower:* A parable of a sower was calculated to appeal to a rural audience of workers. **4.** *the road:* The first of four kinds of ground on which the seed fell. The road could not be plowed, so the seed lay on the surface, where the birds could get at it. **5.** *rocky soil:* Much of Palestine is rocky, and the topsoil is often quite thin. The seed sprouts too soon, unprotected by deeper soil, unable to sink roots. **6.** *scorched:* In the blaze of Palestinian sun, the sprouts burn up and shrivel. **7.** *fell among thorns:* Here the soil is sufficiently deep but another problem arises; it is already occupied by weeds powerful enough to choke the new sprouts. **8.** *good soil:* When the seeds fall on deep, unencumbered soil, they bear abundantly, though not in equal measure. Oddly, the Greek does not actually use the word for seed, *sperma,* anywhere in the parable. **9.** *he who has ears to hear, let him hear:* This common refrain (11:15; 13:43) constitutes an invitation to the listener to think reflectively on the human application of the figure. The audience must participate if the parable is to have its effect. The parable will be explained in vv 18-23. Supposing the explanation had arisen later, we could surmise that the sower is either God, Jesus, one of God's emissaries, even Lady Wisdom. The seed is either divine revelation or the kingdom of God. The different soils represent the different human receptions. The message is that, despite some failures, the sower's work ultimately succeeds for the most part. The sign of success is the fruit bearing of the recipients. The story gives hope and encouragement.

86 **(B) The Purpose of the Parables (13:10-17).** See Mark 4:10-12; Luke 8:9-10. **10.** *why do you speak to them?* The disciples' question intrudes upon Jesus' address to the crowds. If we take the setting in vv 1,2 seriously, the crowds too must hear Jesus' depressing answer. But this is less likely than that Mark inserted a theological consideration at this point. Matthew follows him in this, but without stating that Jesus was alone when they asked (cf. Mark 4:10). **11.** *the mysteries of the kingdom:* Matthew changes Mark's sg. *mystērion* to a pl. and reduces the suggestion of a distinction between an exoteric and esoteric circle of hearers. Mysteries here has the sense of the Semitic word *rāz* found in Dan and QL, the hidden plans or designs of God for history and particularly for establishing his just rule through overcoming the forces of evil (see R. E. Brown, *The Semitic Background of the Term "Mystery" in the New Testament*

[FBBS 21; Phl, 1968]). **12.** *he who has, to him shall be given:* Both here and in the preceding verse the passives are theological (*ZBG* § 236): God will give. The bitter truth of this is not meant economically (though it is often true there too), but spiritually, intellectually: if you open yourself in faith and hope to God's revelation of his plan of salvation, you can make rapid progress in understanding it. If you close yourself to it, you can lose the offer. **13.** *that seeing, they may not see:* There has been a great battle among interpreters to understand the word "that" here: does it mean that Jesus intended that the people should not understand or merely that this was the (unintended) result in many cases? Matthew has clearly softened Mark in the latter sense. But the more difficult Marcan form has its basis in the biblical language of predestination and election, language intended to affirm that God is in ultimate control and will win out in the end. **14–15.** Matthew then quotes the full text of Isa 6:9–10 alluded to in v 13, so that the reader can see its positive intent to save, visible at the very end, "and I heal them." **16.** *blessed are your eyes:* Matthew adds here a related beatitude from Q (Luke 10:23–24), changing kings to just men (one of his great themes is justice). The beatitude expresses the privileged role of the disciples as eyewitnesses.

87   (C) The Parable of the Sower Explained (13:18–23). See Mark 4:13–20; Luke 8:11–15. Apart from changes at the beginning and end, Matthew follows Mark rather closely, yet the overall shaping leads to an important increase in meaning. **19.** *the word:* It is further specified as the word "of the kingdom," and failure to receive it is a failure of "understanding," not of hearing. *the evil one:* So Satan is more vaguely called; and the locus of the failure is "his heart." **23.** *understanding:* Again inserted as the characteristic of the good disciple, along with "doing." In v 21 the cause of failure is "tribulation or persecution"; in v 22 the cause is "delight in riches." Both are from Mark. The whole adds up to the same teaching as in 4:11. Only one who loves God with heart, soul (to the point of martyrdom during persecutions), and strength (wealth) (Deut 6:5; *m. Ber.* 9:5) truly receives his word. The failures come from defects of the heart, soul, or strength (Gerhardsson). Thus, all is centered on the pure love of God as the way to receive and understand the word of the kingdom. For a Jewish parallel, see 2 Esdr 8:41–44.

88   (D) The Parable of the Weeds among the Wheat (13:24–30). As traditionally understood, this parable has no parallel, but it is becoming recognized today as Matthew's rewriting of Mark 4:26–29, the parable of the seed growing secretly. Matthew has not only updated the older parable to suit the needs of his community, but he has also provided it with an elaborate allegorical interpretation (vv 36–43). Viewed in itself it is a kingdom parable, the first explicitly so (cf. v 19). The remaining five parables will all begin with the kingdom too. **24.** *a man:* He turns out to be a "householder" with "slaves" (v 27). The slaves are scandalized that there are weeds. **30.** *let both grow together until the harvest:* This is the crucial part of the answer, advocating patience and tolerance until the final sorting. The mention of "gathering" four times suggests that the parable is concerned somehow with the community. For the application, see vv 36–43.

89   (E) The Parables of the Mustard Seed and the Leaven (13:31–33). See Mark 4:30–32; Luke 13:18–21. These parables are paired in Matt and Luke, one about a man, the other about a woman, reflecting the evenhanded fairness of Jesus to both sexes. Source-critically, the situation is complex: the first parable is preserved in Marcan and Q forms; the second is a Q

parable. Matthew draws on both sources. **31–32.** The point of the parable of the mustard seed is the sudden, surprising shift from the near invisibility of the kingdom to its full grandeur and its universal, all-embracing hospitality. Verse 32 contains allusions to Ps 104:12; Dan 4:9,12,18,21,22; Ezek 17:22–24; 31:2–9. **33.** *like leaven which a woman took:* At a time when it was the privilege of the chief woman of the household to knead the bread for the entire family and staff the sight of dough rising as a result of the catalytic effect of the bit of leaven mixed with it was a familiar domestic experience. Here Jesus uses it to point to the surprising effect a small movement can have on the whole of society, God's plan working almost invisibly to bring about its purposes. Leaven in Jewish tradition often had the symbolic meaning of evil, the proneness or tendency to sin in an individual, connected with the rituals of Passover as the feast of Unleavened Bread (Exod 12:19; 13:7; Deut 16:3; 1 Cor 5:6–8). But here Jesus uses leaven positively, as a symbol for the power of God. A side effect of this parable is that it is possible to see God present and active in everyday things if one looks at them with wonder.

(Crossan, J. D., "The Seed Parables of Jesus," *JBL* 92 [1973] 244–66. Dahl, N. A., *Jesus in the Memory of the Early Church* [Minneapolis, 1976] 141–66.)

90   (F) Jesus' Use of Parables (13:34–35). See Mark 4:33–34. **34.** *in parables:* This verse is almost poetic in its carefully balanced structure of antithetical parallelism. Matthew omits Jesus' need to explain everything to his disciples because they generally understand his teaching (contrast v 36 with vv 51,52). **35.** *that might be fulfilled:* Another fulfillment citation is added (→ 7 above), this time from Ps 78:2, to explain why Jesus, the Son of David, spoke in parables. The first line follows the LXX exactly, but the second, "I will utter what has been hidden since the foundation," is an independent reworking that returns to the idea of the hidden mysteriousness of the kingdom of vv 10–17. Jesus is privy to the divine mind, says Matthew. The unit serves as a buffer which breaks the series of parables and invites the hearer to reflect on what has been heard so far.

91   (G) The Interpretation of the Parable of the Weeds (13:36–43). Matthew now reveals in full allegorical detail the meaning of vv 24–30. In vv 37–39 he gives eschatological equivalents to seven elements in the parable, in a rather static fashion. In the second part of the explanation (vv 40–43) he gives a dynamic presentation of the last judgment and the separation it entails of the "evildoers" (lit., those performing lawlessness) from the "just." **38.** *the field is the world:* The *kosmos* here refers to the human world, humanity. *the evil one:* Evil is here personified, as in 5:37; 6:13; 13:19; but it is named "the devil" in the next verse. **41.** *his kingdom:* This phrase has in the past been used to make a distinction between the kingdom of the Son (the present church) and the kingdom of God, but this distinction seems unfounded. The kingdom of God is given to the Son of Man, and he will bring it to earth in its fullness "at the close of the age" (vv 39,40). **42.** *furnace of fire:* This is a gen. of quality, equivalent to "fiery furnace." Matthew here and elsewhere (e.g., 25:31–45) pastorally applies the apocalyptic vision of hell. *weeping and gnashing:* Almost a cliche in Matt (8:12; 13:50; 24:51; 25:30); cf. Luke 13:28. **43.** *then the just:* This cheerful phrase echoes Dan 12:3 but with several important changes: it is the "just," rather than the wise, who will shine; the place of their shining is "the kingdom." The details should not obscure the main point of the parable: the kingdom is a mixed body of saints and sinners on earth, until the final sifting by God's agents. Therefore patience, tolerance, and forbearance are necessary. No one should usurp divine judgment. This view may appear as commonplace, but in fact it differs somewhat from Paul's view of a church of "saints," a view that has led some later theologians to speak of the true church as being hidden or invisible, while others insist on its visibility. Puritanical groups who try to exclude all sinners end up with small or short-lived communities. Taken as a whole, Matthew's view urges preparation for the judgment and protects the community from charges of hypocrisy. The problem with his view is that it can be stretched to read: nothing can be done about the evil in our midst; the only response in that case would be passive indifference. But this cannot be the whole truth. Weeds left unchecked can choke the wheat (v 7), so they must be kept under control even if not eliminated entirely. The church needs constant reformation and positive action including the quest for holiness, yet must avoid unrealistic purism or angelism. This is the elusive but needed balance. A single parable cannot say everything. The parable of the dragnet (vv 47-50) makes the same point, that the kingdom is a mixed body; patience is necessary, and one must leave the sifting to God.

92   (H) The Parables of the Treasure, the Pearl, and the Dragnet (13:44-50). All three are peculiarly Matthean kingdom parables. In the first two the problem of interpretation is to decide whether the point is the priceless value of the treasure or the pearl, or the behavior of those who sell all to possess the object found. The latter emphasis is clear in the story of the pearl merchant and probably holds also for the treasure. **44.** *joy:* This note must not be overlooked: the kingdom is such a priceless treasure that a wise man would gladly give all for the chance to seize it; it is the chance of a lifetime. Half measures will not do for the kingdom of God (see J. Dupont, "Les paraboles du trésor et de la perle," *NTS* 14 [1967-68] 408-18; J. D. Crossan, *Finding is the First Act* [Phl, 1979]). **47.** *like a dragnet:* The parable proper runs through vv 47-48, and the interpretation follows in vv 49-50. The point is the same as in the parable of the weeds (vv 24-30) and its interpretation (vv 36-43): the kingdom is a mixed body of saints and sinners (good and rotten fish). The final sorting out must be left to God and his angelic agents. In the meantime patient tolerance must guide the practice of those in it.

93   (I) Old and New (13:51-52). 51. *have you understood:* The disciples boldly answer yes. Understanding is a characteristic of the good disciple in Matt (cf. Mark 8:17-21). **52.** *every scribe who has been discipled:* This verse is important from several points of view. First, in its immediate context, it is a kind of parable that concludes the chapter of seven other parables. It is a parable about making parables, a metaparable that invites the reader/hearer to enter the parabolic process through creating new parables to add to the ones just given. *new and old:* The problem of interpretation turns on the meaning of this phrase. The most common view takes the old as the OT, the new as Jesus' teaching about the kingdom. But A. Schlatter (*Der Evangelist Matthäus* [4th ed.; Stuttgart, 1957] 450-51) argues that the old includes both OT and Jesus' teaching, the new is what lies ahead, the crucifixion, etc. J. Dupont objects that this view is far from the mind of Matthew (5:17-19). Here a distinction is necessary: Matthew does not envisage innovation in moral law (*halaka*), but he does practice and encourage storytelling to make the law appealing and understandable (*haggada*). Second, the verse suggests the existence and activity of Christian scribes in Matthew's church (23:34). Third, the verse has rightly been taken as the

autobiography or pen portrait of the evangelist. It would also fit Paul.

(Dupont, J., *Etudes sur les évangiles synoptiques* 2. 920-28. Zeller, D., "Zu einer jüdischen Vorlage von Mt 13,52," *BZ* 20 [1976] 223-26.)

94   (VII) Acknowledgement by Disciples (13:53-17:27).
(A) The Rejection of Jesus in His Own Country (13:53-58). See Mark 6:1-6; Luke 4:16-30. A new section of the Gospel begins at this point, consisting of narratives mostly derived from Mark, in which Matthew develops the elements relating to Peter (14:28-31; 16:16-19; 17:24-27). Here Jesus begins the road to the cross more explicitly and predicts his passion, at the same time forming his disciples to carry on after his passing. Not unfittingly, the section begins with a story of rejection. **53.** *when Jesus had finished:* See comment on 7:28a. **54.** *their synagogue:* From here on in the unit Matthew follows Mark closely. Again he changes "the" synagogue to "their" (see comment on 4:23; 10:17). **55.** *carpenter's son:* Matthew changes the Marcan phrase from Jesus as carpenter (or mason) to the less ignoble "carpenter's son." In the Talmud carpenters or joiners (*naggār*) are praised for their knowledge of Torah (y. *Yebam.* 8.9b; y. *Qidd.* 4.66b). *brothers:* The term could refer to half brothers or kinsmen in general (see *FGL* 723-24; *MNT* 65-72; → NT Thought, 81:142). **56.** Familiarity breeds contempt. Jesus' countrymen fail to perceive God's presence in him simply because they know his humble human origins and context, of which they are a part. In despising him they despise themselves. **57.** *a prophet is not without honor:* The saying may have been proverbial, but it identifies Jesus as a prophet. **58.** *he did not do:* Matthew changes Mark's "could not do" (involuntary failure) to "did not do" (voluntary, free decision).

(Batey, R. A. "Is Not This the Carpenter?" *NTS* 30 [1984] 249-58.)

95   (B) The Death of John the Baptist (14:1-12). See Mark 6:14-29; Luke 9:7-9. Matthew abbreviates Mark in this story as he does in the miracles. The story is told from a less intimate and moral but more political point of view in Josephus, *Ant.* 18.5.2 § 116-19. **1.** *Herod the tetrarch:* Antipas, son of Herod the Great and Malthace (→ History, 75:165). **3.** *Herodias:* The niece of Herod the Great and daughter of Aristobulus IV, she married her uncle "Philip," a son of Herod who lived privately in Rome. Josephus calls her first husband Herod Boethus. Her only known daughter was Salome. After Herodias met Antipas, she was as ambitious as he, left her husband and followed him. Herod Antipas divorced his wife, the daughter of Aretas IV, king of the Nabateans, to marry her (→ History, 75:165). **4.** *it is not lawful:* JBap judged that Herod had sinned by taking his brother's wife while his brother was still alive, thereby committing adultery and incest, prohibited in Lev 20:10,21. **5.** *he feared the people:* Matthew rewrites Mark heavily here, suppressing the feminine intrigue and changing the object of the fear from JBap to the people, as in Josephus. **7.** *he promised with an oath:* This oath may have been binding in law. To break it would involve perjury or political inconvenience. Matthew minimizes Herod's extravagance but still shows him as light-minded and a prey to intrigues. Note the echoes of Esth 5:3,6; 7:2; 1 Kgs 13:8; 19:2,10,14. **10.** *beheaded in prison:* Josephus identifies the prison as Machaerus in Transjordan. **12.** *told Jesus:* By adding this clause, Matthew relates the whole episode to his central figure. JBap was beheaded without even the pretense of a trial.

(Derrett, J. D. M., *Law in the New Testament* [London, 1970] 339–58).

96   (C) The Feeding of the Five Thousand (14:13–21). See Mark 6:30–44; Luke 9:10–17. Another feeding miracle occurs in 15:32–39. **13.** *when Jesus heard this:* The death of JBap is the motive for Jesus' withdrawal; cf. Mark 6:30,31. **14.** *cured their sick:* Jesus' compassion leads to healing, not to teaching as in Mark. **16.** *you give them something to eat:* Jesus trains the disciples to have self-confidence, to show initiative, to be leaders (cf. v 19). **17.** *two fish:* Since the fish do not fit eucharistic overtones, Matthew will mention them only once again; Mark thrice more. **19.** *blessed, broke, and gave:* The ritual of the daily Jewish meal; but the formula points forward to the Last Supper (26:26). The disciples act as mediators between Jesus and the crowds. **20.** *and all ate:* The crowds represent all Israel gathered by Jesus. *twelve baskets:* The baskets represent the 12 tribes under the 12 disciples (cf. 19:28). **21.** *besides women and children:* Matthew's addition is very important, because the total figure could well come to 20 or 30 thousand; and it happens again (15:38). Since the total Jewish population of Palestine at the time is estimated at half a million, Jesus is presented as feeding a tenth of the population. This gives to the two feeding stories a social character, which makes them different from healing stories. Besides nature miracles or moral miracles (the people shared their provisions so that all had enough), we must see the social miracle. The events are described so as to echo Exod 16, Num 11 (the manna and the quails), as well as 2 Kgs 4:1–7,42–44 (Elisha multiplying the oil and bread). As Israel is here fed, the doublet in chap. 15 is often said to represent the feeding of the Gentiles. As the feedings anticipate the eucharist, the eucharist anticipates the messianic banquet in the kingdom.

(Fowler, R. M., *Loaves and Fishes* [Chico, 1981]. Masuda, S., "The Good News of the Miracle of the Bread," *NTS* 28 [1982] 191–219.)

97   (D) Walking on the Water (14:22–23). See Mark 6:45–52; John 6:15–21. **22.** *go ahead of him to the other side:* The disciples cross over into Gentile territory. **23.** *to pray by himself:* Jesus' solitary nocturnal prayer is a model for Christians, who besides prayer in common also at times need periods of silent personal prayer in contact with nature. **24.** *the wind was against them:* In this ideal scene the wind represents the hostile forces of the world. **25.** *walking on the sea:* In Canaanite myth and the OT the Lord overcomes the waves of death (Ps 77:19; Job 9:8; 38:16; Isa 43:16; Sir 24:5–6). **27.** *it is I:* Lit., "I am." Jesus shares in the divine power to save (Ps 18:17–18; 144:7; Exod 3:14; Isa 43:10; 51:12). **29.** *Peter . . . walked on the water:* The four-verse insertion (28–31) by Matthew into his Marcan source gives prominence to Peter, as do two other Matthean special traditions (16:17–19; 17:24–27). Peter's conduct does not make sense except as a combination of impulsive love and faith weakened by doubt. Elements of the uniquely personal and the typical intertwine here (cf. John 20:28, 29). **33.** *you are the Son of God:* In contrast to the Marcan ending, the disciples here understood and believe; they also anticipate in part Peter's confession in 16:16. The story as a whole relates a nature miracle that has been classed in the genre of sea-rescue epiphanies. It resembles 8:18–27, the stilling of the storm, in being a parable of the church besieged and offering symbols of a faith that is bold, stepping out into the unknown, yet vulnerable.

(Heil, J. P., *Jesus Walking on the Sea* [AnBib 87; Rome, 1981].)

98   (E) The Healing of the Sick in Gennesaret (14:34–36). See Mark 6:53–56. A summary report which Matthew abbreviates from Mark, this little pericope generalizes Jesus' healing activity into a social event and provides a transition to the discussion of ritual purity which follows. **34.** *Gennesaret:* This was a fertile plain lying between Capernaum and Tiberias. **36.** *touch the fringe:* Cf. 9:20. The fringes were attached to Jesus' prayer shawl. By touching them the people made an implicit act of faith, but at the same time, from a Pharisaic point of view, they in some cases communicated their ritual uncleanness to Jesus.

99   (F) Jesus and Pharisaic Tradition on Purity and Vows (15:1–20). See Mark 7:1–23. Matthew has carefully and subtly rewritten Mark here so as to make it clear that, while Jesus (and Matthew's church) broke with Pharisaic halaka, he (and they) nevertheless remained faithful to Torah, when interpreted his way (see comment on 5:17–20). Matthew has done this by suppressing two Marcan clauses: 7:18, "cannot defile him," and the anachronistic gloss 7:19b, "Thus he declared all foods clean." In historical fact Jesus did not clearly abolish the ceremonial law as such, since otherwise the struggles of the early church recorded in Gal 2, Acts 10 and 15 would be unintelligible. Matthew has also added in 15:20b the words "To eat with unwashed hands does not defile a man." This concentrates the reader's attention on two points of peculiarly Pharisaic practice that are not in the written law, handwashing and *qorbān* vows, while drawing attention away from the sensitive issue of kosher food laws that are in the law. Matthew retains the radical saying in v 11, but tries to limit its application so that it makes a moral point without undermining the law. There may also be an allusion to the commandment to love God (Deut 6:5) with heart (v 18), soul (vv 13,14?), and wealth (v 5) as the guiding light for all legal observance. **2.** *the tradition of the elders:* The Pharisees believed their tradition or oral law came from Sinai, i.e., from God (*m.* '*Abot* 1:1). For Jesus as the recipient of divine tradition, see 11:27. The basic rabbinic treatment of handwashing is found in *m. Yad.* **3.** *the commandment of God:* Jesus makes the crucial distinction between the Torah and Pharisaic tradition. **4.** See Exod 20:12; Deut 5:16; Exod 21:17; Lev 20:9. **5.** The tractate *m. Ned.* treats of *qorbān* vows; see also J. A. Fitzmyer, *ESBNT* 93–100. **8–9.** See Isa 29:13. **11.** *what comes out:* Kosher food laws are less important than moral conduct and speech. By adding the word "mouth" twice to the Marcan source, Matthew limits the range of the saying. **13.** *every plant:* This saying and v 14 are a Matthean editorial addition (cf. Luke 6:39); it stresses that the Pharisees are no longer to be followed. **19.** *evil thoughts:* Matthew, unlike Mark, limits the list to biblical vices. Note that the whole pericope is structured according to the addressees: scribes (vv 1–9), people (vv 10–11), disciples (vv 12–14), Peter (vv 15–20).

(Neusner, J., *The Idea of Purity in Ancient Judaism* [Leiden, 1973].)

100   (G) The Canaanite Woman's Faith (15:21–28). See Mark 7:24–30. Matthew shifts the focus from the miracle to the dialogue. **22.** *a Canaanite woman:* Matthew chooses this archaic biblical name in place of Mark's contemporary "Syrophoenician" to remind us of 1:5. The woman is doubly marginal: a woman alone in a man's world; a Gentile and hence unclean, a "menstruant from the cradle" (*m. Nid.* 4:1; cf. Matt 15:1–20). *Son of David:* See comment on 9:27. **23.** *did not reply:* Jesus' strange silence is explained in the next verse: he did not wish to exceed his divine mission. **24.** *except to the lost sheep of the house of Israel:* Cf. 10:6. This statement reflects the normal policy of the historical Jesus, his mission to gather all Israel for the end-time events; but cf. 28:19. **26.** *to the dogs:* Matthew retains the harsh saying from Mark, but without the softening "Let the children first be fed," which includes a salvation-historical perspective: first the Jews, then the Gentiles (Rom 1:16). **27.** *the dogs too:* The woman is quick to pick up the imagery of Jesus' reply and twist it to her advantage, yet without arrogance. Her bold humility bests him in debate. **28.** *your faith is great:* Jesus is generous in his praise (only she is said to have "great faith" in Matt) and in his healing power. On the redactional level we hear two voices from Matthew's community, particularist and universalist (see A. Dermience, *ETL* 58 [1982] 25–49).

101   (H) The Healing of Many People (15:29–31). See Mark 7:31–37. This is another summary report of healing (cf. 14:34–36). **29.** *he went up the mountain and sat down:* Recall 5:1. Jesus heals various kinds of sick people, but the deaf are not mentioned; cf. Mark 7:32–36, where Jesus heals a deaf-mute. The kinds of illness recall Isa 35:5–6; 29:18–19. **31.** *they glorified the God of Israel:* This is Matthew's ending, perhaps influenced by Isa 29:23. The people healed are possibly Gentiles, so that through Jesus' ministry they become part of regathered Israel. The same crowd is fed in the next pericope.

102   (I) The Feeding of the Four Thousand (15:32–39). See Mark 8:1–10. Although a doublet of 14:13–21, the shaping of the details makes it a feeding of the Gentiles. **32.** *summoned his disciples:* The event is motivated by the compassion of Jesus, as he takes the initiative. **33.** *bread in the desert:* The phrase is reminiscent of the feeding of the Israelites with manna (Exod 16:4–12). **36.** *giving thanks:* The ptc. *eucharistēsas* points to the eucharist. **37.** *seven baskets:* The number recalls the nations of Canaan (Acts 13:19) and the Hellenist table servers (Acts 6:5; 21:8); thus, the Gentiles who have been incorporated into the fullness of Israel. **38.** *besides women and children:* Matthew adds this phrase, which makes of it an even more significant social event; see comment on 14:21. **39.** *Magadan:* The site is unknown.

103   (J) The Demand for a Sign (16:1–4). See Mark 8:11–13; Luke 12:54–56. There is also an internal parallel in Matt 12:38–39. Text-critically, vv 2–3 are not read with certainty. Only the first and last verses parallel Mark 8:11–12. Matthew seems to be conflating sources here. These are sayings of warning or threat. **1.** *Pharisees and Sadducees:* This is an odd combination of two hostile parties, not found in Matthew's sources. The Sadducees had ceased to exist by Matthew's day. Together the two party names symbolize Jewish leadership in opposition to Jesus. *a sign:* See comment on 12:38; cf. 1 Cor 1:22, "Jews demand a sign." **2.** *fair weather:* Agrarian discernment about the weather should lead to or be a model for discernment about God's activity in history in his agent Jesus, but it often does not. **3.** *the signs of the times:* God gives hints of his will in each age, but believers must be attentive to them. The saying is an invitation to the hermeneutics of history and as such a permanent challenge to the church. **4.** *the sign of Jonah:* A Matthean cross-reference (to 12:39) added to the Marcan source; the sign is probably Jesus' ministry (see comment on 12:39).

104   (K) The Leaven of the Pharisees and Sadducees (16:5–12). See Mark 8:14–21. As in the preceding unit Matthew again conflates his sources, editing out what he judges to be Mark's excessive harshness about the disciples' lack of understanding, and adding v 12 to make his own polemical point against his rivals at Jamnia. All the Gospel versions are warnings. Matthew warns against false teaching, Luke against

hypocrisy. Mark's original point seems to be a concern for open table fellowship between Gentiles and Jews, wherein "one loaf" would be sufficient (so N. A. Beck, *CBQ* 43 [1981] 49–56). **6.** *leaven of the Pharisees and Sadducees:* On leaven as a symbol for corruption, see comment on 13:33. On the two parties, see comment on v 1. **9.** *do you not understand?:* Matthew abbreviates Mark here, because in v 12 he will make his point that the disciples do understand. **12.** *they understood:* For Matthew a good disciple is one who understands and remains faithful to the teaching of Jesus as opposed to that of the emerging rabbinate, and as opposed to any nostalgia for the temple as represented by the Sadducees.

105   (L) Peter's Confession (16:13–20). See Mark 8:27–30; Luke 9:18–21. This unit constitutes the high point of the Marcan Gospel, together with 8:31–9:13. Matthew adds here vv 16b–19, which amount to a famous ecclesiological complement to Peter's confession. **13–16.** On these verses, which contain Peter's great confession of faith in Jesus, see comments on Mark 8:27–30 (→ Mark, 41:55). But note the following points peculiar to Matthew. **13.** *the Son of Man:* This replaces Mark's "I." Matthew has inherited the identification of the earthly Jesus with the Son of Man (cf. Dan 7:13) from Q. **14.** *Jeremiah:* Matthew mentions this prophet here because he is the prophet who in his own experience of rejection and suffering announces the rejection and suffering of the Messiah (M. J. J. Menken, *ETL* 60 [1984] 5–24). **16.** *the Son of the living God:* Matthew adds this clause (cf. 14:33) to Mark's stark "the Christ," to interpret it in the direction of Jesus' unique consciousness of sonship (11:27). By invoking the Father–Son relationship, Matthew directs our attention away from the military-national connotations of the title "messiah." **17–19.** Mark's version has no satisfactory response by Jesus to Peter's confession, only a command to silence. Matthew undertakes to supply one, probably out of an earlier source. Formally, v 17 is a macarism, while vv 18,19 could be viewed as an etiological legend explaining Peter's change of name. Together, vv 17–19 provide a foundation story about post-Easter authority in the church and a commission to leadership. **17.** *revealed this to you:* This may counter Paul's claim in Gal 1:15,16 (J. Dupont, *RSR* 52 [1964] 411–20). **18.** *rock:* A pun on Peter's name (*Petros, petra*); in Aramaic both would be *kêpā'* (cf. Isa 28:14–22; 51:1,2; 1QH 3:13–18; 6:25–27; see J. A. Fitzmyer, *TAG* 112–24). *church: Ekklēsia* is found only here and in 18:17 in the four Gospels. It refers to the assembly of the people of God. *gates of hell:* Cf. Isa 38:10; Job 38:17; Ps 9:14; Wis 16:13. **19.** *keys:* Isa 22:22,23; Job 12:14; *1 Enoch* 1–16 (G. W. E. Nickelsburg, *JBL* 100 [1981] 575–600). *kingdom:* Here Matthew relates church to kingdom: the church is an interim arrangement which mediates salvation in the time between the earthly ministry of Jesus and the future coming of the kingdom. *shall be bound:* This and the parallel "shall be loosed" are theological passives (*ZBG* § 236); God shall bind and loose what Peter binds and looses. This verse gives enormous authority to Peter. What is the nature of this authority? Binding and loosing are rabbinic technical terms that can refer to binding the devil in exorcism (R. H. Hiers, *JBL* 104 [1985] 233–50), to the juridical acts of excommunication and of definitive decision making (a form of teaching through legislation, policy setting). See J. Jeremias, *TDNT* 3. 744–53. The authority to bind and loose is given to the disciples in 18:18, but to Peter alone are accorded the revelation, the role of the rock of foundation (Eph 2:20), and esp. the keys. In *Gos. Thom.* 12 the key role is accorded to James, the leader of the Jewish Christians. For Gentile Christians Paul would have been the preferred candidate for leadership. Peter thus represents a compromise that can hold both tendencies in the early church in an uneasy synthesis. Matthew here shows his ecumenical good sense. There is also involved the historical reminiscence that Peter was the spokesman for the disciples during the ministry of Jesus. As a whole vv 17–19 represent a blend of OT poetic imagery and institutional legislation. Such a combination is not unusual in rabbinic literature, but here it attains a remarkable density. **20.** *that he was the Christ:* Matthew sums up the main revelation at the end to tie the whole together. See further *PNT* 83–107.

106   (M) First Prediction of the Passion and Sayings on Discipleship (16:21–28). See Mark 8:31–9:1; Luke 9:22–27. The other two predictions will follow in 17:22–23; 20:17–19; cf. 26:1–2. **21.** *from then on:* With this clause Matthew, unlike Mark, separates the passion prediction from the confession. *Jerusalem:* This is the city where the prophets die (23:29–39). *elders, chief priests, scribes:* The three groups of leaders compose the sanhedrin; the elders were lay leaders. Note that Pharisees as such are not mentioned. *the third day:* An allusion to Hos 6:2. It is unlikely that Jesus would have spoken in such precise terms of his fate (though neither crucifixion nor Gentiles are mentioned). In this sense it is a prophecy after the fact. But Jesus did very likely reflect on his future death at the hands of the authorities and on its meaning in God's plan of salvation (H. Schürmann, *Jesu ureigener Tod* [Freiburg, 1975]). **22.** *rebuke:* Peter wants only a theology of grace and glory, to separate Christ from his cross. **23.** *Satan:* To this harsh appellation Matthew adds: "You are a stumbling stone to me," ironic after 16:18. **24–28.** See the parallels in 10:38–39,33. In Matt the five sayings are addressed only to the disciples. The first three, on the cost of discipleship, can be understood as a commentary on the great commandment to love God with all one's heart, soul, and strength (Deut 6:5; see comment on Matt 4:1–11). **24.** Self-denial means submission of one's will to God's. *take up one's cross:* This is not an allusion to Jesus' crucifixion. This horrible death was common in antiquity, and the cross was a proverbial term for suffering, agony. **25.** *save one's soul (life):* By avoiding martyrdom. **26.** *gain the whole world:* I.e., to acquire great wealth. Striking is the transfer of the commandment to love God into a commandment to love (follow) Jesus. The sayings express a profound psychological truth that happiness eludes those who seek it directly rather than seeking first the will of God, i.e., what is right. **27–28.** The last two sayings involve an apocalyptic picture of the rewards of discipleship. The Son of Man acts as judge and the kingdom is his. **27.** *requite:* An allusion to Ps 62:13. **28.** *shall not taste death:* The time frame is incorrect if it refers to the coming of the kingdom in its fullness (cf. Mark 13:32). But some have seen the promise fulfilled in the Transfiguration (17:1–9, described as a vision in v 9).

107   (N) The Transfiguration (17:1–13). See Mark 9:2–13; Luke 9:28–36. **1.** *after six days:* Cf. Exod 24:13–16, where God reveals himself to Moses after six days; Deut 16:13–15, the last day of the feast of Tabernacles. *Peter, James, John:* The triad will reappear in Gethsemane (Matt 26:37). *a high mountain:* A mountain symbolic of revelation, a kind of Galilean Sinai, perhaps then Carmel rather than the traditional Tabor or the visually appropriate Hermon, though no localization is necessary. **2.** *he was transfigured:* This motif of metamorphosis is so common in classical paganism (cf. Ovid, *Metamorphoses*) that Luke judged it best to avoid the term altogether. Thus it is not essential to the event. *as the light:* Jesus becomes a being of light; his nature becomes luminous, transparent to the disciples' gaze. This is the central point (cf. Exod 34:29,35). **3.** *Moses and Elijah:* The

preeminent seers of God in the OT, both connected with Sinai-Horeb, representative respectively of the law and of (Galilean, itinerant, wonder-working) prophets. **4.** *Lord:* Matthew correctly translates Mark's *rabbi,* which in Mark does not refer to a Jewish teacher but represents an older Aram usage, lit., "my great one," an address of respect to God, angels, and earthly sovereigns. *three tents:* Doubtless a reference to the Jewish feast of Tabernacles, Tents, or Booths (in the sense of *Sukkôt,* "sheds," Lev 23:42; Neh 8:14–18). This liturgical setting is the clue to the meaning of the event. **5.** *a lightsome cloud:* This stands for the divine presence, the *shekinah,* the cloud of unknowing in which God is met and heard; see the black cloud in the Beth Alpha mosaic for a visual representation (see E. L. Sukenik, *The Ancient Synagogue of Beth Alpha* [Jerusalem, 1932]). *This is my beloved son:* To Mark's references to Ps 2:7 and Deut 18:15, Matthew has added one to Isa 42:1. Jesus is here designated Son of God, Suffering Servant, and prophet like Moses. Law, Prophets, and Wisdom books bear witness to Jesus. **6.** *they feared greatly:* Matthew transfers their fear here as a reaction to the divine command, rather than to the vision itself (Mark). **7.** *touching them:* Jesus' touch overcomes their fear and perhaps consecrates them to further service. **8.** *Jesus himself alone:* Moses and Elijah have withdrawn, i.e., diminished in significance before the fuller revelation in Jesus. **9.** *the vision:* By labeling the event a vision, Matthew may give a clue to the nature of the event: some have regarded it as a vision accorded to Peter in the context of a study of Scripture during the feast of Tabernacles, through which he receives insight into the role of Jesus. Thus the story is seen as the externalization of an inner spiritual event—whether pre- or post-Easter it is impossible to say. Note the apocalyptic influence of Dan 8:17; 10:9–10. Applications of the event to the destiny of the Christian occur in Rom 12:2; 2 Cor 3:18; cf. 2 Pet 1:16–18; 2 Tim 1:8,10,11. *Elijah:* See Mal 3:23–24 (Eng 4:5–6). *must come first:* This does not mean before the Messiah comes but before the rising from the dead (Dan 12:2) or before the Son of Man rises from the dead (see J. A. Fitzmyer, *JBL* 104 [1985] 295–96). **12.** See 1 Kgs 19:2,10; Ps 22:6; Isa 53:3. **13.** JBap has already been identified with Elijah in 11:14. In Matt the disciples understand, whereas in Mark nothing is said of that.

(Chilton, B. D., "The Transfiguration," *NTS* 27 [1980–81] 115–24. Nützel, J. M., *Die Verklärungserzählung im Markusevangelium* [Würzburg, 1973].)

108   (O) The Healing of the Moonstruck Boy (17:14–20). See Mark 9:14–29; Luke 9:37–43. Here again Matthew much abbreviates his Marcan source. **15.** *Lord:* Matthew changes Mark's "teacher" to the more reverent "Lord" and has the man kneel to show his faith. *moonstruck:* Gk *selēniazesthai,* "be struck by the moon," was an ancient way of describing epilepsy, a nervous disorder that causes temporary violent seizures. If unaided, the epileptic can die from the effects of such a seizure, e.g., by falling into fire or water. **16.** *could not cure him:* A hint that the disciples of Jesus will not be as effective at healing as was Jesus himself here emerges, but cf. John 14:12. **17.** *faithless:* See Deut 32:5,20. In the case of the disciples, v 20 will soften the charge to "little faith." **20.** *faith as a grain of mustard seed:* The disciples have a faith of understanding and assent but not of sufficient trust. Matthew derives this image from Q (Luke 17:6). The image of casting the mountain into the sea is shared with Mark 11:23. *Nothing will be impossible:* Cf. Mark 9:23. The whole episode thus becomes an instruction to the disciples on the power of trusting faith.

109 **(P) Second Passion Prediction (17:22–23).**
See Mark 9:30–32; Luke 9:43–45. This is the shortest
and vaguest of the predictions (see 16:21; 20:18,19) and
perhaps represents the earliest type. **22.** Matthew suppresses the Marcan secrecy motif here. The Son of Man
is identified with Jesus and is destined to suffer, an idea
not found in Dan 7:13. *is to be handed over:* The passive
may connote divine agency (through Judas). *men:* Here
neither Jews nor Gentiles are singled out for blame. **23.**
kill him: No mention of the means of execution is made.
he will be raised: Again, God is the agent. *very sorrowful:*
The disciples' sorrow suggests that they understand, at
least in part, Jesus' tragic destiny.

110 **(Q) The Stater in the Fish's Mouth (17:24–
27).** This puzzling episode is found only in Matt. Most
authors assume that the tax in question was the Temple
tax, but in fact four different taxes have been proposed
as the subject of the narrative. If it was a civil tax, the
meaning of the story is the same as in 22:15–22. If the
story reports an incident in the life of Jesus, the tax could
be a religious tax for the upkeep of the Temple (see Exod
30:13–14). If the story comes from Matthean redaction
and refers to the post-70 situation, as seems most likely,
then the tax could refer to one to support the temple of
Jupiter Capitolinus in Rome (which, as contributing to
pagan worship, would be offensive to Jews and Christians), or to a collection to support the (rival) scholars in
Jamnia, as a sign of solidarity with other Jews (so W. G.
Thompson). This last sense would be highly paradoxical, since Jamnia had already banished the Jewish Christians. In this sense as well as in the sense of being under
the lordship of Jesus Christ, Matthew's church had
broken with the "other" synagogue; yet in other ways,
such as devotion to the law and a sense of being the true
fulfillment of Israel, it had not yet broken. The payment
to Jamnia may therefore be the tax intended, but it is impossible to be certain. The scene unfolds in two parts:
first comes the dialogue between the tax collectors and
Peter (v 24); then comes the dialogue between Jesus and
Peter, making it a school discussion (vv 25–27). **26.**
therefore the sons are free: A very Pauline way of thinking
emerges (Rom 14:13; 1 Cor 8:13; 9:1). Here the freedom
at issue is not from the law but from Jamnia (and Roman
authority). **27.** *lest they be scandalized:* Here Matthew
shows his ecumenical diplomacy and pastoral good
sense. Scandal will be a major theme in chap. 18, to
which this unit is a prelude. This is not a miracle story
because the miracle is not described (R. J. Cassidy, *CBQ*
41 [1979] 571–80).

111 **(VIII) Community Discourse (18:1–35).**
Chapter 18 contains Matt's fourth great discourse,
addressed to Peter and the other leading disciples, and is
about community relations. It gives rules for God's
household until the kingdom comes. The different
sections of the discourse concern relations to outsiders,
to those who are led, and to all within the community.

(Thompson, W. G., *Matthew's Advice to a Divided Community*
[AnBib 44; Rome, 1970].)

112 **(A) True Greatness (18:1–5).** See Mark
9:33–37; Luke 9:46–48; Matt 20:20–28. This unit relates
standing in the present community to the final goal of
life in the kingdom (vv 1,3,4). **1.** *the disciples:* Scholars are
divided on whether "disciples" refers to the whole community or to the church leaders. Note the presence of the
"little ones" in vv 6,10,14, which sets up a contrast
between the leader-disciples and those who are led.
There was no "hierarchy" in Matthew's church, but there
were authoritative leaders (23:34). The contrast continues till v 21, where a shift to "brother" occurs, sug-

gesting that all are on the same level when it comes to
forgiveness. Thus both opinions have a basis in part of
the text. **2.** *a child:* Here a real child serves as a symbol
for humility, not because children are naturally humble,
but because they are dependent. **3.** *if you do not turn:*
"Turn" is a Semitism for change, conversion (cf. Matt
19:14). **4.** *whoever humbles himself:* This is the full answer
to the question in v 1. To humble oneself is to set a self-
imposed limit; self-regulation checks the tendency to
arrogance built into positions of authority. This solution
does not always work, in which cases various forms of
rebellion occur. **5.** Cf. 10:40–42.

113 **(B) Leaders Who Cause Little Ones to Sin
(18:6–9).** See Mark 9:42–48; Luke 9:49–50; 17:1–2.
Matthew here weaves his sources and omits the admonition to tolerance. **6.** *believe in me:* Matthew heightens the
christological object of faith by adding "in me" to his
source. *drowned in the deepest part of the sea:* By changing
the vocabulary a bit, Matthew heightens the tone of
anger while refining the language. **7.** *it is necessary:* Matthew has carefully reshaped his Q source, framing the
central assertion with two woes which form an inclusion. Why is it necessary that sins come? Because God
created people with moral freedom and the capacity for
moral struggle and mutual influence, and they have, as
a matter of experience, used that freedom to sin. The
necessity is not metaphysical, as can be seen from v 14.
8–9. See 5:29–30. *life:* This term is used to refer to the
fullness of life in the kingdom of God.

114 **(C) The Parable of the Lost Sheep (18:10–
14).** See Luke 15:3–7. **10.** *do not think little of one of these
little ones:* The "little ones" are minor community
members, and the warning is against the arrogance of
leaders. *their angels:* The little ones have powerful connections, angels and God. Matthew here individualizes
the idea of the angels of the nations (Dan 10:13,20–21).
Cf. Gen 48:16; Acts 12:15. *behold the face:* An expression
borrowed from oriental court ceremonial, which designates the presence of courtiers before the sovereign
whom they serve (cf. 2 Sam 14:24; 2 Kgs 25:19; Tob
12:15). **12.** *has gone astray:* In Matt the sheep is not lost,
as in Luke, but has wandered away from the flock, a sign
of adventuresomeness. *does he not leave:* It seems to be a
shocking lack of pastoral prudence to risk all for the one.
In real life the dog, other shepherds, or the native timid-
ity of the other sheep might keep them together, but that
is not the point here. The risk is the point. *on the mountains:* See Ezek 34:12–16. *seek the one who has wandered off:*
In Matt the parable is an example of right concern for a
community member who has gone astray, whereas in
Luke it answers the question, How can Jesus associate
with sinners? **13.** *the ninety-nine who did not wander:*
Pastorally it is sometimes worth risking the fate of un-
adventurous members for one great-souled person who,
once won, can win or hold others. **14.** *your Father in
heaven:* Matthew has carefully framed the little parable in
vv 12,13 with his own favorite terminology: heavenly
Father, angels, little ones.

115 **(D) Trial Procedures (18:15–20).** On the
basis of a brief admonition to fraternal correction in Q
(Luke 17:3), Matthew constructs in vv 15–17 an entire
three-stage trial procedure for disciplining a recalcitrant
brother. In vv 18–20 he provides divine backing for
these judicial decisions, moving from law to theology.
15. The first stage is private confrontation and rebuke.
have gained your brother: "Gained" is here a technical
rabbinic term for missionary conversion (Lev 19:17,18).
16. *two or three witnesses:* This is a citation from Deut
19:15. The Qumranites (1QS 5:26–6:1; CD 9:2–4,
17–22) and the rabbis (*m. Mak.* 1:6–9) debate the problem, What happens when you have only one witness?

The text here answers that even one is sufficient, a legal difference from these other traditions. **17.** *tell it to the church:* "Church" here has the sense of a local community. *let him be to you as a Gentile or a publican:* This is a way of saying, let him be excommunicated, excluded from the community, a drastic step to be taken only in serious matters where the welfare of the community is at stake. Jesus welcomed tax collectors but only when they showed faith and repented their sins (9:9–13). See Gal 6:1; Tit 3:10; Jas 5:19–20. **18.** *shall be bound:* This is a theological passive (*ZBG* § 236); God shall bind. The disciple leaders are given the same power as Peter to bind and loose, but not the power of the keys. On binding and loosing, see comment on 16:19. **19.** *if two . . . arrive at an accord . . . concerning any claim that they may be pursuing, it shall be ratified:* This transl. stresses the legal senses of the terms as they would be used in a lawsuit or settlement out of court by mutual agreement. The vb. *symphōnein,* "accord," "agree," suggests a harmony of voices. **20.** *Where two or three are convened in my name:* This gathering can be for prayer, study, or, as in context, decision making (cf. John 15:7). In view of the parallels in *m. 'Abot* 3:2,6; 4:11, this verse identifies Jesus both with the Torah and with the divine presence (1:23; 28:20).

(Caba, J., "El poder de la petición comunitaria (Mt. 18,19–20)," *Greg* 54 (1973) 609–54. Derrett, J. D. M., "'Where Two or Three Are Convened in My Name': A Sad Misunderstanding," *ExpTim* 91 [1979] 83–86. Forkman, G., *The Limits of the Religious Community* [ConBNT 5; Lund, 1972]. Galot, J., "'Qu'il soit pour toi comme le païen et le publicain,'" *NRT* 96 [1974] 1009–30. Murphy-O'Connor, J., "Sin and Community in the NT," *Sin and Repentance* [ed. D. O'Callaghan; Dublin, 1967] 18–50. Neusner, J., "'By the Testimony of Two Witnesses,'" *RevQ* 8 [1972–75] 197–217.)

116   **(E) The Parable of the Unforgiving Servant (18:21–35).** See Luke 17:4. Matthew turns an instruction by Jesus in Q into a Peter–Jesus dialogue in which the bloodthirsty boast of Lamech is reversed (Gen 4:15,24); see comment on the sin against the Spirit in Matt 12:31. The parable that follows in vv 23–35 is only loosely attached to this teaching. It is properly a homiletic midrash on the instruction in Matt 6:12,14,15, probably composed by the evangelist himself to make part of the Lord's Prayer vivid to his people. **23.** It is a parable of the kingdom. *servants:* This is an OT way of referring not only to slaves but also, as here, to court officials or ministers. In this parable the servants could refer to tax gatherers or finance ministers. **24.** *a debtor of ten thousand talents:* Lit., "a myriad of talents." Since the silver talent was worth over $1,000.00, this is a way of saying an immensely large sum. **26–27.** Already we see that the parable concerns not abusing the divine patience and mercy. **28.** The parable unfolds in three acts: the first is between the king and his minister; the second between the royal ministers themselves; the third returns to the king and his minister. **34–35.** The divine patience is not infinite. The parable teaches the need to imitate the divine mercy (see B. B. Scott, *JBL* 104 [1985] 429–42).

117   **(IX) Authority and Invitation (19:1–22:46).**
(A) Teaching about Divorce (19:1–12). See Mark 10:1–12. As Jesus leaves Galilee a new geographical phase of his ministry begins. But he continues to form his disciples by teaching them about marriage and celibacy, children, rich and poor, his future passion, and the temptation to wrongful ambition (chaps. 19–20). Matthew picks up the Marcan narrative thread again and will follow it to the end of the passion, adding other material as he goes along. **1.** *when Jesus had finished:* See comment on 7:28a. *into the region of Judea beyond the Jordan:* It is not obvious that Judea ever extended beyond

the Jordan; perhaps an "and" has dropped out between "Judea" and "beyond"; cf. Mark 10:1. The point is that Jesus avoided Samaria; cf. 10:5. **2.** *he cured them:* In Mark it says that he "taught" them; in Matt he teaches too, but the effect is viewed as therapeutic for the crowds, the start of the new people of God (14:14). **3.** *to divorce:* See comments on 5:31–32. *for any cause:* This phrase, based on Deut 24:1, suggests the debate between Hillel and Shammai (*m. Git.* 9:10; → 31 above). **4.** See Gen 1:27; 5:2. **5.** See Gen 2:24. *the two:* This subject is not in the MT, but it is in the LXX; → 32 above. **6.** *let no one separate:* Jesus bases his stress on the permanent union of the married couple on the original will of the Creator. **7.** See Deut 24:1. **8.** *your hardheartedness:* A similar concession is found in 1 Sam 10:17–19. *from the beginning:* Note the *inclusio* with v 4. **9.** Matthew shifts Jesus' private explanation to the disciples to a public one, adds the exceptive clause, and omits the case of a woman initiating the divorce. *except for unchastity:* Jesus opposed divorce simply. On the exceptive clause, see comment on 5:32. **10.** Matthew begins the private part of the school dialogue at this point. **11.** *to whom it is given:* Note the theological passive (*ZBG* § 236); it is God who gives the capacity to remain single for the sake of the kingdom. **12.** *eunuchs:* Three kinds are listed: physically malformed; castrated through the cruelty of men, for use as harem guards and courtiers (disapproved in Deut 23:1); those who voluntarily refrain from marriage (*eunouchizein* is here used metaphorically) in order to devote themselves more fully to the urgent demands of the kingdom (so too 8:22; 1 Cor 7:17,25–35). The Jewish background of this strong teaching is found in Isa 56:3–5 and Qumran (see A. Sand, *Reich Gottes und Eheverzicht im Evangelium nach Matthäus* [SBS 109; Stuttgart, 1983]).

118   **(B) Little Children Blessed (19:13–15).** See Mark 10:13–16; Luke 18:15–17. **13.** *lay his hands on them and pray:* Matthew turns Mark's familiar or therapeutic touch into a solemn religious rite. Jesus is unique among ancient religious and philosophical teachers in receiving children as significant. His disciples were unprepared for this. **14.** *forbid them not:* This was used in the early church to permit the baptism of infants. **15.** See 2 Kgs 4:8–37 (see S. Légasse, *Jésus et l'enfant* [Paris, 1969]).

119   **(C) The Rich Young Man (19:16–30).** See Mark 10:17–31; Luke 18:18–30. The pronouncement story begins in Mark with a dialogue that scandalized later Christians because it contained a denial by Jesus that he was God (cf. John 1:1). Matthew carefully rewrites the dialogue so as to avoid this scandal, while showing full reverence for God on Jesus' part. *one is good . . . eternal life:* Parallel equivalents are vv 21,23,25. "Entering life" is the same as entering the kingdom (v 23). **18–19.** To the second table of the Decalogue (Exod 20:13–16; Deut 5:17–20) is added the command to love one's neighbor (Lev 19:18). On the use of the Decalogue in early Christianity, see R. M. Grant, *HTR* 40 (1947) 1–18. **20.** *young man:* Matthew alone makes it clear that he is young and that he senses some incompleteness in his life. **21.** *if you would be perfect:* This is Matthew's major addition to the story. *Teleios* can mean "complete, mature," or observant of all God's laws (cf. 5:48). The phrase in later times led to a distinction between the commandments (addressed to all believers) and counsels of perfection (addressed to a few). In Matt 5:48 the invitation to perfection is addressed to all. The distinction comes in the degrees of obligation: all are held to keep the commands (with forgiveness for repentant sinners), but not all are held to be celibate (19:12) or to sell all. **23.** *a rich person will find it hard:* Riches pose spiritual dangers because crime is sometimes involved in gaining them; and, once possessed, they can distract one from God, cut us off from others, and lead to exploitation and oppression. But they can also be used to do much good. **24.** *camel through the eye of a needle:* This is an extreme Oriental exaggeration, a colorful image for an insuperable difficulty. **26.** *with God all things are possible:* See Gen 18:14; Job 42:2. Hope is held out for the salvation of the rich through the primacy of the divine initiative. The rich are ultimately not saved in a way different from others. **27.** Matthew has Jesus answer Peter's question in two stages: a special promise for the Twelve (v 28; cf. Luke 22:28-30 = Q); a general promise for all the disciples (v 29). **28.** *in the regeneration:* Though a rare word (*palingenesia*) is used here, the sense is the same as "in the kingdom." *Son of Man sits upon his throne:* The promise looks toward a future apocalyptic judgment scene (25:31; Rev 21:1-22:5). *upon twelve thrones judging the twelve tribes:* In this form the promise is restricted to the Twelve, but in 1 Cor 6:2 it is made to all the saints. Judging could mean trying cases or, more broadly, ruling. Jesus will share his authority with his followers. The twelve tribes no longer existed as such, but Jesus came to gather the scattered of Israel (10:6; 15:24) for the endtime, to fulfill Ezek 47:13; and this may have been a way of including believing Gentiles. The Twelve are to judge collegially with Jesus all twelve tribes, not one each. The authenticity of the verse has been challenged by its archaic character, dependence on Dan 7, and eschatological expectancy suggest its dominical origin. A mention of the Twelve and the tension with 20:23 are not decisive arguments against this, since both could be preresurrectional. The verse does not directly address problems of church government, but can provide analogies for it. **29.** This verse promises a reward to all the radical disciples (see 10:37), but only in the next eon (unlike Mark), and without mentioning the wife (unlike Luke). **30.** *the last first:* The pattern is that of eschatological reversal of fortune (20:16; see J. Dupont, *Bib* 45 [1964] 355-92).

120   (D) The Parable of the Laborers in the Vineyard (20:1-16). Cf. the other vineyard parable in 21:33-44. This parable is linked with the preceding by the clamp in 19:30 and 20:16 and is probably a midrash to illustrate the themes of rewards for the disciples and the reversal of fortune of first and last (v 8). But once the story develops its own momentum, it becomes a story of God's generosity. **1.** *vineyard:* It is a symbol for Israel (cf. Isa 5; Jer 2:10). **2.** *denarius:* This was a normal day's wage. **3.** The boss hires at 6 A.M., 9, 12, 3 P.M. and 5. In the Levant it is normal for those who seek work to look for it at a crossroads or market. **4.** *whatever is right:* The wage is just but unspecified. **6.** *the eleventh hour:* About an hour before sundown, when work ceased. **7.** *no one has hired us:* They want to work but suffer the curse of unemployment; their idleness is not identical with laziness. Work is here viewed as more honorable than doing nothing. **8.** *beginning with last:* This phrase makes the parable a midrash on 19:30. **10.** *they thought:* The early workers are victims of the revolution of rising expectations; hence their discontent. **11.** *they murmured:* Cf. Exod 16:3-8. **12.** *equal to us:* The wage is the same, yet it is not truly equal because the boss is more generous to the latecomers. Did he count their intention to work? Cf. 21:31. **13.** *I do you no wrong:* The householder commits no injustice. **14.** *take what is yours:* This reflects a classic definition of justice: to render to each his own, his due. **15.** *generosity:* The reversal of fortunes is attributed to the generosity and goodness of God, his love for the most needy, not to any class vindictiveness. **16.** See 19:30, where the saying occurs in reverse order, making a chiasm.

121   (E) The Third Prediction of the Passion (20:17-19). See Mark 10:32-34; Luke 18:31-34. **17.** *apart:* Matthew omits the fear and wonder of the disciples. **18.** *will be handed over:* This prediction is more explicit than the second one in 17:22-23. The responsible agents are Jewish leaders; see comment on 16:21. **19.** *the Gentiles:* The leaders collaborate with the Romans, viewed as foreign oppressors. *crucified:* Matthew makes precise the form of death, but omits the undignified spitting (mentioned in Mark 10:34; cf. Matt 26:67; 27:30).

122   (F) The Request of the Sons of Zebedee (20:20-28). See Mark 10:35-45. This pericope unites a dialogue in vv 20-23 with an originally separate collection of sayings (Luke 22:24-27) on Christian styles of leadership. **20.** *the mother of the sons of Zebedee:* Matthew places the initial request in the mouth of a woman (27:56) to spare the disciples, but goes further in not mentioning their names, James and John, either here or in v 24 (cf. 26:37; 27:56). He thus protects the honor of a hero of the Jewish Christians, James. His model was 1 Kgs 1:11-31, including the act of obeisance. **21.** *sit:* Not at the messianic banquet but at the end-time judgment, as coregents (19:28). **22.** *the cup:* The cup is a symbol of suffering (Isa 51:17,22; Jer 25:15,17,28; 49:12; Lam 4:21; Ps 75:8; cf. Matt 26:39, Gethsemane). Matthew omits Mark's baptism as confusing. **23.** *for whom it has been prepared:* Jesus does not rebuke the sons. He assures them a share in his fate (perhaps an allusion to martyrdom; cf. Acts 12:2) and that the glorious future has already been planned by God. **24.** *the ten:* Ambition is not unique to the two. **25.** *the rulers of the nations:* Secular political models are not suited to the kingdom. **26-27.** Jesus offers two other models of authority, free service and involuntary slavery, the second more radical than the first, but both important. These lessons are next grounded in his own example. **28.** *not to be served but to serve:* Jesus himself is the model of humble service of the community as a leadership style, in contrast to the usual hunger for power and domination. *to give his life as a ransom for many:* Though well soldered into its present context, this highly condensed reflection on the meaning of Jesus' death may have had a separate history (it is missing from the Lucan parallel). It reflects the martyr theology of 1 Macc 2:50; 6:44, as well as the vicarious suffering of the Servant of Yahweh (Isa 53:10-12). *Lytron,* "ransom," is a rare word, often used to refer to money for the manumission of slaves, but also for rescue; cf. 1 Tim 2:5-6. (See S. Légasse, *NTS* 20 [1973-74] 161-77; J. Roloff, *NTS* 19 [1972-73] 38-64; W. J. Moulder, *NTS* 24 [1977-78] 120-27.)

123   (G) The Healing of Two Blind Men (20:29-34). See Mark 10:46-52; Luke 18:35-43; Matt 9:27-31. Matthew abbreviates the Marcan story and doubles the number of blind men, perhaps to overcome the impression that it is a merely private affair. Two are already a social relationship. **29.** *Jericho:* Only 15 mi. from Jerusalem (→ Biblical Geography, 73:66). **30.** *Lord, have mercy:* Three times (here [see *app. crit.*], vv 31,33) the blind men address Jesus as Lord; not so in Mark, who uses the archaic *rabbouni,* which meant almost the same thing, "Master." The address quickly entered liturgical use. *Son of David:* See comment on 9:27. **32.** *what do you want:* Jesus humbly asks (cf. vv 24-28 above), though the answer was obvious. **33.** *our eyes may be opened:* Besides the literal meaning, the request suggests a desire for understanding faith on the part of many potential disciples. **34.** *touched:* Matthew adds the notes about the compassion and healing touch of Jesus, while eliminating the words about saving faith. Discipleship to the cross is the result of the healing (see V. K. Robbins, *JBL* 92

[1973] 224–43; E. S. Johnson, *CBQ* 40 [1978] 191–204; R. A. Culpepper, *JBL* 101 [1982] 131–32).

124   (H) The Triumphant Entry into Jerusalem (21:1–11). See Mark 11:1–11; Luke 19:28–38; John 12:12–19. Matthew follows Mark here, yet all is altered by the insertion of the fulfillment citation in vv 4,5. The whole describes a joyous festal procession with messianic overtones. **1.** *Jerusalem:* The capital of Judea, identical with Zion, was the religious center of the people because of the presence of the Temple there (→ Biblical Geography, 73:92–94). *the Mount of Olives:* It towered to the E above the city but had no water supply of its own; so it had only a few villages, like Bethphage, on it. **2.** *the village opposite:* Probably Bethany. There are two animals because of Matthew's overliteral understanding of the prophecy. **3.** *the Lord:* Jesus' foreknowledge and lordship are stressed here to an uncommon degree. Matthew has no time for Mark's petty consideration that the ass would be returned. A messianic revolutionary law prevails, along with festal largesse. **4.** *Tell:* This is the first fulfillment citation since 13:35, and the second to the last (27:9; → 7 above). **5.** Matthew conflates Isa 62:11 with Zech 9:9. *behold your king:* Matthew shapes the quotation to stress the humility and peacefulness of the king. The Hebr parallelism would refer to a single animal in two different ways, "ass, even a colt," but Matthew mistakenly posits two animals. **7.** *he sat on them:* Matthew envisages Jesus riding two animals at once, hard to imagine. The difficulty may be avoided by referring "them" to the garments. **9.** *Hosanna to the Son of David:* Hōsanna means, "Help (or save), I pray." Here it is part of a quotation from Ps 118:25,26, where it has simply become a liturgical acclamation, Hail! or Blessing! This psalm is used in the liturgy of Jewish feasts. *the highest:* This could refer to God. The two hosannas form an *inclusio* around the central blessing. Matt omits Mark's second blessing with its mention of the kingdom (cf. *Did.* 10:6). **10.** *the whole city shook:* Cf. 2:3. The question of Jesus' true identity is posed. **11.** *this is the prophet Jesus from Nazareth:* The crowds have a low christology, and this lends their view historical verisimilitude (see B. A. Mastin, "The Date of the Triumphal Entry," *NTS* 16 [1969–70] 76–82).

125   (I) The Cleansing of the Temple (21:12–17). See Mark 11:15–19; Luke 19:45–48; John 2:13–22. **12.** *cast out all who sold and bought:* This prophetic action is the only incident in the Gospel that connects Jesus with violence. Matthew omits the Marcan description of a blockade of the Temple to soften the new image of Jesus. The court of the Gentiles, where pigeons and other animals were sold for sacrifice and where debased currency was exchanged for "hard" Tyrian shekels, was quite large. How one person could control this whole area is difficult to imagine. The event remains uncertain in historical detail but expresses Jesus' zeal as a religious reformer and his disgust with a bankrupt system; it also expresses Matthew's judgment on a Temple already in ruins when he wrote. **13.** *it stands written:* The OT quotations must be read in their full context. *house of prayer:* It comes from Isa 56:7, but see 56:3–8. *den of thieves:* This comes from Jer 7:11, but the great speech in Jer 7:1–5 denounces excessive trust in the Temple. Cf. Zech 14:21. Matthew omits Mark's "for all nations"; cf. 28:19. **14.** *the blind and lame came to him in the Temple:* This verse is Matthew's great contribution to the unit. In context it calms down the effect of the preceding event. Against the background of Lev 21:16–23 and 2 Sam 5:6–8, it shows the immense differences Jesus has made in human lives—his quiet revolution, which troubles the leaders in v 15. Jesus calls the marginal in Israel to salvation (9:10–13; 11:5; and the children in v 15). **15.** *chief priests*

and scribes: The priests see the danger Jesus poses to the status quo, their collaboration with the Romans. **16.** Jesus quotes Ps 8:3 LXX, historically improbable. **17.** *Bethany:* A village on the Mt. of Olives, it was the home of Mary, Martha, and Lazarus, according to John 11:1 (→ Biblical Geography, 73:95).

126   (J) The Cursing of the Fig Tree (21:18–22). See Mark 11:12–14,20–24. Matthew unites the two parts of Mark's sandwich and abbreviates. Luke omits this story in its historicized form because he has already recorded a parabolic form of it in 13:6–9. **19.** *a fig tree:* A tree is a symbol of life; the fig as the sweetest of Levantine fruits is a biblical symbol of beatitude. Thus, a barren fig tree is a symbol of blighted promise, failure. Perhaps it here represents the failure of the Pharisees and Sadducees to renew the life of the people (21:43). Matthew omits Mark's detail that it was not the season for figs, because this would make Jesus' expectation unreasonable and capricious, and changes a wish into a curse. He heightens the miraculous by having the withering occur immediately rather than overnight. **20.** Strangely, Matthew omits the role of Peter. **21.** *if you have faith and do not doubt:* For Matthew faith is usually mingled with doubt (14:31; 28:17). **22.** *ask in prayer:* Faith leads to prayer, which is the expression of faith.

127   (K) The Authority of Jesus Questioned (21:23–37). See Mark 11:27–33; Luke 20:1–8. Matthew follows Mark closely. The relation of this passage to what follows is that we have the basic dispute over divine authority (vv 23–27), then three harsh parables of judgment (vv 28–32; 33–46; 22:1–14), after which come four more controversy dialogues on particular points: taxation, resurrection, the great commandments, the Son of David (22:15–22,23–33,34–40,41–46). Together they build up the conflict between Jesus and the Jerusalem leaders, which will lead to his excruciating death. **23.** *chief priests and elders:* These refer to the religious and civil lay leaders respectively. *by what authority:* The Gk word *exousia* means both power and authority. In religious matters this is difficult to establish for an outsider. Jesus was not a Jewish priest of the tribe of Levi. The usual methods are a direct appeal to God supported by miracles or an appeal to the tradition of the ancestors. In John, where the question is debated at length (chaps. 5–10) Jesus appeals to his works (10:25,38). *these things:* The reference is to his ministry in general, cleansing the Temple, healing, receiving praise from the crowds, teaching. In rabbinic fashion Jesus asks a counterquestion. **25.** *John:* Jesus appeals to the prophetic tradition in a recent example, JBap. This tradition is a real one in Israel (and in the church), but it is difficult for administrators to handle since it falls outside the law. The law did try to set up tests (Deut 13:1–5), but the debates in Jeremiah (e.g., 29:21,23,31) show how difficult they were to apply. **27.** *we do not know:* By this answer the administrators confess their incapacity in religious matters. This will not prevent them from taking part in the death of Jesus (see Daube, *The New Testament and Rabbinic Judaism* 151–57, 217–23 [→ 76 above]).

128   (L) The Parable of the Two Sons (21:28–32). This parable is the first in a trilogy of parables of judgment. It is a product of Matthean redaction; the second stems from Mark, the third from Q. While thus pointing forward, it is also closely related to the preceding dispute. It is, in fact, a midrashic commentary on 21:23–27. It is transitional, a narrative hinge. All three parables are addressed to the same audience, chief priests and elders (v 23). This passage pronounces their guilt. **28.** *had two sons:* Who are the two sons? The distinction is not between Jews and Gentiles, but between two kinds of Jews, faithless leaders and faithful outcasts (v 31), false and true Israel. But, from this perspective, Gentile converts can also be included among the believing sinners. *vineyard:* See comment on 20:1. **30.** *I go, Lord:* Cf. 7:21. **31.** *did the will of the father:* Obedient faith is always the final test for Matthew. The tax collectors and prostitutes are part of the Jewish *'am hā-'āreṣ*, ignorant and unclean sinners. The shocking paradox that they will enter the kingdom ahead of the others is the heart of the Gospel; cf. Luke 7:29-30. **32.** *the way of righteousness:* This is a phrase common in wisdom literature (Prov 8:20; 12:28; Ps 23:3), not to mention the doctrine of the two ways in QL. The reference to JBap relates the whole to 21:23-27. *you did not repent afterward:* This ending contains an ironic twist. The public sinners (the son who first said no) knew they needed to repent. The leaders by contrast thought they were righteous and thus had no need of repentance. The parable, like its better known counterpart in Luke 15:11-32, the Prodigal Son, contains a psychological truth: the son who first says no resolves his Oedipal conflict by first rebelling and then obeying (see Dupont, *Béatitudes* 3. 213-25; H. Merkel, *NTS* 20 [1973-74] 254-61; A. Ogawa, *NovT* 21 [1979] 121-49).

129   (M) The Parable of the Vineyard and the Wicked Tenants (21:33-46). See Mark 12:1-12; Luke 20:9-19. **33.** *householder:* A favorite Matthean word, which refers to an absentee landlord. There is a loose quotation from Isa 5:1-7. **34.** *when the time of fruit drew near:* Matthew shapes this clause to make the reader think of the near approach of God's kingdom (v 43). **35.** *beat one:* Matthew adds killing and stoning (James?) at this point. **36-37.** Matthew summarizes Mark and omits the adj. "beloved" from "son." **38.** *kill him:* The servants leap to an unreal conclusion; the owner is still alive and can punish them. **39.** Matthew inverts the order of events to fit the view that Jesus died outside the city (John 19:17; Heb 13:12-13). **40-41.** Matthew creates a dialogue in which the harsh answer is ironically given by the very chief priests incriminated by the story. **42.** Ps 118:22-23 is quoted. **43.** *the kingdom of God will be taken from you and will be given to a people producing the fruit of it:* This is Matthew's chief contribution to the interpretation of the parable, which in its present form is an allegory of salvation history. The emissaries are the prophets who have been killed by the people of Israel, culminating in Jesus as the son. "Kingdom" could mean something like the present possession of God's favor and protection, but the fut. pass. vbs. make it probable that it refers to the promise of the full end-time blessing. "People" refers to the church, made up for Matthew primarily of believing Jews but also of converted Gentiles, who together form the new people of God, the true Israel. This conclusion is milder than the parable; the wicked tenants are not destroyed, but the promise is taken from them.

(Dillon, R. J., "Toward a Tradition-History of the Parables of the True Israel," *Bib* 47 [1966] 1-42. Hengel, M., "Das Gleichnis von den Weingärtnern Mc 12:1-12 im Lichte der Zenonpapyri und rabbinischen Gleichnisse," *ZNW* 59 [1968] 1-39. Hubaut, M., *La parabole des vignerons homicides* [Paris, 1976]. Snodgrass, K., *The Parable of the Wicked Tenants* [WUNT 27; Tübingen, 1983].)

130   (N) The Parable of the Marriage Feast (22:1-14). See Luke 14:15-24. The parable unfolds in three acts: (a) vv 2-7, two calls to the proper guests; (b) vv 8-10, a call to the outcasts; (c) vv 11-14, a sorting out at the wedding party. **2.** *a marriage feast:* The kingdom is depicted in its aspect as the messianic banquet, derived from Isa 25:6-10. **3.** *his servants:* The prophets. *the invited:* An invitation is a free act of kindness; God is not obliged to invite. **4.** *all is ready:* The concept "ready, prepared" occurs three times—twice here and once in v 8. It connotes extreme eschatological urgency; the dishes are hot. **5.** *made light of it:* In effect, the invited deny the urgency, they become careless with the things of God. **6-7.** These verses break the logic of the story. They represent an intrusion which historicizes the parable, alluding to the Roman capture of Jerusalem in AD 70. **8.** *worthy:* The guests must show an appropriate moral and spiritual response: cf. 10:10,11,13,37-38. **9.** *road outlets:* The gates and markets of an oriental city, where the crowds swarm. The people there are the outcasts of Israel, the tax collectors and people in despised trades. **10.** *the bad and the good:* Sinners too are invited, and the church in history is a mixed body of saints and sinners, as in 13:37-43,47-50. **11.** *wedding garment:* This represents a converted life full of good deeds. Sinners are invited but are expected to repent. **13.** *bind him hand and foot:* This harsh conduct fits the pattern of salvation history, but does not fit the story line, though large parties do at times require the expulsion of a rowdy guest (cf. 18:17; *m. 'Abot* 4:16). **14.** *the invited are many:* Matthew distinguishes between the initial call of salvation and final election and perseverance. The latter are not automatic. Believers are thus warned against complacency. Matthew has modeled his tradition on the parable of the wicked tenants in 21:33-46 (see further *FGL* 1058-59; C.-H. Kim, *JBL* 94 [1975] 391-402).

131   (O) Paying Taxes to Caesar (22:15-22). See Mark 12:13-17; Luke 20:20-26. This is the first of four units containing controversies with various kind of Jewish leaders—Pharisees, Herodians, Sadducees. **15.** *ensnare:* Entrapment even today is a legal offense. **16.** *with the Herodians:* See comment on Mark 3:6. Matthew subordinates them to the Pharisees because they no longer posed a threat to his church, unlike the heirs of the Pharisees. *you are true:* This means "faithful to your word." The compliment is so fine, the better to conceal their guile. *you do not regard the position of men:* This odd idiom expresses a basic aspect of the biblical idea of justice, an impartiality that refuses to take a bribe and tilts in favor of the poorer litigant. This is the biblical basis for the preferential option for the poor; cf. *TDNT* 6. 779-80. **17.** *is it lawful to pay taxes:* This would have been a true question of conscience for Pharisees, but not for Herodians. To pay meant to acknowledge a foreign pagan sovereignty over Israel. **18.** *hypocrites:* Matthew shifts the offensive word into the direct dialogue. See comment on 6:2; cf. 23:13-29. **19.** *denarius:* See comment on 20:2. **20.** *inscription:* This read "Tiberius Caesar son of the divine Augustus, great high priest." **21.** *render therefore to Caesar:* This is the logion that contains the point of the apophthegm. It is meant neither ironically (which would encourage zealotic violent rebellion) nor quietistically (cf. Hillel, *m. 'Abot* 1:12). It accepts the state as it is as the lesser of two evils, the worse being anarchy. Cf. *m. 'Abot* 3:2: "Pray for the peace of the ruling power, since but for fear of it men would have swallowed up each other alive." It does not accept the state's claim to be divine. (The state can even be demonic; see Rev 13.) Jesus looked to nonviolent social change (5:38-48) and to the kingdom of God as soon to come. God's claim is greater than the state's. Cf. 17:24-27; Rom 13:1-7; 1 Pet 2:13-17; see further O. Cullmann, *The State in the New Testament* (NY, 1957).

132   (P) The Question about the Resurrection (22:23-33). See Mark 12:18-27; Luke 20:27-40. **23.** *Sadducees:* These were the conservative party, which accepted only the Pentateuch as revealed. The Pentateuch and the OT generally did not directly teach resurrection (the great exception is Dan 12:2, late). Cf. Acts

23:8, which means that they did not accept either the Gk understanding of the afterlife as immortality of the soul or the Pharisaic view of it as resurrection of the body. **24.** Deut 25:5,6; Gen 38:8 are conflated; they refer to the levirate institution (→ Deuteronomy, 6:41), as does Ruth 4:1-12. **25-28.** A hypothetical case to show the problems with a belief in resurrection. **29.** *neither the Scriptures nor the power of God:* Book learning does not suffice; you must have faith in a God who acts (cf. 1 Cor 1:24,30). **30.** *like angels in heaven:* Jesus answers their question in Pharisaic fashion. Life in the eschaton will be different (cf. 1 Cor 15:44). **31.** *have you not read?:* Jesus now shifts the conversation to the basic question: Is resurrection taught in the Torah? **32.** Jesus answers by citing Exod 3:6 and building an argument on it, which concludes that the patriarchs are immortal. Since the Sadducees deny this form of afterlife as well, they are fairly hit. But they will soon work their revenge, at the passion.

133   **(Q) The Great Commandment (22:34-40).** See Mark 12:28-34; Luke 10:25-28. **34.** Matthew creates this verse as a transition. **35.** *lawyer:* The Gk word *nomikos* is found only here in Matt, but six times in Luke; it means the same as scribe, one learned in the Torah. **36.** *greatest:* The request is, in effect, a request for a summary of Israel's law or, even deeper, for its center. The Pharisees as the popular party were interested in popular education and summaries were indispensable to that end. The Pharisaic overdevelopment of minor laws, however, threatened a grasp of the essentials (cf. 7:12). **37.** *you shall love:* Jesus cites Deut 6:5. The "love" is not primarily a feeling but covenant fidelity, a matter of willing and doing. *with all your heart . . . soul . . . mind:* The rabbis stressed this part of the commandment: heart meant will, soul meant life, and strength meant wealth. Here Matthew has not translated "strength" but given another translation of "heart" as mind; cf. on 4:1-11. **38.** Jesus sees the law as a unified whole. From the love of God all the other laws can be derived and supported. **39.** *love your neighbor as yourself:* Jesus now cites Lev 19:18, a less central text in Jewish liturgy, but one that becomes important in the NT (Matt 5:43; 19:19; Rom 13:8-10; Gal 5:14; Jas 2:8). The commandment includes a right form of self-love. The combination of these two commands is not clearly attested before Jesus and marks an important moral advance; cf. 1 John 3:17. **40.** *on these two commandments hang all the law and the prophets:* The rabbis said that the world hangs on Torah, Temple service, and deeds of loving-kindness — or, on truth, judgment, and peace (*m. 'Abot* 1:2,18). Matthew makes the law itself depend upon deeds of love.

(Moran, W. L., "The Ancient Near Eastern Background of the Love of God in Deuteronomy," *CBQ* 25 [1963] 77-87. Wallis, G., *TDOT* 1. 101-18.)

134   **(R) The Question about David's Son (22:41-46).** See Mark 12:35-37; Luke 20:41-44. Jesus now interrogates the Pharisees. In this controversy dialogue Matthew clarifies his Marcan source and increases the dialogue. **42.** *what do you think about the Christ?:* As the passion approaches the focus narrows somewhat from the kingdom to the Christ. The question is a real one, since messianic speculation was not unified at the time in Judaism; a variety of messianic figures were expected (→ OT Thought, 77:152-54). The Pharisaic answer here fits Matthew's own view, which from 1:1 on affirms Jesus as son of David. **43,45.** *if David . . . calls him Lord, how is he his son?:* The twice-repeated question reflects the basic conflict between the superiority of the past (traditions and ancestors) and the new work that God is working and will complete (the

kingdom of God and the Christ), between the myth of origins and the power of the future. Both have value, as do old and new wine, but Jesus fights for an openness to the new, the superiority of David's son to David himself. **44.** *the Lord said to my Lord:* The quotation is from Ps 110:1, a text that had an immense influence on the early church; see Acts 2:29-36; Heb 1:13; 1 Cor 15:25-28. **46.** *no one was able to answer him:* The doctrinal helplessness, not to say bankruptcy, of the religious leaders of the time on the major issues of kingdom and Christ is the presupposition for the great attack that follows (chap. 23) and the great discourse on the end-time woes that will usher in the kingdom. Their only response is the passion. The counter-response is the resurrection and the great commission (see further J. A. Fitzmyer, "The Son of David Traditions and Mt 22:41-46 and Parallels," *ESBNT* 113-26).

135   **(X) Woes and Eschatological Discourse (23:1-25:46).**

(A) Woes against the Scribes and Pharisees (23:1-36). See Mark 12:38-40; Luke 11:37-52; 20:45-47. This chapter is a hinge which concludes the series of parables of judgment and controversies with the Jewish leaders, which began in 21:23, and at the same time introduces the last great discourse in chaps. 24-25, on the parousia. It is composed of material from Mark, Q, and Matthew's own special material. Although it contains some ugly controversy, it is of historical interest both because it helps us to see the background of the crucifixion and, on a second level, because it shows us the Matthean community in polemical dialogue with the rival academy in Jamnia. **2.** *sat on Moses' seat:* The past tense suggests that their authority is also past. Moses' seat is a metaphor for Moses' authority. The Pharisees claimed to stand in his succession (*m. 'Abot* 1:1). The phrase may refer to their "seat" at Jamnia. **3.** *do all:* Much of their teaching was sound, at least in showing zeal for God and the OT, but for Matthew their practice does not follow. Except as irony this is a puzzling verse. **4.** Cf. 11:28-30. **5.** Cf. 6:1,5,16. **6.** Cf. Luke 14:7-11. **8.** *do not be called rabbi:* Verses 8-10 contain a critique of titles carefully constructed by Matthew. Rabbi (lit., "my great one") had only recently come into use (AD 60-80) as a technical term for an authorized Jewish teacher-sage. Its rejection is part of Matthew's feud with those who bore it. **9.** Saul ben Batnith (*ca.* 80-120) was the first known Jewish sage to bear the title *Abba,* father. Despite this prohibition the title crept back into Christianity through the monastic movement, where it first served as a term for a spiritual director. Matthew's own list of preferred titles comes in v 34. **10.** *teacher:* Christians have only one teacher, Christ, in the sense that they are lifelong disciples of him alone. Other teachers play a transitory role. **11.** *greatest:* Matthew reinforces the teaching on humility with references to 20:26,27 and use of Q (Luke 14:11). **13-33.** Now comes a terrible section of seven woes, corresponding to the Beatitudes in chap. 5 and modeled on Isa 5:8,11,18,20,21,22. **13.** *woe to you, scribes and Pharisees, hypocrites:* Matthew flattens out the opposition to Jesus, which, in fact, came from several directions, and unifies it to correspond to the opponents of his own church. But these woes are addressed also to his church to warn it against complacency. On "hypocrites," see comment on 6:2. Ultimately here the Pharisees are accused of being false teachers because they do not accept the teaching mission of Jesus as the Christ. **15.** *you travel sea and land:* This is a great backhanded compliment to the Pharisees for their Diaspora mission, on whose foundations Paul built (see B. J. Bamberger, *Proselytism in the Talmudic Period* [Cincinnati, 1939]). **16-22.** Cf. 5:33-37. **23.** Cf. Lev 27:30; Deut 14:22,23; Zech 7:9;

Mic 6:8. *the weightier matters of the law:* Against this the rabbis resisted distinguishing light and heavy precepts (*m. 'Abot* 2:1; 3:19; 4:2; *m. Ḥag.* 1:8). *without neglecting the others:* This represents Matthew's Jewish-Christian viewpoint that the whole Torah is to be observed, but as interpreted by Jesus (5:17-20). **25-26.** These verses take up a debate current in the houses of Hillel and Shammai and turns the debate into a moral matter; people, not utensils, are what matter (J. Neusner, *NTS* 22 [1975-76] 486-95). **34.** *behold, I send you prophets and wise men and scribes:* This contains a list of leaders in Matthew's church. *Apostellō,* "send," alludes to apostles. See comments on 10:40-42. The titles come from the OT. **35.** *Abel:* See Gen 4:8,10. *Zechariah the son of Barachiah:* There is confusion here. He bears the name of the eleventh of the 12 minor prophets, who is also called "son of Iddo" (Ezra 5:1), but he is not known to have been slain. Zechariah, son of Jehoiada (2 Chr 24:20-22) may be the person meant. Some commentators think it is Zechariah, son of Baris or Baruch, known from Josephus, *J.W.* 4.5.4 § 334-44.

136   (B) The Lament over Jerusalem (23:37-39). See Luke 13:34-35; cf. Luke 19:41-44. This Q passage forms the poignant climax of chap. 23. It portrays Jesus as personified divine wisdom bearing a message of salvation from God (cf. 11:28-30; Sir 24:7-12; Lam). Matthew omits the story of the widow's mite to join this chapter to chap. 24. *Jerusalem:* An apostrophe with a double vocative is OT style. By this time the violent death of the prophets had become a convention (Acts 7:52). *how often:* Jesus visited Jerusalem frequently though Matthew records only one visit. The image of the mother hen nestling her brood of chicks suggests care, protection, and love (cf. Isa 31:5; Deut 32:11; Ps 36:7). **38.** *house:* An allusion to Jer 22:5 and the events of AD 70. **39.** Notice the *inclusio* with 21:9, where Ps 118:26 is also cited. The prophetic warning looks forward to the coming of the Son of Man with judgment and the kingdom. Notice the repetition of "from now on" in 26:29,64.

(Frankemölle, H., *Biblische Handlungsanweisungen* 133-90. Garland, D. E., *The Intention of Matt 23* [NovTSup 52; Leiden, 1979]. Stanton, G. N., "The Gospel of Matthew and Judaism," *BJRL* 66 [1984] 264-88.)

137   (C) The Eschatological Discourse (24:1-25:46).
    (a) THE DESTRUCTION OF THE TEMPLE AND THE BEGINNING OF THE WOES (24:1-14). See Mark 13:1-13; Luke 21:5-19. The apocalyptic discourse proper now begins (→ OT Apocalyptic, 19:3-4,23); it will run to the end of chap. 25 and is arranged concentrically around the actual description of the parousia in 24:29-31 (J. Dupont). Matthew depends on Mark 13 but expands his source by two thirds, primarily through his parenetic emphasis, which culminates in the great description of the last judgment. **1,2.** Cf. 21:23. Matthew shifts our attention away from the Temple and the beauty of its Herodian masonry to the fate of the whole city (cf. Mic 3:12). **3.** *the Mount of Olives:* From there one has a good view of the city and Temple. Matthew broadens the audience for the discourse from Mark's four to "the disciples" as a group. He also introduces the term *parousia,* "coming," "arrival," here and in vv 27,37,39. He is the only evangelist to use it, though it is common in the epistles. It originally referred to the majestic entry of a Hellenistic king. The focus of the discourse is the parousia of the Son of Man. *close of the age:* Cf. 28:20. **5.** *I am the Christ:* For Matthew the great danger of error is in christology. **6.** *the end:* Cf. Dan 2:28. The war that would rage AD 66-70 was already brewing. **7.** *nation*

against nation: Cf. Isa 19:2; 2 Chr 15:6. **8.** *all these are the beginning of the woes:* The woes are called the birthpangs of the Messiah in Jewish apocalyptic. **9.** Matthew departs from Mark here because he has already used this material in 10:17-22. *all the nations:* Cf. 28:19. **10.** *shall fall away:* Cf. Dan 11:41. The woes that will afflict the community—scandal to the point of apostasy, betrayal, and internal divisions to the point of hatred—are those that afflict any religious group under stress, but they will be extreme at the end. **11.** *false prophets:* These are a special concern of Matthew (7:22). **12.** *because lawlessness is increased the love of many will grow cold:* With a pastor's expert eye, Matthew diagnoses the sickness of the community in chilling terms (see further J. Dupont, *Les trois apocalypses synoptiques* [LD 121; Paris, 1985]).

138   (b) THE GREAT TRIBULATION (24:15-28). See Mark 13:14-23; Luke 21:20-24. 15. *the abomination:* An allusion to the violation of the sanctuary described in 1 Macc 1:54; 6:7; the terms come from Dan 9:27; 11:31; 12:11. Matthew makes precise the grammar and the references to Daniel and to the place. In his context "the reader" should consult Daniel, not Jesus' speech. **16.** *flee to the mountains:* Judea consists of small mountains. The point could be: valley-dwellers, move to the hills: to the smaller towns, desert caves, and hills of Moab across the Jordan. **18.** *not turn back:* An allusion to Lot's wife (Gen 19:26,17). **19.** This leads to further advice to women. **20.** *nor on the sabbath:* This note added by Matt suggests that his community observed the sabbath. **21.** Cf. Dan 12:1. Matthew adds "great." **22.** *those days will be shortened:* Matthew uses the theological passive (*ZBG* § 236): God will shorten. The verse is concentrically constructed. "The elect" are those whom God loves, esp. those who suffer. God is in control, so that there is no reason for despair even in the midst of tribulations. **24.** Cf. v 11. **25.** *I have told you beforehand:* The point of the discourse is to enable believers to prepare themselves for the trial. **26.** Cf. v 23. The Messiah's coming this time will not be humble or hidden. **27.** *the parousia of the Son of Man:* This is Matthew's label for the whole event, which will be universal and all-encompassing in its scope. **28.** *there will the eagles gather:* A proverbial way (Job 39:27-30) to refer to a public event.

139   (c) THE COMING OF THE SON OF MAN (24:29-31). See Mark 13:24-27; Luke 21:25. This section is the centerpiece of chap. 24, which answers, while correcting, the question in v 3. Matthew expands Mark by a fuller use of the OT and a heightening of christology in v 30. **29.** *the sun will be darkened:* The end is described with cosmic portents from Isa 13:10. **30.** *the sign of the Son of Man:* The sign is the Son of Man himself. Matthew produces a Gk pun: *kopsontai,* "beat the breast," *opsontai,* "see." *with power and much glory:* This is a way of referring to the kingdom of God. The combined quotation from Zech 12:10 and Dan 7:13,14 recurs in Rev 1:17. **31.** *his angels:* God's angels will become the agents of the Son of Man at the gathering of the elect from the entire universe. Cf. Isa 27:13; Zech 2:6; Deut 30:4.

140   (d) THE LESSON OF THE FIG TREE (24:32-35). See Mark 13:28-31; Luke 21:29-33. The concentric ring returns to the idea of v 15. *when you see:* This refers to the time just before the parousia. **32.** *summer is near:* The language of nearness reminds us of the initial proclamation of the nearness of the kingdom (3:2; 4:17). Here the Greek could be translated, "he is near" (so the RSV) or "she/it is near." Luke takes it to refer to the kingdom. Actually kingdom of God and Son of Man are inseparable; one implies the other. **34.** *this generation shall not pass away until:* This is a troublesome verse. The death and resurrection of Jesus as an anticipated parousia fulfill part of it, as does the fall of Jerusalem in AD 70, but neither fulfills "all these things." The greatest event, the coming of the Son of Man with the kingdom, is still to come (5:18). Matthew's answer to this difficulty begins in v 36 and continues to the end of chap. 25, concerning the unknown day and hour and the delay of the parousia. **35.** *my words shall not pass away:* Cf. Isa 40:8. Jesus' word is like God's word in the OT, abiding in truth and sureness.

141   (e) THE UNKNOWN DAY AND HOUR (24:36–44). See Mark 13:32–37; Luke 17:26–30,34–36. In this section Matthew draws upon Q except for vv 36 and 42 (from Mark). **36.** *nor the Son but only the Father:* This verse states the principle that no one knows the exact time of the parousia. The principle will dominate the entire passage, while v 42 will begin to draw parenetic consequences, which will continue to 25:13. In itself, the verse blocks calculations of the end. Matthew stresses that "only" the Father knows. Since the Son (of God) is ignorant of the hour, this verse has a lower christology than v 30, yet the absolute use of the term Father and Son reminds us of 11:27 and points to a Marcan-Q overlap of idiom, a criterion of authenticity. Sharing our human condition, the Son shared also our partial ignorance. **37.** *Noah:* Cf. Gen 6:11–13 and note the *inclusio* with v 39. **38.** The men of Noah's day drew the wrong conclusion from their ignorance of the time of the flood and were careless in the things that pertain to God. **39.** *they did not know:* Matthew makes their foolish and culpable ignorance explicit. **40,41.** These verses mark a transition to moral exhortation. **40.** *in the field:* Matthew chooses a more dignified setting than Luke's two men in a bed. **41.** *two women:* The pattern of twinning parables of men and women continues here. **42.** *watch therefore:* Watchfulness, eschatological alertness to the will of God, will be the main theme to 25:13. **43.** *if the householder had known:* Another little parable makes explicit the connection with watchfulness (in Matt, not in the Lucan parallel). **44.** *you also must be prepared:* Matthew draws the conclusion of the unit, employing a new term, *hetoimoi,* "ready," "prepared," to vary the terminology of vigilance.

142   (f) THE FAITHFUL OR THE UNFAITHFUL SERVANT (24:45–51). See Luke 21:41–48. Matthew now presents a parable from Q, which contrasts two ways of being a servant of the Lord during the time of waiting for his return. We can think of them as two different persons or, better, as one and the same person who can react to his situation in different ways. **45.** *wise and faithful:* In the context of chap. 24 these qualities mean the same as vigilant (v 43) or prepared (v 44). **46.** *blessed is that servant:* The servant who remains faithful during the delay of the master is praised with a macarism and rewarded. **48.** *if that wicked servant:* Matthew cannot wait to moralize. He calls the servant wicked before he has shown him misbehaving. *my master is delayed:* The central problem is the delay of the return of the Lord: the servant errs in calculating on the delay, as though he knew when the Lord would return or that the delay would be long. **49.** *beats his fellow servants:* The servant errs through lack of charity and responsibility. He does not imitate God's forbearance. **50.** *does not expect him:* The servant is in for a surprise, and his miscalculation is shown to have been presumptuous. **51.** *will cut him into pieces:* I.e., the master will punish him with the utmost severity. *weeping and gnashing:* Matthew repeats this eschatological threat, which he found once in his source (Matt 8:12 = Luke 13:28), five times: 13:42,50; 22:13; 24:51; 25:30 (see further F. W. Burnett, *The Testament of Jesus-Sophia* [Lanham, 1981]).

143   (g) THE WISE AND FOOLISH VIRGINS (25:1–13). This is another twin parable, giving the feminine coun-

terpoint to 24:45–51. Partially an allegory, it is a Matthean redactional development of the hint found in Luke 12:35–38 together with the general eschatological teaching of Jesus. The precise matrimonial situation is impossible to reconstruct (e.g., Are the ten virgins betrothed to the one groom? Where is the bride?). Nuptial imagery, employed in Cant, was applied by the rabbis to the relationship between God and his people; cf. Matt 9:14,15; 22:1–14. **1.** *ten virgins:* They represent the disciples, expectant believers (2 Cor 11:2). **2.** *foolish . . . wise:* These premature labels recall 7:24,26; 10:16; 23:17,19; 24:45. The wisdom in question is a practical wisdom about salvation. **5.** *delaying:* The delay of the parousia sets up the problem, the danger of love growing cold (24:12). *all . . . slept:* Thus, absolute vigilance is not so much the point (despite v 13) as readiness (v 10). **6.** *in the middle of the night:* The Son of Man is the Lord of surprises. The cry expresses the longing of the early church for the consummation of the kingdom. **8.** The oil stands for good works (cf. *Num. Rab.* 13:15,16). The foolish ones lack sufficient good works. **9.** *not enough:* The refusal by the wise does not constitute lack of charity or helpfulness. Their good works are not completely transferable. Others can help, but readiness to accept salvation is ultimately a matter of personal responsibility. **10.** *ready:* I.e., for the groom; this is the point of the parable. The shut door means that admission is not automatic. **11–12.** Cf. 7:22,23. **13.** Cf. 24:42.

(Donfried, K. P., "The Allegory of the Ten Virgins . . . ," *JBL* 93 [1974] 415–28. Puig i Tàrrech, A., *La parabole des dix vierges* [AnBib 102; Rome, 1983].)

144   (h) THE PARABLE OF THE TALENTS (25:14–30). A most interesting and many-sided story, it doubtless derives from Q, although there is a germ or vestige of it in Mark 13:34. It could also be understood as a commentary on Mark 4:25. Matthew preserves the simpler, earlier version, whereas Luke conflates it with another story about a throne claimant (Archelaus, 4 BC?). But Luke is likely to be original in the sums of money involved, pounds or minas worth $20.00 each, rather than talents worth $1,000.00 each. The message of the parable can also be read in several ways. In its present context it offers a life-style for the interim before the Son of Man returns, urging us to a responsible use of the master's goods in view of the judgment to come. Moralizing points can also be drawn from the situation, as in 24:48–51. But at an earlier stage, the story may have contained a reproach of a static (Sadducean?) attitude to religious tradition, which refuses to develop it. This view is based on the presence of the word "hand over" in vv 14,20,22, a technical term for tradition. **15.** *talent:* See comment on 18:24. *to each according to his ability:* The combination of the fiscal term "talent" in proximity with the term "ability" has led in modern languages to the use of the term "talent" for gift, aptitude, flair. The recognition of human diversity of abilities and rewards is typically Matthean (13:23). **16.** *worked with them:* The vague vb. allows for trading or investing. *gained:* This vb. is used in religious contexts for winning converts. **18.** *dug in the ground:* He hid his light, guarding the tradition in a static way ('*Abot R. Nat.* 14). **19.** *after much time:* This hints at the delay of the parousia and the settling of accounts at the last judgment. **21.** *faithful:* Here it means trustworthy, risk-taking, as well as believing. *joy of your lord:* This refers to the kingdom of God (Rom 14:17). **24–25.** Cf. Job 23:13–17; *m. 'Abot* 1:3; 2:15; 3:17. **27.** *with interest:* This seems to favor usury and moderate capitalism. **29.** *to him who has:* Cf. Mark 4:25; Matt 13:12; Luke 8:18. The pass. vbs. refer to God's actions. See further L. C. McGaughy, *JBL* 94 (1975) 235–45.

145 (i) THE JUDGMENT OF THE NATIONS (25:31-46). The form of the unit is that of an apocalyptic revelation discourse with much dialogue. It is not a parable, except for vv 32,33. The passage is a masterpiece, the high point and grand finale of the fifth discourse and of the public ministry. But does it stem from Jesus, from Matthew, from the early church, or, as Bultmann has suggested, from Judaism? It has no Synoptic parallels (cf. John 5:29), fits well with Matthew's theology, and employs some characteristic Matthean vocabulary (angels, my Father, just); thus, it could be of Matthean composition. These arguments are not decisive, except for the final form, and in any case the passage reflects Jesus' own concern for preparing oneself to enter the kingdom. This much-loved text presents a practical religion of deeds of loving-kindness, love of neighbor. It has been overinterpreted to say that neither faith in Christ nor membership in the church is necessary for salvation; but, in fact, it is addressed to Christian disciples, and discipleship is understood in a very bold way as identical with care of the needy. This is not a denial of faith; it is of the essence of faith. **31.** *Son of Man:* Cf. Dan 7:9,13,14; Zech 14:5. The Son of Man here acts in the place of God. **32.** *will be gathered:* God will gather (a theological passive [*ZBG* § 236]). *all the nations:* Cf. 24:9,14; esp. 28:19. It refers to all nations, Israel included, not just the Gentiles. *goats:* The word used, *eriphos,* normally means "kid." It may, therefore, represent an animal of less value. **34.** *king:* The Son of Man as king is executing his Father's will. With a blessing he invites the saved to enter the kingdom, which always exists but which we enter when he decides to bring it and admit us to it. **35-36.** This list provides six of the seven corporal works of mercy in the catechetical tradition (the additional one is to bury the dead, despite 8:22). *sick and you visited me:* Both the *RSV* and the *NAB* ("comforted") undertranslate the Gk vb. *episkeptomai,* better taken as "look after," "nurse." Cf. *m. Pe'a* 1:1. **37-39.** Matthew labels them as "just," and they show surprise. They were not trying to buy off God or to force his hand. **40.** *as you did it to one of the least of these my brethren, you did it to me:* This great answer identifies service to the needy with love of Christ. There is currently much debate over whether the "brethren" refers only to Christians or to any people in need. Note that in v 45 the word "brethren" is dropped. A glance at Matthew's usage of the term in nonsibling contexts shows two senses: in one series (12:48-50; 18:15,21,35; 23:8; 28:10) *adelphos* refers to a member of the Christian community; in the other (5:22,23,24,47; 7:3,4,5) it refers to any human being as the object of ethical duty. Verse 40 should be taken in this broader ethical sense. **41-43.** This binary thinking may offend some. It stems from the deuteronomistic theology of a covenant conditioned by human obligation (as opposed to the covenant of unconditional divine commitment, represented in the NT by Paul's theology). It presupposes human moral responsibility and conscience and God taking human actions seriously. **46.** Cf. Dan 12:2.

(Agbanou, V. K., *Le discours eschatologique de Matthieu 24-25* [EBib; Paris, 1983]. Brandenburger, E., *Das Recht des Weltenrichters* [SBS 99; Stuttgart, 1980]. Donahue, J. R., "The Parable of the Sheep and Goats," *TS* 47 [1986] 3-31. Marguerat, D., *Le jugement dans l'évangile de Matthieu* [Geneva, 1981].)

146 (XI) **Death and Rebirth (26:1-28:20).** The passion-resurrection narrative now begins. In the story of the passion, chaps. 26-27, Matthew follows closely his one source, Mark (Q has no passion narrative). His several expansions, at the Last Supper, the arrest, the fate of Judas, at the trial before Pilate (the blood cry, Pilate's

wife's dream, the handwashing), the cosmic portents at the death of Jesus, generally flow from Mark's narrative logic. The guard at the tomb (27:62-66) and their report (28:11-15) he adds for apologetic reasons. The Gospel ends with a brief but magnificent commissioning scene. Matthew develops three main themes that he found in his source: christology (esp. through prophetic knowledge and fulfillment), a polemical emphasis on the responsibility of Jewish leaders and their supporters, and a series of moral examples, primarily that of Jesus, but also of Peter and Judas, the women, other disciples, and the Gentile soldiers.

(Benoit, P., *The Passion and Resurrection of Jesus Christ* [NY, 1970]. Senior, D. P., *The Passion Narrative according to Matthew* [BETL 39; Leuven, 1975].)

147 (A) **The Suffering and Death of Jesus (26:1-27:66).**
(a) THE PLOT TO KILL JESUS (26:1-5). See Mark 14:1-2; Luke 22:1-2; John 11:45-53. **1.** *when Jesus had finished:* See comment on 7:28a. Here the word "all" is added. It refers to the entire public ministry of Jesus, esp. the teaching. Ministry and passion are thus linked. **2.** *the Son of Man is handed over to be crucified:* Jesus shows prophetic knowledge of his destiny (note the prophetic present tense). Matthew adds this prediction to the three he inherited from Mark (Matt 16:21; 17:22; 20:17). The passive "is handed over" shows that God is in control; the passion is part of the divine plan. **3.** *the chief priests and the elders:* See comment on 16:21. Matthew, following Mark, does not mention the Pharisees during the passion story. As such, they were not responsible for what happened. They return in 27:62, after the burial.

148 (b) THE ANOINTING AT BETHANY (26:6-13). See Mark 14:3-9; John 11:1-8. Matthew abbreviates here. The whole is a prophecy in action of Jesus' death. **6.** *Simon the leper:* Perhaps the Pharisee of Luke 7:36-50. In John the man is called Lazarus, and the woman is his sister Mary. **7.** *as he reclined:* This is a Hellenistic posture while dining. The woman's gesture is one of excess, appropriate to love and festivity, which the disciples do not understand. **10.** *a beautiful work:* Jesus affirms that the utilitarian and everyday are not to have exclusive sway. **11.** *the poor you have with you always:* Matthew here eliminates Mark's middle cl., "and when you wish, you can do good to them." He has thus achieved a clearer parallelism between the two clauses that remain. But he has thereby damaged the doctrine of Jesus' answer, based on Deut 15:11, and given a dangerous handle to those who would remain indifferent to the poor. **12.** *toward my burial:* The interpretation of the deed given here sees it as a burial anointing. Others see in it a messianic anointing (1 Sam 10:1; 2 Kgs 9:6; Acts 10:38) or, anachronistically, an extreme unction. **13.** *this gospel:* This refers specifically to the message of the suffering, death, and resurrection. *in memory of her:* Historically women's work has usually gone unrecorded (and unrewarded). Jesus sets himself against this injustice. His recognition of women is returned at the cross (27:55,56).

(Holst, R., "The One Anointing of Jesus," *JBL* 95 [1976] 435-46. Schüssler-Fiorenza, E., *In Memory of Her* [→ 71 above].)

149 (c) JUDAS' AGREEMENT TO BETRAY JESUS (26:14-16). See Mark 14:10-11; Luke 22:3-6. **14.** *one of the Twelve:* Matthew sets up a contrast between the woman's loyal love and the apostle's betrayal. **15.** Matthew turns the transaction into a dialogue. Judas bargains away his Messiah and the priests pay immediately (cf. Mark). *they weighed out thirty pieces of silver:* This alludes to Zech 11:12 (see Matt 27:3,9); Exod

21:32; all occurs according to the divine plan. **16.** *and from then on:* This formula marks important turning points in the life of Jesus (4:17; 16:21). A new phase opens; the cast of characters has been introduced, and the drama can begin.

150   (d) THE PASSOVER WITH THE DISCIPLES (26:17–25). See Mark 14:12–21; Luke 22:7–14,21–23; John 13:21–30. **17.** *prepare . . . to eat the Passover:* The whole feast lasted a week and a day. The city was jammed with pilgrims who rented space. The city's normal population was about 30,000; the pilgrims are calculated at about 130,000. Thus, reservations were necessary. See J. Jeremias, *Jerusalem* 77–84. **18.** Matthew abbreviates by omitting Mark's sign, which has no biblical warrant (cf. 21:1–9, based on Zech 9:9). *my time is near:* The passion is not part of the parousia, but it is a climactic moment in salvation history and is oriented to the *eschaton.* In this broad sense it is eschatological. *I keep the Passover:* A prophetic present. **19.** *as Jesus had charged them:* Matthew emphasizes the disciples' obedience in carrying out Jesus' command. He is in charge. **20.** *he reclined with the twelve disciples:* This notice is important because it makes clear that no one else was present for the Last Supper, contrary to the usual family character of the seder meal, with women and children present. On "disciples," see *app. crit.* In vv 21–24 Matthew follows Mark closely, but in v 22 the loyal disciples address him as Lord, in contrast to Judas' address, rabbi (v 25). **23.** *he who dips with me:* The verse is tightened to make clear that Jesus knows exactly who the traitor is; cf. Mark 14:20. **25.** This verse is unique to Matthew and serves the direct confrontation of the betrayer and the betrayed.

151   (e) THE INSTITUTION OF THE LORD'S SUPPER (26:26–30). Mark 14:22–26; Luke 22:15–20; 1 Cor 11:23–25. Matthew follows Mark closely, but in v 26 he adds the command to "eat," and in v 27 he turns the statement that they drank into another command, "drink." He thus strengthens the authority of Jesus and the impression of a liturgical rite. **28.** *poured out for the forgiveness of sins:* Matthew adds the last phrase, derived remotely from Lev 17:11 (rules for sacrifice), to relate the eucharistic rite to the impending death on the cross, as of atoning saving significance (cf. Exod 24:8; Jer 31:31–34). He had denied this significance to John's baptism in 3:2 (cf. Mark 1:4), now to attach it to the cross and eucharist. **29.** *from now on:* Matthew adds this phrase to signify a decisive turning point in salvation history. After the passion and resurrection believers have nothing more to look for from God save the kingdom in its fullness. *with you:* Matthew adds this phrase as an echo of the Emmanuel prophecy in 1:23 (cf. 18:20; 28:20). The phrase is also a reference to the covenant formulary of the OT, whose full form runs, "I shall be your God and you shall be my people." Matthew thus stresses the covenantal nature of the meal, already stated in v 28. The meal as a whole is presented as a reinterpreted Passover supper. Jesus identifies the elements of the meal with his broken and bleeding body on the cross. Since this implies foreknowledge, some critics question the authenticity of these words. But all agree that v 29 authentically reflects Jesus' kingdom faith and anticipation of the messianic banquet (Isa 25:6). The meal is the culmination of Jesus' earlier meals with his disciples and with sinners (9:9–13). **30.** *when they had sung a hymn:* The hymn in question is the Hallel, Pss 115–18. *Mount of Olives:* Cf. David's flight there from Absalom's revolt (2 Sam 15:30,31). According to *Tg. Neof.* Exod 12:42, four great events of salvation history took place or were to take place on Passover night: the creation of the world, the binding of Isaac (Gen 22), the exodus from

Egypt, and the coming of the messiah (see R. Le Déaut, *La nuit pascale* [AnBib 22; Rome, 1963]).

152   (f) PETER'S DENIAL FORETOLD (26:31–35). See Mark 14:27–31; Luke 22:31–34; John 13:36–38. In this short passage Jesus makes three predictions, and they will all be fulfilled in the rest of the story. Recall the earlier prediction about Judas (26:20–25). Here two predictions are of cowardly betrayal and one of resurrection and its aftermath. **31.** *all:* Jesus' first prediction is of a general betrayal. Matthew adds a more precise reference to the one betrayed and to the time when it will occur ("this night"). He will insert the personal reference again in v 33, and the time reference in v 34; cf. Mark 14:27. Jesus cites Zech 13:7. Striking the lead dog on the snout to cow the pack is a classical political maneuver but does not work in this case because of the resurrection and Peter's residual faith and courage, despite his momentary betrayal. The prediction is fulfilled in 26:56. **32.** *I shall go before you:* The second prediction will be referred to again in 28:7,10 and fulfilled in 28:16–20. The resurrection is here subordinate to the implied command to regroup in Galilee. **34.** *you will deny me:* The third prediction is addressed to impulsive Peter personally. It will be fulfilled in 26:69–75. **35.** *all the disciples:* Their highly touted boast is ironically chided and unmasked; they all flee in 26:56.

153   (g) THE PRAYER IN GETHSEMANE (26:36–46). See Mark 14:32–42; Luke 22:39–46. Matthew remains close to Mark yet makes the three moments of Jesus' prayer stand out more sharply and shifts attention away from Jesus' return to the disciples and to his withdrawal for prayer. **36.** *with them:* Again Matthew hints at the covenant formulary; see comment on 26:29. *Gethsemane:* The name means "oil press," and it was located in the Kidron Valley. This passage and 6:5–15 are the great prayer texts of this Gospel (cf. 14:23). **37.** *Peter and the two sons of Zebedee:* As in 20:20, Matthew drops the names of the two sons. **38.** *very sorrowful:* Jesus' prayer echoes Ps 42:6,12; 43:5. **39.** *but not as I want:* Jesus submits his will in obedience to the divine will. The cup is the bitter cup of his death (cf. 20:22; 26:27,28). **40.** *could you not watch with me:* Not for the last time his disciples disappoint him. **41.** *the spirit . . . the flesh:* These correspond to the two tendencies or *yĕṣārîm,* the good and the evil, of rabbinic psychology. **42.** *prayed:* Matthew models the second prayer on 6:10. **45–46.** The concluding sentences are symmetrically balanced and rounded. The first speaks of Jesus' "hour" of destiny, truth, and supreme trial. The second personalizes that hour in the figure of Judas, "my betrayer." God has tested his Son to see what was in his heart (cf. 2 Chr 32:31). The effect of the prayer is that Jesus can now face his enemies. As with the temptation (4:1–11), the whole scene, as well as the whole passion, can be read as a commentary on the command to love God with all one's heart, soul, and strength, in which Jesus loves his heavenly Father perfectly with his will (v 39), his soul (v 38), and his external well-being (v 45).

(Barbour, R. S., "Gethsemane in the Tradition of the Passion," *NTS* 16 [1969–70] 231–51. Feuillet, A., *L'Agonie de Gethsemani* [Paris, 1977]. Gerhardsson, B., "Jésus livré et abandonné d'après la passion de Saint Matthieu," *RB* 76 [1969] 206–27. Stanley, D. M., *Jesus in Gethsemane* [Ramsey, 1980].)

154   (h) THE BETRAYAL AND ARREST OF JESUS (26:47–56). See Mark 14:43–50; Luke 22:47–53; John 18:3–12. In Matthew this scene is climactic; it is the hour of Jesus' tragic destiny. **47.** *chief priests and elders:* Matthew eliminates the scribes from the list of villains (but cf. 26:57; 27:41); thus, the Pharisees are exonerated implicitly. **48.** *a sign:* By using a kiss as a signal for arrest,

[42:155-160] Matthew (26:49-27:19) 671

Judas perverts a gesture of friendship. **49.** *hail:* Matthew adds this word as a further token of falseheartedness. **50.** Matthew adds a bit of dialogue. *friend:* This slightly formal and ironical address is also used in 20:13 and 22:12. *for this have you come:* The cl. *eph' ho parei* is difficult to translate. "It is the kiss (of betrayal which will start the events of the passion) for which you are come"—this has been suggested as the best way to understand it. From this moment Jesus loses control over his body. **51.** *drew his sword:* A disciple cuts off the earlobe of the high priest's servant. This is not an accident in a scuffle but a deliberately intended symbolic gesture. The servant was not a minor domestic but vice-president of the Temple administration. He thus represents the high priest. A mutilated ear, according to Lev 21:18 LXX, disqualifies one from serving as high priest. Thus, the gesture says that a priest who would arrest God's emissary is unfit for office, spiritually bankrupt. **52-54.** This expansion encapsulates many Matthean redactional emphases, didactic and ethical; also interest in the divine paternity, angels, and scriptural fulfillment. The logion in v 52 reflects Jesus' preference for nonviolent resistance (5:39). Cf. Rev 13:10. Different from Luke, the ear is not healed. **56.** Matthew makes clear that the Scriptures are prophetic. All is happening according to divine plan. *then the disciples, all of them, leaving him, fled:* This abandonment by his followers was cause for pain equal to his physical suffering.

155 (i) JESUS BEFORE THE SANHEDRIN (26:57-68). See Mark 14:53-65; Luke 22:54-55,63-71; John 18:12-14,19-24. The historicity of the hearing before the sanhedrin is disputed. There probably was such a hearing, which, however, fell short of a full-scale trial and may have involved some Roman share in its planning. Matthew's account is more compact than Mark's. **57.** *Caiaphas:* Matthew alone so identifies the high priest. Cf. John 18:13. **58.** *to see the end:* This Matthean formulation is more solemn than Mark's "warming himself." **61.** Cf. Mark 13:2. **63.** *adjure you:* Matthew introduces the high priest's question with an oath formula. **64.** *you have said so:* This puzzling formula probably gives a half-affirmative answer, as is easier to see in 26:25. Thus, it would agree with the "I am" of Mark 14:62. Jesus then points to his future exaltation. This part of his answer conflates parts of Dan 7:13 and Ps 110:1. **65.** *he has blasphemed:* Matthew adds this statement to explain the high priest's gesture of tearing his robes. **66.** *deserves death:* Blasphemy was punishable by death (Lev 24:16). **67-68.** By omitting the blindfold and the servants of Mark 14:65, Matthew creates some confusion. The sanhedrin members themselves appear to slap Jesus. Their expanded question shifts from asking him to identify unseen mockers to asking him about unknown mockers.

(Sloyan, G. S., *Jesus on Trial* [Phl, 1973].)

156 (j) PETER'S DENIAL OF JESUS (26:69-75). See Mark 14:66-72; Luke 22:56-62; John 18:15-18,25-27. The threefold accusation-denial schema is not useless repetition. In the Jewish moral theology of apostasy during persecution a private denial was less grave than a public one, and an evasive denial was less grave than an explicit one. In Mark this casuistry works toward an escalation of gravity in Peter's sins: first a private, evasive denial; then a public, evasive denial; finally a public and explicit denial. Matthew has obscured this pattern by introducing a public denial in v 70, an oath in v 72, and a vaguer form of denial in v 74. But he has artistically framed the pericope with the adv. "outside" (vv 69 and 75) and added the emotional word "bitterly" at the very end. The whole fulfills exactly Jesus' proph-

ecy in v 34. This is the last time Peter is mentioned by name (but cf. Mark 16:7); he must also be among the Eleven of 28:16 (see further D. Daube, "Limitations on Self-Sacrifice in Jewish Law and Tradition," *Theology* 72 [1969] 291-304).

157 (k) JESUS BROUGHT BEFORE PILATE (27:1-2). See Mark 15:1; Luke 23:1-2; John 18:28-32. Matthew has composed this editorial bridge with care. He again omits the scribes from the list of decision makers, makes explicit the content of their decision, "to put Jesus to death" (cf. 26:59), and gives the impression that the hearing of 27:57-68 has gone on all through the night. **2.** *Pilate:* He is here mentioned for the first time, and his generic title "governor" accompanies him (→ History, 75:168).

158 (l) THE DEATH OF JUDAS (27:3-10). See Acts 1:18-19. This complex pericope is peculiar to Matt. It probably began as an etiological legend to explain how the potter's field came to be called "the field of blood." It is based on local oral traditions and shares with the version in Acts that Judas suffered a violent death and that there was a connection between his death and the field of blood. The two versions differ on the form of death: hanging in Matt, falling headlong and bursting in Acts. Matthew has introduced the story here to make explicit the fulfillment of the prophecy in 26:24. **3.** *thirty pieces:* See comment on 26:15; cf. 27:9. **4.** *innocent blood:* Cf. 27:24. **5.** *hanged himself:* Judas' suicide can be understood as a case of anomie, a loss of moral bearings once he had betrayed his center of meaning (see E. Durkheim, *Suicide* [Paris, 1897]; and 2 Sam 17:23). **7.** *a burial ground for strangers:* The place was also used for plague victims, criminals, and paupers. **9.** This is the last of the 11 fulfillment citations (→ 7 above). It is a complex use of Zech 11:12,13; Exod 9:12; Jer 32:6-15, esp. v 7; 18:2; 19:1-2; 7:30-34. Although Jeremiah is only alluded to, the introduction mentions him because he was a man of sorrows, a prophet of judgment and condemnation.

(Benoit, P., *Jesus and the Gospel* [NY, 1973] 1. 189-207. Senior, D. P., *Passion Narrative* [→ 147 above] 343-97.)

159 (m) JESUS QUESTIONED BY PILATE (27:11-14). See Mark 15:2-5; Luke 23:3-5; John 18:33-38. **11.** Matthew introduces the Roman trial in a formal juridical way. *are you the king of the Jews?:* Pilate's question is suited to a Gentile magistrate and contrasts with the high priest's question, "Are you the Christ?" (26:63). But the title "Christ" reappears in vv 17 and 22. For "king of the Jews," see 2:22; 27:29,37,42-43. Jesus' answer is half-confirmatory, as in 26:25,64. In effect, he says to Pilate: you have answered your own question. **12.** If no one presses specific charges, there can be no trial; only Luke 23:2 gives a concrete list (cf. John 11:48).

160 (n) JESUS SENTENCED TO DIE (27:15-26). See Mark 15:6-15; Luke 23:13-25; John 18:39-19:16. **15.** *release one prisoner:* The so-called *privilegium paschale* or custom of amnesty for a prisoner at Passover is not attested outside the Gospels, though the idea of amnesties on special occasions was not unknown, and *Papyrus Florentinus* 61.59-64, from Egypt, may contain a partial parallel. Matthew has overinterpreted Mark by making it a custom. **16.** *Barabbas:* A few early mss. read "Jesus Barabbas." *Barabbas* means "son of the father." Thus there is a contrast between Jesus Barabbas and Jesus Christ. Instead of "Jesus called the Christ," Mark reads "king of the Jews" (Mark 15:9). **18.** *out of envy:* This aside about the unworthy motive on the part of these Jewish authorities leads Matthew to develop a contrast in the next verse. **19.** *his wife:* Pilate's wife's dream represents a redactional insertion. Dreams in Matt furnish divine guidance. Here the message that Jesus is "just" suggests that he should be released (cf. v 24). **20.** *the crowds:* They are implicated in the miscarriage of justice for the first time, to culminate in their cry in v 25. Matthew makes explicit the alternative to the release of Barabbas, viz., the death of Jesus. **21.** *which of the two:* Matthew's editing accents the free choice of the crowd. **22.** Matthew changes Mark's "king of the Jews" to "Jesus . . . Christ." *be crucified:* This is the first of three cries for the death penalty (cf. vv 23,25). **23.** *what evil has he done?* This is an indirect statement of Jesus' innocence. The second cry for his death carries a graver guilt since his innocence has just been suggested. **24-25.** These verses represent Matthew's principal redactional intervention in this scene. **24.** *washed his hands:* This gesture at a trial is not a Roman, but an OT practice: Deut 21:6-9; Ps 26:6; 73:13. By both gesture and word Pilate declares his innocence before God, though this declaration is not impressive in view of his acquiescence in v 26. *see to it yourselves:* Cf. v 4. **25.** *all the people:* This includes the priests, the lay elders, and the crowd. *his blood be upon us:* Cf. 2 Sam 1:16; Jer 26:15; 51:35; 1 Kgs 2:33. Matthew sets up a contrast between Pilate's claim to be innocent and the people's claim to be responsible. The blood curse contains no "forever" cl., unlike 1 Kgs 2:33. The bitter, ugly character of the verse can only be understood as the result of contemporary polemic and in the light of Matthew's historical perspective (see comment on 21:43). It is a human being's word, not God's or Jesus'; 26:28 gives Jesus' word on the meaning of his blood. **26.** *scourged:* Prisoners were flogged to weaken them so as to shorten the horrid agony on the cross. *he delivered him:* Pilate remains ultimately and concretely responsible, despite Matthew's redactional efforts.

(Kampling, R., *Das Blut Christi und die Juden* [NTAbh 16; Münster, 1984]. Mora, V., *Le Refus d'Israël* [LD 124; Paris, 1986].)

161   (o) THE SOLDIERS MOCK JESUS (27:27-31). Mark 15:16-20; John 19:2-3. The mocking of Jesus as a king is a gesture of momentary moral chaos with affinities to the Roman Saturnalia festival and to all the mock king occasions going back to ancient Babylonia. Jesus has already been rudely mocked in 26:67-68. Matthew tidies up Mark's order: first Jesus is stripped (though he must have already been stripped for the flogging in v 26), then he is clothed in the scarlet cloak, then stripped again, then garbed in normal clothes. **28.** *scarlet cloak:* It was worn by soldiers and is thus historically more probable than Mark's purple. **29.** *a reed:* Matthew adds this as a scepter to increase the grotesquerie.

162   (p) THE CRUCIFIXION OF JESUS (27:32-44). See Mark 15:21-32; Luke 23:26-43; John 19:17-27. Matthew follows Mark closely here, but strengthens the references to Pss 22 and 69. Three groups deride Jesus: passers-by, the authorities, and the robbers. The humiliating, inglorious excruciating death shatters any mythic tendency in the life of Jesus. A slave's death on the cross is not poetry but bitter historical reality. Matthew's editing will introduce some mythic details in vv 51-53 in order to interpret the cross, but the cross itself remains firmly historical. **32.** *Simon:* Matthew omits the names of the sons of this man from Cyrene (cf. Mark 15:21). *to carry his cross:* In John 19:17 Jesus carries his own cross. **33.** *Golgotha:* A small stone hill just outside the city walls near an abandoned quarry. **34.** Matthew gives a closer allusion to Ps 69:22 and thus omits Mark's pain-killing drug. See the further reference in v 48. **35.** See Ps 22:19. **36.** Matthew stresses the watching of the guards, as in 27:62-66; 28:11-15. **37.** *This is Jesus:* Matthew adds these words to the Marcan form of the title on the cross,

which states the legal grounds for his execution. *king of the Jews:* This title would be read differently by Jews and Romans, the first seeing it as a claim to be messiah, the second as the token of rebellion against the emperor. **39.** Cf. Ps 22:8; 109:25; cf. Lam 2:15. **40.** *if you are the Son of God:* Matthew adds these words to elevate the theological level of the derision; cf. the devil's taunts in 4:3,6. **41.** Matthew provides a full list of the leaders responsible for the death of Jesus; see comment on 16:21. **42.** From the viewpoint of Christian faith Jesus is savior not by evading the cross but by enduring it. **43.** Cf. Ps 22:9. **44.** *robbers:* Matthew clarifies the reviling by an explicit reference to those of v 38.

(Hengel, M., *Crucifixion* [Phl, 1977]. Kuhn, H.-W., "Die Kreuzesstrafe," *ANRW* II/25.1, 648-793; "*Stauros, ou,*" *EWNT* 3. 639-49.)

163   (q) THE DEATH OF JESUS (27:45-56). See Mark 15:33-41; Luke 22:44-49; John 19:28-30. **45.** *darkness:* Cf. Gen 1:2; Exod 10:22; Amos 8:9. According to Mark 15:25,33-34, Jesus suffered on the cross for about six hours. Matthew omits the first time-reference. **46.** *Eli, Eli:* Jesus' cry of dereliction comes from Ps 22:1. Matthew may quote it in Hebrew except for the last word, Aram *šĕbaq,* "leave," "abandon." The words express Jesus' feeling of abandonment, but not despair, since they are a prayer to God. **47.** *calling Elijah:* There is a play on '*Elî,* "my God," and '*Eliyyâ,* "Elijah." **48.** Cf. Ps 69:22 and v 34 here. **49.** *save:* Matthew changes Mark's "take down" to the theologically more appropriate "save." **50.** Cf. v 46. *yielded up his spirit:* Matthew's wording stresses the voluntary nature of Jesus' death. **51.** *veil of the Temple:* The torn veil symbolizes a new era of salvation history, in which the Temple would not be a building. **51b-53.** These verses constitute a Matthean midrashic gloss in paratactic style. For a similar cosmic portent, see 2:2. The OT apocalyptic background is found in Joel 2:10; Ezek 37:12; Isa 26:19; Nahum 1:5-6; Dan 12:2. Together these verses answer the mockery of 27:43 and begin the process of divine vindication: Jesus' death is life-giving. **54.** *the centurion:* Matthew integrates this man's confession (identical with that of the disciples in 14:33) into his own perspective by motivating it through the events narrated in vv 51-53 and turns it into a chorus by associating others with it. **55.** *many women:* Matthew straightens out Mark's text by placing the general statement before the particulars, and he adds a reference to the mother of James, Joseph, and the sons of Zebedee (see comment on 20:20). The presence of the faithful and courageous women contrasts with the absence of the Twelve and shows the power of love.

(Senior, D. P., "The Death of Jesus and the Resurrection of the Holy Ones (Mt 27:51-53)," *CBQ* 38 [1976] 312-29.)

164   (r) THE BURIAL OF JESUS (27:57-61). See Mark 15:42-47; Luke 23:50-56; John 19:38-42. Matthew changes his Marcan source quite a bit here, besides abbreviating. He makes the details less Jewish and more Christian and escalates the dignity and grandeur of the proceedings. In general the burial serves to underline the reality of the death of Jesus (against gnostics and others who would deny it) and to prepare for the account of the resurrection. **57.** *evening:* Matthew shifts Mark's reference to the sabbath to v 62, and even there it is oblique. *Joseph of Arimathea:* From Ramathaim north of Lod; he is no longer said to be a member of the sanhedrin, which was after all responsible for the death of Jesus, but is rather "a disciple of Jesus" (cf. Luke 23:51), a more specifically Christian way of looking for the kingdom of God (Mark). He is said to be "rich" to explain the enhanced status of the tomb. **58.** *went to Pilate:* Matthew omits Pilate's interrogation of the centurion in Mark 15:44 because he will use the military in vv 62-66; 28:11-15 for a different purpose. **59.** *shroud:* The vulgar Marcan detail that the shroud was bought is replaced by the dignified detail that it was "clean." **60.** *tomb:* The tomb is now "new" (contrast Mark 15:46) and intended for Joseph himself, who had it cut; and the stone in front of it is now "great" (a detail from Mark 16:4). These magnifying details lack verisimilitude, since according to recent excavations the tomb was undoubtedly in an abandoned quarry, i.e., not a splendid location (→ Biblical Archaeology, 74:150). Mark's more modest account fits the site better. Criminals were to be buried the same day (Deut 21:22-23). **61.** The faithful women are present as witnesses to the correct site, not only as mourners. Since women's testimony was of little value in Jewish law, this detail is worthy of historical credence.

(Coüasnon, C., *The Church of the Holy Sepulchre in Jerusalem* [Oxford, 1974]. Parrot, A., *Golgotha and the Holy Sepulchre* [London, 1957]. Smith, R. H., "Holy Sepulcher, Church of the," *IDBSup* 413-15.)

165 (s) THE GUARD AT THE TOMB (27:62-66). This and its companion piece (28:11-15) are peculiarly Matthean passages motivated by late apologetics. Matthew had already mentioned a guard (vv 36,54). Here the key words are "secure" (three times), "fraud" (twice), and the surprising latinism *custodia*, "guard" (twice). **62.** *after the day of Preparation:* Some interpreters think the visit to Pilate would have been a violation of the sabbath, but this is not certain and is not stressed by the text. Both the time and the guard are developed out of Mark 15:42,44,45. The Pharisees reappear (the last mention of them was in 23:26), perhaps as a hint of the polemical situation in Matthew's own day. **63.** See 16:21; 17:23; 20:19; cf. 12:40; 26:61; 27:40. **66.** The sealing of the tomb may allude to Daniel in the lions' den (Dan 6:17).

166 (B) **The Resurrection and Great Commission (28:1-20).**
(a) THE RESURRECTION OF JESUS (28:1-10). See Mark 16:1-8; Luke 24:1-12; John 20:1-10. After the anticipated general vindication in 27:51-54 comes the personal vindication of Jesus through God's raising him from the dead bodily. This event, accessible only to faith, is not yet the fullness of the kingdom on earth, but it points to the permanent kingdom in heaven. Matthew's presentation is characterized by an increase in dignity and splendor over against the Marcan source. **1.** *toward the dawn:* The luminous event begins in the predawn darkness. Again Matthew eliminates the buying (of spices, this time) as well as the anointing, since the guards would make this impossible. The women (two, to fit with 27:61, not three as in Mark) come to gaze and to mourn. **2.** *great earthquake:* It reminds us of 27:51-54. *an angel:* Mark's "young man" has become such. *rolled back the stone:* The stone blocking the tomb was the victory monument of death. Rolled back and with the angel sitting upon it, it becomes the symbol of victory over death. Like the virginal conception it is a small outward sign of a greater invisible reality. **3.** *white:* The angel's appearance reminds one of the transfigured Christ (17:2). **4.** Cf. 27:54. Fear and awe are a theme that recurs in vv 5,8. **5.** *I know:* Matthew stresses the angel's knowledge; in this he is like a good disciple (13:51). **6.** *as he said:* See comment on 27:63. Matthew adds the note of prophetic fulfillment, one of his special interests (cf. 12:40; 16:21; 17:23; 20:19; 26:32). **7.** *he has been raised from the dead:* Matthew adds this creedal formula to make the resurrection message explicit. He omits the mention of Peter, perhaps because this has been treated in 16:17-19, but also because he plans a final address to the disciples as a group in vv 16-20. That they will see the risen Lord in Galilee suggests (a) that they have been forgiven their betrayal, (b) that Galilee is a place of vision and grace. **8.** *ran:* Matthew hastens the tempo, but mingles the women's "fear" with "great joy" (in place of Mark's ecstasy). The psychological incongruity of simultaneous fear and joy has been likened to the emotions of one about to be married. The women become apostles to the apostles, and their testimony, precisely because discountable in rabbinic law, becomes historically credible. **9.** *Jesus met them:* The tradition of a christophany or appearance of the risen Christ to the women was known elsewhere in early Christianity (John 20:11-18), but Matthew adds v 10. The women's gesture is one of worship but also attests the reality of the resurrection body (cf. 1 Cor 15:44). **10.** The message is a doublet of vv 5,7, but Jesus now calls his followers "brothers," as in John 20:17; Matt 12:46-50. Forgiveness is implied in this. The discovery of the empty tomb is not absolutely essential to the bare minimum of Christian faith (it is not mentioned in the creeds or early kerygma, e.g., 1 Cor 15:3-5), but it is an external support for that faith. In strict logic, empty tomb and resurrection do not necessarily entail each other: Jesus could have risen and the corpse be in the tomb; Jesus could have not risen and the tomb be empty (the corpse could have been stolen). But the two fit together well and are asserted by the evangelists.

(Fuller, R. H., *The Formation of the Resurrection Narratives* [Phl, 1980]. Perkins, P., *Resurrection* [GC, 1984].)

167 (b) THE REPORT OF THE GUARD (28:11-15). This peculiarly Matthean section picks up the thread of 27:62-66; 28:4, and, together with them, reflects the apologetics and polemics of the AD 80s or 90s, as v 15 suggests, though administrative cover-ups and hush money are familiar to many historical periods. **11.** *some of the guard:* The emissaries are contrasted with the women evangelists. This shows that the same message can be received by some as good news, by others as disastrous. **12.** *sufficient money:* Cf. 27:3-10. **13.** *tell the people:* In addition to asking the soldiers to take a bribe, the leaders now ask them to lie and offer an alibi for their dereliction of duty, which could entail maximum penalties. There is an ironic contrast with 27:64. **14.** *to the governor's notice:* The elaborate contingency planning for a worst-case scenario manifests the difficulties in the tangled operation. **15.** *did as they were instructed:* The leaders have become teachers of sin. Spiritual bankruptcy commonly endeavors to cover its emptiness with financial clout. *among Jews to this day:* The lack of the article in front of "Jews" could mean "some Jews," since the word Jews normally takes the article in Gospel usage. Some of Matthew's community still regarded themselves as Jews (10:6; 15:24), even though Jews who followed Jesus rather than the Pharisaic halaka and believed in his gathering of the renewed people of God in view of the kingdom; but those Jews who followed the rabbis of Jamnia were obliged to reject his claims. Matthew's church has been excommunicated by the Jamnian synagogue, yet it remains in polemical dialogue with it. Still, there is here a hint of the usage of late NT books (Acts and John) in which Christians are presented as a body standing over against Jews, rather than as a renewal movement within Judaism. The whole passage offers a negative witness to the dangerous power of the resurrection, which some feel must be suppressed at all costs.

168 (c) THE GREAT COMMISSION (28:16–20). See Mark 16:14–18; Luke 24:36–49; John 20:19–23; Acts 1:9–11. This brief ending is so rich that it would be hard to say more or greater things in the same number of words. It has been called an anticipated parousia, a partial fulfillment of Daniel's vision of the Son of Man. Its genre combines elements of an OT enthronement pattern with an apostolic commissioning. **16.** *the eleven disciples:* This number alludes to Judas' sorry end. *the mountain where Jesus had appointed them:* This is the mountain of revelation (17:1), where Jesus touched them (17:7). **17.** *saw:* The disciples see an appearance of the risen Jesus, but his words rather than looks are stressed. There is no mention of an ascension because that has coincided with the resurrection. Their worship shows their faith, yet this is mingled with doubt, a common psychological experience which gives hope to moderns. **18–20.** The farewell words of Jesus may be divided into three parts, which refer respectively to past, present, and future. **18.** *all authority . . . has been given:* Note the past tense and the theological passive (*ZBG* § 236); it is God who has bestowed divine authority on Jesus as Son of Man. This authority is that of the kingdom of God (cf. Dan 7:14; 2 Chr 36:23; Matt 6:10). **19.** *go therefore . . . :* The great missionary commission concerns the present. It contains a general command to go forth and make disciples and then two subordinate clauses which explain how this is to be done. *all nations:* This universal call applies to all peoples including their cultures, and even Jewish people who are not yet disciples. After the par-

ticularism of 10:6; 15:24, this command comes as somewhat of a surprise, yet the Gentile mission had been hinted at in 2:1–12; 4:15,16,23–25; 8:5–13; 10:18; 15:21–28; 22:1–10; 24:14; 25:32; 26:13. *Father . . . Son . . . Spirit:* This triadic formula may have its OT roots in the apocalyptic triad of God, Son of Man or Elect One, and Angel found in Dan 7, Ezek 1 (cf. *1 Enoch* 14). Circumcision is not mentioned, probably because of Acts 15:1–29. **20.** *teaching them to observe all that I have commanded you:* The disciples are to carry on Jesus' teaching ministry, thus laying the foundation for Christian education, theology, and other intellectual work. The subject matter of their teaching is the great discourses of Matthew's Gospel, but esp. the Sermon on the Mount, which interprets the OT. The entire task is so daunting that the last verse must offer a promise of future support. *I am with you:* I.e., I am and will continue to be. The covenant formulary forms an *inclusio* with 1:23; cf. 18:20. Jesus is Emmanuel, the divine presence (*shekinah*) with his people as they make decisions, study, pray, preach, baptize, and teach. The gift of the Spirit is not explicitly mentioned, in contrast to John 20:22; Acts 2:1–4, but in Paul the Spirit is the presence of Jesus among us (2 Cor 3:17). *the close of the age:* This refers to the coming of the kingdom of God in its fullness.

(Hubbard, B. J., *The Matthean Redaction of a Primitive Apostolic Commissioning* [SBLDS 19; Missoula, 1974]. Lange, J., *Das Erscheinen des Auferstandenen* [Würzburg, 1973]. Schaberg, J., *The Father, the Son and the Holy Spirit* [SBLDS 61; Chico, 1982].)

43

THE GOSPEL ACCORDING TO LUKE

Robert J. Karris, O.F.M.

BIBLIOGRAPHY

1 Bovon, F., *Luc le théologien* (Neuchâtel, 1978). Cadbury, H. J., *The Making of Luke-Acts* (2d ed.; London, 1958). Caird, G. B., *The Gospel of St. Luke* (PC; Baltimore, 1963). Conzelmann, H., *The Theology of St. Luke* (London, 1960). Creed, J. M., *The Gospel according to St. Luke* (London, 1930). Danker, F. W., *Jesus and the New Age According to St. Luke* (St. Louis, 1972). Ellis, E. E., *The Gospel of Luke* (NCB; GR, 1974). Ernst, J., *Das Evangelium nach Lukas übersetzt und erklärt* (RNT; Regensburg, 1977). Fitzmyer, J. A., *The Gospel According to Luke* (AB 28, 28A; GC, 1981, 1985). Ford, J. M., *My Enemy is My Guest* (Maryknoll, 1984). Grundmann, W., *Das Evangelium nach Lukas* (THK 3; 2d ed.; East Berlin, 1961). Jeremias, J., *Die Sprache des Lukasevangeliums* (MeyerK; Göttingen, 1980). Jervell, J., *Luke and the People of God* (Minneapolis, 1972). Karris, R. J., *Luke: Artist and Theologian* (TI; NY, 1985). Klostermann, E., *Das Lukasevangelium* (HNT 5; 3d ed.: Tübingen, 1975). Lagrange, M.-J., *Évangile selon Saint Luc* (EBib; 8th ed.; Paris, 1948). LaVerdiere, E., *Luke* (NTM 5; 2d ed.; Wilmington, 1982).

Maddox, R., *The Purpose of Luke-Acts* (Studies of the New Testament and Its World; Edinburgh, 1982). Marshall, I. H., *The Gospel of Luke* (NIGTC; GR, 1978). O'Toole, R. F., *The Unity of Luke's Theology* (GNS 9; Wilmington, 1984). Plummer, A., *A Critical and Exegetical Commentary on the Gospel according to St. Luke* (ICC; 5th ed.; NY, 1922). Richard, E., "Luke—Writer, Theologian, Historian," *BTB* 13 (1983) 3-15. Schneider, G., *Das Evangelium nach Lukas* (ÖTK 3/1-2; Gütersloh, 1977). Schürmann, H., *Das Lukasevangelium* (HTKNT 3/1; Freiburg, 1969). Schweizer, E., *The Good News According to Luke* (Atlanta, 1984). Talbert, C. H., *Literary Patterns, Theological Themes, and the Genre of Luke-Acts* (SLBMS 20; Missoula, 1974); *Reading Luke* (NY, 1982). Thompson, G. H. P., *The Gospel according to Luke in the Revised Standard Version* (NClarB; NY, 1972). Tiede, D. L., *Prophecy and History in Luke-Acts* (Phl, 1980).

DBSup 5. 545-94. *IDBSup* 588-60. Kümmel, *INT* 122-51. Wik-Schm, *ENT* 247-72.

INTRODUCTION

2 (I) Authorship; Date and Place of Composition. There are seven major, ancient witnesses about the author: Muratorian Canon, Irenaeus, late 2d-cent. Prologue to the Gospel, Tertullian, Origen, Eusebius, and Jerome. From their testimony one should separate out those items which cannot be deduced from the NT (the author was Luke, a Syrian of Antioch, who wrote a Gospel derived from Paul; he wrote it in Achaia [or Rome or Bithynia]) from those which can be deduced from the NT (he was a physician, a companion or collaborator of Paul). One should accept the tradition that Luke composed this Gospel, for there seems no reason why anyone in the ancient church would invent this datum and make a relatively obscure figure the author of a Gospel. There is no reason to deny that Luke was from Syrian Antioch. Since Luke in Acts shows little acquaintance with Paul's theology and no acquaintance with Paul's letters, it seems that his association with Paul was early and thus before Paul's theology was fully developed, before Paul engaged in serious letter writing to his communities, and before the Jerusalem "Council."

In any case, one looks in vain for more than a trace of Pauline theology in Luke-Acts. Since Luke seems to hail from Syrian Antioch, there is no compelling reason not to place the composition of Luke-Acts in this, the third-largest city in the Roman Empire with a varied population including Jews. Despite the attempt by W. K. Hobart (*The Medical Language of St. Luke* [Dublin, 1882]) to confirm the ancient tradition by proving that Luke's language was indeed that of a physician, subsequent studies have shown that Luke's language was not more technical in scope than that of other authors of his time who we know were not physicians.

3 The tradition of the ancient witnesses is of little help in dating Luke's Gospel. For that we must turn to internal considerations. Luke used Mark, which was written a little before the Jewish War of AD 66-70. Luke 21:5-38 presupposes that Jerusalem has been destroyed; thus, a date after AD 70 is required. Luke-Acts does not reflect knowledge of the bitter persecution of Christians from the latter part of Domitian's rule (AD 81-96). Luke-Acts does not reflect the severe controversy that existed between church and synagogue after the Pharisaic reconstruction of Judaism at Jamnia (AD 85–90). From these considerations one arrives at a date of AD 80–85 for the composition of Luke-Acts. (See *FGL* 35–62; for a differing view, see Maddox, *Purpose*.)

4   (II) Literary Style and Characteristics. The talents of Luke, artist and theologian, include the following, many of which will be emphasized in this commentary. Luke is a master of Greek and can write the elegant Greek of 1:1–4 and the Septuagintal Greek of 1:5–2:52. He adapts Gk literary forms to convey his message, e.g., the symposium genre in 7:36–50; 11:37–54; 14:1–24; the farewell discourse genre in 22:14–38 (and Acts 20:17–38).

Luke uses his sources creatively. By means of parallelism, e.g., the birth announcements and the births of JBap and Jesus, Luke joins together various traditions in 1:5–2:52 to convey his christology. In his account of Jesus' ministry he uses Mark, the sayings source, Q, and his special materials, L, in service of his theology. Thus, while adopting some 60 percent of Mark, he omits Marcan redundancy and, e.g., takes over only one of Mark's feeding stories. He adapts the Marcan theme and structure of Jesus' journey to Jerusalem (8:27–10:52), combining them with materials from Q and L to fashion his own incomparable theology of Jesus' and Christians' journey to God (9:51–19:27). In his account of Jesus' last days Luke redacts Mark and recapitulates many of the themes he has been developing in his Gospel (→ Synoptic Problem, 40:13).

Luke is particularly adept at employing various literary devices to link traditions and sources together. Events predicted in the narrative do come to pass as Luke engages in literary promise and fulfillment. See, e.g., Simeon's prediction that Jesus is set for the rising and fall of many in Israel (2:34), which is fulfilled ofttimes in the rest of Luke-Acts. Luke delights in literary inclusions, e.g., the Gospel begins and ends in the Temple. He revels in parallelism, e.g., Jesus calls for Jerusalemites to repent as he is about to enter Jerusalem and as he exits the holy city. A careful reading of all 52 chapters that comprise Luke-Acts would reveal even more parallelisms, e.g., the prayer of the dying Jesus that his enemies be forgiven corresponds to that of Stephen. Luke employs a dominant geographical schema in his kerygmatic story: from Galilee Jesus journeys to Jerusalem and to God; from Jerusalem the church, gifted by the promised Holy Spirit, journeys to the ends of the earth (Acts 1:8). And even when dealing with theological geography, Luke maintains his bent for parallelism, as he shows that Paul, in Acts, journeys to Jerusalem according to God's will in imitation of Jesus, his Lord. Lucan themes also hold materials together. Take, for example, the theme of prayer: the prayer of praise radiates throughout 1:5–2:52; Jesus' ministry begins and concludes with prayer; the promised Holy Spirit comes upon the primitive community at prayer.

5   (III) Luke's Theology and *Sitz im Leben*. Writing in pluralistic Syrian Antioch in the first years of the ninth decade of the Christian era, Luke addresses a primarily Gentile audience with well-to-do members who are painfully rethinking their missionary thrusts in a hostile environment. Internal and external controversies contribute to the hostile environment. The key question of Luke's communities deals with theodicy: If God has not been faithful to the promises made to God's elect people and has allowed their holy city and Temple to be destroyed, what reason do Gentile Christians, who believe in this God, have to think that God will be faithful to promises made to them? Luke's answer takes the form of the kerygmatic story, which we call Luke-

Acts. In it Luke demonstrates that God through Jesus was faithful to promises made to Israel, but in an unexpected way to include Gentiles, the unclean, the poor, women, Samaritans, rich toll collectors, and assorted other outcasts as well as elect people who are repentant of their initial rejection of Jesus, God's prophet and Chosen One. This Israel is called reconstituted Israel. In it is found continuity with the old.

6   (A) Continuity with the Old. In his Gospel Luke depicts a Jesus who, while at times laying aside prescriptions of the law, is nevertheless an upholder of the validity of the law (see, e.g., 16:17). Paul, too, in Acts defends himself against accusations that he is against the law and the Temple. For the Lucan Paul Christianity stands in the best tradition of Judaism, viz., that of Pharisaism (see the trials of Paul in Acts 21–26). Judaism had a long and fine tradition of prayer. Jesus and the community that follows his way stand in this noble tradition. Judaism is founded on the twelve tribes. In narrating God's establishment of reconstituted Israel, Luke tells how Jesus selected Twelve (6:12–16) and how this Twelve was restored after the death of Judas (Acts 1:15–26). The Gospel begins in Jerusalem and in the Temple. Acts 1–3 details the origins of reconstituted Israel in Jerusalem and in the Temple. From Jerusalem God's word goes out to all the nations (Acts 1:8).

7   (B) Internal and External Controversies. Luke wages theological battles on two fronts. Internally he engages in polemic against Jewish Christians who seek to apply overly strict entrance requirements to those who want to join reconstituted Israel. These Jewish Christians are the "Pharisees" of the Gospel, who object to Jesus' eating habits and association with sinners and toll collectors. Against them Luke employs the symposium genre and has them invite Jesus to dinner only to hear him answer their objections. Against them Luke also develops his view of who are the children of Abraham (e.g., 13:10–17; 19:1–10) and therefore heirs of God's promises. Luke further attacks their position by expanding the notion of who belong to "the poor of God," an image used in the OT and in QL to describe the elect. Social status, ethnic heritage, and religious self-justification do not qualify for membership in this exclusive group. The lame, blind, and maimed now belong to this elect group (see 14:13,21) as well as well-to-do Gentile Christians who share their possessions with those in need (6:17–49). See also the comments on 1:51–53; 4:18–19,25–28; 16:23. Finally, in reconstituted Israel the outcast class, women, plays a prominent role, e.g., 7:36–50. Needless to say, such internal objections, if sustained, would greatly limit the missionary endeavors of Luke's communities. For further detail on the Lucan Pharisees, → 75–77 below.

**8   ** The main external problems which Luke's communities face are those of harassment, primarily from local Jewish synagogue leaders. See 21:11–19 and the problems of Peter, John, Stephen, Barnabas, and Paul in Acts. As the sermons of Peter, Stephen, and Paul further indicate, these problems involve the interpretation of Scripture, esp. how Jesus is the fulfillment of God's promises. And such Scripture interpretation is no small concern for mission to Jews.

9   (C) The Lucan Jesus. As we have already implied in (A) and (B) above, Luke's main answer to the question of theodicy agitating his communities is his portrayal of Jesus. In his compassionate mission to all and by his selection of the Twelve, Jesus laid the foundation for reconstituted Israel. Jesus' mission is an inclusive one as he seeks out the lost and sinners and restores them to union with God. The ministry of Jesus the prophet seems wasted as he is rejected by the religious leaders.

The people (*laos*), however, are not as stubborn and blind in their rejection of Jesus as their leaders. They contemplate the meaning of Jesus' crucifixion (23:35) and ultimately repent of their sin of rejecting Jesus in preference for Barabbas (23:48). From these repentant people Jesus forms the bond of continuity between the old and the new in reconstituted Israel.

Luke's theme of the rejected prophet brings out a further nuance of his portrayal of Jesus. The schema of rejected prophet has four components: God's mercy in sending a prophet; rejection of the prophet; punishment; sending of another prophet. For specifics, → 61 below. Jesus may have been rejected by the religious leaders, but such rejection does not close the door to God's offers of mercy. For as the schema of rejected prophet makes clear, after punishment comes another offer of mercy. Luke narrates this further offer of mercy (e.g., in Acts 2), which records the repentance of 3,000 Jewish people from all over the world after Peter's Pentecost sermon. These help to form reconstituted Israel.

There is a final nuance to Luke's portrait of Jesus, and this deals with the fidelity of Jesus' God. Luke begins his Gospel with this theme as he tells how promises have been fulfilled in the birth of Jesus; he ends it with the theme as he tells how God has fulfilled promises in raising Jesus from the dead. This God, who did not allow God's Holy One, Jesus, to see corruption (Acts 2:27), will surely be faithful to promises made to Jesus' followers who journey from all corners of the globe to take up their places at the heavenly banquet with Abraham, Isaac, and Jacob. See J. Jervell, *Luke and the People of God;* L. T. Johnson, *The Writings of the New Testament* (Phl, 1986) 197–240; R. J. Karris, *CBQ* 41 (1979) 80–97.

10   (IV) Outline. The Gospel according to Luke is outlined as follows:

(I) Preface (1:1–4)
(II) Dawn of God's Fulfillment of Promise (1:5–2:52)
  (A) Gabriel's Annunciation of the Birth of John to Zechariah in the Temple (1:5–25)
  (B) Gabriel's Annunciation of the Birth of Jesus to Mary in Obscure Nazareth (1:26–38)
  (C) Elizabeth's and Mary's Pronouncements about the Meaning of Jesus in God's Plan of Salvation (1:39–56)
  (A′) Zechariah's Pronouncement of the Meaning of John in God's Plan of Salvation (1:57–80)
  (B′) The Angels' Pronouncement about the Meaning of the Baby Jesus Lying in the Manger (2:1–20)
  (C′) Simeon's Pronouncement of the Meaning of the Baby Jesus Who Has Come into the Temple (2:21–40)
  (D) Bridge Passage: Conclusion to Luke's Overture, Jesus' Pronouncement about Himself, and Anticipation of the Future Journey of Jesus, God's Son, from Galilee to Jerusalem (2:41–52)
(III) Preparation for Jesus' Public Ministry (3:1–4:13)
  (A) John the Baptist's Preaching (3:1–20)
  (B) Jesus' Baptism (3:21–22)
  (C) Jesus, Culmination of God's Plan in Creation and Salvation History (3:23–38)
  (D) Jesus, God's Son and Servant, Conquers the Devil (4:1–13)
(IV) Jesus' Galilean Ministry (4:14–9:50)
  (A) Anticipatory Description of Jesus' Galilean Ministry (4:14–15)
  (B) God's Promises Fulfilled in Jesus for All (4:16–30)
  (C) God's Kingdom Restores Men and Women to Wholeness (4:31–44)
  (D) Positive Response to Jesus' Kingdom Message (5:1–11)
  (E) Jesus' Boundary-Breaking Ministry for Outcasts (5:12–16)

  (F) Religious Leaders Oppose Jesus' Kingdom Message (5:17–6:11)
    (a) Jesus' Power to Forgive Sins (5:17–26)
    (b) Jesus' Mission Is for Sinners (5:27–32)
    (c) Jesus is the Bridegroom and Provider of New Wine (5:33–39)
    (d) The Sabbath Is Subordinate to Jesus (6:1–5)
    (e) Compassionate Jesus Cures on the Sabbath (6:6–11)
  (G) The Gathering of Reconstituted Israel (6:12–49)
    (a) Jesus' Selection of Twelve Apostles (6:12–16)
    (b) The Sermon on the Plain (6:17–49)
  (H) Jesus' Kingdom Message Is for Men and Women and Shatters the Boundaries of Clean and Unclean (7:1–9:6)
    (a) Unclean Gentiles Are Open to Jesus' Kingdom Message (7:1–10)
    (b) God's Prophet, Jesus, Has Compassion on a Widow (7:11–17)
    (c) The Roles of John and Jesus in God's Plan of Salvation (7:18–35)
    (d) A Woman Sinner Responds to God's Gift of Forgiveness (7:36–50)
    (e) The Women Disciples of Jesus (8:1–3)
    (f) Diverse Ways of Hearing God's Word (8:4–21)
    (g) Jesus Conquers Chaos (8:22–25)
    (h) Jesus Restores a Demented Gentile to Human Community (8:26–39)
    (i) Jesus' Power Goes beyond Ritual Purity and Gives Life to Two Women (8:40–56)
    (j) The Twelve Continue Jesus' Kingdom Mission (9:1–6)
  (I) Responses to Jesus as His Galilean Ministry Draws to a Close (9:7–50)
    (a) The Fate of Jesus' Forerunner Is His Fate and That of His Disciples (9:7–9)
    (b) Jesus' Gift of Food Is Linked to His Cross (9:10–17)
    (c) The Cross in the Lives of the Messiah and His Disciples (9:18–27)
    (d) Jesus' Transfiguration and the Divine Confirmation of the Way of the Cross (9:28–36)
    (e) How the Cross Interprets Jesus' Merciful Deeds (9:37–45)
    (f) The Disciples' Misunderstanding of the Meaning of Following Jesus (9:46–50)
(V) Jesus' Journey to Jerusalem (9:51–19:27)
  (A) First Part of Instruction on the Meaning of the Christian Way (9:51–13:21)
    (a) The Samaritan Rejection and Nonretaliation (9:51–56)
    (b) The Cost of Discipleship (9:57–62)
    (c) Jesus' Teaching about Mission (10:1–24)
    (d) The Christian Mission and Observance of the Law (10:25–37)
    (e) Discipleship for Men and Women (10:38–42)
    (f) Jesus' Disciples and Prayer (11:1–13)
    (g) Controversies Reveal the Meaning of Jesus' Journey (11:14–36)
    (h) Almsgiving Makes One Clean before God (11:37–54)
    (i) Disciples Meet with External and Internal Opposition (12:1–59)
    (j) All Need to Repent (13:1–9)
    (k) An Illustration of the Nature of God's Kingdom (13:11–17)
    (l) Despite Opposition God's Kingdom Grows (13:18–21)
  (B) Second Part of Instruction on the Meaning of the Christian Way (13:22–17:10)
    (a) The Need for Repentance Stressed Again (13:22–30)
    (b) Jesus Obediently Journeys to Jerusalem (13:31–35)
    (c) The Inclusive Nature of Jesus' Kingdom Banquet (14:1–24)
    (d) The Demands of Discipleship Repeated (14:25–35)

COMMENTARY

11 **(I) Preface (1:1-4).** Luke alone of the evangelists introduces his work with a finely crafted, periodic Gk sentence. Verses 1-2 provide the "since" clause of the sentence; v 3 is the main clause; v 4 is a purpose clause. As a comparison with Josephus, *Ag. Ap.* 1.1 § 1-3; 2.1 § 3; and *Ep. Arist.* 1 indicates, much of the Lucan vocabulary is conventional. The meaning of the words is to be obtained primarily from parallel vocabulary in Luke's two-volume work and from its theology. Thus, words like *diēgēsis,* "narrative account," must not be interpreted solely from prefaces similar to Luke's and taken to mean that Luke has not penned kerygma, but a historical foundation for the Gospel. **1.** *inasmuch as:* This literary word, *epeidēper,* occurs only here in the Gk Bible. *narrative account: Diēgēsis,* in literary parallels (e.g., *Ep. Arist.* 1) means an orderly account and not merely a stringing together of anecdotes or notes. Within Luke-Acts itself the root verb *diēgeisthai* is found in a pregnant meaning in Luke 8:39; Acts 12:17 and is equivalent to "to proclaim." *Diēgēsis* might be translated as "kerygmatic narrative." Although Luke, unlike Mark, does not call his work "gospel," his intent is the same: to elicit faith. *events accomplished among us:* That Luke's purpose is not to write mere history is clearly evidenced in this phrase, which anticipates a dominant Lucan motif (see 4:16-21; 22:37; 24:25,27,44-47). Luke narrates events

that are interpreted as having been brought to fulfillment by God for human salvation. **2.** *became ministers of the Word:* One group is in view. As the Lucan theme of seeing makes clear, esp. in chap. 24, sight is not sufficient for the witness. The integration in faith of God's promises and their fulfillment in the risen Jesus makes one a proclaimer of the Word. **3.** *sequenced account: Kathexēs* can refer to a chronological, spatial, or logical sequence. The parallel in Acts 11:4 indicates that the meaning here is "logical sequence." The order of the account is determined by the "logic" of Luke's promise-and-fulfillment view of God's action. Thus, e.g., Luke 4:16-30 appears out of chronological order, but it is orderly because it sets up Luke's program of how God's promises of salvation have been fulfilled in Jesus' ministry to the poor and unfortunate. *Theophilus:* Perhaps Luke's patron; he is also representative of a wider audience which needs upbuilding in faith. **4.** *assurance: Asphaleia* seems best interpreted by Acts 2:36. Thus, Luke's purpose is not to present true teaching over against heretics or to present an uninterpreted chronicle of past events. Rather, he (like Peter in Acts 2) assures his readers that the events he proclaims fit into God's plan of salvation and invites his readers to respond in faith to his kerygmatic narrative. Such a narrative, however, will not extricate readers from the risk of deciding that God's promises have been fulfilled among us and for our salvation. See R. J. Dillon, *CBQ* 43 (1981) 205-27. Contrast Conzelmann (*TSL* 11-15).

12 **(II) Dawn of God's Fulfillment of Promise (1:5-2:52).** Although it is customary to denote 1:5-2:52 as "infancy narrative," this tag is inaccurate. For only 2:1-40 deals with Jesus' infancy, and the thrust of 1:5-2:52 lies not in narrative but in the pronouncements of Gabriel, Mary, Zecharaiah, the angel who appears to the shepherds, Simeon, and the 12-year-old Jesus. 1:5-2:52 is better seen as an overture to the Gospel. In it Luke's major theological themes are sounded, esp. that of God's fidelity to promise. The 20 Lucan themes investigated by J. Navone (*Themes of St. Luke* [Rome, 1970]) are already enunciated in 1:5-2:52: banquet, conversion, faith, fatherhood, grace, Jerusalem, joy, kingship, mercy, must, poverty, prayer, prophet, salvation, spirit, temptation, today, universalism, way, witness. This overture is gospel as it seeks to elicit from its readers a more intense confession of faith in God as faithful and trustworthy and in Jesus as Christ, Savior, and Son of God (see Schürmann, *Lukasevangelium* 24). What R. Tannehill (*JBL* 93 [1974] 265) has said of Mary's Magnificat (1:46-55) holds true for all of 1:5-2:52, these pronouncements stop the action and generate in the reader a deeper awareness of what is happening.

As the chart in *BBM* (248-49) shows, there have been many attempts to outline the artistic structure of 1:5-2:52. The outline used here stresses content (see Ellis, *Luke* 67).

13 On the issue of the historical reliability of the materials of 1:5-2:52, the sage advice of I. H. Marshall (*Gospel* 51) is to be followed: "Despite Lewis Carroll, it is impossible to have the Cheshire cat's grin without the Cheshire cat as its bearer." Luke used traditions in creating his overture. But Luke has marvelously and with deep faith in God's fidelity to promise interpreted these traditions by the pronouncements of Gabriel, Mary, Zechariah, the angel, and Simeon. In interpreting these traditions thus, he writes similarly to the way he does in the speeches of Acts (→ Acts, 44:7). The traditions are generally to be derived from those twelve elements which Luke and Matthew, despite great discrepancies (e.g., Luke has no story of the Magi), have in common:

(1) Jesus' birth is related to the days of Herod the Great (Luke 1:5; Matt 2:1).
(2) Mary, Jesus' future mother, is a virgin espoused to Joseph, but they have not yet come to live together (Luke 1:27,34; 2:5; Matt 1:18).
(3) Joseph is from the house of David (Luke 1:27; 2:4; Matt 1:16,20).
(4) An angel from heaven pronounces the coming birth of Jesus (Luke 1:28-30; Matt 1:20-21).
(5) Jesus himself is said to be a son of David (Luke 1:32; Matt 1:1).
(6) Jesus' conception will take place through the holy Spirit (Luke 1:35; Matt 1:18,20).
(7) Joseph is not involved in Jesus' conception (Luke 1:34; Matt 1:18-25).
(8) The name "Jesus" is given by heaven before Jesus' birth (Luke 1:31; Matt 1:21).
(9) The angel says that Jesus is "Savior" (Luke 2:11; Matt 1:21).
(10) Jesus is born after Mary and Joseph begin living together (Luke 2:4-7; Matt 1:24-25).
(11) Jesus is born in Bethlehem (Luke 2:4-7; Matt 2:1).
(12) Jesus settles, along with Mary and Joseph, in Nazareth in Galilee (Luke 2:39,51; Matt 2:22-23).

See *FGL* 307; *TAG* 41-78, esp. pp. 53-54. The commentary proper will treat the Lucan modification of these and other traditions.

14 Amidst heated discussions about the historicity of individual details in 1:5-2:52 (see R. Laurentin, *The Truth of Christmas Beyond the Myths* [Petersham, 1985]), one must never lose sight of the fact that Luke is writing for the purpose of deepening the faith of Theophilus and his fellow Christians (see 1:1-4). Luke invites Theophilus and friends to see in faith that in Jesus all God's promises have come to fulfillment. Luke invites them to confess faith in Jesus as Savior, Christ, and Lord not only in their reflections upon the resurrection and the baptism of Jesus but also in their reflections upon the beginning of Jesus' life in God. Luke seeks to elicit from them a deeper faith in a God whose grace is sovereign and generous beyond measure and who reverses human expectations and creates human possibilities in impossible situations. In their reflections on 1:5-2:52 Luke wants his readers to imbibe hearty draughts of the joy, trust, faith, hope, endurance, expectation, and exultation of those who responded to the faithful God's actions in their lives. See P. S. Minear, "Luke's Use of the Birth Stories," *StLA* 111-30. Among those who responded to God's actions Luke focuses on Mary, the slave woman, the humiliated one, the model believer. See *MNT* 105-77.

15 **(A) Gabriel's Annunciation of the Birth of John to Zechariah in the Temple (1:5-25).** Regarding the historicity of this account, Marshall (*Gospel* 50) is correct: "There is nothing improbable in the view that Zechariah and Elizabeth had a child comparatively late in life, and that this event was seen in the light of similar events in the OT." To his view should be added the observation that vv 13-17 probably stem from Luke's reworking of the traditions about JBap he has in 3:1-20 and 7:18-35 and do not stem from a separate Baptist source (*BBM* 272-79). Luke has set the information about John's birth, given him by tradition, into the pattern of an OT annunciation of birth. *Pace* R. E. Brown (*BBM* 156, 272), this pattern does not have five parts, but three: *annunciation of birth* (vv 11-13d), *giving of the child's name* (v 13e), and *specification of the child's destiny* (vv 14-17). See E. W. Conrad, *CBQ* 47 (1985) 656-63. This ABND pattern is found in Gen 16:11-12 (Ishmael); Gen 17:19 (Isaac); 1 Kgs 13:2 (Josiah); Isa 7:14-17 (Immanuel); 1 Chr 22:9-10 (Solomon). It should be noted that the last three texts concern the birth of a Davidic king. It should further be noted that the ABND pattern recurs in Luke 1:28-33, which deals with the birth of a Davidic king, Jesus. Luke has also interpreted the tradition about John's birth by painting Zechariah and Elizabeth (see also Mary) in the colors of childless OT couples, esp. Abraham and Sarah (Gen 16 and 18) and Elkanah and Hannah (1 Sam 1-2), whose children Isaac and Samuel had key roles in salvation history as patriarch and prophet respectively. God does again, in fulfillment of promise, what God has done in the past: the impossible, giving a child to an aged sterile couple. The final OT means which Luke used to interpret the tradition about John's birth (and events in Jesus' life) is taken from Dan 9:20-24; 10:7-17; and Mal 2:6; 3:1, 23-24: with the events of 1:5-2:52 has begun the messianic age of justice, the coming of the Day of the Lord for forgiveness, and the entrance of Jesus as Lord into the Lord's Temple. J. A. Fitzmyer (*FGL* 316) has given the instances of these key but often subtle OT allusions: Luke 1:12-13 = Dan 10:7,12; Luke 1:16 = Mal 2:6; Luke 1:17 = Mal 3:1,23-24 (see Sir 48:1,3,10); Luke 1:19 = Dan 9:20-21; Luke 1:26-29 = Dan 9:21-24; Luke 1:64-65 = Dan 10:16-17; Luke 1:76 = Mal 3:1,23; Luke 2:11,22, 42 = Mal 3:1.

16 **5.** *Herod:* The time indication is vague, for Herod the Great ruled from 37-4 BC. *Zechariah:* The name means "Yahweh has remembered." *Elizabeth:* Her name means either "My God is the one by whom to swear" or "My God is fullness." Luke may have intended some in his audience to capture the meaning behind these names and those of John, Gabriel, Joseph, Mary, Jesus, Simeon, and Anna and to praise the God who has acted in behalf of his people. More importantly, Luke uses these people, along with the shepherds of 2:8-20, to represent expectant Israel responsive to God's revelation. **6.** *righteous:* This priestly couple lives in conformity with God's will, esp. as seen in the law. In describing John's parents in this way, Luke begins a theme that will run the length of his Gospel and culminate in the centurion's confession of Jesus as "righteous" (23:47) and in the good deed of Joseph of Arimathea, who is righteous and waiting for the kingdom of God (23:50-51). In Luke's Gospel many of Israel's religious leaders, in contrast to righteous Zechariah the priest, turn out not to be righteous. See Karris, *Luke* 23-46. "Combining priestly origins and blameless observance of the Law, Zechariah and Elizabeth were for Luke the representatives of the best in the religion of Israel; and as a remnant which received the 'good news' (1:19), they personified the continuity in salvation history" (*BBM* 268). **7.** *they had no children:* As v 25 will confirm, to be childless in Judaism was a misfortune, even a disgrace, for a couple. Echoes of OT barren women, esp. Sarah, who later bore famous children, surface: Sarah (Gen 16:1), Rebekah (Gen 25:21), Rachel (Gen 30:1), the mother of Samson (Judg 13:2), and Hannah (1 Sam 1-2).

17   **8-10.** With his description of Zechariah's offering of incense at the evening sacrifice in the holy place of the Temple, Luke introduces his theme of Temple, which he will develop in 1:21-23 and 2:21-42. "The 'good news' of the inauguration of God's definitive plan of salvation was to be heralded first in the Holy Place associated with His presence in Israel" (*BBM* 270). **11.** The name of the angel is withheld until v 19. In Dan 9:21 Gabriel appeared to Daniel at the time of the evening sacrifice. **13.** *John:* Although Luke does not provide the meaning of John's name — Yahweh has shown favor — the importance of the name of the child reappears in 1:57-67. **14.** The theme of joy in the wake of God's fulfillment of promise finds expression here. **15.** That John will abstain from intoxicating beverages seems an allusion to Num 6:3 and to the figures of Samuel and Samson, who were set apart from birth for the Lord as Nazirites. **16-17.** John's coming is in fulfillment of Mal 3:23-24.

18   **18-20.** In those analyses of biblical annunciations of birth which champion five steps, v 18 is step 4 (objection) and vv 19-20 are step 5 (sign). It seems more likely that vv 18-20 are Luke's redaction of a three-step ABND pattern. Using questions like those of Gen 15:8 and 17:7 to enliven his narrative, Luke added vv 18-20 (1) to introduce the name of Gabriel (God is my warrior) from Dan 9:21-24 and 10:15; (2) to prepare for the completion in 1:57-80 of the annunciation of John's birth; (3) to prepare for Mary's parallel question in 1:34; (4) to prepare for 24:50-53. Thus, the silencing of Zechariah by Gabriel is not a punishment for an objection of disbelief, but is the Lucan counterpart of the silencing of Daniel by Gabriel in Dan 10:15. Luke 1:57-80 is not really the confirmatory sign indicated in 1:20, but is an instance of what might be called Lucan redundancy: what is important should be repeated. It is important that the child be once more called "Yahweh has shown favor" and that human beings acknowledge their God as one who is faithful even in the face of human impossibilities. Zechariah's question (1:18), like that of Mary in 1:34, is Luke's artistic and theological way of moving

the drama to its next act and is not to be seen as an "objection." And this next act features the Lucan theme of Temple and is perhaps the most important reason for not seeing vv 18-20 as parts 4 and 5 of a stereotyped pattern. By depicting Zechariah as dumb, Luke in effect says that he is unable to complete the liturgy he began, for he cannot bless the people (1:21-23). Through this element of story theology, Luke forms the first pole of an *inclusio* whose second pole is found in 24:50-53. In 24:50-53 Jesus, who has taken over God's Temple and is God's Temple (19:28-44), who is the cornerstone of the Temple of reconstituted Israel (20:9-19), and who is God's presence among people (23:44-45), now blesses his disciples after he has completed the liturgy of his life. And his disciples are found in the Temple, the Lucan symbol of continuity between OT promise and God's fulfillment in Jesus. **24-25.** Luke mentions Elizabeth's seclusion to prepare for 1:36 and thus more tightly connects the annunciation of the birth of John with that of Jesus.

19   **(B) Gabriel's Annunciation of the Birth of Jesus to Mary in Obscure Nazareth (1:26-38).** The traditions behind these verses are numbers 2-8 in 13 above. In brief, the historical base on which Luke builds is that Mary became pregnant before she had sexual relations with Joseph. That base has been expanded in various ways. (1) The pre-50 AD creed incorporated in Rom 1:3-4 provides evidence for Christian reflection upon Jesus as descended from David and designated Son of God through the holy Spirit at his resurrection. The christological reflection behind 1:31-35 is more developed than that behind Rom 1:3-4 and proclaims that the Davidic Jesus is Son of God through the holy Spirit at his very conception. Thus, Mary's conception is virginal and through the power of the holy Spirit. See *BBM* 517-33; J. A. Fitzmyer, *A Christological Catechism* (NY, 1982) 67-71. (2) Through his use of the same ABND pattern in 1:5-25 and 1:26-38 Luke compares and contrasts John and Jesus, esp. in part D: whereas John is to be great before the Lord (1:15), Jesus is Son of the Most High, occupant of the throne of David, whose reign will not end (1:33). John's birth may have been extraordinary because he is born to aged parents; Jesus' is more extraordinary still because he is born to a virgin. (3) The figure Gabriel links the annunciations together and invites reflection on the significance of Jesus' birth as fulfillment of Dan 9:24-27: the 70 weeks (490) of years is being fulfilled (after the 180 days of Elizabeth's pregnancy, Mary's pregnancy of 270 days begins, to be followed, after 40 days, by Jesus' entry into the Temple); the reign of justice is beginning. Finally, the faith of Mary is highlighted as Luke draws on the tradition of 8:19-21 to paint a picture of Mary, the model believer. In all of 1:26-38, Luke plays mightily upon his theme of "grace alone." See W. Klaiber, "Eine lukanische Fassung des *sola gratia:* Beobachtungen zu Lk 1:5-56," *Rechtf* 211-28.

20   **26.** *Nazareth.* The naming of this obscure town (see John 1:45) of some 150 people contributes to Luke's theme of God's sovereign grace active in human history. **27.** *Joseph:* The name means "May Yahweh add." *Mary:* The name means "Excellence." **28.** *O Graced One:* Of the three greetings given to Mary *kecharitōmenē* is the most significant. It prompts Mary to question (v 29) in what way she is graced or favored by God. Gabriel will supply the answer in vv 30-33. **31.** *Jesus:* The name means "God saves." **32-33.** The remainder of Luke's Gospel will spell out how Jesus is king. See esp. how Jesus embodies God's kingdom, which has come for outcasts, and how frequently Jesus is called king (e.g., 23:3,37,38) in the passion account when his power is apparently at its nadir. **34.** *how:* Mary's question parallels Zechariah's (1:18) and is the Lucan means of moving his drama to its next phase. **35.** Mary's conception is pure gift from God through the power of God's spirit. **36.** *your relative:* Luke connects the two annunciations and provides an advance link to the events of 1:39-56. With another reference (see 1:25) to the month of pregnancy Luke invites reflection upon how the promise of Dan 9:24 is being fulfilled. **37.** An allusion to the birth annunciation of Isaac (Gen 18:14) sounds here and repeats the Lucan theme that God creates something out of nothing. **38.** Mary of Nazareth is the model believer and slave who responds wholeheartedly to God's plan and is the forerunner of Luke's rogues' gallery, i.e., women, sinners, little people whom no one would expect to respond favorably to God's revelation.

21 **(C) Elizabeth's and Mary's Pronouncements about the Meaning of Jesus in God's Plan of Salvation (1:39-56).** The meaning of God's inauguration in Jesus of the final stage of salvation history is so rich theologically that Luke interprets it twice more, in 1:39-45 and 1:46-56. **39.** *journeyed with haste:* Luke's intent in vv 39-56 is missed if one accentuates Mary's charity and social concern in visiting her aged, pregnant relative Elizabeth. If Luke were intent on presenting Mary as a model of charity, he would not have written v 56, which portrays Mary as departing from Elizabeth at the time of greatest need. It also strains credulity to imagine a fourteen-year-old Jewish virgin making a four-day journey by herself. Rather Luke's intent in the "Visitation" is literary and theological. He brings together the two mothers-to-be (1:25 and 1:36), so that both might praise the God active in their lives and that Elizabeth's child might be presented as the "precursor" of Mary's child. Luke removes Mary from the scene before the birth of John, so that each birth narrative might have solely the three main characters proper to it: Zechariah, Elizabeth, and John; Joseph, Mary, and Jesus. **41.** *leapt:* The "leaping" of Esau and Jacob in Rebekah's womb (Gen 25:22 LXX) presents a parallel to the "leaping" of John: such activity is a foreshadowing of future relationships. The context, esp. v 44, makes clear that by leaping, John recognizes his Lord, Jesus. Through the gift of the holy Spirit Elizabeth is empowered to interpret the leaping of John. **42.** In words recalling Jael's (Judg 5:24) and Judith's (Jdt 13:18) liberation of their people, Elizabeth praises Mary, whose contribution to liberation is the birth of the bringer of peace (2:14). **43.** *my Lord:* John has leapt in Elizabeth's womb because Mary is carrying their Lord. **44.** *joy:* John's joy is the appropriate response to God's fulfillment of promise in Jesus. **45.** *blessed:* Mary, as model believer (see 1:38), is praised for her trust in the fidelity of God.

22 Mary's Magnificat (1:46-55), which elicits reflection upon the nature of the God active in Jesus' conception, can be easily divided into 1:46-50 and 1:51-55. The first stanza deals with Mary, and the second universalizes from Mary's experience to reflect upon God's dealing with all humanity. See R. C. Tannehill, *JBL* 93 (1974) 263-75. These verses have many OT parallels, esp. the Song of Hannah in 1 Sam 2:1-11 (see *BBM* 358-60). They stem from a pre-Lucan Gk source. Luke has modified the reversal theology of this revolutionary canticle by creating v 48 and by situating it within the flow of his Gospel, which admonishes the rich to share their possessions and which enjoins peace and love of enemies.

23 **46.** *Mary said:* Although the content of the canticle may fit Elizabeth's situation more than Mary's, that is not sufficient reason for gainsaying the evidence of all the Gk mss., which read that Mary is the speaker, and

accepting three copies of the OL version, which say that Elizabeth is the speaker. Mary extols God for what God is doing for women and men through her child. **47.** *extolls:* The theme of rejoicing in God's fulfillment of promise again bubbles forth. **48.** This verse is plausibly seen as a Lucan insertion into a traditional canticle in order to join it more closely to its new setting. See how *doulē,* "slave, handmaid," recalls 1:38 and how "blessedness" recalls 1:45. The lowly slave woman Mary will be hailed by all in the new era of salvation begun by God in her son. **49.** *mighty:* The lowliness of Mary is contrasted with the might of God, for whom nothing is impossible (see 1:37). **50.** This verse concludes the first stanza and leads into the second: what God has done for Mary is universalized into what God does for "those who fear God." **51-53.** Problems abound. Luke uses six vbs. in the Gk aor. (past) tense: shown power and scattered (v 51); brought down and exalted (v 52); filled and sent away (v 53). Since it is not easy to see how God has accomplished (past tense) all this in the mere conception of Jesus, scholars explain the six past vbs. differently. Preferable is the view that the six past-tense vbs. describe God as one who characteristically performs these actions (gnomic aor.) and is beginning to do so now in the conception of Jesus (inceptive aor.). See J. Dupont, *NRT* 102 (1980) 331-35. Another issue is the question of who the rich (arrogant/mighty) are and who the lowly (hungry) are. R. E. Brown (*BBM* 350-65) argues that the lowly are Jewish Christian *anawim.* D. P. Seccombe (*Possessions and the Poor in Luke-Acts* [SNTU B/6; Linz, 1982] 70-83) maintains that the lowly are Israel and that the rich are her Gentile oppressors. For J. A. Fitzmyer (*FGL* 361), the poor are the physically poor in Israel plus unfortunate people, lowly, sick, and downtrodden; the rich are the physically rich as well as the proud, the arrogant, and those who experience no need of God. J. M. Ford (*My Enemy* 19-23) underscores the militant, holy-war character of vv 51-53. F. W. Horn (*Glaube und Handeln in der Theologie des Lukas* [GTA 26; Göttingen, 1983] 137-44, 181-83) holds that vv 51-53 contain Ebionite views, i.e., the rich are rejected solely because they are rich and the poor are exalted solely because they are poor. Being poor is a condition of receiving God's grace. By his insistence on the absolute gratuity of God's salvation in 2:1-20 Luke modifies this view, which is present also in 6:20-26 and 16:19-26. There is much to commend in Horn's view. By retaining this "Ebionite" tradition, Luke agrees that the God whose powerful arm (v 51) has created a new exodus does show a preference for the downtrodden, a preference that will be manifested in Son Jesus and in the mission of Jesus' disciples. The situation of the downtrodden (in the person of Mary; see Luke's modification in 1:48) will be reversed. But as Luke narrates in the immediate context, the downtrodden, too, have to respond to God's good news (see the shepherds of 2:6-20). As Luke's Gospel develops, further modifications of 1:51-53 will be made, esp. in Luke's themes of the rich sharing possessions, peace, and forgiveness of enemies. See Ford, *My Enemy* 36; and Karris, *RR* 42 (1983) 903-8. For Luke, membership in "the poor of God" does not come with social status or ethnic heritage. **54-55.** Again the theme of God's fidelity to promises appears. *Abraham:* This is the first occurrence of an extensive Lucan theme. See 1:72-73; 3:7-11,34; 13:16; 13:28-29; 19:9; 20:37; Acts 3:13,25; 7:17,32; 13:26; 26:6; 28:20. While it is true that God builds the new of salvation history upon the old promises made to Abraham, membership in reconstituted Israel is God's gift which elicits the response of appropriate conduct and is not contingent solely on one's ethnic heritage as a child

of Abraham. **56.** *Mary returned:* This is Luke's literary
way of ushering Mary off the scene, so that only the
appropriate characters will be present for the next scene
of John's birth and naming.

**24   (A') Zechariah's Pronouncement about
the Meaning of John in God's Plan of Salvation
(1:57–80).** This section has two parts. After Luke has
provided sufficient narrative detail to keep his drama
moving (1:57–66), he stops the action and interprets it
by means of the canticle in 1:67–80. Both parts are
redolent of Luke's theology that God has acted in history
in fulfillment of former promises.

25   58. *rejoiced with her:* What Gabriel had promised
in 1:14 has come to pass. Again the response to God's
merciful action in the face of human impossibility is one
of joy. **59.** *to circumcise:* The event of the circumcision and
naming of John parallels that of Jesus in 2:21. Through
circumcision both John and Jesus are incorporated into
Israel. Since for Luke Christianity is a logical outgrowth
of Judaism, "those who inaugurate it and found it must
be shown to be part of Judaism" (*FGL* 376). **60.** *John:*
What is astonishing in the eyes of all is that Elizabeth and
then Zechariah, who is deaf and thus unable to hear what
Elizabeth said, both say that the child's name shall be
John: Yahweh has shown favor. **64.** *blessing:* The first
words spoken by Zechariah, now able to speak in fulfillment of 1:20, are those of praise of God. **65–66.** The
question of the future role of John will be answered in
1:76–79 initially and then more fully in 3:1–20 (see also
7:17–35).

26   Zechariah's Benedictus (1:67–79) is widely
acknowledged not to be a unitary piece, for it begins by
praising God for what God has done in Jesus for Israel
(1:68–75) and then changes theological gears and
foretells the future role of JBap (1:76–77) and then again
changes gears to proclaim the role of Jesus (1:78–79).
Solutions to this problem are many. R. E. Brown (*BBM*
377–92) argues that into a pre-Lucan Jewish Christian
anawim canticle Luke has inserted vv 76–77, concerning
JBap, to connect the canticle to its new context (Luke
redacted similarly in the Magnificat by joining that pre-
Lucan canticle to its context by means of 1:48).
Preferable is the solution of Schürmann (*Lukasevangelium*
84–94): Luke has adopted and joined together two
Jewish Christian hymns: 1:68–75 and 1:76–79. The
latter material stresses John's role as precursor of Jesus.
67. *filled with the holy Spirit:* This is the same description
Luke used of Elizabeth, Zechariah's wife, in 1:41. Just as
Elizabeth spoke of the greatness of Jesus (1:41–44), so
too does Zechariah (1:68–75). It is Lucan artistry and
theology that all the speakers of the canticles in 1:5–2:52
tell of Jesus. **68.** *God of Israel:* This entire canticle stays
within the orbit of Judaism and God's dealings with the
elect people. *visited:* With its use of past tenses the hymn
of 1:68–75 resembles the Magnificat and probably stems
from the same group which composed that pre-Lucan
canticle. These Gk aor. tenses are to be seen as gnomic
and inceptive. They, thus, depict how God
characteristically acts (gnomic) and what God is inaugurating (inceptive) in Jesus. **69.** *David:* The theme of
promise and fulfillment fleshes out what Gabriel said in
1:32. As in 1:51–53, the effect of the coming of the
Davidic Messiah is painted in military imagery. David's
heir will effect salvation from enemies. In his next story
about Jesus, the Davidic Messiah, Luke will present him
as pacific (2:1–20). In Jesus, God conquers enemies by
bringing them peace. **70–73.** Again the theme of God's
fidelity to promise surfaces. As in 1:55, God's fidelity to
Abraham's covenant is highlighted. **76.** This and the
following verses recall Gabriel's words in 1:16–17 and
answer the question of 1:66. Again there is an echo of

Mal 3:1. **77.** See the description of the ministry of JBap
in 3:1–20. This passage stems from traditions embedded
in 3:1–20. **78.** For a close parallel to this verse, see
T. Zeb. 9:8, which incorporates its two key words: "And
after these things the Lord himself will arise (*anatelei*) for
you, the light of righteousness, with healing and mercy
(*eusplanchnia*) in his wings." *will visit:* Following the best
Gk mss., we should read a fut. tense here and not an aor.
R. E. Brown (*BBM* 373) argues for the validity of the
textual tradition which reads the past (aor.) tense and
thus finds support for his solution to the nonunitary
character of the Benedictus. Rather than being the conclusion of the original hymn, into which Luke inserted
vv 76–77 with their fut. tenses, vv 78–79 continue the
description of John. He whom vv 76–77 depicted as a
prophet is now portrayed, in vv 78–79, as the precursor
of Jesus, "the dawn from on high." **79.** *peace:* This is the
first instance of an important theme, which courses
strongly in Luke. Peace is not merely the cessation or
absence of hostilities. Its focus is on wholeness, harmony, well-being, prosperity, and security. In Luke it
interconnects with the theme of love of enemies. Verse
79 forms an *inclusio* with 24:36, which narrates that the
first word of the crucified and raised Jesus was "peace."
80. *in the desert:* Luke removes John from the scene and
prepares his readers for a future act of his drama when
he will tell of John's prophecy to Israel.

**27   (B') The Angels' Pronouncement about
the Meaning of the Baby Jesus Lying in the Manger
(2:1–20).** This section is the epitome of Lucan artistry.
He takes the traditions that Mary and Joseph stem from
Nazareth and that Jesus is born in Bethlehem (see
numbers 9–11 in 13 above). He ties these events to the
figures of Herod the Great, Caesar Augustus, and
Quirinius, under whom a census took place. And around
and through these traditions and figures he weaves eight
of his themes (food, grace, joy, lowliness, peace, salvation, today, universalism) to fashion an exquisite theological tapestry.

**28   This section can be outlined as follows: 2:1–7
(setting and birth of Jesus); 2:8–14 (angelic pronouncement of the meaning of Jesus); 2:15–20 (responses to the
angelic pronouncement). The key to the meaning of
2:1–20 lies in 2:11–14. In these verses we hear Luke's
voice. In 1:51–53 and 1:69–71 he quoted traditions that
could be viewed as presenting Jesus as a militaristic
Davidic Messiah. In his typical way of juxtaposing and
thereby bringing out the lasting value of diverse understandings of Jesus and his ministry (see H. Flender, *St.
Luke* [Phl, 1967] 8–35; E. Schweizer, *Luke* [Atlanta,
1982]), Luke now presents Jesus as the Davidic Messiah
who will bring about the eschatological gift of peace.
Toward the end of his narrative of Jesus' ministry of
peace, Luke will in 19:38 recall what the choir of angels
said of Jesus at his birth (2:14). In the powerlessness of
his babyhood Jesus is Savior and bringer of peace to all
in contrast to the mighty Roman ruler, Caesar Augustus,
whom imperial cult celebrated as the inaugurator of
peace. The angels' revelation of the meaning of Jesus is
accepted by lowly shepherds and pondered by Mary,
who models for believers the necessity of reflecting
upon and embodying peace. See Schneider, *Lukas* 64–68.

29   1–3. There are historical problems in vv 1–3:
Quirinius was governor of Syria in AD 6–7 and not
during the reign of Herod (see 1:5), who ruled from
37–4 BC; there is no extra-Lucan evidence that under
Caesar Augustus a worldwide census occurred or that
people were required to register in their ancestral towns.
As Luke showed also in Acts 5:37, he has not a well informed memory about the census. In any case, Luke's
purpose in mentioning the census is not to follow the

canons of historical order, but those of the order of promise and fulfillment (see 1:1–4). The census provides Luke with a means of getting Mary and Joseph from Nazareth to Bethlehem, the city of David wherein the promised heir of David is to be born (Mic 5:1). See BBM 547–56. **1.** *Caesar Augustus:* Luke makes a subtle contrast between this Roman ruler (27 BC–AD 14), who was fabled as an inaugurator of peace, and Jesus, the Savior (2:11) and bringer of peace (2:14). The Priene inscription praises Augustus as "[a Savior] who has made war to cease and who shall put everything [in peaceful] order" (F. W. Danker, *Benefactor* [St. Louis, 1982] 217). When Luke wrote his Gospel some 70 years after Augustus's death, the imperial cult and the Asian calendar, whose New Year was the birthday of Augustus (September 23), kept Augustus's memory alive as the benefactor of the whole world. See S. R. F. Price, *Rituals and Power* (Cambridge, 1984) 54–56, 61, 106. **4.** Jesus' Davidic background is spotlighted; see 1:27,32–33,69–71. **7.** *firstborn:* It has been suggested (E. LaVerdiere, *Emmanuel* 89 [1983] 544–48) that *prōtotokos* would fit better in the christological context of 1:5–2:52 if it were translated by "firstborn" (of God). See the parallels in Col 1:15,18; Heb 1:6; Rev 1:5. This seems less subtle than to see *prōtotokos* as Luke's way of preparing for the dedication of the "firstborn" in 2:23. *swaddling clothes:* See Wis 7:4: like King Solomon, his predecessor on the Davidic throne, Jesus wears the trappings of humanity. *manger:* In accord with Luke's overriding interest in the theme of food (see Karris, *Luke* 47–78) it seems best to interpret the manger, which recurs in 2:12,16, as a symbol that Jesus is sustenance for the world. *inn:* There does not seem to be any significant difference between the Gk word (*katalyma*) used here and in 22:11 and the Gk word (*pandocheion*) used in 10:34. By "inn" is probably meant a two-story caravansary 40 ft. by 70 ft. The animals stayed in the inner courtyard. Kitchen and other facilities were on the first floor. Bedrooms, some of which were large, were on the second floor. See L. Casson, *Travel in the Ancient World* (Toronto, 1974) 197–218. In order to create and underline the important and symbolic value he places on the thrice-mentioned manger (2:7,12,16), Luke says there was no room in the inn. Although born in lowly circumstances and without hospitality, Jesus is the one who will be host to starving humanity. Fully grown and about to lay down his life as a servant, Jesus hosts in an inn (22:11) a meal that his disciples will continue in his memory.

30   **8.** *shepherds:* There is an echo of David's humble origins as a shepherd (see 1 Sam 16:1–13) in the description of those who are privileged with a vision of David's successor. More generally and in accord with Luke's theme of poverty, the shepherds are the lowly. "Mangy, stinking, bathless shepherds are in their ritual uncleanness an encouragement for all who lack religious status" (Danker, *Jesus and the New Age* 27). See also Marshall, *Gospel* 96. **10.** The Lucan theme of joy in the face of God's salvific inbreaking into human history sounds again (see 1:28,46,58). *today:* God's salvation is not in some distant future, but is already being inaugurated. This Lucan theme is played out in the length and breadth of the Gospel: 4:21; 5:26; 12:28; 13:32,33; 19:5,9; 22:34,61; 23:43. *Savior:* Jesus, and not the peace-bringing Caesar Augustus, is Savior of humanity. This Lucan theme is well studied by I. H. Marshall, *Luke: Historian and Theologian* (GR, 1971). For Luke salvation means restoration to wholeness, rescue from sin and alienation from God (see *FGL* 222) and also includes a dimension of immanence: in Jesus God is present *with* sinners (19:5,10; 23:43); Jesus saves (8:36) from destructive self-isolation to union *with* nurturing human

community. See R. J. Karris, *CurTM* 12 (1985) 346–52. **12.** The sign of the manger recurs. **14.** *glory:* In Jesus God has effected God's end-time gift of peace. Deeds of peace and not worldly weapons grace the escutcheon of King Jesus. As Jesus completes his journey to Jerusalem, he will be hailed with a greeting of peace (19:38). *men and women favored by God:* The Lucan theme of God's grace toward human beings brings out another dimension of the Davidic birth.

31   **15.** The shepherds respond eagerly to the angelic good news. **16.** *manger:* The shepherds find the sign given by the angel (v 12). But this "sign" does not merely attest the truthfulness of the angel's message. Rather it bears out and exemplifies the message that Jesus is Savior (v 11). "The one who has been born is also a savior. To this feature corresponds his significant presence in the manger, the sign of God's being the sustenance of his people" (C. H. Giblin, *CBQ* 29 [1967] 100). **17.** *made known:* The shepherds tell others, Mary and Joseph included, about the good news, which is complementary to that announced to Mary in 1:31–33, by Mary in 1:46–55, and by Zechariah in 1:68–79. The meaning and destiny of the infant Jesus are like a diamond whose facets Luke illumines from different perspectives. **19.** *pondering:* Mary rolls the events, esp. the angelic good news, around in her head, trying to hit upon their meaning. Mary does not capture the full significance of God's action in Jesus immediately. Verse 19 becomes a refrain in 2:51 and signals Mary's journey of faith (see 8:19–21; 11:27–29; Acts 1:14). Mary is the model believer.

32   **(C')** **Simeon's Pronouncement of the Meaning of the Baby Jesus Who Has Come into the Temple (2:21–40).**   Besides the Nunc Dimittis (2:29–32) Luke has used as a source for this section the narrative of Hannah and Elkanah in 1 Sam 1–2. To Elkanah and his barren wife Hannah is born Samuel, who is presented to the Lord. The old man and priest, Eli, accepts the dedication of their son at the sanctuary of Shiloh and blesses Samuel's parents. Luke has expanded these sources with his themes of fulfillment of promise, temple, universalism, rejection, witness, and women. He structures his story as follows: 2:21–24 is the setting for the dual witness of Simeon and Anna in 2:25–38 and 2:39–40 forms the conclusion. The theological centerpiece of the whole is found in 2:29–32. As is evidenced in his composition of speeches in Acts, Luke has a talent of blending tradition with his own theology and of relating speech to speech. See P. Schubert, *JBL* 87 (1968) 1–16. That same talent is evident in the contrasts and development in the pronouncements of 1:5–2:52: 1:46–55; 1:68–79; 2:14; 2:29–32: the Davidic Messiah, Jesus, is not just Savior for some people, although these are chosen, but for all; he conquers his enemies by efforts at peace. In 2:29–32 Luke sounds the theme of universalism which is his hallmark.

33   **21.** *to circumcise him:* Jesus, like his precursor John, is circumcised (1:59) and "formally stamped as a member of God's chosen people, through whom world salvation was to be achieved" (C. Stuhlmueller, *JBC* art. 44 § 21). Luke refers to 1:31 and Jesus' name ("God saves"). **22.** *Mosaic law:* See also 2:23,24,27,39. Luke's "aim is to stress fidelity to the Mosaic Law. The new form of God's salvation comes with obedience to this Law" (*FGL* 421). The law for purification is found in Lev 12:2–8: Lev 12:6 is alluded to in 2:22 and Lev 12:8 in 2:24. The law for consecration of the firstborn male is found in Exod 13:1–2. When the child was a month old, he was to be redeemed for five shekels (Num 3:47–48; 18:15–16). Luke does not mention this last regulation, but instead introduces Jesus' presentation, about which there is no regulation in the OT. It seems that Luke accentuates the presentation of the consecrated one in order to bring in echoes of Samuel's presentation in 1 Sam 1:22–24 and of two of his favorite interpretive OT passages: the Lord has come into his Temple (Mal 3:1–2); Jesus is in the Temple as the Most Holy One who was to come at the end of 70 weeks of years (Dan 9:24). See *BBM* 445–46. *Jerusalem:* Luke uses here the form *Hierosolyma,* which he will employ also in 13:22; 17:28; 23:7 and 25 times in Acts. In 2:25 he will use the Gk *Ierousalēm,* a form he will use 26 more times in the Gospel and 39 times in Acts. Attempts to make precise theological distinctions between these two Gk usages have failed. The juxtaposition of the two different forms for Jerusalem in 2:22,25 and Acts 1:4,8 may be revelatory of Luke's literary intent. By using the indirect type of etymology common in the ancient Mediterranean world, Luke shows via juxtaposition that *Hierosolyma,* which occurs first and means "holy Salem" or "holy space," is the etymology of *Ierousalēm,* which occurs second. See D. D. Sylva, *ZNW* 74 (1983) 207–21. Jerusalem is a very important theme and symbol in Luke for God's blessings and continuity between promise and fulfillment, between Judaism and reconstituted Israel, which journeys forth from Jerusalem to the ends of the earth (Acts 1:8). **34   25.** *Simeon:* This old man, whose name means "God has heard," is described in much the same way as JBap's parents (1:6). *consolation of Israel:* Isa 40:1 LXX and 66:12–13 LXX are background for this expectation of God's saving deed. *holy Spirit:* The gift of this creative life "does not bring religious satiety but hunger and thirst for the consummation. . . . The imminence of the fulfill-ment dominates Simeon's life and that of those who hear him" (Schweizer, *Good News* 56). **27.** *Temple:* Although Simeon is not a priest, both he and later Anna embody the heart of Temple cult: service of God. The stage is now set for Simeon's Nunc Dimittis, for "the Law, the prophetic Spirit, and the Temple cult have all come to-gether to set the scene for the greatness of Jesus" (*BBM* 53). **29.** The vocabulary of vv 29–32 seems drawn from the prophet Isaiah: 52:9–10; 49:6; 46:13; 42:6; 40:5 (ibid. 458). **30.** *salvation:* Throughout the pronouncements of 1:5–2:52 this theme has sounded, sometimes in creative theological tension: 1:47; 1:71,77; 2:11. **31–32.** God's sal-vation in Jesus moves out and embraces God's people Israel and then encircles the others, the nations (see 24:44–47). The nations cannot be seen simply as rulers to be put down (1:51–53) or as enemies to be vanquished (1:69–71); they are heirs of God's promises. **34.** In antici-pation of a large theme in his Gospel, Luke notes that many of God's elect will reject Jesus (see 4:16–30). In a stage whisper Luke announces the cross. **35.** *sword:* The most illuminative OT parallel is Ezek 14:17 and the sword of discrimination. "The image is of a selective sword of judgment, destroying some and sparing others, a sword for discrimination and not merely for punish-ment . . ." (*BBM* 464). Mary, too, the model believer, will have to decide for or against God's revelation in Jesus; family ties do not create faith. **36.** *Anna:* Her name means "Grace, Favor." Like Simeon, she is the embodiment of waiting for the Lord. She gives her silent witness to the meaning of Jesus for those who long for redemption. The pairing of Simeon and Anna corresponds to that of Zechariah and Elizabeth in chap. 1 and foreshadows an impressive theme in Luke: "Luke expresses by this arrangement that man and woman stand together and side by side before God. They are equal in honour and grace, they are endowed with the same gifts and have the same responsibilities (cf. Gen. 1.27; Gal. 3.28)" (Flender, *Luke* [→ 28 above] 10). Other pairings include the widow

of Sarepta and Naaman (4:25–28), the healing of the demoniac and Peter's mother-in-law (4:31–39), the cen-turion of Capernaum and the widow of Nain (7:1–17), Simon and the sinful woman (7:36–50), the women at the tomb and the Emmaus disciples (23:55–24:35), Lydia and the Philippian jailer (Acts 16:13–34). **39.** *Nazareth:* Luke concludes his thematic development of the mean-ing of Jesus' presentation in Jerusalem's Temple by having the holy family journey to Nazareth. To that Temple they will return in 2:41–52. **40.** *he became strong:* See the description of John in 1:80. *God's favor:* There are echoes here of 1 Sam 2:21,26, the story of Samuel, which has informed so much of Luke's narrative in 2:21–40.

35   (D) Bridge Passage: Conclusion to Luke's Overture, Jesus' Pronouncement about Himself, and Anticipation of the Future Journey of Jesus, God's Son, from Galilee to Jerusalem (2:41–52). The source of this passage seems to be a pre-Lucan pro-nouncement story that did not know of Jesus' virginal conception and whose focus is Jesus' pronouncement about his relationship to his Father in v 49. The kernel of this story would be 2:41–43,45–46,48–50. Modifica-tions are found in vv 44,47,51–52, and the "must" theme of v 49. See *MNT* 157–62. The story may have its origin in the human tendency to find the man in the boy. A helpful parallel is found in Josephus, *Ant* 5.10.4 § 348, wherein Samuel, the son born to Elkanah and Hannah, is described as beginning to prophesy at the age of 12 although 1 Sam 3 does not mention any age whatsoever. Luke used this story because it allowed him to dwell on his themes of cross, faith, fatherhood, must, temple, and way/journey.

36   41. *Passover:* Regulations for the feast of Pass-over are found in Exod 23:17; 34:23; Lev 23:4–14. There is also an allusion to the yearly pilgrimages of Elkanah and Hannah (see 1 Sam 1:3,21; 2:19). **42.** *they journeyed up to Jerusalem according to custom:* Stress is laid on Jesus' family and its devout adherence to the law as the environment in which he was brought up. This story anticipates Jesus' later journey to Jerusalem (9:51–19:27), which he makes with his disciples, and reveals in word and deed his relationship to his Father. See LaVerdiere, *Luke* 39. **44.** This verse seems to be a literary device by which Luke heightens for his readers the anxiety of the parents. **46.** *in the Temple:* Luke began his overture in the Temple in Jerusalem (1:5–25). He concludes his overture in the Temple. This large *inclusio* prepares for the end of the Gospel, which describes the disciples in the Temple praising God. **47.** The connection with the "wisdom" motif of 2:40 should be noted. **49.** The entire story has been leading up to this "punch line" in which Luke records Jesus' first words. No longer does Gabriel, or Mary, or Zechariah, or angels, or Simeon pronounce who Jesus is, but Jesus himself pronounces who he is. *must:* The Gk word *dei* conveys the theme of necessity, which occurs frequently in the Gospel (18 times) and Acts (22 times) and "expresses a sense of divine compul-sion, often seen in obedience to a scriptural command or prophecy, or the conformity of events to God's will. Here the necessity lies in the inherent relationship of Jesus to God which demanded obedience" (Marshall, *Gospel* 129). See further C. H. Cosgrove, *NovT* 26 (1984) 168–90. *in my Father's house:* This seems to be the sense of the difficult Gk phrase *en tois tou patros mou,* which could also mean "(involved) in my Father's affairs" or "among those belonging to my Father" (see *FGL* 443–44). Jesus has not underlined the meaning of his words in v 49 by miracles as in the apocryphal Gospels, esp. the *Infancy Gospel of Thomas.* Rather he underlines them by a hidden life of participation in the everyday life of his family "in the almost unimaginably narrow and primitive environment of a small near Eastern town" (Schweizer, *Good News* 64). **50.** *did not understand:* Jesus' parents do not comprehend that his relationship to his God takes precedence over his relationship to them. The sword of discrimination spoken of by Simeon in 2:35 is at work. **51.** *was submissive to them:* God's Son willingly submits to obedience. Thus this story "foreshadows the cross by insisting that Jesus preserved his identity in the role of a servant" (R. E. Brown, *Worship* 51 [1977] 485). Mary, the model believer, continues her journey of faith as she ponders the meaning and destiny of her son (see 2:19). **52.** See the refrain in 2:40.

37   (III) Preparation for Jesus' Public Ministry (3:1–4:13). After a section on JBap (3:1–20), in which Luke shows that the responses given to John's ministry are similar to those which will be given to Jesus' ministry, he devotes three sections to the question of who is the Jesus who ministers in Galilee, on the way to Jerusalem, and in Jerusalem. He is God's beloved Son and agent of the holy Spirit (3:21–22); the culmination of God's plan for creation (3:23–38); the faithful Son who conquers the powers of evil (4:1–13).

38   (A) John the Baptist's Preaching (3:1–20). This section is divided into four parts. Luke 3:1–6 describes John's call to prepare the way of the Lord. In 3:7–14 Luke depicts how ordinary and outcast folks prepare themselves for the Lord. Luke 3:15–18 highlights the difference between the one who prepares the way of the Lord and the Messiah. In 3:19–20 Luke concludes his presentation of John.

39   The quest for the historical JBap cannot be pursued in detail here. Important elements in that quest would be the independent witness of Josephus (*Ant.* 18.5.2 § 116–19) to the extensive influence that John had among the people and the hypothesis of J. A. Fitzmyer (*FGL* 453–54) about John's relationship to the Essenes at Qumran, who used Isa 40:3 of themselves, lived in the desert, and employed water rituals. The concern here is how Luke has adapted traditions about John into his proclamation of the good news of Jesus Christ. See W. Wink, *John the Baptist in the Gospel Tradition* (SNTSMS 7; Cambridge, 1968) xii.

40   Luke's adaptation of Johannine traditions is controlled by his christology and has the following components. John's ministry, as well as that of Jesus, is set in the matrix of world and religious history, with all its joys and sinfulness (3:1–2). John is God's prophet (3:2), who does not belong to the period of promise but inaugurates the period of fulfillment (Acts 1:22; 10:37), whose central figure is Jesus. As John completes his preparation (1:80) and becomes an itinerant preacher who prepares the way of Jesus, he does so in fulfillment of God's prophecy: that of Gabriel (1:15–17), that of his father Zechariah (1:76–79), and that of Isaiah (3:4–6). In fulfilling promises, God directs the ministry of John (and also that of Jesus). As will also be true of Jesus, John's ministry is for all (3:7–14). John is not Jesus, the Messiah (3:15–17). His baptism, which is preparatory for the way of Jesus, must be completed by Jesus' Way (Acts 18:25–26) and by faith in Jesus and the gift of the Spirit (Acts 19:3–5). John will meet a violent death (3:19–20; 9:7–9) because of his preaching; a similar fate awaits the one whose path he prepares.

41   Luke raises up John as a model for his churches. They, too, prepare for Messiah Jesus and are not the Messiah. They, too, are the pioneers leading others to the frontiers of faith in Jesus. Whenever John's story is preached as part of the good news, they are challenged to repent, so that they, too, may be prepared for the advent of the Lord Jesus. See Wink, *John the Baptist* (→ 39 above) 113–15.

42   1–2. These verses, one long periodic sentence in Greek, are an elegant beginning to Luke's story of how John affects world history. But just beneath the surface of literary finesse lies the tragic reality of negative response to God's word and its messengers. **1.** *Tiberius Caesar:* The 15th year of Tiberius Caesar seems to be August/September AD 28–29 (see *FGL* 455). *Pontius Pilate:* In the person of Pontius Pilate (prefect of Judea from AD 26–36 [→ History, 75:168]) Roman authority will bring about the crucifixion of Jesus. Luke gives additional attention to Pilate in 13:1; 23:1–6, 11–13,20–24,52; Acts 3:13; 4:27; 13:28, underscoring his association with the death of Jesus, God's messenger. Luke mentions two sons of Herod the Great next. Even the power of someone as mighty as Herod the Great came to an end with his death, as the Romans carved up his kingdom and gave it to his sons (→ History, 75:163–66). *Tetrarch Herod:* This is Herod Antipas, 4 BC to AD 39. Luke will have much to say about him, none of it good: 3:19; 9:7,9; 13:31; 23:7–15; Acts 4:27. Neither John nor Jesus fares well at Herod's hands. Philip, 4 BC to AD 34, and Lysanias, whose dates and identity are quite obscure (see *FGL* 457–58), complete Luke's account of petty secular rulers. *Annas:* Among the religious rulers, Annas was high priest from AD 6–15; Caiaphas, his son-in-law, AD 18–37. Like the petty rulers just mentioned, these men held authority only because Rome so willed it. By means of a completing analepsis or "flashback" in 20:5 Luke tells how the high priests rejected John's baptism. The response of the high priests to Jesus is even more hostile: 9:22; 19:47; 20:1,19; 22:2,4,52,66; 23:4,10,13; 24:20. The response of the high priests to the preaching of Jesus' followers is also hostile: Acts 4:1,6,23; 5:17,21,24,27; 7:1; 9:1,14,21; 22:5,30; 23:2,4,5,14; 24:1; 25:2,15; 26:10,12. Into this bleak scenario of how humanity responds to God's messengers, God sends John, son of Zechariah (see 1:5–25, 57–80), as the inaugurator of the gospel's new time of grace. For God's gracious word will not allow human perversity the last word in salvation history. In terms reminiscent of the call of the prophet Jeremiah (Jer 1:1) Luke describes John's call. *in the desert:* Although Luke does not exploit the rich symbolism of "desert" as the exodus from slavery to new life, he frequently associates "desert" with John (see 1:80; 3:4; 7:24). If the Qumranites lived in the desert awaiting God's deliverance, the fact that John also exercises his ministry in the desert may be another instance of Qumran influence on the historical John. See comment on 3:4.

43   3–6. In this passage the evangelist has dressed JBap in Lucan theological clothing, some original and some cherished "hand-me-downs" from Mark. **3.** *all the neighborhood:* Unlike the Marcan JBap, but very much like the Lucan Jesus, Paul, and Barnabas, the Lucan John is an itinerant preacher. *Jordan:* Though one needs water for baptism, this factor does not necessarily explain the selection of the Jordan River. Is there a historical tradition here that John's baptism was associated with a covenant renewal before people crossed over the Jordan into the "promised land"? *repentance:* A turning from sin and turning over a new leaf of moral behavior. *forgiveness of sins:* The imagery stems from the cancellation of economic debts and release from slavery or imprisonment. See 5:31–32. While retaining "traditional" language about John's role as a baptizer, Luke puts his own stamp on the content of his preaching. In many passages Luke accentuates John's relationship to baptism: he is called "the baptizer" in 7:20,33; 9:19; his mission from God is summarized as "John's baptism" in 7:29; 20:4; Acts 1:22; 10:37; 18:25 and "baptism of repentance" in Acts 13:24; 19:4. But the content of

JBap's preaching in v 3, although identical in wording to Mark 1:4, betrays Lucan theology. "Repentance" and "forgiveness of sins" are among Luke's treasured ways of detailing what Jesus Christ has achieved for humanity (see, e.g., 24:47). Although Luke clearly separates John's baptism from Christian baptism in 3:16 and Acts 18:25-19:5, he closely unites the two "because what John preaches inaugurates the Period of Jesus" (*FGL* 459). **4.** *it is written:* What John is about is in fulfillment of God's promise of a new exodus, which will be from the exile of death and sin and will be accomplished by Jesus, whose way John prepares. It should be noted that the Qumranites applied Isa 40:3 to themselves as they prepared the Lord's way by living in the desert, by studying the law, and by separating themselves from outsiders (see 1QS 8:13-14). While abiding in the desert, John is not engrossed in study of the law and accepts all for baptism. Whereas the LXX of Isa 40:3 has "prepare the way of our God," Luke has "prepare his way," a clear reference to John's preparation of the way of Jesus and one he shares with Mark 1:3.

44   **5.** *make paths straight:* This and similar expressions in v 5 seem metaphorical and may be read ethically as radical changes in a person's life-style. See Marshall, *Gospel* 136-37. This verse of Isaiah (40:4) is not found in Mark 1:3. **6.** The Lucan theme of universality sounds forth in this quotation from Isa 40:5, which is not found in the parallel Mark 1:3. On this theme, see 2:31-32. *salvation:* See comment on 2:10.

45   **7-9.** These verses provide strong evidence for the existence of Q, for 60 out of Luke's 64 words are identical with the 63 words in Matt 3:7-10. This sample of John's eschatological preaching shows that he did not understand repentance as the adoption of his way of life: living in the desert (1:80; 3:2,4; 7:24), forgoing alcoholic beverages (1:15; 7:33), praying and fasting (5:33; 11:1). **7.** *crowds:* Whereas Matt 3:7 has "Pharisees and Sadducees," Luke has "crowds." Two points should be made. In Luke "crowds" (*ochloi*) is interchangeable with "people" (*laos*). See 3:15; 7:29; Conzelmann, *TSL* 164 n. 1; P. S. Minear, *NovT* 16 (1974) 86. By means of the literary technique of completing analepsis or "flashback," Luke will show in 7:30 and in 20:5 that the Pharisees and the high priests respectively rejected John's baptism. At this juncture in his story Luke wants to focus on those who accepted John's baptism. *wrath:* God's judgment by which he deals with evil in the world. **8.** Verses 10-14 will give examples of behavior that corresponds to repentance. *Abraham:* See comment on 1:54-55. Appreciation of God's dealings with humanity does not flourish in the soil of presumption. God will fulfill his promises to Abraham in unexpected ways. **9.** *axe:* Another forceful image of the either-or eschatological situation about which John preaches.

46   **10-14.** These verses are peculiar to Luke and betray his theology and *Sitz im Leben*. It is not the religious leaders (see 7:30; 20:5) who are willing to repent, but the ordinary Jewish people and those who, at best, are on the fringes of Jewish society: toll collectors and soldiers. These are the same people who respond positively to Jesus' preaching. In his baptismal catechesis Luke reminds his churches that they should be as open to finding goodness outside the acceptable ways of life as John and Jesus were. See P. W. Walaskay, *'And so we came to Rome'* (SNTSMS 49; Cambridge, 1983) 28-32. **10.** *what shall we do?:* This question is repeated in vv 12 and 14. It occurs twice more in the Gospel: 10:25 and 18:18, in which a lawyer and a ruler respectively ask Jesus for an authoritative response about what they must do to inherit eternal life—and they receive different answers. Thrice in Acts this question occurs and in each

instance Christian baptism is part of the answer: 2:37 (the Jewish people after Peter's Pentecost sermon); 16:30 (the Gentile Philippian jailer); 22:10 (the Pharisee and persecutor Paul whom the Lord Jesus has halted on the Damascus road). **11.** John does not enjoin the offering of sacrifices or the performance of ascetical practices like fasting. His injunctions are far more radical: a selfless concern for one's disadvantaged brothers and sisters. Here Luke once again plucks on the chord of his theme of the proper use of material possessions, as John preaches, in advance, what Jesus will preach. People who share half of their clothing are like Zacchaeus, who gives half of what he possesses to the poor (19:8). **12.** *toll collectors:* It is surprising that toll collectors come to John for baptism, for little ethical seriousness was expected of this group, which was despised by both Jews and Gentiles. Again and again in Luke normal expectations and deep-seated prejudices are turned upside down. Toll collectors will eagerly respond to Jesus' preaching too: 5:27,29-30; 15:1; 19:2; see also the parable of the Pharisee and the toll collector (18:9-14). **13.** *no more:* The Roman tax system was ridden with abuses, which Augustus tried to eliminate. The high ideals of the Augustan age are reflected in the admonition John gives to these Jews, who were involved in collecting indirect taxes (customs, tolls, tariffs, imposts) from various parts of Palestine for the Romans. See Walaskay, *'And so we came to Rome'* 29-30. **14.** *soldiers:* It seems that these soldiers are Jewish men in the service of Herod Antipas. Since they helped to enforce Rome's will in a subject country, they too were despised. As embodiments of Luke's themes of reversal of expectations and God's love for the despised, they present themselves for baptism. In the course of his gospel story Luke will present two other soldiers, centurions at that, who respond favorably to Jesus (7:1-10; 23:47). The first Gentile converted in Acts is the centurion Cornelius (Acts 10-11). These passages provide evidence for Luke's positive view of Roman military authority, but see 20:25. The injunctions John gives to the soldiers reflect Augustan ideals of how the military should conduct itself. It does not seem within Luke's vision of reality to promote explicitly reforms of unjust tax systems and conscientious objection. His diverse responses to the question What must I do? could indicate that "even the clearest response never relieves anyone of the responsibility of asking again and struggling for an answer. Simple obedience to the instructions of Luke 3:13-14, for example, would be guaranteed in a well-administered system of taxation and a disciplined army. This is not to be despised; it is probably much more a fruit of the gospel than we realize. But it is not identical with the gospel. Only hearts that have been deeply affected by the gospel are always open to what God expects as the next concrete requirement after the present one" (Schweizer, *Good News* 75-76).

47   **15.** *the messiah:* There may be a historical nucleus present in v 15: "Luke's comment implies that there were Palestinian Jews who awaited the coming of a messiah, i.e., an 'anointed' agent of Yahweh sent for the restoration of Israel and the triumph of God's power and dominion . . ." (*FGL* 471). *all:* Here and in v 16 this expression indicates the Lucan theme of universalism. **16.** *baptize with water:* John is inferior to Jesus. John uses the purifying agent of water; Jesus will use the superior purifying and refining agents of the holy Spirit and fire. In Acts 2 Luke shows how the fire of the holy Spirit accomplishes its work in human beings. *more powerful one:* Though this phrase clearly refers to Jesus, its exact meaning is elusive. Within the Lucan story it may refer to the thematic of 11:20-22: Jesus is more powerful than

John in repulsing the powers of evil. John is not even fit
to perform the work of a slave for Jesus by unfastening
his sandal strap (see Acts 13:25). **17.** The imagery of the
winnowing fork separating the fruitful from the unfruitful is of a piece with that of 3:7 (wrath) and of 3:9 (axe).
All three may reflect the view of the historical John and
explain why in 7:18-23 John raises questions about the
ministry of Jesus and his less dramatic repulsion of evil
by healing, exorcism, reconciliation, and preaching to
the poor. **18.** *preached good news:* In the Lucan perspective
there are so many similarities between John and Jesus
that Luke can say that John preaches the good news as
he inaugurates the new time of salvation.

48   **19-20.** These verses form an *inclusio* with 3:1.
Herod Antipas rejects the preaching of the good news
and imprisons its preacher. Jesus' preaching of God's
kingdom will meet with similar success, and Luke's
churches are reminded of the possible consequences of
preparing the way of the Lord.

49   **(B) Jesus' Baptism (3:21-22). 21.** *all the*
people: They admit their need to respond to God's plan
as unfolding in the preaching of John (see 7:29-30). *Jesus*
was also baptized and was praying: Jesus submits to baptism
to show his solidarity with John's proclamation of God's
salvific plan. The fact that Jesus was baptized, presumably by John, is mentioned in a Gk gen. absol. clause.
Evidence for a Lucan tripartite view of salvation history
has been found in the fact that Luke has removed John
from the scene, into prison, in 3:19 before he narrates
Jesus' baptism (see Conzelmann, *TSL* 19-27). A more
simple, literary explanation seems correct. In accord
with his literary style of removing one figure from the
stage before his description of a new scene (see 1:56),
Luke removes John from the stage. Onto the stage
vacated by John steps Jesus, upon whom God's eschatological gift of the holy Spirit descends. It is important to
note that John, Jesus' forerunner, goes to prison for his
ministry. The same will be true for the one whose
sandals John was unworthy to untie. Although many of
the features of Luke's account of Jesus' baptism are
mythological and therefore do not provide a basis for the
view that Luke is presenting Jesus as a model for Christians undergoing baptism, there is one feature that is
patient of this interpretation: Jesus is at prayer. In Luke
Jesus' ministry begins with prayer and ends with prayer
(22:46). Jesus prays in connection with healings (5:16)
and before selecting the 12 apostles (6:12), before his
prediction of his passion (9:18), before his transfiguration (9:28-29), and before he teaches his disciples how
to pray (11:1-2). He prays for Peter (22:32). He prays to
his Father once on the Mt. of Olives (22:39-46), and
twice from the cross (23:34,46). As 11:13 makes clear, the
holy Spirit will be given in response to prayer. But Jesus
at prayer is not only the model for Christians, but also the
mediator of salvation. The figure of Jesus at prayer is a
symbol that Jesus' power to effect salvation stems from
God. In this instance that power comes through God's
gift of the Spirit. Furthermore, Jesus at prayer as he
prepares to embark on his mission in the Spirit is paralleled in Luke's description of the missionary church
aborning in Acts 1:14; 2:1-13. See L. Feldkämper, *Der*
betende Jesus als Heilsmittler nach Lukas (Veröffentlichungen
des Missionspriesterseminars St. Augustin bei Bonn 29;
St. Augustin, 1978). *the heaven was opened:* This prophetic
and eschatological symbol indicates that divine revelation is to be made (see Ezek 1:1; Isa 64:1). While the
audition of 3:22 is given solely to Jesus, it seems that the
heavens being opened (3:21) and the dove descending in
bodily form (3:22) constitute a theophany visible to
all—who have the eyes of faith. **22.** *holy Spirit:* As Joel
3:1-5 indicated, God's eschatological coming to his

people is characterized by an outpouring of the creative
and prophetic Spirit. That Spirit rests upon Jesus now.
In Acts 2:1-41 Luke will narrate the gift of the same
Spirit at Pentecost and interpret that gift via Peter's sermon, which employs Joel 3:1-5. As Acts 10:37-38 and
Luke 4:16-21 show, the Spirit that rests upon Jesus is for
the fulfillment of God's will: to liberate those bound by
Satan and to preach the good news to the poor. This narration of a new gift of the Spirit is related to 1:35 in this
wise: Jesus is depicted as receiving the holy Spirit, not
because he did not have that gift before, but because
Luke is describing a new stage in Jesus' career. See
J. D. G. Dunn, *Baptism in the Holy Spirit* (Phl, 1970) **28.**
bodily form: This phrase is found only in Luke and means
"really." *as a dove:* It has been shown that Mark's Jewish
simile of "dovelike descent" has been changed by Luke
for a Hellenistic audience into "dovelike form" (see L. E.
Keck, *NTS* 17 [1970-71] 41-67, esp. 63). Although
Jewish allusions to a dove in Gen 1:2; 8:8; and Deut
32:11 do not carry conviction as interpretive background, there is much food for thought in E. R. Goodenough's analysis of the polyvalent nature of the dove in
antiquity: its gentleness, its moaning cry like those in
birth pangs, its flight on high (*Jewish Symbols* [NY, 1958]
8. 27-46). The dove symbolized the hopes of men and
women for love, life, and union with God. These hopes
are now realized in Jesus, who in the Spirit breaks down
barriers that separate people from life and who, raised
from the dead to be at God's right hand, will send the
life of the promised Spirit upon those who call upon his
name. *you are my beloved Son, in you I am well pleased:* This
audition, a combination of Ps 2:7 and probably Isa 42:1,
calls upon Jesus as Son and Servant to assume the power
that was his since his conception (1:32,35). Thus, at this
junction in the story, when Jesus is about to journey
through Galilee proclaiming God's kingdom in word
and deed, Luke reminds his readers who Jesus is. In the
revelation of Jesus' sonship in 9:35, Luke will again
remind his readers that Jesus, about to journey to
Jerusalem for death and vindication, is God's Son. In
3:22 and 9:35 Jesus does not become something he was
not before, but Luke's readers are told something more
about Jesus, God's Son, and about God's plan than they
knew before.

50   **(C) Jesus, Culmination of God's Plan in**
Creation and Salvation History (3:23-38).   There are
more differences than similarities between Luke's
genealogy and Matthew's (1:1-16). Major similarities:
Jesus' lineage is traced through Joseph; same names for
the lineage between David and Amminadab (3:31-33;
Matt 1:3-5); same names for lineage between Hezron
and Abraham (3:33-34; Matt 1:2-3). Major differences:
Luke makes no explicit reference to women; Luke traces
Jesus' lineage back to "Adam, son of God" whereas Matthew goes back to Abraham; Luke uses the "ascending
order" of beginning with Jesus and ascending to "Adam,
son of God" whereas Matthew has the "descending
order" of beginning with Abraham and descending to
Jesus; Luke places the genealogy after his account of
Jesus' baptism, whereas Matthew begins his Gospel with
it. These differences are explicable from two insights.
(1) Luke has drawn upon a Davidic-ancestry source
different from Matthew's. This source, which has 36
unique names completely unknown in Matthew and the
OT, used the sacred biblical number of seven in its
theology. From Joseph to God there are seven times
eleven names. Jesus is the culmination of what God has
done for creation and God's elect people, since he begins
the twelfth and final set of seven (see 4 Ezra 14:11 for an
indication of such eschatological speculation). In this
view God enjoys the doubly perfect number of 77, and

David is number 42 (six times seven). (2) Genealogies were composed for different purposes: to prove identity in a tribe; to prove lineage of a king or a priest and thus authenticate these office holders; to structure history into epochs; to show that as was the character of the ancestor, so too the character of the descendant. Luke's genealogy clearly proves Jesus' identity as Davidic and shows how he fits into God's plan, which is traceable to God's creation of humanity. These two insights point to the nature of Luke's genealogy: it does not intend to provide archival or family records, but to preach who Jesus is and what he means for the salvation of all women and men.

51   **23.** *was beginning:* This is an important but difficult phrase. References to *archē* and cognates occur in 1:2; 23:5; Acts 1:1,22; 10:37. The meaning of Jesus' "beginning" is not simply chronological (after his baptism) and geographical (in Galilee), but especially theological. See E. Samain, "La notion de *APXH* dans l'oeuvre lucanienne," *L'Evangile de Luc* (Fest. L. Cerfaux; ed. F. Neirynck; BETL 32; Gembloux, 1973) 299–328. Jesus is the beginning of God's new eschatological humanity. *about thirty years old:* Thirty is a round number and seems indicative of the time when a person embarks on an important phase of life (see Gen 41:46: Joseph; 2 Sam 5:4: David). *as assumed:* This phrase links the genealogy to 1:26–38 and its proclamation that Jesus' origin is from a virgin and thus from God. This subtle cross-reference shows again that God adjusts the normal patriarchally centered way of viewing God's dealings with humankind. *Joseph:* In 1:27 Joseph's Davidic lineage was noted. **31.** *Nathan, the son of David:* In Matthew's descending genealogy (1:6) Solomon is singled out as David's son. Luke underlines David's third son, Nathan (see 2 Sam 5:14). Like David himself, Nathan is not the firstborn, but is selected to manifest God's free election and grace. David's role in God's plan for humankind was mentioned earlier (1:32,69; 2:11). **34.** *Abraham:* See 1:54–55,72–73, wherein it was announced that what God was doing in Jesus is in fulfillment of promises made to Abraham. **38.** *son of Adam, son of God:* The universal significance of Jesus for all—men and women, rich and poor, slave and free—is emphasized. Looking back over Luke's genealogy, one realizes that the line, begun with Adam and flowing through Israel's history of faith and failing, has come to its definitive fulfillment in Jesus. As God's eschatological beginning, Jesus is the leader of those who belong to God not because of blood relationships but because they are gifted by the Spirit (see 3:21–22). See *BBM* 64–94; W. S. Kurz, "Luke 3:23–38 and Greco-Roman and Biblical Genealogies," *Luke-Acts* (ed. C. H. Talbert; NY, 1984) 169–87.

52   **(D) Jesus, God's Son and Servant, Conquers the Devil (4:1–13).** Luke, basing his account on Mark and Q, changes the order of the temptations and places the final one in Jerusalem. When Jesus is on the cross in Jerusalem, he will again encounter temptations like those of 4:1–13 (see 23:34b–39) and will conquer them and evil by his faith. See J. Neyrey, *The Passion According to Luke* (TI; NY, 1985) 156–92. Speculation about the end-time included the mythological element of the overthrow of the devil (*As. Mos.* 10:1; *1 Enoch* 69:29). Luke also gives evidence of this type of thinking in 10:17–20; 11:22; 22:3,53; Acts 10:38; 26:18, wherein he describes Jesus' and the church's ministry. But since 4:1–13 contains such a mythological way of thinking, it is difficult to assess its historicity. It is somewhat plausible that Jesus himself used these apocalyptic thought patterns of his day to tell his disciples about the testings of his faith engendered by the conflicts he encountered as he preached the kingdom. In addition to the christo-

logical message that Jesus, Son and Servant, is the paradigm of the new humanity who vanquishes the powers of evil through the Spirit and obedient faith, there is an ecclesiological message present. Jesus' trust and faith in the graciousness of his God and Father and his reliance on God's word as his secure weapon in conflict (see Eph 6:17) provide models for Christians, who are also gifted with the holy Spirit.

53   **1.** *full of the holy Spirit:* This phrase occurs only here and in Acts 6:5 and 7:55 (Stephen) and 11:24 (Barnabas). Jesus is the model for Christians under duress. *from the Jordan:* A clear link is made with Jesus' baptism in the Jordan (3:21–22) at which he was revealed as Son and Servant. *led by the Spirit:* The Spirit, given Jesus at his baptism (3:22), does not lead him into temptation, but is the sustaining power with him during temptation. A similar baptismal tradition may be at the base of Rom 8:14. *in the desert:* Perhaps a reference to the Judean wilderness. In 8:29 and 11:24 the desert is the place of demons. A reference to Israel's desert experience does not seem present. **2.** *forty days:* In the biblical tradition "forty" refers to a sufficiently long period of time (see Jonah 3:4). It is Matthew, not Luke, who evokes Israel's desert experience (see Matt 4:2 and Exod 34:28) in his account of Jesus' temptation. In Luke Jesus is neither a new Moses nor a new Israel. *tempted by the devil:* Unlike Matthew, who mingles "Satan" and "devil" in his account, Luke refers to God's prosecuting attorney (see Job 1–2) consistently as *diabolos*. Jesus' destiny as Son and Servant is challenged amid the risks and ambiguities of day-to-day human existence. *he ate nothing:* This is not a penitential fast. Nor is the reference to Israel's experience in the desert, which lasted for 40 years, not 40 days. Fasting is symbolic of Jesus' fullness of the Spirit and of his helplessness, contingency, and humbling of self before an omnipotent God who generously gives and sustains life. See J. F. Wimmer, *Fasting in the New Testament* (TI; NY, 1982). **3.** *if you are the Son of God:* Both here and in v 9 Jesus is called "Son of God," a reference to his baptism (3:22) and to "Adam, son of God" (3:38). Jesus, God's Son and Servant, who fulfills God's plan in creation and in Israel's history (3:23–38), is faithful to God's plan, whereas both Adam and Israel failed. *this stone:* Luke, more realistically than Matthew, mentions one stone. He does not envision turning the rock-filled Judean desert into a bakery. **4.** *a human being shall not live on bread alone:* Having refrained from human nourishment for a long time, the human Jesus is obviously famished and vulnerable to the devil's temptation. Jesus' response to the devil is taken from Deut 8:3. His responses in vv 8 and 12 are also from Deut (6:13,16). Jesus combats the devil with the armament of God's authoritative word as found in Israel's mature reflection upon its exodus experience, wherein it learned about God's fidelity to promise, sovereignty, and graciousness and about what was required of a covenant and elect people. Jesus, endowed with God's Spirit and able to provide food for himself, trusts in his sovereign and gracious God to sustain him with life and food. Jesus' obedience as Son, symbolized by fasting, is now verbalized. Jesus trusts that his Father will sustain him during all conflicts and trials. **5.** *took him up:* The text is cryptic. It seems that Luke has suppressed "mountain" and added "in an instant" to make the temptation more realistic. From no mountain could Jesus see all the kingdoms of this earth. He could see them "in a flash." **6.** *power:* Power in a political sense (*exousia*) is proper to Luke (see 20:20; 23:7). **8.** *it is written: you shall worship the Lord, your God, and serve only him:* Jesus quotes from Deut 6:13. The devil assails the fasting Jesus from another angle. Drawing upon Israel's experience of God's jealousy with regard to God's elect, Jesus again verbalizes what it means for him to fast: his God is the sole sustainer of true life. By means of his reference to "political power" in v 6, Luke may also be drawing on one dimension of Jesus' servanthood. In 22:24–27 Jesus, obedient to his Father's will, is the Servant and commands his disciples to eschew political power as a model of being servant. **9.** *Jerusalem:* The Lucan order makes this the last temptation. In Jerusalem, Jesus will complete his *exodus* (see 9:31) to God via cross, resurrection, and ascension in obedience to his Father's will and plan. In Jerusalem, Satan seizes Judas (22:3); in Jerusalem the powers of darkness (22:53) are mightily at work. *Son of God:* See the parallel in v 3. Again reference is being made to 3:22 and 3:38.

54   10–11. *it is written:* The devil now takes up Jesus' armament and quotes Scripture (Ps 91) in an attempt to prove to the fasting Jesus that God will sustain him even if he goes his own way in Jerusalem and does something extraordinary. **12.** *you shall not tempt the Lord, your God:* Obedient to God's will, Jesus quotes from Deut 6:16. Again Jesus verbalizes what his fasting symbolizes: God's plan and will are decisive—even if that plan means suffering and an ignominious death for the innocently suffering Jesus in Jerusalem. **13.** *for some time:* That the devil departs from Jesus for some time does not mean that there exists a period between Jesus' temptations and his arrival in Jerusalem and that that period is devil-less (*pace* Conzelmann, *TSL* 27–29). During his ministry Jesus will continue to encounter the powers of evil, who know who he is (4:41; 8:29), and will vanquish them. Thus, 4:1–13 is programmatic as it describes Jesus' ministry: Jesus, Son and Servant and human culmination of God's plan, will overcome hostility to his mission by obedient faith and will liberate women and men held captive by the devil (Acts 10:38).

55   (IV) Jesus' Galilean Ministry (4:14–9:50).
(A) Anticipatory Description of Jesus' Galilean Ministry (4:14–15). *in the power of the Spirit:* Jesus' proclamation in word and deed of God's kingdom stems from God's creative Spirit (see 3:21–22). *into Galilee:* Not only does Jerusalem (the city of God's fulfillment of promise) have theological significance for Luke, but so too does Galilee. Galilee is the territory wherein Luke begins his description of the meaning of God's kingdom. As J. Nützel has observed (*Jesus als Offenbarer Gottes nach den lukanischen Schriften* [FB 39; Würzburg, 1980] 28–30), 4:14–44, esp. 4:43 provides a potent summary of Jesus' Galilean ministry of preaching the kingdom of God. That preaching involves fulfillment of God's promises (4:16–30), restoring both men and women to health and casting out demons (4:31–44). Galilee is also the place where Jesus gathers witnesses to his ministry (see Acts 1:11: "men of Galilee"; 1:21–22: the criteria for an apostle; 10:37–38: Peter's kerygma about Jesus, whose mission began in Galilee). Finally, Galilee is the site where the disciples do not comprehend Jesus' person and mission, but marvel at his mighty deeds and vie among themselves about who is the greatest (9:43–46). Once their eyes have been opened by Jesus as he journeys to the cross (9:51–19:27) and by the crucified and risen Jesus (24:45), they will comprehend Jesus' role in God's plan and will not go back to Galilee (24:7; contrast Mark 16:7). Their journey will be from Jerusalem to all the nations (24:47). See R. J. Dillon, *From Eye-Witnesses to Ministers of the Word* (AnBib 82; Rome, 1978) 37–38.

56   15. *was teaching:* Luke introduces a pervasive theme: Jesus as teacher. The vb. *didaskein* is used of Jesus 14 times: 4:15,31; 5:3,17; 6:6; 11:1; 13:10,22,26; 19:47; 20:1,21; 21:37; 23:5; a number of these passages refer to

Jesus teaching in synagogue and Temple. Jesus is called teacher (*didaskale*) 13 times: 7:40; 8:49; 9:38; 10:25; 11:45; 12:13; 18:18; 19:39; 20:21,28,39; 21:7; 22:11. He is called master (*epistata*) 6 times: 5:5; 8:24 (2 times); 9:33,49; 17:13. Through this theme Luke emphasizes Jesus' authority in addressing people about God and God's plan; he also implies that Jesus, the teacher, has disciples for whom the master's way is normative. *their synagogues:* Note how often interpretation of who Jesus is occurs in a synagogue, both in Luke (e.g., 4:16–30) and in Acts (e.g., 13:13–52). By means of this motif of synagogue, Luke underlines how Jesus stands in continuity with God's promises of old. But there are also persecution and opposition from within the synagogue to Jesus (e.g., 4:16–30) and his disciples (e.g., 12:11; 21:12; Acts 18:1–11). Jairus, a ruler of a synagogue (8:41), is favorably disposed to Jesus, whereas the unnamed ruler of a synagogue in 13:14 is hostile to him. The Lucan community struggles to dialogue with its Jewish brothers and sisters about Jesus, the fulfillment of their common Scriptures. The story of Luke-Acts is not an unbroken success story of how the Word of God journeyed from Galilee to Jerusalem and thence to the ends of the earth. The cross tempers any Lucan tendency to write a theology of glory. See Tiede, *Prophecy and History.*

57   (B) God's Promises Fulfilled in Jesus for All (4:16–30). This programmatic account of Jesus' ministry is a prime example of Luke's ordering of materials according to the theological principle of promise and fulfillment (see 1:1–4). For his description of Jesus' inaugural preaching Luke uses as one of his sources Mark 6:1–6a, a passage that does not describe the beginning of Jesus' ministry. Luke also uses traditional materials in vv 23 and 25–27. Verses 17–21 and 28–30, which evidence Lucan theological motifs, come from his hand. See *FGL* 526–27.

58   16. *where he had been raised:* It is important for the interpretation of the reaction of the townspeople in the troublesome v 22 to stress at the outset that Jesus' compatriots in obscure and tiny Nazareth (see John 1:46) think that they know him and his origins. *synagogue:* It seems that the sabbath synagogue service during the first century AD consisted of the singing of a psalm, the recitation of the *Shema* and the Eighteen Benedictions, a reading from the Torah and a reading from the prophets, a sermon on the meaning of the readings, a blessing by the president, and the priestly blessing of Num 6:24–27. It is highly controverted whether there was a triennial cycle of readings at this time. *sabbath:* This is the first of six incidents dealing with Jesus' activity on the sabbath; see 4:31–37; 6:1–5; 6:6–11; 13:10–17; 14:1–6. This account is programmatic for the interpretation of the activities Jesus performs on the sabbath: the sabbath is subordinate to Jesus because he is the eschatological fulfillment of God's promises for the hungry, the sick, and the imprisoned. Cf. S. G. Wilson, *Luke and the Law* (SNTSMS 50; Cambridge, 1983) 35. *as was his custom:* Luke emphasizes the continuity between the old and the new; Jesus stands in the finest line of Israel's traditions.

59   17. *he found the passage:* Here we are dealing with Lucan theology of promise and fulfillment. As the analysis of vv 18–19 will make clear, this Isaiah text is not to be found on a synagogue scroll. It is an artistic text, woven from Isa 61:1–2 and Isa 58:6, and resplendent with the colors of Luke's christology. **18–19.** This text consists of Isa 61:1a,b,d; 58:6d; 61:2a. In quoting from Isa 61, which was also used by the Qumranites about themselves in 11QMelch, Luke omits those elements which would spiritualize the text or narrow its focus on "true" Israel. Thus, he omits Isa 61:1c: "to heal the broken-hearted" and Isa 61:2b–3a: "(to announce) a day of vindication, to console those who mourn, to give those of Zion who mourn glory instead of ashes." He adds Isa 58:6, which occurs in a passage describing the true fast Yahweh desires and which refers to releasing those who are burdened by indebtedness. See R. Albertz, *ZNW* 74 (1983) 182–206. *Spirit of the Lord:* From 1:35 and 3:22 the reader knows that Jesus has the Spirit. Now the goal of that gift of the Spirit is underlined: it is for the benefit of those who are economically, physically, and socially unfortunate. *good news to the poor:* By his modifications of Isaiah 61, esp. through the introduction of Isa 58:6, Luke shows that "the poor" is not to be interpreted metaphorically as "Israel in need," the object of God's favor as the "new restoration" occurs. Luke will reinforce this message of universalism in vv 25–27. As analyses of 6:20–26; 7:22; and 14:13,21 will make manifest, "the poor" is to be interpreted by context. *release to those in prison:* At times this aspect of Jesus' ministry is seen fulfilled in 13:10–17 and 23:39–43, but it may be better to see this as a reference to those who may be imprisoned because of debts. Jesus will address words to those who may be responsible for such imprisonment in 6:35,37. The image of the biblical jubilee also rises to the surface in this phrase. The jubilee year was held every 50 years. During it fields lay fallow, persons returned to their homes, debts were canceled, and slaves were set free. The image derived from it underscored restoration, beginning, faith in the sovereignty of God, and conviction that the structures of social and economic life must reflect God's reign. See S. H. Ringe, *Jesus, Liberation, and the Biblical Jubilee* (OBT; Phl, 1985); R. B. Sloan, *The Favorable Year of the Lord* (Austin, 1977). The Gk word for "release" is *aphesis.* The LXX of Lev 25:10 uses *aphesis* to translate the Hebrew for jubilee; in Deut 15:1–11 the sabbath year is described by *aphesis* in the LXX (see also Exod 23:10–11). That such jubilee reflections were contemporary to Luke is evident at Qumran. In their reflections upon the end-time, the Qumranites associated Isa 61:1 with Lev 25:10–13 and Deut 15:2 (see 11QMelch) and identified the "release" as that of debtors during jubilee year. Although this socioeconomic background of jubilee is very much present in this passage, one should also recall that *aphesis* is the word used by Luke for "forgiveness" (of sins), e.g., 24:47. *release for those downtrodden:* This phrase from Isa 58:6 also contains the word *aphesis.* The Gk *thrauō,* behind "downtrodden," literally means "to break in pieces" (as a rock). In a figurative sense it means "to break," "oppress in spirit." See *BAGD* 363. It is plausible from Neh 5:1–10 that the "downtrodden" are those oppressed by debts and imprisonment. *to proclaim the Lord's acceptable year:* Luke has changed the LXX's vb. in Isa 61:2a from *kalesai,* "call," to *kēryxai,* "proclaim." For Luke the proclamation is that, in Jesus, God has fulfilled ancient promises. Again jubilee imagery seems present. The Gk word for "acceptable" is *dektos,* and it will recur in v 24, concerning the "acceptable" prophet. Jesus' ministry is only acceptable to God provided he does not limit his words and deeds to his own people, who because of his limitless mission will not find him or his words acceptable. See D. Hill, *NovT* 13 (1971) 169.

60   **21.** *today this Scripture has been fulfilled:* The word "today" introduces an important Lucan theme (see also 2:11; 22:61; 23:43) and should not be taken as a reference to the historical then of Jesus' time. Rather, the reference is to the present today of the time of fulfillment (*pace* Conzelmann, *TSL* 36; cf. Schweizer, *Good News* 89). The adult Jesus' first words in Luke deal with the theme of God's fidelity to promise. **22.** This notoriously difficult verse needs to be treated verb by verb. See F.

Ó Fearghail, *ZNW* 75 (1984) 60–72. *they all were giving favorable testimony to him:* There is no evidence in Luke or other Gk writings that the vb. *martyrein* is patient of a negative meaning: they were bearing witness against him. Inscriptional evidence points to the meaning of "favorable testimony borne by people who lived with the person under consideration." This meaning is supported by v 16, "where he was reared." *but were astonished at the words of salvation which came from his mouth:* Parallels from Acts 14:3; 20:24,32 suggest that *hoi logoi tēs charitos* should be translated not as "gracious or winsome words," but as "words of salvation." Deut 8:3 helps to explain the import of "came from his mouth." There the reference is to the word of God. The townspeople are amazed that one whom they have known all along is the messenger of such news. *is this not Joseph's son?:* This question gives the reasons for the astonishment of the townspeople and is ironic for readers who know of 1:32, 35; 3:21–22; 4:1–13. **23.** As in 11:37–54, Luke describes Jesus as taking the offensive with his audience. Jesus charges them with a lack of faith in him as the fulfillment of God's promises and as desirous of having him effect powerful deeds for their curiosity and benefit.

61   **24.** *no prophet is acceptable:* Luke refers to the theme of the "rejected prophet" here and in vv 25–27. See also 6:22–23; 11:49–51; 13:34–35; Acts 7:35,51–52. This theme highlights God's boundless compassion as he continues to send prophets to a rebellious people. The pattern of the "rejected prophet" thematic is found clearly in Neh 9:26–31: (1) rebellion and killing of the prophets; (2) punishment: (3) mercy through sending of new prophets; (4) sin and rejection of prophets. The first part of this pattern is found in Luke 1–23, and the second part dominates Luke 24 and Acts. Because of this thematic, the rejection given Jesus in 4:16–30 should not be seen as God's final answer in Jesus to Israel. See R. J. Dillon, "Easter Revelation and Mission Program in Luke 24:46–48," *Sin, Salvation, and the Spirit* (Fest. Liturgical Press; ed. D. Durken; Collegeville, 1979) 240–70. **25–27.** By these references to God's mercy for non-chosen, needy people through the prophets Elijah (1 Kgs 18:1) and Elisha (1 Kgs 17:9) Luke provides further support for his universalizing of Isa 61:1–2 in vv 18–19. Note also that God's mercy is for both men and women. **62**   **28.** *they were all filled with rage:* Their reaction is of a piece with that in v 22. But now they know clearly, because of Jesus' examples in vv 25–27, that God's offer of salvation in the prophet Jesus is not restricted to them. God's grace is unconditional. They are not "God's poor," who can claim special treatment. **29–30.** Jesus continues his journey to God according to God's plan, which opposition cannot squelch. Jesus' escape points ahead to Easter victory. See J. A. Sanders, "From Isaiah 61 to Luke 4," *Christianity, Judaism and Other Greco-Roman Cults* (Fest. M. Smith; ed. J. Neusner; SJLA 12; Leiden, 1975) 1. 75–106; *God Has a Story Too* (Phl, 1979) 67–79; *Int* 36 (1982) 144–55.

63   **(C) God's Kingdom Restores Men and Women to Wholeness (4:31–44).** This section, based on Mark 1:21–39, is a well-knit unity. Luke uses a group of Jesus' activities, which seem inadequately described as a typical day within Jesus' ministry, to create a christological catechism for his churches. **31–37.** This is the first of many exorcisms in Luke-Acts. In addition to the healing story of 4:38–39 and the stilling of the storm at sea in 8:22–25, which use the technical term for exorcism *epitiman* (4:39; 8:24 respectively), Luke has three other exorcisms: 8:26–39; 9:37–43a; 13:10–17. Only 13:10–17 is proper to Luke; the others stem from Mark. In his summaries Luke refers to Jesus' exorcisms: 4:40–41; 6:17–19; 7:21; 13:32; Acts 10:38.

The first two are taken from Mark; the third from Q; the last two from L. Jesus' followers are released from demons (8:1-3) or share in his power over evil: 9:1-6, 49-50; 10:17-20; Acts 5:16; 8:7; 16:16-18. Of these references all are proper to Luke except Luke 9:1-6, 49-50. In the Q passage, 11:14-26, Jesus engages in controversy with the religious leaders about the source of his power over evil. Luke and the traditions known to him could not describe Jesus without emphasizing that in him God is freeing creation from those powers which are strangling it. There is much truth in the position of those who view Luke 11:20 and Acts 10:38 as keys to all that Luke has to say about Jesus and evil: in his exorcisms Jesus shows the nature of God's rule; his whole ministry can be described as the liberation of all those who are oppressed by the powers of evil. See W. Kirchschläger, *Jesu exorzistisches Wirken aus der Sicht des Lukas* (Österreichische biblische Studien 3; Klosterneuburg, 1981).

64 **31.** *Capernaum:* In 4:23 Luke anticipated part of what he wanted to say about this important trade center, which was located on the northwestern shore of the Sea of Galilee (→ Biblical Geography, 73:61). He will complete his story about it in 7:1 and 10:15; the latter verse is ominous. Capernaum had a population of 15,000. See L. J. Hoppe, *What Are They Saying About Biblical Archaeology?* (NY, 1984) 58-78, esp. 58. *polis:* Luke has a proclivity for situating stories about Jesus and Paul in cities, which are the cultural, economic, political, and social centers of an area. *teaching on the sabbath:* See 4:14-15. **32.** *his word:* Here this refers to his teaching. In the *inclusio* of 4:36 it will refer to his word over unclean spirits. Jesus' teaching has as much power as an exorcism. **33-34.** *synagogue:* What was implicit in vv 31-32 is made explicit. See 4:14-15. The theme of purity unites three concepts here: sabbath, unclean spirit, Holy One of God. Jesus cleanses a man of an unclean spirit on the day that separates ordinary from holy because Jesus stands in intimate relationship to God, holiness itself. The relationship of Jesus to God conveyed here echoes 1:32-33,35; 2:11,30,49; 3:22-23; 4:1-13 and points ahead to Luke's christological emphasis in 4:41: Son of God and Messiah. **35.** *commanded:* This is the Gk *epitiman,* one of the means Luke uses to interconnect the materials in 4:31-44; it recurs in 4:39,41. It is a technical term and "denotes the pronouncement of a commanding word whereby God or his spokesman brings evil powers into submission. It is part of the vocabulary belonging to the description of the final defeat of Belial and his minions" (*FGL* 546). Jesus exorcizes the unclean spirit within a man in the presence of all; in 4:38-39 he will exorcize a fever within a woman in a private house. His liberating power is for men and women and is not limited to sacred or secular space. On the theme of women in Luke, see comment on 2:36-38. Luke, in contrast to Mark 1:26, underlines the fact that after Jesus' command the unclean spirit has no power to harm the man. **36.** *with authority:* The power of Jesus' word to restore to wholeness those who are fractured by evil is highlighted, as v 36 forms an *inclusio* with 4:32. In contrast to Mark, Luke balances Jesus' miraculous activity and his teaching and gives them equal weight. See P. J. Achtemeier, *JBL* 94 (1975) 547-62.

65 **38-39.** *Simon:* In Luke the call of Simon is first narrated in 5:1-11, whereas Mark narrated his call in 1:16-20, a passage occurring before the sequence in Mark (1:21-39) which Luke redacts in this section. Two reasons have been given for Luke's order. (1) Luke, esp. in Acts (e.g., 8:4-12), develops the thesis that faith and discipleship grow out of an encounter with miracle. On this reading, Simon, having seen the miracle Jesus

performed for his mother-in-law, is ready to follow Jesus when he calls him. (2) This reason builds upon the fact that one of Luke's literary techniques is to mention the name of a character early on in the story and only later to give more details about that person. Thus, Luke mentions Barnabas early on in Acts 4:36-37, but only fills out that first sketch in Acts 13. Similarly, Paul's first mention in Acts 7:58-8:3 is teasing. From Acts 9 on Paul plays a dominant role in Luke's story. *high fever:* Luke intensifies the fever and thereby underscores the power of Jesus' word. Because of its sudden advent and deleterious effects, esp. delirium, fever was feared in antiquity. **39.** *standing over her:* In contrast to Mark 1:31 and Acts 28:8, Luke does not mention the use of hands. In 4:40 Luke will stress how Jesus lays his hands on the sick. Here his redaction puts onto center stage the power of Jesus' word. *commands the fever:* Luke again uses *epitiman,* the technical word for an exorcism. The cure is instantaneous. There is no long recuperation to regain strength; Simon's mother-in-law assumes her social obligations in full stride.

66 **40-41.** This summary is similar to 6:17-19, in both of which Jesus' exorcisms are subsumed under the more general term "cure" (*therapeuein*). **40.** *each and every one:* Luke highlights Jesus' compassion for all. **41.** *came out of:* This is the same Gk construction (*exerchesthai apo*) that Luke employed in 4:35 (twice) and 4:36 and is one of his means of unifying 4:31-44. In contrast to Mark 1:34 Luke adds two christological titles: Son of God and Messiah. It is because of Jesus' origin in God (see 1:32-33,35) and because he is God's anointed agent of salvation that he casts out demons. From the start the demons know who Jesus is and what he is about. It will take humans the long journey of faith to appreciate the role of the cross in the Messiah's life (see 24:26).

67 **42-44.** These verses, esp. v 43, are an important recapitulation of 4:14-43: Jesus' first mission in Galilee. **42.** Luke will hold over until 5:16 the mention of Jesus at prayer found in Mark 1:35. See J. Dupont, *RSR* 69 (1981) 45-55, esp. p. 46. The response to Jesus given by the people of Capernaum stands in sharp contrast to that of the folks of Nazareth (4:16-30). But does it? See 10:15. Perhaps the people of Capernaum were not led to faith in Jesus by the mighty deeds Jesus performed for them. **43.** *kingdom of God:* Luke's story in 4:16-42 provides a descriptive definition of this term. God's rule means the conquest of evil for all, for both men and women, for outcasts and poor, for blind and lame. And that rule is effected by the preaching and the mighty deeds of Jesus, the Holy One of God, God's Son, God's Anointed. *I have been sent:* By observing what Jesus does, one can arrive at a clear view of the one who sent him. The sender, too, is for life and for the elimination of evil. He is, moreover, trustworthy because he is faithful to promises (4:16-21). **44.** *Judea:* One would expect to read "Galilee." Galilee is part of the larger Judea, land of the Jews. See U. Busse, *Die Wunder des Propheten Jesus* (FB 24; Stuttgart, 1977) 66-90.

68 **(D) Positive Response to Jesus' Kingdom Message (5:1-11).** This passage makes four major points, all of them interrelated. (1) Peter's positive response to Jesus, along with that of James and John, is the first such in the gospel story. Jesus' hometown folks in Nazareth responded hostilely to his preaching of promise and fulfillment (4:16-30). As 10:15 will indicate, the response of the people of Capernaum was not totally positive (4:31-43). (2) Now that Luke has demonstrated via his stories in 4:16-44 what Jesus' preaching of the kingdom of God involves, he tells a story of how Jesus enlists Peter as a helper in his kingdom activity and calls Peter, James, and John to follow his kingdom life-style.

Their response is total as they abandon all for Jesus. (3) In this story, esp. in 5:10, Luke paints the first strokes of his very flattering and deeply appreciative portrait of Peter. (4) Peter's missionary success, like his catch of fish, is not his own doing, but the Lord's.

69   Luke's redactional hand has been busily at work in 5:1-11. For the opening of his story in 5:1-3 he employs Mark 4:1-2. For the material in 5:4-9,10b he draws on a source that also lies behind John 21:1-11. For 5:10a he draws on Mark 1:19; for 5:11 he draws on Mark 1:18,20. A quick comparison of Luke 5:1-11 with Mark 1:16-20 will show how unique Luke's version is.

70   **1-3.** See Mark 4:1-2, in a context of Jesus preaching parables. **1.** *God's word:* This phrase occurs 14 times in Acts (e.g., 4:31; 16:32) and generally refers to the Christian message. By using it of Jesus' own preaching, Luke "roots the Christian community's proclamation in the teaching of Jesus himself" (*FGL* 565). In 4:31-39 Luke accentuated the power of Jesus' word. **2.** *two boats:* Throughout 5:4-11 the Lucan spotlight will be on Simon Peter, but his companions are always in the shadows, ready to help. See the pl. vbs. in 5:4,5,6,7. The fishermen described here are middle-class artisans. See W. Wuellner, *The Meaning of "Fishers of Men"* (Phl, 1967) 26-63. **3.** *Simon:* Before 6:14 Jesus' first-called bears this name. Luke has the deepest respect for Simon Peter, describing his founding role in the primitive church in Acts. Besides 5:4-9,10b, he alone of the Synoptics has 22:31-32 (Jesus' prayer for Peter) and 24:34 (the risen Jesus' appearance to Peter alone). Luke eliminates the negative remarks found about Peter in Mark 8:32-33 and 14:37. For more details, see *PNT* 39-56, 109-28.

71   **4-9.** J. A. Fitzmyer (*FGL* 560-61) notes eleven points of similarity and seven points of dissimilarity between 5:4-9 and John 21:1-11. It seems that both Luke 5:4-9,10b and John 21:1-11 bear independent witness to a post-Easter appearance of Jesus to Peter. John develops the tradition in his own way by introducing the Beloved Disciple. Into his account of Jesus' earthly ministry and his call of his first followers, Luke has transposed a story that once told of Peter's recognition of the Lord in the miraculous catch of fish, his reconciliation with the Lord after denial, and his commission to head up Jesus' postresurrection mission.

72   **10-11.** Luke draws on Mark 1:18-20 to fill out his story. **10.** *from now on:* This particular Lucan phrase occurs in 1:48; 12:52; 22:18,69; and Acts 18:6 and denotes the beginning of a new period of salvation. *catching human beings and in so doing bringing them new life:* This transl. is an attempt to capture the nuance behind the peculiar Lucan vb. *zōgrōn.* The symbol of fishing has a rich background in antiquity. Writing for those familiar with Greco-Roman traditions, Luke singles out that aspect of the symbol which was exploited by teachers who lured students to themselves and through their education of them transformed their lives. That aspect is the bait. Peter will be catching men and women with the bait of God's word and thereby bringing them new life. If one focuses on the aspect of water in the symbol, one is caught in the difficulty of presenting Peter as one who does something destructive to human beings on the analogy of what happens to fish once they are taken from the water. A remnant of Luke's meaning may be found in our expression "they took the bait—hook, line, and sinker." The people who took the bait were not killed, but won over to a new point of view. See Wuellner, "Fishers of Men" (→ 70 above) 70-71, 217, 237-38; and Lucian, *Fisherman* 48-52. **11.** *everything:* This is Lucan redaction and is of a piece with 5:28; 12:33; 14:33; 18:18-23. See W. E. Pilgrim, *Good News to the Poor* (Minneapolis, 1981) 87-102. *followed:* Companions on Jesus'

journeys, Peter, James, and John have committed themselves to his message and destiny. See S. O. Abogunrin, *NTS* 31 (1985) 587-602.

73   **(E) Jesus' Boundary-Breaking Ministry for Outcasts (5:12-16).** Lev 13-14; Num 5:2-3; 2 Kgs 7:3-9; 15:5 provide essential biblical background for an appreciation of the christology of this passage. Persons with skin diseases were not clean or holy and therefore were isolated from concourse with the holy people of God in cities and were banned from participation in the Temple worship of God, the Holy One. Jesus, the Holy One of God (4:34), steps across the boundaries separating clean from unclean, touches the unclean, and restores that person to the nurture of human community. See Mark 1:40-45.

74   **12.** *one of the cities:* This phrase connects this story with 4:43, but raises the problem of what the afflicted person was doing in a city (see Lev 13:45-46). Is the man breaking boundaries to encounter the ultimate boundary-breaker? The disease the person has is not leprosy, Hansen's disease, but a skin disorder like psoriasis. The *NJB* has "skin-disease." See 7:22 and 17:11-19 for other instances of Jesus' ministry for these social outcasts. **13.** *touched him:* Contact with the unclean renders one unclean. Human concern, and not religious taboos, prompts Jesus' behavior. *I will:* By removing the references to Jesus' mercy (Mark 1:41) and Jesus' anger (Mark 1:43) in his source (Mark 1:41-45), Luke underlines the power of Jesus' will and word. The cleansing takes place immediately. **14.** *tell no one:* There is a tension in the text. The man is already clean, made holy by Jesus, God's Holy One. Why does he have to be declared clean by the Temple priests? Jesus, the new wine (5:37-39), acknowledges the presence of the old wine; but see 19:44-45. **15.** *the word spread about him:* Luke changes Mark 1:45, so that the man is not disobedient to Jesus, who remains in charge of the entire situation. Although the story dealt solely with a cure, Luke characteristically adds "to hear" Jesus' teaching. **16.** *praying:* The motif of prayer, not used from Mark 1:35 in Luke 4:42, appears here. See 3:31-32. In two ways 5:12-16 prepares for the controversies of 5:17-6:11. Luke 5:14 shows Jesus' fidelity to the law, a point disputed in the controversies. Luke 5:16 shows that the one attacked in 5:17-6:11 maintains an intimate relationship with God. See Busse, *Wunder* (→ 67 above) 103-14; J. J. Pilch, *BTB* 11 (1981) 108-13.

75   **(F) Religious Leaders Oppose Jesus' Kingdom Message (5:17-6:11).** This section is based on Mark 2:1-3:6 and is a "ring composition." Both the first (5:17-26) and the fifth (6:6-11) stories concern healing. Both the second (5:27-32) and the fourth (6:1-5) deal with eating. The third passage explains why Jesus has engaged in such controversial activities as those narrated here. The stories are interconnected in other ways, too: 5:17-26 and 5:27-32 treat forgiveness of sins; 6:1-5 and 6:6-11 take place on a sabbath.

76   The Pharisees appear here (5:17,21,30,33; 6:2, 7) for the first time (→ History, 75:146-48) and are Jesus' opponents. Although it is easy to count the 35 times Luke mentions the Pharisees in Luke-Acts, it is more difficult to ascertain their function in his story. In Acts the Pharisee Gamaliel seems favorably disposed to the Way (5:34). Paul is described as a Pharisee (23:6; 26:5) who is on trial for his faith in the resurrection of the dead. The Pharisees, who along with the Sadducees make up the sanhedrin and who also believe in the resurrection of the dead, find nothing wrong with Paul (23:6-9). These texts indicate that Lucan Christianity with its belief in the resurrection of the dead stands in line with Pharisaic teaching. In Acts 15:5 Christian Pharisees demand that Gentile converts to Christianity be circumcised and charged to obey the law of Moses. If we suppose that the rigoristic and sectarian Jewish Christian views espoused in Acts 15:5 are those of members of Luke's communities, we may have a key to unlocking many unique references to the Pharisees in Luke's Gospel. In brief, in his Gospel he is not writing about the Pharisees at the time of Jesus of Nazareth but of Christian Pharisees in his communities, who limit universal forgiveness.

77 The Pharisees in Luke's Gospel criticize Jesus and his disciples for eating with sinners (5:27-32; 15:1-2). The Pharisees invite Jesus to dine with them. During these meals Jesus is twice critical of their narrow views of who belongs to God's holy community (7:36-50; 14:1-24); once he upbraids them for neglecting justice and the love of God for supererogatory practices (11:37-54). The Pharisees are self-righteous and have no need of repentance (5:32; 7:29-30; 18:9-14). Because of their narrow view of who belongs to God's community, they repudiate Jesus' teaching of giving alms to all and thus show their greed (16:14). They are not able to see that God's kingdom has come in Jesus' extension of mercy to Samaritans, half-Jews at best (17:11-20). They want Jesus to prevent his disciples from rejoicing over the mighty deeds that he has performed for all (19:37-39). Their narrow-mindedness is the leaven of which Luke's readers must beware (12:1). See J. T. Sanders, "The Pharisees in Luke-Acts," *The Living Text* (Fest. E. Saunders; ed. D. E. Groh and R. Jewett; Lanham, 1985) 141-88. For other views, see J. B. Tyson (*The Death of Jesus in Luke-Acts* [Columbia, 1986] 64-72), who emphasizes the positive aspects of Luke's portrait of the Pharisees; and R. J. Karris (*Luke* 23-44), who puts the Pharisees and high priests under the category of "religious leaders" who oppose Jesus.

78 Questions about the fine points of the controversies in this section should not obscure Luke's major focus, which is christology. Jesus, the bridegroom and dispenser of new wine, has come to reconcile sinners with God and one another. Even the sabbath is subordinate to him.

(a) JESUS' POWER TO FORGIVE SINS (5:17-26). From 4:31-5:16 Luke has been depicting Jesus' kingdom power of effecting cures and exorcisms. Now in this composite story of healing (5:17-20a,24c-26) and pronouncement (5:20b-24ab) he will narrate something strange indeed (see 5:26): Jesus forgives sins, something which God alone can do. **17.** *Pharisees:* They come from all around. Their reactions to the activities of the Lucan Jesus will heat up in negative intensity throughout this "ring composition." In the end they are furious with Jesus (6:11). **20.** *their faith:* The paralytic's friends have deep confidence that God is operative for healing in Jesus. Before all the dust generated by the paralytic's unusual approach to Jesus can settle down, Jesus restores the ill man to union with God. **21.** *who can forgive sins?:* The Pharisees do not miss the implication of Jesus' action: he is equal to God. **22.** Jesus' foreknowledge is also underscored in 6:8, the companion to this story in Luke's "ring composition." **24-26.** Restoration to full health, an externally visible action, is testimony to Jesus' authority to perform the action of forgiveness of sins which is not visible to human eyes. The man's new way of life is symbolic of what forgiveness entails.

79 (b) JESUS' MISSION IS FOR SINNERS (5:27-32). Jesus' universal kingdom message draws fire from the Pharisees, who have a narrow view of who can be saved. **27.** *toll collector:* Jesus calls a despised toll collector, and he responds wholeheartedly. See 3:12-13. **28.** *everything:* Such abandonment is indicative of his interior change of

heart and total commitment to Jesus. See 5:11; 12:33; 14:33; 18:18-23. **29.** *great feast:* Luke's theme of food, which runs throughout his Gospel, surfaces here. God's desire to be with his creation is symbolized by a feast with all its joy, celebration, friendship, and merriment; see Karris, *Luke* 47-78. **30.** *Pharisees:* The presence of the Pharisees at such a gathering is incongruous at one level of the story, for what would these purists be doing sharing food with sinners? But on the level of Luke's theology it is highly significant that they are present. These Christian sectarians demand of Luke's community, Jesus' disciples, the rationale for their liberal membership policies. **31.** Jesus answers the objections thrown in the face of his disciples. **32.** *I have come:* The pf. tense of this verse indicates that the effect of Jesus' action continues into the present. Luke adds another brush stroke to his compelling portrait of the compassionate Jesus. *righteous:* In the Lucan context the use of this word is ironic. It may legitimately be translated as "self-righteous." The theme of Pharisaic self-righteousness may also be found in 7:29-30; 16:15; 18:9. *repentance:* The grace of God's call is free, but not cheap. A change of life is required. This *metanoia* is represented in this story by Levi's forsaking of all and by his sharing of the good news of Jesus with his friends at a banquet. "Thus, in Luke's story the good news of Jesus' identification with sinful humanity is incomplete without the invitation to a reorienting of life" (D. L. Tiede, *Int* 40 [1986] 61).

80 (c) JESUS IS THE BRIDEGROOM AND PROVIDER OF NEW WINE (5:33-39). As the key passage in Luke's "ring composition," this passage provides additional christological underpinning for Jesus' forgiveness of sins (5:17-26; 5:27-32) and his authority over the sabbath (6:1-5; 6:6-11). **34.** *bridegroom:* This figure was applied in the OT and Judaism to represent God's union with his people. See Hos 2:18,21; Ezek 16; Isa 54:5-8; 62:5; Jer 2:2. The images of joy, beginning of new life after estrangement, deep love and concern, and fidelity shine forth from this powerful symbol. In Jesus, God is united with his people. **38.** *new wine:* In Jesus, God has done something new. The symbol of new wine teases the imagination to think of life triumphing over death. The harvest has been productive, and life has vanquished the forces of death in drought, disease, and flood. From grapes, pulverized and inedible, surges bubbling, hearty, heady new wine to rejoice the heart. **39.** *the old is good:* This unique Lucan proverb curbs one line of interpreting vv 37-38. The old is not to be cast aside, for the sabbath and the law and the prophets also contain God's will.

81 (d) THE SABBATH IS SUBORDINATE TO JESUS (6:1-5). **1.** *sabbath:* This is the second of six stories concerned with Jesus' liberating actions on a sabbath. See 4:16-30; 6:6-11; 13:10-17; 14:1-6. **3-4.** *what David did:* Jesus answers the Pharisees with an argument from analogy, which is not too forceful, for David's action did not occur on a sabbath and his action dealt with forbidden food and not with working on a forbidden day. The main point of the analogy is that both David and Jesus' disciples did something forbidden, but that is to concede the Pharisees' point. **5.** *the Son of Man is Lord of the sabbath:* Luke presents Jesus' ultimate argument for the actions of Luke's communities in neglecting provisions of sabbath regulation. Jesus, God's eschatological agent or Son of Man (see also 5:24), has subordinated God's sabbath to himself and his kingdom mission and given such power to his followers. "The claim to lordship over the sabbath ultimately subordinates the sabbath to Jesus and does not merely establish him as the arbiter of sabbath disputes. If the sabbath is subordinate to Jesus so is the law" (Wilson, *Luke and the Law* [→ 58 above] 35).

82   (e) COMPASSIONATE JESUS CURES ON THE SABBATH (6:6–11). **9–10.** *is it lawful to do good on the sabbath . . . ?:* Jesus and his disciples are not bound by sabbath regulations when it is a question of doing good for people or saving a person's life. Jesus, the Son of Man, enunciates the principle of compassion. **11.** *the Pharisees were filled with wrath:* Luke softens Mark 3:6, which says that the Pharisees plot how to destroy Jesus. In Luke the Pharisees do not participate in the high priests' plot to kill Jesus, for after 19:39 they no longer appear in the Gospel. Luke is dealing with the rigorist Christian Pharisees within his communities, who cannot tolerate the lenient views obtaining in these communities: association with sinners and neglect of sabbath regulations, whose purpose is to prevent the holy from being contaminated by the unholy. Luke's main argument against them is christological: the Lord Jesus, the Son of Man, made us do it.

83   **(G) The Gathering of Reconstituted Israel (6:12–49).** After presenting Jesus as encountering hostility from the Pharisees because of his kingdom ministry (5:17–6:11), Luke now depicts Jesus' choice of twelve intimates who symbolize reconstituted Israel. They are also Jesus' apostles or emissaries, who continue his kingdom proclamation. In 6:17–49 Jesus details what membership in reconstituted Israel entails.

84   (a) JESUS' SELECTION OF TWELVE APOSTLES (6:12–16). **12.** *mountain:* Jesus ascends to the place where the religious man communes with God. His selection of the Twelve apostles stems from God. **13.** *twelve:* For Luke the Twelve symbolize continuity with Israel. In Acts 1 the number twelve must be completed after the death of Judas, so that the Twelve, thus reconstituted, might be present to receive the promised holy Spirit and begin preaching to the ends of the earth. In Acts 26:6–7 Paul talks about the resurrection promise made to the twelve tribes and now fulfilled in Jesus. *apostles:* This is a "technical term for a Christian emissary or missionary commissioned to preach the Christ-event, or in Lucan terms, 'the word of God'" (*FGL* 617). Among the other evangelists this is a rare word (→ NT Thought, 81:137–57). It occurs some 30 times in Luke-Acts. Luke is almost without parallel also in linking the Twelve with the apostles (cf. Matt 10:2; Rev 21:14). Put another way, Luke goes against the grain of other NT writers by so linking the Twelve with the apostles. See further 1 Cor 15:5–9, where Paul lists those to whom the risen Lord has appeared: Cephas, the Twelve, 500 brethren, James, all the apostles, Paul. Paul is an apostle, although not one of the Twelve. One key to the Lucan usage of twelve apostles is found in Acts 1:21–22: the one to replace Judas has to have accompanied Jesus from the baptism of John to the ascension and thus become a witness of his resurrection. Thus, for Luke the Twelve become the bond of continuity between Jesus' kingdom proclamation and the church's preaching of God's word. Luke's definition, however, raises additional problems, because Paul, although featured in the last half of Acts, is not called an apostle (save in Acts 14:4,14). The Lucan view of Jesus' associates is further complicated by a felicitous inconsistency. Witnesses to Jesus' ministry are not just the apostles, but also the disciples, a much larger group that includes men and women. See the Lucan account of the Last Supper, where Luke interchanges "disciples" (22:11) and "apostles" (22:14). See further 24:1–10, where Luke depicts women disciples as the first witnesses of Jesus' resurrection and has them proclaim the resurrection gospel to the apostles. **14–16.** Other lists of the Twelve occur in Mark 3:16–19; Matt 10:2–4; Acts

1:13. What a symbol of unity from diversity: fishermen, a zealot, Galileans, a Judean (Judas of Iscariot), a toll collector, one with a Greek name (Philip), and one who betrayed Jesus' offer of deep intimacy. It is sobering to reflect that little is remembered later of most of this group that was so important at one time. As a matter of fact, the lists of the Twelve keep mixing their names up. Even Luke in 6:14–16 and Acts 1:13 does not follow the same order of names (→ NT Thought, 81:137–46).

85   (b) THE SERMON ON THE PLAIN (6:17–49). There are four key problems in Luke's counterpart of Matthew's Sermon on the Mount (see Matt 5–7). These problems are sources, audience, meaning of poor and rich, and Luke's intention; these problems intersect on the theme of sharing possessions. Luke's version of the sermon is shorter than Matthew's; the following verses are derived from Q and thus also found in Matthew: 20b–23,27–33,35b–36,37a,38b,39bc,40–42,43–45,46–49. The major Lucan redaction occurs in vv 24–26 (the woes), 27c,28a,34–35a,37bc,38a,39a. See further *FGL* 627. In vv 34–35a,37bc, and 38a Luke makes reference to the sharing of possessions. Lending money, pardoning financial debts, and giving unstintingly are hardly commands one gives to impoverished disciples (see comment on 6:20–23). They are commands to people with possessions.

86   It is widely held that although Luke explicitly says in v 20a that Jesus is speaking to his disciples, he cannot be addressing these same disciples in 6:24, for they are hardly "rich." The Lucan Jesus must be addressing rich people, who are not present to hear his sermon. But as A. Plummer (*Luke* 182) advised decades ago, "We have no right to assume that no persons were present to whom these words would be applicable." Luke tells us who was present: see 6:17,19, which refer to a large crowd present; see further 6:27a: "but to you who listen I say"; 7:1 says that Jesus spoke the words of 6:20–49 to the people. H. Flender (*Luke* [→ 28 above] 23–25) has correctly explained the Lucan fluidity between disciples (6:20a) and people (6:17,19,27; 7:1) thus: the division between the people and the disciples is not final; discipleship must be constantly renewed through hearing and responding to Jesus' word (see Luke 12, where a comparable distinction is made between people and disciples). In vv 47–49 both disciples and people will be challenged to respond to Jesus' words. The well-to-do prospective Christian disciple is addressed in vv 24–26; and in vv 34–35a,37bc, and 38a is admonished to lend, pardon debts, and give unhesitatingly.

87   The entire context of 4:16–6:19 sheds light on the meaning of the terms "poor" and "rich" and "kingdom" in vv 20–26. Jesus' inaugural sermon in 4:16–30 clearly proclaimed that membership in "the poor of God" was not restricted to an ingroup. 4:31–44 showed that the nature of the God whose kingdom Jesus preached was to show mercy to ill men and women and to conquer the forces of evil. In 5:1–11 Jesus is depicted as calling Peter and others as disciples and sharers in his kingdom ministry. In 5:17–6:11 Luke described Jesus' controversies with the religious leaders over the question of who speaks and acts authoritatively in God's name. In 6:12–16 Jesus is portrayed as selecting the Twelve to symbolize the reconstituted Israel. Jesus, the gatherer of the reconstituted Israel, preaches (6:20–49) to those who would belong to God's kingdom. Those who want to belong to "the poor of God," that group which acknowledges its need of his salvation, will become recipients of the kingdom provided they confess Jesus, the bringer of the kingdom (6:23). Put another way, although God's fulfillment of promise in Jesus is an invitation for all to become "the poor of God" (see

4:16–30), only those who confess that God's kingdom is effected by Jesus form "the poor of God." The rich are those who do not want to commit themselves to Jesus and the kingdom he effects. They are content with their present, comfortable existence. Further, in 6:20 Luke is not extolling poverty, but praising the God who in Jesus' kingdom ministry, as narrated in 4:16–6:19, has a special love for the unfortunate. See J. Dupont, "The Poor and Poverty in the Gospels and Acts," *Gospel Poverty* (Chicago, 1977) 25–52.

88 Through Jesus' sermon Luke preaches to his Gentile Christians, some of whom are well-to-do, about their place in reconstituted Israel and about the nature of the God whose kingdom Jesus enacted. In imitating this generous God (6:35–36), these Christians will lend money, forgive debts, and give generously to those inside and outside the community. In so doing, they will not fall back into the reciprocity ethic in which they were reared and expect their beneficiaries to return the favor. Cf. Horn, *Glaube und Handeln* (→ 23 above) 177–81; Seccombe, *Possessions* (→ 23 above) 84–93.

89 The sermon can be outlined as follows: 6:20–26: beatitudes and woes; 6:27–38: contemporizing of 6:20–26 for Luke's community; 6:39–49: parabolic reinforcements of the message of 6:20–38. **20–23.** *blessed:* The Lucan Jesus is not declaring a social class blessed. The blessed condition comes from and will come from the kingdom which Jesus is effecting. Moreover, membership in the Israel being reconstituted by Jesus depends on one's becoming a disciple of Jesus (6:20). Such discipleship may have dire consequences which will, in turn, prove the depth of the commitment to Jesus and his kingdom message (6:23). Verse 23 prepares for 6:27–38, esp. its twice-repeated command to love one's enemies (6:27,35).

90 **24–26.** *woe:* The woes are Luke's redaction and are meant to caution against a too facile understanding of who does or can belong to "the poor of God." The "woe" form is minatory in character. Its purpose is to elicit reform. Thus, a social class is not being condemned. As v 20a indicates, the woes are addressed to would-be disciples who have possessions. They are challenged that wealth, stomachs filled with select foodstuffs, carefree times, and being held in high esteem by the right people are ephemeral when compared with following Jesus and his kingdom message. As Luke will teach in vv 34–35a,37bc,38a, those with possessions can only become members of "the poor of God" provided they share their possessions with those in need.

91 **27–38.** Contemporizing of vv 20–26 for Luke's community. **27a.** *to you that hear:* Luke's message is addressed to would-be disciples. **27b–29.** These verses refer to 6:22 and spell out in more graphic detail how disciples are to respond to persecution. The love of enemies proposed here is radical. The imagery of turning the other cheek for a further insulting blow and of stripping oneself naked (v 28) flies in the face of the natural human tendency to place self-protection first. This command suggests that another pattern of conduct replace that of self-protection. See R. C. Tannehill, *The Sword of His Mouth* (SBLSS 1; Phl, 1975) 67–77. The Lucan theme of love of enemies, introduced here, is a pervasive one, e.g., in Luke's stories of Samaritans: 9:51–56; 10:25–37; 17:11–17; Acts 8:4–25. See Ford, *My Enemy;* W. Klassen, *Love of Enemies* (OBT; Phl, 1984) 80–102. **30.** *to all:* Whereas Matt 5:42a has "give to the one who begs," Luke, in addressing would-be disciples who have possessions, radicalizes the command and makes it universal. Whereas Matt 5:42b has "do not turn away a person who wants to borrow from you," Luke radicalizes the command: "Do not demand your posses-

sions back from the person who takes them." See J. Piper, *'Love your enemies'* (SNTSMS 38; Cambridge, 1979) 157–62. **31.** *do likewise to them:* The Lucan version of the "golden rule," introduced here, will be interpreted by vv 32–36, lest Luke's Gentile audience construe it according to the dominant reciprocity ethic of their culture. See W. C. van Unnik, *NovT* 8 (1966) 284–300. Through the teaching of 6:32–35ab Luke, moreover, interprets the command to love one's enemies (6:27) to mean that disciples must share their possessions with them (6:35). **32–35.** *and if you . . . :* According to the reciprocity ethic, the one who received some good was obliged to reciprocate. Such reciprocation does not engender "thanks" (*charis*) because it stems from obligation. Only when one "does good" (*agathopoiein,* the Lucan way of stressing the concrete, active nature of love) even though one has not been given anything and only when one expects nothing in return, does one get—quite unexpectedly—not only "thanks" but also reward from God. See also 14:12–14. **35c–36.** Seen within its context of disciples sharing possessions with others, the motif of imitation of God translates thus: "As God stands to the needy world with the gracious gift of salvation, so the disciples should stand to the poor of society in generous open-handedness" (Seccombe, *Possessions* [→ 23 above] 196). **37–39.** Luke continues to interpret traditional material from Q by means of his teaching of sharing possessions. **37c.** *pardon your debtors and you will be pardoned:* The Gk *apolyein* should not be translated "forgive" (the one who has wronged you). As BAGD 96 demonstrates, the verb has an economic force; in that sense, it fits well with the Lucan teaching in 6:27–39. **38.** *lap:* The arresting image of one's lap not being able to contain a cascade of goodies illumines God's superabundant response to human generous sharing of possessions. With many variations on the one theme of sharing possessions, Luke has given a unity to disparate materials in 6:27–38 and has actualized the meaning of the beatitudes and woes for disciples and would-be disciples.

92 **39–49.** Parabolic reinforcements of the message of vv 20–38. The parables of 6:39–40,41–42,43–45, 46–49 should not be interpreted as general messages to disciples. Luke has given specific meaning to these largely traditional parables by his context of calling disciples and would-be disciples to join "the poor of God" by sharing their possessions, even with enemies. **39–40.** *blind:* These verses are not addressed to false teachers in the Lucan community. See Marshall, *Gospel* 267–68. The disciples are blind until they have their eyes opened by Jesus' teaching in 6:20–38. Once they have been fully trained in what Jesus means by sharing possessions (see 5:11; 18:28; Acts 2:41–47; 4:31–34), then they will be able to instruct others. See A. J. Mattill (*NovT* 17 [1975] 15–46), who, however, argues that 6:40 refers to disciples having learned the meaning of suffering and persecution from the Lord Jesus. **41–42.** *speck in your brother's eye:* An admonition for those who see their lapses in the area of sharing possessions as being minute compared with the gross failures of others. **43–45.** *good tree:* Effective compliance with the teaching in 6:20–38 can come only from a heart that has been converted to the gracious God proclaimed in Jesus' kingdom ministry. Be converted! **46–49.** *and do not do what I say:* The conclusion to Jesus' sermon again addresses would-be disciples. Hearing and even calling Jesus Lord, although important (see 8:4–21), are not enough. Disciples will join the Israel being reconstituted by Jesus only if they build their lives on effective implementation of Jesus' teaching on lending with no strings attached, pardoning debtors, and generous giving—even to the enemy. See J.

Lambrecht, *The Sermon on the Mount* (GNS 14; Wilmington, 1985) 19-79, 206-33.

93   (H) Jesus' Kingdom Message Is for Men and Women and Shatters the Boundaries of Clean and Unclean (7:1-9:6). This section, which highlights Jesus as crossing over boundaries separating clean from unclean to restore people to life and community, begins with stories of Jesus curing a sick man and raising a dead man to life (7:1-17). It ends with stories of Jesus curing a sick woman and raising a dead woman to life (8:40-56). Throughout this section pulsates the theme of who does and who does not respond generously to God's messengers. Gentiles, toll collectors, sinners, and the hopelessly sick acknowledge Jesus' authority; they hear his word and do it. They form reconstituted Israel. At the end of this entire section Jesus sends forth the Twelve to heal and preach as he has (9:1-6). We readers, on the basis of 7:1-8:56, know full well what that healing and preaching involve and who will respond to them.

94   (a) UNCLEAN GENTILES ARE OPEN TO JESUS' KINGDOM MESSAGE (7:1-10). This story is a foreshadowing of Christianity's full-scale movement to the Gentiles. In it Luke plays on the theme of who is worthy to receive the benefits of Jesus, God's prophet in Israel (see 7:16). See Matt 8:5-13; John 4:46-54. **2.** *centurion:* This centurion is a Gentile officer, perhaps in the employ of Herod Antipas. One should note the parallel between this story and Luke's story of the first Gentile convert, a centurion by the name of Cornelius (Acts 10). Through his alms this centurion cared for God's people (10:2, 4,31). In him God showed to Peter that he shows no partiality (10:34-35). For the generous and unexpected response soldiers give to God's messengers, see 3:14. Is it indicative of the exemplary character of the centurion that he is concerned about a servant? **3-5.** *elders of the Jews:* This is the first of two delegations; see 7:6b-8. It sets up the thematic of what constitutes worthiness to receive a benefaction from Jesus. In effect, the Jewish elders say: Because of all he has done for God's elect, do not consider him a Gentile and thus outside the scope of your blessings for Israel. **6-8.** In contrast to what the Jewish elders say, the centurion claims that he is not worthy. He is not such a holy or good individual that Jesus should come into his house and thus break a rule of ritual purity. Arguing from the analogy of his own experience of authority, the centurion acknowledges Jesus' power over the forces of death. Jesus' mere word will restore his servant to health. **9.** *such faith:* The centurion is worthy not because he has done good deeds for Israel but because he believes that God in Jesus conquers death. His unexpected faith is contrasted with that of those who were expected to believe and did not.

95   (b) GOD'S PROPHET, JESUS, HAS COMPASSION ON A WIDOW (7:11-17). This peculiarly Lucan story prepares for 7:22 and proclaims that the God Jesus preaches liberates those who are in death's prison. **12.** *only son:* For similar Lucan coloring, see 8:42 (only child) and 9:38 (son, an only child). For a woman to have lost her only son in a patriarchal society meant that she was without any male agency. Her fate was grim. **13-14.** Jesus' compassion for someone in such dire need bypasses laws of ritual purity which dictate that one should not touch a corpse (Num 19:11,16). **15.** *he gave him to his mother:* These same words occur in 1 Kgs 17:23 LXX, the story about Elijah restoring to life the son of the widow of Zarephath. God's mercy in Jesus is again stressed. **16.** *a great prophet:* The audience recalls the mighty deeds of Elijah. The theme of Jesus as prophet is a broad one in Luke-Acts. There are three types of passages. In the first Jesus acts like a prophet although

the text does not actually call him a prophet (9:22-23; 9:43b-45; 11:20,29-32,50; 13:32,34; 18:31-34; 19:41-44; 20:9-18; 21:20-24; 22:64; 23:28-30,43; 24:19-20; Acts 3:22-23; 7:37-53). In the second Jesus uses the title "prophet" for himself (4:24; 13:33). In the third the title of prophet is used to describe Jesus' power (7:16,39; 9:8-9,19). See A. Büchele, *Der Tod Jesus im Lukasevangelium* (FrTS 26; Frankfurt, 1978) 91-92. In many of these passages the prophet Jesus is rejected. *visited:* God has drawn near to needy people in and through Jesus' kingdom mission.

96   (c) THE ROLES OF JOHN AND JESUS IN GOD'S PLAN OF SALVATION (7:18-35). Luke pauses in his story to ponder the roles that JBap and Jesus play in God's plan of salvation and the responses these messengers of God have received. This material is closely connected with 3:1-20 and is paralleled in Matt 11:2-6,7-11,16-19. **18-23.** This section harks back to 4:16-21 and reinterprets Jesus' kingdom ministry of 4:31-7:17 in terms of God's fulfillment of promise. **18.** *all these things:* In the story line the reference is to what Luke has depicted Jesus doing in 4:16-7:17. *two disciples:* They will serve as eyewitnesses (Deut 19:15) to God's power working in Jesus for the needy. **19-20.** *the one who is to come:* See 3:15-18. Is Jesus the one who comes with wrathful eyes and axe and winnowing fork in hand? **21.** Jesus gives his answer in actions that benefit the unfortunate. **22.** This verse echoes 4:18. Jesus' deeds of mercy are done in fulfillment of God's promises; allusions to Isa 26:19; 29:18-19; 35:5; and 61:1-2 course through this verse. **23.** *scandalized:* The answer John receives challenges him, Luke's communities, and us, for all have preconceived notions of how God should act and for whom. Jesus' God is not for vengeance, but for mercy.

97   24-30. Luke supplements what he said about John's baptism and desert living in 3:1-20. **25.** *clothed in soft garments:* Luke is attuned to the symbolism of clothing. See 2:7,11; 8:35; 16:19; 23:11. **26-28.** John's role in God's plan is spotlighted. He is a prophet, the forerunner of Jesus, the greatest of human beings; but he is not Jesus, who, although less than John, is greater than he in God's kingdom. **29-30.** This unique Lucan material is a completing analepsis or "flashback" to 3:10-14, where the Pharisees and lawyers were not mentioned. Having seen how they responded to Jesus, God's messenger (5:17-6:11), the reader is not surprised to learn that they did not give a favorable response to God's other messenger, John. The Pharisees do not want to accept God's plan of righteousness as revealed in John or Jesus. They have their own righteousness. But the people and toll collectors readily acknowledge their need for God.

98   31-35. John is not subordinated to Jesus in this section. Both are God's messengers and are included among wisdom's children. **31-32.** *like children:* The comparison centers on childish stubbornness to have things one's own way. **33.** John's ascetic life-style is too rigorous. Yet this is not the dimension of his preaching which Luke has mentioned in 3:10-14. Were John's contemporaries really hearing what he was saying? **34.** *a glutton and a drunkard:* Perhaps, a reference to Deut 21:20 and the rebellious one who must be killed. Jesus does not use food and drink as a means of marking what and who is holy, but as a means of uniting himself with all, clean and unclean alike. See Wimmer, *Fasting in the New Testament* (→ 53 above) 112. **35.** *justified:* This is a catchword link with 7:29. Those who find fault with John and Jesus are actually foolish and not wise as they think. In their stubbornness they keep their minds closed and ignore wisdom, who wants to befriend men and women (see Wis 6:16). *all her children:* John and Jesus are not the only ones in view. Wise people like the sinner in 7:36-50 also belong to wisdom's family.

99 (d) A WOMAN SINNER RESPONDS TO GOD'S GIFT OF FORGIVENESS (7:36-50). This story is eloquent in its proclamation of God's love for sinners, inspiring in its description of the generosity of the forgiven sinner, and sober in its presentation of religious self-righteousness. Luke is heir to a tradition that is found also in Mark 14:3-9; Matt 26:6-13; John 12:1-8. He has modified this tradition in two major ways. In accordance with his pervasive theme of care for the poor, Luke has eliminated Jesus' statement that the poor you have always with you (Mark 14:7; Matt 26:11; John 12:8). He has set the tradition within the framework of a Hellenistic symposium genre, which he employs also in 11:37-54 and 14:1-24. The *dramatis personae* of this genre are host, chief guest, and other guests. The structure is invitation (v 36), gradual revelation of who the host (v 40) and other guests (v 49) are, the *fait divers* or action that prompts the speech of the chief guest (v 39, Simon's unspoken reaction), and the speech of the chief guest (vv 40-50). See E. S. Steele, *JBL* 103 (1984) 379-94.

100 **36.** *Pharisees:* → 76-77 above. The Pharisees represent Jewish Christians who espouse rigoristic criteria for membership in the Lucan communities and for participation in their meals. Implicit in the offer of hospitality is the *Weltanschauung* of clean and unclean. "The problem then is how to admit a representative of the outside into the purity lines of the community for a while and then allow the outsider to return to his/her proper place without altering the social fabric.... Hospitality necessarily must put the guest in a liminal or marginal position since the guest is an outsider now on the inside, and yet not an insider since s/he must return to the outside" (B. J. Malina, *Semeia* 35 [1986] 182). In allowing the sinner to touch him (vv 37-39), Jesus shows that his norms for clean and unclean conflict with those of the Pharisee. **37.** *sinner:* There is no convincing evidence that the woman is a prostitute. See the generic "sinners" in 5:30; 7:34; 15:2. Both men and women can be guilty of sins other than sexual ones. **38.** The woman's treatment of Jesus is generous. See how her actions are picked up in vv 44-46 and are made examples of her great love. **39.** *prophet:* See 7:16. Jesus is, indeed, a prophet, but one who forgives sinners. **40.** The speech of the chief guest, Jesus, commences. **43.** *more:* In true Socratic style Jesus draws the correct answer out of Simon. **44-46.** Though Simon is not guilty of any infraction of the rules of hospitality, he had not shown Jesus any special acts of hospitality. The generosity of the sinner is contrasted with the stinginess of Jesus' host. **47.** The first part of this troublesome verse can be paraphrased: Because she has performed such acts of love for me, it is obvious that her many sins have been forgiven. The text does not say when she received the gift of forgiveness, but it was before she encountered Jesus at this meal. J. J. Kilgallen (*JBL* 104 [1985] 675-70) argues that her sins were forgiven in John's baptism. *loves a little:* Jesus brings home the message of the parable of vv 40-43 and challenges the Pharisee for his self-righteousness. **48.** *forgiven:* Jesus articulates in words what had been obvious in the sinner's actions. **49.** *even forgives:* The theocentric thrust of the story is given a christological orientation as Luke gives Jesus' fellow guests a voice. One hears echoes of 5:17-32 and is being prepared for the "Who is this?" questions of 9:7-50. **50.** *peace:* On this beloved Lucan theme, see 1:79.

101 (e) THE WOMEN DISCIPLES OF JESUS (8:1-3). This summary passage is unique to Luke and accords with the important role he assigns to women. See 2:36-38. **1.** *kingdom of God:* God's rule is preached in

word and is embodied in Jesus' traveling band. The first members of that band are the Twelve, all men, who symbolize God's intent to reconstitute, through Jesus, twelve-tribe Israel (see Acts 26:7). **2.** *women:* Women comprise the second element of the band, and this is strange. For the mention of women would strike Luke's Greco-Roman readers with as much force as the reality it described struck Jesus' Jewish contemporaries: "It was not uncommon for women to support rabbis and their disciples out of their own money, property, or foodstuffs. But for her to leave home and travel with a rabbi was not only unheard of, it was scandalous. Even more scandalous was the fact that women, both respectable and not, were among Jesus' traveling companions" (B. Witherington, *ZNW* 70 [1979] 244-45). The physical well-being of these women, who had been healed of evil spirits and maladies, is visible proof of the power of God's kingdom in Jesus. Jesus' power over evil is especially manifest in the restoration to health of Mary, from the small Galilean town of Magdala, from whom seven (number of totality) demons have been removed. **3.** *Joanna:* She is the wife of Chuza, the manager of Herod Antipas's estate, and a person of position and means. This evangelical traveling band images God's kingdom, in which there is reconciliation between men and women, married and single, healthy and ailing, those with much and those with little. Besides this christological dimension, these verses have a challenging ecclesiological one. This passage should be read in conjunction with 23:49-24:12, which is another instance of a Lucan completing analepsis or "flashback" and shows that when readers read of "disciples" in 8:4-23:54 they should include women in that group. These faithful women are witnesses of what Jesus has done in Galilee, on the road to Jerusalem, and in Jerusalem, even at the Last Supper. They preach the gospel meaning of what they have witnessed (24:7-10) and receive the promised holy Spirit (Acts 1-2).

102 (f) DIVERSE WAYS OF HEARING GOD'S WORD (8:4-21). In this section Luke returns to Mark (8:4-18 = Mark 4:1-25; 8:19-21 = Mark 3:31-35) and plays on the motif of hearing the Word of God, which is the Christian message and, in doing so, spins out many a lesson about the meaning of discipleship. **4-15.** This section contains one of Luke's 50 parables. See J. Drury, *The Parables in the Gospels* [NY, 1985] 108-57). **5.** *his seed:* Luke stresses the seed which is sown; see v 11. **8.** While the initial seeding seemed to lead to disastrous results, the harvest is unbelievably plentiful. This parable of the historical Jesus paints a word picture of a trustworthy God, who will ultimately bring God's kingdom to fruition. *ears to hear:* Hearing becomes the leitmotif and challenge of the rest of this section. See vv 10,12,13,14, 15,18,21. See J. Dupont, "La parabole du semeur dans la version de Luc," *Apophoreta* (Fest. E. Haenchen; ed. W. Eltester and F. H. Kettler; BZNW 30; Berlin, 1964) 97-108. **10.** *the others:* Luke has toned down Mark's harsh treatment of the "outsiders" and of Jesus' disciples (see Mark 4:11-13). It is a hallmark of Lucan discipleship that disciples not only hear the parables of God's kingdom, but are recipients of the singular grace of knowing what God's kingdom means for everyday Christian living. The context, esp. vv 16-18, shows that the Lucan communities have not ceased to preach the word of God to the others, who are locked in on the level of merely hearing the word. **11.** *the word of God:* The explanation of Jesus' original parable reflects the experience of Luke's communities as they struggled to preach the word to others and to deepen their own response to it. On the theme of the word of God, see Acts 6:7; 12:24; 19:20. **12.** The various kinds of soil occupy center stage in Luke's interpretation in this and the following verses. *be saved:* The goal of Christian preaching is powerfully and challengingly presented. **13.** *apostasy:* This is Gk *peirasmos.* Luke is taken up with the alternatives of apostasy from and perseverance in the Christian way of life. See S. Brown, *Apostasy and Perseverance in the Theology of Luke* (AnBib 36; Rome, 1969). **14.** *anxieties, riches, and pleasures of life:* The opponents of the word found in this Lucan triad are formidable. Luke 12:19 and 16:19 present the dangers of riches and the pleasures of life in dramatic form. In Luke 21:34 Luke returns to the problems for Christian discipleship created by anxieties over worldly concerns. **15.** Two strengths characterize the disciples of Jesus: their generosity and perseverance in responding to God's word.

103   **16-18.** These proverbial sayings continue Luke's reflection on hearing the word (see v 18). **16.** This Lucan version of the proverb adjusts it to the types of houses Luke knew, i.e., those with vestibules. The disciple must make manifest to the "others" of v 10 the light of God's word. **17.** Knowledge of the "mysteries of God's kingdom" (v 10) is not esoteric or gnostic, reserved for a sect. It is to be shared with the "others." **18.** *be careful how you hear:* Hearing without understanding the word, especially the understanding that originates in the effort to communicate the word to others, leads to total loss of hearing.

104   **19-21.** Again "hearing the word" (v 21) is the link with the preceding. In contrast to Mark 3:31-35 Luke does not depreciate Jesus' mother and relatives. Echoes of Luke 1:38; 2:19,51 sound in v 21: Mary is the model disciple who ponders God's word and acts on it. Christian disciples become God's family neither by birth, nor by being male, nor by observing laws of ritual purity, but by hearing and acting on God's word.

105   (g) JESUS CONQUERS CHAOS (8:22-25). This passage continues the Lucan teaching about Jesus' power to save and about the meaning of discipleship. See Mark 4:35-41. **22.** *the disciples:* Both men and women followers are in view (see 8:1-3). In contrast to Mark 4:36 Jesus, not the disciples, is in charge and commands the disciples to go across to Gentile territory (see 8:26-39). **23.** In the OT, watery storms were symbols of chaos. In creation God conquered them (Ps 29:3-4). At the exodus God conquered the forces of the Red Sea (Ps 106:9). God would rescue the faithful who were on a ship in a storm-tossed sea (Ps 107:23-32). The power of the storm is engulfing the disciples. **24.** *rebukes:* This technical term from the vocabulary of exorcism of unclean spirits was used earlier in 4:35,39. Jesus, like the God praised in the Psalms, saves his disciples who are perishing from the chaos of the storm. **25.** *where is your faith?:* This provocative question is less harsh than its counterpart in Mark 4:40, but is nevertheless pointed. Luke plays on the intimate connection he made between faith and salvation in 8:12. *who is this?:* The pericope comes to its christological conclusion and challenge. Will disciples and readers, who believe in Jesus' kingdom power, hold onto their faith when in the future chaos reigns? See Busse, *Wunder* [→ 67 above] 196-205.

106   (h) JESUS RESTORES A DEMENTED GENTILE TO HUMAN COMMUNITY (8:26-39). In this awesome exorcism Luke redacts Mark 5:1-20 in such a way as to make explicit Mark's implicit contrasts: outside the city (8:27) inside the city (8:39); living in the tombs (8:27) living in a house (8:27,39); unclothed (8:27) clothed (8:35); demented (8:27) of sound mind (8:35); living in the desert (8:29) living in a house (8:39). These contrasts involve transfers, transfers from destructive isolation to nurturing human community, transfers which Luke identifies as "being saved" (8:36) and which are effected

by Jesus, "Son of the Most High God" (8:28). Even the pigs, whose presence in this exorcism is at first blush puzzling, contribute to Luke's christological teaching: not only the demon world but also the powers of pagan religion and Roman rule, symbolized by the pigs, are subject to Jesus' authority. It is he and not they who restore human beings to wholeness of life.

107   **26.** *Gerasenes:* This is the correct reading and refers to people from Gerasa, one of the cities of the Gentile Decapolis, 33 mi. SE of Lake Gennesaret (→ Biblical Geography, 73:52). Since pigs do not have sweat glands, they would not have survived a stampede of 33 mi. The story is moving on a symbolic level. *opposite Galilee:* In this roundabout way of speaking, Luke can foreshadow the church's later mission to the Gentiles while maintaining his story line of Jesus' mission in Galilee, Jewish territory. **27.** *city:* From the viewpoint of Luke's culture, to be outside the city was to be in danger of losing one's existence. Jesus will liberate the possessed man from his isolation and restore him to the city, where he will find security from bodily harm and have a meaningful existence with his fellow men and women. *unclothed:* Persons whose liberty had been definitively taken away lost the capacity to wear clothing. Such people are prisoners and slaves (see Deut 28:48; Isa 20:2-4), prostitutes (Ezek 16:38-40), demented people (1 Sam 19:23-24), and damned folks (1 Sam 28:14). To be deprived of one's clothing was to lose one's identity. By being clothed (8:35), the demented man has an identity and control over his life. See E. Haulotte, *Symbolique du vêtement selon la Bible* (Théologie 65; Paris, 1966) 79. *did not live in a house:* The Gk *oikos/oikia,* "house," is a Lucan favorite and refers to "my house and home with all its personnel and property, my family and lineage, my 'given identity,' the place where I 'belong' and exercise my personal and communal rights and responsibilities, my moral obligations" (J. H. Elliott, *A Home for the Homeless* [Phl, 1981] 24). By restoring the man to his home (v 39), Jesus gives the man back his identity. He now belongs. He has a past, enjoys the present within his family, and will have a future through the household. *tombs:* An unclean place. **28.** *fell down:* Luke leaves no doubt that Jesus is in charge. See also v 29: Jesus commands. **29.** *the desert:* The desert is the locus of demons and their destructive forces. Jesus restores the man to his home and city. **30.** *legion:* A legion consisted of 6,000 Roman foot soldiers. The legion will be sent into the pigs. Roman might was symbolized by a very fecund white sow who gave birth to 30 piglets and by the wild boar. The symbol of *Legio X Fretensis,* which had been transferred to Syria under Tiberius and which participated in the Jewish war of AD 66-70, was the wild boar. "The presence of a foreign political power was always the presence of a threatening numinous power, a pollution of the land. Roman rule could thus be interpreted as a threat from a demonic power.... This made the activity of the exorcist a 'sign' of future liberation" (G. Theissen, *The Miracle Stories of the Early Christian Tradition* [Phl, 1983] 255). **31.** *abyss:* This word, which is unique to Luke's account, refers to the realm of Satan and Satan's power. See Rev 20:1-3. By picturing Jesus destroying the demon legion, Luke underscores Jesus' power over evil. **32.** *pigs:* These animals recur in Luke 15:15-16. The pig was the most frequently used sacrificial animal in Greek and Roman worship. In Jewish eyes eating pork was equivalent to paganism and apostasy from Judaism (see 2 and 4 Macc; Isa 65:1-5). It was also the symbol of Roman might (see v 31). **35.** *at the feet of Jesus:* This is the posture of a disciple of Jesus; see 10:39; Acts 22:3. *sound mind:* Another Lucan contrast. Because of Jesus this madman is now rational, able to utter words that will be intelligible to his fellow men and women, able to make reasonable decisions in a city and within a household (see v 39). **36.** *was saved:* One ascertains what Luke means by salvation by seeing what transformations the Lord Jesus has effected in the former madman's life. **37.** Whereas people greet many of Jesus' exorcisms with wonderment and praise, they greet this one negatively. Even though their ways of dealing with the madman had been ineffectual (v 29), they find it hard to cope with the transforming powers Jesus has unleashed in their midst. **39.** The man becomes a missionary as he gives voice to what he experiences in his person and proclaims to his fellow Gentiles what God in Jesus had done for him. See F. Annen, *Heil für die Heiden* (FrTS 25; Frankfurt, 1976).

108 (i) Jesus' Power Goes beyond Ritual Purity and Gives Life to Two Women (8:40–56). In this passage Luke builds on Mark 5:21–43 and concludes his presentation which has run from 7:1 and has had as its major theme Jesus' power over destructive forces for the benefit of men and women. Jesus does not allow laws of ritual impurity to hinder his kingdom mission for all: "The young woman who begins to menstruate, like the older woman who experiences menstruation as a pathological condition, are both 'given' new life. The life-creating powers of women manifested in 'the flow of blood' are neither 'bad' nor cut off in death but are 'restored' so that women can 'go and live in *shalom*'" (E. Schüssler Fiorenza, *In Memory of Her* [NY, 1983] 124).

109 **41.** *Jairus:* This leader of a synagogue is an exception to Luke's generally negative picture of Jewish leaders. **42.** *only child:* Luke invites the reader to recall a similar story in 7:11–17, where Jesus raised to life the only son of a widow. *twelve:* The child was at marriageable age. **43.** The story of another woman in dire straits is linked via the catchword "twelve." **44–46.** Jesus is touched by an unclean person. **47.** The woman has moved from lying to a confession of grateful faith in the presence of the people. **48.** *your faith:* She has faith in God's power in Jesus to restore her to health. She is no longer an outcast, separated from life and cult by the uncleanness of her menstrual flow of blood, but is a daughter who belongs to reconstituted Israel. **54.** Jesus touches the unclean corpse. *rise up:* Jesus' command is couched in the same Gk word (*egeirein*) that Luke uses for Jesus' resurrection (e.g., 9:22). Jesus' raising up of Jairus's daughter is a sign of his resurrection power. **55.** *to eat:* Luke's theme of food surfaces: a hearty appetite is a sign of restoration to health.

110 (j) The Twelve Continue Jesus' Kingdom Mission (9:1–6). This passage, based on Mark 6:7–13, must be read in conjunction with the entire section (Luke 7:1–8:56) of which it is the culmination. For in chaps. 7–8 we learn the nature of Jesus' kingdom mission in which the Twelve now share. **1–2.** In 6:12–16 Luke narrated the selection of the Twelve, who now experience firsthand the power of Jesus' proclamation and healing. **3.** The starkness of their provisions and their dependence on God's providence are in focus. See 10:1–12; 22:35–38. **5.** The rejection shown Jesus, noted in 7:31–35, is also in store for those sent by Jesus. *dust:* See Acts 13:51. **6.** *everywhere:* The Lucan theme of universalism sounds forth.

111 (I) Responses to Jesus as His Galilean Ministry Draws to a Close (9:7–50). This section functions as a literary and theological switching station between Jesus' Galilean ministry (4:14–9:6) and his journey to Jerusalem (9:51–19:28). In 9:7–50 by means of the cross Luke switches the focus by which one views the familiar themes of Jesus' Galilean ministry (see comment on 4:14–15): Jesus' power over evil and his status as God's son, discipleship, opposition, and food. When

these themes recur in 9:51–19:27, they are to be seen from the perspective of the cross.

112 (a) The Fate of Jesus' Forerunner Is His Fate and That of His Disciples (9:7–9). See Mark 6:14–16. This is the meat of the sandwich formed by the sending out of the Twelve (9:1–6) and their return (9:10–17). Just as the missions of JBap and Jesus met with opposition, so too will that of the church. **7.** *Herod:* See 3:1–20 (→ History, 75:165). In Luke's Gospel Herod Antipas is hostile to both John and Jesus (see 13:31–32; 23:6–12). *all that had happened:* Luke's way of summarizing 4:16–9:6. The Twelve, whom Jesus had sent out (9:1–6), and Jesus are in view. **9.** *who is this?* This question, which echoes those of 5:21; 7:49; 8:25, serves to summarize 4:14–9:6. In 9:10–50 Luke will introduce the cross as an essential and new ingredient to an answer. *see:* In 23:8 Luke will thrice use "see" of Herod's desire to see Jesus. Herod's curiosity will be contrasted in 23:35–49 with the seeing of those who are open to God's revelation in Jesus' death on the cross.

113 (b) Jesus' Gift of Food Is Linked to His Cross (9:10–17). See Mark 6:30–44; 8:1–10; Matt 14:13–21; 15:32–39; John 6:1–15. Jesus gives his disciples, who have just returned from preaching and curing God's people, a new charge: they are to feed reconstituted Israel—with the eucharist. **11.** Preaching about the kingdom of God and healing summarize Jesus' Galilean ministry. **12–15.** The Lucan theme of food recurs. In 4:16–9:6 this motif largely surfaced in stories dealing with Jesus' joyful table fellowship with sinners (e.g., 5:27–32). Here a further dimension shines forth: In Jesus' kingdom mission God is fulfilling his promises of feeding hungry creation. See Isa 25:5–6 and Karris, *Luke* 52–57. **16.** *blessed, broke, gave:* These words match almost verbatim those in the Lucan account of the institution of the eucharist (22:19) and in the Emmaus story (24:30). Luke, of all the evangelists, immediately links this feeding account with Jesus' prediction of his passion and his instructions about bearing one's cross daily (9:18–27). To celebrate the eucharist in memory of Jesus (22:19) is to share not only his mission (9:1–6) but also his dedication and destiny, symbolized by the cross (9:18–27). *disciples:* The same word occurs in v 14, whereas v 10 has "apostles" and v 12 has "the Twelve." See comments on 6:12–16 and 8:1–3. Male and female disciples feed God's people.

114 (c) The Cross in the Lives of the Messiah and His Disciples (9:18–27). See Mark 8:27–9:1. Luke does not use Mark 6:45–8:26. His reasons for this Great Omission stem from his own theology of when God's word goes to the Gentiles, of clean and unclean, and of food. In this passage the theme of opposition to Jesus and his disciples, seen in 4:16–9:6, takes on a new perspective, that of the cross. **18.** Luke's reference to Jesus at prayer indicates that something very important theologically is about to occur. **19.** These answers concur with those given Herod in 9:7–8. **20.** *Christ of God:* Peter is the spokesperson for the disciples. See comment on 5:1–11. In the Lucan story line Peter's answer ("confession" is a misleading term and is more Matthean than Lucan) is dependent on what he has seen Jesus do and what he himself has done in Jesus' name. Thus, Peter's answer focuses on Jesus' power to save needy people from the forces of evil. That this is the dimension of Jesus' ministry highlighted in Peter's answer is corroborated by the immediate context, which modifies the understanding of "Christ of God" by reference to Jesus' rejection (9:22,43–45), and by Luke 23:35, where the same title is used with reference to Jesus' power to save others. **21–22.** These verses form one sentence in Greek, as Luke gives (v 22) the reason for the command to silence in v 21: Jesus as Christ of God must be viewed from a new perspective, that of the cross. In 4:16–9:6 the reader met a Jesus who successfully withstood opposition (5:17–6:11; 7:31–35). Now Luke alerts his readers that opposition will mount and eventually lead to Jesus' death. *Son of Man:* The title, which Luke had employed to depict Jesus' authority to forgive sins (5:24) and to change sabbath regulations (6:5), is now used to describe his humiliation. See 9:26. *must:* Behind the deepening opposition to Jesus stands God's plan and the vindication of Jesus in the resurrection. Luke eliminates Mark's presentation of Peter as one who rebukes Jesus for predicting that he will suffer (8:32–33). **23.** *all:* Jesus extends his invitation to follow him to all. In contrast to the call stories of 5:1–11 or 5:27–32, the cross is embossed in the center of the invitation. In 5:30,33 and 6:2 Jesus defended his disciples in the face of opposition. Now they, like him, may be defenseless. *cross:* Not the headaches and other vicissitudes of life, but Jesus' commitment to and his disciples' participation in God's kingdom in word and deed. *each day:* Martyrdom is not in view, but daily steadfast loyalty to the master and his way of life. **24.** *for my sake:* Only a profound commitment to Jesus is a basis for losing one's life to help bring about God's kingdom. **25.** Luke's theme of the dangers of possessions is couched in terms of discipleship. **26.** *will be ashamed:* Luke introduces the eschatological consequences of relinquishing one's attachment to Jesus and his teaching about God's kingdom. In contrast to the lowly Son of Man (9:22), Luke presents the exalted Son of Man (cf. 22:69). **27.** In its Lucan context, this difficult verse refers to the disciples, to whom a new understanding of God's kingdom will be given after Jesus' resurrection (Acts 1:3).

115   (d) Jesus' Transfiguration and the Divine Confirmation of the Way of the Cross (9:28–36). See Mark 9:2–9. The teaching that Jesus has given in 9:22–27 is so different from what he had taught in 4:16–9:6 that it needs divine sanction. The disciples are commanded by God to listen to this new teaching. Jesus, who was proclaimed Son of God at his baptism (3:21–22) and whom Luke has portrayed (4:16–9:6) as bodying forth God's glory in his kingdom ministry of vanquishing the forces of destruction, is Son of God as he goes to the cross.

116   **28.** *after these words:* Luke tightly connects the transfiguration on God's mountain with Jesus' teaching in vv 22–27. *praying:* See comment on 3:21. **29.** *white, dazzling:* Luke uses symbols of the transcendent. **30.** *Moses and Elijah:* The road upon which Jesus is embarking is in accord with the law and the prophets (24:26–27), i.e., God's will. These two OT figures were rejected prophets. **31.** *exodus:* The topic of the conversation between the heavenly triad is mentioned only by Luke. He refers to the next phase of Jesus' ministry, his journey to Jerusalem and his passage from this world to God. **32.** *glory:* Associated with the risen and heavenly life (24:26), glory is also manifested in Jesus' cures, which cause people to glorify God (5:26; 7:16). **33.** *three booths:* Peter apparently did not understand the conversation of v 31 and interprets the event in the light of the harvest festival of Tabernacles, the abundance of which came to symbolize God's consummation of history. **34.** *cloud:* Symbol of God's presence. **35.** *my son:* These words recall God's voice at Jesus' baptism (3:21–22). *hear him:* Perhaps this is a reference to the prophet like Moses of Deut 18:15 (see D. P. Moessner, *JBL* 102 [1983] 575–605), but, more importantly, disciples are commanded to be attentive to this new phase of God's revelation of who the Son is: one who returns to God via the cross. The implications for disciples of Jesus' journey to the cross will be spelled out in 9:51–19:27.

117   (e) How the Cross Interprets Jesus' Merciful Deeds (9:37–45). See Mark 9:14–29. In streamlining this story, Luke has closely connected it with the transfiguration and underscored Jesus' mercy. He links it and all Jesus' mighty deeds intimately with his second prediction of the passion, thus showing that in the future the mercy of mighty deeds will come from the mercy of the cross. **37.** *mountain:* The first of three contrasts is sounded. Jesus comes from the mountain of God's presence into a needy world. **38.** *look with compassion:* See 1 Sam 1:11 and Luke 1:48. *only child:* See 7:12; 8:42. Luke highlights the man's need and Jesus' mercy. **39.** The miserable condition of the sick child enhances Luke's depiction of Jesus' power and mercy. **40.** A second contrast is drawn: the master, Jesus, is more powerful over the forces of evil than his disciples. **41.** *faithless and perverse generation:* This cry of exasperation is difficult to interpret in the Lucan context, for (1) neither the boy's father nor the disciples have shown lack of faith; (2) "generation" involves more than the boy's father and the disciples. This generalization seems best explained in two ways: (1) Luke is providing a third contrast: the fidelity of Jesus to God in contrast to general human infidelity. (2) Behind this exasperation lies the fact that Jesus' deeds of mercy will be greeted with disbelief, which will eventually lead to the cross. See Busse, *Wunder* (→ 67 above) 249–67. **42.** *gave him back to his father:* Cf. 7:15. At this point Luke does not share the Marcan teaching (9:28–29) on prayer and fasting as means of casting out such powerful demons. Luke's attention is on Jesus' power. See J. Dupont, *RSR* 69 (1981) 45–55. **43.** *all the miracles:* Luke universalizes from one miracle to all that had been described in 4:16–9:6. All Jesus' mighty deeds must be seen from the vantage point of the crucifixion. **44.** *to be handed over:* More marvelous than Jesus' deeds of mercy is his merciful death on the cross. This second passion prediction is referred to in 24:7, where women disciples remember its significance. **45.** I. H. Marshall (*Gospel* 393) sees this verse as an expression of Luke's "suffering secret": only after Jesus' resurrection and his gift of insight (see 24:13–35) will the disciples understand the meaning of his cross.

118   (f) The Disciples' Misunderstanding of the Meaning of Following Jesus (9:46–50). See Mark 9:33–41. **46–48.** Close upon the heels of Jesus' second prediction of his powerlessness before human beings (9:44) and Jesus' instructions about taking up one's cross and following him (9:23–27) comes Luke's story of the disciples' quest for power. In a dramatic way Luke shows that the lessons of discipleship, newly introduced in 9:7–50, will not be assimilated overnight. Building on the figure of the child, a prime example of powerlessness, Jesus teaches that greatness comes from being the least. **49–50.** Disciples misunderstand their relationship to Jesus if they think that theirs is an exclusive one. They must be open and tolerant of others who work "in Jesus' name" and do not adhere to their group.

119   (V) Jesus' Journey to Jerusalem (9:51–19:27). With 9:51 Luke begins a new part of his kerygmatic narrative. He has adapted the theme of Jesus' journey to Jerusalem from Mark 8:26–10:52, adding (1) some 15 references to Jesus traveling and (2) materials from Q and L. The result of Luke's creative adaptation is a multidimensioned view of journey. In obedience to God's will (9:22,44) Jesus goes on his way to Jerusalem, the city that symbolizes the continuity between the old and the new in God's plan. In Jerusalem, Jesus will complete his exodus (9:31) to God, and from Jerusalem the Christian mission will travel to the ends of the earth (Acts 1–2). On his way to Jerusalem, Jesus is the supreme teacher of his disciples, his witnesses, in the meaning of his way (see Acts 9:2; 18:26; 24:22, where Christianity is called "the Way"). Jesus instructs his disciples about missionary travels (10:1-24), about the use of possessions (16:1-31), about prayer (11:1-13), and delivers challenging parables like those of the Good Samaritan (10:25-37) and the Prodigal Son (15:11-32). Neither Jesus' journey nor that of the Christian will be free from trials. The Samaritans reject Jesus (9:51-56); the religious leaders object to his teaching and way of life (13:11-17; 14:1-24). In brief, Luke's "journey narrative" paints a captivating portrait of Jesus, the faithful and resolute Son (9:35), who in word and deed teaches the way that leads to life with God. As readers walk with Jesus on his way to Jerusalem, they should be mindful of the divine imperative: "Listen to him!" (9:35).

Luke's travel narrative is divided into three sections: 9:51-13:21; 13:22-17:10; 17:11-19:27. The verse that commences each of these sections mentions explicitly that Jesus was on his way to Jerusalem.

120   (A) First Part of Instruction on the Meaning of the Christian Way (9:51-13:21). This part contains many lessons about the nature and demands of discipleship.

(a) THE SAMARITAN REJECTION AND NONRETALIATION (9:51-56). **51.** This Lucan composition is replete with theologically weighty vocabulary. *days being completed:* God is the one who is completing or filling up (*symplērousthai*) the days and thus bringing the salvific plan closer to fulfillment. *assumption:* The verb-form of the noun *analēmpsis* used here occurs in Acts 1:2,11,22. The reference is to all phases of Jesus' exodus to God: death, burial, assumption, and sending of the holy Spirit. *set his face:* This unique expression indicates Jesus' obedient resoluteness to fulfill God's will despite all opposition. **52-53.** *Samaritans:* Samaritans were not friendly to Jews (see John 4:9), esp. when the Jews were passing through their territory on the way to the holy city, Jerusalem. Later on in his travel narrative (10:30-35; 17:11-19) Luke will use the despised Samaritans to teach further lessons about discipleship. In Acts 8:4-25 he will narrate how these folks, who are inhospitable now, accept the message of the Christian Way with open hearts. Ever sensitive to parallelism, Luke shows that Jesus meets with opposition at the initial stages of his journey to Jerusalem just as he encountered opposition at the beginning of his Galilean ministry (4:16-30). **54.** *fire come down from heaven:* The wording of this verse echoes that of 2 Kgs 1:10,12, which narrates how Elijah twice called down fire to destroy his enemies. **55.** Jesus lives out in deed his teaching about nonretaliation against enemies (6:27-29,35).

121   (b) THE COST OF DISCIPLESHIP (9:57-62). 57. *along the road:* Discipleship as following Jesus on his way is illustrated by three hyperbolic proverbs. The function of normal proverbs is to help people make sense out of life, to show how the world coheres, e.g., an hour of sleep before midnight is worth two after midnight; spare the rod and spoil the child. In the proverbs of vv 58, 60,62 Jesus uses hyperbole or exaggeration to jolt listeners out of their staid way of ordering their universe and to view existence from an entirely new angle—that of discipleship in response to the kingdom of God preached by Jesus. To literalize these proverbs is to strip them of their power. See W. A. Beardslee, *Int* 24 (1970) 61-73. **58.** The exaggeration highlights the lowliness of Jesus, the Son of Man. **60.** *dead bury their own dead:* This proverb has been so successful in subverting the way people normally order their moral universe that endless discussion reigns that Jesus could not have meant what he said. The ways of God's kingdom are not necessarily in step with our human ways. The common interpreta-

tion is that the proverb means that the spiritually dead should bury the physically dead. **62.** *the plow:* The modern tractor and plow are not in view, but a very light Palestinian plow, which was guided by one hand while the other hand drove the unruly oxen. "This primitive kind of plough needs dexterity and concentrated attention. If the ploughman looks round, the new furrow becomes crooked" (J. Jeremias, *The Parables of Jesus* [NY, 1963] 195). *fit for:* The proverb challenges expectations of who would be fit to receive the reign of God into their lives.

122   (c) JESUS' TEACHING ABOUT MISSION (10:1-24). This section is Luke's longest meditation on mission and has parallels in Q (Matt 9:37-38; 10:7-16; 11:21-23) and in Luke 9:1-6; 22:35-38; 24:44-49. Luke gives no attention to the actual mission of the disciples, but rather concentrates his reflections on the nature of mission and the causes of its joys and sorrows. **1.** *seventy(-two):* Application of the principles of text criticism does not lead to an indisputable decision of whether 70 or 72 is the original text; trustworthy, ancient mss. support both readings. The OT text behind the number seems to be Gen 10:2-31, the table of the nations of the world: the MT reads 70 whereas the LXX has 72. In any case, Luke roots the universal mission of his church in the ministry of Jesus. *two by two:* Three reasons for pairing are involved: mutual support; bearing of witness to the truth of their testimony (see Deut 19:15); living embodiment of the gospel of peace (see vv 5-6). Perhaps, the most famous NT missionary pair was that of Paul and Barnabas (see Acts 13). **3.** *lambs among wolves:* This powerful image has two dimensions: the missionaries may be defenseless before hostile people; the Christian mission inaugurates a new era of peace and reconciliation in which the lamb will lie down with the wolf (see Isa 11:6; 65:25). **4.** *greet no one:* This socially shocking symbolic action, akin to that of the prophets (Ezek 4-5), would call attention to what genuine peace involves. See Klassen, *Love of Enemies* (→ 91 above) 92-93. **6.** *son of peace:* This unique expression is part and parcel of the Lucan emphasis on the Christian message of reconciliation and means one who is dedicated to the pursuit of peace. **9.** In the Christian missionary preaching and curing of the ill the reign of God is manifest.

123   10-16. To this point Luke has been accentuating the largely positive character of the Christian mission. He now gives voice to the negative side: just as Jesus met with hostility and rejection, so too will his missionaries. But as the story of Paul in Acts will demonstrate, the word of God will triumph even though its preachers may be dispensable. **13-15.** In their Lucan context these verses function as warnings to Luke's communities to respond favorably to God's word and not to imitate the responses given to Jesus' mission by some Galilean cities. **16.** *who hears you, hears me:* The meaning of Christian mission finds lapidary expression: hearing the word of the disciple is hearing the word of Jesus; hearing the word of Jesus is hearing that of God. See v 22 for an equally deep foundation for Christian mission.

124   17-20. The effects of mission in Jesus' name are in focus. **17.** *demons:* Recall Jesus' power over the demons in Galilee (8:26-39) and the power Jesus gave the Twelve (9:1-2). The 70 (72) disciples share that same authority. **18.** In Jesus' ministry and that of his church the powers of evil are attacked and overcome. **19.** "The serpent and the scorpion were not only well-known sources of physical evil in Palestinian life, but were OT symbols of all kinds of evil" (*FGL* 863). In Acts Luke frequently narrates how the Lord Jesus rescued his missionaries from the forces of destruction (e.g., 28:1-6).

20. Luke tempers enthusiasm for missionary success with insistence on a more enduring gift: to have one's name inscribed on the roster of the citizens of heaven. **125   21–24.** From the universe of discourse of wisdom, which differs from that of representation found in v 16, Luke concludes his reflections on mission. His perspective seems to be postresurrectional, for Jesus' disciples are gifted with the knowledge of and truly see, in contrast to 9:45 and 18:34, Jesus as the revelation of the Father. **21.** *these things:* In the Lucan context the references are to the nature of God's kingdom, the union of Jesus' disciples with him in mission, and Jesus' relationship to God. The terminology is different, but the thought is the same as that of 8:10. *wise . . . babes:* The familiar wisdom contrast between those who have no need for God and the little ones, the disciples who approach God with open minds and hearts. **22.** Christian mission finds its deepest foundation in the Son's relationship to his Father and the Son's pure gift of revealing to his disciples who the Father is. *all things:* "Again, if the sense of *panta* (10,22) in its original setting escapes us, it refers in the Lucan (and Matthean) context to the knowledge that the Son has about the Father and the knowledge that only he can transmit to his followers, the 'little children'" (J. A. Fitzmyer, "*Abba* and Jesus' Relation to God," *À cause de l'évangile* [Fest. J. Dupont; ed. R. Gantoy; LD 123; Paris, 1985] 36). **23–24.** In the new age of fulfillment inaugurated by Jesus, his disciples witness with insight his missionary activity and share in its power for good. What these "little children" experience was not granted the mighty religious leaders and political rulers of times past. **126** (d) THE CHRISTIAN MISSION AND OBSERVANCE OF THE LAW (10:25–37). This passage is two-pronged. While providing a powerful lesson about mercy toward those in need, it also proclaims that non-Jews can observe the law and thus enter into eternal life. This involved controversy story has the following components: 10:25, the question of a lawyer; 10:26, Jesus' counterquestion; 10:27, the lawyer's answer; 10:28, Jesus' imperative; 10:29, a further question of the lawyer; 10:30–36, Jesus' counterquestion, which has the story of the Good Samaritan; 10:37a, the lawyer's answer; 10:37b, Jesus' imperative. **25.** *test him:* It seems that the lawyer has been present to hear what Jesus has just said about Christian mission in 10:1–24. The testing concerns the role of God's law in the salvation preached by missionaries. Luke gives two answers: the law is valid; non-Jews who observe the law inherit eternal life. In 18:18–30 Luke will provide a more specifically Christian answer to the same question about inheriting eternal life. On this Lucan dual view of the law, see Wilson, *Luke and the Law* (→ 58 above) 28–29. **27.** The lawyer's answer comes from Deut 6:5 and Lev 19:18. **28.** Jesus confirms the validity of the law for salvation and accentuates the doing (see also vv 25,36) of the twin commandment. **29.** *neighbor:* The lawyer's question stems from debates about who belongs to God's people and therefore is an object of neighborly love. **30–35.** Jesus' counterquestion in v 36 has the long lead-in of this famous example story, which is meant to arrest the readers' attention and impel them to imitate the conduct of a pariah, a Samaritan. *a priest . . . a Levite:* These leading examples of law-observant people do not aid the stripped and apparently dead man for fear of becoming defiled. **36.** *who . . . neighbor . . . ?:* Jesus' question turns the lawyer's question on its head: Don't ask about who belongs to God's people and thus is the object of my neighborly attention, but rather ask about the conduct incumbent upon a member of God's chosen people. **37.** *the one who did mercy:* The lawyer cannot bring himself to

say "Samaritan." Because he did the law, the outcast Samaritan shows that he is a neighbor, a member of God's people, one who inherits eternal life. See G. Sellin, *ZNW* 65 (1974) 166–89; 66 (1975) 19–60. **127** (e) DISCIPLESHIP FOR MEN AND WOMEN (10:38–42). To the fore is Luke's universalism as he depicts Jesus thrice acting contrary to Jewish cultural norms: Jesus is alone with women who are not his relatives; a woman serves him; Jesus is teaching a woman in her own house. See B. Witherington, *Women in the Ministry of Jesus* (SNTSMS 51; Cambridge, 1984) 100–3. **38.** *into her house:* Certain mss. seem to have omitted this phrase in an effort to make this passage conform to 19:6; cf. Acts 17:7, where Luke uses *hypodechesthai*, "receive," without such a prepositional phrase. The emphasis on "house" in this uniquely Lucan episode is of a piece with Luke's redaction of Q and Mark, to which he has added 28 references to "house/home" (e.g., 8:27; 14:23). In view is household Christianity; women host the church in their houses. See J. Koenig, *New Testament Hospitality* (OBT 17; Phl, 1985) 103–7. **39.** *at the feet of the Lord:* For this posture of the disciple, see 8:35; Acts 22:3. **40.** *serving:* At the time of Luke's Gospel *diakonein* refers to Christian ministry (see 1 Cor 4:1; Rom 16:1). As happens frequently in his narrative of Jesus' table fellowship (5:29–39; 7:36–50; 11:37–54; 14:1–24; 19:1–10; 24:13–35), Jesus, the guest, becomes the dominant figure, or host, and answers questions about community life. **42.** *one thing:* The lesson is not that one should prepare a casserole rather than a seven-course meal. One thing undergirds all following of Jesus: listening to his word (v 39; see 8:4–21), and that is the best part. **128** (f) JESUS' DISCIPLES AND PRAYER (11:1–13). See Matt 6:9–13; 7:7–11; Luke 18:1–8. Luke writes a catechism on prayer for Gentile Christians, whose knowledge of the God of Jesus and of OT revelation needs development and who need encouragement to persevere in prayer in a hostile environment. See J. Jeremias, *The Prayers of Jesus* (SBT 2/6; Naperville, 1967) 88–89. **1.** *teach us to pray:* To have its own distinctive form of prayer was the mark of a religious community. This ancient way of recognizing a religious community is also true today, e.g., the consecration to Mary of Marianists; the "We adore you" of Franciscans. Jesus' bequest of the Our Father to his disciples will not only teach them how to pray, but especially how to live and act as his followers. **2.** The Lucan form of the Our Father has five petitions. *Father:* This distinctive feature of Jesus' prayer, viz., his personal, individual address to God as caring, provident, gracious, and loving parent, finds expression also in 10:21; 22:42; 23:34,46. It is Jesus' gracious revelation to his "little ones" as they face the evils presupposed in petitions three through five: disunity of peoples who need to be brought into unity at meals; their own sinfulness and the perversity of others; the ever-present danger of apostasy. *may your name be sanctified:* May all the evils which defile your creation be removed, esp. those in our hearts, so that the gracious love, witnessed to in your name, may be manifested. *your kingdom:* From 4:14 to this point in the Gospel Luke has been narrating the nature of God's kingdom, which breaks boundaries separating rich and poor, hale and halt, men and women, clean and unclean, saint and sinner. See the comments on 4:14–30. May that kingdom come, and not cheap human imitations of it. **3.** *bread:* The meaning of the otherwise unattested adj. *epiousios,* which modifies "bread," is highly controverted. Seen from the perspective of the Lucan motif of food, the adj. refers, on the one hand, to the food which is necessary to sustain life and is God's gracious gift. On the other hand, "bread" should not be interpreted individualistically, but should be seen as shared with others, sinners included, at meals of reconciliation, esp. the eucharist. **4.** *sins:* Jesus' community, composed of sinners, prays in confidence to its gracious Father-God for forgiveness. Disciples who are closed to forgiving each and every person who has sinned against them do not have a proper view of Jesus' God, who is merciful to all (6:35-36). *temptation:* In Luke, temptation does not have a positive outcome, e.g., strengthening of character. Temptation is always bad. Disciples pray that their ever-loving God will preserve them from apostasy from the Christian Way. See 22:39-46.

129 **5-13.** Various instructions on the necessity of perseverance in prayer. Presupposed are God's graciousness and readiness to respond to the needs of God's children on the Christian journey. If a friend will aid a friend, if the father will provide for his child, how much more will God care for the disciples of God's Son, Jesus. **13.** *holy Spirit:* Matt 7:9 has "good things." In Luke's theology "good things" can get the disciple in trouble, e.g., 12:18-19; 16:25. In answer to the prayers of disciples, who want to pray, live, and act as Jesus did, God gives them the postresurrection gift of the holy Spirit. "The gift of the Holy Spirit sums up all that is given to the community of Jesus: joy, strength, courage for witness and therefore for life" (Schweizer, *Good News* 192). See P. Edmonds, *ExpTim* 91 (1980) 140-43; E. LaVerdiere, *When We Pray...* (Notre Dame, 1983).

130 (g) CONTROVERSIES REVEAL THE MEANING OF JESUS' JOURNEY (11:14-36). Luke reveals his artistry as he creates the unity of this passage by linking disparate passages, esp. vv 24-26,33-36, around controversies about the source of Jesus' kingdom power. The result of his creativity is an A (11:15), B (11:16), A' (11:17-28), B' (11:29-36) pattern in which vv 23-28, with their dual themes of responding to Jesus' healing power and his word, form a bridge between A' and B'. Luke further manifests his creativity in the way he alternates his teachings on christology and discipleship in this section. Luke 11:14-23 is paralleled in Matt 12:22-30; Mark 3:22-27; Luke 11:24-26 in Matt 12:43-45; 11:29-32 in Matt 12:38-42; 11:33-36 in Matt 5:15; 6:22-23 (Luke 11:33 is a doublet of 8:16). **14.** *he was casting out a demon:* The exorcism is narrated in one verse. The fact of Jesus' exorcism is not debated. Rather, the source of Jesus' power, and that of those who follow on his way, is in question. **15.** *some:* Note the generalization of the opposition. In the controversy of 11:37-54 the Pharisees and lawyers are the opponents. *Beelzebul:* This word probably means "Lord of heaven." Luke has set up the A part of his pattern; he will pick up Jesus' answer to this objection in vv 17-28. **16.** *others:* The Lucan generalization of the opposition, which seeks for some extraordinarily powerful sign, is to be noted. Luke introduces B of his pattern; he delays giving an answer to their demand until vv 29-36. **17.** Luke stresses Jesus' foreknowledge. See other controversy stories (5:22; 6:8; 7:36-50). **20.** *finger of God:* The reference is to Exod 8:15 LXX. What God has done in the past to rescue God's people from the oppression of slavery is being continued by Jesus, in whose ministry God's kingdom power is being manifested. See comments on 4:14-43. **21-22.** Luke deepens his christological reflection and uses the symbolism of riches (courtyard of a palace, possessions, confidence in material security) to depict the strong man. Jesus, the stronger one (see 3:16), vanquishes the forces of evil. See S. Légasse, *NovT* 5 (1962) 5-9. **23.** *the person who is not with me is against me:* Luke strikes his theme of discipleship. While living in a hostile environment, Luke's communities are comforted by Jesus' power over evil and exhorted to continue to adhere to him and his

way. **24-28.** The puzzling vv 24-26 must be seen in the context Luke the artist has created for them: God's conquest of evil in Jesus does not take away the need for disciples to respond to Jesus' preaching of God's word. To hear and keep the word of God is the necessary help disciples need to avoid falling back into the clutches of the demonic (see Grundmann, *Lukas* 240). Luke contrasts the responses of the disciples with that of the objectors of vv 15-16. Verses 23-28 form a transition to the final part (vv 29-36, B') of Luke's pattern.

131 **29.** Luke returns to the request for a sign, first introduced in v 16. *sign of Jonah:* Matt 12:38-42 should not be read into this passage; Luke is not concerned about Jonah's three-day sojourn in the whale's belly. Verses 30,32 will make very clear that Luke's concern is with Jonah's preaching of God's word as the sign, for that accords with his insistence on hearing and keeping God's word proclaimed by Jesus. **31.** *Queen of the South:* See 1 Kgs 10. Again Luke ponders the meaning of Jesus: his wisdom is greater than that of Israel's fabled wise king, Solomon. **32.** *preaching of Jonah:* The power of God's word in Jonah is demonstrated by the mass conversion of the Ninevites. In Jesus, God's spokesperson, greater power is present. Luke holds up for imitation by his Gentile readers and all disciples the generous response given to God's word by nonelect people. **33-36.** Luke has creatively welded these wisdom sayings to his context of how one should respond to God's word preached by Jesus. **33.** *those entering may see the light:* Disciples, who preach Jesus as the light, must let that light shine for men and women who are searching for a way to come in out of the darkness. **34.** *sincere... evil:* The Gk *haplous... poneros* is to be taken in a moral sense as is the contrast between "light and darkness." A sincere and generous response to God's word leads to the moral goodness of the entire person. **36.** Jesus' and the church's preaching of the word of God will find a ready reception in the hearts of those who sincerely seek God's ways. See John 3:19-21.

132 (h) ALMSGIVING MAKES ONE CLEAN BEFORE GOD (11:37-54). As Christian communities journey on Jesus' Way, they will encounter internal and external controversy. On the meaning of "Pharisees," → 76-77 above. On the literary form of the symposium, → 99 above. Note the structure: gradual revelation of guests (lawyers are first mentioned in 11:45; scribes and other Pharisees in 11:54) and *fait divers* (the host's unspoken amazement at Jesus' failure to wash before the meal in 11:38 provides the occasion for Jesus' speech). The narrative framework (11:30-32) into which Luke has set this symposium accounts for its one anomaly, i.e., Jesus' discourteousness toward his host overshadows his wisdom. "There is a chief guest who, at least from the redactor's perspective, bests his opponents and is wiser than Solomon" (E. Steele, *JBL* 103 [1984] 389). This pericope is largely paralleled in Matt 23. **39-41.** There is a subtle play on the meanings of inside/outside in these verses: inside and outside of vessels and of human beings created by God. **41.** *the inside:* Three meanings are possible: "give the contents [food and drink] as alms"; "so far as what is inside is concerned, give alms"; "give alms from the heart" (see Marshall, *Gospel* 495). *alms:* Apart from Matt 6:2-4, only Luke-Acts in the NT mentions almsgiving. See also 12:33; 18:22; Acts 9:36-43; 10:2,4, 31; 24:17. "Thus almsgiving constitutes an essential part of the Christian ethical life for Luke. Here again we meet the Lucan challenge to those who have, to share with those who have not" (Pilgrim, *Good News to the Poor* [→ 72 above] 136; see also L. T. Johnson, *Sharing Possessions* [OBT; Phl, 1981]). Luke enjoins on his Gentile Christians the Jewish practice of almsgiving, of which their culture was almost totally ignorant. *all things are clean:* To the legalists in Luke's communities this statement is revolutionary: crossing boundaries to care for those in need renders one clean, and not established ritual practices. Examples of the way Luke has previously dealt with the issue of cleanliness may be found in 6:1–11; 8:26–56. **42.** The first of Luke's three woes against the Pharisees. *without neglecting the others:* It should be noted that Luke does not repudiate the supererogatory practices of the legalists in his community. "Luke apparently saw nothing objectionable in a Pharisaic lifestyle *per se,* including the commitment to an expanded legal system; he objects only to the neglect of central commands, whose centrality they themselves recognized (Lk. 10:25f)" (Wilson, *Luke and the Law* [→ 58 above] 19). **45.** *lawyers:* The other guests, who are legal experts among the Pharisees, are introduced. They, too, will receive three woes. **48.** *you build their tombs:* The meaning of this verse is not crystal clear because one normally builds a monument with the laudatory intent of honoring a person. Since the context indicates that the lawyers are accused of not listening to God's past or present spokespersons, v 48 may be ironic: you only honor dead prophets, not living ones; by erecting a monument over them, you have made sure they are truly dead and will not bother you now. Your building of a monument is honorable, but you are no more open to listening to God's spokespersons than your ancestors were. **49.** *prophets and apostles:* Luke refers to Christian spokespersons within his own communities. **51.** *Abel . . . Zechariah:* A contrast seems to be implied between the first book of the Bible (Gen 4:8–10) and one of the last books (2 Chr 24:20–22): you recapitulate in your response to God's word in Jesus what has occurred during the length of God's dealings with God's people. **52.** *key of knowledge:* Amid the heat of the polemic, a positive note sounds: the lawyers in Luke's communities do possess the key of knowledge. See also v 42. Their conduct seems to have prevented them from using it for themselves and others. **53–54.** The hostility on the part of the religious leaders against Jesus mounts. See also 6:11; 19:47; 20:19–20; 22:2.

133   (i) Disciples Meet with External and Internal Opposition (12:1–59). Luke constructs this section mainly from Q and L. His connections are chiefly thematic and catchword. Via 12:1–3 Luke links the opposition that the Pharisees, whose leaven is hypocrisy, give Jesus (11:37–54) to that to be experienced by his disciples (12:4–12). The opposition Jesus' "little flock" experiences finds an ally in the human desire for possessions (12:13–34). Besides the external problems caused Jesus' disciples by opposition, there are the internal problems caused by selfish church officials (12:35–48). In 12:49–53 Luke gives the christological rationale for opposition experienced by Jesus and his disciples. In 12:54–59 Luke brings the crowds into his total picture of those who oppose Jesus and the disciples by forming an *inclusio* in 12:56 with 12:1: both the Pharisees and the crowds are guilty of hypocrisy. **1–3.** *Pharisees:* Luke continues his polemic against the Pharisees or rigorist teachers in his community, whose actions do not conform to their words. The disciples should not let themselves be contaminated by their leaven or corrupting influence (v 1). No matter how persuasive and influential the teachings of the Pharisees may seem now, the false nature of their position and the destructive character of their persons will eventually be revealed (vv 2–3). Verses 1–3 seem to contain stereotyped polemic against false teachers (→ 150 below; cf. R. J. Karris, *JBL* 92 [1973] 549–64). **4–12.** Luke alternates messages of comfort and admonition as he develops the theme: if the master's teachings met with opposition, so too will those of his disciples. **4.** *my friends:* This comforting expression occurs only here in the Synoptics. **5–7.** Disciples are admonished to be faithful to God and the message of God's Son (9:35). It is God who has control over one's entire life. *five sparrows . . . hairs of your head:* With a bit of humor Luke argues from the lesser to the greater: if God cares for the least expensive items on the menu and counts the hairs that fall from the heads of balding men and women, how much more will God care for Jesus' disciples. **8–9.** *Son of Man:* The stakes of discipleship are high: those who are faithful to Jesus receive his support as Son of Man at the judgment. **10–12.** Verse 10 should be read with vv 11–12. The so-called unforgivable sin has two aspects: a stubborn refusal to entertain the Christian message (see 8:10; 11:14–26) which the church, gifted with the holy Spirit, preaches to all.

134   **13–21.** This passage commences a long meditation, which continues through 12:34 and has echoes in 12:45, on the deleterious effects possessions can have on disciples. **15.** *greed:* Part of the polemic against false teachers was that they were greedy (→ 150 below). The example story that follows in vv 16–21 warns disciples about the futility of seeking refuge from opposition by amassing possessions. **17.** Note how frequently in this verse and vv 18–19, the "fool" uses "I" and "my." His egotistical concerns eliminate God and neighbor from sight. **19.** *eat, drink:* This description of the dissipated life finds an echo in 12:45. **20.** The death of the individual as a time of reckoning is in view. *to whom shall it go?:* This is the punchline of the example story and forces readers to ask the basic question: What is life all about? **21.** Luke gives his own answer to the question of v 20: Find the meaning in life by acknowledging God and giving alms to the needy (→ 132 above).

135   **22–34.** In these verses, which are often romanticized, Luke continues his reflections on possessions and opposition. His meditation points are: "little faith" (v 28) and "fear not, little flock" (v 32). **24.** *ravens:* These birds are unclean (Lev 11:15; Deut 14:14). "They were known in antiquity as careless creatures that even fail to return to their nests" (*FGL* 978). Why a raven rather than a lion? **27–28.** *lilies:* The splendor of the lily is extolled in one breath; its ephemeral character in the next breath. Why a lily rather than a cedar of Lebanon? Through these images Luke is directing his readers' imaginations to situations in which their existence seems as helpless and as short-lived as that of ravens and lilies. One such situation is that of opposition to the message of God's word which they preach (see 8:11–15). See P. S. Minear, *Commands of Christ* (Nash, 1972) 132–51. In such a situation Jesus authoritatively assures his "little-faith" disciples of God's gracious care for them. **32.** *little flock:* To his struggling, opposed, and small group of disciples Jesus promises what is all-important, the kingdom, the powers of which are operative in it. **33–34.** *give alms:* Having warned disciples about anxiety over material goods in vv 22–32, Luke returns to the necessity of sharing material goods through almsgiving, which he introduced in v 21.

136   **35–48.** These "servant" parables are given an ecclesiological interpretation by Luke: community officials must be faithful and not create internal problems for the church. One key to Luke's meaning is the fact that the Gk *doulos,* "servant," "slave," which occurs in vv 37,43,45,46,47, means one who gives service to the Christian community (see Rom 1:1; 1 Cor 7:22; Gal 1:10; cf. Acts 4:29; 16:17). Another key is the fact that *oikonomos,* "steward," occurs in the Gospels only in Luke (12:42; see 16:1,3,8) and means one who gives service to the Christian community (1 Cor 4:1–2; Titus 1:7; 1 Pet

4:10). **37.** *he will serve them:* This role reversal is significant and underscores God's absolute gratuity. The servant who is faithful during the time of fulfillment before the parousia will share in the eschatological banquet. Contrast 17:7–10, which underlines the responsibility of the servant. See further Luke's presentation of Jesus as servant in 22:24–27 and as Suffering Servant in 23:6–25. **41.** *Peter:* He is the spokesperson for questions about church officials (→ 70 above). **42.** *measure of food:* More seems to be involved here than mere foodstuffs. Is there reference to communal meals? And the eucharist? **45.** *to eat, drink, and become intoxicated:* Echoes of v 19 sound: the church official has taken on some of the characteristics of the "fool." **47–49.** The punishments for unfaithful and negligent church officials are stark.

137 **49–53.** With a flashback to 3:16 Luke gives the rationale for opposition to Jesus, his disciples, and within the church. **49.** *fire:* The nature of Jesus' message is to purify and to cause people to distinguish dross from the genuine product. **50.** *baptism:* To baptize "is here used without primary reference to the rite of baptism, but in the metaphorical sense of being overwhelmed by catastrophe . . ." (Marshall, *Gospel* 547). In obedience to God's will Jesus goes on his journey to Jerusalem and his exodus (9:31), resolutely facing all opposition. **53.** *father will be divided against son . . . :* Perhaps Mic 7:6 provides the background for this verse. More important, it seems that Luke has hedged on his theme of peace in this verse and v 52. These verses should be read, however, with the programmatic 2:34–35 in mind. Peace will not be obtained at any cost, esp. at the cost of compromising God's word. Yet even in nonpeaceful situations the Lucan Jesus calls for forgiveness and reconciliation (e.g., 9:51–56) and love of enemies (6:27–36). **54–59.** The Pharisees, because of their hypocrisy (12:1), do not accept Jesus. The crowds, because of their hypocrisy, refuse to see God's key moment of salvation history (*kairos*) present in Jesus' kingdom ministry (12:56). Ironically, the crowds have sufficient intelligence, e.g., in legal matters, to seek reconciliation and freedom from imprisonment. If only they would apply that ingenuity to reading the signs of the times in Jesus (12:57–59)!

138 (j) ALL NEED TO REPENT (13:1–9). This passage, found only in Luke, teaches disciples that Jesus is compassionate but not wishy-washy. He demands that sinners repent before it is too late. Jesus' dual injunction to repent (vv 3,5) will form the basis for the later question about whether few will be saved (13:23). **1.** *Galileans whose blood Pilate had mingled with their sacrifices:* This incident is not otherwise attested. **2–3.** The catastrophe of v 1 (and also of v 4) did not overwhelm these folks because they were notorious sinners. In his counsel that disciples learn from the unexpected death of others that they should repent and be ready for judgment, Luke connects this passage with the judgment theme of chap. 12, e.g., vv 20,40,46. **3.** *unless you repent, you all will perish in a similar way:* This verse is repeated almost verbatim in v 5 and is a refrain. Luke also develops his theme of peace and nonviolence: ". . . Jesus shows no sign whatsoever of hatred or vengeance when he is told of Pilate's cruelty to his compatriots" (Ford, *My Enemy* 101). **6–9.** *fig tree:* On the one hand, this is a parable of compassion, which produces comfort in the disciple who stumbles along the Christian Way. On the other hand, it is a parable of crisis, which should light a fire under procrastinators and other unproductive disciples.

139 (k) AN ILLUSTRATON OF THE NATURE OF GOD'S KINGDOM (13:11–17). In this rich passage, found exclusively here, Luke shows in action the meaning of God's kingdom, which he will illustrate through parables in

13:18–21. **10.** *synagogue:* → 56 above. *sabbath:* → 58, 81 above. **11.** *woman:* God's kingdom is not just for males. This "little one," who responds to God's kingdom power in her life by praising God (v 13), is contrasted with the religious leader, whose views of when God can act blind him to the presence of that kingdom and his need for repentance. **15–16.** Jesus argues from the lesser to the greater: If you loose animals on the sabbath, why can't I loose a human being on the sabbath? *daughter of Abraham:* The Jewish religious heritage is not restricted to the healthy or to males. This woman belongs to reconstituted Israel (→ 23 above). See also 19:9, where Jesus declares that the chief toll collector, Zacchaeus, another outcast, is a "son of Abraham." What Jesus has done for this woman is in fulfillment of his commission of releasing captives from the bonds of evil (4:18). *sabbath:* What Jesus does on the sabbath is truly a celebration of its deep meaning, i.e., release from the effects of the fallen order. The sabbath's purpose, as Jesus sees it, is fulfilled not by forbidding works of compassion, but by encouraging them. See Busse, *Wunder* (→ 67 above) 289–304; Wilson, *Luke and the Law* (→ 58 above) 37; Witherington, *Women* (→ 127 above) 68–71.

140 (l) DESPITE OPPOSITION GOD'S KINGDOM GROWS (13:18–21). These two kingdom parables, the only ones found in Luke, are paralleled in Matt 13:31–33. These parables do not stress the contrast between the smallness of the beginning and the greatness of the end product. What is in the limelight is growth, which ineluctably takes place. In the immediate context before these parables Luke emphasized opposition to Jesus (see 11:13–13:17); and in what follows the theme of opposition will be no less strong (14:1–24; 15:1–2). These parables comfort disciples who, as they continue their master's journey, will also face fierce opposition. They also show why Jesus' kingdom mission was opposed. **19.** *birds of the air build their nests in its branches:* This composite reference to Ps 104:12 and Dan 4:9,18 refers to the diverse human beings who find refuge in God's kingdom. Luke's theme of universalism surfaces. Jesus suffered opposition because he accepted outcasts at meals that symbolized God's kingdom (see 13:28–29). **21.** *leaven which a women took and hid:* A woman is paired with the man of the previous parable. R. W. Funk (*Int* 25 [1971] 149–70) has called attention to three strange items in this parable: (1) God's kingdom is compared to something that is unclean and corrupts, leaven; (2) God's kingdom under the image of leaven is hidden; (3) it is hidden in the amount of flour used to respond festively to a divine epiphany (Gen 18:6; Judg 6:19). The comparison of God's kingdom to something that is unclean challenges ordinary conceptions of what is clean and rings true in Luke's Gospel (e.g., 8:26–56). That kingdom is indeed hidden, esp. from the wise and learned (10:21). In the kingdom Jesus proclaims in word and deed that there is an epiphany of God for those who open their eyes and ears to see and hear it. Disciples can be confident that God's kingdom, like the powerful corrupting agent, leaven, is operative and will achieve its goal despite all indications to the contrary.

141 **(B) Second Part of Instruction on the Meaning of the Christian Way (13:22–17:10).** Luke continues to exploit the rich symbolism of Jesus' journey to Jerusalem and his rendezvous with God's will and instructs disciples on the various dimensions of the Christian way.

(a) THE NEED FOR REPENTANCE STRESSED AGAIN (13:22–30). Perhaps using Q material for vv 24–29, Luke builds on the injunctions to repentance found in 13:3,5 and stresses that the Christian way demands total allegiance to Jesus and provides travel companions from all over the globe as well as places at the eschatological banquet. **24.** *narrow gate:* The implied contrast seems to be between large city gates through which throngs can pass at one time and one slight passage. **25–27.** *closes the door:* Luke changes the image to a door that Jesus locks on those who were content with boasting that they were acquainted with him and his message. Casual eating and drinking with Jesus is not enough. One must share in his life as symbolized by his table fellowship with the lowly. **28–29.** *Abraham, Isaac, and Jacob:* The kingdom of God (see 13:18–21) is now imaged by the eschatological banquet (see Isa 25:6–8). Those who do not want to commit themselves to Jesus' way find themselves on the outside. In graciousness God opens the banquet to all peoples. These now form reconstituted Israel. **30.** Luke sounds his familiar theme of reversal.

(b) Jesus Obediently Journeys to Jerusalem (13:31–35). In this passage Luke accentuates Jesus' obedience to God's will (see 9:51) and his loving care for God's city, Jerusalem, and its people. Underneath these larger themes Luke plays on his familiar motif of opposition to Jesus, God's spokesperson. **31.** *some Pharisees:* This may well be the only positive reference to the Pharisees in this Gospel. **32.** *fox:* Jesus considers Herod Antipas (see 3:1,19–20; 9:7–9; 23:6–10) a tricky, sly person. One should not miss the import of this criticism of a political figure. In Luke's Gospel there is nothing sacrosanct about the Roman social order or those, like Herod, who uphold it. Jesus criticizes them freely. "Moreover, Jesus does not submit to the social patterns and practices to which the Romans and their allies are committed. He rejects the violence and exploitation that they accept as a normal part of living, and his teachings and conduct run counter to many of the other patterns that they accept and endorse" (R. J. Cassidy, *Jesus, Politics, and Society* [Maryknoll, 1978] 61–62). → 170 below. *on the third day I reach my goal:* Herod will not impede Jesus from carrying out his kingdom mission from day to day. In God's own time Jesus will attain to Jerusalem and will be raised up there in vindication by God on the third day. **33.** *I must journey:* Jesus resolutely embraces God's will as signified by "must" (Gk *dei*). Jerusalem is not only the place of Jesus' murder, but its agent. On the motif of "rejected prophet," by means of which Luke has been able to make sense out of Jesus' death in Jerusalem, → 61 above. **34.** *hen:* Through this image of loving care and warm protection the Lucan Jesus speaks of his compassion for his own people. **35.** *house:* This is not necessarily a reference to the Temple. The OT background seems to be Jer 22:1–9 where "house" means the king's household of leaders. In Luke's passion account it is primarily the religious leaders, the high priests, who are responsible for Jesus' death. See F. D. Weinert, *CBQ* 44 (1982) 68–76. *blessed:* Within the Lucan story line the reference is to 19:38 (→ 163 below).

142   (c) The Inclusive Nature of Jesus' Kingdom Banquet (14:1–24). This passage continues the note of opposition on which chap. 13 concluded. Jesus is the host (14:24) of God's eschatological banquet, to which all, elect and nonelect, are invited. **1–6.** This story, unique to Luke, is the *fait divers,* which triggers Jesus' wisdom discourses in vv 7–24. The Pharisees should have invited needy people like the man with dropsy to their feast (see vv 12–14). **1.** *Pharisees:* → 76–77 above. *sabbath:* → 58 above. This is the final Lucan controversy on a sabbath. *to take a meal:* → 99–100, 132 for information on the nature of the symposium genre that Luke adapts here to give answers to problems his communities face with the "Pharisees": should they associate with the unclean (7:36–50); what renders one clean

(11:37–54); who should be invited to Christian meals (14:1–24). In each instance Luke gives the answers, radical ones at that, in a meal setting. **2.** *dropsy:* Dropsy or edema, the disease whereby the body retains too much fluid with attendant problems of swelling and poor blood circulation, is known in Western societies, where it is often caused by excessive sodium consumption. **4–6.** Jesus again shows himself to be "Lord of the sabbath" (6:5), who champions works of compassion on the sabbath.

143   **7–15.** This is the first part of the wisdom teaching of Jesus, the chief guest. Luke builds on a theme that was a set piece in literature about symposia: places of honor (see Lucian, *Convivium* 8–9). **7.** *invited:* Gk *keklēmenoi.* J. A. Sanders has called attention to the double entendre involved in this Gk vb. throughout 14:1–24: "*Keklēmenoi* ('those invited') in Luke means 'apparently elect' or 'those who consider themselves elected'" ("The Ethic of Election in Luke's Great Banquet Parable," *Essays in Old Testament Ethics* [Fest. J. P. Hyatt; ed. J. L. Crenshaw, *et al.;* NY, 1974] 259). Thus, in vv 16–24 we will have a contrast between those considered elect and those deemed nonelect. **11.** *everyone who exalts:* Luke gives secular wisdom a theological orientation: God will not be fooled by one's self-promotion. **12–14.** Luke's communities do not maintain a strict Greco-Roman reciprocity ethic or *do ut des* mentality, whereby friends, who have all things in common, come to one another's aid in the hope that when they are down on their luck the friend will come to their aid. In Luke's communities people from different walks of life and from different nations are like friends as they have all things in common (Acts 4:32). See W. C. van Unnik, *NovT* 7 (1966) 284–300. **13.** *the poor, maimed, lame, blind:* The needy folks mentioned in this verse will reappear in v 21. There is good evidence that during Jesus' and Luke's time both Jewish and Greco-Roman society spurned these unfortunate people, e.g., 1QSa 2:5–22 lists the following people as those forbidden entry to the eschatological banquet: those who are afflicted in flesh, crushed in feet or hands, lame, blind, deaf, or dumb; those who suffer from defective eyesight or senility. See further W. den Boer, *Private Morality in Greece and Rome* (Mnemosyne 57; Leiden, 1979) 129–32. Luke seems to be the one who has added "the poor" to this list. Why? "In both Hebrew Scriptures and the literature of Qumran, 'the poor' is frequently used as a designation for Israel, and especially for the elect within Israel" (Ringe, *Jesus* [→ 59 above] 59). May it be that Luke, by introducing "the poor" into a list of those deprived of social and economic influence, is ironically expanding the notion of who are elect? **14.** *resurrection of the just:* Verses 12–14 have made it clear that the righteous to be repaid at this resurrection are those who have shared the food of life with the disadvantaged. **15.** *one of Jesus' table companions:* One of the "other guests" of the symposium genre speaks up, self-assuredly, and provides Luke with the opportunity to introduce the final element of Jesus' speech in vv 16–24.

144   **16–24.** This parable, which concludes Luke's extensive use of food symbolism in 14:1–24, is paralleled in Matt 21:1–10 and *Gos. Thom.* 64 and continues the Lucan motif of the elect failing to respond to God's kingdom (vv 16–20,24) which is open for all others (vv 21–23). As has been evident before (5:27–32), Jesus, the guest at a meal, becomes the host (v 24). **18–19.** *a field . . . five yoke of oxen:* As one would expect from Luke, the first two excuses involve the pursuit of mammon. It should be noted that the story line is based on threes: three invited, three excuses, three sendings. This factor rules out observations that the nonelect who are called in the second and third sendings rate less in God's eyes. Without the servant's second and third rounds there would be no story. **20.** *I have married a wife:* This verse will be paralleled in v 26 and gives evidence of a certain ascetic strain in Luke-Acts. While having a positive attitude to marriage (see Elizabeth and Zechariah [1:5–25] and Aquila and Priscilla [Acts 18]), Luke also favors celibacy. This emphasis does not contradict Luke's positive portrayal of women disciples, for in a patriarchal society not being married can be emancipatory. Besides 14:20,26; 18:29; and 20:34–36, see his portraits of Mary, Jesus, Paul, and the four prophetess daughters of Philip (Acts 21:9). Women like Mary Magdalene (8:3; 24:10), Mary and Martha (10:38–42), Tabitha (Acts 9:36), Lydia (Acts 16:14–15), and Damaris (Acts 17:34) may have been unmarried. Luke is against remarriage after divorce (3:19–20; 16:18; Acts 24:24–25). He presents widows in a positive light (2:36; 7:12; 18:3; 21:2; Acts 9:39). It does not seem fortuitous that in a number of the passages singled out (esp. 14:26; 18:29) Luke makes a connection between abandoning possessions and being celibate. See H.-J. Klauck, *Claretianum* 26 (1986) 39–43. **23.** *force them to come in:* One should not overinterpret this language, which is rooted in the ways of Middle Eastern hospitality: "even the poorest, with oriental courtesy, modestly resist the invitation to the entertainment until they are taken by the hand and gently forced to enter the house" (Jeremias, *Parables* 177). **24.** *my banquet:* The Lucan Jesus is Lord of the eschatological banquet.

145 (d) THE DEMANDS OF DISCIPLESHIP REPEATED (14:25–35). In this material, which is on the whole unique to him, Luke again lays down the conditions for discipleship. See 9:23–27,57–62. If 14:16–24 placed emphasis on the absolute gratuity of God's election, these verses develop the flip side of that election, full-hearted response on the part of disciples. **26.** *hate:* The total commitment Jesus demands of his disciples is stated starkly. *wife:* → 144 above. *my disciple:* This forms the refrain for vv 27,33. **28–32.** These two parables concentrate on the necessity of reflection before action. Those who want to follow Jesus on the way must weigh the costs. **33.** This troublesome verse is introduced by Gk *houtōs oun,* normally translated "similarly," and shows that in v 33 a conclusion is being drawn from the parables of vv 28–32. But what is the point of comparison? The comparison drawn between vv 28–32 and 33 is this: the fate of those who are not able to see something through to completion. Jesus' followers must not recoil before any sacrifice required of them to see their following of him through to the end, even if this means the sacrifice of all their possessions. See J. Dupont, *NRT* 93 (1971) 561–82. A. Plummer (*Luke* 366) captures Luke's meaning: "All disciples must be ready to renounce their possessions." Thus, v 33 is not a command that all disciples willy-nilly renounce their possessions. **34–35.** *salt:* Disciples must beware of letting their allegiance to Jesus deteriorate and become inactive. "A ruined builder, a conquered king, spoiled salt—these are the unpleasant pictures Luke uses to illustrate the situation of a disciple who from discouragement or any other cause withdraws from the profession he has once made" (C. E. Carlston, *The Parables of the Triple Tradition* [Phl, 1975] 89).

146 (e) GOD'S MERCY FOR SINNERS THRICE ILLUSTRATED (15:1–32). In three parables Luke champions the theme that God's mercy breaks through all human restrictions of how God should act toward sinners. God's mercy, indeed, is as foolish as a shepherd who abandons 99 sheep to save one, as a woman who turns her house upside down to recover a paltry sum, and as a Jewish father who joyfully welcomes home his wastrel

son who has become a Gentile. Because disciples have such a merciful God, they can embark trustingly and joyfully on Jesus' way to this God. **1–10.** Luke images God's love for sinners through a man and a woman. **2.** *Pharisees:* → 76–77 above. Although Luke does not place this Pharisaic criticism of Jesus at a meal or symposium (see 7:36–50; 11:37–54; 14:1–24), there is still reference to Jesus' indiscriminate table fellowship. The basic issue between Jesus and the Lucan Pharisees remains the same: Are some people outside the limits of God's mercy? **4–7.** A parallel to this parable is found in Matt 18:12–14. **5.** *rejoicing:* The theme of joy suffuses this chapter (see also 15:6,7,9,10,23,24,29,32) and has four emphases: (1) The motifs of universality, community, and soteriology are inextricably commingled. (2) Conversion is a requisite for finding joy. (3) Happiness consists essentially in a willingness to share in God's own joy in dispensing salvation. (4) The call to participate in God's love and joy is issued through Jesus Christ (see P. L. Bernadicou, *ScEs* 30 [1978] 76–78). **6.** *lost:* This becomes a refrain in the chapter: lost sheep, lost coin (v 9), lost son (v 24), lost brother (v 32).

147 **11–32.** This parable plays upon the hearers' knowledge of two-brothers stories, in which the younger brother triumphs over the older brother(s). See, e.g., Esau and Jacob (Gen 25:27–34; 27:1–36); Joseph and his brothers (Gen 37:1–4). Jesus doubly reverses expectations: the prodigal son is a parody of the successful younger brother; the elder son is not vanquished, but invited to the feast. **15–16.** *to feed swine:* The younger son has sunk to the depths of engaging in Gentile ways. See 8:26–39 on the symbolism of pigs. **17–19.** The son articulates the stirrings of repentance agitating his person. **20.** *ran:* This is undignified behavior for an elderly Oriental gentleman. **22–23.** The father's forgiveness of his son who had become a Gentile is acted out: there is a ceremonial robe; a signet ring; shoes, which betoken the status of free people. Meat, which is rarely eaten, marks this as a special occasion. **24.** The refrains of "lost and found" and rejoicing flood this verse. **25–32.** Although often ignored, these verses are an integral part of the two-son parable and address the issue of self-righteousness (see 15:2 on "the Pharisees" and 15:7, where "righteous" can ironically mean "self-righteous"). **30.** *this son of yours:* The elder son does not want to accept his "dead" brother as alive and as his brother. **32.** *your brother:* The refrains of "lost and found" and rejoicing crowd together around the father's plea that his older son accept the repentant son as his brother. The challenge of this parable is enhanced by its open ending: will righteous people enter the banqueting hall to make merry with sinners and the God who delights in their company? For a possible parallel to 15:11–32 from oral haggadic tradition about Rabbi Eliezer ben Hyrcanus, see R. D. Aus, *JBL* 104 (1985) 443–69.

148 (f) THE NECESSITY OF SHARING POSSESSIONS WITH THE NEEDY (16:1–31). The unifying theme of this apparently disunified chapter is that of using possessions to benefit others, esp. the needy. See Karris, "Poor and Rich," *PerspLA* 121–23; Horn, *Glaube und Handeln* (→ 23 above) 68–88. The chapter is divided into four, interrelated sections: 16:1–8a; 16:8b–13; 16:14–18; 16:19–31. **1–8a.** The parable of the "dishonest steward" ends with v 8a; the master spoken of in v 8a is not Jesus, but the rich landowner of vv 1,3,5. The legal system presupposed by the parable is a widely attested one and is contrary to the OT ban of usury. The steward was authorized to make binding contracts for his master. The usurious interest on oil and wheat, for example, would not be listed separately in the contract. It would be included in the one lump sum mentioned in the contract. Thus, a person may have obtained only 450 gallons of olive oil, but because of the 100 percent interest charged, had to have 900 gallons written on his contract (see v 6). There is no evidence that the steward could pocket the interest as his commission; the steward's job was to make money for his master. See J. D. M. Derrett, *NTS* 7 (1960–61) 198–219. **1.** *rich man:* This designation makes clear what the story presupposes; see also 16:19. The master is an absentee landlord and not a beloved figure in Palestinian or Greco-Roman society. *charges were brought against the steward with hostile intent:* This is the usual, negative meaning of *diaballein.* **2.** The master believes the calumny and prepares to dismiss his steward. **3–4.** *I know what I shall do:* In his soliloquy, which attracts the reader to identify with him, the unjustly treated steward does not engage in self-pity or some other tactic of indecision. He will act decisively. **5.** *his master's debtors:* Twice it is mentioned that the sums are owed the master. There is no evidence that the steward is forgoing his commission. The steward is going to get even with his master at the master's expense. He cancels the usurious profit of his master. Surely, the debtors will reciprocate such largess (see v 4). **8a.** *dishonest steward:* This is not a simple repetition of what is implied in vv 1–2, but a reference to the dishonest conduct depicted in vv 5–7. *praised:* The steward is not beaten or otherwise punished (contrast 12:46). *prudently:* "The adverb *phronimos* refers to practical action aimed at accomplishing some particular end. It does not have anything to do with virtue in the more general sense of justice" (P. Perkins, *Hearing the Parables of Jesus* [NY, 1981] 166).

What are the meanings of 16:1–8a? Since Luke is fond of using "example stories" instead of parables (see 10:29–37; 12:16–21; 16:19–31; 18:9–14) to arrest his readers' attention and drive home a lesson, 16:1–8a is often taken to be an example story, and this interpretation is taken in two directions. Its popular version generates enormous problems, for it maintains that Jesus is teaching that his disciples should imitate the unjust actions of the steward. Such teaching is morally repugnant. The scholarly version maintains that what is to be imitated is the steward's shrewdness in the use of possessions (even though these possessions were not his own).

Others take 16:1–8a to be a genuine parable about the kingdom of God. One viewpoint maintains that the point of contact between the actions in the parable and in Jesus' audiences on his journey to Jerusalem is similar and is this: the steward was decisive when faced with a crisis, so too should Jesus' listeners who are wavering in their decision to follow him and his kingdom message. Another viewpoint holds that the point of contact is one of dissimilarity: the sense of justice normally implied in the symbol kingdom does not accord with the behavior of the master in v 8a. How can the master praise such unjust conduct perpetrated on himself and not have the rascal punished? Are normal standards of justice being denied in the kingdom Jesus preaches? Yes, in Jesus' kingdom of justice and power, masters do not get even. This view of the meaning of the parable accords with the Lucan Jesus' command to love enemies (6:27–35) and his teaching about nonretaliation and love of enemies (see 9:51–55; 10:29–37; 17:11–19; 22:47–55; 23:34). See B. B. Scott, *Bib* 64 (1983) 173–88.

149   8b–13. Various interpretations of the parable are provided, via catchwords. They focus on the use of possessions and present a prime example of Luke's two-sided thinking: mammon can seduce disciples away from God, yet disciples must use mammon—now—for alms! **8b.** *children of this age are shrewder:* The steward represents the enthusiastic response which people of this age show in their dealings with one another and contrasts sharply with the lackluster response of disciples to Jesus' kingdom. **9.** *unrighteous mammon:* All mammon ("that in which one puts one's trust") belongs to this evil age. Disciples are to convert mammon into heavenly capital by sharing it with others, particularly the needy. See 12:33–34. This command of Jesus on almsgiving affirms the abiding validity (see 16:16–17) of what the law and the prophets command about almsgiving (16:29–31). On the parallel between 16:9 and 1 Tim 6:18–19, see S. G. Wilson, *Luke and the Pastoral Epistles* (London, 1979) 50. **10.** *faithful:* This application of the parable highlights the necessity of daily fidelity. **11.** If disciples do not share possessions, they will not be entrusted with the true, heavenly reality. **12.** If disciples do share possessions, which are on loan from another, i.e., God, they will be given the treasure of heaven as their own inalienable possession. See Marshall, *Gospel* 624. **13.** *you cannot serve both God and mammon:* The disciple must give exclusive loyalty to God or succumb to the enslavement of mammon, and one is loyal to God by sharing mammon with others, esp. those in want.

150   14–18. After H. Conzelmann published his view that 16:16 conveys Luke's tripartite view of salvation history (see *TSL* 16–17), more attention was given to arguing the pros and cons of his position than to ascertaining how 16:14–18 connects with 16:1–13 and 16:19–31, which are obviously thematically interrelated. See Wilson, *Luke and the Law* (→ 58 above) 43–51. **14–15.** *Pharisees:* The connections of 16:14–18 with 16:1–13 and 16:19–31 are three. (1) Verses 14–15 treat the sectarian Christian Pharisees as types of the rich (see 16:19–31), who mock Jesus for his teaching about sharing possessions with the needy, who are not members of their community (16:1–13). Luke has previously used the Pharisees as negative examples (→ 76–77, 99–100, 132, 142). In describing the Pharisees as greedy and exalting themselves (vv 14–15), Luke is drawing on Greco-Roman polemical tradition against false teachers as evidenced in 1 Tim 6:10 (greed) and 1 Tim 6:17 (exaltation). In other NT authors greed is linked with sexual sins (see Eph 4:19; 5:3,5). Luke also links greed and sexual sins in 16:14 and 16:18; note a similar connection in 8:14 and Acts 24:25–26. (2) Jesus' teaching is in fulfillment of and continues the Law and the Prophets (16:16; see v 29), i.e., their teaching about aid to the needy (16:1–13; 16:27–31). Furthermore, what God has done in raising the lowly Jesus (16:31) shows that God's action is in fulfillment of God's will to save the poor (16:16). See J. Dupont, *Les Beatitudes* (EBib; Paris, 1973) 3. 62–64. (3) The gospel is not a restrictive message for some rich who think they are elect (16:15,19–26). It is for all (16:16). In sum, Luke warns the well-off members of his community to avoid greed (and immorality) by following Jesus' teaching about almsgiving, which accords with God's will. In 16:19–31 Luke will continue that exhortation with the negative example of the rich man.

151   19–31. This is a two-tiered (vv 19–26,27–31) example story which focuses on the rich man, his five brothers, and the readers. It asks: Will the five brothers and readers follow the example of the rich man or heed Jesus' teaching and that of the OT about care of the needy like Lazarus and thus be children of Abraham? If the five brothers and the readers do not follow that teaching, they will not have a place at the messianic banquet. **19–26.** There are parallels in Egyptian folklore and the story of Bar Ma'yan for this part of the example story (see *FGL* 1126–27). What these parallels of reversal in the next life of the conditions one had in the present life do not account for are the dialogue between the rich man and Abraham (vv 23,24,25,27,29,30) and the fact that the poor in the person of Lazarus does not gloat over the punishment of the rich man. Contrast *1 Enoch* 92–105; *Apoc. Pet.* 13. See M. Himmelfarb, *Tours of Hell* (Phl, 1983). **19–20.** *rich man . . . poor man:* Despite attempts to show that vv 19–26 depict the rich man as doing wrong (see Seccombe, *Possessions* [→ 23 above] 176–78), the text gives no indication that he was guilty of moral wrong or, for that matter, that Lazarus was morally right. Thus, there is reason to hold that vv 19–26, by itself, may condemn the rich because they are rich and bless the poor because they are poor (see 1:51–53; 6:20–26). **23.** *bosom of Abraham:* A reference to the choice position when one reclines with Abraham at the messianic banquet (13:28–29; see John 13:22). **24.** *tongue:* See Himmelfarb, *Tours* 68–105, for examples of this "measure for measure" punishment. **27–31.** This second tier of the example story continues the dialogue between the slow-witted rich man and Father Abraham and clearly shows that the rich man's failure to care for Lazarus was not in accord with the OT (16:29–31) and with Jesus' teaching (16:9). **27.** *Father (Abraham):* The reference to Abraham draws upon a Lucan theme (→ 23 above). Mere words do not make one a child of Abraham and therefore a member of reconstituted Israel. "Dives' claim that Abraham is his father is of no effect, for he has not produced the deeds of loving kindness that would have signified repentance from his self-centered, callous way of life" (G. W. E. Nickelsburg, *NTS* 25 [1978–79] 338). **31.** *rise from the dead:* The well-off of Luke's community are exhorted to help the Lazaruses in their midst. Although 16:19–31 teaches that the poor are saved *sola gratia,* they, too, will need to respond to the Lucan Gospel of God's raising up of the lowly in the death and resurrection of Jesus (16:31). See *FGL* 1129.

152 (g) THE INWARD RENEWAL OF DISCIPLES (17:1–10). Most of the second segment of Luke's travel narrative (13:22–17:10) has been taken up with opposition to Jesus and his disciples. As he concludes this segment, Luke returns to the note on which he commenced in 13:22–30: renewal. The material in vv 1–6 is largely from Q; vv 7–10 is proper to Luke. **1–2.** A stern warning is given to disciples not to cause their brothers and sisters to abandon the Christian journey. **1.** *temptations:* As they journey on Jesus' way, disciples, like everyone else, will be subject to bad example, disedification, and scandal. **2.** *millstone:* Perhaps a reference to the basalt millstone common in Palestine and weighing hundreds of pounds. Wearing a millstone as swimming attire would quickly cause the name of the seducer to be scratched from the list of the living. *one of these little ones:* Disciples can be as helpless as small children in the face of the mighty force of the person who makes them plummet into apostasy. Are church officials the cause of the scandal? See vv 7–10; → 136 above. **3–4.** *forgive:* Disciples are not only to pray the Our Father but also to live it out as they forgive one another without limit (→ 128 above). **5–6.** What disciples on the way need more than anything else is a deepening faith in the God of Jesus Christ, who can and will rescue them from opposition and other destructive forces. **6.** *mulberry tree:* A relatively large tree with an extensive root system. It would be difficult not only to uproot this tree but also to grow it in deep water. Genuine faith can bring about quite unexpected things. **7–9.** *servant:* This is the other side of the coin of 12:35–37, which underscored God's unmerited graciousness to disciples (→ 136 above). Stressed here is responsible ministry on the part of church officials who till the field of the church and shepherd its flock. **10.** *unworthy:* The point is not that disciples are not worth anything in themselves or in their work for the Lord. The fact that disciples have

done their duty does not empower them to lay a claim upon God that they are worthy of God's graciousness. That graciousness is and remains sheer gift.

153 (C) **Third Part of Instruction on the Meaning of the Christian Way (17:11–19:27).** On the last legs of his journey to God, Jesus concludes his instructions about what it means to follow him.

(a) THE GRATITUDE AND FAITH OF A SAMARITAN LEPER (17:11–19). This miracle is proper to Luke and the fourth in his travel narrative (see 11:14; 13:10–17; 14:1–6). "In each case the theme of the episode is not the miraculous act but the teaching-word arising from it" (Ellis, *Luke* 209). In this instance the teaching-word will have christological, soteriological, eschatological, and parenetic import. **11.** *between Samaria and Galilee:* One should not press the text for geographical exactitude. Two things are important to Luke: Jesus is making for Jerusalem and his rendezvous with God's will; since he is near Samaria, he can encounter a Samaritan leper. **12.** *ten lepers:* → 73–74 above. High, solid boundaries separate these men from their brothers and sisters. **14.** See Lev 13:49. **15.** *seeing:* "Only the Samaritan sees and fully understands what has happened. His seeing leads him to understand not only that he is healed, but that he has found God's salvation. His return to Jesus amounts to his conversion" (H. D. Betz, *JBL* 90 [1971] 318). *praised God:* This is Luke's favorite response to a manifestation of divine power and mercy (see 2:20; 5:25, 26; 7:16; 13:13; 18:43; 23:47; Acts 4:21; 21:20). Here and in v 18 christology is to the forefront: the Samaritan leper praises God for what Jesus, God's agent, has done. Prominent also is eschatological fulfillment. What was promised in 2 Kgs 5:8–19a and repeated in 4:27 and 7:22, has come to fulfillment in Jesus: God's salvation is for all peoples. See W. Bruners, *Die Reinigung der zehn Aussätzigen und die Heilung des Samariters Lk 17,11–19* (FB 23; Stuttgart, 1977). **16.** *gave thanks:* Luke contrasts ingratitude and gratitude as he makes a parenetic point. *a Samaritan:* This phrase stands in an emphatic place in the Gk text. On the role of the Samaritans, see 9:51–55; 10:25–37; Acts 8:4–25. From outside the chosen people Luke draws his hero. **19.** *your faith has saved you:* Luke's soteriological message sounds. Jesus is the one who saves from disease and restores one to human concourse. In him disciples find the fullness of human wholeness.

154 (b) FIDELITY WHILE WAITING FOR THE COMING OF THE SON OF MAN (17:20–18:8). From eschatological materials Luke creates exhortations for disciples on the journey as he mixes his unique material with largely Q material (17:20–37). The delay of the coming of Jesus, the Son of Man, causes little problem for disciples when days are bright and cheery. Problems abound when persecution arises (17:25,33), and Jesus' God delays vindication of the elect (18:1–8). **20–21.** *Pharisees:* → 76–77 above. These narrow-minded Christians are not able to see God's kingdom present and within their comprehension in such events as Jesus' cure of the unclean lepers and the grateful faith of a Samaritan (17:11–19), events that foreshadow the church's mission to the Gentiles. **22–37.** In 21:5–36 Luke will present an additional eschatological discourse. Whereas that one accentuates the events that lead up to the coming of the Son of Man, this one emphasizes the suddenness of Jesus' coming (vv 22–25) and the unpreparedness of people (vv 26–37) for it. See Flender, *Luke* (→ 28 above) 13–15. **25.** *he must suffer many things:* This verse stems from Luke and gives a christological orientation to traditional eschatological material. After the humiliation of the cross, Jesus, the Son of Man, has been glorified (see 9:22). On their road to glory disciples will not be able to escape suffering for the name (see Acts 5:41; 14:22). **26.** The focus changes from the suddenness of Jesus' coming to the need for disciples on the Way to be prepared. **27–30.** *they ate, drank . . . :* Disciples should beware lest everyday concerns replace active, personal waiting for Jesus' return. **31–32.** Disciples are ready for Jesus' return when they have renounced their attachment to possessions. **33.** *whoever loses life:* See 9:24–25 in the context of Jesus' prediction of his rejection and vindication (9:22). As they experience opposition because of their allegiance to Jesus, disciples are admonished to ponder once again what life is all about. **34–35.** *taken . . . left:* The context of Noah and Lot indicates that these disciples will be taken away from destruction whereas others will be left behind. Luke again uses examples of both men and women. "The closest intimacy in this life is no guarantee of community of condition when the Son of Man comes" (Plummer, *Luke* 409). **36.** This verse is not found in the most reliable manuscripts. **37.** *eagles:* The Son of Man's coming is as certain as the fact that a corpse is present when one sees birds of prey flocking overhead. **155   18:1–8.** Luke has closely tied this parable to 17:20–37 by referring in v 8 to its major theme, the coming of the Son of Man. He draws out lessons for his beleaguered communities: God will not abandon them, the elect; they must remain faithful and therefore people of steadfast prayer until Jesus comes. **1.** *to pray:* See the similar parable in 11:5–8. As v 8 will make clear, mere continual prayer is not meant. Fidelity to the God of Jesus must be the engine of prayer. **3.** *widow:* Such a woman, whose male agency in a patriarchal society has been stripped away, is a frequent image of powerlessness in Luke-Acts (7:11–17; 20:45–21:4). **6.** *hear what the unjust judge says:* Two lessons are drawn via the argument from the lesser to the greater: if the persistent pleading of the helpless widow triumphs over an unjust judge, how much more will the persistent praying of Christian disciples achieve; if an unjust judge yields to the entreaties of a widow, how much more will a gracious God. **8.** *will he find faith?:* The decisive question is not about God's vindication of God's persecuted community; God will vindicate them. The decisive question is whether Jesus' disciples will remain faithful to him during the long haul caused by the delay of his return.

156   (c) DISCIPLES MUST DEPEND ON GOD RATHER THAN ON THEMSELVES (18:9–17). Jesus instructs disciples who journey on the way that their touted virtuous works will not earn them entrance into God's kingdom. **9–14.** *parable:* This pericope, unique to Luke, is another example story (see comment on 16:1–8a). Disciples are to concretize in their conduct the attitude of the toll collector. *righteous:* Since the opening of his Gospel (1:6) Luke has been playing on the theme of who is righteous, unrighteous, and self-righteous (e.g., 5:32; 15:7). Luke's view is not that of Paul, for Luke does not relate righteousness to faith, the law, and the cross, as Paul does. Luke's emphases are three: self-confident boasting of one's good deeds will not achieve acquittal at God's judgment; like Jesus, one must engage in deeds of righteousness, e.g., almsgiving; God has vindicated his innocently suffering righteous one, Jesus the Christ (see 23:47; Acts 3:14; 7:52; 22:14). See J. Reumann, *"Righteousness" in the New Testament* (Phl, 1982) 135–43; R. J. Karris, *JBL* 105 (1986) 70–74. **10.** *Pharisee:* → 76–77 above. *toll collector:* → 46 above. **11.** *unrighteous:* Lucan irony is red-hot as he places in the Pharisee's mouth a Gk word (*adikoi*) from the same stem as "righteous" (*dikaios*): Who really is the unrighteous one? **12.** Works of supererogation are carefully spelled out. **13.** *beat his breast:* This is a sign of repentance. The same phrase recurs at 23:48 and should be taken in the same sense there. **14.** *justified:* The toll collector is acquitted at God's court of justice;

he has recognized his need of God's mercy and has shown sorrow for his sins. The Pharisee, however, does not need God's free gift of justification, for he has justified himself. **15–17.** In 9:51 Luke departed from the order of Mark's Gospel to develop his travel narrative. He now resumes contact with Mark. See Mark 10:13–16; Matt 19:13–15. *infants . . . children:* In 9:46–48 Jesus used a child to caution his disciples about their desire to be "the greatest." In 10:21 he praised his Father for revealing the meaning of his ministry to "little ones." Now he uses the tiny ones of human society to teach another lesson. In contrast to the boasting Pharisee of 18:9–14 disciples should approach God as a little child: with spontaneity, a spirit of dependence, a sense of wonderment, with no plaques of achievement. The doors of the kingdom do not swing open to those who comport themselves differently. In contrast to Mark 10:16 Luke does not say that Jesus blessed the children. In Luke Jesus blesses people only after he has completed the liturgy of his exodus (→ 198 below).

157   (d) THE WEALTHY HAVE GREAT DIFFICULTY ENTERING GOD'S KINGDOM (18:18–30). At the conclusion of his travel narrative Luke draws together the strands of the various themes that comprise it. In this pericope and its contrast, 19:1–10, he singles out the themes of possessions and entry into the kingdom of God. See Mark 10:17–31; Matt 19:16–30. **18.** *ruler:* This individual may be a religious leader; see the parallel usage in 14:1; 23:13,35; 24:20. *eternal life:* → 126 above. Observing the commandments of love of God and love of neighbor leads to eternal life (10:25–37); so too does abandoning all one's possessions, giving them to the poor, and following Jesus. Verse 30, which also has a reference to "eternal life," forms an *inclusio* with v 18. This *inclusio* is just one instance of the artistic couplings that pervade the entire pericope. See H.-J. Klauck, *Claretianum* 26 (1986) 28. **19.** *no one is good except God alone:* God is the source of all goodness, even that of Jesus' ministry. **20.** These are the commandments that govern human relationships. In v 29 reference is made to the new human relationships created by commitment to the kingdom of God. **21.** *all these I have observed:* The ruler speaks from deep conviction. In v 28 Peter, as representative, speaks of the deep commitment involved in following Jesus. **22.** *distribute to the poor:* The ruler must adopt a life-style of caring for those in need as exampled in selling all his possessions and distributing them to the poor; he must follow Jesus. Peter and his companions have already done this (v 28); from their actions one can argue to the possibility of such actions. **23.** *grew sad:* In contrast to Mark, the exceedingly rich ruler does not depart. He, as an example to rich people in Luke's community, is present to hear Jesus' further words of challenge. **24.** *how hard:* It is difficult for a rich person to enter the kingdom of God, but God can liberate individuals from their slavish attachment to possessions (v 27). **25.** *eye of a needle:* This hyperbole, which contrasts the largest Palestinian animal with the smallest opening, should not be denuded of its force. One will search Luke's Gospel in vain for evidence that the rich will be easily saved. **26.** *who can be saved?:* This question issues from social and religious expectations that possessions are a sure sign of God's blessings both now and hereafter. **27.** *is possible with God:* ". . . even the rich man can be saved by God; God can break the spell that wealth exercises over such people" (*FGL* 1205). **28.** *what is our own:* The Gk phrase *ta idia* recurs in Acts 4:32 in Luke's description of the primitive church's sharing of possessions. **29.** *wife:* → 144 above.

158   (e) JESUS' PASSION AND VINDICATION PREDICTED AGAIN (18:31–34). Luke connects this passage closely with the preceding and indicates that the commitment Jesus demands of disciples in 18:18–30 is not any more than has been demanded of him. See Mark 10:32–34; Matt 20:17–19. **31.** *Jerusalem:* The end of Jesus' journey to God is in sight. *will be fulfilled:* God's plan of saving human beings spurs Jesus on. **32–33.** Although this is often called the third prediction of the passion (see 9:22,44), Luke has made references to Jesus' death before this point in his travel narrative (see 12:50; 13:32; 17:25). In assessing Luke's stance toward the Roman authorities, one should note that v 32 mentions the Gentiles only (→ 46 above). **34.** Thrice Luke states the incomprehension of the disciples. It is only after Jesus' death and resurrection that they will comprehend his significance (→ 117 above and 196 below).

159   (f) SUMMARIES OF JESUS' MINISTRY TO THE OUTCASTS (18:35–19:10). As Luke brings Jesus to Jericho and the end of his journey, he tells two stories which summarize all of Jesus' ministry, and, not unexpectedly, there is opposition to that ministry (18:39; 19:7). **35–43.** See Mark 10:46–52. **35.** *blind:* Twice before Luke has stated that Jesus' ministry brings sight to the blind in fulfillment of God's promises for these afflicted ones (4:18; 7:22). Twice Luke has taught that one should invite the blind to share the bounty of one's table (14:13,21). Now Luke uses a story of Jesus' mercy toward a blind beggar to conclude his travel narrative and to summarize Jesus' ministry for society's unfortunates. As the contrast of the persistence and faith of the blind man with the disciples (18:31–34) shows, there is another dimension to this story. It is only the sight of faith which opens eyes to see who Jesus is and to follow him. See Busse, *Wunder* (→ 67 above) 333; → 196 below. **38.** *Son of David:* See 1:27,32; 2:4; 20:41,44 on Jesus' Davidic status. To reign on David's throne is to have compassion for society's poor ones. **43.** The sighted man follows Jesus on the way, giving praise to God for what Jesus has done for him.

160   19:1–10. This story is proper to Luke. **2.** *Zacchaeus:* The name means "clean." He straddles two Lucan symbolic worlds: he is a toll collector, one who responds generously to God's call (see 3:12–13; 5:27–32; 7:29–30; 15:1–2; 18:9–14); he is also a rich man, one who finds great difficulty liberating himself from attachment to possessions (18:24–27). **5.** *today:* See also v 9 and the comment on 2:11. *must:* In accordance with God's plan Jesus extends himself hospitality in Zacchaeus's house; see the comment on 2:49. **7.** *all murmured:* The generic "all" murmur against Jesus' crossing of the boundaries separating clean from unclean. **8.** Whereas Jesus had earlier answered objections made against him and his disciples for associating with toll collectors (5:27–32), it is now the toll collector who answers the objections. *I give . . . I repay:* There is controversy over the transl. of these vbs. in the pres. tense. If one views the pres. tense as futuristic, then Zacchaeus is saying that he is no longer a sinner; he resolves to change his ways. If one views the pres. tense as iterative or customary, then Zacchaeus is arguing that he is not a sinner because it is his customary conduct to be generous and just. In the latter interpretation Jesus in v 9 vindicates the good reputation of Zacchaeus. See R. C. White, *ExpTim* 91 (1979) 21. The first interpretation is to be preferred. The second interpretation reduces the depth of the soteriological statements of vv 9–10, for it says that Zacchaeus has achieved salvation on his own and makes Jesus extraneous to salvation. **9.** *salvation . . . today:* Because of Jesus' offer to stay with Zacchaeus, his acceptance of Jesus, and his change of life, salvation has come to his entire household. ". . . The presence of Jesus makes possible what is humanly impossible. A wealthy man gets

through the needle's eye! But not without some radical change" (Pilgrim, *Good News to the Poor* [→ 72 above] 133). *son of Abraham:* This outcast is not outside the pale of God's chosen people (→ 23 above). **10.** *to save the lost:* Like God portrayed as a shepherd in Ezek 36:14, Jesus seeks out the lost to save them. Thus Luke summarizes his view of Jesus, the preacher of God's mercy.

161   (g) DISCIPLES MUST TAKE RISKS IN FOLLOWING JESUS THE KING (19:11–27). This parable, which stems from Q (see Matt 25:14–30) and Luke's own hand, should be interpreted via its context: What are the responses to be given to Jesus, the king? See L. T. Johnson, *NovT* 24 (1982) 139–59. **11.** *they heard these things:* The "they" seems to include Jesus' disciples, the people, and his opponents. "These things" refers at least to 19:1–10. In that pericope and in this one, at issue is how one uses one's material possessions in response to the advent of Jesus in one's life. *kingdom of God:* In 18:17,24–25,29 Luke had taught about conditions for entrance into God's reign. Here he lays the foundation for a new aspect of his teaching on the kingdom of God. There is to be no spectacular manifestation of the kingdom of God in Jerusalem. What will be present in Jerusalem is the steadfastness and fidelity of Jesus the king (19:38; 22:29–30; 23:3,11,37–38), obedient to his Father's will. Seen from this perspective, the king of the parable can indeed seem exacting and demanding (see vv 21–26), for he himself has taken the risk of faith, gone through the crucible of suffering, and wears as his regal trappings the marks of the cross. **12.** *journeyed to a distant country to acquire kingly power for himself:* The materials that follow in vv 12–27 do not refute the expectation voiced in v 11: Jesus is going to appear as king in the story line; the people, religious leaders, and disciples will respond differently to Jesus as king. There is no great delay envisioned in the story. **14.** *we do not want this one to rule over us:* Note how often in what follows Luke contrasts the positive response of the people (*laos*) with the negative response of the religious leaders to Jesus, the king (19:47–48; 20:1,19; 21:37–38; 22:2,52–53,66; 23:10,13, 27,35). **15–19.** *servants:* This is the third of the Lucan "servant" parables, which bear on Christian discipleship (→ 136, 152 above). Disciples who are faithful to Jesus on the way will be rewarded abundantly and given even greater responsibility. "There is no 'safe' position. The only road to success is to take the risks of the first two servants" (Perkins, *Parables* [→ 148 above] 150). **20–23.** The third servant has been paralyzed by fear, been disobedient, and unproductive. **24–26.** The king's generosity is bounteous. **27.** *slaughter them before me:* The imagery of destruction for those who refused to accept the king shows that accepting God's rule over oneself is a great moment of decision. Unfortunately, some decided against the life that King Jesus brings. The christological import of this parable is profound: Jesus, the king, has a decisive role in human destiny, for responses to him determine life and death.

162   (VI) **Jerusalem Rejects God's Prophet and Son and Temple (19:28–21:38).** In this section Luke is largely dependent on Mark 11:1–13:37, but develops his own themes, primarily by the *inclusio* of 19:47–48 and 21:37–38: Jesus was teaching the people (*laos*) daily in the Temple and the religious leaders opposed him. Jesus, the king who brings God's peace (19:28–40), which is rejected by the religious leaders (19:41–44), takes possession of the Temple and is the Temple (19:45–46). All that Jesus teaches in 20:1–21:36 occurs in the Temple and highlights who Jesus is, what true worship of God is, and who forms reconstituted Israel. This teaching occurs amid controversy and predicts controversy for members of reconstituted Israel, whose cornerstone is Jesus, the rejected one.

163   (A) Jesus Takes Over the Jerusalem Temple (19:28–48). It is important to note that the first act of the Lucan Jesus upon the completion of his journey to Jerusalem (see 9:51–19:27) is to enter the Temple (19:45).

(a) Jesus Is Hailed as King (19:28–40). **28.** *Jesus kept journeying:* Jesus is completing his journey back to his Father, which he commenced in 9:51. The instructions in 9:51–19:27 about the meaning of discipleship and mission for those who journey along Jesus' way will be deepened by Jesus' final actions in Jerusalem. The Christian journey is empowered by Jesus' exodus (9:31) of passion, death, resurrection, ascension, and sending of the holy Spirit. *Jerusalem:* Since 9:51 Jesus has been journeying to this city of destiny; from it the Christian mission will journey to the ends of the earth. "Jerusalem becomes almost a 'geographical symbol' of the continuity of God's actions" (Schweizer, *Good News* 301). **29–30.** Through the theologoumenon of Jesus' foreknowledge Luke shows that Jesus is in control of his journey to his Father, knows God's will, and is faithful and obedient to him. *colt on which no one has yet ridden:* This phrase is taken over from Mark and seems to be a reference to Zech 9:9. Luke, however, will not exploit this OT text on kingship. He has his own view of how Jesus is king—by life-giving death. **35–36.** *cloaks:* Instead of palms, Luke mentions the use of a person's costliest piece of clothing. True to his theme of rich and poor, Luke describes people's response to Jesus the king by means of the use of their possessions. All one has is at the disposal of one's king. See Marshall, *Gospel* 714. **37.** *mighty deeds:* This is a summary statement of Jesus' ministry to the blind, lame, crippled, and poor in fulfillment of Scripture (see 4:18–19; 7:22); it shows that Jesus' kingly rule is over the enemies of peace—sickness, demons, death. Also, Jesus' previous ministry is now linked (see v 38) to King Jesus, whose kingly rule of glory for outcasts will now be shown to be through suffering (see 23:42–43). **38.** *king:* The pilgrim psalm (118:26) is used as a basis for the Lucan proclamation of Jesus' kingly status. The theme of Jesus as king, which was foreshadowed in 1:32 and 18:38,40 ("Son of David [the King]") will be developed in Luke's final chapters. See 22:16,18,29–30; 23:3,37,38,42. *one who comes:* This phrase alludes to 7:19 and JBap's question which was answered by Jesus' mighty deeds in fulfillment of God's promises in Isaiah (7:20–22). Jesus is, indeed, the one to come (into God's Temple), foretold by Mal 3:1 LXX, but he is such not only by mighty deeds but also by teaching what true worship of God means and by ruling and saving outcasts from the cross. *peace in heaven:* This cross-reference to and *inclusio* with 2:14 indicates that Jesus' entire mission is to bring heaven's gift of peace to men and women. If "in heaven" is a surrogate for "God," the meaning may be "that the impending death of Jesus is that event which will create peace between alienated humanity and God" (J. R. Donahue, *The Way* 22 [1982] 95). **39.** The Pharisees oppose Jesus the teacher. During his ministry in the Temple Jesus will frequently be referred to as teacher (of God's way). See 20:21,28,39; 21:7. At each phase of Jesus' ministry Luke shows how Simeon's prediction of rising and falling (2:34) comes true. See 4:16–30 (Galilee); 9:51–55 (journey to Jerusalem). **40.** *stones will cry out:* The Scripture background for this difficult verse seems to be Hab 2:11. The meaning is: If the disciples were to keep silence, then the stones, which personify witnesses for God's vindication of injustices, would proclaim the arrival of Jesus, God's agent of vindication. The witness of these stones against those who

have not responded to God is given further dramatic expression in 19:44; 21:6; 20:17. See *FGL* 1252.

164   (b) Jesus Weeps over Jerusalem (19:41–44). Before entering the Temple, Jesus pauses. In contrast to 4:16–30, where the theme of universality overrode that of rejection, and in contrast to 9:51–55, where the theme of nonretaliation overshadowed the theme of rejection, 19:41–44 dwells on the theme of Jesus' rejection by the religious leaders (19:39). The city, whose name means peace, does not recognize the visitation of Jesus, God's agent for peace (see 13:34–35). Jesus' lament has a prophetic prehistory. It is "the sympathy of the suffering prophet, of Deuteronomy's Moses, of Jeremiah, Isaiah, and Hosea, caught up in the rage, anguish, frustration, and sorrow of God for Israel that constitutes the pathos of this story" (Tiede, *Prophecy and History* 78). Jesus' great love for God's people, evidenced in 19:41–44 as he prepares to enter Jerusalem, is paralleled by 23:27–31 as he leaves Jerusalem—to die. **43–44.** *your enemies will erect an embankment . . . :* Although this description of the fall of Jerusalem may draw on the actual historical events in AD 70, its meaning lies deeper. The fact that vv 43–44 are heavily dependent on the prophets' description of the fall of Jerusalem (see *FGL* 1258–59) indicates that the religious leaders are repeating their forebears' mistake with severe consequences.

165   (c) Jesus Takes Possession of the Temple and Is the Temple (19:45–46). As H. Conzelmann (*TSL* 76) has well said, the sole purpose of Jesus' entry is that he may take possession of the Temple. The presence of Jesus in the Temple has been prepared for earlier (1:9–10; 2:27,49; 4:9; see Ernst, *Lukas* 530); his entry is in fulfillment of Mal 3:1 LXX. *entering the Temple, he began to cast out the sellers:* Because the Temple was the place for true worship of God, for instruction on the meaning of God's will, for the treasury, and especially the place where God was present, then Jesus' taking possession of the Temple implies much about Jesus. "When Jesus enters the Temple or is in the Temple, the Temple is really the Temple" (K. Baltzer, *HTR* 58 [1965] 275). In his teaching within the Temple in 20:1–21:36 Jesus will teach what God's will is and what true worship is. He will base the reconstituted Israel upon himself, the cornerstone. As 23:44–45 will reveal, through him God is present for all people. A final note that sounds in this passage is that of money: Jesus "purpose is to purge his Father's house (2:49) of all unsuited service of mammon" (*FGL* 1266).

166   (d) The Responses of the People and Religious Leaders to Jesus (19:47–48). This is the first part of the Lucan *inclusio;* the second part is 21:37–38. All Jesus' teachings occur in the Temple. The people (*laos*) who will form reconstituted Israel hang on Jesus' words, whereas the religious leaders plot against him. See J. Kodell, *CBQ* 31 (1969) 327–43, on this important and pervasive contrast within chaps. 19–23.

167   (B) Jesus Affirms His Authority to Speak for God (20:1–21:4). This section presents the final major controversy between Jesus and the religious authorities in the Gospel. Previous controversies occurred in 4:14–9:50 and 9:51–19:27 and dealt primarily with Jesus' ministry to the sick and needy. They can be grouped as follows: sabbath controversies (4:16–30; 4:31–37; 6:1–5; 6:6–11; 13:10–17); controversies at a meal or over the meaning of eating (5:27–39; 6:1–5; 7:36–50; 11:37–54; 14:1–24); synagogue controversies (4:16–30; 4:31–37; 6:6–11; 13:10–17). What is new in this controversy is that it occurs within the Temple and is not directed against the Pharisees. The high priests, scribes, elders, and Sadducees are now Jesus' opponents. Part and parcel of this controversy is a profound revelation of who Jesus is: "It is in the Temple that the final manifestation of who Jesus is is now given in view of his imminent Passion" (Conzelmann, *TSL* 78). As G. Schneider (*Lukas* 393) correctly observes, Jesus, who uses nonviolence during his controversies in the Temple and is not bested in debate, will be vanquished by violence (22:49-53).

168 (a) JESUS IS A PROPHET COMMISSIONED BY GOD (20:1-8). **1.** *the people:* The people (*laos*) are contrasted with the religious leaders. **2.** *these things:* While the ostensible reference of *tauta* seems to be the events of 19:28-46, more may be implied. The high priests and elders, who have not been mentioned before the Jerusalem segment of the Gospel, now respond to "these things," i.e., all that Jesus has done since 4:14. **5.** In this completing analepsis or "flashback" (→ 42 above), Luke shows that the high priests did not accept John's baptism. Their response to Jesus will be similar to the response they and the Pharisees and lawyers gave to JBap (7:29-30). Recall that in 7:29-30 the religious leaders rejected God's messenger whereas the people welcomed him. **8.** One must tease the christological meaning out of this controversy by stressing the nature of its argumentation: If JBap's authority comes from God, a fortiori so does Jesus'. In the Temple, Jesus, as God's commissioned agent, teaches God's will and the meaning of true worship.

169 (b) JESUS IS GOD'S SON AND THE CORNERSTONE OF RECONSTITUTED ISRAEL (20:9-19). In this allegorized parable Luke again contrasts the responses to Jesus of the people (20:9,16) and the religious leaders (20:19). **9.** *vineyard:* Although Luke has shortened the Marcan version (Mark 12:1), the allusion to Israel as God's vineyard (Isa 5:1-5) still shines through. **10-19.** *owner . . . tenants . . . son . . . others:* The key to the allegory is this: the owner is the faithful and abundantly gracious God who continues to send messengers to his beloved. The tenants who reject God's messengers and Son are the religious leaders. The son, who is killed outside the vineyard, is Jesus. The others are those who respond to Jesus' preaching and that of his disciples and make up reconstituted Israel. Chief among the "others" are the people who say "God forbid" (20:16). The rejected stone is the rejected Jesus, who becomes the cornerstone of God's new building, the reconstituted Israel. The Temple imagery of this pericope accentuates Jesus' role as he teaches in the Temple: Jesus takes the place of what the Temple symbolized, for as God's Son and vindicated cornerstone he is God's presence among human beings (see 23:44-45).

170 (c) JESUS TRULY TEACHES THE WAY OF GOD (20:20-26). Again Luke contrasts the religious leaders (20:20) and the people (20:26). The christological meaning of this passage adheres in the ironic v 21: Jesus does indeed teach the way of God. **25.** *render to Caesar . . . to God:* J. A. Fitzmyer captures well how Jesus' teaching relates to Jesus' presence in the Temple and to what true worship of God means: "A human being belongs to God, whose image he/she bears; God has not only a right of possession over human beings, but also a claim to a basic recognition of his lordship" (*FGL* 1293). For centuries "render to Caesar" has been the subject of debate. There are two contemporary nuances of this debate. One stresses that Luke wrote an apologetic on behalf of the empire to his church and was urging them to pay taxes. See P. Walaskay, *'And so we came to Rome'* (→ 46 above) 36: "Christians, according to Luke, would do well to come to terms with their fiscal obligation to the government." The other approach seeks to interpret v 25 within the flow of a Gospel that has revealed a social pattern of care for the needy, which is contrary to

the social pattern of mighty Rome. This approach also emphasizes that the two parts of v 25 are not coordinate; rather, Caesar is dependent on God. See R. Cassidy, *Jesus* (→ 141 above) 58: "Thus, the only areas in which Caesar can expect allegiance are those in which his patterns are in conformity with God's desired patterns." Cassidy's view is worthy of consideration. During Jesus' trial before Pilate the religious leaders will refer to this episode and accuse Jesus of perverting the people by his teaching (see 23:2,5,14).

171 (d) JESUS' GOD IS THE GOD WHO GIVES AND SUSTAINS LIFE BEYOND THE GRAVE (20:27-40). In the Temple the controversy continues as the Sadducees, who do not believe in the resurrection or angels and who hold only the Pentateuch (Torah) as authoritative, question Jesus, the teacher (20:28,39). Jesus will not only show his authority in interpreting the Mosaic law, but he will also demonstrate his faith and confidence in the life-giving power of the God he proclaims in the Temple. **28-33.** *Moses wrote for us:* The Sadducees, basing themselves upon the levirate marriage legislation of Deut 25:5, propose to Jesus a *reductio-ad-absurdum* argument against the late doctrine of bodily resurrection. **34-36.** Jesus' answer attacks the basic premise of the Sadducees: The life of the age to come is a continuation of this life and therefore needs human propagation lest it die out. **37-38.** *God of Abraham . . . :* Jesus bolsters his argument from other places in the Torah (Exod 3:2,5): Since God is the God of the living, God must have sustained the dead Abraham, Isaac, and Jacob in life by resurrecting them. To the argument from the resurrection Luke adds one from immortality in v 38b: "for all are alive to him" (see the very close parallel to this expression of immortality in 4 Macc 7:19). **39.** The scribes who maintain that there is a resurrection from the dead are pleased with Jesus' answer. See Acts 23:6-10 on how Jesus' teaching in the Temple in 20:27-40 is in continuity with that of the Pharisees.

172 (e) JESUS THE MESSIAH IS DAVID'S SON AND LORD (20:41-44). This passage builds on earlier statements about Jesus' Davidic role (1:32; 18:38,40). **41.** *the Messiah is David's son:* Jesus, the Messiah, who is gathering reconstituted Israel around him in the Temple, challenges the beliefs of the religious leaders from the psalms sung in the Temple liturgy. In his interpretation of the psalms, Jesus proclaims that as Messiah he himself is both David's son and Lord.

173 (f) WORSHIP OF GOD AND A LIFE-STYLE OF JUSTICE (20:45-21:4). Two segments (20:45-47; 21:1-4) have been joined together via the theme of "widow" (20:47; 21:2-4). True worship of God, in the prophetic tradition, demands care of and justice to society's neediest and weakest members represented by the widows. **2.** *this poor widow:* In a lament interpretation of 21:1-4 Jesus decries the religious teaching which has caused a widow to give up all she has to preserve a decaying religious institution. Jesus lauds the generosity of the widow, who prepares the reader to note the generosity of Jesus, the self-effacing servant (see 22:24-27). See A. G. Wright, *CBQ* 44 (1982) 256-65.

174 (C) The Consequences for Jerusalem for Not Heeding God's Prophet (21:5-38). See Mark 13:5-37; Matt 24:1-36. This pericope opens up two windows. Through one the reader may look back on 19:47-21:4 and see the consequences of the religious leaders' rejection of Jesus and his teaching in the Temple. Through the other window the reader looks beyond the events of Luke 22-23 and sees God's vindication of the rejected Son of Man and Jesus' strengthening of his disciples, who will be rejected because of their allegiance to him. This complex passage may be outlined as follows: (1) introduction (21:5-7); (2) opening exhortation (21:8-9); (3) cosmic disasters (21:10-11); (4) events that occur before the end of the world: Christians are persecuted (21:12-19); destruction of Jerusalem (21:20-24); (5) cosmic disasters (21:25-33); (6) concluding exhortation (21:34-36); (7) *inclusio* with 19:47-48 (21:37-38). See J. Dupont, *AsSeign* ns 64 (1969) 77-86. This outline shows how the events of the end of the world are related to the destruction of Jerusalem and thus underlines a powerful christological point: the crisis which Jerusalem faced in Jesus' ministry is "a harbinger of the crisis which Jesus and his message, and above all, his coming as the Son of Man, will bring 'to all who dwell upon the entire face of the earth' (21:35)" (*FGL* 1329).

175   **5-6.** The Lucan Jesus looks back on the destruction of the Temple. In what follows the horizon will broaden to include Jerusalem (vv 20-24) and the end of the world (vv 25-33). **7.** *these things:* With the Gk word *tauta* Luke achieves a certain degree of unity in this complex passage by means of his frequent use of this generic word (see vv 9,12,28,31,36). The antecedent of "these things" changes from the destruction of the Temple to the destruction of Jerusalem and then to the destruction of the entire world. *sign:* The cosmic disasters in vv 9-10 and 25-33 are referred to as "signs" (Gk *sēmeion,* vv 11,25). These references bracket the key Lucan materials in vv 12-19 about persecution and in vv 20-24 about Jerusalem's destruction. **8.** Disciples should not confuse the destruction of the Temple with Jesus' return (as Son of Man). **12.** *before all these things:* I.e., before the end of the world. The Jesus who had met controversy throughout his ministry and especially in Jerusalem now predicts the same treatment for his disciples. But the rejected Jesus has been vindicated and will strengthen his beleaguered disciples. See 12:11-12 and the stories of Stephen (Acts 7) and Paul (Acts 21-26), who speak boldly and eloquently when persecuted. **19.** Jesus exhorts his disciples to perseverance amid duress. As in 12:35-48 and 17:20-18:8 Luke uses eschatological material for hortatory purposes. **20-24.** Luke has nuanced the description of God's destruction of Jerusalem by means of the tradition of the rejected prophet (→ 61 above). **22.** *vengeance:* "The same *vengeance* that requires the *vindication* of God's faithfulness at the expense of an unfaithful people also produces the *vindication* of the people called by God's name in the presence of the Gentiles" (Tiede, *Prophecy and History* 93). For an example of the theological pattern involved here, see Deut 32:20,35, 36,39. **24.** *time of the Gentiles:* The fact that God has used Gentiles to punish unfaithful people does not mean that the Gentiles have replaced Israel or that God will not fulfill his longstanding promises to Israel (ibid., 95). **25-33.** Luke resumes his narration of the cosmic signs, but now introduces a christological dimension: Jesus, the victorious Son of Man, is in control of the forces of evil whether these are wars (v 9) or sea (v 25); he is the judge. **28.** *your redemption is near:* This verse bursts with a message of confidence and hope for disciples. In contrast to the cowardly actions of other men and women (vv 26-27), faithful disciples stand erect with heads held high to greet their faithful judge, Jesus, Son of Man (see 9:26; 12:9; Acts 7:56). **33.** *my words will never pass away:* Again Lucan christology bursts forth: the one who will meet a violent death in Jerusalem utters words that have eternal significance. **34-38.** Luke gives exhortation the final word. **34-36.** *take care of yourselves:* Luke uses this eschatological setting as a vehicle for a mini-catechesis of admonitions. For parallels to these exhortations, see 8:11-15; 11:5-8; 12:22-31,45; 18:1-8. **37-38.** By means of these verses Luke forms his *inclusio* with 19:47-48.

The people, the basis of reconstituted Israel, are open to hearing God's prophet, Jesus, who will die in Jerusalem (see 13:33).

176   (VII) Jesus' Last Meal and Association with Sinners (22:1-23:56a). Two interrelated issues pulse through this material: Luke's sources and his theology. His basic source for the passion account is Mark 14:1-15:47. In those places (e.g., 22:35-38 and 23:44-48) where he differs from Mark the explanation is not to be found in a separate, continuous passion account, but rather in other possibilities: Luke's special traditions and Lucan redaction of Mark. See the conclusion of F. J. Matera, *Passion Narratives and Gospel Theologies* (TI; NY, 1986) 155: "But I suspect that nearly all of the differences between Luke and Mark can be accounted for by Luke's editorial activity and the availability to him of special traditions not employed by or known to Mark." On the sources of Luke 22, see M. L. Soards, "The Scope, Origin, and Purpose of the Special Lucan Passion Narrative Material in Luke 22," (Ph.D. thesis; NY, 1984). On the sources of Luke 23, see the test case of 23:44-48 in F. J. Matera, *CBQ* 47 (1985) 469-85.

Although it is widely repeated that Luke presents Jesus' passion as a martyrdom, this view is inaccurate. See J. A. Fitzmyer, *FGL* 1367-68; R. J. Karris, *JBL* 105 (1986) 65-74; Matera, *Passion Narratives* 150-52. Rather, Luke's passion account is to be seen as a theological drama that emphasizes the saving power of Jesus, the innocently suffering righteous one, and underscores God's graciousness in vindicating this righteous one (see 23:47; Acts 3:15; 7:52; 22:14) and Son from the powers of darkness. Through this drama Luke seeks to elicit from his readers a response of deeper faith in Jesus and a more eager commitment to follow his way to God. See Karris, *Luke* esp. 116-17 n. 4 for bibliography; Neyrey, *Passion* (→ 62 above); Matera, *Passion Narratives* 150-220, 239-44.

177   (A) Jesus' Farewell Discourse at a Meal (22:1-38).

(a) PREPARATION FOR JESUS' FAREWELL DISCOURSE TO HIS DISCIPLES (22:1-13). The first part of what Jesus had predicted in 9:22 is now coming to pass: rejection of the Son of Man by the elders, chief priests, and scribes. As he will do throughout his passion account, Luke depicts Jesus going to his death obediently and freely and exhorts disciples to listen to his last words and to imitate his example. See Mark 14:1-2,10-16. **1.** *the feast of Unleavened Bread, which is called Passover:* Passover was celebrated at the sunset which indicated the beginning of 15 Nisan. The Passover meal was eaten with unleavened bread; and unleavened bread was to be eaten during the seven days after Passover. Strictly speaking, the feast of the Unleavened Bread referred only to this period of seven days (→ Institutions, 76:122-29). Luke combines the two feasts; see 22:7 and contrast 2:41. Jesus' last earthly meal as he journeys to complete his exodus (9:31) will celebrate the exodus of God's people from slavery. **2.** *high priests:* In 19:39 Luke mentioned the Pharisees for the last time (→ 76-77 above). From 19:47 on he spotlights the high priests and separates the people (*laos*) from them. On the significance of the "high priests" in Luke-Acts, see Tyson, *Death of Jesus* (→ 77 above) 84-113, esp. 110: "We conclude that, in Luke's writing, the rejection of Jesus by the chief priests, their refusal to recognize him as lord of the temple, and their refusal to grant him his rightful control of the temple led to his death." **3-6.** *Judas:* Simeon's prediction that Jesus was set for the rise and fall of many (2:34) had earlier affected Jesus' townspeople (4:28-29), the Pharisees (11:53-54), and the high priests (19:47);

now it affects Jesus' select band of Twelve as Judas leaves the journey of Jesus and betrays him for money. On Luke's view of the seductive force of money, see 12:15-21; 16:1-31. For Luke's conclusion of his story of Judas, see Acts 1:15-20. After his description of Jesus' conquest of the devil's temptations (4:1-13), Luke prepared for his story of Jesus' passion by noting that the devil departed until an opportune moment (4:13). That moment now takes place in Jerusalem; in the events of Jesus' last hours Satan and the power of darkness (22:53) are active. But as Jesus was victorious in the desert, so too will he be in Jerusalem (see 23:44-45). The plot to betray Jesus forms the first part of an *inclusio* whose second part is found in the accomplishment of that plot in 22:47-53. Highlighted between the poles of that *inclusio* are Jesus' legacy to his church (22:14-38) and his obedience to his Father's will (22:39-46), both of which show how Jesus preserves his church and himself from the power of Satan.

178   **8.** *he sent Peter and John:* Jesus initiates the action, showing that he is in control of his destiny. Peter and John, who had been selected by Jesus to accompany him in 8:51 and 9:28 and who will be depicted as leaders in Acts (3:1,3; 4:11,13,19; 8:14), go forth, in contrast to Judas, as faithful servants to prepare the meal. Their actions thus anticipate Jesus' injunctions about leaders as servants in 22:26-27. See Schneider, *Lukas* 442-43. **11.** *householder of the house:* This is the transl. of the pleonastic Gk *oikodespotē tēs oikias.* By using a pleonasm, which he usually eschews, Luke seems to be interpreting Jesus' last meal from the perspective of his own communities' meals, which took place in house-churches owned by either men or women. See A. Vööbus, *The Prelude to the Lukan Passion Narrative* (Papers of the Estonian Theological Society in Exile 17; Stockholm, 1968) 20-21. *inn:* The usual translation of the Gk *katalyma* as "guest room" is misleading and masks the unmistakable cross-reference to 2:7. See Fitzmyer, *FGL* 1383: "The reader of the Greek text would catch it as an echo." When Jesus' parents came to Bethlehem, the city of David, there was no place to stay or to eat in an inn (2:7) for them and the one who is savior and Christ the Lord (2:11). When Jesus now comes to Jerusalem, the city of David and of his rendezvous with God, he is shown hospitality. From the inn (v 11) Jesus hosts a meal which is symbolic of his servant life for others and which his disciples will do in his memory. See also the comment on 2:7. *my disciples:* Last Supper paintings, e.g., Leonardo da Vinci's are so ingrained in our memories that it is difficult for us to read Luke's account accurately. Luke does not describe a supper with just Jesus and the Twelve apostles present. He is painting on a much larger canvas with many more subjects—women and men of his own communities who continue Jesus' ministry of feeding people. See the fluctuating terminology: Judas, one of the Twelve (22:3; see 22:30,47); disciples (22:11; see also 22:39,45; see further 22:32, where "brothers" equals disciples; and 22:35-36, where the reference is to the sending out of the 70 [72] disciples); apostles (22:14); → 84, 101 above. **13.** *they found things just as he had told them:* Since the predictions Jesus gave in vv 10-13 did come to pass, the disciples can be confident that what Jesus promises later at the meal will also come to pass.

179   (b) THE EUCHARIST AS JESUS' LEGACY TO THE CHURCH (22:14-20). These verses introduce the Lucan version (see John 13-17) of Jesus' farewell address to the church. This address, which concludes in 22:38, imitates those of significant personages who are about to die. The most telling biblical parallels deal with David (1 Kgs 2:1-10) and Mattathias (1 Macc 2:49-70). Through Jesus' farewell address about the past and the future,

about the meaning of his life, Luke provides exhortations for his communities, e.g., about how to prepare for the eucharist (22:21-23). He also justifies and illustrates: (1) the divine plan of history, e.g., Jesus' fate was determined by God (22:22,37); (2) transitions in authority (22:24-34) and missionary praxis (22:35-38) after Jesus, the founder, has died; (3) the soundness of the foundations that Jesus laid for the future church, e.g., the eucharist (22:15-20). In contrast to the parallel farewell address of Paul in Acts 20:17-38, which is a monologue, 22:14-38 is partly dialogue (see 22:23,24,38), dialogue in which the disciples' misunderstanding and weaknesses predominate. Luke invites readers to reflect on what it means for a church to follow—courageously, with halting pace, and during changed circumstances—in the footsteps of Jesus, the leader, who is about to die. See W. S. Kurz, *JBL* 104 (1985) 251-68. Cf. Mark 14:17-18a,22-25. **14.** *the hour:* Luke approaches the Johannine understanding of "hour": the completion of Jesus' exodus and return to God. *reclined at table:* The common designation of this meal as the "Last Supper" should not blind readers of Luke's Gospel to the fact that this is the last meal in a long series of meals in which Jesus, "the glutton and drunkard, friend of toll collectors and sinners" (7:34) has been involved (see 5:27-32; 7:31-34; 15:1-2; 19:7). This meal Jesus shares with his apostles and disciples, who also are sinners in need of his forgiveness, mercy, and protection. For in Luke's account, their sinfulness becomes manifest as one of them betrays him; all of them squabble over their greatness; one of them denies that he knows him; and they misunderstand his word about swords and purchase these weapons of destruction. Earlier at meals Jesus had engaged in controversy with the Pharisees and their role of spokesmen for God's will in the community (see 7:36-50; 11:37-54; 14:1-24). This meal, too, will have its controversy over the roles of church officials in the community. *apostles with him:* See comment on 22:11. One should not miss the community dimension of this meal which Jesus shares. **15.** *Passover:* → 177 above. The sequence of a 1st-cent. Palestinian Passover meal will help illumine the complex sequence of vv 15-20: (1) preliminary course, during which one cup of wine was drunk and a second cup was poured; (2) the Passover liturgy itself, in which the head of the family retold the story of the exodus; the second cup of wine was drunk; (3) the meal proper, which commenced with breaking of bread; after the meal a third cup of wine was blessed. This meal celebrated God's liberation of his people from slavery and looked ahead to his future definitive liberation. This sequence can illumine vv 15-20 thus: v 16 refers to the entire Passover meal about to take place; vv 17-18 refer to the first (or second cup of wine); v 19 refers to the bread, with which the Passover meal proper begins; v 20 refers to the cup of blessing after the meal. See *FGL* 1390. Verses 15-18 are Jesus' reinterpretation of the Passover in terms of God's eschatological banquet (see 13:29); vv 19-20 are Jesus' reinterpretation of the Passover in terms of the salvific meaning of his death, which inaugurates a new covenant. **17-18.** *take this:* Till his dying breath Jesus continues to feed his disciples; this cup is a pledge that they will share life with him at the eschatological banquet. The implicit christology is noteworthy. Jesus, who is about to die, has the power to ensure places for his own at God's feast. **19.** The most reliable Gk mss. should be followed, which include 22:19b-20 as part of Luke's account of the institution. *took bread:* See 9:16; 24:30. In the Passover liturgy the head of the house took the bread for distribution as a symbol of how he provided for his own. Jesus now provides not bread but himself for his own. This is the meaning of the Gk *sōma,* which does not mean the mere human body, but one's entire life, the whole human being. *is given for you:* Jesus' gift of himself has salvific meaning. *do this in memory of me:* If one views this meal in a sequence of meals with sinners, then the word "this" should not be limited to mere repetition of Jesus' words. As Jesus has given up his entire life for others and symbolized that by sharing meals with them, so too must disciples give their lives in service to others. See Karris, *Luke* 68. **20.** *new covenant in my blood:* Allusions to Exod 24:3–8; Jer 31:31 are at hand as Jesus establishes a new bond between God and people. This bond or covenant has been created by Jesus' life, now symbolized by his blood poured out to save people. Thus, Luke ends the first part of his farewell address. The dying Jesus has bequeathed to his community of reconstituted Israel the eucharist to replace the Passover meal. At that meal they experience liberation from destructive forces and a foretaste of the eschatological banquet.

180   (c) WILL FUTURE DISCIPLES BETRAY JESUS? (22:21–23). As Luke continues his farewell discourse, he addresses a searching challenge to his communities: Will they, who communicate at the Lord's table, betray Jesus? Whereas Mark 14:18b–21 places this betrayal before the institution account, Luke places it after it. **21.** *at this table:* Perhaps there is a reference here to Ps 41:9 and its lament that a cherished friend, who ate at my table, has gone against me. Judas's name is not mentioned; it seems that Luke is generalizing for hortatory purposes. **22.** *as it has been determined:* In this part of the farewell discourse Luke shows that the betrayal did not come upon Jesus unexpectedly; it was foreseen by God. **23.** In contrast to Mark 14:19, the disciples do not question Jesus about betrayal, but one another. Luke's parenetic intention clearly surfaces.

181   (d) THE MEANING OF LEADERSHIP IN LUKE'S COMMUNITIES (22:24–30). See Mark 10:42–45 and Matt 19:28 for some slight parallels to this largely unique Lucan material. By means of his literary genre of a farewell discourse Luke addresses the issue of transition of authority after Jesus has died. **24–27.** What Mark places during Jesus' journey (10:42–45), Luke places at Jesus' last meal as he concludes his use of the imagery of "servants" (see 12:35–48; 17:7–10; 19:11–27). **24.** *dispute:* Recall other "controversies" at meals (7:36–50; 11:37–54; 14:1–24). **26.** *leader:* The Greek is *hēgoumenos.* Perhaps there is reference here to church officials. See Acts 15:22; Heb 13:7,17,24. **27.** A cross-reference to 12:37 seems obvious: the master will wait on table for his faithful servants. *among you as one who serves:* This phrase might be more at home in John 13:1–21 after Jesus had washed the feet of his disciples. In Luke, although it is not literally related to its context, it is christologically very much part of a context that accentuates Jesus' soteriological significance for others (see 22:19–20). Leaders are to adopt Jesus' life-style of leadership: ". . . leaders are to be called to repentance and to the obligation to recognize that their talents as leaders are gifts of a beneficent Creator to relieve the lot of the oppressed and to set at liberty the captives enchained by social patterns, custom, and economic necessity" (F. W. Danker, *Luke* [Phl, 1976] 61). **28–30.** Verses 24–27, in stressing how authority should be exercised in Jesus' name after his death, did not present the disciples in the most positive light. Verses 28–30, by contrast, are more complimentary. **28.** *trials:* These have been brought on by the opposition Jesus has received during all phases of his ministry: in Galilee, e.g., 5:17–6:11; during his journey to Jerusalem, e.g., 11:14–35; in Jerusalem, e.g., 19:47–21:4. His disciples have stood and continue to

stand steadfastly by him. **29.** *I bequeath:* The Gk *diatithesthai* comes from the same root as *diathēkē,* "covenant." The language of farewell address or last will and testament is very much in evidence. The christology implied in this imagery is profound: Jesus, the king (see comment on 19:11), has gone through death and been vindicated by his Father with the gift of kingly rule. "In the conferral of the kingdom on the apostles we see that the church participates in the kingdom through Jesus' death. Luke rarely speaks of the death of Jesus in the manner in which we might expect, especially when we come to him from reading Paul, but in his own way he makes clear that that death was a death 'for us'" (R. C. Tannehill, *ATR* 43 [1961] 203). **30.** As Acts will show, the apostles, esp. Peter and John, will have authority over reconstituted Israel, and that authority is rooted in Jesus' farewell gift to the church.

182   (e) PETER'S ROLE IN THE CHURCH (22:31–34). There is a parallel in Mark 14:29–30 to Luke 22:33–34. The authoritative role of Peter, to be described in Acts, is also anchored in Jesus' farewell address (→ 70 above). **31.** *Satan:* See 22:3. Luke contrasts the effects Satan's attacks have on Judas and Peter. Jesus' efficacious prayer saves Peter from the fate of Judas (see Acts 1:15–19). *you all:* The Greek here is pl. whereas in v 32 it is sg. Peter is representative of Satan's sifting (see Amos 9:9) of all. **32.** The implicit christology is deep, and the church is consoled that its Lord can save it too from the power of Satan. *turned back, converted:* The Gk *epistrepsas* does not mean locomotion, but moral conversion (see 17:4; Acts 3:19; 9:35; 11:21; 14:15; 15:19; 26:18,20). *your fellow Christians:* As Acts 15:23,32 show, this is the transl. of *adelphous,* lit., "brethren." Examples of Peter's strengthening of the church can readily be seen in Acts 1–11,15. Having shown how Peter's authority is founded in the last words of Jesus, Luke moves on to another of his favorite concerns in vv 33–34: *exhortation.* **33–34.** In vv 24–27 there was much ado about who was the greatest. Now we see how the greatest is tested and fails. "The Lucan Jesus is making it clear to the reader of the Gospel that no disciple, not even the one for whom Jesus has prayed, will be safe from a test to his/her loyalty and fidelity" (*FGL* 1423). *that you know me:* Luke softens Peter's denial. See the story of the fulfillment of this prediction in 22:54–62, esp. vv 61–62: Jesus' merciful glance leads to Peter's repentance.

183   (f) THE JUSTIFICATION FOR THE CHANGED MISSIONARY PRAXIS OF LUKE'S COMMUNITIES (22:35–38). This passage is proper to Luke and anticipates his story of Paul in Acts and justifies the way missionaries operate in Luke's communities. In changed and hostile circumstances they cannot abide by the regulations of 9:1–6 and 10:1–11. **35.** *purse, knapsack, sandals:* The actual reference is not to the sending out of the apostles in 9:3, but to the sending out of the 70 (72) disciples. **36.** *from now on:* A new time within the era of fulfillment is dawning. Hostility will be the church's bedfellow. Jesus has told them so. *sword:* The reference to this destructive weapon must be taken in the total context of Luke-Acts and the immediate context of vv 38,47–53. Since Luke narrates in his Gospel that Jesus not only preached love of enemies (6:26–36) but also lived that teaching (9:51–55; 23:34), and since he narrates in Acts that Paul and other missionaries never use swords, he cannot mean by "sword" here a lethal weapon. Since in v 38 Luke depicts Jesus' disgust with the disciples' literal understanding of his words in v 36 and since he reprimands the use of a sword in 22:47–53 and even heals the wounded person, Luke cannot mean by "sword" here a destructive weapon. Rather "sword" is a symbol for crisis. A paraphrase of the latter part of v 36 is: Sell your mantle and buy trouble. **37.** Again Luke underlines in this discourse that what Jesus is about is according to God's plan. He is the new Servant of Yahweh (Isa 53:12). If Jesus is treated this way, so too will be his disciples. **38.** *that's enough!:* The reader should not miss the Lucan irony. See D. M. Sweatland, *BTB* 13 (1983) 23-27; G. W. H. Lampe, "The two swords (Luke 22:35-38)," *Jesus and the Politics of His Day* (ed. E. Bammel *et al.;* Cambridge, 1984) 335-51.

184 **(B) Jesus' Fidelity and the Disciples' Failure during Trial (22:39-71).** Luke continues his contrast between Jesus' eager and obedient journey to his gracious God and the disciples' lethargic and misinformed following of Jesus.

(a) JESUS AND HIS DISCIPLES CONTRASTED IN PRAYER (22:39-46). See Mark 14:26,32-42; Matt 26:30,36-46. Unlike Mark, Luke does not limit his narrative to Peter, James, and John. Because of his hortatory intent Luke focuses on all disciples. The chiastic structure of this passage helps Luke make his christological and parenetic points: after the introductory v 39 Luke has (A) v 40, pray lest you enter into temptation; (B) v 41, Jesus removes himself from the disciples, kneels down, and prays; (C) vv 42-44, the content and resoluteness of Jesus' prayer; (B') v 45, Jesus rises from his prayer and returns to his disciples; (A') v 46, pray lest you enter into temptation. **39.** *custom:* See 21:37. *the disciples:* See comment on 22:11. *followed him:* This phrase conveys Luke's hortatory goal. **40.** *pray:* See comment on 3:21. *temptation:* See comment on 11:4. Involved is entry into Satan's field of force with the result of apostasy. **41.** Jesus does not use the normal posture for prayer, standing; rather, he assumes a posture of humility and kneels. **42.** *Father:* See comment on 11:1. *cup:* This is a reference to Jesus' destiny as described in this Gospel: he will die in Jerusalem because God has sent him to do kingdom ministry for the needy, oppressed, and unfortunate of this world (see 4:43; 9:51; 13:33). Jesus will continue to drink of that cup as he heals a servant (22:51), forgives his enemies (22:34), and promises a place in paradise to a repentant evildoer (23:39-43). **43-44.** The authenticity of these verses is highly disputed. Since the text-critical or external evidence for authenticity does not seem decisive, one must turn to internal evidence or Lucan theology. J. H. Neyrey makes a plausible case that Luke is contrasting Jesus (vv 43-45) with the disciples (v 46). Jesus engages in the contest or *agōnia* of seeking to know God's will and accepts that will obediently, not as a victim, nor out of control, not subject to irrational passion. The angel strengthens Jesus in this contest. His sweat is that of the moral athlete seeking victory in the contest. The disciples, however, succumb to *lypē* (v 46), which is crippling fear in the face of impending conflict and leads to loss of strength, shrinking to the ground, and contraction in sleep. See Neyrey, *Passion* (→ 52 above) 49-68; for a contrary view, see D. M. Stanley, *Jesus in Gethsemane* (NY, 1980) 205-8. **45-46.** *rose . . . rise:* There is a conscious play on the word for resurrection here (see 24:7). "Only by the power of the risen Jesus will his followers be able to throw off their lethargy and despondency in the trials they will have to face and so obtain strength to *pray continually* to avoid the *temptation* that would lead inevitably to apostasy . . . 'Now he has risen, and they are to rise with him to face in the constant spirit of his prayer all that lies before them'" (ibid., 220).

185 **(b)** INFIDELITY AND FIDELITY CONTRASTED (22:47-53). This section forms the second part of the *inclusio* which began in 22:1-6. The announcement of the betrayal and its fulfillment at this point bracket 22:7-46 and illumine their content. For Luke draws a contrast between Judas's infidelity and Jesus' fidelity to those he has chosen (22:7-38) and to the God who has commissioned him (22:39-46). In this passage Luke draws a further contrast: Jesus' fidelity to his ministry of compassion and Judas's infidelity to his master. See Mark 14:43-52; Matt 26:47-56; John 18:2-11. **47.** *one of the Twelve:* As in 22:3, Luke draws his readers' attention to Judas's privileged position. *was leading:* An implicit contrast is drawn between Peter, the leader (see 22:31-34, 54-62), and Judas, the leader. **48.** *kiss:* A sign of intimacy becomes the sign of treachery. *hand over:* When language about "handing over the Son of Man" was used in the predictions of 9:44 and 18:32, religious and political authorities were mentioned, but not Judas (see, however, 24:7, which refers to "sinful human beings"). The powers of darkness, which come under cover of night (see v 53), do not restrict their prey to religious and political leaders. They also pursue disciples. **49-50.** Fortified by prayer, Jesus does not succumb to the temptation of abandoning his nonviolent ministry and using violence (→ 183 above). **51.** *healed:* This is the only miracle in the passion and demonstrates that Jesus is not only the savior in his pre-Jerusalem ministry, but also during his passion. He even heals an enemy! Such is the nature of the compassionate God proclaimed by Jesus. See Busse, *Wunder* (→ 67 above) 336; J. Drury, *Tradition and Design in Luke's Gospel* (Atlanta, 1977) 111. **52.** *swords:* Nonviolence is overcome—for the moment—by violence. **53.** *Temple:* See 19:47-48 and 21:37-38. In contrast to Mark 14:50 the disciples do not abandon Jesus. They will be present with him at his cross (23:49).

186 (c) THE FIDELITY OF JESUS, SON OF GOD, AND OF PETER CONTRASTED (22:54-71). See Mark 14:53-15:1; Matt 26:57-27:1; John 18:13-27. Instead of Mark's sequence of arrest, night trial, mockery, denial, Luke has arrest, denial, mockery, and morning trial. Thus, for mainly parenetic reasons Luke first spotlights Peter's abandonment of Jesus and then Jesus' fidelity to his prophetic calling. With deep christological import Luke ends the scene with the church's witness to Jesus on the lips of Jesus himself, the model witness: Jesus is Messiah, vindicated Son of Man, Son of God. **54-62.** What Jesus had predicted in 22:31-34 is coming to fulfillment. **54.** The contrast is set up between faithful Jesus and unfaithful Peter. **56-57.** *a woman servant:* Luke softens Peter's denial, for the Lucan Peter does not deny Jesus, but denies that he knows Jesus (see 22:34). **58-59.** Two men now hound Peter. This Lucan touch may be in accord with Deut 19:15, which requires the witness of two males in a trial. **60.** *a cock crowed:* Jesus' prophecy in 22:34 is fulfilled. **61.** The Lord's glance is one of compassion. *remembered:* Peter recalls the meaning of 22:34. For other significant references to "remembering" in Luke-Acts, see 24:6-7; Acts 11:16; 20:35. "By recalling the words of the Lord, believers will be saved from the fate which befell Peter" (Matera, *Passion Narratives* [→ 176 above] 172). **62.** *wept bitterly:* Jesus' prayer has been effective by preserving Peter in his sifting. There is an implicit contrast with Judas: Peter repented of his deed; Judas did not (see Acts 1:15-19). **63-65.** What Jesus predicted in 18:32 now comes to pass: he is mocked (see also 23:11). **64.** *prophesy:* Luke plays on his theme of Jesus, the rejected prophet (→ 61 above). Luke's irony is supreme. Jesus is mocked as a prophet just after one of his prophecies, that of Peter's denial, has been fulfilled. **65.** *blaspheming him:* The Gk ptc. *blasphēmountes* is usually translated as "reviling." In Luke's account of the trial, Jesus is not accused of blasphemy. His opponents, however, blaspheme him, the Son of God. **66-71.** The Lucan account of the trial differs markedly from Mark's: Luke's is a morning trial; there are no false witnesses;

there is no charge that Jesus claimed to destroy the Temple (see, however, Acts 6:12–14); the entire assembly or sanhedrin handles Jesus' trial in contrast to Mark's singling out of the high priest as spokesman. Lucan theology, and not another source, accounts for these differences. "Luke's purpose [is] to describe a solemn, valid, and formal trial of Jesus by Israel" (Neyrey, *Passion* [→ 52 above] 71). Jesus' witness at his trial becomes the model for the witness of Peter (Acts 4–5), of Stephen (Acts 6–7), and of Paul (Acts 21–26) at their trials, trials predicted by Jesus in 12:8–12; 21:12–15. **67–68.** *the Messiah:* See 1:32–35; 2:11; 3:1; 23:35; Acts 2:32. This is the church's confession of Jesus as the fulfillment of God's promises to David. Jesus' answer to the assembly's question is similar to that of the prophet Jeremiah when he was on trial (see 45:15 LXX). *Son of Man:* When he is apparently powerless, Jesus foretells God's vindication of him and his ministry. This, too, is the church's confession of faith in Jesus (see Acts 2:32–34,36; 7:56). **70.** *all:* Luke underlines the point that the rejection of Jesus, God's prophet, is done by the entire official leadership of Israel (but see 23:50–53). *Son of God:* This is the final and fundamental confession of faith in Jesus. Until this point in the Gospel Luke has informed his readers that unearthly beings have recognized Jesus as Son of God (see 1:32,35; 3:22; 4:3,9,41; 8:28; 9:35), and that is Jesus' true nature. Luke gives "his story a special twist as Jesus' enemies from the Temple . . . mistake his true identity but at the same time inadvertently recognize him for who he is" (J. M. Dawsey, *BTB* 16 [1986] 147).

187   (C) To the End, the Innocent Jesus Associates with Sinners (23:1–56a). Throughout this section Luke will emphasize the loving fidelity to God of Jesus, the innocently suffering righteous one, who to his dying breath extends God's mercy to sinners.

(a) THE WRONGED AND RIGHTEOUS JESUS IS HANDED OVER TO CRUCIFIXION (23:1–25). The innocence of Jesus is a refrain that pulses through this section (vv 4,14,15,22): he the wronged one, who is righteous. See Mark 15:1–15. **1.** Jesus, unbound, journeys to his Father freely and obediently, as his predictions of 9:22, 44; 18:32 are being fulfilled. Pilate, the Roman prefect (→ 42 above), has the authority to pronounce a sentence of death by crucifixion upon a criminal. **2.** *they started to accuse him:* The charges against Jesus are not based in reality. Jesus did not forbid the payment of the imperial tax (see 20:20–25). His kingship (see 19:38; 22:24–35; 23:35,37,39) is not a political one. In fact it consists of serving (22:24–27). With irony Luke will stress that it is the Jews themselves who not only approve of insurrection (23:18–19,25) but even incite riots (see Acts 13:50; 14:19; 17:5–8,13; 18:12–17; 21:27). See G. Schneider, "The political charges against Jesus (Luke 23:2)," *Jesus and the Politics of His Day* (→ 183 above) 403–14. **4.** *I find no crime in this person:* Pilate pronounces acquittal for Jesus. **6–12.** This material, proper to Luke, has been prepared for by 3:1,19–20; 9:7–9; 13:31–32. **8.** Thrice Luke mentions "seeing," thus setting up a contrast between the type of seeing Herod brings to Jesus and the type of seeing required for faith (see 23:35,47–49; 24:12, 16,24,31,32,39,45; Acts 26:17–18). **9.** As will be true of his next session with Pilate (22:13–25), Jesus remains silent. It is the silence of the innocently suffering righteous servant of Isa 53:7; it is silence born of profound trust in a faithful God. **11.** *white gorgeous robe:* Since Herod is a tetrarch, this robe is not kingly. Two levels of meaning may be present. Jesus, the innocent one, is clothed in white, the symbol of purity. Jesus is clothed in a garment worn by candidates for office: Will the Jewish nation select him or Barabbas? **12.** *became friends:*

Even when he seems powerless, Jesus is able to effect a saving work, that of reconciliation between enemies. See M. L. Soards, *Bib* 66 (1985) 344–63.

188   13–25. Pilate first declares Jesus innocent, in a legally correct trial, but plays the coward when all Israel demands Jesus' death. **13.** All Israel, leaders and people (*laos*), are present. **14–16.** The fullness of the juridical procedure engaged in by Pilate is manifest: arrest (v 14a); charges (v 14b); examination or *cognitio* (v 14c); verdict of innocence (v 14d); supporting verdict from Herod (v 15a); acquittal of Jesus (v 15b); judicial warning (v 16). "Luke has taken considerable pains to present Jesus' hearings before Pilate as forensic trials, legally correct in all aspects, and readily recognizable as such" (Neyrey, *Passion* [→ 52 above] 81). **17.** This verse is to be omitted on external and internal grounds. **18.** *take him away:* Twice more (in vv 21 and 23) entire Israel will demand Jesus' death. Five times Luke will describe the choice of all Israel that Jesus be condemned: vv 18,23,24,25a,25b. *Barabbas:* "A substitute criminal is demanded in place of a criminal! The irony of the scene is apparent. Moreover, they scream for the release of one called Barabbas, 'son of the father,' and reject him who is really the Father's son (recall 2:49; 10:21–22; 11:2; 22:29,42)" (*FGL* 1489). **19.** *had been thrown into prison for insurrection and murder:* Here and in v 25 Luke underscores Barabbas's nefarious character. Jesus will die that such persons may be liberated from prison (see 4:18–19). **22.** For the last time Pilate pronounces Jesus innocent. Although Pilate mentions the light beating or *fustigatio,* Luke never says that Jesus was beaten or scourged. He goes to his cross in full command of the situation. **23.** *their voices prevailed:* As 23:35,48 will make clear, the people of God (*laos*) repent of their action against Jesus, whereas the religious leaders remain firm in their decision. **25.** *handed over to their will:* This is not a juridical sentence. The Lucan Pilate had already given that: Jesus is innocent. Thus, Luke lessens Roman involvement in Jesus' condemnation and crucifixion. In what follows readers see that God does not allow human perversion of the noble institution of Roman law and justice to hinder his plans of bringing about new life, the resurrection, and reconstituted Israel. See Walaskay, *'And so we came to Rome'* (→ 46 above) 38–49.

189   (b) JESUS, REJECTED PROPHET, CALLS FOR REPENTANCE (23:26–31). When Jesus was about to enter Jerusalem (19:41–44), he called upon Jerusalemites to repent. Now as he is leaving Jerusalem to be crucified, he again calls for repentance.

26. See Mark 15:20b–21. *they led away:* Luke uses the ambiguous "they," whose grammatical antecedent is "the high priests, leaders, and the people" of 23:13. Luke softens Roman involvement. *laid friendly hands upon:* Luke's purpose is hortatory. In Luke-Acts the Gk word *epilambanesthai* has the meaning "to compel" (Acts 16:19; 18:17; 21:30,33); it also has the positive meaning "to lay friendly hands on" a person for healing or for recommendation (9:47; 14:4; Acts 9:27; 17:19; 23:19). No one is compelled to become a disciple; the call is free. As in Simon's case, it can come quite unexpectedly. *behind Jesus:* This is discipleship terminology (see 9:23; 14:27). **27–31.** Jesus issues a stern warning that Jerusalemites repent of their rejection of him, the innocent and righteous one, God's prophet. Otherwise, God's punishment will visit them. As the pattern of rejected prophet shows, however, punishment is not God's final word to his people. In 23:34a and in the preaching of Acts, Luke shows that God once again extends the offer of forgiveness to those who have rejected Jesus. See comment on 4:24. **29.** Luke expresses the tragedy in language which startles those who consider bearing children a singular blessing. See 1:25. **30.** *fall on us:* See Hos 10:8. **31.** The meaning of this proverb is cloudy. Does the "they" of "they do this" refer to Romans, Jews, God, or the power of evil? Wherein lies the contrast between "green" and "dry": half-grown/fully grown; hard to burn/easy to burn; alive/dead? A paraphrase of v 31, which gives the rationale for vv 28–30, is: For if they have done this to Jesus, one who is life-giving, what will happen to dead, unrepentant Jerusalem? **190** (c) Jesus, among Sinners, Prays for Forgiveness (23:32–34). What prophet Jesus had foretold in 22:37 now comes to fulfillment: he is among transgressors. See Mark 15:22–24. **34a.** *Father, forgive them:* Manuscripts, many and of diverse origin, omit Jesus' prayer for forgiveness, which is unique to Luke. Internal evidence weighs heavily, however, for its authenticity. The language and thought are Lucan: Father (see 10:21; 11:2; 22:42; 23:46); forgiveness of sins because of ignorance (Acts 3:17; 13:27; 17:30). Luke balances Stephen's prayer (Acts 7:60) with that of Jesus. Luke has sayings of Jesus in each main section of the crucifixion narrative (23:28–31,43,46). The inclusion of a saying here conforms to Lucan artistry. Jesus' prayer is part and parcel of Luke's theology of rejected prophet and of a Jesus who teaches and practices forgiveness of enemies (6:27–28; 17:4). Jesus' prayer could have been excised by later copyists because it conflicted with their interpretation of 22:28–31 or because they felt that the destruction of Jerusalem showed that Jesus' prayer was ineffective or because of anti-Jewish sentiment. See Marshall, *Gospel* 867–68; Talbert, *Reading Luke* 219–20. Jesus, who had come to call sinners to repentance (5:32), continues that ministry to the end as he prays to his Father. **34b.** *dividing up his garments:* What happens to Jesus is in fulfillment of Ps 22:18, one of the psalms of the innocently suffering righteous one. On the indignity of being stripped naked, → 107 above. There does not seem to be any evidence that the Romans allowed a loincloth on the Jewish crucified lest Jewish sensitivities be offended. **191** (d) Negative and Positive Reponses to Jesus (23:35–49). In vv 35–39 hostile but ironically true responses will be given to God's revelation in Jesus crucified. In vv 40–43,47–49 (see also 23:50–53) God's revelation is truly seen and met with the positive responses of faith and repentance. See Mark 15:25–39. **35–39.** There is a downward progression in Luke's narration of those who humiliate Jesus: religious leaders, soldiers, a criminal. **35.** *the people . . . the religious leaders:* Luke draws a contrast between the people (*laos*), who contemplate the last events of Jesus' life, and the religious rulers, who scoff at Jesus. Inspired by what they see, the people will repent of their rejection of Jesus (see 23:13–25). As he did earlier in 23:34b, Luke now draws on Ps 22 to describe what is happening to Jesus (see Ps 22:7–8; Wis 2:18). *saved:* This becomes a refrain of taunting (see vv 37,39). These taunts recall Jesus' temptations in 4:1–13 as Jesus is now tempted to save his life not by giving it away but by holding on to it (see 9:24). What will save Jesus is his faith in a gracious God and Father, who will raise him from the dead (see Jesus' predictions of his passion and resurrection in 9:22 and 18:33; see also 20:27–40; 22:69). *Christ of God:* This taunt is ironically true (see Peter's confession in 9:20). *his Chosen One:* This bit of mockery is also ironically true (see 9:35). **36.** *sour wine:* The soldiers' actions accord with another of the psalms of the innocently suffering righteous one, Ps 69:21. **37.** *King of the Jews:* Ironically this, too, is true (see 19:38). **39.** *Christ:* Luke concludes the Christian confession of faith which he has ironically placed on the lips of Jesus' mockers. Those who contemplate this scene in

faith know that Jesus crucified is all that is denied of him. **192** **40–43.** The "good" criminal initiates the positive responses to Jesus. Luke's soteriology and theology of the cross find powerful dramatic expression in this "gospel within the Gospel." **41.** *this man has done nothing wrong:* Again the theme of Jesus' innocence is sounded. **42.** *Jesus:* Luke continues his confession, via titles, of the meaning of Jesus crucified: only in the name of Jesus is there salvation (see Acts 4:12). *into your kingdom:* The reading of "into" rather than "in" is not only supported by reliable mss., but fits Lucan theology (see 22:30) where Jesus' kingly rule is begun by his death and resurrection; see also 24:26. The criminal has deep faith that the dying Jesus is truly a king and can dispense the pardon and mercy which only a king can. **43.** Jesus, who will experience God's victory over death, declares the repentant criminal free from sin. "It is an acquittal uttered by him who is 'the one ordained by God to be the judge of the living and the dead' (Acts 10:42)" (*FGL* 1508). *today:* Jesus' salvific death has meaning for the present. *with me:* This aspect of salvation is also present in Jesus' table fellowship *with* sinners and his restoration of unclean folk to be *with* their fellow human beings. See R. J. Karris, *CurTM* 12 (1985) 346–52. *paradise:* This rich image encompasses the return to original creation, eating of fruit of the tree of life, and fellowship with the righteous. The gates of paradise have been reopened by the obedience and faith of the New Adam. See Neyrey, *Passion* (→ 52 above) 156–92. **44–45.** God's creation and the Jewish Temple give their response to the meaning of Jesus' death. **44.** *darkness:* In Joel 2:31 and Amos 8:9 the Day of the Lord, a day of judgment, comes with darkness. In Amos 8:9 that darkness occurs at noon. God's judgment against evil occurs in Jesus' death. **45.** *curtain of the Temple was torn in twain:* Since Luke has a positive view of the Temple, this verse cannot mean the destruction of this sacred place (→ 165 above). As Jesus dies, the outer curtain of the Temple, which separated all but the priests from God, is torn in two. In Jesus all now have access to God. For a different view, see D. D. Sylva, *JBL* 105 (1986) 239–50. **193** **46.** *Father, into your hands I commend my spirit:* Jesus' prayer is based on another psalm of the innocently suffering righteous one, Ps 31:5. With profound faith in his gracious Father, who raises the dead to life, Jesus concludes his life of obedience to God's will. He has drunk the cup God had mixed for him (see 22:42). **47–49.** Luke continues his narration of positive responses to Jesus' death as he returns to his theme of sight (see 22:8,35). **47.** *centurion:* → 46 above, on Luke's positive view of soldiers. The positive response of this Gentile should be joined to that of the Jews (vv 40–43,48,49) as a sign of the universal meaning of Jesus' death. *saw what happened:* With the free gift of faith this Gentile sees the inner significance of Jesus' forgiveness of his enemies, his fidelity to God during temptation, and his mercy to a repentant criminal. *praised God:* In Luke–Acts this phrase signifies a response to a revelation of God's power and mercy present in a mighty deed (see 2:20; 5:25,26; 7:16; 13:13; 17:15; 18:43; Acts 4:21; 21:20). The mighty deed that the centurion sees is not the healing of a leper (17:15); rather, he sees that God's mercy and power for the benefit of human beings occur in the death of a powerless individual, Jesus of Nazareth. *this man was righteous:* Through his insistence on Jesus' innocence (23:4,14–15,22,41) and his use of the psalms of the innocently suffering righteous one, Luke has prepared his readers for this confession of faith. Through his righteous conduct Jesus has shown that he is God's Son. By being faithful to Jesus, God has shown that Jesus is his Son and that God cares for unrighteously treated creation typified in Jesus. The logic of this theme of God's righteous one (see also Acts 3:14–15; 7:52; 22:14) is eloquently expressed in Wis 2:18: "For if the righteous one is God's son, he will help him, and will deliver him from the hand of his adversaries." See R. J. Karris, *JBL* 105 (1986) 65–74. **48.** *crowds:* → 45 above, on the interchangeability of "crowds" and "people." Thus, v 48 has as its cross-reference 23:35. Thrice Luke uses a word for "sight" to underline that those who once preferred Barabbas to Jesus have now seen the inner meaning of Jesus' death as a death for them (see 22:19–20). They repent by beating their breasts (see 18:13). **49.** *acquaintances:* This group includes Jesus' disciples who, in Luke's account, do not flee from Jesus. They along with the women see the meaning of what has been happening. As chap. 24 will make clear, their insight will be immeasurably enhanced. *women who had followed Jesus from Galilee:* This refers not merely to geographical following, but to the following of discipleship. This completing analepsis or "flashback" to 8:2–3 requires the reader to re-read and include women disciples in passages where they are not present. See further on 24:6–8.

194   (e) JESUS IS GIVEN A KINGLY BURIAL (23:50–56a). Joseph of Arimathea and the faithful women provide additional positive responses to God's revelation in Jesus crucified. **50.** *assembly:* Despite 22:70 and 23:1 the decision of the religious leaders against Jesus was not unanimous. **51.** *the kingdom of God:* This theme has streamed through the Gospel (e.g., 4:43 and 23:42). Jesus, even in death, is the bringer of God's kingdom. **53.** *linen:* At the time of Luke, linen was the symbol of immortality, for it came from flax, which came from life-giving earth. See J. Quasten, *AJP* 63 (1942) 206–15. In the hope of the resurrection Joseph clothes Jesus in linen. In 24:12 Peter will find the linen clothes by themselves. The symbol of resurrection life gives way to the reality of the risen Lord Jesus, who reveals what God has in store for all creation. *no one had yet been laid:* The crucified innocent and righteous Jesus is not tossed into a common grave, but is given a burial fitting one who is God's Messiah, Chosen One, and king of the Jews. **55.** See comments on 23:49 and 24:1–12.

195   **(VIII) Jesus' Vindication, Promise of the Spirit, and Ascension (23:56b–24:53).** Luke has come to the conclusion of the first part of his kerygmatic story of the events that have been accomplished among believers (see 1:1–4, and the emphasis on promise and fulfillment in 24:5–8,25,27,32,44–47). Through appearances of the risen Christ in Jerusalem the disciples journey from sorrow to joy, from perplexity to understanding, from disbelief to belief and finally have their eyes opened to see in the risen Lord what God has in store for all creation.

(A) Women as Evangelists (23:56b–24:12). See Mark 16:1–8; Matt 28:1–8; John 20:1–13. Luke grounds his insistence on the important role of women in the church's life in their commission to be the first proclaimers of Easter faith. **1.** *early dawn:* The power of darkness (22:53) gives way to the light of the dawn of Jesus' victory over death (see 1:78–79). **5.** *he is not here, but has been raised:* In fulfillment of his promise of vindication (9:22), God has vindicated his faithful, innocently suffering righteous Son, Jesus. This is the Easter gospel. **6.** *remember:* See also v 8. The meaning of this key Lucan and OT word should not be watered down and taken to mean the mere recollection of the content of a previous conversation. Remembering is bringing to bear in the present, with power and new and deepened insight, the meaning of past actions and words in salvation history. The same Gk word *mimnēskesthai* is found in a pregnant sense in 1:54,72; 23:42; Acts 10:31; 11:16.

Luke uses related Gk words in 22:19; 22:61; Acts 17:32; 20:31,35. See *TDNT* 4. 677; P. Perkins, *Resurrection* (GC, 1984) 154–55; R. H. Smith, *Easter Gospels* (Minneapolis, 1983) 109. *Galilee:* In accord with Luke's theological geography, all appearances occur in Jerusalem and its environs. From Jerusalem, the bond of continuity between promise and fulfillment in God's revelation, the Christian kerygma will spread to the ends of the earth (see Acts 1:8). **7.** The closest parallels to this saying are found in 9:22 and 9:44. Recall that at both those places it was not explicitly stated that women disciples were present (→ 101 above, on Luke's use of concluding analepsis or "flashback"). **8.** The revelation of Jesus' vindication gives new meaning and power to the women's recollection of Jesus' words. **9.** *proclaimed:* The faithful women disciples are the first to proclaim the Easter gospel. The Gk *anēngeilan* used here is usually undertranslated as "told." See the parallels in 9:36; Acts 26:20; and the observation of J. Schniewind, *TDNT* 1. 66. The vb. connotes "the message of resurrection in a specialized sense." **11.** *did not believe:* Luke employs the same Gk vb. *ēpistoun* to describe the apostles' response to the women's Easter message that he uses in Acts (e.g., 28:24) to describe a negative response to the Christian proclamation. The apostles have a way to go on their odyssey from misunderstanding to understanding and faith. **12.** This verse is to be retained as it is found in the most reliable mss. and is consonant with Lucan theology. *saw:* Peter's seeing is still not that of faith. See 24:34. *linen:* → 194 above. *what had happened:* This general clause is found in 23:47,48; 24:18. Eyes opened by the risen Lord Jesus will see the significance of what God has wrought for all in his Chosen One.

196   **(B) Emmaus and Return to the Journey of Discipleship (24:13–35).** This exquisite story, found only in this Gospel, sparkles with Lucan themes, esp. those of journey, faith as seeing, and hospitality. **13.** *were journeying:* The two disciples have abandoned the way of Jesus, for he did not meet their expectations (see v 21). Their infidelity is contrasted with the fidelity of the women (23:49–24:12). The reader should recall the Lucan theme of journey which was so predominant as an image for discipleship in 9:51–19:27. This story is shot through with journey language (vv 15,17,28,29,32,33, 35) and narrates how the risen Jesus reconciles two wayfarers, who, once they are forgiven and enlightened, immediately journey back to Jerusalem. **16.** *their eyes were held so that they did not recognize him:* Throughout his Gospel Luke has played on the theme of seeing (9:45; 18:34; 23:8,35,47–49). Now he articulates this theme in vv 23–24,31,32,35 as he tells how the risen Christ opens the eyes of disciples to see his true meaning in God's plan. But as the story will narrate, the disciples' eyes are only fully opened after they have shown hospitality to a stranger. **19.** *Jesus of Nazareth:* With theological irony Luke develops his theme of faith as seeing, for what the disciples say in this verse is the Christian creed (see Acts 2:22–24; 10:38). Mere recital of that creed will not create the sight of faith. **20–21.** *handed him over:* Luke's irony deepens as the facts being narrated by the disciples fulfill Jesus' prophecies in 9:22; 13:32–33; 18:31–33. To recite the facts of Jesus' life and to demonstrate how they mesh with his predictions do not open the eyes of faith. **22–24.** *some women from our band:* Luke relentlessly drives home his ironic message. The faithful women disciples' proclamation of the Easter gospel is resisted and does not open eyes to faith. **25–27.** *commencing from Moses:* What does positively contribute to faith (see v 32) is Jesus' interpretation of his life as the fulfillment of all God's promises from one end of the Scriptures to the other. God has exalted to glory his rejected prophet, the innocently suffering righteous Son. **29.** *stay with us:* Luke now adds his final touches to his theme of faith as seeing. Disciples who entertain the stranger will have their eyes opened. "So the lordship of Jesus is not known or manifested in acts of war or vengeance or in dreadful and mighty signs, but is attained through a cross and expressed in a meal—an act of hospitality, peace, brotherhood and sisterhood" (R. H. Smith, *Easter Gospels* [→ 195 above] 122). **30.** *reclined with them . . . took bread:* This instance of eating should not immediately be interpreted as eucharist, but should be linked with the thematic of eating which Luke has been developing throughout his Gospel. Through this thematic he has shown that God's kingdom has come in Jesus' sharing of food with others, esp. outcasts. Jesus, who at his last meal said that he would not share food with his disciples until God's kingdom came (22:16,18), now shares food with them and thereby shows that God's kingdom has indeed come. Now his table companions are not toll collectors, but his own disciples who have strayed from his way; they are forgiven and sent back on their way, which is his way. But all this happens to them only because they have been hospitable. **32.** *hearts burning:* Through their concern to provide hospitality to a stranger, the disciples' sadness, foolishness, and slowness of heart are transformed into joy, insight, and joyful recommitment to Jesus' way. **34.** *appeared to Simon:* Jesus' prayer has been efficacious. Simon Peter has also been forgiven and is now empowered to strengthen his fellow Christians on the way (see 22:31–34). See Dillon, *From Eye-Witnesses to Ministers of the Word* (→ 55 above) 69–155; R. J. Karris, *Int* 41 (1987) 57–61; B. P. Robinson, *NTS* 30 (1984) 481–97.

197 **(C) Commissioning and Ascension (24:36–53).** The themes of peace (v 36), table fellowship (vv 41–43), God's promises fulfilled in Jesus (vv 44–47), forgiveness of sins (v 47), Jerusalem (vv 47,52), witness (v 48), holy Spirit (v 49), Jesus' completion of his journey to God (v 51), and Temple (v 53) intermingle in this final section of Luke's Gospel. The entire Gospel culminates in Luke's description of the posture of the disciples: they worship Jesus (v 52). The vast majority of this material is uniquely Lucan. **36.** *he said to them: Peace to you:* This text is supported by the majority of ancient mss. and should be considered authentic. It, along with all or parts of 22:19b–20; 24:3,6,12,40,51,52, is, however, omitted by other ancient mss., esp. D. The evidence is not convincing for the authenticity of these eight readings (and also Matt 27:49), which were called "Western non-interpolations" by Westcott and Hort. See B. M. Metzger, *TCGNT* 191–93. K. Snodgrass, *JBL* 91 (1972) 369–79. *peace:* The blessings of wholeness and fullness of life, promised in 2:14, effected by Jesus' kingdom ministry (see, e.g., 7:50), and proclaimed in 19:38, are now the risen Jesus' permanent gift to his disciples. **38.** *why are you terrified?* The Emmaus story (24:13–35) with its journey from disbelief to belief is not referred to here. We have a fresh story: this time from doubts to worship (v 52). **43.** *at their table:* This is the way the Gk *enōpion autōn*, lit., "before them," should be translated. The evidence for this transl. is drawn from LXX usage (e.g., 2 Kgs 11:13; 3 Kgdms 1:25), from Luke's usage (13:26; Acts 27:35), and from Luke's account of the risen Lord's eating with his disciples (Acts 1:4; 10:41). Thus, the main point of this verse is not apologetic insistence on the reality of Jesus' body, but rather Jesus' victory over death as symbolized by his renewal of table fellowship with his disciples. See Dillon, *From Eye-Witnesses to Ministers of the Word* (→ 55 above) 200–1. **44.** All the Scriptures—the Law, the

Prophets, and the Writings—find their fulfillment in the risen Jesus. **45.** *opened their minds to comprehend:* Luke continues his theme of revelation as opening eyes and minds. See comment on 24:16. **47.** *forgiveness of sins . . . to all nations:* Acts 26:23 helps one answer the question raised by this verse: How is it possible for Jesus Messiah to preach to all nations in fulfillment of Scripture? He will do it through Paul and the church. Thus, Luke achieves his christological universalism. "Jesus is Messiah in a real and total sense only if God's salvation goes 'to the ends of the earth' through him" (J. Dupont, "La portée christologique de l'évangélisation des nations d'après Luc 24,47," *Neues Testament und Kirche* [Fest. R. Schnackenburg; ed. J. Gnilka; Freiburg, 1974] 143). **48.** *you are witnesses:* This commission is addressed to a larger group than the Eleven (see 24:9,33). The Lucan context would also indicate that women were included. See Perkins, *Resurrection* (→ 195 above) 166–67. **49.** *promise of my Father:* The holy Spirit is the animator of the continuation of Luke's story of how God has fulfilled promises. See Acts 1–2.

198 **50–53.** These verses contain numerous cross-references to 1:5–2:52 as Luke rounds off his themes via inclusion. **50.** *led them out:* Luke plays on the exodus theme and uses the Gk vb. *exagein,* which is used in the LXX to describe God's leading the people from Egyptian slavery in the exodus. Jesus is about to complete his exodus (see 9:31) to his Father. *lifting up his hands . . . blessed them:* There seems to be conscious allusion to Sir 50:20–24, which has the sequence of Simon the high priest's blessing, worship, and congregational response of praise. This is the only time in Luke's Gospel where he mentions that Jesus blessed people. At the conclusion of the liturgy of his life Jesus blesses his disciples. Contrast Zechariah (1:21–22). **51.** *was carried up into heaven:* In Acts 1:6–11 Luke provides another account of the ascension. This one has been helpfully called his "doxological" account, which stresses the worship of Jesus. The account of Acts is rather an "ecclesiastical" interpretation, which leads up to Luke's narrative of how God's *ekklēsia* must leave a posture of joyful worship and travel the highways of the world with the good news. See P. A. van Stempvoort, *NTS* 5 (1958–59) 30–42. Luke also "wishes to show that the journey Jesus made did not end . . . in absolute nothingness but in the heart of the One whom Jesus called his Father" (G. Lohfink, *Death is not the final word* [Chicago, 1977] 18). See also J. A. Fitzmyer, *TS* 45 (1984) 409–40. **52.** *worshiped him:* The christological high point of vv 36–53, indeed of the entire Gospel, has been reached, for this is the first and only time that Luke says that the disciples worship Jesus. Luke's christology is close to that of John 20:28. *Jerusalem:* The Gospel begins and ends in the holy city, but much has happened in between to alter readers' perception of this city's meaning. *joy:* See the angels' message in 2:10. "Clearly it is Lk's purpose to coordinate beginning and end, birth and departure. By doing this, he makes it very clear that the promise of the beginning is fulfilled at the end, and moreover that this entire life brings human beings great joy" (G. Lohfink, *Die Himmelfahrt Jesu* [SANT 26; Munich, 1971] 253). **53.** *Temple:* The Gospel begins and ends in the Temple, which, for Luke, is the bond of continuity between old and new. The primitive community of Acts is found worshiping in the Temple (Acts 3). *praising God:* See 1:64; 2:28. This is the response Luke wishes to elicit from his readers as they take to heart his kerygmatic narrative and confess with deepened conviction that God has done these things in Jesus for us and our salvation (see 1:1–4).

44

ACTS OF THE APOSTLES

Richard J. Dillon

BIBLIOGRAPHY

1 Bauernfeind, O., *Kommentar und Studien zur Apostelgeschichte* (WUNT 22; Tübingen, 1980). *The Beginnings of Christianity* (ed. F. J. Foakes Jackson and K. Lake; 5 vols.; London, 1920–33) Part 1, *The Acts of the Apostles.* Cadbury, H., *The Making of Luke-Acts* (2d ed.; London, 1958). Conzelmann, H., *Die Apostelgeschichte* (HNT 7; 2d ed.; Tübingen, 1972); *The Theology of St. Luke* (NY, 1960). Dibelius, M., *Studies in the Acts of the Apostles* (NY, 1956). Dömer, M., *Das Heil Gottes* (BBB 51; Bonn, 1978). Dupont, J., *Études sur les Actes des Apôtres* (LD 45; Paris, 1967); *The Salvation of the Gentiles* (NY, 1979); *Nouvelles études sur les Actes des Apôtres* (LD 118; Paris, 1984). Haenchen, E., *The Acts of the Apostles: A Commentary* (Phl, 1971). Hengel, M., *Acts and the History of Earliest Christianity* (Phl, 1980). Holtz, T., *Untersuchungen über die alttestamentlichen Zitate bei Lukas* (TU 104; Berlin, 1968). Keck, L. E. and J. L. Martyn (eds.), *Studies in Luke-Acts* (Nash, 1966). Kränkl, E., *Jesus, der Knecht Gottes* (Regensburg, 1972). Kremer, J. (ed.), *Les Actes des Apôtres* (BETL 48; Leuven, 1979). Lohfink, G., *Die Sammlung Israels* (SANT 39; Munich, 1975). Maddox, R., *The Purpose of Luke-Acts* (Studies of the New Testament and Its World; Edinburgh, 1982). Marshall, I. H., *The Acts of the Apostles* (TynNTC 5; GR, 1980). Munck, J., *The Acts of the Apostles* (AB 31; NY, 1967). Neil, W., *The Acts of the Apostles* (GR, 1973). O'Neill, J., *The Theology of Acts in Its Historical Setting* (2d ed.; London, 1970). Plümacher, E., *Lukas als*

hellenistischer Schriftsteller (SUNT 9; Göttingen, 1972). Radl, W., *Paulus und Jesus im lukanischen Doppelwerk* (Bern, 1975). Rese, M., *Alttestamentliche Motive in der Christologie des Lukas* (SNT 1; Gütersloh, 1969). Roloff, J., *Die Apostelgeschichte* (NTD 5; 17th ed.; Göttingen, 1981). Schmithals, W., *Die Apostelgeschichte des Lukas* (Zurich, 1982). Schneider, G., *Die Apostelgeschichte* (2 vols.; HTKNT 5; Freiburg, 1980, 1982). Talbert, C. H. (ed.), *Perspectives on Luke-Acts* (Danville, 1978); *Luke-Acts* (NY, 1984). Trocmé, É., *Le "Livre des Actes" et l'histoire* (Paris, 1957). Weiser, A., *Die Apostelgeschichte* (2 vols.; ÖTK 5/1–2; Gütersloh, 1981, 1985). Wilckens, U., *Die Missionsreden der Apostelgeschichte* (WMANT 5; 3d ed.; Neukirchen, 1974). Wilson, S. G., *The Gentiles and the Gentile Mission in Luke-Acts* (SNTSMS 7; Cambridge, 1973). Zingg, P., *Das Wachsen der Kirche* (OBO 3; Göttingen, 1974).

Surveys: Bovon, F., *Luc le théologien* (Neuchâtel, 1978). Bruce, F. F., *BJRL* 65 (1982) 36–56. Gasque, W. W., *A History of the Criticism of the Acts of the Apostles* (GR, 1975). Grässer, E., *TRu* 41 (1976–77) 141–94, 259–90; 42 (1977) 1–68. Neirynck, F., *ETL* 59 (1983) 338–49; 60 (1984) 109–117. Plümacher, E., *TRu* 48 (1983) 1–56; 49 (1984) 105–69.

DBSup 1. 42–86. *IDBSup* 7–9. Kümmel, *INT* 151–88. Wik-Schm, *ENT* 344–79. *CBLAA.* Mills, W. E., *A Bibliography of the Periodical Literature on the Acts of the Apostles 1962–1984* (NovTSup 58; Leiden, 1986).

INTRODUCTION

2 **(I) Identity and Credentials of the Author.** Like the four Gospels, Acts is an anonymous book, which means that the author's identity is nowhere asserted in the text. The earliest attributions of the Third Gospel and Acts to Luke, the Antiochene and companion of Paul, occur in writings of the late 2d cent.: the Anti-Marcionite Prologue to Luke; Irenaeus, *Adv. Haer.* 3.1.1; 3.14.1; and the Muratorian Canon (see SQE 533–38). Although the continuity of literary plan and authorship between the two books dedicated to Theophilus is not seriously contested, the credentials of the author and the historical source-value of his work are matters of a standoff dispute between more or less institutionalized schools of thought. The one school, in which English-language authors predominate (but cf. Hengel, *Acts* 66), insists on the full factual basis of the

familiar "we" passages of Acts (16:10–17; 20:5–8,13–15; 21:1–18; 27:1–28:16), in which the book's author appears to take a position among Paul's companions on mysteriously sporadic portions of his missionary journeys. The other school, of which adherents are mostly German-speaking (but cf. Cadbury, *The Making* 219, 274–76; O'Neill, *Theology* chap. 1; V. Robbins, in *PerspLA* 241–42), emphasizes the considerable differences between the Acts portrait of Paul and the apostle's firsthand testimonies in his authentic letters (see P. Vielhauer, in *StLA* 33–50). The entire value of Acts as a historical source need not hang in the balance between these positions, but many consider the author's canonical authority to be inadmissibly compromised by any denial of his credentials as a Pauline eyewitness.

Both sides of the debate find it difficult to process the

evidence submitted on the opposite side. Those who deny Luke's personal connection with Paul cannot agree on whether the "we" passages come from intermittent source material or the author's own literary technique, or on what, in any case, the author intended by introducing the "we" so unpredictably (see E. Plümacher, *ZNW* 68 [1977] 9–12). Those who maintain that it was Paul's companion who wrote the book and expressed himself in the "we" (cf. Col 4:14; Phlm 24) tend to make light of the unfamiliar features of the Lucan Paul, urging Luke's limited participation in his journeys (cf. 2 Tim 4:11!) and the effect of 30 years' interval, or making the convergences outweigh the differences—even though the latter include such momentous issues as Paul's missionary methods, his attitude toward the Mosaic law, and the motive of his fateful last journey to Jerusalem (in which the "we" participated [21:1–18]; → 102, 126 below).

3 In this writer's opinion, the interpretation of the distinguishing traits of Luke's Paul is not assisted by the view that a companion of the apostle wrote Acts. Saying this does not mean (1) that one can minimize the difficulties of explaining the "we" otherwise, or (2) that one becomes programmatically committed to accentuating the Luke–Paul discordances while underplaying their harmonies. Regarding (1), the "we" is more likely a stylistic device than a signal of roughly inserted source material. The appearance of the first person, notably in Paul's sea travels, could certify the authenticity of Luke's material in a special way (cf. Luke 1:3–4), thus addressing a concern for eyewitness warranty that is also shown by contemporary historians like Polybius and Lucian. It was not necessarily himself as world traveler that Luke meant to accredit in this way (*pace* Plümacher, *ZNW* 68 [1977] 17–22; Weiser, *Apg.* 392), but rather the pedigree of his narrative, particularly at crucial turns of Paul's missionary path, each traveled by sea (Robbins, in *PerspLA* 237) and each reported by an eyewitness (Schneider, *Apg.* 1. 93–94). See comment on 27:1–44; → 126–27 below.

Regarding (2), the hypothesis that the "we" is Luke's own certifying device does not compromise the historical value of the accounts given in that form. "What is fictional is the first-person plural form alone, not necessarily the story that is told in it" (E. Plümacher, *TRu* 49 [1984] 124). The sections of 1st-pers. narration, and indeed much of the rest of the Acts story, can be based on traditions of great historical value, perhaps even a connected strand of it, as in the Pauline chapters. But the fact that Luke himself looks back on Paul is powerfully argued by the numerous factors that are wanting in his portrayal of him: any acquaintance with his letters, "the picture, drawn large in the epistles, of Paul as the center of controversy in the church," and nearly any degree of difference between Paul's mission and, say, Peter's, or Stephen's, or Philip's (Maddox, *Purpose* 70). Luke is the historian digesting and contouring the past; he is not an actor in the story told in either of his books.

4 The immense importance accorded Paul in the Acts history suggests its composition in a community of the Pauline mission ambit, but one in which the personal legend of the apostle had far outdistanced any assimilation of his writings. The exact location of this community is guesswork, but the dating parameters would have to include the Third Gospel's composition well after AD 70 and the probable circulation of a letter corpus *ca.* AD 100. The dating of Acts somewhere between AD 80 and 90 is thus a widely accepted convention (see Kümmel, *INT* 185–87; Wik-Schm, *ENT* 376–79; H. Conzelmann, in *StLA* 298–316).

5 **(II) Literary Form and Purpose.** The crucial questions of why Luke produced this companion volume to his Gospel, and what the two-volume combination was meant to accomplish, are closely related to the vexed problem of the literary genre of the books. Some insist that Acts, like the Gospels, created a new literary form and conformed to no existing one (Kümmel, *INT* 116). Where the genre question has been pursued, this has usually redounded to the separation of the two Lucan volumes, with scholars assuming that the Gospel's purpose was self-evident whereas the purpose of Acts needed explaining (Maddox, *Purpose* 19). Then, because this author delights in imitating a wide range of postclassical literary conventions, it became tempting to generalize recurrent partial comparisons to define the genre of Acts as a whole. Suggestions have included Greco Roman biography (C. H. Talbert; cf. D. L. Barr and J. L. Wentling, in *Luke-Acts* [ed. C. H. Talbert] 63–88), the aretalogical romance exemplified in apocryphal *praxeis*-literature (*KINT* 2. 51–52), even the Greco-Roman novel (S. M. Praeder, "Luke-Acts and the Ancient Novel," *SBLASP* [1981] 1. 269–92; R. J. Karris, "Widows and Mirrors," *SBLASP* [1979] 1. 47–58). The uncomfortable fact for all these positions is that our author's first line of interest is not individual human actors and their feats or fortunes, but the progress of the word of salvation on its appointed course (1:8). Numerous attempts, however, to classify Acts as an apologetic or controversial treatise (see Maddox, *Purpose* 19–21), defending the gospel against Paul's detractors, or Christianity's, or perhaps heretical currents within the fold, all risk inflating partial concerns of the author into his overall purpose; and they ignore the fact repeatedly demonstrated by the text (cf. Luke 1:3–4) that "Luke-Acts is in every way a book dedicated to clarifying Christian self-understanding," not an evangelistic or polemical address to outsiders (ibid., 181).

A more promising, and lately more popular, approach to this issue involves two firm principles: (1) that their literary relationship shows Luke and Acts to constitute "a historical and literary unity" (Hengel, *Acts* 37); (2) that the most reliable clues to the character and purpose of his work are offered by Luke's unique prologues, which stand alone in the NT as expressions of self-conscious authorship (Dibelius, *Studies* 123). To judge by his prologues, Luke intended to write history and to do so with unexceptional procedure (Luke 1:3), measuring his task by the stature of his subject matter (Plümacher, *Lukas* 22–31, 137). A closer definition of the genre ventured by some is the "historical monograph" (Conzelmann, *Apg.* 7; Hengel, *Acts* 36), of which the distinguishing feature is the exposition of the driving forces and consequences of a longer historical process through treatment of one or more of its key episodes in a reduced narrative framework (E. Plümacher, in *Les Actes* [ed. J. Kremer] 462–63). Both Lucan volumes, self-enclosed but interrelated, argue the author's view of the entire process of salvation history, embracing the epochs of promise and fulfillment, Israel and the church, which are understood, and therefore "monographically" expounded, at the vantage point of their historic intersection.

Indeed, the continuity of salvation history through its central crossroads, the life of Jesus and the birth of the church, is now understood with increasing consensus to be the principal argument of Luke-Acts, and consequently to offer the best clues to the community setting and purpose of the work (E. Grässer, *TRu* 42 [1977] 51–58; E. Plümacher, *TRu* 48 [1983] 45–51). Exegetes project an "identity crisis" or "continuity crisis" in Luke's constituency, aroused by the persistent rejection of the gospel by Jewish audiences (Acts 13:46–47; 28:24–28) and the gradual alienation of a predominantly Gentile Christendom from the biblical people of promise. Luke was concerned not to explain as such the reasons for the failure of the Jews to embrace the gospel, "but to counter the real theological difficulty that such a failure presented to Christians" (E. Franklin, *Christ the Lord* [Phl, 1975] 111). How could non-Jews find value in something which had its roots in Judaism but which most Jews repudiated? (Maddox, *Purpose* 184). To argue his "continuity" thesis in the face of this, Luke had to establish the historical nexus between Israel and Jesus on the one hand (the Gospel) and between Jesus and the church on the other (Acts), and thus to demonstrate the full scope of the divine plan in which the church of the present proves to be the proper destination of God's way with Israel (cf. 15:14–21).

6   (III) Tradition and Composition. Luke's appropriation of the models of historiography practiced by such contemporaries as Polybius, Dionysius of Halicarnassus, Tacitus, Livy, Sallust, and Flavius Josephus involved the compositional stratagems of inserted speeches and letters, generalizing summaries, and mimicry of classical discourse patterns, as well as the "dramatic-episode" texture of presentation. Let us address this last feature first.

(A) Dramatic-Episode Style. The debate over the historical value of Acts is sharpened by the fact that the author concentrates on bringing "historical reality vividly before the eyes of the reader by concentrating on particular paradigmatic events" and mostly ignoring the chronological sequence between them (Hengel, *Acts* 55–56; cf. Plümacher, *Lukas* 100–11). Some think that this method makes Luke more an edifying storyteller than a historian (so E. Haenchen, in *StLA* 260); but Hengel insists that the method is not "peculiar" but stands "in a broad tradition of hellenistic historiography" which did not sacrifice truth to "edification" just because it singled out the typical, the exemplary, the programmatic, amid a flow of events much larger than the sources at hand (so also E. Grässer, *TRu* 41 [1976] 192). The clearest examples of these freestanding dramatic episodes are the Pentecost (chap. 2), Stephen's martyrdom (chaps. 6–7), the Cornelius conversion (chap. 10), the Jerusalem agreement (chap. 15), Paul's Athens mission (17:16–34), and successive trials (chaps. 21–26). Each of these has been shaped as a vehicle for an important theorem of Luke's theology of history, whose significance reaches far beyond the scene itself (Plümacher, *Lukas* 86, 92, 101), so each has to be judged on its own merits as a source of historical information.

7   (B) Speeches. The centerpiece of most of the great scenes listed above is a speech, whether a mission sermon (chaps. 2, 17), a prophetic indictment (chap. 7), a didactic commentary on the event at hand (chaps. 10, 15), or an apologia before public authority (chaps. 22, 26). The popularity of speeches as historiographical devices is well documented in Hellenistic literature, notably in works of the Jewish tradition (1–3 Macc; Josephus). Following the celebrated maxim of Thucydides (1.22; cf. Dibelius, *Studies* 140–42), historians inserted speeches as part of the sustained dialogue between themselves and their readers; hence, the speeches are "to be understood less from the historical situation than from the context of the book as a whole . . . , for the book has a theme and the speeches play their part in developing it" (ibid., 174–75). The speeches in Acts thus all have Luke as their author and his readers as their audience; whether the audience on the scene would have grasped the argument is often beside the point (e.g., 17:22–31!).

A special case, thought by Dibelius to limit his Hellenistic analogy, are the so-called missionary discourses, six to Jewish audiences (2:14–39; 3:12–26; 4:9–12; 5:29–32; 10:34–43; 13:16–41), two to Gentiles (14:15–17; 17:22–31). Here the content is held within the traditional contours of the early Christian kerygma, which accounts for the repetitive feature of these passages but does not make tracing their precise traditional background an easy exercise. Some think that they reproduce the historic pattern of the apostles' preaching (C. H. Dodd), or perhaps an established kerygmatic schema used in Luke's day (Dibelius, *Studies* 165); others consider the schema a product of Luke's design for his own argumentative purposes (Plümacher, *Lukas* 33–35). In the Jewish sermons, the audience hears itself (or its forebears) accused: "you killed him whom God has raised up," and this motivates a summons to repentance which climaxes the argument. This "contrast schema" may go back to an old preaching formula (Roloff, *Apg.* 50), perhaps a pattern of repentance-parenesis developed in the Hellenistic synagogues out of the deuteronomic reproaches of Israel for its resistance to the prophets (Wilckens, *Missionsreden* 200–8; Weiser, *Apg.* 100). But the mission sermons are not really an exception to the Hellenistic analogy verified elsewhere in the speeches of Acts; they do not preach the gospel directly but illustrate, together with their scenic frameworks, how the apostolic preaching and its reception carried earliest Christian history toward the outcome intended by God (Plümacher, *Lukas* 35). Closer determination of the sermons' traditional background remains an open question (see Plümacher, *TRu* 49 [1984] 131–35).

8   (C) Mimesis. The archaic flavor and Semitic idiom of the speeches to Jews have been taken as pointers to older tradition, but they more often pertain to writing techniques widely practiced in the postclassical culture, viz., imitation (*mimēsis*) of classical models and stylistic affectation of the "atmosphere" of the venerated past (archaism). In the section of Acts dealing with the mission under the Twelve, just as in Luke's Gospel, the classical model is the LXX, "the Bible" of Greek-speaking Jews. Not his formal or allusive quotation of biblical passages, but his adaptation of their style and idiom for his own writing constitutes the mimetic procedure distinctive of Luke. Yet this is not his invention but "characterizes a whole epoch of hellenistic literature," for instance the classisistic mimesis of historians Dionysius of Halicarnassus, Josephus, *et al.* With his LXX mimicry, as with his archaizing kerygmata, Luke cultivates the impression of the church's beginnings as a *sui generis* "sacred time," hallmarked by "sacred speech" (Plümacher, *Lukas* 68, 74, 78). The LXX mimesis is suspended after chap. 15, when the Twelve likewise exit Luke's stage (but see 20:18–35). The aura of classical Athens, however, is exquisitely conjured up in 17:16–34.

9   (D) Summaries. To fill the gaps between his freestanding episodes, Luke used the generalizing summary, which he had been able to observe in Mark's composition of the episodic Jesus tradition (Mark 1:32–34,39; 3:10–12). The summary generalizes single incidents and circumstances of the narrated episodes, making them into the usual and typical traits of a period (Dibelius, *Studies* 9–10; Cadbury, *The Making* 58; *Beginnings* 5. 392–402). The major summaries of Acts all occur in the first five chapters, where Luke's information was probably most fragmentary (2:42–47; 4:32–35; 5:11–16). Minor summaries, usually only a single verse, occur at 1:14; 6:7; 9:31; 12:24; 16:5; 19:20; 28:30–31. The summaries are not mere stopgap devices; they are important compositional stratagems for sustaining the author's argument concerning the history he is telling. They idealize the period of the apostles' ministry in Jerusalem and sustain the reader's impression of a steady growth of the Christian movement punctually plotted by the will of God (Zingg, *Wachsen* 36–40). Like his stylistic mimesis, Luke's idealizing of the earliest community surrounds that period with the glitter of a "golden age," just as did much contemporary retrospect on the classical period (Plümacher, *Lukas* 16–18).

10   (E) The Sources of Acts. Luke's skills as a resourceful Hellenistic author must not discourage the quest for his source material, which has come back into its own after 20 years or so of redaction-historical enthusiasm (see E. Grässer, *TRu* 41 [1976] 186–94; E. Plümacher, *TRu* 49 [1984] 120–38). Stylistic criteria alone will not trace continuous source substrata because of the author's consistently strong hand in rewriting his sources (see Dupont, *Sources* [→ 11 below]; Hengel, *Acts* 61–62). He demonstrated this vis-à-vis Mark and Q in the Gospel, and we should be as hard put there to identify his sources if we did not know them from Synoptic comparison. Most scholars do not subscribe to a continuous source basis for the first half of Acts, except that the old hypothesis of an "Antiochene" source underlying chaps. 6–15 has recently been exhumed (Hengel, *Acts* 65–66; Lüdemann, *Paul* [→ 11 below] 25). After chap. 15, the book gives surer footing for source analysis, above all in the reports of Paul's second and third mission journeys, for which M. Dibelius formulated the durable hypothesis of the "itinerary" (*Studies* 5–6, 197), which was perhaps a travel diary written by a companion of Paul. In countless forms, that idea has renewed vigor at present (E. Plümacher, *TRu* 49 [1984] 123–28, 138), and some believe comparison of the journey stations in chaps. 16–21 with Paul's letters will give analytical support to the pre-Lucan documentation there (Lüdemann, *Paul* [→ 11 below] 156; Weiser, *Apg.* 388–90). G. Schneider's laconic appraisal is just: such a source is "as hard to deny as it is to delineate!" (*Apg.* 1. 91).

11   (IV) The Gk Text of Acts. This book is unique in the NT for the fact that it was transmitted from early on, perhaps as far back as the early 2d cent., in two text types, the "Egyptian" (Alexandrian) and the "Western," neither of which can be consistently derived from the other. The "Western" text, of which the Codex Bezae (D), African Lat version, and Harclean Syr (*apparatus*) are the principal witnesses, is nearly 1/10 longer than the "Egyptian," which has its purest form in the Codex Vaticanus (B), less so in the Boh and Vg versions. 20th-cent. scholarship has increasingly favored the "Egyptian" text as consistently closer to Luke's autograph, principally because the lengthened "Western" text and its occasional omissions betray tendencies of conscious revision (J. H. Ropes, *Beginnings* 3. ccxxiv–ccxl; Haenchen, *Acts* 51–59). These include stylistic alterations and rather uninhibited glossing to enrich religious expressions (6:8; 7:55; 8:39; 13:32; 15:32), to clarify wording or situations (15:34 *l.v.;* 16:35), to smooth out inconsistencies or anomalies (3:11; 20:15), and to "update" the text to suit present practices and perceptions (15:20,29). The astonishing scope of these initiatives testifies to an atmosphere of unconstraint in rewriting the text and thus points to a period before the learned recensions, when the scribe "did not yet consider Acts to be 'holy writ' which no one was allowed to alter" (Haenchen, *Acts* 52). All the same, but for 15:20,29 and 21:25, the Western "plus" does not bring substantial novelties to the book (C. Martini, in *Les Actes* [ed. J. Kremer] 29); it mostly augments, polishes, even belabors what was already there. By way of exception, it might occasionally outbid rivals to represent Luke's hand (12:10?

19:1? 27:5? cf. Haenchen, *Acts* 384 n. 6; 698 n. 7), but one's attitude toward it should still be systematic skepticism, not "eclectic" ambivalence (*pace* Schneider, *Apg.* 1. 168).

(Boismard, M.-É. and A. Lamouille, *Le texte occidental des Actes des Apôtres: Reconstitution et réhabilitation* [2 vols.; Synthèse 17; Paris, 1984]. Brodie, T., "Greco-Roman Imitation of Texts as a Partial Guide to Luke's Use of Sources," *Luke-Acts* [ed. C. H. Talbert] 17–46. Dibelius, *Studies* 1–25, 84–92, 102–8, 123–85, 192–214. Dodd, C. H., *The Apostolic Preaching and Its Developments* [NY, 1962]. Dupont, J., *The Sources of Acts* [NY, 1964]. Haenchen, E., in *StLA* 258–78. Kränkl, *Jesus* 1–81. Lüdemann, G., *Paul, Apostle to the Gentiles* [Phl, 1984] 23–43. Martini, C., in *Les Actes* [ed. J. Kremer] 21–35. Metzger, B. M., *TCGNT* 259–503. Plümacher, E., in *Les Actes* [ed. J. Kremer] 457–66; "Wirklichkeitserfahrung und Geschichtsschreibung bei Lukas," *ZNW* 68 [1977] 2–22. Robbins, V., "The We-Passages in Acts and Ancient Sea Voyages," *BR* 20 [1975] 5–18; in *PerspLA* 215–42. Schneider, G., "Der Zweck des lukanischen Doppelwerkes," *BZ* 21 [1977] 45–66. Schweizer, E., in *StLA* 208–16. Talbert, C. H., *Literary Patterns* [SBLMS 20; 1974] 125–40. Unnik, W. C. van, in *StLA* 15–32; in *Les Actes* [ed. J. Kremer] 37–60. Vielhauer, P., in *StLA* 33–50. Wilckens, *Missionsreden* 7–31, 187–224.)

12   (V) Outline. Acts may be outlined as follows:

COMMENTARY

13   **(I) Introduction to the Era of the Church (1:1–26).** The whole of chap. 1 forms an introduction to Acts inasmuch as it forges the connection between Jesus' time and the time of the church that is the basic rationale of the two-part Lucan opus. The controlling perspective of continuity between the two periods is well served by the structure of this passage, which passes from a review of the first volume (vv 1–2) directly into the narrative of the second (v 3) without the balancing announcement of the second volume's contents which vv 1–2 made us expect. Had he structured this prologue mechanically true to form, with successive résumés of both books (see P. van der Horst, *ZNW* 74 [1983] 17–18), Luke would have given the impression of separate stories and eras, whereas he was intent on showing that the first flowed directly and coherently into the second. So it is that the story of Acts takes up right amid the retrospect on Jesus' story, without any formal introduction. The program of Acts can therefore be given at best indirectly in the concluding testament of the heaven-bound *Kyrios* (vv 7–8), the passage that carries the main weight of the section (Pesch, "Anfang" [→ 17 below] 9).

The axis for this joining of the periods is, of course, the Easter–Ascension sequence, whose restatement in vv 3–14 resumes and varies Luke 24:36–53, now with accents fine-tuned to the perception of a beginning rather than a conclusion. The fact that Luke and Acts overlap at the Easter story confirms that these are not two independent books telling separate stories, but two tightly meshed installments of one comprehensive history (Dömer, *Heil* 94–95). The parallelism with Luke 24 assures us that the caesura for the first section does not come until after v 14 (Schneider, *Apg.* 1. 187; Weiser, *Apg.* 46–47) since vv 12–14 resume Luke 24:52–53. Dividing Acts 1 thus into vv 1–14 and 15–26, we find that the two sections present two necessary steps in the incorporation of the church's time into the greater sweep of salvation history: (1) the witnesses' preparation and commissioning by the departing Christ; (2) their deployment as a formally accredited sacred community, gathered around the reconstituted circle of twelve "witnesses of his resurrection" (v 22).

14   **(A) Witnesses' Commission and Jesus' Ascension (1:1–14).**

(a) PROEMIUM (1:1–8). **1.** *the first book:* The particle *men* at the head of the first sentence makes the reader expect a correlative *de* subsequently introducing the new book's contents. The fact, however, that such does not follow is not a syntactical anomaly (cf. the solitary *men* at 3:21; 4:16; 27:21; 28:22), and secondary prefaces occasionally lack the matching content statement for the story to follow after their résumé of what was told heretofore (cf. Josephus, *Ant.* 8.1.1 § 1–2;

13.1.1 § 1–2; Cadbury, *The Making* 198–99). Recapitulation of the Gospel in terms of its bid for completeness (*peri pantōn*) recalls the evangelist's accreditation of his project in Luke 1:3 (*parēkolouthēkoti anōthen pasin*). Jesus' total ministry of deed and word forms the necessary foundation and point of reference for the great mission of which Acts will tell. This already suggests that it will be necessary to heed parallels between the two books and their leading personages as a vehicle of the author's argumentation. *began to do and teach:* In view of Luke's emphasis on the "beginning" of Jesus' work, to which his account and its sources reach back (Luke 1:2–3; 3:23; 23:5; Acts 1:22; 10:37), *ērxato*, "began," is no mere pleonasm (Schneider, *Apg.* 1. 191), but emphasizes either Jesus' ministry as the "beginning" of the work he is now to continue after his ascension (Marshall, *Acts* 56) or the completeness of the former account in covering its subject "from the beginning" (*Beginnings* 4. 3). The latter meaning would make the recapitulation include both Lucan termini of Jesus' work (v 22): *a quo* and *ad quem*, his baptism and his ascension (Pesch, "Anfang" [→ 17 below] 21; Roloff, *Apg.* 19). **2.** *the apostles whom he had chosen:* The vb. *exelexato* echoes Luke 6:13, the selection of the Twelve to be named "apostles," and yet the retrospect is clearly to Luke 24:44–49, where the broader circle, "the Eleven and those who were with them" (24:33), received the risen Lord's final instruction. Here we experience the intriguing alternation of emphasis by Luke, now on the broader group of Easter witnesses (Luke 24:9,33; Acts 1:14–15; 2:1), now on the Twelve as somehow the key "witnesses of his resurrection" (Acts 1:2,13,21–26; cf. Lohfink, *Sammlung* 64–67; Dömer, *Heil* 134). The concentric association of the Twelve and the larger disciple corps, begun back at Luke 6:17, is nowhere interrupted in the Easter–Pentecost sequence, for it represents a kind of blueprint of the church and certifies its direct lineage with Israel (Luke 22:30). *he was taken up:* The slender "Western" ms. tradition against *anelēmphthē* was concerned, as was the more considerable one against Luke 24:51b (→ Luke, 43:198), to eliminate apparently conflicting dates of the ascension (Benoit, *Jesus* [→ 17 below] 1. 237–40). In view of the reference of the ptc. *enteilamenos* to Luke 24:44–49, *anelēmphthē* certainly refers to Jesus' ascension here (Luke 24:50–53), just as its ptc. does in v 11. Cf. the same verb applied to bodily ascension in the LXX: 2 Kgs 2:9; 1 Macc 2:58; Sir 48:9; 49:14. It serves here, as in v 22, to define the boundary of the time of Jesus by Lucan reckoning (cf. Dupont, *Études* 477–80).

15 **3.** *alive after his passion:* A freestanding relative clause continues the first book's recapitulation just where we were expecting the present book's program. "Living" recalls the angels' word at the tomb (Luke 24:5,23) and will become a capsule expression of the Easter kerygma at 25:19 (cf. Rom 14:9). For the full expression, see 9:41. The inf. *paschein* connoting Jesus' integral passion–death experience is distinctively Lucan (Luke 22:15; 24:26,46; Acts 3:18; 17:3; 26:23). But cf. Heb 9:26; 13:12; 1 Pet 3:18. *with many convincing proofs:* All the weight of the "proofs" should not be thrown on the physical demonstrations of the Easter story (Luke 24:39–43; *pace* Lohfink, *Himmelfahrt* [→ 17 below] 152–53; Dömer, *Heil* 112). The articulating ptcs. "appearing" and "speaking" reflect the structure of the two appearance stories of Luke 24, where the disciples were rescued from utter perplexity before the physical evidence by the risen One's words of instruction (24:25–27, 44–49; cf. Dillon, *Eye-Witnesses* [→ 17 below] 198–99). *during forty days:* The number is symbolic, whether Luke derived it from an existing tradition concerning the duration of the appearances (Haenchen, *Acts* 174; Pesch,

"Anfang" [→ 17 below] 10, 14), or invented it himself (Lohfink, *Himmelfahrt* [→ 17 below] 176–86; Weiser, *Apg.* 49–50). The period is understood as the sufficient space of the witnesses' preparation (13:31), and the LXX furnished precedents for such a rounded period of preparation, e.g., Exod 24:18; 34:28 (Moses); 1 Kgs 19:8 (Elijah); Num 13:25; 14:34. Cf. also 4 Ezra 14; 2 *Apoc. Bar.* 76. Closer to hand is the period of Jesus' temptation, which preceded his first preaching (Luke 4:2,14–15), even though the Gospel did not stress its preparation aspect. The "kingdom of God" is a constant as subject matter of the preaching: of Jesus (Luke 4:43; 8:1; 9:11; 16:16), the Seventy-two (Luke 10:9,11), and hereafter of Paul (Acts 19:8; 20:25; 28:23). Both it and the "40 days," therefore, enhance Luke's argument for the direct continuity between the two seasons of the one saving message (Dömer, *Heil* 113). A relationship between the 40 days and the 50 of Pentecost will be suggested by v 5, "after not many days." **4.** *as he was eating with them:* This meaning of the vb. *synalizō* is assured by Luke 24:43 and Acts 10:41 (*synephagomen*). The sg. number and pres. tense of the ptc. (root *hals*, "salt") discourage the alternate meaning of "come together" (BAGD 791). *not to depart from Jerusalem:* Cf. Luke 24:49. Jerusalem is the spatial symbol of the continuity between the times of Jesus and the church, just as the Twelve and the stable Easter gallery around them are personal embodiments of it. By editing out the disciples' flight from Jesus' side (Mark 14:50–52) and all provisions for Galilean appearances (Mark 16:7; cf. Luke 24:7), Luke made Jerusalem the theater of the entire Passion-to-Pentecost sequence and the stable situs of the principal tradition bearers, the Twelve (cf. 2:43 *l.v.;* 5:16,28; 8:14; 16:4), who will linger there even when persecution has scattered the rest of the community (8:1). Jerusalem's centrality in the Lucan history exhibits the continuity between Israel and the church and does so with particular reference to the city's historic role of prophet-murderer (Luke 13:33–35; 18:31 [Mark 10:33]; Acts 13:27–28), which will make it the first venue of the gospel's recruitment of repentant sinners (Luke 24:47; Acts 2:36–41; 3:17–21) as well as a keynote beginning for a Christian mission fertilized and universalized by successive persecutions (cf. Lohfink, *Himmelfahrt* [→ 17 below] 264–65, citing Isa 2:3; Dillon, *Eye-Witnesses* [→ 17 below] 214–15). On the variation of Gk spellings of the city's name—now the sacred, transliterated *Ierousalēm,* now the hellenized *Hierosolyma* favored by profane Gk authors (possibly prompted here and in v 6 by the formal proemium style)—see J. Jeremias, *ZNW* 65 (1974) 273–76; I. de la Potterie, *RSR* 69 (1981) 57–70. *the promise of the Father:* This fills out and varies the reprise of Luke 24:49 in this verse. Fulfillment of the "promise" (*epangelia;* cf. Gal 3:14; Eph 1:13) will be announced at 2:33, rounding off the speech which began with its foundation in OT prophecy (Joel 3:1–5/2:17–21). The same "promise" was transmuted into a Jesus logion at Luke 11:13. *which you heard:* Non-indicated metabasis from indirect to direct speech is compositional technique. Cf. Luke 5:14; Acts 14:22; 17:3; 23:22; 25:5, and Hellenistic parallels in P. van der Horst, *ZNW* 74 (1983) 19–20. Readers have now forgotten their expectation of an explicit program for the book at hand but are being prepared imperceptibly for the indirect program statement of vv 6–8. **5.** The "promise" is articulated in the familiar Baptist logion of Mark 1:8 (cf. 11:16), which is actualized here by the addition of "after not many days." The analogy between JBap's bath ritual and the outpouring of the Spirit on Jesus' disciples crosses over from the literal ("immerse") to a metaphorical ("endow fully") sense of the vb. and also varies the sense of the instrumental dats. (whereby, wherewith). The conjunction of water baptism and Spirit outpouring (cf. Ezek 36:25-26; John 7:37-39) will recur at 2:38; 8:14-16; 10:47-48; 19:5-6. Recourse to JBap's prophecy in connection with the Pentecost, here and at 11:16, precisely demonstrates the prophecy's fulfillment and makes JBap the herald of the church as well as of the Messiah.

16   **6-8.** The dialogue in these verses is the pro-emium's center of gravity. The question posed is: What is to happen in this new period at hand? The answer will state the new book's program, outlined in the geographical schema of v 8b (Haenchen, *Acts* 145-46; Pesch, "Anfang" [→ 17 below] 27). The substance of v 7 comes from Christian tradition about the incalculable last day (Mark 13:32; 1 Thess 5:1), and v 8 is again part of the Easter story cross-reference (Luke 24:48-49). The shaping of the dialogue, with leading question tailored to the answer and the latter programming the book (v 8), shows these verses to be Luke's composition without any continuous tradition underneath (Lohfink, *Himmelfahrt* [→ 17 below] 154-58; Weiser, *Apg.* 51-52). **6.** The tailoring of the disciples' question to Jesus' answer extends to all three phases of both, with the answer correcting, respectively, the temporal, personal, and spatial assumptions of the question (Dömer, *Heil* 115-17). Thus, the question of a time for the great restoration is disqualified (v 7); the question of what the Lord will do is answered in terms of his "witnesses" under the Spirit (v 8a); and the question of the kingdom restored to Israel is recast in the prospect of their mission "to the end of the earth" (v 8b). The delay of the parousia is surely part of the concern (Conzelmann, *TSL* 136), but it is not correct to isolate that issue from the other two. *those who had come together:* The circle of witnesses-to-be appears to broaden beyond the chosen Eleven (v 2) to the larger gallery (Luke 24:33) from which the twelfth apostle will be chosen (vv 21-22). *at this time:* "This time" must be that of v 5, "after not many days." It is the time to be begun by Pentecost, and so the question aims at the meaning of that new period, which will be designated "the last days" in 2:17 (Pesch, "Anfang" [→ 17 below] 28-29). The purpose of the present exchange can therefore not be to de-eschatologize the time of the church (Lohfink, *Himmelfahrt* [→ 17 below] 260-61). *restore the kingdom to Israel:* See Jer 33:7; Pss 14:7; 85:2; Hos 6:11; Sir 48:10. *Apokathistanō,* "restore," relates this prospect to the "restoration of all things" in 3:21; hence, it is not disowned altogether (*pace* Maddox, *Purpose* 106-8). For Luke, the realization of "the hope of Israel," for which Paul will also toil (28:20), involves the accession of the Gentiles to it (15:14-19), hence the entire process of "the last days" (Lohfink, *Sammlung* 79). **7.** *times or seasons:* The two Gk words (cf. 1 Thess 5:1) denote, respectively, time's duration and its opportune moments, both of which are God's domain and beyond human inquiry. This combination of temporal perspectives will be further unfolded at 3:20-21, where the argument closely parallels 1:6-11. **8.** *but you will receive the power of the holy Spirit:* The *ouch-alla,* "not . . . but rather," structure of vv 7-8 turns on the business of the disciples (*hymōn estin*), not the location of the parousia, so it is inexact to speak of the Spirit as parousia-*Ersatz;* nor, in view of 2:17, does the Spirit cease being the "power of the end-time" (*pace* Conzelmann, *Apg.* 27; rightly Schneider, *Apg.* 1. 202). Comparison of this Spirit "baptism" with JBap's rite (v 5) shows it to be the equipment for the task of "the last days," not a mere immunization against the judgment (Kremer, *Pfingstbericht* [→ 17 below] 186). *you will be my witnesses:* The full content of their testimony was stated at Luke 24:46-48, the Gospel's account of this

appointment. Included was the full christological testimony of the Scriptures, even the still future ingredient of the universal mission in Jesus' name, which forbids any reading of "witness" in terms merely of a "voucher for the facts" (*pace* Lohfink, *Himmelfahrt* [→ 17 below] 267-70; Kränkl, *Jesus* 167-75). Intended is a much more comprehensive personal representation of Jesus through reenactment of his life's "journey" (cf. 10:39; 13:31), esp. the journey's destination in fatal contest with this world's rulers (Dömer, *Heil* 135-36; Dillon, *Eye-Witnesses* [→ 17 below] 215-17). The fact that the witness function becomes possible only with the bestowal of the Spirit's power accounts for the word's absence prior to Luke 24:48-49 and already implies what 5:32 will plainly declare: the "witness" shares the risen Lord's embassy with the holy Spirit before the hostile tribunals of the world (cf. Luke 12:12). *Jerusalem . . . to the end of the earth:* This does, in fact, delineate the movement of the story of Acts—if, i.e., Rome, the imperial capital, can qualify as "the end of the earth." This phrase anticipates 13:47, with its quotation of Isa 49:6 LXX and its programmatic announcement of the Pauline mission to the Gentiles. Rome, capital of the pagan world and geographic destination of Luke's story, is situated at "the end of the earth" in the religious sense expressed in the parallel stichs of Isa 49:6 (cf. Dupont, *Salvation* 17-19).

17   (b) THE ASCENSION (1:9-14). The debate over whether Luke derived the accounts of a visible ascension from existing Christian tradition (so Haenchen, Conzelmann, Schneider; R. Pesch, "Anfang" 16-19) or not (Lohfink, *Himmelfahrt* 208-10, 244, 276; Kremer, Weiser) has to be governed by recognition of the difference between the old kerygma of Christ's heavenly exaltation (Phil 2:9-11; Rom 8:34) and the interpretation thereof in terms of bodily translation (Lohfink, *Himmelfahrt* 74-79). To the latter idea belongs a literary form of which numerous components are represented in Luke 24:49-53 and Acts 1:9-12: the departing figure's testament, the earthbound scenario, the transporting cloud, and the interpreting angels. This passage sounds direct verbal echoes of the accounts of Elijah's ascension in 2 Kgs 2:9-13 and Sir 48:9,12 and, together with Third Gospel passages showing Elijah parallels, may attest Luke's debt to Christian circles that celebrated Jesus' earthly ministry as the climax of Israel's colorful tradition of charismatic prophecy. Other possible traces of the ascension's tradition history include Eph 4:8-10; 1 Tim 3:16; John 20:17; *Barn.* 15:9. **9.** *as they looked on:* This is the first of five references to the witnesses' vision in just vv 9-11. The visibility and historicity of Jesus' ascension are being argued, along with an essential ingredient of the apostolic witness (v 22; Lohfink, *Himmelfahrt* 269-70); yet the need of an angelic interpretation (as in Luke 24:4-7; cf. 24:25-27,44,49) reassures us that the ascension is not conceived of as an event fully "within history," accessible and comprehensible on terms set by its witnesses. **10.** *two men:* This designation for the angels (cf. 10:22,30), together with the reproach-explanation sequence of their message, puts this passage in close parallel with Luke 24:4-9 (cf. Mark 16:5-8) and strongly suggests the origin of both at Luke's hand (Lohfink, *Himmelfahrt* 195-98; Dömer, *Heil* 120). Cf. also the "two men" and "the cloud" at Luke's transfiguration (9:30,34 [cf. Mark 9:4,7]). Jesus transfigured, attended by the once-translated Elijah (and Moses?), was thus already a prefiguration of the ascended Christ: the ultimate prophet, the ultimate apotheosis. **11.** *will come in the same manner:* The point of the comparison seems to be the transportation by the cloud, which was also to be the conveyance of the Son of Man at his coming (cf. the sg.

"cloud" [Luke 21:27] with the pl. in Mark 13:26; Dan 7:13–14). The correspondence between Jesus' ascension and his parousia suggests that these events are to circumscribe the period now beginning, which was just programmed in v 8 (hence the angels' reproachful question). "The ascension becomes a prefigurement of the parousia," and thus the conclusion of Jesus' time anticipates the conclusion of the church's (Lohfink, *Himmelfahrt* 262). The view that the ascension thus begins a period of Jesus' absence (3:21) and prompts an "absentee Christology" in Acts that features mediating substitutes for his presence (so C. F. D. Moule, in *StLA* 179–80; Bovon, *Luc* 144–45) seems to underestimate the effective *praesentia Christi* that Luke will bring out in recounting the activity of his witnesses (cf. Kränkl, *Jesus* 177–86; R. F. O'Toole, *Bib* 62 [1981] 471–98). **12.** *the mount called Olivet:* This location and the "Bethany" of Luke 24:50 were contiguous and, in Luke's geography, interchangeable. The importance of Olivet in Jewish eschatology (cf. Zech 14:4) accounts for its belated mention in the wake of the parousia's evocation in v 11. *a sabbath journey's distance:* I.e., negligible (*ca.* ½ mi.). As in Luke 24:13, this relational geography promotes the impression of no real change of place. Jerusalem remains the theater of all the paschal events (Cadbury, *The Making,* 248; Lohfink, *Himmelfahrt* 207). **13.** According to the alternating pattern noted at v 2, the Eleven are reintroduced, but only by part of a reintroduction to the larger community surrounding them (vv 14,15). The list of names agrees with Luke 6:14–16 (cf. Mark 3:16–19), minus Judas and in a different order. Appearing first are three apostles about whom we shall hear more in Acts: Peter, John (3:1–11; 4:13,19; 8:14; 12:2), and James (12:2). **14.** The chapter's first section concludes with a summarizing statement portraying an ideally harmonious and prayerful community life (cf. Luke 24:53; → Luke, 43:198). *Homothymadon,* "of one accord," is a refrain in the summaries (2:46; 4:24; 5:12). The wider group around the Eleven harks back to Luke 23:49; 24:9–10,33. Of Jesus' mother and brothers we heard in Luke 8:19–21, though we shall hear no more of them in Acts, save for James, who will not be identified as a brother (cf. Gal 1:19). In view of the gift of the Spirit which they now await, this plenary assembly's prayer effectively illustrates Luke 11:13 (cf. Matt 7:11; see Schneider, *Apg.* 1. 207–8).

(Benoit, P., *Jesus and the Gospel* [NY, 1973] 1. 209–53. Brown, S., in *PerspLA* 99–111. Dillon, R., *From Eye-Witnesses to Ministers of the Word* [AnBib 82; Rome, 1978] 157–225. Dömer, *Heil* 94–122. Fitzmyer, J. A., "The Ascension of Christ and Pentecost," *TS* 45 [1984] 409–40. Grässer, E., *TRu* 42 [1977] 1–6. Kremer, J., *Pfingstbericht und Pfingstgeschehen* [SBS 63/4; Stuttgart, 1973] 179–90. Lake, K., in *Beginnings* 5. 1–7, 16–22. Lohfink, G., *Die Himmelfahrt Jesu* [SANT 26; Munich, 1971]. Pesch, R., "Der Anfang der Apostelgeschichte," *EKKNT Vorarbeiten 3* [Zurich, 1971] 9–35. Van der Horst, P., "Hellenistic Parallels to the Acts . . . 1:1–26," *ZNW* 74 [1983] 17–26. Van Stempvoort, P., "The Interpretation of the Ascension in Luke and Acts," *NTS* 5 [1958–59] 30–42. Wilson, *Gentiles* 88–107; "The Ascension," *ZNW* 59 [1968] 269–81.)

18   (B) The Restoration of the Twelve (1:15–26). The pericope has two components, deftly interwoven: a tradition about the death of Judas (vv 18–20), of which see the variants in Matt 27:3–10 and a Papias fragment quoted by Apollinaris of Laodicea (*SQE* 470), and an account of the selection of Judas's successor in the circle of the Twelve (vv 23–26). Comparison with Matt and Papias shows that the two elements were not combined before Luke's writing (*pace* M. Wilcox, *NTS* 19 [1972–73] 452; cf. Holtz, *Untersuchungen* 46; Weiser, *Apg.* 64–65). The linkage between the traditions is effected by the two citations of Pss in v 20, which were

announced in v 16 but delayed for the updating of Judas's tragic story. Peter's discourse (vv 16–22) accomplishes the merger of the two stories and gives us a first example of an Acts discourse, properly speaking. Its instruction for the reader is focused on vv 21–22, which state the Lucan theology of the apostolate. **15.** *in those days:* The episode is carefully located between the ascension and Pentecost and can therefore be expected to affect the all-important continuity between the periods delimited by those events. Cf. the same time notice in other election scenes (Luke 6:12; Acts 6:1). *Peter stood up:* The ptc. *anastas,* a LXX-style pleonasm, often signals the beginning of a speech (13:16; 15:7; cf. *statheis,* 2:14). Peter's prompt accession to leadership is related to Jesus' mandate in Luke 22:32 (cf. Dietrich, *Petrusbild* [→ 19 below] 173–74). *together:* The phrase *epi to auto,* "in the same place," "in unity," is part of a tissue of mimetic (LXX) expressions in this verse, including *anastas, en mesǭ, onoma* as person. *one hundred and twenty persons:* The number can scarcely be accidental, considering the number of twelve to be restored. Even if Luke is not thinking of ancient Israel's "leaders of tens" (Exod 18:12; 1 Macc 3:55), the tenfold structure of the apostolic assembly around its leaders recalls the relationship of the Twelve to the wider circle of disciples when they were first chosen (Luke 6:17). Luke must be demonstrating the continuation of the chosen twelve tribes (Lohfink, *Sammlung* 72; E. Grässer, *TRu* 42 [1977] 8–9), just as when he has Peter "with the Eleven" (2:14) address "the whole house of Israel" (2:36). **16.** *my brothers:* The assembly's character of brotherhood is reinforced, as is the cross-reference to Luke 22:32. The vocative *andres* with pl. substantives in apposition is a stylistic hallmark of the Acts discourses. *the Scripture had to be fulfilled: Dei,* "it is necessary," in Luke combines the Gk sense of fated necessity with the biblical conviction of a personal God's irresistible and unconditional control of events. David's authorship and the impf. *edei* point to the psalm text in v 20a (Ps 69:26), not, however, to Ps 109:8 in v 20b, whose fulfillment is still to come (Dupont, *Études* 318–19). After the parenthesis of v 17, the actual events that fulfilled Ps 69:26 are related in vv 18–19. But that psalm verse could not stand alone as David's prophecy since it would leave the impression that the vacant place could never be filled; thus the addition to it (*kai*) of Ps 109:8, which generates a new "necessity" unexpressed in *edei.* This will require the quick *dei oun* of v 21, forging a partnership of *edei* (v 16) and *dei* (v 21) matching the combination of texts in v 20 and the fusion of Judas and Matthias episodes in the pericope (Dömer, *Heil* 126). All this bespeaks compositional plan, not haphazard splicing of traditions (Dupont, *Études* 315). **17.** *for he was numbered among us:* Cf. Luke 22:3 (Mark 14:10). The *hoti* is causal, supporting the application of the Davidic Scripture to Judas and his property, whereas the actual citation of the Scripture is postponed in favor of our reintroduction to Judas and his tragedy. **18.** *falling headlong:* No rare meaning for *prēnēs* need be sought. Papias has *prēstheis,* "swollen" (cf. 28:6); but then, his version extravagantly develops the traitor's loathsome condition at death. At work in all versions, of course, is the popular imagination of condign endings for infamous lives. Cf. 12:23; 2 Macc 9:7–12; Wis 4:19(!); Sir 10:9–18; Josephus, *Ant.* 17.6.5 § 168–70 (Herod); *J.W.* 7.11.4 § 451–53; *Beginnings* 5. 29–38; Benoit, *Jesus* 1. 193–95. **19.** *in their own language:* Is anything else needed to show that Peter's words are informing Luke's readers rather than the apostle's hearers? *Akeldama:* The Gk form transliterates an Aram name *ḥāqēl-dĕmā'* (→ Matthew, 42:158), whose etiology here is based on Judas's death on the property, not its purchase with the betrayal money (Matt). The "blood" in question is that of the betrayer; in Matt, that of the betrayed. **20.** The first psalm text was found among the curses of his enemies by the suffering righteous one of Ps 69, a composition elsewhere influential in the passion tradition (the vinegar drink). Pre-Lucan tradition had altered the wording to fit the single enemy and his purchased property (MT: an abandoned campsite of pl. enemies), with the assistance of the LXX version (Haenchen, *Acts* 161) or without it (E. Nellessen, *BZ* 19 [1975] 215–16). *his superintendency:* Ps 109:8 LXX offered the scriptural rationale for Judas's replacement in the apostolate (*episkopē*). This text may have been associated with an original Matthias tradition, just as its partner was with the Judas tradition (E. Nellessen, *BZ* 19 [1975] 217); otherwise Luke added it as a *ductus* from Judas's fate to Matthias's accession (Schneider, *Apg.* 1. 214–15).

19   21. The Election of Matthias. *one of the men who accompanied us:* G. Klein's oft-quoted characterization of vv 21–22, the "Magna Charta of the apostleship of the Twelve" (*Die zwölf Apostel* [FRLANT 59; Göttingen, 1961] 204), attributes too much of the standardized apostle concept to Luke's invention (Haenchen, *Acts* 124–25) and assumes that his concern was mainly to define the source of church authority and tradition. Although Paul could not have claimed the status of apostle if Luke's norm prevailed in his time, Luke neither initiated the restriction to Jesus' earthly companions (cf. Mark 3:14; 6:7,30; Matt 10:2; Rev 21:14) nor does he work very hard to suppress Paul's claim (cf. 14:4,14). His purpose is different: to demonstrate in the twelvefold apostolate the precise continuity between Jesus' and the church's claims upon "the whole house of Israel" (2:36; cf. vv 2,15 above; Lohfink, *Sammlung* 77–84). Jesus' "comings and goings" with the Twelve involved the fateful journey to Jerusalem as a framework for "all that he did in the territory of the Jews" (10:39), following the law that governed the fate of all Israel's prophets (Luke 13:33–35 [cf. Matt 23:37–39]). That is why those certain men who "journeyed up with him from Galilee to Jerusalem" qualify to be "his witnesses to the people" (13:31 – Paul's sermon!), summoning them to repentance (10:41–43) under risk of their murderous opposition to all prophets (7:51–52). **22.** *beginning from:* The delimitation of Jesus' earthly ministry will be recognized as a condensing cross-reference to vv 1–5. *witness of his resurrection:* Parallelism with 13:31 suggests that we might measure this phrase by "witnesses to the people" there. Luke's prerequisite for an Easter *martys* (cf. 1 Cor 15:15), viz., total exposure to Jesus' earthly works, shows that this cannot be primarily an eyewitness testimony of the resurrection as fact, but rather a vouching for the identification of the risen Christ with the earthly Jesus (Roloff, *Apg.* 33–34; Schneider, *Apg.* 1. 225), and this by a comprehensive reenactment of Jesus' embattled mission "to the people" of Israel (Dömer, *Heil* 135–36). "Witness" as embodiment of the risen *Christus praesens* makes possible the term's later application to Stephen (22:20) and Paul (22:15; 26:16) under accusation by the Jews. **23.** Of neither candidate do we hear anywhere else in the NT. The very specific information about Joseph Barsabbas (Palestinian tradition) tricks the reader into expecting his election! **24–25.** The prayer, like the one in 4:24–30, carries the author's argument under a garnishment of venerable formulas, such as "knower of all hearts" (cf. 15:8; *Beginnings* 4. 15). *the place:* The nuance of locality strengthens the ironic counterpoint between the office Judas vacated and the ill-fated "territory" he acquired in exchange for it. *this ministry and apostolate:* The *kai* is epexegetical as the language of v 17 is echoed. Apostleship as *diakonia* (1 Cor 12:5,28; Eph 4:11–12),

however, is not yet ecclesiastical office. The basic "service" of the Twelve is the "ingathering of Israel," which Jesus had begun and which their own number prophetically symbolized (Lohfink, *Sammlung* 79). **26.** *they gave in lots for them:* This was no casting of votes, for "it is God who is choosing" via the incalculable lots (Haenchen, *Acts* 162). Cf. the OT institution in Lev 16:7–10; G. Lohfink, *BZ* 19 (1975) 247–49. *with the eleven apostles:* The anachronism becomes apparent in a reading of 1 Cor 15:5–8.

(Benoit, *Jesus* 1. 189–207. Dietrich, W., *Das Petrusbild der lukanischen Schriften* [Stuttgart, 1972] 166–94. Dömer, *Heil* 122–38. Dupont, *Études* 309–20. Holtz, *Untersuchungen* 43–48. Lake, K., in *Beginnings* 5. 22–30. Nellessen, E., "Tradition und Schrift in der Perikope von der Erwählung des Mattias," *BZ* 19 [1975] 205–18; *Zeugnis für Jesus und das Wort* [Bonn, 1976] 128–78. Wilcox, M., "The Judas-Tradition in Acts 1,15–26," *NTS* 19 [1972–73] 438–52.)

20   (II) The Mission in Jerusalem (2:1–5:42). (A) The Appeal to Israel (2:1–3:26).
    (a) THE PENTECOST EVENT (2:1–13). The bestowal of the Spirit upon the first community takes the form of a vivid scene that furnishes a splendid example of Luke's "dramatic episode" historiography (Plümacher, *Lukas* 107–8). Pentecost presses the question of the historical foundation of these episodes since neither the miracle of the tongues nor the chronological distance of the outpouring of the Spirit from Easter (cf. John 20:22!) is supported by any other NT author. The quest for a historical kernel often fastens on the ostensibly dual signification of *glōssai*, "tongues," now glossolalia, or ecstatic speech "in tongues" (vv 12–13; cf. 1 Cor 14:23), now *xenolalia*, or intelligible speech in foreign "tongues" (vv 4,6–11), the two senses possibly coinciding with two stages of the story's development (so Trocmé, Lohse, Grundmann; Dömer, *Heil* 139–42; Weiser, *Apg.* 81, 86). Other scholars reverse this picture and hold that Luke reinterpreted a foreign-language miracle in terms of glossolalia (G. Kretschmar, *ZKG* 66 [1954–55] 236; Roloff, *Apg.* 38–39). J. Kremer thinks of an older story of polyglot preaching (vv 1–4) reinterpreted by Luke as a prolepsis of the universal mission (vv 5–13; see *Pfingstbericht* [→ 17 above] 165–66, 262–63). Consequently, neither the tradition history nor the historicity of the narrative can be considered settled questions, though it remains plausible that the Pentecost after Jesus' death saw the very first stroke of the apostolic mission, marked by the enthusiastic Spirit phenomena known from other early Christian sources and first given the character of a miraculous preaching "in other tongues" by Luke (Schneider, *Apg.* 1. 245).
    1. *when the day was fulfilled:* The sg. "day" distorts the usual LXX formula in which the pl. "days" signifies a period of waiting now ended (Gen 25:24; Lev 8:33; Jer 25:12; Luke 2:6; 9:51). In view of these comparisons, the present phrase cannot mean merely the conclusion of the festival period (*pace* Haenchen, Conzelmann, Schneider) but must mean that the awaited "day" of the prophets' forecast (vv 17–21) and the Master's promise (1:5–8; Luke 24:49) has come to pass. Awkward as it is, the formula introducing the festival dating declares a salvation event of the highest importance to be at hand, "the actual turning point at which the true Israel begins to separate itself from unbelieving Jewry to become the church" (Lohfink, *Sammlung* 83–84). To demonstrate this, Luke will assemble a vast representation of "all Israel" to hear the apostles (vv 5–11,14, 36), standing in direct continuity with the constituency of the earthly Jesus (Luke 6:17; 19:47–48; 20:1; 21:37–38). The pathos of fulfilled expectation has thus been engendered by an editorial

continuum between the Gospel and Acts. *the Pentecost:* Considering the importance of this annual pilgrimage festival in Judaism, the presence of Jesus' disciples in Jerusalem on the Pentecost after his death is historically quite plausible. The Gk name of the feast means "fif-tieth," expressing its distance in days from the "Un-leavened Bread"/Passover, which was the first agrarian pilgrimage of the year. The Hebr names were *ḥaqqāṣîr,* "the (grain) harvest" (Exod 23:16), and *ḥag šābū'ôt,* the "feast of weeks" (Exod 34:22; cf. Lev 23:15), and it received the historical rationale of the gift of the land in Deut 26:1-11 (→ Institutions, 76:130-32). Of the earliest Christian associations of the feast, we know only that Paul knew of the observance in the Diaspora (1 Cor 16:8), not necessarily that Pauline Christians celebrated it with a content of their own (Kremer, *Pfingstbericht* [→ 17 above] 23). Nor does 20:16 demonstrate more than Luke's concern to present Paul as an observant Jew. Luke's story could, indeed, rest upon the factual basis of an inaugural mission event on this festival (so Kretschmar, Menoud, Lohse; Roloff, *Apg.* 39); but some insist that Luke invented the dating, based on his 40-day period of Easter appearances (Haenchen, *Acts* 173-74; Dömer, *Heil* 152-53). Beyond these simplest alterna-tives, there is the difficult question of a Pentecost sym-bolism, based on Jewish interpretations of the feast, which might have influenced the telling of the "tongues" story, if not an invention of the dating. In fact, this annual celebration of the promised land did shift to a commemoration of the giving of the law on Sinai among the rabbis of the 2d cent. (see E. Lohse, in *TDNT* 6. 48-49); this may be related to echoes of Sinai traditions that many discern in vv 2-3 (Dupont, *Salvation* 35-45; but cf. Schneider, *Apg.* 1. 245-47). However, that new content of the festival, partially rehearsed in sectarian writings (*Jub.* 6:17-21; QL), probably came too late to explain the Christian Pentecost, throwing us back on an actual mission experience as its likelier basis (Kremer, *Pfingstbericht* 261-64). Closer to Luke is Eph 4:8 (= *Tg. Ket.* Ps. 68:19, differing from the MT), applying the Sinai ascent of Moses to Jesus' ascension and gifts of the Spirit (Eph 4:9-16). Such christological appropriation of Sinai tradition implies that Luke might not have invented the sequence of the ascension and the outpouring of the Spirit (G. Kretschmar, *ZKG* 66 [1954-55] 216-22; Kremer, *Pfingstbericht* [→ 17 above] 232). *all together in the same place:* 120 people (1:15) in the same "house" (v 2)? **2-3.** Parallel sentences, articulated in biblical-style para-taxis, depict a theophany of the Spirit with striking resemblance to the theophany marking the gathering of Israel in Isa 66:15-20 LXX. With storm wind and fire (1:5) the heavenly origin of the Spirit is expressed, and with the fire's division, its destination in all members of the assembly. For related traditions of the Sinai theoph-any (Exod 19:16), see Philo, *De dec.* 33, 46; Str-B 2. 604-5; Conzelmann, *Apg.* 32-33. **4.** *filled with the holy Spirit:* The reality cloaked by the physical imagery of vv 2-3 ("like" . . . "as if") now comes to direct expression. The Spirit in the pre-Lucan story was surely the charis-matic power of early Christian enthusiasm (1 Cor 12-14), source of miracles and ecstasies, of wondrous insight and exalted speech, wholly recognizable in the religious environment of late Hellenism (Kremer, *Pfingst-bericht* [→ 17 above] 72-77). Luke himself does not con-centrate on this feature of the Spirit (*pace* Roloff, *Apg.* 42; cf. Bovon, *Luc* 253) but broadens it into a comprehen-sive expression of the dynamism of the mission (4:8,31; 6:10; 8:29,39; 10:19-20; 11:12; 13:2-4; 20:22-23; 21:4, 11). The Spirit will be the principal mover of the event which opens the church to the uncircumcised (10:19; 11:12), and the apostles' confident belief in this is

remarkably expressed in their decree in 15:28. As against the "absentee-Christology" theorists who make the Spirit Christ's surrogate on earth (Schmithals, *Apg.* 24; E. Grässer, *TRu* 42 [1977] 13), one should recall that the Spirit as the driving force of the mission is a continuum between the ministries of Jesus (Luke 3:22; 4:1,18; 10:21; Acts 1:2) and the apostles, not something that begins upon his departure (G. W. MacRae, *Int* 27 [1973] 160-61). Moreover, 16:6-7 identifies "the holy Spirit" and "the Spirit of Jesus" in parallel statements, coherently with the kerygma that the exalted One himself pours forth the Spirit (2:33). The Pentecost tradition may thus be taken to express the belief that the miracle of the tongues inaugurated the discourse of the heavenly Kyrios through his witnesses (cf. 26:22-23; Kremer, *Pfingstbericht* [→ 17 above] 267; Franklin, *Christ the Lord* [→ 5 above] 46; R. F. O'Toole, *Bib* 62 [1981] 484-86). *in other tongues:* The content of the miraculous speech is given first in v 11: "the mighty works of God," the same as when the Gentile converts speak "in tongues" in 10:46 (*megalynontōn ton theon*). Because 10:46 and 19:6, where speaking "in tongues" is equated with prophesying, both refer to Pentecost, they confirm Luke's consistent inter-est in reinterpreting the "tongues" prompted by the Spirit in terms of inspired and intelligible preaching of the Word (Dömer, *Heil* 141; Kremer, *Pfingstbericht* [→ 17 above] 122). It is conceivable that Luke's outlook had been influenced by Paul's critique of the glossolalia in 1 Cor 14:2-19, comparing their incomprehensible sounds unfavorably with the edifying words of proph-ecy. This view would have sanctioned a reinterpretation of the ecstatic experience of the first Pentecost in terms of its lasting significance: the inauguration of a mission that would cross all language barriers.

21 5. *Jews . . . from every nation:* A startling change of scene from the "house" to some unnamed arena where this vast throng could gather signals the shift of argu-ment from the theophany to its effects. The reference is to foreign-born Jews who have returned to reside in Jerusalem (*katoikountes*), and their ethnic universality (vv 9-11) portends "the ingathering of Israel from their dis-persion amongst all the nations" (Kremer, *Pfingstbericht* [→ 17 above] 131). The originality of *Ioudaioi* in the text should not be doubted (*pace* E. Güting, *ZNW* 66 [1975] 162-63); there can be no question yet of any mission to Gentiles in Luke's linear schema. "Both Jews and pros-elytes" are included (v 11). 6. *they were bewildered:* The miracle, therefore, is not understood as one of hearing; the Spirit is in the speakers. *each in his own language:* *Dialektos* is the language of a people or region (1:19; 21:40; 22:2; 26:14); hence the adj. *idia,* "one's own" (vv 6,8). 7. *they were beside themselves:* A crescendo of crowd reaction, moving from the bewilderment of v 6 over parallel statements in vv 7-8,12, shows that the whole second paragraph of this story expands on the typical choral conclusion of a miracle story (cf. Luke 4:36; 5:26; 7:16; Kremer, *Pfingstbericht* [→ 17 above] 138, 164-65). *Galileans:* The awestruck observers speak at some length (vv 7-11) and, by recognizing the homeland of the poly-glot preachers, they reaffirm for us the geographic origin of the apostolic testimony (13:31; Luke 23:5) even as they foreshadow its universal destination. **9-11.** The list of their nationalities is put right on the lips of the marveling crowd, as befits the "dramatic episode" style. The list itself is a puzzle, amazing for "what it includes, and even more (for) what it omits" (Dupont, *Salvation* 57). The absence of regions where much of the Acts story will unfold, e.g., Syria and Cilicia, Macedonia and Achaia, accounts for the *opinio communis* that Luke did not originate it himself (but cf. E. Güting, *ZNW* 66 [1975] 169). Indeed, the inscrutable combination of countries, provinces, and ethnic groups suggests a stylized catalogue long in use, no doubt serviceable for its broad sweep from E to W (Haenchen, *Acts* 169-70). Its original conception cannot be retrieved (cf. attempts by Conzelmann, Güting; J. Brinkman, *CBQ* 25 [1963] 418-27), though its Lucan application is unmistakable. The strange additions of "Judea" (v 9) and "Jews and proselytes" (v 11) will best be credited to the author, who thus keeps in focus the original destination of the apostolic preaching to "the whole house of Israel" (v 36), even as he allows the ultimate universality of the mission to be foreshadowed (Kremer, *Pfingstbericht* [→ 17 above] 154-56). *settlers from Rome:* A point at which Luke perhaps breaks through the confines of the older list, expanding his horizons to his (Conzelmann, *Apg.* 31). *Cretans and Arabs:* As a conclusion to the list: "westernmost and easternmost," maybe; or "isle and continent"? **13.** *others mocking:* A part of the crowd nurtures a different reaction (cf. 17:32; 28:24). This division of a Jewish audience is already programmatic of all Israel's encounters with the kerygma (28:24). Since this misunderstanding, with the perplexed question of v 12, builds a bridge between the narrative and the discourse (v 15), it more likely originated at Luke's hand than in the older tradition (see I. Broer, *BibLeb* 13 [1972] 273; but cf. Dörner, *Heil* 140).

22 (b) THE PENTECOST SERMON (2:14-41). The first of the "missionary discourses" to Jews illustrates their typical outline (→ 7 above): (1) an introduction relating the sermon to the narrative framework (vv 14-21); (2) the Jesus kerygma, framed as an accusation of the audience, replete with arguments from Scripture (vv 22-36); (3) a call for repentance and conversion based on the kerygma (vv 38-39). Argumentation from Scripture already functions in the first part here, with Joel 3:1-5 LXX forming "the carefully placed and aptly chosen link joining situation and sermon" (Wilckens, *Missionsreden* 34). The elaborate exegesis which the Joel text receives in the framework of the Lucan Pentecost furnishes a key ingredient of the argument of Acts—hence, gives us a showcase example of Luke's art of composition (Zehnle, *Discourse* [→ 28 below] 123-31). Moreover, since no form of this discourse ever existed without its arguments from Scripture, the fact that all of them depend on the LXX version (e.g., *Kyrios* in vv 21,36) proves that the sermon was first conceived and composed in Greek (Conzelmann, *Apg.* 33). **14.** *with the Eleven:* The Twelve represent the gospel's claim on Israel (1:21); and all Israel (v 36), including the Jews of the Diaspora, is to be confronted with the apostolic kerygma (Lohfink, *Sammlung* 49). The "ingathering of Israel" is under way, prefigured in the Gospel's introduction to the Sermon on the Plain (Luke 6:17 [cf. Mark 3:7-8]) by the same concentric gathering around the Twelve. *all who dwell in Jerusalem:* Not a different group from "Jewish men," but rather stressing "the Jerusalem connection" between the audiences of Jesus and the apostles (Lohfink, *Sammlung* 47-48). "All Israel" is globally represented by its capital, as in Luke 13:34-35. This is the public that will be accused of murdering its Messiah (vv 23,36; 13:27-28); but it is also the selfsame public that left the crucifixion scene ready for repentance (Luke 23:48, added at Mark 15:39), and that is what really counts toward the denouement of this Pentecost (vv 37-41). **15-16.** For the observers' misunderstanding as a "lead-in" to Acts discourses, see 3:12; 14:15; also 4:9; 17:20, 22-23; E. Schweizer, in *StLA* 211, 214.

23 **17-21.** Joel 3:1-5 LXX, including the formula identifying the quoted words as God's own (cf. Ellis, *Prophecy* [→ 28 below] 182-87), contains a threefold affirmation pertinent to the event at hand: (1) the eschatological outpouring of the Spirit, which begets a generalized charism of prophecy; (2) cosmic signs of "the Day of the Lord" before its dawning; (3) the arrival of that day, with salvation for all who call upon the name *Kyrios.* A most important guide to the author's intentions is the series of alterations he (or his source?) has made in the quoted text to produce a pertinent testimony (cf. Rese, *Motive* 46-55; Holtz, *Untersuchungen* 5-14). *in the last days:* This phrase replaces the simple "afterwards" (*meta tauta*) of the LXX in all but a few mss. (including B), but it only makes the prophecy more plainly the eschatological vision it already was (cf. v 18, "in those days"). No recent commentary endorses Haenchen's preference for the LXX phrasing (*Acts* 179); the copyists' reflex to restore the latter makes the option for the novel wording methodologically inescapable (Kränkl, *Jesus* 190-91). "The last days" are understood in the expanded sense of a "time of the church" (cf. 1:6-8) rather than narrowly the "turn of the age" (cf. 2 Tim 3:1; 2 Pet 3:3; Schneider, *Apg.* 1. 268; E. Grässer, in *Les Actes* [ed. J. Kremer] 119-22). The dramatic act of salvation by the *Kyrios* (v 21) is interpreted in terms of the outpouring of the Spirit (v 33), which empowers the mission (v 4) and enacts conversions (vv 38-39). **18.** *they shall prophesy:* Luke adds this phrase to Joel 3:2 *in fine,* and it is no mere mechanical repetition (*pace* Holtz) but represents a special Lucan interest, even though it is not explicitly enlarged upon in the sermon (Schneider, *Apg.* 1. 269; Roloff, *Apg.* 53). The prophet status of Jesus' witnesses is never more than obliquely affirmed in Luke-Acts, but neither is the risen Lord's status as a prophet like Moses (3:22-26; 7:37; Luke 24:19), and yet that is a most important ingredient of Luke's theory of the necessity of the passion (Luke 13:33) and the nature of Jesus' earthly ministry (Luke 4:18-30; *pace* Bovon, *Luc* 193). The fact that the apostolic mission is part of the eschatological prophecy of Jesus himself will be brought out through the exegesis of Deut 18:15-16 in the Temple sermon (3:22-26), illustrating the very close partnership of the two sermons. **19.** *wonders . . . and signs:* The words "signs," "above," and "below" are added to the Joel text, and this touch is closely related to the accentuation of the witnesses' prophecy just added v 18. This interpolated wording produces the biblical formula "wonders and signs" (usually in reverse order), which signified the accreditation of the prophet (Deut 13:1-3) in which no Israelite had ever rivaled Moses (Deut 34:10-12; cf. F. Stolz, "Zeichen und Wunder," *ZTK* 69 [1972] 125-44). The formula, in word order prompted by the edited prophecy, is given punctual application to the ministries of Jesus and the apostles by the context (vv 22,43; Weiser, *Apg.* 92), as Luke cumulatively instructs his readers concerning the apostles' collaboration with their risen Lord in prophetic wonder-working (cf. also Stephen, 6:8; Paul, 14:3; 15:12; Moses, 7:36). "Above" and "below" include the Pentecost event itself in this continuing thaumaturgy of the Spirit. **21.** *the name Lord:* The bearer of this name will be declared in v 36, based on God's actions through him (vv 22-35), whereupon "shall be saved" will be interpreted in terms of baptism, forgiveness, and the gift of the Spirit in vv 38-39.

24 **22-24.** The Jesus kerygma is the central component of the missionary discourse schema. The discursive climax of that schema is uniformly the call (or announcement) of repentance (Dibelius, *Studies* 111, 165; Wilckens, *Missionsreden* 54; Zehnle, *Discourse* [→ 28 below] 35-36), and that explains the puzzling grammatical structure of the statement at hand. It has one main clause ("you killed . . . this Jesus") and several subordinates, including the resurrection statement in merely a rel. cl. (v 24). The sentence as a whole, therefore, works as an accusation of the audience, citing the antithesis of their murderous action and the divine attestation (*apodedeigmenon*) toward the same Jesus. This basic declaration of Jewish guilt is a mainstay of the missionary sermons to Jews (3:13b–15a; 4:10–11; 5:30; 10:39–40; 13:27–30), but it is not the message they convey to the reader. The collision of divine and human actions in Jesus is rather in complete accord with God's plan attested in the Scriptures — hence the extended argumentation of vv 25–35 — and works consistently to motivate the speaker's concluding invitation to or announcement of penance and forgiveness (vv 38–39; 3:19–26; 5:31; 10:42–43; 13:38–41; Wilckens, *Missionsreden* 119). The kerygma of the discourses is therefore neither a rehearsal of the actual preaching of the earliest days nor the burden of the instruction Luke is giving his reader. Its function is strictly historiographic: to make intelligible "the procedure of the apostles' preaching as the decisive historical fact which got church history under way" (Plümacher, *Lukas* 35); and specifically here to demonstrate how the church's first membership was recruited from "all Israel," summoned to be unburdened of the very guilt of their Savior's death. **22.** *which God did through him:* The overall concern to show history under God's sovereign direction at its every turn (1:7) creates a "subordinationist" idiom in the discourses (Conzelmann, *TSL* 173–76), which is one of their most persistent features. **23.** *by the definite plan and foreknowledge:* The Lucan semantics of salvation history favors words with the prefix *pro-* to express God's antecedent disposition of events (1:16; 3:18,20; 4:28; 10:41; 13:24; 22:14; 26:16). God's foreordination of Jesus' death does not diminish the people's guilt; rather, by disguising the salvation process as nonsalvation, it asserts God's sovereignty in dialectical independence of human designs, triumphing through them rather than despite them. This draws out the sense of the "passion secret," so markedly developed in Luke's editing of Mark's passion formulas (esp. Luke 22:22 [cf. Mark 14:21]; see H. Flender, *St. Luke* [Phl, 1967] 30–35). Absent, of course, is any suggestion of the expiating or sacrificial significance of Jesus' death, and many generalize this as a hallmark of Lucan soteriology (cf. Cadbury, *The Making* 280; P. Vielhauer, in *StLA* 45; Conzelmann, *TLS* 201). The context of accusation, however, in which the death of Jesus partakes of his definitive prophecy in Israel (Luke 13:33; 24:19–20), is not particularly congenial to the redemption motif, which was not employed in the Marcan passion formulas either (save Mark 10:45 [cf. Luke 22:27]). **24.** *raised up:* The trans. *anistanai* (v 32; 13:33–34; 17:31), rather than the traditional *egeirein*, "arouse" (3:15; 4:10; 5:30; 10:40; 13:30,37), is an Acts property, related, perhaps, to the Marcan usage of the intrans. forms (Wilckens, *Missionsreden* 138–40), more palpably to Deut 18:15 LXX, explained in 3:22–26. *having loosed the pangs of death:* This Septuagintalism (Pss 18:5; 116:3) is derived from the Hebr "cords of death," *concretum per abstractum* (A. Schmitt, *BZ* 17 [1973] 244–45); the same translation policy will explain "corruption" at v 27 (Ps 16:10). Contemporary Jewish usage gave *ōdines*, "pangs," the connotation of the messianic woes (Mark 13:8; Matt 24:8; 1 Thess 5:3). **25** **25–31.** Proof from Scripture: Ps 16:8–11 LXX (cf. A. Schmitt, *BZ* 17 [1973] 229–48; D. Juel, *CBQ* 43 [1981] 543–56). The same basic argument from the psalm occurs here and in 13:34–37, Paul's sermon; nor is the psalm cited elsewhere in the NT. Remarkable liberties were taken by the Gk translator with the original Hebrew: *proorōmēn*, "I saw before(hand)," renders *šiwwîtî*, "I put"; *ep' elpidi*, "in hope," for Hebr *lābeṭaḥ*, "securely"; *diaphthora*, "corruption," for *šaḥat*, "hole/pit."

A systematic readjustment of the prayer to the prospect of the worshiper's immortality thus took place under the translator's pen (Schmitt), making the LXX version indispensable to Peter's argument. Use of the psalm as a resurrection testimony thus probably began among Greek-speaking apologists (Dupont, *Salvation* 147), just as it functions here in an argument devised by a Greek-language author. **25.** *David says:* The Jewish tradition that David wrote all the psalms (cf. 1:16) and the divine pledge of his everlasting dynasty (2 Sam 7:12–16) play a key role in the Scripture proofs of the Lucan kerygma (cf. v 30; 13:22–23,32–37; R. F. O'Toole, *JBL* 102 [1983] 245–58). The consecutive logic of *gar* involves vv 22–24, not the resurrection statement alone, since what is argued is not the fact of the resurrection but, as the conclusion of v 36 requires, the fact that the crucified and risen Jesus is really the Messiah whose voice is heard in the psalm (cf. vv 29–31; Dupont, *Salvation* 109). **26.** *my flesh shall dwell in hope:* "Flesh," which meant earthly human beings in their totality to the psalmist, meant only the transitory part of humans to the translator; and "soul," equivalent to the personal pronoun in Hebrew, involved the human component destined for immortality in Gk anthropology. Thus, the psalmist's "securely," motivated by rescue from a premature death, shifts to the Gk "in hope," implying even a future prospect for the "flesh" (A. Schmitt, *BZ* 17 [1973] 237). In Peter's sermon, it is the Messiah who expresses this hope, based on the assurance expressed in v 27. **27.** *to see corruption:* "Corruption" for "pit" was not a translator's mistake, any more than *ōdines* in v 24; it was an abstract substitution for the concrete Hebr idiom, necessary for the latter to be intelligible to the Gk reader. **29.** The grave of David (1 Kgs 2:10; Josephus, *Ant.* 7.15.3 §392–93; *J.W.* 1.2.5 §61) disqualifies the patriarch from being the reference point of his own messianic testimony (cf. 2:34–35; 8:30–35; 13:35–37). **30.** *prophet that he was:* David was never called a "prophet" in the OT; but cf. 11QPs^a 27:11; Josephus, *Ant.* 6.8.2 §166 (J. A. Fitzmyer, *CBQ* 34 [1972] 332–39). As a prophet, David could speak for the Messiah, perhaps as a type of the latter (M. Rese, in *Les Actes* [ed. J. Kremer] 76). Cf. the use of Ps 16 with a different Davidic catena in 13:33–37. *set one of his descendants:* The trans. *kathisai* coheres with God's action as subj. in vv 32, 36 and matches the pass. *hypsōtheis*, "exalted," in v 33 (cf. Eph 1:20). For the "oath" in question, see Ps 132:11.

26 **32–36.** Kerygmatic summation. Having been interrupted by the scriptural argument in v 24, the resurrection kerygma is resumed and complemented by the witness formula (as in 3:15; 5:32) and the exaltation kerygma (as in 5:31; cf. 3:21). *witnesses of this:* Not, indeed, of the fact alone, but of the argument that has shown it to be the work of God in conformity with his promises recorded in the OT (cf. Luke 24:44–48). The "witnesses" thus carry forward the instruction of the earthly Jesus uninterrupted (see Luke 18:31–34 and comment on 1:22). **33.** *having been exalted:* This kerygmatic formula antedates Luke's writing (Phil 2:9; cf. Rom 8:34; Eph 1:20), but he has interpreted it in terms of Christ's bodily ascension (so v 34). The phrase "at God's right hand," derived from Ps 110:1 (v 35), employs the dat. locatively to designate the position of the king as God's viceroy in OT royal ideology. *having received the promise of the holy Spirit:* Cf. the same formula in Gal 3:14. In all events of the kerygma God remains the actor, Jesus his instrument (cf. v 22), who is now enabled to pour forth what he has received. This statement should therefore not be weighed against 10:38 or Luke 4:1,14. *he has poured out:* The verb establishes the empirical connection between the Pentecost event and the prophecy of Joel (vv 17,18). The pains taken to preserve both the theocentrism of the kerygma and the dominical action of the "outpouring" must be aimed at asserting the Lord's direct action in the apostles' mission. The Spirit is medium, not *Ersatz,* for the *Christus praesens* (Kränkl, *Jesus* 180–81; see comment on 2:4). **34.** *David did not ascend:* The same *via-negativa* argumentation as in vv 29–31 introduces the "locus classicus" for the exaltation kerygma (Wilckens, *Missionsreden* 152) and shows that Luke understands the traditional "exalted" in the new dimension of "ascended" (Lohfink, *Himmelfahrt* [→ 17 above] 228–29; Kränkl, *Jesus* 149–50). Peter's case is not that Ps 110:1 proves the exaltation, for that is now a matter of empirical evidence (v 33c); it is rather that the Exalted is the one whom Israel's prophet-king named *Kyrios* (cf. Mark 12:35–37 par.; Rese, *Motive* 62). The psalm citation brings the argument full circle from its beginnings with the saving *Kyrios*-name of Joel 3:5 (v 21), and we are fully prepared for the summation of v 36. **35.** *until I make your enemies:* These words of the psalm verse reintroduce Peter's audience, "the whole house of Israel" (v 36), grimly known to Luke's reader as violent adversary of all the prophets, including the Messiah (7:51–52; Luke 11:47–51; 13:33–35). **36.** *the whole house of Israel:* The "ingathering of Israel" has reached a decisive pass, and that Israel which now remains obstinate in rejecting Jesus will have lost its claim to the honorific title and status of God's people (Lohfink, *Sammlung* 55). *God has made both Lord and Messiah:* This summation perfectly coordinates the *Kyrios*-testimonies of Joel 3 and Ps 110 with the Messiah argument of Ps 16 (v 31). The reference of "God has made" is not to the proximate exaltation context alone (*pace* Kränkl, *Jesus* 159–63; Kremer, *Pfingstbericht* [→ 17 above] 175, 208), but to the whole series of divine actions introduced at v 22 (cf. 10:38; Wilckens, *Missionsreden* 36, 173; Rese, *Motive* 65–66). Here, as in v 22, the aor. *epoiēsen* is complexive, not punctual. The refrain of conflict between God's action and the people's execution was already struck in vv 22–23, and that sentence surely participates in the present summation. *whom you crucified:* When the speaker next calls for repentance (v 38), the attentive reader will remember Luke 23:48 (cf. Mark 15:39–40), where Luke had recorded the Jerusalem crowd's readiness for repentance after their collusion with their leaders in obtaining Jesus' crucifixion (Luke 23:4–23).

27 **37–41. Call for repentance and response. 37.** *they were cut to the heart:* The continuum with Luke 23:48 probably accounts for the audience initiative in place of a regular discursive conclusion of the sermon. This paragraph is nevertheless the precise target of the argumentation which began at v 14; and since it is historiographic, it requires mention of the preacher's success in recruiting the first baptized from Israel's ranks. Several reprises of the Joel prophecy in vv 38–40 confirm that the argument begun with the prophecy has here come to its plotted conclusion. **38.** *repent:* Like the OT prophets' reproaches, the apostles' accusation of "all Israel" bestirs the listeners to "dispositions of compunction leading to forgiveness" (Dupont, *Salvation* 69). Here, as also in Paul's preaching to the pagans (17:29–31), the kerygma awakens the consciousness of sin (cf. 3:17) and therewith the state of mind necessary for forgiveness (cf. 3:19; 5:31). *in the name of Jesus:* As a formula with *baptisthēnai,* with varying preposition (8:16; 10:48; 19:5), it is found only in Acts. Use of *epi* here is prompted by *epikalesētai,* "call upon," in v 21, showing that the formula has a confessional sense (Matt 28:19) rather than the Pauline

incorporative sense (Gal 3:27; Rom 6:4; → Pauline Theology, 82:119). *the gift of the holy Spirit:* Christian baptism and this gift (10:45; cf. 8:20; 11:17) are inseparable (1:5; 10:44–48; 11:15–16; 15:8), but for the "justified exceptions" (8:15–16; 19:2,6) which will bring out the indispensable mediation of the apostles and their tradition (Haenchen, *Acts* 184). **39.** *as many as the Lord our God summons:* This likely allusion to Joel 3:5b, which was excluded from the end of Peter's original quotation (v 21), strikes the theme of God's control over the young church's growth (vv 41,47), which will be illustrated repeatedly in the chapters to follow. It effects the only limitation on the offer of salvation to "all Israel" (cf. Roloff, *Apg.* 63). **40.** *be saved:* Here we observe, with yet another Joel reprise and the mimetic "from this perverse generation" (Deut 32:5; Ps 78:8), the process of separation between "the true Israel" and unbelieving Jewry that is still under way at the end of Acts (28:24–28). **41.** *about three thousand souls were added:* "Added" presumably to the 120 (1:15). The vb. *prosetethēsan* is a "theological passive" in view of vv 47,39b (cf. 5:14; 11:24; *ZBG* §236). The large number is historically implausible, more likely a round number dramatizing the extraordinary success of the Spirit-filled Pentecost mission (cf. 4:4; 21:20; Zingg, *Wachsen* 165–68).

28 (c) FIRST MAJOR SUMMARY (2:42–47). In the three major summaries (→ 9 above) a certain repetitive phraseology and overlapping of contents recall Luke's reworking of the Marcan summaries (cf. *Beginnings* 5. 397–98). Some contents of this passage seem, in fact, to anticipate the later points where they will be more pertinent: e.g., "fear" (v 43 = 5:11) and shared possessions (vv 44–45 = 4:32,34). The summaries of chaps. 4 and 5 together practically equal the content of the present one; and although individual elements of these passages derive from traditions Luke has used, he is finally to be recognized as their composer (Schneider, *Apg.* 1. 284). It clearly suits his purpose to have the most comprehensive summary here at the keynote position of his history. **42.** This compendium of the principal norms of church life incumbent upon the newly baptized probably reflects Luke's time. His portrayal of the first community as unwavering in all of them (*proskarterountes*) begins the pattern of idealization that marks all the summaries and attests the author's distance from his subject matter (Schneider, *Apg.* 1. 106). *the teaching of the apostles: Didachē* includes proclamation to outsiders (5:28; 13:12; 17:19), so this phrase is a generalization of the sermon just ended. Faithful continuity in *didachē* from Jesus to the apostles is one of the principal arguments of Luke-Acts (1:1–8; Luke 1:1–4). *common life: Koinōnia,* used only here in Luke's writing, but 13 times in Paul's, connotes the bond of responsibility for one another enjoined on believers by their assent to the gospel (2 Cor 8:4; 9:13; Gal 2:9–10). *breaking of the bread:* Originally the ritual opening of a festive Jewish meal, this was the gesture of the risen One at Emmaus (Luke 24:35) and recalls the earlier dominical instructions with bread-breaking as well (Luke 9:11–27; 22:14–38). We can consider the phrase a *terminus technicus* for the eucharist in Luke-Acts (with Weiser, *Apg.* 104–5). Cf. v 46; 20:7,11; 27:35. **43.** *many wonders and signs:* An effective transition to 3:1–11, but also a consolidation of the credentials of the eschatological prophecy (v 19 = Joel), in which his witnesses collaborate with the risen Lord (3:12,16). **44–45.** See comments on 4:34–37. **46.** *in the Temple:* Having served as Jesus' forum in Jerusalem, the Temple becomes the appropriate venue for the apostolic assembly (cf. Luke 2:27,49; 19:45; 22:53; 24:53). This principal institution of OT Judaism can be appropriated by Christians under the Twelve, along with the OT itself, as a powerful expression of Luke's continuity thesis. *having favor with all the people:* This "Jerusalem spring" is the setting for an initial success of the "ingathering of Israel." It will not last beyond the Stephen episode, when the people rejoin their leaders in murderous opposition to the witnesses (7:51–52), and thereupon Luke's story will concentrate on the hardening of Jewry against the kerygma (cf. Lohfink, *Sammlung* 95). *the Lord was adding* (cf. v 41): Like other "growth" notices, this one ends the literary unit to which it belongs (as 2:41; 4:4; 6:7; 9:31; 12:24; 19:20). The notices have the literary function of "inserting individual scenes and circumstances into the dynamic course of the gospel's spread," directed by an attentive and irresistible providence (Weiser, *Apg.* 106).

(Bovon, *Luc* 235–44. Broer, I., "Der Geist und die Gemeinde," *BibLeb* 13 [1972] 261–83. Chevallier, M., "Pentecôtes lucaniennes et 'Pentecôtes' johanniques," *RSR* 69 [1981] 304–14. Dömer, *Heil* 139–59. Dupont, *Salvation* 35–59. Ellis, E. E., *Prophecy and Hermeneutic in Early Christianity* [GR, 1978] 182–208. Grundmann, W., *SE II* 584–94. Grässer, E., *TRu* 42 (1977) 9–15. Güting, E., "Der geographische Horizont der sogenannte Völkerliste des Lukas," *ZNW* 66 [1975] 149–69. Kremer, *Pfingstbericht* [→ 17 above]. Lake, K., in *Beginnings* 5. 111–21. Lohse, E., *Die Einheit des Neuen Testaments* [Göttingen, 1973] 178–92. Marshall, I. H., "The Significance of Pentecost," *SJT* 30 [1977] 347–69. Menoud, P., "La Pentecôte lucanienne et l'histoire," *RHPR* 42 [1962] 141–47. Weiser, A., "Die Pfingstpredigt des Lukas," *BibLeb* 14 [1973] 1–12. Zehnle, R., *Peter's Pentecost Discourse* [SBLMS 15; Nash, 1971]. Zimmermann, H., "Die Sammelberichte der Apostelgeschichte," *BZ* 5 [1961] 71–82.)

29   (d) THE HEALING IN THE TEMPLE (3:1–11). The first miracle story of Acts has a clear connection with 2:43 and the prophetic thaumaturgy foreseen by Joel with the outpouring of the Spirit (2:19). Regular formal elements, familiar from the Synoptic stories, include the exposition (vv 1–5), healer's word and gesture (vv 6–7), demonstration of the cure (v 8), and effect upon the bystanders (vv 9–10). These traits suggest the story's origin in local (Jerusalem) tradition (Weiser, *Apg.* 107), while elements of symmetry between this event and healings of Jesus (Luke 5:17–26) and Paul (14:8–13) will have been supplied by Luke with the overall course of his history in mind (F. Neirynck, in *Les Actes* [ed. J. Kremer] 172–88). **1.** John's inactive presence, like Barnabas's in 14:12, may not be original to the story (cf. vv 6–7; Dibelius, *Studies* 14). Is he supplied by Luke as a second witness to the healing before the sanhedrin (4:20; Haenchen, *Acts* 201)? **2.** *the gate called the Beautiful:* This name appears in no Jewish source. Many scholars suggest that it was the Nicanor Gate, made of Corinthian bronze, probably separating the courts of the women and the Gentiles (Josephus, *Ant.* 15.11.5 §410–25; *J.W.* 5.5.2–5 §190–221). **6.** *in the name of Jesus Christ:* "Name" and "power" are parallel concepts (4:7); hence, Peter's invocation of Jesus' name gains him empowerment by the Lord to work the cure (cf. Mark 9:38–39 par. Luke 9:49–50; 10:17). The name is not a magical surrogate for Jesus subject to earthlings' control, but the medium of the heavenly Christ's direct action, granted only upon confession of faith in him (cf. 4:10; 3:16; G. W. MacRae, *Int* 27 [1973] 161–62; R. F. O'Toole, *Bib* 62 [1981] 488–90). **11.** *at the porch called Solomon's:* We recognize Luke's hand in the assembly of "the whole people" (= Israel!) before the apostles, and we may suspect that his faulty information about the Temple topography made him reckon the portico as part of the temenos (v 8; thus the "Western" *l.v.*—see *Beginnings* 3. 28–29).

30   (e) PETER'S TEMPLE SERMON (3:12–26). The Pentecost and Temple sermons are continuous and complementary, despite their different ingredients (Conzelmann, *Apg.* 39; F. Hahn, in *Les Actes* [ed. J. Kremer] 137–38). A clue to their relationship is the connection between the arguments from Scripture that frame their combined contents: the Joel prophecy beginning the first, and the deuteronomic promise of the prophet like Moses (Deut 18:15–16) concluding the second (vv 22–26; see R. Dillon, *NTS* 32 [1986] 544–56). The combined statement of these two scriptures forms a christological framework around the two sermons, declaring that the kerygma of the apostles represents the eschatological renewal of prophecy, and in it the voice of the risen Christ is heard as the awaited voice of Moses' successor. This framework of the eschatological prophecy also accommodates the accreditation of the Mosaic prophet by the healing miracle, which Peter emphatically attributes to his action in vv 12–16. This explanation includes the familiar kerygmatic schema contrasting God's and his people's actions toward his "servant" (vv 13–15); and once again the goal of the discourse is the call to repentance (vv 19–26), motivated by that contrast and confirmed by the argument from Deut, the only Scripture argument used in this sermon. — Outline of the sermon: (1) misunderstanding as *ductus*, v 12; (2) Easter kerygma honed to the situation, vv 13–16; (3) appeal for repentance and conversion, vv 17–21, reinforced by the argument from Moses' testimony, vv 22–26.

12. Misunderstanding as *ductus. men of Israel:* The audience is the "people" (*laos*, v 11), no distinction made between participants in Jesus' execution and any others (Schneider, *Apg.* 1. 319). *why do you marvel:* The misunderstanding to be corrected is, we might say, that of an "absentee christology." **13–16.** Easter kerygma. **13.** Hallowed titles of the OT Deity echo the revelation to Moses (Exod 3:6,15) and show that the speaker stands within Israel even as he bids it repent. The Exod echo already anticipates the Mosaic christology of the sermon's conclusion, and the latter may also have prompted the choice of titles, "servant" (v 13; cf. 4:26–27,30) and "leader" (v 15; cf. 5:31), as if to systematize and round off the Moses typology (Zehnle, *Discourse* [→ 28 above] 47–52). *has glorified his servant:* It is unusual that the exaltation kerygma should come first, before the passion, with an echo of the Isaian Servant's vindication (Isa 52:13); but this is so that the preacher can take up the experience of the miracle directly, in counterargument (with vv 13b–15) to v 12b. The "glorifying" is not the miracle itself (*pace* Haenchen, *Acts* 205), but Christ's entry into "glory" (Luke 24:26), the heavenly sphere whence mighty effects are wrought on earth (cf. 7:55; 22:11; Luke 9:31–32). *before Pilate, who had ruled for his release:* A precise cross-reference to Pilate's threefold declaration in Luke 23:15,20,22 (cf. Mark 15:12,14); cf. 13:28 and, *e contra*, 4:27. **14.** *the holy and just one:* These messianic titles, with their archaic ring, serve effectively the rhetoric of contrast between what God and the people had wrought. We now better understand the centurion's acknowledgment of "a just man" (Luke 23:46 [cf. Mark 15:39]), based on the "just man's" lamentation in Ps 31. For "the holy one," see 4:27,30; Mark 1:24; Luke 4:34; John 6:69. For "the just one," see 7:52; *1 Enoch* 38:2; 53:6; 1 Tim 3:16. **15.** *leader to life:* The gen. is of direction, in view of 26:23 and the Moses typology (cf. 7:35; Heb 12:2; BDF 166). "Life," as the goal to which Jesus opened the way for all (cf. 4:2; 17:31), contributes to the clashing terminology (vs. "killed," "dead") by which the accusation of the audience is orchestrated. **16.** *on the basis of faith in his name:* This overweighted sentence identifies the risen and exalted Servant with the agent of the miraculous deliverance witnessed by all.

Since faith in the healer is a healing-story commonplace we missed in vv 1-10, part of v 16 may be transposed from the pre-Lucan narrative (so Wilckens, *Missionsreden* 41; but cf. F. Neirynck, in *Les Actes* [ed. J. Kremer] 205-12).

31   17-26. Appeal for repentance and conversion. 17. *acted in ignorance:* The apostolic kerygma marks the end of ignorance, both here (cf. 13:27) and in Paul's preaching to the pagans (17:30). Their *agnoia* does not diminish the listeners' guilt (Wilckens, *Missionsreden* 134), especially since the Scriptures revealing God's plan were read to them every sabbath (13:27; cf. comment on 2:23). *as did your leaders:* The people's collusion with the leaders in obtaining Jesus' execution was brought out by Luke's editing of the passion narrative (Luke 23:4-5, 13-23), as was their subsequent withdrawal from that alliance and readiness for repentance (Luke 23:35,48). The "leaders" are prototypes of impenitent Jewry, placing itself resolutely outside the sphere of salvation (4:4-5, 16-17; cf. comment on 2:46). **18.** See comment on 2:23. The adv. *houtōs,* "in this way," gives a positive salvational moment to the death of Christ (*pace* E. Käsemann, *Jesus Means Freedom* [Phl, 1969] 125). *Pathein ton Christon,* expressing the total christological testimony of Scripture, is Luke's own summary of the Marcan passion-prediction formulas (cf. Luke 24:26-27; Acts 17:3; 26:22-23; M. Rese, *NTS* 30 [1984] 341-44). **19-21.** The three verses contain a grammatically integral sentence, with a dual impv. (v 19) flowing into a final cl. (*hopōs an*) in v 20 and the rel. cl. of v 21. The sentence offers the first of two motivations to respond to Peter's appeal for conversion, the second being the scriptural argument of vv 22-26. As against the older hypothesis of an integral Elijah or Baptist tradition quoted in vv 20-21 (Bauernfeind, *Apg.* 473-83; Roloff, *Apg.* 72-73), G. Lohfink has argued for the historiographical function of the statement, hence its basically Lucan authorship (*BZ* 13 [1969] 223-41): it addresses not a Jewish audience but Luke's Christian readers, showing them the splendid prospect which a repentant Israel could have obtained but impenitently refused (Kränkl, *Jesus* 197-98; F. Hahn, in *Les Actes* [ed. J. Kremer] 139-40). Because so many "men of Israel" would reject the kerygma and incur the exclusion from "the people" threatened in v 23, v 20 paints a picture that would not come to realization during the Acts history; and vv 20-21 together restate the rationale for the period of the church which was differently unfurled in 1:6-11, heavenly ascension and parousia portent included (E. Grässer, in *Les Actes* [ed. J. Kremer] 119). **20.** *times of refreshment:* An era (pl. "times") of surcease for Israel, crowned by the parousia of Jesus as the Messiah destined for it (cf. 4 Ezra 11:37-12:3; 2 Apoc. Bar. 73), was contingent upon Israel's response to the kerygma. Just like the disciples' question in 1:6, this expectation, too, must be reinterpreted in terms of the extended time of mission that follows upon the Jewish refusal (implied in vv 21,25; cf. 13:46; 28:28). *Messiah foreordained for you:* This was to be the fruit of Israel's election, which is also the basis of the *prōton,* "first," in v 26. **21.** *heaven must receive him:* Like the other *assumpti*—Enoch, Elijah, Ezra, Baruch—Jesus has been taken to heaven to be held there until the advent of final salvation (1:11). *the times of restoration:* Cf. 1:6; Mal 3:22-23 LXX. Accent is now on the end of the period (= pl. *chronōn*) because (a) *achri* with gen. pl. can pinpoint the end of a time span (cf. 20:6), hence, it favors the sense "as long as"; (b) the antecedent of the rel. cl. "of which God spoke," is "all things," not "the times" (W. Kurz, in *SBLASP* [1977] 309-11; Schneider, *Apg.* 1. 326-27). These "times" can thus be equated with the "times of refreshment" (v 20), only that such language of Jewish

apocalyptic is being stretched to apply to the age of the church's mission (1:6-8; 2:17).

32   22-26. Argument from Moses' testimony. Prophecy from Moses' lips is now adduced to support the call to conversion and refine the definition of the church's time just advanced in vv 19-21. The citation is actually a "spliced" Scripture, Deut 18:15-16, joined by an editorial *estai de,* "but it shall be" (cf. 2:21), to part of Lev 23:29 (v 23). In view of this "splicing," and the fact that the Deut text is twice quoted in Acts in word order diverging from the LXX, the argument at hand may be borrowed from a Christian *testimonia* booklet (cf. 4QTestim 5-8; Holtz, *Untersuchungen* 74; R. Hodgson, *JBL* 98 [1979] 373-74; J. A. Fitzmyer, *ESBNT* 59-89). The grammatical coordinates *men* and *de* (vv 22 and 24) show how the merged Scripture works in this sermon's peroration, as the first step of a logic carried forward in v 24 (Rese, *Motive* 68-69). The point is: Moses and the whole prophetic tradition, of which he was founder, have foretold this time of Israel's ultimate opportunity for conversion, proffered by the awaited "prophet like Moses" (v 26). Verse 23 quotes Moses' provision for the fate of all Israelites who discard this opportunity. **22.** Comparison with Deut 18:15 LXX shows that *anastēsei,* "will raise up," has been moved up to the lead position behind *prophētēn hymin,* an adjustment directly serving the use of the passage as an Easter testimony (cf. R. F. O'Toole, *ScEs* 31 [1979] 85-92). Stephen's speech (7:37) will confirm the importance of this Mosaic-prophet christology applied to the risen One (*pace* Kränkl, *Jesus* 199) and recall the Gospel's preparations for it at Luke 7:16 and 24:19 (cf. Acts 7:22). **23.** *every person:* An original reference to doing penance on the Day of Atonement in Lev 23:29 LXX has been replaced here by "does not listen to that prophet." The Mosaic punishment of unrepentant Israelites—extirpation from the chosen people's ranks—applies now to such as reject the kerygma of the risen Christ (C. Martini, *Bib* 50 [1969] 12). **24.** *these days:* Cf. the "times" in v 21; also 1:6; 2:17. The time of the apostolic preaching is interpreted eschatologically as the fulfillment of all OT prophecy (Luke 24:44-47; Acts 26:22-23). **25.** *in your offspring:* Yet another "Mosaic" testimony, whose wording comes closest to Gen 22:18 = 26:4 LXX (only with *patriai,* "families," replacing *ethnē,* "nations"), reiterates Israel's privilege as the first audience of the kerygma (vv 20,26). "Families" (cf. Gen 12:3) is suitably unspecific for the mere intimation of the mission beyond Israel which the author intends (Rese, *Motive* 73; Marshall, *Acts* 96). **26.** *raising up his servant:* The combination of the ptc. *anastēsas* (cf. v 22) with *apesteilen,* "sent," appears to favor the application of the prophet figure of Deut to the earthly Jesus' mission (so Haenchen, Wilckens, Kränkl, Roloff). But Luke's distinctive use of the trans. *anistanai* in resurrection kerygmata (2:26 etc.), plus the obvious function of vv 22-26 as scriptural support for Peter's present appeal, make the verb's reference to Jesus' resurrection in this passage much more likely (cf. Dupont, *Études* 249; C. F. D. Moule, in *StLA* 169). The "servant" title, interpreting "prophet" (Deut) and "your seed" (Gen), rounds out the Moses-Christ typology which has shaped the sermon. The risen Christ is depicted as the active exponent of the apostolic summons to repentance (so also 26:23; cf. R. F. O'Toole, *ScEs* 31 [1979] 90), just as he, rather than the apostles, was the healer in the miracle that prompted the sermon (vv 12,16).

(Dietrich, *Petrusbild* [→ 19 above] 216-30. Hahn, F., in *Les Actes* [ed. J. Kremer] 129-54. Kränkl, *Jesus* 193-202. Kurz, W., "Acts 3:19-26 as a Test of the Role of Eschatology in Lucan Christology," *SBLASP* [1977] 309-23. Lohfink, G., "Christologie und

Geschichtsbild in Apg 3,19–21," *BZ* 13 [1969] 223–41. MacRae, G. W., "'Whom Heaven Must Receive until the Time,'" *Int* 27 [1973] 151–65. Martini, C., "L'esclusione dalla communità del popolo di Dio e il nuovo Israele secondo Atti 3,23," *Bib* 50 [1969] 1–14. O'Toole, R. F., "Some Observations on *Anistēmi*, 'I Raise,' in Acts 3:22,26," *ScEs* 31 [1979] 85–92. Rese, *Motive* 66–77. Zehnle, *Discourse* [→ 28 above] 19–26, 41–60, 71–94.)

33   (B) The Life and Trials of the Apostolic Church (4:1–5:42).

(a) PETER AND JOHN BEFORE THE SANHEDRIN (4:1–22). The arrest of the apostles at the moment of their appeal for Israel's conversion begins the tide of opposition that will culminate in the dispersal of the community (8:1) and, ultimately, in the proclamation of the message to the Gentiles (chaps. 10–28). This narrative has troubling improbabilities (v 4) and inconsistencies, including the motive of the arrest (vv 2,7) and the release of the unbowed preachers (vv 18–20), which make it difficult to explain as a straightforward historical account. Nor have source analyses (Bauernfeind, Jeremias) produced any abiding result (Haenchen, *Acts* 222; Weiser, *Apg.* 123–24). Luke is clearly about his usual confection of a "dramatic episode," although the memory of real and bitter repressions of the infant mission by Jerusalem's religious aristocracy may give our passage a respectable historical foundation. **1.** *speaking to the people:* The "people" (*laos*) and their leaders are again separately presented (cf. 3:17), and their reactions to the message about Jesus are sharply contrasted (vv 2,4). *Sadducees:* Quite plausibly the apostles' Easter kerygma fueled the quarrel over the hermeneutics of the Torah that raged for generations between Jewish leadership factions (23:6–7; → History, 75:149–50); hence, Luke can be trusted when he portrays the Sadducees, the literalists who opposed "unscriptural" doctrines like resurrection (cf. 23:8; Luke 20:27–40), as the apostolic church's severest repressors (5:17–18; 23:6–10; Hengel, *Acts* 96). It is odd, however, not to find mention of the Pharisees here, though they were surely the sanhedrin's most influential constituents in the apostles' time (E. Schürer, *HJPAJC* 2. 213, 401–3). Although this Pharisaic party would have been more congenial to the eschatological fervor of the earliest Christians, their systematic defense of the missionaries (5:34–40; 23:9), from their platform of "most exact" Jewish observance (26:5), is undoubtedly part of a certain schematizing of the record in the service of Luke's "continuity" thesis (→ 5 above). **2.** *the resurrection of the dead in Jesus:* The phraseology explains the Sadducees' opposition and is itself elucidated in 26:23 (cf. 3:15). **4.** *five thousand:* The extravagant headcount amplifies the contrast between persecuting leaders and believing commonfolk (cf. comment on 2:41). **5–6.** On the sanhedrin's composition, see Luke 22:66; → Luke, 43:186); for the house of Annas, see Luke 3:2 (→ Luke, 43:42). *John and Alexander:* Otherwise unknown. **7.** *by what power or in what name:* The question is framed as a precise introduction to the discourse that follows. The issue of the arrest appears to have changed (v 2), but not really, for the apostles' activity in Jesus' "name" displays the active power of the resurrected Lord (see comment on 3:6). Questions about the judicial power of the sanhedrin, or whether belief in a resurrection could justify an arrest, are quite beside the point of our text.

34   8–12. Peter's first discourse before the sanhedrin, like the second (5:29–32), is an *apologia* rather than a sermon; and yet the schema of the mission sermons to Jews is unmistakable (→ 7 above), but for a contextual adjustment of the usual appeal for repentance in v 12 (Wilckens, *Missionsreden* 44–45). As a whole, the little speech gives a precise answer to the question put by the interrogators (v 7). **8.** *filled with the holy Spirit:* The reader is reminded of Luke 12:11–12 (cf. Matt 10:19): the promise of the Spirit's "teaching" *in statu confessionis.* **10.** *whom you crucified, whom God raised:* In these two clauses, condensing 3:12–15, we have the christological kerygma of the Jewish sermons in its tersest formulation (L. Schenke, *BZ* 26 [1982] 11). But can it be traced to earliest Christian usage (so Schenke, Roloff; → 7 above)? There is, of course, a necessary connection between "whom God raised" and the *en toutǭ*, "through this man," that proclaims the agent of the healing. As an answer to v 7, *en toutǭ* (= *houtos*, v 11) shows how the name and person of the risen One are interchangeable (*pace* Conzelmann, *Apg.* 43). **11.** Ps 118:22, as expression of the risen One's triumph over his enemies, was quoted in Luke 20:17 and is perfectly suited to the contrast schema of the kerygma of Acts. "Despised" (*exouthenētheis;* cf. Mark 9:12) is a change in the LXX wording introduced, perhaps, in earlier Christian exegesis of the psalm verse (Holtz, *Untersuchungen* 162). An ecclesiological application, only implied here (v 12), is explicit in 1 Pet 2:4–5 (cf. Matt 21:42–43). **13.** *boldness:* Gk *parrēsia* connotes the freedom and confidence which the divine Spirit gives its spokesmen despite all dangers. It is a hallmark of the apostles' preaching (2:29; 4:29,31) and of Paul's (9:27–28; 13:46), to the point of being practically the last word of Luke's history (28:31). *unlettered, common men:* This is literary counterpoint to the power of Peter's Spirit-filled speech, not a historical record (Schneider, *Apg.* 1. 349). **16–17.** The leaders' consultation effectively illustrates the finality of their unbelief, resistant to even the universal acclaim of the healing miracle among the differently disposed populace (v 21). **20.** *what we have seen and heard:* The apostolic witness to all Jesus had "done and taught" (1:1; 10:39) is under divine obedience (5:29), which quite improbably nullifies the proceeding against them (v 21).

(Barrett, C. K., "Salvation Proclaimed: Acts iv. 8–12," *ExpTim* 94 [1982] 68–71. Dupont, *Sources* 33–50. Jeremias, J., *Abba* [Göttingen, 1966] 241–47. Schenke, L., "Die Kontrastformel Apg 4,10b," *BZ* 26 [1982] 1–20.)

35   (b) THE APOSTLES' PRAYER (4:23–31). The regrouped apostolic community (*hoi idioi*) raises a prayer which is fitted precisely (vv 29–30) to the miracle-arraignment sequence of 3:1–4:22 and shows Luke's hand in practically all its expressions. Nevertheless, an intriguing exegesis of Ps 2:1–2 forms its center, and the fact that the application turns on the action of Herod and Pilate against Jesus, by way of analogy to the apostles' present peril, clashes with the finding for Jesus' innocence credited to the two rulers in the Lucan passion narrative (23:14–15). This may be explained by a pre-Lucan Christian interpretation of the psalm utilized here, without precise echo elsewhere in the NT (so Dibelius, Haenchen; cf. Rese, *Motive* 95–97), or, less persuasively, as a casual cross-reference to Luke 23:12 amid a wholly Lucan composition mimicking OT models like Isa 37:16–20 (2 Kgs 19:16–19; so Dömer, *Heil* 63–66). **24.** *Sovereign Lord:* The invocation *despota* is a Hellenistic (Jewish and Christian) prayer idiom favored where God's dominion over the cosmos is invoked (cf. Jdt 9:12; 3 Macc 2:2; *1 Clem.* 59:4; 60:3; 61:1–2; *Did.* 10:3). A juxtaposition of ptc.-predications in vv 24–25, *ho poiēsas,* "who made," and *ho eipōn,* "who spoke," has its effect blunted by the overladen construction of v 25 (cf. ms. variants). **25.** Cf. psalm-text introductions at 1:16; 2:25; Luke 20:42. **27.** *whom you anointed:* Cf. etymology of the Christ title (v 26) also at 10:38; Luke 4:18. "Holy servant" echoes 3:13–14 (and v 25). *Herod and Pontius*

Pilate: King and ruler (v 26), together with "nations and peoples" (v 25), pointedly apply the psalm and are obviously dictated by it. **28.** *to do:* The aor. infin. can only refer to Jesus' crucifixion (cf. 2:23; Kränkl, *Jesus* 110), elsewhere charged to the people's doing without Pilate's assent (3:13). **29.** *and now, Lord:* This conforms to the *wĕʿattâ* hinge of OT prayers (2 Kgs 19:19), but the symmetry of the apostles' and Jesus' situations is imperfect. **31.** The association of the earthquake, signaling the prayer's answer, with the bold proclaiming of the Word artistically matches the two divine functions, creator and speaker, invoked at the beginning of the prayer (vv 24–25; Schneider, *Apg.* 1. 357).

36   (c) SECOND MAJOR SUMMARY (4:32–35). This passage offers an insight into "summary" composition (→ 9 above), since it adjoins two single cases, drawn from Luke's tradition, which it generalizes into a community-wide ideal of renunciation (vv 36–37; 5:1–4; cf. 2:44–45). The literary relationship between the single cases and the summary is manifest, and the latter's generalization of freewill offerings nurtures the "golden age" impression of the apostolic era, not unrelated to Hellenistic visions of primal days and political utopias (Conzelmann, *Apg.* 37; Plümacher, *Lukas* 16–18). However, since the ideal certainly reflects his Gospel's strong emphasis on Jesus' commands to renounce possessions (12:33; 14:33; 18:22), Luke can hardly be excluding all sense of example for the church of the present (Schneider, *Apg.* 1. 294; *pace* Conzelmann, *TSL* 233). *all things in common:* The language echoes the Gk proverb about friends (Plato, *Rep.* 4.424a; 5.449c), which Luke will typically interpret by way of the biblical exclusion of poverty in Israel (v 34a = Deut 15:4). **33.** *with great power:* That the apostles' deeds of power marked their "testimony of the resurrection" (cf. 3:12–16) confirms our interpretation of the apostle's function in terms of the ongoing activity of the risen One (see comment on 1:22). **35.** *as any had need:* This qualification (2:45) betrays a certain ambivalence over against Jesus' call for total divestiture (Luke 14:33; Schneider, *Apg.* 1. 293). Luke understands the surrender of goods as voluntary (5:4) and related to need, not mandatory or systematic.

37   (d) SINGULAR CASES (4:36–5:11). **36.** *Joseph . . . Barnabas:* His Cypriot origin seems to suggest that he will belong among the "Hellenists" (6:1); but cf. Hengel, *Acts* 101–2. Luke will, in any case, rely on his membership in the original community to establish Paul's dependence thereon (9:27; 11:25–26). **37.** *sold a field:* The deed would hardly have been memorable if everyone was obliged to do the same!

The chilling tale of Ananias and Sapphira (5:1–11) is a lone NT example of "rule-miracles of punishment" (G. Theissen, *The Miracle Stories of the Early Christian Tradition* [Phl, 1983] 109). These are miracles that reinforce divine ordinances, either by wondrously saving one who observes them or uncannily punishing one who violates them. Here, as in most Jewish examples of the punishment genre, divine prescription is reinforced as a matter of life and death. Ananias's guilt is no less than denying the holy Spirit's presence in the church by lying to it (vv 3,8; Schneider, *Apg.* 1. 372), thus serving Satan's intolerable challenge to the testimony of the Spirit through the voluntary sharing of goods by believers (Weiser, *Apg.* 146–47). Inconsistencies in the text, as to where the sin lies (in the withholding or the lying) and how v 7 can credibly follow v 5, may result from subsequent expansions of an old Palestinian-Christian story (A. Weiser, *TGl* 69 [1979] 151–57). Qumran analogies, suggesting that the couple sought to enter a circle of *perfecti* of whom total surrender of goods was required, are wholly

inconclusive (cf. Haenchen, *Acts* 241). **2.** *held back:* The rare vb. *nosphizō* suggests the influence of Achan's sin and punishment (Josh 7:1 LXX) and may be a secondary embellishment by someone who saw this as the sinful act. **3.** *Satan:* His entry on the apostolic scene and clash with the divine Spirit operating there parallel the same development in the life of Jesus (Luke 4:1–2). The symmetry enhances this strange episode's contribution to the Lucan history (Weiser, *Apg.* 146). **4.** Peter's remonstrance may be from Luke's pen, stressing that the sale of property and surrender of proceeds were strictly voluntary; hence, the generalized practice (4:34) was a mark of the Spirit's fervor in the first church (Schneider, *Apg.* 1. 375). In any case, this verse conclusively locates the sin in the lie. **5.** *fear:* It is a stylistically requisite conclusion to the original "rule-miracle." **6.** This verse makes possible the addition of the Sapphira episode, closely configured to vv 1–5. **11.** *the whole church:* The first occurrence in Acts of the biblical term *ekklēsia* for the local assembly of believers (cf. 8:1; 9:31; → Pauline Theology, 82:133).

(Derrett, J. D. M., *Studies in the New Testament* [Leiden, 1977] 1. 193–201. Lake, K., in *Beginnings* 5. 140–51. Menoud, P., "La mort d'Ananias et de Saphira," *Aux sources de la tradition chrétienne* [Fest. M. Goguel; Neuchâtel, 1950] 146–54. Noorda, S., *Les Actes* [ed. J. Kremer] 475–83. Weiser, A., "Das Gottesurteil über Hananias und Saphira," *TGl* 69 [1979] 148–58.)

38   (e) THIRD MAJOR SUMMARY (5:12–16). This passage has the apostles' "signs and wonders" as its theme (cf. 2:43) and the dreadful Ananias event as its point of departure. Verses 12–13 weave the connection with what has preceded: v 12 to the prayer of 4:29–30, v 13 to the "fear" engendered by the dissemblers' fate (v 11). Verses 14–16 invite comparison with the summary in Mark 6:53–56, which Luke's Gospel did not reproduce, perhaps because he intended to adapt it here. **12.** *through the hands of the apostles:* The foregoing miracles featuring Peter (3:1–11; 5:1–11) are thus generalized as part of a routine performance by all the apostles. **13.** *none dared join them:* The "zone of godly awe" surrounding them (v 11) kept outsiders from approaching on their own (Roloff, *Apg.* 98); but this is only in counterpoint to the "adding" to their ranks that God was doing (v 14). The positive disposition of "the people" persists. **14–15.** The two assertions, the expansion of believers' ranks and the scramble for cures, are connected by the consecutive conj. *hōste,* subordinating the latter to the former. Any magical implication of Peter's shadow (cf. P. van der Horst, *NTS* 23 [1976–77] 204–12) is thus drastically modified: its power is a function of faith in the living *Kyrios* (Dietrich, *Petrusbild* 238–39). The expression *kan hē skia,* "even just the shadow," gives this the same role as the hem of Jesus' garment (Mark 6:55–56) and Paul's handkerchiefs (19:11–12).

39   (f) THE SECOND PERSECUTION (5:17–42). This sequence illustrates Luke's predilection for symmetrical pairing of passages, esp. for the effect of augmenting and surpassing the elements of the first in the second ("climactic parallelism"; cf. Flender, *St. Luke* [→ 24 above] 25–27). The second sanhedrin arraignment parallels the first (4:1–22), but with recurring elements dramatically intensified: (1) the hostile Sadducees (v 17) stand in sharp contrast this time to the supportive Pharisee (v 34); (2) expression of the irresistible divine will directing the preaching is strengthened (vv 29, 38–39) and illustrated by the miraculous escape (vv 19–20); (3) the charges and resolution of the sanhedrin are augmented from the relatively mild inquiry and warning of 4:7–21 to the angry accusations (v 28), the wish to put the preachers to death (v 33), and the admonition with scourging (v 40), which mark this proceeding; (4) the embattled preachers are now all the apostles (vv 18,29,40), not Peter and John only. This exercise of literary parallelism for intensification shows that the duplicate arraignments do not result from doublet sources, much less historical circumstance, but come from Luke's own design, which thus arranges his fragmentary information into a historiographic statement: the preaching of the gospel, under God's direct control, waxed ever stronger, and with it, by concurrent necessity, the tide of its opposition (Weiser, *Apg.* 155). **40   19–20.** The miraculous escape, which gets no mention in the subsequent hearing, will have been condensed and transposed here from the Peter tradition in 12:6–17 (cf. 16:25–34). **25.** Verisimilitude is sacrificed to dramatic effect: the sanhedrin must learn from "someone" that its quarries are preaching to "the people" in the Temple! The Word is still out to Israel (*ho laos*), and popular favor is still with the preachers (vv 26,13). **28.** *you have filled Jerusalem with your teaching:* The accusation articulates salvation-historical necessity (see comment on 1:4); hence Peter's rejoinder. **29–32.** Peter's second sanhedrin discourse illustrates Luke 21:13 (cf. Mark 13:9): the *status confessionis* is the opportunity of bearing "witness" (v 32). **29.** *we must obey God:* More closely than in 4:19 does Peter's imperative now echo Socrates' (Plato, *Apol.* 29d). **30.** *hanging him on a tree:* The allusion to Deut 21:22 is clear (cf. 10:39; 2:23; Gal 3:13). Paul's recourse to the exposed body's curse was to declare the means of salvation apart from the law, whereas Luke's purpose is to argue from the law itself the magnitude of this people's shame in "laying violent hands" on their Savior (Wilckens, *Missionsreden* 126; Rese, *Motive* 116). **31.** *leader and savior:* These functions (cf. 3:13; 13:23) are explicated by the substantive cl. *tou dounai,* "to give," etc., which, in the light of 2:32–33, ought to have Christ as its subject. **32.** On the joint "witness" of the apostles and the holy Spirit, see Luke 12:12; and comment on 1:8. **41   33–40.** The Intervention of Gamaliel. Historically factual is at least the career of Gamaliel I—"the Elder" and descendant of the great Hillel—who surely was a most respected Jewish scholar in Jerusalem in the period AD 25–50 (*IDB* 2. 351). His meager recorded teaching would qualify him as a Pharisee (Str-B 2. 636–39), and it is conceivable that such an influential rabbi might intervene in support of a law-abiding sect whose apocalyptic enthusiasms could be a common cause against the Sadducees (cf. 23:6–9; Zingg, *Wachsen* 127–28). **34.** *a teacher of the law:* This credential contributes to Luke's "continuity" thesis. That Gamaliel's student, Paul, became a fierce antagonist of the gospel (22:3–5) is understood as an aberration (26:9–14), not a natural consequence of zeal for the law. **36–37.** The precedents of Theudas and Judas the Galilean may be anachronistic (*Beginnings* 4. 60–62; Dibelius, *Studies* 186–87), but their point is clear: those leaders perished and their movements died with them, but that has not been the case with Jesus' following. **38.** *this plan or this work:* The analogy of short-lived gatherings of "people" (v 37) suggests that we are to understand the "work" as the ingathering of Israel, under way in the mission of the apostles (see comments on 1:15,21; 2:14,36). **39.** *if it is from God:* The shift from an eventual (v 38) to a real condition already implies the conclusion: the real founder and gatherer of the apostolic church is God (Lohfink, *Sammlung* 86–87). *opponents of God: Theomachoi,* "Godfighters," a word of Euripides' coinage (*Bacchae* 45) and Luke's Hellenistic schooling, denotes exactly what the Jerusalem audience has perennially been (cf. 7:51). **41–42.** The apostles emerge as models of fearless confession under persecution (cf. Luke 6:22–23; 12:4–12), surely one of the guiding compositional motifs of this section.

42   (III) The Mission's Outward Path from Jerusalem (6:1–15:35).
(A) The Hellenists and Their Message (6:1–8:40).
(a) THE COMMISSION OF THE SEVEN (6:1–7). After the idealized portrait of the apostolic community that Luke has drawn for us, we are unprepared for the conflict that breaks out here; and that in itself is evidence that his source material is wrinkling the smooth surface of his historical tableau at this point (Hengel, *Between Jesus* [→ 43 below] 3–4; Weiser, *Apg.* 168; J. Lienhard, *CBQ* 37 [1975] 231). "The Hellenists," who are suddenly before us, without introduction, as a constituency separate from "the Hebrews," will certainly hold the key to young Christianity's advance beyond the borders of its Palestinian homeland (cf. 11:19–21; E. Grässer, *TRu* 42 [1977] 23). In this, Luke's story is true to fact. How this other constituency emerged, however, and how its leadership, including two of Luke's principal actors, was duly constituted, are factors which his linear argument cannot directly disclose. It seems, indeed, that the conflict of which we are told so little was not the cause of the appointment of new leaders after all, but rather the result of an already existing division in the Jerusalem church, with one segment led by the Twelve, the other by the men we are meeting here for the first time (v 5). The features of the account that make these newcomers subordinate to the Twelve, obtaining the lesser ministry of table service (v 2) by the imposition of the apostles' hands (v 6), are likely the result of Luke's editing (Schneider, *Apg.* 1. 421; N. Walter, *NTS* 29 [1983] 372–73). Other information, including the dissension and the seven names, perhaps the substance of vv 5–6, comes from an untraceable source account. In view of the sharp difference between the table service assigned the Seven here and the properly apostolic "ministry of the word" which Stephen and Philip exercise in the account of their missions (6:8–8:40), it was probably Luke who first joined the commissioning account to the Stephen–Philip sequence as the latter's introduction, thus stationing the two "Hellenistic" missionaries in appropriate subordination to the Twelve Apostles from the outset (J. Lienhard, *CBQ* 37 [1975] 230; U. Borse, *BibLeb* 14 [1973] 189).
43   1. *Hellenists against the Hebrews:* The most successful explanation of these groups is also the simplest (best argued by M. Hengel [*Between Jesus* 4–11]): they are the separate language groups of Jerusalem Jewry, the one speaking the Aramaic of Palestine, the other consisting of immigrants from the Diaspora who have settled in Jerusalem (cf. 2:5) but speak only Greek. The existence of several Greek-language synagogues in 1st-cent. Jerusalem is securely documented by contemporary inscriptions (e.g., the noted Theodotus inscription, ibid. 17, 148 n. 119; cf. R. Hestrin, *et al., Inscriptions Reveal* [2d ed.; Jerusalem, 1973] §182); and the zeal for ancestral institutions which propelled the immigrants' "homecoming" probably made most of them fierce Mosaic loyalists, like Saul (9:1–2), ready to defend their traditions vigorously in debate with Stephen (v 9) and Saul (9:29). Only this explanation can coordinate the present use of "Hellenists" with 9:29, its single remaining occurrence in the NT. It is better not to add any peculiar theological stripe to the word's meaning (O. Cullmann), or any pejorative note of syncretistic (M. Simon) or libertine praxis (W. Schmithals, *Apg.* 65). With its linguistic meaning alone, "Hellenists" can include Jews and Christians in a city-wide constituency, rather than designating exclusively a Christian faction in ferment over issues of gospel and mission. *the daily distribution:* This refers more likely to a day-to-day survival effort by the unworldly,

enthusiastic Christian community (cf. 4:34–37; 11:29; 12:25; so Hengel, Roloff) than to any assistance program of the Jewish society at large (so N. Walter, *NTS* 29 [1983] 379–82; cf. Haenchen, *Acts* 261–62). We easily imagine why widowed immigrants faced special economic hardships and why they might be "overlooked" in a food distribution run by the native contingent. **2.** *serve at tables:* The expression *diakonein trapezais* presumably connotes the whole community effort to give sustenance to the needy. The noun *diakonos* is not used, though Luke may well be thinking of that early and important ministry (Phil 1:2; 1 Tim 3:8,12). The Seven will not, in fact, be shown in that capacity hereafter in Acts, so they are not called "deacons" here for good reason. **2–6.** The commissioning sequence conforms to an OT model (cf. Gen 41:29–43; Exod 18:13–26; Deut 1:9–18) which might have been followed already in Luke's source (cf. Richard, *Acts 6:1–8:4* 269–74; E. Plümacher, *TRu* 49 [1984] 140). It is clearly the product of later reflection on the event, and not the protocol of an apostolic ordination. **3.** *seven men:* They apparently became known as "the Seven" (21:8), and their number may reflect the institution of the Jewish town council (Deut 16:18; Str-B 2. 641). **4.** *the service of the word:* In obvious contradistinction to the "table service," this is nevertheless the "apostolic" activity in which we shall find Stephen (v 10) and Philip "the evangelist" (21:8) engaged as Luke's story continues. **5–6.** The seven names, with Stephen at the head, are all Greek and widely documented in Hellenistic sources. They give handy support to our explanation of this group's background. *laid their hands on them:* The Jewish ritual expressed both transfer of function and bestowal of powers (cf. Num 27:18–23), and it is an ecclesiastical practice of Luke's own time (1 Tim 4:14; 5:22; 2 Tim 1:6) read back into the story of the church's beginnings (also 13:2–3; [14:23]; cf. J. Coppens, in *Les Actes* [ed. J. Kremer] 405–38). It graphically expresses, for Luke, the subordination of this originally independent Hellenistic leadership to Jesus' chosen apostles. **7.** *increased:* A "growth" notice concludes the episode (cf. 2:47) and proclaims its contribution to the story's momentum. The "priests" offer a concrete illustration without follow-up.

(Bihler, J., *Die Stephanusgeschichte im Zusammenhang der Apostelgeschichte* [MTS 1/16; Munich, 1963]. Borse, U., "Der Rahmentext im Umkreis der Stephanusgeschichte," *BibLeb* 14 [1973] 187–204. Cadbury, H., in *Beginnings* 5. 59–74. Cullmann, O., "Von Jesus zum Stephanuskreis . . . ," *Jesus und Paulus* [Fest. W. G. Kümmel; ed. E. E. Ellis and E. Grässer; Göttingen, 1975] 44–56. Grässer, E., *TRu* 42 (1977) 17–25. Hengel, M., *Between Jesus and Paul* [Phl, 1983] 1–29; *Acts* 71–80. Lienhard, J., "Acts 6:1–6: A Redactional View," *CBQ* 37 [1975] 228–36. Richard, E., *Acts 6:1–8:4* [SBLDS 41; Missoula, 1978]. Simon, M., *St. Stephen and the Hellenists in the Primitive Church* [London, 1958] 1–19. Walter, N., "Apg. 6.1 und die Anfänge der Urgemeinde in Jerusalem," *NTS* 29 [1983] 370–93. Wilson, *Gentiles* 129–53.)

44   (b) THE TESTIMONY OF STEPHEN (6:8–8:3). The narrative about Stephen in 6:8–15 has its organic continuation in 7:55–8:3, with the great speech probably a secondary insertion in the middle of the story (Dibelius, *Studies* 168). The narrative, which Luke received at least in part from his source, fluctuates in its portrayal between a judicial proceeding and a lynching, presumably because Luke augmented the source account with elements of a sanhedrin trial in order to configure the protomartyr's death to Jesus' (Conzelmann, *Apg.* 51; Schneider, *Apg.* 1. 433–34). The parallelism between the two "martyrdoms" is typically Lucan in that ingredients of the Synoptic passion story omitted in Luke 22–23 are brought forward here for the process against Stephen

(e.g., vv 13–14 = Mark 14:57–58). The reprise of Jesus' passion in Stephen's will include the false witnesses, the high priest's question, the "Son-of-Man" vision (7:56), and the dying prayers (7:59–60; cf. Richard, *Acts 6:1–8:4* 281–301). At the same time, the sanhedrin-trial setting permits Stephen's martyrdom to fall into a climactic series with the earlier persecutions in Acts, the first having ended in mere threats (4:17,21), the second with scourging (5:40) and a resolve to kill (5:33) which will now reach fruition (Haenchen, *Acts* 273–74).

(i) *Mission and trial* (6:8–7:1). **8.** *full of grace and power:* This portrait of an exemplary Spirit-bearer (cf. v 5), with accrediting miracles (2:22,43) and irresistible speech charisma (v 10), is a point where Luke's source breaks through with essential information about Stephen and his movement. The combination of their Spirit enthusiasm and the influence of Jesus' teachings accounts for the sharp criticism of Jewish institutions which Stephen's accusers cite (vv 11,13). "The decisive factor is the spirit-inspired interpretation of the message of Jesus in the new medium of the Greek language" (Hengel, *Between Jesus* 24). **9.** On Jerusalem's Hellenistic synagogues (also 24:12), see comment on 6:1. **12–14.** Different from the generalized Jewish charges against Paul (21:21,28), the accusations against Stephen include specific points of teaching which his circle undoubtedly propounded. Luke, protective of his continuity thesis, brands the accusers "false witnesses," but the substance of v 14 (cf. Mark 14:58; Acts 7:48) need not be merely the product of his configuring of the passion if it attests the reception of the Temple logion by congenial spirits disposed to question the centralization of Jewish worship (cf. 7:48; 17:24; Roloff, *Apg.* 113; *e contra*, G. Schneider, in *Les Actes* [ed. J. Kremer] 239–40). **15.** *like the face of an angel:* Stephen's "transfiguration" (cf. Luke 9:29) is a prelude to his vision (7:55–56), and the formal integrity of the sequence has been strategically broken by his speech (cf. Richard, *Acts 6:1–8:4* [→ 43 above] 298–99).

45   (ii) *The speech of Stephen* (7:2–53). Opinions on this longest and grandest of the discourses of Acts run the entire gamut from a completely traditional (M. Simon) to a completely compositional (J. Bihler) product. The truth should, of course, be sought somewhere in between. This is the first of two speeches (with 13:16–41) featuring a sweeping recapitulation of Jewish history, a genre of which other examples abound in the OT and Judaism (cf. Richard, *Acts 6:1–8:4* [→ 43 above] 141–45). Particularly interesting analogies to this text are presented by Jdt 6:6–18; Neh 9:6–31; Ps 105, but it is not directly dependent on any of these. The sharp polemical climax of Stephen's argument draws upon a historical schema developed by the deuteronomic historians (cf. O. Steck, U. Wilckens, whose insistent counterpoint between God's gracious acts and his people's obstinate resistance (Neh 9:6–31; cf. 2 Kgs 17:7–18) included the motif of Israel's murderous rejection of her prophets (Neh 9:26; Josephus, *Ant.* 9.13.2 §265), which resounds in Stephen's incendiary conclusion (vv 51–53). M. Dibelius believed that the historical synopsis and polemical conclusion of the speech represented separate literary strands, the first pre-Lucan and basically irrelevant to Stephen's circumstance (vv 2–34), the second supplied by Luke to turn the history to the controversy at hand (vv 35–53; cf. *Studies* 167–69; similarly Haenchen, Conzelmann, Holtz). The better probability, however, is that the historical summary came to Luke already augmented by themes of penitential preaching inspired by the deuteronomic tradition and its prophet-murder dogma (Steck, *Israel* [→ 50 below] 266; Wilckens, *Missionsreden* 216–19). Clues to the text's layered development may be offered by its noticeably different modes of OT (LXX) employment: now in freewheeling narrative survey, now word-for-word quotation (vv 3,5,6–7,27,32,33–34,35,37,40), now formal citation (vv 42–43,48–50), now studied typology (vv 22,25,35,37; cf. Weiser, *Apg.* 179–80; *pace* Richard, *Acts 6:1–8:4* [→ 43 above] 253). Of these, especially the last produces cross-references to related passages elsewhere in Luke-Acts and hence points to Luke's editorial activity. From the vantage point thus gained, we can suggest the following stages of development: (1) the historical summary, drawn from a model used in the Hellenistic synagogues; (2) the addition of the penitential reproaches, concentrated in vv 39–42a and 51–53, and derived by pre-Lucan Christian expositors from a tradition of deuteronomic parenesis echoed in familiar words of Jesus (Luke 11:47–51; 13:34–35); (3) the Moses-prophet typology, and perhaps the formal OT citations (vv 42b–43,48b–50), introduced at Luke's writing and keyed to the broader thematic harmonies of his history. Attempts to trace the scriptural argument to Palestinian tradition, either Samaritan (M. Simon, M. Scharlemann, C. Scobie) or Qumranite (O. Cullmann), have faltered for inadequate assessment of the breadth of the speech's traditional currents (G. Schneider, in *Les Actes* [ed. J. Kremer] 225–37).

46 Stephen's argument may be divided as follows: (1) God's way with Abraham, vv 2–8; (2) God's way with Joseph, vv 9–16; (3) God's way with Moses, vv 17–43; (4) God's dwelling with his unfaithful people, vv 44–50; (5) Conclusion: Israel's perennial resistance to the holy Spirit and its messengers, vv 50–53. The historical survey moves from Abraham's call over the careers of Joseph and Moses, which saw Israelite resistance to God's designs grow into a sustained counterpoint, finally to the building of the Temple, treated as the climax of the former generations' infidelities. The invective of vv 51–53 then makes a withering peroration for the present audience, illustrating the nation's perennial disobedience in its violence against all the prophets and showing the logical conclusion of this in the murder of the "Mosaic" prophet (v 37), the Messiah, by the listeners. **2–8.** God's Way with Abraham. The biblical synopsis contains intriguing divergences from the pentateuchal accounts and the MT and LXX textual traditions. These include the location of Abraham's call in "Mesopotamia" (cf. Gen 11:31; 12:1; but cf. Philo, *De Abr.* 62), the timing of his migration to Canaan (cf. Gen 11:26,32; 12:4; but cf. Philo, *De migr. Abr.* 177), the word "inheritance" in v 5 (Deut 2:5), and the adaptation of Exod 3:12 to Gen 15:14,16 in v 7 ("this place"). **4.** *he removed him:* With Abraham's migration to Canaan, God becomes the actor, and the whole history of the promise will ride on his action alone. To emphasize this, v 5 records that Abraham had neither land nor offspring of his own when the promise was given (cf. Heb 11:8–12). **6–7.** The quotation of Gen 15:13–14, with words from Exod 3:12, creates a prophecy of succeeding events in Stephen's historical summary (N. Dahl, in *StLA* 143–44): the story of Joseph (vv 9–16) will show how Abraham's posterity became aliens in a foreign land, where they were enslaved and ill-treated (vv 18–19); the story of Moses (vv 20–36) will tell how they were led out as God judged their captors; and, finally, vv 44–47 will complete the story with the worship of God in the land of promise, under David and Solomon. **7.** *in this place:* Exod 3:12 has "this mountain" (Horeb); cf. Gen 15:16: "and they shall come back here." The promise to Abraham included worship of God in the land, but this was not to be fulfilled by the building of the Temple (vv 47–48), to which Luke's speech-setting would seem to make "this place"

refer (6:13–14; but cf. vv 33,49d; Richard, *Acts 6:1–8:4* [→ 43 above] 326).

47 **9–16.** God's Way with Joseph. Joseph began the settlement in a land belonging to others (v 6), the situation that presaged the great Diaspora (v 43d). His importance goes beyond that, however, as v 9 immediately shows: he is the first focus of the summary's thematic counterpoint, envied and sold by his brothers whereas "God was with him" (cf. 10:38). **10.** The contrast between God's deliverance and extraordinary endowment of Joseph, on the one hand, and Joseph's "afflictions" from human hands on the other, echoes the familiar kerygmatic schema (cf. 2:22–24; 10:38–40) as well as the circumstance of the similarly gifted Stephen (6:8–10). **14.** *seventy-five persons:* Cf. Gen 46:27; Exod 1:5 LXX, as against the MT (also Deut 10:22). **16.** *they were taken to Shechem:* This tradition results from a commingling of Abraham's Hebron purchase (Gen 23:17–20; cf. 50:13) and Jacob's Shechem purchase (Gen 33:18–19; cf. Josh 24:32). Oddly, no Samaritan testimonies support the Shechem burial tradition against Hebron (G. Schneider, in *Les Actes* [ed. J. Kremer] 451).

48 **17–43.** God's Way with Moses. In many respects, the Moses portion is the center and fulcrum of the speech. Verses 17b–19 closely report Exod 1:7–10 LXX; then, in freer summaries of the LXX text, Exod 2:2–10 (vv 20–22); Exod 2:11–22 (vv 23–29); and Exod 3:1–10 (vv 30–34). The deuteronomic-style commentary in vv 39–43 expands the dark side of the record, already shown in vv 27–29,35. Luke's editorializing can be seen in the introduction (v 17) and in his enrichments of the all-important Moses–Christ typology (vv 22,25, 35,37; cf. Weiser, *Apg.* 182, 185). **22.** *mighty in his words and deeds:* The charismatic portrait of Moses continues the analogy with Stephen (6:8,10) but contradicts Exod 4:10! The phraseology is a nearly exact reprise of Luke 24:19, where the Emmaus traveler inferentially describes the "Mosaic" prophet in the latter's unsuspected presence. **23.** *forty years old:* Moses' 120-year life-span (Deut 34:7) is here divided into 40-year periods (vv 30,36), symbolizing God's close direction of each phase (v 30). **25.** *they did not understand:* The narrative is interrupted by reflection on a theme dear to Luke: the understanding (Luke 24:45) vs. nonunderstanding (Luke 2:50; 8:10; 18:34; Acts 28:26,27) of the message of salvation. Cf. also 3:17–18; 13:27. **29.** *Moses fled:* The summary's thematic counterpoint directs that the flight be prompted by the compatriots' opposition, not the pharaoh's threat (as Exod 2:15). **32.** *the God of your fathers:* The shift from sg. "father" (MT, LXX) has some support in the textual tradition (E. Richard, *CBQ* 39 [1977] 200–2) and, in any case, better serves the coherence of the summary. **35.** Who could miss the structural conformity of this sentence to the central assertion of the Acts kerygma (2:36; 3:13–15; 5:30–31)? Note the change of style: "the placid flow of historical narrative gives way to passionate, rhetorically heightened indictment" (Haenchen, *Acts* 282). **36.** *wonders and signs:* The historical cycle of these hallmarks of "Mosaic" prophecy is here rounded off at its beginning (cf. 2:19,22,43; 6:8). **37.** Cf. 3:22–26, where Deut 18:15 has its full discursive function. Here it seems an insertion, whether Lucan (A. Weiser) or pre-Lucan (G. Schneider), meant to strengthen the Mosaic typology in preparation for v 52. **39–41.** *refused to obey him:* The rel. pron. *hō* accentuates the disobedient people's personal rejection of Moses, and *apōsanto*, "thrust aside," repeated from v 27, shows the continuity of their resistance. This section, expanding on the original summary in deuteronomic style, develops the analogy between Moses and Jesus under rejection by the Israelites; hence, it turns the history told thus far toward the polemical climax of vv 51–53 (Schneider, *Apg.* 1. 464). **42–43.** For the "talion" between idolatry and its punishment, see Wis 11:16; also the *paredōken,* "handed over," in Rom 1:24–28. The quotation of Amos 5:25–27 LXX substitutes "Babylon" for Damascus, thus declaring the ultimate fulfillment of the dire oracle.

49   44–46. As God's dwelling in the wilderness and Canaan, the "tent of witness" was precisely willed by God, built according to the "model" he showed Moses (Exod 25:9,40). This lasted until David, whom God favored, prayed to find a "habitation" (of God), in which his people might worship (Ps 132:5) in accordance with the divine promise in v 7. **47.** *but Solomon built:* The adversative *de* already strikes the counterpoint: Solomon's Temple was not the fulfillment of the promise to Abraham or of David's prayer (N. Dahl, in *StLA* 146). **48.** Here at the conclusion of the old historical summary, Diaspora Jewry found that, to encounter a God who does not dwell in shrines made by human hands, it did not have to go back to Jerusalem! (Schneider, *Apg.* 1. 467). **49–50.** Isa 66:1-2 backs this judgment with the very words of God, which are made to conclude with the salient point in the form of a rhetorical question (cf. 17:24).

51–53. Stephen's polemical peroration follows a "classic" specimen of the deuteronomic prophet-murder parenesis (Wilckens, *Missionsreden* 215–16; Steck, *Israel* [→ 50 below] 265–69): (1) all Israel, generations present and past, is accused of obstinate resistance to God's word; (2) God repeatedly sent prophets to correct their ways; but (3) they rejected, persecuted, (and murdered) the prophets; for which (4) God visited terrible judgment upon them in the form of the end of the kingdoms of Israel (2 Kgs 17:18) and Judah (Neh 9:27). The final element is missing here but was anticipated in v 43 (cf. Dillon, *From Eye-Witnesses* [→ 17 above] 257–60). **52.** *the just one:* Cf. 3:14; 22:14; Luke 23:47. **53.** *you did not keep them:* Association of the present generation with their fathers' sins is steadfast in this tradition (2 Kgs 17:14; Neh 9:32-35; Luke 11:50-51; 6:22-23). Messiah-murder culminated a perennial disobedience to the law (15:10).

50   (iii) *The martyrdom of Stephen* (7:54–8:3). The conclusion of the protomartyrdom, resuming the thread of 6:15, recounts the lynching that we suppose belonged to the pre-Lucan stratum (→ 44 above). Luke's hand will be seen in two series of embellishments (Schneider, *Apg.* 1. 471): the parallels to Jesus' sanhedrin trial (vv 55, 56,58b) and dying words (vv 59–60), and the supernumerary presence of Saul with preview of his persecutor's role (v 58b; 8:1a,3). **55.** *gazing into heaven:* Taking up 6:15, this Lucan statement interprets Stephen's angelic countenance in terms of a heavenly vision; and coming right after the speech, the vision ratifies what was spoken: the indictment of the listeners and the location of God's "glory" in heaven, with the risen Christ, rather than in the Temple made by humans (Mussner, "Wohnung Gottes," 286). **56.** *the Son of Man standing:* Remarkable for both this "standing" posture and for being the very rare Son-of-Man saying on other than Jesus' lips, this word of the martyr is likely Luke's variation on Luke 22:69 in further elaboration of v 55 (so Conzelmann, Schneider, Weiser, Sabbe, Mussner). "Standing" may bespeak the Lord's welcome to his martyr in an individualized parousia (Barrett), or his intercession for his confessor true to Luke 12:8 (Schneider), or his exercise of judgment against recusant Jewry (Pesch); or, least plausibly, it could be a "meaningless" variation upon the risen One's sitting at God's right hand (2:33–35; Mussner, Sabbe). **58.** *they stoned him:* Stoning "outside the city" (Lev 24:14; Num

15:35–36; *m. Sanh.* 6:1) pertains to the prophet-murder tradition received by Luke (cf. Luke 4:29; 13:34; 20:15). "Witnesses" will hardly have been appointed for a lynching; they are evidence of Luke's hand in v 58b, introducing the young "Saul" (so named 15 times in 7:58–13:9). It is doubtful that this Stephen-Saul nexus comes from pre-Lucan tradition (*pace* Burchard, *Der dreizehnte Zeuge* 28–30); we should rather credit exquisite literary design for the great Gentile missionary's first appearance at the precise point where the mission's outward movement from Jerusalem begins. Cf. the further association of the two "witnesses" in 22:15–20. **8:1.** *all were scattered:* Underlying this schematic Lucan picture is the persecution that drove the Christian Hellenists from Jerusalem and along the first pathways of the Gentile mission (cf. 11:19–20; Hengel, *Acts* 73–75). The regions "Judea and Samaria" show how this turn of events fulfilled the risen Lord's directive of 1:8. Luke's reader well knows why "the apostles" could not be among the dispossessed (see comment on 1:4); undoubtedly the native "Hebrew" contingent was not included either. **3.** *Saul strove to destroy the church:* Cf. 9:21; Gal 1:13,23. Could it be that he had a hand in the end of the Hellenists' church in Jerusalem (Hengel, *Acts* 74)? What of Gal 1:22?

(Barrett, C. K., "Stephen and the Son of Man," *Apophoreta* [Fest. E. Haenchen; ed. W. Eltester and F. H. Kettler; BZNW 30; Berlin, 1964] 32–38. Bihler, J. *Die Stephanusgeschichte* [→ 43 above]. Burchard, C., *Der dreizehnte Zeuge* [FRLANT 103; Göttingen, 1970] 26–31, 40–42. Dahl, N. A., in *StLA* 139–58. Grässer, E., *TRu* 42 [1977] 35–42. Holtz, *Untersuchungen* 85–127. Kilgallen, J., *The Stephen Speech* [AnBib 67; Rome, 1976]. Kliesch, K., *Das heilsgeschichtliche Credo in den Reden der Apostelgeschichte* [Bonn, 1975] 5–38, 110–25. Mussner, F., "Wohnung Gottes und Menschensohn nach der Stephanusperikope," *Jesus und der Menschensohn* [Fest. A. Vögtle; ed. R. Pesch, et al.; Freiburg, 1975] 283–99. Pesch, R., *Die Vision des Stephanus* [SBS 12; Stuttgart, 1966]. Richard, *Acts 6:1–8:4* [→ 43 above]; "Acts 7," *CBQ* 39 [1977] 190–208. Sabbe, M., in *Les Actes* [ed. J. Kremer] 241–79. Scharlemann, M., *Stephen, A Singular Saint* [AnBib 34; Rome, 1968]. Scobie, C., "The Use of Source Material in the Speeches of Acts III and VII," *NTS* 25 [1978–79] 399–421. Steck, O., *Israel und das gewaltsame Geschick der Propheten* [WMANT 23; Neukirchen, 1967]. Stemberger, G., "Die Stephanusrede," *Jesus in der Verkündigung der Kirche* [ed. A. Fuchs; SNTU A/1; Linz, 1976] 154–74. Wilckens, *Missionsreden* 200–24.)

51   (c) PHILIP AND THE ADVANCE OF THE WORD (8:4–40).

(i) *The gospel's triumph in Samaria* (8:4–25). Philip, "the evangelist" from Caesarea Maritima (21:8), one of the Hellenist Seven (6:5), was apparently associated with the Samaritan mission by the same tradition that furnished the eunuch story (vv 26–40). It is remarkable, however, that his activity is depicted only in very general terms (vv 5–8) and that he has no role in the encounter between Simon Magus and Simon Peter (vv 18–24). Either Luke rewrote a tradition that told of the magician's attempt to purchase the power of the Spirit from Philip (Dibelius, *Studies* 17; Haenchen, *Acts* 308), or he connected Philip's mission secondarily with a "Peter story" through the redactional vv 12–13 (Weiser, *Apg.* 200; Hengel, *Acts* 78–79). In any case, most agree that his concern to subordinate the Hellenists' mission to "the apostles in Jerusalem" (v 14) has produced the curious separation of baptism from the bestowal of the Spirit noted in v 16 (but cf. C. K. Barrett, in *Les Actes* [ed. J. Kremer] 293). Hereafter, Philip will mostly work in the "Gentile Hellenistic areas of the coastal plain" (v 40; Hengel). **4.** *preaching the word:* An echo of this in v 25, at the end of the Samaria story, shows the guiding editorial interest in between: the unity of the dispersed Hellenists with the apostles in the mission. **5.** *the city of*

Samaria: This uncertain reference (Sebaste? Shechem?) is perhaps owing to the person of Simon Magus, whose home was the Samaritan village of Gitta (Justin, *Apol.* 1.26.1–3). **6–8.** This account, though editorial and schematic (cf. 5:16; Luke 6:18), is true to the character of the Hellenists' mission and indicative of the proselytizing strategies in which they had to outdo their rivals. **9.** *Simon . . . practiced magic:* In the NT, only Acts takes notice of magic (cf. 13:6,8; 19:19), and this to cast it in the role of an adversary power conquered by the gospel. Simon's stature of archheretic and founding gnostic (Irenaeus, *Adv. Haer.* 1.23; Justin, *Apol.* 1.26.1–3; Hippolytus, *Ref.* 6.9–20; Epiphanius, *Haer.* 21.1–4) goes unmentioned, either because Luke "demoted" him to keep the apostolic period pure of heresy (C. H. Talbert, *Luke and the Gnostics* [Nash, 1966] 92–93), or because the heresiologists demonized him by making him the author of a later, full-blown heterodoxy (cf. R. Wilson, in *Les Actes* [ed. J. Kremer] 485–91). **10.** *the power of God called Great:* This sounds like the self-designation of a revelation bearer, which would mean that Simon was already more than a magician, perhaps a monger of gnosis in its birth-stage (Conzelmann, *Apg.* 60–61). **13.** *believed:* Simon's conversion by Philip consolidates the impression of the latter's overwhelming success (vv 6,8). **14–17.** In Luke's plan, new communities are bonded to the mother church by the visitation of her delegates (cf. 11:22). This editorial interest helps us to understand the anomaly of Philip's baptism without conferral of the Spirit (v 16). Whether received after (19:6) or even before (10:47–48) the rite, the holy Spirit operates only where there is communion with the apostles, who, as "witnesses of his resurrection" (1:22), certify the risen One's continued activity on earth. This is only *in via* toward an "early Catholic" conception; the Spirit is not controlled by ritual or office (v 15), and Simon's comeuppance will reaffirm its inviolable "gift" character (v 20; cf. 2:38; 10:45; 11:17). **21.** *part nor lot in this word:* This may mean "excommunication" (Haenchen), though it is vulgar pagan religiosity, not heresy, that is disowned. **52** (ii) *Philip and the Ethiopian eunuch* (8:26–40). The underlying tradition here was doubtless an account of the first Gentile conversion, told in Hellenist circles and rival to the Cornelius story (chap. 10), told in Jerusalem about Peter's discovery (Dinkler, "Philippus" 88). For the purposes of his history, Luke has left the religious status of the eunuch vague so as not to preempt the Gentile overture by Peter; but the deep African origin of this convert, conjuring readers' visions of dark-skinned hordes beyond civilization's outer boundaries, gave expressive evidence that the gospel, having conquered Samaria, was truly on its way to "the end of the earth" (1:8). **26.** *angel of the Lord:* Whether by an angel (5:19), or by the Spirit itself (v 39; 10:19; 11:12; 13:2), the initiatives of the mission are God's. Philip appears the merest pawn in the Spirit's program, much as the perplexed Peter is in 10:19–20. *southward from Jerusalem:* Having followed the mission northward to Samaria, we now appropriately sense an expanding circle, with Jerusalem as center, by taking the road that finally meets the great desert separating Palestine from Egypt. **27.** *eunuch:* Deut 23:1 ruled out admission of *castrati* into the racial and religious community of Israel. But cf. the promise to faithful eunuchs in Isa 56:3–5. **30–31.** The story's centerpiece, the Scripture instruction, is replete with Lucan cross-references. The Isa reading recalls Luke 4:16–21, and the fellow traveler's instruction (v 35), with sacramental outcome, strongly resembles the Emmaus walk (Luke 24:13–35). **32–33.** The pilgrim's text is Isa 53:7b–8c, cut off tantalizingly short of the Isaian Servant's death "for the transgressions of my

people" (v 8d)! Such cropping is not accidental; Luke's "theology of the cross" does not include atonement for sins (Rese, *Motive* 98–99). Christological interpretation here is more *eisegesis* than exegesis: the humiliated One has become the Exalted (cf. 4:11; 5:30f.; Luke 24:26) and obtained an innumerable following ("his generation"; Kränkl, *Jesus* 114–15). **34.** The eunuch's question, not too obviously prompted by the text, follows Luke's familiar *via negativa* in the OT (2:29–31,34–35; 13:34–37). "The eunuch questions as the ideal non-Christian reader should but only the Christian reader can" (Conzelmann, *Apg.* 63). [**37.**] An old Western variant (Irenaeus) adds a baptismal dialogue here from current practice. **39.** *caught up:* The vb. is from the vocabulary of heavenly assumptions (2 Cor 12:2,4; 1 Thess 4:17; Rev 12:5; 2 Kgs 2:16). **40.** We leave Philip in Caesarea Maritima, his home, where Paul will be his houseguest (21:8).

(Barrett, C. K., in *Les Actes* [ed. J. Kremer] 281–95. Casey, R., in *Beginnings* 5. 151–63. Dietrich, *Petrusbild* [→ 19 above] 245–56. Dinkler, E., "Philippus und der *anēr Aithiops,*" *Jesus und Paulus* [Fest. W. G. Kümmel; ed. E. E. Ellis and E. Grässer; Göttingen, 1975] 85–95. Grässer, E., *TRu* 42 [1977] 25–34. Hengel, *Between Jesus* [→ 43 above] 110–16. Unnik, W. C. van, "Der Befehl an Philippus," *ZNW* 47 [1956] 181–91. Wilson, R. M., in *Les Actes* [ed. J. Kremer] 485–91.)

53   **(B) The Persecutor Becomes the Persecuted (9:1–31).**
(a) THE CONVERSION OF SAUL (9:1–19a). The Ethiopian pilgrim's conversion has symbolically restated the goal of the mission, and Luke now turns to one of its largest milestones, the conversion of that fearsome enemy who was to become the greatest missionary and, therewith, the hero of the book's remaining chapters. Saul's conversion stands with that of Cornelius's household at the pivotal center of the history of Acts, each of these events having its extraordinary importance demonstrated through a twofold subsequent retelling by the protagonist. The story of Saul is told a second and third time in his speeches of self-defense (22:3–21; 26:2–23), and this shift of genres in recording the one event affords a rare opportunity to gauge Luke's editorial interests over against his source material. Recalling that the speeches are historiographical instruments for this author (→ 7 above), we shall sooner look for the pre-Lucan Saul story in its first telling, whereas "replays" in the speeches will likely be Luke's rewriting of the tale under viewpoints of his own (Löning, *Saulus-tradition* [→ 54 below] 18–19; C. W. Hedrick, *JBL* 100 [1981] 427–28).

The story told in chap. 9 is of a conversion, not a vocation. It records no commission given the blinded persecutor, only a prognosis of his future as persecuted Christian confessor (vv 15–16) delivered to the local church's representative, Ananias, who cures and baptizes him. As against this portrayal, the speech versions diminish the intercessor's role until he disappears altogether (26:13–18), and they draw Saul's vocation as the risen Lord's witness into the conversion event, so that Ananias delivers his mandate in 22:14–16, then he receives it directly from Christ in 26:15–18. By the third telling, therefore, conversion and vocation fully coincide, and we may identify this merger as a principal Lucan interest in rewriting the story (Burchard, *Der dreizehnte Zeuge* [→ 54 below] 120–21; Löning, *Saulustradition* [→ 54 below] 109–13). Many variations of detail among the three versions will be found to serve that interest, such as the suppression of the legendary blindness–healing sequence, differences in the sensory effects of the appearance, and the final suppression of

Saul's baptism (v 18; 22:16). Still others will be merely literary variations, such as regularly accompany Lucan repetitions (H. J. Cadbury, in *StLA* 88–97).

The first account of the Damascus experience, where the Saul tradition shows through most clearly, is too complex to derive from a single genre. It shares certain features of the punitive epiphany which deters the enemy of religion (e.g., Heliodorus, 2 Macc 3:27–29), the conversion legend told by Jewish propagandists (*Jos. Asen.* 14), and the OT epiphany dialogue (Gen 31:11–13; Gen 46:2–3; cf. Weiser, *Apg.* 217–19). Moreover, a feature in which the conversions of Saul and Cornelius are similar is the "double vision," in which the convert and his inductor are drawn together by cross-referential visions (vv 10–12; 10:3–20), a device sooner found in Hellenistic than OT-Jewish literature (Lohfink, *Conversion* [→ 54 below] 76). The close parallelism between the transactions in Acts 9 and 10 — convert's vision, reluctant inductor's vision, then their encounter, followed by the convert's baptism and reception of the Spirit — suggests that Luke has assimilated the two stories to some extent so that the foremost Gentile missionary and the first Gentile conversion could stand side by side at the pivotal center of his composition.

54   **1.** *still breathing threats:* Editorial connection is made with 8:3 and Saul's first appearance in the story. **2.** *letters to the synagogues in Damascus:* Such authority of the high priest over Diaspora communities cannot be documented by the witnesses usually cited: 1 Macc 15:15–21; Josephus, *Ant.* 14.10.2 §190–91; *J.W.* 1.24.2 §474. Paul's own testimonies of his persecution of the churches (1 Cor 15:9; Gal 1:13–14,23; Phil 3:6) may intersect with the Saul tradition used by Luke (cf. v 21). **3–4.** In the genre of the original Saul story, the light of the appearance was a blinding weapon against the persecutor, not a medium of revelation (Löning, *Saulustradition* 95–96). **4.** *why do you persecute me?:* This reproach is identical in all three versions (22:7; 26:14). In his disciples the Lord himself is persecuted (v 5), a conception peculiar to these passages but true to a *Christus praesens* theory of the mission (cf. comment on 2:4,33; R. F. O'Toole, *Bib* 62 [1981] 490–91). **5.** *who are you, Sir?:* Paul's counterquestion underscores the nonrevelatory nature of the dazzling light. His persecuting was a consequence of his failure to recognize the living *Kyrios* as his victim (cf. 3:17). **7.** The reaction of Saul's companions is precisely the reverse in 22:9: sight but no hearing (see comment there). **8–9.** The dreaded persecutor, completely immobilized and made a remorseful penitent, belongs to the pathos of the original appearance story. **11.** *Straight Street:* A well-known colonnaded thoroughfare of Damascus lends some local color to the Saul tradition, as do Ananias and the householder, Judas. **13.** It is probable that Ananias obeyed promptly in the original story, hence that v 12 led directly to v 17 (Löning, *Saulustradition* 27–28). Ananias's protest, which contains a typical Lucan retrospect (to 8:3; 9:1–2), follows awkwardly upon vv 11–12, and the reassurance of v 15 reduplicates that of v 11. Verses 13–16, therefore, belong to a redactional enlargement of the old story, with vv 13–14 allowing the insertion of the all-important vv 15–16. **15–16.** These verses contain Luke's principal comment on the Damascus event, even if they are not completely his creation (cf. Burchard, *Der dreizehnte Zeuge* 123; Radl, *Paulus* 69–81). To reassure the hesitant Ananias, the risen One lays down, but only in metaphor and inference, the program of Saul's future, to be carried out "point by point" in Acts (Conzelmann, *Apg.* 66). **15.** *my chosen one:* Lit., "vessel of election," a hebraistic adj. gen. (BDF 165). Cf. Rom 9:22–23, where the potter simile employs "vessels" in the sense of objects

of divine wrath or mercy (Burchard, *Der dreizehnte Zeuge* 101). The expression is artfully unspecific since it is to be unfolded gradually, by Lucan "intensification," over the other accounts (22:14–15; 26:16; Lohfink, *Conversion* 94). *to bear my name:* This phrase, usually misunderstood in terms of mission journeys, means only to confess the name publicly before (prep. *enōpion*) Gentiles and Jews. The articular infin. expresses purpose, hence "chosen to confess," and provides for the concrete situation of public arraignment before the specified groups, just as chaps. 22–26 will record it. **16.** *how much he must suffer:* The *gar* up front makes this application of the messianic passion imperative to Saul the direct corollary of his election as confessor. What is announced is not yet Paul's missionary work, but the harsh experience before the world's tribunals that was forecast for all Jesus' disciples in Luke 21:12–19. Ananias's protest is thus allayed with irony: the fierce persecutor is now to become the one fiercely persecuted (Burchard, *Der dreizehnte Zeuge* 103). **17.** *Jesus, who appeared to you:* The Easter-appearance terminology (*ophtheis soi;* cf. 1 Cor 15:8) hardly fits what we have been told, but it will figure prominently in Luke's speech adaptations of this story (22:14; 26:16). **18–19.** The old story ended with Saul's healing and baptism, without provision for his mission as "witness" (22:15; 26:16); yet this is the very role he will immediately play at Damascus (v 20). As for his baptism, unmentioned in the epistles, see R. Fuller, in *Les Actes* [ed. J. Kremer] 503–8.

(Burchard, C., *Der dreizehnte Zeuge* [Göttingen, 1970] 51–136. Hedrick, C. W., "Paul's Conversion/Call," *JBL* 100 [1981] 415–32. Léon-Dufour, X., "L'Apparition du ressuscité à Paul," *Resurrexit* [ed. E. Dhanis; Rome, 1976] 266–94. Löning, K., *Die Saulustradition in der Apostelgeschichte* [Münster, 1973]. Lohfink, G., *The Conversion of St. Paul* [Chicago, 1976]. Steck, O., "Formgeschichtliche Bemerkungen zur Darstellung des Damaskusgeschehens in der Apostelgeschichte," *ZNW* 67 [1976] 20–28. Stolle, V., *Der Zeuge als Angeklagter* [Stuttgart, 1973] 155–212.)

55   (b) SAUL'S PREACHING AND PERIL IN DAMASCUS (9:19b–25). This paragraph and vv 26–30 are similarly structured since Saul's preaching in Damascus and Jerusalem is countered both times by Jewish rejection and designs on his life, prompting hasty flight from both cities. Echoes of Gal 1:13–24 in vv 20–21, and of 2 Cor 11:32–33 in v 25, do not come from use of those letters but from the "Pauline legend," which was already developing in Damascus and Jerusalem (cf. Gal 1:23–24) and which flowed highly developed into Acts (H. Schenke, *NTS* 21 [1974–75] 511–12). The main divergence here from Paul's account of his early period is the omission of his sojourn in Arabia (Gal 1:17), which moves the conversion and first Jerusalem visit much closer together (v 23) than the "three years" reported in Gal 1:18. **20.** *the Son of God:* The rarity of this title in Acts (13:33) confirms Luke's reliance on Pauline tradition here (Gal 1:16), as in "destroyed" (*porthēsas,* v 21; Gal 1:13,23). **23–25.** The risen Lord's demonstration of the harsh consequences of Saul's election (v 16) gets under way promptly with his preaching. In 2 Cor 11:32 it was the Damascus deputy of the Nabatean king, Aretas, whose onslaught caused Saul's hasty flight. Our account probably reflects Luke's systematic view of the Jews as the foremost enemy of his mission from beginning to end (cf. 28:25–28; but cf. Hengel, *Acts* 85).

56   (c) SAUL'S CONFRONTATIONS IN JERUSALEM (9:26–31). **26.** *all feared him:* Disbelief of his discipleship could hardly be lingering three years later (Gal 1:18). Luke may be disguising their discomfort with the antinomian theologian as an outdated fear of the strongman (Hengel, *Acts* 86). **27.** *Barnabas:* His role need not be

Luke's invention but could result from his source's anticipation of the later comradeship. **29.** *Hellenists:* Clearly the traditionalists among Jerusalem's immigrant Jews (cf. comment on 6:1). **31.** *peace:* As a summary concluding vv 1-31, this statement attributes the peace of the Palestinian churches to the change in Saul's career!

57 (C) Peter as Missionary (9:32-11:18).
(a) MIRACLES IN LYDDA AND JOPPA (9:32-43). After the dramatic outreach of the Hellenist Philip and the conversion of the world mission's hero, all is in readiness for the conclusive phase of Luke's history, the mission to the Gentiles. But in his schema, this must be inaugurated by Peter, not Paul, and so two miracles fix our attention on the leading apostle as prelude to his epoch-making conversion of Cornelius. The miracles, particularly the second, evoke similar feats of Jesus (Luke 5:24-26; 8:49-56; cf. F. Neirynck, in *Les Actes* [ed. J. Kremer] 182-88), and so contribute a sense of continuity between Master and apostle which will help integrate the Gentile conversion into the christocentric plan of history. **32.** *Lydda:* Gk form of Lod, a town on the old Joppa road some 25 mi. NW of Jerusalem. The area had already been evangelized, and the Aeneas healing remained in local tradition. **34.** *heals you:* Once again, the one who heals is the *Christus praesens,* not Peter (cf. 3:6,16; 4:10,30). **36-43.** The resurrection story has OT models (1 Kgs 17:17-24; 2 Kgs 4:32-37) and sustains a continuum of this ultimate thaumaturgy from Elijah through Jesus down to Paul (20:9-12). **36.** *Joppa:* Yāpô, Jaffa, an ancient port city *ca.* 12 mi. farther NW from Lod. St. Peter's Church, spectacularly mounted on a coastal cliff south of the beaches of modern Tel Aviv, commemorates the apostle's Joppa sojourn. *Tabitha:* Dorcas, the transl. of the Aram name, together with LXX borrowings (3 Kgs 17:17,19; 4 Kgs 4:33,35), show this to be a Jewish-Christian story transmitted by hellenized Christians. **40.** *putting them all outside:* Cf. Mark 5:40 with Luke 8:51. *Tabitha, stand up:* Cf. *talitha koum[i]* (Mark 5:41). **41.** *he presented her alive:* Cf. 1:3. **43.** *with one Simon, a tanner:* The stage is set for the momentous event to follow (10:6).

58 (b) THE CONVERSION OF CORNELIUS AND HIS HOUSEHOLD (10:1-11:18). The Cornelius sequence, which is the pivot of Luke's argument in Acts, comprises five scenes: (i) Cornelius's vision, vv 1-8; (ii) Peter's vision, vv 9-16; (iii) Peter's reception of the centurion's messengers in Joppa, vv 17-23; (iv) the proceedings in Cornelius's house, vv 24-48; (v) the accounting of the event by Peter at Jerusalem, 11:1-18. M. Dibelius (*Studies* 109-22) argued that the basic tradition here was a pietistic conversion story, similar to that of the Ethiopian in chap. 8 and typical of the tales of prominent conversions that edified many early communities. To this older legend Luke made four additions, including the two interpretive speeches (10:34-43; 11:5-18), Peter's vision of animals proffered for eating (10:9-16), and the intrusive "flashback" to the vision in 10:27-29a (so also Weiser, *Apg.* 253-62). The speeches are a Lucan staple, of course, but the vision represents a separate tradition, originally told to dispel inherited food taboos, which Luke adduced here in symbolic application to people taboos (10:28b) so as to elevate the Cornelius episode to the "classic" or foundational status it has in 15:6-18. This feature of Dibelius's criticism has been disowned by more recent contributors, who contend that the apostle's vision is indispensable to the economy of the larger story (K. Löning, *BZ* 18 [1974] 3-6) and completely dependent on the interpretation it receives in that context, which relates it closely to the issue of Peter's liability in 11:3 and Gal 2:12 (K. Haacker, *BZ* 24 [1980] 240-41). Consensus is also wanting on the first of the two

speeches, where an apparent overreaching of the kerygmatic schema of the earlier Petrine sermons convinces some of the text's pre-Lucan provenance (P. Stuhlmacher, R. Guelich). There is broader agreement that 11:1-18 contains a Lucan summation of the meaning of the centurion's conversion, making it a "classic" precedent for the whole church (15:7) and thus preparing for Luke's version of the Jerusalem conference (chap. 15; Conzelmann, *Apg.* 69).

59 (i) *The vision of Cornelius* (10:1-8). **1.** *Caesarea:* This magnificent Hellenistic port city, *ca.* 30 mi. N of Joppa, was the capital of Palestine for nearly 600 years after Herod the Great built it in 37-34 BC. The Roman prefects and procurators, including Pontius Pilate (AD 26-36), had their headquarters and residence here after AD 6, when they came to rule Judea directly. The "Italian cohort" seems, however, to be an anachronism since it is documented for the first time in Syria *ca.* AD 69, and Roman soldiers cannot have been quartered in Caesarea prior to the death of Agrippa I (AD 44; cf. Josephus, *Ant.* 19.9.1-2 §354-66). **2.** *a pious man and God-fearer:* The eulogy of the officer is in good Lucan style (Weiser, *Apg.* 253-54) and is related to the recognition word inaugurating Peter's discourse (vv 34-35), where the heightened significance of the conversion reaches full expression. Luke is the only NT author to use the phrase *phoboumenos/sebomenos ton theon* technically to designate the Gentile fringe of synagogue attendance (cf. 13:16,26; 17:4,17), and although one should not apply this meaning everywhere (K. Lake, in *Beginnings* 5. 86), Cornelius's synagogue connection seems to be indicated by his observance of the appointed "ninth-hour" prayer (v 3; cf. 3:1). **3.** *angel of God:* Heavenly beings direct the earthly action throughout the Cornelius story, illustrating the abiding truth of the affair: that "God made it his business" to accept Gentiles as his people (15:14); it did not happen on human initiative. The narrative will return to this vision three times (vv 22,30-32; 11:13-14), underscoring by repetition its decisive causality at the start of the proceedings. **4-6.** The heavenly direction includes commands but no explanations; the humans are pawns in a turn of events wholly enacted from above (Haenchen, *Acts* 347; K. Löning, *BZ* 18 [1974] 8). **4.** *have gone up as a memorial:* This mimetic phraseology is equivalent to "are remembered" (v 31; cf. Sir 50:16; Tob 12:12). The pagan's piety is to be rewarded without the entitlement of membership in the elect! **6.** *Simon, a tanner:* Connection is made with and information added to 9:43, where Luke editorially anticipated data of the Cornelius tradition.

60 (ii) *The vision of Peter* (10:9-16). **9.** *as they neared the city:* The synchronizing (v 17) is from above, whence even the timing of our story's action is determined. Prayer is the prelude to vision, as in 22:17; Luke 1:10; 3:21; 9:28-29; 22:41-43. **11.** *the heavens opened:* Cf. 7:56; Luke 3:21. This vision, like the centurion's, will be magnified through repetition (v 28; 11:5-10). *a receptacle resembling a great cloth:* Responding to Peter's hunger (v 10), this is apparently a table setting, though its contents are hard to visualize. **12.** *fourfooted beasts and reptiles and birds:* This listing echoes Gen 1:24(28,30; 6:20) and has obviously become a rhetorical commonplace (Rom 1:23). It already hints that a theology of creation (Gen 1:31; 1 Tim 4:4) annuls all food taboos (Weiser, *Apg.* 264). **13.** *slaughter and eat:* The "voice" ignores the strictures against certain species in Lev 11:2-23 and Deut 14:3-20. **14.** *unclean:* Peter's demurral, echoing Ezek 4:14, correspondingly ignores the presence of clean animals on the cloth! Some scholars (Haenchen, Löning, Haacker) insist that this shows that the vision was never told separately to dispel food restrictions but can only have the figurative sense of voiding distinctions between clean and unclean humans (v 28). **15.** *declared clean:* The causative vb. has a forensic meaning, as in Lev 13:13 LXX. All creatures' purity is thus promulgated, not effectuated, by the vision, and that is its very point (cf. 15:9).

61   (iii) *Reception of the messengers* (10:17–23a). In this scene the strands of the previous two are united. **17.** *inwardly baffled:* Peter's vision is now shown to be a riddle, whether or not it was intended as such when first related (cf. K. Löning, *BZ* 18 [1974] 11); its solution must follow in the figurative interpretation Peter learns from subsequent happenings (v 28). **19.** *the Spirit:* With the apostle perplexed and the messengers seeking him, a new intervention from on high is needed to bring the principals together, so punctually is divine control plotted throughout the story. Strangely, the speaker makes no reference to the foregoing vision, which may confirm the latter's secondary addition to the context (with vv 17a,19a). **23a.** Peter, though himself a guest, makes the visitors his guests! Thus does the story concentrate on its principals.

62   (iv) *Proceedings in Cornelius's house* (10:23b–48). **23b.** *brothers from Joppa:* They are numbered six in 11:12 and are important parti-pris witnesses to what follows (10:45). **24.** *his relatives and closest friends:* If this story was a foundation legend for the local church, these would presumably be the first Christians of Caesarea (Haenchen, *Acts* 361). **25.** *worshiped him:* Prostration before the apostle, which he wards off here, will become a commonplace suppliant's gesture in the apocryphal Acts (e.g., *Acts Pet.*), which will not limit their heroes to mere human status. Cf. 14:11–15; 28:6. **27–29.** If one holds Peter's vision to be an extraneous addition to the older story, these verses, which include the specific solution to the vision's enigma (v 28), must also be such (Dibelius, *Studies* 113; but cf. Schneider, *Apg.* 2. 72). **27.** *conversed with him:* There is scant room for this, given Peter's query in v 29b. **28.** *call no person common or unclean: Anthrōpon* reveals the allegorical meaning attributed to the animals Peter saw. "Common or unclean" is a hendiadys; what is "common" is accessible and permissible to all, whence the nuance of "profane," "unholy." **29b.** This question may resume the original narrative from v 26 (Dibelius). Like v 21, it introduces a reprise of vv 1–8 in direct discourse and sounds rather obtuse after all Luke has told us.

63   Peter's Sermon (10:34–43). Nowhere is the question of tradition vs. Lucan composition raised more acutely than in this passage, which alters both beginning and end of the mission-discourse schema we came to know in chaps. 2 and 3 (→ 7 above). In place of the familiar call for repentance comes a kerygma of universal forgiveness under the auspices of the one appointed judge of the world (vv 42–43), matching the conclusion of Paul's speech to Gentile Athenians (17:30–31) and the argument of 1 Thess 1:10. Up front, the expanded Jesus kerygma begins with the concept of God's "good news" to Israel (v 36), based on Isa 52:7 (Nah 2:1), thus associating the "gospel" (ptc. *euangelizomenos*) with a schematic account of Jesus' earthly activity after John's baptism (v 37), much as Mark (1:1) would apply the term *euangelion* to his account of the public life. The crucial issue is joined with the question: Does this sermon represent a traditional preaching pattern out of which the Synoptic Gospels developed (C. H. Dodd, *New Testament Studies* [Manchester, 1953] 1–11; P. Stuhlmacher, in *Das Evangelium* [→ 65 below] 22–23, 181–82; Guelich, "Gospel Genre" [→ 65 below] 208–16), or has Luke here reshaped the Petrine kerygma into an outline of the narrative gospel in his own literary version (Wilckens, *Missionsreden* 69; Weiser, *Apg.*

258–59)? The first position probably makes too much of the indubitable tradition layer underlying the sermon, for the hand of Luke is heavy throughout (better Roloff, *Apg.* 167–68). **34–35.** A word of recognition by Peter connects discourse to situation. Thought by some to be the climax of the original legend (Bauernfeind, Löning), it is nevertheless filled with good Lucan expression. *accepter of persons:* On *prosōpolēmptēs,* see comment on Rom 2:11. The antonym is *kardiognōstēs,* "knower of hearts" (15:8; cf. 1 Thess 2:4). The universalist thought pattern goes back to Paul. **36–37.** The grammar is confusing here. Rather than make "the word" the object of the subsequent "you know" (v 37), or strike "which" as a copyist's error, it is better to read them in apposition to the "that"-clause in the previous statement (v 34), hence as a continuation of Peter's solemn "I understand" (Schneider, *Apg.* 2. 75–76). Verse 37 is then a new sentence. The content of "the word" is, in any case, the confession, "He is Lord of all," to be understood in the light of Rom 10:12 and as the creed of Greek-speaking Christians, who made *Kyrios* the name of the unpredisposed *Pantokratōr* (v 42; cf. Hengel, *Acts* 104–5). *proclaiming peace:* The tradition of the eschatological prophecy based on Isa 52:7 and 61:1 (v 38) was applied to Jesus' ministry with redoubled emphasis in Luke's Gospel (7:22; 4:17–20), and his commission of disciples as "peace" harbingers in the same tradition was prominent in the mission instruction (Luke 10:5–6). *beginning from Galilee:* With v 39, this forms the geographical delimitation of the authentic Jesus tradition, keyed to accrediting the apostolic witness (13:31) just as 1:22 did in chronological terms. Mention of baptism has particular relevance to the Pentecost "replay" in vv 44–46, since JBap was made the prophet of the Pentecost in 1:5 (cf. 11:15–16). Peter's kerygma is thus not so irrelevant to its narrative context, as Dibelius thought (*Studies* 162). **38.** *God anointed him:* The allusion to Isa 61:1 recalls Jesus' investiture with the "power" of the Spirit at his baptism (Luke 3:22; 4:14,18). This introduces *topoi* of the Hellenistic "divine man" (Conzelmann, *Apg.* 73), depicting Jesus' ministry as his "witnesses" carry it forward (v 39). For them, as for him (2:22), powerful deeds are the proof of God's saving action through earthly agents. **39.** *suspending him:* Cf. 5:30. **40–41.** *he gave him to be manifested:* Luke 24:31,45 offer commentary on this unusual expression, which serves the kerygma's focus on God's sovereign action. On Luke's alternation of the apostles and a wider circle of Easter witnesses at center stage, see comment on 1:2. **42.** *to the people:* The special responsibility of the Twelve to Israel (*ho laos*) is reaffirmed (cf. 13:31; comment on 1:21). *judge of the living and the dead:* The universality of Jesus' judgment, as of his lordship (v 36), is thus a bracketing motif for the sermon and its principal point of connection with the context (likewise v 43: "all who believe"). **43.** This verse completes the text's reprise of Luke 24:44–48.

64   Reception of the Spirit and Baptism (10:44–48). **44.** *still speaking:* Does 11:15 therefore recall a stage of the Cornelius tradition as yet lacking Peter's discourse? *fell upon:* The vb. emphasizes the Spirit's unmediated action, thus its "gift" character (v 45), independent even of baptism (v 48; cf. comment on 8:14–17). **45.** *poured out:* This vb. is an explicit echo of Joel's prophecy applied to Pentecost (2:17–18,33); 11:15 will formally state the connection implied here (v 47). **46.** *speaking in tongues:* An accompanying phrase makes this surpass mere glossolalia, as in 19:6 (cf. comment on 2:4). **47.** *can anyone forbid:* Here is the target of the story's several notices of the divine control of its action. The Spirit has moved, the institution can only follow (cf. 11:17). **48.** *to remain:* Peter's sojourn creates the space and issue for what follows.

65 (v) *Peter's Accounting at Jerusalem* (11:1–18). This section gives the Cornelius story its foundational status and full Lucan context. **2.** *those of the circumcision:* I.e., Jewish Christians, not a faction (15:5), although the adj. "faithful" (10:45) is missing. **3.** *ate with them:* This was not mentioned in chap. 10, but that does not mean a phase of the old story has been eliminated (so K. Löning, *BZ* 18 [1974] 10–11). Table fellowship is but the ultimate affront to Mosaic sensibilities given by one who becomes a Gentile's houseguest (10:48). This was also the issue in Gal 2:12 (K. Haacker, *BZ* 24 [1980] 240). **4.** *in order:* Cf. Luke 1:3. As in the Gospel prologue, the "order" is that of salvation history's logic, not a mechanical chronology. **5–14.** Peter's account covers the story from his vantage point, and the author hones the coverage to fashion his own balance sheet. **15.** *as I began to speak:* Since the sermon we heard at this point was for our consumption as readers, it can be omitted from the review of essential happenings (cf. comment on 10:45). *in the beginning:* Pentecost gets *archē*-status comparable to Jesus' baptism by JBap (1:22): in the two events, the Spirit inaugurated the successive phases of Luke's history. **16.** Peter recalls JBap's prophecy that originally connected the two "beginnings" (1:5). **18.** *to the Gentiles too:* Here is the story's final upshot for Luke's history, the definitive authorization of its new phase (Zingg, *Wachsen* 197).

(Bovon, F., "Tradition et rédaction en Actes 10,1–11,18," *TZ* 26 [1970] 22–45. Busse, U., *Die Wunder des Propheten Jesus* [FB 24; Stuttgart, 1977] 337–72. Dibelius, *Studies* 109–22. Dietrich, *Petrusbild* [→ 19 above] 256–95. Dupont, *Études* 75–81; *Salvation* 24–27. Guelich, G., "The Gospel Genre," *Das Evangelium* [ed. P. Stuhlmacher] 183–219. Haacker, K., "Dibelius und Cornelius," *BZ* 24 [1980] 234–51. Löning, K., "Die Korneliustradition," *BZ* 18 [1974] 1–19. Nellessen, *Zeugnis* [→ 19 above] 180–97. Stuhlmacher, P., "Zum Thema: Das Evangelium und die Evangelien," *Das Evangelium* 1–26; "Das paulinische Evangelium," ibid. 158–82; idem (ed.), *Das Evangelium und die Evangelien* [Tübingen, 1983]. Wilckens, *Missionsreden* 46–50, 63–70.)

66 **(D) Between Jerusalem and Antioch (11:19–12:25).** Luke interrupted the story of the fleeing Hellenists by design in order to insert the events to which he gave foundational significance for the worldwide mission: the conversions of Saul and Cornelius. He can now continue the refugees' story, since the beginning they are about to make (v 20) has been safely inserted into the "apostolic tradition" by the "detour" taken in 9:1–11:18. The firm bond between the first Gentile church, Antioch, and the apostolic mother church will be the editorial motif of this new section, which will recount the "inspection" visit by Jerusalem's delegate, Barnabas, his conduct of Saul to Antioch, and their joint mission to bear the new community's relief offerings back to Jerusalem. This mission, in fact, appears to frame the account of the apostolic church's persecution and deliverance in chap. 12, bordered by 11:30 and 12:25. Luke will rely here on disparate traditions which he works up into an overall picture; he is hardly using an integral "Antioch source" (*pace* Hengel, *Acts* 99; cf. Weiser, *Apg.* 275).

(a) THE FIRST CHURCH OF THE GENTILE MISSION (11:19–30). **19.** *those scattered:* Connection is made editorially with 8:1,4, retrieving the thread of the Hellenists' story. Their path has led up the Mediterranean coast N of Palestine (Phoenicia) and to the nearby island of Cyprus, then to the capital of the Roman provincial government of Syria, Antioch on the Orontes, where there was a strong Jewish community (see W. A. Meeks and R. Wilken, *Jews and Christians in Antioch* [SBLSBS 13; Missoula, 1978] 1–18). That only Jews were evangelized is Luke's preface to the report that

follows. **20.** *to the Greeks also:* Despite the authoritative reading in ms. B, "Hellenists," which is rejected by commentators as often as it is preferred by editors (e.g N-A[26]), the better choice is *hellēnas*, "Greeks," properly contrasting with *Ioudaiois*, "Jews," in v 19 (Zingg, *Wachsen* 205–7). We meet Luke's source material here, for the report takes no cognizance of the precedent of Cornelius. Verse 21 typically generalizes the information as evidence of the divine force propelling the mission. **22–24.** Barnabas (4:36) performs the visitation which, like 8:14, secures the new church's ties to the mother church. **25–26.** Barnabas's conduct of Saul from his hometown is hard to credit; it looks like a Lucan stratagem to pick up the dangling thread of Saul's mission (9:30; but cf. Gal 1:21) and to reiterate his subordination to the apostolic church (cf. 9:27; Schneider, *Apg.* 2. 88, 91–92). That Barnabas and Saul were among Antioch's prophets and teachers is, however, assured by the traditional listing in 13:1. *Christians:* The use of this name by outsiders attests that at Antioch the "Christ-people" first stood out as a sect distinct from Judaism (see Meeks and Wilken, *Jews* 15–16; Zingg, *Wachsen* 217–22). **27.** *prophets:* Jerusalem is even the source of the prophetic charism (1 Cor 14:1,3) in its offspring congregation. On wandering prophets in earliest Christianity, see G. Theissen, *Sociology of Early Palestinian Christianity* (Phl, 1978). **28.** *Agabus:* See 21:10. *a great famine:* This subject matter and its universal dimension fit the conventions of apocalyptic prophecy; cf. Mark 13:8; Rev 6:8. (For a possible historical reference, → Paul, 79:11.) **30.** *to the elders:* Abruptly and without introduction, we encounter the postapostolic leadership of the mother church (15:2–6,22–23; 16:4; 21:18). This purported visit of Saul to Jerusalem cannot be identified with either his first (9:26; Gal 1:18) or his fateful council visit (15:2; Gal 2:1); Paul's account in Gal excludes others in between. This relief mission is hardly Luke's invention, but Saul's part in it may be (→ Paul, 79:25).

67 (b) HEROD'S PERSECUTION AND PETER'S ESCAPE (12:1–25). Divine custody of the apostle and vengeance against the persecutor are the exquisite counterpoint of this section, which is sandwiched between the dispatch and return of Antioch's envoys (similarly Mark 6:7–13,30). Its centerpiece is the rescue story (vv 6–11), which goes on to tell with relish the miracle's effects on fellow believers (vv 12–17) and captors (vv 18–19), and all within a framework formed by the account of the doomed Agrippa (vv 1–5,20–23). Both the rescue and the impious king's demise are told in conventional forms known from the literature of religious propaganda (Weiser, *Apg.* 284–86). **1.** *Herod the King:* Herod Agrippa I, grandson of Herod the Great (→ History, 75:173). **2.** *James:* Son of Zebedee (→ NT Thought, 81:139). At this point, with the mission to homeland Jewry behind us, there will be no move to replace James, as there was Judas (1:15–26), in the circle of the Twelve. **6–19.** Peter's rescue, its effect heightened by the "four squads" guarding him (v 4) and augured by the church's prayer (v 5), belongs to the genre of rescues by divine epiphany, which argue the validity of a revelation by reason of its prevailing over humanly insuperable powers of nature or state (cf. 5:17–25; 16:25–34; Theissen, *Miracle Stories* [→ 37 above] 99, 101). The local color and *nominatim* personal references (vv 12–13) indicate that this story came to Luke among other "Peter stories" and was possibly reworked by him in composing 5:17–25 (→ 40 above). **11.** *expectation of the Jewish people:* This statement, carrying the author's assessment of the miracle, documents the further development of the process that began at the stoning of Stephen: the defection of "the people" who once welcomed the apostolic ministry (2:47; 5:13) into unbelieving Jewry and, therewith, "the true Israel's" outreach to the Gentiles (W. Radl, *BZ* 27 [1983] 83–84). **12.** *John called Mark:* Cf. 1:25; 15:37; → Mark, 41:2. **17.** *report this to James:* This is "the brother of the Lord" (Gal 1:19), who will emerge as the leader of the Jerusalem church as the apostles fade from Luke's pages (cf. 15:13; 21:18; → NT Thought, 81:143). **20–23.** Cf. the account of Herod Agrippa's death in Josephus, *Ant.* 19.8.2 §343–54 (→ History, 75:176). The king's fate is condign because the persecutor's sin is the same as the blasphemer's: contention with God (5:39). **24–25.** Lucan framework (cf. 11:30). **24.** A growth summary appraises the persecutor's demise (cf. 9:31). Since unbelieving Jewry stood behind the king (v 3), the end of his threat to the church coincides with the end of her confinement within Judaism—something of a symbolic overtone to Peter's release (W. Radl, *BZ* 27 [1983] 87). **25.** *Barnabas and Saul returned:* The connection with 11:30 requires "from Jerusalem," but the mss. are divided between "from" (*ex* or *apo*) and "to" (*eis*, which can also mean "in" in NT Greek); → Paul, 79:25. Since the better codices show *eis* and it is the *lectio difficilior,* one might take it with *plērōsantes,* "having completed their service *in* Jerusalem" leaving "returned" without destination (as in 8:28; 20:3). Other instances where a finite aor. form of *hypostrephein* is left without adverbial complement, when a succeeding prep. phrase is construed with a ptc. following it are Luke 12:25; 10:17, both exemplary of this author's stylistic freedom (cf. Dupont, *Études* 235–41, along with Haenchen, Schneider, and Weiser).

(Dupont, *Études* 217–41. Hengel, *Acts* 99–107. Radl, W., "Befreiung aus dem Gefängnis," *BZ* 27 [1983] 81–96. Zingg, *Wachsen* 180–228.)

68   (E) The First Missionary Journey of Paul (13:1–14:28). Based on Luke's literary management of his raw materials, it is conventional to differentiate three "journeys" in his account of Paul's missions (→ Paul, 79:28–45): (I) chaps. 13–14, in the company of Barnabas and limited to Cyprus and SE Asia Minor; (II) 15:40–18:22, with principal stations in Greece, Paul alone as protagonist; (III) 18:23–21:16, dubiously articulated at the beginning, with sweep of Asia Minor and Macedonia, ending in Jerusalem. Whereas Missions II and III have good support in Paul's letters (→ Paul, 79:6), Mission I is never referred to by him (but see Gal 1:21–23), nor does he report mission activity in Barnabas's company (but see Gal 2:1). Some scholars doubt the historicity of Mission I on this basis (Conzelmann, Schneider), but the same sequence of (Pisidian) Antioch (13:14–50), Iconium (13:51–14:5), and Lystra (14:6–20) is attested independently of Luke in 2 Tim 3:11. In view of this remnant of an itinerary and the several traditions Luke found associated with it, many now defend Mission I as a correctly situated but fragmentary record of the 13-year interval mentioned in Gal 1:21; 2:1 (Hengel, *Acts* 108–10; Roloff, *Apg.* 194–95; Weiser, *Apg.* 308–10). Of course, this section does not intend to retail information; it serves Luke's reader as an introduction to the method and schedule of Paul's activity ("Jew first, and then Greek," cf. Rom 1:16!), and it thus sharpens the crucial issue to be resolved by the Jerusalem Council (chap. 15).
69   (a) Prelude to the Journey (13:1–3). **1.** *prophets and teachers:* The list of resident "prophets and teachers" of the Antioch congregation comes from Luke's tradition and agrees with lists of leading community functions in Rom 12:6–7; 1 Cor 12:28. Persons other than Barnabas and Saul are otherwise unknown. Paul's reticence about his Antioch ties in the letters, where the city is mentioned but once, must be due to the

fateful parting of ways that occurred there (Gal 2:11–14). **2–3.** This solemn and stylized account of the two missionaries' deputation plainly shows Luke's hand (Weiser, *Apg.* 304–5) but rests on solid historical evidence of their partnership as Antiochene envoys (Gal 2:1,9) and fellow apostles (1 Cor 9:6; Acts 14:4,14). In fact, the early rationale of the apostleship as delegation by the risen Lord is echoed in this report of vocation by the Spirit. **2.** *as they were worshiping:* The cultic sense of *leitourgein,* "perform a service," is favored by Luke's LXX mimesis (cf. Exod 28:35,43; 29:30; Num 18:2). The revelation was delivered through prophetic utterance in the assembly gathered for worship (cf. 1 Cor 14:26–33). **3.** *laying on their hands:* It is hard to trace this rite to the period in question, even as a commissioning after the rabbinic model of the *šālîaḥ,* "commissioned emissary" (→ NT Thought, 81:150–52; *pace* J. Coppens, in *Les Actes* [ed. J. Kremer] 417–20). Here it is at most a blessing by peers (v 1), certainly not an ordination rite (Schneider, *Apg.* 2. 115). As in other cases (6:6; 8:17; 19:6), Luke may be reading back the broader ritual practice of his own day (Roloff, *Apg.* 194).
70   (b) A Contest Won by Paul in Cyprus (13:4–12). **4.** *sent out:* The holy Spirit launches the journey in which, by its final assessment, God "opened a door of faith to the Gentiles" (14:27). **4–5.** Seleucia was the seaport of Antioch, 16 mi. distant, and Salamis was the E port of the island of Cyprus, homeland of Barnabas (4:36). *in the synagogues:* This "Jews first" schedule (13:46) will be programmatically broken by the conversion of the proconsul (v 12). *John as assistant:* His modest role forestalls any chagrin over v 13. **6.** *magician:* The mission meets its competitor in the arena of thaumaturgy and divination, both included in a broad Hellenistic usage of *magos* (A. Nock, in *Beginnings* 5. 175–82). The adversary's double name (v 8) and double billing could result from a fusion of traditions (Dibelius, *Studies* 16), but not necessarily (Weiser, *Apg.* 313). **7.** *Sergius Paulus:* The propraetor, resident in the provincial capital, Paphos, apparently has the sorcerer in his retinue; but as a "man of intelligence," he is in the wrong company. That such prominent men embraced the gospel serves the apologia for it as a socially respectable movement (Haenchen, *Acts* 403). **8.** *Elymas:* The second name's etymology is inscrutable, but the issue of the contest is unmistakable: God's "ways" (v 10) vs. quackery. **9.** *Paul:* Luke's shift from the Jewish sobriquet, Saul, to the Roman family name (→ Paul, 79:3) coincides with the first conversion of the missionary's journeys. "Saul" reappears hereafter only in replays of the conversion (chaps. 22, 26). **9–11.** *filled with the holy Spirit:* Paul now succeeds Peter and Stephen (4:8; 6:5) as exemplary "Spirit-bearer." He first exercises pneumatic scrutiny of the sinner (cf. 8:20–23), then performs something like a "rule miracle" (cf. 5:1–11), reinforcing the divine stricture against sorcery. Since the magician's blindness is nevertheless of limited duration ("for a time"), the miracle seems aimed at repentance rather than retribution (cf. 5:5,10).
71   (c) Mission and Rejection at Pisidian Antioch (13:13–52). Verses 13–14a, which move the scene to the Asia Minor mainland, also move Paul into the position of principal actor ("Paul and his company"). Verses 14b–43 and 44–52 constitute a "dramatic episode" with two related scenes, situated on successive sabbaths (vv 14,44). The first scene features Paul's one and only missionary sermon to Jewish listeners (vv 16–41); the second brings "nearly the whole city" to hear the missionaries, who now meet with blasphemous rejection from the Jews and are forced to leave town. The sharp contrast between the eager listeners of the first scene (vv

42-43) and the jealous antagonists of the second (v 45) is not explained by the narrative because the logic of it is that which underlies the whole of Acts: the Word goes to the Jews first by salvation-historical necessity, and their rejection of it begets the mission to the Gentiles (v 46). Luke illustrates this theorem, inherited from Paul (Rom 11:11-12), in a bipartite episode which opens the door to the whole Pauline section of Acts (cf. 18:6; 28:26-28; Radl, *Paulus* 92-94; Haenchen, *Acts* 417). In this respect, it compares closely with Jesus' inaugural preaching at Nazareth (Luke 4:16-30), which is similarly structured: synagogue instruction on the sabbath, contrasting public reactions, scriptural argument for the mission beyond Israel, preacher's flight from town. Both episodes enunciate the program of the ministry they inaugurate, and their parallelism implies the essential continuity of the two ministries (Radl, *Paulus* 385-86).

(i) *Mise-en-scène and sermon* (13:13-43). **13.** *John left them:* Cf. 15:37-38. **14.** *Pisidian Antioch:* Administrative center for the Roman province of Galatia, with a sizable Jewish community, but reachable from Perga (100 mi.) only by a hazardous mountain journey. *entering the synagogue:* That this is invariably Paul's first visit in a town (9:20; 14:1; [16:13]; 17:1-2,10,17; 18:4,19; 19:8) is based on good historical probability but has become, for Luke, a stereotypical expression of the theorem of v 46. **15.** *a word of exhortation:* An address after the readings is true to synagogue protocol. Cf. Heb 13:22.

72   Paul's Sermon (13:16-41). The text is neatly divisible into sections marked off by repeated words of salutation (vv 16,26,38); hence (1) a summary of OT history, the era of promise (vv 16-25); (2) the Jesus kerygma with scriptural argument demonstrating fulfillment of the promise (vv 26-37); (3) the concluding summons to faith and forgiveness (vv 38-41), conforming to the schema of earlier sermons (2:38-40; 3:19-26). The OT summary reminds us of the raw material of Stephen's speech (→ 45 above), although here Luke's shaping is obvious in the concerted emphasis on God's action as prelude to the characteristically theocentric Jesus kerygma. In addition, the demarcation of the OT period after JBap (vv 24-25) coheres with the boundary drawn in Luke 16:16 (cf. Matt 11:13). The preacher, however, does not segregate the two periods; the Jesus-event belongs to the history of Israel (v 23), and that is why it must be proclaimed to Israel "first" (v 46). The "hinges" of this argument are vv 23,26,32-33,38 (Dupont, *Études* 359; Buss, *Missionspredigt* [→ 76 below] 30), each verse serving connective, resumptive, and actualizing functions. They make Paul's recited history of salvation into kerygma for the present; "the history of Israel right down to the preacher's situation is a living unity," grounded in God's fidelity to his promise (ibid. 25). Rather than treat portions of this argument, whether the historical summary (Kliesch) or the Davidic scriptural catena (Bowker, Ellis), as keys to the overall conception and origin of the sermon, we do better to view it as essentially a Lucan composition that has made skillful use of these traditional ingredients to forge a statement in which Paul can illustrate the "first" principle of his labors (v 46; so Buss, Weiser).

73   The era of promise (vv 16-25). **16.** *God-fearers:* Now the phrase has its technical meaning (see comment on 10:2): Gentiles frequenting the synagogue through philosophical congeniality with Judaism, but without circumcision or total Mosaic commitment (also v 26). This class was particularly fertile soil for the Christian mission. **17.** *this people Israel:* The dem. pron. makes the synagogue assembly representative of the whole "people" (v 15), and Paul begins with the theme of their election, echoed in the honorific "Israelites" (v 16). This already

lays the foundation of the *prōton*, "first," in v 46 and is typical of the sermon's sustained focus on its present situation. **18.** *he sustained them:* Mss. waver between the vb. *etrophophorēsen* and the pejorative *etropophorēsen*, "put up with them"; the difference is made by an exchange of one consonant (*phi* for *pi*). In Deut 1:31 LXX the first is used, and this conforms to the Lucan summary's positive tone (contrast 7:2-49). **19.** *seven nations:* Cf. Deut 7:1. **20.** *four hundred and fifty years:* Apparently an awkward timing for the whole sequence from v 17, including the 400 years before the exodus (Gen 15:13). **20b-22.** Whereas no patriarchs or judges have been named, now we hear the names connected with the beginning of the royal dynasty in Israel, whose tradition supplies the sermon's central argument from prophecy (vv 23, 33-37). Samuel's role (cf. 3:24) in inaugurating the kings' line is matched by JBap's, heralding Jesus from the end of the old prophets' line (vv 24-25). **22.** *raised up David:* The use of the vb. *egeirein* serves, with v 23, to make David a type of Jesus (v 30). God's testimony to David combines Ps 89:21 and 1 Sam 13:14, the latter a prophecy of Samuel. **23.** *from this man's progeny:* The influence of 2 Sam 7:12 is clear; it is less clear that the whole summary from v 17 constitutes a midrashic commentary on the full oracle of Nathan (so Lövestamm, Dumais). *true to his promise:* Since this was given to "the fathers" (v 32), it cannot refer to Nathan's oracle alone (2 Sam 7). It includes all the OT promises of a "savior," which came to fulfillment in the resurrection of David's descendant (v 33; 26:6-8; Buss, *Missionspredigt* [→ 76 below] 46). **24.** *before his coming:* Lit., "before the face of . . . ," this phrase is an excellent example of Lucan mimesis (→ 8 above). **25.** *as John was finishing:* This coincides with the end of "the Law and the Prophets," according to Luke 16:16. Cf. 20:24; Luke 3:16.

74   Jesus kerygma (vv 26-37). We now move into material largely familiar from the Petrine sermons. **26.** *to us:* Corresponding to "for Israel" in v 23, this reiterates the identification of the Word's audience made in vv 16-17. **27.** See comment on 3:17-18 (also 15:21). Unlike Peter in Jerusalem, Paul cannot accuse the Diaspora listeners of Jesus' murder nor invite their repentance of it; hence the alteration of the schema in vv 38-41. Still, Jerusalem did act according to plan (Luke 13:33) as the representative of a perennially disobedient people (7:51-53; 15:10). **28.** Cf. 3:13-14. **29.** *laid him in the tomb:* This seems to ignore the pious Arimathean's service (Luke 23:53), but the allusion to Deut 21:22-23, which we have met before (5:30; 10:39), probably encouraged adding the burial to the taking down "from the tree" among the guilty deeds of Jerusalem. The change of actor can now be the more rhetorically effective in v 30. **31.** See comment on 1:21-22 (also 1:3). **33.** *God has fulfilled:* The striking pf. tense form reflects that Luke knew only two eras of history, promise and fulfillment, and all Israelites living in the latter era are included in "us, their children." *raising up Jesus:* This refers unmistakably to the Easter event (cf. 26:6-8), and so does Ps 2:7 (*pace* Rese, *Motive* 81-86), whose contribution to the Easter kerygma can already be observed in Rom 1:4 (cf. Heb 1:5). Paul quotes the psalm as a step in the reasoning that shows the resurrection to be the fulfillment of the ancient promise in this Davidic descendant. Nathan's oracle, promising the filial adoption of the descendant (2 Sam 7:14), is the self-understood fulcrum of this logic (cf. v 23). **34.** *the holy and sure (blessings):* This fragment of Isa 55:3 LXX could be linked to Ps 16:10 LXX (v 35) by the catchword *hosios*, "holy." Since its citation is prefaced by the claim that the risen One will "no more return to corruption," it must be assumed that David's blessings included Nathan's promise of his descendant's everlasting reign (1 Sam 7:13,16). "I will give you" (pl.) reaffirms that the blessings are destined for the whole people (vv 23,33), not the risen One alone; and on that depends the logical nexus with v 38. **36–37.** See comment on 2:25–31.

75   Exhortation (vv 38–41). **38.** *by this man:* Here is the point of the logical nexus asserted by *oun,* "therefore": the resurrected heir of David is the one "by whom" forgiveness is proclaimed to this audience (cf. 3:22–26; 26:23; Buss, *Missionspredigt* [→ 76 below] 124). The parallel relationship between *dia toutou* and *en toutǭ* (v 39) suggests that we give the same instrumental sense to both. Paul, preaching forgiveness "in his name" to complete the plan of salvation (Luke 24:47), acts *in persona Christi,* just as when miracles are done in his name (3:12,16). *by the law of Moses:* The law is not accorded even a power of partial justification (*pace* P. Vielhauer, in *StLA* 41–42), for this clause explicates the "forgiveness of sins" announcement of the first clause. Luke is retailing Pauline tradition faithfully enough, even though in equating "justify" and "forgive" he does not rise to the Pauline conception (cf. Rom 6:7; 1 Cor 6:11; → Pauline Theology, 82:68–70, 75). **41.** The use of Hab 1:5 to reinforce Paul's exhortation is already a preview of its widespread rejection. Editorial repetition of "work" (*ergon*) seems to assure its reference to the Gentile mission, about to enter the wake of Jewish rejection. **43.** *Godfearing proselytes:* Does this not commingle separate groups: converts and nonconverts (cf. comment on v 16)? Perhaps Luke wished to prepare for v 46 by specifying that only Jews heard the instruction in the synagogue.

76   (ii) *Beleaguered missionaries turn to the Gentiles* (13:44–52). **44–48.** The plastic oversimplification in this scene is obvious even on casual reading. It has been woven out of the program of v 46, which has been the historian's target throughout the Antioch episode. **45.** *jealousy:* On the change of Jewish temper, → 71 above. **46.** *to you first:* The whole discursive structure of Paul's sermon has illustrated this divine schedule of salvation. **47.** Cf. comment on 1:8, where the Isa text quoted here (49:6 LXX) was alluded to in the commission of the risen One. We are obviously at a milestone in the enactment of his plan. **48.** Lucan style par excellence. Cf. 2:47. **51.** Cf. Luke 9:5; 10:11. This serves missionary typology better than it fits the situation at hand (cf. v 48; 14:21–22). *Iconium:* Capital of the province of Lycaonia (modern Konya), located 87 mi. ESE of Pisidian Antioch.

(Bowker, J., "Speeches in Acts," *NTS* 14 [1967–68] 96–111. Buss, M., *Die Missionspredigt des Apostels Paulus in Pisidischen Antiochien* [Stuttgart, 1980]. Dumais, M., in *Les Actes* [ed. J. Kremer] 467–74. Dupont, *Études* 337–59. Ellis, *Prophecy* [→ 28 above] 198–208. Holtz, *Untersuchungen* 131–45. Kliesch, *Das heilsgeschichtliche Credo* [→ 50 above]. Lövestamm, E., *Son and Saviour* [Lund, 1961]. O'Toole, R. F., "Acts 13,13–52," *Bib* 60 [1979] 361–72. Radl, *Paulus* 82–100. Rese, *Motive* 80–93. Schmitt, J., in *Les Actes* [ed. J. Kremer] 155–67.)

77   (d) MIXED RECEPTIONS IN CENTRAL ASIA MINOR (14:1–20).

       (i) *Iconium* (14:1–7). **1.** *in the same way: Kata to auto* could also mean "together," but since the pattern of mission set at Antioch, under the rule of 13:46, is to become a mainstay of Luke's composition, the phrase would effectively declare his intention if it expressed the "like" priority of Iconium's synagogue on the mission agenda. Repeated here, too, is the quick sequence of success and rejection (v 2). **2–3.** Grammar and logic suggest that the order of these sentences might once have been the reverse. Note the continuity of the authenticating "signs and wonders" (2:43; 6:8). **4.** *the Jews:* After the *schisma* at Antioch, they are ever more cohesively the

mission's principal antagonists. *the apostles:* We probably hear Luke's tradition at this point (also v 14), since he elsewhere reserves this status to the Twelve (cf. comment on 1:21).

78   (ii) *Lystra and Derbe* (14:8–20). To the slender thread of the itinerary, Luke appends a miracle story (vv 8–15a), mostly traditional material, and a miniature discourse (vv 15b–17), his own version of an inherited schema (Wilckens, *Missionsreden* 81–91). The miracle closely parallels Peter's temple healing (3:1–11), and the speech is a rehearsal of the *tour de force* at Athens (17:22–31); hence, both serve Luke's cross-referential pedagogy. **8–11.** The healing story has standard ingredients of the form (cf. comment on 3:1–11). Paul again seizes the initiative as a charismatic man of God and discerns the patient's disposition by pneumatic scrutiny. **8.** *Lystra:* A town about 25 mi. SSW of Iconium, shown by coins found at the site to have been made a Roman colony by Augustus (*Colonia Iulia Felix Gemina Lustra*). Variation between the pl. (v 8) and sg. (v 6) forms of the name is repeated in 16:1–2. **12.** *gods:* The Anatolian legend of Philemon and Baucis (Ovid., *Metamorph.* 8.611–28) has in common with this story the Hellenized deity names, the miracle-epiphany, and the concluding cultic scene (v 13). Hermes is, in any case, the name that fits Paul as Luke's current "spokesman of the gods." **14.** *Barnabas and Paul:* This protocol, abandoned at 13:46 and hereafter, is prompted by v 12. **15.** *men:* See comment on 10:26. **15b–17.** The little sermon contains the invitation to turn from benighted idolatry to nature's self-disclosing Creator, which early Christian preachers inherited from Hellenistic-Jewish counterparts (cf. 1 Thess 1:9); but there is no christological conclusion here (as 17:30–31; 1 Thess 9:10), perhaps because monotheistic conversion was still wanting among the Lystrans (v 18). In any case, this passage is but a preview of the Gentile kerygma which will be heard in its cameo setting on the Areopagus (chap. 17). **19.** *Jews:* They are now not only recusant prospects of the mission but aggressive enemies stalking it. It is hard to credit this report of their travel from adjacent regions to make common cause with superstitious pagans. Cf. comment on 7:58. **20.** *Derbe:* 60 mi. E of Lystra; lacking in 2 Tim 3:11. This town probably got mere mention in the log of Paul's travels that Luke used.

79   (e) RETURN TO ANTIOCH (14:21–28). **21–22.** *Lystra and Iconium:* The fact that the travelers revisit towns that had violently expelled them suggests that Luke artificially contoured the conclusions of the last three episodes according to his typology of the beleaguered witness, like Jesus (cf. Luke 4:29–30). This major interest is confirmed by the content of their exhortation, which applies Luke 24:26 existentially. **23.** *hand-picking elders:* Is it remotely possible that this report is true to fact (cf. 20:17), despite the fact that Paul's letters never mention *presbyteroi* and they were a fixed institution by Luke's time (cf. 1 Tim 5; Titus 1:5; 1 Pet 5:1,5)? One might argue the special circumstances of this early mission, esp. the guiding role of Barnabas, shortly to leave Paul's side (15:39), and the mandate of Antioch which both men were under (so Nellessen, "Die Einsetzung," 184–85, 189). Most will likely continue to vote for Luke's reading back contemporary church structure (Haenchen, Conzelmann, Roloff, Weiser). **26.** *sailed to Antioch:* I.e., to Antioch in Syria. This verse signals the literary closure of the section begun at 13:1–3. **27.** *all that God had accomplished:* Cf. 15:4,12; 21:19. *the door of faith:* Cf. 1 Cor 16:9; 2 Cor 2:12. This verse draws the conclusion of the journey for the progress of Luke's history. **28.** *some time:* An interval separated the journey's end from the Jerusalem proceedings to follow. The first missionary journey is usually dated AD 46–49 (→ Paul, 79:29).

(Nellessen, E., "Die Einsetzung von Presbytern durch Barnabas und Paulus," *Begegnung mit dem Wort* [Fest. H. Zimmermann; ed. J. Zmijewski, *et al.*; BBB 53; Bonn, 1979] 175–93. Schnackenburg, R., "Lukas als Zeuge verschiedener Gemeindestrukturen," *BibLeb* 12 [1971] 232–47. Zingg, *Wachsen* 240–45.)

80   (F) The Jerusalem Conference and Resolution (15:1–35). The Lucan argument which began with the emergence of "the Hellenists" at 6:1 is now brought full circle as their church's representatives return to Jerusalem to seal the legitimacy of the mission to the uncircumcised. Luke's account of these proceedings includes the same meeting as Paul recounted in Gal 2:1–10 (→ Paul, 79:36); but because of his idyllic view of the apostolic church under the unwavering guidance of the Spirit (v 28), Luke will not tell us of the subsequent conflict ignited by the Jerusalem agreement at Antioch (Gal 2:11–14), when Paul upbraided Peter for backing away from meal fellowship with Gentile converts under Jewish rigorists' pressure and cut his ties with Barnabas and the rest of the Antiochenes (cf. Hengel, *Acts* 122–23). This traumatic falling out, which reverberates faintly at v 39, has been finessed by a clever historiography that blends its issue into the original Jerusalem agenda, relegating it thus *ad acta!* This is accomplished in two steps: after Peter's discourse has resolved the circumcision issue, which stood alone on the conference agenda reported by Paul (Gal 2:3 = vv 7–11), a second speech, by James, prematurely settles the meal-sharing controversy (Gal 2:12 = vv 13–21; cf. 11:3) by laying on the "four clauses" of minimal Gentile observance (vv 20,29) for which Paul's account left no room (Gal 2:6; cf. Strobel, "Das Aposteldekret" [→ 85 below] 90).

Historically, the "decree" formulated by James was a compromise on the common-table controversy reached either before the crisis at Antioch (P. Achtemeier, *CBQ* 48 [1986] 19–21) or, more likely, after it and in response to it (Hengel, *Acts* 117; Wilson, *Gentiles* 189–91). That the compromise now appears as the original Jerusalem resolution is a *tour de force* by Luke, reinforcing his unilinear view of the universal church's origins (Schneider, *Apg.* 2. 189–90; Weiser, *Apg.* 368). Accordingly, the "classic" precedent of the Cornelius conversion by Peter becomes the keystone of the settlement (vv 7,14). At the same time, the partnership of Peter and James as decisive actors at the conference, with Paul reduced to a "friend-of-court" witness (vv 4,12), signals the imminent departure of the apostles from the scene and the accession of James and the elders to custody of the norm-setting mother church.

Earlier scissors-and-paste theories of Luke's sources for this chapter have been superseded by studies that stress his integrating plan of composition (Dibelius, *Studies* 93–101; Haenchen, *Acts* 457). Yet the source question will not go away because the convergences between Luke's information and Paul's are too substantial to pass over. The speeches will be, as usual, the more direct statements of this author (Dömer, *Heil* 182–85), while the "decree" will have come from his tradition, perhaps carrying the memory of an actual compromise solution initiated by James (Roloff, *Apg.* 227).

81   (a) PREHISTORY (15:1–5). The introduction seems to include competing accounts of the immediate impetus for the conference: the advent of Judaizing teachers in Antioch (vv 1–2) and the upsurge of Pharisaic sentiment in Jerusalem (v 5). Of the two, vv 1–2 seem to fill the editorial requirement of connection with the setting of the antecedent narrative (14:26), whereas v 5

is more likely the point where we touch the conference tradition Luke used. By the same token, the report of the delegation and its purpose (v 2) is true to Gal 2:1–2 and thus to Luke's source, whereas vv 3–4, showing the envoys retracing the steps of the fleeing Hellenists (8:1; 11:19) and repeating for the Jerusalem assembly the account of their mission given at Antioch (14:27), are clearly from Luke's pen (cf. Dömer, *Heil* 174–75; differently, Dietrich, *Petrusbild* [→ 19 above] 308). **1.** *after the custom of Moses:* This means, of course, that circumcision was prescribed by the Pentateuch, which came from Moses. But Jewish tradition traced the rite to Abraham, not Moses (see Gen 17:9–14; cf. Rom 4:9–12). **2.** *dissension and dispute:* For once, Luke reports a conflict that Paul does not (cf. Gal 2:1). **3.** *great joy to all the brothers:* This unanimous acclaim shrinks the stature of the missionaries' opponents to that of a splinter faction in the church. **4.** *the apostles and the elders:* First- and second-generation directorates of the mother church will share the deliberations (v 6), showing how these overreach the moment at hand to affect all Christian posterity. *what God had done:* The familiar theocentric perspective on history (vv 6–10,12,14) minimizes any dependency of the Gentile mission on the outcome of human deliberations. **5.** *party of the Pharisees: Hairesis,* "faction," "school," is applied across the spectrum of Judaism: Sadducees (5:17), Pharisees (26:5), even Christians (24:5). Luke's interest in Pharisees is mostly to promote his continuity thesis (see comment on 4:1), so there is good reason to trace the present report to his source (*pace* Weiser, *Apg.* 369–70). *circumcise them:* The only antecedent for "them" in the context is Gentiles of the Antioch delegation (v 4; cf. Gal 2:3).

82   (b) PETER'S APPEAL TO PRECEDENT (15:6–12). The apostolic voice appropriately sounds first, and the little speech shows its literary origin and function in the fact that only Luke's reader could grasp its allusions to the Cornelius sequence (vv 7–9; Dibelius, *Studies* 94–95; Borse, "Beobachtungen" [→ 85 below] 201–2). **7.** *from days of old:* The Cornelius event now belongs to the "classical" past (Dibelius), even at this relatively short temporal distance. *God decided:* In the matter before it, the mother church can only acknowledge and obey the election (*exelexato*) already made by God (Roloff, *Apg.* 230; see comment on 10:3,47). James's argument will build on the same divine initiative (v 14: *epeskepsato,* "provided for"), showing the structural parallelism and complementarity of the two speeches (J. Dupont, *NTS* 31 [1985] 323). *the word of the gospel:* Cf. 10:36. The noun *euangelion* is rare in Luke; cf. 20:24 (on Paul's lips). **8.** *knower of hearts:* See comment on 10:34–35. *just as to us:* Cf. 10:47; 11:15–17. **9.** *made no distinction:* God himself had removed the law's distinction between clean and unclean people (10:34–35), and this was revealed in Peter's vision (see comment on 10:14–15). **10.** *test God:* The biblical expression (Exod 17:2) means to challenge the manifest will of God. This rhetorical question is pressed by the theocentric recital of vv 7–9. *a burden on the shoulders:* This view of the law as an unbearable yoke is neither Pauline nor mainstream Jewish; it is the perspective of a Christian for whom the break with Judaism lies well in the past (Conzelmann, *Apg.* 91). **12.** *grew silent:* Does this imply that the controversy (*zētēsis*) which prompted Peter's words (v 7) was settled by them? *signs and wonders:* As prophetic certification (2:19,22), this testimony by "Barnabas and Paul" (their order in the chain of apostolic tradition) is not at all extrinsic to the issue (*pace* Haenchen, "Quellenanalyse" [→ 85 below] 158–60).

83   (c) JAMES'S CONFIRMATION AND AMENDMENTS (15:13–21). James (12:17) follows the steps of Peter's argument from the divine action toward Cornelius (v 14) to the conclusion that there must be no imposition on the converts (v 19; see comment on v 7). The first step he augments with a Scripture quotation (Amos 9:11–12 LXX), and the second he qualifies with four minimal requirements for Jewish–Gentile coexistence based on Israel's "holiness code," Lev 17–18 (v 20). Paul is on hand to learn this resolution of Luke's conference and, in fact, to become one of its promulgators (vv 22–29); and yet Luke will hint that his sources had it differently when he records James's announcement of the "four clauses" to Paul as something new in 21:25 (see comment there; cf. Borse, "Beobachtungen" [→ 85 below] 198–200). **14.** *Symeōn:* The Gk form of Hebr *Šimĕ'ôn,* introduced mimetically, along with the heavy biblical phrasing of the two speeches, recreates the sacred "atmosphere" of the conference (→ Paul, 79:36). *God first saw to the taking:* The divine initiative and its "classic" (*prōton*) relationship to the present are the restatement of v 7; but "saw to" (*episkeptesthai*) belongs to the OT vocabulary of divine saving actions (Hebr *pāqad*), and so it introduces an important enlargement of our perspective on the Cornelius event and its effects. *a people from among the nations:* As part of the substantive clause acting as obj. of *epeskepsato,* this phrase asserts for the new Gentile constituency of the church no less than full participation in the "people of God." *Laos,* "people," has its pregnant sense of God's elect, as it so consistently does in Luke's writing, and as it will have again in reference to Gentile converts at 18:10 (cf. J. Dupont, *NTS* 31 [1985] 324–29). The oxymoron combining *laos* with *ethnē* (Gentiles) brings out the sharp surprise factor in God's provision. *for his name:* The sense of this phrase is found in the quoted words of Amos 9:12 (at v 17b), which is, in fact, the only other biblical use of this terminology to signify God's rule of pagan nations. The Amos citation will now clarify the relation of the newly elect "people" to Israel. **16–17.** The Amos lines do not reproduce the LXX exactly, so they may come from a Christian testimonia booklet, where words from Isa 45:21 were added at the end (Dömer, *Heil* 179). James's use of the passage will work only in the LXX version, where MT's *yîrĕšû,* "possess," was exchanged for *yidrĕšû,* "seek," and *'dm,* "Edom," for *'dm,* "humanity." The Gk translator's prophecy can now explain how the risen Lord could reinterpret the restoration of Israel (1:6) in terms of the universal mission (1:8): David's "fallen tent" is to be rebuilt so that (v 17) all nations may "seek the Lord" (Richard, "The Divine Purpose" [→ 85 below] 195; Dömer, *Heil* 185). The rebuilding, therefore, does not mean the risen Christ's fulfillment of the Davidic promise (*pace* Haenchen, Schneider), but the "ingathering of Israel" begun with the apostolic preaching, now expanding to embrace the Gentiles (Roloff, Weiser; see comment on 2:1,14). **20.** *but should instruct them:* The adversative connection of this to "trouble" (v 19), and the reprise of vv 10–11 in v 19, demonstrate that the "decree" is a concession rather than an imposition, making common life and table possible without laying any onus on the newcomers. The four clauses (also v 28; 21:25) seem to be four of the things proscribed by Lev 17–18 for aliens residing in Israel: meat offered to idols, the eating of blood and of strangled animals (not ritually slaughtered), and intercourse with close kin (see Lev 17:8–9,10–12,15 [Exod 22:31]; 18:6–18). The mention of *porneia,* "unchastity," disturbs the sequence of the other three items, which concern diet; and if it is understood in the light of Lev 18, it corresponds to the Jewish term *zĕnût,* lit., "fornication," often applied specifically to incestuous unions (see J. A. Fitzmyer, *TAG* 91–97). Exegesis of the clauses from Lev 17–18 well fits the

Lucan view that Gentiles embracing the gospel gained access to the terrain of the chosen people, kept sacred by the "holiness code." **21.** Supporting the four clauses (*gar*) is their recognition factor, based on universal Torah instruction.

84   (d) RESOLUTION (15:22–29). This passage, in which Luke records the consequence of the conference newly conceived by him, is mainly his own composition, but the dual embassy, Judas and Silas alongside Paul and Barnabas, may preserve a tradition of the decree's publication in which the latter pair had no part (cf. Strobel, "Das Aposteldekret" [→ 85 below] 92–93). **22.** *with the whole church:* In view of the negotiations in private reported by Paul (Gal 2:2; cf. v 6), the resolution's authorship by the plenary mother church can be judged part of Luke's own perspective. *Judas . . . and Silas:* Of the former we hear nowhere else, but Silas will be a companion of the second journey (15:40–18:5; cf. "Silvanus," 1 Thess 1:1; 2 Cor 1:19), and for Luke he is one more link binding Paul's mission to the mother church. **23.** The apostolic letter is a "document" of our author's confection, quite in keeping with Hellenistic historians' convention (Plümacher, *Lukas* 10; Cadbury, *The Making* 190–91; → 6 above). The prescript is standard in all Hellenistic letters (→ NT Epistles, 45:6). *Syria and Cilicia:* The letter is destined beyond the inquiring church (v 2) to its expanding mission territories (cf. v 41; Gal 1:21). It will subsequently be published in the towns of Mission I (16:4), whose successes hastened the deliberations. **26.** *men who have given over:* The dat. refers this to Barnabas and Paul (*pace* Schneider; cf. 9:16). **28.** *the holy Spirit and us:* This suitably tallies up the deliberations, which have so emphasized the divine initiative. Church authority does not act on power or agenda of its own; it is legitimate only in carrying out the saving will of God. **29.** The "decree" puts the clauses in an order corresponding to Lev 17–18. As for the addition of the "golden rule" here in ms. D, → 11 above.

85   (e) AFTERMATH (15:30–35). The closing paragraph of the conference account paints an ideal picture of Antioch's joyous reception of the resolution. **33.** *they were sent back:* Yet Silas seems still to be at Antioch in v 40, accounting for the addition of v 34 in ms. D (Vg.): "But Silas decided to stay there, and only Judas left for Jerusalem." **35.** Historically, Paul had more likely left Antioch for new mission frontiers when the new norms came to be established there.

(Achtemeier, P., "An Elusive Unity," *CBQ* 48 [1986] 1–26. Bammel, E., in *Les Actes* [ed. J. Kremer] 439–46. Borse, U., "Kompositionsgeschichtliche Beobachtungen zum Apostelkonzil," *Begegnung mit dem Wort* [→ 79 above] 195–212. Dibelius, *Studies* 93–101. Dietrich, *Petrusbild* [→ 19 above] 306–21. Dömer, *Heil* 173–87. Dupont, *Études* 361–65; "Un peuple d'entre les nations," *NTS* 31 [1985] 321–35. Haenchen, E., "Quellenanalyse und Kompositionsanalyse in Act 15," *Judentum—Urchristentum—Kirche* [Fest. J. Jeremias; ed. W. Eltester; BZNW 20; Berlin, 1964] 153–64. Hengel, *Acts* 111–26. Jervell, J., *Luke and the People of God* [Minneapolis, 1972] 185–207. Kümmel, W. G., *Heilsgeschehen und Geschichte* [Marburg, 1965] 278–88. Lake, in *Beginnings* 5. 195–212. Richard, E., "The Divine Purpose," *Luke-Acts* [ed. C. H. Talbert] 188–209. Strobel, A., "Das Aposteldekret als Folge des antiochenischen Streites," *Kontinuität und Einheit* [Fest. F. Mussner; ed. P.-G. Müller; Freiburg, 1981] 81–104. Weiser, A., "Das Apostelkonzil," *BZ* 28 [1984] 145–67. Wilson, *Gentiles* 178–95.)

86   **(IV) Paul's Path to Rome (15:36–28:31).**
    (A) The Major Missions of Paul (15:36–20:38). We agree that the familiar division of the text into second and third "missionary journeys," separated at 18:23, is analytically unsound (Weiser, *Apg.* 387; but → Paul, 79:38–45). A more evident caesura is 19:21,

which points Paul toward Jerusalem and Rome, echoing
Luke 9:51 (Radl, *Paulus* 116–24). Since mission activity
continues after that point, however, we prefer to terminate the major-mission sequence with Paul's farewell at
Miletus (20:17–38), which includes a more explicit
announcement of the dominical way of suffering now
before him (vv 22–24).

87 (a) MISSION JOURNEYS RESUMED (15:36–41).
This is a transitional passage which both announces a
new phase of Paul's career and gathers loose threads
from previous ones. **37–39.** A "sharp disagreement"
between Paul and Barnabas ends their association, but
apart from cryptically connecting it with the defection
of John Mark from Mission I (13:13), Luke leaves us
wondering about its deeper causes. Gal 2:13 tells the real
story, of course, as Luke follows his usual policy of
mollifying early-church conflicts (→ 80 above).

88 (b) THE ROAD TO EUROPE (16:1–10).
(i) *Timothy's circumcision* (16:1–5). **1.** *Timothy:*
→ Pastorals, 56:3. *a Jewish woman:* Eunice (2 Tim 1:5).
Mixed marriages were illegal (Deut 7:3), but if the
mother was Jewish, her offspring was considered Jewish
(Str-B 2. 741). Is the situation, therefore, that Timothy
should have been circumcised but was not, requiring this
proof of Paul's loyalty to the law as binding upon Jews
(cf. 21:21; 25:8)? **3.** *circumcised him:* The reason given
seems to relate this deed, so surprising after 15:5–11, to
Paul's missionary ideal, "all things to all people" (1 Cor
9:20–22). But Timothy was already baptized (v 1), and
Paul could hardly have compromised the stand he consistently took against the Judaizers (Gal 5:2–3), even to
win converts (G. Bornkamm, in *StLA* 203). Most commentators therefore question the reliability of this report
(save Marshall, Schmithals); it may derive from a tradition that echoed misconceptions like Gal 5:11, or
perhaps a faulty account of the Titus episode, Gal 2:3
(W. Walker, *ExpTim* 92 [1981] 231–35). Luke's use of
the tradition serves his intense concern to show a Paul
standing squarely within observant Judaism, rigorously
faithful to the Torah (22:3; 26:5) and thus forging the
continuity between Israel and the worldwide church
which the conference resolution programmed (v 4). **4–5.**
Note the consecutive logic: "decree" propagation, strong
and growing churches.

89 (ii) *Paul's vision* (16:6–10). **6–8.** The route
through N Asia Minor (the original "Galatian country";
→ Galatians, 47:3–5) toward the seaport of Troas, is a
datum of the travel diary which many scholars trace
behind chaps. 16–21 (→ 10 above). The Spirit's direction
of the journey in headlong haste to Europe (v 6) is an
expression of Luke's theological perspective, which
leaves no room for the founding of Pauline communities
in the area (cf. Gal). **9.** *a vision at night:* This is the first of
five visions for Luke's Paul (cf. 18:9–10; 22:17–21;
23:11; 27:23–24), all but one (chap. 22) of which come "at
night" and fit into a broad stream of biblical and extrabiblical dream lore, though they do not match the
ecstatic heavenly transports Paul claimed for himself
(2 Cor 12:1–7; cf. Weiser, *Apg.* 406–15). Like other
venerated figures, Paul gets instruction and encouragement from heaven in dreams that precede momentous
stages of his mission, particularly amid dangers about
its successful completion in doubt. *man of Macedonia:* He
represents the new Gk audience whom Paul was being
hastily propelled to evangelize. **10.** *we sought to go on:* The
unheralded first appearance of the "we" narrator (→
2 above) joins the report of Paul's dream and confirms its
revelational content. The close conjunction of the two
suggests that they are both author techniques lending
special significance to the mission's crossover to Greece
and Europe. Like the eyewitness narrator, the vision

assuring success despite all hazards is a staple of
Mediterranean sea-voyage literature (V. Robbins, in
PerspLA 230).

90 (c) THE MISSION IN GREECE (16:11–18:17).
(i) *The evangelization of Philippi* (16:11–40).
Upon the account (vv 11–12) of the N Aegean itinerary
to Philippi follow four scenes of Paul's ministry there:
the conversion of Lydia (vv 13–15), the expulsion of the
divining spirit (vv 16–18), the missionaries' miraculous
release from prison (vv 19–34), and their vindication by
the authorities (vv 35–40). Rather than an independent
tradition detachable from the context (Dibelius, *Studies*
23), the wondrous release is more likely an addition of
Luke's to a source account that featured the jailer's conversion and authorities' recognition (Kratz, *Rettungswunder* [→ 91 below] 482; Roloff, Schmithals, Weiser).
The release miracles form an augmented continuum in
Acts, involving the apostles (5:19–20), Peter (12:6–11),
and now Paul. **11–12.** The voyage from the NW Anatolian port of Troas proceeded by "direct route" to the
island of Samothrace, and thence to the port of Neapolis,
which served Philippi and marked the E terminus of the
strategic Via Egnatia, systematized by the Romans in 27
BC as the main highway from the Adriatic to Asia.
Philippi gained importance from the highway and,
under the name *Colonia Julia Augusta Philippensis,* was
settled by veterans of the great battle in which Antony
and Octavian routed the republican forces in 42 BC (→
Philippians, 48:2). **13.** *a place of prayer:* Though the word
proseuchē could connote "synagogue," this is presumably
an outdoor meeting place used by Jews for want of one.
Gentile women of circumstance were attracted to
Judaism in some number (cf. 13:50; Josephus, *J.W.*
2.20,2 § 560). The fabric of genuine local tradition continues in the account of Lydia, and the "we" narration
confirms its eyewitness pedigree. **14–15.** *Lydia:* Her
name is also that of her native region in W Asia Minor
(cf. Rev 2:18,24), and she is a "God-fearer," or Gentile
patron of Jewish worship (13:16). In respect to both this
affiliation and her hospitality to the travelers (cf. Luke
10:7; 24:29), she is an exemplary case of the success of
the early Christian household mission. Other household
baptisms occur in vv 31–34; 11:14; 18:8; 1 Cor 1:16.
16–18. Terminating this first "we"–narrative (to resume
at 20:5, in the selfsame location) is an encounter with a
divining spirit, to which Luke has given a standard exorcism format reminiscent of the Marcan stories in Luke
4:31–37 and 8:26–39. **16.** *a spirit of divination:* The Gk
word *pythōn* originally designated the serpent guardian
of the Delphic oracle slain by Apollo; it later came to
mean the power of soothsaying, sometimes associated
with ventriloquism. This account serves to distance the
charismatic Christian mission from both mantic arts (cf.
13:6–11) and mercenary ambitions (cf. 8:18–20;
19:23–27; 24:25–27). **17.** *cried out:* Both the cry and its
content are redolent of the gospel exorcisms (cf. Luke
8:28; 4:33–34). Just as there, the doomed spirit utters the
truth of salvation to betoken his defeat. **18.** Cf. Luke
8:29 and Mark 5:8. *in the name of Jesus Christ:* As in 3:6,
16; 4:10,30, the risen One is he who works the saving
deed. **19–24.** The antinomy of gospel and material gain
is confirmed by the role of the disenfranchised slave
owners in securing the missionaries' arrest. **20.** *the
magistrates:* The *stratēgoi* are probably this colony's *duum-
viri,* responsible for trying court cases. **21.** *us Romans:*
Contrast the vindication of the accused as Roman
citizens in vv 37–39. Their accusers attack them as Jews,
based on the known Roman contempt for Jewish
customs (cf. Tacitus, *Ann.* 5.5). **22.** Cf. 1 Thess 2:2;
2 Cor 11:25. **23–24.** *guard them securely:* The adv. *asphalōs*

and the vb. *ēsphalisato,* "secured," build a foil for the wondrous events to follow (cf.12:6).

91   **25–34.** The miraculous release is only a prelude to the jailer's conversion, which is "the real deliverance-miracle" here (Kratz, *Rettungswunder* 484). Indeed, the inconclusiveness of the release argues for its secondary addition to the context. **30–33.** A familiar question-and-answer framework of faith instruction and baptism (cf. 2:37–41; 8:34–38; 10:33–48) shows Luke's hand in the telling of the conversion, which is the solid historical core of this section. **34.** *set food:* A meal shared in jubilant gladness (*agalliasis*) is the sign of salvation received and recreates in the jailer's home the atmosphere of the first church (2:46). **35.** A motive for the lictors' mission is a deficit remedied in ms. D, which adds that the magistrates were in terror over the earthquake; it thus sews a seam between pre-Lucan and Lucan stages of the story. **37.** *Roman citizens:* Paul appeals to the *Lex Porcia,* which forbade under heavy penalty the flogging of a *civis Romanus* (cf. 22:25; Livy, *Hist.* 10.9.4; Cicero, *Pro Rabirio* 4.12–13; Conzelmann, *Apg.* 102–3). That the appeal is lodged only after the punishments shows Lucan artifice in pressing the apologetic rejoinder to v 21. **38.** *alarmed to hear:* Cf. 22:29. **39.** *apologized:* The reader can conclude with the officials: the preaching of the gospel in no way undermined the Roman state (cf. Maddox, *Purpose* 93–96). **40.** *visited Lydia:* The return to Lydia's rounds off the dramatic episode, which has argued what could not bear direct statement against facts: the mission's invulnerability to earthly opposition (Plümacher, *Lukas* 95–97).

(Kratz, R., *Rettungswunder* [Frankfurt, 1979] 474–99. Unnik, W. C. van, *Sparsa collecta* [NovTSup 29; Leiden, 1973] 374–95.)

92   (ii) *Paul in Thessalonica and Beroea* (17:1–15). The log of Paul's travels takes us some 140 mi. SW along the Via Egnatia, supplying the information of vv 1a,10a, 14a,15. To this strand Luke added two scenes, at Thessalonica and Beroea respectively, both highly schematic and of parallel structure: customary synagogue beginning, discussion of the Scriptures, success with (especially) women of high standing, outbreak of persecution under Jewish instigation. Our impression is that Luke builds schematically on slender source material, including the itinerary and the local tradition of Jason's travail (cf. 1 Thess 2:14; Schneider, *Apg.* 2. 222–23). **1.** Amphipolis and Thessalonica (modern Saloniki) were district capitals according to the Roman division of Macedonia in 167 BC. The latter was the largest and most important city of the province (→ 1 Thessalonians, 46:2). **2.** *his usual custom:* See comment on 13:14. *three sabbaths:* The impression of at most a month-long stay results from Luke's schematizing and hardly measures up to 1 Thess 1:2–2:9; Phil 4:16. **3.** *disclosing and expounding:* Paul's argument is an illation from Scripture's prescription for the Messiah's destiny to the sole claimant to fit that prescription (W. Kurz, *CBQ* 42 [1980] 179). Cf. 18:28; Luke 24:25–35,44–46. **4.** *became convinced:* The vb. *epeisthēsan* befits the logical appeal and expresses the Lucan concept of Easter faith as insight into the divine plan of salvation fully expressed in Scripture. "Godfearing" women continue to stand out in the tumultuous story of Paul's mission (cf. 13:50; 16:13–14). **5.** *the Jews:* Their comportment, motivation, and allies further document Jewry's consolidation as enemy of the gospel (cf. comment on 12:11) and disqualify the accusations of vv 6–7. **7.** Cf. Luke 23:2–5; Mark 15:2–5. Luke continues his political apologetic (cf. 16:37–39). **11.** *more highminded:* Verses 1–9 form the backdrop for the brief Beroea account, which can function only in counter-

point to the Thessalonian experience (J. Kremer, in *Les Actes,* 12). *received the word:* I.e., they became believers (2:41; 8:14; 11:1). *examining the Scriptures: Anakrinein* has the sense of critical study here, elsewhere that of judicial inquiry (4:9; 12:19; 24:8; 28:18). The "nobler" Beroean converts become models of Christian belief, to which critical reasoning and responsible judgment rightfully pertain (J. Kremer, ibid. 19–20). **14–15.** His companions remain behind as Paul proceeds to Athens, contrary to 1 Thess 3:1–2 but preparatory to vv 16–34.

93   (iii) *Paul in Athens* (17:16–34). As perhaps no other passage, this one shows us the potency of historical argument through "dramatic episodes" (→ 6 above). Structure and division are determined by the centrality of the speech (vv 22–31), for which the scenario prepares (vv 16–21) and from which the ending results (vv 32–34). The key word of the philosophers' challenge is "foreign" (vv 18,20), to which the words "unknown," "unknowing," and "ignorance" (vv 23,30) present the preacher's rejoinder. The sermon, in proclaiming the true God hitherto "unknown," makes a threefold criticism of pagan religiosity from a standpoint shared with the Hellenistic enlightenment: temples (v 24), sacrifices (v 25), and idols (v 29). As M. Dibelius recognized (*Studies* 57), the speaker is interrupted at precisely his argument's target: "raising him from the dead" (v 31), the point where propaedeutic theodicy reaches out to Christian kerygma, and likewise the point where the kerygma predictably repels many of its educated prospects (Schneider, *Apg.* 2, 233). Once again, this is not Paul speaking to pagan thinkers (*pace* Marshall, *Acts* 283); it is Luke instructing his reader about the great opportunity and the immense stumbling block of any mission to the Hellenistic intelligentsia. **16–21.** The Athens "cityscape" is painted larger than life, yet with each element carefully calibrated to the sermon's content: a nervously devout populace frequenting ubiquitous shrines, philosophers of famous schools dialoguing in the agora, new gods introduced from time to time, and everyone athirst for things novel and different. In painting this tableau, Luke relies on his own generation's view of classical culture and its mecca, rather than any special records of Paul's ministry. **16.** *idol-ridden:* Cf. similar impressions of the city in Livy, *Hist.* 45.27; Pausanias 1.17.7; Strabo, *Geogr.* 9.1.16. **17.** *synagogue:* More than the divinely established mission schedule noted before (13:14,46; 17:2), this first stop attests the Jewish auspices under which the sermon's accommodation of philosophical and biblical ideas have been developed (cf. W. Nauck, J. Dupont). *public square:* The agora, whose famous ruins lie just NW of the Acropolis, was the city's governmental and commercial hub and the meeting place par excellence for all matters of community life. **18.** *Epicurean and Stoic philosophers:* These are not plastic scenery props; their doctrines echo in the sermon's critique of popular religion (Barrett, "Paul's Speech" 72). With the followers of Epicurus (342–271 BC) the preacher shares a fervent opposition to common people's groveling superstition (*deisidaimonia;* cf. v 22) and a conviction that the gods are unaffected by human maneuvering (v 25). From the Stoics, members of the "painted portico" school (*Stoa poikilē*) founded by Zeno of Cyprus (*ca.* 320 BC), he draws several key ideas, including the unity of humanity (v 26) and the natural kinship of humans with God (v 28). *babbler:* Lit., "seed-picker" (*spermologos*), like a browsing bird—a bit of "atmospheric" vocabulary for the encounter. *promoter of foreign gods:* This echoes the charge leveled against Socrates (Plato, *Apol.* 24b; Xenophon, *Mem.* 1.1.1); it will be countered by the sermon's "ignorance" motif (vv 23,30). *Jesus and the Resurrection:* The climax of the sermon is presaged here (vv

30-31; Conzelmann, in *StLA* 224). Is it implied that the Athenians took the fem. noun *Anastasis,* "Resurrection," to be the name of a consort to the foreign deity Jesus? **19.** *Areopagus:* The "hill of Ares," now a bare-rock promontory just W of the Acropolis, was once the meeting place of the supreme Athenian council, which also bore the name. Luke means the hill rather than the council, which met elsewhere and had mainly judicial functions in his day. The ptc. *epilabomenoi* means "taking him along" (9:27), not "seizing him" (16:19). No verdict or sentence follows the sermon; its setting is learned disputation rather than judicial defense. **94**   Paul's Sermon (vv 22-31). Since the composition develops an older schema — conversion from idolatry, resurrection faith, judgment/rule of the world by the Resurrected (cf. 1 Thess 1:9-10; 1 Cor 8:6) — the christological conclusion is no ill-fitting appendix to a theodicy (*pace* Schweizer, in *StLA* 213), but the climax of an established, two-pronged kerygma to pagans in which the summons to monotheism, nourished by Hellenistic-Jewish apologetics, formed the necessary premise of the proclamation of Christ (Legrand, "Areopagus Speech" [→ 95 below] 342-45). Use of natural theology as a positive threshold to the gospel contrasts with Paul's use of it to convict sinful humanity in Rom 1:18-32 (P. Vielhauer, in *StLA* 34-37). **22.** *scrupulously religious:* Ostensibly courting the audience, this portrayal of them carries a hidden reproach to be insinuated in what follows (cf. 25:19; comment on v 18). **23.** *to an Unknown God:* Literary references to altars to "unknown gods" (Pausanias 1.1.4; Philostratus, *Life of Apol.* 6.3.5) may have inspired Luke's recasting in the singular, which furnishes an ideal fulcrum for the parrying of the "strange gods" accusation. **24.** *the world and everything:* The divine predications here show how freely the preacher mingles Gk concepts (unitary, all-embracing cosmos) with biblical ones (bipartite universe). This merger had been effected by Jewish apologists like Philo, Aristobulus, and Pseudo-Solomon (Wis 9:9-10). Compare 14:15; Isa 42:5 LXX. *does not dwell in temples:* This protest was *ex principiis* in the Stoa, where God and cosmos were coextensive. The idea is in the OT (Isa 66:1-2), but *cheiropoiētos,* "handmade," does not occur with "temples" in the LXX. Cf. 7:48; Philo, *De vita Mosis* 2.88. **25.** The Stoics, e.g., Seneca, argued from God's nature to the manner of his worship (see Dibelius, *Studies* 53-54; Conzelmann, *Apg.* 107). *gives life and breath:* Cf. Isa 42:5. The basic thought that God, as Creator, is giver rather than receiver implies his freedom from all need, a refrain of Gk philosophy going back to the Eleatics (Dibelius, *Studies* 42-43), but only late in the LXX and as a premise of thanksgiving for the Temple (2 Macc 14:35; 3 Macc 2:9). **26.** *he made from one:* The context is against construing "he made" modally with "dwell" ("he made them dwell"), but (in continuation of v 24) as "he created." This then governs "to dwell" and "to seek" as asyndetic infins. of purpose. Biblical and Stoic perspectives merge in *ex henos,* "from one," which could mean "one stock" (neut.) or "one ancestor" (masc.). The Gen allusion (1:27-28) is the stronger. *seasons and boundaries:* According to the same merging perspectives, these could be either the epochs and territories of the world's nations (a biblical slant; cf. Dan 8; Deut 32:8; Schneider; Wilson, *Gentiles* 201-5), or the seasons of nature's cycle and the earth's habitable zone (a philosopher's view; cf. Dibelius, *Studies* 29-34; Eltester, Haenchen, Weiser, and most commentators). Context and comparison with 14:17 favor the latter reading. **27.** *to seek God:* This is obviously the philosopher's intellectual quest (Dibelius, *Studies* 32-33), not primarily the OT expression for obedience and service (Deut 4:29 etc.). **28.** *one of your*

poets: Viz., Aratus, in his *Phaenomena,* probably influenced by the early-Stoic hymn of Cleanthes (E. Lohse, *New Testament Environment* [Nash, 1976] 245). **29.** The nonsequitur of images of God carved by God's human kin again reflects a blending of ideas: the Jewish, that the Creator cannot be represented by anything created; the Greek, that only living beings can represent a living Being (Conzelmann, in *StLA* 224). **30.** *times of ignorance:* As in the sermons to Jews (3:17; 13:27), the kerygma brings the end of ignorance, when a choice must be made and one's fate in the judgment is sealed. **31.** Cf. 10:42; Pss 9:9; 96:13; 98:9. *he has given a guarantee: Pistis* as "proof" or "warranty" is distant from Paul's use of the word for self-renouncing trust (Dibelius, *Studies* 62). **95**   Response (vv 32-34). **32.** Interruption of the speaker before the Resurrected is even named confirms the literary origin of the speech (→ 93 above). **34.** This sermon, like others in Acts, results in a divided audience. It can therefore not be classified as a failure in order to harmonize it with 1 Cor 1:18-2:5 (Legrand, "Areopagus Speech" 339). Converts' names will be from the log of Paul's travels.

(Barrett, C. K., "Paul's Speech on the Areopagus," *New Testament Christianity for Africa and the World* [ed. M. Glasswell; London, 1974] 69-77. Calloud, J., "Paul devant l'Aréopage d'Athènes," *RSR* 69 [1981] 209-48. Conzelmann, H., in *StLA* 217-30. Dibelius, *Studies* 26-83. Dupont, *Études* 157-60; "Le discours à l'Aréopage," *Bib* 60 [1979] 530-46. Eltester, W., "Gott und die Natur in der Areopagrede," *Neutestamentliche Studien* [Fest. R. Bultmann; ed. W. Eltester; BZNW 21; Berlin, 1954] 202-27. Legrand, L., "The Areopagus Speech," *La notion biblique de Dieu* [ed. J. Coppens; Leuven, 1976] 337-50. Mussner, F., *Praesentia Salutis* [Düsseldorf, 1967] 235-44. Nauck, W., "Die Tradition und Komposition der Areopagrede," *ZTK* 53 [1956] 11-52. Schneider, G., "Apg 17,22-31," *Kontinuität und Einheit* [→ 85 above] 173-78. Taeger, J., *Der Mensch und sein Heil* [Gütersloh, 1982] 94-103. Wilckens, *Missionsreden* 81-91. Wilson, *Gentiles* 196-218.)

96   (iv) *Paul in Corinth* (18:1-17). This account offers detailed and reliable information on one of Paul's most important missions, though it is silent about any developments that would later evoke the reproaches and polemical fulminations of 1-2 Cor (cf. Bornkamm, *Paul* [→ 97 below] 68). His arrival in this prosperous, ethnically diverse portage city, capital of the Roman province of Achaia (the Peloponnesos), can be dated in early AD 51 (→ Paul, 79:9; differently Lüdemann, *Paul* [→ 11 above] 157-77; → 1 Corinthians, 49:8). **2.** *Aquila:* Though he is called a Jew, context (v 18) and data of the letters (1 Cor 16:19; Rom 16:3) suggest that he and his wife Priscilla (called "Prisca" by Paul) were already Christians at this point, refugees from Rome residing temporarily in Corinth. They are not mentioned as converts of Paul there (cf. 1 Cor 1:14-16; 16:15). *edict of Claudius:* AD 49 (→ Paul, 79:10). **3.** *tentmakers:* See R. F. Hock, *The Social Context of Paul's Ministry* (Phl, 1980). Thus far the report could come straight from the logbook which furnished Luke's best information on Paul's travels (so Roloff, Schneider, Weiser). *in the synagogue:* See comment on 13:14. **5.** *Silas and Timothy:* Only now do they arrive (cf. 17:14-15). *testifying to the Jews:* The summary of his testimony (cf. 9:22; 17:3; 18:28; 28:31), together with the Jewish reaction (13:45) and Paul's prophetic rejoinder (13:46,51; 20:26), makes clear the sound of Lucan refrains, editorial in origin (Weiser, *Apg.* 485). **6.** *your blood be upon your heads:* A sacral law formula (Judg 9:24; 2 Sam 1:16): the consequences of a deed befall its doer. **7-8.** At least the names come from local tradition, though maybe not the exuberant generalizing relative to Crispus (cf. 1 Cor 1:14), which documents v 10b. **9-10.** The dream-vision of the exalted Lord (cf. 16:9) is the centerpiece of the Corinth account, interpreting a carefully planned intensification of the action up to its culmination in Paul's victory before Gallio (vv 14–16; cf. Haenchen, *Acts* 537–41). The vision conveys Luke's interpretation of this momentous mission, confirming its brilliant success (v 8) and deriving that from the active presence of the *Kyrios.* **10.** *people: Laos,* the hallowed designation of Israel, is now being used in the expanded sense declared in 15:14. **11.** *a year and half:* AD 51–52 (→ Paul, 79:9). The vision makes this extended sojourn amid vigorous opposition intelligible. **12–17.** Paul is accused before the proconsul Gallio, elder brother of the philosopher Seneca (→ Paul, 79:9). Verse 18 indicates that this occurred toward the end of Paul's sojourn in the city, showing how that period has been telescoped in Luke's telling. The account of the Jewish accusers' debacle, with its strong local color and element of burlesque, was probably passed down in the local church to recall its origin (Roloff, *Apg.* 269). There is no good reason to doubt Paul's part in the episode (*pace* Lüdemann, *Paul* [→ 11 above] 160–61). **12.** *to the tribunal:* The *bēma,* or monumental rostrum, recently unearthed and on display in the ruins of the Corinthian agora, may be the structure Gallio used (see J. Murphy-O'Connor, *St. Paul's Corinth* [GNS 6; Wilmington, 1983] 28, 141). **13.** *contrary to the law:* The charge seems deliberately ambiguous as to whose law had been violated. If so, the proconsul was not to be misled. **14.** *Gallio spoke:* Preempting Paul's self-defense, Gallio rules in a manner Luke considered exemplary for public officials involved in controversy between Jews and Christians: their concern is not religious law but wrongdoing against the state, and of this the Christian preacher could not be accused (Lüdemann, *Paul* [→ 11 above] 158). Here again is the apologetic front of the historiography of Acts (cf. 16:37–39), which will be broadly developed in the accounts of Paul's trials, chaps. 21–26. **17.** *Sosthenes:* Apparently a Gentile crowd turns upon the Jews, and "the blows come back to the smiter" (Conzelmann). Nothing suggests that this is he of 1 Cor 1:1.

97   (d) RETURN TO ANTIOCH AND JOURNEYS RESUMED (18:18–23). A rapid travelogue brings us back to Syria via Ephesus, and just as abruptly thereafter Paul is back in Asia. The account of each stop is drastically brief, and the demarcation of a "third missionary journey" in v 23 makes no effective content division in the text (→ 86 above; but → Paul, 79:28, 40–45). Verse 22 and the Nazirite-vow ritual (v 18; Num 6:13–20) hint that Paul's journey to "Syria" had Jerusalem as its destination, though the city is never mentioned and there is no room in Paul's own testimonies for an extra visit between those of chaps. 15 and 21 (Weiser, *Apg.* 501). Most agree that Luke has taken the travelogue of these verses from his Pauline source, but the pilgrimage of "ascent" in v 22 will more likely be his own thematic concentration on Paul's bond to the mother church (*pace* Lüdemann, *Paul* 141–57). **18.** *Priscilla and Aquila:* Their transfer to Ephesus is supported by 1 Cor 16:19, written from there. *Cenchreae:* Seaport of Corinth (see Rom 16:1). *a vow:* According to the Nazirite law for personal consecration, the cutting of hair grown long during the period of the vow was to be done amid Temple ritual (Num 6:1–21). One wonders whether, in coloring his portrait of Paul as Mosaic loyalist, Luke left his imperfect knowledge of the ritual showing (cf. 21:23–26). **19.** *Ephesus:* Capital of the Roman province of Asia, residence of the proconsul, and a commercial city of first importance. It was a Greek (Ionian) settlement that retained, under the Romans, its strategic role as the Aegean terminus of the main trade across lower Asia from the

Euphrates. This briefest epitome of Paul's first Ephesian activity (vv 19b–21a) safeguards his founding mission vis-à-vis Apollos (vv 24–27), whereas the promise to return anticipates chap. 19 and the longest of his sojourns (19:10; 20:31). **22.** *Caesarea:* Why this port (cf. 10:1), if the destination were Antioch (cf. 13:4)? Unfavorable winds, perhaps (Haenchen), but better that the different destination was already being hinted (Conzelmann). *going up:* The unqualified ptc. can only mean the pilgrimage to lofty Jerusalem (11:2; 15:2; 21:15; 24:11; 25:1,9), whence one "goes down" to elsewhere (8:5; 9:32). **23.** *from place to place:* Lit., "in order" (cf. Luke 1:3), i.e., through the region of 16:6–8.

(Bornkamm, G., *Paul* [NY, 1971] 43–77. Lüdemann, *Paul* [→ 11 above] 141–77.)

98   (e) THE MISSION IN EPHESUS (18:24–19:40). (i) *The ministry of Apollos* (18:24–28). A series of episodes united by the Ephesus locale begins with one that was a potential disturber of Luke's order. Assuming that it originally told of a mission in Ephesus before Paul (*contra* v 19; so Conzelmann, Schneider), we observe how Luke utilizes it to show how movements on the fringe of his linear history were integrated into the mission charted by the apostles (cf. 6:1–6; 8:14–17). This argument unites the Apollos episode with the one that follows it (19:1–7). **24.** *Apollos:* His learning is worthy of his provenance: the leading center of Jewish culture in the Diaspora (→ Biblical Geography, 73:25). There is no trace here of the rivalry with Paul suggested in 1 Cor 3:4–11; 4:6. **25.** *the way of the Lord:* Luke, if not his source (so Roloff, *Apg.* 279), understood that Apollos was already "instructing" (Luke 1:4) as a Christian teacher. *burning with the Spirit:* This despite his acquaintance with only John's baptism, a step short of Spirit-baptism (1:5; 19:2–3). Does this reflect that he was first a disciple of JBap (Roloff)? Luke does not subordinate his "Spirit" to the institution, in any case (cf. comment on 8:14–17; 10:47). **26.** *more accurately:* The zealous couple is his link with Paul and historical legitimacy. Luke could not allow Apollos to appear as an authorized Christian teacher until he had in some way integrated him into the apostolic fellowship (Käsemann, *ENTT* 147). Yet he could not report the rebaptism of such a celebrated missionary (cf. 19:5). **27.** *Achaia:* This is a preview of his "building upon" Paul's work in Corinth (1 Cor 3:10). **28.** Cf. 18:5; his kerygma is now fully at one with Paul's.

99   (ii) *Paul and the Baptist's disciples* (19:1–7). The Apollos episode illumines this otherwise incomprehensible situation, and vice-versa. Since, with the entire gospel tradition, Luke knows JBap as precursor and herald of Jesus (v 4), he cannot give a plausible rationale for the existence of Baptist disciples, who gave a messianic acclaim to John which the latter reserved for Jesus (Luke 3:15–17; Käsemann, *ENTT* 142–43). Such a phenomenon could only be portrayed as an immature Christianity: "disciples" (v 1) who, like Apollos, knew only John's baptism but, unlike him, had no experience yet of the holy Spirit (8:16) and had still to undergo the Jesus baptism. **1.** *the upper country:* Cf. 18:23, where Paul's itinerary was interrupted for the parenthesis on Apollos. Mention of the latter here emphasizes his connection to what follows. **2.** *never even heard:* Such a species of Christianity, or even a Baptist sect, is inconceivable. This is Lucan editorializing: like the Samaritans (8:15–16), these "disciples" gain access to the holy Spirit only with entry into the apostolic fellowship (Käsemann, *ENTT* 145). **3.** *into John's baptism:* This is Luke's circumlocution for the actual following of JBap. Just as he avoided suggesting an Apollos–Paul rivalry, so here he suppresses any between John's movement and Jesus'. The two were related in direct salvation-historical continuity (v 4), hence John's followers already stood in the "vestibule" of the Christian church. **4.** *that is, Jesus:* Christian interpretation has applied JBap's proclamation of "the coming One" to Jesus, not Yahweh (13:25; Mark 1:7; Luke 3:16); hence, faith in Jesus was demanded out of very obedience to John. **5-6.** See comment on 8:14-17; 2:38. The argument is not that humans control or dispense the Spirit, but that this gift is bestowed in the church, which began at Jerusalem with the first outpouring of the Spirit (which echoes here) and is represented by the apostles (8:17) or accredited witnesses (v 6; Weiser, *Apg.* 518). *spoke in tongues:* Cf. 10:46 and comment on 2:4.

(Böcher, O., "Lukas und Johannes der Täufer," SNTU A/4 [1979] 27-44. Käsemann, E., *ENTT* 136-48.)

100 (iii) *Paul's mighty word and wonders in Ephesus* (19:8-20). The section comprises three smaller units, the outer two having the nature of summaries (vv 8-12, 17-20), the inner one a pre-Lucan anecdote with legendary and comic features (Dibelius, *Studies* 19). The three sections obtain a literary unity from the relationship between Paul's thaumaturgy and the conquest of his competitors that gets summarized in vv 18-20. The material shows good local color, but for such a lengthy and important Pauline mission, Ephesus does not have a quality of information given about it comparable to Corinth in chap. 18 (Bornkamm, *Paul* [→ 97 above] 78-79). **8.** *kingdom of God:* In the historical schema of Luke 16:16, this proclamation came after JBap, so the theme sounds here by design following his disciples' baptism. **9.** *the Way:* This unqualified expression for Christian life and teaching is found at 9:2; 19:9,23; 22:4; 24:14,22. *withdrew from them:* We recognize Lucan schematism: synagogue preaching, opposition, separation, new forum. The whole course of Paul's mission is thus condensed in its individual stations. *Tyrannus:* Otherwise unknown owner or resident teacher. Paul is portrayed as a wandering philosopher on a teaching sojourn. **10.** *two years:* The lengthy duration of the Ephesus stay is reliable information (→ Paul, 79:40-42), as is the report that from here a large Asian area was evangelized (e.g., Colossae, Laodicea, Hierapolis). There is, however, no room in Luke's linear history for mention of troubling events in other communities which evoked the literary activity of this period: 1-2 Cor, Gal, Phil. **11-12.** Introducing the Sceva anecdote is a summary portrait of the Paul of legend, cherished in a later generation and not particularly consonant with Paul's self-portraits (cf. 2 Cor 10:10; Haenchen, *Acts* 562-63). Cf. 5:12-16, with which this passage strikes the theme of continuity. **13-17.** Since we know from elsewhere of exorcists who invoked Jesus' name outside his followers' circle (Mark 9:38-40), the original story here may not have involved Paul. The high priest with a Latin name is otherwise unknown, but his stature augments the disgrace of his seven sons. Certain fixtures of the exorcism genre get a novel twist here: the demon's recognition of would-be conquerors is withheld, spelling their defeat (v 15), and a concluding acclamation (v 17) records paradoxical victory for the misused name. Distancing the gospel from magic is the fact that this name will not work automatically for just any wielder (Conzelmann, *Apg.* 120). **18-20.** The edge of this summation cuts against Christian syncretism. True to the *genius loci* is the popularity of magic and its formula books (*Ephesia grammata*) in Ephesus (PW 5. 2771-73).

101 (iv) *The silversmiths' riot and Paul's departure*

(19:21-40). **21.** *Rome:* The first announcement of Paul's fated itinerary to Jerusalem and Rome precedes rather than follows the tumult which could otherwise be taken as the cause of his leaving Ephesus (20:1). **22.** *to Macedonia:* The path of eventual martyrdom and the dispatch of two messengers pointedly evoke the moment of Jesus' embarking on his final journey in Luke 9:51-52. Disciple and Master walk together to their shared destiny (Radl, *Paulus*). Historic factors prompting these travels (→ Paul, 79:43-44), including Corinthian ferment (1 Cor 16:5-7) and the bearing of the collection to Jerusalem (Rom 15:25-28; 1 Cor 16:1-4), are absorbed into the theological aegis (*dei*—cf. 1:16) that propels every movement in Luke's story. **23.** *no small disturbance:* A "dramatic episode" (vv 23-40), easily detached from its context and typically enlivened by principals' speeches, serves both to illustrate Paul's tribulations at Ephesus and to mollify them (cf. 1 Cor 15:32; 2 Cor 1:8-10). A link with the real story is Aristarchus (v 29), mentioned as coworker of the imprisoned apostle in Phlm 24: his part in the present episode hints that Luke knew of worse troubles at Ephesus than he recorded (cf. Bornkamm, *Paul* [→ 97 above] 79-84). In any case, it tells against the hypothesis that Paul, kept offstage in the Demetrius story, originally had no part in it (Weiser, *Apg.* 543-44; *pace* Roloff). **24.** *silver shrines of Artemis:* This implies small models of the goddess's famous shrine, which was one of the seven wonders of the ancient world (cf. Strabo, *Geogr.* 14.1.20). On Artemis, see *Beginnings* 5. 251-56; R. Oster, JAC 19 (1976) 24-44. **25-27.** The Speech of Demetrius. Luke tips his hand in this with the argument that the survival of the goddess cult depends on the profitable commerce surrounding it (cf. 5:1-11; 8:18-20; 16:16-20). Too, it is a measure of the gospel's flourishing power (v 20) that it now threatens the very existence of pagan cults. For v 26, cf. 17:24-25; and v 27 is usually compared with Pliny the Younger's assessment of Christianity's impact in Asia (*Ep.* 10.96.10). **29.** *Gaius and Aristarchus:* Cf. 20:4; on the latter, see also 27:2; Phlm 24; Col 4:10. **31.** *Asiarchs:* Leaders of uncertain capacity (see *Beginnings* 5. 256-62), they are part of the story's local color and an argument for Paul's social standing. **33.** *Alexander:* His intention is unclear, but as a would-be defense (*apologeisthai*) it might have been to disclaim any association of Jews with the accused (cf. 16:20). **35-40.** The Speech of the Town Clerk. This official articulates Luke's apologetic argument: Christian faith entails no subversion of public order or sacrilege against other cults. Paul's Ephesian triumph thus culminates in this official recognition that no judicial cause exists against him (cf. 16:37-39; 18:12-17; 25-26; Plümacher, *Lukas* 100).

102 (f) FINAL TRAVELS BETWEEN ASIA AND GREECE (20:1-16).

(i) *To Greece and back to Troas* (20:1-6). **1.** *for Macedonia:* Departure from Ephesus came according to plan (19:21), not under duress, probably in mid AD 57 (→ Paul, 79:43). What follows is a summary travel report, resumed in vv 13-16 and 21:1-18, interrupted by the insertion of the Eutychus anecdote (vv 7-12) and the farewell discourse at Miletus (vv 17-38). The travel diary (→ 10 above) has probably furnished the hard details, which are highly simplified and purged of reversals and conflicts vis-à-vis 1 Cor 16:1-9; 2 Cor 2:12-13; 7:5-7. The material's eyewitness pedigree is certified by the reappearance of the "we" narrator at v 5. **2.** *Greece:* Only here in the NT does the classical name *Hellas* appear. Popular parlance applied it to the province of Achaia, esp. Corinth and environs, where Paul spent three winter months (in AD 57-58) and wrote Rom with his imminent Jerusalem visit in mind (Rom 15:25;

→ Paul, 79:43-44). **4.** Listing of the seven companions with their home districts suggests that they were bearers of the collection for Jerusalem (Rom 15:26-27; 2 Cor 8-9), who had convened at Corinth with their proceeds. Luke's limited and belated attention to the collection (24:17) explains why we never learn of their trust from him. **6.** The "we" narrator associates himself with the part of Paul's retinue that lingered at Philippi. That is, in fact, where he left us at 16:17. *Unleavened Bread:* Cf. v 16.
103 (ii) *Eutychus resurrected* (20:7-12). This miracle, which local tradition might have made out of a wondrous recovery (Roloff), wins a place for Paul in the tradition which now includes Elijah, Elisha, Jesus, and Peter (9:36-43). It rests uncomfortably in the framework of a night-long Sunday worship preceding Paul's departure on his journey of no return (vv 22-23, 38). Since the portentous departure and the bread-breaking are confined to vv 7 and 11 and represent sustained interests of Luke, those verses may be his additions to an older story, adapting it with limited success to the ongoing itinerary (so Conzelmann, Schneider, Weiser). **7.** *first day of the week:* This is, by Jewish reckoning, Sunday, "the Lord's day" (Rev 1:10; *Did.* 14:1), and the custom of a eucharistic service in the evening (not on the eve) is probably a reflection of Luke's own time (W. Rordorf, *ZNW* 68 [1977] 138-41). Cf. Luke 24:29-30 with 24:1. *to break bread:* See comment on 2:42. Since this gesture adjoined Jesus' explanations of his destiny as shared by his followers (Luke 9:12-27; 22:19-38; 24:25-35), we sense that, at this crucial juncture of Paul's career, it is intended to further the assimilation of the two figures (cf. 19:21). **9.** *fell:* On possible symbolisms of the boy's fall, which discourage its "comic" assessment, see B. Trémel, *RTP* 112 (1980) 359-69. **10.** *fell upon him:* Cf. 1 Kgs 17:21 (Elijah); 2 Kgs 4:34-35 (Elisha); Luke 8:52 (the reassurance). **12.** This conclusion would naturally follow v 10; the redactional v 11 is intrusive.
104 (iii) *Troas to Miletus* (20:13-16). The travelogue now plots a southward route along the W coast of Asia Minor and the offshore islands (Lesbos, Chios, Samos). The displacement of an Ephesus reunion to Miletus (v 16) is historically probable, but Luke again avoids the real troubles that put the big city off limits to Paul (see comment on 19:23). The "Pentecost" deadline is not taken up hereafter.
105 (g) PAUL'S FAREWELL TO HIS MISSIONS (20:17-38). Over against the other speeches of Acts, Miletus represents a new genre, the farewell discourse (Michel, *Abschiedsrede* [→ 108 below] 68-72; Prast, *Presbyter* [→ 108 below] 36-38), to which analogies abound in the Bible and intertestamental writings (NT: John 13-17; Matt 28:16-20; Luke 24:44-52). This "testament" for all the churches he leaves behind (v 25) is the only speech to Christians by Luke's Paul. It announces both the end of his missions and the onset of his trials and imprisonments (vv 22-24), serving thus as a "hinge" between the two segments, mission and passion, in which Paul's career parallels the Lord's (Prast, *Presbyter* [→ 108 below] 21). The voice we hear is Luke's (Dibelius, *Studies* 158), but some nuggets of broad-based Pauline tradition (vv 24,28,34) bring the air of authenticity (J. Lambrecht, in *Les Actes* [ed. J. Kremer] 319-23). Luke uses this biographical *caesura* to mark the end of the church's first generation, that of the founding witnesses, and to document the orderly transition from their ministry to the later life of the church (Michel, *Abschiedsrede* [→ 108 below] 76).
106 The articulation of the text is unclear (J. Dupont, *Discours* [→ 108 below] 21-22), but the repetition of *kai (ta) nyn,* "and now," suggests the follow-

ing: a backward look (vv 18b-21); a forward look (vv 22-24); a testament (vv 25-31); a concluding commendation (vv 32-35). **17.** *the elders:* See comment on 14:23. This collegial leadership is casually associated with the *episkopos,* "overseer," function in v 28. **19.** *serving the Lord:* The *Kyrios* throughout the speech is Jesus, and "serving" (*douleuōn*) echoes Paul's self-depiction as *doulos* of Christ (Rom 1:1; Gal 1:10; Phil 1:1). *plots of the Jews:* 9:24; 20:3; 23:30. **20.** *I held nothing back:* The completeness and full publicity (*dēmosiᾳ̦*) of Paul's preaching disqualify in advance all heretical and secret doctrines later promoted in his name (cf. v 30). This clearly cuts against movements of Luke's own time. **22-24.** Sharply augmented over 19:21 is the forecast of Paul's destined "passion" at Jerusalem. **22.** *bound by the Spirit:* The dat. is instrumental, as usually with the vb. *deō,* "bind." Luke's reader recalls the "appointed" journey of the Son of Man prefacing a similar last discourse before Jesus' death (Luke 22:22-38). Concrete Spirit testimonies concerning Paul's fate at Jerusalem will come in the prophecies of 21:4,10-11. **24.** *complete my course:* In context, this is a circumlocution for his death (cf. v 25; 21:13; Radl, *Paulus* 147-48). The way of suffering fulfills the "service" (cf. Luke 22:27) of preaching the gospel.
107 **25.** *and now, behold:* A new section is marked in LXX style, appropriate to the "classical" era that is ending herewith. *the kingdom:* As message content, this is a key continuum between Jesus and the postapostolic church (cf. comment on 1:3). **26.** *I am innocent:* The self-exculpating formula belongs to the farewell genre (Michel, *Abschiedsrede* [→ 108 below] 51-52) and stresses the followers' accountability for their own adherence to God's "plan" of salvation (v 27). **28.** *take heed:* This earnest exhortation (5:35; Luke 12:1; 17:3; 21:34) brings the high point of the speech, at which vv 28-31 form an integral argument under the metaphor of the "flock" (1 Pet 5:1-3; Mark 6:34). *overseers:* This single Lucan use of *episkopoi* merges a rank instituted in some Pauline churches (Phil 1:1; 1 Tim 3:1-6) with the "elders" better known in the Asia of Luke's day (cf. Titus 1:5-9; J. A. Fitzmyer, in *StLA* 247-48). This "church office" provision is not yet the institutionalized apostolic succession of the Catholic Church (Prast, *Presbyter* [→ 108 below] 199-211). *the church of God:* This reading (ms. B) should be preferred to "of the Lord" (mss. A,D), even though it forces us to render the last phrase of the verse: "the blood of his Own" (Son; cf. Rom 8:32). Mechanical insertion of hallowed Pauline phrases may account for the problem, as for the rare emergence of expiation theology in Luke's writing (J. Lambrecht, in *Les Actes* [ed. J. Kremer] 322; cf. comment on 2:23; 8:32-33). **29-30.** With pneumatic foresight, Paul predicts heresy in the period following his departure (death?), with "wolves," an early-Christian cipher for heretics (Conzelmann, *Apg.* 129), coming from without and within Paul's churches. The halcyon days of harmony under the one gospel (2:44; 4:32) will end when he departs. **31.** *be watchful:* In prospect of the heresies, Paul furnishes the antidote of a vigilant church office, founded on the tradition of his own ministry.
108 **32.** *I commend you:* Notice that the church is confided to the Word, not vice-versa, fending off the early-Catholic interpretation. Office is in the service of the Word but is not its proprietor (Weiser, *Apg.* 583-85). **33-34.** Cf. 18:3; 1 Thess 2:9; 1 Cor 4:12; 9:3-18. **35.** *words of the Lord:* A common proverb has probably been attributed to Jesus here (Prast, *Presbyter* 155-56). The ideal of detachment is, of course, a Lucan refrain. **36-38.** All elements here belong to the genre of farewell scenes. That Paul will be seen no more confirms that his speech has been a last testament.

(Barrett, C. K., "Paul's Address to the Ephesian Elders," *God's Christ and His People* [Fest. N. A. Dahl; ed. J. Jervell and W. A. Meeks; Oslo, 1977] 107-21. Dömer, *Heil* 188-202. Dupont, J., *Le discours de Milet* [Paris, 1962]. Lambrecht, J., in *Les Actes* [ed. J. Kremer] 307-37. Michel, H., *Die Abschiedsrede des Paulus an die Kirche* [Munich, 1973]. Prast, F., *Presbyter und Evangelium in nachapostolischer Zeit* [Stuttgart, 1979]. Radl, W., *Paulus* 127-68.)

109   (B) Paul as Prisoner and Defendant in Palestine (21:1-26:32).
(a) THE RETURN TO CAESAREA (21:1-14). The "we" resumes after the Miletus interlude (cf. 20:15). Verses 1-10 illustrate the tissue of unassimilated facts that Luke found in the chronicle he certifies with the "we" (cf. G. Lohfink, *The Bible* [NY, 1979] 107-9). **2.** *Phoenicia:* See 11:19. **4.** *through the Spirit:* Cf. 20:22-24. The warning does not forbid the journey but continues the prophecy of what it portends (cf. v 12). Here and in vv 5,10-14, Luke fashions an introduction to his account of Paul's arraignments in Jerusalem and Caesarea, deftly building a taut expectancy for what lies ahead (Stolle, *Zeuge* [→ 54 above] 72-74). **7.** *Ptolemais:* → Biblical Geography, 73:80. **8.** *Caesarea:* Maritima, cf. 8:40; comment on 10:1. *Philip:* See 6:5; → 51 above. **9.** *daughters prophesying:* Cf. 2:17. **10.** *Agabus:* The same as in 11:28. **11.** Like some OT prophets he acts out his message (cf. Isa 20:2; Ezek 4:1; Jer 13:1). *into the hands of the Gentiles:* A clear echo of Jesus' passion prediction (Luke 18:32), which it fits better than it does Paul's case (vv 30-33; cf. Radl, *Paulus* 155-56). **12.** *not to go up:* See comment on v 4; 20:22-24. **13.** *for the name:* Cf. 9:16; 5:41. **14.** *the Lord's will be done:* Cf. Luke 22:42, rounding out a striking cross-reference to Jesus facing his appointed destiny (Radl).
110   (b) PAUL'S IMPRISONMENT AND TESTIMONY IN JERUSALEM (21:15-23:11).
(i) *Paul's reception by the church* (21:15-26). J. Roloff compares this account to a musical rendition in which the instrument playing the melodic line stays silent (*Apg.* 312). Luke omits crucial circumstances of this last Jerusalem visit, esp. the consignment of the collection and the grounds Paul had for fearing it might be rejected (Rom 15:31). The fever pitch of Jewish nationalism during the mid 50s AD put pressure on the vulnerable Christian community, whose relations with compatriots could hardly be improved by the arrival of Paul and his gifts from *gôyîm*. This is the framework in which the accusation of v 21 and the token of Paul's fidelity to the law (vv 23-24) gain their meaning. Luke's belated mention of the relief mission at 24:17 shows that he knew of this purpose of Paul's return to Jerusalem; that he is silent about it here may be due to his "passion-journey" motif (Weiser, *Apg.* 597) or may conceal the fact that this gesture of unity with the mother church failed after all to gain the latter's acceptance (P. Achtemeier, *CBQ* 48 [1986] 25). In any case, it is in the proof of Paul's Mosaic devotion, not in the crisis requiring it, that Luke is mainly interested (cf. 22:3; 24:13-15; 25:8; 26:4-5). **15-18.** The travelogue underlying chaps. 20-21 (→ 102 above) ends with these verses, and so the "we" rests until travel resumes in 27:1. The information we get is historically solid. The Jerusalem church was under the postapostolic leadership of James and the elders at this time (*ca.* AD 58; → Paul, 79:47), and James, once the Jewish rigorist (Gal 2:12), is probably now the voice of moderation amid rising Jewish fundamentalism (v 20). **19.** Cf. 15:4,12. A typical Lucan picture of harmony and incredible growth (v 20) prefaces the problem to be solved. **21.** *defection from Moses:* Like the charges against Stephen (6:11-14), Luke judges these to be without foundation, and so his record has shown (cf. 16:3; 18:18). Presumably Paul's attitude toward "Moses" as a

way of salvation was the basis of the charge (Gal 3:10-25; 5:6; 6:15; Rom 3:20-21; 10:4); but as for his advice to Jews, see 1 Cor 7:18-20. **22-24.** Solution: Nazirite purification (see comment on 18:18). Paul's participation in this private ritual in order to reassure his critics is based on a source account and is quite credible (cf. 1 Cor 9:20), even though it can hardly carry all the weight Luke puts on it (v 24; cf. G. Bornkamm, in *StLA* 204-5). See the requirements for terminating the vow in Num 6:14-15. **25.** *we have sent:* With this announcement of the decree (15:20,29) Luke may be tacitly admitting that it grew up after the agreement to which Paul was a party (Hengel, *Acts* 117; → 80 above). Addressed to the reader, the reprise reiterates the *de iure* foundation of the unity of Jews and Gentiles in the one church. **26.** *next day:* The timing is apparently that of Num 6:13, but it is unlikely that Paul undertook the Nazirite separation. The "seven days" (v 27) is too short for that (Num 6:5) and sooner pertains to a general-purpose purification (e.g., Num 19:12), such as might have been prescribed for a Jew returning from Gentile territory (Str-B 2. 759; Haenchen, *Acts* 612).
111   (ii) *Riot and imprisonment* (21:27-36). **28.** Cf. 6:13; 18:13. The whole issue of the trial section is formulated here (Conzelmann, *Apg.* 132). *brought Greeks into the Temple:* Stone inscriptions, in Latin and Greek, bounded the Court of the Gentiles, warning foreigners of the death penalty for breaching the temenos (*J.W.* 5.5.2 §194; *Ant.* 15.11.5 §417; *NTB* §47, 205). **29.** *Trophimus:* See 20:4; 2 Tim 4:20. Luke exculpates Paul according to the declaration of 25:8. **30-36.** The tumult scene is modeled after 19:28-32. **31.** *the commander of the cohort:* This reflects the assignment of a force of 1,000 soldiers to the Fortress Antonia, at the NW corner of the Temple area, for the purpose of quelling disturbances in that volatile district. The commander is named at 23:26. **36.** *away with him:* Cf. Luke 23:18.
112   (iii) *Paul's defense and appeal to Roman law* (21:37-22:29). The first of three *apologiae* by Paul in the trial chapters (22:3-21; 24:10-21; 26:2-23) is framed by introductory and concluding narratives that constitute a literary unit with it; most of the contents are the creation of the author (Weiser, *Apg.* 606-7). A series of disclosures at the beginning answers the question of who this is, just as the speech will answer the soldier's other query, what he had done (v 33). Speech and narrative framework together argue Paul's equal footing with his accusers; thus his language (v 40), the address "brothers and fathers" (22:1), and the topical affirmation, "I am a Jewish man" (22:3). Paul claims full membership in the sacral community of the chosen people, right here in Judaism's historic center. Moreover, as a Jewish rigorist, Paul is speaking to his peers, and the burden of his solidarity argument is that the Damascus event, rehearsed a second time in 22:6-16, would have brought any one of them to the selfsame conclusion as it had him: Christian conversion and mission (Löning, *Saulustradition* [→ 54 above] 174-75). **38.** *that Egyptian:* The commander's conclusion from Paul's use of Greek sounds like a contrivance of the author. Is Luke evoking the memory of contemporary Jewish uprisings in order to distance Christianity from them (Conzelmann)? Cf. *Ant.* 20.8.6 §169-70; *J.W.* 2.13.5 §254-55; → History, 75:179. **39.** *Tarsus:* A Roman provincial town with the right of citizenship (→ Paul, 79:16-17). Paul's citizenship is left unspecified so that it can come out climactically at the end of the sequence (22:25). **40.** *in Hebrew:* I.e., Aramaic, the popular tongue in Palestine at the time (see J. A. Fitzmyer, *WA* 38-43). **22:1.** *my defense:* Apologia (vb. *apologeisthai* at 24:10; 26:1) announces the genre of

vv 3-21. See Stolle, *Zeuge* [→ 54 above] 237-41; F.
Veltman, in *PerspLA* 243-56.
113 Paul's *Apologia* (22:3-21). The speech typically
does not address the charge that caused the riot (21:28-
29) but augments the reader's understanding of Paul's
vocation, building on the account in 9:1-19 (Dibelius,
Studies 159-60). Luke applies his own perspective to the
Damascus event in this speech and chap. 26, steadily
remodeling the conversion story as a vocation story (→
53 above). The speaker is once again interrupted at his
precise target (v 21; cf. 17:31), just as he will be at 26:23.
These corresponding devices show that the Temple
speech defends Paul's mission, that of chap. 26, his
message. **3.** *in this city: Pace* M. Hengel (*Acts* 81-82), this
is not very plausible (→ Paul, 79:18). *educated:* Luke's
Paul gives an "unreservedly positive" portrayal of his
Jewish formation, as against the "loss" and "refuse"
assessment of the apostle himself (Phil 3:4-11; Löning,
Saulustradition [→ 54 above] 167). This is because law
and promise are identified by Luke (24:14-15; 26:5-7),
whereas they were contraries for Paul (Gal 3:16-29;
Rom 4:13-17). *the law of our fathers:* Cf. Gal 1:13-14; Phil
3:6. **4-5.** On the persecutor's role (8:3; 9:1-2), see comment on 26:9. **6-8.** See comment on 9:3-5, and note the
typical augmentation of detail in the retelling. **9.** *saw the
light:* The companions did precisely the reverse in 9:7;
they heard but did not see. The change is intentional; the
light is revelatory rather than combatant, and the voice
now begins a message meant for Paul alone. The Saul
tradition is being deftly reworked as the story of his
direct commissioning by the risen Christ. **11.** *the
brilliance of that light:* This qualification further reduces
the old story's moment of divine combat against the
persecutor, as does the near elimination of the healing (v
13; cf. 9:17-19). **12.** *Ananias:* His Jewish credentials are
new vis-à-vis 9:10 and are prompted by the apologist's
forum and audience. **13.** Cf. 9:17. **14.** *to see . . . and to
hear:* These words are not merely anticipatory of the
Temple vision (v 18; so Stolle, *Zeuge* [→ 54 above] 108)
or solely interpretive of the Damascus vision (vv 6-9; so
Burchard, *Der dreizehnte Zeuge* [→ 50 above] 107-8);
they refer to both events and fashion a linkage between
them. We thus learn the full size of Paul's commission
cumulatively from the three passages, and the conclusive
word is reserved to the Lord's own instruction of Paul
(v 21; so also 26:15-18). *the Just One:* Cf. 3:14; 7:52. **15.**
witness: This designation reinterprets the "chosen vessel"
of 9:15 in reference to the forensic situation at hand.
Constitutive of the "witness" role is the defendant status
(Luke 21:12-13), where contradiction and conflict make
the spokesman's testimony a direct continuation of Jesus'
own (Löning, *Saulustradition* [→ 54 above] 149; Stolle,
Zeuge [→ 54 above] 140-54). The destination "to all
humanity" contrasts with the original "witnesses to the
people" (13:31), indicating that Paul carries the apostles'
testimony onward to the worldwide audience ordained
for it in 1:8. **17-21.** Paul's vision in the Temple may be
a separate tradition (Burchard, *Der dreizehnte Zeuge* [→
50 above] 163-65) but is hardly a full-fledged rival to
the Damascus tradition (*pace* Conzelmann, *Apg.* 135). It
is best taken as a Lucan construct, arguing the historical
legitimacy of Paul's Gentile mission from his mandate
received right at the religious heart of Judaism (Weiser,
Apg. 411). The text presupposes 9:19b-30 but relates
something quite new vis-à-vis that passage. **17.** *in the
Temple:* The God whom Paul served as a Jew (v 14) and
he who directs the Gentile mission are one and the same
(Dibelius, *Studies* 161). **18.** *they will not accept:* The Jewish
refusal as prelude to the Gentile mission is a recurrent
Lucan argument (13:46-48; 18:6; 28:25-28) and shows
the author's hand in the shaping of this vision. Since

Paul's mission will finally validate Isaiah's oracle on the
blinding of Israel (28:26-27), Luke may intend his
Temple vision to evoke the prophet's (Isa 6; so Betz,
"Die Vision" [→ 114 below] 118-20). **19-20.** *I said:* This
response has the place of the subject's protest of unworthiness in a divine commissioning (cf. Isa 6:5). On
Luke's partiality to this form, see T. Mullins, *JBL* 95
[1976] 603-14; B. Hubbard, in *PerspLA* 187-98. **20.**
your witness Stephen: This completes the reprise of
7:58-8:3 and brings Stephen to the "witness stand" next
to Paul, just as the latter was on the scene of the *proto-
martyrium.* **21.** *to nations afar:* No more than 13:47 or 18:6
does this imply a restriction of Paul's audience to Gentiles. Rather, it reiterates the dynamic of a mission propelled ever outward by the obstinate refusal of its
primary audience.
114 Prisoner's Appeal to Roman Law (vv 22-29).
22. *up to this word:* Paul's *apologia* is complete with "this
word"; so the interruption is the historian's stratagem.
The renewed outcry confirms the Lord's word to Paul (v
18). **23.** *to fling dirt:* Cf. *Beginnings* 5. 269-77. **24.** *examined
under the lash:* This step in the commander's pursuit of
clarity was legal only toward aliens and slaves, so Paul's
assertion of his citizenship promptly cancels the procedure (cf. *Beginnings* 4. 282; 5. 305). **25.** *to flog a Roman:*
Paul again appeals to the *Lex Porcia* (see comment on
16:37). A dramatic intensification builds between 21:39
(Tarsus provenance) and 25:10, the appeal to Caesar,
with this text as a middle stroke. **28.** *I was born one:* →
Paul, 79:15-17. Paul even stands higher than the officer
in Roman social station! Dio Cassius (*Rom. Hist.*
60.17.5-6) gives an idea of the financial outlay for purchased citizenship.

(Betz, O., "Die Vision des Paulus im Tempel von Jerusalem,"
Verborum Veritas [Fest. G. Stählin; ed. O. Böcher, *et al.;* Wupper-
tal, 1970] 113-23. Burchard, *Der dreizehnte Zeuge* [→ 50 above].
Jervell, *Luke and the People of God* [→ 85 above] 153-83. Löning,
Saulustradition [→ 54 above]. Stolle, *Zeuge* [→ 54 above].)

115 (iv) *Paul before the sanhedrin* (22:30-23:11).
Amid "a bundle of historical improbabilities unparalleled in the rest of Luke's work" (Roloff, *Apg.* 326), we
puzzle here over the commander's recourse to the
sanhedrin, his unlikely competence to convene them and
prepare their agenda, the character of the assembly
(meeting or trial, vv 30,6), the striking of Paul and the
latter's curse, then his incredible protestation of not
having recognized the high priest, and finally his manipulation of the ruling factions' *odium theologicum* to his
own advantage. Whatever its historical basis, the
account is clearly cross-referential to the sanhedrin
arraignments of Jesus (Luke 22:63-71), Peter and John
(4:5-22), the apostles (5:26-40), and Stephen
(6:12-7:60), and builds a historical continuum with
them. Thus the judicial process against the earthly Jesus
has been continued in four trials of Acts where the
accused is the Christ of the kerygma (Stolle, *Zeuge* [→ 54
above] 234). **30.** *the whole sanhedrin:* → Luke, 43:167.
23:1. *a clear conscience:* Cf. 24:16; 2 Cor 1:12. *I have lived:*
The Gk vb. *politeuesthai* means "to fulfill one's role in
society" (cf. Phil 1:27). *to this very day:* This covers Paul's
life as both Jew and Christian, implying that there is no
break between the two phases (v 6; 26:4-7). **2.** *high priest
Ananias:* This is the son of Nedebaeus, who held office
from AD 47 to 59 (Josephus, *Ant.* 20.5.2 §103; 20.9.2-3
§204-8; → History, 75:155). **3.** *it is you God will strike:* Is
this curse written with hindsight of Ananias's assassination at the beginning of the first Jewish revolt (*J.W.*
2.17.6 §429; 2.17.9 §441))? *you violate the law:* Cf. Lev
19:15. **5.** *I did not know:* This highly improbable
response, with its citation of Exod 22:27, keeps Luke's

hero faithful to the law even as he clashes with the highest Jewish leadership. **6.** *Sadducees and . . . Pharisees:* See comment on 4:1. *I am a Pharisee:* That he was such as a Jew, Paul himself reports (Phil 3:5); but that he is still such as a Christian is Luke talking, and for the benefit of the argument he caps at 26:5-8 (cf. J. Ziesler, *NTS* 25 [1978-79] 146-48). *the hope and the resurrection:* This is hendiadys: Paul's hope is the resurrection (24:15; 26:6-8). This illustrates again the identification of law and promise which Luke has made, as against Paul's strict dissociation of these (see comment on 22:3; 24:14-15). **8.** *no resurrection, nor any angel or spirit:* Only the first denial is supported in Jewish sources (*Ant.* 18.1.4 §16; *J.W.* 2.8.14 §165); the other items complete a counterpoint to the Pharisees' contention in Paul's favor (v 9). Because Luke does not disclose the basis of the Sadducees' views in their Torah rigorism, he makes them sound like scoffing rationalists (cf. Luke 20:27-33). **9.** *spirit or an angel:* Paul's supporters refer to his Damascus vision (22:6-10), and their acknowledgment of its reality falls thus in full accord with their theology (v 8). **11.** *the Lord appeared:* This consoling vision (cf. 18:9; 27:24) erects a major milepost in Luke's story: Paul's Jerusalem testimony is finished, and his mission's goal at Rome comes into view, both under the "necessity" (*dei*) of the very plan of God (cf. 19:21).

116 (c) PAUL BEFORE GOVERNOR AND KING AT CAESAREA (23:12-26:32).

(i) *Transfer to Caesarea* (23:12-35). The Jewish conspiracy against Paul and his hasty transport to Caesarea get a broad description, perhaps from a freestanding anecdote which Luke has augmented with the commander's letter (vv 25-30) in order to adapt it to his literary sequence. **12.** *hatched a plot:* This story's discomfort as sequel to the failed sanhedrin hearing (vv 1-10) is felt when the plot turns on a pretense of the same kind of inquiry (vv 15,20), even though the commander could hardly have been so prone to repeat the fiasco (v 21). The situation is inherently plausible, however, since lynching of traitors to the Jewish cause by fanatical patriots occurred often in the years just prior to the Jewish wars. *bound themselves by an oath:* Lit., "put themselves under anathema." This will leave us wondering over the fate of the frustrated conspirators (v 21). **16.** *the son of Paul's sister:* That Paul had relatives in Jerusalem is apparently rooted in local tradition (cf. 22:3). The family's rigoristic piety suggests that the nephew had zealot connections whereby he learned of the plot (Roloff, *Apg.* 331). **23.** *two hundred footsoldiers:* The fantastic numbers given here would have required half the troops assigned to the Fortress Antonia (cf. 21:31). *to Caesarea:* The governor's seat, 60 mi. distant (NW); see comment on 10:1. *third hour of the night:* About 9:00 PM. **24.** *the governor Felix:* This Roman freedman, with friends close to Claudius and Nero, obtained this position despite his background (cf. Suetonius, *Claudius* 28; Tacitus, *Hist.* 5.9; *Ann.* 12.54; Conzelmann, *Apg.* 139). His term was roughly AD 52-59/60 (→ History, 75:179) and was marked by cruelty and cupidity (cf. 24:26). **25-26.** The letter's redactional origin is universally admitted. A standard Hellenistic prescript is used (cf. 15:23; → NT Epistles, 45:6), and we learn the commander's name for the first time. **27-30.** The letter corpus offers an assessment of the prisoner's situation from the Roman viewpoint: he has no juridical guilt, and his case is a matter of religious disputes to which the imperial authority is extraneous. This view is the same as Gallio's (18:15; cf. 25:18-19) and is, in fact, Luke's main argument on the issue of public authority versus the gospel: the missionaries are repeatedly victims of conspiracy but are themselves innocent of any conspiratorial designs (Maddox, *Purpose* 95-96). **30.**

directing his accusers: This could not have been done until after the writing; but Luke's reader is this letter's real addressee. **31.** *Antipatris:* → Biblical Geography, 73:76. **34.** *Cilicia:* Cf. 21:39; 22:3. *Herod's praetorium:* The provincial governor had resided in the old palace of Herod the Great (37-4 BC) since AD 6.

117 (ii) *The governor's hearing* (24:1-23). Typically of Luke's dramatic episodes, this account is dominated by speeches, not one but two: a statement of accusation by the "pleader" (Gk *rhētōr*) for Jerusalem Jewry (vv 2-8), and Paul's second speech of self-defense (vv 10-21). The latter responds pointedly to the former and is structured in parallel with it: an initial *captatio benevolentiae* (v 10 = 2-4), rebuttal of the accusations (vv 11-18 = 5-6), and an invitation to the governor to pursue the evidence (vv 19-21 = 8). Parallelism will also be noted between Paul's arraignments and Jesus' (Luke 22:66-23:25): the succession of sanhedrin and procurator hearings (cf. Luke 21:12), the pressing of charges by Jewish spokesmen, the editorially refined combination of religious and political charges (cf. 25:8; Luke 23:2), and the ultimate Jewish failure to convince the Roman of the prisoner's guilt (cf. Radl, *Paulus* 211-21; Weiser, *Apg.* 627). **1.** *Ananias:* Cf. 23:2. *Tertullus:* The *rhētōr* was presumably a lawyer schooled in Roman as well as Jewish law. The punctiliar correctness of their procedure will only accentuate the accusers' failure to make their case. **2.** Felix's favor is courted in an elegant rhetorical style whose actual points of historical reference were better not pursued. Tacitus (*Hist.* 5.9) and Josephus (*Ant.* 20.8.5-9 §160-84) give the opposite impression of this governor's reign. **5.** *a pest:* The charges involve sedition and defilement of the Temple, but Luke's larger argument is hinted in the expansion of Paul's sphere of influence and his designation as Christian "ringleader." *the sect of Nazoreans:* "Sect" (*hairesis*) could imply a "school" within Judaism (26:5) but is usually pejorative on adversaries' lips (v 14; 28:22). "Nazorean" is Jesus' title in the kerygma (2:22; 4:10) and as the one Paul persecuted through his followers (22:8; 26:9), so it easily becomes a designation of the followers whom Paul now leads. **6.** *to desecrate our Temple:* Here is probably the historical core of Luke's dramatization of the governor's inquest (cf. 21:28-29). **6b-7.** The Western text (Vg) adds an invective against Lysias which ill fits the Paul reference of v 8 and is wanting in the better Gk mss.

118 Paul's Apologia (vv 10-21). **10.** *for many years:* This is the flourish of a speaker courting favor, not a real timing of Felix's career. **11.** *twelve days:* The sum of 12:27 and 24:1. The point is the ease of investigating such a short sojourn, hence a seizing of the gauntlet thrown down in v 8. This was the sojourn of a pilgrim, not an agitator undermining public order (v 12). **13.** *nor can they prove:* Appeal is to the legal principle that guilt must be proved, not innocence. **14-15.** *I confess:* This central statement of the apology is a definition of Christian life wholly in terms of OT Jewish faith (Stolle, *Zeuge* [→ 54 above] 120-21). The strict continuity of the two rests on Luke's identification of law and promise (see comment on 22:3; 23:6), and this is his most concise statement of that very un-Pauline equation. *the Way:* The contrariety between this term (see comment on 19:9) and the pejorative *hairesis* lies in the renunciation of any narrowing of the ancestral faith ("all that is written"), of which Christian faith is therefore no sectarian distortion but the fully logical conclusion, "the true Israel" (Weiser, *Apg.* 629). *having a hope:* The general resurrection, without christological specification (4:2), is foreseen in the terms of Dan 12:2, thus within the vision of the Pharisees. As goal of "the way," it fits the kerygma of

3:15 and 26:23. **16.** *a clear conscience:* Cf. 23:1. **17.** *alms and offerings:* At long last, the principal purpose of his final Jerusalem journey given by Paul himself (→ 110 above) is introduced to support his rebuttal of the charges against him (v 18). "The Acts reader will hardly understand this allusion; Luke clearly knows more than he tells" (Conzelmann, *Apg.* 142). **18.** *in the midst of these:* I.e., offerings. Paul was engaged in prescribed purification rites, not defiling the Temple (cf. 21:26–27). **19.** *but some Jews:* We should understand: "Not I stirred people up, but . . ." (cf. 21:27–28). The sentence begun in v 18 is not completed, and the anacoluthon both bespeaks the accusers' quandary and clears the agenda for the single issue that matters to Luke. This must be intruded through abrupt retrospect on the sanhedrin hearing (vv 20–21); Stolle, *Zeuge* [→ 54 above] 122–23). **21.** *resurrection of the dead:* Cf.23:6. Adjournment (vv 22–23). **22.** *accurately informed:* This surprising information has an apologetic dividend: the governor's favorable attitude was based on real knowledge, not deception. Given this disposition and the judgment of Lysias already communicated to him (23:29), Felix's postponement of a verdict of acquittal has to be a tactical concession to the Jews — or, in Luke's case, a concession to the fact that Paul never quite regained his freedom. **23.** The conditions of Paul's detention are similar to those that will be imposed on him in Rome (28:16,30).

119 (iii) *Paul's confinement at Caesarea* (24:24–27). **24.** *his Jewish wife:* Details of this adulterous union with Herod Agrippa's daughter are given in Josephus, *Ant.* 20.7.2 §141–44. It may explain the matters of Paul's discourse and Felix's reaction thereto (v 25). **26.** *money:* This fits the portrait of Felix drawn by the historians (cf. comment on 23:24) but also the Lucan motif seen in 8:18–20; 16:16–20; 19:23–27. *frequently . . . conversed with him:* This is a Lucan summary of an obscure period, based more on the popular narrative commonplace of the head of state instructed by the man of God than on any source account (cf. Mark 6:20; Weiser, *Apg.* 632). **27.** *two years:* The period is probably AD 58–60 (→ Paul, 79:47) and pertains to Paul's detention prior to the change of governor. Postulating a different referent in Luke's source (Haenchen, *Acts* 68) is unfounded and does not solve Felix's dating problems. *Porcius Festus:* Meager information in Josephus, *J.W.* 2.14.1 §271; *Ant.* 20.8.9–11 §182–96 (→ History, 75:180).

120 (iv) *Appeal to Caesar* (25:1–12). This initiative by Paul and its acceptance by Festus are the solid historical foundation of Luke's account. The circumstances of the appeal, however, and its sequel in the intervention of King Agrippa II are likely Lucan products, bringing this climax of Paul's self-defense into a close parallel with the unique Pilate–Herod sequence in the Lucan passion narrative (23:1–25; cf. Radl, *Paulus* 220–21; A. Mattill, *NovT* 17 [1975] 32–37). Historical implausibilities result from the heavy editorial hand, including the absence of a governor's verdict, his ostensible readiness to abdicate his judicial competence (v 11?) despite the crime against Caesar among the charges (v 8), and the strange matter of the trial's venue (v 9). Paul's historic appeal was, in all likelihood, against an official verdict unfavorable to him, but Luke preferred to keep Roman officialdom on Paul's side, leaving the appeal and the governor's role without plausible motivation (Haenchen, *Acts* 668–70; but cf. Schneider, *Apg.* 2. 356). **3.** The same assassination procedure is plotted as in 23:12–15. **7–8.** This brief summary of the proceedings shows that both sides have nothing new to say beyond what they contended before Felix (24:1–23). Paul's words resume the charges and, in different order, the defense he made against them in 24:11–19. Leading an uprising (24:11–

12) was classified as a *crimen laesae maiestatis* against the emperor's person; hence, the governor's remand of the case to a Jewish tribunal would be unthinkable. **9.** *a favor for the Jews:* Instead of the acquittal we are expecting after v 7, Festus moves to shift the venue to Jerusalem and thus becomes responsible for prolonging Paul's captivity. Does his inscrutable proposal cloak the historical fact that he ruled in the accusers' favor (Roloff, *Apg.* 342)? *tried before me:* Though Festus is to retain jurisdiction, Paul foresees his deliverance into Jewish hands (v 11). Luke is apparently thinking of a sanhedrin adjudication under the governor's aegis, as in 22:30–23:10. But such a proposal is just as unrealistic as that scene was (Roloff, *Apg.* 343). **11.** *I appeal to Caesar:* On the still murky legal background, see *Beginnings* 5. 312–19; Conzelmann, *Apg.* 144–45. What Paul employs is apparently a developed version of the old (republican) *provocatio,* whereby a citizen could win trial in Rome rather than the provinces. **12.** *to Caesar you shall go:* This declares the final directional thrust of the trial sequence toward the goal of Paul's story (19:21; 23:11) and Luke's (1:8).

121 (v) *Festus informs King Agrippa II* (25:13–22). After v 12, it remained only to put Paul on board ship for his Roman journey. In fact, two scenes delay that turn of our story, and both seem to be free compositions of Luke rather than material from his sources (so Conzelmann, Roloff, Schneider, Weiser). The first, containing the governor's review of his hearing of Paul's case for the king's benefit, seems to be superfluous, and only at v 26, in the following scene, do we learn that Festus is seeking Agrippa's help in examining the prisoner so as to be able to introduce his appeal to the emperor. The two Agrippa scenes are united by the motif of Paul's innocence, progressively articulated by governor and king (vv 18,25; 26:31–32); moreover, the king's hearing will evoke a final and conclusive statement of Paul's legitimacy under the Jewish tradition, of which Agrippa is a knowledgeable representative (26:3). With him, Paul's realization of the missionary *status confessionis* charted by Jesus (Luke 21:13) is complete, having run the gamut of synagogue, governor, and now king. **13.** *Agrippa the king:* Marcus Julius Agrippa II, son of the "Herod" of 12:1, with his sister, Bernice (→ History, 75:177). Theirs is a courtesy call (aor. ptc. of subsequent action; BDF 339.1) on the new representative of the *imperium.* **14.** *Festus presented Paul's case:* Like other Lucan reprises, this speech supplies details not given in the first telling: vv 15c,16,19 over against vv 1–12. **15.** *demanding his condemnation:* It now appears that the Jews wanted this without a fair hearing. **16.** *not the custom:* The principle Festus invokes was among the most fundamental of Roman jurisprudence; cf. *Digestae* (in *Cod. Iuris Civilis*) 48.17.1; Tacitus, *Hist.* 1.6; Dupont, *Études* 541–50. **19.** *disputes concerning their own religion:* With his august Jewish guest, Festus uses *deisidaimonia* with the meaning "religion" (cf. 17:22), not "superstition" (*RSV*). His report reiterates a major Lucan argument of the trial section (see comment on 18:14; 23:27–30). *whom Paul claimed to be alive:* The big issue of controversy previously identified in Jewish apocalyptic terms, "resurrection of the dead" (23:6; 24:15,21), is now stated in language more suitable to the Roman, ostensibly distanced from the kerygma but, as we know, still redolent of it (cf. 1:3; 3:15; Luke 24:5,23), and adding to those previous trial scenes the name of Jesus as the Resurrected. **20.** *at loss:* This statement confirms that Festus intended to abdicate judgment of Paul's case (contrast v 9). **21.** *a decision of the August One:* The Gk title *Sebastos* (Lat *Augustus*) was first accorded the Roman head of state by the senate in 27 BC (*OCD* 124).

122 (vi) *Paul before King Agrippa* (25:23-26:32). **23.** *with great pomp:* An idyllic description of the king's arrival sets the scene for Paul's last and fullest apologia, which completes the schedule of his persecuted confessions set by the Lord in 9:15. **26.** *to write about him:* With tactical delay, Luke finally tells us why Agrippa too must hear the case. The ensuing apologia will certainly not add practical items for Festus's report to Caesar (cf. 26:24!). That is not Luke's true objective in chap. 26; he intends rather to finish his answer to the nagging question of the gospel's relation to Judaism (26:2-3; → 5 above). *to the Sovereign:* Lit., "to the Lord," the earliest known application of an unqualified *ho kyrios* to the Roman emperor (see *TDNT* 3. 1055; Conzelmann, *Apg.* 147; J. A. Fitzmyer, *WA* 115-42).

123 Paul's Final Apologia (26:1-29). The speech before Agrippa is the plotted climax of Paul's self-defense in chaps. 22-25 and his summation, as defendant, on the issue of the Jewish suit against him, viz., his interpretation of the promise around which Mosaic Scripture and piety revolve (vv 6-8; cf. Löning, *Saulustradition* [→ 54 above] 177-78). A strategically placed interruption (v 24) identifies the discursive goal of the composition, which is the digest of Paul's kerygma in v 23. There his proclamation of the promise fulfilled asserts that it is finally the resurrected Christ himself, speaking through his "witness" (v 16) to Jew and Gentile, who stands on trial before the knowledgeable king (Stolle, *Zeuge* [→ 54 above] 133, 140). Because Paul's gospel is thus his final answer to the Jewish case against him, his apologia and his kerygma coincide (vv 28-29); he is witness precisely as defendant (Stolle, *Zeuge* [→ 54 above] 134). Moreover, for the benefit of the argument validating his kerygma, Paul's conversion and his vocation must now fully coincide in the one christophany. Accordingly, Luke's revisions of the Saul legend that were under way in 22:3-21, notably the suppression of Ananias's mediating role and the blinding-healing sequence, are brought to completion in this third telling (→ 53, 113 above).

124 The consecutive expressions *men oun* (vv 4,9) and *hothen* (v 19; BDF 451) signal points of articulation in the speech, hence: vv 4-8, Paul and the hope of Israel; vv 9-18, Paul's experience of Christ; vv 19-23, Paul's testimony as Christ's witness. The rejoinder to Festus (vv 25-27) doubles back on the beginning of the speech, and vv 28-29 show the apologist and the evangelizer as one. **1.** *extending his hand:* Cf. v 29! *made his defense:* See comment on 22:1. **2.** *before you, King Agrippa:* Agrippa's favor is courted with *captatio benevolentiae* as an informed and objective representative of Jewry (vv 26-32), unlike the hostile sanhedrin. **4-5.** *my way of life:* See comment on 22:3. Paul's Pharisaic piety weighs positively (cf. Phil 3:4-9) inasmuch as this is the "most exact" Jewish belief—consequently, the most reliable witness to the truth of his message. Support for this contention follows in the statement of his cause. **6.** *hope in the promise:* According to Paul's letters, God's promise remained outside and independent of the law throughout biblical history from Abraham on (Rom 4:13-17; Gal 3:15-18). For Luke's Paul, however, the law contains the promise and is understood as such in its entirety; thus his zeal for the law demonstrated a faithful adherence to the promise, and no futile Mosaic rigorism or misguided zeal for the law could be conceived (Löning, *Saulustradition* [→ 54 above] 168-69). **8.** *God raises the dead:* In this definition of the promise, the first *nekros,* "dead man," to be resurrected, according to Paul's kerygma (v 23), is clearly implied among the pl. *nekrous* (pace O'Toole, *Climax* [→ 125 below] 47-48). **9.** *Now I thought:* An important corollary of Luke's merging of law and promise is the separation of Paul's zealous Jewish piety from his activity as

persecutor. Whereas the latter was a logical consequence of the former and a symptom of its error in Paul's writing (Gal 1:13-14; Phil 3:5-6), here it becomes an aberrant personal conviction "kicking against the goad" of the Jewish fidelity that was propelling him into Christ's service (cf. v 14; Löning, *Saulustradition* [→ 54 above] 170). **10-11.** *I imprisoned:* The persecutor's portrait is much intensified vis-à-vis 8:1,3; 9:1-2; 22:4-5. This creates a foil for the correspondingly intensified appearance that overwhelms him in the very midst of his depredations (*en hois,* v 12). **13-14.** The light-motif (9:3; 22:6) rises to overcome the darkened persecutor's portrait, but the part played by Paul's companions (9:7; 22:9) is all but suppressed. Quite as the context requires (vv 16-18), Paul alone sees and hears (Burchard, *Der dreizehnte Zeuge* [→ 54 above] 109-10). **14.** *kick against the goad:* Though this is supposed to be said in "Hebrew" (cf. 21:40), the proverb is recognizable only as a commonplace of the Gk tragedians (e.g., Euripides, *Bacchae* 795; cf. Lohfink, *Conversion* [→ 54 above] 77-78). It is applied here to the persecutor's fury, which vainly resisted his Jewish piety's thrust toward Christ (see comment on v 9). **15.** *I am Jesus:* This mainstay of the three accounts (cf. 9:5; 22:7) interprets the expression "against the name . . ." in v 9 (see comment on 9:4; 3:6). **16.** *stand up:* Cf. Ezek 2:1-2. Parallels with earlier versions of the story end as the Lord commissions Paul directly. *I have appeared:* See comment on 9:17. *servant and witness:* These terms and their direct communication by the risen One place Paul's commission now on a par with that of the Twelve (cf. 1:8; Luke 1:2; 24:48; Burchard, *Der dreizehnte Zeuge* [→ 54 above] 112, 124-25). Without, of course, sharing their unique historical position, Paul directly continues their functions of authoritative witness for the risen One (22:15) and medium of his living message; indeed, he will carry these to the destination appointed for them in 1:8 (Dupont, "La mission" [→ 125 below] 297). Luke has thus brought the conversion story around to Paul's own viewpoint on it (→ 53 above; Roloff, *Apg.* 349-50). *of what you have seen and what I will give you to see:* The difficult double gen. seems to embrace the continued visionary experience of Paul: Damascus to begin with, then the later visions by which his career will be guided (18:9-10; 22:17-21; 23:11; so Stolle, *Zeuge* [→ 54 above] 130; O'Toole, *Climax* [→ 125 below] 69). **17.** *rescuing you:* An allusion to Jer 1:8 promises protection of the witness from his very clientele. This meant that his testimony would always be as defendant (→ 123 above). **18.** *to open their eyes:* Echoes of the language of yet another prophet to the Gentile nations, the Dt-Isa (42:7,16). *darkness to light:* This stock metaphor of NT baptismal parenesis (Col 1:12-14; Eph 5:8; 1 Pet 2:9) gains all the greater meaning in this context (v 13), where Paul's conversion and commission coincide. *forgiveness:* Cf. 2:38; 5:31; 10:43; 13:38. **19.** Renewed direct address of the listener signals the end of the Lord's words and return to Paul's *vita.* **20.** Cf. 9:19-30. "All the country of Judea" belongs to a familiar geographical sweep (1:8), but not to what Luke has reported. **22.** *I stand testifying:* Compare "I stand condemned" (v 6); witness and defendant situations coincide (cf. v 17). *saying nothing other:* This digest of Paul's message, directly continuous with the apostles' (Luke 24:44-48), proves that its rejection by the Jews is disobedience toward their own tradition. *the Christ would suffer:* See comment on 3:18. *first to rise:* See comment on 3:15. This formula links up with the definition of the promise in v 8. *he would proclaim light:* The invitation to conversion, clad in the metaphor of v 18 and in standard Israel-Gentile sequence (cf. 13:46-47; Isa 49:6), has the *Christus praesens* as its speaker (O'Toole, *Climax* [→ 125 below] 119–21; see comment on 3:26). As in Luke 24:47, the preaching partakes of the saving event.

125   24. *Festus spoke out:* The planned interruption works much as it did in 22:22 (cf. 17:32; → 113 above). The Roman's befuddlement is as it should be (cf. 18:15; 25:19–20), but Agrippa is the right target here (v 26), as his reaction confirms (v 28). **26.** *done in a corner:* A Gk proverb (Epictetus 2.12.17) carries Luke's assertion of the full publicity and accessibility of the Jesus-event (cf. 2:22; Luke 24:18). **27.** Reaffirmation of vv 6–7. **28.** Agrippa at once acknowledges the force of the argument and withdraws from its sway. **29.** *short or long:* Paul elegantly turns the king's aloof irony into an earnest objective. **31.** *nothing deserving death:* This is the final word of the trial section (cf. 23:29!) and one of the two prongs of its argument, the other being stated in vv 22–23. **32.** Ironic! See comment on 25:12; 27:24.

(For bibliography, → 114 above; also: Cadbury, H., in *Beginnings* 5. 297–338. Dupont, *Études* 527–52; "La mission de Paul d'après Actes 26.16–23," *Paul and Paulinism* [Fest. C. K. Barrett; ed. M. D. Hooker and S. G. Wilson; London, 1982] 290–301. Lohfink, *Conversion* [→ 54 above]. Neyrey, J., "The Forensic Defense Speech and Paul's Trial Speeches," *Luke–Acts* [ed. C. H. Talbert] 210–24. O'Toole, R. F., *The Christological Climax of Paul's Defense* [Rome, 1978]. Radl, *Paulus* 198–220. Veltman, F., in *PerspLA* 243–56. Wilson, *Gentiles* 161–70.)

126   (C) Paul's Last Journey and Ministry in Rome (27:1–28:31).

(a) THE JOURNEY TO ROME (27:1–28:16).

(i) *Sea voyage, shipwreck, and deliverance* (27:1–44). It is widely agreed that chap. 27 was composed after a popular Greco-Roman literary model, the adventurous sea voyage, which owed its vogue to the classic tales of Odysseus and Aeneas (cf. V. Robbins, in *PerspLA* 217–28). The 1st pers. pl. narrative form became conventional in the sea-voyage literature, again recommended by the prototypes, the *Odyssey* and the *Aeneid;* and, accordingly, the "we" narrator reappears in v 1 (cf. 21:18) and speaks until 28:16, the arrival in Rome. Exegetes disagree on the matrix account, whether it was a preexisting nautical tale taken over by Luke with insertions featuring his hero (Dibelius, *Studies* 204–6; Weiser, *Apg.* 391), or whether it records the actual memories of a Pauline companion, perhaps Aristarchus (v 2), whose voice Luke transmits in the "we" (E. Haenchen, in *StLA* 276; Roloff, *Apg.* 359). The first view is favored by the intrusiveness of the Paul insertions, particularly vv 9–11 and the loose-hanging clause in v 43 (cf. also vv 21–26, 31,33–36). Furthermore, a striking array of seafaring *termini technici* in the description of the journey's toils points to its origin in literature rather than experience (as E. Haenchen admits, "Acta 27" [→ 129 below] 250). We sense, too, the improbability of Paul's role as advisor to the ship's officers and leader of fellow passengers when, as a prisoner, he would more likely have been below deck in chains! As for Luke's purpose in "paulinizing" a nautical yarn, he expresses it plainly in vv 22–25: Paul must reach his (and the book's) destination in the world capital, and the terrors of the contrary sea and elements only accentuate the invincible divine plan that directs his journey (Schneider, *Apg.* 2. 382).

127   1. *we were to set sail:* The "we" is awkward: it seems detached from "some other prisoners," yet it has become part of them at v 6. This suggests that it is the literary device of the sea-voyage genre (V. Robbins, in *PerspLA* 229), even though other details in vv 1–8 may come from an actual record of Paul's transfer to Rome. **2.** *Adramyttium:* The ship's home port, in NW Asia Minor E of Troas. *Aristarchus:* See comment on 19:19; 20:4. **3.** *Julius treated Paul kindly:* Cf. v 43. **4–5.** The

panorama of passing ports and islands is true to the genre, and v 4 introduces the motif of adverse elements which will build the drama of this voyage (V. Robbins, in *PerspLA* 233). The headwinds of autumn (v 9; → Paul, 79:48) would have come from the NW, so the "lee," or sheltered side, of Cyprus was its E shore. *Myra in Lycia:* On the S coast of Asia Minor, E of Patara (21:1). **6.** *an Alexandrian ship:* This grain vessel (v 38) came from the Egyptian port almost directly S of Myra. **7.** *Cnidus:* The difficulty of making this port might have been due to its position on one of the rocky fingertips of SW Asia Minor. *Salmone:* A town on the NE tip of Crete. **8.** *Fair Havens:* The ancient name is preserved in the modern Kali Limenes, on the S coast of Crete. **9.** *the fast was already over:* This Jewish timing (cf. 20:6) refers to the Day of Atonement observance (Lev 16:29–31; → Institutions, 76:147–50), therefore late Sept. or early Oct. The point is, it was perilously near the season (Nov. to Mar.) when sea travel was suspended because of winter storms. **9(b)–11.** First Paul Insertion. As man of God, he foresees the grave danger in resuming the voyage (cf. Philostratus, *Life of Apol.* 5.18) and will be proved right. His intervention is scarcely conceivable for a prisoner, needless to say. Shipowner and captain appear only here; elsewhere just "sailors." **12.** *Phoenix:* Best identified with the modern Phineka, a harbor facing SW/NW.

128   14. *northeaster:* Gk *eurakylōn,* composed of Gk *euros,* "E wind," and Lat *aquilo,* "N wind." On wind terms in these verses, see *Beginnings* 5. 338–44; PW 20. 431–35. **16–17.** Off the island of Cauda, 25 mi. S of Crete, things come to a full emergency. The lifeboat, towed hitherto, is secured on deck, the hull is "trussed" (*Beginnings* 5. 345–54), and fear of the Syrtis shoals off Africa prompts a lowering of the drift-anchor for controlled drift (Haenchen, "Acta 27" [→ 129 below] 245). **18–20.** Frantic jettisoning of cargo and tackle, amid an extended period without sun or stars to help plot the path of sail, brings the story to its nadir: all hope is lost. All is ripe for a second intervention by the man of God. **21–26.** Second Paul Insertion. As against Jonah 1:9, salvation can be promised the seafarers because the prophet is on board (Kratz, *Rettungswunder* [→ 91 above] 328). **21.** *long without food:* This was for seasickness, not shortage. *Paul stood:* Gale blowing and ship listing, what a time for a speech! The argument moves from reproach to reassurance, centering on the angel's "fear not" (v 24), which remains the watchword of Paul's Rome journey from beginning (23:11) to end (28:15). **23.** *an angel of the God I . . . worship:* This is phrased for pagan shipmates, and so it replaces the less easily explicable christophany (23:11). Rescue from sea peril by a god's intervention was a cliché of the Gk mysteries (Isis, Serapis, the Dioscuri; cf. PWSup 4. 295–97). **24.** *destined to appear before Caesar:* With the typical formula of heavenly visitors' reassurance, the "necessary" (*dei*) completion of Paul's harried travels is reaffirmed (cf. 19:21; 23:11; P. Pokorný, *ZNW* 64 [1973] 240–41). In the context of chaps. 27–28, the completed voyage will also be a confirmation of Paul's innocence (26:31–32). *and behold:* In LXX idiom, the angel promised deliverance of all on Paul's account, betokening his role in God's wider plan. **26.** *shipwrecked on some island:* Spoken in prophetic foreknowledge of vv 41–44.

129   27. This verse is a sequel to v 20. *the Adriatic:* The name was applied in Luke's day to the waters between Crete and Sicily as well. *nearing land:* Indicated by the sound of breakers? **30–31.** By intervening to prevent the sailors' flight, Paul appears again as instrument of the "saving" of his shipmates. **31.** Third Paul Insertion. **33–36.** Fourth Paul Insertion. **34.** *this will help* to save you: "Salvation" (sōtēria) is thematized in this passage (cf. v 31), so the food's physical effect may well betoken something deeper. not a hair of his head: An OT expression (1 Sam 14:45; 2 Sam 14:11), echoed in Luke 21:18. **35.** taking some bread: The eucharistic character of this meal is hard to deny, given the "salvation" augury, the punctual echo of Luke 22:19, and the Lucan development of the "bread-breaking" (see comment on 2:42; so Schneider, Weiser, contra Haenchen, Conzelmann, Roloff). The disjunction between vv 35 and 36 (cf. 2:46) forestalls the impression of a communio infidelium; Luke means only that all partook of the saving power of the risen Lord made present in the eucharistic meal (cf. Kratz, Rettungswunder [→ 91 above] 331). **37.** two hundred seventy-six persons: This information may well have resumed the original story (from v 32). **38.** Cf. v 18. **39.** a bay: A "St. Paul's Bay" is found today on the NE coast of the island of Malta (28:1), which is the unrecognized land revealed by the light of dawn. **40.** cast off the anchors: These maneuvers with anchors, rudder lines, and small foresail were for easier management of the vessel through the shallow bay waters to the shore. **41.** a shoal: Lit., a "place of two seas" (topos dithalassos), a sandbank with deep water on both sides. The loss of the lifeboat (v 32) weighs heavy here, for it might have borne the passengers through the shallow waters without running aground, as the vessel now does. **42.** kill the prisoners: This, too, is a panic reaction of the soldiers (cf. v 32), who would have been held responsible for their captives' flight. **43.** wishing to save Paul: Paul's instrumentality in his shipmates' salvation (v 24) is now fully apparent. Luke's interpolation of this clause into an older story is confirmed by the fact that we never learn which of the bidden courses, swimming or clinging to flotsam, Paul actually took. **44.** all came safely ashore: Thus is Paul's faith finally vindicated (v 25).

(Haenchen, E., "Acta 27," Zeit und Geschichte [Fest. R. Bultmann; ed. E. Dinkler; Tübingen, 1964] 235–54. Kratz, Rettungswunder [→ 91 above] 320–50. Ladouceur, D., "Hellenistic Preconceptions of Shipwreck and Pollution as a Context for Acts 27–28," HTR 73 [1980] 435–49. Miles, G. and G. Trompf, "Luke and Antiphon," HTR 69 [1976] 259–67. Pokorný, P., "Die Romfahrt des Paulus und der antike Roman," ZNW 64 [1973] 233–44. Radl, Paulus 222–51.)

130   (ii) Paul on Malta (28:1–10). A strand of typical travelogue in the "we" style (vv 1–2,7,10; cf. 27:1–8) is complemented by two miraculous episodes (vv 3–6, 8–9), both remarkable for their concentration on Paul's personal prowess without the usual disclaimer in favor of the real agent of the miracles (3:12,16). The composite effect is to carry forward the perspectives already instilled by chap. 27: Paul must reach his destination under divine decree and protection; his deliverance from mortal danger disproves his guilt of any capital crime (now explicitly in vv 4–6); salvation comes to others through Paul (vv 8–9). **1.** having reached safety: The ptc. diasōthentes links up with 27:44 and echoes the theme word sōzesthai, "be saved," of chap. 27. Malta: A large island S of Sicily, off the main shipping route (cf. 7:39), where a form of the Semitic Punic language was spoken. See Strabo, Geogr. 17.3.16. **2.** the natives: Lit., "the barbarians"; see comment on Rom 1:14 (cf. 1 Cor 14:11; H. Windisch, TDNT 1. 546–53). **3.** a viper: It is as fruitless to inquire after this species of "clinging" snake as it is to wonder whether the Punic language spoken by the Maltese had any equivalent to the Gk "Justice" (v 4). The story gained all its color from narrators on other shores. **4.** Justice has not allowed: The Gk hē dikē here connotes the goddess "Justice" pursuing a murderer. The islanders, to whom the story attributes this Gk "theology," imagine

that she has allowed her quarry to escape shipwreck only to strike him down in this unheroic and anticlimactic circumstance. **5.** no ill effect: Cf. Luke 10:19; Mark 16:18. Besides dispelling the natives' misapprehension, the episode accredits Paul as an authorized emissary of Jesus, who had bestowed this very immunity with his commission. **6.** he was a god: So far from a fugitive from "Justice"! Paul does not disown this accolade as he did in 14:15; his prayer before the cure (v 8) is the closest this passage comes to citing the true agent of its miracles (contrast 3:6; 9:34; 14:3; 16:18; 19:11; cf. W. Kirchschläger, in Les Actes [ed. J. Kremer] 516). **7.** Publius: The legate of the praetor of Sicily was the "first citizen" of Roman Malta. He illustrates again the mission's success with people of the upper classes (cf. 8:27; 10:1; 13:7,50; 16:14,38; 17:4,12; 19:31; 24:24; 25:23; 26:26). **8.** laying his hands on him: The combination here of the afflicting fever, curative imposition of hands, and subsequent mass healing (v 9), suggests a conscious reprise of Jesus' first cures (Luke 4:38–41), hence a literary rounding off of the charismatic ministries Luke has narrated (W. Kirchschläger, ibid. 520). The direct continuity of these ministries is the point being pressed. **10.** when we set sail: Cf. v 11.

131   (iii) Paul's arrival in Rome (28:11–16). The Pauline travelogue in the "we" style will now conclude at Paul's appointed destination. **11.** three months later: I.e., after the winter spent on Malta (see comment on 27:9; → Paul, 79:49). Twin Brothers as figurehead: The Gk Dioskouroi (Lat Castor and Pollux), brothers of Helen and sons of Zeus, were venerated as astral deities, hence sailors' protectors (Beginnings 4. 343–44). Their images appropriately adorned the prow of this ship. **12.** Syracuse: Important port city in SE Sicily, once the powerful and successful enemy of invading Athens (Thucydides, Pelopon. War 7), but rather in sleepy decline when Paul arrived. Rhegium: The Reggio di Calabria of today, on the tip of the Italian boot. Puteoli: Modern Pozzuoli, on the Gulf of Naples W of that city, still 125 mi. SE of Rome. This was the regular port of entry to Rome from the E, though it would shortly yield that status to a freshly dredged Ostia. **14.** brothers: A Christian congregation (see 1:15) already existed there, as in Rome (v 15). The invitation makes it hard to remember that Paul is coming to Rome as a prisoner. we came to Rome: This notice seems premature and duplicated by v 16a, but its purpose is to set the stage for the encounter of v 15 (Hauser, Abschlusserzählung [→ 133 below] 14). Paul's arrival at Jerusalem the last time (21:15–18), a comparably momentous milepost of his journeys, was likewise weighted with dual notices of arrival (21:15,17) and meetings with fellow Christians on the penultimate stops (21:16). **15.** Forum of Appius: The five-day journey on foot from Puteoli followed the Via Campania to Capua, then the Via Appia northward. Two stations of the great highway are mentioned here, respectively 43 and 33 mi. from the capital. Only at these liminary stations is the existing community of Rome referred to; hereafter Luke shrinks the spotlight to Paul, his trailblazing missionary. took courage: Tharsos, "courage," echoes the risen Lord's tharsei at 23:11, thus editorially rounding off the Rome journey that Luke has plotted. **16.** live on his own: This apparently means that Paul was under house arrest in rented quarters (v 30). This sentence sets the stage for the concluding episode and brackets it, together with the statement that echoes and complements it in vv 30–31. Nevertheless, the exit of the "we" narrator at this point confirms that v 16 is the organic conclusion of Paul's journeys, not the introduction to his final sojourn (pace Hauser, Abschlusserzählung [→ 133 below] 12–16).

132   (b) PAUL IN ROME (28:17–31). With the end of the journey record, Luke's own hand designs a rounding finale of his work. It is a bipartite dramatic episode, parallel to 13:13–52 in its sequence of instruction, Jewish rejection, and turning to the Gentiles (→ 71 above); it thus condenses Paul's two-year Roman sojourn in a reprise of the stages his mission has followed at all of its principal stations (cf. esp. 18:1–6; 19:8–10; J. Dupont, in *Les Actes* [ed. J. Kremer] 383–86). The two parts of the sojourn account are two encounters with the capital's Jewish leadership, the first resuming the full argument of the trial chaps. 22–26 (vv 17–22), the second summarizing the problem that has motivated the whole work (→ 5 above): the Jewish no vs. the Gentile yes to the Christian gospel (vv 23–28). The concluding sentence resembles other summary statements that closed earlier sections of the book (1:13–14; 5:42; 15:35). None of these ingredients gives evidence of any integral source account underlying the episode, which thus appears to have been composed from disparate strands at best (cf. Weiser, *Apg.* 677–79). Nor is there any evidence to support the old hypothesis of a missing conclusion to the book or of a projected third Lucan volume (cf. Schneider, *Apg.* 2. 411–13). The plan of the risen Lord for his witnesses is, in fact, complete at vv 30–31 (see comment on 1:8). The end of an epoch is reached when Paul, the last of the witnesses directly commissioned by the risen One, completes his missionary odyssey from Jerusalem, city of the true Israel's first assembly, to Rome, center of a vast and fertile world of the Gentiles (Roloff, *Apg.* 371; Wilson, *Gentiles* 236–37). Only our thirst for an ending to Paul's biography does Luke leave unslaked, quite as he did in the case of Peter and the apostles, unceremoniously removed from his story after 16:4 (→ 5 above). It is the exalted Christ, the true prophet of salvation to all the nations (26:23; 3:22–26), whose path has been plotted in Acts; his witnesses have come and gone in its pages only as needed.

133   **17.** *the Jews:* On the important Jewish community of the capital, gradually and painfully regrouped after the expulsion decree of Claudius in AD 49 (cf. 18:2; → Paul, 79:10), see W. Wiefel, "The Jewish Community in Ancient Rome . . . ," *The Romans Debate* (ed. K. P. Donfried; Minneapolis, 1977) 100–19; R. Penna, *NTS* 28 (1982) 321–47. *nothing against our people:* The charge of 21:21 has been disproved long since (see 25:8; 26:31). *handed over to the Romans:* This new version of the process, as against 21:31–33, makes Jesus' trial echo in Paul's (cf. 21:11; Luke 18:32; 24:7; Radl, *Paulus* 264–65; J. Dupont, in *Les Actes* [ed. J. Kremer] 381). **18.** See 23:29; 25:25; 26:31. One detail here, the Roman wish to release Paul (*eboulonto apolysai*), was not recorded in the trial sequence and belongs rather to the editorial retrospect on Jesus' trial (cf. 3:13; Luke 23:20; Radl, *Paulus* 255–56, 262). **19.** *appeal to Caesar:* See 25:11; 26:32. *not having any accusation:* Though unfaithful Israel has made itself Paul's adversary, he is no adversary of Israel but the beleaguered exponent of its "hope" (v 20). **20.** *the hope of Israel:* This is a restatement of 23:6 (cf. 24:15,21; 26:6–8) and refers, at least primarily, to the resurrection. Yet one should not exclude a second line of reference, the "ingathering" that is effected by the kerygma of the resurrected Christ (see comment on 1:6; 15:16–17). That process is obviously still under way in Rome (see comment on v 28). *I wear this chain:* See 26:29; but all indications of chaps. 27–28 are otherwise to the contrary (see comment on v 14; → 126 above). **21–22.** The Jews speak as if they were all but isolated from the rest of Jewry, and as though there were no Christian community in Rome (cf. v 15). This is Lucan artifice, obtaining the result of a completely unpredisposed hearing of what

Paul had to say (Roloff, *Apg.* 373). The division of this audience (v 24) will therefore be a matter of divine determination, not contingencies of the situation. *to hear your views:* This is the first of a series of occurrences of the vb. *akouein,* "hear," that includes three in the Isa citation (vv 26–27) and Paul's augury of the Gentiles' "hearing" (v 28). The text from Isa illustrates the range of the verb's meaning, from "listen" to "heed," which lies in between the unfaithful Jews' inquiry and the obedience of the Gentiles (cf. Hauser, *Abschlusserzählung* 69–81). **23.** *the kingdom of God:* This message has been the hallmark of the epoch of fulfillment (Luke 16:16), and it is to remain the principal continuum between the messages of Jesus and his church (v 31; see comment on 1:3). Close parallelism between vv 23 and 31 indicates that the focal point of this concluding passage is the indomitable kerygma about Christ, not the person and fate of Paul (J. Dupont, in *Les Actes* [ed. J. Kremer] 365, 371–72; Schneider, *Apg.* 2. 413). *about Jesus:* Cf. 26:22–23. The two components of Paul's instruction thus link the message preached by Jesus with the message about him. **24.** *some were convinced:* Divided Jewry has been a constant in Paul's mission (14:1–2; 17:2–5; 18:5–6; 19:8–9; 23:9–10) and persists even here as a sign of the continuing discernment of the true Israel (cf. Luke 2:34; see comment on 2:40). **25.** *one word:* This is Paul's last, quoting Isa 6:9–10 LXX on the blinding of Israel. This was apparently already a Christian missionaries' *testimonium* before Luke's writing, a ready resort to explain the gospel's repudiation by the great majority of Jews (cf. Holtz, *Untersuchungen* 35–36). NT authors mostly reproduce the milder, predictive wording of the LXX version, as against the mandated blinding in MT (cf. Matt 13:14–15 [Mark 4:12; Luke 8:10]; but cf. John 12:40). The predictive version suits Luke's purpose in the present passage, where the Spirit's forecast shows Jewry's persistent refusal to be a matter of salvation-historical necessity. **28.** *let it be known to you:* The conclusion of this argument from prophecy is solemn and definitive: any prospect of conversion for the Jewish people at large has faded completely (differently Rom 11). Nay-saying Jewry has lost the status of the chosen; the believing portion has become the cornerstone of the true Israel, into which the Gentiles are being incorporated (Lohfink, *Sammlung* 93; Jervell, *Luke* [→ 85 above] 62–64; differently J. Dupont, in *Les Actes* [ed. J. Kremer] 376–80). This picture undoubtedly reflects the experience of Luke's generation: the church was now predominantly Gentile, and Jews, almost without exception, were unresponsive to the gospel (Wilson, *Gentiles* 232; → 5 above). *they will heed it:* See comment on vv 21–22.

30–31. Epilogue. *two full years:* This implies Luke's knowledge of the fatal turn that Paul's fortunes took thereafter (cf. 20:25,38; *1 Clem.* 5:5–7). The period is roughly AD 61–63 (cf. 24:27). *rented quarters:* This meaning of *misthōma* (mostly understood as "contract price," "rent") is unattested elsewhere but is recommended by the context, which pictures Paul receiving interested visitors (*pantas tous eisporeuomenous*). It is used by the *JB* and *NAB,* but not by the *RSV* or *NEB* ("at his own expense"). Cf. Hauser, *Abschlusserzählung* 153–57. *preaching . . . and teaching:* The argument is continuous; see comment on v 23. *very forthrightly:* Lit., "with all boldness" (*parrhēsia*). This hallmark of apostolic preaching (2:29; 4:29,31) illustrates the continuity between what the Romans heard and what had rung out in Jerusalem at the very beginning. One last time, and as its very last assertion, Acts portrays the indomitable Christian message in its "world-conquering power" (Hauser, *Abschlusserzählung* 144). *unhindered:* Cf. the words elsewhere attributed to Paul in chains: "the word of God is not fettered" (2 Tim 2:9). As the reader closes Acts, Paul's personal fate is overshadowed by this open-ended triumph of the gospel over its powerful opposition. But that, after all, rather than the "acts of apostles," was the real subject matter all along.

(Dupont, J., in *Les Actes* [ed. J. Kremer] 359–404. Hauser, H., *Strukturen der Abschlusserzählung der Apostelgeschichte* [Rome, 1979]. Holtz, *Untersuchungen* 33–37. Jervell, *Luke* [→ 85 above] 41–74. Maddox, *Purpose* 42–46. Müller, P., in *Les Actes* [ed. J. Kremer] 523–31. Radl, *Paulus* 252–65. Stolle, *Zeuge* [→ 54 above] 80–89. Wilson, *Gentiles* 226–38.)

45

INTRODUCTION TO THE NEW TESTAMENT EPISTLES

Joseph A. Fitzmyer, S.J.

BIBLIOGRAPHY

1   Deissmann, G. A., *Bible Studies* (Edinburgh, 1901) 3–59; *LAE* 228–29. Doty, W. G., "The Classification of Epistolary Literature," *CBQ* 31 (1969) 183–99; *Letters in Primitive Christianity* (Phl, 1973). Fascher, E., "Briefliteratur, urchristliche, formgeschichtlich," *RGG* 1. 1412–15. Fitzmyer, J. A., "Aramaic Epistolography," *Studies in Ancient Letter Writing* (ed. J. L. White; Semeia 22; Chico, 1982) 22–57. Hercher, R., *Epistolographi graeci* (Paris, 1873; repr. 1965). Kim, Chan-Hie, *Form and Structure of the Familiar Greek Letter of Recommendation* (SBLDS 4; Missoula, 1972). Koskenniemi, H., *Studien zur Idee und Phraseologie des griechischen Briefes bis 400 n. Chr.* (Helsinki, 1956). Mullins, T. Y., "Disclosure: A Literary Form in the New Testament," *NovT* 7 (1964) 44–50; "Formulas in New Testament Epistles," *JBL* 91 (1972) 380–90; "Greeting as a New Testament Form," *JBL* 87 (1968) 418–26; "Petition as a Literary Form," *NovT* 5 (1962)

46–54; "Visit Talk in New Testament Letters," *CBQ* 35 (1973) 350–58. Oppenheim, A. L., *Letters from Mesopotamia* (Chicago, 1967). Pardee, D., "An Overview of Ancient Hebrew Epistolography," *JBL* 97 (1978) 321–46; *Handbook of Ancient Hebrew Letters* (SBLSBS 15; Chico, 1982). Schneider, J., "Brief," *RAC* 2. 563–85. Schnider, F. and W. Stenger, *Studien zum neutestamentlichen Briefformular* (NTTS 11; Leiden, 1987). Stirewalt, M. L., Jr., "The Form and Function of the Greek Letter-Essay," *The Romans Debate* (ed. K. P. Donfried; Minneapolis, 1977) 175–206. Stowers, S. K., *Letter Writing in Greco-Roman Antiquity* (Phl, 1986). White, J. L., "New Testament Epistolary Literature in the Framework of Ancient Epistolography," *ANRW* II/25.2, 1730–56; *Light from Ancient Letters* (Phl, 1986) — see *BR* 32 (1987) 42–53.

See also Kümmel, *INT* 247–52; Wik-Schm, *ENT* 380–86; *IDBSup* 538–40; *DBSup* 7. 329–41.

OUTLINE

GENERAL REMARKS

3   **(I) "Epistolē" as a Literary Form.** Of the 27 NT books 21 are called *epistolai*, whereas not one OT book is so designated. There are letters in the OT; but the use of this form of writing for a religious purpose, though it owes much to the popularity of the letter in the Hellenistic world, becomes particularly prominent with Paul, who was imitated by later Christian writers.

Letter writing is an ancient practice, attested for official, business, royal, and private correspondence for millennia in Egyptian and Mesopotamian areas antedating

the OT (*ANET* 475–90), as well as in Aram and Hebr forms contemporary with it. In the OT, there are summaries of official correspondence in the era of the preexilic kings (2 Sam 11:14–15; 1 Kgs 21:8–10; 2 Kgs 5:5–6; 10:1–6). Further summaries are found in the exilic and postexilic periods, but in the latter period they tend to preserve the form of the ancient (Aram) letter (Ezra 4:11–16,17–22; 7:12–26). In Esth 9:20 a memorandum of Mordecai and a letter of the king about Purim are mentioned; the deuterocanonical additions to the book appropriately supply the text of such documents, a Gk literary effort (12:4; 13:1–7). Similarly, Bar 6 preserves the so-called Letter of Jeremiah (see Jer 29:1). Many letters preserved in Maccabees (1 Macc 5:10–13; 8:23–32; 10:18–20,25–45; 2 Macc 1:1–2:18), written by Jews, Romans, Seleucid rulers, and Spartans, deal with national or political aspects of Palestinian Jewish life. Though the religious use of the letter form is found in Jer 29:4–23, such use was not prominent; it became so in NT times. Some NT letters, however, are no more specifically religious than many in the OT (Acts 23:26–30).

4   (II) "Letter" or "Epistle." Since the studies of G. A. Deissmann one has often distinguished a "letter" from an "epistle." "A letter is something nonliterary, a means of communication between persons who are separated from each other. Confidential and personal in its nature, it is intended only for the person or persons to whom it is addressed, and not at all for the public or any kind of publicity" (*LAE* 228). In style, tone, and form it can be as free, intimate, familiar, or frank as conversation; it can also be an official letter intended for a group or several groups. It generally has an ad hoc purpose. Ancient "letters" exist in thousands of Gk papyri from Egypt (A. S. Hunt and E. E. Edgar, *Select Papyri* [LCL; Cambridge MA, 1952]; D. Brooke, *Private Letters Pagan and Christian* [London, 1929]). Most of the OT examples cited above are "letters" in this sense.

"An epistle is an artistic literary form, a species of literature, just like the dialogue, the oration, or the drama. It has nothing in common with the letter except its form; apart from that one might venture the paradox that the epistle is the opposite of a real letter. The contents of an epistle are intended for publicity — they aim at interesting 'the public'" (Deissmann, *LAE* 229). The epistle is a careful literary composition possibly but not necessarily occasioned by a concrete situation, and destined for a wide audience. Developed in Greek philosophical schools of the 4th cent. BC, it resembles a treatise, a dialogue, or an essay devoted to an instructive or polemical discussion of some theme. Ancient "epistles" are found in Seneca's *Ad Lucilium epistulae morales,* in Epicurus's epistles preserved by Diogenes Laertius (*Lives of Eminent Philosophers* 10), and in such Jewish writings as Aristeas (in reality, an apologetic narrative; → Apocrypha, 67:32), Bar 6:1–73 (a homily), and 2 Macc 1:1–2:18. Today one hears discontent with Deissmann's distinction: is it not too sharply drawn? The real problem is to decide whether a given writing should

be classed as a "letter" or as an "epistle."

5   Though the NT *epistolai* constitute a corpus in the Bible, this does not mean that they were originally intended to be "epistles." The private letters of famous litterateurs have become at times part of a country's literature, and the collection of Paul's letters into a corpus did not radically change their specific character. Nor does inspiration, by which letters were destined by the Spirit for the edification of the Christian church, alter a human author's destination of them to one person or group or to handle one problem or other. Hence, the literary form of the writing must be respected.

6   (III) Ancient Letter Form. The contemporary Greco-Roman letter had at least three parts: (1) *Opening Formula.* This is not the address (which was usually written on the outside of the folded papyrus), but the *praescriptio,* an elliptic sentence giving the name of the sender (nom.) and of the addressee (dat.) and a short greeting (usually *chairein,* an inf. with the stereotyped meaning, "Greetings!"). See 1 Macc 10:18, 25; 11:30; in the NT, only in Acts 15:23; 23:26; Jas 1:1. (2) *Message.* The body of the letter. (3) *Final Greeting.* Usually *errōsō* (pl. *errōsthe,* "Goodbye" [lit., "be well"; cf. Lat. *vale, valete*]). See 2 Macc 16:21,33,38; in the NT, Acts 15:29 (and 23:30 in some mss.). In the case of dictated letters the final greeting was sometimes penned by the sender; it often took the place of a signature in modern letters. In official letters a date was often added. In many ancient letters a 4th part could also be found, a *Thanksgiving,* which served as an introduction to the body of the letter and expressed a religious or nonreligious sentiment of gratitude. It often began with either *eucharistō,* "I thank," or *charin echō,* "I am grateful."

7   The form of contemporary Jewish letters, written either in Aramaic or Hebrew and derived from older Assyrian, Babylonian, or Canaanite models, was not very different from the Greco-Roman form. Although a thanksgiving only rarely appears, the opening formula was either like the Greco-Roman form, but with *šālôm* or *šĕlām,* "Peace," instead of *chairein* (see Mur 42,43,44,46), or more frequently with a double sentence. The first part named the sender and the addressee ("To our lord Bagohi, governor of Judah, your servants Yedaniah and his colleagues, the priests. . . .") and the second part expressed a blessing ("May the God of Heaven seek the welfare of our lord at all times"). See *ANET* 322, 491–92; cf. Dan 4:1; *2 Apoc. Bar.* 78:3 (*OTP* 1. 648); Fitzmyer, "Aramaic Epistolography."

NEW TESTAMENT LETTER WRITING

8   (I) Form of the Pauline Letter. The Pauline letter shares features of the contemporary Greco-Roman and Semitic letters.

(A) Opening Formula. The *praescriptio* is normally an expansion of the Greco-Roman form, using Semitic elements; Paul (nom.) to X (dat.) with appropriate epithets in Semitic fashion to express the relation between him and the addressee(s). Co-senders are sometimes mentioned: Timothy (2 Cor 1:1; Phil 1:1; Phlm 1); Silvanus and Timothy (1 Thess 1:1); Sosthenes (1 Cor 1:1). Paul never uses simply *chairein,* but expresses a wish involving *charis kai eirēnē* (1 Thess 1:1), usually expanded: "Grace and peace be yours from God our Father and the Lord Jesus Christ" (Gal 1:3; Phil 1:2). At first sight, *charis kai eirēnē* looks like a Pauline adaptation or combination of the Greek *chairein* and Semitic *šālôm/šĕlām;*

but more may be involved, for the greeting uses the notions of *charis* (covenant favor) and *eirēnē* (peace) found in the old priestly blessing of Num 6:24–26. Further, *charis* has the Pauline connotation of God's merciful bounty manifested in Christ Jesus (cf. Rom 5:1–11). Thus, the words may be Paul's summation of the *bona messianica* of the Christian era, the spiritual gifts that he begs for his readers. This formula occurs also in 2 John 3 and Rev 1:4; it is modified in 1 Pet 1:2 and 2 Pet 1:2 and is sometimes found in later Christian letters.

(B) Thanksgiving. In common with many Greco-Roman letters, most of Paul's letters have a thanksgiving. Structurally, it is often a periodic sentence, the function of which is to "focus the epistolary situation, i.e., to introduce the vital theme of the letter" (Schubert, *Form* [→ 15 below] 180). In Gal,

Paul replaces the thanksgiving with a rebuking *thaumazō,* "I am amazed . . . ," (1:6-9), which more effectively sets the tone of that letter. In 2 Cor he appropriately uses an extended blessing on the Corinthian church, striking the chord of reconciliation with the congregation that caused him much pain, a note that is the burden of part of 2 Cor. In this section Paul is usually at prayer; and though it resembles the Greco-Roman thanksgiving, the sentiments expressed are often phrased in characteristic Jewish "eucharistic" formulas, sometimes recalling even the Qumran *Hôdāyôt* (Thanksgiving Psalms, → Apocrypha, 67:86). Often it is not easy to decide where the thanksgiving ends and the body of the letter begins (so in 1 Thess).

(C) **Message.** Undoubtedly reflecting early Christian preaching, which often joined an ethical exhortation to its doctrinal exposé, the body of the Pauline letter is usually divided into two parts—one *doctrinal,* presenting truths of the Christian message, the other *hortatory,* giving instructions for Christian conduct.

(D) **Conclusion and Final Greeting.** The final section of a Pauline letter often contains personal news or specific advice for individuals. It is followed by Paul's last greeting—never the ordinary Greek *errōsō,* but a characteristic blessing, "The grace of our Lord Jesus Christ be with you" (1 Thess 5:28; Gal 6:18; Phil 4:23; 1 Cor 16:23; 2 Cor 13:13; Rom 16:20,[24]; Phlm 25).

9   (II) Paul's "Letters." Having set up the categories of "letter" and "epistle," Deissmann classed Paul's writings as letters, not literary epistles. Though guilty of a certain oversimplification, he was basically correct, for Paul's writings are fundamentally "letters," composed for an occasion, often produced in haste, and mostly written in complete independence of each other. Phlm is a private letter sent to an individual; Gal a letter addressed to a group of local churches and imbued with Paul's personal concern for his converts. Similarly, 1 Cor, 1 Thess, Phil, despite all the great truths they discuss, are basically "letters" handling concrete issues in the churches addressed. Much of the difficulty of 2 Cor comes from its letterlike character; it contains many allusions no longer fully understood and yet so expressive of Paul's feelings about his relations with that church. Of the genuine letters of Paul, Rom comes closest to being an epistle sent to a church that Paul had not yet evangelized (→ Romans, 51:3-6); it might best be called an essay-letter.

10   Even with Deissmann's characterization, it must be remembered that Paul rarely wrote his letters as a private individual; he was primarily an apostle, a missionary, a preacher. His letters were sent to communities and individuals to express his apostolic presence and authority in building up Christian churches. He used the letter form as a means of spreading his understanding of the Christian gospel and especially of applying it to the concrete problems that arose in areas that he could not then visit personally. Part of his genius was to adopt a manageable form of writing for his evangelistic purposes. His writings are then best characterized as "apostolic letters." Though Paul is often called the first Christian theologian, he did not write with the precision of one presenting systematic theology, conciliar definition, or canonical legislation. More simply, he was casting his apostolic teaching in letter form.

11   Into this form Paul often introduced—sometimes in unpolished ways—other literary subforms: fragments of the early kerygma (1 Thess 1:9-10; 1 Cor 15:1-7; Rom 1:3-4; 4:25; 10:8-9); homilies (Rom 1:18-32); exhortations (Gal 5:19-24 [list of vices and virtues]; cf. 2 Cor 12:20); hymns (Phil 2:6-11; Rom 8:31-39; 1 Cor 13:1-13); liturgical formulas (1 Cor

11:24-25; 12:3; 16:22); midrashim (Gal 4:21-31; 2 Cor 3:4-18; Rom 4:1-24); "testimonia" (i.e., chains of OT proof texts, Rom 3:10-18; 15:9-12); "diatribes" (in the ancient sense, Rom 2:1-3:9). In many cases the material so introduced was derived from the church's nascent tradition (1 Cor 11:23; 15:3) but was reshaped by Paul's own preaching and teaching (Rom 3:24-26). Hence, though a Pauline composition is basically a "letter," careful scrutiny of its parts often discloses other homiletic, rhetorical, and literary formulations that are to be respected in interpretation.

12   (III) The Pauline Corpus. In the NT 13 letters are attributed by name to Paul. This number appears too in the Muratorian Canon (lines 39-63; *EB* 4; → Canonicity, 66:84). Since the time of Cyril of Jerusalem (*Catech.* 4.36; PG 33. 499 [*ca.* AD 348]), 14 letters have been ascribed to him, including Heb. Modern scholars, however, following the lead of ancients like Origen, abandon the Pauline authorship of Heb (→ Hebrews, 60:2). As for authenticity, Paul's letters fall into three categories: (a) genuine writings: 1 Thess, Gal, Phil, 1-2 Cor, Rom, and Phlm; (b) doubtfully genuine writings: 2 Thess, Col, and Eph—sometimes called "Deutero-Pauline," i.e., written by a disciple of Paul; and (c) pseudonymous writings: 1-2 Tim, Titus (see introductions to the various letters for details; → Canonicity, 66:87-89).

13   Several Pauline passages suggest, however, that he wrote other letters beyond the 13 so attributed to him. In 1 Cor 5:9 Paul refers to a letter previously written to the Corinthian church; 2 Cor 2:3-4 mentions a "letter written in tears," composed apparently between 1 Cor and 2 Cor. Since the latter is undoubtedly conflate, the "letter written in tears" may be part of it (→ 2 Corinthians, 50:3). In Col 4:16 a letter to the Laodiceans is mentioned; a letter so entitled and another addressed to the Alexandrians are rejected as noncanonical in the Muratorian Canon (line 64; *EB* 5). It is debated whether Rom 16 was intended as a separate letter (→ Romans, 51:10), and Phil is possibly also a conflate letter (→ Philippians, 48:4). References in Paul's canonical letters to other letters gave rise to the literary fabrication of apocryphal Pauline letters (see *HSNTA* 2. 128-66). 2 Thes 2:2 may even refer to such fabrication.

14   Paul himself was aware (2 Cor 10:10) that some of his letters were being widely read and causing comments. By the end of the 1st cent. AD the letters were already being gathered (→ Canonicity, 66:58). 2 Pet 3:15-16 refers to "all the letters" of "our dear brother Paul" and may allude to a collected Pauline corpus. The earliest clear indication of a corpus comes to us from Marcion, who drew up at Rome *ca.* AD 144 a canon in which he admitted 10 letters apparently in the following order: Gal, 1-2 Cor, Rom, 1-2 Thess, Eph (= for him "To the Laodiceans"), Col, Phil, Phlm (see Epiphanius, *Pan.* 42.9.4; GCS 31. 105).

15   Of the 13 letters ascribed to Paul in the canon, Phil, Phlm, Col, and Eph are often called "Captivity Letters" because imprisonment is mentioned in them (Phil 1:7,13,14; Phlm 1,9,10,23; Col 4:3,18; Eph 3:1; 4:1; 6:20). "Pastoral Letters" is the title for 1-2 Tim and Titus because of their concern for the establishment of ecclesiastical, even hierarchical discipline. The order of the Pauline letters in the modern Bible follows that of the Vg and is not chronological; the letters to the seven churches precede those to the four individuals. This order has often been considered one of dignity—a plausible explanation for the overall precedence of Rom, but not for the precedence of Gal over Eph or of Phil over 1 Thess. The purely material factor of length is more likely the reason for the order within the groups, for the length of the letters decreases from Rom to Phlm. According to some counts, Eph is slightly longer than Gal (see O. Roller, *Das Formular* 38); and Eph precedes Gal in the Chester Beatty Papyrus (P⁴⁶ from 3d cent., → Texts, 68:179). Note that Heb, despite its length, greater than most of the letters, is significantly left outside the Pauline group traditionally so ordered; in P⁴⁶, however, it follows Rom.

(Bahr, G. J., "Paul and Letter Writing in the Fifth [*sic!*] Century," *CBQ* 28 [1966] 465–77; "The Subscriptions in the Pauline Letters," *JBL* 87 [1968] 27–41. Berger, K., "Apostelbrief und apostolische Rede / Zum Formular frühchristlicher Briefe," *ZNW* 65 [1974] 190–231. Bjerkelund, C. J., *Parakalô* [Oslo, 1967]. Dahl, N. A., "The Particularity of the Pauline Epistles as a Problem in the Ancient Church," *Neotestamentica et patristica* [Fest. O. Cullmann; ed. W. C. van Unnik; NovTSup 6; Leiden, 1962] 261–71. Finegan, J., "The Original Form of the Pauline Collection," *HTR* 49 [1956] 85–103. Friedrich, G., "Lohmeyers These über das paulinische Briefpräskript kritisch beleuchtet," *TLZ* 81 [1956] 343–46. Funk, R. W., "The Apostolic *Parousia*: Form and Significance," in *Christian History and Interpretation* [Fest J. Knox; ed. W. R. Farmer, *et al.*; Cambridge, 1967] 249–68. Gamble, H. "The Redaction of the Pauline Letters and the Formation of the Pauline Corpus," *JBL* 94 [1975] 403–18. Knox, J., "A Note on the Format of the Pauline Corpus," *HTR* 50 [1957] 311–14. Lohmeyer, E., "Briefliche Grussüberschriften," *ZNW* 36 [1927] 158–73. Mitton, C. L., *The Formation of the Pauline Corpus of Letters* [London, 1955]. O'Brien, P. T., *Introductory Thanksgivings in the Letters of Paul* [NovTSup 49; Leiden, 1977]. Roller, O., *Das Formular der paulinischen Briefe* [BWANT 58; Stuttgart, 1933]. Schubert, P., *Form and Function of the Pauline Thanksgivings* [BZNW 20; Berlin, 1939].)

16   (IV) Hebrews and the Catholic Epistles. "Epistle" is a title better suited to Heb and the other seven NT epistles, except for 2 John and 3 John, which are "letters" (even though the "chosen lady and her children" [2 John 1] may refer to a community rather than to an individual). Heb is rather a hortatory sermon, rich in theological discussion and Alexandrian exegesis of the OT; unlike the Pauline letters, its exhortations are scattered throughout the writing. There is no evidence that it ever had an opening formula, and the concluding section with its final greeting and request (13:24) gives it a bit of epistolary form, but that may be secondary to the whole composition (→ Hebrews, 60:5). Jas, 1–2 Pet, and Jude are "epistles," because they are homilies in letter form: 1 Pet may be an outgrowth of a homily for a baptismal liturgy; Jas is written in the style of Hellenistic Jewish parenesis; Jude and 2 Pet are didactic homilies full of admonition and exhortation. 1 John is harder to classify since it lacks all elements of the letter form (see *BEJ* 86–87).

17   The "Catholic Epistles" (Jas, 1–2 Pet, 1–3 John, and Jude) are distinguished by the name of the writer to whom they are textually or traditionally ascribed, rather than by that of the addressees. Eusebius (*HE* 2.23.25; GCS 9. 174) was the first to speak of "the seven called catholic." The number seven for these epistles was arrived at only after a long, varied history (→ Canonicity, 66:70–80).

The title *katholikē epistolē* was apparently first used of 1 John by Apollonius, an anti-Montanist (*ca.* AD 197; see Eusebius, *HE* 5.18.5; GCS 9. 474; cf. the corrupt text of the Muratorian Canon, line 69; *EB* 5). From 1 John the title seems to have spread to the group. The Sixto-Clementine Vg, however, uses it only for Jas and Jude. The title's meaning is debated: in the East it meant "addressed to all the churches," whereas in the West the seven were called *epistulae canonicae,* suggesting that "catholic" there was understood as "canonical," i.e., recognized in *all* the churches. If the title in the Eastern sense be considered more appropriate, it is harder to justify, since 2–3 John and 1 Pet are addressed to specific communities.

18   In Eastern lists (see Athanasius, *Ep.* 39.85; PG 26. 1177, 1437) the Catholic Epistles follow Acts and precede the Pauline corpus; they seem to have been considered more important, being attributed to original apostles or members of the Jerusalem mother church. In Lat lists, however, they follow Paul's letters, which are considered older and more important. Within the group the present order (Jas, 1–2 Pet, 1–3 John, Jude) may depend on the order of the names in Gal 2:9. A different order found in the decrees of the councils of Florence and Trent (*EB* 47, 59; DS 1335, 1503) reflects an estimate of dignity in use in the West: 1–2 Pet, 1–3 John, Jas, Jude.

19   (V) Writing or Dictation. Four modes of letter writing were used in antiquity: (1) to write oneself; (2) to dictate word for word, syllable for syllable; (3) to dictate the sense, leaving the formulation to a secretary; (4) to have someone write in one's name, without indicating the contents. The most commonly used modes were (1) and (3). Ancient writers complained of the wearying mode of dictation (2), especially when the scribe was not skilled.

20   What method did Paul use? Rom 16:22 suggests dictation to Tertius (does it refer only to Rom 16? [→ Romans, 51:10–11, 134]). In 1 Cor 16:21 Paul adds the greeting in his own hand, which may imply that the rest was dictated. See too Gal 6:11, where he compares his handwriting with that of the trained scribe, who has written what preceded. Cf. 2 Thess 3:17; Col 4:18. Was the dictation of the sort (2) or (3)? Impossible to say. The latter could explain the difference in style in the Deutero-Paulines. Phlm 19 may mean that Paul has written the whole letter in his own hand. Anacolutha, inconsistencies of style, and the lack of consistent terminology may be explained by dictation; distractions must have occurred that would also have affected the style. A long letter like Rom or 1 Cor would scarcely have been finished in one sitting or one day. Little can be said about the writing of other NT epistles. 1 Pet 5:12 may imply writing by Silvanus as scribe.

21   Did the NT writers dictate to scribes who used shorthand? Shorthand was known in the Roman world. It is usually thought that it was not practiced by Gk scribes before *ca.* AD 155. See, however, the as yet undeciphered stenographic Gk text in Mur 164 (DJD 2. 275–79) from a possibly earlier date (→ Apocrypha, 67:119).

46

THE FIRST LETTER
TO THE THESSALONIANS

Raymond F. Collins

BIBLIOGRAPHY

1 Best, E., *A Commentary on the First and Second Epistles to the Thessalonians* (HNTC; NY, 1972). Black, D. A., "The Weak in Thessalonica," *JETS* 25 (1982) 307–21. Boers, H., "The Form-Critical Study of Paul's Letters: 1 Thessalonians as a Case Study," *NTS* 22 (1975–76) 140–58. Broer, I., "'Antisemitismus' und Judenpolemik im Neuen Testament," *BN* 20 (1983) 59–91. Bruce, F. F., *1 & 2 Thessalonians* (WBC 45; Waco, 1982). Collins, R. F., *Studies on the First Letter to the Thessalonians* (BETL 66; Leuven, 1984). Ellis, P. F., *Seven Pauline Letters* (Collegeville, n.d. [1982]). Friedrich, G., *Die Briefe an die Galater, Epheser, Philipper, Kolosser, Thessalonicher und Philemon* (NTD 8; 15th ed.; Göttingen, 1981) 203–51. Harnisch, W., *Eschatologische Existenz* (FRLANT 110; Göttingen, 1973). Henneken, B., *Verkündigung und Prophetie im 1. Thessalonicherbrief* (SBS 29; Stuttgart, 1969). Hock, R. F., "The Working Apostle: An Examination of Paul's Means of Livelihood" (diss., Yale; New Haven, 1974). Klijn, A. F. J., "1 Thessalonians 4,13–18 and Its Background in Apocalyptic Literature," *Paul and Paulinism* (Fest. C. K. Barrett; ed. M. D. Hooker and S. G. Wilson; London, 1982) 67–73. Koester, H., "1 Thessalonians:

Experiment in Christian Writing," *Continuity and Discontinuity in Church History* (Fest. G. H. Williams; SHCT 19; Leiden, 1979) 33–44. Laub, F., *Eschatologische Verkündigung und Lebensgestaltung nach Paulus* (BU 10; Munich, 1973). Marshall, I. H., *1 and 2 Thessalonians* (NCB; GR, 1983). Marxsen, W., *Der erste Brief an die Thessalonicher* (ZBK NT 11/1; Zurich, 1979). Pearson, B. A., "1 Thessalonians 2,13–16: A Deutero-Pauline Interpolation," *HTR* 64 (1971) 79–94. Plevnik, J., "The Parousia as Implication of Christ's Resurrection," *Word and Spirit* (Fest. D. M. Stanley; Willowdale, 1975) 199–277; "1 Thess 5,1–11: Its Authenticity, Intention and Message," *Bib* 60 (1979) 71–90. Reese, J. M., *1 and 2 Thessalonians* (NTM 16; Wilmington, 1979). Rigaux, B., *Les épitres aux Thessaloniciens* (EBib; Paris, 1956); "Tradition et rédaction dans 1 Th. v. 1–10," *NTS* 21 (1974–75) 318–40. Staab, K., *Die Thessalonicherbriefe* (RNT 7; 4th ed.; Regensburg, 1965) 7–63. Whiteley, D. E. H., *Thessalonians in the Revised Standard Version* (NClarB; London, 1969).

IDBSup 900. Kümmel, *INT* 255–62. Wik-Schm, *ENT* 399–404.

INTRODUCTION

2 **(1) The Church at Thessalonica.** Thessalonica was a port city in Macedonia (the N of modern Greece). Located at the head of the Thermaic Gulf, it was founded about 315 BC on the site of ancient Therma by Cassander, a general of Alexander the Great. Cassander named the city after his wife, the half sister of Alexander. Once the Romans had assumed control of the city, after the battle of Pydna (168 BC), it increased in importance. In 146 BC Thessalonica became the capital of the Roman province of Macedonia. The city supported Octavius at the battle of Philippi (42 BC) and thereby achieved the status of a "free city," having its own magistrates and serving as the seat of government.

At the time of Paul, Thessalonica was an important city for economic, commercial, and political reasons. Because of its harbor and its location on the Egnatian Way, the main Roman road across the Balkans, Thessalonica had become a thriving commercial center. Commerce attracted a cosmopolitan population. The Jewish population of Thessalonica had a synagogue, in

which according to Acts 17:1–2 Paul preached. Egyptian and Roman sanctuaries have been discovered among the archaeological remains. Isis, Serapis, Osiris, and Anubis were among the Oriental deities venerated, but there was also some emperor worship.

3 According to Acts, Paul, Silvanus, and Timothy came to Thessalonica during Paul's Mission II, most probably in AD 50. Having been expelled from Philippi (Acts 16:16–40), almost 100 mi. E of Thessalonica, they passed through Amphipolis and Apollonia but did not linger in either of these places, apparently because neither of them had a synagogue. The Jewish population of Thessalonica was, however, large enough to support one. Luke relates that Paul and his companions found lodging in the house of Jason, that he preached in the synagogue for three weeks, and that a riot ensued among the Jewish population because of the success of his preaching. Paul and Silvanus were expelled from the city, from which they came to Beroea (Acts 17:1–9). Luke's account of Paul's activity in Thessalonica is composed according to the stylized manner of Acts; it does not provide a full or accurate historical description of Paul's activity in Thessalonica. From the intensity of Paul's affection for the Thessalonian Christians, it would appear that he remained in the city for more than the brief period of two to three weeks allowed by Acts. Paul's letter does not support the notion that Jesus as Messiah was the primary focus of his preaching. The letter is, in fact, silent about Paul's preaching in the synagogue there. It does, however, clearly suggest that Thessalonian Christians were Gentiles, i.e., converts from paganism.

4   **(II) Occasion, Date, and Place of Composition.** According to Luke, Paul's Jewish opposition followed him to Beroea. Unaccompanied, Paul escaped to Athens (Acts 17:10–15). Silvanus and Timothy later joined Paul there, where he yearned to visit again the Thessalonians. Unable to do so, Paul sent Timothy in his stead (1 Thess 2:17–3:3). In the meantime Paul moved on to Corinth, where he was eventually joined by Timothy (Acts 18:5). Timothy brought good news about the situation of the church in Thessalonica but apparently indicated that there was some misunderstanding of the faith among the Thessalonian community, viz., about the fate of those who had died (4:13). Whereas many who hold this view think that the question was contained in Timothy's oral report (e.g., B. N. Kaye, F. F. Bruce), a few (e.g., E. Fuchs) think that the question was addressed to Paul in written form.

5   1 Thess was occasioned by Timothy's report to Paul. It is virtually certain that it was written from Corinth almost immediately after Timothy's arrival there from Thessalonica. The impression given in Acts that the events of Paul's Mission II were moving quickly at this point in his life is confirmed by 1 Thess. Paul writes about being separated from the Thessalonians for a short while (1 Thess 2:17). He frequently recalls his personal presence within the Thessalonian community (the "recall motif," 2:1). It would seem, then, that only a relatively short time, probably a few months, intervened between Paul's evangelization of Thessalonica and his writing of 1 Thess. Most probably the letter was written in AD 50 (B. Schwank, A. Suhl), but some scholars continue to date it in AD 51 (→ Paul, 79:39).

6   **(III) Authenticity, Unity, and Integrity.** Although a few late-19th-cent. scholars, notably F. C. Baur and some members of his Tübingen School (G. Volkmar, C. F. Holsten), doubted the authenticity of 1 Thess, the Pauline authorship of 1 Thess is almost unanimously affirmed at the present time.

7   Less unanimity exists among scholars concerning the unity and integrity of the letter (Collins, *Studies* 96–135). In 1909, R. Scott divided the letter into two parts, chaps. 1–3 and 4–5, in which he discerned respectively the influence of Timothy and Silvanus. Since 1961 more serious doubts about the unity of 1 Thess have been raised by a group of scholars (esp. K.-G. Eckart, W. Schmithals, H.-M. Schenke, K. M. Fischer, and R. Pesch), who maintain that canonical 1 Thess represents a compilation of two letters written by Paul to the Thessalonians. Such scholars vary among themselves about the parts of 1 Thess that come from one or other of the hypothetical earlier letters. Schmithals assigns 1:1–2:12 and 4:2–5:28 to one letter and 2:13–4:1 to the other; but the views of others are more complicated. W. G. Kümmel (1965) raised serious objections against the compilation theories of the time. Relatively few scholars outside the German world maintain that 1 Thess is a composite of earlier texts, but the view continues to be held by some Germans.

8   Quite another issue is that of the integrity of

the letter. Throughout the 20th cent. a substantial scholarly opinion has held that 2:13–16 is an interpolation (e.g., J. Moffatt, M. Goguel, K.-G. Eckart, B. A. Pearson, D. Schmidt, and H. Koester). The main arguments for this view are the strong anti-Jewish tone of the pericope and the fact that 2:17 seems to follow naturally on 2:12. Debate on the issue continues. Those scholars who maintain the Pauline authorship of 2:13–16 generally draw attention to the fact that the main arguments against Pauline authorship are more of a theological and ideological nature than of the historical and literary variety (e.g., J. Coppens, G. E. Okeke).

The appurtenance of 5:1–11 to the letter has also been questioned in recent times (G. Friedrich, W. Harnisch). The principal arguments in support of the view that it was not an original part of 1 Thess are based on an analysis of the passage's vocabulary and style. It is also said that 5:1–11 is a doublet of 4:13–18. Serious critiques of this view have been made by J. Plevnik, among others. The number of authors who believe that 5:1–11 represents a later addition to the letter is far smaller than the number of those who opt for the inauthenticity of 2:13–16. Friedrich's commentary is virtually alone in maintaining that 5:1–11 is an addition, while the view that 2:13–16 is an addition is supported by several modern commentaries.

9   **(IV) Significance of the Letter.** The date at which 1 Thess was composed makes it the earliest written book in the NT. Since it uses traditional material, particularly the creedal formulas (1:9–10; 4:14; 5:10), it serves as a significant witness to the gospel in the period between the death and resurrection of Jesus and the written works of the NT (i.e., AD 30–50). The letter provides the oldest literary evidence of the significance attached to the death and resurrection of Jesus by the early Christians.

10   From a doctrinal point of view it is the eschatological sections of the letter (4:13–18; 5:1–11) that are discussed most frequently. Paul has written about the parousia (4:13–18) and the Day of the Lord (5:1–11). These passages speak of the eschatological expectations of the early Christians, but they are couched in apocalyptic terminology. To a very large extent, apocalyptic language is symbolic. There is considerable distance between the symbol and that to which the symbol points. Thus, the passages cannot be taken as a literal description of end-time events. Nonetheless, conservatives and fundamentalists understand the passages as if they provide literally a factual description of the end times.

11   From the literary standpoint, 1 Thess is especially valuable as the oldest extant Christian document. After the death and resurrection of Jesus, a variety of historical, social, and religious factors coalesced to prevent the development of a specifically Christian literature. These factors did not prevent the writing of letters, which are literature (because they are written) but not literary (in the sense of particularly artful compositions). Hence they are called *Kleinliteratur* (lit., minor literature) in German scholarship. As the oldest of the extant Christian letters, 1 Thess is an "experiment in Christian writing" (H. Koester). Contrary to the views of those scholars who consider 1 Thess a parenetic letter (esp. A. J. Malherbe), it is preferable to see the letter as a type of personal letter which Paul has written according to the norms of personal letter writing in the Hellenistic world (→ NT Epistles, 45:4–8). The essential structure of 1 Thess is similar to the personal letters of the times, although the content is decidedly Christian and evangelical. Because it has the form of a personal letter, it must be read as a letter, i.e., an essentially *ad hoc* communication.

12   (V) Outline. 1 Thess may be outlined as follows:

(I) Salutation (1:1)

(II) Thanksgiving (1:2–3:13)
  (A) First Thanksgiving Period: The Thessalonians' Reception of the Gospel (1:2–2:12)
  (B) Second Thanksgiving Period (2:13–3:13)

(III) Exhortation (4:1–12)
  (A) On Chastity (4:1–8)
  (B) On Charity (4:9–12)

(IV) Eschatology (4:13–5:11)
  (A) First Apocalyptic Disclosure: The Parousia (4:13–18)
  (B) Second Apocalyptic Disclosure: Eschatological Existence (5:1–11)

(V) Final Exhortation (5:12–22)
  (A) First Period: Call for Order in the Community (5:12–13)
  (B) Second Period: Call for Various Functions (5:14–22)

(VI) Closing Wishes and Salutation (5:23–28)

COMMENTARY

13   (I) Salutation (1:1). Paul's first letter begins in the typical fashion of Hellenistic letters, with mention of the writer(s), the recipient(s), and a greeting. 1 Thess is presented as having been written by Paul, Silvanus, and Timothy. The use of the 1st pers. pl. throughout the letter (except for 2:18; 3:5; 5:27) shows that not only the greetings but also the contents come from all three (2:7). The occasional use of the sg. shows that Paul actually composed the letter, though an unnamed scribe was probably responsible for the physical writing of the letter. *Silvanus:* To be identified with "Silas" of Acts 17:4, one of the leading members of the Christian community in Jerusalem. Initially sent to Antioch (Acts 15:22), Silas accompanied Paul on his missionary voyages after the separation of Barnabas and Mark from Paul (Acts 15:36–41). *Timothy:* "One who honors God"; Paul's chief aid and trusted emissary in the work of evangelization. *the church of the Thessalonians:* The letter is addressed to a group rather than to a single individual. The expression suggests that the recipients were assembled or gathered together (5:27), probably in the home of one of the Thessalonian Christians. It is unlikely that the recently evangelized Thessalonians would have been aware of the rich biblical (LXX) connotations of the word "church" (→ Pauline Theology, 82:134). *of the Thessalonians:* This suggests that the Christians were an elect group (1:4) among the Thessalonians. *Father:* Mention of the relationship of the church to the Father and to Jesus Christ distinguishes the Christian gathering from other gatherings of Thessalonians, specifically, perhaps, the Jewish synagogue. God is recognized as Father in biblical and extrabiblical literature, but Paul specifically relates the fatherhood of God to his relationship with Jesus. *Jesus Christ:* Jesus is the name of the historical Jew from Nazareth; the titles "Christ" and "Lord" identify him respectively as the object of messianic expectations and as the risen One. *grace and peace:* Paul's greeting is unusual in epistolary literature. Rather than use the simple *chairein* of Hellenistic letters, Paul has probably employed a liturgical formula (→NT Epistles, 45:8A).

14   (II) Thanksgiving (1:2–3:13).
  (A) First Thanksgiving Period: The Thessalonians' Reception of the Gospel (1:2–2:12).
2–5. In Paul's Gk text, vv 2–5 form a single sentence. Paul begins his letter with an expression of thanksgiving (→ NT Epistles, 45:8B). Paul's thanksgiving is different from other epistolary thanksgivings because of its addressee and the reason for his thanks. *God:* Paul addressed his thanks to "God," i.e., the monotheistic God of the Jewish tradition; his reason is the fruitful reception of the gospel by Thessalonian Christians. *Ho theos* is normally a personal name, designating God the Father. **2–3.** Paul's thanksgiving is expressed in formal prayers, where God's name is invoked. *prayers: Proseuchē* is a general word that implies invocation. In prayer Paul commemorates the Christian ethos of the Thessalonian community—their active faith, their manifested love, and their steady hope. *before our God and Father:* Paul believes that the Christian life of the Thessalonians takes place under the providence of God. Their life is one of a dynamic faith: i.e., belief expressed in life; manifested love, i.e., a love expressed in actions that are sometimes difficult; and a steady hope, i.e., a patient expectation of the coming of the Lord Jesus despite the tribulations of the age (1:6; 3:3). **4.** *brethren:* Paul's manner of addressing the Thessalonians reflects his affection for them. Used 19 times in 1 Thess, *adelphos* also reflects the socioreligious situation of the 1st cent. *beloved of God:* This epithet recalls the biblical description of Yahweh's relationship with Israel and emphasizes the constancy of God's love for the Thessalonians. That love is the source of God's election of the church at Thessalonica. *election of you:* This term is rich with the nuances of salvation history (Deut 7:6–8). The proof of the election of the Thessalonian church is their reception of the gospel. **5.** *our gospel: Euangelion* designates the act of proclaiming the good news; at other times it designates the content of the good news (→ Pauline Theology, 82:31–36). The last part of the verse stresses the apostles' life-style as an important witness to the authenticity of their message. Paul emphasizes that the power of the gospel lies not in the force of his own rhetoric but in the power of the Spirit of God (1 Cor 2:1–5). *Power, holy Spirit, full force:* Three virtually synonymous expressions. For Paul the proclamation of the gospel is as much an expression of God's power as is the working of miracles.

15   6–8. These verses form one sentence in Paul's Gk text. *imitators:* The faith of the Thessalonian Christians is expressed in their having become imitators of the apostles and of the Lord (1 Cor 11:1). Although W. Michaelis (*TDNT* 4. 659–74) highlights the Thessalonians' obedience, most authors emphasize their sharing in eschatological affliction and/or the proclamation of the gospel. As the Thessalonians had become imitators of Paul and the Lord, they in turn became examples for other "believers" (*pisteuousin*, a pres. ptc.; cf. v 3, "active faith"). *affliction: Thlipsis* is almost a technical term to denote eschatological distress, sometimes described in other literature as a final battle, the onslaught of both physical and moral evil, or the messianic woes. *Joy.* This is an eschatological reality, the gift of the Spirit (Gal 5:22). The experience of joy suggests that one is in the presence of God (3:9); it denotes the proleptic realization of an eschatological gift because of the proclamation of the good news. **7.** *Macedonia and Achaia:* Paul writes enthusiastically and hyperbolically of the effect of his evangelization of the Thessalonians. That the gospel is received in affliction and yet with joy affirms that the proclamation and reception of the gospel are an eschatological event. **16** **9-10.** Paul notes that the conversion of the Thessalonian Christians was a part of the good news announced in Macedonia and Achaia: the spread of the gospel is part of the gospel message. Paul's description of the conversion of the Thessalonian Christians makes use of formulas traditionally employed in the missionary discourses of Hellenistic Judaism. *turned:* The language focuses on a real conversion (the biblical *šûb,* "turn back," "return"), i.e., a movement from and a movement toward. *idols:* The Thessalonians' conversion was a movement "from" idols, a term which of itself means representations but which had acquired pejorative connotations in the preaching of the prophets for whom "idols" were false gods. For Paul idols were "no gods" (1 Cor 8:4-5); he would relate idol worship to demons (1 Cor 10:20). *to God:* The Thessalonians' movement "toward" focused on the one God (monotheism). *living and true:* In apologetic usage these qualifications distinguished the monotheistic God from inert (Ps 15) and false gods. Paul's biblical background would have meant that the terms had a far richer significance in his own mind. "Living" is a typically biblical description of God, connoting his activity in human history as well as his role as creator. "True" suggests God's fidelity (5:24), especially his covenant fidelity. For Paul conversion to the living and true God has a christological and eschatological implication. **10.** This verse is a Christian complement to the traditional categories of Hellenistic Jewish apologetics. *Son: Huios* is used as a title for the risen Christ (cf. Rom 1:4); this title does not occur elsewhere in this letter (→ Pauline Theology, 82:50). *he raised from the dead:* Paul makes use of an early Christian creedal formula to affirm that God has raised Jesus from the dead. On the resurrection of Jesus as an act of the Father, → Pauline Theology, 82:59. In Judaism (e.g., 1 Macc 2:60) God himself is presented as the deliverer. The resurrection identifies Jesus as the one by whom God will effect salvation. *who delivers:* Paul uses a pres. ptc. to emphasize not only that Jesus is God's agent in the deliverance but that deliverance is already begun, even though its final manifestation has not yet occurred. *wrath to come:* God's eschatological wrath, already operative in history (2:16; Rom 1:18; → Pauline Theology, 82:38). With the resurrection, God enables Jesus to fulfill a divine function; because of the resurrection, Christians are enabled to perceive who Jesus is. **17** **2:1-12.** Paul's autobiographical confession. The Gk text of v 1 recapitulates some of the terminology of chap. 1, thereby showing the close link between this section and the preceding chapter. The tendency of the older exegesis of the passage was to consider it an *apologia,* as if Paul had need to defend himself (v 2). W. Marxsen (*Der erste Brief* 43) takes the passage to be an apology for the gospel. The similarities between Paul's presentation of himself in this pericope and the descriptions that some Hellenistic philosophers provided of themselves make it preferable to regard vv 1-12 as an "autobiographical confession," similar in some respects to the confessions of Jeremiah. **18** **1.** *you know:* Paul reflects on his presence among the Thessalonians (1:9a) and notes, using litotes and a pf. tense, that his evangelization of the Thessalonians continues to have an effect. He appeals to their own experience as evidence of the fruitfulness of his proclamation of the gospel. **2.** *we suffered:* Mention of the apostles' physical and moral suffering at Philippi (Acts

16:19-40) serves not only to remind the Thessalonians of the circumstances that brought the apostles into their midst but also to underscore Paul's earlier affirmation that the power of the gospel lies with God (1:5). *in the midst of opposition:* Paul's first use of athletic imagery (see 1 Cor 9:24-27) to describe the spread of the gospel. The *agōn* motif (or struggle motif) recalls similar usage among the Stoic and Cynic philosophers who compared philosophical exposition to a gladiator's struggle. *courage: Parrhēsia,* in the categories of Gk rhetoric, usually suggests the freedom of speech enjoyed within democratic assemblies. Within the NT, *parrhēsia* connotes prophetic boldness. It suggests God's gift to prophetic figures whereby they proclaim his message with inner freedom and exterior courage (Acts 4:13,29,31; Matt 10:20,26; cf. S. B. Marrow, *CBQ* 44 [1982] 431-46). **19** **3-4.** Paul twice uses *contradictio* ("not this, but that") to emphasize his point, viz., the integrity of the gospel which he and his companions have proclaimed. His words offer an explanation for his boldness. *our appeal:* The message that had been proclaimed is described as *paraklēsis,* a word commonly used in early Christian literature in reference to Christian preaching (2 Cor 5:20; Acts 2:40), probably in dependence on Dt-Isa's announcement of consolation for Israel (the vb. *parakaleō* is used in Isa 40:1). *error:* Paul affirms that his message of consolation has neither been corrupted by error nor compromised by base motives. Since Paul's vocabulary is comparable to that of Stoic-Cynic literature, he is implicitly comparing his proclamation of the gospel with the preachments of itinerant philosophers. *gospel:* What is singular about the proclamation of Paul and his companions—he continues to employ the pl. number—is that they have been entrusted with the gospel. Paul's language recalls that of the Athenian court. Public officials are first scrutinized before they are entrusted with political responsibility. In similar fashion, Paul and his companions have been scrutinized by God before being entrusted with the mission of proclaiming the gospel. The language used suggests that the apostles are God's trusted aides. *to please:* Paul, in fact, affirms their loyalty to God. They are not pleasers of human beings, but of God. An allusion to Jer 11:20 suggests that the role of the apostles is similar to that of the biblical prophets. **20** **5-8.** One complicated Gk sentence focuses attention on the relation between the apostles and the Thessalonian Christians. In vv 3-4 Paul explained what it meant for him and his companions to be apostles, to have been sent by God. In vv 5-8 Paul describes the implications of the apostolate for those to whom apostles are sent. He uses a mild oath to emphasize the truthfulness of what is being said. **5.** *flattery:* Paul rejects the notion that the apostles had flattered the Thessalonians or that they were looking for money or for glory. Although Paul affirms the rights of the apostles to be supported (1 Cor 9:4-15), they have not looked to the Thessalonians for financial support. **6.** *glory: Doxa* may refer to money in this context (1 Tim 5:17). **7.** *apostles: Apostoloi* appears in the Gk text, but in v 6 in many modern transls.; as a pl. noun, it describes Paul, Silvanus, and Timothy. **8.** *our very lives:* Rather than being a burden on the Thessalonians, the apostles were ready to share with them not only their message but also their very lives. Such was the intensity of the apostles' love for the Thessalonians. In v 7 Paul employs a mixed metaphor to describe the situation of the apostles among the Thessalonians. Paul uses the image of the wet nurse. Some Gk mss. read *ēpioi,* "gentle," at the beginning of the verse; others read *nēpioi,* "little children." On either reading, the suggestion is that the Thessalonians have not been coerced by the apostles.

21   **9.** *you remember:* Use of the recall motif invites the Thessalonians to consider realistically the conduct of the apostles among them. Paul reminds them that the apostles were self-supporting. In Judaism, rabbis were expected to exercise a trade, but Paul probably made use of the leatherworker's shop (Acts 18:3) as a locale for proclaiming his gospel (R. Hock). *the gospel of God:* I.e., the gospel that comes from God and that proclaims what God has done. **10.** *and God too:* Another mild oath supports the affirmation of the apostles' personal integrity. *holy, pious, and innocent:* Virtually synonymous. Use of such synonymous repetition is characteristic of an oratorical style often found in 1 Thess (e.g., 1:5; 2:3). **11.** *father:* Another image highlights the nature of the apostles' relation with the Thessalonians. Nurses nourish (v 7); fathers instruct. **12.** *walk worthily:* The father's instruction bears on the conduct (*peripatein,* "to walk," reflects Hebr *hālak* as a description of behavior) of his children (4:1–2). The purpose of this instruction is that the Thessalonians may faithfully respond to God's call to enter his kingdom and glory. *Basileia* is rarely used by Paul, but is frequent in the Synoptics. Both "kingdom" and "glory" refer to God's eschatological reign.

22   **(B) Second Thanksgiving Period (2:13–3:13). 13.** Paul's thanksgiving essentially repeats the notions of 1:2–10. *you received God's word which you heard from us:* In the Greek, a complicated expression employs a technical term, *paralabontes,* "receive," used for the acceptance of traditional teaching (1 Cor 15:1–3) to highlight the fact that the gospel ("God's word," Rom 9:6; 1 Cor 14:36; 2 Cor 2:17; 4:2) comes from God through a message that is heard (lit., "word of hearing"; see Rom 10:14–17; → Pauline Theology, 82:31–36, 109).

23   **14.** *imitators:* As churches in Macedonia and Achaia imitated the Thessalonian church (1:7), so the Thessalonian church imitated the churches of God in Judea. The movement of the gospel is effected by word and by example. *church of God:* This phrase, perhaps reflecting the biblical *qĕhal yhwh,* "assembly of Yahweh," originally designated the Jewish Christian community in Jerusalem (1 Cor 15:9; Gal 1:13). By extension it was applied to other churches as well, especially those in Judea. *you also suffered:* Acceptance and proclamation of the word of God imply the real possibility of persecution (Matt 5:11–12; John 15:20). In Judea the persecution of Christians came from Jews (Acts 8:1–3; 9:1–2; 12:1–4), as it also did in Thessalonica (Acts 17:5,13).

In a passage (vv 13–16) that many scholars judge to be inauthentic, Paul lists a series of complaints against the Jews: killing Jesus and the prophets, persecuting Paul and his companions, being disobedient to God, displeasing humans, preventing the gospel from attaining the Gentiles, where it serves their salvation. Some of these complaints are similar to those articulated even by some Jews (cf. Luke 11:49; 1QS 1:21–26; 1QH 4:30; CD 20:29) but also by some pagan writers (e.g., Tacitus, *Hist.* 5.5; Philostratus, *Life of Apol.* 5.33). This is the only place in Paul's writings where the death of Jesus is attributed to the Jews (cf. 1 Cor 2:8). **15.** *Lord:* This title highlights the seriousness of the deed. **16.** *to fill up the measure of their sins:* Jewish terminology (Dan 8:23; 2 Macc 6:13–16) expressing a specific view of history; God has appointed certain moments for the punishment of sins and others for the rewarding of righteous conduct. Delay in punishment is a strong sign of divine displeasure. Paul's language reflects an apocalyptic perspective. *wrath:* God's eschatological wrath (see comment on 1:10) The use of apocalyptic language makes it impossible to affirm that a specific historical event is intended (e.g., any of a number of tumultuous

events about AD 49: the famine, the edict of Claudius expelling Jews from Rome, the massacre in the Temple courts at Passover). Those who interpret vv 13–16 as an interpolation frequently identify the destruction of Jerusalem as the event that manifests divine wrath. *until the end:* The phrase *eis telos* is sometimes translated "at last" or "finally" and sometimes "in full" or "to the utmost." Cf. Rom 9–11 for another Pauline view of Israel; in 2:13–16 his thoughts are directed to the Jews who have hindered the spread of the gospel, not to all Jews.

24   The apostolic parousia (2:17–3:13). One of the functions of the Hellenistic letter was the expression of the writer's desire to be present to the recipients of the letter. Paul relativizes the theme of presence by suggesting that he wants to be present in his apostolic function. A second relativization occurs at the end of the pericope where the apostle's presence is transcended by the presence (parousia) of Christ.

25   **17–20.** Paul resumes his review of the apostles' relation with the Thessalonians. **17.** *physically separated from you:* The apostles feel like parents who have lost their children. The number of words amassed emphasizes the intensity of their emotions. **18.** *I:* Paul highlights his personal desire to visit the Thessalonians, as distinct from that of Silvanus and Timothy, perhaps because of the decision to send Timothy to Thessalonica (3:1–5). *Satan hindered us:* The real nature of the obstacle to Paul's realization of his desire is unknown; he attributes it to Satan, a hostile force personified in late Jewish theology. **19–20.** Paul's rhetorical questions articulate his pride in his converts (3:9), his crown and joy (Phil 4:1). **19.** *crown of boasting:* Another athletic metaphor (2:2; see Gal 2:2; 1 Cor 9:25). These verses provide a commentary on vv 17–18 by highlighting an underlying aspect of the apostles' desire.

26   **3:1–5.** Timothy's Mission. **1–3a.** The vocabulary of v 1 continues to express the intensity of the apostle's desire. Verse 2 is a mission statement, containing an announcement of the mission, a description of the credentials of the emissary, and the purpose of the mission. *our brother and God's coworker in the gospel of Christ:* These credentials stress the emissary's relationship to the other apostles and his relationship to God (2:4). "God's coworker" is so striking a description that it has been replaced by less forceful language in many Gk mss. *Christ:* The content of the good news. **3.** *these afflictions:* The purpose of the mission is to provide support for the Thessalonians living out their faith in the midst of eschatological affliction (1:6). *our lot:* Eschatological affliction will inevitably reach those who proclaim the gospel. **5.** This verse is essentially a résumé of 2:17–3:4. *I:* A second time (2:18) Paul emphasizes the intensity of his emotions. *Labor: Kopos* is almost a technical term to describe apostolic activity (see 1:3; cf. 1 Cor 3:8; 2 Cor 6:5), which ought not to be without fruit (2:1; Phil 2:16). *fearing that:* Paul's anxiety is that the tempter, the Satan of 2:18 (cf. 1 Cor 7:5), would make the proclamation of the gospel fruitless by inhibiting the dynamic faith of the Thessalonians.

27   **6–10.** Report on the Mission. **6.** Rejoining Paul and Silvanus at Corinth, Timothy is the bearer of good news. *faith and love:* These epitomize the Christian life (1:3; 5:8; Gal 5:6). *you remember us:* The Thessalonians have intense feelings for the apostles. **7.** *distress and affliction:* The accumulation of terms is typical of apocalyptic language. **8.** *stand firm:* Paul frequently writes about standing firm in the faith (1 Cor 16:13; Gal 5:1; Phil 1:27). Verses 9–10 are a "prayer report," which introduces Paul's first prayer of intercession (vv 11–13). The motivation of his thanksgiving (1:2–5) is now the Thessalonians' continued perseverance in faith. **10.** *praying:* The apostles' prayer is mixed; it is both thanksgiving and supplication. The apostles' desire to visit the Thessalonians was confirmed, and perhaps intensified, by Timothy's report. *supply what is needed:* Instead of merely assuaging the apostles' anxiety, the desired visit would have a specific purpose, viz., to give further instruction in specific areas. **28**   **11–13.** Prayer of intercession. Ancient epistolary style precluded the inclusion of a direct prayer in a letter, so the prayer is couched in the form of a blessing. It contains three petitions: for a return visit, an increase in love by the Thessalonians, and fulfillment of the Thessalonians' Christian life. **11.** *our God and Father himself and our Lord Jesus:* The first petition is addressed to the Father and to the Lord Jesus, but the vb. is sg., as if the Father and Jesus are to act as one. **12.** *the Lord:* The second petition is addressed to Christ, as the risen and eschatological Lord, and asks for a superabundance of love (1:3; 3:6; 5:8) directed within (4:9–10) and beyond the community. *as we do:* The apostles serve as an example (1:5–6) in this regard. **13.** *strengthen:* The third petition focuses on the parousia of Jesus as Lord (1:10; 4:16–17). *parousia:* Lit., "presence." This technical term is used by Paul (2:19; 4:15; 5:23) and some later NT writings (2 Thess 2:1,8,9; Matt 24:3,27,37,39; Jas 5:7,8; 2 Pet 1:16). *with all his holy ones:* See 4:17; cf. Zech 14:5 LXX. *your hearts:* → Pauline Theology, 82:106. Blamelessness and holiness are qualities of fully realized eschatological existence.

29   **(III) Exhortation (4:1–12).**
(A) On Chastity (4:1–8). **1–2.** Introduction to Paul's parenesis. **1.** *Finally:* A transitional expression. *ask and exhort:* Paul's diplomatic language implies his authority. *the Lord Jesus:* This designates the source of that authority. *as you received:* Paul recalls his earlier instruction, identified as traditional teaching (see comment on 2:13), apparently presented within a Jewish frame of reference—the twice repeated "conduct yourselves" (lit., "walk," *hālak*) as a description of behavior, "pleasing God," i.e., with obedience to God, as its aim. Paul's attitude is pastoral; he commends and encourages. **2.** *you know:* The recall motif; Paul reiterates earlier instructions. **3–6.** Paul's theme is sanctity, whose source is the Holy Spirit (v 8). Verses 3–6 are one sentence in Greek, involving the use of five participles. **3.** *the will of God:* This idea belonged to late Judaism's vocabulary of moral discourse. *unchastity:* Sanctification involves the avoidance of *porneia,* "unchastity." **4.** *to take a wife:* Lit., "to get a vessel." *Skeuos ktasthai* probably reflects a Hebr idiom with the meaning "to take a wife," but some commentators interpret Paul's metaphor in the sense of "keeping one's body (or, more specifically, the male organ) under control" (see Collins, *Studies* 311–19, 326–35). *in holiness:* For Paul, marriage is sanctifying (1 Cor 7:7,14; cf. Eph 5:22–32). **5.** *who do not know God:* Because of their lack of experience of God, it is presumed that pagans fall into immorality (Rom 1:18–32). **6.** *this matter:* Lit., "the thing"; probably in the sense of chastity, but some commentators interpret *to pragma* as "in business affairs." *exceed due limits and cheat one's brother:* Probably in the sense that adultery was considered a violation of a husband's rights, though some commentators take it to mean economic fraud. *avenging:* The last part of the verse introduces the first element of a threefold motivation: the coming judgment (v 6b), the call to holiness (v 7), and the gift of the Spirit (v 8). *Lord:* This title probably refers to the parousiac Jesus, although some take it to be a reference to God because of the allusion to Ps 94:2 LXX. **7.** God's call (2:12; 5:24) is

consequent upon his election-sanctification. **8.** *rejects God:* Sexual offenses are not simply offenses against other human beings; they are offenses against God. For a later development, see 1 Cor 6:16–20. *giving the holy Spirit:* The use of a pres. ptc. underscores the continuity of the gift of the Spirit. The holy Spirit is a present and active reality in the lives of the Thessalonians.
30   **(B) On Charity (4:9–12). 9–10a.** *concerning brotherly love:* Paul introduces a new topic (*philadelphia*) by means of a classic formula ("concerning") and emphasizes it by means of preterition. Love of fellow Christians is a hallmark of Christian existence (Rom 12:10; John 13:34; 15:12,17) and was probably a topic in baptismal catechesis. *taught by God:* Perhaps a reference to this catechesis (see, however, Isa 54:13; Jer 31:33–34). *Philadelphia* does not exclude love of others; indeed, it should overflow into a love for others (3:12). The apostles' attitude continues to be one of pastoral commendation. **10b.** *we exhort:* The exhortation continues (see v 1) as the apostles spell out some of the implications of love within the community. **11.** *make it a point to:* Oxymoron ("be ambitious to be without ambition") is used for emphasis' sake. Although some commentators see here an allusion to gnostic "enthusiasm," it is not necessary to do so; the apostles simply urge the Thessalonians to remain calm in their new religious situation. As a concrete expression of their concern for one another, the Thessalonians are urged to pursue their own trades (see comment on 2:9). **12.** *outsiders:* Although there is a sharp distinction between Christians and outsiders (4:5; 1 Cor 5:12), the Christian way of life is expected to make an impression on those outside (1 Cor 14:23,25,40; cf. John 13:35; 1 Tim 3:7; Col 4:5). *have no need of anyone:* Self-sufficiency is a first expression of concern for others (Rom 13:8; cf. 2 Thess 3:6–15; 1 Tim 5:13), rather than an expression of independence and autonomy.
31   **(IV) Eschatology (4:13–5:11).**
(A) First Apocalyptic Disclosure: The Parousia (4:13–18). The pericope is easily divided into four sections, corresponding to its four sentences in Greek: (a) announcement of the topic and purpose of the exposition (v 13); (b) recollection of the creed and a statement of its implications (v 14); (c) explanation based on a word of the Lord (vv 15–17); (d) final exhortation (v 18). **13.** The topic, those who are asleep, is formally introduced ("concerning"). *asleep:* A biblical image for those who have died (Ps 13:4 LXX). Paul probably has in mind the Christian dead (v 16). A few of the Christians at Thessalonica had apparently died in the interval between the apostles' evangelization and Timothy's visit. The apostolic kerygma did not address itself to a consideration of death. The lack of hope may well have included an element of concern about their own fate on the part of the Thessalonian Christians. Outsiders may not hope, but Christians are expected to be a hopeful people (1:3).
32   **14.** *we believe:* Paul employs a formal lemma to introduce an early Christian creedal formula. The two-part formula highlights the death and resurrection of Jesus and implicitly attributes Jesus' resurrection to an act of God (see comment on 1:10). Although an expanded creedal formula is found in 1 Cor 15:3–7, a simple formula is used here. The introductory formula highlights the common faith of the apostles, the recent converts at Thessalonica, and earlier Christian communities. *Jesus died and rose:* Use of the creedal formula grounds Paul's exposition of Christian hope. As God has raised Jesus from the dead, so he will bring with Jesus those who have died in him (→ Pauline Theology, 82:59).
33   **15–17.** In explanation, Paul cites a word of the

Lord and makes use of various apocalyptic motifs. **15.** *word of the Lord:* Although some commentators continue to think of sayings of the historical Jesus, either one akin to Matt 24:30 or an agraphon, and others suggest a personal revelation to Paul, it is preferable to think that Paul is making use of a dictum of early Christian prophecy. The prophetic statement is to be found in vv 16-17, while v 15b offers Paul's own reflection on the situation about which he has become aware. *we who are alive:* Paul assumes that the parousia will soon take place, "the imminent expectation." He affirms that the living will have no advantage over the dead when it occurs (v 17). **16-17.** The prophetic statement, rife with apocalyptic motifs, may be an outgrowth of an earlier Jewish apocalyptic statement about the coming of the Son of Man. *command, the archangel's call, trumpet sound:* (See Rev 14; 17; 19; 20.) These details stress the divine initiative in the event. *meet the Lord:* One current of exegesis, the "Hellenistic interpretation," cites the solemn entrance of kings into a (conquered) town as the model for the scenario (E. Peterson). Another current of exegesis maintains that the biblical description of the theophany at Sinai provides the exemplar for this description of the parousia (J. Dupont, M. Sabbe). *the dead in Christ will rise:* The same vb. is used of the resurrection of Christian dead in v 16 as is used of the resurrection of Jesus in v 14; thus, both the similarity of the events, as acts of God, and the resurrection of Christians in consequence of the resurrection of Jesus are stressed. The resurrection of the dead is cited as the means employed by God to ensure the accompaniment of the parousiac Lord by those who have died in him. *first:* Order is a typical feature of apocalyptic descriptions; in vv 16-17 order is expressed in processional fashion. *we shall always be with the Lord:* The reality of ultimate salvation is being with the Lord (4:14; Phil 1:23; cf. 1 Thess 5:10). *clouds:* Typically a means for heavenly transport (Dan 7:13). The meeting of Christians with the Lord implies both rapture and some form of transformation (1 Cor 15:51-54a). **18.** *encourage one another:* An invitation to mutual encouragement is found also in 5:11; here the aspect of mutual comfort is especially important.

34   (B) Second Apocalyptic Disclosure: Eschatological Existence (5:1-11). The pericope is readily divided into three subunits: (a) announcement of the topic (vv 1-3); (b) parenesis (vv 4-10); (c) final exhortation (v 11). Because this pericope appears to be a doublet of 4:13-18, albeit from a somewhat different perspective, some authors consider it to be a corrective interpolated into the letter by a later author (→ 8 above). It is better to interpret the pericope as an instructive complement to 4:13-18. There Paul commends the fate of the dead to God; here he reflects on the implications of the *eschaton* for those who are alive.

35   1-3. Announcement of the topic. **1.** Paul uses preterition to introduce his topic: the Day of the Lord. **2.** *the Day of the Lord:* A biblical image taken over from the prophetic tradition (Amos 5:18; Joel 2:1; Zeph 1:7) and used in the NT (Acts 2:20; 1 Cor 5:5). In later Pauline writings it is identified as the Day of the Lord Jesus (Phil 1:6,10). The traditional nature of "Day of the Lord" implies that *kyrios* = God, rather than Jesus. Speculation about the coming of the end times is characteristic of an apocalyptic world view; some apocalyptic writings focus on this coming by the periodization of human history (Dan 9:2,24-27; 2 Esdr 14:5). *thief in the night:* The traditional image (Matt 24:43-44; Luke 12:39-40) symbolizes the suddenness of the event. **3.** *peace and security:* The saying has a proverbial ring (Jer 6:14; Ezek 13:10,16) and may be a traditional apocalyptic motif taken over by Paul (B. Rigaux). *pregnant woman:*

In contrast to the complacency implied by the saying, the motif of the pregnant woman adds dimensions of suddenness, precariousness, and inevitability to the coming of the Day of the Lord.

36   4-10. Parenesis. **4-5.** *light, darkness:* Paul's metaphorical description of the Christian condition uses the theme of light and darkness (common in religious literature, e.g., Job 22:11; 1QS 3:13-14; 1QM passim; *T. Naph.* 2:7-10) and day and night (perhaps his own creation). *sons of light:* A Semitism is used to set the Christian condition off from others' (sons of darkness); this exclusionary language is found also in QL (1QS 1:9-10; 3:13-22; 1QM 1). **6-8.** In vv 6-7 Paul draws on typical apocalyptic language to exhort Christians to vigilance. *sleepers, drunkards:* Traditional metaphors. **8.** *breastplate, helmet:* The imagery of the warrior's panoply is an accommodation of Isa 59:17 (cf. Wis 5:17-23; Eph 6:14). Characterizing Christian existence by faith, love, and hope, the image may suggest that Christians are involved in a final, eschatological confrontation. Many scholars believe that this exhortation (vv 4-8) reflects Christian baptismal catechesis. **9.** *destined us:* In his exposition of the christological foundation of Christian existence, Paul uses a Semitic expression to indicate that Christians are destined (but not predestined) for salvation (as distinct from eschatological wrath). Salvation is effected through the Lord Jesus Christ (1:10). The special relationship between Christians and the Lord is the ground of their salvation. **10.** Paul uses another fragmentary creedal formula (see 1:10; 4:14) to attribute salvific value to Jesus' death. Salvation accrues to all, whether they are alive or not (4:14,16-17). **11.** *encourage one another:* The pericope's concluding exhortation is similar to 4:18, but adds both a reflection, that mutual encouragement builds up the community, and a pastoral commendation (4:1,10).

37   (V) Final Exhortation (5:12-22).
(A) First Period: Call for Order in the Community (5:12-13). 12-13. These verses relate to the building up of the community (v 11). *laboring* (3:6), *caring* (Rom 12:8), *admonishing:* Though many commentators distinguish among these three functions and attribute them to the leaders of the Thessalonian community, J. Hainz (*Ekklesia* [BU 9; Munich, 1972] 37-42) claims that they speak cumulatively of the ministry of caring for the community and imply that all the members of the community are involved in that ministry. *in the Lord:* The authority and norm for ministry (4:1-2). **13.** *love:* A dimension of *philadelphia* (see comment on 4:9). *peace:* This implies the biblical notion of complete well-being, not simply the absence of dissension within the community.

38   (B) Second Period: Call for Various Functions (5:14-22). A series of instructions is given in staccato fashion (C. Roetzel: "shotgun parenesis"). **14.** *the idle:* A general type of behavior rather than a specific vice (= unruly, C. Spicq). *the fainthearted:* A *hapax legomenon* in the NT. *the weak:* I.e., those who need steadfastness in the midst of affliction and who are exhorted to vigilance in vv. 1-11 (D. A. Black). Patience is a fruit of the Spirit (Gal 5:22). **15.** A similar exhortation to nonretaliation is found in Rom 12:17 (Matt 5:44-48; Luke 6:27-36). Christian charity is to be put into practice (1:3; 4:10-11); it is directed both to community members and those outside (3:12; 4:9-10). **16-18.** General exhortations on the Christian way of life (God's will, cf. 4:3). **16.** *rejoice always:* See Phil 4:4; joy is a fruit of the Spirit (Gal 5:22; cf. Rom 14:17). **17.** *pray incessantly:* See Luke 18:1; Eph 6:18; prayer proceeds from the Spirit (Rom 8:15-16). *give thanks:* Thanksgiving and prayer are closely associated (3:9-10); see Phil 4:6; cf.

Col 2:7; 3:15–17. **19–22.** Exhortations on charisms and discernment. **19–20.** *Spirit, gift of prophecy:* Jewish and Hellenistic parallels indicate that the passages refer to the charismatic activity of oneself and of others. The community at Thessalonica may be "charismatically" ordered, but Paul does not as yet use the technical term "charism" to describe the gifts of the Spirit (1 Cor 12:4–11). **21–22.** *test:* The discernment of charisms is itself a charismatic activity (1 Cor 12:10). *good, evil:* Some authors interpret vv 21b–22 of true and false prophecy, while others think that the reference is to moral discernment (Isa 1:16,17).
39   **(VI) Closing Wishes and Salutation (5:23–28).** **23.** *A second wish prayer* (see 3:11–13) has the form of a homiletic benediction. Its two parts are characterized by synonymous parallelism, i.e., the basic content is the same in each of the two parts. *God of peace:* A traditional epithet (Judg 6:24) taken over by Paul (Rom 15:33; 1 Cor 14:33). All blessings come from God, including ultimate sanctification (4:1–8). *kept sound and blameless:* The second part of the prayer uses the "theological" passive (*ZBG* § 236) to speak of ultimate salvation (i.e., at the parousia). *spirit, soul, body:* Commentators, both ancient and modern, have suggested that Paul expressed a tripartite form of anthropology.

More common is the opinion that the three terms designate the whole human person under one or other aspect. This would be consistent with typical Jewish anthropology (see comment on 3:13), where "spirit" essentially identifies the person as a creature; "soul," the person as a vital being; and "body," the person as a corporal and social being. Other commentators (e.g., P. A. van Stempvoort, J. O'Callaghan) would see the human person identified as "soul and body" and would give an independent nuance to "spirit."
40   **24.** An affirmation of God's fidelity, already implicit in the epithet "God of peace." **25.** *pray for us:* As Paul has prayed for the Thessalonians (1:2; 3:11–13; 5:23), he requests their prayers (Rom 15:30–32; Phil 1:19; Phlm 22). **26.** *holy kiss:* See comment on Rom 16:16. *all:* This may be emphatic if, indeed, the community was beginning to be divided, as some authors think (see comment on gnostic enthusiasm at 4:11). **27.** *I adjure you:* For the third time (2:18; 3:5). Paul writes in the sg., and his language is authoritative. The reading of a Christian text was apparently a new practice in the Christian assembly (cf. Col 4:16; see Collins, *Studies* 365–70). **28.** A solemn greeting concludes all of the authentic Pauline letters (→ NT Epistles, 45:8D).

47

THE LETTER
TO THE GALATIANS

Joseph A. Fitzmyer, S.J.

BIBLIOGRAPHY

1 Barrett, C. K., *Freedom and Obligation: A Study of the Epistle to the Galatians* (London, 1985). Betz, H. D., *Galatians* (Herm; Phl, 1979). Bonnard, P., *L'Épître de saint Paul aux Galates* (CNT 9; 2d ed.; Neuchâtel, 1972). Borse, U., *Der Brief an die Galater* (RNT; Regensburg, 1984); *Der Standort des Galaterbriefes* (BBB 41; Bonn, 1972). Brinsmead, B. H., *Galatians—Dialogical Response to Opponents* (SBLDS 65; Chico, 1982). Bruce, F. F., *The Epistle to the Galatians* (NIGTC; GR, 1982). Burton, E. DeW., *The Epistle to the Galatians* (ICC; NY, 1971). Ebeling, G., *The Truth of the Gospel: An Exposition of Galatians* (Phl, 1985). Eckert, J., *Die urchristliche Verkündigung im Streit zwischen Paulus und seinen Gegnern nach dem Galaterbrief* (BU 6; Regensburg, 1971). Guthrie, D., *Galatians* (NCB; London, 1974). Howard, G., *Paul: Crisis in Galatia* (SNTSMS 35; Cambridge, 1979).

Lietzmann, H., *An die Galater* (HNT 10; 4th ed., rev. P. Vielhauer; Tübingen, 1971). Lyonnet, S., *Les épîtres de Saint Paul aux Galates, aux Romains* (SBJ; 2d ed.; Paris, 1959). Mussner, F., *Der Galaterbrief* (HTKNT 9; 2d ed.; Freiburg, 1974). Oepke, A., *Der Brief des Paulus an die Galater* (THKNT 9; 2d ed., rev. E. Fascher; Berlin, 1964). Ridderbos, H. N., *The Epistle of Paul to the Churches of Galatia* (NICNT; 8th ed.; GR, 1953). Roux, H., *L'Evangile de la liberté* (Geneva, 1973). Schlier, H., *Der Brief an die Galater* (MeyerK 7; 14th ed.; Göttingen, 1971). Schneider, G., *The Epistle to the Galatians* (NTSR 15; NY, 1969). Viard, A., *Saint Paul: Epître aux Galates* (SB; Paris, 1964).

DBSup 7. 211–26. *IDBSup* 352–53. Kümmel, *INT* 294–304. Wik-Schm, *ENT* 409–20.

INTRODUCTION

2 **(I) Authenticity.** Apart from a few stray questioners (F. R. McGuire, *HibJ* 66 [1967–68] 52–57; G. Ory, *CahCER* 32 [1984] 139–47), no one seriously queries the Pauline authorship of Gal today, just as it was not questioned up to the 19th cent. (see Kümmel, *INT* 304; Wik-Schm, *ENT* 419).

3 **(II) Destination.** Paul writes to the "churches of Galatia" (1:2). The *Galatai,* originally an Indo-Aryan tribe of Asia, were related to the Celts or Gauls ("who in their own language are called *Keltae,* but in ours *Galli*" [J. Caesar, *Bell. gall.* 1.1]). About 279 BC some of them invaded the lower Danube and Macedonia, descending even into the Gk peninsula. After they were stopped by the Aetolians in 278, a remnant fled across the Hellespont into Asia Minor. They harassed that area widely until Attalus I, king of Pergamum, defeated them (*ca.* 239 BC) and fixed their land between the Sangarius and Halys rivers around the three towns of Ancyra, Pessinus, and Tavium. They continued to annoy their neighbors until the Roman Manlius Vulso subdued them in 189 BC. Rome subsequently used them as a buffer state against Pergamum. In the Mithridatic wars they remained loyal to Rome, and as a reward their territory was gradually expanded. About 40 BC some areas of Pisidia, Phrygia, Lycaonia, and Isauria became

part of Galatia. When the last Galatian king, Amyntas, willed his land to Rome, it was incorporated into the empire in 25 BC, becoming a province, *Galatia*. As such, it took in more than the original "Galatian country" in northern Asia Minor, including a large part of the south and center as well. In the southern area were situated Pisidian Antioch, Iconium, Lystra, and Derbe. The population of the whole area was quite mixed: Galatians, Greeks, *Gallograeci,* Romans, and Jews (see *DKP* 2.666–70; *OCD* 453–54).

4 In what sense did Paul use "Galatia"? In antiquity commentators understood the term to refer to N Galatia, the area about Ancyra, Pessinus, and Tavium. In 1748, J. J. Schmidt proposed the "South Galatian theory," later espoused by E. Renan, T. Zahn, and W. M. Ramsay; it still enjoys considerable vogue among NT scholars. According to it, Paul would have written to the churches of Antioch, Iconium, Lystra, and Derbe (founded on Mission I [Acts 13:14,51; 14:6] and visited again on Mission II [Acts 16:1–2]). The reasons for the South Galatian theory are mainly these: (1) Unlike Luke, Paul normally uses the official Roman province names for regions of which he speaks rather than names of countries (e.g., Achaia [Rom 15:26], Macedonia [1 Thess 1:7–8], Asia [Rom 16:5]). (2) Neither Acts 16:6 nor

18:23, both of which mention Paul's passage through Galatia, suggests the foundation of any Christian communities in N Galatia. (3) Paul probably did not speak the Galatian language, which in Jerome's time was still a form of Celtic. (4) Gal 3:2–3,13–14,23–24; 4:2,5; 5:1 seem to presuppose Jewish-Christian readers, who would only have been found in the hellenized towns of S. Galatia.

5 But is any of these reasons really valid? Apropos of (1), in Gal 1:21 Paul uses "Syria and Cilicia," names of countries, not of provinces; in Gal 1:17 he speaks of "Arabia," which became a province only in AD 106. If one hesitates about "Galatia" (1:2), there is little room for hesitation about the meaning of *Galatai* (3:1), the name of a barbarian race, which Paul himself, a native of S Asia Minor, would scarcely apply to inhabitants of the hellenized cities of Pisidia and Lycaonia. (2) The argument proceeds from silence in Acts, in which many of Luke's accounts are known to be telescoped résumés. Acts 18:23, in fact, presupposes communities already established. Again, the natural explanation of Acts 16:6 is that Paul passed from Lystra and Iconium into Phrygia and "the Galatian country"—note the expression, also found in 18:23. (3) If the Galatians of the N spoke a different language, it probably was not the only place where Paul might have had to use an interpreter; cf. Acts 14:11. (4) Finally, none of the verses of Gal cited need be so interpreted as to mean that Jewish Christians apart from the Judaizers were really members of the Galatian communities. In fact, Gal 4:8; 5:2–3; 6:12–13 suggest rather the pagan background of the majority of the readers. In Antioch, Lystra, etc., where Jews are known to have lived, it is not unlikely that the problem of the relation of Christianity to the law would have been faced even earlier. The fascination with Jewish practices presupposed by Gal 1:6 seems to have been of recent vintage. Hence Paul more likely wrote Gal to the predominantly Gentile communities of N Galatia. In the long run, this question is of minor importance, since Paul's message comes through, whether the destination can be definitely settled or not.

(Betz, *Galatians* 1–5; Bonnard, *Galates* 9–12. Bruce, F. F., "Galatian Problems: 2. North or South Galatians?" *BJRL* 52 [1970] 243–66; *Galatians* 3–18. Kümmel, *INT* 296–98. Wik-Schm, *ENT* 410–13.)

6 **(III) Date.** Gal is not easily dated—4:13 may suggest that it was written after a second visit to Galatia (probably that of Acts 18:23 on Mission III). Ephesus is the likely place of writing. At any rate, Gal belongs to the period of Paul's major struggle with the Judaizers in the early church, when he also wrote 1 Cor, 2 Cor, Rom, and probably Phil. Almost certainly Gal preceded Rom (*ca.* AD 58); its relation to 1 Cor and 2 Cor is problematical, but probably it preceded them too. A not unlikely date is *ca.* AD 54, not long after Paul's arrival in Ephesus at the beginning of Mission III (→ Paul, 79:40). An earlier date is often given for Gal by proponents of the S Galatian theory (see Bruce, *Galatians* 43–56), but it is difficult to reconcile that with all the data. C. H. Buck (*JBL* 70 [1951] 113–22) and C. E. Faw (*BR* 4 [1960] 25–38) argue for a date situating Gal between 2 Cor and Rom.

7 **(IV) Occasion and Purpose.** Shortly after Paul's second visit to the Galatian churches he learned in Ephesus that "some agitators" (1:7) in Galatia were impugning his authority as an apostle (1:1,12—apparently on the grounds that his commission did not come from Christ); they further claimed that he was not preaching the true gospel (1:7), because he did not insist on observance of Mosaic regulations: circumcision (even for

Gentile Christians, 6:12), celebration of Jewish feasts (4:10, days, months, seasons, and years). They may have further accused him of opportunism for having once permitted circumcision (5:11). Thus he was watering down the requirements of the gospel for the sake of Gentile converts. Having learned of the activity of such agitators and the confusion that they were creating in the Galatian churches, Paul wrote this strong letter to warn his Christian followers there against this "different gospel" (1:7) that was actually being preached to them by such people. He defended his position as an "apostle," and stoutly maintained that the gospel he had preached, without the observance of the Mosaic practices, was the only correct view of Christianity, as recent events had shown. Gal thus became the first exposé of Paul's teaching about justification by grace through faith apart from deeds prescribed by the law; it is Paul's manifesto about Christian freedom. Though he called the Galatians "senseless" (3:1), he still found room in his heart for "my children" (4:19) and "brothers" (4:12; 5:11; 6:18).

8 Who were the agitators in Galatia? Though some commentators (M. Barth, J. Munck) have tried to make them out to be Gentile Christians or even gnostics (W. Schmithals), they are best identified as Jewish Christians of Palestine, of an even stricter Jewish background than Peter, Paul, or James, or even of the "false brethren" (2:4) of Jerusalem, whom Paul had encountered there. (The account in Acts 15:5 would identify the latter as "believers who had belonged to the sect of the Pharisees.") It is, moreover, unlikely that they had anything to do with "the people from James" (Gal 2:12), who caused trouble in Antioch. The agitators in Galatia were Judaizers, who insisted not on the observance of the whole Mosaic law, but at least on circumcision and the observance of some other Jewish practices. Paul for this reason warned the Gentile Christians of Galatia that their fascination with "circumcision" would oblige them to keep "the whole law" (5:3). The agitators may have been syncretists of some sort: Christians of Jewish, perhaps Essene, background, affected by some Anatolian influences. (Long before the discovery of the Qumran scrolls, J. B. Lightfoot related the "Colossian heresy" to Essenism [*Saint Paul's Epistles to the Colossians and to Philemon* (London, 1890) 80–103; his suggestion has found support in some of the QL: on Col 1:12–13, see 1QS 11:7–8; on Col 2:16, see 1QS 10:1–8; CD 8:15].) Even though Col may be Deutero-Pauline (→ NT Epistles, 45:12), the teachings of the Galatian agitators may have been related to similar Anatolian influences. See Gal 4:10.

(Eckert, *Die urchristliche Verkündigung.* Jewett, R., "The Agitators and the Galatian Congregation," *NTS* 17 [1970–71] 198–212. Schmithals, W., "Die Häretiker in Galatien," *ZNW* 47 [1956] 25–66; "Judaisten in Galatien?" *ZNW* 74 [1983] 27–58.)

9 **(V) Relation of Gal to Rom.** Clearly, Gal is not merely an outline or rough draft of Rom, for a difference of perspective marks the two letters. In Rom, Paul presents irenically his apostolic and missionary reflections on the historic possibility now offered humanity through the preaching of the gospel—an exposé of the righteousness and love of God that brings about human justification and salvation, a way of Christian life that must be inaugurated by faith. In Gal, however, Paul writes a polemical letter, warning the Galatian churches against the Judaizing error: there is no other gospel than the one that he has preached to them. He insists on the freedom from the law that has been won for humanity in Christ Jesus. Though, as in Rom, justification by faith is taught, Paul's emphasis in Gal falls rather on the freedom that the Christian has won in

Christ Jesus. Again, nothing in Rom corresponds to Gal 1:1-2:14, but the résumé of Paul's gospel in Gal 2:15-21 sounds like an outline of Rom 1-8, with the same positive progress of thought.

(Hübner, H., "Identitätsverlust und paulinische Theologie: Anmerkungen zum Galaterbrief," *KD* 24 [1978] 181-93. Kertelge, K., "Gesetz und Freiheit im Galaterbrief," *NTS* 30 [1984] 382-94. Mood, D. J., "'Law,' 'Works of the Law,' and Legalism in Paul," *WTJ* 45 [1983] 73-100. Stagg, F., "Freedom and Moral Responsibility without License or Legalism," *RevExp* 69 [1972] 483-94.)

10   (VI) Outline. Gal may be outlined thus (I am following with slight adaptation the rhetorical analysis of H. D. Betz, *NTS* 21 [1974-75] 353-79):

(I) Introduction (1:1-11)
   (A) *Praescriptio:* Opening Formula (1:1-5)
   (B) *Exordium:* Amazement (1:6-7), Anathema (1:8-9), Transition (1:10-11)
(II) *Narratio:* Paul's Historic Call to Preach the Gospel (1:12-2:14)
   (A) Paul's Gospel Not of Human Origin (1:12-24)
   (B) Paul's Gospel Approved by Jerusalem Church Leaders (2:1-10)

(C) Paul's Gospel Challenged Peter's Inconsistency at Antioch (2:11-14)
(III) *Propositio:* Paul's Gospel Set Forth (2:15-21)
(IV) *Probatio:* In God's Plan Humanity Is Saved by Faith, Not by the Law (3:1-4:31)
   (A) Proof 1: Experience of the Galatians in First Receiving the Spirit (3:1-5)
   (B) Proof 2: Experience of Abraham and God's Promises to Him (3:6-26)
   (C) Proof 3: Experience of Christians in Baptism (3:27-29)
   (D) Proof 4: Experience of Christians as Children of God (4:1-11)
   (E) Proof 5: Experience of Galatians in Their Relation to Paul (4:12-20)
   (F) Proof 6: The Allegory of Sarah and Hagar (4:21-31)
(V) *Exhortatio:* Hortatory Section (5:1-6:10)
   (A) Counsel: Preserve the Freedom That You Have in Christ (5:1-12)
   (B) Warning: Walk Not according to the Flesh, but according to the Spirit (5:13-26)
   (C) Advice: The Right Way to Use Christian Freedom (6:1-10)
(VI) *Postscriptio:* Paul's "Signature" and Résumé; Farewell Blessing (6:11-18)

COMMENTARY

11   (I) Introduction (1:1-11).
(A) *Praescriptio:* Opening Formula (1:1-5).
Paul expands the *praescriptio* by incorporating into it motifs of the letter itself: the defense of his apostolate (its independence and divine origin); God's plan for the justification of humanity through Christ. **1.** *Paul an apostle:* Paul argues against the idea that because he was not one of the Twelve he has no real authority. Here he deliberately assumes the title "apostle" to emphasize his equality with them, for his authoritative commission comes from the risen Lord. The word *apostolos,* rarely found in extrabiblical Greek or the LXX, developed a specific Christian nuance under the influence of the contemporary Jewish institution of the šělîaḥ, "one sent": a commissioned agent sent with full powers to carry out a definite (legal, prophetic, or missionary) charge (see K. H. Rengstorf, *TDNT* 1. 437-43; → NT Thought, 81:149-52). *God the Father who raised:* Paul's commission to preach the gospel is directly from God and not delegated by human beings. Its origin lies in him who put the final seal of approval on the very mission of Christ himself (4:4). Note that Christ's resurrection is attributed to the Father (→ Pauline Theology, 82:59). **3.** *grace and peace:* Paul's grace invokes a share in the messianic blessings (→ NT Epistles, 45:8), derived from both the Father and Christ; contrast his anathema (1:8-9). **4.** *who offered himself:* The letter's dominant chord is sounded: salvation through Christ according to the Father's plan or will (→ Pauline Theology, 82:41). *the present wicked world [age]:* Contemporary Jewish theology contrasted "this world (age)" with "the world (age) to come." Paul echoes that contrast and sees the former dominated by Satan (see 2 Cor 4:4). Christ's "giving" of himself has brought about the meeting of the two ages (1 Cor 10:11) and freed human beings from "this age."
12   (B) *Exordium:* Amazement (1:6-7), Anathema (1:8-9), Transition (1:10-11). Instead of his customary thanksgiving (→ NT Epistles, 45:8B) Paul voices his surprise and shock at Galatian fickleness. Denouncing any other teaching as a spurious gospel, he affirms that his alone is the real "gospel of Christ." **6.** *so*

quickly: Either in the sense of "so soon after your conversion (and my evangelization)" or "so easily." His amazement is mild, when compared with the curse invoked on those who mislead the Galatians. *him who called you:* The Father, since Paul normally makes *theos* the subject of "to call" (Gal 1:15; 1 Cor 1:9; Rom 4:17; 8:30; 9:24); the Father's plan is executed through the grace (benevolence) of Christ. A possible, but less probable, interpretation: "turning away from Christ, who has called you in grace." **7.** *any other (gospel):* Since the gospel is a "force for salvation" (Rom 1:16), emanating from Christ, who is not divided (1 Cor 1:13), there can be only one gospel. This Paul has already proclaimed to them. *some people:* The agitating Judaizers (→ 7-8 above). **8.** *an angel from heaven:* Cf. 2 Cor 11:4. In Gal 3:19-20 Paul refers to the Jewish belief that the Mosaic law was enacted by angels. Even if one of *them* were to appear again with a modified gospel, he is not to be heard—in fact, Paul curses such a being. *anathema:* The word originally denoted a "votive offering set up in a temple" (cf. Luke 21:5; cf. BAGD 54), but in time, esp. under LXX influence (Num 21:3; Deut 7:26), it came to mean an "object of a curse." So Paul uses it to utter a solemn curse on the Judaizers (see 1 Cor 12:3, 16:22; Rom 9:3). **10.** This and v 11 are transitional. *am I courting the favor of men—or of God?:* Paul rejects an implied accusation that he is watering down the gospel to win converts (see 1 Thess 2:4; 2 Cor 5:11). *still trying to please men:* As formerly, in the time before his conversion, when he persecuted God's church (1:13). Now service of Christ has delivered him from such motivation and vainglory. *a slave of Christ:* His conversion has freed him from the "yoke of slavery," which was the Mosaic law (5:1), with its emphasis on human achievement. He has become a slave of Christ, prompt to obey him (Rom 6:16-20). There may also be a further nuance. In Phil 1:1; Rom 1:1, Paul calls himself a "slave," possibly like great OT figures who served Yahweh faithfully (Moses, 2 Kgs 18:12 LXX; Joshua, Judg 2:8; Abraham, Ps 104:42). If he were courting human favor, he would not be true to such a calling. **11.** *I would have you know:* The same solemn affirmation introduces the kerygmatic fragment that Paul "received" and "passed on" in 1 Cor 15:1. But his "gospel" is from Christ; as in 1 Thess 2:13, its origin is "from God." *the gospel I have preached:* The essence of what Paul likes to call "my/our gospel" (1 Thess 1:5; 2 Cor 4:3; Rom 2:16) is that salvation is possible for all human beings alike through faith in Christ (→ Pauline Theology, 82:31-36).

13   (II) *Narratio:* Paul's Historic Call to Preach the Gospel (1:12-2:14). The Judaizers apparently had accused Paul of having derived his message not from Christ, because he had never witnessed the ministry of Jesus, but from other preachers, and of having watered it down for Gentiles by eliminating the obligation of Jewish practices. He replies by reaffirming his historic apostolic commission and by explaining his relation with the mother church of Jerusalem.

14   (A) Paul's Gospel Not of Human Origin (1:12-24). It comes rather from God himself. **12.** *through a revelation of Jesus Christ:* The gen. can be either objective (revealing Christ, see 1:16) or subjective (Christ revealing the gospel, not human beings). The revelation near Damascus (→ Paul, 79:20-22) illumined Paul about Christ and his meaning for humanity — about the essential character of the gospel, not necessarily about its "form." Verse 12 does not mean that facts about Jesus' life were communicated to Paul so that he never had to depend on an early tradition emanating from the Jerusalem church (→ Pauline Theology, 82:16-20).

15   13. *my former conduct as a Jew:* Paul's former way of life hardly provided the psychological background from which his gospel would naturally have developed. As a Pharisee (Phil 3:5-6), he would have rejected resolutely what was opposed to the Mosaic law and the traditions of the Fathers (i.e., Pharisaic interpretations of the Torah; see Mark 7:1-13). *I persecuted the church of God:* See 1 Cor 15:9 (cf. Acts 8:3; 9:1-2). On the phrase "church of God," → Pauline Theology, 82:134-35. **15.** *from my mother's womb:* A Septuagintal phrase. As was Jeremiah (Jer 1:5) or even the Servant of Yahweh (Isa 49:1), Paul had been destined for the call by the Father that antedated his very existence. Did Paul consider himself another Servant of Yahweh? (see D. M. Stanley, *CBQ* 16 [1954] 385-425). **16.** *to reveal his Son to me:* Lit., "in me"; but *en* with the dat. can equal the dat. of indir. obj. (BDF 220.1; cf. 1:12; 2:20; 1 Cor 15:10). Paul insisted that he had "seen" the Lord (1 Cor 9:1; 15:8) and was therefore an apostle. Another transl., "through me," is possible, but seems redundant in view of the following clause. *that I might announce good news of him among the Gentiles:* See 2:7. Paul connects his apostolic commission with the revelation of Christ, but his words do not force one to conclude to a historical simultaneity of these two events (see B. Rigaux, *The Letters of St. Paul* [Chicago, 1968] 40-67). For Christ as the content of the gospel, see Rom 1:2-5. *I consulted no human being:* Lit., "flesh and blood," an OT expression (Sir 14:18; 17:31), used again in 1 Cor 15:50. The emphatic denial of the human origin of his commission is explained by the chronological and geographical details that follow. **17.** *to Jerusalem:* His basic insight into Christ did not stem from the traditional center from which the "word of the Lord" went forth (Isa 2:3; Luke 24:48). *apostles before me:* Paul was conscious that he was the "least important" of the apostles (1 Cor 15:9), but that does not mean that he was an apostle of only second rank. *to Arabia:* Probably the Nabatean kingdom of Aretas IV Philopatris (2 Cor 11:32; cf. G. W. Bowersock, *JRS* 61 [1971] 219-42; *Roman Arabia* [Cambridge MA, 1983]; J. Starcky, *DBSup* 7. 886-1017) in Transjordan, E and S of Damascus, and stretching westward S of Palestine toward Suez. The nature and duration of

this withdrawal are not stated, and Paul's sojourn there is passed over in Acts (→ Paul, 79:7-8).

16   18. *then after three years:* To be reckoned from Paul's return to Damascus after his journey to Arabia. *to get information from Cephas:* The meaning of the Gk infin. *historēsai* is disputed; lit., it means "to inquire about, into" (a person, thing), "to go and examine" (a thing). Many ancient Gk and Lat interpreters understood it simply as "to see" (Vg, *videre*) often interpreted as "to pay a (social) call on" Cephas. Yet there is little evidence for such a meaning. The preferable interpretation: Paul visited Cephas for the purpose of inquiry (LSJ 842), to get information from him about Jesus' ministry (see G. D. Kilpatrick, "Galatians 1:18, *historēsai Kēphan,*" *New Testament Essays* [Fest. T. W. Manson; Manchester, 1959] 144-49; cf. J. D. G. Dunn, *NTS* 28 [1982] 461-78; *ZNW* 76 [1985] 138-39; O. Hofius, *ZNW* 75 [1984] 73-85). During the 15 days spent with Cephas, Paul probably learned "traditions" of the Jerusalem church (1 Cor 11:2,23-25; 15:3-7). Though the identity of Cephas and Peter has been questioned (by K. Lake, D. W. Riddle, C. M. Henze; see Betz, *Galatians* 97), it is widely accepted (see O. Cullmann, *Peter* [Phl, 1953] 18 n. 7; *TDNT* 6. 100-12). *Kēphas,* a Gk form of Aram *kēpā',* "rock," "stone," "crag," now known to have been used as a personal name (see *BMAP* 8:10; cf. J. A. Fitzmyer, *TAG* 112-24), was given to Simon as a title and denoted the quality of the bearer (like Maccabee, "hammer"). In virtue of this title Simon is a "rock" in the eschatological temple (= the church); he is also one of the "pillars" (2:9) of the Jerusalem church. **19.** *but only James:* Or possibly "except James." The conj. *ei mē* can be either adversative, "but" (as in Gal 2:16; Matt 12:4), or exceptive (see *ZBG* §470). In the former meaning, which seems preferable, James is distinguished from the apostles; in the latter, James is said to be an apostle. But then he is not to be identified with either James, son of Zebedee, or James, son of Alphaeus, members of the Twelve (Mark 3:17-18). Paul calls him "the brother of the Lord," who was regarded as the first "bishop" of Jerusalem (Eusebius, *HE* 2.23.1; → NT Thought, 81:143). *the brother:* In classical and Hellenistic Greek, *adelphos* means "blood brother." In the LXX it translates Hebr *'āḥ,* even when used in the sense of "kinsman" (Gen 13:8; 29:12-15; see BAGD 16); in Gk papyri from Egypt it also has the wide sense of "relative" (see J. J. Collins, *TS* 5 [1944] 484-94; cf. J. A. Fitzmyer, *WA* 221). In view of the problem created by Mark 6:3 and 15:40,47; 16:1, where "Mary, the mother of James the Little and Joses" can scarcely be used by the evangelist to designate the mother of the person crucified on Calvary, *adelphos,* used of James, is best understood as "kinsman, relative." **21.** *Syria and Cilicia:* This probably includes Tarsus, Paul's native town, which was the place of a sojourn for several years, possibly even of apostolate; as a result he was not personally known as a Christian to the "churches of Judea."

17   (B) Paul's Gospel Approved by Jerusalem Church Leaders (2:1-10). 1. *once again in fourteen years:* The usual translation, "14 years later," has been questioned (e.g., by S. Giet, *RSR* 41 [1953] 323-24) because elsewhere Paul uses *dia* with the gen. to mean "during (the course of)." This meaning, plus the use of "again," seems to imply a reckoning of the date from Paul's conversion (*ca.* AD 36). Correlation of this visit to Jerusalem with the data in Acts is one of the most difficult exegetical problems in the NT. However, one cannot escape the impression that Gal 2 refers to the same event as that in Acts 15 (at least vv 1-12) — all other attempts to identify it otherwise notwithstanding. Yet many problems remain

(→ Paul, 79:25, 32, 35–37). *Barnabas:* See 1 Cor 9:6. According to Acts 4:36, he was a Cypriote Levite, named Joseph, called Barnabas by the apostles (with the popular etymology "son of consolation"). Acts 13:1 presents him as a prophet or teacher of Antioch, who becomes Paul's companion during Mission I (up to the Jerusalem "Council"). *Titus:* A Gentile Christian (see v 3), companion of Paul during Mission III, who smooths over Paul's relations with the Corinthian community (see 2 Cor 2:13; 7:6,13–14; 8:6,16,23; 12:18). **2.** *because of a revelation:* Who had it? If Paul, he is mentioning it at least to show that he has not been summoned by the Jerusalem apostles. (In Acts 15:2 the reason for the visit is given as a decision of the Antiochene community.) *privately to those of repute:* His argument slightly disparages the Jerusalem "pillars," who were apostles before him (1:16). **3.** *not compelled to be circumcised:* Does Paul mean that Titus was in fact not circumcised or that he was not "compelled" to be, but agreed to submit to it? The general tenor of the passage would favor the former answer, i.e., Paul won his case for the noncircumcision of Gentile converts. **4.** *false brothers:* In Acts 15:5 similar Jewish-Christian converts, said to be of Pharisaic background, press for the circumcision of Gentiles and their obligation to observe the Mosaic law. *the freedom we have in Christ Jesus:* The Magna Charta of Gal: In Christ Jesus we have been freed of the law (5:1, 13). **5.** *not even for a moment did we yield:* Paul boasts as if he had influenced the assembly. Acts 15:7–11, however, gives the credit to Simon. **6.** *the men of repute:* James, Cephas, and John (2:9). *what kind of people they were:* A difficult, parenthetical statement that seems to mean that Paul was not overawed by the prestige gained by the "pillars" for having been eyewitnesses of Jesus' ministry. Such an experience and such prestige could not outweigh the truth of the God-given gospel. *added nothing to me:* Paul's gospel was recognized by the pillars as not deficient, despite the claims of the Judaizers. (For the relation of "nothing" to Acts 15:19–29, → Paul, 79:33, 35–37.) **7.** *as Peter was for the circumcised:* So Paul was acknowledged as Peter's peer, and the mission field was divided between them (Rom 15:17–21; cf. Acts 15:12). The division must be understood geographically, not ethnically, for Paul often began his evangelization of an area with the Jews (1 Cor 9:23–24; Rom 2:10–11; cf. Acts 13:46; 17:1–8; 18:4). Whereas Paul normally uses "Cephas" (1 Cor 1:12; 3:22; 9:5; 15:5; Gal 1:18; 2:9,11, 14), he uses here "Peter" (2:7–8), perhaps quoting the terminology used in the assembly's debate (see Betz, *Galatians* 97). **9.** *James, Cephas, John:* James, the "bishop" of Jerusalem, is given precedence over Cephas and John, son of Zebedee. The order further suggests that even the head of the Jerusalem community agreed to Paul's gospel and mission. Are the three called *styloi,* "pillars," because they were a triumvirate ruling the Jerusalem mother church? (See C. K. Barrett, in *Studia paulina* [Fest. J. de Zwaan; ed. J. N. Sevenster, *et al.;* Haarlem, 1953] 1–19.) **10.** *remember the poor:* The only added charge of the "Council." They are probably the "poor among the saints in Jerusalem" (Rom 15:26), i.e., those economically poor when compared with Gentile Christians of Hellenistic cities, but also those of Palestinian Jewish-Christian *'ănāwîm* piety (see J. Dupont, *Les Béatitudes* [3 vols.; Paris, 1958–69] 2. 13–51). On whether they can be related to former Qumran *'ebyônîm* or not, see L. E. Keck, *ZNW* 56 (1965) 100–109.

18   (C) Paul's Gospel Challenged Peter's Inconsistency at Antioch (2:11–14). Not only did the pillars of the Jerusalem church approve Paul's gospel, but in the Antiochene church of Gentile and Jewish backgrounds it proved to be the only answer. **11.** *opposed*

him to his face: Though frank in his assertion, Paul apparently regarded Cephas as a person of greater consequence than himself (see *PNT* 24–32). Presumably both Cephas and Paul came to Antioch shortly after the decision on circumcision at the Jerusalem "Council." *because he stood condemned:* By his own actions, explained in 2:12–13. Paul makes no reference here or elsewhere to what Luke recounts about his having Timothy circumcised (Acts 16:3) or about his later submitting himself to the Nazirite vow ritual (Acts 21:20–26). Though he states a guiding principle in 1 Cor 9:20 (cf. Rom 14:21), a greater issue was at stake in Antioch, involving the unity of the church itself. **12.** *some people from James:* They are scarcely the "false brothers" of 2:4, for the issue now concerns Jewish dietary laws, quite distinct from the issue of circumcision, which had been settled at Jerusalem (2:3–9; cf. Acts 15:1–12). At the "Council" the dietary issue had not come up and had not been resolved (even though the composite account in Acts 15 may suggest this prima facie; → Paul, 79:33–37). *he withdrew:* Cephas refused to eat further with the Gentile Christians and gave the impression that only Jewish Christians, still observing such laws as Lev 17:8–9,10–12,15, were the real Christians. *fearing those of the circumcision:* Why Cephas "feared" is not clear; but it is taken by Paul as a sign of his lack of conviction about the gospel. **13.** *the other Jews:* Jewish Christians. *played the hypocrite along with him:* Though Cephas's influence on a minority of the Antiochene community might be explained in various ways, Paul saw it as inconsistency and political compromise. So he rebuked Cephas for it publicly. **14.** *the truth of the gospel:* The "freedom we have in Christ Jesus" (2:4–5), not only from the custom of circumcision, but also from Jewish dietary laws. Paul found fault with Cephas because he was not "walking straight" according to this truth, i.e., was unorthodox in his conduct (see G. D. Kilpatrick, in *Neutestamentliche Studien* [Fest. R. Bultmann; ed. W. Eltester; BZNW 21; Berlin, 1954] 269–74). *if you, a Jew, live like a Gentile:* See 2:12. *why do you force Gentiles to live like Jews?:* Since Cephas's example had already misled Barnabas and others, it would tend to affect Gentile Christians analogously. Was Paul's rebuke effectual? The passage implies that it was; he cites his opposition to Cephas in order to establish the validity and logic of his own gospel. He made his point with Cephas. Whether the issue of dietary regulations was settled in Antioch by that incident is another matter. It seems to have arisen again after the departure of both Cephas and Paul, and the Antiochene church sent for instructions from James in Jerusalem (Acts 15:13–33; → Paul, 79:35–37).

19   (III) *Propositio:* Paul's Gospel Set Forth (2:15–21). Paul now proposes a concise summary of his teaching on faith and Jewish observances; it may represent a reformulation of Paul's address to Cephas at Antioch. **15.** *we:* Primarily Cephas and Paul. *Jews by birth:* Lit., "by nature," or natural condition (see Rom 2:27). Paul thus acknowledges his own Jewish background. *not sinners of pagan origin:* Paul ironically contrasts his privilege (echoing the claim of his Judaizing opponents) with the lot of pagans, who not only failed to observe the Mosaic law, but did not even possess it. Being *anomoi,* "law-less," they were sinners (Rom 2:12); yet Paul knew that both the Jew and the Greek were equally sinners (Rom 3:9,23). **16.** *no one is made upright:* The pass. of the vb. *dikaioun* expresses the status of human beings standing before God's tribunal; it expresses the juridical aspect of what only divine benevolence can accomplish for humanity as a result of faith (→ Pauline Theology, 82:68–70). *by deeds of the law:* I.e., by performing acts prescribed by the Mosaic law. On this slogan-like phrase, → Pauline Theology, 82:100. *through faith in Christ Jesus:* Lit., "through (the) faith of Christ Jesus," the gen. usually being taken as objective, because of the following clause; cf. Rom 3:22, where a similar gen. is found and in the context of which (3:28) the "faith" is that of a believing human being (*anthrōpos*). See further Betz, *Galatians* 117; Bonnard, *Galates* 53. For attempts to understand the phrase of the "fidelity of Christ," see G. Howard, *HTR* 60 (1967) 459–65; L. T. Johnson, *CBQ* 44 (1982) 77–90. *even we believed:* Paul appeals to the conviction shared by him and Cephas at their conversion that a Jew fully realizes his inability to achieve righteousness by the "deeds of the law." *no mortal is made upright:* Ps 143:2 is implicitly quoted: "No living being is righteous before you." Paul omits "before you," diminishing the psalmist's forensic nuance, but he adds, "by (doing) the deeds of the law." The sense of the psalm is thus greatly restricted (cf. Rom 3:20).

20 **17.** *through Christ:* At first sight, *en Christō* seems to be the Pauline formula for union with Christ (→ Pauline Theology, 82:121); but here in contrast to "by deeds of the law," it is more likely instrumental. *we too turn out to be sinners:* I.e., like the pagans (2:15), because as "Christians" we are "law-less." *does that make Christ an agent of sin?:* This transl. understands the particle *ara* as interrogative (BAGD 104), but it could also be inferential (BAGD 103): "Then Christ is. . . ." Because of the following exclamation the question is preferred. *by no means!:* A strong negative used after rhetorical questions (see Rom 3:4,6,31). Paul resolutely rejects the suggestion and turns it back on the imaginary objector. To submit to the law again would be to become involved again with sin. **18.** *if I (try to) rebuild what I tore down:* The first reason to justify the rejection. Commentators dispute its precise meaning: either Paul would admit that in restoring the law as a norm of conduct he had sinned in abandoning it; or, less probably, he would commit himself, in setting up the law as a norm again, to a life of certain transgression (Rom 7:21–23; 4:15). In either case, it emerges that not Christ, but the Judaizer, is the real "agent of sin." **19.** *because of the law I died to the law:* The second reason. The clue to this difficult verse lies in recognizing that Christ himself is not "an agent of sin," and that the Christian, crucified with him, now lives for God. Living for God is hardly sinful, but this status of the Christian has been made possible through crucifixion with Christ. So crucified, one has died to the law ("is dead to the law," Rom 7:6; cf. 2 Cor 5:14–15). But how has this status resulted "because of the law"? Its proximate cause is the crucifixion of Christ himself, but its remote cause is the law, the curse of which was leveled against Christ (3:13). The Mosaic law and the mentality that it produced among human beings were responsible for the refusal to put faith in Christ and for the crucifixion of him—and thus indirectly for the emancipation of Christians who believe in him. *I have been crucified with Christ:* See Rom 6:8–11. Through faith and baptism the Christian has been identified (pf. tense, expressing the status of identification) with the phases of Christ's passion, death, and resurrection (→ Pauline Theology, 82:120), and so can "live for God." **20.** *Christ lives in me:* The perfection of Christian life is expressed here; it is not merely an existence dominated by a new psychological motivation ("living for God"), since faith in Christ does not substitute a new goal of action. Rather, it reshapes human beings anew, supplying them with a new principle of activity on the ontological level of their very beings. A symbiosis results of the Christian with Christ, the glorified *Kyrios,* who has become as of the resurrection a "vivifying Spirit" (1 Cor 15:45), the vital principle of Christian activity. *I live by faith in the Son of*

God: Paul's profound insight into the Christian experience: the reshaping of even physical human life by the transcendent influence of Christ's indwelling. It must penetrate to one's psychological awareness so that one realizes in faith that true life comes only from the redemptive and vicarious surrender of the Son of God. **21.** *I am not nullifying the grace of God:* As were the Judaizers, who insisted on legal obligations and human achievement, and implied thereby the inefficacy of Christ's surrender.

21 **(IV) Probatio: In God's Plan Humanity Is Saved by Faith, Not by the Law (3:1–4:31).** Paul now provides the basis for the thesis that he has just propounded in vv 15–21. He will appeal to the experience of the Galatians and make use of arguments from Scripture to establish his thesis about the reign of faith and Christian freedom.

(A) Proof 1: Experience of the Galatians in First Receiving the Spirit (3:1–5). The first argument is proposed in five rhetorical questions. **1.** *portrayed before your very eyes crucified:* Paul had preached Christ crucified (1 Cor 1:23; 2:2) so eloquently as even to "placard" him before the Galatians, perhaps like Moses with the bronze serpent (Num 21:9). The position of the ptc. "crucified" at the end is emphatic; its pf. tense expresses the status initiated on Calvary. **2.** *did you receive the Spirit?* Paul appeals to the conversion experience of the Galatians, when they received the Spirit by accepting in faith his message (see 4:6; Rom 8:7–17). In this they were like other Christian communities (2 Cor 1:22). Some commentators restrict the meaning of *pneuma* to charismatic gifts, as in 1 Cor 12:4–11; but Paul does not make the clear distinction of later theology between the created gifts and the uncreated gift of the indwelling Spirit; *pneuma* here designates rather the outpoured Spirit in a pregnant, eschatological sense (→ Pauline Theology, 82:65). Having mentioned *pneuma,* Paul proceeds, using catchword bonds, to another meaning of the word, now in contrast to *sarx,* "flesh." Because "deeds of the law" can never be on the same level as the Spirit (2 Cor 3:6–8), they must belong to the realm of the "flesh," i.e., earthly unregenerate human beings. Yet "flesh" has still another connotation here, for Paul alludes scornfully to the Judaizers' demand for circumcision, something done to the flesh. Whereas *pneuma* was the power with which they began to live as Christians (5:18; Rom 8:14–15), how can they abandon this gift for a sign in the flesh? **4.** *experienced so much in vain:* A return to "the deeds of the law" would mean that the Spirit was received to no avail. *if it is really in vain:* A cryptic afterthought, revealing Paul's hope that the Galatians will not yield to this new fascination. Another possible translation: "inasmuch as it would really be in vain" (BAGD 152). It would then express Paul's regret. **5.** *when he supplies you with the Spirit and works wonders among you:* The subject is God, as in 1 Thess 4:8; Gal 4:6; 1 Cor 12:6; 2 Cor 1:22. Here the *dynameis,* "miracles," are given along with the Spirit; elsewhere they come from the Spirit (1 Cor 12:11; Rom 15:19). They are used in a complementary sense, for neither gift came to the Galatians because they performed "deeds of the law." So their own experience testifies.

22 **(B) Proof 2: Experience of Abraham and God's Promises to Him (3:6–26).** Paul will now develop his scriptural argument for his thesis; it is a midrashic development of details of the Abraham story in Gen. It probably represents a recasting of a theological argument often used in his missionary work among Gentiles or Gentile Christians under pressure of Jewish opposition. In writing to the Galatians, he adapts the argument to his situation (see W. Koepp, *WZUR* 2 [1952–53] 181–87). The theme of his first argument: the people of faith are the real children of Abraham and the heirs of the promises made by God to him. The Christians of Galatia are like Abraham, who was upright in God's sight not because of "deeds" but because of faith. Paul does not imply that Abraham was a sinner before he believed in Yahweh, and then only was considered upright by some legal fiction. He merely insists that Abraham's righteous status was the result of faith (cf. Rom 4:3). Note the inclusion marking the first part of this argument: *ek pisteōs* (3:7a) and *dia tēs pisteōs* (3:14c). **6.** *just as Abraham put faith in God . . . :* An implicit quotation of Gen 15:6. **7.** *people of faith:* Lit., "those of faith," thus vaguely expressed, without any obj. being specified. **8.** *Scripture foresaw . . . and proclaimed:* A well-known Jewish personification of Scripture (Str-B 3. 358) implies its divine origin; thus Paul hints that even from of old righteousness through faith was part of the divine plan for the salvation of all human beings. His gospel, now preached alike to Jews and Greeks (Rom 1:16), was first announced to Abraham, the patriarch. *will be blessed in you:* Allusion to Gen 18:18 or 12:3. In Gen, Yahweh's promise immediately meant a numerous progeny and the possession of Canaan. The meaning of the vb. in the Hebr form of the blessing in Gen is disputed (→ Genesis, 2:20). Paul understands it as passive, reflecting a common Jewish understanding of the text (see Gen 48:20; cf. Jer 29:22). Gentiles were to share in the blessings promised to Abraham, provided they would worship Yahweh and submit to circumcision. Paul, however, insists that Scripture foresaw the share of Christians in the blessings of Abraham, as the children of Abraham through faith in Christ Jesus. **9.** *with Abraham, the believer:* A favorite Jewish epithet for Abraham, *pistos,* "faithful," "loyal" (1 Macc 2:52; 2 Macc 1:2; Sir 44:20; Philo, *De post. Caini* 173), is used by Paul with his own nuance: those who *believe* like Abraham are his "children" (3:7) and will thus share in his promised blessings.

23   10. *all who insist on deeds of the law:* Paul's phrase (lit., "those [who are] of the deeds of the law") is a parallel to his other expression, "those [who are] of faith" (3:7). *are under a curse:* Explained by Deut 27:26; cf. 28:58–59. For Paul the law could not transmit the blessings of Abraham; it rather imposed a curse, obliging those under it to the burden of having to observe every word of it. This obligation was laid on humanity extrinsically, without help being given to observe it (see Rom 8:3). Having cited the OT text that lays a curse on those who do not obey the law, Paul proceeds to show that the OT itself teaches that real life comes through faith. **11.** *the upright will have life through faith:* The Scripture argument continues with the quotation of Hab 2:4, quoted as in Rom 1:17 (→ Romans, 51:21; cf. J. A. Fitzmyer, *TAG* 236–46). Life for an upright person is derived from faith, not from the observance of the law. Paul is using the LXX and understands *pistis* in his own pregnant sense of Christian faith. Such "faith" will produce "life" in the fullest sense. **12.** *the law does not depend on faith:* Its principle is rather the universal observance of its prescriptions; cf. Lev 18:5, "The one who carries them out shall find life through them." Though the Lev text teaches that life comes to the observer of the law, and Paul in another context might admit this (Rom 2:13), his attention here is centered on the phrase "through them" (i.e., through the detailed "deeds of the law"). These things, Paul insists, have nothing to do with faith. Gentile Christians, who believe in Christ and have come to faith in him as *Kyrios,* cannot now have recourse to a quest of righteousness through the observance of such details, whether few or many. **13.** *Christ has bought us [Jewish Christians especially] from the curse of the law:* The law with its manifold prescriptions enslaved Jews (5:1), and from

this enslavement humanity has been delivered by Christ's "purchase" (1 Cor 6:10; 7:23). As Yahweh in the OT through his setting the Hebrews free from Egyptian bondage and through his covenant "acquired" his people (Exod 19:5–6; Isa 43:21; Ps 73:2), so Christ with his covenant blood, shed on the cross, "bought" his people. This purchase emancipated God's people from the law and its curse (5:1). On the vb. *exagorazein,* → Pauline Theology, 82:75. *becoming a curse for us:* With free association, Paul now passes from one meaning of "curse" to another: from the "curse" uttered on the one who does not observe all the law's prescriptions (Deut 27:26) to the specific "curse" uttered in the law on one hung on a tree (Deut 21:23, which Paul then quotes). The latter was directed against the corpse of an executed criminal displayed as a deterrent to crime (Josh 10:26–27; 2 Sam 4:12). As accursed in God's sight, it defiled the land of Israel; hence it was not to remain suspended beyond sunset. In Roman times, when crucifixion became a frequent punitive measure, the OT verse was applied to it (see J. A. Fitzmyer, *TAG* 125–46). The early church considered crucifixion a "hanging" on a tree (Acts 10:39; cf. 1 Pet 2:24), and this idea underlies Paul's reference to Christ crucified as a "curse." In citing Deut 21:23, Paul delicately omits "by God," and so clearly excludes the suggestion offered by later commentators that Christ was cursed by the Father. Paul's image is bold; even though it offers only "a remote and material analogy" (Lyonnet) with a corpse suspended after death, it should not be watered down. The verse must be understood in connection with 2:19: Christ was crucified "through the law." In dying as one on whom a curse of the law fell, Paul sees Christ embodying the totality of the law's curse "for us" (just how he does not say!). Christ died to the law, and in his death we died vicariously (2 Cor 5:14). **14.** *we might receive the promised Spirit:* Promised not to Abraham, but to the people of Israel through the prophets (Ezek 36:26; 37:14; 39:29; Joel 2:28).

24   15. Another midrashic development of the Abraham story (3:15–26). *no one can annul or alter a man's will:* Only the testator can do so, by cancellation or a codicil, but no one else. A fortiori, God's will, made manifest in his promises and covenant, cannot be altered by the law, which came in later and was administered by angels (3:19). Paul plays on the meaning of *diathēkē,* which in Hellenistic Greek meant a "last will and testament." The LXX translators had used it (instead of *synthēkē,* "treaty") to express Hebr *běrît,* "covenant," probably because it characterized more closely the kind of covenant that God had made with Israel, in which, as in a vassal treaty, stipulations were set by the overlord that Israel was expected to obey. Paul begins his discussion by using *diathēkē* in the Hellenistic sense, but he gradually shifts to the LXX sense (3:17). **16.** *to Abraham and his lineage:* Lit., "his seed" (coll. sg.). Cf. Gen 15:18; 17:7–8; 22:16–18. In Hebrew the pl. of *zera‘* is not used to designate human descendants, but in Greek the pl. *spermata* is so used. Paul, therefore, plays on the difference and interprets the Hebr sg. *zera‘* as a reference to the historical Christ. This verse interrupts the argument begun in 3:15, but it is preparing for 3:19b, insinuating that the covenant promises are the real basis of the relation of human beings with God. **17.** *four hundred and thirty years later:* The time given in Exod 12:40–41 (MT) for Israel's sojourn in Egypt. The LXX gives the same time span for Israel's sojourn in both Egypt and Canaan; but cf. Gen 15:13; Acts 7:6. Actually, the calculation may be inaccurate by some 200 years (→ Exodus, 3:24), but this does not affect Paul's argument. The unilateral disposition (*diathēkē*) made to Abraham was not altered by subsequent obligations imposed in the Mosaic law. The Judaizer's contention is thus rejected that the covenant promises were subsequently made conditional to the performance of "deeds of the law." **18.** *if the inheritance [of the promise] depends on the law:* It would become a bilateral affair, destroying the very notion of a promise. In the LXX *klēronomia* is the term par excellence for the "inheritance" of the land of Canaan; here it denotes rather the blessings promised to Abraham in general. **19.** *added to produce transgressions:* Lit., "for the sake of transgressions." Some ancient commentators tried to interpret this phrase to mean "to curtail transgressions," but its sense is clear from Rom 4:15; 5:13-14,20; 7:7-13. A law is made to stop crimes, but not to stop transgressions of a legal prescription, which can only begin with the law. *until the descendant came:* The law was a temporary measure used by God; see 3:24-25. *enacted through angels:* An echo of a contemporary Jewish belief that angels, not Yahweh himself, gave the law to Moses (see Deut 33:23 LXX; Josephus, *Ant.* 15.5.3 §136; *Jub.* 1:27-29; Acts 7:53; Heb 2:2). Not only was the law an interim measure, but its mode of promulgation reveals its inferiority, when it is compared with promises made directly by God. *through an intermediary:* Moses; see the vague allusions in Lev 26:46; Deut 5:4-5. This is the most likely interpretation of a highly disputed phrase (see A. Vanhoye, *Bib* 59 [1978] 403-11 for another interpretation). **20.** *an intermediary is not needed for one party:* As a principle, this is not necessarily true because an individual can use an agent, but Paul thinks of the angel promulgators as a plurality and as dealing with Israel, another plurality. So they needed a mediator. Thus the law is inferior to the covenant promises, which Yahweh made directly without a mediator (see J. Bligh, *TS* 23 [1962] 98). **21.** *which could bestow life:* Paul's view of the basic deficiency of the law: it tells people what they must do, but cannot "give life"; see 3:11; Rom 8:3. **22.** *Scripture:* Esp. the law and the texts quoted in Rom 3:10-18. *has imprisoned all in sin:* Rom 11:32 would suggest that "all" refers to human beings, but *panta,* being neut., may refer to the wider effects on all creation of the state in which people existed before Christ (cf. Rom 8:19-23). **23.** *in view of the coming revelation of faith:* The reign of law was divinely ordained to prepare for the reign of Christian freedom (see 4:3). **24.** *our custodian:* Lit., "boy-leader," "disciplinarian," a slave charged to lead a boy to and from school and to watch over his studies and conduct while he was still a minor. The termination of such discipline came with Christ, the "end of the law" (Rom 10:4). Freedom from such discipline came with righteousness through faith in Christ. **26.** *sons of God:* Filial adoption is the new relation of Christians to God, achieved "through Christ Jesus," or possibly "in union with" him. The phase *en Christō* does not depend on *pisteōs;* it does not mean "faith in Christ Jesus." The formula suggests rather the mode of union with Christ the Son as a result of faith and baptism (see A. Grail, *RB* 58 [1951] 506.

25 **(C) Proof 3: Experience of Christians in Baptism (3:27-29).** The experience that the Galatians have had in faith and baptism supports Paul's contention. **27.** *baptized into union with Christ:* Baptism is the sacramental complement of faith, the rite whereby a person achieves union with Christ and publicly manifests his commitment. For the prep. *eis* expressing an initial movement of incorporation, → Pauline Theology, 82:119. *put on Christ:* As a garment. Paul either borrows a figure from Gk mystery religions, in which the initiate identified himself with the god by donning his robes (see BAGD 264), or uses an OT expression for the adoption

of another's moral dispositions or outlook (Job 29:14; 2 Chr 6:41). As Paul uses it in Rom 13:14, it seems to have the latter nuance (see V. Dellagiacoma, *RivB* 4 [1956] 114-42). **28.** *you are all one:* Secondary differences vanish through the effect of this primary incorporation of Christians into Christ's body through "one Spirit" (1 Cor 12:13); see further M. Boucher, *CBQ* 31 (1969) 50-58; J. J. Davis, *JETS* 19 (1976) 201-8. Such unity in Christ does not imply *political* equality in church or society.

26 **(D) Proof 4: Experience of Christians as Children of God (4:1-11).** This section contains a further scriptural defense of Paul's gospel, another midrashic development of the Abraham story. To become an heir to the promises made to Abraham, performance of the "deeds of the law" is not required, but rather faith, which makes one his offspring in the real sense. This is illustrated by Hellenistic and Palestinian legal customs of inheritance. **1.** *a child:* Paul uses *nēpios,* "infant," i.e., one who does not speak; in its minority it does not speak for itself. **2.** *under guardians and managers:* A comparison of the status of human beings with that of a freeborn, orphaned son explains the interim character of the law. Paul is not thinking of Roman law, but of Palestinian usage. The father would have appointed an *epitropos,* "guardian," who handled the child's possessions in his interest (see S. Belkin, *JBL* 54 [1935] 52-55; cf. J. D. Hester, in *Oikonomia* [Fest. O. Cullmann; Hamburg, 1967] 118-25). Outwardly and for a time, the minor son was not free. **3.** *spirit-elements of the world:* The meaning of *stoicheia tou kosmou* (4:9; Col 2:8,20) is quite disputed: *stoicheia* could mean "elements," "rudiments" (of learning, as in Heb 5:12); or "elemental substances" (earth, air, fire, water); or "elemental signs" (of the zodiac); or "spirit-elements" (celestial beings controlling the physical elements of the world; cf. Rev 16:5). In the first instance, it would connote "slaves to rudimentary ways of thought and conduct." But opinion today seems to favor the last meaning, "slaves to the spirit-elements" (see Betz, *Galatians* 204-5), since they seem to be envisaged as personal beings parallel to the "guardians and trustees" and are described as "by nature not gods" (4:8). **4.** *fullness of time:* From the "date set" by the parent (4:2), Paul widens the application of his comparison to the point in history when God's salvific intervention took place. Human freedom came with Christ. *God sent forth his Son:* The vb. *(ex)apostellein* developed in the early church a specific religious meaning: to send someone in the service of the kingdom with authority fully grounded in God (see *TDNT* 1. 406). The "sending" is functional; the mission of the Son is expressed in the purpose cl. Nothing is said explicitly about the Son's preexistence, which is at most implied (→ Pauline Theology, 82:49-50). *born of a woman:* The ptc. *genomenon* is aor., emphasizing the assumption of human condition for the mission. The phrase is derived from the OT (Job 14:1; 15:14; 25:4; cf. 1QH 13:14). So born, Jesus submitted to the law by being circumcised and thus became capable of falling under its curse. But lest the Galatians draw a wrong conclusion, Paul does not mention Jesus' circumcision. Instead of *genomenon,* "born," some patristic writers read *gennōmenon,* and understood this ptc. as referring to Mary's virginal conception; but this is anachronistic interpretation (see *MNT* 37-38, 42). **6.** *the proof that you are sons:* The conj. *hoti* can mean "because," and then adoptive sonship would be the basis for the gratuitous sending of the Spirit. However, Rom 8:14-17 seems to suggest that the gift of the Spirit constitutes Christian sonship; hence, many commentators prefer that sense here too, "the fact that" (cf. S. Zedda, *L'adozione a Figlio di Dio* [Rome, 1952]). *the Spirit of his Son:* The

Spirit is also the object of a mission from the Father (*ho theos*); elsewhere it is the gift of the risen *Kyrios*. (For the pertinence of this phrase to Paul's lack of a clear distinction between Son and Spirit, → Pauline Theology, 82:61–64.) *Abba, Father:* The vivifying Spirit of the risen Son is the dynamic principle of adoptive sonship (see Rom 1:3; 8:15–17). It empowers the Christian's inmost conviction, as one exclaims of God, "Father!" Without the Spirit the Christian would never be able to utter this cry. The Aram emph. *'abbā'*, lit., "the father," was used as a voc.; when the word was taken up in Gk communities, its literal Gk equivalent, *ho patēr*, was added, and the combination became a liturgical formula (see J. A. Fitzmyer, "*Abba* and Jesus' Relation to God," *A cause de l'évangile* [Fest. J. Dupont; ed. R. Gantoy; LD 123; Paris, 1985] 57–81). **7.** *no longer a slave:* The Christian is free of the law. *through God:* Inferior mss. read "through Christ" or "an heir of God through Christ." **8.** *in your ignorance of God:* The Galatians' pagan background is recalled (cf. 5:2–3; 6:12–13). Like the Jews before Christ's coming, the pagans were also enslaved, but to idols (1 Thess 4:5; 1 Cor 12:2). **9.** *known by him:* Cf. 1 Cor 8:3. The Galatians' knowledge of God did not spring merely from within them; it is the result of divine predilection (an OT idea, see Gen 18:19; Amos 3:2; Jer 1:5; Ps 139). *how can you return?:* To adopt Jewish practices is not outright paganism, but regard for such material practices, subjecting the practitioners to the angels of the law (3:19), would be a reversion to reverence for the spirit-elements. **10.** *you keep (special) days, months, seasons, and years:* Days like the sabbath and *Yôm hakkippûrîm* are meant; months like the "new moon"; seasons like Passover and Pentecost; years like the sabbatical years (Lev 25:5). Such observances would be the material practices of 4:9; Paul can see no reason for a Gentile Christian to observe these.

27   (E) Proof 5: Experience of Galatians in Their Relation to Paul (4:12–20). **12.** *I have become like you:* Freed from enslavement to the law, and hence "law-less" (1 Cor 9:21), Paul began to preach to Gentiles. He now appeals to the Galatians directly (vv 12–20), as one who saw fit to abandon it all: "Be imitators of me, as I am of Christ" (1 Cor 11:1; cf. D. M. Stanley, *Bib* 40 [1959] 859–77). **13.** *physical illness:* Paul's first evangelization of the Galatians was occasioned by some (unknown) affiction (BDF 223.3). *the first time:* The phrase *to proteron* may imply that more than one visit to Galatia preceded the writing of this letter (see Heb 4:6; *Herm. Vis.* 3.12.1; *Sim.* 9.1.3; cf. BAGD 722). **14.** *what might have been a trial for you:* An allusion to some repulsive physical ailment? Paul never explains it further (cf. 2 Cor 12:7). *an angel of God:* Paul uses *angelos* not in the sense of "messenger" but of "angel" (1:8; 3:19; 1 Cor 4:9; 11:10; 13:1). This instance is surprising in view of his attitude toward angels elsewhere in Gal. **15.** *would have torn out your eyes:* Though this might suggest that Paul was suffering from an eye ailment, the hyperbole is obvious: they would have given him what was most precious to them. **16.** *telling you the truth:* The Galatians were once overjoyed at his evangelization; now Paul fears that this letter, in which he warns them of the Judaizing danger, will alienate them. **17.** *want to shut you out:* Of the Christian community, by preaching to you "another gospel." Their aim is that you regard them as authorities and masters. **19.** *I am in labor again until Christ be formed in you:* The reshaping of Christians after the form or model of Christ is the goal of Paul's missionary endeavors. His concern for his spiritual "children" springs from an almost maternal instinct; cf. 1 Thess 2:7–8; 1 Cor 3:2.

28   (F) Proof 6: The Allegory of Sarah and Hagar (4:21–31). Perhaps the use of the metaphor of a mother suggested to Paul another midrashic development of the Abraham story, an allegory on Sarah, the mother of the true heir, Isaac. **22.** *Abraham had two sons:* Ishmael, born to Hagar, the Egyptian slave girl (Gen 16:1–6); Isaac, born to his wife Sarah (Gen 21:2–5). Paul ignores Abraham's children by Keturah (Gen 25:2). **23.** *in the normal course of nature:* Gen 16:4,15. *through the promise:* Not the generic one made to Abraham (Gen 12:2), but the special one in Gen 15:4; 17:16–21. God's intervention, consequent on the promise, brought Isaac to life. **24.** *are meant allegorically:* Paul tells his readers that the historic figures of the Gen story have for him a deeper significance (on *allēgorein*, see *TDNT* 1. 260–63; *NIDNTT* 2. 754–56). *the women represent two covenants:* Hagar represents the Sinai covenant, and Sarah represents the one made with Abraham. Jews and Judaizers may take pride in the Sinai pact; for Paul it "enslaved" the children born of Abraham "according to the flesh" — like Hagar's offspring, born into slavery. Christians boast of the real covenant made by God with Abraham, for they are sons of Abraham "according to the promise" — like Sarah's offspring, "law-less" and free. **25.** *now Hagar is Mt. Sinai in Arabia:* This is the *lectio difficilior*, preferred by N-A[26]. But the oldest ms. of the Pauline letters (P[46]) and several others read: "for Sinai is a mountain in Arabia." In either case, wishing to emphasize that the slavery the law introduced was the condition of the rejected son of Abraham, Paul identifies Hagar with the Sinai pact and the "present Jerusalem." Verse 25a is a geographical detail that explains how Hagar, though connected with a holy place outside of the promised land, is yet equated with the "present Jerusalem." Geographically, Hagar represents a place in Arabia, but even so she stands for enslavement and corresponds to Jerusalem. But why does Paul mention Arabia at all? Possibly because Mt. Sinai is in Arabia, which is Ishmaelite territory; he thus associates the Sinai pact with the eponymous patriarch of Arab tribes (see Gen 25:12–18). Paul thus suggests that the law itself stems from a situation extrinsic to the promised land and to the real descendants of Abraham. Paul's Jewish former co-religionists would not have been happy with this allegory. *corresponds to the present Jerusalem:* The earthly Jerusalem was for the Jews what Sinai once was, the place whence "the word of the Lord" goes forth (Isa 2:3; Mic 4:2). **26.** *the Jerusalem above:* The "heavenly" Jerusalem (Rev 3:12; 21:2; cf. Ezek 40; Zech 2; Hag 2:6–9) is implicitly identified with Sarah and her offspring, the freeborn children of Abraham. **27.** *it stands written:* Lit., "it has been written," a common introductory formula; see J. A. Fitzmyer, *ESBNT* 9. Isa 54:1 is quoted from the LXX (close to the MT). The prophet's words are addressed to deserted Zion, bidding it rejoice at the return of the exiles. Paul applies Isaiah's words to the allegorized Sarah, to "Jerusalem above." **29.** In Gen 21:10 Sarah, seeing Ishmael "playing" with Isaac and viewing him as the potential rival to Isaac's inheritance, drives him and his mother out. Nothing in Gen is said of Ishmael's "persecution" of Isaac, but Paul may be interpreting the "playing" as did a Palestinian haggadic explanation of Gen 21:9 (see Josephus, *Ant.* 1.12.3 §215; Str-B 3. 575–76). **30.** *"cast out the slave girl":* Paul quotes Sarah's words (Gen 21:10), as if they were God's. Accommodating the text, Paul bids the Galatians rid themselves of the Judaizers — and, ironically enough, obey the Torah itself. **31.** *children of the free woman:* Thus the OT itself supports Paul's thesis that in Christ God's new freedom reigns. To adopt the practices of the

Judaizers is to forfeit this Christian freedom. Cf. M. McNamara, *MStud* 2 (1978) 24–41.

29   (V) *Exhortatio*: Hortatory Section (5:1–6:10). From the foregoing exposé Paul draws certain practical conclusions. This section has three parts.

(A) Counsel: Preserve the Freedom That You Have in Christ (5:1–12). 1. *for freedom Christ has set us free:* The emphatic position of the dat. of purpose (*eleutheriā*) sums up the doctrinal section of the letter: not license, but freedom from the law and its material observances. **2.** *Christ can do nothing for you:* Cf. 2:21. The Galatians must choose one or the other: Christ and freedom, or the law and slavery. **3.** *the whole law:* The Judaizers insisted on the adoption of certain Jewish customs (→ 7 above), but Paul warns: If you accept the "sign" of a Jew, you oblige yourselves to the whole way of life (cf. Jas 2:10). This is not to walk according to the truth of the gospel (2:14). **5.** *the hope of righteousness:* The full measure of human righteousness is still a thing of the eschatological future (cf. Rom 5:19). *Elpis* is a "thing hoped for," and *dikaiosynēs* is an epexegetical gen. (*ZBG* §46). **6.** *neither circumcision nor the lack of it matters:* Lit., "neither circumcision nor the foreskin." One might retort, "Then why oppose circumcision?" Paul's words have to be understood in the light of 5:2 (cf. 3:28). *only faith active in love:* The principle of righteousness is faith working through love after the fashion of Christ himself (2:20; Rom 5:5–8; → Pauline Theology, 82:111). In NT Greek, *energein* with an impersonal subj. occurs always in the middle voice, hence "faith working (expressing) itself through love" (BAGD 265; cf. BDF 316.1) **7.** *running well:* Paul often compares Christian effort to that of a runner in a race (2:2; 1 Cor 9:24–26). But the Judaizers have been getting in the way. To follow their advice is to ignore God's call (see 1:6). **9.** *a little leaven:* A proverb (cf. 1 Cor 5:6) stresses the power of the Judaizing influence to spread. **11.** *still advocating circumcision:* The Judaizers may have claimed that Paul himself admitted the validity of circumcision, when it suited his purpose (1 Cor 9:20). Paul answers: If he were still of that mind he would not be opposed by the Judaizers (cf. 2:3). *the stumbling block of the cross:* The preaching of the cross has made circumcision unnecessary, even if it has become a stumbling block to Jews (cf. 1 Cor 1:23, for another reason; Phil 3:18). **12.** *would that they would castrate themselves:* Paul's sarcasm (cf. Phil 3:2) may allude to the ritual emasculation of the *galloi*, priests of Cybele-Attis, undoubtedly known to the Galatians.

30   (B) Warning: Walk Not according to the Flesh, but according to the Spirit (5:13–26). Paul's admonition illustrates the love of which he spoke in 5:6. **13.** *an incentive for the flesh:* Supply *poieite*, "Do not make freedom an incentive." If the law is done away with, Christians may not abandon themselves to earthly, material, Godless conduct. Their freedom must rather be one of service of love, a freedom for others. **14.** *the whole law:* See Lev 19:18. Is Paul thinking directly of Lev, of a well-known Jewish summary (see Str-B 1. 907–8), or of Jesus' summary (Matt 7:12)? Whatever the answer, neither here nor in Rom 13:8–10 does Paul include the love of God. In Lev the "neighbor" is a fellow Israelite; for Paul "there is no distinction between Jew and Greek" (Rom 10:12). **16.** *live by the Spirit:* Lit., "walk by," in the Semitic sense: "conduct oneself." The Spirit, as the principle of Christian sonship, is also the principle of Christian activity (5:18; cf. Rom 8:14). **17.** *you do not do:* The Christian in union with Christ and endowed with the Spirit still struggles with the "flesh" (→ Pauline Theology, 82:103), the symbol of all human opposition to God. See Rom 7:15–23. **18.** *guided by the Spirit:* Under the influence of the indwelling Spirit, the Christian has an

interior principle to counteract the "flesh" and is no longer merely confronted with the extrinsic norm of the law. **19–21.** A catalogue of vices (→ Pauline Theology, 82:142). **22–23.** A catalogue of virtues (cf. 2 Cor 6:6–7). Note how Paul speaks of the "deeds" (*erga*) of the flesh, but of the "fruit" (*karpos*) of the Spirit; "fruit" can be applied to the flesh, but never "deeds" to the Spirit (cf. Rom 6:21; 7:5). This catalogue shows that "good deeds" are important in Christian life. *against such there is no law:* There is no need to enact a law against such "fruits," for the law was "added because of transgressions" (3:19). **24.** *have crucified the flesh:* The Christian, crucified with Christ (2:19) in faith and baptism, has died not only to the law but also to the *sarx*-self, to its earthbound, degrading tendencies (6:14). Paul speaks on the ontological level, i.e., the basic reorientation of a Christian to God, and not merely of psychological awareness. That is why one must continue to "mortify the ways of the body" (cf. Rom 6:6; 8:9,13).

31   (C) Advice: The Right Way to Use Christian Freedom (6:1–10). 1. *you who are spiritual:* Mature Christians are addressed, those guided by the Spirit (1 Cor 3:1); they are to correct the one "detected in some sin." **2.** *the law of Christ:* On the figurative use of *nomos*, → Pauline Theology, 82:90.2. Freed of obligation to the Mosaic law, the Christian becomes *ennomos Christou*, "under the law of Christ" (1 Cor 9:21). The "law of Christ" is the "law of the Spirit of life" (Rom 8:2). In this context it is specified as the law of love, as Christians must bear the burdens of one another in fraternal correction. **3.** *thinks he is somebody:* Either because he believes he is without sin or because he is charitable enough to correct an erring Christian. **5.** *own load:* Not to be confused with the "burdens" of 6:2, this "load" is probably to be understood of ordinary responsibilities of daily life. **6.** *share all good things:* A practical manifestation of love to be shown to the catechist of the community; cf. 1 Cor 9:11,14; Phil 4:15; Rom 15:27. **8.** *will reap eternal life:* This verse sums up 5:16–26. "Eternal life" is the equivalent here of "kingdom of God" (5:21). The former expression is characteristically Johannine, occurring only rarely in Paul (Rom 2:7; 5:21; 6:22–23).

32   *Postscriptio*: Paul's "Signature" and Résumé; Farewell Blessing (6:11–18). 11. *with my own hand:* Thus far the letter has been dictated to a scribe (→ NT Epistles, 45:20); now Paul himself adds the conclusion by way of his "signature." **12.** *not to be persecuted for Christ's cross:* The Judaizers fear that if they preach the real "message of the cross" (see note on 5:11) they might be persecuted for it by Jews or other Judaizers; they prefer to make a good showing before others by preaching circumcision. **13.** *not even the circumcised:* The pf. ptc. *peritetmēmenoi* seems to be the preferable reading (P[46], B, Koine text-tradition); other mss. read the pres. ptc., "those who are being circumcised." In this context it must refer to the Judaizers. *do not observe the law themselves:* Though the Judaizers insist on circumcision and other legal obligations, they do not observe the law in its entirety (hence Paul's warning in 5:3). **14.** *to boast in anything but the cross:* To the vanity (6:12) of the Judaizers Paul opposes his own boast: not self-reliance, but dependence on the grace and favor of God (cf. 1 Cor 3:31; 2 Cor 11:16–12:10). *cross:* The whole Christ-event (→ Pauline Theology, 82:67). *through which* (or *whom*) *the world has been crucified to me and I to the world:* Here *kosmos* denotes all that stands at enmity with God, the sphere of pleasure and ambition related to the flesh, in which the Judaizers find their boast. To all this Paul has died (2:19; 5:24), not by some interior psychological or mystical experience, but through the historic event of Calvary, which is the realization of the Father's plan of salvation for humanity. The pf. tense expresses the condition in which Paul finds himself through his share in the Christ-event by faith and baptism (Rom 6:3–11). **15.** *circumcision means nothing:* An echo of 5:6; cf. 1 Cor 7:18–19. *but a new creation:* This new ontological reshaping of human existence comes not through some extrinsic norm of conduct, but through an energizing principle that re-creates life (see 1 Cor 15:45; → Pauline Theology, 82:79). The word *ktisis* has the active sense of "creation" only in Rom 1:20; here and elsewhere the stress is rather on "creation" as the "created thing" (cf. 1 Cor 7:19; 15:47–49; Rom 6:3–4). **16.** *the Israel of God:* The Christian people of God, as the new "offspring of Abraham" (3:29; cf. Phil 3:3; Rom 9:6), in contrast to "Israel according to the flesh" (1 Cor 10:18). Thus Paul modifies

the last words of Ps 125:5 or 128:6, "Peace be upon Israel." **17.** *the marks of Jesus:* The Gk *stigmata* did not mean what this word often means in English today. Paul had suffered so much from illness (4:13; 2 Cor 12:7), floggings (2 Cor 11:25), "beasts" (1 Cor 15:32), and "affliction" (2 Cor 1:8) for Christ's sake that he could speak of the evidence of such suffering as "brands" marking him forever as "the slave of Christ Jesus" (Gal 1:10; cf. Rom 1:1). In antiquity *stigmata* often designated the branding used to mark a slave or an animal as someone's possession. Of such "marks" in his flesh Paul would gladly boast to those who try to glory in a different mark in the flesh (circumcision). **18.** Cf. Phil 4:23; Phlm 25. *brothers:* → 7 above (end).

48

THE LETTER
TO THE PHILIPPIANS

Brendan Byrne, S.J.

BIBLIOGRAPHY

1 Barth, G., *Der Brief an die Philipper* (ZBK NT 9; Zurich, 1979). Barth, K., *The Epistle to the Philippians* (London, 1962). Beare, F. W., *A Commentary on the Epistle to the Philippians* (BNTC; London, 1959). Bonnard, P., *L'épître de Saint Paul aux Philippiens* (CNT 10; Neuchâtel, 1950). Caird, G. B., *Paul's Letters from Prison* (Oxford, 1976). Collange, J.-F., *The Epistle of Saint Paul to the Philippians* (London, 1979). Dibelius, M., *An die Thessalonicher I,II; an die Philipper* (HNT 11; 3d ed.; Tübingen, 1937). Friedrich, G., *Der Brief an die Philipper* (NTD 8; 9th ed.; Göttingen, 1962). Getty, M. A., *Philippians and Philemon* (NTM 14; Wilmington, 1980). Gnilka, J., *Der Philipperbrief* (HTKNT 10/3; 3d ed.; Freiburg, 1980). Houlden, J. L., *Paul's Letters from*

Prison (Harmondsworth, 1970). Lohmeyer, E., *Der Brief an die Philipper* (MeyerK 9/1; 14th ed. [W. Schmauch]; Göttingen, 1974). Martin, R. P., *Philippians* (NCB; GR, 1980). Mengel, B., *Studien zum Philipperbrief* (Tübingen, 1982). Michael, J. H., *The Epistle of Paul to the Philippians* (MNTC; 5th ed.; NY, 1928; repr. 1954). Pesch, R., *Paulus und seine Lieblingsgemeinde* (Freiburg, 1985). Schenk, W., *Die Philipperbriefe des Paulus* (Stuttgart, 1984). Vincent, M. R., *The Epistles to the Philippians and Philemon* (ICC; 3d ed.; Edinburgh, 1897; repr.1922).

DBSup 7. 1211–33. *IDBSup* 665–66. Kümmel, *INT* 320–35. Wik-Schm, *ENT* 496–507.

INTRODUCTION

2 (I) Philippi: the City and the Christian Community. In the time of Paul, Philippi was a leading town in the Roman province of Macedonia, situated in the plain E of Mt. Pangaeus on the Via Egnatia (linking the Adriatic with the Aegean). Founded in 358–357 BC by Philip II of Macedon, it came under Roman rule in 167 BC and won fame as the site of M. Antony's defeat of Brutus and Cassius in 31 BC. In due course veterans of Roman armies were settled at Philippi, and the city, now made up of Romans and Macedonians, received the prized status of a Roman *colonia,* enjoying thereby the *ius italicum*—a dignity noted in Acts 16:12 and important for the understanding of Phil. In Philippi Paul began the European phase of his missionary work (*ca.* AD 50 on Mission II; → Paul, 79:39). Acts 16:11–40 describes, with some legendary embellishments, the foundation of the church. Since the city lacked a Jewish synagogue, Paul began his preaching at a "prayer-place" by the river Crenides. His exorcism of a slave girl led to his being arrested, flogged, and imprisoned. An earthquake during the night gave Paul an opportunity to escape. Instead, he publicly vindicated his cause by revealing his Roman citizenship. Women seem to have played a leading role in the community from the start (notably Lydia [Acts 16:14–15, 40]; Euodia and Syntyche [Phil 4:2–3]). Personal names appearing in Phil suggest that the community makeup was predominantly Gentile.

(Collart, P., *Philippes, ville de Macédoine* [Paris, 1937]. Davies, P. E., "The Macedonian Scene of Paul's Journeys," *BA* 26 [1963] 91–106. Lemerle, P., *Philippes et la Macédoine orientale à l'époque chrétienne et byzantine* [2 vols.; Paris, 1945].)

3 (II) Authenticity. The Pauline authorship of Phil, contested by the Tübingen School (19th cent.), is not in question today.

4 (III) Unity. There is today a widespread, though far from unanimous, view that Phil represents a conflation of two or three originally separate letters. The 2d-cent. writer Polycarp does indeed mention "letters" which Paul wrote to the Philippians—though this use of the pl. is not conclusive (*Phil.* 3:2). More suasive is the internal evidence. (1) Following what seems to be a typical conclusion to a Pauline letter, a sharp change in tone and content occurs at 3:2, where Paul begins a polemical passage warning against a set of adversaries as yet unmentioned. (2) After a similar conclusion in 4:2–9, Paul seems to make a fresh start at 4:10, acknowledging at length the Philippians' gift. (3) The injunction to "rejoice" in 4:4 flows very naturally from the similar theme in 3:1. A typical division may be set out as follows: *Letter A:* 4:10–20 (a letter acknowledging a gift); *Letter B:* 1:1–3:1a; 4:4–7,21–23 (a letter urging unity and joy); *Letter C:* 3:1b–4:3,8–9 (the body of a polemical letter). Defenders of the unity of Phil point out the considerable links in language, ideas, and formal construction across the supposed parts and also the difficulty of accounting for the process of compilation; but the sharp break at 3:2 remains a grave obstacle.

(Garland, D. E., "The Composition and Unity of Philippians," *NovT* 27 [1985] 141–73 [extensive bibliography]. Mengel, B., *Studien zum Philipperbrief* [Tübingen, 1982]. Rahtjen, B. D., "The Three Letters of Paul to the Philippians," *NTS* 6 [1959–60] 167–73.)

5   (IV) The Philippian Letters in the Setting of Paul's Life.   At least two of the letters contained in Phil (A and B) presuppose that Paul is in prison. Traditionally, this imprisonment has been identified with the "house arrest" in Rome mentioned at the close of Acts (28:16–30). References to the *praetorium* (1:13) and "Caesar's household" (4:22) seem to confirm this. Though the Roman origin of Phil has had its defenders in recent years (F. W. Beare; C. O. Buchanan; G. B. Caird; L. Cerfaux; C. H. Dodd), this view is largely rejected today. (1) The doctrinal affinities of Phil seem to lie with letters stemming from an earlier stage of Paul's life such as Rom and 1–2 Cor. (2) Phil presupposes an ease of communication between Philippi and the place of writing inconsistent with the distance between Macedonia and Rome. (3) Paul's confinement as reflected in Phil seems more restrictive than the "house arrest" of Acts 28. (4) Letters A and B suggest that Paul has not revisited Philippi, whereas Acts 20:1–6 records two subsequent visits prior to the journey as a captive to Rome. (5) In Phil 1:26 and 2:24 Paul hopes to revisit Philippi, whereas the plan outlined, prior to the Roman imprisonment, in Rom 15:23–28 suggests that he considers his work in the E to be finished.

6   As alternatives to Rome as the place of imprisonment Caesarea and Corinth have been proposed, but most modern scholars assign the imprisonment to the apostle's lengthy stay in Ephesus in the course of Mission III (Acts 19:1–20:1; → Paul, 79:40). (1) We have no explicit Pauline record of an Ephesian confinement, but he recalls multiple imprisonments (2 Cor 11:23) and speaks (doubtless metaphorically) of having "fought with beasts in Ephesus" (1 Cor 15:30–32; cf. 2 Cor 1:8–10). (2) Inscriptions at Ephesus mention *praetoriani* and also a "guild" of civil servants making up the *familia Caesaris*. (3) Philippi lay within easy reach of Ephesus.

7   (V) The Purpose and Occasion of the Letters to Philippi. *Letter A*, Phil 4:10–20: The Philippians had sent money to Paul in prison via one of their number, Epaphroditus. Phil 4:10–20 represents Paul's immediate acknowledgment of this gift.

8   *Letter B,* Phil 1:1–3:1a; 4:4–7,21–23: This letter followed some weeks after Letter A. Epaphroditus had fallen ill, but was now recovered and anxious to return to Philippi. Paul composes a more extended response to what he has heard about the situation in Philippi. The Philippians are experiencing considerable antagonism from their fellow citizens (1:28–30). Paul sees their capacity to withstand gravely weakened by internal divisions, caused by self-seeking and pride.

With great love he urges them to close ranks and find a deeper unity through unselfishness. At the same time, reflecting upon his own fate, he evolves for their comfort a mystique of suffering in behalf of the gospel: as they share in his suffering they should share also in the joy emanating from the deeper union with Christ that such suffering brings. The letter revolves around the idea of *koinōnia,* "common participation": *koinōnia* in suffering intensifies the union between apostle and community; at the same time, the basic *koinōnia* in Christ should shape and determine their mutual relationships.

9   *Letter C,* 3:1b–4:3,8–9: This polemical warning seems to stem from a period after Paul's release from prison and to follow the visit to Philippi proposed in 2:24 (cf. 1:26; Acts 20:1–2). Paul sees a grave threat to the community posed by itinerant Christian missionaries of a Judaizing stamp. So he writes (possibly from Corinth: cf. Acts 20:2–6; Rom 15:24–26) to counter this danger, building his case upon his own discovery of what conversion to Christ means and wherein true "perfection" lies.

10   (VI) Date. On the schema outlined above, Letters A and B would date from the closing period of Paul's stay in Ephesus (AD 54–57) with Letter C following some months later (AD 57–58).

(Buchanan, C. O., "Epaphroditus' Sickness and the Letter to the Philippians," *EvQ* 36 [1964] 157–66. Duncan, G. S., "Were St. Paul's Imprisonment Epistles Written from Ephesus?," *ExpTim* 67 [1955–56] 163–66. Koester, H., "The Purpose of the Polemic of a Pauline Fragment (Phil III)," *NTS* 8 [1961–62] 317–32. Pesch, R., *Paulus.* Schmithals, W., in *Paul and the Gnostics* [Nash, 1972] 65–122.)

11   (VII) Outline. The letter to the Philippians may be outlined as follows.

(I) Introduction (1:1–11) [L. B]

(A) Opening Formula—Address and Greeting (1:1–2)
(B) Thanksgiving (1:3–8)
(C) Prayer (1:9–11)

(II) Part I: News and Instructions (1:12–3:1a) [L. B]
(A) Paul's Own Situation (1:12–26)
(B) Exhortation for the Community (1:27–2:18)
   (a) Unity and Steadfastness (1:27–30)
   (b) Humility and Selflessness (2:1–11)
   (c) Obedience and Witness to the World (2:12–18)
(C) Announcements about Timothy and Epaphroditus (2:19–30)
(D) Conclusion (3:1a)

(III) Part II: Warning against False Teachers (3:1b–4:1) [L. C]

(IV) Part III: Exhortations to Unity, Joy, and Peace (4:2–9)
(A) Call to Unity (4:2–3) [L. C]
(B) Call to Joy and Peace of Mind (4:4–7) [L. B]
(C) Call to Imitation of Paul (4:8–9) [L. C]

(V) Part IV: Acknowledgment of Community's Gift (4:10–20) [L. A]

(VI) Conclusion (4:21–23) [L. B]

COMMENTARY

12   (I) Introduction (1:1–11).
(A) Opening Formula—Address and Greeting (1:1–2).   The introduction follows a pattern, familiar from epistolary convention in the ancient world, employed by Paul (with some modification) in all his

letters (→ NT Epistles, 45:8A). *Paul and Timothy:* Timothy is not a coauthor of the letter, but Paul includes him in the address so as to enhance the stature of one who is, according to 2:19–24, to be his accredited representative. *to all the saints in Christ Jesus in Philippi:* Christians are "saints" in that they make up "in Christ" God's holy people, the eschatological Israel. *the bishops and deacons:* Only in this letter does Paul single out a distinct group of officeholders, *episkopoi* and *diakonoi,* within the wider community — perhaps because they saw to the gift sent to him. Both terms had widespread secular usage in the Greek-speaking world, *episkopos* denoting oversight or administration (cf. the Qumran *mĕbaqqēr* [1QS 6:11,20; CD 14:8–11]), and *diakonos* having the sense of "minister" or "attendant." The *episkopoi* here correspond to the *presbyteroi,* "elders," of the post-Pauline churches (Acts 20:17,28; 1 Pet 5:1,2; Tit 1:5–9). The *diakonoi* may have seen to the relief of the poor, though Paul also regards preaching as a *diakonia.* While remote from the use of these terms in the later church, their mention here marks the dawn of permanent ministry.

13   (B) Thanksgiving (1:3–8). 3. *I thank my God:* Paul's thanksgiving follows a standard formula: → NT Epistles 45:8B. **4.** *with joy:* Joy is pervasive in Phil (1:18,25; 2:2,17,18,28,29; 3:1; 4:1,4,10). **5.** *your participation in the gospel:* The Philippians have had a share (*koinōnia;* see J. Hainz, *EWNT* 2. 749–55) in the gospel through their conversion, their support of Paul, and their own costly witness to the faith. **6.** *the day of Christ:* I.e., the "parousia," when, his task of "subduing" the world to God's glory (Phil 3:21) complete, Christ will appear in glory to hand over the kingdom to the Father (1 Cor 15:24–28). **7.** *in the defense and confirmation of the gospel:* Paul's coming trial will provide an occasion for the power of the gospel to be displayed. *you have been participants in my grace:* The transl. is difficult. Two points emerge: (1) Paul's being in chains is not an evil but a special grace, conformed to the mystery of the gospel, which displays its power in external weakness and suffering (2 Cor 4:7–15; 6:3–10). (2) The Philippians share in this grace not merely through their concern and tangible support for Paul but also because as a community they have similarly borne the cost of evangelization (1:29–30). **8.** *with the affection:* The Gk *splanchna* denotes the inward organs (heart, lungs, liver) seen as the seat of deepest emotion.

(C) Prayer (1:9–11). 10. *the day of Christ:* See comment on 1:6. **11.** *the fruit of righteousness:* Righteousness for Paul is the eschatological right-standing with God already granted to believers (Rom 5:1). Christian ethical life is entirely the fruit of this new relationship (→ Pauline Theology 82:68–70, 140).

14   (II) Part I: News and Instructions (1:12–3:1a).

(A) Paul's Own Situation (1:12–26). Presuming the community to be informed about the external details of his situation, Paul shares with them his deeper reactions and reflections. **12.** *to advance the gospel:* Far from being a hindrance, Paul's imprisonment has furthered the work of evangelization. *my chains have become manifest in Christ:* Paul's imprisonment has achieved notoriety, and this, through Christ's disposition, has served to advance the gospel. *throughout the praetorium:* As usually in the NT (Matt 27:27 par.; John 18:28,33; Acts 23:35), *praitōrion* refers to the precincts of the Roman governor's palace, where the guard was quartered and prisoners held. **14.** *have been emboldened to speak the word:* God's grace has emboldened others to fill the "vacuum" in the work of preaching created by the restriction of Paul. **15.** *Some:* Paul's quarrel in this short excursus (vv 15–18) is not with the content of the preaching but with the motives of some preachers. They seem to have taken advantage of his imprisonment in a calculating and insensitive way, perhaps regarding it as a disgrace. **17.** *add affliction:* They cause Paul mental distress over and above the burden of his physical constraint. **18.** *in this*

I rejoice: Zeal for the gospel converts Paul's personal hurt to joy.

15   19–26. Paul now turns to reflect upon what lies ahead for him. **19.** *to my salvation:* Paul echoes Job 13:16 LXX, identifying with both Job's plight and his hope. "Salvation" here does not mean acquittal at his coming trial but vindication at the eschatological tribunal, which, whatever the earthly verdict, will uphold his faithfulness in God's sight. *the support provided by the Spirit:* The Synoptic tradition also pledges the Spirit's aid to Christians arraigned before earthly tribunals (Mark 13:11; Matt 10:20; Luke 12:12). **20.** *Christ may be glorified:* The power of the risen Christ, operative through the Spirit, will be so effective as to demand public acknowledgment. *in my body: Sōma* here, as frequently in Paul, denotes not merely the physical body but the entire outward presentation of a person (→ Pauline Theology 82:102). The meaning here is "in my whole public appearance." *whether through life or death:* Paul confronts both the gravity and the uncertainty attaching to his trial. **21.** *to me life means Christ:* Through baptism Paul has died to his former life and lives now an existence entirely taken over by Christ (Gal 2:19–20; 3:27–28; Phil 3:7–11; Rom 6:3–11), one that transcends the barrier of physical death. *death means gain:* Death is gain, not — as in certain strands of Greek philosophy — in the sense of welcome release from bodily existence, but as intensifying the union with Christ, who has already passed through death to resurrection. Resurrection remains the ultimate goal (3:11,21). **22.** *productive toil:* Remaining alive provides further opportunity for preaching the gospel and reaping its fruits. **23.** *depart:* This means simply "die" — with no implication of the separation of the soul from the (burden of the) body. *be with Christ:* Paul seems to envisage here a "being with Christ" in some (disembodied) state prior to the general resurrection (cf. 2 Cor 5:2–4). Whether this represents a movement away from Jewish eschatology in the direction of Gk ideas is doubtful. (See F. W. Beare, *NTS* 17 [1970–71] 314–27. P. Siber, *Mit Christus Leben* [Zurich, 1971] 86–94). *a far better thing:* See comment on v 21. **24.** *is more necessary for your sake:* The pragmatic, but no less worthy, consideration of the demands of the apostolate overrides Paul's personal option for death. **25.** *I know:* The conviction about what is "more necessary" from a pastoral point of view turns into (despite 1:20) a confidence about survival. **26.** *my being with you once again:* Subsequent visits of Paul to Philippi are mentioned in Acts 20:1–6.

16   (B) Exhortation for the Community (1:27–2:18). Paul's interpretation of his own situation in the light of the gospel serves as prelude for the exhortation which now follows. The gospel makes similar demands on the Philippians.

(a) UNITY AND STEADFASTNESS (1:27–30). **27.** *let your communal pattern of life:* The Gk vb. *politeuesthai* carries its original specific sense of "discharge one's duty as a citizen" (E. C. Miller, *JSNT* 15 [1982] 86–96). Cf. the use of the cognate *politeuma,* "citizenship," in 3:20, also the civic status of Philippi (→ 2 above). *worthy of the gospel:* For Paul, Christian ethics flows from the status before God brought about through faith in the gospel. *stand firm in one spirit:* Paul appeals for the kind of steadiness that comes from closed ranks in a line of battle. *for the faith of the gospel:* To both defend and propagate the faith they have received. **28.** *your opponents:* Day-to-day harassment from non-Christian fellow citizens was probably involved rather than outright persecution. *an omen of destruction, but (a sign) of your salvation:* The united and unshakable front presented by the community signifies to the opponents that they are opposing a more-than-human force, God himself, a fact that presages at one and the same time their eschatological doom and the community's destiny to salvation. **29.** *to believe . . . also to suffer:* Commitment to Christ through faith leads inevitably to sharing the conflict in which he was engaged and so suffering at the hands of the as yet unreconciled world. Within the perspective of faith, such suffering leads not to bitterness but to a sense of being graced. **30.** *same struggle:* Paul's experience is paradigmatic for the community, since he and they share (*koinōnein*) the same suffering and the same grace.

17   (b) Humility and Selflessness (2:1–11). **1.** *if anything is meant by . . . :* Paul invokes a series of qualities which for him essentially characterize life "in Christ" and so should regulate community relations. *fellowship in the Spirit:* "Fellowship" between Christians rests on a common participation (*koinōnein*) in the eschatological gift of the Spirit (cf. 1 Cor 12:13; for *koinōnia*, see comment on 1:5; cf. also 1:7; 3:10; 4:13,15). **2.** *having the same . . . one mind:* The Gk *phronein* in Paul's usage goes beyond rational reflection to include the "mindset" that issues in a determined pattern of behavior. **3.** *humility:* In the Greco-Roman world *tapeinophrosynē*, "lowliness," denoted simply a despised and abject condition, in the OT an appropriate human stance before God. In Christianity (with some foreshadowing at Qumran: 1QS 5:3–4) the free adopting of a lowly, unassertive stance before fellow human beings became a distinctive virtue, after the pattern established by Christ (vv 5–11). **4.** *not looking to one's own interest:* For Paul, Christian love flows from the free disposition to unseat concern for self as the driving force of life and replace it with a practical concern for others (cf. 1 Cor 13:5). **5.** *have this mind among you:* See comment on v 2. *which was also in Christ Jesus:* On this interpretation the terse relative clause introduces Christ's historic example of humility and selfless love, recounted in the passage to follow, as a model for Christian imitation; cf. 2 Cor 8:9; Rom 15:1–8; 1 Cor 11:1. But "in Christ Jesus" may have the technical Pauline sense denoting the sphere of influence emanating from the risen Lord in which Christian life is lived out (→ Pauline Theology, 82:121). So one would translate (supplying some form of the verb *phronein*): "which it is also appropriate for you to have in view of your existence in Christ Jesus."

18   The Christ-Hymn (vv 6–11). The distinctive qualities of this passage—rhythmic character, use of parallelism (as in OT psalms and poetry), occurrence of rare and uncharacteristic language—have led, since E. Lohmeyer's foundational study (*Kyrios Jesus: Eine Untersuchung zu Phil. 2.5–11* [SHAW Phil.-hist. Kl. 1927–

28/4; 2d ed.; 1961]), to the widespread view that Paul supports his exhortation to selflessness by quoting a hymn composed independently of Phil (possibly originally in Aramaic: see P. Grelot, *Bib* 54 [1973] 176–86). The hymn has a basic twofold structure: vv 6–8 describe Christ's abasement; vv 9–11 his exaltation. Beyond this fundamental division scholars offer a great variety of more detailed analyses. The one below adheres closely to that of Lohmeyer. It sees the original hymn as composed of six strophes, each containing three cola and each summing up one complete stage of the drama. Strophes 1–3 (vv 6–8) are each built around one main vb., qualified by participial phrases. In strophes 4–6 (vv 9–11) the verbal pattern alters to express the goal or consequence of the divine action.

19   **6.** *his condition was divine:* Lit., "being in the form (*morphē*) of God." *Morphē* denotes the mode of being or appearance from which the essential character or status of something can be known. What is said here of Christ is that he enjoyed a Godlike way of being. *En morphē theou* recalls the description of human dignity in the creation account of Gen 1:26–27 (cf. 2:15), but the LXX wording, *kat' eikona theou*, is different. *being like God:* The Gk wording (adv. *isa* rather than *ison*) indicates, again, likeness to God rather than strict equality. In the Jewish tradition, being like God meant immunity to death (Wis 2:23). *something to exploit for selfish gain:* The rare word *harpagmos* is elsewhere attested only in the active sense of "robbery," which is meaningless in the present context. By analogy with the cognate and more common *harpagma*, a passive sense is preferable, either in the sense of something seized (*res rapta*) or something to be seized (*res rapienda*). The context really demands for the former the sense of something seized and clung to (*res rapta et retinenda*). The latter (*res rapienda*) is favored by those who see Christ's attitude being contrasted here with that of Adam. But what did Christ, already "in the form of God," have to seize? In fact, the entire phrase (including "did not consider") probably reflects a proverbial expression meaning "exploit something for one's own (selfish) advantage" (see R. W. Hoover, *HTR* 64 [1971] 95–119). The phrase then means that the Godlike one did not use his exalted status for purely selfish ends. A contrast with Adam at this point (so P. Bonnard, O. Cullmann, J. Héring, M. D. Hooker, J. Murphy-O'Connor) is difficult to prove (see T. F. Glasson, *NTS* 21 [1974–75] 133–39).

20   **7.** *he emptied himself:* This expression has contributed to the development of "kenotic" christologies, but here it probably has a metaphorical sense along the

		The Christ-Hymn	
I	(6)	Who, though his condition was divine, did not consider being like God something to exploit for selfish gain.	Original status and attitude
II	(7)	But rather he emptied himself, adopting the condition of a slave, taking on the likeness of human beings.	Humiliation 1
III		And being found in human form,	Humiliation 2
	(8)	He lowered himself further still, becoming obedient unto death [even to death upon a cross].	
IV	(9)	Wherefore God has highly exalted him and graciously bestowed upon him the name that is above every other name,	Exaltation
V	(10)	So that at the name of Jesus every knee should bend, in heaven, on earth, and under the earth,	Homage 1
VI	(11)	And every tongue confess that Jesus Christ is Lord to the glory of God the Father.	Homage 2

lines of Paul's use of the same vb. (*kenoun*) in the pass. to mean "be rendered powerless, ineffective" (cf. Rom 4:14). The meaning would then be that Christ freely rendered himself powerless — exactly as a slave is powerless. *adopting the condition of a slave:* In the thought of the hymn (cf. Gal 4:1-11; 4:21-5:1; Rom 8:15) unredeemed human existence is essentially a slavery, a bondage to spiritual powers, ending in death. Some translate *doulos* here as "servant," rather than "slave," finding also in the preceding phrase an allusion to the "Servant" of Isa 53:12 ("He poured out his soul [= "himself"] unto death"). Although linguistically plausible, this disturbs the sequence of ideas in that it precedes rather than follows the reference to becoming human in the next phrase; it also nullifies the contrast the hymn appears to be setting up between the extremities of lordship (vv 9-11) and slavery. *taking on the likeness of human beings: Homoiōma* can mean both "identical copy" and "(mere) resemblance." The former is most likely intended here, bringing out the paradox of the Godlike and hence immortal One taking on full human existence with its destiny in death. The clear implication in this and the following phrase that the Godlike One "took on" the human condition "from outside," as it were, creates a grave difficulty for those (e.g., C. H. Talbert, J. Murphy-O'Connor) who see the hymn as having solely the earthly existence of Christ in view. *being found in human form:* The language (*heurētheis*, "being found," *schēma*, "form") stresses the manner in which he now appeared in the sight of both God and human beings, i.e., simply as a man. **8.** *he lowered himself:* The selfless attitude of Christ, shown in his original disposition to take on the slavelike, mortal human condition, continues in his human history. On "lowering" (Gk *tapeinoun*), see comment on v 3. *becoming obedient unto death:* Throughout his whole life, Christ lived out perfectly the demands of human existence before God. Death was not simply the terminal point of his obedience; it was the inevitable consequence of being both fully human and totally obedient in a world alienated from God. *even to death upon a cross:* This phrase, somewhat intrusive in the structure of the hymn as outlined above, was probably added to the original by Paul. Crucifixion, the form of execution reserved for slaves and those who had totally forfeited all civic rights, marked the extremity of human abasement.

21   **9.** *wherefore God:* The self-denying act of Christ is matched by the active response of God. His obedience is "rewarded," not in the sense that it forced God's hand but that God in his fidelity moved to vindicate, "justify," the one who had placed himself so totally at the divine disposition. *highly exalted:* Beyond the exaltation of all the just, Christ is given the unique status of lordship over the whole universe. There is no mention of resurrection; the hymn moves in other categories of contrast: abasement/exaltation; slavery/lordship. *graciously bestowed:* The selflessness of Christ has given scope to God's victorious grace, which has full play where the human will is not grasping. *the name that is above every other name:* Explicit mention is held back till the climax (v 11), but the "name" is clearly *Kyrios,* "Lord," which came to be substituted for the ineffable *yhwh* in Christian copies of the LXX. If God himself has "graciously bestowed" the name *Kyrios* upon him, Jesus bears it without cost to strict monotheism. **10.** *at the name of Jesus:* Mention of "Jesus" now inextricably connotes also the title and authority of universal Lord. *every knee should bend:* Alluding to Isa 45:23, the hymn transfers to the exalted Christ the universal eschatological homage there given to God alone (cf. Rom 14:11). *in heaven, on earth and under the earth:* The threefold enumeration emphasizes the universality of the homage. **11.** *that Jesus Christ is Lord:* The climax of the hymn

encapsulates an early Christian confession (see 1 Cor 12:3; Rom 10:9). He who in selfless obedience took on the powerlessness of a slave now through divine commission and investiture holds universal lordship (1 Cor 3:21-23; Rom 14:9). *to the glory of God the Father:* The ultimate goal of the entire sequence is the reclaiming of the universe to God's sovereignty and glory. Christ's role and dignity are instrumental and subordinate to this (see 1 Cor 15:28; Rom 6:10-11).

22   Conclusion: Whether Paul composed this hymn remains an open question (cf. the poetic quality of passages such as 1 Cor 1:20-25; 13:1-13). In its original form the hymn theologically situates the "story" of Jesus within the overall framework of God's eschatological design to reclaim the universe for himself, seeing the historical selfless obedience of Christ foreshadowed in his pretemporal "career." Although an aspect of ethical imitation is not necessarily excluded, Paul more likely quotes the hymn to summon the Philippians to live out the selfless attitude (*phronein*) that should well up within them on the basis of their being "in Christ." In this way their lives will be caught up in the rhythm, scope, and ultimate victory of the same divine plan.

(Georgi, D., "Der vorpaulinische Hymnus, Phil 2.6-11," *Zeit und Geschichte* [Fest. R. Bultmann; ed. E. Dinkler; Tübingen, 1964] 263-93. Henry, P., "Kénose," *DBSup* 5. 7-161. Hofius, O., *Der Christushymnus Philipper 2, 6-11* [WUNT 17; Tübingen, 1976]. Käsemann, E., "A Critical Analysis of Philippians 2.5-11," *God and Christ* [*JTC* 5; NY, 1968] 45-88. Martin, R. P., *Carmen Christi: Philippians 2.5-11 in Recent Interpretation* [rev. ed.; GR, 1983] [full bibliography]. Murphy-O'Connor, J., "Christological Anthropology in Phil., II.6-11," *RB* 83 [1976] 25-50. Wright, N. T., "*Harpagmos* and the Meaning of Philippians 2:5-11," *JTS* 37 [1986] 321-52.)

23   (c) OBEDIENCE AND WITNESS TO THE WORLD (2:12-18). **12.** *as you have always been obedient . . . :* Paul reinforces his exhortation to unity through humble deference by appealing to the Philippians' as yet unblemished obedience to himself. His physical absence should increase, rather than weaken, their fidelity in this respect. *with fear and trembling:* This standard OT expression simply denotes in Paul's letters a humble and lowly attitude before fellow human beings (see 1 Cor 2:3; 2 Cor 7:15; cf. Eph 6:5; see S. Pedersen, *ST* 32 [1978] 1-31). *work out your own salvation:* The injunction is communal: a humble attitude toward one's fellow Christians (cf. vv 3-4) enters essentially into the community's collective passage to salvation. **13.** *for God is at work in you:* The divine creative power will more than compensate for the apostle's absence (cf. v 12). *goodwill:* The context suggests that "goodwill" toward each other (rather than God's goodwill) is meant. **14.** *without murmurings and questionings:* Such complaints were characteristic of the exodus community: see esp. Exod 15-17; Num 14-17. Paul alludes to the difficulties Moses had with Israel to highlight, by way of negative contrast, the cooperation (i.e., obedience) he expects of the Philippians. **15.** *children of God without blemish . . . :* The language here comes from Moses' castigation of Israel in Deut 32:5 (LXX). Paul summons the Philippians to be what the Israelites of old were not, applying the final denunciation ("crooked and perverse") to the surrounding unbelieving world. *lightbearers:* God has kindled the light of his gospel in a darkened world and elected Christians to be its bearers (cf. Matt 5:14,16). For Paul this is an essential element of the Christian journey to salvation. **16.** *holding out the word of life:* This ("missionary") transl. suits the context better than the alternative "holding fast to." *day of Christ:* See comment on 1:6. **17.** *poured out as a libation:* The image is standard in the ancient world for death freely accepted.

added to the sacrifice of your faith: The libationary cup was poured out over or around sacrifices. Paul, hinting that his "absence" (v 12) might be final, suggests that his death, should it occur, will garnish in this way the sacrifice already constituted by the Philippians' life of faith, which has its own costly aspect (see 1:29–30).

24   (C) Announcements about Timothy and Epaphroditus (2:19–30). 19. *Timothy:* See Acts 16:1–3; 17:14–15; 19:22. For similar commendations of Timothy as Paul's trusted representative, see 1 Cor 4:17; 1 Thess 3:2. **23.** *how it will go with me:* Timothy's departure depends on the outcome of Paul's trial. **25.** *Epaphroditus:* The bearer of the community's gift to Paul (4:18). Paul seems to feel constrained to justify his return to Philippi. **26.** *he was sick:* The cause of this illness we do not know, but cf. v 30.

25   (D) Conclusion (3:1a). *rejoice:* The Philippians, united with Paul in his suffering (1:5,30), are summoned once more (see 2:18), as Letter B concludes, to share also in his joy.

26   (III) Part II: Warning against False Teachers (3:1b–4:1). The abrupt change of tone and content that now occurs suggests that this segment of Phil stems from a later communication of Paul (Letter C; → 4, 9 above). The adversaries would seem to be itinerant Christian preachers, who in the name of a higher "perfection" (vv 12–16) seek to impose upon Gentile converts what is in Paul's eyes the essence of a Judaism outdated by God's act in Christ. **2.** *the dogs:* Paul's applying to fellow Christians this stock term of contemptuous abuse—reserved in Jewish circles for Gentiles, the unclean, and outsiders generally—reflects the intensity of his conviction about their perversion of the gospel; cf. v 18. *mutilate:* The adversaries are not allowed even the term "circumcision." The fleshly rite they vaunt is simply "mutilation" (*katatomē*) of the flesh; cf. the practice of the prophets of Baal (1 Kgs 18:28). **3.** *we are the true circumcision:* A spiritual and moral "circumcision of the heart," more pleasing to God than the external rite, is foreshadowed in the Jewish tradition (Jer 4:4; 9:24–25; Lev 26:41; Deut 10:16; 30:6; Ezek 44:7; cf. 1QS 5:5,26). Paul admits only this inward circumcision as valid for the eschatological age and appropriates it to the Christian community (Rom 2:25–29; cf. Col 2:11). *serve by the Spirit of God:* One is qualified for the "acceptable worship" of daily life (Rom 12:1) not by physical marks but by the circumcision of heart (new moral life), which the Spirit creates in those who are "in Christ" (Rom 2:29; 8:1–13). *no trust in the flesh: Sarx* denotes human nature as unredeemed and unresponsive to God's eschatological grace (→ Pauline Theology, 82:103). Physical circumcision belongs irremediably to this realm. **4.** *I myself:* Paul refutes the Judaizing claims by recounting his own discovery of how totally and irreversibly they were replaced by Christ. He heightens the impact by accepting for a moment the key Jewish criteria: on such terms he has impeccable, indeed superior credentials. **5.** *circumcised . . . :* Cf. the similar list in 2 Cor 11:22. *a Hebrew:* I.e., a Greek-speaking Jew who also spoke "Hebrew" (= Aramaic; cf. Acts 21:40). *Pharisee:* Paul adhered to that religious party in Judaism most distinguished in zeal for the law and its application to everyday life. **6.** *a persecutor:* Paul's ultimate "credential"; see Acts 8:3; 9:1–2; 22:4–5; 26:9–11; 1 Cor 15:9; Gal 1:13. *righteousness based on law:* The eschatological right-standing in God's sight based on faithful adherence to the law. *blameless:* This claim cautions us against understanding the struggle under the law recorded in Rom 7:7–25 in a strictly autobiographical way. **7.** *I came to reckon:* Using "loss-and-gain" language, reminiscent of bookkeeping, Paul now recounts the total turnaround in his life that

took place at the time of his conversion. *because of Christ:* Over against the mass of privileges and allegiance associated with his former life there is placed simply the person of Christ. **8.** *knowing Christ Jesus my Lord:* Such "knowing" goes beyond intellectual knowledge to include, in the OT sense, experience and deep personal involvement; it also transforms the subject into the likeness of the one known (cf. 2 Cor 3:18). *suffered the loss of all:* The commercial image continues: such "knowledge" of Jesus relativizes the value of all former ties, so that one can freely, indeed joyfully, let them go (cf. Matt 13:44–46). *refuse:* The Gk word *skybala,* means either "rubbish" or "excrement"—in either case something that is disposed of irrevocably. **9.** *be found in him:* Paul hopes to appear before God at the eschatological judgment as one totally identified with Christ. *not having as my righteousness:* Here begins a concise but remarkably adequate summary of the doctrine of justification so central to Rom and Gal (→ Pauline Theology, 82:68–70). *that which comes from the law:* The law for Paul is in itself "holy, just, and good" (Rom 7:12), but because of sin, which it cannot remedy, it remains a fatally flawed way to righteousness and leads to death. *that which comes through faith:* The gospel proclaims that true eschatological right-standing comes solely through accepting in faith God's offer of renewed relationship with himself made freely and graciously in Christ (Rom 3:21–26). *in Christ:* The Greek could also be understood in the sense of Christ's own faith; cf. his "obedience" (Rom 5:19; Phil 2:8). *the righteousness from God:* All human righteousness stems ultimately from God's own righteousness, i.e., his saving fidelity to creation, which has impelled him to reach out and freely offer acceptance and salvation to an undeserving world. Believers have their righteousness "from God" in that, eschewing all independent claims to right-standing, they allow themselves to be drawn in Christ into the sphere and scope of God's own righteousness (2 Cor 5:21). **10.** *to know him and the power of his resurrection:* To "know Christ" means to experience him as "life-giving Spirit" (1 Cor 15:45; 2 Cor 3:17), the one who here and now is conquering the forces of death and readying Christians for resurrection (cf. v 21; see Fitzmyer, *TAG* 202–17). *participation in his sufferings:* It is precisely in the weakness of suffering that one experiences most forcefully the power that is working resurrection; see esp. 2 Cor 4:7–18. *conformed to his death:* The path to resurrection for the Christian follows that of Christ: the more perfect the "conformity," the surer the arrival at the goal (cf. Rom 6:3–4; 8:17).

27   12. *not . . . already perfect:* Against the adversaries' false claims, Paul contests that "perfection" is something attainable in this life. He uses the image of a race to show that what matters is to leave past achievements irrevocably behind and focus attention on what lies ahead. **14.** *the prize of the upward call:* At the end of a race the judge summoned the winner by name and title to ascend to receive the victor's crown. By "call" here Paul means God's summons to the Christian, when the eschatological "race" is complete, to ascend and join Christ in eternal life; this and this alone is the moment of "perfection" (see V. C. Pfitzner, *Paul and the Agon Motif* [NovTSup 16; Leiden, 1967] 139–53). **18.** *enemies of the cross:* The adversaries are "enemies of the cross" in that preaching something (circumcision) which denies its efficacy, they void Christ's costly self-sacrifice (Gal 2:21). **19.** *destruction:* Eschatological ruin. *whose god is the belly:* This refers either to zeal for Jewish food laws or to selfishness in general (Rom 16:18). *their shame:* To boast of circumcision (vv 2–3) is to "glory" in something (the sexual organ), which otherwise one modestly covers (cf. 1 Cor 12:23). *earthly things:* All that belongs to the old age now superseded by Christ. **20.** *our citizenship is in heaven:* Though not yet fully arrived in the new age, Christians are already enrolled as citizens of the "heavenly city" (cf. Gal 4:24-27; Eph 2:19); see comment on 1:27. **21.** *transform our lowly body:* The bodies of Christians, now partaking in the mortality of present life, cannot enter the final glory without "transformation"; see 1 Cor 15:50. *conformable to his glorious body:* The risen Christ is exemplar as well as agent of the true humanity God intended for human beings from the start (Rom 8:19-21,29-30). *subject all things to himself:* Paul alludes to Ps 8 (v 7), which for him tells of the messianic reign of Christ (1 Cor 15:25-28; Rom 8:20; cf. Eph 1:22; Heb 2:6-9; 1 Pet 3:22). **4:1** *stand firm:* A concluding exhortation not to be seduced away from the new existence now enjoyed "in the Lord."

28   (Part III) Exhortations to Unity, Joy, and Peace (4:2-9).
(A) Call to Unity (4:2-3). 2. *Euodia and Syntyche:* Two women, prominent in the community (v 3), otherwise unknown to us (W. D. Thomas, *ExpTim* 83 [1971-72] 117-20). **3.** *Syzygus:* Again unknown. The word may simply be Paul's affectionate title, "yoke-fellow," for some leading person in the community. *book of life:* The heavenly record of God's eschatological people (cf. Dan 12:1).
(B) Call to Joy and Peace of Mind (4:4-7). **5.** *the Lord is near:* Cf. the early acclamation, *marana tha* (1 Cor 16:22; cf. Rev 22:20). **7.** *God's peace . . . :* This "surpasses all understanding" either as beyond the power of the human mind to grasp or as accomplishing more than we can conceive of (cf. Eph 3:20).
(C) Call to Imitation of Paul (4:8-9). 8. *whatever . . . :* Paul commends to the community, who must bear witness before the world (cf. 2:15-16), a set of distinctively Gk (Stoic) virtues.
29   (V) Part IV: Acknowledgment of the Community's Gift (4:10-20). This segment of Phil contains the initial response of Paul to the community (→ 7 above). **10.** *I rejoice greatly:* Paul is clearly most

appreciative of the concern that prompted the gift (see also v 14). But there is no explicit word of thanks for the gift itself. This lends a certain ambivalence to his entire response. **11-13.** *I have learned to be independent:* Paul reasserts in a small excursus his principle of financial independence for the sake of the gospel (1 Thess 2:5-9; 1 Cor 9:4-18; 2 Cor 11:7-10; 12:13-18). **14.** *you did well:* Though strictly counter to this principle, what the Philippians did was right. **15-16.** *in the beginning of the (preaching of the) gospel:* Paul began the European phase of his missionary work in Philippi (Acts 16:9-10). *no other church:* That Paul received—and was willing to accept—support from the Philippians marks the uniqueness of his relationship with them (→ Paul, 79:29). *entered into partnership of giving and receiving:* Paul uses commercial language, alluding perhaps to a form of legal partnership (consensual *societas*) widespread in Greco-Roman society (see J. P. Sampley, *Pauline Partnership in Christ* [Phl, 1980]). **17.** *the credit accruing to your account:* The Philippians' material gift has brought them spiritual "credit." **18.** *I am paid in full:* Employing an expression used for endorsing a receipt, Paul hints that he would be embarrassed by further gifts at this point. *a fragrant offering . . . :* The sacral language, taken from the OT, suggests that the true recipient of the favor is God himself. **19.** *richness in glory:* God, in his fidelity, will repay the Philippians in that in which he is supremely rich, viz., glory. Glory is the divine power and presence, working the eschatological transformation of human beings into God's own likeness (3:21; cf. 2 Cor 3:17-18; Rom 5:2; 8:18-25, 29-30).

30   (VI) Conclusion (4:21-23). This includes a farewell (4:21-22) and a final blessing (4:23; → NT Epistles, 45:8D). **22.** *Caesar's household:* The body of officials and servants, mostly freedmen or slaves, involved in the imperial household and administration, not only in Rome but also in the great cities. Inscriptions record their presence in Ephesus (*CIL* 3. 6082, 6077; *CIL* 6. 8645, 8653, 8654).

49

THE FIRST LETTER TO THE CORINTHIANS

Jerome Murphy-O'Connor, O.P.

BIBLIOGRAPHY

1 Allo, E.-B., *Saint Paul: Première épître aux Corinthiens* (EBib; 2d ed.; Paris, 1956). Barrett, C. K., *The First Epistle to the Corinthians* (HNTC; NY, 1968). Conzelmann, H., *1 Corinthians* (Herm; Phl, 1975). Fascher, E., *Der erste Brief des Paulus an die Korinther: Kapitel 1–7* (THK 7/1; 2d ed.; Berlin, 1980). Godet, F., *La première épître aux Corinthiens* (2d ed.; Neuchâtel, 1965). Hurd, J. C., *The Origin of 1 Corinthians* (NY, 1965). Lietzmann, H., *An die Korinther I–II* (HNT 9; 4th ed.; Tübingen, 1949). Murphy-O'Connor, J., *St. Paul's Corinth: Texts and Archaeology* (GNS 6; Wilmington, 1983). Robertson, A. and A. Plummer, *The First Epistle of St. Paul to the Corinthians* (ICC; 2d ed.;

Edinburgh, 1914). Ruef, J., *Paul's First Letter to Corinth* (PC; Phl, 1977). Senft, C., *La première épître aux Corinthiens* (CNT 2/7; Neuchâtel, 1979). Theissen, G., *The Social Setting of Pauline Christianity: Essays on Corinth* (Phl, 1982). Thrall, M. E., *I and II Corinthians* (Cambridge NEB; Cambridge, 1965). Weiss, J., *Der erste Korintherbrief* (MeyerK; Göttingen, 1910; repr. 1970). Wendland, H. D., *Die Briefe an die Korinther* (NTD 7; Göttingen, 1963). Wolff, C., *Der erste Brief des Paulus an die Korinther: Kapitel 8–16* (THK 7/2; Berlin, 1982).

DBSup 7. 171–83. *IDBSup* 180–83. Kümmel, *INT* 269–79. Wik-Schm, *ENT* 420–32.

INTRODUCTION

2 **(I) Corinth.** Situated on a plateau at the southern end of the narrow isthmus and backed by the 1,750-ft.-high Acrocorinth, Corinth controlled the land route from the Peloponnesus to the Gk mainland and had access to the Aegean and the Adriatic seas through its ports at Cenchreae and Lechaeum respectively. From remote antiquity the taxes levied on both N-S and E-W trade won for it the title "wealthy" (Homer, *Iliad* 2.570; J. B. Salmon, *Wealthy Corinth* [Oxford, 1984]). Excavations begun in 1896 by the American School of Classical Studies at Athens (published in the series *Corinth*) supplement the many classical texts that reveal its history.
3 Destroyed by the Roman general Lucius Mummius in 146 BC, the city was restored by Julius Caesar in 44 BC and named *Colonia Laus Julia Corinthiensis*. The first settlers were mostly freedmen (Strabo, *Geogr.* 8.6.23; Appian, *Hist.* 8.136) hailing originally from Greece, Syria, Egypt, and Judea. Within 40 years some of the merchants had become sufficiently wealthy to sponsor the Isthmian games, which had been transferred to Sicyon in 146 BC. Celebrated every second year in the spring at the sanctuary of Poseidon at Isthmia, this great panhellenic festival was second in importance only to the Olympic games. The intense competitiveness that inspired such commercial success gave rise to the proverb "Not for everyone is the voyage to Corinth" (Horace, *Ep.* 1.17.36; Strabo, *Geogr.* 8.6.20). Its ethos was that of a wide-open boom town without

the burdens of a weighty tradition or a hereditary patrician class. Despite many projects from the 6th cent. BC on, the wealth of Corinth never sufficed for the construction of a canal; instead, small boats were wheeled across the isthmus on the *diolcos* (Pliny, *Nat. Hist.* 4.10).
4 Indirect evidence indicates that Corinth was the capital of the senatorial province of Achaia, governed by a proconsul sent annually from Rome. In AD 51–52 the office was held by Lucius Iunius Gallio (→ Paul, 79:9). The municipal government was a miniature of that of republican Rome. Citizen voters elected four annual magistrates, who on retirement became members of the city council. The *duoviri*, the senior magistrates, were assisted by two *aediles*. An inscription on a pavement east of the theater reads, "Erastus in return for his aedileship paved (the area) at his own expense." This individual is identified with the Erastus who was city treasurer at the time of Paul and a Christian (Rom 16:23).
5 By the early 1st cent. AD Corinth had a vital Jewish community (Philo, *De legat.* 281), but the only material remains are an undated lintel with the inscription [Syna]gōgē Hebr[aiōn]. Other religious groups are well represented. Temples dedicated to the cult of the emperor, to the various Gk deities, and to Egyptian gods highlight both the religious diversity and the ethnic complexity of the city that Paul was to make one of the most important centers of early Christianity.

6   Corinth's reputation as Sin City par excellence is based on Strabo's assertion that the temple of Aphrodite had over 1,000 sacred prostitutes (*Geogr.* 8.6.20) and on the use of the city's name as a component in words denoting sexual license, e.g., *korinthiastēs*, "a whoremonger," *korinthiazesthai*, "to fornicate," *korinthia korē*, "a prostitute." Such words, however, appear only in the works of Athenian writers of the 4th cent. BC and never became part of current speech. Strabo's story, which, moreover, is told of the pre-146 BC city, has been shown to be totally devoid of foundation. Aphrodite's very secondary position in the pantheon of Corinth is underlined by the fact that the two temples dedicated to her, one on Acrocorinth, the other in the agora, were small and not specially significant. In terms of sexual morality, Corinth was no worse than any other Mediterranean port.

(Conzelmann, H., "Korinth und die Mädchen der Aphrodite: Zur Religionsgeschichte der Stadt Korinth," *NAWG* 8 [1967] 247-61. Furnish, V. P., *II Corinthians* [AB 32A; GC, 1984] 4-22. Murphy-O'Connor, J., *St. Paul's Corinth*. Roux, G., *Pausanias en Corinthie (Livre II, 1 à 15)* [Paris, 1958]. Saffrey, H. D., "Aphrodite à Corinth: Réflexions sur une idée reçue," *RB* 92 [1985] 359-74. Wiseman, J., "Corinth and Rome I: 228 BC-AD 267," *ANRW* II/7.1, 438-548.)

7   **(II) The Composition of the Church.** More data are available on the social makeup of the Corinthian church than of any other. The names of 16 members are known from Acts 18, 1 Cor 16, and Rom 16, and details given or implied about them can be analyzed in various ways. There was a solid nucleus of Jews but many pagans. The very top and bottom of the Greco-Roman social scale are absent. The social status of most is shot through with ambiguity; they rate high in some areas, low in others, e.g., rich but female (Phoebe), a city official but an ex-slave (Erastus), a skilled artisan but a Jew with a wife of higher social rank (Aquila). Fueled by frustration, such individuals did not cease to question and explore once they had accepted Christianity, and so generated a greater diversity of problems for Paul than any other church. In particular they welcomed other visions of Christianity and competed with one another for spiritual prestige.

(Judge, E. A., *The Social Pattern of Christian Groups in the First Century* [London, 1960]. Meeks, W. A., *The First Urban Christians* [New Haven, 1983]. Theissen, G., *The Social Setting of Pauline Christianity*.)

8   **(III) Date and Place of Origin.** Paul himself tells us that 1 Cor was written in the spring from Ephesus (16:8), but the year is a matter of some dispute. The suggested dates range from AD 52 to 57 with the majority opting for a date close to the middle of that span. When all of Paul's complex relations with the Corinthians are taken into account, the most probable date is the spring of AD 54 (so also Barrett, Furnish, Georgi, *KINT* 2. 120-26; but → Paul, 79:41). The authenticity of 1 Cor is undisputed.

9   **(IV) Occasion and Purpose.** 1 Cor is a complex reaction to two sets of data about the situation in Corinth. In a letter (7:1), probably carried by Stephanas and others (16:17), the Corinthians brought to Paul's attention a series of problems on which they wanted his advice. Such official information was supplemented by gossip. Chloe's people (1:11), on their return to Ephesus from a business trip to Corinth, recounted to

Paul those aspects of the life of the church there that surprised them, but which apparently were not problematic for the Corinthians. These observations revealed to Paul certain basic flaws in the Corinthians' understanding of Christian community. In consequence, he integrated his replies to their questions into an effort to bring them to a true appreciation of authentic life in Christ.

10   **(V) Outline.** The contents of 1 Cor are arranged as follows:

(I)   Introduction: Greeting and Thanksgiving (1:1-9)
(II)   Part I: Divisions in the Community (1:10-4:21)
    (A)   Rival Groups in the Community (1:10-17)
    (B)   God Has Different Standards (1:18-31)
    (C)   The Power of Paul's Preaching (2:1-5)
    (D)   True Wisdom and the Language of Love (2:6-3:4)
    (E)   The Right Attitude toward Pastors (3:5-4:5)
    (F)   Application to the Corinthians (4:6-13)
    (G)   The Visit of Timothy (4:14-21)
(III)   Part II: The Importance of the Body (5:1-6:20)
    (A)   A Case of Incest (5:1-8)
    (B)   Clearing Up a Misunderstanding (5:9-13)
    (C)   Lawsuits among Christians (6:1-11)
    (D)   Casual Copulation (6:12-20)
(IV)   Part III: Responses to Corinthian Questions (7:1-14:40)
    (A)   Problems of Social Status (7:1-40)
       (a)   Sexual Relations in Marriage (7:1-9)
       (b)   Marriage and Divorce (7:10-16)
       (c)   Changes in Social Status (7:17-24)
       (d)   Changes in Sexual Status (7:25-40)
    (B)   Problems Arising from Pagan Environment (8:1-11:1)
       (a)   Food Offered to Idols (8:1-13)
       (b)   Paul Renounces His Rights (9:1-27)
       (c)   The Dangers of Over-Confidence (10:1-13)
       (d)   The Significance of Social Gestures (10:14-22)
       (e)   The Scruples of the Weak (10:23-11:1)
    (C)   Problems in Liturgical Assemblies (11:2-14:40)
       (a)   Dress at Liturgical Assemblies (11:2-16)
       (b)   The Eucharist (11:17-34)
       (c)   The Gifts of the Spirit (12:1-11)
       (d)   The Body Needs Many Members (12:12-31)
       (e)   Love the Greatest Gift (13:1-13)
       (f)   Prophecy More Important than Tongues (14:1-25)
       (g)   Order in the Use of Spiritual Gifts (14:26-40)
(V)   Part IV: The Resurrection (15:1-58)
    (A)   The Creed of the Church (15:1-11)
    (B)   The Consequences of Different Theses (15:12-28)
       (a)   The Corinthians' Thesis (15:12-19)
       (b)   Paul's Thesis (15:20-28)
    (C)   Ad Hominem Arguments for Resurrection (15:29-34)
    (D)   The Resurrected Body (15:33-49)
    (E)   The Need for Transformation (15:50-58)
(VI)   Conclusion (16:1-24)
    (A)   The Collection for Jerusalem (16:1-4)
    (B)   Paul's Travel Plans (16:5-9)
    (C)   Some Recommendations (16:10-18)
    (D)   Final Greetings (16:19-24)

COMMENTARY

11   (I) Introduction: Greeting and Thanksgiving 1:1–9). 1–3. The opening formula follows a standard pattern (→ NT Epistles, 45:8A). **1.** *apostle:* This title underlines Paul's authority as an emissary of Christ. *Sosthenes.* Possibly the individual mentioned in Acts 18:17. The absence of Timothy's name (2 Cor 1:1) suggests that he was already on his way to Corinth (4:17; 16:10–11). **2.** *church of God:* → Pauline Theology, 82:134–35. *saints in virtue of a divine call:* The highly condensed formula *klētois hagiois* means that believers have been set apart by God, not that they are intrinsically holy. It is in this sense that they have been "sanctified" through Christ (→ Pauline Theology, 82:77) and must strive to be worthy of the opportunity given them (1 Thess 4:3–7). *with all those who in every place call on the name of our Lord Jesus Christ:* Diverse interpretations are possible (Barrett), but the general thrust of 1 Cor suggests that Paul is simply reminding the Corinthians that they are not the only Christians (11:16; 2 Cor 1:1). This would exclude the possibility that "place" means house-church (Barrett; see U. Wickert, *ZNW* 50 [1959] 73–82). *theirs and ours:* "Place" is the proximate antecedent, but this would be banal. All Christians serve one Lord.

12   4–9. A thanksgiving is normal at this point in a Pauline letter (→ NT Epistles, 45:8B) **4.** *grace:* The basis of Paul's gratitude is the gift of God mediated by Christ, which must be manifest. **5.** *with all speech and all knowledge:* The suggestion that they were endowed with spiritual gifts (see 1 Cor 12–14) would have flattered the Corinthians, but here Paul is damning them with faint praise. In other communities grace is manifest as faith, hope, and charity (1 Thess 1:3), faith (Rom 1:8), or partnership in the gospel (Phil 1:5) — all qualities that were not conspicuously evident at Corinth. **6.** *the testimony of Christ:* Since the context demands that this be something that God has effected — note the theological passive "was confirmed" (*ZBG* § 236) — in the Corinthians, it is probable that this much-disputed phrase means "bearing witness to Christ" (see G. W. MacRae in *Harry M. Orlinsky Volume* [ErIsr 16; Jerusalem, 1982] 171–75). **7.** *you come short in no gift of grace:* The Corinthians are adequately equipped with spiritual gifts. *as you wait:* The Corinthians tended to focus on the excitement of the present, so Paul has to remind them that completeness is reserved to the future. *revelation:* The parousia or second coming of Christ. **8.** *who will confirm:* Here we have the act. form of the vb. in v 6. God is again the subject. *irreproachable:* If believers are to receive a favorable eschatological judgment, it is due to God's assistance. See comment on 10:13. *day of our Lord:* The Christian adaptation of the Day of Yahweh (Amos 5:18; Joel 3:4 = Acts 2:20); see also 1 Cor 3:13; 4:3. **9.** *God is faithful:* God will not abandon what he has begun (1 Cor 10:13; 1 Thess 5:24). *by whom you were called:* Members of the church are frequently termed *hoi klētoi,* "the called ones" (1 Cor 2:2,24; Rom 1:6,7; 8:28), and *kalein* is a technical term for the whole process of salvation (see K. L. Schmidt, *TDNT* 3. 492). Implicit in the call to salvation (1 Cor 7:15,22; Gal 1:6; 5:13; 1 Thess 4:7) is the call to glory (Rom 8:28–30; Phil 3:14; 1 Thess 2:12), whose author is always God *ho kalōn* (Gal 5:8; 1 Thess 5:24; see J. Murphy-O'Connor, *Paul on Preaching* [Chicago, 1964] 21–26). *common union:* Paul uses *koinōnia* to mean the vital union of believers among themselves,

which is their union with Christ. Their shared existence as members of his body (1 Cor 12:12–27) is highlighted in the eucharist (1 Cor 10:16–17). (See G. Panilulam, *Koinōnia in the New Testament* [AnBib 85; Rome, 1979].)

13   (II) Part I: Divisions in the Community (1:10–4:21).

(A) Rival Groups in the Community (1:10–17). Since the basis of Christian life and its only authentic expression is *koinōnia,* Paul is particularly sensitive to any lack of unity in the community and so deals first with this aspect of the situation at Corinth. **10.** *that all of you say the same thing:* The reference is to the slogans in v 12, which show that the Corinthians are "brothers" only in name. They do not share a common vision. **11.** *quarreling:* The factions were hostile to one another. As yet there was no complete breakup. *Chloe's people:* These were employees or slaves of a Gentile businesswoman (cf. Acts 16:14), most probably based in Ephesus, and thus sensitive to aberrations in another community. **12.** *Paul:* This group probably formed as a reaction to the others. Paul could stress his own example (1 Cor 4:17; 11:1), without always noting that it was modeled on that of Christ (Phil 4:9; Gal 4:12). *Apollos:* Originally from Alexandria (Acts 18:24–19:1), he preached in Corinth in Paul's absence (1 Cor 3:6) and was with Paul in Ephesus when this letter was written (1 Cor 16:12). Would-be sophisticates may have found his eloquence more to their taste than the bluntness of Paul. He may have been the channel whereby Philonic wisdom speculation penetrated the community; → 18–21 below. *Cephas:* From Aram *kēpā',* "rock" (John 1:42; Matt 16:18; see J. A. Fitzmyer, *TAG* 112–24); Paul's habitual name for Peter (1 Cor 3:22; 9:5; 15:5; Gal 1:18; 2:9,11,14), but he can also use the Gk form, *Petros* (Gal 2:7–8). It is not impossible that Cephas visited Corinth. If not, Judeo-Christians may have invoked his name to legitimize a more law-observant form of Christianity than Paul found palatable (see C. K. Barrett, "Cephas and Corinth," *Abraham unser Vater* [Fest. O. Michel; ed. O. Betz et al.; AGJU 5; Leiden, 1963] 1–12). *Christ:* This is the most mysterious of the factions. Ultra-spirituals may have repudiated the mediation of church or kerygma and given their allegiance to Christ directly.

14   1. *is not Christ divided?:* The form of the question demands an affirmative answer, which is intelligible only if "Christ" means the community as in 1 Cor 6:15; 12:12. The church prolongs the mission of the historical Jesus; it is the presence in the world of the risen Christ. The following two questions contain the particle *mē,* which indicates that a negative answer is expected. **14–16.** No one is to claim a privileged position because baptized by Paul. He presumably baptized the first converts in a given area and then delegated the responsibility to others. **14.** *Crispus:* The president of a synagogue at Corinth (Acts 18:8). *Gaius:* A wealthy man whose house could contain the whole church (Rom 16:23; 1 Cor 14:23), an assembly made up of a number of smaller house-churches (1 Cor 16:19). **15.** This expresses the practical result, not Paul's intention at the time. **16.** *Stephanas:* See comment on 16:15. *household:* Since the household almost certainly included children, this text has been used to prove that the early church baptized infants (see J. Jeremias, *Infant Baptism in the First Four Centuries* [Phl, 1960–]). This meaning, however, is excluded by the limitation of the *oikos* of Stephanas to adults in 16:15 (see A. Strobel, *ZNW* 56 [1965] 91–100; P. Weigandt, *NovT* 6 [1963] 49–74). **17.** Only from this perspective of Paul's understanding of his primary obligation is baptism somewhat disparaged. *not with wisdom of speech:* Authentic preaching (see comment on 2 Cor 4:7–12) releases the power of the gospel (Rom 1:16). That power is nullified by attempts to make it reasonable by clever arguments or attractive by rhetorical artifices, which bring it down to the level of fallen humanity.

15   (B) God Has Different Standards (1:18–31). Believers must detach themselves from the standards of fallen humanity—the cause of the divisions at Corinth—if they are to understand the way God relates to them. Various attempts (surveyed by V. Branick, *JBL* 101 [1982] 251–69) to show that Paul here begins to reuse material composed for a different audience are unconvincing. **18.** The fact of acceptance or rejection is the basis of the division of humanity into two groups. God has not predestined some to salvation and others to condemnation. In the future the status of a member of either group could change (1 Cor 5:5; 10:12). **19.** The worldly wisdom that rejects the gospel has been condemned by God in Isa 29:14 (LXX). **20.** The meaning of the rhetorical questions (inspired by Isa 19:11; 33:18; 44:25; Job 12:17) is clarified only by the two following verses, each introduced by *epeidē*, "since." **21.** *in the wisdom of God:* This does not mean a divine plan, for that would rob the argument of all force, but the organization and beauty of creation (Rom 1:19–20). *through wisdom:* Rational speculation, which in the world passes for wisdom, had failed to perceive that God acted through a suffering savior. *the folly of what we preach:* This is the word of the cross (1:18). **22.** *ask for signs:* The demand for miracles is a refusal to trust God and camouflages contentment with the status quo. *Greeks:* Since *ethnoi* occurs in the next verse, the reference must be to Gentiles in general (Gal 3:28). *seek wisdom:* They construct a religious system, the demands of which they are prepared to accept. **23.** God's foolishness is a crucified Christ, who is refused by Jews because of their messianic expectations and by Gentiles because of their rationalism. **24.** *those who are called:* Even though the gospel is addressed to all, Paul reserves the term *klētoi* to those who have accepted it (see comment on 1:9). *Christ:* The authentic humanity of Jesus makes visible God's intention for the human race and radiates an attractive force that enables response. **25.** Paradox is forced to the extreme to underline that God's ways are not the ways of human beings (Rom 11:33).

(K. Müller, "1 Kor 1:18–25: Die eschatologisch-kritische Funktion der Verkündigung des Kreuzes," *BZ* 10 [1966] 246–72. R. Penna, "La *dynamis theou:* Riflessioni in margine a 1 Cor 1:18–25," *RivB* 15 [1967] 281–94. U. Wilckens, *Weisheit und Torheit* [BHT 26; Tübingen, 1959] 21–41.)

16   26–31. The membership of the Corinthian community illustrates the paradox of 1:25. God did not call those whom the world would have selected to further his plan for humanity. **26.** This verse could be construed as a question expecting an affirmative answer (so W. H. Wuellner, *SE VI* 666–72), but to do so would destroy Paul's argument. *according to the flesh:* By the standards of fallen humanity. **27–28.** *of the world:* According to the common estimation. **29.** *boasting:* In Paul's lexicon this means sinful self-reliance, which ignores the question in 1 Cor 4:7. What has been achieved at Corinth is not due to any qualities of the believers. **30.** *from him you are through Christ Jesus:* The vb. should be accented *esté* (Allo) because it is question of a new mode of existence, fundamentally a new way of looking at reality. *wisdom for us:* This new perception is communicated to believers by the wisdom revealed in the humanity of Christ, whose content is clarified by the three terms standing in apposition. Through being separated from sinners (sanctification), believers are removed from the control of sin (redemption), and so become what they should be before God (righteousness; see W. Bender, *ZNW* 71 [1980] 263–68; → Pauline Theology, 82:68–70, 75, 77). **31.** Though presented as an OT quotation, only *ho kauchōmenos* and *kauchasthō* come from Jer 9:24 or 2 Sam 2:10. *in the Lord:* The reference is to God's activity in history. The same formula appears in 2 Cor 10:17 (see Meeks, *First Urban Christians* 51–73).

17   (C) The Power of Paul's Preaching (2:1–5). Paul shows his fidelity to the principle enunciated in the last section by developing 1:17. **1.** *testimony of God:* The reading *martyrion*, "testimony," is more probable than the equally well-attested *mystērion*, "mystery" (Barrett). The testimony given by God, or the secret revealed by God, is Christ, whom Paul refused to adorn with rhetorical artifices or clever arguments. **2.** *I did not think it fit to know:* All Paul's attention was focused on the crucified Christ, who was not the type of savior that either Jews or Gentiles expected. **3.** Paul's comportment was the antithesis of that of the itinerant philosophers who made a good living from the credulity of the simple. **4.** *in persuasive words of wisdom:* Some witnesses insert the adj. "human" before wisdom in order to underline that this latter term has a pejorative connotation here. *in a demonstration of spirit and power:* Paul again argues from effect to cause. The power of the Spirit (hendiadys) is the only explanation of the conviction that gripped the Corinthians when Paul spoke. **5.** A faith based on a persuasive presentation is at the mercy of better arguments. *the power of God:* The object of Christian faith is not God *in se* but as active in history.

18   (D) True Wisdom and the Language of Love (2:6–3:4). The suggestion that 2:6–16 is an interpolation (M. Widmann, *ZNW* 70 [1979] 44–53) is less probable than the view that Paul here turns against his opponents their own ideas and terminology. They were influenced not by gnosticism (*pace* W. Schmithals, *Gnosticism in Corinth* [NY, 1971]) but by the Hellenistic-Jewish wisdom speculation associated with Philo, which Apollos (Acts 18:24–28) may have introduced into Corinth. Some Christians believed they possessed a "wisdom" that made them "mature" or "perfect" and gave them the right to look down on others as "children." These latter were "soul-people" concerned only with the body and its needs, whereas the perfect were "spirit-people" who speculated on Christ as "the Lord of Glory" and prized eloquence.

(Davis, J. A., *Wisdom and Spirit* [Lanham, 1984]. Horsley, R. A., "*Pneumatikos* versus *Psychikos:* Distinctions of Status among the Corinthians," *HTR* 69 [1976] 269–88; "Wisdom of Word and Words of Wisdom in Corinth," *CBQ* 39 [1977] 224–39. Pearson, B., *The Pneumatikos–Psychikos Terminology in 1 Corinthians* [SBLDS 12; Missoula, 1973]. Winter, M., *Pneumatiker und Psychiker in Korinth* [MarTS 12; Marburg, 1975].)

19   6. The opening words are pure irony intelligible only in the light of 3:1; among believers there are no distinctions based on knowledge reserved to a few chosen souls. *wisdom:* The Pauline meaning appears in the next verse. Paul's judgment on the speculation that attracted the Corinthians appears in the two qualifying phrases. *of this age:* See comment on Gal 1:4. *of the leaders of this age:* Of the three current interpretations—human rulers, demonic powers, and human rulers as the instruments of demonic powers—the first is the most probable (see M. Pesce, *Paolo e gli arconti a Corinto* [Testi e ricerche di scienze religiose 13; Brescia, 1977].) The opinions of fallen humanity are reflected in the structure of a corrupt society, which is only being brought to nothing. **7.** *wisdom of God:* God's plan of salvation is the only authentic wisdom, which is inaccessible to rational speculation (2:11–12). *for our glory:* Through the Fall, humanity lost the ability to glorify God (*Apoc. Mos.* 20:1-2; 21:6; Rom 3:23). Christ had this capacity, and those who belong to him grow into it gradually (2 Cor 3:18). It is in this sense that glory is the goal of the plan of salvation (see J. Coppens, *ETL* 46 [1970] 389–92). **8.** *which:* The proximate antecedent is glory, but common sense indicates that the reference is to the plan of salvation. Had the arrogant authorities known that it would be achieved through the humiliating death of Jesus, they would have tried to frustrate it by letting him live. *lord of glory:* This appears as a divine title in *1 Enoch* 63:2 and equivalently in Ps 24:8, but here it indicates the aspect of Christ on which the "spirit-people" in Corinth preferred to concentrate. The crucified Jesus, however, is the truth of the risen Christ (Eph 4:21; see I. de la Potterie, *SPC* 2. 45–57). **20**   **9.** *as it is written:* Contrary to Paul's usual practice (1:31; 2 Cor 8:15; 9:9; Rom *passim*), the formula here does not introduce an OT citation. The earliest attestation of the first part is Ps.-Philo, *Bib. Ant.* 26.13 (for later versions, see K. Berger, *NTS* 24 [1977–78] 271–83), which may be inspired by Isa 64:3. The combination of the two parts may reflect a complicated evolution (see H. Ponsot, *RB* 90 [1983] 229–42), but the awkwardness of *hosa,* the rel. pron. in v 9b, suggests rather that the second part does not belong to the quotation but is Paul's commentary. It was very much to his purpose to make love the criterion (Rom 8:28; see J. B. Bauer, *ZNW* 50 [1959] 106–12). **10.** *God revealed:* The object is expressed in v 9. **11.** The argument is based on human separateness. In each person there are areas into which no outsider can penetrate. Only one's self-consciousness can reveal them. Similarly, only the divine self-consciousness (Spirit of God) can penetrate the profundity of God. **12.** *the spirit of the world:* If this is the mentality of a corrupt society, "this spirit which is from God" can only be the mentality of an authentic Christian community. Mysteries are grasped only through commitment. **13.** The means of communication correspond to the mode of knowledge. *words taught by the Spirit:* The new being of believers (1:30) is due to God's initiative, and so both the instinctive knowledge given with it and the language in which it is expressed must be attributed to him. *pneumatikois pneumatika synkrinontes:* Different combinations of meanings are possible (see Robertson-Plummer, *First Epistle* 47), but the context suggests "interpreting spiritual truths in spiritual terms" (so Barrett, Conzelmann). **14.** Paul turns the Corinthians' own distinction (→ 18 above) against them. If the "spirit-people" do not understand him, it is they who are "soul-people." The principle underlying the distinction is explained by Philo in *Quod det.* 86. **15.** In context this Corinthian principle (Philo, *Leg. alleg.* 1.94), which has had a most pernicious influence in church history, must mean that Paul is immune to the judgments of his opponents; see comment on 4:3–5. **16.** The force of Isa 40:13 LXX becomes clear only if vv 10 and 12 are kept in mind. If Paul's opponents have not known God, how can they understand his works, viz., the spiritually perfect? *the mind of Christ:* God is known only through Christ, whose mind is not concerned with speculation but with obedience and service (Phil 2:5–7). **21**   **3:1–4.** Abandoning the mental gymnastics intended to bemuse the Corinthians, Paul now articulates his basic objection to their attitude. They cannot be mature Christians since they have not grasped the nature of authentic community. **1.** *fleshly people:* Those

still dominated by the standards of a fallen world; see R. Bultmann, *TNT* 1. 232–39. **3.** *you walk according to man:* In opposition to *kata theon* (2 Cor 7:9–10), *kata anthrōpon* (1 Cor 9:8; 15:32; Gal 3:15; Rom 3:5) means the common human estimation. By accepting envy and strife as normal they betray their acceptance of the common judgment of what is possible for humanity. **4.** *are you not men:* Through their use of party slogans (1:12), they show themselves to be ordinary and not the enlightened spiritual leaders they claim to be. **22**   **(E) The Right Attitude toward Pastors (3:5–4:5).** The main theme enunciated in 3:5–9 returns again in 4:1–5. In between (3:10–23) is a digression that is less directly relevant to the point at issue. **5.** *what:* One would expect "who," but the neuter is used deliberately here and in v 7 to underline the instrumental character of ministry. *through whom you believed:* Though a divine gift (12:9), faith does not bypass incarnational channels. A defective instrument can impede or distort the action of the principal cause (1:17). **6.** Chronologically Paul and Apollos were related as evangelist and catechist. **7.** God does not need human instruments, but in his wisdom had decided to employ them. **8.** *are one thing:* In view of their effect Paul and Apollos form a single complex instrument. How silly, then, to set them against each other! *each shall receive his wages:* Even though all the credit must go to God, this acknowledges the reality of the ministers' contribution. **9.** *God's coworkers:* Pace V. P. Furnish (*JBL* 80 [1961] 364–70), the idea is divine–human cooperation (1 Thess 3:2), the mode of divine activity inaugurated in Christ. *tillage/building:* The association of these images is widespread (see Conzelmann, *1 Corinthians* 75). In stony Palestine, clearing fields meant building walls (Jer 1:10). **23**   **10.** The building image sidetracks Paul into a digression on the quality of ministerial contributions, which he expects others to make. **11.** A parenthetical allusion to a claim of the Cephas party that the church should be founded on Peter (Matt 16:18); see comment on 1:12. **13.** *the Day:* Fire is a consistent element (Isa 26:11; Dan 7:9–11; Mal 4:1) in the scenario of the eschatological Day of Yahweh (Isa 2:12; Jer 46:10; Amos 5:18), which Paul here uses to denote the second coming of Christ (4:5; 5:5). **14.** *a reward:* God's approval for the full use of one's talents in contributions appropriate to the nature of the church. **15.** To give mistakenly (e.g., the attempt of the Cephas party to impose Jewish customs on the church) or inadequately in terms of one's talents will merit salvation — but only just, as one who runs out of a burning house. There is no reference to purgatory (see S. Cipriani, *RivB* 1 [1959] 25–43; J. Gnilka, *Ist 1 Kor 3:10–15 ein Schriftzeugnis für das Fegfeuer?* [Düsseldorf, 1955]. J. Michl, *SPC* 1. 395–401). **16.** From construction Paul jumps to the edifice itself. *a temple of God:* In opposition to the Essenes, who relate the concept to spiritual sacrifice (1QS 8:4–9; 9:3–5), Paul makes the presence of God the basis (6:19; 2 Cor 6:16; see G. Klinzing, *Die Umdeutung des Kultus in der Qumrangemeinde und im Neuen Testament* [SUNT 7; Göttingen, 1971] and my review, *RB* 79 [1972] 435–40). **17.** *holy temple:* The community is destroyed by lack of sanctity (see I. de la Potterie and S. Lyonnet, *La vie selon l'Esprit* [Paris, 1965] chap. 7). **24**   **18.** Sanctity is loving service, the antithesis of the divisions promoted by Corinthian wisdom speculation that followed worldly standards. *become a fool:* By accepting the foolishness of the cross (1:18–25). **19.** Here, as in Rom 11:35, Paul uses a non-LXX transl. of Job 5:13. What the Corinthians think of as wisdom is only craftiness. **20.** In citing Ps 94:11, Paul substitutes "wise" for "men." **21–22.** Following the Stoic principle "All things belong to the wise" (Diog. Laertius, *Vit.* 7.125), the Corinthians should have reversed their slogans (1:12). **23.** The *ad hominem* character of the argument in vv 21–22 is underlined by the formal statement of the relation of all to Christ, and his subordination to God (15:28). **25** **4:1.** In conclusion Paul flatly states how the Corinthians should view their pastors. *servants: Hypēretēs* often has the connotation of "official witness" (see Murphy-O'Connor, *Paul on Preaching* 60–64). *stewards:* This term was also applied to religious functionaries (see H. Cadbury, *JBL* 50 [1931] 47–51; J. Reumann, *JBL* 77 [1958] 339–49). **2–3.** Since Paul did not appoint himself and the Corinthians did not name him, their judgments are meaningless. **4.** *my conscience is clear:* Paul does not experience the pain of transgression (see C. A. Pierce, *Conscience in the NT* [SBT 15; London, 1955] 21, 28), but this is no guarantee that the one true judge agrees. **5.** *the time:* This moment is fixed by the following reference to the parousia. "In view of this *last* judgment, all human verdicts must be *pre*-judice" (Barrett, *First Epistle* 103). An element of hyperbole is evident.

26 **(F) Application to the Corinthians (4:6–13).** **6.** Paul's application of metaphors (3:6; 4:1) to himself and Apollos was to clarify their role (see M. Hooker, *NTS* 10 [1963–64] 131). *the "not" is above what is written:* J. Strugnell has shown (*CBQ* 36 [1974] 555–58) that *to mē hyper ha gegraptai* is the marginal comment of a copyist whose exemplar lacked a *mē*, "not," which he inserted before *heis*. **7.** Of themselves the Corinthians have nothing to recommend them to a party leader. **8–13.** From sarcasm Paul turns to bitter irony. In contrast to the preachers, who are conscious only of suffering and struggle, the Corinthians imagined themselves to be in possession of the eschatological kingdom of God. Their faulty eschatology (see A. C. Thiselton, *NTS* 24 [1977–78] 510–26) was reinforced by the Stoic idea that the wise are kings (Weiss).

27 **(G) The Visit of Timothy (4:14–21).** **14.** After severity, sweetness. **15.** *paidagōgos:* Lit., "boy-leader," usually a slave who superintended a youth's conduct, but was not his teacher (see comment on Gal 3:24). *I begot you:* The effect of the power of Christ (1:24) mediated by Paul's gospel (1:17) is new life (1:30; see P. Gutierrez, *La paternité spirituelle selon saint Paul* [EBib; Paris, 1968].) **16.** See comment on 11:1. **17.** *I sent Timothy:* The aorist is not epistolary, as 1:1 and 16:11 show. Timothy was known in Corinth (1 Thess 3:2). His mission in May AD 54 was probably Paul's initial reaction to the gossip brought by Chloe's people (1:11). *my ways in Christ:* My manner of life as a Christian. **18.** Fear for Timothy makes Paul angry again. **19.** *I will come shortly:* This heated declaration is not in contradiction to Paul's detailed travel plan in 16:5–9. **20.** The reality of the kingdom of God is in its transforming power, not in speculation (Rom 14:17–18). **21.** Paternal love may be expressed in tenderness or chastisement (Job 37:13; see C. Spicq, *RB* 60 [1953] 509–12).

28 **(III) Part II: The Importance of the Body (5:1–6:20).** The three problems, which fall into the pattern sex–lawsuits–sex, all illustrate the Corinthian belief that no physical action has any moral significance (6:18b). For Paul the body is the sphere in which commitment to Christ becomes real; there is no such thing as a purely spiritual Christianity.

29 **(A) A Case of Incest (5:1–8).** **1.** Marriage or concubinage with a stepmother was condemned by both Jews (Lev 18:8; 20:11; *m. Sanh.* 7:4) and Gentiles (Caius, *Inst.* 1.63). **2.** *you are puffed up:* The community took infantile (3:1) pride in thus being different, whereas they should have gone into mourning and showed their sincerity (the *hina* is explicative) by expelling the sinner. Since the woman is not mentioned, she was probably not a Christian. **3.** *present in spirit:* Since it was the duty of the community to purify itself, Paul could give himself a

voice in their council only by claiming spiritual presence. *on the man who has done such a thing in the name of the Lord Jesus:* The Corinthians justified the act as an expression of their new freedom in Christ (see J. Murphy-O'Connor, *RB* 86 [1977] 239–45). **4.** *assembled:* The decision is to be made by the whole community. **5.** *to deliver: Chrē* or *dei,* "it is necessary," must be understood before the infin. *paradounai.* Paul is indicating the decision he wants, not imposing it. *Satan:* A personalized evil force related by Paul exclusively to believers (see T. Ling, *The Significance of Satan* [London, 1961]). *destruction of the flesh:* The negative goal of the man's expulsion from the community is the extinction of his false orientation, not necessarily by death or sickness (see A. C. Thiselton, *SJT* 26 [1973] 204–28). *that his spirit may be saved:* Positively, excommunication is designed to promote an authentic orientation toward God. The action of Satan is also productive of good in 2 Cor 12:7. *the Day:* See comment on 1:8; 4:5. **6.** *a little leaven:* The bad example of one risks infecting all others; every sin has a social dimension (Rom 14:7; cf. Gal 5:9). **7.** *old leaven:* The remnants of our sinful past, which should already have been purged (3:17).

(Collins, A. Y., "The Function of 'Excommunication' in Paul," *HTR* 73 [1980] 251–63. Derrett, J. D. M., "'Handing over to Satan': An Explanation of 1 Cor 5:1–7," *RIDA* 26 [1979] 11–30. Forkman, G., *The Limits of the Religious Community* [ConBNT 5; Lund, 1972]. Roetzel, C. J., *Judgement in the Community* [Leiden, 1972].)

30 **(B) Clearing Up a Misunderstanding (5:9–13).** **9.** This earlier letter has been lost. **10.** The Corinthians had given an overly rigorous interpretation to his directive in order to ignore it. **11.** The church cannot fulfill its mission unless its behavior is distinctively better than that of society. *the name of brother:* One known as a merely nominal Christian by his behavior. **12.** *outsiders:* Association with nonbelievers is not forbidden (10:27). **13.** *the evil man:* The individual condemned in vv 1–5. The formulation evokes Deut 17:7.

(Dahl, N. A., "Der Epheserbrief und der verlorene, erste Brief des Paulus an die Korinther," *Abraham unser Vater* 65–77. Zaas, P. S., "'Cast Out the Evil Man from Your Midst' (1 Cor 5:13b)," *JBL* 103 [1984] 259–61.)

31 **(C) Lawsuits among Christians (6:1–11).** The mention of judgment and outsiders recalls to Paul an issue unrelated to sexual problems (*pace* P. Richardson, *NovT* 25 [1983] 37–58). **1.** *the unjust:* Not corrupt judges but merely nonbelievers. The community should witness to a divisive world by exhibiting its ability to reconcile its own members (see W. C. van Unnik, "Die Rücksicht auf die Reaktion der Nicht-Christen als Motiv in der altchristlichen Paränese," *Judentum — Urchristentum — Kirche* [Fest. J. Jeremias; ed. W. Eltester; BZNW 20; Berlin, 1960] 221–34). **2.** If the elect are to participate in the eschatological judgment (Dan 7:22; Wis 3:8; 1QpHab 5:4; *Jub.* 24:29; Matt 19:28; 1 Thess 4:16–17), they are certainly competent to arbitrate ordinary cases. **3.** Wicked angels will be judged at the parousia (Jude 6; 2 Pet 2:4; cf. *1 Enoch* 91:15). **4.** *those despised by the church:* For the sake of his argument Paul adopts the perspective of those Corinthians who looked down on their fellow Christians (→ 18 above). A fortiori they would have held nonbelievers in contempt. **5.** The pretentiousness of the "wise" and "perfect" is brutally revealed; they avow themselves incapable of a simple judgment! **7.** Having stated how cases should be handled, Paul goes on to say they should not even arise. *you have lawsuits with your own selves:* This is the basic incongruity. Such is the unity of the body (12:12–27) that a Christian who sues a brother sues himself (Rom 12:5). The two questions evoke Matt

5:39–42. 9–10. The vice list of 5:10–11 is expanded by four terms. If "thieves" is well in place here (v 7), "adulterers" will appear in 6:12–20, and "catamites" and "sodomites" (see D. F. Wright, *VC* 38 [1984] 125–53) may prepare for 11:2–16 (see S. Wibbing, *Die Tugend- und Lasterkataloge im NT* [BZNW 25; Berlin, 1959]). *kingdom of God:* Here a future reality as in 15:50 and Gal 5:21, but it can also be present (4:20; 15:24; Rom 14:17; 1 Thess 2:12). **11.** *such were some of you:* Another hint of the background of the Corinthian community; the list is not mere repetition of traditional material. *you have had yourselves washed:* They asked for baptism. *you were sanctified and justified:* God set them apart in Christ (1:2) and thus made them pleasing to him in principle. God, Christ, and Spirit are mentioned, but the thought is not yet trinitarian.

(Delcor, M., "The Courts of the Church of Corinth and the Courts of Qumran," *Paul and Qumran* [ed. J. Murphy-O'Conner; London, 1968] 69–84. Meurer, S., *Das Recht im Dienst der Versöhnung und des Friedens* [ATANT 63; Zurich, 1972]. Vischer, L., *Die Auslegungsgeschichte von I Kor. 6:1–11* [BGBE 1; Tübingen, 1955].)

32   (D) Casual Copulation (6:12–20). The theme of sexual license in the vice list brings Paul back to the type of problem dealt with in 5:1–8. **12.** *all things are lawful to me:* A Corinthian slogan (see Hurd, *Origin* 68), the application of which Paul restricts, because not everything builds up the community; some things destroy it (Gal 4:9). **13a.** *Food . . . both one and the other:* A second Corinthian slogan designed to prove that physical actions have no moral value. **13b–14.** Paul's response matches each element of the slogan. If our bodies are to be raised, God must attach importance to actions performed in and through the body. Though used interchangeably with "us" and "you," *sōma* is always physical (see R. H. Gundry, *Sōma in Biblical Theology* [SNTSMS 29; Cambridge, 1976]); it is as such that it is a medium of communication (see B. Byrne, *CBQ* 45 [1983] 608–16). **15.** *Christ:* As in 12:12, "Christ" designates the Christian community, the physical presence of him in the world. Commitment to his mission is negated by the use of another person in casual copulation. **16.** Transitory pleasure without real communication denies the full union which is the Creator's intention for the physical act in Gen 2:24. **17.** A purely formal contrast inspired by "one flesh" in v 16, and designed to be evocative of the Corinthian commitment to Spirit (→ 18 above). **18.** *shun fornication:* This is Paul's conclusion, but he immediately recalls a third Corinthian slogan. *every sin which a man commits is outside the body:* Only motives count, not actions (see v 13a). *the fornicator sins against own body:* By refusing to get involved with the other person he perverts the intention of the most intimate physical act. **19.** *your body:* Because *sōma* is sg. and *hymōn* pl., there could be a reference to the body of Christ, but this is excluded by the context; *sōma* is a distributive sg. (2 Cor 4:10; Rom 8:23). *temple of the holy Spirit:* The holiness of the community (3:16–17) must be reflected in the comportment of each member. *you are not your own:* Because possessed by the Spirit and belonging to Christ (3:23). **20.** *you were bought:* The image is that of the ransoming (1:30) of a slave or a prisoner (Gal 5:1). *glorify God:* By using the body in its intended sense sexually (v 16), but also to serve others (Gal 5:13).

(Kempthorne, R., "Incest and the Body of Christ: A Study of 1 Cor 6:12–20," *NTS* 14 [1967–68] 568–74. Miller, J. I., "A Fresh Look at 1 Cor 6:16f.," *NTS* 27 [1980–81] 125–27. Murphy-O'Connor, J., "Corinthian Slogans in 1 Cor 6:12–20," *CBQ* 40 [1978] 391–96. Romaniuk, K., "Exégèse du Nouveau Testament et ponctuation," *NovT* 23 [1981] 195–209.)

33   (IV) Part II: Responses to Corinthian Questions (7:1–14:40). In replying to the Corinthian letter (7:1) Paul deals with a wide variety of questions, but the treatment is not haphazard. He deals first with problems of social status (7:1–40), then with those arising from contact with the pagan environment (8:1–11:1), and finally with those related to the liturgical assemblies (11:2–14:40). Tone and treatment are modified according to the nature of the problem.

34   (A) Problems of Social Status (7:1–40). Paul begins (7:1–16) and concludes (7:25–40) with sexually related problems, but the central portion (7:17–24) considers the situation of circumcised/uncircumcised and slave/freeman. The combination is evocative of Gal 3:28; cf. Col 3:11.

35   (a) Sexual Relations in Marriage (7:1–9). 1. *now concerning:* New questions raised by the Corinthians are introduced by *peri de* in 7:25; 8:1; 12:1; 16:1. *it is good for a man not to touch a woman:* This is not Paul's opinion but that of certain Corinthians who idealistically believed that married couples should abstain from sexual relations (see Hurd, *Origins* 68; W. E. Phipps, *NTS* 28 [1982] 126–31). **2.** *have:* As in 5:1, *echein* has a sexual connotation. It is a question not of being married but of normal relations within marriage. **3–4.** In terms of sexual relations (the only aspect of marriage with which Paul is here concerned), the body of each is gifted to the other; it is thus owed to the other, creating a "debt" (see B. Bruns, *MTZ* 33 [1982] 177–94). **5.** Hence, abstention can only be by mutual agreement and for a limited time. In Jewish law the husband could make a unilateral decision (Str-B 3. 37–72). *for prayer:* One example of the type of thing that would justify abstention. *Satan:* See comment on 5:5.

36   6. *this:* The pron. *touto* (as in vv 26,35) points forward, not backward (see N. Baumert, *Ehelosigkeit und Ehe im Herrn* [FB 47; Würzburg, 1984] 48–63). Paul is merely giving advice. **7.** *as I myself am:* At the time of writing Paul was single, but J. Jeremias (ZNW 25 [1926] 310–12; 28 [1929] 321–23) argues that he was a widower (→ Paul 79:19). *each has his own gift:* Paul will no more impose celibacy than insist on marriage. What people instinctively choose manifests God's gift. Thus he takes it for granted that the married are not called to celibacy. **8–9.** The single have a choice, which must be based on practical considerations. *it is better to marry than to burn:* Flaming frustrated passion (so rightly F. Lang, *TDNT* 6. 948–51; *pace* M. L. Barré, *CBQ* 36 [1974] 193–202) is a hindrance to Christian living.

37   (b) Marriage and Divorce (7:10–16). 10–11. These verses are not a general statement of principle but the application of the dominical directive on divorce to a highly specific case (see J. Murphy-O'Connor, *JBL* 100 [1981] 601–6). **10.** *not I but the Lord:* The invocation of the dominical directive is an afterthought. *she should not permit herself to be separated:* For this sense of the passive, see BDF 314. The wife should resist being divorced. **11.** *if she should have been put away:* The pending divorce could have been finalized by the time the letter reached Corinth. *let her remain single or else be reconciled to her husband:* Having been forcibly divorced by a husband who accepted the Corinthian principle (v 1b), the wife would naturally think of remarriage, but this would make it impossible for her to forgive him fully (see *Herm. Man.* 4.1), when, as Paul hoped, the husband came to his senses. *the husband should not divorce his wife:* Jesus' prohibition of divorce (Matt 19:9; Luke 16:18) is addressed to the husband, who in Jewish law had the sole right to initiate a divorce (*m. Yebam.* 14:1; *m. Ketub.* 7:9–10; *m. Giṭ.* 9:8).

38   12–16. Some at Corinth were proposing that marriages in which only one partner had become a

Christian should be broken up, presumably because they felt it brought the world of sin too close to the church (2 Cor 6:14–7:1). Paul's response is to make a distinction. **12–13.** The good will shown by the pagan who consents to live with the convert should be capitalized on (see v 16). Hence, the marriage should be maintained. **13.** In contrast to vv 10–11, the wife is here considered capable of initiating a divorce, as in Greek and Roman law (see *RAC* 4. 707–19). **14.** *the unbeliever is sanctified:* There are many different interpretations (see G. Delling, *Studien zum Neuen Testament und zum hellenistischen Judentum* [Göttingen, 1970] 257–60); the simplest is that Paul considered the unbeliever holy because, by deciding to maintain the marriage, he or she is acting in conformity with the divine plan (Gen 2:24 = 1 Cor 6:17) and the dominical directive in 7:10–11 (see J. Murphy-O'Connor, *RB* 84 [1977] 349–61). *on account of the believer:* The decision to maintain the marriage necessarily involved the Christian partner. *your children are not unclean but holy:* In order to clarify the application of "holy" to a pagan on the basis of his comportment, Paul evokes the children of the community who, as unbelieving and unbaptized, were theoretically "unclean." But since their behavior was modeled on that of Christian parents, they were in fact "holy." *Akatharsia* and *hagiōsynē* (or a cognate) characterize the two modes of being open to humanity in 1 Thess 4:3–7 and Rom 6:19–22 (cf. Rom 12:1–2). **15.** In flat opposition to Jesus' prohibition, which was addressed to Jews (Matt 19:3) and applied to all humanity (Matt 19:4–6), Paul permits a full divorce, which in both pagan (see PW 5. 1241–45, 2011–13) and Jewish law (*m. Giṭ.* 9:3) was essentially the right of remarriage (*pace* D. Dungan, *The Sayings of Jesus in the Churches of Paul* [Phl, 1971] 89–99; J. K. Elliott, *NTS* 19 [1972–73] 223–25). *is not bound:* The writ of divorce was a deed of liberation (*m. Giṭ.* 9:3). *God has called us to peace:* The absence of *gar* indicates that this goes with what follows. **16.** *perhaps you will save:* The intention of the phrase is positive (see J. Jeremias, "Die missionarische Aufgabe in der Mischehe (I Kor 7:16)," *Neutestamentliche Studien für R. Bultmann* [ed. W. Eltester; BZNW 21; Berlin, 1954] 255–60; *pace* S. Kubo, *NTS* 24 [1978] 539–44). The situation is illustrated by 1 Pet 3:1–2.

39 (c) CHANGES IN SOCIAL STATUS (7:17–24). The essential irrelevance of every social-legal situation is shown by the fact that God's call (see comment on 1:9) comes to individuals in all situations. No change, therefore, will raise one in God's estimation. Paul's views on social equality (e.g., Gal 3:28) may have been interpreted as a program for social action by some Corinthians (see E. Neuhäusler, *BZ* 3 [1959] 43–60.) **21.** To make *mallon chrēsai* intelligible an object must be understood. Many supply *tē douleiā;* e.g., "But even if you can become free, remain the more readily as you are" (Conzelmann). In conformity with the principle of v 20, a slave, even if offered freedom, should remain in slavery. A slave, however, had no choice in the matter of manumission; it was a change of status over which he had no control (and thus parallels v 15). Hence, it is preferable to supply *tē eleutheriā;* e.g., "Yet, if you can become free, make use of the opportunity" (Robertson-Plummer; S. S. Bartchy, *Mallon Chrēsai* [SBLDS 11; Missoula, 1973; P. Trummer, *Bib* 56 [1975] 344–68). A slave should not try to refuse manumission beause of the principle in v 20. **22.** In terms of response to the divine call it does not matter whether one is a slave or a freeman. **23.** *you were bought with a price:* The idea of redemption (6:20; → Pauline Theology, 82:75) evokes the prebaptismal state of slavery to sin (Rom 3:9). *slaves of men:* This is not a criticism of slavery as such, but of the attitudes of fallen humanity (see comment on 3:3–4).

40 (d) CHANGES IN SEXUAL STATUS (7:25–40). **25.** *concerning virgins:* The formulation introduces a new topic raised by the Corinthians (see on 7:1). The meaning of *parthenoi* is disputed, and certitude is hardly possible. The choice is between engaged couples and those committed to celibacy in marriage, but each may be in view at different points. **26.** *it is good for a man to stay as he is:* This practical principle is the thesis of the section, but Paul will permit exceptions. **28.** *does not sin:* This seems to imply the breaking of a vow (Weiss) and thus points to spiritual marriage (see comment on v 36). *affliction for the flesh:* At least a more complicated life, but perhaps also criticism from the ascetics at Corinth (see comment on 7:1). **29–30.** Paul expected an imminent parousia (1 Thess 4:16–17; 1 Cor 15:51–52), and recommended not pretense but detachment. It would be silly to make new commitments when all is going to end. **32.** *free from care:* Anxious concern is a characteristic of unredeemed existence (see R. Bultmann, *TDNT* 5. 589–93). *the unmarried man:* Even though it is directed to the things of the Lord, his care is not a good thing; it suggests a fawning servility rooted in a lack of confidence in God's love. Barrett rightly sees this as a criticism of the asceticism in vogue at Corinth. **33.** *the married man:* Paul does not have in mind the love of husband and wife (Gal 5:13–14) but the complete absorption in one another of the newly married. Since the married man is a member of a community of love, his wife has only the first, but not the exclusive, claim on his affection. **34.** Paul's view of the equality of men and women is highlighted by the fact that he says precisely the same thing to the woman. *the unmarried woman or virgin:* The formulation suggests that *parthenos* is being used in a technical sense. If so, it can only mean one who has entered into a spiritual marriage (see *Herm. Sim.* 9.11). **35.** Paul gives clear advice but does not impose solutions. His attitude stands in vivid contrast to the doctrinaire positions adopted by some at Corinth. **36–38.** Opinions are sharply divided on the import of the particular case discussed here (see W. G. Kümmel, "Verlobung und Heirat bei Paulus (I Kor 7,36–38)," *Neutestamentliche Studien für R. Bultmann* 275–95; J. J. O'Rourke, *CBQ* 20 [1958] 292–98). **36.** *his virgin:* It is taken to mean either his daughter, his fiancée, or his spiritual wife. Though the most traditional, the first is the least likely; its only support is *gamizein* (v 38), but this does not necessarily mean "to give in marriage" (see BDF 101). The probability of the fiancée meaning is seriously diminished by the allusion to sin (see v 28). Why should anyone have thought it sinful for an engaged couple to marry? Moreover, this problem has been dealt with in 7:8–9. Hence, the case concerns a spiritual marriage; Paul advises that if they cannot control their sex drive they should have no scruple about entering into a normal married relationship. He wants them to be without care (v 32), undistracted (v 35). **37.** *being under no necessity:* Those capable of sustaining a spiritual marriage should maintain their commitment. **38.** *does well:* It is a question of what is good for the individual, not of what is better in principle, but Paul cannot resist mentioning his personal preference for the single state (7:7–8). The reason is not intrinsic superiority but the time factor (7:28–31). **39.** *free to be married:* Through the association of ideas Paul moves to the question of second marriages, even though he has already dealt with the problem in 7:8–9. The ideal is permanency in marriage, but death confers full freedom on the surviving partner (Rom 7:2). *only in the Lord:* I.e., remembering that she is a Christian, perhaps a hint not to enter into a mixed marriage. **40.** *I think that I also have the Spirit of God:* A massive understatement tinged with irony.

(Adinolfi, M., "Motivi parenetici del matrimonio e del celibato in 1 Cor 7," *RivB* 26 [1978] 71–91. Byron, B., "1 Cor 7:10–15: A Basis for Future Catholic Discipline on Marriage and Divorce?" *TS* 34 [1973] 429–45. Cartlidge, D. R., "1 Cor 7 as a Foundation for a Christian Sexual Ethic," *JR* 55 [1975] 220–34. Ford, J. M., "St. Paul the Philogamist (I Cor. VII in Early Patristic Exegesis)," *NTS* 11 [1964–65] 326–48. Glazer, J. W., "Commands-Counsels: A Pauline Teaching?" *TS* 31 [1970] 275–87. Moiser, J., "A Reassessment of Paul's View of Marriage with Reference to 1 Cor 7," *JSNT* 18 [1983] 103–22. Niederwimmer, K., *Askese und Mysterium* [FRLANT 113; Göttingen, 1975].)

41   (B) Problems Arising from Pagan Environment (8:1–11). Paul begins (8:1–13) and ends (10:23–11:1) with a discussion of the Christian attitude toward meat offered to idols. The theological principles involved are deepened in the examination of apparently extraneous topics in 9:1–10:22. Generally speaking, meat was available in the ancient world only after great festivals, when the priests sold the surplus of the meat of the sacrificial victims that was their share (see J. Casabona, *Récherches sur le vocabulaire des sacrifices en Grec* [Paris, 1966] 28–38). At Corinth the "strong" and the "weak" (the terminology comes from Rom 15:1) were divided on the morality of eating such meat; the former approved, the latter were revolted. The problem is also dealt with in Rom 14:1–15:13.

(Fee, G. D., "*Eidolothyta* Once Again: An Interpretation of 1 Cor 8–10," *Bib* 61 [1980] 172–97. Horsley, R. A., "Consciousness and Freedom among the Corinthians: 1 Cor 8–10," *CBQ* 40 [1978] 574–89. Lorenzi, L. de [ed.], *Freedom and Love* [Benedictina 6; Rome, 1981].)

42   (a) Food Offered to Idols (8:1–13). 1. *concerning idol-meat:* A new question raised by the Corinthians (see 7:1). *we all have knowledge:* A statement of the strong at Corinth, which will be clarified in v 4. *love builds up:* Authentic Christian knowledge must be rooted in love (Phil 1:9–10). **3.** *one is known by him:* Divine election (Rom 8:28–30) is manifested by the response of love. Paul plays down the importance of knowledge. **4.** In order to justify the eating of idol-meat, the strong based themselves on monotheism, which is expressed positively and negatively. *an idol is nothing in the world:* If an idol has no real existence (see C. H. Giblin, *CBQ* 37 [1975] 530–32), food offered to it cannot have been changed. *there is no God but one:* The basic OT conviction (Deut 6:4; Isa 44:8; 45:5). **5.** *so-called gods:* While objectively idols did not exist, for many they were subjectively real. The strong had ignored this practical point. **6.** *one God:* Paul corrects the abstract monotheism of the strong by citing an acclamation (see E. Peterson, *Heis Theos* [FRLANT 41; Göttingen, 1926]), probably from a baptismal liturgy, which highlights the role of Christ. Verbs of motion ("come" and "go") should be supplied rather than forms of "to be" (see F. M. M. Sagnard, *ETL* 26 [1950] 54–58). *all things:* The cosmological interpretation (see E. Norden, *Agnostos Theos* [Leipzig, 1913] 240–50) is less probable than the soteriological interpretation, which is more conformed to Pauline usage (Rom 11:36; 1 Cor 2:10–13; 12:4–6; 2 Cor 4:14–15; 5:18; see J. Murphy-O'Connor, *RB* 85 [1978] 253–67). There is no allusion to the preexistence of Christ (see J. D. G. Dunn, *Christology in the Making* [London, 1980] 179–83).

43   7. *having until now been accustomed to idols:* Gentile converts had not yet emotionally assimilated their intellectual conversion to monotheism. *their weak conscience:* The strong may have so qualified the objectively erroneous response of the weak. *Syneidēsis,* here used for the first time by Paul, means the awareness that one has sinned (see R. Jewett, *Paul's Anthropological Terms* [AGJU

10; Leiden, 1971] 402–39; → Pauline Theology, 82:146). **8.** *food will not bring us before (the judgment-seat of) God:* In keeping with their principle (6:13) the strong proclaim food to be morally neutral. *we are neither better off if we do not eat, nor worse off if we do eat:* This is the preferable reading, and the allusion is to charisms. They are neither increased in the case of those who abstain nor diminished for those who eat idol-meat (see J. Murphy-O'Connor, *CBQ* 41 [1979] 292–98). **9.** Paul refuses to accept the criterion proposed by the strong. The impact of one's action on others should guide a Christian's decision. **10.** *reclining in an idol's temple:* The fact that the strong participated in temple banquets put the weak in an impossible position as regards invitations, e.g., to family reunions at which idol-meat would be served (see J. Murphy-O'Connor, *St. Paul's Corinth* 161–65). *the conscience of the weak person:* No longer the "weak conscience" of v 7. Paul is trying to inspire concern for an individual in need. *will be built up:* The tone is heavily ironic and is explicable only if the strong were insisting that "the weak conscience should be built up." They thought it could be done by education, but Paul realized that the reaction of the weak had much deeper roots in the personality. **11.** *the brother:* The "weak person" of v 10 now becomes a brother in Christ, and so deserving of the same love that Christ displayed. *destroyed:* Torn apart by the unresolved tension between instinct and action. **12.** *you sin against Christ:* In context this is equivalent to destroying Christ, and so "Christ" must designate the community (see comment on 6:15; 12:12), which is torn apart by the lack of charity that binds all together in perfect harmony (cf. Col 3:14). **13.** Paul does not impose a course of action on the strong. He simply focuses the elements of reflection that he has given them by informing them of what he would do.

44   (b) Paul Renounces His Rights (9:1–27). In order to drive home the point of the last verse, Paul highlights other areas of his life in which he has accepted limitations on his freedom for the good of others. The topics are introduced by the two opening questions, with which he deals in inverse order. He discusses his apostolic ministry in vv 1c–18, and his freedom in vv 19–27.

45   1–2. Paul is an apostle because he has seen the risen Lord (15:8) and been commissioned by him (Gal 1:15–16). The Corinthians should have deduced this, since he was the channel of divine power (2:4; 2 Cor 4:7) that brought the community into being. **3.** *my defense:* Paul's personal status as an apostle has come under attack. **4.** *the right:* Since Paul had not used an apostle's right to be supported by the community, some concluded that he did not have the right and in consequence was not an apostle. **5.** The irrelevant mention of a wife was occasioned by the previous reference to eating and drinking. "Eat, drink, and be merry" (Luke 12:19) was a common triad, in which the last element was a euphemism for sexual intercourse (2 Sam 11:11; Tob 7:10; see comment on 1 Cor 10:6; see J. B. Bauer, *BZ* 3 [1959] 94–102). The individuals mentioned for comparison suggest that the opposition to Paul originated in Jerusalem. *the brothers of the Lord:* The only one named by Paul is James (Gal 1:19; cf. Mark 3:31; 6:3; Acts 1:14). *Cephas:* See comment on 1:12. **6.** *Barnabas:* See Gal 2:1,13. Since the initial *monos,* "alone," is sg., Paul suddenly must have remembered another apostle whose practice mirrored his own. *the right not to work:* Paul employs four arguments (vv 7,8,13, 14) to justify the right to support. **7.** The argument from common sense is used also in 2 Tim 2:3–6. **8.** *according to man:* This characterizes the argument in v 7 as the common estimation (see comment on 3:3; cf. C. J. Bjerkelund, *ST* 26 [1972] 63–100; D. Daube, *The New Testament and Rabbinic Judaism* [London, 1956] 394–400). **9–10.** The

citation from Deut 25:4 is interpreted on the principle that if God cares for animals he cares more for human beings (Matt 6:26). **11.** The conclusion to the first two arguments is stated as a *quid pro quo* (Gal 6:6). **12a.** The reciprocity just spoken of has in fact been accepted by the Corinthians. Missionaries other than Paul, and opposed to him (see on vv 4–5), had at least passed through Corinth. **12b.** In order to give his commitment witness value and to distinguish himself from the charlatans, who made a good living preying on the credulity of the simple (see A. D. Nock, *Conversion* [Oxford, 1933] 77–98), Paul supported himself (4:12; cf. 1 Thess 2:9).
46   **13–15.** The structure is identical to that of vv 7–12. **13.** An argument based on the cultic practice of antiquity, both Jewish and pagan. **14.** *to live from the gospel:* The command, which is addressed to the preachers and not to their hearers, summarizes a directive given for the Palestinian mission (Mark 6:8–9 par.; cf. 1 Tim 5:18). Here we catch another hint of the origin of Paul's opponents. **15.** *I have not used any of these:* The arguments in vv 7, 8, and 13 gave Paul a privilege that he was free to waive, but the dominical directive imposed an obligation. The fact that he did not obey indicates that for him even commands of the Lord were not binding precepts (see comment on 7:15). **16.** *I preach:* Preaching is the expression of Paul's being as a Christian; for this, then, he deserves no special credit. **17–18a.** *if I preached spontaneously, I merit a reward, but if unwillingly I have been commissioned, what reward can there be?* The point of v 16 is made again in a complicated way that has given rise to much discussion. **18b.** *free of charge:* Paul answers the question with a feeble joke. The wages of one not entitled to any is to work for nothing! *not making full use:* The compound verb *katachraomai* (BAGD 420) is used deliberately to disguise a mental reservation, because while at Corinth Paul was being subsidized from Macedonia (2 Cor 11:7–9).

(Dautzenberg, G., "Der Verzicht auf das apostolische Unterhaltsrecht: Eine exegetische Untersuchung zu 1 Kor 9," *Bib* 50 [1969] 212–32. Dungan, D., *Sayings of Jesus* 3–80. Käsemann, E., *NTQT* 217–35. Lüdemann, G., *Paulus, der Heidenapostel: II. Antipaulinismus im frühen Christentum* [FRLANT 130; Göttingen, 1983] 105–15. Pesch, W., "Der Sonderlohn für die Verkündiger des Evangeliums," *Neutestamentliche Aufsätze* [Fest. J. Schmid; ed. J. Blinzler *et al.*; Regensburg, 1963] 199–206. Theissen, G., *Social Setting* 27–67.)

47   **19.** Paul now turns to the theme of freedom announced in v 1. *free from all men:* He is not subject to the constraints of the financially dependent, because he assures his own livelihood. **20.** *as a Jew:* When among those who believed themselves to be under the law Paul behaved as a Jew both socially and religiously. His principle is expressed in Gal 4:12. *though not being under the law:* The law of Moses had no relevance for Christians. **21.** *those outside the law:* The primary reference is to Gentiles, but the next verse shows that there is also an allusion to the "law-less" strong at Corinth, who proclaimed *panta exestin* (6:12; 10:23). *under the law of Christ:* The reference is not to a new code of precepts (*pace* C. H. Dodd, *More New Testament Studies* [GR, 1968] 134–48) but to the law of love exemplified by Christ (Gal 6:2). *Christou* is a gen. of content (BDF 167). **22.** *I became weak:* In 8:13 Paul submits himself to the conscience of the weak. *to win the weak:* As will become clear in 10:23–11:1, the hearts of the weak also needed to be changed. *all things to all people:* The basis of Paul's integrity is love for individuals, whatever their religious or social situation. **23.** *to be a joint-partaker of it:* Since his being is to be an apostle (9:16), Paul can share in the fruits of the gospel only by bringing it to others. **24–27.** In addition to

subordinating himself to the needs of others, Paul's freedom is restricted by the need for self-discipline. Conversion is but the beginning of a process, which may be aborted by sin (see comment on 10:1–22). **27.** *I buffet my body:* The boxing metaphor must not be pushed to make Paul an advocate of penitential practices. The body for him was not evil, but the vehicle of commitment and the instrument of love. It must be trained to be more responsive to the needs of others than of its own.

(Bornkamm, G., in *StLA* 194–207. Broneer, O., "The Apostle Paul and the Isthmian Games," *BA* 25 [1962] 1–31. Chadwick, H., "'All Things to All Men' (1 Cor ix.22)," *NTS* 1 [1954–55] 261–75. Pfitzner, V. C., *Paul and the Agon Motif* [NovTSup 16; Leiden, 1967]. Richardson, P., "Pauline Inconsistency: 1 Cor 9:19–23 and Gal 2:11–14," *NTS* 26 [1979–80] 347–62.)

48   (c) THE DANGERS OF OVER-CONFIDENCE (10:1–13). Using OT examples, Paul warns the Corinthians that even those called by God can be condemned for infidelity. **1–4.** Paul establishes a parallel between the situation of the Israelites in the desert and the Corinthians. He takes it for granted that his readers are familiar with the Exodus narrative, whose order he follows: the cloud (Exod 13:21), the sea (14:21), the manna (16:4, 14–18), the water (17:6), and the rebellion (32:6). **1.** *under the cloud:* As in Ps 105:39 LXX. **2.** *baptized into Moses:* A purely Christian interpretation inspired by "baptized into Christ" (Gal 3:27; Rom 6:3). **3–4.** *spiritual food/drink:* The adj. *pneumatikon* evokes their miraculous origin, and the allusion is evidently to the eucharist. *the rock which followed them:* There is no hint of movement of the rock in the OT, but a legend developed on the basis of a Jewish interpretation of Num 21:17 (see E. E. Ellis, *JBL* 76 [1957] 53–56). *the rock was Christ:* To heighten the Corinthians' appreciation of the parallel situations, they should see the rock then as an equivalent of Christ now; the middle term is continuity of giving, not Philo's identification of the rock as Wisdom (*Leg. alleg.,* 2.86). The past tense is used not because Christ existed in the past but because the rock is not in the present (see Dunn, *Christology* 183–84). **6.** *these things were types of us:* Paul has been basing himself on the typical sense of Exod (→ Hermeneutics, 71:46–48). **7.** *do not be idolaters:* Though the Corinthians did not offer worship to pagan gods, some participated in pagan cult meals (see 8:10; 10:14–22). *stood up to play:* Jewish tradition explained the Hebr. vb. underlying *paizein* in various ways (*t. Soṭa* 6:6), including sexual immorality, which the following reference to fornication indicates must be the sense here (see 9:5). **8.** According to Num 25:1–9 the number was 24,000. **9.** Num 21:4–6. The Corinthians were testing God by their childish self-centeredness. **10.** Probably Num 17:10. *the Destroyer:* The term does not appear in the LXX. On the basis of Exod 12:23; 2 Sam 24:16; 1 Chr 21:15; Wis 18:20–25 the rabbis believed that there was a special destroying angel (Str-B 3. 412). **11.** See comment on v 6. *on whom the ends of the ages have come:* There is no really satisfactory explanation of the pl., but the meaning is that Christians are living in the last period of human history (→ Pauline Theology, 82:42). **12.** This is the point of the whole section. **13.** *except what is human:* The Corinthians, some of whom thought themselves spiritually so superior, have failed the tests that commonly beset humanity. But they could have resisted. God will permit them to be tested, but never in such a way that failure is inevitable.

(Goppelt, L., "Paul and Heilsgeschichte: Conclusions from Rom 4 and 1 Cor 10:1–13," *Int* 21 [1967] 315–26. Martelet, G., "Sacrements, figures et exhortation en 1 Cor x, 1–11," *RSR* 44 [1956] 323–59, 515–59. Meeks, W. A., "'And Rose up to Play': Midrash and Paraenesis in 1 Cor 10:1–22," *JSNT* 16 [1982]

64–78. Perrot, C., "Les exemples du désert (1 Co 10,6–11)," NTS 29 [1983] 437–52.)

49   (d) THE SIGNIFICANCE OF SOCIAL GESTURES (10:14–22). By participating in temple banquets (8:10) the strong had no intention of worshiping idols, but Paul believed that such social gestures had an objective significance that was independent of the intentions of those who made them. He had argued in the same way apropos of the act of sexual intercourse in 6:12–20. **14.** *shun:* Note the parallel with 6:18a. **15.** *reasonable people:* The appeal is to reason, but the basic premise is a matter of faith. **16.** *a sharing:* Paul begins by establishing common ground. The Corinthians accept the identification of the bread and wine of the eucharist with Christ and believe that the sharing of this meal produces a common-union or shared-union (*koinōnia*), so named because it has two focuses, Christ and other believers. The usual order of bread and cup (11:23–29) is inverted to facilitate the transition to the next verse. **17.** *one bread:* Sharing the one life-source, the loaf that is the body of Christ, believers are constituted a body whose diversity is rooted in an organic unity. **18.** *Israel:* As a further illustration of the same type of phenomenon Paul evokes the Israelite sacrifice of communion (see R. de Vaux, *Studies in Old Testament Sacrifice* [Cardiff, 1964] 27–51), in which the victim was divided between God (represented by the altar), the priest, and the offerer (Lev 3 and 7; 1 Sam 9:10–24). The sharing was understood to create a bond between all involved. **19.** *is an idol anything:* Paul forestalls an objection. The nonexistence of idols (8:4) does not affect the validity of his analogy. **20–21.** The absence of a real vertical dimension in idol-worship did not destroy the horizontal dimension established by the gesture of sharing. Thus, by participating in temple banquets, the strong entered into a "common-union" with pagans who by their belief gave idols a subjective existence, which facilitated the activity of the anti-God forces at loose in the world ("demons"). The strong were "partners with demons" insofar as they destroyed other Christians and initiated the destruction of the community (8:10–12). This they never intended but it was in fact the consequence of their action. **22.** God is stronger than the strong.

50   (e) THE SCRUPLES OF THE WEAK (10:23–11:1). Having dealt with the attitude of the strong toward idol-meat, directly in 8:1–13 and indirectly in 9:1–10:22, Paul now turns to the position of the weak, which also has blameworthy aspects. **23.** The Corinthian slogan of 6:12 is again criticized, but this time from a community perspective. *helpful:* This is explained by "build up" (*oikodomein*), which refers primarily to the edification of the community (see chaps. 12–14). **24.** *the other:* In context this means the one with whom I instinctively disagree (Barrett); it applies equally to both strong and weak. **25.** *whatever:* The utter pragmatism of this advice ("what you don't know won't hurt you") shows how far Paul had moved from the Jewish principle that "an ignorant person cannot be saintly" (*m. 'Abot* 2:6; cf. 4:13). **26.** The citation of Ps 24:1 was used by Jews to justify the blessing of food (see E. Lohse, *ZNW* 47 [1956] 277–80), but certainly not to legitimize the eating of anything and everything. **27.** *if you are invited by a pagan:* In the light of the prohibition in 10:20–21 this must be to a meal in a private house. **28–29a.** Paul suddenly adverts to the fact that his words would also be read by the strong, and so digresses to remind them that the rule of conduct enunciated in 8:13 remains in force. *out of consideration for the informant:* As in 8:11 Paul emphasizes the person (10:24), but adds a reference to *syneidēsis* (see comment on 8:7), the term preferred by the Corinthians, but which he has to

qualify immediately in order to avoid a misunderstanding. To eat such meat would have been painful only to the conscience of the weak, to whom the informant belonged. **29b–30.** Paul shifts to the 1st pers. sg. as in 8:13 and speaks from the perspective of the strong who had been attacked by the weak. *what good does it do for my freedom to be judged by the conscience of another?:* The weak assumed that the strong were also acting against their consciences and defamed them publicly (see J. Murphy-O'Connor, *RB* 85 [1978] 555–56). To which the strong responded with the shocked question, "Why am I blamed?" The fact that they blessed their food by giving thanks to God indicated that they were acting in good faith. By taking the position of the strong Paul indicted the lack of charity of the weak. **31.** *do all for the glory of God:* Note the parallel concluding exhortation in 6:20; see comment on 2:7. **32.** *be blameless as regards Jews and Gentiles:* As the next verse indicates the community has a missionary responsibility (14:3; Phil 2:14–16). It must positively empower conversion and not merely avoid creating stumbling blocks. **33.** *I seek to please:* This summary of his missionary stance (see comment on 9:19–23) does not contradict Gal 1:10 or 1 Thess 2:4. **11:1.** Christ is the ideal of humanity toward which all believers strive, but since they cannot see him, Paul's comportment must mirror "the life of Jesus" (2 Cor 4:10). This is the only authentic hermeneutic. The theme appears with reference to every community that knew Paul personally (1 Cor 4:16; Gal 4:12; Phil 3:17; 4:9; 1 Thess 1:6; 2:14).

(See bibliography, → 41 above. Betz, H. D., *Nachfolge und Nachahmung Jesu Christi im Neuen Testament* [BHT 37; Tübingen, 1967]. Cadbury, H. J., "The Macellum of Corinth," *JBL* 53 [1934] 134–41. De Boer, W. P., *The Imitation of Paul* [Kampen, 1962]. Stanley, D. M., "'Become Imitators of Me': The Pauline Conception of Apostolic Tradition," *Bib* 40 [1959] 859–77.)

51   **(C) Problems in Liturgical Assemblies (11:2–14:40).** In contrast to the question concerning spiritual gifts (12:1) the two issues dealt with in 11:2–34 were not raised in the Corinthian letter (7:1). They are the sort of thing reported to Paul orally (1:11; → 9 above). Paul, however, refers to the letter in 11:2 (see Hurd, *Origins* 68). The Corinthians may have concluded their discussion of idol-meats by saying, "We remember everything you told us and maintain the traditions as you delivered them to us. In particular we come together for prayer and the celebration of the eucharist." This neatly explains the transition, but, having just dealt with social occasions involving pagans (10:14–22,27), Paul may simply have decided to treat social occasions within the Christian community at this point.

52   (a) DRESS AT LITURGICAL ASSEMBLIES (11:2–16). The attempts by W. O. Walker (*JBL* 94 [1975] 94–110) and G. W. Trompf (*CBQ* 42 [1980] 196–215) to prove that this section is not from the pen of Paul are not convincing (see J. Murphy-O'Connor, *JBL* 95 [1976] 615–21; *CBQ* 48 [1986] 87–90). The way in which certain men, and possibly some women, dressed their hair suggested homosexual tendencies. Paul's response is to stress the importance of the difference between the sexes (for more detail on all points, see J. Murphy-O'Connor, *CBQ* 42 [1980] 482–500).

53   **3.** *head:* Gk *kephalē* never connotes authority or superiority (*pace* S. Bedale, *JTS* 5 [1954] 211–15); "source" (LSJ 945) is the only appropriate meaning here. *the source of every person's new being is Christ:* Paul evokes the role of Christ (see comment on 1:30; 4:15) in the new creation (2 Cor 5:17). The general context of Paul's thought demands that *anēr* be understood generically (see A. Oepke, *TDNT* 1. 360–62). *the source of every woman's being is man:* See comment on v 8. *the source of Christ's being is*

God: For Paul, Christ is the one who is sent (Gal 4:4–5; Rom 8:3) in view of a saving mission (1 Thess 1:10; Gal 2:20; Rom 8:29,32); it is a question of his being as Savior. **4.** *prays:* Aloud and in public, possibly with a leadership role. *prophesies:* A ministry of the word (14:3,22,31) deriving from a profound knowledge of the mysteries of God (13:2) based on the Scriptures (see C. Perrot, *LumVie* 115 [1973] 25–39). *with something hanging down from the head:* The reference is to long hair as in v 14, which male homosexuals grew in order that it might be dressed elaborately (see Philo, *De spec. leg.* 3.36). *dishonors himself: Kephalē* here means the whole person (see H. Schlier, *TDNT* 3. 674). **5.** The parallel structure indicates that the common terms have the same meaning as in v 4. *with unbound head:* Her hair is not properly dressed (see on v 15). *as if her head were shaven:* She looks mannish. Paul has to go on to explain himself. **6.** *for if a woman is unbound, let her be shorn:* Disordered hair on a woman was unfeminine only in a very generic sense. It did not connote deviant sexuality, as long hair on the male did, but Paul puts the two cases in parallel. If a woman will not tend her hair, she may as well go to the other extreme and appear as a man, whose normally short hair was sometimes shaved off for certain festivals (see Apuleius, *Metamorphoses* 11.10).

54 **7–10.** Paul's first argument against the Corinthian practice is based on the divine intention as revealed in Gen 2; the variation in the mode of creation proves that God intended men and women to be different. **7.** *a man ought not to bind up his head.* This would be unmasculine. The parallel conclusion regarding the woman appears in v 10. *he is the image and glory of God:* Since humanity lost the glory of God through the Fall (see comment on 2:7), Paul is here invoking the pristine state of humanity. *woman is the glory of man:* In Jewish tradition, with which Paul was perfectly familiar, woman was also the image (Gen 1:27; see J. Jervell, *Imago Dei* [FRLANT 76; Göttingen, 1960]) and glory of God (*Apoc. Mos.* 20:1–2). But Paul could not say so here. He had to find a formula that underlined the difference between the sexes, and the idea that woman gave glory to man (see A. Feuillet, *RB* 81 [1974] 161–82) was justified by Gen 2:18, to which he refers in v 9. According to Gen 2:21–23, woman was made from man's rib, whereas man was made from the dust of the earth (Gen 2:7). Paul wants to insinuate that if God had intended men and women to be indistinguishable, he would have created them in the same way. **10.** *a woman ought to have authority on her head:* Paul's formulation is so condensed that the meaning can only be deduced from the context. *Exousian echein* can only mean authority to be exercised, and Paul takes it for granted that women play a leadership role in the community (v 5). She enjoys this authority precisely as a woman, and so must stress her sex by her hairdo. *on account of the angels:* In order not to scandalize envoys from other churches. Same usage in Gal 4:14; Luke 7:24; 9:52; contrast Gal 1:8. **11–12.** The basis of Paul's argument in vv 7–10 was the creation account, which Jews used to prove that woman was inferior to man (Josephus, *Ag. Ap.* 2.24 § 201; see J. B. Segal, *JJS* 30 [1979] 121–37). Paul now flatly excludes such an interpretation. **11.** *woman is not otherwise than man:* In the Christian community woman is no whit inferior to man (see J. Kürzinger, *BZ* 22 [1978] 270–75). **12.** *all things are from God:* The fact that woman is the source of man (contrast v 3b) is also a manifestation of the divine intention and nullifies the Jewish interpretation of Gen 2:21–23 (see Philo, *Quaest. Gen.* 1.16).

55 **13–15.** Paul's second line of argument is based on the canonization of current convention that often passes for natural law. **14.** *long hair is degrading:* It is a sign of homosexuality. **15.** *her long hair is given to her as a*

wrapper: 1st-cent. illustrations show women with long hair wrapped around the head in plaits (see E. Pottier, M. Albert, and E. Saglio, "Coma," *Dict. des antiquités grecques et romaines* [Paris, 1887] 1361, 1368–70). **16.** Paul's final argument is the practice of other churches. He could be sure that all would agree that men should look like men and women like women.

(Adinolfi, M., "Il velo della donna e la rilettura paolina di 1 Cor 11:2–16," *RivB* 23 [1975] 94–110. Boucher, M., "Some Unexplored Parallels to 1 Cor 11:11–12 and Gal 3:28," *CBQ* 31 [1969] 50–58. Martin, W. J., "1 Cor 11:2–16: An Interpretation," *Apostolic History and the Gospel* [Fest. F. F. Bruce; ed. W. W. Gasque *et al.*; Exeter, 1970] 231–41. Meier, J. P., "On the Veiling of Hermeneutics (1 Cor 11:2–16)," *CBQ* 40 [1978] 212–26. Padgett, A., "Paul on Women in the Church: The Contradiction of Coiffure in 1 Cor 11:2–16," *JSNT* 20 [1984] 69–86. Pagels, E., "Paul on Women: A Response to Recent Discussion," *JAAR* 42 [1974] 538–49. Scroggs, R., "Paul and the Eschatological Woman," *JAAR* 40 [1972] 283–303; "Paul and the Eschatological Woman: Revisited," *JAAR* 42 [1974] 532–37.)

56 (b) THE EUCHARIST (11:17–34). Paul passes to another problem in Christian social assemblies (→ 51 above). The essence of his reaction is that there can be no eucharist in a community whose members do not love one another. **17.** *while insisting on this:* The rather awkward transition looks back to v 16 in this phrase, whereas the remainder looks forward to what is to come. **18.** *there are divisions among you:* The situation has been reported to Paul, presumably by Chloe's people (1:11). The divisions in this instance (vv 21–22) have a different origin from the party factions of 1:12. *I partly believe it:* He gives unwilling acceptance to the news. **19.** *there must be factions:* This is not simple resignation to the inevitable, but the articulation of an eschatological necessity (note the use of *dei* in 15:25, 53), which here functions as a warning. The behavior of inadequate Christians highlights the comportment of authentic believers and so facilitates God's judgment. **20.** *it is not possible to eat the Lord's Supper:* Even though the ritual words (vv 24–25) were said, the lack of love (vv 21–22) meant that in reality there was no eucharist. **21.** The meal was celebrated in a private house (Rom 16:23) whose rooms were too small to contain the whole community in one area. The division thus imposed may have been exacerbated by the Roman custom of classifying guests socially and giving little or nothing to those considered inferior (see J. Murphy-O'Connor, *St. Paul's Corinth* 153–61). *each takes his own supper before the rest:* Only the wealthier members of the community could afford to arrive early and were concerned exclusively with the gratification of their own desires. *one is hungry:* Poorer members of the community might have worked all day without eating. **22.** *do you not have houses to eat and drink in?:* If all they were interested in was eating and drinking they should have stayed at home and not indulged in the mockery of a common meal. *the have-nots:* Many Corinthian believers were poor (1:26), and the humiliation of dependency was intensified by contemptuous neglect.

57 **23.** Paul presents himself as a link in the chain of tradition reaching back to Jesus, whose authority remains present in the church. **24–25.** Paul's version of the words of institution is closest to that of Luke (22:15–20), but not dependent on it. The apostle introduced minor modifications into a text that had already undergone liturgical development (see *EWJ*). On the meaning of the eucharist, → Pauline Theology, 82:128–32. **25.** In contrast to Luke, who mentions *anamnēsis* only apropos of the bread (22:19), Paul also has an exhortation (for which he may be responsible) apropos of the cup. The meaning of the formula "Do this as my memorial" has given rise to much discussion (see

F. Chenderlin, *"Do This as My Memorial"* [An Bib 99; Rome, 1982]), but the sense in this context is determined by v 26, which is Paul's commentary designed to confront the Corinthians with the existential meaning of the eucharist. **26.** *you proclaim the Lord's death:* The death of Jesus, which is an act of love (Gal 2:20), is proclaimed existentially (2 Cor 4:10–11) in and through the shared eating and drinking (10:16). Authentic remembering is imitation of Christ (11:1), whereby God's saving love (Rom 8:39) is made present effectively in the world. From this perspective it is clear why the comportment of the Corinthians (v 21) made an authentic eucharist impossible (v 20). *until he comes:* Until Christ returns in glory (15:23).

58   **27.** Paul now applies this understanding of the eucharist to the situation at Corinth. *whoever eats the bread or drinks the cup of the Lord unworthily:* Paul has in mind the lack of loving concern for one another displayed by the Corinthians (v 21). The gen. *tou kyriou* obviously applies to the bread as well as to the cup. *will be guilty of the body and blood of the Lord:* If participants in the eucharistic meal are not united in love (v 26), they class themselves among those who murdered Jesus (Deut 19:10; cf. Heb 6:4–6; 10:29). **28.** Hence, the importance of self-examination leading to reconciliation (Matt 5:23–24) prior to participation in the eucharist. **29.** *discerning the body:* This is the criterion by which believers must judge themselves. They must evaluate the authenticity of their relationships to other members of the body of Christ, a theme already known to the Corinthians (6:15) and mentioned in 10:17. **30.** *weak and sick:* Against the Jewish background of the association of sin and sickness (Mark 2:1–12; John 9:1–2) Paul interprets an epidemic at Corinth as divine punishment. *a large number:* Many (*hikanoi*, see BAGD 374) had died, and many had been enfeebled. **31.** *if we made a practice of assessing ourselves:* Self-correction is the only way to forestall divine punishment. **32.** *being judged by the Lord we are disciplined:* Acceptance of unpleasant experiences as educative warnings is an incentive to avoid the type of behavior that merits condemnation. *together with the world:* The selfishness displayed by some Corinthians was typical of the comportment of "those perishing" (1:18). **33.** *wait for one another:* This is one practical way of "discerning the body" (v 29) and avoiding the selfishness (v 21) that destroyed the sharing that should characterize the eucharist. **34a.** When taken in conjunction with v 22 this appears as a compromise designed to diminish the impact of social differences on community life. The wealthy might indulge themselves at home, but at the eucharistic meal they should limit themselves to the common fare. **34b.** *the other matters:* Paul was unhappy with other aspects of the liturgical assemblies, but these were minor and could wait until he arrived.

(Käsemann, E., "The Pauline Doctrine of the Lord's Supper," *ENTT* 108–35. Klauck, H.-J., *Herrenmahl und hellenistischer Kult* [NTAbh 15; Münster, 1982]. Léon-Dufour, X., *Le partage du pain eucharistique selon le Nouveau Testament* [Paris, 1982]. Murphy-O'Connor, J., "Eucharist and Community in 1 Cor," *Worship* 50 [1976] 370–85; 51 [1977] 56–69. Theissen, G., *Social Setting* 145–74.)

59   (c) The Gifts of the Spirit (12:1–11). The *peri de* introduction indicates a question raised by the Corinthians. Paul's response, which runs to 14:40, suggests that it concerns the hierarchy of spiritual gifts. He discerned an egocentric competitiveness that was detrimental to church unity. **1–3.** The criterion by which manifestations of the Spirit are to be judged. **2.** *as if you were carried along:* At one stage ecstasy had authenticated the pagan Corinthians' worship of idols. **3.** *Jesus is anathema:* There were overtones of contempt in the way

the "spirit-people" neglected the lessons of the life of the historical Jesus (2 Cor 5:15), and Paul probably created this shocking formula to crystallize the implications of their attitude. *Jesus is Lord:* Paul undermines any spiritual elitism by reminding them that all had made this baptismal confession (Rom 10:9). See J. M. Bassler, *JBL* 101 (1982) 415–18; → Pauline Theology, 82:52–54. **4–7.** Since all the gifts have a common origin they should serve a common purpose. **8–10.** The list of gifts (cf. 12:27–30; Rom 12:6–8; Eph 4:11) is not exhaustive and precise definitions are impossible. Many of the meanings assumed by charismatic groups are arbitrary. **11.** Since the Spirit both gives and "operates" the gift no one should be puffed up with pride (see J. Koenig, *Charismata* [Phl, 1978].)

60   (d) The Body Needs Many Members (12:12–31). Though widespread in the ancient world, the idea of society as a body is unlikely to have been the source of the Pauline concept (→ Pauline Theology, 82:122–27). He saw society as, above all, characterized by divisions (Gal 3:28), and he predicated "body" of the Christian community to emphasize its organic unity. His use of the concept may have been triggered indirectly by ex-votos of parts of the human body in the Asclepion at Corinth (see Murphy-O'Connor, *St. Paul's Corinth* 165). **12.** *many members:* Diversity is rooted in unity. The different members all share a common existence. *Christ:* As in 6:15 the name is predicated of the community. **13.** *one Spirit to drink:* The fact that the vb. *potizein* is aor. militates against a reference to the eucharist (3:6–8). The Spirit is within the church (3:16; 6:19). **14.** *one member:* In context this is the key statement. Just as the human body needs different members (vv 14–20), so the church needs a diversity of spiritual gifts, and each one makes a specific contribution. **21.** *do not need you:* The perspective changes slightly. Now the point is that members need each other. **23–25.** In terms of clothing, the genitals receive more attention than ears or nose. The instinct of modesty reveals the divine plan to ensure that the eyes (for example) should not command all consideration. **27.** *taken singly:* The precise force of *ek merous* is unclear. Collectively the Corinthians are the body, but individually they are its members (cf. Rom 12:5). **28–30.** Paul makes the application of v 14 to spiritual gifts. **28.** The first three gifts, set off from the others by being numbered and personalized, constitute the fundamental threefold ministry of the word by which the church is founded and built up. *prophets:* See comment on 14:3. *teachers:* Their role may have differed from that of prophets by being exercised outside the framework of the liturgical assembly (see comments on Rom 12:6–7). **31.** *the higher gifts:* Either the first three in v 28, if the verb is imperative, or those gifts mistakenly esteemed by the Corinthians, if the verb is indicative.

61   (e) Love the Greatest Gift (13:1–13). At first sight chap. 13 appears to break the connection between chaps. 12 and 14. Hence, it has been considered: (a) a non-Pauline interpolation (E. L. Titus, *JBR* 27 [1959] 299–302); (b) a misplaced part of one of the letters combined into 1 Cor (W. Schenk, *ZNW* 60 [1969] 219–43); (c) a text composed for another occasion and inserted here by Paul (Barrett, Conzelmann). The first two hypotheses are without foundation. The third is recommended by the quality of the writing (Weiss) and the use of the Hellenistic literary form "praise of the greatest virtue" (cf. U. Schmid, *Die Primael der Werte im Griechischen von Homer bis Paulus* [Wiesbaden, 1964]), which made its way into the Jewish sapiential tradition (e.g., Wis 7:22–8:1; 1 Esdr 4:34–40). Nonetheless, the links with the immediate context and the Corinthian situation are so specific as virtually to impose the view that chap. 13 was written for its present place in 1 Cor.

62 **1–3.** The three statements are all constructed on the same model. In each case the conditional protasis contains an allusion to a charism mentioned in chap. 12, viz., tongues (v 1 = 12:28), prophecy (v 2 = 12:10,28), knowledge (v 2 = 12:8), faith (v 2 = 12:9), helping (v 3 = 12:28). There is a progression from the lowest gift, tongues (14:6–12), via the intellectual gifts and miracle-working faith, to acts of supreme devotion benefiting others. **2.** *I am nothing:* Only by loving does the Christian exist authentically (1:30). **3.** *to be burned:* The reading *kauthēsomai* is to be preferred to *kauchēsōmai* (R. Kieffer, *NTS* 22 [1975–76] 95–97). After the surrender of possessions, only that of the body remains. Burning was considered the most horrible of deaths. **4–7.** Rather than define love Paul personifies it. The 15 verbs all involve another person and were chosen in order to highlight virtues neglected by the Corinthians. The strong were not "patient and kind" (8:1–13). The sexual ascetics tended to "insist on their own way" (7:1–40). The community "rejoiced at wrong" (5:1–8). **8–13.** Paul contrasts the present ("now") in which the Corinthians overvalue spiritual gifts with a future ("then") in which they will give supreme importance to the essential virtues of faith, hope, and love (see E. Miguens, *CBQ* 37 [1975] 76–97). **10.** *when maturity comes, immaturity will be abolished:* This interpretation of the *to teleion—to ek merous* contrast is recommended by the following verse. Paul considered the Corinthians childish (3:1; 14:20) and desired them to be "mature" (14:20). **12.** *to see face to face:* The metaphor says no more than *epignōsomai,* "I shall really know," and is used in the OT to express the quality of Moses' knowledge of God (Exod 33:11; Num 12:8; Deut 34:10) in this present life. There is no reference to the beatific vision. *as I have been known:* See 8:3; Gal 4:9; Rom 8:29. **13.** Faith and hope are incompatible with the beatific vision, but with love are essential to Christian life (1 Thess 1:3; 2 Thess 1:3–4; Col 1:4–5).

(Kieffer, R., *Le primat de l'amour* [LD 85; Paris, 1975]. Sanders, J. T., "1 Cor 13: Its Interpretation since the First World War," *Int* 20 [1966] 159–87. Spicq, C., *Agapè dans le Nouveau Testament,* II [EBib; Paris, 1959] 53–120.)

63 (f) PROPHECY MORE IMPORTANT THAN TONGUES (14:1–25). Paul's criticism of tongues indicates that the Corinthians attached undue importance to this gift. The mysterious babble of unintelligible sounds was seen as the clearest sign of possession by the Spirit and so offered enhanced social prestige. The latent individualism is brought out by Paul's assessment in terms of utility to the community, which he highlights by contrasting tongues with prophecy. **1.** *eagerly desire:* There is a certain realism in the hint that believers tend to get the gift they want. **2.** *tongue:* Though audible, glossolalia is intelligible only to God, the author of the gift, and so is quite different from the foreign languages of Acts 2:4–11 (*pace* R. H. Gundry, *JTS* 17 [1966] 299–307). **3.** *prophesies:* Prophecy is defined by its effect on the community. Revelation in the sense of a new insight into the mystery of salvation is actualized in pastoral guidance and instruction; see comment on 1 Thess 5:19–21; Rom 12:6. **5.** *unless the latter can put it into words:* In this case there is no difference between glossolalia and prophecy; see comment on v 13 and vv 27–28. **6–12.** Paul uses three arguments to prove that sound without intelligibility contributes nothing: his own ministry (v 6); musical instruments (vv 7–8); and foreign languages (vv 10–11). **11.** *I shall be a foreigner to the speaker:* Yet in the community of faith the other should be a brother (8:11–12)! Glossolalia breaks the unity of the community. "Foreigner"

translates *barbaros,* "barbarian"; → Romans, 51:18. **13–19.** Tongues can make a contribution to the community provided they are accompanied by the exercise of the mind, which makes them intelligible. **13.** *he who speaks in a tongue should pray for the power to produce articulate speech:* There is no gift of "interpretation" given to others distinct from the speakers in tongues. The latter should aspire to a further gift that would make their inchoate experience of God intelligible (see A. C. Thiselton, *JTS* 30 [1979] 15–36). **14.** *my spirit:* The holy Spirit active in the person as gift and working through psychological channels distinct from the rational *mind.* **15.** The inarticulate activity of the Spirit should overflow into the mind and become intelligible. *sing with the mind also:* See Col 3:16. **16.** *if you bless:* God is praised in "thanksgiving" (*eucharistia*) for his grace, e.g., 2 Cor 1:3–4; 2:14. *the one who has the status of an outsider:* A believer confused about what is going on or a non-Christian. *say the Amen:* Christianity inherited from Judaism the custom of assenting to prayer by responding "Amen" (Deut 27:14–26; 1 Chr 16:7–36; Neh 5:13; 8:6). "The responsibility of the church as a whole to hear, understand, test, and control is underlined" (Barrett). **20–25.** Having dealt with the intracommunal dimension of glossolalia, Paul now turns to its relationship to the apostolate of the community. **21.** Paul cites Isa 28:11–12 in a transl. close to that of Aquila. Since the Israelites will not listen to the prophet, he threatens them with "the terrible gibberish of foreign invaders" (Robertson-Plummer), which they cannot understand. **22.** In diatribe style (→ Pauline Theology, 82:12) Paul places an inference from the citation in the mouth of an imaginary opponent, who claims that if glossolalia (in contrast to prophecy) is ineffective within the church, its purpose must be to serve as an apologetic sign to those without (see B. C. Johanson, *NTS* 25 [1978–79] 180–203). **23.** Paul resumes his argument (for this sense of *oun,* see BDF 451.1) and contradicts his interlocutor. *outsiders or unbelievers:* The two terms refer to the objective (outsider) and subjective (unbelieving) aspects of the same group; the order is reversed in the next verse. *you are raving:* A judgment that would put Christianity on the same level as the ecstatic pagan mystery cults. **24–25.** The mutual concern expressed in edification, encouragement, and consolation (14:3) is so obviously good and so evidently at variance with the self-centeredness of the "world" that the outsider is effectively challenged to perceive the active presence of God in the community.

64 (g) ORDER IN THE USE OF SPIRITUAL GIFTS (14:26–40). Liturgical assemblies that were disorderly or too long would not build up the community. Paul, in consequence, has to discount the view that possession of a gift entitled one to impose oneself on a meeting. **26.** *a hymn:* Not an OT psalm, but a spontaneous composition, as perhaps Phil 2:6–11 or 1 Tim 3:16. *a revelation:* The basis of prophetic speech. **27b–28.** *let one of them put it into words. But if he cannot put it into words, let him remain silent in the assembly:* See comment on 14:13. **29.** *let the others evaluate:* Paul has all present in mind (14:16; 1 Thess 5:19–22) and not merely other prophets (*pace* D. E. Aune, *Prophecy* 219–22). The criterion is certainly the harmony between what is said and the faith of the community. **34–35.** These verses are not a Corinthian slogan, as some have argued (N. Flanagan and E. H. Snyder, *BTB* 11 [1981] 10–11; D. W. Odell-Scott, *BTB* 13 [1983] 90–93), but a post-Pauline interpolation (G. Fitzer, *Das Weib schweige in der Gemeinde* [TEH 110; Munich, 1963]). Not only is the appeal to the law (possibly Gen 3:16) un-Pauline, but the verses contradict 11:5. The injunctions reflect the misogynism of 1 Tim 2:11–14 and probably stem from the same circle. Some mss. place these verses after v 40. **36.** *what!:* The rhetorical questions, intensified by the disjunctive particle *ē,* are a negative reaction to the situation implied in vv 26–33. **37.** *is of the Lord:* Paul had the authority of his commission (15:8–11) and the mind of Christ (2:16). Though attested by P⁴⁶, *entolē,* "command," is not authentic (see G. Zuntz, *The Text of the Epistles* [London, 1953] 139–40). **38.** *he is not recognized:* Paul refuses to admit that he is inspired (cf. v 29).

(Aune, D. E., *Prophecy in Early Christianity and the Ancient Mediterranean World* [GR, 1983]. Cothenet, E., *DBSup* 8. 1222–337. Grudem, W. A., *The Gift of Prophecy in 1 Cor* [Washington, 1982]. Hill, D., *New Testament Prophecy* [Atlanta, 1979].)

65   (V) Part IV: The Resurrection (15:1–58). There are different views of the problem that Paul faced (see J. H. Wilson, *ZNW* 59 [1968] 90–107), but the most probable hypothesis (see R. A. Horsley, *NovT* 20 [1978] 203–31) is that the denial of resurrection (v 12) came from the "spirit-people" (→ 18 above), who, under the influence of Philonic wisdom speculation, believed that they already possessed eternal life (e.g., *De spec. leg.* 1.345). Resurrection of the body would have been meaningless to those who attached no importance to the body (see 6:12–20). How the problem came to Paul's attention is unclear.

66   (A) The Creed of the Church (15:1–11). 1. *the gospel:* The basis of Paul's response is the church's belief in the resurrection of Jesus. Since he really rose from the dead, resurrection is no longer just a possible theory concerning the mode of survival after death (→ OT Thought, 77:173–74). **2.** Extreme concision makes an exact translation impossible; at least six different constructions have been proposed (see Conzelmann, *1 Corinthians* 250). *with what form of words I preached:* The precise formula Paul used is important. **3a.** *I delivered:* An introduction to the creed that Paul received and passed on. **3b–5.** Nothing proves that this earliest creed is a transl. from a Semitic language, but it almost certainly originated in a Palestinian community. Paul inserted the triple *kai hoti,* "and that." **3b.** *died for our sins in accordance with the Scriptures:* The interpretation of Jesus' death in terms of Isa 53:5 may go back to Jesus himself (see *JNTT* 287–88). **4.** *was buried:* This guaranteed the reality of his death. *raised on the third day in accordance with the Scriptures:* The only precise reference is Hos 6:2, but later Jewish tradition considered the third day the day of salvation (*Gen. Rab.* 5b on Gen 22:4–5; H. Friedman and M. Simon, *Midrash Rabbah* [London, 1939] 1. 491). **5.** *he showed himself:* The vb. *ōpthē* is to be understood not as passive but as middle voice (see A. Pelletier, *Bib* 51 [1970] 76–79). The emphasis is on the initiative of Jesus, not on the subjective experience of the beneficiaries. **6.** The point of this addition by Paul is to underline that eyewitnesses were still available for questioning. It is not a doublet of the Pentecost event (see C. F. Sleeper, *JBL* 84 [1965] 389–99). **7.** *to James, then to all the apostles:* A traditional fragment inserted by Paul to serve as a transition to his own experience. Like Paul, James, "the brother of the Lord" (Gal 1:19), had not been a disciple of Jesus (cf. Acts 1:21–22). An appearance to James is narrated in *Gos. Hebrews* 7 (*HSNTA* 1. 165). **8.** *as if to an abortion:* Possibly a term of abuse used by Paul's opponents, who mocked his physical appearance (2 Cor 10:10) and denied his apostleship (1 Cor 9:1–18). **10.** *I labored more abundantly than any of them:* The polemic note indicates an allusion to the situation dealt with in 9:1–18.

(Kremer, J., *Das älteste Zeugnis von der Auferstehung Christi* [SBS 17; Stuttgart, 1966]. Lehmann, K., *Auferweckt am dritten Tag nach der Schrift* [QD 38; Freiburg, 1968]. Murphy-O'Connor, J., "Tradition and Redaction in 1 Cor 15:3–7," *CBQ* 43 [1981] 582–89.)

67   (B) The Consequences of Different Theses (15:12–28). Having laid the foundation, Paul now confronts the Corinthians with the consequences of their denial and the benefits of his affirmation.

(a) THE CORINTHIANS' THESIS (15:12–19). Paul points out to the Corinthians that if their thesis (v 12) is correct, four conclusions must be drawn: (1) Christ has not been raised (vv 13,16); (2) Paul's preaching is in vain (v 14) and he is open to the charge of misrepresenting God (v 15); (3) the faith of the Corinthians is meaningless and they are still sinners (vv 14,17); (4) those who died as Christians are definitively lost (v 18). He concludes on a rather effective emotional note (v 19). **12–13.** If here and in vv 15–16 Paul draws a conclusion concerning a specific individual, Christ, the sense of the Corinthian claim must be that there is no such thing as resurrection from the dead; it was not part of God's plan for humanity. **14.** *in vain:* In Paul's lexicon (1 Cor 15:10,58; 2 Cor 6:1; Phil 2:16; 1 Thess 2:1; 3:5) *kenos* means "nonproductive." His preaching brought nothing new into being, and the Corinthians are unchanged. **17.** *ineffective:* By using *mataia* (see 3:20), Paul intensifies the force of *kenos.* This verse is the key argument and the one most likely to reach the Corinthians. They thought of themselves as wisdom-filled (→ 65 above) precisely as Christians (see 2:8; 6:4). Through conversion to Christ they had been changed, raised to a new level of being (see comment on 1:30; 4:15), but if Christ was not as Paul said, then nothing had altered. They were as the rest of humanity. Their denial of the resurrection sapped the foundations of their cherished status (see comment on 2:6–16). **18.** *those who have fallen asleep in Christ:* Those who have died (1 Thess 5:10) as Christians (1 Thess 4:16) are lost (the same verb is used in 1:18 to designate nonbelievers), even if they thought of themselves as "spirit-people." This is a further conclusion from v 17. **19.** *if in this life we who are Christians have only hope:* Many pagans had what was for Paul an unfounded hope in a future state of beatitude. To deny the resurrection of Christ (which for Paul transformed survival after death from a theoretical possibility into a real possibility) reduced Christians to the same miserable level.

(Bachmann, M., "Zur Gedankenführung in 1 Kor 15:12ff.," *TZ* 34 [1978] 265–76. Bucher, T. G., "Die logische Argumentation in 1 Kor 15:12–20," *Bib* 55 [1974] 465–86; "Nochmals zur Beweisführung in 1 Kor 15:12–20," *TZ* 36 [1980] 129–52.)

68   (b) PAUL'S THESIS (15:20–28). Human logic here gives way to the passion of the prophet proclaiming a conviction that transcends reason and experience. **20.** *the firstfruits:* What was done for Christ can be done for others, and God's goodness indicates that it will. **21–22.** See Rom 5:12–21. The parallel between Adam and Christ is founded in the ideas of belonging (to Adam by nature; to Christ by decision) and causality (through Adam, who infected society with sin and death; through Christ who gives life). **23.** *at his appearance:* The general resurrection will take place at the second coming of Christ (1 Thess 4:16). **24–26.** Having been exalted to the status of Lord through his resurrection (15:45; Rom 1:3–4; 14:9), Christ must continue his work by destroying the hostile powers (2:6b), who hold the living captive, and then Death, the master of the dead. The kingdom is not yet perfect, and the Corinthians do not yet reign (4:8). **24.** *rule, authority, and power:* These are mythological expressions for forces hostile to authentic humanity. See Rom 8:38; cf. Col 1:16; 2:10; Eph 1:21. **25.** *he must continue to reign:* The necessity is that of the divine plan as revealed in a prophetic psalm, Ps 110:1b, which is quoted implicitly. **26.** The personification of Death is well attested in the OT, e.g., Pss 33:19; 49:14; Jer 9:20–22; Hab 2:5; see N. J.

Tromp, *Primitive Conceptions of Death and the Netherworld in the OT* (BibOr 21; Rome, 1969). **27.** Ps 8:7 is also associated with Ps 110:1 in Eph 1:20–22. In both psalm citations the emphasis is on "all," which permits the extension to Death but might create a misunderstanding. Thus, Paul continues, "It is plain that this is with the exception of him (God) who subjected all things to him (Christ)." **28.** *the Son himself:* Within history Christ exercises the sovereignty of God, but once history comes to its end (v 24a), there will be no more struggle (v 24b), and so he will remit into the hands of his Father the authority given him for his mission of salvation. The subordination of Christ to God (3:23) creates problems for dogmatic theologians.

(Barth, G., "Erwägungen zu 1 Kor 15:20–28," *EvT* 30 [1970] 515–27. Cothenet, E., *DBSup* 10. 173–80. Lambrecht, J., "Paul's Christological Use of Scripture in 1 Cor 15:20–28," *NTS* 28 [1982] 502–27. Schendel, E., *Herrschaft und Unterwerfung Christi* [BGBE 12; Tübingen, 1971]. Wilcke, H. A., *Das Problem eines messianischen Zwischenreiches bei Paulus* [Zurich, 1967].)

69   (C) Ad Hominem Arguments for Resurrection (15:29–34). Abruptly Paul switches back to a hard-nosed approach similar to that in vv 12–19. He argues (1) from his own apostolic commitment (vv 29–32a) and (2) from the inevitable consequences for ethics of a denial of resurrection.
70   29. Interpretations of this verse are legion (Foschini, Rissi), but the most common view sees Paul as referring to members of the community who had themselves baptized on behalf of dead friends or relatives who had died unbelievers (so Barrett, Conzelmann, Senft, *et al.*). Paul's sacramental theology, however, would never have permitted him to condone such superstition, much less to use it as an argument. Moreover, the antecedent context suggests that v 29 should evoke Paul's ministry in a general way, and this is confirmed by vv 30–32a. In this perspective one would translate, *Why are they destroying themselves on account of those dead (to higher spiritual truths)? If those who are really dead are not raised, why are they being destroyed on their account?* The "spirit-people" at Corinth—those who denied the resurrection (→ 65 above)—had mocked Paul for the effort he expended on those whom they considered merely "soul-people" (→ 18 above). By radicalizing the gibe in the second question, Paul draws their attention to the implications of such effort. He would not be working himself to death, were he not absolutely convinced that the dead would be raised.

(Foschini, B. M., "'Those Who Are Baptized for the Dead' [1 Cor 15:29]," *CBQ* 12 [1950] 260–76, 379–99; 13 [1951] 46–78, 172–98, 276–83. Rissi, M., *Die Taufe für die Toten* [ATANT 42; Zurich, 1962]. Murphy-O'Connor, J., "'Baptized for the Dead' [1 Cor 15:29]. A Corinthian Slogan?" *RB* 88 [1981] 532–43.)

71   30. *we are in danger every hour:* The wearing effect of such tension confirms the well-attested sense postulated for *baptizontai* in v 29 (see Oepke, *TDNT* 1. 530). **31.** *your boasting which I have:* The apparent contradiction has suggested an interpolation (D. R. MacDonald, *HTR* 93 [1980] 265–76), but the possessive adj. *hymetera* embodies the ambiguity of the gen. (BDF 285) and must be understood objectively as in Rom 11:31. The Corinthians are Paul's boast (9:2; 2Cor 3:2). **32a.** *speaking popularly:* By this phrase (see comment on 9:8) Paul indicates that the allusion to fighting with beasts at Ephesus should be understood figuratively, as "to be saved from the lion's mouth" (Ps 22:21; 1 Macc 2:60; 2 Tim 4:17; 1QH 5:9,11,19). See A. J. Malherbe, *JBL* 87 (1968) 71–80. **32b.** *if the dead are not raised:* If this life is the

only one, why should one dedicate it to others? The immediate referent is Paul, but the application is much wider. The citation from Isa 22:13 would have evoked Epicurean sayings, and the "spirit-people" at Corinth would not have wanted to be associated with such materialists. **33.** *no longer permit yourselves to be deceived:* Paul here addresses the community as a whole. The citation from Menander (*Thaïs* frg. 218) had the status of a proverb, and here "bad company" means those who deny the resurrection. **34.** *what some have is ignorance of God:* An allusion to the slogan of 8:1 is probable and suggests a certain overlap between the strong and the "spirit-people" to whom this verse is addressed.
72   (D) The Resurrected Body (15:33–49). Paul deals with two associated questions. What is the resurrected body like (vv 35–44a)? What reason is there to think that such a body really exists (vv 44b–49)?
73   35. The diatribe-style questions (→ Pauline Theology, 82:12) are really an objection. If nothing can be said about the risen body, it is pointless to talk about resurrection. *with what sort of body do they come?:* This question was first raised in Judaism in *2 Apoc. Bar.* 49:2, written some 30 years after 1 Cor. **36–38.** The plant that emerges has a body different from the seed that was buried. The form of the plant body is determined by God, and no one could guess his intention from the form of the seed body, particularly since so many different plants come from seeds that look very much alike. **39–41.** The point here is that words like "flesh," "body," and "glory" are not univocal terms. There are different types of each, and so the realities to which we apply such terms may not be the only realities to which they may be applied. **40.** *celestial bodies:* In Jewish tradition the stars were considered animate beings (*1 Enoch* 18:13–16; 21:3–6; Philo, *De plant.* 12). **42–44a.** With his imaginary interlocutor's mind thus prepared, Paul answers the question of v 35 by simply transforming four negative qualities of the present body into positive qualities. The negative qualities selected would all have been heartily approved by his opponents, and the choice may have been a tactful gesture on Paul's part. The vb. "sow" is used to apply the idea developed in vv 36–38, viz., that continuity may be accompanied by radical change. The image, of course, derives from burial. **44a.** *physical body:* The adj. is derived from *psychē*, "soul," which could be conceived of as a purely material principle of animation (Philo, *Quis rer. div.* 55). "Earthly body" would have been a less ambiguous expression, but Paul had already used it (and its antithesis) in another sense in v 40. *spiritual body:* The human body as adapted by the Spirit of God for a completely different mode of existence (see comment on vv 51–53).
74   44b. *also a spiritual one:* Paul here begins to answer the question, How do we know that there is in fact a resurrection body? The form of his thesis implies some common ground with his opponents, which he can use as a starting point. In order to reconcile the two accounts of creation Philo distinguished the heavenly man of Gen 1 from the earthly man of Gen 2 (*Leg. alleg.* 1. 31–32) and argued that the second, historical man was a copy of the first ideal man (*De op. mund.* 134). Paul accepts the distinction but maintains (obviously with Christ in mind) that the relationship should be understood differently. **45.** *the first man Adam became a living soul:* By adding "Adam" to the citation of Gen 2:7b, Paul accepts the historical character of this figure. By adding "first" he departs from the exegesis of Philo. *the last Adam became a life-giving spirit:* In virtue of a belief that the end would correspond to the beginning, Jewish theology granted Adam a role in the eschaton (*1 Enoch* 85–90; *Apoc. Mos.* 21:6; 39:2; 41:1–3). This permitted Paul to present

Christ as the last Adam. Through his resurrection he became Lord (Rom 1:3–4; 14:9) and so, in contrast to the first Adam, is presented as a giver, not a recipient, of life. **46.** *first:* Since for Philo the heavenly man was both incorporeal and incorruptible (*De op. mund.* 134), his body could be described as "spiritual." For Paul this quality could be predicated only of the risen body of Christ. Hence, he reverses Philo's order, thus overturning the position of his opponents, who would have accepted the idea of a heavenly man, and so confirming his thesis in v 44b. **47.** Paul amplifies what he has just said, but in terms that echo Philo's terminology. *from earth, from heaven:* In context these multivalent phrases are intended to indicate the sphere to which Adam and Christ belong, e.g., certain qualities are implied by saying that someone is "from Ireland." **48–49.** These verses reiterate the thought of vv 21–22, but from a slightly different perspective. Adam and Christ each represent a possibility of human existence, possibilities that are real since all are what Adam was and can become what Christ is. **49.** *to bear the image:* To have the same sort of body.

(Altermath, F., *Du corps psychique au corps spirituel* [BGBE 18; Tübingen, 1977]. Barrett, C. K., *From First Adam to Last* [London, 1961]. Dunn, J. D. G., "1 Cor 15:45—Last Adam, Life-giving Spirit," *Christ and Spirit in the New Testament* [Fest. C. F. D. Moule; ed. S. S. Smalley, *et al.;* Cambridge, 1973] 127–41. Morissette, R., "La condition de ressuscité. 1 Cor 15:35–49: Structure littéraire de la péricope," *Bib* 53 [1972] 208–28. Pearson, B., *The Pneumatikos–Psychikos Terminology in 1 Corinthians*. Scroggs, R., *The Last Adam* [Oxford, 1966]. Sharp, J. L., "The Second Adam in the Apocalypse of Moses," *CBQ* 35 [1973] 35–46. Stemberger, G., *Der Leib der Auferstehung* [AnBib 36; Rome, 1972].)

75   (E) The Need for Transformation (15:50–58).   50. J. Jeremias (*NTS* 2 [1955–56] 151–59) sees the two parts of the verse as complementary, because he takes "flesh and blood" as meaning the living, and "corruption" as meaning those who have already died. It is perhaps more likely that "corruption" explains why "flesh and blood" are incompatible with an eternal kingdom. **51.** *mystery:* A hidden truth revealed to and through Paul about what is to happen at the end (Rom 11:25). *all (of us) we shall not sleep:* Unless *pantes ou* is assumed to be identical with *ou pantes* (BDF 433), Paul expected the parousia to come before any more Corinthians died. Some witnesses delete the negative in order to remove Paul's unfulfilled expectation that he would live to see the parousia. **52.** The distinction between living and dead serves only to stress the equality in the destiny of both groups; it is related to the nature of the human person. *at the trumpet of the eschaton:* The trumpet was part of Jewish apocalyptic imagery (Joel 2:1; Zeph 1:16; 4 Ezra 6:23; cf. 1 Thess 4:13–18). **53.** Strictly speaking, *aphtharsia,* "incorruption," and *athanasia,* "immortality," are not synonyms. The former is applicable only to material beings (Wis 2:23; cf. J. Reese, *Hellenistic Influence on the Book of Wisdom and Its Consequences* [AnBib 41; Rome, 1970] 65–66), but Paul predicates it of God in Rom 1:23. Here he specifies the type of change the living must undergo. **54b.** For his climax Paul combines two OT texts. Only Theodotion comes close to Paul's version of Isa 25:8 (see A. Rahlfs, *ZNW* 20 [1921] 182–99), which influenced him to insert "victory" in Hos 13:14. **56.** Sin, death, and law have played no role in Paul's theology up to this point, but they are key concepts in Rom (→ Pauline Theology, 82:82–100). The verse may have originated as a post-Pauline marginal note. **57.** Typically Paul stresses that our victory over death is due to Jesus Christ. **58.** *be steadfast, immovable:* The exhortation evokes "if you hold fast" (v 2), creating a neat inclusion.

76   (VI) Conclusion (16:1–24).
        (A) The Collection for Jerusalem (16:1–4).
1. *now concerning:* The formula indicates a question raised by the Corinthians (7:1). The collection for the impoverished of Jerusalem (Rom 15:26) was decided at the Jerusalem Conference (Gal 2:10) in early fall AD 51, after the journey described in Acts 15:36–18:22 (see J. Murphy-O'Connor, *RB* 89 [1982] 71–91; or possibly in AD 49; → Paul, 79:31–33). Paul hoped that this good-will gesture would bridge the growing gap between the Jewish and Gentile wings of the church (Rom 15:25–31). *the churches of Galatia:* Paul must have informed the Galatians when he visited them for the second time (Acts 18:23) on his way overland to Ephesus. *so you are also to do:* The aid of the Corinthians must have been solicited during his long stay in Ephesus (Acts 19:8–10), possibly in the previous letter (1 Cor 5:9), because their question concerned the mechanics of the collection. No direct contact between Corinth and Galatia is implied, for Paul goes on to repeat the instructions given the latter. **2.** *the first day of the week:* Sunday (see W. Rodorf, *Sunday* [Phl, 1968]). The fellowship expressed in the liturgical assembly was to serve as a reminder to be generous to others. *each of you:* No believer at Corinth was destitute (1:26), but the impression is that spare cash was limited. In order that the total might do honor to the church, a little was to be put aside each week. As to how they responded, see comments on 2 Cor 8–9. **3–4.** These instructions reflect Paul's concern that money should not obscure the witness value of his ministry (9:15; 1 Thess 2:5–9). Suggestions that he had been accused of financial mismanagement are unfounded.

(Georgi, D., *Die Geschichte der Kollekte des Paulus für Jerusalem* [TF 38; Hamburg, 1965]. Nickle, K. F., *The Collection* [SBT 48; London, 1966].)

77   (B) Paul's Travel Plans (16:5–9).   5–7. Circumstances forced Paul to change this plan (→ 2 Corinthians, 50:9). **8.** This fixes the place of composition of 1 Cor.
78   (C) Some Recommendations (16:10–18).
10–11. Timothy has already left, and Paul's worry about his reception at Corinth is manifest (4:17). **12.** *Apollos:* The Corinthians had set Apollos against Paul (1:12; cf. 3:5–9; 4:6); Paul makes it clear that Apollos's failure to return to Corinth was not due to any refusal on his part. **15–18.** Stephanas, Fortunatus, and Achaicus may have brought the letter from Corinth (7:1). If so, they could have confirmed the gossip brought by Chloe's people (1:11). **15.** *the household of Stephanas:* Mentioned as having been baptized by Paul (1:16), thus one of the first converts at Corinth (cf. Acts 17:34). *Achaia:* The southern and central portion of Greece, a Roman province since 27 BC (Strabo, *Geogr.* 17.3,25). *they appointed themselves for the service of the saints:* Seeing a need, they met it. **16.** The basis of Christian authority is effective service to the community. Paul urges the Corinthians to recognize the *de facto* situation implied in v 15. **17.** *Achaicus:* This nickname ("the man from Achaia") suggests that he was a freedman who had lived outside Greece for some time.
79   (D) Final Greetings (16:19–24).   19. *Aquila and Prisca.* Prisca is mentioned before her husband in Rom 16:3 (→ Romans, 51:132) as well as in Acts 18:18,26. The implication is that she had higher status than her husband (see Meeks, *First Urban Christians* 59). *the church in their house:* This type of gathering is to be distinguished from the assembly of the whole church (14:23; Rom 16:23). Subgroups were a virtual necessity in view of the amount of space available in the average house (see comment on 11:21). **20.** *with a holy kiss:* See comment on Rom 16:16.

The kiss was definitely part of the Christian liturgy in the 2d cent. AD (see K.-M. Hofmann, *Philema Hagion* [BFCT 2; Gütersloh, 1938]), but it was only possibly so at the time of Paul (see G. Stählin, *TDNT* 9. 139–40). Thus, the injunction does not guarantee that his letters were read in the liturgical assembly. **21.** Since letters were written by different secretaries (Rom 16:22; see G. Bahr, *CBQ* 28 [1966] 465–77), they had to be authenticated by Paul (Gal 6:11; Phlm 19; Col 4:18; see G. Bahr, *JBL* 87 [1968] 27–41). Forgeries were not unknown (2 Thess 2:2; cf. 3:17); → NT Epistles, 45:19–22. **22.** *if anyone does not love the Lord:* The use of *philein* rather than Paul's usual *agapan* indicates the presence of a traditional Christian formula, possibly of liturgical origin (see C. Spicq, *NovT* 1 [1956] 200–4). *let him be anathema:* See comment on 12:3. *our Lord, come:* The much discussed *maranatha* (*Did.* 10:6) is probably a transcription of an elision of the Aramaic *māránā' 'āthā'*. So far there is no contemporary evidence for the impv. form, but the suffixal substantive is attested in 4QEn[b] 1 iii 14 (see Fitzmyer, *TAG* 223–29). The formula derives from the liturgy and prays for the second coming (4:5; 5:5; 11:26; 15:23). **24.** *my love be with you all:* Despite all the problems that the Corinthians caused him, the note of paternal affection is evident (4:14–15; 2 Cor 12:14).

50

THE SECOND LETTER TO THE CORINTHIANS

Jerome Murphy-O'Connor, O.P.

BIBLIOGRAPHY

1　　Allo, E.-B., *Saint Paul: Seconde épître aux Corinthiens* (EBib; 2d ed.; Paris, 1956). Barrett, C. K., *The Second Epistle to the Corinthians* (HNTC; NY, 1973). Bultmann, R., *The Second Letter to the Corinthians* (Minneapolis, 1985). Collange, J.-F., *Enigmes de la deuxième épître aux Corinthiens* (SNTSMS 18; Cambridge, 1972). Fallon, F. T., *2 Corinthians* (NTM 11; Wilmington, 1980). Furnish, V. P., *II Corinthians* (AB 32A; GC, 1984). Hanson, R. P. C., *The Second Epistle to the Corinthians* (TBC; London, 1967). Héring, J., *The Second Epistle of St. Paul to the Corinthians* (London, 1967). Hughes, P. E., *Paul's Second Epistle to the Corinthians* (NICNT; GR, 1962). Martin, R. P., *2 Corinthians* (WBC; Waco, 1986). Plummer, A., *The Second Epistle of St. Paul to the Corinthians* (ICC; Edinburgh, 1915). Prümm, K., *Diakonia Pneumatos* (2 vols.; Rome, 1960, 1967). Rissi, M., *Studien zum zweiten Korintherbrief* (ATANT 56; Zurich, 1969). Schelkle, K. H., *The Second Epistle to the Corinthians* (NY, 1981). Tasker, R. V. G., *The Second Epistle of Paul to the Corinthians* (TynNTC; GR, 1958). Windisch, H., *Der zweite Korintherbrief* (MeyerK 6; 9th ed.; ed. G. Strecker; Göttingen, 1970). For commentaries combining 1 and 2 Cor, → 1 Corinthians, 49:1.

DBSup 7. 183–95. *IDBSup* 183–86. Kümmel, *INT* 279–93. Wik-Schm, *ENT* 432–48.

INTRODUCTION

2　　**(I) Authenticity and Unity.** With the exception of 6:14–7:1, which many consider a post-Pauline interpolation, the authenticity of 2 Cor is unquestioned. Its unity, however, is a matter of some controversy. Although the integrity of 2 Cor has its defenders (Allo, Hughes, Lietzmann; W. H. Bates, *NTS* 12 [1965–66] 56–69; N. Hyldahl, *ZNW* 64 [1973] 289–306), the majority of commentators see it as a collection of Pauline letters. The most influential view is that of G. Bornkamm (*NTS* 8 [1961–62] 258–64), who divides 2 Cor into five letters dated in the following order: (A) 2:14–7:4 minus 6:14–7:1; (B) 10–13, the sorrowful letter; (C) 1:1–2:13 plus 7:5–16, the letter of reconciliation; (D) 8:1–24, a letter to Corinth concerning the collection for Jerusalem; (E) 9:1–15, a circular letter to Achaia about the collection. This hypothesis is based on what are viewed as hard transitions in the present text of 2 Cor. The details will be discussed in the commentary, but with many interpreters I do not find that the breaks in chaps. 1–9 involve such a degree of discontinuity as to demand a partition hypothesis. Chaps. 10–13, however, cannot be the continuation of chaps. 1–9; it is psychologically impossible that Paul should suddenly switch from the celebration of reconciliation (1–9) to a savage reproach and sarcastic self-

vindication (10–13). Thus, 2 Cor is certainly a combination of two letters.

3　　Because of the harsh tone a number of scholars (Bornkamm, Georgi, *KINT* 2. 126–30) identify chaps. 10–13 with the sorrowful letter (2 Cor 2:4; 7:8), and so date it before chaps. 1–9. This hypothesis is untenable. The sorrowful letter was occasioned by the behavior of a single individual (2 Cor 2:5–8), who is not even alluded to in chaps. 10–13, which are concerned with the damage done to the community by false apostles. It is more probable (Barrett, Furnish, Windisch) that chaps. 10–13 (Letter B) were occasioned by some development at Corinth subsequent to the dispatch of chaps. 1–9 (Letter A). The seeds of the trouble that necessitated Letter B can be detected in Letter A.

4　　**(II) Time and Place of Composition.** The sequence of events between 1 Cor and 2 Cor is treated elsewhere (→ Paul, 79:41–43), but I would lower the dates given there by three years. Letter A was written a year after 1 Cor (2 Cor 8:10; 9:2; cf. 1 Cor 16:1–4), therefore in the spring of AD 55, from Macedonia (2 Cor 2:13; 7:5; 8:1; 9:2), where Paul had wintered at Thessalonica or Philippi. Titus, who had been the bearer of the no longer extant sorrowful letter (2 Cor 7:6) because he had been at the Jerusalem Conference (Gal

2:1; see comment on 1 Cor 16:1) and could report authoritatively on the attitude of the mother church to the Gentile mission, was also entrusted with Letter A (2 Cor 8:16–17), which brought to a happy conclusion a distasteful episode in Paul's relations with Corinth.

Having spent the winter with the churches of Macedonia, there was little more for Paul to do there, so in the summer of AD 55 he moved on to virgin territory (2 Cor 10:16) in Illyricum (Rom 15:19). At some point news reached him there of a drastic deterioration in the situation at Corinth. Letter B was written in the heat of his disappointment and anger.

5   (III) The Opponents. Letters A and B reflect different stages of a developing situation at Corinth. Opposition to Paul that is only hinted at in Letter A is brought out into the open in Letter B. There is a consensus on two points: the intruders were Jewish Christians, and they attacked Paul's apostolic authority. Disagreement, however, persists concerning the adversaries' origins and role at Corinth, because the evidence points in different directions. Some hints indicate Judaizers of Palestinian origin, whose attitude toward the law was more positive than Paul found palatable. Other clues, however, are thought to suggest Hellenistic-Jewish wandering preachers, who were convinced that their possession of the Spirit showed itself in their eloquence, their ecstatic experiences, and their power to work miracles. There has been a tendency to emphasize one set of clues at the expense of the other, with the result that there are two dominant schools of thought. For one the opponents are Judaizers; for the other Hellenistic-Jewish propagandists. The ways in which each group strives to integrate elements unsympathetic to its basic hypothesis defy systematic presentation. The position adopted here is a modification of approaches first suggested by Windisch and Barrett. The intruders were Palestinian Judaizers. In Corinth they developed links with the "spirit-people" (→ 1 Corinthians, 49:18), who had previously created problems for Paul. In the process both groups were somewhat changed. The situation was further complicated by the fact that the Corinthian church, which had to decide between Paul and his rivals, tended to adopt the criteria by which their pagan contemporaries judged religious figures. This in turn influenced not only Paul's opponents but the apostle himself. They adapted their modes of presentation in varying degrees to meet the expectations of the community.

(Barrett, C. K., "Paul's Opponents in II Corinthians," *NTS* 17 [1970–71] 233–54. Friedrich, G., "Die Gegner des Paulus im

2 Korintherbrief," *Abraham unser Vater* [Fest. O. Michel; ed. O. Betz, et al.; AGJU 5; Leiden, 1963] 181–215. Georgi, D., *The Opponents of Paul in Second Corinthians* [Phl, 1984]. Lüdemann, G., *Paulus, der Heidenapostel: II. Antipaulinismus im frühen Christentum* [FRLANT 130; Göttingen, 1983] 125–42. Machalet, C., "Paulus und seine Gegner," *Theokratia* 2 [1973] 183–203.)

6   (IV) Outline. In both of the letters combined in 2 Cor, Paul is on the defensive. Outbursts of passion, stimulated by a sense of injury, replace the cool logic that permitted clear divisions in 1 Cor. Themes are strung together by means of associative links that give rise to digressions and repetitions, which make a precise outline impossible. The proposed divisions are legion, and the one presented here intends only to set in relief what seems to be the dominant aspect of the various parts of the letters.

Letter A (1–9)
(I) Introduction: Greeting and Blessing (1:1–11)
(II) Part I: A Canceled Visit to Corinth (1:12–2:13)
  (A) Paul's Plan (1:12–22)
  (B) The Consequences of a Change of Plan (1:23–2:13)
(III) Part II: Authentic Apostleship (2:14–6:10)
  (A) The Apostolate: Theory and Practice (2:14–3:6)
  (B) Ministry: Old and New (3:7–4:6)
  (C) Ministry and Mortality (4:7–5:10)
    (a) The Manifestation of Jesus (4:7–15)
    (b) Facing the Fear of Death (4:16–5:10)
  (D) Reconciliation in a New Creation (5:11–6:10)
    (a) The New Creation (5:11–17)
    (b) The Ministry of Reconciliation (5:18–6:10)
(IV) Part III: Relations with Corinth (6:11–7:16)
  (A) An Appeal for Openness (6:11–7:4)
  (B) The Results of the Mission of Titus (7:5–16)
(V) Part IV: The Collection for Jerusalem (8:1–9:15)
  (A) A Challenging Request (8:1–15)
  (B) The Recommendation of Representatives (8:16–9:5)
  (C) The Rewards of Generosity (9:6–15)

Letter B (10–13)
(VI) Part I: An Appeal for Complete Obedience (10:1–18)
  (A) The Consequences of Disobedience (10:1–6)
  (B) Paul's Authority as Founder of the Community (10:7–18)
(VII) Part II: Paul Speaks like a Fool (11:1–12:13)
  (A) His Justification for Being Foolish (11:1–21a)
  (B) Paul's Boasts of Himself (11:21b–12:10)
    (a) His Sufferings (11:21b–33)
    (b) His Visions and Revelations (12:1–10)
  (C) Further Justification for His Foolishness (12:11–13)
(VIII) Part III: A Warning Prepares a Visit (12:14–13:10)
  (A) Again the Question of Financial Support (12:14–18)
  (B) The Corinthians Must Correct Themselves (12:19–13:10)
(IX) Conclusion: Final Words and Greeting (13:11–13)

COMMENTARY: LETTER A

7   (I) Introduction: Greeting and Blessing (1:1–11). 1–2. The address is stereotyped (→ NT Epistles, 45:8A). *Timothy:* See comment on 1 Cor 4:17. *saints:* See comment on 1 Cor 1:2. *Achaia:* See comment on 1 Cor 16:15. Nothing is known about communities other than in Corinth. 3–11. The use of a blessing in place of the usual thanksgiving (→ NT Epistles, 45:8B) betrays Paul's recognition of God's goodness in saving him from deadly peril in Asia. 3. *comfort:* This noun and its corresponding verb appear 25 times in Letter A. It implies not sympathetic consolation but active strengthening to endure "affliction," which is mentioned 12 times in Letter A. 4. Paul can strengthen others because he himself has

been strengthened. 5. *the sufferings of Christ:* The sufferings of the community (Phil 3:10–11; Col 1:24), which is "Christ" (see comment on 1 Cor 6:15; 12:12), reflect those of the historical Jesus (see B. Ahern, *CBQ* 22 [1960] 1–32; C. M. Proudfoot, *Int* 17 [1963] 140–60). *our comfort also abounds:* God strengthens Paul in proportion to his sufferings, which brought the community into being and of which they are part. Affliction does not imply disgrace or defeat. 7. Those who have shared pain and comfort can face the future confidently despite current problems. 8–11. Paul makes the theme of strength in affliction more concrete by evoking a terrifying personal experience in Asia. 8. *we do not want you to be ignorant:* This disclosure formula (see T. Y. Mullins, *NovT* 7 [1964] 44–50) introduces new information. *affliction in Asia:* Details are lacking because it was the meaning that was important for Paul. The formulation excludes a serious illness (as in Gal 4:13). Paul had been imprisoned in Ephesus (→ Philippians, 48:5–6), the capital of the Roman province of Asia (in modern western Turkey), but this is less likely than a violent episode such as the revolt of the silversmiths (Acts 19:23–20:1). *we even despaired of survival:* There seemed to be no way out of the predicament. **9.** *sentence of death:* The formulation suggests less a juridical condemnation than Paul's conviction that his days were numbered. *that we should no more rely on ourselves:* Confidence in God is based on experience of his power. **10.** *from such deadly dangers:* The episode in Ephesus was but the latest of many threats to Paul's life (4:11; 11:23). The pl. reading of P[46] is preferable to the widely accepted sg. **11.** As yet no one has succeeded in unraveling the syntax of this verse. Paul hopes that the Corinthians' intercessory prayer and his own in view of a future deliverance will be transformed into thanksgiving for a successful rescue.

(Hofius, O., "'Der Gott allen Trostes': *Paraklēsis* und *parakalein* in 2 Kor 1:3–7," *TBei* 14 [1983] 217–27. Watson, N. M., "'. . . to Make Us Rely not on Ourselves but on God Who Raises the Dead': 2 Cor 1:9b as the Heart of Paul's Theology," *Die Mitte des Neuen Testaments* [Fest. E. Schweizer; ed. U. Luz, *et al.;* Göttingen, 1983] 384–98.)

8   (II) Part I: A Canceled Visit to Corinth (1:12–2:13). Paul's problems with the Corinthian community had been exacerbated by a broken promise to visit them, which his enemies had distorted into evidence of his untrustworthiness.

(A) Paul's Plan (1:12–22). 12–14. Paul introduces the delicate topic by an appeal for an attentive and sympathetic reading of this letter. **12.** *the testimony of our conscience:* Paul has nothing with which to reproach himself (see on 1 Cor 4:4). *with godly candor and sincerity:* Pace M. E. Thrall (*Studies in NT Language and Text* [Fest G. D. Kilpatrick; ed. J. K. Elliott; NovTSup 44; Leiden, 1976] 366–72), the context demands the reading *haplotēti* (8:2; 9:11,13; cf. J. Amstutz, *Haplotēs* [Theophaneia 19; Bonn, 1968]). Paul had been accused of deceitfulness. *not with fleshly wisdom but by grace:* His decisions are rooted in his sense of mission not in the calculations typical of fallen humanity. *in the world:* Toward unbelievers, as the contrast with "you" indicates. **13.** The Corinthians are to pay attention to what Paul actually says and not misread him (e.g., 1 Cor 5:9–11) or find offense where none was intended (e.g., 1 Cor 4:14). **14.** *we are your boast as you are ours:* Without Paul the church would not have come into being (1 Cor 3:5; 4:15); its existence authenticates his ministry (1 Cor 9:2; 2 Cor 3:2–3).

9   15. *grace: Charis* here means the spiritual and human benefit of Paul's presence as in Phil 1:25–26 and Rom 1:11; 15:29. **16.** *that is:* The initial *kai* is explanatory (see BDF 442.9), for this verse explains the cryptic "first" and "second" of v 15. The reference is to the intermediate visit (12:14; 13:1–2). Paul had gone by sea to Corinth from Ephesus and, while there, had informed the community of this plan to return after a visit to Macedonia (a Roman province in northern Greece), where there were churches at Thessalonica (the capital) and Philippi. He did not carry out this project (v 23), which was already a modification of the plan announced in 1 Cor 16:5–6. **17.** The rhetorical questions articulate the reaction of the Corinthians to such chopping and changing; it would have been reported by Titus (7:7). *yes, yes and no, no:* Though evocative of Matt 5:37 and Jas 5:12, the meaning is different. Paul did not say "yes, yes" eagerly

when he thought his readers expected agreement, or "no, no" when they wanted a negative response. What he said he meant sincerely. **18–22.** A theological digression. The faithful God, revealed in a totally dedicated Christ and an unambiguous gospel, would not have commissioned Paul were he not completely dependable. **18.** *our word:* It refers primarily to Paul's preaching (v 19), but in this context also to his travel plans in the service of that gospel. The former participated in the dependability of the latter. **19.** *Son of God:* Only here is this traditional title (Rom 1:4; Gal 2:20) combined with the name Jesus Christ, which facilitates the transition from v 18 to v 21. *Silvanus:* A Latinized form of Silas. His presence at Corinth is attested by 1 Thess 1:1 and Acts 18:5; cf. Acts 15–17. *Timothy:* See comment on 1 Cor 4:17. *an enduring yes:* The adj. brings out the force of the perfect *gegonen.* Christ did not waver in his commitment. The gospel is equally unambiguous. **20.** *all God's promises have their yes through him:* Christ brought to reality in history all the varied forms in which God had promised salvation. He is the seed of Abraham (Gal 3:16), the Davidic Messiah (Rom 1:4), the last Adam (1 Cor 15:45), life, wisdom, righteousness, and sanctification (1 Cor 1:30). *the customary Amen:* The liturgical assent of the community (1 Cor 14:16; cf. G. Delling, *Worship in the New Testament* [Phl, 1962] 71–75) prolongs the assent of the Son that proclaims the fidelity of the Father. **21.** *the one confirming us with you for Christ:* God's ongoing communication of his fidelity conforms both Paul and the Corinthians to the faithful Christ. *having anointed us:* To bring out the play on words (*chriein/Christos*) one should translate "having christed us." Believers are other Christs (4:10; Rom 8:29). They are anointed by faith. **22.** *having sealed us and given the first installment:* The language of commerce is used to express the effect of baptism (Eph 1:13–14), which marks believers publicly as belonging to Christ (1 Cor 3:23; 6:19) and gives the Spirit (5:5) as a promise of future fulfillment.

(Fee, G. D., "Charis in II Corinthians 1:15: Apostolic Parousia and Paul-Corinth Chronology," *NTS* 24 [1977–78] 533–38. Dinkler, E., "Die Taufterminologie in 2 Kor 1:21f.," *Neotestamentica et patristica* [Fest. O. Cullman; ed. W. C. van Unnik; NovTSup 6; Leiden, 1962] 173–91. Hahn, F., "Das Ja des Paulus und das Ja Gottes," *Neues Testament und christliche Existenz* [Fest. H. Braun; ed. H. D. Betz, *et al.;* Tübingen, 1973] 229–39. Lampe, G. W. H., *The Seal of the Spirit* [London, 1951]. Potterie, I. de la, "L'Onction du chrétien par la foi," *Bib* 40 [1959] 12–69. Unnik, W. C. van, "Reisepläne und Amen-sagen," *Studia paulina* [Fest. J. de Zwaan; ed. J. N. Sevenster, *et al.;* Haarlem, 1953] 215–34.)

10   (B) The Consequences of a Change of Plan (1:23–2:13). After the digression of 1:18–22 Paul has to explain why he substituted a letter for the proposed visit. He is clear on his subjective reaction, but what actually happened during the intermediate visit (v 16) has to be deduced from slender hints in 2:5–11 and 7:8–12. Apparently he was insulted by a visiting Christian, and the Corinthians did not come to his defense but took a neutral position. See C. K. Barrett, "*Ho Adikēsas* (2 Cor 7:12)," *Verborum Veritas* (Fest. G. Stählin; ed. O. Böcher, *et al.;* Wuppertal, 1970) 149–57. **23.** The reason is given in 2:1. **24.** Again Paul digresses because of a fear of being misunderstood. "The power to spare implies the power to punish, and this seems to imply a claim to control everything. He hastens to assure them that he makes no such claim" (Plummer). **2:1.** Once away from Corinth, Paul recognized that to return in his hurt and angry mood would do more harm than good. The risk of widening the rift was too great. Hence, he continued on from Macedonia (1:16) to Ephesus (v 12). **2.** *who?:* The sg. denotes a typical Corinthian. If Paul made the Corinthians sad, they could not communicate joy to him. **3–4.** In place of the planned visit Paul wrote the (now lost) sorrowful letter (→ 3 above). *having confidence in all of you:* Paul's profession of love for the entire community that had hurt him suggests that its members were not primarily responsible for the situation — hence the hypothesis that a visiting Christian was the culprit. **11** **5–11.** Most ancient and a few modern commentators wrongly identify the offender with the man condemned in 1 Cor 5:1–5. The differences are highlighted by Furnish, *II Corinthians* 164–66. **5.** Though Paul was the ostensible victim, in his view the real victim was the whole community (v 10; 7:12). **6.** *this punishment:* The Gk term *epitimia* could cover anything from a verbal reprimand (Barrett) to excommunication (Windisch), but the hint of duration (v 7) suggests that the community refused to associate with the individual (1 Cor 5:11). *by the majority:* The community as such had finally taken action, delayed perhaps by a dissenting minority. *enough:* In terms of duration (v 7) not severity. **7–8.** Punishment ceases to be remedial if unduly prolonged. **9–10.** The absence of any mention of the offender's repentance underlines that the attitude of the community to Paul is his major concern. **11.** Paul's reconciliation with the Corinthians made them less vulnerable to hostile forces doing the work of God's archenemy (see on 1 Cor 10:20; 2 Cor 11:12–15). *Satan:* See comment on 1 Cor 5:5. **12** **12–13.** The break with the foregoing is not as abrupt as it might seem. Paul's concern for Titus (7:6–7), for whom he sacrificed a promising mission, is indirect evidence of his love for the Corinthians. He longed to hear about them. **12.** *Troas:* A large coastal city (Acts 16:6–10; 20:1–12) about 300 km. NNW of Ephesus, which became a Roman colony under Augustus (see C. J. Hemer, "Alexandria Troas," *TynBul* 26 [1975] 79–112; J. M. Cook, *The Troad* [Oxford, 1973]). The move from Ephesus must have been dictated by extraordinary circumstances (see comment on 1:8). *a door was opened:* By using the passive Paul gives God the credit for the fruitful mission field he found at Troas (1 Cor 16:9; cf. Col 4:3). **13.** Only the imminent end of the sailing season in October (Acts 27:9) explains the abrupt move to Macedonia (Acts 16:11). Were he to leave it too late, he would be separated from Titus returning overland from Corinth for several months. *Titus:* The bearer of the sorrowful letter (→ 4 above). *Macedonia:* See comment on 1:16. In Paul's mind this term evoked churches whose very being was apostolic (1 Thess 1:6–8; Phil 1:5,27; 2:14–16), and so set off the train of thought developed in the next section (see J. Murphy-O'Connor, *JSNT* 25 [1985] 99–103). Thus there is no necessity to see 2:14 as the beginning of a new letter (→ 2 above). **13** **(III) Part II: Authentic Apostleship (2:14–6:10).** Paul's reflections on his ministry are a reply to attacks on his authority by intruders, who compared him unfavorably with themselves and highlighted his weaknesses.

(A) The Apostolate: Theory and Practice (2:14–3:6). Beginning with a lofty vision of the apostolate (2:14–16), Paul is quickly drawn back to the reality of his current situation (2:17–3:6). **14.** *who parades us everywhere:* From the much-discussed vb. *thriambeuein,* which connotes a Roman triumph, Paul retains only the idea of motion in complete dependence on a higher authority. *the odor which is knowledge:* The image is influenced by Sir 24:15; cf. *2 Apoc. Bar.* 67:6. *of him:* God as revealed in Christ (4:6). **15.** *we are the aroma of Christ:* Christ, as the wisdom of God (1 Cor 1:24), is not only preached by (5:20) but also manifested in (4:10–11) his ministers. *those being saved . . . those perishing:* See comment on 1 Cor 1:18. *from death to death:* From inauthentic existence (Col 2:13)

to ultimate destruction (Rom 7:5). *from life to life:* From authentic existence (4:10) to eternal beatitude (5:4; Rom 2:7). This multilayered use of the life–death contrast is well attested in Philo (e.g., *De fuga et inv.* 55). *who is competent?:* A resigned reaction (cf. Joel 2:11) to the awesome responsibility thrust on Paul (1 Cor 9:16–18).

(Carrez, M., "Odeur de mort, odeur de vie à propos de 2 Cor 2:16," *RHPR* 64 [1984] 135–42. McDonald, J. I. H., "Paul and the Preaching Ministry," *JSNT* 17 [1983] 257–70. Marshall, P., "A Metaphor of Social Shame: *thriambeuein* in 2 Cor 2:14," *NovT* 25 [1983] 302–17. Thrall, M. E., "A Second Thanksgiving Period in II Corinthians," *JSNT* 16 [1982] 101–24.)

14 **17.** *adulterating the word of God:* The connotation of *kapēleuein* was extremely derogatory (see H. Windisch, *TDNT* 3. 603–5). For Paul, his opponents chose ministry for personal profit and gave false value, but he, mandated by God, spoke as Christ (12:19; 13:3; 15:18). **3:1.** *to commend ourselves:* Paul's opponents accused him of recommending himself, which he had done to distinguish himself from other itinerant preachers (1 Thess 2:1–12), whereas they had come recommended by another church, probably Jerusalem. *letters of recommendation:* Illustrated by Rom 16:1–2 and mentioned in Acts 9:2; 18:27. **2.** The existence of the community guaranteed the authenticity of Paul's ministry (1 Cor 9:2). *written in your hearts:* The better-attested "our hearts" produces only nonsense (Barrett, Bultmann). The heart is understood as the source of all human activity. **3.** *Christ's letter:* As Paul's letter is different in kind, so it comes from a much higher authority. *serviced by us:* A vague formula implying only mediation. *tablets of stone:* See Exod 24:12; 31:18. The shift from the expected "not on skins" (to correspond to "not with ink") is due to the opponents' insistence on the law. *fleshy hearts:* See Ezek 11:19; 36:26; Jer 31:33. **5.** God empowers Paul (4:7) to carry out his mission, which is beyond the capacity of fallen human nature. **6.** *a new covenant not of the letter but of the spirit:* Paul is forced to distinguish two types of new covenant (1 Cor 11:25), because his opponents were using the new covenant theme to insist on the law (Jer 31:33). To this extent the new covenant participated in the destructive power ("the letter kills"; cf. Rom 7:10) of the old covenant (3:14). *the Spirit gives life:* Christ (1 Cor 15:45) gives the new life (2:16) of authentic humanity.

(Baird, W., "Letters of Recommendation: A Study of 2 Cor 3:1–3," *JBL* 80 [1961] 166–72. Chan-Hie Kim, *Form and Structure of the Familiar Greek Letter of Recommendation* [SBLDS 4; Missoula, 1972]. Käsemann, E., *PP* 138–68. Kremer, J., "'Denn der Buchstabe tötet, der Geist aber macht lebendig,'" *Begegnung mit dem Wort* [Fest. H. Zimmermann; ed. J. Zmijewski, *et al.;* BBB 53; Bonn, 1979] 219–50. Luz, U., "Der alte und der Neue Bund bei Paulus und im Hebräerbrief," *EvT* 27 [1967] 318–36. Westerholm, S., "Letter and Spirit: The Foundation of Pauline Ethics," *NTS* 30 [1984] 229–48.)

15 **(B) Ministry: Old and New (3:7–4:6).** Paul highlights the characteristics of his ministry (splendor, boldness, power) by contrasting it with that of Moses in Exod 34:27–35. The prominence given to Moses is probably due to an emphasis of his adversaries. It is not a midrash in the strict sense (*pace* Windisch), still less one composed by Paul for another occasion (*pace* Lietzmann, Fitzmyer); nor is he correcting a preexistent document of his opponents (*pace* Schulz, Georgi). **16** **7–11.** In unusually impersonal language Paul contrasts the splendor (*doxa*) of his ministry, not of his person (cf. v 1), with that represented by Moses. **7a.** *the ministry of death:* Called the "ministry of condemnation" in v 9. The Jews' understanding of the role of the law (Rom 7:10) made them existentially "dead" (see comment on 2:16). **7b.** *fading:* With the exception of the splendor

of Moses' face, what Paul says contradicts Exod 34:29–35 but has a link with Philo's interpretation (*De vita Mosis* 2.70). **8–9.** The basis of Paul's position is made apparent. What was true of the lesser must be even more fully verified in the greater (in rabbinic terms *qal wāḥômer;* cf. H. L. Strack, *Introduction to the Talmud and Midrash* [NY, 1969] 94). **8.** *the ministry of the Spirit:* Paul has abandoned the concept of new covenant. **9.** *the ministry of righteousness:* Because permeated by the Spirit it sets humanity in its correct relationship to God (5:21). **10.** *what has had splendor has not had splendor:* In contrast to the glory of the ministry of the Spirit, the glory of the Mosaic ministry is so negligible as to be nonexistent. **11.** *what was being annulled:* Moses' fading glory is here transferred to the whole dispensation he represented (v 7). *what is permanent:* Christ is God's definitive revelation (1 Cor 1:24), so what preceded must have been essentially transitory, however exalted it may have been.
17   12–13. Paul contrasts his attitude with that of Moses; a polemic or apologetic intention should not be dismissed too lightly. **12.** *such a hope:* The greater glory of the Christian ministry empowers Paul to speak and act with authoritative plainness (*parrhēsia*). See S. B. Marrow, *CBQ* 44 [1982] 431–46. **13.** *a veil:* Moses' veiling of his face is the only element of Exod 34:33–35 retained by Paul, whose interpretation of Moses' action is based on his position in vv 7–11. Moses was forced to dissimulate because he knew his ministry was transitory. **14–18.** Corresponding to the difference between Paul and Moses, there is a difference between their followers. One group is open, the other closed. **14.** *the same veil:* Those who do not see the hidden person of Moses are themselves blind. *their thoughts were hardened:* See Isa 6:9–10; 29:10; Deut 29:3; Rom 11:7. *the old covenant:* This term for the law was invented by Paul to underline the outdated character of Mosaic dispensation. *in Christ it is being annulled:* Deliverance from the bondage of the old covenant takes place only through and in relation to Christ. **15.** *over their hearts:* The veil image again shifts, nuancing the critique of the law in v 14. *Moses is read:* As in Acts 15:21, this is a way of speaking of "the book of Moses" (2 Chr 25:4; Neh 13:1; Mark 12:26). **16.** *turns to the Lord:* I.e., to be converted (1 Thess 1:9; cf. Deut 4:30; Sir 5:7; Isa 19:22) to the God revealed in Christ (v 14; 4:6). Only from this perspective is God's intention in his word perceived. There is an implicit critique of those (vv 3–6) who gave the law an interpretation that Paul denied. **17.** *the Lord is the Spirit:* Opinion is divided, but it is probable that Paul has God directly in view (but → Pauline Theology, 82:61). God is identified with the Spirit in order to deny that he still operates through the letter of the law (v 6). *there is freedom:* Those who are led by the Spirit are no longer under the law (Gal 5:18). A polemic note is evident. **18.** *we all with unveiled face:* Those who have fulfilled the condition of v 16, i.e., all believers, and not merely Paul and his collaborators. *beholding as in a mirror:* The linguistic evidence (BAGD 424) is against rendering *katoptrizomenoi* by "reflecting as in a mirror" (the view defended by J. Dupont, *RB* 56 [1949] 392–411). *the glory of the Lord:* As the last Adam (1 Cor 15:45) Christ is the image and glory of God (1 Cor 11:7). God is mirrored in Christ (4:6). *are being transformed into the same image:* Salvation is a process whose goal is conformity to Christ (Rom 8:29; for the antithesis, cf. Rom 12:2). His authentic humanity must become progressively manifest in believers (see on 4:10–11). *from glory to glory:* The meaning of *doxa* shifts from "splendor" to "giving glory" (see 1 Cor 2:7). As believers are conformed to Christ, they become ever more capable of rendering him the honor that is God's due. *as from the Lord, the Spirit:* The agent of transformation is God acting through the Spirit.

(Carrez, M., "Présence et fonctionnement de l'AT dans l'annonce de l'évangile," *RSR* 63 [1975] 325–41. Eckert, J., "Die geistliche Schriftauslegung des Apostels Paulus nach 2 Kor 3:4–18," *Dynamik im Wort* [ed. Kath. Bibelwerk; Stuttgart, 1983] 241–56. Hanson, A. T., "The Midrash in 2 Cor 3: A Reconsideration," *JSNT* 9 [1980] 2–28. Hickling, C. J. A., "The Sequence of Thought in 2 Cor 3," *NTS* 21 [1974–75] 380–95. Hugedé, N., *La métaphore du miroir dans les épîtres de saint Paul aux Corinthiens* [Neuchâtel, 1957]. Lambrecht, J., "Transformation in 2 Cor 3:18," *Bib* 64 [1983] 243–54. Molina, M. A., "La remoción del velo o el acceso a la libertad," *EstBib* 41 [1983] 285–324. Schulz, S., "Die Decke des Moses," *ZNW* 49 [1958] 1–30. Ulonska, H., "Die Doxa des Mose," *EvT* 26 [1966] 378–88. Wagner, G., "Alliance de la lettre, alliance de l'Esprit: Essai d'analyse de 2 Cor 2:14–3:18," *ETR* 60 [1985] 55–65. Wong, E., "The Lord is the Spirit (2 Cor 3:17a)," *ETL* 61 [1985] 48–72.)

18   4:1–6. In both theme and tone this section recalls 3:1–6. Paul strikes back at those who have denigrated his ministry. **1–2.** The point introduced in 3:12 is developed. **1.** *as we obtained mercy:* Prior to his conversion (3:5–6) Paul had persecuted Christians (1 Cor 15:9; Gal 1:13,23). *we are not fainthearted:* Another way of expressing the *parrhēsia* of 3:12, which refutes the charge in 10:9–11. **2.** *we for our part have renounced:* The rare middle voice of *apeipon* distances Paul from his opponents (2:17; 3:13), even though it involves self-praise (3:1). The meaning is that they should have renounced the following practices rather than that he ever employed them (cf. 1 Thess 2:1–12). *shameful hidden things:* The things that one hopes will never be brought to light. The next two clauses explain what Paul has to refute (12:16). *operating without scruple:* By writing 1 Cor 9:19–23, Paul had laid himself open to the charge of unscrupulous readiness to adopt any means to achieve his end. *adulterating the word of God:* The vb. *doloun* is different from that in 2:17, but the meaning is the same. *displaying the truth openly:* Paul's is a full and complete disclosure of the gospel (Gal 2:5, 14), with nothing disguised or omitted, as his opponents claimed. *conscience:* Here the faculty of authentic discernment (see M. E. Thrall, *NTS* 14 [1967–68] 123–25), perhaps equivalent to "the love of truth" (2 Thess 2:10). **3.** *even if our gospel is veiled:* The concession that his preaching has been partly ineffective implies an accusation, possibly that he failed to make many Jewish converts (3:14–15). *those perishing:* Identified in v 4 as unbelievers (see comment on 2:15). **4.** *the god of this age:* Possibly Beliar (6:15), who is to be distinguished from Satan (see comment on 1 Cor 5:5). But it is more likely a gen. of content (BDF 167), so one would translate, "the god who is this world" (cf. Phil 3:19). Sin plays the same role in Rom 3:9; 6:6–23. *blinded the thoughts:* Contrast 3:14. *the enlightenment of the gospel:* The gospel is an illuminating force (Rom 1:16), because it presents the *glory of Christ,* who reflects (3:18) the glory of God (4:6), and is contrasted with Moses (3:7), the mediator of the old covenant (3:14). *the image of God:* The definition of authentic humanity (Gen 1:26–27) is applied only to Christ and to Adam before the Fall (1 Cor 11:7). **5.** *it is not ourselves we preach:* A hint that others gave themselves more prominence than Christ in their message (see comment on 12:12). *Christ Jesus as Lord:* Paul appropriates a confessional formula (1 Cor 12:3; Phil 2:10–11; Rom 10:9). **6.** *the god who said:* The free citation of Gen 1:3 identifies the Creator, who remains active to illuminate (Isa 9:2). The deliberate contrast with the god of this age (v 4) highlights the necessity of grace in the reception of the gospel. *in the face of Christ:* The contrast with Moses (3:7) is deliberate. In effect, Paul is saying to his opponents that it is not he who should be compared with Moses but Christ.

(Fitzmyer, J. A., "Glory Reflected on the Face of Christ [2 Cor 3:7–4:6] and a Palestinian Jewish Motif," *TS* 42 [1981] 630–44.

Lambrecht, J., "Structure and Line of Thought in 2 Cor 2:14–4:6," *Bib* 64 [1983] 344–80. Richard, E., "Polemics, OT, and Theology: A Study of 2 Cor 3:1–4:6," *RB* 88 [1981] 340–67. Theobald, M., *Die überströmende Gnade* [FB 22; Würzburg, 1982] 167–239.)

19   (C) Ministry and Mortality (4:7–5:10). Paul's opponents interpreted his trials and tribulations as contradicting his claim to be an apostle. Such weakness could not minister the saving power of God. In reply Paul insists that suffering is integral to authentic apostleship and to Christian life.

20   (a) THE MANIFESTATION OF JESUS (4:7–15). What is offered here is "an interpretation of the *curriculum vitae Pauli* as the *curriculum mortis et vitae Iesu*" (Furnish, *II Corinthians* 288). Paul's sufferings assimilate him to Jesus and enable him to demonstrate the authentic humanity that Jesus embodied. **7.** *earthen vessels:* The weakness and frailty of human existence contrasts so vividly with what the apostles have achieved that divine power must have been at work (3:5; 13:4). **8–9.** Similar catalogues of hardships occur in 6:4–5; 11:23–29; 12:10; 1 Cor 4:9–13, but the antithetical formulation here is designed to confirm v 7. **10.** *the dying of Jesus:* The earthly existence of the historical Jesus as a being given up to death. *the life of Jesus.* The authentic humanity manifested by the historical Jesus (2:16). *in the body/in our bodies:* It is a question of Paul's comportment (1 Cor 11:1) as complementing his verbal preaching. **11.** *we the living:* Those who are both physically and existentially alive (Rom 6:11; Col 2:13) are continuously in mortal danger. This explains v 10a. *in our mortal flesh: Sarx* has the same meaning as *sōma* in v 10 and was chosen because of the adj. It highlights the vulnerability of physical existence. **12.** *death is made active in us:* Paul is being ground down by suffering (v 16), but this is part of God's plan. *life in you:* The new being of authentic humanity (v 10) is the goal of ministry (1 Cor 4:15c; Gal 4:19). **13.** *spirit of faith:* An active faith imbued with the power of the Spirit. *according to what was written:* This introduces an exact citation of Ps 116:10 (LXX 115:1). *we believe and therefore we speak:* Paul's interpretation of his sufferings (vv 10–11) is rooted in faith, not in reason. **14.** *will raise us:* The thought of death leads Paul to the reward of resurrection, which robs death of its power. **15.** The thanksgiving of the community grows in proportion to the increasing number of those who accept Paul's grace-filled message (3:5–6) and so become capable of giving glory to God (see 1 Cor 2:7).

(Fridrichsen, A., "Zum Thema 'Paulus und die Stoa,'" *ConNT* 9 [1944] 27–31. Spicq, C., "L'Image sportive de 2 Cor 4:7–9," *ETL* 13 [1937] 209–29.)

21   (b) FACING THE FEAR OF DEATH (4:16–5:10). Paul affirms his confidence by contrasting what is of permanent value with what is only transitory. **16.** *we are not fainthearted:* See comment on 4:1. *outer/inner person:* The whole person considered in terms of visibility (v 18). Paul's increasing disability can be seen, his ever-growing faith and hope cannot. The use of "inner person" in Rom 7:22 is different (see H. P. Rüger, *ZNW* 68 [1977] 132–37). **17.** The vast disproportion between humiliation and reward is articulated in terms of time and weight. **18.** *things seen/unseen:* The distinction is between the unimportant (e.g., external appearances), on which Paul's opponents tend to focus (5:12), and the things that really matter (Phil 1:10).

22   5:1–10. Very divergent interpretations of this paragraph have been proposed because of disagreement concerning the topic discussed (see Allo, *Seconde épître* 137–55; F. G. Lang, *2 Kor 5:1–10 in der neueren Forschung* [BGBE 16; Tübingen, 1973]). The majority would

perhaps see the problem as that of bodily existence between burial and resurrection and would so interpret the images anthropologically and individualistically. The context, however, would suggest that Paul is concerned with showing that present sufferings are not a valid criterion of apostleship because the true home of all believers is elsewhere. The images, in consequence, should be interpreted existentially.

23   1. *we know:* What follows is an explanation of 4:18. There is an alternative to earthly existence. *a tentlike house:* The image highlights the impermanence and fragility of the human body, the "earthen pot" of 4:7. *is destroyed:* By death as the culmination of sufferings (4:8–9,16). *a building from God:* The antithetical image may have been influenced by the idea of the eschatological temple (*2 Apoc. Bar.* 4:3; 2 Esdr 10:40–57) under the stimulus of Mark 14:58 and John 2:19–21. It symbolizes a new existence (Phil 3:12–21) rather than the resurrection body. *we have:* The pres. tense expresses the certitude of hope. **2.** *for in this:* This phrase is probably causal (1 Cor 4:4) and thus = "therefore." *we sigh:* I.e., with hopeful longing, as "desiring" makes clear. *to put on over:* The clothing metaphor of 1 Cor 15:53–54 fits badly with the building image. The common denominator is a new modality of existence; cf. "to put on Christ" (Gal 3:27; Rom 13:14), which, however, refers to this life. **3.** *presupposing: Ei* followed by *kai* introduces a necessary assumption (see M. E. Thrall, *Greek Particles in the New Testament* [NTTS 3; GR, 1962] 86–91); it thus expresses assurance, not doubt. *not be found naked:* The image does not suggest the stripping off of the body in death, as in the Gk philosophical tradition, but in conjunction with the clothing metaphor refutes the view that there is no life after death. **4.** A reiteration of the thought of v 2. *being in the tent:* Living in this world. *being burdened:* This refers not to the weight of the body (as in Wis 9:15), but to Paul's apostolic sufferings, which intensify his longing for another mode of existence. *not to take off but to put on over:* He hopes that the parousia will arrive before he is killed (1 Cor 15:51; 1 Thess 4:15). **5.** Paul's hope is based on what God has already done through the Spirit (1:22).

(Lambrecht, J., "La vie engloutit ce qui est mortel," *La pâque du Christ* [Fest. F. Durrwell; ed. M. Benzerath, *et al.;* LD 112; Paris, 1982] 237–48. Thrall, M. E., "'Putting on' or 'Stripping off' in 2 Cor 5:3," *New Testament Textual Criticism* [Fest. B. Metzger; ed. E. J. Epp, *et al.;* Oxford, 1981] 221–37. Wonneberger, W., *Syntax und Exegese* [BBET 13; Frankfurt, 1979] 180–201.)

24   6–7. The anacoluthon in v 6a was caused by Paul's recollection that what he has just said (vv 1–5) could be interpreted as a denigration of bodily existence in a sense congenial to some at Corinth (see comment on 1 Cor 6:18b). So he cites a Corinthian statement introduced by *eidotes hoti*, "knowing that" (1 Cor 8:1,4), to the effect that bodily existence is an obstacle to union with Christ (see J. Murphy-O'Connor, *RB* 93 [1986] 214–21). **8.** *rather we think it good:* Paul indicates his preference for a reformulation of the Corinthian slogan. By substituting *ek* and *pros* for *en* and *apo* he transforms a static opposition into a unified movement. **9.** *whether at home:* The utility of the residence image is denied. What is important is to please the Lord (1 Thess 2:25; 4:1). **10.** *judgment seat:* This stresses the significance of the body by making its activities the basis of the final judgment.

(Aono, T., *Die Entwicklung des paulinischen Gerichtsgedankens bei den Apostolischen Vätern* [EHS 23/137; Bern, 1979]. Baumert, N., *Täglich sterben und auferstehen: Der Literalsinn von 2 Kor 4:12–5:10* [SANT 34; Munich, 1973]. Lillie, W., "An Approach to 2 Cor 5:1–10," *SJT* 30 [1977] 59–70. Penna, R., "Sofferenze apostoliche, anthropologia ed escatologia in 2 Cor 4:7–5:10," *Parola e Spirito* [Fest. S. Cipriani; ed. C. C. Marcheselli; Brescia, 1981] 1. 401–31.)

25   (D) Reconciliation in a New Creation (5:11–6:10). Paul concludes his long development on authentic apostleship by highlighting its christological foundation and ultimate objective.

(a) THE NEW CREATION (5:11–17). **11.** *we persuade:* In 1 Cor 2:4 and Gal 1:10 *peithein* has a pejorative connotation. In using it here Paul accepts and qualifies his opponents' description of his ministry. *your conscience:* See comment on 4:2. **12.** *we do not commend ourselves:* See comment on 3:1. *with regard to those whose boasting concerns the face:* Paul intends to give arms to the Corinthians against his opponents, who focus on superficial appearances. **13.** *if ever we were mad:* The assertion that religious ecstasy concerns only God may be a refutation of those who claimed that it validated their ministry. Full possession of one's senses is the prerequisite for love. **14.** *the love of Christ:* The love shown by Christ (Gal 2:20; Rom 8:35–38) as the model of authentic existence (v 15). *constrains us:* Paul feels that he has no choice but to imitate the selflessness of Christ. *one has died for all:* This modification of a traditional formula (see comment on 1 Cor 15:3) highlights the number who benefited by Christ's death. *all have died:* The effect of Christ's saving act, new life (1 Cor 15:22; Rom 5:12–21), is expressed in terms of its prerequisite, death to all that is hostile to God (Rom 8:13). **15.** That new life (4:10–12) must be expressed in behavior that is other-directed, as was Christ's (Gal 2:20). How he died is how Christians must live. **16.** *we judge no one in a fleshly way:* Paul condemns an assessment of others based on the conventional criteria of a fallen world (see comment on 1 Cor 3:1–4). The humanity of Christ is the true touchstone. *we once knew Christ in a fleshly way:* As a Pharisee, Paul had judged Christ falsely because of his uncritical acceptance of current Jewish opinion. *we know him so no longer:* There must be a similar radical shift in the way believers assess other human beings. **17.** *if anyone is in Christ:* Anyone who belongs to the believing community, which is Christ (1 Cor 6:15; 8:12; 12:12). *a new creation:* To link this to what precedes one must supply either "he/she is" or "there is" (→ Pauline Theology, 82:79). The former highlights the effect, the latter the causality, of a new act of creation, which in apocalyptic Judaism (*1 Enoch* 72:1; *2 Apoc. Bar.* 32:6; *Jub.* 4:26; 1QS 4:25; 1QH 11:10–14; 13:11–12) inaugurated the *eschaton*. *the old things have passed away, new things have come:* Given the epistemological context, the primary referent must be the standard of judgment. Radical change takes place through the lived acceptance of the standard of humanity represented by Christ (v 15).

(Fraser, J. W., "Paul's Knowledge of Jesus: 2 Cor 5:16 Once More," *NTS* 17 [1970–71] 293–313. Kuhn, H.-W., *Enderwartung und gegenwärtiges Heil* [SUNT 4; Göttingen, 1966] 48–52, 75–78. Martyn, J. L., "Epistemology at the Turn of the Ages: 2 Cor 5:16," *Christian History and Interpretation* [Fest. J. Knox; ed. W. R. Farmer, *et al.;* Cambridge, 1967] 269–87. Sjöberg, E., "Wiedergeburt und Neuschöpfung im palästinischen Judentum," *ST* 4 [1951] 44–85; "Neuschöpfung in den Toten-Meer-Rollen," *ST* 9 [1955] 131–36. Stuhlmacher, P., "Erwägungen zum ontologischen Charakter der *kainē ktisis* bei Paulus," *EvT* 27 [1967] 1–35.)

26   (b) THE MINISTRY OF RECONCILIATION (5:18–6:10). Paul now spells out the process whereby God's saving love touches human lives. In the divine plan human agents mediate grace (see 1 Cor 3:5–9). **18–19.** Paul cites and interprets a traditional formula (v 19ab), which mentioned the initiator (God), the agent (Christ), and the means of reconciliation (forgiveness of sins). Only when restored to authenticity is humanity at peace

with God. Paul answers the question how, arising out of the pres. ptcs. in the formula, by introducing the mediators who make the action of Christ real to their contemporaries. **20.** *ambassadors for Christ:* Ministers are not merely official representatives (1 Cor 1:17; Rom 10:15) but prolong the mission of Christ in a unique way (see 4:10–11). *God appealing:* The verb underlines God's respect for the freedom of his creatures, which is maintained in Paul's own words "we beg." *be reconciled:* The impv. corresponds to the indic. in vv 18–19 (→ Pauline Theology, 82:72). **21.** This verse expands vv 18–19 by explaining the role of Christ in reconciliation. *he made him sin who knew no sin:* As Messiah (Isa 53:9; *Pss. Sol.* 17:40–43; *T. Jud.* 24:1; *T. Levi* 18:9), Christ was acknowledged as sinless (Heb 4:15; 1 Pet 2:22; John 8:46; 1 John 3:5); yet through God's choice (Rom 8:3) "he came to stand in that relation to God which normally is the result of sin" (Barrett). He became part of sinful humanity (Gal 3:13). *so that we through him might become the righteousness of God:* "Through God's loving act in Christ, [we] have come to stand in that relation to God which is described by the term righteousness, that is, we are acquitted in his court, justified, reconciled" (Barrett). Humanity is what it can and should be only as righteous (→ Pauline Theology, 82:68–70).

(Hahn, F., " 'Siehe, jetzt ist der Tag des Heils': Neuschöpfung und Versöhnung nach 2 Kor 5:14–6:2," *EvT* 33 [1973] 244–53. Hofius, O., "Erwägungen zur Gestalt und Herkunft des paulinischen Versöhnungsgedankens," *ZTK* 77 [1980] 186–99; " 'Gott hat unter uns aufgerichtet das Wort von der Versöhnung' [2 Kor 5:19]," *ZNW* 71 [1980] 227–32. Hooker, M. D., "Interchange in Christ," *JTS* 22 [1971] 349–61. Lyonnet, S. and L. Sabourin, *Sin, Redemption, and Sacrifice* [AnBib 48; Rome, 1970] 187–296. Thrall, M. E., "2 Cor 5:18–21: Reconciliation with God," *ExpTim* 93 [1981–82] 227–32. Walter, N., "Christusglaube und heidnische Religiosität in paulinischen Gemeinden," *NTS* 25 [1978–79] 422–42.)

27   6:1. *working together with him:* Paul, Timothy, and Apollos are God's coworkers (1 Cor 3:9; 1 Thess 3:2). *not to accept the grace of God in vain:* Human cooperation is essential if the power of the gospel (Rom 1:16) is to act effectively (1 Cor 15:10). For *kenos,* see comment on 1 Cor 15:14. The implicit warning is developed in 1 Cor 10:1–13. **2.** The citation reproduces Isa 49:8 LXX exactly. The parenthetical character of this verse is underlined by the series of ptcs. in vv 3–10 dependent on "we beseech" in v 1. **3.** *obstacle:* Ministers can nullify the power of the gospel (see 1 Cor 1:17). **4a.** Paul's self-recommendation (3:1; 4:2) is the antithesis of that of his opponents (5:12), stressing suffering (see 4:10–11) and internal attitudes rather than the external trappings of spiritual power (→ 5 above). **4b–10.** Another catalogue of apostolic sufferings (see 4:8–9) divided into four strophes (vv 4b–5,6–7a,7b–8a,8b–10). An apologetic note is particularly clear in the last strophe. **8b.** *deceivers:* See comment on 1:15–2:2. **9.** *unknown:* See 3:1; cf. 1 Cor 4:13. *dying, and behold we live:* This epitomizes 4:7–5:10. **10.** *sorrowful:* See comment on 2:1–4. *poor:* Paul's refusal to accept support from the Corinthians had been used by his opponents to prove that he was not an apostle (see comment on 1 Cor 9:1–18; 2 Cor 11:7–11; 12:14–18; cf. W. Schrage, "Leid, Kreuz und Eschaton," *EvT* 34 [1974] 141–75).

28   (IV) Part III: Relations with Corinth (6:11–7:16). Paul returns to the theme of 1:1–2:13. Having been reconciled with God, the Corinthians should be reconciled with those who brought them the gospel.

(A) An Appeal for Openness (6:11–7:4). The line of thought is complicated by the interweaving of two themes. The salvific appeal of 6:1–2 is prolonged in 6:11 and 6:14–7:1, where the focus is on the Corinthians' relation to God, who has acted so graciously in their behalf. In vv 12–13 associated ideas lead Paul to mention his sense of injury; this theme is resumed in 7:2–4. The status of 6:14–7:1 is controverted (Furnish, *II Corinthians* 375–83), but recent studies (Fee, Lambrecht, Murphy-O'Connor, Thrall) conclude that it is not anti-Pauline (Betz) or un-Pauline (Fitzmyer), but cited by the apostle (Furnish); nor is it part of the letter mentioned in 1 Cor 5:9 (Hurd). Paul wrote it for this place in 2 Cor.

(Betz, H. D., "2 Cor 6:14–7:1: An Anti-Pauline Fragment?" *JBL* 92 [1973] 88–108. Derrett, J. D. M., "2 Cor 6:14ff: A Midrash on Dt 22:10," *Bib* 59 [1978] 231–50. Fee, G. D., "2 Cor 6:14–7:1 and Food Offered to Idols," *NTS* 23 [1976–77] 140–61. Fitzmyer, J. A., "Qumran and the Interpolated Fragment in 2 Cor 6:14–7:1," *ESBNT* 205–17. Hurd, J. C., *The Origin of 1 Cor* [NY, 1965] 235–39. Lambrecht, J., "The Fragment 2 Cor 6:14–7:1: A Plea for Its Authenticity," *Miscellanea Neotestamentica* [ed. T. Baarda, *et al.*; NovTSup 48; Leiden, 1978] 2. 143–61. Murphy-O'Connor, J., "Relating 2 Cor 6:14–7:1 to Its Context," *NTS* 33 [1987] 272–75. Thrall, M. E., "The Problem of 2 Cor 6:14–7:1 in Some Recent Discussion," *NTS* 24 [1977–78] 132–48.)

29   11. Paul speaks freely (3:12) and from a generous heart (Deut 11:16 LXX). *Corinthians:* Cf. Gal 3:1; Phil 4:15. **12.** Any constraint in the relationship comes from their feelings toward him. **13.** *as to children:* This could be critical (1 Cor 3:1; 14:20) or affectionate (12:14–15; 1 Cor 4:14). **14–16a.** Response to God must be exclusive. There may also be an implicit critique of the Corinthians' use of worldly standards to judge ministers (→ 5 above). **14.** *with unbelievers:* The "spirit people" (→ 5 above) displayed practical unbelief through involvement with iniquity, idols, and demons (1 Cor 5:1; 8:10; 10:20). Philo uses the same antitheses (*De spec. leg.* 1.279; 2.204) and applies Lev 19:19 in *De spec. leg.* 4.204. **15.** *Beliar:* An evil spirit (*T. Levi* 19:1). *believer/unbeliever:* See Philo, *Her.* 93–94; *De Abr.* 269. **16a.** *temple of God:* See 1 Cor 3:16; 6:19 (cf. 1QS 2:11; 8:5–9). **16b–18.** The affirmation of v 16b is supported by a collection of OT texts (Lev 26:12 or Ezek 37:27; Isa 52:11; Jer 51:45; Ezek 20:34; 2 Sam 7:14,27; → Romans, 51:35). **7:1.** The warmly pastoral concluding imperative is rooted in the indicative of v 16b. **2a.** Paul reverts to 6:13. **2b.** Charges of his opponents are denied. **3.** *not in condemnation:* Paul appears to distinguish between the community and his adversaries (see 3:1). *I said before:* Probably something like 2:4c. *to die together and to live together:* A formula of abiding friendship, the order of which may have been inverted by Paul to give it a more profound meaning (Rom 6:8). **4.** *comfort/affliction:* See comment on 1:3–7.

(Ker, R. E., "Fear or Love? A Textual Note," *ExpTim* 72 [1960–61] 195–96. Lambrecht, J., "'Om samen te sterven en samen te leven' uitleg von 2 Cor 7:3," *Bijdr* 37 [1976] 234–51. Olivier, F., "*Synapothnēskō:* D'un article de lexique à saint Paul, 2 Cor 7:3," *RTP* 17 [1929] 103–33. Stählin, G., "Um mitzusterben und mitzuleben,'" *Neues Testament und christliche Existenz* [Fest. H. Braun; ed. H. D. Betz, *et al.*; Tübingen, 1973] 503–21.)

30   (B) The Results of the Mission of Titus (7:5–16). The mention of divine comfort (v 4) recalls to Paul's mind the outstanding recent example of God's benevolence, the good news brought by Titus of the effects of the sorrowful letter (2:4). There is no justification for considering 7:5 the continuation of 2:13 (→ 1 above). That connection is both grammatically awkward (the shift from sg. to pl.) and psychologically implausible. The aspect of the situation dealt with here (the repentance of the Corinthians) is logically prior to the aspect dealt with in 2:5–11 (the action taken with regard to the culprit). **31   5.** *without/within:* The reference could be either Paul personally or the communities with which he

worked. **6.** *Titus:* See comment on 2:13. **7.** If Paul was delighted to see Titus safe, he was overjoyed at the reaction of the Corinthians to his delicate mission. **8.** *the letter:* The definite article identifies it with that of 2:4. Paul's embarrassment and worry are betrayed by the complicated sentence structure in which he tries to express both regret and joy. **10.** *godly/worldly grief:* The former produces repentance (*metanoia*), which is life-giving (v 11), whereas the latter produces destructive resentment. **11.** The repeated *alla,* "but," gives the sentence tremendous rhetorical force (BDF 448.6). *what defense:* They vindicated themselves (*apologia*) by showing that they had neither abetted the culprit nor condoned his offense. *what fear:* Nervous apprehension concerning the outcome of the whole sorry affair (v 15). *what reprisal:* The action taken in 2:6. *you showed yourself innocent:* Their repentance (vv 9–10) was not for "a wrong they had themselves committed, but for a wrong committed by another" (Barrett). **12.** *the one wronged:* Certainly Paul himself. Timothy may also have suffered, but it was his report that caused the intermediate visit during which the incident occurred. At this point Timothy was in Macedonia (Acts 19:22) replacing Paul (1 Cor 16:5). *the one who did the wrong:* A particular individual was at fault (2:5–8). Paul's positive response to the community as a whole (v 14) suggests that the culprit was not a permanent member, but this is disputed (Furnish). **32   13.** *the joy of Titus:* Chapters 10–13 show that either Paul or Titus was over optimistic. There have been hints that Paul was still the object of criticism (1:15–22). **14.** *I boasted to him about you:* This implies that Titus' mission was his first contact with Corinth and in no way suggests that his mission (8:6) was totally unrelated to the sorrowful letter episode. In this latter hypothesis Paul's anxiety (2:13) becomes inexplicable. **15.** *fear and trembling:* Paul's failure to return as he had planned (1:16,23) induced a nervous apprehension regarding his intentions (had he abandoned them for ever?), which was relieved by the arrival of his emissary. **16.** *every confidence in you:* An apt summary of Paul's present frame of mind, which prepares the way for the following appeal.

(Barrett, C. K., "Titus," *Neotestamentica et semitica* [Fest. M. Black; ed. E. E. Ellis, *et al.*; Edinburgh, 1969] 1–14; "*Ho Adikēsas* (2 Cor 7:12)," *Verborum Veritas* [Fest. G. Stählin; ed. O. Böcher, *et al.*; Wuppertal, 1970] 149–57.)

33   Part IV: The Collection for Jerusalem (8:1–9:15). Chapters 8–9 are a key element in the debate about the integrity of 2 Cor (→ 1 above). Although no serious arguments have been invoked to separate chap. 8 from chaps. 1–7, those who deny the unity of chaps. 8–9 (Georgi, *Kollekte* 56–57) demand careful consideration. (1) 9:1 is not the continuation of 8:24 and announces a new subject. (2) The relation between Macedonians and Corinthians is reversed in 8:1–5 and 9:2. (3) The purpose of sending the delegates differs in 8:20 and 9:3–5. (4) Achaia, mentioned in 9:2, appears nowhere in chap. 8. Though they highlight different emphases, the commentary will show that none of these points implies the type of contradiction that would demand that chap. 9 be considered a separate letter. For the nature of the collection and the initial Corinthian reaction to it, see comment on 1 Cor 16:1–4. **34   (A) A Challenging Request (8:1–15).** Using the example of Macedonian generosity, Paul delicately challenges the Corinthians to move from eager acceptance of the idea of the collection to actual giving. Titus must have informed him that the mechanism set up in 1 Cor 16:2 was not operative (see v 12), and Paul was able to contrast this with the selflessness of the Thessalonians and the Philippians, among whom he had lived for six months (→ 4 above). **1.** *the grace of God:* Given the situation outlined in vv 2–3, only divine power could explain the response of the Macedonians. **2.** *their extreme poverty:* Possibly as a result of persecution, or by comparison with the wealth of Corinth. **3.** *beyond their means:* There is a deliberate contrast with what he demanded of the Corinthians (v 12; cf. 1 Cor 16:2). Rom 15:26 seems to suggest that the contribution of Macedonia exceeded that of Achaia. **5.** *not merely as we had hoped:* The reference point is Paul's expectation. *first:* This implies that donations had in fact been made. *they gave themselves:* In theological terms their gift had value as an expression of love (v 8). **6.** Titus must have brought up the matter of the collection when he saw the response of the Corinthians (7:15). It would have been an appropriate moment to suggest that they act on a matter that Paul had very much at heart.

35   **7.** *faith, speech, knowledge:* To mention spiritual gifts (1 Cor 12:8–9) is really to damn with faint praise (see on 1 Cor 1:5), but the Corinthians would not have seen it that way. *the love we have for you:* This reading (P⁴⁶, B) is certainly more difficult than the widely attested "your love for us" and reflects Paul's realistic assessment of the situation (6:11–13). **8.** *not as a command:* Paul does not want to give the impression that he is bullying them (1:12; 1 Cor 7:6), but the theological reason is given in 9:7 (cf. Phlm 8,14). *the reality of your love:* Paul has his doubts. Love is earnestness in action. **9.** Choosing an image appropriate to the situation, Paul enunciates the theological principle of 5:21, whose practical meaning is given in 5:15. The preexistence of Christ is not implied (see J. D. G. Dunn, *Christology in the Making* [London, 1980] 121–23). **10.** *it is expedient:* To preserve the honor of the community. Paul avoids direct criticism of their failure. *not only the doing but also the willing:* One would expect the reverse order (Phil 2:13). The aor. *to poiēsai* seems to refer to a particular action, i.e., the beginning of a collection that was aborted for some reason (v 12), whereas the present *to thelein* evokes a continuing desire to act. The latter was more important to Paul. *from last year:* Paul is unlikely to have had a specific calendar in mind. "As long ago as last year" best renders his intention (9:2). **11.** Desire should be translated into action. **12.** *according to what one has:* Paul's assertion that anything they can afford to give is acceptable seems to imply that the Corinthians had postponed the collection until they could offer a great sum. **13–14.** The Corinthians are not expected to beggar themselves, but to share their surplus wealth, however little it may be. Now Jerusalem is in need, one day it could be themselves. **15.** Exod 16:18 is cited, in which the vb. "gathered" has to be supplied from the context.

36   **(B) The Recommendation of Representatives (8:16–9:5).** As a practical step toward the realization of v 11, Titus and two brethren are sent to Corinth to assist in the organization of the collection (vv 16–24), and Paul explains why it has to be done now (9:1–5). **17.** The principal reason for Titus's return to Corinth is not Paul's request, but his own love for the community. **19.** *appointed by all the churches:* The churches in question are presumably those of Macedonia, but the individual is unlikely to have been a native of that region (9:4). He may have been a Corinthian who had settled there as a missionary (v 18) and who would have been recognized in Corinth. *for the glory of the Lord and our readiness:* The collection gives glory to God and manifests Paul's willingness to aid Jerusalem. **20–21.** This individual was probably selected at Paul's urging (1 Cor 16:3) as a guarantee that no impropriety might even be suspected. From the beginning Paul took precautions against being accused of self-seeking (1 Thess 2:1–12; 1 Cor 9:1–18).

21. There is an allusion to Prov 3:4. **22.** *our brother:* The second delegate was also a member of one of the Macedonian churches (v 23) and may have assisted Paul during his sojourn there. *his great confidence in you:* Such knowledge of the community at Corinth suggests that he might have been known there. **23.** *my partner and coworker:* "My" sets Titus apart from the other two. He was a permanent member of Paul's entourage, as was Timothy (1 Cor 16:10; Phil 2:19–22; cf. 1 Thess 3:2). *envoys of the churches:* This use of *apostoloi* parallels that of Phil 2:25 and Rom 16:7. *the glory of God:* They honor God by their integrity. **24.** The appeal of vv 7,11 is reiterated. The Corinthians' response to Paul's love will confirm the claim he has made about them (9:2).

37   **9:1.** *concerning: Peri de* followed by a genitive is common in 1 Cor as the introduction to a new topic (1 Cor 7:1; 8:1,4; 12:1; 16:1). But here Paul is not responding to a question, and, in opposition to the stereotyped formula of 1 Cor, the phrase contains *gar* and *men.* The former looks back to 8:24 and should be translated "certainly, indeed" (BAGD 152). Paul does not have to recommend the collection because the Corinthians are enthusiastic about the idea (v 2; cf. 8:10–11). The *men* looks forward to the *de* of v 3. **2.** *Achaia has been prepared since last year:* Paul cites the phrase he has been using to stimulate Macedonian generosity, but which he now knows to be untrue (8:10–12; 9:5). He had taken the will for the deed. The use of Achaia (see 1 Cor 16:15) was prompted by the mention of Macedonia. **3–5.** Far from being a contradiction, these verses presuppose 8:16–24. The definite article before "brethren" assumes that they have been identified. **4.** Were the Corinthians unprepared, they would make Paul a liar and show themselves lacking in love (8:8,24). **5.** *not as an exaction:* A third reason for sending the delegates ahead. Were Paul to ask for money in the presence of members of other churches (v 4), it might look like extortion. The response would be due to pressure, and therefore not a gift (v 7).

38   **(C) The Rewards of Generosity (9:6–15).** To the very human arguments based on pride (8:8–10) and concern for his reputation (9:3–5), the apostle now adds the promise of reward. **6.** *sows . . . reaps:* A commonplace of popular wisdom (Gal 6:7–9) answers the question of how much to give. **7.** Turning to the attitude of the giver, Paul insists on a personal decision taken in complete freedom (8:8; Phlm 8,14; Rom 12:8). A gift offered simply because commanded would not please God. *God loves a cheerful giver:* Almost a citation of Prov 22:8a LXX, not in the MT (cf. Sir 35:9; Deut 15:10). **8.** *have enough of everything:* The term *autarkeia* expresses the Gk ideal of "self-sufficiency," the freedom and contentment deriving from being beholden to no one. Paul introduces two modifications. Wealth is God's gift (Deut 8:17–18), and its purpose is to do good for others (Rom 14:7). **9.** The citation is from Ps 112:9. Those who help the poor participate in the righteousness of God (see 5:21). **10.** *seed to the sower and bread for food:* The implicit citation of Isa 55:10 refers to rain, which is used to illustrate the effectiveness of the divine word, and so points to God as the subject. The imagery echoes v 6. *the harvest of your righteousness:* An allusion to Hos 10:12. **39**   **11–15.** Paul's thought moves from the idea of reward to a wider and more theological horizon. Generosity glorifies God. **11–12.** Since grace is its cause (8:1), the reaction to Corinthian generosity will be thanksgiving addressed to God (cf. 1:11; 4:15). **13.** *through the proof provided by this ministry:* The collection is a demonstration of the reality of authentic love (8:8). *glorifying God:* The ptc. could apply either to the Corinthians or to the recipients of their gift. The latter is recommended by vv 11–12. To thank God is to acknowledge his power and thereby give him glory. *the obedience of your confession of the glory of Christ:* The meaning is explained in the next phrase. Generosity to others in imitation of Christ (5:15; 9:9) is the existential proclamation of the obedience of faith (Rom 1:5). Paul hoped that the collection would prove to Jerusalem believers that Gentiles were as Christian as they. Such optimism had somewhat abated by the time he wrote Rom 15:31 in Corinth. **14.** Paul hoped that the response of the poor of Jerusalem would be intercessory prayer for them and recognition that Gentiles have been graced by God. **15.** *his indescribable gift:* The grace of God (8:1), which empowers the generosity of love.

(Berger, K., "Almosen für Israel: Zum historischen Kontext der paulinischen Kollekte," *NTS* 23 [1976–77] 180–204. Betz, H. D., *Second Corinthians 8 and 9* [Phl, 1985]. Buchanan, G., "Jesus and the Upper Class," *NovT* 7 [1964] 195–209. Georgi, D., *Die Geschichte der Kollekte des Paulus für Jerusalem* [TF 38; Hamburg, 1965]. Morgan-Wynne, J. E., "2 Cor 8:18f. and the Question of a Traditionsgrundlage for Acts," *JTS* 30 [1979] 172–73. Nickle, K. F., *The Collection* [SBT 48; London, 1966].)

LETTER B

40   As in Letter A (→ 1–2 above) the fundamental theme is Paul's apostleship, but it is approached in a radically different way. In contrast to the measured tone and careful language of Letter A, in which polemic and apologetic elements are subordinated to the didactic exposition of Paul's understanding of his ministry, Letter B is an explosion of outrage in which both self-vindication and abuse of opponents are bitterly intemperate. The kindly tact of Letter A, which betrays Paul's feeling of being in control of the situation, is replaced by a desperate anxiety regarding the future of the community. Expressions of confidence in the Corinthians, which characterized Letter A, are conspicuously lacking in Letter B. No author who expected the appeal of chaps. 8–9 to succeed would have followed it by such an attack on the potential contributors. Hence, something very serious must have happened in Corinth in the four to five months since Letter A was written.

41   The polemic is directed against a group of intruders, whose presence is already hinted at in Letter A (3:1–6). What they did to gain such ascendancy over the Corinthians is a matter of speculation, but a very plausible scenario has been suggested by Furnish (*II Corinthians* 45). Noting the Corinthians' unwillingness to participate in the collection (8:10–12), the intruders took advantage of Letter A (see comment on 10:9–10) to draw attention to what appeared to be Paul's suspiciously ambiguous attitude toward money. He had refused to demand financial support from the community (1 Cor 9:1–18) but, nonetheless, had twice solicited it for funds (1 Cor 16:2; 2 Cor 8–9). Perhaps he intended to use the money for his own purposes (12:14–18)! Jerusalem-based intruders may even have professed to have no knowledge of the arrangement made at the Jerusalem conference (Gal 2:10). In a world where the giving of money was a sign of prestige and power, to refuse a gift was a serious affront to the benefactor (see R. MacMullen, *Social Relations* 106–7). Given this social convention, it would have been easy for the intruders to present Paul's refusal to accept support as a calculated insult to the community, particularly if it had become known that while in Corinth he had been a secret client of Macedonia (11:7–9). With Paul thus discredited, the intruders' claim to be the authentic apostles began to be listened to on a wider scale than ever before (→ 5 above). This was the most worrying aspect of the situation, and so his concern is to reestablish his authority.

(Betz, H. D., *Der Apostel Paulus und die sokratische Tradition* [BHT 45; Tübingen, 1972]. Forbes, C., "Comparison, Self-praise and Irony: Paul's Boasting and the Conventions of Hellenistic Rhetoric," *NTS* 32 [1986] 1–30. Fuchs, E., "La faiblesse, gloire de l'apostolat selon Paul," *ETR* 55 [1980] 231–53. Käsemann, E., "Die Legitimität des Apostels," *ZNW* 41 [1942] 33–71.

MacMullen, R., *Roman Social Relations, 50 BC–AD 284* [New Haven, 1974]. Travis, S. H., "Paul's Boasting in 2 Cor 10–12," *SE* VI 527–32.)

42   **(VI) Part I: An Appeal for Complete Obedience (10:1–18).** The address, which must have been similar to 1:1–2, was omitted by the editor who combined Letters A and B. Given Paul's anger (as in Gal), it is unlikely that Letter B ever had a Thanksgiving or a Blessing (→ NT Epistles, 45:8B). Paul goes straight to the heart of the matter, backing an appeal for obedience by an assertion of his authority. His opponents are a group (vv 2,12), which is sometimes evoked by means of the typical sg. (vv 7,10).

43   **(A) The Consequences of Disobedience (10:1–6).** The appeal for obedience is designed to pave the way for an impending visit, which will be like a military campaign if the situation in Corinth is not rectified. **1a.** *I, Paul:* The phrasing betrays intense urgency (1 Thess 2:18; Gal 5:2). *by the gentleness and forbearance of Christ:* Apparently a curious way to assert authority, but *praytēs* is a characteristic of the messianic king (Zech 9:9 LXX = Matt 21:5; cf. Matt 11:29) and *epieikeia* is predicated of God in Wis 12:18 and 2 Macc 2:22; 10:4. Paul thus prepares his readers for a correct understanding of his "weakness." It might camouflage the same power. **1b.** In a parenthesis Paul ironically notes the charge specified in v 10. *I who cringe:* This translation of *tapeinos* is demanded by the context (contrast 7:10; 11:7). When he seemed servile and weak he was only reflecting the attitude of Christ (Phil 2:8; see comment on 13:3–4). **2.** *toward certain persons who reckon that we walk according to the flesh:* Paul never dignifies his opponents by naming them (3:1). They are distinguished from the community ("you"). In Letter A Paul twice used *kata sarka* in contexts that imply criticism of his behavior (1:12,17). The meaning is not the usual Pauline one (for which, see *TNT* 1. 236–38), but "nonspiritual," i.e., lacking the ecstatic experiences his opponents claimed (12:1). **3.** *walking in the flesh:* En *sarki* is a neutral formula that expresses the corporeity of human existence; it = "in the world" (1:12). **4.** *powerful for God in the demolition of strongholds:* The underlying image is the tactic of siege warfare (1 Macc 5:65), also used metaphorically in Prov 21:22. "Strongholds" is clarified in the next verse. **5.** *we demolish reasonings and every great height:* Paul alludes to the reasoning of his opponents, who adopted false criteria of the apostolate and a false wisdom. They might seem as solid as the bulwarks that constitute a stronghold, but they cannot resist his God-given power. *the knowledge of God:* Defined in this verse as "obedience to Christ," who is the wisdom of God precisely as crucified (1 Cor 1:23–24). This aspect of Christ, emphasized in v 1, was refused by the "spirit-people" at Corinth (1 Cor 2:8). *taking every thought captive:*

Inhabitants are rounded up, once the fortifications have been breached, and forces stand ready to repress any uprising. **6.** When the Corinthians' obedience to Christ as presented in his gospel is perfect, the apostle will deal with those who preach another gospel (11:4).

(Leivestad, R., "'The Meekness and Gentleness of Christ' 2 Cor 10:1," *NTS* 12 [1965–66] 156–64. Malherbe, A. J., "Antisthenes and Odysseus, and Paul at War," *HTR* 76 [1983] 143–73. Tanner, R. G., "St. Paul's View of Militia and Contemporary Social Values," *Studia biblica 1978, III* [ed. E. A. Livingstone; JSNTSup 3; Sheffield, 1980] 377–82.)

44   (B) Paul's Authority as Founder of the Community (10:7–18). The polemic of vv 1–6 is sharpened. Paul carries the war into the enemy camp by explaining to the Corinthians what has been going on under their noses. **7.** *anyone:* A typical member (v 10) of the group of opponents (vv 2,12). *he belongs to Christ:* A reference either to the Christ-party (1 Cor 1:12) or to the status of a Christian (1 Cor 3:23; 15:23) is implausible. The opponents must have claimed a unique relation to Christ (11:13,23), possibly based on acquaintance with the historical Jesus (5:16) or on their commissioning by those who had known him. *as he is Christ's, so are we:* Jerusalem opposition to Paul was centered on James (Gal 2:12), whose status vis-à-vis the earthly Jesus was identical with that of Paul (see comment on 1 Cor 15:7–8). **8.** *our authority which the Lord gave:* As in 13:10, Paul evokes his commission by Christ (1 Cor 9:1; Gal 1:12) to found communities (vv 13–16) in terms drawn from Jer 1:9–10. **9.** *lest I should seem:* The connection with v 8 is not entirely clear. **10.** Paul cites a sneering Corinthian critique, which contrasts his strong, demanding letters with his unimpressive physical presence and his unsophisticated oratory (1 Cor 2:3–4). The opponents were appealing to the Hellenistic expectation that speakers should combine rhetorical skills with dignified presence (e.g., Lucian, *Dream* 13) in order to highlight Paul's lack of the power given by possession of the Spirit. **11.** *when absent:* If Paul wrote a severe letter (2:4; 7:8), it was simply because he could not be present, not because he was afraid to appear. **12.** With sharp irony Paul distances himself from his rivals. They can recommend themselves because they compare themselves with one another, ignoring the true criterion, which is Christ (see comment on 5:16–17; 13:5). *are without understanding. We however:* These words were accidentally omitted in the Western text (→ Texts, 68:167, 173).
45   13–18. From the idea of limitless boasting (v 8) Paul moves to another sense of "limit," the territory assigned to him by God, in which his opponents are intruders without mandate. **13.** *the measure of the jurisdiction:* Furnish's formulation is perhaps the best rendering of the difficult *to metron tou kanonos,* which implies both the standard and what is measured out. *to reach even to you:* Paul's divine authorization to evangelize the Gentiles was approved by Jerusalem, but in a formula that did not exclude a Judeo-Christian mission to Jews in the Diaspora (Gal 2:9). **14.** *we are not overextending ourselves:* But his opponents were by appearing at Corinth. *we came all the way to you with the gospel of Christ:* This gave Paul paternal rights (12:14; 1 Cor 4:15), which no one who came later could enjoy. **15.** *in the labors of others:* In opposition to Paul, who sought virgin territory (Rom 15:17–20), his rivals were like thieves who try to take over another's property. Missionary expansion should not take the form of poaching. *we may grow in your estimation in conformity with our jurisdiction:* Since authentic faith is obedience to Christ (v 6; 13:5; cf. Rom 1:5), Paul's hope is that the Corinthians may develop a correct understanding of his relation to Christ (4:10–11) and thus free

him for his real work, the setting up of new communities, not the maintenance of established ones (1 Cor 1:17). **16.** *to preach the gospel in lands beyond you:* Paul may have already set his mind on Spain (Rom 15:23–24; cf. Phil 3:13–14). *not boasting . . . in another's jurisdiction:* Another gibe at his opponents (v 15), who were claiming his success as their own. **17.** Paul's favorite quotation from Jer 9:21 (1 Cor 1:31), which implies that there is an authentic form of boasting (Phil 3:3; Gal 6:4). **18.** This verse is clearly directed at the intruders, who had drawn attention to qualifications that Paul deemed irrelevant (v 12; 4:18; 5:12) and who challenged him to produce the same type of proof (13:3).

(Henning, J., "The Measure of Man: A Study of 2 Cor 10:12," *CBQ* 8 [1946] 332–43. Krämer, H., "Zum sprachlichen Duktus in 2 Kor 10:9 und 12," *Das Wort und die Wörter* [Fest. G. Friedrich; ed. H. Balz, *et al.;* Stuttgart, 1973] 97–100. Strange, J., "2 Cor 10:13–16 Illuminated by a Recently Published Inscription," *BA* 46 [1983] 167–68.)

46   (VII) Part II: Paul Speaks like a Fool (11:1–12:13). In defiance of his own refusal to boast (10:17) or to accept comparison as a valid criterion (10:12), Paul decides to adopt the procedure of his adversaries. The situation at Corinth (11:3) left him little choice. Even though he knew it to be foolishness (11:1,16; 12:13), he had to show that he could beat his rivals at their own game (4:18; 5:12; 11:18), as he had already done to the "spirit-people" (see comment on 1 Cor 2:6–16). In so doing, he contradicts the charge of 10:10c (cf. 11:6) by displaying his knowledge of the rhetorical conventions of his day, notably, self-display, comparison, irony, and parody. His form of preaching (1 Cor 2:1–5) was by choice, not by necessity.

(Spencer, A. B., "The Wise Fool (and the Foolish Wise)," *NovT* 23 [1981] 349–60. Zmijewski, J., *Der Stil der paulinischen "Narrenrede"* [BBB 52; Cologne, 1978].)

47   (A) His Justification for Being Foolish (11:1–21a). Paul's apprehension regarding the dangers of the tactic he has chosen is betrayed by the "nervous prolixity" (Furnish) of this introduction to the "fool's speech" proper (11:21b–12:10). He in fact digresses to the point that he has to begin again in 11:16. **1.** *bear with me:* To beg indulgence at the outset implies that what follows might not please his readers. **2.** Paul justifies his fatherly concern (12:14; 1 Cor 4:15) for his virgin community in terms of Jewish marriage customs (Gen 29:23; Deut 22:13–21; cf. Eph 5:23–32). **3.** *the serpent deceived Eve:* In Jewish tradition (v 14) the serpent is identified with the devil (Wis 2:24; Rev 12:9), whose interest in Eve was sexual (*2 Enoch* 31:6). Eve here symbolizes the gullibility of the whole community (contrast 1 Tim 2:13–14). *seduced from a total and pure commitment to Christ:* Paul's quarrel with his opponents is that they were preaching an inauthentic gospel (Rom 16:17–18), which presented a false vision of Christ.
48   4. This is perhaps the most important clue in the quest for the identity of Paul's opponents. *if someone comes:* His adversaries were from outside Corinth (3:1; 10:14–16). *preaches a Jesus other than the one we preached:* The sudden switch from "Christ" (10:1,5,7,14; 11:2,3) gives "Jesus" a special significance; the emphasis is on his earthly existence. Since the intruders claimed to "belong to Christ," they must have shared the tendency of the "spirit-people" to downgrade the importance of Christ's humanity, which was displayed in service, suffering, and death (see comment on 1 Cor 2:8; 12:3). The moral posture of this group (1 Cor 3:3–4; 6:12–20) is evoked in 12:20–21. *a different Spirit . . . a different gospel:* Here the latent polemic of 3:1–18 surfaces. The Judaizers (3:3)

preached a different gospel (Gal 1:6–9). Since Paul's gospel was a "ministry of the Spirit" (3:8) and of freedom (3:17), his opponents must have given their allegiance to a different Spirit, viz., that of the new covenant, which they understood in a way that Paul could not accept (see comment on 3:6). The Judaizers would have shared common ground with the "spirit-people" (→ 1 Corinthians, 49:18) insofar as the wisdom tradition of the latter was rooted in the law. **5.** *the super-apostles:* Opinion is divided on whether these are the intruders or their masters in Jerusalem, i.e., the "pillar" apostles led by James (Gal 2:9). The context recommends the former, but Paul's acceptance of their status as equal to his own (12:11) indicates a rather more positive attitude than he displays toward the intruders (11:13–15). **6.** Though Paul may not be able to express himself very well (→ 46 above), he does know what he is talking about, and his spiritual insight has been manifested in various ways.
49   **7–11.** Paul offers a particular example of his insight taken from his dealings with the Corinthians, and in the process deals with a point on which he was attacked. **7.** *commit a sin:* Ironic exaggeration designed to force his readers to evaluate the social convention under which he had been judged (→ 41 above). *in demeaning myself:* The manual labor by which Paul supported himself (1 Cor 4:12; 1 Thess 2:9) was seen by many as servile and degrading (see R. F. Hock, *JBL* 97 [1978] 555–64). **8.** *I plundered other churches:* This could be a mere rhetorical flourish, but if Paul knew that the Corinthians were already aware that he had been receiving support from Macedonia (v 9), it would be a claim that he had not become a client of those churches by accepting a gift. **9.** *was in want:* Any artisan of the period found it hard to make ends meet (see R. F. Hock, *The Social Context of Paul's Ministry* [Phl, 1980] 34). Paul had other demands on his time and energy, even when trade was good. *did not burden:* This is Paul's view of his position (12:14), which the Corinthians interpreted very differently (12:16–18). Apparently his principle was to accept subsidies only from churches in which he was not physically present (Phil 4:15–16). This diminished the dangerous side of the patron-client relationship. *will refrain from burdening you:* Given the current state of their relations, he would not touch their money if they were the last church on earth. **10.** *this boast:* It can only refer to his financial independence, which confirms the second interpretation of v 8. **11.** Paul's motive in acting as he did was the opposite of the one the Corinthians imputed to him (12:15). See W. Pratscher, "Der Verzicht des Paulus auf finanziellen Unterhalt durch seine Gemeinden," *NTS* 25 (1978–79) 284–98.
50   **12–15.** The attitude that Paul has just been explaining becomes the basis of an attack on his opponents. **12.** *the claim:* Unless the intruders adopt the same attitude toward support, they will always be inferior to Paul in disinterestedness. The clear implication is that they were being supported by the Corinthians, as were the opponents in 1 Cor 9:1–18. **13.** Paul repudiates the claim of the intruders to be *apostoloi Christou* (cf. v 23) by dismissing them as "false-apostles" and "deceitful workers." His basis is their activity as reported in v 4. **14.** In Jewish tradition (cf. v 3) Satan transformed himself into a shining angel in order to seduce Eve (*Apoc. Mos.* 17:1–2; *Adam and Eve* 9:1 [Latin]; 38:1 [Slavonic]). **15.** *his servants:* They do the work of Satan (see 1 Cor 10:20; Rom 16:17–20). In Paul's view they are flatly opposed to God's plan of salvation (Gal 1:8). *servants of righteousness:* This is evocative of 3:9 and suggests that Paul has the same situation in view (see comment on v 4).

(Barrett, C. K., "*Pseudapostoloi* (2 Cor 11:13)," *Mélanges bibliques*

[Fest. B. Rigaux; ed. A. Descamps, *et al.;* Gembloux, 1970] 377–96. McClelland, S. E., "Super-Apostles, Servants of Christ, Servants of Satan: A Response," *JSNT* 14 [1982] 82–87. Thrall, M. E., "Super-Apostles, Servants of Christ, and Servants of Satan," *JSNT* 6 [1980] 42–57.)

51   **16.** Realizing that he has digressed, Paul restates the appeal of v 1. **17.** *I speak, not according to the Lord:* He recognizes that such boasting is "worldly" (v 18); contrast "speaking in Christ" (2:17; 12:19). **18.** *many boast according to the flesh:* They stress external appearances (4:18; 5:12). **19.** *you gladly endure fools:* They have listened to Paul's opponents, a curious thing for "wise" people to do (1 Cor 2:6–16; 4:10; 6:4–5). **20.** The Corinthians who had set themselves up as judges between Paul and his rivals (13:3) and who were tending to take the latters' side are presented with vicious irony as the willing victims of tyranny and exploitation. None of the verbs should be taken literally. **21a.** But if that is the sort of thing that the Corinthians prefer, Paul ironically regrets that he was too "weak" to domineer.
52   **(B) Paul Boasts of Himself (11:21b–12:10).** One must presume that Paul's claims in some way echo those of his rivals. Hence, these must have stressed (1) their Jewishness, (2) their achievements, and particularly (3) their visions and revelations. A strong element of parody betrays his refusal to take the competition seriously.
(a) His Sufferings (11:21b–33). **22.** His rivals' claim to "good breeding"—a rhetorical commonplace—is quickly dealt with. *Hebrew . . . Israelite:* The terms are also juxtaposed in Phil 3:5. "Hebrew" here, because of the association with "Israelite," probably has a linguistic connotation, i.e., Hebrew- or Aramaic-speaking (Acts 6:1), and points to Palestinian origin (see W. Gutbrod, *TDNT* 3. 388–91). *the seed of Abraham:* Jewish Christians could have based a law-observant mission to Gentiles on the promise to Abraham (Gen 12:1–3). See J. L. Martyn, *Michigan Quarterly Review* 22 (1983) 221–36. **23.** *servants of Christ:* Paul has already said what he thought of their claim to represent Christ (see v 13), and so develops the idea of service not in terms of honors won (as his rivals did) but in terms of pain endured.
53   **24–27.** Similar catalogues of suffering have already appeared in 4:8–9; 6:4–5, and will again in 12:10 (cf. 1 Cor 4:9–13; Rom 8:35). **24.** *40 lashes less one:* The legal basis is given in Deut 25:1–3. The offenses are unknown. **25.** *beaten with the rod:* A specifically Roman form of punishment. One instance is known from Philippi (1 Thess 2:2; Acts 16:37). *stoned:* At Lystra by a mob (Acts 14:19). **26.** *frequent journeys:* The journey from Jerusalem to Corinth and back was approximately 3,000 miles. *danger from robbers:* Army units were occasionally used to wipe out robber bands, but no forces anywhere carried out police duties (see F. Millar, *JRS* 71 [1981] 66–69). *danger in the city:* Paul was always the vulnerable outsider. *danger from false brethren:* In Gal 2:4 *pseudadelphoi* means those who try to impose the law on Gentile Christians (see comment on 12:7). **27.** The problems of a traveler in rough country who fails to make it to an inn before nightfall. **28.** His worries (v 29) about the churches he founded and had to leave were an internal suffering that accompanied all the external pains. **30.** Just in case his readers did not grasp the thrust of his parody, Paul states the perspective from which the whole speech is to be understood. **32–33.** This incident is perfectly in place as a graphic illustration of humiliation (against those who consider it an interpolation, e.g., Windisch, Betz). It is the one episode mentioned by Paul which can be dated (→ Paul, 79:8, where, however, the specification of AD 39 is questionable; it could be a year or two earlier;

see R. Jewett, *A Chronology of Paul's Life* [Phl, 1979] 30–33, 99).

(Barré, M. L., "Paul as 'Eschatological Person': A New Look at 2 Cor 11:29," *CBQ* 37 [1975] 500–26. Casson, L., *Travel in the Ancient World* [London, 1974]. Collins, J. N., "Georgi's 'Envoys' in 2 Cor 11:23," *JBL* 93 [1974] 88–96. Knauf, E. A., "Zum Ethnarchen des Aretas, 2 Cor 11:32," *ZNW* 74 [1983] 145–47. Murphy-O'Connor, J., "On the Road and on the Sea with St. Paul," *Bible Review* 1 [Summer 1985] 38–47.)

54   (b) HIS VISIONS AND REVELATIONS (12:1–10). Paul now moves on to another area in which his rivals claimed superiority. **1.** *visions and revelations:* The absence of articles indicates a general topic. The formula may have come from his opponents. *of the Lord:* Probably a gen. of origin, "granted by the Lord" (vv 2–4). **2a.** *I know a Christian:* Paul speaks of himself in the 3d pers. (v 5) because he is unwilling to claim a private religious experience as proof of an apostolic mandate. *fourteen years ago:* This would be roughly midway between his conversion and his arrival in Corinth. The precision is intended to underline the reality of the experience, which is identical with that in v 3. **2b–3.** *caught up:* The agent is God (cf. 1 Thess 4:17; Wis 4:11; *1 Enoch* 39:3–4). The journey to another world is a common theme in apocalyptic literature (see *Semeia* 14 [1979]). *to the third heaven:* Here identified with paradise, as in *2 Enoch* 7 and *Apoc. Mos.* 37:5. The number of heavens varies widely in Jewish literature. **4.** Paul was forbidden to express the unutterable. This could be simply in conformity to the convention of sealed revelation (cf. Dan 12:4; Rev 10:4; 13:2–3), but it could also be a way of showing the irrelevance of the experience in apostolic terms (cf. 1 Cor 14:19).

(Bietenhard, H., *Die himmlische Welt im Urchristentum und Spätjudentum* [WUNT 2; Tübingen, 1951]. Crownfield, D. R., "The Self Beyond Itself," *JAAR* 47 [1979] 245–67. Lincoln, A. T., "'Paul the Visionary': The Setting and Significance of the Rapture to Paradise in 2 Cor 12:1–10," *NTS* 25 [1978–79] 204–20. Price, R. M., "Punished in Paradise (An Exegetical Theory on 2 Cor 12:1–10)," *JSNT* 7 [1980] 33–40. Saake, H., "Paulus als Ekstatiker," *Bib* 53 [1972] 404–10. Schäfer, P., "NT and Hekhalot Literature: The Journey into Heaven in Paul and the Merkavah Mysticism," *JJS* 35 [1984] 19–35. Spittler, R. S., "The Limits of Ecstasy: An Exegesis of 2 Cor 12:1–10," *Current Issues in Biblical and Patristic Interpretation* [Fest. M. C. Tenney; ed. G. F. Hawthorne, *et al.*; GR, 1975] 259–66.)

55   **6.** The reality of the experience in vv 2–4 leads Paul to say that he could truthfully boast of things other than his weaknesses, if he wished. *anything more than what he sees in me or hears from me:* The only authentic test of an apostle is the extent to which he manifests Christ, primarily in comportment (4:10–11) and secondarily in speech (2:17; 12:19; 13:3). **7a.** The syntax is problematic (see J. Zmijewski, *BZ* 21 [1977] 265–72). **7b.** *a thorn in the flesh:* This is widely interpreted as a psychic or physical ailment, which, in Jewish tradition, was caused by a demon or by Satan (see K. L. Schmidt, *TDNT* 3. 819). The two phrases, however, are not causally related but stand in apposition, suggesting an external personal source of affliction, which is confirmed by the use of "thorns" in the OT to mean enemies (e.g., Num 33:55; see T. Y. Mullins, *JBL* 76 [1957] 302). The allusion could be to the type of persecution evoked by the catalogues of sufferings, but the link with 11:14–15 ("servants of Satan") suggests that Paul has in mind hostility coming from within his own communities. **8.** *I asked:* Paul had prayed fervently for release at one stage but no longer does. **9a.** The formulation of the insight as a divine oracle is not an explanation of how Paul came to it. *grace:* Defined as "power," but its relation to "weakness" is diversely interpreted (see G. O'Collins, *CBQ* 33 [1971]

528–37). The context illuminated by 4:7 suggests that "weakness" (v 10) is the condition that the power displayed in Paul may be recognized as of divine origin. *is made perfect:* I.e., becomes effectively present (cf. 1 John 4:12). **9b.** *my weakness:* Acceptance of weakness now appears as the means whereby power is acquired. *to take up residence with:* The same verb (*episkēnoun*) appears in John 1:14. **10.** *when I am weak, then I am powerful:* He does not mean that weakness is power, or that the weak will become powerful (as in Luke 1:46–55), but that his apostolic weaknesses disclose the power accorded to him for his ministry (3:5–6).

(Barré, M. L., "Qumran and the 'Weakness' of Paul," *CBQ* 42 [1980] 216–27. Betz, H. D., "Eine Christus-Aretalogie bei Paulus (2 Kor 12:7–10)," *ZTK* 66 [1969] 288–305. Minn, H. R., *The Thorn that Remained* [Auckland, 1972]. Park, D. M., "Paul's *skolops tē sarki:* Thorn or Stake?" *NovT* 22 [1980] 179–83.)

56   (C) **Further Justification for His Foolishness (12:11–13).** This epilogue to the "fool's speech" echoes the justification for boasting given in its introduction (11:1–21a). **11.** *commended by you:* Such honor as Paul claims for himself should have been offered by the Corinthians. *I was in no way lacking with respect to the super-apostles:* The aor. *hysterēsa* must be understood as constative (BDF 332) to bring it into line with the pf. *hysterēkenai*, which must be understood as a pres. (BDF 341) in 11:5 (see comment). It is most unlikely that Paul has in mind the intermediate visit (→ 10 above), the only occasion when he could have been compared with the intruders. This verse is not an objection to the identification of the "super-apostles" with the James group in Jerusalem. *nothing:* His opponents may have described Paul as a complete nonentity (cf. 10:10b). **12.** *the signs of an apostle:* The Corinthians, in an attempt to judge between Paul and his rivals (cf. 13:3), had set up criteria, one of which was the ability to work miracles. This is an inference from Paul's reaction. *were performed:* A theological pass.; see *ZBG* § 236. Paul takes no personal credit. *with utmost endurance:* In the context of weakness and sufferings, the dominant characteristics of Paul's ministry. *signs, wonders, mighty works:* The first two are often combined in the OT (e.g., Exod 7:3; Deut 34:11; Isa 8:18; cf. Rom 15:19), and the three appear together in Acts 2:22; 2 Thess 2:9; Heb 2:4. **13.** Paul's comportment in Corinth was the same as in all other churches, a salutary reminder to the Corinthians that they were not the only Christians (see comment on 1 Cor 1:2). The sole exception to this rule was that Paul made no financial demands on them even when absent (see 11:7–11).

(Nielsen, H. K., "Paulus Verwendung des Begriffes *Dynamis*," *Die paulinische Literatur und Theologie* [ed. E. Pedersen; Teologiske Studier 7; Aarhus, 1980] 137–58.)

57   (VIII) **Part III: A Warning Prepares a Visit (12:14–13:10).** Two problems preoccupy Paul as he prepares for the crucial visit that will settle the fate of the Corinthian church: (1) the financial question that had so poisoned the atmosphere, and (2) indications that the way of life of some members was incompatible with the gospel.

58   (A) **Again the Question of Financial Support (12:14–18). 14a.** *I am ready to come to you for the third time:* This interpretation of the somewhat ambiguous Gk text is required by 13:1–2 (against N. Hyldahl, *ZNW* 64 [1973] 303). This is the visit he had planned (1:16) but postponed after the painful visit (2:1). **14b.** He will maintain the decision stated in 11:9 and justifies it in terms of the parental relationship explained in 1 Cor 4:15. **16.** If Paul understood his own refusal to accept support as an act of love, which should have been reciprocated (v 15), it was given a different interpretation in Corinth. *being unscrupulous I took you in by deceit:* The way this accusation is repudiated in vv 17–18 would appear to imply that Paul was aware only of a generic imputation of dishonesty, not of a specific charge. **17.** Knowing his own innocence, Paul first considers the possibility that one of his agents solicited funds for him. The way the question is framed shows that he expected a negative answer. **18a.** *Titus:* The reference is to his mission to get the collection moving (see 8:6). *the brother:* Probably Paul's nominee to accompany Titus (8:22), since the other was appointed by the churches (8:18–19) and was thus above suspicion. **18b.** The form of the first question demands a negative response, that of the other two an affirmative answer. Paul is in effect challenging the Corinthians to produce evidence of fraud.

59   (B) The Corinthians Must Correct Themselves (12:19–13:10). The sudden appearance of a warning about improper conduct, both social and sexual, is surprising. In order to maintain the unity of theme of Letter B one must infer that Paul has in mind that segment of the community most receptive to the intruders. **19.** Paul denies any apologetic intent in what he has written, lest it appear that the charges have substance or that he was motivated less by concern for the community than by self-interest. **20a.** *find you not what I wish:* This is explained in the two vice lists. *you may not find me what you wish:* In a mood to punish rather than to show paternal love (13:2,10; cf. 1 Cor 4:21). **20b.** The eight vices are in a sense conventional, and the first four appear in the same order in Gal 5:20. In the light of the next verse and of 13:2 this is less significant than the appearance of "jealousy," "strife," and by implication "factiousness" in 1 Cor 3:3–4, which is part of Paul's critique of the "spirit-people" (→ 1 Corinthians, 49:18). **21.** *many of those who continue to sin:* This excludes the possibility that Paul is thinking of the pre-baptismal state of the community (as in 1 Cor 6:9–10). The "to all the rest" in 13:2 confirms that he has in mind a particular group in Corinth. *sexual immorality:* 1 Cor 6:15–16 furnishes a perfect illustration of *porneia*. *lasciviousness:* 1 Cor 5:1–5 is a case of flagrant public immorality. In Corinth, the first was certainly justified by the attitude of the "spirit-people" to the body (see comment on 1 Cor 6:18), and so very probably was the second.

60   13:1. *by the testimony of two or three witnesses must every point be substantiated:* The context makes an allusion to the charges against Paul (12:16) improbable. Deut 19:15 was extended to mean that wrongdoers were to be warned of the possibility of punishment (see H. van Vliet, *No Single Testimony* [Studia theologica rhenotraiectina 4; Utrecht, 1958] 43–62), and this fits perfectly with the next verse. **2.** Two time frames complicate the sentence. "I said earlier" goes with "being present the second time," and refers to a time before the present. "I say beforehand" goes with "being absent now," and evokes the present contrasted with the future. The point is that

the Corinthians have been given the requisite warnings, and in consequence Paul will be free to punish them if they have not changed by his arrival. *Hoti,* "that," introduces what Paul said during his second visit. **3.** *you desire proof that Christ is speaking in me:* Paul's claim (2:17; 5:20; 12:19) will be verified by the exercise of his authority to punish. **4.** As Christ is both weak and strong, when viewed from different perspectives, so is Paul. If the Corinthians are convinced about the former (10:10b), they should have no doubts about the latter.

(Jackson, B. S., "Testes Singulares in Early Jewish Law and the New Testament," *Essays in Jewish and Comparative Legal History* [SJLA 10; Leiden, 1975] 172–201.)

61   5. *examine yourselves:* To those who would examine him, Paul points out that it would be more appropriate for them to examine themselves. Have they understood Christ correctly? Only when they have come to a correct understanding of Christ (see comment on 1 Cor 2:8) will they appreciate the way in which Paul carries out his ministry. **6.** Paul applies the same criterion to himself. **7.** *we pray:* His concern, however, is for their success, not for his own. Paul's anger has almost run out of steam. **8.** *the truth:* In context this general maxim (cf. 1 Esdr 4:35,38) must modify the possibility of Paul's failure as suggested in v 7. **9.** Paul does not mind them thinking of him as weak (contrast 1 Cor 4:10), as long as they are strong in faith (v 5). **10.** This summary of the thrust of chaps. 10–13 is quite incompatible with the contents of chaps. 1–9, and thus confirms the division of 2 Cor into two letters. The formulation echoes 10:8.

62   (IX) Conclusion: Final Words and Greeting (13:11–13). 11. *rejoice, be restored, heed my appeal, be of one mind, be at peace:* The impvs. betray both Paul's concern for the Corinthians and his recognition of the problem in their relationship. **12a.** *with a holy kiss:* See comment on Rom 16:16. **12b.** *all the saints:* Most Protestant translations (e.g., *RSV, NEB, NIV*) number this sentence v 13. *saints:* The Christians (see comment on 1 Cor 1:2) in western Macedonia or Illyricum (→ 4 above). **13.** Only Eph 5:23 is comparable to this triadic benediction, which is not a trinitarian formula in the dogmatic sense. *the grace of our Lord Jesus Christ:* See 1 Cor 16:23; Phil 4:23; 1 Thess 5:28; Rom 16:23. *the love of God:* The love flowing from God is manifest in the power-laden grace (12:9) given by Christ, which creates "the common union of the Holy Spirit." The force of the gen. is disputed, but fellowship given by the Spirit must result in *koinōnia* with the Spirit (cf. Phil 2:1).

(Panilulam, G., *Koinōnia in the NT* [AnBib 85; Rome, 1979]. Riesenfeld, H., "Was bedeutet 'Gemeinschaft des heiligen Geistes'? Zu 2 Kor 13:13; Phil 2:1 und Rom 8:18–30," *Communio Sanctorum* [Fest. J.-J. von Allmen; ed. A. de Pury; Geneva, 1982] 106–13. Schneider, B., "*Hē koinōnia tou hagiou pneumatos* (2 Cor 13:13)," *Studies Honoring I. G. Brady* [ed. R. S. Almagno, et al.; Franciscan Inst. Pub. Theol. Series 6; NY, 1976] 421–47.)

51

THE LETTER
TO THE ROMANS

Joseph A. Fitzmyer, S.J.

BIBLIOGRAPHY

1 Achtemeier, P. J., *Romans* (Interpretation; Atlanta, 1985). Althaus, P., *Der Brief an die Römer* (NTD 6; 9th ed.; Göttingen, 1959). Barrett, C. K., *A Commentary on the Epistle to the Romans* (BNTC; London, 1971). Cranfield, C. E. B., *A Critical and Exegetical Commentary on the Epistle to the Romans* (2 vols.; ICC; Edinburgh, 1975, 1979); *Romans: A Shorter Commentary* (GR, 1985). Huby, J., *Epître aux Romains* (rev. ed., S. Lyonnet; VS 10; Paris, 1957). Käsemann, E., *Commentary on Romans* (GR, 1980). Kertelge, K., *The Epistle to the Romans* (NTSR 12; NY, 1972). Kuss, O., *Der Römerbrief* (3 parts, never finished; Regensburg, 1963–78). Lagrange, M.-J., *Epître aux Romains* (EBib; Paris, 1950). Leenhardt, F., *The Epistle to the Romans* (London, 1961). Lietzmann, H., *An die Römer* (HNT 8; Tübingen, 1928). Lyonnet, S., *Epître aux Romains* (SBJ; Paris, 1954) 43–132; *Quaestiones in epistulam ad Romanos* (2 vols.;

Rome, 1962). Michel, O., *Der Brief an die Römer* (MeyerK 4; Göttingen, 1966). Pesch, R., *Römerbrief* (NEchtB 6; Würzburg, 1985). Robinson, J. A. T., *Wrestling with Romans* (Phl, 1979). Sanday, W. and A. C. Headlam, *The Epistle to the Romans* (ICC; 5th ed.; Edinburgh, 1902). Schlatter, A., *Gottes Gerechtigkeit* (2d ed.; Stuttgart, 1952). Schlier, H., *Der Römerbrief: Kommentar* (HTKNT 6; Freiburg, 1977). Schmidt, H. W., *Der Brief des Paulus an die Römer* (THK 6; Berlin, 1962). Taylor, V., *The Epistle to the Romans* (London, 1955). Viard, A., *Epître aux Romains* (SB; Paris, 1975). Wilckens, U., *Der Brief an die Römer* (3 vols.; EKKNT 6; Neukirchen, 1978–82). Zeller, D., *Die Brief an die Römer* (RNT; Regensburg, 1985).

DBSup 10. 739–863. IDBSup 752–54. Kümmel, INT 305–20. Wik-Schm, ENT 449–62.

INTRODUCTION

2 **(I) Date and Place of Writing.** Though these questions are involved in the problem of the integrity of Rom (→ 10 below), chap. 15 suggests that Paul wrote Rom shortly before he made his last trip to Jerusalem (15:25). He probably wrote it in Corinth or in Cenchreae, sometime in the winter of AD 57–58, after an evangelization of Illyricum (15:19) and of Macedonia and Achaia (15:26; cf. 1 Cor 16:5–7; Acts 20:3). Rom 16:23 speaks of Gaius as his host; cf. 1 Cor 1:14.
3 **(II) Occasion and Purpose.** Paul wrote Rom, conscious that his apostolate in the eastern Mediterranean area was over. Having preached "all the way from Jerusalem to Illyricum" (15:19), he looked westward to Spain. He planned to visit the Roman church en route, to fulfill the desire of years (1:13; 15:22,24,28). Before heading west, he had to attend to one last matter: to carry personally to Jerusalem the collection taken up in Gentile churches that he had founded (15:25; cf. 1 Cor 16:1) in order to manifest to the Jewish Christian mother church the solidarity existing between the "poor" of that community and the Gentile Christians of Galatia, Macedonia, and Achaia. These Gentile Christians contributed to that collection, realizing that they had

"shared in the spiritual blessings" of the mother church (15:27). So before he departed from Corinth for Jerusalem, Paul wrote to the Roman church to announce his coming visit. Writing as "the apostle of the Gentiles" (11:13), he wanted to introduce himself to this church that did not know him personally. Conscious too of his apostolic commission, he fashioned this letter of introduction, as an extended exposé of his understanding of the gospel (1:16–17), which he was also eager to preach at Rome (1:15), about which he had heard so much.
4 Rom is not "a compendium of Christian doctrine" (P. Melanchthon), or Paul's "last will and testament" (G. Bornkamm), or even a summary of Paul's own doctrine. Some of his significant teachings (e.g., on the church, the eucharist, the resurrection of the body, even eschatology) are missing from it. Rather, it is an essay-letter presenting his missionary reflections on the historical possibility of salvation, rooted in God's uprightness and love, now offered to all human beings through faith in Christ Jesus. In view of his eastern apostolate, and especially of the Judaizing crisis (now of past history), Paul came to realize that justification and salvation depended not on deeds prescribed by the law,

but on faith in Christ Jesus, the Son whom the Father's love did not spare. Through faith and baptism human beings share in the effects of the Christ-event, in the plan of salvation conceived by the Father and brought to realization in the death and resurrection of Jesus Christ (→ Pauline Theology, 82:41–48).

5   A climax of Paul's eastern ministry was the personal delivery of the collection to Jerusalem. Concerned about how it would be accepted, Paul begged the Roman Christians to pray that the help being taken might be well received by the people there (15:31). In Jerusalem Paul was distrusted, still known among Jews as the former Pharisee who was doing away with the law. So the collection was not simply to help the poor; it was to be a sign of solidarity of his Gentile converts with the first Jewish Christians. Would it be accepted in the right spirit? Rom may also (indirectly) represent a formulation of Paul's "gospel" such as he would present to Jewish Christians in Jerusalem still suspicious of him.

6   Rom discusses some of the same topics as Gal (→ Galatians, 47:9), but whereas Gal was composed in a context of polemics, Rom was written in an irenic mood. It is more of a treatise than a letter; it introduces elements of Greek literary style, rhetoric, and Stoic diatribe. Rom is no longer dealing with the Judaizing claim as such, even though it implicitly seeks to vindicate Paul's apostolic commission to evangelize the Gentile world. It stands to Gal as the Deutero-Pauline Eph does to Col. Though Paul is writing to a church that he does not know personally and parts of the hortatory section of Rom reflect problems that he has already had to contend with elsewhere in his ministry, his instructions to the "weak" and the "strong" (14:1–15:13) are probably his comments on the Roman situation about which he has had hearsay information. These two groups have plausibly been identified with the Jewish Christians and the Gentile Christians of Rome. Their conflicting differences were no longer the Judaizing problem of old (as in the churches of Galatia), but rather a problem of dietary and calendaric nature. When the Jews and Jewish Christians had to leave Rome because of Claudius's edict (AD 49; → Paul, 79:10), the Gentile Christians would have remained behind. This Gentile Christian community would have then developed on its own independently of Jewish Christian influence. But when the Jewish Christians returned to Rome, after the death of Claudius (AD 54) when the wife of the next emperor (Nero) was favorably disposed toward Jews, they probably found a situation different from what they had left behind. The Gentile Christians by now felt no qualms about dietary and calendaric regulations; they were the "strong," whereas the Jewish Christians, for whom such regulations were important, represent the "weak." Paul would have somehow heard about this situation in the church of Rome and writes about it. See further W. Marxsen, *Introduction to the New Testament* (Phl, 1968) 99–101; K. P. Donfried (ed.), *The Romans Debate* (Minneapolis, 1977).

7   **(III) The Roman Church.** Paul's habit in the east was to establish Christian communities in important cities of the empire (Philippi, Thessalonica, Corinth, Ephesus). Though eager to preach the gospel in Rome too, he knew that its church had been founded by someone else (15:20; cf. 1:8,13). Who it was he does not say. Writing Rom as he did, it is unlikely that he considered Peter its "founder" (cf. Gal 2:7–8). Most likely the community there was formed of converts from Palestine or Syria at an early date (cf. Acts 2:10; Ambrosiaster, *In ep. ad Rom.,* prologue; PL 17. 47–48; Tacitus,

Ann. 15.44). Peter probably did not arrive in Rome before the 50s; he was still in Jerusalem for the "Council" (*ca.* AD 49). Aquila and Prisca, Jewish Christians compelled to leave Italy by Claudius's edict, came to Corinth (*ca.* AD 49). See Wik-Schm, *ENT* 588.

8   Commentators often maintain that the composition of the Roman church is important for the understanding of Rom. In modern times the Tübingen School, E. Renan, T. Zahn, W. Manson, F. Leenhardt have considered it to have been predominantly Jewish Christian. Their main argument is derived from the abundant use of OT quotations, and especially the Abraham story. This might suggest that Paul envisaged his readers as predominantly of Jewish origin. There was certainly a large Jewish segment of the population in 1st-cent. Rome (see S. Lyonnet, *Quaestiones* 1. 17–23; H. J. Leon, *The Jews of Ancient Rome* [Phl, 1960]), which would have been a natural matrix for the Christian church. Though expelled in great numbers by Claudius, they could have returned to Rome after his death. However, many others (C. K. Barrett, S. Lyonnet, O. Michel, J. Munck) believe that the Roman church was predominantly Gentile. This seems preferable, since Paul includes his readers among the Gentiles for whose salvation he has been commissioned an apostle (see 1:5–7,12–14; 11:11–13; 15:16).

9   **(IV) Authenticity and Integrity of Rom.** The Pauline authorship of Rom is universally admitted today, as it was in antiquity. The dissenting voices of the 19th cent. (E. Evanson, B. Bauer, A. D. Loman) have been "relegated to a place among the curiosities of NT scholarship" (Cranfield, *Romans* 2).

The authenticity of the final doxology (16:25–27) is, however, questioned. (1) Its position varies in Gk mss.: in the Hesychian (ℵ, B, C) and Western (D) text-traditions after 16:23; in the Koine text-tradition (L and minuscules) after 14:23; in P⁴⁶ (the oldest text of Rom) after 15:33; in mss. A, P, 5, 33 after both 14:23 and 16:23; and in mss. G, g, and Marcion it was wholly omitted (though a space for it was left after 14:23 in G, g). (2) Its style is periodic, redolent of liturgical, hymnic phraseology—a feature otherwise absent from Rom. (3) The "mystery" applied to the salvation of the Gentiles is found in the Deutero-Paulines, but not in Rom. None of these reasons yields certainty about the matter, but the majority of commentators tend to regard the doxology as an addition made to Rom at a later date, possibly when the corpus of his letters was gathered. See J. Dupont, *RBén* 58 (1948) 3–22; H. Gamble, *The Textual History of the Letter to the Romans* (SD 42; GR, 1977).

10   Rom 16:1–23 presents another problem. Its Pauline authorship is normally admitted, but is it an integral part of Rom? Marcion and some patristic writers (Tertullian, Cyprian, Irenaeus) knew of a form of Rom without chaps. 15–16. In P⁴⁶ the doxology follows 15:33, a verse that sounds like the conclusion of a letter (cf. 1 Cor 16:23–24; 2 Cor 13:11; Phil 4:9). Again, Rom 16:1–16 reads like a letter of recommendation for Phoebe, a deacon of the church of Cenchreae. It resembles an ancient letter of recommendation (*epistolē systatikē*). See comment on 16:1. Was it originally addressed to the Roman church? An Ephesian destination has often been maintained (by D. Schulz, J. Moffatt, T. M. Taylor, *et al.*). It would thus have been sent to a church with which Paul was well acquainted. In 16:3 he greets Prisca and Aquila, who had settled in Ephesus (Acts 18:18,26), where they were with a community gathered about them (1 Cor 16:19). 2 Tim 4:19 may imply that they were still in Ephesus later on. Again,

Paul greets Epaenetus, "the first convert for Christ in Asia" (16:5). Besides, Paul greets at least 25 others (23 by name) — a large number of acquaintances in a church he does not know personally! He is even familiar with groups that meet in the house-church (16:5). Finally, the warning in 16:17-20, so different in tone from the rest of Rom, seems strangely addressed to a church that he does not know intimately. Yet none of these arguments is cogent in the last analysis. The way Prisca and Aquila moved around, they could be in Rome itself again at the time that Paul writes (after Claudius's death). Why did Epaenetus, the first convert in Asia, have to stay there? Paul could have learned of the house-church from Prisca and Aquila. 16:17-20 is not entirely admonitory in tone; it may merely echo his hortatory style in other letters (cf. 1 Cor 5:9,11). But the main reason for regarding 16:1-23 as an integral part of Rom is that otherwise Rom 1-15 would be the sole letter in the Pauline corpus to lack an epistolary ending. See H. Gamble, *The Textual History*, 56-95.

11 The problematic ending of Rom, together with the omission of *en Rōmē*, "at Rome," at 1:7,15 in some mss. (G, g, 1908), has evoked the theory that Rom was really composed as a "circular letter," destined for more than one church (T. W. Manson, *BJRL* 31 [1948] 197-200). In this view, Rom 1-15, with the doxology as in P[46], would have been sent to Rome, whereas the 16-chapter form would have been sent to Ephesus. The phrase *en Rōmē* would then represent the real address in the first instance, but its omission in some mss. would come from other copies destined for elsewhere. But this intriguing suggestion is based on slim ms. evidence, since the best Gk mss. attest Rom in a 16-chapter form. Nor is there any real parallel in this case between Rom and Eph (→ Ephesians 55:2).

12 **(V) Significance of Rom.** Rom has affected later Christian theology more than any other NT book. Scarcely an area of theological development has not been influenced by its teaching. Its influence is manifest even in other NT writings (1 Pet, Heb, Jas) and subapostolic works (Clement, Ignatius, Polycarp, Justin). Patristic and scholastic commentaries on Rom abound, beginning with Origen; the chief interpreters were Chrysostom, Theodoret, John Damascene, Oecumenius, Theophylact, Ambrosiaster, Pelagius, Hugh of St. Victor, Abelard, and Thomas Aquinas. Immeasurable is the part Rom played in the Reformation debates. Famous commentaries on it were penned by M. Luther, P. Melanchthon, and J. Calvin. Modern religious thinking has also been greatly affected by the theological commentaries by K. Barth (*Epistle to the Romans* [London, 1933]), A. Nygren (*Commentary on Romans* [London, 1952]), H. Asmussen (*Der Römerbrief* [Stuttgart, 1952]), and E. Brunner (*Der Römerbrief* [Leipzig, n.d.]). The contribution that Rom has made to Western Christian thinking is inestimable.

13 **(VI) Outline.** Many modern commentators agree about the obvious divisions of Rom (Introduction, Doctrinal Section, Hortatory Section, Conclusion [with or without chap. 16]), but debate centers on the subdivision of the doctrinal section. Is it to be divided into two or three subsections? Does chap. 5 go with what precedes or with what follows? Has Paul incorporated into Rom certain pieces formulated for other occasions and already used as units (3:10-18; 5:12-21; 9:1-11:36)? These passages seem to some commentators to be

abruptly introduced, but, as they stand now, they are to be taken as integral parts of the development of Rom. See appropriate places below for further comments. The outline used here is a modification of that of Lyonnet, but it is very close to those of Cranfield and Käsemann.

(I) Introduction (1:1-15)
    (A) Address and Greeting (1:1-7)
    (B) Thanksgiving (1:8)
    (C) Proemium: Paul's Desire to Come to Rome (1:9-15)
(II) Part I: Doctrinal Section — God's Gospel of Jesus Christ Our Lord (1:16-11:36)
    (A) Through the Gospel the Uprightness of God Is Revealed as Justifying the Person of Faith (1:16-4:25)
        (a) The Theme Announced: The Gospel Is the Powerful Source of Salvation for All, Disclosing God's Uprightness (1:16-17)
        (b) The Theme Negatively Explained: Without the Gospel God's Wrath is Manifested toward All Human Beings (1:18-3:20)
            (i) God's wrath against the Gentiles (1:18-32)
            (ii) God's judgment against the Jews (2:1-3:20)
        (c) The Theme Positively Explained: God's Uprightness is Manifested through Christ and Apprehended by Faith (3:21-31)
        (d) The Theme Illustrated: In the OT Abraham Was Justified by Faith (4:1-25)
    (B) The Love of God Assures Salvation to Those Justified by Faith (5:1-8:39)
        (a) The Theme Announced: The Justified Christian, Reconciled to God, Will Be Saved, Sharing with Hope in Christ's Risen Life (5:1-11)
        (b) The Theme Explained: New Christian Life Brings a Threefold Liberation (5:12-7:25)
            (i) Freedom from sin and death (5:12-21)
            (ii) Freedom from self through union with Christ (6:1-23)
            (iii) Freedom from the law (7:1-25)
        (c) The Theme Developed: Christian Life is Lived in the Spirit and Is Destined for Glory (8:1-39)
            (i) Christian life empowered by the Spirit (8:1-13)
            (ii) Through the Spirit the Christian becomes a child of God, destined for glory (8:14-30)
            (iii) Hymn to the love of God made manifest in Christ (8:31-39)
    (C) This Justification/Salvation Does Not Contradict God's Promise to Israel of Old (9:1-11:36)
        (a) Paul's Lament for His Former Coreligionists (9:1-5)
        (b) Israel's Plight Is Not Contrary to God's Direction of History (9:6-29)
        (c) Israel's Failure Is Derived from Its Own Refusal (9:30-10:21)
        (d) Israel's Failure Is Partial and Temporary (11:1-36)
(III) Part II: Hortatory Section — The Demands of Upright Life in Christ (12:1-15:13)
    (A) Christian Life Must Be Worship in the Spirit Paid to God (12:1-13:14)
    (B) Charity Is Owed by the Strong to the Weak (14:1-15:13)
(IV) Conclusion (15:14-33)
(V) Letter of Recommendation for Phoebe (16:1-23)
(VI) Doxology (16:25-27)

COMMENTARY

14 **(I) Introduction (1:1-15).** The opening formula, Paul's greeting to the Romans, is the most solemn *praescriptio* in his letters (→ NT Epistles, 45:8). He alone sends the letter. Because he writes to a church not yet personally acquainted with him, he desires to introduce himself and his preaching. The first sentence of the opening formula (1:1-7a) is expanded to include a triple description of himself, echoes of the primitive kerygma, and motifs to be treated in the letter (gospel, appeal to the OT, divine favor, election, faith, the risen Christ).
15 **(A) Address and Greeting (1:1-7). 1.** *slave of Christ Jesus:* The first description of Paul. *Doulos* designates him not only in a generic way as a Christian, a "slave of Christ" (1 Cor 7:22), but more specifically as a preacher of the gospel serving the Christian community (cf. Gal 1:10; Phil 1:1; 2:22). His use of *doulos* reflects not only the OT custom of certain persons calling themselves "slaves" of Yahweh (Ps 27:9; 31:17; 89:51) but also the use of it to describe great figures who served Yahweh in salvation history (Moses, 2 Kgs 18:12; Joshua, Judg 2:8; Abraham, Ps 105:42). Paul, as the "slave of Christ," belongs to the same line. *called as an apostle:* The second description stresses the divine origin of his mission. The event near Damascus may be regarded as his call to the apostolate (see B. Rigaux, *The Letters of St. Paul* [Chicago, 1968] 40-67). In Gal 1:15 Paul regards his "call" as the continuation of the divine vocation of OT figures (Jeremiah, the Servant of Yahweh). On "apostle," see comment on Gal 1:1. *set apart for God's gospel:* The third description of himself: Gal 1:15 explains that he was destined for this role from before his birth. The ptc. "set apart" may be playing on Aram *pĕrîš*, "separated," the word that underlies "Pharisee." Paul may be implying that his Pharisaic past was a divinely ordained background for this apostolate. It at least means that even before his birth he was marked by God for this role in salvation history. It is "God's gospel" because its ultimate source is the Father (15:16; 2 Cor 11:7). **2.** *which he promised previously:* From the beginning of Rom Paul stresses that this "gospel" of salvation is part of a divine and ancient plan, in which even the OT had a part. He is no Marcionite but sees the new dispensation growing out of the same source as the old. *through his prophets:* Not just the three major and twelve minor prophets of the OT, but all the OT persons whom the early church regarded as uttering statements applicable to Christ. **3.** *about his Son:* God's gospel and the promises made by him in the OT refer to Jesus, who stands in a unique relation to God as "his Son" (cf. 8:3,32; Gal 4:4). Paul is not referring to the ontological makeup of Christ, but is going to affirm two things about the risen Christ: he enjoys a filial relation to God and his preexistence is implied. Here too begins the fragment of the primitive kerygma that Paul introduces. *descended from David according to the flesh:* The first affirmation asserts that Jesus was a Davidid in the order of natural, physical descent (cf. Rom 4:1; 9:5); he was a scion with a right to the sacral anointing of a Davidic heir. The phrase *kata sarka,* "according to the flesh," stands in contrast to *kata pneuma hagiōsynēs,* "according to a Spirit of holiness," the basis of Paul's second affirmation; from this point of view the risen Christ possesses a still greater quality.
16 **4.** *set up as the Son of God with power:* Three problems complicate the understanding of this phrase:

(1) What does the aor. ptc. *horisthentos* mean? (2) What does *en dynamei* modify? (3) What is the sense of "Son of God"? (1) Certainly to be rejected as the meaning of *horisthentos* is "predestined" (Vg, Augustine, Pelagius), since *horizein,* "limit, define," is not the same as *proorizein,* "predetermine." Chrysostom and other Gk writers explained the ptc. as "manifested, displayed." This meaning, though tolerable, was all too often understood in terms of the later discussion of the natures of Christ. Modern commentators usually prefer the meaning "appointed, installed, set up" (see Acts 10:42; 17:31). (2) The phrase *en dynamei* has been taken as an adv. modifier of the ptc., "decisively declared" (Goodspeed, Sanday-Headlam), or "by a mighty act" (*NEB*); but the position of the phrase is against such an interpretation. Paul's contrast demands that, though Jesus was Son descended from David on the natural level, he was set up as "the Son of God with power" on the level of the Spirit (as of the resurrection). (3) In saying "Son of God with power," Paul is not thinking of the inner-trinitarian relation of the Father and the Son (of later theology), but of the unique relationship of Christ to God in the salvific process. For Paul the resurrection made a difference in that process, though it did not *make* Christ the Son of God (cf. 2 Cor 4:4; 8:9; Phil 2:6). Before, Jesus was the Son born of Davidic lineage; now he is the "son of God with power" (on the omission of the article before *en dynamei,* see BDF 272). Just as the early church looked on the resurrection as the event in Jesus' existence when he became "Lord" and "Messiah" (Acts 2:36) and applied to him apropos of it Ps 2:7 ("You are my son; today I have begotten you"), so for Paul Christ was endowed with a power of vivification at the resurrection (Phil 3:10) and became a "vivifying Spirit" (1 Cor 15:45; → Pauline Theology, 82:60-64). *according to a Spirit of holiness:* This expression is found nowhere else in Paul's writings and is part of the primitive formula being used. It could mean "the holy Spirit," as a literal translation of *rûaḥ haqqōdeš* (Isa 63:11), an expression used at times in QL (1QS 4:21; 9:3), revealing its Palestinian usage. Some patristic and modern commentators have understood it of the activity of the Holy Spirit unleashed, as it were, by the risen Christ. But the obvious parallelism of the phrase with *kata sarka* suggests that Paul regards it as something belonging to Christ himself. It is not simply his divine nature (R. Cornely, J. Bonsirven), but rather the transcendent, dynamic source of holiness in his glorified state in virtue of which he vivifies human beings (cf. 1 Cor 15:45). *from his resurrection from the dead:* The prep. *ex* denotes either time or causality. Understood temporally, it would express Christ's new mode of dynamic existence as of his resurrection; understood causally, it would designate the resurrection itself as an influence in Christ's salvific activity (see M.-E. Boismard, *RB* 60 [1953] 5-17; D. M. Stanley, *Christ's Resurrection in Pauline Soteriology* [AnBib 13; Rome, 1961] 165; J. A. Fitzmyer, *TAG* 202-17). **5.** *the grace of apostleship:* Lit., "grace and apostleship." Paul's call to be the apostle to the Gentiles came to him through the risen Christ (Gal 1:12,16). *in view of the commitment of faith:* The gen. is appositional. Paul conceives of faith as a something that begins with *akoē,* "hearing" (10:17), and ends with a personal commitment or submission (*hypakoē;* → Pauline Theology, 82:109). **7.** *in Rome:* The capital of the Greco-Roman

world of Paul's day (→ 11 above). *holy people:* Lit., "called saints," or possibly, "called (to be) saints." Paul's pl. expression echoes the sg. *klētē hagia* of the LXX (= Hebr *miqrā' qōdeš*), "a holy called gathering," used of the Israelites at the exodus (Exod 12:16). It designated them as a people set apart, dedicated to Yahweh (Lev 11:44; 19:2). Paul flatters the Roman Christians by adapting the OT expression and insinuating the new sense in which they are now the "holy called ones."

17   (B) Thanksgiving (1:8). Paul uses an epistolary formula (cf. 1 Thess 1:8) similar to that found in contemporary Gk letters (→ NT Epistles, 45:8B). His prayer for the Romans is addressed to God through Christ (cf. Rom 7:25; 11:36; 1 Cor 15:57).

18   (C) Proemium: Paul's Desire to Come to Rome (1:9–15). Paul's coming visit to the Roman church will be a source of mutual benefit, but also an opportunity to preach the gospel there. **9.** *whom I serve:* Paul compares his work in the service of the gospel with a priestly act of worship offered to God; cf. 15:16. *in my spirit:* This phrase is variously interpreted, but it most likely means that Paul put his whole self into evangelization. **10.** *by God's will:* Though Paul sensed that his coming trip to Jerusalem was not without risks (15:31–32), his eventual trip to Rome is destined by God himself. **13.** *I want you to know:* Lit., "I do not want you to be ignorant," a favorite Pauline phrase of emphasis (11:25; 1 Thess 4:13; 1 Cor 10:1; 12:1; 2 Cor 1:8). *prevented up till now:* By what? In 15:18–22 he cites his apostolate in the east and his respect for a community not founded by him. Since the passive is often used as a circumlocution for God (the "theological passive," *ZBG* § 236), Paul may be hinting that the delay is divinely ordained. **14.** *to Greeks and to barbarians:* As the apostle to the Gentiles, he must bring the gospel to all non-Jews. He designates the non-Greek world by a Gk onomatopoeic word *bar-bar-oi*, dividing the Gentiles into those who spoke Greek (many Romans included at this period) and those who did not. **15.** *in Rome:* → 11 above.

19   (II) Part I: Doctrinal Section—God's Gospel of Jesus Christ Our Lord (1:16–11:36). The introduction has already mentioned God's gospel and Paul's role in proclaiming it. This section expounds the unique, historic possibility of salvation for all human beings that God makes known in this gospel. This section is best divided into three main parts: (A) 1:16–4:25; (B) 5:1–8:39; (C) 9:1–11:36.

20   (A) Through the Gospel the Uprightness of God is Revealed as Justifying the Person of Faith (1:16–4:25). Paul's pride in his role of proclaiming this gospel introduces the theme of the first part.

(a) THE THEME ANNOUNCED: THE GOSPEL IS THE POWERFUL SOURCE OF SALVATION FOR ALL, DISCLOSING GOD'S UPRIGHTNESS (1:16–17). Given what the gospel is, Paul is not ashamed of preaching it even in the capital of the civilized world—a grandiose understatement (cf. 1 Cor 2:3–6). **16.** *the gospel:* See comment on 1:3; → Pauline Theology, 82:31–36. *God's power:* This initial description of the gospel stresses that it is not just a message, a philosophy, or a system of thought to be learned; it is the "story of the cross" (1 Cor 1:18). "God's power" is an abstraction, expressive of the force (*dynamis*) with which God affects the course of human history (cf. 1 Cor 2:4; 4:20). *for the salvation of everyone who has faith:* The divine force, which is the gospel, is destined for the "salvation" of the believer. Significantly, Paul expresses the purpose of the gospel in terms of "salvation," and not of "justification," in this formulation of the proposition of Rom. *Sōtēria* means "deliverance, rescue" from evil (of any sort; → Pauline Theology, 82:71). In the NT it normally connotes deliverance from dangers to Christian

destiny and (positively) the fostering of those conditions that ensure its attainment. Elsewhere in Rom (5:9–10; 8:24; 10:9,13; 11:11,26; 13:11) it refers to a future, eschatological reality, conceptually distinct from justification or reconciliation. *for the Jew first and (then) the Greek:* "First" is lacking in some mss. (B, G). It is to be retained, however, since it agrees with Paul's conviction about Israel's privilege (2:9–10; 3:9). To it the Messiah was promised (9:5), and Jews were the first to turn to him in faith. Fully aware of this historic privilege, Paul nevertheless asserts the possibility now given to all human beings to share by faith in that salvation (10:12; 1 Cor 1:24; 12:13).

21   17. *God's uprightness is disclosed:* The gospel now manifests, as never before, God's basic attitude toward human beings, his power and activity in their behalf in acquitting them through Christ, for apart from this gospel only divine wrath is revealed from heaven (1:18–3:20). The contrast of "uprightness" (1:17) and "wrath" (1:18) suggests that Paul is speaking of a quality or attribute in God. Here in 1:17 Paul speaks of *dikaiosynē theou*, "the uprightness of God." It is often translated "the righteousness of God," which sometimes sounds like his self-righteousness. The Vg translated this Gk phrase as *iustitia Dei*, which often appears in older Catholic versions (or in romance-language translations) as "the justice of God." This transl., however, was often misunderstood as God's "vindictive or punitive justice," as Luther the monk once understood it (see LWks 34:336–37). Because of such problems, I follow E. J. Goodspeed's transl., "the uprightness of God" (Rom 3:5; *The Complete Bible: An American Translation* [Chicago, 1960] NT, 143). It denotes the divine quality whereby God acquits his people, manifesting toward them his gracious power in a just judgment. The meaning of the phrase as an attribute of God is further found in 3:5,21, 22,25,26; and probably in 10:3 (→ Pauline Theology, 82:39), even though it does not always mean that in Paul's letters (cf. 2 Cor 5:21 and Phil 3:9—where it clearly denotes a gift from God). Here Paul means that the gospel is the means whereby this aspect of God is revealed. *from faith to faith:* This literal transl. reveals the problem of a much-debated phrase. Certainly inadequate is the interpretation of Tertullian and Origen, "from faith in the law to faith in the gospel," since the use of the two preps. *ek* and *eis* with the same word usually supposes the identical meaning of the word so governed (cf. 2 Cor 2:16; 3:18). Two interpretations are mainly current: (1) "from a beginning faith to a more perfect faith" (Lagrange, Huby). This exploits the notion of progress often associated with this kind of prep. expression (Ps 84:8); God's economy of salvation is shared more and more by a human being as faith grows. (2) "Through faith and for faith." This interpretation presupposes the development in 3:21–22, where a similar development of thought is found: "through (*ek*) faith" would express the means by which a human being shares in salvation; "for (*eis*) faith" the purpose of the divine plan. In either case, salvation is a matter no longer of law but of faith from start to finish, and God's uprightness is disclosed only in the sphere of faith (E. Käsemann, *Romans*, 31). *as it is written:* In Scripture. Paul introduces an OT quotation by using a current Jewish introductory formula (see J. A. Fitzmyer, *ESBNT* 8–10). *the upright shall live by faith:* Hab 2:4, quoted neither according to the MT ("The upright shall live by his fidelity") nor according to the LXX (mss. B, S: "The upright shall live by my faithfulness"; mss. A, C: "My upright one shall live by faith"). In the original, the coming Chaldean invaders, whose god is their might, are contrasted with Judah, whose deliverance lies in fidelity to Yahweh. Habakkuk is ordered to record Yahweh's message: One who is puffed up (with confidence) will fail, but the upright one will live by his fidelity (to Yahweh). Paul, however, omits the possessive pron. and adopts the LXX transl. of Hebr *'ĕmûnâ*, "fidelity," Gk *pistis*. The "life" promised to Judah was temporal deliverance from the invader. Paul extends the sense of both "life" and "faith" in terms of Christian destiny. See J. A. Emerton, *JTS* 28 (1977) 1–18; J. A. Fitzmyer, *TAG* 236–46; O. P. Robertson, *Presbyterian* 9 (1983) 52–71. Some interpreters (e.g., Cranfield, Kuss) link "by faith" to "upright" (i.e., he who is justified through faith [*NEB*]). This may agree with Paul's thought, but it forces the meaning of the phrase in Hab and is not as satisfactory; see H. C. C. Cavallin, *ST* 32 (1978) 33–43.

22 (b) THE THEME NEGATIVELY EXPLAINED: WITHOUT THE GOSPEL GOD'S WRATH IS MANIFESTED TOWARD ALL HUMAN BEINGS (1:18–3:20). The proposition of 1:16–17 is explained first by an antithetical consideration: what happens to human beings without the gospel. Paul indicts both paganism and Judaism for failing to enable people to achieve moral uprightness. Left to himself, the pagan Greek did not come to acknowledge God and consequently lapsed into moral depravity. Without the gospel, the Jew does not succeed in achieving uprightness before God, despite the advantage of possessing the Mosaic law. In both cases the result is estrangement from God; divine wrath is displayed toward both. Such is the human condition without the gospel of Jesus Christ.

23 (i) *God's wrath against the Gentiles* (1:18–32). O. Michel (*Römer* 60) plausibly suggests that this paragraph is an example of a missionary sermon such as Paul delivered to pagans. In it he echoes a judgment of the pagan world current among Jews of his day. His topic sentence is v 18; his summary judgment: "they deserve to die" (1:32).

18. *God's wrath:* God's reaction to human sin and evil conduct is vividly expressed by the use of an OT anthropomorphic image (Isa 30:27–28; → Pauline Theology, 82:38; OT Thought, 77:99–102). It was a protological way of describing the living God's steadfast reaction to Israel's breach of the covenant (Ezek 5:13; Hos 5:10) or to the nations' oppression of his people (Isa 10:5–11; Ezek 36:5–6). It is a way of saying that God "leaves pagan society to stew in its own juice" (Robinson, *Wrestling* 18). Related to the "Day of Yahweh" (Zeph 1:14–18), it acquired an eschatological nuance. Now Paul asserts that it is revealed "from heaven" against pagans who are without the gospel. **19.** *what can be known of God:* Elsewhere in the NT (and in the LXX) *gnōstos* means "known," not "can be known," and Chrysostom and the Vg preferred the meaning "what is known of God." But this creates a tautology with the predicate "is clear to them." So most modern commentators follow Origen, Thomas Aquinas, *et al.,* in interpreting it as "capable of being known" (BAGD 164; Bultmann, *TDNT* 1. 719; Cranfield, *Romans* 113). *is clear to them:* Lit., "is clear in them." But "in them" scarcely means "to their minds" (Lyonnet, Huby). Rather, either (1) "among them," since Paul insists on the externality of the manifestations (Michel, Cranfield), or better (2) "to them," since *en* with the dat. occasionally = the simple dat. (Gal 1:16; 2 Cor 4:3; 8:1; BDF 220; ZBG § 120). Paul explains the "knowable" in v 20.

24 **20.** *his invisible qualities:* Lit., "his unseen things," the specific qualities being named at the end of the verse. *since the creation of the world:* Cf. Job 40:6–42:6; Ps 19:1–6; Isa 40:12–31. Often in the NT, *ktisis* means "what is created, creature" (so Vg, *a creatura mundi*). Since

that would be tautological here, many commentators prefer the temporal, active sense of "creation" (as in Matt 24:21; 25:34; cf. Cranfield, *Romans* 114). *perceptible to the mind:* Lit., "being intellectually apprehended are perceived." An oxymoron, *pace* Käsemann, *Romans* 40. Contemplating the created world and reflecting on it, a human being perceives through its multicolored façade the great "Unseen" behind it—the omnipotence and divine character of its Maker. Though essentially invisible, these qualities are mirrored in the "great works" (*poiēmata*) produced by him. There is no question here either of knowledge through a positive primal revelation or of knowledge by faith. *so they have no excuse:* Paul echoes a current Jewish idea of the culpability of pagans in not acknowledging and reverencing God as they should have; see Wis 13:1–9; *As. Mos.* 1:13 (*AOT* 607). The Gk phrase could express either purpose or result. Sanday-Headlam, Barrett, Michel prefer the idea of (conditional) purpose: God did not intend that pagans should sin; but if they did, he intended that it would be without excuse. Many scholars (Cornely, Lietzmann, Cranfield, *et al.*), recognizing that in NT Greek the consecutive sense of the phrase encroaches on the final (ZBG § 351–52; BDF 402.2) argue that the sense of result better suits the present context. In either case, the human condition since creation argues against an atheistic attitude. **21.** *though they knew God:* After the general principle enunciated in 1:20, Paul proceeds to the specific sin of the pagans. Here he seems to admit that in some sense they "knew God"—despite what Jews normally thought (Jer 10:25; Ps 79:6; Wis 14:12–22) and what Paul himself seems to say in 1 Cor 1:21, "the world with all its wisdom did not come to know God." What is denied in these passages is a real, affective knowledge of God that includes love and reverence. In this quasi-philosophical discussion the word *gnontes* connotes an inceptive, speculative sort of information about God that Paul thinks that the pagans could not help but have. The inconsequential character of that knowledge, which did not develop into real religious recognition, is the root of their sin. Paul is not speaking merely of pagan philosophers, much less of some primitive positive revelation (e.g., of the law, 2 Esdr. 7:21–24) or just of some first pagans (*pace* A. Feuillet, *LumVie* 14 [1954] 71–75). He is speaking of all pagans, at least up to his day. *did not honor him:* Paul's complaint is centered not only on pagan ignorance but also on the failure to manifest reverence and gratitude, which should have sprung from the knowledge they had of him; instead their reverence was paid to created things. *indulged in vain speculations:* Three consequences of their failure follow: the futility of self-sufficient reasoning, the obscuring of vision in other religious matters, and idolatry. **23.** *exchanged the glory of the immortal God for images:* Allusion to Ps 106:20, "They exchanged their glory for the image of a grass-eating bullock," which refers to the golden calf of Exod 32. Paul applies the allusion to pagans. Idols are preferred to Yahweh's *doxa*, the resplendent external manifestation of his presence (Hebr *kābôd*, Exod 24:17; 40:34–35). Paul is echoing Deut 4:16–18 here.

25 (In the dogmatic constitution of Vatican Council I *De fide catholica*, Rom 1:20 is cited in support of the thesis that God can be known with certainty by the natural light of human reason from created things [DS 3004]. Such a use of this text does not mean that Paul is saying exactly the same thing. The council was opposing Fideism and Traditionalism and asserted the possibility of such knowledge of God, apart from faith and apart from positive revelation. The difference in the texts of Paul and Vatican I is that the latter deals with the *capability* (active potency) of the human mind to know

God and prescinds from the *de facto* use of it, whereas Paul asserts the fact that God is intellectually perceived and known from created things. He also speaks of human "impiety and wickedness" [1:18] and of human failure to acknowledge God properly [1:28]; from such attitudes the council prescinded. The further theological question about the human capability to know God without any divine assistance [e.g., grace] is beyond Paul's perspective. See Lyonnet, *Quaestiones,* 1a ser., 78–88.)

26   **24.** *abandoned them:* Lit., "handed them over to." The rhetorical triple use of the vb. *paradidonai* (see also vv 26,28) introduces the punishment protologically ascribed to God's wrath. Paul seeks to establish an intrinsic relation between sin and punishment; impiety brings its own retribution (see Wis 11:15–16; Ezek 23:28–30). Idolatry, the consequence of failure to honor God duly, is the source of immorality, for it is the "big lie" (Wis 14:22–31). **25.** *exchanged the truth of God:* An echo of 1:18,22–23. What is, is true; what is not, is falsehood (see Jer 10:14). *who is blessed forever, Amen!:* Paul betrays his Jewish background in spontaneously uttering a doxology at the climactic mention of God the creator (see 2 Cor 11:31). **26.** *have exchanged their natural function:* The contrast between "females" and "males" (1:27) shows that the sexual perversion of which Paul speaks is homosexuality. (Only modern eisegesis could distort Paul's words and refer them to female contraception.) The depravity of the perversion is the merited consequence of pagan impiety; having exchanged the true God for a false one (1:25), pagans inevitably changed their true natural functions for perverted ones (cf. Philo, *De Abr.* 135; *De spec. leg.* 2.50; 3.37). **28.** *what is not proper:* Idolatry leads not only to sexual perversion, but to all sorts of immoral conduct. Pauls adds a catalogue of vices (→ Pauline Theology, 82:142), an echo of the early church's *didachē.* **32.** *God's decree:* In 2:14–15 Paul will show that the pagan conscience perceives at times some of the injunctions prescribed in the Mosaic law. Echoing 1:21 (*gnontes, epignontes*), he formulates his verdict against the pagans and explains why they are "without excuse." *deserve to die:* This phrase might seem at first to refer to physical death as a punishment for the vices listed, but it is difficult to establish that pagan consciences would recognize this for all of them. Paul is probably thinking of total death (5:12,19), the lot of all sinners; it amounts to exclusion from God's kingdom (1 Cor 6:10; Gal 5:21). *approve those who practice them:* The abysmal state of the pagan is thus revealed, not only in failure to honor God and live uprightly but in approbation of the same conduct in others.

27   In this entire section Paul is not saying that every individual pagan before Christ's coming was a moral failure. He speaks collectively and describes a *de facto* situation; he does not mean that paganism was *de iure* incapable of moral uprightness. When Christian theologians teach the need of divine assistance for perseverance in a good, natural life, they go beyond Paul's perspective and have in mind the individual's fallen condition. The basis of their teaching, however, is Pauline: Humanity cannot do without the gospel (see 7:7–25).

28   (ii) *God's judgment against the Jews* (2:1–3:20). Paul turns to an imaginary listener who loudly applauds his description of the pagans' moral failure. Such a one is no better than the pagan, for in spite of a superior moral culture he does not do what is expected. Hence, he shall not escape divine judgment.

The identity of *anthrōpos* in 2:1–16 is disputed. For Chrysostom and Theodoret it was the secular judge or Roman authority; for Origen, the Christian bishop, priest, or deacon; for T. Zahn, the pagan philosopher or moralist. But many modern interpreters identify him as a Jew that judges himself superior to the pagan because of his people's privileges. In 2:17 the Jew is explicitly mentioned, and vv 1–16 seem to be only a buildup to this identification. Verses 12–16 show that a knowledge of divine ordinances is not exclusive to the Jew; some prescriptions of the Torah are known even to pagans. The Jew is thus implicitly compared. Again, these verses support 2:9–10, where Jew and Greek are put on an equal footing before God; vv 1–8 prepare for this view. Hence, 2:1–16 is an indirect indictment of Judaism that becomes overt in v 17; it eventually forces the Jew to pronounce sentence against himself. In developing his argument, Paul enunciates the general principle of God's impartial judgment (2:1–11), showing that possession of the law is no guarantee against divine wrath (2:12–16) and announcing that it will condemn the Jew as well as the Gentile (2:17–24)—and this, in spite of circumcision (2:25–29). See Wis 11–15; cf. Cranfield, *Romans* 137–42; J. M. Bassler, *Divine Impartiality* (SBLDS 59; Chico, 1982). Verses 1–11 and 17–29 are often regarded as an example of *diatribē* (→ Pauline Theology, 82:12).

29   **1.** *So:* Normally the particle *dio* introduces a conclusion from what precedes; here it is transitional and introduces a new topic. *O you who judge:* Lit., "O every man who judge." Such a use of *anthrōpos* in an address is characteristic of diatribes in Epictetus (see also 2:3; 9:20). *you condemn yourself:* The topic sentence in this section: You are yourself a sinner and an object of God's wrath. **2.** *God's judgment:* The noun *krima* can mean merely "lawsuit" (1 Cor 6:7) or "decision, judgment" (Rom 11:33); but it frequently connotes "condemnation, adverse sentence" (3:8; 13:2; Gal 5:10), as here. Such condemnation falls on all evil-doers "rightly" (lit., "according to the truth"), without respect of persons (2:11). **3.** *who sit in judgment:* The first of two questions highlights the critic's illusion; once asked, it answers itself. **4.** *do you make light of . . . :* It is not only a question of illusion, but even of contempt. To make light of the delay on God's part to punish sin—which should lead to repentance—is to manifest one's culpable negligence (see Wis 11:23; 2 Esdr. 7:74). **5.** *you store up wrath:* I.e., reason for the adverse reaction of God; see comment on 1:18. *God's just judgment:* The word *dikaiokrisia* stresses the equity of the divine decision to be given on the day of wrath; it is clearly something other than *dikaiosynē theou* (see comment on 1:17). Paul implies that the impenitent Jew fails to realize the relation of the present to the coming judgment of God. **6.** *repay everyone according to one's deeds:* Allusion to Ps 62:13 or Prov 24:12. Paul does not simply borrow this affirmation in a moment of ardent rhetoric; it is an important part of his teaching. Significantly, it is affirmed here in Rom even prior to his discussion of justification by grace through faith (3:23–26; cf. 14:10; 2 Cor 5:10). But retribution according to deeds must be understood against the backdrop of justification by faith (Käsemann, *Romans* 58; → Pauline Theology, 82:138). **7.** *life eternal:* The reward of those who patiently perform good deeds is a life to be enjoyed "forever with the Lord" (1 Thess 4:17; cf. Rom 5:21; 6:22–23). For the OT background, see Dan 12:2. It is life in the *aiōn,* "age," to come. **8.** *but for self-seeking people:* A difficult phrase, often misunderstood by commentators. Etymologically, *eritheia* is related to *erithos,* "mercenary's pay"; Aristotle (*Pol.* 5.3) used *eritheia* to denote "selfishness, selfish ambition" in a political context (see Barrett, *Romans* 47). But it often occurs in contexts of "strife" (*eris*) and was often confused with the latter in popular usage (see Gal 5:20; Phil 1:17; 2:3; 2 Cor 12:20). Hence, some commentators understand it here to mean "rebellious people" (Lagrange, Lietzmann, Lyonnet). Either meaning actually suits the context: they are not those who patiently pursue the good, and their lot is divine wrath. **9.** *trouble and distress:* A protological OT phrase (Deut 28:53,55,57), expressive of divine displeasure manifested toward human beings in this life (cf. Rom 8:35). Verses 9–10 reformulate vv 7–8, applying in reverse order the effects of wrath to all who do evil; they also recast in terms of Jews and Greeks what was said in 1:18. *on every human being:* Lit., "soul" (*psychē*). According to Lagrange these punishments are to affect specifically the "soul," but that is too Hellenistic an interpretation. Paul is more likely using *psychē* like OT *nepeš* (Lev 24:17; Num 19:20) for an aspect of "human being" (→ Pauline Theology, 82:104). *the Jew first and the Greek too:* See comment on 1:16. Having received unique privileges in the history of salvation, the Jew is more responsible when he sins; but when he does what is right, he is the first to receive his reward. The Gentile is not neglected. **11.** *God has no favorites:* Lit., "there is no partiality in God." Paul uses *prosōpolēmpsia*, "partiality," a word found only in Christian writings but coined from a LXX expression, *prosōpon lambanein*, a transl. of Hebr *pānîm nāśā'*, "lift up the face." It denotes the gracious act of someone who lifts a person's face by showing him favor (Mal 1:8; Lev 19:15). Such lifting-up-the-face is not found in God. So Paul sums up the principle underlying his discussion in 2:1–11: God is no respecter of persons; despite their privileges, Jews will be no better off than Gentiles, unless they do what is expected of them.

30 **12.** *without the law:* Not simply "without a law," but specifically without the Mosaic law. The context deals with Gentiles who lived without the benefit of Mosaic legislation. If they sin without knowledge of its prescriptions, they may perish without respect to it; their sin brings its own condemnation, even though the law is not applied to them. In this, Paul goes against current Jewish notions. *all who sinned under the law:* The phrase *en nomō* (without the article) refers to the same Mosaic law. Commentators have at times tried to establish a distinction between Paul's use of *ho nomos,* "the (Mosaic) law," and *nomos,* "law" (in general, or even "natural" law); but this distinction is without sound philological support (*pace ZBG* § 177; → Pauline Theology, 82:90). What human beings do is the criterion by which they will be judged, and this is explained in the two following verses. **13.** *hearers of the law:* The Jew is not upright before God simply because he knows the prescriptions of the Torah from hearing it read every Sabbath. Paul uses a well-known hortatory distinction between knowledge and action. *the doers of the law:* Paul adopts a Jewish perspective as he argues and implicitly echoes Lev 18:5 ("whoever observes these things shall find life"). *shall be made upright:* The fut. vb. betrays the eschatological forensic nature of justification expected at the judgment in accordance with the adopted Jewish perspective (→ Pauline Theology, 82:68). **14.** *when Gentiles who do not have the law:* This and the following verse explain why Gentiles without a knowledge of the Mosaic law will be punished (2:12). *instinctively observe:* Lit., "by nature" (*physei*), i.e., by the regular, natural order of things (BAGD 869), prescinding from any positive revelation. Following the guidance of *physis,* the Gentiles frame rules of conduct for themselves and know at least some of the prescriptions of the Jewish Torah. *what the law prescribes:* Lit., "the things of the law," a phrase not to be understood too rigidly, as if each of the precepts of the Torah was meant. For, though Paul admits that Gentiles do observe "the things of the law," his statement is couched in a general temporal clause, "Whenever. . . ." *even though they have not the law:* I.e., the benefit of a revealed legislation, such as the Jews had. *they are (a/the) law to themselves:* Because they have in them *physis*

as a guide for their conduct, a guide that is "not only relative or psychological, but absolute and objective" (Michel, *Römer* 78). Paul speaks of *ethnē,* "Gentiles"; he does not mean "all Gentiles," nor does he imply the perfect observance of all the precepts. He uses *physei* in a context referring primarily to knowledge: Even without the law Gentiles know instinctively what is to be done. His term does not mean "by nature," as distinguished from "by grace"; so his viewpoint is not that of the later theological problem, whether the pagan's will suffices *physei* to obey the natural law. **15.** *they show that what the law requires is written in their hearts:* Lit., "the deed of the law is written." Paul uses the sg. of the expression that he employs elsewhere in the pl. in a pejorative sense, *erga nomou,* "the deeds of the law" (3:20, 28; Gal 2:16; 3:2,5,10), or simply *erga* (4:2,6; 9:12,32; 11:6). They are the deeds that the law prescribes. For the slogan-like phrase, → Pauline Theology, 82:100. Paul affirms such knowledge as a present real condition of the Gentile conscience. *their thoughts argue their case pro and con:* This version of a difficult sentence takes *metaxy allēlōn,* "between one another," to refer to the mutual debate of inward thoughts in the Gentile conscience; the debate would concern the Gentile's conduct (so Cranfield, *Romans* 162; Käsemann, *Romans* 66). Some commentators (Sanday-Headlam, Lyonnet) take it to refer to thoughts that criticize or defend the actions of others, "in their dealings with one another." This, however, is farfetched. **16.** Logically, this verse follows 2:13; some commentators suggest that vv 14–15 are parenthetical or even misplaced. The ms. tradition, however, is constant. Paul does not mean that the Gentile conscience will function only on judgment day, but that it will especially bear witness on that day. "Such self-criticism anticipates the last judgment, as in Wis 1:5–10" (Käsemann, *Romans* 66). *when God will judge through Jesus Christ:* Contemporary Jews expected Yahweh to exercise judgment through an Elect One (*1 Enoch* 45:3–6). Paul applies this belief to Jesus. The prep. phrase *dia Christou* refers to the mediation of Christ in his eschatological role (→ Pauline Theology, 82:118). *according to my gospel:* The proclamation of Christ's role in eschatological judgment forms part of Paul's "good news" of salvation (→ Pauline Theology, 82:31–36). For Paul it is salvific judgment.

31 **17.** *you call yourself a Jew:* The imaginary critic is now identified by the common diaspora name for a member of the chosen people. This is the first of two series of five and four paratactically aligned, taunting phrases in which Paul sums up the Jewish claim: I am a Jew; I rely on the law; my boast is in Yahweh (cf. Jer 9:23; *Ps. Sol.* 17:1); I understand his will; instructed by the law, I know what is right and wrong. **19–20.** Four more taunts reveal the Jew's attitude toward others. Paul does not deny Israel's privileges (9:4–5) but sees all too clearly the lie in normal Jewish complacency. **21.** *do you refuse to teach yourself?:* The complex sentence begun in 2:17 is not finished; Paul breaks off and addresses the Jew directly with five pointed questions (2:21–23) that reveal the rift between the Jew's teaching and his own deeds (Ps 50:16–21). *you must not steal:* Exod 20:15.

32 **25.** Paul forestalls an objection, "Perhaps we Jews do not observe the law as we should, but at least we are circumcised." This argument too Paul rejects. *circumcision:* The "sign of the covenant" (Gen 17:10–11; *Jub.* 15:28; cf. Rom 4:11) incorporated a man into God's chosen people and assured him of life in the age to come (J. P. Hyatt, *IDB* 1. 629–31). Paul does not deny the value of circumcision and Israel's heritage denoted by it; but it means little without the observance of the law (Lev 18:5; Deut 30:16). **26.** *uncircumcision be regarded as circumcision:* Paul's courageous question, equating a good pagan with a circumcised Jew, would have been an abomination to Pharisaic ears (cf. Gal 5:6). **27.** Recall 2:14–15. **28.** *the real Jew:* Paul's climax: he pits against contemporary Jewish religious attitudes the principle of interior motivation of human actions—the circumcision of the heart, already proclaimed in the OT (Deut 10:16; 30:6; Jer 4:4; 9:24–25; Ezek 44:9). For God deals not with human beings according to outward appearances but "judges the secrets" they cherish "through Christ Jesus" (2:16). **29.** *real circumcision is of the heart, a thing of the Spirit, not of the letter:* In 2 Cor 3:6 the contrast of the Spirit and the letter is a succinct way of summing up the different realities of the two dispensations, the new and the old. The latter was governed by a written code, an extrinsic norm to be observed and esteemed; the former is vitalized by God's gift of the Spirit, an intrinsic principle reshaping human beings and remolding their conduct. Thus the OT idea of the circumcision of the heart takes on a new nuance; it is not just a spiritual circumcision of the human heart, but one that springs from the Spirit of Christ himself. *his praise is not from human beings but from God:* The real Jew is the Israelite with a circumcised heart, who will be known as such by God and receive his praise from him. Such a one cares not for the praise of mortals who might notice his Torah-fidelity. Paul may be playing on the meaning of the Hebr name for "Jew," *Yĕhûdî,* derived from the patriarchal name Judah (*Yĕhûdâ*). In popular etymology it was explained as the passive of *hôdâ,* "praised." The person with the circumcised heart is the one "praised" in God's sight, the real "Jew."

33   Paul's foregoing exposé might imply that Jews really have no advantage over Gentiles, despite his willingness to accord them a certain precedence (1:16; 2:9–10). Now in chap. 3 he answers an imaginary objector, pressing his point and returning to his thesis: Despite the divine oracles of salvation recorded in their sacred books, the wrath of God will burst upon Jews too. Verses 1–9 form the first paragraph in chap. 3. This paragraph is an integral development of Paul's argument, in which he considers objections that might come from a fellow Jew. It is neither a digression (*pace* M. Black, *Romans* [GR, 1981] 62; C. H. Dodd, *The Epistle of Paul to the Romans* [NY, 1932] 46; Käsemann, *Romans* 78), nor does it lack unity or coherence. It is a dialogic argument in which Paul pits his teaching about Christian faith over against the Torah-fidelity of a contemporary Jew. Paul controls the dialogue and, like an ancient teacher using diatribe (→ Pauline Theology, 82:12), guides the discussion with an imaginary Jewish interlocutor. Verse 3 poses the leading question that dominates the whole discussion. Verses 1–4 set forth the Jew's advantage in God's fidelity to his own promises and oracles; vv 5–8 handle the objection of libertinism, and v 9 enables Paul to reformulate his basic thesis in the whole negative development of his theme: all human beings, both Jews and Greeks, are under the power of sin when they are without the gospel. Throughout these nine verses the 1st pl. (we, our) is to be understood of Paul and the imaginary Jew with whom he is in dialogue. See S. K. Stowers, *CBQ* 46 (1984) 707–22.

34   **1.** *what advantage, then, is there in being a Jew?:* If possession of the law and circumcision mean nothing, what advantage does a member of the chosen people have? **2.** *in the first place:* Thus Paul admits much advantage, as he begins his explanation, but he never gives a second or a third point. Instead, his first advantage evokes further comments on the infidelity of Israel. *the utterances of God:* The possession of these is an obvious advantage. In the LXX *ta logia tou theou* (Ps 106:11; Num 24:4,16) denotes the "oracles of God" given to prophets to be communicated to his people; they include not only

revelations and promises but also rules of conduct. As elsewhere in the NT (Heb 5:12; 1 Pet 4:11), the phrase refers to the OT in general as God's words about salvation. Nothing in the phrase itself or in the context restricts its meaning to messianic promises. **3.** *What then? If some of them were unfaithful:* Since *apistein* can mean either "refuse to believe" or "be unfaithful" (BAGD 85), either or both senses could be intended here, for numerous OT examples could be cited of Israel's historic incredulity (Num 14; Exod 15:22–16:36) or infidelity (1 Kgs 18:21; Hos 4:1–2). Only "some" have been unfaithful. Paul does not restrict it in any way temporally; nor is he thinking of the "remnant" (9:27; 11:5) that did accept Christ and become the Jewish Christian church. *can their faithlessness nullify the faithfulness of God?:* As depositaries of the divine utterances, the Jews possessed Yahweh's protestations of fidelity to the people of his covenant (Exod 34:6–7; Hos 2:19–23; Num 23:19). Did his fidelity to such utterances not depend on Israel's fidelity to him? **4.** *By no means!:* The suggestion of God's infidelity is rejected by the indignant negative *mē genoito* (really a negative oath, "Let it not be so!" BDF 384). In the LXX it translates Hebr *ḥālîlâ,* "far be it from (me)." God's fidelity is not measured by human fidelity—this is basic in Paul's teaching on uprightness. God is always upright and will justify Israel (3:26). *God must be true though every human be a liar:* In using *alēthēs* of God, Paul plays on its two meanings: (1) "true, honest"; (2) "faithful, loyal." Though the second is obviously intended in the context, the first cannot be excluded, because of the allusion to Ps 116:11 (LXX 115:2), which calls human beings liars. *as it is written:* See comment on 1:17. Paul quotes Ps 51:6, not according to the MT ("that you may be justified in your sentence, vindicated when you condemn") but according to the LXX ("that you may be justified in your words, and win out when you are judged"). In the MT the psalmist admits that even when the divine sentence falls on David for his sin with Bathsheba, people will know that God is upright. But in the LXX, the connotation of "sentence" is lost, and "in your words" refers to "utterances" (as in Rom 3:2), so that even in his infidelity David learns of God's fidelity, "I will not be false to David" (Ps 89:36). Paul cites the psalmist to bear out his contention that Yahweh is ever shown to be faithful to his utterances. **5.** *if our wickedness brings out God's uprightness:* The diatribe moves to a logical conclusion that could be drawn from Paul's contention. If David's infidelity did not nullify God's fidelity but rather made it manifest, then human wickedness brings about the manifestation of God's uprightness (the attribute; see comment on 1:17; cf. A. Schlatter, *Gottes Gerechtigkeit*). *is God unjust to inflict his wrath (on us)?:* There is no contradiction in the manifestation of divine uprightness and wrath. Underlying the objection is the suggestion that if human wickedness brings out God's acquitting uprightness and fidelity, then he would be unjust in inflicting wrath. **6.** *By no means!:* Paul again emphatically rejects the notion of cheap grace for Israel; see comment on 3:4. *otherwise how is God to judge the world?:* A fundamental Jewish belief regarded Yahweh as the eschatological judge of the world (Isa 66:16; Joel 3:12; Ps 94:2; 96:13). **7.** *if the truth of God . . . :* This is really the same objection as 3:5, involving merely a third attribute. **8.** Paul does not take pains to refute the sophism involved in the accusation leveled against him (or Christians in general). In a parenthetic aside he simply rejects the allegation (see Cranfield, *Romans* 185–87). **9.** *What then? Are we (Jews) at a disadvantage? Not at all!:* Three difficulties are involved in v 9a. (1) A textual problem. The preferred reading in critical editions of the

NT is *tí oun; proechometha; ou pantōs* (two questions and an answer, as in mss. **א**, B, 0219 and the Koine text-tradition). But mss. A, L read the subjunc. *proechōmetha* (as a deliberative question), whereas mss. D, G, Ψ, 104 and some patristic writers have *prokatechomen; perisson,* "Do we have a previous advantage? Abundantly!" The last reading was substituted because of the ambiguity in *proechometha*. (2) The punctuation. Should a question mark follow *tí oun* (marking off a diatribic expostulation) or not (thus making *tí* the object of the verb, "what advantage, then, do we have?")? The former is preferred by most commentators. (3) The voice of the vb. *proechometha*. In the active, *proechein* means "jut out, excel, have an advantage" (see Josephus, *Ant.* 7.10.2 § 237). But *proechometha* is a middle-passive form, and many commentators have tried to take it as a middle with act. force (so Barrett, Cranfield, Käsemann, Lagrange, C. Maurer, *TDNT* 6. 692-93), "Have we (Jews) any advantage? Not at all!" Though, in general, such use of the middle voice is possible (BDF 316.1), no instance of this use is attested for *proechein*. With a minority of commentators (Good-speed, Lightfoot, Sanday-Headlam, Stowers), I prefer the pass. meaning of *proechometha*: "Are we (Jews) excelled (by others)?" Such a meaning is not inappropriate after vv 1-8; rather, it is the climactic question in Paul's dialogue with a contemporary Jew, enabling him to assert what he does in v 9b. *we have already charged that all are under (the power of) sin:* Paul's fundamental thesis about the human condition without the gospel (3:23; 5:12). "Sin" is thus mentioned for the first time in Rom. Paul personifies it as a master who dominates a slave; it holds humans in bondage to it (→ Pauline Theology, 82:82-88; OT Thought, 77:125-31).

35   10-18. After the dialogue with a fellow Jew in vv 1-9 Paul cites a catena of OT texts to prove his point. Paul uses a literary subform, called "testimonia," which strings together OT verses to illustrate a common theme. It was in use in pre-Christian Palestinian Judaism and has been found in QL (4QTestim; → Apocrypha, 67:91; cf. Fitzmyer, *ESBNT* 59-89). Here passages from the Pss and the prophets are strung together to illustrate the theme of the sinfulness of all human beings. Possibly Paul makes use of a catena that was already in existence (so M. Dibelius, *TRu* 3 [1931] 228). The texts are drawn from Ps 14:1-3 (or 53:2-4); 5:10; 140:4; 10:7; 36:2 and Isa 59:7-8; they are linked by the mention of parts of the body: throat, tongue, lips, mouth, feet, eyes. Thus, all of a human being is found involved in sin in God's sight. In citing such texts, Paul uses the Jews' own oracles to show that they as well as the Gentiles are "under sin."

36   19. *the law:* Though none of the quotations in 3:10-18 comes from the Torah, Paul here calls the whole OT "the law" (cf. 1 Cor 14:21), naming it in Jewish fashion after its most authoritative part. *to those under the law:* In the OT itself, which speaks above all to Jews, Paul finds the support of his thesis. *that the whole world may be accountable to God:* Lit., "may be liable to judgment by God." The universality of human moral failure without the gospel is emphasized by the threefold use of *pas,* "all, every," in 3:19-20. Thus v 9b is solemnly rephrased. **20.** *by observing the law:* Lit., "from the deeds of the (Mosaic) law"; see comment on 2:15. These are not simply "good deeds," but those performed in obedience to the law and regarded by Jews as the means of attaining uprightness before God. *no human being will be made upright in his sight:* An implicit quotation of Ps 143:2, a psalm of personal lament, in which the psalmist, conscious of his sinfulness and God's transcendent uprightness, confesses his inability to vindicate himself. Instead, he appeals for his vindication to God's characteristic

"fidelity" (Gk *alētheia* = Hebr *'ĕmûnâ*) and "uprightness" (Gk *dikaiosynē* = Hebr *ṣedeq*). See comment on 1:17. The MT of the Ps says, "Before you no living being is upright"; but Paul cites the LXX, which has the fut. tense, and he changes "living being" to "flesh," using a hebraism (Isa 40:5). Moreover, he significantly adds, "by deeds of the law." He therefore accommodates the psalmist's cry to a specific problem: the attainment of uprightness through the law. Cf. Gal 2:16. That no human being is upright before God is also an Essene tenet in QL (1QS 11:9-12; 1QH 4:29-31; 7:16; 12:19). *through the law (comes) the real knowledge of sin:* The developed discussion of the role of the law in human history (7:7-8:4) is foreshadowed here. The law gives human beings a real perception (*epignōsis*) of sin; → Pauline Theology 82:94. Without the law human beings did evil, but their wrongs were not recognized as transgressions (4:15; 5:13), i.e., acts of rebellion against the expressed will of God. But if the law declares all people sinners and makes them conscious of their condition, then a fortiori the Jew to whom the law is addressed is just as much an object of God's wrath as the pagan, whose moral perversion and degradation reveal his condition.

37   (c) THE THEME POSITIVELY EXPLAINED: GOD'S UPRIGHTNESS IS MANIFESTED THROUGH CHRIST AND APPREHENDED BY FAITH (3:21-31). Paul has developed his theme antithetically by showing how the very condition of human beings without the gospel calls forth God's wrath, impartially on Jew and Greek alike. Now he will show that a new period in human history began with the coming of Jesus Christ, whose mission was a manifestation of divine uprightness. The gospel proclaiming his coming and its effects are thus "the power of God for the salvation of everyone who has faith" (1:16). Paul now explains positively how this is so. Verses 21-31 are the most important part of Rom, formulating in effect the essence of Paul's gospel: salvation through faith in the Christ-event. In them the theme of the manifestation of divine uprightness is developed, as Paul treats of (1) its relation to the law (3:21); (2) its universal destination (3:22); (3) its necessity (3:23); (4) its nature and gratuity (3:24a); (5) its mode of manifestation (3:24b-25a); (6) its finality (3:25b-26); and (7) its polemical consequences (3:27-31).

38   21. *but now:* The adv. "now" is temporal, marking the new era inaugurated. It supersedes the law, circumcision, and the promises. The period of wrath also gives way to that of God's uprightness. This is the first use of the "eschatological 'now'" in Rom; see further 3:26; 5:9,11; 6:22; 7:6; 8:1,18; 11:5,30,31; 13:11. *independently of the law:* Paul insists the Mosaic law has nothing to do with this new manifestation of God's uprightness—at least directly (cf. Gal 2:19). The Christian dispensation of justification is independent of and destined to supersede and fulfill the law (Rom 10:4). *God's uprightness has been manifested:* I.e., the divine quality of uprightness is revealed; see comment on 1:17 (cf. U. Wilckens, *An die Römer* 1. 187). It is God's bounteous and powerful uprightness whereby he acquits his sinful people in a just judgment (→ Pauline Theology, 82:39). *though the law and the prophets bear witness:* The OT was privileged to prepare for this manifestation of God's uprightness (Rom 1:2; Gal 3:23-25). In fact, it still bears witness (pres. ptc., expressing contemporaneity with the main vb.); Rom 4:1-25 will illustrate this. For the "law and prophets" representing the OT, see Acts 13:15; 24:14; 28:23; Matt 5:17; 7:12; 11:13 (cf. Käsemann, *Romans* 93). **22.** *through faith in Jesus Christ:* Lit., "through the faith of Jesus Christ." The sense of the gen. is disputed. Some would understand it as subjective (G. Howard, *HTR* 60 [1967] 459-65; *ExpTim* 85 [1973-74]

212–15; L. T. Johnson, *CBQ* 44 [1982] 77–90), so that it would mean "through the fidelity (or obedience) of Jesus Christ." While this might seem plausible, it runs counter to the main thrust of Paul's theology, and so many commentators prefer to understand the gen. as objective, as in 3:26; Gal 2:16,20 (so Cranfield, *Romans* 203; Käsemann, *Romans* 94; Wilckens, *An die Römer* 1. 188, *et al.*). Paul is not thinking of Christ's fidelity to the Father; nor does he propose it as a model of Christian conduct. Christ himself is rather the concrete manifestation of divine uprightness, and human beings appropriate to themselves the effects of that manifested uprightness by faith in him. Indeed, that divine uprightness is comprehended only by those who have the eyes of faith (→ Pauline Theology, 82:109–10). *for all who have faith:* The universal destination of the effects of God's uprightness. This short form of the phrase (*eis pantas*) is normally preferred to an inferior reading in some mss. (D, G) and the Vg, "for all and upon all who . . ." (*eis pantas kai epi pantas*). *without distinction:* Of Jew or Greek (see 10:12).

39   **23.** *all have sinned:* Christian salvation, embracing all human beings, copes with the universality of sin among them. Paul is thinking primarily of the two historic groups of humanity, Jews and Greeks; yet his absolute formulation connotes the idea of "all individuals." Gk *hamartanein* retains in the NT its basic meaning, "miss the mark" (i.e., to fail to attain the moral goal), as in classical Greek and the LXX; but it also connotes transgression against custom, law, or divine will. "To sin" means to commit personal, individual acts in thought or execution from which evil results (*TDNT* 1. 296–302, 308–11; *EWNT* 1. 157–65; → Pauline Theology, 82:82). (There is no reference here to original sin or to sin as a *habitus.*) *fall short of the glory of God:* All human beings remain, because of their sins, without a share in God's glory. On "glory," see comment on 1:23. For Paul, it becomes a way of expressing the eschatological destiny of human beings; *doxa* is understood as communicated to them as they draw close to God (2 Cor 3:18; 4:6). Estranged from the intimate presence of God by sin, they are deprived of that for which they were destined; hence they fall short of their destined share in God's presence. Gk *hysterein* means "come too late, miss through one's own fault"; hence "lack, fall short of" (the middle voice used here implies that human beings by their actions have fallen short of this moral goal). There does not seem to be any reason to think that Paul is referring to the contemporary Jewish notion of Adam (and Eve) robed in glory before their sin (*Apoc. Mos.* 20:2 [*AOT* 163]; cf. 1QS 4:23; CD 3:20).

40   **24.** Verses 24–26a are frequently regarded as an insertion of a pre-Pauline statement about justification that ran as follows: "Being justified gratis through the redemption that is in Christ Jesus, whom God put forth as a means of expiation with his blood, for the manifestation of God's uprightness, for the sake of the remission of bygone sins (committed) in the forbearance of God" (see J. Reumann, *"Righteousness" in the New Testament* [Phl, 1982] 36–38; cf. K. Kertelge, *"Rechtfertigung" bei Paulus* [NTAbh ns 3; Münster, 1967] 48–62). Paul's modifications of this statement consist of the addition of the phrases "by his grace" (added after "gratis" in v 24a), "(to be received) through faith" (added after "blood" in v 25a), and "for the demonstration of his uprightness at the present time so that he might be upright even while justifying the one (who lives) on faith in Jesus" (v 26b–c). See further S. K. Williams, *JBL* 99 (1980) 241–90; *Jesus' Death as Saving Event* (HDR 2; Missoula, 1975); B. F. Meyer, *NTS* 29 (1983) 198–208. *(but are) being justified:* Or "made upright" through God's powerful declaration

of acquittal. Human beings achieve that status of uprightness before God's tribunal at which the Jew of the dispensation of yore aimed in trying to observe the deeds of the law. They find, however, that this is not achieved by something that is within them or within their own power. Paul affirms this in the light of his own conversion experience and the subsequent Judaizing controversies and continues to express the new relationship of human beings with God in terms that are legal and juridical. Paul means that a sinful human being is not only "declared upright," but is made upright (see 5:19), for justification as an effect of the Christ-event can also be seen as a "new creation," in which the sinner becomes the very "uprightness of God" (2 Cor 5:17–21; → Pauline Theology, 82:68–70). *gratis:* I.e., "freely, for nothing." This pre-Pauline term excludes the possibility of the meriting of justification on one's own; it is a sheer gift of God. *by his grace:* This redundant explanation of "gratis" has been added by Paul to the adopted formulation. He sees the Christian dispensation as owing wholly to the merciful and gratuitous benevolence of God the Father. In using *charis,* Paul is not thinking of the OT notion of *ḥesed,* "benevolence," the root of the covenant relationship of God with his people. A similar idea is found in QL (1QH 6:9; 7:27). *through the redemption that is in Christ Jesus:* In using this pre-Pauline formulation, Paul adopts a second mode of expressing an effect of the Christ-event; human beings are not only "justified" by Christ Jesus, but they are also "redeemed" by him. Gk *apolytrōsis,* "redemption," denoted in the Greco-Roman world the buying back of a slave or captive by the payment of a ransom (*lytron,* BAGD 96; cf. *EWNT* 1. 331–36). Whether the notion is solely of Greco-Roman background is disputed; → Pauline Theology, 82:75. In any case, the term denotes a liberation or ransoming of humanity by Christ Jesus (see 8:23; 1 Cor 1:30), an extension of that achieved by God himself for Israel at the exodus (Ps 78:35). This ransoming has already taken place in principle in the death and resurrection of Jesus (3:25), but its definitive phase is still awaited (8:23). This is insinuated even here, where Paul uses the title "Christ," a title with eschatological connotations (→ Pauline Theology, 82:51).

41   **25.** *whom God put forth:* The sense of the vb. *proetheto* is not clear and has been debated since antiquity. It could mean "God designed him to be . . ." (Origen, Lagrange, *NEB,* Cranfield, i.e., proposed him to himself, as he planned human salvation. But if more stress is put on the prefix *pro-,* then it would mean "God set him forth," i.e., displayed him publicly. It would then be a reference not so much to the divine plan of salvation as to the crucifixion (cf. Gal 3:1); it is so understood by Sanday-Headlam, Michel, Käsemann, and F. F. Bruce, and is preferred because of other references to public manifestation in these verses. In any case, the redemption is ascribed to the Father (*ho theos*). *as a means of expiation:* God set forth Christ on the cross as *hilastērion.* If this Gk word is understood as a masc. adj., it would mean "as expiatory"; if understood as a neut. noun, it would mean "as a means of expiation." But in what sense? Though the word is related to Gk *hilaskesthai,* "appease, propitiate" (an angry god), neither the OT background nor the Pauline usage suggests that *hilastērion* has such a meaning, well attested in classical and Hellenistic Greek. It does not mean a "propitiatory sacrifice" (*pace* Cranfield, *Romans* 201, 214–18; → Pauline Theology, 82:73–74). In the LXX *hilaskesthai* refers either to God's pardon of sin or to a ritual removal of cultic defilement that hinders the communion of a person or object with God. Since *hilastērion* is the name for the "mercy seat" in the Holy of Holies (Lev 16:2,11–17; → Institutions, 76:32), Paul is undoubtedly saying that Christ crucified has become the mercy seat of the new dispensation, the means of expiating (= wiping away) the sins that have estranged human beings from God. *through faith:* This cryptic phrase, difficult to translate, disrupts Paul's exposition. He has added it to the inherited statement, and it is crucial to his argument: Even though the most important aspect of Christian salvation is what Jesus did in dying and rising, the benefits of it are shared in only "through faith." *for the manifestation of his uprightness:* This is the first of two parallel statements revealing the finality of the cross. Christ's expiatory death makes public the Father's bountiful acquittal, and human uprightness flows from the uprightness of God himself. The Essenes of Qumran also attributed the acquittal of sinners to God's uprightness (1QH 4:37; 11:30-31); indeed, it is rooted in the OT itself (Ps 143:1-2,11; Ezra 9:13-15; Dan 9:16-18). In QL it is an acquittal awaited in the *eschaton,* but in Paul the act of acquittal has taken place in Christ. *for the sake of the remission of bygone sins:* In this difficult phrase the rare word *paresis* is used; it was understood by ancient commentators as "remission," a meaning found in extra-biblical Greek (BAGD 626) and preferred by Lietzmann, Kümmel, and Käsemann. Accordingly, Christ's death would have been a demonstration of divine uprightness that remitted the sins committed in bygone times—sins that awaited expiation on this great Day of Atonement (cf. Acts 13:38-39; Heb 9:15). Many commentators, however, prefer to translate the phrase "for the sake of passing over bygone sins" (so *RSV,* Barrett, Cranfield, Huby, Kuss, Michel). This etymological meaning is derived from the cognate vb. *parienai,* "pass over, let go," a meaning that is only doubtfully attested for the noun. In this case, Christ's death would demonstrate God's uprightness in wiping out sins, in contrast to the forbearance previously shown in passing over human sins of the past. See W. G. Kümmel, *ZTK* 49 (1952) 165; J. M. Creed, *JTS* 41 (1940) 28-30; for another more complicated but less convincing interpretation, see S. Lyonnet, *Bib* 38 (1957) 40-61; *Romains* 83. **26.** *(committed) in the forbearance of God:* Though up to Christ's coming sinful human beings were subject to God's wrath (1:18), that wrath did not always manifest itself in the punishment of sin, for it is really eschatological. God's tolerance was based on his plan, according to which he knew that these sins would be expiated in the death of Christ in due time. Even the expiation of sin on the yearly Day of Atonement made sense only in prefiguring that manifested by the shedding of Christ's blood on the cross.

42   *for the demonstration of his uprightness in the present:* The "eschatological 'now'" (see comment on 3:21) is coupled with *kairos,* "(critical) time," as in 11:5. This verse contains the second statement about the finality of the cross of Christ; it had effect not only in the past but also "now." *(to show) that he is upright himself:* Through the public exposure of Christ, his Son, on the cross, God vindicated his claim to be the acquitter and savior of his people (Isa 59:15-20). He thereby brought human beings into a status of rectitude, innocence, and acquittal. *even in making upright the one who has faith in Jesus:* Earlier commentators, who understood *dikaiosynē theou* of God's vindictive justice, often gave a concessive force to the ptc. *dikaiounta,* "in order to be just, even though he justifies. . . ." This involved the demand that Christ die in satisfaction for human sins. The context, however, seems to be against such an interpretation. Paul is rather saying that the recent divine intervention in human history proves that God is upright; he even makes human beings upright through faith in Christ's expiatory death.

43   **27-31.** The polemical consequences of the manifestation of God's uprightness, in particular the role of faith. No human beings can boast of achieving their salvation. **27.** *on what principle?:* Lit., "through what law" are human boasting and self-confidence excluded? Paul plays on the word *nomos.* The Jew could boast of observance of the law, but Paul rules out a "law of deeds" and admits only a "law of faith," in reality no law at all; hence the transl., "the principle of faith" (→ Pauline Theology, 82:90). **28.** *is made upright by faith:* See Gal 2:16; Phil 3:9. This is the main tenet of Pauline justification. Human beings cannot boast, because their rectitude before God is not the product of achievement. At this point Luther introduced the adv. "only" into his transl. of 1522 ("alleyn durch den Glauben"). This became a major Reformation issue, but it was not done without precedent in the earlier theological tradition (see Hilary, *Comm. in Matt.* 8.6; PL 9. 961; Ambrosiaster, *In ep. ad Rom.* 3.24; CSEL 81/1. 119; Thomas Aq., *Expos in I ad Tim.* 1.3; Parma 13.588). How much of that tradition was influenced by Jas 2:24? Did Luther and his predecessors mean the same thing by it? *without observing the law:* Lit., "without the deeds of the law" (see comment on 2:15). Paul never denied the relation of deeds performed after Christian conversion to salvation (see Gal 5:6; Rom 2:6; Phil 2:12-13; → Pauline Theology, 82:111), but because he sometimes omits the gen. *nomou,* his phrase acquired a more generic meaning, "deeds." This apparently happened even in the early church, for Jas 2:24 represents a protest not against Paul's teaching but against a caricature of it to which the unguarded phrase was open (see Reumann, *"Righteousness"* § 270-75, 413). **29.** *does God belong to the Jews alone?:* No Jew would have denied that Yahweh was the God of all human beings; but though his salvation was for all, Israel was favored. Paul makes capital of such a conviction for his own purpose. **30.** *only one God:* The one mode of salvation open to all, Jew and Greek alike, is traced to its monotheistic origin. **31.** *do we do away with the law by (this) faith:* The question that ultimately had to be asked. There is a sense in which Paul's gospel "confirms" or "upholds" the law. Paul will devote chap. 4 to an explanation of this and will return to it later in chap. 10. *Nomos* here means the whole OT. In insisting on one principle of salvation—faith—and linking it to the one God, Paul affirms the basic message of the whole OT, and in particular that of the Mosaic law itself, rightly understood.

44   (d) THE THEME ILLUSTRATED: IN THE OT ABRAHAM WAS JUSTIFIED BY FAITH (4:1-25). To show that the justification of all human beings by grace through faith confirms the law, Paul argues that the principle was already operative in the OT. Abraham is used as an example: He was reckoned upright because of his faith (4:1-8); not because of his circumcision (4:9-12), nor in dependence on the law, but in virtue of a promise (4:13-17). As a result, he is our father; his faith is the "type" of Christian faith (4:18-25).

45   **1.** *what then shall we say about Abraham?:* The Gk text is not certain. Many commentators (Leenhardt, Lyonnet) and versions (Goodspeed, *RSV, NEB*) read the text as given, omitting the problematic infin. *heurēkenai* (of mss. B, 6, 1739). The more difficult reading (of mss. א, A, C, D, E, F, G) retains the infin.: "What shall we say Abraham found," i.e., what sort of uprightness was his? (so Cranfield, Käsemann, Wilckens). Another group of mss. (K, L, P) links the infin. with *kata sarka:* "What shall we say Abraham . . . found according to the flesh?" i.e., what did he achieve by natural powers? The last reading, besides being weakly attested, is inconsistent with Pauline teaching. Much can be said for either of the other two. *our natural forefather:* Lit., "according to the flesh" (see

1:3). Descent from Abraham was a source of pride among the Jews (Matt 3:9; Luke 3:8). **2.** *because of deeds:* Contemporary Judaism depicted Abraham as an observer of the law in advance (Sir 44:20 [a midrash on Gen 26:5]; *Jub.* 6:19), and even in a broader sense spoke of his "deeds" (his defeat of the kings [Gen 14]; his trial [Gen 22:9–10]) as a source of his uprightness (1 Macc 2:52; Wis 10:5; cf. Jas 2:21). But in saying *ex ergōn* only, Paul means "deeds of the law" (see comment on 2:15); this sense alone fits this context. In effect, Paul rejects the contemporary Jewish view that Abraham was an observer of the law. *reason to boast:* Before human beings. **3.** *put faith in God, and it was accredited to him as uprightness:* Gen 15:6 (cf. Gal 3:6). Abraham believed in Yahweh's promise of a numerous progeny, and this faith was "booked to his credit." The quotation comes not from the MT ("Abram believed Yahweh, who credited it to him as uprightness"), but from the LXX (with the pass. vb.). By "faith" is meant Abraham's acceptance of Yahweh at his word and his willingness to abide by it. It involved his personal confidence and included hope in a promise that no mere human could guarantee (4:18). The OT text proves for Paul that Abraham was justified apart from deeds and had no reason to boast. The vb. *elogisthē*, "was accredited," is a bookkeeping term figuratively applied to human conduct (Deut 24:13; Ps 106:31); it was thought that good and evil deeds were recorded in books (Esth 6:1; Dan 7:10). For Paul, Abraham's faith counted as uprightness, because God sees things as they are. The manifestation of Abraham's faith is *de se* justifying (→ Pauline Theology, 82:70). **4.** *not as a gift, but as his due:* The laborer working for pay has a strict right to it. Paul introduces this comparison to illustrate v 2. God was never in Abraham's debt, and his justification is not a matter of something owed. **5.** *believes in him who justifies the ungodly:* This is not a theoretical expression of Abraham's belief, nor does it mean that Abraham was himself *asebēs*, "ungodly," before he put faith in Yahweh. Jewish tradition considered Abraham a *gēr*, "stranger, alien" (Gen 23:4), one called from paganism. Since at the moment of belief in Yahweh, of which Paul speaks, Abraham had already been called and was scarcely "godless," the phrase "who justifies the ungodly" is a generic Pauline description of God.

46   **6.** *David:* Like his Jewish contemporaries, Paul regarded David as the author of the Pss, even though the Ps to be quoted is usually considered a late one (of personal thanksgiving). In the MT it bears the ancient title "Of David." *apart from deeds:* These important words are placed in the emphatic final position of the sentence, immediately preceding the words of the Ps itself. **7.** *blessed are they . . . :* Ps 32:1–2 (LXX). The text continues Paul's argument that began with Gen 15:6. Just as God credited Abraham with uprightness independently of meritorious deeds, so too a human being can be acceptable to God even without such deeds. In the first case Paul argued by prescinding from deeds; now he argues by showing that the absence of deeds of merit is not an obstacle to justification by God. The vbs. in the Ps quoted, "forgive, cover, take no account of," are ways of expressing the removal of sin, the obstacle to human rectitude before God. They express, as it were, the negative side of the Christian experience. But the Ps also emphasizes the gratuity of divine mercy; it is only the Lord (Yahweh; cf. 9:28) who can produce these effects, and human beings must trust in him and be surrounded by his kindness (Ps 32:10). The words of the Ps do not necessarily mean that the sins remain, whereas God's benevolence merely covers them up. These are metaphors for the remission of sins. Thus both witnesses, Abraham and David, show that the OT itself supports Paul's thesis of graced justifi-

cation through faith. In this way his teaching "upholds" the law (3:31).

47   **9–12.** Abraham was justified before his circumcision, therefore, independently of it. **9.** *upon the uncircumcised too:* The beatitude uttered by David was not reserved exclusively for the circumcised Jew, despite the teaching of some rabbis (Str-B 3. 203). To prove his point, Paul employs a Jewish exegetical principle, *gĕzĕrâ šāwâ* (that identical words, occurring in two different places in Scripture, are the basis for mutual interpretation). The vb. *logizesthai* is found in Ps 32 and in Gen 15:6, said of Abraham while still uncircumcised. Hence the "blessedness" of Ps 32 can also be applied to uncircumcised sinners (see J. Jeremias, *Studia paulina* [Fest. J. de Zwaan; Haarlem, 1953] 149–51). **10.** *before he was circumcised:* Paul argues from the sequence in Gen itself: in Gen 15 Abraham's faith was counted as uprightness, but only in Gen 17 was he circumcised. Therefore, circumcision has nothing to do with his justification. **11.** *the seal of uprightness:* In Gen 17:11 circumcision is called the "sign of the covenant" between Yahweh and Abraham's family (cf. Acts 7:8). Later rabbis regarded it as the sign of the Mosaic covenant, for it served to distinguish Israel from the nations (Judg 14:3; 1 Sam 14:6). Significantly, Paul avoids mention of the covenant, and the "sign of the covenant" becomes for him the "seal of uprightness." He seems to have identified the covenant too much with the law; here he insinuates that God's true covenant was made with people of faith. *father of all who believe:* When Abraham put faith in Yahweh and was justified, he was as uncircumcised as any Gentile. His spiritual paternity is thus established vis-à-vis all believing Gentiles (Gal 3:7). **12.** Jews too must follow the footsteps of their forefather, imitating his faith, if they are to be regarded hereafter as his children. Abraham's spiritual paternity is an important aspect of God's salvific plan for all. Hence the purpose expression at the end of v 11 (*eis to* + infin.; see BDF 402.2).

48   **13–17.** Abraham received a promise independently of the law. **13.** *the promise:* The promise of an heir to be born of Sarah (Gen 15:4; 17:16,19) and of numerous posterity (Gen 12:2; 13:14–17; 17:8; 22:16–18) was extended in Jewish tradition on the basis of the universality of "all the families of the earth" (Gen 12:3) to mean that "the whole world" was Abraham's inheritance (see Str-B 3. 209). *not through the law:* I.e., the Mosaic law (see comment on 2:12); Paul implicitly assails the Judaizing view that all blessings came to Abraham because of his merit in keeping that law, which he knew in advance (see comment on 4:2). *through the uprightness of faith:* I.e., that based on faith. In 4:11 Paul had set this cardinal tenet over against the claim of circumcision; now he pits it against the Mosaic law itself. **14.** *if adherents of the law are the heirs:* If the only condition for such inheritance were the observance of the law, then faith would mean nothing; God's promise would be no promise, for an extraneous condition, foreign to the very nature of a promise, would have been introduced (cf. Gal 3:15–20). **15.** *the law brings wrath:* This verse is parenthetical, but it expresses Paul's profound conviction. The prescriptions of the law are honored more in the breach than in the observance; in thus furthering transgressions (Gal 3:19), it promotes the reign of sin. It thus provokes the retribution described in Rom 2–3 (see 7:7–11; → Pauline Theology, 82:94). *where there is no law, there is no violation:* Without law an evil may be only vaguely apprehended, but not as *parabasis*, "transgression" (cf. 3:20; 5:13). Since transgression, which calls down divine wrath, arises only in a legal context, Paul implicitly concludes that the world needs a dispensation independent of the law. **16.** *for this reason it all depends on faith:* This cryptic statement picks up the thought of 4:13.

Since the law and the promise cannot exist side by side, the law must yield. Faith is the all-important element, involving God's gracious promise. The one who lives by faith, lives by grace, and the promise holds good not only for the Jew but for all who share Abraham's faith, as the OT teaches. **17.** *the father of many nations:* Gen 17:5 (LXX). In Gen the patriarch's name first appears as *Abram,* "Exalted as to the Father," i.e., this child's father is great. The P source preserved the story of the change of Abram to Abraham and its popular etymology: *'Abrāhām* means "Father of a throng of nations" (*'ab hămôn gôyîm,* which exploits the *h* but neglects the *r*). The "many nations" refers to the descendants of Isaac, Ishmael, and the children of Keturah (Gen 25:1–2). Paul, however, understands it of Gentiles in general, who are children of Abraham by faith. *in the sight of God:* Though the argument ends with the OT quotation, Paul adds a thought, alluding to Abraham's colloquy with God (Gen 17:15–21). *who makes the dead live:* This and the following phrase may be derived ultimately from a Jewish liturgical formula. This one is similar to *Shemoneh Esreh* 2: "You, O Lord, are mighty forever, you who make the dead live" (*NTB* 159). In Paul's context, however, it refers to the divine power by which the barren Sarah came to conceive Isaac (Gen 17:15–21). Remotely, it prepares for 4:24–25. *calls into being what does not exist:* A formula similar to *2 Apoc. Bar.* 48:8, "With a word you call to life what was not, and with mighty power you hold back what has not yet come to be" (*AOT* 866). In this context it refers to the unborn Isaac; remotely it connotes the influence of God on the numerous Gentiles destined to be sons of Abraham.

49   18–25. Abraham's faith is the "type" of Christian faith. **18.** *hoping against hope, he believed:* Lit., "contrary to (all human) expectation, in hope he believed (God)." Though Abraham had many human motives for despairing of ever having posterity, he believed, confident about what the divine promise inspired in him. He took God at his word and believed in his creative power to do what seemed impossible. Isaac thus became one "born of a promise" (Gal 4:23; cf. Gen 17:16,19; 18:10). **19.** *his own body was as good as dead:* Disregarding Gen 25:1–2, which mentions six other children born to Abraham by Keturah, Paul alludes only to Gen 17:1–21: Abraham fell on his face and laughed when he heard that he, a man of 99 years and with a body near death, would have a son. Sarah too was 90, and barren. **20.** *did not waver in disbelief about God's promise:* Paul passes over the fact that Abraham was convulsed with laughter. Later in Jewish tradition it becomes his great joy (*Jub.* 16:19). *gave glory to God:* An OT expression (1 Sam 6:5; 1 Chr 16:28) formulates Abraham's reaction of grateful recognition to God. His uprightness is now ascribed to this reaction. For a third time Paul quotes Gen 15:6 (see 4:3,9). **24.** *but for our sake too:* Paul has recalled the Abraham incident to apply it to his readers. He thus employs a feature of midrashic interpretation, the tendency to modernize or actualize the OT by applying it to a new situation (R. Bloch, *DBSup* 3. 1263–65). Compare the later midrash: "All that is recorded of Abraham is repeated in the history of his children" (*Gen. Rabb.* 40:8). See further 1 Cor 9:9–10; 10:6–11. Abraham's faith is the pattern for Christian faith, because its object is the same: belief in God who makes the dead live. *it will be credited to us too:* Uprightness will be booked to our credit at the eschatological judgment, provided we have the faith of Abraham. *who raised Jesus our Lord from the dead:* Abraham's faith in God, who makes the dead live (4:17), foreshadowed the Christian's faith in God, who in a unique sense raised Jesus from the dead. The efficiency of the resurrection is ascribed to the Father (as often in Paul;

→ Pauline Theology, 82:59). The risen Christ is also hailed as *Kyrios* (see 10:9). **25.** *handed over for our offenses and raised for our justification:* This verse is most likely a fragment of pre-Pauline kerygmatic preaching. It alludes to Isa 53:4–5,11–12 and suggests the vicarious character of Christ's suffering in his role as the Servant of Yahweh who takes away human sin and achieves justification for human beings. In Isa 53:11 (LXX) sins (*hamartias*) and justification (*dikaioun*) are similarly contrasted, and in 53:12 the Servant "was handed over for their sins." The two pass. vbs. used by Paul are probably to be understood as "theological passives," a periphrasis for God (*ZBG* § 236). The dual use of the same prep. *dia* makes Paul's parallelism clear. The sense of the prep. is, however, disputed. Taylor translates it "because of" in both cases, without further explaining it. Michel is right in rejecting the meaning in the second part that Jesus was raised up because we were justified through his death (Schlatter). Many commentators distinguish the use, understanding the first *dia* as causal ("because of our offenses") and the second as final ("for the sake of our justification"); thus Cranfield, Käsemann, Kuss, Leenhardt, Michel, Wilckens. Since the cross and the resurrection are two intimately connected phases of the same salvific event, their juxtaposition here is the result of the rhetoric of antithetical parallelism (Käsemann, *Romans* 129). It is not to be pressed as if Christ's death were destined only for the removal of human sin and his resurrection for justification. Paul does not always explicitly relate justification to the resurrection (3:24–26; 5:9–10). The affirmation of the part played by Christ's death and resurrection in the objective redemption of humanity forms a fitting conclusion to this part A of the doctrinal section of Rom. See S. Lyonnet, *Greg* 39 (1958) 295–318; Stanley, *Christ's Resurrection* 171–73,261.

(Käsemann, E., "The Faith of Abraham in Romans 4," *Perspectives on Paul* [Phl, 1971] 79–101. Oeming, M., "Ist Genesis 15,6 ein Beleg für die Anrechnung des Glaubens zur Gerechtigkeit?" *ZAW* 95 [1983] 182–97. Wilckens, U., "Die Rechtfertigung Abrahams nach Römer 4," *Rechtfertigung als Freiheit: Paulusstudien* [Neukirchen, 1974] 33–49.)

50   (B) The Love of God Assures Salvation to Those Justified by Faith (5:1–8:39). Having established the justification of human beings through faith in Christ Jesus, Paul begins to discuss the Christian experience in itself and explains how salvation is assured for the upright.

The position of chap. 5 in the literary structure of Rom is a matter of debate, in which four main views are held: (1) Chap. 5 concludes part A. Justification is the subject matter of 1:18–5:21; sanctification of 6:1–8:39 (Feine-Behm, M. Goguel, Huby, Lagrange, Pesch, Sanday-Headlam, Wilckens). (2) Chap. 5 introduces part B. Justification is treated in 1:18–4:25; the condition and life of the justified in 5:1–8:39, which some extend even to 11:36 (Cerfaux, Cranfield, Dahl, V. Jacono, Käsemann, Kümmel, Lamarche, Michel, Minear, F. Prat, Viard, Wikenhauser-Schmid). (3) 5:1–11 concludes part A, whereas 5:12–21 introduces part B (P. Bonnard, Feuillet, Leenhardt, Zahn). (4) Chap. 5 is an isolated unit (Althaus, Barrett, J. Cambier, Dupont, Kuss, Taylor). Certainty in this debate is impossible.

The chief reasons for relating chap. 5 to what follows are: (1) 5:1–11 announces briefly what 8:1–39 develops (see N. A. Dahl, *ST* 5 [1951] 37–48; cf. Jeremias, *Studia paulina* 146–49). (2) The discussion in 1:16–4:25 centers on Jews and Greeks, who are not mentioned at all in 5:1–8:39. (3) Whereas the divine attribute dominating 1:16–4:25 is *dikaiosynē,* "uprightness," it is *agapē,* "love," in the following section (5:5,8; 8:28,35,37,39). (4) Divisions within chaps. 5–8 are indicated by variations of the same concluding formula, which echoes 1:5; thus 5:21, "grace . . . through Jesus Christ our Lord"; 6:23, "gift . . . in Jesus Christ our Lord"; 7:24–25, "thanks be to God! Through Jesus Christ our Lord"; 8:39, "the love of God in Christ Jesus our Lord." (5) 1:18–4:25 has a juridical tone, whereas 5:1–8:39 is more ethical (see S. Lyonnet, *RSR* 39 [1951] 301–16; P. Rolland, *Bib* 56 [1975] 394–404).

51   (a) The Theme Announced: The Justified Christian, Reconciled to God, Will Be Saved, Sharing with Hope in Christ's Risen Life (5:1–11). Once justified, the Christian is reconciled to God and experiences a peace that distressing troubles cannot upset, a hope that knows no disappointment, and a confidence of salvation. **1.** *justified through faith:* A summary of part A (→ 13 above) serves as the transition to the new topic. *we enjoy peace with God:* The first effect of justification the Christian experiences is peace; reconciliation replaces estrangement. The pres. indic. *echomen,* "we have (peace)," is the preferred reading; the pres. subjunc. *echōmen,* "let us have," though better attested, is an obvious copyist's correction. The indic. asserts the effect, whereas the subjunc. would mean, "Let us now give evidence of this justification by a life of peace with God." *through our Lord Jesus Christ:* In some form or other, Paul makes frequent use of this phrase in chap. 5 (vv 2,9,11, 17,21; cf. 1:5; 2:16) The prep. phrase *dia Christou* expresses the mediation of Christ in the Father's salvific plan (→ Pauline Theology, 82:118); it affirms his present actual influence on human beings as the risen *Kyrios.* **2.** *we have secured an introduction:* The peace that Christians experience is derived from being introduced into the sphere of divine favor by Christ, who has, as it were, reconciled Christians by leading them into the royal audience chamber and the divine presence. Some mss. add "by faith," but the reading is not solidly attested. *we boast of the hope of the glory of God:* The second effect of justification is confident hope. This statement is a typically Pauline paradox: the Christian who boasts puts the boast in something that is wholly beyond ordinary human powers—in hope. Yet hope is really as gratuitous as faith itself; in the long run the boast relies on God. What the Christian hopes for is the communicated glory of God (see comment on 3:23), still to be attained, even though the Christian has already been introduced into the sphere of "grace." The relation between *charis* and *doxa* should be noted here, but it should not be transferred too readily (and without proper distinctions) to the later theological categories of *gratia* and *gloria.* **3.** *even in (our) troubles:* Divine favor, as the basis of Christian hope, is mighty enough to give confidence even in the face of *thlipseis,* "hardships," that might tend to separate human beings from Christ's love (see 8:35; 1 Cor 4:11–13; 7:26–32). Paul is not advocating here some form of Pelagianism, when he says that tribulation produces endurance, endurance character, and character hope, for the basis of it all is divine grace. **5.** *(such) hope does not disappoint:* An illusion to Pss 22:6; 25:20 stresses that the hope of God's glory is not illusory; it is founded on God's love of human beings. Hence the Christian will never be embarrassed by a disappointed hope; implicit is a comparison with merely human hope, which can deceive. *the love of God:* Not "our love of God," as many older commentators understood it, but "God's love of us" (subjective gen.), as the following context makes clear (→ Pauline Theology, 82:40). In the OT the "pouring out" of a divine attribute is a commonplace: "mercy" (Sir 18:11); "wisdom" (Sir 1:9); "grace" (Ps 45:3); "wrath" (Hos 5:10; Ps 79:6); see esp. Joel 3:1–2, the outpouring

of the Spirit. *through his holy Spirit:* The gift of the Spirit is not only the proof but also the medium of the outpouring of God's love (8:15–17; Gal 4:6). It signifies par excellence the divine presence to the justified (→ Pauline Theology, 82:64).

52   **6.** *when we were still helpless:* So Paul describes the status of the unjustified person: incapable of doing anything to achieve rectitude before God. *then:* The phrase *kata kairon* probably means no more than this, despite attempts to interpret it as "at that decisive time, at the right time" (see J. Barr, *Biblical Words for Time* [SBT 33; Naperville, 1962] 47–81; J. Baumgarten, *EWNT* 2. 572). *Christ died:* Paul affirms the historical event in a theological setting of vicarious suffering. The whole context stresses the gratuitous, spontaneous character of that death. **7.** *hardly for an upright person:* To prove his point, Paul argues a fortiori. However, he quickly corrects himself, allowing that possibly for a really good person, a benefactor, one might give up one's life. The comment brings out the sheerly gratuitous character of the altruism involved, when Christ died for the "godless." The verse is much disputed, whether the second part is a gloss, a correction made by Paul and allowed to stand by Tertius, the scribe, etc. (see G. Delling, *Apophoreta* [Fest. E. Haenchen; BZNW 30; Berlin, 1964] 85–96; L. E. Keck, *Theologia crucis–Signum crucis* [Fest. E. Dinkler; ed. C. Andresen and G. Klein; Tübingen, 1979] 237–48; F. Wisse, *NTS* 19 [1972–73] 91–93). **8.** *God proves his love for us:* This statement completely rules out any doctrine of the cross that sets God and Christ over against each other (Taylor, *Romans* 38). Since *ho theos* is the Father and it is his love that is poured out "through the Spirit" (5:5) and is now manifested in Christ's death, this triadic text is a Pauline starting point for later trinitarian dogma. There is no *quid pro quo* in the love manifested: divine love is demonstrated toward the sinner without a hint that it is repaying a love already shown. **9.** *by his blood:* Whereas in 4:25 justification was ascribed to Christ's resurrection, it is here attributed to his death. On blood, → Pauline Theology, 82:74. *we shall all the more be saved:* A still greater favor will be manifested to the justified Christian in the eschatological salvation to come. **10.** A repetition of 5:8 in a more positive way; the sinner is not just "weak" or "ungodly," but actually an "enemy" of God. Yet the death of Christ brings about the reconciliation of such an enemy; this is but another way of expressing the "peace" of 5:1, for "reconciliation" is the restoration of the estranged and alienated sinner to friendship and intimacy with God (2 Cor 5:18–20; → Pauline Theology, 82:72). *we shall be saved by his life:* The third effect of justification is a share in the risen life of Christ, which brings salvation. Though justification is something that happens now, salvation is still to be achieved—it is rooted in Christ's risen life (→ Pauline Theology, 82:71). **11.** *we also boast of God:* The third climactic boast in the paragraph, following up those in 5:2,3. The effect of justification is that the Christian even boasts of God himself, whereas before one stood in fear of his wrath. Having experienced God's love in the death of Christ, one can now exult at the very thought of God.

(Fitzmyer, J. A., "Reconciliation in Pauline Theology," *TAG* 162–85. Furnish, V. P., "The Ministry of Reconciliation," *CurTM* 4 [1977] 204–18. Käsemann, E., "Some Thoughts on the Theme 'The Doctrine of Reconciliation in the New Testament,'" *The Future of Our Religious Past* [Fest R. Bultmann; ed. J. M. Robinson; NY, 1971] 49–64).

53   (b) The Theme Explained: New Christian Life Brings a Threefold Liberation (5:12–7:25).
(i) *Freedom from death and sin* (5:12–21). Paul begins his description of the condition of the justified and

reconciled Christian by comparing it with the status of humanity before Christ's coming. It involves a comparison of Adam, the first parent, with Christ, the head of the new humanity. But it is not a smoothly worked out comparison, for Paul also wants to clarify the dissimilarity and the superabundance of Christ's grace that now reigns instead of sin and death, which had been in control since Adam. Just as sin came into the world through Adam (and with it death, which affects all human beings), so through Christ came uprightness (and with it life eternal). So the comparison should run, but Paul felt the need of explaining his novel teaching about Adam and broke into the parallelism to assert emphatically that it was Adam's *sin* that has affected all human beings (5:12c–d,13,14; → Pauline Theology, 82:84–85). Because of this insertion, anacoluthon appears at the end of 5:14, and his real conclusion is expressed only indirectly. The comparison involves an antithetical parallelism between the death wrought by Adam and the life brought by Christ. The antithesis is reformulated in 5:15–17, where Paul emphasizes the surpassing quality of what Christ did, when it is compared with Adam's influence. Christ, the new Adam and new head of humanity, was incomparably more beneficent toward human beings than Adam was maleficent. This is repeated again in 5:18–19, and the latter verse is an echo of 5:12. In 5:20 the antithesis is again proposed, this time in terms of the law. Except for the formulaic ending in 5:21, Paul does not use the 1st pers. pl. in 5:12–21, as he does in 5:1–11 and 6:1–8. This fact, plus the unified impression that this paragraph makes in Paul's treatment of Adam and Christ, suggests to many that he may be incorporating here part of a writing composed for another occasion.

54 The main exegetical problems are met in 5:12d and center on the meaning of three expressions: "death," "they sinned," and the phrase *eph' hō*. **12.** *so:* The paragraph begins with *dia touto*, "for this reason," and might at first seem to be a conclusion to v 11; but it should rather be understood as a conclusion to vv 1–11 (Cranfield, *Romans* 271). If the paragraph were actually composed for another occasion, then the antecedent of this phrase is lost; consequently, it may now be merely transitional (see comment on 2:1). *just as:* So the comparison begins; its conclusion is not introduced by *kai houtōs*, "and so," of v 12c, though L. Cerfaux (*ChrTSP* 231–32) and Barrett (*Romans* 109) have tried to take it that way. That would rather be *houtōs kai*. The conclusion to the comparison is implied in the last cl. of v 14. *through one man:* Note the emphasis on "one man," which occurs 12 times in this paragraph. The contrast between "one" and "many" or "all" brings out the universality of the influence involved. Here the "one man" is Adam, the man in Gen 2–3 whose disobedient transgression unleashed into human history an active evil force, sin. *sin entered the world:* Harmartia is a personified malevolent power (capital *S*?), hostile to God and alienating human beings from him; it strode upon the stage of human history at the time of Adam's transgression (6:12–14; 7:7–23; 1 Cor 15:56; → Pauline Theology, 82:84–85). *through that sin, death:* Another personification is *Thanatos*, an actor on the same stage, playing the role of a tyrant (5:14,17) and dominating all human beings descended from Adam. "Death" is not merely physical, bodily death (separation of body and soul), but includes spiritual death (the definitive separation of human beings from God, the unique source of life), as 5:21 makes clear (cf. 6:21,23; 8:2,6). It is a cosmic force (8:38, 1 Cor 3:22), the "last enemy" to be vanquished (1 Cor 15:56). Paul may be alluding to Wis 2:24, "Through the devil's envy death came into the world," where *thanatos* has the same sense.

55 Paul alludes to the story of Gen 2–3, but he prescinds from its dramatic details to utilize the theological truth of the enslavement of human beings to sin and death. The unmistakeable etiological character of that story (→ Pauline Theology, 82:83) insinuates that the sin of Adam and Eve was the cause of universal human misery. Paul's statement, however, is the first clear enunciation of the universal baneful effect of Adam's *sin* on humanity. Paul does not explain how that effect takes place; he makes no mention of its hereditary character (as Augustine later would). In 1 Cor 15:21–22 the effect of "death" is explained by the incorporation of human beings "in Adam," but here he goes further and asserts a causal connection between the transgression of "one man" and the sinful status of all humanity. Though Paul is primarily interested in the contrast of the universality of sin and death with the universality of life in Christ, he does indicate not only the beginning of such universal phenomena but also the causality of the head (Adam or Christ). But he is also aware that not all human sinfulness is owing to Adam alone; he makes this clear in 5:12d.

56 *and in this way:* The adv. is important; it establishes the connection between Adam's sin and "all human beings." *death spread to all human beings:* That "all" would include infants is a precision born of later controversy, which Paul did not envisage. *since:* Or, "inasmuch as." The meaning of the phrase *eph' hō* is much disputed. The least convincing interpretations treat it as a strict rel. phrase: (1) "In whom," a meaning (incorporation) based on the OL transl. *in quo* and commonly used in the western church since Ambrosiaster and Augustine (see G. I. Bonner, *SE V* 242–47). This interpretation was unknown to the Gk Fathers before John Damascene. If Paul had meant "in whom," he would have written *en hō*, as in 1 Cor 15:22; moreover, the pers. antecedent of the rel. pron. is quite removed from it. (2) "On the grounds of which," an interpretation that takes "death" as the antecedent (so Zahn, Schlier). This meaning is hard to reconcile with 5:21; 6:23, where death is the result of sin, not its source. (3) "Because of the one by whom" (= *epi toutō eph' hō*), an interpretation that spells out the elliptical phrase and refers the pron. to Adam. It would thus imply "a relationship between the state of sin and its initiator" (Cerfaux, *ChrTSP* 232). But it is not clear that the phrase is elliptical, and the prep. *epi* would have two different meanings, "because of" and "by." (4) Most modern commentators understand *eph' hō* as the equivalent of a conj., "since, because, inasmuch as," an interpretation commonly used by the Gk Fathers and based on 2 Cor 5:4; Phil 3:12; 4:10 (BAGD 287; BDF 235.2). It would thus also ascribe to all human beings an individual responsibility for death (so Bruce, Cranfield, Huby, Käsemann, Lagrange, Pesch, Wilckens.) (5) "In view of the fact that, on condition that," an interpretation that employs the proviso cl. meaning of the conj. in classical and Hellenistic Greek (so R. Rothe, J. H. Moulton, S. Lyonnet, *Bib* 36 [1955] 436–56). But *eph' hō*, expressing a proviso, governs an infin. or a fut. indic. (occasionally a subjunc. or opt. in later Greek). The only example of it with an aor. indic., to parallel Paul's usage here, is found in a letter of a 4th-cent. Bp. Synesius (*Ep.* 73) — scarcely a valid parallel. Moreover, it seems to make Paul say that death spread to all on the condition that they would sin after its entry; however, if one stresses the past indic., then this sense differs little from the fourth. The difficulty felt in the fourth meaning, "since," is that it seems to make Paul say in 5:12c–d something contradictory to what he says in 5:12a–b. In the beginning of v 12 sin and death are ascribed to Adam; now death seems to be owing to human acts. Yet one must not lose sight of the adv. *houtōs,* "in this way" (5:12c), which establishes a connection between the sin of "one man" and the death of "all human beings." Thus Paul in v 12 is ascribing death to two causes, not unrelated: to Adam and to all human sinners.

57   *all have sinned:* See comment on 3:23. The vb. *hēmarton* should not be translated "have sinned collectively" or "have sinned in Adam," since these would be additions to the text. The vb. refers to personal, actual sins of human beings, as Pauline usage elsewhere suggests (2:12; 3:23; 1 Cor 6:18; 7:28,36; 8:12; 15:34) and as the Gk Fathers understood it (see S. Lyonnet, *Bib* 41 [1960] 325–55). The last cl. of v 12 thus expresses a secondary causality that the actual sins of human beings play in the condemnation of them to "death." The universal causality of Adam's sin is presupposed in 5:15a, 16a,17a,18a,19a. It would, then, be false to the thrust of the whole paragraph to interpret 5:12 as though it implied that the human condition before Christ's coming were due solely to personal sins.

58   **13.** *before the law sin was in the world:* The continuation of the digression introduces a further precision. From Adam to Moses, the source of "death" was Adam's sin. Human beings did, of course, commit evil (see Gen 6:5–7, to which Paul never alludes), but they were not charged with it in that period. *sin is not imputed where there is no law:* Paul enunciates a general principle that agrees with 4:15; 3:20 but that explains the reign of death. **14.** *from Adam to Moses:* Paul saw human history divided into three periods (→ Pauline Theology, 82:42). The first period from Adam to Moses was law-less (5:13; cf. Gal 3:17), when human beings did evil, but did not transgress a law. In the second period, from Moses to the Messiah, "the law was added" (Gal 3:19; cf. Rom 5:20), and human sin was understood as a transgression of it. In this period there was, in addition to the influence of Adam's sin, the contributing factor of individual transgressions now imputed because law existed. In the third period (that of the Messiah) there is freedom from the law through the grace of Christ (8:1). *who had not sinned as Adam had:* Lit., "in the likeness of Adam's transgression." Here *hamartia,* "sin," and *parabasis,* "transgression," are distinguished; the latter is the formal aspect of an evil deed considered as a violation of a precept. Adam had been given a precept (Gen 2:17; 3:17), but those who lived in the first (law-less) period did not do evil as he had done, for they violated no precepts. Again, Paul passes over the so-called Noachic legislation (Gen 9:4–6) and discusses only the problem of the Mosaic law. His perspective here has nothing to do with that of 2:14, even though it does not contradict that view. The sentence ends in anacoluthon, as Paul tries to conclude the comparison begun in 5:12. *so Adam foreshadows the future (Adam):* Lit., "who is the type of the coming (Adam)," i.e., Christ, the "last Adam" (1 Cor 15:45) or the Adam of the *eschaton.* Though Adam prefigures Christ as the head of humanity, the resemblance between type and antitype is not perfect. Differences exist, and the rest of the paragraph brings them out; the antitype reproduces the type in a sense, but in a more perfect way.

59   (Rom 5:12–14 has been the subject of a centuries-long theological debate, because Paul seems to affirm in it the existence of hereditary sin. Indeed, Roman Catholic exegetical tradition has almost unanimously interpreted it, esp. 5:12, in terms of the universal causality of Adam's sin in the sinfulness of human individuals. This tradition found its formal conciliar expression in the Tridentine *Decretum de peccato originali,* Sess. V,2–4. Echoing canon 2 of both the 16th Council of Carthage [AD 418; DS 223] and the 2d Council of Orange [AD 529; DS 372], it decreed that "what the Apostle says, 'Through

one man sin entered the world, and through that sin, death, and thus death passed to all human beings, in whom all have sinned,' is not to be understood in any other way than as the Catholic church spread all over has always understood it" [DS 1514; cf. 1512]. This decree gave a definitive interpretation to the Pauline text in the sense that his words teach a form of the dogma of Original Sin—a rare text that enjoys such an interpretation [see *DAS* § 47; *RSS* 102; → Hermeneutics, 71:83].

Care must be had, however, to understand what Paul is saying and not to transform too facilely his expression into the precision of later dogmatic development. He does not speak of "original sin," a term that betrays its western theological origin in the time of Augustine as a transl. of *peccatum originale.* Trent appealed in its decree to the sense of Paul's words as they were understood in the church at all times and places. Differences existed in its tradition regarding details or the understanding of individual words, but there was agreement on the fact of the sin and on its extent. However, those very differences are important, for they show that Paul's formulation has to be understood for what it is. As *Humani generis* 21 [DS 3886] put it: Theologians must make it clear in what way [*qua ratione*] the church's teaching is contained in Scripture. In this case Paul's teaching is seminal, open to the later dogmatic development.)

60   **15.** *the mass of humanity:* Lit., "the many," which means "all" (cf. 5:18; 12:5; 1 Cor 10:17). *the free gift:* God's benevolent favor, assuring justification (see comment on 3:24). *all the more lavish:* Lest the comparison with Adam should seem an affront to Christ, Paul stresses the surpassing quality of Christ's influence on humanity. The first mode of expressing that superabundance is the manifestation of God's favor far in excess of any mercy that sin might have otherwise evoked. **16.** *(God's) gift (arose) out of many offenses (and issues) in acquittal:* The second mode contrasts the verdict of condemnation for one sin, which fell on all human beings, with the justification (or verdict of acquittal) for all those condemned not only through Adam's transgression but also through their offenses. **17.** *all the more will they reign and live:* Lit., "reign in life." The third mode contrasts death as the effect of the offense of one man (Adam) with the gift of upright life obtained through one man (Christ). Note the stress on "one man" in these verses; herein lies the similarity between Adam and Christ. The relation between "one" and "the many" is parallel, for both Adam and Christ exercised causality on the latter.

61   **18.** *through the offense of one man . . . so through the upright act of one man:* Given the preceding context, in which the pron. *henos* refers to "one man," it is better to preserve that sense and take it here as masc. However, Paul may be varying his formulation and intending *henos* to be neut., "through one offense . . . so through one upright act." *for acquittal and life:* Lit., "for the justification of life" (the gen. is appositional). The gracious act manifesting God's gift of uprightness (5:17) not only cleared human beings of guilt but also granted them a share in "life." This "life" is explained in chap. 8. **19.** The climax of the comparison is reached; it echoes 5:12 and formally enunciates the basic contrast of Adam and Christ. *were made sinners:* The formal effect of Adam's disobedience (Gen 3:6) was to make humanity not only liable to punishment, but actually sinners. So astute a commentator as Taylor has remarked, "No one can be made a sinner or made righteous" (*Romans* 41). And yet that is what Paul says, and he is not speaking of personal sinful acts. The vb. *katestathēsan* does not mean "were considered (to be sinners)," but "were made, were caused to be" (BAGD 390; cf. J.-A. Bühner, *EWNT* 2. 554–55; F. W. Danker, "Under Contract," *Fest. to Honor F. Wilbur*

Gingrich [Leiden, 1972] 106–7). Adam's disobedience placed the mass of humanity in a condition of estrangement from God; the text does not imply that they became sinners merely by imitating Adam's transgression; rather they were affected by him. *the mass will be made upright:* Elsewhere the process of justification seems to be regarded as past (5:1); here the fut. tense refers to the eschatological judgment, when the final phase of that process will be achieved in glory. "The many will be constituted righteous through Christ's obedience in the sense that, since God has in Christ identified Himself with sinners and taken upon Himself the burden of their sin, they will receive as a free gift from Him that status of righteousness which Christ's perfect obedience alone has deserved" (Cranfield, *Romans* 291). **20.** *the law slipped in:* As in Gal 3:19, the Mosaic law is regarded as a means of multiplying offenses in the religious history of humanity. This it does by supplying human beings with a "knowledge of sin" (3:20; cf. 7:13). As in the case of *Hamartia* and *Thanatos,* so too *Nomos* is personified and treated as an actor on the stage of human history. Instead of being a source of life for the Jews, it proved only to be their informer and accuser, bringing condemnation (→ Pauline Theology, 82:91–94). **21.** *eternal life through Jesus Christ our Lord:* The mediation of Christ (see comment on 5:1), the head of reconciled humanity, is stressed at the end of the first subdivision of this part of the letter (→ 50 above). The risen *Kyrios* brings to humanity a share in "eternal life," the life of the Son of God, in which vitality is derived from his Spirit. The adj. "eternal" indicates the quality of that life rather than its duration; it is the life of God himself.

(Caragounis, C. C., "Romans 5.15–16 in the Context of 5.12–21: Contrast or Comparison?" *NTS* 31 [1985] 142–48. Castellino, G. R., "Il peccato di Adamo," *BeO* 16 [1974] 145–62. Cranfield, C. E. B., "On Some of the Problems in the Interpretation of Romans 5.12," *SJT* 22 [1969] 324–41. Grelot, P., *Péché originel et rédemption* [Paris, 1973]. Haag, H., *Is Original Sin in Scripture?* [NY, 1969] 95–108. Muddiman, J., "Adam, the Type of the One to Come," *Theology* 87 [1984] 101–10. Vanneste, A., "Où en est le problème du péché originel?" *ETL* 52 [1976] 143–61. Wedderburn, A. J. M., "The Theological Structure of Romans v. 12," *NTS* 19 [1972–73] 339–54.)

62 (ii) *Freedom from self through union with Christ* (6:1–23). The description of the Christian experience proceeds a step further. The Christian has been endowed with a new life through Christ (5:12–21), who now reigns supreme instead of sin and death. But this new life means a reshaping of human beings. Through baptism, they are identified with Christ's death and resurrection, and their very being or "self" is transformed. The outlook of the newly justified person is such as to exclude sin from his or her conduct. As an introduction to his explanation, Paul takes up a question broached in 3:5–8: Why not do evil so that good may come of it? If human sin evokes God's uprightness (3:23–24), then why not give God greater scope to manifest it? If God brings about the salvation of humanity through Christ and all this is sheer gift, then why should one try to exclude evil from one's life? This Paul rejects vehemently: If one is in union with Christ, one is "dead to sin and alive to God."

63 **1.** *persist in sin?:* An imaginary objection echoes 3:5–8. If uprightness comes from faith, not deeds, then why does the Christian have to worry about evil acts? *by no means:* See comment on 3:4. **2.** *we who died to sin:* Christians have died to sin (5:12–21) and have nothing more to do with it. It is not they who live but Christ who lives in them (Gal 2:20). **3.** *do you not know?:* Roman Christians, instructed in the apostolic catechesis, should

be acquainted with the sublime effects of baptism. *we who were baptized:* In the NT *baptizein* refers either to Jewish ritual washings (Mark 7:4; Luke 11:38) or to JBap's washing or to Christian baptism (John 1:25,28; Gal 3:27). Here Paul's discussion of the last is most easily understood of immersion, but it is not certain that early Christian baptism was so administered (see C. F. Rogers, "Baptism and Christian Archaeology," *Studia biblica et ecclesiastica* [Oxford, 1903] 5. 239–361; cf. E. Stommel, *JAC* 2 [1959] 5–14). *into Christ:* The phrase *eis Christon* does not simply reflect the imagery of immersion, nor is it merely an abbreviation of a borrowed bookkeeping term (*eis to onoma Christou,* "to the name, account, of Christ"), as if baptism established Christ's proprietorship over the baptized person. Like other Pauline prep. phrases, it formulates an aspect of the relationship of the Christian to Christ, occurring most often with words denoting "faith" or "baptism" and connoting the movement of incorporation by which one is born to life "in Christ" (→ Pauline Theology, 82:119). *baptized into his death:* The rite of Christian initiation introduces a human being into union with Christ suffering and dying. Paul's phrase is bold; he wants to bring out that the Christian is not merely identified with the "dying Christ" who has won victory over sin, but is introduced into the very act by which that victory has been won. Hence the Christian is "dead to sin" (6:11), associated with Christ precisely at the time when he formally became Savior.

64 **4.** *buried with him in death:* The baptismal rite symbolically represents the death, burial, and resurrection of Christ; the convert descends into the baptismal bath, is covered with its waters, and emerges to a new life. In that act one goes through the experience of dying to sin, being buried, and rising, as did Christ. Paul uses one of his favorite compound vbs., *synthaptein,* a compound of *syn-,* "with" ("co-buried"). As a result, the Christian lives in union with the risen Christ, a union that finds its term when the Christian will one day "be with Christ" in glory (*syn Christō,* → Pauline Theology, 82:120). *through the Father's glory:* The efficiency of the resurrection is ascribed to the Father (see comment on 4:24), and specifically to his *doxa,* "glory." As in the OT (Exod 15:7,11; 16:7,10) exodus miracles were ascribed to Yahweh's *kābôd* (see comment on 3:23), so too is the raising of Christ (see Fitzmyer, *TAG* 202–17). Indeed, the *doxa* of the Father shines on the face of the risen Christ (2 Cor 4:6) and invests him with "power" (Rom 1:4) that is "life-giving" (1 Cor 15:45). This transforms the Christian (2 Cor 3:18), who is glorified together with Christ (Rom 8:17). *we too may live a new life:* Lit., "may walk in newness of life." Baptism brings about an identification of the Christian with the glorified Christ, enabling him or her to live actually with the life of Christ himself (Gal 2:20); a "new creation" is involved (→ Pauline Theology, 82:79). "To walk" is another favorite Pauline expression, borrowed from the OT (2 Kgs 20:3; Prov 8:20), to designate the conscious ethical conduct of the Christian. Identified with Christ through baptism, he or she is enabled to lead a new conscious life that can know no sin.

65 **5.** *for:* Verses 5–8 affirm of the baptized Christian what Paul will say of Christ himself in vv 9–10. The latter thus supply the christological basis for the truth set forth about Christian life. *we have grown (into union) with (him):* The pron. "him" is supplied as the logical complement of *symphytoi,* "grown together"—as a young branch grafted onto a tree grows together with it and is nourished by it. This bold image expresses the communication of Christ-life to the Christian. *through a death like his:* Lit., "by a likeness of his death," the dat. of instrument. Baptism (6:3) is the means by which Christians grow together with Christ, who died and rose once for all. Some commentators (Käsemann, Kuss, Lietzmann, Sanday-Headlam, Wilckens) understand the dat. *tō homoiōmati* to depend directly on *symphytoi* and translate, "if we have been conformed to the image of his death . . . ," i.e., have grown into union with the death-like rite. Grammatically, this understanding is possible; but how does one grow together with an image or a likeness? Normally, for Paul the Christian is united with Christ himself (or his "body"), not with an image of the salvation-event (cf. F. A. Morgan, *ETL* 59 [1983] 267–302). *also through a resurrection like his:* Lit., "we shall then be (grown together with him) through (a likeness of) the resurrection too." Since the context describes the present experience of the Christian, the fut. tense is probably logical, expressing a sequel to the first part of the verse, for baptism identifies a person not only with Christ's act of dying but also with his rising. But the fut. may also refer to a share in eschatological destiny. **6.** *the self we once were:* Lit., "the old man," the self under the domination of sin and exposed to divine wrath, as opposed to the "new man," who lives in union with Christ and is liberated through him from sin and from any consideration of it. *was crucified with him:* See Gal 2:20; 5:24; 6:14. *to do away with our sinful self:* Lit., "with the body of sin." This phrase denotes not merely the material part of a human being, as opposed to the soul, but the whole of an earthly being, dominated by a proneness to sin (as the rest of the verse shows). In 7:24 Paul will speak of a "body of death" (cf. Col 1:22). In each case the gen. expresses the element that dominates the earthly, natural human being (→ Pauline Theology, 82:102). *that we might no longer be enslaved to sin:* The real answer to the objection posed in 6:1. The destruction of the sinful "self" through baptism and incorporation into Christ means liberation from enslavement to sin. Hence one's outlook can no longer be focused on sin.

66   **7.** *the one who has died has been acquitted of sin:* Two explanations are current for the difficult vb. *dedikaiōtai*. Understood in a forensic sense, it would mean that from the standpoint of law a dead person is absolved or acquitted, since sin no longer has a claim or a case against him or her. Possibly Paul is thus echoing a Jewish notion: the death of a guilty person ends all litigation (see Str-B 3. 232; cf. K. G. Kuhn, *ZNW* 30 [1931] 305; G. Schrenk, *TDNT* 2. 218). The other explanation seeks to interpret the vb. without forensic connotation (so Lyonnet, *Romains* 89; Cranfield, *Romans* 310–11): The one who has died has lost the very means of sinning, "the body of sin," so that he or she is definitively freed of sin. In either case, a change of status has ensued; the old condition has been brought to an end in the baptism-death, and a new one has begun. **8.** *died with Christ:* I.e., through baptism. *we believe:* The new life of the Christian is not the object of sensible perception or immediate consciousness; it is perceived only with the eyes of faith, in token of which baptism has been undergone. *we shall also live with him:* Paul thinks primarily of the future definitive form of new life *syn Christō,* "with Christ" (→ Pauline Theology, 82:120). However, the Christian already enjoys a share in that life, as 6:4 suggests (2 Cor 4:10–11). **9.** *never to die again:* The resurrection of Christ has brought the Christian into the sphere of "glory," freed from the sphere of sin and death. Though Christ came in the likeness of sinful flesh (8:3), he broke sin's dominion by his own death and resurrection. This victory is the foundation for the liberation of the baptized Christian. For Christ was raised from the dead not merely to publicize his good news or to confirm his messianic character, but to introduce human beings into a new mode of life and give them a new principle of vital activity, the Spirit.

death no longer lords it over him: I.e., having himself become *Kyrios* at the resurrection (Phil 2:9–11), he, not the personified *Thanatos,* reigns supreme. **10.** *died to sin once for all:* His death was a unique event, never to be repeated (*ephapax*), for through it he entered the definitive sphere of his glory as *Kyrios.* In so doing, he died to sin, "though he knew no sin" (2 Cor 5:21). This is the christological basis for the answer that Paul gives in 6:6 to the imaginary objector of 6:1. *he lives for God:* Since the resurrection, Christ enjoys a new relationship with the Father, into which he also introduces those who are baptized (Gal 2:19). **11.** *think of yourselves as dead to sin:* The conclusion of Paul's argument. He expresses his view of the problem of the integration of Christian life. Ontologically united with Christ through baptism, the Christian must deepen his or her faith continually to become aware psychologically of that union. Thus consciously oriented to Christ, one could never again consider sin without a basic rupture of that union. *in Christ Jesus:* The paragraph ends with the significant phrase of union, a brief description of Paul's view of the relation of the Christian to the risen *Kyrios.* "In Christ," the Christian is incorporated into the body of Christ through the holy Spirit and thereby shares in his vitality (see E. Schweizer, *NTS* 14 [1967–68] 1–14).

67   **12–23.** An exhortation, based on the preceding doctrinal exposé of baptism and its effect. Does it reflect a sermon once uttered at a baptismal liturgy? **12.** *do not let sin reign over your mortal body:* Though the Christian has been baptized and freed from sin, this freedom is not yet definitive. The Christian can still be tempted and can succumb to sin's seduction. (The Council of Trent, following Augustine, explained "sin" here as concupiscence [DS 1515]; however, as Lagrange notes [*Romains* 153], this might be an exact theological transposition, but it is a precision not yet found in the text.) For Paul *hamartia* is that personified active force that came into human history with Adam, has reigned over human beings up to Jesus' coming, and seeks to continue to reign. It can entice the Christian too. *make you obey its cravings:* I.e., the body's cravings. This is the preferred reading, but in P[46] (oldest text of Rom), D, G, Irenaeus, Tertullian, the text is rather "obey it," i.e., sin. This might be more logical in the context, but the variant does not change the sense much. **13.** *as instruments of evil:* Or, "as weapons of wickedness." The expression is a military figure, as the second part of the verse also suggests. The "arms of uprightness" allude to the OT (Isa 11:5; 59:17). Christians are supposed to be instruments in God's service, not in the cause of evil. The contrast of "iniquity" and "uprightness" is also found in QL (1QS 3:20–21); but there *ṣedeq,* "uprightness," is closely linked to the observance of the law, whereas for Paul it has assumed all the connotations of the "new" Christian life. **14.** *sin must no longer lord it over you:* Related as it is to death. The fut. tense expresses a categorical prohibition (BDF 362). *not under law, but under grace:* The law is never far from Paul's mind; here he links it with sin momentarily. He will develop the relationship at length in chap. 7. The new Christian condition can be called "uprightness," but it is not associated with the law; rather it is the effect of God's benevolent favor (see 3:24).

68   **15.** The question of 6:1 is repeated and again vehemently rejected. **16.** *slaves:* The military figure of 6:13 gives way to one from the social institution of slavery, which better suits the idea of law. But what underlies Paul's comparison is not so much "slavery" as such, but service. He insists on the freedom of the Christian from the law (Gal 5:1); yet he never conceives of it as license, a freedom to sin (Gal 5:13). It is rather a service of Christ, to which the Christian is now dedicated. There has been a change of *kyrioi*, and the Christian through baptism has become "the slave of Christ" (see comment on Rom 1:1; cf. 1 Cor 6:11). **17.** *you obeyed the pattern of teaching to which you have been given over:* This part of v 17 and v 18 are sometimes regarded as a non-Pauline gloss, but their Pauline authenticity is often stoutly maintained (see Cranfield, *Romans* 323). The difficulty is that the cl. is elliptical in the Gk text; it is here taken to mean *hypēkousate . . . tō typō didachēs eis hon paredothēte.* The crucial word is *typos,* which basically means the "visible impression" (of a stroke or die), "mark, copy, image." But it was also used to designate a "compendious, terse presentation" of some topic (Plato, *Rep.* 414a, 491c). Coupled with *didachē,* "teaching," it would seem to be used by Paul in the latter sense. He seems to refer thereby to a succinct baptismal summary of faith to which the convert freely was handed over after he or she had renounced all enslavement to sin. In this case, the vb. "handed over" would refer not to the transmission of traditional doctrine (cf. 1 Cor 11:23; 15:3) but to the transfer of slaves from one master to another, without a pejorative connotation (cf. 1 Cor 5:5; Rom 1:24). The allusion would be to the custom of the Hellenistic world in which the transfer of slaves was often accomplished with their consent (see J. Kürzinger, *Bib* 39 [1958] 156–76; F. W. Beare, *NTS* 5 [1958–59] 206–10, where other less likely interpretations are noted). **18.** *freed from sin:* This verse makes explicit the idea contained in the preceding verses, and indeed in the whole chapter. For the first time in Rom Paul speaks of Christian liberty, which from now on becomes an operative notion (6:20, 22; 7:3; 8:2,21; → Pauline Theology, 82:76). Actually, he has been speaking of some form of Christian freedom since 5:12. **19.** *familiar human terms:* Paul apologizes for using a figure derived from a social institution to express a Christian reality, but he wants to be sure that his talk of Christian liberty is not misunderstood. It is not license, but a service of Christ motivated by love, proceeding "from the heart.' *impurity and lawlessness:* These may seem to be typically pagan vices (see Gal 2:15), but Qumran Essenes repudiated the same in their members (1QS 3:5; 4:10,23–24). *sanctification:* The end result of consecration to God in Christ Jesus (→ Pauline Theology, 82:77).

69 **20.** *free of uprightness:* A play on the word "freedom" in this and the following verses stresses that a human being can be deluded by what one thinks is freedom. Verses 20–23 emphasize the incompatibility of two ways of life. **21.** *what profit did you get then?:* The punctuation of this verse is disputed. One could translate, "What profit did you then get out of the things you are now ashamed of?" The sense, however, is little affected in either case. The important affirmation is that death results from such things—not just physical death, but spiritual death too. **22.** *your profit is sanctification:* Being enslaved to God means a dedication to him that brings with it a withdrawal from the profane and from the attachment to sin. Such dedication does not remove one from this world, but it makes one live in it as one dedicated to God. The goal of this dedication is "life eternal," a share in the sphere of divinity itself (see comments on 2:7; 5:21). Though it has already begun in a sense, its "end" is yet to come. **23.** *the wages of sin is death:* Paul reverts to a military figure and uses *opsōnion,* "ration (money)" paid to a soldier. Underlying it is the idea of regularly recurrent payment. The more one serves sin, the more pay in the form of death one earns. These "wages" are paid out as death to those who serve sin (see H. Heidland, *TDNT* 5. 592; C. C. Caragounis, *NovT* 16 [1974] 35–57). *the free gift of God:* In contrast to the "wages of sin" that are due (4:4), "eternal life in Christ

Jesus our Lord" is graciously given to the Christian by God himself. There is no *quid pro quo,* and God's grace eventually brings about an assimilation of the Christian to God himself (2 Cor 3:18). *in Christ Jesus:* Concluding formula (→ 50 above).

(Byrne, B., "Living out the Righteousness of God: The Contribution of Rom 6:1–8:13 to an Understanding of Paul's Ethical Presuppositions," *CBQ* 43 [1981] 557–81. Dunn, J. D. G., "Salvation Proclaimed: VI. Romans 6:1 – 11: Dead and Alive," *ExpTim* 93 [1981–82] 259–64. Schlier, H., "Die Taufe nach dem 6. Kapitel des Römerbriefes," *Die Zeit der Kirche* [5th ed.; Freiburg, 1972] 47–56. Tannehill, R. C., *Dying and Rising with Christ* [BZNW 32; Berlin, 1967] 7–43. Wagner, G., *Pauline Baptism and the Pagan Mysteries* [Edinburgh, 1967]. Wedderburn, A. J. M., "Hellenistic Christian Traditions in Romans 6?," *NTS* 29 [1983] 337–55.)

70 (iii) *Freedom from the law* (7:1–25). Paul began his description of the justified Christian's new situation by explaining how Christ put an end to the reign of sin and death (5:12–21) and then how the "new life in Christ Jesus" meant a reorientation of the self so that one could no longer even think of sinning (6:1–23). In 6:14 he introduced the relation of the law to this freedom, haunted by the problem it posed: What role did it still have in human life? Earlier in Rom (3:20,31; 4:15; 5:13, 20) he had betrayed his preoccupation with this problem, but now he tries to face it squarely. What is the relation of the law to sin? How can it be the minister of death and condemnation (2 Cor 3:7,9)? What is the Christian's relation to this law? Verses 1–6 are the introduction to his answer, asserting the Christian's freedom from the law; vv 7–25 explain the relation of the law and sin. Here Paul asserts the law's basic goodness and shows that it has been used by sin as an instrument to dominate the person of "flesh." He finds the answer to his problem, then, not in the law itself but in the inability of weak, natural, earthly human beings to cope with its demands.

71 In 7:1–6 Paul interweaves two arguments: (1) The law binds only the living (7:1,4a); consequently, the Christian who has died "through the body of Christ" is no longer bound by it. (2) A wife is freed by the death of her husband from the specific prescriptions of the law binding her to him; the Christian is like the Jewish wife whose husband has died. Just as she is freed from "the law of the husband," so through death the Christian is freed from the law (7:2,3,4b). The second argument is only an illustration of the first, and a perfect one at that. It should not be forced into an allegory, as Sanday-Headlam once proposed (*Romans* 172): The Wife = the true self (Ego); the (first) Husband = the old state of man; the "Law of the Husband" = the Law condemning the old state; the New Marriage = union with Christ. For Paul's argument is different; it is the same person who dies and is freed from the law. He uses the illustration for one point only: that the law's obligation ceases when death occurs. Since the Christian has experienced death, the law has no more claim on him or her. So he argues here in chap. 7.

72 **1.** *brothers:* This is the first use of this address since 1:13. *who know the law:* Though Weiss, A. Jülicher, and E. Kühl thought that Paul, in addressing Roman Christians, was thus referring to Roman law, and a few others (Lagrange, Lyonnet, Sanday-Headlam, Taylor) interpreted *nomon* (without the article) as "law in general," most commentators rightly understand the expression to refer to the Mosaic law (see comment on 2:12), because there are allusions to it in 7:2,3,4b and the verse resumes 5:20; 6:14. As Leenhardt noted (*Romans* 177), if Paul's argument were based on a pagan juridical principle, it would lose much of its demonstrative force. Paul argues in effect that Moses himself foresaw a situation in which the law would cease to bind. *the law binds an individual as long as one lives:* Lit., "lords it over," i.e., keeps a person in bondage by the obligation to observe it. The conclusion from this is drawn in v 4a. It is now illustrated by the marriage law. **2.** *a married woman:* Cf. Num 5:20,29; Prov 6:29. By OT law the wife was considered the property of her husband; her infidelity was adultery (Exod 20:17; 21:3,22; Lev 20:10; Num 30:10–14; cf. R. de Vaux, *AI* 26). *the law of the husband:* The individual prescription of the Mosaic law, binding the wife to her owner (husband). **3.** *if she lives with another man:* Lit., "belongs to another (man)." The expression is derived from Deut 24:2; Hos 3:3. The freedom of the wife comes with the husband's death and has obviously nothing to do with divorce. **4.** *through the body of Christ:* I.e., through the crucified body of the historical Jesus (see Gal 2:19–20). By baptism the Christian has been identified with Christ (6:4–6), sharing in his death and rising. When Christ died for all "in the likeness of sinful flesh" (8:3), then all died (2 Cor 5:14). *may belong to another:* The "second husband" is the glorified risen Christ, who as *Kyrios* lords it over the Christian henceforth. *bear fruit for God:* The union of Christ and the Christian was just depicted in terms of marriage. Paul continues the figure: such a union is expected to produce the "fruit" of reformed life.

73 **5.** *we were living merely natural lives:* Lit., "we were in the flesh," in the past without Christ. That mode of existence is contrasted implicitly with life "in the Spirit" (8:9), to which Paul alludes in 7:6. *sinful passions:* The propensity to sin following upon strong sense impressions (see Gal 5:24). *aroused by the law:* The law spurs on human passions dominated by "flesh" and so becomes an occasion for sin. Another aspect of it appears in v 7. *to bear fruit for death:* The phrase expresses result, not purpose (see comment on *eis to* + infin., 1:20). The passions were not destined to contribute to death, but abetted by the law they did so (see 6:21). **6.** *but now:* In the new Christian dispensation (see comment on 3:21). *we have died to what once held us captive:* Though some commentators try to refer the pron. "what" to the domination of the passions, it is rather another reference to the law just mentioned. *so as to serve with the newness of Spirit:* The spirit as the dynamic principle of the new life begun in baptism (6:4) is radically different from the written code. The phrase has been suggested to Paul by the mention of "flesh" (v 5); flesh and Spirit thus served as the springboard for another contrast, the Spirit and the letter (= life under the Mosaic law; cf. 2 Cor 3:6–8, an excellent commentary on this verse).

74 In vv 7–13 Paul deals with the relation of the law to sin. **7.** *is the law sin?:* Paul is clearly thinking of the Mosaic law (see 7:1), for he even quotes it at the end of this verse. But some commentators have tried to understand *nomos* here as either (1) the natural law (Origen, E. Reuss), or (2) all law given from the beginning, including even the "command" laid on Adam (Theodore of Mopsuestia, Theodoret, Cajetan, Lietzmann, Lyonnet). To support this, appeal is made to Sir 17:4–11, which is supposed to show that contemporary Jews extended the notion of law to all divine precepts, even those imposed on Adam (Sir 17:7, echoing Deut 30:15,19) and on Noah. Sir 45:5(6) speaks of the law given to Moses in terms of *entolai,* "commands," the very word used in 7:8. Abraham is said to have observed God's law (Sir 44:20), and in the later *Tg. Ps.-Jonathan* (on Gen 2:15) Adam is said to have been put in Eden to observe the law's commandments (a view held also by Theophilus of Antioch, *Ad Autolycum* 2:24; PG 6. 1092; Ambrose, *De Paradiso* 4; CSEL 32. 282). However, none of these reasons shows

that Paul had a concept of law wider than that of the Mosaic law. They echo at most the belief of some Jews that the Mosaic law was itself already known to Abraham or people of earlier times. Paul does not share this belief (4:13; Gal 3:17–19). Rather, he is worried about the conclusion that might be drawn from some of his remarks on the law. It might seem to be sinful itself, since it "slipped in" to increase offenses (5:20), furnishes "knowledge of sin," and "brings down wrath" (4:15). Such a conclusion he resolutely rejects (see comment on 3:4). *I did not know of sin except through the law:* What was grasped by the conscience as evil came to be regarded as formal rebellion and transgression through the law. As in 3:20, the law appears as a moral informer.

75 Paul now shifts to the 1st pers. sg., and this shift has posed a historic exegetical problem. What is meant by the Ego? (1) According to A. Deissmann, Dodd, Bruce, Kühl, *et al.,* Paul speaks autobiographically. Yet this is unconvincing, since it conflicts with what Paul says about his own psychological background as a Pharisee and his preconversion experience with the law (Phil 3:6; Gal 1:13–14). It also misses an all-important generic perspective he adopts here, as he reflects on phases of human history. (2) According to P. Billerbeck, Davies, M. H. Franzmann, *et al.,* Paul would be thinking of the pious young Jewish boy who at 12 years became obligated to observe the law. Yet this idea of childish innocence is too restrictive for Paul's whole discussion. (3) According to Methodius of Olympia, Theodore of Mopsuestia, Cajetan, Dibelius, Lyonnet, Pesch, *et al.,* Paul would be referring to Adam confronted with the "command" of Gen 2:16–17. Yet, though this gives to the passage a comprehensive perspective that it needs and though Paul may allude to Gen 3:13 in 7:11, it does not explain why he would refer to Adam as Ego; and the allusion in v 11 is isolated. Indeed, when he quotes a divine precept, it is not that of Gen 2:16 or 3:3, but one of the Sinai commandments. (4) According to Augustine, Thomas Aq., Luther, Barth, Althaus, Nygren, *et al.,* Paul would be speaking of his own experience as a Christian confronted with regulations of his new life as a convert. Yet one must ask in such a case why all the talk about the law. Such a view tends to make of Paul a young Luther. (5) According to Käsemann and many others, Paul is making use of a rhetorical figure, Ego, to dramatize in an intimate, personal way the experience common to all unregenerate human beings faced with the Mosaic law and relying on their own resources to meet its obligations. Instead of using *anthrōpos,* "human being," or *tis,* "someone," he chose to speak of Ego, somewhat as in 1 Cor 8:13; 13:1–3,11–12; 14:6–19; Rom 14:21; Gal 2:18–21. This rhetorical device "is encountered not only in the Greek world but also in the OT psalms of thanksgiving when divine deliverance from guilt and peril of death is confessed" (Käsemann, *Romans* 193).

Trivial insistence on one aspect of the Ego problem tends to obscure Paul's profound insight. The confrontation of Ego with sin and the law is not considered by him on an individual, psychological level, but from a historical and corporate point of view. Paul surveys human history as it was known to him through Jewish and Christian eyes—without Christ and with Christ (see E. Stauffer, *TDNT* 2.358–62). Some of his statements in this passage are susceptible of application to experiences beyond his own immediate perspective. What he says in vv 7–25 is undoubtedly the experience of many Christians faced with divine, ecclesiastical, or civil law; when these verses are read in such a light, few will fail to appreciate their significance. But in attempting to understand what Paul meant, it is important to keep *his* perspective in mind.

76   *you shall not covet:* Thus the Mosaic law is epitomized (Exod 20:17; Deut 5:21). It expresses the essence of the law, teaching human beings not to let themselves be drawn by created things rather than the Creator. By such a command the sluggish moral conscience is made aware of the possibility of a violation of the will of God so manifested. **8.** *sin found its opportunity through that command:* The "command" may sound like an allusion to the injunction laid on Adam in Gen 2:16, but it refers to the specific prohibition of the Mosaic law just cited. Here one should recall Paul's view of salvation history (→ Pauline Theology, 82:42). From Adam to Moses people did evil, but they did not violate precepts, as did Adam. Their evil deeds became violations with the coming of the law. The latter then became an *aphormē,* "occasion, opportunity" (BAGD 127), for formal sin. *without the law sin was lifeless:* Like a corpse, it was powerless to do anything—powerless to make evil into a flagrant revolt against God (see 4:15; 5:13b). **9.** *alive without the law:* This is not an allusion to Paul's happy, innocent childhood or an allusion to Adam's state before he ate the fruit, but an ironic reference to the life led by everyone without Christ and ignorant of the real nature of evil conduct. The expression "lifeless," used of sin (v 8), probably suggested to Paul the contrast "I was alive"; but the main emphasis is on the phrase "without the law." The life so lived was, indeed, not that of union with God in Christ; nor was it an open rebellion against God in formal transgression. *sin became alive:* With the intervention of the law, the human condition before God changed, for "desires" now became "coveting," and its pursuit a revolt against God. If the vb. *anezēsen* were taken literally, "came to life again," it would be difficult to see how this could apply to Adam, but it may mean only "sprang to life" (BAGD 53). Sin "was live" in Adam's transgression; it "sprang to life" again in the transgressions of the Mosaic law. **10.** *then I died:* The death meant here is not that of Gal 2:19, whereby the Christian dies to the law through Christ's crucifixion, so that it no longer has any claim on him or her. This death is rather the condition resulting from sin as a violation of the law. Through formal transgressions, human beings are thrust under the domination of *Thanatos* (5:12). *the command that should have meant life:* The Mosaic law promised life to those who would observe it: "by the observance of which one shall find life" (Lev 18:5; cf. Deut 4:1; 6:24; Gal 3:12; Rom 10:5). *in my case meant death:* The law itself did not kill, but it was an instrument used by sin to bring human beings to death. It was not only an occasion of sin (7:5) or a moral informer (7:7), but it also leveled a condemnation to death against the one who did not obey it (Deut 27:26; cf. 1 Cor 15:56; 2 Cor 3:7,9; Gal 3:10). **11.** *sin deceived me:* Just as the command of God gave the tempting serpent its opportunity, so sin used the law to deceive human beings and entice them to go after what was forbidden. Paul alludes to Gen 3:3, but by no means so explicitly as in 2 Cor 11:3. The deception developed when human autonomy was confronted with the divine demand for submission. As the serpent did, so sin enticed human beings thus confronted to assert their autonomy and make themselves "like God." **12.** *holy, just, and good:* Because the law was God-given and destined to give life to those who would obey it (7:10,14; Gal 3:24). The law never commanded human beings to do evil; in itself it was good. **13.** *did what was good prove the death of me?:* The anomaly of the law! Again, Paul vehemently rejects the thought that a God-given institution was the direct cause of death (see comment on 3:4). *it was sin, so that it might be shown to be sin:* The real culprit was sin, the direct cause of everyone's death (5:12; 6:23). It used the law as a tool. Once this is understood,

then it is clear that the law was not the equivalent of sin (cf. 2 Cor 3:7) and that sin is shown up to be what it really is, revolt against God.
77   **14-25.** Paul's explanation is not yet complete; he now probes more deeply. How could sin use something good in itself to destroy human beings? The problem is not with the law, but with human beings themselves. **14.** *the law is spiritual:* Because of its God-given origin and its purpose of leading human beings to God. Thus it did not belong to the world of earthbound, natural humanity. As *pneumatikos,* it belonged to the sphere of God; it was opposed to what is *sarkinos,* "carnal, belonging to the sphere of flesh." *what I do I do not understand:* The enigma is derived from a conflict in the inmost depths of humanity, the cleavage between reason-dominated desire and actual performance. *I do not do what I want to, and what I do I detest:* Moral aspiration and performance are not coordinated or integrated. Often quoted in this connection are the plaintive words of the Roman poet Ovid, "I perceive what is better and approve of it, but I pursue what is worse" (*Metamorph.* 7.19). The Essenes of Qumran explained the same inner conflict by teaching that God had put two spirits in human beings to rule until the time of his visitation, a spirit of truth and a spirit of perversity (1QS 3:15-4:26). Paul, however, attributes the rift not to spirits but to human beings themselves. **16.** *I agree that the law is good:* The desire to do what is right is an implicit recognition of the goodness and excellence of the law in what it imposes. **17.** *sin that dwells in me:* Hamartia came into control to "reign" over humanity (5:12,21) and by lodging itself within human beings it has enslaved them. This verse is really a corrective to 7:16a: Sin is responsible for the evil that human beings do. Paul may seem almost to absolve human beings from responsibility for sinful conduct (see 7:20); but it is human sin (5:12d). **18.** *good does not dwell in me—in my natural self:* Lit., "in my flesh." The additional qualification is important, for Paul finds the root of the difficulty in the human self considered as *sarx,* the source of all that is opposed to God. From the Ego considered as *sarx* proceed the detestable things that one does. But the Ego as the true willing self is dissociated from that self that has fallen victim to "flesh" (→ Pauline Theology, 82:103). **19-20.** A repetition of 7:15,17 from a different standpoint.
78   **21.** *I detect, then, the principle:* From experience everyone learns how things stand. In 7:21-25 *nomos* undergoes a shift in nuance. Paul is playing on other meanings of the word he has used so far to mean the Mosaic law. Now *nomos* denotes a "principle" (BAGD 542), or the experienced "pattern" of one's activity. **22.** *in the depths of me I find delight in God's law:* This is not the Christian speaking, but, as the following verses make clear, the "mind" (*nous*) of unregenerate humanity. Though dominated by sin when considered as "flesh," everyone still experiences that one desires what God desires. The mind or reason recognizes the ideal presented by the law—God's law. **23.** *another principle is at war with the law of my mind:* The *nomos* in which the reasoning self finds delight is opposed to another *nomos* that ultimately makes the self a captive (6:13,19). This *nomos* is none other than indwelling sin (7:17) that enslaves a human being so that the willing self, which delights in God's law, is not free to observe it. **24.** *miserable wretch that I am!:* The agonizing cry of everyone weighted down with the burden of sin and prevented by it from achieving what one would; it is a desperate cry to God for help. *who will save me from this doomed body?:* Lit., "this body of death," see comment on 6:6. Threatened by defeat in this conflict, a human being finds deliverance in the merciful bounty of God manifested in Christ Jesus. **25.** *thank God!:* In the ms. D and in the Vg,

the answer to the question in v 24 is "the grace of God," but this is an inferior reading. Verse 25 is an exclamation, expressing the Ego's gratitude to God, which anticipates the real answer to be given in 8:1–4. Gratitude is expressed "through Jesus Christ our Lord," using the refrain of this part of Rom (→ 50 above). It may be preferable to separate the exclamation (Thank God!) from the following phrase, understanding the latter as an initial expression of the answer to the question of v 24: "(It is done) through Jesus. . . ." *with my mind:* The reasoning self willingly submits to God's law and stands in contrast to the carnal self, the person enslaved to sin. Thus Paul terminates his discussion of the three freedoms achieved for humanity in Christ Jesus.

(Benoit, P., "The Law and the Cross according to St Paul, Romans 7:7–8:4," *Jesus and the Gospel, Volume 2* [London, 1974] 11–39. Bornkamm, G., *Early Christian Experience* [Phl, 1969] 87–104. Bruce, F. F., "Paul and the Law of Moses," *BJRL* 57 [1974–75] 259–79. Hübner, H., *Law in Paul's Thought* [Edinburgh, 1984]. Kümmel, W. G., *Römer 7 und die Bekehrung des Apostels* [UNT 17; Leipzig, 1929]. Räisänen, H., *Paul and the Law* [WUNT 29; Tübingen, 1983].)

79   (c) The Theme Developed: Christian Life is Lived in the Spirit and Is Destined for Glory (8:1–39). In 5:1–11 Paul announced that justified Christians have been empowered to live a new life as the result of God's love manifested in the liberating acts of Christ. Now that liberation from sin, death, and the law has taken place, they are able to live this life "for God," whose love is poured out through the dynamic principle of such life, the Spirit of God himself. Chapter 8 begins by answering the question posed in 7:24: Christ has rescued human beings from enslavement and made it possible for them to live "according to the Spirit" (8:1–4). This answer serves to introduce a development of the theme announced in 5:1–11, explaining how Christian existence is dominated by the Spirit, not the flesh (8:5–13). Because of the gift of the Spirit the Christian is a child of God, adopted and destined for the glory of God's intimate presence (8:14–30). Finally, as Paul contemplates this plan of salvation, he indulges in rhetoric and extols the love of God made manifest in Christ Jesus (8:31–39).

80   (i) *Christian life empowered by the Spirit* (8:1–13). **1.** *no condemnation for those united with Christ Jesus:* Condemnation is no longer leveled by the law against those not observing it, nor is there any condemnation resulting from sin. "Condemnation" means the same as the "curse" of Gal 3:10 (cf. Deut 27:26). It clung to unregenerate human beings torn in two, because they were "flesh" and were dominated by sin (5:16–18), but still had a "mind" that recognized God's law. But this condition does not affect the Christian, who no longer lives under that dispensation of "condemnation" (2 Cor 3:9) or of "death" (2 Cor 3:7). **2.** *the law of the Spirit of life:* Thus qualified, *nomos* no longer refers to the Mosaic law. Paul indulges in oxymoron and applies *nomos* to the Spirit, the dynamic "principle" of the new life; but the Spirit is not really *nomos* at all, for it supplies the vitality that the Mosaic law could never give. It is the life-giving power of God himself. "Spirit" occurs 29 times in chap. 8, but only 5 times in chaps. 1–7. *has freed you:* Christian freedom is achieved either "through" Christ (instrumental) or "in Christ" (unitive). The better reading is "you" (sg.), even though some important mss. read "me," which is a more direct answer to the Ego's cry in 7:24, yet clearly a copyist's correction. *from the law of sin and death:* Again *nomos* is used in a wide sense, "principle," but one should not fail to note the collocation of the three key words—law, sin, and death. They sum up the

discussion of chaps. 5–7; and their tyranny is broken.

81   **3.** *what the law could not do:* "This God has done," or a similar phrase, must be understood to clear up the anacoluthon. Paul refers to the inability of the Mosaic law to put human beings in a state of rectitude before God and free them from sin and death. *because it was weakened by the flesh:* Or, "as long as it was. . . ." The good that the law might have achieved was rendered ineffective by the human self dominated by indwelling sin (7:22–23). Though it told human beings what to do and what not to do, it supplied no power to surmount the opposition to it coming from the human inclination to sin. *God sent his own son:* The emphatic phrase "his own son" is stronger than the stereotyped formula "Son of God" and highlights the divine origin of the task to be accomplished by one in close filial relationship with God. Implied is a unique bond of love between the two that is the source of human salvation; also implied is the divine preexistence of Christ (→ Pauline Theology, 82:50). His task was to accomplish what the law could not do. The "sending" refers not to the whole redemptive incarnation, but to its climax in the cross and resurrection (Gal 3:13; 2 Cor 5:19–21; Rom 3:24–25). *in a form like our sinful flesh:* This is not a docetic description, implying that the Son only appeared to be human. Rather, he was sent as a man, born of a woman, born under the law (Gal 4:4). Paul avoids saying that the Son came with sinful flesh, just as in 2 Cor 5:21 he qualifies his statement that God made Christ "sin" for us, by adding "who knew no sin" (cf. Heb 4:15). He came in a form like us in that he experienced the effects of sin and suffered death as one "cursed" by the law (Gal 3:13). Thus in his own self he coped with the power of sin. *to conquer sin:* Lit., "and for the sake of sin," i.e., to take it away, expiate it (BAGD 644; cf. Gal 1:4; 1 Pet 3:18; Num 8:8). This was the purpose of the Son's mission. Some commentators, however, take *peri hamartias* to mean "as a sin offering," since *hamartia* occurs in this sense in the LXX (Lev 4:24; 5:11; 6:18; cf. 2 Cor 5:21). Though the image would be different, the underlying idea would still be the same. *condemned sin in the flesh:* The Father thus passed definitive judgment on the force that Adam's transgression unleashed in the world (5:12) and thereby broke its dominion over human beings. He accomplished this "in the flesh." How? According to Kühl, Lagrange, and Zahn, Paul refers to the incarnation, when the Father by sending the Son "in the flesh" implicitly passed sentence on sin. It was a condemnation in principle, in that the Son assumed the human condition without sin and lived a sinless life. But since elsewhere Paul associates the redemptive activity of Jesus with his passion, death, and resurrection, the phrase is better understood of the crucified and risen "flesh" (so Benoit, Käsemann, *et al.*). In the flesh that he shared with humanity he underwent the experience of death on its behalf and was raised from death by the Father. Identified with Christ in baptism, the Christian shares that destiny and victory, which marks the end of the reign of sin in human life.

82   **4.** *that the requirement of the law might be met:* Through the power of the Spirit, the divine principle of new life, the uprightness that the law demanded is finally obtained. The key word here is *dikaiōma*, the meaning of which is disputed; most likely it means "requirement, commandment" of the law, i.e., an ideal requirement (see 2:26; cf. BAGD 198; K. Kertelge, *EWNT* 1. 809). *in us . . . who live according to the Spirit:* The law proposed an ideal but did not enable human beings to achieve it; now all this is changed. The Spirit enables them to surmount the flesh and arrive at the goal that the law once proposed. The Gk ptc. with the negative *mē* gives a proviso or conditional force to the expression, "provided we walk not according to the flesh." It thus insinuates that Christian living is not something that flows automatically from baptism; cooperation with the grace of God thus conferred is required. The contrast of "flesh" and "Spirit" is developed in vv 5-13. **5.** *who live according to the flesh:* I.e., whose motivation in life is a self-centered interest. **6.** *death is the aspiration of the flesh:* All striving of natural human beings is focused on death (total death; see comment on 5:12). Compare Gal 5:21, "People who do such things have no share in the kingdom of God." Radically opposed to this is the aspiration of the Spirit, "life and peace." Paul implies that the tendency of unregenerate humanity is to enmity with God; he formulates this explicitly in 8:7. Through the Spirit, however, human beings can find reconciliation and peace with God. **7.** *does not submit to God's laws:* This verse recasts 7:22-25 but goes further in asserting that the earthly-minded human being is fundamentally unable to obey God's law, lacking the power to transcend the inner conflict, when confronted with the law. This hostility to God is responsible for the open transgression of the law's commands. **8.** *cannot please God:* Paul chooses a neutral way of expressing the goal of human life: to please God. It is a goal aimed at by both Jew and Christian (cf. 2 Cor 5:9), yet it cannot be attained by one who is dominated by self ("in the flesh"); one must be "in the Spirit," i.e., live "according to the Spirit" (8:5).

83   **9.** *since the Spirit of God dwells in you:* The Spirit, as the new principle of Christian vitality, is derived from "God," the same source as all other manifestations of salvation. The baptized Christian is not only "in the Spirit," but the Spirit is now said to dwell in him or her. Such expressions of the mutual relationship of the "spiritual" person and the Spirit forestall any facile interpretation of human participation in divine life in a too local or spatial sense. Both modes express the same basic reality. At the beginning of the cl. Paul used the conj. *eiper,* translated "since," but it can also mean "if, in reality." *Christ's Spirit:* Note how Paul interchanges "the Spirit of God," "the Spirit of Christ," and "Christ," as he tries to express the multifaceted reality of the Christian experience of participation in divine life (for the implications of this multiple use in the development of trinitarian theology, → Pauline Theology, 82:61-62). *does not belong to him:* Attachment to Christ is only possible by the "spiritualization" of human beings. This is no mere external identification with the cause of Christ, or even a grateful recognition of what he once did for humanity. Rather, the Christian who belongs to Christ is the one empowered to "live for God" (6:10) through the vitalizing influence of his Spirit. **10.** *if Christ is in you:* Or the Spirit (8:9); cf. Gal 2:20; 2 Cor 5:17. *your spirit is alive:* Paul plays on the meanings of *pneuma.* In 8:9 it clearly meant the Spirit of God, but he is aware of its sense as a human component that can be contrasted with "flesh" (→ Pauline Theology, 82:105). Without the Spirit, the source of Christian vitality, the human "body" is like a corpse because of the influence of sin (5:12), but in union with Christ the human "spirit" lives, for the Spirit resuscitates the dead human being through the gift of uprightness (see Leenhardt, *Romans* 209; cf. M. Dibelius, *SBU* 3 [1944] 8-14). **11.** *the Spirit of him who raised Jesus:* As in 8:9, *pneuma* is the Spirit of the Father, to whom the efficiency of the resurrection is attributed (see comments on 4:24; 6:4). The power vivifying the Christian is thus traced to its ultimate source, for the Spirit is the manifestation of the Father's presence and power in the world since the resurrection of Christ and through it. *will give life to your mortal bodies:* The fut. tense expresses the

role of the vivifying Spirit in the eschatological resurrection of Christians. At his resurrection Christ became through the Father's glory (6:4) the principle of the raising of Christians (see 1 Thess 4:14; Phil 3:10,21; 1 Cor 6:14; 2 Cor 4:14; → Pauline Theology, 82:58-59). *through his Spirit:* Modern editors of the Gk NT read *dia* with the gen., which expresses the instrumentality of the Spirit in the resurrection of human beings (so mss. ℵ, A, C). Another strongly attested reading is *dia* with the acc., which would stress the dignity of the Spirit (so mss. B, D, G, and the Vg), "because of his Spirit." In either case, "his" refers to Christ (*ZBG* § 210; BDF 31.1), for it is the Spirit as related to the risen Christ that is the vivifying principle. **13.** *if you put to death the accomplishments of the body:* This verse and v 12 conclude the preceding discussion and form a transition to the next section. Paul implies that the baptized Christian could still be concerned about the "deeds, acts, pursuits" of one dominated by *sarx.* Hence his exhortation: Make use of the Spirit received; this is the debt that is owed to Christ.

84   (ii) *Through the Spirit the Christian becomes a child of God, destined for glory (8:14-30).* The Spirit not only gives new life but also establishes for human beings the relationship of an adopted son and heir. Material creation, hope itself, and the Spirit all bear witness to this glorious destiny. **14.** *sons of God:* Mortification, necessary though it is to Christian life (8:13), does not really constitute it. Rather, the Spirit animates and activates the Christian and makes one a child of God. This is the first appearance of the theme of sonship in Rom; by it Paul attempts to describe the new status of the Christian in relation to God. **15.** *not a spirit of slavery:* Paul plays on the meanings of *pneuma* (Spirit/spirit). Christians have received the Spirit (of Christ or God), but this is not a "spirit" in the sense of a disposition or a mentality that a slave would have. Animated by God's Spirit, the Christian cannot have the attitude of a slave, for the Spirit sets free. True, at times Paul speaks of the Christian as a "slave" (6:16; 1 Cor 7:22), but that is to make a point. In reality, he considers the Christian a son (cf. Gal 4:7), empowered by the Spirit to call upon God himself as Father. *the spirit of adoption:* Or, "the Spirit of adoption." Because Paul has been playing on the word *pneuma,* it is hard to say just which nuance he intends here; perhaps both are meant. The Spirit constitutes adoptive sonship, putting Christians in a special relationship to Christ, the unique Son, and to the Father. The word *huiothesia,* "adoption," is used of Israel in 9:4, with special reference to its being chosen by God (cf. Exod 4:22; Isa 1:2; Jer 3:19; Hos 11:1), but it is not found in the LXX, probably because adoption was not a widely practiced institution among the Jews. Paul has borrowed the word from current Hellenistic legal language and applied it to Christians (cf. M. W. Schoenberg, *Scr* 15 [1963] 115-23). It denotes that the baptized Christian has been taken into the family of God and has a status in it—not that of a slave (who belonged indeed to the ancient household) but of a son. The Christian's attitude should, then, correspond to the status that he or she enjoys. *which enables us to cry:* Lit., "in which (or by which) we cry." Though the vb. *krazein* is used in the LXX of various life situations in which one calls upon God (Pss 3:5; 17:6; 88:2,10), it also means to "cry aloud" in proclamation (Rom 9:27). This may be the sense here: through the Spirit the Christian proclaims that God is Father. *Abba, Father:* See comment on Gal 4:6. The cry used by Jesus in the moment of his supreme earthly confidence in God (Mark 14:36), preserved by the early Palestinian community, became for Paul even in Gentile communities the mode of address distinctive of Christians.

85   **16.** *the Spirit joins with our spirit in testifying:* The vb. *symmartyrein* means either "testify along with" or simply "testify, certify." The latter would denote that the Spirit makes the Christian aware of adoptive sonship, "testifies to our spirit that. . . ." But the former reckons more with the compound vb. Paul would not mean that an unregenerate person, without the influence of the Spirit, could come to the knowledge of adoptive sonship, so that the Spirit would just concur with the human spirit recognizing this. The preceding context makes it clear that the vital dynamism of the Spirit constitutes the sonship itself and bestows the power to recognize such a status. Now Paul goes further and stresses that the Spirit concurs with the Christian as one acknowledges or proclaims in prayer this special relation to the Father. Paul is going beyond Gal 4:6. **17.** *if sons, then heirs:* The Christian, as an adopted son, is not only admitted into God's family, but by reason of the same gratuitous adoption receives the right to become the master of his Father's estate. Though he has no natural right to it, he acquires title by adoption (cf. Gal 4:7). *joint heirs with Christ:* Christ, the unique son, has already received a share of the Father's estate (glory); the Christian is destined one day to share in that glory too (see comment on 3:23). Note the connection explicitly asserted between Christ's passion and his resurrection. The double use of verbs compounded with *syn-,* "with," expresses once again the share of the Christian in these phases of Christ's redemptive activity (→ Pauline Theology, 82:120).

86   **18.** *for I consider . . . :* This verse introduces the threefold testimony given to the Christian destiny, which is sharply contrasted with the sufferings just mentioned. *the glory to be revealed for us:* Paul reminds his readers that, although suffering is a sign of the authentic Christian experience, it is only a transition to the assured glory that awaits them in the *eschaton.* **19.** *creation waits with eager expectation for God's sons to be revealed:* Paul discloses his view of the created world, which in its chaotic state manifests its cosmic striving toward the very goal set for humanity itself. He thus affirms a solidarity of the human and the subhuman world in the redemption of Christ. It recalls Yahweh's promise to Noah of the covenant to be made "between myself and you and every living creature" (Gen 9:12-13). In this context the noun *ktisis* denotes "material creation" apart from human beings (see 8:23; cf. Cranfield, *Romans* 414; Wilckens, *An die Römer* 2. 153). Created for human beings, it was cursed as a result of Adam's sin (Gen 3:15-17); since then material creation has been in a state of abnormality or frustration, being subject to corruption or decay itself. Yet Paul sees it sharing in the destiny of humanity, somehow freed of this proclivity to decay.

87   **20.** *but by him who subjected it with (the) hope,* **21.** *that creation itself would be freed from the bondage of decay:* Three items are problematic in these clauses: (1) the sense of the prep. *dia* in the phrase *dia ton hypotaxanta;* (2) the meaning of the phrase *eph' helpidi,* "in/with hope"; and (3) the meaning of the conj. *hoti* or *dioti* (v 21). One interpretation, used with some variation by Chrysostom, Zahn, W. Foerster, Lyonnet, Wilckens, *et al.,* takes *dia* as causal, the sense it often has in Pauline writings (2:24; Gal 4:13; Phil 1:15), "because of him who subjected it." This would refer to Adam, whose transgression caused the disorder of material creation. But then the question is raised, how Adam subjected it "in/with hope." This phrase, which is not found in the Gen story, is then understood to be elliptical, "(yet it was) with hope." The conj. preferred in v 21 is *dioti* (read by mss. ℵ, D*, F, G, 945), "because (creation itself . . .)." Though this explanation seems defensible, it does not really explain the source of the hope that Paul has added to the Gen allusion. Another explanation, used by Käsemann, Lagrange,

Leenhardt, J. Levie, Lietzmann, Pesch, Sanday-Headlam, *et al.,* takes *dia* as denoting agency, "by him who subjected it," which would refer neither to Adam nor to Satan (serpent), but to God, who cursed the ground and to whom Paul now ascribes the "hope" (that was not expressed in Gen). Then the cl. in v 21, introduced by the conj. *hoti* (read by mss. P⁴⁶, A, B, C, D², etc.), would express the object of that hope, "that (creation itself . . .)." This interpretation seems to make better sense, even though the use of *dia* + acc. to denote agency is rare (see BAGD 181; cf. Sir 15:11; John 6:57). Paul would be saying that God, though he cursed the ground because of Adam's sin, still gave it a hope of sharing in human redemption or liberation. This "hope" should not be facilely identified with Gen 3:15, which expresses rather lasting enmity; Paul is actually the first biblical writer to introduce the note of "hope." *decay:* Not just moral corruption, but the reign of dissolution and death found in physical creation. Material creation is thus not to be a mere spectator of humanity's triumphant glory and freedom, but is to share in it. When the children of God are finally revealed in glory, the material world will also be emancipated from the "last enemy" (1 Cor 15:23-28).

88   **22.** *all creation has been groaning in travail together till now:* Gk philosophers often compared the vernal rebirth of nature to a woman's travail. Paul adopts this image to express the tortuous convulsions of frustrated material creation, as he sees it. It groans in hope and expectation, but also in pain. The compound vb. *synōdinei* expresses the concerted agony of the universe in all its parts. Some commentators maintain that it expresses the groaning of creation, "with humanity," as it too awaits the revelation of glory. This is possible, but the former interpretation seems better because humanity may only be introduced in the next verse. **23.** *we ourselves:* Not only material creation bears testimony to the Christian destiny, but Christians themselves do so by the *hope* that they have, a hope based on the gift of the Spirit already possessed. *the firstfruits of the Spirit:* The Spirit is compared with the firstfruits of the harvest, which, when offered to God (Lev 23:15-21), betokened the consecration of the whole harvest. But "firstfruits" was often used in the sense of a "pledge, guarantee" of what was to come (cf. *arrabōn,* 2 Cor 1:22; 5:5; cf. G. Delling, *TDNT* 1. 486; A. Sand, *EWNT* 1. 278-80). *we groan within ourselves:* The second testimony to Christian destiny is the hope that Christians themselves have of it. *await the redemption of our bodies:* The Gk text of this verse is disputed. Mss. P⁴⁶, D, F, G, 614, etc. omit the noun *huiothesian,* "adoptive sonship." Though it is difficult to explain how it got into the text of other mss., its omission seems preferable because Paul nowhere else speaks of such sonship as a form of eschatological redemption. The Christian is already son of God (cf. 8:15), made so by the Spirit received. With such "firstfruits," the Christian looks forward to the full harvest of glory, the redemption of the body (so Lyonnet, *Romans* 98; P. Benoit, *RSR* 39 [1951-52] 267-80). If, however, "sonship" is to be retained as the *lectio difficilior,* then Paul would be referring to a phase of it still to be revealed. **24.** *in hope we were saved:* The aor. tense expresses the past aspect of salvation already wrought by Christ's death and resurrection; but it may also be a gnomic aor., expressing a general truth (BDF 333). "In hope" enhances such "salvation" with an eschatological aspect (→ Pauline Theology, 82:71). *who hopes for what he sees?:* The preferred reading of this poorly transmitted text is *ho gar blepei tís elpizei* (P⁴⁶, B*), translated here. Others read, "For how can anyone still hope for what he sees" (mss. D, G). In the long run, the sense is little affected. **25.** *we await it with patience:* Hope enables the Christian to bear with "the sufferings of the present" (8:18), but it also makes him or her a witness to the world of a lively faith in the resurrection (see 1 Cor 2:9; 2 Cor 5:7). **89** **26.** *the Spirit too helps us in our weakness:* The third testimony to the new life and glorious destiny of Christians. Human aspirations risk being inefficacious because of the natural weakness of the flesh, but the Spirit adds its intercession, transcending such weakness (*hyperentynchanei,* "intercedes over and above"). The result is that the Christian utters what would otherwise be ineffable; to pray "Abba, Father," the Spirit must dynamically assist the Christian (8:15; Gal 4:6). The Christian who so prays is aware that the Spirit manifests its presence to him or her. **27.** *who searches the hearts:* An OT phrase for God (1 Sam 16:7; 1 Kgs 8:39; Pss 7:11; 17:3; 139:1). Only God himself comprehends the language and the mind of the Spirit and recognizes such Spirit-assisted prayer. *according to God's will:* Lit., "according to God." It was part of his plan of salvation that the Spirit should play such a dynamic role in the aspirations and prayers of Christians. This plan is now briefly sketched in vv 28-30.

90 **28.** *in everything God works for good with those who love him:* The addition or omission of *ho theos,* "God" (as subj. of the vb.), in various mss. has resulted in three different interpretations of this verse: (1) If *ho theos* is read (with mss. P⁴⁶, B, A) and the vb. *synergei* is taken intransitively with an indir. obj., "works together with," then one gets the transl. given above: God cooperates "in all things" (*panta,* adv. acc.) with those who love; this is seen as the realization of his loving plan of salvation. This interpretation is used by many patristic and modern commentators. (2) If *ho theos* is read, but the vb. *synergei* is taken transitively with *panta* as the dir. obj., then "God makes all things conspire for the good of those who love him." So BDF 148.1, Lagrange, Levie, Prat; but no parallel of the transitive use of *synergein* is offered. (3) If *ho theos* is omitted (with mss. ℵ, C, D, G, and the Koine text-tradition; Vg) and *panta* is taken as the subj. of the vb., then "all things work together for good for those who love God." The first and second interpretations add an explicit nuance to what is implicit in the third: God's purpose and plan are what is really behind all that happens to Christians, for he is really in control. *who are called according to his purpose:* God's "plan" is described in vv 29-30—and from the divine perspective. This phrase must not be restricted only to such Christians as are predestined; the application of it to individual predestination comes in with the interpretation of Augustine. Paul's view is rather corporate, and the phrase is a complement to "those who love him," i.e., Christians who have responded to a divine call (cf. Rom 1:6; 1 Cor 1:2). **29.** *he foreknew...he predestined:* Paul stresses the divine prevenience of the process of salvation. His anthropomorphic language should not be too facilely transposed into the *signa rationis* of a later theological system of predestination. *be conformed to the image of his Son:* According to the divine plan of salvation, the Christian is to reproduce in himself or herself an image of Christ by a progressive share in his risen life (see 8:17; 2 Cor 3:18; 4:4-6; Phil 3:20-21; cf. A. R. C. Leaney, *NTS* 10 [1963-64] 470-79). **30.** *he also glorified:* Another effect of the Christ-event is thus indicated (→ Pauline Theology, 82:80). God's plan, involving call, election, predestination, justification, is aimed at the final destiny of glory for all who put faith in Christ Jesus.

91 **31-39.** Having discussed various aspects of the new life in union with Christ and his Spirit and the reasons that provide a basis for Christian hope, Paul concludes this section with a rhetorical (hymnic?) passage about the love of God made manifest in Christ Jesus. No little emotional language and some rhythmic phrasing mark the passage. **31.** *who can be against us?:* The terminology is that of a lawcourt, similar to the debates in Job or Zech 3. God's salvific plan makes it clear to Christians that God is on their side. **32.** *did not spare his own Son:* See 5:8; 8:3. This may be an allusion to Gen 22:16, to Abraham, who did not spare Isaac. God the judge has thus already pronounced sentence in our favor; hence there is no reason to expect anything different from him hereafter. **33-35.** The punctuation of the sentences in these verses is disputed. Taking them all as rhetorical questions is preferred; but cf. the *RSV* for a different punctuation. **33.** *who shall accuse God's elect? Is it God who justifies?:* The answer implied, of course, is no. A possible allusion to Isa 50:8-9 makes some commentators take this sentence as a statement, to which the following is a question in reaction. **34.** *rather was raised:* Attention is shifted to the resurrection of Christ (cf. 4:24-25), to which Paul adds a rare reference to the exaltation of Christ (without alluding to the ascension). *intercedes for us:* Paul ascribes to the glorified Christ an activity that continues the objective aspect of human redemption: he still presents his supplication to the Father on behalf of Christians. In Heb 7:25; 9:24 this intercession is linked with Christ's priesthood, a notion not found in the Pauline corpus. Cf. 1 John 2:1. **35.** *from the love of Christ:* I.e., from the love that Christ has for us. None of the dangers or troubles of life can make the true Christian forget the love of Christ made known to human beings in his death and resurrection. **36.** *as Scripture says:* Lit., "as it was written" (see comment on 1:17). Paul quotes Ps 44:23, a community lamentation, bemoaning the injustice done to faithful Israel by its enemies, recalling its fidelity to Yahweh and seeking his aid and deliverance. The psalm is cited to show that tribulations are not proof of God's not loving the persecuted; rather, such things are a sign of his love. **37.** *through him who loved us:* Either Christ, as in 8:35, or God, as in 5:5,8. **38.** Two series of obstacles for the love of God (or Christ) have been cited in vv 33-34,35-37; a third is now given. *angels...principalities...powers:* Spirits of different ranks; whether they are good or evil is not clear, but in any case even such beings will not separate Christians from God's love. Paul may be listing such forces that ancient peoples regarded as hostile to human beings. **39.** *neither height nor depth:* These are probably terms of ancient astrology designating the greatest proximity or remoteness of a star from the zenith, by which its influence was measured. Even such astrological forces cannot separate Christians from this divine love. *from the love of God in Christ Jesus our Lord:* The love of God manifested in the Christ-event is thus the unshakable basis of Christian life and hope. This ending sums up the theme of this section (developed from 8:1); once again Paul ends with the refrain noted earlier (→ 50 above).

(Coetzer, W. C., "The Holy Spirit and the Eschatological View in Romans 8," *Neotestamentica* 15 [1981] 180-98. Dahl, N. A., "The Atonement—An Adequate Reward for the Akedah? (Ro 8:32)," *Neotestamentica et semitica* [Fest. M. Black; Edinburgh, 1969] 15-29. Goedt, M. de, "The Intercession of the Spirit in Christian Prayer," *Concilium* 79 [1972] 26-38. Gibbs, J. G., *Creation and Redemption* [NovTSup 26; Leiden, 1971] 34-47. Isaacs, M. E., *The Concept of the Spirit* [London, 1976]. Osten-Sacken, P. von der, *Römer 8 als Beispiel paulinischer Soteriologie* [FRLANT 112; Göttingen, 1975]. Rensburg, J. J. J. van, "The Children of God in Romans 8," *Neotestamentica* 15 [1981] 139-79. Vögtle, A., *Das Neue Testament und die Zukunft des Kosmos* [Düsseldorf, 1970].)

92   **(C) This Justification/Salvation Does Not Contradict God's Promises to Israel of Old (9:1–11:36).** Having developed in chap. 8 the theme announced in 5:1–11, Paul now turns to a further specific problem that his gospel of the new uprightness, obtained through faith in Christ Jesus, has raised. It is the relationship of Judaism to this mode of justification or salvation. Paul's discussion of this problem is heavily scriptural, as he tries to relate the teaching of the OT to his gospel. In effect, this part of Rom turns out to be a biblical illustration of the theme developed in part B, resembling somewhat the discussion of Abraham's justification and the law in chap. 4 and its relation to chaps. 1–3. For some commentators, however, Rom 9–11, though an authentic Pauline composition, is a "foreign body" in the letter, added perhaps by some later editor, since it is thought to interrupt the continuity of Rom 12–15 with Rom 5–8. The reasons, however, for regarding Rom 9–11 as a foreign body have scarcely been convincing. Centuries ago, J. Calvin succinctly stated the connection of Rom 9–11 with the preceding part of the letter: "If this [the teaching of chaps. 1–8] be the doctrine of the Law and the Prophets, why is it that the Jews reject it?" (*Comm. in Rom.* 9.1). The same question must have been put to Paul himself by contemporaries. This part of Rom may be subdivided into four sections: 9:1–5; 9:6–29; 9:30–10:21; 11:1–36. It is important to realize from the outset in this part of Rom that Paul's perspective is corporate; he is not discussing the responsibility of individuals. Moreover, he is not discussing the modern problem of the responsibility of the Jews for the death of Jesus. Neither of these questions should be imported into the interpretation of these chapters.

(Aageson, J. W., "Scripture and Structure in the Development of the Argument in Romans 9–11," *CBQ* 48 [1986] 265–89. Campbell, W. S., "The Freedom and Faithfulness of God in Relation to Israel," *JSNT* 13 [1981] 27–45. Davies, W. D., "Paul and the People of Israel," *NTS* 24 [1977–78] 4–39. Käsemann, E., *NTQT* 183–87. Lorenzi, L. de [ed.], *Die Israelfrage nach Rom 9–11* [Benedictina Abt. 3; Rome, 1977]. Munck, J., *Christ & Israel* [Phl, 1967]. Stendahl, K., *Paul among Jews and Gentiles* [Phl, 1976].)

93   **(a) PAUL'S LAMENT FOR HIS FORMER CORELIGIONISTS (9:1–5).** Paul begins this part of Rom with an expression of his anguish at the plight of the Jews, his "brothers" and "kinsmen," who have not accepted Jesus as God's Messiah. His sadness is poignant because he is aware of Israel's past prerogatives as God's chosen people. In expressing this anguish, he briefly states the problem that confronts him in preaching his gospel. **1.** *in Christ:* Paul speaks out sincerely as a Christian, without any resentment against Jews who may have caused him trouble or charged him with disloyalty (2 Cor 2:17; 11:31; 12:19). **3.** *accursed:* Lit., "anathema" (see comment on Gal 1:8). Paul would willingly undergo the worst possible fate, "to be cut off from Christ," for the sake of his fellow Jews. In this he echoes Moses' prayer for the unruly Israelites (Exod 32:32), "to be blotted out from the book of life," that they might be forgiven. **4.** *Israelites:* Instead of the common political title *Ioudaioi,* "Jews," Paul readily makes use of their honorific religious title, bestowed of old by Yahweh himself on his people (Gen 32:28; cf. 2 Cor 11:22). Then he proceeds to recount the historic prerogatives associated with this name—seven of them. *sonship:* The adoption of Israel as the "son of God" (Exod 4:22; Deut 14:1; Hos 11:1); see comment on *huiothesia,* 8:15. *glorious presence:* The second prerogative was the resplendent manifestation of Yahweh's presence to Israel in the desert and in the Jerusalem Temple (Exod 16:10; 40:34; 1 Kgs 8:10–11); see comment on *doxa,*

3:23. covenants: If the pl. *diathēkai* is read, the third prerogative would be the "covenants" made with the patriarchs (Gen 15:18; Exod 24:7–8; Sir 44:12,18). But important mss. (P[46], B, D, G) read the sg. *diathēkē,* which would then refer to the pact of Sinai. *the law:* The fourth prerogative was the *tôrâ,* the expression of God's will given to Moses (Exod 20:1–17; Deut 5:1–22). *the cult:* The awesome worship of Yahweh in the Temple, so different from the idolatrous worship of Israel's neighbors, which often included prostitution and human sacrifice, was Israel's fifth prerogative. *the promises:* The sixth prerogative consisted of the promises made to Abraham (Gen 12:2; 21:12), Moses (Deut 18:18–19), David (2 Sam 7:11–16). **5.** *the patriarchs:* Israel's seventh prerogative was its ancestral heritage, for it still worshiped the God of its fathers, Abraham, Isaac, and Jacob (see Rom 11:28). To this summary of Israel's historic privileges Paul himself adds an eighth, the climax: *Christ,* the descendant par excellence. The Messiah is their greatest title to glory, but unfortunately is not recognized as such.

94   *who is above all, God blessed forever! Amen:* Part of the problem in this half verse is the punctuation of it; there are four main possibilities: (1) ". . . from whom is the Christ by physical descent, who is above all things, God blessed forever! Amen." So the vast majority of the interpreters of Rom in the first eight centuries and many modern commentators (Althaus, Cranfield, Cullmann, Kuss, Leenhardt, Michel, Pesch, Nygren, Sanday-Headlam). This punctuation (comma before "who") proclaims Christ as God (though not as *ho theos*) and as blessed forever. (2) ". . . from whom is the Christ by physical descent. God who is over all be blessed forever! Amen." So a few writers from the 4th cent. on, Erasmus (who introduced the modern discussion), and many exegetes today (Barrett, Bultmann, Cerfaux, Dodd, Feine, Goodspeed, Käsemann, Lietzmann, Robinson, Wilckens; *NEB, RSV*). This punctuation (period before "God") creates a doxology addressed to God in the manner of Jewish doxologies; Paul blesses God at the mention of the Messiah. (3) ". . . from whom is the Christ by physical descent, who is over all. God be blessed forever! Amen." This punctuation (comma after "descent" and period before "God") divides the praise between Christ and God. (4) ". . . from whom is the Christ by physical descent, and to whom belongs God who is over all. Amen." So J. Weiss and the early K. Barth. This interpretation conjecturally inverts the words *ho ōn* (to *hōn ho theos*) and introduces yet another privilege, making God himself Israel's prerogative. The last two interpretations are improbable and have little to commend them; the choice lies between (1) and (2). The preference of (1) is mainly based on three considerations: (i) The normal sense of this half verse in its context; the phrase *to kata sarka,* "by physical descent," calls for some contrast. (ii) The normal wording of a doxology is not used; "blessed" should precede *theos.* In Paul's writings such a doxology is never joined asyndetically with what precedes or with the subject expressed first (see Gal 1:5; 2 Cor 11:31; Rom 1:25; 11:36; cf. Eph 3:21; 2 Tim 4:18; 1 Pet 4:11; Heb 13:21). (iii) The use of *theos* of Christ is compatible with Paul's teaching, even though the appellation is not found elsewhere. Other statements of his make this attribution not unjustifiable (see 1 Cor 8:6; Phil 2:6; cf. Titus 2:13 for a possible later extension of his thought). In any case, one cannot argue apodictically about this matter (see O. Cullmann, *Christology* 311–14; Cranfield, *Romans* 464–70; Kuss, *Römerbrief* 679–96; Michel, *Römer* 197–99).

95   **(b) ISRAEL'S PLIGHT IS NOT CONTRARY TO GOD'S DIRECTION OF HISTORY (9:6–29).** Paul's first explanation of the problem that caused his anguish emphasizes God's role in the predicament. (1) God's promises to Israel all stem from his gratuitous election of it as his people; hence his word has not failed (9:6-13). (2) Through the OT example of Moses with Pharaoh Paul insists on God's sovereign right over his creatures; he even makes use of human indocility to accomplish his ends (9:14-24). (3) God does not act arbitrarily, for Israel's call, infidelity, and remnant are all part of what has been announced in the OT (9:25-29).

96   **6-13.** The problem of Israel's rejection does not mean that God's word has failed; his promises stem from his gracious election of Israel as his people. **6.** *God's word has not failed:* This is the proposition of the subsection. Paul rejects the notion that the *logos* addressed to Israel in Yahweh's promises (9:4,9) has somehow been thwarted by his kinsmen's refusal to accept the Christ. *not all the descendants of Israel are really Israel:* The argument runs thus: God promised that Israel would be the recipient of blessings; but now that Gentiles are becoming the recipients, it might seem that God's promises vacillate. If Paul's development in Rom 1-8 depends on God's promises, then maybe it is all as shaky as they are. No, Paul replies, the OT promises were not made to Israel in the sense of physical descent, but to the Israel of faith. **7.** *children of Abraham:* Physical descent alone does not ensure inheritance, for Abraham had many sons (Gen 15:2; 16:15; 21:2; 25:1), but the patriarchal promise of salvation was transmitted only through Isaac (Gen 21:12). **8.** *children of God:* Abraham's true progeny are those born to him in virtue of a promise, not a connection *kata sarka*, "according to the flesh," i.e., physical descent. **9.** *the promise:* Paul is not thinking of the generic promise of numerous progeny (Gen 15:5) but of the specific promise of Isaac's birth (Gen 18:10,14 conflated). Had it depended on *sarx* alone, Isaac would never have been born to barren Sarah. **10.** *Rebecca too:* Another example confirms Paul's contention: God freely bestows favor on whom he wills. In this case it is no longer a choice between mothers (Sarah and Hagar, allegorized in Gal 4:21-31), but between sons of the same mother, between the twins Jacob and Esau, born to the patriarch Isaac. Yet God showed favor to Jacob, making a choice that freely conditioned Israel's history (Gen 25:21-23). **11.** *before the children had done anything, good or evil:* The choice of Jacob was entirely gratuitous and did not depend on merits or demerits; this verse is crucial to Paul's argument, for the call of Gentiles to Christian faith is equally gratuitous. *that God's elective plan might continue:* Lit., "that the purpose of God according to election might continue." Jacob was favored in order to make known the execution of a divine plan proceeding according to gratuitous election. **12.** *she was told:* See Gen 25:23. Of twins, the firstborn was to serve the other. Israel was descended from favored Jacob, and Esau became the ancestor of Edom (and the later Idumeans). The latter were never considered real Jews, even though John Hyrcanus I defeated them (*ca.* 108 BC) and forced them to be circumcised and to follow the Mosaic law; Josephus (*Ant.* 13.9.1 § 257; 14.15.2 § 403) calls them "half Jews." How different then was their destiny from that of Israel! **13.** *Jacob I loved:* See Mal 1:2. The prophet records Yahweh's love of Israel and then gives the reason for the five great reproaches that follow this protestation of love. Paul uses this quotation to emphasize Israel's role in the salvific plan in contrast to Edom's. Jacob and Esau are the representatives of their ethnic groups and are tools in the execution of the divine plan. *Esau I hated:* I.e., "loved less" — ancient Near Eastern exaggeration.

97   **14-24.** The example of Moses with Pharaoh also reveals God's sovereign right to choose. **14.** *is injustice in God then?:* God might seem to be involved in *adikia* in choosing one brother over the other — or in choosing Gentiles as his people after centuries of service from the Jews. **15.** *said to Moses:* Paul quotes Exod 33:19, Yahweh's answer to Moses after the incident of the golden calf. After such infidelity Yahweh could still manifest his mercy, favoring Israel as his chosen instrument. Through Israel he would continue to make his will known to humanity. This verse is explained in 9:18. **16.** *depends on God's mercy:* Paul's conclusion is drawn from the fact that only God's "mercy" is mentioned in the OT text cited. Without it all human efforts are in vain. Paul, however, does not say that once given God's assistant grace, such efforts are useless; elsewhere he stresses the need of them. His emphasis is rather on God's grace because of the specific problem that he is treating. **17.** *Scripture says to Pharaoh:* Whereas the transcendent God of Israel spoke directly to Moses (9:15), he speaks to the heathen only indirectly, through Scripture. *showing my power in (dealing with) you:* See Exod 9:16, esp. according to the LXX, ms. A. The Pharaoh thus became an instrument in God's plan, just as Moses was. His very obstinacy was a means God used to deliver Israel. Ultimately, the hardhearted Pharaoh contributed to the proclamation of God's name in the world. **18.** *hardens the heart:* In the OT the hardening of Pharaoh's heart is ascribed at times to God (Exod 4:21; 7:3; 9:12) and at times to Pharaoh himself (Exod 7:14; 8:15,19,32). The "hardening of the heart" by God is a protological way of expressing divine reaction to persistent human obstinacy against him — a sealing of a situation that he did not create. It is not the result of some arbitrary or even planned divine decision; it is the OT way of expressing God's recognition of a situation arising from a creature that rejects divine invitation. But it brings out God's utter control of human history. The exodus from Egypt was a phase in salvific history, and Pharaoh who opposed Israel's departure was a figure setting the stage for the divine control of events. See further E. Brandenburger, *ZTK* 82 (1985) 1-47. **19.** *why does he still find fault?:* If God can make use of human indocility to accomplish his ends, why should he complain about human beings? Recall the objections in 6:1,15. **20.** *who are you?:* Paul does not try to silence his imaginary objector, but rather to put the discussion on its proper level. God's control of the world cannot be judged by a human myopic view. *can what is molded say to its molder?:* A familiar OT figure is used; see Isa 29:16; 45:9; 64:8; Jer 18:6; Wis 15:7; cf. 1QS 11:22. Paul adapts it to his own purpose. The figure is intended to depict God as creator and governor of the universe. Ancient potters used a wheel, set in rapid motion by the foot, while deft fingers quickly drew from the shapeless lump of clay slender and exquisite vessels. From such a feat the ancients derived the notion of God as a potter fashioning the world and human beings as he would (see *ANEP* 569); it stressed God's power, dominion, and freedom. *why have you made me thus?:* Not "Why did you make me clay?" but "Why did you make me an unshapely pot rather than a beautiful vase?" The emphasis is on the function of the molded object. **21.** *lump:* The Gk *phyrama* was translated as Lat *massa*. From this came the pejorative term *massa damnata* in the predestinarian controversies (see Augustine, *Ep.* 190.3-9).

98   **22.** *desiring:* Though some commentators (Jerome, Thomas Aq., Barrett, Cranfield, Michel) understand the ptc. *thelōn* causally, "because he desired," it seems better in the context (especially in view of the phrase "with much patience") to understand it concessively, "though he desired," i.e., though his anger might have led him to make known his power, his lovingkindness restrained him. God gave Pharaoh time to repent. *vessels of wrath:* Paul uses a phrase from Jer 50:25, which suits the pottery context (9:21, "vessel"). At the same time he plays on the wider sense of *skeuos,* which can also mean "object, tool, instrument" (see A. T. Hanson, *JTS* 32 [1981] 433-43). Pharaoh was an "object" toward which divine anger could be displayed. *prepared for destruction:* The pf. ptc. expresses the state in which such "vessels" find themselves, "suited, fitted out" for the rubbish heap. This verse expresses God's radical incompatibility with rebellious, sinful human beings. It also contains a nuance of predestination, and Paul's formulation is more generic than the example with which he began; this is why his words served in the later predestinarian controversies. One should, however, not lose sight of his corporate perspective. **23.** *to make known the wealth of his glory:* Those chosen for a role in salvation history have been destined by God for a share in his abundant glory (see comments on 3:23,29); this destiny is not limited to the Jewish people. But, as 11:22 shows, it is not an absolute predestination. If God has been patient, it is because he wants to allow Israel time to repent so that he might manifest his mercy toward it all the more. **24.** *even us whom he called:* Anacoluthon. To the questions posed in vv 19-21 Paul never gives a direct answer; he merely insists on God's freedom of election and his patience in waiting for instruments he would use to manifest their utility. The "vessels of mercy" include not only Jews, but Gentiles too.

99   **25-29.** Israel's call, infidelity, and remnant are all announced in the OT itself. Paul makes use again of the literary subform "testimonia" (see comment on 3:10). The conflated quotations are derived from Hos and Isa (mentioned in v 27). **25-26.** See Hos 2:25 (which Paul adapts to his own purpose, since his wording agrees with neither the MT nor the LXX nor any ancient version) and 2:1 (from the LXX). In the original text the words refer to God's restoration of the ten tribes of Israel after they have committed "adultery" (= idolatry) and ceased to be his people. Hosea promised their restoration, but for Paul the words refer to the Gentiles. As he applies them, they illustrate God's election, and especially his choice of those who were unworthy to become the privileged ones. **27.** *Isaiah:* See Isa 10:22-23 (abridging the LXX). Paul is interested in only the one phrase "a remnant shall be saved." Through all of Israel's infidelities and consequent punishments a ray of hope has gleamed. The words were used originally by Isaiah of the Assyrian captivity; Paul applies them to the Jews called to accept Christ and to the remnant that did so. **29.** See Isa 1:9 (according to the LXX). The prophet was speaking of the punishment of faithless Israel. The burden of these OT quotations is that the OT, the book that gives Israel its basis of hope, has testified that Israel would fare as did Sodom and Gomorrah of old, except for a remnant that would preserve its name and seed. See J. A. Battle, *GTJ* 2 (1981) 115-29.

100   (c) ISRAEL'S FAILURE IS DERIVED FROM ITS OWN REFUSAL (9:30-10:21). Paul has concluded the first part of his argument, and he now argues that the cause of Israel's failure is to be found not with God but in Israel itself. His argument proceeds in four steps. (1) Israel has preferred its own way of uprightness to that of God (9:31-33). (2) Paul expresses his sorrow that Israel has failed to recognize that Christ is the end of the Law and that uprightness has been made attainable through him (10:1-4). (3) The old way of attaining uprightness was difficult, whereas the new way is easy, within the reach of all and announced to all, as Scripture shows (10:5-13). (4) Israel has not taken advantage of this opportunity offered by the prophets and the gospel; and so the fault lies with her (10:14-21).

31-33. Israel has preferred its own way of uprightness. **31.** *have obtained it:* Paul stresses the irony of the situation in that Gentiles have succeeded in the pursuit of uprightness by putting their faith in Christ Jesus. **32.** *faith . . . deeds:* See 3:20,28; and comment on 2:15. **33.** A conflation of Isa 28:16 and 8:14-15 disregards the contexts of the original and strings together phrases that makes the OT almost say the opposite of what it actually says. The stone laid by Yahweh in Zion (the eastern hill of Jerusalem on which the Temple was built) was a symbol of salvation for those who trusted in him. As Paul uses it, the "stone" refers to Christ, and neglect of him makes the stone a stumbling block. But those who believe in him (the remnant and the Gentiles) will not come to grief over that stone. The Essenes of Qumran also applied Isa 28:16 to themselves, looking upon their community as a temple (1QS 8:5-8).

(Barrett, C. K., "Romans 9:30-10:21: Fall and Responsibility of Israel," *Die Israelfrage* 109-21. Bring, R., "Paul and the Old Testament," *ST* 25 [1971] 21-60. Cranfield, C. E. B., "Romans 9:30-10:4," *Int* 34 [1980] 70-74; "Some Notes on Romans 9:30-33," *Jesus und Paulus* [Fest. W. G. Kümmel; Göttingen, 1975] 35-43. Refoulé, F., "Note sur Romains IX, 30-33," *RB* 92 [1985] 161-86.)

101   **1-4.** An expression of sorrow opens chap. 10, as Paul states that Israel has failed to recognize that uprightness comes through Christ, the end of the law. **1.** *that they may be saved:* Paul's prayer explicitly includes the Jews in his view of God's plan of salvation (cf. 1 Thess 5:9; Rom 1:16). **2.** *a zeal for God:* Paul could speak from experience (Gal 1:13-14; Phil 3:9; cf. 1 Macc 2:26-27). *not intelligent:* Lit., "not according to knowledge" (*epignōsis*), i.e., a real knowledge that recognizes the actual relation of humanity to God as it has now been revealed in Christ Jesus. **3.** *in their ignorance of God's uprightness:* This has often been understood of a communication of uprightness to human beings, i.e., the Jews do not realize that the genuine status of uprightness before God is not achieved by their efforts but is conferred by God as a gift. This is the sense of Phil 3:9, "an uprightness (that comes) from God" (cf. 2 Cor 5:21; → Pauline Theology, 82:39). But Paul does not use the prep. phrase here and speaks rather of a misunderstanding of "God's uprightness," the divine attribute (as elsewhere in Rom: 1:17; 3:5,21-26). The Jews have missed the real meaning of God's acquitting power and hence have refused to submit to it. **4.** *Christ is the end of the law:* The meaning of this cl. is quite disputed. Gk *telos* can mean (1) "termination, cessation," (2) "last part, conclusion," or (3) "goal, purpose, *finis*" (BAGD 811). Meaning (2) is irrelevant here, and the dispute centers on whether Christ is the "termination" of the law or the "goal or purpose" of the law. In the first sense *telos* is understood temporally, the "end" of the period of *tôrâ;* Christ would be the termination of all human striving to achieve uprightness before God through observance of the Mosaic law (so *NEB,* Bultmann, Käsemann, Pesch, Robinson). Even though Paul never uses this cl. in Gal, this sense of it would suit Gal 4:2-6 (→ Pauline Theology, 82:96-97). But one may ask whether it suits the discussion in Rom, and hence other commentators prefer the third sense: Christ would be the goal of the law, that at which it was aimed in a purposive or final sense (so Cerfaux, Cranfield, Flückiger, Howard). This final sense is based on the connection between 10:4 and 9:31-33, where the "pursuit" of uprightness by Gentiles implies a "goal." Again, the "zeal" in 10:2 implicates this sense, and this is probably the reason why Paul insists in 3:31 that his gospel of justification by grace through faith "upholds" or "confirms" the law. For a right understanding of Pauline faith, "working itself out through love" (Gal 5:6), which is "the fulfillment of the law" (Rom 13:10; → Pauline Theology 82:98), explains how Paul could not only regard Christ as the goal of the law but also look upon uprightness through faith in him as a way to fulfill the law itself and uphold all that it stood for. *for the uprightness of anyone who has faith:* The prized status of uprightness before God is now available to everyone through faith (see 1:16).

(Campbell, W. S., "Christ the End of the Law: Romans 10:4," *Studia biblica III* [JSOTSup 3; Sheffield, 1978] 73–81. Cranfield, C. E. B., "St. Paul and the Law," *SJT* 17 [1964] 43–68. Flückiger, F., "Christus, des Gesetzes *telos*," *TZ* 11 [1955] 153–57. Howard, G. E., "Christ the End of the Law," *JBL* 88 [1969] 331–37. Refoulé, F., "Romains, X,4: Encore une fois," *RB* 91 [1984] 321–50. Rhyne, C. T., "*Nomos dikaiosynēs* and the Meaning of Romans 10:4," *CBQ* 47 [1985] 486–99.)

102   **5–13.** The new way of uprightness, open to all, is easy, as Scripture shows. **5.** *Moses writes:* Lev 18:5, also quoted in Gal 3:12, promises life to those who strive for legal uprightness. The practical observance of the law's prescriptions was a necessary condition for the life so promised. Implied in the quotation is the arduous nature of that condition. In contrast to such a demand, the new way of uprightness does not ask of human beings anything so arduous. To illustrate his point, Paul alludes to Moses' words in Deut 30:11–14. Just as Moses tried to convince the Israelites that the observance of the law did not demand that one scale the heights or descend to the depths, so Paul plays on Moses' words, applying them in an accommodated sense to Christ himself. The heights have been scaled and the depths have been plumbed, for Christ has come to the world of humanity and has been raised from the dead. No one is asked to bring about an incarnation or a resurrection; one is asked only to accept in faith what has already been done for humanity and to identify oneself with Christ incarnate and risen. Paul adds an allusion to Ps 107:26 in his midrashic explanation of Deut. In this explanation "Christ" is substituted for the "word" of the Torah. **9.** *if you acknowledge:* One must utter the basic Christian confession of faith and mean it. Paul proceeds to cite the creedal (perhaps even kerygmatic) formula of the early Palestinian church, *Kyrios Iēsous,* "Jesus is Lord" (cf. 1 Cor 12:3; Phil 2:11). An inward faith is demanded that will guide the whole person; but it also includes an assent to an expression of that faith. Paul again asserts the activity of the Father in Christ's resurrection (→ Pauline Theology, 82:58–59). **10.** This verse formulates rhetorically the relation of human uprightness and salvation to faith and the profession of it. The balance stresses different aspects of the one basic act of personal adherence to Christ and its effect. One should not overstress the differences between justification and salvation. **11.** *no one who believes in him will be put to shame:* Isa 28:16 is used again; cf. 9:33. Paul modifies the quotation by adding *pas,* "all," thus emphasizing the universality of the application: "not . . . all" = "no one." In Isa the words referred to the precious cornerstone laid by Yahweh in Zion; they are accommodated by Paul to faith in Christ and used as an assurance of salvation for the Christian believer. The addition of *pas* prepares for the next verse. **12.** *no distinction between Jew and Greek:* All have the opportunity to share alike in the new uprightness through faith (3:22–23). *the same Lord:* At first, *Kyrios* seems to refer to Yahweh, since Paul uses Jewish expressions, "the Lord of all" (Josephus, *Ant.* 20.4.2 § 90), "call upon the name of" (1 Sam 12:17–18; 2 Sam 22:7), and refers explicitly in v 13 to Joel 3:5. But in the context (esp. after 10:9) *Kyrios*

can refer only to Jesus, who is the risen Lord of Jew and Greek (cf. 9:5; Phil 2:9–11). In the OT those who "call upon the name of the Lord" denoted sincere and pious Israelites; in the NT it is transferred to Christians. Verses 12–13 are an eloquent witness to the early church's worship of Christ as *Kyrios.*

103   **14–21.** Israel, however, did not take advantage of the opportunity offered to it by the prophets and the gospel; so the fault lies with it. The opportunity to believe in Christ was offered to all, but especially to Israel; it cannot claim that it did not hear his gospel. Paul proposes to himself four difficulties or objections, perhaps echoing comments from missionary sermons among Jews, and to each he proposes a brief answer by quoting Scripture: (1) How can people believe the gospel unless it has been fully preached? (10:14–15). (2) But it has not been accepted by everybody! (10:16–17). (3) But perhaps the Jews did not hear it! (10:18). (4) Perhaps they did not understand! (10:19–21).

104   **14.** *have not believed:* The first difficulty is multiple and begins with the assumption that the cult of Christ must be founded on belief in him. *whom they have never heard:* The question does not refer to Jews of Palestine, who might have witnessed the ministry of Jesus, but to those who had not listened to him directly. *unless someone preaches to them:* Faith is founded on an authorized preaching, on the testimony of those who have been charged with the mission to make known the word of God. Here, as in v 17, the initial step in all faith is a "hearing" of the proposed message; the object of faith, propositionally formulated, is thus first presented (→ Pauline Theology, 82:109). **15.** *unless they are sent:* Authoritative preaching, the basis of faith, presupposes a mission. In expressing the latter, Paul uses the vb. *apostellein,* alluding to the apostolic origin of the testimony of the Christian church and its authorized preaching of the Christ-event. To this objection Paul answers with Isa 52:7 (in a form closer to the MT than to the LXX). *who bring good news:* In Isa the text refers to the good news announced to Jews left in ruined Jerusalem that deliverance from Babylonian Captivity was coming and that Jerusalem's restoration was close at hand. As used by Paul, the text takes on the overtones of his good news, the "gospel." His answer to the first difficulty, then, is to quote Isaiah and show that the "gospel" has indeed been preached to Israel. **16.** *not everyone has heeded the good news:* The second difficulty. Paul replies by quoting Isa 53:1. Indirectly, he states that, because not everyone among the Jews has accepted the good news, it does not mean that it has not been preached to them, for a comparable refusal to believe has been foreseen by Isaiah in his own mission. **17.** *through Christ's message:* This vague expression can be variously interpreted, and Paul does not explain it. It could mean the message that Christ himself brought or (more likely in this context) the message about Christ. See R. R. Rickards, *BT* 27 (1976) 447–48. **18.** *have they not heard?:* The third difficulty, the sense of which is: Maybe they have not had the opportunity to hear the good news; maybe the apostolic preachers have not done their job. Paul answers with Ps 19:5. In the original the psalmist sings of nature proclaiming the glory of God everywhere. Paul accommodates the words to the preaching of the gospel. In effect, he denies that Israel has lacked the opportunity to believe in Christ. **19.** *did Israel not understand?:* The fourth difficulty: Maybe apostolic preachers spoke in an unintelligible fashion, and Israel did not comprehend their message. Again Paul answers with Scripture, quoting Deut 32:21 and Isa 65:1–2, first the Torah, then the Prophets. The words of Deut are from the Song of Moses, in which Yahweh — through Moses — tries to educate Israel and announces that it will be humiliated by heathens. In thus quoting Deut, Paul implies a comparison of Israel's situation with what it was at the time of the exile. If it was humiliated then, how much greater should its humiliation be now; Gentiles understand the gospel message, but Israel is uncomprehending. **20.** In the original context of Isa 65:1–2 the same people are envisaged by the prophet's words in vv 1–2, be they Samaritans, apostate Jews, or simply Jews (disputed among OT commentators). But Paul, influenced by the LXX that speaks of *ethnos,* "nation," in v 1 and of *laos,* "people," in v 2, splits up the reference in the two verses. The first is applied to the Gentiles, the second to the Jews. The contrast is obvious between the Gentiles, "the foolish nation," accepting Christ in faith, and the Jews, "a disobedient and obstinate people," refusing belief in him. So ends Paul's indictment of Israel.

(Black, M., "The Christological Use of the Old Testament in the New Testament," *NTS* 18 [1971–72] 1–14. Delling, G., "'Nahe ist dir das Wort,'" *TLZ* 99 [1974] 401–12. Howard, G. E., "The Tetragram and the New Testament," *JBL* 96 [1977] 63–83. Lindemann, A., "Die Gerechtigkeit aus dem Gesetz," *ZNW* 73 [1982] 231–50. Suggs, M. J. "'The Word is Near You': Romans 10:6–10 within the Purpose of the Letter," *Christian History and Interpretation* [Fest. J. Knox; ed. W. R. Farmer, *et al.;* Cambridge, 1967] 289–32.)

105   (d) ISRAEL'S FAILURE IS PARTIAL AND TEMPORARY (11:1–36). The picture painted thus far in chaps. 9–10 by Paul is not pleasant: Israel's disbelief suits the plan of God based on gratuitous election (chap. 9); but actually its cause rests not with him but with Israel itself (chap. 10). But even in 9:27 Paul had hinted at a ray of hope, when he said that "a remnant of them shall be saved." Now he returns to this aspect of the problem and further explains that Israel's disbelief is only partial (11:1–10), that it is only temporary (11:11–24), and that in God's plan mercy is to be shown to all, the Jews included (11:25–32). At the end of this section Paul bursts into a hymn to the merciful wisdom of God (11:33–36).

106   1–10. Israel's disbelief is only partial. **1.** *has God rejected his people?:* If God's plan is one of gratuitous election and Israel has been unfaithful, and if Gentiles are now accepting the gospel, whereas Israel is not, then apparently God has repudiated those who were once his chosen people (cf. Ps 94:14). *by no means!:* Emphatic, almost indignant denial; see comment on 3:4. *Israelite:* See comment on 9:4. *descendant of Abraham:* "According to the flesh"; see comment on 1:3. *of the tribe of Benjamin:* See Phil 3:5. Benjamin was often regarded as the most Israelite of the tribes, the "beloved of the Lord" (Deut 33:12); from it came Saul, the first king of the undivided monarchy, Paul's namesake. Paul and other Jewish Christians have been called and invited to belief in Christ; this shows that God has not rejected his people. **2.** *Elijah:* See 1 Kgs 19:9–18. After his journey of 40 days and nights to reach Horeb, the mount of God, the prophet took shelter in a cave where he complained bitterly to Yahweh of Israel's infidelities. Yahweh announced the coming chastisement of his people, but also the deliverance of 7000 in Israel who had not bent their knees to Baal. Just as Elijah was not alone, so Paul is not alone among the Jews in his belief in Christ Jesus. **3.** Paul uses 1 Kgs 19:10 in abbreviated and inverted form. The example of Elijah is drawn from Israel's history to reveal God's plan in the present situation too. **4.** Here 1 Kgs 19:18 is quoted freely, according to neither the MT nor the LXX. Paul is interested in only one point: 7000 remained faithful to Yahweh. Israel has not been entirely repudiated, then or now. **5.** *a remnant, chosen*

by grace: Lit., "a remnant according to the selection of grace," i.e., without any regard of their fidelity to the law. The Essenes of Qumran also regarded themselves as *běhîrê rāṣôn,* "those chosen by (divine) benevolence" (1QS 8:6; cf. E. Vogt, "'Peace among Men of God's Good Pleasure' Lk 2.14," *The Scrolls and the New Testament* [ed. K. Stendahl; NY, 1957] 114–17). **6.** *not on the basis of deeds:* See 3:24; 4:4; 9:16. The existence of this remnant is evidence of God's benevolence rather than of human merit. **7.** *Israel failed to get what it desired:* The majority of the Jews apart from the remnant did not attain the uprightness they pursued (9:30–31). This is the source of the sorrow that Paul expressed in 9:1–2. *but those whom God chose attained it:* Lit., "the election," i.e., the abstract for the concrete is used. Though those chosen embrace the Gentiles and the remnant, Paul is thinking only of the latter when he contrasts it with *hoi loipoi,* "the rest." *became callous:* Lit., "were hardened." This effect on the Jews results from their resistance to the gospel; but even it has its providential function in God's plan. **8.** *as it is written:* See comment on 1:17. On the conflated OT quotations used here, see comment on 3:10. Paul links together Deut 29:3; Isa 29:10; Ps 69:23–24. The words of Deut 29:3, not quoted literally, were addressed by Moses to Israel, which had witnessed all the portents sent by God against Pharaoh on its behalf but had never appreciated their full significance: "But to this day Yahweh has not given you a mind to understand, or eyes to see, or ears to hear." Paul modifies his free quotation with an addition from Isa 29:10, "a spirit of stupor," drawn from a passage in which Isaiah spoke of the spiritual blindness and perversity of Israel. The conflated texts serve Paul's purpose of describing Israel's reaction to Christ, but one should not miss the way in which Paul uses the OT (see J. A. Fitzmyer, *ESBNT* 44–45; J. Schmid, *BZ* 3 [1959] 161–73). **9.** *David:* David's name stands at the head of Ps 69 in the OT, where it is a lament for deliverance from personal tribulation. The catchword bond linking these verses with the preceding is "eyes that see not." One need not try to decide to what the other details refer (feasting, etc.); the main point is the sealing by God of the situation that exists (see comment on 9:18) — a situation that is neither entire nor final.

107   11–24. Israel's disbelief is only temporary. **11.** *stumbled so as to fall:* Israel has stumbled over Christ, but it has not fallen down completely so that it cannot regain its footing. Indeed, its stumbling has been providential in that the apostles turned from it to the Gentiles (cf. Acts 13:45–48; 18:6). In the long run Israel's stumbling would arouse in it a jealousy of the Gentiles, who were attaining the uprightness before God that Israel itself had been pursuing. **12.** *their full number:* The meaning of Gk *plērōma* is disputed. It most likely means "that which is brought to fullness, full number, complement," as in 11:25. But some commentators understand it as "their fulfilling (the divine demand)" (see BAGD 672). Paul hints at the untold benefits for the world that would come with the full acceptance of Jesus as Messiah by the Jews; if their action has so far resulted in such incredible benefits, then what will their full acceptance mean?

108   13. *to you Gentiles:* See 1:5. The Gentiles are not to be presumptuous or haughty because they have accepted Christ; they have no right to look down on Israel. *apostle of the Gentiles:* The epithet commonly given to Paul stems from his own writings (see Gal 2:7–8; cf. Acts 9:15; 22:21). He spends himself in this ministry with one purpose: to stimulate his kinsmen and thus save some of them. Though a Christian, Paul still looks on himself as a member of the race of the Jews. He calls them literally "my flesh," and thereby gives vivid expression of

his solidarity with them. **15.** *their rejection:* Though some commentators (Cranfield, Wilckens) take this as an objective gen., God's (temporary) "rejection of them," it is better understood as a subjective gen., the Jews' rejection of the gospel, in view of what Paul exclaims in 11:1. *the reconciliation of the world:* See 2 Cor 5:19. The providential aspect of Israel's "rejection" has been the reconciliation of all others to God — and possibly even a cosmic extension of that effect of reconciliation to the whole universe (→ Pauline Theology, 82:72). This reconciliation will have the effect of making Jews jealous and of drawing them to Christ. *life from the dead:* The meaning of this phrase is quite disputed. Origen, Cyril of Alexandria, many medieval commentators, Barrett, Cranfield, Käsemann, Lagrange, Lietzmann, Lyonnet, Michel, and Sanday-Headlam, understand *zōē ek nekrōn* to refer to the general resurrection of the dead at the end of time. If the conversion of the Gentiles represents the first phase of redemption, viz., "reconciliation," then the "acceptance" of the gospel by the Jews will represent its definitive stage. Appeal is made to vv 25–26 to support this reference to the general resurrection at the parousia; commentators who use it often add that Paul is not necessarily asserting a temporal connection here. Other interpreters, such as Theophylact, Photius, Euthymius, Cornely, Huby, and Wilckens, understand *zōē ek nekrōn* in a figurative sense: "The conversion of Israel en masse will be for the Gentiles an event of great utility and happiness" (Huby). This is preferred because Paul does not write *anastasis nekrōn,* the expression that he uses elsewhere for "resurrection of the dead" (1 Cor 15:12,13, 21,42; Rom 6:5), when he means that. Still others, such as Leenhardt and Stanley, consider the image to refer to the Jewish people themselves; their acceptance of the gospel will mean for them the passage from the status of death to life. There would be an allusion to the effect of their identification with Christ, as in baptism (6:4), and above all to the new life that would be theirs as a result of their "acceptance." The last interpretation seems preferable. **16.** *if the first handful of dough is consecrated:* Paul's figure is mixed (dough and root). First, he means, "If the firstfruits are holy, then the whole lump of dough is," referring to Num 15:18–21. Because the first portion of the meal is set aside for the Lord (i.e., given to the Temple priests [Josephus, *Ant.* 4.4.4. § 70]), the whole batch acquires a legal purity, making it fit to be consumed by the people of God (cf. Lev 19:23–25). Then he uses another image. *if the root is consecrated:* See Jer 11:16–17. This image expresses the same idea as the previous one, but to what does "root" refer? For Origen and Theodore of Mopsuestia the first handful of dough and the root are Christ, whose holiness guarantees blessings for all Israel. For Barrett and Weiss they refer rather to the converted remnant — an interpretation that suits the preceding context. For Käsemann, Lagrange, Michel, Pesch, Sanday-Headlam, and Wilckens the "root" means the patriarchs, because in v 17 it will be used again to designate ancient Israel, onto which the Gentiles have been grafted. Either of these interpretations is possible, but perhaps it is better to divide the images between two interpretations (with Cranfield, Leenhardt): the first handful of dough representing the "remnant," which has already accepted Christ, and the root representing the "patriarchs." Thus a link is established with both the preceding and following contexts.
109   **17.** *some of the branches were broken off:* Paul, still addressing Gentile Christians, warns them not to be smug about their favored situation. They are not to look down on the unbelieving Jews who have been cut off from the source of life. *a wild olive shoot:* In part the figure depends on the OT (Jer 11:16; Hos 14:6), but also on the

practice among ancient horticulturists of grafting a young wild olive branch onto an old, worn-out olive tree that had been giving good fruit (Columella, *De re rustica* 5.9,16). The Gentiles are the wild olive shoot grafted onto Israel, in place of the lopped off branches (= unbelieving Jews). **18.** *the root supports you:* Israel of old still occupies the privileged position of the carrier of salvation to the world. **20.** *that is true:* Paul does not deny that the defection of Israel has facilitated the conversion of the Gentiles, but Israel was not broken off in order that the Gentiles might be grafted onto the stock. Rather, its disbelief has resulted in their being lopped off, but that had no intrinsic connection with the election of the Gentiles actually grafted on in its place. *only through faith you stand where you do:* The situation of the Gentiles is owing to God's gratuitous election and their response in faith, not to any merits of which Gentile Christians can boast. **21.** *did not spare the natural branches:* If branches belonging to the tree *kata physin,* "by nature," could be lopped off (because of infidelity), so can those that have been simply grafted onto it (if they prove unfaithful). **22.** *God's kindness and severity:* These two notions come closest to what has traditionally been called God's "mercy and justice," but to express them Paul uses Gk *chrēstotēs* and *apotomia.* Significantly, he does not use *eleos* or *dikaiosynē,* which because of their OT background have a notably different connotation (→ Pauline Theology, 82:39). *provided you continue in his kindness:* God's election, though gratuitous, is conditioned by the Gentile Christians' responsible fulfillment of their obligations. **23.** *will be grafted on:* Paul finally explains how the lopped off branches will be able to find life in the parent stock of Abraham. *God has the power to graft them on again:* A fortiori — if he were able to graft on a wild olive branch. Throughout the argument based on the wild olive shoot Paul implies that the lopped off natural branches have not yet been cast on the rubbish heap. Israel has not been definitively rejected by God (11:1). **24.** *from a wild olive tree . . . onto a cultivated one:* The contrast suggests the transcendent nature of the vocation to which the Gentile Christians have been called. The restoration of the Jews, however, will be easier than the call of the Gentiles. So Israel's rejection is not definitive, but temporary.

(Bourke, M. M., *A Study of the Metaphor of the Olive Tree in Romans XI* [Studies in Sacred Theology 2/3; Washington, 1947]. Rengstorf, K. H., "Das Ölbaum-Gleichnis in Rom 11.16ff," *Donum gentilicium* [Fest D. Daube; ed. E. Bammel, *et al.;* Oxford, 1978] 127–64.)

110   **25–32.** In God's plan mercy is to be shown to all, including the Jews. **25.** *wise in your own way of thinking:* Gentile Christians should not conclude that their view of human history is the only valid one; Paul prefers to disclose to them aspects of the divine *mystērion* long hidden in God but now revealed (→ Pauline Theology, 82:33–34). This "secret" has three aspects: (1) the "partial insensibility" of Israel (see comment on 11:7; Paul reverts to what he said in 11:1–10); (2) "the full complement of the Gentiles" (the third aspect will await the *plērōma* of the Gentiles, i.e., their "entering" as a graft onto the stock of the olive tree that is Israel; see comment on 11:12). (3) **26.** *in this way all Israel will be saved:* Thus Paul expresses his firm conviction about the definitive corporate destiny of his kinsmen — an echo of Isa 60:21–22. But *how* will they all "be saved"? Two explanations are current: (1) theological and (2) christological. According to the first, espoused by F. Mussner (*Kairos* 18 [1976] 241–55) and K. Stendahl (*Paul among Jews and Gentiles* [Phl, 1976] 3–4, the vb. *sōthēsetai* would be taken as a theological passive (*ZBG* § 236), "will be saved," i.e., by God, in a merciful act independent of any acceptance of Jesus as the Messiah or of a mass conversion prior to the parousia. They would be rescued from their "partial hardening" (v 25c) by "the Deliverer" (v 26b; cf. Isa 59:20), who would be Yahweh himself, since Christ has not been mentioned in this entire section since 10:17. The "covenant" (v 27) would be understood as one different from Jer 31:33. This would then be a salvation of the Jews apart from Christ. According to the christological explanation, espoused by W. D. Davies (*NTS* 24 [1977–78] 23–29) and many modern commentators, the vb. *sōzein* would be used in the sense of 1 Cor 9:22 (with a nuance of conversion); the "Deliverer" of Isa 59:20 would be applied to Christ at the parousia (as in 1 Thess 1:10); and the "covenant" of v 27 would be that of Jer 31:33 in its definitive stage. Thus, at the parousia "all Israel" would be pardoned its culpable "hardening," would accept Jesus as the Messiah, and would have its sins "taken away" in the fulfillment of the covenant of Jer 31:33 (cited in 1 Cor 11:25; 2 Cor 3:6). The christological explanation is preferable, because Paul is scarcely envisaging two different kinds of salvation—one achieved by God for Jews and one by Christ for Gentiles; that would be to go against his entire thesis about justification by grace through faith. Earlier in this section Paul quoted the OT against Israel; now he does so in its favor. The quotation is again composite; see comment on 3:10. Isa 59:20–21 (quoted according to the LXX with slight changes) is joined to Isa 27:9 to illustrate the "secret" hidden in God and now revealed. The words show that God, in announcing his new covenant, reckoned with Israel's infidelity; they are now applied to Christ. See further C. M. Horne, *JETS* 21 (1978) 329–43; D. G. Johnson, *CBQ* 46 (1984) 91–103; F. Refoulé, "... *et ainsi tout Israel sera sauvé: Romains 11,25–32* (LD 117; Paris, 1984); P. Stuhlmacher, "Zur Interpretation von Römer 11,25–32," *Probleme biblischer Theologie* (ed. H. W. Wolff; Munich, 1971) 555–70. **28.** *they are enemies of God:* Because of their temporary and partial failure to accept Jesus as Messiah. *on your account:* A summation of 11:11–14. *they are beloved by him because of their forefathers:* The election of Israel is irrevocable in human history, manifested in the favor shown to its patriarchs—a claim that the Gentiles lack. **30.** *you once disobeyed God:* Paul's view of the former Gentiles agrees with that of his Jewish kinsmen. Gentile disobedience was disbelief in God. The attitude of Jews toward Christ represents the same sort of disobedience. But as Jewish disobedience has been a factor in the display of divine mercy toward Gentiles, so the mercy shown to the latter will be used toward the Jews. **32.** *God has consigned all human beings to disobedience:* All, Jews and Greeks, have as groups been unfaithful to God, who makes use of such infidelity to manifest to all of them his bounty and mercy—to reveal just what kind of God he really is (see 3:21–26; Gal 3:22). Now Paul passes to an exclamation about the merciful wisdom of God.

111   **33–36.** Hymn to the merciful wisdom of God. **33.** *how inexhaustible are God's resources:* Paul exclaims, not in awe and fear but in wonder and gratitude, at the boundless providence of God in arranging the mutual assistance of Jews and Gentiles in attaining salvation. Israel's role in the divine plan of salvation may never have been suspected otherwise. **34.** Paul joins Isa 40:13 and Job 41:3(?) to stress that God is no one's debtor, either for his plans or for his gifts to humanity. All proceeds from his gracious bounty; he needs neither consultants nor research assistants. Paul cites the Isa text according to the LXX, with a slight change of word order. In Isa the words refer to the deliverance of the Jews from exile by Yahweh and extol his greatness for it. The passage in Job is not certain; 41:3 is corrupt in the

MT, and it is almost impossible to decide what text Paul might have been following. Some commentators think that he is alluding to Job 35:7 or 41:1. **36.** A doxology to God (the Father) as the creator, sustainer, and goal of the universe. The prep. *ex* denotes "origin," *dia* (with the gen.) the "originator" of an action or condition, and *eis* (with the acc.) the "end, goal." The prayer expresses the absolute dependence of all creation on God. Paul's formulation may be influenced by Hellenistic philosophical thought (cf. Marcus Aurelius, *Medit.* 4.23; H. Lietzmann, *An die Römer* 107). Cf. 1 Cor 8:6; 11:12.

112   **(III) Part II: Hortatory Section—The Demands of Upright Life in Christ (12:1–15:13).** Paul now adds to the doctrinal section an exhortation addressed to the Roman church, even though it is practically unknown to him. Rom 12–13 form a catechetical unit, rather similar to 1 Thess 4–5. It reflects the tendency in the early church to join parenesis to a kerygmatic or doctrinal exposé. This hortatory section is not exactly an ethical treatise, for it is quite unsystematic and somewhat rambling. As it stands in Rom, it implies that Mosaic legal prescriptions may no longer be the norm for Christian conduct, but there are demands on Christians, and the principle at work in all of them is love or charity. Many of the topics in this section are generalities, reflecting problems with which Paul had to cope in the past in other churches founded by him, perhaps even at Corinth from which he sends this letter. Though the topics are not closely related, they concern in general the relation of justified Christians to the society in which they live.

113   **(A) Christian Life Must Be Worship in the Spirit Paid to God (12:1–13:14).** The unity of the Christian community demands that individuals strive to overcome evil with good. The common pursuit of the good is expected of those who are members of the body of Christ and whose lives are to be a sacrifice offered to God. **1.** *I urge you:* Paul speaks as an authorized apostle (1:5; 11:13). *by the mercy of God:* Lit., "mercies," the pl. suggesting the multiple manifestations of mercy just described in chaps. 9–11, esp. in 11:30–32. *to offer yourselves:* Lit., "your bodies" (→ Pauline Theology, 82:102). The verb not only means to place something at the disposition of another but also has the nuance of "offering, presenting" something in a sacrificial setting (BAGD 628). *as a living sacrifice:* Christians who strive to do what is right give a cultic sense to their lives. Paul implicitly compares them with animals slaughtered in Jewish or pagan cults, but he adds a distinguishing note: their offering of themselves is "alive and living," not accomplished through dead animals. *spiritual worship:* It is guided by *logos,* "reason," and befits a human being. **2.** *do not be conformed to this world:* "This world" is passing and imperfect (1 Cor 7:31). Paul alludes to the Jewish distinction of "this world/age" and the "world/age to come," which was adopted by the early church and given a Christian nuance. Paul himself thinks of the "world/age to come" as already begun; the "ages" have met at the start of the Christian dispensation (1 Cor 10:11). Hence the Christian, though in "this world," must live for God and not be conformed to any other standard. *be transformed:* See 2 Cor 3:18. The metamorphosis is not external but inward, involving the renewal of the human *nous,* and is effected by the presence of God's indwelling Spirit.

114   **3–13.** The cult to be paid to God should manifest itself concretely in a life in society based on humility and charity. It calls for a proper, unselfish use of spiritual gifts received. As an apostolic founder of Christian churches, Paul realized only too well the danger to the community of elements in it that overestimated their worth. **3.** *the grace given to me:* See 1:5;

15:15. *according to the standard of faith:* Lit., "the measure of faith." The norm of one's judgment is to be *pistis*. This is not the charismatic "faith" of 1 Cor 13:2, since the exhortation is addressed to all Christians, but may be either the active response of the believer (*fides qua creditur*) or, better, the object believed in (*fides quae*), which in the concrete is Christ Jesus. Each one, instead of thinking too highly of oneself, should measure oneself by the standard of what one believes in (see Cranfield, *NTS* 8 [1961–62] 345–51). **5.** *we are one body in Christ:* In earlier letters Paul referred to the union of Christians with Christ and to their mutual unity in him under the figure of the body of Christ (1 Cor 6:15–20; 10:16–17; 12:12–31). As in 1 Cor 12:12–31, the phrase "one body" probably does not suggest anything more than a moral union of the members who conspire together for the common good of the whole, as in the body politic. We have to look elsewhere for further nuances of his thought on the subject (→ Pauline Theology, 82:122). Note that here Paul does not say that we are "the body of Christ" or mention the "one body" in any connection with the church. We are "one body" because we are "in Christ." One should preserve the nuances of his thought in various passages.

115   **6.** *we have gifts:* The different gifts of grace that Christians receive from the Spirit as a result of faith are destined for the community's benefit. Each one must realize the social character of the God-given talents or gifts and make use of them for the common good without envy or jealousy. Paul enumerates seven of them, at first in abstract terms, then later in names for persons. *inspired preaching:* Lit., "prophecy," understood in the NT sense (1 Cor 12:10; 13:2; 14:3–6,24; 1 Thess 5:20). *in proportion to (our) faith:* Gk *analogia* means "right relationship, proportion" (BAGD 56) and creates little problem here. The word *pistis* is more problematic; see comment on v 3 above. It is best understood here as *fides quae*, the body of Christian belief. **7.** *service:* The second gift is *diakonia,* which probably refers to the administration of material aid or the distribution of alms of the community (see 1 Cor 16:15; Acts 6:1). Nothing in this context relates it to a distinct class of persons (= "deacons"). *if one is a teacher:* The third gift is the teaching of Christian doctrine, a task distinct from preaching and service previously mentioned (see also 1 Cor 12:28; cf. Eph 4:11). **8.** *if one exhorts:* The fourth gift is possessed by the "spiritual father" of the community. *if one contributes:* The fifth gift is possessed by the one who "shares" private wealth by way of alms; such a philanthropist is expected to exercise it "with a generous simplicity" (see 2 Cor 9:11,13 and comment on 2 Cor 8:2). *if one is a leader:* The sixth gift belongs to *ho proistamenos,* "the one who is at the head" of the community, an official or administrator (see 1 Thess 5:12). If the order of the gifts be significant, the "leader's" place in the list is noteworthy. Another transl. is sometimes used, "the one who contributes" (*RSV;* cf. BAGD 707); but then it is difficult to distinguish this gift from the second or the fifth. *with diligence:* Diligent attention should characterize the leader's governance. *a merciful helper:* The seventh gift belongs to the person who performs acts of mercy; such a one is expected to do them cheerfully. The spirit in which they are done is more important than the acts.

(Ellis, E. E., "'Spiritual' Gifts in the Pauline Community," *NTS* 20 [1973–74] 128. Käsemann, E., *ENTT* 63–94.)

116   **9.** *let love be genuine:* Love without sham or hypocrisy is explained by a series of instructions or maxims about charitable acts. **10.** *with brotherly affection:* Unfeigned charity must be shown above all to members of the Christian community. Paul uses *philadelphia* to distinguish it from the wider obligation of *agapē. eager to show one another honor:* The sense of this phrase is disputed; the transl. used here follows that of several ancient versions. It could, however, be: "As far as honor is concerned, let each one esteem the other more highly" (see BDF 150). **11.** *serve the Lord:* This is the motive for all Christian conduct. Instead of *kyriō* some mss. (D, G) read *kairō,* "serve the hour." If this were right, Christians would be called upon to meet the demands of the time in which they live (see O. Cullman, *Christ and Time* [Phl, 1950] 42). **13.** *the needs of the saints:* Is Paul hinting to the Roman Christians that they too should think of helping the Jerusalem Christian community with alms (see 15:25)?

117   **14–21.** In these verses Paul recommends charity to all, even one's enemies. **14.** *bless your persecutors:* This counsel echoes Jesus' words (Matt 5:44; Luke 6:27–28). Some important mss. (P⁴⁶, B, 1739) omit "your," and the sense would be more general, "Bless (all) persecutors." There is no reason to think that Paul is aware of any official persecution of Christians in Rome at this time. **16.** *have the same regard for one another:* A recommendation of mutual esteem for the concord of the community (see 15:5); it is also a warning against any false self-esteem. *associate with lowly folk:* This transl. understands Gk *tapeinois* as masc., but in view of the preceding injunction (not to set one's mind on lofty things), it could mean, "Give yourselves to lowly tasks" (neut.). *do not be conceited:* See Prov 3:7, quoted freely. **17.** *no evil for evil:* Paul's warning may echo the words of Jesus (Matt 5:39, 43–44). *aim at what is honorable:* Prov 3:4 adapted (cf. 2 Cor 4:2; 8:21). **19.** *look not for revenge:* Both the desire for revenge against (outside) enemies and the pursuit of it are excluded from Christian conduct. The right to avenge oneself is not part of the conquest of evil, despite any first impression. Charity must reign in everything. *make place for the wrath:* Give scope to God's (eschatological) wrath, which will manifest itself against sin. Paul immediately quotes Deut 32:35 (in a form close to the MT). The quotation makes the reference to God's wrath certain. The Christian should leave to God the retribution of evil and pursue only the good. **20.** Paul cites Prov 25:21–22 (LXX, ms. B), making it his own recommendation. *heaping burning coals upon his head:* The meaning of this OT phrase is obscure. In following the LXX, Paul clearly speaks of heaping coals "upon" the "head" (*pace* M. Dahood, *CBQ* 17 [1955] 19–23; L. Ramaroson, *Bib* 51 [1970] 230–34). Various explanations are given for the figure used: (1) For Ambrosiaster, Augustine, and Jerome the coals were a symbol of burning pangs of shame. The enemy would be moved by kindness to shame and regret, which would burn upon his head like coals of fire. But such a symbolic meaning is not attested elsewhere. (2) For S. Morenz (*TLZ* 78 [1953] 187–92) the coals are a symbol of repentance. This symbolic meaning he derives from a remote allusion to an Egyptian ritual described in a 3d-cent. BC Demotic text according to which a penitent carries on his head a dish of burning charcoal to express such repentance, when he had wronged someone. So kindness to an enemy would make him express his repentance before God (cf. W. Klassen, *NTS* 9 [1962–63] 337–50, for a nuanced use of Morenz's explanation). (3) Some Gk Fathers (Origen, Chrysostom) understood the coals as a symbol for a more noble type of revenge: If one feeds one's enemy and he remains hostile, one makes him liable to more serious punishment from God; thus one heaps coals of divine punishment on the enemy's head. Again, such a symbolic meaning is not elsewhere attested. (4) K. Stendahl (*HTR* 55 [1962] 343–55) has modified the last interpretation by comparing Paul's general principle with statements in QL advocating the nonretaliation of evil done by enemies and the deferring of retribution to God's day of vengeance (see 1QS 10:17–20; 9:21–22; 1:9–11). Paul's use of Deut 32 and Prov 25, then, would suggest a qualified way of adding to the measure of an enemy's sins.

(Cranfield, C. E. B., *A Commentary on Romans 12–13* [Edinburgh, 1965]. Culpepper, R. A., "God's Righteousness in the Life of His People: Romans 12–15," *RevExp* 73 [1976] 451–63. Schelkle, K.-H., "Der Christ in der Gemeinde: Eine Auslegung von Rom 12," *BK* 28 [1973] 74–81.)

118   **13:1–7.** The duties of Christians toward civil authorities. As Paul writes to the Roman church, he is aware that this community more than others would be conscious of imperial authority. Up to the time that Paul writes Rom, there has been no official persecution of Christianity in Rome, but an internal strife in the Jewish community there (probably between Jews and Jewish Christians; → Paul, 79:10) was settled by Claudius's expulsion of the Jews from Rome (Acts 18:2). This was known to Paul, yet his discussion of the duties of Christians toward civil authorities remains on the level of general principles. As citizens of another world (Phil 3:20), they might be inclined to question their relation toward civil authorities, especially when these were pagans. Paul's solution of the problem is related to the principles of Prov 8:15 and Matt 22:16–21.

119   **1.** *every person:* Lit., "every soul," a hebraism (see comment on 2:9). The injunction is not restricted to Christians. In some mss. (P⁴⁶, D*, G) and the OL "soul" is omitted, and there is a simple impv., "obey all higher authorities." *higher authorities:* Lit., "highly placed, governing authorities" (BAGD 841). The pl. noun *exousiai* is commonly used for human "authorities" in profane Greek and in the NT (Luke 12:11). O. Cullmann, however, has maintained that *exousiai* has another meaning, the "invisible angelic powers that stand behind state government," or even a double meaning, "the empirical state *and* the angelic powers" (*The State in the New Testament* [NY, 1956]); cf. 1 Cor 2:8; 1 Pet 3:22. It is, however, hardly likely that Paul is referring to anything like that; he means ordinary human civil authorities, on whom Christians are dependent and whom they must obey. *there is no authority except from God:* Even Rome's imperial authority comes from God, though Rome may be reluctant to admit it. Indirectly, Paul acknowledges the Father as the source of all the welfare and peace brought by imperial Roman rule. **2.** *anyone who resists authority opposes what God has ordained:* A general principle is deduced from the foregoing. Obedience to civil authorities is a form of obedience to God himself, for the relation of human beings to God is not limited to the religious or cultic sphere. The supposition running through vv 1–7 is that the civil authorities are conducting themselves rightly and are seeking the interests of the community. The possibility is not envisaged either of a tyrannical government or of one failing to cope with a situation where the just rights of individual citizens or of a minority group are neglected or violated. Paul insists on merely one aspect of the question: the duty of subjects to legitimate authority. He does not discuss here the duty of civil authorities. **4.** *for they are God's agents working for (your) good:* This is a reformulation of v 1, stressing the delegated character of civil authority; it envisages only a civil government properly fulfilling its functions. The phrase *eis to agathon,* "for the good," expresses the *finis* of civil activity. *they do not carry the sword for nothing:* The sword is introduced as the symbol of penal authority, of

the power legitimately possessed by civil authorities to coerce recalcitrant citizens in the effort to maintain order and strive for the common goal. *God's agent to execute (his) wrath on wrongdoers:* The context shows that the wrath is divine, as in 12:9; otherwise such authorities would not be God's agents. **5.** *for conscience' sake:* Another motive for obedience is introduced; Paul realizes that fear of punishment will not always deter citizens from violating civil regulations. His appeal to conscience suggests a moral obligation for obedience to civil laws, and not one that is simply legal or penal. It links human reaction to civil rulers with the divine origin of civil authority itself. **6.** *why you also pay taxes:* Paul takes it for granted that Roman Christians have been paying taxes. For the third time he stresses the delegated nature of civil authority (13:1,4)—here in the matter of taxes. **7.** cf. Mark 12:17.

(Bruce, F. F., "Paul and 'the Powers That Be,'" *BJRL* 66 [1983–84] 78–96. Dyck, H. J., "The Christian and the Authorities in Romans 13:1–7," *Direction* 14 [1985] 44–50. Hultgren, A. J., "Reflections on Romans 13:1–7: Submission to Governing Authorities," *Dialog* 15 [1976] 263–69. Hutchinson, S., "The Political Implications of Romans 13:1–7," *Biblical Theology* 21 [1971] 49–59.)

120   **8–10.** From the Christian's duty to civil authorities Paul moves on to the obligation of charity that sums up the whole Mosaic law in the new dispensation. **8.** *owe no one anything, except mutual love:* In this all the obligations of Christian life find their summation. Paul is not making love or charity a sort of duty owed to someone, but he expresses it thus to stress its role in all Christian conduct; it is not restricted only to fellow Christians. *has fully satisfied the law:* As elsewhere in Rom (see comment on 2:12) the Mosaic law is meant, as the following quotations make clear. **9.** *commandments:* Paul cites phrases from the Decalogue (Exod 20:13–17; Deut 5:17–21). The order of individual prohibitions differs from that of the MT, but it is the same as that of the LXX of Deut 5:17–18 (ms. B); cf. Luke 18:20; Jas 2:11; Philo, *De dec.* 120, 132. *summed up in this saying, "Love . . . :* Paul may be echoing a saying of Jesus (Mark 12:28–34) that sums up the Mosaic law with Deut 6:4–5; Lev 19:18. Other Jews were also accustomed to epitomizing the law in similar ways (see Str-B 1. 907–8), as they regarded the specific regulations (613 commands and prohibitions of the Torah) as developments of such OT passages. In Lev 19:18 "neighbor" means, however, fellow Jews, but as it is used by Paul it has a wider extension. **10.** *love is the fulfillment of the law:* Though this may seem to be only an abstract formulation of the preceding, Paul is enunciating his own basic principle. If Christ is the "goal of the law" (10:4), then "love," which motivated his whole existence and soteriological activity (8:35), can be said to be the law's fulfillment. It becomes the norm for Christian conduct and, when properly applied, achieves all that the law stood for. See A. L. Bencze, *NTS* 20 (1973–74) 90–92.

121   **11–14.** An eschatological exhortation addressed to the Christians of Rome: they must realize that they are already living in the *eschaton,* for the two ages have met (1 Cor 10:11). **11.** *critical time:* The period of Christian existence is *kairos,* a time when Christians are called upon to manifest by their actions that they are such and to conduct themselves suitably. Elsewhere Paul uses eschatological motivation in moral exhortations (1 Thess 5:6; 1 Cor 7:26,28–30); cf. Col 4:5; Eph 5:16. Even though what Paul says in 11:25 about the conversion of Israel might suggest that the definitive stage of salvation is still something of the future, nevertheless the *kairos* has begun—with the death and resurrection of Christ. Now is the time for Christians to appropriate to themselves by their faith, "working itself out through love" (Gal 5:6), the effects of what Christ Jesus once achieved for all. *awake from sleep:* See 1 Thess 5:6; 1 Cor 15:34; cf. Eph 5:14. *salvation is nearer:* The eschatological deliverance of Christians as the fulfillment of the pledge (2 Cor 1:22) or of the firstfruits (Rom 8:23) has been guaranteed by the indwelling Spirit. It is now nearer than it was when they first put their faith in Christ. **12.** *the night is far spent:* Paul implies that not too long a time separates Christians from their eschatological destiny. *let us throw off the deeds of darkness:* The contrast of day and night, of light and darkness, is symbolic of good and evil, just as in 1 Thess 5:5–8 (cf. Eph 5:8–11). These pairs are commonly used in current Jewish apocalyptic writings, esp. in the Essene QL (1QS 2:7; 3:20–4:1; 1QM 15:9, "in darkness are all their deeds," i.e., the deeds of the sons of darkness who are dominated by the prince of demons, Belial). *don the armor of light:* Christians cannot afford to remain in the unprotected condition of scantily clothed sleepers at a time when the situation calls for "armor." The armor is not described here, but in 1 Thess 5:8 it is described as faith, charity, and hope; cf. Eph 6:15–17. **13.** A list of vices that are the "deeds of darkness" (see comment on 1:28; → Pauline Theology, 82:142). **14.** *put on the Lord Jesus Christ:* Let Christ be your armor. Through baptism the Christian has already "put on" Christ (Gal 3:27). But that ontological identification of the Christian with Christ must bear fruit in one's conscious life; as one becomes more and more aware of Christian identity, one should withdraw more and more from sin. Such a psychological outlook once cultivated will stifle all the desires of the Ego subject to Sin. See E. Lövestam, *Spiritual Wakefulness in the New Testament* (Lund, 1963).

122   (B) Charity is Owed by the Strong to the Weak (14:1–15:13). The second part of the hortatory section is immediately concerned with such minor questions as the eating of meat and the observance of holy days. But more fundamentally it deals with the age-old problem of the scrupulous vs. the enlightened conscience, or the conservative vs. the progressive. Paul seems to have heard something about the Roman church, and in this part of Rom addresses himself to a problem there (→ 6 above). However, he deals with it only in generic terms, probably because he is not intimately acquainted with this church. Though unimportant in itself, it gives Paul the opportunity to formulate prudent principles based on conviction (14:1,22,23), love (14:15), the example of Christ (14:9,15; 15:3,7–8), and the Christian's loyalty to him (15:13). Paul's discussion ends with a plea for unity based on important ideas of the doctrinal section.

1. *welcome the one who is weak in conviction:* Paul has probably heard of scrupulous Jewish Christians whose judgments are based on an insufficiently enlightened faith. Such persons have not really grasped what is meant by uprightness through faith and have sought instead to find assurance by added practices. And yet even such persons belong to the Christian community. On *pistis,* "conviction," see comment on 14:23. *without debating minor points:* Lit., "not for the purpose of quarrels about opinions." The "weak" person should be welcomed as God would welcome him; he should not be subjected to idle disputes, since such disputes undermine confidence on all sides. **2.** *vegetables:* Paul's first example involves a food taboo. Whereas the "strong" eat food of all sorts, the "weak" eat only vegetables, perhaps because of their pre-Christian background (cf. Dan 1; Jdt 8:6). Once it is seen that such an issue is not related to the essentials of Christian faith, the obligation of mutual charity becomes clear. Each must accept the other as God would. **4.** *to criticize*

someone else's servant: A warning is addressed to the "weak" Christian: the person one would regard as lax is actually a member of God's household. God alone, as that person's master, will judge his failure or success. From God come both the acceptance of the weak and the status of the strong.

123   5. *distinguishes one day from another:* Another example of scrupulosity has to do with the celebration of holy days or fast days (see Zech 7:5; 8:19). Early Christians came to fast on Wednesdays and Fridays (*Did.* 8:1; *Herm. Sim.* 5.3.7). In any case, the "weak" Christians of Rome continued to distinguish such days from ordinary days, whereas the "strong" Christians were not that concerned about them. There is no evil in entertaining different convictions about such matters, and Paul resolutely excludes disputes or critical judgment about them. **6.** *for the Lord:* What matters in all of this is the motivation, whether the days be observed or not, as long as the Lord is served thereby. A member of the Lord's household is expected to serve his Lord. **7.** *none of us lives for himself:* The liberating act of Christ, freeing human beings from bondage to law, sin, and death (8:2), has enabled them to live for God (6:10–11; Gal 2:19). This implies the service of God in all things, and it is the basis of life in Christian society. **8.** *we are the Lord's:* Christians belong to and must acknowledge their relation to the risen Christ as *Kyrios* (see 1 Cor 6:20; 7:23; 8:6). **9.** *Lord of both the dead and the living:* Paul formulates the finality of the passion, death, and exaltation of Christ, stressing his sovereignty over the dead and the living, which became his as of the resurrection. It is a universal dominion proper to the *Kyrios* of all (cf. 1 Thess 5:10; Phil 2:11). The Christian, who shares in that redemption through faith and baptism, will eventually share the glory of the risen Lord himself (2 Cor 5:14–15). **10.** *judge:* The Christian must not judge other Christians, be they weak or strong. *we shall all stand before God's tribunal:* A further argument is introduced, echoing the sentiments of 14:4. **11.** It is supported by a conflated OT quotation, from Isa 49:18 and 45:23 (LXX). The latter has been used in Phil 2:10–11 in a form quite close to the meaning of the original, as Paul acknowledges Christ as *Kyrios.* But here the vb. *exomologēsetai* is taken in the sense of "admitting, confessing" what one has done before God as judge: bending the knee and confessing sins are what Christians do before God. If so, then they should not presume to judge one another.

124   14:13–15:6. The main part of Paul's exhortation, addressed to the "strong," is given here. The principles enunciated, however, are generic and can be applied to all. **14.** *nothing is unclean in itself:* This verse is somewhat parenthetical and sets forth a principle that is operative in the rest of the discussion. The principle may be related to that in 14:6. It may echo Jesus' saying (Matt 15:11) about the Pharisaic distinction between "clean" and "unclean" ("common" or "uncommon") things (cf. Lev 17:15; Str-B 1. 718). The created thing in itself is neither, but the estimate of it by a person becomes the guide to his or her actions. **15.** *your conduct is no longer ruled by love:* This verse resumes the idea of 14:13, but Paul now introduces the prime consideration, charity or love. Though to the strong no food is unclean, concern for a "brother" (= fellow Christian) will make the strong consider the social aspects of judgment and actions. *do not destroy with your food one for whom Christ died:* The weak "brother," who follows the dictates of his conscience, may be distressed at the sight of Christians partaking of certain kinds of food. The strong, in vaunting their enlightened or emancipated consciences before the weak, are not making professions of charity. Paul calls on Christians to relinquish their legitimate claim of freedom

for the sake of one who is weak (see 14:20). **16.** *do not let your privilege be criticized as evil:* Lit., "let not your good be spoken of as evil." The "good" is Christian liberty, which Paul recognizes fully, but he refuses to allow it to be asserted at the expense of distress to another. It might lose its esteemed quality and be brought into disrepute.
125   **17.** *uprightness, peace, and joy in the holy Spirit:* The essence of the kingdom does not consist in freedom from such things as dietary regulations, but in the freedom of the Christian to react to the promptings of the indwelling Spirit. Three qualities—two of which echo key ideas of the doctrinal section of Rom, uprightness (chaps. 1–4) and peace (5:1; 8:6)—proceed from the Spirit's promptings and are the conditions of Christian conduct in the kingdom. In Gal 5:13 Paul counsels Christians to be slaves to one another in love because of their new-found Christian freedom (see 1 Cor 8:1; 10:23). **20.** *for the sake of food:* Paul repeats v 15b substantially. Of more importance than the right to eat or celebrate is the Christian's obligation not to destroy the "work of God" by making a weak brother stumble. In the context, the "work of God" probably refers to the weak brother, but it may refer to the unity of the Christian community, which could be undone by insistence on extravagant claims of freedom without respect for others (cf. 1 Cor 3:9). **21.** See 1 Cor 8:13. **22.** *keep the conviction you have between yourself and God:* The clear insight and the firm conviction the "strong" Christian has of the moral goodness of a certain deed should guide one whenever one scrutinizes one's conduct in the sight of God. This is the norm, when an action is considered between oneself and God. But social considerations may compel one to modify one's conduct before others. *who has no reason to condemn himself for what he approves:* A beatitude is uttered over the one who has no qualms of conscience for a practical decision, whether to eat or not. **23.** *all that does not proceed from conviction is sin:* Lit., "all that is not of conviction." *Pistis* here has the same force as in vv 1,22. Pace E. Käsemann (*Romans* 379), it does not mean the faith that justifies. It is rather to be understood as "conviction" (with O. Bardenhewer, E. Best, Cranfield, Lietzmann, Sanday-Headlam). Moreover, "all" is to be understood in a restricted sense as referring to the examples that Paul has cited in the paragraph. *Pistis* is, then, the perspective that enables the Christian to judge actions in such cases in the sight of God. Whatever is thus done against the conviction of one's conscience would be sinful. (→ 9 above.)
126   **15:1.** The example of Christ is proposed to the "strong," who are now mentioned for the first time, even though the exhortation to them began at 14:13. Paul identifies himself with them. *to put up with weaknesses:* The vb. *bastazein* means either "to bear" (a burden) or "to endure, put up with" (BAGD 137). The former would imply that the strong are called upon to help the weak in shouldering the burden of their scruples; the latter would counsel patient forbearance of the immature attitude of the weak. **2.** *to build up:* I.e., the life of the community. The phrase *pros oikodomēn* is often taken to mean "to edify him," referring to the personal development of a Christian neighbor. But because Paul often uses the building metaphor in a corporate sense (see 1 Cor 14:12; Rom 14:19; cf. G. W. MacRae, *AER* 140 [1959] 361–76), the phrase undoubtedly has a social, corporate sense here too. **3.** *Christ did not please himself:* Christ's sacrifice of his life was motivated by his love for human beings (8:32–35). Love, then, should motivate the Christian to seek to please others and to contribute to the upbuilding of all. Paul applies to Christ Ps 69:10, a verse from a psalm of personal lament uttered by an upright Israelite who has sustained opprobrium because of his zeal for

God's house. As applied to Christ, it means that he bore the reproaches addressed to God. But the original sense of the Ps is not too pertinent to the situation envisaged by Paul; therefore he tries to justify the accommodated sense that he gives to it. **4.** See Rom 4:23, which makes the same point that the OT Scripture has meaning for Christians of today. *we might have hope:* When Jesus' suffering is viewed against sacred history, it takes on a deeper meaning. Seen in this larger perspective, it gives Christians a basis for their hope. **5–6.** Paul's prayer for harmony.
127   **7–13.** An appeal for unity, based on the pattern set by Christ. **7.** *as Christ has welcomed you:* The conclusion that follows from Christ's own command (John 13:34; 15:12). *for the glory of God:* The motive behind all of Christ's redemptive activity (see Phil 1:11; 2:11; cf. 1Q19 13:1; 1QSb 4:25; 1QS 10:9). **8.** *became a servant of the Jews:* Lit., "of circumcision" (see Gal 2:8–9 for the same way of designating the Jewish people). Jesus had to be a Jew and minister to the Jews in order to confirm God's promises to the patriarchs and thereby give evidence of divine "truth" (= fidelity; see comment on 3:4). But as Paul understands these promises, both Jews and Gentiles share in them. In this Paul finds the unity of the Christian community despite its ethnic background. **9.** *that the Gentiles might praise God for his mercy:* They too were included in the OT promises, as the Scripture texts to be cited will show. Even though Christ's ministry was directed to the Jews, the Gentiles were to be included in his kingdom in due time, as the OT promises indicate. *I will praise you among the Gentiles:* Ps 18:50 (= 2 Sam 22:50). Again Paul uses testimonia from the Torah, Prophets, and Pss to support his contention (see comment on 3:10). Note the linking idea *ethnē,* "nations," or *laoi,* "peoples." **10.** See Deut 32:43 (LXX). **11.** See Ps 117:1. **12.** See Isa 11:10 (LXX). **13.** *hope . . . joy . . . peace:* The final blessing, which concludes the hortatory section, employs key ideas of the OT passages just cited; in addition, it echoes those of the doctrinal section. *God of hope:* The God on whom both Jews and Gentiles center their hope.
128   **(IV) Conclusion (15:14–33).** Paul sends news about himself, his apostolate, and his plans. Now that his labors in the East have come to an end, he must visit Jerusalem with the token of good will and solidarity that his Gentile churches are offering to the mother church. Once this is done—and he asks the Roman Christians to pray that this will be accepted in the right spirit—he plans to visit Rome on his way to evangelize the West. Paul takes the occasion to compliment the Romans on the good things he has heard about them. He is proud to write to them as the "apostle of the Gentiles," even though he has so far had no influence on their belief in Christ. **14.** *I am convinced:* Although he has just finished exhorting the Roman Christians to unity (15:7–13), Paul points out the abiding conviction (pf. tense) that he has of their goodness and their understanding of Christian faith. **15.** *I have written rather boldly:* As in 1:5,13, he apologizes for writing to a church not founded by him, but he is emboldened to do so because he has received a commission to evangelize Gentiles, and the Roman Christians thus fall under his apostolic care. *because of the grace given to me:* The God-given charism (= *gratia gratis data* of later theology) to summon Gentiles to faith in Christ (1:5; 12:3; Gal 2:7–8; 1 Cor 4:6). **16.** *to be a minister of Christ Jesus:* Paul describes his role in liturgical language, using neither *diakonos,* "servant," as in 2 Cor 3:6, nor *oikonomos,* "steward," as in 1 Cor 4:1, but *leitourgos,* "cultic minister." In his mission to the Gentiles he sees his function to be like that of a Jewish priest serving in God's Temple. If all Christian life is to be

regarded as a worship paid to God (12:1), the spreading of Christ's gospel is easily compared to the role of a sacred minister in such worship (see K.-H. Schelkle, *TQ* 136 [1956] 257–83). Paul implies that the preaching of the word of God is a liturgical act in itself. If Clement of Rome (*Ad Cor.* 8:1) could look on the OT prophets as cultic ministers of God's grace, this can be applied even more to the apostles and prophets of the NT (cf. 11:13; 2 Cor 3:3; Phil 2:17). *the offering of the Gentiles:* Objective gen.; it is the evangelized Gentiles who are consecrated and offered to God as an acceptable sacrifice. Since the *finis* of all sacrifice is to bring about in some way the return of sinful human beings to God, Paul looks on his work among Gentiles as a form of sacrifice, for their conversion has achieved that very purpose. The apostle offers to God not slaughtered animals, but repentant human beings. **17.** *in what pertains to God:* Paul's pride and boast are rooted where they should be, in Christ (see 5:2).
129 **18.** *what Christ has accomplished through me:* Paul is aware that he is only an instrument in the conversion of the Gentiles; Christ really brings about their turning to God. **19.** *by the power of signs and miracles:* Paul's rhetoric, physical stamina, and especially the extraordinary deeds performed by Christ through him have been elements that served the evangelization of the Gentiles. For the phrase *sēmeia kai terata,* see 2 Cor 12:12; cf. Acts 2:19, 22,43; 15:12. *from Jerusalem to Illyricum:* The two terms of Paul's apostolic activity in the East. It began in Jerusalem, the city from which "the word of the Lord" goes forth (Isa 2:3), and reached as far as the Roman province of Illyricum (on the west coast of the Balkan peninsula, including lower Yugoslavia and Albania today). **20.** *on another's foundation:* Paul is not thinking of Christ as the sole foundation of Christian life, as in 1 Cor 3:11, but of the work of other apostles and prophets who founded churches. His ambition is to carry Christ's name to areas where it is unknown (2 Cor 10:15–16). **21.** Isa 52:15 is quoted according to the LXX, which introduces "about him" into its translation. The LXX text is thus more suited than the MT to Paul's use of the verse with reference to Christ. In Dt-Isa the verse is part of a song of the Servant of Yahweh (cf. Rom 10:16).
130 **22.** See Rom 1:10–13. **23.** *no longer an opportunity in these parts:* Paul knows, of course, that he has not yet converted all the Gentiles in the eastern Mediterranean area, but he seems to regard his function as that of laying foundations. Others may build on them (1 Cor 3:6,10). **24.** *on my way to Spain:* As in 15:28, we learn only of Paul's plans to visit Spain. Did he ever get there? (→ Paul, 79:52). *to be sent from there by you:* To be dispatched at least with their prayers and good wishes, if not also with their alms. **25.** *to take help to God's holy people:* Lit., "to the saints." The collection, taken up in the Gentile churches founded in Galatia, Achaia, and Macedonia (Gal 2:10; 1 Cor 16:1–4; 2 Cor 8:1–9:15), must be carried by Paul personally to Jerusalem, despite his desire to head west. He attached much importance to this collection, intended to establish good relations between the Jewish Christian mother community of Jerusalem and the newly founded Gentile Christian churches. It would be a token of their solidarity. *the poor:* This is a term for the needy among Jerusalem Christians; it is not a title for that community as such (like the use of the term *'ebyônîm* for the Qumran Essenes, 4QpPs a 1–2 ii 9; 1,3–4 iii 10); see L. E. Keck, *ZNW* 56 (1965) 100–29. **27.** *they are indebted to them:* Even though the collection was the result of freewill offerings, the Gentile Christians are acknowledging thereby their indebtedness to the mother church of Jerusalem. The Gentile Christians have shared in the spiritual benefits of the Jewish

Christians, the first converts to Christ; so they now share their material benefits with the poor of Jerusalem. Underlying this sharing is the recognition that "salvation comes from the Jews" (John 4:22; cf. Rom 9:4–5). Paul may also be hinting delicately to the Romans that they too should think similarly (see 12:13). **28.** *delivered the proceeds under my own seal:* Lit., "having sealed or stamped the fruit." Paul makes use of a figure from tenant farming. When the tenant delivered the harvested fruit to the owner, it was marked with the farmer's seal as identification. Paul wants the collection to be known as coming from the churches founded by him in the Lord's harvest. He also implies that he is still under suspicion in Jerusalem. This prompts him to ask the Roman church to pray for three things (vv 30–32): that no danger may befall him from unbelievers in Judea, that his collection may be received by the saints in the proper spirit, and that he may eventually come to Rome with a joyous heart. **33.** Paul's final blessing on the Romans.

(Cranfield, C. E. B., "Some Observations on the Interpretation of Romans 14,1 – 15,13," *ComViat* 17 [1975] 193–204. Dupont, J., "Appel aux faibles et aux forts dans la communauté romaine [Rom 14,1–15,13]," *SPC* 1. 357–66. Lorenzi, L. de [ed.], *Freedom and Love* [Benedictina 6; Rome, 1981]. Nickle, K. F., *The Collection: A Study in Paul's Strategy* [SBT 48; London, 1966].)

131   **(V) Letter of Recommendation for Phoebe (16:1–23).** For the relation of this chapter to the whole of Rom, → 9–11 above. **1.** *I commend to you:* Paul uses *synistēmi,* a current epistolary expression to introduce a friend to other acquaintances (see 1 Macc 12:43; 2 Macc 4:24; cf. C.-H. Kim, *Form and Structure of the Familiar Greek Letter of Recommendation* [SBLDS 4; Missoula, 1972]. *Phoebe:* An otherwise unknown Christian woman, the bearer of this letter. *our fellow Christian:* Lit., "our sister," see 1 Cor 7:15; 9:5; Phlm 2. She is not an imposter. *a deacon:* Perhaps (common gender) *diakonos* designates a member of a special group in the church of Cenchreae, or perhaps it is only a generic designation, "servant, assistant." There is no way of being sure that the term already designates a special "order" of ministers. For the generic use, see 1 Thess 3:2; 2 Cor 3:6; 11:23. However, Phil 1:1 and 1 Tim 3:8,12 begin to point in the direction of a specific group or function. *church at Cenchreae:* Cenchreae was one of the two ports of ancient Corinth; it was situated on the east side of the Isthmus of Corinth, on the Saronic Gulf, whereas Lechaeum was the port on the west side (see J. Murphy-O'Connor, *St. Paul's Corinth* [Wilmington, 1983] 17–21). The letter of recommendation may have been written from either Corinth or Cenchreae. In Rom, Paul uses *ekklēsia* only in chap. 16 and always in the sense of the "local church" (vv 1,4,5,16,23). **2.** *in the Lord:* Phoebe is to be welcomed into the community as one of its members. *in a manner worthy of God's holy people:* Lit., "of the saints" (see comment on 1:7). Paul flatters his readers by associating them with the "holy ones," formerly called and chosen, and with the early mother church of Jerusalem, which enjoyed this title par excellence (see 1 Cor 16:1; 2 Cor 8:4; 9:1). *she has been of great assistance:* Lit., "a patroness." Paul acknowledges the service that Phoebe has shown to him and to other Christians at Cenchreae. We can only speculate about the kind of assistance: hospitality? championing their cause before secular authorities? furnishing funds for his journey to Jerusalem?
132   **3–16.** Paul sends personal greetings to at least 26 acquaintances. **3.** *Prisca and Aquila:* In 1 Cor 16:19; 2 Tim 4:19 Aquila's wife is called *Priska,* as here, but the diminutive *Priskilla* is used in Acts 18:2,18,26. They were Jewish Christians, expelled from Rome by Claudius (→ Paul, 79:10). Having settled in Corinth, they engage in

tentmaking. When Paul first arrives in Corinth, they extend him hospitality (Acts 18:1–2). Later on they travel with him to Ephesus, where they take up residence and instruct among others Apollos, the Alexandrian rhetor (Acts 18:26). When 1 Cor was written from Ephesus, Paul sent greetings to the Corinthian church from the Christians who gathered in the house-church of Prisca and Aquila (16:19). This notice in Rom suggests that the two have already returned to Rome. *my fellow workers in Christ:* Either at Corinth (Acts 18:3) or at Ephesus (Acts 18:26). *who risked their necks for me:* Paul gratefully recalls some valiant intervention of Prisca and Aquila on his behalf either in Ephesus (at the riot of the silversmiths, Acts 19:23) or during some Ephesian imprisonment, to which he may refer in 1 Cor 15:32; 2 Cor 1:8–9. Cf. Rom 16:7. **5.** *the church at their house:* Local communities gathered for cult at the large house of some early Christian (before special buildings were erected for such purposes); see 1 Cor 16:19; Phlm 2. Cf. M. Gielen, *ZNW* 77 (1986) 109–25. *Epaenetus:* Otherwise unknown. *first convert for Christ in Asia:* Lit., "firstfruits of Asia unto Christ." Paul reflects on the conversion of Epaenetus as that which sparked the conversion of many others in the Roman province of Asia (the western end of Asia Minor, with its gubernatorial seat at Ephesus). His conversion "consecrated" the rest of Asia to Christ (see comment on 11:16). **6.** *Mary:* Otherwise unknown.
133   **7.** *Andronicus and Junia(s):* Early Jewish Christian converts, otherwise unknown but related to Paul as "kinsfolk." Junias is a man's name, but *Iounian* could also be the acc. of "Junia," a woman's name, which ancient commentators at times took as the name of Andronicus's wife. Moreover, ms. P⁴⁶ and some versions (Vg, bo, eth) read "Julia." *fellow prisoners:* At Ephesus (1 Cor 15:32), or at Philippi (Acts 16:23), or elsewhere (2 Cor 11:23)? *eminent among the apostles:* This may suggest that Andronicus and Junia(s) enjoyed the esteem of those who were apostles, or it may mean that they were, indeed, among those who were "apostles"—for the latter title was given in the early church to more than just the Twelve (→ NT Thought, 81:154–57). **8–16.** *Ampliatus, Urbanus, Stachys, Apelles, Aristobulus, Herodion, Narcissus, Tryphaena, Tryphosa, Persis, Rufus, Asyncritus, Phlegon, Hermes, Patrobas, Hermas, Philologus, Julia, Nereus, Olympas:* Many of these names are well-known slave names, found on inscriptions throughout the Roman empire. It is sheer speculation that identifies Rufus as the son of Simon of Cyrene (Mark 15:21) and Narcissus as the famous freedman of Claudius's household, put to death in Nero's reign (Tacitus, *Ann.* 13.1). **16.** *a holy kiss:* See 1 Thess 5:26; 1 Cor 16:20; 2 Cor 13:12. Paul often ends a letter in this way, perhaps using in an epistolary context a liturgical gesture (used at the Lord's Supper, according to Justin, *Apol.* 1.65,2).

134   **17–20.** A warning to the community against the influence of strangers who would introduce dissension and scandal. In tone this paragraph differs from the rest of Rom; it sounds much like Gal 6:12–17. **18.** *slaves of their own appetites:* Lit., "of their own belly." See Phil 3:19; Gal 5:7–12 for similar sarcasm in the polemic with Judaizers. "Belly" may be a sarcastic reference to the dietary problem of chaps. 14–15. W. Schmithals (*ST* 13 [1959] 51–69) would identify these strangers as Jewish-Christian gnostics; but were there such at this time? **19.** *your obedience:* I.e., faith (see 1:5; 15:18; cf. 16:26). **20.** *God of peace:* See 15:33. *will crush Satan:* Satan is to be understood as the personification of all disorder, dissension, and scandal in the community. God, who shapes human ways in peace, will do away with such dangers threatening it. An illusion here to Gen 3:15 is not unlikely. After the farewell with which this verse ends, one finds further greetings, but they are greetings from persons present with Paul (vv 21–23). **21.** *Timothy:* See comments on Acts 16:1–3; 2 Cor 1:1. *Lucius:* Not necessarily Lucius of Cyrene (Acts 13:1). *Jason:* Not necessarily Jason of Thessalonica (Acts 17:5–9). *Sosipater:* The same as Sosipater of Beroea (Acts 20:4)? **22.** *Tertius:* Paul's scribe, who may be adding these few verses. **23.** *Gaius:* Probably the same as Gaius of 1 Cor 1:14 (cf. Acts 19:20). *Erastus:* The city commissioner is possibly the same as the aedile Erastus, who at his own expense paved a square in 1st-cent. Corinth, according to a Lat inscription still *in situ* (see Murphy-O'Connor, *St. Paul's Corinth* 37). **24.** Omitted in the best Gk mss., since it is simply a repetition of 16:20b.
135   **(VI) Doxology (16:25–27).** On the position of this doxology in various mss. of Rom, → 9 above. *to him who can strengthen you:* "Paul" blesses God, who assures the gospel of Christ to human beings and also constancy in Christian life. *my gospel:* The good news that "Paul" makes known (→ Pauline Theology, 82:31–36). *preaching of Jesus Christ:* The proclamation that announces Christ Jesus. *according to the revelation of the mystery:* → Pauline Theology, 82:33–34. *prophetic writings:* The OT and Jewish apocalyptic writings that bear on the mystery mentioned. *according to the command of the eternal God:* "Paul" may be alluding to his commission as an apostle to the Gentiles so that he could make this mystery, now revealed, known to all the nations. *the obedience of faith:* Appositional gen.; see comment on 1:5. **27.** *to God who alone is wise:* This is the climax of the doxology (see 11:33–36; cf. Jude 24; Rev 15:4). Praise is paid once again to God the Father, through his Son, Jesus Christ. (See J. Dupont, *ETL* 22 [1946] 362–75; *RBén* 58 [1948] 3–22; L.-M. Dewailly, *NTS* 14 [1967–68] 111–18; J. K. Elliott, *ZNW* 72 [1981] 124–30.)

52

THE LETTER TO PHILEMON

Joseph A. Fitzmyer, S.J.

BIBLIOGRAPHY

1 Benoit, P., *Les épîtres de saint Paul aux Philippiens, à Philemon, aux Colossiens, aux Éphésiens (SBJ;* 3d ed.; Paris, 1959) 39–46. Caird, G. B., *Paul's Letters from Prison* (NClarB; Oxford, 1976). Carson, H. M., *The Epistles of Paul to the Colossians and Philemon* (TynNTC; GR, 1960) 103–12. Ernst, J., *Die Briefe an die Philipper, an Philemon . . .* (RNT; Regensburg, 1974) 123–39. Friedrich, G., "Der Brief an Philemon," *Das Neue Testament deutsch* (14th ed.; Göttingen, 1976) 8. 277–86. Gnilka, J., *Der Philemonbrief* (HTKNT 10/4; Freiburg, 1982). Lohse, E., *A Commentary on the Epistles to the Colossians and to Philemon* (Herm; Phl, 1971) 185–208. Moule, C. F. D., *The Epistles of Paul the Apostle to the Colossians and Philemon* (CGTC; Cambridge, 1957) 140–49. Müller, J. J., *The Epistles of Paul to the Philippians and to Philemon* (NICNT; GR, 1961). Scott, E. F., *The Epistles of Paul to the Colossians, to Philemon and to the Ephesians* (MNTC; London, [1930]). Stöger, A., *The Epistle to Philemon* (NTSR; NY, 1971) 54–100. Stuhlmacher, P., *Der Brief an Philemon* (EKKNT 18; Einsiedeln, 1975). Thompson, G. H. P., *The Letters of Paul to the Ephesians, to the Colossians and to Philemon* (CBC; Cambridge, 1967) 172–92.

DBSup 7. 1204–11. *IDBSup* 663. Kümmel, *INT* 348–50. Wik-Schm, *ENT* 475–79.

INTRODUCTION

2 **(I) Philemon.** The addressee was a young, well-to-do, respected Christian of a town in the Lycus Valley of Asia Minor, probably Colossae. Paul greets him along with Apphia (probably Philemon's wife) and Archippus (their son?), and "the church that meets in your house" (2). Philemon was apparently converted by Paul (19), possibly in Ephesus.

3 **(II) Occasion and Purpose.** The slave Onesimus had run away, having caused his master considerable damage (11,18). In his flight he came to where Paul was imprisoned, perhaps knowing of the esteem his master held for Paul. Somehow Paul managed to give him refuge (see E. R. Goodenough, *HTR* 22 [1929] 181–83) and ultimately converted him to Christianity ("whose father I have become in my imprisonment," 10). Eventually, Paul learned that Onesimus was Philemon's slave, and though he wanted to keep him with himself for help in evangelization, he recognized Philemon's right and decided to send Onesimus back (14,16). In a letter similar to one written by Pliny the Younger (*Ep.* 9.21 and 24) Paul begged Philemon to take the runaway slave back, "no longer as a slave, but . . . as a beloved brother" (16). In effect, Paul asked Philemon not to inflict on Onesimus the severe penalties permitted by law (see Coleman-Norton, "The Apostle Paul" [→ 11 below] 174–77; cf. Gnilka, *Philemonbrief* 54–81). Paul

also promised to restore the damage that Onesimus had caused—how he would do this from prison is not said. Paul further suggested that he would like to have Onesimus come back to work with him (20). Did Paul mean by this that Philemon should emancipate the slave? This may be implied.

4 **(III) Onesimus.** From Col 4:9 one usually concludes that he was a Colossian. J. Knox (*Philemon among the Letters of Paul* [rev. ed.; NY, 1959]) has maintained that he was the slave of Archippus, also mentioned in Col 4:17, that Col and Phlm were composed at the same time, that Phlm is actually "the letter from Laodicea" (Col 4:16), that Philemon was rather an inhabitant of that town, to whom Paul sent this letter to use his influence with Archippus of Colossae. Finally, Knox suggested that Onesimus would have returned to Paul as a helper, would have eventually become the bishop of Ephesus (see Ignatius, *Eph.* 1:3–6:2) and would have played a major role in collecting Paul's letters into a corpus. The last suggestion may have some plausibility, but the rest of this hypothesis is quite tenuous. For it is unlikely that Phlm and Col were written about the same time; they are "at least 15 years apart" (J. Gnilka, *Philemonbrief* 5; → Colossians, 54:7). Any ordinary reading of Phlm 1–4 would note that Philemon is considered the master of Onesimus and that the "you"

(2,4) refers to Philemon. Again, would Paul write for Onesimus in such delicacy in Phlm, only to pressure Archippus himself (by name) in a separate, public letter (Col) to fulfill a "ministry received in the Lord," i.e., the emancipation of Onesimus (see F. F. Bruce, *BJRL* 48 [1965–66] 91–96; Lohse, *Colossians and Philemon* 186–87).

5 (IV) Date and Place of Composition. From Marcion on, the Pauline authenticity of Phlm has been generally admitted; there is no reason to question it. Paul wrote Phlm from prison (1,9–10,13,23), but it is almost impossible to say where that imprisonment was. The traditional view (held in modern times by W. Bieder, F. F. Bruce, C. F. D. Moule, *et al.*) makes it the Roman house-arrest (AD 61–63). Some commentators, however, have preferred the Caesarean imprisonment (M. Dibelius, H. Greeven), i.e., *ca.* AD 58–60. More recently, commentators have been favoring the Ephesian imprisonment of Paul (→ Paul, 79:40), i.e., *ca.* AD 56–57 (so G. A. Deissmann, G. Friedrich, J. Gnilka, E. Lohse, *et al.*). This last opinion has the advantage of keeping Philemon (in Colossae) and Paul (in Ephesus) within a plausible range (about 108 mi.). It also explains more easily Paul's plan to visit Philemon (22), which is difficult for the Roman hypothesis.

6 (V) Significance. Ancient commentators wondered why an ostensibly private letter with little corporate pastoral concern should have become canonical (see Jerome, *In Ep. ad Philem.*, prol.; PL 26. 637). But Phlm is addressed to others than Philemon himself, even to a house-church. If Paul does not invoke his apostolic authority to demand obedience of Philemon (8), he does

confront him with a plea for love (8–11,21). Despite the surface character as a letter dealing with a private matter, Phlm embodies an attitude toward slavery that merits Christian attention. First, it manifests Paul's pastoral and warmhearted affection for Onesimus. Second, in sending him back to Philemon, Paul does not try to change the existing social structure. Modern Christians are repulsed by the idea of slavery, but this outlook is perhaps a development of a principle that Paul tries to advocate in this letter, while realizing the futility of trying to abolish the system of slavery. Third, Paul's own solution was to transform or interiorize the social structure; recall 1 Cor 7:20–24; 12:13. He urges Philemon to welcome Onesimus back as a "brother," for he is a "freedman of the Lord" (1 Cor 7:22), especially in view of what Paul teaches in Gal 3:27–28. Moreover, this plea is made "for love's sake" (8), but it took centuries for the Pauline principle to be put into practice, even in the Christian West. Because of this principle Phlm is rather "an apostolic writing" about a private individual (see U. Wickert, *ZNW* 52 [1961] 230–38).

7 (VI) Outline. Phlm is structured as follows:

(I) Introduction: Prescript and Greeting (1–3).
(II) Thanksgiving: Thanks to God for Philemon's Faith and Love (4–7).
(III) Body: Appeal to Philemon's Goodwill to Welcome Back Onesimus and a Hint at His Usefulness to Paul (8–20).
(IV) Conclusion: Final Instructions, Greetings, and Blessing (21–25).

COMMENTARY

8 (I) Introduction: Prescript and Greeting (1–3). 1. *prisoner:* Paul does not write as an apostle, as in Rom, 1–2 Cor, or Gal; he appeals as one in a lowly condition to Philemon (see 9–10). *Timothy:* The cosender; see comment on Phil 1:1; 2 Cor 1:1. **2.** *Archippus:* See Col 4:17. There is no clear reason to regard him as Onesimus's master. **3.** *grace and peace:* → NT Epistles, 45:8A.

9 (II) Thanksgiving: Thanks to God for Philemon's Faith and Love (4–7). 5. *all God's holy people:* Lit., "all the saints"; see comment on Phil 1:1. **6.** *their sharing in your faith:* The meaning of this phrase is obscure; see Moule, *Colossians and Philemon* 142–43, for various interpretations. It seems to mean: Paul prays that a sense of solidarity with Philemon through faith in Christ will be productive of a deeper knowledge of all the good that comes to "the saints" through incorporation into Christ (→ Pauline Theology, 82:116–27). This is a faith involving active love (Phlm 5; cf. Gal 5:6).

10 (III) Body: Appeal to Philemon's Goodwill to Welcome Back Onesimus and a Hint at His Usefulness to Paul (8–20). 8. Paul does not demand obedience from Philemon, but appeals to his love and goodwill. **9.** *an old man:* All mss. read *presbytēs,* "an elderly man," between 50 and 60 years of age (→ Paul, 79:14); cf. Luke 1:18. In virtue of his senior status Paul pleads with young Philemon. Some commentators prefer to read *presbeutēs,* making Paul "an ambassador" of Christ (cf. 2 Cor 5:20) or insist that *presbytēs* itself can have this meaning (see 2 Macc 11:34). But this meaning is unlikely in this context (see G. Bornkamm, *TDNT* 6. 683). **10.** *on behalf of my child . . . whom I have begotten in prison:* Paul alludes to Onesimus's conversion (cf. 1 Cor 4:15,17; Gal 4:19). Another possible transl.: "whom I have begotten

as Onesimus," playing on the name of the slave, for *Onēsimos* means "Profitable One" and stands in contrast to the adj. *achrēstos,* "useless" (11). Paul implies that this slave, now a Christian, will live up to his name. Another play on this name, involving Philemon himself, may be found in v 20. **14.** *without your consent:* Paul acknowledges the master's right to the slave, but hints that he would like to have Onesimus back to work with him (see 21). **15.** *forever:* The sense of this adv. is double. The providential separation of Onesimus from Philemon means that the slave is now returning more faithful than ever, but Paul also alludes to the new relationship existing between them. Both are now Christians, related in a way that not even death can undo. **16.** *brother:* Onesimus is such because he is, like Philemon (20), an adopted child of God through baptism (Gal 4:5; Rom 8:15). **18.** *I, Paul, write this:* Probably the whole of this short letter (→ NT Epistles, 45:20).

11 (IV) Conclusion: Final Instructions, Greetings, and Blessing (21–25). 21. *even more than I ask.* Is Paul begging Philemon to emancipate Onesimus? He hints that Philemon should allow Onesimus to return to work with him. **22.** Paul hopes for his own speedy release from prison. **23.** *Epaphras, Mark, Aristarchus, Demas, Luke:* See Col 4:10–14. **25.** See comment on Gal 6:18.

(Coleman-Norton, P. R., "The Apostle Paul and the Roman Law of Slavery," *Studies in Roman Economic and Social History* [Fest. A. C. Johnson; Princeton, 1951] 155–77. Preiss, T., *Life in Christ* [SBT 13; London, 1954] 32–42. Rollins, W. G., "Slavery in the NT," *IDBSup* 830–32. Westermann, W. L., *The Slave Systems of Greek and Roman Antiquity* [Phl, 1955] 150.)

53

THE SECOND LETTER
TO THE THESSALONIANS

Charles Homer Giblin, S.J.

BIBLIOGRAPHY

1 Aus, R. D., "God's Plan and God's Power: Isaiah 66 and the Restraining Factors of 2 Thess 2:6–7," *JBL* 96 (1977) 537–53; "The Liturgical Background of the Necessity and Propriety of Giving Thanks According to 2 Thes 1:3," *JBL* 92 (1973) 432–38. Bailey, J. A., "Who Wrote II Thessalonians?" *NTS* 25 (1978–79) 131–45. Barnouin, M., "Les problèmes de traduction concernant II Thess. ii. 6–7," *NTS* 23 (1976–77) 482–98. Bassler, J. M., "The Enigmatic Sign: 2 Thessalonians 1:5," *CBQ* 46 (1984) 496–510. Best, E., *A Commentary on the First and Second Epistles to the Thessalonians* (HNTC; NY, 1972). Coppens, J., "Miscellanées bibliques LXVI: Les deux obstacles au retour glorieux du Sauveur," *ETL* 46 (1970) 383–89. García-Moreno, A., "La realeza y el señorío de Cristo en Tesalonicenses," *EstBib* 39 (1981) 63–82. Giblin, C. H., *The Threat to Faith: An Exegetical and Theological Re-examination of 2 Thessalo-

nians 2* (AnBib 31; Rome, 1967). Kaye, B. N., "Eschatology and Ethics in 1 and 2 Thessalonians," *NovT* 17 (1975) 47–57. Laub, F., *1. und 2. Thessalonicherbrief* (NEchtB; Würzburg, 1985). Marín, F., "2 Tes 2,3–12: Intentos de comprensión y nuevo planteamiento," *EstEcl* 54 (1979) 527–37. Marshall, I. H., *1 and 2 Thessalonians* (NCB; GR, 1983). Marxsen, W., *Der zweite Thessalonicherbrief* (ZBK NT; Zurich, 1982). Rigaux, B., *Les épîtres aux Thessaloniciens* (EBib; Paris, 1956). Scott, J. J., "Paul and Late-Jewish Eschatology — A Case Study, I Thessalonians 4:13–18 and II Thessalonians 2:1–12," *JETS* 15 (1972) 133–43. Trilling, W., *Untersuchungen zum zweiten Thessalonicherbrief* (Erfurter theologische Studien 27; Leipzig, 1972); *Der zweite Brief an die Thessalonicher* (EKKNT; Neukirchen, 1980).

IDBSup 900–1. Kümmel, *INT* 262–69. Wik-Schm, *ENT* 404–9.

INTRODUCTION

2 **(I) Authenticity.** By the first third of the 2d cent., the letter was accepted as Pauline. Literary criticism (mainly German) has recently tended to regard 2 Thess as a pseudepigraph, i.e., its author appealed to Paul's authority to maintain against deceivers Pauline or other authentic traditions regarding Christ's second coming.
3 Intrinsic literary evidence, taken not only cumulatively but also with regard to the integrated composition of the whole letter, decidedly weighs in favor of pseudonymity. Nonetheless, whether one opts for Paul himself as the author or for a pseudonymous author, the precise circumstances of the central issue (the Lord's triumphal coming [*parousia*]) remain open to debate. The dating of 2 Thess (between AD 51 and 100) poses difficulties to any critical hypothesis. Lastly, the mode of interpreting the letter is itself affected by hypotheses concerning authenticity, since there is question of the author's theological position: whether, as Paul would, he writes directly from his own standpoint, or, like a pseudonymous author, from his own understanding of Paul and of wider ecclesial tradition.
4 On first perusal, certain remarkable similarities between the two letters occur in structure, vocabu-

lary, and general theme. Structural similarities emerge at the beginning, in the opening formula (2 Thess 1:1–2; 1 Thess 1:1) and in an opening thanksgiving (2 Thess 1:3–12; 1 Thess 1:2–10); in the middle, with a repeated thanksgiving (2 Thess 2:13–14; 1 Thess 2:13) and prayer for steadfastness (2 Thess 2:16–17; 1 Thess 3:11–13); and within the closing, hortatory sections (2 Thess 3:1–18; 1 Thess 4:1–5:28), with an introductory [*to*] *loipon*, "for the future," a wish for peace (2 Thess 3:16; 1 Thess 5:23–24), final greetings (2 Thess 3:17; 1 Thess 5:26–27), and a blessing (2 Thess 3:18; 1 Thess 5:28). The similarity in vocabulary is also striking, especially given the relatively short length of 2 Thess (see J. A. Bailey, *NTS* 25 [1978–79] 133–34). Both letters show a salient concern with the eschatological perspective of requital for persecution (2 Thess 1:4–10; 1 Thess 1:10; 2:14–16) and final reunion with the Lord at his coming (2 Thess 2:1–15; 1 Thess 1:10; 2:19; 4:13–18). Both letters also attend to a problem peculiar to the Thessalonian correspondence, viz., the *ataktoi*, "disorderly" (2 Thess 3:6–13; 1 Thess 5:14).
5 Upon further examination, however, the similarities mask considerable differences. These affect the substance and scope of the second letter vis-à-vis the

first. Thus, the marked similarities in vocabulary occur in those portions of 2 Thess which serve as formal elements of the structure (e.g., opening formula and concluding blessing) and as "frame passages" for themes developed in a distinctive way (as, e.g., 2 Thess 1:3–4 and 1:11–12 encompass 1:5–10). The thanksgiving in 2 Thess 2:13–14, although reminiscent of Pauline usage, is uncharacteristically embedded (de, v 13) within a much larger context, which is defined by a double inclusion (vv 2 and 15; see Giblin, *Threat to Faith* 45–46). Although 2 Thess uses parallelism extensively, the parallelism is primarily synonymous, more rarely synthetic, and almost never antithetic; accordingly, it is contrary to Paul's own style (Trilling, *Untersuchungen* 52–53). The language of 2 Thess (e.g., "we ought to give thanks" [2:13] and "to be thought worthy" [1:5]) suggests the terminology of a later period (see J. A. Bailey, *NTS* 25 [1978–79] 134). Even the theological emphasis on Christ as the Lord (*kyrios*) rather than insistently on the Father (*ho theos*) as the originator of a given action or blessing (1 Thess 1:4 and 2 Thess 2:13; 1 Thess 5:24 [cf. 1 Cor 1:9; 10:13] and 2 Thess 3:3; 1 Thess 5:23 [cf. 1 Cor 14:33; 2 Cor 13:11; Rom 15:33 and 16:20; Phil 4:9] and 2 Thess 3:16; 1 Thess 3:11 and 2 Thess 3:5) and the order of the blessing in 2 Thess 2:16 speak for authorship a generation or two after Paul's time.

6   Furthermore, although eschatology emerges as a major theme in both letters, it is handled differently in each. In 1 Thess, Paul expressly supposes that the Thessalonians are not preoccupied with the clock-and-calendar time of the Day of the Lord (5:1–3). He goes on to encourage them to continue being prepared (5:4–11). He has already assured them (4:13–18) that the deceased faithful do or will enjoy a definite priority over those who still hopefully look forward to the Lord's coming, probably (as Paul optimistically envisaged the future) within their own lifetime. In contrast, while retaining an even stronger focus on the Day of the Lord, making it the central doctrinal issue, 2 Thess almost officiously disapproves of enthusiasm concerning the clock-and-calendar presence or nearness of the Lord's parousia. The second letter draws attention to the signs or prerequisite conditions for the Lord's triumphal coming and presents these in a grimly sobering way (1:5–10; 2:1–15). It also treats the topic more from the standpoint of official, traditional teaching than from that of a shared, eager hope. Unlike 1 Thess 5:19–20, 2 Thess does not encourage sound prophecy and holding fast (*katechein*) what is good; rather, it confronts specifically the threat that false prophecy poses to the doctrinal stability and ongoing patient endurance of the community.

7   Typically Pauline touches like personal travel plans and even his own signature appear in a different light in 2 Thess. 2 Thess 3:7–9 speaks briefly and quite dispassionately about previous contacts with the Thessalonians (contrast 1 Thess 1:6–2:12) and bypasses reference to the fulfillment or frustration of Paul's earnest desires for further personal contacts with the Thessalonians (1 Thess 2:17–20; 3:9–11). Elsewhere, when Paul concludes in his own script (Gal 6:11–18; 1 Cor 16:21–24), he includes a spirited personal message; 2 Thess 3:17, however, adduces the signature only to authenticate the document with a view to the tradition

that it contains (cf. 2:2,15; 3:6). Accordingly, the author of 2 Thess modifies the appeal to the example of "Christ's apostles" (in 1 Thess 2:7), not arrogating to himself personally the founding of churches; he appeals more insistently to "imitation" of a traditionally recognized model (*typos*, 2 Thess 3:9). Lastly, in contrast to Pauline letters (even 1 Thess 4:14; 5:10; cf. 1:6; 2:15), vivid awareness of the "theology of the cross" is surprisingly absent throughout 2 Thess. Even in recalling basic instruction, the tone of 2 Thess (2:5; cf. 1 Thess 1:5; 2:5) lacks Pauline vitality. In short, contrasted with Paul himself, the writer of 2 Thess is not as personally engaged in the process of communication.

8   In contrast to what one infers from Paul's own correspondence, the close references to 1 Thess in this letter suppose that the author of 2 Thess had at hand a copy of a previous letter to the community and drew on it mainly to provide a context for his own advice in view of a new situation. That situation concerned eschatological expectation, a topic most easily developed in the context of 1 Thess. Whether the author of 2 Thess is countering an incipiently gnostic view that the Day of the Lord has already occurred (and the parousia is therefore irrelevant) or a resurgence of apocalyptic expectation of its imminence in clock-and-calendar time remains debatable (depending largely on the way one construes *enestēken* in 2:2). In either case, the author himself stands in an apocalyptic tradition which he intends further to authenticate. He is hardly trying to replace 1 Thess (as Marxsen holds) in developing without contradiction but with a new focus the language and themes of 1 Thess. In addressing a problem of "the Thessalonians," he writes from a wider perspective of other Pauline letters as well (3:17, "in every letter"). The probable circumstance of his communication, as scholarly guesses go, is Asia Minor in the last decade of the 1st cent., when the Pauline corpus of letters was taking shape.

9   Pseudonymous authorship does not justify doctrinally negative evaluation. Precisely as a pseudepigraph, 2 Thess attests to a process of theological development, consciously pursued with regard to the finality of Christian life: the ultimate divine judgment against the wicked (deceivers and the unrepentant deceived) and the final security of the faithful through the coming of the Lord Jesus Christ. Such theological development draws on past tradition even as it may fail to recapture its zest. Nonetheless, it meets key issues anew in order to foster sober understanding of faith (1:10; 2:2a) and sound hope in the practical conduct of life (2:16–17).

10   **(II) Outline.** 2 Thessalonians is outlined as follows:

(I) Opening Formula (1:1–2)
(II) Test of Persecution Leading to the Lord's Glory in Judgment (1:3–12)
   (A) Thanksgiving (1:3–10)
   (B) Prayer (1:11–12)
(III) Proper Understanding of the Parousia (2:1–17)
   (A) The Lord's Triumph over Deception (2:1–15)
   (B) Prayer for Strengthening (2:16–17)
(IV) Two Sets of Closing Exhortations and Prayers (3:1–5,6–16)
(V) Final Greetings (3:17–18)

COMMENTARY

11   **(I) Opening Formula (1:1–2). 1.** *to the church . . . in God our Father and Jesus Christ, Lord:* The

status of the church provides the grounds for the similarly amplified greeting. **2.** *grace and peace:* Messianic blessings now and to come find their source in both persons, the Father and Jesus Christ, Lord, as the basis for the community's existence (→ NT Epistles, 45:8A).

12 (II) Test of Persecution Leading to the Lord's Glory in Judgment (1:3–12).

(A) Thanksgiving (1:3–10). The thanksgiving (vv 3–10) and prayer (vv 11–12) form one long, involved sentence. The trials of persecution (v 4) help indicate God's forthcoming judgment in proving the Thessalonians worthy of their calling (vv 5,11). Accordingly, the author prays that God will bring about in them the personal glory of the Lord Jesus. The thanksgiving arises from what is right (vv 3b–5) and just (vv 6–10). Its formulation suggests that of standard Jewish and Christian prayers in times of trial (see R. D. Aus, *JBL* 92 [1973] 432–38).

13 3b–5. *give thanks to God at all times for you, brothers, as is* (only) *right:* The reason is twofold: the increase of their faith and love (v 3cd) and the writer's grounds for taking credit among the churches of God for their patient endurance and fidelity in the persecutions and tribulations, which they are undergoing. **4.** *patient endurance: Hypomonē,* the passive aspect of *elpis,* "hope," is intrinsically associated (by the same article) with *pistis,* "fidelity." Persecutions have a generic quality here; in 1 Thess 2:14–16 Paul himself was more specific. *we boast:* Paul's own boasting regularly looks to the final stage of the eschatological period (e.g., 1 Thess 2:19); the writer looks to the present situation as well. For he considers current trials as related to their future resolution. **5.** *advance indication of God's righteous judgment:* The ultimate purpose of their sufferings is not just survival, but being able to be judged worthy of God's kingdom, i.e., to qualify as those admitted to enjoy God's fully achieved governance at the parousia. Although the gift of faith is not conditioned on human accomplishments, faith once received must be worked out in fidelity and patient endurance.

14 6–10. *it is just on God's part:* The twofold, anticipated aspect of God's just judgment (see v 5) is carried forward with regard both to persecutors and to the faithful. *rest with us:* Final respite (*anesis*) for both the writer and his readers will come only with the Lord's self-manifestation. For "rest with us" is conceived mainly in terms not of a life after death but of a clear demonstration of God's condemnation of the wicked. As for Paul, God's condemnatory judgment, executed through the Lord Jesus (Rom 1:18–2:16), is conceived as a good thing, merited, not capriciously imposed. **7–8.** *from heaven, with his mighty angels, in blazing fire:* Standard, apocalyptic descriptive phrases are used sparingly, just enough to indicate a climactic, public manifestation of divine power, with irresistible, consuming force. **8–10.** The author directs more attention to the basis for the divine requital. **8.** *those who have not known God:* Pagans throughout the ages are considered culpably ignorant of not religiously acknowledging the Lord (Rom 1:18–32; Wis 13:1–9). *those who have not heeded the gospel of our Lord Jesus:* A more extensive class (ethnically, if not numerically) is added in the framework of the worldwide preaching of the gospel. **9.** *everlasting just punishment:* The writer does not speak of physical torment (as if "blazing fire" [v 8] were being applied), but refers to a definitive, everlasting dismissal upon confronting the face of the Lord. The Lord's glory is his unique, sovereignly effective power. **10.** *to be held in awe:* The Lord's glory is shown especially in the transforming power of his resurrection. Although, by itself, "holy ones" may suggest angels, parallelism with v 10b and a subsequent phrase in 2:14 suggest the resurrection of the faithful, as appreciatively acknowledged (v 10b). As made immortal

(not "as spirits"), they will share an "angelic" status (cf. Luke 20:35–36; 1 Cor 6:2). *our testimony to you was believed:* Parenthetically, but emphatically, this manifestation of the Lord's glory is rooted in Christians' faithful adherence to apostolic testimony.

15 (B) Prayer (1:11–12). *every good purpose and every effort of faith:* Moral fulfillment depends on God's own power. It is his grace that will make the faithful worthy of the Father's call. Accordingly, this fulfillment will amount to mutual glorification (mighty manifestation) at the parousia of their intimate personal relationship to the Lord Jesus. The latter (v 12a) is described in language borrowed from Isa 66:5 and used there of the one God, Yahweh himself. Similarly, *charis,* "grace," in v 12b describes the sovereign gift both of God (the Father) and of the Lord Jesus Christ. The two personal subjects (under one article, developing 1:1–2) function as one being.

16 (III) Proper Understanding of the Parousia (2:1–17).

(A) The Lord's Triumph over Deception (2:1–15). The major, central portion of the letter (chap. 2) consists of an explained warning held together by an inclusion in vv 2 and 15 and followed by a prayer for strengthening (vv 16–17). The writer shows concern consistently to instill a Christian (Pauline) tradition by presenting his addressees' experience, even its dangers, as part of an ultimately salutary divine process, countering diabolical deception. He deals pastorally with a surmountable threat to faith and does not speculate about an end-time scenario or provide a "countdown" for it.

17 1–3a. *concerning the parousia:* The writer appeals for sober judgment about Christ's triumphal coming, which he regards not as a date, but (by linking it with "our being gathered together to [meet] him" under one article) as the fulfillment of Christian life. **2.** *not suddenly to be shaken from your wits or be upset:* He warns them about being shaken from their wits (*apo tou noos*). His unusually strong language could well allude to a kind of Dionysiac mania. The allusion is ironic, much as in Paul's reference to witchcraft ("the evil eye") in Gal 3:1 (cf. Gal 1:6–7; 5:10b). Possible sources of this unhealthy alarm suggest a liturgical context (cf. 1 Cor 14:26–33a; 1 Thess 5:27). *a spirit:* Either a false oracle or, rather, its supposed superhuman agent; cf. 1 Cor 12:2–3. *a word:* Either an oral report (*logos*) or a sermon, or a forged letter. **3a.** *let no one deceive you in any way at all:* Danger of deception at the end of the end-time and even before it always figures prominently in NT apocalyptic (Mark 13:5–7; Luke 21:8–9; 17:22–24; Rev 13:13–34; 20:7–8; 2:24–25).

18 In apocalyptic thinking, evil must reach a certain fullness before the time is ripe for God's just judgment [see Giblin, *Threat to Faith* 131–39; cf. Rev 22:11]. A prior necessity for the Lord's coming is the manifestation of evil in its worst conceivable form, according to the writer's creative, biblical imagination and his pastoral purpose. "Signs" must be construed accordingly. **3b–4.** *for, unless the apostasy comes first and the Man of Rebellion is manifested, the Doomed One, the one who asserts himself against and opposes everyone called divine and every sacred object so as to (try to) seat himself in God's sanctuary passing himself off as divine:* These signs function as preconditions for what v 4 leaves unstated, viz., "the Day of the Lord is not at hand." "The apostasy" is a loss of faith even on the part of believers (or of those hitherto assumed to be such). Defection from true worship of God was extensive in the time of the persecutions of Antiochus IV Epiphanes (1 Macc 2:15; Dan 9:14). Description of the "Man of Rebellion" is indebted to a prophetic depiction of the historical despot who caused apostasy (Dan 11:36–37). As vv 8–10 will make clear, this rebel (*ho* *anomos*) is an imagined, symbolic figure representing a real evil, the antithesis of faith. He is at once Anti-God (v 4), Anti-Christ (vv 8–9a) with a pseudo parousia, and false prophet par excellence (vv 9b–10). "God's sanctuary" (*naos*) may refer to the Christian community as the Anti-God's objective, since "so as to" (*hōste* + infin.) in the context of the rebel's act of self-aggrandizement may be taken as conative, not as fully achieved. However, it may function simply as a "classical image" referring to the rebel's usurping God's prerogative. No concern for the physical Temple of Jerusalem (destroyed in AD 70) is required by this visionary scenario. **5.** *do you not recall:* In breaking off his statement (anacoluthon, v 4) the writer hastens to remind his addressees of basic Christian instruction: not details of a given apocalyptic scenario, but a warning of what the faithful must be prepared to face, especially the threat to their faith (cf. Mark 13; Matt 24–25; Luke 21:5–36).

19   **6–7.** The author alludes to a current, nonclimactic manifestation of the Anti-God, a pseudo-prophetic threat discernible in the context of previous instruction. He then indicates the continuity between this current, pseudo-prophetic threat and its future, climactic manifestation and closes by noting the current threat's elimination. **6.** *you know the seizing power, so that the rebel himself will be manifested at his own proper time:* "The seizing power" translates *to katechon* (neut. sg. ptc. of *katechein*, which regularly means "to possess," "hold fast," "hold on to" and not "to restrain"). It never, in fact, has the sense of "hold off," "prevent from coming" (which would be a form of *kōlyein*). *now, then:* This refers to the logical and also temporal consequence of previous instruction about the danger of deception. The writer hardly alludes to a cryptic figure known only from his Gk readers' supposedly esoteric, previous instruction, particularly if this entailed allusion to a Hebr word. *you know:* Oidate looks particularly to experiential knowledge, not to mere identification (for the writer does not say what *to katechon* is, which would require *tí to katechon* [*estin*]). Other interpreters suppose the transl. "restraining force," which they identify either as the preaching of the gospel, God's power, civil authority, or, in some way, as a beneficent power. The substantivized ptc. *to katechon* need suppose no object. Most interpreters supply "him" (meaning the Man of Rebellion), but "you" is no less likely if one feels the need to construe an object. Present experiential knowledge of attempted, manic "possession" is loosely but integrally related to the future, more overt manifestation of a "classical" Anti-God, Anti-Christ, a pseudo-prophetic figure (*eis to* + articular infin., "so that," i.e., "with a view to"). The "seizing power" is more plausibly taken as an allusion to a kind of demon or spirit (cf. v 2) of manic, Dionysiac character which has shaken the readers out of their wits. Such an allusion accords with the writer's pastoral interest in dealing with the problem at hand and does not suppose a speculative excursus, much less one that cannot reasonably be construed by his readership. *manifested at his own proper time:* The author refers to the timely moment (*kairos*) of the rebel's destruction, linking the mention of the "Doomed One" (v 2) with what will be developed in vv 8–10a. **7.** The writer then explains the continuity between the present, afflicting experience and what lies ahead. *the mystery of rebellion is active already:* Energeitai, "is active," figures as a key term; the identical notion (*energeia*) is repeated in vv 9 and 11. The explanatory v 7a militates against identifying *to katechon* as beneficent or neutral. The present threat to stability in faith is a foretaste of the much worse future one, which the Lord will triumphantly resolve (cf. present tribulations as an indication of the coming just judgment, 2 Thess

1:4c–5). *but the seizer must be for the present, until ousted:* The writer now uses the masc. ptc., *ho katechōn* (which, again, fits well as an allusion to a deceptive "pseudo spirit" or its human agent). The VL rightly perceived that the clause (introduced by Gk *monon*) had to be imperatival, and so added *teneat*. The seizer must be or must (try to) "seize," "possess" for the present until he is put out of the way or otherwise disappears. Such a disturbance, like divisions within the community (1 Cor 11:19), is inevitable, as are false reports (cf. Luke 21:7–9: *dei . . . genesthai prōton*). In a sense, the community may be freed from the problem simply by being alerted to it. In any event, the author, like Paul in Gal 5:10, takes no further measures to resolve the problem, perhaps for the same reason: he does not know the one(s) responsible.

20   **8–10.** After relating (vv 6–7) the present phase of deception to its future, apocalyptic fulfillment, which he had recalled to their minds (vv 3b–5), the writer takes up his description of the Day of the Lord as the triumph over deception. **8.** *at that point, the rebel will be manifested:* He will have a pseudo parousia (conceived as a foil to the Lord's own, actual coming) and will be eliminated effortlessly by the Lord's Spirit (cf. Isa 11:4). *by the éclat of his own parousia, the Lord will completely inactivate him:* The Lord's undoing (*katargēsei*) the rebel again plays on the term *energeia*. **9–10.** The rebel's pseudo parousia is the result of a satanic activity (*energeia*). Thus, the rebel's self-manifestation or disclosure proves to be the unmasking of the process of deception ("mystery of rebellion") which is already at work and amounts to pseudo prophetic activity (cf. "power [miracles], signs, wonders"). This process is not necessarily fatal. **10.** *in every wicked deceit among those who are being brought to ruin because they have not welcomed the love of the truth for their salvation:* In spite of humans' own faults, salvation remains a real prospect, given a free, loving response to the gospel.

21   **11–14.** *that is why God sends them . . . ; but we must give thanks concerning you:* Contrasted actions on God's part show that, ultimately, it is he who controls the total process (under the aspect of governance and invitation rather than "predetermination"). **11–12.** One line of God's action results in condemnatory judgment, which is a good thing, granted that it is deserved. Employing imagery reminiscent of 2 Kgs 22:19–23, the author indicates God's control even over the power of deception (his "sending" it). At the same time, he supposes that human beings can pass this test, if they genuinely welcome the truth (cf. vv 11,12) and do not delight in wrongdoing, which follows from a distorted understanding of God (cf. Rom 1:18–32). **13–14.** The other line, phrased encouragingly as a thanksgiving, looks to salvation. **13.** *called from the beginning:* This phrase (rather than the *l.v.,* "called as the firstfruits") stresses God's initiative. **14.** *to possess the glory of our Lord Jesus Christ:* Salvation, equivalently "becoming the Lord's glorious possession," follows from moral holiness and doctrinal fidelity according to the Christian vocation. **15.** *stand firm and hold fast to the traditions which you were taught either orally or by our letter(s):* Communication by "a spirit" (cf. v 2) seems pointedly to be omitted. *Epistolē* is generic here; the writer supposes more than one letter (cf. 3:17).

22   **(B) Prayer for Strengthening (2:16–17).** Without prayer, constantly included in this letter, the writer seems to think that his advice and exhortations would be sterile. Once more, he looks to stability (v 16; cf. v 15a) in contrast to instability (v 2) arising from deception in any form. **16.** *good hope in* (his) *grace: Elpis agathē,* "good hope," was used by the mystery religions for bliss after death, but is given a Christian dimension by being joined with "has given (us) everlasting consolation" and "in (his) grace." The new, Christian context refocuses "good hope" on the Lord's parousia (cf. 1:12).

23 **(IV) Two Sets of Closing Exhortations and Prayers (3:1–5,6–16).** The third part of 2 Thess consists of two sets of rather conventional exhortations, each closing with a prayer.

1–5. In the first set, the writer asks for prayers for the continued success of his apostolic work in the face of malevolent unbelievers. That work is not so much his as it is the progressive triumph of the Lord's word. Similarly, his confidence for the continued good work of the faithful is grounded in the Lord's own fidelity in strengthening and guarding them.

24 **6–16.** The second set of exhortations concerns treatment of the disorderly (*ataktoi*, not merely "the idle"). These people do not accept in practice the tradition on which the writer insists and may well be among those who created the religious confusion mentioned in 2:1–3a. Apostolic example itself is a practical norm of tradition. The disorderly not only fail to model themselves after it by not working, but also interfere with the stable lives of others. The prayer for peace in v 16 appropriately balances the prayer for progress in v 5.

25 **(V) Final Greetings (3:17–18).** The rather effusive greetings characteristic of Paul's own letters (except, understandably, for Gal) are notably absent here. The writer is concerned rather to authenticate his communication on the basis of a tradition that must refer to more than one of the Pauline letters we have. **17.** *in every letter:* He not only assumes 1 Thess (which Paul does not note as one he signed) but also supposes at least two other letters in which Paul penned his own comments (of which we have clear evidence only in 1 Cor, Gal, Phlm). His final blessing, minimally amplified, is precisely patterned on 1 Thess 5:28.

54

THE LETTER TO THE COLOSSIANS

Maurya P. Horgan

BIBLIOGRAPHY

1   Benoit, P., *Les épîtres de saint Paul aux Philippiens, à Philémon, aux Colossiens, aux Éphésiens* (SBJ; 3d ed.; Paris, 1959). Bruce, F. F., *The Epistles to the Colossians, to Philemon, and to the Ephesians* (NICNT; GR, 1984). Caird, G. B., *Paul's Letters from Prison* (NClarB; London, 1976). Cannon, G. E., *The Use of Traditional Materials in Colossians* (Macon, 1983). Conzelmann, H., *Der Brief an die Kolosser* (NTD 8; 14th ed.; Göttingen, 1976). Dibelius, M., *An die Kolosser, Epheser; an Philemon* (HNT 12; 3d ed., rev. H. Greeven; Tübingen, 1953) 1–53. Gabathuler, H. J., *Jesus Christus: Haupt der Kirche—Haupt der Welt* (Zurich, 1965). Gnilka, J., *Der Kolosserbrief* (HTKNT 10/1; Freiburg, 1980). Houlden, J. L., *Paul's Letters from Prison* (PC; Phl, 1978). Lähnemann, J., *Der Kolosserbrief* (SNT 3; Gütersloh, 1971). Lightfoot, J. B., *St. Paul's Epistles to the Colossians and to Philemon* (London,

1892). Lindemann, A., *Der Kolosserbrief* (ZBK NT 10; Zurich, 1983). Lohmeyer, E., *Die Briefe an die Philipper, an die Kolosser und an Philemon* (MeyerK 9/2; 11th ed.; Göttingen, 1956) 1–170. Lohse, E., *A Commentary on the Epistles to the Colossians and to Philemon* (Herm; Phl, 1971). Martin, R. P., *Commentary on Colossians and Philemon* (NCB; GR, 1981). Masson, C., *L'Épître de Saint Paul aux Colossiens* (CNT 10/2; Neuchâtel, 1950). Moule, C. F. D., *The Epistles of Paul the Apostle to the Colossians and to Philemon* (CGTC; Cambridge, 1958). Percy, E., *Die Probleme der Kolosser- und Epheserbriefe* (Lund, 1946). Schweizer, E., *The Letter to the Colossians* (Minneapolis, 1982).
         DBSup 7. 157–70. IDBSup 169–70. Kümmel, *INT* 335–48. Wik-Schm, *ENT* 463–75.

INTRODUCTION

2   **(I) Colossae.** Located in S Phrygia in the upper valley of the Lycus River, Colossae was an important city in late antiquity (Herodotus, *Hist.* 7.30.1; Xenophon, *Anab.* 1.2.6). It had a flourishing wool and textile industry, and its name was used for a dark red dye for wool (*colossinus*) (Strabo, *Geogr.* 12.8.16; Pliny, *Nat. Hist.* 21.51). The ruins of Colossae were discovered in 1835, but the site has not been excavated. By the beginning of the Christian era, Colossae had been eclipsed in stature by its neighboring city Laodicea (→ Apocalypse, 63:28). An earthquake in AD 60/61 destroyed parts of the Lycus Valley, including probably Colossae. There is no evidence of the extent of rebuilding in Colossae, but it is known that Laodicea was restored (Tacitus, *Ann.* 14.27.1; *Sib. Or.* 4:101–2; cf. 3:471; 5:318).

3   The population of Colossae comprised native Phrygians, Greeks, and a sizable community of Jews—perhaps as many as 10,000 in the Lycus Valley (Cicero, *Pro Flacc.* 28; Josephus, *Ant.* 12.3.4 §149–50). The Christian community in Colossae, made up principally of Gentiles (1:21,27; 2:13), was probably founded by Epaphras (1:7; 4:12), a native of Colossae. The slave Onesimus was also from Colossae, and probably also his master, Philemon (→ Philemon, 52:2–4; see F. F. Bruce,

BSac 141 [1984] 3–15; B. Reicke, *RevExp* 70 [1973] 429–38).

4   **(II) Authenticity.** The earliest evidence for Pauline authorship, aside from the letter itself (1:1,23; 4:18), is from the mid to late 2d cent. (Marcionite canon; Irenaeus, *Adv. Haer.* 3.14.1; Muratorian Canon). This traditional view stood unquestioned until 1838, when E. T. Mayerhoff denied the authenticity of Col, claiming that it was full of non-Pauline ideas and dependent on Eph. Thereafter others have found additional arguments against Pauline authorship. Debate has focused on two areas of comparison with the undisputed Pauline letters: language and style, and theological ideas.

5   The vocabulary of Col shows the following peculiarities: 34 *hapax legomena* in the NT, 28 words that do not appear in the undisputed Pauline letters, 10 words in common only with Eph, 15 words that occur in Col and Eph but not elsewhere in the NT. In addition, some of the most characteristically Pauline terms do not appear in Col: righteousness, to believe, law, to save, and many of the usual Pauline connectives and particles. The address "brothers" or "my brothers," frequent in the undisputed writings (e.g., Rom 1:13; 1 Cor 1:10; 2 Cor 1:8; Gal 1:11), does not appear in Col or Eph. References to the Spirit are infrequent in Col. These peculiarities are balanced somewhat by other evidence: typically Pauline expressions are used in the introduction, thanksgiving, greetings, and conclusion. Moreover, many of the unique terms in Col appear in the traditional hymn (1:15-20) and in the polemical section (2:6-23), which draws its vocabulary from that of the opponents.

Non-Pauline features of the style of Col include the following: the liturgic-hymnic style in contrast to the debating style of Rom and Gal; frequent coordination of synonyms (1:9,11,22,23,26; 2:7; 3:8,16; 4:12); strings of dependent genitives (1:5,12,13,20,24,27; 2:2,11,12); nouns attached to phrases with *en* (1:6,8,12,29); loosely joined infinitives for purpose or result (1:10,22,25; 4:3, 6); long sentences with many subordinate clauses. Some suggest that these differences represent Paul's style as it developed in later years or that the differences are the result of the incorporation of a great amount of traditional material into the letter. (See Lohse, *Commentary* 84-91; Percy; and W. Bujard, *Stilanalytische Untersuchungen zum Kolosserbrief* [Göttingen, 1973].)

6 The theological areas usually singled out for comparison are christology, eschatology, and ecclesiology. The christology of Col is built on the traditional hymn in 1:15-20, according to which Christ is the image of the invisible God (1:15; cf. 2 Cor 4:4), the firstborn of all creation (1:15; cf. Rom 8:29), before all things (1:17), the beginning (1:18), the firstborn from the dead (1:18); the one in whom, through whom, and for whom all things were created (1:16), the one in whom the fullness dwells (1:19; cf. Eph 3:19), the one through whom all things are reconciled (1:20; cf. Rom 5:10; 2 Cor 5:18-19), the head of the body, the church (1:18; cf. Eph 1:22; 4:15; 5:23). These themes are developed throughout the letter, and other christological statements that have no parallel in the undisputed Pauline writings are added: that Christ is the mystery of God (1:27; 2:2-3); that believers have been raised with Christ (2:12); that Christ forgives sins (1:13-14; 3:13; cf. Eph 1:7); that Christ is victorious over the principalities and powers (2:15). However, some characteristically Pauline christological ideas do appear in the letter: Christ is the Son in whom believers have redemption (1:13-14; cf. Rom 3:24; 1 Cor 1:30); believers are buried with Christ in baptism (2:12; cf. Rom 6:4); Christ is seated at the right hand of God (3:1; cf. Rom 8:34) (→ Pauline Theology, 82:48-60, 67-80; see J. C. O'Neill, *NTS* 26 [1979-80] 87-100; W. A. Meeks, "In One Body," *God's Christ and His People* [Fest. N. A. Dahl; ed. J. Jervell and W. A. Meeks; Oslo, 1977] 209-21; F. O. Francis, "The Christological Argument of Colossians," ibid. 192-208).

The eschatology of Col is described as realized. There is a lessening of eschatological expectation in Col, whereas Paul expected the parousia in the near future (1 Thes 4:15; 5:23; 1 Cor 7:26). The idea of the future return of Christ does appear in Col (3:4), but believers are encouraged to make "the things that are above" a present reality (3:1-2). The congregation has already been raised from the dead with Christ (2:12; 3:1), whereas in the undisputed letters resurrection is a future expectation (1 Cor 6:14; 2 Cor 4:14). In Col, hope, which is the content of the gospel (1:23) and the mystery (1:27), is already laid up in heaven (1:5), whereas in Paul (e.g., Rom 5:2; 8:24; 2 Cor 1:10; Gal 5:5) hope is within the believer and oriented to the future (→ Pauline Theology, 82:44-47). The difference in eschatological orientation between Col and the undisputed letters results in a different theology of baptism (→ Pauline Theology, 82:112-15). Whereas in Rom 6:1-4 baptism looks forward to the future, in Col baptism looks back to a completed salvation. In baptism believers have not

only died with Christ but also been raised with him.

The chief difference in ecclesiology between Col and the undisputed Pauline writings is that, whereas in the Pauline writings the term "church" usually designates the local church in a specific and concrete way, in Col the church is a universal entity, the body of which Christ is the head (1:18,24; 2:19; 3:15; but cf. 4:15,16, which refer to local churches). In this, ecclesiology is connected to christology, and what is said of Christ as the head of the body can be inferred to have significance for the members of that body. The role of believers in the church is to hold fast to the head (2:19), to teach and admonish one another (3:16). There is no description of special offices or structures within the church. Paul refers to himself as an apostle (1:1), and he, Epaphras, and Tychicus are called ministers (1:7,23; 4:7).

7 The cumulative weight of the many differences from the undisputed Pauline epistles has persuaded most modern scholars that Paul did not write Col (Lohse, Gnilka, Meeks, Francis, Käsemann, Lindemann [→ NT Epistles, 45:12-15]). Those who defend the authenticity of the letter include Martin, Caird, Houlden, Cannon, and Moule. Some, e.g., Masson and Benoit, describe the letter as Pauline but say that it was heavily interpolated or edited. Schweizer suggests that Col was jointly written by Paul and Timothy. The position taken here is that Col is Deutero-Pauline; it was composed after Paul's lifetime, between AD 70 (Gnilka) and AD 80 (Lohse) by someone who knew the Pauline tradition. Lohse regards Col as the product of a Pauline school tradition, probably located in Ephesus.

8 **(III) The Opponents.** The purpose of Col was to bolster the faith of the community (1:3-14; 2:2-3) and to correct errors reported about the church in Colossae (2:4,8,16,18-22). One of the chief areas of study about Col has been the attempt to identify the opponents who were misleading the community in Colossae. According to the letter, the false teaching is a philosophy and an empty deceit (2:8), a human tradition (2:8); it concerns the elemental spirits of the universe (2:8) and angels (2:18); it demands observance of food regulations and festivals, new moons, and sabbath (2:14, 16,20,21); and it encourages ascetic practices.

Since the opponents are charged with "not holding fast to the head," the error must have arisen within the believing community. Jewish and Hellenistic elements seem to be interwoven in what can be inferred of the error. A complex syncretism that incorporated features of Judaism, paganism, Christianity, magic, astrology, and mystery religion forms the cultural background of the letter (Lähnemann, *Kolosserbrief* 82-100), and, consequently, it may be impossible to identify the opponents in Colossae with a particular group.

Features that suggest some relation of the error to pagan cults or mystery religions include the apparent reference to an initiation rite (2:11); the phrase *stoicheia tou kosmou*, "elements of the universe," well attested in Oriental, Hellenistic, and gnostic speculation (→ 20 below); and the word "mystery" (1:27; 2:2; 4:3). Moreover, Hierapolis, the neighboring city of Colossae and Laodicea, is known to have been a center of Phrygian mystery cults (Strabo, *Geogr.* 13.4.14). Parallels to Hellenistic philosophy have been noted by Schweizer, who refers to a Pythagorean text containing all the elements of the Colossian error except the regulations about drink and sabbath.

Many elements in the Colossian error have been connected with gnosticism, e.g., asceticism, fullness of God, wisdom, knowledge, dualism, negation of things of the world; however, most commentators caution that the use of the term gnosticism may be misleading, since it properly refers to the 2d-cent. heresy. The descriptions "proto-gnostic," "pre-gnostic," "incipient gnosticism" are used to describe this tendency in Col.

Most scholars connect the error with Judaism in some form, since even the elements that can be connected with pagan cults, mystery religion, Hellenistic philosophy, or "incipient gnosticism" can also be found in the very diverse early Judaism of the time, as evidenced in the later writings of the OT, Jewish apocalyptic writings, wisdom literature, the DSS, and in other intertestamental writings. In 1875, long before the discovery of the DSS, J. B. Lightfoot suggested that the Colossian opponents had some connection with Essenism. Indeed, there are points of contact between the QL and what can be inferred about the opponents from Col: dietary regulations, concern with the calendar, festivals, and sabbath.

(Bruce, F. F., *BSac* 141 [1984] 195–208. Evans, C. A., *Bib* 63 [1982] 188–205. Francis, F. O., *LTQ* 2 [1967] 71–81. Francis, F. O. and W. A. Meeks [eds.], *Conflict at Colossae* [Cambridge MA, 1973]. Gunther, J. J., *St. Paul's Opponents and Their Background* [Leiden, 1973]. Rowland, C., *JSNT* 19 [1983] 73–83.)

9   (IV) Composition and Structure of the Letter. Col is a carefully composed letter that incorporates the main structural features of the undisputed Pauline letters (greeting, thanksgiving, exposition, exhortation, messages, and closing; → NT Epistles, 45:8) and also blocks of traditional material (a hymn, 1:15–20;

baptismal catechesis, 2:6–15; lists of vices and virtues, 3:5–17; a household code, 3:18–4:1). The traditional materials are integrated into the letter by means of sections of application and transition (1:12–14,21–23; 2:1–5; 3:1–4; 4:2–6), which summarize the themes that precede, usually with specific reference to the community in Colossae, and introduce the topic that is to be taken up in the next section.

(V) Outline.

   (I) Greeting (1:1–2)
  (II) Thanksgiving and Prayer (1:3–23)
      (A) Thanksgiving (1:3–8)
      (B) Prayer (1:9–11)
      (C) Application and Transition (1:12–14)
      (D) Hymn (1:15–20)
      (E) Application and Transition (1:21–23)
 (III) Paul's Ministry (1:24–2:5)
      (A) The Apostle's Hardships (1:24–25)
      (B) The Mystery Revealed and Preached (1:26–29)
      (C) Application and Transition (2:1–5)
 (IV) Life in the Body of Christ in Teaching (2:6–3:4)
      (A) The Tradition of Christ Jesus (2:6–15)
      (B) The Human Tradition (2:16–23)
      (C) Application and Transition (3:1–4)
  (V) Life in the Body of Christ in Practice (3:5–4:6)
      (A) Vices (3:5–10)
      (B) Virtues (3:11–17)
      (C) Household Code (3:18–4:1)
      (D) Application and Transition (4:2–6)
 (VI) Messages and Closing (4:7–18)

COMMENTARY

10   (I) Greeting (1:1–2). Following the form of ancient letters, Col begins by naming the sender(s) and the addressee(s) and by including a greeting (→ NT Epistles, 45:6, 8A). **1.** *Paul an apostle:* See comment on Gal 1:1. The content of the letter, esp. the instruction to correct false teaching, is presented with the authority of Paul's apostleship, which is the theme of 1:24–2:5. **2.** *to the holy and faithful brethren:* In contrast to the beginnings of other letters (Rom 1:7; 1 Cor 1:2; 2 Cor 1:1; Eph 1:1; Phil 1:1), "holy" is an adj. coordinated with "faithful" rather than the substantive "saints." In the OT, Israel is a holy (*qādôš*) people, but *qĕdōšîm* ("holy ones") often refers to the heavenly assembly (e.g., Zech 14:5; Ps 89:6). The members of the Qumran community referred to themselves as the "holy ones" (1QM 3:5; 6:6; 10:10; 16:1). *in Christ:* → Pauline Theology, 82:121. The phrase *en Christǭ* expresses the union of the believer with Christ on many levels, and this is an important theme in Col (1:4,14,16,17,19,28; 2:3,6,7,9,10,11,12; 3:18,20; 4:7).
11   (II) Thanksgiving and Prayer (1:3–23).
(A) Thanksgiving (1:3–8). The thanksgiving, a common feature of Greco-Roman letters, is a part of most of the NT epistles (→ NT Epistles, 45:8B). These verses form one long sentence that includes facts about the relationship between the sender(s) and the addressee(s), about the community, and about the situation of the letter: the gospel was brought to the community by Epaphras (1:7); the community is growing and bearing fruit (1:6); a report of this has been brought to Paul (1:4). **3.** *our Lord Jesus Christ:* → Jesus, 78:42; → Pauline Theology, 82:51–54. **4–5.** *faith, love, and hope:* This triad appears frequently in NT epistles and probably was part of early pre-Pauline tradition (Caird). The triad becomes a theme that is expanded in the teaching of the letter. Faith in Christ Jesus (1:4; see also 2:5,7) is

developed in 1:23 as the condition for being presented holy and blameless before Christ, and in 2:12 as one of the means by which believers have been raised with Christ. Love is the practice within the Christian community that holds the body together (1:4,8; 2:2; 3:14). Hope, in contrast to the former two dispositions of the believers, is something outside the believer (1:5,23,27; → 6 above; see Rom 8:24 and comment).
12   (B) Prayer (1:9–11) and **(C) Application and Transition (1:12–14).** Grammatically these verses are a unit in which the main vb., "we have not ceased," is followed by three ptcs., "praying" (1:9), "asking," and "giving thanks" (1:12). Picking up the themes of the thanksgiving section, the prayer expands on the ideas of faith, love, and hope. **9.** *knowledge, wisdom, and understanding:* These key words indicate a practical, not a speculative, goal: knowledge demands obedience to God's will. The three corresponding Hebr terms *da'at, ḥokmâ,* and *bînâ,* are found very frequently in the QL (1QH 1:19–21, where the three are connected with the revelation of mysteries [cf. Col 1:27–28; 2:2–3], 1QS 4:2–8, which recounts the ways of the Spirit of Truth, which include humility and forbearance; understanding, knowledge, and wisdom; zeal for just ordinances, a firm inclination, and discretion concerning the mysteries [cf. Col 2:18,23; 3:12–13]). **12.** *share in the lot of the saints in light:* This calls to mind again the teachings of the QL: the ethical dualism of "light and darkness" (see Col 1:13) and the "portion" or "lot" (Hebr *gôrāl* [1QM 13:9–10; 1QH 3:22–23; 6:12–13; 11:11–12]), which is a predetermined destiny meted out to human beings (see P. Benoit, "Qumran and the NT," *Paul and Qumran* [ed. J. Murphy-O'Connor; Chicago, 1968] 18–24; "Hagioi in Colossiens 1.12," *Paul and Paulinism* [Fest. C. K. Barrett; ed. M. D. Hooker and S. G. Wilson; London, 1982]

83–101; in the latter article he suggests that "saints" refers perhaps both to the faithful community and to heavenly beings). **12–14.** These verses, taken by some as an introduction to or actually a part of the christological hymn in vv 15–20, form one of the transition sections of the letter (→ 9 above). They are tied both in grammar and in content to the preceding thanksgiving section and to the following hymn. **14.** *forgiveness of sins: Aphesis hamartiōn* does not occur in the undisputed Pauline writings; see Eph 1:7; Heb 9:22; 10:18; → Pauline Theology, 82:75 (end).

13 (C) Hymn (1:15–20). However vv 12–14 are interpreted, it has long been recognized that vv 15–20 are an independent unit that has the character of a primitive Christian hymn. Other poetic passages in the NT letters can be found in Phil 2:6–11; 1 Tim 3:16; 1 Pet 2:22–25; they probably had their origins in the liturgy (see B. Vawter, *CBQ* 33 [1971] 68–70). Both the style and the content of these verses may also be compared with the Qumran hymns or *Hôdāyôt* (1QH) and with the prologue to the Gospel of John (J. M. Robinson, *JBL* 76 [1957] 278–79; *BGJ* 20. Differences in language, style, and thought from the rest of Col and from the undisputed Pauline letters suggest that this hymnic section was not composed by the author of the letter but rather that it was, for the most part, traditional material adapted by the author of Col to serve the instructional purposes of the letter. (But Benoit thinks that the author of Col composed the hymn, and E. Käsemann has argued that the origins of the hymn were gnostic, not Christian.)

The many attempts to identify the background of the hymn include the following descriptions of the material: a stoic hymn mediated by Hellenism (E. Norden); a Jewish midrash on Gen 1:1 in the light of Prov 8:22 (C. F. Burney, followed by W. D. Davies); Jewish material related to the Day of Atonement (Lohmeyer); a Christianized hymn to a gnostic redeemer figure (Käsemann); Jewish wisdom speculation (J. T. Sanders); Jewish and Christian missionary theology growing out of OT thought (N. Kehl). These descriptions, like those of the Colossian error, must be weighed against the atmosphere of syncretism that pervaded Asia Minor at this time. Many elements from diverse settings may be interwoven in the hymn, but most commentators would agree that Jewish wisdom motifs are prominent.

Although it is agreed that a hymn is present here, there are many different suggestions concerning its structure. The two chief issues are: (1) whether the hymn begins with v 12 (→ 12 above; so, e.g., Lohmeyer, Norden, Käsemann, Lohse, Schille, and Kehl) or with v 15 (so, e.g., Schweizer, Bruce, Martin, Masson, Gnilka, Benoit, Conzelmann, Gabathuler, Lindemann, Aletti); (2) which elements in the hymn are redactional. The latter question, however, does not affect the hymn as it stands in Col, but is of importance for those who attempt to recover the original hymn or to determine the theology of the redactor. (For a summary of the views of modern commentators concerning redactional elements, see the chart in Benoit, "L'hymne" 238.) Almost all (except Kehl) agree that "the church" in 1:18a is an addition, and most regard "through the blood of his cross" in 1:20b as redactional. There are some repetitions within the hymn that are clear indications of the main divisions: the rel. pron. *hos estin* (1:15a,18b); *prōtotokos*, "firstborn" (1:15b,18b); clauses beginning with *hoti en autō*, "for in him" (1:16,19); clauses with *di' autou*, "through him" (1:16b,20).

15 Who is the image of the invisible God,
     Firstborn of all creation,

16 For in him was created everything,
     in heaven and on earth,
     the seen and the unseen,
     whether thrones or dominions,
     whether principalities or powers;
   everything through him and for him
       was created.
17   He is before everything;
     and everything in him exists.
18   He is the head of the body,
     the church.
Who is the beginning,
Firstborn from the dead,
     so that in everything he is preeminent.
19 For in him all the fullness was pleased to dwell,
   and through him to reconcile everything to him,
     making peace through the blood of his cross,
       whether on earth
       or in heaven.

15–16. The theme is the role of Christ in creation, which alludes to wisdom motifs in the OT. In Prov 3:19 wisdom is described as an agent in creation; in Prov 8:22–31, wisdom, created first, is a partner in the work of Yahweh (cf. Wis 7:22; 9:2–4). *image:* For Christ as the image of God, see 2 Cor 4:4; elsewhere Paul speaks of human beings in the image of Christ or of God (Rom 8:29 [see comment]; 1 Cor 11:7; 15:49; 2 Cor 3:18). *thrones or dominions . . . principalities or powers:* These created entities are presented in Col as angelic beings that are subordinate to Christ (these terms are used also to refer to earthly powers [see comments on 2 Pet 2:10; Jude 8]). In the false teaching in Colossae, these entities may have been thought of as rivals of Christ or beings that provided supplementary power to that of Christ (2:10,15). Such a belief grew out of a complex and highly developed angelology that was widespread at this time. This is the only place in the NT where "thrones" is a category of angelic beings; the other terms do appear: "dominions," Eph 1:21; "principalities," Rom 8:38 [see comment]; 1 Cor 15:24; Eph 1:21; "powers," 1 Cor 15:24; Eph 1:21; 2:10 (→ Pauline Theology, 82:89; see also W. Carr, *Angels and Principalities* [Cambridge, 1981]; M. Black, *"Pasai exousiai autō hypotagēsontai," Paul and Paulinism* [→ 12 above] 74–82). **17.** *before everything:* The hymn presents Christ as preexistent, another reflection of wisdom speculation in Hellenistic Judaism (→ Pauline Theology, 82:49–50; see comment on 1 Cor 8:4–6; R. G. Hamerton-Kelly, *Pre-Existence, Wisdom, and the Son of Man* [Cambridge, 1973]). **18.** *the head of the body, the church:* See also 2:19. The redactional phrase "the church" alters the idea of Christ as the head of the cosmic body to Christ as the head of the church, an important theme in Col (1:24,27; 2:17,19; 3:15). The community as the body is a theme present also in the undisputed Pauline writings (1 Cor 6:15; 10:16–17; 12:12–27; Rom 12:4–5 [see comment]), but the image of Christ as the head of the body represents a development over the Pauline idea (Eph 1:23; 4:15–16; 5:23; → Pauline Theology, 82:122–27). *the beginning:* There may be a play on words here between *archē*, "beginning," referring to Christ's preexistence and role in creation, and *archē*, "principality," which proclaims Christ the ruler par excellence over the entities named in v 16 (see 2:10,15). *firstborn from the dead:* Cf. Rom 8:29; 1 Cor 15:20; Rev 1:5. **19.** *all the fullness was pleased to dwell:* Cf. 1 Cor 8:6. Some commentators explain "fullness" as "of God" from 2:9 (so *RSV*), but "fullness" is used here without a qualifying genitive. The *plērōma* would have had special significance if gnostic ideas formed part of the false teaching in Colossae. In gnosticism, the *plērōma* was the whole body of heavenly powers and spiritual emanations that came forth from God (J. Ernst, *Pleroma und Pleroma Christi*

[Regensburg, 1970]). **20.** *to reconcile:* The vb. *apokatallassō* occurs only in Col and Eph. Paul uses *katallassō* with the same meaning in Rom 5:10; 2 Cor 5:18,19 (→ Pauline Theology, 82:72).

(Aletti, J.-N., *Colossiens 1,15–20* [AnBib 91; Rome, 1981]. Benoit, P., "L'hymne christologique de Col 1,15–20," *Christianity, Judaism and Other Greco-Roman Cults* [Fest. M. Smith; ed. J. Neusner; Leiden, 1975] 1. 226–63. Bruce, F. F., *BSac* 141 [1984] 99–111. Deichgräber, R., *Gotteshymnus und Christushymnus in der frühen Christenheit* [Göttingen, 1967] 146–52. Gabathuler, *Jesus Christus.* Käsemann, E., "A Primitive Christian Baptismal Liturgy," *ENTT* 149–68. Kehl, N., *Der Christushymnus im Kolosserbrief* [Stuttgart, 1967]. Norden, E., *Agnostos Theos* [Leipzig, 1913]. Schille, G., *Frühchristliche Hymnen* [Berlin, 1965]. Vawter, B., *CBQ* 33 [1971] 62–81.)

14   (E) Application and Transition (1:21–23). This section returns to the themes of the prayer (vv 9–14) and of the hymn (vv 15–20) and demonstrates their relevance to the community. **21.** *alienated and hostile in mind, in evil deeds:* Before the gospel was brought to the community by Epaphras, their situation was the opposite of what the author prays for in vv 9–14: knowledge, wisdom, and spiritual understanding (v 9), in contrast to their having been alienated and hostile in mind; doing "every good work" (v 10), in contrast to their evil deeds. **22.** *his fleshly body:* See also 2:11. K. G. Kuhn ("New Light on Temptation, Sin, and Flesh in the New Testament," *The Scrolls and the New Testament* [ed. K. Stendahl; NY, 1957] 107) calls this a *terminus technicus* in Judaism with the neutral meaning of ordinary human body or bodiliness (cf. 1QpHab 9:2). In Col, the importance and dignity of Jesus' human body in its saving function contrast with the depreciation of the body that seems to have been part of the false teaching of Colossae (2:18, 21,23), recalling again the important theme of the body of Christ. *through death:* Reconciliation through the death of Jesus is a frequent idea in the Pauline writings; see comment on Rom 5:10. **23.** *hope of the gospel:* That is, the hope and the gospel are the same (→ 6 above). *in all creation:* The gospel is universal, in contrast to the exclusiveness of secret cults. *I, Paul, became a minister:* The Deutero-Pauline author injects a note of authenticity and completes the transition to the next section, which treats Paul's ministry (→ 6 above).

15   (III) Paul's Ministry (1:24–2:5). Paul's apostolic authority is established before the main christological instruction and the warnings that will be presented in 2:6–23. As in the preceding section, this part of the letter interweaves themes that have been presented earlier (the church as the body of Christ; the triad of faith, hope, and love; wisdom, knowledge, and understanding) and introduces new themes that will be developed throughout the rest of the letter: the mystery (1:26,27; 2:2; 4:3) and false teaching (2:4,8–23).

16   (A) The Apostle's Hardships (1:24–25). **24.** *I complete what is needed of the Christian sufferings in my flesh for his body:* This is usually translated, "I fill up in my flesh what is lacking in the afflictions of Christ." Interpreters have debated two issues: (1) the meaning of filling up what is lacking; and (2) the meaning of "afflictions of Christ." Since the hymn proclaimed Christ as the one through whom all are reconciled—restated by the author in 1:22—v 24 should not be thought to say that Christ's work was somehow insufficient. The word *thlipsis,* which is never used of Jesus' passion but is regularly used of the hardships of those proclaiming the gospel (Rom 5:3; 8:35; 2 Cor 1:4,8; 2:4; 4:17; 6:4; 7:4), suggests that the afflictions are Paul's, not Christ's (Schweizer, Lindemann). (A similar use of the gen. "of Christ" can be found in 2:11, "the circumcision of

Christ," i.e., not Jesus' circumcision, but the metaphorical circumcision of the Christian community [W. A. Meeks, "In One Body" [→ 6 above] 217 n. 8]). This verse reflects the belief that those who proclaim the gospel would have to endure hardships and afflictions.

17   (B) The Mystery Revealed and Preached (1:26–29). **26.** *the mystery:* In contrast to "the mysteries," i.e., Hellenistic or Jewish syncretistic cults in which knowledge of cosmic or religious secrets was available to a few privileged initiates, "the mystery" here is a universal revelation open to all, the word of God, Christ among you, the glorious hope. Mystery is a key idea also in the sectarian writings of the QL (Hebr and Aram *rāz;* cf. Dan 2:18,19,27–30,47; 4:6). In QL *rāz* is a mystery revealed by God to certain persons, e.g., the Teacher of Righteousness (1QpHab 7:1–5). The mystery in Jewish prophetic, apocalyptic, and wisdom writings is associated with the ancient prophets' being introduced in their visions into the heavenly assembly and there learning the secret divine plans for history (see R. E. Brown, *CBQ* 20 (1958) 426–48; 40 (1959) 70–87; J. M. Casciaro Ramirez, *Scripta Theologica* 8 (1976) 9–56; Benoit, "Qumran and the New Testament" [→ 12 above] 21–24). The mystery refers to the divine plan of history, in contrast to its use in the so-called mystery cults, where mysteries were cosmic, metaphysical, or philosophical secrets. *God wished to make known:* The revelation of the mystery is from God (cf. 1QpHab 7:1–5). *the richness of the glory of this mystery:* Cf. Rom 9:23. *the glorious hope:* → 6 above. **28.** *admonishing and teaching:* Here this is the task of the apostle, but in 3:16 the members of the community are instructed to admonish and teach one another.

18   (C) Application and Transition (2:1–5). 1. *I want you to know:* This strong assertion begins the transition to the direct confrontation with the Colossian error (cf. similar formulations: Rom 11:25; 1 Cor 10:1; 11:3; 1 Thess 4:13). This section repeats the themes of love (cf. 1:4,10); wisdom, understanding, and knowledge (cf. 1:9); Christ as the mystery of God; the joy of the apostle (1:24); and the faith of the community (1:4,23).

19   (IV) Life in the Body of Christ in Teaching (2:6–3:4). The main christological teaching of the letter (2:6–15) is followed by the refutation of the false teaching at Colossae (2:16–23). After a transition (vv 6–8) that exhorts the community to hold fast to the teaching that they have received and warns them of the danger of the error, the christological section builds on the themes of the hymn (the fullness of the deity dwelling in Christ; Christ as the head) and culminates in vv 11–15 in the teaching about baptism, much of which is drawn from traditional baptismal material (Schille, Cannon, Lohse, Käsemann). In the encounter with the opponents in vv 16–23, catchwords, regulations, and practices of the opponents are interwoven with the author's response to them.

20   (A) The Tradition of Christ Jesus (2:6–15). **6.** *therefore:* The particle *oun* marks the transition, as it does in 2:16; 3:1,5,12. *as you received Christ Jesus the Lord:* The vb. *paralambanō* is a technical term for receiving a tradition, and the choice of this word here is significant. It follows the section on Paul's ministry, which establishes the authority from which they have received the tradition. Moreover, the content of the tradition is Christ Jesus the Lord, in contrast to the human tradition of the opponents (2:8). *live in him:* The result of receiving the tradition is practical: the believers will "walk," i.e., manifest in their conduct, the close union described as being "in Christ" (→ 10 above). **8.** *be on your guard:* The community is here warned of the danger, and the opponents are described by the rare vb. *sylagōgeō* as ones who "capture" them "and carry them off as booty." *elements of the universe:* The meaning of *stoicheia tou kosmou* is quite disputed; see comment on Gal 4:3. In Hellenistic syncretism the word referred to spirits that were conceived of as personal powers, and this must have been a feature of the Colossian error. These "elements" were viewed as angelic powers that performed some function of mediation between God and the world and had some control over cosmic order (Lohse, *Commentary* 96-98; A. J. Bandstra, *The Law and the Elements of the World* [Kampen, 1964]). In Col these powers are set in contrast to Christ. **9-10.** *in him:* This phrase is in an emphatic position and thus connects the proclamation forcefully to the contrast expressed immediately preceding between "the elements" and Christ. The phrase is repeated several times in the baptismal teaching in vv 11-15. *the fullness of the deity:* Whereas in the hymn the fullness was pleased to dwell in Christ, here "fullness" is explained as divine fullness. *you have been filled:* In Rom 15:13 Paul prays that the community might be filled (in the future). Here what Paul prayed for has been accomplished. *the head:* In the hymn (1:18) Christ is the head of the body, the church; here he is the head of every rule and power. All the spirits that the philosophy revered are subject to Christ. **11-15.** It is generally recognized that some sort of liturgical or hymnic formulations lie behind these verses (Lohse, Cannon, Schille, Martin, Gnilka, Käsemann). The theme is participation in the death and resurrection of Christ through baptism. Verse 11 identifies baptism with circumcision, a figurative equation not made elsewhere in the NT. Circumcision is used figuratively in the OT (Deut 10:16; Jer 4:4; Ezek 44:7), in QL (1QS 5:5), and in the NT (Rom 2:28,29; Phil 3:3). The Christian circumcision spoken of by the author of Col is not made with hands; it is a putting off or a stripping off of human bodiliness. This idea of "putting off" may allude to practices of the mystery cults in which the garments of the one being initiated were laid aside during the rite (Lohse). A similar practice may have been part of a baptismal ritual (Gal 3:27 [see comment]). **12.** *buried with him in baptism . . . raised with him through faith:* See comment on Rom 6:3-6. Whereas in Rom 6:5 those who have died with Christ in baptism will in the future be united with him in resurrection, in Col this resurrection has already happened. **13.** *and you:* A change to 2d pers. pl. directs the christological proclamation to the members of the community, describing the result of being in union with Christ, the forgiveness of sins (1:14; cf. Acts 2:38, where forgiveness of sins is connected with baptism; see also Matt 6:9-15 par.). **14.** *cancelled the note of debt that was against us:* The subject is God, who has brought about the union with Christ. *Cheirographon,* "handwritten note," occurs nowhere else in the NT. It introduces the image of debtor and creditor, used frequently in the OT and NT to describe the relationship between God and human beings. This may be a traditional formulation (Lohse), and the phrase "regarding the regulations it was against us" may be a redactional interruption for the purpose of focusing the meaning of the formula specifically on the Colossian situation. The regulations, the requirements of the philosophy, will be attacked in vv 16 and 20. The forceful images of victory in this verse—disarming the principalities and powers, making a public spectacle of them, and leading a triumphal procession—recall the warlike image of the danger with which this section began (v 8), that those of the philosophy might capture them and carry them off as booty.

21   **(B) The Human Tradition (2:16-23).** Again, the particle *oun,* "therefore," marks a transition to a new section. **17.** *a shadow of the things that are coming,*

namely, the body of Christ: The criterion for judgment in v 16, the observance of regulations, is a shadow of what is to come, the ultimate criterion for judgment, viz., belonging to the body of Christ (cf. 1 Cor 13:10). This builds up to v 19, in which the opponents are charged with not holding fast to the head. (The explanatory use of the particle *de* is paralleled in Rom 3:22; 9:30; Phil 2:8). The second half of this verse is usually translated, "but the substance (*sōma*) belongs to Christ." The verse is interpreted as an example of the shadow/substance contrast well attested in Hellenistic philosophical writings. There may be a play on this contrast here, but since the body of Christ is an important theme in this letter, the primary meaning of the verse should be sought in the development of that theme (Lähnemann, *Kolosserbrief* 135-37). This is, then, a forceful eschatological statement about the community that is further elaborated in 2:19, which speaks of the growth of the body, and in 3:4, when the believers are told that they will appear with Christ in glory (cf. Rom 5:14). **18.** *let no one condemn you, insisting on humility and religion of angels:* In 3:12 "humility" is one of the Christian virtues, but here it has something to do with the objectionable practices of the philosophy. Lohse translates it "readiness to serve," suggesting that it is a cultic attitude. It could also mean fasting or some kind of self-abasement. Humility was one of the practices required of the Essenes (1QS 2:24; 3:8; 4:3; 5:3,25; N. Kehl, *ZKT* 91 [1969] 364-94). *religion of angels:* The question raised by this gen. "of angels" is whether the angels are the object of worship or whether the opponents see themselves as joining angels in worship of the deity. Most take this as an objective gen. and connect it to the prominence of heavenly beings in the false teaching—the elemental spirits, the principalities and powers. This would suggest that the adherents of the philosophy worshiped these beings. The phrase is taken here as a subjective gen. that refers to joining angels in worship (see F. O. Francis, "Humility and Angelic Worship in Col 2:18," *Conflict at Colossae* [→ 8 above] 163-95). There is evidence from Qumran of a belief in hierarchies of angels worshiping God (see C. Newsom, *Songs of the Sabbath Sacrifice* (HSS 27; Atlanta, 1985). This verse charges that the opponents were practicing certain disciplines in order to gain access to heaven to join the angelic worship (F. O. Francis, *LTQ* 2 [1967] 71-81; C. Rowland, *JSNT* 19 [1983] 73-83). **20-23.** The constraints of the philosophy are contrasted with the liberty of believers, who have been freed from the human tradition of regulations by dying with Christ in baptism.

22   **(C) Application and Transition (3:1-4).** The beginning of a new section is signaled again by the particle *oun.* These verses sum up the teaching of the preceding section as a foundation for the detailed ethical instruction that follows. **1.** *at the right hand of God:* This creedal statement, based on Ps 110:1, was used in the early church to show that the messianic promises had been fulfilled in Christ. **3-4.** Although the resurrection has already taken place, all the conditions of the end-time are not present. There is still a gap between what is on earth and what is in heaven, and the fulfillment of the body of Christ is hidden "with Christ in God"; but, finally, Christ and the believers will appear in glory.

23   **(V) Life in the Body of Christ in Practice (3:5-4:6).** The hortatory section is a standard part of NT letters (→ NT Epistles, 45:8C). This section consists of two lists of vices, a list of virtues, and a household code, all of which are chiefly traditional material. Lists of vices and virtues were common in Hellenistic philosophical writings, and similar lists occur also in the DSS, e.g., 1QS 4:3–5; CD 4:17–19. There are a number of examples in the NT: vices, Rom 1:24,26,29–31; 13:13; 1 Cor 5:10,11; 6:9,10; Eph 4:31; 5:3–5; 1 Pet 4:3,4; virtues, Matt 5:3–11; 2 Cor 6:6,7; Eph 6:14–17; Phil 4:8. In the NT these lists are general and are not intended to offer instructions that are specific to the context in which they occur.

24   (A) Vices (3:5–10). In Col, the lists of vices (vv 5,8) are set in an eschatological context (v 6), and the baptismal imagery that was part of the instruction in the letter is repeated: "put to death," "put off the old nature," "put on the new nature." The first list (v 5) enumerates sins of the body and passions, and the second (v 8) includes sins that would arise in the intellect. On account of these sins—which are part of the old nature, not the body of Christ—the wrath of God is coming.

25   (B) Virtues (3:11–17). The exhortation to virtue begins with the formula that W. A. Meeks calls the "baptismal reunification formula" (cf. Gal 3:28; 1 Cor 12:13; Gal 6:15; 1 Cor 15:28; Eph 1:23; see Meeks, *HR* 13 [1974] 180–83) and builds to the proclamation "Christ is all and in all."

26   (C) Household Code (3:18–4:1). Like the lists of vices and virtues, the household code is a general type of exhortation and instruction that can be found in popular Hellenistic philosophy. It has been incorporated into the NT in several places (Eph 5:22–6:9; 1 Pet 2:13–3:7; Titus 2:1–10; 1 Tim 2:8–15; 6:1–2; see also *1 Clem.* 21:6–9; → Pauline Theology, 82:145) and has been given a Christian ethical perspective. The code reflects the social mores of the time and is not directed at the specific situation of Colossae. Three pairs are addressed: wives and husbands, children and parents, and slaves and masters. The subordinate member of each pair is first admonished to "be subject," and then the other member of the pair is charged with responsibility.

All of these customs are to be practiced "as is fitting in the Lord" (3:18), "for this pleases the Lord" (3:20), "fearing the Lord" (3:22), "serving the Lord" (3:24). W. A. Meeks views the inclusion of such codes in the later NT writings as evidence that Deutero-Pauline parenesis was concerned with the structure of Christian groups in an orderly society and with the household as the basic cell of the Pauline mission (*The First Urban Christians* [New Haven, 1983] 76–77, 106).

(Balch, D., *"Let Wives Be Submissive"* [SBLMS 26; Chico, 1981]. Crouch, J. E., *The Origin and Intention of the Colossian Haustafel* [FRLANT 109; Göttingen, 1972]. Müller, K., "Die Haustafel des Kolosserbriefes und das antike Frauenthema," *Die Frau im Urchristentum* [Freiburg, 1983] 263–65. Verner, D. C., *The Household of God* [SBLDS 71; Chico, 1983].)

27   (D) Application and Transition (4:2–6). The final exhortation is to pray and be watchful. In the transition to the final messages, the author of Col, adopting the identity of Paul, asks for prayers, refers again to his ministry of declaring the mystery of Christ, and mentions his imprisonment (4:3).

28   (VI) Messages and Closing (4:7–18). 7–9. Tychicus and Onesimus are sent to the Colossians to bring news and encourage the community. **10–14.** Greetings are sent from Aristarchus, Mark the cousin of Barnabas, Jesus who is called Justus, Epaphras, Luke the beloved physician, and Demas. **15–16.** Greetings are sent also to Laodicea with the instruction that the two churches exchange letters. **17.** A specific message is sent to Archippus. **18.** The Deutero-Pauline author closes with a final note of authenticity (cf. Gal 6:11; 2 Thess 2:2; 1 Cor 16:21; → NT Epistles, 45:8D). The similarities between the messages here and those at the end of Phlm suggest that the author of Col may have imitated the authentic letter in this closing section.

55

THE LETTER
TO THE EPHESIANS

Paul J. Kobelski

BIBLIOGRAPHY

1 Allan, J. A., *The Epistle to the Ephesians* (London, 1959). Barth, M., *The Epistle to the Ephesians* (2 vols.; AB 34, 34A; GC, 1974). Beare, F. W. and T. O. Wedel, "The Epistle to the Ephesians" IB 10 (1953) 595–749. Benoit, P., *Les épîtres de saint Paul aux Philippiens, à Philémon, aux Colossiens, aux Éphésiens (SBJ;* 3d ed.; Paris, 1959). Bruce, F. F., *The Epistles to the Colossians, to Philemon, and to the Ephesians* (NICNT; GR, 1984). Caird, G. B., *Paul's Letters from Prison* (NClarB; Oxford, 1976). Conzelmann, H., *Der Brief an die Epheser* (NTD 8; 9th ed.; Göttingen, 1962). Dibelius, M., *An die Kolosser, Epheser; an Philemon* (HNT 12; 3d ed.; rev. H. Greeven; Tübingen, 1953) 54–100. Foulkes, F., *The Epistle of Paul to the Ephesians* (TynNTC; GR, 1963). Gnilka, J., *Der Epheserbrief* (HTKNT 10/2; 3d ed.; Freiburg, 1982). Goodspeed, E. J., *The Key to Ephe-*

sians (Chicago, 1956); *The Meaning of Ephesians* (Chicago, 1953). Houlden, J. L., *Paul's Letters from Prison* (PC; Phl, 1978). Käsemann, E.,"Epheserbrief," *RGG* 2. 517–20. Kirby, J. C., *Ephesians: Baptism and Pentecost* (Montreal, 1968). Mitton, C. L., *Ephesians* (NCB; Greenwood, 1976); *The Epistle to the Ephesians* (London, 1951). Percy, E., *Die Probleme der Kolosser- und Epheserbriefe* (Lund, 1946). Schlier, H., *Der Brief an die Epheser* (6th ed.; Düsseldorf, 1968). Schnackenburg, R., *Der Brief an die Epheser* (EKKNT; Neukirchen, 1982). Swain, L., *Ephesians* (NTM 13; Wilmington, 1980). Zerwick, M., *The Epistle to the Ephesians* (NTSR; New York, 1969).

DBSup 7. 195–211. *IDBSup* 268–69. Kümmel, *INT* 350–66. Wik-Schm, *ENT* 479–96.

INTRODUCTION

2 **(I) Destination.** Since the late 2d cent., Christian tradition has identified this letter as being "To the Ephesians" (Muratorian Canon, Irenaeus, Clement of Alexandria). Although the superscription "To the Ephesians" is present in all NT mss., the phrase "in Ephesus" is absent from 1:1 in P[46] (the earliest text of Eph), from the original hand of the important 4th-cent. codices Vaticanus and Sinaiticus, and from minuscules 424 (corrected) and 1739.

Early patristic citations of Eph indicate awareness of the absence of "in Ephesus" from 1:1 (Marcion, Tertullian, Origen), and Basil (*Adv. Eunom.* 2.19) stated that the words were not present in texts known to him. Marcion (according to Tertullian, *Adv. Marc.* 5.11.16) understood the letter as addressed to the Laodiceans (see Col 4:16).

The absence of "in Ephesus" is best explained if Eph is understood as an encyclical, a circular letter destined for several churches in the Roman province of Asia. This theory was first proposed by Abp. J. Ussher in the 17th cent. Ussher's further contention that a blank space was intentionally left in the address in 1:1 to be filled in by the community using the letter has not been widely followed because of the lack of parallels to this phenomenon elsewhere in the ancient world. The introduction of

"in Ephesus" in 1:1 and the later superscription "To the Ephesians" may be traced to the importance of Ephesus among the churches for whom the letter was intended, or to the addition of "in Ephesus" in a copy of the original used in Ephesus, or to the joining of Eph 6:21–22 with the notice in 2 Tim 4:12 that "I have sent Tychicus to Ephesus."

3 **(II) Authenticity.** From the 2d cent. to the 18th, the attribution of Eph to the apostle Paul was largely unquestioned. In the late 18th cent., Pauline authorship began to be challenged. Among modern scholars who defend authorship of the letter by Paul are Barth, Benoit, Bruce, Caird, Dahl (*STK* 21 [1945] 85–103; *TZ* 7 [1951] 241–64), Foulkes, Percy, Rendtorff, Schlier, and Zerwick. Some proponents of authenticity modify their position by arguing that a Pauline core of the letter was expanded or altered by a disciple, scribe, or interpolator (Benoit; L. Cerfaux, in *Littérature et théologie pauliniennes* [ed. A. Descamps; RechBib 5; Bruges, 1960] 60–71; M. Goguel, *RHPR* 111 [1935] 254–85; 112 [1936] 73–99; A. van Roon, *The Authenticity of Ephesians* [NovTSup 39; Leiden, 1974] 205–6; Swain). Among those who argue for pseudonymity are Allan, Beare, Conzelmann, Dahl (*IDBSup*), Dibelius, Gnilka,

Goodspeed, Käsemann, Kirby, Mitton, and Schnackenburg (→ NT Epistles, 45:12, 15, 19-20). The questioning of Pauline authorship is based on content, vocabulary and style, theological differences from the undisputed Pauline letters, literary dependence on the Pauline corpus, and literary dependence on Col.

4   (A) Content. That Paul is mentioned as the writer of the letter (1:1; 3:1) and that there are references to his personal experiences must be viewed against what is known of pseudonymity in antiquity (see K. Aland, *JTS* 12 [1961] 39-49; B. M. Metzger, *JBL* 91 [1972] 3-24; see also Gnilka, *Epheserbrief* 20-21 and 20 n. 3). Furthermore, there are statements in the letter, such as "I have heard of your faith" (1:15) and "I am sure you have heard of the stewardship . . . given to me" (3:2), that suggest an audience that had no firsthand acquaintance with the preaching of Paul (see also 3:5; 4:21).

5   (B) Vocabulary and Style. The frequency of *hapax legomena* in Eph is not unusual when compared with their frequency in undisputed Pauline letters of comparable length (P. N. Harrison, *The Problem of the Pastoral Epistles* [London, 1964] 20-48). More significant are terms such as *ta epourania,* "heavenly places" (1:3,20; 2:6; 3:10; 6:12), alongside the more usual Pauline *hoi ouranoi,* "the heavens"; *diabolos,* "devil" (4:27; 6:11), in place of the Pauline *satanas;* words that occur in late NT writings and early Church Fathers (e.g., *asōtia, hosiotēs, politeia;* see Schnackenburg, *Der Brief* 22 and n. 19; Kümmel, *INT* 358); and words such as *mystērion, oikonomia,* and *plērōma* that occur with meanings other than those attested in the undisputed Pauline letters.

The letter is marked by long and complex sentences (1:3-4,15-23; 2:1-7; 3:1-9; 4:1-6; 5:7-13), an abundance of interwoven relative clauses and participial constructions (e.g., 1:3-14; 2:1-7), and the joining of synonyms with the gen. case (e.g., *eudokian tou thelēmatos autou* [1:5]; *en tǭ kratei tēs ischyos autou* [6:10]). Many of these characteristics of vocabulary and style can be paralleled in isolated cases in the undisputed Pauline writings (Percy, *Probleme* 19-35), but there is no undisputed letter marked by so many such verbal and stylistic traits.

6   (C) Theological Differences.
(a) THE CHURCH. In Eph, the church is viewed as a universal phenomenon, cosmic in extent and influence, embodying all creation (1:21-23; 3:9-11), whereas in the undisputed Pauline letters the view of the church as the local community predominates (see 1 Cor 1:2; Gal 1:2; Phlm 2; but see 1 Cor 12:28; 15:9; Gal 1:13 for a wider understanding of church). In Eph the church is "built upon the foundation of the apostles and prophets"—a stance that would require more distance from the first generation of church leadership than was possible for Paul; in 1 Cor 3:11, Christ is identified as the only foundation of the church. The understanding in Eph of Christ as the head of the church, which is his body (1:22-23; 5:23), is a significant development beyond the image of the varied members making up the body of Christ in 1 Cor 12:31; Rom 12:4-8.

7   (b) THE GENTILES. Polemics about admission of Gentiles into the Christian community are not a concern for the author of Eph. The author does not regard the conversion of Gentiles as a means of making Israel jealous so that one day all Israel might be restored to its rightful position (Rom 11; → Pauline Theology, 82:43). In place of this hope for a future restoration of Israel, one finds that in Eph Jew and Gentile together have been "reconciled to God in one body through the cross" (2:16), "becoming one new person instead of two" (2:15), now that "the dividing wall of hostility" has been breached (2:14).

8   (c) ESCHATOLOGY. In Eph there are no explicit references to the expectation of the parousia nor to the imminent end of the world. The emphasis is on the present-day sharing in the resurrection by Christians who have been "made alive," "raised up," and who now "sit with [Christ] in the heavenly places" (2:5-6), and for whom a long future in the church is envisioned (2:7; 3:21). In the undisputed Pauline letters, Christians are said to share in the death of Christ, but their participation in the resurrection is still an unfulfilled hope (Rom 6:5; Phil 3:10-11; → Pauline Theology, 82:46-47, 58-60).

9   (d) MARRIAGE. The image of the church as the bride of Christ and the exalted conception of marriage in Eph 5:22-31 stands in contrast to the presentation of marriage in 1 Cor 7:8-9,25-40.

10   (D) Relationship to Colossians. Structural and verbal similarities are evident in the address (Eph 1:1-2; Col 1:1-2), in the Thanksgiving (Eph 1:15-17; Col 1:3-4,9-10), and in the conclusion (Eph 6:21-22; Col 4:7-8). Certain doctrinal and parenetic elements in Eph are developed in dependence on the thought of Col: resurrection with Christ (Eph 2:5-6; Col 2:12-13); putting off the old nature and putting on the new (Eph 4:17-24; Col 3:5-15); Spirit-filled worship (Eph 5:17-20; Col 3:16-17); household codes (Eph 5:22-25; 6:1-9; Col 3:18-4:1); need for unceasing prayer (Eph 6:18; Col 4:2); request for prayer for the preacher (Eph 6:19; Col 4:3). Many of the verbal similarities occur in sections of Eph that have no thematic parallel in Col (e.g., in the Blessing [*hagious kai amōmous:* Eph 1:4; Col 1:22]; in the section on the reconciliation of Jews and Gentiles in Christ [the use of *apallotrioō* in Eph 2:12 and Col 1:21 and of *apokatallassō* in Eph 2:16 and Col 1:20,22]).

Yet the verbal relationship cannot hide differences in perspective. The doctrinal focus of Eph is ecclesiology, not christology as in Col. This difference can be detected not only in the rich imagery used of the church but also in the distinctive way in which terms that have a christological meaning in Col, such as *mystērion* and *plērōma,* are applied to the church in Eph. Likewise, in the parenesis of Eph the emphasis has shifted from exhortation to "heavenly" conduct (as opposed to "earthly" conduct) to conduct that distinguishes itself from that of the pagan world (Eph 4:17-19; 5:7-8; cf. Col 3:1-2,5; see Schnackenburg, *Der Brief* 28). The author of Eph used Col as a source for the composition of Eph but freely and independently developed themes and introduced ideas to fit his own purposes.

11   (III) Authorship. These considerations (→ 4-10 above) argue for the Deutero-Pauline composition of this letter. The suggestion that the many differences in style and theology reflect the development of Paul's thought in his later years raises problems: it does not account for the time during which such an evolution could have taken place, and it does not reckon with the impression that the letter looks back to an earlier revered generation of apostles (among whom was Paul) and prophets who provided the foundation for the household of God in the post-Pauline period (2:20; 3:2-11; 4:11-14).

The Deutero-Pauline author of Eph was thoroughly schooled in the Pauline literature. There are clear reminiscences of Pauline thought throughout Eph (cf. Eph 2:8 and Rom 3:24; Eph 2:17-18; 3:11-12 and Rom 5:1-2; Eph 4:28 and 1 Cor 4:12; Eph 3:14; 4:5 and 1 Cor 8:5-6; see Mitton, *The Epistle* 120-33). Like the author of Col, the author of Eph may have belonged to a Pauline school (in Ephesus?) that was imbued with the thinking of Paul and was conversant with the liturgical, parenetic, and catechetical traditions that had developed in Pauline mission areas in the post-Pauline period.

12   (IV) Interpretation of the Letter. H. Schlier and E. Käsemann began the modern debate about the gnostic interpretation of Eph. They viewed the language as a reflection of a pre-Christian gnostic myth of the heavenly man who descends to earth to redeem himself and his members. The problem with the various forms of the gnostic theory is the difficulty of showing that such developed gnostic thought, particularly the redeemer myth, existed before the 2d cent. (See H. Schlier, *Christus und die Kirche im Epheserbrief* [Tübingen, 1930]; but his earlier views are modified in *Der Brief* 19-20, esp. 19 n. 1, where he qualifies his understanding of gnostic elements with Qumran dualism]; E. Käsemann, *Leib und Leib Christi* [BHT 9; Tübingen 1933]; A. Lindemann, *Die Aufhebung der Zeit* [Gütersloh, 1975]).

Eph has also been interpreted as a document representative of early catholicism. E. Käsemann, in particular, has championed a negative view of early catholicism — that Eph, along with other writings such as Luke-Acts, the Pastorals, Jude, and 2 Pet, represents a regression in the theology of the NT church characterized by a universal, abstract church that is the object of its own theology; by the disappearance of the expectation of an imminent end; by an emphasis on church structure and authority at the expense of enthusiasm and charism; and by a stress on orthodoxy and sacramentalism. More positive assessments of the early catholicism of Eph can be found in H. Merklein, *Christus und die Kirche* (Stuttgart, 1973); J. H. Elliott, *CBQ* 31 (1969) 213-23, and J. Gager, *Kingdom and Community* (EC, 1975) 66-92.

(Harrington, D. J., "Ernst Käsemann on the Church in the New Testament," *Light of All Nations* [GNS 3; Wilmington, 1982]; "The 'Early Catholic' Writings of the New Testament," ibid. 61-78. Käsemann, E., "Paul and Early Catholicism," *NTQT* 236-51; "Ephesians and Acts," *StLA* 288-97.)

Recent study of Eph has emphasized its connections with the world of Hellenistic Judaism and, in particular, its close contact with a type of Judaism represented by the DSS. Ideas such as the world view of Eph, the cosmic man, *logos*-speculation, and sacred marriage may also be related to philosophical speculation represented by Philo of Alexandria (see, e.g., Gnilka, *Epheserbrief* 38-45, 63-66, 122-28, 290-94; see also C. Colpe, "Zur Leib-Christi-Vorstellung im Epheserbrief," *Judentum — Urchristentum — Kirche* [Fest. J. Jeremias; ed. W. Eltester; 2d ed.; Berlin, 1964]; H. Hegermann, *Die Vorstellung vom Schöpfungsmittler im hellenistischen Judentum und Urchristentum* [TU 82; Berlin, 1961]). Similarly, the contribution that the QL makes in clarifying the language of Eph has been noted (Gnilka, *Epheserbrief* 123-25, 27-29; K. G. Kuhn, "The Epistle to the Ephesians in the Light of the Qumran Texts," *Paul and Qumran* [ed. J. Murphy-O'Connor; Chicago, 1968] 115-31; F. Mussner, "Contributions

Made by Qumran to the Understanding of the Epistle to the Ephesians," *Paul and Qumran* 159-78). Also in recent years greater attention has been paid to the diversity of liturgical and catechetical traditions used by the author of Eph. The recognition of this diversity of traditions — Pauline, Colossian, OT, Jewish, liturgical, catechetical — led E. Käsemann to this description of Eph: it is "a mosaic composed of extensive as well as tiny elements of tradition, and the author's skill lies chiefly in the selection and ordering of the material" ("Ephesians and Acts" 288; see also M. Barth, *NTS* 30 [1984] 3-25; A. T. Lincoln, *JSNT* 14 [1982] 16-57).

13   (V) Date and Purpose. The author's use of the genuine letters of Paul and of Col suggests a date late in the 1st cent. (AD 80-100) after the collection of the Pauline writings into a corpus.

Though Eph possesses the structural elements of a letter (→ NT Epistles, 45:6, 8) it is a theological discourse addressed to several churches (probably in Asia Minor, because of its relationship to Col). The discourse recalls to readers, in terms familiar to them from catechetical and liturgical traditions, the exaltation of Christ and the church over all heavenly and earthly powers and the reconciliation of Jews and Gentiles in the church under the headship of Christ; and it encourages them to celebrate their unity by appropriate conduct.

14   (VI) Outline. The first half of the letter (1:3-3:21) is structured as an extended prayer of intercession with a pattern that can be detected in Jewish and early Christian devotional literature: blessing-thanksgiving-prayer of intercession-concluding doxology (Gnilka, *Epheserbrief* 26-27; Dahl, *IDBSup* 268-69). The second half (4:1-6:20) exhorts Christians to behavior that is in keeping with their exalted status as children of light and members of the church — God's household and the bride of Christ.

(I) Introduction: Address and Greeting (1:1-2)
(II) Part One: God's Plan Revealed and Accomplished (1:3-3:21)
    (A) Blessing (1:3-14)
    (B) Thanksgiving and Prayer of Intercession (1:15-23)
    (C) Once Dead, Now Alive with Christ (2:1-10)
    (D) Union of Jews and Gentiles (2:11-22)
    (E) Paul as Interpreter of the Revealed Mystery (3:1-13)
    (F) Prayer (3:14-19)
    (G) Concluding Doxology (3:20-21)
(III) Part Two: Exhortations to Worthy Conduct (4:1-6:20)
    (A) Unity and Diversity in the Church (4:1-16)
    (B) Christian and Non-Christian Conduct (4:17-5:20)
    (C) Code of Conduct for the Household of God (5:21-6:9)
    (D) Christian Life as Warfare with Evil (6:10-20)
(IV) Conclusion: Personal News and Blessing (6:21-24)

COMMENTARY

15   (I) Introduction: Address and Greeting (1:1-2). The identification of the sender as Paul in this pseudonymous letter mediates his authority and presence to a post-Pauline generation. The address and greeting follow the usual pattern (→ NT Epistles, 45:6, 8A). **1.** *to the saints and to those faithful:* The author addresses the readers as both "saints" (a designation used throughout this letter [1:4,15,18; 2:19; 3:8,18; 4:12; 5:3; 6:18] and in the Pauline letters [e.g., Rom 1:7; 1 Cor 1:2; 6:2]) and faithful ones (cf. 1:15). Their identification as

saints not only makes them members of God's holy people but also suggests their participation in the heavenly assembly — a theme to be developed later in Eph (see comment on 1:18). Important mss. support the omission of *en Ephesō*, which leaves a very awkward construction (→ 2 above), but even its presence after *tois hagiois* would be unusual because the following *kai pistois* would then appear to identify a group different from "the saints." The proposal that a blank space was left after *tois hagiois* that was then filled in with the name of the community using the letter still does not solve the syntactical problem.

(Best, E., "Ephesians 1.1 Again," *Paul and Paulinism* [Fest. C. K. Barrett; ed. M. D. Hooker and S. G. Wilson; London, 1982] 273-79. Dahl, N., "Adresse und Proömium," *TZ* 7 [1951] 241-64. Lindemann, A., "Bemerkungen zu den Adressaten und zum Anlass des Epheserbriefes," *ZNW* 67 [1976] 235-51.)

16   (II) Part One: God's Plan Revealed and Accomplished (1:3-3:21).
    (A) Blessing (1:3-14). A great blessing (cf. 1 Cor 1:3-7; → NT Epistles, 45:8B) precedes the thanksgiving. The blessing is the composition of the author and echoes phrases from Col and announces themes that will be developed in the first half of Eph (P. T. O'Brien, *NTS* 25 [1978-79] 504-16). Attempts to discern a formal strophic arrangement in the blessing have not been satisfactory (Dibelius, Schille). A more productive area of inquiry has been to compare the blessing to the Qumran *Hôdāyôt,* which show similarities of language, content, and structure (J. T. Sanders, *ZNW* 56 [1965] 215-32, esp. 227-28). **3.** *blessed be:* The blessing begins with a formula known from the OT and common in Jewish and early Christian prayers (cf. Tob 13:1; 1QH 7:20; 10:14; 1 Pet 1:3). *with every spiritual blessing:* Cf. 1QSb 1:5. *in Christ:* This important phrase occurs frequently throughout the letter (in various forms — *en autǭ, en hǭ*) in contexts referring to the unity of Jews and Gentiles (e.g., 2:15; 3:11). J. Allan (*NTS* 5 [1958-59] 54-62) has argued that *en christǭ* should be understood instrumentally in Eph rather than in its typical Pauline sense of incorporation in Christ (→ Pauline Theology, 82:121). *in the heavenly heights:* The Gk *en tois epouraniois* can also be translated "among the heavenly beings"; its spatial meaning elsewhere in Eph (1:20; 2:6; 3:10; 6:12) suggests that it indicates a location here too. It is a phrase quite distinctive to Eph and introduces the theme of the union of the heavenly and earthly worlds. **4.** *because he chose us:* The comparative conj. *kathōs* is used in a causal sense (BDF 453.2) at the beginning of the enumeration of reasons for blessing God. The motif of God's chosen people is taken over from the OT (e.g., Deut 14:2; → OT Thought, 77:81) and developed extensively in pre-Christian Judaism (1QH 13:10; 15:23; 1QS 1:4; 11:7; 1QSb 1:2; 1QM 10:9). *holy and unblemished:* Cf. Col 1:22. The same phrase is used in 5:27 to describe the spotless bride of Christ, the church, cleansed in baptism. The terms in Eph refer to the moral qualities of holiness and purity demanded of God's chosen ones. In the Qumran community, the requirement to be without physical blemish was "because of the presence of the angels in the congregation" (1QSa 2:8-9). Such thinking is related to that of Eph, which also emphasizes the church's involvement with the heavenly realm (2:6; 3:10). **5.** *out of love he predestined us:* The phrase *en agapę* can also be taken with "holy and spotless before him" at the end of v 4. Taking it with "he predestined us" makes it refer to God's love and creates a formal parallel to "with all wisdom and understanding he made known to us" in v 9. The idea of predestination is not foreign to Pauline thought (see Rom 8:28-29 and comment) and is also found in QL (e.g., 1QH 15:14-17; cf. 1QS 3:15-18 for the idea that God has determined the fate of all through his unalterable plan). *his adopted children:* Through their association with Christ and the church, Christians are members of the family of God (see Rom 8:14-17 and comment). *good pleasure:* Cf. CD 3:15. **6.** *through his Beloved:* The identification of Christ as God's Beloved recalls the baptism scene in the Gospels, in which the voice from heaven identifies Jesus as *ho agapētos* (Mark 1:11 par.). Note also

the use in the baptismal scene of *eudokeō* ("I take pleasure") and its cognate *eudokia* in v 5.
17   7. *redemption through his blood:* Cf. Col 1:14,20. Redemption and forgiveness are possible because of Christ's death, into which the Christian is incorporated through baptism. The mention in vv 5-7 of adopted children, the Beloved, good pleasure, forgiveness of transgressions, and the later reference to being sealed with the Spirit (1:13) suggest dependence on baptism traditions. The baptismal resonances throughout the letter led N. Dahl to hypothesize that the purpose of Eph was to recall to new converts the implications of their baptism (*TZ* 7 [1951] 241-64). He characterized the letter as baptismal *anamnēsis* (remembrance) and *paraklēsis* (exhortation) (*Zur Auferbauung des Leibes Christi* [Fest. P. Brunner; Kassel, 1965] 64). *riches of his grace:* The Hebr equivalent of this phrase occurs frequently in QL in various forms (e.g., 1QS 4:4; 1QH 1:32). **8-9.** *with all wisdom and understanding he made known to us:* See comment on v 5. Wisdom and understanding are divine qualities underlying the revelation of the mystery of God's will. It is not impossible, however, to construe them with the preceding "he caused to abound in us," as does the *NEB,* and to see them as human qualities bestowed through "the riches of his grace." Eph 3:10 supports interpreting them as divine qualities because it explicitly connects the wisdom of God with the revelation (*gnōristhē*) of the mystery to humanity and to the heavenly powers (3:9-10). **9.** *the mystery of his will:* The content of the mystery has an ecclesiological focus in Eph: in 1:10 it refers to the summing up of all things in Christ on behalf of the church (1:22-23); in 3:4-6 it refers to the union of Gentiles and Jews in the church; in 5:32 it refers to the interpretation of Gen 2:24 as the union of Christ and the church. The proper background for understanding *mystērion* in Eph is the belief in Judaism of late antiquity that everything is regulated according to God's mysteries (R. E. Brown, *The Semitic Background of the Term "Mystery" in the New Testament* [FBBS 21; Phl, 1967]). The God of knowledge is in control of all things, because the unalterable course of events has been decreed by him before all eternity (1QS 3-4, esp. 3:9-10). Not only the human world (1QH 1:15) but also the angelic (1QM 14:14) and cosmic (1QH 1:11-15) realms have been determined by him. These mysteries have been revealed to chosen interpreters (1QH 1:21; 1QpHab 7:4-5; cf. Eph 3:4-6; → Pauline Theology, 82:33-34). **10.** *as a plan:* In Col 1:25 *oikonomia* refers to Paul's commission or appointment to preach the word; here in Eph the term describes the arrangements or measures that make up God's plan to sum up all in Christ. In Col 1:19; 2:19 *plērōma* refers to the totality of divinity; here in Eph it identifies the time when God's eternal purposes are accomplished and brought to fulfillment. *to sum up all . . . things:* The cosmic embrace of Christ encompassing heavenly and terrestrial realities has been the goal of God's eternal plan. All reality finds its meaning and completeness in Christ. **11-14.** The author describes the position in God's plan occupied by the recipients of the letter, who are the beneficiaries of God's plan in Christ. The section is composed using words and phrases from Col 1:13-14: "lot," "hope," "word of truth," "gospel," "will," "glory," "redemption." The contrast in these verses between "we" and "you" has been taken to refer to Jews ("we") and Gentiles ("you"). If this were so, the phrase *hēmas . . . proēlpikotas en tǭ Christǭ* in v 12 should be translated "we who hoped in the Messiah [before the Gentiles did, or in advance of Christ's coming]." It is also possible to interpret "we" as a reference to all Christians and "you" as a reference to the recipients of the letter. In this case, the *proēlpikotas*

may be translated "we who set our hope [on fulfillment] in Christ" (BAGD 705). The latter interpretation of "we" and "you" is supported by the first part of the hymn, which uses *hēmeis* to refer to all Christians. Moreover, the author of Eph certainly includes Gentiles among those that were "predestined and appointed by lot."

18 **11.** *we were predestined and appointed by lot:* See comment on 1:5. The verb *klēroō,* translated here "appointed by lot," recalls the recurring identification of the children of light in QL as belonging to "the lot of God" (e.g., 1QS 2:2; 1QM 1:5; cf. Eph 5:8). There is a close parallel in 1QH 3:22-23: "You have cast an eternal lot for man . . . in order that he might praise your name together in joy." **13.** *you heard . . . you believed . . . you were sealed:* The sequence of verbs is a reflection of missionary reports such as those in Acts 8:12-17; 10:34-48; 19:2. The connection between believing and receiving the holy Spirit and baptism in these passages underscores the baptismal allusions in this part of the blessing. The idea of being sealed with the holy Spirit, "the pledge of our inheritance," occurs also in 2 Cor 1:22. As a pledge of our future inheritance, the sealing with the Spirit makes salvation a present reality. **14.** *for the setting free of (enslaved) property:* The meaning of the phrase is difficult to determine. *Apolytrōsis* may be used in the sense of "buying back" that which was enslaved property and may be a reference to the freedom achieved by the death of Christ from the malevolent spirits of the universe (see Eph 2:2-3).

(Cambier, J., "La bénédiction d'Éphésiens 1,3-14," *ZNW* 54 [1963] 58-104. Coutts, J., "Eph. 1:3-14 and 1 Pet. 1:3-12," *NTS* 3 [1956-57] 115-27. Deichgräber, R., *Gotteshymnus und Christushymnus in der frühen Christenheit* [Göttingen, 1967] 146-52. Lyonnet, S., "La bénédiction de Éph 1:3-14 et son arrière-plan judaïque," *À la rencontre de Dieu* [Fest. A. Gelin; Le Puy, 1961] 341-52. Maurer, C., "Der Hymnus von Eph 1 als Schlüssel zum ganzen Briefe," *EvT* 11 [1951/52] 151-72. Schille, G., *Frühchristliche Hymnen* [Berlin, 1965] 65-73.)

19 **(B) Thanksgiving and Prayer of Intercession (1:15-23).** The thanksgiving and beginning of the prayer (vv 15-16) have been composed in imitation of Phlm 4-5 (cf. Col 1:3-4,9-10). The rest of the prayer draws freely on the vocabulary of Col and of the blessing in Eph (cf. Eph 1:18 and Col 1:12,27; Eph 1:20 and Col 2:10,12; Eph 1:21 and Col 1:16; Eph 1:22-23 and Col 1:18-19,24) but also incorporates ideas from Pss 110 and 8 to make distinctive statements about the exaltation of Christ and the church. **18.** *among the holy ones:* In Eph, *hagioi* may refer to the earthly congregation (1:1, 15) or to the heavenly congregation, the angels (see P. Benoit, "Hagioi en Colossiens 1:12," *Paul and Paulinism* [→ 15 above] 83-101). Here the reference is to the angels with whom the earthly congregation has been joined in Christ. The thought has close parallels in QL (1QSb 3:25-4:26; 1QH 3:21-23). **19.** *his mighty power:* Cf. 1QH 4:32; 1QS 11:19-20. **20-23.** God's might is revealed in the resurrection and ascension of Christ and in his exaltation over all angelic forces. The author uses early Christian creedal statements that formulated the Christ-event in terms of Ps 110:1 and 8:7 to impress upon the readers the glorious position to which they have been called in Christ. *above every ruler . . . :* See comment on Col 1:15-16. **22.** *he appointed him head:* The author announces an important metaphor that will pervade this letter: Christ is the head of the body, the church. This is a development of the Pauline concept of many diverse members together forming the body of Christ (1 Cor 12:12-17; → Pauline Theology, 82:122-27). The church is the beneficiary of God's all-embracing

plan, and, as beneficiary of his lordship over all things and over all angelic powers, the church — Christ's body — shares in the dominion of the head. **23.** *his body, the fullness of the one who fills all in all:* The ptc. *plēroumenou* could be either pass. ("the one who is filled") or middle ("the one who fills"). Eph 4:10 ("that he might fill all") supports interpreting the ptc. here as middle. In either case the image is a difficult one to comprehend, but may refer to Christ as the source and the goal of the body's growth, such as is described in 4:15-16.

(Bates, R., "A Re-examination of Ephesians 1²³," *ExpTim* 83 [1972] 146-51. Benoit, P., "The 'plērōma' in the Epistles to the Colossians and the Ephesians," *SEA* 49 [1984] 136-58. Howard, G., "The Head/Body Metaphors of Ephesians," *NTS* 20 [1974] 350-56. De la Potterie, I., "Le Christ, plérôme de l'église (Ep 1,22-23)," *Bib* 58 [1977] 500-24.)

20 **(C) Once Dead, Now Alive with Christ (2:1-10).** This is God's grand scheme as it affects humanity (cf. 1QH 11:8-14; 3:19-23; F. Mussner, "Contributions Made by Qumran" [→ 12 above] 174-76). As with 1:11-14, there is a problem here in interpreting "we" and "you." Though the "we" may be Jewish Christians and the "you" Gentile Christians, there is no clear allusion to the Jewish-Gentile distinction before 2:11-22. All unambiguous uses of "we" in this letter refer to all Christians (2:14; 3:20; and frequently in chaps. 4-6), and "we" should be taken here in the same way. The author uses "you" when the recipients of the letter are addressed directly. In language reminiscent of Eph 2:1-3, the QL speaks of a period of time when the spirit of darkness would be allowed to exercise authority over humanity (1QS 3:20-23; 11QMelch 2:4-6) until evil is destroyed and righteousness prospers (1QS 4:18-23; 1QM 13:14-16; 17:5-9). Against this background the author of Eph describes the sinful condition of humanity, which walks under the power of evil. **1.** *dead because of your transgressions:* See Rom 12:21 and comment. **2.** *the Aeon of this world:* The apposition of Prince of the realm of air with *Aeon* suggests that *aiōna* is an evil power (BAGD 28; cf. 2 Cor 4:4). *the spirit now operating:* Cf. 1QS 3:20-25. **3.** *desires of the flesh:* → Pauline Theology, 82:103. *children of wrath:* Cf. 1QH 3:27-28. **5-6.** *he made us alive:* What was said of Christ in 1:20 is now said of all Christians: they are raised and enthroned with him in the heavenly heights. Their solidarity with him and his exaltation is indicated by Gk verbs used in 1:20 but now compounded with the prep. *syn,* "together with" (→ Pauline Theology, 82:120). **8-10.** With dependence on Pauline vocabulary ("grace," "faith," "works," "boasting"; see A. T. Lincoln, *CBQ* 45 [1983] 617-30) — but with a shift in emphasis from Paul's description of justification by faith apart from works of the law — Eph speaks of salvation as the result of God's gift alone (→ Pauline Theology, 82:71). The dichotomy is no longer faith vs. works (Rom 3:28) but God's grace vs. human good deeds.

21 **(D) Union of Jews and Gentiles (2:11-22).** Gentiles and Jews now form one new humanity, created in Christ and reconciled to each other and to God (vv 13-18). **11.** *circumcision:* Circumcision, a recognized feature of Judaism in the Hellenistic world, symbolizes the distinction between Jews and Gentiles. **12.** *alienated from the commonwealth of Israel:* The author uses the political imagery of citizenship to describe the Gentiles' exclusion from the people of God. Estranged from the God of Israel, the Gentiles had no access to the covenant, which promised salvation (see Rom 9:4-5; → OT Thought, 77:81; → Pauline Theology, 82:43). **13.** *far off . . . near:* Spatial images (see Isa 57:19 and Zech 6:15) describe the former condition of the Gentiles and the new situation resulting from the death of Christ. In Pauline writings (Rom 5:10–11; 2 Cor 5:18–20) the reconciliation accomplished through the death of Christ brought peace and union with God (→ Pauline Theology, 82:72). In Eph, this understanding of reconciliation is expanded to include peace and unity between Gentiles and Jews. **14.** *he is our peace:* This may be the beginning of a fragment of an early Christian hymn extending to 2:16 that the author has incorporated into the letter (see Schille, *Frühchristliche Hymnen* [→ 18 above] 23–27; J. T. Sanders, *ZNW* 56 [1965] 216–18). **14.** *he has torn down the barrier wall:* Although this may be a figurative reference to the wall separating Gentiles from the inner court of the Jerusalem Temple (Josephus, *Ant.* 15.11.5 §417), the noun in apposition, *echthron,* "enmity," suggests that the image is intended to depict the end of ethnic hostility between the two groups (see Acts 10:28). **15.** *that he might create in himself:* The old humanity was flawed and alienated from God because of the sin of Adam (Rom 5:12–17), but the new humanity created in Christ has been reconciled to God through the cross. The author employs the Adam–Christ typology of the Pauline writings (→ Pauline Theology, 82:82–85) to describe the new situation of Gentiles and Jews together forming the one new humanity in one body. **16.** *in one body:* Cf. Col 1:22. By omitting the specification of Col that this body is the crucified body of Christ, the author interprets *sōma* as the one new humanity, the church. **17.** *peace to those far off:* See Isa 57:19. (See N. J. McEleny, *NTS* 20 [1973–74] 319–41; P. Tachau, *"Einst" und "Jetzt" im Neuen Testament* [FRLANT 105; Göttingen, 1972]). **19–22.** A series of powerful and interpenetrating metaphors for the church describes the situation of the new humanity. **19.** *fellow citizens:* Citizenship in God's *polis* transcends the political boundaries of city and province and extends to fellowship with the angels (see 1:18). *household of God:* The basic social unit of Greco-Roman society was the household, within which were included parents, children, and slaves. Christians, as members of God's household, are called God's beloved children (5:1), entitled to the rich inheritance (1:18; 2:7) that their father lavishes upon them (1:7–8). **20.** *built on the foundation:* The social unit of the household is concretized as a building—the apostles and prophets provide the foundation stones and Christ is the cornerstone (cf. 1 Cor 3:11). **21.** *whole building is joined together:* The church-as-building metaphor merges with the body image to create the picture of a building being constructed of living stones that grow and develop into God's place of dwelling, the Temple (cf. 4:15–16; 1 Pet 2:4–5). The understanding of the community as God's temple develops the Pauline idea of the body being the temple of God and is closely paralleled by the Qumran community's understanding of itself as the temple of God (B. Gärtner, *The Temple and the Community in Qumran and the New Testament* [SNTSMS 1; Cambridge, 1965]; R. Schnackenburg, "Die Kirche als Bau: Epheser 2:19–22 unter ökumenischen Aspekt," *Paul and Paulinism* [→ 15 above] 258–70).

22   (E) Paul as Interpreter of the Revealed Mystery (3:1–13). Paul's insight into the mystery of Christ is that Gentiles are full participants in the church. The section depends on Col 1:23–29. **1.** *therefore, I, Paul:* The beginning is an anacoluthon. The thought begun in v 1 is resumed in the prayer in v 14; the connection is made in v 14 by *toutou charin,* "therefore," repeated from v 1. The authority of Paul, the prisoner of Christ Jesus, and the hardships he suffered are recalled to a post-Pauline Gentile audience to assure them of their place in God's eternal plan. **2.** *for you must have heard:* Lit., "if indeed you have heard." The author assumes that what he

is going to tell them about Paul's role in the announcement of God's plan is something they should already be aware of. **3.** *the mystery was made known to me:* Cf. 1QpHab 7:4–5; 1QH 1:21. *as I have written above:* Lit., "in brief." The reference is to the revelation of the mystery of Christ mentioned in 1:9; 2:13–17. Goodspeed interpreted *en oligō* as a reference to the collection of Paul's letters and found in this interpretation support for viewing Eph as an introduction to that corpus. **4.** *my insight:* The content of Paul's insight is stated in v 6—the full and equal participation of Gentiles in the church. **5.** *to his holy apostles:* Cf. Col 1:26; the author of Eph wishes to recall the solid foundation upon which the church is built (2:20) and underscores the role played by the apostles and prophets. **6.** *coheirs, comembers . . . , copartners:* Three nouns compounded with the prefix *syn,* "together," depict the full and equal participation of Gentiles with Jews in the one body. **7–9.** The practical application of Paul's insight made him the apostle of the Gentiles. **8.** *very least:* Cf. 1 Cor 15:9. **9.** *in God the creator:* At creation God established his providential control of the cosmos and only in the present age, because he has revealed the mystery to his chosen interpreters, are his designs becoming known. **10.** *through the church:* Not only is the church the content and the beneficiary of the mystery; it is also the means of announcing to the heavenly powers the wisdom of God that lies behind the plan. The heavenly powers identified here are malevolent forces (see Eph 6:12) that prior to the death of Christ exercised authority over humanity (see comment on 2:1–3; cf. 1 Cor 2:6–8). But God's wisdom put an end to their dominion (cf. 1QS 4:18–23) through the subjection of all things to Christ (1:20). This end is revealed through the church, which signals the end of alienation of humans from God (2:16) and of Gentiles from Jews (2:15; 3:6). Cf. 1 Cor 2:6–8. **12.** *in him we have confidence:* Christians, freed from the domination of the heavenly powers, now are able to approach God with boldness.

23   (F) Prayer (3:14–19) and **(G) Concluding Doxology (3:20–21).** The section resumes the intercessory prayer, which was begun in 1:15–20, taken up again in 3:1, only to be interrupted in 3:2–13 by the description of Paul's role in the revelation of the mystery. It concludes with a solemn doxology that also brings the doctrinal portion of Eph to a close. **15.** *from whom every family:* God, the creator of all the families of beings, established his power and control over all creation in the act of naming them (Ps 147:4; Isa 40:26; cf. Gen 2:19–20). **16.** *in your inner selves:* The phrase is Pauline (Rom 7:22–23; 2 Cor 4:16) and is to be seen as parallel to "heart" in v 17 (→ Pauline Theology, 82:106). **18.** *width and length . . . :* It is not clear to what these dimensions refer. They have sometimes been taken to refer to the dimensions of the Jerusalem Temple or of Jerusalem (Ezek 42, 47, 48; Rev 21:9–27). In this context, however, they may describe God's plan of salvation or, more likely, the love of Christ, which is mentioned in the preceding and following verses. **19.** *fullness of God:* The final petition in the intercessory prayer specifies the goal of humanity in the church: growth into the fullness of divinity. The author has come full circle from his identification of God at the beginning of the prayer in v 14 as the source of all life to God as the goal of humanity. **21.** *in the church and in Christ Jesus:* The mention of both the church and Christ preserves the distinction between the body and the head yet identifies both as the sources of God's glory.

24   (III) Part Two: Exhortations to Worthy Conduct (4:1–6:20). The exhortations to worthy conduct issue from earlier statements about the unity of all things in Christ and the subjection of all things to him

(1:10,22–23), about the new humanity created through the sacrifice of Christ (2:15–16), and about the unity of Gentiles and Jews in the church (3:4–6). These earlier themes are kept before the readers' attention with reminders to preserve the unity of the church (4:3–6), to live lives subject to one another (5:21), to renounce former ungodly ways (4:17–18), and to acknowledge the lordship of Christ (5:21; 6:10–12). The hortatory section is particularly rich in baptismal language (W. A. Meeks, "In One Body," *God's Christ and His People* [Fest. N. A. Dahl; ed. J. Jervell and W. A. Meeks; Oslo, 1977] 209–21).

25 (A) Unity and Diversity in the Church (4:1–16). 1–6. At the beginning of the hortatory section, the image of Paul, the prisoner in the Lord, is again invoked to confer his authority upon the exhortations. The unity of the new humanity created in Christ (2:14–16) is exemplified by the church's unity, fostered by the virtues that make life in common a reality: humility, gentleness, patience, and forbearance. The inspiration for the passage is Col 3:12–15. **4–6.** *one body:* The mention of being called in one body in Col 3:15 leads to a seven-part statement of the pervasiveness of the unity that must characterize Christian life. **5.** *one Lord:* Cf. 1 Cor 8:6. This is particularly important because of the Gentile background of the readers and because of the author's stress on the subjection of all the heavenly powers to Christ (1:20–22). *one faith, one baptism:* Unity in faith may be regarded in this letter as unity of belief. It denotes the teachings to which all members of the church subscribe. As institutional Christianity emerges in the postapostolic period, faith becomes the acceptance of an authoritative apostolic tradition (see 2:20), which can be distinguished from false doctrine (4:14). The reference to unity in baptism is fitting here within the ecclesiological perspective of Eph (→ Pauline Theology, 82:125–26). The new life to which Christians are called in the church (4:1) is entered into at baptism, the formal initiation into the body (cf. Col 2:9–12). **6.** *above all . . . through all . . . in all:* A statement of monotheism (cf. Deut 6:4; Rom 3:30; 1 Cor 8:5–6) culminates the series. The transcendence and all-pervasiveness of God are described by the fourfold repetition of *panta,* "all." **7–16.** The unity of the body in vv 3–6 provides the setting for the discussion of the diversity of church offices. **8.** *when he ascended:* The author cites Ps 68:19 in a form that does not correspond to any Hebr or Gk biblical mss. (which read "you received" in place of "he gave"). Later rabbinic tradition interpreted the passage as Moses ascending Mt. Sinai and giving the law (Str-B 3. 596). The author of Eph interprets it in a related fashion as a reference to Christ's ascension and subsequent bestowal of gifts on the church. **9.** *lower regions:* Either descent into Hades, the abode of the dead (cf. Rom 10:7; Phil 2:10; 1 Pet 3:19; 4:6), or incarnation on earth is meant by the "lower regions." The author's cosmology, in which all nonhuman beings, beneficent and malevolent, are located in the heights (1:20–22; 3:9–10; 6:10–20) supports interpreting *tēs gēs,* "the earth," as an appositional gen. ("the lower regions," i.e., "the earth" (for a different opinion, see BDF 167) and the descent as the incarnation. The lower regions, *ta katōtera,* are contrasted to the heavenly heights, *ta epourania.* **11.** *he gave apostles:* After a christological interpretation of the Scripture citation, the author adds the ecclesiological dimension by interpreting the "gifts" of Ps 68:19 as church offices. First are apostles and prophets, who for the author belong to the past and are the foundation of the church (2:20). They are followed by preachers of the gospel, shepherds, and teachers, which are church offices prominent in the period of the writer. This list of offices

is to be distinguished from similar lists in the Pauline letters (Rom 12:6–8; 1 Cor 12:8–11,28), which enumerate charisms bestowed on individuals by the Spirit. *shepherds:* As a title for a church official, "shepherd" (or pastor) is not used elsewhere in the NT. Allusions to such an office, however, occur in exhortations to church leaders (Acts 20:28; John 21:15–17; 1 Pet 5:7) to tend the flock and in the image of Jesus as the good shepherd (John 10:11). These offices equip the church for ministry and contribute to the growth of the body. **13.** *to full-grown adulthood:* The emphasis of the Gk *anēr* in this context is not on maleness but on adulthood, in contrast to the childhood mentioned in the following verse (BAGD 66[2]). This full adulthood is measured in relation to "the stature of the fullness of Christ." **14.** *every wind of doctrine:* False doctrine poses a threat to the unity in the faith; see comment on 4:5. **15–16.** *grow up . . . into the head:* The author returns to images first used in 1:23 and 2:20–22, depicting the body as a living organism that has Christ as the source and goal of its growth. **16.** *when each part is working properly:* The growth and development of the body depend on each member performing the tasks proper to him or her.

26 (B) Christian and Non-Christian Conduct (4:17–5:20). This long parenetic section contrasts ungodly ways of Gentiles to the ethical implications of life in the body of Christ. The admonitions are largely traditional and are phrased for the most part as negative injunctions. They deal with general expectations of Christian conduct and show no trace of addressing specific problems. **17–19.** The passage reiterates the common Jewish view of pagan moral conduct; see Rom 1:21–25. **22–24.** *put off the old humanity:* Cf. Col 3:9–10. In baptismal language (→ Pauline Theology, 82:112–14) the author exhorts the readers to conduct befitting the new humanity (2:14–16). **4:25–5:2.** These verses present a series of moral exhortations that illustrate the type of conduct proper to Christians who in baptism have put on a new nature (4:24). The motivation is common membership in the one body (4:25), care for the poor (4:28), edification of one's fellows (4:29), and especially imitation of God (5:1) and of Christ (5:2). **30.** *do not offend the holy Spirit:* The community-centered nature of the exhortations suggests that any offense against a fellow member is an offense against the holy Spirit, for all Christians together form a living temple in which the Spirit dwells (2:21–22). *in whom you were sealed:* See Eph 1:13. **31.** *all animosity . . . :* Elements of a traditional list of vices are incorporated into the parenesis; such lists are common in Hellenistic moral tracts as well as elsewhere in the NT (e.g., Rom 1:29–31; Gal 5:19–21) and in the QL (e.g., 1QS 4:3–5; CD 4:17–19; see S. Wibbing, *Die Tugend- und Lasterkataloge im Neuen Testament* [BZNW 25; Berlin, 1959]). The vices listed here are those that are disruptive of communal life. **32.** *forgive one another:* The thought is reminiscent of the petition in the Lord's prayer that God forgive those who forgive others, but the imperative and the condition are reversed. **5:1.** *be imitators of God, as beloved children:* Cf. 1 Cor 11:1; 1 Thess 1:6. There is a manner of life that characterizes membership in God's household (2:19); one of the characteristics defining Christians as members of God's household is love of neighbor, modeled on the love that the Son of God manifested in his sacrificial death (5:2). **3–5.** In portraying the conduct of those outside God's family, the author incorporates again a list of vices (see comment on 4:31), which includes three NT *hapax legomena: aischrotēs,* "shamefulness," *mōrologia,* "foolishness," and *eutrapelia,* "buffoonery." Cf. 1QS 10:22–24; 7:9,14; see Kuhn, "The Epistle to the Ephesians" (→ 12 above) 122. **6–20.** Using a vocabulary in vv 6–17 that is reminiscent of language in the QL, the author contrasts the children of disobedience/darkness to the children of light (cf. 1QS 5:1–2; 3:10–11; 1:5; 2:24–25). As at Qumran the light–darkness dualism is wholly ethical and not ontological, as in later gnosticism. **11.** *reprove them:* The responsibility to correct sinners was also important at Qumran (1QS 5:24–6:1; cf. Matt 18:15–17). **14.** *awake, O sleeper:* The words *dio legei,* "therefore it says," introduce what appears to be a portion of an early baptismal hymn. **15–17.** *wise . . . foolish:* Cf. 1QS 4:23–24. **18–19.** Further admonitions to be filled with the Spirit of God and an exhortation to practices associated with a Spirit-filled life (cf. Col 3:16–17) conclude the section.

27   (C) Code of Conduct for the Household of God (5:21–6:9).   Cf. Col 3:18–4:1. Household codes, found in the NT only in the Deutero-Paulines and 1 Pet, were adapted from Greco-Roman popular philosophy by NT authors to assist in the moral instruction of Christians. The codes depict the Christian household as a hierarchically ordered social unit and may have served the function of responding to accusations that Christianity undermined the social fabric by advocating equality among its adherents. In Greco-Roman literature, as here in Eph, the household codes treated relations between husbands and wives, children and parents, and slaves and masters as relationships of subordinates to superiors. In the NT, specifically Christian motivation is presented as the basis for the imperatives expressed in the code. The code in Eph, similar to that in Col, is integrated into the overall thought of the letter by the expansion relating to Christ and the church in 5:22–23. Christ's lordship over the body is presented as the model for the husband as head of the wife. A further expansion in vv 25b–33 focuses on Christ's love for the church and the image of the church as the bride of Christ. Against the background of the ancient Near Eastern sacred marriage of the gods, the author presents Jesus as the bridegroom (cf. Mark 2:19–20 par.) who cleanses the church, his bride, in the waters of baptism so that clothed in her dowry of holiness and purity, she may now appear before him (see J. P. Sampley, *"And the Two Shall Become One Flesh"* [SNTSMS 16; Cambridge, 1971]). *with the word:* This may be an allusion to a baptismal formula that accompanied the ritual washing. *holy and blameless:* See comment on 1:4. **28.** *husbands ought to love their wives:* Christ's love for his body, the church, is the model for the husband's love of his wife. **31.** *for this reason, a man will leave:* The author quotes Gen 2:24 and continues with an interpretation that is similar to the interpretations of Scripture found in the Qumran *pěšārîm.* **32.** *this is a great mystery:* The pesharim state that the mysteries of God's plan, which lay hidden in Scripture, are revealed to God's chosen interpreters. The true meaning of the Scripture passage was not to be found in its original

setting but in the present day or at the end of days. For the author of Eph, the true meaning of the mystery of the two becoming one flesh that lies hidden in Gen 2:24 is the union of Christ and the church, which in the household code is the model for the union in one flesh between husbands and wives. **6:1–4.** The admonition to children is expanded by the author's citation of the OT command to honor father and mother (Exod 20:12; Deut 5:16). The exhortation to fathers to provide for their children a good Christian upbringing suggests that the expectation of the imminent return of Jesus no longer provided the motivation for instruction and conduct. Rather, Christian life was accommodating itself to the ongoing life of the human community. **6:5–9.** Though the injunctions to slaves are more fully developed than those to masters, the author concludes this section by reminding masters of the equality of all in the sight of God.

28   (D) Christian Life as Warfare with Evil (6:10–20).   The concluding parenesis underscores the tension in Eph between the doctrinal and parenetic sections. The doctrine has emphasized the triumph that God accomplished in Christ, the subjection of all things, including the heavenly powers, to Christ (1:19–22), the participation of the church in the exaltation of Christ in the heavens (2:5–6), the church as the sign to the heavenly powers that God's plan has been accomplished in Christ (3:9–12). The parenesis has reminded the readers that the triumph must still be appropriated by individual members of the body in the human sphere. Christian existence is portrayed as a constant warfare against the malevolent spirits in the heavens (see comment on 2:2). Christians are enjoined to put on the armor of God in order to withstand the onslaughts of the evil one. **11.** *armor of God:* The very armor with which God clothes himself in the OT (Isa 11:5; 59:17; see also Wis 5:17–20) is to be the armament of Christians (6:14–17). Such divine armament is the Christian's guarantee of success. **20.** *I am an imprisoned ambassador:* The final verses of this concluding parenesis recall the image of Paul as a prisoner for the sake of the gospel. Though he is "in chains," he proclaims the gospel freely. This paradox is intended to confront readers with the paradox of their own situation: though they are under the sway of the spiritual forces of evil (6:12), they, as members of the body of Christ, have actually been freed from the dominion of evil and are sharers in the triumph of Christ (1:22–23; 2:5–7). Paul as prisoner thus serves as the model for Christian existence (see R. A. Wild, *CBQ* 46 [1984] 284–98).

29   (IV) Conclusion: Personal News and Blessing (6:21–24). 21–22. The personal news reproduces almost verbatim Col 4:7–8. **23–24.** A Pauline greeting concludes the letter (→ NT Epistles, 45:8D).

56

THE PASTORAL LETTERS

Robert A. Wild, S.J.

BIBLIOGRAPHY

1 Barrett, C. K., *The Pastoral Epistles* (NClarB; Oxford, 1963). Brox, N., *Die Pastoralbriefe* (RNT 7/2; 4th ed.; Regensburg, 1969). Dibelius, M. and H. Conzelmann, *The Pastoral Epistles* (Herm; Phl, 1972). Hanson, A. T., *The Pastoral Epistles* (NCB; GR, 1982). Hasler, V., *Die Briefe an Timotheus und Titus (Pastoralbriefe)* (ZBK NT 12; Zurich, 1978). Holtz, G., *Die Pastoralbriefe* (THKNT 13; 2d ed.; Berlin, 1972). Houlden, J. L., *The Pastoral Epistles* (PC; Harmondsworth, 1976). Jeremias, J. and A. Strobel, *Die Briefe an Timotheus und Titus. Der Brief an die Hebräer*

(NTD 9; Göttingen, 1975). Karris, R. J., *The Pastoral Epistles* (NTM 17; Wilmington, 1979). Kelly, J. N. D., *The Pastoral Epistles* (London, 1963). Lock, W., *The Pastoral Epistles* (ICC; Edinburgh, 1924). Spicq, C., *Les épîtres pastorales* (EBib; 4th ed.; Paris, 1969). Trummer, P., *Die Paulustradition der Pastoralbriefe* (BBET; Frankfurt, 1978). Verner, D. C., *The Household of God: The Social World of the Pastoral Epistles* (SBLDS 71; Chico, 1983). DBSup 6. 1–73. Kümmel, *INT* 366–87. Wik-Schm, *ENT* 507–41.

INTRODUCTION

2 **(I) Name, Recipients, Order of the Letters, and Situation.** Because these letters are the only NT documents addressed to shepherds or "pastors" of Christian communities and because they deal with church life and practice (i.e., with "pastoral" theology), 1 Tim, 2 Tim, and Titus since the 18th cent. have been called the "Pastoral Letters."

3 Their ostensible recipients, Timothy and Titus, were two of Paul's closest companions. According to Acts 16:1–3 Timothy, who was born of mixed Jewish and pagan parentage, had at sometime become a Christian and began to follow Paul after meeting him at Lystra. Timothy served as Paul's representative on missions to Thessalonica (1 Thess 3:2,6), to Corinth (1 Cor 4:17; 16:10–11), and probably also to Philippi (Phil 2:19–23). He was in close contact with Paul during the latter's imprisonment at Ephesus (Phlm 1) and was also with him at Corinth when Rom was written (Rom 16:21). He is listed as a coauthor of four of Paul's genuine letters (2 Cor 1:1; Phil 1:1; 1 Thess 1:1; Phlm 1). (Acts 17:14–15; 18:5; 19:22; 20:4; Col 1:1; 2 Thess 1:1; and Heb 13:23 also mention Timothy.) Titus, a Gentile convert, came with Paul to the Jerusalem conference *ca.* AD 49, and Paul subsequently claimed that he had refused at that time to have him circumcised (Gal 2:1,3–5). Titus later accomplished a delicate mission to Corinth to patch up relations between Paul and that community (2 Cor 12:18; 2:13; 7:6–7,13–16) and then served there as Paul's delegate for the gathering of the Jerusalem collection (2 Cor 8:6,16–24).

4 The present sequence of the Pastorals, 1 Tim–2 Tim–Titus, almost certainly is not original but probably derives from stichometry, i.e., in a given grouping of texts those with more *stichoi* or lines precede those with fewer (e.g., 1–3 John). Since 2 Tim is in the form of a spiritual last will and testament and predicts the imminent death of Paul (2 Tim 4:6–8), it once must have been the final letter. Brief as it is, Titus has a greeting (Titus 1:1–4) that is 65 words long. Of the NT epistles only Rom and Gal have longer greetings (Rom 1:1–7; Gal 1:1–5). This suggests that Titus was intended as the first letter in the Pastorals corpus, a conclusion that is strengthened by the observation that 1 Tim has no proper concluding section and so leads easily into 2 Tim. The Pastorals, therefore, were originally read in the order Titus–1 Tim–2 Tim.

5 The original narrative sequence of the Pastorals (for its actual historical value, → 13 below) presumes a lapse of time of at least two years. Paul is depicted as leaving Crete (Titus 1:5) apparently to journey to Ephesus. Paul's plan of possibly sending Tychicus to Crete (Titus 3:12) implies such an Ephesian destination, for that individual is normally in the NT associated with Asia Minor and with Ephesus (Acts 20:4; Col 4:7; 2 Tim 4:12). Paul then moved N and W toward Macedonia–1 Tim is depicted as being sent at this time (1 Tim 1:3)–and then still farther W toward Nicopolis in Epirus, where he proposed to spend a winter (Titus 3:12). From there he went (with Titus–see Titus 3:12; 2 Tim 4:10) to Rome. Others also joined Paul in Rome

(2 Tim 4:10-12) before or during the time of his imprisonment and trial (2 Tim 4:16-18, etc.). News of Paul's misfortune then reached Ephesus; many there turned away from him (2 Tim 1:15), but Onesiphorus left his family and joined his master in Rome (2 Tim 1:17). 2 Tim reports that Paul had recently sent Tychicus, who had come to him (from Crete? from Ephesus?), back to Ephesus (2 Tim 4:12). In 2 Tim itself Paul asked Timothy to come quickly to Rome via Troas before winter set in (2 Tim 4:9,13,21). Two winters are clearly mentioned in the Pastorals. It is all this journeying back and forth across the Mediterranean that requires the passage of at least one more winter in the narrative time scheme and thus the lapse of two or more years in all.

(Quinn, J., "Paul's Last Captivity," *Studia Biblica 1978* [JSOTSup 3; Sheffield, 1980] 289-99.)

6   (II) Authorship. If Paul were the actual author of the Pastorals, the above chronological reconstruction would then need to be fitted into the full life history of the apostle. However, although there is not complete unanimity on the matter, since the early 19th cent. very many exegetes have argued that these letters are the pseudonymous creations of a later follower of Paul. These arguments seem quite convincing. Although quite similar to one another in vocabulary, grammatical usage, and style, 1-2 Tim and Titus diverge sharply in all these respects from the clearly genuine letters of Paul. Numerous key theological terms used in the Pastorals do not appear in Paul (e.g., "piety," "good conscience," "epiphany," "sound teaching," "trustworthy word"), and many words important in Paul's writings are not found in the Pastorals even where they would be expected (e.g., "body" [of Christ, etc.], "cross," "freedom," "covenant"). The collective absence of these latter terms is striking. As a group, further, the Pastorals contain a very high number of words not found elsewhere in the Pauline corpus or in the NT. Most important to note is the divergence between Paul and the Pastorals in the usage of various commonplace and recurrent Gk adverbs, conjunctions, and particles, for such linguistic features are less subject to conscious control. For example, the manner in which the Pastorals use *kai,* "and," differs considerably from Paul's typical usage. Overall, whereas Paul ordinarily favored a passionate and explosive style sprinkled with interjected thoughts and unfinished sentences, the Pastorals are much more formal and subdued. They depict Paul explaining basic matters in rather sharp language to longtime colleagues whom he has just left (1 Tim 1:3; Titus 1:5) and whom he shortly will see again (1 Tim 3:14; Titus 3:12), a phenomenon that can only be called odd if in fact Paul himself were the author.
7   Those who defend the authenticity of the Pastorals offer various explanations of these features. Some suggest that Paul's advancing age and his sufferings in prison account for the changes. However, according to the usual reckoning adopted by the defenders of authenticity, these letters would have been composed no more than five years after Rom. This makes it difficult to explain all the divergencies, esp. the grammatical and syntactical shifts, on the basis of such psychological determinants.
   More popular, therefore, has been the hypothesis that Paul told a secretary what themes he wished covered and handed over to that individual the actual work of composing the three letters (→ NT Epistles, 45:19-20). However, when Paul did make use of secretaries (see Rom 16:22; 1 Cor 16:21; Gal 6:11-18), his own typical style remained unaltered. If a secretary composed the Pastorals—the Pastorals themselves offer no reference to

such a person—that individual was given unusual freedom by Paul. Furthermore, Paul had to have made use of the same secretary both in the E and in Rome over the whole period of time required for the composition of the Pastorals, for these three letters possess remarkable stylistic consistency. This type of secretary theory, an unlikely hypothesis at best, ends up in any case quite akin to actual pseudonymous authorship.
8   The Pastorals do not fit well into the biographical framework of Paul's life and so are also suspect on that account (→ Paul, 79:49-51). All agree that the Roman imprisonment of 2 Tim cannot be correlated with the imprisonment of Acts 28. Paul must then have been released from that earlier imprisonment, have traveled back to Crete and Ephesus (1 Tim and Titus), and then have returned to Rome where he was again put in jail (2 Tim) and finally executed. However, Paul spoke only of going to Spain and strongly implied that his work in the E was completed (Rom 15:17-29). Further, the close parallelism found in Luke-Acts between Jesus' journey to Jerusalem to undergo his crucifixion and Paul's journey to Rome seems to suppose that the latter's travels had also brought him to his death.
   The Pastorals also present a much more developed church order than is found in the clearly genuine letters of Paul, a somewhat less heightened expectation of an imminent *eschaton,* and a christology that stressed Jesus' birth and resurrection but not, at least as much as in Paul, his crucifixion. Although developments certainly occurred within Christianity even during Paul's lifetime, changes such as these, taken together, tend to point to a later period than Paul's own age. See Brox, *Pastoralbriefe* 22-60; Hanson, *Pastoral Epistles* 2-11.
9   (III) Purpose of the Letters. Although written by someone else under Paul's name, the Pastorals are not "forgeries." Within the Greco-Roman philosophical tradition, the writing of pseudonymous epistles was a long-standing tradition. In such case the writer sought to extend the thought of his or her intellectual master to the problems of a later day. The writer said in effect, "The master would surely have said this if faced with this set of problems or issues." It is quite likely that the original readers of the Pastorals knew very well that Paul himself was not the "actual" author and that the letters represented an effort to extend his heritage to a later generation (→ Canonicity, 66:87-89).
   Although the word *philosophia* does not appear in the Pastorals, the vocabulary, manner of argumentation, parenetic thrust, and general style of these letters situate them firmly within the general milieu of Greco-Roman philosophical discourse. The author of the Pastorals views Pauline Christianity as the only true philosophy or way of life. He calls church leaders, and, by extension, all Christians (note the plural blessing formula at the end of each letter), to a renewed commitment and enthusiasm for this teaching. What Paul said and what Paul did are proposed as the exemplification of this way of life; indeed, the Pastorals make no reference to the existence of any apostle except Paul. Those who oppose Paul and his gospel—1 and 2 Tim in particular engage in polemic against such heretical teachers—are treated as "sophists," and much of the language used against them is stock invective found also in a variety of contemporary philosophical writings.
10   Only those features in the polemics of the Pastorals that are not commonplace in character will help to identify the heresy or heresies in question. The opponents called themselves "teachers of the law" (1 Tim 1:7), and the author of Pastorals attacked them as fomenters of "legal debates" (Titus 3:9) and proponents

of "human commandments" (Titus 1:14). They also were interested in "Jewish myths" (Titus 1:14; see 1 Tim 1:4). Yet though these features point to some aberrant form of Jewish Christianity, other elements do not fit this picture as well: the promotion of an extreme asceticism which opposed marriage and called for abstinence from food (1 Tim 4:3–5), the belief that the resurrection of believers was an already accomplished fact (2 Tim 2:18), and an interest in "genealogies" (Titus 3:9). Because such concerns are found in 2d-cent. gnosticism, scholars have supposed that the author of the Pastorals was struggling against some kind of gnosticizing Jewish Christianity. Yet since those same 2d-cent. gnostics had a very negative view of the law and of the (lower) God who gave the law, it is more probable that the author of the Pastorals was either concerned with several different heresies or else wished to offer a kind of all-purpose polemic against heresy in general. He had, in any case, no interest in refuting such teachings but only in pointing out their folly.

11 What the author of the Pastorals did intend was to urge church leaders to value and maintain ecclesial and societal structure and order. For him true (i.e., Pauline) Christianity was no countercultural movement akin to early Cynicism. It upheld, rather, the fundamental value of Roman society, *eusebeia*, "piety," i.e., the due maintenance of proper relationships between the divine realm and the human and between the various orders of human society among themselves. Both the author's understanding of God's salvific intent ("God wishes to save every human being" [1 Tim 2:3–4]) and his concern to resist heresy and division pushed him in this direction. He envisioned Christianity as a worldwide and fully unified movement that fulfilled the deepest aspirations of contemporary culture for civic and familial harmony.

Titus and 1 Tim each set forth in rather reduplicative fashion procedures for the proper maintenance of "God's household," the church (1 Tim 3:15). Some argue that the rules in Titus may have been directed toward newer churches and those in 1 Tim toward more established communities. Though this remains a possible reason for the duplication in the two letters, these texts differ more clearly with respect to the theological motivations they propose. Titus stresses the theme of salvation—the words "savior" and "salvation" recur with frequency—while 1 Tim forcefully upholds the goodness of all of God's creation (1 Tim 4:1–5). As a spiritual "testament," 2 Tim proposes Paul as a model for all teachers who seek to hand on his tradition.

(Foerster, W., "*Eusebeia* in den Pastoralbriefen," *NTS* 5 [1958–59] 213–18. Johnson, L., "II Timothy and the Polemic Against False Teachers," *JRelS* 6–7 [1978–79] 1–26. Karris, R. J., "The Background and Significance of the Polemic of the Pastoral Epistles," *JBL* 92 [1973] 549–64. Quinn, J., "Parenesis and the Pastoral Epistles," *De la Tôrah au Messie* [Fest. H. Cazelles; ed. M. Carrez, *et al.*; Paris, 1981] 495–501. Wilken, R., *The Christians as the Romans Saw Them* [New Haven, 1984] 48–67).

12 **(IV) Time and Place of Composition.** In terms of geography, the Pastorals focus on Christian churches in the Aegean area and especially in Asia Minor. This has led most scholars to suppose that the Pastorals originated somewhere in this region, perhaps in Ephesus.

The dates proposed for these letters, however, have a very wide range (*ca.* AD 60 to AD 160). Both the more developed church order found in the Pastorals (an ordination ritual; rules for the appointment of bishops,

deacons, and widows; etc.) and the use of language drawn (though almost certainly via Jewish sources) from contemporary Greco-Roman philosophy suggest a later rather than an earlier date. Yet, Titus 1:7 notwithstanding, the Pastorals do not yet seem to know of the monepiscopacy, an institution already found in some of the churches of Asia Minor when Ignatius of Antioch wrote letters to them (*ca.* AD 110). On balance, a date of composition somewhat before or around AD 100 seems a reasonably solid conjecture.

13 **(V) Sources Utilized.** The author of the Pastorals certainly drew on the writings of his master, Paul, although it is not certain that he knew all of his letters. The Pastorals offer numerous clear allusions to Rom and 1 Cor and possibly have a reference or two to Phil. Titus 3:3–7 makes use of Eph 2:3–12 or a closely related tradition. There are many allusions to and citations of Scripture (i.e., the OT), and 1 Tim 2:11–14 makes use of an extensive argument based on Gen 2–3. At one point a proverbial saying of the pagan sage Epimenides of Crete is directly quoted (Titus 1:12). In addition, the Pastorals cite—often with the formula "The saying is trustworthy"—various hymnic and creedal fragments, traditional sayings, etc.

A 2d-cent. Christian text, *Acts of Paul and Thecla* (hereafter *Acts P. Thec.*), shares in significantly large measure with 2 Tim a common cast of characters and a common geographical setting (→ Apocrypha, 67:54). Furthermore, the Pastorals oppose precisely the sort of teaching ascribed to Paul by *Acts P. Thec.*, the demand that all Christians refrain from marriage and practice strict asceticism. Although for various reasons it is unlikely that either text used the other as a direct source, the author of the Pastorals probably drew on traditions also employed by *Acts P. Thec.* They represented a perspective on Paul's teaching that had developed over a period of time. What was at stake, therefore, was a struggle over the Pauline heritage. The author of the Pastorals signaled by the use of these traditions his awareness of this competing view of Paul, a view that he then proceeded to reject as inauthentic.

The numerous biographical references to Paul found in the Pastorals have led some to suppose that these letters contain sections drawn from now-lost letters of Paul (= the so-called fragments hypothesis). Stated in this fashion, the theory is difficult to maintain, since the style of the Pastorals is consistent throughout. Therefore, the beginning and end points of these supposed source texts cannot be detected. It is likely, however, that the author of the Pastorals did draw on traditions about Paul known to him yet not recorded in other NT sources. Yet his interest was not to correct extant Pauline biographical accounts but to develop a theologically useful image of Paul, and he used the biographical traditions that he had, whether historically accurate or not, to achieve this end. Because biography constantly serves theological rather than historical ends, it is difficult to evaluate the historical worth of the information supplied in the Pastorals. Some of it may possibly record authentic memories of Paul's activities.

(Brox, N., "Zu den persönlichen Notizen der Pastoralbriefe," *BZ* 13 [1969] 76–94. Collins, R., "The Image of Paul in the Pastorals," *LTP* 31 [1975] 147–73. Lindemann, A., *Paulus im ältesten Christentum* [BHT 58; Tübingen, 1979] 134–49. MacDonald, D., *The Legend and the Apostle* [Phl, 1983]. Trummer, P., "'Mantel und Schriften' (2 Tim 4,13)," *BZ* 18 [1974] 193–207; *Paulustradition.* Wild, R. A., "Portraits of Paul Created by Some of His Early Christian Admirers," *Chicago Studies* 24 [1985] 273–89.)

COMMENTARY ON TITUS

14   Outline. The letter to Titus may be outlined as follows:

15   (I) Address and Greeting (1:1–4). This disproportionately lengthy greeting served to introduce the Pastorals as a group rather than just Titus (→ 4 above). *servant of God:* The NT limits this common OT title to individuals with a prophetic mission (Lk 2:29; Rev 1:1; 22:6; Acts 4:29; 16:17). *in accord with* [and/or *for;* the Gk prep. *kata* means both] *the faith of God's elect:* Paul's teaching stands in continuity with the faith of all those chosen by God (the "elect" = the Christian community) and extends and supports that faith. *the clear knowledge of the truth:* A formula in the Pastorals referring to truth revealed by God (see 1 Tim 2:4; 2 Tim 2:25; 3:7; in Epictetus [*Diss.* 2.20.21] a synonym for "true philosophy"). Such knowledge is opposed to the so-called knowledge (1 Tim 6:20) taught by the false teachers. *in accord with piety:* Eusebeia, "piety" or "reverence," i.e., right behavior toward God and human society, is an essential demand of God's revelation. **2.** *a hope for eternal life:* Cf. 3:7. It is this life which God has promised and which is both the support and the goal of ethical life. *before the eternal ages:* I.e., from all eternity. **3.** *as his message:* It is God who promises eternal life. *with which I was entrusted:* Paul's mission is seen as integral to the divine plan of salvation. **4.** *to Titus, my legitimate child in accord with* [and/or *for*] *the common faith:* Titus is Paul's true heir because he accepts and will promote the faith proclaimed by Paul. This connects him with the developing chain of tradition (for further links in this chain, see 1:5; 2 Tim 2:1–2). *Christ Jesus our Savior:* The Pastorals use the title "Savior" both of God and of Christ. The mention here of Christ's role as Savior is unique in the introductory blessings of the Pauline letters and so serves to signal the centrality of the salvation theme in Titus.

16   (II) Leaders for the Church on Crete (1:5–9).

(A) The Charge to Titus (1:5). This is the sole mention of a missionary visit by Paul to the island of Crete; Acts 27:8–12 records only a brief stopover at the harbor of Fair Havens. *establish presbyters city by city:* Collegial groups (see 1 Tim 4:14) of elders or presbyters were to be established in each city. This ecclesial structure was borrowed from Judaism. *as I commanded you:* Paul's authority, insists the author, supports this institution. Cf. Acts 14:23.

17   (B) Qualities Required of the Presbyter (1:6–9). Verses 6–8 (cf. 1 Tim 3:2–4) may draw upon an already traditional listing of requirements for this office. If so, v 9 was added by the author of the Pastorals. **6.** *husband of one wife:* Probably not, as some think, an exclusion of widowers who have remarried but a demand for ordinary marital fidelity. That the candidate would be married was assumed. His children, further, had to be believers and not insubordinate or wild and dissipated (traditional language; see Prov 28:7). The would-be manager of God's household (1:7) had to be able to manage his own family (1 Tim 3:5). **7.** The author of the Pastorals equated (as in Acts 20:17,28) presbyters and *episkopoi,* i.e., "overseers" or "bishops." Paul does not mention *presbyteroi,* but he did know of *episkopoi* (Phil 1:1); the two offices may have had a separate history. Verse 7 does not refer to a single bishop in charge of an entire city. However, since (wealthy) ancient households were managed by a single *oikonomos,* "steward," the reference to "God's steward" suggests that each house-church may have been led by just one presbyter/bishop. *not an alcoholic:* The Pastorals often show concern about alcoholism (see 2:2,3; 1 Tim 3:2,3,8,11), but the author rejects the view that liquor as such is evil (see 1 Tim 5:23). *not greedy for money:* See also 1 Tim 3:3,8; 6:17–19; but note in 1 Tim 5:17–19 the concern that church leaders receive sufficient financial support. Greediness for money, a charge leveled against the false teachers in the Pastorals (Titus 1:11; 1 Tim 6:6–10), functions as a polemical commonplace in Greco-Roman philosophical attacks on sophists. **8.** *moderate, just, devoted, self-controlled:* A version of the four cardinal virtues of Greco-Roman antiquity. The candidate must be a fully virtuous man. **9.** For the author of the Pastorals fidelity to Pauline teaching and the ability to communicate it was of paramount importance.

18   (III) False Teaching vs. True Teaching (1:10–3:8).

(A) The Nature of the False Teachers (1:10–16). The mention of "opponents" in v 9 leads into this section, but the argument rapidly shifts to a contrast between Pauline truth and heretical falsehood. Many of the charges, e.g., "talkers of nonsense" (v 10), teaching "for the sake of base gain" (v 11; see 1 Tim 6:5), were commonplaces leveled by one school of philosophy against another. **10.** *insubordinate:* As people who disobey church authority and tradition, the false teachers are likened to "disobedient children" (1:6). *those of the circumcision:* Jewish Christians. **11.** *they overturn whole households:* House-churches rather than ordinary families may well be in view here (cf. 2 Tim 3:6). *for the sake of shameful gain:* See 1:7. **12.** The author here cites Epimenides of Crete (6th cent. BC), a diviner and sage whom he calls a prophet. *Cretans always are liars:* The author's emphatic agreement with this sentiment is a good indication that this is not a real letter intended to be read to Cretan Christians. The archetypal lie of the ancient Cretans was the claim that Zeus was dead and had been buried on Crete (Lucian, *Philopseudes* 3; *Anth. Pal.* 7.275). Cretans therefore probably appear here as types of the Christian heretics. **13–14.** The Pastorals have no interest in a debate with false teachers. Yet hope for their conversion is never abandoned (see also 2 Tim 2:25–26). *that they may be healthy:* The true philosopher was often looked upon as a physician of the soul. The Pastorals share the view that falsehood is a disease which only the truth can remedy. (See A. Malherbe, in *Texts and Testaments* [ed. W. March; San Antonio, 1980] 19–35.) *Jewish myths:*

Although "to teach myths or fables" was a stock charge leveled by philosophers against poets (cf. Plato, *Phd.* 61B; *Tim.* 26E; Plutarch, *De glor. Ath.* 348A-B), the Jewish-Christian nature of the false teachers is again emphasized. **15.** *everything is pure:* A saying accepted by Paul but only with qualification (Rom 14:20; cf. 1 Cor 6:12; 10:23). The Pastorals ground this principle in the goodness of God's creation (1 Tim 4:4). *their mind and conscience:* The means respectively to discover truth in the theoretical and practical realms; if they were "defiled," truth was unattainable. **16.** *unqualified for any good work:* The ironic state of heretics who show such interest in law observance. "Readiness for every good work" (2 Tim 2:21; 3:17; Titus 3:1; cf. 1 Tim 5:10) is a hallmark of true believers.

19   (B) What the True Teacher Is to Teach (2:1-3:8).

(a) CHRISTIAN DUTIES WITHIN THE HOUSE-HOLD (2:1-15).

(i) *The basic charge* (2:1). By contrast Titus must offer "sound (i.e., healthy) teaching." The recurrence of the key word "speak" (*lalei*) in 2:15 demarcates the textual unit.

20   (ii) *Duties of the household members* (2:2-10). In this *Haustafel,* "list of household duties" (cf. Col 3:18-4:1; Eph 5:21-6:9; 1 Pet 2:18-3:7), the virtues and vices are stereotypical with respect to the five groups addressed. All but one group is called to the cardinal virtue of "moderation" (2:2,4,5,6). **2.** *in faith, love, and endurance:* "Endurance" replaces "hope" in the traditional triad (1 Cor 13:13). **3.** *teachers of virtue:* The author of the Pastorals, however, did not want women teaching men or teaching in a worship context (1 Tim 2:11-12). **4-5.** The stress here on domestic virtues is not unrelated to the fact that some of the younger women apparently had become involved in spreading false teaching (1 Tim 5:13). Ancient social morality assumed as a given the submission of wives to their husbands. **7.** *a model:* Like Timothy (1 Tim 4:12; 5:1; 2 Tim 2:22) Titus is depicted as a young man, probably in order to make him a type of the next generation of church leaders after Paul. **9.** *slaves:* Although 1 Tim 6:1-2 implies that many slave masters were not Christian, the community of the Pastorals had wealthier members (cf. 1 Tim 2:9; 6:17-19) who presumably owned slaves. **10.** The mention of a stereotypical slave vice like "pilfering" and the failure to list the duties of masters suggest a lurking bias in favor of the slaveholders.

21   (iii) *Reason: God's saving action* (2:11-14). We Christians, says the author of the Pastorals, are enabled to live virtuously in the present and with hope for the future by the saving power of God in Christ. Both popular Hellenistic philosophy (see vv 11-12) and the Bible (v 14) have influenced the language of this section (see S. Mott, *NovT* 20 [1978] 22-48). **11.** *the saving favor of God has appeared to all human beings:* As in Philo, an abstract divine attribute, God's "favor" or "grace," is personified. Elsewhere in the Pastorals it is always Christ who "appears" (2:13; 1 Tim 6:14; 2 Tim 1:10; 4:1, 8); so he becomes here the historical actualization of "God's saving favor." This saving gift is not just for some, but for "all human beings" (see 3:2,8; 1 Tim 2:1,4; 4:10). **12.** *educating us:* God achieves for the believer what was so valued in Greco-Roman society, true education (*paideia*). It both counters "impiety," the vice opposed to piety/loyalty/devotedness (*eusebeia*), and promotes the living of a fully virtuous life (the three cardinal virtues of moderation, justice, and piety stand for the virtues in general). **13.** *our great God and Savior Christ Jesus:* The Pastorals view Christ as subordinate to God yet accord

him, as a past and also yet-to-come manifestation of God, the same titles as God. Here he receives the very name of God. **14.** Formulaic language to which the author has added a reference to the need for an ethical response to Christ's redemptive work. *that he might redeem us from all lawlessness and cleanse for himself a chosen people:* Biblical promises made by God (Ezek 37:23; Ps 130:8; Exod 19:5) are accomplished through Christ's self-giving.

(iv) *The basic charge restated* (2:15). See 2:1. *let no one despise you:* A reference here to Titus's youth? Cf. 1 Tim 4:12. Those who pass on the teaching of Paul deserve the respect accorded to the apostle himself.

22   (b) CHRISTIAN DUTIES WITHIN SOCIETY (3:1-8).

(i) *Duties* (3:1-2). **1.** *be subject to the ruling authorities:* This is developed further in 1 Tim 2:2 (cf. Rom 13:1-7; 1 Pet 2:13-17). *ready for every good work:* See 1:16. **2.** The Pastorals insist that Christians deal with others, including nonbelievers, in an unassuming and gentle manner.

(ii) *Reason: God's saving action* (3:3-8). The use here of the common "then/now" schema (its vocabulary reflects Eph 2:1-10; cf. also Rom 6:17-18; 1 Cor 6:9-11; Col 3:7-8) serves to remind Christians that they were once like those nonbelievers but were gratuitously rescued by God's power. **3.** *fools:* A number of the evils listed here are attributed also to the false teachers (see 1:16; 1 Tim 6:4; 2 Tim 3:3,6). **4.** As in 2:11, manifestations of God are personified and linked via "appearance" language with the coming of Christ. This passage, however, depicts Christ as God's instrument (v 6). *kindness and love for humanity:* These divine characteristics are directly related to the ethical demands of 3:1-2. **5.** *uprightness:* The language of justification found here probably is derived not directly from Paul himself, but from Eph 2:8-9 (or a prior popular summation utilized by both texts). *through a bath of rebirth:* I.e., baptism. The author uses a commonplace from Hellenistic religious language, *palingenēsia*, "rebirth," to express Paul's notion of "new creation." **7.** A formulaic summary of Paul's teaching on justification (→ Pauline Theology, 82:68-70). **8.** *the saying is reliable:* A formula used in the Pastorals (see 1 Tim 1:15; 3:1; 4:9; 2 Tim 2:11) to declare that Paul himself guarantees the tradition in question (3:3-7). *good works:* They are again emphasized as the task of believers; but they are a response to God's prior saving work (see Phil 2:13).

23   (IV) Strife and Division to Be Avoided (3:9-11). As the model of a church leader, Titus is instructed what his own behavior should be toward false teachers and their message. **9.** *genealogies:* The reference is uncertain. In 1 Tim 1:4 the word is coupled with "myths" in a negative context; 2d-cent. gnosticism developed extensive accounts of families of divine aeons within the "fullness" (of divinity). *legal fights:* Conservative Jewish Christians continued to press for the full applicability of the law.

24   (V) Business Matters and Closing Blessing (3:12-15). On the geography and the temporal movements ascribed to Paul, → 5 above. **12.** *Artemas:* Not mentioned elsewhere. *Tychicus:* He appears in various texts as a companion of Paul (Acts 20:4; Col 4:7; Eph 6:21; 2 Tim 4:12). **13.** *Zenas:* Not mentioned elsewhere. *Apollos:* Possibly identical with the rather independent colleague of Paul (1 Cor 1:12; 3:4-6). **14.** *for their urgent necessities:* Probably ironic. The truly "urgent necessities" are not bodily concerns, but the demands of Christian ethical life. **15.** *greetings:* The final formula envisions a wider audience for the letter than just Titus. Col, 1 Tim, and 2 Tim use the same final blessing, but omit the word "all."

COMMENTARY ON 1 TIMOTHY

25   Outline. The first letter to Timothy may be outlined as follows:

(I) Address and Greeting (1:1–2)
(II) Introduction: Main Themes of the Letter (1:3–20)
    (A) Paul's Command to Timothy (1:3–5)
    (B) The Opponents as False Teachers (1:6–11)
    (C) Paul as the True Teacher (1:12–17)
    (D) Summary (1:18–20)
(III) Worship and Leadership in the Church (2:1–3:13)
    (A) The Community's Conduct at Worship (2:1–15)
        (a) Prayer Intentions (2:1–7)
        (b) How Men Should Act (2:8)
        (c) How Women Should Act (2:9–15)
    (B) Leadership for the Community (3:1–13)
        (a) Basic Principle (3:1)
        (b) Requirements for Bishops (3:2–7)
        (c) Requirements for Deacons (3:8–12)
        (d) Conclusion (3:13)
(IV) Purpose and Theological Perspective of 1 Tim (3:14–4:10)
    (A) Purpose: Conduct in God's Household (3:14–16)
    (B) Perspective: The Goodness of Creation (4:1–10)
        (a) The Basic Statement (4:1–5)
        (b) These Things Must Be Taught (4:6–10)
(V) Teachings for Different Groups in the Church (4:11–6:2)
    (A) Introduction (4:11)
    (B) Timothy as Type of the Church Leader (4:12–16)
    (C) The Leader and Various Age Groups (5:1–2)
    (D) The Widows (5:3–16)
    (E) The Elders (5:17–25)
    (F) Slaves (6:1–2)
(VI) Summation (6:3–16)
    (A) The Situation of the False Teachers (6:3–10)
    (B) How Timothy Is to Act (6:11–16)
(VII) Supplementary Reflection on the Rich (6:17–19)
(VIII) Final Exhortation to Timothy (6:20–21a)
(IX) Closing Blessing for the Community (6:21b)

26   (I) Address and Greeting (1:1–2). 1. *by command of:* By using *kat' epitagēn*, the author designates divine revelation as opposed to human ordinance (1 Cor 7:6,25; cf. also Rom 16:26). *God our savior and Christ Jesus our hope:* Both titles pick up the salvation theme that is so prominent in Titus (cf. Titus 1:1–4). **2.** *to Timothy, my legitimate child:* Like Titus, Timothy is also Paul's true heir (cf. Titus 1:4). *grace, mercy, peace:* Only here and in 2 Tim 1:2 does "mercy" appear in the opening formula of a Pauline letter (→ NT Epistles, 45:8A).
27   (II) Introduction: Main Themes of the Letter (1:3–20).
    (A) Paul's Command to Timothy (1:3–5).
3. *as I urged you . . . Macedonia:* The Gk sentence has no main vb., but the introductory *kathōs*, "as," can signal an implied command ("As I urged you, so do" [BAGD 391]). On Paul's geographical movements, → 5 above. *that you might instruct some people:* The Gk vb. *parangellō*, "I teach, instruct, admonish," and its related noun, *parangelia*, "command, precept, instruction," are key words in 1 Tim (verb: 1:3; 4:11; 5:7; 6:13,17; noun: 1:5, 18) but do not appear in 2 Tim or Titus. Verse 5 defines the purpose of such instruction. **4.** *myths and endless genealogies:* On "myths," see comment on Titus 1:14; on "genealogies," see comment on Titus 3:9. These may well be stock charges rather than descriptions of a specific heresy. *speculations rather than the plan of God:* The Pastorals insist that a valid Christian theology must affect behavior in the real world (e.g., Titus 1:1). The "plan of God" is literally the "way of managing the

household of God" (*oikonomia theou*). 1 Tim intends to set forth the proper conduct to be followed in "God's household" (3:15). **5.** *the goal of instruction is love deriving from a clean heart, a good conscience, and sincere faith:* A summary of the purpose of Christian ethical instruction. The expression "a clean heart" probably comes from Ps 51:10 (there it is viewed as a gift from God). Two synonymous phrases follow: the more Hellenistic expression "a good conscience" (see Titus 1:15; 2 Tim 1:3; 2:22) and the reference to "sincere faith," i.e., a faith that is lived out.
28   (B) The Opponents as False Teachers (1 Tim 1:6–11). 7. *teachers of the law:* The context indicates that these are Jewish Christians ("they have turned aside," i.e., from the truth of Christianity), and this is their self-description. In the view of the author they are not such, since they lack true knowledge altogether. **8.** *we know that the law is good:* A combination of Rom 7:14 and 16. However, a different point is made here, viz., that the good do not need a law to guide their conscience (so also Gal 5:18). Only evildoers have such a need. **9–10.** The list of vices almost certainly is based on the commandments although in several cases extreme instances serve as examples. The four pairs ending with "patricides and matricides" illustrate the first "table" of the commandments (cf. Philo, *De Dec.* 51). The final two commandments are not mentioned (see N. McEleney, *CBQ* 36 [1974] 204–10). **11.** As generally in the Pastorals, Paul is here depicted as having unique responsibility for transmitting the gospel (see Titus 1:3).
29   (C) Paul as the True Teacher (1:12–17). A ring construction formed by the two (quasi) doxologies (vv 12 and 17) and the repeated statement "but I received mercy" (vv 13 and 16) serves to focus attention on the "reliable saying" about Christ's saving work (v 15). The "then/now" schema (see Titus 3:3–8) is here applied to Paul. He himself never depicted his conversion in quite such stark terms (see Gal 1:11–16; Phil 3:4–8; but cf. Acts 9:1–19). **13.** *blasphemer:* Paul was what the heretics are now (v 20). Unlike them, however, Paul then had "ignorance" (v 13) as an excuse (cf. Acts 3:17; 17:30). Yet the comparison points forward to the hope for their conversion as expressed in v 20. **15.** *Christ Jesus came into the world to save sinners:* Gospel variants of this "reliable saying" include John 3:17; Luke 19:10; Matt 9:13 par. **16.** *as prototype of those who would come to believe:* Paul is "first" (v 15) to be delivered by Christ; his conversion is a model for all believers who come after him (see also 2 Tim 1:13). **17.** The transcendence of God is highlighted.
30   (D) Summary (1:18–20). The task of "instruction" (see v 5) is now formally "entrusted" (*paratithemai*—for the related noun *parathēkē*, "deposit," see 1 Tim 6:20; 2 Tim 1:12,14) by Paul to Timothy (v 18). The latter is reminded of the need for "faith and a good conscience" (v 19; cf. v 5). Timothy's efforts are to stand in sharp contrast with those of the false teachers. **18.** *in accord with the prophecies which pointed beforehand to you:* A reference to Timothy's ordination (1 Tim 4:14). **20.** *Hymenaeus and Alexander whom I handed over to Satan to be trained:* Hymenaeus is paired with Philetus in 2 Tim 2:17 as a false teacher. The same Alexander (probably) is depicted in 2 Tim 4:14 as Paul's enemy and accuser. On the procedure of "handing over to Satan," see 1 Cor 5:4–5; in both cases the eventual salvation of the individual is hoped for.
31   (III) Worship and Leadership in the Church (2:1–3:13).

(A) The Community's Conduct at Worship (2:1-15).

(a) PRAYER INTENTIONS (2:1-7). The stress in this section is upon God's desire to save every human being (see also 1 Tim 4:10; Titus 2:11; 3:2,8). Verses 5-6 provide theological reasoning for this insistence, and v 7 indicates that Paul specifically accepted this mission. **1.** *I urge:* Every human being is to be included in the intercessory and thanksgiving prayer intentions of the community. **2.** *for kings:* Like the Jews, Christians did not participate in civic worship of the gods and so were suspect on that account. In part to offset such suspicion both groups made it clear that they did pray for the welfare of the emperor and other civic authorities. The author of the Pastorals, however, does not urge such prayer out of a concern for patriotism as such but out of a desire that such authorities might allow the Christians to live in peace ("that we might lead a peaceful and quiet life" [v 2]) and out of an (implied) hope that these authorities might come to "a clear knowledge of the truth" (vv 3-4). *piety:* See Titus 1:1. **4.** *clear knowledge of the truth:* See Titus 1:1. **5-6.** Much or all of this seems to be a traditional formula. *one God:* If God is one, he must be concerned with all peoples, not just with this or that group or nation. *and one intermediary between God and humanity, the human being Christ Jesus:* The repetition of the word "one" links Christ with God. Yet his humanity is here stressed both by the use of the word *anthrōpos,* "human being," and by the designation "intermediary" (used of Moses in Gal 3:19-20; cf. Philo, *De vita Mos.* 2.166). **6.** *as a ransom for all:* Cf. Mark 10:45. The stress again is on the universality of Christ's work. *the testimony at the proper times:* Christ's "testimony" certainly refers to his death (see 2 Tim 1:8) but probably also, given the plural formulation, "proper times," to the whole of his activity. What Christ did witnesses to the fulfillment of God's promise (see Titus 1:2-3; 2 Tim 1:1). **7.** *I speak the truth, I do not lie:* Paul's integral role in God's plan of salvation (Titus 1:3; 2 Tim 1:11) is here underscored by this formula of asseveration drawn from Rom 9:1.

32 (b) HOW MEN SHOULD ACT (2:8). *in every place:* A formulaic expression used in worship legislation (cf. also *Did.* 14.3) and drawn from Mal 1:11. *raising holy hands:* In early Christian art this is the normal posture of a person at prayer, i.e., standing, with hands outstretched, and with palms turned upward toward heaven to indicate receptivity of God's gifts. *without anger and strife:* Cf. Phil 2:14. According to the author of the Pastorals, the false teachers typically promote debates and arguments (1 Tim 6:4; 2 Tim 2:14,23).

33 (c) HOW WOMEN SHOULD ACT (2:9-15). As in 1 Cor 11:5, women are assumed to have the right to pray aloud at Christian worship. But the author is clearly concerned about the conduct of women, for some of them seem to have exercised a teaching and preaching role (see 1 Tim 5:13). Women in the Pauline churches held responsible positions (e.g., Phoebe [Rom 16:1-2], Prisca [Rom 16:3; 1 Cor 16:19], Junia [? Rom 16:7]) and are depicted as preaching (1 Cor 11:5) and teaching (Acts 18:26; cf. *Acts P. Thec.*). **9-10.** Concern about attire that is too rich and contrived is a commonplace in Greco-Roman philosophy. Nonetheless, the community of the Pastorals presumably had wealthier members who could afford pearls, gold jewelry, etc. **11-12.** 1 Cor 14:33b-35, a probable early addition to the original text of 1 Cor, is close in language and sentiment to this text. The author of the Pastorals speaks explicitly only of women's behavior at Christian worship but may intend a more general application. *nor to have authority over a man:* In the author's view, a violation of Gen 3:16. **13-14.** *Adam:* A scriptural argument drawn from, and

using the language of Gen 2-3 LXX. Two points are made: The male has priority because he was created first and, as in Gen 3:13 where "deception" is explicitly predicated of the female but not of the male, women are more likely to be led astray and so should not be teachers (see also Sir 25:24). Paul himself prefers to assign blame to Adam (as a counterpart of Christ—see Rom 5:12-21; 1 Cor 15:45-49; → Romans, 51:53). *she will be saved through childbearing:* Not a purely chauvinistic sentiment, but to be read in the light of 1 Tim 4:3-5: the false teachers prohibit marriage, but true faith insists upon the goodness of human sexuality as something created by God. Indeed women are to be saved, says the author of the Pastorals, by the very thing that the false teachers reject!

34 (B) Leadership for the Community (3:1-13).

(a) BASIC PRINCIPLE (3:1). Some suggest that the "reliable saying" (see Titus 3:8) refers to 2:13-14 but it seems rather to underscore as genuine Pauline tradition what immediately follows. *overseership: Episkopē* is generic and does not yet mean "bishopric" in our modern sense.

(b) REQUIREMENTS FOR BISHOPS (3:2-7). Both this text and Titus 1:6-8 appear to draw on an earlier listing of requirements. The author of the Pastorals has probably edited this earlier tradition in various ways. Verse 7 seems certainly to be such an addition. **2.** *the bishop:* I.e., any bishop/overseer. This individual probably was a kind of "pastor" in charge of a house-church (see v 5 and Titus 1:7), but he possibly also had wider responsibilities. *husband of one wife:* See Titus 1:6. *sober:* This refers primarily to temperance in food and drink but can have a more general meaning. See Titus 1:7. **3.** *not a lover of money:* See Titus 1:7. **4-5.** The bishop is presumed to be married and with children. Since the author of the Pastorals views the assembly of believers as "God's household" (1 Tim 3:15), the candidate's management of his own household is deemed a fine indicator of his probable performance as bishop. **7.** The characteristic concern of the Pastorals that the Christian community be attractive to outsiders derives from the realization that God wants every person to be saved (see 1 Tim 2:1-7).

(c) REQUIREMENTS FOR DEACONS (3:8-12). **8.** *deacons:* Normally in the NT the Gk word *diakonos* bears the general sense of "servant" or "minister" but occasionally, as here, it refers to a church office (as also in Phil 1:1 and possibly also Rom 16:1; cf. Acts 6:1-6). The precise role of deacons in this early period is difficult to determine, for the deacons / "table waiters" of Acts 6 also engaged in preaching (Acts 7; 8:4-8,26-40). **9.** *mystery of the faith:* Deacons must be believers in and doers of the word. **11.** *women:* Since the qualities required of the "women" (or "wives" [i.e., of the deacons—the Gk *gynaikas* is ambiguous]) are virtually identical to those listed in vv 8-9, and since there is no similar reference to the wives of bishops or elders, the author probably refers here to women deacons. **12.** Male deacons are also presumed to be married and with children (see Titus 1:6-7; 1 Tim 3:4-5).

(d) CONCLUSION (3:13). Although linked by the ptc. "ministering" to the preceding discussion of deacons, this verse apparently serves to explain why desiring an "overseership" (3:1) is a "good work."

35 (IV) Purpose and Theological Perspective of 1 Tim (3:14-4:10).

(A) Purpose: Conduct in God's Household (3:14-16). **15.** *but if I delay:* The original readers knew that Paul's death had caused a very long delay! Yet he has provided the church with proper instructions for its conduct. *God's house* [or *household*]: A biblical phrase referring to Israel but more often to the Temple in Jerusalem. Here it also deliberately reflects the familial character of the early Christian communities, which typically met in private homes. **16.** *who appeared . . . in glory:* An early poetic formulation of the kerygma. Three pairs of phrases are arranged so as to juxtapose heavenly/spiritual and earthly events. With one exception the six Gk phrases have almost the same number of syllables. *mystery:* As in Col 1:26–27 and 2:2, the "mystery" of God's revelation (i.e., the revelation in time of the once-hidden moment of salvation) is equated with Christ. *who appeared in flesh:* Some type of divine preexistence seems involved. *vindicated* [or *justified*] *in spirit:* This refers to Christ's resurrection.

Reumann, J., *"Righteousness" in the New Testament* [Phl, 1982] 30. Schweizer, E., "Two Early Christian Creeds Compared," *CINTI* 166–77.

36   (B) Perspective: The Goodness of Creation (4:1–10).
(a) THE BASIC STATEMENT (4:1–5). **1.** As also in 2 Tim 3:1–5, the activities of the false teachers (here clearly identified as being within the Christian community) are viewed as signs of the end-time foretold by the prophetic spirit of God. **2.** *branded:* Slaves, esp. fugitives, were sometimes branded with a red-hot iron. The image points to the unfree, enslaved status of those who reject the truth. **3–4.** The false teaching, now identified with precision, turns out to be very much like the teaching attributed to Paul in *Acts P. Thec.* (→ 13 above). There Paul is depicted as proclaiming a doctrine of "continence and the resurrection" (5), and he and his followers are found living in a tomb and subsisting upon bread, vegetables, and water (23–25). Apparently, since the author of the Pastorals used Gen 1:4,10,12 to insist that all of God's creation is good and therefore to be utilized by believers, the false teachers had urged a withdrawal from the material world as something evil, a widespread perspective found in gnosticism and elsewhere. **5.** *it is sanctified:* Creation is good in itself. God's word and prayer and thanksgiving (vv 3–4) are all means enabling the Christian to recognize that the created world is from the hand of God.
(b) THESE THINGS MUST BE TAUGHT (4:6–10). Timothy and all Christian leaders are to follow Paul's example (v 10) in teaching the point of view advanced in vv 3–5 ("these things," v 6) and in rejecting the heresy. **6.** *which you have followed closely:* This is developed further in 2 Tim 3:10. **7.** *old wives' tales:* While this phrase is stereotypical (cf. Epictetus, *Diss.* 2:16.39; Lucian, *Philops.* 9), the author is concerned about the involvement of women in the false teaching (e.g., 1 Tim 5:13). **8.** *piety:* See Titus 1:1. *the saying is reliable:* The double-member proverb in v 8a seems to be traditional. It is not a rejection of athletic exercise but of the "bodily exercise" (i.e., bodily abstinence) advocated by the heretics. **10.** *the savior of every human being, especially of believers:* One of the strongest biblical affirmations of God's universal salvific will. Believers enjoy a special, but not a unique, claim. See Titus 2:11; 3:2,8; 1 Tim 2:1,4.

37   (V) Teachings for Different Groups in the Church (4:11–6:2).
(A) Introduction (4:11). 1 Tim 6:2 ends with very similar language; the two verses therefore frame the section.
(B) Timothy as Type of the Church Leader (4:12–16). Although specific ecclesial duties are enumerated (v 13), what is emphasized is the exemplary life-style required of the church leader. **12.** *let no one despise your youth:* That Timothy was a "youth" (so also 1 Tim 5:1) is historically unlikely. Instead, his "youth"

makes him a symbol of every church leader who comes after Paul (i.e., each "new generation"). Cf. Titus 2:15. *in purity:* See 1 Tim 5:2 for specifics. **13.** *in the reading, encouragement, and teaching:* The "reading" was the public reading of the OT, and "encouragement" refers to the homily. Both practices derive from the Jewish synagogue. **14.** *laid hands on:* 2 Tim 1:6 emphasizes Timothy's direct link with Paul in the chain of tradition. This text, however, reflects the ordination rites known to the community of the Pastorals, i.e., the use of prophecy to discover a candidate's charism and the missioning of the candidate through the (Jewish) ritual of the elders laying on their hands (cf. Num 27:18–23; Deut 34:9). **15.** *progress:* See Phil 1:25. The leader, too, cannot stand still but must progress and so encourage others.

38   (C) The Leader and Various Age Groups (5:1–2). 1. *an older man:* The Gk word *presbyteros,* here contrasted with *neōterous,* "younger men," refers to "an older man" rather than to an "elder" or "presbyter."

(D) The Widows (5:3–16). The community of the Pastorals was familiar with the institution of "enrolled widows"; in vv 9–10 the author probably cites older regulations regarding their enrollment. Clearly the author believes that this institution has overexpanded, and he indicates three ways (vv 3–8,9–15,16) for limiting its membership to "those who are truly widows" (vv 3,5). His concern derives not only from financial exigencies (v 16) but also from the activity of some present "widows" in the spreading of error (vv 13,15; see J. Bassler, *JBL* 103 [1984] 23–41). **4.** *let them first learn:* I.e., the children or grandchildren. Widows with living family relatives should be cared for by them. **5.** *true widow:* She is defined as someone truly alone in the world. Although it is more probable that such women had specific duties of prayer, etc., within the community and so formed a kind of "religious order," the language of v 5b may merely serve to underscore their absolute dependence on God alone. **6.** Such widows must not form irregular sexual relationships. **7–8.** Directed at the living relatives of widows. **9–10.** The fact that the form of these regulations is reminiscent of Titus 1:6–9 and 1 Tim 3:2–7,8–12 strengthens the impression that the "enrolled widows" constituted a specific office within the community. *wife of one husband:* Not a prohibition of a second marriage (see v 14). On the meaning, see Titus 1:6. *brought up children . . . every good work:* As elsewhere in the Pastorals, care of the family, hospitality, and the corporal works of mercy are stressed. **11–12.** The author wants younger widows (i.e., those under age 60) to remarry and to return to the organized life of the household (see v 14). *they want to remarry:* Celibacy was apparently required of enrolled widows. It is easy to see why teachers who "forbade marriage" (1 Tim 4:3) might have wanted to expand the number of such widows. **13.** *saying what they must not:* In Titus 1:11 almost the same words are applied to the false teachers. *going from house to house:* This almost certainly (cf. Titus 1:11) involved not simple gossip but the spreading of teachings abhorrent to the author of the Pastorals (cf. v 15). **14.** The disciplined structure of the Greco-Roman household is viewed as an effective antidote to such activities (cf. also 1 Tim 2:9–15). **16.** *if any believing woman has widows in her house: Pistē* refers to a Christian woman who has undertaken to support one or more widows who are not her relatives.

39   (E) The Elders (5:17–25). 17. *presiding elders:* Some "older men" (*presbyteroi*—see v 1) "preside" and so are church leaders in the formal sense. Those who carry out this ministry "well" deserve "double compensation" from the community. This especially applies in the case of those presiding elders who have special responsibility for the "word" and for "teaching." (See J. Meier, *CBQ* 35 [1973] 325-37.) **18.** The author follows Paul (1 Cor 9:9) in using Deut 25:4 to urge financial support for the church's ministers. *the worker . . . his pay:* In Luke 10:7 this is a saying of Jesus. Here this saying is treated as a scriptural text (cf. 1 Cor 2:9). **19.** *witnesses:* Biblical law (Deut 19:15; cf. 2 Cor 13:1; Matt 18:16) governs the reception of charges against elders. **20.** Those guilty must be rebuked so that the remaining elders may refrain from wrongdoing. **21.** Favoritism should not govern the treatment of elders. **22.** *do not readily lay hands on anyone:* As in 1 Tim 4:14 and 2 Tim 1:6 a reference to ordination. *keep yourself pure:* Probably the false teachers claimed "purity" as a special virtue; the digression of v 23 therefore insists that true "purity" is not a world-negating asceticism (see 1 Tim 4:3-5). **24.** *sins:* The good and bad deeds of some presbyteral candidates are evident while those of others come to light only after careful investigation.

(F) Slaves (6:1-2). For the general perspective, see Titus 2:9-10. **1.** *lest God's name . . . be slandered:* A reference to Isa 52:5 as cited in Rom 2:24; the author has added the phrase "and the teaching." **2.** Although in the experience of the Pastorals most slave masters were non-Christian (v 1), there were some wealthier Christians who did own slaves (see comment on Titus 2:9). *teach and exhort these things:* This picks up the language of 4:11 and so concludes the unit of thought.

40   (VI) Summation (6:3-16).

(A) The Situation of the False Teachers (6:3-10). Much of the language of this section, esp. the charge of money-grubbing, is stock invective drawn from the polemic of philosophers against their opponents. As in the Platonic dialogues, these latter are regularly depicted as "sophists" who teach for pay and seek to please rather than to present the truth. **3.** Several words recall 1:3-4. *the healthy words:* On the application of health/sickness imagery—note also v 4—to teaching, see Titus 1:13; 2:1. *in accord with piety:* See comment on Titus 1:1. **4.** *having understood nothing:* In the philosophical tradition *epistēmē* is the highest form of knowledge, knowledge of truth itself. The false teachers lack this altogether. Cf. Titus 1:1. *envy . . . wrangling:* A state of affairs directly opposed to the love produced by "instruction" referred to in 1:5. **6.** *Piety that encompasses self-sufficiency is a matter of great profit:* The sophistlike false teachers, says the author, teach a so-called piety to acquire monetary profits. They lack the philosophical virtue of *autarkeia,* "self-sufficiency," i.e., contentment with the goods they have (see v 8), and so do not obtain true (i.e., spiritual) profit. **7.** This sentiment appears in many ancient sources (cf. Job 1:21; Philo, *De spec. leg.*

1.294-95; *Anth. Pal.* 10.58; Seneca, *Ep.* 102.25). **8.** *content:* 2 Tim 4:13 depicts Paul as exemplifying simplicity in his clothing needs. **10.** *the love of money . . . evils:* A commonplace saying in antiquity.

41   (B) How Timothy Is to Act (6:11-16). The true church leader will act very differently from the false teacher. **11.** *man of God:* The use of an appellation applied often in the OT to prophets (e.g., Deut 33:1; 1 Sam 2:27) calls attention to the spiritual power possessed by the church leader. **12.** *the good fight:* Paul's own life exemplified how this fight should be carried out (2 Tim 4:7). *the good profession:* Probably a reference to the profession of faith made at baptism rather than, as some think, to ordination. **13.** *testimony:* Jesus' own conduct in facing his passion and death when Pilate was governor exemplifies proper fidelity. **14.** *the mandate:* The Gk word *entolē* does not here, as often, refer to a specific "commandment" from God but to the entire divine "mandate" given to Timothy. *until the appearance:* See Titus 2:11,13. **15-16.** A doxology in praise of God somewhat parallel to that found in 1:17. It is Hellenistic Jewish in inspiration and stresses both God's transcendence and his superiority to all earthly rulers.

42   (VII) Supplementary Reflection on the Rich (6:17-19). The raising of the issue of money in 6:6-10 may have led to the inclusion of this parenetic digression directed to the more prosperous members of the community, apparently a not insignificant group (see 2:9; 6:2; Titus 2:9-10). **17.** *to God who richly supplies us with everything for enjoyment:* Following the thought of 4:3-5, money is included among God's created gifts. **18-19.** Money even offers spiritual opportunities to its possessors if it is rightly used. The increasing prosperity of the Christians encouraged the development of such views.

43   (VIII) Final Exhortation to Timothy (6:20-21a). **20.** *guard that which has been entrusted:* The Gk word *parathēkē* can refer to a "deposit," e.g., of money, which a person is to hand back exactly as received (see comment on 1:18). Given the dynamic way in which the Pastorals deal with Pauline tradition, the emphasis here is on the "preservation of a trust." *the so-called knowledge:* The false teachers apparently called their teaching "knowledge" (*gnōsis*), a name that may connect them with developing gnosticism (→ 10 above). For the author of the Pastorals, true Christianity is by contrast "clear knowledge" (*epignōsis*—cf. Titus 1:1; 1 Tim 2:4; 2 Tim 2:25; 3:7).

(IX) Closing Blessing for the Community (6:21b). A blessing for a wider group of readers; the "you" is plural (as also in Titus 3:15 and 2 Tim 4:22).

COMMENTARY ON 2 TIMOTHY

44   Outline. The second Letter to Timothy may be outlined as follows:

(I) Address and Greeting (1:1-2)
(II) Thanksgiving (1:3-5)
(III) Call to Timothy to Renew the Spiritual Gifts of Power, Love, and Ethical Instruction (1:6-2:13)
  (A) Introduction: Rekindle the Divine Charism (1:6-7)
  (B) Power Enables the Endurance of Sufferings (1:8-12)
  (C) Love Enables Fidelity to Paul (1:13-18)
  (D) Ethical Instruction Enables the Steadfast Handing on of the Gospel (2:1-10)

    (a) Need to Preserve the Deposit of Faith (2:1-2)
    (b) Three Examples for Imitation (2:3-6)
    (c) Paul's Exemplary Fidelity to Christ (2:7-10)
  (E) Summary: The "Reliable Saying" (2:11-13)
(IV) True Teaching vs. False Teaching (2:14-4:8)
  (A) Four Antitheses That Distinguish the True Teacher from the False (2:14-26)
  (B) Resources Available to the Church Leader amid the Evils of the Last Days (3:1-17)
    (a) The Behavior of the False Teachers vs. the Virtuous Example of Paul (3:1-12)
    (b) The Errors of the False Teachers vs. the Truth of Scripture (3:13-17)

45   **(I) Address and Greeting (1:1–2).** **1.** *through God's will:* Paul's role as Christ's emissary was for the Pastorals a part of the divine plan of salvation (cf. 1 Tim 2:7; 2 Tim 1:11; Titus 1:3). *in accord with* [and/or *for*] *the promise of life:* A shorthand summary of Titus 1:2–3. On the double meaning of the Gk prep. *kata,* see comment on Titus 1:1. *in Christ Jesus:* I.e., not just any "life" but that found within the Christian community. **2.** *to Timothy, a beloved child:* As in 1 Cor 4:17, the language stresses Timothy's close relationship to Paul.

    (II) Thanksgiving (1:3–5). A typical epistolary thanksgiving (→ NT Epistles, 45:6, 8B), developed with the help of Rom 1:8–11. The faith of both Paul and Timothy depends on chains of tradition reaching back even to the faith of Israel. **3.** *as did my ancestors:* Paul recalls his (Jewish) fathers and mothers in the faith (cf. Acts 24:14–15; 26:6). **4.** *mindful of your tears:* Probably a reference to a departure scene similar to that recorded in Acts 20:37–38. **5.** *in your grandmother Lois and in your mother Eunice:* Acts 16:1 indicates that Timothy's mother was "a believing Jewish woman," i.e., a Jewish Christian, but is silent about his grandmother. The Pastorals and Acts here utilize common tradition; presumably because he was a pagan (Acts 16:1,3), Timothy's father received no mention. The "chain of tradition" (cf. also 2:1–2; Titus 1:4–5) exemplifies how the faith is properly handed on (cf. 3:14–15).

46   **(III) Call to Timothy to Renew the Spiritual Gifts of Power, Love, and Ethical Instruction (1:6–2:13).**

    (A) Introduction: Rekindle the Divine Charism (1:6–7). **6.** *to rekindle God's charism:* 2 Tim depicts Paul as in his final days; his spiritual heirs must carry on his mission. *through the laying on of my hands:* Not a reflection of the ordination practice used in the community of the Pastorals (see 1 Tim 4:14) but an effort to make clear that Paul alone authenticated Timothy's mission. Nothing is said here that restricts charismatic gifts to the laying on of hands. **7.** The structure of the sentence closely parallels Rom 8:15. *a spirit . . . of ethical instruction:* The word *sōphronismos* literally refers to the communication of the cardinal virtue of moderation (*sōphrosynē*) and then, by extension, to the capable teaching of virtue in general. This capacity is seen as a gift from God.

47   **(B) Power Enables the Endurance of Sufferings (1:8–12).** Following the example of Paul, who is "not ashamed" in the face of suffering—the vocabulary in vv 8 and 12 is reminiscent of Rom 1:16—Timothy, as the type of the church leader, is not to be "ashamed" but is to join with Paul in suffering for the Gospel. References to God's "power" in vv 8 and 12 and the recollection of the kerygma provide a basis for confidence. **8.** *the testimony of our Lord:* Despite this reference to Jesus' passion, it is Paul and not Jesus who is proposed as the prime model for imitation. *nor of me his prisoner:* This is a bit ironic; if Paul is Christ's prisoner, he is actually free (cf. 1 Cor 7:22). **9–11.** Much of the language of this "schema of revelation" is found elsewhere in the Pauline corpus; for the pattern, see Titus 1:2–3; Eph 3:5–7,9–11; Rom 16:25–26. *who has saved us:* For Paul himself salvation is normally a future event (but see Rom 8:24–25; → Pauline Theology, 82:71). *not according to our works . . . in Christ Jesus:* A very Pauline sentiment (see Rom 9:11; Gal

2:16; cf. Eph 2:8–9). *before the eternal ages:* See Titus 1:2. *the appearance of our Savior:* See comment on Titus 1:4; 2:11,13. *who has abolished death:* In 1 Cor 15:26 this is described as a future event. **11.** *I was made herald:* On Paul's essential role in the economy of salvation, see Titus 1:3; 1 Tim 2:7. **12.** *to guard that which has been entrusted to me:* On *parathēkē,* see comment on 1 Tim 6:20.

48   **(C) Love Enables Fidelity to Paul (1:13–18).** Verse 15 illustrates negatively, and vv 16–18 positively, the principle enunciated in vv 13–14. Paul and his teaching remain the exemplar for the Christian community. **15.** *all turned away from me:* Titus 1:14 views "turning away" as apostasy. Presumably this occurred when the report of Paul's arrest reached Ephesus (→ 5 above). *Phygelus:* Not known from any other source. *Hermogenes:* With Demas (see 4:10), he appears in *Acts P. Thec.* as an apostate follower of Paul. **16.** *Onesiphorus:* Known otherwise only from *Acts P. Thec.,* where he is also depicted as a faithful friend of Paul. **18.** *may the Lord grant that he find mercy from the Lord:* Probably the first use of "Lord" refers to Christ and the second to God, but the matter is not clear. Onesiphorus is spoken of as though he is dead.

49   **(D) Ethical Instruction Enables the Steadfast Handing On of the Gospel (2:1–10).**

    (a) NEED TO PRESERVE THE DEPOSIT OF FAITH (2:1–2). The author envisions Paul looking ahead to (at least) three further generations of Christian leaders: Timothy ("my child," v 1), the "reliable people" (v 2), and the "others" who will in turn be taught by them. Cf. *1 Clem.* 42, 44. **2.** *in the presence of many witnesses:* Perhaps a reference to Timothy's ordination (1:6; 1 Tim 1:18; 4:14), but see also Deut 19:15. *entrust these things:* See 1 Tim 1:18; 6:20.

    (b) THREE EXAMPLES FOR IMITATION (2:3–6). The examples are commonplaces from the philosophical tradition (cf., e.g., Epictetus, *Diss.* 3.10.8; 3.24.31–37) and were employed also, although in a somewhat different sense, by Paul (1 Cor 9:7,24–27). Here the soldier teaches the need for single-mindedness, the athlete self-denial, and the farmer intense effort.

    (c) PAUL'S EXEMPLARY FIDELITY TO CHRIST (2:7–10). **7.** God's power enables understanding of the external word of revelation. **8.** The Pauline parentage of this creedal formula is explicit. *in accord with my gospel:* See Rom 1:1; 2:16; 16:25. The wording probably derives from Rom 1:3–4. Curiously, Christ's resurrection is mentioned before his birth. **9–10.** There is no thought in the Pastorals of other apostles who would act if Paul's own work were impeded.

    (E) Summary: The "Reliable Saying" (2:11–13). A portion of a hymn used in the Pauline churches. It is in the form a,b,a′,b′,c,d,c′,d′ with a coda (*for he cannot deny himself*) added, perhaps by the author of the Pastorals. **11.** *the saying is reliable:* See Titus 3:8. The remainder of v 11 is linguistically quite similar to Rom 6:8. **13.** The (d′) element (*he remains faithful* [i.e., to God]) is the theological basis for the (d) element (*he will deny us*); the other parallel elements in the hymn are synonyms.

50   **(IV) True Teaching vs. False Teaching (2:14–4:8).** See L. Johnson, *JRelS* 6–7 (1978–79) 1–26.

    (A) Four Antitheses That Distinguish the True Teacher from the False (2:14–26). Each of the antitheses (2:14–15,16–21,22,23–26) points out actions to be avoided and urges either directly or by implication the contrary correct behavior. This style of antithetical parenesis ("do this, avoid that") follows a common ancient pattern. **14.** *adjuring them before God:* The recurrence of this phrase in 4:1, i.e., at the end of the major unit, helps to link the argument together. *not to battle over *words:* According to 1 Tim 6:4–5 a characteristic activity of teachers who are without true understanding. **15.** *guiding the word of truth aright:* The Gk image is that of "cutting a straight line" or "hewing out a straight path" for the word. **16.** *profane and empty talk:* This phrase, repeated from 1 Tim 6:20, describes a feature of the "so-called knowledge" possessed by the false teachers. *impiety: Asebeia,* the opposite of the *eusebeia,* "piety," praised so often by the author (see Titus 1:1). **17.** *Hymenaeus and Philetus:* In 1 Tim 1:20 Hymnaeus also appears as an opponent of Paul; there he is paired with Alexander. Philetus is not otherwise known. **18.** *the resurrection has already happened:* In *Acts P. Thec.* 14 a different pair of opponents of Paul, Demas (see 2 Tim 4:10) and Hermogenes (see 2 Tim 1:15), teach that "the resurrection, which Paul says is to come, has already taken place in the children whom we have, and that we are risen again [i.e., already] because we have come to know the true God." **19–20.** Language from 1 Cor 3:10–12 and Rom 9:21 is combined to create the somewhat mixed image of a great house (i.e., the church) built on a firm foundation and containing various types of vessels. **19.** *God's foundation:* Whereas 1 Cor 3:10–11 identifies this simply as "Jesus Christ," Eph 2:20 thinks rather of the "apostles and prophets" with Christ as the foundation's "cornerstone." Here the idea probably is that the church is built on God's true revelation. *seal:* Two texts serve as a "seal" or distinguishing mark upon this "firm foundation." The first, Num 16:5, is from the account of God's destruction of Korah and the other opponents of Moses: "God knows his own"—and destroys those who are not! The second, possibly a combination of Sir 35:3 (or 7:2) with Lev 24:16, warns true believers to shun wrongdoing. **21.** *vessel:* Although the church is a mixed body containing both valuable and ignoble members (the various "vessels," the latter through "cleansing" can also become valuable. *ready for every good work:* For the Pastorals this is a hallmark of the true believer (see Titus 1:16; 3:1; 2 Tim 3:17). **22.** The third antithesis: Flee passion and pursue virtue. *with a clean heart:* See 1 Tim 1:5, cf. 1 Tim 3:9; 2 Tim 1:3. **23.** Close in language to Titus 3:9–10 (cf. 1 Tim 6:3–5), which refers specifically to the behavior of the false teachers. **24–26.** By contrast the true church leader ("servant of the Lord," v 24) is not to be a contentious debater but a gentle teacher. **25.** *God may give them a change of heart:* Despite the hostility of the author of the Pastorals to the false teachers (e.g., Titus 1:10–16; 3:9–11; 1 Tim 1:19–20; 6:9–10), he remains convinced that "God wants to save everyone" (1 Tim 2:4; cf. 1 Tim 1:12–17). *the clear knowledge of the truth:* See 1 Tim 2:4 and comment on Titus 1:1. **26.** *by him for his own purpose:* The Gk pronouns are ambiguous as to their antecedent(s), but both probably refer to the devil.

51   **(B) Resources Available to the Church Leader amid the Evils of the Last Days (3:1–17).**
(a) THE BEHAVIOR OF THE FALSE TEACHERS VS. THE VIRTUOUS EXAMPLE OF PAUL (3:1–12). The evildoers are signs of the "last days" (3:1–5), people who "have the outer form of piety" (v 5) but not the reality. These turn out to be real personages, the false teachers at work within the community of the Pastorals (3:6–9). Timothy (and every other church leader) is to follow not their example but that of Paul (3:10–12). **2–5.** Assonance and alliteration rather than a deeper logical or biblical order govern the organization of this Gk list of vices. *boastful, haughty, . . . disobedient to parents, . . . unloving:* These vices are mentioned in almost the same order in Rom 1:30–31. *having the outer form of piety:* Rom 2:20 employs a rather similar phrase. By these parallels with Rom, the author of the Pastorals may wish to imply that those who turn away from the truth fall back into the

evil state of people prior to the coming of Christ. **6.** *into houses: Oikia,* "house," "household," or "family," clearly refers in 2:20 to the "household" of believers; it may well also mean that (i.e. "house-church") in its other two appearances in the Pastorals, 1 Tim 5:13 and here. *silly little women: Gynaikaria* is a contemptuous diminutive. Although to contend that false teaching appealed to women was a stock charge in antiquity, 1 Tim 5:13 suggests that some women helped to spread the unorthodox Christian teaching opposed by the author of the Pastorals (cf. 1 Tim 2:9–15; 5:15; perhaps also 4:7). *multifarious passions:* The state of slavery proper to non-believers rather than to Christians (see Titus 3:3). **8–9.** *Jannes and Jambres:* The names given in later tradition (CD 5:18–19; see also Pliny, *Nat. Hist.* 30.11; Apuleius, *Apol.* 90; Numenius, frg. 9 [= Eusebius, *Praep. evang.* 9.8.1–2]) to the magicians who opposed Moses in Exod 7:11–12. Just as neither these men nor Korah and his allies (2:19 above) could long succeed against God's true representative, so likewise the false teachers are doomed to failure (v 9). **10–11.** The true church leader will imitate Paul especially in enduring whatever suffering comes as a result of upholding the gospel. *at Antioch, Iconium, and Lystra:* Paul himself never singles out his activities in these cities. See instead Acts 13:50; 14:5–6, 19. In *Acts P. Thec.* Paul's work focused on these three localities. *the Lord rescued me from all of them:* Probably a reference to Ps 34:20, which insists on the vindication of the righteous individual. Like Moses (2:19; 3:8) Paul also was vindicated by God. Cf. 4:18. **12.** A generalized principle: All true Christians will suffer persecution. *to live in a reverent manner:* See Titus 1:1; 2:12.

52   (b) THE ERRORS OF THE FALSE TEACHERS VS. THE TRUTH OF SCRIPTURE (3:13–17). **13.** The wretched state of the false teachers. *sorcerers:* I.e., they are like Jannes and Jambres (3:8). The word also is a stock epithet used of philosophical opponents. *being led astray:* They are in the same state as nonbelievers (see 3:6; Titus 3:3). **14.** *as for you, abide:* "To abide, stand fast, remain" (*menein*) is opposed to the state of the false teachers, "wandering about" or "being led astray." *from whom you learned:* "From whom" is pl.; Timothy was taught not only by Paul but also by his family (1:5). **15.** *through the faith which is in Christ Jesus:* Scripture—the author is thinking of the OT—is able to offer true instruction but only if read in the context of the faith of the Christian community. **16.** *every text of Scripture is inspired by God and is useful:* Since the author probably could not have imagined any scriptural texts that were not inspired, the other possible transl., "Every God-inspired text of Scripture is also useful," should be rejected because of the context. On *theopneustos,* see *TDNT* 6. 453–55. Verse 16 is regularly referred to in discussions of biblical inspiration (→ Inspiration, 65:9–16). **17.** *man of God:* See 1 Tim 6:11. *equipped for every good work:* See Titus 1:16.

53   **(C) Concluding Exhortation (4:1–8). 1.** *I adjure you before God and Christ Jesus:* Repetition of the language of 2:14 closes off the thought unit. *his appearance:* See Titus 2:11,13. **2.** *when timely and when not:* This is unusual advice, since the ancients commonly urged speech only when it would be "timely." But the "times" are in God's hands (see Titus 1:3; 1 Tim 2:6; 6:15), and the speaker therefore can leave "timeliness" to God (see A. Malherbe, *JBL* 103 [1984] 235–43). **3–4.** *there will be a time:* Cf. 3:15. This "time" is in fact part of the community's present experience. *sound teaching:* See Titus 1:13; 2:1. **4.** *myths:* See Titus 1:14. **5.** *be sober in every respect:* The language is reminiscent of 3:14. Verses 3–5 continue the pattern of exhortation by antithesis characteristic of 2 Tim. *endure hardship, do the work of an evangelist:* In 2:9 Paul speaks of "my gospel for which I endure hardship even unto chains." In 1:8 Timothy was invited to "join (with Paul) in enduring hardships for the gospel." Responsibility for the Christian message is being passed from Paul to the next generation of church leaders. *your ministry:* Previously it was Paul's "ministry" (1 Tim 1:12). **6–8.** Paul's death is depicted as being at hand and so he hands on his legacy to Timothy and to other future leaders. The images are found in Paul's own letters: libation (Phil 2:17); contest and crown (1 Cor 9:25); race (1 Cor 9:24; Phil 3:12).

54   (V) Paul's Situation and Needs (4:9–21). This is one of the longest closing sections found in the Pauline corpus (→ NT Epistles, 45:8D). Given the fact that Paul did not write the Pastorals, this section is probably best interpreted as providing vignettes of Paul as worthy models for imitation. On the geographical setting and proposed course of events, → 5 above.

(A) Timothy Is to Come to Paul (4:9–13). 10. *Demas:* In Phlm 24; Col 4:14 a faithful follower of Paul; but see comment on 2:18. *Crescens:* Not known from other sources. *Galatia:* The region in Asia Minor. Some mss. read *Gallia,* "Gaul." **11.** *Luke:* See Phlm 24; Col 4:14 ("Luke the physician"). As death approaches, Paul suffers abandonment by almost everyone, just as Jesus did (Matt 26:56; Mark 14:50). *Mark:* Probably the Mark of Phlm 24; Col 4:10, "the cousin of Barnabas." John Mark, a colleague of Barnabas (Acts 12:12,25; 15:37–39), is probably the same person, though he is said to have abandoned Paul at one point (Acts 13:13; 15:38). **12.** *Tychicus:* See Titus 3:12. **13.** This verse is illustrative of Paul's own practice of the philosophic virtue of self-sufficiency (see 1 Tim 6:6–8 and compare, e.g., Epictetus, *Diss.* 3.22.47–48) and of his interest in

the things of the mind and spirit rather than of the body. Paul's sole material need is for his coarse winter cloak; beyond that he asks only for his books and parchments. *Carpus:* Not known from other sources.

55   (B) Paul's Legal Situation (4:14–18). 14–15. The relationship of Alexander's hostility to Paul's initial legal defense (v 16) is uncertain, but the vb. *enedeixato,* "he showed, offered in proof," can carry a legal sense. If that is correct, v 15b should then be translated, "for he very strongly opposed our arguments." *Alexander the coppersmith:* The same one as mentioned in 1 Tim 1:20? In *Acts P. Thec.* 1 Hermogenes "the coppersmith" opposes Paul (→ 13 above). *will repay him according to his works:* Cf. Prov 24:12; Ps 62:12. **16–18.** Paul is imagined as writing 2 Tim in the interval between his first and his second trial. Although abandoned by "everyone" (see comment on 4:11), he is not abandoned by his Lord. Yet his life remains in peril (see 4:6–8). *from the lion's mouth:* See Ps 22:22. Ps 22 tells how God vindicates the just person who suffers persecution. *will rescue me:* See 3:11. Such "rescuing" did not exclude the possibility of physical death for Paul!

56   (C) Greetings and Other Matters (4:19–21). 19–20. *Prisca and Aquila:* A married couple that worked closely with Paul (see Rom 16:3; 1 Cor 16:19; Acts 18:2, 18,26). *Erastus:* See Rom 16:23; Acts 19:22. *Trophimus:* Probably Trophimus of Ephesus (Acts 20:4; 21:29). Miletus is quite close to Ephesus. **21.** The four individuals mentioned are not known from other sources.

(VI) Closing Blessings to Timothy and to the Readers (4:22). *with your spirit:* This "you" is sg. *grace be with you:* See Titus 3:15; 1 Tim 6:21; the "you" is pl. here.

57

THE FIRST EPISTLE OF PETER

William J. Dalton, S.J.

BIBLIOGRAPHY

1   Beare, F. W., *The First Epistle of Peter* (3d ed.; Oxford, 1970). Best, E., *1 Peter* (NCB; London, 1971). Bigg, C., *The Epistles of St. Peter and St. Jude* (ICC; 2d ed.; Edinburgh, 1902) 1–198. Brox, N., *Der erste Petrusbrief* (EKKNT 21; Zurich, 1979). Cranfield, C. E. B., *The First Epistle of Peter* (London, 1958). Dalton, W. J., *Christ's Proclamation to the Spirits: A Study of 1 Peter 3:18–4:6* (AnBib 23; Rome, 1965). Elliott, J. H., *A Home for the Homeless* (Phl, 1981). Franco, R., "Primera carta de San Pedro," *La Sagrada Escritura* (BAC 214; Madrid, 1962) 219–97. Goppelt, L., *Der erste Petrusbrief* (MeyerK 12/1; ed. F. Hahn; Göttingen, 1978). Hunter, A. M., "The First Epistle of Peter," (*IB* 12; NY, 1957) 75–159. Kelly, J. N. D., *A Commentary on the Epistles of Peter and Jude* (London, 1969) 1–221. Leaney, A. R. C., *The Letters of Peter and Jude* (CBC; Cambridge, 1967) 3–73. Margot, J. C., *Les épîtres de Pierre* (Geneva, 1960) 1–91.

Michl, J. C., *Die katholischen Briefe* (RNT 8/2; 2d ed.; Regensburg, 1968) 94–152. Perrot, C. (ed.), *Études sur la première lettre de Pierre* (Paris, 1980). Reicke, B., *Epistles of James, Peter and Jude* (AB 37; GC, 1964) 67–139. Schelkle, K. H., *Die Petrusbriefe; der Judasbrief* (HTKNT 13/2; 3d ed.; Freiburg, 1967) 39–99. Schrage, W., *Der erste Petrusbrief* (NTD 10; Göttingen, 1973) 59–117. Schweizer, E., *Der erste Petrusbrief* (Prophezei; 3d ed.; Zurich, 1972). Selwyn, E. G., *The First Epistle of Peter* (2d ed.; London, 1947). Spicq, C., *Les Épîtres de Saint Pierre* (SB; Paris, 1966) 9–182. Stibbs, A. M. and A. F. Walls, *The First General Letter of Peter* (TynNTC; GR, 1959). Windisch, H., *Die katholischen Briefe* (HNT 15; 3d ed., rev. H. Preisker; Tübingen, 1951) 49–82.

DBSup 7. 1415–55. Kümmel, *INT* 416–24. Wik-Schm, *ENT* 589–602.

INTRODUCTION

2   **(I) Authorship.** The epistle's claim to have been written by Peter (1:1) was accepted from Eusebius (*HE* 4.14.9) up to the 19th cent. Many modern scholars, however, do not accept the Petrine authorship. They either explain the epistle as the later work of a Petrine "school" (e.g., Best, Goppelt, Elliott) or regard it as a purely pseudepigraphical work (e.g., Brox). Arguments against authenticity are the following: (1) The Gk style in 1 Pet and the OT citations from the LXX could not come from Peter. (2) There is a heavy dependence on Pauline writings. (3) It is unlikely that Peter knew the addressees in Asia Minor. (4) There was no universal state persecution of the church in Peter's time (see 5:9). (5) The churches to which 1 Pet was sent would not have existed in the time of Peter. As for (1), it was common practice in NT times for a person to give a secretary considerable freedom in the composition of letters (e.g., 5:12; → NT Epistles, 45:19; cf. W. G. Doty, *Letters in Primitive Christianity* [Phl, 1973] 41). As for (2), the influence of Paul in the early church has been exaggerated (see R. E. Brown and J. P. Meier, *Antioch and Rome* [NY, 1983] viii). As for (3), Peter was certainly at Rome and died there. As in the case of *1 Clem.*, personal acquaintance with the addressees was not required. With the beginnings of the Jewish revolt, the Roman church could well have begun to exercise the leadership formerly provided from Jerusalem. As for (4), the persecution was an example of the harassment of Christians by the local population generally experienced throughout the whole church. As for (5), there is evidence for early Christian development in Bithynia (see Pliny, *Ep.* 10.96). We simply do not know how soon the church developed in other places in Asia Minor. In favor of authenticity, there is the primitive theology of 1 Pet (eschatology, servant christology) and church order. Also, if 1 Pet were written shortly after Peter's death, it is hard to explain why there is no hint of the horrendous persecution of the Roman church by Nero in AD 64 or of Peter's martyrdom (cf. 4:12; 2 Pet 1:14–15; *1 Clem.* 5:4). Those who prefer to see in 1 Pet a later pseudepigraphical work should establish the conditions that would have made this feasible (see N. Brox, *Der erste Petrusbrief* 43–47; "Tendenz und Pseudepigraphie im ersten Petrusbrief," *Kairos* 20 [1978] 110–20; *Fälsche Verfasserangaben: Zur Erklärung der frühchristlichen Pseudepigraphie* [Stuttgart, 1975]).

3   **(II) Date, Occasion, Purpose.** We have seen that there is good reason for dating 1 Pet just before Peter's death, which took place probably in AD 65 in the persecution of Nero (Eusebius, *HE* 2.25.5). The letter is addressed to "visiting strangers" (1:1), "resident aliens" (2:11), terms that indicate the precarious condition of Christians in the pagan world. They were mainly of pagan origin (see 1:14,18; 2:9,10; 4:3–4), probably recently converted (see 1:14; 2:2; 4:12), and in danger of giving up the Christian faith in the face of pagan hostility. There is no indication of an official state persecution: the letter counsels respect for government and emperor (2:13–17). By recalling the greatness of their vocation and by showing that persecution is a sign of their calling, the writer encourages and exhorts his readers to stand firm (5:12). Those who are regarded by the world as aliens and strangers have found a home in the Christian community.

4   (III) Literary Genre.   There has been much discussion since the time of A. von Harnack about the literary genre of 1 Pet. Some scholars have seen in 1:3–4:11 a baptismal homily or liturgy, with 1:1–2 and 4:12–5:14 as later additions. R. Bultmann claimed to have discovered in the text a hymn (2:21–24) and a creedal confession (3:18–19,22) ("Bekenntnis- und Liedfragmente im ersten Petrusbrief," *ConNT* 11 [Fest. A. Fridrichsen; 1947] 1–14), and M.-É. Boismard developed this line of research to discover four hymns (1:3–5; 2:22–25; 3:18–22; 5:5–9); see his *Quatre hymnes baptismales dans la première épître de Pierre* (Paris, 1965).

Modern scholars admit that much creedal and hymnic material is incorporated into 1 Pet, but they see in it a real letter with its own literary unity and purpose (see Dalton, *Christ's Proclamation* 76–77; Kelly, *A Commentary* 21).

5   (IV) Doctrine.   1 Pet is a pastoral document. By emphasizing the dignity of the Christian vocation, which provides a God-given "home" (*oikos*, 2:5; 4:17) for the "homeless" (*paroikoi*, 2:11; cf. 1:17), and the positive value of sharing the passion of Christ through persecution, the writer encourages his readers to remain faithful. These two themes run through the whole letter, but reach high points in texts such as 2:4–10 (the "spiritual house") and 2:18–25 (directly dealing with slaves but valid for all Christians). The climax of the letter seems

to come in 3:18–4:6, where Christians' confidence in persecution is seen as based on the story of Christ's salvific acts.

(For a general view of the theology of 1 Pet, see A. Vanhoye, "1 Pierre au carrefour des théologies du Nouveau Testament," *Études* [ed. C. Perrot] 97–128.)

6   (V) Outline.   1 Pet may be outlined as follows:

(I) Introduction: Address and Greetings (1:1–2)
(II) Part I: The Dignity of the Christian Vocation and Its Responsibilities (1:3–2:10)
  (A) The Christian Vocation (1:3–25)
    (a) Salvation Wrought by the Father, through the Son, Revealed by the Spirit (1:3–12)
    (b) Exhortation to Holiness (1:13–25)
  (B) Responsibilities of the Christian Vocation (2:1–10)
    (a) Exhortation: Live as God's Children (2:1–3)
    (b) The New Household of God (2:4–10)
(III) Part II: Witness of Christian Life (2:11–3:12)
  (A) Conduct in a Pagan World (2:11–12)
  (B) Traditional Catechesis (2:13–3:7)
    (a) Toward Civil Authority (2:13–17)
    (b) Domestic Code (2:18–3:7)
  (C) Above All, Love and Humility (3:8–12)
(IV) Part III: The Christian and Persecution (3:13–5:11)
  (A) The Christian Approach to Persecution (3:13–4:11)
    (a) Confidence in Persecution (3:13–17)
    (b) Christ Is the Basis for Confidence (3:18–4:6)
      (i) Christ's victory over sin applied to Christians by baptism (3:18–22)
      (ii) The Christian through suffering renounces sin (4:1–6)
    (c) Christian Life and the Parousia (4:7–11)
  (B) Persecution Faced Realistically (4:12–5:11)
    (a) Joy in Actual Persecution (4:12–19)
    (b) Exhortation to Elders and Faithful (5:1–5)
    (c) Final Exhortation: Trust God, Who Brings You through Suffering to Glory (5:6–11)
(V) Conclusion: This Is the True Grace of God: Stand Firm in It; Farewell (5:12–14)

(For a discussion of the plan of 1 Pet, see Dalton, *Christ's Proclamation* 72–83.)

COMMENTARY

7   (I) Introduction: Address and Greetings (1:1–2).   Here we have a form of opening formula common in Jewish official correspondence (→ NT Epistles, 45:6–8A). **1.** *Peter:* The Gk version of the Aram *Kēpā'*, "rock" (see Matt 16:17–18). His central position in the early church is reflected in the Gospels (e.g., Matt 16:16–19; Luke 22:32; John 21:15–19). He is the leader of the original apostles (Mark 3:16 par.; Gal 1:18). *to the chosen sojourners:* The last term means, more technically, "visiting strangers." This, with the "resident aliens" of 2:11, designates Christians as an inferior social class without the rights of citizens. *of the Diaspora:* This is a technical term for Jews living in groups outside the holy land in Hellenistic times (Deut 28:25 LXX; 30:4), applied to Christians (Jas 1:1) and here to largely Gentile Christian communities. *Pontus, Galatia, Cappadocia, Asia, Bithynia:* Either Roman provinces (Pontus and Bithynia forming one province) or names denoting earlier districts. **2.** *according to the foreknowledge of God the Father, by the sanctifying action of the Spirit, for obedience and for sprinkling of the blood of Jesus Christ:* The election of the Christian to the new covenant (cf. Exod 24:8) involves

the cooperation of Father, Spirit, and Son. This trinitarian reference is expanded in 1:3–12. *grace and peace:* In addition to the regular greeting, the typically Jewish "be multiplied to you" is added (see Dan 4:1; 6:25).

8   (II) Part I: The Dignity of the Christian Vocation and Its Responsibilities (1:3–2:10).
  (A) The Christian Vocation (1:3–25).
    (a) Salvation Wrought by the Father, through the Son, Revealed by the Spirit (1:3–12). **3.** *blessed be the God and Father of our Lord Jesus Christ, who . . . caused us to be born again:* The Father's initiative in the Christian's election is celebrated in the form of a blessing common in Jewish tradition (see Gen 9:26; Pss 66:20; 68:20; 72:18; 1 Kgs 1:48; 2 Macc 15:34). He is revealed and does all things through his Son. Christians enter into the new divine life through "the living and abiding word of God" (1:23), "the word which was preached to them" (1:25). *to a living hope:* A dominant theme of 1 Pet, much deeper than a word-count suggests (1:3,13,21; 3:5,15). *through the resurrection:* This refers not only to "living" but also to "caused to be born again." **4.** *for an imperishable inheritance:* The promises made to

Israel are seen as fulfilled also in the Christian church. In the OT the inheritance is primarily the land of Israel (Deut 15:4). As opposed to the land, the Christian inheritance is "imperishable." *kept in heaven for you:* Cf. Col 1:5; Phil 3:20; Gal 4:26. **5.** *through faith:* "Faith" has a wide range of meanings in 1 Pet (1:5,7,9,21; cf. 1:8,21; 2:6,7). Here it refers to that trust in God which is essential for salvation. *salvation ready to be revealed:* Eschatological salvation (see 1:9,10; 3:21) is imminent (see 1:20; 4:5,13,17; 5:10). **6.** *in this you rejoice:* "This" refers to the whole thought of 1:3–5. "Rejoice" expresses religious, eschatological joy (see 4:13; Matt 5:12; Jude 24; Rev 19:7). Note the *inclusio* formed by this verse and 4:12–13. *trials:* In 1 Pet, Christian experience of social dislocation in a pagan world is normally called "suffering" (in both noun and vb. forms): 1:11; 4:13; 5:9; 2:19,20; 3:14,17; 4:1,15,19; 5:10. This is linked with the "sufferings" of Christ (5:1; 2:21,23; 3:18; 4:1). **8.** *without having seen him:* The author of 1 Pet is presented in 1:1 as one of the original apostles who had "seen" Jesus (cf. Acts 1:21–22). **9.** *receiving as the goal of your faith the salvation of your souls:* Eschatological realities are inaugurated now in the church by faith. "Soul" in 1 Pet (1:9,22; 2:11,25; 3:20; 4:19) has the meaning of "self" or "person" (→ Pauline Theology, 82:104). **10.** *about this salvation:* The link word "salvation" indicates a new topic, the role of the Spirit (1:10–12; cf. 1:2). *prophets:* Not Christian prophets but those of the OT (see Matt 1:22–23; Rom 1:2; 4:23; Acts 3:18). **11.** *the Spirit of Christ:* This refers more probably to the holy Spirit (see 1:12; Rom 8:9; Phil 1:19; Acts 16:7). *the suffering destined for Christ and the subsequent glories:* The passion of Christ and the stages in his glorification bear on the message of 1 Pet (see 1:6–7; 4:13; 5:1,10). **12.** *to them it was revealed:* The prophets were to serve a people to whom "now," in the age of the church, the gospel has been proclaimed. *things into which the angels yearn to look:* The image is that of peering through a window (cf. 1 Enoch 9:1 Gk).

9 (b) EXHORTATION TO HOLINESS (1:13–25). **13.** *gird up your minds:* The picture of a man tucking up his long robe into his belt and preparing for action (see 1 Kgs 18:46; Jer 1:17; Luke 17:8) is here applied to readiness for the parousia (see Luke 12:35). **14.** *obedience:* The Christian is to obey the law of holiness of the new covenant (cf. 1:2). *former ignorance:* The majority of the addressees had been pagans (see 1:18; 4:3–4). **15.** *holy:* The basic meaning is "separated," "dedicated," the opposite of "profane." The covenant relationship with God not only set Israel apart but also required ethical standards. **16.** See Lev 11:44; 19:2; 20:7,26. **17.** *invoke as Father:* Christians' intimacy with God as Father is not an excuse for careless conduct (cf. 4:17; Heb 12:5–11; Acts 10:34; Rom 2:10–11). *the time of your existence as resident aliens:* This does not refer to an "exile from heaven," but to the social dislocation that Christians experience in a pagan world. **18.** *not ransomed . . . with silver:* An allusion to Isa 52:3 (see comment on Rom 3:24). **19.** *precious blood of Christ:* In the Jewish concept of sacrifice, blood represented life (see Lev 17:14). Here the reference is to the blood of the Passover lamb (see Exod 12:7,13; Rev 5:9; Eph 1:7; Heb 9:12; cf. 1 Cor 5:7; John 1:29; 19:36). *like a lamb without blemish:* This was required for every victim (see Lev 22:19–25) and in particular for the Passover lamb (see Exod 12:5). **20.** *predestined . . . made manifest:* This is probably a fragment of an ancient creed or hymn (cf. 2 Tim 1:9–10; see M.-É. Boismard, *Quatre hymnes* 57–109). God's eternal plan (cf. Rom 16:25–26; 1 Cor 2:7; Col 1:26; Eph 3:9–10; Titus 1:2–3) is "made known" by the incarnation at the inauguration of the "last times" (see comment on Rom 5:14; 1 Cor 10:11).

21. *so that your faith may also be your hope in God:* Or, "so that your faith and your hope are in God" (see W. J. Dalton, " 'So that Your Faith May Also Be Your Hope,' " *Reconciliation and Hope* [Fest. L. L. Morris; ed. R. J. Banks; Exeter, 1974] 262–74). 1:22–25 is added to complete the triad of faith, hope, and love. **23.** *born anew:* The reception of the gospel by faith (cf. 1:24) brings about the new birth (cf. 1:3). *living and abiding:* These epithets should be taken with "word" rather than with "God." **24.** Isa 40:6–8 LXX.

10 (B) Responsibilities of the Christian Vocation (2:1–10).

(a) EXHORTATION: LIVE AS GOD'S CHILDREN (2:1–3). **1.** *put off:* This is a technical term of baptismal exhortation (cf. Rom 13:12; Eph 4:22,25; Col 3:8; Jas 1:21). **2.** *newborn infants:* The image of 1:3,23 is developed. The implication is that those addressed are recently converted Christians. *pure milk of the word:* "Pure" also means "without deceit" and is thus opposed to the "deceit" of 2:1. *Logikos* here means "of the word" rather than "spiritual" (cf. 1:23–25). **3.** *seeing that you have tasted that the Lord is good:* From Ps 34:9, a psalm much used in 1 Pet, e.g., 2:4; 3:10–12.

11 (b) THE NEW HOUSEHOLD OF GOD (2:4–10). **4.** *the living stone . . . chosen, honored:* The writer anticipates his citation of Isa 28:16 and Ps 118:22 in 2:6–7 in beginning his picture of the church as a new "spiritual household" (2:5). **5.** *living stones . . . spiritual household:* By sharing the life of the risen Lord, Christians become with him a household formed by the holy Spirit (cf. 4:17). *to be a holy priesthood . . . spiritual sacrifices:* Christians, viewed corporately as a body of priests (cf. 2:9), present their lives of faith and love to God as a sacrifice (cf. Rom 12:1; Eph 5:2; Phil 4:18). **6.** An adapted form of Isa 28:16 LXX. **7.** *to you who believe belongs the honor:* "Honor" echoes the adj. "honorable" ("precious") of 2:6. Citations from Ps 118:22 and Isa 8:14 indicate the lot of those "who do not obey the word" (2:8). **8.** *as they were destined to do:* The unbelievers are destined by God to "stumble." In this context, these are the pagan persecutors (cf. 4:5,17–18).

12 **9.** *chosen race:* In this verse four OT titles of Israel are now applied to the new household of God to indicate its unique dignity. The first is taken from Isa 43:20. Basic to this dignity is divine election (cf. 1:1; 5:13). *a royal house, a body of priests:* See comment on 2:5. This phrase is better taken as two nouns than as a noun with an adj., "royal priesthood" (cf. Rev 1:6; 5:10; Exod 19:16 LXX). *a holy nation:* The third title is also taken from Exod 19:6. As Israel was holy, chosen, and loved by God (Deut 7:6–9), so also is the new people of God. For "holy," see comment on 1:15. *God's own people:* Lit., "a people for possession," a combination of Isa 43:21 and Mal 3:17 (cf. Acts 20:28; Titus 2:14). Christians have become God's "possession" by the shedding of the precious blood of Christ (see 1:19). *that you may proclaim the mighty deeds:* An adaptation of the second part of Isa 43:21 LXX. For God's new household his mighty deeds are found in the death and resurrection of Jesus. This proclamation refers to the Christian witness to the gospel (cf. 2:5). *of him who called:* It is God, not Christ, who calls (cf. 1:15; 2:21; 3:9; 5:10). *out of darkness . . . into light:* This is more aptly applied to converts from paganism (1:18; 4:3). **10.** *no people . . . God's people:* An application of Hos 1:6,9,10; 2:25 to the Christian church.

(Sandevoir, P., "Un royaume de Prêtres?" *Études* [ed. C. Perrot] 219-29. Elliott, J. H., *The Elect and the Holy* (NovTSup 12; Leiden, 1966). Brox, *Der erste Petrusbrief* 108–10.)

13   Part II: Witness of Christian Life (2:11–3:12).
(A) Conduct in a Pagan World (2:11–12).
11. *visiting strangers and resident aliens:* See comment on
1:1. By becoming Christians, the addressees were
reduced to the level of an inferior social class (cf. Heb
10:32–34). In 1 Pet, unlike in Heb, the true home of the
Christian is not so much the world to come as the Christian community. **12.** *conduct:* A favorite word of 1 Pet
(1:15,18; 2:12; 3:1,2,16; vb., 1:17). Christian witness
may bring pagans finally to God.
14   (B) Traditional Catechesis (2:13–3:7).
(a) TOWARD CIVIL AUTHORITY (2:13–17).**13.** *be
subject:* This is the basic Christian attitude in social
behavior (cf. 2:18; 3:1; 5:5), reflecting the God-given
order of society. *every human institution:* In ordinary
Greek, *ktisis* is used for the "founding" of a city. In the
LXX and the NT it indicates something created by God.
Here both ideas seem to be included: human institutions
come from God (cf. Rom 13:1). *for the Lord's sake:* The
risen Christ is meant. **15.** *the ignorance of foolish people:*
Christians should aim at making a good impression on
hostile pagans by blameless lives (cf. 3:15–16). **16.** *live as
free human beings:* Cf. Matt 17:26; Luke 4:18–21; John
8:32; Rom 8:2; 1 Cor 7:22; 2 Cor 3:17; Gal 5:1. *as slaves
of God:* Christian freedom is liberation from sin and
readiness to do God's will. Unsocial behavior under the
pretext of freedom is an aberration. **17.** *honor all people:*
These commands fall into two pairs, the last pair being
an adaptation of Prov 24:21 (cf. Matt 22:21). The favorable attitude shown in this passage to public authority
throws light on the dating of 1 Pet (cf. Rom 13:1–7; →
3 above).
15   (b) DOMESTIC CODE (2:18–3:7). In this
section we have instruction on the behavior of Christian
slaves (2:18–28), wives (3:1–6), and husbands (3:7).
Similar codes are found in Col 3:18–4:1; Eph 5:22–6:9
(cf. 1 Tim 2:1,8–15; 6:1–2; Titus 2:1–10). See Goppelt,
Der erste Petrusbrief 163–79; D. L. Balch, *Let Wives Be
Submissive* (SBLMS 26; Chico, 1981). **18.** *house-slaves:*
Despite the NT teaching on freedom (see comment on
2:16), the early church did not see the inherent social evil
of slavery (cf. 1 Cor 7:21; Eph 6:5–8; Col 3:22–25). See
M. Carrez, "L'Esclavage dans la Première Épître de
Pierre," *Études* (ed. C. Perrot) 207–16. *fear:* Reverence
for God, not fear of human beings. **19.** *because of your
consciousness of God:* The Gk *syneidēsis,* commonly translated "conscience," can have various meanings according
to the context (cf. 3:16,21; → Pauline Theology,
82:144). **21.** *to this you have been called:* This introduces a
section (2:21b–25) that is commonly understood as part
of a primitive Christian hymn based on Isa 53:4–12 (see
Goppelt, *Der erste Petrusbrief* 204–7). **22.** Cf. Isa 53:9.
23. *he entrusted everything to the One who judges justly:* In the
Gk text, there is no object of the vb. "entrusted." The
sense is best left vague. **24.** *he bore our sins to the tree in his
body:* Cf. Isa 53:4,12. "Tree" or "wood" is a very early
term for the cross (see Acts 5:30; 10:39; 13:29; Gal 3:13).
so that we might cease from sins: Cf. Rom 6:10–11. *healed:*
Cf. Isa 53:6. **25.** *shepherd and guardian:* The Suffering
Servant, vindicated by God in the resurrection (cf. Isa
52:13; 53:11), becomes the Good Shepherd (cf. John
10:11; 13:10; for the OT background, see Ps 23; Isa
40:11; Ezek 37:24). "Shepherd" and "guardian" (*episkopos*) later became ecclesiastical terms (cf. 5:2–4; Acts
20:28).
16   3:1 *who disbelieve the word:* Christian wives may
still hope to win over their pagan husbands, not by
preaching but by good example. **2.** *pure and reverent
behavior:* Lit., "pure behavior with fear (of God)." **3.** *your
adornment:* Cf. 1 Tim 2:9. **4.** *the hidden person of the heart:*
"Person" translates *anthrōpos,* "human being." (Cf. the

"inner human being" in Rom 7:22; 2 Cor 4:16; Eph
3:16). **6.** *Sarah:* The mother of Israel (cf. Isa 51:2). *calling
him lord:* In Gen 18:12, the title "lord" is merely conventional, but Jewish tradition interpreted it as an indication
of Sarah's obedience to Abraham. **7.** *live with your wives
considerately:* The husband is not to exercise the absolute
rights given to him by pagan society, but to act with
understanding love (cf. 1 Thess 4:4–5; Eph 5:25). *giving
honor to the female as the weaker sex:* This attitude
represents the patriarchal system of the ancient world,
according to which women, because weak, were given
special honor (cf. 1 Cor 12:22–23). *joint heirs of the gift of
life:* This concept helped to transform marriage in Christian society (cf. Gal 3:28). *your prayers may not be hindered:*
Proper marital relationships cannot be separated from
relationship with God expressed in prayer.
17   (C) Above All, Love and Humility (3:8–12).
8. *united in mind . . . :* In the Gk text, five adjs. sum up the
traditional ideal of Christian community life. **9.** *do not
return evil for evil:* Cf. Rom 12:17; 1 Thess 5:15; 1 Cor
4:12. *bless:* The vb. here means "invoke God's blessing."
that you might inherit a blessing: Christians are the heirs of
the OT blessings (cf. Gen 27:29; 49:25–26). **10–12.** Ps
34:13–17 (LXX, with slight changes). The terms
"peace," "life," "good days," are given a deeper meaning
as realities of Christian existence.
**18   (IV) Part III: The Christian and Persecu-
tion (3:13–5:11).** After early vague references to
persecution (1:6–7; 2:12,15,19–20; 3:9), the author now
treats the topic explicitly.
**(A) The Christian Approach to Persecu-
tion (3:13–4:11).**
(a) CONFIDENCE IN PERSECUTION (3:13–17).
13. *who will harm you?:* The "harm" here is the weakening
or loss of Christian faith. **14.** *if indeed you should suffer:*
The "if" does not imply that the possibility of suffering
is remote, but rather is a gentle introduction to a painful
subject. *blessed:* Cf. Matt 5:10–11. **15.** *reverence Christ as
Lord:* The "Lord" of Isa 8:13 is God; here the title is
applied to Christ. *a defense:* This does not imply a court
of law. *the hope that is in you:* Cf. Col 1:27. **16.** *may be put
to shame:* The pagan accuser, being "put to shame," will
desist from harassing Christians. **17.** *better to suffer for
doing right . . . than for doing wrong:* In this text, "better"
means "more suitable," not "morally better." The writer
is aware of the fact that some Christians may, by their
bad conduct, give ground for pagan hostility.
**19   (b) CHRIST IS THE BASIS FOR CONFIDENCE
(3:18–4:6).**
(i) *Christ's victory over sin applied to Christians by
baptism* (3:18–22). The context is that of an exhortation
to Christians, in danger from their social alienation, to
remain faithful. In the interpretation offered here, the
spirits to whom Christ made proclamation are the
archetypal angelic sinners, who, according to Jewish
tradition, instigated the "original sin" of human beings
at the time of the flood and who continue to induce
humans to do evil. Christ's proclamation to these
sinners, on the occasion of his ascension, is a mythical
way of saying that, by his death and resurrection, he has
conquered all evil: he proclaimed himself the risen One.
The association of these spirits with the flood gives the
writer an opportunity of a typological development
(3:20–22): just as Noah was rescued from the evil world
of his day by water, so are Christians rescued through
the water of baptism. In the new covenant, Christians
make a pledge to live in keeping with God's will. This
is effective only through the power of the risen and
triumphant Christ (3:21–22).
20   In the Apostles' Creed we read: "He descended
into hell." This is a way of saying that Jesus really died,

that he went to the abode of the dead (cf. Rom 10:6–7; Heb 13:20; Acts 2:24,31; Matt 12:40). Later speculation was concerned with the activity of Christ in the abode of the dead. The interpretation presented here maintains that 1 Pet 3:19 has nothing to do with Christ's descent.

The following is a sketch of the history of the text's interpretation. (1) Up to the time of Clement of Alexandria (AD 150–215), there is no clear link between 1 Pet 3:19 and Christ's descent. (2) Clement understood the text as a preaching of the gospel by the soul of Christ, in the world of the dead, to the souls of the sinners of the flood (*Strom.* 6:6; GCS 15. 454–55). This view, in modified form, is proposed by some modern scholars (Goppelt, Vogels). (3) According to Augustine, Christ, in his divine preexistence, preached through Noah to the sinners of the flood (*Ep.* 164; CSEL 44. 521–41). (4) Robert Bellarmine supposed that the sinners of the flood had repented of their sins before death. Christ's soul, on the occasion of the descent, announced their liberation from limbo. (5) A later view, proposed by F. Spitta (*Christi Predigt an die Geister* [Göttingen, 1890]), held that the disobedient spirits were not the souls of human beings, but the rebellious angels who, in Jewish tradition, instigated the human sin that provoked the flood. Some authors place Christ's proclamation during his descent (Selwyn, Reicke); others (Gschwind, Dalton) on the occasion of Christ's ascension. The last explanation is used here. Verses 18–22 are probably a conflation of a creedal statement or hymn (3:18,22) and a catechetical section on baptism (3:19–21).

21   18. *Christ too suffered:* The better-attested reading *apethanen,* "died," is probably due to harmonization with the regular NT creedal statement: "Christ died for our sins" (cf. Rom 5:6; 6:10). The vocabulary of 1 Pet and the context require the reading "suffer" (cf. 3:14,17; 4:1). *in the flesh . . . in the spirit:* This distinction is not that of "body" and "soul" as found in Gk philosophy. Thus, 3:19 does not refer to the activity of Christ's "soul." The text refers to two spheres of Christ's existence, that of his earthly life and that of his state as risen Lord transformed by the Spirit (cf. Rom 1:3; 1 Cor 15:45; 1 Tim 3:16). **19.** *in which:* Some translate *en hō kai* as "on this occasion," but the proximity of the rel. pron. *hō* to the noun "spirit," the very common NT phrase "in the spirit," and the universal interpretation of the early Greek-speaking commentators all point to taking "in which" as the equivalent of "and in this spirit." Christ made his proclamation as the risen Lord. *to the spirits in prison:* In NT usage, "spirits," without a qualifying phrase (cf. Heb 12:23), means "supernatural beings," not "human souls." In *1 Enoch,* a book very popular in early Christian times, Enoch, on a mission from God, went and announced to the rebellious angels (cf. Gen 6:1-2) that they were condemned to prison (see *1 Enoch* 6–11; 12–16; cf. *OTP* 1. 15–22). In this tradition, the rebellion of the angels is expressly linked with the flood (*T. Naph.* 3:5 [*OTP* 1. 812]). In a later development, Enoch passes through the heavens and meets the rebellious angels imprisoned in the second heaven (*2 Enoch* 7:1-3; 18:3-6 [*OTP* 1. 113–14, 131–32]). The story of Enoch is applied in 1 Pet 3:19 to the risen Christ, who in his ascension passed through "all the heavens" (see Eph 4:8–10; Heb 4:14; cf. 1 Tim 3:16; Phil 2:9; Eph 1:20; 6:12; Heb 7:26). All hostile spirits were made subject to him (cf. Eph 1:20–22; 4:8; 1 Pet 3:22). *he went:* This refers to the activity of Christ after his bodily resurrection. Such a "going" is naturally taken as his ascension into heaven (cf. 3:22; Acts 1:10–11). *made proclamation:* The vb. *ekēryxen* means "act as a herald" (*kēryx*). It is commonly used in the NT of the proclamation of the gospel. Here, Christ proclaims himself as "Lord" (cf.

Phil 2:11). As in 3:22, the power of the hostile spirits is declared to be at an end. Both in 3:19 and in 3:22, the writer is concerned not with the psychological reaction of the spirits but only with the liberation of human beings from their power.

22   20. *who disobeyed:* In later Jewish tradition, the obscure text of Gen 6:1-2 is developed into an elaborate story. The "sons of God" were angels who sinned with women and were responsible for the moral corruption of human beings that provoked the flood. This is one version of the primeval or "original" sin: "The whole earth has been corrupted by Azaz'el's teaching of his actions; and write upon him all sin" (*1 Enoch* 10:8 [*OTP* 1. 18]; cf. Josephus, *Ant.* 1.3.1 § 73; *1 Enoch* 15:1–11; *Jub.* 5). The word *apeithein,* "disobey," is used elsewhere in 1 Pet (2:8; 3:1) for the rejection of the gospel. *while God's patience waited:* In late Jewish tradition, "God cursed the watchers (angels) at the flood" (*T. Naph.* 3:5). Their story and that of human sinners are inextricably bound together. Noah (see 2 Pet 2:5) warned his sinful contemporaries of the coming punishment, in the hope that they might repent. *eight persons:* The number eight (cf. 2 Pet 2:5) is a symbol of the resurrection (cf. Justin, *Dial.* 138.1–2). *were brought safely to the ark through water:* The picture is that of Noah and his family passing through the rising waters (cf. 1 Cor 10:1–2; *Midr. Gen. Rab.* 7:7). **21.** *baptism:* Christians are saved by "passing through" the waters of baptism. In this sense, the water of baptism is a counterpart, "antitype," of the water of the flood. *not the removal of the dirt of the body:* Lit., "not the putting aside of the dirt of the flesh." This would be a strange way of referring to the act of mere washing. The language is better suited to the Jewish rite of circumcision. As the church of Rome was probably founded from Jerusalem, this comparison could be a regular part of its catechesis (cf. Col 2:11; 3:8–9; Eph 4:22; Dalton, *Christ's Proclamation* 215–24). *a pledge to maintain a right attitude:* The Gk *eperōtēma* means "question," but it became a technical term for making a contract. The Gk *syneidēsis,* often translated "conscience," does not refer here to a subjective state, but to an objective disposition or attitude. *resurrection:* See 1:3; 3:18; cf. Rom 6:3–9). **22.** *gone into heaven:* The Gk vb. *poreutheis* is used here, as in 3:19. *God's right hand:* An application to Christ of Ps 110:1 (cf. Matt 22:24; Acts 2:33–35; Rom 8:34; Heb 8:1). *angels . . . made subject to him:* A similar theme to that of the "proclamation to the spirits" of 3:19. Christians by baptism share the victory of Christ over all hostile spirits (cf. Phil 2:10; 1 Cor 15:24,27; Eph 1:21; 6:2; Col 2:10,15).

(Dalton, *Christ's Proclamation.* Gschwind, K., *Die Niederfahrt Christi in die Unterwelt* [NTAbh 2/3–5; Münster, 1911]. Reicke, B., *The Disobedient Spirits and Christian Baptism* [Copenhagen, 1946]. Vogels, H.-J., *Christi Abstieg ins Totenreich und das Läuterungsgericht an den Toten* [FTS 102; Freiburg, 1976]. Perrot, C., "La descente aux enfers et la prédication aux morts," *Études* 231–46. Brox, *Der erste Petrusbrief* 182–89.)

23   (ii) *The Christian through suffering renounces sin* (4:1-6). **1.** *Christ has suffered:* The theme of Christ's suffering (3:18) is taken up again as a motive for Christian life. *the same thought:* This is better taken as referring to the preceding context. The following *hoti* is thus to be translated "because" (cf. 2:21; 3:18). The Christian who takes up a life of suffering (*pathōn*) with Christ is thereby dedicated to a moral life which rejects sin (cf. 1 John 3:6; Rom 6:1–11). **4.** *they are surprised:* Here we have a graphic picture of the situation of newly converted Christians and of the pressure put on them to return to pagan ways. **5.** *judge the living and the dead:* A creedal formulation that presents the risen Christ at the parousia as judge of all human beings, both those living on earth and those already dead (cf. Acts 10:42; Rom 14:9; 2 Tim 4:1). **6. he was preached:** NT usage favors the translation given here (see Acts 5:42; 8:35; 11:20; Gal 1:16; cf. 1 Cor 15:12; 2 Cor 1:19; 1 Tim 3:16). *even to the dead:* The preaching about Christ is the normal preaching of the gospel on earth. The point of the text is to vindicate those Christians who had accepted the gospel on earth but who had since died (cf. 1 Thess 4:13–18). This text has quite a different theme from that of 3:19.

24 (c) CHRISTIAN LIFE AND THE PAROUSIA (4:7–11). **7. the end:** Cf. 1:5,7; 2:12; 4:5,17; 5:4,10; Luke 21:36; 1 Cor 7:29; 10:11; Jas 5:8. **8. love covers a multitude of sins:** A Christian proverb derived from the MT of Prov 10:12. In the latter, the sins that are "covered" are those of the people loved; here they are those of the person who loves (cf. Jas 5:20; Luke 7:47; 1 Cor 13:7). **9. hospitable:** Cf. Rom 12:13; Heb 13:2; 3 John 5–8; Matt 25:23; Luke 7:44-47; 11:5-10; 14:12. *stewards:* Christians are stewards (*oikonomoi*) in the household (*oikos*) of God (see 2:5; 4:17). **11. whoever speaks:** Teachers and preachers in the community should communicate the genuine message of the gospel (cf. 1 Thess 2:13; 2 Cor 5:20). *to whom:* This doxology is addressed to the Father (as in Rom 16:27; Rev 1:6).

25 **(B) Persecution Faced Realistically (4:12–5:11).** Throughout the letter the writer has prepared the readers for this confrontation with persecution (see 1:6-7; 2:12,21–24; 3:14,17; 4:1).

(a) JOY IN ACTUAL PERSECUTION (4:12–19). **12. do not be surprised:** This indicates a time before regular state persecutions: *ordeal by fire:* The image of 1:6-7 is taken up again. **13. share the suffering of Christ:** We go beyond the imitation (2:21) of Christ's sufferings to a deeper participation (2:24–25; 3:18; 4:1). **14.** Cf. 3:14. *the Spirit of glory and of God:* The text, which is inspired by Isa 11:2 LXX, is difficult and may be corrupt. We have here an echo of 1:8: "You exult with joy . . . full of glory." **15. mischief-maker:** The Gk *allotriepiskopos* is a very rare term indicating a person who meddles in another's business (cf. Acts 16:20–21). **16. as a Christian:** Cf. Acts 11:26; 26:28. This does not mean that being a Christian was a public crime. The situation is that of 2:15; 3:16; 4:4. *do not be ashamed:* Christians are not facing death but public opprobrium. **17. judgment:** The present sufferings of Christians are the beginnings of the eschatological judgment, a purification of "God's household" (cf. Mark 13:8-13; 1 Cor 11:31-32; Mal 3:1-6). This judgment will be terrible for the unbelieving pagans (cf. 2 Thess 1:5-10). **18.** Prov 11:31 LXX. **19. commend their souls . . . Creator:** There is no reference to martyrdom. Here alone in the NT God is called Creator.

26 **(b)** EXHORTATION TO ELDERS AND FAITHFUL (5:1-5). This addition to the code of 2:13–3:7 (cf. 1 Tim 3:13; 5:4-19) reveals a relatively undeveloped church structure. *elders:* This office of pastoral leadership was taken from contemporary Judaism. *fellow elder:* A term coined by the author to indicate solidarity between apostle (see 1:1) and elders, like Paul's "fellow workers"

(Rom 16:3,9,21; Phil 2:25; 4:3; Phlm 24; Col 4:11; 2 Cor 8:23). *witness:* One who testifies, not necessarily "eyewitness" (cf. Luke 24:48; Acts 1:8; 22:15,20; Rev 2:13; 17:6). **2. tend the flock of God:** In 5:2–33 we have the picture of an ideal pastor (cf. John 21:15-17; Acts 20:28; Eph 4:11). Church leaders were paid (cf. Acts 20:33-34; 1 Cor 9:7-14; 2 Cor 12:13-18; 1 Tim 5:17-18; Matt 10:10); hence, the warning against greed (cf. Titus 1:7; 1 Tim 3:8). Some mss. add *episkopountes,* "overseeing" (cf. 2:25). **4. chief shepherd:** Cf. 2:25. Christ calls other shepherds to share his ministry and glory. **5. younger:** "Elder" designates both age and office. "Younger," as contrasted here with "elder," refers to age rather than to some subordinate ministry. *clothe yourselves:* The image behind the rare Gk verb *enkombōsasthe* is that of a slave putting on an apron for menial work. The citation is from Prov 3:34 LXX; cf. Jas 4:6-10.

27 (c) FINAL EXHORTATION: TRUST GOD, WHO BRINGS YOU THROUGH SUFFERING TO GLORY (5:6–11). **6. Humble yourselves:** A link word with "humble" of 5:5. *God's mighty hand:* An image recalling God's great acts of deliverance (see Exod 3:19; 6:1; Deut 9:26), but here even more the discipline he exercises over his people (see Job 30:21; Ps 32:4; Ezek 20:34-35). **7.** Citation from Ps 55:23 LXX with an echo of Wis 12:13 (cf. Matt 6:25-34). **8. be watchful:** Cf. 1:13; 1 Thess 5:6; Matt 24:42; Luke 21:34-36; Rom 13:11-12). *your adversary:* Gk *antidikos* means "opponent" in a lawsuit. *the devil:* In the LXX the Gk term *diabolos,* "devil," translates the Hebr *śāṭān,* "accuser" (Job 1-2) and was later applied to the leader of the fallen angels. *a roaring lion:* See Ps 22:14; as such, the devil incites pagans in their persecution of Christians. **9. your brotherhood in the world:** Christians everywhere were facing the same problem of alienation and harassment. **10. the God of all grace:** This verse sums up some of the chief elements of the letter, "suffered," "grace," "calls," "glory."

28 **(V) Conclusion: This Is the True Grace of God: Stand Firm in It; Farewell (5:12-14).** These verses could well have come from Peter's hand (cf. 1 Cor 16:14; Gal 6:11; Col 4:18; 2 Thess 3:17). **12. Silvanus:** The companion of Paul (cf. 1 Thess 1:1; 2 Thess 1:1; 2 Cor 1:19; called "Silas" in Acts 15:22,27,32,40; 16:19, 25,29; 17:4,10,14,15; 18:5). *I have written:* In Greek "to write by means of someone" can mean "to send a letter using someone as a courier." *briefly:* This refers to the composition of the letter. *the true grace:* Persecution is a gift of God (cf. 2:19). *stand firm in it:* Here alone in NT letters the Gk *eis* means "in," a possible sign of Peter's imperfect Greek (cf. ZBG § 99–111). **13. she who is at Babylon:** The church at Rome (cf. 2 John 13). "Babylon" was a cryptogram for "Rome" (cf. Rev 14:8; 2 Apoc. Bar. 11:1-2; 67:7; 2 Esdr. 3:12,28; Sib. Or. 5:143,159). *Mark, my son:* John Mark, originally of Jerusalem (Acts 12:12-17), associated later with Peter in the writing of Mark's Gospel (see Eusebius, HE 3.39.15), otherwise known in the NT as Paul's fellow worker (Acts 12:25; 2 Tim 4:11). **14. kiss:** See comment on Rom 16:16.

58

THE EPISTLE OF JAMES

Thomas W. Leahy, S.J.

BIBLIOGRAPHY

1   Adamson, J. B., *The Epistle of James* (NICNT; GR, 1976); *James: The Man and His Message* (GR, 1986). Cantinat, J., *Les épîtres de Saint Jacques et de Saint Jude* (SB; Paris, 1973). Chaine, J., *L'Epître de Saint Jacques* (EBib; Paris, 1927). Davids, P., *Commentary on James* (NIGTC; GR, 1982). Dibelius, M., *James* (rev. H. Greeven; Herm; Phl, 1975). Francis, F., "The Form and Function of the Opening and Closing Paragraphs of James and I John," *ZNW* 61 (1970) 110–26. Hoppe, R., *Der theologische Hintergrund des Jakobusbriefes* (FB 28; Würzburg, 1977). Hort, F. J. A., *The Epistle of St. James* (London, 1909). Kugelman, R., *James and Jude* (NTM 19; Wilmington, 1980). Laws, S., *The Epistle of James* (HNTC; SF, 1980). Luck, U., "Die Theologie des Jakobusbriefes," *ZTK* 81 (1984) 1–30. Mayor, J.,

The Epistle of St. James (London, 1892). Mussner, F., *Der Jakobusbrief* (HTKNT 13/1; Freiburg, 1964). Ropes, J. H., *A Critical and Exegetical Commentary on the Epistle of St. James* (ICC; Edinburgh, 1916). Sidebottom, E. M., *James, Jude and 2 Peter* (NCB; London, 1967). Vouga, F., *L'Epître de Saint Jacques* (CNT 2/13a; Geneva, 1984). Ward, R. B., "The Communal Concern of the Epistle of James" (diss., Harvard; Cambridge MA, 1966). Wuellner, W., "Der Jakobusbrief im Licht der Rhetorik und Textpragmatik," *LB* 8/43 (Sept. 1978) 5–65. Zmijewski, J., *Christliche 'Vollkommenheit': Erwägungen zur Theologie des Jakobusbriefes* (SUNT A5; Göttingen, 1980).

DBSup 4. 783–95. *IDBSup* 469–70. Kümmel, *INT* 403–16. Wik-Schm, *ENT* 563–77.

INTRODUCTION

2   **(I) Authenticity.** According to its opening verse, this first of the Catholic Epistles (→ NT Epistles, 45:17) is written by "James, a servant of God and of the Lord Jesus Christ." Who is this James? Is he actually the author of the epistle? The use of the title "servant," which suggests a church official, his presuming to address "the twelve tribes in the Dispersion," and the unmistakable tone of authority throughout the letter all indicate someone of authority, well known in the church. This conclusion is confirmed by Jude 1, where the writer refers to himself as "brother of James." Such a person is identifiable in the NT as James, "brother of the Lord" (Gal 1:19; cf. Matt 13:55; Mark 6:3) and leader of the early church in Jerusalem (Acts 12:17; 15:13; 1 Cor 15:7; Gal 2:9,12), known to later tradition as "James the Just" (Eusebius, *HE* 2.23.4). This identification has been traditionally accepted in the church and is generally held by modern scholars. Although the Western church traditionally identified this James of Jerusalem with the apostle James (son) of Alphaeus (Mark 3:18; Acts 1:13), this view is now largely abandoned (Wik-Schm, *ENT* 574).

3   Did this James write the epistle attributed to him? Modern opinion is divided: A growing majority of contemporary scholars opt for pseudonymity (→ Canonicity, 66:88), basing this largely on the following

reasons: the excellent Gk style of the letter; the lack of attestation to its canonicity before the 3d cent. (and even later); indications of a date substantially after Paul (whereas James died *ca.* AD 62); and the apparent absence from the letter both of specifically Christian teaching and of the strict legalism and ritualism that the traditions about James the Just might lead one to expect. Although penetrating answers to each of these points individually have been provided by Davids, Mussner, Chaine, and their predecessors, the most widely held view today is that a Christian versed in both Hellenism and Judaism wrote the letter under the name of James of Jerusalem, in the latter part of the 1st cent. AD. The mediating view (Davids, Cantinat) that early tradition stemming from James of Jerusalem was updated and published by an unknown Christian teacher of a later Christian generation, has much to commend it.

4   **(II) Purpose and Destination.** The epistle consists of a long series of exhortations, mostly brief and loosely connected, some developed at length. The one common trait, which gives the letter its distinctive quality, is a concern that the faith of the recipients be not merely theoretical or abstract, but implemented in action, in every aspect of their lives. In a situation where trials and temptations abound and where the poor suffer at the hands of the rich, Jas exhorts them to joy, endurance, wisdom, confident prayer, and faithful response to the liberating word of God in a hostile world, as they wait for the coming of the Lord. Judging from the letter as a whole, the recipients would seem to be a group of Jewish-Christian communities outside Palestine, but living in an area where the name of James would have authority.

5 (III) Date and Place of Composition. A likely date would seem to be the early or middle sixties, after Paul's teaching on faith and works, but before the destruction of Jerusalem in AD 70. In that case, Jerusalem could well have been the place of origin. If, however, the letter dates from after AD 70, Antioch or Alexandria would be candidates.

6 (IV) Outline. The Epistle of James may be outlined as follows:

(I) Opening Formula (1:1)
(II) Opening Exhortation (1:2–18)
    (A) Joy in Trials (1:2–4)
    (B) Unwavering Prayer for Wisdom (1:5–8)
    (C) Attitudes of the Lowly and the Rich (1:9–11)

    (D) Endurance Gains the Crown of Life (1:12)
    (E) Genealogy of Sin and Death (1:13–15)
    (F) Our Birth in God's Word (1:16–18)
(III) Be Doers of the Word (1:19–27)
    (A) The Proper Disposition (1:19–21)
    (B) The Precept: Be Doers, Not Mere Hearers (1:22)
    (C) Simile of the Mirror (1:23–25)
    (D) Genuine Religion (1:26–27)
(IV) Avoid Partiality (2:1–13)
    (A) The Precept (2:1)
    (B) Hypothetical Example (2:2–4)
    (C) Various Arguments (2:5–13)
(V) Faith without Works Is Dead (2:14–26)
    (A) Main Thesis (2:14–17)
    (B) Various Examples (2:18–26)
(VI) Guard of the Tongue (3:1–12)
(VII) Qualities of Wisdom (3:13–18)
(VIII) Causes of Strife; Remedies (4:1–12)
(IX) Against Mercantile Presumptuousness (4:13–17)
(X) Woe to the Rich (5:1–6)
(XI) Patient Waiting for the Coming of the Lord (5:7–11)
(XII) Directions for Various Circumstances; End of Letter (5:12–20)

COMMENTARY

7 (I) Opening Formula (1:1). *James:* Gk *Iakōbos* = Hebr *Ya'ăqōb* (on the identity of James, → 2–3 above). *servant of God:* The writer applies to himself a title given in the OT to such religious leaders as Moses, Abraham, Jacob, and the prophets. He thus indicates the basis of his authority, in virtue of which he will exhort his readers. *the Lord Jesus Christ:* The applying to Jesus of the title *Kyrios,* "Lord," and the close pairing of God and Christ indicate the author's share in the Christian faith. This is of particular significance in view of the paucity of specific references to Christ in Jas. *to the twelve tribes:* Since the Assyrian captivity of the 10 northern tribes, this expression had come to represent the eschatological hope of the restoration of Israel. It is here applied to the Christian church as the continuation of God's people. *dispersion:* See 1 Pet 1:1. *greeting:* The Gk formula (*chairein*) used here is found nowhere else in the NT (except Acts 15:23 and 23:26), although it was normal in Hellenistic epistolary style (→ NT Epistles, 45:6).

8 (II) Opening Exhortation (1:2–18). A series of short exhortations, linked together more by studied verbal connections than by concept, introduces topics that will be resumed and developed later in the letter.

(A) Joy in Trials (1:2–4). 2. *all joy:* The word "joy," *chara,* not only provides a verbal link with the preceding "Greeting" (*chairein*) but also, by its strategic position at the beginning of the letter, introduces a dominant tone of Christian optimism, serving to balance the condemnatory tone of much of the letter. *my brothers:* Jas uses this normal form of Christian address (taken from Judaism) 11 times, including 4 times with "beloved," conveying a sense of affectionate earnestness. *various trials:* The theme of rejoicing in trials is widespread in the NT, originating in Jesus' "beatitudes" (Matt 5:10–12; Luke 6:20–23; Acts 5:41; Rom 5:3; 1 Thess 1:6). The subject of patient endurance, here briefly introduced, will be taken up at greater length in 5:7–11. **3.** *testing of your faith:* Gold tested and purified by fire is the implied image (as in the OT and 1 Pet 1:7), referring to trials or persecutions that endangered faith. *steadfastness:* The word *hypomonē* implies not mere passive endurance, but an active spirit of resistance to defection characteristic of the

martyrs. **4.** *let steadfastness have its full effect:* Lit., "have a perfect work." The Gk expression is vague, but its intent is clarified by the following: "that you may be perfect and complete." Both present striving and eschatological fulfillment are in view. The concept of perfection is important in Jas (occurring also in 1:17,25; 3:2), as it is in the OT, at Qumran, and elsewhere in the NT. It includes aspects of maturity, completion, fulfillment. J. Zmijewski (*Christliche 'Vollkommenheit'* 50–78) considers perfection to be the key concept and unifying principle of Jas. (See also B. Rigaux, *NTS* 4 [1957–58] 237–41, 248.) Verses 3–4 employ the stylistic device of "climax," in which the end of one phrase is echoed at the beginning of the next. The similarities of vocabulary and thought between these verses and 1 Pet 1:6–7 and Rom 5:3–5 are probably due not to literary dependence, but to a primitive common stock of parenetic material. (See Dibelius, *James* 74–77.)

9 (B) Unwavering Prayer for Wisdom (1:5–8). This section introduces several topics that will be developed later: wisdom (3:13–18), prayer (4:2–3; 5:13–18), God as giver of all good (1:17–18), faith (2:14–26), instability (4:1–8). **5.** *lacks wisdom:* The verbal interlinking of sentences continues, with "lacks" (*leipetai,* 1:5) harking back to "lacking" (*leipomenoi,* 1:4). The logical connection is less apparent, but seems dependent on OT wisdom themes, which closely connect wisdom, testing by trials, and perfection (see Wis 9:6; Sir 4:17) and stress the need of wisdom (Wis 9:10–18). *generously and without reproaching:* This characteristic of God contrasts with the grudging type of giving reprehended in Sir 18:15–18; 20:10–15. **6.** *ask in faith:* The implied object of this faith is God's readiness to answer prayers (see 1:5). *with no doubting:* This probably depends on sayings of Jesus, such as Matt 21:21–22; Mark 11:23–24.

10 (C) Attitudes of the Lowly and the Rich (1:9–11). The author's interest in the religious significance of lowliness and poverty on the one hand and wealth on the other, first seen here, comes out also in 1:27; 2:1–7,15–17; 4:10,13–16; 5:1–6. It is a dominant theme of the letter. It derives from the OT understanding of the poor and oppressed — the *'ănāwîm* — who are the objects of God's special concern and who see in God their only hope of refuge from affliction. This theme, widely and diversely represented in the intertestamental period, is found in QL and in the NT, esp. in Luke (→ 43:23). This concern includes condemnation of oppression or neglect of the poor, affirmation of their actual exaltation, and assurance of their eschatological vindication. **9.** The connection of this verse with the foregoing may be that it is a particular application of the general exhortation of 1:2, and perhaps also a paradoxical insight gained through the wisdom described in v 5. *exult:* The note of joy of v 2 reechoes. See Rom 5:3. The basis for this exultation is given in 2:5. **10a.** *the rich:* The parallelism of vv 9 and 10 indicates that the rich are also members of the community. *in his humiliation:* I.e., in the transitory nature of his wealthy status, described in the following phrases. From the viewpoint of Christian eschatology, the rich man's only hope is in the realization of his utter poverty and nothingness before God. **10b-11.** The imagery of the quickly fading grass — particularly appropriate in Palestine — is well known in the OT (see Isa 40:6-7; for a different use, see 1 Pet 1:24-25). *in the midst of his pursuits:* The word for "pursuits" can also mean "journeys." See the similar imagery in 4:13-15.

11   **(D) Endurance Gains the Crown of Life (1:12).** This verse forms a kind of climactic *inclusio* with vv 2-4, providing a sense of coherence to the section. *blessed is the one who:* The form of this "beatitude" reflects the OT (Ps 1:1) and the Gospels (Matt 5:3-10 par.). *crown of life:* The crown is eschatological, but the blessedness is a present reality. *who love him:* This phrase, recurring in 2:5, is traditional in the context of divine reward for fidelity (Exod 20:6; Deut 5:10; Rom 8:28; 2 Tim 4:8; in QL, see 1QH 16:13). The similarity of thought and expression in 1:2-3,12 to that of 1 Pet 1:6-9 and Rom 5:3-5 may indicate dependence on an early Christian hymn, perhaps from the baptismal liturgy (see M.-É. Boismard, *RB* 64 [1957] 162-67).

    (E) Genealogy of Sin and Death (1:13-15). **13.** *I am being tempted by God:* The author points out the age-old fallacy of blaming one's sins on God instead of on oneself. See Sir 15:11-20; 1 Cor 10:13. **14.** *by his own passion:* Temptation is caused by something interior to a person; yet this is represented as somehow distinct from him, because it lures him as a hunter lures his prey. **15.** The image changes to that of genealogical descent. *when it has conceived:* I.e., when consent is given to the temptation. *when it is full grown:* This indicates the eschatological destiny toward which sin is growing. The sequence of passion, sin, and death is the negative counterpart of trial, proved endurance, and crown of life (1:12). The verse partially echoes Ps 7:15.

12   **(F) Our Birth in God's Word (1:16-18).** **17.** Since a well-known poetic proverb is perhaps being quoted, it seems better (following H. Greeven, *TZ* 14 [1958] 1-13) to take these words as a complete sentence: "Every gift is good, and every present is perfect." Its meaning would be the familiar sentiment: What counts in a gift is not its value but the giver's intention. A deeper meaning is added, explaining the source of all created goodness: Every gift comes from above. *Father of lights:* The expression seems intended to refer to God as creator of the heavenly luminaries, the prime instance of his giving good gifts. This same title occurs in *Apoc. Mos.* 36:5. *shadow due to change [to turning]:* Unlike heavenly bodies, whose movements according to times and seasons result in corresponding variations in the light they send forth, their creator is unchanging; therefore, his goodness never diminishes. **18.** *of his own will:* The freedom of the divine initiative with which God gives birth to his children contrasts with the blind force of desire that

gives birth to sin (vv 14-15). *he gave birth:* Of itself, this expression can be understood in the OT context of Deut 32:18. That it is rather to be understood in the specifically Christian sense (as in John 1:12-13) is indicated by a comparison of v 18 with 1 Pet 1:23, in which the sense is obviously Christian. However, an allusion to creation may likewise be intended. Just as the first creation (in Gen) took place through God's word, so likewise does the new creation. *by the word of truth:* This probably refers to the acceptance of the gospel message. On the use of "word," see comment on 1:21.

13   **(III) Be Doers of the Word (1:19-27).** The word in which we were given birth by God must be heard, obstacles must be removed, and the word must be implemented in deed.

    (A) The Proper Disposition (1:19-21). **19.** *be quick to listen, slow to speak, slow to anger:* These three admonitions are of a type that frequently occurs in the OT and in QL (Sir 5:11-13; 1QH 1:34-37). They will be developed respectively in 1:22-25; 3:13-18; and 1:20 + 4:1-2. *slow to speak:* This theme is resumed in 1:26 and developed at length in 3:1-12. **20.** The reason is given for the last of the three admonitions of v 19. *the righteousness of God:* I.e., demanded by God, as in Matt 5:20; 6:33. **21.** *receive the implanted word:* Gk *emphytos,* "implanted," normally means "inborn" — a meaning that seems logically inadmissible in the present context. This implantation of the word refers rather to the acceptance of the Christian faith at baptism, including the ethical demands involved. The use of "word" (*logos*) in 1:18,21-23 reflects typical NT usage. It is God's saving revelation, foreshadowed in the word given to the prophets and in the word that is a synonym for law (*tôrâ*), but fully expressed only in Christ and the gospel.

14   **(B) The Precept: Be Doers, Not Mere Hearers (1:22).** This verse is an apt summary of the whole letter. It is strikingly similar to Rom 2:13. The general theme of a "religion of deed," so characteristic of Jas, is prominent in other NT writings. See Matt 7:24-27 par.; Luke 8:21; 11:28. For OT background, see Deut 4:5-6; 28:13-15; Ezek 33:31-32. *deceiving yourselves:* For an example of this self-deception, see v 26.

    (C) Simile of the Mirror (1:23-25). **23.** *in a mirror:* The "word" is like a mirror: by presenting ideal human conduct, it reveals the hearer's shortcomings, just as a mirror reveals facial blemishes or untidiness. If the one using the mirror forgets what has been seen, one will fail to remedy the situation — one will not be a "doer." **25.** Once again Jas introduces a theme ("law") that will also recur later in a lengthy treatment in 2:8-12 and in a brief mention in 4:11. *perfect law of liberty:* Because of the close connection of this verse with the preceding, the "law" (as in 2:8-12; 4:11) is to be identified with the "word" of the preceding verses. Jas lacks Paul's distinction between the law and the gospel, showing rather an affinity to the spirit of Matt 5:17-19 as specified in the Sermon on the Mount. That he does not refer simply to the Old Law seems indicated by the qualifications "perfect" and "of liberty" (see 2:12), as well as by the absence in the letter of any emphasis on the fulfillment of ritual prescriptions. In fact, Jas manifests no rigid legalism of the type attributed to "James the Just" by later tradition (see Eusebius, *HE* 2.23).

15   **(D) Genuine Religion (1:26-27).** The exhortation of v 22 is now given practical application. **26.** *bridle his tongue:* The concern for restraint in speech, which already surfaced in 1:19, will be developed at length in 3:1-12. See also 4:11. *deceives himself:* Lit., "his heart" — a Hebraism derived from LXX usage. **27.** *pure and undefiled:* These qualities, usually ritual and cultic, are aptly applied to the practice of external works of charity and to inner integrity. No complete definition of religion is attempted here, but only an emphasis on certain aspects without which the practice of religion has no meaning. (See Isa 58; Matt 23.) *before God the Father:* The title is chosen in view of God's fatherly care of widows and orphans (Ps 67:6). *orphans and widows:* These are the natural objects of charity in the community; see Deut 27:19; Sir 4:10; Acts 6:1. *from the world:* This pejorative sense of "world" (opposition to God) occurs also in Paul, 2 Pet, John, 1 John (see BAGD 7).

16   (IV) Avoid Partiality (2:1–13). This section is a further explanation of the exhortation of 1:22: "Be doers of the word." The brief mention of widows and orphans in 1:27 leads to a fuller consideration of the poor in the community. The development: warning against partiality (2:1); concrete example (vv 2–4); reasons against partiality (vv 5–13).

(A) The Precept (2:1). 1. *my brothers:* See comment on 1:2. *partiality:* See comment on Rom 2:11. *our glorious Lord:* Lit., "our Lord of glory." The great glory of the Lord in whom we believe should nullify all such ideas of worldly rank or status as would lead to partiality in conduct.

(B) Hypothetical Example (2:2–4). The vivid character of the example may not allude to an actual incident. Such examples are characteristic of the rhetorical style of "diatribe" (see Dibelius, *James* 124–26; → Pauline Theology, 82:12). *into your synagogue:* This example, unique in the NT, of a Christian extension of the term *synagōgē* is an indication of Jewish-Christian background. Both the rich man and the poor man are envisaged as strangers to the community, so that their social status is known only by their appearance. **3.** The rich man is being offered a seat of honor (see Matt 23:6; Mark 12:39; Luke 11:43; 20:46).

(C) Various Arguments (2:5–13). 5. *has not God chosen the poor:* See 1:19 and comment. The OT belief that the poor are the object of God's special care (Ps 35:10) and of messianic blessings (Isa 61:1) is prominent also in QL (1QM 13:14; 1QH 18:14) and in the Gospels (Matt 5:3; Luke 6:20; Matt 11:5). 1 Cor 1:17–29 gives Paul's explanation of this divine "preferential option." The poor, by reason of their faith, are rich. *heirs of the kingdom:* This unique reference to "the kingdom" is reminiscent of the first beatitude (Matt 5:3; Luke 6:20). *which he has promised:* The concept of divine promise, with the closely associated ideas of election and inheritance, as well as that of the response of love toward God, is the very basis of OT and NT theology. *who love him:* See comment on 1:12. *dishonored the poor one:* Their conduct is the very antithesis of that attributed to God in the preceding verse. *who oppress you:* This implies that the readers rank with the poor. The oppressive rich are considered as a class, characterized not only by wealth but also by oppressiveness and impiety, in terms reminiscent of OT prophets (Amos 8:4; see Wis 2:10). *drag you into court:* In view of v 7, reference to religious persecution is probably included, along with various forms of social and economic oppression. **7.** *blaspheme that honorable name by which you are called:* To be called by a name (lit., "to have a name called over one") is to be designated as belonging to the person named. To persecute Christians baptized in the name of Jesus (Acts 2:38) is to dishonor his exalted name (see Phil 2:10).

17   8. *royal law:* Since the Mosaic law comes from God, the universal king, it is rightly called royal. James is likewise alluding to the command of love of neighbor (Lev 19:18) cited in Jesus' preaching of the kingdom (Matt 22:39; L. Johnson, "Leviticus 19 in James," *JBL* 101 [1982] 391–401.) By fulfilling the command of love of neighbor, one fulfills the whole law. This was made

explicit in Rom 13:8–10; Gal 5:14. **9.** A balanced antithesis to the preceding. The implied relationship among sin, the law, and transgression seems to be in basic harmony with Paul's more elaborate development (see Rom 4:15; 5:13–14; 7:7–21; Gal 3:19). **10.** *guilty in respect to all of it:* The transgression of even a single precept of the law puts one into the category of transgressors of the law. This principle is implied in Matt 5:18–19; Gal 3:10; 1QS 8:3; it is found in rabbinic tradition. According to M. O'R. Boyle ("The Stoic Paradox of James 2.10," *NTS* 31 [1985] 611–17), it also reflects Stoic tradition. **12.** *going to be judged:* In 1:12 James appealed to the motive of future reward; now he appeals to the motive of future judgment (see 3:1; 4:12; 5:9). This motivation in connection with the precept of love of neighbor occurs also in Matt 5:22,25; 7:1–2; 25:31–46. *under the law of liberty:* See comment on 1:25. Only a free self-dedication to the law as being God's will (and opposed to mere external constraint) is adequate to assure an integral observance of all the precepts. This spirit of joyful free dedication to God's law finds expression in the OT (Pss 1:2; 40:9; 119:21) and in QL. **13.** *mercy wins out over judgment:* This echoes the teaching of Jesus in Matt 6:15; 18:23–35; 25:41–46, a teaching occurring also in OT and apocryphal wisdom literature.

18   (V) Faith without Works Is Dead (2:14–26). This section is unique for its unified and relatively lengthy development of a single theme. It is the heart of the letter, giving the theoretical basis for the practical exhortations. Nevertheless, the appearance of a contradiction of Paul's teaching on justification by faith has tended to give exaggerated prominence to this section. It was largely because of this apparent contradiction that Luther wished to exclude Jas from the canon (see Mussner, *Jakobusbrief* 42–47).

19   (A) Main Thesis (2:14–17). 14. *says he has faith:* James does not here imply the possibility of true faith existing apart from deeds, but merely of the making of such a claim. To judge by the present passage and by 1:3,6; 2:1,5; 5:15, James means by faith the free acceptance of God's saving revelation. *has not works:* By "works" is meant the obedient implementation of God's revealed will in every aspect of life, as illustrated by the numerous practical exhortations in the epistle. *can his faith save him:* I.e., can such a "faith" save him from judgment (see 2:13 and comment on 5:15). **17.** *thus:* The point of the preceding analogy is made explicit. *faith by itself:* Unaccompanied by deeds—thus the contrary of the "faith working through love" (Gal 5:6). *is dead:* It is unable to save him for eternal life (see 2:14). Note that James is not opposing faith and works, but living faith and dead faith.

20   (B) Various Examples (2:18–26). 18. *but someone will say:* The interpretation of this verse is considerably disputed. It seems best to consider this a genuine objection. Understand "you" and "I" not as, respectively, James and the objector, but as signifying simply that some specialize in faith, others in works. The next phrase, "Show me your faith . . ." is James's reply to the objector, challenging him to give evidence of the existence of faith apart from works. His next assertion, "I by my works," claims that where works might be supposed to exist without faith, a closer examination would show that faith underlies them. **19.** *you believe that God is one:* The OT emphasis on the oneness of God as the basic truth of faith (Deut 6:4) is found likewise in the NT (Mark 12:29; 1 Cor 8:4,6; Eph 4:6). *you do well:* The tone of *kalōs,* "well," is ironic (see Mark 7:9; John 4:17; 2 Cor 11:4). *even the demons believe and tremble:* They are objects of God's wrath, in spite of their barren "belief" in God's oneness. The point of this example is that mere knowledge of religious truths is of no avail when the will is alienated from God. **20.** *faith without works is barren:* In Greek, this involves a wordplay between "without works" (*chōris ergōn*) and "barren" (*argē*—from *a-ergos*). The verse serves as an introduction to the following Scripture proofs. **21** 21. *Abraham our father:* A favorite title for Abraham among the Jews. According to Paul (Rom 4; Gal 3-4), Abraham is the father of all believers. In spite of the different emphasis to be found in Jas and in Paul, both are following a venerable line of Jewish tradition in citing Abraham as an example of fidelity and righteousness before God (Sir 44:19-21; Wis 10:5; 1 Macc 2:52; *Jub.* 17-19; CD 3:2; Heb 11:8-12,17-19). *justified by works:* The pass. voice implies divine agency. The "works" are the offering of Isaac. The "justification" seems to mean Abraham's being found pleasing to God and therefore being confirmed in the promise (Gen 22:16-18). James has combined the statement about Abraham's justification (Gen 15:6) with that of his obedience (Gen 22). The basis for this combination follows. 22. *faith was active along with his works:* Abraham's obedience to God's difficult word indicates the activeness of his faith. *faith was completed by works:* Believing God's promise of offspring in the face of the slaying of the only visible source of offspring made perfect his faith in God's initial promise. This demonstrates the inseparability of faith and works. **23.** *Scripture was fulfilled:* Gen 15:6 is taken as a prophecy fulfilled by the events of Gen 22 (see 1 Macc 2:52). *friend of God:* This title of Abraham, not found in Gen, occurs in Isa 41:8; 2 Chr 20:7; and in QL (CD 3:2). **24.** *a person is justified:* A conclusion is now drawn from Scripture: What was true in the case of Abraham is true universally. *by works and not by faith alone:* As is clear from context, this does not mean that genuine faith is insufficient for justification, but that faith unaccompanied by works is not genuine. There is thus no basic disagreement of James with Paul, for whom faith "works through love" (Gal 5:6).

Yet a problem remains. Not only is there a strong difference of emphasis in Paul and James regarding faith and works, but there is such a striking quasi identity of wording, and of emphasis on Abraham (with each quoting Gen 15:6 in his own favor), along with a superficial appearance of mutual contradiction (see Rom 3:28; also 1:17; 3:20-27,30; 4:2-5,16-24; Gal 2:16; 3:6-12,24), that some kind of connection, by way of refutation or correction, seems postulated. The most satisfactory hypothesis is that James seeks to correct a current perverted understanding of Pauline teaching on justification by faith, one that would, unlike genuine Pauline doctrine, make no moral demands on the believer. **22** 25. *Rahab the harlot:* James does not mention her faith, since it is evident from Josh 2:11. Her fellow citizens also had a kind of faith (2:9-11); but she alone acted on her belief and so was justified—was found pleasing before God and was saved (Josh 6:22-25). A similar use of the Rahab example in Heb 11:31 and (at greater length) in *1 Clem.* 12 indicates the ancient popularity of this theme. **26.** The body—spirit comparison sums up the treatment, neatly indicating the indispensability of both faith and works. Forming a Semitic *inclusio* with v 14, it indicates the close of the section.

(Burchard, C., "Zu Jakobus 2:14-16," *ZNW* 71 [1980] 27-45. Burtchaell, J., "A Theology of Faith and Works: The Epistle to the Galatians—A Catholic View," *Int* 17 [1963] 39-47. Jacobs, I., "The Midrashic Background for Jas ii.21-23," *NTS* 22 [1975-76] 457-64. Jeremias, J., "Paul and James," *ExpTim* 66 [1954-55] 368-71. Mussner, *Jakobusbrief* 133-36, 146-50, 152-57. Reumann, J., *"Righteousness" in the New Testament* [Phl, 1982] 270-75, 413.)

23 **(VI) Guard of the Tongue (3:1-12).** This is a clearly defined, closely developed section, developing the theme briefly mentioned in 1:19 and 26. **1.** *let not many . . . become teachers:* The role of teachers in the early church was important and honorable (Acts 13:1; 1 Cor 12:28; Eph 4:11), yet liable to abuse if sought for unworthy motives. James echoes the warnings of Jesus (Matt 5:19; 23:7-8). *we who teach:* James regards himself as a "teacher" in the church. **2-12.** Since teaching is exercised through speech, Jas now enters upon a lengthy admonition on the use of the tongue. **2.** *all of us often go wrong:* A well-known theme in Scripture (Eccl 7:20; Sir 19:16; 1 John 1:8,10; 2 Esdr 8:35). *not offend in speech:* Counsel about the right and wrong use of speech is frequent in OT wisdom literature (see Prov 15:1-4,7,23, 26,28; Sir 5:11-6:1; 28:13-26) and in QL (1QS 7:4-5; 10:21-24). *a perfect man:* The word *teleios* is used specifically of Christian moral perfection (Matt 5:48; 19:21; Col 1:28; 4:12). See comment on 1:4. **3-4.** Two analogies illustrate the assertion of the preceding verse. The bit and the rudder are compared to the tongue because, though small (see v 5a), both are instruments of the will (of the rider and of the pilot). **24** **6.** This verse is a harsh denunciation of the evils of the tongue. It contains obscurities of structure and meaning that baffle exegetes. *a fire:* See Sir 28:22-23. *the unrighteous world:* The obscure phrase *ho kosmos tēs adikias* could mean "the sum total of iniquity" (see BAGD 8). *setting on fire the wheel of birth: Phlogizousa ton trochon tēs geneseōs* is "one of the hardest phrases in the Bible" (Hort). Similar phrases are found in Hellenistic literature, esp. in connection with Orphic rites. The *RSV* understands it of nature's cycle. *hell:* The Gk form *geenna* (= Hebr *gê hinnōm,* "Valley of Hinnom") occurs in the NT only in the Synoptics and here in Jas. The verse thus makes a sudden transition from Gk ways of speaking to Jewish. **7.** The four categories of animals are biblical (occurring in the same order in Gen 9:2; Deut 4:17-18; 1 Kgs 4:33). **9.** *bless the Lord and Father:* In Jewish custom "Blessed be he" was added to any mention of God, as well as to other liturgical blessings. *in the likeness of God:* See Gen 1:26; 9:6; Sir 17:3; Wis 2:23. **10.** The exhortation follows the Christian tradition of Luke 6:28; Rom 12:14; 1 Pet 3:9. **11.** The imagery is characteristic of Palestine, where springs are of great importance in the dry season. In 4 Ezra 5:9 a combination of sweet and brackish waters is regarded as a sign of the approaching end. **12.** The imagery of the fig, olive, and vine is also typical of Palestine, as it is of other Mediterranean countries. The figure is similar—without being identical to that of Matt 7:16 par. **25** **(VII) Qualities of Wisdom (3:13-18).** The theme of wisdom, briefly mentioned in 1:5, is now resumed in a clear-cut self-contained unit. It may also hark back to the "teacher" theme of 3:1, since from a Jewish point of view the teacher is almost identical with the "wise man." **13.** *who is wise:* A real understanding of wisdom is clearly expressed in these verses. Essentially that of OT wisdom literature, it is also reminiscent of Paul's understanding in 1 Cor 1-4. *let him show:* This structure of an imperative following an interrogative, having the force of a conditional, is biblical; see Deut 20:5-8. *his works:* The teaching of 2:14-26 is being applied to the concept of wisdom. *with the meekness of wisdom:* The important Christian concept of "meekness" (*praytē* includes gentleness, moderation, courtesy, humility). It occurs frequently in Paul (2 Cor 10:11; Gal 5:23) and is prominent in the teaching (Matt 5:5) and example (Matt 11:29) of Jesus. **14.** *the truth:* Judging from the present context, as well as from 1:18 and 5:19, "truth" means the Christian revelation, as put in practice by the Christian "wise man." **15.** *comes from above:* On the heavenly origin of wisdom, see Prov 2:6; 8:22–31; Wis 7:25; 9:4,9–10; Sir 1:1–4,24. *earthly, unspiritual, devilish:* In 1 Cor, the wisdom opposed to divine wisdom is that "of the world" (1:20); it characterizes the man who is "unspiritual" (2:14). Divine wisdom is unknown to "the rulers of this age" (2:8)—an expression that may include sinful angels. **16.** *jealousy . . . selfish ambition . . . disorder:* These expressions occur in the list of vices of 2 Cor 12:20; they were a feature of early Christian parenesis. **17.** In terms that emphasize the contrast with earthly wisdom, James here gives a masterful sketch of Christian wisdom, redolent of the Synoptics (see the Beatitudes, Matt 5:3–10) and of Paul (see Gal 5:22–23). **18.** Although "wisdom" is not mentioned in the verse, the phrasing is reminiscent of Septuagintal association of wisdom, peace, and righteousness (Prov 3:9,17,18; 11:30 LXX). The verse is also reminiscent of the beatitude of Matt 5:9 and forms an apt conclusion to this little treatise on wisdom.

26   (VIII) Causes of Strife; Remedies (4:1–2). Since faults of the tongue (3:2–12) and false wisdom (3:13–16) lead to strife in the community, James now considers the root causes (4:1–6) and remedies (4:7–10) thereof, concluding with a consideration of law and judgment (4:11–12). **1.** *wars, fightings:* The two Gk words often occur together in the figurative sense of contentions, disputes, and the like. They form an emphatic contrast with the last word of the preceding section, "peace." *your passions:* Lit., "your pleasures" (see Titus 3:3). **2.** The generality of v 1 is now specified with concrete examples. *because you do not ask:* This echoes, in negative form, the Gospel exhortations on prayer (Matt 7:7–11 par.; Mark 11:24; John 14:13–14; 1 John 3:22). **3.** *you ask wrongly:* The proper approach to prayer is indicated below (4:7–10). See also 1 John 5:14; Matt 6:33. (On prayer in Jas, see also 1:5–8; 5:13–18 and comments.) **4.** *adulterers:* This surprisingly harsh epithet reflects OT prophetic representation of unfaithfulness to God as adultery (Jer 3:9; Ezek 16; Hos 3:1), perhaps echoing the usage of Jesus (Matt 12:39; 16:4; Mark 8:38). *world:* See comment on 1:27. *makes himself an enemy of God:* A state of enmity between God and people differs from that of ordinary human relations, because the permanent attitude of love on God's part is not thereby interrupted.

27   5. *Scripture says:* No such text can be found in the OT. James may be quoting an apocryphal work or a lost variant from a Gk OT version. *the spirit:* This is the inner, God-given life breathed into man at his creation (see 2:26). **6.** *God resists the proud, but gives grace to the lowly:* Jas quotes Prov 33:4 LXX in v 6, and will then comment on and apply that text in vv 7–10—a procedure that A. Alonso Schökel calls "thematic announcement" (*Bib* 54 [1973] 73–76). **7–10.** These verses with their 10 imperatives form a highly structured development based on Prov 33:4 (see Davids, *James* 165). The fact that 1 Pet 5:5–9 quotes the same passage from Prov in a similar context of submission to God and rejection of the devil is a prime example of the dependence of these two letters (and other early Christian writings) on a common stock of Scripture-based parenesis. **10.** *humble yourselves before the Lord, and he will exalt you:* The first part of this verse forms a unifying *inclusio* with v 7. The verse as a whole echoes the teaching of Jesus (Matt 23:12; Luke 14:11; 18:14).

28   11–12. The theme of sins of speech, already treated in 1:26 and 3:2–10, is resumed, in connection with the judging of others, since these practices also contribute to strife in the community. In vocabulary and structure these two verses form a self-standing, well-unified section. **11.** *brothers:* The term of affection contrasts with the preceding harsh "adulterers" (v 4). *one who disparages a brother or judges the brother:* The stricture against judging is found elsewhere in the NT (Matt 7:1–5; Luke 6:37–42; Rom 2:1; 14:4,10), but the reason given for it here—that this is to disparage and judge the law—is unique to Jas. The "law" that one judges by speaking against a brother is the "second great commandment," love of neighbor (see 2:8). **12.** *save and destroy:* See Matt 16:25; Luke 6:9; in the OT, God is he who kills and makes live (Deut 32:39; 1 Sam 2:6; 2 Kgs 5:7). *but who are you:* The rhetorical question emphasizes the enormity of presumption hidden in the all-too-common practice of judging one's neighbor. Such a one has equivalently "usurped the role of God" (Davids, *James*).

29   (IX) Against Mercantile Presumptuousness (4:13–17). This passage and the following (5:1–6) are parallel in that each is introduced identically—"Come now" (*age nyn*)—and employs direct address. They differ in that 4:13–17 is a strong admonition, probably aimed at Christians, while 5:1–6 is an extremely harsh condemnation of the oppressive rich who are apparently not viewed as Christians. **13.** Although this verse may seem to introduce an abrupt change of subject, it may be considered as a development of the preceding question "Who are you?" **14.** *you do not know about tomorrow. What is your life?:* See Prov 27:1; Matt 6:34. The letter's complaint is not against trade and commerce as such, but against a false sense of security. *you are a mist:* This image of the fragility and transitory nature of human existence is common in the OT (Ps 39:6,7,12; Wis 2:1–5). *appears . . . disappears:* In Greek, this constitutes a play on words (*phainomenē . . . aphanizomenē*). **15.** *if the Lord wills:* Expressions similar to this famous *conditio Jacobaea* were in common use among the early Greeks and Romans. The formula does not occur in the OT or in rabbinic writings. It was apparently borrowed from pagan use and "christened" by NT writers. It is expressed in the common Muslim *inshallah.* **17.** This "advice to *méchants*" concludes with a pithy proverb, similar to Luke 12:47; John 9:41; 15:22,24. It is a more abstract expression of the truth that faith without works is dead (2:26).

30   (X) Woe to the Rich (5:1–6). See comment on 4:13–17. This severe denunciation of the unjust rich is reminiscent of OT prophets (e.g., Amos 8:4–8). It is not intended to influence the rich to whom it is rhetorically addressed, but is rather a salutary warning to the faithful of the terrible fate of those who abuse riches and perhaps also a consolation to those now oppressed by the rich (2:5–7). **1.** *miseries that are coming:* The loss of wealth (vv 2–3) and the dread judgment that will avenge their heartless injustices (vv 3–6). **2.** *have rotted:* The pf. tense of this and the two following vbs. probably indicates the present worthlessness of wealth. *garments:* These were a principal form of wealth in antiquity (see Horace, *Ep.* 1.6.40–44; Matt 6:19; Acts 20:33). **3.** *have rusted:* Although silver and gold do not actually rust, this expression indicates their basic worthlessness. *evidence against you:* The rust and decay of their possessions will be evidence that their owners failed to put them to good use at the service of the poor. *eat your flesh like fire:* The objects of accumulated wealth are, by metonymy, represented as instruments of vindictive punishment—no doubt, with allusion to "the Gehenna of fire" (Matt 5:22). *the last days:* In view of the allusion to the coming of the Lord in vv 7 and 9, James probably points out the absurdity of excessive concern for this age, since the last days are at hand (see Acts 2:16–17). Others understand it

to refer to the future judgment of wrath that the rich man has "stored up" for himself.
31 **4.** *wages of the laborers:* Denunciation of the withholding of wages or otherwise defrauding workers is an important theme in both OT and NT (see Lev 19:13; Deut 24:14; L. Johnson, *JBL* 101 [1982] 391–401; Davids, *James*). *to the ears of the Lord of Hosts:* These words are taken verbatim from Isa 5:9 LXX, which is in a context similar to that of Jas. **5.** *day of slaughter:* This phrase, taken from Jer 12:3, emphasizes the proximity of the eschatological judgment. It is ironic that their excessive indulgence makes the rich more vulnerable to coming torments. **6.** *killed the righteous man:* James may allude to Sir 34:22, "To take away a neighbor's living is to murder him; to deprive an employee of his wages is to shed blood." This climactic charge may likewise allude to Wis 2 and 3, in which the godless plot the destruction of the righteous poor (see esp. Wis 3:3–5:16). Finally, there may also be included here a reference to the death of Christ. *does he not oppose you?* The meaning is uncertain. Since the word *antitassetai*, "oppose"—rare in the NT—occurs also in 4:6, the verb in 5:6 may well be intended to evoke the earlier occurrence, where God is explicitly the subject, and thereby to unify and round off the intervening section (see L. Alonso Schökel, "James 5:2 [*sic*—read 5:6] and 4:6," *Bib* 54 [1973] 73–76).
32 **(XI) Patient Waiting for the Coming of the Lord (5:7–11).** **7.** *be patient:* The opening word sums up the whole section. It applies not only in the face of outrageous injustice (5:4–6), but in the ordinary trials of life (5:9,12,13,14,19). *the coming of the Lord:* The parousia of the Lord is often referred to in the NT (1 Thess 2:19; 4:15; 2 Thess 2:1,8,9; Matt 24:3; 2 Pet 1:16; 3:4,12; 1 John 2:28). Probably "the Lord" here means Christ, as elsewhere (thus Ropes, Chaine, Dibelius, Mussner, Law, Davids), rather than God the Father (thus *JB*; see vv 10 and 11). *the farmer:* Again James employs an imaginative illustration (see 1:6,11,23–24; 3:3–4,11–12). *the early and the late rain:* An OT expression used often in the enumeration of God's gifts (e.g., Deut 11:14). The importance of the early (October–November) and late (April–May) showers to the farmer was distinctive of Palestine and S Syria. James thus manifests an awareness of this aspect of Palestinian life. **8.** *be patient:* Repeating the opening precept of the section, James now applies the preceding illustration to his hearers. Is the object of patience only various sufferings, or is it also the delay in the coming of the Lord? Verses 7–8 seem to indicate the latter (see 2 Pet 3:3–13). *make firm your hearts:* See 1 Thess 3:13. *the coming of the Lord is near:* Other expressions of the nearness of the parousia occur in Phil 4:5; Heb 10:25,37; 1 John 2:18; Rev 22:10,12,20. In most of these cases, it is a motive of hope and strength amid present trials. Since parousia in the NT refers to the coming of the risen Christ, this passage is one of the few in Jas to present explicitly a specifically Christian doctrine (see 1:1; 2:1), one that clearly goes beyond the teachings of OT and contemporary Judaism. The extensive echoing, however, of sayings of Jesus and other parts of the NT identifies Jas as a thoroughly Christian document.
33 **9.** The exhortation changes rather abruptly to the theme of mutual relations in the community, harking back to 4:11–12 (see 1:19; 3:2–10). The coming of the Lord is now viewed as the coming of the judge. *may not be judged:* See Matt 7:1–2. *at the doors:* See Rev 3:20; Mark 13:29 par. **10.** *as an example:* Jas has already used OT characters as examples (Abraham and Rahab, 2:21–25); now the prophets are represented as martyrs (see Matt 23:29–31; Acts 7:52). The persecution of Christians is seen as a prolongation of that of the prophets in Matt 5:12 and 23:29–39. **11.** *we call those blessed who were*

steadfast: James has himself done this (1:12). Combinations of "blessed" (*makarios*) and "steadfastness" (*hypomonē*) occur also in Dan 12:12 (Theodotion); 4 Macc 7:22. *the steadfastness of Job:* Ezek 14:14,20 illustrates the fame of Job as an example of virtue, even independently of the book that bears his name. See also the apocryphal *Testament of Job. the outcome of which the Lord brought about:* This is the probable meaning of the compendious *to telos kyriou* (a Semitism—see Davids, *James*). It implies that the readers are familiar with the details of Job's trials, patience, and providential deliverance. *the Lord is compassionate and merciful:* An OT phrase: Exod 34:6; Pss 103:8; 111:4; 145:8. James departs from the LXX by introducing the word *polysplanchnos*, "compassionate," unattested in earlier Gk usage, but an apt rendering of the Hebr *rāḥûm* of the MT. In contrast to the self-sufficient virtue of Stoicism, Christian steadfastness is based on a conviction of the divine mercy and the hope of the coming of the Lord.
34 **(XII) Directions for Various Circumstances; End of Letter (5:12–20).** Three topics conclude the letter: instruction on oaths (5:12); on prayer (5:13–18); and on converting the wayward (5:19–20). **12.** *before all:* The Gk expression (*pro pantōn*) occurs in the closing section of some of the Hellenistic papyrus letters discovered in Egypt (see F. X. Exler, *The Form of the Ancient Greek Letter* [Washington, 1923] 110). This brief admonition is unconnected with what precedes and follows, except that the warning about falling under condemnation is similar to that of 5:9. However, Exler (*Form* 127–32) has pointed out that an "oath formula" often occurs in the concluding section of Hellenistic letters. *do not swear:* See Matt 5:33–37. Thought and expression are similar, although the Greek of Matt is more Semitic. In both passages, oaths are not absolutely forbidden, but only their abuse (see Sir 23:9–11). *let your yes be yes, your no be no:* James does not specify the mode of asseveration, as does Matt 5:37 ("Let your speech by 'Yes, yes' or 'No, no'"). It exhorts only to truthfulness. Thus, not the use of oaths, but untruthfulness is said to bring on danger of falling under judgment. If both Jas and Matt present variant forms of one original saying of Jesus, Jas's form of the "Yes–No" section is probably more original.
35 **13–18.** The topic of prayer, mentioned briefly in 1:5–8 and 4:2–3, is now developed into a well-organized and widely inclusive treatment. **13.** *is any one cheerful?:* Since suffering and cheerfulness, as general terms, may be considered to include the vicissitudes of human life, and since "singing praise" is a form of prayer, the advice here corresponds to the "pray at all times" of Eph 6:18. Joy and prayer are associated in Rom 12:12; 1 Thess 5:16–17. **14.** *sick:* The vb. *astheneō* is sometimes used of those near death (John 4:46–47; 11:1,4,14; Acts 9:37). *among you:* The reference is to members of the Christian community. *let him call for:* The man is sick enough to be confined to bed, but not yet *in extremis. elders of the church:* In the early Christian community, the *presbyteroi*, "elders," were closely associated with the apostles in authority (Acts 15:2,4,6,22–23; 16:4). Elders were likewise appointed over the missionary churches (Acts 14:23; 20:17; 1 Tim 5:17,19; Titus 1:5). Thus the term does not signify merely advanced age, but an official position of authority in the local church. *let them pray over him:* Prayer for healing in time of illness is recommended in Sir 38:9–10, together with repentance for sin. *anointing him with oil:* The use of oil as a therapeutic agent is found in the OT as well as in rabbinic literature and among the Greeks. A NT instance occurs in Luke 10:34. *in the name of the Lord:* Thus the anointing is not a mere medical remedy, but as in Mark 6:13, it symbolizes the healing presence and power of the Lord, i.e., of Jesus

Christ (cf. the baptizing "in the name of the Lord," Acts 19:5). **15.** *the prayer of faith:* Here again, no mere medical treatment is envisaged. *will save the sick one:* Elsewhere in Jas *sōzein,* "to save," refers to eschatological salvation of the person (1:21; 2:14; 4:12; 5:20). In the Gospels it is used both of salvation of the person and of restoration to health (see BAGD) and frequently in connection with "faith" (Mark 5:34 par.; 10:52 par.; Luke 7:50; 17:19; Rom 10:9). In the present context, the emphasis is on restoration to health. *the Lord will raise him up:* The same vb. is used of Jesus' cures in Mark 1:31; 9:27. As in v 14, "the Lord" probably refers to Christ, although in both cases the wording may have been adapted from Jewish expressions referring to God. *if he has committed sins:* In view of 3:2, the sins are apparently something more than the unavoidable faults committed by all. *will be forgiven him:* Physical healing and forgiveness of sins are closely associated also in Mark 2:3–12 and John 5:14. The wording of the former bears a strong resemblance to this passage.

36   The Council of Trent, Session XIV, defined Extreme Unction as "truly and properly a Sacrament instituted by Christ our Lord and promulgated by blessed James the apostle" (DS 1716; see 1694–1700). This is not to say that all the precisions of later sacramental theology are to be found in Jas. However, the following points are important with regard to the substantial identity of what James is here recommending with the sacrament of Anointing of the Sick in the church: the distinction from mere charismatic healing (1 Cor 12:9,28,30), as evinced by the cultic role of the *presbyteroi;* the anointing with olive oil; the invoking of the name of the Lord and the prayer of faith; the ensuing recovery and forgiveness of sins. It is also significant to note, as M. Dibelius points out, that, in accordance with his parenetic style, James is clearly not intending to introduce a new procedure, but presupposes its existence.

(Coppens, J., "Notes exégètiques: Jacques 5,13–15," *ETL* 53 [1977] 201–7. Cothenet, E., "La maladie et la mort du chrétien (Jc 5,13–16)," *EspV* 84/41 [1974] 561–70. Empereur, J., *Prophetic Anointing* [Wilmington, 1982].)

37   **5:16–18.** The connection with the preceding is obscure. Having spoken of the forgiveness of the sick person's sins, James seemingly turns to the members of the community in general, to remind them of how their sins are to be forgiven. The ideas of prayer and healing provide further appearance of continuity with the preceding. **16.** *confess your sins:* Confession of sins is an OT theme (Lev 5:5; Num 5:7; Ps 32:5; Dan 9:4–20; Ezra 9:6–15), also known in the NT (Matt 3:6; Acts 19:18) and the early church (*Did.* 4:14; *Barn.* 19:12; *1 Clem.* 51:3). *to one another:* This probably means "in the liturgical assembly," as in the *Did.* Since in the *Did.* and *Barn.* the confession of sins is considered a necessary preparation for effective prayer, the same relationship may be intended here. *pray for one another:* This basic Christian precept (implied in Matt 5:44 and in the petitions of the second half of the Lord's Prayer [Matt 6:11–13] and exemplified in Acts 12:5; Col 3:4; 1 Thess 5:25; 2 Thess 3:1; Heb 13:18, as well as in Paul's frequent assertions that he prays for his readers) is apparently given explicit formulation in Scripture nowhere outside of the present verse. In the present context, mutual prayer is probably to be understood as being motivated by the mutual confession of sins (as is now exemplified in the "penitential rite" at the opening of the Liturgy). *that you may be healed:*

In accordance with the intepretation that James is now addressing not merely the sick but the community in general, the word "heal" is to be understood in the spiritual sense of forgiveness of sins—a sense it bears elsewhere in the NT and in the Apostolic Fathers. A secondary reference to the healing of the sick may also be intended. *the fervent prayer of a righteous person is very powerful:* Others translate: "The prayer of a righteous person is powerful in its effects." The general idea is found in Ps 34:16,18; Prov 15:29. The intent of the verse is both to encourage confidence in the power of Christian prayer, and to exhort to fervor in its practice (see G. Bottini, "Confessione e intercessione in Giacomo 5,16," *SBFLA* 33 [1983] 193–226; F. Manns, "Confessez vos péchés les uns aux autres," *RSR* 58 [1984] 233–41.)

38   **17.** *Elijah:* The OT examples of Abraham and Rahab were used as models of good works (2:21–25), and Job as one of patience (5:11); Elijah is now presented as a model of efficacious prayer (see 1 Kgs 17:1,7; 18:1, 41–45). His role in connection with the famine is recalled also in Sir 48:2–3 and 4 Ezra 109. *a man like us:* The nuance of the Gk *homoiopathēs* is well expressed by the *NEB* paraphrase: "was a man with human frailties like our own." James anticipates the objection that the prayer of that heroic saint is to be admired rather than imitated. *he prayed fervently:* 1 Kgs narrates Elijah's prophecy of the drought and the rain, without stating that they were due to his prayer. James follows the tradition of Sir and 4 Ezra. *three years and six months:* This specification of the duration of the drought is more precise than 1 Kgs 18:1. It reflects a Jewish tradition found also in Luke 4:25, and probably connected with the apocalyptic "three and a half," the half of seven (Dan 7:25; 12:7; Rev 11:2,9; 12:6, 14; see G. Bottini, *La preghiera di Elia in Giacomo 5:17–18* [Studium Biblicum Franciscanum, Analecta 16; Jerusalem, 1981]).

39   **5:19–20.** Although this final passage, like several earlier ones, begins abruptly, there is continuity of subject matter in the themes of sin and forgiveness. **19.** *strays from the truth:* Alētheia here, as already in 1:18 and 3:14, and frequently in the Gospel and Epistles of John, has the OT sense of efficacious fidelity to God's word, rather than the Gk emphasis on intellectual comprehension of reality. **20.** *will save his soul* (= "person" or "self") *from death:* Spiritual and eschatological death is meant, as in Rom 5:12. Commentators differ as to the reference of "his": Is it to the sinner, or to the rescuer? In view of a probable influence of Ezek 3:20–21 and 33:9, it may very well include both. *will cover a multitude of sins:* The wording is very similar to 1 Pet 4:8. Probably both derive from a Jewish parenetic tradition based on Prov 10:12 (MT, not LXX). The "covering" of sins is a metaphor for forgiveness. (See Ps 32:1–2 LXX and its use in Rom 4:7–8.) The sins thus "covered" include those of the straying brother, but may also be understood more inclusively. Jas lacks a final epistolary salutation. But F. X. Exler (*Form* 69) has pointed out that a large number of official ancient Gk letters are found without any final epistolary salutation. The final verses of Jas serve well as a conclusion. In the threatening problems addressed in the letter, there is reflected the grim possibility of apostasy; but the opening note of joy in the beginning of the letter is recaptured in the concluding prospect of Christians, as doers and not mere hearers of the word, rescuing the endangered ones in a common hope of ultimate salvation.

59

THE EPISTLE OF JUDE

Jerome H. Neyrey, S.J.

BIBLIOGRAPHY

1 Bigg, C., *Epistles of St. Peter and St. Jude* (ICC; 2d ed.; Edinburgh, 1902). Ellis, E. E., *Prophecy and Hermeneutic in Early Christianity* (GR, 1978) 221–36. Eybers, I. H., "Aspects of the Background of the Letter of Jude," *Neot* 9 (1975) 113–23. Kelly, J. N. D., *The Epistles of Peter and of Jude* (London, 1969). Osborn, C. D., "The Christological Use of I Enoch i.9 in Jude 14–15," *NTS* 23 (1976–77) 334–41; "The Text of Jude 5," *Bib* 62 (1981)

107–15. Rowston, D. E., "The Most Neglected Book in the New Testament," *NTS* 21 (1974–75) 554–63. Wisse, F., "The Epistle of Jude in the History of Heresiology," *Essays on the Nag Hammadi Texts* (Fest. A. Böhlig; ed. M. Krause; Leiden, 1972) 133–43.

DBSup 4. 1285–98. Kümmel, *INT* 425–29. Wik-Schm, *ENT* 579–84.

INTRODUCTION

2 **(I) Authenticity.** The stated author is "Jude . . . brother of James" (v 1), who is presumably James, "the brother of the Lord" (Gal 1:19) and leader of the Jerusalem church (Acts 15:13–21). Jude is not the apostle Jude (Luke 6:16). Scholars judge this to be a pseudonymous letter because of (1) the late date of the letter (v 17 speaks of "the apostles of our Lord" as though they were figures of the distant past); (2) the sense of the formalization of "the faith, handed on once for all" (v 3), a characteristic of "early catholic" writings; (3) the excellent Gk style, not thought possible for a Jewish follower of Jesus; and (4) the convention in the later church of validating teaching by attribution to an early church personage.

3 **(II) Occasion, Purpose, Destination.** The author scores the presence of scoffers in the community (v 18) who contest central doctrines such as God's authority (v 4) and whose bad theology leads to immorality. Yet as F. Wisse notes ("Heresiology"), Jude's description of them is too general to allow us to reconstruct their heresy. As for the letter's occasion, an old prediction of false teachers is said to be fulfilled (vv 17–18), a convention invoked to magnify what Jude perceives as a crisis. This letter is addressed not to any specific church but to all churches, describing no particular heresy in a given church but alerting all the churches to a general problem. Nothing in Jude allows us to date it with any precision, so we are left regarding it as a pseudonymous letter expressing general concern at the presence of divergent viewpoints in the churches of the late 1st cent.

4 **(III) Type of Church.** As E. E. Ellis pointed out (*Prophecy and Hermeneutic*), Jude shows a remarkable knowledge of diverse materials, both documents and widespread traditional perceptions and expressions. It alludes to the *Assumption of Moses* (v 9), cites *1 Enoch* (vv 14–15), and quotes apostolic predictions (vv 18–19); Jude dips into Gen for examples (vv 5–7) and knows Jewish lore (v 11). This suggests a sophisticated church with rich resources which is in the process of affirming the consistency of a "faith given once for all" with both Christians and biblical materials. Nothing in Jude allows for a secure dating. Since it was used by 2 Pet, tentatively dated *ca.* AD 100, Jude must have been written earlier, probably in the 90s.

5 **(IV) Relationship of Jude to 2 Peter.** Since it is generally agreed that 2 Pet borrowed Jude's text, the issue of the close relationship of these two documents is best studied in the context of the commentary on 2 Pet (→ 2 Peter, 64:5).

6 **(V) Outline.** According to epistolary conventions Jude may be outlined as follows:

(I) Letter Opening (1–2)
(II) Occasion of the Letter (3–4)
(III) Judgment Warnings (5–15)
  (A) Past Judgments of God (5–7)
  (B) Declaration of God's Judgment (8–10)
  (C) Examples of Judgment (11–13)
  (D) Prediction of Judgment (14–15)
(IV) Sinners and Saints (16–23)
  (A) Traits of Sinners (16–19)
  (B) Characteristics of Saints (20–23)
(V) Letter Closing: Doxology (24–25)

COMMENTARY

7   (I) Letter Opening (1-2).   1. *Jude:* As servant
of Jesus Christ, Jude stands alongside other servants
such as Moses (Deut 34:5), David (2 Sam 7:5-29), Paul
(Phil 1:1) and Peter (2 Pet 1:1), and so he is an authorized, faithful agent of Jesus. *brother of James:* Jude claims
orthodoxy in virtue of his intimate relationship with a
"pillar of the church" (Gal 2:9). *called:* No specific church
is addressed, but "those who have been called" suggests
the catholic or universal intent of the document. The
church addressed is a well-defined group, clearly distinguished from other groups in the world: (a) "called by
God," therefore a specific group; (b) "loved," i.e.,
members of a covenant group; and (c) "guarded by Jesus
Christ," viz., insiders in Jesus' group. These group-
specific labels should be linked with other tags in the
document which dialectically serve to distinguish this
group from a heterodox group. *mercy, peace, and love:* An
increase of covenant love, community agreement, and
group solidarity is prayed for, an understandable prayer
in light of the evident division in the group (→ NT
Epistles, 45:8A).

8   (II) Occasion of the Letter (3-4).   3. *necessary:* The author highlights his role of expounder of the
faith with a sense of necessity to exhort them to strive
to defend the faith, a clear system of teachings. *delivered:*
A technical term for "tradition" (see 1 Cor 11:23 and
15:3). In a culture that accepts the past as normative,
appeal to the faith handed on once for all serves as a
claim for orthodoxy against novel teaching (see v 5; cf.
Mark 7:13). **4.** *stealthily entered in:* If the past was a time
of agreement, heterodox teachers did not belong from
the beginning, but sneaked in later like seducers or
thieves. Inasmuch as they are "destined from of old" for
appropriate judgment, their appearance was already
taken into account (see vv 17-18). *ungodly:* A synonym
for sinners (Prov 11:31; 1 Tim 1:9), who are always censured (Rom 1:18); judgment on these godless persons
will become a prominent theme in vv 15,18. *turn grace
into wantonness:* The worst vice is the perversion of grace
(see 2 Pet 2:20-22); although called and saved, the
heretics transform grace into sin. Typical of this culture,
the end result of bad theology is the fall from spirit back
into flesh, even into sexual debauchery (see Rom 1:24-
27). *disown our master:* As in 2 Pet 2:1, these heretics are
like the scoffers of the Psalms who either deny that God
knows what they do or imply that God is impotent to
judge them; lack of respect for the Lord's laws is perceived as "denial" of the Lord's power and jurisdiction.
It is not clear whether the heretics formally deny Jesus'
judgment or whether the author perceives this to be the
implication of their error.

9   (III) Judgment Warnings (5-15).   There is
less interest in refuting heterodox doctrine than in calling down judgment on its proponents. Jude appeals to
the Scriptures as well as other traditions as illustrations
of the coming judgment of the heretics.

        (A) Past Judgments of God (5-7).   5. *remind
you:* If the tradition of faith is a fact of the past, then
"remembering" it correctly becomes the premier task of
the church (see John 2:22; Luke 24:6). The scriptural
examples in vv 5-7 serve as proof against present sinners.
Echoing the warning in 1 Cor 10:5-13, Jude alludes to
examples of God's just judgment of the exodus generation. Freed from slavery and made God's holy people,
they sinned and were destroyed in the desert. **6.** *angels:*
They too fell from grace, from heaven to hell, from light

to gloom (Gen 6:1-4). The exemplary nature of these
references lies in the fact that they are already incarcerated, awaiting the Great Assize. *kept in chains:* A *quid-
pro-quo* principle underlies v 6; the angels did not keep
their place and so are "kept" by God in another place. **7.**
Sodom and Gomorrah: A third example emphasizes not so
much a fall from grace as simply crime and punishment:
Sodom indulged in the worst vices (homosexuality—
"going after other flesh" [Gen 19:4-8]—and fornication),
vices of which the author accuses the heretics in vv
4,8,12. *punishment of fire:* Destroyed by fire, Sodom can
serve as proof of the Lord's fiery judgment (see Matt
3:10; Mark 9:43-48), a judgment that is definitive and
never-ending.

**10   (B) Declaration of God's Judgment (8-10).
8.** *in like manner:* Verse 8 drives home the lesson of vv
5-7: the heretics are like those judged in the OT in terms
of (a) their crime (as did Sodom and the fallen angels,
these people "defile the flesh") and (b) their punishment.
They are "dreamers," a label used of false teachers in
Deut 13:1-5 and Jer 27:9. *disregard authority:* They deny
authority, probably Jesus' future judgment of sinners
(see v 4); this leads to sexual license, i.e., "defilement of
the flesh." Verses 4 and 8, then, form an *inclusio:*

Verse 4	Verse 8
A. sexual immorality	A. defile the flesh
B. deny our only Master	B. reject authority.

deride the glorious ones: A third sin; since "blasphemy" is
not the same as "defiling" the church's holiness, the
glorious ones are not the saints of the church (v 3).
Rather they are God's angels, the cherubim of glory
(Heb 9:5; *T. Levi* 18:5). Blaspheming God's angels
means denying the Lord and rejecting authority; so if the
heretics reject God's law and judgment, they deny as
well any mention of angels as givers of God's law or
agents of heavenly judgment (see v 14). **9.** *Michael . . . the
devil:* The argument in vv 9-11 may allude to As. Mos. (→
Apocrypha, 67:49). A glorious one, Michael, disputed
with Satan—a traditional cosmic battle situation (see
Dan 10:13; Rev 12:7). Michael's word is the point of the
allusion, a declaration of God's judgment: "The Lord
rebuke you" (cf. Zech 3:2). The scenario symbolizes the
situation of the author: like Michael, the author affirms
the Lord's judgment (see vv 5-7,11,14). Unlike Michael,
who did not "dare to pronounce a judgment on blasphemy," this author censures the heretics for their
"blasphemy" against all agents of judgment. As in v 8,
the example is brought home: as they blasphemed against
the glorious ones, so now they blaspheme against what
they do not know; vv 8,9, and 10 are stitched together
by the catchword "blaspheme." **10.** *dumb beasts:* Calling
his opponents ignorant and irrational, the author considers them less than human, "brute animals," whose
nature is to be captured or killed (or judged).

11   (C) Examples of Judgment (11-13).   11.
woe to them: Like the judgments in Isa 5:8,11,18 or Matt
11:23-24, a curse is pronounced upon these heretics.
This verse compares the heretics with three biblical sinners, a trio occasionally lumped together as "those who
have no share in the world to come" ('*Abot R. Nathan*
41). This comparison is in strict parallelism: "in the
manner of Cain . . . in the deceit of Balaam . . . in the
rebelliousness of Korah." Why these three? According to
tradition, Cain denied God's just judgment (see Gen
4:13; cf. "deny the Lord," v 4); Balaam, a prophet of

God, perverted his office to curse Israel for money (see Num 22–24; 31:16; cf. "swapping vice for grace," v 5); and Korah rebelled against Moses, God's legitimate authority in the covenant community (see Num 16; cf. "spurn dominion," v 8). As God punished this trio of sinners, so will he punish the heretics. **12.** *stains:* The view expressed here is quite similar to Paul's perspective in 1 Cor 5 of pollution corrupting a holy community: just as the sinful leaven corrupted a holy batch (1 Cor 5:6–8), these heretics are blots on the sacred meals and they act unscrupulously at its solemn feasts. *looking to themselves:* Like certain Corinthians, they ignore the group's holiness and integrity, looking only after themselves (see 1 Cor 13:5; 10:29; Phil 2:4,21). Divisiveness, then, is a threat to a whole and holy body (see 1 Cor 1:11–13). *clouds without water . . . unfruitful trees:* Balancing the previous comparison, four metaphors now label the heretics: clouds, trees, waves, and stars. The choice is determined by several factors: (a) the clouds are moistureless, the trees fruitless; and since by their fruits one shall know them, the heretics are sterile, fruitless, and condemned; (b) the clouds are "blown hither and yon," the waves dash "wildly," and the stars "wander," suggesting the heretics' maverick lawlessness and uncontrolled behavior; (c) the waves soil with foam, just as the heretics pollute (v 12); and (d) as the tree is uprooted and the stars are locked up, so a judgment will be pronounced on these sinners.
12   (D) Prediction of Judgment (14–15). 14. *Enoch:* The importance of Enoch lies in the content of his citation and its function in the argument. *1 Enoch* (1:9), like Mark 8:38 and 13:24, describes the Lord's coming with angels to judge sinners (see *AOT* 185; → Apocrypha, 67:7–15). Jude even claims that Enoch was "prophesying" against these very heretics, and so the citation functions as one more traditional judgment against Jude's opponents, alongside the biblical examples of judgment in vv 5–7,11. *the seventh:* I.e., the seventh generation from Adam (see Gen 5:18–23 for the biblical story of Enoch; cf. his position in the Lucan genealogy of Jesus [Luke 3:27; *FGL* 494, 503]). **15.** *impious:* Three times the heretics are called *asebeis,* which links this with previous charges of their godlessness (v 4) and with predictions of it (v 18). Godlessness connotes rebellion (Isa 1:28; see Korah in v 11) and lawlessness (see denial of authority and dominion in vv 4,8).
13   (IV) Sinners and Saints (16–23). The heretics are contrasted with the ideal members of Jude's holy church.
     (A) Traits of Sinners (16–19). In these verses we find a summary of the evils attributed to the heretics, juxtaposed to the list of the positive characteristics of the orthodox members of the group in vv 20–23. Two summaries of their vices (vv 16 and 19) form an *inclusio* around an apostolic prediction of their coming: (A) first list of evils (v 16), (B) prediction of such evils (vv 17–18), (A′) second list of evils (v 19). **16.** *murmurers:* So are the heretics (see Exod 15:24; 17:3):

disgruntled complainers, libertines, verbose flatterers; they do not fit into the regulated, obedient church. **19.** *spirit-less:* Hence fleshly sensualists and, worst of all, dividers of the one church (see 1 Cor 1:11–13; 3:3). **18.** *scoffers will come:* The presence of heretics is disturbing, but this is eased by remembrance of a conventional apostolic prophecy: the Lucan Paul predicted wolves attacking the church (Acts 20:29–30), as did Peter (2 Pet 3:3). Heresy, it is argued, does not belong in the ideal beginning of the church (see v 3), but creeps in later, "in the last days." The prophecy, then, functions as a conventional warning of troubled times, a way of labeling the opponents (scoffers, godless), and an appeal to hold to the early, correct tradition of the faith given once for all.
14   (B) Characteristics of Saints (20–23). 20. *you:* The faithful are described in stark contrast with the heretics. *holy:* Believers are holy in virtue of their correct faith and because they pray in the holy Spirit. Heretics do not have the Spirit (v 19) and are unholy or godless. **21.** *keep:* The faithful keep God's love, as opposed to those who do not keep God's grace and favor (vv 4,6a) and so are kept for judgment (vv 6,13). *looking for:* The saints wait for Christ's mercy by obeying God's law and by preparing for a divine audit (2 Cor 5:10), whereas heretics deny God's judgment (v 4). *life everlasting:* Jude's Christians enter eternal life, in contrast to the eternal darkness prepared for the wicked (v 13). **22–23.** How ought holy folk deal with the impious? Jude distinguishes between those who are remediable and those who are not (see 1 John 5:16–17). The former should be saved from the fire of judgment. The latter are another case: the church should deal "in fear" with them and hate contact even with their mere surface, either clothing or skin. Jude twice tells the church to "have pity on them." Later editors of this text read this as "convict them," which, while not the correct textual reading, conveys the sense of the injunction. Those being convicted are disputants (see v 9). They have soiled their clothing, an echo of v 12 that they are soiled people who soil the church.
15   (V) Letter Closing: Doxology (24–25). Like Rom 16:25–27, this letter closes with a doxology. **24.** *preserve:* The Christian God is the one God, who can guard us (see v 1). *without sin:* God guards us from stumbling, i.e., from lapsing from the true faith (see 1 Cor 10:32); God makes us stand, i.e., approach the divine judgment seat unhumbled and confident. God keeps us unblemished or sinless (1 Thess 5:23). **25.** *glory, majesty, dominion, authority:* Glory is regularly given to God, to which Jude attaches three other attributes — majesty, power, and authority — probably affirming what the heretics deny (see vv 4,8) and confirming the traditional doctrine of God's just judgment (see vv 5–7, 9,14–15). *before all time, now and forever:* It belongs to the true God to be both eternal in the past and everlasting in the future, a theological note found in Isa 41:4 as well as in Rev 1:4,8 and 4:8.

60

THE EPISTLE
TO THE HEBREWS

Myles M. Bourke

BIBLIOGRAPHY

1 Attridge, H. W., *Hebrews* (Hermeneia; Phl, 1989). Bonsirven, J., *Saint Paul: Epître aux Hébreux* (VS 12; Paris, 1943). Bruce, F. F., *The Epistle to the Hebrews* (NICNT; GR, 1964); "Hebrews," *IDBSup* 394–95. Buchanan, G. W., *To the Hebrews* (AB 36; GC, 1972). Grässer, E., "Der Hebräerbrief 1938–1963," *TRu* 30 (1964) 138–236. Héring, J., *The Epistle to the Hebrews* (London, 1970). Hughes, P. E., *A Commentary on the Epistle to the Hebrews* (GR, 1977). Kuss, O., *Der Brief an die Hebräer* (2d ed.; RNT 8/1; Regensburg, 1966). Manson, W., *The Epistle to the Hebrews* (London, 1951). Michel, O., *Der Brief an die Hebräer* (6th ed.; MeyerK 13; Göttingen, 1966). Moffatt, J., *A Critical and Exegetical Commentary on the Epistle to the Hebrews* (ICC; NY, 1924). Montefiore, H., *A Commentary on the Epistle to the Hebrews* (HNTC; NY, 1964). Spicq, C., *L'Epître aux Hébreux* (2 vols.; EBib; Paris, 1952–53); *L'Epître aux Hébreux* (SB; Paris, 1977). Strobel, A., *Der Brief an die Hebräer* (NTD 9; Göttingen, 1975). Vanhoye, A., *La structure littéraire de l'Epître aux Hébreux* (StudNeot 1; Paris, 1963). Westcott, B. F., *The Epistle to the Hebrews* (London, 1909). Windisch, H., *Der Hebräerbrief* (2d ed.; HNT 13; Tübingen, 1931).

DBSup 3. 1409–40. *IDBSup* 394–95. Kümmel, *INT* 388–403. Wik-Schm, *ENT* 542–62.

INTRODUCTION

2 **(I) Authenticity.** The identity of the author of Heb is unknown. With the exception of 1 John, it is the only NT epistle that begins without a greeting mentioning the writer's name. Its ascription to Paul goes back at least to the end of the 2d cent. in the church of Alexandria. According to Eusebius, it was accepted as Paul's work by Clement, who, in this matter, followed the view of Pantaenus. Clement believed that Paul had written it in Hebrew for Hebrews and that Luke had translated it into Greek (*HE* 6.14.2–4). Origen accepted its Pauline authorship only in a wide sense, for he remarked that "everyone who is able to discern differences of style" would not fail to see the dissimilarity with Paul's writings. He felt that the thoughts were Paul's, but "the style and composition belong to one who called to mind the apostle's teaching"; who that was, "God knows" (quoted by Eusebius; *HE* 6.25.11–14). The views of Alexandria influenced the rest of the East, and, ultimately, the West. Clement of Rome most probably used Heb in his epistle to the Corinthians (*ca.* AD 95; see chap. 36), but he gives no clue to its authorship. It is not listed in the Muratorian Canon (*ca.* AD 200; → Canonicity, 66:84). The earliest known view of its authorship is that of Tertullian, who ascribed it to Barnabas. However, by the end of the 4th cent. and the beginning of the 5th, the Western church had accepted it as Pauline and canonical. In 1516 Erasmus raised serious doubts about Paul's authorship, "probably the first" to do so "after Hebrews had been accepted into the canon" (cf. K. Hagen, *A Theology of Testament in the Young Luther* [Leiden, 1974] 23). That Paul is neither directly nor indirectly the author is now the view of scholars almost without exception. For details, see Kümmel, *INT* 392–94, 401–3.

3 The principal arguments against Pauline authorship are the differences of vocabulary and style from those of Paul, the different structure of the epistle (the interweaving of doctrine and exhortation), the different manner of introducing OT citations, and the author's usually observed rule of citing Scripture according to the LXX (with preference for the form of text represented by the Codex Alexandrinus [→ Texts, 68:96]). Although there are important theological differences from Paul, not all of these are such decisive arguments against Pauline authorship as is sometimes thought; e.g., the author's emphasis on Jesus' entrance into heaven rather than on the resurrection is evidently dictated by his concern with the heavenly priesthood of Christ. However, most of the reasons given for denying Pauline authorship are of such weight as to be compelling. Certain theological similarities between Heb and the Pauline letters (e.g., in respect to christology) do not necessarily point to an influence of Paul or of the Pauline kerygma on the author, for he and Paul could both have drawn on a common tradition (see Grässer, "Hebräerbrief" 186–88).

Among the reasons for thinking that the author was of Hellenistic background is his consistent use of the contrast between heavenly and earthly spheres of reality, the latter being understood as a mere shadow of the former. This is a Platonic conception, and although it has parallels in ancient Near Eastern sources, in the OT (Exod 25:9,40), and in apocalyptic Judaism (*T. Levi* 5:1) in respect to comparison between heavenly and earthly cult places (cf. G. W. MacRae, "Heavenly Temple and Eschatology in the Letter to the Hebrews," [*Semeia* 12 (1979) 179–99]), Heb's extensive use of the contrast between the eternal, stable, and abiding nature of heavenly reality and the transitory and imperfect nature of all that is outside that sphere has led many scholars to maintain that the intellectual world of the author was that of Middle Platonism, the same as that of the Hellenistic Jewish philosopher Philo of Alexandria (see S. Sowers, *The Hermeneutics of Philo and Hebrews* [Basel Studies of Theology 1; Richmond, 1965]; L. Dey, *The Intermediary World and Patterns of Perfection in Philo and Hebrews* [SBLDS 25; Missoula, 1975]; J. Thompson, *The Beginnings of Christian Philosophy* [CBQMS 13; Washington, 1982]). That may explain the many verbal similarities between Heb and the writings of Philo, although it is not probable that Heb depends on them directly (*pace* Spicq, *Hébreux* 2. 39–91). In any case, the author's strong historical concern with respect to the redemptive work of Christ, as well as his faithfulness to Judeo-Christian eschatology, makes a great difference between his understanding of OT fulfillment and Philo's philosophically oriented allegorism; see G. Hughes, *Hebrews and Hermeneutics* (SNTSMS 36; [Cambridge, 1979] 26): ". . . whatever echoes of Platonic ideas we may find in the author's conception of heavenly archetype and earthly copy, the fact is undeniable that the two covenants . . . also stand in sequential or horizontal relationship as earlier and latter."

Because the author was a Hellenistic Christian whose work has literary merit and shows acquaintance with the devices of Gk rhetoric, many since M. Luther have thought that he was Apollos (cf. Acts 18:24). The most that can be said for that view is that it is plausible; nothing speaks decisively in its favor.

Although hypotheses have been advanced about the loss of the original ending and of the later addition of chap. 13, the integrity of Heb is generally admitted; a few scholars still hold that 13:22–25 is an addition intended to give a Pauline touch to the work.

4   (II) The Addressees.   Heb's demonstration that the old covenant, specifically the worship of the old covenant, has been superseded by the sacrifice of Jesus is joined with exhortation against abandoning the Christian faith (e.g., 2:1–3; 3:12; 6:4–6). This makes reasonable the assumption that the epistle was meant for Jewish Christians, although many scholars propose a Gentile Christian group; and the view has even been put forth that the work was intended for a group of Jews who had broken with orthodox Judaism but were not convinced that Jesus was the Messiah. The arguments for the latter position are not persuasive, but Gentile Christian addressees may be supposed if the attraction to OT sacrificial worship manifested by those addressed can in fact be predicated of them, as it can be in the case of the Gentile Christian recipients of the *Epistle of Barnabas*. But whether the addressees were Jewish or Gentile Christians, the author's insistence on the imperfect and transitory nature of OT sacrifice is hard to explain on the view that it is "nowhere to be perceived" that "the readers evidenced an inclination to Judaism" (so Kümmel, *INT* 399). Although the question of the ethnic origin of the addressees can be left open without

prejudice to the view that their attitude toward OT sacrifice was seen by the author as a danger to their Christian faith, it is more likely that such an attitude would exist among Jewish rather than Gentile Christians. (For a valuable discussion of the theological varieties within different Jewish and Gentile Christian groups in the 1st-cent. church, see R. E. Brown and J. P. Meier, *Antioch and Rome* [NY, 1983] 1–9.) The title "To [the] Hebrews" is found for the first time in P⁴⁶ (Chester Beatty ms., 3d cent. [→ Texts, 68:179]). The often repeated observation that it was derived from what its author thought the content of the epistle to be (Wik-Schm, *ENT* 547) is most probably right, but the attempts to show that that was a wrong understanding are unconvincing to many scholars who hold that the title is an accurate deduction from the content.

For the view that Heb was addressed to former Jewish priests converted to Christianity (Acts 6:7), among whom some may even have been Essenes, and for affinities of Heb with QL, see Y. Yadin, ScrHier 4 (1958) 36–55; C. Spicq, *RevQ* 1 (1958–59) 365–90; cf. J. Coppens, *NRT* 84 (1962) 128–41, 257–82 (= ALBO 4/1).

5   (III) Literary Form, Date, and Place of Composition.   Because of its careful and involved composition and its major theme of the priesthood of Christ, Heb has been regarded as a theological treatise. However, the author's principal purpose was not to expound doctrine for its own sake, but to ward off the apostasy that was a real danger for those to whom he wrote. The work is called a "word of exhortation" (13:22), a designation that is also given to a synagogue sermon in Acts 13:15. Probably, Heb is a written homily to which the author has given an epistolary ending (13:22–25). Because there are references to "speaking" (e.g., 2:5; 5:11; 6:9; 9:5), some have suggested that the homily was intended for oral delivery. That is unlikely, and the ending, which is probably the original one, is clearly against that hypothesis.

The fact that the work was most probably used by Clement of Rome provides the *terminus ad quem* for the time of its composition. The references in 10:32–34 and 12:4 to persecution undergone by the addressees are too imprecise to be an indication of a particular persecution that can be dated with certainty. Some see a possible reference in 10:32–34 to the Neronian persecution of Roman Christians (AD 64) and find there support for dating the epistle around AD 85 (see R. H. Fuller, *A Critical Introduction to the New Testament* [London, 1966] 145). But since that passage says nothing about martyrdom, it hardly suits the suggested reference. Since in his description of the worship offered under the old covenant the author relies mainly on the OT account of the Mosaic tabernacle and its liturgy and does not mention the Temple of Jerusalem, the pres. tense used in describing that worship cannot prove that he wrote before the destruction of the Temple in AD 70 and that Temple worship was still going on at the time of writing. Many commentators favor a date later than 70, usually AD 80–90. But the reason for the author's speaking of the liturgy of the tabernacle rather than of the Temple is dictated by his purpose in writing. He wishes to show that the sacrifice of Jesus has replaced the OT sacrificial worship, and he refers to the latter in its most venerable and authoritative expression, the legislation of the sacred biblical text. As far as its value is concerned, whether it is still going on or has ended because of the destruction of the Temple is irrelevant. However, the destruction of the Temple would have been a confirmation of his position, and if he wrote after that event his silence about it is difficult to explain.

The greetings sent to the readers by "those from Italy" (13:24) have been taken as showing that Heb was written in Rome, but the text may mean no more than that people who were natives of Italy were in the author's company when he wrote. See F. V. Filson, 'Yesterday' (SBT 2/4; Naperville, 1967) 10–11; BAGD 87; cf. Grässer, "Hebräerbrief" 156. For a strong case for the Roman destination of the epistle, see Brown and Meier, Antioch and Rome [→ 4 above] 142–49.

6   (IV) Outline. The Epistle to the Hebrews is outlined as follows:

(I)   Introduction (1:1–4)
(II) The Son Higher than the Angels (1:5–2:18)
    (A) The Son's Enthronement (1:5–14)
    (B) Exhortation to Fidelity (2:1–4)
    (C) Jesus' Exaltation through Abasement (2:5–18)
(III) Jesus, Merciful and Faithful High Priest (3:1–5:10)
    (A) Jesus, the Faithful Son, Superior to Moses (3:1–6)
    (B) A Warning Based on Israel's Infidelity (3:7–4:13)
    (C) Jesus, Merciful High Priest (4:14–5:10)
(IV) Jesus' Eternal Priesthood and Eternal Sacrifice (5:11–10:39)
    (A) An Exhortation to Spiritual Renewal (5:11–6:20)
    (B) Jesus, Priest according to the Order of Melchizedek (7:1–28)
      (a) Melchizedek and the Levitical Priesthood (7:1–10)

      (b) The Levitical Priesthood Superseded (7:11–28)
    (C) The Eternal Sacrifice (8:1–9:28)
      (a) The Old Covenant, Tabernacle, Worship (8:1–9:10)
        (i)   The heavenly priesthood of Jesus (8:1–6)
        (ii) The old covenant contrasted with the new (8:7–13)
        (iii) The old covenant tabernacle (9:1–5)
        (iv) The old covenant worship (9:6–10)
      (b) The Sacrifice of Jesus (9:11–28)
        (i)   Sacrifice in the heavenly sanctuary (9:11–14)
        (ii) The sacrifice of the new covenant (9:15–22)
        (iii) The perfect sacrifice (9:23–28)
    (D) Jesus' Sacrifice, Motive for Perseverance (10:1–39)
      (a) The Many Sacrifices and the One Sacrifice (10:1–18)
      (b) Assurance, Judgment, Recall of the Past (10:19–39)
(V)   Examples, Discipline, Disobedience (11:1–12:29)
    (A) The Faith of the Ancients (11:1–40)
    (B) God's Treatment of His Sons (12:1–13)
    (C) The Penalties of Disobedience (12:14–29)
(VI) Final Exhortation, Blessing, Greetings (13:1–25)

(For another mode of outlining Heb, see A. Vanhoye, *Structure littéraire.*)

COMMENTARY

7   (I) Introduction (1:1–4). 1. *incompletely and in varied ways:* Some commentators see no difference between these two manners of designating God's speaking in times past and regard the expression as an example of hendiadys. However, it is more likely that each refers respectively to the fragmentary nature of the OT revelation and to the varied ways in which it was given. *the fathers:* The ancestors of Israel. This does not necessarily mean that the epistle was addressed to people of Jewish origin, for the same language is used in 1 Cor 10:1 to Gentile Christians. By their conversion to Christ, the descendant of Abraham, the Gentiles have been brought into the commonwealth of spiritual Israel (Gal 3:29). *the prophets:* Not only those whose message is preserved in the OT books bearing their names, but all in Israel's history through whom God spoke, e.g., Abraham (Gen 20:7), Moses (Deut 18:18), Nathan (2 Sam 7:2), and Elijah (1 Kgs 18:22). **2.** *in these, the last days:* Lit., "at the end of these days"; the Gk phrase translates in the LXX the Hebr *bě'aḥărît hayyāmîn,* "in the end of days." Here "these" is added to the LXX formula, which does not always mean the "end-time," the final age; but that is its usual meaning (cf. Isa 2:2; Jer 23:20; Ezek 38:16; Dan 10:14). The author of Heb, together with primitive Christianity in general, regarded the final age as inaugurated by the Christ-event, preeminently by Jesus' redemptive sacrifice (cf. 9:26), and he speaks of the Christians as those who have experienced "the powers of the age to come" (6:5). *through his Son:* Lit., "through a son," i.e., one who is Son. God's speaking through his Son is primarily the revelation of his saving purpose in respect to the human race through the coming of Jesus and the "eternal redemption"(9:12) achieved through his death and exaltation. "Christ is God's last word to the world; revelation in him is complete, final and homogeneous" (Moffatt, *Hebrews* 2). *heir of all things . . . through whom he created the worlds:* The Son's role as redeemer and mediator of creation. Although it comes at the end of the ages, the former is mentioned first. His being made heir

was not an event outside of time, previous to the incarnation; it took place when he entered glory after his passion (cf. Rom 8:17). The connection of "heir" with the "inherited" of v 4 shows that the Son's being made "heir of all things" is associated with his inheriting the "more excellent name" that he received after his humiliation (Phil 2:6–11). Yet he existed before he appeared as human: through him God "created the worlds" (*tous aiōnas*). The Gk word *aiōn* can mean either "world" or "age," but its use in 11:3 in connection with the creation of the universe suggests the former meaning here. Unless the pl. should be regarded as lacking significance (BDF 141.1), there appears here the conception of a number of worlds, the visible and the invisible, the latter being the several heavens (cf. T. *Levi* 3:1–9; 2 Cor 12:2; Heb 4:14; see J. Bonsirven, *Le judaisme palestinien* [2d ed.; Paris, 1934] 1. 158). J. D. G. Dunn (*Christology in the Making* [Phl, 1980] 51–56, 206–9) has argued that the designation of the Son as mediator of creation and the subsequent assertions of v 3 point to "the pre-existence perhaps more of an idea and purpose in the mind of God than of a personal divine being" (56). Against this, see J. P. Meier, "Symmetry and Theology in the Old Testament Citations of Heb 1,5–14," *Bib* 66 (1985) 504–33, esp. 531–33.

8   Many scholars think that vv 3–4 (some would include v 2) contain a liturgical hymn that the author has incorporated (cf. U. Luck, "Himmlisches und irdisches Geschehen im Hebräerbrief," *Charis kai sophia* [Fest. K. H. Rengstorf; Leiden, 1964]) 192–215), or at least the elements of such a hymn (cf. J. Jervell, *Imago Dei* [FRLANT 76; Göttingen, 1960] 198 n. 99); for criticism of this, see Meier, "Symmetry" 524–28. The description of the Son as mediator of creation assimilates him to the personified Wisdom of the OT (Prov 8:30; Wis 7:22), and this verse continues in that vein. He is the "refulgence" (*apaugasma*) of the Father's "glory" (Wis 7:26). *Apaugasma* can be understood either actively (radiance) or passively (reflection, refulgence); in view of the dependence on Wis 7:26 and of the following designation, the passive meaning is more likely here. *the very imprint (charaktēr) of his substance:* This recalls the further description of Wisdom as the "image" (*eikōn*) of God's goodness (Wis 7:26). *Charaktēr* probably means the same as *eikōn,* which is applied to Christ in Col 1:15 (see R. Bultmann, *TNT* 1. 132; E. Käsemann, *The Wandering People of God* [Minneapolis, 1984] 102-4). *supporting all things:* He guides and sustains all that has been created through him (cf. Col 1:17), just as Wisdom "reaches from end to end mightily and orders all things well" (Wis 8:1). *having made purification from sins:* Attention is now turned from the cosmological role of the preexistent Son to the redemptive work of the glorified Jesus. A similar juxtaposition is found in Col 1:15-20; in the OT, Wisdom's role is both cosmological and soteriological (Prov 8:22-36; Wis 9:9-18). *the Majesty:* A reverent periphrasis for God, like "the Power" of Mark 14:62 (for this Jewish usage, see Bonsirven, *Judaïsme* [→ 7 above] 1. 128-49). Jesus' enthronement "at the right hand" of God is seen in 1:13 as the fulfillment of Ps 110:1. This text is frequently used in the NT to describe the glorification of Jesus (Acts 2:34-36; Rom 8:34; Col 3:1; 1 Pet 3:22); see D. M. Hay, *Glory at the Right Hand* (SBLMS 18; Nash, 1973). That glorification is connected immediately with the resurrection, and no significance should be seen in the fact that Heb does not explicitly refer to the resurrection except in 13:20, for it is presupposed when Jesus' exaltation is mentioned (see O. Kuss, *Auslegung und Verkündigung* [Regensburg, 1963] 1. 320; Thompson, *Beginnings* [→ 3 above] 131 n. 15).

9   **4.** *made superior to the angels:* At his exaltation Jesus "inherited a more excellent name than they." In Semitic thought the name designated what a person was, and reception of a new name indicated some change in the person who received it. Here the name is "Son"; cf. O. Hofius, *Der Christushymnus Philipper 2, 6-11* (WUNT 17; Tübingen, 1976) 79; J. Dupont, "Filius meus es tu," *RSR* 35 (1948) 522-43. A. Vanhoye rightly points out that this cannot be concluded from vv 1-4 alone and that the fact that the name "Son" is "inherited" by Jesus at his exaltation becomes clear only from the following verse (see *Situation du Christ* [Paris, 1969] 93-148). That this receiving of a name at his exaltation is not to be understood in an adoptionist sense is well expressed by the statement of Hofius (cited above) that "the Son becomes as the Exalted One what he already is as the Pre-existent One." The reason for introducing Jesus' superiority to the angels is connected with the purpose of Heb: the addressees are in danger of falling away from the word of God spoken through his Son. The consequences of that would be fearful, much worse than the punishment received by those Hebrews who disobeyed the word spoken through angels (2:2), the Mosaic law, because the Son is superior to the angel mediators of the law. (For angels as mediators of the law, see Acts 7:53; Gal 3:19, Josephus, *Ant.* 5.15.3 §136.) However, the primary contrast that Heb draws between the old and the new covenant is that the latter has a new, superior priesthood, whose sanctuary is not on earth but in heaven (8:1-2). The priesthood of the old covenant with which that of the new is contrasted is the levitical priesthood; but the author may also have taken into account the Jewish conception that the ministering priests of the heavenly sanctuary were angels (cf., e.g., *T. Levi* 3:4-6; also *b. Ḥag.* 12b, where that function is ascribed to the archangel Michael). In emphasizing Jesus' superiority to the angels, he possibly has in mind the major concern of Heb, the heavenly priesthood of Jesus, and wishes to say that Jesus, and not an angel, is the priest who functions in the heavenly sanctuary (see H. Bietenhard, *Die himmlische*

Welt im Urchristentum und Spätjudentum [WUNT 2; Tübingen, 1951] 129 n. 1). Finally, these introductory verses of Heb have remarkable similarities with the writings of Philo, in which the Logos is the image (*eikōn*) of God (*De spec. leg.* 1.81) and the instrument through whom the universe was created (*De cher.* 127; *De sacr. Ab.* 8). The Gk word *charaktēr,* which occurs in the NT only in Heb 1:3, is frequent in Philo, used often of the human soul but also of the Logos (*De plant.* 18).

10   **(II) The Son Higher than the Angels (1:5-2:18).**

(A) The Son's Enthronement (1:5-14).   5. Jesus' superiority to the angels is now shown by a catena of seven OT texts. The first, Ps 2:7, belongs to one of the royal Pss celebrating, most probably, the enthronement of the king of Judah. According to 2 Sam 7:14, the second text of the catena, the relationship between God and the Davidic ruler was that of father to son; consequently the day of the king's accession to power was the day on which he was "begotten" as the son of God. The messianic interpretation of these texts, a result of the belief that the Messiah would be of the Davidic line, is found in the pre-Christian 4QFlor 1:11-13 (→ Apocrypha, 67:92), explicitly for 2 Sam 7:14, implicitly for Ps 2:7, since the Florilegium refers to vv 1-2 of that psalm, but the "Anointed One" of those verses is the one to whom v 7 is addressed. The author of Heb understood the "today" of Ps 2:7 as the day of the exaltation of the risen Christ (cf. Acts 13:33). **6.** The third quotation, a combination of Deut 32:43 LXX and Ps 97:7, is introduced by "he says" (for the justification of the transl. "he" rather than "it" [the book] and its significance, see M. Barth, "The Old Testament in Hebrews," *CINTI* 58-61). It is not certain to what event v 6a refers. Some scholars think that it is the parousia (Héring, *Hebrews* 9). If "again" is taken as modifying the verb ("when he again leads his firstborn into the world"), that interpretation receives strong though not conclusive support. However, "again" may be simply the introduction to a new scriptural argument, as in 1:5 (cf. 2:13; 10:30); the fact that it occurs within the temporal clause does not rule out that possibility (cf. Wis 14:1). In that case, the reference is probably to the exaltation of Jesus; the world into which he is led is the "world to come" that is made subject to him, and not to the angels (2:5). Since the incarnate Son was "for a little while made lower than the angels" (2:9), it is not probable that the birth of Jesus (cf. Montefiore, *Hebrews* 45) is meant.

11   **7.** The LXX wording of Ps 104:4 furnishes the author with a statement about the angels that serves to bring out their contrast with the Son. The meaning of the LXX text, different from that of the MT, is probably that God changes the angels into wind and fire, a concept found in 4 Ezra 8:21-22. This is well suited to the purpose of the author: the angels are mutable, transitory beings, unlike the Son, whose rule is everlasting. **8.** *your throne, O God:* This might be translated "God is your throne." Since the Son is seated at God's right hand (1:3,13), such a transl. would not suit the context; nor is it easy to see what it might mean. The principal reason for the author's quoting Ps 45:7 seems to be simply to bring out the permanence of the Son's kingdom. Of itself, the application of the name "God" to him is of no great significance; the Ps had already used it of the Hebr king to whom it was addressed. Undoubtedly, the author of Heb saw more in the name than what was conveyed by the court style of the original, but his understanding must be derived from what he has already said about the preexistent Son. The theme of the entire section suggests that what the author envisages is the Son's everlasting rule consequent upon his enthronement.

10–12. The next quotation, taken from Ps 102:26–28, attributes to the Son the work of creation; the Ps itself addresses these words to God. Since the author has spoken of the Son as the mediator of creation, that is not surprising. The permanence that the Ps attributed to God is here predicated of the Son: the heavens will perish, but he remains (cf. Isa 51:6). **13.** The final OT quotation is Ps 110:1, to which the author has already alluded in v 3. These words were not spoken to any angel. **14.** In contrast with the enthroned Son, the angels are only servants, "ministering spirits" (cf. Philo, *De virt.* 73). Perhaps the mention of their ministry being on behalf of human beings is directed against a tendency to regard them as proper objects of worship (cf. Col 2:18). See K. J. Thomas, "The Old Testament Citations in Hebrews," *NTS* 11 (1964–65) 303–25.

12 Some hold that vv 5–13 reflect a hymn in which, similarly to Phil 2:9–11 and 1 Tim 3:16, the stages of Jesus' exaltation are given in the order corresponding to that of ancient Near Eastern (esp. Egyptian) enthronement ceremonies (see J. Jeremias, *Die Briefe an Timotheus und Titus* [NTD 9; Göttingen, 1975] 27–29; F. Schierse, *Verheissung und Heilsvollendung* [MTS 9; Munich, 1955] 96 n. 100; Hay, *Glory* [→ 8 above] 86). The three stages of the ceremony are: (1) the elevation of the new king to divine status; (2) his presentation to the gods of the pantheon; (3) his enthronement and reception of kingly power. With the modification demanded by a monotheistic religion, that sequence is said to be discernible in these verses: (1) Jesus' elevation to the rank of Son of God whom the angels must adore (vv 5–6); (2) the proclamation of everlasting lordship (vv 7–12); (3) the enthronement (v 13). Against Heb's use of such a ritual pattern, see Meier, "Symmetry" [→ 7 above] 521 n. 55.

13   (B) Exhortation to Fidelity (2:1–4). Here the author passes from exposition to exhortation. The alternating transition from one to the other is characteristic of the epistle. The warning against apostasy (2:1–3a) is repeated several times in Heb, and the a fortiori argument in these verses is frequently used (cf. 7:21–22; 9:13–14; 10:28–29; 12:25; see Spicq, *Hébreux* 1. 53 for parallels in Philo). Here it is based on the inferiority of the "word spoken through angels" (the Mosaic law; see comment on 1:4) to that which the Christians have received. **3–4.** The salvation they are to inherit (cf. 1:14) had its origin in the word "spoken through the Lord" and "confirmed for us by those who had heard it." The author is clearly in the same position as those whom he is addressing in respect to knowing that word: he received it from witnesses. But the distinction between "us" and "those who heard" should perhaps not be pressed as an argument that the author and his contemporaries belonged to the second generation of Christians (see B. Hunt, *SE II* 410). The confirmation came not only through those who had heard but also through God's setting his seal on its truth "by signs, wonders, many kinds of miracles, and the gifts of the holy Spirit distributed according to his will." Signs and wonders are mentioned in Acts as confirmation of the apostolic preaching (4:30; 14:3; 15:12); the triad "miracles, wonders, signs" is the attestation given by God to Jesus himself (Acts 2:22) and is given by Paul as indication of his true apostleship (2 Cor 12:12).

14   (C) Jesus' Exaltation through Abasement (2:5–18). **5.** *the world to come:* It has been made subject to the glorified Son as the climax of an ascending movement that began in the humiliation of his earthly life, suffering, and death. (For the conception that the present world was under the dominion of angels, see Deut 32:8 LXX; Dan 10:13). **6–9.** The OT citation, Ps 8:5–7, is

introduced by the formula "Someone has testified somewhere." Its imprecision is due to the author's indifference to the human author of the text—all Scripture is the word of God. A similar mode of introduction is found in Philo (*De ebr.* 61). The Ps is also applied to Jesus in 1 Cor 15:27; Eph 1:22; and probably in 1 Pet 3:22. This use by such a variety of authors suggests that the application belonged to a common early Christian tradition of OT interpretation (see C. H. Dodd, *According to the Scriptures* [NY, 1953] 32–34). Possibly the origin of the application was that v 5 speaks of "the son of man." That expression is in synonymous parallelism with "man" of the previous line, but to Christians it would have recalled the designation of Jesus as the Son of Man (→ Jesus, 78:38–41). The Ps begins by contrasting God's greatness with the relative insignificance of human beings but proceeds to reflect on how great humans are in respect to the rest of creation; they are indeed "a little lower than the angels" but all else has been made subject to them. The author of Heb takes that asserted subjection as the starting point of his argument. At the moment "we do not yet see all things subject" to humanity, except in the case of Jesus, the Son of Man. **7.** *for a little while:* The Gk words (*brachy ti*) can mean either little in degree or little in time; the first is their meaning in the psalm, but Heb takes them in the second sense. Jesus was for a little while made lower than the angels, in the days of his earthly life, but now he is crowned with glory and honor; and all things, angels included, are subject to him. Here the author regards all things as already subject to Jesus in virtue of his exaltation; for the same conception, see Eph 1:22. Paul uses Ps 8 in 1 Cor 15:25–27 with a different meaning: Jesus' reign has begun, but the subjection of all things (specifically, of "all [his] enemies") will not be complete until his final triumph at the parousia. That view is found also in Heb 10:13, although there Ps 8 is not used in connection with it. Since the supremacy and triumph of Jesus can be regarded from different perspectives, the two views are not incompatible; and it is not surprising to find both held by the same author. **9.** *in order that he might taste death on behalf of everyone:* This is a purpose clause, but what is meant by saying that Jesus was crowned with glory and honor in order that he might taste death etc.? H. Strathmann's opinion that the crowning refers not to Jesus' exaltation but to his consecration as high priest in preparation for his sacrificial death (*Der Brief an die Hebräer* [NTD 9; Göttingen, 1968] 85) is difficult to accept in view of the preceding part of the verse in which Jesus' crowning appears to be the consequence of his having suffered death ("because of the suffering of death"); cf. also 5:4–5, where his honor and glory as high priest are connected with his exaltation; and 12:2. J. Héring suggests that the purpose clause should be understood as connected with the phrase "because of the suffering of death," as explanatory of the latter (*Hebrews* 17); see also the discussion in P. Hughes (*Hebrews* 90), where v 9 is seen as chiastically constructed, with the purpose clause (the fourth element in the chiasmus) connected in sense with the first ("who for a little while was made lower than the angels"). *by the favor of God:* This reading (*chariti theou*) has excellent ms. attestation and fits in well with v 10, which speaks of God's initiative in Jesus' saving work. However, a few mss. read *chōris theou,* "apart from God." In spite of its poor attestation this may be correct, on the principle that the more difficult reading should be preferred, especially since a scribe might easily have changed it through theological scruple. It expresses Jesus' feeling of abandonment in death (cf. Mark 15:34). *taste death:* A Semitism for experiencing death (cf. Mark 9:1).

15   **10.** *it was fitting:* This use of the argument *ex convenientia* in regard to God is "an innovation in the Bible" (Spicq, *Hébreux* 2. 36), although it occurs often in Philo (e.g., *Leg. alleg.* 148; *De conf. ling.* 175). *for whom and through whom all things exist:* This concept of God as the Creator in whom all that he has made finds its purpose is found also in 1 Cor 8:6 and Rom 11:36. *in bringing many sons to glory, to make their leader to salvation perfect through suffering:* The Gk ptc. *agagonta,* "in bringing," probably refers to God, although some apply it to Jesus ("to make perfect through suffering their leader to salvation, the one who brings many sons to glory"). The argument for the latter interpretation is based on the fact that the ptc. is in the acc. case, whereas the pron. referring to God ("it was fitting for him") is in the dat. But this is not conclusive (see ZBG § 394; BDF 410). The tense of the ptc. is best explained as an ingressive aor. indicating the starting point of God's action (Michel, *Hebräer* 148; Héring, *Hebrews* 18-19). The designation of Jesus as leader announces an important theme of Heb: the journey of the people of God to the place of rest (4:11), the heavenly sanctuary, in the footsteps of Jesus, their "forerunner" (6:20). R. Bultmann sees this as related to the gnostic motif of the soul's journey to the world of light (*TNT* 1. 177), as does E. Käsemann (*Wandering* 87-96, 128-33). *to make perfect:* The Gk vb. *teleioō,* "make perfect," occurs nine times in Heb, three of which have to do with Jesus' being made perfect (2:10; 5:9; 7:28). It is used in the LXX of priestly consecration, translating a Hebr phrase, "to fill [the hands]" (Exod 29:9,29,33,35; Lev 16:32; 21:10; Num 3:3); for the corresponding noun "perfection" (*teleiōsis*), see Lev 8:33. This cultic notion of perfection is certainly present in Heb (see G. Delling, "*Teleioō,*" *TDNT* 8. 82-84; M. Dibelius, *Botschaft und Geschichte* [Tübingen, 1956] 2. 106-76; Vanhoye, *Situation* [→ 9 above] 325-27). But Jesus' priestly consecration involved his obedience learned through suffering (5:8-10) and his being perfected means also that through that obedience he was brought "to the full moral perfection of his humanity" (Westcott, *Hebrews* 49). D. Peterson argues for a "vocational" understanding of the concept of perfection in Heb, meaning by that Jesus' being qualified, through the sufferings of his obedient life and death and through his exaltation, to be the source of salvation for those who obey him; and he maintains that although "hints" of "cultic perspective" are given in 2:11-12, they are "not sufficient to demand a cultic understanding of perfection in 2:10" (*Hebrews and Perfection* [SNTSMS 47; Cambridge, 1982] 72). But he goes on to say that "the transition to the presentation of the work of Christ in high-priestly terms at 2:17 is highly significant" (p. 73). Do not those terms throw light on the meaning of 2:10? **11.** *for he who consecrates and those who are consecrated:* Jesus is the one who consecrates. The Gk vb. *hagiazō,* "consecrate," is, like "make perfect," a cultic term; cf. Exod 28:41; 29:33. Jesus' being perfected as high priest enables him to perfect his people (cf. 10:4 [where the terms "make perfect" and "consecrate" are used together]; 11:40; 12:23). "Through Christ's priestly consecration the believers themselves are perfected and consecrated" (Dibelius, *Botschaft* 2. 172). The author of Heb emphasizes the uniqueness of Jesus' priesthood and does not attribute to his followers what is uniquely his. But the common element of the two consecrations is that each brings about the possibility of access to God. As high priest, Jesus has entered into the Holy of Holies (9:12), into heaven itself, there to appear before God on our behalf (9:24); the believers are able confidently to make their entrance after him and draw near to God (7:19). *all have the same father:* Lit., "are all of one." Most commentators identify God as the "father"; others, Abraham (cf.

2:16), but the argument suggests that Adam is meant (cf. O. Procksch, "*Hagiazō,*" *TDNT* 1. 112). It is not true that there is an implication that "Christ's common tie with mankind goes back to the pre-incarnate period" (Moffatt, *Hebrews* 32); the incarnation of the Son is what makes human beings his brothers (cf. 2:14). Because he has associated himself with them by becoming "blood and flesh" as they are, he is able to be their high priest (2:17). The basis of the argument is that he is able to help them because he shares their lot and is one of them, i.e., because like them he is a son of Adam. *he is not ashamed to call them brothers:* Because he shares the nature of those whom he has consecrated. **16**   **12-13.** Three OT texts are now cited that show the union between the Son and those he came to save. The first is Ps 22:23, taken from a psalm widely applied in the early church to Christ in his passion (cf. Matt 27:43,46; Mark 15:34; John 19:24). The Ps belongs to the "individual lament" category; in v 23 the "certainty of hearing" motif, common to that category, begins. The author of Heb places the sufferer's joyous praise of Yahweh upon the lips of Jesus. Probably the principal reason for doing so was the use of "brothers" in that verse, but it is not an exaggeration to say that the author thinks of the praise given to God by the glorified Christ "in the midst of the assembly (*ekklēsia*)" of those whom he has consecrated. The second and third citations are from Isa 8:17 and 18, respectively. The purpose of the second is not clear. If one accepts Dodd's view that when OT texts are cited in the NT the reference is not simply to the verse(s) cited but to their context (*According to the Scriptures* [→ 14 above] 61), the reason for the citation may be that Isaiah was stating his confidence in the truth of the divine oracles that most of the people had rejected. Similarly here, the exalted Christ is presented as looking forward to the vindication of his work, the significance of which is not apparent now except to those who believe in him (cf. 10:13). However, it seems unlikely that that is the point of the citation; at this stage of Heb the author is dealing with the solidarity existing between Jesus and his followers. It is more probable that he wishes to present Jesus as an example, in his mortal life, of that confidence in God that is necessary for those whom he has consecrated and who are now in need of a like confidence in order that they may not "slip away" (2:1). The third citation is surprising for it seems to mean that the believers are children of Jesus. Such a concept is found nowhere else in the NT (John 13:33 and 21:5 are not exceptions). Various are the attempts to accept that meaning and to explain satisfactorily its peculiar usage (see Bruce, *Hebrews* 48; Michel, *Hebräer* 154). The children are God's own, or, more likely, Adam's; "the same father" (2:11) is Adam rather than God. In either case, there is a departure from the meaning of the OT text, where the children are Isaiah's. **17**   **14.** *since the children have blood and flesh in common, he likewise shared them:* In the biblical sense, "flesh" means human nature considered in its weakness and frailty, and as such it is contrasted with "spirit" and God (cf. Pss 56:5; 78:39; Isa 31:3; 2 Chr 32:8). The expression "flesh and blood" meaning human beings occurs in the OT only in Sir 14:18; 17:26; for the NT, cf. Matt 16:17; Gal 1:16; Eph 6:12. Here the author speaks of human nature under the ban of death and sees death as associated with the devil. It is difficult to think that he does not relate that notion with the story of the fall and that he does not stand in a tradition that saw a connection between death and the sin of Eden (Sir 25:23; 4 Ezra 3:7; *2 Apoc. Bar.* 23:4). Consequently, one must question the view of E. Schweizer that in Heb the concept of flesh is never linked with the thought of sin ("*Sarx,*" *TDNT*

4. 142). *that . . . he might destroy him who holds the power of death, that is, the devil:* The conception that death was no part of God's plan for human beings and that it had been brought into the world by the devil was held in Hellenistic Judaism (Wis 1:13; 2:23–24). Because of that connection between sin and death, the power of death was broken when Christ through his high-priestly work removed sin (2:17). The paradox that death was nullified by Christ's death is similar to that of Rom 8:3, where Paul says that God condemned sin by sending his Son "in the likeness of sinful flesh." The author gives no reason beyond saying that it was fitting for God to act thus.

18 **15.** *free those who through their whole life were slaves because of the fear of death:* This fear of death should not be regarded as the natural fear that is generally experienced by human beings. (Nor is there any suggestion that the freedom meant is freedom from a constraint to do evil in order to avoid death [so Bruce, *Hebrews* 51].) It is, rather, a religious fear based on the belief that death is a severance of one's relations with God (cf. Isa 38:18; Ps 115:17–18) but also on a proper recognition that death, because connected with sin, is more than a physical evil (cf. 1 Cor 15:26, where death is the "last enemy" to be destroyed by Christ). The fear that Jesus felt at the prospect of death (cf. 5:7) can be explained only by his realizing the latter better than anyone else. But by his death the way to unending life with God was opened to all who obey him. **16.** *for certainly he does not take hold of angels, but of the descendants of Abraham:* The vb. *epilambanetai* is taken as a reference to the incarnation by C. Spicq (*Hébreux* 2. 46), following many patristic commentators. The entire section deals with the incarnation, but it seems that this verse has a wider reference. The vb. *epilambanomai* is used in 8:9 (in a citation of Jer 31:32 [LXX 38:32]) with the meaning "to take hold of" a person in order to help him, which may well be the meaning here. The pres. tense suggests a continuing help rather than the single event of the incarnation. Abraham's descendants are those who believe in Christ. **17.** *that he might be a merciful and faithful high priest:* This is the first mention of the central theme of Heb: Jesus' role as high priest. In designating him as "faithful," the author follows a tradition that demands that quality of a priest (cf. 1 Sam 2:35), but that he must be "merciful" is a notion peculiar to Heb. When the motif of the high priest's mercy is taken up again in 4:15 and 5:1–3, it is based, as here, on his solidarity with human beings. Nothing in the OT tradition emphasizes that quality; it is probably derived from the author's reflection on the manner of Jesus' earthly life, suffering, and death. In respect to mercy, Christ did not fit into a preconceived definition; rather, the definition (5:1–3) was based on the author's knowledge of what Jesus had been. *that he might expiate the sins of the people:* The Gk vb. *hilaskesthai,* "expiate," occurs frequently in the LXX, where it usually translates Hebr *kippēr.* It expresses the removal of sin or defilement, by God or by a priest through the means set up by God for that purpose (see C. H. Dodd, *The Bible and the Greeks* [London, 1935] 82–95; → Pauline Theology, 82:73–74); Dodd's view that the word does not also express the idea of "placating" the wrath of God, i.e., the idea of "propitiation," has been contested; cf. L. Morris, *The Apostolic Preaching of the Cross* (GR, 1955) 125–85; D. Hill, *Greek Words and Hebrew Meanings* (SNTSMS 5; Cambridge, 1967) 23–48. **18.** The temptations (testings) of Jesus, which have qualified him to help those undergoing temptation, were not only the prospect of the sufferings of his passion but the temptations experienced throughout his life (4:15; Luke 22:28). Gospel tradition indicates that fidelity to his mission was a principal object of

temptation (Matt 4:1–11; Luke 4:1–13; cf. J. Dupont, *NTS* 3 [1956–57] 287–304). The temptation of those here addressed was to apostasy, fundamentally the same urge to infidelity that he experienced.

19   (III) Jesus, Merciful and Faithful High Priest (3:1–5:10).

(A) Jesus, the Faithful Son, Superior to Moses (3:1–6). The author now begins a consideration of Jesus' mercy and faithfulness in inverse order to that stated in 2:17. **1.** *holy brothers who share a heavenly calling:* Christians are "holy" because they are consecrated by Jesus, and "brothers" because of their common relation to him (2:11). They are called to follow him into the heavenly sanctuary where he now functions as high priest on their behalf. *fix your eyes on Jesus:* The vb. is an ingressive aor. The danger of falling away from Christianity is due to forgetfulness of what Christ has done for them; now he must be constantly in their spiritual vision. *the apostle and high priest:* This is the only place in the NT where Jesus is called "apostle." The meaning is that he is the one sent by God, as his final word to human beings (1:2). Since the author's interest is principally in the work of Jesus as priest rather than in his teaching, the word-event is the primary reference. That may account for the omission of the article with "high priest"; the two titles probably constitute a unity (K. Rengstorf, "*Apostolos,*" *TDNT* 1. 423–24); not precisely, however, as Rengstorf conceives the unity (apostle-revealer-word :: high priest-expiator-work). *whom we confess:* Lit., "of our confession." Here for the first of three times (cf. 4:14; 10:23), the author speaks of a *homologia,* "confession," made by those whom he addresses. He probably refers to a baptismal acknowledgment of Jesus as Son of God (note the baptismal tone of the context). His teaching on Jesus as "apostle and high priest" is meant as a new interpretation of what Christians have confessed at their baptism (cf. G. Bornkamm, *Studien zu Antike und Christentum* [BEvT 28; Munich, 1963] 188–203; Michel, *Hebräer* 173). However, the author's concern here is not with the content of the confession, but with its power to give his addressees strength and support in their trials (cf. V. Neufeld, *The Earliest Christian Confessions* [NTTS 5; GR, 1963] 133–37).

20   2. The comparison between Jesus and Moses is probably due to Jesus' being mediator of the new covenant (9:15) as Moses was of the old. Moses' mediatorship was not unconnected with priesthood and sacrifice; his sacrifice at the time of the establishment of the covenant is recalled in 9:19–20, although the designation "priest" is not given to him in Heb. When the author deals with Jesus' sacrifice, the OT antitype is not Moses but the Aaronic high priest in his function on the Day of Atonement (9:6–15). However, Philo speaks of Moses' high priesthood (*Quis rer. div.* 182; *De praem.* 53), and possibly the author thinks of this when he makes the Jesus–Moses contrast here. *who made him:* This is not a reference to the origin of Jesus but to his appointment to office (cf. Schierse, *Verheissung* [→ 12 above] 109). The vb. is used with that meaning in 1 Sam 12:6, "The Lord . . . who made Moses and Aaron. . . ." Moses' faithfulness "in all his [God's] house" is derived from Num 12:7; this section has been called a midrash on that verse (Montefiore, *Hebrews* 72). While seeing an allusion to that text here, M. R. D'Angelo considers that the OT text cited is 1 Chr 17:14 LXX, and that the citation is "a deliberate reference to the Nathan oracle" (*Moses in the Letter to the Hebrews* [SBLDS 42; Missoula, 1979] 69); that view is rejected by E. Grässer (*ZNW* 75 [1984] 15 n. 66). The "house" of God in which Moses was a faithful servant is Israel.

21   3. *as the builder of a house has greater honor than* *the house:* If this verse and the following were not present and vv 5 and 6 followed v 2 immediately, Jesus' superiority over Moses would seem to be sufficiently indicated: Moses was the faithful servant in God's house (v 5), Christ is the faithful Son over the house (v 6). Yet v 3 is closely connected with the different positions stated in vv 5–6. Moses as servant in the house (Israel) was part of the house; Christ as Son over it was, together with God, its builder. As preexistent Son, he shared in God's creative work (1:2–3); cf. Kuss, *Hebräer* 49; O. Michel, "*Oikos*," *TDNT* 5. 126–27. For a similar view ("Jesus as Son . . . belongs to the family of the builder"), see W. Loader, *Sohn und Hoherpriester* (WMANT 53; Neukirchen, 1981) 77–78. **4.** *every house is built by someone, but he who built all is God:* Some scholars understand v 4b as a parenthesis (Héring, *Hebrews* 25; Moffatt, *Hebrews* 42; Spicq, *Hébreux* 2. 67), yet it seems that, only if one extends the parenthesis to the entire verse and understands it not as an "edifying aside" (Moffatt) but as demanded by the argument, the author's thought flows naturally. The house of v 2 is God's house, but in using Num 12:7 the author has changed the possessive pron. from the first to the third pers. ("my house" to "his house"). This change, made necessary by the transfer from the direct discourse of the OT, could be misinterpreted; "his house" might be misunderstood as Moses' house rather than God's. To avoid that misunderstanding and thus to reinforce the argument of v 3 that Moses was not the one who built it but merely part of that house, the author recalls him who did built it—God, who built all things. **5.** *as a servant, to witness to what would be spoken:* It is not Moses' role as mediator of the old covenant and as lawgiver that is emphasized here; rather, Moses is the one who foretold the Christian dispensation. *what would be spoken:* I.e., through God's Son (1:2; 2:3). **6.** The "house" is the Christian community. Its continuity with ancient Israel is indicated by the fact that there are not two houses but one; the old continues in the new. (For the metaphor of the Christians as "the house of God," see 1 Tim 3:15; 1 Pet 4:17; Eph 2:19; as "the temple of God," see 1 Cor 3:6; in QL, see 1QS 8:5–9; 9:6). For the full implication of Christ's being the Son who is "over" the house, see comment on v 3. *if we hold fast our confidence and pride in what we hope for:* The majority of mss. add "firm to the end," but this is not found in B or P⁴⁶ and appears to be an interpolation derived from v 14. Although the Gk *parrhēsia*, "confidence," might mean "boldness" and point to open acknowledgment of the faith in the face of danger and trial (Montefiore, *Hebrews* 73), Heb's exhortations to faithfulness do not seem to be motivated by the danger of persecution, calling for bold confession, but rather by the danger of "drifting away" (2:1), which calls for confidence.

22   (B) A Warning Based on Israel's Infidelity (3:7–4:13). 7. *the holy Spirit:* The spirit of God, inspirer of the Scriptures, speaks through them. Trinitarian concepts should be not read into the expression. The verse begins a section of warning based on Israel's experience during the wandering. The argument rests on the early Christian concept of the redemption wrought by Christ as a new exodus. In the OT the exodus had served as a symbol of the return of the Jews from the Babylonian Exile (Isa 42:9; 43:16–21; 51:9–11); in the NT the redemptive work was regarded as a new exodus, experienced first by Jesus himself (Luke 9:31) and then by his followers (1 Cor 10:1–11). The addressees are still en route to the goal of their exodus: the heavenly sanctuary, where Jesus has gone before them (6:20). They have grown weary and are in danger of discontinuing their journey. Hence the warning lest they, like those

Hebrews who rebelled against God, fail to achieve the goal. The quotation in vv 7b–11 is from Ps 95:7b–11, but it differs in many ways from the LXX reading. The principal difference is that whereas the LXX (and the MT) connect the "forty years" (v 10) with God's anger, it is here taken with the previous phrase, "they saw my works," although in v 17 the LXX order is followed. The reason for the transposition is not clear. **9.** *your fathers tested:* Cf. Exod 17:7; Num 20:2–5. **11.** Cf. Num 14:1–23. *my rest:* The land of Palestine; cf. Num 20:12; Deut 12:9. Käsemann sees Heb's motif of the journey of the people of God to their appointed rest as a gnostic theme (*Wandering* [→ 8 above] 67–75; against this, see C. Colpe, *Die religionsgeschichtliche Schule* [FRLANT 78; Göttingen, 1961]), but the OT counterpart seems to be an adequate explanation of the source on which the author of Heb drew. (For the view that Heb is not concerned with Israel's journey as such but solely with the refusal of the Hebrews to enter the promised land because of their fear of being slain by the inhabitants [Num 14:11–12,21–23,27–35], see O. Hofius, *Katapausis* [WUNT 11; Tübingen, 1970] 116–46; similarly Strobel, *Hebräer* 112). **12.** *the living God:* The designation of God as "living" means that he manifests himself in his works (cf. Josh 3:10; Jer 10:10). The expression "to apostatize from the living God" is frequently taken as indication that Heb was written not to Jewish Christians in danger of relapsing into Judaism, but to pagan converts; for a return to Judaism would not, it is argued, be called an "apostatizing from the true God." However, the author speaks not of the true God simply, but of the true God as living, i.e., acting, and specifically manifesting himself in Christ. To fall away from Christianity, then, is apostasy from the living God, even if it should be a return to Judaism, where the supreme act of God is ignored. **13.** *while it is still today:* The author anticipates what he will say in 4:2–11. The "rest" into which Israel was to enter was only a foreshadowing of that rest to which the addressees are called; and it is still open to them provided that they persevere in the faith with which they began their lives as Christians. *we have become partners of Christ:* Probably the participation means sharing the common destiny of entering the heavenly sanctuary.

23   16–19. Cf. Num 14:1–38; Deut 1:19–40. Because they were fearful at the prospect of battle with the Canaanites, the Hebrews refused to go into the land of Canaan. In punishment, the Lord decreed that all except the scouts Caleb and Joshua and those who had been born since the departure from Egypt would die in the desert and never enter the promised land. The author emphasizes the connection of disobedience (v 18) and unbelief (v 19). **4:2.** *the gospel has been preached to us as it was to them:* Because the promise to the Hebrews of entering Palestine foreshadowed the promise given to Christians of entering heaven, the author uses NT terminology to describe what Israel had heard; it was "gospel." **3–4.** The "rest" of God is seen in deeper dimension than Palestine. Ps 95:11 calls that land God's rest ("my rest") because it was the place of rest that he would give his people (against G. von Rad, who sees the spiritualization of the concept in the psalm itself; see *Gesammelte Studien zum Alten Testament* [Munich, 1965] 101–8). The author understands it as a share in the rest upon which God entered after the work of creation had been completed. Those who are faithful will enter into God's abode, described here as a place of rest rather than as the heavenly sanctuary (the author's usual designation) or as the lasting city (13:14).

24   6–9. The author attempts to read his meaning of God's rest into the psalm. The Hebr noun for "rest"

in Ps 95:11 is *měnûḥâ* and is different from the vb. "rest" in Gen 2:2 (*šābat*), but the LXX uses a word derived from the same Gk stem in each case: *katapausis* (Ps 95:11) and *katapauō* (Gen 2:2). Hence the author of Heb finds a basis in the text of the psalm for his interpretation. He argues that what was promised to the Hebrews was not Palestine, but a share in God's own postcreation rest; cf. the Jewish concept that the sabbath, which reflects that rest, is "the image of the world to come" (*Gen. Rab.* 17 [12a]). Because of unbelief many of the Hebrews of the exodus period were excluded from that rest, and even those who did enter Palestine under Joshua (v 8) did not enter into the promised rest, which is something greater than the promised land. (Since the Gk form of "Joshua" is the same as that of "Jesus," the name itself brings out both the similarity and the contrast between the OT figure, who led the Hebrews into Palestine, and Jesus, who leads his followers into the heavenly rest of God). If that were not so, then God would not still be offering the promise long after Palestine had been occupied. Yet he does do, as "David's" injunction to the Israelites of his day shows. This injunction is also addressed to the Christians: "Today if you hear his voice, harden not your hearts" (Ps 95:7–8). Because the promise is still good, "there still remains a sabbath rest for the people of God" (v 9), a share in the sabbath rest of God himself.
25   **11.** *let us strive to enter:* Although the vb. *spoudazō*, "strive," may also mean "hasten," the context does not suggest the latter meaning. There is no thought of hurrying into the rest, but rather of persevering in the effort needed to achieve it. **12–13.** These two verses continue the warning to persevere, for the Word of God judges rightly, since nothing is unknown to it; in its light, those of the present generation will be judged worthy or unfit to enter God's rest. **12.** *the word of God:* This refers to v 7. It is the Word that speaks to human beings, inviting them to belief and perseverance. It is a saving Word, but also one that judges, since it condemns those who refuse to hear it. *living and effective:* The Word is described in a way calculated to bring out its efficacy: it produces life (cf. Deut 32:47) and it achieves its purpose (cf. Isa 55:10–11). It does not seem that the author intends more than a personification of the Word, although some would see here a reference to the Word of God incarnate in Jesus (cf. H. Clavier, "*Ho logos tou theou* dans l'épître aux Hébreux," *New Testament Essays* [Fest. T. W. Manson; ed. A. J. B. Higgins; Manchester, 1959] 81–93; R. Williamson, *ExpTim* 95 [1983–84] 4–8). *sharper than any two-edged sword:* Cf. Isa 49:2; Prov 5:4; Wis 18:16. The penetrating power of the Word is described in Philonic language (cf. *Quis rer. div.* 130–31), but in that context Philo is not speaking of its power in respect to judgment, as is the case here. *soul and spirit:* Some see here the conception of the human being as composed of body, soul, and spirit (E. Schweizer, "*Pneuma,*" *TDNT* 6. 446); it is difficult to agree with F. F. Bruce that "it would indeed be precarious to draw any conclusions from these words about our author's psychology" (*Hebrews* 82). These human components, like the correlative "joints and marrow," are intimately connected, and the statement that the Word is sharp enough to separate them is made simply to emphasize its penetrating power. *able to judge the reflections and thoughts of the heart:* The author attributes to the Word that knowledge of human beings which only God has (cf. Acts 1:24; 15:8). **13.** *bare and exposed:* The Gk ptc. *tetrachēlismena*, "exposed," is related to the noun *trachēlos*, "neck." The context suggests that it is synonymous with "bare," but none of the explanations of how it came to have that meaning is really satisfactory. The Gk words of the last phrase of this verse may mean "about whom

we are speaking," or "to whom we must render an account." The latter is better suited to the context. Williamson (see comment on v 12) thinks it probable that the meaning is "with whom the Logos (Word) is present on our behalf," and he compares the phrase to John 1:1.
26   **(C) Jesus, Merciful High Priest (4:14–5:10). 14–16.** These verses recall 2:16–3:1 and prepare for the development on Jesus' priesthood that follows. **14.** *great high priest:* This is the only place in the epistle where Jesus is so designated; usually the author speaks of him as high priest or simply priest; it may be that he wishes to emphasize here Jesus' superiority to the Jewish high priest, with whom he constantly compares him. The same designation is used by Philo for the Logos (cf. *De somn.* 1. 214,219). *who has passed through the heavens:* See comment on 1:2; also *2 Enoch* 3–20. *let us hold fast to our confession:* See comment on 3:2. **15.** *tempted in every way as we are, although he did not sin:* The only difference that the author remarks between Jesus' temptations and those of his followers is that he never succumbed to them. **16.** *the throne of grace:* The throne of God (cf. 8:1; 12:2). The reign of the exalted Jesus is a theme of Heb, as the frequent use of Ps 110:1 shows, and in 1:8 the author speaks of Jesus' throne. But the similarity of this verse and 10:19–22 shows that the author is thinking of the confident access to God that has been assured by the redemptive work of Jesus: "Through Jesus Christ, the true high priest, God's throne has become the throne of grace" (Michel, *Hebräer* 209–10).
27   **5:1.** *to offer gifts and sacrifices for sins:* Some think that "gifts" refers to grain offerings and "sacrifices" to animal offerings, but probably the author did not intend any such distinction. As appears later (chap. 9), the Day of Atonement rite is the OT type with which he is principally concerned; it is an atonement for "sins," rather than for "sin" (cf. Lev 16:30,34); hence the pl. here. **2.** *he is able to deal gently with the ignorant and erring:* The Gk word *metriopathein*, "deal gently," does not occur elsewhere in the Bible; it corresponds to a term of Stoic philosophy signifying "the right mean between passion and lack of feeling" (Michel, *Hebräer* 217). The designation of sinners as "the ignorant and erring" does not mean that the author was thinking only of those who were not aware of the sinful nature of their deeds or who committed less serious moral offenses or ritual violations. The only sins for which sacrificial atonement was impossible were those designated in Num 15:30 as sins committed "with a high hand." Those sins are probably sins perpetrated of set purpose, rather than those into which one "fell" through human weakness (see H. H. Rowley, *BJRL* 33 [1950–51] 74–100); so "the ignorant and erring" seems to mean all sinners except those who sin "with a high hand." *since he is himself subject to weakness:* The weakness is principally that which leads to sin, as v 3 shows (cf. Lev 16:6). **6.** Although Ps 110:1 is frequently used in the NT of the exalted Jesus, v 4 (here quoted) is used only in Heb (cf. also 7:17,21).
28   **7–8.** Just as v 6 shows how the requisite of a call from God to the high priesthood is verified in Jesus, these verses show that he is qualified as one who can sympathize with sinners. The author does not use here the word "weakness" of Jesus and later specifically contrasts him with the Jewish high priest in that respect (7:28). It is important, however, to notice that the contrast applies to the present exalted state of Christ. The reason for avoiding the word here is probably that in v 3 weakness and sin are made correlative, and it is clear that Jesus did not sin (4:15). There is no doubt, however, that the author, while avoiding the word, does consider that Jesus' ability to sympathize with sinners is based

precisely on the fact that he knew temptation, as they do, and "shared in blood and flesh" (cf. 2:14–18; 4:15). He was acquainted with the trials of human nature, i.e., he experienced its weakness, particularly its fear of death. After his exaltation, he no longer knows weakness, but having experienced it he can sympathize with those who do. This concept of Heb is similar to that of Paul: "He died on the cross through weakness, but he lives through the power of God" (2 Cor 13:4). **7.** *in the days of his flesh:* I.e., the time of his mortal life, when he lived in the sphere of the flesh. *he offered prayers . . . to him who was able to save him from death:* If this be taken as a single incident, it is probably a reference to Gethsemane (cf. Mark 14:35–36). Apart from John 12:27, there is no single incident in the Gospel tradition that is similar to it, and the view that the author knew of "a number of incidents in the life of Jesus" not found in the Gospel narratives to which he might also be referring (Bruce, *Hebrews* 98) is at best conjectural. Apart from that proposal, Bruce also sees, together with the Gethsemane reference, "a more general reference to the whole course of our Lord's humiliation and passion (*Hebrews* 100; similarly, A. Vanhoye, *Prêtres anciens, prêtre nouveau selon le Nouveau Testament* [Parole de Dieu 20; Paris, 1980] 146–47). *heard because of his reverence:* R. Bultmann ("*Eulabeia*," *TDNT* 2. 753) accepts A. von Harnack's emendation of the text, "He was not heard," because Jesus did die. But that purely conjectural reading is unnecessary if one supposes that the author takes Jesus' deliverance from death as a reference to his resurrection. Since the prayer of Jesus in Gethsemane was that he might be kept from dying rather than be rescued from death once he had undergone it, the author uses "save from death" with a double meaning. The justification for that supposition is that the context deals with Jesus' priesthood (it is even possible that 5:7–10 reflects a hymn to "Jesus the High Priest" [cf. G. Friedrich, *TZ* 18 (1962) 95–115]). In 7:23–24 his priesthood is contrasted with that of the levitical priests precisely insofar as they were prevented by death from remaining in office, whereas Jesus has a priesthood that does not pass away, in virtue of the "indestructible life" that he received in his resurrection. His death was essential for his priesthood, but if he had not been saved from death by the resurrection, he would not now be the high priest of his people. **8.** *Son though he was:* See comment on 1:4. The author considers Jesus' sonship in two ways: he became Son when exalted; he always was Son because he existed with the Father even before he appeared on earth. (In terms of later theology, the resurrection–exaltation gave Jesus' human nature full participation in his divine nature.) The two concepts are entirely compatible, but apparently that of the preexistent Son was arrived at later, as the relative lateness of the texts in which it is expressed shows. However, if the hypothesis is correct that 5:7–10 is in substance an ancient hymn, similar to Phil 2:6–11, the lateness of the concept must not be exaggerated. There is no reason to regard the later concept as more congenial to the author of Heb than the former, as R. H. Fuller does (*The Foundations of New Testament Christology* [NY, 1965] 187). *he learned obedience from what he suffered:* The learning-through-suffering motif is common in Gk literature, but this text, Rom 5:19, and Phil 2:8 are the only places in the NT where the obedience of Christ in his passion is explicitly mentioned. **9.** *when perfected:* See comment on 2:10. *the source of eternal salvation . . . obey him:* Jesus' obedience leads to his priestly consecration, which in turn qualifies him to save those who are obedient to him. The expression "source of salvation" is common in Philo (*De agric.* 96; *De virt.* 202; *De vita contemp.* 86), but it is not distinctively

Philonic. The salvation that Jesus brings his followers is eternal because it is based on his eternal priesthood (7:24–25). With the exception of 6:2, the cases where the author uses "eternal" (here and in 9:12,14,15; 13:20) have to do with realities that endure because they belong to the heavenly sphere, which is characterized by permanence, as opposed to the transitory realities of earth. **29**   **(IV) Jesus' Eternal Priesthood and Eternal Sacrifice (5:11–10:39).**

(A) An Exhortation to Spiritual Renewal (5:11–6:20). The central section of Heb begins with a long exhortation that is at the same time a rebuke. Jesus' priesthood is a difficult subject to treat; all the more so because those who are addressed have become listless and forgetful of even elementary Christian truths. **11.** *about which we have much to say and it is difficult to explain:* The antecedent of the rel. pron. is not certain. There are three possibilities: Jesus, Melchizedek, and Jesus' designation as high priest according to the order of Melchizedek. As the neut. transl. indicates, the last has been chosen here. **12.** *although you should be teachers by this time:* This has been used as an argument that Heb was addressed to converted Jewish priests (cf. Acts 6:7); their position in the Christian community should be similar to that which they held in Judaism (see Spicq, *Hébreux* 1. 228). But the function of teacher in Judaism was not particularly associated with the priesthood. In any case, the notion that those who are advanced should be teachers of others is so well attested that no background of previous teaching position before conversion need be supposed (see Moffatt, *Hebrews* 70; D. Peterson, *Hebrews and Perfection* [→ 15 above] 178, 286 n.4). *you need someone to teach you again the basic elements of God's oracles:* The Gk word *stoicheia*, "elements," has none of the pejorative sense that it has in Gal 4:3,9 (cf. Col 2:8,20); here it means elementary, but necessary, teaching, beyond which the addressees should long since have passed. The expression "God's oracles" is used in Rom 3:2, where it probably means the OT Scriptures; here it includes God's speaking in the OT and, preeminently, his speaking through his Son (1:2). *of milk not of solid food:* The contrast between milk and solid food as metaphorical designations of teaching suitable for the spiritually immature and mature, respectively, is found also in 1 Cor 3:1–3 and is common in Philo. The words that Paul uses in 1 Cor to designate either class (children— the perfect) are also found here (vv 13–14). **13.** *no experience of the word of righteousness:* He has not come to an appreciation of the deeper aspects of Christian belief. It is possible, however, that the expression continues the child metaphor and means that one in such a state is not able to speak intelligibly ("has no experience in the right way of speaking"). H. P. Owen has suggested a third possibility: the expression means "a principle of righteousness," i.e., a standard whereby one exercises moral judgment (*NTS* 3 [1956–57] 243–53). He finds in these verses not two stages of the Christian life, but three, and thinks that this standard, gained by asceticism, belongs to the second stage. **14.** *solid food is for the perfect:* For Owen, "the perfect" are those in the second stage of Christian life, the practice of virtue, which results in the ability to discern what is morally good, to have a "principle of righteousness." "By a series of correct moral choices he builds up a moral standard" (p. 244). Such people may then proceed to the third stage, the assimilation of advanced doctrine, which is like solid food.

30   **6:1.** *therefore . . . move towards perfection, not laying again the foundation:* Since the author has just declared his addressees in need of instruction in the rudiments of doctrine (5:12), it is strange that he now not only proposes to pass over these and give teaching for the mature, but that his proposal begins with the conjunction "therefore." H. Kosmala solves the difficulty by proposing that 5:11b–14 are a later addition, which in their sharpness of tone and loosely connected construction do not suit either the context or the style of the author (*Hebräer-Essener-Christen* [SPB 1; Leiden, 1959] 17–21). This radical treatment has no mss. support. Of the various explanations given for the author's paradoxical method, the best seems to be that he considers that nothing less than the challenge offered by difficult doctrine (5:11) will serve to move the addressees out of their spiritual lethargy. "The originality of Hebrews is to emphasize intellectual progress as a condition for moral perfection" (Spicq, *Hébreux* 2. 146). He now mentions six elementary teachings: repentance from dead works, faith in God, teaching about ritual washings ("baptisms"), laying on of hands, the resurrection of the dead, and eternal judgment. The list probably comes from a traditional catechism and is not meant to be exhaustive. **31** Kosmala holds that there is nothing specifically Christian about the catechism. "The Christ" in v 1 does not mean Jesus, but simply "the Messiah," and the six teachings are only those accepted by a group that expects the coming of the Messiah. A closer inspection of the points would indicate that the group in question was the Qumran sect and that the addressees, prospective converts to Christianity, already believed in the teachings (*Hebräer* [→ 30 above] 31–38). However, it is doubtful that a non-Christian catechism, or any part of it, would have been designated by the author of Heb as the foundation of Christian life, even when belief in its contents might be presupposed in those who turned to Christianity from the group that followed it. In any case, if the exegesis of "instruction about baptisms" given below is correct, it is impossible to regard the teachings merely as a Jewish sectarian foundation of Christian belief. *repentance from dead works and faith in God:* Repentance and faith are, respectively, the negative and positive sides of the first response of humanity to God's word. (For a similar coupling of these correlatives, see Mark 1:15.) Dead works do not mean the works demanded by the Mosaic law, but sins that lead to spiritual death and from which the conscience needs cleansing (cf. 9:14). A similar expression is found in 4 Ezra 7:49 [119], "deeds that bring death." **2.** *instruction about baptisms:* The Gk word translated "baptisms" is not *baptisma* (probably of Christian coinage and regularly used in the NT for Christian baptism and that of JBap) but *baptismos*, which in the two other instances of its occurrence in the NT means Jewish ritual washings; 9:10; Mark 7:4 (Josephus uses it in reference to the baptism of John; see *Ant.* 18.5.2 § 117). That fact, as well as the word's being used in the pl., shows that here it does not mean simply the Christian sacrament. As a water rite, that sacrament could be so designated; hence the reason why instruction about ritual washings would have formed part of Christian catechesis seems to lie in the necessity of instructing converts about the difference between the Jewish washings (including proselyte baptism, the baptism of John, and the water purifications of Qumran; cf. 1QS 3:4–9) and the Christian sacrament (cf. A. Oepke, "Baptismos," *TDNT* 1. 545; R. Schnackenburg, *Baptism in the Thought of St. Paul* [NY, 1964] 8–9). O. Michel remarks that "since the plural is unusual in the language of the Church, it must be understood as polemic" (*Hebräer* 239). **32** In P⁴⁶ and B "instruction" is read in the acc. (*didachēn*), a reading accepted by G. Zuntz (*The Text of the Epistles* [London, 1953] 93) and other scholars. This reading might suggest that "instruction" is in apposition to "foundation," as Montefiore thinks (*Hebrews* 105; also Bruce, *Hebrews* 110 ["probably in apposition"]). If the

foundation is simply repentance and faith in God, then the content of the "foundation" and that of the "instruction" are quite different, a fact that argues against regarding the two nouns as being in apposition. One should either follow the gen. reading (*didachēs*), "of instruction," and see that as part of the foundation, or, accepting the acc. reading, take the "instruction" as different in content from the foundation, although similar insofar as each deals with the rudiments of Christian life. **33** *laying on of hands:* This rite is mentioned in Acts 8:17; 19:6 (in connection with the coming of the holy Spirit) and in Acts 6:6; 13:3; 1 Tim 4:14; 5:22; 2 Tim 1:6 (in connection with the conferral of some ministry or mission in the church). Presumably what is meant here is the rite connected with the giving of the Spirit. (For discussion of the relation between the rite and the coming of the Spirit, see J. Oulton, *ExpTim* 66 [1955] 236–40; D. Daube, *The New Testament and Rabbinic Judaism* [London, 1956] 224–46). *resurrection of the dead and eternal judgment:* The last pair of rudimentary truths concerns the eschatological term of the Christian life. The judgment is "eternal" because it is definitive (cf. Matt 25:46). **3.** *and this we shall do, God permitting:* Evidently the author means not that he will "lay the foundation again," which he has said that he will not do (v 1), but that he will now pass on to the doctrine suitable for the mature. He is not suggesting that he will deal with the rudiments later; the verses that follow exclude that possibility. **4–6.** These verses have created much difficulty, for they deal with the impossibility of repentance after apostasy. Many attempts have been made to avoid their apparent import, e.g., the suggestion that so far as human experience is concerned, apostates are beyond the possibility of repentance, although nothing is said of what may happen if they receive an extraordinary grace (cf. Bruce, *Hebrews* 118) or that "they are normally indisposed for penance" (B. Poschmann, *Penance and the Anointing of the Sick* [NY, 1964] 13). "Such interpretations go against the plain meaning of the Greek and the whole tenor of the author's argument" (Montefiore, *Hebrews* 109). Kuss thinks that the absolute statement should be judged in the light of the author's pastoral concern: he speaks in an exaggerated manner in order to set his readers firmly against apostasy (*Hebräer* 199–201); similarly C. Carlston (*JBL* 78 [1959] 296–302). **34** **4.** *for it is impossible, when men have been once enlightened and have tasted the heavenly gift and have become sharers in the holy Spirit:* The ptcs. in vv 4–5 are all aor., and *hapax,* "once," probably modifies them all, not simply the first. It is disputed whether there are direct sacramental references here or whether these four experiences of the Christian refer simply to one's coming to the faith. The designation of baptism as "enlightenment" and of the baptized as the "enlightened" is at least as early as Justin Martyr (*Apol.* 1.61.12; 65.1), and it is possible that "enlightened" here refers to the reception of that sacrament (cf. Bornkamm, *Studien* [→ 19 above] 190; Käsemann, *Wandering* [→ 8 above] 187–88). In support of that view, cf. Eph 5:14, which is probably a fragment of a baptismal hymn (or "cult saying"; so H. Schlier, *Der Brief an die Epheser* [Düsseldorf, 1958]; cf. discussion in J. Gnilka, *Der Epheserbrief* [HTKNT 10/2; Freiburg, 1971] 259–63). However, the enlightenment spoken of here may mean simply the illumination given by faith in Christ (2 Cor 4:6). In 1QH 4:5, the covenant is a light by which God illumines the face of his disciple, and Philo speaks of the divine commandment as enlightening the soul (*De fuga et inv.* 139). Nor should the possible influence of Ps 34:6 be overlooked, where the LXX (Ps 33:6) reads "Come to him and be enlightened." Such influence is suggested also because the author of Heb goes on to speak of those who "have tasted the heavenly gift," and v 9 of that psalm speaks of tasting how good the Lord is. In any case, the single-event nature of the tasting makes it unlikely that tasting the heavenly gift means receiving the eucharist, although the expression has been so interpreted (Héring, *Hebrews* 46; J. Betz, *Die Eucharistie in der Zeit der griechischen Väter* [Freiburg, 1961] 2. 156–57. "Taste" is a common metaphor for "experience" and the phrase probably means only that Christians have experienced the power of the salvation brought by Jesus (cf. Rom 5:15; 2 Cor 9:15). This gift is termed heavenly because it is an eschatological reality possessed in an anticipatory manner by the believer. "Sharers in the holy Spirit" means those who possess the Spirit as a guarantee of the full possession of the eschatological blessings in the future (cf. 2 Cor 1:22; Eph 1:14, where the Spirit is called the *arrabōn*, the "first installment").

35   5. *and have tasted the good word of God and the powers of the age to come:* The preaching of the gospel was accompanied by manifestations of the presence of the Spirit (cf. 2:3–4; 1 Cor 2:4). This activity of the Spirit is seen as indication of the presence even now of the "age to come." This designation of the eschatological future is contrasted with "this age" in both apocalyptic and rabbinic Judaism (see Bonsirven, *Judaïsme* [→ 7 above] 1. 312). In late Judaism, the "tasting of the powers of the age to come" was attributed to Abraham, Isaac, and Jacob (Str-B 3. 690), but there is a profound difference between the two conceptions. What Judaism believed to be the privilege of a chosen few is a common Christian experience; but even more important, the age to come, while absolutely future in Jewish thought, is a present reality for the Christian, though not yet realized in its fullness. 6. *they are crucifying for themselves the Son of God and holding him up to contempt:* A vivid portrayal of the malice of apostasy, which is conceived of as a crucifixion and mockery of the Son of God. The apostates' rejection of the Christian faith means that "they put Jesus out of their life . . . he is dead to them" (Moffatt, *Hebrews* 80). 7–8. The sharp warning ends with a comparison between two kinds of ground. Each drinks in the rain sent by God, but one bears fruit and is blessed; the other bears thorns, verges on being cursed, and finally is burned. The application to the faithful Christian and the apostate, respectively, is obvious.

36   9. *beloved . . . we are persuaded of better things in your regard:* With this verse the tone of the exhortation becomes mild. For the first and only time in Heb the addressees are called "beloved." It is difficult to agree, however, that the author does not believe that there are even potential apostates among his readers (so Bruce, *Hebrews* 126); the purpose of his writing is to avert a danger that is very real. The new approach seems to be dictated by the belief that his purpose may be best achieved by mildness and, more important, by the fact that in spite of their lukewarm faith there is one sign that gives reason to hope that the calamity of their apostasy may not take place. That sign is their charity to their fellow Christians, of which v 10 speaks. 10. *he will not forget your work and the love you have shown for his name by your service:* The services that they rendered in times past are mentioned in 10:33b–34a. Such services are fundamentally a manifestation of love for God. Here and in 13:24 the author uses the common early Christian designation of those who believe in Christ, "the saints." 11. *the same zeal in respect to persevering:* Their zeal for works of charity should be matched by their zeal in persevering in their Christian vocation, a perseverance founded upon hope. 12. The author begins a theme that he will develop in chap. 11. His readers should imitate

the confident faith of the holy ones of the OT, "who are inheriting the promised blessings." The reference does not seem to be to any other persons than those mentioned in chap. 11, although Montefiore thinks that the author "points to the example of contemporaries" (*Hebrews* 112). This exegesis is presumably based on the fact that the pres. ptc. of "inherit" is used here. Yet since the Gk *epangelia* can mean either the promise itself or the thing promised (see J. Schniewind and G. Friedrich, "*Epangelia,*" *TDNT* 2. 582 n. 59), the author seems to be saying that the OT holy ones, who did not receive the promised blessings during their lifetime (11:13), are now in possession of them (see comment on 11:40). The fact that he passes on to the case of Abraham confirms the view that he means not contemporaries of the addressees, but those of whom he will speak in chap. 11.

37   13. *he swore by himself:* Cf. Philo, *Leg. alleg.* 3.72. The secure basis for hope is God's promise, confirmed by his oath; this is affirmed in the case of Abraham. The episode of the patriarchal history to which this refers is Gen 22:16–18, the sequel to the story of Abraham's obedience in his readiness to sacrifice Isaac. God then confirmed by oath his promise that he would have numerous descendants, who would inherit the cities of their enemies and would be a source of blessing for all the nations of the earth. **15.** *he obtained the promised blessings:* For some commentators, this refers to the partial fulfillment of the promise during Abraham's lifetime (Montefiore, *Hebrews* 114), but the fulfillment which the author probably means is that to which he has referred in v 12: the present eschatological blessings enjoyed by the OT patriarchs, to which the promises of blessing in this world were subordinate. **17.** The reason for the oath confirming the promise was to "make assurance doubly sure" (cf. Philo, *De Abr.* 46). The author's interest does not seem to be directly in the oath made to Abraham, but in that which it recalls to him, viz., the oath by which Jesus was constituted eternal high priest after the manner of Melchizedek. The importance of that oath is emphasized in chap. 7, and the priesthood that it confirms, rather than the promises to Abraham, is the basis of the hope to which the author exhorts his readers. The theme of Jesus' priesthood had been set aside so that the author could make his warning about apostasy; now he is about to return to it. **18.** *through two unchangeable things:* God's promise and his oath. *we who have fled to grasp the hope that lies before us:* The beneficiaries of the promise are Christians ("we"). Nothing is said about the flight except that its term is hope. It does not seem that a reference is intended to the city that they are seeking (13:14), conceived of as a city of refuge (so Montefiore, *Hebrews* 116). **19.** The author here uses a mixed metaphor to describe Christian hope: it is an anchor, and it extends into the inner sanctuary. By speaking of the sanctuary, the author alludes to what he will later develop as a central point in his theology of Christ's priesthood: the Mosaic tabernacle as an earthly replica of the heavenly sanctuary, and the Holy of Holies, beyond the veil that separates it from the Holy Place (Exod 26:31–33), as the earthly counterpart of the heavenly abode of God. Into that sacred place, "heaven itself" (9:24), Jesus our high priest has entered; there he has brought his atoning sacrifice to its climax. Christian hope lies in what Jesus has done in the eternal order by his sacrifice. He has not only entered the heavenly sanctuary, but entered it as the "forerunner" (v 20) of his brothers, whose destiny it is to join him there.

38   **(B) Jesus, Priest according to the Order of Melchizedek (7:1–28).**

(a) MELCHIZEDEK AND THE LEVITICAL PRIESTHOOD (7:1–10). **1.** This verse introduces a midrash on

Gen 14:18–20 that serves to demonstrate the superiority of Jesus' priesthood to that of the OT by a detailed demonstration of the similarity between Jesus and Melchizedek (see J. A. Fitzmyer, *ESBNT* 221–43). The assumption that Melchizedek was a priest of the God of Israel (cf. Gen 14:22, where "Yahweh" and "God Most High" are in apposition) is accepted by the author of Heb. **2.** *tithes:* The OT does not make clear who paid tithes to whom; by adding "Abraham" as subject of the verb the author follows a contemporary understanding (cf. 1QapGen 22:17; Josephus, *Ant.* 1.10.2 § 181), as is necessary for his argument. He also accepts the popular etymology of Melchizedek's name, "king of justice" (cf. *Leg. alleg.* 3.79) and of his title, "king of peace" (ibid.). No further mention is made of these qualities; they are probably given here because Melchizedek is regarded as a prototype of Jesus, the Messiah, and the messianic blessings include justice and peace (cf. Isa 9:5–6; 32:1,17). **3.** Many commentators hold that here the author quotes from a hymn about Melchizedek. *without father . . . end of life:* The OT does not speak about Melchizedek's ancestors, birth, or death. According to a principle of rabbinic exegesis, what is not mentioned in the Torah does not exist (cf. Str-B 3. 693–95). This is a partial but probably insufficient explanation for the ascription of eternal life to Melchizedek (see P. J. Kobelski, *Melchizedek and Melchireša'* [CBQMS 10; Washington, 1981] 123. In 11QMelch Melchizedek appears as a heavenly being "in the congregation of God," who is to exact vengeance and atone for sins in a jubilee year (see M. de Jonge and A. S. van der Woude, *NTS* 12 [1965–66] 301–26). While no direct influence of that text on Heb can be established (see J. A. Fitzmyer, *ESBNT* 267; Kobelski, *Melchizedek* 128), both documents present Melchizedek as a heavenly being, and Kobelski proposes that Ps 110:4 led to the ascription of eternity to Melchizedek in both (ibid. 124). *made to resemble . . . a priest forever:* The resemblance (Melchizedek's being an eternal priest) is found in what the OT says of him (cf. Moffatt, *Hebrews* 93); thus Melchizedek is seen as a foreshadowing of Jesus (cf. Peterson, *Hebrews and Perfection* [→ 15 above] 107; similarly Vanhoye, *Prêtres anciens* [→ 28 above] 175). But though Melchizedek's "eternity" furnished the author with a typology that suited his purpose since it provided not only a foreshadowing of Jesus' priesthood but a contrast with that of the sons of Levi (v 8), it also creates a problem, viz., are there, then, two eternal priests, Melchizedek and Jesus? W. Loader suggests that the author thought of Melchizedek as a priest who still lived, but without exercising any priestly function (*Sohn und Hoherpriester* [→ 21 above] 214–15). But does a priest who ceases to function fit Heb's comparison between Melchizedek and Jesus? And for all the subordination of Melchizedek to Jesus found in the phrase that he was "made to resemble the Son of God," a point on which Kobelski rightly insists (*Melchizedek* 127, 129), that subordination does not eliminate Melchizedek's eternal priesthood. Perhaps one must conclude that the Melchizedek–Jesus typology, for all its usefulness to the author of Heb, raises also a difficulty that he simply ignored. Certainly one must agree with O. Michel that for him the only eternal priesthood is that of Christ (*Hebräer* 260). It should also be noted that the author's use of the title "Son of God" when speaking of the resemblance between Jesus and Melchizedek does not mean that it is not the incarnate Jesus but "the eternal being of the Son of God which is here in view" (so Westcott, *Hebrews* 173). Heb does not ascribe any priesthood to the Son of God other than that which belongs to him through his passion and exaltation (cf. 5:5–10).
39   **4–5.** *tithe:* The tenth of the booty, which

Abraham paid Melchizedek, recalls to the author the tenth of all products of the land which the Israelites had to pay the levitical priests (cf. Num 18:20–32). That this payment is made according to the Mosaic law is stated explicitly because the author will say later (7:12) that the priesthood and the law are so closely connected that the passing away of the priesthood involves the passing away of the law. Although their fellow Jews are descended from Abraham as they are, the superiority of the priests is evident because they are authorized to demand tithes from them. (For "to come out of the loins" of someone as a way of expressing descent from him, see Gen 35:11.) **6.** Similarly, Melchizedek's superiority to Abraham is seen by his receiving tithes from the patriarch. The Gen account does not suggest that Melchizedek had any right to the tithes Abraham gave him; they were a pure gift. But the supposition of the author is that just as the other Israelites were obliged to pay tithes to the priests, so Abraham paid his to Melchizedek in acquittal of duty. The fact that Abraham was the recipient of God's promises is mentioned in order further to emphasize Melchizedek's superiority: he received tithes even from the patriarch who was so highly favored by God. **7.** *he who is inferior is blessed by him who is superior:* In spite of the axiomatic tone of these words, this contradicts what is said in the OT (cf. 2 Sam 14:22; Job 31:20), but possibly the author gives not a general principle but a liturgical rule (see O. Michel, *Hebräer* 267). That the blessing of Abraham is seen by the author as a blessing bestowed on the levitical priesthood by the priest Melchizedek is sufficient explanation why a liturgical consideration should be introduced here. **8.** *he lives:* The superiority of Melchizedek consists in his being "eternal," whereas the levitical priests, who receive tithes from their fellow Hebrews, are "men who die." **9–10.** *Levi, who receives tithes . . . his father's loins:* "Levi" stands not only for the "historical" son of Jacob but for the priestly tribe descended from him.
40   (b) THE LEVITICAL PRIESTHOOD SUPERSEDED (7:11–28). **11.** *if, then, perfection were achieved by the levitical priesthood:* The perfection spoken of is not priestly consecration as in 2:10; 5:9; and 7:28, but cleansing from sin and the consequent ability to approach God (7:19). *on the basis of which the people received the law:* The law was given to Israel as a means of union with God, and the priesthood was the instrument by which the law was meant to achieve its purpose. Spicq regards the principle expressed by this phrase as the foundation of the entire argument of Heb (*Hébreux* 2. 227). **12.** *when there is a change of priesthood . . . change of law:* This is not a truism; it is peculiar to the situation of Israel where the priesthood and the Mosaic law were inseparably linked. **13.** *him about whom these things are said:* Jesus, the priest according to the order of Melchizedek, about whom Ps 110:4 speaks (v 17). **14.** *Judah . . . concerning which tribe . . . about priests:* The author knows and accepts the tradition that Jesus was of the family of David (cf. Rom 1:3); he does not share Qumran's expectation of a priestly Messiah descended from Aaron and a royal Messiah descended from Judah through David (see R. E. Brown, *CBQ* 19 [1957] 53–82). It is doubtful that Judaism had any expectation such as that of the author of Heb, in spite of the statement in *T. Levi* 8:14, ". . . from Judah a king will arise and shall found a new priesthood." That priesthood is said to be "according to the gentile model," and H. C. Kee suggests that the text alludes "to the Maccabean priest-kings, with their increasingly secular discharge of the dual role" (cf. *OTP* 1. 791 n. d).
41   **15–16.** *another priest is set up after the likeness of Melchizedek:* The argument is that Jesus' priesthood has supplanted that of the Levites. Melchizedek's "eternity"

is plainly the principal point of comparison between him and Jesus. *a commandment about the flesh:* The legal requirement that provided for the OT priestly succession confined it to those descendants of Levi who were of the family of Aaron (cf. Num 3:3,10). *a life that cannot be destroyed:* Not that which Jesus possesses because of his divinity (against Westcott, *Hebrews* 185; Montefiore, *Hebrews* 125–26) but the life he possesses because of his resurrection; he is priest not through his "divine nature," but in virtue of his exaltation (cf. 5:5–6). The author cannot have been unaware that Exod 40:15 states that the Aaronic priesthood is to be eternal, although he does not deal with that objection to his argument. The problem is implicitly solved by the contrast drawn between the transitory life of individual Jewish priests and the eternal life of Jesus (vv 23–24), and by the fact that Jesus' eternal priesthood was confirmed by God's oath (vv 20–21) while the Aaronic priesthood was not. But the main reason for the transfer of priesthood was that the priesthood of Jesus had achieved that of which the OT priesthood was incapable: "From the fact, accepted through faith, that perfection has been brought about by Jesus, the author concludes to the imperfection of the Levitical priesthood" (O. Kuss, *Hebräer* 95). **18.** *the former commandment has been annulled . . . uselessness:* The commandment setting up the OT priesthood was useless because the priesthood it established was powerless to cleanse people from sin and unite them with God. **19.** *a better hope has been introduced . . . near to God:* The better hope is based on the accomplished sacrifice of the Son of God, through which we have access to the Father (4:16). The similarity between this verse and 6:19–20 should be noticed. "Better" is a characteristic designation of Heb for the new order (cf. 1:4; 7:22; 8:6; 9:23; 10:34). "Draw near to God" is used in the OT for priestly service; in Lev 10:3 the priests are described simply as "those who approach God" (the Gk vb. is the same as here). Here the Christian life is spoken of in priestly terms; what the OT reserved to the priesthood is attributed to all believers. **42**   **20.** *not without [God's] taking an oath:* Jesus' priesthood is superior to that of the OT priests because of its being confirmed by God's oath (cf. Ps 110:4); hence he is priest forever and they are not. **22.** *thus far has Jesus become the guarantee of a better covenant:* The covenant of the OT to which this "better" one is contrasted is the Mosaic covenant (cf. 9:18–20), and the central part of the Mosaic law in the life of Israel must be seen in the context of that covenant (cf. P. A. Riemann, *IDBSup* 192–97; L. Goppelt, *Theology of the New Testament* [GR, 1982] 2. 256). Hence, if a change of priesthood involves a change of law (7:12), a new covenant has come into being with the new priesthood of Jesus. It is "better" than the old, because it will remain as long as the priesthood on which it is founded remains, and the eternity of that priesthood has been confirmed by God's oath. Thus, Jesus, the priest of this covenant, is himself the guarantee of its permanence. **24.** The Gk word *aparabaton* may mean "permanent" or "untransferable"; the context, which speaks of Jesus' eternal priesthood, seems to favor the former meaning, but the ideas are so closely connected that, in any case, the one involves the other. **25.** *hence he is forever able to save those who draw near to God through him . . . to make intercession for them:* The intercession of the exalted Jesus has been interpreted as the sequel of his completed sacrifice; it is understood as a priestly work but different from the sacrifice, which is regarded as past and over; see O. Cullmann, *The Christology of the New Testament* (Phl, 1959) 99–104. The reason for this view is principally that those who hold it regard the work of atonement as coextensive with Jesus' death on the cross, evidently an event of the past.

But the comparison drawn in the following chapters between Jesus' sacrifice and that offered by the high priest on the Day of Atonement suggests that the sacrifice of Jesus cannot be thought of as limited to his death; his exaltation is an essential part of it. Consequently, the sacrifice cannot be considered past, since its climax takes place in the heavenly sanctuary, where the time sequences of earth are surpassed. S. Lyonnet has shown that in late Judaism expiatory sacrifice was regarded as intercession (*Bib* 40 [1959] 855–90); if that concept is reflected in this verse, the intercession of the Exalted One should not be regarded as the sequel to his sacrifice but as its eternal presence in heaven. J. Moffatt, who does not favor this view, concedes that in this verse "language is used which has suggested that in the heavenly *skēnē* this sacrifice is continually presented or offered" (*Hebrews* xxxviii). The intercession of Jesus is mentioned also in Rom 8:34 in a formulary that is closely similar to that of Heb.

43   **26.** This verse appears to be a hymn in honor of the exalted Jesus, the high priest, that corresponds to the Melchizedek hymn of v 3. *separated from sinners:* This may be related to a prescription of the Mishna (*Yoma* 1:1) that the high priest be prepared for the offering of the Day-of-Atonement sacrifices by being separated from his own house for seven days (cf. Michel, *Hebräer* 280). But the comparison seems forced, for Jesus' separation from sinners is not presented as a preparation for his sacrifice but is connected with his ascension. *higher than the heavens:* This seems to be a reference to Jesus' passage through the intermediate heavens into the heavenly sanctuary, the abode of God (4:14; 9:24; cf. H. Koester, *HTR* 55 [1962] 309). **27.** There is no prescription in the law that the high priest had to offer sacrifice daily, first for his own sins and then for those of the people. That prescription applied only to the Day of Atonement (cf. Lev 16:6–19), and none of the commanded daily offerings fits the description given here (cf. Exod 29:38–42; Lev 6:1–6, 7–11,12–16; Num 28:3–8). Many solutions of the difficulty have been proposed (see Michel, *Hebräer* 281–83). Possibly the least unsatisfactory is the suggestion of O. Kuss that the author, wishing to contrast most strikingly the insufficiency of the OT sacrifices and the all-sufficient sacrifice of Jesus, "chose a formulation ('day by day') which does not suit exactly the actual circumstances" (*Hebräer* 104). *this he did . . . himself:* Since the author has just said that the high priests offered sacrifices first for their own sins, then for those of the people, D. Peterson rightly speaks of "a certain technical inexactitude" in his now saying that Jesus did "this," which, if taken exactly, would mean that he offered sacrifice for his own sins as well as for the sins of the people (*Hebrews and Perfection* [→ 15 above] 117). The view that that is what the author did mean has been defended by G. W. Buchanan (*Hebrews* 129–31) and R. Williamson (*ExpTim* 86 [1974–75] 4–8), who take 4:15, where Jesus is declared to have been "without sin," as referring not to his whole life but to his obedient acceptance of death. Against that limitation of the scope of 4:15, see D. Peterson, *Hebrews and Perfection* 188–90. Here for the first time Heb speaks of the victim of Jesus' sacrifice: himself. The absolute sufficiency of that sacrifice is emphasized by the "once for all" (*ephapax*), an adv. which, together with the simple form *hapax,* occurs 11 times in Heb. **28.** *the word of the oath . . . after the law:* The author deals with the possible objection that the Mosaic law set aside the priesthood of which Ps 110 speaks. On the contrary, the promise of the new nonlevitical priesthood came long after the law that established the OT priesthood, and it set up as high priest not the weak, transitory high priests of the OT, but the Son who has been consecrated priest forever.

44   (C) The Eternal Sacrifice (8:1-9:28).
(a) THE OLD COVENANT, TABERNACLE, WOR-
SHIP (8:1-9:10).
(i) *The heavenly priesthood of Jesus* (8:1-6).   **1.**
the main point . . . is this: The Gk *kephalaion,* here
translated "main point," may also mean "summary," but
there are many elements in what has preceded that are
not mentioned here even summarily, so "main point"
seems preferable. *we have such a high priest:* Cf. 7:26-28.
who has taken his seat . . . Majesty in heaven: The reference
to Ps 110:1 recalls 1:3 and the theme of the enthronement developed in 1:5-14. **2.** *minister of the sanctuary:*
This phrase is found in Philo (*Leg. alleg.* 3.135) but with
a different sense, in reference to the "toil and discipline"
of priestly service, the latter interpreted allegorically.
The Gk *ta hagia,* here translated "the sanctuary," may
also mean "holy things," and the use of the pl. might
seem to favor that interpretation. But in all the other
texts in Heb where the same neut. pl. form occurs (9:2,
8,12,24,25; 10:19; 13:11) it designates a place of
worship. *of the true tabernacle which the Lord . . . set up:* The
heavenly tabernacle in which Christ functions as priest
is called "true" in contrast to the earthly tabernacle of
Judaism; that earthly counterpart is, for the author, not
the Temple of Jerusalem, to which he never refers, but
the Mosaic tabernacle. For the source of the concept that
what belongs to the heavenly sphere is "true," or "real,"
and that what belongs to the earthly is only a shadow of
the real (v 5), → 3 above. In contrast to the earthly tabernacle set up by Moses (Exod 25:8-9), the heavenly one
was set up by God. That Jesus, its ministering priest, is
described as seated (v 1) does not mean that his sacrifice
is "done and over" (so Moffatt, *Hebrews* 140). The author
is using the imagery of Ps 110 and is dealing with the
double role, royal and priestly, that the exalted Jesus exercises. His being seated should not be used as an argument against his present offering as ministering priest.
45   3. *hence the necessity of this man's having something
to offer:* A. Vanhoye has rightly emphasized that the
author does not say here that Jesus is now offering his
sacrifice in heaven, but simply states the necessity of his
offering sacrifice since he is high priest (*VD* 37 [1959]
32-38). The time of that offering cannot be determined
from this verse. It is also true that here, as elsewhere
when speaking of Jesus' sacrifice, the author uses the
aorist, which suggests completed action, whereas when
dealing with priesthood in general or with the liturgy of
the OT he uses the present (7:27; 9:7,9,14,25,28; 10:1,2,
8,12). Moreover, he insists on the once-for-all character
of Jesus' one sacrifice (7:27; 9:12,26,27,28; 10:10). From
these facts, and particularly from a consideration of
9:24-28, Vanhoye concludes that the author nowhere
affirms or insinuates that the sacrificial offering of Jesus
continues in heaven (ibid., 36) but that, on the contrary,
the texts where the aor. indic. is used to express the act
of offering show conclusively that it is an act of the past.
Vanhoye's argument has been accepted by E. Grässer
(*TRu* 30 [1964] 222), but it appears to lose its force when
one considers the heavenly-earthly contrast that is the
background of the author's thought. Jesus' sacrifice is
completed in the heavenly sanctuary; it perdures in its
moment of completion because eternity is a quality of
the heavenly sphere. The aorists and the emphasis on the
unicity of the sacrifice serve, respectively, to show that
the sacrifice is complete and that no further sacrifice of
Jesus is either necessary or possible. This is in contrast
to the constantly repeated sacrifices of the OT, none of
which was perfect. An action completed in the earthly
sphere would be an event of the past, but that is not so
of one completed in the heavenly, eternal order.
Although 8:3 does not by itself determine the time of

Jesus' sacrifice, if that sacrifice is now ended one of two
equally unacceptable conclusions has to be drawn.
Either the author means that the sacrifice ended after
reaching its climax, or he means that it was not a heavenly event. In the former case, the time sequence of earth
would be attributed to heaven; in the latter, Jesus would
be the heavenly high priest in respect to everything
except the distinctively priestly act (F. Schierse's position that Jesus' death on the cross was a heavenly event
[*Verheissung und Heilsvollendung* (→ 12 above) 160 n. 73;
similarly Peterson, *Hebrews and Perfection* (→ 15 above)
192] is without basis). The comparison that the author
will draw in chap. 9 between Jesus' sacrifice and that of
the Jewish high priest on the Day of Atonement will
indicate in detail how he conceives the relation between
the offering begun on the cross and its heavenly
completion.
46   4. *if he were on earth, he would not be a priest:* The
earthly priesthood is the levitical; Jesus is not a priest of
that sort. **5.** *who are serving in a copy and shadow of the
heavenly* [*sanctuary*]: The fact that the OT priestly worship is spoken of in the pres. tense does not necessarily
mean that Heb was written before the destruction of the
Temple, for the earthly sanctuary to which the author
always refers is the Mosaic tabernacle. Since he finds no
difficulty in using the pres. tense of priestly service in the
tabernacle, which was certainly no longer in existence,
it is clear that his description is conceptual rather than
historical. **6.** *he has obtained a ministry as superior* [*to the old*]
as the covenant is better: The intimate connection between
priesthood and covenant is similar to that between priesthood and law mentioned in 7:12. The old covenant had
its own priesthood; Jesus' priesthood is an element of the
new and better covenant of which he is mediator. The
title "mediator" belongs to him because his sacrifice has
been the means of union between God and human
beings; it has taken away sin, the barrier to that union,
and thus made possible the new covenant relationship
(9:15). In 7:22, the superiority of the new covenant was
seen in the permanence of its priesthood; here the superiority is based on better promises. What these are is made
explicit in the citation of Jer 31(LXX 38):31-34.
47   (ii) *The old covenant contrasted with the new*
(8:7-13).   **7-8.** *if the first had been faultless . . . he says:* The
faults of the people are regarded by the author as ultimately due to the faultiness of the covenant itself, i.e., to
its inability to give them the power to keep its laws. His
view is similar to that of Paul in Rom 7:11-24. **8-12.**
The citation from Jer follows the LXX in all but a few
points. In vv 8-9 the Gk *diatithēmi,* "dispose," which the
LXX uses for God's establishing the new and old covenants, is replaced by, respectively, *synteleō,* "conclude,"
and *poieō,* "make." J. Swetnam has maintained (*CBQ* 27
[1965] 373-90) that the latter is a significant change and
throws light on the vexed question whether in 9:15-18
the author, as most believe, uses different meanings of
diathēkē: "covenant" (in vv 15,18) and "testament" (in vv
16-17). Swetnam's position is questionable, as will be
seen in the discussion of those verses. Moreover, the
change from *diatithēmi* to *synteleō* occurs in v 8 where the
prophet is speaking of the new covenant, in which, as
Swetnam holds, God is the one who "disposes," and
where the LXX vb. would have been quite suitable for
the author's argument. This change, then, was quite
unimportant, which suggests that the change to *poieō*
may have been equally insignificant. That is particularly
so if the differences in the quotation in Heb from the
LXX are not due to the author of Heb but were already
found in the OT text that he was using. **10.** *with the house
of Israel:* For the author, the Israel with which the new
covenant will be established is the Christian community.

I will be their God . . . my people: This relationship does not constitute the newness of the covenant, for it existed even under the old (Deut 7:6). Its newness consists rather in its interiority (God's laws will become part of the very being of the covenanted people), in the immediacy of the people's knowledge of God (v 11), and in the forgiveness of sins (v 12). These are the "better promises" (v 6) upon which the covenant is based. **13.** *what is becoming obsolete . . . close to disappearing:* The author's comment was written from the prophet's perspective, not from his own; he knew that the old covenant had already disappeared (v 6).

48   (iii) *The old covenant tabernacle (9:1–5).* **2.** *in it were the lampstand . . . this is called the Holy Place:* The author begins to describe the Mosaic tabernacle (cf. Exod 25–26). This was divided into two parts, separated by a veil (Exod 26:31–35); but rather than speak of the outer and inner section of the one tabernacle, the author speaks of the first and second tabernacle. The Gk *hagia,* "the Holy Place," presents difficulties. Normally, the author uses that term (with the definite article, however, unlike here) for the inner part of the tabernacle (cf. vv 8,25; 13:11), the part that he calls in v 3 "the Holy of Holies" and in v 7 "the second [tabernacle]." If it is used here with the meaning "the Holy Place" as contrasted with "the Holy of Holies" (v 3), it is strange that the author did not maintain that terminology instead of applying to the inner part in succeeding texts the designation that he gives here to the outer part. Attempts have been made to deny the apparent inconsistency (see Vanhoye, *Structure littéraire* 144, n. 1; Montefiore, *Hebrews* 144). However, the similarity in this respect between vv 2,3 and Exod 26:33 suggests that *hagia* and *hagia hagiōn* in these verses mean the same, respectively, as *to hagion* and *to hagion tōn hagiōn* of the LXX Exod, i.e., "the Holy Place" and "the Holy of Holies." **3.** *the second veil:* The veil separating the Holy Place from the Holy of Holies is called "the second" because there was a curtain at the entrance to the former (cf. Exod 26:36). **4.** *having a golden altar of incense:* The Gk word *thymiatērion,* "altar of incense," means "censer" in the three places where it occurs in the LXX (2 Chr 26:19; Ezek 8:11; 4 Macc 7:11); some have supposed that the reference is to that cult object, used in the Day-of-Atonement rite (Lev 16:12; cf. Michel, *Hebräer* 299–301). However, most commentators think that he is speaking of the altar of incense (cf. Exod 30:1–10). Although *thysiastērion* is the LXX word for that altar, Philo (*Quis rer. div.* 226) and Josephus (*Ant.* 3.6.8 § 147) designate it as *thymiatērion,* the same word as that used here. But whereas Heb puts that altar in the Holy of Holies, the OT puts it in the Holy Place, the "first tabernacle" (Exod 30:6). It seems that the author made a mistake here, misinterpreting the Exod text. Similarly, the OT does not say that the objects that the author locates in the ark of the covenant were actually within it, except for the tablets on which the Ten Commandments were written (Deut 10:5). (For the jar, cf. Exod 16:32–34; for the rod of Aaron, cf. Num 17:16–26). **5.** *above the ark were the cherubim of glory . . . place of expiation:* The gold "place of expiation" (Gk *hilastērion*) was so called because the blood of the sacrifices of the Day of Atonement was sprinkled on it (Lev 16:14–15), and thus the sins of the previous year were "expiated" or wiped out. (For the concept of expiation, see comment on 2:17.) *Hilastērion* is often translated "propitiatory," but that transl. may be thought to imply that God was "appeased" by the sprinkled blood. "Mercy seat," another transl., is better, but perhaps too vague (→ Pauline Theology, 82:73–74).

49   (iv) *The old covenant worship (9:6–10).* **6.** *the priests go into . . . continually:* The cultic duties performed

in the outer tabernacle were the care of the lamps on the lampstand (Exod 27:21), the burning of incense on the incense altar every morning and evening (Exod 30:7), and the weekly replacing of the loaves on the table of showbread (Lev 24:8). **7.** *into the second the high priest alone [enters], once a year:* The reference is to the two sacrifices of the Day of Atonement offered by the high priest (Lev 16:1–14), one to expiate his sins and those of his family, the other to expiate the sins of the people. The sins for which atonement was made are called "sins of ignorance." In 5:2 (see comment) the author had spoken of the compassion of the high priest for "the ignorant," meaning those who had committed sins of that sort (see Bonsirven, *Judaïsme* [→ 7 above] 2. 92–93; *ETOT* 1.161 n. 6; Montefiore, *Hebrews* 148). (For the Mishna's understanding of the sins expiated by the Day-of-Atonement rites, see *Yoma* 8:8,9.) In this verse the author speaks for the first time of sacrificial "blood," a subject with which he will be preoccupied in this and the following chapter. It is now generally recognized that the death of the sacrificial animal was not intended to symbolize that the one in whose name the sacrifice was offered deserved death, if for no other reason than that most of the sins for which sacrifice was offered were sins to which the death penalty was not attached (cf. R. de Vaux, *AI* 158; *ETOT* 1. 165 n. 2). The purpose of the slaughtering of the animal was to release its blood. The significance of the blood was expressed in Lev 17:11,14. The blood was the element in which life resided. Insofar as it is life, the blood is the peculiarly divine element in the human person, and by reason of its sacred character, it was, when poured out on the altar or sprinkled on the place of expiation, an effective symbol of the purification of sin and of the reestablishment of union between God and the offerer. "By the outpouring of the blood, life was released, and in offering this to God the worshiper believed that the estrangement between him and the Deity was annulled, or that the defilement which separated them was cleansed" (W. D. Davies, *Paul and Rabbinic Judaism* [London, 1962] 235; cf. D. McCarthy, *IDBSup* 114–17; L. Sabourin, *DBSup* 10. 1494–97. For a different meaning of the sacrificial blood, see L. Morris, *Apostolic Preaching* [→ 18 above] 108–24). The blood ritual was an element of all the OT animal sacrifices; since expiating power is attributed to the blood (Lev 17:11), the notion of expiation is present in all the various kinds of sacrifice, and the removal of sin was the purpose of all, even though not the only purpose (see R. de Vaux, *AI* 453). But in the OT it is not said that the blood is "offered." Although some scholars speak of the blood ritual as an offering (W. D. Davies, *Paul* 235; *ETOT* 1. 164), others, while emphasizing that ritual as part of—and indeed the essential element of—the sacrifice, refuse to regard it precisely as an offering (L. Moraldi, *Espiazione sacrificale e riti espiatori* [Rome, 1956] 249–52). The point is perhaps unimportant, but if the latter view is right, the fact that Heb here speaks of the blood as being offered means that the author is introducing into his description of the Day-of-Atonement sacrifice a conception that is not found in the OT. From what source did he derive it? Possibly he was using the technique of speaking of the OT type in terms that apply properly only to the NT antitype (e.g., in 1 Cor 10:2 the passage through the sea is called a baptism "into Moses" because of its antitype, baptism "into Christ").

50   **8.** *the way into the [inner] sanctuary has not yet been revealed:* The goal of the worship was access to God. The fact that only the high priest could enter that part of the tabernacle, the earthly counterpart of God's heavenly abode, showed that the goal had not been attained by OT worship. **9.** *this is a symbol of the present time:* The "present time" is not merely a chronological indication. It means the same as the "present age," in contrast to the "age to come." Even now the latter is present, in an anticipatory way, and Christians have experienced its powers (6:5). *not able to make perfect the conscience of the worshiper:* I.e., to cleanse it of sin (cf. v 14). **10.** *only [to cleanse] in respect to food and drink and various kinds of ritual washings:* The author limits the efficacy of OT sacrifices to a cleansing from defilements caused by the violation of ritual laws, viz., the dietary prescriptions (cf. Lev 11; Num 6:1–4) and ritual washings (cf. Lev 14:8; Num 19:11–21). This low estimate of their efficacy would hardly have been accepted by any Hebrew. For the Hebrew, sacrifice "was not merely an expression of the spirit of the offerer, and certainly not an empty form that neither added nor subtracted anything. It required the spirit to validate it, but once validated it was thought to be charged with power. It was never merely a plea, whether for aid or for forgiveness or for communion. It was potent to effect something, either within or on behalf of the offerer or of another" (H. H. Rowley, *BJRL* 33 [1950] 87).

51 (b) THE SACRIFICE OF JESUS (9:11–28).

(i) *Sacrifice in the heavenly sanctuary* (9:11–14). **11.** *high priest of the good things that have come to be:* The Gk reading here adopted and translated as "the good things that have come to be" (*tōn genomenōn agathōn*) is different from that of many mss. which read *tōn mellontōn agathōn,* "the good things to come." For the reading here followed, see *TCGNT* 668. *through the greater and more perfect tabernacle not made by hands, that is, not of this creation:* This tabernacle is regarded by A. Vanhoye as the risen body of Christ, "the temple raised up in three days" (*Structure littéraire* 157 n. 1). In pointing out that it is not simply the body of the incarnate Son without further qualification, he rightly remarks that during his mortal life Jesus' body could not be called "not of this creation"; the resurrection made it the spiritual, heavenly body (cf. 1 Cor 15:46–47). But the opinion seems preferable that sees this tabernacle as the heavenly regions, the heavenly counterpart of the earthly outer tabernacle, through which Jesus passed (4:14) into the highest heaven, the abode of God (9:24), the counterpart of the inner tabernacle, the Holy of Holies (see Michel, *Hebräer* 311–32; H. Koester, *HTR* 55 [1962] 309; Peterson, *Hebrews and Perfection* [→ 15 above] 143–44). An objection made to that interpretation is that it involves taking the prep. *dia,* "through," in a local sense, whereas the same preposition is used twice in the latter part of the sentence (v 12) in an instrumental sense, although the case of the nouns governed by the prepositions is the same (gen.) in all three instances. H. Montefiore declares that such a procedure would be "bad style and unparalleled in NT usage" (*Hebrews* 152). J. Moffatt's attempt to explain the fluctuation in sense as a literary technique found elsewhere in Heb is not to the point, for in the cases that he cites in justification of his claim (*Hebrews* 121), the difference in sense comes from the fact that the preposition governs different cases. Yet the striking parallel between 9:11 and 10:20, where *dia* is used with a local sense, confirms the view that it has that sense in 9:11 also; both the greater and more perfect tent of this verse and the veil of 10:20 are "spheres" through which the passage of Christ is made. There is no need to see in this conception of Christ's passage through the heavens any influence of the gnostic myth of the journey of the redeemed redeemer back into the world of light. The author's cosmological views, which he shared with apocalyptic Judaism (see comment on 1:2), are sufficient explanation of the origin of the concept. The objection that the intermediate heavens would not be designated as "not of this

creation" has no weight, for that is plainly an explication of "not made by hands"; the greater and more perfect tent is not made by human hands, unlike the earthly sanctuary.

52 **12.** *by his own blood:* Just as the high priest had right of access to the Holy of Holies because he bore the blood of the sacrificial animals, so Jesus' life offered in sacrifice gives him the right of access to the heavenly sanctuary. As the Day-of-Atonement sacrifice cannot be conceived of apart from the essential element of the blood sprinkling, so here it is impossible to regard Jesus' entrance into the sanctuary as the consequence of his sacrifice completed in his death on the cross rather than as a part of that sacrifice, begun on earth and completed in heaven. Since the author draws an exact parallel between the two entrances, it is difficult to see how F. F. Bruce can say that "there have been expositors who, pressing the analogy of the Day of Atonement beyond the limits observed by our author, have argued that the expiatory work of Christ was not completed on the cross," but in heaven (*Hebrews* 200–1; similarly N. H. Young, *NTS* 27 [1980–81] 198–210). The limits observed by the author in his comparison between the two are precisely the reason why one must look for the heavenly counterpart of the high priest's sprinkling of the blood, which was not a sequel to the sacrifice but its essential part. *achieved eternal redemption:* The vb. translated in the indic. mood is a Gk aor. ptc.; it is here understood as an aor. of coincident action (BDF 339). The word *lytrōsis,* "redemption," must be understood in the light of its OT usage. It belongs to a word group (*lytron, lytrousthai, apolytrōsis*) that expresses the notion of deliverance (cf. Dan 4:34 LXX), frequently in reference to the deliverance of Israel from Egypt (Exod 6:6; Deut 7:8) and from the Babylonian Captivity (Isa 41:14; 44:22, 24). It is used in Ps 130:7–8 of deliverance from sin. In none of these cases is there any notion that the payment of a price was demanded as a condition for deliverance, and there is no reason to see such a concept in this verse (cf. F. Büchsel, "*Lytrōsis,*" *TDNT* 4. 354) in spite of the view of those who would see the blood of Christ as the price paid (to God) for the redemption of humanity (cf. A. Médebielle, *DBSup* 3. 201; A. Deissmann, *LAE* 331; → Pauline Theology, 82:75). Like the salvation of 5:9, the redemption is "eternal" because it is based on the eternally acceptable sacrifice of Jesus.

53 **13.** *a heifer's ashes:* These ashes were mixed with water and used to cleanse those who had become defiled by contact with corpses, human bones, or graves (cf. Num 19:9,14–21). *sanctify the defiled in respect to cleansing of the flesh:* The blood of the sacrifices and the lustral water conferred external ritual purity on the defiled. **14.** *through the eternal spirit offered himself spotless to God:* This spirit is neither the holy Spirit nor the divine nature of Jesus (so Spicq, *Hébreux* 2. 258). Like Paul, the author sees Jesus' earthly life as one lived in the sphere of the flesh (cf. 2:14; 5:7; 10:20); and although, unlike Paul, he does not explicitly characterize the life of the risen Christ as life "in the spirit," the flesh–spirit contrast is too deeply rooted in the Bible (see comment on 2:14) for the second member of the contrast not to be implied by his use of the first. A comparison of this verse with 7:16 shows that "eternal spirit" corresponds to the "life that cannot be destroyed" of that verse (cf. Montefiore, *Hebrews* 155). In 7:16 the emphasis is on Jesus' eternal priesthood (eternal not in the sense that it had no beginning, but because it will never end) in contrast to the transitory OT priesthood; here, the emphasis is on the eternity of Jesus' one and only sacrifice, in contrast to the annually repeated sacrifices of the Jewish high priest on the Day of Atonement (v 25). This suggests that Jesus' "life that cannot be destroyed" and his "eternal spirit" are the same. This verse is another statement that Jesus' self-offering is a heavenly, not an earthly, reality, since it is offered through the eternal spirit, i.e., in that new sphere of existence that he enters at the time of his exaltation. Clearly, the author does not question the importance of the cross, nor does he mean that the sacrifice lies wholly within the heavenly sphere, but only that the sacrifice is consummated there. To avoid the consequences of that conception by holding that Jesus' death "took place in the eternal, absolute order" (Moffatt, *Hebrews* 124), or that it was a heavenly event (see comment on 8:3), is to ignore the fact that Jesus' "human nature is axiologically earthly until it enters heaven at the term of the Ascension" (A. Cody, *Heavenly Sanctuary and Liturgy in the Epistle to the Hebrews* [St. Meinrad, 1960] 91). The designation of Jesus as the "spotless" victim of his own sacrifice recalls the prescription of the law that the sacrificial animal should be physically unblemished (Exod 29:1); the word is used here in a moral sense, as in 1 Pet 1:19. *will cleanse our conscience from dead works:* Whereas the OT blood-sprinkling produced only ritual cleanness, the purifying power of Jesus' sacrifice extends to the defiled conscience and purifies it from dead works; see comment on 6:1. *worship the living God:* Primarily a sharing in Jesus' sacrificial worship, through which Christians have access to God (4:16; 7:25; 10:19-22). It also designates the entire conduct of Christian life as a cultic action, a manner of speaking that recalls the usage of Paul (cf. Rom 12:1).

54   (ii) *The sacrifice of the new covenant* (9:15-22). **15.** Jesus' sacrifice is the basis on which he is mediator of the new covenant (cf. 8:6). Through it he has brought deliverance ("redemption," *apolytrōsis*) from the sins committed under the old covenant, sins that were not taken away by the OT sacrifices. As long as they remained, men could not possess the inheritance promised by God, i.e., the "better promises" (8:6), the "good things that have come to be" (v 1), which, like the sacrifice that has made its possession possible, is eternal. **16-17.** *where there is a testament, . . . it has no force while the testator is alive:* In these verses the author speaks of the new order introduced by Jesus' sacrifice as that produced by "a testament" (= a will), which has come into force because of the testator's death. Since the Gk word *diathēkē* can mean both "covenant" and "testament" and is used in these verses with the latter meaning, but in vv 15 and 18 with the former, the author has been charged with inconsistency; or his consistency has been defended either by the claim that at the time when Heb was written *diathēkē* always meant "testament" (A. Deissmann, *LAE* 341) or by holding that both concepts are expressed in each use of the word in vv 15-18 (J. Swetnam, *CBQ* 27 [1965] 389). As for Deissmann's view, since the LXX used *diathēkē* to translate the Hebr *bĕrît,* "covenant," it is hardly likely that any NT author could have regularly disregarded the LXX meaning, "covenant," whatever change of meaning the evolution of the language had brought to the word (cf. MM 148-49). However, it is difficult to see how the concept will-testament could be applied to the old covenant. One of the differences between the old covenant and the new is that the latter has the aspect not only of a covenant but also of a testament, whereas the former has not. What verifies the testament concept in the case of the new covenant is that it did involve the death of the one who initiated it; hence he is not only one who established the covenant, but also the testator. The death of the animal victims in the sacrifice that sealed the old covenant (Exod 24:5-8) can in no way be considered as even imperfectly verifying the concept of a testator's death (*pace* J. Swetnam, *CBQ*

27 [1965] 378). But since God is the one who establishes the new covenant (cf. 8:10), how can it be at the same time a testament, which requires the death of the testator? The answer is that Jesus, the eternal Son, who, with the Father, has established the new covenant, is at the same time the testator whose death has brought it into force. In that respect it is quite unlike the old covenant; hence the difference in meaning between *diathēkē* in vv 15,18 and 16-17.

55   **18.** *hence neither was the first covenant inaugurated without blood:* The particle "hence" creates difficulty. It seems to indicate that the author is drawing a conclusion from vv 16-17, in which case it would appear that in his mind the death of the animals sacrificed at the inauguration of the old covenant corresponded in some way to the death of a testator. But if the illative force of the particle applies to the general argument of the chapter rather than to the statements of the two preceding verses, the problem largely disappears. The major interest of the chapter is in the blood of Christ, i.e., in his sacrifice, through which atonement was made and the new covenant inaugurated. Since the new is the fulfillment of the old, the author seeks a parallel in the inauguration of the two and finds it in the account of the sacrifice related in Exod 24:5-8. **19-20.** The description of the inaugural sacrifice of the old covenant differs from that found in Exod. The sacrificial animals are goats as well as bulls; water, scarlet wool, and hyssop are spoken of (these are derived probably from the purificatory rites found in Lev 14:3-7 and Num 19:6-18); Moses sprinkles the book (of the covenant) rather than the altar. The book is here regarded as representing God; the signification therefore would be the same (see comment on 9:7). The words attributed to Moses are slightly different from those of Exod; they recall the words of Jesus over the eucharistic wine (Mark 14:24). If this was an intentional change, it would be an argument against the common opinion that the author never alludes to the eucharist. **21.** *the tent:* In Exod 24 there is no mention of this sprinkling of the tabernacle with blood, because it had not yet been constructed. In the account of its dedication (Exod 40:16-28) nothing is said of a blood-sprinkling, although that is mentioned by Josephus (*Ant.* 3.8.6 § 205). The purpose of this blood-sprinkling was cathartic, closely related to what L. Moraldi calls the "sacramental" aspect of the blood rite, which expressed the reestablished union between God and humanity (*Espiazione* [→ 49 above] 231, 248). However, the cathartic aspect comes closer to magical conceptions and is less susceptible of being interpreted in a symbolic manner that would eliminate a religiously primitive understanding of the rite. **22.** *without the shedding of blood there is no forgiveness:* This ignores the other means of forgiveness known to the OT: fasting (Joel 2:12), almsgiving (Sir 3:29), contrition (Ps 51:19). But the author is thinking of the sacrificial cult, and in that case the statement is true. He does not mean, however, that the sacrificial shedding of blood was regarded as vicarious punishment for the sins of the offerer; it is the expiatory, unitive power of the blood that is envisaged, and the necessity of its being shed so that the blood ritual might be performed (cf. T. Thornton, *JTS* 15 [1964] 63-65).

56   (iii) *The perfect sacrifice* (9:23-28). **23.** *the heavenly things themselves need better sacrifices than these:* It is difficult to attribute to the heavenly tabernacle a need for purification; C. Spicq holds that in this second part of the verse the author is speaking not of purification but of dedication (*Hébreux* 2. 267). But the parallel with the purification of the earthly tabernacle, to which the first half of the verse refers, makes that interpretation improbable. If one applies the statement to the intermediate heavens, which correspond to the outer part of the earthly tabernacle, the statement of Job 15:15, "the heavens are not clean in his sight," may be pertinent (see H. Bietenhard, *Die himmlische Welt* 130 n. 1). The pl. "sacrifices" is strange, since the author knows of only one purificatory heavenly sacrifice, but it may have been used to correspond to the pl. "heavenly things." **24.** *an antitype of the true one:* "Antitype" is used here with the meaning "copy." *to appear now before God on our behalf:* Cf. 7:25; Rom 8:34. **25–26.** If Jesus' sacrifice had not been definitive and final but had demanded constant repetition, like the annually repeated Day-of-Atonement sacrifices, he would have had to suffer many times since the creation of the world. The author rejects the notion of repeated sacrifices of Jesus, not the eternal presence of his one sacrifice. The statement that that sacrifice took place "at the end of the ages" is another indication of the author's fidelity to the time sequence of Jewish and Christian eschatology; cf. C. K. Barrett, "The Eschatology of the Epistle to the Hebrews," *BNTE* 363–93. His acceptance of the Platonic conception of eternal heavenly reality contrasted with temporal earthly shadow is modified by his strongly historical Christian faith. For him, the heavenly sanctuary always existed, but the heavenly sacrifice, now eternally present there, entered into the eternal order at a determined point of time. **28.** *to bear the sins of many:* Cf. Isa 53:12. By taking the sins upon himself, Jesus has taken them away. "The idea of vicarious sin-bearing is prominent, but there is no hint of vicarious punishment" (Montefiore, *Hebrews* 162). For the Semitic use of "many" meaning "all," see J. Jeremias, *"Polloi,"* *TDNT* 6. 536–45. *will appear a second time, not to deal with sin but to bring salvation to those who eagerly await him:* A reference to the parousia, with perhaps an allusion to the Day-of-Atonement ritual; the appearance of Jesus will be like that of the high priest coming out of the Holy of Holies (cf. Sir 50:5–10). The parousia will bring complete and final salvation (cf. 1:14).

57   (D) Jesus' Sacrifice, Motive for Perseverance (10:1–39).

(a) THE MANY SACRIFICES AND THE ONE SACRIFICE (10:1–18). **1.** *the law, having only a shadow of the good things to come:* Here the author is not using "shadow" as he does in 8:5, where the Platonic heavenly–earthly contrast is intended, but in the sense of a foreshadowing of that which is to come through Christ (Col 2:17; cf. Vanhoye, *Prêtres anciens* [→ 28 above] 240). *not the very image:* P⁴⁶ reads "and the image," practically equating the two. But the normal meaning of "image" (*eikōn*) is a representation that in some way shares the reality of which it is image (cf. H. Kleinknecht, *"Eikōn,"* *TDNT* 2. 388–90). Consequently, the reading that contrasts it with "shadow" is preferable. The annually repeated Day-of-Atonement sacrifices were not able to remove sin; they simply foreshadowed the sacrifice of Jesus. **2.** *to be offered:* The very repetition of the sacrifices proves their impotence. If they had taken away sins, the worshipers would no longer have had any consciousness of guilt and the sacrifices would have ceased. The argument is weak and ignores the evident objection that those sacrifices could have expiated past sins, but new sins would have called for further sacrifices. But it is merely an overstatement of what the author's faith assures him to be true: the one sacrifice of Jesus has brought deliverance from past sins (9:15) and because of it he is forever the source of salvation (5:9); because of its perfection no further sacrifice is necessary or possible. **3–4.** *year after year:* The annual atonement sacrifices brought past sins into "remembrance" (*anamnēsis*) but could not efface them. This statement of inability contradicts the belief

expressed in *Jub.* 5:17–18. It does not seem, however, that the "remembrance" of sins means that the author believed that "the cultic rites actually bring past sins into the present" (so Montefiore, *Hebrews* 165; similarly J. Behm, *"Anamnēsis,"* *TDNT* 1. 348–49). For the Semitic concept of remembrance, which is often invoked in this connection, see W. Schottroff, *"Gedenken" im alten Orient und im Alten Testament* (Neukirchen, 1964) 117–26, 339–41. It is not clear whether God or the offerer is the one who "remembers" the sins. The former interpretation is suggested by 8:12, which points to the time of the new covenant when God will no longer remember the sins of his people, and by the statement of Philo (*De plant.* 108) that the sacrifices of the wicked "put Him in remembrance" of their sins. But in that case, the author would mean that all the sacrifices, whether offered by the repentant or the unrepentant, served only to remind God of sin and actually called forth punishment of the offerer; and v 4, as well as other texts of Heb, speaks only of the inefficacy of these sacrifices rather than of their positive harmfulness for the offerer. *it is impossible for the blood of bulls and goats to take away sins:* L. Goppelt calls this judgment about the value of Israel's sacrificial cult one that "could hardly have been more radical" (*Theology* [→ 42 above] 2. 256).

58   **5–7.** The words of Ps 40:7–9a are here attributed to the Son at his incarnation. The quotation follows the LXX in substance. In v 7b of the psalm, the MT reads "ears you have dug for me" (to hear and obey God's will). The majority of LXX mss. have the reading given in Heb: "a body you prepared for me." The meaning of the psalm is that God prefers obedience to sacrifice; it is not a repudiation of ritual but a statement of its relative inferiority. Since Jesus' obedience was expressed by his willing offering of his body (i.e., himself) in death, the LXX reading of v 7b is peculiarly applicable to him, so much so that it has been thought that the reading may be have been introduced into the LXX under the influence of Heb (cf. Héring, *Hebrews* 88 n. 8). **8.** *sacrifices and offerings, holocausts and sin offerings:* These terms for sacrifice are probably meant to cover the four main types, i.e., peace offerings ("sacrifices"), cereal offerings ("offerings"), holocausts, and sin offerings. The last includes the guilt offerings (cf. Lev 5:6–7, where in the MT the names of the two are interchanged). *which are offered according to the law:* This prepares for the statement of v 9 that the law has been annulled in this respect. **9.** *then he says, Behold, I have come to do your will. He abolishes the former in order to establish the latter:* God's preferring obedience to sacrifice is interpreted as his repudiation of the OT sacrifices and their replacement by the self-offering of Jesus. **10.** *it is by this will that we have been consecrated:* "This will" is the will of God, carried out by Christ, that he offer in death the body that God "prepared" for him. The offering of Jesus' body means the same as the shedding of his blood; each expresses the total self-offering of Christ.

59   **11.** *every priest stands performing his service daily:* The fact that the author speaks here of "every priest" rather than of the high priest alone, and that he speaks of a priestly service performed daily, indicates that he is no longer thinking of the Day of Atonement but of all the OT sacrificial ritual. **12.** *but this man offered one sacrifice for sins and took his seat forever at the right hand of God:* The contrasting postures of the standing Jewish priests and the seated Christ have frequently been invoked against the view that the sacrifice of Jesus perdures in heaven (see comment on 8:2–3). But one must recognize that the different images used in Heb to depict the functions of Christ overlap. As in 8:1, Jesus' being seated here refers to his enthronement. His being seated as king is contrasted to the standing position of the OT priests in their constantly repeated sacrificial work. Is it meant also to say that Jesus' own sacrificial work is over? The answer to that depends on how seriously one takes the previous Day-of-Atonement typology used to portray Jesus' sacrifice. To exclude priestly sacrificial activity as an essential aspect of Jesus' heavenly existence is to make questionable why the author should have used that typology at all (as, e.g., in W. Loader's view [see *Sohn und Hoherpriester* (→ 21 above) 182-222] that Heb locates Jesus' expiatory sacrifice only in the cross and sees his heavenly priesthood solely as intercession for his people). But if the Day-of-Atonement typology offers a vision of Jesus' sacrifice as both earthly and heavenly, can the latter be conceived of as ever ending? For Heb, eternity is a quality of all heavenly reality. In this connection one may recall a comment of Philo, who, following the Platonic distinction of *aiōn* as timeless eternity and *chronos* as the successive time of the earthly world (*Quod Deus imm.* 32), says, "The true name of eternity is 'today'" (*De fuga et inv.* 57). It can hardly be doubted that Jesus' being seated is an allusion to Ps 110:1 (cf. 1:3; 8:1; 12:2). W. Stott compares it to David's sitting and praying before the Lord (2 Sam 7:18), meaning that Jesus is now "claiming the fulfillment of the covenant promises to his seed" (*NTS* 9 [1962-63] 62-67). But if the author had intended the comparison, it is strange that in spite of all he has to say about the heavenly activity of Jesus, there is not a single unmistakable allusion to that text of 2 Sam. **13.** *to wait:* The time between Jesus' enthronement and the parousia is described by an allusion to Ps 110:1b. Unlike Paul, the author does not indicate whom he understands by the enemies yet to be made subject to Christ (1 Cor 15:24-26). **14.** *by one offering he has forever made perfect those who are being consecrated:* Through the cleansing of their consciences so that they may worship the living God (9:14), Jesus has given his followers access to the Father; they share in his own priestly consecration (see comment on 2:10-11). **15-17.** What has been said is now confirmed by the testimony of Scripture ("the holy Spirit"; see comment on 3:7). The text cited is an excerpt from the prophecy of Jer 31:31-34 concerning the new covenant, already used in 8:8-12. The two citations are slightly different in the verses in which they coincide, but the variants do not affect the meaning. **18.** *where there is forgiveness of these, there is no more offering for sin:* The conclusion is drawn from the last words of the prophecy, that God will remember sins no more. They will be no longer remembered because they will have been forgiven. The fulfillment of this has come about through Jesus' sacrifice; there is now no more offering for sin. W. G. Johnsson objects to the transl. of the Gk word *aphesis* as "forgiveness," maintaining that the latter "is a category outside the conceptual scheme of Hebrews" (*ExpTim* 89 [1977-78] 104-8; against this, see L. Goppelt, *Theology* [→ 42 above] 2. 257).

60   (b) ASSURANCE, JUDGMENT, RECALL OF THE PAST (10:19-39). **19.** *confidence to enter the sanctuary:* Cf. 3:6; 4:16; 6:19-20. **20.** *the new and living way that he opened for us:* The Gk *enkainizō*, "open," also can mean "inaugurate" or "dedicate" (cf. 9:18; 1 Kgs 8:63). *through the veil, that is, his flesh:* See comment on 9:11. Christ's flesh is not the means of access to the sanctuary but, like the veil before the Holy of Holies, an obstacle to entrance (Kuss, *Hebräer* 155). It should be noted that the author speaks not of Christ's "body," but of his "flesh." E. Käsemann's view on the pejorative meaning of the latter is to be accepted (*Wandering* [→ 8 above] 225-26); see also comments on 2:14; 5:7; 9:13. There may be a connection between this text and the rending of the Temple veil at the death of Christ (Mark 15:38). For a different inter-

pretation of the verse, see O. Hofius, "Inkarnation und Opfertod Jesu nach Hebr 10,19f.," *Der Ruf Jesu* (Fest. J. Jeremias; ed. C. Burchard, et al.; Göttingen, 1970) 132-41. **21.** *the house of God:* The Christian community (cf. 3:6). **22.** *with hearts sprinkled [clean] from a bad conscience, and bodies washed with clean water:* The sprinkling is a metaphorical designation of the purifying power of the sacrifice of Christ. Whereas the Jewish ritual sprinkling of lustral water produced only external purity (9:13), thoe who have been sprinkled with the blood of Christ are cleansed in respect to conscience (9:14). "Washed with clean water" probably refers to baptism (cf. 1 Cor 6:11; Titus 3:5). **23.** *the confession of hope:* This probably means the confession made at baptism (see comment on 3:1). **24.** *to stimulate each other to love and good works:* The mention of love in this verse may be intended to complete the triad, faith (v 22), hope (v 23), and love (so Westcott, *Hebrews* 322). **25.** *our assembly:* Probably the gathering together of the community for worship. Possibly the neglect of these gatherings was due to the fear of persecution, but more likely it was simply another manifestation of the slackening of fervor verging on apostasy against which Heb is directed. The assembly is seen by the author as a situation peculiarly suitable for the stimulation of love and for mutual encouragement. *the day:* The parousia; cf. Rom 13:12; 1 Cor 3:13.

61   **26.** *if we sin willfully:* The reference is to the sin of apostasy, as is clear from v 29 (cf. 3:12). The author's reflections on the consequences of that sin resemble 6:4-8. **28.** *anyone who has set aside the law of Moses is put to death without mercy on the testimony of two or three witnesses:* The "setting aside" of the law envisaged is evidently not any sin against it, but idolatry, for which the death penalty was enjoined, provided two or three witnesses could testify to it (Deut 17:2-7). **32.** *when you had been enlightened:* See comment on 6:4. The persecution of which the author speaks here and in vv 33-34 is hard to identify (→ 5 above). **37-38.** The author now cites an OT text in support of what he has said. He uses Hab 2:3-4, introducing it by a short citation from Isa 26:20, "a very little while." The Hab citation is almost identical to the text of Codex Alexandrinus of the LXX, but the author inverts the first and second lines of v 4. "He who is to come" is Jesus; his coming is the parousia, which is now a matter of only "a very little while." In the meantime, the righteous man must live in faith, waiting for the return of Christ. If he loses faith and falls away, he will incur the displeasure of God. The Hab text was used at Qumran as referring to the deliverance of those who had faith in the Teacher of Righteousness (1QpHab 8:1-3), and was used by Paul as an OT support of justfication by faith rather than by works (Rom 1:17; Gal 3:11). It is not certain how the author understands the word "faith" (Gk *pistis*) in his use of the Hab text (see J. A. Fitzmyer, *TAG* 235-46). He may mean "faithfulness," but in view of what he says about *pistis* in the following chapter, "faithfulness" cannot be its sole or even principal meaning here. **39.** *we have faith and will possess life:* As in 6:9-12, after a warning the author sounds a note of encouragement.

62   (V) Examples, Discipline, Disobedience (11:1-12:29).

(A) The Faith of the Ancients (11:1-40). **1.** The meaning of the two Gk words *hypostasis* and *elenchos* is much disputed. While many commentators take *hypostasis* as "assurance" and *elenchos* as "conviction," H. Koester thinks that neither of those "subjective" meanings is correct, and that the words mean, respectively, "reality" and objective "demonstration" (cf. "Hypostasis," *TDNT* 8. 572-89). Faith (*pistis*), then, is here said to be "the reality" of the goods hoped for, the "proof" of things one cannot see, the latter being the heavenly world, and the former, those of that world. J. A. Fitzmyer is "inclined to agree" with that view (cf. J. Reumann, J. A. Fitzmyer, and J. D. Quinn, *Righteousness in the New Testament* [Phil, 1982] 222–23). That *hypostasis* means "reality" (or "substance") in at least Heb 1:3 is clear, but L. Goppelt considers Koester's reading of 11:1 in the light of that text "a semantic short-circuit" (*Theology* [→ 42 above] 2. 264). Moreover, as J. Thompson points out, the context of 11:1 (10:32–39; 11:3–40) indicates "an emphasis on the believer's experience." While agreeing with Koester that faith, for Heb, is "reality" and "proof," Thompson argues that it is also knowledge and realization of the invisible world, and he plausibly proposes as the meaning of the repeated *pistei* ("by faith") of chap. 11 "in the recognition of what constitutes true reality." This recognition is also intimately connected with hope (cf. *Beginnings* [→ 3 above] 70–75). **3.** *the worlds were fashioned by the word of God:* See comment on 1:2; Ps 33:6; Wis 9:1. This verse seems to break the continuity of the argument, for it deals with the author's faith and that of his addressees, rather than with that of the ancients; but it exemplifies the second aspect of faith mentioned in v 1.

63   **4.** For a list of heroes similar to that which begins here, cf. Sir 44:1–50:21. *by faith Abel offered a sacrifice:* The OT says nothing about the motive of Abel's sacrifice; probably the author was influenced by his own conviction that without faith it is impossible to please God (v 6) and the statement of Gen 4:4 that God was pleased with Abel's sacrifice. *though dead, he still speaks:* Possibly a reference to Gen 4:10, but more likely an indication of the enduring witness to faith given by Abel's example. **6.** *must believe that he is, and that he rewards those who seek him:* The two objects of faith should probably be understood as synonymous, i.e., not the mere fact of God's existence but his existence as the One who has entered into gracious relations with humans. For the opposite view that God is unconcerned with human conduct, see Ps 53:2, where the fool's statement expresses practical, not speculative, atheism. **7.** *warned about things not yet seen:* Cf. Gen 6:13. *condemned the world:* The author seems to have drawn on a tradition alluded to in 2 Pet 2:5, that Noah warned his contemporaries of the imminent flood and urged them to repentance, though without success. The event vindicated his faith, which was a condemnation of their unbelief.

64   **8–9.** Cf. Gen 12:1,4; 15:16,18; 26:3; 35:12). **10.** *he was looking forward to the city with foundations:* Abraham's sojourn in Canaan is interpreted as an indication of his realization that his permanent dwelling would be nowhere on earth, but in the heavenly city; in this he is made to resemble the Christian believer (cf. 13:14). **11.** *by faith Sarah herself received power for the sowing of seed:* The Gk text seems to attribute to Sarah the male role in the conception of Isaac (cf. Gen 18:1–15). Some understand the text to mean "although Sarah was barren, (Abraham) received . . ." or "(Abraham), together with Sarah, received . . ."; cf. *TCGNT* 672–73.

65   **13–16.** It was Abraham who said that he was a stranger and sojourner (Gen 23:4), but here the author attributes to all the patriarchs the acknowledgment that their homeland is in heaven. For God's not being "ashamed" to be called their God, cf. Exod 3:6. **17–18.** The last example of Abraham's faith is his obedience to the command to offer Isaac in sacrifice (Gen 22:1–19). It is disputed whether the later-attested Jewish belief in the vicariously atoning power of the sacrifice, with Isaac as a willing victim, existed at the time of the composition of Heb; against that, see P. Davies and B. Chilton, *CBQ* 40 (1978) 514–46; in favor, see J. Swetnam, *Jesus and*

Isaac (AnBib 94; Rome, 1981). **19.** *as a symbol:* Some take the Gk *en parabolē* to mean "figuratively speaking," since Isaac did not actually die. But it seems more likely that his deliverance from death is seen as a symbol of Jesus' resurrection.

66   **23–28.** Four instances follow of faith connected with the history of Moses. The glorification of Moses in vv 24–27 does not correspond to the OT account (Exod 2:11–15). *the reproach of the Messiah:* A christological interpretation of Moses' choosing to share his people's suffering. **32–38.** The author passes summarily through other heroes of the OT, some named, others not. It is impossible to know in all instances to whom the references apply. The sufferings of vv 35b–38 are principally those endured by faithful Israelites in the persecution that preceded and accompanied the Maccabean revolt (cf. 1 Macc 1:60–63; 7:34; 2 Macc 6:18–31; 7:1–42). **40.** *so that without us they should not be made perfect:* The fulfillment of the promise did not take place until the saving work of Christ had been completed. Now they have obtained (6:12) what Christians still on earth possess only in an anticipatory way.

67   **(B) God's Treatment of His Sons (12:1–13).** **2–3.** Jesus is the model for endurance of hardship. *for the sake of the joy:* Some take the Gk *anti* to mean "instead of" rather than "for the sake of." But the exhortation that the addressees persevere in view of the triumphant end of the race suggests that the author understands Jesus' example in the same way. **5–6.** Cf. Prov 3:11–12. **9.** *the father of spirits:* Cf. Num 16:22; 27:16.

68   **(C) The Penalties of Disobedience (12:14–29).** **15.** An exhortation to watch over one another to avert the danger of apostasy. *lest any bitter root spring up and cause trouble:* Cf. Deut 29:17 LXX. **16.** *no fornicator or profane person like Esau:* It is not certain that "fornicator" refers to Esau. His profaneness is shown by his giving up his birthright for a single meal (Gen 25:29–34). **17.** Esau is an example not only of apostasy but of the impossibility of repentance after that sin (cf. 6:4–6). **18–21.** The first part of a contrast between the assembly of Israel when the old covenant was made and that of those who have entered into the new. The former took place on earth; for its awesome circumstances, cf. Exod 19:12–13, 16–19; 20:18–21. **22.** The assembly of the people of the new covenant is in heaven. The author speaks to those who are still on the journey there, yet since they already possess the benefits of Jesus' sacrifice, he can speak of them as having already arrived. **23.** *the firstborn:* These may be the angels of v 22 (so Spicq, *Hébreux* 2. 407), or the entire assembly of the Christian faithful (so J. Lécuyer, *SPC* 2. 161–68). *the spirits . . . made perfect:* The saints of the OT; cf. 11:40. **24.** The blood of Abel cried out for vengeance (Gen 4:10); that of Jesus brings access to God (10:19). **25.** There will be greater punishment for those who reject God's warning from heaven than for those who rejected his warning given at Sinai. **26.** Cf. Hag 2:6.

69   **(VI) Final Exhortation, Blessing, Greetings (13:1–25).** **2.** Cf. Gen 18:1–8. **7–8.** The community's former leaders, whose faith is to be imitated, have died, but Jesus remains its high priest forever (cf. Filson, 'Yesterday' [→ 5 above] 30–35). **9.** *diverse and strange teachings:* These are connected with "foods," which, in contrast to grace, cannot benefit those who live by them. The Gk word *brōma* "food," is used elsewhere in Heb only in 9:10. G. Theissen sees both verses as a denigration of Christian sacramental cult; the apparent anti-Jewish polemic of 9:9–10 is only a way of reducing the Christian eucharist to the level of OT ritual (*Untersuchungen zum Hebräerbrief* [SNT 2; Gütersloh, 1969]

69–79). H. Koester holds that "what is attacked here as *bromata* is the Christian—but heretical—doctrine of direct communion with the divine in the sacrament or in any other regulations and rituals" (*HTR* 55 [1962] 315). For criticism of these views, see J. Thompson, *Beginnings* (→ 3 above) 141–51. Verse 10 suggests that the useless "foods" may be the sacrificial meals of Judaism. **10.** *we have an altar . . . have no right to eat:* The emphatic position of the first words implies that this is an answer to the charge that Christians are at a disadvantage in respect to sacrifice. The "altar" probably means the sacrifice of Christ, in which the believers participate. There is no convincing reason for taking this as a reference to the eucharist (cf. Kuss, *Auslegung* [→ 8 above] 1. 326–28; R. Williamson, *NTS* 21 [1974–75] 300–12. If, as it seems,

the author does not speak of the eucharist either here or elsewhere, the reason may be that he did not consider it a sacrifice. This seems more probable than the suggestion (Williamson, ibid. 309–10) that he belonged to a community that did not have any eucharistic celebration. **11.** Cf. Lev 16:27. **12.** A rather inexact comparison between the Day-of-Atonement ritual and Jesus' suffering "outside the gate" of Jerusalem. **20.** The only explicit reference in Heb to the resurrection; but see comment on 1:3. *the great shepherd of the sheep:* Cf. Isa 63:11. **22–25.** These verses, together with v 19, may constitute the epistolary ending of Heb, added when the homily was being sent to some group of Christians (→ 5 above). **22.** *word of exhortation:* → 5 above. *Timothy:* → Pastorals, 56:3. **24.** *those from Italy:* → 5 above.

61

THE GOSPEL ACCORDING TO JOHN

Pheme Perkins

BIBLIOGRAPHY

1 Barrett, C. K., *The Gospel according to John* (2d ed; Phl, 1978). Becker, J., "Aus der Literatur zum Johannesevangelium," *TRu* 47 (1982) 279–312. Boismard, M.-É. and A. Lamouille, *L'Evangile de Jean* (Paris, 1977). Brown, R. E., *The Community of the Beloved Disciple* (NY, 1979); *The Gospel according to John* (AB 29, 29A; GC, 1966, 1970). Bruce, F. F., *The Gospel of John* (GR, 1983). Bultmann, R., *The Gospel of John* (Phl, 1971). Carson, D. A., "Recent Literature on the Fourth Gospel," *Themelios* 9 (1983) 8–18. Cullmann, O., *The Johannine Circle* (Phl, 1976). Culpepper, R. A., *The Johannine School* (SBLDS 26; Missoula, 1975). Dauer, A., *Johannes und Lukas* (Würzburg, 1984). Dodd, C. H., *Historical Tradition in the Fourth Gospel* (Cambridge, 1963); *The Interpretation of the Fourth Gospel* (Cambridge, 1953). Dunn, J. D. G., "Let John Be John," *Das Evangelium und die Evangelien* (ed. P. Stuhlmacher; WUNT 18; Tübingen, 1983). Forestell, J. T., *The Word of the Cross* (AnBib 57; Rome, 1974). Gnilka, J., *Johannesevangelium* (Würzburg, 1983). Haacker, K., *Die Stiftung des Heils* (AzT 1/97; Stuttgart, 1972). Haenchen, E., *John* (2 vols.; Herm; Phl, 1984). Jonge, M. de, *Jesus: Stranger from Heaven* (SBLSBS 11; Missoula, 1977). Käsemann, E., *The Testament of Jesus* (Phl, 1968). Klein, G., "'Das wahre Licht scheint schon': Beobachtungen zur Zeit und Geschichtserfahrung einer urchristlichen Schule," *ZTK* 68 (1971) 261–326. Kysar, R., *The Fourth Evangelist and his Gospel* (Minneapolis, 1975); "The Gospel of John in Current Research," *RelSRev* 9 (1983) 314–23. Langbrandtner, W., *Weltferner Gott oder Gott der Liebe* (BBET 6; Frankfurt, 1977). Lindars, B., *The Gospel of John* (NCB; London, 1972). Maier, G., *Johannes-Evangelium. 1 Teil* (Stuttgart, 1984). Martyn, J. L., *History and Theology in the Fourth Gospel* (2d ed.; Nash, 1979). Potterie, I. de la, *La vérité dans saint Jean* (AnBib 73–74; Rome, 1977). Schnackenburg, R., *The Gospel According to St. John* (3 vols.; NY, 1968–82); *Das Johannesevangelium, IV. Teil* (HTKNT 4; Freiburg, 1984). Segovia, F. F., *Love Relationships in the Johannine Tradition* (SBLDS 58; Missoula, 1982). Smalley, S. S., *John* (Nash, 1978). Smith, D. M., *The Composition and Order of the Fourth Gospel* (New Haven, 1965); *Johannine Christianity* (Columbia, 1984). Thyen, H., "Aus der Literatur zum Johannesevangelium," *TRu* 42 (1977) 211–70; 43 (1978) 328–59. Vouga, F., *La cadre historique et l'intention théologique de Jean* (Paris, 1977). Witacre, R. A., *Johannine Polemic* (SBLDS 67; Chico, 1982).

DBSup 4. 815–43. *IDBSup* 482–86. Kümmel, *INT* 188–247. Wik-Schm, *ENT* 299–344.

INTRODUCTION

2 **(I) Sources and Composition.** The Johannine Gospel differs from the Synoptics in the style and content of Jesus' words, which no longer focus on the kingdom of God, use proverbs and parables, or appear in apophthegms. Instead, Jesus speaks in symbolic discourses, which often refer to his relationship to the Father. Chronologically, John differs in presenting the ministry of Jesus over a period of three years and having Jesus' death on the day of preparation before Passover. Geographically, John presents the ministry of Jesus alternating between Galilee and Judea, with its major focus on the confrontations in Judea. This pattern departs from the Synoptic picture of a relatively extensive ministry in Galilee followed by a brief period in Jerusalem before Jesus' arrest at Passover.

John agrees with the Synoptics that Jesus healed persons, multiplied the loaves, and rescued the disciples from a storm at sea, but he never includes exorcism among the healings of Jesus. Many of the miracles in the Johannine Gospel provide the occasion for symbolic insight into Jesus' identity. The Synoptics make the perception that Jesus is Messiah the climax of Jesus' Galilean ministry (Mark 8:31), whereas the disciples in John have confessed this truth from the beginning (1:41–49).

Despite its differences, John clearly draws on traditions about Jesus' ministry which are related to those found in the Synoptic Gospels and their sources. Awkward geographical, chronological, and literary transitions within the Gospel make it likely that various sources were worked into the composition of it. Although the precise determination of what was taken from a source and what has been composed by the evangelist is disputed, several types of source material appear to have been used. The miracle stories have probably been derived from a collection of Jesus' miracles.

Individual miracles may already have been elaborated with discourse about their significance by Johannine Christians before they were incorporated into the Gospel. The miracles source is often referred to as the Signs (or *sēmeia*) Source. Some scholars have suggested that the discourses in John might have resulted from the expansion of a collection of Jesus' sayings different from that behind the Synoptic Gospels. Others have proposed that John took over a well-formed pattern of revelation discourses from non-Christian sources, referred to as the Revelatory Discourse Source. Rather than assume such a source, it seems more plausible that the discourse material reflects patterns and units of preaching that had been developed within the Johannine community. Finally, John must have drawn on an earlier account of Jesus' passion and traditions about the empty tomb and resurrection appearances of Jesus.

3 At various points, John has links with traditions in Mark, Luke, and, to a lesser extent, Matthew. Some scholars hold that John did depend on on one or more of the Synoptics, most commonly Mark. Others suggest that the impulse to put the Johannine traditions about Jesus in the form of a gospel was the result of the appearance of Gospels in other communities, that the evangelist may have had some acquaintance with one or more of the Synoptics, but that the Fourth Gospel is based on an independent line of tradition preserved in the Johannine churches. That is the hypothesis adopted here. Some of the major episodes which occur in both John and the Synoptics are: ministry and testimony of JBap (John 1:19–36; Mark 1:4–8); cleansing of the Temple (John 2:14–16); feeding the multitude (John 6:1–13; Mark 6:34–44); walking on the sea (John 6:16–21; Mark 6:45–52); request for a sign (John 6:30; Mark 8:11); Peter's confession (John 6:68–69; Mark 8:29); anointing of Jesus (John 12:1–8; Mark 14:3–9); entry into Jerusalem (John 12:12–15; Mark 11:1–10); Last Supper and predictions of betrayal (John 13:1–30; Mark 14:17–26); arrest (John 18:1–11; Mark 14:43–52); passion (John 18:12–19:30; Mark 14:53–15:41); burial and empty tomb (John 19:38–20:10; Mark 15:42–16:8); Jesus appears to women (John 20:11–18; Matt 28:9–10); Jesus appears to disciples in Jerusalem (John 20:19–23; Luke 24:36–49); Jesus appears to disciples in Galilee (John 21:1–19; Matt 28:16–20, a Galilean appearance; Luke 5:1–11, a miraculous catch of fish). The healing of the royal official's son in John 4:46–54 is more distantly related to the healings in Matt 8:5–13 and Luke 7:1–10, and the healing of the man born blind in John 9 parallels healings of the blind in the Synoptics (e.g., Mark 8:22–26; 10:46–52).

Some of the sayings of Jesus also appear in Synoptic and Johannine versions: words of JBap (John 1:27; Mark 1:7 par.; John 1:33; Mark 1:8 par.; John 1:34; Mark 1:11 par.); the name "Cephas" for Peter (John 1:42; Mark 3:16 par.); a Son-of-Man saying (John 1:51; Mark 14:62 par.?); saying about the Temple (John 2:19; Mark 14:58 par.; Mark 15:29 par.); a saying about "becoming a child" to enter the kingdom (John 3:3,5 ["newborn" instead of child]; Mark 10:15; Luke 18:17?); comment on the plentiful harvest (John 4:35; Matt 9:37–38); prophet in his own country (John 4:44; Mark 6:4 par.); losing and saving one's life (John 12:25; Mark 8:35 par.); servant and master (John 13:16; 15:20; Matt 10:24); envoy and sender (John 13:20; Matt 10:40; Luke 10:16; Mark 9:37; Luke 9:48); forgiving sins (John 20:23; Matt 18:18; 16:19).

John does not quote the OT frequently. Of the 18 explicit citations (1:23; 2:17; 6:31,45; 7:38,42; 8:17; 10:34; 12:15,38,40; 13:18; 15:25; 17:12; 19:24,28,36,37), only five are clearly parallel to quotations in the Synoptics:

JBap as a "voice crying in the wilderness" (Isa 40:3; John 1:23; Mark 1:3 par.); "king is coming," entry into Jerusalem (Zech 9:9; John 12:15; Matt 21:5); hardening of hearts (Isa 6:9–10; John 12:40; Mark 4:12 par.); the traitor (Ps 41:10; Mark 14:18 [allusion]); casting lots for Jesus' clothing (Ps 22:19; John 19:24; Mark 15:24 par. [without identification as a citation]). Some of the other citations are derived from passages that were frequently used in the early church: John 2:17; 15:25; 19:28 and 19:29 refer to Ps 69, a commonly cited psalm of suffering; John 6:31 and perhaps 7:38 refer to Ps 78:16,20,24.

4 Exegetes have pointed to problems of transition and duplications within the Gospel as evidence that it is the result of several stages of editing. The clearest examples of additions to the Gospel occur with chaps. 15–17 and 21. Both follow on what appear to be formal conclusions (14:31; 20:30–31). John 16:5 contradicts John 14:4. The functions attributed to the Paraclete in John 14:16–17 and 14:26 differ from those in John 16:7–11 and 16:13–14. John 21:20–23 contains a reference to the death of the Beloved Disciple, who is identified as the witness behind the Johannine tradition in 21:24. These passages would seem to be material that had been circulating within the Johannine community and was added to the Gospel in the appropriate locations in order to preserve it. The relative "age" of any particular element in the tradition would have to be determined on other grounds.

It is also frequently suggested that some shorter passages which seem to be left hanging may have been added in the editing process. John 3:31–36, which suddenly breaks in without any transition to a passage in which JBap has been speaking, may represent an editorial summary to conclude the chapter. But it is also seen to parallel an earlier switch to the voice of the narrator away from the words of Jesus in John 3:16–21. John 6:51–59 expands the discourse on the bread of life with a clear reference to the eucharistic celebration; it also situates the discourse in the synagogue at Capernaum (v 59) rather than by the sea (v 22). The affirmation in 5:24–26 that the present response to Jesus' word is the time of judgment in which one passes to eternal life sits awkwardly next to a reference to the future coming of the Son of Man (5:27–29). John 12:44–50 is an isolated piece of discourse, since the public ministry would appear to conclude with the pericope on the hardness of heart that kept "the Jews" from accepting Jesus' preaching (12:36b–43).

Many scholars solve the difficulties created by the juxtaposition of a healing in Jerusalem in John 5, the feeding miracle and associated discourses in Galilee in John 6, and then discourses back in Jerusalem in John 7, which refer to the issues of John 5 (in 7:15–24), by presuming that John 6 has been "dislocated" from a sequence of Galilean stories. It has also been proposed that at one time the account of Jesus' public ministry ended with the withdrawal of Jesus in 10:40–42. Later, the tradition about the raising of Lazarus was elaborated into an affirmation of Jesus as "resurrection and life" and made the precipitating cause for Jesus' death, which led to the insertion of 11:1–12:11,20–50. Perhaps, the story of the cleansing of the Temple, which John, contrary to the Synoptics, now has at the beginning of the public ministry, was displaced when this new material was added.

The prologue which opens the Gospel (1:1–18) seems to elaborate on an early hymn. Comments about JBap have been inserted in vv 6–8,15 and about revelation through Jesus in contrast to Moses in vv 17–18. The rest of the Gospel does not speak of Jesus as the preexistent, creative Word. Therefore, some interpreters suggest that the hymnic introduction was added after the Gospel had been completed.

This commentary is based on the Johannine text in its present form. The difficulties that have led to the various theories of sources and editions make it probable that the Gospel has been reworked in the Johannine community, but it is difficult to separate editing of the Gospel from the development of Synoptic-like stories and discourses into their Johannine form prior to the composition of a gospel narrative. Nor does it seem possible to derive the "wording" of pre-gospel sources from the Gospel as it stands. This commentary also assumes that the editing of the Gospel took place in accord with the orientation of the Johannine material and was not, as some exegetes suppose, a way of making a heterodox Christian writing more acceptable to some undefined ecclesiastical standard.

5   (II) Background of the Fourth Gospel. Exegetes have sought for the background to the Gospel in the diverse religious movements of the 1st cent. The complexity of this quest is due, in part, to the universality of the symbols in John. The Gospel affirms that whatever a person's understanding of salvation is, that expectation is fulfilled (and corrected) by the unique revelation of God in Jesus (see G. W. MacRae, *CBQ* 32 [1970] 13–24).

Although the term *Logos,* "Word," is linked with the immanent divine spirit that pervades and orders the cosmos in Stoic philosophy, there is no other hint of philosophic terminology in the Gospel. Nor do the contrasts between "above" and "below," "heavenly" and "earthly" function in the way that they do in Platonic philosophy. Therefore, suggestions that part of John's unique perspective was shaped by philosophy, even of a popular sort, are unlikely.

Links between the Gospel and pagan religious cults are also fairly tenuous. The Synoptic tradition has nothing comparable to turning water into wine (John 2:1–11). But the god Dionysus was said to be responsible for transforming water into wine (e.g., Euripides, *Bacchae* 704–7; Pausanias, *Descr. of Greece* 6.26.1–2). This miracle appears to have been "enacted" in rituals at Dionysus shrines, and some readers of the Fourth Gospel may have associated the Cana miracle and the Dionysus cult (see E. Linnemann, *NTS* 20 [1973–74] 408–18). But short of the substances transformed, there is nothing else in the Johannine story to suggest that the Dionysus cult was responsible for the attribution of such a miracle to Jesus.

The Johannine image of "rebirth" (1:13; 3:3,5) and the affirmations that the believer possesses eternal life are sometimes linked with the mystery cults or with the Hermetic writings. However, the story of Jesus is quite different from the enactment of a mythic story of the death or captivity in Hades and restoration (usually partial) of the deity, which constitutes what is publicly known of the gods and goddesses of such cults. In addition, some scholars feel that the promises held out to the initiate in the mysteries had much less to do with immortality than is commonly supposed. Prosperity, friendship with the god or goddess, and protection in this life are equally important themes in the mysteries (see R. MacMullen, *Paganism in the Roman Empire* [New Haven, 1981] 133–37). Some of the links between John and the Hermetic writings, such as the use of Logos in a creation myth (*C.H.* 1.5–6), are due to the incorporation of Gen into the syncretistic system of the Hermetic work. The mystery of rebirth in *C.H.* 13 presumes a salvific vision in which the initiate is transformed into the deity. The Fourth Gospel never suggests that the

Christian is transformed "into God." Only Jesus has such a special relationship with the Father.

6   As scholars recover the diversity of 1st-cent. Judaism, the Jewish background of the Gospel comes more sharply into focus. Though John does not cite the OT as frequently as the Synoptics do, allusions to OT texts and images often appear to be woven into the discourses (see G. Reim, *Studien zum alttestamentlichen Hintergrund des Johannesevangeliums* [SNTSMS 22; Cambridge, 1974]). The references to the patriarchs Jacob (4:5–6; 1:51) and Abraham (8:31–58) reflect traditions that had developed in 1st-cent. Judaism. The exposition on the bread of life in 6:30–59 has been compared with the homiletic exposition of the *midrāšîm* (see P. Borgen, *Bread from Heaven* [NovTSup 10; Leiden, 1965]). Other references to the OT in John may have been derived from targumic traditions (see G. Reim, *BZ* 27 [1983] 1–13). Mosaic traditions are taken up in the covenant allusions of John 1:17–18; the typology of the serpent in 3:14; the discourse on the manna/bread of life and the imagery of the people "murmuring" against Jesus in John 6; the subordination of Moses to Jesus in 5:45–47 and 9:28–29, and the affirmation that Jesus is the Mosaic prophet of Deut 18:15 (1:21,25; 4:19; 6:14; 7:40).

Even the Johannine expressions for Jesus' special relationship with God are rendered intelligible against a Jewish background. The hymnic affirmation of Jesus as divine Word active in creation reflects the tradition's portrayal of God's Wisdom as agent of creation (Prov 8:22–30; Wis 9:1–9). Wisdom is described as coming forth from her dwelling with God to be with humans. As Jesus is rejected by "his own" (John 1:11), Wisdom finds no dwelling among humans (*1 Enoch* 42:2). Although the OT traditions do not speak of Wisdom as "Word," the two are equated in Philo of Alexandria, and Wisdom and Word or the law often appear in parallelism. The Johannine Jesus also identifies himself with the divine "I Am" (e.g., 8:24,28,58; 13:19). The LXX of Dt-Isa clearly understands the expression *egō eimi,* "I Am," as the divine name (Isa 51:12; 52:6). OT symbolism also underlies the other class of "I Am" sayings, in which a predicate provides the figurative description of Jesus (6:35,51; 8:12 [9:15]; 10:7,9; 10:11,14; 11:25; 14:6; 15:1,5; → Johannine Theology, 83:41–49).

Finally, the Gospel advances Jesus' claims to speak for God and to be received as God on the grounds that Jesus is God's agent. The Jewish legal traditions about agency held that the agent is "like the one who sent him." The agent has the authority to function as though he were the sender (see P. Borgen, "God's Agent in the Fourth Gospel," *Religions in Antiquity* [Fest. E. R. Goodenough; ed. J. Neusner; Leiden, 1968] 137–47).

The DSS have provoked further questions about the relationship between the Fourth Gospel and Jewish traditions. Similarities between the dualism of light and darkness in the DSS and John suggest that some of the symbolism of the Gospel derives from sectarian Jewish circles. The group of antitheses, light–darkness (1:5; 3:19–21; 8:12; 12:35–36,46), truth–lie (8:44–45), spirit–flesh (1:13; 3:6; 6:63), all have parallels in the religious imagery of the DSS. The Johannine image of an adversary, "ruler of this world" (12:31; 14:20; 16:11), or the "devil," master of those who belong to him (8:41, 44), has a counterpart in the DSS image of the "angel of darkness," who is master of the "children of darkness" and attempts to mislead the "children of light" (1QS 3:18b–4:1; → Johannine Theology, 83:31–32).

Other similarities have been suggested between the doctrine of the Spirit in the Fourth Gospel and the DSS. The DSS contain hints of the relationship between water and the giving of the Spirit (cf. John 3:5; 7:37–38; 1QS

4:19-28). The expression "Spirit of Truth" (John 14:17; 15:26; 16:13) appears in 1QS 3:6-7. Some exegetes have suggested that the mysterious figure of the Paraclete, esp. as it comes to convict the world in John 16:8-11, has been derived in some way from DSS images of the heavenly, angelic defenders of Israel, Michael or Melchizedek.

Differences between John and the DSS make it unlikely that the evangelist forged his theological vision by simply taking over the symbol system of a 1st-cent. Jewish baptismal sect. The life-death antithesis, which is prominent in John (e.g., 5:24; 8:51; 6:49,58; 11:25), does not play such a striking role in the DSS. Whereas purity and obedience to the law distinguish the "children of light" from those of darkness in the DSS, the Fourth Gospel makes belief in Jesus as the one who has come from God and who reveals God the dividing point. There are, however, enough similarities to support the suggestion that at some time there must have been contact between the Johannine tradition and the type of religious symbolism that had developed in such sectarian Jewish circles.

7 The story of Samaritan converts in John 4:7-42 may provide a clue to yet another religious tradition which lies in the background of the Fourth Gospel. This story reflects Samaritan expectations of a "prophet like Moses" and of the eschatological restoration of the true worship of God on Mt. Gerizim. Josephus reports that such expectations had led a crowd to follow a man who promised to reveal where Moses had buried the vessels (*Ant.* 18.4.1 § 85; see M. F. Collins, *JSJ* 3 [1972] 97-116). The expectation of a "prophet like Moses" was not limited to the Samaritans. It is also found in the DSS (4QTestim, 1QS 9:11). The charge that Jesus is a "demon-possessed" Samaritan in John 8:48 has been taken to imply that the early Johannine church had incorporated a group of Samaritan converts (Brown, *Community* 37-38). Since the details of 1st-cent. Samaritan beliefs about the prophet to come are unclear, some exegetes caution against elaborate inferences about the influence of Samaritan expectations on the Fourth Gospel (see M. Pamment, *ZNW* 73 [1982] 221-30).

8 Certain features of the Johannine picture of Jesus do not appear to be completely represented in the background material from Jewish sources. The most striking is the Gospel's focus on Jesus as the one who has come from heaven with a revelation of God that was not "known" by anyone else. The "I Am" proclamations of the Gospel have counterparts in the revelatory declarations of gnostic revealer figures. Since the extant gnostic writings postdate the Gospel, their value in providing background for the emergence of Johannine christology and soteriology is disputed. First-person, revelatory discourse by a heavenly revealer, which employs pronouncements in the "I Am" style, is well represented in such works as *Thunder, Perfect Mind,* and *Trimorphic Protennoia* (*NHLE* 271-77, 461-70). Both *Trimorphic Protennoia* and *Tripartite Tractate* employ "Word" as one of the manifestations of the divine revealer. But these revelatory discourses are attached to heavenly figures derived from a divine triad of Father—Mother—Son and are embedded in a mythic context. Any contact between the Fourth Gospel and gnosticism would have to be between Johannine traditions and those strands of heterodox Jewish exegesis and pagan myth making and philosophy that were welded together in later gnostic syntheses (see G. W. MacRae, "Nag Hammadi and the New Testament," *Gnosis* [Fest. H. Jonas; ed. B. Aland; Göttingen, 1978] 144-57; Y. Janssens, "The Trimorphic Protennoia and the Fourth Gospel," *The New Testament*

and Gnosis [Fest. R. McL. Wilson; ed. A. H. B. Logan, et al.; Edinburgh, 1983] 229-44).

Jewish wisdom traditions also played a role in shaping gnostic stories of the divine Sophia (Wisdom) and of rejected revelation (see G. W. MacRae, *NovT* 12 [1970] 86-101). Some scholars argue that the gnostic writings of the 2d cent. already presuppose a myth of a heavenly revealer, who comes to save humanity by bringing "knowledge of God and the divine world" to humans trapped in ignorance. This story was, they suggest, attached to Seth or to the heavenly Adam or to Wisdom. It emerged from heterodox Jewish traditions of exegesis of Gen sometime in the 1st cent. (see K. Rudolph, *Gnosis* [SF, 1983] 113-59). Though it is possible to distinguish the christology of the Fourth Gospel from the gnostic systems of the 2d cent., its picture of Jesus as divine revealer may stand much closer to the redeemer stories that were emerging in gnosticizing circles at the end of the 1st cent.

However, it is often possible to argue that the process of gnostic mythologizing was influenced by the development of Christian claims about Jesus as revelation of God. One finds a heightening of the connection between Jesus, the Logos, and the redeemer as gnostic writers of the 2d cent. seek to present a more explicitly Christian front. Thus, the "Christian" gnostic author of *Concept of Our Great Power* says of Jesus: "Who is this? What is this? His Logos has abolished the law of the eon. He is from the Logos of the power of life. And he was victorious over the command of the archons, and they were not able to rule over him" (42.4-11). The Logos is victorious over the powers of the lower world (cf. John 12:31; 14:30-31; 16:11,33b). In *Apocalypse of Adam,* which has hardly been christianized, we find the Logos assigned to the thirteenth generation, the last of the lower world (92.10-17). It has been suggested that this Sethian work is aware of Johannine christology and has placed Jesus' kingdom squarely in the material world ruled by Sakla. Only the gnostics are not enslaved by Sakla, are a race without a king over them (92.19-20). This author, then, appears to be rejecting the possibility of assimilating the Johannine Logos to gnosticism in such a way as to claim that redemption came through a gnostic Jesus (see G. A. Stroumsa, *Another Seed* [NHS 24; Leiden, 1984] 96-103).

9 **(III) The Johannine Community.** One approach to "ordering" the complex patterns of sources, editing, and backgrounds presented by the Fourth Gospel is to formulate a set of hypotheses about the origins, development, and social setting of the Johannine church (as in W. A. Meeks, "The Man from Heaven in Johannine Sectariansm," *JBL* 91 [1972] 44-72; Martyn, *History and Theology;* Brown, *Community;* → Johannine Theology, 83:9-14).

The most characteristic division in the Gospel is that between Jesus as the one who is "from above" and what is from this world. The second half of the Gospel focuses on Jesus' return to the Father from whom he came. The pattern of descent and return also establishes the identity of the Johannine community (see G. C. Nicholson, *Death as Departure: The Johannine Descent-Ascent Schema* [SBLDS 63; Chico, 1983]). The Gospel suggests at least three groups that the community had to draw its boundaries against: (a) followers of JBap (1:35-37; 3:22-30; 4:1-3; 10:40-42); (b) the Jews, who had taken measures to expel those who believed in Jesus from the synagogues (9:22-23; 16:1-4a), and (c) other "Christians," who had been followers of Jesus but who have now separated themselves from the community, apparently over the christological affirmations of the divinity of Jesus (6:60-65).

Further hints about the "social world" of the Johannine community have been drawn from the Fourth Gospel. John 4:4–42 alludes to the conversion of a significant group of Samaritans. The coming of the Gentiles in John 12:20–26 suggests that the community had turned from the largely futile mission to the Jews and sought to evangelize the Gentiles. Despite the Jewish ban on Christians in the synagogues, an event that some scholars link to the formulation of the benediction against heretics (*birkat hammînîm*) around AD 90, John insists that there were believers and sympathizers within the Jewish community (12:42–43). John 16:1–4a implies that persecution continued beyond the Jewish expulsion from the synagogue (see B. Lindars, "The Persecution of Christians in John 15:18–16:4a," *Suffering and Martyrdom in the New Testament* [Fest. G. M. Styler; ed. W. Horbury, *et al.;* Cambridge, 1981] 48–69).

Finally, the figure of Peter in the Fourth Gospel appears to represent Christians of apostolic communities outside the Johannine church. Peter is characterized as the leader of the Twelve. The final edition of the Gospel establishes Peter's place as "shepherd" in a commissioning by the risen Lord (21:15–17). At the same time, Peter's "faith" and closeness to Jesus are always inferior to that of the Beloved Disciple (13:23; 20:4,8; 21:7). While Acts 1:14 claims that the mother of Jesus was part of the circle of the Twelve in Jerusalem, John 19:26–27 asserts that Jesus entrusted his mother to the Beloved Disciple, the only disciple present at the cross. Some exegetes hold that John 21 was created to moderate the rejection of a Petrine pattern of authoritative shepherds in the Johannine community, which had based its tradition of leadership on the "Paraclete-inspired" Beloved Disciple (see A. H. Maynard, *NTS* 30 [1984] 531–48).

10 R. E. Brown (*Community*) has forged a hypothesis linking the development of the Johannine church with the tradition history of the Gospel. The Gospel was composed after the crisis caused by the expulsion of Christians from the synagogue. The severity of its condemnation of "the Jews" indicates that the persecution had been a costly one. Perhaps it was even followed by a geographic move from the Palestine of the original Johannine community to a location in the Diaspora such as Ephesus, the locale assigned to Johannine Christianity in later church traditions.

Preservation of authentic details about Palestine not found in the Synoptics and the emphasis on proper evaluation of JBap point to the origins of the community among the diverse sects of Palestinian Judaism. Two important sources of the Gospel go back to this period: (a) the collection of Jewish messianic titles and the affirmation that Jesus fulfills the Scripture, which now form the basis of John 1:19–51; (b) the initial collection of the miracles of Jesus, which at this period were probably expounded as evidence for belief in Jesus as Messiah and Son of God (see M.-É. Boismard, *ETL* 58 [1982] 357–64).

At some point members of the Johannine community converted a number of Samaritans. The mission in Samaria may have coincided with the emphasis on Jesus as the replacement for the Temple (2:13–22), the rituals of purification (2:6) and the other feasts of the Jewish calendar such as Passover and Tabernacles. It would also have brought to the fore the Mosaic themes: Jesus is the true source of the covenant blessings, the only one to have "seen God," and the Mosaic prophet who restores true worship of God.

After expulsion from the synagogue and possibly a relocation from Palestine to Ephesus(?), the missionary effort of the community is focused on Gentiles. John 7:35 and 12:20–22 may indicate the initial success of that endeavor. This period (in the 90s) also sees the elaboration of the community's tradition in writing. The extensive homiletic expansion on the miracle traditions, the Logos hymn in the prologue, and the carefully crafted passion narrative probably preceded the composition of a narrative account of Jesus' mission. Some of the discourse material now preserved in chaps. 15–17 may also have taken shape during this period.

Finally, close to the turn of the century, we see the Johannine community torn by schism in the Johannine Epistles. Some scholars trace echoes of that schism back into the Gospel (e.g., in the exhortation to remain on the vine in 15:1–17; so F. F. Segovia, *JBL* 101 [1982] 115–28). The final editing of the Gospel acknowledging the "shepherd" in the Petrine churches may also have taken place at this time.

11 The Johannine epistles present a picture of the Johannine church as a collection of "house churches" clustered around a central area and linked together by traveling missionaries. They suggest that the schism between Johannine Christians resulted from divergent interpretations of the meaning of the inherited tradition. Some exegetes see this inner-directed schism as evidence that the Johannine community had played out the logic of its dualistic symbol system and become a sect. The schism may only intensify the process of rigid self-identification and isolation. The acknowledgment of Petrine authority in John 21 may have made it possible for some Johannine churches to amalgamate with Christians from other churches. But for others the Johannine symbol system could lead to the kind of "mythologizing ontology" provided by the 2d-cent. gnostics.

12 **(IV) Authorship of the Fourth Gospel.** The "writing down" of Johannine traditions was clearly part of the ongoing life of the community. It may have been the result of a "Johannine school" of disciples of the Beloved Disciple and teachers within the Johannine churches. There is a sufficient unity in the literary composition and the narrated point of view in the Gospel to justify the claim that a single individual was responsible for the structure of the gospel narrative. But the importance of the community's history of faith in shaping the Johannine tradition makes preoccupation with a single Johannine author inappropriate today.

Appropriation of John by gnostics made it important for the ancient church to pursue the question of its apostolic authorship. Some Christians were suspicious of John because it was so popular with heretical groups and was so different from the other Gospels. If it could be shown that the Gospel had apostolic origins, then orthodox Christians could adopt it. One of the strongest opponents of gnosticism, bishop Irenaeus of Lyons (d. 202), defended the apostolicity of John and its inclusion in the Christian canon of four Gospels by appealing to the tradition that was circulating in Asia Minor in his time. He affirms that it was composed by the Beloved Disciple, named John, at Ephesus toward the end of his life. Irenaeus has heard that John had lived until the time of Trajan, i.e., the beginning of the 2d cent. AD (*Adv. Haer.* 3.1.2; 3.3.4; 2.33.3; also Eusebius, *HE* 3.23.3; 5.20.4–8). However, Irenaeus also appears to have confused the apostle, John the son of Zebedee, with a presbyter from Asia Minor known as John. Since Irenaeus claims to have received his information as a child from Polycarp, the bishop of Smyrna (d. 156), we should not be overly surprised at the confusion. The church historian Eusebius also recognized that Irenaeus had confused two different persons known as "John."

Christians at Ephesus venerated John, the son of Zebedee, in the 2d cent. In fact, Eusebius reports that they had two different tombs, both of which were said to be his resting place. Eusebius suggests that perhaps the extra tomb was really that of the Christian prophet named John who had written Rev (*HE* 3.31.3; 3.39.6). By the end of the 2d cent. variants of the tradition that the Fourth Gospel was composed by the apostle John at Ephesus are known in Alexandria (see Eusebius, *HE* 6.14.7) and Rome (Muratorian Canon 9-16, 26-33). Once this apostolic identification was made, the place of the Fourth Gospel in the orthodox Christian canon was assured. Even in antiquity, Eusebius recognized that there was confusion over various persons named John associated with Christianity at Ephesus. The author of John 21 clearly does not identify the Beloved Disciple, who is the source of the Johannine tradition, with John the son of Zebedee. John 21:2 refers to "the (sons) of Zebedee," whereas 21:7,20 refer to the Beloved Disciple. Elsewhere, the Gospel also appears to separate the Twelve from other disciples of the Lord, including the Beloved Disciple. Another difficulty for the view that John the son of Zebedee was the author of the Fourth Gospel is the presumption of Mark 10:39 that both brothers would suffer martyrdom. John 21:20-23 asserts quite clearly that the Beloved Disciple did not die a martyr's death as Peter did. Finally, modern exegetes observe that the developments in christology and the realized eschatology of the Fourth Gospel are well beyond what would be likely for a Galilean fisherman.

Although scholars today give quite a different answer to the question about the authorship of the Fourth Gospel, this solution need not undermine the basic point that affirmation of apostolic authorship made. The Fourth Gospel is not an inherently heretical work, a covert "baptizing" of a non-Christian redeemer myth, or a docetic portrayal of Jesus as the heavenly Christ. It is a witness to the legitimate development of apostolic faith. As such, it had a rightful place within the orthodox gospel canon just as Irenaeus insisted.

13   **(V) Literary Features of the Fourth Gospel.** Scholars also seek to understand the Gospel as it stands before us. What special features of composition and style has the author used? How are characters and their relationships depicted? What is the "plot" that guides the story from its beginning to its conclusion? (See R. A. Culpepper, *Anatomy of the Fourth Gospel* [Phl, 1983].)

A Johannine discourse is shaped by the repetition of set words, the formulation of antitheses, inclusion, and the structuring of verses within a unit in a chiastic pattern. These features are illustrated by John 8:12-20. An "I Am" saying introduces the discourse about testimony and judgment (v 12). Jesus opposes the Pharisees' objection with a contrary thesis. The passage then develops around a series of catchwords. Verse 14 introduces an opposition, "I know . . . you do not know [where Jesus has come from and is going]." Verse 15 creates a variant opposition: "You judge according to the flesh; I do not judge." Verse 16 returns to the objection from v 13 that Jesus would not testify "truly" and also introduces what the Johannine reader knows to be true of Jesus' origins, his link with the Father. At the same time the reference to true judgment retains its link to the previous verse. Verse 17 then invokes the law that pronounces the testimony of two witnesses to be true. Verse 18 opens with the "I Am" expression and names the two witnesses. Both v 16 and v 18 place the word "Father" in an emphatic position at the end of the sentence. Verse 19 opens with an objection phrased as a question, "Where" is your Father, which Jesus answers with another statement that distinguishes himself from the Pharisees in terms of knowledge, "You do not know me or my Father," an expression that is further emphasized by being repeated, "If you knew me, you would know my Father." Then

the evangelist/narrator steps in to bring the unit to a conclusion (v 20). At the same time he directs our attention to the goal of the plot, the "hour" when Jesus will be seized and return to the Father at the crucifixion.

This passage also reflects another Johannine technique, deliberate misunderstanding by Jesus' protagonists of what he says. The misunderstanding is evident in the question "Where is your Father." Misunderstandings often turn on a double meaning that can be assigned to a particular word or phrase used by Jesus. The main examples of such misunderstanding are: 2:19-21, "the Temple," Jesus' death and resurrection; 3:3-5, "born again/from above," becoming a child of God; 4:10-15, "living water," the Spirit that comes from Jesus [7:38]; 4:31-34, "food," doing the will of the Father; 6:32-35, "bread from heaven," Jesus' saving revelation; 6:51-53, "my flesh," Jesus' saving death; 7:33-36, "I go . . . you cannot," Jesus' glorification; 8:21-22, "I go away," glorification; 8:31-35, "make you free," given by Jesus to those who become children of God; 8:51-53, "death," eternal life; 8:56-58, "see my day," Jesus reveals God; 11:11-15, "sleep," death and eternal life; 11:23-25, "brother will rise again," Jesus is life; 12:32-34, "lifted up," glorification on the cross; 13:36-38, "I am going," glorification; 14:4-6, "where I am going," glorification, Jesus as the way; 14:7-9, "you have seen Him," Jesus reveals God; 16:16-19, "little while," Jesus' death and return to the disciples (see G. W. MacRae, "Theology and Irony in the Fourth Gospel," *The Word in the World* [Fest. F. L. Moriarty; ed. R. J. Clifford, *et al.;* Cambridge MA, 1973] 83-96; D. A. Carson, *TynBul* 33 [1982] 59-91).

It is also characteristic of the narrator to break into the narrative and speak in his own voice. He explains names (1:38,42) and symbols (2:21; 12:33; 18:9); corrects possible misapprehensions (4:2; 6:6); reminds the reader of related events (3:24; 11:2), or reidentifies characters (7:50; 21:20). The narrator's interjections make him the authoritative interpreter of Jesus' words (2:21; 6:6,71; 7:39; 8:27; 12:33; 13:11; 18:32; 21:19,13). Sometimes the narrator provides a retrospective comment that indicates the understanding which the Johannine community has achieved after the resurrection (2:22; 12:16; 13:7; 20:9).

14   The plot of the Gospel is focused on the "hour" of Jesus' glorification, his return to the Father at the crucifixion. Summary statements remind the reader of the mission that Jesus has been sent by the Father to accomplish (1:11-12; 18:37). The significance of Jesus' ministry in revealing the Father and bringing about the "grace and truth," the blessings of the covenant (not brought by Moses), is stated in 1:14,18. The prayer in John 17 is the triumphant announcement that Jesus' mission has reached its goal. He has revealed the Father to the community of disciples, and through them to others. He now returns to the "glory" which he had had with the Father (17:4,6,26).

At the same time that the plot moves toward the glorification of Jesus, the narrative moves through cycles of acceptance and rejection. The first half of the Gospel, chaps. 1-12, falls into two sections. Although there are proleptic hints of "the hour," of inadequate faith and rejection of Jesus, chaps. 1-4 are essentially positive statements of Jesus' coming to those who receive him. Though Nicodemus fails to become a believer, he remains positively disposed toward Jesus and will even suffer the accusation of being one of Jesus' disciples (3:1-15; 7:45-52; 19:39). The dialogues with Nicodemus and the Samaritan woman introduce the reader to the "double meaning" of Johannine discourse and to the idea that Jesus is the locus of all salvation. Chaps. 5-12,

however, tell the story of conflicts over Jesus' identity
and his progressive rejection. The tale is one of escalat-
ing conflict over belief/unbelief. Unlike the Synoptic
stories, there is no other form of conflict in the plot: no
demons to defeat, no struggle with hostile forces of
nature, no conflict with the disciples. The misunderstandings that arise on the part of the disciples are
presented as a necessary component of a faith that must
remain incomplete until Jesus has concluded his mission
and returned to the Father.

Chaps. 13–17 provide an interlude, though one
clearly marked by the impending departure of Jesus
(13:2). Once Judas has left the supper room, "it is night"
(13:30). Jesus turns to speak with his disciples about his
departure, their grief, and their future joy when he
"returns" to dwell with them, when the Paraclete comes
to guide them, or when they eventually come to see the
glory which Jesus has had with the Father since the
beginning. After that, the events of the passion begin to
unfold in a carefully crafted series of short scenes until
the dying Jesus pronounces his mission completed
(19:30). The resurrection traditions appended to the
Gospel then carry the reader into the future mission of
the disciples, for which they had been commissioned in
the supper discourses. The commissioning themes are
stronger in the present arrangement of the Gospel,
which includes chaps. 15–17 and 21, than they would
have been in the proposed initial version, which included only John 13:31–14:31. That discourse is primarily directed toward internal relationships between the
disciples, Jesus, the Father, and the Paraclete. The resurrection stories in John 20 can also be said to establish
faith within the community. The Thomas episode paves
the way for the narrator's statement that the gospel is to
lead us to faith in Jesus (20:30–31). But the discourses of
John 15–17 establish the community of disciples in that
pattern of struggle over belief/unbelief in the "world"
which had marked the ministry of Jesus.

15   None of the characterizations in the Fourth
Gospel stirs as much dispute as its portrayal of "the
Jews" (see W. A. Meeks, "'Am I a Jew?' Johannine
Christianity and Judaism," *Christianity, Judaism and Other
Greco-Roman Cults* [Fest. M. Smith; ed. J. Neusner; SJLA
12; Leiden, 1975] 1. 163–86; U. von Wahlde, *JBL* 98
[1979] 231–53; J. Ashton, *NovT* 27 [1985] 40–75). By
the time the Gospel was composed any possibility of
conversions from among "the Jews" appears to have
been over. With the exception of traditional expressions
like "king of the Jews" or passing references to Jewish
feasts or customs (2:6,13; 7:2), the generic references to
"the Jews" appear to be the work of the evangelist. Both
the narrator and Jesus speak of "the Jews" as outsiders.
"The Jews" cause fear in the people (9:22); they are
sharply distinguished from the disciples (13:33), and
they follow "their law" (7:19; 8:17; 15:25; cf. 10:34).

When the phrase "the Jews" has nothing to do with
ethnic (Jewish as opposed to Samaritan, 4:22), religious,
or geographical differentiation (inhabitants of Judea
rather than Galilee, some of whom do believe in Jesus,
11:19,31,33,36; 12:9,11), it is emblematic of unbelief.
Some of the shifts between an apparently neutral use of
the phrase "the Jews" and "the Jews" as hostile enemies
of Jesus may be dictated by the narrative's emphasis on
the growing crisis of unbelief. John's blanket use of "the
Jews" as protagonists in the story has erased much of the
diversity of Jewish persons in the Synoptic traditions.
Explanations of disbelief are not grounded in the peculiarities of Judaism but in the fundamental oppositions of
the symbolic world created by the Gospel. They have
not "heard or seen the Father" (5:37); do not want to
"come to Jesus in order to have life" (5:40); have the

"love of God in themselves" (5:42); receive Jesus (5:43),
or seek God's glory (5:44). Ultimately, they are "from
below," whereas Jesus is "from above" (8:23). Not all
who are Jews in the narrative fall into these negative
categories, since some do believe. Further, the hints that
belief must be "given" by the Father (6:37,39,44,65;
10:3) mitigate some of the harshness in the description
of unbelief. Since the evangelist has clearly shaped the
characterization of "the Jews" to the plot of his story of
belief and unbelief, one cannot derive from his statements canonical warrant for anti-Semitism among
Christians today.

16   **(VI) Christology in the Fourth Gospel.**
Investigation of Johannine christology is demanded by
the focus of the Gospel itself. John 20:31 points to faith
in Jesus as "Son of God" as the source of eternal life. The
same link is made in the first prediction of Jesus' "lifting
up" as "Son of Man" in John 3:15. The call to "believe"
that echoes throughout the Fourth Gospel characteristically has Jesus as its object (e.g., with "me," 6:35;
7:38; 11:25,26; 12:44; 14:1,12; 16:9; with "him," 2:11;
4:39; 6:40; 7:5,31,39,48; 8:30; 10:42; 11:45,48; 12:37,
42; with "Jesus," 12:11; with "his name," 1:12; 2:23; "the
one he sent," 6:29; "the light," 12:36; "the Son," 3:15,
16,18,36; "Son of Man," 9:35). The Gospel makes it
clear that this faith is the condition of salvation. It
presumes that "believing in" Jesus implies perceiving the
special relationship between Jesus and the Father, which
is the focus of the discourses in the Gospel (→ Johannine
Theology, 83:24–37).

John 1:19–50 gathers together a number of the traditional messianic titles that had formed the basis for
christological assertions in the earliest Christian communities, Messiah, Elijah, the prophet, Lamb of God,
Son of God, king of Israel. Such messianic affirmations
are then relativized by the promise of "greater things" in
a logion promising a vision of the Son of Man on whom
the angels of God ascend and descend (1:51). This saying
transforms the apocalyptic imagery of the Son of Man
and the angels from heaven and the story of Jacob's
vision at Bethel into an expression by which Jesus has
both "fulfilled" and transcended any expectations that
might have been linked to such traditional messianic
hopes. John's reinterpretation is governed by his larger
vision of Jesus as the Logos/"Son" sent as the saving
revelation of the Father (see F. J. Moloney, *The Johannine
Son of Man* [Biblioteca di Scienze Religiose 14; 2d ed.;
Rome, 1978]).

This pattern of transformation is evident in the
disputes in which the expectations of Jesus as Messiah or
Mosaic prophet are under discussion. A midrashic discussion of the initial assertion culminates in a Son-of-
Man saying (e.g., 3:13–14; 6:35,38,53,62;8:28;
9:35–41). A similar process may be found in the collection of "I Am" revelatory sayings. They form a vehicle
whereby Jesus appropriates great religious symbols, but
in the absolute sense as the "name of God" they show
that Jesus is the one who reveals God in contrast to the
competing claims to "know God" (8:24,28,51). The connection between the divine "I Am" and the glorification
of Jesus on the cross (8:24,28) is presupposed in the use
of "I Am" as consolation in John 13:19.

17   Johannine christology seems to be more than
a simple expansion of possibilities already in Jewish or
earlier Christian sources. One cannot escape the novelty
of the evangelist's use of categories previously felt appropriate only to the transcendent reality of God in conjunction with a narrative which describes the earthly
career of a human being. Johannine christology poses
the problem of redefining monotheism (see Dunn, "Let
John Be John" 309–39).

With the introduction of a Logos christology into the prologue of the Gospel, John presents the reader with an image of preexistence which implies the personal being of Jesus with God. John 1:18 makes the link between the Logos and Son christologies. The references to Jesus' return to the glory he had had with the Father (17:4,24) secure the connection between the preexistent Word and the Jesus of the narrative. The Fourth Gospel rejects "simple" solutions to the problem of Jesus' identity. It does not limit its affirmation about Jesus to predicates like the eschatological prophet, which might be understood of any human, albeit one whose role in God's plan of salvation has a certain ultimate or final position. Nor does the Gospel solve the problem as the gnostics would later do by simply making Jesus the earthly costume for a heavenly redeemer figure, who is essentially without any connection with the historical or human realities of this world. By refusing either antithesis, the Fourth Gospel sets the parameters for an incarnational christology. It may also have exhausted the possibilities of narrative to express such a christology, since storytelling depends on our ability to connect events and persons in patterns from human experience. But the Johannine Jesus does not come to clarify human experience. He comes to reveal the Father (see J. D. G. Dunn, *Christology in the Making* [Phl, 1980] 213–68).

18   (VII) Text of the Fourth Gospel. The major 4th- and 5th-cent. NT codices, Vaticanus, Bezae, and Sinaiticus, which is closer to Vaticanus in John 1–7 and elsewhere closer to Codex Bezae, have been supplemented by a number of Gk papyri from the 2d through the 7th cents. which contain significant sections of the Gospel. The most important papyrus witnesses are P[52] (*ca.*AD 130; contains 18:31–33,37–38); P[66] (beginning 3d cent. AD; contains chaps. 1–14 fairly complete; frgs. of chap. 21); and P[75] (*ca.* AD 200; contains chaps. 1–12 almost complete; frgs. of chap. 13, and 14:9–30; 15:7–8). P[75] is closest to Vaticanus, whereas P[66] is somewhat closer to Sinaiticus. Agreement between these two papyri may constitute a strong argument for a reading, but their divergence shows that different forms of the text of John were already in circulation. P[66] may itself be the result of a scribal attempt to create a version of the text out of an Egyptian text-type and a form of the Western text. (→ Texts, 68:179).

The antiquity of the fragment of John in P[52] has had an important impact on dating the Gospel. Before its discovery, the complex christology of John and the lack of clear citations of the Gospel in early 2d-cent. Fathers led some to argue that the Gospel had actually been composed in the 2d cent. Now that the papyrus evidence suggests circulation of variant texts of the Gospel in Egypt from the first quarter of the 2d cent. on, such theories have to be rejected as implausible. If one further presumes that John was composed in Asia Minor, not Egypt, and in a relatively closed community, one must also allow time for it to have passed into general circulation in Egypt. Therefore, the latest plausible date for the composition of the Gospel would be *ca.* AD 100. But if the synagogue expulsion referred to in the Gospel is to be associated with the promulgation of the benediction against heretics sometime around AD 90, then the period in which the Gospel was written is most likely to have fallen in the 90s.

Some passages that were later incorporated into the text of the Gospel are not supported by the older witnesses. The most significant is the pericope about the woman taken in adultery (7:53–8:11). Literarily, this story is more in the style of the Synoptics than of the Fourth Gospel. It will be treated here as a "free-floating" *agraphon*, which happens to have been copied into Johan-

nine mss. Nor do the oldest mss. support the presence of 5:4, the explanation of the angel stirring up the water of the pool, which is now omitted from Gk editions of the text and appears as a footnote in some translations as well.

19   (VIII) Destination and Purpose of the Fourth Gospel. Treatments of the destination and purpose of the Gospel are dependent on one's decisions about the sources and composition of John and about the history of the Johannine community. Though the "miracle source" used in the Gospel may have been shaped to serve the purpose of converting others to a belief in Jesus as Son of God, its present use as part of a complex presentation of Jesus' identity as Son in conflict with Jewish objections hardly seems appropriate to a missionary tract. Nor does the formulation of the argument with "the Jews" in the discourses appear to be intended to win persons who are Jews to belief in Jesus. If anything, the intensification of the claims about Jesus' identity in the discourses appears designed to confirm the worst fears of those presented as Jesus' antagonists. The literary dynamics of the Gospel, both in its use of a special language of double meaning and symbolism and in the asides by the narrator, suggest a work intended for circulation in the community of Johannine Christians. The farewell discourses clearly speak to the inner experiences of the Johannine community. The issues of Jesus' return, the guidance of the community by the Paraclete, the mission of the community "in the world" to which it no longer belongs, and the problem of continued persecution are all well beyond the difficulties posed by Jewish hostility and the expulsion from the synagogue.

We can also gain some perspective on the audience to which the Gospel is directed from an analysis of the implied reader in the Gospel itself. What does the narrative presume that that reader knows? It is presumed that the readers know who the "we," which we have linked with the Johannine school, are (1:14,16; 21:24). They are apparently familiar with the Logos hymn used in the prologue. The readers may also be familiar with JBap. Perhaps the care with which the narrator sets the place of JBap as a witness to Jesus indicates that he thinks the audience may have too high an estimate of him. The reader also knows that JBap was imprisoned (3:24). Perhaps the evangelist also wishes to correct an impression that that event had occurred before the beginning of Jesus' ministry.

The audience's knowledge of Judaism is presumed to vary. Passages from Scripture, esp. prophetic quotations, are familiar, as are some symbols from Scripture, and the major heroes of the patriarchal period and Moses. However, the way in which Jewish feasts are identified suggests that neither the author nor the readers observe such feasts. The reader must have some minimal knowledge about Passover, the significance of the sabbath, institutions like the high priesthood and sanhedrin, though purification rites and burial customs are not necessarily familiar. Though the reader does not know the meaning of "Messiah," other christological titles like "Son of Man" go unexplained.

The Fourth Gospel apparently presumes that much of the story about Jesus, its persons and places, is already familiar to the readers. They would also apparently be familiar with such Christian beliefs as those represented in the christological titles, baptism, the Lord's Supper, and the Spirit. The Johannine reader, then, must be envisaged as a Christian. Whether that Christian reader has to have shared all the nuances of Johannine theology or might have been a person whose faith was in some way being "built up" or "corrected" by the Gospel is more difficult to say. It has been suggested that, given the strong christological point of view advocated in the Gospel, the reader may not have shared that view. Perhaps the readers of the Gospel are envisaged as falling into one or more of the misunderstandings represented by characters in the story (see Culpepper, *Anatomy* [→ 13 above] 206–27).

20   (IX) Outline. The Johannine Gospel is outlined as follows:

(I) Prologue: The Word Coming into the World (1:1–18)
(II) Book of Signs: "His Own Did Not Receive Him . . ." (1:19–12:50)
  (A) Gathering Disciples (1:19–4:54)
    (a) At John's Testimony (1:19–51)
      (i)   John is not the Messiah (1:19–28)
      (ii) Jesus is the Lamb of God (1:29–34)
      (iii) Andrew and Peter (1:35–42)
      (iv) Philip and Nathanael (1:43–51)
    (b) Cana: Disciples See His Glory (2:1–12)
    (c) Judea: Temple Cleansing (2:13–25)
      (i)   Sign of the resurrection (2:13–22)
      (ii) Comment: Faith rejected (2:23–25)
    (d) Nicodemus: Rebirth and Eternal Life (3:1–36)
      (i)   Dialogue: Receiving eternal life (3:1–15)
      (ii) Comment: God sent the Son to give life (3:16–21)
      (iii) John testifies to Jesus (3:22–30)
      (iv) Comment: God sent Jesus to give life (3:31–36)
    (e) Withdrawal to Galilee (4:1–3)
    (f) Samaria: Savior of the World (4:4–42)
      (i)   Dialogue: Living water (4:6–15)
      (ii) Dialogue: The Messiah-prophet (4:16–26)
      (iii) Dialogue: The harvest (4:27–38)
      (iv) Samaritan believers (4:39–42)
    (g) Galilee: The Official's Son (4:43–54)
      (i)   Jesus' return to Galilee (4:43–45)
      (ii) The official's son healed (4:46–54)
  (B) Disputes over Jesus' Deeds and Words: Is He from God? (5:1–10:42)
    (a) Jerusalem: Healing the Cripple: Life and Judgment (5:1–47)
      (i)   A cripple healed on the sabbath (5:1–18)
      (ii) The Son's authority to give life (5:19–30)
      (iii) Testimony to Jesus (5:31–40)
      (iv) Unbelief condemned (5:41–47)
    (b) Galilee: The Bread of Life (6:1–71)
      (i)   Feeding the five thousand (6:1–15)
      (ii) Walking on water (6:16–21)
      (iii) Dialogue: Jesus is bread from heaven (6:22–40)
      (iv) Dispute over Jesus' origins (6:41–51a)
      (v) The bread is Jesus' flesh (6:51b–59)
      (vi) Dispute: Jesus loses disciples (6:60–66)
      (vii) Peter's confession (6:67–71)
    (c) Jerusalem at Tabernacles (7:1–8:59)
      (i)   Galilee: Rejects advice to go to the feast (7:1–9)
      (ii) Jesus goes secretly to the feast (7:10–13)
      (iii) Jesus teaches in the Temple (7:14–24)
      (iv) Division: Is this the Messiah? (7:25–31)
      (v) Soldiers sent to arrest Jesus (7:32–36)
      (vi) Jesus is the living water (7:37–39)
      (vii) Division: Is this the prophet? (7:40–44)
      (viii) Authorities reject Jesus (7:45–52)
    [*Agraphon:* Woman Taken in Adultery (7:53–8:11)]
      (ix) The Father testifies to Jesus (8:12–20)
      (x) Jesus is returning to the Father (8:21–30)
      (xi) The seed of Abraham hear the truth (8:31–47)
      (xii) Before Abraham was, I Am (8:48–59)
    (d) Jesus Restores Sight to the Blind (9:1–41)
      (i)   Healing a man born blind (9:1–12)
      (ii) Pharisees question the man: Jesus is a prophet (9:13–17)

      (iii) Jews question the parents: Fear of being expelled from the synagogue (9:18–23)
      (iv) Second interrogation and expulsion from the synagogue (9:24–34)
      (v) Jesus is Son of Man (9:35–38)
      (vi) Blindness of the Pharisees (9:39–41)
    (e) Jesus, the Good Shepherd (10:1–42)
      (i)   Parable of the sheepfold (10:1–6)
      (ii) Jesus, the gate and the good shepherd (10:7–18)
      (iii) Division: Is Jesus possessed? (10:19–21)
      (iv) Jesus' sheep know his identity (10:22–30)
      (v) Attempt to stone Jesus for blasphemy (10:31–39)
      (vi) Jesus withdraws across the Jordan (10:40–42)
  (C) Jesus Gives Life and Receives Death (11:1–12:50)
    (a) Raising of Lazarus (11:1–44)
      (i)   Jesus waits to go to Lazarus (11:1–16)
      (ii) Jesus, the resurrection and the life (11:17–27)
      (iii) Jesus loved Lazarus (11:28–37)
      (iv) Jesus raises Lazarus (11:38–44)
    (b) Jewish Leaders Condemn Jesus to Death (11:45–53)
    (c) Jesus Has Withdrawn (11:54–57)
    (d) Jesus Is Anointed for the Hour (12:1–8)
    (e) Plot against Lazarus (12:9–11)
    (f) Entry into Jerusalem (12:12–19)
    (g) The Hour Is at Hand (12:20–36)
      (i)   Greeks come to Jesus (12:20–26)
      (ii) I am to be lifted up (12:27–36)
    (h) Condemnation of Unbelief (12:37–50)
(III) Book of Glory: ". . . He Gave Them Power to Become Children of God" (13:1–20:31)
  (A) The Last Supper Discourses (13:1–17:26)
    (a) The Last Supper (13:1–30)
      (i)   Washing the disciples' feet (13:1–20)
      (ii) Jesus predicts his betrayal (13:21–30)
    (b) Jesus Returns to the Father (13:31–14:31)
      (i)   Announcement of the hour (13:31–38)
      (ii) Jesus is the way to the Father (14:1–11)
      (iii) The Paraclete and Jesus' return (14:12–24)
      (iv) Conclusion: Jesus' departure (14:25–31)
    (c) Jesus, the True Vine (15:1–16:4a)
      (i)   Jesus is the true vine (15:1–11)
      (ii) Disciples are friends of Jesus (15:12–17)
      (iii) The world will hate the disciples (15:18–25)
      (iv) The Paraclete as witness (15:26–27)
      (v) Persecution of the disciples (16:1–4a)
    (d) Consolation for the Disciples (16:4b–33)
      (i)   The Paraclete will convict the world (16:4b–11)
      (ii) The Paraclete will guide you into all truth (16:12–15)
      (iii) Jesus' departure and return (16:16–24)
      (iv) Jesus has overcome the world (16:25–33)
    (e) Jesus' Prayer for the Disciples (17:1–26)
      (i)   Jesus returns to glory (17:1–5)
      (ii) Jesus sends the disciples into the world (17:6–19)
      (iii) That they may be one (17:20–26)
  (B) The Passion Narrative (18:1–19:42)
    (a) The Arrest of Jesus (18:1–11)
    (b) Before the High Priest (18:12–27)
      (i)   Jesus is brought to Annas (18:12–14)
      (ii) Peter denies Jesus (18:15–18)
      (iii) Annas interrogates Jesus (18:19–24)
      (iv) Peter denies Jesus (18:25–27)
    (c) Trial by Pilate (18:28–19:16a)
      (i)   Scene one (18:28–31[32])
      (ii) Scene two (18:33–38a)
      (iii) Scene three (18:38b–40)
      (iv) Scene four (19:1–3)
      (v) Scene five (19:4–7)

COMMENTARY

21   (I) Prologue: The Word Coming into the World (1:1-18). The parallel structure of the sentences in this section of the Gospel, the use of *logos*, "word," which is not part of the rest of the Gospel, the narrator's interruptions in the structure (vv 6-8,[9?],13,15), and the use of "his own" in v 11 contrary to its meaning in 13:1, all suggest that the prologue has adapted earlier traditional material. The tradition used by the evangelist appears to fit the pattern of a christological hymn (against the view that the tradition came as a hymn, see E. L. Miller, *NTS* 29 [1983] 552-61). Reconstructions of the pre-Johannine hymn differ (see G. Rochais, *ScEs* 37 [1985] 5-44), though a variant of the following outline would be common: v 1, [v 2], vv 3-4, [v 5], [v 9ab], [v 10ab], v 10c-11, v 12ab, v 14a[b]c, v 16. The hymn celebrates the preexistent Word and its activity in creation (vv 1-5); the activity of the Word in guiding and illuminating humans, who often reject divine wisdom (vv 9ab,10-12); and the incarnation of the Word, which has enabled humans to partake of divine fullness (vv 14, 16; → Johannine Theology, 83:19).

22   1-2. *in the beginning . . . the Word was with God:* This recalls Gen 1:1 as well as the traditions of Wisdom with God at the creation (Prov 8:30; Wis 7:25). In Hellenistic Greek *pros* can be used for simple accompaniment without any implications of motion "toward," though some exegetes find a hint of the dynamic relationship between the Word and God in it. *Theos,* "God," used without the article is a predicate. John goes beyond the careful formulations of the Wisdom tradition, which would never suggest that Wisdom has any form of equality with God (cf. *theos* used of Jesus in 1:18[?]; 20:28; 1 John 5:20). **3-4.** *all things came into being through him:* It is unclear whether "what came to be" should be attached to the end of v 3 or form the beginning of v 4. Attaching the phrase to the beginning of v 4 can be understood as a reading influenced by the gnostic picture of a number of eons coming to be in the Word (see *Tri. Trac.* 76.2-104.3, for an elaborate account of the realms that came into being in the Logos). Attaching the phrase to v 3 makes the expression parallel to 1QS 11:11: "And by His knowledge all has come to be, and by His thought He directs all that is, and without Him not a thing is done." Both life (11:25; 14:6) and light (8:12; 9:5; 12:46) take on a soteriological meaning when they are identified with Jesus in the Gospel. **5.** *the light shone in darkness:* Some exegetes think that this expression was added by the evangelist in anticipation of the darkness of unbelief (8:12; 3:19; 12:35,46). Wis 7:29-30 speaks of a beauty that surpasses sun and stars; sin cannot prevail over Wisdom.

23   6-8. *a man sent from God:* The first of a series of passages on the role of JBap; he is not a messianic figure but a witness. This insertion into the hymn at this point shifts the focus of what follows from the activity of the Logos in salvation history to the incarnation. **9.** *the true light:* This may be an addition by the evangelist referring what follows to the incarnation. *Alēthinos,* "true," is used to designate the "real" (= divinely given reality): worshipers (4:23); bread from heaven (6:32), vine (15:1), and God himself (17:3; cf. 7:28).

24   10-11. *his own did not receive him:* Rejection of the Logos/light upon coming to its own place (*ta idia*) and its own people (*hoi idioi*) recalls the rejection of Wisdom in *1 Enoch* 42:2: "Wisdom went out to dwell with the children of the people, but she found no dwelling place; (so) Wisdom returned to her place and she established herself among the angels." **12.** *he gave them the power to become the children of God:* This may have originally referred to Wisdom finding a dwelling in the souls of the righteous (e.g., Sir 1:9-10). It has been recast to reflect the soteriology of the Gospel (2:23; 3:18, believe in his name; → Johannine Theology, 83:55-56). **13.** *begotten from God:* John 3:3-8 attributes divine "rebirth" to the activity of the Spirit. According to Wis 7:2 the human born of "blood," the "seed of man," and the "pleasure of marriage" is identical with every other mortal and must ask God for Wisdom (Wis 7:7).

25   14. *the Word became flesh:* Reference to the Word becoming flesh (*sarx*) goes beyond the OT images of divine glory and Wisdom dwelling with Israel (Exod 25:8-9; Joel 3:17; Zech 2:10; Ezek 43:7, the "name" of God is to dwell with Israel forever; Sir 24:4,8,10). It also counters any suggestion of a docetic christology. *Monogenēs* reflects the Hebr *yāḥîd,* "only," "precious," "unique" (see Gen 22:2,12,16; Heb 11:17; cf. *EWNT* 2. 1082-83). *We have seen . . . :* This refers to the witnesses of the Johannine community. Some think that v 14b is an expansion of the original verse. "Glory" appears throughout John as God's glory seen in Jesus; also Jesus' preexistent "glory with the Father" (17:5,24). *full of grace and truth:* Originally appended to v 14a, this phrase probably reflects the *ḥesed we'ĕmet* of the covenant, God's mercy and loving kindness to the people. **15.** *John testified:* Reference to JBap's testimony alludes to the words in 1:30.

26   16. *from his fullness we have received:* The only use of *plērōma,* "fullness," in John probably alludes to the fullness of God's grace (Pss 5:8; 106:45) or mercy (Ps 51:3). Cf. 1QS 4:4, "the fullness of his grace." *Charin anti charitos,* "grace upon grace," may either be a variant of the first expression or suggest that the old grace of the covenant is replaced by the new. **17.** *grace and truth through Jesus:* Contrast between Moses and Jesus suggests that the evangelist understands v 16 as referring to the replacement of the "old" revelation by Jesus. **18.** *no one has ever seen God:* The superiority of Jesus is grounded in his relationship with God. John consistently rejects the claims of others to knowledge of God (5:37; 6:46; 8:56; see G. Neyrard, *NRT* 106 [1984] 59–71; J. Painter, *NTS* 30 [1984] 460–74; M. Theobald, *Im Anfang War das Wort* [SBS 106; Stuttgart, 1983]).

27   (II) Book of Signs: "His Own Did Not Receive Him . . ." (1:19–12:50). The narrative of Jesus' ministry will culminate in the rejection of Jesus by "his own," those whose hearts have been hardened. They refuse to believe in the light and so do not become "sons of light" (12:36).

28   (A) Gathering Disciples (1:19–4:54). In the first section of the public ministry Jesus gathers together disciples, persons who believe in him, though with an inadequate faith; persons sympathetic to him; and such non-Jewish followers as the Samaritans and the royal official and his household. Judea, Galilee, and Samaria are all represented. This section is tied together with chronological indicators (1:29,35,43; 2:1,12,13; 3:24; 4:40,43).

29   (a) At John's Testimony (1:19–51). JBap fulfills his role as witness referred to in the prologue first by denying any messianic claims about himself, then by pointing to Jesus as the "Lamb of God," and finally by sending his own disciples to Jesus. This section is built around a collection of messianic titles.

30   (i) *John is not the Messiah* (1:19–28). The evangelist frequently creates "double scenes" out of a tradition that had only a single episode. He has created dual introductions in vv 19 and 24 by dividing groups of Jewish authorities, "priests and Levites," (v 19) and "those from the Pharisees" (v 24). **19.** They come at the bidding of "the Jews," an expression which John later uses for authorities who instigate opposition to Jesus, esp. the Pharisees and high priests (5:10,15,16,18; 7:1, 13; 8:48,52,57; 9:18,22; 10:24,31,33; 11:8; 18:12,14,31, 36,38; 19:7,12,14,31,38; 20:19). The formal references to Jerusalem as their place of origin and to Bethany (not the one near Jerusalem, but a town in Transjordan of which there is no remaining trace) as the place of the testimony in v 28 gives the whole section a juridical tone. **20.** *Messiah:* *Māšîaḥ* first appears for a future anointed agent of God in Dan 9:25. This usage is developed in the DSS (1QS 9:11; 1QSa 2:14,20; CD 20:1; 4QPBless 2:4; 4QFlor 1:11–13; → Pauline Theology, 82:51). Luke 3:15 also has the people wonder whether JBap is "the Messiah." **21.** *Elijah:* Expectation of Elijah's return was based on Mal 3:1,23; the messenger sent to prepare the Day of the Lord; he is identified as Elijah in 3:23. Synoptic traditions identify Elijah with JBap in order to make John the forerunner of Jesus (Mark 9:13; Matt 17:12; cf. Luke 1:17; 7:27; the Baptist is to act in the manner of Elijah). Only in Christian sources does Elijah become the forerunner of the Messiah rather than of Yahweh's day of judgment. *the prophet:* Presentation of Jesus as the Mosaic prophet from Deut 18:18 (in the DSS, see 1QS 9:11, "until the coming of a prophet and the messiahs of Aaron and Israel") formed an important element in the christological tradition of the Johannine community and may have been developed under the influence of Samaritan expectations (→ 7 above). **22–23.** *a voice crying in the wilderness:* The citation from Isa 40:3 is used about JBap in the Synoptics (Mark 1:3 par.), but the Johannine form differs from the Synoptics and the LXX, having *euthynate* instead of *hetoimasate* for "prepare," and may reflect the next part of the verse, *eutheias poieite,*

"make straight," which John omits. By omitting the second part, John adapts the citation to the role of witnessing that is assigned JBap.

31   24–25. The evangelist creates a second scene of testimony by having Pharisees question John's authority to baptize if he is not a messianic figure. The question presumes that such baptism would both express repentance and provide purification through the Spirit, as in the OT and the DSS (Ezek 36:25–26; Zech 13:1–3; 1QS 4:20–21). Baptism had evidently been a point of contention between Johannine Christians and the followers of JBap (e.g., 3:22–23; 4:1–2). **26–27.** Synoptic traditions distinguished Jesus and JBap by contrasting water baptism and purification by the Spirit and appending the saying about John's unworthiness in comparison to Jesus (Mark 1:7–8 par.). The Fourth Gospel seems to have modified this tradition so that JBap's answer points to Jesus as the one who is "unknown" to the Pharisees. Thus are anticipated the coming exchanges between Jesus and "the Jews" who do not "know" Jesus or his Father (e.g., 8:14,19; 7:27 points to Jesus as the hidden Messiah). The logion in v 27 is an independent variant of that found in the Synoptics, having the sg. "sandal strap" and *axios,* "worthy," instead of *hikanos,* "fit," "able." John 1:15,30 give a more sharply christological interpretation to the saying about Jesus as the one who "comes after" JBap. **28.** *Bethany beyond the Jordan:* Unknown, and for this reason it becomes *Bethabara* in some Gk mss. (see Judg 7:24).

32   (ii) *Jesus is the Lamb of God* (1:29–34). Whereas the Synoptic tradition has the baptism of Jesus and the coming of the Spirit upon him (Mark 1:11; Luke 3:22; Matt 3:17), the Fourth Gospel has a scene in which JBap gives double testimony before "Israel" (see G. Richter, *ZNW* 65 [1974] 43–52). The coming of the Spirit is the divine sign to JBap that Jesus is the one designated by God. The early Christian contrast between "baptism with the spirit" and John's baptism with water appears here (v 33). **29.** *the lamb of God who takes away the sin of the world:* Since the Fourth Gospel does not stress atonement for sin as the primary purpose of Jesus' crucifixion/exaltation, JBap's affirmation must reflect earlier tradition in the community. 1 John rejects those who claim that Jesus' death was not an atonement for sin (1 John 3:5). Jesus as the "lamb" probably represents a primitive Christian combination of two images: (a) the Suffering Servant of Isaiah 52:13–53:12, who is led to slaughter like a lamb (53:7) and bears (*pherein*) our sins (53:4); and (b) the death of Jesus as that of the Passover lamb (John 19:36; 1 Cor 5:7 shows that this interpretation of Jesus' death is early). **33.** *the Spirit coming down and resting:* This version of the descent of the Spirit stems from an independent tradition which the evangelist has shaped to make the Baptist its witness. He also speaks of the Spirit "resting/remaining" on Jesus. The verb *menein* belongs to John's special vocabulary. It describes the permanent relationship between Father and Son and the Son and believers. It is applied to the "indwelling" of divine attributes. Here, the Spirit is said to "remain with" Jesus, who will be shown to be the one who dispenses the Spirit (3:5, 34; 7:38–39; 20:22). Isa 52:1 describes the Spirit "resting" (*katapauein*) on the servant. **34.** A textual variant in v 34 replaces "Son of God" with "elect of God." Since this passage would be the only Johannine use of "elect" and since "Son of God" would more likely to be introduced into the tradition, many scholars take that to have been the original reading. "Elect" appears as a title in some of the later sections of *1 Enoch* (e.g., 45:3; 49:2; 50:5) and in Isa 42:1 for the Suffering Servant.

33   (iii) *Andrew and Peter* (1:35–42). JBap's testimony achieves its goal when two of his own disciples

follow Jesus. This section is divided into two episodes as
are the parallel events on the next day. In the first
episode of each day initial disciple(s) are invited by Jesus
to follow him (vv 35-39,43-44). In the second, the new
disciples bring another person to Jesus while confessing
their faith in Jesus as the promised Messiah; Jesus looks
at the newcomer and greets him with a special name (vv
40-42,45-50). **38-39.** *Rabbi:* Not a designation for a
teacher in Jesus' time. John makes extensive use of the
title in chaps. 1-12, where it is frequently a sign of
respect combined with a statement or question which
will require that the individual's understanding of Jesus
be corrected (1:49, correction: Son of Man; 3:2, correction: rebirth through the Spirit; [3:26, correction:
relationship between Jesus and the Baptist clarified];
4:31, correction: food is doing the will of the Father;
6:25, correction: Jesus is the bread of life from heaven;
9:2, correction: the miracle will show that Jesus is light;
11:8, correction: the miracle will show that Jesus is life).
The "correction" in vv 38-39 is carried by the double
meaning of *menein,* "to dwell" and "to remain" in the
special Johannine sense. The promise *opsesthe,* "you will
see," is repeated in 1:51, where its christological content
is evident. Both "coming to Jesus" (e.g., 3:21; 5:40; 6:35,
37,45) and "seeing" (e.g., 5:40; 6:40,47) are indications
of faith in the Fourth Gospel.
34   **40-42.** The scene with two anonymous
disciples is linked with the call of Andrew and Peter by
identifying Andrew as one of the anonymous pair. *we
have found the Messiah:* The summons to conversion is
based on confession that Jesus is "Messiah" (→ Jesus,
78:34; OT Thought, 77:152-54). The "we" reflects the
testimony given by the early community. Only in John
and Matt (16:16-18) is Jesus responsible for Simon's
nickname, "Rock," which Matt explains as an indication
of Peter's future role in the community. The Johannine
tradition appears to have used "shepherd" for the ecclesiological role assumed by Peter (e.g., 21:15-17).
35   (iv) *Philip and Nathanael (1:43-51).* The
second scene is marked by both a temporal shift and an
impending geographical shift back to Galilee. **43.** *follow
me:* Jesus' call to discipleship resembles the Synoptic call
stories (e.g., Mark 2:14 par.). **45-46.** *him of whom Moses
in the law and the prophets wrote:* Not a christological title
(though some have suggested a link to the "prophet-
like-Moses" christology), but an affirmation of an early
Christian confession about Jesus (Luke 24:27, which indicates that it was a postresurrection development of
faith). *anything good from Nazareth:* The query has the
sound of a local proverb. The expression also hints at
later attempts to reject Jesus on grounds of his origins
(6:42; 7:52) by those who do not know that he comes
"from God." Philip's "come and see" echoes v 39.
36   **47.** *a genuine Israelite:* The adv. *alēthōs,* "truly,"
placed before "Israelite" appears equivalent to John's use
elsewhere of *alēthinos,* "true," "genuine." Nathanael is the
exemplary Israelite because he does come to Jesus rather
than reject him as do others who invoke the law and the
prophets (e.g., 7:15,27,41; 9:29). *Dolos,* "guile," "falsehood," has negative religious overtones in the OT (e.g.,
Pss 17:1; 43:1; Prov 12:6); and in the prophets it can
imply unfaithfulness to God (Jer 9:5; Zeph 3:13; denied
of the servant of Yahweh in Isa 53:9). With the addition
of v 51 the "naming" of Nathanael may also be understood in the context of traditions about the patriarch
Jacob, who received the name "Israel," "one who sees
God" (Gen 32:28-30). But according to John, no one has
"seen God" except the Son and those who will receive
the revelation brought by the Son. "Guile" was also an
attribute of the patriarch Jacob (Gen 27:35). **48-49.** A
satisfactory parallel for the reaction produced by Jesus'

saying about "sitting under a fig tree" has not been
found. The best suggestion is that it may be related to a
later tradition that the rabbis studied the law "under a fig
tree" (*Midr. Rab. Eccl.* 5:11).
37   **49.** *Son of God, king of Israel:* In the OT, the
king is referred to as "son of God" (e.g., 2 Sam 7:14; Pss
89:27; 2:6-7; → Johannine Theology, 83:35-37). The
2 Sam passage appears in connection with a figure described as the "Shoot of David" in the DSS (4QFlor 1-2
i 10), though without any clear indication that the king
so described is a messianic figure. Pilate's inscription
"King of the Jews" on the cross (e.g., John 19:19) may
have led to the early Christian portrayal of Jesus as
Messiah/King. The Fourth Gospel will return to the
theme of Jesus' kingship in the trial before Pilate. **50.**
you shall see greater things: This promise parallels the invitation to "come and see" in v 39. The pattern of subordinating a claim which could be derived from a Jewish
tradition to a "greater one," which is only accessible to
the Johannine believer, is often repeated in the Gospel
(e.g., 3:12; 4:21-23; 11:40). Some think that the "greater
things" point forward to the signs that show the disciples Jesus' glory (e.g., 2:11).
38   **51.** *the angels of God ascending and descending on
the Son of Man:* The formal "Amen, amen" and the shift
from v 50 "you (sg.) will see" to "you (pl.)" suggest that
this saying was added to the Nathanael story in a subsequent edition of the Gospel. John 3:12-15 makes a
similar move from earthly to heavenly things by allusion
to the Son of Man (→ Johannine Theology, 83:38-40).
Verse 13 is particularly close to this verse: "No one has
gone up into heaven except the one who has come down
from heaven, the Son of Man." This verse is to be linked
with the same christology: there is no one who could
have "seen God" except the Son. Consequently, Jacob's
vision (Gen 28:11-12) has been transformed into a
future vision promised to the believers in which Jesus is
the link between heaven and earth. John 5:37 rejects
Moses' visions on Sinai. Elsewhere the Gospel suggests
that those who are said to have seen God in Scripture
actually saw the Son (e.g., 8:56,58; 12:41).
39   *Son of Man:* The Synoptic Son-of-Man sayings
link the heavenly "Son of Man," "accompanying angels,"
and "glory" with the parousia (e.g., Mark 14:62; Matt
26:27-28). The judgment saying in John 5:27 (cf. Mark
8:38; 13:26, the Son of Man as judge) shows that such
traditions were part of the Johannine heritage. But the
Johannine farewell discourses never apply "Son of Man"
to the expectation of Jesus' return. The three Son-of-
Man passion predictions (3:14; 8:28; 12:34) differ from
their Synoptic counterparts (e.g., Mark 8:31) in not
stressing the necessity of suffering for the Son of Man
but the necessity that one believe in Jesus as the one who
has been exalted/glorified in order to attain salvation. A
similar point is made in John 6:62: after some have abandoned Jesus, the disciples are warned, "if you do not see
the Son of Man ascending to where he was before." The
pattern of descent, rejection, and ascent to a prior place
in heaven was evident in the Wisdom theme of the
prologue. These passages suggest that the Johannine
community has developed an independent tradition of
Son-of-Man sayings. Those which may originally have
referred to rejection and suffering have been recast in
light of the Gospel's preexistence, descent/ascent patterns, and its understanding that Jesus is the only revelation of the Father. John 1:51 represents a similar
recasting of the tradition. The vision is now promises is
fulfilled in the believing community (see J. Neyrey, "The
Jacob Allusions in John 1:51," *CBQ* 44 [1982] 586-605).
40   (b) CANA: DISCIPLES SEE HIS GLORY (2:1-12).
The first of the miracles in the Gospel is referred to as

one of Jesus "signs" and is made the occasion for a revelation of Jesus' glory that leads his disciples to believe in him (v 11). Though some readers may have noted a link with Dionysus, the story appears to have been taken by the evangelist from an earlier source, more likely to have been of Palestinian origin. Two themes can be linked to a "Jewish" context: (a) the necessity for Jesus to "replace" the water of the Jewish purification rituals in the "empty" stone jars; (b) the imagery of wine as part of the messianic wedding feast (Isa 54:4–8; 62:4–5). Both themes have occurred in the Synoptic tradition independently of any miracle story (e.g., Mark 2:19,22, which include a saying about "new wine"; 7:1–7). Abundant wine is frequently a sign of restoration or of the *eschaton* (cf. Amos 9:13; Hos 2:24; Joel 4:18; Isa 29:17; Jer 31:5; *1 Enoch* 10:19; *2 Apoc. Bar.* 29:5). Some have suggested that the miracle story should be considered a variant of the "feeding type" in the Elijah-Elisha cycle (loaves, 2 Kgs 4:42–44; oil, 1 Kgs 17:1–16; 2 Kgs 4:1–7).

41   Whatever its origins, the Gospel uses the story for its symbolism about Jesus. The actual miraculous occurrence is mentioned almost in passing (v 9) and never becomes a public demonstration of Jesus' power. Much of the narrative is free from John's special language, though v 4 refers to Jesus' "hour." In addition, the miracle is described as the "beginning" in v 11, and in John 4:54 we are told that the healing of the official's son was the "second sign which Jesus did coming from Judea into Galilee." Perhaps the unusual numbering of these two "signs" was derived from a source used by the evangelist (→ Johannine Theology, 83:55–57). In addition to v 4, the evangelist is certainly responsible for the temporal marker in v 1, which continues the sequence of days begun with 1:35; and for the explanatory comments such as the identification of the purpose of the jars (v 6b), the comment that the steward did not know "whence the water had come" (v 9b), and the conclusion, at least identifying the place and the miracle as a manifestation of Jesus' "glory" (v 11; → Johannine Theology, 83:25). The original collection of miracles may have contained some reference to the miracle resulting in faith, perhaps as a demonstration of Jesus' "power" rather than his "glory." **1.** *Cana:* → Biblical Archaeology, 74:146. **4.** *what has your business to do with me?:* Both Mary's request in v 3 and Jesus' reply are ambiguous. Verse 5 suggests that Jesus' mother (she is never named in the Gospel) does believe in Jesus, as she will when she next appears at the foot of the cross (19:25). The evangelist may have added the explanation that Jesus' "hour" (i.e., his crucifixion/glorification) had not come, in order to resolve an ambiguity that he felt in his source. The expression "what to me and to you, woman" could represent the Hebr expression *mâ-lî wālāk*, which does carry overtones of refusal or at least unwillingness to get involved in whatever the petitioner is concerned about (e.g., Judg 11:12; 1 Kgs 17:18; 2 Kgs 3:13; Hos 14:8). Persistence after apparent rejection appears in the other Cana miracle as well (4:47–50). It reminds the reader that no human agency, only the Father's will, guides what Jesus does in his ministry.

42   (c) JUDEA: TEMPLE CLEANSING (2:13–25). The Fourth Gospel departs from the Synoptics by placing this episode at the beginning of Jesus' ministry rather than as the cause of official hostility against Jesus during the passion (e.g., Mark 11:15–19 par.). Here, Jesus' authority to act as he does is challenged immediately, whereas the Synoptics have some time elapse between the incident and the challenge (Mark 11:27–28). The charge that Jesus predicted destruction of the Temple appears as part of the false testimony against Jesus (Mark 14:58). John has reinterpreted this tradition

to apply it to Jesus' resurrection. Its criticism of the Temple prepares for the saying on "true worshipers" in 4:21. A sharp attack on the Temple provides a more plausible occasion for the authorities to arrest Jesus than the raising of Lazarus.

43   (i) *Sign of the resurrection* (2:13–22). The evangelist appears to have relocated the Temple episode in order to make the Lazarus episode the cause of Jesus' death. Lack of extensive verbal parallels between John and the Synoptics shows that his version of the story came from an independent tradition: he mentions "sheep and oxen" along with the doves; he has Jesus make a whip out of cords and then turn to address the dove-sellers separately (in the Synoptics he overturns their tables too). Unlike the Synoptics, Jesus' justification is not a Scripture citation (cf. Isa 56:7; Jer 7:11) but a saying directly from the Lord. **17.** *his disciples remembered the word of Scripture:* "Remembering" is a technical term in John for the process by which the community came to see Jesus as the fulfillment of Scripture after the resurrection. They supply an OT citation, Ps 69:10, though the evangelist has changed the present tense of the Psalm text into the future, probably thinking of the bitter hostility that is to erupt between Jesus and "the Jews" (5:16,18).

44   **18–20.** Requests for "a sign" appear during the public ministry in both John (6:30) and the Synoptics (Mark 8:11–12; Matt 12:38–39; 16:11; Luke 11:16,29–30). The request here appears to be closer to the question of Jesus' authority to act as he has (also Mark 11:27–33). Jesus' answer is formulated as an enigmatic revelation saying that could not have been intelligible in the situation from which the story stems. As will be typical of Johannine misunderstandings, the authorities presume that Jesus has threatened to destroy the magnificent Temple, which Herod had begun *ca.* 20 BC (→ History, 75:158) and on which construction continued until shortly before the Jewish revolt (*ca.* AD 62; cf. Josephus, *Ant.* 15.11.1 § 380). Taken literally, Jesus' saying is absurd. **21–22.** The evangelist clarifies for the reader the symbolic meaning of Jesus' saying: the new temple will be Jesus' resurrected body. The DSS speak of the community as the true "temple" of God's Spirit (e.g., 1QS 5:5–6; 8:7–10; 1QH 6:25–28; 4QpPs^a 2:16), an image which also appears in Paul (e.g., 1 Cor 6:19–20). A quite different appeal to the resurrection appears as an answer to the request for a sign in Matt 12:38–40, the prophet Jonah. However, the evangelist does not think of the community as the new Temple, but of Jesus. This pattern dominates the Gospel's use of symbols. We have already seen that Jesus is "the light." Only once do we find the democratizing term "sons of light" for the community (12:36). For John, Jesus is the reality of all the great religious symbols of Israel. Verse 22 also makes the word of Jesus parallel to that in Scripture. John 20:9 will speak of the disciples prior to their resurrection faith not yet knowing "the Scripture that it was necessary for him to rise from the dead."

45   (ii) *Comment: Faith rejected* (2:23–25). The evangelist has created these verses to provide a bridge to the Nicodemus story in the next chapter. Some have suggested that the reservations expressed about a faith based on miracles, here referred to as "signs," was intended as a warning about the type of faith that the "miracle source" had engendered. (It may have proved quite unreliable when the Johannine community had to face persecution itself.) A similar rejection of faith engendered by a miracle appears in 6:14–15 when the crowd reacts to the miracle of the loaves by attempting to make Jesus king. There the ensuing dialogue will reveal the inadequacy of their faith (see Z. Hodges, *BSac*

135 [1978] 139–52; F. J. Moloney, *Salesianum* 40 [1978] 817–43). **25.** *he himself knew what was in a person:* Knowledge of what is in the heart of a person is one of God's attributes (cf. 1QS 1:7; 4:25). Jesus demonstrated this link with God in a positive way in naming Simon and Nathanael (1:42,47).

46   (d) NICODEMUS: REBIRTH AND ETERNAL LIFE (3:1–36). The evangelist breaks into this section with an exposition of the Johannine kerygma (vv 16–21, 31–36). Some begin the first section of discourse with v 13 in order to bring the opening of the two sections into parallelism, since vv 31–32 pick up the theme of v 13. However, vv 13–15 also have a role in "concluding" the story of Nicodemus. They specify the "heavenly things" that one must "see" and move the story to a christological perspective. This pattern parallels 1:50–51 and represents a stage in the editing of the Gospel, which recast traditional narratives to show the necessity of the christology of Jesus as "unique Son." Ending the dialogue with Nicodemus at v 12 makes the question an implicit condemnation of the latter's failure to understand the truth. John 5:47 concludes on such a note directed against Jesus' Jewish opponents (see J. H. Neyrey, *NovT* 23 [1981] 115–27).

47   The editing of the passage also raises questions about the sacramental theology of the evangelist. John 1:12 associates belief in Jesus with the power to become "children of God" (M. Vellanickal, *The Divine Sonship of Christians* [AnBib 72; Rome, 1977]). Birth "from above" of John 3:3 could also refer to faith as divine gift. The explanations of what is necessary for salvation in vv 13–15 and 16–21 fit a similar pattern. One must believe in the crucified/exalted Son of Man in order to have life (M. Pamment, *JTS* 36 [1985] 56–66). John 3:6–8 speaks of the Spirit as the source of the birth "from above." Therefore, the only textual support for a reference to baptism in this passage lies in "unless someone is born of water and the Spirit" (v 5) and in the connection between the Nicodemus episode and the narrative section (vv 22–30). Had the two episodes followed one after the other, one could hardly have avoided concluding that the Nicodemus episode referred to baptism. Omitting vv 31–36 brings the narrative back to the question of baptism with 4:1, where the Pharisees' concern with the baptismal activity of John (1:25) is matched by their concern with the "even greater numbers" of Jesus. Though it is sometimes argued that the baptismal allusion in v 5 was the creation of a final redactor who sought to provide a foundation for later church views, this section moves in the opposite direction. What was originally a set of stories about baptism, the Spirit, and purification, contrasting Christian practice with Judaism, has become the occasion for an opening statement of the Johannine combination of christology and soteriology (R. Fortna, *Int* 27 [1973] 31–47). Belief in the one who has come from heaven and has returned in exaltation from the cross is the key to salvation.

48   (i) *Dialogue: Receiving eternal life* (3:1–15). Nicodemus is a sympathetic but "unbelieving" Jewish teacher (7:50–51; 19:39). Though a Gk name, "Nicodemus" was a loanword in Aramaic and is attached to an aristocratic Jerusalem family (*Naqdîmôn*). Some exegetes think that the sequence of Nicodemus scenes is intended to depict a development toward faith. Nicodemus is certainly distinguished from the superficial faith rejected in 2:23, and the designation "teacher of Israel" (v 10; cf. 1:47, "true Israelite") may be intended to distinguish Nicodemus from "the Jews," the hostile authorities who explicitly reject Jesus.

49   **1–2.** Nicodemus is identified as *archōn,* "leader," of the Jews, presumably a member of the sanhedrin, which formed the civic "council" for the Jewish community in Jerusalem. *at night:* This note would have symbolic overtones for the reader of the Gospel. John 3:19–21 will establish the symbolism of two groups, those who "come to the light (Jesus)" and those who will not do so. Others have suggested that the nighttime visit is already a hint that people will be afraid to associate with Jesus because of the Jews (e.g., 19:38). Or the time may indicate Nicodemus's stature as a true teacher, since he studies the law at night (e.g., 1QS 6:7). Nicodemus's salutation allows that Jesus' "signs" show him to be a teacher from God on a par with himself. This acknowledgment contrasts with the crowd's false understanding of signs in 2:23 and with the later rejection of Jesus because he is "unlettered" (7:15).

50   **3–5.** *unless a person is born from above:* An enigmatic saying initiates the dialogue (cf. 4:10; 5:17,19; 6:26). Use of the double Amen in the Gospel falls into distinct groups of sayings: (1) christological affirmations (5:19; 8:58; 10:7); (2) formal judgments against Jesus' protagonists (3:11 [spoken in the name of the community]; 6:26; 8:34; 10:1; 6:32 [implied]); (3) conditions for salvation using a positive affirmation (5:24,25; 6:47; 8:51); (4) conditions for salvation using a negative affirmation (3:3,5; 6:53; 12:24 [adapted proverb?]); (5) references to future experiences of salvation in the community (1:51; 13:16,20; 14:12; 16:20,23); (6) predictions (13:21,38; 21:18). Jesus' saying turns on the ambiguity of the word *anōthen,* which can mean "from above," "from the beginning," or "again." The reader knows that the first meaning is intended (1:12). Nicodemus employs a typical opening for debate by taking the most literal meaning possible: a person would have to emerge from the womb again. Repetition of the saying in v 5 makes the Spirit the agent of rebirth. This saying may have been the more traditional one, since it speaks of "entering the kingdom of God," phraseology typical of the Synoptic kingdom sayings, whereas v 3 uses "see the kingdom" (cf. "you will see heaven opened" in 1:51). The discourse in 3:31 will shift from the Spirit to Jesus as the one who comes "from above." Some scholars have suggested that these Johannine sayings are variants of Synoptic sayings about "becoming like a child" in order to enter the kingdom (e.g., Matt 18:3; → Johannine Theology, 83:58–61).

51   **6–8.** *what is born from the Spirit:* Verse 6 recalls the distinction between flesh and "becoming a child of God" in 1:12. Jewish apocalyptic writings (e.g., *Jub.* 1:23, "I will create in them a holy spirit and I will cleanse them so that they will not turn away from me from that day unto eternity") associated cleansing by God's Spirit with the messianic age. The DSS speak of entry into the community with this inward purification (e.g., 1QS 4:20–24; 1QH 3:21; 11:10–14) and of "flesh" to describe the human being as subject to weakness, sinfulness, and alienation from God (1QS 9:7; 1QH 4:29; 8:31; 9:16). Verse 8 invokes a short proverb about the "wind," the same word as "Spirit" in both Hebrew (*rûaḥ*) and Greek (*pneuma*), to explain the mysterious activity of the Spirit. The identification of Spirit and water reappears in 7:38–39, where it is given the full christological sense of Jesus as the source of the "Spirit/living water." **9–10.** The 1st-cent. Jewish parallels to Jesus' imagery make Jesus' rebuke of Nicodemus plausible. **11.** *we bear witness to what we have seen:* The "we know" in this saying, probably created by the evangelist, picks up the "we know" used by Nicodemus in v 2. Jewish teachers will not accept the true Christian testimony about Jesus.

52   **12.** *if I tell you earthly things and you do not believe:*

The rebuke is a proverbial one with parallels in both Jewish and Gk writers. In Jewish writings, it can refer to the limits of human wisdom, which force it to rely on the Wisdom of God (cf. Prov 30:3–4; Wis 9:16–18). **13.** The discourse turns to the Johannine claim that Jesus is the only source of knowledge about the heavenly world. *no one has ascended to heaven:* This negates the claims of other visionaries to have knowledge of what is in heaven (e.g., 1 *Enoch* 70:2; 71:1 have Enoch ascend into heaven, where he is identified with the Son-of-Man figure from Dan 7:14). The Son-of-Man saying in 1:51 promises the believer this heavenly vision as a vision of Jesus. **14–15.** The first of the three Son-of-Man sayings to refer to Jesus' exaltation (→ Johannine Theology, 83:28,38). The allusion to Num 21:9–11 may be a typology created in the Johannine church. Wis 16:6–7 speaks of the event as turning Israel toward the Torah and toward God as Savior. The Johannine connection between believing and having eternal life is applied to the story in v 15.

53   (ii) *Comment: God sent the Son to give life* (3:16–21). The evangelist breaks into the narrative with a discourse on the sending of the Son to bring life to the world. The realized eschatology of Johannine theology is evident in the connection between believing in the Son and not being judged but having eternal life (cf. John 12:46–48). Some exegetes have suggested that there is OT typology at work in this passage as well. These are the only verses outside the prologue (1:16,18) to speak of the Son as *monogenēs*. They may be thinking of Isaac as the "only son" whom Abraham loved but was willing to sacrifice. Though the Fourth Gospel does not focus on the death of Jesus as a sacrifice, the expression "he [= God] gave his only Son" (v 16) would be understood as a reference to Jesus' being given up to death (cf. Gal 1:4; 2:20; Rom 8:32). **19–21.** *those who do the truth come to the light:* Using an ethical dualism of light and darkness, this explains why people reject God's salvation. In the DSS, "do the truth" is an idiom for being righteous. Responsiveness to the truth is a function of one's righteousness. In a passage that occurs in the context of a teaching about purification by the Spirit, we find, "According as one's inheritance is in truth and righteousness, so he hates evil; but insofar as his heritage is in the portion of perversity, so he abominates the truth" (1QS 4:24). This piece of Johannine discourse may have reworked earlier Jewish material (→ Johannine Theology, 83:21,50–54).

54   (iii) *John testifies to Jesus* (3:22–30). Two comments by the evangelist have been inserted into the scene (vv 24,28) to remind the reader about JBap's life and earlier testimony (1:20). His imprisonment is never described in the Fourth Gospel. **22–23.** The introduction is awkward and may represent a fragment of early geographical tradition, though the identification of the sites named is not certain. John 4:2 will correct the impression that Jesus baptized. **25–26.** The reference to a controversy over purification is also unclear. It may be intended to raise the issue of the relative value of the baptism of Jesus and that of JBap, though what follows does not speak directly to the issue of purification, but about the relative success of the two men. **27,29–30.** John's first response takes the form of an aphorism. Is the subject the Baptist or Jesus? Applied to Jesus, a variant of this aphorism appears in 6:65 after followers have abandoned Jesus. The Gospel consistently insists that "believers" are given to Jesus by God (6:37). Mark 2:18–19 has Jesus use an aphorism about the presence of the bridegroom to justify the fact that his disciples do not fast like those of JBap. That imagery applied to him implies that his function as "best man" is over. Consequently, the difference in response to the two missions is to be expected.

55   (iv) *Comment: God sent Jesus to give life* (3:31–36). This segment of discourse can be seen as a summary of the whole section. JBap clearly cannot be said to have spoken "earthly things," since he has fulfilled the role that he had from God, testifying to Jesus. **31.** *from above:* This adv. recalls vv 3 and 7: Jesus is now seen to be the one "from above." *earthly things:* The contrast between "speaking earthly things" and the one "from heaven" who can speak heavenly things reflects v 13. **32.** Testimony to what he has seen as well as refusal to accept that testimony recalls v 11 rather than the immediate testimony of JBap. **33–34.** The abrupt shift from condemnation of unbelief to the believer occurs in 1:11–12. Rejecting Jesus' testimony is rejecting God (5:23; 8:50; 12:44–45). *he gives the Spirit without measure:* The words Jesus speaks are God's. God is also the source of the measureless gift of the Spirit. This reference to the Spirit recalls vv 6–8. **35.** The Father's love for the Son (cf. 5:20; 10:17; 15:9–10; 17:23–26) appears here for the first time, though it may be implied in the *monogenēs* of 3:16. Among the things that the Gospel says God gives the Son are judgment (5:22,27), life (5:26), power over "all flesh" to give life (17:2), his followers (6:37; 10:29; 17:6), what he says (12:49; 17:8), the divine name (17:11–12), and glory (17:22). **36.** The whole comes to its close on a note of division between the believers, who have eternal life (e.g., 12:48) and unbelievers, who are under divine judgment, an ominous note in this presentation of persons coming to discover who Jesus is and to believe in him.

56   (e) WITHDRAWAL TO GALILEE (4:1–3). As the Gospel progresses, we see Jesus "withdrawing" from hostility or, as here, from false popularity (6:15b; 7:1–2, 9; 8:59; 10:40; 11:54). **2.** A parenthetical comment has been added to dispel the impression that Jesus had baptized people in imitation of JBap.

57   (f) SAMARIA: SAVIOR OF THE WORLD (4:4–42). The conversion of large numbers of Samaritans culminates in the christological insight that Jesus is "Savior of the world." Samaritan messianic expectations are represented in the portrayal of Jesus as the Mosaic prophet. Whereas the earlier stories described the conversion of individuals by a disciple who had come to believe in Jesus, this episode presents the Samaritan woman as the first missionary. Jesus' exchange with the disciples (vv 31–38) also focuses on the task of evangelization. **4–5.** The usual route from Judea to Galilee lay through Samaria. The journey took about three days (Josephus, *Life* 52 § 269; → Biblical Archaeology, 74:114). The well of Jacob lay at the major fork in the road, one branch turning W to Samaria and western Galilee; the other NE toward Beth-shan and the Lake of Gennesaret. Mt. Gerizim is to the SW. The village, Sychar, is probably modern Askar, half a mile NE from the well.

58   (i) *Dialogue: Living water* (4:6–15). **6–9.** The scene, Jacob's well, provides the basis for the symbolism in which Jesus proves to be greater than Jacob. We have already seen hints of such Jacob typology in 1:51. The woman responds to Jesus' request on the literal level by referring to the strained relationships between Jews and Samaritans. Luke 9:51–55 refers to an episode in which Jesus and his disciples were refused hospitality by a Samaritan village (a serious clash in AD 52, which even required Roman intervention, is reported by Josephus [*Ant.* 20.6.1–3 § 118–36; *J.W.* 2.12.3–5 § 232–46]).

59   **10–12.** *Are you greater than our father, Jacob?:* Jesus' assertion that he is the "gift of God" and source of "living water" leads to the first christological insight of the passage—Jesus is greater than Jacob. John 8:53 has the Jews repeating the same question in connection with Abraham. Gen 33:19; 48:22 speak of Jacob giving

Shechem to Joseph. Later legends about the patriarch Jacob associated him with a "traveling well" (*Pirqe R. El.* 35). Lack of a cup would be no problem, since Jacob was also associated with a miracle in which the water would bubble to the top of the well and continuously overflow (*Tg. Yer. I* Num 21:17–18; 23:31; *Tg. Neof.* Gen 28:10. Targumic traditions also show that Num 21:16–20 had been interpreted so that the place-name "Mattanah" was read in terms of its root *ntn,* "gift," combined with the promise in 21:16c, "I (= God) will give them water." Jesus' comment, that he is the "gift of God," may echo this tradition. The crucified/exalted Jesus becomes the source of living water, the Spirit (7:37–39; 19:34). **13–15.** *the water which I will give:* Jesus responds that he is not only "greater than" Jacob, but that he supplants the reality that had been described in the OT (cf. 6:49–51; 11:9–10). Permanent possession of "living water" within a Jewish symbolic system could either refer to the purifying of God's Spirit in the righteous community (e.g., 1QS 4:21, "like purifying waters he will sprinkle upon him the Spirit of Truth"), a connection implied in 3:5. Or to God, the "fountain of living waters" (Jer 2:13), from which worshipers drink (Ps 36:8); or to the law (as in CD 19:34; 3:16; 6:4–11); or to Wisdom, who says of herself, "He who eats of me will hunger still; he who drinks of me will thirst for more" (Sir 24:23–29). Jesus' saying may even be a deliberate reversal of Wisdom's claim.

60   (ii) *Dialogue: The Messiah-prophet* (4:16–26). **16–18.** *call your husband:* Jesus' demand appears to shift the issue. No completely satisfactory explanation has been offered for the "five husbands." The reader of the Gospel is not surprised at Jesus' unique insight into persons (see 1:42,48; 2:24–25). It appears that the reader is to infer that the woman's past would be considered sinful. However, the Jacob theme may still be implicit in this passage, since the well is the place of courtship in the Jacob story. Jesus replaces the numerous "husbands" which the woman has had.

61   **19–20.** *you are a prophet:* Samaritan tradition expected "the prophet" to uncover the lost Temple vessels and to vindicate its own tradition of worship, not in Jerusalem but on Mt. Gerizim, which they took to be the location of Jacob's heavenly vision in Gen 28:16–18. The woman's words may be intended as a challenge. **21–22.** *neither on this mountain nor in Jerusalem:* Jewish traditions enlisted Jacob's vision as legitimation for the Jerusalem cult. *Jub.* 32:21–26 has the angel who shows Jacob the heavenly tablets warn against building a temple at Bethel. 4QPBless has Jacob foresee the coming of a messianic ruler from Judah along with the Interpreter of the Law. A midrash on Gen 27:27 has God show Jacob the building, destruction, and rebuilding of the Jerusalem Temple (*Gen. Rab.* 65:23). Jesus proclaims that in the messianic age, which has now dawned, worship of God will not be tied to a holy place. Any priority of Jews over Samaritans implied in v 22 will quickly be wiped away, as it becomes clear that the true standard of worship is belief in Jesus. He has already supplanted Jewish purification rites (2:6–11; 3:25–30). The reader has been told that the "risen Lord" supplants the Jerusalem Temple (2:13–22).

62   **23–24.** *worship in Spirit and in truth:* Though the importance of the cultic site has been relativized, worship has not. We have already seen that John understands "Spirit" to be the Spirit of God, which purifies the believer and is a permanent possession. God's truth can also be spoken of as purifying the sinfulness and perversity of humanity (1QS 4:20–21). The Essenes described the Torah as a well dug by their teachers from which they drew their knowledge of truth (CD 6:2–5). For

John, Jesus is the truth, since he is the revelation of God (8:45; 14:6; 17:17–19). **25–26.** The discourse reaches its conclusion when the woman suggests that Jesus might be the messianic prophet and Jesus responds "I Am." Though the context leads one to supply a predicate "Messiah" for "I Am," any Johannine Christian would have recognized the absolute use of the expression "I Am" to indicate Jesus' divine being (→ Johannine Theology, 83:41–49). This link will be made explicit when Jesus is shown to be greater than Abraham (8:24,28). The basis for true worship in the Johannine community is the confession of Jesus as prophet, Messiah, Savior of the world, and equal to God (see J. H. Neyrey, *CBQ* 43 [1979] 419–37).

63   (iii) *Dialogue: The harvest* (4:27–38). The discourse concludes on the theme of mission. **27–30.** Jesus' disciples return as the woman goes into the town to bring people to Jesus, the Messiah. Her action reflects the pattern established in the discipleship stories (1:40–49). **31–34.** Jesus will complement the giving of water with giving bread in chap. 6. Here the disciples misunderstand Jesus' words about food just as the woman misunderstood "water." Jewish tradition could describe the Torah as food (e.g., Prov 9:5; Sir 24:21). Jesus makes doing the will of the one who sent him his "food." This expression is a common one for Jesus' ministry (cf. 5:30,36; 6:38; 17:4; → Johannine Theology, 83:22). *to complete his work:* This will be echoed at the conclusion of Jesus' ministry (17:4; 19:30), and the dying Jesus says, "It is completed."

64   A series of proverbial sayings (with parallels in the agricultural imagery of the Synoptics) directs the disciples toward their own task in "harvesting" those who are yet to come to Jesus. **35.** *yet four months:* Jesus corrects a proverb about the time between sowing and harvest by announcing that the field is already ripe. (Remember the approaching Samaritans, v 30.) A similar saying appears in Matt 9:37–38. Some exegetes also point to the theme of harvest in Synoptic kingdom parables (Mark 4:3–9,26–29,30–32), where the contrasts are drawn in terms of the perilous conditions, hidden growth or small seed and the abundance of the harvest. **36.** Sower and reaper receiving their wages together is another sign of the new age. Lev 26:5 describes the ideal reward as a time in which wheat harvest, grape harvest, sowing, all follow consecutively (also Amos 9:13). In John the missionary "harvest" does not begin until the hour of Jesus' crucifixion/exaltation (e.g., 12:32). The phrase "for eternal life" added to "fruit" makes it clear that the "harvest" is conversion to belief in Jesus. **37–38.** *one sows another reaps:* Jesus uses the proverb without its pessimistic overtones (e.g., Mic 6:15). It is difficult to determine how the proverb is being applied to the disciples. Does it allude to a "mission" of the disciples during Jesus' ministry (e.g., they will "reap" what the woman has sown among the Samaritans)? Or does it refer to the postresurrection "sending" of the disciples (e.g., 17:18; 20:21)? The narrative structure of the Gospel favors the latter. The saying cautions the community against taking credit for its missionary success. It merely reaps the fruits of others' labor: primarily that of Jesus, but reference to the first generation of Christian missionaries could also be implied. Acts 8 distinguishes two phases in the conversion of Samaria, the preaching of Philip and the arrival of Peter and John to confer the Spirit on the new converts.

65   (iv) *Samaritan believers* (4:39–42). The Samaritans believe first on the basis of the word of the woman who testified about Jesus and then on the basis of their own experience of Jesus' words. The story envisages the mission of the community after the resurrection. John

17:20 has the departing Jesus pray for "those who will believe in me through their word," and John 20:29b has the risen Lord pronounce a blessing on those who have "not seen and (yet) believed." **42.** *truly the Savior of the world:* The title "Savior" occurs only here in John and in 1 John 4:14. "Savior" is not a title derived from the Samaritan expectations but might be intended to show that the Samaritans have transcended their particularized expectations just as the Jewish protagonists of Jesus are challenged to do in discourses that culminate with the Son-of-Man sayings. John prefers to speak of Jesus coming or giving himself for the "life of the world" (e.g., 1:29; 6:33,51). The only two occurrences of the verb "save" are in what appear to be fragments of a discourse inserted into the narrative (3:17; 12:47). "Savior" is infrequent as a title for Jesus in the earlier NT writings. It appears in the infancy narrative of Luke (2:11) and in reference to the exalted Lord as "Savior" in Acts (5:31; 13:23). *Sōtēr* appears in the LXX to translate Hebr *môšia'*, which is used of God (e.g., Isa 45:15,21; Wis 16:7; Sir 51:1; 1 Macc 4:30). It was also current in the pagan world as a designation for deities, kings, emperors, and others who might be perceived to function as benefactors of the people. An inscription found at Ephesus from AD 48 speaks of the deified Julius Caesar as "god manifest and common savior of human life." Phil 3:20 uses "Savior" for the exalted Jesus when he comes in judgment at the parousia. However, "Savior" appears to have become a common title for Jesus only toward the end of the 1st cent., as is evident in its use in the Pastoral Epistles (e.g., 1 Tim 4:10; 2 Tim 1:10; Tit 1:4; 2:13; 3:4,6; also 2 Pet 1:1,11; 2:20; 3:2,18).

66   (g) GALILEE: THE OFFICIAL'S SON (4:43–54). Jesus' return to Galilee brings this section to a conclusion with a second "sign" at Cana. The cure of the royal official's son has parallels with the centurion's request for the cure of his "child" (Matt 8:5–13) or "slave" (Luke 7:1–10; see F. Neirynck, *ETL* 60 [1984] 367–75). The Synoptic story concludes with a contrast between the faith of the centurion and the lack of faith that Jesus finds in Israel. A similar contrast is "enacted" during the Johannine narrative. The reader has just witnessed the spectacular response of the Samaritans. The curing of the official's son culminates in what appears to have been a stock epithet for early conversion stories, "he believed and his whole household" (cf. Acts 10:2; 11:14; 16:15, 31; 18:8). Jesus' next miracle, in Jerusalem (5:1–18), will evoke hostility.

67   (i) *Jesus' return to Galilee* (4:43–45). Verses 43–45 are awkward. The evangelist appears to have inserted a traditional saying of Jesus (Mark 6:4, "A prophet is not without honor except in his own country;" Luke 4:24, "No prophet is welcomed in his own country") into an otherwise positive scene. Some exegetes conclude that Judea is Jesus "own country," though the hostile use of "Galilean" to accuse Nicodemus of being a follower of Jesus (7:52) hardly supports the view that the evangelist was confused about the country of Jesus' origin. Luke's version of the rejection of Jesus at Nazareth shows a similar tension: those who welcome Jesus' words turn against him. It appears that the evangelist, looking toward the conflict between Jesus and the Galilean crowd in chap. 6, where he will again pick up a sequence of materials with parallels in Mark 6 and 8, has created a transitional passage by inserting the traditional saying of v 44. This transition is of the same sort as that in 2:23–25.

68   (ii) *The official's son healed* (4:46–54). Although this story is a variant of the healing of the centurion's child/slave, there are few verbal parallels between John and Matt/Luke, making this episode

evidence of independent, Synoptic-like Johannine tradition. All versions locate the episode at Capernaum (→ Biblical Geography, 73:61). The "son" in John and the "slave" in Luke could both be variants of a tradition that originally had *pais*, "child," which could mean either an offspring or a slave. Whereas Matt/Luke make the petitioner a centurion, and consequently a representative of "Gentiles" coming to believe in Jesus, John's version has "royal official," presumably a Jewish functionary of Herod's court. The interaction between the petitioner(s) and Jesus varies. Both Luke and John have a "second scene." In Luke the father sends friends to dissuade the petitioners from bothering Jesus; in John the servants meet the father to report the boy's cure. Both Matt and John correlate the father's "belief" with the healing of the boy at the moment Jesus speaks. John's version also uses the second scene as an opportunity to emphasize the "word" of Jesus, in which the man believed by repeating both the words and the affirmation that he believed. This repetition is linked to the conversion of the whole household, which appears only in John.

69   **48.** Jesus' rejection of the request differs from the other versions of the story, though the healing of the Syrophoenician woman's daughter (Mark 7:24–30 par.) does contain an initial rejection, which the woman must overcome. That motif may have been part of the Johannine tradition. Since all the father does is repeat his request, it is also possible that this verse is inserted to remind the reader of the inadequacy of faith based on miracles. As the evangelist tells the story, the miracle is less important than the fact that the official believes in the word which Jesus spoke. The story has not been edited to bring out the symbolism of that "word," but any Johannine Christian would certainly connect Jesus giving "life" to a boy near death and the concluding miracle in the Gospel, the raising of Lazarus.

70   (B) **Disputes over Jesus' Deeds and Words: Is He from God? (5:1–10:42).** These chapters have undergone a complex process of editing, which saw the addition of chaps. 11–12 and, some scholars think, either the relocation of chap. 6 from a position following chap. 4 or its insertion between chaps. 5 and 7. Chaps. 5–12 have a parallel set of double miracle stories. The healings in chaps. 5 and 9 bring Jesus into conflict with the authorities as one who breaks the sabbath. In the first, the healed man's eventual conversion to belief in Jesus is left in doubt, whereas in the second, the healed man becomes a prototype for the Christian persecuted by the authorities. The second pair consists of stories in which Jesus, the source of life, is rejected. The miracle of the loaves, Jesus as "bread of life," eventuates in a loss of disciples. The raising of Lazarus, Jesus as "resurrection and life," is the occasion for his death.

Jesus now steps onto the public stage in confrontation with "the Jews" (5:10,15; 6:41,52; 7:15,35; 8:22, 31,48,57; 10:19,24,33; 11:54). Every chapter contains some form of hostility against Jesus. His life is frequently threatened (e.g., 5:16,18; 6:15a; 7:32,45; 8:59; 9:34b [against a follower of Jesus]; 10:31,39; 11:16 [impending], 45–54 [condemnation by Jewish authorities]; 12:9–11, against Lazarus because Jesus healed him). Chapters 5–12 are also linked together by a series of feasts beginning with the unnamed feast in chap. 5, which scholars who transpose chaps. 5 and 6 suggest could be identified with Pentecost prior to the feast of Tabernacles in chap. 7.

71   The narrative sequence of chaps. 4–6 is so awkward that many scholars think the chapters were once in the sequence 4, 6, 5. Since our earliest papyri support the present order, one can only presume that any reordering of the chapters took place during the final editing of the Gospel within the Johannine community. Geographically, the location of chap. 6 fits the end of 4:54: Jesus has gone from the W to the E bank of the sea. Similarly, the warning voiced in 7:1 seems more appropriate in the context of the hostility expressed in 5:18 than following on chap. 6. If chap. 6 at one time followed chap. 4, then the chronological outline of Jesus' ministry is closer to that in the Synoptics. Jesus conducts a mission in Galilee, which has the feeding of the multitude, walking on water, and confession by Peter as its high point; then Jesus turns toward Jerusalem. The present sequence follows the pattern of alternation between Galilee and Judea and the lengthening of Jesus' ministry with visits to Jerusalem prior to the passion, which has already been established in chap. 2.

72 (a) JERUSALEM: HEALING THE CRIPPLE; LIFE AND JUDGMENT (5:1–47). The miracle serves as the occasion for a discourse on Jesus' relationship to the Father and his power to give life. The discourse also illustrates the point implied in John 4:50: Jesus' word is the real source of faith, not the signs.

73 (i) *A cripple healed on the sabbath* (5:1–18). This miracle does not have a direct Synoptic parallel, though Jesus heals a paralytic in Mark 2:1–12: Jesus' words in v 8 are similar to Mark 2:9 and probably indicate a stereotyped pattern in oral tradition; the rare word *krabattos*, "pallet," appears only in Mark and John, and the assessment of the illness as a consequence of sin appears in Mark 2:5; in John 5:14 it serves as a nucleus to create a second scene between Jesus and the cripple in the Temple. As was the case in 4:4–42, and to a lesser degree in 1:19–51, we see the evangelist's practice of elaborating on traditional material to form short scenes within the larger whole. A second element, the conflict over Jesus' breaking the sabbath (vv 9c–10), has been added to the story, but is also found in connection with some of Jesus' miracles in the Synoptic tradition (e.g., Mark 2:23–28).

74 **2.** Archaeological research has thrown some light on the location. We can resolve disagreement in the mss. over the name of the site in favor of "Bethesda," thanks to a reference in the Copper Roll from Qumran Cave 3: "By Bethesdatayin, in the pool where you enter is a smaller basin" (3Q*15* 11:12–13). The structure found by archaeologists had five porticoes with two pools—a smaller one to the north and a larger one on the southern side—enclosed by four porches with a fifth one between the two pools. The structure was sunk seven to eight meters into the ground and gathered a great deal of rainwater. Its name, "Sheep Pool," suggests that originally it had a different use, but the reference in the Copper Roll (AD 35–65) shows that it has been turned into quite an elaborate structure, probably by Herod the Great. The excavations do not shed any light on the man's remark that in order to be healed one must be the first person into the pool when the water is stirred (v 7). Some interpreters think that there may have been confusion between it and the spring at Siloam, which ejected water several times a day during the rainy season, twice in summer and once in the autumn; or that the effect may have been caused by a system of pipes used to move the water from one pool to the other. A solution to this problem was given by later mss., including Alexandrinus, which have a verse (v 4) explaining that an angel of God came to stir the waters.

75 **9c–15.** A series of short encounters shifts our attention away from the miracle to Jesus as one who violates the sabbath. The forgiveness theme was probably part of the tradition. It appears in Mark 2:5–10. For John, the "sin" is failing to believe in Jesus (e.g., 16:9). John has used that theme to create a second encounter between the man and Jesus in the Temple area, the site of Jesus' major controversies with "the Jews" (e.g., 7:28; 8:20,59; 10:23). *lest something worse befall you:* Jesus' warning may also cast the man's action in reporting Jesus to the authorities in a negative light. He has "sinned again" by reporting Jesus. The contrast between this man and the believing response to a gift of healing will become evident in John 9 when the blind man defends Jesus. Within the context of Johannine symbolism this man stands condemned in the judgment (e.g., 3:36).

76 **16–18.** *the Jews persecuted him:* The real issue, as it was for Johannine Christians, becomes Jesus' claim to equality with God; it may have occurred in the pre-Johannine tradition. Mark 2:7 has Jesus accused of blasphemy for claiming a prerogative, forgiving sins, which belongs to God alone. These verses are addressed to the reader, who already knows that Jesus was "persecuted" and "killed" by the Jews (vv 16,18). The saying in v 17 is awkwardly inserted between the editorial comments to introduce the theme of Jesus' reply to the charges: he works just as his Father does on the sabbath.

77 (ii) *The Son's authority to give life* (5:19–30). Two sections describe the activity of the Son, giving life and judging, as the reflection of what he has "seen" the Father doing. Verses 19–20a may have been derived from a short parable about a father and an apprentice son. Jesus will insist that he is the true agent of the Father. He never acts on his own authority but only on what he hears from the Father (7:18; 8:28; 14:10). **20b–23.** *greater things than these:* "Greater things" in John express Jesus' relationship to God (20b; cf. 1:50). They are defined in what follows, "giving life" and "judging." John 3:31–36 has already instructed the reader that the Son's mission from the Father is to "give life" to those who believe. Those who refuse to believe are under judgment. This eschatological perspective is repeated in this section. Where the earlier passage had spoken of "eternal life," this one incorporates the theme of restored life through resurrection of the dead. Both expressions will return in the "greater work" which will enact the promise that the audience will see a "greater thing" from Jesus, viz., the raising of Lazarus (11:1–44). The claim that honoring the Son is honoring the Father invokes the image of Jesus as the agent of God, who therefore deserves a reception appropriate to the one from whom he comes (see W. A. Meeks, "The Divine Agent and His Counterfeit," *Aspects of Religious Propaganda* [ed. E. Schüssler Fiorenza; Notre Dame, 1976] 43–67).

78 **24–25.** The double Amen sayings sharpen the perspective of realized eschatology in the Fourth Gospel. The person who does hear and believe "has life." Death and judgment are not the future of such a person. *passed from death to life:* A stock expression of coming to salvation in the Johannine community (cf. 1 John 3:14). Verse 25 makes the Johannine reinterpretation of the traditional eschatological message even more evident by speaking of the resurrection of those who have died in the present tense. *the hour is coming and now is:* This appeared in 4:23 of the realization of messianic worship in the Son. Only the dead who hear the voice of the Son of Man are raised to life.

79 Gnostic mythology used "death" as a metaphor for the state of the unawakened souls trapped in this world. They [= those who become gnostics] are said to hear the revealer's call to awaken from death, drunkenness, sleep. *Apocryphon of John* 30.33–31.25 describes the call of awakening and salvation issued by the heavenly *Pronoia* (forethought, providence). It shows how the gnostic revelation dialogue parallels themes from Johannine revelation discourse but incorporates them into an ontological structure of the earthly prison vs. the heavenly light world that is not yet part of the symbolic world of the Fourth Gospel (see Rudolph, *Gnosis* [→ 8 above] 119–21).

80   **26.** *just as the Father has life:* This parallels v 21 and repeats its assertion that the Father has given this power to the Son. **27a.** *has given him power to judge:* This echoes 22b. **27b.** *because he is Son of Man:* The only anarthrous Son-of-Man expression in the Gospel jumps to the saying about the call to the dead in v 25. This image of Son of Man goes back to the early Christian use of the figure from Dan 7:13 to describe Jesus coming as judge. However, none of the other Son-of-Man sayings in John refers to Jesus as future eschatological judge. **27b–29.** The Son-of-Man saying in these verses is a future prediction of resurrection to judgment, which had its origins in postexilic Judaism (Dan 12:2; *1 Enoch* 51; *4 Ezra* 7:32; *2 Apoc. Bar.* 42.7; *Apoc. Mos.* 10:41) and which had commonly been associated with Jesus as "Lord" or as "Son of Man" in primitive Christianity (e.g., 2 Cor 5:10). While some writings use resurrection as reward for the righteous (e.g., Phil 3:20), others envisage a dual resurrection, which makes the judgment possible (e.g., Dan 12:2). Verse 29 adopts the latter view, whereas v 21 has linked resurrection of the dead and "giving life," thus suggesting the former. The tension between the "future eschatology" of bodily resurrection to judgment and the "realized eschatology" of judgment by one's response to the present call embodied in the word that Jesus speaks suggests that these verses are an independent piece of tradition. Verse 28 uses wording characteristic of John; so the saying itself appears to have been shaped and circulated in the Johannine communities. Some exegetes think that it was used to provide a repetition of the earlier discourse, which then reaches its final conclusion with the repetition of v 19 in v 30. But others follow Bultmann's lead in thinking that this piece of tradition was added during the final editing of the Gospel by a disciple. Perhaps it was necessary to counteract the misinterpretations of Johannine eschatology being put forward by the successionists of the Johannine epistles.

81   (iii) *Testimony to Jesus* (5:31–40). Suddenly the discourse shifts to the issue of testimony to Jesus. The objection which such an assertion answers is not voiced until 8:13, where the legal principle that no one can testify on his own behalf is invoked (Deut 19:15 holds that no one can be convicted on the testimony of one witness; *m. Ketub.* 2:9 cites the legal principle that no one can be a witness on his own behalf). The question of "witnesses" shifts the language of judging from judgment passed on others to that which they pass on Jesus. Thus, the narrative tensions of the Gospel can be seen as a double-sided trial. On one side, humans judge and condemn Jesus, since they reject those whom he brings forward as witnesses. On the other, Jesus' word is the trial and condemnation of an unbelieving world, since those who testify on his behalf are in fact "true." The real witness to Jesus is the Father (vv 32,37).

82   **33–35.** The testimony of the Baptist before those sent from Jerusalem (1:19–28) is invoked only to be suddenly cut off as mere "human" testimony. *you rejoiced for a while in his light:* This may refer to the popularity of JBap among the people (cf. Josephus, *Ant.* 18.5.2 § 118). Verse 35 seems to presuppose the Baptist's death, though the evangelist does not mention it directly. **36.** Jesus points to his "works" as greater testimony than that of JBap, alluding indirectly to the cure of the paralytic. The direct connection between a "work" of Jesus and his being "from God" is made by the blind man (9:33). Jesus' works are again invoked as testimony in

10:25; 14:10–11. In the Synoptic tradition, Jesus' "works" are given as evidence that he is the expected one in response to a query made by the Baptist's disciples on behalf of their imprisoned master (Matt 11:5). **37–38.** *you do not have His word:* The real "witness" on Jesus' behalf is the Father. Failure to receive God's envoy is cause for condemnation. The two negative clauses suggest that Jesus' protagonists are incapable of receiving that testimony, since they have not "heard his voice," "seen him," or possessed his word "abiding with them." **39–40.** *you search the Scriptures:* Lacking access to knowledge of God that can come only through Jesus, even the commendable activity of studying the Scriptures in order to have life is fruitless. "Search" represents Hebr *dāraš*, which is used for study of the Scriptures. Verses 39–40 thus return the discourse to the theme of life with which it began and set forth the rather grim expectation (one grounded in the experiences of the Johannine community) that the religious leaders of Judaism would not turn to Jesus.

83   (iv) *Unbelief condemned* (5:41–47). The judgment pronounced in vv 39–40 is sharpened in this section as Scripture will indict those who do not believe Jesus' words. **41.** *glory from human beings:* Again the theme shifts abruptly to a topic that will be repeated in later controversies. The charge of seeking human glory, currying favor with an audience, etc. was widely used in antiquity to castigate Sophists and false teachers. Dio says that the ideal Cynic is a person who "with purity and without guile speaks with a philosopher's boldness, not for the sake of glory, nor making false pretensions for the sake of gain" (*Or.* 32.11). The question of "human glory" over against speaking the truth originated in forensic contexts, since the rhetorician was able to make the audience accept as "truth" what is in fact false. The contrast between those who seek their own glory and Jesus, coupled with the charge that Jesus' opponents are not heeding Moses, reappears in 7:18. **42–44.** The consequences of false perceptions of glory are spelled out. They do not show love for God by receiving the one God sends. Instead, they would prefer to accept any charlatan. John 12:43 reiterates the claim that desire for human glory kept many who were sympathetic to Jesus from believing.

84   **45–47.** *Moses will condemn you:* Jewish tradition pictured Moses as the intercessor for the people, pleading before God day and night (*As. Mos.* 11:17; 12:6; "the good advocate," *Exod. Rab.* 18:3 on Exod 12:29; Philo, *De vita Mos.* 2.166; *Jub.* 1:19–21); he pleads on Sinai that the "spirit of Beliar" will not "master" the people so that they are accused before God. Moses, the advocate or "paraclete" (*synergos; paraklētos*) of the people is suddenly turned into their accuser. Moses testifies to Jesus (1:45), yet those who claim to place their hope in Moses and his writings show that they do not really believe Moses when they reject Jesus (see U. von Wahlde, *CBQ* 43 [1981] 385–404).

85   (b) GALILEE: THE BREAD OF LIFE (6:1–71). This section parallels the sequence of events in Mark 6:30–54 and 8:11–33 (omitting the duplicate feeding miracle in Mark 8:1–10): (1) feeding 5,000 (John 6:1–15; Mark 6:30–44); (2) walking on the sea (John 6:16–24; Mark 6:45–54); (3) request for a sign (John 6:25–34; Mark 8:11–13); (4) comment on bread (John 6:35–59; Mark 8:14–21); (5) Peter's confession (John 6:60–69; Mark 8:27–30); (6) passion (John 6:70–71; Mark 8:31–33). The symbols of Jesus as the one who provides "living water" in John 4 (also 7:38–39) and the heavenly bread were developed along with the Johannine christology of Jesus as the Mosaic prophet-king. The discourse on the bread was probably a homiletic midrash before its use in the Gospel. For the evangelist, the whole discourse becomes another confrontation between an unbelieving crowd and the one who has come from heaven with the word of life. Finally, some exegetes think that the section on Jesus as bread in the eucharist (vv 51–59) was added during the final editing of the Gospel to supply an etiology for the Johannine eucharistic celebration (L. Schenke, *BZ* 29 [1985] 68–89).

86   (i) *Feeding the five thousand* (6:1–15). **1–4.** The evangelist has expanded the introduction by adding (1) the vague chronological marker "after these things"; (2) the specification of the place, (lake of) Tiberias (→ Biblical Geography, 73:60–61), though this specification may be the result of the addition of 21:1, where it is the place of the appearance of the risen Lord; (3) the motivation for the crowd — they had seen Jesus' healings (signs); (4) and the reference to the impending "Passover of the Jews." **5–10.** *how are we to buy bread?:* As in other Johannine miracle stories, the initiative lies with Jesus. John lacks the reference to the lateness of the hour or to the distress of the people (Mark 6:35; [8:2–3]). Jesus puts the question to Philip as a test. Philip does not perceive that this question is an appeal to his faith and simply refers to the amount of money required.

87   **11–13.** *he distributed them:* The comment that Jesus gave out the bread points forward to the discourse on Jesus as the bread of life. *he gave thanks:* John's use of *eucharistein* (also in the summary of Jesus' actions in 6:23) has eucharistic overtones, though the expression reflects the Jewish custom of a blessing before meals. *so that nothing would be lost:* The symbolic intent of the added phrase is made evident in 6:27, "Do not labor for food which perishes." The large amount left over is taken from the tradition.

88   **14–15.** *this is truly the prophet:* The crowd responds correctly that Jesus is the messianic prophet but misunderstands that statement. The true nature of Jesus' kingship, which is not that of a national liberator, can only be revealed at the trial (18:33–37; 19:12–15).

89   (ii) *Walking on water* (6:16–21). This traditional episode further separates Jesus and the crowd. *Jesus had not yet come to them:* This presumes that the story is familiar to the reader. Unlike the Synoptics, John does not tell the story as one which emphasizes the disciples' faith. *it is I (I Am); do not be afraid:* Johannine Christians might understand this story as an epiphany, since "I Am" can be used to identify Jesus and God (e.g., 8:28). The conclusion shifts away from Jesus as divine savior in a sea-rescue miracle to the instantaneous crossing. The storm had driven the disciples out into the middle of the lake. They arrive suddenly at their goal. Some have suggested that the Passover/exodus theme in this chapter would remind the reader of the crossing of the sea under Moses (see C. H. Giblin, *NTS* 29 [1983] 96–103; H. Kruse, *NTS* 30 [1984] 508–30).

90   (iii) *Dialogue: Jesus is bread from heaven* (6:22–40). The biblical citation in v 31 forms the backbone of the discourse and its expansions through v 59. **22–25.** *on the next day:* A characteristic transition (e.g., 1:29,35,43). These verses form an awkward transition between the feeding and the discourse. The large number of textual variants in this section shows that it had created problems in antiquity. The link between Tiberias and the feeding miracle (v 23) may have been created by later editors. The crowd infers a mysterious crossing by Jesus on the grounds that there was only one boat, which the disciples had taken, while they had had to cross in boats from Tiberias. The geography is complicated by the presumption that the next discourse takes place in Capernaum, which is not "across the sea" but on the N

shore, slightly W of Tiberias. The confusion suggests a lack of familiarity with the region.

91   **26–29.** The crowd's question of "when" Jesus came (v 25) is bypassed. Jesus' saying distinguishes between "seeing the sign" and concern with the material elements. The crowd's first response, "to make Jesus king" (v 14), was rejected by Jesus' withdrawal. **27.** *do not work for food which perishes:* Recalls the discourse about Jesus as living water (4:14; 6:35 combines both images). In both the key to receiving the gift of Jesus is faith that he is the one from God. Thus, this verse does not refer primarily to the "bread" of the eucharist, but to Jesus' word of revelation. *on him God the Father has set his seal:* This recalls 3:33: whoever accepts the testimony of the one who has come "from above" sets his seal on the truthfulness of God. The phrase anticipates the coming polemic by emphasizing that it is God who attests to Jesus' role. **28–29.** *works of God:* This can refer to what God does and requires (e.g., CD 2:14–15). Jesus speaks of himself as doing the "works" of the one who sent him (9:4). He insists that only one "work" is necessary, that of believing in the one sent by God.

92   **30–31.** *sign that we may believe:* The traditional demand for a sign presumes that the crowd understands Jesus to be making a claim for himself and reminds the reader of Jesus' statement in v 26 that the crowd has not "seen the sign." They challenge Jesus by alluding to Exod 16:4–5. John's citation conflates Exod with Ps 78:24. Evidence for the expectation that in the eschatological age the "manna" would again become available derives from later Jewish writings. E.g., 2 *Apoc. Bar.* 29:8: "the treasury of manna shall again descend from on high and they will eat of it in those years" (for later examples, see *Midr. Rabb. Eccl* 1:9; *Midr. Tanḥuma* [*Beshallah* 21:26]). **32–33.** Jesus' response reformulates the citation by insisting: (1) not Moses, my Father; (2) not gave, "gives"; (3) the true (*alēthinos*) bread from heaven. Then the "true bread" is defined not as food but as "bread from God," the one who comes to give life to the world (e.g., 3:15–16; 5:24). **34–35.** The crowd's request parallels that of the Samaritan woman (4:15). It is met with the decisive affirmation, "I Am the bread of life." Both thirsting and hungering are picked up in the promise made to the one who believes in Jesus. *bread of life:* The expression used for the bread has gradually been shifted away from the OT "bread from heaven" first to "bread of God" and now, in connection with the claim that the "bread of God" gives life to the world (v 33), to "bread of life."

The expression "bread of life" does not appear in Jewish texts about the manna. But there are parallel expressions in *Joseph and Aseneth.* The God-fearing Jew "eats blessed bread of life and drinks blessed drink of immortality and is anointed with the blessed oil of imperishability." The honeycomb which is given the converted Aseneth to eat is described as "white as snow, full of honey like dew from heaven" (*Jos. Asen.* 16:8–9), a description that shows it is considered to be like the manna in the desert (e.g., Exod 16:14,31; Wis 19:21; *Sib. Or.* 3:746). She has received this heavenly food from an angelic figure who descends from heaven in answer to her prayers (*Jos. Asen.* 14:7–11). The angel also promises immortality to those who eat from the heavenly food which he provides, "And all the angels of God eat of it, and all the chosen of God and all the sons of the Most High, because this is the comb of life, and everyone who eats of it will not die, for ever (and) ever" (*Jos. Asen.* 16:14). Unlike *Jos. Asen.* John's christology makes it possible for him to identify Jesus as "the bread," not merely as an angelic being which gives a heavenly substance to the pious on earth.

93   **36–40.** These verses break into the discourse, which is resumed with the audience's reaction to the "I Am" statement in v 41. They pick up the condemnation of the audience for their unbelief (v 30). They also point forward to the division that is to come. Only those given by the Father come to Jesus, but none of them are lost. Therefore, the disciples who are offended and leave do not belong to those given by the Father; nor does Judas (6:66,70). Nor does Jesus cast out any who come to him—unlike the Jews, who will cast those who believe in Jesus out of the synagogue (9:34–35). The passage also looks to the discourse on Jesus as the source of life in 5:24–30. **40.** *raise him on the last day:* This may be an editorial expansion to bring the saying into line with the dual eschatology: "having eternal life" and "being raised on the last day" in John 5.

94   (iv) *Dispute over Jesus' origins* (6:41–51a). By murmuring, Jesus' audience shows up like the Israelites in the desert. "Murmuring" provoked the Mosaic gift of water (Exod 15:24) and of manna (Exod 16:2,7,12). It was an example of "unbelief" (Isa 10:12; Ps 106:24–25). **42.** John has taken a traditional episode, rejection of Jesus because his origins are known (e.g., Luke 4:22; Mark 6:3), to provide the crowd's assertion that Jesus cannot be "from heaven" (in 7:27–28, it represents the type of objection lodged against Johannine Christians). *his father and mother:* There is no evidence that John knew any of the traditions about Jesus' conception or birth in Bethlehem. Such a tradition would be irrelevant in any case, since the point is that Jesus has come from heaven. **95**   **43–47.** Jesus' command to stop murmuring is followed by a series of sayings which encapsulate the Johannine theology of belief. Verses 44–45 reiterate the statement that only those "drawn by God" believe in Jesus. Again in v 44c (as in v 40c) we find an editorial expansion that makes Jesus the agent of "resurrection on the last day." **45.** John appears to have created another Scripture quote, perhaps conflating Isa 54:13 and Jer 31:34, to demonstrate the claim that God is responsible for the faith of those who believe in Jesus. **46.** *not that anyone has seen the Father:* There is no knowledge of God apart from Jesus (e.g., 1:18; 3:33; 5:37). One cannot be "taught by God" apart from hearing and believing the word of Jesus. **47.** The series concludes with another affirmation that the believer has eternal life. **96**   **48–51a.** Division of the discourse in v 51 is problematic. With the concluding sentence in v 51, "the bread I shall give is my flesh," the topic shifts from Jesus as revealer of the Father, who has come from heaven, to specifying the bread that Jesus gives in eucharistic terms. This new theme continues through v 59. Some prefer to conclude the first section with v 50 and assign all of v 51 to what follows. We have chosen to divide v 51 on the grounds that it is at least possible that vv 51b–59 were not part of the original discourse but were added during the final editing of the Gospel (see M. Gourges, *RB* 88 [1981] 515–31; M. Roberge, *LTP* 38 [1982] 265–99). **48–49.** *the fathers ate and died:* Return to vv 32–35. Reference to the Israelites "eating" the manna in the desert completes exposition of the Scripture citation in v 31. **50.** The life that comes through eating the bread from heaven is contrasted with the death of the wilderness generation. This sequence repeats the pattern of vv 32–33: (a) a negative statement in reference to the exodus tradition, "not Moses . . . ," "your fathers died . . ."; (b) followed by a definition, "bread of God is . . . ," "bread which comes from heaven is. . . ." **51a.** This completes the passage by picking up the sequence in v 35: (a) I Am saying; (b) condition: "anyone comes . . . ," "anyone eats . . ."; (c) salvation: ". . . not hunger . . . ,"

". . . live forever." Verse 51a makes clear what is implied by the images of not hungering and thirsting, viz., eternal life.

97   (v) *The bread is Jesus' flesh* (6:51b–59). The suggestion that these verses may have been added to the Gospel during its final editing need not imply that they represent a "correction" of the Gospel to make it acceptable to the sacramental theology of an emerging orthodoxy, as Bultmann had suggested. The refrain "I will raise him up on the last day," which appears to reflect later editing, appears again in v 54. Verses 57b and 58b speak of having life in the future tense, but vv 54a and 56b use the language of realized eschatology. Verse 56 uses the language of remaining, *remains in me and I in him,* that appears in the farewell discourses (15:4–5; cf. 17:21, 23, without the vb. *menein*). It also appears to represent additional material from the evangelist that has been added to the Gospel. R. E. Brown (*BGJ* 287–91) has proposed that this material was originally part of the Johannine supper traditions. He suggests that it has been extensively recast so that those traditions now fit the pattern of the preceding discourse on Jesus as the bread of life.

This text continues the exposition of the vb. "to eat" in such a way that the symbolic meanings of "eating and drinking" established in the first part of the discourse can now be applied to the "bread" of the eucharistic celebration. When this process is appreciated, one need not conclude that this section somehow demeans the spiritual insights of the discourse on Jesus the revealer as bread with some lesser form of "magic sacramentalism" that replaces faith with ritual (see U. Wilckens, "Der eucharistische Abschnitt der johanneischen Rede vom Lebensbrot," *Neues Testament und Kirche* [Fest. R. Schnackenburg; ed. J. Gnilka; Freiburg, 1974] 220–48). The Jews quarrel because they take Jesus' words on the literal level (v 52; → Johannine Theology, 83:58–61). **98**   **53–56.** These verses expand the original saying (v 51b) about the bread as Jesus' flesh with the expression "flesh and blood." Each verse follows the same pattern of referring first to eating the flesh and drinking the blood. The assertion that they are "real" (*alēthēs*) food and drink recalls v 35. The other sayings follow the claim that it is necessary to "eat his flesh and drink his blood" with a reference to salvation: (a) have life in you (v 53); (b) "have eternal life" [and "I will raise him up on the last day"] (v 54); (c) "remain in me and I in him" (v 56). In light of the strong negative warning of v 54 and the immanence formula "remain in me" in v 56 (cf. 15:4–5), one might see here a saying directed toward a later crisis in the community. John 15 speaks about the necessity for the disciples to remain attached to Jesus, the vine (also a eucharistic symbol; cf. Mark 14:25). This warning may be directed toward Christians who would separate from the Johannine community, whether as a result of external persecution or as a result of the later split within the community that is evidenced in the Johannine Epistles. **99**   The parallel sayings about flesh and blood appear to represent the eucharistic formula used in the Johannine community. Unlike the formulas in the Synoptics and Paul, the body of Christ is referred to with the word *sarx*, "flesh," not *sōma*, "body." "Flesh" also appears in the formulas of Ignatius of Antioch (*Rom.* 7:3; *Phld.* 4:1; *Smyrn.* 7:1). The Johannine formula probably also contained a "for, on behalf of" clause, which may be represented in the "for the life of the world" of 6:51b. **100**   **57.** The unusual expression, "the living Father," may have been formed on analogy with "the living bread" of v 51. The reader knows that the Father sent the Son to give life (3:16–17), and that the life which the Son has is the Father's own life given to the Son (5:26). Verse

57 extends that type of relationship between Father and Son to the believer who partakes of the eucharist. This verse, too, uses a pattern of relationships between Father–Son and believer that belongs in the context of the farewell discourses (cf. 14:20–21; 17:21a). Immanence formulas, developed on the basis of Johannine christology, express the relationship between the believer and Jesus established in the eucharist. **58.** *the one who eats the bread will live forever:* These words conclude the discourse and bind it to the larger context by drawing a sharp contrast between the community that possesses the "bread from heaven" and its Jewish opponents, whose ancestors had only the manna and died (vv 49–50). **59.** This brief note on the place of the teaching, the Capernaum synagogue, may have been derived from the tradition that Jesus had taught there (e.g., Luke 4:31; 7:5).

101   (vi) *Dispute: Jesus loses disciples* (6:60–66). Jesus' words cause a division in the crowd, but this division is not among the Jewish "crowd," in which one side suspects that Jesus' messianic claims may be true, while others reject them (e.g., 7:11–12,26–27,31,40–43). This division addresses the Christian community. Some disciples now desert Jesus. Their departure provides the occasion for the Johannine equivalent to "Peter's Confession" in the Synoptic tradition. The reader is also reminded of the community setting by the references to the one who betrays Jesus (vv 64b,71). The departure of a group of disciples emphasizes the demands for remaining within the eucharistic community that were implied in the previous section. No Johannine reader could have overlooked the connection between the loss of disciples in the narrative and the community's own experiences of betrayal and desertion. **60.** *a hard saying:* The introduction does not say what was scandalous about Jesus' speech. The communal concerns of the previous section, Jesus' claim to give his flesh as the bread of life, and the fact that disciples are being addressed all suggest that the eucharistic discourse is the source of division. However, Jesus' claim to "give life," also a source of contention in 5:19–47, and an identification of his revelatory word with the "bread from heaven" in the earlier part of the discourse might also be the focus of such concerns. **61–62.** Jesus' reply, contrasting a "lesser thing" which scandalizes the audience with a greater truth, inclines us to consider the whole earlier discourse as the object of these comments. It is characteristic of such "lesser truths" that they can be understood as images used within Judaism. A combination of wisdom language and speculation about heavenly manna might be said to make the earlier part of the discourse intelligible. Not surprisingly the "greater thing" that remains to be seen is the Son of Man ascending back to his heavenly glory (e.g., 1:51; 3:13).

102   **63.** Verse 63a points back to the contrast between what comes from the flesh and from the Spirit in 3:6. Only the person "born of the Spirit" will be capable of accepting the truth of Jesus' words. Verse 63b points back to the life-giving power of Jesus' word which had been the subject of the previous discourse. **64–65.** These verses appear to relativize the destructive effects of disbelief among Jesus' own disciples by repeating the affirmation that faith is only possible for the person drawn to Jesus by the Father (cf. 5:38; 6:37; 8:25,46–47; 10:25–26). **66.** As if to illustrate the truth of Jesus' words, a group of disciples depart. This verse not only ends the section on the loss of disciples; it also serves as the introduction for the final piece of traditional material that has been taken over in the narrative sequence, Peter's confession.

103   (vii) *Peter's confession* (6:67–71). In the Synoptic parallel, Peter's confession served to show that

the disciples had begun to perceive Jesus as Messiah. In John such traditional christological titles have been acknowledged from the beginning. Here, Peter's confession echoes Jesus' own words in v 63b. This is the first explicit reference to "the Twelve." The narrator presumes that the reader knows who that group is, that Jesus had chosen them, and that Peter serves as their spokesman. The Synoptic story of Peter's confession ended on the ominous note of Jesus' suffering and the rebuke directed at Peter as "Satan" for resisting Jesus' passion prediction. Here Jesus' choice would appear to confirm his earlier words about the divine source of faith. Yet they are immediately qualified. Jesus knows that one of those chosen is not so "chosen." The narrator speaks in the final verse to remind the reader of the name of the person to whom Jesus refers. He also notes the horrifying fact that Judas, the betrayer, was one of the Twelve.

104   (c) JERUSALEM AT TABERNACLES (7:1–8:59). The editing of the material in these chapters appears to have been a complex process, which is evident in awkward transitions, sudden shifts in theme, and the lack of setting for 8:12–59. Only the introductory "I Am the light of the world" (v 12) and the concluding reference to the Temple (v 59) suggest that this discourse occurs at the end of the feast of Tabernacles, which provides the structure for chap. 7. (Later copyists may have been attempting to remedy this narrative difficulty when they inserted the non-Johannine controversy story about the woman taken in adultery at 7:53–8:11.) John 8 is the high point of Jesus' self-identification in his controversy with "the Jews," since he there claims the divine "I Am" (vv 28,58).

The sudden reappearance of debate over Jesus' healing of the paralytic in 7:19–23 and remarks about a plot against Jesus, not part of their immediate narrative context (vv 1,19,25,30,32), point to a quasi-judicial proceeding against Jesus at the end of the chapter (vv 44–52), which creates the isolation of the discourse material that follows. The defense of the sabbath healing in 7:19–23 is much less christologically oriented than in 5:19–47. Instead of insisting that he does what the Father does on the sabbath, Jesus employs an argument from a lesser to a greater case in the law, a procedure used in the Synoptic stories of sabbath controversies (cf. Mark 2:23–26; Matt 12:5). The dispute over where Jesus obtained his "learning" (7:15–17) might also derive from this context. This section of John 7 may have belonged to the context of a sabbath healing at one time and been displaced when the lengthy discourse on Jesus' relationship to God in giving life and judging was attached to the miracle. The division of opinion and the plot against Jesus in 7:43–44 could also have been part of the original account of that miracle. Insertion of the Passover theme in John 6 provides for the ministry of Jesus between the unnamed feast of John 5, really a sabbath controversy, and Jesus' return to Jerusalem for Tabernacles. John uses the occasion of this "going up" to Jerusalem to show the reader that Jesus will indeed manifest himself in Jerusalem, but he will not be glorified from the cross until the hour has arrived. All the plots against his life are futile apart from the time for Jesus' return to the Father. (See H. W. Attridge, *CBQ* 42 [1980] 160–70.)

105   (i) *Galilee: Rejects advice to go to the feast* (7:1–9). **1–2.** Jesus' presence in Galilee is linked to the danger of death from "the Jews" in Judea (cf. 5:18). **2.** Tabernacles: → Institutions, 76:133–38. **3.** Jesus' "brothers" and "disciples" were last mentioned in 2:12 as staying in Capernaum, the setting of the bread-of-life discourse. The tradition that Jesus' relatives failed to comprehend his mission also appears in the Synoptics

(Mark 3:21,31–32; 6:4). The reader already knows that Jesus' signs will not win him the approval in Judea that is presumed by the brothers' request (see 2:23–24). **4.** *show yourself to the world:* Demand for a public demonstration of Jesus' powers seems equivalent to the political reading of the feeding miracle in 6:14–15. But the dichotomy between a Jesus whose "signs" are only open to the believer and the requirement that his works be manifest to the world may also reflect a Jewish argument against the Christian claim that Jesus is the Messiah. R. E. Brown (*BGJ* 308) finds a pattern in these messianic challenges that corresponds to the Synoptic tradition of the temptation by Satan: (a) people wish to make Jesus king (John 6:15; offers kingdoms of the world, Matt 4:8); (b) people demand manna miracle (John 6:31; change stones into bread, Matt 4:3); (c) public demonstration of Jesus' powers (John 7:4; cast yourself from the Temple tower, Matt 4:5). **5.** The narrator's comment reminds the reader that such a request shows disbelief. **6–7.** *my time has not arrived:* The hatred that will lead to attempts on Jesus' life (e.g., 8:59) already exists. When the "hour" of Jesus' crucifixion/exaltation does come, it will represent the conclusion of the cosmic trial that has been initiated by his testimony and will prove the world guilty of sin (this work is brought to its conclusion by the Paraclete, 16:8–10).

106   (ii) *Jesus goes secretly to the feast* (7:10–13). Jesus' "secret" departure for Jerusalem sets the stage for the murmuring (cf. 6:41,61) in Jerusalem. Divisions of opinion (also 7:40–41; 10:20–21) often introduce charges against Jesus that had emerged during debates between Johannine Christians and their opponents. Verse 13 reflects that situation in referring to the "fear of the Jews" that prevents people from speaking openly about Jesus. The passage introduces three groups, none of them believers, who will appear as protagonists in Jesus' ministry at Jerusalem: (a) "disciples," persons with an inadequate belief in Jesus based on his earlier "signs"; (b) the crowd, usually of divided opinion about Jesus; (c) "the Jews," sometimes represented by the Pharisees whom the evangelist thinks of as their leaders, who are already declared enemies of Jesus.

107   The critical accusation that Jesus may be a deceiver, one who leads the people astray (v 12) is repeated in 7:47 (cf. its use as a legal charge in Luke 23:2). Later Jewish (*b. Sanh.* 43a) and Christian (Justin, *Dial.* 69:7; 108:2) sources report that the Jews condemned Jesus as a "sorcerer" and one who "leads the people astray." Jesus is thus condemned as a "false prophet" under the law in Deut 18:18–22 (also Deut 13:1–16; *m. Sanh.* 11:5). Apocalyptic writings described the coming of false prophets who would lead the people astray and work signs (Mark 13:22; Matt 24:11; 1QpHab 2:2; 5:9–12 on the "man of lies"). John 7 answers such accusations. (The evangelist has already given an answer in 6:14–15 by showing that Jesus does not try to gather large crowds and lead them astray through his signs.)

108   (iii) *Jesus teaches in the Temple* (7:14–24). The basic elements of Jesus' self-defense have already been stated: he does not speak on his own but for God (vv 17–18; 5:19,30); he does not do his own will (7:17; 5:30); he does not seek his own glory (7:18; 5:41,44). The contrast between Jesus' "learning" (*grammata*) and what his opponents understand to be the "teachings" (*grammata*) of Moses is also part of the earlier debate (7:15; cf. 5:47). Jesus challenges his opponents with a desire to kill him, which is contrary to the law of Moses they claim to uphold (v 19; 5:18). **20.** *who seeks to kill you?:* The crowd takes Jesus' words as an indication that he "has a demon." The Synoptic tradition has that charge shortly after Jesus has healed on the sabbath and in

conjunction with disbelief by Jesus' relatives, which is possibly its context in the pre-Johannine tradition as well (Mark 3:20–22). **22–23.** *if a man is circumcised on the sabbath:* Jesus responds with a more conventional style of Jewish argument than in John 5. He argues from the "lesser case," permitted by his opponents, the circumcision of a child on the sabbath, to the "greater case," making a person whole. Thus, he demonstrates his "learning" and the injustice of the judgment passed against him (v 24).

109   (iv) *Division: Is this the Messiah?* (7:25–31). **25–27.** *when the Messiah comes no one will know where he is from:* Justin refers to such a belief: the Messiah is hidden among humans until he is "revealed" by the anointing of Elijah (*Dial.* 8:4; 110:1). **28–29.** The reader already knows what the answer to this objection will be. Jesus is not "from" the "place/parents" which the crowd associates with him but comes from heaven (6:41–42). Only those who "know" the Father who sent Jesus can recognize Jesus' origins (cf. 6:43–45). **30–31.** The scene concludes with another division: those who would make an attempt on Jesus' life and those who "believe" on the basis of his "signs."

110   (v) *Soldiers sent to arrest Jesus* (7:32–36). The division in the crowd brings Jesus' popularity to the attention of the Pharisees (cf. 4:1,3), who are consistently linked to efforts to suppress faith in Jesus (7:47–48; 9:13–16,24–29,40; 11:46; 12:19,42). **33–34.** *you will seek me and not find me:* The "hour" is approaching (cf. 11:9–10). A similar announcement at the end of the public ministry serves as a judgment saying against those who have not believed (12:35–36). This threat is spelled out in 8:21,23: they will die in their sins. **35–36.** The reader can discern the hidden meaning in the crowd's words. When Jesus returns to the Father, he will draw others, "the Greeks," to him (cf. 12:20–22).

111   (vi) *Jesus is the living water* (7:37–39). The water symbolism in the Gospel reaches its climax. On the seventh day of Tabernacles, the priests took water from the spring of Siloam and circled the altar seven times. The crowd carried branches of myrtle and willow twigs tied with palm in the right hand and a citron or lemon in the left as signs of harvest. After the circumambulation the priest went up the ramp to the altar and poured the water through a silver funnel onto the ground. Such a ritual would provide an appropriate setting for Jesus' words. **37b–38.** The saying of Jesus contains three interrelated problems: (a) Does "the one who believes in me" belong with 37b or with what follows it in v 38? (b) What Scripture text does John have in mind? (c) Does the image imply that the waters flow from the believer or from Jesus? The parallelism between the invitation to come to Jesus if one thirsts (cf. 4:14; 6:35) and the "out of him" in the following verse suggests that the source of the water in both cases is Jesus. This theme can be seen as repeating the parallelism between Jesus and divine wisdom (Prov 9:5; Sir 24:19–21; 51:23–24). "The one who believes in me" is awkward whether taken with v 37b or v 38. It is probably an addition by the evangelist to remind the reader that only the believer can receive such salvation from Jesus.

112   Identification of Johannine citations from Scripture is notoriously difficult when they do not correspond to any specific passage. Some suggestive parallels are provided by references to the manna and water in the desert (a combination mentioned in the connection with the manna in John 6:35; e.g., Ps 105:40–41; Ps 78:15–16, 24). One may also point to prophetic texts about rivers of water coming from the Temple mount in the last days (e.g., Ezek 47:1–11; Zech 14:8). Targumic materials have also shown that allusions to the eschatological water flowing from the Temple rock and the water from the rock in Exodus could be combined (e.g., *Tos. Sukk.* iii 3:18). **39.** *about the Spirit:* The evangelist then adds his own comment, explaining that the saying referred to the Spirit, which the risen Christ bestows upon believers (e.g., John 20:22).

113 (vii) *Division: Is this the prophet?* (7:40–44). The relentless series of questions about Jesus' identity continues. This section is the antitype of the short episodes in which Jesus gathered disciples around a series of christological titles at the beginning of the Gospel. Here the messianic questions are constantly repeated. They will reach their climax in the "I Am" sayings of the next chapter. Yet the outcome is increasing disbelief and hostility. **40–41a.** These verses propose two titles, "the prophet" and "the Messiah." **41b–42.** *from Bethlehem:* Once again, Jesus' origins seem to disqualify him from being the anointed Davidic Messiah (Mic 5:1 links the Messiah with Bethlehem; cf. Matt 2:4–6). Nathanael had come to believe in Jesus after initial skepticism over his Nazareth origins (1:45–46). This question was clearly part of anti-Christian polemic directed at the Johannine community. **43–44.** Again, division among the people contains the seeds of hostility.

114 (viii) *Authorities reject Jesus* (7:45–52). **45–46.** *the guards:* In their excuse for not having arrested Jesus, the guards refer to the unusual character of Jesus' speech (cf. Mark 1:22; 6:2; 7:37; 11:18). The Johannine reader knows that they speak the truth, not knowing that Jesus' words are from a source unlike any other (cf. 8:40). **47–49.** *have you been led astray?:* The Pharisees repeat the accusation that Jesus is someone who leads the people astray. The hostility between the Jewish leaders and "the crowd," pronounced ignorant of the law, is dramatically enacted in the blind man's testimony to Jesus in John 9 and probably reflects the experiences of Johannine Christians when they were persecuted. **50.** *Nicodemus:* He suddenly reappears on the scene. The evangelist reminds us of the encounter between Jesus and Nicodemus in 3:1–12. He highlights the "illegality" of the proceedings against Jesus, condemning a person without a hearing (cf. *Exod. Rabb.* 21:3). *from Galilee too?:* The response of the others is to brand Nicodemus with a disdainful epithet, "Galilean," suggesting that he is no better than the rabble who follow Jesus, and to repeat the objection that the Scriptures rule out any possibility of "the prophet" coming from Galilee.

115 [AGRAPHON: WOMAN TAKEN IN ADULTERY (7:53–8:11)]. This story did not find its way into mss. of the Gospel until the 3d cent. Though it fills a "gap" by providing a narrative before the discourse of 8:12–59, it has none of the characteristic features of Johannine style or theology. The copyist who inserted the story here may have thought that it illustrated 8:15, "I pass judgment on no one," and 8:46, "Can anyone convict me of sin." The story is a "biographical apophthegm," in which Jesus' opponents set a "trap" that he must escape through a wise saying or action (e.g., Mark 12:13–17, on the tribute coin). The setting presupposes the "daily teaching in the Temple" connected with Jesus' Jerusalem ministry in Luke 20:1; 21:1,37; 22:53. Some NT mss. have this story after Luke 21:38. Its interest in Jesus forgiving a sinful woman reflects a theme that appears in Luke's special tradition (e.g., Luke 7:36–50; 8:2–3). **8:1.** *Mt. of Olives:* Jesus' going to the Mt. of Olives reflects Luke 21:37. Thus, many exegetes think that this story is a piece of the special Lucan material that was circulating in the tradition. **5.** *in the law:* Deut 22:23–24 prescribes stoning for a married woman who commits adultery. If John 18:31 is correct in insisting that the Romans had deprived

the Jews of the right to carry out the death penalty in cases where their law required it, then the "trap" may have been similar to that implied in the tribute money story (Mark 12:13–17). Jesus must, so his opponents think, reject either the law of Moses or the authority of Rome. **6.** *wrote with his finger:* There is no clear indication of why Jesus wrote on the ground. Patristic authors suggested Jer 17:13, "those who turn away from you shall be written in the earth, for they have forsaken the Lord," as the text that governed Jesus' action. If so, it is an indirect reminder of the "guilt" of those who are condemning the woman. **7.** *first to throw:* The warning in Jesus' words may have carried a reference to the law. Deut 17:7 acknowledges that those who are witnesses against an accused person have special responsibility for that person's death. **11.** *neither do I:* After the accusers have left, Jesus makes it clear that he is not ranked among them. The woman is free to go but not to sin again.

116 (ix) *The Father testifies to Jesus* (8:12–20). The image of light may have been associated with the lighting of four huge golden lamps in the courtyard of the women on the first night of Tabernacles (*m. Sukk.* 5:2–4). The reader knows that Jesus is the light of the world (1:9), whose coming has divided humanity into those who "come to the light" and those whose "evil deeds" lead them to prefer darkness (3:19–21). But the purpose of his coming was to bring life (3:16). The discourse does not focus on the symbolism but on Jesus' testimony to himself and the authority of his "true judgment" (cf. 5:30–31). Jesus' defense is framed with sayings which ground the truth of his testimony in his origin, "from the Father," which goes unacknowledged by his protagonists (vv 14,19). Between these familiar affirmations, the theme of the "trial" of the world which claims to judge Jesus is invoked. **16.** *my judgment is true:* Jesus was sent for salvation, not judgment (or "condemnation"; cf. 3:17; 12:47). At the same time, the Father has entrusted judgment to the Son (5:22; 9:39). Unlike false human judgments (7:27), that judgment is true (5:30). **18.** *I testify and the Father who sent me testifies:* Jesus provides witnesses (Deut 17:6; 18:15 require two witnesses) by appealing to himself and the Father (cf. 5:37–38). **19.** *where is your Father?:* Such testimony cannot be received by those who do not "hear the Father" in Jesus' words; so Jesus' antagonists ask for his Father with the same bitter irony that Pilate will ask about truth (18:38). **20.** This episode concludes with another reference to the impossibility of acting against Jesus.

117 (x) *Jesus is returning to the Father* (8:21–30). **21.** *you will die in your sin:* Unbelief is the sin for John (cf. 16:9). **22a.** *will he put himself to death?:* As in the previous "riddle" of Jesus' departure (7:34–36), the crowd's words contain a truth which they cannot understand. Jesus will not commit suicide, which deprived a person of any share in the age to come (e.g., Josephus, *J.W.* 3.8.5 § 361–82). But Jesus will freely give up his life (cf. 10:11,17–18). **23.** *you are from below, I am from above:* The sharp contrast between Jesus' heavenly origins and the earthly origins of his enemies, which makes it impossible for them to go where he is going, comes close to the dualism of heavenly and earthly origins in gnostic mythologies. Gnostic writers might also use this dualism to explain what separates them from their ecclesiastical adversaries, as is the case in *Apocalypse of Peter.* Peter sees the essence of the docetic Christ depart from the cross, filled with light and surrounded by angels (82.5–16). These truths can only be given to persons who themselves are of "immortal substance" (83.6–26). What is lacking in the Fourth Gospel is any trace of "like substances" between Jesus, the light from above, and those who are saved. Such a suggestion would be contrary to the Gospel's focus on Jesus as the unique revelation of God. The sharp separation of spheres in this passage points forward to the confession that Jesus is the divine "I Am." **24.** *you will die in your sins:* The first occurrence of Jesus' "I Am" is introduced by a judgment pronouncement. Use of the divine "I Am" in a covenant lawsuit with the world links the Johannine "I Am" sayings and the prophetic traditions of Dt-Isa. Isa 43:10–11 LXX is particularly appropriate, "that you may know and believe me and understand that I am He (*egō eimi*) . . . I am the Lord, and besides me there is no savior." (→ Johannine Theology, 83:41–49.)

118 **25.** *who are you?:* The crowd's response is expected from those who are unable to hear Jesus' words. What follows in vv 25b–27 is awkward. *tēn archēn ho ti kai lalō hymin* (v 25b) is a difficult expression in Greek. *Tēn archēn,* acc. of *archē,* "beginning," is sometimes translated as though it were the Johannine expression *ap'* or *ex archēs,* "from the beginning" (e.g., 8:44; 15:27; 16:4) and the pres. tense of the vb. *lalō* is ignored. So the *RSV:* "(I am) what I have told you from the beginning." The Gk Fathers understood *tēn archēn* as an adv., as though it were equivalent to *holōs,* "at all." This usage is more common in negative clauses, though a negative may be implied by the interrogative context here. In that case the expression might be one of exasperation, "What is it that I am saying to you at all?" or "Why am I talking to you at all?" Difficulty with this phrase is evident from an early period. P⁶⁶ has *eipon hymin,* "I was saying," before *tēn archēn* to create the sense, "I told you at the beginning, what I am saying to you now" (see E. L. Miller, *TZ* 36 [1980] 257–65). **26–27.** These verses break into the context with remarks about Jesus' generation. His word comes from the Father in judgment against those who have not recognized that God is addressing them (see 5:30). *I have many things to say (and to judge) concerning you:* This will be echoed in the farewell discourses (e.g., 14:30; 16:12). In both contexts, we find reference to the impending judgment of the unbelieving world, which results from Jesus' crucifixion. John 14:31 also points toward the crucifixion as the final demonstration of his unity with the Father, which has guided his actions. These verses may represent a double expansion: (a) an explication of Jesus' speaking in the language of the farewell discourses, which points forward to the further judgment to be spoken against "the world"; (b) a remark by the final editor to clarify the reference of Jesus' remarks.

119 **28a.** *then you will know that I Am:* Jesus' identity is finally stated in a second Son-of-Man passion saying. **28b–29.** The crucifixion is the manifestation of Jesus' unity with God (see 10:18; 14:31). But it is not a moment of victory for Satan (and those opposed to Jesus); nor is it a sign that God has abandoned him (cf. 14:30; 16:32–33). Inserted into the context of a bitter dispute, the Son-of-Man saying in v 28a has overtones of judgment, which differ from the promise of salvation attached to the saying in 3:14 and 12:32,34. **30.** *many believed:* The "salvific" overtones of the parallel sayings may be the reason that the section comes to the surprising conclusion that "many believed."

120 (xi) *The seed of Abraham hear the truth* (8:31–47). **31.** The reference to "Jews who believed" seems to stem from a layer of the tradition in which "the Jews" was simply used to designate inhabitants of Judea (e.g., 1:19; 3:1; 6:52). Speaking of this group as "disciples" and the injunction to "remain in my word" (cf. 6:56b; 14:21, 23–24; 15:4–10) suggest that the narrator is thinking of Jewish Christians in his own time faced with a choice of remaining Jesus' disciples or abandoning their loyalty as "disciples of Moses" (cf. 9:27–28). As the dialogue

progresses these "Christian Jews" are merged with "the Jews" who are actively seeking Jesus' life (v 37; cf. 7:19). **32.** *the truth will make you free:* Jesus posits the challenge to his opponents in an unusual assertion connecting truth and freedom. Some exegetes have turned to the Pauline controversies over the law to provide the background for the polemic in this section of the Gospel (e.g., Gal 4:21–31; 2 Cor 11:20–22; Rom 9:6–13; see T. Dozeman, *CBQ* 42 [1980] 342–58). Dispute over who constitutes the true "seed of Abraham" is evident in Gal 3:16,19,29; Rom 4:13,16. John uses "truth" elsewhere to contrast the salvation that has come through Jesus with that from Moses (1:14,17). Predicated of Jesus, it indicates that he is the only way to salvation (14:6; 17:17).

121 **33.** *no one has ever enslaved us:* Clearly, the crowd's claims of "freedom" cannot be grounded in the political situation. Perhaps the evangelist has that irony in mind, since Pilate will force the "Jews" to claim that they have "no king but Caesar" (19:15). **34.** Rejection of Jesus will ensure that the antagonists remain slaves to sin (8:21,24). **35.** *slave does not remain . . . son remains forever:* A contrast between the "son" and the "slave" appears in other early Christian examples of the superiority of Christ to the law/Moses (Gal 4:1–2; Heb 3:5–6). Reference to the son remaining while the slave leaves the household might have been a polemic against presuming salvation based on one's status as "descendant of Abraham" (cf. Matt 3:9; 8:11). **36.** *if the Son makes you free:* This is a return to the Johannine theme that only the Son can make one free. **37–38.** The audience is now identified with those who are seeking Jesus' death (cf. 7:19,20,25) because they do not keep the commandments of God or recognize that Jesus speaks on God's behalf.

122 **39.** *you would do the works of Abraham:* Killing the one who speaks for God cannot be a work of Abraham. Those who do such things must have a different "Father" than the one who has sent Jesus to testify to the truth (cf. 5:33; 8:26,28b; 18:37). **41.** *we were not born of immorality:* Israel was described as "God's (firstborn) son" (e.g., Exod 4:22; Deut 14:1; Jer 3:4,19; 31:9; Isa 63:16; 64:7). *Porneia,* "sexual immorality," is commonly associated with the Gentiles (e.g., 1 Thess 4:3,5). This response may be drawn from slogans of Hellenistic Jewish propaganda. The Jews are proud of the separation from the sins of idolatry and sexual immorality that characterize the pagans. They will not accept the suggestion that they have some other "Father." **42–43.** These verses reiterate the view that all those who are "from God" accept the one sent from God. Therefore, the hostile audience cannot be God's children. **44.** *you are from the devil as father:* The only "father" that those who seek to kill Jesus can claim is the one who is Cain's father, the devil. Targumic tradition understood Cain to have been faced with the choice of mastering the "evil inclination" within and thereby being righteous or commiting sin (see *Tg. Neof.* Gen 4:7; G. Reim, *NTS* 39 [1984] 619–24). 1 John 3:8–12 shows us how this tradition was applied within the Johannine community. The dualism of being "from God" or "from the devil" like Cain is made evident in a person's deeds. In 1 John the "deeds" in question refer to loving/not loving fellow Christians. Here, the decisive factor is loving/not loving Jesus (v 42). The DSS contrast the "sons of light" who "walk in God's truth" with the sons of Belial (e.g., 1QS 1:18,23–24; 2:19; 3:20–21; 1QM 13:11–12). Opponents of the sect are also described as led astray by the Man of Lies or Interpreters of Error (1QpHab 2:2; 5:11; CD 20:15; 1QH 2:13–14; 4:10). Truth lies with God; sin and deceit with humanity (1QH 1:26–27). It is important for Christians to recognize that this dualism can be used within Judaism itself to separate those who walk according to God's law from those who are sinners. 1 John adapts it from general ethical exhortation among Christians to meet the situation in which Christians were divided among themselves. The farewell discourse in John 14 returns to this theme from the point of view of the disciples who "love Jesus" and through him are brought into a new relationship with the Father (see F. F. Segovia, *CBQ* 43 [1981] 258-72). These statements do not imply divine condemnation of the Jews as a people.

123   45-47. This section repeats the claim that those who are "of God" accept Jesus (3:6,31; 8:23,43). Verse 46 also points to the opponents' side of the great "trial." Jesus cannot be charged with any sin. Blindness to Jesus convicts his opponents of sin (9:41; 15:22,24; 16:9; 19:11).

124   (xii) *Before Abraham was, I Am* (8:48-59). **48-51.** These verses take up a variant of the tradition that Jesus was accused of being "possessed" (cf. Mark 3:22-23), with the negative epithet that Jesus is a "Samaritan." His opponents have "insulted Jesus' origins" and linked him with the devil. *I honor my Father:* Jesus replies by appealing to God as the one who will vindicate him (cf. 5:23,41-42). Jesus' proclamation that the believer will never die (cf. 5:24-25) serves to provoke the misunderstanding that will finally reveal Jesus' superiority to Abraham.

125   52-53. In a passage reminiscent of the exchange with the Samaritan woman (4:11-12), the Jews accuse Jesus of claiming to be greater than Abraham and the prophets. **54.** *if I glorify myself:* Before making the claim that constitutes blasphemy to his Jewish opponents (5:18), Jesus repeats once again the defense that he is the one who knows and honors God while those who claim to be "defending God" are in fact "liars." **56.** *rejoiced:* Jewish tradition interpreted the "laugh" of Gen 17:17 to be rejoicing over the promise of his "son" Isaac (*Jub.* 15:17; Philo, *De mut. nom.* 154; 175), or as joy over the birth of Isaac, whose name was interpreted to mean "laughter," (e.g., Philo, *De mut. nom.* 131; also *Jub.* 14:21; 15:17; 16:19-20). The "rejoicing" of Abraham may also have links with the eschatological rejoicing of the patriarchs linked to the coming of the Messiah and the final defeat of Satan, as in *T. Levi* 18, which uses a number of themes familiar in the Fourth Gospel to describe the messianic priest: he will "shine like the sun and take away all darkness" (v 4; John 1:9); "knowledge of the Lord will be poured out on the earth like the water of the seas" (v 5; John 1:18; 8:55); "heavens will be opened and from the temple of glory sanctification will come upon him, with a fatherly voice, as from Abraham to Isaac" (v 6; John 1:32,51); "the glory of the Most High shall burst forth upon him" (v 6; John 8:54); "he shall give the majesty of the Lord to those who are his sons in truth forever" (v 7; John 8:32,36; 17:22); "there shall be no successor for him" (v 8; John 12:34); "he will grant to the saints to eat of the tree of life. The spirit of holiness shall be upon them" (vv 10-11; John 8:51; 7:39); Beliar shall be bound by him (v 11; John 12:31); "the Lord will rejoice in his children; . . . then Abraham, Isaac, and Jacob will rejoice" (vv 12-13). Thus, Abraham's "joy" is linked to seeing the day of salvation.

126   56-58. *before Abraham was I Am:* Another misunderstanding by the "Jews" elicits the final christological affirmation in this section. Jesus is indeed greater than Abraham: he bears the divine name, "I Am" (→ Johannine Theology, 83:41-49). **59.** *picked up stones:* The crowd understands the claim Jesus has made as they prepare to execute the punishment for blasphemy, stoning (cf. *m. Sanh.* 7:5a).

127   (d) JESUS RESTORES SIGHT TO THE BLIND (9:1-41). The task of witnessing to Jesus is taken on by the blind man. Jesus must be "from God"; not the sinner that the Jewish teachers claim Jesus is. After the man's expulsion from the synagogue, Jesus reveals that he is the "Son of Man," and the blind man comes to worship Jesus. Healing, hostility from the authorities, and a second encounter with Jesus repeat the pattern of 5:1-18, but this man comes to true faith in Jesus (see M. Gourges, *NRT* 104 [1982] 381-95). One can hardly avoid the conclusion that this story is an example for the Johannine Christian of how one ought to react when confronted with hostile authorities.

128   (i) *Healing a man born blind* (9:1-12). Similar miracles occur in the Synoptics (e.g., Mark 10:46-52 par.; Mark 8:22-26). Verses 1,2,3a,6,7 probably represent the story derived from the evangelist's source; vv 3b-5 are the evangelist's addition. They make the symbolism of Jesus as light clear and point to the approach of the hour when that light will depart. They may have replaced a different answer to the question of the miracle's purpose. The narrator has also supplied the reader with an interpretation of the name of the pool in v 7. **11.** *the man called Jesus:* Unlike the paralytic, the blind man is able to tell those who ask him that Jesus is the one responsible for healing him, though he cannot say "where" Jesus is.

129   (ii) *Pharisees question the man: Jesus is a prophet* (9:13-17). To create grounds for the interrogation, the miracle is secondarily linked to the sabbath. **16.** *the Pharisees asked again:* The first attempt by the Jewish authorities to quell belief in Jesus by insisting that one who breaks the sabbath (by making clay) cannot be "from God" creates a division of opinion. How could a sinner do such signs (cf. 5:36, Jesus' "works" testify to him; also 10:25,32,33; cf. the affirmative statement about Jesus' signs in 3:2). **17.** *he is a prophet:* The man answers the Pharisees' question with the conclusion that Jesus is a prophet. "Prophet" probably does not refer to the messianic prophet of John 4 or 7:52 but to Jesus as someone whose power comes from God.

130   (iii) *Jews question the parents: Fear of being expelled from the synagogue* (9:18-23). Questioning the man's parents establishes the identity of the blind man with the man born blind (contrast the division in vv 8-9). The parents' refusal to become further involved enables the evangelist to connect this story with the crisis that had been faced by members of the Johannine community (vv 22-23).

131   (iv) *Second interrogation and expulsion from the synagogue* (9:24-34). The scene which culminates in the Pharisees calling the man one "born in sin" (cf. Jesus' denial of this interpretation in vv 2-3) and expelling him from the synagogue shows the full power of the evangelist's irony. **24.** *give glory to God:* A formula used when people are to confess their guilt (e.g., Josh 7:19; 1 Sam 6:5; 2 Chr 30:8; Jer 13:16; *m. Sanh.* 6:2). The Johannine reader knows that no one can give "glory" to God by calling Jesus a sinner. One must believe that Jesus is the one to whom God gives glory (e.g., 5:41,44; 7:18; 8:54). **26-28.** *I have already told you:* The request for a repetition of how the man was healed leads to a sharp exchange that sets the man among the "disciples of Jesus" and the Jews as "disciples of Moses." **29-33.** The arguments against Jesus probably reflect the disputes between Johannine Christians and Jewish opponents. *if this person were not from God:* The "Jews" claim that Moses has spoken with God, but Jesus' origins are unknown. The reader knows that Jesus is the one who speaks what he hears from his Father (8:26) and is the only one who has seen God (1:18). *from God:* Unlike his interrogators, the man understands the "sign" given by healing one born blind and so reaches the conclusion that Jesus is "from God."

132   (v) *Jesus is Son of Man* (9:35–38). The man's faith in Jesus is not complete until the second encounter reveals that Jesus is "Son of Man." Jesus' coming to find the man may also be an enactment of Jesus' saying in 6:37, "Everyone the Father gives me will come to me, and the one who comes to me, I will not cast out." The use of "Son of Man" here must carry the overtones of the expression for the Johannine Christian since it results in the man's worshiping Jesus. John 12:32,34 promises that the exalted Son of Man will draw all to himself.

133   (vi) *Blindness of the Pharisees* (9:39–41). The trial motif returns as Jesus' coming has divided those who truly see from those like the Pharisees who claim to see but are blind. **41.** *your sin remains:* This reminds the reader that the "sin" is disbelief (e.g., 8:24) and recalls the condemnation of 3:36b, "the one who does not believe in the Son will not see life, but the wrath of God remains on him."

134   (e) JESUS, THE GOOD SHEPHERD (10:1–42). A new clash between Jesus and the Jews occurs at the feast of Dedication three months after Tabernacles (→ Institutions, 76:151–54). Division among the people (vv 19–21), points to the healing of the blind man. The shepherd imagery reappears in vv 26–29, so that taking vv 1–21 as a continuation of the events connected with Tabernacles will not account for the literary complexity of the chapter. None of the proposals to rearrange blocks of text has gained widespread agreement.

135   (i) *Parable of the sheepfold* (10:1–6). **6.** *they did not understand:* The evangelist tells the reader that Jesus has told a *paroimia,* "proverb," or more generally a *māšāl* in Hebrew, which can mean "proverb," "riddle," or, using the familiar synoptic term, a "parable." This comment may be based on a tradition like Mark 4:10–12. Parabolic discourse keeps those "outside" from understanding and repenting, while the disciple knows what Jesus is speaking about. Shepherd imagery appears in the Synoptics: (a) the crowds are compared with sheep who have no shepherd (Mark 6:35); (b) the parable of the lost sheep is directed against Pharisaic criticism of Jesus' ministry to sinners in Luke 15:3–7; (c) the believers are compared with sheep who must watch out for wolves (Matt 7:15, against false prophets within the community; 10:16); (d) the righteous are "sheep" who are saved in the judgment (Matt 25:32–34). In addition there is a rich tradition from the OT. The Lord is the shepherd of the people (Gen 49:24; Ps 23). Ezek 34 castigates the leaders of the people as bad shepherds who fatten themselves at the cost of the sheep. The sheep are left wandering and scattered as prey for the wolves (34:1–10). The Lord promises to go and gather his sheep, who are scattered throughout the lands, and bring them back to good pasture (34:11–16). This chapter of Ezek may have been particularly attractive to John because it concludes with the affirmation that the people will know God in this activity: "And they will know that I Am (*egō eimi*) the Lord their God, and they, house of Israel, are my people, says the Lord. You are my sheep and the sheep of my pasture and I Am the Lord your God," (Ezek 34:30–31 LXX). (See P.-R. Tragan, *La parabole du "Pasteur" et ses explications* [SAns 67; Rome, 1980].)

136   Some exegetes find two separate parables in vv 1–5: (a) vv 1–3a contrast approaches to the sheep. Anyone who does not come through the gate is malevolent; (b) vv 3b–5 focus on the relationship between the sheep and shepherd. They will only respond to the voice of their own shepherd. For the reader who has just heard the blindness of the Pharisees condemned, it would be evident that one was being warned not to respond to their teaching.

137   (ii) *Jesus, the gate and the good shepherd* (10:7–18). The interpretation picks up both metaphors. Jesus is the gate through which persons have access to the sheep (vv 7–10); and the "good" (= ideal, model) shepherd (vv 11–19). Each of these images is repeated twice. **8–10.** The choice of "door" as a messianic symbol may have been taken from Ps 119:20. Other verses of Ps 119 were used as messianic prophecies in early Christianity (cf. John 12:13; Mark 1:10; Matt 23:39). John insists that Jesus is the only source of salvation. Those who came before him, probably a reference to the Jewish teachers and the tradition to which they appealed, are rejected as thieves (v 8). The contrast with the thieves who will not bring salvation recalls Ezek 34. John has recast the saying in his own language: Jesus has come that they might have life (cf. 14:6, Jesus is "the way, truth, and life").

138   **11–13.** *the good shepherd:* Gk *kalos,* "good," means "good" in the sense of "noble" or "ideal," not simply "good at" something. Unlike bad shepherds who let the sheep be eaten by wolves, Jesus dies for the sheep. Mark 14:27 has Jesus refer to Zech 13:7 about the slaying of the shepherd and the scattering of the sheep. Thus, the image of Jesus as shepherd who dies for the sheep belongs to the early Christian passion tradition. **14.** *I know my own:* The second saying is more typically Johannine, since it speaks of the relationship between the shepherd and the sheep as analogous to the close relationship between Jesus and his Father. This relationship is the basis for the sacrifice that Jesus makes on behalf of the sheep. John 15:12–17 uses the imagery of friendship to describe Jesus' death in the context of such a relationship. **16.** *other sheep not of this fold:* This saying breaks into the reflection on the relationships involved in the shepherd/sheep image to refer to "other sheep" who will also hear Jesus' voice. Elsewhere in the Gospel these breaks refer to the future generations of believers (e.g., 17:20; 20:29). It is also possible to relate this saying to the future coming of the Gentiles, "the Greeks," which is referred to twice (7:35; 12:20–22). By the time the Gospel was completed, the Johannine community is also conscious of the existence of other Christian communities, esp. those which trace their tradition back to Peter (21:15–19), who is given the title of "shepherd." This reference might also be a reference to those Christians who are not part of the Johannine fold.

139   **17.** *the Father loves me because I lay down my life:* Primitive Christianity emphasized the fact that Jesus offered his life in willing obedience to God (thus reversing the disobedience of Adam; cf. Phil 2:8; Rom 5:19; Heb 5:8). The Johannine transposing of the theme emphasizes the love that exists between the Father and Son (cf. 3:35) and the sovereign freedom of Christ's death. That freedom is evident in the fact that unlike humans condemned to mortality unless they receive life from Christ, Christ can "take up his life again." The stress on the fact that Christ offers his life for the sheep should make it clear that the Fourth Gospel does not interpret Christ taking up his life again as a gnosticizing docetism in which the "spiritual essence" of the Lord never suffers death. John also guards against the misperception that Jesus' death is the victory of his enemies. It is likely that Johannine Christians found their opponents arguing that Jesus could never have had the unity with the Father he claimed or been the source of life for humans (e.g., 5:21) if he himself was executed among the lowest criminals.

140   (iii) *Division: Is Jesus possessed?* (10:19–21). Though these verses refer to the healing of the blind man, the evangelist uses them as a "scene of division" to highlight the importance of what Jesus has just said. **20.** *has a demon:* The accusation that Jesus is "possessed" has appeared in 7:20, where the crowd rejects Jesus' claim that people are seeking to kill him only to admit it in 7:25; and in 8:48,52 in connection with Jesus' claim to be "greater than Abraham."

141 (iv) *Jesus' sheep know his identity* (10:22-30). **22.** The setting not only makes another Jewish feast the occasion for an attempt on Jesus' life, but brings him back to the Temple precincts, which he had left after the attempt to stone him in 8:59. **23.** *Solomon's portico:* It ran along the outer wall on the E side of the Temple (see Acts 3:11; Josephus, *J.W.* 5.5.1 § 185). **24.** *frankly:* The demand for a "public" answer (*parrhēsia*) to the questions about whether Jesus is "Messiah" or not brings the reader back to the disputes of John 7-8. Jesus refused his brothers' demand to do signs in Jerusalem that would show his messianic status publicly (*parrhēsia;* 7:4). People would not speak publicly about Jesus "for fear of the Jews" (7:13). Jesus' public appearance in Jerusalem leads to speculation that he is the Messiah (7:26). **25.** *I have told you and you do not believe:* This does not point to a specific statement to the crowd; such a direct statement can only be heard by a believer. Jesus has told the Samaritan woman that he is "the Messiah" and the blind man that he is "Son of Man." Both passages also emphasize the fact that Jesus, "the one speaking with you," is the one about whom such claims are made. He has, of course, made a public statement about his identity in the Temple area on the previous feast, the divine "I Am" in 8:24,58. The evangelist makes sure we remember that fact by having this section end with a reaffirmation of the unity between the Father and Son (v 30). Jesus' works are also taken as testimony to his identity (cf. 5:36, a fact correctly understood by the blind man and repeated in the questions of the crowd in 10:21).

142 **26-29.** The shepherd image returns as Jesus explains the failure of belief with another metaphor of "origins," though one less hostile than 8:42-47. There the separation between two groups, "children of Abraham" and "of the Devil," rested on the charge that the latter sought Jesus' death. The crowd addressed here, though they will be offended by Jesus, are not part of that plot. In 6:44 no one can come to Jesus who has not been "called by the Father," and 6:65 refers to that saying to explain why some who had been disciples left Jesus. These examples suggest that the Johannine community has used sayings about God's calling persons to faith in order to make its experiences of rejection, of failed discipleship, and of active persecution intelligible. These experiences have also left their mark on this passage. Since God is the one who has "given" these sheep to Jesus no one (even religious leaders acting in God's name like those of chap. 9) can take them from him. They cannot frustrate Jesus' purpose, the gift of eternal life for those who believe (cf. 17:2,6). **30.** *I and the Father are one:* In the farewell discourses the unity of Father and Son is shown to include the community of believers (cf. 17:11; → Johannine Theology, 83:50-54).

143 (v) *Attempt to stone Jesus for blasphemy* (10:31-39). **31.** *to stone him:* As the reader has grown to expect, Jesus' claim of unity with the Father provokes a charge of blasphemy. **32-33.** Jesus' appeal to his "good works" is rejected on the grounds that he has blasphemed (cf. 5:16-18). **34.** *is it not written:* Jesus gives a scriptural argument from a "lesser to a greater" case; if Scripture can speak of humans as "gods" (Ps 82:6 LXX), how much more of the consecrated agent of the Father. The reader may have also been expected to recall the continuation of the quote, "and all of you are sons of the Most High." **37-38.** Though Jesus has claimed scriptural warrant for

calling one who is God's agent, "son of God," he must still show that the audience should consider him God's agent. That case is made on the grounds of Jesus' works (cf. 5:36), but his works are nothing if they do not lead a person to the recognition that he and the Father share the relationship expressed by "indwelling" (cf. 14:10-11; 17:21).

144 (vi) *Jesus withdraws across the Jordan* (10:40-42). Some think that an earlier edition of the Gospel ended Jesus' public ministry at this point. It brings the events to a conclusion where they had begun in the territory where JBap had first been active. It also completes JBap's mission, since people there do accept his testimony and believe in Jesus.

145 **(C) Jesus Gives Life and Receives Death (11:1-12:50).** Jesus' greatest "sign," the gift of life, leads to the decisive act of unbelief, the formal decision that Jesus must "die for the people" (11:1-57). John 12 builds around two traditional episodes from the passion narrative, the anointing of Jesus (12:1-8) and the entry into Jerusalem (12:12-16), the theme of plots against Lazarus and Jesus.

146 (a) RAISING OF LAZARUS (11:1-44). The healing of the blind man had demonstrated that Jesus was the "light" of the world. John now takes another traditional miracle; Jesus is its "life" as well (see C. F. D. Moule, *Theology* 78 [1975] 114-25). The Lazarus episode can even be seen as an enactment of the promises in 5:24-29. This sign demonstrates that the Father has given power over life and death to the Son (5:26).

147 (i) *Jesus waits to go to Lazarus* (11:1-16). The Synoptic stories in which Jesus restores to life a person who has died (Mark 5:22-23; Luke 7:11-16) concern one who has just died. But the Lazarus miracle is to be a sign that Jesus really is the power of life evident in resurrection. He calls to life a person buried in the tomb. This section creates the necessary time between the death of Lazarus and Jesus' arrival so that there can be no mistake. Lazarus was not in a coma. He had been dead for a long enough time that rabbinic authorities would have said that the soul had left the vicinity of the body and decay would have definitely set in. **1.** *Lazarus of Bethany:* The way in which the narrator identifies Lazarus suggests that he expects the reader to know "Martha and Mary." Two sisters, Martha and Mary, appear in Luke 10:38-42, where Jesus is a guest who teaches in their house. *Bethany:* → Biblical Geography, 73:95. **2.** *Mary:* John 12:1-8 has Mary be the one (unnamed in Mark 14:3-9) who anoints Jesus before the passion.

148 Part of the identification of Lazarus from v 1 may have belonged to the evangelist's source, which would also have contained a message that Lazarus had died or was at the point of death (v 3). After that, the source may have jumped to Jesus' arrival (vv 17-18) and the question about the location of the tomb and going there (vv 33-34,38-39). Annoyance with mourners appears in Mark 5:38-39. The miracle concludes with Jesus' cry and Lazarus' emergence (vv 43-44). The source might also have had the crowd's reaction. John has taken that reaction as the cause for the authorities to condemn Jesus. Some exegetes argue that, if there was any exchange between Jesus and one of the sisters, it would have been with the better-known Mary. However, Luke's tradition had an exchange between Jesus and Martha. Mary is the heroine of the anointing story. It seems more likely that the evangelist has made Martha the key figure in this story on the basis of a tradition which already had some exchange between her and Jesus. Some also see a connection between Lazarus in this story and the Lazarus of the parable, the rich man and Lazarus (Luke 16:19-31). However, interpreters of that parable suspect that both the name "Lazarus" and the development of a resurrection theme at the end of the parable (vv 30–31) result from Lucan redaction, which might even have been influenced by a story that was circulating in the tradition about Jesus raising a "Lazarus."

149 4. *it is for the glory of God:* The illness has a special purpose: it is to make the "glory of God" manifest so that the Son will be glorified (cf. 9:3). This theme recalls John 2:11 and points toward the real glorification on the cross (cf. 13:31–32; 17:1). 5. *Jesus loved:* This points to the community of Christian disciples as those whom Jesus (and the Father) love. John 15:13–15 shows that "friends" had become a term for Christians in the Johannine community (also 3 John 15). The story may have also been told to console Johannine Christians who themselves faced death for being disciples (16:1–4a). 7. *let us go to Judea:* This suggestion brings the objection that his life is in danger there. Jesus' reply uses the image of his coming (and impending departure) as light of the world (cf. John 9:4–5). 13. *Jesus had spoken about his death:* The exchange turns on a misunderstanding of "sleep" as a metaphor for death (cf. Mark 5:39). Jesus is "glad" because the sign will provide an occasion for the disciples to believe (cf. v 40). The dialogue concludes with a partially correct perception by the disciples: when Jesus does return to Judea, he is going to his death. 16. *Thomas:* → NT Thought, 81:140.

150 (ii) *Jesus: The resurrection and the life* (11:17–27). 17–20. The evangelist may have taken the geographical note about the location of Bethany from his source, but he has used the detail to explain that a large number of witnesses were from Jerusalem. They provide the link to the Jerusalem authorities. Because Lazarus had been buried for four days, no one could question the fact that Lazarus has come back "from death." 21. *if you had been here:* Martha voices the common expectation that even the crowd has. One who is well known for his miracles should have been able to heal Lazarus (cf. vv 32,37). Martha thus confesses a faith in Jesus that has recognized that God is the source of Jesus' powers. It separates her from those crowds that are amazed by Jesus' deeds and divided over his identity. 23. *your brother will rise again:* Jesus' words elicit from Martha an expression of her belief in the eschatological resurrection of the dead (e.g., 5:28–29; cf. the eschatological confession in 4:25). 25–26. Jesus' "I Am" follows the confession of faith. Verses 25b–26b then explain "resurrection and life" in terms of the promises of life to the one who believes, more characteristically Johannine phrasing (cf. 1:4; 3:15, 16,36; 5:24,26; 6:27,40,47; 10:10,28). "Resurrection" (*anastasis*) appears only here and in the reference to future resurrection in 5:29. With the exception of 20:9, the corresponding vb. *anistēmi* is limited to phrases that refer to the "last day" (5:29; 6:39,40,44,54). Thus, the expression "resurrection and life" links together a traditional word with the Johannine epithet for Jesus, "life." 27. *you are the Messiah, the Son of God, the one coming into the world:* These words do not point to what Jesus has just revealed but to three christological affirmations made in the gospel.

151 (iii) *Jesus loved Lazarus* (11:28–37). The evangelist creates a second scene in which Mary comes out to Jesus. Repetition of Martha's opening comment frames a demonstration of deep emotion on Jesus' part (vv 33b,35). The vb. *embrimasthai* (v 33b) refers to a reaction of anger, which may have been derived from a demonstration of anger at the mourners in the source. The evangelist understands it as inner anger or agitation. Even the crowd is able to recognize that Jesus "loved" Lazarus (v 36).

152 (iv) *Jesus raises Lazarus* (11:38–44). 39. *he will stink:* Jesus' command provides one last occasion to remind the reader of how long Lazarus has been buried. 40. *if you would believe:* Only the disciples had been explicitly told that the death of Lazarus is for the "glory of God" (v 4). Mark 5:36 has a parallel injunction to Jairus. 41b–42. Gestures of prayer on Jesus' part are always expressions of the relationship between Jesus and the Father. The reader already knows that the Father has given Jesus "life." The evangelist makes it clear that Jesus' gesture is a form of instruction to the crowd. Jesus' words also remind the reader of Martha's assertion that God grants Jesus whatever he asks (v 22) and that Jesus is always doing the will of the Father. 43–44. After all the interpretation is completed the miracle itself need only be recounted briefly to indicate that it had indeed occurred. 43. *cried out in a loud voice:* The events recall the words of 5:28–29: the hour is coming when all in the tombs (as Lazarus is) will hear his voice and will come forth, those who have done what is good to resurrection of life. Thus, the reader can also see this episode as a fulfillment of Jesus' earlier words.

153 (b) JEWISH LEADERS CONDEMN JESUS TO DEATH (11:45–53). According to the Gospel, this last "sign" leads to an outburst of belief in Jesus, which continues through the entry into Jerusalem (cf. 11:56; 12:9,12,17–19). But the Gospel also pictures Jerusalem as a place where the authorities are monitoring all activities. They check on JBap (1:19,24) and investigate Jesus' miracles (5:10,15; 9:13; 11:46). We have already seen that most scholars think it unlikely that the raising of Lazarus would have been the historical cause for the death of Jesus. The attack on the Temple implied by the cleansing episode is a much more likely cause. However, in the Fourth Gospel, one never gets to the "truth" of a saying or event on the literal level. The evangelist has already laid the groundwork for the view that the "good works" which Jesus does from the Father, preeminently giving life, are also the cause for hostility against him. John 7:45–52 has shown an earlier assembly of "Pharisees and high priests" declaring Jesus a blasphemer.

154 49. *Caiaphas, high priest that year:* It is not clear whether the evangelist has a confused understanding of the appointment of the high priest and thinks that they held office only for a one-year term or means that Caiaphas was high priest "in that year." John 18:13 suggests that Annas, Caiaphas's father-in-law, was high priest. Although controlled by aristocratic families from Jerusalem, the occupant held office for as long as he enjoyed Roman favor (→ History, 75: before 156). Caiaphas had been high priest since AD 18 and would continue in office until shortly after Pilate's fall from power in AD 36. Though the evangelist may not be clear about the details, the sudden introduction of concerns about a Roman reaction to a popular leader like Jesus are appropriately introduced in connection with a council that included members of the Jerusalem priestly aristocracy. Jesus' trial before Pilate will provide the occasion for him to contrast his kingship with that of an earthly ruler. Caiaphas's words are the height of Johannine irony. 50. *it is expedient:* I.e., that Jesus "die for the people," but the Johannine reader can hardly fail to observe that Jesus' death did not prevent the Romans from coming and destroying the "place" (= the Temple). That tragedy was brought on by the Jewish leadership during the revolt against Rome (AD 66–70). Early Christians considered the destruction of Jerusalem punishment for failure to recognize Jesus as the Messiah (cf. Luke 13:34–35; 19:41–44; Mark 12:9–11).

155 51. *he prophesied that Jesus should die for the people:* This tells the reader that Caiaphas's statement was made out of a prophetic inspiration associated with the office of high priest (cf. Josephus, *J.W.* 1.2.8 § 68; *Ant.* 13.10.7

§ 299). It shows that the death of Jesus "for the people," an expression of the sacrificial character of Jesus' death, does not apply simply to the Jewish nation. Jesus dies so that all who are "children of God" can be gathered into one (cf. 1 John 2:2, Jesus dies "for the world"). **53.** Finally a death sentence is passed against Jesus, one which the reader might suspect from 7:51 is illegal. The plot against Jesus is brought to its conclusion. **156** (c) JESUS HAS WITHDRAWN (11:54–57). Although it is not explained how the council's decision became public, the reader is clearly to presume that that hostility motivates Jesus' withdrawal to the village of Ephraim (modern eṭ-Ṭaiyibeh, 12.5 mi. NW of Jerusalem), a day's journey away from it. **55–56.** Now that the feast of Passover approaches, the crowd begins to wonder just as they had at Tabernacles (7:11–13) whether or not Jesus will appear. **57.** *had given orders:* The authorities put out a notice that if anyone knows where Jesus is, the authorities are to be told so that they can arrest him. **157** (d) JESUS IS ANOINTED FOR THE HOUR (12:1–8). Jesus' anointing appears in Mark 14:3–9 par. (and Luke 7:36–50, during his Galilean ministry). It is preceded by secret plots to arrest and kill Jesus (Mark 14:1–2; Matt 26:3–4, at the home of Caiaphas). John's tradition seems related to that behind Mark, with details that are found in Luke: the meal setting and the fact that the woman anointed Jesus' feet and dried his feet with her hair (though in Luke the latter is done to wipe off her tears before the anointing). The rare word *entaphiasmos,* ("burial preparation," v 7) is the nominal form of the verb used in Matt 26:12. John has derived the location, Bethany, and the time, "before Passover," from his source. The number of days varies: Mark has "two" days; John, "six." The oil is described as genuine *pistikos,* "spikenard oil." Its great value is described as *polytelēs* in Mark and *polytimos* in John. Mark and John also agree that the oil is valued at 300 denarii. Both have Jesus tell the disciple(s) to "let her alone." Matt, Mark, and John all agree that the woman's action is preparation for Jesus' burial. They all have the saying about the poor (cf. Deut 15:11); though in John the saying is the climax of the story, the Synoptics all conclude with words about what the woman has done. **158** **1.** *to Bethany:* The evangelist has connected this story with the previous account of Lazarus, Martha, and Mary. The detail of Martha serving echoes Luke 10:40. **3.** *spikenard oil:* Derived from the roots of a plant grown in the mountains of northern India, it would not normally be used to anoint the feet. Mark has the woman anoint Jesus' head, whereas Luke has her cleanse Jesus' feet, thus making up for the deficient hospitality of Jesus' host. The Johannine version may have resulted from the confusion of two originally independent stories of Jesus being anointed. John also specified the weight of oil used just as he will specify the quantity of spices used for Jesus' burial (cf. 19:39). **4–6.** *Judas Iscariot:* Although the evangelist may have found "Mary" as the woman's name in his tradition, he almost certainly has cast Judas in the role of the one who protests. He identifies him as the betrayer and then explains that he has no concern for the poor but is a thief (cf. Matt 26:15; also John 13:27–29). Judas and Mary are contrasting characters: (a) Mary, Jesus' "friend" (true disciple), who has provided costly burial preparations for Jesus, and (b) Judas, Jesus' betrayer (false disciple), a thief, whose departure will be misunderstood as the need to make provisions for the Passover or to give something to the poor (13:29)! **7–8.** *let her be:* By shifting the order of the traditional sayings, the poor who are "always with you" come into sharper contrast with Jesus, who is not always to be with the disciples (12:35–36). **159** (e) PLOT AGAINST LAZARUS (12:9–11). These verses bring the anointing story into the plot against Jesus' life which resulted from the raising of Lazarus. The crowd is as curious about Lazarus as they are about Jesus. Their shallow reaction to the sign is benign when contrasted with the viciousness of those who would not only kill Jesus but also Lazarus. **160** (f) ENTRY INTO JERUSALEM (12:12–19). The crowd which witnessed the Lazarus miracle is identified as those acclaiming Jesus on his entry into the city (vv 17–18). Their behavior gives the Pharisees further reason for their desire to kill Jesus (cf. Luke 19:39). **19.** *look, the whole world has gone after him:* They state an ironic truth. John had left the crowd wondering whether Jesus would come to the feast in 11:55–56. The evangelist also reminds the reader that the application of Scripture to what Jesus does in Jerusalem comes only after Jesus has been glorified (v 16: cf. 2:22). Either John's source was more abbreviated than the Synoptics (Mark 11:1–11; Matt 21:1–11; Luke 19:28–40), or he has deliberately abbreviated a longer account in order to focus attention on the heart of the issue: Jesus is now entering Jerusalem in fulfillment of the two prophecies. **13.** *the king of Israel:* So Jesus now enters Jerusalem; this is an expression that the evangelist has added to Ps 118:25–26 in v 13 in order to parallel the reference to the coming of the king in v 15. **14.** John speaks only of Jesus "seated" on the ass's colt, not "riding" or "mounted." **15.** He also conflates citations from Zech 9:9 and Zeph 3:16. The quotations portray the Messiah as one who comes in peace, not with a war chariot. Introduction of palm branches may have been symbolic victory. Not native to Jerusalem, they had to be imported for Tabernacles (2 Macc 10:7). During the second Jewish revolt palm branches were used on coins. The crowd going out to meet Jesus may have been copying the welcome accorded a visiting king or dignitary (cf. Josephus, *J.W.* 7.5.2 § 100). The real truth of Jesus' kingship will not be evident until the crucifixion. **161** (g) THE HOUR IS AT HAND (12:20–36). We see Jesus accepting his destiny and making one final appeal to the crowd, which remains divided and unable to square his claims with its own conceptions about the Messiah. **162** (i) *Greeks come to Jesus* (12:20–26). **20.** *some Greeks:* The ironic words of v 19 are immediately fulfilled. "Greeks," i.e., Gentiles, come seeking Jesus. Josephus (*J.W.* 6.9.3 § 427) reports that "God-fearing" Gentiles came to Jerusalem to worship at Passover. Their arrival also points back to the crowd's question in 7:35, whether Jesus would go teach "the Greeks" in the Diaspora. Their presence may also hint at the transition from evangelization among the Jews and Samaritans to a Gentile mission that had occurred in the Johannine church. **21.** *Philip:* See 1:43–48; 6:5–7. *Bethsaida:* → Biblical Archaeology, 74:144. **23.** *the hour has come:* Jesus' words are addressed to the disciples. The "now" of that announcement will be repeated in vv 27 and 31. Each speaks of what it means for the Son to be glorified: the hour is the culmination of his mission, and it is also the condemnation of "this world" and its ruler. **163** **24.** *unless a grain of wheat falls into the ground:* This saying is echoed in 1 Cor 15:36. It was probably a common proverb, which John has shaped to the situation of Jesus' death by emphasizing the fact that the seed "remains alone" above ground. Only Jesus' death makes salvation possible for others. The community will not "remain alone" after Jesus' death but will attain a new unity with him and the Father (e.g., 14:18,28; 16:22).

25. *the one who loves his life will lose it:* This saying occurs in a number of variants (cf. Luke 9:24//Mark 8:35//Matt 16:25; Matt 10:39//Luke 17:33). The Synoptic contexts apply it to the suffering and loss of discipleship. John may also have had the future sufferings of his community in mind (cf. 15:18–21). **26.** *where I am, there my servant will be:* The identity of Jesus and his followers will be emphasized in the farewell discourses (cf. 13:13,16; 15:20). Verse 26a echoes Mark 8:34. The conclusion, "if someone serves me, the Father will honor him," reappears in the love language of the farewell discourses (14:23; 16:27). Synoptic judgment sayings have the Son of Man confess or deny before God persons who have confessed or denied him (Mark 8:38; Matt 10:32//Luke 12:8).

164   (ii) *I am to be lifted up* (12:27–36).   The third Johannine passion prediction forms the center of a public announcement that Jesus is to be "lifted up" and of a final appeal for faith. **27–30.** The second "now" section in the chapter clearly reminds the reader of the Gethsemane story in the Synoptics (e.g., Mark 14:34–36). **28.** *Father, glorify your name:* Cf. Luke 11:2. For John it expresses the unity of Jesus' purpose with God's will. Jesus will glorify God on the cross and will, in turn, be glorified by the Father (cf. 13:31–32; 17:4). *a voice:* The crowd which cannot "hear" God's response to Jesus thinks the voice that of an angel. As in the Lazarus story, the prayer is also an example to them. **30.** *for your sake:* John has thus transformed the "private agony" tradition into a public manifestation of Jesus' obedient service.

165   **31.** *now is the judgment of this world:* Judgment (cf. 3:18–19) culminates in the crucifixion. The thunder of the divine voice in the previous scene also carries overtones of God's coming in judgment to cast out the "prince of this world." Here, John uses the expression "the world" not as the object of God's love, as in 3:16, but as a symbol for all that is unbelieving and hostile to God (e.g., 8:24; 15:18–19; 16:8–11). Satan as the ruler of "the world" in its opposition to God is a frequent figure in Jewish apocalyptic (e.g., 1QM 1:1,5,13; 4:2; 11:8; 1QS 1:18; 2:19; 3:20–21). But John only uses the figure of Satan to account for Judas's betrayal (6:70; 13:2,27) and in sayings which announce Jesus' victory (14:30; 16:11). Luke 10:18 preserves an independent saying of Jesus that announces Satan's fall from heaven. **32.** *lifted up from the earth:* Primitive Christian traditions had seen Jesus' exaltation to God's right hand as the foundation for his cosmic lordship (e.g., Phil 2:9–11). The final Son-of-Man saying speaks of the exalted Christ drawing all to him, clearly a reformulation of this early confession. **33.** *by what death:* The evangelist reminds us that Christ's exaltation is at his death on the cross.

166   **34.** *the Messiah remains forever:* Though Jesus had used the first person, the crowd reformulates his words as a Son-of-Man saying, understands that they refer to death or departure, and counters with a common expectation that the Messiah would "remain" forever (e.g., *T. Levi* 18:8). It is the last objection to Christian claims for Jesus as Messiah in the Gospel: (a) no one is to know where the Messiah comes from (7:27); (b) will he do more signs than this person (7:31); (c) not from Galilee, but from Bethlehem, seed of David (7:41–42); (d) the Messiah remains forever (12:34). These objections represent early Christian polemic concerning Jesus as Messiah (see M. de Jonge, "Jewish Expectations about the Messiah according to the Fourth Gospel," *NTS* 19 [1972–73] 246–70). **35.** *walk while you have the light:* Jesus has already answered the messianic question in his revelation to the blind man (9:35–38). Instead, he picks up the image of "light" to make one final appeal for faith.

167   (h) Condemnation of Unbelief (12:37–50). The evangelist has taken over Isaian texts that were already traditional explanations of the disbelief of Israel (v 38 = Isa 53:1, see Rom 10:16; v 40 = Isa 6:10, see Matt 13:13–15; Rom 11:8; Acts 28:26–27). **41.** *Isaiah said these things when he saw his glory:* Just as Abraham did (8:56), Isaiah was able to see Jesus' glory and prophesy about him. **42–43.** *many even of the authorities believed:* Suddenly, the evangelist modifies this picture of universal rejection. Nicodemus (3:1–2; 7:50–52; 19:38–42) and Joseph of Arimathea (19:38–42) serve as examples of such sympathizers. The evangelist concludes that more persons would be willing to admit to believing in Jesus if the synagogue ban and concerns for "human glory" did not prevent them from confessing their faith (see K. Tsuchido, *NTS* 30 [1984] 609–19).

168   **44–50.** A final, isolated revelatory discourse has been added to the conclusion of the public ministry. Its content is close to the fragment in 3:16–19. Its final verses may be an allusion to Deut 18:18–19 and 31:19,26 in which those who refuse to heed the prophet sent by God are condemned. Thus, this section is a ringing affirmation of the theme of Jesus as the agent of God. To reject him is to reject the Father who sent him, to resist the command of the Father, and to stand condemned (see P. Borgen, *NTS* 26 [1979–80] 18–35).

169   (III) **Book of Glory: ". . . He Gave Them Power to Become Children of God"** (13:1–20:31). The account of Jesus' passion is dwarfed by the discourse material, which appears to have been expanded during the editing of the Gospel and may well represent different situations in the later history of the Johannine community. Throughout the concluding chapters of the Gospel we find the same distinctive use of traditional passion/resurrection material that we have already seen in chap. 12. It often remains difficult to determine how much of the Johannine passion account derives from pre-Johannine sources and how much is the work of the evangelist (→ Johannine Theology, 83:27–30).

170   (A) **The Last Supper Discourses** (13:1–17:26). Though there is a clear break at 14:31, the establishing of other divisions within these chapters remains difficult. Since prediction of Peter's denial belongs to the Last Supper in Luke 22:31–34, some would defer the beginning of the first discourse to 14:1. Since John 15:1–17 stresses the necessity of remaining in union with Jesus and loving one another, some exegetes see in that discourse a reflection of the situation that faced the community when the Johannine epistles were written. Since the theme of hatred by the world is suddenly introduced in 15:18, some would begin a new discourse there. It might then be held to conclude with the reference to persecution in 16:1–4a, or might continue through the condemnation of the world by the Paraclete in 16:11 or with the second Paraclete saying in 16:15. Most agree that Jesus' prayer in John 17 constitutes an independent unit. Finally, analysis of the theology of individual sections of these discourses has produced a number of complex hypotheses about the development and redaction of the discourses within the Johannine circle of teachers (see J. Becker, *ZNW* 61 [1970] 215–46; J. P. Kaefer, *NovT* 26 [1984] 253–80). We shall adopt R. Schnackenburg's division of the discourse material: (a) 13:31–14:31, an announcement of the hour and farewell to the disciples; (b) 15:1–16:4a, a discourse of exhortation to the disciples concerning relations within the community and in the face of external hostility; (c) 16:4b–33, consolation for the sorrowing disciples; and (d) 17:1–26, Jesus' prayer for the disciples. The frequent echoes of farewell discourse material in the Johannine Epistles (→ see below, 62:4–5), presume that the audience is already familiar with these discourses, whereas the Gospel is intelligible without reference to the epistles. Therefore, it seems unlikely that major sections of the discourse material were composed to counter that crisis. Shorter passages may have been added in the final editing of the Gospel, to emphasize themes which the later community had found crucial.

171 (a) THE LAST SUPPER (13:1-30). Comparison of John's Last Supper account with the Synoptics raises major questions: When did the supper and consequently the crucifixion of Jesus take place? Was the supper a Passover meal? Why is there no account of the institution of the eucharist in John? What is the significance of the footwashing? Who were the participants in the supper? The Johannine tradition holds that Jesus died on the Day of Preparation (18:28), not during Passover (in contrast to the Synoptics, e.g., Mark 14:12-16; Luke 22:15). Attempts at harmonizing the two traditions by claiming that the Johannine version followed an Essene calendar which began with Passover on Tuesday evening and that Jesus' trial had been extended over two days have no support in the narrative. The evangelist is interested in Jewish feasts and would have exploited a tradition of Jesus replacing the Passover meal had he known it. The suggestion that John rearranged the chronology in order to have Jesus' death coincide with the slaughter of Passover lambs is only a deduction from his chronology and use of the expression "Lamb of God" in 1:29,36. The simplest hypothesis may be to conclude that the tradition in John's community was that Jesus had been crucified on Friday, Nisan 14, the day before Passover.

We have seen in the discourse on the bread of life that some exegetes consider authentic Johannine soteriology to be focused on the Word. Salvation is grounded in one's obedient hearing of the Word of revelation and not in sacramental practices. Others have proposed that 6:51b-58 was detached from its location in the Last Supper narrative when the discourse material was added or that the Johannine community presumed that the eucharist was originally independent of the supper and is derived from Jesus' meal fellowship with his disciples. The difficulty with presuming that the eucharist stems from such communal meals lies in the links between the eucharist and the passion that are evident both in the words of institution and in Paul's assertion in 1 Cor 11:23 that the eucharist is linked to the betrayal of the Lord. It seems evident that there was an account of the institution of the eucharist in the Johannine community, which is presupposed by 6:51b-58. (See H. Thyen, "Johannes 13 und die 'kirchliche Redaktion' des vierten Evangeliums," *Tradition und Glaube* [Fest. K. G. Kuhn; ed. G. Jeremias, *et al.;* Göttingen, 1971] 343-56.)

Concern over the circle of participants in the supper is often tied to a desire to include or exclude particular persons, frequently women, as "ordained" celebrants of the eucharist in contemporary churches. Mark 14:17,20 speak explicitly of the Twelve as sharing the supper. Luke speaks of the disciples in 22:11 but later calls them "the apostles" (22:14), which suggests that he also has the Twelve in mind (see Luke 6:13). John, who knows of the existence of the Twelve as a group led by Peter (see 6:67-68), maintains the more indeterminate circle of "disciples" (13:5,22-23), a group not limited to the Twelve, as the presence of the Beloved Disciple shows (D. J. Hawkin, *LTP* 33 [1977] 135-50). John's interest throughout the discourses is not ecclesial authority but the including of the later community, which is to look back on Jesus' words and actions as a guide for its own life.

172 (i) *Washing the disciples' feet* (13:1-20). The first section falls into three parts: Jesus' action (vv 1-5) and two interpretations (vv 6-11,12-20). The second interpretation generalizes the action so that it teaches a lesson to all of Jesus' later disciples. **1-3.** The account opens with an awkward sentence which stretches over three verses (cf. 6:22-24). Verses 1 and 3 are summary statements in which the evangelist and perhaps a later editor have compressed the significance of Jesus' departure. The Father handed over all to the Son-agent (3:35; 7:30,44; 10:28-29), so that the Son might bring them salvation, in dying on their behalf and thus showing his love (10:17). The reference to Judas's betrayal may have been introduced from 13:27 in a later editing. **5.** *began to wash the disciples' feet:* Footwashing was a sign of hospitality (Gen 18:4; 1 Sam 25:41; Luke 7:44). It might be performed by the master's slaves when welcoming a dignitary to the house as in *Jos. Asen.* 7:1. In *T. Abr.* 3:7-9 Abraham and Isaac wash the feet of their angelic visitor, Michael.

173 **6-8.** Peter appropriately questions Jesus' action, since he is not a superior for whom Jesus (who has no human superior) might perform this task as a sign of respect. Jesus' initial response reminds the Johannine reader of other events: Jesus' saying about the Temple or his entry into Jerusalem, which the disciples could not understand until they "remembered" them after his death and resurrection (2:22; 12:16). **8.** *you have no part in me:* Peter's persistence is met with the assertion that he cannot share the "place" which Jesus offers his disciples (cf. 14:3; 17:24), if he is not washed. **9.** *also my hands and head:* Such literalism is typical of Johannine misunderstandings. The evangelist has linked this story to Jesus' love for his own to the end. Jesus' action represents his coming sacrifice on behalf of his disciples. In line with the soteriological emphasis of the Gospel, we see Jesus as the means of salvation. Verse 10 obviously created difficulties in antiquity, since some mss. lack the expression "except the feet." Without that phrase, Jesus would appear to be citing a proverb to imply that the disciples are sufficiently cleansed (except Judas, who will not have a "share with Jesus"). The narrator then breaks in to remind the reader that Jesus knows what Judas is going to do.

174 **14.** *you ought also wash each other's feet:* Instructions that the disciples must follow in the path shown by Jesus occur in the Synoptics (e.g., Mark 10:42-45 par.). Luke 22:24-30 links the disciples' share in the eschatological banquet with their share in the trial of Jesus and their willingness to follow Jesus' example of being servant (*diakonos*). **16.** *a servant is not greater than his master:* A Johannine variant of the saying in Matt 10:24; Luke 6:40. It picks up the theme of sender and agent from the christology of the Gospel. **17.** *blessed are you:* A macarism is added to underline the seriousness of the exhortation.

175 **19.** *I tell you this now before it takes place:* The Scripture citation (Ps 41:9), applied to the prediction of betrayal, belongs to the passion tradition (cf. Mark 14:18). Verse 19 cannot mean that the betrayal itself will manifest Jesus' divine "I Am." It must refer to the fulfillment of Jesus' word in the crucifixion (cf. 8:28). **20.** *whoever receives the one I send receives me:* This refers to v 16, but it seems somewhat out of place. Its Synoptic counterpart refers to the reward due those who receive the disciples who are sent in Jesus' name (cf. Matt 10:40).

176 (ii) *Jesus predicts his betrayal* (13:21-30). **21-22.** The announcement of the betrayal is very close to that in the Synoptics (Mark 14:18; Matt 26:21). This is the third time that we see Jesus "being troubled" as the events of the passion begin to unfold (11:33; 12:27). **23-25.** As though to replace the traitor, the Beloved Disciple, who is the source of the community's tradition, appears. He is the one closest to Jesus, and his question brings about the revelation of the traitor. **26.** *he to whom I shall give this morsel:* A saying that the betrayer is one who dips his hand in the common dish occurs in Mark 14:20. In Luke 22:3 Satan is also responsible for Judas's action. But John is the only Gospel in which Jesus actually hands Judas the morsel. The evangelist may wish to underline the horror of betrayal in the face of Jesus' act of hospitality. However, Jesus' words show the reader that even Satan has not gained power over Jesus (e.g., 10:18). Jesus knows what is to happen and dispatches Judas. **28–29.** These verses appear to be an explanatory addition to the narrative, which indicates that the other disciples are not aware of the purpose behind Judas's actions. **30.** *it was night:* Judas's departure brings the words whose symbolic sense could hardly be lost on the reader of the Gospel (9:4; 11:10). (See A. J. Hultgren, *NTS* 28 [1982] 539–46; G. Richter, *Die Fusswaschung im Johannesevangelium* [Regensburg, 1967]; F. F. Segovia, *ZNW* 73 [1982] 31–51.)

177   (b) JESUS RETURNS TO THE FATHER (13:31–14:31). The basic structure of this discourse is repeated in the third discourse (16:4b–33): Jesus announces his departure (13:33; 16:5); there is a question about where he is going (13:36; 16:5b); a statement about the sorrow of the disciples (14:1; 16:6); each has two sayings about the Paraclete (14:16–17; 16:7–11; 14:26; 16:13–15); each refers to Jesus' return to the disciples (14:18–20; 16:16); each speaks of the love which the Father has for the disciples (14:21; 16:27); each promises that whatever the disciple asks the Father will be granted (14:13; 16:23); each predicts the infidelity of the disciples during the passion (13:38; 16:32).

R. E. Brown (*BGJ* 597–601) draws extensive parallels between the themes of the Johannine discourses and the literary genre of a farewell discourse by a dying patriarch, Moses or some other revealer figure, such as we find in *T. 12 Patr., 1 Enoch,* and *Jub.* The Johannine farewell discourses differ from their Jewish models in having a picture of the future of the "children" whom Jesus is leaving behind that includes a renewed presence of the departing revealer. And, as in the Gospel itself, they do not have extensive exhortations to moral virtue or obedience to the law. Only the love command appears as the foundation for the behavior required of believers toward each other.

178   (i) *Announcement of the hour* (13:31–38). These verses mark a transition between the supper and the discourses that follow. The solemn reintroduction of the theme of glorification in vv 31–32 suggests that the discourse ought to begin here rather than with 14:1. **31–32.** These verses make five statements about the coming glorification of Jesus, though v 32a is textually uncertain. If v 32a is omitted, then they fall into two groups of statements, the proclamation that the Son of Man has been glorified and God has been glorified in him (v 31) and that God will very soon glorify him. Verse 32a makes the future glorification of the Son contingent on the fact that the Son has already glorified God (by fulfilling his mission; cf. 17:1,4–5). **33.** *little children:* The only occurrence of *teknia* in the Gospel. It is used for Christians in 1 John (2:1,12,28; 3:7,18; 4:4; 5:21), probably as a variant of *tekna,* "children" (cf. John 1:12; 11:52; 1 John 3:1,2,10). The term might also be introduced here from the farewell discourse genre in which the departing patriarch addresses his descendants. *as I said to the Jews:* This refers to 7:33–34 and 8:21. Those sayings functioned as judgment oracles against unbelief.

179   **34–35.** *a new commandment . . . love one another:* The commandment fits awkwardly into this position, since what follows deals with the theme of Jesus'

departure. The commandment returns in 15:12–17 and is identified as the criterion of salvation and of knowledge of God in 1 John (e.g., 1 John 2:7–8; 3:11,23). John 13:1 (also 10:11,17) has established the coming death of Jesus as the ultimate example of love. God's "command" has also been mentioned in connection with Jesus' self-offering in 10:18 (also 14:31; implied in 12:49,50). Loving Jesus and "keeping his commandments" are referred to in 14:15,21. Thus, these verses may have been added to specify the reference of "commandments" in these passages. This "commandment" is "new" because it is grounded not in the love commands of the Jewish tradition (e.g., Lev 19:18; 1QS 1:9–11) but in the self-offering of Jesus. The formulation of the commandment as the distinctive mark of Christian community among outsiders in v 35 (cf. 17:23b) differs from its use in 1 John to castigate those who create internal division within the community.

180   **37.** *why can I not follow you?:* The first question of a series that demonstrates the inevitable misunderstanding of Jesus' words by the disciples prior to his glorification (14:5,8,22). Jesus' answer alludes to 12:26 and contains an implicit prediction of Peter's death (cf. 21:18–19). The evangelist uses a version of the tradition that Jesus predicted Peter's denial (Mark 14:29; Luke 22:31–32) to refute Peter's claim.

181   (ii) *Jesus is the way to the Father* (14:1–11). This section is framed by two strongly worded commands to believe in God and in Jesus (vv 1,11). They make the claim that, if one will not believe Jesus' words, then his "works" should provide the grounds for knowing that Jesus and the Father are one (cf. 10:37–38). **2.** *many dwellings:* Traditional imagery would understand the "Father's house" to mean heaven (e.g., Philo, *De somn.* 1.256). The apocalyptic tradition of heavenly journeys described the "dwelling places of the holy" in the heavens (e.g., *1 Enoch* 39:4; 41:2; 45:3). 4 Ezra says the wicked "shall see how the habitations of the others [= the righteous] are guarded by angels in profound peace" (7:85). **5.** *Thomas:* See 11:16; 20:24–28. **6.** *I am the way, truth, and life:* Jesus himself, not a course in apocalyptic heavenly geography, is the "way." "Truth" and "life" qualify the expression "way" with two of the basic soteriological images of the Gospel. Jesus is not just a guide to salvation; he is the source of life and truth (5:26; 10:10,28; 11:25–26; see I. de la Potterie, *NRT* 88 [1966] 907–42). Verse 6b repeats the Johannine theme that there is no access to God except through Jesus (1:18; 3:13).

182   **9.** *whoever has seen me has seen the Father:* Philip's request for a vision of the Father prompts another assertion of the unity between Father and Son, which makes it clear that when John speaks of Jesus as "the Way," he is not thinking of Jesus as a heavenly figure who simply brings people into the realm of the Father or, as the gnostics would have it, leads them into the pleroma (as in *1 Apocalypse of James* 33.1–36.1). Jesus is the revelation of God (cf. 6:40, "everyone who sees the Son and believes will have eternal life"; 12:45, "the one who sees me, sees the one who sent me"). The link between Jesus' words and those of the Father who sent him is grounded in the picture of Jesus as the agent of the Father (e.g., 3:34; 7:17–18; 8:28,47; 12:47–49).

183   (iii) *The Paraclete and Jesus' return* (14:12–24). Attention now shifts to the first set of promises which Jesus makes to the believer. **12.** *he will do even greater works than these because I go to the Father:* This saying may have originally referred to the possibility of the disciples doing miracles in the name of Jesus (e.g., Luke 17:6; Matt 17:20). **13.** *whatever you ask in my name I will do:* This saying appears in a number of variants (Matt 7:7//Luke

9:9; Matt 7:8//Luke 9:10; Matt 18:19; 21:22). Different forms of this promise appear in 14:13,14; 15:16 and 16:23; 16:24 and 15:7; 16:26; and in 1 John 3:21-22; 5:14-15. Sometimes Jesus is the one who answers the request; sometimes the Father, when asked in Jesus' name; sometimes the Father is addressed directly, and sometimes neither is specified but one would presume that the Father is meant. Some have suggested that the evangelist has attached the words on Jesus' glorification and the necessity of acting in Jesus' name to the saying about "greater works" to counter a tendency toward charismatic identification with the Paraclete on the part of members of the Johannine community. The only significance that any "works" of the disciple can have is the same as Jesus' works: they must serve to testify to the unity between Jesus and the Father.

184   The next section of promises reflects the special way in which Jesus remains present with the believing community. The passage contains three sequences in which we hear of (a) love of Jesus (14:15,21a,23a [and 24a, no love of Jesus]); (b) reward for such love (14:16-17a,21b,25-26), and (c) opposition between the disciples and the world (14:17bc,18-20,22). Insertion of the love command in 13:34-35 leads the reader to identify "keeping the commandments" of Jesus with the command to love one another. However, the expression "keep the word" of Jesus occurs in the earlier controversies as a condemnation of unbelief (e.g., 5:38; 8:51; 12:37). This language of indwelling presence may have originally been attached to the question of "loving" or "hating" Jesus during the period of persecution by Jewish authorities. The question posed by Judas in v 22: "How are you going to show yourself to us and not the world?" also fits a wider context of Christian polemic (cf. Acts 10:40-41; repeated by 2d-cent. polemicists; see Origen, *Contra Celsum* 2.63-65).

185   In its present form, the three promises of "return" and indwelling are not limited to vindication of a community under persecution. They unite three traditions which the Johannine community had developed in speaking about its own relationship with God. In each case, the "divine presence" is evident only to the believers, not to outsiders (vv 17b,19,23b, implied in the Father who is "not seen except through the Son" and Son coming to make their dwelling with the believer). **16.** *another Paraclete:* The permanence of the Paraclete is contrasted with Jesus' departure. *Paraklētos* appears only in the five sayings in 14:16-17,26; 15:26; 16:7b-11,13-15, and as a designation for the exalted Christ as intercessor for Christians in 1 John 2:1-2. Though some scholars have attempted to argue that the five Paraclete sayings were interpolated into the farewell discourses as a group, the sayings have clearly defined functions within their individual discourses. We have already seen that the saying in 14:16-17 is required by the threefold structure of this section. As a heavenly intercessor, "Paraclete" would attribute to Jesus a function like that attributed to Moses in Jewish writings, pleading for the sinful people before God. John 5:45 makes a savage attack on Jesus' opponents using that tradition. Moses will turn and accuse those who fail to believe in Jesus. The "Paraclete" in 16:7b-11 performs a similar function of convicting the world. However, the other Paraclete sayings in the Gospel show that the title had taken on a number of other functions, some of which may be paralleled with those attributed to the holy Spirit in the Synoptics and others which may have developed out of the apocalyptic figure of an angelic protector of the righteous (→ Johannine Theology, 83:52-54). *the Spirit of Truth:* In the DSS the "Spirit of Truth," described both as an angelic figure and as one of two "spirits" struggling within a person,

is sometimes spoken of as an angel (of light) opposed to Beliar (1QS 3:18-4:26). The "Spirit of Truth" is clearly known only to the Qumran sectaries, not to those being led astray by the "Angel of Darkness." Use of "two spirit" language to divide opposing groups is evident in 1 John 4:6. Internalization of the "two spirits" also made it possible to ascribe a forensic function to the "Spirit of Truth." *T. Jud.* 20:1-5 equates its operation with conscience. The Paraclete in vv 16-17 is not assigned any particular functions, but it is described as "successor" to Jesus, "another Paraclete." Thus, the Paraclete may be seen as continuing the functions of Jesus' earthly ministry for the disciples. (See O. Betz, *Der Paraklet* [AGJU 2; Leiden, 1963]; K. Grayston, *JSNT* 13 [1981] 67-82; G. Johnston, *The Spirit-Paraclete in the Gospel of John* [SNTSMS 12; Cambridge, 1970]; E. Malatesta, *Bib* 54 [1973] 539-50; U. B. Müller, *ZTK* 71 [1974] 31-77.)

186   **20.** *you will know that I am in my Father and you are in me:* This saying follows the pattern of 8:28 and 10:38. But the conclusion points to the glorification as the time when the disciples will know not only Jesus' relation to the Father, but that such a relationship exists between Jesus and themselves. A similar expression, including references to living through Jesus (cf. v 19), appears in connection with the eucharistic formula in 6:56. The result of this new relationship is not merely the presence of Jesus. It also brings the believer into a new relationship with the Father. **23.** *we will come and make our dwelling:* The final reference to this new relationship recovers the word "dwelling" from v 2. There is no longer any "separation" of the believers from God/Jesus, so they need not look to heavenly habitations to experience salvation in the presence of God.

187   (iv) *Conclusion: Jesus' departure* (14:25-31). Having established the future life of the community he is leaving, Jesus finally admonishes them to rejoice at his return to the Father (v 28). His words are to keep them from being shaken by the events that are to take place (v 29; cf. 14:1). **26.** *the Paraclete, the holy Spirit:* The words of Jesus are to be complemented by the activity of the Paraclete, here identified with the holy Spirit. The reader knows that "remembering" refers to the ability of the disciples to understand the true significance of words and deeds of Jesus after the resurrection (2:22; 12:16). These verses make it clear that the Paraclete's teaching involves understanding what Jesus had taught and done. The Paraclete does not bring teaching that is independent of the revelation in Jesus. **28b.** *the Father is greater than I:* During the Arian controversy, this saying was used to support a subordinationist christology (C. K. Barrett, "The Father is Greater than I," *Neues Testament und Kirche* [→ 97 above] 144-59). The Fourth Gospel, which is clearly able to affirm a unity of Father and Son, could hardly have had such questions in view. The expression, like the proverb in 13:16, is part of the Gospel's portrayal of Jesus as God's agent. He acts in perfect obedience to what he has seen and heard from the Father and is thus not blasphemously claiming to "be God" as his opponents charged. **31.** *that I love the Father:* The final words of the discourse remind us that the death of Jesus is not even a temporary—i.e., until the resurrection—"victory" for Satan, but a sign of the Son's loving obedience to the Father.

(Leaney, A. R. C., "The Johannine Paraclete and the Qumran Scrolls," *John and Qumran* [ed. J. H. Charlesworth; London, 1972] 38-61. Segovia, F. F., "The Love and Hatred of Jesus and Johannine Sectarianism," *CBQ* 43 [1981] 258-72; "The Structure, Tendenz and *Sitz im Leben* of John 13:31-14:31," *JBL* 104 [1985] 471-93. Woll, B., "The Departure of 'The Way': The First Farewell Discourse in the Gospel of John," *JBL* 99 [1980] 225-39.)

188   (c) JESUS, THE TRUE VINE (15:1–16:4a). This section contains two main divisions: (1) 15:1–17, the necessity of remaining with Jesus, the vine, and of mutual love; (2) 15:18–16:4a, the "hatred" Christians can expect from "the world." Some argue that the first deals with the division within the community that is reflected in 1 John, whereas the second treats the persecution of Christians by the Jews referred to in the Gospel (see F. F. Segovia, *JBL* 101 [1982] 115–28; *CBQ* 45 [1983] 210–30). The persecution envisaged in 16:1–4a appears to be even more intense than the expulsion from the synagogue. John 16:2 may mean that the persecution has entered a new stage, in which Christians are in danger of death, and that the community may suffer further apostasy. The author seeks to meet the situation by paralleling the new situation with that faced by Jesus and already known to them in some form of the gospel story (15:20 refers to 13:16). The description in the first half of the discourse of the community, of its mutual love, and of its willingness to emulate Jesus' death can be seen as an ecclesiology suited to meet just such an external threat. At the same time, it also has within it the symbolic possibilities of generating a closed community, focused on its internal affairs and using the language developed against persecutors on its opponents that we find in 1 John (see B. Lindars, "The Persecution of Christians" [→ 9 above] 48–69).

189   (i) *Jesus is the true vine* (15:1–11). **1.** *the true vine:* John 4:23 and 6:32 use "true" in connection with a symbol that proclaims Jesus as the replacement of the OT reality. The images of Israel as "vine" (e.g., Isa 5:1–7; 27:2–6; Jer 2:21; 5:10; Hos 10:1; Ezek 15:1–6; 17:5–10; 19:10–14; Ps 80:8–15) provide the basis for Johannine use of the symbol (R. Borig, *Der wahre Weinstock* [SANT 16; Munich, 1967]). The shepherd symbol in chap. 10 was used to insure that no one would "seize" any of the sheep belonging to Jesus (10:28–29); and the eucharistic tradition in 6:51b–58, which might also have been a carrier of "vine" imagery in the Johannine community, was linked with teaching about the necessity of remaining with Jesus. Just as God is responsible for the sheep who come to Jesus, so God is also the one who tends the vine. **2.** *he prunes:* OT traditions spoke of pruning fruitless vines (Jer 5:10; Ezek 17:7). This saying may have been formulated as a warning to Christians who attempted to "hide" their faith under persecution (e.g., 12:43). **3.** *you are pure because of the word:* A parenthetical remark, perhaps alluding to 13:10, seems intended to reassure the disciples that they are not in danger of being pruned. **5.** *the one who remains in me and I in him bears much fruit:* This brings the vine imagery into the "indwelling language" of the farewell discourses (e.g., 14:10–11,20). John 4:36 and 12:24 suggest that "bearing fruit" implies missionary activity, though within the context of the discourse it may be intended simply as a general characterization for Christian life. Eschatological warnings that fruitless branches and weeds will be burned appear in the Synoptics (e.g., Matt 3:10; 13:30). The relationship of "remaining in Jesus" is the basis for confidence in prayer (cf. 14:13). **8.** *in this my Father is glorified:* The disciples now represent Jesus in the world (cf. 13:35) so they are also seen as "glorifying the Father." **9.** *as the Father has loved me, I have loved you:* This mutual love is grounded in the fact that both Jesus and the disciples keep the commandments and abide in the love of the superior party. **11.** *my joy:* This verse makes the transition to Jesus' death as the highest example of love by invoking the theme of "joy" from 14:28.

190   (ii) *Disciples are friends of Jesus* (15:12–17). Jesus' love "for his own," shown in his death (13:1), provides the foundation for love among the disciples. The reader has already seen the love that Jesus has for his "friends" demonstrated in the Lazarus story (11:3,11,36). The term "friends" appears in Philo as a designation for the "wise" who are "friends of God" and not "slaves" of God (e.g., *De sobr.* 55; *De migr. Abr.* 45; *Leg. alleg.* 3.1). Wis 7:27 also speaks of the "wise" as God's friends. Here, this tradition is applied to all who believe. It is not the privilege of a select few. The tradition of being "friends" rather than "slaves" may have been apparent to Johannine readers in the polemic of John 8:32–36, which promised that the Son would make persons free. Another characteristic of Moses as "friend" of God was that he could speak to God with "boldness" (*parrhēsia*). This tradition may be implied in the second saying about prayer (v 16). As has been the case elsewhere in the Gospel, one does not "choose Jesus" but has already "been chosen" or drawn by him or by the Father (e.g., 6:70; 13:18). But while the earlier parts of the Gospel linked salvation and believing, this section stresses "bearing fruit" as the result of receiving the new status as "friend."

191   (iii) *The world will hate the disciples* (15:18–25). In the earlier discourse we found a sharp division between the community of disciples to which Jesus "returns" and "the world" which cannot receive him (14:19,22,27). Here, the dualism of the imagery picks up the hints of "hatred" and "love" of Jesus found in the previous discourse (14:24) to a new pitch. The world will "hate" the disciples just as it did Jesus, since they are now the "agents" whom Jesus has sent. As vv 18–25 repeat this theme, the reader is constantly reminded of the hostile exchange between Jesus and "the Jews" in 8:12–59. The "sin" which the world incurs in persecuting Jesus' disciples is the same sin and hatred of God demonstrated in its treatment of Jesus. Verse 25 has a rather awkward and unusual introduction to a Scripture citation referring to this hatred. Apparently the passage intended is Ps 69:5. (Citations from Ps 69 are connected with Jesus' death in Mark 15:36; John 2:17; 19:29.)

192   (iv) *The Paraclete as witness* (15:26–27). References to persecution of Christians in the Synoptics contain sayings about the function of the holy Spirit (Mark 13:9,11; Matt 10:20). These verses coordinate "testimony" by the Paraclete with the "testimony" which the disciples will be required to give about Jesus. If this discourse was composed as the second half of the previous discourse, then "testimony" about Jesus would seem to be implied in the injunction to bear fruit.

193   (v) *Persecution of the disciples* (16:1–4a). Whereas 14:29 saw Jesus' words as confirming the disciples' faith in the face of Jesus' crucifixion, 16:1 speaks of the possibility that some will be "scandalized." The verb is used in 6:61 to describe those "disciples" who will take offense at the bread of life discourse. The danger against which this discourse seeks to guard the community is that severe persecution will cause people to deny their faith in Jesus. They are reminded that those who persecute Christians have not known God (or Jesus) even though they may base their persecution on religious grounds (as in the charges of blasphemy and impiety lodged against Jesus in the Gospel; cf. 5:37b–38; 7:28; 8:27,55). Some interpreters think that v 2 refers to the same expulsion from the synagogue mentioned earlier in the Gospel. Others point to hints of persecution by Jews in Asia Minor found in Rev 2:3,9; 3:9 (and later the Jews are agents in the *Mart. Pol.* 13:1), as a context for a second episode of persecution that affected the Johannine community. Whatever the particulars, John 15:18–16:4a presumes that hostility from an unbelieving world will be a permanent facet of Christian life.

194   (d) CONSOLATION FOR THE DISCIPLES (16:4b–33). This discourse is closely related to the first farewell discourse, but it also presumes the condemnation of a hostile world evident in 15:18–27. Verses 16–24 contrast the disciples' grief and tribulation with the rejoicing of "the world." It presupposes not just a single "little while" before the disciples see Jesus again (as in 14:19) but a double "little while": during the first, they are sad and persecuted; then, they see Jesus again and rejoice (vv 16–17). This double scheme appears closer to traditional language about the parousia of Jesus. This discourse appears to have been composed independently of its present location. John 16:5b contradicts the extensive questions about "where" Jesus is going in 13:36–14:6. While the conclusion of the first discourse sought to strengthen the disciples' faith, 16:29–32 carries a warning against false confidence. The Paraclete sayings in the first discourse are completely oriented toward the function of the Paraclete within the community. Here, the first saying recovers the forensic associations of the term to present the Paraclete as continuing Jesus' lawsuit with the world (E. Bammel, "Jesus und der Paraklet in Johannes 16," *Christ and Spirit in the New Testament* [Fest. C. F. D. Moule; ed. B. Lindars, *et al.*; Cambridge, 1973] 199–217; D. A. Carson, *JBL* 98 [1979] 547–66). This discourse serves as consolation in suffering, but it may also serve to moderate the danger of sectarian isolation by integrating that suffering into the ongoing pattern of witness to the world (J. Painter, *NTS* 27 [1980–81] 535–43).

195   (i) *The Paraclete will convict the world* (16:4b–11). **4b–6.** The introduction to this section picks up some of the phrasing of the previous discourses: (a) a reference to Jesus *tauta lalein*, "telling these things" (14:25; 15:11; 16:1,4a) becomes "I did not say these things" (*tauta eipon*) in 16:4b, picking up the *eipon* from 16:4a; (b) the contrast between when Jesus was "with you" and his impending departure is repeated (cf. 14:27c–28,30; 16:4b–5; (c) *ex archēs*, "from the beginning," in v 4b reflects the *ap' archēs* of 15:27. Jesus' words as a cause of grief for the disciples, "because I have spoken these things grief has filled your heart" (v 6), are the opposite of 15:11, "I have spoken these things so that my joy may be in you, and your joy may be fulfilled." **7.** *it is good for you:* Jesus' insistence that the disciples should be rejoicing in his departure (cf. 14:27b–28) is repeated, where the expression "it is good for you" refers to the fulfillment of the divine plan (cf. 11:50). *if I do not go, the Paraclete will not come:* The coming of the Paraclete might be associated with the gift of the Spirit that is only possible after Jesus has been glorified (7:39; enacted in 20:17,22). **8–11.** The functions attributed to the Paraclete in these sayings are forensic. The expression *elenchein peri* can mean: (a) "bring to light," "expose"; (b) "convict of." Although "Paraclete" usually suggests an advocate or defender, the Johannine tradition had turned the "defender" of Israel, Moses, into Israel's accuser. The expression "Spirit of Truth," linked with Paraclete in the Johannine community, could refer both to an angelic guide for the righteous and to the internal operation of conscience which "convicts" the sinner. John 3:20 speaks of the persons whose evil deeds keep them from coming to the light lest those deeds be condemned (*elenchein*), whereas in 8:46 Jesus uses the same word in challenging his audience to convict him of sin. John 12:31 announces that the hour of the crucifixion is the hour of judgment for the "prince of this world." With the coming of the Paraclete, the legal suit of Jesus against the world is decided in Jesus' favor. The "sin" of which it is convicted has been "unbelief" throughout the Gospel (e.g., 3:19,36; 8:21–24; 15:22–25). **8.** *righteousness:* This term appears only here; but John 5:30 affirms that Jesus, who always does the will of the one who sent him, judges with "just" (*dikaia*) judgments, and the reference to

that episode in 7:24 challenges those who would condemn Jesus for healing on the sabbath not to judge by appearances but with "just" judgment. Since Jesus returns to the Father, he is proved to be God's agent. The "righteousness" of those who have condemned him is thus proved false. **10.** *you no longer see me:* These words contradict the experience of the community (cf. 14:19, where it "sees" Jesus and has life from him), but echo the judgment pronounced against those who have condemned Jesus in 8:21. **11.** *ruler of this world:* This verse links the false judgments made by the world to "its ruler," who is also condemned (cf. 8:42–47, those who seek to kill Jesus are doing the works of their father, the devil).

196   (ii) *The Paraclete will guide you into all truth* (16:12–15). As in 14:25–26, the Paraclete plays an important role within the community. It must guide the disciples in the future, since Jesus has not been able to tell his disciples everything they must know. Nor have they been able to understand his words and actions prior to his glorification (2:22; 12:16; 13:7). **13.** *in all truth:* The "truth" in which the Paraclete guides the community must have the same sense as "truth" elsewhere in the Gospel: belief in Jesus as the sole revelation of God and the one who speaks the words of God (e.g., 3:20,33; 8:40,47). The Paraclete helps the community fulfill the injunction of 8:31–32, "if you remain in my word, you are truly my disciples, and you will know the truth and the truth will make you free." *declare things to come:* The vb. *anangellein*, "declare," is used in apocalyptic writings for the revelation of the mysteries of the "end-time." In 4:25 the Samaritan woman speaks of the coming prophet in similar terms. We have seen that one of the manifestations of the Paraclete's activity was making what Jesus said or did intelligible, often by associating it with Scripture. A similar expression is associated with the messianic interpretation of prophetic texts in 1QpHab 7:1–3, which says of the prophet: "God told him to write down the 'things that were to come,' but he did not tell them when that moment would come to fulfillment." It may be that revelation of "things to come" had acquired a technical sense early in the history of the Johannine community. It did not mean that the Paraclete could make any sort of prophetic revelations about the future but that the Paraclete guided the community in its understanding of Jesus as the fulfillment of everything that had been promised in Scripture. The author of this section has made it clear that the Paraclete is not the source of new or divergent revelation by insisting that, like Jesus, the Paraclete does not speak "on his own" (7:17–18; 8:28; 14:10). His function is to glorify Jesus and take what the Father has given Jesus and declare it to the disciples.

197   (iii) *Jesus' departure and return* (16:16–24). Jesus returns to the theme of sorrow and departure (vv 5–7). **16.** *little while:* Cf. 14:19; 13:33; 7:33; it becomes the focus of a new riddle, not "where" Jesus is going but what does "little while" mean (vv 16–19). **20.** *you will weep and lament but the world will rejoice:* A revelatory pronouncement is structured on a pattern of apocalyptic reversal (cf. Matt 5:4). **21.** The reversal is illustrated with a "parable" of the woman in labor; this image has been applied to the messianic age in the OT (e.g., Isa 26:17–18 LXX; 66:7–10, the "birth pangs" of Zion in the Day of the Lord). Though *thlipsis*, "pangs," can also refer to the "trials" faced by the faithful in the last days (e.g., Zeph 1:14–15; Hab 3:16; Mark 13:19,24), the image here serves simply as an analogy to describe the reversal. **23.** *in that day:* The new situation of the disciples is reflected in the promises of what will come. **24.** *your joy:* No one can take their "joy" from them, possibly a reference to the persecution that they will suffer (15:11); they will finally "understand" what remains unclear until after the glorification (and coming of the Paraclete); and their new relationship with the Father will enable them to approach him confidently in prayer (14:13–14; 15:7,16; for the expression "ask and you shall receive," also see Matt 7:7; Jas 4:3; 1 John 3:22).

198   (iv) *Jesus has overcome the world* (16:25–33).   As the time of Jesus' glorification approaches the "parables" in which he had been speaking will be made clear. Jesus has come from the Father and is returning there again. **27.** *the Father himself loves you:* His disciples, who have believed that he came "from God," will find their reward in the love which God has for those who love the Son. **29.** *now you speak plainly:* The author has one last twist of misunderstanding. The disciples think that they already understand what Jesus is saying to them. Yet they do not understand the way in which he is to depart and be glorified. They confess only the first part of the pattern that Jesus has come "from the Father" (v 30b; 6:69). Their expression of confidence parallels Peter's claim to be ready to die for Jesus in 13:36–37. **32.** *you will be dispersed:* Jesus meets their claim with a reference to the flight of the disciples (cf. Mark 14:31; Matt 26:31). The Johannine passion story does not depict the fulfillment of this prophecy, since the Beloved Disciple is present at the foot of the cross (19:26–27) and the disciples have remained gathered together in Jerusalem (20:19). The tradition that they had returned to Galilee is represented in the additional resurrection story of 21:1–14. *am not alone:* The author quickly corrects any possible impression that Jesus might really be "alone" by reminding the reader that the Father is always with him. **33.** *in me you may have peace:* As in 14:27–31, this discourse concludes with a promise of peace to the disciples and a further affirmation that Christ has "conquered the world." The crucifixion is not a victory for those who are hostile to Jesus. Nor should the persecution suffered by the community be a sign of their victory. Once the disciples understand what has taken place in Jesus' glorification, then they will see both as evidence that Jesus has been victorious.

199   (e) JESUS' PRAYER FOR THE DISCIPLES (17:1–26). Some parallels have been noted between this prayer and the "Our Father": (a) use of "Father" as the form of address to God; (b) glorification of God and use of the divine name (17:1,11–12); (c) doing the will of God (v 4); (d) a petition to be delivered from the "evil one" (v 15; see W. O. Walker, *NTS* 28 [1982] 237–56). Like the other Johannine scenes of Jesus' prayer (11:41–42; 12:27b–28a), it reflects the unity of Father and Son and Jesus' complete dedication to his mission. This prayer also picks up the previous hints of a unity of the Father and Son with the disciples as the basis on which they continue to be "in the world." The presence of an extensive prayer at the conclusion of the discourse section may be another reflection of the "farewell discourse" genre (→ 177 above). The prayers uttered by the departing patriarch usually point toward the future (Deut 32:43–47; *Jub.* 1:19–21; *Jub.* 20–22). But the language of this prayer has no obvious parallels in such prayers. It is thoroughly Johannine. Some have connected this prayer with the imagery of Jesus as God's agent. The prayer represents his "report" of the mission he has accomplished. Consequently, Jesus even speaks as though he has already "left" the world (v 11). After an opening request for glorification (vv 1–5), Jesus turns first to his immediate disciples, the implied audience for the prayer (vv 6–19), and then includes all those who will come to believe in him (vv 20–26). The readers of the Gospel are directly included in this prayer. Some exegetes wonder whether its emphasis on unity, on God "sanctifying" the disciples, and on the need to keep to what Jesus has revealed reflects dangers that the author detects in the church of his day.

200   (i) *Jesus returns to glory* (17:1–5).   **1.** *the hour:* The opening announcement of the hour, the affirmation that Jesus is to be "glorified" because he has completed the work (→ Johannine Theology, 83:23) of "glorifying" the Father in giving eternal life, and the request that God "glorify the Son" are already familiar from 13:31–32. **2.** *power over all flesh:* This directs attention back to the affirmation in 5:20–27 that the Father has given the Son power to give life and to judge. **3.** This verse is clearly a gloss giving a Johannine definition of "eternal life" as knowing the "one true God" and "Jesus Christ." It is reminiscent of the command to believe in 14:1 and may have been an independent creedal formula in the Johannine community. **5.** *now glorify me:* This goes beyond the previous affirmations about Jesus' glory in the narrative and discourses and recalls the "glory" of the Word in the prologue (1:14), which will ultimately be shared by the disciples (v 24). By returning to the prologue, the author makes it clear that Jesus is much more than a righteous, perfectly obedient human being, commissioned by God, who has been exalted and glorified "in heaven." He is instead "from God" in a much more radical sense than his opponents could ever have imagined.

201   (ii) *Jesus sends the disciples into the world* (17:6–19).   The first part of this section summarizes what has been given to those who have been chosen by God and received the revelation which Jesus brought. They are the successful result of Jesus' mission (vv 6–11a), but they are also "in the world," whereas Jesus is not. The intercessions of the second half correspond to the promises of return and indwelling in the earlier discourses. However, such language is noticeably lacking here. Instead, we find Jesus requesting that the Father keep and sanctify the disciples, who will now assume the place "in the world" that he has held (vv 11b–19). **8.** *they have received them and know truly that I have come from you:* Verses 6–8 reverse the condemnations of unbelief in the public ministry (8:23,28,58). Jesus' disciples do know his true origins and know that God is the source of everything he has said and done. The discourses have been using "the world" as symbolic of the unbelief and hatred which Jesus' revelation encounters. Therefore, the disciples are described as being given to Jesus "from the world" (v 6). **9.** *I am not praying for the world but for those you have given me:* An important division underlies this statement. Just as the sayings about the disciples' new relationship to the Father in the earlier discourses presumed that only those who "loved" and "believed in" the Son could approach the Father, so "the world" that rejects Jesus (and thereby God) has no place in this prayer. **11a.** *I am no longer in the world:* These words describe the situation that exists with Jesus' return to the Father and are also the precondition for the new role which the disciples must play as those "sent by" Jesus.

202   **11b.** *holy Father:* This unusual expression in John may represent liturgical usage (cf. *Did.* 10:2). *keep them in my name:* Jesus had been able to "keep the disciples" in the "name" of God when he was with them. This expression may refer to the image of Jesus as shepherd in 10:28. **12.** One, however, Judas, has perished (6:70; 13:2,27). *the Scripture:* This may be the citation in 13:18. Verse 11 also introduced the theme of unity, which will be picked up again when future believers are introduced in vv 20–23. The reader of the Gospel in its present form may well find echoes of the "vine" language of 15:6–10, where believers are exhorted to keep Jesus' words/commands and remain in his love just as he remains in the Father's love. The language of "being one" may have roots in the early history of the Johannine community. The Essenes spoke of their new covenant as *yaḥad*, "a unity," which implied a group of persons, separated from "outsiders." The process of entering the covenant is described as *h'spm lyḥd*, "their being gathered into the unity" (1QS 5:7). But the Johannine perception of Christ has transformed the grounds of any such unity from a sociological or covenantal context to a reflection of the relationship between Jesus and God.

203 **13–16.** After a reference to the joy which Jesus' departing words are to bring to the disciples (cf. 15:11; 16:20–22,24), the discourse returns to the basis for the hostility which the disciples experience "in the world." **14.** *your word:* The disciples now have the "word of God" from Jesus and are not "of the world" (cf. 15:18–25). **15.** *the evil one:* Unlike Jesus, who is not touched by the "ruler of this world" (12:31; 14:30; 16:33), the disciples could be, and they must be kept safe from the "evil one." Though the believers are not "of the world," since they have accepted Jesus, they still remain "in the world" and are at least potentially subject to its influence.

204 **17.** *sanctify them in truth:* The climax of this section of the prayer comes with the commissioning of the disciples to take Jesus' place "in the world." The image of sanctification has strong overtones in the tradition of cult (Exod 28:41; 40:13; Lev 8:30) and sacrifice (Exod 13:2; Deut 15:19). Cultic interpretations of the death of Jesus like that in Heb attribute sanctifying power to the blood of Jesus (e.g., Heb 2:11; 10:10,14,29). John 10:36 speaks of the Father having "sanctified" and sent the Son into the world. That mission was to witness to what he had seen and heard from the Father (8:26; 3:32). Now that the disciples have accepted the word which Jesus has spoken (17:6,14; 15:3 speaks of Jesus' word "cleansing" the disciples), they are sent to bear witness to that word (J. Suggit, *JTS* 35 [1984] 104–17). **19.** *on their behalf:* When Jesus speaks of thus sanctifying himself, he is describing his death (cf. 6:51; 10:11,15; 15:13).

205 (iii) *That they may be one* (17:20–26). Jesus suddenly looks beyond the immediate circle of disciples to those who will believe as a result of their testimony. There are two dimensions to expressions of unity as they emerge in the Fourth Gospel. The vertical dimension grounds unity in the relationship between Jesus and God. The horizontal dimension sees in the command to love one another the expression of that relationship among members of the community (13:34–35; 15:12,17). Neither of these sources of unity should be taken simply as an expression of human solidarity or the creation of an institutional structure, since for John both are rooted in the revelation of the Father which occurs in Jesus. Nor does the author presume that this "unity" is a private experience of the believing community, since it poses a challenge to the world in the same way that Jesus' unity with the Father had posed a challenge of salvation or judgment (vv 21,23). Its object is not to challenge the world with some program of communal reform but with the gospel message about the relationship between Jesus and the Father. **24–26.** Jesus is the one who brings the disciples into community with God (10:38; 14:10–11,23; 15:4–5). **24.** *they may see my glory:* The culmination of that new unity would be sharing the "glory" that Jesus had with the Father from the beginning. This verse makes it clear that the foundation of that relationship between Jesus and the Father is their mutual love. In this way, the community can continue to sing that it has seen the glory of the incarnate word (1:14). At the same time, this verse also suggests that until the Christians have come to be with God as Jesus is, they have not fully experienced the reality of Jesus' relationship with God.

206 **(B) The Passion Narrative (18:1–19:42).** The Johannine passion narrative is cast in separate scenes: 18:1–11; 18:12–27; 18:28–19:16a; 19:16b–30; 19:31–42. It presents complex questions about the extent of John's sources and his redaction of them (see T. A. Mohr, *Markus- und Johannespassion* [ATANT 70; Zurich, 1982]). We have already encountered elements of the Synoptic "agony in the garden" in 12:27–28 and puzzles in Johannine chronology and understanding of the high priesthood. There is no formal proceeding before a Jewish body, the proceedings in 11:45–53 have decided the issue of Jesus' fate. A hearing before Annas appears in place of a Jewish trial or hearing. Annas lays the groundwork for a religious charge. His questions point toward the charge of being a "false prophet" or deceiver (cf. Deut 18:28). The trial before Pilate focuses on the political dangers of Jesus' popularity, the motive given in 11:45–53 for seeking Jesus' death. The question becomes one of the nature of Jesus' kingship. While it remains a matter of no little dispute among historians whether the preponderance of the gospel evidence suggests that those responsible for Jesus' death acted on religious or political grounds, one cannot either use the Johannine material to decide that question or consider it sufficiently answered to use as a criterion for distinguishing tradition and redaction in the Johannine narrative. In the trial before Pilate, Jesus acts as he has throughout the Gospel. He shows that Pilate is really the one who is on trial, and with supreme irony, Pilate forces the Jews to show their own disloyalty to God by declaring Caesar their king (19:14–15). The reader of the Gospel is already well aware that Jesus' death is not a humiliation or defeat but a glorious return to the Father.

207 (a) THE ARREST OF JESUS (18:1–11). John 18:1 appears to belong directly after 14:31, since the evangelist immediately establishes their destination and the fact that Judas is familiar with the location. The evangelist may also have highlighted the fact that Judas and his party had to come to arrest Jesus with lights as well as weapons, just as he dramatically referred to the fact that it was night when Judas left the supper room in 13:30. The question of whether or not Roman soldiers would have been included in such a party, clearly not a "cohort" (*speira* usually means a cohort) in any case, depends on the likelihood of collusion between Jewish and Roman authorities. Many scholars think that it would be unlikely even for Caiaphas to turn so vehemently against a fellow Jew. Pilate seems unacquainted with the case when Jesus is brought before him. John 18:12 repeats the term in question and even mentions the military tribune of a cohort. Therefore, the addition of Roman soldiers may be due either to a modification in a source that originally referred to Jewish police or to a desire on the evangelist's part to demonstrate unequivocally that Jesus is in control of what happens to him.

208 **4–9.** The core of the scene consists in the double confrontation between Jesus and those who have come to arrest him, clearly the work of the evangelist. **4.** *then Jesus:* He goes to meet the party, asks whom they seek, and when he identifies himself by saying "I Am," they all fall to the ground. Jesus repeats the question (vv 7–9) and uses the opportunity to secure release of his followers, thus fulfilling the promise of safety for those entrusted to him (6:39; 10:28; 17:12) — except Judas, who has been lost to the circle of disciples since Jesus commanded him to depart (13:27). **10.** *Malchus:* An independent development of the story that one of Jesus' disciples cut off the ear of one of the high priest's slaves (Mark 14:47; John and Luke 22:50 agree in specifying the right ear). John and Matt have Jesus speak to the disciple. Matt 26:53–55 appeals to a proverb about "living by the sword," Jesus' power to summon heavenly angels, and the necessity to fulfill Scripture. **11.** *Peter:* John has already demonstrated Jesus' power to stop the proceedings; he instructs Peter to put the sword away and alludes to the necessity of drinking the "cup" that the Father has given. This allusion would appear more appropriate to a source that contained a "cup word" in the garden (e.g., Mark 14:35-36 par.).

209   (b) BEFORE THE HIGH PRIEST (18:12-27). The evangelist has shaped the episode of Jesus' questioning before Annas, the "high priest," actually the former high priest whom the Romans had deposed in favor of Caiaphas, so that the lack of understanding shown by Peter's use of the sword in 18:10-11 pales beside his explicit denial of Jesus. Given the persecution faced by Johannine Christians, Peter must have served as a negative example for the Gospel's readers.

210   (i) *Jesus is brought to Annas* (18:12-14). While in Matt 26:57-68 and Mark 14:53-65 Jesus is brought to a formal trial, Luke 22:54,63-65, has an episode of mockery at the high priest's house before Jesus is led to the sanhedrin, where he is questioned about his messiahship, though no verdict is reached (Luke 22:66-71). **14.** *Caiaphas:* John has already recounted a "trial" by the sanhedrin (11:47-50). He may have known an independent tradition about Jesus being questioned at the house of the high priest and used it to set up the dramatic contrast between Peter's denial and Jesus' "confession" (R. T. Fortna, *NTS* 24 [1977-78] 371-83).

211   (ii) *Peter denies Jesus* (18:15-18). Peter's denial is even more striking in John than in the Synoptics because he is not a scared disciple, following along to see what happened to Jesus after all the others had fled. Nor does the setting suggest that Peter is in danger of his life if he answers truthfully. **15.** *another disciple:* Peter enters the house in the company of a disciple of Jesus who is known to the high priest. Though some exegetes think that this unnamed disciple was the Beloved Disciple, one would expect him to have been so designated if the evangelist had intended that we make such a connection (see F. Neirynck, *ETL* 51 [1975] 113-41).

212   (iii) *Annas interrogates Jesus* (18:19-24). **19.** *the high priest:* Annas's questions appear to represent an attempt to show that Jesus is a false prophet and leads the people astray (as charged in John 7:45-52). **20.** *answered him:* Jesus' answer appeals to the great controversies which make up his public ministry in the Gospel narrative. The reader will not miss the overtones of Jesus' mission in both testifying and bringing "the world" to judgment for its unbelief in Jesus' words, "I have spoken openly" (or "boldly," *parrhēsia*) "to the world." **21.** Jesus challenges Annas to answer his own questions by interrogating the crowds who heard him. Yet the reader of the Gospel knows that they did not really "hear" Jesus and that the true "witness" about the Son is the Father (5:30-40). **22.** *struck Jesus:* The physical attack and mockery of Jesus derive from the evangelist's source (cf. Mark 14:65). **23.** *Jesus answered:* The response is purely Johannine. Jesus has given a similar answer to those who attempted to stone him in 10:32, and he challenges "the Jews" to convict him of sin in 8:46. **24.** This verse shows that John knows of an interrogation before Caiaphas.

213   (iv) *Peter denies Jesus* (18:25-27). **25.** *Simon Peter:* Ironically, one of those who should be most able to "testify" to the "good" which Jesus has done will continue to deny that he has anything to do with him. The bold-faced lie involved in Peter's action is intensified by the fact that John has identified Peter as the disciple who cut off the slave's ear (v 10). **26.** *a kinsman:* Even when confronted by a relative of the wounded man, who is presumed to have witnessed the episode, Peter persists

in his denial (see C. H. Giblin, *Bib* 65 [1984] 210-31).

214   (c) TRIAL BY PILATE (18:28-19:16a). The trial before Pilate can be divided into scenes marked off by the alternations between "the accusers" outside and Jesus inside (18:29,33,38b; 19:1 [implied],4,8-9,13). Only in the last scene is Jesus brought "outside," still clothed in the "royal robes" of the soldiers' mockery. To increase the irony, 19:13 leaves it unclear whether Jesus or (more likely) Pilate sat on the judgment seat. Only when the Jews have renounced all kings but Caesar is Jesus handed over to "them" (another ambiguity), for crucifixion (19:15-16). The confession that Jesus is indeed "king of Israel" was made at the beginning and end of the narrative (1:49; 12:13,15). Jesus rejected the desire of the crowd to make him king (6:15). Now that Jesus has come to trial, the issue of his kingship can be raised. Since the reader knows that Jesus is "from God," the political issue of Jesus as "king" can only serve as an ironic mask for the real issue; rejection of the "king of Israel" is rejection of God. Just as earlier stories had been structured around ascending statements of belief, so the accusations made at the trial are forced to become sharper. They move from: (a) he is an "evildoer," whom we have no authority to kill (18:30); to (b) he made himself "Son of God" (19:7); to (c) he makes himself "king," implying rebellion against Caesar (19:12).

215   (i) *Scene one* (18:28-31[32]). The introductory scene contains several unresolved historical problems. **28.** *early:* In addition to the question of the day itself, v 1 suggests that Jesus was brought to Pilate around dawn. While some have suggested a symbolic reference to Jesus as light after all that has taken place during the "night," dawn would be a common time for the Roman governor to conduct such a hearing. But then the condemnation of Jesus at noon (19:14) seems out of order. Some suggest a symbolic reference to the slaughter of the Passover lambs. *did not enter:* There is no coherent explanation for the claim that the accusers would have been "defiled" by entering the praetorium. Mere contact with a Gentile in a legal setting would not have constituted such a defilement. **29.** *Pilate went out:* While a Roman governor could conduct a trial *extra ordinem* according to his own rules, the accused does have to be handed over with a more "formal charge" than that given by Jesus' accusers. **31.** There is much dispute over the question of whether this verse preserves an accurate piece of historical information. Jews were permitted to execute those Gentiles who violated the Temple precincts. Some Roman historians think that they are unlikely to have been allowed to carry out any other capital sentences, esp. in Judea. For the Johannine reader, this verse is highly ironic, since Jesus has already charged "the Jews" with acting against their own law in seeking to kill him (8:37-47); Nicodemus accuses them of condemning Jesus illegally (7:51). Now they show a sudden concern for "Caesar's law." **32.** The evangelist's comment reminds the reader that Jesus had predicted he would die by being "lifted up" (3:14-15; 12:32-33), i.e., crucified.

216   (ii) *Scene two* (18:33-38a). **33-34.** Jesus' exchange with Pilate about kingship is the final time that we hear the word "truth" in the Gospel. The reader already knows that Jesus testifies to the "truth" (5:33; 8:40,45,46) and that "the Jews" have rejected the truth (8:44), while the disciples receive it from Jesus (14:6; 17:17,19). The reader also knows that such dialogues between Jesus and an antagonist quickly turn to showing up the character of the latter. Pilate is not being "excused" for his role in the death of Jesus. **35.** *Am I a Jew?:* Pilate's scorn for the Jews is made evident. **36.** *my kingship:* Jesus' answer to the question separates his kingship from anything that could threaten Pilate, since he claims that it can be proved that his kingship is not of this world. He has no followers fighting to secure his release. At the same time, Jesus' reference to "the Jews" puts a gulf between himself and "the Jews," whom the reader knows have already rejected him. **37.** *you are a king then?:* Jesus must also testify to the truth. He was sent as "king," but Pilate's question, "What is truth?" shows that he is ranked with "the Jews" as one of those who cannot hear Jesus' voice.

217 (iii) *Scene three* (18:38b–40). Though Pilate cannot hear Jesus' words as those which reveal the truth, his actions can still create further levels of irony in the narrative. **39.** *you have a custom:* John uses the Barabbas episode, probably from a source (e.g., Mark 15:9,13), to confront the Jews with a choice: their real king or a "robber." The reader of the Gospel will recall that 10:1,8 contrasted the behavior of the true shepherd with that of "robbers." The term *lēstēs*, "robber," was often used for persons who stirred up rebellion, a charge that Jesus has explicitly denied. Pilate seems to have declared Jesus innocent in v 38b (so Luke 23:4). His scorn for the Jews may be reflected in the choice he offers them. The reader may also see this episode as an example of the type of "justice" for which the world is condemned (16:9–11). An innocent person is exchanged for one who is guilty.

218 (iv) *Scene four* (19:1–3). **1.** *flogged him:* Scourging a prisoner would normally have been part of the punishment, as it is in Mark 15:16–20 par. John has abbreviated and relocated the tradition of Jesus being flogged and mocked as "king" to the center of the trial so that for the rest of the proceedings he appears as "king."

219 (v) *Scene five* (19:4–7). Again Pilate claims to have found nothing for which to condemn Jesus and shows him to the people, with the comment, "Look, the man!" Directed toward Jesus, who has been beaten and is still attired in the crown and robe, the expression may be one of contempt for the wretched victim. Others have found a second meaning in the words, since normally a "new king" would be presented to his subjects in royal attire, his throne-name would be announced, and the people would offer cheers acclaiming their new ruler. It has been suggested that "the man" (*anthrōpos*, which can mean simply "human being") is an ironic throne-name derived from a prophecy in Zech 6:12, "Behold, a man whose name is branch." **6.** *crucify him:* Those who brought Jesus to Pilate demand his death. *take him yourselves:* For a second time, Pilate throws the case back at the Jews. **7.** They now specify the charge more precisely: according to their law Jesus ought to die for making himself "Son of God" (cf. 10:31–39). The issue of Jesus' claim to a special relationship with God is the one that has been contested throughout the Gospel (e.g., 5:18; 8:59).

220 (vi) *Scene six* (19:8–11). **8.** *feared even more:* The reason for Pilate's fear is not clear. It may be a reaction to the truth that Jesus is "Son of God" (cf. 18:6). **9.** *where are you from?:* The focus of controversies in 7:27–28; 8:14; 9:29–30. *gave him no answer:* While Jesus' silence before Pilate is taken from the tradition (e.g., Mark 15:5), the Johannine reader knows that it has a deeper significance. Jesus cannot reveal that truth to Pilate, who has already shown himself unable to "hear" Jesus' voice (see comment on 18:37). But Jesus can reply to Pilate's false claim to power. **11.** *unless it had been given from above:* Jesus' answer reminds the reader once again that his death is not the victory of his enemies but follows the divine plan (10:17–18). On the other hand, Jesus' willing self-offering does not exempt any of those involved in bringing about his death from sin.

221 (vii) *Scene seven* (19:12–16a). **12.** *if you release him, you are not Caesar's friend:* In later times, "friend of Caesar" was an honorific title bestowed on persons in recognition of their special service to the emperor. The circle around a Hellenistic king, known as "friends of the king," usually comprised persons of special influence. Coins of Herod Agrippa I bear an inscription *philokaisar*, "friend of Caesar." In order to compel Pilate to execute Jesus, the authorities have shifted away from their real charge against Jesus, religious claims, to a political charge that he "makes himself king" against Caesar, and they threaten to report Pilate as a "traitor" to the emperor. Pilate gains his revenge by forcing the Jews, whose original actions had been predicated on the claim that Jesus would bring Roman retaliation and destruction of their Temple (11:48,50), to renounce any king but Caesar. **14.** *look, your king!:* Pilate ironically repeats the "truth" that Jesus is "king." He also leaves the death sentence to be pronounced by the "Jews"—a sentence that the reader knows they had already passed (11:53; see D. Rensberger, *JBL* 103 [1984] 395–411).

222 (d) THE CRUCIFIXION OF JESUS (19:16b–30). As in the previous sections, John's account of the crucifixion goes its own way. The crucified is the exalted Son. There is no mockery by the crowd or abandonment. Instead, Jesus dies with his mother and the Beloved Disciple at the foot of the cross. In some incidents where John parallels the Synoptics, he emphasizes different elements of the story. Jesus carries his own cross (v 17); Pilate has deliberately formulated the charge on the cross (vv 19–22); Jesus' tunic was seamless, so that the soldiers had to cast lots for it (v 23); Jesus' thirst is predicted in Scripture (v 28); Jesus' death is described as "handing over" the Spirit (v 30).

223 (i) *The charge on the cross* (19:16b–22). John has none of the episodes associated with the journey to the place of crucifixion in the other Gospels. Either he had no tradition about such incidents as Simon being enlisted to carry Jesus' cross (e.g., Mark 15:21), or he chose to have Jesus carry his own cross as a sign that he was still in control of his fate. **19.** *the King of the Jews:* Instead of the inscription leading to mockery by the crowd (as in Mark 15:26–32), it provokes a final confrontation between Pilate and "the chief priests" (v 21). **22.** *what I have written . . . :* By insisting that his inscription will stand as written, Pilate affirms the truth about Jesus that Jesus' opponents desperately seek to reject. He also emphasizes the public and universal character of the inscription, since it could be read by all: Jews, Greeks, and Romans.

224 (ii) *At the foot of the cross* (19:23–27). Whereas the Synoptics have a number of words and actions take place around Jesus on the cross in which outsiders react to Jesus, John focuses on Jesus and "his own." They are not at a distance as are the women in Mark 15:40–41. **23.** *took his garments:* The evangelist has expanded the tradition that the soldiers divided Jesus' garments (Mark 15:24) into a double action of dividing the clothes and then rolling dice for the seamless tunic. This double action is then presented as fulfillment of the Scripture (Ps 22:19). **25.** Expansion of the garments-scene makes it a doublet with the second scene in which Jesus speaks to the Beloved Disciple and his own mother. In the Synoptic tradition the women who followed Jesus stood at a distance, and all the other disciples were in flight; John has the women at the foot of the cross. **27.** *behold your mother:* John 2:3–5,12 is the only other place where Jesus' mother is mentioned (see I. de la Potterie, "Das Wort Jesu, 'Siehe deine Mutter' und die Annahme der Mutter durch den Jünger," *Neues Testament und Kirche* [→ 97 above] 191–219). It is impossible to decide what the relationship is between this tradition that she comes under the care of the Beloved Disciple and that in Acts 1:14, which places her and the brothers of Jesus in the circle gathered around the Twelve. Nor is it entirely clear how much symbolism should be attached to the figure of the mother of Jesus. Clearly, entrusting the Beloved Disciple and his mother to each other shows that Jesus' mission is completed in the care and provision that Jesus has made for "his own." Other suggestions rely on importing symbols, which are not directly hinted at in this passage, such as that of a new Eve or of the messianic Zion giving birth to her children. Both interpretations of the passage became extremely prominent in the mariological piety of the 12th cent.

225 (iii) *Jesus dies* (19:28–30). Jesus remains in control of his death until the end. **28.** *I thirst:* His thirst, which John must have derived from his source, and the drink of vinegar are mentioned only to show that everything is accomplished. John does not actually cite the Scripture that is linked with that episode. Possibly he has Ps 69:22 in mind, though that psalm understands the offering of sour wine as a hostile gesture. Exegetes have also suggested that this gesture was understood in John as fulfilling the words about drinking the "cup" which the Father has given (John 18:11). **30.** *it is finished:* Announcing that his mission from the Father is now completed (cf. 8:29; 14:31; 16:32; 17:4), Jesus "hands over" his spirit. This expression once again reminds the reader that no one has "taken" Jesus' life. He has given his life willingly (e.g., 10:18).

226 (e) THE BURIAL OF JESUS (19:31–42). John's narrative shows considerable development in the burial account. Some of the details, like the soldiers' treatment of the body, may have come from John's source. Skeletal remains of a crucified man have suggested that the legs of victims might be broken near the time of death in order to hasten the process of suffocation. Verse 33 may correctly reflect that procedure. Others, like the authentication of the "blood and water" from the side of Jesus may have found their way into the Gospel as part of its final editing (vv 34b–35).

227 (i) *Authorities certify his death* (19:31–37). This section appears to be based on a source, which comprises vv 31 (without the explanation about the sabbath), 32–34,36,37(?). **34.** *blood and water:* In the original story, these elements, flowing from the side of the victim, may have simply been a detail of a martyr story. 4 Macc 9:20 has blood and water flow out of the side of one of the martyrs. However, the Gospel has already interpreted "water" as the Spirit, which the glorified Jesus will bestow on his followers (John 7:39). **35.** This verse has been attached to that detail by its final editor. It sets the groundwork for the affirmation made in 1 John 5:6–7 that makes the "blood" (death) of Jesus necessary for salvation (also 1 John 1:7). **36–37.** The passage is unusual in having two Scripture citations at the end. The second, Zech 12:10, can only apply to the detail given in this tradition, that the soldiers pierced Jesus' side. It may have been added by the evangelist in order to provide a citation for each of the soldiers' actions. If the citation came from the source, then as in Rev 1:7 it must have referred to the crucifixion as "piercing." The people will see the crucified one (in judgment). For John, the judgment has already been accomplished in Jesus' death. The citation does not function as an oracle of judgment against the people. The source of the first citation is not as clear. If the passage intended to parallel Jesus with the Passover lamb then the rule against breaking the lamb's bones would be its origin (Exod 12:10 LXX; 12:46; Num 9:12). If the author just looks to the image of the suffering righteous one, then one of the psalms

traditionally associated with the passion may be the source of the citation (e.g., Ps 22:19 [John 19:24]; 69:22 [John 19:28]).

228 (ii) *Joseph and Nicodemus bury Jesus* (19:38–42). The account of Jesus' burial by Joseph appears to have been derived from a different tradition than the previous story. Here, Joseph is responsible for obtaining the body from Pilate. There is no reference to the actions by the "Jews" in the previous account (cf. Mark 15:42–45). Mark makes Joseph a member of the sanhedrin who is seeking the kingdom; in John he is a secret disciple (12:42). **39.** *Nicodemus:* Some think that the figure of Nicodemus originally came into the Johannine tradition through this story. The evangelist reminds the reader that this is the Nicodemus of the earlier episode (3:1–12; 7:50–51). *myrrh and aloes:* The large amount of spices (cf. the amount of precious ointment used by Mary in 12:3) may have been intended as a sign of the great honor due to Jesus. **40.** *linen cloths:* Unlike the tradition in Mark 15:46, which presumes that the body was placed in a single linen shroud, John's tradition holds that it was anointed and wrapped in strips of linen (as was Lazarus 11:43–44). **41.** *a new tomb:* The detail that the tomb was in a nearby garden and had never been used may have come into the story as a piece of resurrection apologetic: when Mary and the disciples went there on Easter morning, they could not have been mistaken about the location of the tomb.

229 (C) **Jesus is Raised** (20:1–29). All four Gospels report that women visiting Jesus' tomb found it empty (cf. Mark 16:1–8). Matt 28:9–10 appends an appearance of the Lord to the women. Though the tradition that the Lord appeared to the disciples is very ancient (1 Cor 15:3b–5), the narratives of appearances are so divergent that it is difficult to assess the probable antiquity of individual accounts. John 20:1–29 embodies three types of tradition: (1) finding the tomb empty (vv 1–2,11–13); (2) confirmation of the report about the tomb by Peter (vv 3–10; cf. Luke 24:12,24); (3) stories of appearances of Christ to disciples (vv 14–18,19–23, 24–28 [?]). Inconsistencies in the narrative make it evident that the evangelist has edited earlier sources (see F. Neirynck, *NTS* 30 [1984] 161–87). In 20:1 Mary Magdalene comes to the tomb alone, but her report in v 2 uses the plural "we," appropriate to traditions in which several women visited the tomb. When Mary is back at the tomb in v 11, she had apparently not yet looked inside, though she had reported the body stolen in v 2. As in the Synoptic accounts, Mary sees angels in the tomb (v 12), but they do not deliver the Easter message. Mary is already facing Jesus (vv 14–15), when she is again said to turn toward him (v 16). When Peter and the Beloved Disciple had looked into the tomb (vv 6–7), they saw the grave clothes but no angels. The evangelist appears to have added the Beloved Disciple to the story about Peter checking the tomb (see R. Mahoney, *Two Disciples at the Tomb* [Bern, 1974]). In v 2 a second "to . . ." phrase is added to accommodate him. Verse 3 begins, "Peter went out," then adds reference to the Beloved Disciple and shifts to a pl. vb., "they were coming." The description of the contents of the tomb is duplicated (vv 5 and 6). The faith ascribed to the Beloved Disciple in v 8 has no relationship to the action. Verse 9 asserts that "they did not understand."

The appearance of Jesus to Thomas in John 20:24–29 has no analogies elsewhere. The physical demonstration that the risen One is identical with the crucified Jesus appears in the appearance to the disciples in Luke 24:39–43. The evangelist may have created the Thomas scene out of such a tradition.

230 (a) THE EMPTY TOMB (20:1–10). Whereas

the Synoptics have an expanded account of the women coming to the tomb, finding it open, Jesus' body missing, and receiving the Easter kerygma and a message for Jesus' disciples (Mark 16:1–8a par.; Luke 24:12,24 refer to a visit by Peter or some disciples to check the report), John has a brief account of Mary's discovery followed by a more lengthy account of Peter and the Beloved Disciple at the tomb. The structural parallel to their visit is the second episode in which Mary encounters the risen Lord (vv 11–18). This episode also contains details that were associated with the finding of the empty tomb in the other traditions: the angelic figures, and the message to deliver to the disciples. For the Fourth Gospel, neither the tomb nor the appearances carry the full meaning of Easter. Jesus' mission is completed only in his return to the Father and the glory that he had "before the foundation of the world" (20:17; 3:13; 6:51; 7:33; 13:2–3; 14:4, 28; 16:5,17,28; 17:13). The Spirit comes when Jesus has been glorified (7:39; 16:7).

231   **1.** *Mary Magdalene:* One of the group standing at the foot of the cross in 19:25. She is the first named in the list of women who come to the tomb in the Synoptics (e.g., Mark 16:1; Matt 28:1; Luke 24:10). The pl. in v 2 suggests that John's source had several women come to the tomb. He may have reduced the number to Mary Magdalene to fit the tradition in which she sees the risen Lord. *while it was still dark:* Reference to dawn on the day after the sabbath is traditional. The evangelist may have added darkness to incorporate the scene into the light symbolism of the Gospel. Since the anointing of Jesus was completed in the Johannine burial scene, it is not a motive for her visit (cf. Mark 16:1; Luke 24:1). Some exegetes think that this short episode represents the most primitive tradition of the finding of the empty tomb, since the stone is moved away, but there are no elements of angelophany in either this story or the visit by Peter. The disciples will not have any understanding of the significance of these events until the risen Lord has appeared to them. **2.** *they have taken the Lord from the tomb:* Mary expresses concern three times that Jesus' body had been taken (vv 2,13,15). In the first episode in the Johannine burial account the body is released to the custody of "the Jews" (19:31). While John's source may have taken Mary's concern as evidence that the disciples had not robbed the tomb (cf. Matt 28:13–15), the evangelist may intend the reader to think that "the Jews" could have removed Jesus' body. "Fear of the Jews" is mentioned both in the story of the actual burial (19:38) and in connection with the disciples gathered in hiding (20:19,26). *we do not know where they have laid him:* The report can then be seen as an echo of the earlier references to not knowing "where" Jesus is going in the controversies with the Jews (7:11,22; 8:14,28,42) as well as the disciples' ignorance of "where" Jesus is going in the farewell discourses (13:33; 14:1–5; 16:5). The Gospel has already given two answers to the question of where Jesus is going. He returns to the Father (13:1–3; 14:12,28; 17:21–26) and to "abide with" his disciples (14:3,18,20, 23,28). Some exegetes have also proposed a final Mosaic theme in these verses, since no one knows where Moses is buried (Deut 34:10). Any objections to Jesus as Mosaic prophet would be answered by these verses. He does "remain forever" (e.g., John 12:34; see P. Minear, *Int* 30 [1976] 125–39).

232   **3.** *Peter with the other disciple:* Though the evangelist appears responsible for inserting the figure of the Beloved Disciple into this story, it is possible that one version of the tradition had an unspecified group of disciples visit the tomb. Just as the Beloved Disciple was closest to Jesus at the supper (13:25), so his exemplary love for Jesus leads him to arrive at the tomb first (v 4)

5. *did not go in:* By delaying his entry into the tomb, the evangelist makes the Beloved Disciple's affirmation of faith the climax of the visit. **7.** *the napkin . . . not lying with the linen cloths:* The positioning of the grave clothes shows that the body had not been stolen. **9.** *the Scripture:* The original conclusion of the episode probably left the disciples perplexed. As is characteristic of the early creed in 1 Cor 15:4, Jesus' resurrection is spoken of as fulfilling Scriptures, but there is no indication of which OT passage was applied to this expectation. Until Jesus' glorification is complete, the disciples will not be able to "remember" and understand the significance of the events which have occurred (e.g., 14:25–26; 16:12–15). The Beloved Disciple is introduced as an example of faith which immediately perceives the truth of the resurrection events (also 21:7). He serves as a sharp contrast to the doubts expressed by Thomas (20:24–29).

233   (b) THE LORD APPEARS TO MARY MAGDALENE (20:11–18).   The appearance of angels in the tomb (v 12) and the mission to report the resurrection to the disciples (v 17) are both part of the empty-tomb tradition. In Matt 28:9–10 the risen Christ appears to the women as they are leaving the tomb and repeat the message given them by the angels. In that episode the women fall down before the Lord and grasp his feet in a gesture of worship (v 9). Here, Jesus prohibits a similar gesture by forbidding Mary to touch him, since his return to the Father is not yet complete (v 17). This verse is also the only place in which the disciples are referred to as "brothers," an expression used in Matt 28:10. The evangelist has reworked a traditional story in which the risen Christ appeared either to Mary Magdalene alone or in the company of the other women near the tomb. He has recast the resurrection message so that it is clear that Jesus' return is not to the disciples in the various appearance stories. His return (14:18–19; 16:22) is his exaltation to his place with the Father (e.g., 3:13; 6:62). **11–16.** The double scene with the angels and Jesus enables the evangelist to emphasize the fact that the body of Jesus has not been taken. It forms the prelude to forbidding Mary to cling to the risen Lord as though that were the substance of resurrection faith. **17.** *I am ascending:* John sees Jesus' crucifixion, resurrection, exaltation, and return to heavenly glory as part of a single event (12:32–33). One is not to think of Jesus' resurrection as though Jesus had returned to life and then later ascended into heaven. Rather, Jesus has passed into an entirely different reality. John 14:22–23 answers the question of how Jesus will manifest himself to the disciples and not to the world in terms of love and the indwelling presence of Father and Son with the disciples. The message which Jesus sends to the disciples is cast in Johannine terms. They are now the "children" of God (1:12). **18.** *I have seen the Lord:* Mary's report uses traditional resurrection language rather than that of the farewell discourses or the ascent/return schema in the Gospel.

234   (c) THE LORD APPEARS TO THE DISCIPLES (20:19–23).   The evangelist has taken a traditional account of Jesus' appearance to the disciples in Jerusalem to show that the promises of Jesus' return were being fulfilled in the "hour" of his exaltation/glorification (cf. Luke 24:36–43,47–48). **19.** *fear of the Jews:* The evangelist has added this phrase to the introduction of the story. Jesus' sudden appearance in the midst of the disciples gathered in the room and the greeting "Peace" are both derived from the tradition (cf. Luke 24:36, accepting the longer reading, which includes the "peace" formula). **20.** *showed them:* Demonstration that the risen One is the crucified was also part of the tradition (e.g., Luke 24:39). Within the context of the Johannine narrative, this demonstration also answers the question, "Where have they put him?" "They" (= the Jews?) have not put the body of Jesus anywhere. It is taken into the heavenly glory of the exalted Jesus. The disciples' joy fulfills the promises of renewed joy (14:19; 16:16–24). 21. *Peace:* Also a promised gift (14:27). Commissioning of the disciples appears in other stories of Jesus' resurrection appearances (e.g., Luke 24:47–48; Matt 28:19–20a). Here it takes the Johannine form of "sending" the disciples who now represent Jesus to the world (e.g., John 13:16,20; 17:18). 22–23. *Receive the Holy Spirit. If you forgive anyone's sins . . . :* This instruction appears to be derived from the evangelist's source, since the words are not used in the Gospel. There the Spirit is one expression of divine indwelling (14:17) and flows from the exalted Jesus as a source of eternal life (7:39). Luke 24:47–49 links the commissioning of the disciples as "witnesses," their preaching forgiveness, and the Spirit, which is to be received on Pentecost. 1 John shows that the Johannine tradition did speak of forgiveness of sins (e.g., 1:9; 2:19), but the Gospel speaks only of the "sin" of disbelief (8:24; 9:41). The double formula parallels the saying on binding and loosing in Matt 18:18; 16:19. Since John uses only the general expression "disciples," the commissioning in these verses may be intended to apply to the believing community as a whole, not to some specific group within that community such as "the Twelve." This "power" of forgiveness is probably expressed in the bestowing of the Spirit on those who believe as a result of the disciples' "mission" and who join the community rather than in a process of dealing with Christians who have committed sin (as in Matt 18:19).

235   (d) THE LORD APPEARS TO THOMAS (20:24–29). While Luke 24:41–43 lengthened the demonstration of Jesus' physical identity with the crucified in response to disbelief, John creates a separate story of Jesus' appearance to Thomas (→ NT Thought, 81:128). Verse 25 draws on v 20, and v 26 paraphrases v 19. The remaining elements of the scene are all characteristically Johannine: (a) the summons to become a believer (v 27); (b) Thomas's confession, "my Lord and my God" (v 28); (c) the blessing on future believers (v 29). Thomas's confession is the culmination of the Gospel's christology, since it acknowledges the crucified/exalted Jesus as "Lord and God" (cf. other acclamations in the Gospel, 1:49; 4:42; 6:69; 9:37–38; 11:27; 16:30). Thomas is reprimanded for demanding such a sign before he will believe (v 25; cf. 4:48). He should believe on the basis of the word which has been spoken to him by others (e.g., 17:20). 29. *blessed are . . . :* The concluding blessing insists that all those Christians who have believed without seeing have a faith which is in no way different from that of the first disciples. Their faith is grounded in the presence of the Lord through the Spirit.

236   **(D) Conclusion: The Purpose of the Gospel (20:30–31).** These verses are similar to the conclusions in John 21:24–25 and 1 John 5:13. They appear to have stood as the conclusion to the Gospel before the edition which appended chap. 21. 30. *many other signs:* This verse characterizes the content of the work as "signs," which has led some to suggest that it was originally the conclusion to the collection of miracles used by the evangelist. In that context Jesus' resurrection would have been understood as the final "sign" of his relationship with the Father, though the evangelist seems to limit the "signs" to the miracles which structure Jesus' testimony before the world in the first part of the Gospel (e.g., 12:37). Verse 31 then summarizes the purpose of the Gospel as having fatih in Jesus as Messiah

and Son of God as the source of eternal life (e.g., 3:15–16,36).

237   **(IV) Epilogue: The Lord Appears in Galilee (21:1–25).** This chapter has drawn on several pieces of independent tradition: an appearance of the risen Lord by the Sea of Tiberias (cf. Matt 28:16–18; → Biblical Geography, 73:60–61), a miraculous catch of fish (cf. Luke 5:1–11), a meal scene (cf. Luke 24:30–31,41–43), the commissioning of Peter (cf. Luke 5:10b; Matt 16:18), the prediction of Peter's martyrdom and the fate of the Beloved Disciple (cf. Matt 10:23; 16:28; Mark 9:1; 13:30). These pieces of tradition have been brought together around Peter as the central figure. His relationship to Jesus as a primary witness to the resurrection, as a missionary, as a shepherd of the sheep, as a martyr, and his relationship to the Beloved Disciple are all spelled out in these stories. Though the author of John 21 presupposes the stories in chap. 20 (e.g., vv 1,14; as well as the reference to Thomas as *Didymos* in v 2, cf. 20:24), the Gospel itself does not call for such a continuation. The decidedly ecclesial focus of chap. 21 with its emphasis on recognition of the risen Lord in a meal and the role of Peter in relationship to Jesus' sheep has led to the suggestion that it reflects a final editing of the Gospel in light of the crisis of the period of the epistles. It may represent an accommodation between Johannine Christianity, which had seen Jesus' "own" entrusted to the Beloved Disciple (19:26–27) and the Petrine authority recognized in other churches (so R. E. Brown, *Community* 161–62; H. Thyen, "Entwicklungen innerhalb der johanneischen Theologie und Kirche im Spiegel Joh 21," *L'Evangile de Jean* [ed. M. de Jonge; BETL 44; Gembloux, 1977] 259–99). Verses 24–25 have been added as a conclusion to the whole.

238   **(A) Appearances beside the Sea of Galilee (21:1–14).** Verses 1 and 14 have been used to incorporate this material into the Gospel narrative, which already included appearances in Jerusalem. An early tradition held that Jesus appeared in Galilee (Mark 16:7), but the only other narrative associated with such an appearance is the commissioning scene on a mountain in Matt 28:16–20. The fishing scene in John's tradition has ties to the Lucan story of a miraculous catch and the commissioning of Peter as "fisher of men" (Luke 5:1–11). It has sometimes been assumed that Luke's story is a misplaced resurrection story (see *FGL* 561). Although that view brings the Lucan and Johannine traditions into closer proximity, the independent development of the Johannine tradition makes it equally probable that the two traditions have developed a story of a miraculous catch in different contexts.

239   (a) THE MIRACULOUS CATCH (21:2–8,10–11). 2. *Simon Peter, Thomas . . . :* The list of names may also stem from the editor of the Gospel, since both Thomas and Nathanael are identified for the reader in terms of their identities in the Gospel. 3. *I am going fishing:* The decision to go fishing, not surprising if the story had originally been about the first (only?) appearance to Peter and the disciples, now seems awkward, since the commissioning in 20:21 is apparently ignored. 4. The theme of nonrecognition, typical of appearance stories (e.g., John 20:15; Luke 24:14–15), is also better suited to an independent appearance story. Several details of the catch have parallels in the Lucan miracle story: disciples have been fishing all night with no success; Jesus' command to cast the nets; the great haul of fish; Peter's spontaneous reaction to the haul; fish as symbolic of the mission; and reference to the condition of the net. However, the stories diverge in the location of the boat, the position of Jesus with regard to the boat, the nature of Peter's reaction, the actual condition of the net, and the presence of other boats to help with the catch. **7.** *it is the Lord!:* John has made the Beloved Disciple's recognition of the stranger on the shore the motive for Peter's action. Some exegetes draw a parallel with the Mary Magdalene scene; she recognizes the Lord when he calls her name (20:16). Jesus has addressed the disciples with the Johannine community's self-designation, "children" (v 5; cf. 1 John 2:13,18; 3:7). **10.** *bring some of the fish:* This contradicts v 9, but links the catch to the meal scene. **11.** *153 fish:* The symbolism of the 153 fish is disputed. The parallel with the Lucan story suggests that it refers to the universality of the mission (cf. 10:16). The narrator may have emphasized the fact that the net did not break to point to the unity of these diverse believers in contrast to the divisions over Jesus that had occurred in the unbelieving crowds (e.g., 7:43; 9:16; 10:19).

240   (b) The Meal (21:9,12-14). The story of the miraculous catch becomes a resurrection appearance story in combination with the tradition that Jesus is recognized in a meal. In Luke 24:43 Jesus himself eats some fish to dispel doubts. In Luke 24:30 Jesus opens the disciples' eyes by blessing, breaking, and distributing bread. Bread and fish were the food blessed in the feeding miracle of John 6:9. Other echoes of that scene may be found in the fact that both meals take place by the Sea of Tiberias (the only times it is mentioned in the Gospel) and the action of Jesus in taking and giving the food to his disciples (v 13). John 6:11 has Jesus distribute the food to the crowd. It seems likely, then, that recognition at the meal would remind the Johannine reader of Jesus' presence at the eucharistic meal (see R. Pesch, *Der reiche Fischfang: Lk 5,1-11/Jo 21,1-14: Wundergeschichte — Berufungserzählung — Erscheinungsbericht* [Düsseldorf, 1969]).

241   (B) Jesus' Words about Peter and the Beloved Disciple (21:15-23). At the supper, Peter's question about the betrayer was placed through the Beloved Disciple (13:23-25); whereas Peter had denied the Lord, the Beloved Disciple was present at the cross to receive/be received by Jesus' mother (19:26-27); the Beloved Disciple reaches the tomb first and has faith in the risen Lord without having seen him (20:4-8); the Beloved Disciple recognizes the Lord on the shore and thus provides the occasion for Peter to go to him (21:7). But in this section, Peter's role as shepherd and martyr is established by the risen Lord. The Beloved Disciple's special position is acknowledged but also apparently ended with his death.

242   (a) Peter, Shepherd and Martyr (21:15-19). **15-17.** *Simon, son of John, do you love me?:* Peter reverses his triple denial in 18:17,25-26. Luke 22:31-34 associates a prediction that Peter would "turn and strengthen his brothers" with Jesus' prediction of the denial at the supper. This turning is often linked to Peter's position as the first to see the Lord (e.g., 1 Cor 15:4; Luke 24:34), a tradition that was never narrated unless the appearance story in John 21:1-14 goes back to a story of an appearance just to Peter. The Gospel links loving Jesus with keeping his commands (14:15; 15:10). Here the command establishes Peter as the one to "feed" and "shepherd" Jesus' sheep. This tradition seems to presume

the development of an ecclesial office of "overseer." Shepherding the flock is also used for bishops and elders in 1 Pet 5:2-4 and Acts 20:28. The Gospel had emphasized Jesus' own concern for his flock, which had been entrusted to him by God (10:3-4,14,27-30; 17:6,9-12). Peter is now entrusted with those concerns. A related Petrine tradition is preserved in the saying about Peter as "rock" in Matt 16:18-19, which many exegetes think was also taken from a postresurrection commissioning scene. **18.** *I say to you:* Jesus now declares that Peter will fulfill his earlier promise (13:37-38) to follow Jesus even to death. *1 Clem.* 5:4 testifies to the fact that Peter had suffered death as a martyr under Nero. *when you were young, you girded yourself and went where you wished, but when you are old . . . :* A proverbial saying. The narrator's comment in v 19 interprets it as a reference to Peter's death. However, it is unclear whether "stretching out your hands" simply refers to the act of being bound as a prisoner or whether the narrator has the tradition that Peter was crucified in mind. That tradition is not attested until Tertullian (*Scorpiace* 15.3).

243   (b) The Beloved Disciple (21:20-23). This section is built around an older saying of Jesus that applied to the Beloved Disciple a tradition similar to the sayings about the Son of Man coming before all of Jesus' generation had seen death (v 22; cf. Mark 9:1). The narrator has created a rather lengthy introduction in v 21 to remind the reader of the special relationship between Jesus and the Beloved Disciple. Peter's mission will include glorifying God as martyr (vv 22b,19), but the Beloved Disciple did not die a martyr's death. The Johannine community used "remain" in a variety of senses. It can refer to the new relationship between the disciples and the Father/Son. Here it is the occasion for misunderstanding. **23.** *the saying:* This verse tells the reader that a saying had been going around that the Beloved Disciple would not die. The narrator corrects that misunderstanding in light of the fact that the Beloved Disciple has died. He may have intended the reader to understand that the Beloved Disciple does "remain" with the community in the Spirit-inspired interpretation of the tradition, which goes back to his testimony and is the foundation of the Gospel.

244   (C) Conclusion: Testimony to Jesus (21:24-25). The concluding words of the Gospel remind the reader that the Gospel owes its truth to the testimony which the Beloved Disciple had given to Jesus (cf. 19:35). **24.** *these things:* They need not refer to the whole Gospel, but may imply that the oral tradition stemming from the Beloved Disciple and perhaps some written embodiment of that tradition underlie the Gospel. The author of these words asserts that the Beloved Disciple's testimony was true in a phrasing very much like that used for the truth of Jesus' testimony in the Gospel (e.g., 5:31-32). **25.** *many other things:* This verse may have been added by yet another hand. It is clearly dependent on 20:30, though without its christological focus. Some have suggested that it serves to justify the additional material that had been included in the Gospel.

62

THE JOHANNINE EPISTLES

Pheme Perkins

BIBLIOGRAPHY

1 Balz, H. D., "Die Johannesbriefe," *Die katholischen Briefe* (NTD 10; 11th ed.; Göttingen, 1973) 150–216. Bogart, J., *Orthodox and Heretical Perfectionism* (SBLDS 33; 1977). Bonnard, P., *Les épîtres johanniques* (Geneva, 1983). Brown, R. E., *The Epistles of John* (AB 30; GC, 1982). Brox, N., "'Doketismus'—eine Problemanzeige," *ZKG* 95 (1984) 301–14. Bultmann, R., *The Johannine Epistles* (Herm; Phl, 1973). Cooper, E. J., "The Consciousness of Sin in 1 John," *LTP* 28 (1972) 237–48. Dodd, C. H., *The Johannine Epistles* (MNTC; London, 1946). Grayston, K., *The Johannine Epistles* (NCB; GR, 1984). Houlden, J. L., *A Commentary on the Johannine Epistles* (HNTC; NY, 1973).

Malatesta, E., *Interiority and Covenant* (AnBib 69; Rome, 1978). Marshall, I. H., *The Epistles of John* (NICNT; GR, 1978). Nauck, W., *Die Tradition und der Charakter des ersten Johannesbriefes* (WUNT 3; Tübingen, 1957). O'Neill, J. C., *The Puzzle of 1 John* (London, 1966). Schnackenburg, R., *Die Johannesbriefe* (HTKNT 13; 3d ed.; Freiburg, 1965; Suppl. 5th ed. 1975). Smalley, S. S., *1,2,3 John* (WBC 51; Waco, 1984). Wengst, K., *Häresie und Orthodoxie im Spiegel des ersten Johannesbriefes* (Gütersloh, 1976).

DBSup 4. 797–815. *IDBSup* 486–87. Kümmel, *INT* 434–52. Wik-Schm, *ENT* 613–30.

INTRODUCTION

2 **(I) Relationship of the Epistles.** The Johannine Epistles represent different types of communication between churches. 2 and 3 John are short letters from a person called "the presbyter" to other communities. 2 John prohibits association between members of the church and a separatist group of Johannine Christians. 3 John seeks to secure hospitality for missionaries associated with the presbyter from Gaius after another leading Christian, Diotrephes, had refused it. Parallel phrasing in the opening ("whom I love in truth," 2 John 1; 3 John 1; "I rejoiced greatly to find . . . following truth," 2 John 4, 3 John 3), and closing (2 John 12; 3 John 13) shows that the letters are by the same person.

1 John is not a letter but an exhortation to Johannine Christians (→ NT Epistles, 45:16). No designation is given for the author. He speaks as the authoritative representative of a group of "witnesses" to the true Johannine tradition (1 John 1:4). 1 John warns the community against the views of the dissidents. The opponents are castigated for failing to observe the commandment of love, for being deceivers and antichrists, for not acknowledging "the coming of Jesus Christ in the flesh" (2 John 5–7; 1 John 2:7; 5:3; 3:7; 2:23; 4:2; 2:18). Some exegetes hold that the awkwardness of expression in 2 John implies that it was not written by the author of 1 John but by one of the other Johannine teachers referred to by the "we" of 1 John 1:4. (Compare the charge

against those who have "gone beyond" the teaching in 2 John 9 with the parallel in 1 John 2:23–25.) Others attribute the difference to the fact that 2 John is a private letter, not a public exhortation.

The severity of the action against the dissidents recommended in 2 John 10–11 is only intelligible in light of the crisis among Johannine Christians found in 1 John. Therefore, the most common view of the relationship between these letters should be maintained. 1 John was composed prior to 2 John. Some scholars think that a copy of 1 John might have been sent to those addressed in 2 John. 3 John could have been written at any time during this period, since it does not address the issue of the dissidents directly. Many exegetes presume that missionaries from the author's group were being denied hospitality because of the confusion created by dissident preaching.

3 **(II) Authorship, Date, and Community Setting.** Although the epistles have traditionally been attributed to the author of the Fourth Gospel, their lack of authoritative status in the first two centuries suggests that they were not always closely associated with the Gospel. 1 John is only clearly cited in the West and the East at the end of the 2d cent. 2 John also received acceptance by AD 200. Mid-3d cent. is the earliest attestation for 3 John (see *BEJ* 5–13).

Comparisons between 1 John and the Fourth Gospel suggest that 1 John (and consequently 2 and 3 John) was not by the author of the Gospel. In some instances, 1 John appears to reach back to theological traditions from the Johannine community that did not play a significant part in the Gospel or to use traditions in a less theologically developed way than the Gospel does. As a result, it is sometimes claimed that 1 John should be considered earlier than the Gospel.

The decisive argument against making 1 John early lies in the community setting which it presupposes. The Fourth Gospel addresses itself to the challenges posed by Judaism and others outside Johannine circles who have rejected the community's vision of Jesus as preexistent Son, sent by the Father. The epistles describe the fracturing of the Johannine community itself. Further, the shock of that breakup, the priority of the command to love one another, and the persistent appeals to remain with "what you have heard from the beginning" are only intelligible in light of the shape that the Johannine tradition had taken in the Fourth Gospel.

Therefore, many exegetes propose that 1 John was composed to provide a framework for understanding the tradition in the Gospel. Some identify the author of 1 John as the Johannine teacher who did the final editing of the Gospel materials. They detect his hand in such editorial touches as the emphasis on "blood and water" at the crucifixion (John 19:34b–35; cf. the emphasis on the testimony of blood and water in 1 John 5:6). This view, however, suggests that the canonical form of the Fourth Gospel and 1 John represent a unified theological perspective.

If the Gospel stems from *ca.* AD 90, the epistles would represent the situation of the Johannine communities *ca.* AD 100. It seems difficult to push their composition much later. Writing around AD 110, Ignatius of Antioch opposes Christians in Asia Minor who deny the importance of Jesus as a human being by advocating a docetic christology, one which denies that the divine Savior really took on humanity. The opponents of the epistles do not seem to have reached such a theoretical position. Ignatius reflects an Asia Minor in which the Petrine episcopacy has become the norm for community organization. The Johannine communities of the letters lack such centralized authority. The community seems to have had established teachers and may have designated such persons "presbyters." But the author of 1 John cannot appeal to an apostolic office to ground his claims to be the true teacher of the tradition. The community must acknowledge that what the author writes represents what they have heard from the beginning (→ Johannine Theology, 83:14).

Some scholars have suggested that the emphasis on Peter's rehabilitation in John 21:15–19 enabled Johannine Christians to acknowledge the authority of the presbyter-bishop. In the rest of the Fourth Gospel, only Jesus (or the Paraclete) guides the community (10:1–18); only he lays down his life for the sheep (10:14–18). The shepherd image was a popular one for the presbyter-bishop in Asia Minor (Acts 20:28; 1 Pet 5:2; Ign. *Rom* 9:1). If this section stems from the final editor of the Gospel, then he would appear to have a different solution to the crisis from 1 John (see *BEJ* 110–12) and would accept church office modeled on the example of Jesus as shepherd.

4   (III) Relationship to the Fourth Gospel. The view that the epistles were written after the traditions in the Fourth Gospel had taken shape (though perhaps not their final form) seems best suited to the community setting presupposed by the Gospel and the epistles. Though it is difficult to speak of any passage in 1 John as a direct quotation of the Gospel, the persuasive power of many of the passages in 1 John depends on echoing what is clearly established in the Gospel as the Johannine tradition. For example, 1 John 1:1–4 alludes to both the prologue of the Fourth Gospel, in which Jesus is light and life from the Father made manifest (1:1–18), and to elements in the farewell discourses of the Gospel such as the importance of the disciples as Jesus' witnesses "from the beginning" (15:27). In the Gospel, Jesus' discourses are spoken "so that your joy may be full" (15:11). Here the author writes so that the audience will "have fellowship with us" and "our joy may be complete."

Some scholars are troubled by the difference in theological elaboration between the Gospel and 1 John. In contrast to the Gospel, 1 John omits any direct mention of the glory of Jesus. Even the stress on his identity with God is missing in 1 John. Often the theological language of 1 John appears to derive from the type of tradition which the Gospel had moved beyond or reformulated. For example, "Paraclete" (1 John 2:1) refers to Jesus as heavenly advocate rather than to the "return" of Jesus realized in the coming of the Paraclete as a permanent presence guiding the community. The titles used for Jesus are Righteous One (1 John 2:7–8), Messiah (2:22), and Son (1:3; 3:23). Rather than find in Jesus' cross the revelation of his "glory," 1 John reaches back to the older tradition of the death of Jesus as expiation (1:7; 2:2; 3:16; 4:10).

5   Such differences have led some to argue that 1 John was written earlier than or in the context of one of the later sections (such as crises reflected in the farewell discourse) of the Gospel. The following sections have been proposed as preliminary versions of material which received its final shape in the Gospel: (1) 1:1–4, as preliminary to the prologue of the Gospel; (2) 2:20,25 and 3:22, teaching about the Spirit; (3) 3:12–13, Judas; (4) 3:18, a parenetic attack on speech which is dropped in the Gospel's picture of the power of speech; (5) 3:23 on believing; (6) 4:14, the world; (7) 5:14–17, asking anything of Christ, and (8) 5:20–21, true knowledge of God (see Grayston, *Epistles* 12–14).

However, the number of passages in 1 John that are intelligible only on the presumption that the author and audience are familiar with formulations in the Gospel (see *BEJ* 19–35 755–59) makes it difficult to sustain such proposals. The farewell discourses appear to have played a particularly important role in establishing the images on which 1 John draws. 1 John echoes the relationships between God (Father, Son, Spirit) and the Christian: the Father loves the Christian (John 14:21; 1 John 4:16); the Son abides in the faithful Christian (John 15:4; 1 John 3:24); gift of the Spirit (John 14:16–17; 1 John 4:13). Important factors in the way in which the Christian relates to God are: mutual indwelling (John 14:20; 1 John 3:24); forgiveness (John 15:3; 1 John 1:9); eternal life (John 17:2; 1 John 2:29); righteousness (John 16:10; 1 John 2:29). Basic conditions for Christian discipleship are reasserted: the believer is not "in sin" (unlike the unbelieving "world," John 16:8–9; unlike the false perfectionism of the dissidents, 1 John 1:8; 3:4–9); one must love Jesus, keep commandments (John 14:15; 1 John 2:3 ["know him" instead of love]; 3:10, 22–24); reject behavior that is "of the world" (John 15:18, world's hatred of believers; 1 John 2:15, not "love the world"; 4:1, false spirits gone out into world); belief "overcomes the world" (John 17:8–9; 1 John 2:13–14; 5:5). (See Smalley, *1,2,3 John* xxx.)

It has been suggested that 1 John has followed the structure of the Gospel. After a prologue that echoes the Gospel (1 John 1:1–4), there are two major sections in the epistle. The first, parenesis on the obligation to "walk in the light" (1 John 1:5–3:10) reflects the "book of signs" (John 1–12). Walking in light, the authentic response to the Gospel that has been preached "from the beginning" separates Johannine Christians from the dissidents. The second section, on the obligation of mutual love (1 John 3:11–5:12), reflects the "book of glory" (John 13–21), esp. the farewell discourses, in which the love commandment is established and Jesus' death is presented as the exemplary embodiment of divine love. A concluding statement of the author's purpose also parallels the Gospel (cf. John 20:30–31 and 1 John 5:13). (See BEJ 124–25, 765.) However, only the introduction and the statement of purpose echo language of the Gospel directly. One might expect the Gospel to be echoed in the transition between the two sections of the body of 1 John, though it might be proposed that the concluding judgment on the world which does not receive Jesus' revelation (John 12:44–50) is related to the separation of "children of God" and "children of the devil" in 1 John 3:10.

6   (IV) The Johannine Opponents. 1 and 2 John mention persons who had been part of the Johannine fellowship but have now separated themselves from that community (1 John 2:19; 4:1; 2 John 7). The statement that persons have separated from the community is linked with a failure to "confess" the truth about Jesus and with an assertion that such persons are "deceivers and antichrists," who must be overcome. While 1 John 4:1–5 speaks positively—the community addressed will reject such "false spirits"—2 John 8–11 issues a command that Christians not even greet those associated with dissident teaching (→ Johannine Theology, 83:14).

7   If some time has elapsed between 1 John and 2 John, the sharper tone might suggest that the situation had worsened. Though some interpreters have proposed that the opponents had begun to preach a docetic understanding of Jesus as the earthly instrument of the heavenly revealer such as we find in 2d cent. gnostic writings, no peculiarly gnostic views are attributed to the dissidents (→ Early Church 80:64–80). If the emphases of 1 John are a clue to the dissident views, then they seem to have held to a soteriology that proclaimed the believer sinless and rendered any representation of the death of Jesus as sacrifice useless. They also appear to claim to have received "knowledge of God" and the Spirit. How such views led them to separate from the Christians addressed in 1 and 2 John, we do not know.

8   By refusing to grant hospitality to those who come from the presbyter, Diotrephes (3 John 9–10) appears to be turning the presbyter's rule for dealing with the dissidents (2 John 10–11) against him. For some exegetes this is evidence that the Johannine fellowship of house churches linked by traveling missionaries has been shattered. 3 John does not imply that Diotrephes was sympathetic to the dissidents. He is the leader of a local community, who has decided to exclude all traveling missionaries.

9   (V) Literary Form of the Epistles. 2 and 3 John correspond to the conventions of ancient letter writing (→ NT Epistles, 45:8). They are atypical in not giving a personal name for the sender and, in 2 John, not stating where the church addressed is located. However, the content of both letters addresses concrete problems. They should not be taken as "fictional" letters. 2 John has the characteristic "grace, mercy, and peace," of NT letter greetings but uses them as a statement rather than in a greeting formula. 3 John lacks a greeting. Concluding greetings from the church in which the letter originates to the addressees is typical.

The closest NT analogies to 1 John are in treatises like Heb and Jas. But unlike those writings, 1 John appears to have been directly provoked by the desire to refute positions advocated by the dissidents. The elements of general instruction in 1 John stem from the tradition which the author has turned to this purpose rather than being the primary purpose behind the composition of the work. (For the view that the 1 John is primarily exhortation, see J. M. Lieu, NovT 23 [1981] 210–28.) The internal structure of 1 John is more difficult to discern beyond the general agreement that 1 John opens with a prologue (1:1–4) and concludes with a parallel to the end of the Gospel at 5:13, which leads many commentators to consider 5:14–21 an appendix. The majority will also agree that some transition is implied in 2:28–29. Those who divide the body of the work into three sections usually begin the third with 1 John 4:1.

10   The existence of formally structured units within 1 John has led to a number of theories that 1 John represents a reworking of an earlier source. Such units include: (a) 1:6–2:2, "if we say . . . ," with contrasting "but if . . ."; (b) 2:4–11, three sentences with "the one who says . . . ," followed by development; (c) 2:12–14, parallel instructions to "children, fathers, young men"; (d) 2:15–17, parenesis against love of the world; (e) 2:29–3:10, seven clauses, "everyone who . . ." followed by a participle; (f) 5:18–20, three "we know . . ." clauses. There is little to hold these units together as a single source. They probably represent stylized units of traditional teaching.

1 JOHN

11   Outline. 1 John may be outlined as follows:

(I) Prologue (1:1–4)
(II) Walking in Light (1:5–2:29)
   (A) Two-way Exhortation (1:5–2:17)
      (a) God Is Light (1:5)
      (b) Freedom from Sin (1:6–2:2)
      (c) Keeping the Commandments (2:3–11)
      (d) Address to Three Groups (2:12–14)
      (e) Reject the World (2:15–17)
   (B) Reject the Antichrists (2:18–29)
      (a) Division as a Sign of the Last Hour (2:18–19)
      (b) Anointing Preserves True Faith (2:20–25)
      (c) Anointing Teaches the Community (2:26–27)
      (d) Confidence at the Judgment (2:28–29)
(III) Love as the Mark of God's Children (3:1–24)
   (A) The Father Makes Us Children Now (3:1–10)
      (a) We Are God's Children Now (3:1–3)
      (b) Those Born of God Do Not Sin (3:4–10)

   (B) Christians Must Love One Another (3:11–18)
      (a) Cain: Hatred Is Death (3:11–15)
      (b) Christ's Death: Model for Love (3:16–18)
   (C) Our Confidence before God (3:19–24)
      (a) God is Greater than Our Hearts (3:19–22)
      (b) God Abides in Those Who Keep the Commandments (3:23–24)
(IV) Commandments to Love and Believe (4:1–5:12)
   (A) Reject the Antichrists (4:1–6)
      (a) They Do Not Confess Jesus (4:1–3)
      (b) They Have Not Overcome the World (4:4–6)
   (B) God is Love (4:7–21)
      (a) Christ Has Shown Us God's Love (4:7–12)
      (b) We Know God's Love through the Spirit (4:13–16a)
      (c) Our Confidence: Abiding in God's Love (4:16b–21)
   (C) Belief in the Son (5:1–12)

(a) Faith Overcomes the World (5:1–5)
(b) Testimony: The Son Came in Water in Blood (5:6–12)

(V) Conclusion (5:13–21)

(A) Confidence in Prayer (5:14–17)
(B) Three Confidence Sayings (5:18–20)
(C) Keep Yourselves from Idols (5:21)

COMMENTARY

12   (I) Prologue (1:1–4). In the Gospel the pre-existent Word in God's presence is the life and light of the world (John 1:1,4). Here "from the beginning" refers to the "word of eternal life," the testimony about Jesus given in the community from the beginning (vv 1–3; cf. 2:7, 24; 3:11). **1.** Belief in the Son as the source of eternal life stems from the Gospel and appears in the conclusion (1 John 5:13). *we have heard, seen . . . felt with our hands:* As in the Gospel, testimony interrupts the affirmations about what "was from the beginning." 1 John stresses the physical character of the revelation that the community has received. **2.** *eternal life which was with the Father and was made manifest:* The description of "eternal life" as "with the Father" echoes the Gospel's description of the Word as "with the Father." Jesus is the "life," which is made manifest (cf. the "I Am" sayings in John 11:25; 14:6). 1 John 3:5,8 also uses the aor. pass., "was revealed" (*ephanerōthē*) of Jesus' incarnation. **3.** *may have fellowship with us . . . fellowship with the Father and his Son:* Koinōnia, "fellowship," "partnership," "communion," appears in 1 John 1:6–7 as a correction of a false claim to *koinōnia* with God and the verbal form in 2 John 11 against "sharing" the evil works of the dissidents by greeting them. In the Pauline Epistles *koinōnia* was used of sharing material goods in a missionary partnership or sharing its blessing (1 Cor 9:23). It was expanded to the divine "fellowship of the Spirit" (2 Cor 13:13). The term may have been used among the missionaries of the Johannine community. This verse makes the purpose of writing the securing of *koinōnia* between the author and audience so that they can enter into salvation, the *koinōnia* shared with the Father and Son (see P. Perkins, *CBQ* 45 [1983] 631–41). Other expressions are more frequently used in the Johannine writings to express this relationship between believers and God, such as "to be in God" (1 John 2:5; 5:20); to "remain/abide" in God or God in the Christian (e.g., 2:6,24; 3:24; 4:13,15–16; or "to have God/Son" (2:23; 5:12; 2 John 9; → Johannine Theology, 83:35–37). **4.** *our joy may be complete:* This echoes John 15:11 and 16:24, where Jesus' discourses are to complete the joy of the disciples. John 17:13 makes this joy that of Jesus.

**13   **The various expressions for *koinōnia* with God point to a reciprocal relationship between the believing community and God. "Abiding in" can be understood as the Johannine expression of the covenant relationship applied to the Christian community. This *koinōnia* has a christological origin, since it is only possible through the Son (e.g., 1 John 2:23; 5:12,20). But, contrary to the view of the dissidents (?), it is not the automatic result of claiming to believe in Jesus. There is a moral dimension that is reflected in the conditions which must obtain to claim *koinōnia* with God. These conditions are also reflected in the association of "indwelling" formulas with attributes of God: "truth" (1:8); "his word" (1:10; 2:14, cf. 2:24; 5:10); "love" (4:12).

**14   **Testimony-statements play an important role in grounding faith throughout the Johannine tradition. Here the author associates himself with an authoritative group of witnesses, "we," in contrast to the recipients.

The realistic language need not imply that the author was an associate of the earthly Jesus, only that the tradition handed down in the community attests the reality of eternal life manifested in "Jesus Christ come in the flesh" (1 John 4:2). The author of 1 John uses "we" when associating himself with the guardians of the tradition (including eyewitnesses of Jesus) and handing on the tradition to others or when identifying himself with his readers in terms of their basic Christian experience. He often uses "I" in direct address or exhortation.

15   (II) Walking in Light (1:5–2:29). The first attack on the dissidents' position enlists preformulated elements from the initiatory parenesis of the community. One must live a life in accord with the attributes of God, the real source of all that the community has, light (1:5), fidelity, and righteousness (1:9).

(A) Two-ways Exhortation (1:5–2:17). The dichotomy between light and darkness reflects the ethical division between those who live according to God's commandments and those who do not. The ethical contrast between the "two ways" of darkness and light is well represented in the QL (e.g., 1QS 3:13–4:26; → Johannine Theology, 83:31–32).

(a) GOD IS LIGHT (1:5). **5.** *Message: Angelia* occurs here and in 1 John 3:11; the vb. is used for Mary's announcement in John 20:18. It refers to the "gospel" preached by the Johannine teachers and reminds the readers of what they have heard when they became Christians. *God is light:* One of three descriptions of God: Spirit (John 4:24); love (1 John 4:8,16b). John 1:4,5,9 described the Word as the "light of humanity." Believers walk in light. Those who prefer evil are in darkness (e.g., John 3:19; 8:12; 12:35,46). Here, the focus is on God. What follows draws ethical applications from this affirmation.

(b) FREEDOM FROM SIN (1:6–2:2). If no darkness is associated with God, then Christians must free their lives of sin. The three disapproved conditions (vv 6,8,10) point to false claims about freedom from sin. Each assertion is "corrected" in the context with an affirmation that the Christian should make (vv 7,9; 2:1). **6–7.** Walking in darkness, lying, and "not doing the truth" are all equivalent expressions for a life opposed to God in the two-ways type of exhortation. The concern that a Christian might claim "fellowship with God" without a corresponding "life-style" may reflect the origins of this section in initiation parenesis. Or it may represent claims made by the dissidents. **7.** *fellowship with one another, and the blood of Jesus purifies us:* Additional conditions for freedom from sin are remaining within the community and the cleansing of sin by the expiating death of Jesus. The Gospel does not elaborate on the sacrificial death of Jesus (John 1:29). Elsewhere we find Christ's death understood as an offering for the sins of humanity (Rom 3:25; Heb 9:12–14; 10:19–22; Rev 1:5). **8–9.** Reference to sin at the end of the previous verse provides the key word for the second boast. *faithful and righteous . . . :* Attributes of God associated with the covenant are invoked to affirm that God cleanses those who acknowledge their sinfulness. The author would appear to have some public expression of sinfulness in mind. **1:10–2:2.** The final pair focuses on the affirmation of Christ as expiation for sins and heavenly intercessor (*paraklētos*) with God. The theology of Christ's death as perfect sin offering by one who was not a sinner coupled with the conviction that the Christian can turn to Christ as heavenly intercessor is elaborately developed in Heb 9–10. Christ is seated at God's right hand, and his blood continues to purify (9:14). Christians are exhorted to have confidence in approaching the "heavenly high priest" (Heb 4:16; 10:19). This section of 1 John contains all the elements of this tradition. Representation of Christ's death as expiating sacrifice may have been developed in the Jewish Christian phase of the Johannine tradition.

16   *Paraclete:* "Advocate," "intercessor," "counselor" is unique to the Johannine tradition. In the Gospel (→ John, 61:185), the Spirit/Paraclete is modeled on Jesus, "another Paraclete" (14:16), suggesting that the earthly Jesus had been a "Paraclete" for the community. 1 John 2:1 reflects a more primitive stage of the tradition that Jesus is "Paraclete," the exalted Jesus as a heavenly advocate for the faithful (→ Johannine Theology, 83:52).

17   The original setting of this material seems to have been for initiation into the community. The initiation ceremony described in 1QS 1:18–3:22 included a covenantal liturgy with public confession of the sinfulness of the people; admonition that no one could enter who had not turned from walking in darkness to walking in the ways of God. A person who had not turned toward God could not be purified either by water or expiation. One who joined the sect would become part of an eternal communion (1QS 3:11–12). The sectarians are then warned to follow the Spirit of Truth, and walk in light—not to follow the Angel of Darkness, who seeks to deceive the children of light. The NT does not contain a description of such a ceremony, but parallels are found to some of the major elements: conversion as transfer from Satan to God, from darkness to light, along with forgiveness of sins (Acts 26:18; Col 1:13–14; Eph 5:6–11; 1 Pet 1:16–23).

18   (b) KEEPING THE COMMANDMENTS (2:3–11). This section emphasizes the biblical view that "to know God" means "to keep God's commandments." In the Gospel, "knowing God" separated those who believed in Jesus from the hostile world (1:10–13; 14:7). That tradition could be distorted to divorce knowledge of God from a person's ethical conduct. The section is structured around three claims. Each is "corrected" by the addition of an ethical dimension: (a) one says, "I know him" [= "Jesus Christ, the righteous," v 2]; such a one must be obedient (vv 4–5); (b) one says, "I abide in him"; such a one must walk as he walked (v 6); (c) one says, I am "in the light"; he must love his brother (v 9). **4.** *a liar; truth is not in him:* This rephrases 1:6,8. This section has the final use of the "two ways" of light and darkness in 1 John. **5.** *love of God is perfected:* The gen., "of God," may refer to human love for God or God's love for humans; or possibly to love as the essence of the revelation of God. 1 John 4:8,16,20; 5:2–3 all refer to God's love for humanity as the source of love within the Christian community. The connection between love, keeping the commandments, and indwelling appear in John 14:23–24. God's love is fulfilled in the community whose love is expressed in keeping Jesus' word and thus has the Father/Son abiding with it. **6.** *ought to walk as Christ walked:* Christ's example to the believer is one of love in dying for us (1 John 3:16; 4:11).

19   **7.** *new commandment:* The love commandment as the mark of the community and the foundation of any claim to knowledge of God is introduced as the "commandment" that is "old" because it has been part of the instruction that Johannine Christians received from the beginning. Cf. John 13:34. The association made there between this commandment and Jesus' example (also see John 15:12) provides the link joining this section with v 6. **8.** *the true light is shining already:* This expands v 7 by reminding the reader of the "realized eschatology" of the Gospel, in which Christ is the light shining in darkness (1:5; 8:12; 9:5). **11.** *darkness has blinded his eyes:* Several passages in the Gospel refer to those who fail to believe in the light as walking in darkness or as blinded (9:39–41; 11:9–10; 12:35,46). 1 John insists that the believer who fails in love is just as "blind" as those who had rejected Jesus. 1 John 2:11; 3:15; 4:20 all make "hatred" the contrast to "love." In the Gospel, "the world"—persons outside the community who were actively engaged in the persecution of Christians—is described as "hating you" (15:18–16:4a; 17:14). This hatred represents the "hatred of God" expressed in the rejection of Jesus. Here, that complex of images is transposed to relationships between Christians. 1 John 2:19 will make it clear that the dissidents have left the fellowship of the author and those whom he addresses. Their departure is an expression of the hatred to which 1 John refers.

20   (d) ADDRESS TO THREE GROUPS (2:12–14). These verses are the first of two pieces of parenetic tradition that break into the continuity between the general warning about hating one's fellow Christian and the application of the warning to the situation of the community fractured by the departure of the dissidents, the "antichrists" of 2:18. This section prepares for that apocalyptic image by its exhortation to Christians as those who know the Father, know the Son, have the word of God abiding in them and so have overcome "the evil one." The pattern of three groups based on age, "children, fathers, young people," is suggestive of wisdom exhortation directed at persons in different stages of life. Some exegetes maintain that they are perhaps now being used to refer to the community as a whole ("children" is frequently used for the addressees in 1 John) and to two groups within the community, older and more recent converts. The admonitions apply to all members of the community, since they recall entry into the church.

21   (e) REJECT THE WORLD (2:15–17). Once again 1 John associates "belief" with practice by immediately introducing a piece of ethical preaching from Christian initiation. **15.** *do not love the world:* Love of the world and its associated vices reflects attachment to what is transitory. Love of God brings the Christian into relationship with what "remains" forever. (Jas 4 is an example of Jewish Christian preaching on this theme.) **16.** *desire of the flesh, desire of the eyes, pride of life:* A traditional list of vices. "Desire/lust of the flesh" can refer to all human passions that are against God (cf. Eph 2:3; 1 Pet 2:11; *Did.* 1:4, for the condemnation of lust in the context of baptismal preaching). *desire/lust of the eyes:* This can refer to sins of pride (Isa 5:15), greed (Wis 14:9), and sexual immorality (Matt 5:28). *pride: Alazoneia* refers to an arrogant, boastful pride that has no basis; *bios,* "life" means the external aspects of life, material wealth (e.g., 1 John 3:17; Mark 12:44). The expression "pride of life" can encompass both the arrogant boasting of the wealthy and the inflated sense of security placed in material possessions (Wis 5:8; Jas 4:16).

22   (B) Reject the Antichrists (2:18–29). 1 John leaves off the dualism of light and darkness to address the problem of the dissidents. Those who have received "anointing" will not be led astray by their teaching.

(a) DIVISION AS A SIGN OF THE LAST HOUR (2:18–19). The author shifts to an eschatological warning against those who have left the community, referred to as deceivers (2:26) and false prophets (4:1–4). Apocalyptic sayings (cf. Mark 13:21–23) make the emergence of false christs and prophets a sign of the last days. **18.** *antichrist:* This term for the opponent of God's messianic purpose occurs only here in the NT. **19.** *not that they were from us:* The idea that apocalyptic division proves who the genuine Christians are also appears in Paul (1 Cor 11:19).

23 (b) ANOINTING PRESERVES TRUE FAITH (2:20–25). The anointing that Christians received upon entry into the community should confirm the truth of the author's presentation of the tradition. 1 John apparently refers to the Spirit/Paraclete who is to guide the community into all truth (John 16:13). **22–23.** *deny Jesus is the Christ, deny Father and Son:* 1 John invokes the christological confession that the readers made when they entered the community rather than the formula that reflects the dissidents' views, "deny Jesus the Messiah come in the flesh." The author is establishing the fact that the Christians must hold onto this tradition if they are to remain "in the Son and in the Father" and are to obtain the promised reward of eternal life.

(c) ANOINTING TEACHES THE COMMUNITY (2:26–27). Since an even more expanded affirmation of "anointing" as teacher of the community is appended to the warning about the dissidents as deceivers, it would appear that they may have grounded their teaching in a claim to the Spirit. Like John 14:26, 1 John insists that what the Spirit teaches is what Jesus has taught "from the beginning."

24 (d) CONFIDENCE AT THE JUDGMENT (2:28–29). An affirmation of confidence when Christ appears in judgment concludes the section. Just as loving one's fellow Christians is a sign of belonging to God and walking in light, so one who "does righteousness," knowing that God is righteous, has been born of God. Verse 29 provides a transition to the second half of the letter (3:9; 4:7; 5:1,5,18).

25 (III) Love as the Mark of God's Children (3:1–24). The reference to divine begetting (in baptism, John 3:5) evokes the community's self-designation as "children of God." 1 John uses themes from the previous section to contrast the "children of God" and the "children of Satan."

(A) The Father Makes Us Children Now (3:1–10). Christians have already experienced God's goodness in becoming children of God.

(a) WE ARE GOD'S CHILDREN NOW (3:1–3). Affirming the present reality of God's love in making the Christians "children of God" has three consequences. Christians do not belong to the world, which failed to receive Jesus (John 15:18–19; 17:14–16). Christians will lead lives of holiness like Christ (John 17:17–19). Christians are confident of an even greater salvation in the future (John 17:24). **2.** *we shall be like him because we shall see him as he is:* A common theme in Hellenistic religion was that "like would know like," the human being who knows God is divinized. For the Johannine tradition this experience is mediated through Jesus. Jesus possessed the divine name and equality with God (17:11–12). He has shared this name with the disciples (17:6,26). They have shared Jesus' fate at the hands of the world (John 15:21) and will witness his preexistent glory (17:24). Paul refers to expectations of a future vision of God or divine glory (1 Cor 13:12; 2 Cor 3:18).

(b) THOSE BORN OF GOD DO NOT SIN (3:4–10). This section is patterned on a sharp division between those who belong to Christ, are righteous, and do not sin and the "lawless," the children of the devil. **4.** *sin is lawlessness:* 1 John appears to be referring to the "lawlessness" associated with Satan's rule at the end of

the age. Sinning proves that one is really a child of Satan. **6.** *no one who sins has seen him:* 1 John implies that the person who sins is not really a Christian (cf. 2:5). **9.** *God's seed abides in him, and he cannot sin:* The emphasis on the inherent sinlessness of the Christian appears to stand in sharp contrast to the earlier claim that one should not say, "We have no sin" (1:8,10). This section deals with the certainty of divine election and indwelling over against those who persist in doing evil. It presumes that the Christian is living in a way that coheres with being a child of God (v 7, is righteous; v 10, loves fellow Christians). Compare the distinction between those who are hostile to Jesus (= children of Satan) and those who are real children of Abraham (= rejoice in Jesus) in John 8:39. (J. du Preez, *Neot* 9 [1975] 105–12).

26 (B) Christians Must Love One Another (3:11–18). **11.** *the message:* A second announcement of the "gospel" (cf. 1:5) returns to the love command of 2:7–11. Here the readers are addressed in the 2d pers. pl. as those who embody love.

(a) CAIN: HATRED IS DEATH (3:11–15). **12.** *Cain:* The only OT reference in 1 John takes Cain as an example of hatred of the brother which leads to death. Jude 11 refers to evil people as "walking in the way of Cain." Jewish traditions preserved in gnostic writers (*Valentinian Exposition* 38.24–38) make Cain an example of those who murder. 1 John evokes the image of those "children of Satan" who seek Jesus' death (8:39–44) and of Judas, whom Satan induced to betray Jesus (13:2,27). The Gospel accuses Jews of killing Christians (16:2) at the conclusion of a section that began with the parallel to 1 John 3:13, "Do not be surprised that the world hates you" (John 15:18). (See H. Thyen, "'. . . denn wir lieben die Brüder' [1 Joh 3,14]," *Rechtf* 527–42.).

(b) CHRIST'S DEATH: MODEL FOR LOVE (3:16–18). **16.** *his life for us:* According to John 15:13, Christ's death is the highest model of friendship (cf. also 10:11,15). Christians ought to be willing to show as much love for one another. **17.** *worldly goods:* Christians can demonstrate the appropriate depth of love by sharing material goods with those in need; a commonplace of early Christian ethical exhortation (cf. Jas 2:14–17).

27 (C) Our Confidence before God (3:19–24). Just as the previous section ended with evidence of the confidence Christians are to have before God (2:28–29), this section closes on a note of assurance (see W. Pratscher, *TZ* 32 [1976] 272–81).

(a) GOD IS GREATER THAN OUR HEARTS (3:19–22). **19.** *reassure our hearts before him:* Since God, the source of forgiveness (1:8–2:2), is "greater than our hearts," the possibility of the conscience condemning us does not shatter Christian confidence. Even if the Christian is not conscious of sin, one is assured that God hears prayer (cf. John 16:26–27). The test of acceptance by God is willingness to "do what pleases him" (cf. John 8:29).

(b) GOD ABIDES IN THOSE WHO KEEP THE COMMANDMENTS (3:23–24). A summary of the commandments is given in typical Johannine form: **23.** *believe in his Son's Name . . . and love one another:* This may be the Johannine version of the double love command of Mark 12:28–31, since in the Johannine tradition "to believe" in the Son whom God sent is equivalent to loving God (→ Johannine Theology, 83:55–57). **24.** *he abides in us by the Spirit:* 2:27 has pointed to the "anointing" received upon entering the community (cf. John 3:5). The Spirit is a pledge elsewhere in the NT (Rom 8:14; 2 Cor 1:22). This passage also prepares for the next section, in which the Spirit inspires the true confession which unmasks false teachers (1 John 4:2-6: → Johannine Theology, 83:50–54).

28   (IV) Commandments to Love and Believe (4:1–5:12). Two sections on belief frame the final exhortation to love, making the double command to believe in Jesus and to love the concluding theme.

(A) Reject the Antichrists (4:1–6). Opposition between the spirit of truth and the spirit of error reflect that between the spirit of truth and the "prince of this world" in John 16:11. A sharp division between those who "know God" and hear his true witnesses and the "world" under Satan, which only hears what belongs to it, stems from John 15:19,21. The spirit of truth is sent to bear witness to Jesus for the Christian community (15:27).

(a) THEY DO NOT CONFESS JESUS (4:1–3). **1.** *test the spirits:* This refers to the spirit which inspires what Christian teachers say. The "test" in question may have involved a public confession. **2.** *Jesus Christ come in the flesh:* The point at issue is not whether Jesus was a human being but whether there is any relation between Christ's being "in the flesh" and salvation. 1 John has modified the traditional confession "Jesus is the Christ" to attack the dissidents (cf. 2 John 7). **3.** *the spirit of the Antichrist:* The "last days" were to see an increase of false teachers, who would lead people astray (cf. 1QH 4:7,12–13; *T. Judah* 21:9; Mark 13:32; Matt 7:21–23; 24:11,24; 1 Tim 4:1).

(b) THEY HAVE NOT OVERCOME THE WORLD (4:4–6). **4.** *you are of God:* The parenetic traditions of the community taught that the Christian in whom the word of God abides has overcome the evil one (2:13–14). Jesus has conquered the world (John 16:33) and the Spirit/Paraclete has convicted it by showing that its prince is condemned (John 16:8–11). **5.** *the world listens to them:* The author implies that the opponents' success in preaching reflects the spirit of error. The world rejects Jesus, who comes from God, and those who preach the true gospel (John 1:10; 15:19; 8:43–44). Everyone who belongs to the truth hears Jesus (John 18:37; 8:47; 10:26–27).

29   (B) God is Love (4:7–21). This section takes up the second half of the double commandment. An intensive concentration of love language centers on God as the source of the love to be shown by Christians; → Johannine Theology, 83:20–21.

(a) CHRIST HAS SHOWN US GOD'S LOVE (4:7–12). Love distinguishes the person who "knows God" from the one who does not (cf. 2:4–5; 3:1,11). Christ's death in expiation of sin is again invoked as the example of the obligation that Christians must follow (cf. 3:16). **9.** *revealed in us:* Not only is God's love revealed to the Christian in Jesus, but it can also be said to be revealed "in" the Christian community, which now has life through that love (John 5:26; 6:57; 1 John 5:11). **10.** *he loved us:* The new emphasis in this section lies in its insistence that love must be seen as God's initiative. Johannine writings contrast God's love with the hatred of the world. The love of God can only be known through Jesus, whom God has sent (e.g., John 1:16–18; 3:16–17). **11.** *we ought also to love:* The author never forgets the obligation for Christians that follows from the divine attributes to which he refers. **12.** *no one has ever seen God:* A general maxim that the Johannine tradition had employed to insist that only Jesus reveals the Father (e.g., John 1:18; 5:37; 6:46). The abiding divine presence in those who keep the command of love can be understood as God's love reaching its perfection (cf. 2:5). The contrast between the maxim and the reality of divine indwelling highlights the divine origin of love (cf. 3:1).

(b) WE KNOW GOD'S LOVE THROUGH THE SPIRIT (4:13–16a). **13.** *his Spirit:* 3:24 introduced the gift of the Spirit as evidence of God's indwelling. That theme is associated with the testing of spirits in 4:1–6. God's Spirit is evident in the witness to the sending of the Son, which goes back to the beginning (1:1–4). **16a.** *we know and believe the love that God has for us:* This expands the confession of v 15 to draw the conclusion emphasized in this section: We are to believe in and act on God's love.

(c) OUR CONFIDENCE: ABIDING IN GOD'S LOVE (4:16b–21). Once again 1 John brings a unit to its close with the theme of confidence. **17.** *this is love perfected . . . perfect love casts out fear:* This returns to the affirmation that divine love is perfected in the believing community (1 John 2:5; 3:12). Here 1 John emphasizes the positive result: Christians need not fear judgment. This reaffirms 1 John 3:19–21 on the relationship between the Christian conscience and God. **20–21.** *he who does not love his brother . . . cannot love God.* This picks up the example of hating/loving one's fellow Christian from 3:15 and of love as the representation of God, whom we have not seen from 4:12. As in 3:23, this section includes a double command to love God and fellow Christians. In 1 John there is really only one commandment, since one cannot claim to love God if one does not love others (cf. a related judgment tradition in Matt 25:40).

30   (C) Belief in the Son (5:1–12). In a final argument against the dissidents, 1 John will bring together obedience to the love command, belief in Jesus as Son, and the conviction that Jesus' death for sin brings us eternal life.

(a) FAITH OVERCOMES THE WORLD (5:1–5). This section links the christological confession Jesus is Son of God (vv 1,5) and the love command. **1.** *loves the parent loves the child:* A conventional maxim repeats the association between love of God and love of fellow Christians from 4:20–21. **4.** *the victory that overcomes the world, our faith:* The victory over the world was won when Christians were converted (2:13,14). The word of God or the "anointing" is the source of this victory (4:4), a share in the victory won by Jesus.

(b) TESTIMONY: THE SON CAME IN WATER AND BLOOD (5:6–12). The affirmation that belief is the source of eternal life is expanded in two directions: (i) belief must include his coming in water and blood; (ii) belief in the Son is grounded in God's own testimony. **6.** *not with water only but with water and blood:* In John 1:31–32, the Baptist testified that revelation of Jesus as preexistent Son was linked to the descent of the Spirit and to baptism. (1 John 5:7 refers to the testimony given by the Spirit.) Jesus' sending is associated with the boundless gift of the Spirit (John 3:34; 7:38–39.). The dissidents might have associated salvation and the coming of the Spirit with water (baptism) and not with blood (crucifixion). John 19:35 may have been added to the Gospel to emphasize that this conviction about the death of Jesus goes back to the beloved disciple. **9.** *God's testimony is greater:* The claim that God is the real witness to Jesus derives from the controversies in the Fourth Gospel. Those who reject Jesus' testimony about his relationship to the Father are confronted with lists of witnesses (cf. John 5:31–40; 8:14–19). **10.** *has the testimony in himself:* A number of passages in the Gospel speak of the ways in which the believer could be said to "have testimony." God is responsible for a persons' believing response to Jesus (John 6:44; 10:3–4). The Spirit/Paraclete dwelling within the community serves as witness (John 14:16) and also enables the community to witness to the world (John 15:26–27). **12.** *the one who has the Son has life:* The theme that the Son has been sent to give life to those who believe runs through the Fourth Gospel (e.g., 3:36; 5:24,26; 6:57; 20:31).

31   *Comma Ioanneum:* Some Lat witnesses contain

an expansion of 1 John 5:7–8: "because there are three who testify *in heaven, Father, Word, and Holy Spirit; and these three are one; and there are three who testify on earth,* the Spirit, the water, and the blood, and these three are unto one." This expanded reading, the so-called Johannine Comma, is not attested before the end of the 4th cent. AD. It begins to appear in mss. of the Vg of Spanish provenience in the 8th cent. and in some Carolingian copies of the Vg, though more mss. prior to AD 1200 lack the expansion than contain it. Its presence in the Vg led to the inclusion of a Gk rendering of it in Erasmus's 3d ed. of the Gk NT (1522), whence it found its way into the *textus receptus* (1633) and the *KJV* and Rheims translation. Modern textual critics would agree with Erasmus's judgment that this Lat reading does not represent an original variant of the Gk text of 1 John. It follows a theological tradition attested from 3d cent. Church Fathers (Cyprian, *De ecclesiae catholicae unitate* 6; CC 3. 254; Augustine, *Contra Maximinum* 2.22.3; PL 42. 794–95), appealed to this text in combination with John 10:30 to provide scriptural evidence for the orthodox doctrine of the equality and unity of persons in the Trinity. (See further the Declaration of the Holy Office, *EB* 135–36 [1897]; DS 3681–82 [1927].)

32   (V) Conclusion (5:13–21). The letter ends with a conclusion reminiscent of the Gospel and a collection of appended sayings about confidence. **13.** *that you possess eternal life:* Cf. John 20:31. Unlike the former, 1 John 5:13 presumes that the readers are indeed believers. Verse 13 introduces the theme of certainty taken up in the remaining sayings.

(A) Confidence in Prayer (5:14–17). General sayings about confidence in prayer set the stage for an assertion of how prayer is to be applied to the Christian who sins. **14.** *he hears us:* The assertion that Christians can be confident that God hears their prayer reflects Jesus' promises in John 15:7; 16:24 as well as 1 John 3:22. **16.** *he will ask and He will give him life, for the ones whose sin is not mortal:* 1 John 2:1–2 presented the exalted Jesus as an advocate for the sinful Christian before God. Now the believing community can do the same for its sinful members except in the case of a person whose sin is mortal. (For a similar example of prayer for the sinful Christian, see Jas 5:15–16,20.) *a sin which leads to death:* This phrase is difficult to interpret. The author has insisted that the "sinful Christian" has forgiveness through the expiating death of Jesus and Jesus' advocacy before God (1 John 1:6–2:2; 4:10) and that the true Christian does not sin (1 John 3:6,9). The best solution to the difficulty is to argue that the sin in question refers to the dissidents, who have separated themselves from the community. Such persons "abide in death" (1 John

3:14). However, in 2:19, the author seems to deny that the dissidents could ever be considered to have been part of the community. Therefore, some exegetes consider this verse a general teaching against prayer for those who deliberately refuse to fulfill the conditions for walking in light and being a child of God quite apart from any connection with the dissident group (e.g., S. S. Smalley, *1,2,3 John* 298–99; D. Scholer, "Sins Within and Sins Without," *Current Issues in Biblical and Patristic Interpretation* [Fest. M. C. Tenney; ed. G. F. Hawthorne; GR, 1975] 230–46). The reference to seeing a fellow Christian committing sin suggest a general community rule for dealing with sinful Christians such as that in Matt 18:15–17. A rule similar to this one may also have been invoked in the crisis occasioned by expulsion from the synagogue. Application of such a rule to the dissidents would be in line with the rule in 2 John 10–11 that Christians are to refuse such persons hospitality or even a greeting.

33   (B) Three Confidence Sayings (5:18–20). 1 John concludes with three affirmations that Christians "know" their salvation is based on gifts that God has given the Christian. **18.** *anyone born of God does not sin:* This repeats 3:9a and then follows it with an explanation related to 4:4. Christian sinlessness is based on God's gift, protecting the Christian from the evil one. This extension makes it clear that the "seed" of 3:9 is not understood as some inherent divine spark that is incapable of sin. **19.** *we are of God; the whole world is in the power of the evil one:* This rephrases the distinction between the children of God and of Satan (3:8–10). The "world" which belongs to sin is that into which the dissidents have gone (4:1,5) and which the Spirit/Paraclete condemned for its failure to believe in Jesus (16:8–11). The evil one is its prince (John 12:31; 14:30; 16:11). **20.** *the Son of God has come and given us understanding . . . and we are in him who is true:* This summarizes the work of the Son and contrasts the sphere to which the Christian belongs ("in God," "in the Son") with the world. Knowing God and Jesus Christ is the basis for eternal life (cf. John 17:3). Some exegetes have also seen a connection of the sequence "has come, truth, life" with the "way, truth, and life" of John 14:6.

34   (C) Keep Yourselves from Idols (5:21). A peculiar conclusion, since the Johannine writings do not mention "idols" elsewhere. "Idols" may be intended as a contrast to the "true God" in 1 John 5:20. The readers are exhorted to remain faithful to the relationship with God that has been made possible through Jesus. If the phrase is directed toward the situation that provoked the treatise, then the views of the dissidents are seen as little more than idolatry (J.-L. Ska, *NRT* 101 [1979] 860–74).

2 JOHN

35   Outline. 2 John may be outlined as follows:

(I) Opening Formula (vv 1–3)
(II) Body of the Letter (vv 4–11)
    (A) Faithfulness of the Addressees (vv 4–6)

(B) Warning against the Dissidents (vv 7–9)
(C) Take Action against the Dissidents (vv 10–11)
(III) Letter Closing (vv 12–13)

COMMENTARY

36   (I) Opening Formula (vv 1–3). 2 John reflects the influence of Christian letter tradition in the greeting, "Grace, mercy, and peace . . . from God the

Father and from Jesus. . . ." One would more commonly find a "wish" statement rather than the assertion in 2 John (→ NT Epistles, 45:6). **1.** *elder:* It is difficult to determine whether *presbyteros* refers to an ecclesial office and teaching authority as head of a local church such as we find elsewhere in Asia Minor at this time (e.g., 1 Tim 5:17; Tit 1:5; 1 Pet 5:1). If this letter is by the author of 1 John, teaching authority seems to derive from a group of authoritative witnesses to the tradition. "Elder" may have been a general term used for members of that group. *to the elect lady with her children:* A designation for the members of the church to which the letter is directed rather than for a particular person. For "elect" as a term for Christians, see 1 Pet 1:1. **1–2.** *whom I love in truth . . . the truth which abides in us:* The expansion of the greeting around the themes of love and truth which abides eternally in the community points forward to the subject matter of the letter: rejection of the dissident teachers. Some exegetes see a reference to the work of the Spirit in guiding the community (cf. John 14:16; 1 John 4:6). **37**   **(II) Body of the Letter (vv 4–11).** The conditions for living as God's children from 1 John are alluded to: "remain" in God (vv 1,2,4,9); obey the love command (vv 5–6); avoid the deceivers and those associated with "the world" (v 7). The only new elements are the measures taken against the dissidents. **38**   **(A) Faithfulness of the Addressees (vv 4–6).** A *captatio benevolentiae* prior to the business of the letter. The traditional character of the love language may be intended to distance the elder's view from the deviations of those who have left the community.

(B) Warning against the Dissidents (vv 7–9). The characterization of the dissidents as those who have gone out into the world, as antichrists and as persons who will not confess "Jesus Christ coming in the flesh," parallels the description given in 1 John 4:1–6. **9.** *anyone who is "advanced" and does not abide in the doctrine of Christ does not have God:* The only use of *proagein,* "go ahead," "make progress," "advance," in the Johannine

writings. It may represent a claim that the dissidents made for their teaching. *doctrine of Christ.* Although *didachē* refers to the teaching given by Jesus in John 7:17, 19; 18:19, the meaning here appears to be teaching about Christ, the true confession authoritatively handed down by the tradition of witnesses. Exegetes who hold that this expression refers to the teaching that comes from Christ emphasize the role of the Spirit/Paraclete in continuing that teaching (John 14:16,26) and in constituting the presence of Jesus among Christians.

(C) Take Action against the Dissidents (vv 10–11). **10.** *do not receive him into the house and do not greet him:* A ban against dissident preachers. The presbyter clearly considers them a threat to other communities, not merely a group that has left the "fellowship." Their missionaries may have been spreading their views by claiming to teach Johannine tradition. **11.** *shares his evil works:* The vb. *koinōnein,* "share," recalls *koinōnian echein,* "have fellowship, communion," (1 John 1:3–7). In the language of an association for missionary purposes all who contributed "shared" the fruits of that association (cf. Phil 1:5–7). Hospitality for traveling missionaries was important to the Johannine fellowship. Those who aid the dissidents thus become partners in deeds that are like Cain's, from the evil one (1 John 3:12).

39   **(III) Letter Closing (vv 12–13).** Letters often included promise of future contact between the parties. This formula is repeated at 3 John 13–14. Reference to fulfilling the author's joy forms an *inclusio* with the opening of the body of the letter (v 4). It may have been conventional in Johannine circles (cf. 1 John 1:4). The conclusion invokes the presence of those Christians who are "in fellowship" with the elder. He does not speak on his own, but as a representative of a larger community.

3 JOHN

40   **Outline.**   3 John may be outlined as follows:

   (I) Opening Formula (vv 1–2)
  (II) Body of the Letter (vv 3–12)
    (A) Render Hospitality to Missionaries (vv 3–8)

    (B) Diotrephes' Refusal of Hospitality (vv 9–10)
    (C) Request for Hospitality (vv 11–12)
  (III) Letter Closing (vv 13–15)

COMMENTARY

41   **(I) Opening Formula (vv 1–2).**   A personal letter to a Christian, Gaius, known for his hospitality to missionaries. The opening greeting and wish for the health of the recipient follow the conventions for a private letter (→ NT Epistles, 45:6). **1.** *whom I love in truth:* The expression may mean simply "truly," but given the use of "truth" in Johannine writings, it suggests that Gaius is a true "fellow Christian" (cf. 2 John 1b). **42**   **(II) Body of the Letter (vv 3–12).** The crisis created by Diotrephes' refusal of hospitality is framed by the positive example in Gaius's past behavior and the expectation that he will continue to show such hospitality.

(A) Render Hospitality to Missionaries (vv 3–8). **3–4.** *I greatly rejoiced when some of the brethren arrived and testified . . . to hear that my children follow the truth:* Thanksgiving for the report given by traveling missionaries that Gaius is a faithful member of the Johannine

fellowship (cf. 2 John 4; 1 John 1:6–7; 2:6,11). *children:* A term for Johannine Christians (2 John 1,4: 1 John 2:1, 12,28; 3:7,18; 4:4; 5:21) that does not imply that the elder had converted Gaius. **5–6.** *you do a loyal thing . . . you will do well:* Gaius has shown hospitality to traveling missionaries from the elder's community. The obligation for Christian missionaries to depend upon hospitality goes back to sayings of Jesus (e.g., Matt 10;10; 1 Cor 9:14). Persons who showed kindness to them were showing it to Jesus (e.g., Matt 10:40; John 13:20). The elder's praise contains an exhortation to continue showing such beneficence. **7.** *have been accepting nothing from pagans:* The Johannine missionaries were to depend on the generosity of fellow Christians. This restriction may have been an innovation, since the earlier sayings contain no such rule. It may have been intended to remove any suspicion that Christians sought personal gain from preaching. **8.** *that we may be fellow workers in the truth:*

"Fellow worker" is used of persons involved in the Pauline mission (cf. Rom 16:3; Phil 2:25). One who supports the mission shares its "fruits," a rule the elder used to forbid hospitality for the dissidents in 2 John 11.

(B) Diotrephes' Refusal of Hospitality (vv 9-10). The "brothers" who reported on Gaius's hospitality may have been turned away by Diotrephes, who refused to accept a letter (of recommendation for them?) written by the elder. 9. *Diotrephes who loves to put himself first does not acknowledge us:* Diotrephes has not acknowledged the authority of the elder. Some exegetes presume that Diotrephes is a local bishop, who has refused to have anything to do with outside authority such as that of the Johannine school represented by the elder. Others have attempted to associate him in some way with the dissidents and suggest that he is now repaying the elder with some of his own medicine. The issue presented in 3 John turns on hospitality, not teaching. Diotrephes' authority in his local community may well reflect a transition toward the type of local leadership embodied in the presbyter bishops of other churches (e.g., 1 Tim 3:2; Tit 1:8, on the bishop's obligations for hospitality). 10. *I will bring up what he is doing, talking against us with evil words:* Refusal to accept the elder's authority is coupled with some form of malicious gossip, presumably connected with the actions Diotrephes has taken against missionaries. *stops those who want to receive them and puts them out of the church:* Diotrephes appears to employ the same tactics against missionaries generally that the elder has proposed against dissidents in 2 John 10-11. In addition, he is said to expel (*ekballein*) from the community those who would offer hospitality. John 9:34-35 uses *ekballein* for the banning of Christians from the synagogue. It seems unlikely that Diotrephes would have had sufficient authority to take such a formal act. He might be said to do so by turning the rest of the community against traveling missionaries.

(C) Request for Hospitality (vv 11-12). The author turns to traditional language of Johannine exhortation. Hospitality is "doing good" (by showing love to fellow Christians) and hence a sign that one is "from God" and "knows/has seen" God (cf. 1 John 3:6, 10: 4:4,6f,20). 12. *Demetrius is vouched for . . . by the truth itself:* The elder requests hospitality for Demetrius (possibly the bearer of the letter), who is recommended by all. Demetrius may have been a well-known member of the missionary circle associated with the elder. The elder's additional testimony brings the weight of the whole Johannine fellowship to bear in this request.

43 (III) Letter Closing (vv 13-15). This repeats the pattern of 2 John 12-13. Reference to a visit "fulfilling the author's joy" is omitted, while the possibility of such a visit being "very soon" is added. Perhaps the elder's community is closer to Gaius than to that addressed in 2 John and such a visit is impending. The concluding greetings add the Christian wish for peace to the greetings from the Christians ("friends," cf. John 15:13-15; 1 John 4:11) in the elder's church to those associated with Gaius.

44 The confusion caused by traveling missionaries from the different factions in the Johannine churches may have prompted Diotrephes to ban them from the house churches in which he enjoyed some authority. However, this letter does not refer to the teaching of the dissidents as the problem. Rejecting the elder's request on behalf of traveling missionaries associated with the Johannine circle of teachers that he represents, speaking evil of the elder, and prohibiting other Christians from receiving the missionaries would seem to have put Diotrephes' allegiance to the truth and his "love of the brothers" in question. Gaius had apparently made up for the former's refusal of hospitality. 3 John encourages him to continue that practice and so continue in Christian love and truth (see K. P. Donfried, "Ecclesiastical Authority in 2-3 John," *L'Evangile de Jean* [ed. M. de Jonge; BETL 44; Gembloux, 1977] 325-33; A. Malherbe, "The Inhospitality of Diotrephes," *God's Christ and His People* [Fest. N. A. Dahl; ed. J. Jervell, *et al.;* Oslo, 1977] 222-32).

63

THE APOCALYPSE
(REVELATION)

Adela Yarbro Collins *

BIBLIOGRAPHY

1 Allo, E.-B., *Saint Jean: L'Apocalypse* (EBib; 4th ed.; Paris, 1933). Barclay, W., *The Revelation of John* (2 vols; Phl, 1976). Beasley-Murray, G.R., *Highlights of the Book of Revelation* (Nash, 1972). Böcher, O., *Die Johannesapokalypse* (Darmstadt, 1975). Bousset, W., *Die Offenbarung Johannis* (MeyerK 16; 6th ed., Göttingen, 1906). Caird, G. B., *A Commentary on the Revelation of St. John the Divine* (HNTC; NY, 1966). Charles, R. H., *A Critical and Exegetical Commentary on the Revelation of St. John* (2 vols.; ICC; NY, 1920). Farrer, A., *The Revelation of St. John the Divine* (Oxford, 1964). Ford, J. M., *Revelation* (AB 38; GC, 1975). Kiddle, M. and M. K. Ross, *The Revelation of St. John* (MNTC; London, 1940). Kraft, H., *Die Offenbarung des Johannes* (HNT 16a; Tübingen, 1974). Lohmeyer, E., *Die Offenbarung des Johannes* (HNT 16; 2d ed., Tübingen, 1953). Minear, P. S., *I Saw*

a New Earth (Washington, 1968). Mounce, R. H., *The Book of Revelation* (NICNT; GR, 1977). Prigent, P., *L'Apocalypse de Saint Jean* (CNT 14; Lausanne, 1981). Quispel, G., *The Secret Book of Revelation* (NY, 1979). Rist, M., *The Revelation of St. John the Divine* (IB 12; NY, 1957). Schüssler Fiorenza, E., *Invitation to the Book of Revelation* (GC, 1981). Sweet, J. P. M., *Revelation* (Phl, 1979). Swete, H. B., *The Apocalypse of St. John* (3d ed.; London, 1909). Wikenhauser, A., *Die Offenbarung des Johannes* (RNT 9; 3d ed.; Regensburg, 1959). Yarbro Collins, A., *The Apocalypse* (NTM 22; Wilmington, 1979). Zahn, T., *Die Offenbarung des Johannes* (2 vols.; Leipzig, 1924–26).

DBSup 1. 306–25. *IDBSup* 744–46. Kümmel, *INT* 455–74. Wik-Schm, *ENT* 631–58.

INTRODUCTION

2 **(I) Literary Character.** Rev is unique within the NT. The Gospels and the Acts of the Apostles are, for the most part, realistic narrative. The epistles are basically expository and hortatory prose. Rev differs from all of these in being narrative of a special kind. It narrates extraordinary visions and auditions that concern things normally unseen and unheard by human beings. Rev is unique in the NT, but not in the ancient world. Similar texts have been preserved in the OT, in other Jewish literature, and in extracanonical Christian literature (→ OT Apocalyptic, 19:19–23; Apocrypha, 67:4–77). In genre Rev is (a) an apocalypse, although it has affinities with (b) prophecy, (c) letters, and (d) drama as well.

3 (a) Rev begins with the words "(The) revelation of Jesus Christ. . . ." In this context the Gk word *apokalypsis,* "revelation," expresses the idea that God through Jesus Christ, John, and this written text, has unveiled secrets about heaven and earth, past, present, and future.

The ancient genre of apocalypse seems to have been fluid and imprecise. Any text that revealed secrets about heaven or the future fitted under this rubric, whether its form was oracular or visionary. Modern scholars have attempted to define the genre more precisely. A recent definition defines as essential elements of the genre a narrative framework about how the revelation was received and the mediated character of the revelation (*Semeia* 14 [1977] 9). The revelation is mediated in the sense that the visionary does not receive it directly from the deity, as an oracle, but only through another heavenly being, such as an angel or the risen Christ.

The revelation may be mediated in a variety of forms: epiphanies, visions, auditions, otherworldly journeys, or access to a heavenly book. The content of the revelation has two focuses: secrets of the cosmos and secrets of the future. Secrets of the cosmos involve the nature and workings of the stars, sun, and moon, including the fixing of the calendar and the causes of the weather. The names and activities of angelic beings are very important, as are places of reward and punishment. On the places of punishment, see M. Himmelfarb, *Tours of Hell* (Phl,

*The author is grateful to the University of Notre Dame, Institute for Scholarship in the Liberal Arts, for a stipend to support the research and writing of this commentary.

1983). Secrets of the future involve political and historical events as well as the ultimate destiny of the people of God, humanity, heaven, and earth.

The function of apocalypses is a question requiring further study. The most common view is that the genre's function was to console people in distress during a time of crisis, like persecution. This view is too simple. Social crisis is a factor in the setting of some apocalypses, but it is probably not always a significant factor. It is important to recognize the ideological or propagandistic factor that seems to be universal in apocalypses. Secrets are revealed in order to present a particular interpretation of the times and to persuade the hearers or readers to think and live in a certain way.

4   (b) Rev refers to itself as a prophecy (1:3; 22:7,10,18–19). John never refers to himself as a prophet but is indirectly suggested to be one. The angel who mediates revelation to John refers to his "brothers the prophets" (22:9). On another occasion John is told that he must "prophesy again" (10:11). Prophecy was an important phenomenon in early Christian communities (1 Cor 11:2–16; 14:1–40; Matt 7:22; 10:41; Acts 21:9; 1 Tim 1:18, 4:14; *Did.* 11–13). It seems reasonable then to understand Rev in a context of early Christian prophecy. Although the book as a whole is an apocalypse, it contains smaller prophetic forms. The messages to the seven congregations, for example, are prophetic oracles. See D. E. Aune, *Prophecy in Early Christianity and the Ancient Mediterranean World* (GR, 1983) 274–88.

5   (c) Rev also contains epistolary elements. The opening references to the book as a revelation or apocalypse (1:1) and as a prophecy (1:3) occur in the prologue in which John is spoken about in the third person. In most of the rest of Rev John speaks in the first person. At the point of transition from third to first person, epistolary elements are introduced (1:4). Verses 4–5a have the standard form of the opening formula of the typical ancient letter (sender, addressee, greeting; → NT Epistles, 45:6). The greeting is elaborated in a way similar to the greeting in Gal (1:3). In many Pauline and Deutero-Pauline letters, the greeting is followed by a thanksgiving or a benediction. In Rev the greeting is followed by a doxology, another type of liturgical element (vv 5b–6). In Gal the greeting concludes with a doxology (1:5).

The usual body of a letter does not follow the doxology in Rev as one would expect. Rather, it is followed by two isolated prophetic sayings (1:7 and 8) and then by a report of an epiphany of Christ to John (1:9–3:22) and by reports of other visions and auditions (4:1–22:5). Various isolated sayings follow in 22:6–20. The book closes with a benediction (22:21), which is a typical element in the ending of the conventional ancient letter. The epistolary framework, therefore, does not determine the genre of Rev. It is a kind of envelope in which the apocalypse is enclosed.

The use of the epistolary form may be explained in various ways. It may be the result of necessity. Used to communicating in person in oral form with the congregations in western Asia Minor, John may have resorted to writing and to the letter form because of his banishment to the island of Patmos (1:9). Another possibility is that the letter was the form authoritative Christian leaders were expected to use. Paul may have established this precedent, perhaps influenced by Jewish or imperial Roman models. Ignatius of Antioch and Polycarp of Smyrna also wrote letters to Christian communities in Asia Minor. The combination of apocalyptic and epistolary forms is found also in *2 Apoc. Bar.* This work as a whole is an apocalypse, but it concludes with a letter

from the visionary (Baruch) to the nine and a half tribes of Israel (78–87).

6   (d) Drama is literature in which the author presents all the characters as living and moving before the audience. Rev clearly does not belong to the genre of drama, because it is narration rather than direct action. In Rev the author describes events, speaking in his own person. Rev does, however, have some affinities with drama, esp. with tragedy. According to Aristotle the subject matter of tragedy is serious rather than trivial or ordinary, as in comedy (*Poetics* 4.7–10.6,2). The subject matter of Rev is certainly grave and great, as in tragedy.

Greek tragedies were performed by actors, usually three in number, and a chorus (after the 5th cent. BC, usually 15 in number). The drama alternated between episodes or acts performed by the actors and songs performed by the chorus. Besides the songs between acts, there were occasional short, lively songs expressing sudden joy and other types of involvement of the chorus in the action. Occasionally an individual member of the chorus sang a few words (G. Norwood, *Greek Tragedy* [NY, 1960] 78).

As he describes his visions of the heavenly world and of things to come, John often portrays groups and individuals speaking in direct discourse. On two occasions what is said is identified as a song (5:9–10; 15:3–4). In many cases the sayings comment on the actions reported in the vision (12:10–12; 16:5–7; 18:10,16–17,18–19). Calls for rejoicing and the expression of joy appear in 18:20 and 19:6–8. This interplay of reported action and songlike commentary by groups and individuals may well have been influenced by Gk tragedy.

Aristotle also comments on the function of tragedy: "through pity and fear effecting the proper purgation of these emotions" (*Poetics* 6.2). The plot should depict the change of fortune from good to bad of a person who is decent but in error or frail. The audience is to pity him for his misfortune and fear that something similar could happen to them. Rev, like other apocalypses, also excites fear. It clarifies and emphasizes the danger facing the faithful in this world, but it also portrays the terrors of the next world for those who prove unfaithful. See H. D. Betz, in *Apocalypticism in the Mediterranean World and Near East* (ed. D. Hellholm; Tübingen, 1983) 577–97 and A. Yarbro Collins, *Crisis and Catharsis* (Phl, 1984) 152–54.

7   **(II) Authorship.** In the prologue of Rev (1:1–3) the author is referred to simply as God's servant (v 1). He does not call himself an apostle or a disciple of Jesus. He does not even claim the title prophet, although he is closely associated with prophets and prophecy in the text (10:11; 22:9). He authorizes his message by describing its heavenly origin.

The earliest Christian writer to comment on the authorship of Rev is Justin Martyr. In *Dial. Tryph.*, written about AD 160, he identifies the author of Rev as John, one of "the apostles of Christ" (81). Irenaeus is the earliest known writer to say that both Rev and the Fourth Gospel were written by John, the disciple of the Lord (*Adv. Haer.* 3.11.1–3; 4.20.11). Hippolytus, Tertullian, and Origen took the same position as Irenaeus, perhaps in dependence on him. Rev was widely known and accepted as Scripture in the 2d half of the 2d cent. in East and West (Swete, *Apocalypse* cviii–cxi).

Nevertheless, the case for the authorship of Rev by one of the Twelve is not very strong. Conceivably, John the son of Zebedee moved to Asia Minor and survived until about 95; it is not, however, very probable. The issue is complicated by a tradition that John the son of Zebedee was martyred, probably before 70 (Charles, *Commentary* 1. xlv–xlix).

8   The relationship between Rev and the Gospel of John is also a complicated issue. Many have pointed out the differences between the two works in the style and diction of the Greek and in theology, esp. eschatology. These differences are so great that theories attempting to explain them by the use of different scribes or secretaries or by the passage of time have not been compelling. There are certain similarities between the two, such as the use of the title "Lamb" for Christ (but the Gk words are different: John 1:29,36; Rev 5:6; 6:16; etc.) and phrases like "living water" (John 4:10–11; 7:38) and "water of life" (Rev 7:17; 21:6; 22:1,17). These similarities, however, can be explained adequately by the dependence of both works on earlier Christian tradition or even by their independent adaptation of Jewish tradition (see E. Schüssler Fiorenza, NTS 23 [1976–77] 402–27).

9   Theories that Rev is pseudonymous or that it was written by John the Elder (or Presbyter; see Eusebius, HE 3.39) have not won wide support. It seems best to conclude that the author was an early Christian prophet by the name of John, otherwise unknown. The authority of the book lies in the effectiveness of the text itself and in the fact that the church has included it in the canon.

10   **(III) Date.** Most early Christian writers who comment on the matter say that Rev was written toward the end of the reign of Domitian (AD 81–96: Irenaeus, Adv. Haer. 5.30.3; Clement of Alexandria, Quis dives 42; Origen, In Matt. 16.6; Victorinus, In Apoc. 10.11; 17.10; Eusebius, HE 3.18,20,23; Jerome, De Viris Illustr. 9). A few ancient, but not early, sources date Rev differently. Epiphanius places John's exile and return during the reign of Claudius (Haer. 51.12,32; → History, 75:175). The titles of both Syriac versions of Rev locate the banishment in the reign of Nero. Jerome (Adv. Jovin. 1.26) says that Tertullian attests the dating of the exile in the reign of Nero (cf. Tertullian, Scorp. 15). Theophylact associates John's banishment with Trajan (In Matt. 20.22).

11   These comments by ancient writers constitute external evidence for the date of Rev. Internal evidence is also important, viz., allusions within the text to historical situations and events that indicate the time of writing. Such allusions must be used carefully, however, because of the possibility that John incorporated earlier traditions, even sources with fixed wording, into his work. An appropriate methodological principle is that a work should be dated in accordance with the latest historical allusion it contains.

Rev 11:1–2 seems to imply that the earthly, historical Temple in Jerusalem was still standing when Rev was written. J. A. T. Robinson argued, primarily on the basis of this passage, that Rev as a whole was written before AD 70 (Redating the New Testament [Phl, 1976] 238–42). Robinson did not succeed, however, in refuting the arguments of previous exegetes who had concluded that this passage is a source taken over by John. It is likely that he reinterpreted the reference to the Temple in a spiritual sense (see Yarbro Collins, Crisis [→ 6 above] 64–69).

Other internal evidence makes it highly unlikely that Rev as a whole was composed before the destruction of Jerusalem in 70. This evidence is the frequent use of "Babylon" and the implication that Rome is the earlier city's antitype (14:8; 16:19; 17:5; 18:2,10,21). Most commentators have recognized that Babylon in Rev is a symbolic name for Rome, but they have not seen the implications for dating the book. The name "Babylon" is usually seen as a symbol of political power, great luxury, or decadence. A historically sensitive interpretation of this typological symbol, however, should take into account Jewish typological language about Rome from the same general period. "Egypt," "Kittim," and "Edom" are other types of Rome besides "Babylon" in Jewish sources from the Second Temple period and in rabbinic literature. Most of the uses of Babylon as a type of Rome occur in 2 Esdr 3–14, 2 Apoc. Bar. and Sib. Or. 5. In each occurrence in these three works, the context makes clear why Rome is portrayed as the antitype of Babylon (2 Esdr 3:1–2,28–31; 2 Apoc. Bar. 10:1–3; 11:1; 67:7; Sib. Or. 5:143,159). The similarity between the two is their common role as destroyer of the Temple and Jerusalem. It is likely that John either learned this tradition from his fellow Jews or that his thinking was analogous to that expressed in the texts cited above. Thus, the use of this typology strongly implies that Rev in its present form was composed after 70. The rest of the internal evidence is compatible with a post-70 date. It seems, therefore, that there is no compelling reason to doubt the traditional dating of Rev attested by Irenaeus and other early Christian writers, viz., the end of the reign of Domitian (AD 95–96).

12   Acceptance of the traditional dating, however, does not imply confirmation of the tradition that Rev was written in response to a great persecution of Christians during Domitian's reign. Early Christian tradition has it that Nero was the first emperor to persecute Christians and that Domitian was the second. The earliest known writer to take this position was Melito of Sardis, who was bishop there in about 160–170. A passage from his lost book To Antoninus is quoted by Eusebius (HE 4.26.5–11). This work was an apology for Christianity dedicated to the emperor Marcus Aurelius. Its presentation of the emperors' attitudes toward Christians is tendentious. Melito's thesis is that only those emperors who had a bad reputation among Romans themselves persecuted Christians, not because there is something wrong with Christianity but because those emperors were men of poor judgment or ill will. Nero in fact did persecute Christians and was unpopular with Romans of senatorial rank. Domitian was called a second Nero by some Latin writers (Juvenal, Sat. 4.38; Pliny, Paneg. 53.3–4). After Domitian died, the senate passed a decree of damnatio memoriae against him. This meant that his first name might not be perpetuated by his family, that images of him had to be destroyed, and that his name had to be removed from inscriptions. It would have been tempting and easy for Melito to associate the two emperors and to exaggerate the occasional local actions against Christians into a systematic persecution.

Names of Christians persecuted by Domitian are sometimes given, but critical assessment leads to the conclusion that they may have been sympathizers with Judaism, but were probably not Christians (E. M. Smallwood, CP 51 [1956] 1, 7–9; A. A. Bell, NTS 25 [1978–79] 94–96). Once Melito had characterized Domitian as a persecutor, the characterization became traditional. Details were added and particular names cited as victims (see J. Moreau, NClio 5 [1953] 125). When read in light of this tradition, Rev does seem to reflect a situation of severe persecution. But a closer look reveals very few incidents of actual persecution: John's banishment (1:9), Antipas's execution (2:13), and the expectation of the arrest of some Christians in Smyrna (2:10). These incidents are clearly local and probably close to the time of writing. The allusions to persecution in the visions do not necessarily reflect local and contemporary events. They are more appropriately interpreted as reflections of persecutions of the past, such as Nero's, and of the expectation of intense persecution in the near future.

13   (IV) Composition and Structure. There is little consensus among exegetes on the overall structure of Rev. Its structure is problematic because of the presence of numerous parallel passages and repetitions within the book and because of occasional breakdowns in consecutive development. Particularly striking parallel passages are the seven messages, seven seals, seven trumpets, and seven bowls. The parallels between the trumpets and bowls are especially close. The events associated with the sixth bowl (16:12-16) seem to repeat those following the sixth trumpet (9:13-21). The sequence of one event logically following another breaks down especially between 11:19 and 12:1 and between 19:10 and 19:11. A fundamental question is whether these anomalies are best explained by the compilation of sources (source criticism), by a series of editions of the text (redaction criticism and composition criticism), or as part of the author's original literary design.

The oldest surviving commentary on Rev is by Victorinus of Pettau (*ca.* 275-300). He recognized the similarity of the trumpets and bowls and concluded that both series predict the eschatological punishment of unbelievers. This assumption of purposeful repetition was also made by the Donatist Tyconius and by Augustine. This approach, which has been called the recapitulation theory, dominated the exegesis of Rev for centuries.

In the 19th cent., source criticism had proven very fruitful in the analysis of the Pentateuch and the Synoptic Gospels (→ Pentateuch, 1:6-8; → Synoptic Problem, 40:13-34). Many scholars came to believe that source criticism could explain the repetitions and other anomalies in Rev better than the recapitulation theory. They argued that Rev was composed by the compilation of various sources only superficially edited by the author (see the summary by R. H. Charles, *Studies in the Apocalypse* [2d ed.; Edinburgh, 1915] 185-90). This approach has been taken by a few scholars in this century. M.-É. Boismard (*RB* 56 [1949] 507-41; 59 [1952] 178-81) argued that John wrote three separate compositions, an apocalypse written during Nero's reign, another apocalypse from Domitian's time, and the letters to the seven churches; near the end of Domitian's reign (*ca.* 95) an editor combined the three to give Rev its present form. J. M. Ford (*Revelation*) proposed that chaps. 4-11 was originally a Jewish apocalypse which took oral form in the time and under the influence of JBap. Chaps. 12-22, in her view, was also an originally independent Jewish apocalypse composed in the 60s. A Jewish-Christian disciple of JBap combined these sources and added chaps. 1-3 and 22:16a, 20b, 21.

14   At the end of the 19th cent. and in the early part of the 20th, several commentators argued against the source critics' theories because of the consistency throughout Rev of theological perspective, images and symbols, style and language (e.g., Bousset, Swete, Charles). Recent linguistic studies have confirmed the fundamental unity of Rev (e.g., G. Mussies, *The Morphology of Koine Greek as Used in the Apocalypse of John* [NovTSup 27; Leiden, 1971]). This overall unity suggests that Rev owes its present form to a single author, but it does not exclude the possibility that the author used oral or even written sources or that the work was edited by the author once or more times.

15   When the basic unity of Rev was reestablished among scholars, the recapitulation theory was revived in modified form as a key to understanding the composition of Rev (G. Bornkamm, *ZNW* 36 [1937] 132-49; A. Yarbro Collins, *The Combat Myth in the Book of Revelation* [HDR 9; Missoula, 1976] 8-13, 32-44). The number seven has been seen by many as a key organizing principle (Lohmeyer, *Offenbarung*; J. W. Bowman, *The*

Drama of the Book of Revelation [Phl, 1955]; Farrer, *Revelation*). Others have taken a more thematic approach, attempting to understand form and content as a unity (e.g., E. Schüssler Fiorenza, *CBQ* 30 [1968] 537-69; *CBQ* 39 [1977] 344-66).

Others have attempted to explain the structure of shorter units and even the composition of Rev as a whole as based on patterns embodied in older Jewish prophetic and apocalyptic texts. A. Feuillet has proposed that the organizing principle of Rev is the pattern of woes against Israel followed by woes against the nations, a pattern he found in Ezek 25-32. In his view Rev 4-11 describes God's wrath against Israel and chaps. 12-22 depict the destruction of the Gentile opponent, Rome (*Johannine Studies* [Staten Island, 1965] 183-256; *The Apocalypse* [Staten Island, 1964]). The destruction of Babylon/Rome is certainly a major theme of chaps. 12-22. The destruction of Jerusalem is at least alluded to in chap. 11. But there is no indication that the seals and trumpets are directed against Israel. Cf. M. Hopkins, *CBQ* 27 (1965) 42-47.

16   (V) Outline. The following outline is based on the convictions that the structure of Rev is the author's literary design and that recapitulation and the number seven are important ordering devices. It also recognizes that the narrative at times begins anew, rather than depicting events always as following clearly from what has gone before.

(I) Prologue (1:1-3)
    (A) Description of the Book (1:1-2)
    (B) Beatitude Regarding the Reception of the Book (1:3)
(II) Epistolary Framework (1:4-22:21)
    (A) Prescript (1:4-6)
    (B) Two Prophetic Sayings (1:7-8)
    (C) Report of a Revelatory Experience (1:9-22:5)
        (a) Setting of Scene (1:9-10a)
        (b) The Revelatory Experience Proper (1:10b-22:5)
            (i) First cycle of visions (1:10b-11:19)
                (1) Epiphany of Christ to John with seven messages (1:10b-3:22)
                    (a) To Ephesus (2:1-7)
                    (b) To Smyrna (2:8-11)
                    (c) To Pergamum (2:12-17)
                    (d) To Thyatira (2:18-29)
                    (e) To Sardis (3:1-6)
                    (f) To Philadelphia (3:7-13)
                    (g) To Laodicea (3:14-22)
                (2) The scroll with seven seals (4:1-8:5)
                    (a) The heavenly court (4:1-11)
                    (b) The scroll and the Lamb (5:1-14)
                    (c) The first four seals (6:1-8)
                    (d) The fifth and sixth seals (6:9-17)
                    (e) Two inserted visions (7:1-17)
                      (1') 144,000 sealed (7:1-8)
                      (2') Salvation of a multitude (7:9-17)
                    (f) The seventh seal and vision of an angel offering the prayers of the saints (8:1-5)
                (3) The seven trumpets (8:2-11:19)
                    (a) The first four trumpets (8:2,6-12)
                    (b) The eagle and the three woes; the fifth and sixth trumpets (8:13-9:21)
                    (c) Two inserted visions (10:1-11:13)
                      (1') A mighty angel and a little open scroll (10:1-11)
                      (2') The temple and two witnesses (11:1-13)

(d) The seventh trumpet (11:15-19)
(ii) Second cycle of visions (12:1-22:5)
  (1) Symbolic visions revealing secrets of the past, present, and future (12:1-15:4)
    (a) The woman and the dragon (12:1-17)
    (b) The beast from the sea (13:1-10)
    (c) The beast from the earth (13:11-18)
    (d) The Lamb and the 144,000 (14:1-5)
    (e) The three angels (14:6-13)
    (f) Harvest and vintage (14:14-20)
    (g) Salvation of the conquerers (15:2-4)
  (2) The seven bowls (15:1-19:10)
    (a) Seven angels with the last plagues (15:1,5-16:1)
    (b) The first four bowls (16:2-9)
    (c) The last three bowls (16:10-21)
    (d) Elaboration of the seventh bowl: The nature and fall of "Babylon" (17:1-19:10)
      (1') A woman on a scarlet beast (17:1-18)
      (2') Apocalyptic prediction of divine judgment on "Babylon" (18:1-24)
      (3') Rejoicing in heaven (19:1-10)
  (3) Visions of the last things (19:11-22:5)
    (a) The second coming of Christ (19:11-16)
    (b) Call to the "banquet" (19:17-18)
    (c) The final battle (19:19-21)
    (d) The binding of Satan (20:1-3)
    (e) The thousand-year reign (20:4-10)
    (f) The last judgment (20:11-15)
    (g) New heaven, new earth and new Jerusalem (21:1-8)
    (h) Elaboration of the vision of the new Jerusalem (21:9-22:5)
      (1') The city, its gates and walls (21:9-21)
      (2') The inhabitants of the city (21:22-27)
      (3') The river of life and the tree of life (22:1-5)
(D) Isolated Sayings (22:6-20)
  (a) Saying about the Nature and Origin of the Book (22:6)
  (b) An Oracle Implicitly Attributed to Christ Which Is an Apocalyptic Prediction (22:7a)
  (c) A Beatitude Regarding the Reception of the Book (22:7b)
  (d) Identification of the Visionary by Name (22:8a)
  (e) Reaction of the Visionary and Angelic Response (22:8b-9)
  (f) Directive to the Visionary from the Revealing Figure (22:10)
  (g) Threat of Judgment and Promise of Salvation (22:11-12)
  (h) Self-disclosing Oracle Implicitly Attributed to Christ (22:13)
  (i) Promise of Salvation and Threat of Judgment (22:14-15)
  (j) Self-identification of the Revealing Figure, Jesus (22:16)
  (k) Invitations to the Water of Life (22:17)
  (l) Threat of Judgment against Those Who Violate the Integrity of the Book (22:18-19)
  (m) An Oracle Implicitly Attributed to Christ Which Is an Apocalyptic Prediction (22:20a)
  (n) Response to the Oracle (22:20b)
(E) Concluding Epistolary Benediction (22:21)

(On the literary form of the dream-vision report, see J. S. Hanson, *ANRW* II/23.2, 1395-1427.)

COMMENTARY

17 **(I) Prologue (1:1-3).**
(A) Description of the Book (1:1-2). 1. *(the) revelation of Jesus Christ:* The Gk descriptive phrase may mean either revelation about Jesus Christ or the revelation that Jesus Christ gives. The immediate context suggests that the meaning is the revelation which Jesus Christ gives, because it is revelation "which God gave to him." This interpretation is supported by the book as a whole. Although Jesus Christ as one in human form, the Lamb, and Word of God plays an important role in the book, its revelations are not primarily about him, but about "what must happen soon." **2.** *who testified:* John bore witness by writing this book. *to the word of God and the testimony of Jesus:* This formula appears also in 1:9 and 20:4. In those passages it indicates the Christian proclamation which evokes opposition from the authorities. Here the qualification "all that he saw" shows that the "word" and "testimony" refer to the content of Rev.
(B) Beatitude Regarding the Reception of the Book (1:3). This is the first of seven beatitudes in Rev (14:13; 16:15; 19:9; 20:6; 22:7,14). **3.** The contrast between the sg. "one who reads" and the pl. "those who hear" suggests that Christians in Asia Minor gathered in groups in the various cities to hear Rev read publicly. The setting may have been liturgical. *the time of crisis is near:* The addressees are urged to heed the book, because the judgment is approaching.

18 **(II) Epistolary Framework (1:4-22:21).**
(A) Prescript (1:4-6). 4. *the seven spirits which are before his throne:* These are seven angels of high rank (cf. Tob 12:15; *1 Enoch* 90:21). The number seven here may show a connection with the seven planets, which in John's time were held to be heavenly beings. **5.** *the firstborn of the dead:* The resurrection of Jesus is the event that has inaugurated the new age; it is the sign that the time of crisis has dawned. *the ruler of the kings of the earth:* The resurrection of Jesus is equivalent to his installation as universal king (cf. 1 Cor 15:20-28). *to him who loves us and freed us from our sins by means of his blood:* The precise wording of this phrase is unique in the NT to Rev, but the basic idea is early Christian tradition (cf. Rom 3:21-26; 8:37; Gal 2:20). **6.** *he made us a kingdom and priests:* Jesus' work fulfills the promise of Exod 19:6. Being a kingdom means being under God's rule rather than Satan's. All those who hear and obey God's word are priests: mediators between God and the rest of humanity. This doxology may reflect in part early Christian liturgy; see E. Schüssler Fiorenza, *Priester für Gott* (Münster, 1972).
(B) Two Prophetic Sayings (1:7-8). 7. The first saying is an apocalyptic prediction which combines and adapts Dan 7:13 and Zech 12:10, older sayings interpreted as prophecies of the return of the risen Jesus as judge (cf. Matt 24:30). Rev 1:7 and Matt 24:30 reflect

early Christian exegetical activity (B. Lindars, *New Testament Apologetic* [Phl, 1961] 122-27). **8.** The second saying is a divine oracle. This is the first of only two passages in Rev in which God is explicitly identified as the speaker (21:5-8 is the other). "I am" is typical of oracles in which the revealer identifies himself or herself. **19 (C) Report of a Revelatory Experience (1:9-22:5).** This unit, which includes most of Rev, is a single account of a visionary experience in the sense that only one setting is given (place, time, circumstances) for the entire book. The account is, however, divided into various visions and auditions.

(a) SETTING OF SCENE (1:9-10a). **9.** *in the tribulation:* A general word for physical and mental distress, tribulation often refers to the sufferings related to the crisis of the end-time (Dan 12:1; Matt 24:21). *kingdom:* The kingdom established by Jesus' death (v 6). *endurance in Jesus:* Endurance, which has connotations of patience and perseverance, is a virtue emphasized in several of the messages to the seven congregations. In 13:9-10 the context suggests that one aspect of endurance is patient acceptance of oppressive measures taken by the authorities against Christians. Another aspect is perseverance in loyalty to the way of life advocated by Rev to avoid eternal punishment (14:9-12). *was on the island called Patmos because of the word of God and the testimony of Jesus:* John was on the island as a consequence of his communication of the Christian message (Charles, *Commentary* 1. 21-22). Christianity as such was offensive to many at the time, but the eschatological character of John's teaching may have been viewed as subversive by authorities (R. MacMullen, *Enemies of the Roman Order* [Cambridge MA, 1966] 142-62). Patmos is a small, rocky island off the coast of Asia Minor. Roman authorities occasionally banished individuals to such islands for threatening the public interest (Yarbro Collins, *Crisis* [→ 6 above] 102-4). **10a.** *on the Lord's day:* Sunday, as the day of Jesus' resurrection, had special, perhaps liturgical, meaning for John. *a loud voice like a trumpet:* The sound of a trumpet was traditionally used to describe a theophany (Exod 19:16,19). In early Christian literature it is often associated with the end-time (Matt 24:31; 1 Thess 4:16).

20 (b) THE REVELATORY EXPERIENCE PROPER (1:10b-22:5).

(i) *First cycle of visions* (1:10b-11:19). These visions are linked by transitional phrases, resumptions of previous motifs, and the logical sequence of one event following another. No such connective devices link 11:19 and 12:1.

(1) Epiphany of Christ to John with seven messages (1:10b-3:22). An epiphany is a vision whose focuses on the appearance and speech of the revealing figure. **11.** The seven localities mentioned were located in sequence on a major road. So this apocalypse in the form of a circular letter could have been carried easily from one place to the next (W. Ramsay, *The Letters to the Seven Churches of Asia* [NY, 1904]). **13.** *one in human form:* Lit., "like a son of a human being," often translated "like a son of man." The phrase reflects a Semitic idiom: a "son of man" means simply "a man." Here the depiction of a heavenly being in human form alludes to Dan 7:13; in that passage such a figure is given dominion by God, "one that was ancient of days" (Dan 7:9). In the Synoptic tradition this figure is identified with Jesus (Matt 8:20; Mark 8:31; Luke 6:5). **14-15.** *his head and hair were white, like white wool, like snow:* This is an adaption of the description of God in Dan 7:9. *his eyes were like a flame of fire and his feet were like bronze:* Allusions to the angel of Dan 10:6. **16.** *seven stars:* These are angels associated with the seven congregations (v 20). The image of the

seven stars may allude to a particular constellation, such as the Little Bear (Little Dipper) or the Pleiades, or to the seven planets. The angels of the congregations are their heavenly patrons and protectors (cf. Dan 10:20-11:1; 12:1). *a sharp two-edged sword was proceeding from his mouth:* The word of God carries the sharp sword of God's command (Wis 18:14-16; cf. Rev 19:13,15). The description of the revealer in vv 13-16 is ambiguous. Some elements suggest that he is God; some that he is an angel, and some that he is the risen Jesus. This assimilation of Jesus to God suggests that the risen Messiah has been exalted to divine status (cf. 3:21). **18.** The allusions to the death and resurrection of Jesus make clear finally that (the) "one in human form" (v 13) is the risen Lord. **19.** *write then what you see and what is and what is about to happen afterward:* This command is an elaboration of the commission given by the revealer to John in v 11. It is a common formula describing prophecy (W. C. van Unnik, *NTS* 9 [1962-63] 86-94).

21 The seven messages belong to the speech of the revealer to John in his epiphany. They further specify the command to write in vv 11 and 19. It is highly unlikely that these messages ever existed independently as actual letters sent to the seven congregations because they do not manifest the literary form of the ancient letter. Rather, they are prophetic speeches (F. Hahn, in *Tradition und Glaube* [Fest. K. G. Kuhn; ed. G. Jeremias, et al.; Göttingen, 1971] 357-94). Each message begins with a prophetic commissioning formula. In the OT this formula has the basic pattern: "Go and say to X, thus says Y." Since John was unable to leave Patmos, the command to "go" is replaced by the command to "write." The speaker (Y) in each message is the risen Jesus. The central portion of each message is introduced by "I know." This section consists of exhortation and has similarities to the postexilic Jewish salvation-judgment oracles. Such an oracle may contain (1) praise, (2) censure, (3) call to repentance, (4) threat of judgment, (5) promise of salvation. Each message ends with two formulaic sayings whose order varies. One is a call for attention ("whoever has ears to hear . . ."). This formula is similar in function to the prophetic proclamation formula in the OT (e.g., "Hear the word of the Lord" in 1 Kgs 22:19). The other is a promise of eschatological salvation to the conqueror (see D. E. Aune, *Prophecy in Early Christianity* [→ 4 above] 275-78). Another reason for concluding that these messages were composed for their present context is the artful way in which they are related to their immediate context, the epiphany of Christ, and to Rev as a whole. In each message, the speaker in the commissioning formula is identified as the risen Jesus by phrases taken from the description in 1:13-16. The promises to the conqueror anticipate the description of salvation in chaps. 21-22.

22 (a) To Ephesus (2:1-7). **2.** *having tested those who call themselves apostles and are not, you have found them to be false:* Traveling charismatic leaders who were visiting Ephesus considered themselves commissioned by the risen Lord or by particular congregations to this work. Such itinerant leadership was common in the early church; Paul and John himself fit into that pattern (cf. *Did.* 11-13; Matt 10:41; 1 Cor 9:1-7). John calls these apostles false because he rejects their teaching or because they rival his leadership or both (cf. 2 Cor 11:12-15). **5.** *I will move your lampstand from its place:* This figurative threat alludes to the description of the revealer in 1:13 and to the identification of the speaker in 2:1. The allegorical meaning of the threat may be that the congregation will lose its prominent position if its way of life does not regain its once exemplary character. **6.** *the Nicolaitans:* Ancient commentators connected this group with the proselyte Nicolaus from Antioch, who, according to Acts 6:5, became a Christian deacon in Jerusalem. Modern commentators tend to reject this interpretation as a guess. The name may be allegorical, meaning "conqueror(s) of the people." More is said about them in the message to Pergamum. **7.** *what the Spirit says:* The speaker is identified here and in the other messages as the Spirit, although each of the commissioning formulas identifies the speaker as the risen Jesus. The implication is that the glorified Jesus and the Spirit are equivalent, at least in their relations with Christians (cf. 2 Cor 3:17–18). *to the conqueror:* The basic meaning of "conquer" is to prevail in battle, in athletic games, or in any contest. In Rev it symbolizes the goal of prevailing in the battle against Satan which God, the glorified Jesus, the Spirit, and the faithful are waging (cf. *Apoc. Zeph.* 7:9; 9:1 [*OTP* 1. 513–14]). Although Christians have been transferred to the kingdom of God and freed from their sins and the kingdom of Satan (1:5,9), God's kingdom is under attack by Satan and his allies. So Christians will have "tribulation" (1:9), but if they "conquer" through their endurance and perseverance (1:9), they will be rewarded (cf. Matt 11:12; Eph 6:10–20). *the tree of life, which is in the Garden of God:* This promise alludes to the tree of life which was in the Garden of Eden (Gen 2:8–9). It anticipates the description of the new Jerusalem, which will contain the tree of life (22:2). The eschatological salvation of the end is modeled on the ideal state of the beginning.

23 (b) To Smyrna (2:8–11). **8.** *the first and the last, who died and returned to life:* The identification of the speaker in the commissioning formula alludes to 1:17–18. Since members of the congregation at Smyrna were in danger of arrest by the authorities, which could lead to execution, the image of their dying and rising Lord serves as a model, an exhortation, and a comfort. **9.** *your poverty:* Christians at Smyrna may have been poor because they were immigrants from Galilee or Judea, uprooted by the Jewish War (AD 66–74). A 2d-cent. inscription from Smyrna refers to a group called "the former Judeans" (A. T. Kraabel, *JJS* 33 [1982] 455). *those who say that they are Jews and are not, but are a synagogue of Satan:* Some have taken the statement "and are not" literally and concluded that the reference is to Judaizing Christians, citing Ignatius in support (*Phld.* 6:1; 8:2; *Magn.* 8:10). It is more likely that these remarks are rhetorical and that the right of the local Jewish community to the name "Jew" is being challenged (so Bousset, Charles, and most commentators). These words attributed to Christ reflect a situation in which the name "Jew" is being claimed by Christians as a self-designation as the true heirs of the Jewish heritage (and perhaps also as immigrants from Judea, "Jew" and "Judean" being equivalent in Greek [*Ioudaios*]). The attack on the local Jewish community as "a synagogue of Satan" shows that local Jews and Christians were at least hostile to one another and probably engaged in conflict. Their conflict is analogous to that between the community at Qumran and other Jews (cf. 1QS 5:1–2,10–20; 9:16; CD 1:12; 1QM 1:1; 4:9–10; 1QH 2:22; → Apocrypha, 67:97–105). *the blasphemy:* The Jews' "blasphemy" could be simply their claim to the name "Jew." More likely, it is their criticism of Christian teaching. **10.** *the devil is about to cast some of you into prison:* The devil, "the slanderer," is identical with Satan, "the adversary." Behind the human beings who oppose John's followers, the chief of the evil spirits is seen as the ultimate power and agent. The close connection between vv 9 and 10 suggests that the Jews had accused John's followers before Roman authorities (cf. Acts 17:1–9). The Christians expected an arrest and detention in prison pending

trial to follow shortly. **11.** *the conqueror will not be injured by the second death:* The "second death" is death of the soul or spirit, death of the resurrected person, or eternal punishment (cf. Matt 10:28; *1 Enoch* 108:3–4).

24 (c) To Pergamum (2:12–17). **12.** *the one who has the sharp, two-edged sword:* The identification of the speaker prepares for the threat in v 16. **13.** *the throne of Satan:* Satan's throne has been interpreted diversely as the altar dedicated to Zeus on the acropolis of Pergamum, the shrine of Asclepius, the temple dedicated to Roma and Augustus, and the seat of the Roman governor. The immediate context associates "Satan's throne" with the death of Antipas, whom Christ calls "my faithful witness." As in the message to Smyrna, Satan is seen as the ultimate instigator of actions taken against Christians by local authorities. The word "witness" suggests that Antipas was arrested and interrogated by the Roman governor. *who was killed among you:* These words suggest that the result was his execution. "Satan's throne" then is the judgment seat of the Roman governor. This interpretation is supported by the association of Satan with Rome in chaps. 12–13. Although Pergamum was no longer the capital of Asia in John's time, it was one of the cities in which the governor regularly heard legal cases and made decisions. As in all provinces, the governor alone held the right of capital punishment. The sharp, two-edged sword of Christ (vv 12,16) contrasts with the "sword" of the governor, whose right to execute was called the "law of the sword" (cf. 20:4, where those who died for their faith are those who have been beheaded). **14.** *the teaching of Balaam:* A typological relationship is expressed between John's rival teacher and the Canaanite diviner whose interaction with ancient Israel is recounted in Num 22–24. *who taught Balak to place a stumbling block in the path of the descendants of Israel:* This is an allusion to Num 31:16, which suggests that Balaam and Balak incited the Israelites to intermarry with the Moabites and to worship their gods (cf. Num 25:1–2). *to eat food sacrificed to idols:* This act seems to be what "Balak" has taught some of the Christians in Pergamum to do (cf. 1 Cor 8–10). A whole range of issues is involved here: Could a Christian buy meat in the market which may have come from an animal sacrificed to a Greco-Roman or Asiatic deity? Could a Christian participate in dinner parties with non-Christians, in meals which often would consist of food offered to such deities and involve prayers and hymns to them, or sometimes take place on temple grounds? (see R. MacMullen, *Paganism in the Roman Empire* [New Haven, 1981]). The underlying issue is religious and cultural assimilation: What degree of exclusiveness does fidelity require and when does assimilation become idolatry? *to be sexually immoral:* Unlike eating food sacrificed to idols, this part of his teaching should probably not be taken literally. Sexual immorality is a metaphor in the OT for idolatry. The term is frequently used metaphorically in Rev (14:8; 17:2,4; 18:3,9; 19:2). It is used literally in only one passage (9:21); even there sexual immorality is closely linked to idolatry (v 20). The metaphorical meaning here is to participate in non-Christian, non-Jewish worship or to associate with Gentiles in a way that seems to imply participation in their worship. **15.** *Nicolaitans:* Their teaching is apparently identical with that of "Balaam." **17.** *some of the hidden manna:* According to Jewish apocalyptic tradition, the treasury of manna would descend in the messianic age (*2 Apoc. Bar* 29:8). *I will give him a white stone and upon the stone a new name will be written, which no one knows except the one who receives it:* This promise can be understood best in the context of popular magic (Charles, *Commentary* 1. 66–67). The white stone is an amulet, and the "new name" is a powerful magical formula. Its power is greater if no one else knows it, since then no one else may use it. This name is probably a name of the risen and glorified Jesus (cf. 3:12 and 19:12).

25 (d) To Thyatira (2:18-29). **20.** The congregation is chastised for permitting another rival of John's teaching to be active in their community. *Jezebel:* A typological relationship is expressed between this Christian leader and Jezebel, the daughter of the king of Sidon who married Ahab, king of Israel (1 Kgs 16:31). As a Canaanite, she advocated the worship of Baal. *who calls herself a prophetess:* It is likely that she was recognized as such, at least by some Christians in Thyatira. *to commit sexual immorality and to eat food sacrificed to idols:* Her teaching was the same as Balaam's (v 14). **24.** *the deep things of Satan, as they say:* Some have argued that the followers of Jezebel were taught "the deep things of God" and that the speaker implies that what they know is rather the mysteries of Satan, a rhetorical move analogous to the claim in v 9 that the synagogue of God is really the synagogue of Satan. The problem with this interpretation is the phrase "as they say." The speaker is apparently quoting them, not saying what they really know. If they claimed to know "the deep things of Satan," they may have taught magical formulas and practices which could control evil spirits. **26-27.** The promise to the conqueror makes use of imagery from one of the royal psalms (Ps 2:8-9). The same imagery is used to describe the work of Christ in 12:5; 19:15. In the context of this message, the promise implies that the future authority and power of Christians over non-Christians makes their attempt to assimilate with them appear misguided (cf. 1 Cor 6:1-6). **28.** *give the conqueror the morning star:* Giving the morning star may mean making one like the morning star: the faithful will be glorified and immortalized (cf. Dan 12:3; Matt 13:43; 1 Cor 15:40-44).

26 (e) To Sardis (3:1-6). **1.** *the seven spirits of God and the seven stars:* See 1:4,16,20. The risen Jesus has power over angels (cf. Phil 2:10; Heb 1:4-14; 2:5-9). **3.** *come like a thief . . . upon you:* In 16:15 the image of the thief is used for the general crisis of the end. Here a more particular judgment seems to be threatened, like the one against "Jezebel" and her followers (2:22-23). **4.** *a few names in Sardis:* The use of the word "name" suggests a register or list. The allusion may be to the book of life (see 3:5; 13:8; 17:8; 20:12,15; 21:27). *who have not soiled their garments:* Soiled garments may be a general symbol for sinfulness (cf. Zech 3:3-5). Another possibility is that the clean garments symbolize the purification and new beginning of baptism, which a few in Sardis have maintained. *they will walk with me in white garments, for they are worthy:* The "white garments" symbolize the glorified bodies which the faithful will receive either following their deaths or at the time of the resurrection (see 6:11; 7:9,13; cf. 2 Cor 5:4; *Asc. Isa.* 4:16; *Herm. Sim.* 8.2,3). **5.** *the book of life:* Originally a roster of names of those who would survive the manifestation of God's wrath (Mal 3:16-4:3); in Rev, a list of those who will enter the new Jerusalem (21:27).

27 (f) To Philadelphia (3:7-13). **7.** *who has the key of David, who opens and no one shall shut, and who shuts and no one opens:* This identification of the speaker alludes to Isa 22:22, where a new steward is described as having exclusive authority over personal access to the king. Here the risen Jesus is symbolically portrayed as the only mediator between humanity and God. **8.** *I have placed before you an open door which no one can shut:* This promise continues the imagery of v 7; through Jesus Christians have access to God and no one can deprive them of it. Since the Jews are mentioned in the next verse, the

question of mediators and access to God may have been a matter of controversy between Christians and Jews in this locality. **9.** *the synagogue of Satan:* See comment on 2:9. *I will make them come and worship at your feet:* The congregation is promised public vindication over their opponents in the future. **10.** *I will protect you at the hour of trial:* This promise does not mean that the Christians in Philadelphia are to be rescued from the sufferings of the end-time or from death, but that the speaker will support them in those sufferings in order that they may persevere. **12.** *a pillar in the temple of God:* This promise anticipates the vision of the new Jerusalem, in which there is no temple as a building, but a direct relationship and dwelling together of God and people (21:22; 22:3-4).

28 (g) To Laodicea (3:14-22). **17.** *you say "I am rich":* Apparently the Christians in Laodicea were wealthy and of relatively high social standing in the city. Having a secure social and economic position, they became complacent. *you are miserable, piteous, and poor:* The bold rhetoric here is the reverse of the message to Smyrna, where the economically poor are declared rich. **18.** *buy from me gold refined by fire:* The Christians in Laodicea are exhorted to testify to their Christian faith, even though such testimony will lead to social rejection and possibly to harassment, accusation before authorities and death. **20.** *behold, I stand at the door and knock:* This metaphorical saying at first seems to refer to the future (cf. v 11). What follows, however, refers to the present. *if any one hears my voice and opens the door:* It may be that the indifference of the Laodicean Christians or their concern for their standing had led them to refuse hospitality to John as he traveled in Asia and to reject his teaching. This saying would suggest that whoever receives such a teacher receives Christ (cf. Matt 10:41-42). *I will dine with such a person and he or she with me:* The reference to a meal may allude to the Lord's Supper. **21.** The conqueror will sit with me on my throne as I also conquered and sat with my Father on his throne: The enthronement of Jesus alongside God is a striking image of their equality (cf. 1:14,15,17). At the time John wrote, Christians constituted God's kingdom; they acknowledged God's rule. In the new age, they would share that rule over the new creation (2:26-27; 5:10; 22:5).

29 (2) The scroll with seven seals (4:1-8:5). No conclusion to the epiphany of Christ which begins in 1:10b is recorded. When the seventh message has been dictated, John reports "Afterward I saw . . ." (4:1). The lack of a narrative conclusion to the epiphany, describing the departure of the "one in human form" (1:13) or what John did after this revelatory experience, suggests that the experience whose beginning is recounted in 4:1 occurred on the same occasion. The phrase "Afterward I saw," however, separates the epiphany from a subsequent vision account.

(a) The heavenly court (4:1-11). This vision is closely linked to that of the scroll and the Lamb (5:1-14). Together they introduce the seven seals (6:1-8:5). Chapter 4 is a vision of God enthroned, surrounded by various attendants. Significant precedents of this vision include Isa 6 and Ezek 1. Important analogies are *1 Enoch* 14 and 71; *2 Enoch* 20-21; *Apoc. Abr.* 18. **1.** *a door opened in heaven:* In a Jewish apocalypse, an angel escorts the visionary to the firmament and through a very large door (or doors) into the first heaven (*3 Apoc. Bar.* 2:2; see also 3:1; 11:2; Gen 28:17; 3 Macc 6:18). *the first voice like a trumpet which I had heard speaking with me:* This statement refers to 1:10-11; it links the epiphany of "one in human form" in 1:10b-3:22 with the section 4:1-8:5 by implying that the revealer is the same in both accounts. "Come up here": This command suggests that

4:1-8:5, or even 4:1-22:5, should be understood as a heavenly journey or tour of heaven. Some other books which contain a vision of the enthroned deity are heavenly journeys, e.g., *1 Enoch* 1-36; *1 Enoch* 37-71; *2 Enoch; Apoc. Abr.* But the two major prototypes, Isa 6 and Ezek 1, are not (and 1 Kgs 22:19-23 is not). Rev 4:1-22:5 seems to be a borderline type. The opened door in heaven, the call to ascend, and analogous texts support the conclusion that Rev in part is a report of a heavenly journey. But, unlike the other texts mentioned, John's ascent is not described, nor his movement from place to place within heaven, nor his descent back to earth. In the rest of 4:1-22:5, John's vantage point is not explicit. *what must happen afterward:* A partial resumption of 1:19. **2.** *a throne stood in heaven:* A traditional Jewish notion (1 Kgs 22:19; Isa 6:1; Ezek 1:26; *1 Enoch* 14:18,19). **3.** *a rainbow all around the throne like the appearance of emerald:* The rainbow probably represents the halo or nimbus, the light commonly thought to encircle divine beings (Charles, *Commentary* 1. 115).

30   **4.** *I saw twenty-four thrones and upon the thrones twenty-four elders sitting:* In Jewish apocalyptic and mystical literature, all heavenly beings are described usually as standing, except the seated deity (*b. Ḥag.* 15a; *3 Enoch* 16). The portrayal of the elders as sitting around God may be influenced by the practice of the Roman court. When the emperor heard legal cases orally, he was seated and surrounded by senators, men of consular rank and other friends and advisors (D. E. Aune, *BR* 28 [1983] 8-9). In Babylonian astrology, 24 stars, half to the N and half to the S of the zodiac, were called "judges of the All." If such figures are the prototypes of the 24 elders, their presence and their placement in a circle around the deity symbolize cosmic order and governance. *seven spirits of God:* See comment on 1:4. **6.** *a glass sea like crystal:* In 15:2 the glass sea is described as mixed with fire. This combination recalls *1 Enoch* 14 in which a "great house" (palace or temple) in heaven is described with a ground or floor of crystal and surrounded by flaming fire (vv 10-12). It seems then that in 4:6 and 15:2 the background of the image is Ezek 1 and subsequent elaboration and interpretation of that vision. **6b.** *four living creatures:* The image of the four living creatures is a new literary creation, although individual motifs are borrowed from Isa 6 and Ezek 1 (cf. *Apoc. Abr.* 18:3-5). **10.** *twenty-four elders fall before the one sitting on the throne and prostrate themselves:* An act of reverence that originated in Persia and became part of the ceremony of the ruler cult in Hellenistic kingdoms and eventually of the imperial cult (D. E. Aune, *BR* 28 [1983] 13-14). **11.** *worthy are you:* This hymnlike passage was probably not borrowed from early Christian worship but was composed for this context (K.-P. Jörns, *Das hymnische Evangelium* [Gütersloh, 1971] 178-79). *you created all things:* The conclusion of the "hymn" suggests the underlying theme of chap. 4: God as creator; although God's power and concern for creation may not always be apparent, God is in reality not only Creator but also the Almighty who is coming to restore the creation (v 8).

31   *(b)* The scroll and the Lamb (5:1-14). Chapter 4 set the scene: the heavenly court or council. In chap. 5 the action begins. **1.** *a scroll written upon the inside and on the back, sealed with seven seals:* The context suggests that the scroll with seven seals is a book of destiny in which events of the end-time are recorded (Dan 10:21; *1 Enoch* 81:1-3). Opening the seals is equivalent to causing these events to occur. The eschatological events are depicted in the sequences of seven seals and seven trumpets. **2.** *"who is worthy to open the scroll?":* The heavenly council is faced with a serious problem. Someone must be found to break the seals of the scroll and initiate the events of

the end-time, through which God will be triumphant over preternatural and human adversaries. **3.** *no one in heaven, on earth, or under the earth was able:* No one can be found to accomplish this task. **4.** *I wept a great deal because no one was found worthy to open the scroll:* John's tears express the dilemma of the heavenly council as well as the desire of the faithful to know the events of the end-time and to see them put into effect. **5.** At last a champion is found. *the lion of the tribe of Judah:* A messianic (kingly) title (Gen 49:9-10). *the root of David:* Also a royal title (cf. Isa 11:1,10). *has conquered:* Since Rev is a Christian writing, the messianic titles refer to Jesus. In what sense can Jesus be said to be a conqueror? The allusion must be to his death, resurrection, or both, viewed as closely related events. The image of the lamb which appears in v 6 suggests an emphasis on the death. **6.** *a lamb standing as if slain, having seven horns:* The origin of the symbol "Lamb" for Jesus is uncertain. The description of the Lamb as slain strongly suggests that either Isa 53 or Exod 12 and related traditions have played a role in the formation of this symbol. The depiction of the Lamb as horned, the juxtaposition of the epithet Lamb with the messianic titles in v 5, and the role of the Lamb in Rev as a whole suggest that the apocalyptic messianic symbol of a horned sheep or ram has also had an influence (Dan 8:20-21; *1 Enoch* 89:42; 90:9). *"worthy are you to take the scroll":* Only the Lamb is worthy to possess the scroll and to open its seals. This implies that the death and resurrection of Jesus and the reconstitution of the redeemed people of God are essential prerequisites for the unfolding of the eschatological events. It also suggests that only the Lamb's followers may know the contents of the scroll; only the risen Jesus can mediate knowledge of the future. **11-14.** The acclamations of large numbers of beings of every class and the elders' act of prostration recall the honors given to the Roman emperor (D. E. Aune, *BR* 28 [1983] 14-20). The offering of these honors to God and the Lamb rather than the emperor reflects John's vision of the conflict between the rule of God and the rule of Caesar.

32   *(c)* The first four seals (6:1-8). The traditional interpretation of Rev held that the seven seals represent the past from John's point of view, not the present or the future (for a revival of this type of interpretation, see E. Corsini, *The Apocalypse* [Wilmington, 1983] 118-63). Interpreters of the late 19th cent. and some in the 20th have found allusions in the first four seals to historical events of John's time. Widespread disagreement on which events are depicted suggests that this approach is misguided. The theory that the seals depict world history is supported by the fact that many Jewish apocalypses contain symbolic reviews of history (Dan; *1 Enoch; 2 Apoc. Bar.*). But most commentators have concluded rightly that Rev lacks this feature. This conclusion is supported by the similarities between the seals and the messianic woes as depicted in the Synoptic Gospels (L. A. Vos, *The Synoptic Traditions in the Apocalypse* [Kampen, 1965]). The seals depict in summary form the imminent eschatological future, not the past or present, although past and contemporary events may provide images for describing that future. The other series of visions describes the same events from different perspectives and in varying detail (→ 13-15 above). The major themes in each series are persecution of the faithful, judgment of their adversaries, and salvation of the faithful. The first four seals are unified by the image of the four horsemen (cf. Zech 1:8-11; 6:1-8) and by the common wording of their introductions. **2.** *a white horse:* A symbol of victory; the general celebrating a military triumph often rode a white horse. *holding a bow:* A weapon characteristic of Parthian armies; Parthia was the successor to the Persian empire. *a crown:* A crown was sometimes given as a prize for public service in war. Parthia was Rome's greatest rival in the East. Inhabitants of the eastern provinces, including some Jews, who were unhappy with Roman rule, looked to Parthia as a potential liberator. Chapter 17 suggests that John expected Parthia to invade and defeat Rome. This first seal depicts such a Parthian victory, which would mean the destruction of the enemy of Christians, in John's view. The positive tone of this vision expresses joy at such a prospect. **4.** *a flame-colored horse:* The second horseman represents war, as the description makes clear. **5.** *a black horse:* The color black was associated with death, perhaps because of the darkness of the underworld (LSJ 1095). The description suggests that death by famine is meant. **6.** *a measure of wheat for a denarius and three measures of barley for a denarius:* A denarius was the typical wage of a laborer for one day. Usually a denarius could purchase eight to sixteen times more grain than the amounts mentioned here. *do not harm oil and wine:* This vision predicts a time in which grain, the staple of life, will be scarce, and extras like oil and wine will be plentiful. **8.** *a pallid horse:* The color may signify fear or ill health (LSJ 1995). *Death:* The personification of Death was known in Gk literature (LSJ 784) and in Jewish (Ps 49:1; Hos 13:14). *Hades was following with him:* Hades was a Gk god, lord of the underworld; the nether world as a place was also called Hades. Hebr *še'ôl* was used in the same ways (Ps 49:15–16; Hos 13:14). The usual power of Death and Hades will be allowed to increase so that one-fourth of the earth is affected.

33   (d) The fifth and sixth seals (6:9–17). **9.** *under the altar:* An altar in heaven is probably meant, since the earthly Temple was a copy of a heavenly original (Exod 25:9; Heb 8:5). According to a rabbinic work, the souls of the righteous rest under the heavenly altar (*'Abot R. Nat.;* see Charles, *Commentary* 1. 228). *the word of God and the testimony which they held:* The reason for their death calls to mind the reason for John's banishment (1:9; cf. 12:11,17; 19:10; 20:4). This seal predicts execution in the context of persecution as one of the woes of the end-time. **10.** The souls cry out for their blood to be avenged. **11.** *each of them was given a white robe:* A symbol of the glorified body of the righteous dead (cf. 3:4–5,18). The avenging of their blood cannot take place until the predetermined number of martyrs has been killed; then the judgment can take place (A. Yarbro Collins, *JBL* 96 [1977] 241–56). This response means that the disasters of the end-time are understood as a punishment of those who have persecuted the followers of the Lamb. **12–14.** The juxtaposition of the vision of the sixth seal with that of the fifth suggests that the cosmic destruction is vengeance for the martyrs' death. **16.** *the wrath of the Lamb:* This phrase is paradoxical if the Lamb is thought of entirely in terms of the silent and meek Servant of Yahweh in Isa 53; it is more understandable if the symbol Lamb has incorporated some of the connotations of the messianic ram (see comment on 5:6).

34   (e) Two inserted visions (7:1–17). The fifth seal predicted the persecution of the faithful, and the sixth the punishment of their persecutors. In these inserted visions, the third major theme is expressed: salvation of the followers of the Lamb. The lack of connection between these two visions and the enumeration of the seals makes them stand out.

(1') 144,000 sealed (7:1–8). **1.** *four angels:* In the thought of Second Temple Judaism, God regulates the natural elements through the agency of angelic beings (*1 Enoch* 60:11–22; *Jub.* 2:2). *the four winds of the earth:* The four winds are agents of divine punishment

(cf. Jer 49:36). This function is explicit in v 2. **3.** *until we seal the servants of our God:* This symbolic sealing was inspired by Ezek 9, where an angel makes a mark on the foreheads of those who have avoided idolatry, a mark that causes their lives to be spared. According to the vision of the souls under the altar, at least some of the faithful will die. The sealing in Rev does not symbolize protection "from" death, but protection in and through death (see comment on 3:10). *upon their foreheads:* The seal may be equivalent to the name of God written upon the foreheads of the faithful (cf. 3:12; 14:1; 22:4). **4.** *one hundred forty-four thousand:* The number sealed includes 12,000 from each of the tribes of Israel. The use of the traditional element of the twelve tribes makes the impression of chosenness. The 12,000 from each tribe intensifies the sense of chosenness; a remnant survives, a minority is loyal. These numbers are not meant literally, but are used for their symbolic connotations. The membership in the twelve tribes is probably also meant symbolically and not literally; membership in the Jewish people is not primarily a matter of birth (2:9; 3:9). The use of numbers, however, does suggest that a limited group is meant, not simply all Christians. The identity of this group becomes clearer in 14:1–5. **5–8.** A peculiarity of this list is the absence of Dan, probably for theological reasons. The OT apparently describes the tribe of Dan as idolatrous (Judg 18; 1 Kgs 12:28–30). According to the present form of the *T. 12 Patr.,* the prince of Dan is Satan (*T. Dan* 5:6). A prophecy of judgment is linked to Dan in Jer 8:16–17. These traditions may have been the basis for the development of the Christian tradition that the antichrist would come from this tribe (Irenaeus, *Adv. Haer.* 5.30.2; see Swete, *Apocalypse* 98).

35   (2') Salvation of a multitude (7:9–17). The second inserted vision describes the ultimate salvation of the righteous more clearly and more dramatically than the first (7:1–8). It is thus the climax of the seven seals. **9.** *a great crowd, which no one could count, from every nation:* The people in this vision are deliberately contrasted with those in the previous account; the first group is meticulously numbered, whereas the second is innumerable. The first come from the people of Israel; the second from all nations. Although the details cannot be pressed, the implication is that the second group is all the faithful who are loyal to the end and the first constitutes a select group within the larger body (see comment on 14:1–5). *palm-fronds in their hands:* The palm-frond was a badge of victory (LSJ 1948). **10.** *victory belongs to our God:* Gk *sōtēria,* usually translated "salvation," means victory here. Its Hebr equivalent *yĕšû'â* has the nuances of welfare, deliverance, salvation, and victory. In many passages it means "victory" (1 Sam 14:45; Hab 3:8; Pss 20:6; 44:5 [BDB 447]). The innumerable multitude sings a victory song to God and the Lamb (cf. Exod 15; Judg 5). This scene is the counterpart of chap. 5. There the heavenly council was faced with a dilemma: who would open the scroll, i.e., initiate the events of the end-time through which God's adversaries would be defeated and punished. The first six seals describe those events. The triumph of God and God's agent the Lamb is celebrated here. **13–17.** A brief interpretation of the vision follows in the form of a dialogue between John and one of the 24 elders, who takes the role here of the interpreting angel common in apocalyptic texts (→ OT Apocalyptic, 19:4, 20). **14.** *great tribulation:* The crisis of the end-time, which involves persecution for the faithful (cf. 1:9; 3:10). *made them white by means of the blood of the Lamb:* The robes symbolize the inner or spiritual state of the person, as in the first half of 3:4. The transformation of a person from soiled (sinful) to clean (holy) is closely related to the death of Jesus understood as a sacrifice (cf. 1:5; 5:6,9). The fundamental allusion here seems to be to repentance, conversion, and baptism taken together as a transformation of the person. The reference to tribulation implies that perseverance in that process of transformation is also crucial for those who would share in the victory of God and the Lamb. Perseverance may lead to death (martyrdom), but it is not implied that all Christians will follow the Lamb in that way. **15–17.** A poetic description of salvation. **15.** *before the throne of God:* The greatest blessing is to be in God's presence (cf. 22:3–4). *in God's Temple:* Serving in the Temple symbolizes closeness to God (cf. 3:12). **16–17.** Various metaphors are used to express the meaning of salvation; the satisfaction of physical and emotional needs symbolizes fulfillment of the whole person.

36 (*f*) The seventh seal and vision of an angel offering the prayers of the saints (8:1–5). The climax of the seven seals has already been reached in 7:9–17. The role of the seventh seal is to reestablish a sense of drama and suspense and provide a transition to the next series of visions, the seven trumpets (8:2–11:19). The transition is accomplished through the literary technique of interlocking two sections of the book. The interlocking or connecting of the seals and trumpets is accomplished by assigning to the opening of the seventh seal three effects: (1) the silence (8:1); (2) the appearance of the seven angels with the seven trumpets (8:2); (3) the vision of the angel with the golden censer (8:3–5). Thus the whole series of the trumpets is included in the series of events caused by the unsealing of the scroll (cf. 5:1). The vision of the angel with the censer also links the two series (see below). **1.** *a silence in heaven of about half an hour:* The uneven length of time characterizes the silence not as a time of rest and fulfillment, but as a time of anticipation. **2.** *the seven angels who stand before God:* Seven angels of high rank, perhaps identical with the seven spirits before God's throne (1:4; cf. 5:6) and the seven torches of fire burning before the throne (4:5). *seven trumpets:* On the symbolic significance of the trumpet, see comment on 1:10.

37 The vision of an angel offering the prayers of the saints (8:3–5) is inserted between the introduction of the seven angels (v 2) and the description of their activity which begins in v 6. The inserted vision alludes back to the fifth seal and forward to the first four trumpets. The altar in v 3 recalls the altar in 6:9. The prayers of the saints (v 3) recall the cry of the souls under the altar for vengeance in 6:10. The offering of incense along with the prayers of the saints by the angel in v 4 repeats under a different image the prayer of 6:10. The casting of fire upon the earth in v 5 recapitulates the response to the souls in 6:11, but instead of requiring a wait, the image suggests divine response to their plea (cf. Ezek 10:2). The angel's gesture foreshadows the plagues upon the earth associated with the first four trumpets (8:6–12). Thus, the implication is that the plagues of the trumpets are punishment for the persecution of the faithful.

38 (3) The seven trumpets (8:2–11:19). The seven messages look forward to judgment and salvation from the point of view of particular Christian communities. The seven seals predict eschatological judgment and salvation in a general way, emphasizing the perspective of all humanity, esp. of the faithful. The series of visions associated with the seven trumpets also concerns the events of the last days, but the emphasis here is on the cosmos: heaven, earth, the waters, and the underworld. The content of the trumpet series is a free adaption of the ten plagues against the Egyptians which preceded the exodus (Exod 7–10). The treatment of Christians by Rome is analogous to the enslavement of

the Israelites in Egypt. God's eschatological judgment will be like the plagues on the land and people of Egypt.
39 (*a*) The first four trumpets (8:2,6–12). Like the first four seals, the first four trumpets form a group. Together they affect the cosmos as a totality. Each is brief relative to the fifth and sixth trumpets. **7.** *hail and fire, mixed with blood:* This catastrophe, which affects one-third of the earth, recalls the seventh plague against the Egyptians, heavy hail upon the land with flashes of fire (Exod 9:22–26). **8.** *one-third of the sea became blood:* This disaster is analogous to the first plague against the Egyptians, the turning of the Nile River to blood (Exod 7:14–24). **11.** One-third of the fresh waters will turn to wormwood and thus become bitter. This plague was perhaps inspired by an oracle against God's unfaithful people in Jer 9:15–16. **12.** This plague on heaven may have been inspired by the ninth Egyptian plague of darkness (Exod 10:21–23), but it is closer in imagery to passages like Amos 8:9; Joel 3:15; and Isa 30:26.

40 (*b*) The eagle and the three woes; the fifth and sixth trumpets (8:13–9:21). The first four trumpets were directed against the cosmos. The last three trumpets (which are the three woes according to 8:13) affect humanity more directly. **9:1–11.** The fifth trumpet unleashes a demonic plague which is directed against the enemies of God (v 4). **1.** *a star fallen from heaven to earth:* Pagans believed that stars were divine beings; Jews identified them with angels. The fall of this angel recalls the myths of the fallen angels and the rebellion of Satan (Gen 6:1–4; Isa 14:12–15; *ANET* 140; *2 Enoch* 18, 29; *Adam and Eve* 12–16). *the key to the shaft of the abyss:* Since the angel "is given the key," the opening of the abyss (the underworld) is not a rebellion, but part of God's plan. This vision is analogous to those of 20:1–3 and 7–10. The events described are not identical, but this passage anticipates chap. 20, and the latter recapitulates the former. Both describe the unleashing of chaotic and terrible forces during the last days. **3.** *locusts:* The fifth trumpet alludes to the eighth plague against the Egyptians (Exod 10). The prophet Joel interpreted the natural catastrophe of a swarm of locusts as God's punishment on the Lord's own people. Rev is similar to Exod 10 in presenting the plague as directed against God's enemies (v 4) and similar to Joel in likening the swarm to an army (vv 7, 9; Joel 2:4–9). It goes beyond both in transforming the locusts into demonic creatures with tails like scorpions (vv 3,5,10), heads like humans' (v 7), and teeth like lions' (v 8), who torture the wicked rather than devour foliage (v 4). **7.** *horses prepared for battle:* The military imagery of the fifth trumpet is resumed in the sixth. Compare the chariots of v 9 with the troops of cavalry in v 17; horses (vv 7,9,17,19) and breastplates (vv 9,17) appear in both. *golden crowns:* The only other beings in Rev said to have golden crowns are heavenly beings (4:4; 14:14); as demons or fallen angels, the locusts are "heavenly" also. The "crowns" may also resume the first seal and thus allude to the Parthians (see comment on 6:2). **11.** *Abaddon:* The leader of the demonic locusts is not Satan but the personified underworld, or "the Destroyer." These names resume Hades (underworld) and Death in the vision of the fourth seal (6:8). Here, however, the point is not death, but prolonged torture. **9:13–19.** Like the fifth, the description of the sixth plague vacillates between an account of a battle and a depiction of supernatural beings executing divine wrath on the wicked. The emphasis in both visions is on the work of angelic or demonic beings. **13.** *the golden altar:* The same altar mentioned in 8:3–5. This allusion links the sixth plague to the prayers of the saints for vengeance (6:10). **14.** *at the great river Euphrates:* The mention of the Euphrates anticipates the battle associated with the sixth bowl (16:12–16). It is likely that the sixth trumpet and the sixth bowl allude to the same event from different points of view. The description here is purposely veiled and mysterious (see G. Bornkamm, *ZNW* 36 [1937] 132–49; Yarbro Collins, *Combat Myth* [→ 15 above] 35–36). The Euphrates calls to mind the great empires to the E and N of Judea. In John's day the dominant power in that region was the Parthian Empire (see comment on 6:2). **15.** *kept ready for the hour and day and month and year:* This remark implies a predetermined divine plan. *one-third of humanity:* One-third is a measurement characteristic of the trumpets (8:7–12); it represents an escalation in comparison with the fourth seal (6:8). **20–21.** The typical response of dwellers on earth to the plagues is to curse God rather than to repent (cf. 16:9,11,21). Only in Jerusalem will the people eventually repent (cf. 16:9 with 11:13). **20.** *worship demons:* The gods of the Gentiles are identified with demons (cf. Deut 32:17; 1 Cor 10:19–20). *idols made of gold and silver and bronze and stone and wood, which are able neither to see nor hear nor walk:* This description of idols is very close to Dan 5:23. The context in Dan is the tale about the writing on the wall at Belshazzar's feast. Daniel interprets it as a revelation concerning the future of the Babylonian kingdom, which will involve its division by the Medes and the Persians. This allusion to Dan 5 may indicate that John expected a great battle at the Euphrates which would fulfill Dan 5:28; "Babylon" (Rome) would be conquered by the Parthians (the successors of the Persians). **21.** *their murders and sorceries and sexual immorality and thefts:* A traditional list of vices (cf. Rom 1:29–31; Gal 5:19–21; 1 Cor 6:9–10; Eph 5:3–5; Mark 7:21–22; *Herm. Man.* 8.5).

41 (*c*) Two inserted visions (10:1–11:13). These two visions are not associated with any of the trumpets and so form a kind of double interlude. Their role in the structure of Rev is analogous to that of the visions inserted into the series of seals (7:1–8, 9–17). Unlike the visions of chap. 7, these do not constitute the climax of the series in which they appear; the climax of the trumpets follows the sounding of the seventh (see comment on 11:15–19). Instead they anticipate some themes of the second cycle of visions (12:1–22:5) and provide thereby a link between the two halves of the book.

(1′) A mighty angel and a little open scroll (10:1–11). This vision may be seen as an introduction to the second cycle of visions because in it John receives a new commission, and a new scroll is brought in whose contents are depicted in chaps. 12–22. **1.** *another mighty angel:* The only other "mighty" angel mentioned so far is the angel associated with the sealed scroll (5:2). *his face was like the sun:* This characteristic calls to mind the description of the risen Christ in 1:16; see comment on vv 8 and 11. **2.** *having in his hand a little open scroll:* This remark is parallel to 5:1, where God is depicted as holding a sealed scroll. The sealed scroll is a symbol of the first cycle of visions: fragmentary, obscure, evidently deliberately veiled. The open scroll symbolizes the second cycle of visions, in which the characters of the eschatological drama are more sharply defined and the nature of the conflict of the last days and its resolution is more vividly and coherently depicted. Both 5:1 and 10:2 allude to Ezek 2:8–3:3. Because the scroll of 10:2 is little, some have argued that it refers only to 11:1–13. This hypothesis is very unlikely (see comments on 10:11 and 11:1). *his right foot upon the sea and his left foot upon the land:* Because of the similarity between vv 5–6 below and Dan 12:5–7, it seems likely that the angel of Rev 10 is modeled in part on the angel (Gabriel) who speaks to Daniel in Dan 10–12. Whereas Dan describes three angels, one on each bank of the Tigris River and one

(Gabriel) above its waters, Rev depicts a single angel straddling the land (or earth) and sea. John's vision is more cosmic and universal. **6.** *no more delay:* The fact that the scroll is little or short may symbolize the nearness of the end. **7.** *the mystery of God:* The divine plan for creation; a mystery is a heavenly secret regarding a hidden present reality or the future (see comment on 17:5). *God's servants the prophets:* The reference may be to the prophets of Jewish Scripture, to early Christian prophets contemporary with John, or both (cf. Amos 3:7; 1QpHab 7; 2 Esdr 13:10–12; Rev 22:9). **8–10.** The allusion to the risen Christ of chap. 1 now comes into play. In 1:11,19 and at the beginning of each of the seven messages, John is commanded to write the revelation he has received in a book and to send it to the seven congregations. This command is equivalent to a commission to prophesy. The scriptural prototype of 10:8–10 (Ezek 2:8–3:3) is also a commission to prophesy. Because of the close link between 4:1–2 and 1:10–11, chaps. 2–11 may be seen as fulfilling the commission of chap. 1. The renewed commission of 10:8–10 is then fulfilled in chaps. 12–22. **11.** *you must prophesy again:* The renewed commission to prophesy is made explicit. *about peoples and nations and tongues and many kings:* This description of the content of the renewed prophecy fits chaps. 12–22 much better than 11:1–13 (see comment on v 2).

(2′) The temple and two witnesses (11:1–13). Like chap. 10 this passage is an insertion into the series of trumpets. It does not follow logically from chap. 10, but is simply placed after it as a parallel passage. 11:1–13 is not a unity, but is a combination of two originally independent traditional elements, vv 1–2 and 3–13. As noted above, chap. 10 introduces chaps. 12–22 formally. 11:1–13 prepares for those chapters by introducing two key motifs: the time limit set for the period of eschatological woes (vv 2 and 3) and the beast which ascends from the abyss (v 7). **1.** *a measuring rod like a staff was given to me:* 11:1–13 is probably not intended to represent the content of the little scroll (see 10:2), because this passage begins with its own symbolic action (R. Bultmann, *TLZ* 52 [1927] 505–12). The significance of the measuring is apparent only in v 2. **2.** *do not measure it:* The courtyard of the Temple is not to be measured because the Gentiles are allowed to trample the holy city; this suggests that the measuring of the Temple itself, the altar, and those who worship there signifies their preservation from the Gentiles. This prophecy probably originated during the Jewish War, when the rebels were occupying the Temple and the Romans had broken through the walls of the outer Temple. Josephus reports that certain prophets proclaimed that God would come to the help of the rebels immediately and deliver them from that dire situation (*J.W.* 6.5.2 § 283–86; see Yarbro Collins, *Crisis* [→ 6 above] 64–69). When the prophecy was not fulfilled literally, it was handed on and given spiritual (allegorical) interpretations. John probably reinterpreted the inner/outer contrast of the oracle in heavenly/earthly terms: the earthly Temple has been destroyed, but its heavenly counterpart endures, to which the (true) worshipers of God turn their attention. *forty-two months:* In the passage alluded to in 10:5–6, the angel tells the seer that all these things would be accomplished in "a time, two times, and half a time" (Dan 12:7). A "time" is apparently a year (see Dan 7:25; 8:14; 9:27; 12:11–12). 42 months is equivalent to the 3½ years implied by Dan 12:7. In Rev it refers to the period of eschatological woes. Since it is so difficult to correlate with historical events alluded to in Rev, it is probably not meant literally. **3.** *I will commission my two witnesses to prophesy:* This verse was probably composed by John to link the older, independent traditions now embodied in vv 1–2 and

4–13. There are indications that a written source was used in vv 4–13 (Yarbro Collins, *Combat Myth* [→ 15 above] 195 n. 60). The term "witness" is also used of Jesus (1:5; 3:14), of Antipas (2:13), and others who have died for their testimony (17:6). The term was not yet technical (i.e., meaning "martyr") in Rev, but became so by the middle of the 2d cent. (*Mart. Pol.* 2.2; 17.3; cf. N. Brox, *Zeuge und Märtyrer* [Munich, 1961]). *one thousand two hundred and sixty days:* Equivalent to the 42 months of v 2. **4.** *the two olive trees and the two lampstands:* Cf. Zech 4:12–14. **5.** *fire:* Cf. 2 Kgs 1:9–12; Sir 48:3. The activity of the witnesses recalls Elijah. **6.** *that it may not rain:* Another allusion to Elijah (1 Kgs 17–18). *every plague:* An allusion to Moses (Exod 7–11). **7.** *the beast which ascends from the abyss:* The imagery recalls the fifth trumpet (9:1–11), but here the eschatological adversary is meant. **8–12.** The two witnesses were probably intended to be understood as eschatological agents of God to be active in the near future. It is significant that the pattern of the witnesses' lives, deaths, and afterlives recapitulates that of Jesus Christ and expresses in an extraordinary and public way the hoped-for destiny of the author and receptive readers. Whatever the intended references were, the paradigmatic function of the narrative is apparent.

42 *(d) The seventh trumpet (11:15–19).* Like the series of the seven seals, the seven trumpets depict the eschatological woes, judgment, and salvation in their entirety. The theme of persecution (woes) appears in the vision which introduces the trumpets (8:3–5) through the allusion to the vision of the souls under the altar (6:9–11). Judgment and ultimate salvation are described in the vision following the seventh trumpet. **15.** *the kingship over the world:* In light of 1:5, one could argue that v 15 describes what is already a present reality for John. 12:12, however, indicates that the present was characterized for John by Satan's rule over the earth. This suggests that 11:15–17 describes the eschatological future for John. **18.** *the nations were wrathful:* The mistreatment of the righteous is probably implied here, and thus the eschatological woes. *your wrath came:* The definitive divine punishment of evildoing. *the time for the dead to be judged:* A clear reference to the general judgment, which probably implies a general resurrection. *reward:* The judgment is blessing (salvation) for the righteous. *to destroy:* The judgment involves punishment for the wicked. As in the climax of the seals, the eschatological resolution is acclaimed by heavenly beings (cf. 11:15 with 7:10–12). **19.** *the heavenly temple of God was opened and the ark of God's covenant appeared:* The opening of the Holy of Holies here expresses an extraordinary self-revelation of God. *flashes of lightning . . . claps of thunder and an earthquake:* Typical cosmic manifestations of the self-revelation or theophany of God (J. Jeremias, *Theophanie* [Neukirchen, 1977]; L. Hartman, *Prophecy Interpreted* [ConBNT 1; Lund, 1966]).

43 *(ii) Second cycle of visions (12:1–22:5).* Very little links chap. 12 with the series of the trumpets; therefore, it is preferable to consider the visions of 12:1–15:4 as the first series in a new cycle, rather than to associate them with the trumpets. The symbol of the second cycle is the open scroll (cf. 10:2).

(1) *Symbolic visions revealing secrets of the past, present, and future (12:1–15:4).* These visions are not explicitly numbered. They may be distinguished from one another, however, by noting the combination of the use of visionary formulas (e.g., "X appeared" or "I saw") and a change in characters or subject matter. These transitional devices indicate that the series contains seven visions.

(a) The woman and the dragon (12:1–17). This chapter is not a unitary composition, but is based on two sources: a narrative describing the conflict between a woman with child and a dragon (reflected in vv 1–6 and 13–17) and a narrative depicting a battle in heaven (vv 7–9). It is probable that these sources were composed by non-Christian Jews and that John edited them, making numerous additions, including the hymn of vv 10–12 (see Yarbro Collins, *Combat Myth* [→ 15 above] 101–16). **1.** *a woman clothed with the sun, and the moon beneath her feet, and upon her head a crown of twelve stars:* These attributes are typical of high goddesses in the ancient world (ibid. 71–76), such as Isis (see Apuleius, *Metamor.* 11.2–6). The identity of the woman has been debated. A traditional Roman Catholic interpretation has been that she is Mary, the mother of Jesus, who is also the new Eve. Other suggestions are that she is the heavenly Jerusalem, personified wisdom, or the church. In the source the woman was personified Israel, whose birth pangs (v 2) symbolized the eschatological woes which precede the appearance of the Messiah. In the present form of chap. 12, the woman is the heavenly Israel, the spouse of God (cf. Hos 1:2; 2:4–5 [*RSV* 2:2–3]; 2:16–17 [*RSV* 2:14–15]; Isa 50:1; 54:5–8). Since John claims the name "Jew" for Christians (2:9; 3:9), he does not distinguish between Israel and the church. **3.** *a great red dragon with seven heads and ten horns:* This dragon or sea-serpent is a mythic beast, a very ancient symbol of chaos. Babylonian tradition includes the motif of a serpentine monster with seven heads (*ANEP* 220 no. 691). Canaanite texts mention a similar beast (*ANET* 138). Such a beast is portrayed as God's opponent in the OT (cf. Isa 27:1; 51:9; Pss 74:13; 89:11; Job 9:13; 26:12). In the final form of chap. 12, the dragon is identified with the serpent of Gen 3, who in turn is identified with the devil and Satan (v 9). The "ten horns" derive from Dan 7:7. **4.** *his tail swept one-third of the stars from heaven and cast them upon the earth:* This motif is similar to Dan 8:10. In Gk tradition, the rebellious chaos monster attacks the stars (see Nonnos, *Dionys.* 1. 163–64,180–81). *the dragon stood before the woman . . . in order that . . . he might devour her child:* Many parallels can be found in the OT and other Jewish texts to individual elements of chap. 12. The closest parallel, however, to the plot of the narrative about the woman and the dragon is a Greco-Roman version of the story of Apollo's birth. Leto, a goddess, was pregnant by Zeus. Python, a dragon, foresaw that Leto's son would displace him as ruler over the oracle at Delphi. So he pursued her when she was about to give birth, in order to kill the child. By order of Zeus, the north wind and Poseidon, god of the sea, aided Leto. She gave birth to Apollo and Artemis. Apollo then killed Python. One of the sources used by John was an adaptation of this narrative to describe the birth of the Messiah. Since several emperors, notably Nero, associated themselves with Apollo, John and his source suggested in opposition to such propaganda that the Messiah promised to Israel would bring in the true golden age (see Yarbro Collins, *Combat Myth* [→ 15 above] 61–70, 101–45). **10.** *because the accuser of our brothers [and sisters] has been thrown down:* The hymn in vv 10–12 serves as a commentary on the narrative of vv 1–9 and 13–17. The dragon or serpent of the narrative is identified in the hymn as the "accuser" of Christians before God in the heavenly court. Christians are acquitted in that court because of the death of Jesus (cf. 1:5b). Vindication in the heavenly court is an ironic reversal of condemnation in earthly (Roman) courts ("on account of the word of their testimony," v 11), which leads to execution ("they did not love their lives unto death," v 11). These Christians are "the rest of her [the woman's] seed" (v 17), whom the

dragon pursued after the child was taken up to heaven (v 5). **18.** *he [the dragon] stood on the seashore:* This verse is a transition to the vision of 13:1–10 and associates closely the dragon and the beast from the sea (cf. *MNT* 219–39).

44   (b) The beast from the sea (13:1–10). This beast and the beast from the earth in the next visionary account have both mythic and historical connotations. The pairing of a beast from the sea with one from the earth or land calls to mind the mythic motif of Leviathan (sea monster) and Behemoth (land monster); see Job 40–41. **1.** *a beast rising up out of the sea:* In the LXX *thalassa*, "sea," is often used to translate the Hebr *yām*. In Canaanite myths, *Yam*, "Sea," is a deity in conflict with Baal, the god of the storm and fertility. Similarly, sea is an opponent of God in the OT (e.g., Ps 74:13). The association of the beast of Rev 13:1 with the sea characterizes it as a mythic symbol of chaos and rebellion. The sea as a mythic motif is equivalent to the "abyss" (11:7). The abyss (the deep) in the OT is the original flood, or floods of water, and has mythic connotations (cf. Ps 77:17). Thus the beast of 13:1–10 resumes and is equivalent to the beast of 11:7; it is also linked in two ways to Dan 7. Certain details suggest that it is a combination of the four beasts of Dan 7: the "ten horns" (v 1) link it to the fourth beast (Dan 7:7–8); it is like a leopard, as is the third beast (Dan 7:6); its bearlike feet recall the second beast (Dan 7:5); and its lionlike mouth associates it with the first beast (Dan 7:4). Whereas Dan 7 is interested in four successive kings and kingdoms (Dan 7:17,23), Rev 13 focuses on one great kingdom, the culmination of all the terrors of the former ones. The fourth beast of Dan 7, however, is the primary model for Rev 13:1–10. John likely understood the fourth beast of Dan as a prophecy of the "kingdom" of his own time (Rome), rather than as an interpretation of the Macedonian kingdom in accordance with the original meaning of the text. Besides the "ten horns," other motifs link the beast of Rev 13:1–10 with Dan 7: a mouth speaking great things (v 5; cf. Dan 7:8,11), which in Rev is understood as blasphemy (cf. vv 5 and 6 with Dan 7:7,8,25); and his oppression of the saints (holy ones) for 3½ times (years), which is 42 months (cf. vv 5,7 with Dan 7:25; 8:14; see also Rev 11:2,3). *seven heads:* This motif, like the sea, indicates that the beast is a mythic symbol; cf. 12:3. **3.** *one of its heads appeared to be mortally wounded, but its wound was healed:* As the horns represent individual kings in Dan 7:24, so here the heads represent individual "kings" or emperors. The remark in v 7 that the beast was given authority over every tribe, people, tongue, and nation is a clear indication that, on the historical level of meaning, the beast from the sea signifies the Roman Empire. The visionary motif of the healing of a head's (= emperor's) mortal wound was probably inspired by the legend that Nero, who committed suicide, would return to regain power over Rome (Suetonius, *Nero* 47–57; *Sib. Or.* 4:119–24,137–48; 5:93–110,361–84; see Yarbro Collins, *Combat Myth* [→ 15 above] 176–83). The form this allusion takes deliberately describes the eschatological adversary in terms similar to those used for the Lamb (5:6). Although the term is not used, the eschatological adversary is depicted as an antichrist.

45   (c) The beast from the earth (13:11–18). **11.** *it had two horns like those of a lamb, but it was speaking like a dragon:* The two horns may have been inspired by Dan 8:3, in which the visionary sees a *krios*, "ram," representing the Medo-Persian Empire. The use of *arnion*, "lamb," suggests that this beast is, like the beast from the sea, a counterimage to the Lamb of Rev 5. In 16:13; 19:20; 20:10, the beast from the earth is described as a false

prophet. The characterization in 13:11 is analogous to that of false prophets in Matt 7:15. Whereas Matt 7:15 refers to false Christian prophets (cf. *Did.* 11:2,5–6,8–10), the false prophet of Rev is neither Jewish nor Christian. **12.** *it exercises the whole authority of the first beast . . . and makes . . . those who dwell on earth worship the first beast:* This characterization suggests that, on the historical level of meaning, the beast from the earth represents a deputy or agent of the Roman Empire who plays an important role in the imperial cult. Since Rev was probably written in or near the Roman province of Asia, the most likely reference is to the provincial elite, local leaders of noble family and wealth who by this time had acquired Roman citizenship and exercised political power under the supervision of the Roman provincial governor. The allusion to the imperial cult calls to mind the league of the cities of Asia whose purpose was to promote the cult of the emperor and the goddess Roma. This league elected several Asiarchs each year, officials whose primary duties were to protect and promote the imperial cult. They came from the noblest, wealthiest, and most powerful families (see D. Magie, *Roman Rule in Asia Minor* [2 vols.; Princeton, 1950]). **13.** *it works great signs:* In v 14 the effect of these signs is that the inhabitants of the earth are led astray. In the Synoptic tradition, false Christs and false prophets will show signs and wonders to the same effect (Mark 13:22; Matt 24:24). According to 2 Thess 2:9, the coming of the lawless one will be accompanied by false signs and wonders which will deceive and cause unbelievers to err. In Rev this tradition may be specified with reference to an imperial mystery cult (see S. J. Scherrer, *JBL* 103 [1984] 599–610). **15.** *to cause those who would not worship the image of the beast to be killed:* During the reign of the emperor Trajan (AD 98–117), those who had been accused of being Christian and denied that they were were asked to invoke the gods, worship the image of Trajan, and curse Christ. These commands were designed to test whether they truly were Christians or not (Pliny, *Ep.* 10.96). Such tests were probably used somewhat earlier as well. **15.** This verse reflects such a situation in a heightened way and shows how offensive the imperial cult was to John. **17.** *the mark . . . of the beast:* The "mark" is probably an allusion to coins with the image, name, and insignia of the emperor on them (see A. Yarbro Collins, *JBL* 96 [1976] 252–54). **18.** *six hundred sixty-six:* This puzzle is based on the fact that words in Hebrew and Greek can be given a numerical value, since each letter is also used as a numeral. The sum here is probably an allusion to Nero (see Charles, *Commentary* 2. 364–68; cf. D. R. Hillers, *BASOR* 170 [1963] 65).

46   (d) The Lamb and the 144,000 (14:1–5). In 13:1–10 a vision of the beast and its followers was presented. Here a contrasting vision is reported of the Lamb and his followers. **1.** *the Lamb standing on Mount Zion:* "The Lamb" contrasts with the beast, and "Mount Zion" is a counterimage to the sea (cf. 13:1). *one hundred forty-four thousand:* Those with the Lamb here are those who were sealed in 7:1–8. *having his name and the name of his Father written upon their foreheads:* This remark specifies the nature of the seal (cf. 7:2–3; see also 3:12; 22:4). It also contrasts the followers of the Lamb with the followers of the beast, who have its mark on their foreheads (13:16). A number of details suggest that the 144,000 are a special group within the faithful and not simply all the faithful (see comment on 7:4,9). They do not simply follow the Lamb, but follow him wherever he goes (i.e., unto death; v 4b). They were not simply redeemed like all Christians, but were redeemed from the rest of humanity as firstfruits (cf. v 4c with 5:9). **4.** *Firstfruits:* Fundamentally a technical sacrificial term

(Exod 23:19; Deut 12:6). This level of meaning suggests an association with the souls under the altar (6:9) and the souls of those who had been beheaded because of their testimony to Jesus (20:4). This suggests that the 144,000 are an ideal group representing those who lose their lives because of their faith and who will be rewarded by participation in the first resurrection (20:4–6). The thesis that "firstfruits" alludes to the first resurrection is supported by the analogous use of the term by Paul (1 Cor 15:20–23). *ones who have not defiled themselves with women, for they are virgins:* It is likely that this characterization of an ideal group reflected and reinforced tendencies toward the practice of sexual continence (see Yarbro Collins, *Crisis* [→ 6 above] 129–31). This motif of defilement also serves to contrast the 144,000 with the Watchers. The Watchers are angels who descended or fell to earth, a change of status associated with sexual intercourse. The 144,000 are humans who are exalted to heavenly status, a transition associated with continence. The Watchers are said to have defiled themselves with women (*1 Enoch* 7:1; 9:8; 15:1–7).

47   (*e*) The three angels (14:6–13). **6.** *flying in midheaven:* This phrase is similar to the description of the eagle in 8:13. There is a formal correspondence between the three woes introduced by the eagle and the messages of the three angels. *having an eternal gospel:* The gospel or good news is an announcement of impending judgment (v 7). **8.** *fallen, fallen is Babylon the great:* This cryptic announcement of judgment (cf. Jer 51:8) anticipates chaps. 17–18. **9–12.** The message of the third angel expresses the consequences for humanity of divine judgment. The criterion will be whether one followed the beast or the Lamb. The followers of the beast will suffer continuous and unending punishment by fire (cf. 19:20; 20:10,14–15; 21:8). This description of punishment is not an opportunity for the readers to gloat over their enemies; rather it functions as an incentive for them to "keep the commandments of God and the faith in Jesus" (v 12). The descriptions of hell in apocryphal Christian apocalypses have a similar function (see Himmelfarb, *Tours of Hell* [→ 3 above]). **13.** The implied threat of punishment in vv 9–12 is balanced by the suggestion of reward in the appended sayings of v 13.

48   (*f*) Harvest and vintage (14:14–20). **14.** *upon the cloud was sitting one like a human:* This figure seems to be an adaptation of the angelic being of Dan 7:13, although "cloud" here is sg., as in Rev 10:1, rather than pl. as in Dan 7:13 and Rev 1:7. Unlike the Gospels, Rev uses "one like a human" descriptively, like Dan 7:13, and not as a title (cf. "the Human One" or "the Son of Man" [Mark 14:62]). It is by no means obvious that the figure in Rev 14:14 is to be identified with Christ, esp. since the next verse refers to "another angel." In light of 1:13,18, however, it is likely that this identification was made (cf. Matt 13:36–43). *in his hand a sharp sickle:* This vision with its two scenes was inspired by Joel 4:13. There the images of harvest and winepress are used to describe a holy war between the divine warrior and the nations which have done violence to Judah (v 19). In Rev the images are universalized to refer to divine judgment upon the earth (vv 15,16,18,19). The reference to "the city" in v 20, however, may be a limitation of that universality, or at least a focusing of it. In Joel, the battle is associated with Zion and Jerusalem (vv 16,17). "The city" in Rev 14:20, however, may be an allusion to "Babylon" (cf. 14:8; 16:19; 17:5; 18:2,10,21), i.e., Rome. **15.** *the harvest of the earth has withered:* It is not clear whether the text of Joel known by John was corrupt (see Charles, *Commentary* 2. 22) or whether he deliberately altered the image from "ripe" to "withered." **18.** *having authority over fire:* Cf. *Jub.* 2:2 and *1 Enoch* 60:11–21. **19.**

the great winepress of the wrath of God: The association of a winepress with God's wrath may have been inspired by Isa 63:1–6. **20.** *the winepress was trodden:* The pass. vb. may be an adaptation of the act., "I have trodden the winepress" (Isa 63:3); in that prophetic oracle the divine warrior slays his opponents (Edom and Bozrah, v 1). *blood flowed from the winepress as high as the bridles of the horses:* In Isa 63:3, the divine warrior says, "their lifeblood is sprinkled upon my garments." Rev 14:19–20 makes clear that treading the winepress is an image for judgment in the form of a battle. The battle is hinted at, however, not described. The account seems to break off abruptly. The same imagery is taken up again in 19:13, 15. These characteristics suggest that 14:14–20 anticipates the great battle of 19:19–21.

49   (*g*) Salvation of the conquerors (15:2–4). 15:1 introduces the next series of visions, the seven bowls (15:1–19:10). 15:5 continues the theme introduced by v 1. Verses 2–4 constitute an intercalated vision which serves as the climax of the series which began in 12:1. Like the other series, this one is dominated by the themes of persecution, judgment, and salvation. Persecution is prominent in chaps. 12–13. The theme of judgment comes to expression in a subtle way in 14:14–20. The theme of salvation is introduced in 14:1–5 and comes to fuller expression here in the vision of the conquerors before the divine throne. **2.** *a glass sea mixed with fire:* See comment on 4:6. *the beast:* This vision depicts the eventual triumph of God and the conquerors over the adversary described in 13:1–10. **3.** *the song of Moses:* This remark associates the song of vv 3–4 with Exod 15, the victory song over the Egyptians. **4.** *because your sentences of condemnation have been made manifest:* This remark alludes to the judgments of God announced by the three angels (14:6–13) and depicted in a veiled way in 14:14–20. It shows that, like Exod 15, this song is a victory song.

50   (2) The seven bowls (15:1–19:10). As noted above, 15:1 and 15:5–8 introduce a new series of visions. Persecution was the dominant theme in the previous series (12:1–15:4). The dominant theme in this series is divine judgment upon the earth and the wicked. It resumes and elaborates the announcements of judgment by the three angels in 14:6–13, clarifying especially the announcement of the fall of "Babylon" (14:8). This series also recapitulates the visions of the seven seals and the seven trumpets; that is, it has the same subject matter as they (the events of the end-time), but describes them from a different perspective. As in the seven seals, the themes of justice and vindication are prominent here. As in the seven trumpets, the natural elements and motifs from Exod play a role. The bowls differ from the trumpets by specifying who the adversaries of God are and the reasons for divine judgment.

(*a*) Seven angels with the last plagues (15:1, 5–16:1). **1.** *I saw another great and remarkable sign in heaven:* The wording is close to that of 12:1,3; the parallel indicates that a new series is being introduced. *the seven last plagues:* The same word is used of the effects of the sixth trumpet (9:18,20) and associated with the exodus (Exod 11:1; 12:13 LXX). *in them the wrath of God is completed:* In 14:6–13 the *thymos*, "passionate longing," of "Babylon" was correlated with the *thymos*, "wrath," of God. This theme is resumed here and becomes prominent in this series (see 15:7; 16:1,19; 18:3; cf. 19:15). Verse 1 is an introduction and summary of 15:5–19:10. The actual description of the vision begins in v 5. **7.** *seven golden bowls:* This type of bowl (*phialē*) was used in offerings. The image is taken from the Temple cult and vessels (Exod 27:3). Note that the angels come out of the

Temple (vv 5–6). **16:1.** *pour out the seven bowls of the wrath of God upon the earth:* Cf. 8:5.

51   (*b*) The first four bowls (16:2–9). It is likely that in chaps. 8–9 and 16, the author of Rev made use of sources that consisted of eschatological reinterpretations of the plagues of Exod. In the sources, the purpose of the plagues may have been to bring humanity to repentance; in their present context, the plagues are divine punishment of sinners (H. D. Betz, *JTC* 6 [1969] 134–56; A. Yarbro Collins, *CBQ* 39 [1977] 370–74; H. P. Müller, *ZNW* 51 [1960] 268–78). The first four bowls are associated with natural elements: the earth (v 2), the sea (v 3), the fresh waters (v 4), and the sun (heavenly body) (v 8). These elements represent a traditional Jewish cosmology (A. Yarbro Collins, *CBQ* 39 [1977] 375–76). **2.** *injurious and nasty sores came upon those who had the mark of the beast and worshiped its image:* The effect of the first plague is not upon the earth as such, but on sinners, viz., those who give divine honors to Rome and the emperor (see 13:11–18; 14:9–11), rather than worshiping the true God (see 14:7 where the natural elements are mentioned also). This first plague is an adaptation of the sixth plague upon the Egyptians (Exod 9:8–12). **3.** *[the sea] became blood, like the blood of a corpse:* This plague calls to mind the first of those brought upon the Egyptians by Moses (Exod 7:14–24; cf. Rev 8:8–9). *every living being in the sea died:* This effect is an intensification of the result of the second trumpet (8:9). **4.** Like the second, the third bowl alludes to the Nile and all the waters of Egypt being turned to blood. The story of the exodus is a paradigm for the situation of Rev: as God delivered the Israelites from Egypt, so will Christians be freed from the power of Rome and vindicated. **5–7.** Verse 4 is from a source used by John, whereas vv 5–7 are his own composition, which serves to comment on and interpret the narrative account of the source (cf. the function of vv 10–12 in chap. 12). **5a.** *the angel of the waters:* This angel is analogous to the one associated with fire (14:18); on the duties of the archangels, see *1 Enoch* 20. **5b–6.** The speech of the angel may be defined as a judgment doxology or an eschatological vindication formula (H. D. Betz, *JTC* 6 [1969] 139; P. Staples, *NovT* 14 [1972] 284–85; A. Yarbro Collins, *CBQ* 39 [1977] 368–69). It affirms the justice of God because of the anticipation of God's eschatological intervention to punish the persecutors of the faithful. **6.** *because they shed the blood of holy ones and prophets, you have given them blood to drink:* Offense and punishment are correlated within an eschatological perspective (cf. 22:18b–19; E. Käsemann, *NTQT* 66–81; A. Yarbro Collins, *CBQ* 39 [1977] 370). Cf. 17:6; 18:24; and Isa 49:26.

52   (*c*) The last three bowls (16:10–21). The first four bowls are unified by their association with natural elements representing the whole cosmos (heaven and earth, fresh waters and salt water). The last three bowls are unified by their common historical and political connotations. Compare the structure of the seven seals and trumpets. **10.** *the throne of the beast:* In 13:2 it is said that the dragon (Satan) gave the beast (Rome and the emperors) his power and throne and great authority. Here, as there, "throne" is probably used figuratively to mean dominion or sovereignty. *its kingdom became dark:* "Kingdom" here means the territory ruled or the realm. This vision (the fifth bowl) calls to mind the ninth Egyptian plague (Exod 10:21–29). *they were biting their tongues in pain:* The transition from darkness to pain is not explained; sores are mentioned in v 11, which connects this vision with the first bowl. This link suggests that those who are punished by this plague are the same as the ones mentioned in v 2. **11.** *they did not repent of their works:* The same motif appears in v 9; cf. 9:20–21. In the

present context, there is no expectation that those affected by the plagues (outsiders) will repent (see 22:11 and above on the first four bowls). Insiders who have erred, on the contrary, are expected to repent (2:5,16, 21–22; 3:3,19). The inhabitants of Jerusalem are a special case (see 11:13). **12.** *the sixth [angel] poured out his bowl on the great river Euphrates:* The mention of the Euphrates River links this vision to the sixth trumpet (9:13–21). There four angels are bound at the river. When the trumpet is blown, they are released to kill one-third of humanity. The vision then combines military and demonic imagery. The significance of the vision is not explicit, although idolatry and other vices are mentioned in vv 20–21. The sixth bowl resumes the sixth trumpet, apparently depicting the same event in more coherent imagery and in a way which makes its historical setting clearer. *its water dried up to prepare the way of the kings of the East:* The sixth trumpet and bowl refer to a battle fought both by supernatural beings (the angels and their demonic armies in 9:13–21 and the three unclean spirits of 16:13–14) and by human beings (explicit only in the sixth bowl—the kings of the East and of the earth—vv 12 and 14). This synergistic or two-story battle is typical of ancient notions of holy war (Judg 5:20; Dan 10:13–11:1; 1QM 1; see A. Yarbro Collins, *JBL* 96 [1977] 242). At the time Rev was written, "the kings of the East" would have been understood primarily in terms of the Parthians (F. E. Peters, *The Harvest of Hellenism* [NY, 1970] 740–41). See comments on 6:1–2; 17:12–18. **13.** The mention of the dragon, the beast, and the false prophet suggests that this battle is the same as the one described in 19:11–21 (see esp. vv 19–20). *three unclean spirits like frogs:* As the Egyptian plague of the locusts was transformed into a demonic plague in the fifth trumpet, here the swarm of frogs of Exod 7:25–8:15 is briefly alluded to and similarly transformed. **14.** *working signs:* See comment on 13:13. *the battle of the great day of God the Almighty:* This "great day" seems to be the same as that depicted in 6:17. This day seems to be the first event of the last stage of the final events, probably coinciding with the return of the risen Christ (19:11–16). The "great day," variously formulated in 6:17; 16:14, does not seem to be a fixed term for John, but is related to the traditional notion of the Day of the Lord (see *IDBSup* 209–10; cf. Rom 2:5; 1 Cor 1:8; 2 Thess 2:2). In Rev this day is linked to a great battle or war (cf. 1QM 1). **15.** *I am coming like a thief:* John suddenly shifts from a narrative account to a prophetic saying, the words of Christ. This traditional saying (cf. Matt 24:43–44; Luke 12:39–40; 1 Thess 5:2,4; 2 Pet 3:10) supports the hypothesis that the great day of v 14 is connected with the return of Christ. *his garments:* Cf. 3:4,18. **16.** The text returns to narrative: the unclean spirits assembled the armies of the kings of the earth. *Armageddon:* The place-name probably means "the mountain of Megiddo" (see *IDB* 1. 226–27). The narrative breaks off abruptly, to be resumed later (see 17:12–14; 19:11–21). **17–18.** The conclusion of God's judgment (the seventh bowl) is described in terms of a theophany (cf. 11:19). **19.** The effect of that judgment is described also in political terms: Babylon, indeed all the cities of the Gentiles, has fallen (cf. 14:8). **20–21a.** The text returns to theophanic language. **21b.** The motif of failure to repent appears again (cf. vv 9,11).

53   (*d*) Elaboration of the seventh bowl: the nature and fall of "Babylon" (17:1–19:10). This section is a coda to the seven bowls. The dominant theme of the bowls is judgment upon the beast, its followers, and the cryptic city "Babylon." The beast was introduced in a veiled and fragmentary way in 11:7 and fully depicted later in chap. 13. Similarly, the destruction of "Babylon" is mysteriously announced in 14:8 and 16:19, but a presentation of the nature, character, and role of "Babylon" is reserved for chaps. 17–18. Like the other series of visions, the bowls with their coda express the three main themes of Rev: persecution (the third bowl, 16:4–7), judgment (the seventh bowl, 16:19), and salvation (the climax and conclusion of the coda, 19:1–10).

(1′) A woman on a scarlet beast (17:1–18). **1.** *one of the seven angels who had the seven bowls came and was speaking with me:* The transition from 16:21 to 17:1 shows that 17:1 and following are a coda to the series of the bowls. No visionary formula is used in 17:1 (e.g., "I saw"), and there is no shift in subject matter (cf. 17:1,5 with 16:19). The identification of "one of the seven angels" links the two passages also. The angel interprets for the visionary what he sees; the role of angelic interpreter or mediator of revelation is typical of apocalypses (a protoapocalyptic example is Zech 1:9; see Dan 7:16; 2 Esdr 10:28–59; cf. Rev 5:5). *the condemnation and punishment of the great prostitute seated by many waters:* In v 5 the prostitute is identified as "Babylon." Thus the prostitute represents a city. The personification of cities by the Hebr prophets was very common (Isa 1:21; 66:7–16; Jer 15:9; Ezek 16). Occasionally Jerusalem was denounced by the prophets with the metaphor of a prostitute (Isa 1:21; Ezek 16:15–45). At times the metaphor was used of the enemies of Israel and Judah (Nah 3:4 of Nineveh; Isa 23:16–17 of Tyre). Here the prostitute is the city of Rome (see vv 9 and 18). The identification of Rome with a harlot who is destroyed is not a simple allegory with a one-to-one correspondence between signifier and signified. Rather, the metaphor condemns not only the physical and historical city, but also what it stood for in the author's point of view: the goddess Roma, the claim of the Roman Empire to dominion over the earth, the inequities of the Roman economic system (see v 4 and 18:3), and the violence involved in imposing Roman sovereignty (18:24). These characteristics were manifestations of Rome's misplaced claims to eternity and divinity, which had the evil fruits of human exploitation. The personification of the city as female and the image of prostitution for idolatry and excessive wealth have roots in Hebr tradition as noted above. They are also a response to Roman self-understanding in terms of the goddess Roma (R. Mellor, *Thea Romē* [Göttingen, 1975]; *ANRW* II/7.2, 950–1030). In the 20th cent., such images may not be used uncritically because, e.g., their ill effects on the lives of women have been recognized (T. D. Setel, "Prophets and Pornography," *Feminist Interpretation of the Bible* [ed. L. Russell; Phl, 1985] 86–95). The "many waters" is an attribute of the historical Babylon (Jer 51:13) which is interpreted allegorically in the present context (v 15). **3.** *[the angel] carried me into the wilderness in the spirit:* Cf. Ezek 3:12–15; 8:2–3,7; 11:1; 40:2–4; Rev 1:10. *a woman sitting on a scarlet beast which was full of blasphemous names and had seven heads and ten horns:* Although different Gk words are used, the color of this beast links it with the dragon of chap. 12. The blasphemous names link it with the beast of chap. 13. Seven heads and ten horns are common to both. The context (17:8,10–18) suggests that this beast is either identical to or the equivalent of the beast of chap. 13. **4.** *a golden cup in her hand:* The inhabitants of the earth drink out of this cup (v 2); cf. Jer 25:15–29; 51:7, *Cebes* 5.1–2 (see *The Tabula of Cebes* [ed. J. T. Fitzgerald and L. M. White; Chico, 1983]). **5.** *forehead:* Roman prostitutes wore labels bearing their names on their foreheads (Charles, *Commentary* 2. 65). The image also brings to mind the characterizations of the followers of the Lamb and of the beast (7:3; 9:4; 13:16; 14:1,9; 20:4; 22:4). *a mystery:* In early Christian literature, *mystērion* was used

for a heavenly secret revealed to humanity by God. Such a secret might involve present but hidden realities, the future, or the interpretation of difficult texts (usually Scripture); see Mark 4:11 par.; Rom 11:25; 16:25; 1 Cor 2:7; 15:51; Eph 1:9; Col 1:26; 2 Thess 2:7; Rev 1:20; 10:7 (→ Colossians, 54:17; Ephesians, 55:17). **6.** *the witnesses to Jesus:* See comment on 11:3; cf. A. A. Trites, *NovT* 15 [1973] 72–80. **8.** *the beast which you saw was, and is not, and is about to ascend from the abyss:* The beast, as eschatological adversary, is a counterfeit image of God (cf. 1:8), as well as of Christ (cf. 13:3). This remark suggests also that the "antichrist" in Rev is modeled on the emperor Nero and the legends associated with him (see comment on 13:3). Nero was (he ruled Rome in his lifetime), he is not (at present he is dead), and is to ascend (he will return from the underworld to regain power). *he goes to destruction:* See 19:20. **9.** *a mind with wisdom:* A similar remark introduced the puzzle of 666 in 13:18. This "wisdom" is not the common-sense, experiential wisdom associated with proverbs, but a heavenly wisdom which is knowledge of the mysteries of God (see comment on v 5; cf. 1 Cor 2:6–13; this "mantic wisdom" is characteristic of apocalypticism; see H.-P. Müller, "Mantische Weisheit und Apokalyptik," *Congress Volume: Uppsala 1971* [VTSup 22; Leiden, 1972] 268–93). *the seven heads are seven hills:* The city of Rome was widely known as a city built on "seven hills" (see Charles, *Commentary* 2. 69). *seven kings:* It is likely that vv 9b–10 is a source which John has reinterpreted for the present context. The seven kings are Roman emperors (see Yarbro Collins, *Crisis* [– 6 above] 58–64). **11.** *both an eighth and one of the seven:* This remark suggests that John identified the demonic (associated with the underworld) Nero with the eschatological adversary: the one who would seize power in the last days is one who formerly ruled as emperor. **12.** *the ten horns which you saw are ten kings, who have not yet received royal power, but they [will] receive authority together with the beast for one hour:* When the historical Nero saw that he could no longer remain in power, he considered fleeing to Parthia (Suetonius, *Nero* 47). After his death a legend arose that he had not died and that he would return with Parthian allies to regain power over the Roman Empire and to destroy his enemies (Charles, *Commentary* 2. 80–81). Verses 12–14,16–17 reflect this legend. The legendary expectation was that Nero and his eastern allies would destroy the city of Rome and that the East would regain hegemony over the Mediterranean world (see Yarbro Collins, *Crisis* [→ 6 above] 89–90). John has adapted that legend and incorporated it into his eschatological schema. The battle of Nero and the Parthians against Rome would take place first; this is the divine judgment against "Babylon" (14:8; 16:19). This battle is alluded to in a veiled way in 6:2 (the first seal) and 9:13–21 (the sixth trumpet). The sixth bowl (16:12–16) serves as an introduction both to the battle of Nero and his allies over Rome (whose outcome is described in 17:16–18) and to the immediately subsequent battle between the exalted Christ and "the beast" (the demonic Nero or "antichrist" and his allies). This final battle is alluded to in the sixth seal (6:12–17), the seventh trumpet (11:15–19), and the vision of harvest and vintage (14:14–20). 17:14 begins to describe this ultimate battle; the description, however, breaks off and is resumed in 19:11. Even though John probably linked the eschatological events to specifically expected historical events, he did so in such a way that his vision of present and future is applicable to other situations as well.

54   (2′) Apocalyptic prediction of divine judgment on "Babylon" (18:1–24). In 17:1 the angel offered to show John "the condemnation and punishment" of

"Babylon." 17:17 alludes to the divine condemnation or sentence in its remark that the ten kings were doing God's will. Verse 16 describes the punishment (destruction) briefly. Chapter 18 elaborates both of these themes in an artful and ironic way. **1.** *another angel:* Besides the one who had one of the seven bowls (17:1). See also 10:1 and Ezek 43:2. Verses 1–3 constitute a report of a vision or epiphany of an angel. The focus is on the speech of the angel (vv 2b–3). In form the speech is a dirge, but here it is used as an announcement of judgment (A. Yarbro Collins, "Revelation 18: Taunt-Song or Dirge?" in *L'Apocalypse johannique et l'apocalyptique dans le Nouveau Testament* [ed. J. Lambrecht; BETL 53; Leuven, 1980] 192–93). **2.** *fallen, fallen:* Cf. Rev 14:8; Isa 21:9; Jer 51:8. *become a home for demons and a spot frequented by every unclean spirit and every unclean and hateful bird:* Cf. Isa 13:19–22; 34:11–15; Jer 50:39–40; Bar 4:35. **3.** *all the nations have drunk the wine of the passionate longing of her prostitution:* See comment on 15:1. This image means that the peoples of the earth, esp. the wealthy and politically powerful, have recognized Rome's claims to divine or quasi-divine status and to sovereignty, because they could profit by doing so (see comment on 17:1). *merchants of the earth have become rich from her excessive wealth:* Cf. Isa 23:18. Verses 4–20 are composed of a number of small units, which together constitute a long and loosely connected audition (a heavenly voice—v 4). **4b–5.** Verse 4b is an admonition, and v 5 gives the rationale for it. Both verses allude to old prophecy (Jer 51:45; 51:9). In the present context, however, the warning functions as a call to cultural exclusiveness, i.e., the rejection of assimilation (see comments on 13:16–17; 2:14). **6–8.** This small unit is a command to execute judgment upon "Babylon." The actual commands are given in vv 6–7a; the explanation of these commands appears in vv 7b–8. Given the two-storey nature of holy war, one should probably conceive of the speaker and addressee(s) as heavenly beings (cf. Ezek 9:1,5–6), whose actions constitute the heavenly counterpart of 17:16 (the mention of fire links 17:16 and 18:8). In v 6 the *lex talionis* is at work, the correlation of sin and punishment (see comment on 16:6; cf. also Matt 7:1–2; 18:23–35; Luke 6:37–38). In vv 7–8, the principle is eschatological reversal (cf. Luke 6:20–26). **9.** *the kings of the earth, who practiced prostitution with her and lived in luxury, will weep and mourn over her, when they see the smoke of her burning:* Here John seems to employ a dramatic device, whereby violence is not depicted on stage, but only the results or reactions to violence. Overall vv 9–10 constitute an announcement of judgment upon the minor kings whose rule depended on Roman favor. The announcement is ironic because it contains a dirge spoken by Rome's friends. From the perspective of the author, however, even the dirge functions as an announcement of judgment: "because in one hour your judgment has come" (v 10; compare 17:12). **11–13.** This is an announcement of judgment directed against the merchants of the earth (cf. v 3). Rev does not seem to condemn the profession of merchant (contrast *Gos. Thom.* 64). It does suggest that wealth in this age and true discipleship are at least in tension with each other, if not incompatible (3:17–20). **12.** *cargo:* The cargo of the merchants, which no one will buy when Rome is destroyed, consists mostly of luxury items. One of the reasons for the judgment of Rome is that its merchants were the "great ones" of the earth (v 23). What may be reflected here is unrest and criticism of a situation in which the rich get richer and the poor poorer (cf. 6:6; see Yarbro Collins, *Crisis* [→ 6 above] 88–97, 132–34). **14.** This verse breaks the rhythm of the announcements of judgment against kings (vv 9–10), merchants (vv 11–13), merchants again (vv 15–17a), and those who

make a living from the sea (vv 17b–19). It is a dirge addressed directly to "Babylon" by the heavenly voice (cf. v 4). **15–17a.** This is a second announcement of judgment against the merchants. It is dramatic in form, like the scene involving the kings of the earth (vv 9–10). Their dirge (v 16) alludes to the luxurious clothing and jewelry of the prostitute (17:4). **17a.** *in one hour so much wealth has been ruined:* The "one hour" resumes the "prediction" in 17:12 that the 10 kings will receive authority with the beast for one hour (cf. 14:7,15; 18:10, 19). **17b–19.** This unit is an announcement of judgment against merchant mariners. Its acts of mourning and dirges are perhaps the most vivid of the series. Taken alone, this unit would evoke pathos, even sympathy or regret. But the context (the allusion to judgment in the parallel [v 17a] and the call to rejoicing [v 20]) shows that such sentiments are not seriously intended. **20.** *rejoice over her, O heaven and you saints and apostles and prophets, because God has pronounced on her the judgment she wished to impose on you:* This call for rejoicing is startling after the series of dirges. It is similar in form to 12:12, which celebrates the Christian victory over Satan. Here, vindication of those who have suffered for their testimony to Jesus is envisaged (see 6:9–11; 16:6; 17:6; 18:24). Verse 20 concludes the lengthy audition which began in v 4. The third major section of chap. 18 is a report of a symbolic action performed by an angel (vv 21–24). Thus the middle section (vv 4–20) is framed by two powerfully visual scenes, each involving an angel (cf. vv 1–3). The announcements of the angels are parallel in content. The eerie images of desolation in vv 2b–3 are complemented by the emptiness and silence implied by vv 22–23. Each announcement closes with reasons for judgment. "All nations" and "merchants" are mentioned in each. On prophetic accounts of symbolic actions, see G. Tucker, *Form Criticism of the Old Testament* (Phl, 1971) 66; K. Koch, *The Growth of the Biblical Tradition* (NY, 1969) 203, 210; W. E. March, "Prophecy," *Old Testament Form Criticism* (ed. J. H. Hayes; San Antonio, 1974) 172. For the background of this symbolic act, see Jer 51:59–64; Ezek 26:19–21.

55 (3′) Rejoicing in heaven (19:1–10). This passage is differentiated from chap. 18 by its introductory formula, "Afterward, I heard" (v 1). It is linked to it, however, by the fact that 18:20 contains a call to rejoice; 19:1–8 is the response to that call. 19:1–10 expresses the themes of divine victory and the salvation of the faithful; it is thus parallel to 7:9–17; 11:15–19; 15:2–4; 20:4–6; and 21:1–22:5. This passage has three parts: two choral units (vv 1–5,6–8) and a transitional scene (vv 9–10). **1–5.** The first choral unit has a structure determined, to some degree, by 18:20. The call to rejoice in 18:20 is directed first to heaven; 19:1–4 describes heavenly rejoicing. Second, the saints, apostles, and prophets are urged to rejoice in 18:20. In 19:5 this address to humans is resumed and expanded to all who serve and fear God. This choral unit is divided into four parts: two victory songs (vv 1–2 and 3), a confirmatory heavenly scene (v 4), and a heavenly call for earthly confirmation (v 5). **1.** *victory:* See comment on 7:10. **6–8.** The close verbal parallels between v 1 and v 6 suggest that a new unit begins in v 6. Verses 1–5 focus on God's victory over "Babylon" as divine judge and warrior; vv 6–8 focus on God's kingship and the marriage of the Lamb. The sequence of victory in battle, accession as king, and sacred marriage is an ancient mythic pattern (see Yarbro Collins, *Combat Myth* [→ 15 above] 207–24). Here the marriage of the Lamb symbolizes the eschatological union of the exalted Christ with those faithful who endure to the end. The same idea is expressed in different language in 22:3–5. **8.** *it was granted to her that she be clothed* *in clean, shining linen:* Eschatological salvation is a gift (cf. Isa 61:10). *the linen is the righteous deeds of the saints:* Individuals are nevertheless responsible (cf. 3:4–5,18). **9–10.** Some commentators conclude that the repetition of virtually the same scene here and in 22:8–9 is the result of editing (Charles, *Commentary* 2. 128–29; Kraft, *Offenbarung* 244–45). More likely it is part of the author's literary design (so Caird, *Commentary* 237). **10.** *your fellow servant and the fellow servant of your brothers [and sisters]:* The significance of this transitional scene seems to be the implication that the faithful are equal to angels. **56**   (3) Visions of the last things (19:11–22:5). This is the last series of visions in the book. Like 12:1–15:4 it is unnumbered, but found to consist of seven visions, when introductory formulas and shifts in content are noted. The seven visions themselves are reported in 19:11–21:8. 21:9–22:5 is a coda, similar in form and function to 17:1–19:10, but antithetically parallel to it in content. In this last series, the theme of persecution almost disappears (cf. 20:9). The sequence of judgment and salvation, however, is recapitulated twice (judgment: 19:11–20:3 and 20:7–15; salvation: 20:4–6 and 21:1–22:5).

(*a*) The second coming of Christ (19:11–16). This passage is an epiphany of the exalted Christ as judge of the world. **11.** *I saw heaven opened:* A revelatory formula; cf. Ezek 1:1; *2 Apoc. Bar.* 22:1; Matt 3:16; Acts 7:56; John 1:51. Cf. 4:1. Although this passage is the beginning of a new account of the end, it resumes many previous passages in Rev. *faithful and true:* See 1:5; 3:14. **12.** *his eyes were like a flame of fire:* See 1:14; 2:18. *many diadems:* These show that this judge is superior to Satan (12:3) and to the beast (13:1). The secret name recalls 2:17 (cf. 3:12). Some of these interconnections show that the cosmic judge is the same as the revealer of 1:9–3:22 and of the whole book (cf. 1:5 and 1:1). Others suggest that this last series takes up and completes earlier partial tellings of the last events. Chapter 12 depicted Satan's defeat in heaven; this series, his ultimate defeat (20:7–10). **13.** *clothed with a garment dipped in blood:* This sentence and the one about the winepress in v 15 link this vision to 14:14–20; what was told there with one set of images is told again here with another set. These remarks also suggest that John expected Isa 63:1–6 to be fulfilled in his near future and that he understood Edom to be another symbolic name for Rome (see C.-H. Hunzinger, "Babylon als Deckname für Rom," *Gottes Wort und Gottes Land* [ed. H. G. Reventlow; Göttingen, 1965] 67–77). *the Word of God:* See Wis 18:14–16 (→ John, 61:21). **14.** *the heavenly armies were following him . . . clothed in clean white linen:* The imagery here is that of holy war (cf. 1QM 1; 2 Macc 10:29–31). The holy war tradition apart from Rev would suggest that these heavenly armies consist of angels (cf. 9:14–16; Matt 13:39–42,49; 16:27; 24:30–31; 25:31). There are indications, however, that John conceived of these armies as made up of glorified humans (those who have died for their faith), as well as angels. As indicated above, 17:12–13,16–17 reflect the expectation that *Nero redivivus* and his allies from the East would destroy the city of Rome in the process of gaining control over the empire. 17:14, in the midst of this account, is a foreshadowing of the subsequent battle between Nero as eschatological adversary (the beast) and the Lamb and his forces (recounted in 19:19–21). The remark that the Lamb "is Lord of Lords and King of Kings" (17:14) clearly links that verse with the epiphany of the Word of God in 19:11–16. Thus, the armies of 19:14 would seem to include "those with him," who are "called and chosen and faithful" (17:14). These terms fit humans, not angels.

57   (*b*) Call to the "banquet" (19:17–18). This

vision is a dramatic prelude to the battle described in 19:19–21. It anticipates the carnage that is reported in v 21. It was probably inspired by Ezek 39:17–20; in that passage the corpses of enemy warriors and horses are described as a sacrificial feast. Isa 34:1–7 shares the notion of a sacrificial slaughter with Ezek 39:17–20 and Rev 19:17–18. It also shares with the context of the latter the image of the sword of God (cf. Rev 19:15 with Isa 34:5–6). Isa 34:7 links the sacrificial slaughter with the notion of fertility; this archaic link reflects ancient myth (see Yarbro Collins, *Combat Myth* [→ 15 above] 225). **58**   (*c*) The final battle (19:19–21). This is the last battle before the thousand-year reign of Christ (20:4–6). It is the event hinted at by the fifth and sixth trumpets, fragmentarily described by the sixth bowl and 17:14, and described in a veiled way by 14:14–20. See comments on vv 13 and 14. **20.** *the beast was caught:* Cf. Job 40:25–26 (*RSV* 41:1–2). *the false prophet:* I.e., the beast from the earth; see 13:11–18. *the lake of fire which burns with brimstone:* A place of eternal punishment (cf. 20:14–15 and 21:8 with 14:10–11). See Isa 66:24; *1 Enoch* 18:11–16; 108:3–7,15; *2 Esdr* 7:36–38; on later conceptions of hell, see Himmelfarb, *Tours of Hell* [→ 3 above].

59   (*d*) The binding of Satan (20:1–3). The fifth trumpet involved the descent of an angel from heaven to open the abyss, so that the angel of the abyss and his demons could torture the inhabitants of the earth (9:1–11). Here, after the victory of the exalted Christ over the beast and false prophet, another angel descends in order to confine the beast's patron, the dragon, in the abyss for a thousand years. **2.** *bound:* Since the dragon symbolizes chaos and infertility (see comment on 12:3), the binding symbolizes creative order and fertility (see *PGM* 4.3086–3124; H. D. Betz [ed.], *The Greek Magical Papyri in Translation* [Chicago, 1986] 1. 98). It also symbolizes a respite from the attacks of the nations (v 3). In Rev this binding occurs in the last days. In an early Jewish apocalypse, the evil angels are bound at the time of the flood and will be confined and punished until the last judgment (*1 Enoch* 10:4–8; 18:11–19:3; 21:1–10; cf. Jude 6). **60**   (*e*) The thousand-year reign (20:4–10). This passage has been controversial among Christians from the early church up to the present day. **4.** *I saw thrones and they sat upon them, and authority to judge was given to them:* This is the first judgment; the second, general judgment is described in 20:11–15. The anonymous judges here are probably faithful followers of Jesus, esp. those who have died for their faith, "those beheaded on account of their testimony to Jesus" (see 3:21; cf. Matt 19:28; Luke 22:28–30; 1 Cor 6:1–3). *they came to life and ruled with Christ for a thousand years:* The nature of this rule has been debated in Christian tradition. The past tense is due to the vision form; John is reporting events which he "saw" in a vision, but these events pertain to the future. It is likely that this rule should be understood as an earthly messianic reign. Verse 9 presupposes that the saints, at the end of 1,000 years, will be living on earth, in the beloved city (presumably Jerusalem). The first resurrection is to take place at the beginning of this period (vv 5–6). This is a special reward for those who were faithful unto death (see comment on 14:1–5). They especially share the rule of Christ. Presumably surviving faithful Christians would also participate. Surviving Gentiles would be the subjects of that rule (cf. 22:2). Some early Christians (chiliasts) believed that the thousand-year reign would be an earthly kingdom of blessedness (H. Bietenhard, *SJT* 6 [1953] 12–30). Origen and Augustine understood the passage spiritually rather than historically. Augustine associated the binding of Satan with the life of Jesus and the thousand-year reign with the time of the church (*City of God* 20.1–9). His view was dominant until millenarianism was revived in different ways by Joachim of Fiore and the radical reformers (see *ODCC* 916). **6.** *the second death:* See 21:8. *they will be priests:* A priestly role is important in the messianic reign, but not in the new Jerusalem (cf. 22:5); see E. Schüssler Fiorenza, *Priester für Gott* [→ 18 above] 338–44, 375–89. **7–8.** The release of Satan and his renewed attack on the faithful reflect the cyclical or recapitulative character of Rev's view of history: the struggle between God and Satan, order and chaos, is repeatedly renewed, until its definitive end (v 10; cf. 21:1). **8.** *Gog and Magog:* This renewal of battle was inspired by Ezek 38–39. For the idea of the limited character of the messianic reign, see 2 Esdr 7:28–30.

61   (*f*) The last judgment (20:11–15). This is the second or general judgment (see comment on 20:4). **11.** *from whose face earth and heaven fled and no place was found for them:* The power and majesty of the presence of God in this final theophany will destroy the first creation (see 21:1 and 11:19). **12.** *I saw the dead:* This is the second resurrection (cf. 20:5). It is general, i.e., it involves all the dead (v 13), except those who rose in the first resurrection (vv 4,6). The earliest clear reference to resurrection in Jewish literature is Dan 12:2, where the expectation is that "many" will rise, viz., the especially righteous and the particularly wicked. A general resurrection is expected in *1 Enoch* 51:1; Acts 26:23; 1 Cor 15:20; *Bib. Ant.* 3.10, 2 Esdr 7:32, 2 *Apoc. Bar.* 30:2; 42:8; 49–52. As in this passage, resurrection and judgment are explicitly linked in *Bib. Ant.* 3.10, 2 Esdr 7:32–43, 2 *Apoc. Bar.* 50:1–4. *books were opened . . . and the dead were judged on the basis of what was written in the books in accordance with their works:* In Jewish apocalyptic writings, the idea is attested that angels record the deeds of other angels and of humans as evidence for the final judgment (*1 Enoch* 89:61–64,68–71; 90:20; 2 *Apoc. Bar.* 24:1). *another book was opened, the book of life:* See comment on 3:5. All humanity is divided into those whose names are written in the book of life and those whose names are not written therein. Those who are in were chosen before the foundation of the world (13:8). Those not in worship the beast and therefore will be punished eternally (13:8; 17:8; 14:9–11; 20:15). The image of the book of life is an attempt to explain why some turn to the true God and some do not. This image of election and nonelection is placed side by side with the image of human responsibility (the books in which deeds are recorded). No contradiction is perceived between them. **14.** *Death and Hades were thrown into the lake of fire:* Cf. 1 Cor 15:26.

62   (*g*) New heaven, new earth, and new Jerusalem (21:1–8). This, the seventh vision in the last series, focuses on salvation. **1.** *I saw a new heaven and a new earth:* Cf. Isa 65:17–25. Radical discontinuity is implied here, since the old heaven and earth are destroyed (cf. 20:11). *the sea was no more:* Discontinuity is implied here also. This statement makes clear the mythic, symbolic character of the sea in Rev (see comment on 13:1). The disappearance of the sea is equivalent to the eternal confinement and punishment of the dragon (Satan), the beast ("antichrist"), and the false prophet (19:20; 20:10) and to the elimination of Death and Hades (20:14). The elimination of the sea symbolizes the complete victory of creation over chaos, of life over death. **2.** *I saw the holy city, new Jerusalem, coming down out of heaven from God, prepared like a bride adorned for her husband:* This vision of salvation was written at a time when the historical Jerusalem had been destroyed recently and by a man who was not at home in any city of his culture. It was inspired by Isa 54, but, like 2 Esdr 9:38–10:59, it does not expect a historical restoration. The city is portrayed

as the bride of the Lamb (v 9); thus it is another symbol of eschatological union of the faithful with their Lord (see comment on 19:6–8). **3.** A voice from the throne interprets the vision by resuming and renewing old promises (see Lev 26:11–12; Ezek 37:27; cf. 2 Cor 6:16). **4.** *I will wipe away every tear:* See Isa 25:8 and Rev 7:17. *death will be no more:* See Isa 25:8 and Rev 20:13. **5–8.** For the second time in Rev, words of God are quoted (see also 1:8). **6.** *I will give to the thirsty [water] from the spring of the water of life without payment:* This promise is inspired by Isa 55:1; it does not allude necessarily to baptism (see comment on 7:16–17).

63   (*h*) Elaboration of the vision of the new Jerusalem (21:9–22:5). This section is a coda to the seven visions of 19:11–21:8. It elaborates one of the images of salvation contained in the seventh vision, the new Jerusalem (21:2).

(1') The city, its gates and walls (21:9–21). **9.** *one of the angels who had the seven bowls:* This introduction creates a deliberate parallel between this coda and the one following the seven bowls (17:1–19:10). This literary parallel highlights an antithetical symbolic parallel between two cities and what they represent: "Babylon" and "Jerusalem." **10.** See 17:3. **11.** *like precious stone:* See Isa 54:11–12. **12.** *the twelve tribes of Israel:* See comment on 7:4. **14.** *the twelve apostles of the Lamb:* This remark looks back on the time of the apostles and would not have been written by one of the disciples of Jesus (→ 7–9 above). The mention of the twelve tribes and the twelve apostles suggests that the city symbolizes a people; but there is no simple equation of the new Jerusalem and the people of God. Rather, the city represents a transcendent and future reality: God dwelling with people, face to face. **18–20.** The twelve foundations of the wall are adorned with twelve precious stones. These correspond to the twelve stones on the breastplate of the high priest. In John's time these stones were associated with the twelve constellations of the zodiac. They are listed here, however, in reverse order (Charles, *Commentary* 2. 164–70). This reversal does not necessarily mean that John rejected current beliefs about astral phenomena, but it does suggest that they had to be reinterpreted.

64   (2') The inhabitants of the city (21:22–27). **22.** *I did not see a Temple in it, for the Lord God the Almighty is its Temple, and the Lamb:* Rev was most probably written after the Temple in Jerusalem had been destroyed (→ 10–12 above). In 3:12 there is already a hint that the physical earthly Temple is not of ultimate importance in itself (see comment on 11:1–2). It continues to have importance, however, as a symbol of the hoped-for close relationship between humans and God. In the vision of salvation in 7:9–17, service in the heavenly Temple has the same symbolic significance (v 15). In this vision, the Temple continues to have symbolic significance as a way of expressing the full and direct presence of God and the Lamb (cf. Ezek 48:35). **24–26.** Cf. Isa 60. **27.** *nothing common shall ever enter into it:* A synonym (*bebēlos*) of the Gk *koinon,* "common," is used in Ezek 44:23. The idea of the separation of the holy and the common or profane is still present in Rev. The main point is that the realm of the holy has been extended. Formerly, only the Temple and what entered it had to be holy; now the entire city is holy (see Zech 14:20–21). *no one who practices abomination and deceit:* The reference is primarily to those who worship what is not truly God, i.e., those whose names are not in the book of life (see comment on 20:12).

65   (3') The river of life and the tree of life (22:1–5). **1.** *a river of living water . . . flowing from the throne of God and the Lamb:* In 21:10 it is implied that the new Jerusalem would descend upon a great and high mountain; this mountain is the idealized Mount Zion, identified with the cosmic mountain of ancient myth (Caird, *Commentary* 269–70). The "river of living water" reflects the traditional idea that a sacred stream issues forth from the cosmic mountain (cf. Ezek 47:1–10; J. Levenson, *Theology of the Program of Restoration of Ezekiel 40–48* [Missoula, 1976] 11–14). **2.** *on this side of the river and on that was the tree of life . . . and the leaves of the tree were for the healing of the nations:* This eschatological vision incorporates the original bliss of Eden (Gen 2:9) and the hope for restoration of Ezek (47:12). **3.** *there will no longer be any curse:* This remark may imply a reversal of the curses of Gen 3:14–19. It may mean that the new Jerusalem is no longer threatened with destruction as punishment for idolatry, as in Zech 14:11 (cf. Exod 22:20; Deut 13:12–18). Or the point may be that God is reconciled with the nations, rather than cursing them and dooming them to destruction (cf. Isa 34:2,5).

66   (D) Isolated Sayings (22:6–20). These sayings constitute a kind of epilogue to the book. Many of them deal with the origin and the authority of Rev; others recapitulate aspects of its message.

(a) Saying about the Nature and Origin of the Book (22:6). *he said to me:* At first it appears that the speaker is the angel who showed John the new Jerusalem (cf. 21:9,15; 22:1). But when the speaker goes on to say, "I am coming soon" (v 7), it becomes clear that it is Jesus (cf. v 20). *these words are trustworthy and true:* The content of Rev is reliable because it was given to all Christians (God's servants) through an angel sent by God. *what must happen soon:* The content of Rev refers to what John expected to happen in the near future.

(b) An Oracle Implicitly Attributed to Christ Which Is an Apocalyptic Prediction (22:7a). Cf. 2:16; 3:11; 22:12,20.

(c) A Beatitude Regarding the Reception of the Book (22:7b). This is the sixth of the seven beatitudes in Rev (→ 17 above). Taken together, these three sayings may be seen as a legitimation formula (Aune, *Prophecy in Early Christianity* [→ 4 above] 332–33).

67   (d) Identification of the Visionary by Name (22:8a). This mention of the human authority for the content of Rev complements the remarks about its divine origin in v 6 (cf. 1:1–2).

(e) Reaction of the Visionary and Angelic Response (22:8b–9). This passage is similar to 19:10. Here the prophets are emphasized more, but the end result is still the implication that any human who responds appropriately to God's word revealed through prophecy is equal to the angels.

(f) Directive to the Visionary from the Revealing Figure (22:10). This command is the opposite of Dan 12:4, but the effect is the same, since Dan was actually written near the time of the expected end.

(g) Threat of Judgment and Promise of Salvation (22:11–12). **11.** *let the wrongdoer continue to do wrong and the defiled continue to be defiled, and let the just continue to act justly and the holy continue to be sanctified:* These remarks indicate that John has little hope for the repentance of the wicked (see comments on 9:20–21; 16:2–9; cf. *1 Enoch* 81:7–8).

(h) Self-disclosing Oracle Implicitly Attributed to Christ (22:13). This oracle identifies the risen Christ with God; cf. 1:8,17; 21:6.

(i) Promise of Salvation and Threat of Judgment (22:14–15). **14.** *blessed are those who wash their robes:* In 7:14, the ones who have washed their robes are those who have come out of the great tribulation and who have made their robes white in the blood of the lamb. Although all believers are saved by the blood of the lamb (1:5b), it is especially those who die for the faith who are declared blessed here (cf. 12:11). **15.** See comment on 21:27; cf. also 21:8; 9:20–21.

68   (j) Self-identification of the Revealing Figure, Jesus (22:16). *I, Jesus, sent my angel to bear witness to you [pl.] concerning these things about the congregations:* "You" refers to the members of the seven congregations (cf. 2:10,13). *the root and the stock of David:* See 3:7; 5:5. *the bright morning star:* This star was a deity in ancient Near Eastern and Greco-Roman religion (Yarbro Collins, *Combat Myth* [→ 15 above] 81; *CBQ* 39 [1977] 379–80).

(k) Invitations to the Water of Life (22:17). *the bride:* The bride is not simply a metaphor for the Christian community. Like the Spirit, she is an aspect of the divine which calls humanity to salvation (see comment on 21:6).

69   (l) Threat of Judgment against Those Who Violate the Integrity of the Book (22:18–19). Charles argued that these verses were added to Rev by a later editor (*Commentary* 2. 222–23). His strongest argument was that, since John expected the end in a short time, he hardly would be concerned about the transmission of his book over a long period of time. But the remarks in vv 18–19 say nothing about a long period. If he considered that his work contained divine revelation necessary for the faithful to prepare properly for the end, he may well have been concerned that it be transmitted accurately in the short time remaining. Another function of these remarks is to reinforce the claim made elsewhere in the book that its contents originate with God (see 1:1). In nonapocalyptic Jewish writings older than or roughly contemporary with Rev, a similar attitude is taken toward the Scripture (Deut 4:2; 13:1 [*RSV* 12:32]; *Ep. Arist.* 310–11; Josephus, *Ag. Ap.* 1.8 § 42. In a Jewish apocalyptic work, such an attitude is expressed toward the work itself (*1 Enoch* 104:9–13).

(m) An Oracle Implicitly Attributed to Christ Which Is an Apocalyptic Prediction (22:20a). Imminent expectation of the end is emphasized by placing this prediction so near the end of the book (cf. vv 7,12).

(n) Response to the Oracle (22:20b). This is a Gk form of an early Christian prayer preserved in transliterated Aramaic as *maranatha* in 1 Cor 16:22b (→ 1 Corinthians, 49:79). G. Bornkamm has argued that the end of Rev, like the end of 1 Cor, reflects the eucharistic liturgy (*Early Christian Experience* [NY, 1969] 171–72).

70   (E) Concluding Epistolary Benediction (22:21). This conclusion corresponds to the epistolary elements in chap. 1 and helps to characterize Rev as an apocalyptic letter (→ 5 above). Cf. 1 Thess 5:28; Gal 6:18; Phil 4:23; Phlm 25.

64

THE SECOND EPISTLE OF PETER

Jerome H. Neyrey, S.J.

BIBLIOGRAPHY

1 Bauckham, R. J., "2 Peter: A Supplementary Bibliography," *JETS* 25 (1982) 91–93. Boobyer, G. H., "The Indebtedness of 2 Peter to 1 Peter," *New Testament Essays* (Fest. T. W. Manson; ed. A. J. B. Higgins, Manchester, 1959) 34–53. Danker, F., "2 Peter 1: A Solemn Decree," *CBQ* 40 (1978) 64–82. Fornberg, T., *An Early Church in a Pluralistic Society* (Uppsala, 1977). Hiebert, D. E., "Selected Studies from 2 Peter," *BSac* 141 (1984) 43–54, 158–68, 255–65, 330–40. Hupper, W. G., "Additions to 'A 2 Peter Bibliography,'" *JETS* 23 (1980) 65–66. Käsemann, E., "An Apology for Primitive

Christian Eschatology," *ENTT* 169–96. Kelly, J. N. D., *A Commentary on the Epistles of Peter and of Jude* (London, 1969). Mayor, J. B., *The Epistle of St. Jude and the Second Epistle of St. Peter* (London, 1907). Neyrey, J. H., "The Apologetic Use of the Transfiguration in 2 Peter 1:16–21," *CBQ* 42 (1980) 504–19; "The Form and Background of the Polemic in 2 Peter," *JBL* 99 (1980) 407–31. Spicq, C., *Les épîtres de Saint Pierre* (Paris, 1966).

DBSup 7. 1455–63. Kümmel, *INT* 429–34. Wik-Schm, *ENT* 602–13.

INTRODUCTION

2 **(I) Authenticity.** Despite 1:1,12–15; 3:1, scholars consider this a pseudonymous letter because: (a) 2 Pet incorporates Jude, weakening claims for authenticity; (b) it alludes to a "collection" of Paul's letters (3:15–16), which did not exist until the end of the century, at the very earliest; (c) it refers to "your apostles" (3:2), suggesting that it does not belong with that earlier group; (d) the letter relies on a wide range of traditions about Peter, which come from quite diverse streams of tradition, presuming a later, synthetic appreciation of these materials. No local church is addressed; rather "Peter" writes according to the growing perception of him as the foundation rock of the theological tradition, alongside his leadership role in the early church's missionary and administrative structure (see Matt 16:16–19). Probably written around the turn of the 1st cent., 2 Pet is a "catholic" letter, confirming traditional doctrine for all churches everywhere for all times (→ NT Epistles, 45:17–18).

3 **(II) Contents.** Käsemann's influential essay ("An Apology") negatively evaluates 2 Pet as an "early catholic," tiresome apology for eschatology because of its lack of christological focus and its anthropocentric view of rewards and punishments. Käsemann missed the central issues of this letter, that it addresses the problem of theodicy, God's just judgment, along with the delay of Christ's parousia. 2 Pet should be viewed alongside 1st.-cent. Gk and Jewish debates about God's providence and judgment; we know of standard attacks on

theodicy from Epicureans and Jewish heretics who argue that there is no providence/judgment in God, no afterlife, and, therefore, no post-mortem rewards and punishments (see Neyrey, "Form," 407–14). 2 Pet reflects this polemic and responds in traditional apologies. The issue is God's just judgment (1:3–4; 2:3,4–9; 3:3–7,8–9), not just christology; the concern is with theodicy, not simply the parousia. No gnostic myths, terms, or arguments are mentioned or refuted; rather the occasion is a typical debate over God's providence and just judgment.

4 **(III) Church.** The letter is written to a pluralistic church of Jewish-Christian and Gk converts. The biblical examples cited in chaps. 2–3 have close parallels in Greco-Roman literature (angels and Titans; Noah and Deucalion; Sodom and Phaethon). The language is good Greek with special attention to technical intellectual terms, such as "divine nature" (1:4), "eyewitness" (1:16), "Tartarus" (2:4), and the four cardinal vices. Arguments for and against God's just judgment resemble those found in Plutarch's *De sera numinis vindicta* as well as in the targumic midrash about Cain and Abel in Gen 4. The description of cosmic fire and renewal would sound congenial to Stoic ears as well as those trained in biblical traditions. The pastoral concern to make eschatological traditions equally intelligible to Jew and Greek suggests an urban setting, where a new, mixed church presents itself in continuity with the wisdom of the ages, Jewish and Gk alike. It shows a self-consciousness of its own chain of authority (1:12–15;

3:1–2), the sacredness of its own past tradition — gospel traditions as well as Paul's "letters," and the need to establish by writing a normative interpretation of its tradition (1:12–15). Though there is no firm evidence for dating 2 Pet, *ca.* AD 100 is a plausible date, for 2 Pet closely resembles the argument of Plutarch's *De sera numinis vindicta* (dated AD 96). It also mentions "all of Paul's letters," which scholars argue were collected about the turn of the century (→ NT Epistles, 45:14).

5   (IV) Relation of 2 Peter and Jude. With the flowering of redaction criticism, the relationship of Jude and 2 Peter is raised again (H. C. C. Cavallin, *NovT* 21 [1979] 263–70). Numerous blocks of material in 2 Pet are either identical with or similar to Jude:

2 Pet	Jude	2 Pet	Jude
2:1,3b	4	2:13,15	11–12
4,6	6–7	17	12b–13
5	5	18	16
10–11	8–9	3:1–4	17–18
12	10	10–13	14–15
		14–18	20–25

Who depends on whom? The problem is compounded by the generality of Jude's polemic, which led F. Wisse to despair of describing with any precision Jude's opponents ("The Epistle of Jude in the History of Heresiology," *Essays on the Nag Hammadi Tracts* [Fest. A. Böhlig; ed. M. Krause; Leiden, 1972] 133–43). Yet the version in 2 Pet is carefully descriptive of an attack on and a defense of divine theodicy, so that it would appear that he edited a generalized document (Jude) to fit a specific situation. A longer document is generally thought to be absorbing a smaller one, for it is hard to image how Jude would discard two-thirds of 2 Pet and

reduce what remained to a generic polemic. The absence of *1 Enoch* and *As. Mos.* from 2 Pet probably points to a fixing of traditions with the exclusion of certain unacceptable materials. It also consciously presents itself as a coherent harmony of established traditions from Jesus, Paul, and "your apostles" (3:2), including Jude.

6   (V) Outline. Epistolary conventions serve as the framework for the apology of 2 Pet:

  (I) Letter Introduction (1:1–11)
    (A) Letter Opening (1:1–2)
    (B) God's Deeds (1:3–4)
    (C) Eschatology and Ethics (1:5–11)
      (a) Good Theology Leads to Good Behavior (1:5–7)
      (b) Two Ways (1:8–11)
  (II) Fictive Letter Setting: Peter's Testament (1:12–15)
  (III) First Apology: Prophecy of the Parousia (1:16–21)
    (A) Mythmaking (1:16a)
    (B) Transfiguration and Parousia (1:16b–18)
    (C) Transfiguration as Prophecy (1:19)
    (D) Inspired Interpretation (1:20–21)
  (IV) Polemic against the Heretics (2:1–22)
    (A) God's Sure Judgment (2:1–11)
    (B) Error Leads to Vice (2:12–16)
    (C) False Promises (2:17–19)
    (D) Lapse from Grace (2:20–22)
  (V) Second Apology: End of the World (3:1–7)
    (A) Faithful Remembering (3:1–2)
    (B) Attack on the Predicted Judgment (3:3–4)
    (C) Rebuttal: Proof from History (3:5–7)
  (VI) Third Apology: "Delay" as a Gift (3:8–9)
  (VII) Eschatology and Ethics Again (3:10–13)
    (A) Thief in the Night (3:10)
    (B) God's Day (3:11–13)
  (VIII) Peter and Paul Agree (3:14–16)
  (IX) Letter Closing (3:17–18)

COMMENTARY

7   (I) Letter Introduction (1:1–11).
(A) Letter Opening (1:1–2). The sender identifies himself as Simon Peter, joining the old name, Symeon (Acts 15:14), with the new leadership name, Peter, which Jesus gave him (Matt 16:18). *servant . . . apostle:* In the Hebr tradition "servant" designates an obedient, legitimate agent of God, such as Moses (Deut 34:5) or David (2 Sam 7:5–29); he is also the premier "apostle" of Jesus Christ in virtue of his special commission (Matt 16:16–19; John 21:15–19). The addressees are not specifically identified, an unusual feature of NT letters, which strikes a note of universality and implies that the contents of the letter are addressed to *all* Christians who have the standard faith. **2.** *grace and peace:* This typical greeting (→ NT Epistles, 45:8A) is tailored to the occasion, as the author prays that his hearers grow toward fullness of knowledge about God, which hints at the central purpose of the letter — a definitive exposition of the Christian doctrine of theodicy, God's just judgment. *God and savior:* The foundation of our membership rests on God's righteousness and Jesus as savior, which in the letter's context imply God's just judgment (see Rom 1:17–3:20) and Jesus' role as savior, not only from past sins (Rom 3:21–26) but especially from God's future wrath (Rom 5:9–11; 1 Thess 1:10).
8   (B) God's Deeds (1:3–4). Typical letters contain a thanksgiving prayer (cf. 1 Pet 1:3–9; → NT Epistles, 48:6, 8B) in which the letter's main themes and tone are established. Although the formal prayer is absent in 1:3–4, the author rehearses the benefits God

has bestowed (see F. Danker, *CBQ* 40 [1978] 64–82). **3.** *all things:* The premier benefit is the complex gift of membership in God's covenant in which one finds all things necessary to life and holiness. This is a call to a new and special world, God's own realm of glory and excellence, which gift transfers Christians from a corrupt, passing world to a holy and permanent world, from a realm of passion to one of holiness. **4.** *great promises:* What constitutes a true insider? Correct knowledge of him who called us, which is focused in this letter on the precious and very great promises which have to do with the correct doctrine of God's just judgment and Jesus' parousia. True insiders, then, are those who have full and correct ideas about God.
9   (C) Eschatology and Ethics (1:5–11).
(a) GOOD THEOLOGY LEADS TO GOOD BEHAVIOR (1:5–7). The author exhorts true insiders to be what in fact they are, as he urges them to let their true faith in God replicate itself more and more in the exercise of righteous actions. In an appeal not unlike Jas 2:17–26, he argues that correct doctrine and true faith show themselves in moral uprightness (good "theology" will lead to good "ethics"). So interior excellence must express itself in correct external behavior, a standard NT argument (1 Thess 2:12). *faith, hope, and love:* Faith, i.e., true doctrine, should lead to virtue, esp. to self-control, steadfastness (hope), godliness, and love. Yet even in this chain of good actions, one senses a subtle emphasis on loyalty to the doctrine of God's just judgment: self-control so as to be blameless before God, steadfastness

in watching for Christ's coming, and godliness or holiness of life.

10 (b) Two Ways (1:8–11). Peter contrasts those who act in accord with true faith with those who do not. **8.** *unfruitful . . . blind:* True insiders will not be ineffective or unfruitful, whereas those of inadequate faith are both blind and forgetful (see 3:3,8) of their original transition from outsider status to that of insiders, from being sinners to becoming partakers of the divine nature. **11.** *everlasting kingdom:* The exhortation closes with an appeal to be a genuine insider by confirmation of God's call to holiness with a holy life (see 1 Thess 4:3–7). It is not enough to begin well; perseverance alone will lead to the permanent and full status of an insider, as correct faith and authentic behavior provide for final entrance into the heavenly kingdom (see Matt 25:31–46). Jesus spoke of the kingdom of God (see Mark 10:15; John 3:3), but here the author refers to the kingdom of our Lord and Savior, Jesus Christ.

11 (II) Fictive Letter Setting: Peter's Testament (1:12–15). Both Jews and Greeks knew of a testament genre, the last remarks of a dying leader or patriarch (e.g., Socrates' testament in Plato's *Apology*, the testaments of Jacob (Gen 49), Jacob's twelve sons (*T. 12 Patr.*), Moses (Deut 32–34), Joshua (Josh 24), even of Jesus (John 13–17; Luke 22:14–36) and Paul (Acts 20:17–35). This letter constitutes Peter's testament, given on the occasion of his impending death (1:14); it bequeaths a legacy to the church of accurate remembering of the doctrine of God's judgment and Jesus' parousia. **14.** *putting off:* The author alludes to a tradition in which Jesus predicted Peter's death (John 21:18–19), which is conventionally expressed as a putting off of this earthly "tent" (see 2 Cor 5:1,4). **15.** *call to mind:* The labeling of this legacy as a "reminder" is another convention (see 1 Thess 2:9) which serves to legitimate a statement by appeal to its antiquity, a value in a tradition-oriented society (see 3:1–2).

12 (III) First Apology: Prophecy of the Parousia (1:16–21).

(A) Mythmaking (1:16a). Some reject the traditional prophecies of Jesus' future parousia as myths made up by human beings to control the lives of others, not unlike Greco-Roman stories of rewards and punishments in the underworld (Lucretius, *R. N.* 3.830–1094). By attacking their source, the scoffers would undermine their content as well (see 3:3–4). This common polemical argument (*myth* vs. *truth*) is commonly dealt with by Jewish (Philo, *De fuga et inv.* 121; *De Abr.* 243), Greek (Plutarch, *De Pyth. orac.* 398D), and Christian apologists (1 Tim 1:4; 4:7; Titus 1:14); as this author is charged with mythmaking, he levels the same charge against his opponents in 2:3.

13 (B) Transfiguration and Parousia (1:16b–18). **16b.** *eyewitnesses:* In response Peter offers the best forensic evidence, his own experience of the giving of the parousia prophecy, the transfiguration of Jesus (see Neyrey, "Apologetic Use" 509–14). **17.** *glory:* Like the Synoptic accounts of the transfiguration, Peter describes: a holy mountain, apostolic eyewitnesses, Peter in particular, Jesus' glorious appearance, God's numinous presence, and God's proclamation, "This is my beloved son." Peter is traditionally credited with special revelations (Matt 16:17), special visions (Matt 28:16–20), special prophecies (Mark 13:1–3; 14:27–31), and special presence at Jesus' exercise of power (Mark 5:37–43). He is, then, a specially informed, trustworthy source of traditions about Jesus.

14 (C) Transfiguration as Prophecy (1:19). In the Gospels the transfiguration is linked with a future coming of God's kingdom (Mark 9:1). According to

Church Fathers, Jesus' prediction that some would not taste death until they saw the coming of God's kingdom was fulfilled in the vision of Jesus' power and glory at the transfiguration. But in writings like the *Apocalypse of Peter* (HSNTA 2. 663–83), the transfiguration was itself a prophecy of Jesus' parousia, not a fulfillment of an earlier prophecy. Reminiscent of Jesus' predictions in Mark 13, this text contains Jesus' answer to questions about his parousia and the end of the world; his response is a pastiche of Gospel statements describing the parousia, the return of the Son of Man, but especially future punishments and rewards. The apocalypse ends with Jesus' glorification in the presence of Moses and Elijah, at which final tableau Jesus especially instructs Peter. The story ends with Jesus' ascent to heaven in glory, which serves to describe his future return. According to this, the transfiguration functions not only as the occasion on which Peter was instructed about Jesus' parousia and future judgment, but also as a prediction of that future event. It is this sense of the transfiguration as prophecy of the parousia that the author appeals to in the argument in 1:17–18. *prophecy surer still:* This phrase is best understood as "we have a very confirmed prophetic word" Although *bebaioteros* is a comparative adj., it may be translated in the superlative degree (ZBG § 148) with the result that the transfiguration material in 1:17–18 is not compared with other prophecies (3:3–4) but represents the very best prophecy of the parousia. Confirmation of promises and prophecies is a recurring theme in Jewish writings; God's promises to Abraham (Gen 22:16–17) are "confirmed" by an oath (see Philo, *Leg. alleg.* 3.203–8); this same promise is confirmed just because the truthful and faithful God spoke it (*De Sacr. Ab.* 93). Paul speaks of a confirmed promise of God in Rom 4:16, offering an immediate parallel to 1:19. *morning star:* The transfiguration prophecy of the parousia is confirmed because spoken by God, so that it can function as a light in darkness for those waiting for the final light, "the morning star" (see Rev 2:28), to rise with Christ's parousia (see 1 Thess 5:4).

15 (D) Inspired Interpretation (1:20–21). **20.** *no prophecy in Scripture:* In the OT true prophecies when rightly understood were uncomfortable, even threatening (see Jer 6:14; Ezek 13:10), a tradition repeated by Paul apropos of parousia prophecies. When people say "peace and security," then Jesus comes as the thief in the night (1 Thess 5:2–4). The false teachers whom the author censures are like Israel's false prophets (2:1), who have neither received God's challenging word nor understood it; for example, they twist Paul's words on the topic under discussion (3:16). **21.** *from God:* Unlike them, the author claims inspiration from God both in his receipt of the parousia prophecy and his exposition of it, a claim comparable to the tradition of Peter's receipt of a revelation about Jesus as "Christ, Son of God" (Matt 16:17). His prophecy is not subject to new, charismatic interpretations, a process noted in the reinterpretation of some of Jesus' sayings and deeds (see John 14:26; 16:12–14), but is the same prophecy he has always been inspired to receive and interpret (see Acts 3:18–26). He is, then, suited to the task because he is an eyewitness, inspired to understand what he has received. This serves to counter hints in the tradition that Peter did not understand what he saw or heard (see Luke 9:32–33).

16 (IV) Polemic against the Heretics (2:1–22). Chapter 2, which incorporates most of Jude's generalized polemic, contains this author's traditional attacks on his adversaries, not a detailed examination and refutation of their ideas.

(A) God's Sure Judgment (2:1–11). **1.** *false teachers:* After defending himself, the author contrasts his legitimacy with that of false teachers disturbing the church. He likens them to false prophets, who according to Jeremiah and Ezekiel were not authorized to speak and who preached peace and security when reform and repentance were called for (Jer 5:12; 6:14; Ezek 13:10). *deny the Lord:* The author does not mean that church members are atheists but rather that they reject God's judgment. The Psalms report sinners rejecting God's knowledge of their deeds and so judgment of them (Pss 10:11,13; 14:1; 73:11). According to Titus 1:16, rejection of God's law means rejection of the lawgiver. Verse 1 amplifies the author's charge in 1:16–19 that some deny the tradition of Christ's parousia and God's just judgment. *sects:* These false teachers are scandalizing the church, an evil condemned in Mark 9:42 and 1 Cor 8:11–13. **2.** *lechery:* Bad theology will only lead to bad morals, in this case "lechery," the worst vice according to this culture (see Rom 1:26–27). Destroying themselves, they dishonor the Christian "way of truth" (Acts 18:25–26), both the true God and the ethical ways of honoring that God, and so discredit Christianity before the world (see 1 Thess 4:12; 1 Cor 14:23; Col 4:5). **3.** *deceitful words:* The author calls attention to false doctrine; as his opponents accused him of "concocted myths" (1:16), he returns the favor with criticism of their "fabricated arguments," imputing to them the base motive of greed, a commonplace polemic against bogus philosophers and preachers (1 Tim 6:5; Titus 1:11; R. J. Karris, *JBL* 92 [1973] 549–64). *slumber:* The author quotes back to his opponents their own slogan ("Judgment is idle! Destruction naps!"), but negates it. It was common of slanderers of God's providence to remark mockingly that "God sleeps" (1 Kgs 18:27) but of believers to insist that God does not sleep (Ps 121:4) and will arise to execute judgment (Pss 9:19; 68:1; 74:22). After charging the heretics with evil (v 3a), the author pronounces punishment on them (v 3b).

17   **4.** *God did not spare:* If v 3 claims that divine judgment is not asleep, proof is necessary. Recourse is had to classic examples of divine judgment in the past: if God did not spare these figures in the past, then just judgment should be expected in the present. In vv 4–9 the author borrows material from Jude 5–7, changing the order and significance of the examples:

Jude 5–7	2 Pet 2:4–8
desert generation	angels
angels	Noah and his generation
Sodom and Gomorrah	Lot and Sodom and Gomorrah

2 Pet arranges them chronologically according to the Scriptures; he replaces the judgment on the exodus wanderers with the saving of Noah, and adds the note about Lot's rescue to the judgment of Sodom. Whereas Jude stressed that those blessed by God fell from grace and faced judgment (see 1 Cor 10:5–13), 2 Pet emphasizes God's providence, both to reward the just (Noah, Lot) and punish the wicked (angels, Sodom). Those who "deny the Lord," i.e., deny God's judgment, are simply wrong. Verse 9 summarizes the three examples, asserting the traditional belief that God justly rescues the just but holds the wicked for judgment, even if that reckoning is not evident on earth.

18   **4.** *into Tartarus:* The examples of God's judgment have a universal appeal to Jews and Greeks alike. The angels were "cast into Tartarus," reminiscent of Gen 6:3 and the pagan myth of the Titans; Noah's escape from the flood parallels the escape of Deucalion; the judgment by fire on Sodom resembles the punishment of Phaethon. Jewish writers noted these similarities, arguing for the antiquity, veracity, and universality of the

Scriptures (Philo, *De praem.* 23; Josephus, *Ant.* 1.3.1 § 73). By using common examples, the author continues a catholic argument in defense of a tradition accepted by all peoples at all times.

19   **9.** *the Lord knows how:* The author touches the present crisis by insisting that God especially judges sinners like the ones now disturbing the church. **10.** *deny authority:* This basically repeats the author's understanding of the errors of the false teachers: they despise authority, esp. God's just judgment (see 2:1), but also church authority such as Peter. Tradition indicates that those who reject God's agent also reject God (John 12:48; 1 Thess 4:8). *unclean lust:* They follow a fleshly path into desire and pleasure (2:2,13), two of the famous four vices against which preachers regularly railed (Diogenes Laertius 7.110–15). *pollution:* Bad theology leads to bad morality and pollution; Christians are called to holiness ("Be ye holy as I am holy," 1 Pet 1:16; 1 Thess 4:3–7), which means a complete and permanent separation from all former sins and evil (see 1 Cor 5:8; 1 Pet 4:1–6). If by their fruits one shall know them, these heretics are surely wrong because their errors lead to vices and pollution. The argument is traditional: those who deny God's judgment use it as a pretext for lawlessness and immorality (Pss 13:1–4; 64:6–7). **11.** *whereas angels:* Another aspect of the false teachers' doctrine: they deny that God's angels act as agents of God's judgment (see Matt 13:41–42; 24:31; Rev 8:6–12).

20   **(B) Error Leads to Vice (2:12–16).** The attack on the false teachers continues in general terms. The polemic begins and ends with reference to their coming recompense for evildoing (2:12,15), harping on the judgment which they deny. **12.** *brute animals:* The false teachers are compared with animals because of their ignorance; they are but creatures of corruptible nature, not sharers of God's imperishable nature, as are true believers (1:4); like animals, their nature is to be captured and perish. For doing evil they will suffer evil. **13.** *spots and blemishes:* Sinners are usually ashamed of their sins and do them under cover of night, but these parade their evil in daylight. The author calls them a pollution (2:10), a blot and blemish which pollutes the holy gatherings of God's saints (see 1 Cor 5:7–8), and so they should be exposed as deceivers and judged (1 Cor 5:11). **14.** *eyes full of adultery:* Their false doctrine is shown to lead to immorality, adultery, incessant sinning, and greed, indicating a total corruption of heart. **16.** *a dumb beast of burden:* Balaam is cited as an example, for he was a greedy, false prophet, both rebuked for his malice by a donkey and recompensed for his wickedness by God; he serves as one more traditional instance of God's just judgment of sinners (see Jude 11; Num 22–24; 31:16).

21   **(C) False Promises (2:17–19). 17.** *cisterns . . . mists:* The heretics are likened to empty cisterns, promising something they have not got (Jer 2:13; 14:3) or insubstantial mists driven helter-skelter by passion and greed. Judgment is reserved for such. Their crime? False speech, denial of the tradition (1:16; 2:1; 3:3–4), and propagation of false teaching. **19.** *freedom:* They promise freedom: freedom from law, from authority, and from judgment. In this they are compared with the lawless (2:8) and accused of lawlessness (2:10,21), a singular evil condemned by both the Gospels (Matt 7:23; 13:41) and Paul (Rom 2:12; 6:19). *slaves of corruption:* The author sarcastically describes how their promises of freedom lead instead to slavery, bondage to corruption, and destruction. On the contrary, his promises (1:4; 3:9) teach one to flee corruption and destruction by fidelity to God's law and expectation of God's just judgment. The result of their promise is a return to a world of flesh, not God's undefiled nature.

22   (D) Lapse from Grace (2:20–22). 20. *having escaped:* Conversion means a definitive break with sin (see 1 Pet 4:1–2), a transition from sin to grace, death to life, darkness to light. The worst thing that could happen would be to cross back into the former realm, a horror warned against in the Gospel (Matt 12:43–45), Paul (Rom 6:6–11), and other Christian writings (Heb 6:1–6; 10:38). **22.** *dog . . . sow:* This lapse is likened to a dog returning to its vomit (Prov 26:11) and a pig to its mire, confirming the slander in 2:12 that the heretics are "animals," not sharers of the divine nature. Like Mark 14:21, better never to have been saved.

23   (V) Second Apology: End of the World (3:1–7). The author returns to the scoffers' doctrines, dealing first with their objections to the prediction of the world's end.

(A) Faithful Remembering (3:1–2). 1. *second letter:* The first letter was apparently 1 Pet (Boobyer, "The Indebtedness," 34–53), which was concerned with searching out the correct message of the prophets (see 1 Pet 1:10–13). *your pure mind:* As in 1:13–15, this remembering is focused on the correct interpretation (*eilikrinē dianoia*) of the eschatological tradition, esp. in the face of disputes over it (see 1:16,20; 3:4,16). The tradition about parousia and judgment is in accord with the words of the prophets of old (see OT references in 2:4–8,15–16) as well as the word of the Lord through his apostles. **2.** *your apostles:* This suggests that Peter did not write this letter, for this author senses a gulf between early, authentic spokesmen and himself. *be mindful:* The emphasis on reminding and remembering here distinguishes the author from the scoffers, who are willfully forgetful of the truth (3:5,8).

24   (B) Attack on the Predicted Judgment (3:3–4). 3. *scoffers:* Here is the clearest reference to the heretics' doctrine. According to testament conventions, the dying leader predicts trouble for his followers, even attacks on them (see Acts 20:29). As false teachers (2:1), they scoff at the group's traditions (1:16); the author discredits this by claiming that their scoffing springs from desires, another reference to the four cardinal vices (1:4; 2:10,18). **4.** *promise:* Their scoffing focuses once more on the promises of the parousia, which the author has been defending all along (1:4; 3:9). *where is . . . ?:* A typical query calling in question the power and intention either of a foreign god (Deut 32:37; 2 Kgs 18:34) or Israel's God (Judg 6:13; Ps 42:4,11). Besides attacking the source of the parousia prophecy (1:16), the scoffers offer arguments against it from experience: there is no evidence of God's judgment in the world, not from creation even up to the most recent death of Church Fathers. *fathers:* Probably NT figures who received predictions about the imminence of the parousia which seem not to have been fulfilled (see Matt 10:23; Mark 9:1). Parodying the axiom that "all is in flux," the scoffers argue that "all remains unchanged." And so, they object to the parousia prophecies for two reasons: (a) denial of God's judgment (2:3b; 3:9) and (b) denial of God's action in creation (3:4).

25   (C) Rebuttal: Proof from History (3:5–7). 5. *willfully forgetting:* The author accuses the heretics of culpable ignorance. Their scoffing, which sprang from evil desires (3:3), is a willful forgetting of what everybody knows. *formed:* The apology for the promise of the parousia rests on the traditional Jewish doctrine of God's powers, creative and executive. All of his actions are regularly summarized under these two inclusive headings (Philo, *Leg. alleg.* 2.68; *De cher.* 27–28; Rom 4:17; see N. A. Dahl, *JSJ* 9 [1978] 1–28). Just as God has power to create (v 5), so he has power to judge. *word of God:* Since the issue is the reliability of God's word, the

point is made that by a word God created heaven and earth and by a word he will exercise executive power on them. **6–7.** *water . . . fire:* According to 2:4–8, God judged Noah and his generation with water, and Lot and Sodom and Gomorrah with fire. So God's judgment in the world has already been proved. *stored up:* Deut 28:12 speaks of God's good treasuries of rain and fertility; yet Philo speaks of God's treasury of judgment (*Leg. alleg.* 3.105–6).

26   (VI) Third Apology: "Delay" as a Gift (3:8–9). 8. *one day:* Stressing the surety of God's word (3:7), the author deals with another explicit argument of the scoffers, "God delays (to judge)!" (see 2:3b). When God's providence to bless and judge is attacked, several typical arguments were urged: (1) a provident God could not make useless or harmful creatures; (2) God's foreknowledge would destroy human freedom; and (3) God is slow to reward the just and punish the wicked. By harping on God's delay, heterodox Greeks and Jews argued against God's future judgment (see Plutarch, *De sera num. vind.* 548D, 549D). *with the Lord:* The author responds to the slur about God's delay in two ways. He indicates that divine time is mysterious to humans and incalculable: 1,000 days = 1 year, 1 year = 1,000 days (see Ps 90:4). This text was understood apropos of the delayed judgment of Adam. Although in Gen 2:17 God said, "On the day you eat it you will die . . . ," Adam lived another 1,000 years. This delay of judgment was explained as God's gift of time to Adam to repent and be saved (*Gen. Rab.* 22:1; *Jub.* 4:29–30). **9.** *delay . . . long-suffering:* God's delay should not be seen as an argument against theodicy, but as divine forbearance to sinners, a theme regularly found in the Scriptures (Wis 12:10), Jewish writings (Philo, *Leg. alleg.* 3.106), Christian writings (Rom 2:4) and Greco-Roman discussions (Plutarch, *De sera num. vind.* 551C,D). It is based on the revelation to Moses in Exod 34:6–7 that God is "slow to anger," a phrase that gets translated in the LXX as God's forbearance (*makrothymia:* Num 14:18; Neh 9:17; Ps 86:15). God, who is both creator and executive of the world, is both merciful and just, with a special emphasis on God's forbearance to sinners.

27   (VII) Eschatology and Ethics Again (3:10–13).

(A) Thief in the Night (3:10). *day of the Lord:* Balancing the remark about a delay for repentance is the affirmation of the sure but unknowable coming of Jesus as a thief in the night (Matt 24:43–44; 1 Thess 5:1; Rev 3:3). *heavens . . . earth:* At his coming, all creation—heavens, intermediate elements, and earth—will pass away with a loud noise, possibly the trumpet and cry of command mentioned in 1 Thess 4:16 or the roar of consuming fire. *found out:* The earth will be "found" in the forensic sense of examined and "found out" (see 1 Cor 3:13–15; F. Danker, *ZNW* 53 [1962] 82–86).

28   (B) God's Day (3:11–13). 11. *holy and pious behavior:* Doctrine affects life, and so reference is made to moral behavior consonant with belief in God's just judgment. We are to live lives of holiness and reverence for God, so as to stand on the final day (see 1 Thess 3:13; 5:23; Phil 2:15–16). **12.** *hasten . . . the day:* How different are believers and scoffers: believers await and hasten the day, whereas scoffers mock its delay and disregard it; believers interpret the delay as a gift of God's forbearance, whereas scoffers turn it against God's judgment; believers live blameless lives, whereas scoffers are mired in defiling passions (2:10,13–14). *the day of God:* This phrase stresses a different point from that made in 3:10 about the day of the Lord (Jesus). Now the emphasis is upon God's power to be active in creation and to judge. This day resembles biblical descriptions of God's day (see Isa 43:4; Mark 13:24–25; Rev 16:8–9), where the heavens are predicted to fail and fire to come upon the world. **13.** *new heavens . . . new earth:* The fiery consumption issues in a new creation, new heavens and new earth, just as the prophets foretold (Isa 65:17; 66:22; Rev 21:1; cf. Matt 19:28). Purified by fire, only saints will share in God's kingdom of justice; the wicked will be destroyed (3:7).

29   (VIII) Peter and Paul Agree (3:14–16). **14.** *blameless:* The following verses draw out the implications of belief in God's judgment: Christians are zealous to be spotless and blameless, whereas the scoffers are described in 2:12 as spotted and blameful. *found by him:* Believers will be examined and found worthy, a repetition of the remark in 3:10 that the world too will be scrutinized by God (see Matt 24:46; Mark 13:36). **15.** *forbearance:* Believers know how to interpret delay of judgment as forbearance (3:9), a gift of time to repent and be saved. *the wisdom given him:* The author takes up Paul's letters, evidently because some think to find in them arguments against the tradition defended by Peter. First, the author affirms that Paul was inspired and authorized in virtue of the wisdom given him by God (Rom 12:3; 1 Cor 3:10; Gal 2:9). Inasmuch as Peter is also an inspired prophet (1:12–15,16–21), the tradition about the parousia rests on the word of two reliable witnesses. Second, despite the alleged disagreement between Peter and Paul in Gal 2:12–14, the author affirms that the eschatological tradition has been held always by everyone in all the churches. Third, the author admits that Paul is difficult to understand and is actually being mis-

interpreted by these scoffers, an error perhaps based on a misunderstanding of Paul's proclamation of freedom (Gal 5:1; see 2 Pet 2:19) and his sense of rising with Jesus in baptism (Rom 6:1–11), which implies that believers are already beyond scrutiny and judgment (1 Cor 4:7; John 3:17–19). A correct interpretation (see 3:2) would include Paul's remarks on Christ's coming to judge (1 Cor 1:7), our need to be spotless on that day (1 Thess 3:13; 5:23), and judgment at the judgment bench of God (2 Cor 5:10; Rom 14:9–12). Paul affirmed God's just judgment (Rom 2:5–9), even God's two powers of creation and judgment (Rom 4:17), and God's forbearance as time to repent (Rom 2:4). **16.** *all of his letters:* We cannot tell how many letters of Paul this author knows; it would seem that Rom and 1 Thess are surely known and considered as "Scripture" for this church, a point that suggests a late dating of this writing.

30   (IX) Letter Closing (3:17–18). As in Mark 13:5,23, the letter closes with warnings about future difficulties. **17.** *beware:* The recipients are to stand firm in the tradition (1 Cor 10:12; 1 Thess 3:13) and not be carried away by deceit (2:3a,19; 2 Tim 4:3–4). **18.** *grow in . . . knowledge:* An *inclusio* with 1:3, where knowledge of God bestowed all that pertains to life and holiness; that knowledge now especially includes correct understanding of Jesus' parousia. *day of eternity:* A summary code for the main theme of the letter, the day of God's judgment and the day of Jesus' parousia, which is a day of cosmic destruction, but also of a new heaven and a new earth.

65

INSPIRATION

Raymond F. Collins

BIBLIOGRAPHY

1 Abraham, W. J., *The Divine Inspiration of Holy Scripture* (Oxford, 1981). Achtemeier, P. J., *The Inspiration of Scripture: Problems and Proposals* (Phl, 1980). Alonso Schökel, L., "Inspiration," *Sacramentum Mundi* (ed. K. Rahner, *et al.;* NY, 1969) 3. 145–51; *The Inspired Word: Scripture in the Light of Language and Literature* (NY, 1965); "The Psychology of Inspiration," *The Bible in Its Literary Milieu* (ed. V. L. Tollers and J. R. Meier; GR, 1979) 24–56. Bea, A., "Deus Auctor Sacrae Scripturae: Herkunft und Bedeutung der Formel," *Ang* 20 (1943) 16–31. Benoit, P., "Inspiration," R–T, 9–59; *Inspiration and the Bible* (London, 1965). Bromiley, G. W., "Inspiration, History of the Doctrine of," *ISBE* 2. 849–54. Burtchaell, J. T., *Catholic Theories of Biblical Inspiration since 1810* (Cambridge, 1969). Cassem, N. H., "Inerrancy after 70 Years: The Transition to Saving Truth," *ScEs* 22 (1970) 189–202. Collins, R. F., *Introduction to the New Testament* (GC, 1983) 317–55. Desroches, A., *Jugement pratique et jugement spéculatif chez l'écrivain inspiré* (Ottawa, 1958). Gnuse, R., *The Authority of the Bible* (NY, 1985). Harrington, W., *Record of Revelation: The Bible* (Chicago, 1965) 20–53. Harris, R. L.,

Inspiration and Canonicity of the Bible: Contemporary Evangelical Perspectives (rev. ed.; GR, 1969). Hoffman, T. A., "Inspiration, Normativeness, Canonicity, and the Unique Sacred Character of the Bible," *CBQ* 44 (1982) 447–69. Lohfink, N., "Über die Irrtumslosigkeit und die Einheit der Schrift," *SZ* 174 (1964) 161–81; Eng digest in *TD* 13 (1965) 185–92. Loretz, O., *Das Ende der Inspirations-Theologie* (2 vols.; Stuttgart, 1974–76); *The Truth of the Bible* (NY, 1968). McCarthy, D. J., "Personality, Society, and Inspiration," *TS* 24 (1963) 553–76. Marshall, I. H., *Biblical Inspiration* (London, 1982). Rahner, K., *Inspiration in the Bible* (2d ed.; NY, 1964). Scullion, J., *The Theology of Inspiration* (TToday 10; Cork, 1970). Stanley, D. M., "The Concept of Biblical Inspiration," *ProcCTSA* 13 (1958) 65–95. Synave, P. and P. Benoit, *Prophecy and Inspiration* (NY, 1961) esp. 84–145. Turner, G., "Biblical Inspiration and the Paraclete," *New Blackfriars* 65 (1984) 420–28. Vawter, B., *Biblical Inspiration* (Phl, 1972). Vogels, W., "Inspiration in a Linguistic Mode," *BTB* 15 (1985) 87–93. Warfield, B. B., "Inspiration," *ISBE* 2. 839–49.

OUTLINE

VATICAN COUNCIL II

3   "The Divine Inspiration and the Interpretation of Sacred Scripture" was the title of chap. 3 of Vatican II's Dogmatic Constitution on Divine Revelation (*Dei Verbum,* Nov. 18, 1965). In the text, inspiration is a specific way of speaking about the unique sacred character of the Scriptures, having important implications for the way in which the OT and NT books are to be regarded by believers.

4   The key conciliar affirmation (3:11) is:

Those divinely revealed realities which are contained and presented in sacred Scripture have been committed to writing under the inspiration of the Holy Spirit [*Spiritu Sancto afflante consignata sunt*]. Holy Mother Church, relying on the belief of the apostles, holds that the books of both OT and NT in their entirety, with all their parts, are sacred and canonical because, having been written under the inspiration of the Holy Spirit [*Spiritu Sancto inspirante conscripti*] (cf. John 20:31; 2 Tim 3:16; 2 Pet 1:19–21; 3:15–16), they have God as their author and have been handed on as such to the church herself. In composing the sacred books, God chose men and while employed by him they made use of their powers and abilities, so with him acting in them and through them, they, as true authors, consigned to writing everything and only those things which He wanted. Therefore, since everything asserted by the inspired authors or sacred writers [*quod auctores inspirati seu hagiographi asserunt*] must be held to be asserted by the Holy Spirit, it follows that the books of Scripture must be acknowledged as teaching firmly, faithfully, and without error that truth which God wanted put into the sacred writings for the sake of our salvation. Therefore, 'all Scripture is inspired by God and useful for teaching, for reproving, for correcting, for instruction in justice; that the man of God may be perfect, equipped for every good work' (2 Tim 3:16–17, Gk text).

5   Clearly Vatican II intended to recapitulate traditional teaching on inspiration. The text refers to four NT passages often cited in the history of the church's long discussion on inspiration, esp. 2 Tim 3:16 and 2 Pet 1:19–21. At a relatively late stage of the conciliar discussion on inspiration and in response to an intervention by Dom B. C. Butler, 2 Tim 3:16–17 was incorporated so that there could be no mistaking how the council fathers understood the doctrine of the inspiration of the Scriptures and what they considered its purpose to be. They intended to recapitulate the teaching

of the (NT) Scriptures themselves. In this regard, Vatican II's statement on inspiration concurs with the views of many evangelical Christians, who look to the NT Scriptures, esp. 2 Tim 3:16–17 and 2 Pet 1:19–21, as providing the key witnesses as to how inspiration is to be understood and enunciated.

6   The council fathers' desire to sum up traditional teaching on inspiration is further evidenced by their footnoted references to Heb 1:1; 4:7; 2 Sam 23:2; to Matthew's use of citation formulas (e.g., Matt 1:22); and to Augustine (*De genesi ad litteram* 2.9.20; *Ep.* 82.3) and Aquinas (*De Veritate* 1.12, a.2). The footnotes also refer to Trent and Vatican I, as well as to two major encyclicals which had appeared in the interim between Vatican I and II, viz., Leo XIII's *Providentissimus Deus* (1893) and Pius XII's *DAS* (1943). Vatican II's concern to recapitulate the tradition on inspiration becomes all the more significant in the light of the retrogressive draft (*schema*) on inspiration that had been submitted at the outset of the council, as well as the extensive discussions that led not only to the rejection of that schema but also to several revisions of the text that was eventually to become part of *Dei Verbum* (→ Church Pronouncements, 72:7, 13–16).

7   Nine additional articles in *Dei Verbum* (7,8, 9,14,16,18,20,21,24) make explicit reference to the inspiration of the Scriptures. The conciliar text states that the OT (3:14), the NT (4:16), the Gospels (5:18), Paul's epistles, and other apostolic writings (5:20) are inspired. Some conciliar passages cite inspiration as a quality of the biblical texts (2:8; 6:21,24), whereas others either predicate inspiration of those who were involved in the biblical writing or refer to the texts as having been written under the inspiration of the Holy Spirit (2:9; 4:14; 5:20; cf. 2:7; 5:18). God is "the inspirer and author of both Testaments" (4:16); elsewhere inspiration is specifically attributed to the Spirit (2:7,9; 5:18,20). Repeatedly, inspiration is cited as the ground for the consideration that the Scriptures are (or contain) the word of God (2:9; 4:14; 6:21,24). The Gospels benefit from the charism of inspiration in a singularly pre-eminent fashion (3:11; 5:18)

EARLY CHRISTIAN AND JEWISH TRADITION

8   **(I) New Testament.** What, then, does the tradition say about inspiration? The two most important Scripture passages are 2 Tim 3:16–17 and 2 Pet 1:19–21. In each, the Lat Vg uses *inspirare* (lit., "to breathe in"), from which are derived not only the Eng "inspire" but also its equivalent in most modern romance and Germanic languages. Initially the 2 Tim passage, which speaks of the inspiration of Scripture, would seem more significant than the 2 Pet passage, which speaks of the inspiration of prophecy.

9   **(A) 2 Tim 3:16–17.** "All scripture is inspired by God and profitable for teaching, for reproof, for correction, and for training in righteousness, that the man of God may be complete, equipped for every good

work" (*RSV*). (For the probable post-Pauline pseudonymity of 2 Tim, → Pastorals, 56:6–8).

The immediate context (3:10–17) encourages Timothy, as the man of God and leader of the congregation, to follow the example of Paul and to continue the tradition of Pauline teaching. Timothy is reminded of the "sacred writings" with which he has been acquainted from his youth. These are clearly the Jewish Scriptures (although a definitive Jewish canon had not yet been established when 2 Tim was written; → Canonicity, 66:35). Such sacred writings "are able to instruct you for salvation through faith in Christ Jesus" (2 Tim 3:15). Their purpose is salvific, but the key to their salvific purpose is Christ Jesus.

10 Apart from this reference to Christ, the author's attitude toward the sacred writings has been formed within the Jewish tradition. The two major Hellenistic Jewish authors whose writings have been preserved speak of the Jewish Scriptures as "sacred writings" (Philo, *De vita Mosis* 2.292; Josephus, *Ant.* 10.10.4 § 210). Jewish males were trained in the Scriptures from as early as five years of age, according to the Mishna (*'Abot* 5:21). Although the reference to faith in Christ Jesus (2 Tim 3:15) clearly manifests a Christian perspective, the "actualizing" exegesis implied by 2 Tim is consistent with the scriptural interpretation found in the Qumran pesher and the rabbinic midrash (→ Hermeneutics, 71:31–34).

11 Verses 16–17 provide an explanatory reflection on v 15, i.e., on the utility of the sacred writings for instructional purposes. The author mentions the reason why the sacred writings are valuable (v 16a) and then specifies the use to which they can be put (vv 16b–17). The Gk text is not altogether clear, as the variety of translations shows. There are three major ambiguities: (1) the meaning of *pasa graphē* ("all scripture"), (2) the meaning of *theopneustos* ("inspired"), and (3) the grammatical function of *theopneustos*.

12 The ambiguity of *pasa graphē* is easily grasped from translations ranging from "the whole Bible" (*Living Bible*) to "every inspired scripture" (*NEB*) and a literally accurate "all Scripture." Of itself, *graphē* can mean a single written verse, an entire book, or the entire collection of the Scriptures. *Pasa* can be taken in an inclusive ("the whole") or in a distributive ("every") sense. Since the NT does not use "Scripture" for a single book, that possibility is to be excluded. Since a collection of Christian Scriptures was not yet in existence at the time when 2 Tim was written (→ Canonicity, 66:55), the expression "all Scripture" makes reference to (only) the Jewish Scriptures, as evidenced also by the parallel expression "sacred writings" in v 15. Finally, since *pasa graphē* lacks the definite article, it most likely means every passage of Scripture.

13 *Theopneustos* (a rare word) is typically rendered as "inspired by God," but we also find the simple "inspired" (*NEB*) and the somewhat cumbersome "God-breathed" (*NIV*). Composed of *theo*, from *theos*, "God," and *pneustos*, from *pneō*, "to breathe," it is found once in the NT, never in the LXX, and only four other times in extant Gk writings. Understood in an act. sense, it would suggest that Scripture is filled with God's breath or spirit (= inspiring). Understood in a pass. sense, *theopneustos* suggests that Scripture has been breathed by God (= inspired). The vast majority of ancient and modern commentators and translations understand this adj. passively, so that *pasa graphē theopneustos* means the Scripture which is inspired.

14 There remains the problem of the grammatical function of *theopneustos*. Is it used as a predicate (*RSV*: "all Scripture is inspired") or as an attribute (some ancient versions and *NEB*: "every inspired Scripture")? The grammatical problem is that the Gk verse lacks a principal vb., so that a copulative vb. ("is") must be supplied within the sentence. The weight of the exegetical considerations would seem to favor understanding "inspired" as a predicate. Thus 2 Tim would be affirming that every passage in the Jewish Scriptures is inspired; in consequence whereof, these Scriptures are useful for teaching, reproof, correction, and training in righteousness. Because the Scriptures have come from God, they can be profitably used for purposes both of instruction and of moral exhortation.

15 Since all other known uses of *theopneustos*, "inspired," appear in literature written after 2 Tim (Plutarch, Vettius Valens, Pseudo-Phocylides, and *Sib. Or.*), some think that "inspired" is a word coined by the author of 2 Tim in order to highlight the divine origin of the Scriptures (see C. Spicq, "*theodidaktoi, theopneustos*," *Notes de lexicographie néotestamentaire* [Göttingen, 1978] 1. 372–74). Nonetheless, the dominant opinion of scholars is that "inspired" is a loanword from ancient Hellenistic descriptions of the ecstatic experience of mantic prophets.

16 Although *theopneustos* is not used by Philo, his description of Moses as "a prophet of the highest quality" (*De vita Mosis* 2.187–91) is somewhat similar to the experience encapsulated in *theopneustos* by *Sib. Or.* and other Hellenistic texts. For Philo it was Moses' role as prophet to "declare by inspiration [*thespizē*] what cannot be apprehended by reason." Philo distinguishes three kinds of divine utterances: (1) The prophet serves as the interpreter of the divine utterance. (2) The utterance takes place in a dialogue between the prophet and God. (3) "The speaker appears under that divine possession [*enthousiōdes*] in virtue of which he is chiefly and in the strict sense considered a prophet."

Philo regards other prophets besides Moses as inspired (*Quis rerum* 265; *De vita Mosis* 1.281; *De mutatione nominum* 120). In this regard, he reflects views generally held in 1st-cent. Judaism. Josephus wrote about Balaam: "Thus did he speak by divine inspiration, as not being in his own power [*epetheiazen ouk ōn en heautō tō de theiō pneumati*], but moved to say what he did by the divine spirit" (*Ant.* 4.6.5 § 118). Earlier, the rule of the Essene Qumran community had urged the sectarians to act "according as the prophets revealed by the spirit of his holiness" (1QS 8:16; see 1QpHab 2:2; CD 2:12–13).

As for the early Christians, a traditional logion attributes to Jesus the view that David was inspired by the Holy Spirit (Matt 22:43; Mark 12:36). The Holy Spirit is said to have spoken through David (Acts 1:16) or a prophet (Acts 28:25). God spoke through the prophets (Luke 1:70) or through Moses (Mark 12:26; cf. Matt 22:31; Luke 20:37). These texts indicate that the early Christians shared the view common among the Jews of their times that the prophets, of whom Moses was a singular example, were inspired by the Holy Spirit.

17 **(B) 2 Pet 1:19–21.** "We have the prophetic word made more sure. . . . First of all you must understand this, that no prophecy of scripture is a matter of one's own interpretation, because no prophecy ever came by the impulse of man, but men moved by the Holy Spirit spoke from God" (*RSV*). (For the pseudonymity of 2 Pet, → 2 Peter, 64:2).

The immediate context (1:12–21) guarantees Christian hope. Having reflected on the transfiguration (vv 12–18), the author cites "the prophetic word" (*ton prophētikon logon*, i.e., the entire Law, Prophets, and Writings — the three divisions of the Hebrew Scriptures; → Canonicity, 66:22) as a firm foundation for hope insofar as God has confirmed its truth, and its message was in the process of being realized. The author's thoughts on false prophets (2:1–3) are introduced by the caveat of 1:20–21: it is not permitted to interpret the prophetic dicta contained in the Scripture (*pasa prophēteia graphēs*) according to one's subjective whim. The reason is that prophecy comes from the Holy Spirit.

18 **(II) Judaism.** The inspiration of prophets is one thing; the inspiration of the Scriptures (i.e., written works) another. That the writings which contain the words of the prophets were inspired is never explicitly said in the Jewish Scriptures, even though they constantly affirm that the Holy Spirit was deeply involved in the activity and proclamation of the prophets (2 Sam 23:2; Hos 1:1; Joel 3:1-2, etc.).

19   Philo echoed the traditional belief of Judaism: "A prophet has no utterance of his own, but all his utterance came from elsewhere, the echoes of another's voice. The wicked may never be the interpreter of God, so that no worthless person is 'God-inspired' [*enthousia*] in the proper sense" (*Quis rerum* 259; cf. *De praemiis* 55). Like the author of 2 Pet, Philo distinguishes the true and inspired prophet from the false prophet. He ascribes the gift of prophecy to Moses, Noah, Isaac, and Jacob, but above all to Moses, who is "everywhere celebrated as a prophet" (*Quis rerum* 262).

20   In Philo's opinion, the words of Moses and the patriarchs were inspired, and all things in the sacred books (*hosa en tais hierais bibliois*) are oracles delivered through Moses. Accordingly, the Torah or law traditionally ascribed to Moses contains inspired prophecy. The Babylonian Talmud goes further in speaking of the Torah as "divinely revealed." Indeed, the rabbis taught that the legislation of Num 15:31, "Because he has despised the word of the Lord, and has broken his commandment, that person shall be utterly cut off," applies to the one "who maintains that the Torah is not from heaven" (*b. Sanh.* 99a).

21   Clearly the doctrine of prophetic inspiration lies at the root of the Jewish doctrine of the inspiration of the Scriptures. The entire *Tĕnāk* (i.e., the Torah, the Prophets, and the Writings; → Canonicity, 66:22) was considered inspired since all three units were derived from prophetic utterance. That both the Torah, which has come from Moses, the prophet par excellence (cf. Deut 15:18), and the prophetic books result from prophetic utterance almost goes without saying. Occasional passages suggest that even the utterance of sages should be interpreted along the lines of inspired prophetic utterance (Isa 11:2; Exod 15:20-21; 2 Chr 15:1-5).

22   It is on the basis of this Jewish tradition that the author of 2 Pet affirms that *ton prophētikon logon* is made more sure—"the prophetic word" of Hellenistic Jewish usage, where it indicates the entire *Tĕnāk*. These Scriptures stand fast because they have begun to be realized in Jesus Christ. Thus early Christianity shared with Jewish tradition the notion that the (Jewish) Scriptures were inspired, as attested by the virtual interchangeability of "it is written" (Acts 13:33) and "he [= God] says" (13:34,35).

23   **(III) Fathers of the Church.** The witness of the NT was such that the early Fathers took the inspiration of the Scriptures as almost self-evident, echoing traditional language in their descriptions. During the 2d and 3d cents., however, "the Scriptures" (*hai graphai*) came to be used also of the authoritative Christian writings that would eventually be incorporated into the canon. This extension of the term used for Jewish writings indicated a divine source. In the school of Alexandria, Clement (*ca.* 150-215) wrote about the "sacred writings" (*hiera grammata*) and the "holy books" (*hagiai biblioi*), affirming that the Scriptures were the work of "divine authors" (*theiōn graphōn*). Clement's pupil, Origen (*ca.* 185-254), wrote about the "sacred books" (*hierai biblioi*) derived "from inspiration" (*ex epipnoias*). Contemporaneously, in Antioch, Theophilus was writing about the "holy Scriptures" (*hai hagiai graphai*) and citing their authors as "bearers of the spirit" (*pneumatophoroi*).

24   Such patristic views underscored the authority of the Jewish and Christian Scriptures. Clement of Alexandria, e.g., wrote of the possibility of citing innumerable texts of the Scriptures of which "not a dot would pass away" (Matt 5:18), because they have been spoken by the mouth of the Lord, the Holy Spirit, "who uttered them" (Isa 1:20; *Protrepticus* 9.82.1). While acknowledging that the Scriptures do not provide answers to all our questions, Irenaeus of Lyons (*ca.* 130-200) noted that the Scriptures are perfect because they have been given by the word of 'God and the Spirit (*Adv. Haer.* 2.28.2). Among the Cappadocian Fathers, Gregory of Nazianzus (329-389) wanted attention paid to even the shortest scriptural texts since they are attributable to the exact care of the Spirit (*Oratio* 2.105; PG 35. 504).

25   **(A) Explanations of Inspiration.** Quite another matter was the way in which the Fathers understood inspiration. Some earlier Fathers considered it the result of an ecstatic phenomenon. Theophilus compared the prophets with the sibyls, for they "were possessed by a holy Spirit [*pneumatophoroi pneumatos hagiou*] and became prophets [*kai prophētai genomenoi*] and were inspired and instructed by God himself [*hyp' autou tou theou empneusthentes kai sophisthentes*]" (*Ad Autolycum* 2.9; PG 6. 1064). Justin Martyr (*ca.* 100-165) wrote: "When you listen to the prophecies, spoken as in the person [of someone], do not think that they were spoken by the inspired prophets of their own accord, but by the Word of God who prompts them" (*Apol.* 1.36). Justin, in fact, rarely cites the name of an individual prophet (but see *Dial.* 118, naming Nathan, Ezekiel, and Isaiah). The prediction of future events was a gift to prophets (*Apol.* 1.31; *Dial.* 7), and inspiration was almost a matter of divine dictation. Somewhat similar views were held by Athenagoras, the 2d-cent. Christian apologist. Capitalizing on the Gk root *pneu-* (*pnein,* "to blow"; *pneuma,* "spirit") and anticipating the scholastic doctrine of instrumental causality in the discussion on inspiration, he wrote about the teachings "of Moses or of Isaiah and Jeremiah and the rest of the prophets who in the ecstasy of their thoughts, as the divine Spirit moved them, uttered what they had been inspired to say, the Spirit making use of them as a flautist might blow into a flute" (*Legatio* 9; PG 6. 905-8).

26   **(B) Origen.** In the East, Origen, one of the first Christian writers to take up the notion of inspiration at length, demonstrated a bias against the view that an ecstatic experience was at the origin of prophecy and of scriptural inspiration. His major work, *On First Principles* (*Peri Archon; De principiis*), contained a chapter entitled "Inspiration of Divine Scripture." He wrote of the testimonies "drawn from the Scriptures, which we believe to be divine, both from what is called the Old Testament and also from the New" (4.1; PG 11. 341). Referring to "divine writings" and the "divine character" of the Scriptures, Origen thought it impossible to accept many scriptural statements "as spoken by a man" (4.22; PG 11. 391). "One who approaches the prophetic words with care and attention . . . will be convinced by his own feelings that the words which are believed by us to be from God are not the compositions of men" (4.6; PG 11. 353). The Holy Spirit "illuminated" (*tō phōtizonti pneumati*) the inspired writer (4.14; PG 11. 372) with an action directed to the human mind, will, and memory (*Contra Celsum* 7.3-4; PG 11. 1424-25). Nevertheless, for Origen the biblical prophets "voluntarily and consciously collaborated with the word that came to them" (*Hom. in Ezech.,* frag. 6.11; PG 13. 709), and the evangelists were able to express their own opinions. Indeed, he distinguished between the word of revelation and the commentary on that word which comes from the human author of the Scriptures. This distinction led Origen to admit the possibility of error on the part of an OT prophet or a NT author.

Origen's greatest contribution probably lay in the emphasis that he placed on the inspiration of the text itself as distinct from the previous stress on the inspiration of the prophets. This shift to emphasizing that the text itself was the word of God was due, at least in part, to Origen's struggle with the remnants of Montanism, which overemphasized Spirit-led prophets. Origen also admitted various levels or degrees of inspiration, a position later held by the Antiochene theologian Theodore of Mopsuestia (ca. 350–428), but not generally espoused by the Eastern Fathers.

27   (C) Augustine. Among the Western Fathers, Augustine (354–430) dealt extensively with the significance of the Scriptures, esp. in *The Harmony of the Gospels* and *On Christian Doctrine.* He stressed that meaning of the Scriptures which the author intended: "Our aim should be nothing else than to ascertain what is the mind and intention of the person who speaks" (*Harmony* 2.12; PL 34. 1092; cf. *Christ. Doct.* 1.36; PL 34. 34). By and large, Augustine held that the Scriptures were dictated to human authors by the Holy Spirit: "the author (through whom the Holy Spirit brought Holy Scripture into being)," and the Spirit of God "who produced these words through him" (*Christ. Doct.* 3.27; PL 34. 80). He accorded a large role to the human authors, who "use all those forms of expression which grammarians call by the Greek name *tropes*" (figures of speech; *Christ. Doct.* 3.29; PL 34. 80). The evangelist may introduce a topic without expanding upon it at length or make some additions of his own "not indeed in the subject-matter itself, but in the words by which it is expressed." "He may not be entirely successful . . . in calling to mind and reciting anew with the most literal accuracy the very words which he heard on the occasion" (*Harmony* 2.12; PL 34. 1091).

28   (D) Important Formulas. While the Fathers of both East and West generally affirmed the inspiration of the Scriptures and yet tried to deal realistically with the problems of interpretation, three expressive formulas emerged from their writings that would dominate much later discussion, viz., condescension, dictation, and "God the author of the Scriptures."

(a) CONDESCENSION. Having a forerunner in Origen's "accommodation" (*symperihora*), the notion of "condescension" (*synkatabasis*), stemming from John Chrysostom (ca. 347–407), had the most enduring value in the discussion of inspiration (Vawter, *Biblical* 40). It continues to be cited in ecclesiastical documents, e.g., *DAS* (*EB* 559; *RSS* p. 98) and Vatican II's *Dei Verbum* (3:13). The latter cites Chrysostom on Gen 3:8 (*Homily* 17.1; PG 53. 134) proclaiming the condescension of divine wisdom "that we may learn the gentle kindness of God, which words cannot express, and how far He has gone in adapting His language with thoughtful concern for our weak human nature." It sees this as analogous to the incarnation of the Word of God, an analogy frequently used in explaining inspiration and intimated by Chrysostom himself (*Homily* 15.3 on John 1:18; PG 59. 100). Chrysostom often used divine "condescension" to talk about the Scriptures being written by human authors, who occasionally expressed their thoughts in metaphor and hyperbole or in such a way as to gain a favorable reception from their readers (*captatio benevolentiae*). See R. C. Hill, *Compass Theology Review* 14 (1980) 34–38.

29   (b) DICTATION. That the Scriptures were "dictated" (Lat vb. *dictare*) is found in such Western Fathers as Augustine (e.g., *En. in Ps.* 62.1; PL 36. 748) and Jerome (Paul's Rom was dictated by the Holy Spirit; *Epist.* 120.10; PL 22. 997). Even in the 16th-cent. Reformation disputes, dictation of the Scriptures by the Holy Spirit served to describe inspiration for both sides. For Catholics, in 1546 Trent clearly "perceived that this truth and rule are contained in the written books and unwritten traditions which have come down to us, having been received by the apostles from the mouth of Christ himself, or from the apostles by the dictation of the Holy Spirit [*Spiritu Sancto dictante*], and have been transmitted as it were from hand to hand" (DS 1501)—a passage cited verbatim in 1870 by Vatican I (*Dei Filius;* DS 3006).

30   In the same vein, "the Reformers took over unquestionably and unreservedly the statement on the inspiration, and indeed the verbal inspiration, of the Bible, as it is explicitly and implicitly contained in those Pauline passages which we have taken as our basis, even including the formula that God is the author of the Bible, and occasionally *making use of the idea of dictation* through the Biblical writers" (emphasis added; K. Barth, *Church Dogmatics* 1.2.520). With regard to how far the Bible is the word of God, Barth finds in the Reformers "that God or the Holy Ghost is its *autor primarius;* that its content is 'given' to the prophets and apostles . . . ; that it is *mandata, inspirata, dictata,* etc., by divine 'impulse.' . . . [that] in the composition of their writings the prophets and apostles acted as *amanuenses* . . . or as *librarii* . . . or as *actuarii*" (1.2.523).

John Calvin (1509–1564) frequently used "dictation" to describe the divine authorship of the Scriptures and "scribes" to describe the role of the human authors. Whatever Daniel "uttered was dictated by the Holy Spirit" and the NT authors were "certain and authentic amanuenses of the Holy Spirit" (*Institutes* 4.8.9). Isaiah and Moses were "instruments of the Spirit of God" who offered nothing on their own" (*24th Sermon on 2 Tim; Corpus Reformatorum* 54. 285–86). Nonetheless, when Calvin spoke of the Scriptures as having been "dictated" and of "scribes," for him dictation was not mere stenography. He admits, e.g., that the scriptural authors were affected by the obscurity of the times (*Institutes* 2.11.6) and that even Paul did not cite the Scriptures without error.

31   (c) "GOD THE AUTHOR." Used by a Reformer like Calvin, this terminology is well attested in Catholic church statements of faith and doctrine, e.g., in the 13th cent. to the Waldensians (DS 790) and to the emperor Michael Palaeologus (DS 854), in Trent, Vatican I and II (DS 1501, 3006; *Dei Verbum* 3:11). The first official church usage was in a profession of faith for future bishops in the so-called Ancient Statutes of the Church (AD 450–500): "There is one and the same author and God of the New and Old Testament, that is, of the Law and Prophets and Apostles" (DS 325). The formula seemingly derived from 5th-cent. African controversies with the Manicheans, polemically countering dualism. Thus Augustine wrote of "venerating God as the author of both Testaments" (*Contra Adimantum* 16.3; PL 42. 157). Similarly, Ambrose, showing the correlation between OT and NT, wrote about the one author of knowledge (*Exp. in Ps.* 118 8; PL 15. 1320). These polemical origins are recalled in the 15th-cent. *Decree for the Jacobites,* which explicitly links God as author with inspiration. The Roman church "professes one and the same God as the author of the Old and New Testament . . . since the saints of both Testaments have spoken with the inspiration of the same Holy Spirit. . . . It anathematizes the madness of the Manicheans, who have established two first principles, one of the visible and another of the invisible; and they have said there is one God of the New Testament, another of the Old Testament" (DS 1334).

The "author" formula indicates that God is the ultimate source of both Testaments but does not necessarily ascribe *literary* authorship to him. Lat *auctor* has a much broader range of meaning than Eng "author," describing one who produces something, whether a building, a bridge, or a literary work. In the ecclesiastical tradition about God's authorship of Scripture, *auctor* has the more generic meaning of producer or source, e.g., in the profession of faith for Michael Palaeologos, Lat *auctor* is rendered by Gk *archēgos,* "beginning, founder, originator." (→ Canonicity, 66:89.)

THE PROPHETIC MODEL OF INSPIRATION

32   From the time of NT writing till the Reformation and Trent, a prophetic model of inspiration was dominant, and the inspiration of the Scriptures was considered analogous to (and dependent on) the inspiration of the prophets. This approach is found in the Jewish philosopher Maimonides (1135-1204), in Aquinas (1225-1274), as well as in the 16th-cent. Reformers. W. Whitaker (1548-1595), a Calvinist divine at Cambridge, wrote: "We confess that God has not spoken of himself, but by others. Yet this does not diminish the authority of Scripture. For God inspired the prophets with what they said, and made use of their mouths, tongues, and hands: the Scripture, therefore, is even immediately the voice of God. The prophets and apostles were only the organs of God."

33   **(I) Causal Instrumentality.** Aquinas considered inspiration to be "something imperfect within the genus of prophecy." The scholastics used the categories of Aristotelian philosophy in attempting to understand inspiration, esp. the category of causality and its four types: efficient, material, formal, and final causality. Within the category of efficient causality, one may distinguish between a principal efficient cause (God or the Spirit) and an instrumental efficient cause (human author). In scriptural composition a distinct but conjoined role is attributable to God and to the human writers, just as in sawing lumber a distinct but conjoined role is assignable to the carpenter (principal efficient cause) and the saw (instrumental efficient cause).

34   Although most scholastics before him considered prophecy a *habitus,* i.e., an almost permanent gift conferring a new nature on the prophet, Aquinas held that prophecy is a *motio,* a gift given by God to a prophet on a temporary basis for a specific function. This gift pertains to the human cognitive factors, not placing the prophet in immediate contact with the reality of God (the *speculum aeternitatis*) but providing divine enlightenment through "likenesses" (*Summa* II 2 q.173,1). Prophecy is not bound to a specific manner of acquiring knowledge; rather, it is a matter of judging that some knowledge is the word of God. It is a *gratia gratis data,* i.e., a gift given to the prophet not for the sake of his personal sanctification but for the sake of the community.

35   The prophetic theory of inspiration, with the frequently concomitant notion of dictation, continued to influence Christians throughout the Middle Ages, the Reformation, and Counter-Reformation and is held by many contemporary Christians, esp. the more conservative. It admits of some variation, according to the way in which the relationship between the prophet and God is understood. Alonso Schökel (*Inspired Word* 58-73) distinguishes three possibilities: the speaker is (1) the instrument through whom God speaks, (2) a person to whom God dictates, or (3) a messenger of God who plays a part in phrasing the message. The second possibility has been the most dominant and has given rise to what is known as plenary (verbal) inspiration.

36   **(II) Plenary Verbal Inspiration.** Melchior Cano, the 16th-cent. Dominican systematic theologian, explained: "Everything great or small has been edited by the sacred authors at the dictation of the Holy Spirit [*Spiritu Sancto dictante esse edita*]" (*De locis theologicis* 2.17). Not far removed is the Reformed *Formula Consensus Helvetica* (1675), which held that not only the words but also the very letters of the Scriptures were inspired. The theory of plenary verbal inspiration has significant consequences in the practical order. (1) Every Scripture is the word of God. (2) Since God is not false, every word in Scripture must be true. (3) The truth of the Bible is ultimately propositional. (4) The unity of the Bible bars any real contradictions among the biblical texts. (5) At least for some conservative Protestants, the Bible does not simply contain or bear witness to revelation; rather, the Bible itself is revelation.

37   *Critique:* A serious reading of OT and NT raises cogent objections against a naïve or simplistic theory of plenary verbal inspiration: (1) The theory makes the dubious assumption that the message which the prophets received from God came in the form of a verbal message. Was this usually or ever the case? Certainly the prophets sometimes conveyed the divine message by means of a nonverbal prophetic gesture rather than by means of a verbal oracle. (2) Are not the *events* of salvation history revelatory? Are not the exodus-event and the Jesus-event primary forms of God's communication with his people? (3) The biblical texts themselves clearly suggest that normal human writing processes were at work in the production of the Scriptures. Ezra cited Persian archives (Ezra 7:11-26). There are self-corrections (1 Cor 1:16; John 4:2). Luke surveyed the accounts written about Jesus and took information from eyewitnesses and ministers of the word (Luke 1:1-2). Such objections have led most contemporary critical scholars to abandon the theory of plenary verbal inspiration.

THE TRACT ON INSPIRATION

38   **(I) Within Roman Catholicism.** The patristic era popularized certain formulas for articulating scriptural inspiration (→ 28-31 above); the scholastic era developed prophetic models of inspiration through philosophical notions of causal instrumentality (→ 33-34 above); the Reformers and Counter-Reformers shared much of this heritage, and their successors independently worked out its implications in terms of plenary inspiration of every detail in Scripture (→ 35-36 above). Finally, in 19th-cent. Roman Catholic theology a systematic tract on biblical inspiration made its appearance under the impetus of issues raised by textual criticism and by the historical-critical method, which was a by-product of advances in the historical and physical sciences.

39   (A) Impact of Textual Criticism. The 18th and 19th cents. saw a great increase in the number of texts and versions of the Bible available for study, as well as a maturing skill in comparing the authority of divergent readings. This proved fatal to the simplistic understanding of (plenary) verbal inspiration. In the absence of the autograph of any biblical work, and with the existence of thousands of textual differences, which is the inspired text? Abandoned by most was the idea that the LXX was inspired—an idea commonly held in early Christianity and occasionally thereafter (to this day in some Eastern churches). The mistranslations and other variants in the LXX compared to the MT make it impossible to affirm that either always represents precisely the inspired OT text. Fortunately, the hypothesis of the inspiration of the Vg did not enjoy much popularity, although it was espoused by a few Catholic theologians after Trent. The *textus receptus* of the Gk NT also ceased to be regarded as the surest guide to the original, inspired text (→ Texts, 68:160–61, 168).

40   (B) Impact of Historical Criticism. The advent of higher criticism (→ OT Criticism, 69:6; NT Criticism, 70:5) made scholars aware that not only the Pentateuch but also the Synoptic Gospels were composed by drawing on previous documents or sources, and not simply by dictation. The impact has been varied: a hardening of the position on verbal inspiration within Protestant orthodoxy; practical abandon of the theory of inspiration by liberal Protestants; and the modification of traditional formulations of inspiration by many Roman Catholics. The historical-critical method of scriptural exposition was the child of the Enlightenment, where methodical skepticism was generally characteristic of the scientific revolution. The 17th-cent. "Galileo affair" was an early landmark in the confrontation between scientific truth and the apparent "truth" of the Scriptures, which implied that the sun moved around the earth. Increased data about the origins of the earth and of the human race led to incompatibility between scientific knowledge and a naïve, literal reading of the creation narratives (Gen 1:2–2:25).

41 In defense of tradition, Roman Catholic ecclesiastical authority responded in somewhat negative fashion. Even the mildly progressive *Providentissimus Deus* (1893) of Leo XIII reacted strongly to the difficulties posed by advances in the natural and historical sciences:

> We have to contend against those who, making an evil use of physical science, minutely scrutinize the sacred books in order to detect the writers in a mistake, and to take occasion to vilify its contents. . . . To the professor of sacred Scripture a knowledge of natural science will be of very great assistance in detecting such attacks on the sacred books, and in refuting them. There can never, indeed, be any real discrepancy between the theologian and the physicist, as long as each confines himself within his own lines, and both are careful, as St. Augustine warns us 'not to make rash assertions. . . .' The Catholic interpreter . . . should show that these facts of natural science which investigators affirm to be now quite certain are not contrary to the Scripture rightly explained. . . . The principles laid down will apply to cognate sciences, and especially to history. . . . It follows that those who maintain that an error is possible in any genuine passage of the sacred writings either pervert the Catholic notion of inspiration or make God the author of such error. . . . Let them loyally hold that God, the Creator and Ruler of all things, is also the Author of the Scriptures—and that, therefore, nothing can be proved either by physical science or archaeology which can really contradict the Scriptures. (→ Church Pronouncements, 72:17.)

42   (II) Plenary and Limited Inspiration. Prior to his remarks on the perverse use of scientific dis-

coveries to attack the credibility of the Scriptures, Leo XIII cited the problems caused by some proponents of "higher criticism." He also affirmed the inspiration of the totality of the Scriptures. "It is absolutely wrong and forbidden to narrow inspiration to certain parts only of Holy Scripture or to admit that the sacred writer has erred." This affirmation of plenary scriptural inspiration was to counteract certain Catholic attempts to maintain both a doctrine of biblical inspiration (because it was traditional) and the principle of scientific knowledge (because it was rational to do so) by limiting biblical inspiration in some way or other.

43   (A) Lessius. Roman Catholic reactions against simplistically viewing scriptural inspiration as stenographic dictation had taken place earlier. The theological faculty of Louvain had censured liberalizing propositions of the Jesuit L. Lessius (1554–1623), e.g.: (1) For something to be Holy Scripture, its individual words need not be inspired by the Holy Spirit. (2) The individual truths and statements need not be immediately inspired in the writer by the Holy Spirit. (3) If a book (e.g., 2 Macc) were to be written through purely human endeavor without the assistance of the Holy Spirit, who would later certify that there was nothing false therein, the book would become Holy Scripture. Lessius wrote to the archbishop of Malines pertinent to (2):

> It is enough that the sacred writer be divinely drawn to write down what he sees, hears, or knows otherwise, that he enjoy the infallible assistance of the Holy Spirit to prevent him from mistakes even in matters he knows on the word of others, or from his own experience, or by his own natural reasoning. It is this assistance that gives Scripture its infallible truth.

In the 19th cent. *this negative assistance* theory of inspiration would reappear: the Holy Spirit acts upon a human author in such a way as to preserve him from error. Close to (3) were some 19th-cent. authors with their *subsequent approval* theory of inspiration. The point of (1) is similar to the theory of *content inspiration* (as distinct from verbal inspiration), which also appeared in 19th-cent. expositions on inspiration.

44   (B) Jahn and Haneberg. J. Jahn, an Austrian Premonstratensian, published 2 vols. (1802, 1804) in which he held that inspiration was simply "the divine assistance for avoiding errors"—the negative assistance theory. In the mid-1800s the Benedictine bishop of Speyer, D. B. Haneberg, proposed that, whereas sometimes inspiration was antecedent to the composition of the scriptural works, and sometimes inspiration consisted of a concomitant influence upon a human author preserving him from error, it sometimes happened that inspiration took the form of the church's approval of the work at the time of its canonization—the subsequent approval theory.

45   (C) Vatican I; Pope Leo XIII. Each of these approaches was expressly disapproved by Vatican I: "These [OT and NT books] the church holds to be sacred and canonical, not because, having been carefully composed by mere human industry, they were afterwards approved by her authority, nor merely because they contain revelation without errors, but because, having been written by the inspiration of the Holy Spirit, they have God for their author and have been delivered as such to the church herself" (DS 3006). The conciliar teaching led Haneberg to revise radically the 4th ed. (1876) of his *Versuch einer Geschichte der biblischen Offenbarung.* This teaching was taken over verbatim by *Providentissimus Deus* (*EB* 125; *RSS* p. 24). Leo XIII also took issue with "those who, in order to rid themselves of these difficulties, do not hesitate to concede that divine inspiration regards the things of faith and morals and nothing beyond" (*EB* 124; *RSS* p. 24). Two books espousing such a view appeared in the interim between Vatican I (1870) and Leo's encyclical (1893). In 1872 A. Rohling published *Natur und Offenbarung,* restricting inspiration to matters of faith and morals. In 1880 F. Lenormant published *Les origines de l'histoire d'après la Bible,* limiting inspiration to supernatural teachings.

46   (D) Newman. The writings of J. H. Newman (1801–1890) have been thought to limit inspiration according to content because of his repeated references to the "passing remarks" (*obiter dicta*) found in the Scriptures. In his Anglican period Newman had written:

> In what way inspiration is compatible with that personal agency on the part of its instruments, which the composition of the Bible evidences, we know not; but if anything is certain, it is this—that, though the Bible is inspired, and therefore, in one sense, written by God, yet very large portions of it, if not by far the greater part of it, are written in as free and unconstrained a manner, and (apparently) with as little consciousness of a supernatural dictation or restraint, on the part of His earthly instruments, as if he had no share in the work. (*Tract 85; Lectures on the Scripture Proofs of the Doctrine of the Church* 30)

As late as 1884, almost 40 years after he became a Roman Catholic and five years after he was named a cardinal, Newman averred that the Word was morally separable from the words of the human authors, because the Word consists of those portions of the Bible that treat of faith and morals.

In 1861 Newman observed: "The plenary inspiration of Scripture is peculiarly a Protestant question; not a Catholic" (C. S. Dessain, ed., *The Letters and Diaries of John Henry Newman* [London, 1969] 19. 488). Yet scriptural inspiration continued to fascinate Newman the Catholic. While holding to the inspiration of the written word (the *Verbum Scriptum*), Newman wrote:

> The formula of inspiration runs thus: the Bible is the Word of God *such,* by virtue of its being throughout written, or dictated, or impregnated, or directed by the Spirit of Truth, or at least in parts written, in parts dictated, in parts impregnated, in parts directed, and throughout preserved from formal error, at least substantial, by the Spirit of Truth. (J. Holmes, ed., *The Theological Papers of John Henry Newman on Biblical Inspiration and on Infallibility* [Oxford, 1979] 81)

He noted that inspiration was "a gift attached to the *Verbum Scriptum*" (ibid., 70) and that "a great variety of teaching is both conceivable, and admissible on the subject of the divine inspiration of Holy Scripture" (68), and again that "inspiration proper . . . admits degrees" (74).

47   (E) Franzelin. Some have thought that Newman's ideas on inspiration were rejected by *Providentissimus Deus;* yet they were close to the ecclesiastically approved ideas of J. B. Franzelin (1816–1886), a peritus of Vatican I. In *De Divina Traditione et Scriptura* (1870) Franzelin expounded his key idea of God as author through a theory of instrumental causality that distinguished between scriptural *content* and truth (the *res et sententia,* or formal content) and scriptural *formulation* (the *res,* or words of Scripture).

> Biblical inspiration seems to consist essentially in a freely bestowed charism of enlightenment and stimulus, whereby the mind of the inspired men would propose to write down those truths which God wished to communicate to his Church through Scripture, and their will would be drawn to commit all these truths, and these alone, to writing; and the men thus raised to be instrumental causes at the disposition of God, the principal cause, would carry through this

divine proposal with infallible truthfulness. We thus distinguish between inspiration, which extends to the truths and "formal word," and assistance, which must extend further, even to the expressions and "material words."

48   (F) Lagrange. Although Franzelin's views enjoyed the implicit endorsement of Vatican I and *Providentissimus Deus,* their importance in Catholic scholarship diminished in the 1890s, alongside the rising popularity of the views of M.-J. Lagrange (1855–1938). Lagrange believed that Franzelin's exposition of scriptural inspiration suffered from both a methodological and a historical deficiency. Methodologically, it separated the Bible into two parts, one divine and one human, creating the almost inextricable difficulty of distinguishing between the core content and the relatively unimportant details of its expression. Historically, studies of the Florentine, Tridentine, and Vatican councils led Lagrange to endorse the logical and theological priority of inspiration over against the notion of divine authorship. Lagrange's own theory of verbal inspiration was heavily dependent upon the Thomistic model of prophetic inspiration. As an "intellectual enlightenment" (*illuminatio iudicii*), inspiration was a divine gift enabling the biblical author to choose certain ideas (no matter their immediate source), to understand and judge them, and form them into a literary unit. Thus the Scriptures were totally the work of God and totally the work of the human author. God was the principal efficient cause; the human author the instrumental efficient cause.

49   Official Roman Catholic reaction to Modernism in the early 1900s (→ Church Pronouncements, 72:5) cast a shadow over Lagrange's theory of inspiration. The modernists had compared biblical inspiration to the "inspiration" of gifted poets and orators, and some found a suspicious resemblance in that to Lagrange's emphasis on the human element in biblical composition. Nonetheless, his fundamental ideas would be resurrected and clarified in the work of P. Benoit (→ 59 below) of the Dominican Biblical School at Jerusalem, which Lagrange had founded. It remains to Lagrange's credit to have emphasized that an understanding of inspiration must begin with *the written text itself.* Notions of divine authorship, scriptural authority, inerrancy, and canonicity are but corollaries of this primary datum of all inspiration study, which accordingly must proceed a posteriori rather than a priori.

50   (III) Inerrancy Theories. There are some, nevertheless, who continue to work with the doctrine of biblical inerrancy as the primary datum or focus.

(A) Among Catholics. The theological tract on inspiration was placed within the treatise on theological authorities (*De locis theologicis*), and so there was emphasis on the results rather than on the nature of inspiration. The inerrant "truth" of the Bible was deemed all-important insofar as the Bible is a principal and normative source for theological endeavor. This approach still dominated in the *preparatory* schema *De Revelatione* presented to Vatican II for deliberation, but quickly rejected. As has been seen (→ 4 above; Church Pronouncements, 72:14), Vatican II gave only a sentence to "the books of Scripture . . . teaching firmly, faithfully, and without error that truth which God wanted put into the sacred writings for the sake of our salvation," as a result of inspiration. Since then, inerrant scriptural "truth" has not received primary emphasis in Roman Catholic circles, a change resulting from a more adequate understanding of the nature of the Scriptures (not *primarily* a source for doctrine) as well as from conciliar directive (→ 70–71 below).

51   (B) Among Conservative Protestants. "Both evangelicals and fundamentalists insist on the 'inerrancy of Scripture' as being the most basic of all their fundamentals" (M. Marty, in *The Evangelicals* [ed. D. and J. Woodbridge; Nash, 1975] 180). The role of the human authors is completely overshadowed by the idea of divine power.

> Inerrancy follows from divine authority, period. For whatever God utters is without error. And the Bible is the Word of God. Therefore, the Bible is without error. But if this is so, then the inerrancy of the Bible cannot be lost by simply adding the human dimension. As long as it is God's Word, then it is thereby inerrant, whether or not it is also the words of men. (N. L. Geisler, "Inerrancy and Free Will," *EvQ* 57 [1985] 350-51)

"The scripture cannot be broken" (John 10:36) is cited as a scriptural warrant for the doctrine of inerrancy, since, if a single error is to be found in the Scriptures, the authority of the whole is undermined.

52   Enlightened fundamentalists, however, are not impervious to the discrepancies in biblical mss. (→ 39 above) or in parallel narratives of the OT and the Gospels as detected by historical criticism (→ 40 above). In a seminal article ("Inspiration," *Presbyterian Review* 2 [1881] 225-60) A. A. Hodge and B. B. Warfield formulated three criteria that must be met before some-thing can be considered an error such as to destroy the inerrancy-inspiration of the Scriptures. The error must (1) occur in the "original autograph" of the biblical text; (2) involve the true meaning and intention of the text, "definitely and certainly ascertained"; and (3) render that true meaning "directly and necessarily inconsistent" with some "certainly known" fact of history or science. But these criteria deprive biblical inerrancy of rational verification, for (1) pertains to a text that is no longer extant.

53   In 1978 the International Council on Biblical Inerrancy produced the Chicago Statement, affirming the total truth and trustworthiness of Scripture, which should always be interpreted as infallible and inerrant. God's "penmen" were not limited to the knowledge available at their time. Although inconsistencies, irregularities, and discrepancies must be dealt with, Scripture remains inerrant "in the sense of making its claims and achieving that measure of focused truth at which its authors aimed." A more popular conservative-fundamentalist position maintains that inerrancy is a quality of the biblical texts such as they exist in edited or translated forms (and not only of autographs). Various harmonizations and metaphorical readings can maintain verbal inerrancy.

CONTEMPORARY APPROACHES TO INSPIRATION

54   (I) Among Protestants.
(A) The Concursive Theory. B. B. Warfield (*The Inspiration and Authority of the Bible* [London, 1951]) and J. I. Packer (*Fundamentalism and the Word of God* [London, 1958]) are articulate spokesmen. Packer used "concursive action" to denote the role of the Spirit in the composition of the Bible. Just as the process of cause/effect and the doctrine of creation/providence are different ways of speaking about the existence of the physical universe, so inspiration and human composition are different ways of speaking about the existence of the Scriptures. They are theological and human understandings of the same material phenomenon; they do not exist on the same plane. Just as creation/providence is a theological statement that the cosmos derives its origin from God, so inspiration is a theological statement that the Scriptures derive their origin from God. The doctrine no more provides Christian believers with an explanation of *how* inspiration occurred than does the doctrine of creation/providence provide an explanation of how creation took place.

55   I. H. Marshall explains concursive action:

> On a human level we can describe its [the Bible's] composition in terms of the various oral and literary processes that lay behind it—the collection of information from witnesses, the use of written sources, the writing up and editing of such information, the composition of spontaneous letters, the committing to writing of prophetic messages, the collecting of the various documents together, and so on. At the same time, however, on the divine level we can assert that the Spirit, who moved on the face of the waters at Creation (Gen 1:2), was active in the whole process so that the Bible can be regarded as both the words of men and the Word of God. This activity of the Spirit can be described as "concursive" with the human activities through which the Bible was written. (*Biblical Inspiration* 42)

56   (B) Consequent Behavior. Conservative Protestant scholarship has produced most of the recent literature on inspiration; liberal Protestants often effectively deny inspiration by silence. A unique contribution has been made by W. J. Abraham (*Divine Inspiration*), an evangelical who takes his cue from a meaning of the English word "inspire" rather than from the Scriptures themselves or inerrancy. An excellent teacher can so inspire students that they are led to consequent behavior (including, perhaps, the writing of a text). Analogously, God, through his revelatory and saving activity, so inspired the biblical authors that they were led to consequent behavior, specifically the writing of biblical books.

57   (C) Neo-orthodoxy. The views on inspiration of K. Barth (1886-1968) have been followed by many mainline Protestant thinkers. Barth accords a unique place to the Bible insofar as it witnesses to God's act of revelation in Jesus Christ, who is primarily the Word of God. Inspiration is not a quality of the scriptural text itself, but an affirmation of a divine ability to use the Scripture to communicate revelation to human beings, either individually or in groups.

58   (II) Among Roman Catholics. A realism marks recent Catholic writing on inspiration. Integral to Vatican II's understanding of the biblical texts was an appreciation of their human quality and the processes by which they were produced. These texts, which are the "word of God," are human words. Various exegetical methodologies only serve to highlight the humanity of the Scriptures. With that humanity as a starting point, recent Catholic theories on inspiration focus on one of four aspects.

59   (A) Psychological Theories. The influential P. Benoit has distinguished scriptural inspiration (which lead the authors to produce texts) from dramatic-historical inspiration (which took place in the events of salvation history) and prophetic-apostolic inspiration (which took place in the oral proclamation of these events). Using Thomistic categories (some of which were abandoned in his later writings) and heir to the legacy of Lagrange (→ 48 above), Benoit makes the human psyche the locus of inspiration. Logically subsequent to revelation to which it is related, inspiration is an impulse to write and produce a book. It bears upon the author's judging what matters are to be included, how they are to be formulated and arranged. Throughout the entire process God is active as the originating cause of the scriptural work. (Benoit's emphasis is essentially on the individual biblical authors.)

60   (B) Social Theories. Form criticism (→ OT Criticism, 69:38; NT Criticism, 70:42) has demonstrated that, to a large extent, biblical books cannot simply be considered the literary production of isolated individuals, as modern books are. The individual writers were members of faith communities which had more than a passing influence on the formation of the biblical literature itself. That is the heart of the varied social theories of inspiration, which recapture an earlier view of the author as the functionary of a community, drawing on its traditions and writing to edify it. J. Barr, a critic of fundamentalism, states:

> If there is inspiration at all, then it must extend over the entire process of production that has led to the final text. Inspiration therefore must attach not to a small number of exceptional persons . . . it must extend over a larger number of anonymous persons . . . it must be considered to belong more to the community as a whole. (*Holy Scripture: Canon, Authority, Criticism* [Phl, 1983])

Within Roman Catholic circles, social theories of inspiration have principally been associated with the names of J. L. McKenzie (*CBQ* 24 [1962] 115–24), D. J. McCarthy (→ 1 above), and K. Rahner (esp. *Inspiration*).
61   A form-critical approach emphasizes the interdependence between a biblical author and his community, and the more radical form critics would reduce the "author" to virtually an anonymous scribe. This has led to the practical abandonment of the psychological theories of inspiration. If the biblical literature is the complex expression of community faith, inspiration is much more complex than divine influence upon an individual author. This disconcerting way of looking at biblical composition virtually silenced discussions of inspiration by biblical scholars and theologians within the mainline churches. Fortunately, the emergence of redaction criticism (→ Hermeneutics, 71:28; NT Criticism, 70:80) has redressed some of the inadequacies of an (exclusively) form-critical approach. The writer who produced the final biblical book, even though influenced by and drawing upon predecessors and the community, was an author and a theologian in the proper sense.
62   (C) Literary Approaches. Some recent approaches to biblical study, viz., literary and structural approaches (→ Hermeneutics, 71:55–70), stress the reality of the text itself, thus opening the way for a text-centered form of theorizing about inspiration. Although a text enjoys a certain semantic autonomy, two essential human activities are related to a text: *writing* (and rewriting) and *reading* (almost a form of mental rewriting). The doctrine of inspiration affirms that the Holy Spirit is responsible for the biblical text as text, i.e., with regard to both these human dimensions. As for writing, the Spirit is active in the long process whereby a biblical text has been produced within a faith community (i.e., including formulation of traditions, partial texts, early drafts, and rewriting). As for reading, inspiration is predicated of the biblical text precisely

because there is a faith community who, under the influence of the Spirit, will read and identify with this biblical text. To this extent, a literary theory of inspiration echoes the active meaning of the *theopneustos* of 2 Tim 3:16 (→ 13 above) and accentuates dimensions of inspiration highlighted by Calvin and Barth.
63   Other dimensions of textuality are important for a full understanding of inspiration, e.g., the three basic functions of language: to inform, to express, and to impress. The Bible may inform its readers by imparting knowledge and communicating truth, but that is only one of its functions. It also expresses something of the dynamic reality of God and affects or impresses the recipient(s) of the language communication in a variety of ways. The inspiring Spirit would be involved in the totality of these language functions. Indeed, the greatest contribution of the literary approaches to an understanding of inspiration may be their emphasis on the *total* reality of the text.
64   Another dimension of textuality to which literary analysis draws attention is the fact that text is "a production of significance" (R. Barthes). Frequently texts derive part of their meaning from the larger textual unit to which they belong. An individual saying of Jesus is part of a Gospel, which is part of the NT, which is part of the Bible. This reality resonates with the traditional doctrine that predicates inspiration of "the books of both OT and NT in their entirety, with all their parts" (Vatican II; → 4 above). The Bible as a whole is inspired, and so by implication the parts are inspired. The tradition does *not* state that because the individual sentences (= texts) of the Bible are inspired, the Bible is considered to be inspired. (Concentration on the inspiration of an isolated text can produce a type of fundamentalism.) This holistic understanding of textuality has no small bearing on an adequate understanding of the notion of biblical truth. Inerrancy should be related to the total biblical view of a topic.

Many factors highlighted by recent literary analysis support G. Turner's notion that the doctrine of inspiration qualifies the Bible as "paracletic literature." He explains ("Biblical Inspiration" 427): "The Bible as paraclete is an advocate in the sense that it is a witness to Jesus Christ. It is often used as a sort of counsellor; certainly it is a helper, consoler and comforter."
65   (D) Ecclesial Aspects. Other theories of inspiration focus upon the relationship between the Scriptures and the church, since inspiration is a "charism of the written communication of the word of God as a constitutive element of the church" (Collins, *Introduction* 345). The ecclesial-theological theories of inspiration are not without analogy to the consequent theories of inspiration (→ 43–44 above). Rahner has written:

> Since scripture is something derivative, it must be understood from the essential nature of the church, which is the eschatological and irreversible permanence of Jesus Christ in history. . . . Then he [God] is the inspirer and the author of scripture, although the inspiration of scripture is "only" a moment within God's primordial authorship of the church. (*Foundations of Christian Faith* [NY, 1978] 371, 375)

Rahner's perspective places God's authorship of Scripture in the context of a broader and more accurate understanding of "authorship," but his approach has been criticized by many proponents of composition inspiration as focusing too exclusively on Jesus, to whom the Scriptures bear witness.

COROLLARIES TO THE DOCTRINE OF INSPIRATION

66   (I) Ecclesial Use of the Scriptures.   A first corollary to or consequence of the inspiration of the Scriptures by the Holy Spirit is that they have authority for Christians and the church. This was recognized historically by the formulation of the biblical canon, i.e., the collection that the church would consider a rule (→ Canonicity, 66:5–11). Biblical authority is also reflected in the use of the Scriptures in the church's liturgical worship, as a source and norm for theological endeavors, and for the personal piety and spiritual growth of individual Christians.

67   (II) The Word of God.   A second important corollary is that the Scriptures are the word of God. This traditional formula, apparently simple, is extremely complex and polyvalent. Some Protestant evangelicals affirm an almost physical identity between the Scriptures and words actually spoken by God, rejecting as inadequate the view that the Scriptures *attest* to the word of God. Other Christians can affirm that the Bible is the word of God while maintaining that God has never communicated in words (even internal words; see R. E. Brown, *The Critical Meaning of the Bible* [NY, 1981] 1–44). Some Protestant theologians affirm that the word of God is a dynamic reality; accordingly, Jesus is preeminently the Word of God (so Barth). The Scriptures are truly the word of God when they become alive in proclamation and preaching (so Bultmann).

68   Cardinal C. Martini has helpfully distinguished various senses of the expression "word of God." Basically (esp. as a trinitarian concept) it suggests divine communicability. Thus it can refer to (1) the events of salvific history because Heb *dābār* means "word, event, reality"; (2) the spoken message of divine emissaries, esp. of the prophets and Jesus; (3) the person of Jesus who is the Word of God (esp. John 1:1); (4) Christian preaching; (5) God's general message to human beings; (6) the Bible. (See *La Parola di Dio alle Origini della Chiesa* [Rome, 1980] 56–58.)

69   Though canonized by long usage, "word of God" should not be used of the Scriptures without further hermeneutical reflection. True, it highlights the divine origins of the biblical communication and expresses its reality and force. Nevertheless, the "word of God" in the Jewish and Christian traditions is radically different from the divine oracles of ancient Hellenistic and Near Eastern religions—it is intended not simply to impart truth but to encourage, console, challenge, etc. Since the words contained in the Scriptures are, in the only written reality they possess, human words, "word of God" is necessarily analogous language. A distance is to be maintained conceptually between the scriptural expression and the self-communication of God in itself, even in the case of the prophets. Theologically it is less confusing to state that the Scriptures *witness* to the word of God.

70   (III) The Truth of the Bible.   Although some conservative Protestant theories of inspiration make the truth of the Bible (its inerrancy or infallibility) the nub of biblical inspiration (→ 51 above), I. H. Marshall, an evangelical, has noted some pertinent issues:

1. First, the Bible uses language in a great variety of ways. . . . 2. Then there is the fact that the question of truth may be answered in different ways at different levels of understanding. . . . 3. An understanding of the Bible as "truth from God" may also lead to a failure to appreciate passages where God is not speaking to man. . . . 4. A further question about biblical truth may be—"true for whom?"

He concludes "that the concept of 'truth' is a complex one, and that it is not easy to apply it to every part of the Bible" (*Biblical Inspiration* 54–57).

The concentration on inerrancy tends to reduce theological discussion about inspiration to a concept that was first introduced into the theological discussion in the 19th cent. The term "inerrancy" has never appeared in a conciliar text (although found in papal encyclicals and the original, rejected schema of Vatican II on revelation). At Vatican II Cardinal Koenig pointed out errors in the biblical books, which "are deficient in accuracy as regards both historical and scientific matters" (*Commentary on the Documents of Vatican II* [ed. H. Vorgrimler; NY, 1969] 3. 205). Indeed, the Scriptures themselves never claim to be inerrant. Finally, serious philosophical reflection on the nature of biblical "truth" and "error" must take into full consideration literary form and the level and function of language.

71   Yet there is much to be gained from a positive reflection on the truth of the Bible, which is ultimately salvific truth. Christians of various backgrounds should be able to approve and accept the language of Vatican II about Scripture's teaching without error that truth which God wanted put into the sacred writings for the sake of our salvation (→ 4 above; Church Pronouncements, 72:14)—a compromise between those who wanted to affirm the truth of the Scriptures without further qualification and those of kerygmatic orientation who envisioned the entire reality of the Scriptures within the context of salvation history. The kerygmatic perspective had already been espoused by the PBC "Instruction on the Historical Truth of the Gospels" (→ Church Pronouncements, 72:35): "It is apparent that the doctrine and life of Jesus were not simply reported for the sole purpose of being remembered, but were 'preached.'. . ." As for "truth" in the biblical sense, "The 'truth' (*emeth*) of God is primarily bound up with his faithfulness" (Loretz, *Truth* 83–84). From this perspective the antithesis is not simple error, but deception or infidelity. The truth of the Scriptures lies not so much in that its passages are without error, but in that through them God manifests his fidelity to his people, bringing them into loving union with himself.

72   (IV) Future of Inspiration Theorizing.   Is it still legitimate to theorize about the inspiration of the Scriptures? Loretz has written *Das Ende der Inspirationstheologie*. Even more radically, the Protestant brother-exegetes A. T. and R. P. C. Hanson have declared: "The ancient doctrine of the inspiration and inerrancy of the Bible not only is impossible for intelligent people today, but represents a deviation in Christian doctrine, whatever salutary uses may have been made of it in the past by the Holy Spirit, who often turns human errors to good ends" (*Reasonable Belief: A Survey of the Christian Faith* [Oxford, 1980] 42).

Even if we dismiss this as overreaction, Cardinal C. Martini (*Parola* 42) has correctly noted that a complete treatise on inspiration is still lacking (and very desirable) in the church. Any adequate treatment of inspiration should begin with the reality of the Scriptures themselves. Since the understanding of the Scriptures is very much "in process," an understanding of inspiration must necessarily be "in process" as well.

66

CANONICITY

Raymond E. Brown, S.S. Raymond F. Collins *

BIBLIOGRAPHY

1   **Canon in General:** Carson, D. A. and J. D. Wood-
bridge (eds.), *Hermeneutics, Authority, and Canon* (GR, 1986).
Coats, G. W. and B. O. Long, *Canon and Authority* (Phl, 1977).
Frank, J., *Der Sinn der Kanonbildung* (Freiburg, 1971). Gnuse, R.,
The Authority of the Bible (NY, 1985). Howorth, H. H., "The
Origin and Authority of the Biblical Canon in the Anglican
Church," *JTS* 8 (1906-7) 1-40; "The Origin and Authority of
the Biblical Canon According to the Continental Reformers,"
JTS 8 (1906-7) 321-65; *JTS* 9 (1907-8) 186-230; "The Origin
and Authority of the Canon Among the Later Reformers," *JTS*
10 (1908-9) 183-232. Keck, L. E., "Scripture and Canon,"
Quarterly Review 3 (1983) 8-26. McDonald, L. M., *The Formation
of the Christian Canon* (Nash, 1988). Maichle, A., *Der
Kanon der biblischen Bücher und das Konzil von Trient* (Freiburg,
1929). Preuschen, E., *Analecta; Kürzere Texte zur Geschichte der
alten Kirche und des Kanons* (Tübingen, 1910). Reuss, E. W. E.,
History of the Canon of the Holy Scriptures in the Christian Church
(Edinburgh, 1891). von Campenhausen, H. F., *The Formation of
the Christian Bible* (Phl, 1972). Westcott, B. F., *The Bible in the
Church* (NY, 1905). Zarb, S., *De Historia Canonis Utriusque
Testamenti* (Rome, 1934). Also → Texts, 68:1-3.
2   **Canon of the OT:** Beckwith, R. T., *The Old Testa-
ment Canon of the New Testament Church* (GR, 1985). Blenkin-
sopp, J., *Prophecy and Canon* (Notre Dame, 1977). Childs, B. S.,
Introduction to the Old Testament as Scripture (Phl, 1979). Eissfeldt,
O., *EOTI* 560-71. Freedman, D. N., "Canon of the OT,"
IDBSup 130-36. Henshaw, T., *The Writings* (London, 1963).
Jepsen, A., "Zur Kanongeschichte des Alten Testaments," *ZAW*
71 (1959) 114-36. Jugie, M., *Histoire du canon de l'Ancien Testa-
ment dans l'église grecque et l'église russe* (Paris, 1909). Katz, P., "The
Old Testament Canon in Palestine and Alexandria," *ZNW* 47
(1956) 191-217. Leiman, S. Z., *The Canonization of Hebrew Scrip-
ture: The Talmudic and Midrashic Evidence* (London, 1976). Loisy,
A., *Histoire du canon de l'Ancien Testament* (Paris, 1890). Ruwet,
J., "Le canon alexandrine des Écritures," *Bib* 33 (1952) 1-29.
Ryle, H. E., *The Canon of the Old Testament* (2d ed.; London,
1895). Sanders, J. A., *Torah and Canon* (Phl, 1972). Smith, W. R.,
The Old Testament in the Jewish Church (London, 1902). Sperber,

A., *New Testament and Septuagint* (NY, 1940). Sundberg, A. C.,
The Old Testament of the Early Church (Cambridge MA, 1964).
Tabachovitz, D., *Die Septuaginta und das Neue Testament* (Lund,
1950). Zeitlin, S., *An Historical Study of the Canonization of the
Hebrew Scriptures* (Phl, 1933).
3   **Canon of the NT:** Aland, K., *The Problem of the New
Testament Canon* (London, 1962). Aletti, J.-N., "Le canon des
Écritures. Le Nouveau Testament," *Études* 349 (1978) 102-24.
Best, E. J., "Scripture, Tradition and the Canon of the New
Testament," *BJRL* 61 (1978-79) 258-89. Bewer, J. A., *The
History of the New Testament Canon in the Syrian Church* (Chicago,
1900). Childs, B. S., *The New Testament as Canon* (Phl, 1985).
Dungan, D. L., "The New Testament Canon in Recent Study,"
Int 29 (1975) 339-51. Farmer, W. R. and D. M. Farkasfalvy,
The Formation of the New Testament Canon (NY, 1983). Gamble,
H. Y., *The New Testament Canon* (Phl, 1985). Goodspeed, E. J.,
The Formation of the New Testament (Chicago, 1926). Grant, R.
M., *CHB* 1. 284-307. Gregory, C. R., *The Canon and Text of the
New Testament* (NY, 1907). Grosheide, F. W., *Some Early Lists
of Books of the New Testament* (Textus Minores 1; Leiden, 1948).
Harnack, A. von, *The Origin of the New Testament* (London,
1925). Hennecke, E., *HSNTA* 1. 19-68. Knox, J., *Marcion and
the New Testament* (Chicago, 1942). Lagrange, M.-J., *Histoire
ancienne du canon du Nouveau Testament* (Paris, 1933). Marxsen,
W., *The New Testament as the Church's Book* (Phl, 1972). Metzger,
B. M., *The Canon of the New Testament* (Oxford, 1987). Mitton,
C. L., *The Formation of the Pauline Corpus* (London, 1955).
Moule, C. F. D., *The Birth of the New Testament* (3d ed.; SF,
1981) 235-69. Nicol, T., *The Four Gospels in the Earliest Church
History* (Edinburgh, 1908). Oxford Soc. of Hist. Theology, *The
New Testament in the Apostolic Fathers* (Oxford, 1905). Sand, A.,
Kanon (Freiburg, 1974). Schmidt, K. L., *Kanonische und Apo-
kryphe Evangelien* (Basel, 1944). Souter, A., *The Text and Canon
of the New Testament* (rev. ed.; Naperville, 1954). Wainwright,
G., "The New Testament as Canon," *SJT* 28 (1975) 551-71.
Westcott, B. F., *A General Survey of the History of the Canon of the
New Testament* (London, 1875).

---

* Sections 5-19, 44-47, and 86 of this article are by R. F. Collins; the remainder is by R. E. Brown.

4   OUTLINE

CANON IN GENERAL

5   **(I) The Word "Canon."** A transliteration of Gk *kanōn*, "canon" is derived from a Semitic word for "reed" (*qanû* in Assyrian, *qaneh* in Hebrew, *qn* in Ugaritic). Classically, *kanōn* was a straight rod or bar—a tool used for measuring. A mason's or carpenter's measuring stick, *kanōn* metaphorically connoted a rule, norm, or standard (of excellence). In chronology, *kanones* (pl.) were the principal eras or epochs in history, and *kanōn* (sg.) designated a chronological table. Occasionally, however, *kanōn* simply meant "series" or "list."
6   In the LXX *kanōn* appears only in Mic 7:4; Judg 13:6; and 4 Macc 7:21—the last a metaphorical reference to a philosophical rule. In the NT the term is used four times, always metaphorically. In 2 Cor 10:13, 15,16, it designates territorial limits; in Gal 6:16, the Christian rule of life, apparently in opposition to non-Christian standards.
7   In early ecclesiastical usage *kanōn* referred to the rule of faith, the norm of revealed truth. (See W. R. Farmer, *Second Century* 4 [1984] 143-70.) The "glorious and holy rule [*kanōn*] of our tradition," in contrast to "empty and silly concerns," is the guiding norm for Christian preaching and the Christian ethos (*1 Clem.* 7:2; AD 96). Irenaeus (*ca.* 180) mentioned frequently the "rule of truth" to which the Scriptures and tradition attest, but which is nonetheless perverted by heretics (*Adv. Haer.* 3.2.1; 3.11.1; etc.). In the early 4th cent. Eusebius employed *kanones* for the lists he compiled, e.g., the dates of the monarchs of the Assyrians, Hebrews, Egyptians, *et al.* The famous Eusebian canons are lists of Gospel references contained in his letter to Carpian: the first cites parallel passages found in all four Gospels; the second, parallel passages in the Gospels except John; and so forth until the tenth cites passages found in just one Gospel. Eusebius listed the books of the NT (*HE* 3.25; 6.25), but he called this a "catalogue" (*katalogos*). The decisions of the Council of Nicaea (AD 325) were

designated as canons, as were the disciplinary decisions of synods, which functioned as rules for Christians to live by.
8   In his 39th festal letter (Easter, 367) Athanasius contrasted "the books included in the canon [*ta kanonizomena*], and handed down, and credited as divine," with the "books termed apocryphal [*apokrypha*]," which the heretics mixed up with the books of the divinely inspired Scripture (PG 26. 1436). Athanasius's distinction between "canonical" and "apocryphal" books recalls a threefold distinction that Eusebius (*ca.* 303) had made in reference to "testamentary" books (*endiathēkos; HE* 3.3. and 3.25): the *homologoumena,* which were indisputably accepted by all, the *antilegomena* or disputed works, and the *notha* or clearly spurious works. (Eusebius attributed a similar division to Clement of Alexandria [*ca.* 200], but most contemporary scholars regard that attribution as a fiction by Eusebius, seeking a precedent for his own work.) Athanasius's canonical books and Eusebius's testamentary *homologoumena* are largely but not totally coextensive.
9   In current terminology, a canonical book is one that the church acknowledges as belonging to its list of sacred books, as inspired by God, and as having a regulating (rule) value for faith and morals (→ 17 below). In Roman Catholic terminology OT books are divided into protocanonical books (39) and deuterocanonical books (7). The latter are Tob, Jdt, 1-2 Macc, Wis, Sir, Bar (plus parts of Esth and Dan). This distinction, which seems to have been contributed by Sixtus of Siena (1520-1569), does not imply that protocanonical books are more canonical than deuterocanonical, or were canonized first. Rather, protocanonical books were accepted with little or no debate, whereas there was serious questioning about deuterocanonical books.
10   Athanasius (→ 8 above) distinguished canonical books from apocryphal books. The latter term

originally described hidden or secret writings destined to be read only by those initiated into a given (Christian) sect, but it came to designate books similar (in content, form, or title) to scriptural books but not accepted into the canon (→ Apocrypha, 67:4–6). In Protestant Bibles published "with the Apocrypha," that term covers the deuterocanonical books of Roman Catholic Bibles (but usually printed separately from either Testament and with the addition of 1–2 Esdr, Pr Man, and sometimes 3–4 Macc). Then the term "pseudepigrapha" is given to the nonbiblical books that Roman Catholics call Apocrypha, even though the root meaning of *pseud + epigrapha* suggests that it should be confined to works attributed to authors who did not write them. The unsatisfactory and confusing terminological situation may be (a bit too) simply presented thus:

OT Catholic Protocanonical = Canonical OT Protestant
OT Catholic Deuterocanonical = Apocrypha Protestant
    Catholic Apocrypha   = Pseudepigrapha Protestant

11   (II) Canonical Listing of Scripture. By the end of the 4th cent., "canon" describing a collection of scriptural books had become common ecclesiastical usage in both East and West. There had been earlier lists of biblical books, e.g., in the 2d cent., the Muratorian Fragment (*EB* 1–2) and Melito; and, in the 3d cent., Origen (→ 84 below). But now the lists took on ecclesiastical status and became more set in content, which thus gave rise to the twofold thrust of "canon" that would dominate subsequent theology (*norm* for the church and *list*). In addition to those of Eusebius and Athanasius, lists are found in Cyril of Jerusalem, Epiphanius, Chrysostom, Gregory of Nazianzus, Amphilocius of Iconium, Jerome, Canon 59/60 of the Council of Laodicea (*ca.* 360), and the decree of Pope Damasus (382). A basic list was endorsed by the councils of Hippo (393; *EB* 16–17), Carthage III (397), and Carthage IV (419).
12   In regard to the contents of the list, the debates in Judaism and the church (Marcion) will be discussed below, as will the theological impetus to select and reject. Athanasius is the oldest witness to the citation of 27 NT books. Both he and Jerome list 22 books from the Jewish Scriptures corresponding to the number of letters in the Hebr alphabet. Since the 12 Minor Prophets were considered a single book, and there were 5 double books (= 10: 1–2 Sam; 1–2 Kgs; 1–2 Chr; Ezra-Neh; Jer-Lam), and Ruth was joined to Judg, their 22 books correspond to 39 (protocanonical) books in a modern Bible. In *De doctrina christiana* 2.8.13 (AD 396–97) Augustine listed 44 OT books (= 46, since Lam and Bar are part of Jer) including the deuterocanonical books (→ 9 above), and his great stature tended to close discussion in the West on the extent of the canon. Thus the Western councils mentioned above (→ 11) and the letter of Pope Innocent I in 405 (DS 213; *EB* 21–22) agreed on a list of 46 OT and 27 NT books. Yet the reproduction of several lists in 692 at the Quinisextine Council of Constantinople, known as Trullo II (Grosheide, *Some Early Lists* 20–21) warns against being too simplistic about the fixity of the consensus that existed at the end of the 4th cent. (→ 41 below).
13   In continuity with the dominant tradition, there were 46 OT books and 27 NT books (73 total) listed in the bull *Cantate Domino* of the (ecumenical) Council of Florence, promulgated in 1442 as a document of union between Rome and the Coptic Christians (Jacobites; DS 1335; *EB* 47). The discussions at Trent revealed doubt about the binding force of the bull; and so, reacting to Protestant questioning, in 1546 that council at its fourth session promulgated *De Canonicis*

Scripturis (→ Church Pronouncements, 72:11), "so that no doubt may remain as to which books are recognized." Trent listed as sacred and canonical "with all their parts" and as inspired by the Holy Spirit 73 books, including the OT books (deuterocanonical) not accepted by many Jews and Protestants (→ 35 and 44 below).
14   Vatican I (*Dei Filius,* 1870; → Church Pronouncements, 72:12) spoke of "sacred and canonical books . . . written by the inspiration of the Holy Spirit," but left the identity of those books to the enumeration of Trent. Canonicity involves the church's acknowledging the inspired quality of the books (DS 3006). Vatican II (*Dei Verbum,* 1965; → Church Pronouncements, 72:13–16) stated: "By means of the same [apostolic] tradition the full canon of the sacred books is known to the church" (2:8). Also "Holy Mother Church, relying on the faith of the apostolic age, accepts as sacred and canonical the books of the OT and NT, whole and entire, with all their parts, on the ground that, written under the inspiration of the Holy Spirit . . . they have God as their author and have been handed on to the church itself" (3:11). Without moving much beyond Trent (which gave Catholicism its definitive canon) the council brings together canon, tradition, and inspiration in a way similar to Athanasius (→ 8 above).
15   (III) Theological Reflections. Canonicity and inspiration designate different realities: a book from the biblical period is canonical to the extent that it is part of a closed collection that has unique status in the church; a book is inspired to the extent that the Holy Spirit was its source. Yet there is a somewhat circular relationship: inspiration preceded canonicity but could not be affirmed with surety by all without canonical recognition. In extending that canonical recognition, the church had to reflect on tradition thought to derive from apostolic origins. The NT books, for instance, were composed for 1st-cent. churches; but the "church catholic" (Ignatius of Antioch) or "great church" preserved those books and organized them into collections, using them in her liturgy. In an ongoing process, other works were rejected as not stemming from apostolic times or as containing views not consonant with the rule of faith. Various debates caused a listing of the biblical books. Once solemnly categorized, these books became an even more decisive norm for judging developments in faith and morals.
16   Thus, from composition to canonization the biblical process has had a strong community thrust—a theological observation parallel to the growing stress on the social and communitarian elements in inspiration (→ Inspiration, 65:60–61) and to the development of canonical criticism (→ Hermeneutics, 71:71–74). If one no longer thinks of inspiration solely as God's moving an individual scribe isolated at a writing table, and if one does not define meaning solely as what that scribe intended and conveyed at the moment he wrote, so one does not think that at a given moment in the 1st cent. the apostles could list inspired books by title.
17   K. Rahner (*Inspiration in the Bible* [2d ed.; NY, 1964]) argues that the revelation of the inspired books was implicit and not direct—inherent in the church's knowledge that certain books were authentic reflections of her faith. (Something of the same process would have gone on in Israel in regard to its sacred writings, which the church later accepted as its OT.) The process of articulating the revelation into an official listing would have taken centuries, have been governed by need, connatural to the church's existence and ongoing life. Thus there is an interplay between "canon" as the church's norm or rule of faith (→ 7 above) and the formation of a biblical canon which in turn constitutes a norm of the

church's faith and practice—indeed, an "unnormed norm" (*norma non normata*). An interesting example of the functioning of the norms may be found in a council like Trent, which in a sense exercised the church's sovereignty in recognizing which books were canonical, but constantly cited the biblical books as a definitive guide to the points of faith it was defining. More practically, however, the Scriptures often exercise their normativeness in liturgy, for public reading within the church gives them "a pulpit" from which they can guide the lives of people.

18   The paradox of the history and interrelationships of canonicity may be caught in these statements. Augustine, *Contra epistolam Manichaei* 5.6 (PL 42. 176): "I would not believe the Gospel did not the authority of the Catholic Church move me to this." Vatican II, *Dei Verbum* 2:10: "The living teaching office of the church . . . is not above the word of God but serves it." That same

section of *Dei Verbum* interrelates Scripture and tradition as "one sacred deposit of the word of God."

19   The global theological picture, however helpful, covers over enormous difficulties as to exactly how and why individual books were judged canonical, with decisions sometimes favoring books of no great theological interest (Jude). The lack of formal or universally accepted criteria for canonicity and the facts that some books were really anonymous collections (Mal), that many books were not written by the authorities whose names have been attached to them (all or most of the Gospels), that very diverse theologies are at work within the same canon, that some values were shut out in the rejection of the apocrypha—these and other factors make the study of the canon extremely complicated, as the detailed discussion below will unfold. Once a subject that collected cobwebs and produced yawns, canonicity has become a very provoking investigation.

THE CANON OF THE OLD TESTAMENT

20   As indicated by our discussions of the deuterocanonical books (or Apocrypha; → 9–10 above), the Roman Catholic Church and some Eastern Orthodox churches (→ 47 below) accept a longer OT canon (46 books) than that acknowledged by most Protestants (39) and by Jews (39 also, but arranged differently). The difference centers on Tob, Jdt, 1–2 Macc, Wis, Sir, Bar (including Ep Jer) and parts of Esth and Dan. A classic thesis hitherto espoused to explain this is that by the end of the 1st cent. AD there were in Judaism two canons, or lists of sacred books, a shorter Palestinian canon drawn up by the rabbis at Jamnia, and a longer Alexandrian canon represented by the LXX. The early Christian church adopted the Alexandrian canon; but the Reformers, following a minority view among the Fathers, decided to revert to the Palestinian canon. The respective results were the Roman Catholic and Protestant canons. Almost every detail of this thesis has been subjected to serious challenge and modification.

21   **(I) Formation of Sacred Writings in Judaism.** The composition of the OT was a process that took over 1000 years. The first poetic compositions, e.g., the Song of Miriam (Exod 15:1–18) and the Song of Deborah (Judg 5), probably go back to the 12th cent. BC. The latest books in the Jewish-Protestant canon, Dan and Esth, were composed during the 2d cent. BC; the latest books in the Roman Catholic canon, 2 Macc and Wis, were composed *ca.* 100 BC. During this long period of composition there was a gradual accumulation of material into books and then into collections of books. In addition to the books that found their way into canonical acceptance, there were others, some composed during the period when the biblical books were being written, some composed slightly later. Some of these other books were lost; some were preserved but did not receive acceptance.

22   The division of the Hebr Bible accepted by Judaism is tripartite: the Law, the Prophets, and the Writings. The Law (*Tôrâ*) consists of the five books of the Pentateuch. The Prophets (*Nĕbî'îm*) are subdivided into the Former Prophets (Josh, Judg, Sam, Kgs) and the Latter Prophets (Isa, Jer, Ezek, the Twelve [= Minor Prophets])—eight books in all. The Writings (*Kĕtûbîm*) are 11 in number: Pss, Prov, Job, the five Megilloth or scrolls (= Cant, Ruth, Lam, Eccl, Esth), Dan, Ezra/Neh,

Chr. This gives a total of 24 books, although by various combinations, the number has sometimes been given as 22, the number of letters in the Hebr alphabet. From *Tôrâ*, *Nĕbî'îm*, and *Kĕtûbîm* comes the modern Hebr acronym TNK (vocalized *Tĕnāk*), meaning "the Bible."

When did this tripartite division become standard, and when were the three individual collections fixed? The generally accepted view is that each division or collection—Law, Prophets, and Writings—represents a stage in the development of the Bible, so that the Law was fixed before the Prophets, etc. There is another point of view favored by Hölscher (*Kanonisch und Apokryph* [Naumberg, 1905]) that sees the three divisions growing more or less concurrently and maintains that the determination of the whole tripartite collection was made at one time. Although it is true that individual books belonging to each of the three divisions were being composed at the same time, it is difficult to deny the evidence that one collection was fixed before another. For the dates of the collections, see the chart on the next page, which is section 23.

24   **(A) The Law.** In modern scholarly opinion, the earliest Hebr law codes preserved in the Pentateuch (the Decalogue of Exod 20:1–17, the Covenant Code of Exod 20:22–23:19, and the Ritual Decalogue of Exod 34:11–26) were composed in the 12th–11th cents. BC. The latest law code, the Priestly Collection, was postexilic (*ca.* 5th cent. BC). Thus the Pentateuch was probably complete by *ca.* 400 BC. Actually, earlier there is mention of an existing law book in 2 Kgs 22:8ff., where in 622 the priest Hilkiah discovered in the Temple "the book of the law." This was probably the nucleus of Deut (12–26). Later, *ca.* 400, we are told in Neh 8:1 that Ezra the scribe read to the assembled people "the book of the law of Moses which the Lord had given to Israel," presumably the law that Ezra had brought from Babylon (Ezra 7:14). Many scholars think that this was a recension of the Pentateuch; others think of it as just the Priestly Collection of laws.

25   One argument that has been used to bolster the theory that the Law was a completed collection by *ca.* 400 BC probably should be rejected, even if the theory itself is accepted. We refer to the argument based on the fact that the Samaritans possess a Pentateuch substantially the same as the Hebr Pentateuch. The reasoning is

23   WORKS OF THE OLD TESTAMENT ERA: APPROXIMATE DATES OF COLLECTION OR COMPOSITION

Centuries BC	The Law	The Prophets		The Writings	Deuterocanonicals and Apocrypha *
		Former Prophets	Latter Prophets		
13th–11th	Career of Moses? Traditions underlying Pentateuch taking shape; early law codes. Early Poetry (Exod 15).	Stories of conquest of Palestine. Traditions underlying Judg and 1 Sam. Early Poetry (Judg 5).			
10th	J tradition put into writing.	Stories of David, esp., "Court History" (2 Sam 9–20, 1 Kgs 1–2).		Use of Pss in Temple worship begins. Cultivation of proverbial wisdom in Jerusalem court under Solomon.	
9th	E tradition composed.	Preservation of royal annals of Judah and of Israel (source of 1–2 Kgs, 1–2 Chr); Elijah and Elisha cycles (1 Kgs 17– 2 Kgs 10)		Ruth? Marriage songs, later echoed in Cant.	
8th	J and E merged (under Hezekiah, ca. 700?).	Preservation of royal annals of Judah and of Israel.	Amos and Hosea in Israel. Isaiah and Micah in Judah.	Hezekiah is a traditional patron of proverbial wisdom (Prov 25).	
7th	Nucleus of Deut is made basis of Josiah's reform (ca. 622). Holiness Code (Lev 17–26) edited.	Preservation of royal annals of Judah.	Oracles of Isaiah collected by disciples and edited. Zephaniah, Nahum, and Habakkuk. Jeremiah dictates to Baruch.		
6th	P is compiled from earlier sources and gives structure to emerging Pentateuch.	Deuteronomic History edited in Exile.	Ezekiel in Babylon. Deutero-Isaiah (ca. 550). Editing of preexilic prophetic corpus. Postexilic oracles of Haggai, Zechariah (1–9), and Trito-Isaiah.	Lamentations. Job(?)	
5th	Completion of Pentateuch (ca. 400?)		Malachi Obadiah(?)	Memoirs of Nehemiah and or Ezra. Prov 1–9 written as preface to Prov 10ff.	
4th–3rd			Jonah(?) Joel(?) Isaian Apocalypse (24–27[?]). Deutero-Zechariah (9–14[?]).	Chronicler's History Sayings of Qoheleth (Eccl) edited by students. Collection of Ps(?).	
2d				Esther(?). Daniel.	Sirach (ca. 190) 1 Enoch * Jubilees * Baruch (composite) Tobit Judith Ep. Aristeas * T. 12 Patr. *(?) Gk Esther Gk parts of Daniel 1 Macc
1st					2 Macc Wisdom 3 Macc * 1 Esdras * 3–5 Pss of Solomon *

Jewish writings of the 1st and early 2d cents. AD include: 4 Macc *; *Assumption of Moses* *; 4 Ezra * (2 Esdras 3–14); *2–3 Apoc. Baruch* *; Prayer of Manasseh *; *T. 12 Patr.* *(?); *Sybilline Oracles* * (books 3–5); *Bib. Ant.* * (Ps.-Philo).
(?) = Date uncertain. An asterisk and italics indicate apocrypha.

that since the Samaritan schism took place in the 5th cent. BC, they must have possessed this Pentateuch before they broke off. It was thought that the Old Hebr script in which the Samaritan Pentateuch was written was a sign of this antiquity, and that this script was maintained by the Samaritans as a protest against the Jewish innovation of employing the Aram script (the script we usually associate with the Hebr Bible). The paleographical studies of F. M. Cross on the basis of the Qumran finds have shown, however, that this Old Hebr script was revived in the 2d cent. BC, and that the Samaritan script was an offshoot of the 2d-cent. writing (*BANE* 189 n. 4). These observations make it *possible* that the Samaritan schism may have occurred as late as the 2d cent. BC, a date before which, we know, the Law was accepted in Judaism (→ Texts, 68:17–18, 38–39).

26 If the Law was accepted by 400 BC, perhaps we should qualify our understanding of what this acceptance meant. Even after that date, a book like *Jub.* (→ Apocrypha, 67:17) was composed and read by various groups of Jews, e.g., the Qumran sectarians, although in some points and laws it was not in harmony with the Pentateuch.

27 **(B) The Prophets.** What Jewish tradition calls the *Former Prophets* is identified today as the Deuteronomic History (Josh, Judg, Sam, Kgs), a historical collection completed in the years 600–560 (→ 1–2 Kings, 10:2–3). In 2 Macc 2:13, Nehemiah (*ca.* 440) is credited with collecting "the books about the kings and prophets, and the writings of David, and the letters of kings about votive offerings"—perhaps this reference represents a popular tradition about the collection of the Former Prophets. Besides the historical material that became part of this collection, there was ancient Israelite historical writing that did not survive to become canonical, as the OT itself bears witness. Josh 10:13 speaks of the Book of Jashar. The royal annal material for the reigns of the kings was excerpted from the Books of the Chronicles of the Kings of Judah and of Israel (1 Kgs 14:29; 15:7,31; 16:5). The Chronicler seems to have known of collections of prophetic material, e.g., the history or visions of the prophets Nathan, Ahijah, Shemaiah, Iddo (2 Chr 9:29; 12:15; 13:22). There is no reason to think that such lost works were not once looked upon as holy; indeed, had they survived, they would probably have become part of the OT. Thus, in books written before the exile, survival through the national catastrophe was probably the criterion that determined canonical acceptance. We know of no pre-exilic books that did survive and were not accepted.

The *Latter Prophets* is a more heterogeneous collection whose individual books were composed between 750 (Amos) and *ca.* 400–300 (the last of the Minor Prophets, i.e., Mal, Joel, Jonah, Dt-Zech; and perhaps the "Isaian Apocalypse," Isa 24–27). By the time of Jesus ben Sira (*ca.* 190 BC) it was already customary to think of the Twelve Prophets (Sir 49:10), and this almost certainly means that the collection of the Latter Prophets was complete.

28 By the 2d cent. BC the whole prophetical collection had achieved the rank of sacred books. For example, the author of Dan (*ca.* 165) refers to Jer as one of "the books" (9:2). It was customary to put the Law and the Prophets side by side in mentioning sacred books (Foreword to Sir; 2 Macc 15:9). In evaluating this Jewish attitude toward the Prophets, however, we must be aware that the acceptance may not have been absolute, for the Talmud (*b. Šabb.* 13b; *b. Ḥag.* 13a; *b. Menaḥ.* 45a) reports later objections to Ezek because of apparent contradictions between this book and the Law.

Moreover, we are not certain that all the ancient references to the Prophets are precisely to those books that came ultimately to be accepted as the Former and the Latter Prophets. We shall see that Josephus counted 13 prophetical books, probably including books later regarded as Writings (so Thackeray, LCL 1. 179; Beckwith, *OT Canon* 119).

29 **(C) The Writings.** This is the most miscellaneous of the collections and the one that caused the most dispute. The books ultimately accepted as Writings in the Hebr Bible probably were all postexilic in composition, with Dan and Esth (2d cent. BC) as the latest. By the end of the 2d cent., as the Foreword to Sir testifies, Jews spoke not only of the Law and the Prophets but also of "the rest of the books of our ancestors." The slightly later reference in 2 Macc 15:9, however, mentions only the Law and the Prophets. What constituted "the rest of the books" in the Sir reference we do not know precisely; Sir does not cite Ezra, Esth, or Dan.

In the 1st cent. AD we find a little more specification of what these other books might have been, for Luke 24:44 attests to this combination: "the Law of Moses, the Prophets, and the *Psalms.*" This is harmonious with Philo's reference (*De vita contemp.* 3.25) to the Law, the prophetic words, and "*hymns and other works* by which knowledge and piety may be increased and perfected." Josephus (*Ag. Ap.* 1.8 § 39–41) knows of the 5 law books of Moses, the 13 books of the Prophets, and 4 books containing "*hymns* to God *and precepts* for the conduct of human life." The last mentioned are thought to have been Pss, Cant, Prov, and Eccl. As yet, no name had been attached to this last classification; but later the designation "the Writings" is found in the Talmud (*b. B. Bat.* 14b; *b. Ketub.* 50a), and this may reflect earlier usage. The vagueness of the references to these "other books" in the 1st cent. AD is a sign that Judaism had not yet reached the stage of a sharply defined collection. Also, it may be that, as latecomers, the Writings did not enjoy the same level of respect accorded to the Law and the Prophets. Yet clearly all three are sacred Scriptures.

30 To some, perhaps, Josephus's statement may seem to have settled the question of a canon, or fixed list of books, within Judaism, and for that reason his statement deserves more attention. At least one may say that the 22 books enumerated by Josephus enjoyed wide acceptance among the Jews. It is another question to what extent Josephus meant to exclude other books or reflected universal Jewish thought in so doing. In his own writings Josephus cites the LXX and uses books that almost certainly were not part of his list of 22, e.g., 1 Macc, 1 Esdr, and the additions to Esth. He includes among the Prophets books that were later counted as Writings. A few years after AD 90, the date of Josephus's work, 4 Ezra mentions 24 books publicly accepted by the Jews; it is uncertain whether this is just a different enumeration of Josephus's 22 books or a real difference in the list of books.

Certainly, in Josephus's remarks we find something closer to a canon than anything we have hitherto encountered. It is interesting to see what he says about the books he lists. They are sacred books, to be distinguished from other books because of their divine origin. They may not be tampered with or added to. Josephus thinks that they were composed in the 3000 years between Moses and Artaxerxes I (450 BC—a ruler seemingly connected with Esth). His historical judgment is, of course, inaccurate; several books he includes were not written until 300 years after Artaxerxes.

31 **(II) Closing the Canon in Palestinian Judaism.** If we doubt that Josephus represents a definitively closed canon, we must face the problem of why and how the canon was closed for normative Judaism.

32   (A) Criteria. The problem is difficult because we are not even certain of the exact criterion used for deciding canonicity. Some have supposed that certain books were received because of their legal character or their relation to the Law, for the Law is the canon by which all is judged. Another factor that certainly played an important part was the thought that certain books contained the word of God and were inspired by him, but this attribute is not easily verified in a book.

It has been proposed by G. Östborn (*Cult and Canon* [Uppsala, 1955]) that a book was held to be canonical because of its specific motif, i.e., if it in some way celebrated or reported Yahweh's activity. This motif endowed the book with cultic value and permitted its use in the synagogue service. Östborn's hypothesis, though attractive, fails to carry total conviction because the endeavor to find a fundamental motif that runs through all the books of the OT becomes forced. Attention is rightly given, however, to the cultic use of books as a factor in their acceptance, e.g., the use of the Pss in the Temple liturgy. Yet we do not know that by the 1st cent. AD there was an annual or three-year cycle in the fixed lectionary of pentateuchal and prophetic readings for the synagogue. (See the controversy between A. Guilding, *The Fourth Gospel and Jewish Worship* [Oxford, 1960] and L. Morris, *The New Testament and the Jewish Lectionaries* [London, 1964].) Later the five Megilloth came to be read at the principal Jewish feasts; this custom may reflect earlier practice in some instances.

33   (B) Time. We find in Jewish tradition three main suggestions.

(a) EZRA. It was believed at one time that the collection of the OT books was accomplished decisively by Ezra (*ca.* 400 BC). Josephus's evidence may be related to this theory because he places the termination of the writing of the OT in the 5th cent. The precise evidence comes from 4 Ezra (→ Apocrypha, 67:41), a work written between AD 90 and 120. In 14:45 God is portrayed as speaking to Ezra of 24 sacred books that are available to all the people, as distinct from the 70 books that are to be kept secret (→ 10 above). This late legend obviously has little historical value because many of the canonical books were written after Ezra's time. At most, the historical Ezra completed the collection of the Law.

A unique form of attributing the canon to one man is Beckwith's attribution of it to Judas Maccabeus "who gathered for us all the writings" (2 Macc 2:14–15; see *OT Canon* 152, 312), so that Dan would have become canonical within three years of final composition!

34   (b) GREAT SYNAGOGUE. Another suggestion is that the OT was determined by "the men of the Great Synagogue," working under the impetus of Ezra. A learned Jewish writer, Elias Levita, drawing from passages in the Talmud, first suggested this theory in his book *Massoreth ha Massoreth* (1538); it subsequently received approval from many Christian scholars. Particularly in Protestant thought it held sway until the late 19th cent., justifying Protestant acceptance of the short Hebr canon. Brian Walton wrote of the men of the Great Synagogue, "Their work of establishing the Canon possessed truly divine authority. . ." (Ryle, *Canon* 263). This hypothesis, however, has been shaken by questions about the very existence of the Great Synagogue (→ Apocrypha, 67:135). Even if some form of the Great Synagogue did exist in the years after Ezra, the thought

that it played a decisive role in the canonizing process is most implausible. The OT, Josephus, Philo, and the Apocrypha report nothing of such a body and its canonizing activity. Indeed, the earliest reference to the Great Synagogue is in the Mishna of the 2d cent. AD (*Pirqe Aboth* 1:1). Moreover, the traditional dating of the Great Synagogue (4th cent. BC) would preclude any complete canon.

35   (c) JAMNIA. That the canon was not completed until the Christian era is recognized by most critical scholars today, and many suggest that the rivalry offered by Christian books was a spur for the closing of the Jewish canon. Others prefer to find the stimulus in the disputes within Judaism, particularly between the Pharisees and some of the more apocalyptically minded Jewish sects. In particular, it is often suggested that the canon was closed at Jamnia (Jabneh or Jabneel, a town near the Mediterranean, W of Jerusalem) where Rabbi Johanan ben Zakkai reestablished his school at the time of the fall of Jerusalem. After a decade Gamaliel II became the head of the school, and in the period AD 80–117 he and Eleazar ben Azariah were the predominant teachers. It has been proposed that about 90–100 the council of the rabbis at Jamnia settled once and for all time the definitive list of inspired books, namely, "the Palestinian canon," consisting of the books now called protocanonical. Yet this thesis has been subjected to much-needed criticism (J. P. Lewis, *JBR* 32 [1964] 125–32; Leiman, *Canonization* 120–24).

Four points of caution should be noted: (1) Although Christian authors seem to think in terms of a formal church council at Jamnia, there was no "council of Jamnia." At Jamnia there was a school for studying the Law, and the Jamnia rabbis exercised legal functions in the Jewish community. (2) There is no evidence that any list of books was drawn up at Jamnia. The rabbis, of course, recognized that certain books were uniquely sacred and "soiled the hands," so that purification was necessary after using them (*m. Yad.* 3:2). But this attitude may represent the popular acceptance of 22 or 24 books that we saw in Josephus and in 4 Ezra at roughly the same period. It need not concern a definite canon (see Leiman, *Canonization*). (3) A specific discussion of acceptance at Jamnia is attested only for Eccl and Cant, and even in these instances arguments persisted in Judaism decades after the Jamnia period. There were also subsequent debates about Esth. (4) We know of no books that were excluded at Jamnia. A book like Sir, which did not eventually become part of the standard Hebr Bible (based on the putative Jamnia canon), was read and copied by Jews after the Jamnia period. Tosephta (*Yad.* 2:13) records that Sir was declared as not soiling the hands, but does not say where or when this was decided.

The safest statement about the closing of the Jewish canon is one which recognizes that, although in the 1st cent. AD there was acceptance of 22 or 24 books as sacred, there was no rigidly fixed exclusive Hebr canon until the end of the 2d cent. In this period various Jewish groups continued to read as sacred, books not included in the 22/24 count.

36   (III) The Canon at Qumran. The discovery of the Dead Sea Scrolls (→ Apocrypha, 67:80) has given us much more evidence for our discussion of the canon among Jews in the 1st cent. BC and the 1st cent. AD. The situation apparent in the books preserved from the Qumran collections betrays the very type of freedom about the canon that we sketched above (P. Skehan, *BA* 28 [1965] 89–90). Of the books that would ultimately find their way into the standard Hebr Bible, only Esth is absent from among the Qumran scrolls and fragments.

This could of course be accidental, although several factors suggest that the Qumran Essenes may have rejected the book: it makes no mention of God, and it places emphasis on the Purim festival (which may not have pleased the rigid Qumran outlook on the calendar and feasts). Esth is also absent from some Christian lists up to the time of Gregory of Nazianzus (380). The Law and the Prophets seem to have been accepted at Qumran, with each collection arranged in the order that would become standard, though often in recensions differing from the MT (→ Texts, 68:20). Of the collection that would become known as the Writings, Pss has the best attestation; Ezra/Neh and Chr have the poorest. Although the Essenes probably knew the canonical Psalter, it is an open question whether the collection of Pss was considered rigidly closed during the lifetime of the Qumran community. In several mss., noncanonical psalms are mixed in with canonical ones (→ Texts, 68:31).

37 The really important factor pertaining to the canon is that the Qumran sectarians preserved copies of many other books. Of the deuterocanonical books, the Letter of Jeremiah (Ep Jer = Bar 6), Tob, and Sir are represented, the latter two in several copies. Moreover, there are many copies of *Jub.*, *1 Enoch*, and various sectarian documents. We cannot be sure that an essential distinction was made between these works and "biblical" works. The thesis that a different type of script and format was used by the Qumran scribes in copying the "biblical" books has no validity. In fact, some of the canonical books were copied on papyrus, a practice forbidden later in Judaism, because only parchment (skin) was thought to be fitting for a biblical book (→ Texts, 68:14). The conclusion of Skehan is worth quoting: "All in all, the Qumran library gives the impression of a certain selectivity, but hardly of any fine distinction between a closed canon and all other texts."

38 (IV) The Canon at Alexandria. We spoke of the thesis that there were two canons in ancient Judaism: the shorter Palestinian canon fixed at Jamnia and the longer Alexandrian canon (→ 20 above). Just as the fixing of the canon at Jamnia has been challenged, so also the thesis of an Alexandrian canon has undergone penetrating questioning (see Sundberg, *OT*). This thesis, apparently first proposed by J. E. Grabe *ca.* 1700, is intimately related to the acceptance of the LXX by the early church.

Three arguments for an Alexandrian canon no longer find acceptance. (1) We now recognize the legendary quality of the information supplied by *Ep. Arist.* (→ Apocrypha, 67:33) concerning the composition of the LXX. Neither the Pentateuch nor the entire OT was translated into Greek at one time (i.e., in 72 days, *ca.* 275 BC) by 72 or 70 translators working under the patronage of Ptolemy II Philadelphus (→ Texts, 68:63). If this legend were true, a fixed number of books would be plausible. But when we consider that the LXX was the product of several centuries both of translating and of original composition, the question of a set number of books becomes more problematical. (2) It was once thought that the extra (deuterocanonical) books in the Alexandrian canon had been composed in Greek and not in Hebrew or Aramaic, the sacred languages known in Palestine. Actually, a good number of the deuterocanonical books were originally composed in Hebrew (Sir, Jdt, 1 Macc) or Aramaic (Tob). The Qumran discoveries prove that some of these books were in circulation in Palestine and were accepted by Jewish groups there. The fact that the codices of the LXX do not isolate the deuterocanonical books as a group but

mix them in with the Prophets (Bar) and the Writings (Sir, Wis) shows that there was no awareness that these books had a unique origin, as there would have been if they were thought to be later and foreign additions to an already fixed collection translated from Hebrew. (3) The thesis that the Jews in Alexandria had a different theory of inspiration from the theory shared by the Jews in Jerusalem is gratuitous. (See P. Katz, *ZNW* 47 [1956] 209.)

39 Moreover, the rigid character of the canon in Alexandria is open to question because the Christian witnesses to this supposedly fixed collection, including the great codices of the LXX, are not in agreement. Sundberg (*OT* 58–59) shows this in charts. For instance, on the question of Macc (→ Apocrypha, 67:34), Codex Vaticanus contains no book of the Maccabees, Sinaiticus has 1 Macc and 4 Macc, and Alexandrinus has all four books. Consequently, it is difficult to deny Sundberg's thesis that the Jews in Alexandria did not have a fixed list of books. They were in the same situation as were their cousins in Palestine in the 1st cent. AD, i.e., they had a large number of sacred books, some of which were recognized by all as older and more sacred than others. It was not the Jews of Alexandria but the Christian church that, working with the LXX, ultimately drew up an exclusive canon. In fact, when the Alexandrian Jews eventually did accept a canon, they, like Jews elsewhere, accepted the one fixed by discussions in the late 2d cent. in the rabbinical schools of Palestine. Indeed, after the depopulation of Egyptian Jewry in the revolt of AD 115–117, reestablishment may have come through immigration from Palestine.

40 (V) The Ancient Christian Canon of the Old Testament. The conclusion that there was no rigidly closed canon in Judaism in the 1st and early 2d cents. AD means that when the church was in its formative period and was using the sacred books of the Jews, there was no closed canon for the church to adopt. This is exactly the situation in the NT. The NT writers cite the sacred books that ultimately found their way into the Hebr canon, especially the Law, the Prophets, and Pss. But they also echo some of the deuterocanonical books. The allusions detected by Nestle's Gk NT (Sundberg, *OT* 54–55) include Sir, Wis, 1–2 Macc, and Tob. One may add the apocryphal works *Pss. Sol.*, 1–2 Esdr, 4 Macc, and *As. Mos.* Jude 14 clearly cites *1 Enoch*; and despite the claim that Jude is not citing it as Scripture, we cannot show that the author would have made such a distinction. (*Barn.* 16:5 refers to *1 Enoch* as "Scripture"; cf. 4:3 also.) In 2 Cor 6:14 Paul seems to cite implicitly a work with Qumran affinities (J. A. Fitzmyer, *CBQ* 23 [1961] 271–80).

41 After the NT period (i.e., 50–150), the Christian church continued to cite the Scriptures according to the LXX; and since the LXX itself reflected the lack of a rigidly fixed canon in Judaism, the early Christian writers had no sharp guidelines. The oft-repeated thesis that from the beginning all Christians agreed on the exact canon and that only later doubts arose about certain books has little to recommend it. Such a thesis is based on the assumption that the contents of the canon were revealed to the apostles—an unwarranted assumption, probably flowing from a misunderstanding of the principle that revelation was closed in the apostolic era (→ 17 above).

The first attempts to set up a rigidly closed OT canon for Christendom apparently reflected the Jewish debates about the canon in 2d-cent. Palestine. In the mid-2d cent., we find Justin in his discussions with the Jews sensitive to differences between the Christian OT and the Jewish Scriptures (*Dial.* 68.7–8; 71ff.; PG 6. 631–36, 641–46); and Tertullian (*Apparel of Women* 1.3; PL 1. 1307) is aware that in arguing from *1 Enoch,* he is not using a book accepted by the Jews. The majority of Christian writers (Clement of Rome, Polycarp, Hermas, Irenaeus, and the author of *Barn.*) seem to use freely a large number of Jewish sacred books, including apocryphal works. In the late 4th cent., the Western church, as witnessed in the North African councils of Hippo and Carthage, accepted a fixed number of OT books including some deuterocanonicals found in the LXX mss. But the writers of the Eastern church were more aware of the shorter scriptural canon drawn up by the Jews. Melito of Sardis (170–190) gives us our earliest Christian list of OT books—a list much like the one that eventually became the standard Hebr list (Esth is omitted). Origen mentions that the Hebrews have 22 books; Athanasius, who had Jewish teachers, insists that the Christians should have 22 books just as the Hebrews have; and, of course, Jerome did his best to propagate the Hebr canon in the Western church. Some writers who favor the short canon nevertheless cite the deuterocanonical books. A distinction between "canonical" and "ecclesiastical" was proposed in order to classify the books, with the latter to be understood as works serving the church for edification. Doubts about the deuterocanonical books keep recurring in the history of the church among those who are aware of the Jewish canon. Those who prefer the shorter canon or express some doubt about the full canonical status of the deuterocanonicals include Cyril of Jerusalem, Gregory of Nazianzus, Epiphanius, Rufinus, Gregory the Great, John Damascene, Hugh of St. Victor, Nicholas of Lyra, and Cardinal Cajetan. (See A. C. Sundberg, *CBQ* 30 [1968] 143–55.)

42 **(VI) The Canon at Trent.** As mentioned earlier (→ 13 above), the Council of Trent accepted definitively the deuterocanonicals, and it did so directly in opposition to the Protestant preference for the Jewish canon. Although Catholics accept the statement of the council as binding in faith, it is wise to know some of the difficulties that surround it. (See P. Duncker, *CBQ* 15 [1953] 277–99; H. Jedin, *A History of the Council of Trent* [London, 1961] 2. 52–98.) Even on the eve of the council the Catholic view was not absolutely unified, as the mention of Cajetan in the preceding paragraph clearly indicates. Catholic editions of the Bible published in Germany and in France in 1527 and 1530 contained only the protocanonical books. The fathers of the council knew the 4th-cent. African councils that had accepted the deuterocanonical books, and the position taken at Florence (→ 11–13 above); but at the time of Trent, there were insufficient historical tools to reconstruct the real picture of the canon in the 1st cent. R. H. Charles, a Protestant, recalls the (rather harsh and oversimplified) evaluation given by B. F. Westcott on the ability of the Tridentine fathers: "This decree of the Council of Trent was ratified by fifty-three prelates, 'among whom [Westcott, *Bible in the Church* 257] there was not one German, not one scholar distinguished by historical learning, not one who was fitted by special study for the examination of a subject in which the truth could only be determined by the voice of antiquity'" (*APOT* 1.*x*.n). Yet, curiously, Trent by accepting a wider canon seems to have preserved an authentic memory of the days of Christian origins, whereas other Christian groups in a professed attempt to return to primitive Christianity have settled for a narrower Jewish canon that, if Protestant researchers like A. C. Sundberg and J. P. Lewis are correct, was the creation of a later period. After all, the

Tridentine fathers did not determine the canon on the basis of purely historical reconstruction but on a theological basis: the consistent church usage of certain books.

43 Even at Trent, however, the council fathers did not specifically attempt to press the detail of church usage back beyond the period of Jerome, for they used the Vg as the norm for church usage, condemning "anyone who does not accept these books in their entirety, with all their parts, according to the text usually read in the Catholic Church and as they are in the ancient Latin Vulgate" (DS 1504). There are many difficulties here that demand investigation. (1) In the period before the Vg there was no consistent church usage, as we have seen. Ironically, Jerome, the translator of the Vg, was very clear in his preference for the same short canon that Trent rejected in the name of the Vg. The Vg was introduced into the West over many protests (including that of Augustine) asserting that Jerome's translation from the Hebrew was an innovation against the church's usage of translating from the LXX. (2) From Jerome's time on, the Vg has not been a perfect witness of church usage, for it was several centuries before the Vg won acceptance in the church. And even then, the Vg was a norm only of *Western* church usage. Although Trent was an ecumenical council, the constituency of the fathers was Western, and perhaps insufficient attention was given to the usage of the Eastern churches. (3) If church usage was the norm for selecting the books of the canon, then several books that had been used in the church were omitted. For instance, 1 Esdr was used by the fathers more than was canonical Ezra/Neh, and the requiem liturgy cited 2 Esdr. Copies of the Vg often contained 1–2 Esdr and the Pr Man—books not accepted at Trent. Not one of these difficulties impairs the binding force of the Tridentine decree (the object of faith is the decree, not the argumentation behind it), but perhaps they illuminate the difficulties often voiced by non-Catholics.

44 **(VII) The Canon in Protestantism.** Earlier the Wycliffe Bible (1382) had a 39-book OT canon (like Jerome). Nevertheless, in debating purgatory with J. Maier of Eck (1519), it was Luther who broke with church tradition and began a new era in discussions on the OT canon. (Already in 1518, A. Bodenstein of Karlstadt, arguing against Eck, placed scriptural authority above that of the church.) Confronted by 2 Macc 12:46 (Vg) as "scriptural proof" for the doctrine of purgatory, Luther rejected 2 Macc as Scripture. He denied the right of the church to decide canonicity, arguing that the inherent quality of the biblical book attests to its canonical and scriptural status. Polemics hardened Luther in his position until he recognized as OT books only those 39 cited in Jerome's list (→ 12 above). When he published his Ger Scriptures in 1534, he grouped Jud, Wis, Tob, Sir, Bar, 1–2 Macc, and portions of Esth and Dan as "Apocrypha" (→ 10 above): "Books which are not held equal to the Sacred Scriptures and yet are useful and good for reading." Publishing the Apocrypha immediately after the OT, Luther affected the Protestant canon.

45 The early Reformers were not eager to reject the Apocrypha altogether, since they had been in ecclesiastical use for more than a millennium. By compromise these books were relegated to secondary status as an OT appendix in Zwingli's Zurich Bible (1529), the Calvinist Olivetan Bible (1534–1535), and the Eng Bibles (Coverdale, 1536; Matthew, 1537; 2d ed. of Great Bible, 1540; Bishops' 1568; *KJV,* 1611; → Texts, 68:194–98). But there was also a harder line. The Apocrypha were excluded from the Bible in the Gallican Confession

(1559), Belgian Confession (1561), Anglican Confession (1563), 2d Helvetic Confession (1566), and by Gomarus and Deodatus (Dutch Reformed Synod at Dort, 1618–1619). The Puritan Confession declared the Apocrypha to be of a merely secular nature. The Westminster Confession (1648) stated: "The books commonly called Apocrypha, not being of divine inspiration, are not part of the canon of Scripture; and therefore of no authority to the Church of God, not to be otherwise approved, or made use of, than any other human writings." The distinguished scholar John Lightfoot (1643) spoke of "the wretched apocrypha."

46 Even though an Eng Bible without the Apocrypha was published in 1629, the custom of printing the Apocrypha in Eng-language Bibles continued until 1825 when the Edinburgh Committee of the British and Foreign Bible Society protested that the apocryphal writings should not be translated and sent to the heathen. On May 3, 1827, the society concurred, and so customarily Eng Protestant Bibles appeared after that without the Apocrypha. Since Vatican II, however, "ecumenical Bibles" have been published containing the Apocrypha (→ 10 above; Texts, 68:201). Very widely now Protestant scholarship and seminary teaching stress the importance of the apocryphal (deuterocanonical) books as a key to Jewish religious thought in the period between the two Testaments. This development has been facilitated by growing subtlety about the theology found in the Apocrypha. For instance, with regard to purgatory (→ 44 above), Protestants have come to recognize that the early Jewish view of the afterlife had more complexity than only heaven and hell. Roman Catholics have come to recognize that the purgatory doctrine of the Western church was not exactly the same as any intermediate Jewish view.

47 (VIII) The Canon in the Oriental Churches. The Byzantine church appears to have accepted the deuterocanonical books (see Jugie, *Histoire*). Initially, the Syrian church seemingly omitted 1–2 Chr and the deuterocanonical books. Under the influence of Gk Christianity, however, subsequent common Syrian use (the Peshitta; → Texts, 68:125) was harmonized with the LXX. The Nestorian churches, reflecting Theodore of Mopsuestia (*ca.* 350–428), generally doubted the value of Esth, and they used the shorter canon. In the opposite direction, the Copts gave status (not necessarily canonical) to some apocryphal works as well as to the deuterocanonical books. A similar tendency is found among the Ethiopians, whose 46-book OT canon includes *Jub., 1 Enoch*, 4 Ezra, and Pseudo-Josephus (Josippon).

The Reformation influenced some OT canonical approaches in the Eastern churches. In 1627 Zacharios Greganos, a Greek who had studied at Wittenberg, rejected the deuterocanonical books. Although similar views were held by a few others, the Gk and Slavic branches of the Byzantine church continued to maintain those books. The Synod of Jerusalem, convened at Bethlehem in 1672 by the patriarch Dositheus to repudiate tendencies toward Calvinism, specifically decreed that Tob, Jdt, Sir, Wis, 1–2 Macc, and the additions to Dan are to be considered canonical. At that time the decrees of the synod were intended to be representative of Eastern Orthodoxy as a whole. Within the Gk church, despite occasional demurrals by theologians, the longer OT canon has been accepted, including 2 Esdr and 3 Macc. Since the 19th cent., however, Russian Orthodox theologians generally have not accepted the deuterocanonical books. Yet a Moscow-published Bible of 1956 contains them. A draft statement for the proposed Great Council of the Orthodox Church (*Towards the Great Council* [London, 1972] 3–4) opts for the shorter canon, as does the negotiation between the Orthodox and the Old Catholics (Beckwith, *OT Canon* 14).

THE CANON OF THE NEW TESTAMENT

48 (I) General Observations. Today, Roman Catholics, Orthodox, and Protestants all accept the same canon of 27 NT books. The theory that these books were accepted from the first days of Christianity and that doubts arose only subsequently is untenable; it is related to the idea, no longer accepted, that the specific contents of the canon were known in the apostolic era. The early followers of Jesus had Scriptures that they considered sacred, but these were writings that had come down to them from their Jewish heritage. For about the first 100 years of Christianity (AD 30–130), the term OT is an anachronism (yet see 2 Cor 3:14); the collection of sacred writings of Jewish origin would not have been designated as "Old" until there was a "New" collection from which to distinguish it. (Modern Judaism does not speak of an OT; since the Jews reject the NT, there is for them only one sacred collection.) When did Christians begin writing their own compositions and why? How soon were these put on a par with the ancient Jewish Scriptures? What determined which Christian works were to be preserved and accepted? When did acceptance come? These are the questions we now must deal with.

49 (A) Causes for Writing Christian Works. Christianity, much more than Judaism, is a religion with its origin in a person. What God has done is centered in Jesus, so that the early Christians could say that God was in Christ Jesus (2 Cor 5:19)—Jews would not have thought of Moses in these terms. To preach the kingdom of God, which had made its presence felt in Jesus' ministry, apostles were commissioned (for the difference between the apostles and the Twelve, → NT Thought, 81:153–57). Contrary to some modern theories, the NT portrays the apostles as the living link between Christian believers and the Jesus in whom they believed (→ Early Church, 80:15, 19). Accordingly, in the early days when Christians were close to the apostles—both geographically and chronologically—there was no pressing need for Christian writings. In fact, we have no clear proof of major Christian writings from the period AD 30–50. During this time the Christian faith was communicated, preserved, and nourished by word of mouth (Rom 10:14–15). Preaching had a role in Christianity beyond what it had in Judaism; and for the first Christians what was "canonical" was what Peter (Cephas), James, and Paul preached in continuity with what Jesus had proclaimed (1 Cor 15:11). Distance was probably the most influential factor in changing the situation so that writing became important.

50 (1) Geographical distance. With the decision at Jerusalem in AD 49 to permit acceptance of Gentiles without circumcision (Acts 15), the far-flung Gentile world, already invaded by Paul, became a wide-open missionary field. The founding of Christian communities at great distances from one another and the continual traveling of the apostles made written communication a necessity. A church whose confines were close to Jerusalem was a thing of the past, and apostolic instruction now often had to come from afar. This need was first met with letters and epistles (→ NT Epistles, 45:3–5), and the Pauline letters are the earliest major Christian writings of which we know with certainty.

(2) Chronological distance. The existence of eyewitnesses to Jesus marked the first years of Christianity; but as the apostles dispersed, and after their death, the preservation of the memory of Jesus' deeds and words became a problem. Moreover, catechetical needs required the organization of oral testimonies into compact units. This gave rise to pre-Gospel collections, oral and written, and from such collections the Gospel writers made a selection as source material. But even the Gospels once written were no substitute for oral witness, as we hear from Papias, who in the early 2d cent. was still seeking oral testimony although he knew several Gospels, canonical and noncanonical (Eusebius, HE 3.39.4; GCS 9/1. 286). Other exigencies, such as the threat of heresy, persecution, and the need to reaffirm faith, produced additional Christian writings.

51   (B) Criteria for Preservation and Acceptance. Once there were Christian writings, what factor determined which ones were to be preserved and were to be considered uniquely sacred? For, as we shall see, some 1st-cent. writings were not preserved, and other early works that were preserved were not accepted. The following factors were important. (1) Apostolic origin, real or putative, was very important, particularly for acceptance. The canonicity of Rev and Heb was debated precisely because it was doubted whether they were written by John and Paul respectively. Today we understand that such apostolic origin is to be taken in the very broad sense that "authorship" has in biblical discussion (→ 89 below). Often this means no more than that an apostle had a traditional connection with a given work. By the stricter standards current today, it may be legitimately questioned whether a single NT work comes directly from any one of the Twelve.

52   (2) Most of the NT works were addressed to particular Christian communities, and the history and importance of the community involved had much to do with the preservation and even with the ultimate acceptance of these works. Seemingly no work emerging directly from the Palestinian community has been preserved, although some of the sources of the Gospels and Acts were probably Palestinian. The reason for this loss probably lies in the disruption of the Palestinian Christian community during the Jewish-Roman war of 66–70. Syria seems to have fared better, for apparently Syrian communities were addressed in Matt, Jas, and Jude. The churches of Greece and Asia Minor seem to have preserved the largest portion of NT material, i.e., the Pauline, the Johannine, and perhaps the Lucan writings. The church of Rome preserved Mark, Rom, and perhaps Heb, and the Lucan writings. For Irenaeus (ca. 180), facing the gnostic claims to apostolic origins for their writings, the connection of apostles to known churches in Asia Minor, Greece, and, above all, Rome was an important argument for the canonical NT (see Farkasfalvy, Formation 146).

53   (3) Conformity with the rule of faith (→ 7 above) was a criterion of acceptance. Doubts about millenarianism caused suspicion of Rev, and an apocryphal gospel like Gos. Pet. was rejected precisely as

constituting a doctrinal danger (→ 65 below). Farmer (Formation 35ff.) relates persecution and martyrdom to the rule of faith. The fact that some gnostics questioned the value of martyrdom was met by an appeal to Gospels, Acts, and letters which highlight Jesus' death on the cross and to Peter's and Paul's sufferings.

54   (4) To what extent did chance play a role in preservation? Some would argue from a theory of inspiration that chance could have had no role: God would not have inspired a work and then allowed it to be lost. But this argument presumes that every inspired work had to have permanent value. Could not the task for which God inspired a particular work have been accomplished when it was received? A good example may have been the lost letter of Paul that pronounced judgment on an individual at Corinth (1 Cor 5:3). Moreover, the argument presumes that God always protects against human vicissitudes the works he has motivated—a presumption that is not verified in the history of Israel and of the church. Consequently, many scholars who hold a theory of inspiration still believe that chance had a role in the preservation of less important works, like Phlm, when more important works were lost (part of the Corinthian correspondence, and the logia of Jesus in Aramaic that Papias attributes to Matthew). Even among the works that were preserved, there were disputes about and slowness in universally accepting some important ones (Heb, Rev, James)—more than in the case of Phlm.

55   (II) Composition and Collection of New Testament Works. All the works eventually accepted into the NT were probably written before AD 150. The dates for their collection into recognized groups are hard to specify. (See the chart on the next page.) Moreover, when these works were acknowledged as sacred or inspired writings, they were not necessarily placed in the same category as the OT Scriptures. Even when the latter step was taken, 2d-cent. church writers who did speak of NT works as "Scriptures" sometimes quoted alongside them (but less frequently) other gospels and writings—an indication that a sense of closed canon had not yet developed. Thus one must distinguish the acknowledgment of Christian writings as sacred works, as Scripture, and as canonical (Keck, "Scripture").

56   (A) Pauline Corpus.
(a) WRITING. Most of the Pauline letters and epistles were written as instruction and encouragement to churches that Paul himself had evangelized (Rom is a notable exception). The traditional groups and dates (very common in Roman Catholic textbooks of the pre-Vatican II era) were these: In the early 50s, 1–2 Thess were written, and in the late 50s the Great Letters (Gal, 1–2 Cor, Rom). Sometimes Phil was counted with them; sometimes with the Captivity Letters (Phlm, Col, Eph), written in the early 60s. The Pastoral Letters (1–2 Tim, Titus) were written before Paul's death in the mid-60s. In all, 13 letters or epistles came to bear Paul's name as author (a claim not made by Heb, which was eventually attributed to Paul as the 14th letter). Numerically this corpus constitutes one-half the NT collection of 27 books.

Modern scholarship has challenged Paul's writing of six of these works, often arguing that they were Deutero-Pauline, penned by a disciple of Paul after his death. Critical scholars are almost evenly divided on Col, which has a rhetorical tone and an emphasis on the church that is absent from the undisputed Pauline letters. A majority hold that Eph is post-Pauline, since its author seems to adapt the themes of Col and of other epistles. A high majority of scholars consider the Pastoral Letters

WORKS OF THE NEW TESTAMENT: APPROXIMATE DATES OF COMPOSITION

Early 50s	Mid-/Late 50s	Early 60s	Mid-60s	70s–80s	90s	After 100
1 Thessalonians	Galatians	Philemon (?)	MARK	MATTHEW	JOHN	2 Peter
2 Thessalonians (?)	1 Corinthians	Colossians (?)	Titus (?)	LUKE	Revelation	
	2 Corinthians	Ephesians (?)	1 Timothy (?)	Acts	1 John	
	Romans		2 Timothy (?)	Colossians (?)	2 John	
	Philippians		1 Peter (?)	Jude (?)	3 John	
	Philemon (?)		James (?)	James (?)	Jude (?)	
			Hebrews (?)	Hebrews (?)	2 Thessalonians (?)	
				1 Peter (?)	Ephesians (?)	
					Titus (?)	
					1 Timothy (?)	
					2 Timothy (?)	

PAULINE CORPUS		GOSPELS		CATHOLIC EPISTLES	
EARLY LETTERS	1 Thessalonians 51 2 Thessalonians 51 or 90s	Mark	65–70	1 Peter	64 or 70s–80s
		Matthew	70s–80s	James	62 or 70s–80s
		Luke	70s–80s	Jude	70s–90s
	Galatians 54–57	John	90s	1 John	90s
GREAT LETTERS	Philippians 56–57 1 Corinthians 57 2 Corinthians 57 Romans 58			2 John 3 John 2 Peter	90s 90s 100–150
CAPTIVITY LETTERS	Philemon 56–57 or 61–63 Colossians 61–63 or 70–80 Ephesians 61–63 or 90–100			OTHER WRITINGS	
PASTORAL LETTERS	Titus 65 or 95–100 1 Timothy 65 or 95–100 2 Timothy 66–67 or 95–100			Acts Hebrews Revelation	70s–80s 60s or 70s–80s 90s

(?) Date uncertain. This chart does not attempt to include datings proposed by a small minority. Except for the early Pauline writings, an approximation of a decade governs most of the dating, e.g., Matt and Luke could have been written in the 90s.

to be post-Pauline, with some placing them as late as the mid-2d cent. and moving them away from the immediate Pauline discipleship. That the Pastorals were written to individuals rather than to churches such as those addressed in the other Pauline letters (even Phlm is to a house-church) is not really decisive, for Timothy and Titus are addressed as having authority over churches. More important is the fascination of the Pastorals with an emerging church order of bishops and deacons which goes beyond Paul's life situation (→ Early Church, 80:27). Perhaps a majority still favor the Pauline writing of 2 Thess, even though its reference to "every letter of mine" (3:27) ill fits the traditional dating, which would make it one of the first Pauline letters. The dating depends on the identification of the apocalyptic figures in chap. 2.

57 (b) COLLECTION. There are many difficulties about the formation of the Pauline collection. The letters were written to handle particular problems in particular churches. Only Rom and Eph consciously reveal a larger scope. A later tendency to reduce the particular, local character of Paul's letters in order to make them applicable to a wider church scene is seen in the omission of "in Rome" (Rom 1:7), of chap. 16 of Rom, which is full of names, and of the geographical destination in Eph 1:1. This means that even in antiquity there was an uneasiness about accepting such temporal documents for all times. In Col 4:16 Paul recommends the exchange and circulation of his letters among neighboring churches; but what prompted a wider circulation, so that by the end of the 1st cent. Pauline letters were being read in churches far distant from the original destination? On the one hand, Paul spoke as an apostle with an apoca-

lyptic, eschatological thrust (→ Pauline Theology, 82:45); on the other hand, would Paul himself ever have expected that his correspondence would be read centuries after his death as a guide to universal Christian faith? Some Pauline letters did not escape the doom that their temporal character might have brought to all (→ NT Epistles, 45:13): there was a letter to the Laodiceans (Col 4:16) and probably several lost letters to the Corinthians (→ Paul, 79:41). A. von Harnack posited a deliberate process of selection and rejection in dealing with the Pauline letters, but the preservation of Phlm, in contrast to these losses, makes this improbable.

How then were the Pauline letters gathered together? In the theory of K. Lake, a community took its letter from Paul and added to it letters addressed to neighboring churches. Such a process would have produced several different collections of Pauline writings, and that is confirmed by the lack of agreement in the order of the letters evidenced in Marcion, the Muratorian Fragment, Tertullian, and Origen. This theory, however, explains neither the fact that an edited Pauline letter is the same in several collections nor the existence of post-Pauline writings. Churches scarcely edited or composed anew. Others have turned to an individual disciple of Paul as collector and editor. E. J. Goodspeed proposed that at first there was a lack of interest in Pauline letters and only after AD 90, with the publication of Acts, was the importance of Paul's contribution to Christianity realized. This realization led to a systematic attempt to collect his writings, some of which had already perished. According to J. Knox and C. L. Mitton, Onesimus (Phlm 10), a disciple of Paul, began to collect the writings soon after Paul's death; he composed Eph as an introduction to this corpus. This theory does not explain the other post-Pauline letters nor the fact that Eph does *not* appear as the first letter in the various collections. *GNTI* (1. 255–69) proposes Timothy as the collector of the corpus, whereas H.-M. Schenke thinks of the activity of a Pauline school (*NTS* 21 [1975–76] 505–18). A school of disciples continuing Paul's work could explain the editing of fragments preserved from Paul's correspondence, as well as the composition of a number of post-Pauline letters. That there was an antignostic motif in such a collection has been proposed (with some exaggeration) by W. Schmithals (*Paul and the Gnostics* [Nash, 1972] 239–74); but other motifs would also have been present, e.g., the need to structure pastorally the Pauline churches. It is also possible that the activity of a school of disciples over a period of time could explain the existence of Pauline collections differing in number and order.

58   When were the Pauline letters gathered into a collection? 2 Pet 3:15 indicates that a group of Pauline letters were being read on the same level as "the other Scriptures"; but 2 Pet is notoriously hard to date. Goodspeed insists that the collection took place shortly after the writing of Acts; for if the author of Acts had known the Pauline writings, he would have cited them. But Knox (in *StLA* 279–87) argues that Acts was written *ca.* 125 against a Marcionite misuse of the already extant corpus of Pauline writings. There are references to Pauline letters in early writers like Clement of Rome (96) and Ignatius (110); but D. K. Rensberger ("As the Apostle Teaches" [Ph.D. diss.; Yale, 1981]) argues that these authors knew only two letters each. In the mid-2d cent. there is clear evidence of a larger collection (Polycarp knew at least 8; Marcion, 10). The Pastorals were rejected by or unknown to Marcion and seemingly were absent from P⁴⁶ (*ca.* 200; → Texts, 68:179). The Muratorian Fragment (→ 84 below), presumably representing Roman acceptance *ca.* 200, knew of 13 Pauline letters. Heb as the 14th was Eastern usage. See A. Lindemann, *Paulus im ältesten Christentum* (BHT 58; Tübingen, 1978).

59   Other epistles bearing Paul's name made their appearance. The Muratorian Fragment rejects the *Epistle to the Laodiceans* and the *Epistle to the Alexandrians,* which display a pro-Marcionite tendency. A different *Epistle to the Laodiceans* was the object of attack in the 4th cent. It has been preserved in the Codex Fuldensis, a ms. of the Vg NT completed in 546; in the Middle Ages this epistle continued to appear in Lat Bibles and was accepted as genuine by some Lat writers. In the *Acts of Paul* (*ca.* 150–180) we find a *Third Epistle to the Corinthians,* which was accepted in 4th-cent. Syria and later in the Armenian church. A 3d-cent. Gk copy of this apocryphal Corinthian correspondence appears in Papyrus Bodmer X. Some of the pseudo-Pauline epistles were suggested by Paul's own indications of correspondence that was not preserved (1 Cor 5:9; 2 Cor 2:4; 10:10; Col 4:16).

60   **(B) Gospels.**

(a) WRITING. Paul shows a knowledge of instructions of the Lord that have more authority than his own (1 Cor 7:10,12) and of some details of Jesus' career (11:23–26; 15:3–5). If the words and deeds of Jesus were committed to writing somewhat later than Paul's letters, that is not a reflection on their antiquity nor on what was most sacred for early Christians. Jesus' words could be more authoritative than the Jewish Scriptures (Matt 5:21–48). As for Christian letters, immediate community problems had to be answered by the apostle; there was no similar necessity to commit to

writing the words of the Lord, who himself had not communicated by writing. Indeed, even after words and deeds of Jesus were written, there was an enduring respect for oral tradition about him (→ 50 above).

In the judgment of scholars, written Jesus tradition antedated the canonical Gospels, e.g., "Q," proto-Mark, pre-Johannine sources—plausibly to be assigned to the 50s (*give or take 10 years—a qualification that governs pre-Gospel and Gospel dating*). Also, the collection of the sayings of the Lord assigned by Papias to Matthew was considered pre-Marcan by Irenaeus (Eusebius, *HE* 3.39.16; 5.8.2). Luke 1:1 asserts that many others had already undertaken to compile a narrative of the things that had been accomplished by Jesus. Such pre-Gospel written sources, now lost but sometimes reconstructed by scholars, must already have shown considerable development over the *ipsissima verba et facta* of Jesus. How faithful is the line of development that stretched from Jesus to pre-Gospel writings to the canonical Gospels? (For historical criteria, → Jesus, 78:7; for church teaching, → Church Pronouncements, 72:35.)

61   The canonical Gospels were written in the period 65–100. Mark most likely (→ Synoptic Problem, 40:6–12) was the earliest, having been written between 65 and 75. In it the pre-Gospel written tradition was systematized along chronological and theological lines. The material to be narrated was fitted into a simplified sequence of the public ministry of Jesus (baptism, ministry in Galilee, ministry outside Galilee, journey to Jerusalem, passion, death, and resurrection), with the evangelist placing incidents where they seemed *logically* to fit—not necessarily on the basis of a correct historical chronology. The choice of the material to be incorporated and the orientation given to it were determined by the evangelist's theological outlook and by the needs of the community for which Mark was written.

In the period 75–90, an unknown Christian wrote the Gospel that has come down to us as the Gospel according to Matthew (some have suggested that the name is explicable because the evangelist was a disciple of Matthew or drew on an earlier collection of sayings by Matthew). In the period 80–95, another writer (later identified, correctly or incorrectly, as Luke a companion of Paul) undertook an elaborate project that produced not only a Gospel that had more formal historical pretensions but also a history of the origin and spread of Christianity in the postresurrectional period (Acts). Theological orientation is clearer in Matt and Luke than it is in Mark, precisely because of the changes those evangelists made while using Mark (for redaction criticism, → Hermeneutics, 71:28). The development of pre-Johannine tradition probably lasted several decades, and the Gospel according to John was written in a substantial form *ca.* 90. (A final redaction of John may have taken place some 10 or 15 years later after 1-2-3 John.) Why the name John was associated with this Gospel remains a disputed point among scholars: few would identify the writer as the son of Zebedee, or identify the Beloved Disciple (the source of Johannine tradition) as one of the Twelve. Although John does preserve some historical reminiscences about Jesus (lost or oversimplified in the earlier Gospels), it has profoundly rethought and rewritten the Jesus tradition. Much of the peculiarly Johannine outlook may be explicable in terms of the unique history of the community that preserved this tradition (→ Joannine Theology, 83:9–17).

62   (b) COLLECTION. In the earliest outlook there was only one gospel (2 Cor 11:4; → Pauline Theology, 82:31), and that is implicitly acknowledged in Mark's opening, "The beginning of the Gospel of Jesus

Christ, the Son of God" (1:1). When another Gospel was written, presumably it became *the* Gospel for the community addressed through it. There is no indication that any of the four evangelists expected his audience to read another Gospel besides what he wrote, and that is probably why Matt and Luke incorporated Mark rather than writing supplements. Thus an individual written Gospel was looked on as the local variation of the one basic gospel (as reflected in the title "The Gospel according to . . ."); the pl. usage "Gospels" seemingly belongs to the post-125 era, e.g., Justin, *Apol.* 1. 66–67. The sense of one gospel probably explains the attempt by Tatian *ca.* 170 to harmonize the four Gospels into one in his *Diatessaron* (→ Texts, 68:122), which for a time replaced the four Gospels in Syrian church usage. The church at large, however, took another, extraordinary route of eventually including four different Gospels in its selection of Scripture, doing nothing to harmonize their differences. (See R. Morgan, *Int* 33 [1979] 376–88.) Why?

63 This question is closely related to the problem of other gospels ultimately not accepted as canonical (→ 64 below). In the mid-2d cent. we find one clue to the selection of those that were accepted, i.e., the apostolic identity or association of their authors (Justin, *Dial.* 103.7: "the Memoirs which I say were composed by his apostles and those that followed them"; → 49, 51 above). But that was a growing appreciation—apparently Tatian was not regarded as audacious in his project of a harmonized gospel not composed by any apostle. Moreover, *ca.* 125, Papias, although he knew of written apostolic Gospels, was still anxious to improve upon them with oral material of an eyewitness pedigree. Eventually, however, the apostolic aura won out, and the church took pride in having two Gospels (Matt and John) derived from the Twelve, in addition to Mark related to Peter, and Luke related to Paul. The importance of the communities with which these Gospels were associated may also have figured in their survival (→52 above): Matt was probably directed to a Syrian community in the Antioch area; Mark was thought to have been composed in Rome and preserved in Alexandria; Luke was variously related to Antioch, Greece, or Rome; John was thought to have been composed in Ephesus. Because of the sharp differences of John from the Synoptics and because of the early-2d-cent. use of that Gospel by the gnostics, John had considerable difficulty in being accepted; and there was opposition to it in Rome as late as 200 (Epiphanius, *Panarion* 51 [GCS 31. 248ff.]). But increasingly in the last quarter of the 2d cent. the idea of four, and then of only four, won out (→ 65 below).

64 A corollary of recognizing this gradual development is acknowledging that alongside Mark, Matt, Luke, and John, *oral* Jesus material from the 1st cent. survived into the 2d cent. (Despite extravagant claims it has not been shown that any extant noncanonical *written* Jesus material dates from the 1st cent.; rather, such ancient oral tradition was committed to writing in the 2d cent. and later.) One early Jesus narrative, the story of the adulteress, was preserved by eventually being written into John (7:53–8:11), perhaps 100 years after that Gospel was composed (and into some mss. of Luke following 21:38). Some genuine sayings of Jesus survived in the form of patristic citations; for these "agrapha," see J. Jeremias, *Unknown Sayings of Jesus* (London, 1957). But the most important source for early extracanonical Jesus material is the apocryphal gospels. Some authentic sayings of Jesus are probably preserved in *Gos. Thom.* (→ Apocrypha, 67:67), as well as some less-developed forms of parables that are found more elaborately in the canonical Gospels. (J. D. Crossan [*Sayings Parallels* (Phl, 1986)] compares canonical and apocryphal material.) But extreme caution must be exercised in discerning what might stem from Jesus or the first proclamation of Jesus in the (relatively few) apocryphal writings that plausibly contain early material. The Apocrypha are far more useful for information about 2d-cent. developments in theology, ecclesiology, and popular piety. Media claims about a new Jesus or a new Christianity based on discoveries in the Apocrypha need to be treated with skepticism; past examples of such proposals have failed to win acceptance by the majority of scholars.

65 If even a limited amount of early Jesus material survived in some Apocrypha, on what grounds were they eventually not accepted into the canon? That a claim to apostolic origin was not the decisive factor is seen from the story of Serapion, bishop of Antioch *ca.* 190 (Eusebius, *HE* 6.12.2; → Apocrypha, 67:72). He discovered that in Rhossus people read from *Gos. Pet.;* but upon reflecting that docetists interpreted this gospel to support their theology, Serapion forbade further use of it in church. This story illustrates two things: (1) The public reading of Gospels in church was equivalent to a type of canonical recognition, and that reading was determined by church authorities. (2) Heretical origin or use of writings created suspicion, no matter what apostle's name was associated with those works. Indeed, the position of the archheretic Marcion (*ca.* 150) in accepting only a form of Luke (without chaps. 1–2), even though it echoed the older custom of having but one Gospel, may have been a factor in leading the anti-Marcionite orthodox bishops and theologians to opt for plural Gospels. (Those who argue that such ecclesiastical figures had no right to determine what was orthodox and which writings should be accepted are, in fact, questioning the role of the church in Christianity, for which the canon issue has been a classic test. The objection that the bishops do not represent the church sometimes stems from an oversimplified thesis that Christianity was by Jesus' intention egalitarian and that the development of authority, supervisory over faith and behavior, was a political power play; → Early Church, 80:19–20.) In any case, from *ca.* 200, the acceptance of four and only four Gospels was assured in the Gk and Western churches. Irenaeus (*Adv. Haer.* 3.11.8) had argued that there could be only four, and, as Origen phrased it (Eusebius, *HE* 6.25.4), those Gospels "are alone undeniably authentic in the church of God on earth." The increasing agreement *ca.* 200 between the Gk East and the West on canonical Scripture (not only of what was discussed above but of what will be discussed below [→ 81]) stemmed from increasing contact through travel: e.g., Origen went to Rome; Irenaeus came from the East. (See Farmer, *Formation* 21.) The Syrian church preferred the use of the *Diatessaron* in the 3d and 4th cents., adopting the four Gospels only in the 5th cent.

Thus far we have dealt with the Pauline letters and the Gospels—two separate bodies of early Christian literature. Perhaps the thought that both types of literature stemmed from apostolic witness was a factor in causing them to be joined. The first instance of such a joining appears in Marcion, who accepted 10 Pauline epistles and a form of Luke, using this *Apostolikon* and *Euangelion* to support his thesis that the Hebr Scriptures were to be rejected. Between 150 and 200 the "Great Church" responded by increasingly insisting on a wider collection of apostolic works (at least 13 Pauline epistles) and four Gospels, which it placed in continuity with the Scriptures derived from Judaism.

66   (C) Other Works. We have even less information about the collection of the remainder of what became the NT. This lack of information presents a difficulty similar to that presented by the third group of OT works—the Writings—for the question of the OT canon.

(a) ACTS. The traditional view was that Luke, a companion of Paul, composed Luke and Acts at the same time, *ca.* 63, when the story of Acts comes to an end. The view of common authorship has survived in scholarship, but Luke-Acts is now more usually dated to the 80s or later. Discrepancies between Acts' account of Paul and data in the Pauline letters have caused many to question whether the author really was a companion of Paul (→ Paul, 79:6–13). Luke and Acts were not preserved as a unit. Marcion accepted only Luke, and it is interesting that Acts came to frequent use only after Marcion's heresy. By giving prominence to the Twelve, by holding them up as a standard of apostleship, and by showing a continuity from them to Paul, Acts effectively offset Marcion's one-sided emphasis on Paul. (Relatively few accept J. Knox's theory that Acts was written much later than Luke [ca. 125] to combat proto-Marcion misuse of the Pauline letters and Luke.) There is evidence that Acts was accepted in some circles as canonical from 200 on. Mss. (P^{45} and Codex Bezae; → Texts, 68:179, 157) point to an early association of Acts with the four Gospels—an association that had the effect of placing a history of the works of Jesus' followers on a plane with the accounts of Jesus himself, thus implicitly stressing the role of the church in continuing the role of Christ. On the other hand, the utility of Acts as a companion to the Pauline letters in what might be called the orthodox *Apostolikon* favored the canonization of Acts.

There were also in circulation apocryphal acts of individual apostles (→ Apocrypha, 67:54). Some of them were highly romantic accounts of the careers of people such as John, Andrew, and Thomas; some had gnostic elements. Tertullian (*De baptismo* 17; CSEL 20. 215) tells how sometime before 190 the priest who fabricated the *Acts of Paul* was caught and punished. The Lat list (*ca.* 300) in the Codex Claromontanus included the *Acts of Paul*, but seemingly puts it on a questionable basis along with *Herm.* and *Barn.* Eusebius (*HE* 3.25.4) lists it as spurious.

67   (b) REVELATION. The Gk designation of this work, *Apokalypsis,* gave a name to a genre of literature that would have been familiar to the first Christians as part of their Jewish heritage (→ OT Apocalyptic, 19). Two Jewish apocalypses written about the same time as Rev (late 1st cent. AD), *2 Apoc. Bar.* and *4 Ezra,* are pseudonymous, using names of famous men who lived centuries before. But there is no reason to think that Rev 1:4,9 is not to be taken literally in describing the author as an otherwise unknown Christian prophet named John. (A later period too simply identified him as John, son of Zebedee—who in turn was too simply identified as the author of a Gospel and three epistles). Besides the clearly apocalyptic elements of the book, there is a strong tone of prophecy in a feature that is not found in the Jewish apocalypses, i.e., the prefatory letters admonishing the seven churches of Asia Minor. This feature may indicate that Christians were already accustomed to epistolary writings. The letters have led some to relate Rev to the Pauline corpus; but there are similarities to the Gospel of John as well, and the work may have had *remote* connections with the Johannine tradition.

The first evidence of Christian usage of Rev is in the mid-2d cent. in Justin, *Dial.* 81.4. In the West around the end of that century, it was accepted by the Muratorian Fragment, Irenaeus, and Tertullian, with only the Alogi (*ca.* 200?) attacking it (and the Gospel of John) on theological grounds. In the East, Melito of Sardis (170–190) is supposed to have written a commentary on it (Eusebius, *HE* 4.26.2) and Origen endorsed it. However, Dionysius of Alexandria (*ca.* 250) perceptively maintained that the author of John (whom he thought to be the son of Zebedee) did not write Rev. Dionysius's worry about the use being made of Rev by heretical chiliasts (millenarianists) had the effect of weakening the acceptance of it as a biblical book in the Gk church. Eusebius (*HE* 3.25.2–4) wavered whether to list Rev as genuine or spurious. It was not included in the list of Cyril of Jerusalem (350) or in Canon 59/60 of Laodicea (→ 11 above) or in the list of Gregory of Nazianzus that was accepted in Trullo II (692; → 12 above). Rev was not accepted in the Syrian church. Luther showed hesitancies about the millenarianism of Rev (→ 86 below).

68   There were also apocryphal apocalypses (→ Apocrypha, 67:55). The most important was *Apoc. Pet.,* which the Muratorian Fragment mentioned with a notation that some do not wish to read it in church. Written *ca.* 125–150, it seems to have been accepted as canonical by Clement of Alexandria (Eusebius, *HE* 6.14.1). The Lat list (*ca.* 300) of the Codex Claromontanus listed it last in questionable context, and *ca.* 325 Eusebius (*HE* 3.25.4) placed it among the spurious books, stating (3.3.2) that neither in the earlier days nor in his time had any orthodox writer made use of it. Jerome also rejected it, but in the 5th cent. it was still being used in the Good Friday liturgy in Palestine.

69   (c) HEBREWS. Although a respectable number of scholars date this work in the late 60s because there is no mention of the destruction of the Jerusalem Temple, the majority opt for the 70s–80s. The author was probably a Jewish Christian educated in Gk oratorical style similar to that of Alexandria. His views on the total replacement of the Jewish cult by Jesus' sacrifice of the cross were at the radical end of the spectrum on Jewish–Christian relationships, close to the views of John (→ Early Church, 80:17). Heb has little of the letter format except in the final greeting, but the mention there of Timothy (Paul's companion) and the large number of canonical Pauline letters influenced the way in which Heb was categorized. The work was probably sent to Italy, perhaps Rome (Heb 13:24), and the earliest knowledge of it is in Roman church documents (implicit in *1 Clem.* and *Herm.*). The realization in Rome that Heb was not from Paul (coupled with its severe refusal of forgiveness for serious sin committed after baptismal enlightenment [6:4]) explains why it was not listed as Scripture in Western lists (Muratorian Fragment; Codex Claromontanus [*ca.* 300]; African Canon of 360). In the East, however, Origen's list mentioned Heb, although with a doubt that it was by Paul's own hand (Eusebius, *HE* 6.25.11–14). A wide acceptance of Heb in the East was attested by Eusebius (*HE* 3.3.5, though he knows that the Roman church denies that it is from Paul) and by the canons of Cyril of Jerusalem (350), Athanasius (367), and Gregory of Nazianzus (400). Thus Heb had a fate opposite to that of Rev (which was accepted in the West and rejected in the East). Acceptance of Heb in the West in the late 300s was through the efforts of Hilary, Jerome, and Augustine, who were influenced by Eastern ideas. It appeared in the lists of the North African councils of Hippo and Carthage; it was also accepted by the Syrian church.

In modern times, when the problem of authorship was divorced from that of canonicity (→ 87–89 below), the sharp difference between the style of Heb and that of Paul has convinced almost all that Paul was not the author. The decree of the PBC in 1914 (→ Church Pronouncements, 72:28v) protecting the Paulinity of Heb by stressing that Paul used a scribe to write it is now followed by very few Roman Catholics. At most, the author may have had some acquaintance with thought like Paul's (→ Hebrews, 60:2–3).

70   (d) CATHOLIC EPISTLES. This designation, meaning universal or general, was given to seven works (Jas, 1–2 Pet, 1–2–3 John, Jude) already by AD 300 (Eusebius, *HE* 2.23.25), although apparently the term was applied as early as 200 to 1 John (*HE* 5.18.5). In the East the designation was generally understood to describe the recipients: these works were not addressed to a particular community, as were the Pauline letters, but encyclically to larger, dispersed groups or even to Christians in general (the church catholic). In the West another interpretation appears whereby "universal, catholic" refers to the general acceptance of these works; whence another designation as "Canonical Epistles" (Junilius, PL 68. 19C). Neither explanation works: 1 Pet and 2–3 John are addressed to particular groups; these works were not universally accepted; and 1 John has no characteristic of a letter or epistle. As for the individual names, it is doubtful that any of them was written by the figure to whom it is attributed, with the possible exception of 1 Pet.

71   (i) *Writing. 1 Peter:* A respectable scholarly minority attributes composition to Peter (through the scribe Silvanus, 5:12) *ca.* 65, but the majority opt for the 80s. A veneration for both Peter and Paul, who died in Rome in the 60s, might explain why the Roman church would write in Peter's name a letter with affinities to Paul's theology. The address to Christians in northern Asia Minor may mean that Rome was taking over the responsibility for areas evangelized by the Jewish mission from Jerusalem now that the mother church had been scattered in the Jewish revolt against Rome in the late 60s (R. E. Brown, *Antioch and Rome* [NY, 1983] 128–39). The appeal to a dignity and holiness given Christians through baptism (largely in OT language) may have been meant to reassure Gentiles alienated from their fellow pagan citizens through conversion to this new, despised sect (J. H. Elliott, *A Home for the Homeless* [Phl, 1981]).

72   *2 Peter:* The use of abstract theological language and the reference to all Paul's letters in 2 Pet 3:16 have led most scholars to think that this work may have been written relatively late and well after Peter's life. A date between 100 and 150 is commonly proposed (making this the last NT work), depending on which adversary the author is thought to have had in mind (gnostics, Marcion?). The knowledge of 1 Pet may mean composition in Rome, which would be harmonious with this letter's appeal to Peter as the greater authority, but in a brotherly relation to Paul (3:15). The implicit use of Jude (written by "the brother of James," Jude 1) may reflect the bridge character given to Peter in the late 1st and 2d cents., reconciling traditions related to Paul and James (→ Early Church, 80:26).

73   *1–2–3 John:* These were composed within the same tradition or school as John, but seemingly later (90–100) and not by the evangelist himself. In 1–2 John the struggle is no longer against "the Jews," but against former Johannine Christians who have seceded from the community. The author objects to their overly "high" christology, in which the human career of Jesus has little importance and all that matters is the descent from above of the divine Son into the world. Similarly, the secessionists seem to have attributed little moral value to the

lives lived after the reception of divine life through faith. These secessionist views were probably derived from a (mis)interpretation of John; and 1 John responds by insisting on a christology and an ethics that were held "from the beginning," seemingly before John was written—a christology and an ethics that insist on the importance of "the flesh," i.e., life in the world. In 3 John, much to the displeasure of the author, who reflects the Johannine lack of interest in authority structure, there has emerged in a local Johannine church a supervisor named Diotrephes. This letter may reflect the awkward coming-to-terms of Johannine Christianity with the structure of "the church catholic."

74   *James:* The great "brother of the Lord" was martyred in Jerusalem *ca.* 62, but most scholars do not think of him as the writer (see Jerome, *De viris illustr.* 2; PL 23. 609). The invocation of his name, the address "To the Twelve tribes in the diaspora," the parallels with Matthean tradition, and the competent Greek suggest a Jewish-Christian situation in the Syro-Palestinian area where James had been influential (see Acts 15:23). There is a corrective of Pauline slogans about faith and works which seem to have been quoted without sharing Paul's understanding of faith; yet there is no explicit personal hostility to Paul such as is found in 2d-cent. Jewish Christianity. A date in the 80s is often suggested. The format is similar to that of a Stoic diatribe.

75   *Jude:* Mark 6:3 lists James and Jude among the "brothers" of Jesus, but in this letter Jude identifies himself as "brother of James," not of Jesus. Few would think of Jude as the actual author, but clearly this work was written in an area where James's name would have influence. The polemic against certain ungodly persons who had gained admission to the faith is strong and vivid, but so general that neither these adversaries nor the date of the writing can be identified. References to *1 Enoch* and *As. Mos.* reflect a time in which the confines of the Jewish canon had not yet been sharply fixed.

76   (ii) *Acceptance.* Despite Eusebius's reference to "the seven [epistles] called catholic" (→ 70 above), he himself was not sure of the canonicity of all. General acceptance of the seven in the Gk and Lat churches did not come until the late 4th cent. Before that 1 Pet and 1 John were the first to receive general acceptance. Both seem to have been known by Papias (Eusebius, *HE* 3.39.17) and by Polycarp. The Muratorian Fragment listed "two [epistles] with the title 'John'"; its omission of 1 Pet may stem from poor preservation of the Muratorian text. Origen accepted 1 Pet and a short epistle by John (1 John?). 1 Pet and 1 John appear in all subsequent lists. Along with Jas, they constitute the three accepted by the Syrian church in the 5th cent.

77   Jas was known by Origen's time, but we do not know when it began to receive canonical status. It was absent from the Muratorian Fragment, listed as disputed by Eusebius, included in the Claromontanus list, but absent from the African Canon of 360. In the late 300s it won acceptance in the West through Augustine, Jerome, and the councils of Hippo and Carthage. In the Gk church of the same period it was listed in the canons of Cyril of Jerusalem, Athanasius, and Gregory of Nazianzus.

78   Curiously, the evidence for early knowledge of Jude is better than for Jas. Jude was known by the author of 2 Pet (implicitly), by Polycarp (seemingly), by Clement of Alexandria, and by the Muratorian Fragment. However, Origen was aware that there were doubts about it, and Eusebius placed it among the disputed books. Its acceptance in the latter part of the 4th cent. followed a pattern similar to that of Jas; but Jude did not receive final acceptance by the Syrian church, and a list adopted by Trullo II (692) indicated uncertainty about its status.

79 Perhaps because of their relatively insignificant contents, 2-3 John were not cited frequently by Christian writers. Irenaeus and the Muratorian Fragment knew 2 John. According to Eusebius (*HE* 6.25.10), Origen knew 2-3 John but also that all did not consider them genuine. A century later, Eusebius himself (*HE* 3.24.17) listed 2-3 John among the disputed books, and a continuing dispute over them is apparent in the North African Canon of 360. Ultimately they were accepted in the Lat and Gk churches in the late 4th cent., but not fully in the Syrian church.

80 Of all the Catholic Epistles, 2 Pet had the poorest record of acceptance. It was never clearly cited before Origen, who considered it doubtful (Eusebius, *HE* 6.25.9). Disputes about 2 Pet were recorded by Eusebius himself and the North African Canon; Jerome accepted it, although he knew there were doubts. It had the same final acceptance as the other disputed Catholic Epistles.

81 **(III) Problems about the Formation of the Canon.** By 200, then, the Gospels, the Pauline epistles, Acts, 1 Pet, and 1 John had come into general acceptance. By the end of the 4th cent. in the Lat and Gk churches there was general acceptance of the 27-book canon of the NT. This development cloaks some difficulties which must be discussed and which may help to explain why K. Aland (*A History of Christianity* [Phl, 1985] 1. 111) can state "until the seventh century, in some parts of the church either an abbreviated canon existed or people possessed an expanded canon through accepting apocryphal writings."

(A) Concept of a New Testament. Above (→ 55) we insisted that in discussing the acknowledgment of Christian writings one must distinguish their evaluation as sacred works, as Scripture, and as canonical. Now we ask when the collection of these writings just described was considered to constitute a NT comparable to the Jewish Scriptures, which then became an OT. This issue is complicated by the fact the Gk *diathēkē* means both "covenant" and "testament," and already Heb 8:7 spoke of a first covenant and a second. 2 Pet 3:16 put the writings of Paul on a par "with the other Scriptures," but we are not certain that this indicates total equality with the OT. By the mid-2d cent. Justin (*Apol.* 1.67) witnessed to the fact that the Gospels and the writings of the apostles were being read in conjunction with the OT at Christian liturgical services. *2 Clem.* 4 cited Isa and then Matt as "another Scripture." Marcion, by rejecting the OT in favor of a truncated collection of 10 Pauline epistles and Luke, helped to gel by way of opposition the belief that the Christian writings form a unity with the OT. (Opposition to Marcion catalyzed but did not create this view; see Farkasfalvy, *Formation*.) Ca. 170-190 Melito of Sardis (Eusebius, *HE* 4.26.14) spoke of the Jewish Scriptures as "the books of the Old Covenant," but that was still not clearly a concept of an OT and a NT. Ca. 200 in the East Clement of Alexandria and in the West Tertullian were developing the basic language of the two Testaments. In the same general period, the Muratorian Fragment and Origen gave lists of NT books—a sign that the concept of a collection of Christian *Scriptures* had taken hold.

82 **(B) Value of Patristic Citations.** In discussing the formation of the NT, we frequently resorted to citations of a NT book by one of the Fathers to show that a given book was known and used with some authority. Indeed, patristic citations and lists of books are the two main criteria for judgment of the canon. Yet neither criterion is totally satisfactory. For

instance, when Clement of Rome, or Ignatius, or Polycarp cited a book that ultimately was recognized as canonical, just what authority was he giving to this book, since we do not know that the concept of either a NT or a canon was yet formulated? Past discussions often simply assumed that these early Fathers had a concept of canonical and noncanonical. And, indeed, even later when there was a concept of a NT, we find strange phenomena in patristic citations. Origen cited 2 Pet at least six times; yet in his canonical list (Eusebius, *HE* 6.25.8) he doubted whether 2 Pet should be included. In other words, even a 3d-cent. patristic citation of a book ultimately accepted as canonical does not mean that the Father thought it canonical. On the other hand, absence of a citation of a NT book (e.g., during the 2d cent.) does not necessarily mean that the Fathers did not know the book or did not consider it of value. There would be little occasion to cite some of the shorter NT works like Phlm and 2-3 John.

83 We have already mentioned some apocryphal gospels, epistles, and acts that received acceptance for a certain period. We should note that the subapostolic writings, like *1-2 Clem., Did., Herm.,* and *Barn.* continued to be considered Scripture even into the 4th and 5th cents. The Alexandrian Fathers seem to have thought of *1 Clem.* as Scripture. The 4th-cent. Codex Sinaiticus contained, along with the books we consider canonical, *Barn.* and *Herm.* The 5th-cent. Codex Alexandrinus had *1-2 Clem.* And we can see why such works were highly valued. Many of them bore names of disciples of the apostles, e.g., Barnabas was a friend of Paul; Clement was thought to be the Clement mentioned in Phil 4:3 and a successor of Peter in Rome. Moreover, early subapostolic works, like *1 Clem.* and *Did.,* may well have been written before a NT work like 2 Pet. The real difficulty is not why such works were thought of as canonical, but why the church did not finally accept them as canonical.

84 **(C) Value of the Early Lists.** If patristic citations tell us nothing about canonicity in the strict sense, but only that a book was thought worthy of respect, the canonical lists (→ 11-12 above) are more helpful. The formation of a list implied acceptance of a book so listed as a particular type of book and, since the lists of NT books are at times coupled with lists of OT books, acceptance as Scripture. But past discussions of the canon have sometimes neglected to consider that a list may represent no more than the author's own judgment or the custom of his local church. The fact that lists do not agree from area to area weakens their witness to universal church practice.

What is thought to be our earliest list, the Muratorian Fragment (*HSNTA* 1. 42-45—considered representative of Roman usage in the late 2d cent.), does not include 1-2 Pet, Jas, and one Johannine epistle; but it does include Wis (as a NT book!) and *Apoc. Pet.,* about which, it admits, there is controversy. A. C. Sundberg (*HTR* 66 [1973] 1-41) questioned the usual dating of this fragment and suggested that it belongs in the 4th cent. This would mean that an incomplete canon perdured at Rome even later than formerly thought. Although accepted by some (R. F. Collins), Sundberg's thesis has been widely rejected (e.g., Gamble, *NT Canon* 32; E. Ferguson, *StudP* 17 [1982] 2. 677-83). Origen's *Hom. in Joshua* 7.1 seemed to accept all 27 NT books; but this homily is preserved only 150 years later in the Latin of Rufinus. According to Eusebius (*HE* 6.25.3-14), Origen's list raised doubt about 2 Pet and two Johannine epistles. In the early 4th cent. we have two Eastern canons from Eusebius and Cyril of Jerusalem and two slightly later Lat canons (North African presumably), and these do not agree. Eusebius (*HE* 3.25.3) listed Jas and Jude as disputed; yet elsewhere (2.23.25) he stated that they have been used regularly in many churches, thereby testifying that his list does not represent universal usage. Only with the lists of the late 4th cent., viz., those from Athanasius, Augustine, and the councils of Hippo (393) and Carthage III (397) do we come to evidence of common agreement in much of the church. As we have already indicated, however, there remain exceptions, e.g., Codex Alexandrinus with its noncanonical inclusions, and the Quinisextine council (Trullo II of 692), which included a list of 26 books (no Rev) from Gregory of Nazianzus, as well as another list that raised doubt about Heb, four Catholic Epistles, and Rev.

85   (D) Oriental Churches. In the East, the picture remained more complex. In the 4th cent. when the Greeks and Latins were beginning to move toward a standard canon of 27 books, the NT of the Syrian church included the *Diatessaron* (not the four Gospels), Acts, and 15 Pauline epistles (including Heb and *3 Cor*). Thus a canon of 17 books was used by Ephraem (320–373) and given as authoritative in the *Doctrine of Addai* (*ca.* 370) at Edessa. In the early 5th cent. the four Gospels replaced the *Diatessaron* (→ Texts, 68:123), *3 Cor* was omitted, and three of the Catholic Epistles (Jas, 1 Pet, 1 John) won acceptance. The Syrian church, however, never fully accepted the other Catholic Epistles or Rev. Coptic NT lists contained *1–2 Clem.*; and the Ethiopian church seems to have had a canon of 35 books, the additional eight including decrees, called the Synodus, and some Clementine writings. Moreover, one may legitimately wonder whether such lists represented universal practice in the respective churches. On

the Eth canon, see R. W. Cowley, *Ostkirchliche Studien* 23 (1974) 318–23; S. P. Kealy, *BTB* 9 (1979) 13–26.

These considerations should make it clear to the student just how much one is generalizing in speaking about *the* NT canon of the early church.

86   (IV) The Canon in the Reformation. The Protestant movement generally maintained the traditional 27-book NT canon. Some 16th-cent. humanists, however, revived the earlier hesitations about certain NT books. Erasmus, whose Gk NT essentially served as the basis for Luther's translation into German, was censured by the Sorbonne for not refuting ancient doubts about the apostolic origin of Heb, Jas, 2 Pet, 2–3 John, and Rev. Luther, who judged books to be canonical according to their inherent quality and valued NT books to the extent that they proclaimed Jesus Christ, esteemed Heb, Jas, Jude, and Rev to be of lesser quality than "the capital books," i.e., "the true and certain, main books of the New Testament." Thus he placed these books after the rest of the NT in his earlier Ger editions. Oecolampadius had a lower rank for Rev, Jas, Jude, 1 Pet, and 2–3 John.

Tyndale's prologue to the NT, printed in Cologne in 1525, enumerated 23 NT books. Separated from the list by a space and special indentation, and without an assigned number, were Heb, Jas, Jude, and Rev. Although the preface was omitted from the 1525 Tyndale ed. (Worms), he and his successors followed Luther's early arrangement of NT books, until the Great Bible of 1539 reverted to the traditional order. Subsequently, Eng Bibles have followed the traditional order, and Western Christendom may be said to agree on a NT canon of 27 books.

ENDURING PROBLEMS IN CANONICITY

87   (I) Authorship, Pseudonymity, and Canonicity. We have seen that early-church judgment on the sacred character and canonicity of books was often determined by tradition about their writers. Accepting the canon that emerged from such ancient judgments does not mean being bound to accept the reasoning behind the judgments. Modern scholarship agrees that the Fathers were often quite wrong in identifying the writers of biblical books. The issue of who wrote a book is a historical question to be settled by scientific criteria of style and content; it is not a religious question in the same way that inspiration and canonicity are. Thus the church has wisely refrained from dogmatic statements about the authorship or writing of biblical books. Even the PBC responses of 1905–1915 which dealt with authorship were not dogmatic but precautionary, and subsequently Roman Catholic scholars were given complete freedom with regard to those responses (→ Church Pronouncements, 72:25). The fact that within 50 years of being issued those responses were no longer in harmony with the consensus of centrist scholarship about authorship is a good indication of the complexities of the problem and the danger of taking official positions (even precautionary) on it. In fact, there is no longer an official Roman Catholic position about the identity of the writer of any biblical book.

88   Pseudonymity, i.e., using a false name, is a term employed to describe the self-attribution of a book to someone (usually of renown) who actually did not write it. (Note that pseudonymity is a matter of self-

attribution. If it is certain or probable that Heb was not written by Paul, nor Matt written by Matthew, those are not cases of pseudonymity, because the works themselves make no claim as to who was their author. Scholars of today would simply be rejecting the oversimplified attributions of the 2d cent. in denying the reputed authorship of such works.) When there are cases which match the definition of pseudonymity, that term should be applied with serious reservation to the biblical books. The claim in Jewish and Christian sacred books to authorship by famous figures who did not write them was made without any intention to deceive; rather it reflected a belief that the books were written faithfully in the tradition or school of the named "authors." Thus, to call Eph pseudonymous is a distortion if one implies that the epistle has nothing to do with Paul or his thought. Granted that reservation, the OT certainly contains pseudonymous works: Moses did not write all of Deut (despite 1:1); Solomon did not write Eccl (Qoh–despite 1:1) or Wis (despite chap. 7). If the facts warrant it, then, in principle there can be no objection to designating as pseudonymous 2 Pet, Jas, Jude, the Pastorals, Col, Eph, and 2 Thess.

89   Some distinctions should be made in the concept of authorship as applied to biblical books, esp. in regard to the relationship of authority to writing. (1) An author could write a book with his own hand–perhaps the author of Luke-Acts. (2) An author could dictate a book or letter to a scribe who copied slavishly. This was not a popular way of composing since it was tiring (for

Paul and dictation, → NT Epistles, 45:19–21). (3) An author could supply ideas and statements to another who would write the work (the equivalent of a modern "ghost writer"). Some who do not think that 1 Pet is pseudonymous have argued that Peter, a Galilean fisherman, composed this well-written Gk letter by thus using Silvanus (5:12). These first three categories would merit the designation "author" in modern parlance too. (4) In antiquity one could be considered an author if a work was written by disciples whose thought was guided by both the master's past words and by his spirit (even a long time after his death). Such authorship is exemplified in the composition of parts of Isa and Jer, and probably in 2 Pet and in the Pastorals. Some who have argued that Matthew or the son of Zebedee were sources of tradition would explain the authorship of the final respective Gospels in this way, but this suggestion is more debatable. (5) In the broader sense, someone could be considered an author if a work was written in the literary tradition for which he was famous. The whole Law (Pentateuch) could be attributed to Moses the lawgiver as author, even though the final writing of parts did not take place until 800 years after his death. The Davidic authorship of the Pss and the Solomonic authorship of the wisdom literature fall into this category. In modern estimation, these last two classifications (4 and 5, which clearly involve pseudonymity) do not meet the standards of authorship; the fourth is an issue of authority; the fifth is an issue of patronage.

(On pseudonymity, see articles in *The Authorship and Integrity of the New Testament* [SPCK Theol. Coll. 4; London, 1965] by K. Aland, 1–13; and D. Guthrie, 14–39. Also Brox, N., *Falsche Verfasserangaben* [SBS 79; Stuttgart, 1975]. Idem (ed.), *Pseudepigraphie in der heidnischen und jüdisch-christlichen Antike* [WF 484; Darmstadt, 1977]. Meade, D. G., *Pseudonymity and Canon* [WUNT 39; Tübingen, 1986]. Metzger, B. M., *New Testament Studies* [NTTS 10; Leiden, 1980] 1–22. Smith, M., *Entretiens* 18 [1971] 191–215.)

90   (II) The Finality of the Canon of Trent. This council was firm about which books, along with their parts, should be accepted as canonical and inspired. But Trent did not say that these were the only inspired books, and the question is sometimes raised whether some lost books may have been inspired, e.g., lost Pauline writings. (For the possible role of chance in the preservation of biblical books, → 54 above.) What judgment about inspiration would the church render if a lost epistle of Paul were to be discovered today? The problem becomes academic when we realize that the criterion for inspiration found applicable at Trent was the long use of the books of Scripture in the church (as evidenced in the Vg). Since a newly discovered book would hardly have been in long use, what could be the church's criterion for determining inspiration? Pauline authorship would really not be sufficient, for if lack of apostolic authorship does not exclude inspiration, the existence of apostolic authorship should not automatically imply it. A less romantic problem is that of the possible inspiration of ancient works considered sacred by NT writers or by the early Fathers but not accepted into the canon of Trent (*1 Enoch, Did.,* etc.). By virtue of not having been accepted at Trent, today these books no longer have a claim to continuous use as Scripture in the church, and almost certainly they will never be recognized as inspired. But they remain important witnesses to God's salvific action in the intertestamental and immediately posttestamental periods.

91   (III) The Vulgate and Canonicity. Trent insisted on its list of books "as sacred and canonical in their entirety, *with all their parts,* according to the text

usually read in the Catholic Church and as they are in the ancient Latin Vulgate" (DS 1504). Among the "parts" mentioned in the discussion were Mark 16:9–20; Luke 22:43–44; John 7:53–8:11 (Jedin, *History of the Council of Trent* 2. 81)—pericopes that are absent from many textual witnesses. Although they used the Vg as a yardstick, the council fathers of Trent and the authorities in Rome who approved the decree were aware that there were errors in the Vg transl. and that not all copies of the Vg were in agreement. Even the official Sixto-Clementine Vg (1592), produced in answer to Trent's request for a carefully edited Vg, leaves much to be desired by modern standards; and in many places it is not faithful to Jerome's original Vg (→ Texts, 68:144–47). Which Vg is to serve as a guide when we raise the question of whether certain passages or verses are canonical Scripture?

Both Jerome's Vg and the Sixto-Clementine Vg contained the long ending of Mark and the pericope of the adulteress (John 7:53–8:11), and Roman Catholic scholars have no real problem in accepting these passages as Scripture (although they were not originally parts of their respective Gospels and were added at a much later period—once again the distinction between canonicity and authorship). But in other instances, where the Sixto-Clementine Vg has passages that Jerome's Vg did not have (John 5:4, the angel stirring the waters; 1 John 5:7–8, the Johannine comma), the problem of acceptance should be settled on the grounds of scholarship rather than by any mechanical application of the principle of Trent, which was not meant to solve all difficulties or to end scholarly discussion. (For a clarification of the authority of the Vg by *DAS,* → Church Pronouncements, 72:20). Roman Catholics must solve textual problems as others do, viz., by the laws of criticism—a principle that holds for other questions too (authorship, dating, history). The church's guidance covers primarily the meaning of Scripture for faith and morals.

92   (IV) The Canon within the Canon. As mentioned above (→ 44–46, 86), the Reformation raised acutely the question of degrees of canonicity. And even when it is agreed which books of Scripture are inspired and canonical, are some more authoritative than others? Obviously some have more value than others and treat more directly of formal religious questions than others do. Obviously, too, some books claim to be more directly from God than others do; e.g., the prophets claim to convey the word of God that came to them, whereas the wisdom writers, although inspired, seem to be giving us the fruit of their own human experience. Finally, the church in her liturgy uses some biblical books extensively and others very seldom, thus forming an "actual canon" within the formal canon.

**93   **This question has become more acute as we have recognized that there are dissimilar outlooks and differing theologies in the books of Scripture. When these differences exist between the two Testaments, one can solve them in terms of new revelation, e.g., Job's formal and explicit denial of an afterlife (14:7–22), contrasted with Jesus' clear affirmation of it (Mark 12:26–27). But, even within the NT, works of roughly the same period contain divergent theologies. The outlook on the law in Rom 10:4 certainly is not the same as the outlook in Matt 5:18. One may explain that there is no *contradiction* between Rom 3:28 ("justified by faith apart from the works of the law") and Jas 2:24 ("justified by works and not by faith alone"); but one can scarcely imagine that Paul's attitude was the same as that of Jas. The thesis that there was a uniform and harmonious development of theological understanding from the time of Pentecost to the end of the apostolic era is not supported by the NT critically read (see R. E. Brown, *New Testament Essays* [NY, 1982] 36–47). But then the question arises: If there are two divergent views in the NT, which one is to be considered authoritative? Within the canon of Scripture and in particular within the NT, what is the canon or rule of what we are to believe?

94   Modern NT scholars have made this a major question. (For some the problem is even more acute since they press divergencies, like the one between Jas and Rom, to the point of contradiction, whereas a Catholic understanding of the inspiration of Scripture would seem to preclude contradictions.) If we focus upon the topic of *early Catholicism* in the NT, we can see the importance of the question of the canon in the canon. "Early Catholicism" designates the initial stages of sacramentalism, hierarchy, ordination, dogma—in short, the beginning of the distinctive features of *Catholic* Christianity. A. von Harnack maintained that in the NT there was no early Catholicism; rather, such theology and church organization were a 2d-cent. development distorting the pristine evangelical character of Christianity (to which the Reformation returned; *What is Christianity?* [orig. 1900; Harper Torchbook ed., NY, 1957] 190ff.). But E. Käsemann (→ NT Criticism, 70:65), a Protestant, recognized that there is "early Catholicism" in the NT itself, particularly in 2 Pet, the Pastorals, and Acts. If so, are these early Catholic developments normative for Christianity? Käsemann's solution was to fall back on the canon within the canon, or "the center of the NT." Just as Paul distinguished between the letter and the Spirit (2 Cor 3), so the Christian cannot make an infallible authority out of the canonical NT but must distinguish the real Spirit within the NT. For Käsemann this is not found in such Deutero-Pauline writings as the Pastorals with their early Catholicism, but in the Great Letters such as Gal and Rom with their spirit of justification by faith. There is the really authoritative teaching.

95   A Roman Catholic answer was given by H. Küng (*Structures of the Church* [NY, 1964] 151–69); he accused Käsemann of judging canonicity on the basis of an a priori Protestant bias. Küng reasoned that, if there is early Catholicism in the NT, then only Catholics can accept the whole NT. The theory of a canon within the canon means an implicit rejection of some books. The answer may not be so simple, however; and later in his career Küng would probably have been more nuanced. All we shall attempt to do here is to make some observations. If Roman Catholics accept the "early Catholic" developments in the later NT books and regard them as normative for Christianity, are they not to some extent establishing a canon within a canon; for are they not implicitly rejecting the looser church organization of the primitive period and the less dogmatic theology of the earlier days? In other words, to Käsemann's reduced canon, which depends heavily on the more pristine NT works, does one oppose a canon consisting of the more developed NT works?

Perhaps we are approaching the problem in the wrong terms when we speak of preferring later books to earlier books. If some features of early Catholicism, prominent in the later books of the NT, have become characteristic of the Roman Catholic Church, it was not because the church consciously preferred one group of NT books over the other. Rather it was because features such as sacramentalism, hierarchy, and dogma were meaningful within the life of the church. In a process of development, the church made these features a part of herself, so that what was truly normative was not a group of writings but the Spirit acting within the living church. It was church usage that led Trent to determine which books should be accepted as canonical; so also it is church usage that determines the degree of normative authority (canonicity) to be attributed to a NT practice or doctrine.

96   Yet we must qualify this understanding of church usage as a normative factor. If the Spirit of God has guided the church in her usage, there has been also a human factor in the historical process of Christian development, so that we cannot simply equate church usage with the will of God. Scripture can be a great help in distinguishing between what is of the Spirit and what is human in the development of church usage. Thus we get a two-sided picture: church usage is a guide to what is normative in Scripture; yet in a way the church itself stands under the judgment of Scripture ("This teaching office [of the church] is not above the word of God, but serves it" [Vatican II, *Dei Verbum* 2:10]). In particular, the church must constantly reassess her usage in light of those biblical theologies that she has *not* followed in order to be certain that what God meant to teach her through such theological views will not be lost. For example, if the church has chosen to follow as normative the ecclesiastical structure attested in the Pastorals (bishop/presbyters, deacons), she must ask herself does she continue to do proportionate justice to the charismatic and freer spirit of the earlier period. A choice between the two was necessary, and in our faith this choice was guided by the Spirit of God; but the structure that was not chosen still has something to teach the church and can serve as a modifying corrective of the choice that was made. Only thus is the church faithful to the whole NT. In NT times the church was ecumenical enough to embrace those who, while sharing the one faith, held very different theological views.

97   The recognition that in practice the church does not accept the whole NT as equally normative is related to the problem of distinguishing between the temporal limitations of the biblical writers and the divine revelation they were conveying. The biblical writers spoke as people of their times, and not all their religious statements have enduring value. For instance, the reader of the Bible must exercise discretion about apocalyptic statements. If the NT writers describe the future coming of the Lord in terms of trumpet blasts and celestial cataclysms, such descriptions do not necessarily constitute revelation to be believed. The problem of distinguishing between what is revelation and what is not becomes acute for delicate topics. In the matter of "original sin," how much revelation and how much time-conditioned 1st-cent. outlook do we find in Paul's picture (Rom 5) of an individual Adam who committed a sin that brought death to all? Careful exegesis can uncover what Paul thought; but only the church, guided by and guiding scholarly investigation, can tell us how much of Paul's thought is God's revelation for his people.

Perhaps a word of caution is called for here. The realization that there is much in Scripture that reflects the time-conditioned mentality of its authors should not lead readers to assume that they can quickly or easily recognize this mentality. Often there is the tendency to think that whatever in the Bible does not agree with the spirit of modern times can be dismissed as time-conditioned and irrelevant. For instance, some would do away with all divine moral imperatives on the principle that God's ethical commands in the Bible reflect the customs of the times. Such generalizations are more often based on inclination than on careful exegesis and have the effect of stripping Scripture of its corrective value. A good practical rule for avoiding self-deception in this matter is to pay more attention to Scripture when it disagrees with what we want to hear than when it agrees. When the Bible disagrees with the spirit of our times, it is not always because the biblical authors are giving voice to a limited, out-of-date religious view; frequently it is because God's ways are not our ways.

(On early Catholicism and the canon within the canon, see Best, E. J., *BJRL* 61 [1978-79] 258-89. Elliott, J. K., *Una Sancta* 23 [1966] 3-18. Harrington, D. J., in *The Word in the World* [Fest. F. L. Moriarty; ed. R. J. Clifford and G. W. MacRae; Cambridge MA, 1973] 97-113. Käsemann, E., *ENTT* 95-107. Marxsen, W., *Der Frühkatholizismus in Neuen Testament* [Neukirchen, 1958].)

98 **(V) Recent Reactions to the Canon.** In the last quarter of the 20th cent., there was much scholarly discussion of the canon, sometimes supporting it, sometimes undermining it. B. S. Childs and others, by developing a theory of canonical criticism (→ Hermeneutics, 71:71-74), emphasized the importance of the canon in a unique way. Against an exaggerated source criticism, they insisted that the final form of a biblical book is what we possess and a far more reliable subject of study than disputably reconstructed antecedents. Moreover, even an individual book was not really biblical until it was made part of a Bible in general and an OT or a NT canon in particular. The tendency to treat passages or books in isolation neglects the context of the canonizing community (Israel and the church), which listened to the different theological voices of the authors not in isolation but in constructive tension. In the NT, for instance, the church did not accept the Johannine preexistent Word without the modification of a Marcan Jesus who did not know things and who objected to being called "good" because that was a term that applied to God alone (Mark 10:17-18). This canonical approach was helpful overall, although, in the judgment of many, Childs himself overstated its value by neglecting the considerable theological results obtained by historical analysis.

99 On the opposite end of the scholarly spectrum there were serious challenges to the validity of the NT canon in particular. One type of challenge came from a use of the canonical writings to reconstruct an earlier style of Christianity judged preferable to that reflected in the canonical writings themselves, so that the NT writings might be seen as distorting an earlier (and better) Christianity. The following are some examples of theories that had the effect (not necessarily the intention) of moving in that direction: G. Theissen (*The Social Setting of Pauline Christianity* [Phl, 1982]) argued that,

because the ethical radicalism of Jesus did not serve the organized Pauline congregations, Paul suppressed that radicalism by not quoting Jesus' words. W. Kelber (*The Oral and the Written Gospel* [Phl, 1983]) proposed that Mark's written Gospel narrowed the much wider range of oral presentation about Jesus and indeed discredited the most plausible tradents of the Gospel oral tradition, i.e., the disciples and the family, including Jesus' mother. For L. Schottroff (*EvT* 38 [1978] 298-313) the pre-Lucan Magnificat and Beatitudes represented a theology in which the rich were truly cast down, and Jesus functioned as a would-be destroyer of the existing social order, radically reversing the inequities of wealth and power. Luke spiritualized all this.

100 Another type of challenge to the canon came from an appeal to the apocryphal gospels as a witness to a Christianity that antedated in time or spirit what is found in the canonical writings. H. Koester, followed by J. D. Crossan (*Four Other Gospels* [Minneapolis, 1985]), suggested that works like *Secret Mark* and *Gos. Thom.* belong to so early a stage in the development of gospel literature that in whole or in part they antedated the canonical Gospels. Since the Apocrypha sometimes show little interest in the death and resurrection of Jesus or in the role of the Twelve, but much interest in the fantastically marvelous, their claimed anteriority has been used to reconstruct a primitive Christianity with a theology and ecclesiology very different from that of much of the NT. Thus they have been used adventurously to support themes of proto-Christian egalitarianism, socialism, and feminism.

101 The challenges to the canon described above (→ 99, 100) cannot be dismissed without technical discussion of the evidence that purportedly justifies the proposals. The sensationalism that has surrounded the claims about an earlier and better Christianity has at times made a critical judgment difficult, for those who judge unfavorably can be dismissed as reactionary supporters of traditional theology or ecclesiology. Actually there is as much prejudice in the quest for the novel as there is in an instinctive distrust of the novel. More important, both canonical criticism and the contemporary challenge to the canon have had the effect of underlining an intimate relationship between canon and church. The church that formed the canon is responsible for the canon: change the canon and one is well on the way toward a different church and even a different Christianity and/or Judaism. The issue of the canon has moved from the erudite periphery to the center of scriptural relevance. (See R. E. Brown, *NTS* 33 [1987] 321-43; P. Perkins, *ProcCTSA* 40 [1985] 36-53.)

67

APOCRYPHA; DEAD SEA SCROLLS; OTHER JEWISH LITERATURE

Raymond E. Brown, S.S.　　*Pheme Perkins*
Anthony J. Saldarini *

* Sections 57–61, 64–71, 73–77 of this article are by P. Perkins; sections 124–143 are by A. J. Saldarini; the remainder is by R. E. Brown.

APOCRYPHA

BIBLIOGRAPHY

2   **Jewish Apocrypha:** COLLECTED TRANSLATIONS: *AOT; APOT;* JSHRZ; *OTP*. Riessler, P., *Altjüdisches Schriftum ausserhalb der Bibel* (2d ed.; Heidelberg, 1966). Sacchi, P., *Apocrifi dell Antico Testamento* (Turin, 1981). STUDIES: Bartlett, J. R., *Jews in the Hellenistic World: Josephus, Aristeas, The Sibylline Oracles* (Cambridge, 1985). Caquot, A. et al., *La littérature intertestamentaire* (Paris, 1985). Charlesworth, J. H., *The Pseudepigrapha and Modern Research* (with suppl.; Chico, 1981); *Pseudepigrapha Prolegomena* (SNTSMS 54; Cambridge, 1985). Collins, J. J., *The Apocalyptic Imagination* (NY, 1984). De Jonge, M., *Outside the Old Testament* (Cambridge, 1985). Delling, G. (ed.), *Bibliographie zur jüdisch-hellenistischen und intertestamentarisch Literatur 1900–1970* (TU 106; 2d ed.; Berlin, 1975). Denis, A. M., *Fragmenta Pseudepigraphorum quae supersunt Graeca* (PVTG 3; Leiden, 1970); *Introduction aux pseudépigraphes grecs de l'Ancien Testament* (SVTP 1; Leiden, 1970). *EJMI* 239–436. Harrington, D. J., "Research on the Jewish Pseudepigrapha during the 1970s," *CBQ* 42 (1980) 147–59. Leaney, A. R. C., *The Jewish and Christian World 200 BC to AD 200* (Cambridge, 1984). Nickelsburg, G. W. E., *Jewish Literature Between the Bible and the Mishnah* (Phl, 1981). Rost, L., *Judaism Outside the Hebrew Canon* (Nash, 1976). Rowley, H. H., *The Relevance of Apocalyptic* (3d ed.; London, 1963). Schürer,

HJPAJC 3.1/2. Stone, M. E. (ed.), *Jewish Writings of the Second Temple Period* (CRINT 2; Phl, 1984).
3   **Christian Apocrypha.** Barnstone, W., *The Other Bible* (SF, 1984). Beyschlag, K., *Die Verborgene Überlieferung von Christus* (Munich, 1969). Cameron, R., *The Other Gospels* (Phl, 1982). Charlesworth, J. H. (ed.), *The New Testament Apocrypha and Pseudepigrapha* [Bibliography] (Metuchen, 1987). Crossan, J. D., *Four Other Gospels* (Minneapolis, 1985). De Santos Otero, A., *Los Evangelios Apocrifos* (Madrid, 1984). Erbetta, M. (ed.), *Gli Apocrifi del Nuovo Testamento* (4 vols.; Turin, 1966–81). Finegan, J., *Hidden Records of the Life of Jesus* (Phl, 1969). Funk, R., *New Gospel Parallels* (Phl, 1985). Grossi, V. (ed.), *Gli Apocrifi cristiani e cristianizzati* (Augustinianum 23.1–2; Rome, 1983). *HSNTA*. James, M. R., *The Apocryphal New Testament* (Oxford, 1924). Jeremias, J., *Unknown Sayings of Jesus* (2d ed.; London, 1964). Junod, E., "Apocryphes du NT . . ." *ETR* 58 (1983) 409–21 with bibliog. Koester, H., "Apocryphal and Canonical Gospels," *HTR* 73 (1980) 105–30. Quéré, F., *Évangiles Apocryphes* (Paris, 1983). Resch, A., *Agrapha* (TU 15.3–4; 2d ed.; Leipzig, 1906). Robinson, *NHLE*. For the series CC Apocryphorum, see J.-D. Dubois, *Second Century* 4 (1984) 29–36. For the gnostic apocrypha, → Early Church, 80:4.

JEWISH APOCRYPHA

4   **(I) The Term "Apocrypha."** The rabbis knew of "Outside Books" (*ḥiṣônîm*), i.e., books outside the sacred collection and used by heretics and Samaritans. However, the term "apocrypha" that has come to designate the books being discussed here, derives from the Gk *apokryphos,* "hidden." Originally, the import of the term may have been complimentary in that the term was applied to sacred books whose contents were too exalted to be made available to the general public. In Dan 12:9–10 we hear of words that are shut up until the end of time—words that the wise shall understand and the wicked shall not. In addition, 4 Ezra 14:44ff. mentions 94 books, of which 24 (the OT) were to be published and 70 were to be delivered only to the wise among the people (= apocrypha). Gradually, the term "apocrypha" took on a pejorative connotation, for the orthodoxy of these hidden books was often questionable. Origen (*Comm. in Matt.* 10.18; PG 13. 881) distinguished between books that were to be read in public worship and apocryphal books. Because these secret books were often preserved or even composed in heretical circles, several Church Fathers came to use the term "apocryphal" for heretical works forbidden to be read. By Jerome's time (*ca.* 400), "apocryphal" had taken on the more neutral connotation of noncanonical, and that is how we use it here.

5   In Protestant parlance, "the Apocrypha" are 15 works, all but one of which are Jewish in origin and found in the LXX (parts of 2 Esdr are Christian and Latin in origin). Although some of them were composed in Palestine in Aramaic or Hebrew, they were not accepted by the more exclusive Jewish canon of the late 2d cent. AD (→ Canonicity, 66:31–35). The Reformers, influenced by the Jewish canon, did not consider these books on a par with the rest of the OT Scriptures; thus the custom arose of making the Apocrypha a separate section in the Protestant Bible, or sometimes even of omitting them entirely (→ Canonicity, 66:44–46). The Catholic view, expressed as a doctrine of faith at the

Council of Trent, is that 12 of these 15 works (in a different enumeration, however) are canonical Scripture; they are called the deuterocanonical books (→ Canonicity, 66:10, 20, 42–43). The three books of the Protestant Apocrypha that are not accepted by Catholics are 1–2 Esdras and the Prayer of Manasseh.

6   In Catholic parlance, the term "apocrypha" has come to designate ancient Jewish or Christian books from the biblical period (or pretending to be from the biblical period) that have not been accepted as genuine Scripture by the church. Recent discoveries of hitherto lost ancient books have greatly extended the range covered by the term. If the books that Catholics call deuterocanonical are called the Apocrypha by Protestants, the apocrypha (at least those of Jewish origin) of which we now speak are often called pseudepigrapha by Protestants, whence the title of R. H. Charles's famous collection, *The Apocrypha and Pseudepigrapha of the Old Testament* (= *APOT;* for pseudepigraphy or pseudonymity, → Canonicity, 66:88–89). Actually, neither designation for these noncanonical Jewish works is completely satisfactory. The term "apocrypha" suggests that they deal with secrets or matters esoteric, whereas several of them are relatively unpretentious history (1 Esdr); "pseudepigrapha" is applicable only to the books that falsely present themselves as having been written by a well-known ancient figure, e.g., the Enoch and Baruch literature. However, for want of a better term, we shall henceforth use the term "apocrypha" in the sense common among Catholics. The deuterocanonical books are, of course, commented on among the other books of Scripture (in particular → Daniel, 25:8,35–38; → 1–2 Maccabees, 26:3; → Sirach, 32:6; → Tobit, 38:5, 26,50).

7   **(II) The Enoch Literature.** Enoch ("Henoch" in the *AV*) was the father of Methuselah: "Enoch walked with God; and then he was no longer, for God took him" (Gen 5:24). The idea that Enoch had been taken to heaven (also Sir 44:16; 49:14) produced much

legend about him, and his life-span of 365 years provoked astronomical speculations. (See H. Odeberg,
TDNT 2. 556–59.) Whether the biblical account is the
source or the digest of an exuberant legend is not clear.
Besides what follows, see *Jub.* 4:17–25; 7:38; 10:17;
19:24–27; 21:10; and P. Grelot, *RevScRel* 46 (1958) 5–26,
181–210.

8   (A) Slavonic and Hebrew Books. Of
three Enochic books, the first two below are of lesser
importance and less certainly of the biblical period.

(a) SLAVONIC ENOCH OR 2 ENOCH. Also
called *The Book of the Secrets of Enoch.* Preserved in 14th-
to 17th-cent. Slavonic copies, there are two versions, of
which the shorter is on the whole more original, having
been translated from (lost, semitized, original?) Greek. In
this apocalyptic work with testamentlike elements (→ 25
below), Enoch ascends to the seventh heaven (seeing
paradise and hell on the way), becomes an angel,
epitomizes 366 heavenly books, and then returns to earth
to give ethical instruction to his children and others. In
33:1–2 a duration of seven millennia is given to world
history, with the eighth as the end. In chap. 71 Enoch's
priestly descendant Melchisedek, conceived without
earthly father, is born from his dead mother's body.
2 Enoch came from sectarian circles of the early centuries
AD who, whether Jewish or not, made use of the Enoch
legend. The lack of witnesses before the 14th cent. is
puzzling. Proposals for a late date and dependence on
Zoroastrianism or Christianity (Heb 7) are declining; see
A. Rubenstein, *JJS* 13 (1967) 1–21. A. Vaillant edited the
Slavonic with a French transl. (Paris, 1952); Eng transls.
can be found in *APOT* 2 (Forbes); *AOT* (Pennington);
and *OTP* 1 (Andersen—the best).

(b) HEBREW ENOCH OR 3 ENOCH. *Sepher ha-
Hekhaloth.* An account of how the Palestinian Rabbi
Ishmael (d. AD 132) ascended into the seventh heaven,
saw the celestial palaces (*hêkalôt*), and learned from
Meṭaṭron (supreme archangel, Yahweh's vice-regent,
who is also Enoch). In 1928 H. Odeberg published the
Hebr text and transl., dating *3 Enoch* to the 3d cent. AD;
but J. T. Milik (1976) opts for 10th cent. G. G. Scholem
in *Major Trends in Jewish Mysticism* (NY, 1941) suggests
5th–6th cent.; P. Alexander agrees in a major study
(*OTP* 1).

9   (B) Ethiopic Enoch or 1 Enoch. Often
simply *Enoch* without further specification.

(a) HISTORY AND TEXT. Miscellaneous Enoch
material (mostly in Aramaic) circulated among Jews until
the 2d cent. AD, when the failure of successive revolutionary movements caused the rabbis to distrust extravagant apocalyptic hopes for the future. Consequently,
1 Enoch fell out of favor in Judaism, and the original text
disappeared. In Greek, *1 Enoch* influenced early Christian works (Jude, *Barnabas,* Irenaeus); but although
Tertullian regarded it as Scripture, Hilary, Augustine, and
Jerome did not. The Gk version also disappeared (leaving only abstracts by George Syncellus, the Byzantine
chronicler), but between 350 and 650 Gk *1 Enoch* was
translated for Ethiopian church usage. Not until 1773,
when James Bruce brought the Eth version to Europe,
did the West see *1 Enoch* (1st ed. 1821). The Ethiopic (in
two recensions) is still the most complete; but now
available are Gk fragments of 33 percent of *1 Enoch*
(1–32; 97–107), a Lat fragment of 106, and Aram
fragments of 5 percent from 11 Qumran mss. Major
studies with Eng transl. by M. A. Knibb (from one Eth
ms.; 2 vols.; Oxford, 1978) and esp. by M. Black (from
critically modified Ethiopic; SVTP 7; Leiden, 1985). See
also *APOT* 2 (Charles); *AOT* (Knibb); *OTP* 1 (Isaac).

10   (b) CONTENTS AND DATING. The material
collected in *1 Enoch* is of varying antiquity and origin. As

preserved in Ethiopic, the book can conveniently be
divided into five sections:

Section One (chaps. 1–36). Called by Syncellus "The
Book of the Watchers." Five fragmentary mss. at Qumran
(the oldest paleographically dated to 200–150 BC); probably composed in the 3d cent. BC. *Contents:* Chaps. 1–5:
introductory vision of final judgment. Chaps. 6–16: corruption of humans by the "Watchers" (Dan 4:13) or fallen
angels—composite, once independent, may antedate
final redaction of Gen 6:1–4. Chaps. 17–36: angel-
guided cosmic tours for Enoch showing Sheol, the
Garden of Righteousness, and astronomical phenomena.
See L. Hartman, *Asking for a Meaning: A Study of 1 Enoch
1–5* (ConBNT 12; Lund, 1979); C. A. Newsom, *CBQ* 42
(1980) 310–29.

Section Two (chaps. 37–71). "The Book of Parables or
Similitudes"—elaborate discourses containing visions,
prophecies, and poems that inform Enoch about heavenly realities. No mss. at Qumran; never cited by the
Fathers; no proof of existence before the Ethiopic—
whence the theory of some that this is a Christian addition to *1 Enoch.* Date: Milik suggests AD 270 and
dependence on the *Sibylline Oracles;* but Charles and
Stone argue for the 1st cent. BC; and Black, Collins,
Knibb, Nickelsburg, and Suter for the 1st cent. AD. A
thesis of Jewish origin (Black: in Hebrew) seems to be
gaining ascendancy. *Contents:* First Parable (chaps.
38–44): the coming judgment and some astronomical
secrets, including an equal role for sun and moon in chap.
41 (a factor that could have offended Qumranian
preference for the sun). Second Parable (chaps. 45–57):
the Head of Days and the preexistent Son of Man (→ 15
below). Third Parable (chaps. 58–69): the blessedness of
the saints and judgment by the Elect One. See J. C.
Greenfield and M. E. Stone, *HTR* 70 (1977) 51–65; M.
Delcor, *EstBib* 38 (1978–80) 5–33; D. W. Suter, *Tradition
and Composition in the Parables of Enoch* (SBLDS 47;
Missoula, 1979).

Section Three (chaps. 72–82). "The Astronomical
Book of the Heavenly Luminaries." Four fragmentary
mss. at Qumran (oldest dated paleographically from *ca.*
200 BC) are from a longer account than that preserved in
Ethiopic, probably composed in 3d cent., thus constituting the oldest surviving Enoch material. Chapter 80
predicts disorder of the heavenly bodies at judgment; 82
has a solar calendar similar to that of *Jub.* (→ 18 below)
and Qumran.

Section Four (chaps. 83–90). "The Book of Dreams."
Four fragmentary mss. at Qumran (oldest dated
paleographically to *ca.* 125 BC); perhaps composed before
Judas Maccabeus's death in 161 BC (90:6–15; see 2 Macc
11:1–12). *Contents:* First dream vision (chaps. 83–84)
about the deluge that will punish the world. Second
dream vision (chaps. 85–90) with an animal allegory
covering history from creation to the endtime—it refers
to the New House of Jerusalem replacing the Old
(90:28–29) and to a final white bull (Messiah? Second
Adam?) and a horned buffalo or wild ox who is first
among all (90:38).

Section Five (chaps. 91–108). "The Epistle of Enoch"
is composite. Two fragmentary mss. at Qumran of 100
BC and 50 BC, the latter with a text longer than the
Ethiopic, confirming Charles's guess that the Apocalypse of Weeks needs reordering (91:11–17 after
93:1–10). Although Milik would date the Apocalypse to
ca. 100 BC, a reference in *Jub.* suggests 200–175 BC (Black,
Collins, Nickelsburg)—perhaps once independent, now
amid later material. The earlier Qumran ms. covers part
of chaps. 104–7 including the birth of Noah—perhaps
the original conclusion, since there is no trace of 108 in

Greek or Aramaic. See F. Dexinger, *Henochs Zehnwochen-apokalypse* (SPB 29; Leiden, 1977); M. Black, *VT* 28 (1978) 464–69; G. W. E. Nickelsburg, *JJS* 33 (1982) 333–48; J. C. VanderKam, *CBQ* 46 (1984) 511–23.

11   There are also Qumran fragments of "The Book of the Giants" (offspring of the Watchers), which Milik thinks was originally one of the five books (the Enoch Pentateuch). He suggests that, having been replaced in the Greek and the Ethiopic by the (Christian) "Book of Parables," the "Giants" section was preserved only among the Manicheans. This thesis has been widely criticized—joined to the other Enoch material, "Giants" was not clearly a separate book at Qumran. The five-book structure may have come only in the Gk transl., which involved abridgment and selection.

12   (c) ANALYSIS. Eth *Enoch* (drawn from Greek) collects Jewish Enochic material that had existed in Aramaic (and Hebrew?) in other combinations and forms, composed between 300 BC and AD 70. Although parts of it later passed through Qumranian and Christian redactions, earlier sections took shape before the sectarian Jewish divisions of the 2d cent. BC. (Parallel here is the apocalyptic Daniel tradition, originally larger than biblical Dan and roughly contemporary with Enoch literature.) Other parts of the Enoch legend, in combination with or independent of elements in *1 Enoch,* are reflected in *2 Enoch* and *3 Enoch* and in Manichean writing. Ideas from it (the descent of a revealer from heaven) may resemble or be reflected in Christianity, *Poimandres,* the Prometheus myth, and gnostic writing, sometimes in combination with personified Wisdom motifs (→ Wisdom Lit., 27:15–17). The Watchers' rebellion against God and the sin it produced (a story once independent of Enoch) is a paradigm for rebellion diagnosed by the authors in their time. The deluge (whence the abundant Noah sections) and the future last judgment are twin events. The detailed celestial descriptions function religiously by portraying places of eternal bliss and punishment as part of the fixed order. The knowledge revealed to the righteous Enoch, who ascends to heavenly status, is in contrast to wicked knowledge imparted by angels who wrongly descended to earthly status. The righteous on earth who accept Enoch's revelation are a remnant within Judaism; prominent among the wicked are the kings of this earth (Hellenistic and, later, Roman).

13   (d) IMPORTANT TEACHING. *1 Enoch* is probably the most important of the pseudepigrapha for understanding ideas in the NT. Yet the composite nature of the literature means that theological positions in different "Books" of *1 Enoch* are not always consistent. Afterlife pictures allow *both* a begetting of children and a becoming like angels (10:17; 51:4; cf. Mark 12:18–27). There are four different fates for varying degrees of sanctity and sin (22:9–14), which imply survival of the spirit until judgment, plus an anticipation of resurrection from the dead. Unlike Sir 24:14, in *1 Enoch* 42 there is no place on earth where Wisdom can dwell, so she returns to a dwelling in heaven—this gives revelation to Enoch a status over the Law.

14   ANGELOLOGY. In 54:6 Satan is the one to whom the wicked angels are subject, but more than one angel acts as a satan (pl. 40:7) or chief adversary. Gadreel led Eve astray (69:6); Semhazah is the leader of the Watchers (6:3) who had sex with women and begot the evil giants, while Asael (8:1) revealed forbidden mysteries (*CBQ* 20 [1958] 427–33) to men, who used the resultant weapons for war, and to women, who used jewels and cosmetics to seduce. (These are variant forms of the "original" sin.) The powerful evil forces are counteracted by a myriad of named angels and, above all, by arch-

angels. Besides the three "biblical" archangels—Gabriel and Michael of Dan 8:16; 10:13; Raphael of Tob—Uriel is the heavenly tour guide of Section Three, while Phanuel (Section Two only) has the fourth spot in 54:6. They, rather than God (Gen 6:5), detect evil on earth. Interceding with the Lord of Lords, they are told in 9–10 to bind Asael into a dark pit and pass judgment on Semhazah and the giants, destroying all wrong from earth (C. Kaplan, *ATR* 12 [1930] 423–37).

15   SON OF MAN. In Dan 7:13–14 a "son of man" (human or angel?), representing the saintly people of Israel, is presented on clouds to the Ancient of Days to receive dominion and kingdom. In *1 Enoch* (Section Two) "the Son of Man" is identified with the Elect and Righteous One (= Servant of Isa 42:1; 53:11), the Lord's Anointed (Messiah, 48:10; 52:4), who receives the spirit of wisdom (cf. Isa 11). (The NT also amalgamates expected figures.) Three different Ethiopic expression in *1 Enoch* are translated "Son of Man." In 71:14 Enoch is addressed by this title, while in 48:2–4 the Son of Man is named before creation and is the light of the nations. He is the supreme judge (61:8), destroying the wicked and ruling over all (62:1–6), banqueting with the righteous on the last day (62:13–14). Such diverse views may represent a development where Enoch becomes an angel and the embodiment of God's wisdom. The disputed dating of Section Two leaves uncertainty whether this is a pre-NT view (and so possibly known to Jesus or the evangelists). See J. Coppens, *Le Fils d'homme vétero- et intertestamentaire* (BETL 61; Louvain, 1983); also M. Black, *ExpTim* 88 (1976) 5–8; P. Grelot, *Sem* 28 (1978) 59–83.

(Barr, J., "Aramaic-Greek Notes on the Book of Enoch," *JSS* 23 [1978] 184–98; 24 [1979] 179–92. Black, M., *Apocalypsis Henochi Graece* [Leiden, 1970]. Milik, J. T., *The Books of Enoch, Aramaic Fragments of Qumrân Cave 4* [Oxford, 1976]. Nickelsburg, G. W. E., "The Books of Enoch in Recent Research," *RelSRev* 7 [1981] 210–17. VanderKam, J., *Enoch and the Growth of Apocalyptic Tradition* [CBQMS 16; Washington, 1984].)

16   **(III) Book of Jubilees.** Called "the Book of Divisions of Time into their Jubilees and Weeks" by CD 16:3–4 and also *Little Genesis,* it may be the same as *The Apocalypse of Moses* and (in part) *The Testament of Moses.* Although it presents itself as dictated to Moses on Sinai by an angel of the presence, *Jub.* is really a rewriting of the story in Gen 1 to Exod 14. At times it copies literally, and elsewhere it both omits offensive sections (Jacob's lie that he was Esau) and expands midrashically, incorporating legal ordinances, popular traditions, and apocalyptic. Speakers in the book express the author's viewpoint.

17   **(A) Text, Date, Origin.** The book was originally composed in Hebrew (not Aramaic). There were fragments of a Hebr ms. at Masada (→ 123 below) and of 11 Hebr mss. among the QL (covering chaps. 4,5,12,23,27,35,46; see J. VanderKam, *Textual and Historical Studies in the Book of Jubilees* [Missoula, 1977] 18–91). *Jub.* was translated into Greek (before AD 220, but only patristic citations remain) and Syriac (*ca.* 500). From the Greek a transl. was made into Latin (about one-fourth of the book; 5th cent.?) and into Ethiopic (about 500). Only the latter preserves the entire book and, as we now know, with reasonable accuracy. The Ethiopic was edited by Charles with all the then available evidence (Oxford, 1885; commentary, 1902). His Eng transl. appears in *APOT* 2 (revised by C. Rabin in *AOT*); now see that of O. J. Wintermute in *OTP* 2.

The oldest Qumran copies of *Jub.* are dated paleographically by F. M. Cross to *ca.* 100 BC, and the biblical citations in *Jub.* represent non-MT forms of the Hebrew

Bible—a status consonant with 2d-cent. BC Palestine. Apparently *Jub.* was written after the early astronomical parts of *1 Enoch* (see 4:17) but before parts of the QL, for it was known to the authors of CD, 1QapGen, and 11QPs³. A strong opposition to the pressures of Hellenization (see below) is combined curiously with no specific reference to desecration by Antiochus Epiphanes (→ History, 75:133) or to a break from the rest of Israel. This fits 176-168 BC as the date of composition (Albright, Nickelsburg), but VanderKam (followed by Wintermute) opts for 161-140, seeing references to Judas Maccabeus's victories in *Jub.* 34; 38. The author (who drew upon older traditions) probably belonged to the Hasidim or "pious ones" described in 1 Macc 2:29-42, of whom one strain constituted the immediate ancestry of the Qumran Essene movement, while another eventually flowed into the Pharisee movement.

18   (B) Basic Theme. The most notable characteristic of *Jub.* is a calendric interest. The book divides the history of the world from the creation to the time of the Sinai covenant into 49 periods of 49 years (a jubilee is 49 years, whence the name), enlarging and embellishing the narrative of Gen within that calendric framework. The basic annual calendar supposed by *Jub.* is a solar calendar of 364 days (6:32—12 months of 30 days each, and 4 intercalary days). This is a fixed calendar rooted in the order of creation revealed to Enoch (4:17; *1 Enoch* 72:1, by Uriel), where every year and every week begin on Wednesday, and the same dates fall on the same weekday every year.

A. Jaubert (*The Date of the Last Supper* [NY, 1965]) has argued that this solar calendar was an ancient one, apparently used by the latest redactors of the Pentateuch, by Ezekiel, and by the Chronicler. Perhaps originally from Egypt, the solar calendar may have been the pre-exilic religious calendar, remaining in use in the Temple until Hellenistic times. (However, in postexilic civil life the solar calendar was replaced by a lunar calendar of Babylonian origin.) During the Maccabean period, the pro-Hellenistic party tried to replace the solar calendar in Temple worship; Dan 7:25 refers to the attempt of Antiochus Epiphanes to change "times" and the law *ca.* 170—the composition period of *Jub.* Despite their firm opposition to the Hellenists, upon acceding to the high priesthood (152), the Maccabees seemed to have retained the newly introduced lunar calendar. Like *Jub.* the Qumran (Essene) community, which seceded from the Maccabean movement *ca.* 150 (→ 99 below), strongly defended the solar calendar.

**19   ** *Jub.* shows contempt for the Hellenistic innovations of the early 2d cent. BC by insisting on the sabbath observance (2:17ff.), the dietary laws (6:7ff.; 7:31ff.), and circumcision (15:25ff.); also by attacking idolatry (20:7ff.), marriage with foreigners (30:7-23), and nudity as practiced by the Greeks in athletic contests (3:31)—all burning issues provoking the Maccabean reform. The stress on brotherly love is impressive (36:4: "Love one another; love your brother as a man loves his own soul"), but this is love strictly within Judaism—the impure Gentiles are to be avoided (22:16).

**20   ** The basic style of the book is midrashic, i.e., embellishing the biblical account with traditional lore and legends (e.g., Jacob slew Esau, 38:2) and infusing it with the spirit of the Judaism of the author's time. (For a similar midrashic work on Deut, see DJD 1. 91-97.) Some material in *Jub.* that has no biblical antecedent may draw on lost historical tradition. Albright (*FSAC* 277) suggests that the account of the wars of the Amorite kings against Jacob in *Jub.* 34 reflects the Hebr conquest of north-central Palestine, not described in Josh.

21   (C) Important Teaching. Like Qumran,

which had priestly origins, *Jub.* gives great attention to the PRIESTLY TRIBE OF LEVI. *Jub.* 31:15 promises that the children of Levi "shall be judges and princes and chiefs of all the descendants of the sons of Jacob." The claim to civil as well as religious power reflects the situation in the late postexilic period when the high priest was effectively the ruler of Israel (although under the Maccabees and the Hasmoneans such regal power became more explicit). There is no reference in *Jub.*, however, to a priestly messiah; the sole reference to a messianic figure is to a prince descended from Judah (31:18). *Jub.* puts more emphasis on salvation through observance of the law (23:26-29) than on a messianic deliverer.

**22   ** The ANGELOLOGY is not so prominent as that of *1 Enoch*(→ 14 above). The personal names of angels are not given, but several classes are distinguished. There are two superior classes: angels of the presence and angels of sanctification; there is also an inferior class set over the forces of nature (2:2; 15:27). As in Dan and *1 Enoch* there are Watchers (both good and bad, 4:15,22). *Jub.* 35:17 mentions that Jacob had an angel guardian. As in *1 Enoch,* the bad angels fornicated with women (4:22ff.), and evil on earth is traced to that sin. Mastema (Satan) is the ruler of an organized kingdom of evil angels (10:8-9). Spirits rule the nations and lead them astray, but God alone rules Israel (15:31-32).

**23   ** As for LIFE AFTER DEATH, it is not the resurrection of the body but the immortality of the soul that is stressed (23:31): "Their bones will rest in the earth, but their spirits will have much joy." This is our earliest attestation in Palestine of the idea of an afterlife "immortality," a concept that Wis 2:23ff. shows to have circulated among contemporary Alexandrian Jews.

**24   ** If rabbinic Judaism maintains both a written law (Pentateuch) and an oral law (eventually the Mishna), the law in *Jub.* is looked upon as eternal, written on heavenly tablets (1:29; 3:31; 6:17). The sabbath (and seemingly circumcision too!) has been binding on the angels since creation (2:18-21; 15:26-28). Revelation consists merely in making known the law which is eternal truth. *Jub.* itself contains this perfect and complete law (33:16). However, the author of *Jub.* enunciates individual laws different from those of the Pentateuch (and those of the Mishna). For instance, concerning punishment for killing, the age of marriage, and nudity, *Jub.* reflects a more stringent legal spirit comparable to that of Qumran. In C. Rabin, *The Zadokite Documents* (2d ed.; Oxford, 1958) 85-86, we find an impressive list of parallels between *Jub.* and Qumran CD.

(Berger, K., *Das Buch der Jubiläen* [Gütersloh, 1981]. Davenport, G. L., *The Eschatology of the Book of Jubilees* [SPB 20; Leiden, 1971]. Denis, A. M. and Y. Janssens, *Concordance Latine du Liber Jubilaeorum* [Louvain, 1973]. Endres, J., *Biblical Interpretation in the Book of Jubilees* [CBQMS 18; Washington, 1981]. Testuz, M., *Les idées religieuses du livre des Jubilés* [Geneva, 1960]. VanderKam, J., "Enoch Traditions in Jubilees . . . ," SBLASP [1978] 229-51.)

25   (IV) Testaments of the Twelve Patriarchs. The literary form of testament or farewell discourse was well known in Judaism and the Hellenistic world, i.e., a speech delivered by famous figures just before death in which they leave a legacy, spiritual or material, to children or followers. Often the legacy has been filled in from a later author's knowledge of what actually happened to those who received the legacy. The relationship of testament to covenant is important (see K. Baltzer, *The Covenant Formulary* [Phl, 1971] 137-63; also J. Munck in *Aux sources de la tradition chrétienne* [Fest. M. Goguel; Neuchâtel, 1950] 155-70; A. B. Kolenkow, *JSJ* 6 [1975] 57-71). Moses' blessing upon the tribes in Deut 33 and Jesus' Last Discourse in John 13-17 are other examples of testaments. (On testaments, see *EJMI* 259–85.) The immediate pattern here is Jacob's blessing upon his 12 sons (= patriarchs) in Gen 49. *T. 12 Patr.* gives the testament of each of those 12 to his own sons.

It is preserved in about 20 Gk mss., none older than the 900s. A critical Gk ed. by M. de Jonge, *et al.* (PVTG I,2; Leiden, 1978) supposes that the shorter of two textual traditions is often derived from the longer by editing—a view very different from R. H. Charles's Gk ed. (Oxford, 1908), which favored the shorter and posited that the Greek reflected two different Hebr recensions. A transl. into Armenian in the 6th–10th cents. is found in some 50 mss., none earlier than the 13th cent., representing four different types of text. De Jonge thinks that the Armenian frequently abbreviated the Greek and is not to be used for reconstructing a shorter original. (Cf. M. Stone, *RB* 84 [1977] 94–107.) The oldest Christian citation is by Origen, so Gk *T. 12 Patr.* existed by AD 200. Major commentary: H. W. Hollander and M. de Jonge (SVTP 8; Leiden, 1985); Eng transl.: *APOT* 2 (Charles); *AOT* (de Jonge); *OTP* 1 (Kee).

26   (A) Composition. Fragments of an Aram *Levi-document* were found in the Cairo Geniza (→ Texts, 68:43) and at Qumran (*RB* 72 [1955] 398–406); they have parallels to *inserts* in a Mount Athos Gk ms. of *T. 12 Patr.* This Aram *Levi* was longer than *T. Levi* in *T. 12 Patr.* but may have contained it. (See J. C. Greenfield and M. E. Stone, *RB* 86 [1979] 214–30.) A Hebr fragment of a *Naphtali-document* was also at Qumran, and Milik on debatable evidence would detect other fragments related to Judah and Joseph. Were these various fragments, some of which may represent pre-Qumranian works, from testaments or from other patriarchal literature (e.g., *Levi* related to priestly writings)? Do they favor the likelihood that *T. 12 Patr.* was a pre-Christian Jewish writing (in Greek [Becker, Kee] or in Hebrew [Charles]) edited by Christians? Or do they represent the kind of sources used (directly or indirectly through a Gk transl.) by Christian author(s) in the 1st to 2d cents. who composed *T. 12 Patr.* in Greek (so de Jonge)? The answers to these questions affect the value of *T. 12 Patr.* for *biblical* study. Two facts are certain: No Semitic original of the present *T. 12 Patr.* has yet been found; the present form has both Jewish and Christian elements, although the latter are less than usually found in 2d-cent. Christian writings. Individual sections differ from each other in style and theology (*T. Levi* more apocalyptic; *T. Judah* and *T. Joseph* more narrative; *T. Asher* more dualistic—like the QL). It is safer to report on the *existing work as a whole,* even if we remain uncertain whether that whole work was early Jewish with Christian redaction, or a later Christian composition from Jewish sources.

27   (B) Contents. With an occasional exception, the 12 testaments follow a definite pattern in relating the last words of each of Jacob's sons to his children: (1) a rubric describing the dying patriarch, generally giving his age; (2) a pseudohistorical account of the patriarch's life, trial, and visions; (3) an all-important parenetic section drawing on that life to warn the children against evil and to encourage virtue, with Joseph being particularly virtuous. The lofty ethics, comparable to those of Sir and 4 Macc, are not without problems: all women are evil in *T. Reuben* 5:1; 6:1; and sexual abstinence is superior in *T. Issachar* 2:1; *T. Joseph* 6:7 (on ethics, see H. W. Hollander in Nickelsburg (ed.), *Studies* 47–104; H. C. Kee, *NTS* 24 [1977–78] 259–71); (4) a conclusion instructing the children for the future— this often involves a reference to obeying Levi and Judah and to the coming of the high priest and Messiah, or a reference to apostasy, punishment or exile, and return; (5) a rubric about the patriarch's death. The consistency of format suggests heavy editing or composition by one hand.

28   The Christian material is prominent. *T. Benj.* 10:8 says of the Lord, "When he appeared as God in the flesh to deliver them, they did not believe him." *T. Levi* 14:2 speaks of the chief priests "who shall lay their hands [violently] on the Savior of the world." *T. Simeon* 6:7 says that God had taken a body and eaten with people and saved people. Some material once thought to be Christian, however, may be of intertestamental Jewish origin (now known, for instance, at Qumran) but having NT parallels, e.g., the mention of bread and wine in *T. Levi* 8:4–5 (see Charles, *APOT* 2. 392; M. Philonenko, *Les interpolations chrétiennes des Testaments des Douze Patriarches* [Paris, 1960]). The importance of knowing whether some statements reflect pre-Christian Judaism is paramount, e.g., the reference to the conqueror from Judah as a lamb (*T. Joseph* 19:8). We might have remarkable background for Jesus' doctrine of forgiveness (Matt 18:15) if the passage in *T. Gad* 6:3 is pre-Christian: "Love one another from your heart. If anyone sins against you, speak peaceably to him. . . . If he repents and confesses, forgive him." *T. Dan* 5:3 says, "Love the Lord your God through your whole life, and one another with a true heart" (cf. Mark 12:30–31).

29   (C) Important Teaching. *T. 12 Patr.,* in parts, seemingly supports the expectation of TWO MESSIAHS. There are references both to an expected anointed high priest descended from the tribe of Levi (*T. Reuben* 6:7–12) and to an expected anointed king from Judah (*T. Judah* 24:5–6). *T. Judah* 21:2ff. gives supremacy to the levitical Messiah. Charles attributed these expectations to different stages of composition, but now we have evidence from Qumran of simultaneous expectations of two Messiahs, one priestly and one kingly (→ 117 below). The Christian final level of *T. 12. Patr.* has merged these two figures into one—Christ (*T. Joseph* 19:6; *T. Simeon* 7:2). See G. R. Beasley-Murray, *JTS* 48 (1947) 1–17; M. Black, *ExpTim* 60 (1949) 321–22. Because he works with the final form of *T. 12 Patr.,* in which the one figure Jesus Christ is both priestly and kingly, M. de Jonge has rejected the thesis that taken in itself and without historical reconstruction the work has a theory of two messiahs (in *Tradition and Interpretation* [Fest. J. C. Lebram; ed. J. W. van Henten *et al.;* Leiden, 1986] 150–62).

30   There is an advanced DEMONOLOGY. Beliar (mutation of "Belial"—in the OT an abstract noun meaning "worthlessness") is the personified leader of the forces of evil and an adversary of God. He is the lord of darkness (*T. Joseph* 20:2). Eventually the high priest from Levi will war upon him (*T. Dan* 5:10), bind him, and stamp on the evil spirits (*T. Levi* 18:12) to be cast into eternal fire (*T. Judah* 25:3). The similarities to NT demonology are obvious, and "Beliar" also appears as a name for Satan at Qumran and in 2 Cor 6:15. Elsewhere in *T. 12 Patr.* the opposing forces are internalized spirits of truth and error (*T. Judah* 20:1) or two impulses (*T. Asher* 1:3–5).

As for the RESURRECTION of the just, they will rise on the right in gladness, while the wicked will be on the left (*T. Benj.* 10:6–8). The righteous will reside in the New Jerusalem (*T. Dan* 5:12), though it is not certain whether this is on earth or in heaven. See *T. Judah* 25:1–5; *T. Zeb.* 10:2.

31   (D) Other Testamental Material. The Hebr midrash *Wayyisa'u* has important parallels with *T. Judah* 2ff. A medieval Hebr *T. Naphtali* exists but is not the same as that section of *T. 12 Patr.* Other early testaments include *T. Job* (Greek, 100 BC to AD 100); *T. Abraham* (not really a farewell discourse; Greek, AD

100); and *T. Moses* or *As. Mos.* (→ 49 below). Somewhat later are *T. Isaac, T. Jacob, T. Solomon,* and *T. Adam.* See *APOT* 1. 829–995; *AOT* 393–452; 617–48; 733–52; *OTP* 1. 829–995.

(Becker, J., *Die Testamente zwölf Patriarchen* [JSHRZ 3.1; 2d ed.; Gütersloh, 1980]. De Jonge, M., *Studies on the Testaments of the Twelve Patriarchs* [SVTP 3; Leiden, 1975]; "The Main Issues in the Study of the Testaments . . . ," *NTS* 26 [1979–80] 508–24. Hultgård, A., *L'Eschatologie des Testaments des Douze Patriarches* [2 vols.; Uppsala, 1971]. Nickelsburg, G. W. E. (ed.), *Studies in the Testament of Joseph* [SBLSCS 5; Missoula, 1975]. Slingerland, H. D., *The Testaments of the Twelve Patriarchs: A Critical History of Research* [SBLMS 21; Missoula, 1977].)

32   (V) (Letter of) Aristeas to Philocrates. Thus far we have been dealing with plausibly pre-Christian Palestinian apocrypha; the next works discussed here shift the scene to the Diaspora of Jews living outside Palestine, especially to the large settlement at Alexandria and its pre-Christian apocrypha. In the (deuterocanonical) Bible itself, there are Alexandrian attempts to justify Jewish law and wisdom as a form of philosophy superior to Gk thought (Wis, 2 Macc); the apocryphal works we shall now consider represent further Jewish attempts to achieve toleration, acceptance, or status in the sophisticated Hellenistic world.

33   *Aristeas* presents itself as a small book (not a letter despite the name often given to it) written in Greek to "his brother" Philocrates by Aristeas, a Gentile courtier of the Egyptian ruler Ptolemy II Philadelphus (285–246). Actually the author was a Jew writing at least a century later (2d cent. BC) for fellow Jews. A critical Gk text, Fr transl., and notes have been published by A. Pelletier (SC 89; Paris, 1962). There are Eng transls. in *APOT* 2; *OTP* 2; M. Hadas (JAL; NY, 1951). Bibliography in *HJPAJC* 3/1. 686–87.

The story, which concerns the legendary origin of the Gk transl. of the Pentateuch, will be told in reference to the LXX (→ Texts, 68:63; see also S. Jellicoe, *JTS* 12 (1961) 261–71. It is a legend that gained considerable favor in later Jewish (Philo, Josephus) and Christian tradition. *Aristeas* was popular in Christian circles because it helped to show the miraculous origins of the LXX, the Christian Bible. To give color to his fictional narrative, the author probably availed himself of sources that gave him some knowledge about the 3d-cent. Egyptian background. See N. Meisner, *Untersuchungen zum Aristeasbrief* (2 vols.; Berlin, 1972); O. Murray, StudP 12 (1975) 1. 123–28.

34   (VI) Maccabean Literature. Besides the deuterocanonical 1–2 Macc, there are two noncanonical books that bear the name of the Maccabees. Composed originally in Greek, the text of both is found in Codex Alexandrinus of the LXX (→ Texts, 68:96); 4 Macc appears in Codex Sinaiticus; neither is in the Vg. The Gk text is printed in Rahlfs's *Septuaginta* 1, and with an Eng transl. and notes in M. Hadas's volume in the JAL series (NY, 1953). There is a transl. of 3 Macc in *APOT* 1 (Emmet) and one of 4 Macc in *APOT* 2 (Townshend); and of both in *OTP* 2 (Anderson); also in the *RSV* Apocrypha (since 1977).

35   (A) 3 Maccabees or the *Ptolemaica.* The designation "Maccabees" is a misnomer because all the action takes place in the late 3d cent. BC, 50 years before the Maccabean revolt. The book relates three incidents in the struggle between the Egyptian king Ptolemy IV Philopator (221–203) and the Jews. *First* (1:1–2:24), after his victory over the Syrians at Raphia (217), Ptolemy attempts to violate the Jerusalem Temple but is struck senseless at the intercession of the high priest Simon II (219–196). This is similar to the story about the Syrian

general Heliodorus at the Temple in the year 176, told in 2 Macc 3. *Second* (2:25–33), Ptolemy insists that all citizens of Alexandria sacrifice to the gods, and the Jews who refuse are to lose their citizenship, be branded, and be enrolled as slaves. Only a few Jews acquiesce. Similar attempts to Hellenize Jews under Syrian rule appear in 2 Macc 4:9; 6:1–9. *Third* (3–7), in the hippodrome at Alexandria, the king tries to slay the Jews whose homes are in the Egyptian countryside, but they are spared by fantastic happenings (one episode involves drunken elephants!). The king repents, gives the Jews a feast, and sends them home. The relation to the story of Esther is obvious.

Although the author had access to some historical material about Ptolemy IV and may recall an otherwise forgotten persecution of Jews in Egypt during that reign, most of the material is legendary, stemming from variants of Hellenistic stories (e.g., Esth, 2 Macc) and shaped in the pattern of a Gk romance (e.g., of Chariton). The book was composed in Greek in the 1st cent. BC by an Alexandrian Jew to encourage his fellows (in the face of anticipated difficulties from the Romans?) and as background for a festival similar to Purim. The work received little Christian use.

36   (B) 4 Maccabees or *On the Supremacy of Reason* (falsely attributed under this title to Josephus). This book is a philosophical discourse or "diatribe" on the supremacy of religious reason over human passions and sufferings. It begins: "Thoroughly philosophical is the subject I am going to discuss." In chap. 1 the author explains his general thesis; then he tells stories from the OT and from Jewish history to illustrate his point, e.g., Joseph overcame sexual appetite in the incident with Potiphar's wife; Moses overcame anger. In chaps. 5–6 and 8–18 he tells two stories of martyrdom (Eleazar; the mother with seven children), illustrating how old and young overcame suffering to be given immortality. The fact that these stories of 2 Macc 6–7 constitute three-fourths of 4 Macc explains the title.

The genuineness of sections of 4 Macc (17:23–24; 18:6–19) has been questioned, but as a whole the work was composed in Greek by a Jew of the Diaspora (Antioch? Alexandria?) early in the 1st cent. AD, probably *ca.* 40. The author drew on 2 Macc and possibly also on Jason of Cyrene (the source of 2 Macc). The biblical stories are embellished considerably, and the style of the entire work is declamatory. Seemingly the purpose was to commemorate Jewish martyrs, perhaps for an annual feast in their honor. Along with Wis and Philo, it is an excellent example of how traditional Jewish thought and morality were cast into Gk philosophical patterns (see P. Redditt, *CBQ* 45 [1983] 249–70) and how a system like Stoicism was found wanting in Jewish eyes. We find in 4 Macc 6:27–29 a magnificent illustration of the theology of vicarious suffering in martyrdom (A. P. O'Hagan, *SBFLA* 24 [1974] 94–120). This work gave incentive to the church's practice of commemorating Christian martyrs, and it was quoted favorably by many of the Fathers. There is a Lat paraphrase, *Passio ss. Machabeorum* (*ca.* 4th cent.).

37   (VII) Prayer of Manasseh. Preserved in Greek in *Apostolic Constitutions* and Codex Alexandrinus, this work moves us into the realm of devotional literature. Pr Man is a beautiful penitential psalm of 15 verses, and in some Gk mss. it appears as one of the canticles appended to Pss. It is a pseudonymous attempt to fill in the prayer of King Manasseh (687–642) mentioned in 2 Chr 33:11–13; indeed, in Lat Bibles it has often been attached to the end of 2 Chr. The justice and merciful forgiveness of God extolled here would be much needed by the wicked Manasseh (→ Chronicler, 23:77).

The piety is that of early Judaism, similar to the deuterocanonical Prayer of Azariah (Dan 3:24–90). Although a Semitic original is not impossible, most posit composition in Greek by a Jew in the 1st cent. BC or AD. Our earliest extant form is in Syriac in the 3d-cent. *Didascalia.* Absent from early Vg mss. the Pr Man appears in medieval ones and is a supplement in the Sixto-Clementine Vg (after Trent failed to list it as canonical). Aquinas related it to the sacrament of Penance, and Luther proposed it as a model plea. For Protestants it is one of "the Apocrypha" although it was not part of the LXX. Charlesworth translates it from Syriac in *OTP* 2. 625–33.

38   (VIII) Esdras Literature. The canonical fate of 1–2 Esdras was similar to that of Pr Man. The titles of the various books of Ezra/Esdras are confusing. (The Hebr name of the biblical scribe '*Ezrā*' appears as Esdras in Greek and Latin.) *In the Hebr* Bible there was originally one book of Ezra, containing what are now the canonical books of Ezra and Nehemiah. Only in the Middle Ages did Hebr mss. begin to separate this material into two books. *In the LXX,* as represented in codices Alexandrinus and Vaticanus, there were two books of Esdras: Esdras A—a book that came to be regarded as apocryphal (our 1 Esdras below); Esdras B—a rendition into Greek of the canonical Ezra/Neh of the Hebr Bible.

In the Latin there were four books of Esdras:

I Esdras—canonical Ezra II Esdras—canonical Nehemiah	"Ezra" and "Nehemiah," the standard Eng designation of these books, is now being accepted by Catholics. Increasingly, "Esdras" is being reserved for the Apocrypha.

III Esdras—the apocryphon that is Esdras A in the LXX (1 Esdras below).

IV Esdras—another apocryphon (2 Esdras below); the apocalyptic part of this apocryphon is also known as 4 Ezra.

39   (A) 1 Esdras (the Esdras A of the LXX; the III Esdras of the Latin).   The principal text of this book is in Greek, found in all modern editions of the LXX. The Lat form in the Sixto-Clementine Vg is an OL transl. from the Greek. There is also a Syr transl. from the Greek. For Eng transl., see *RSV* Apocrypha; also *APOT* 1 (Cook).

In substance this book covers material in 2 Chr 35–36, canonical Ezra, and Neh 7–8 (1 Esdras and canonical Ezra present their material in different order). Once thought of as a free Gk rendition of the MT biblical material, 1 Esdras is now generally considered the original LXX transl. of a Hebr recension of Ezra/Neh different from the Ezra/Neh in the MT. (For such a phenomenon in the earliest LXX tradition, → Texts, 68:68.) In this case the Esdras B of the LXX, which is closer to the MT, represents a later recension of the LXX (→ Texts, 68:69–77). Such an explanation makes clear why 1 Esdras (late 2d cent. BC?) precedes Esdras B in the codices Alexandrinus and Vaticanus.

It appears that 1 Esdras enjoyed more popularity than Esdras B among those who cited the Gk Bible. Josephus used it, and the early Church Fathers seem to have thought of it as Scripture. It was really Jerome with his love for the Hebr Bible who set the precedent for rejecting 1 Esdras because it did not conform to Hebr Ezra/Neh. It contains little that is not in canonical Ezra/Neh except the story in 3:1–5:6, which tells of a contest among three Jewish pages at the Persian court of Darius (520 BC). Zerubbabel won: his prize was the permission to lead the Jews back to Jerusalem. The story in its present form

(from *ca.* 100 BC?) may have been adapted from a pagan narrative (→ Chronicler, 23:83), perhaps in Aramaic. The triumph of a Jewish wise man at a pagan court resembles Dan 1–6.

(Eng transl.: *APOT* 1 [Cook]; *RSV* Apocrypha. Coggins, R. J. and M. A. Knibb, *The First and Second Books of Esdras* [CBC NEB; Cambridge, 1979]. Klein, R. W., "Old Readings in I Esdras," *HTR* 62 [1969] 99–107. Muraoka, T., *A Greek-Hebrew/Aramaic Index to I Esdras* [SBLSCS 16; Chico, 1984]. Myers, J. M., *I and II Esdras* [AB 42, GC, 1974]. Pohlmann, K.-F., *3. Ezra-Buch* [JSHRZ 1.5; Gütersloh, 1980].)

40   (B) 2 Esdras (the IV Esdras of the Vg).   This is a composite work of three independent parts dating from the late 1st cent. AD to the 3d cent. The whole work was preserved only in Latin and may be found in the appendix of the Sixto-Clementine Vg. 2 Esdras has nothing to do with the narrative of canonical Ezra/Neh and is pseudepigraphical.

SECTION ONE (chaps. 1–2).   This is clearly a Christian work, composed in Greek, probably in the 2d cent. AD, to serve as an introduction to Section Two below. It is extant only in Latin. In the narrative, God speaks to Ezra and castigates the Jewish people for infidelity in the past. Echoing the theme of the NT, God promises that he will reject Israel and turn to the Gentiles. Seemingly speaking to the church (2:15), God gives her instruction on how to take care of his new people. "Everlasting rest" and "eternal light" are promised in 2:34–35—the source of the phrases used in the church's requiem liturgy—and immortality is the reward of those who confess the Son of God (2:47). See G. N. Stanton, *JTS* ns 28 (1977) 67–83.

41   SECTION TWO (chaps. 3–14). This is the *Apocalypse of Ezra,* generally called 4 Ezra. By far the most important part of 2 Esdras, it is a Jewish work of about AD 90–120. The original Hebr or Aram texts have been lost, and so has the Gk version, which was presumably the basis for all the extant ancient translations. The Latin is the most important, published by B. Violet (GCS 18/1; Leipzig, 1910) and by A. F. J. Klijn (TU 131; Berlin, 1983). The Syriac (ed. R. J. Bidawid in the Leiden Peshitta 4.3 [1973]), the Armenian (M. E. Stone, Univ. of Penn. Armen Texts 1; Missoula, 1979), and the Ethiopic are also of value. For the question of the original language, see J. Bloch, *JQR* 48 (1958) 279–84. The unity of the work has been questioned but probably wrongly; see Rowley, *Relevance* 156–59; E. Breech, *JBL* 92 (1973) 267–74; M. E. Stone, *JBL* 102 (1983) 229–43. The work contains seven scenes (dialogues and visions) involving Salathiel (= Shealtiel of Ezra 3:2 and 1 Chr 3:17, the father or uncle of Zerubbabel), who is identified in the gloss of 3:1 as Ezra (who, in fact, lived at least a century later!). Thus, the work mistakenly sets Ezra 30 years after the fall of Jerusalem in 587. The first four dialogues (chaps. 3–10) concern the problem of evil, Israel's sufferings, God's plan for the last times, and the New Jerusalem. The real crisis in the author's life, for which he finds a parallel in his fictional setting, is the destruction of Jerusalem by the Romans in AD 70. The fascinating story of the lost Lat text following 7:35 is told by B. Metzger in *JBL* 76 (1957) 153–56. The fifth scene or "eagle" vision of chaps. 11–12 uses symbolism to describe the Roman persecutors of the Jews, much as the contemporary NT Rev describes Rome as a dragon. In the sixth vision (chap. 13) a marvelous Man arises from the sea—he is the preexistent Messiah come to wage war with the Gentiles. This passage has some similarities to the picture of the Son of Man in *1 Enoch* (→ 15 above). See G. K. Beale, *NovT* 25 (1983) 182–88. In the seventh vision (chap. 14) Ezra is told to write down the 24 books of the OT and the 70 hidden books (the apocrypha). Ezra is taken up to heaven. This book continues the chain of Jewish apocalyptic that runs from Dan and *Enoch* through the QL to the Baruch literature.

(Eng transl. of 2 Esdr: *OTP* 1 (Metzger); *RSV* Apocrypha. Of only 4 Ezra: *APOT* 2 (Box). In addition to Coggins and Myers under § 39 above: Brandenburger, E., *Die Verborgenheit Gottes im . . . 4 Esrabuch* [ATANT 68; Zurich, 1981]. Schreiner, J., *Das 4. Buch Ezra* [JSHRZ 5.4; Gütersloh, 1981]. Thompson, A. L., *Responsibility for Evil in the Theodicy of IV Ezra* [SBLDS 29; Missoula, 1977].)

42   SECTION THREE (chaps. 15–16). This is a Christian conclusion, perhaps from the 3d cent. AD, added to the above. Of the original Gk only three verses of 15 remain; the Latin is the only extant version. The theme concerns God's judgment against the nations, especially against Rome.

43   **(IX) Baruch Literature.** Just as Ezra, anachronistically antedated to the fall of Jerusalem (587), became the hero of pseudonymous apocalyptic written after the fall of Jerusalem to the Romans (AD 70), so also did Baruch, Jeremiah's secretary, who at least was dated correctly. Besides the deuterocanonical book of Baruch (1 Bar) there are apocryphal books, of which two are of greater importance.

44   **(A) 2 Baruch,** or the *Syriac Apocalypse of Baruch.* The whole work was known in only one ms. of a Syr version made from a lost Gk version (the Oxyrhynchus papyri contain a Gk fragment of chaps. 12–14). Now a free Arabic rendition based on the Syriac has been discovered at the Sinai monastery (#589). Some find a citation of *2 Apoc. Bar.* in *Barn.* 11:9. Eng transl.: *APOT* 2 (Charles); *AOT* (Brockington); *OTP* 1 (Klijn). Fr transl.: P. Bogaert (2 vols.; SC 144–45; Paris, 1969). For text see B. Violet (GCS 18/2; Leipzig, 1924), and S. Dedering in the Leiden Peshitta 4.3 (1973). Most date this Jewish apocalypse to AD 95–120, some positing literary dependence on 4 Ezra, others on a common source. Charles and others have argued for a Hebr original, but Bogaert thinks of a Gk original. Charles posits six separate sources from before AD 70, some pessimistic and some optimistic on Israel's fate; increasingly, however, scholars opt for literary unity and a cohesive plan. The work, consisting of seven parts, has Baruch fasting four times after Jerusalem's fall, lamenting, issuing prophetic warnings, and receiving three visions that explain the tragedy. Chaps. 78–87 contain a letter to the dispersed Jews stressing obedience to God's commands—a letter that had biblical status among Syrian Christians and exists in 36 Syr copies. 4 Ezra and *2 Apoc. Bar.* give different Jewish responses to Rome's conquest of Jerusalem, even as a Christian response is given by Rev (another collection of prophecies, apocalyptic visions, and letters).

(Murphy, F. J., *The Structure and Meaning of Second Baruch* [SBLDS 78; Chico, 1985]. Sayler, G. B., *Have the Promises Failed?* [SBLDS 72; Chico, 1984].)

45   **(B) 3 Baruch,** or the *Greek Apocalypse of Baruch.* M. R. James published one Gk ms. in 1899; a second ms. contributed to J.-C. Picard's edition (PVTG 2; Leiden, 1967). Two Slavonic versions in 12 mss. are drawn from the Greek (ed. H. E. Gaylord, announced as forthcoming). Eng transl.: *APOT* 2 (Hughes); *AOT* (Argyle); *OTP* 1 (Gaylord—from both Greek and Slavonic). Ger transl. from both by W. Hage (JSHRZ 5.1; Gütersloh, 1974). The work was composed in Greek, perhaps in Egypt, between AD 70 and 150. James deemed the work Christian, but most argue for Christian interpolation and/or editing of a basically Jewish composition. There are parallels with *2 Enoch* and *Paraleipomena*

of Jeremiah. In Origen's reference (*De principiis* 2.3.6), he mentions Baruch's passing through seven heavens (see 2 Cor 12:2), but only five heavens are mentioned in the Gk text. *3 Apoc. Bar.* has had influence on Slavic and Bulgarian literature (Bogomil movement).

46   **(X) Psalms of Solomon.** Never cited by Church Fathers but listed in the 5th cent. as having been attached to the end of the NT in Codex Alexandrinus, *Pss. Sol.* appears in some later Christian lists of the canon. Only in the early 17th cent. was the work rediscovered and made available to Western scholars. Written in Hebrew (now lost), it is preserved in whole or part in 11 medieval Gk mss. and in 4 Syr mss. (there always preceded by the *Odes of Solomon*—a 2d-cent. AD Syr [Jewish-Christian] composition with slight gnostic overtones). See J. Begrich, *ZNW* 38 (1939) 131–64; R. R. Hann, *The Manuscript History of the Psalms of Solomon* (SBLSCS 13; Chico, 1982). The Gk text was edited (with different versifications) by H. E. Ryle (Cambridge, 1891) and O. von Gebhard (TU 13.2: Leipzig, 1895; see also A. Rahlfs, *Septuaginta* [5th ed.; Stuttgart, 1952] 2. 471–89). The Syr text was edited by J. R. Harris (Cambridge, 1909; rev. Manchester, 1916); W. R. Barr in the Leiden Peshitta 4.6 (1972). Most think the Syriac was translated from the Greek, but see J. L. Trafton, *The Syriac Version of the Psalms of Solomon* (SBLSCS 11; Chico, 1985); also *JBL* 105 (1986) 227–37. Eng transl.: *APOT* 2 (Gray); *AOT* (Brock); *OTP* 2 (Wright).

47   Two pss. in the canonical Psalter (72; 127) are associated by title with Solomon; and 1 Kgs 4:32 speaks of his 1,005 songs. None of the individual poems in the present apocryphon claims to have been written by Solomon, and the attribution of the collection as a whole to Solomon (a pseudepigraphical attempt to find patronage; → Canonicity, 66:88–89) was probably necessitated by the fact that the more obvious attribution to David was precluded since the Davidic psalter had now been closed. These 18 psalms were actually composed in Palestine (Jerusalem) *ca.* 60–40 BC. *Pss. Sol.* at 8:15–21 refers to the siege of Jerusalem by Pompey in 63 BC, and 2:26–37 seems to imply knowledge of Pompey's death in 48. Not liturgical but didactic and polemic, *Pss. Sol.* sees this foreign invasion as God's punishment of Israel for the worldliness of its rulers (Hasmoneans; → History, 75:139–42). Such opposition to the Sadducean priestly rulers has led most scholars to attribute *Pss. Sol.* to the Pharisees; but other groups, like the Qumran Essenes, were equally opposed to the Sadducees. For some Qumran parallels, see J. O'Dell, *RevQ* 3 (1961) 241–57; R. B. Wright in SBLSCS 2 (Missoula, 1972) 136–54. S. Holm-Nielsen, *Die Psalmen Salomos* (JSHRZ 4.2; Gütersloh, 1977), gives a nuanced explanation of the Pharisee background. For the eschatology of *Pss. Sol.*, → NT Thought, 81:38.

48   The theology of *Pss. Sol.* has been treated by H. Braun, *ZNW* 43 (1950) 1–54; J. Schüpphaus, *Die Psalmen Salomos* (Leiden, 1977). It includes God's righteousness, a free choice between good and evil, divine retribution, afterlife. *Pss. Sol.* 17 and 18 pray for the coming of a Davidic Messiah who shall bring the Gentiles under his yoke. A sinless and perfect man, the Messiah will renew Jerusalem and establish Israel as God's kingdom. This is a type of messianism that we seem to find in the popular expectations implied in the Gospels—a mixture of political and spiritual aspirations that Jesus does not accept (→ Jesus, 78:34).

49   **(XI) Assumption of Moses.** Antiquity knew both of a *Testament of Moses* and of an *Assumption of Moses,* one belonging to testamentary literature (→ 25, 31 above), the other presumably apocalyptic. The untitled Lat work under discussion was called "Assumption" by A. N. Ceriani, who first edited it in 1861, but its contents would suggest more the *Testament* than the *Assumption*. The original was probably written in Hebrew or Aramaic (lost), translated into Greek (also lost), and finally into Latin (preserved in a defective 6th-cent. ms.). Eng transl.: *APOT* 2 (Charles); *AOT* (Sweet); *OTP* 1 (Priest). See E.-M. Laperrousaz, *Le Testament de Moïse* (Semitica 19; Paris, 1970). For the eschatology of *As. Mos.,* → NT Thought, 81:39.

Moses, shortly before his death, speaks to Joshua and reveals to him the future history of Israel from the entrance into Canaan until the dawn of the blessed age. (The popularity of this type of pseudepigraphical "prediction," which is really a summary in retrospect from the author's own time, is attested in the Bible in Dan.) The clearly datable events described come to a conclusion in chap. 6 with Herod the Great's sons and an intervention by the Roman Quintilius Varus in 4 BC. But this is followed in subsequent chapters by details about godless rulers, a second visitation by a king of kings who crucifies those who confess circumcision, and then in chap. 9 by the appearance of a Levite named Taxo with seven sons. His refusal to accede to the king's edict seems to bring about the end times in chap. 10. How to date the work? Some scholars, following the sequence of the chaps., date the persecution by the king of kings to Roman-Jewish struggles in the early 2d cent. AD (see S. Zeitlin, *JQR* 38 [1947–48] 1–45). Most scholars, however, identify the king as Antiochus Epiphanes and fit Taxo into a Maccabean context of about 170 BC. To explain the present sequence, where Taxo follows Herod the Great, Charles dates the work in the early 1st cent. AD, but rearranges chaps., putting 8 and 9 between 5 and 6. J. Licht (*JJS* 12 [1961] 95–103), followed by G. Nickelsburg (*Studies on the Testament of Moses* [SBLSCS 4; Cambridge, MA, 1973]), dates the original composition of the work to the Maccabean revolt and posits an editing in the early 1st cent. AD. Laperrousaz proposes an Essene origin for the work, and M. Delcor (*RB* 62 [1955] 60–66) sees a relation between Taxo and the "Searcher of the Law" of the DSS (CD 8:5).

The lost *Assumption of Moses,* so far as we can reconstruct from patristic references (Denis, *Fragmenta* 63–67), dealt with the death of Moses and his assumption into heaven after a struggle between Michael and Satan for his body. Seemingly, it is to this legend that Jude 9 refers.

50   (XII) Biblical Antiquities of (Pseudo-) Philo. This work is never mentioned by Christians till the Middle Ages or by Jews until the 16th cent. Over 20 whole or partial Lat mss. (all of German/Austrian origin) from the 11th cent. on give the text of *Liber Antiquitatum Biblicarum,* first edited in 1527 by J. Sichardus in a collection of Lat translations of Philo. A landmark analysis was done by L. Cohn, *JQR* 10 (1898) 277–332. The occasionally corrupt Latin stems from Greek (lost), which in turn may have been translated from Hebrew (lost; Hebr extracts in a 14th-cent. Oxford ms. of the *Chronicles of Yerahme'el* are only a medieval retranslation from Latin; see D. J. Harrington, *The Hebrew Fragments of Pseudo-Philo* [SBLTT 3; Cambridge, MA, 1974]). Eng transl.: M. R. James (London, 1917); D. J. Harrington (*OTP* 2, based on Fr ed. with Lat text and commentary in SC 229–30 [Paris, 1976]). The work was composed by a Jew in the 1st cent. AD whether before or after the destruction of the Temple in 70 (19:7). It is unrelated to Philo. Despite some anti-Samaritan indications, there is little distinctively sectarian in *Bib. Ant.;* it is closest to Pharisee thought, showing great appreciation for the law, strongly attacking idolatry, exhibiting a belief in angels and in an afterlife where the soul will be judged for deeds done in

this life (44:10) and will go either to peace or to punishment (51:5).

It retells the biblical history from Adam to David, sometimes abbreviating or omitting, often imaginatively expanding. A stress on God's covenant fidelity to his people is dramatized in the midrashic coloring of the careers of biblical heroes who effected salvation, e.g., Abraham, and even Cenez or Kenaz (Judg 1:13; *Bib. Ant.* 25–28). Kerygmatic speeches are supplied for them interpreting their roles. Such a work illustrates the type of biblical recollection that could have been in the mind of NT writers. E.g., Matt's infancy narrative tells the story of Jesus' birth against the background of Moses' birth and the story of Balaam, but it often supposes expansions of those stories beyond the biblical books; see *Bib. Ant.* chaps. 9 and 18. The closest parallel to such retelling and expansion of the Bible is in Josephus, *Ant.* (→ 129 below), a work contemporary with Pseudo-Philo.

51   (XIII) Sibylline Oracles. About 500 BC Heraclitus of Ephesus mentioned Sibyl, a prophetess of Cumae. Later the concept of (old) women who were filled with the divine spirit to become channels for the oracles of the gods spread throughout the Hellenistic world, and sibyls functioned at at least ten different shrines, e.g., Delphi and Erythrae. The oracles attributed to these sibyls were composed in Gk poetry (hexameter) and collected over the centuries, but most of the official and private collections of great antiquity were destroyed, e.g., the great Roman collection in 83 BC. Jews and Christians imitated the pagans by composing "sibylline oracles" of their own. The Jewish and Christian collection discussed here consists of two editions (1–8 and 9–14) that have been joined, giving a total of 12 books since 9–10 are duplicates of material in 4; 6–8. The range is from *ca.* 150 BC to AD 650; the individual books consist of disparate material; and it is not always possible to distinguish Jewish from Christian oracles. The Greek was critically edited by J. Geffcken (GCS 8; Leipzig, 1902); also A. Kurfess (Berlin, 1951). Eng transl.: *APOT* 2 (Lanchester); *OTP* 1 (Collins). See V. Nikiprowetzky, *La Troisième Sibylle* (Paris, 1970); *HUCA* 43 (1972) 29–76 on books 4 and 5; J. J. Collins, *The Sibylline Oracles of Egyptian Judaism* (SBLDS 13; Missoula, 1974).

**52   The oldest Jewish oracles are found in books 3–5. Book 2 may contain pagan oracles adapted by Jews in the 2d cent. BC and finally edited with other material between 50 BC and AD 70. Book 4 carries us into the late 1st cent. AD and possibly reflects anti-Temple attitudes in vv 24–30 (Collins). Book 5 probably extends to the reign of Hadrian before AD 130. These oracles served as Jewish propaganda. The Sibyl is identified as Noah's daughter-in-law (3:827); her oracles outlined the course of world history, predicted the destruction of Beliar, ultimate Jewish triumph, and the coming of the Messiah. In 3:63ff. and 4:137–39 we may have an interesting parallel to the NT Rev, for Nero Redivivus seems to appear along with the figure of the wicked woman who dominates the world (→ Apocalypse, 63:44,53). There are interesting parallels between Virgil's *Fourth Eclogue* (40 BC) and 3:367, 652,746,788, which speak of a king sent by God to conquer His enemies and bring idyllic peace. *Sib. Or.* may have been a channel by which the Isaian prophetic expectations reached the Gentile world, and in turn Virgil's *Eclogue* created an atmosphere in which Gentiles could appreciate Luke's birth narrative (*BBM* 564–70).

The oracles were very popular among Christian writers. Augustine admitted the Sibyl to the *City of God* (18.23), and Michelangelo painted sibyls in the Sistine Chapel opposite the OT prophets. There is a debate among scholars about how many of the books of this collection are Christian in origin.

CHRISTIAN APOCRYPHAL GOSPELS

53 **(I) Christian Apocrypha.** As we have already seen in the instances of *1 Enoch, T. 12 Patr.,* 2 Esdr, Christians felt free to interpolate Christian motifs into Jewish apocrypha; but here we turn to works of direct Christian composition. If we define Christian apocrypha as literature that once had a claim—plausible or implausible—to being considered canonical, we would have to treat under that heading some ancient postapostolic works, like *Did., 1-2 Clem., Herm.,* and *Barn.,* which were sometimes treated as Scripture in the early centuries (→ Canonicity, 66:83). Today, however, these works are studied as early church writings (→ Early Church, 80:34-43), and "Christian Apocrypha" is used in a narrower sense to refer to noncanonical books more closely related in form or in content to NT writings.

54 **(A) Works Other Than Gospels.** In a famous collection of Christian apocrypha (*HSNTA*) over 100 works are discussed. From this immense literature we have opted to treat only gospels, for this is the section of the apocrypha that has the best chance of preserving authentic material from the NT era. But we shall mention briefly the other forms or genres of Christian apocrypha (*HSNTA,* vol. 2), most of which are closely patterned on forms of literature that appear in the NT. There is pseudo-Pauline correspondence, e.g., *To the Laodiceans, To the Corinthians, To Seneca,* often written under the pretense of being the (lost) letters mentioned by Paul in his canonical correspondence (→ Canonicity, 66:59). Modeled on the canonical Acts of the Apostles (which really treats only of Peter and Paul), there are apocryphal acts of individual apostles, e.g., *of John, of Peter, of Paul, of Andrew, of Thomas,* purportedly describing their careers after the ascension of Jesus and thus filling in history missing in the NT. There were debates about the scriptural status of some of them (→ Canonicity, 66:66). They emphasize the apostle's miraculous powers; the ascetic life to which Christians are summoned, frequently demanding that marriage be renounced; the distant lands to which the apostles travel; their confrontations with enemies and kings; and their martyrdom. Such materials were also read and produced within gnostic circles as elements in the *Acts of Thomas* and *Acts of John* show. Additional "Acts" were found in the Nag Hammadi collection: *Acts Pet. 12 Apost.* and *Ep. Pet. Phil.* Some of these acts have supplied material for the "biographies" of the apostles found in martyrologies and in breviary lessons. See F. Bovon (ed.), *Les Actes apocryphes des apôtres* (Geneva, 1981); *Semeia* 38 (1986).

55 Patterned on the NT Rev, there are apocryphal apocalypses, e.g., *of Peter* (→ Canonicity, 66:68), *of Paul, of Thomas.* These answer a popular curiosity about the "goings on" in the next world by letting imagination satisfy for the lack of revelation. Another type of Christian apocalyptic is seen in the interpolations and additions to Jewish apocrypha. The *Ascension of Isaiah* deserves mention. Just as NT authors found in a free interpretation of the words of Isaiah (proto- and deutero-) some very valuable OT background for understanding the mystery of Jesus, so in this apocryphal work, Isaiah is granted visions of the life of Jesus and of the church. These visions are added to the Jewish apocryphon, the *Martyrdom of Isaiah,* a midrash on 2 Kgs 21:16 telling how Isaiah was sawed in half at the order of King Manasseh. The interpolated visions of Christian origin concentrate heavily, as does the canonical Rev, on

the struggle between the church and the supernatural prince of evil (Beliar or Sammael; → 30 above).

56 **(B) Gospels.** These constitute a large body of literature, filling vol. 1 of *HSNTA.* Many are known only through fragments quoted by early church writers. However, a number of writings designated "gospels" have been made available through a find in Dec. 1945 in the Nag Hammadi region of Egypt, some 300 mi. S of Cairo. This involved a jar containing 13 Coptic codices buried about AD 400, representing some 50 discrete tractates. The codices came probably from a 4th-cent. monastery associated with St. Pachomius (292-348), perhaps Chenoboskion, where he began his life as a hermit, or Pabau, which were within a five-mi. radius of the find. Although Pachomius himself was orthodox, there is evidence that gnostics did infiltrate some monasteries; and many of the Nag Hammadi writings have a gnostic tone (→ Early Church, 80:74). They often represent translations of texts composed in Greek during the flourishing growth of gnostic sects from the mid-2d cent. to the 3d cent. See *BA* 42 (#4, 1979).

57 In the NT, "gospel" refers to the "good news" of salvation (e.g., 1 Thess 3:2; 1 Cor 4:15; 2 Cor 2:12; Rom 1:1; 15:16). It is used in a similar way to refer to Jesus' preaching of the kingdom (Mark 1:1; Matt 4:23). *Ca.* 150 Justin Martyr notes that the "memoirs composed by the apostles" are called "gospels" (*Apol.* 1.66); by this time, then, the genre "gospel" was loosely defined as an apostolic recollection about Jesus. The four canonical Gospels follow a set pattern: (1) JBap and the baptism of Jesus; (2) calling disciples; (3) Jesus' teaching and healing, which involve controversies with Jewish opponents; (4) final days in Jerusalem; (5) passion narrative; (6) empty tomb story; (7) appearance(s) of the Lord to the disciples (except in Mark).

Apocryphal gospels are not bound to this same narrative pattern or to the older meaning of "kerygma." They generally develop particular elements of canonical Gospel tradition: (1) infancy gospels, the miraculous birth and unusual childhood of Jesus; (2) "sayings gospels," collections of Jesus' sayings and teachings; (3) "passion/resurrection" gospels, dealing with those events; (4) "resurrection dialogues," which claim to report revelations and teachings given by the risen Jesus to his disciples, often over an extended period after the resurrection.

58 The importance of these apocryphal gospels for NT study lies in the evidence they give for the growth and appropriation of Jesus traditions. It is not easy to decide when they represent imaginative appropriations and expansions of canonical Gospel material, when they represent combinations of canonical Gospel material with popular oral tradition that was not included in the canonical Gospels, and when they preserve precanonical written material. In particular, some scholars (e.g., Koester, Cameron, Crossan) claim that material in "sayings gospels" represents a primitive variant of the Jesus tradition with affinities to the developing tradition behind John. They argue for a late 1st-cent. date for these writings (discovered in Coptic at Nag Hammadi) or for their "sayings material" source (which had parallels to Q [→ Synoptic Problem, 40:13]). However, the extensive gnostic reworking of material evident in these texts and the lack of secure criteria for analyzing oral and written developments of traditions in this period make the claim for such an early dating difficult to sustain. Each example must be subjected to tradition-historical scrutiny on its own terms. We now turn to an analysis of the various apocryphal gospels. Eng transls. of all of them may be found in *HSNTA* 1, except for the more recent *Secret Mark* (→ 63 below).

59   (II) Fragmentary Gospels. Some gospels are preserved only in fragments and/or brief citations by Church Fathers. In the latter case it is impossible to tell the type of narrative to which these citations belonged; and sometimes the Church Father is vague about whether he has seen a ms. or only heard of the gospel, whether the Jewish Christians who are using the gospel have it in Greek (which may be original or a transl.) or in Semitic, and whether that Semitic (even if he speaks of "Hebrew dialect") is Hebrew, Aramaic, or even Syriac. See A. F. J. Klijn, in *Text and Interpretation* (Fest. M. Black; Cambridge, 1979) 169-77.

(A) Gospel of the Ebionites. This Jewish-Christian work is preserved in a few quotations from Epiphanius (4th cent.), but the original title is lost. It appears to have been based on Matt and Luke. Eusebius's quotes treat the appearance of JBap, Jesus' baptism (JBap's request that Jesus baptize him is located after the heavenly voice), the choice of disciples, the saying about Jesus' true family, a saying against sacrifice, and another about Jesus eating the Passover, where Jesus apparently instructs his disciples not to prepare a paschal lamb.

60   (B) Gospel of the Hebrews. This Jewish-Christian gospel, independent of Matt, apparently was known to Papias. It survives in quotations in Clement of Alexandria, Origen, Cyril, and Jerome. It treats the descent of the preexistent Christ into Mary, the coming of the Holy Spirit on Jesus at his baptism, a resurrection appearance of the Lord to James at a eucharistic meal, and wisdom sayings of Jesus. One of these sayings was apparently a free-floating logion, since it appears also in *Gos. Thom.* (Clement of Alexandria, *Strom.* 2.9.45; 5.14.96; *Gos. Thom.* 2).

61   (C) Gospel of the Nazoreans. This is known to have existed in an Aram or Syr version (Hegesippus, Eusebius, Epiphanius, and Jerome). The sayings preserved in Origen, Eusebius, and Jerome are variants of sayings in Matt, some of them perhaps the product of exegesis. Jesus' mother and brothers initiate the trip to the Baptist for "remission of sins," while Jesus protests his sinlessness (Jerome, *Adv. Pelag.* 3.2). The adjective qualifying the "bread" in the Lord's Prayer is understood to mean "of the future" (Jerome, *In Matt.* on 6.11). The man with the withered hand needs to be restored so that he can earn his livelihood as a mason (Jerome, *In Matt.* on 12:13). References to the passion account are also included in these citations: Barabbas's name is said to mean "son of their teacher"; the veil of the Temple was not torn but a large lintel collapsed.

62   (D) Papyrus Egerton 2. In 1935, H. I. Bell and T. C. Skeat published from a British Museum papyrus codex four *Fragments of an Unknown Gospel,* in a script of no later than *ca.* AD 150. Two of the three legible fragments have canonical Gospel parallels (Synoptic and Johannine) woven together. Most scholars think of memories borrowed primarily from John mixed with a Synoptic Gospel and some noncanonical material that the author judged of value (→ Canonicity, 66:64). Others, like Mayeda, Koester, and Crossan, argue for Egerton independence and priority. See *SGM* and *Gos. Pet.* (→ 63, 72 below) for other early admixtures of the canonical and the noncanonical.

(Braun, F.-M., *Jean le théologien* [Paris, 1939] 1. 87-94, 404-6. Dodd, C. H., *New Testament Studies* [Manchester, 1953] 12-52. Mayeda, G., *Das Leben-Jesu-Fragment Papyrus Egerton 2* [Bern, 1946]; with a response by H. I. Bell, *HTR* 42 [1949] 53-63. Neirynck, F., *ETL* 61 [1985] 153-60.)

63   (E) Secret Gospel of Mark. A fragmentary 18th-cent. copy of a Gk letter by "Clement [of Alexandria] . . . to Theodore" was found in 1958 in the Mar Saba monastery near Bethlehem by M. Smith of Columbia University. With notable exceptions (Nock, Munck, Kümmel, Musurillo, Quesnell), most have accepted authorship by Clement, *ca.* 175-200. He reports that (1) while Peter was at Rome, Mark wrote the "Acts of the Lord" (=canonical Mark) for catechumens but did not report Jesus' secret (*mystikai*) acts; (2) after Peter's death Mark brought to Alexandria his own and Peter's notes to supplement his first book for those progressing in knowledge (*gnōsis*); this secret spiritual gospel (=*SGM*), kept by the Alexandrian church for those "being initiated into the great mysteries," was (3) leaked to Carpocrates (a gnostic, *ca.* 125), who added lies, distorting it for libertine practice. This implies that *SGM* was composed no later than the early 2d cent. The two quoted *SGM* fragments are located after Mark 10:34 and 10:46. Marcan in style, the subject matter resembles John: At Bethany Jesus brought forth from the tomb a woman's brother, who, loving Jesus, came to him six days later at night with a linen cloth over his naked body (see John 11:1-44; Mark 14:51-52). Most scholars judge *SGM* a pastiche from the canonical Gospels. Smith thinks it reflects an early Aram source on which both Mark and John drew and in which Jesus practiced a magical (and perhaps sexual) initiation into the kingdom of heaven. Koester and Crossan claim that canonical Mark eliminated scenes from the more complete *SGM*. Perhaps, as with *Gos. Pet.,* *SGM* preserves tradition that developed independently of the canonical Gospels in an ambience less controlled by apostolic guidance; yet a knowledge (written of Mark, oral of John) of the canonical Gospels influenced the final writing.

(Text, transl., and commentary in M. Smith, *Clement of Alexandria and a Secret Gospel of Mark* [Cambridge, MA, 1973]; bibliography in M. Smith, *HTR* 75 [1982] 459-61. Brown, R. E., *CBQ* 36 [1974] 466-85. Koester, H., in *Colloquy on New Testament Studies* [ed. B. Corley; Macon, 1983] 35-57. Neirynck, F., *ETL* 55 [1979] 43-66.)

64   (III) Infancy Gospels. These tales of the miraculous birth of Jesus and his equally miraculous powers as a child were extremely popular, as the number of fragments and translations into other languages suggests. They provided popular piety and art with affirmations of the perpetual virginity and "royal" origins of Mary.

(A) Protevangelium of James. This work survives in one 3d-cent. Gk ms. (Papyrus Bodmer V), which appears to have already undergone considerable textual development. Numerous later fragments and transls. (Syriac, Armenian, Ethiopic, Sahidic) survive, though the Lat transls. were apparently destroyed when the book was rejected as noncanonical. The tradition that "James, the brother of the Lord" had special information about Jesus' virginal conception and birth appears in a different form in a gnostic account of James's martyrdom (*2 Apoc. Jas.* 50.1-52.1), where Mary is said to have explained that Jesus was James's stepbrother. Another gnostic tract, *Tri. Trac.* (115.9-34), refers to the "sinless incarnation" of the Logos, who is begotten without passion. References by Justin to the birth of Jesus in a cave (*Dial.* 78) and by Clement of Alexandria to the perpetual virginity of Mary (*Strom.* 6.16.93) suggest that *Prot. Jas.* was circulating by the mid-2d cent. It names Mary's parents as Joachim and Anna, describes Mary's miraculous birth to the aged couple and her presentation in the Temple. The work emphasizes Mary's virginity in giving birth by having her subject to tests and scrutiny by suspicious authorities. Joseph had children by a previous marriage, whence "the brothers of Jesus" in the Gospels. *Prot. Jas.* played an important role in the development of mariology.

65   (B) Infancy Gospel of Thomas. The original Greek survives only in a few late mss., which differ in length (14th–15th cent.). Lat and Syr texts survive from the 5th cent., and other fragments remain in Georgian and Ethiopic. The attribution of the work to "Thomas the Israelite" suggests that it did not derive from the Syrian Thomas traditions that spawned the gnostic Thomas literature, *Gos. Thom.* and *Acts Thom.*, where Thomas is described as the twin of Jesus. This gospel consists of a number of legendary episodes designed to show the miraculous powers of the child Jesus from age 5 through 12. See I. Havener, *TBT* 22 (1984) 368–72.

66   (IV) Sayings Gospels. The scholarly hypothesis that Matt and Luke used a written collection of Jesus' sayings as a source (Q) is bolstered by the continued existence of "sayings gospels" in apocryphal material from gnostic circles. Like their Synoptic counterparts, gnostic authors reshaped and expanded sayings collections. Here, however, the context for elaborating sayings of the Lord is not a narrative of Jesus' life but the setting of an esoteric revelation to be preserved for the "elect," i.e., the gnostics as true heirs of Jesus' teaching. This revelation is generally attributed to the risen Lord. In several instances, gnostic authors have used sayings-gospel material as the content of the "revelation dialogue" type.

67   (A) Gospel of Thomas. This collection of sayings of the "living" Jesus is preserved in one Coptic ms. of the NHL and in three Gk fragments (POxy. 1; 654; 655), which parallel the material in *Gos. Thom.* sayings 1–7, 26–39 and are dated to the beginning of the 3d cent. Of the 114 sayings into which modern scholars divide *Gos. Thom.*, 79 have some parallel in the Synoptics. Eleven are variants of Synoptic parables (20; 9a; 65a [66]; 21d; 96; 64a; 107; 57; 109; 76a; 8a; 63a). Three others are unattested parables (21ab; 97; 98). *Gos. Thom.* lacks the interpretations of the Sower (9a) and of the Wheat and Weeds (57) found in the Synoptics. But *Gos. Thom.* 64b interprets the Great Supper (where the Synoptics do not) by adding to it a saying against businessmen entering the kingdom. A similar expansion appears in the sayings about wealth attached to the Unjust Steward in Luke 16:1–13. As in Luke's version of the Great Supper, the excuses are spelled out (though with a related "antibusiness" cast); as in Matt, the servants are sent only once. Such parallels make *Gos. Thom.* an invaluable resource for the study of the evolution of the sayings tradition(s). Other sayings in *Gos. Thom.* reflect the gnostic spirit of the final editor: only Jesus' revelation saves people from the world (28; 29); the soul's dependence on the body is condemned (87; 112); a rite of the "bridal chamber" is referred to (75), and the "female" (exemplified by Mary Magdalene) must be "made male" in order to enter the kingdom (114); Thomas's authority to give esoteric interpretation of Jesus' teaching is established in a variant of "Peter's Confession" (13).

68   (B) Thomas the Contender. This survives only in its Coptic version. Like *Gos. Thom.*, it opens with the claim to represent the "secret words" of the Savior (words copied by Matthias). But here the gnostic concern with esoteric tradition intrudes more directly, and the work shows little connection with the content of the sayings tradition. An ascetic wisdom parenesis urging complete rejection of the body and its lusts forms the basis for the words of the Lord.

69   (C) Apocryphon of James. Extant only in the Coptic version, the writing is prefaced by a letter from James claiming to transmit a secret revelation that the risen Lord had given to him and Peter. It is apparently contrasted with "memoirs" which the disciples were writing about what the earthly Lord had said to them individually and as a group, including one by James (1.29–2.23). The revelation takes place 550 days after the resurrection and is climaxed by the Lord's final ascent into heaven (16.3–30, which reflects dissent about the teaching of Jesus between authorities). *Ap. Jas.* contains a mixed type of sayings tradition, including parallels with Synoptic material (4.22–37, reward of disciples [Mark 10:28–30]; 5.31–6.11, necessity of the cross [Mark 8:31–37]; 7.1–10, speaking in parables [Mark 4:10–12]; 8.10–27, planting seed and zeal for the word [Mark 4:13–20]; 9.24–10.6, woe against false claims to salvation [Matt 3:7–10]; 12.20–30, seed sown in a field [Mark 4:27–29]). There are also sayings that reflect language more characteristic of the Johannine tradition, and *Ap. Jas.* may provide clues about the development of that type of material. It also contains a list of parables that the risen Lord is said to have expounded (8.5–10) and unattested parables such as that about the date palm (7.22–35).

(Cameron, R., *Sayings Traditions in the Apocryphon of James* [HTS 34; Phl, 1984].)

70   (D) Dialogue of the Savior. Extant only in a badly mutilated Coptic ms., this postresurrection dialogue singles out Matthew, Judas, and Mariam for special revelation. Its condition makes interpretation difficult. Cosmological wisdom material, an apocalypse on the ascent of souls, and some cosmogonic mythic material appear to have been included. Its sayings may have been derived from a tradition related to *Gos. Thom.* (e.g., 125.18–126.2 may be a gnostic reinterpretation of Luke 11:34–36 mediated by the *Gos. Thom.* 33 variant). A list of Jesus' sayings (139.8–12) is given as evidence of Mariam's "gnosis."

71   (V) Passion/Resurrection Gospels. Christians also attempted to fill in the lacunae surrounding Jesus' death and resurrection, since neither Jesus' trial nor his actual emergence from the tomb is the subject of an eyewitness account in the canonical Gospels.

(A) Acts of Pilate. This is the first part of the *Gospel of Nicodemus*, a title given to the combination of *Acts Pil.* and a second work on Christ's descent into hell—a combination found in Lat mss. after the 10th cent. Neither the Gk mss. nor Coptic fragments use this title. *Acts Pil.* claims to be old Hebr records made by Nicodemus and found by a converted Roman guard, Ananias. Several miracles that result from the hostile challenges of the Jews should have proved Jesus' innocence. The reference to Pilate's wife (Matt 27:19) is expanded. Pilate also challenges the Jews in Jesus' defense. The account of Jesus' death on the cross expands on Luke and John, while the legends about the guard at the tomb expand on Matt.

72   (B) Gospel of Peter. On the Nile, 60 mi. N of the monastery founded by St. Pachomius at Chenoboskion (Nag Hammadi; → 56 above) was his monastery at Panopolis (Akhmim). In 1886 its necropolis yielded a small 8th- or 9th-cent. codex containing 174 lines or 60 verses of a Gk passion/resurrection narrative in which Peter speaks in the 1st pers. Two Oxyrhynchus papyri fragments from *ca.* 200 (#2949, ed. R. A. Coles [1972]), with some 16 discernible words on about 20 lines, have a close but partial similarity to the Akhmim text, confirming the scholarly guess that the work had origins no later than *ca.* 150. Most scholars have favored identifying the Akhmim text as the *Gospel of Peter* read in the church at Rhossus in Syria *ca.* 190, championed by docetists but rejected by Bishop Serapion of Antioch (Eusebius, *HE* 6.12.2–6). Origen (*Comm. in Matt.* 10.17 [ANF 10.424]) reported that according to *Gos. Pet.* Joseph, husband of Mary, had children by an earlier marriage (= Jesus' brothers). In the Akhmim *Gos. Pet.* Herod puts Jesus to death, and two men come down from heaven on Sunday morning to bring forth from the tomb a Jesus whose head reaches beyond the heavens and whose cross follows by itself behind him! Many scholars think of an imaginative pastiche dependent on all four Gospels, but independence in whole or part is defended by Harnack, Gardner-Smith, Koester, *et al.* Crossan contends that *Gos. Pet.* in part (1:1–6:22; 7:25–11:49) constitutes the original passion narrative on which the four evangelists drew. Perhaps *Gos. Pet.* represents popular, fluid developments of early traditions free from the control of the apostolic kerygma (e.g., Herod's role against Jesus). These imaginatively expanded accounts may have been written down and combined with stories remembered from past hearing or reading of canonical Gospels.

(Text, Fr transl., commentary, and bibliography in M. G. Mara [SC 201; Paris, 1973]. Brown, R. E., *NTS* 33 [1987] 321–43. Denker, J., *Die theologiegeschichtliche Stellung des Petrusevangeliums* [Bern, 1975].)

73   (C) Apocalypse of Peter. Preserved in Coptic (*NHL*), this work narrates a visionary experience in which Jesus shows Peter the true (docetic) events surrounding the crucifixion. The immortal, spiritual Savior laughs at the futile attempt to kill him (81.3–83.15), warns Peter of the opposition to gnostics from church authorities, and establishes him as the foundation of gnostic revelation.

74   (VI) Resurrection Dialogues. This characteristically gnostic genre includes sayings gospels and dialogues in which a postresurrection appearance of the Lord to the disciples provides a framework for gnostic teaching. This teaching has no connection to the sayings or narratives about Jesus beyond the allusions in the "resurrection vision" frame story. In *Ap. John, 1 Apoc. Jas.,* and *Ep. Pet. Phil.* from the NHL the resurrection dialogue is embedded in a larger framework of the "acts" of the apostles who are about to be dispersed to preach; see also *Soph. Jes. Chr.* Resurrection dialogues from a somewhat later period of gnosis have been preserved in the Coptic Askew and Bruce codices: *Pistis Sophia* (two independent revelations); *1 and 2 Jeu* (→ Early Church, 80:73).

75   (A) Gospel of Mary. Preserved only in the Coptic Berlin codex and a Gk fragment (Ryl. 463), this text lacks the opening and several middle pages. Apparently a resurrection dialogue between Jesus and the disciples, with a second vision of the ascent of the soul, it is a private revelation of Jesus to Mary (Magdalene), held together in the framework of the postresurrection commission to the disciples to preach.

76   (B) Epistula Apostolorum. Surviving in Coptic, Latin (fragments), and Ethiopic, this (2d-cent.?) writing was an "orthodox answer" to the gnostic resurrection dialogues. It claims to preserve the authentic revelations of the risen Jesus that were given to the apostles as a group, with allusions to all four Gospels, some NT epistles, and perhaps even early Christian writings such as the Apostolic Fathers.

77   (VII) Gnostic Writings Titled "Gospel." Several NHL texts entitled "gospel" are treatises or discourses on gnostic teaching. *Gos. Truth* uses the expression "gospel" in its opening (16.31) in the sense of "good news" (which appears in Coptic at 34.35). *Gos. Phil.* is provided with this title in the colophon, as is *Gos. Eg.,* the official title of which was probably *The Holy Book of the Great Invisible Spirit.* In these cases, introduction of canonical titles like "gospel" or "letter" probably reflects the christianization of gnostic texts.

DEAD SEA SCROLLS

ANNOTATED BIBLIOGRAPHY

78   The term "Dead Sea Scrolls," used in its widest sense, covers mss. and fragments discovered independently from 1947 on in a half-dozen sites in the cliffs W of the Dead Sea. In its narrow sense it refers to what was discovered near Qumran, the original and most important site. Some of this general bibliography refers exclusively to Qumran finds.

(I) Bibliographies of DSS. Jongeling, B., *A Classified Bibliography of the Finds in the Desert of Judah 1958–1969* (Leiden, 1971). Fitzmyer, J. A., *The Dead Sea Scrolls: Major Publications and Tools for Study* (2d ed.; SBLSBS 8, Missoula, 1979). Koester, C., "A Qumran Bibliography: 1974–1984," *BTB* 15 (1985) 110–20. *RevQ* has a systematic bibliography in each issue.

(II) Texts. Burrows, *DSSMM.* Charlesworth, J. H., Princeton ed. (3 vols.; 1991). Cross, F. M., *et al., Scrolls from Qumran Cave I* (Jerusalem, 1972). De Vaux, R., *et al., DJD* 1 (1955), 2 (1961), 3 (1962), 4 (1965), 5 (1968), 6 (1977), 7 (1982). Sukenik, *DSSHU.* Convenient student eds. of the Hebr text with Lat transl. by P. Boccaccio (Rome): 1QpHab; 1QS; 1QSa; 1QM. For vocalized Hebr text, see E. Lohse (ed.), *Die Texte aus Qumran* (Munich, 1971).

(III) Concordances. Kuhn, K. G., *Konkordanz zu den Qumrantexten* (Göttingen, 1960) with suppl. in *RevQ* 4 (1963) 163–234.

(IV) Translations. Most complete, with scientific notes, is J. Carmignac, *et al., Les Textes de Qumran* (2 vols.; Paris, 1961–63). Best Eng transl. is by G. Vermes, *The Dead Sea Scrolls in English* (3d ed.; Sheffield, 1987). Literary but free is T. H. Gaster, *The Dead Sea Scriptures in English Translation* (3d ed.; GC, 1976). There are transls. in Burrows's 2 vols. mentioned below. Jongeling, B., *et al., Aramaic Texts from Qumran with Translations* (Leiden, 1976).

(V) Studies. General: J. T. Milik, *Ten Years of Discovery in the Wilderness of Judaea* (SBT 26; London, 1959). F. M. Cross, Jr., *The Ancient Library of Qumran* (Anchor; 2d ed.; GC, 1961). E.-M. Laperrousaz, *et al.,* "Qumran," *DBSup* (1978) 9. 737–1014. M. Delcor, *Qumrân: Sa piété, sa théologie et son milieu* (Paris, 1978). G. Vermes, *The Dead Sea Scrolls: Qumran in Perspective* (Phl, 1981). B. Z. Wacholder, *The Dawn of Qumran* (Cincinnati, 1983). M. Wise, "The Dead Sea Scrolls," *BA* 49 (1986) 140–54, 228–43. J. Murphy-O'Connor, *EJMI* (1986) 119–56; M. A. Knibb, *The Qumran Community* (Cambridge, 1987). Long treatments of early views in M. Burrows, *The Dead Sea Scrolls* (NY, 1955); *More Light on the Dead Sea Scrolls* (NY, 1958). Archaeology: P. R. Davies, *Qumran* (CBW; Guilford, 1982). R. de Vaux, *L'archéologie et les manuscrits de la Mer Morte* (Oxford, 1961). E.-M. Laperrousaz, *Qoumrân* (Paris, 1976). Also *BASOR* 231 (1976) 79–80; *RevQ* 10 (1980) 269–91. Convenient summary of theology in H. Ringgren, *The Faith of Qumran* (Phl, 1963).

(VI) Relation to the NT. Surveys by R. E. Brown, *ExpTim* 78 (1966–67) 19–23; J. A. Fitzmyer, *NTS* 20 (1973–74) 382–407; *TD* 29 (1981) 31–37. Collected articles in *The Scrolls and the New Testament* (ed. K. Stendahl; NY, 1957); *La secte de Qumran et les origines du Christianisme* (RechBib 4; Bruges, 1959); *The Scrolls and Christianity* (ed. M. Black; Theological Collections 11; London, 1969); *Paul and Qumran* (ed. J. Murphy-O'Connor; London, 1968); *John and Qumran* (ed. J. H. Charlesworth; London, 1972). Studies in English are by H. H. Rowley (1957); M. Black (1961); L. Mowry (1962); J. Daniélou (1963); highly imaginative are B. E. Thiering's books on the Gospels and on church origins (Sydney, 1980, 1983). H. Braun, *Qumran und das Neue Testament* (2 vols.; Tübingen, 1966) is very comprehensive.

QUMRAN

79   **(I) The Discoveries.** The wadi that the Arabs call Qumrân empties into the NW corner of the Dead Sea 10 mi. S of Jericho. About a mile inland from the sea, on a marly plateau adjacent to the wadi are ruins excavated by R. de Vaux and G. L. Harding between 1951 and 1956. Originally the site of a fortress built in the 8th–7th cents. BC, the ruins at Qumran show evidence of common occupation in an initial period from 135–110 BC to 67–31 BC, and again in the 1st cent. AD to 68. The enclave had edifices and rooms designed to serve a community's needs: a complete water system with conduits and cisterns; a kitchen, pantry, and large dining room; store rooms; a scriptorium; pottery workshops; and cemeteries of 1,200 graves. The buildings of the initial period show a slow start, but then there was an increase in occupation from *ca.* 110 BC on; this period seems to have ended with a fire followed by an earthquake. The second period came to a close with destruction by Roman armies who occupied the site for short intervals thereafter. In 1956 and 1958 de Vaux also excavated another series of buildings 1.5 mi. S of Qumran at a spring called Ain Feshkha; seemingly they were structures built by the Qumran community to serve its economic needs.

80   In 11 caves within a few mi. of the Qumran buildings have been found the remains of some 600 mss., consisting of about 10 complete scrolls and thousands of fragments. Indeed, it was the 1947 discovery of scrolls in cave 1 that focused the interests of archaeologists on the area. About one-fourth of the mss. are biblical. Seven of the scrolls from cave 1 and the Temple Scroll from cave 11 are in Jerusalem's Shrine of the Book; the rest of the material is at the Palestine Museum in East Jerusalem (Israeli controlled since June 1967). At the museum an international and interconfessional "team" of scholars prepared material from caves 2–11 for publication in DJD; these include R. de Vaux †, J. T. Milik, J. Strugnell, P. Skehan †, F. M. Cross, J. Starcky, J. M. Allegro †, D. Barthélemy, and M. Baillet.

81   On the following page is an inventory of the caves numbered according to the order of their discovery; note that the documents are designated by the number of the cave in which they were found. Caves 1, 4, and 11 are "major" caves whose material is abundant and requires separate publication; the rest are "minor" caves whose material was published together in DJD 3. For an explanation of the system used in referring to Qumran documents, → Texts, 68:23; also Fitzmyer's bibliography, 3–8.

82   **(II) Important Qumran Writings.** The biblical mss. of Qumran will be treated by themselves elsewhere (→ Texts, 68:14–33); here we concern ourselves with works of peculiarly sectarian origin. All the works below, except 1QapGen and 3Q15, are writings composed by the Qumran sect and expressive of their theology and piety.

83   **QS:** *Serek ha-Yaḥad* = the Manual of Discipline, or the Rule of the Community. A well-preserved copy of 11 cols. was found in cave 1 and published by M. Burrows in *DSSMM* 2/2 (1951). Studies in English are by W. H. Brownlee (1951), P. Wernberg-Møller (1957), A. R. C. Leaney (1966); in French by J. Pouilly (1976); in modern Hebrew by J. Licht (1965). See bibliography by H. Bardtke, *TRu* 38 (1974) 257–91. A fragment of a ms. from cave 5 is in DJD 3. 180–81. Ten copies from cave 4 are discussed by J. T. Milik in *RB* 67 (1960) 410–16.

Paleographically, 1QS dates from 100–75 BC (Cross, *Library* 119–20); yet comparison with 4QS shows that 1QS had undergone considerable editing, especially in cols. 5, 8, and 9. The ms. 4QS^c is probably to be dated before 100 BC. Thus, a date of composition for QS between 150 and 125 makes it a most ancient sectarian composition. G. Jeremias traces it to the Righteous Teacher (→ 98 below). Yet it may reflect stages of development in community life; see J. Murphy-O'Connor, *RB* 76 (1969) 528–49; also *RB* 82 (1975) 522–51; *RevQ* 11 (1982) 81–96.

Evidently the QS scroll was the essential rule book for the life of the community. Its theme is that the community represents the New Covenant between God and humanity prophesied by Jer 32:37–41. Entrance into the community of the covenant is described in cols. 1–2. There is a graphic description in cols. 3–5 of two opposing ways of life: the way dominated by the spirit of light and truth and the way dominated by the spirit of darkness and falsehood. Then follow the actual rules that govern community life. The pattern is very much that of Israel during Moses' time in the desert wanderings, and the idea is that by withdrawing to the desert (Qumran) this community is preparing itself to be the nucleus of the new Israel that in God's time will be brought to the promised land. This is the first known example of what in Christianity would develop into rules for monastic life.

The QS scroll from cave 1 had two attached appendixes, published in DJD 1. 107–30. These are the following:

84   **QSa:** *Serek ha-ʿēdâ* = the Rule of the Congregation. This work of 2 cols. begins: "This is the rule for the whole congregation of Israel in the last days." Although the rule is patterned on the daily life of the sectarians, this life is seen as having eschatological significance. The document ends with the description of a banquet at which the *priest* who is head of the whole congregation of Israel and the *messiah* of Israel both bless bread and wine. The mention of women and children in this writing (1:4) has led to the suggestion (Cross, *Library* 79ff.) that the ʿēdâ, or congregation, refers to the totality of the sectarians, including both those in the monastic desert community (yaḥad) at Qumran and those in other places and circumstances, e.g., in camps and cities.

85   **QSb:** a Collection of Blessings. This work of 6 cols. has been poorly preserved. It gives the text for the benediction of groups and of individuals in the sect. There seems to be a special blessing for the priest as well

Documents Found in the Qumran Caves

CAVE 1:   discovered by the Bedouin; excavated by G. L. Harding and R. de Vaux in Feb.–Mar. 1949. It yielded relatively complete scrolls (three still in a jar), as well as 600 fragments of some 70 other mss.

1QIsaᵃ—the Hebr text of Isa somewhat divergent in spelling and reading from the MT (→ Texts, 68:17, 27).

1QS—the rule of life for the community that lived at Qumran (→ 83 below).

1QpHab—a free, interpretative commentary (*pēšer*) on Hab, adapting the thought of the book to the Qumran community (→ 89–90 below).

1QapGen—an apocryphal elaboration of Gen in Aramaic (→ 93 below).

(The above four mss. were taken out of Jordan at the direction of Mar Athanasius Yeshue Samuel, a Syrian prelate who had obtained them from the Bedouin. They were published in part in *DSSMM* [except 1QapGen] and later, through an intermediary, sold to Israel for $250,000.)

1QIsaᵇ—a more fragmentary copy of Isa, closer to the MT (→ Texts, 68:27).

1QH—psalms of praise (*hôdāyôt*) composed in the community (→ 86 below).

1QM—an imaginative description of the final war to be waged between the forces of good and evil (→ 88 below).

(The above three mss. were obtained from antiquities dealers by E. L. Sukenik of the Hebrew University before the partition of Palestine. They were published in part in *DSSHU*.)

Fragments of other mss. published in DJD 1. The most important are two appendixes detached from 1QS, viz., 1QSa and 1QSb (→ 84, 85 below).

CAVE 2:   discovered by the Bedouin in Feb. 1952. The most important of the fragments it yielded are from the lost Hebr text of Sir (→ Texts, 68:33).

CAVE 3:   discovered by archaeologists in Mar. 1952. It yielded two badly oxidized copper rolls that were originally part of one scroll. These were sliced open in 1956 and published in DJD 3 (→ 94 below).

CAVE 4:   discovered by the Bedouin and further excavated by archaeologists in Sept. 1952. In many ways the most important of the caves, it yielded fragments from about 520 mss. It was near the settlement and may have served as a hiding place for the community's library when the Romans were coming. For the work on this cave's fragments, see *BA* 19 (1956) 83–96. A few of the finds are:

—Some mss. of OT books going back to the 3d cent. BC, our oldest copies of Scripture (→ Texts, 68:11).

—Biblical mss. with a Hebr text unlike the MT but close to the Hebr text underlying the LXX (→ Texts 68:18–19).

—Fragments of Tob in the (hitherto lost) original Aramaic (→ Texts, 68:33).

—Fragments in the original language (Hebrew or Aramaic) of important apocrypha, hitherto preserved only in later translations, e.g., *1 Enoch; Jub.; T. 12 Patr.* (→ 9, 17, 26 above).

—Fragments of hundreds of mss. throwing light on the belief and practice of the Qumran community, including earlier copies of works found in cave 1 (QS, QH, QM). There are biblical commentaries, calendars, apocalyptic books, books in code.

CAVES 5, 6, 7, 8, 9, 10: published in DJD 3; caves 5 and 6 excavated in 1952 in relation to cave 4; caves 7–10 discovered in 1955 near the Qumran settlement. An attempt by J. O'Callaghan to identify some Gk fragments of 7Q as NT is almost universally rejected; see K. Aland, *NTS* 20 (1973–74) 357–81; P. Benoit, *RB* 80 (1973) 5–12; yet C. P. Thiede, *Bib* 65 (1984) 538–59.

CAVE 11:   discovered by the Bedouin in 1956. This cave, like cave 1, has yielded extensive portions of scrolls. Part of the material was published by Dutch scholars.

11QPsᵃ—a Pss scroll, published by J. A. Sanders as DJD 4; also see his *The Dead Sea Psalms Scroll* (Ithaca, 1967) with a postscript containing the text of an additional fragment (→ Texts, 68:31). On the noncanonical pss., see articles by P. Auffret and J. Magne, *RevQ* 8, 9, 10 (1975–80); E. M. Schuller, *Non-Canonical Psalms from Qumran* (HSS 28; Atlanta, 1986).

11QPsᵇ—another Pss collection (J. van der Ploeg, *RB* 74 [1967] 408–12).

11QPsApᵃ—a work containing both biblical and apocryphal pss. (J. van der Ploeg, *RB* 72 [1965] 210–17; *Tradition und Glaube* [Fest. K. G. Kuhn; ed. G. Jeremias; Göttingen, 1971] 128–39).

11QpaleoLev—part of Lev in paleo-Hebrew script (→ Texts, 68:17).

11QEz—a poorly preserved copy of Ezek from *ca.* 55 to 25 BC with a Hebr text close to the MT (W. Brownlee, *RevQ* 4 [1963] 11–28). Only a few fragments are legible.

11QtgJob—a 1st-cent. AD copy of a targum probably composed in the 2d cent. BC (→ Texts, 68:104).

11QMelch—fragments of an eschatological midrash from *ca.* 50–25 BC. The figure of Melchizedek, now a heavenly being above the angels, appears in a setting drawn from the description of the jubilee year in Lev 25; he is to have a role on the day of judgment. See P. J. Kobelski, *Melchizedek and Melchireša'* (CBQMS 10; Washington, 1981). For NT relevance, → Hebrews, 60:38.

11QTemple—a long sectarian scroll with cultic rules (→ 95 below).

11QJub—fragments of *Jub.* (→ 17 above).

as one for the prince (*nāśî'*) of the congregation; but see R. Leivestad, *ST* 31 (1977) 137–45.

There is no clear evidence that these works were appended to any other copy of QS, and they may well be compositions of the period when the ms. of 1QS was copied (100–75 BC).

86   QH: the *Hôdāyôt* = the Hymns of Thanksgiving. The poorly preserved 1QH was published by H. L. Sukenik in *DSSHU* 35–58, with additional fragments published by J. T. Milik in DJD 1. 136–38. Bibliography by H. Bardtke, *TRu* 40 (1975) 210–26. Studies in English are by S. Holm-Nielsen (Aarhus, 1960), M. Mansoor (GR, 1961), E. H. Merrill (Leiden, 1975), and B. P. Kittel (SBLDS 50; Chico, 1981); in French by M. Delcor (Paris, 1962). A study in modern Hebrew by J. Licht (Jerusalem, 1959) is excellent in its suggestions for filling in lacunae, as verified in fragments of six more copies of the work from cave 4. J. Carmignac (see *Textes*, 1. 145) has established that the material from cave 1 originally came from two scrolls and that Sukenik published the cols. in the wrong order: cols. 13–16 belonged to the first scroll, while cols. 17 and 1–12 belonged to the second scroll. Three scribes copied 1QH, and paleographically it is dated to the period AD 1–50.

QH is a descendant of the biblical hymn book, the Psalter. However, the classical period of Hebr poetry had passed, and QH poems resemble the hymns preserved in 1–2 Macc and the Lucan hymns of the NT (Magnificat and Benedictus). See *EJMI* 411–36. They are largely mosaics of biblical phrases, culled in particular from Pss and Isa—a style called anthological. Frequently a biblical metaphor is developed into full-blown allegory. The hymnist speaks in the 1st pers. and meditates before God on God's goodness to him. There are many historical reflections taken from the hymnist's life (J. Carmignac, *RevQ* 2 [1959–60] 205–22). For the theology of QH, see J. Licht, *IEJ* 6 (1956) 1–13, 89–101.

Holm-Nielsen has suggested an entirely liturgical origin for the hymns, but the personal character of the meditation makes this unlikely. Interesting is what Philo (*De vita contemp.* 29, 80, 83, 84) says about the Therapeutae, seemingly a branch of the Essene movement. These sectarians had hymns composed by the first chiefs of their sect; in particular, hymns were composed by individuals to be recited on the feast of Pentecost (which at Qumran was the great feast of the renewal of the covenant). The corresponding suggestion that the QH were composed in part, at least, by the Righteous Teacher has many adherents. This would mean a date of *ca.* 150–100 BC, probably after QS.

87   D or CD: the Damascus Covenant or the Zadokite Work(s). Two medieval mss. of this work (ms. A with cols. 1–16; ms. B with cols. 19–20; B 19 = A 7–8), dating from the 10th and 12th cents., were found in the Cairo Geniza (→ Texts, 68:43) in 1896–1897, and were edited as *Documents of Jewish Sectaries* by S. Schechter (1910; KTAV ed. 1970, with Prolegomenon by Fitzmyer); see *BARev* 8 (1982) 38–53. Best edition is by C. Rabin (2d ed.; Oxford, 1958). Fragments of nine mss. of the work have been found at Qumran, so clearly the medieval mss. represent a Qumran work. Fragments from 5Q and 6Q are in DJD 3. 181, 128–31; also M. Baillet, *RB* 63 (1956) 513–23. Milik (*Ten Years*, 38, 151–52; *BA* 19 [1956] 89) discusses fragments from seven 4Q mss.; see *RB* 73 (1966) 105; *JJS* 23 (1972) 135–36; *Sem* 27 (1977) 75–81. There were several recensions of CD; the Qumran material tends to agree with medieval ms. A; the oldest Qumran copy dates from 75–50 BC. Major study by P. R. Davies (JSOTSup 23; Sheffield, 1983); see J. Murphy-O'Connor, *RB* 92 (1985) 223–46, 274–77.

The work consists of two parts: (1) Admonitions drawn from history are found in cols. 1–8 of ms. A, plus 19–20 of B. An introduction for this section appears in the unpublished Qumran material. The author searches through the history of Israel until the rise of the Qumran community, drawing lessons to encourage the community. He is repetitious and oratorical but makes useful allusions to the history of the sect. By the time CD is being written the Righteous Teacher has been dead for some years (20:14). (2) In cols. 15–16 and 9–14 of ms. A, there are laws to be observed by those of the community who live in camps. The cols. in A are out of order, and both the beginning and the end of the law section have perished. In the 4Q copies there is material that continues col. 14, as well as a concluding covenant renewal ceremony. These laws cover entrance into the community, behavior, purifications, organization, and punishments. If we take the two parts together, the whole work may well have been a manual for a covenant renewal ceremony with a historical exhortation and a reminder about the laws.

Milik suggests a date of composition *ca.* 100 BC, and two factors support this date: the failure to mention the Romans in the historical section, and the paleography of the oldest copy. The laws differ to some extent from those of QS, but this may be explained either by the difference in time of composition (QS is earlier) or by the difference in circumstances of those living in camps (as distinct from those living in the desert community). CD 6:5 mentions "the converts of Israel who went out from Judah to sojourn in the land of Damascus"; and the work is addressed to the members of the New Covenant in the land of Damascus (7:19; 8:21). Some (Cross, *Library* 82–83) believe Damascus to be a figurative name for the site of Qumran, but Milik takes the term literally and thinks of a branch community from Qumran dwelling in camps in the Damascus/Hauran area. One argument for the former view is the number of copies of CD found at Qumran. J. Murphy-O'Connor (*RB* 77–81 [1970–74]), who equates Damascus with Babylon, argues for a pre-Qumran origin of the first part of CD (Essene missionary document and an encouraging memorandum), which was joined in 100–75 BC to later material. (See M. A. Knibb, *JSOT* 25 [1983] 99–117.) Davies thinks a substantial form of CD existed before the Qumran period.

88   QM: *Serek ha-Milḥāmâ* = the Rule for the War, or the War of the Sons of Light against the Sons of Darkness. The badly mutilated 1QM was published in *DSSHU,* and a detached fragment, 1Q33, was published in DJD 1. There are fragments from six more mss. in the cave 4 material published in DJD 7. Studies in French are by J. van der Ploeg (1957), J. Carmignac (1958), and B. Jongeling (1962); in English by Y. Yadin (1962) and P. R. Davies (BibOr 32; Rome, 1977). Entitled "For the Sage—the Rule for the War," the work proposes a plan for the armies and the campaign of the final 40-years' war, when God will crush the forces of evil and darkness in this world. Although the author seems to have drawn upon the military terminology of his time, the war is conducted according to theological designs rather than according to a scientific military strategy. The dominating theme is that if the forces of good (or of light) are organized according to the proper semiliturgical scheme and if their standards and trumpets are properly inscribed with prayers, God will favor them and victory will be ensured. The camps of the sons of light are organized after the directives of Num 2:1–5:4; the troops receive ardent sermons from the priests, who also sound the battle signals. The angel Michael, with the aid of Raphael and Sariel, leads the forces of light, while Belial guides the forces of darkness. Columns 2–14 give the general rules, and 15–19 seem to forecast the actual battle—although some see here a duplication (the sign that a shorter work has undergone editing).

All the extant copies of QM are from the 1st cent. AD, but J. J. Collins (*VT* 25 [1975] 596–612) posits presectarian origins in Persian dualism (see his debate with Davies in *VT* 28–30 [1978–80]). Proposals for composition extend from 110 BC (Carmignac—by the Righteous Teacher) to 50 BC–AD 25 (most scholars), or to the whole range (Davies). Yadin argues that the military tactics and equipment are Roman, and the opponents are designated as "Kittim," a term for the Romans in other DSS. Some see QM as a joining of two different works (Dupont-Sommer, Gaster, van der Ploeg), but Carmignac and Yadin argue for a single author. If the work is a later sectarian writing, it may have been composed when the group was infected by a more martial spirit. It shows no clear expectation of a Davidic Messiah; the dominant role is that of the high priest.

89   Pesharim, or Commentaries. See M. P. Horgan, *Pesharim* (CBQMS 8; Washington, 1979) for translations and interpretations. At Qumran the biblical commentaries (sg. *pēšer;* pl. *pěšārîm*) exhibit a peculiar exegetical technique. They study the biblical text verse by verse, searching for a meaning applicable to the life of the sect, to its past or present circumstances, or to its future hope. The presumption seems to be that the ancient prophet or psalmist who wrote the biblical work addressed himself not to his own times but to the future, and that that future was the history of the Qumran community. When *ca.* 600 BC Habakkuk spoke of the righteous, he really meant the Righteous Teacher of Qumran. When he spoke of Lebanon, he meant the council of the Qumran community. At times the Qumran commentator reads the words of the text he is commenting on in a way quite different from the grammatical sense intended by the original author. The procedure of the pesharim differs visibly from that of other Bible-related works at Qumran, which in midrashic manner simply expand or embellish the biblical narrative in a direction that is more faithful to the original author's intention. (For the type of interpretation evidenced in isolated quotations of the OT, see the study of J. A. Fitzmyer, *NTS* 7 [1960–61] 297–333.)

The mental background of the pesharim exegesis is that of apocalyptic. Instead of having messages for their own time, the prophets and psalmists are concerned with the last times, of which the Qumran community is the sign. The style of exegesis seems to stem from the Righteous Teacher; for according to 1QpHab 2:8–10 God gave him understanding to interpret all that was foretold through the prophets and (7:4–5) made known to him all the mysteries behind the prophets' words, just as the pesher of a mysterious vision was revealed to Daniel (Dan 5:26). Most of the pesharim date paleographically from after 50 BC. There is never more than one copy of a pesher; this may mean that the mss. that have come down to us are the autographs, i.e., the originals (Cross, *Library* 114–15). Although they are by different writers, the style of exegesis is very similar. This indicates that the various commentators were instructed in a communal tradition of interpretation, perhaps coming down from the Righteous Teacher.

90   The most important pesher is 1QpHab, a 14-col. commentary. It was published by M. Burrows in *DSSMM* 1. Cave 1 also yielded some fragmentary pesharim on Mic, Zeph, Pss 57 and 68, which appear in DJD 1. 77–82; cave 3 had a pesher on Isa (DJD 3. 95–96). Fragmentary pesharim from cave 4 on Isa, Hos, Mic, Nah, Zeph, and Pss are published by Allegro in DJD

5—a volume severely criticized (see J. Strugnell, *RevQ* 7 [1969–71] 163–276).

91   4QTestimonia, or the "Messianic" Testimonies. Published by J. M. Allegro in DJD 5 (4Q*175*). The copy we have is from 100–75 BC by the same scribe who copied 1QS. The work consists of four biblical citations given one after the other.

Allegro identified the citations as follows: (1) Deut 5:28–29, plus 18:18–19, a reference to the Prophet-like-Moses; (2) Num 24:15–17, the oracle of Balaam about a star coming from Jacob and a scepter from Israel; (3) Deut 33:8–11, glorifying Levi; (4) Josh 6:26, accompanied by a pesher taken from "The Psalms of Joshua," a hitherto unknown Qumran work, now attested in cave 4—the pesher condemns the man of Belial and his brother. There is no apparent reason for the order of the texts as they are identified by Allegro; nor is their theme apparent. Allegro suggested an eschatological theme, viz., destruction for those who do not accept the teaching of the messianic figures of the Qumran sect. Other scholars have concentrated on finding a series of messianic figures in the four citations. Thus, they match up the first three citations with the three figures that Qumran expected at the end time: (1) the prophet; (2) the Davidic Messiah; (3) the priestly Messiah (→ 116–17 below). The fourth text is thought to refer to the great enemy. In this interpretation the work belongs to a species of messianic testimonia. ("Testimonia," a term taken from the title of a work by Cyprian, is the designation for systematic collections of OT passages, usually of messianic import, which are thought to have been used by the early Christians in their arguments with the Jews. These were proof texts culled from the OT to show that Jesus was the Messiah. The use of the title for this Qumran work suggests by analogy that the sect collected texts to substantiate its messianic expectations. See J. A. Fitzmyer, *TS* 18 [1957] 513–37; P. Prigent, *Les testimonia dans le christianisme primitif* [Paris, 1961].)

This analysis of the Qumran work is probably incorrect. The first of the four citations was wrongly identified. P. Skehan (*CBQ* 19 [1957] 435–40) has shown that it is a citation of Exod 20:21 according to a proto-Samaritan text tradition (→ Texts, 68:21, 38–39). With this change the reason for the order of the passages becomes clear; they have been chosen from books in their biblical order (Exod, Num, Deut, Josh). The neat lining up of messianic characters also collapses when it is realized that the star and the scepter of the second citation refer to two different characters. The star is a (or the) priest; the scepter is the Davidic royal Messiah (CD 7:18–20). And so the work is not clearly a collection of messianic testimonia, and Allegro's original interpretation of the basic theme as eschatological is more plausible.

92   4QFlorilegium, or Eschatological Midrash. Published by J. M. Allegro in DJD 5 (4Q*174*). Paleographically the copy is dated to AD 1–50. This incomplete work contains biblical texts accompanied by an interpretation. Allegro thinks of the work as belonging to testimonia literature, but in this instance an interpretation is supplied with the biblical citation. Presumably the theme governing the collection would be a reference to the last days.

W. R. Lane (*JBL* 78 [1959] 343–46) has correctly objected to Allegro's analysis (which continues to be reproduced uncritically). The work itself makes clear that there are three principal biblical passages being discussed (2 Sam 7:10–14; Ps 1:1; Ps 2:1)—any other biblical citations are only by way of interpreting these principal passages. Moreover, the work makes a break between the discussion of 2 Sam and that of the Pss. In both sections the interpretation is described as a pesher; the term midrash appears only in introducing the lemma of Ps 1:1. Here the ordinary technique of the pesher (→ 89 above) is slightly modified because the interpretation is not in the words of the author of the document but is supplied by the use of other biblical texts. According to P. Skehan (*CBQ* 25 [1963] 121), the work is a pesher on the first lines of a series of psalms; the 2 Sam passage serves as an introduction, for it is a passage that glorifies David, who is thought of as the composer of the Psalter. See D. R. Schwartz, *RevQ* 10 (1979) 83-91 for the temples mentioned in the work; also G. J. Brooke, *Exegesis at Qumran: 4QFlorilegium* (JSOTSup 29; Sheffield, 1985).

93	**1QapGen:** the Genesis Apocryphon (formerly the Apocalypse of Lamech). Five cols. (2 and 19-22) of the Aram text of this scroll were published with an Eng transl. by N. Avigad and Y. Yadin in 1956; a fragment was published by J. T. Milik as 1Q*20* in DJD 1. 86-87. There is a comprehensive study in English by J. A. Fitzmyer (Rome, 1971). The copy is dated paleographically to 25 BC-AD 25, and no other copy has been found.

The work is a type of haggadic midrash (→ 140-41 below) on Gen 1-15. Various patriarchs (Lamech, Noah, Abraham) recount experiences that are embellishments of the biblical narrative, for the lacunas are filled in by imagination and folklore. The miraculous birth of Noah is described. The work is not a pesher, for there are no historical references to the Qumran community. Indeed, the work is not necessarily of Qumran origin, and may be simply a Jewish apocryphon. It is seemingly dependent on the treatments of Gen found in *Jub.* and in *1 Enoch* 106 (so Fitzmyer; the editors have the dependency in the opposite direction). A 1st-cent. BC date is thus indicated and the quality of its Aramaic confirms this dating (E. Y. Kutscher in ScrHier 4 [Jerusalem, 1958] 1-35).

94	**3Q15:** the Copper Scroll. For the discovery and the cutting of the two pieces of this scroll, see J. M. Allegro, *The Treasure of the Copper Scroll* (2d ed.; Anchor paperback; NY, 1964). For the unhappy history of the publishing, see R. de Vaux, *RB* 68 (1961) 146-47. The official publication of the text is by J. T. Milik in DJD 3. 201ff. Both Milik and Allegro offer translations, quite different in places (see R. E. Brown, *CBQ* 26 [1964] 251-54). The scroll is written in mishnaic Hebrew, i.e., the type of Hebrew employed in the Mishna (→ 136 below), here dialectal and in its early stages; and so the scroll is very important for the history of the Hebr language. Cross dates the script of the document to AD 25-75; Milik dates it to AD 30-130, so that it was not a part of the QL (there are no sectarian references) but an independent deposit put in a cave after the destruction of the Qumran settlement.

The scroll gives a long list of places in Palestine where treasure was hidden and thereby makes an important contribution to our knowledge of Palestinian topography. For instance 11:11-13, a passage that describes an area near the Temple, reads: "At Bet-Eshdatain in the pool, where one enters its smaller basin. . . ." If Milik's reading is correct, this is the first reference in early descriptions to the pool of Bethesda of John 5:2 (→ John, 61:74).

As for treasures, the sums are fantastically large, e.g., some 4,600 talents of silver and gold. Allegro (*Treasure* 44) reduces the value of the denominations listed in the scroll to a sixtieth or a fiftieth of their normal value, which enables him to take the list seriously as a record of the treasures from the Jerusalem Temple hidden in AD 68 by the Zealots who were in control of Jerusalem

before the Roman destruction. Looking for this treasure, Allegro unsuccessfully excavated some of the places mentioned in the scroll. Milik maintains that the list represents folklore based on the fabulous riches of the Jerusalem Temple. For Laperrousaz the treasures are related to Bar Cochba's revolt (→ 119 below).

95	**11QTemple:** the Temple Scroll. This text is perhaps the sectarians' Second Torah or sealed Book of the Law hidden until Zadok arose (CD 5:2-5; 4Q177 [Catena] 1-4:14). The 11Q copy is about 30 ft. long, with the bottoms of 66 cols. preserved; it dates from the 1st cent. AD (but a 4Q fragment suggests composition *ca.* 135 BC). Acquired by the Israeli government in 1967, it was published by Y. Yadin (*The Temple Scroll* [3 vols.; Jerusalem, 1983; Hebrew 1977]). For analysis, see articles by J. Milgrom (Koester's bibliography); Wacholder, *Dawn;* Y. Yadin, *The Temple Scroll* (NY, 1985). The work probably had the status of revelation (to Moses), for God speaks in the 1st pers. The demands for cultic purity are stricter than in the Pharisaic tradition. God describes how the earthly Temple should be built (see 1 Chr 28:19) in three square concentric courts (differs from the Solomonic and Herodian temples; → Institutions, 76:43), with gates in the walls bearing the names of the tribes, and booths in the outer walls (of which 270 were for levitical priests while on duty). In "the city of the Temple" purity allows no latrines. Strict rules bind the king, who is forbidden polygamy and divorce. See *BA* 41 (1978) 105-20; 48 (1985) 122-26; *BARev* 10 (#5, 1984) 32-49.

96	**(III) History of the Sect.**
	(A) Identity. There have been innumerable theories about the identity of the group responsible for the settlement at Qumran and for the mss. found in the caves. They have been identified as Pharisees, Sadducees, Essenes, Zealots, Ebionites, Karaites — in short, as almost every Jewish sect known to have flourished in a period of 1,000 years (200 BC-AD 800). If we may cut through all the debate, there is no serious reason to doubt that the Qumran ruins represent the Essene city in the desert described by Pliny the Elder (*Nat. Hist.* 5.17.73) as being on the western shore of the Dead Sea N of En-gedi (C. Burchard, *RB* 69 [1962] 533-69). What we know of the life of the Qumran community from its documents corresponds very nicely to what we know of the Essenes from Pliny, Philo, and Josephus (J. Strugnell, *JBL* 77 [1958] 106-15; Cross, *Library* 70ff.). There are minor differences, but these can be explained if we make allowance for different forms of Essene life in the course of 200 years of existence and if we remember that an author like Josephus was simplifying the picture of the Essenes to make them intelligible to a Gentile audience. Therefore, we shall assume that the Qumran sectarians were Essenes; no other thesis can so well account for the evidence. (Cf. R. de Vaux, *RB* 73 [1966] 212-35.)

97	**(B) Origins.** The following theory, supported by Cross, Milik, Strugnell, Skehan, de Vaux, Vermes, and others, is the one that has had the most acceptance. Important variants are offered by H. Stegemann, *Die Entstehung der Qumrangemeinde* (Bonn, 1971) and J. Murphy-O'Connor, *RB* 81 (1974) 215-44; *BA* 40 (1977) 100-24; see J. H. Charlesworth, *RevQ* 10 (1980) 213-33.

The movement of religious and national reformation that would ultimately give birth to the Qumran sect came to the fore about 167 BC. A date in the early 2d cent. is suggested by Qumran's own calculation of its history. In CD 1:5-8 we hear that 390 years after the fall of Jerusalem to Nebuchadnezzar (587) God caused a new planting to grow forth from Israel. This would mean about 190 BC, but the figure 390 may be symbolic (see

Ezek 4:5) or approximate. Another passage in the QL suggests that the reign of Antiochus Epiphanes (175–164), the great persecutor of the Jews, was the precise time of the sect's origins. The author of 4QpNah speaks of a period "from the time of Antiochus until the coming of the rulers of the Kittim [Romans]" — this is probably the span of the sect's existence up to the time when the author is writing, i.e., Roman times.

In particular, the Qumran sect is probably to be related to the Hasidean branch of the Maccabean revolt against Antiochus (→ History, 75:134ff.). In 1 Macc 2:42 we hear that Mattathias, the father of Judas Maccabeus, was joined by the Hasideans (Ḥasîdîm, or "pious ones"). They were incensed at the religious blasphemies of the hellenized Jews favorable to Antiochus, and especially by the removal in 172 of Jason, the high priest from the legitimate line of Zadok, in favor of Menelaus, a non-Zadokite. It is interesting to note that most scholars today derive the Gk name Essēnoi (var. Essaioi) from the pl. forms (ḥasēn, ḥasayyāʾ) of ḥasyāʾ, the Eastern Aram equivalent of Hebr ḥasîd; and so even by name Essenes may be the offshoot of the Hasideans (Milik, Ten Years 80 n. 1; Cross, Library 51–52 n.).

For a while the Hasideans supported the Maccabees; but the interest of the Hasideans was primarily religious, whereas the Maccabees became more and more politically oriented, ambitious to establish a dynasty. When ca. 162 the Syrians appointed the treacherous Alcimus high priest, the Hasideans accepted him as "a priest, from the line of Aaron," even though Judas Maccabeus was opposed (1 Macc 7:9–16). This period of halfhearted alliance with the Maccabees is described in CD 1:9–10 as "the twenty years in which they were like blind men groping their way." But then God "raised for them a Righteous Teacher to guide them in the way of His heart." Seemingly the Qumran Essenes derived directly from those Hasideans who abandoned the Maccabees and followed the Righteous Teacher. Murphy-O'Connor argues that conservative Jews returned to Palestine from Babylon after Judas Maccabeus's first victories in 165 BC, and from them was derived the Qumran group.

98   (C) The Righteous Teacher. The identity of the Righteous Teacher remains a mystery. Our sources for this period are pro-Maccabee and give little attention to their enemies within Judaism (at least until ca. 100 and the revolt of the Pharisees). The Teacher was a priest of the Zadokite line. If he was the author of QH, he was a man of great personal piety. The claims that he was a messiah, that he was crucified, that he came back to life, or that he was the forerunner of Jesus Christ are totally unfounded. (For a thorough discussion, see J. Carmignac, Christ and the Teacher of Righteousness [Baltimore, 1962] and G. Jeremias, Der Lehrer der Gerechtigkeit [Göttingen, 1963].) The Hebr title given to this figure, môreh ha-ṣedeq, often translated "Teacher of Righteousness," is probably to be understood both in the sense that he himself is righteous and in the sense that he teaches righteousness. The title is a traditional one, for Joel 2:23 reads: "He has given you the teacher of righteousness [môreh liṣdāqâ]; He has made the rain come down for you"; see also Hos 10:12.

99   The incident that caused the break between the Teacher and the Maccabees probably came during the period of Jonathan's leadership, after the death of his brother Judas (160). In 152 Jonathan accepted appointment as the high priest of the Jews from the hand of the Syrian king Alexander Balas (1 Macc 10:18–21; → History, 75:137). This action by a Maccabee who was not a legitimate Zadokite must have constituted the unforgivable sin in the eyes of those Hasideans who had joined the revolt because of the Syrian attempt to replace the Zadokite priesthood. In 1QpHab we hear of a "Wicked Priest" who was faithful at the beginning of his term but who, when he became ruler of Israel, betrayed the commandments. Although the epithet may have been applied to more than one man, most agree with Milik and Skehan that the Wicked Priest was Jonathan (contra Cross, who opts for Simon Maccabee). Murphy-O'Connor suggests that the Righteous Teacher was the unnamed Zadokite priest who should have succeeded as high priest in 159–152 after the death of Alcimus (→ History, 74:136–37; Josephus, Ant. 20.9.3 § 237). The Wicked Priest persecuted the Righteous Teacher (1QpHab 5:10–11; 9:9) and even pursued him into his place of exile on the Day of Atonement (11:4–8). The mention of this solemn feast day demonstrates that the Priest and the Teacher were following different calendars; for although the day of this outrage may have been the feast of the Atonement for the Teacher, it could not have been a feast day for the Priest — the violation of such a high holy day would have scandalized all. This confirms other evidence (→ 18 above) that the Maccabees offended the Hasidean followers of the Teacher not only over the question of Zadokite succession but also by following the lunar calendar introduced into Temple worship under Antiochus Epiphanes, instead of restoring the old solar calendar.

The Wicked Priest was unsuccessful in his campaign against the Righteous Teacher. God delivered the Priest into the hands of the Gentiles, where he suffered a death by torture (4QpPs37 1:18–20; 1QpHab 9:9–12). This fits the career of Jonathan, who was arrested in 143–142 by the Syrian general Trypho and who died in prison (1 Macc 12:48; 13:23). Simon, the brother and successor of Jonathan, widened the split with the Teacher and his followers; for in 140 Simon accepted from the Jews the high priesthood for himself and his children forever, thus publicly denying the Zadokite claims (1 Macc 14:41–48; → History, 75:139). The text of the "Psalms of Joshua" preserved in 4QTestim 24–29 condemns Jonathan and Simon together: "Behold an accursed man, a man of Belial, has risen to become a snare to his people and a cause of destruction to all his neighbors. And [his brother] arose [and ruled], both being instruments of violence" (cf. P. Skehan, CBQ 21 [1959] 75).

100   The Teacher seems to have outlived his two Maccabee enemies. It is hard to determine the exact moment when he brought his followers to Qumran, an event that seems to be described in CD 6:5: "The converts of Israel went out of the land of Judah to sojourn in the land of Damascus." (If not meant literally, "Damascus" may be a figurative name for the Qumran desert [see C. Milkowsky, RevQ 11 (1982) 97–106] or for Babylon [Murphy-O'Connor].) The earliest coins found at Qumran date from ca. 130. The beginning of this first phase of Qumran occupation was very light (perhaps 50 persons). Probably the Teacher died a natural death during the reign of Simon Maccabee's son, John Hyrcanus (135–104). The Teacher left his followers looking forward to God's ultimate sending of the Messiah(s) to deliver them (CD 19:35–20:1; 20:13–14).

101   (D) Subsequent History.

(a) FIRST CENTURY BC. Toward the end of the reign of John Hyrcanus, just before the turn of the century, the Qumran complex was enlarged (for perhaps 200 persons). Milik (Ten Years 88) plausibly suggests that this influx was the result of Hyrcanus's persecution of the Pharisees. The Pharisees were another offshoot of the Hasideans who had remained faithful to the Maccabean–Hasmonean cause until they could no longer tolerate the rapacity and religious insensibility of Hyrcanus, who was more a secular prince than a high priest

(Josephus, *Ant.* 13.10.5 § 288–98; → History, 75:140, 147). In describing the Wicked Priest as one who robbed wealth and amassed riches, 1QpHab 8:12 may have been attributing the characteristics of John Hyrcanus to his uncle Jonathan; for Josephus (*Ant.* 13.8.4 § 249) recounts Hyrcanus's ruthless means of raising wealth. Milik (*Ten Years* 88) thinks that Hyrcanus is the one referred to in CD 1:14ff. as a liar who persecuted the backsliders (= Pharisees) and suggests that the Qumran sectarians considered Hyrcanus to be a false prophet (Josephus, *Ant.* 13.10.7 § 299, refers to Hyrcanus's gift of prophecy). Many of the disillusioned Pharisees may have joined the Essene cause, recognizing that the Essenes were right in having opposed the Maccabean corruption when it first became evident.

102 During this flourishing period of settlement after 100 BC, the Qumran Essenes continued their opposition to the Hasmonean priest-rulers in Jerusalem. We find in 4QpNah "the furious young lion . . . who hangs men alive" — a reference to Alexander Janneus (103–76), who crucified many Jews, especially the Pharisees (Josephus, *Ant.* 13.14.2 § 380). This same work mentions the attempt of "Demetrius, King of Greece" [Demetrius III Eukairos] to invade Jerusalem in 88 BC at the request of the Jews opposed to Janneus (*Ant.* 13.13.5–14 § 376ff.). A calendar from cave 4 mentions by name Salome Alexandra (76–67), wife and successor of Janneus, and also tells of a massacre by "Aemilius" Scaurus, the first Roman governor of Syria (Milik, *Ten Years* 73). Several Qumran works refer to the coming of the terrible "Kittim," i.e., the Romans, who represented God's judgment on the Hasmonean family (1QpHab 2:12ff.). Clearly, these works were written after Pompey's entry into Jerusalem in 63 BC.

103 Archaeological evidence points to a violent destruction of the Qumran settlement by fire, followed by an earthquake. This induced a 30–40 year abandonment beginning with the Roman invasion in 67–63 BC (Dupont-Sommer, Laperrousaz), or in 40–37 BC and the Parthian invasion (Milik, Mazar), or before the great Jordan valley earthquake of 31 BC (de Vaux). While some would relate the abandonment to Herod the Great (37–4 BC), who might not have wanted religious fanatics so close to his winter quarters at Jericho, others would date the reoccupation of Qumran to his reign. He is supposed to have been generally favorable to Essenes (Josephus, *Ant.* 15.10.4–5 § 372–79); and he was opposed to the Hasmonean high priest enemies of Qumran.

104 (b) FIRST CENTURY AD. This renewal of settlement, which took place before the beginning of the Christian era, lasted until AD 68. We do not know what gave rise to this rebuilding, but the renewed sectarians were now anti-Roman. In QM the Kittim are pictured on the side of darkness in the eschatological war between the sons of light and the sons of darkness. The Qumran settlement was destroyed for the last time in the summer of 68 by the Roman *Legio X Fretensis,* as the conquerors closed the noose about the centers of Jewish resistance. Before this destruction the community mss. were deposited (hidden?) in caves, especially in cave 4, and some coins were buried. Some of the Essenes seem to have gone south to join the last-ditch resistance at the stronghold of Masada (→ 123 below). The Romans, who established military encampments in the ruins of Qumran, evidently stumbled upon the ms. hoards, for many of the documents were brutally mutilated in antiquity.

105 In Origen's time (early 3d cent.) Gk and Hebr mss. were found in a jar near Jericho. Another discovery about 785 is attested in a letter of the Nestorian Patriarch Timotheus. Evidently one such discovery yielded mss.

that reached the Jewish sect of Karaites and influenced their thought. It was among the sealed up remains of the library of a Karaite synagogue at Cairo (the Cairo Geniza; → Texts, 68:43–44) that in 1896–1897 S. Schechter found documents, like CD and Hebr Sir, that we now know to have been related to the Qumran material. (N. Wieder, *The Judean Scrolls and Karaism* [London, 1962].)

106 (IV) Features in Qumran Life and Thought. We take for granted that there were various types of Essenes and that their life must have varied according to whether they were associated with the main settlement at Qumran or whether they dwelt in "camps" and cities. The life at Qumran is best known to us.

(A) Community Life. Evidently, the buildings excavated at Qumran by R. de Vaux were used as the communal center by several hundred sectarians who dwelt in huts and tents (and caves?) nearby. Admission to this community of the New Covenant was strictly regulated. Candidates had to be Israelites and had to be scrutinized by a "supervisor." The ceremony of entry (1QS 1–3) involved taking a binding oath to observe the Law as it was infallibly interpreted in the Zadokite tradition by the Righteous Teacher (5:7–9). A ritual cleansing was also administered in connection with entrance to the covenant (3:6–12; 5:13). However, as 3:4–6 makes clear, such purification by water was no substitute for purity of heart—the two went together: "He shall be cleansed from all his sins by the spirit of holiness. . . . And his flesh shall be made clean by the humble submission of his soul to the precepts of God, when his flesh is sprinkled with purifying water and is sanctified by cleansing water" (3:7–9).

107 For the first year (6:16–17) the initiates took no part in the solemn meals or the purificatory rites of the community. They retained their own possessions. (Vermes suggests that this was not only a stage of advancement but also a permanent stage for many who never advanced further. Such people made their own living and paid dues to the community. They would also be the married members of the community.) At the end of the year (3:18–20) there was another scrutiny, and the novices who passed it were asked to hand their possessions into the care of the "supervisor." They were not admitted to the community meals yet, and only when the second year had expired (3:21–23) were they made full-scale members of the community. Then their possessions were added to the common fund. There were rules for chastising those who violated community precepts and for expelling serious offenders.

108 How extensive was celibacy among the Qumran Essenes? (See H. Hübner, *NTS* 17 [1971] 155–67; A. Steiner, *BZ* 15 [1971] 1–28; A. Marx, *RevQ* 7 [1972] 323–42.) All the ancient authors, Josephus, Philo, and Pliny, mention Essene celibacy. This agrees with the discovery that there were only male skeletons in the main burial ground of the Qumran community. However, there is mention of women and children in CD, QM, and 1QSa; and female skeletons were found on the fringes of the cemetery. Probably one group (the elite, or the priests, or the fully initiated) did practice celibacy, at least for periods of their life—the priestly line had to be continued—but the rest were married. This agrees with Josephus's evidence about nonmarrying and marrying Essenes (*J.W.* 2.8.2 and 13 § 120, 160). Evidently, both in their constant ritual washings and in their celibacy, the full-scale members of the community imitated the purity that the OT demanded of priests before sacrifice. Their dislike for divorce was close to that of Jesus (J. R. Mueller, *RevQ* 10 [1980] 247–56). Whether or not the Essenes practiced animal sacrifice at Qumran is not clear.

(Skeletons of animals have been found buried, but do they represent sacrifice [Duhaime] or refuse [Laperrousaz]?—*RevQ* 9 [1977–78] 245–51, 569–73.) Certainly there was a tendency on the part of the sectarians to regard their whole existence at Qumran as having sacrificial value.

109 Life at Qumran in the fierce heat of the Jordan valley must have been demanding. After their daily work, the sectarians assembled at night for prayer, study, and reading (1QS 6:7–8). Their meals were imbued with religious significance, whence the exclusion of those not fully initiated. In 1QSa a meal of bread and wine is described in an eschatological context, and the possibility of the appearance of the Messiah is mentioned. From this some have inferred that community meals were looked upon as spiritual anticipations of the messianic banquet. See L. F. Badia, *The Dead Sea Peoples' Sacred Meal and Jesus' Last Supper* (Washington, 1979); L. H. Schiffman, *RevQ* 10 (1979) 45–56.

The similarity between Qumran life and that of the Jerusalem church described in Acts has been noted by several scholars (S. E. Johnson, *ZAW* 66 [1954] 106–20, reprinted in K. Stendahl [ed.], *The Scrolls and the New Testament* 129–42; J. A. Fitzmyer in *StLA* 233–57; R. E. Brown, *ExpTim* 78 [1966–67] 19–23).

110   (B) Community Organization. Rank in the community was sharply defined, and at meals the sectarians were required to sit and to speak in order. The chief division was between the House of Aaron (clergy) and the House of Israel (laity). Most of the authority was vested in the priests; only they "have authority in questions of justice and property, and they will have the decisive disposition regarding the men of the community" (1QS 9:8). There was a symbolic division of the community into 12 tribes, as well as a division into numerical units of thousands, hundreds, fifties, and tens (1QSa 1:29–2:1).

Government seems to have been exercised by distinct judicial, legislative, and executive groups. The presence of judges is mentioned, but we do not know much about them. We have more information about the General Assembly of the community and its Supreme Council. The Assembly of all the mature members of the community, "the Session of the Many" (1QS 6:8ff.), was apparently the organ by which the community governed itself, for it had both judicial and executive authority. It met at least once a year, at Pentecost (2:19), to renew the covenant and receive new members. Within this Assembly, there was a higher and more permanent body, viz., the Supreme Council, consisting of 12 men and 3 priests (8:1). It is not clear whether the total was 15, or only 12, with the 3 priests constituting a subdivision. The 12 seem to have been representatives of the 12 tribes, and perhaps the remainder represented the 3 clans of Levi. See J. M. Baumgarten, *JBL* 95 (1976) 59–78.

111 Besides the Assembly and the Council, there were specific officials with authority. Here we must describe the situation in CD and that in QS separately. CD 13:2–7 stresses that even for the smallest groups of sectarians (tens) there are to be two officials: a *priest* learned in the "Book of Meditation," and a *supervisor* (*měbaqqēr*) learned in the law. The priest takes care of the liturgy, and the tasks of the supervisor are spelled out in 13:7ff.: He is to instruct the congregation, to be like a father and a shepherd to them, and to examine and approve newcomers. If this is the arrangement for small groups, CD 14:7–9 proposes a similar arrangement for the whole congregation. Here again, it is the priest who enrolls (*yipqōd*, from the root *pqd*) the congregation and is learned in the "Book of Meditation," and together with him is the supervisor of all the camps. The latter seems

to have had great authority in commanding individual members and in settling disputes among them. The entire earnings of the community were put into the hands of the supervisor, who, aided by the judges, distributed aid to the orphans and to the needy. Vermes suggests that this head supervisor was a Levite (as distinct from the priest) and bore the title of *maśkîl* (i.e., master or instructor; 1QS 9:12ff. gives a set of rules for a *maśkîl*, who is to select, instruct, and judge the members).

If we turn now to the organization proposed in 1QS, we are not certain if the officials are the identical ones proposed by CD or if there is an adaptation to a different community situation. For groups of ten there are once again two officials: the *priest* who presides at deliberations and blesses food, and *the man who studies the law* and is concerned with the conduct of the members (1QS 6:3–7). Presumably the latter is the same as the "supervisor" of CD. However, 1QS is vaguer about the officials of the whole community. It speaks of a "supervisor of the many" (6:12), who has an important role in the assemblies and takes care of community goods (6:20). There is also "one who presides [*pāqîd*, from the root *pqd*] at the head of the many" (6:14) and examines candidates. From 1QS one could easily get the impression that this head *pāqîd* is the same person as the head supervisor (*měbaqqēr*), whereas in CD the priest who enrolls (*yipqōd*) is distinct from the *měbaqqēr*.

112 We have presented the Qumran organization in such detail because it offers extremely important parallels for the organization of the primitive Christian church. This church also had a General Assembly (the "multitude" of the disciples of Acts 6:2,5; 15:12, very similar to the Qumran Session of the Many). It also had a special body of the Twelve, the intimate followers of Jesus. Moreover, the Christian bishop is an excellent parallel to the Qumran supervisor. *Episkopos,* "overseer" or "supervisor," could be a literal translation of either *pāqîd* or *měbaqqēr;* and the functions attributed to the bishop are much the same as those of the Qumran supervisor, e.g., shepherd of the flock, steward and manager of community property, and inspector of the doctrine of the faithful (1 Pet 2:25; Acts 20:28; Titus 1:7–9; 1 Tim 3:2–7; see R. E. Brown, *New Testament Essays* [3d ed.; NY, 1982] 25–30; L. Arnaldich, *Salmanticensis* 19 [1972] 279–322; B. E. Thiering, *JBL* 100 [1981] 59–74; C. K. Kruse, *RevQ* 10 [1981] 543–51).

113   (C) Eschatology and Messianism. The Qumran community lived in an eschatological context. Throughout Israel's entire history, God had prepared for this community of the New Covenant. If Habakkuk (2:4) had promised that the just man would live by faith, 1QpHab 8:1–3 explains that "this concerns all those who observe the law among the Jews whom God will deliver from judgment because of their suffering and because of their faith in the Righteous Teacher." In other words, everyone who is just will eventually join the sect. 1QpHab 7:1–8 identifies the time in which the community lives as the final time, but says that this time is being prolonged according to the mysterious plan of God.

114 The messianism of Qumran has been discussed at great length: J. Starcky (*RB* 70 [1963] 481–505) has sought to trace a development in the messianic thought of Qumran, but there are difficulties (see R. E. Brown, *CBQ* 28 [1966] 51–57; also E.-M. Laperrousaz, *CahCER* 31 [#128, 1983] 1–11).

The Righteous Teacher, although not a messiah in the ordinary sense and not using any messianic title, regarded his work as offering to Israel its great chance of salvation. (Whether or not he drew on the Suffering

Servant imagery of Dt-Isa to explain his role and that of his community is questionable; J. Carmignac [*RevQ* 11 (1961) 365-86] concludes negatively.) Therefore, it is not surprising that the earliest Qumran writings, written in the flush of enthusiasm about what was being accomplished by God through the Teacher, do not speak of the future coming of a messiah. This holds true for the earliest copies of QS and of QH.

115 The death of the Righteous Teacher (*ca.* 120-110 BC) seems to have served as a catalyst to Qumran messianic expectations. An emphasis on messianism in this period may have also been abetted by the entrance of many Pharisees into the sect. And so CD 19:35-20:1 reckons a span of time from the death of the Righteous Teacher until there would arise a messiah from Aaron or from Israel. By the time this document was written (*ca.* 100) the community realized that their deliverance had not been accomplished in the Teacher's lifetime and that they were living in a period before God's final intervention and his raising up the one(s) chosen or anointed (= messiah) to accomplish ultimate victory. At first they probably expected this period to be short. CD 20:14-15 mentions 40 years from the Teacher's death until the destruction of all the men of war who had deserted to the liar (John Hyrcanus?). If taken literally, this means divine victory within a generation. But the sectarians soon learned better; and 1QpHab, written after the appearance of the Romans in 63, speaks of God's prolonging the period.

116 Just what were the messianic expectations in this period? 1QS 9:11 (a copy written in 100-75 BC) contains a passage not found in an earlier copy of QS from cave 4; this passage speaks of "the coming of a prophet and the Messiahs of Aaron and Israel." Who are these figures? (1) "A prophet." The two most plausible identifications for this expectation are the Prophet-like-Moses of Deut 18:15,18, and the prophet Elijah as he is described in Mal 4:5 (3:23). Both expectations were alive in Palestine a century later, as we see from the NT (→ John 1:21; 7:40; Matt 18:10). Since 1QS speaks of keeping the community's law until the coming of this prophet, the context supports identification as the Prophet-like-Moses. However, Qumran was also interested in Elijah, as we know from a document from cave 4 (J. Starcky, *RB* 70 [1963] 497-98) that paraphrases the passage in Mal.

117 (2) "The Messiahs of Aaron and Israel." Note the pl. As a general precaution, we may warn the reader that in any Jewish document "messiah" does not have all the connotations that the term has in Christian writing, where there has been a radical reinterpretation in the light of Jesus. Nevertheless, it is proper to capitalize the word in referring to Qumran expectations, for the sectarians expected particular individuals set aside and

anointed by God to carry out his work. The Messiah of Aaron would be the anointed High Priest, and the Messiah of Israel would be the anointed Davidic king. (The latter is confirmed by 4QPatriarchal Blessings, where a pesher exegesis of Gen 49:10 speaks of "the righteous Messiah, the shoot of David." We should note, however, that not all scholars accept this interpretation of Qumran messianism, e.g., R. Laurin, *RevQ* 4 [1963] 39-52; B. Vawter, *BCCT* 83-99.) R. E. Brown (*CBQ* 19 [1957] 63-66) shows how the expectations of two such figures, one priestly and one Davidic, may have arisen in postexilic Judaism. Zech 4:14 pictures two anointed figures in the presence of the Lord, Zerubbabel of the Davidic line and Joshua the priest; also see the discussion of Zech 6:11. It is quite plausible that in a priestly group like the Qumran community a hope for a priestly Messiah may have accompanied the more general hope for a Davidic Messiah. If the Davidic expectation was based on the eternal covenant between God and David in 2 Sam 7:12-13, there was just as good evidence for an eternal covenant with the priesthood (cf. Sir 45:15,24; Exod 29:9; 40:15).

We hear more of the two extraordinary figures of Qumran expectation in 1QSa, where in the banquet with messianic overtones the two who preside and bless are the Priest and the Messiah of Israel. The blessings in 1QSb seem to include both the Priest (not mentioned by name) and "the Prince [*nāśî'*] of the congregation" — the latter, on the analogy of Ezekiel's use of "prince" and on the usage of CD 7:20, is the Davidic Messiah of Israel. 4QFlor associates at the end of time the Branch of David and the Interpreter of the Law (a figure whose task, at least, is priestly). 4QpIsa[a] seems to have the Shoot of David being instructed by a priest. In the later works of the Qumran community, e.g., QM, a greater role is given to the eschatological High Priest than to the Davidic Messiah; but it is possible that the failure to mention the latter may be because the copies that have come down to us are incomplete.

The theory of the two Messiahs is found also in *T. 12 Patr.* (G. R. Beasley-Murray, *JTS* 48 [1947] 1-17, although de Jonge disagrees), but we are not certain to what extent this apocryphon preserved in Greek is related to the QL (→ 25-29 above). N. Wieder (*JSS* 6 [1955] 14-25) has shown that there was an expectation of two Messiahs among the medieval Karaites, a sect influenced by Qumran thought (→ 105 above). The NT clearly presents Jesus as the Davidic Messiah, but there are also indications of a theology of Jesus as the anointed High Priest of eschatological times, e.g., in Heb. There are some echoes in patristic writings as well of Jesus as a twofold Messiah. See T. A. Donaldson, *JETS* 24 (1981) 193-207.

OTHER SITES

118 The discoveries at Qumran and the realization that ancient mss. could survive in the dry heat of the Dead Sea area resulted in wider searches on the western shore and in the adjacent mountains. We shall discuss these areas proceeding from N to S.

(I) Khirbet Mird. This site, 9 mi. SE of Jerusalem, is in the Buqei'a, the region in the desert of Judah over the cliffs behind Qumran, some 6 mi. W of the Dead Sea. It was once a Hasmonean fortress (Hyrcanion) and later the Christian monastery of

Castellion (or Marda—Aramaic for fortress and the form from which the current name derives). This monastery was founded in 492 by St. Sabas, and its library was the source of ms. fragments found in the ruins in July 1952 by the Bedouin. A Belgian excavation under R. de Langhe of Louvain took place in Feb.–Apr. 1953, when more fragments were found in a cistern. Paleography points to a date from the 6th to the 9th cent. for these fragments.

The mss. represented are in Arabic, Greek, and

Christian Palestinian Aramaic. A. Grohmann published *Arabic Papyri from Ḥirbet el-Mird* (Louvain, 1963). The Gk material included fragments from uncial biblical codices of the 5th–8th cents. (Wis, Mark, John, Acts), some non-canonical works, and a fragment of Euripides' *Andromache* that predates previously known copies by six centuries. The Palestinian Aram material has attracted some attention (→ Texts, 68:130): J. T. Milik published an inscription and a letter in *RB* 60 (1953) 526–39; C. Perrot published a 6th-cent. fragment of Acts in *RB* 70 (1963) 506–55. The archaeology of Khirbet Mird is discussed by G. R. H. Wright in *Bib* 42 (1961) 1–21; also see 21–27.

119   (II) Murabbaʿat. The four caves of Wadi Murabbaʿat are 15 mi. SE of Jerusalem, about 2 mi. inland from the Dead Sea, roughly 12 mi. S of Qumran and 10 mi. N of En-gedi. In 1951 the Bedouin began marketing fragments from these caves, and R. de Vaux and G. L. Harding led an expedition to excavate the inaccessible site in Jan.–Feb. 1952. Two of the caves yielded written material, and it is probable that much more was destroyed in the 1920s when the Bedouin gathered bat dung, a valuable fertilizer, from these caves. The caves were used as dwellings, permanent or temporary, from Chalcolithic to Arabic times; but our prime interest is in their use in the period AD 132–135, the time of the Second Jewish Revolt against the Romans (→ History, 75:191–93; also A. Kloner, *BA* 46 [1983] 210–21). From the earlier period we shall mention only fragment Mur 17, a palimpsest with text from the 8th cent. BC, which is the earliest known papyrus inscribed in a North Semitic language.

These caves, along with the others to be mentioned below, served as places of refuge for the soldiers of Bar Cochba, the leader of the revolt, when the Roman army began to destroy their more permanent camps, e.g., the one at En-gedi. For the story of the Second Jewish Revolt, see J. A. Fitzmyer in *BCCT* 133–68; also *BTS* 29, 33 (1960); 58 (1963); Y. Yadin, *Bar-Kokhba* (London, 1971). These troops brought along with them their religious books, their records of orders received from headquarters, personal documents, etc.; and the fragments of these varied writings have been published in DJD 2.

The Hebr biblical fragments, including a scroll of the Minor Prophets from *ca.* AD 100 found by the Bedouin in 1955, represent a textual tradition very close to that of the MT. (For their importance, → Texts, 68:36.) Several of the documents are part of the correspondence of the Second Revolt, including two letters (#43, 44) from the revolutionary leader Simon ben Kosibah to his lieutenant Yešuaʿ ben Galgula (Mur 43 may be in ben Kosibah's own hand). These letters supply Simon's real name; he has been known to history as Bar Cochba, from the name bar Kôkĕbâ, "son of the star," supposedly given to him by Rabbi Aqiba as a messianic designation (see Num 24:17); later rabbis called him ben Kôzibâ, "son of the lie," because his messianic revolt misled Israel. As Fitzmyer has pointed out, document Mur 24 is important for dating the revolt to 132–135. There are also dated business and legal documents important for understanding the economic and sociological situation, as well as for linguistic and paleographic purposes. A few documents, chiefly grain lists, are written in Greek.

120   (III) Valleys between En-gedi and Masada. In 1960–1961 a group of Israeli scholars (Y. Aviram, N. Avigad, Y. Aharoni, P. Bar-Adon, Y. Yadin) organized expeditions to investigate caves in a number of valleys in this 10-mi. area in Israel. The reports are published in *IEJ* 11 (1961) 3–96; 12 (1962) 165–262; also Y. Yadin, *BA* 24 (1961) 34–50, 86–95; *BTS* 29, 33 (1960); 58 (1963).

121   *Naḥal Ḥever* (Wadi Khabra) is about 3 mi. S of En-gedi and 7 mi. N of Masada. In 1960 and in 1961 Yadin made significant ms. discoveries here from the time of the Second Revolt. (An earlier fragment of Pss 15–16 dates from *ca.* AD 100 and is of the MT textual tradition.) In 1960 in the "Cave of the Letters" (caves 5/6) he found a bundle of papyri inside a waterskin; these contained 15 letters in Aramaic, Hebrew, and Greek from Simon ben Kosibah to his lieutenants in the En-gedi area. One (5/6Ḥev8) has Kosibah's name in Greek and confirms the vocalization. Evidently the revolutionary leader had his camp near Jerusalem (Beth-ter) and made En-gedi his chief port of supply on the Dead Sea. In one letter (5/6Ḥev15) he asks for palm and ethrogs to be brought up for the feast of Tabernacles. In 1961 in this same Cave of the Letters Yadin found a cache of 35 documents representing the family records and legal documents of one Babata, evidently the relative of a soldier who had fled to the cave. These documents, summarized in *IEJ* 12 (1962) 235–48, 258–60, cover a span of years from AD 93 to 132 and are in Nabatean, Aramaic, and Greek. They are important for the study of language and law, and also for the background of ben Kosibah's revolt. Yadin found six other legal documents from the Second Revolt (*IEJ* 12 [1962] 248–57), similar to material found at Murabbaʿat. For a comparison of the Murabbaʿat and Naḥal Ḥever finds, see M. Lehmann, *RevQ* 4 (1963) 53–81. Yadin told the story at length in *The Finds from the Bar Kochba Period in the Cave of the Letters* (Jerusalem, 1963). It is now clear that some biblical fragments and Aramaic, Greek, and Nabatean documents which were brought by the Bedouin into Jordan in the early 1950s and which were published by J. Starcky and J. T. Milik (*RB* 61 [1954] 161–81, 182–90; *Bib* 38 [1957] 245–68) came from the Cave of the Letters in Naḥal Ḥever (→ Texts, 68:36).

In another cave in this valley, the "Cave of Horrors" (cave 8), where many of the Jewish revolutionaries died, the expedition of Y. Aharoni (*IEJ* 12 [1962] 197–98, 201–7) found fragments from a Gk scroll of the Minor Prophets. They were from the same scroll that the Bedouin had taken from this cave (hitherto identified only as an unknown locale in the Judean desert) and that D. Barthélemy had published in *RB* 60 (1953) 18–29 and in *Les devanciers d'Aquila* (VTSup 10; Leiden, 1963).(For the great importance of this Gk scroll for textual studies of the LXX, → Texts, 68:67, 70–72.)

122   *Naḥal Ṣeʾelim* (Wadi Seiyal) is about 8 mi. S of En-gedi and 2.5 mi. N of Masada. Here in 1960 the expedition of Y. Aharoni found some ms. fragments in the "Cave of the Scrolls," another cave that had served as a refuge for the warriors of Bar Cochba. Two phylactery parchments were discovered, one of which has a Hebr text of Exod 13:2–10 close to the Hebr text that underlies the LXX. There were also Gk papyri with lists of names (*IEJ* 11 [1961] 21–24, 53–58).

123   (IV) Masada. Just S of the middle of the Dead Sea, opposite the Lisan peninsula, stands the imposing rock fortress of Masada. Rising steeply with cliffs on all sides, Masada is as impregnable as nature can render a site. Fortified by the Maccabees, adorned with palaces by the Herods, used by the Romans as a stronghold, Masada fell into Zealot hands in AD 66. In a dramatic narrative, Josephus relates the story of Zealot resistance to the Romans (*J.W.* 7.8.1ff. § 252). The Zealots held out until the year 74 and died to a man—the last gasp of the First Jewish Revolt. The Israelis conducted explorations and excavations between 1953 and 1965.

In 1964 an excavation under Y. Yadin found some mss. among the ruins of Zealot occupation, mss. that obviously must predate 74. These include (1) an ostracon or sherd inscribed in Aramaic dealing with money trans-actions; (2) a scroll of Pss 81–85 having a text identical to that of the MT; (3) a 1st-cent. BC copy of the Hebr original of Sir (→ Texts, 68:34); (4) a copy of a work represented in cave 4 of Qumran describing the heavenly liturgies. This work seems to have been a Qumran sec-tarian work, for it presupposes the solar calendar that was a pillar of Qumran theology (→ 18 above). One may argue that others in Palestine followed this calendar and that the work involved may have been common to many

groups, including the Zealots; but this does not seem probable. Josephus (*J.W.* 3.2.1 § 11) reports that Essenes took part in the resistance to the Romans; and thus, after the destruction of Qumran in AD 68, some Essenes may have fled with their mss. to Masada. Therefore, Yadin's discovery does nothing to prove the thesis that the sectarians at Qumran were Zealot rather than Essene. (See Y. Yadin, *IEJ* 15 [1965] 1–120; *Masada: Herod's Fortress and the Zealots' Last Stand* [NY, 1966]; W. Eck, *ZNW* 60 [1969] 282–89.)

OTHER JEWISH LITERATURE

WRITERS OF THE BIBLICAL PERIOD

124   (I) Philo Judaeus. Born *ca.* 25–20 BC of a wealthy Jewish family in Alexandria, Philo died after AD 41. Trained both in Jewish tradition and in Gk secular studies, especially philosophy, he was ideally situated to bridge the two bodies of knowledge. In facing the task of bringing Judaism to terms with a hellenized world, Philo did what Christian writers would also have to do with their Judeo-Christian heritage. Little is known of Philo's life. At first he seems to have devoted himself to study and contemplation, but later he became more in-volved in the active life of the Alexandrian Jewish com-munity. He went to Rome *ca.* AD 40 at the head of a delegation sent to lay before the emperor Caligula the grievances of the Alexandrian Jews who refused to worship the imperial images (→ History, 75:173–74).

125   In all his writings Philo explicitly refers to or implicitly utilizes Scripture and Gk philosophy. His *philosophical treatises* try to integrate philosophy with biblical principles and are only implicitly related to Scripture. Philo's *apologetic works,* defending his coreli-gionists at Alexandria against calumny, reflect the life of an important Jewish Diaspora community contemporary with Jesus and the early church. They also reveal Philo's evaluation of God's providence and the virtuous life. The *Embassy to Gaius* and the *Flaccus* reveal external Jewish social relations, and the *Contemplative Life* describes a group of Jewish ascetics, the Therapeutae, a sect similar to the Essenes of Palestine (and of Qumran; → 86 above).

Philo's *biblical studies* interpret the Bible, especially the Pentateuch, in an allegorical manner in order to show the compatibility of Jewish tradition with the philosophical wisdom of the Greeks, in particular of the Middle Platonists and the Stoics. Since Philo probably knew little or no Hebrew, his biblical interpretations are based on the LXX rather than on the Hebr text. In his *Allegory of the Jewish Law,* originally much longer than the present 21 books, Philo speaks to the initiates who can under-stand the Bible figuratively. The *Questions and Answers on Genesis and Exodus* gives both the literal and the allegorical senses of biblical passages. The *Exposition of the Law* seems addressed to both Jews and Gentiles, systematically aligning Jewish biblical tradition and Gentile thought. Throughout his biblical interpretations Philo maintains the validity of both the literal and the allegorical levels of interpretation. Philonic allegorical exegesis greatly influenced Christian biblical interpreta-tion of the Alexandrian school (→ Hermeneutics, 71:34–35). For the *Biblical Antiquities* wrongly attributed to Philo, → 50 above.

126   Whether Philo influenced NT thought, espe-cially John's Prologue and the description of Christ as the Logos, is debated: affirmatively, see R. G. Hamerton-Kelly, *Pre-existence, Wisdom, and the Son of Man* (Cam-bridge, 1973) 207–15; negatively, see R. M. Wilson, *ExpTim* 65 (1953–54) 47–49. Philo wrote of the Logos (Word), a radiation from the One (God) relating him to human beings; and Philo attributed to this Logos per-sonal attributes of justice and mercy. Probably both Philonic and Johannine Logos are independently related to personified Wisdom (*Sophia*) of Jewish sapiential writings (→ Wisdom Lit, 27:15–17) and the thought world of Hellenistic Judaism. Also debated is the rela-tionship of Philo's thought to Paul and to Heb (→ Hebrews, 60:3).

(Text and transl. in F. H. Colson and R. Marcus, *Philo* [12 vols.; LCL; 1929–53. Analysis by P. Borgen in Stone [ed.], *Jewish Writings* [→ 2 above] 233–82; and in *ANRW* II/21.1, 98–154 [full bibliography; survey of scholarship]. See also Schürer, *HJPAJC* 3.2. 809ff. Of classic status are E. R. Goodenough, *Introduction to Philo Judaeus* [2d ed.; Oxford, 1962] and H. A. Wolfson, *Philo* [Cambridge, MA, 1947]. R. Radice and D. T. Runia, *Philo of Alexandria: An Annotated Bibliography 1937–1986* [Leiden, 1988].)

127   (II) Flavius Josephus. Born in Palestine of a priestly clan in AD 37–38, Josephus ben Matthias died after 94, probably in Rome. As a young man of 16 he claims to have studied the Jewish "sects" of the Pharisees, Sadducees, and Essenes and to have spent three years with the hermit Bannus before ultimately becoming a Pharisee. During a journey to Rome in 64 he made important Roman contacts (e.g., Poppaea, Nero's wife) and became convinced of Rome's power. Although he counseled the Jews against revolt, he ultimately joined the revolt of 66–70 and became commander of the Jewish forces in Galilee (→ History, 75:181–84). Josephus's loyalty in this position was questioned by some of the revolutionaries (e.g., John of Gischala); at any rate, after the defeat of his forces by the Romans at Jotapata in 67 (a defeat of which Josephus was one of the few Jewish survivors), he surrendered to the Roman general Vespa-sian. Vespasian set him free in 69 after he had predicted correctly that Vespasian would become emperor.

Vespasian was the first of the Flavian family of emperors, and from 69 on Josephus was their client, whence the name *Flavius* Josephus. Titus, Vespasian's son and the conqueror of Jerusalem, brought Josephus to Rome and installed him in a royal palace, granting him an imperial pension and the rights of a citizen. His writings at Rome are our chief source of knowledge for

Jewish history in the period from Maccabean/Hasmonean times to the fall of Masada in AD 73.

128   THE JEWISH WAR. This book, written in the 70s as propaganda to show the futility of revolting against the Romans, is an edition in Greek, translated with the help of collaborators, of a work that Josephus first wrote in Aramaic. The Slavonic version, erroneously thought by some scholars to represent more faithfully the Aram original, is a secondary work based on the Gk text. Book 1 surveys the history of the Jews in the Hellenistic-Roman period, drawing on a (lost) life of Herod by Nicolas of Damascus. Books 2–7 tell of the Jewish war against Rome and are drawn from Josephus's own memories as well as from the Roman military records made available to him. Most of the account is reliable, although the tone is deliberately pro-Roman and Josephus's own role is presented in a sympathetic light.

129   JEWISH ANTIQUITIES. Modeled on the *Roman Antiquities* by Dionysius of Halicarnassus, Josephus's 20-vol. work appeared in AD 93 or 94. This major undertaking is a history of the Jews from patriarchal to Roman times. Books 1–10 cover the period up to the Babylonian Captivity. The information is drawn largely from the LXX Bible, supplemented by later popular Jewish traditions. In Books 11–20 Josephus had not only postbiblical material but also information from Gk and Roman histories. The reference to Jesus in *Ant.* 18.3.3

§ 63–64, the *Testimonium Flavianum*, has been considered an interpolation by many scholars; but L. H. Feldman, the translator of the pertinent vol. in the LCL, concludes (9. 49): "The most probable view seems to be that our text represents substantially what Josephus wrote, but that some alterations have been made by a Christian interpolator" (→ Jesus, 78:5). In times past this reference contributed toward making *Ant.* a companion to the Bible in many Christian homes. The work supplies indispensable knowledge of the intertestamental period.

130   MINOR WORKS. Written as an appendix to *Ant.*, Josephus's *Life* is a self-justification for his behavior as commander in Galilee. *Against Apion*, in 2 books, is a defense of Judaism against contemporary pagan slanders.

(The Eng transl. by William Whiston (1734) became almost *the* transl. of Josephus. It is now supplanted by the 9-vol. LCL transl. by H. St. J. Thackeray, R. Marcus, A. Wikgren, and L. H. Feldman [1926–65] based on the critical Gk text of B. Niese [Berlin, 1885–95]. TOOLS: Feldman, L. H., *Josephus and Modern Scholarship* [bibliography; Berlin, 1984]. Rengstorf, K. H., *A Complete Concordance to Flavius Josephus* [5 vols.; Leiden, 1973–83]. STUDIES: Attridge, H. W., "Josephus and his Works," in Stone [ed.], *Jewish Writings* [→ 2 above] 185–232; *The Interpretation of Biblical History in the Antiquitates* [HDR 7; Missoula, 1976]; *EJMI* 311–43. Cohen, S., *Josephus in Galilee and Rome* [Leiden, 1979]. Rajak, T., *Josephus: The Historian and His Society* [Phl, 1984]. Thackeray, H. St. J., *Josephus, the Man and the Historian* [NY, 1929].)

RABBINIC LITERATURE

131   **(I) General Observations.** Because of the Gospel opposition to the Pharisees, Paul's attitude toward the law in Rom, and modern prejudices against legalism, Christians often have a one-sided and incorrect understanding of rabbinic literature and of the tremendous spiritual and religious contributions that the study of the law has made to Judaism (B. S. Jackson, *JJS* 30 [1979] 1–22). In the spirit of Deut (e.g., 30:15) the law has been the source of life for Judaism. In rabbinic literature Torah refers not just to law but to all sacred literature (the Bible, the Mishna, midrashim, and Talmuds with later commentaries and codes), to study and interpretation of these documents, and to revelation itself. Torah became the central symbol of Judaism and the summary of what Jews believe and how they live. Christian misunderstanding of the nature of the law and its role in Judaism has persisted in NT studies and theology until the present, so that rabbinic Judaism is falsely evaluated as "late," decadent, or legalistic (see E. P. Sanders, *Paul and Palestinian Judaism* [Phl, 1977] 33–59; C. Klein, *Anti-Judaism in Christian Theology* [Phl, 1978]).

132   Law develops in every society as that society faces new situations. In the beginnings of Israel, from the exodus (*ca.* 1250 BC) to the early postexilic period (*ca.* 500 BC), there is a development of law that has left its marks in the Bible. The Decalogue represented the core of the Sinaitic covenantal experience. The application of the spirit of the Decalogue to new situations in the life and history of Israel produced the various law codes preserved in the Pentateuch, from the Covenant Code to the Priestly Collection (→ OT Thought, 77:86ff.). Even after the completion and collection of the Pentateuch (5th cent. or later) new laws and customs came into force as the emerging Judaism faced situations such as Hellenization, conquest by Rome, the Christian movement, and the task of survival as a homeless people in the Roman and Sassanid empires. The legal development of this period is almost a chronicle of the history of Judaism

and a remarkable attestation of the vigor of the people that God chose as his own. Traces of the developing laws after 500 BC can be found in the relatively few biblical books of that period, but more often in the noncanonical literature. In discussions of the Apocrypha (e.g., *Jub.*) and the DSS above, we saw legal stances taken by various Jewish sects. Here we are concerned with a particular development that would lead to the flourishing rabbinic literature of the Christian centuries.

133   The main bodies of rabbinic literature are the Mishna, Tosepta, the Palestinian and Babylonian Talmuds, and the midrashic collections, esp. the Halakic Midrashim, the *Midrash Rabbah*, the *Pesiqta de Rab Kahana*, and *Pesiqta Rabbati*. This literature received its written form between AD 200 and the early Middle Ages, but even when the texts were written they continued to undergo change. For instance, the Mishna was revised for several centuries after its formation (J. N. Epstein, *Mabo le-Nusah Ha-Mishna* [Jerusalem, 1964]), and the Babylonian Talmud contains revisions and additions by the scholars known as the *seboraim*. Different mss. of these works may contain variants whose relation to the development of the documents has not yet been worked out. Indeed, some mss. of midrashim contain an entirely different version of the work rather than simply a variant of an original text. In terms of content, this rabbinic literature contains more than what we would normally call law. A traditional way of describing the content is as *halaka* (from the vb. "to walk"), which refers to legal material, and *haggada* or *agada* (from the vb. "to tell"), which covers the nonlegal, homiletical materials such as stories, exhortations, etc. Most rabbinic literature contains both kinds of material.

134   A major scholarly difficulty in dealing with rabbinic literature involves the task of probing behind the self-presentation of the documents. The rabbis from *ca.* 200 on conceived of the laws that they had developed and codified in the Mishna as laws which were given to

Moses on Sinai and passed on orally (in distinction from the written law, which was preserved in the Pentateuch). They conceived of the "oral law" as both protecting and specifying the written biblical law by determining exactly what was demanded and by ensuring that actual practice did not infringe on the biblical law. (The same phenomenon has occurred within Catholicism in the development of customs and then a code of Canon Law which in its self-understanding is often a specification of and protection for the revelation given in Christ. Secularly, U.S. law is often looked on as interpreting and applying the Constitution to new situations.) In fact, as stated above, the oral law really represented new decisions in the face of new situations. Despite the relatively late date of the rabbinic documents, some laws, customs, midrashic traditions and stories in this literature date from centuries prior to commitment in writing, as parallels with the NT, Josephus, DSS, and other intertestamental literature witness. Nevertheless, redaction in the Mishna and in the midrashim is thorough and constant, so that the literary identification of earlier strata and traditions is very difficult. Attributions of traditions to a named sage or rabbi (which often vary by work and ms.) are *not* reliable historical guides. Hypotheses regarding 1st- and 2d-cent. AD sources for rabbinic documents have not been adequately substantiated. Consequently, rabbinic literature must be used with great caution in NT studies and never be *assumed* to reflect the social, religious, and intellectual situation of the 1st cent. AD (see P. A. Alexander, *ZNW* 74 [1983] 237–46; and J. Neusner, *Ancient Judaism* [Chico, 1984]). Even more specifically, an application of rabbinic information to the situation of Jesus' time must take into account the major reorientation in Judaism that followed the destruction of the Temple and Jerusalem in AD 70. It is very difficult to jump back from rabbinic literature of AD 200 to a pre-70 situation (see G. Vermes, *Jesus and the World of Judaism* [Phl, 1983] 58–88). A general rule is that texts submitted from rabbinic literature should be subjected to literary, historical, and redactional criticism, and their specific meaning in context should be ascertained before they are marshaled as evidence for NT interpretation.

135 If the rabbinic literature cannot be used without great care for the reconstruction of the Christian situation, neither can it be used uncritically for the reconstruction of Jewish history in the period from Ezra to AD 200. This later literature of "normative" or "formative" Judaism tended to retroject its own customs and social structures into previous generations. Thus, the sages or the rabbis of the 2d cent. AD and later appear in the guise of the scribes (*sopherim*) of the pre-Christian period in Judaism. A rabbinic sanhedrin is retrojected creatively as the Great Assembly or Synagogue. Pairs of teachers are pictured as social leaders before AD 70, as the Pharisees with their schools of Hillel and Shammai are given roles identical to those of the later rabbis. In fact, however, the rabbis did not begin to gain real power over the whole Jewish society until the 3d cent. AD, and the Pharisees and similar groups never achieved direct control over the Temple or government dominated by the priests and by the elders of powerful families. Jewish social structures, leadership groups, and modes of living the law varied locally and temporally. The Pharisees, functioning both as a sect and as a political party, were not uniform over time, either in internal form or in external relations.

136   (II) Specific Writings
(A) Mishna (Hebr "repetition, study"). This collection of 63 tractates of rabbinic laws is arranged in six topical divisions covering agricultural tithes, feasts,

marriage (including economic arrangements and divorce), torts (including judicial procedure), sacrifices at the Temple, and ritual purity. The Mishna was edited by Rabbi Judah the Prince in Palestine *ca.* AD 200. The tractates repeat biblical laws, expand the laws into new areas, and develop new legal topics which are only loosely based on the Bible. The Mishna as a whole has similarities to both a law code and a textbook. Some laws and legal opinions are presented anonymously, and others are in the names of sages of the 1st and 2d cents. Controversies and conflicting opinions manifest the many sides of legal interpretation, and lists of cases make clear the application of legal principles. Though some stories are told as part of the legal argument (haggada; → 133 above), the bulk of the material is halakic. Generally, the acceptance of the overriding principles of Jewish life and thought, derived from the Bible, is presumed rather than expounded, and attention is focused on the detailed application of particular points of the law.

137 J. Neusner (*Judaism: The Evidence of the Mishnah* [Chicago, 1981]) has argued that the Mishna has been thoroughly redacted into a unified whole to present an ideal Judaism with the holy Temple at its center and a pure people worshiping in it and living in the holy land. Consequently, no 1st- or 2d-cent. Mishna collections can be detected in the present text; and the talmudic theory that Aqiba, Meir, and other sages developed Mishna collections that were used by Judah the Prince in making his Mishna cannot be verified by form-critical methods. The logic of argument in the Mishna and its attested traditions allow only an uncertain glimpse at some of the laws that were developed before 200. The development of some laws depends logically on others. If a law is placed in a period earlier than 200 and is presumed by laws attributed to a later generation, or if a tradition is attributed to an earlier scholar and then cited by a later scholar, it is probable that the *logically* prior or attested tradition is earlier. Neusner's work suggests that only the division of Mishna concerned with ritual purity had a full agenda before AD 70. Other interests partially developed were concerned with tithing produce for meals, killing animals for food, sabbath observance, and marriage, divorce and attendant property rules. Neusner theorizes that these rules were developed by a sectlike group. Between the First Revolt (AD 66–70) and the Bar Cochba War (132–135) and especially later in the 2d cent., a fuller agenda for the nation at large was developed.

138   (B) Tosepta (Aram "addition"). This collection of laws and comments is arranged in tractates parallel to those in the Mishna. Clearly meant as a supplement to the Mishna, it also presents traditions contradictory to the Mishna or gathers stories and scriptural exegeses connected to mishnaic themes. Probably collected in the 3d or 4th cent., the Tosepta has been traditionally associated with Rabbi Hiyya and Rabbi Oshaia (early 3d cent.), though no proof exists for their authorship. The literary relationships between the Tosepta and the Talmuds, where some of the same traditions appear, are not clear.

139   (C) Talmud (Hebr "teaching, study, learning, a lesson"). The two Talmuds, Palestinian and Babylonian, are lengthy and disparate commentaries on the Mishna. The commentary, called the *Gemara* (Aram "completion," "tradition"), consists of an atomistic analysis of the words and sentences of the Mishna, minute comparisons of one mishna with another, dialectical exposition of all the possible interpretations of the Mishna, along with a selection of traditions complementary to the Mishna, interpretations of Scripture, stories about the rabbis, and long digressions on a variety of topics. The talmudic commentaries are written in the vernaculars of the time, Palestinian and Babylonian Aramaic; but many a *Baraita* (Aram "outside" tradition) and other materials are quoted in Hebrew. The Palestinian Talmud covers the first four orders of the Mishna and was completed in the 5th cent. The Babylonian Talmud covers orders 2 through 5 of the Mishna and was completed in the 6th cent. with some additions and editing done later. The Babylonian Talmud is more thoroughly edited and polished than the Palestinian and became normative for most of Judaism because of the dominance of the Babylonian community into the Islamic period. See J. Neusner, *BTB* 14 (1984) 99–109.

140   (D) Midrash (Hebr "inquiry, interpretation"). Generically this term can refer to a type of biblical interpretation found in rabbinic literature; specifically, midrashim are rabbinic Scripture commentaries or collections of interpretations. R. Bloch (in *Approaches to Ancient Judaism* [ed. W. S. Green; Missoula, 1978] 29–75), followed by R. Le Déaut and with modifications by G. Vermes and J. A. Sanders, understands midrash as a set of attitudes and a process which results in various interpretations of Scripture (see *Midrash and Literature* [ed. G. Hartmann and S. Budick; New Haven, 1986]). Rabbinic midrash may be defined as "a type of literature, oral or written, which stands in direct relationship to a fixed, canonical text, considered to be authoritative and the revealed word of God by the midrashist and his audience, and in which this canonical text is explicitly cited or clearly alluded to" (G. Porton, "Defining Midrash," in *The Study of Ancient Judaism* [ed. J. Neusner; NY, 1981] 1. 62). Midrashic interpretation clarifies peculiarities and obscurities in the biblical text and more often uses such reflections to make the text relevant to the questions, needs, and interests of its audience. Many midrashic techniques have been pointed out in the NT, and some scholars have claimed that sections of NT books are based on earlier midrashim or even that whole books are themselves midrashim. In such discussion the term midrash is not self-explanatory, and any scriptural interpretation so identified must be described clearly and evaluated in comparison with other early biblical interpretation, including rabbinic midrash. For a specific example of the problem, see *BBM* 557–62.

141   The older (halakic) midrashim (*Mekilta* to Exod, *Sipra* to Lev; *Sipre* to Num and Deut) comment verse by verse on sections of the biblical books. They have much halakic discussion along with substantial haggadic sections (→ 133 above). These midrashim and several similar discovered in mss. have been attributed to the 2d-cent. schools of Ishmael or Aqiba, but variations of terminology and content are better explained by different authors, editors, and traditions of transmission.

These midrashim mention only tannaitic (1st–2d cent.) sages and are usually dated from the 3d to the 5th cent., though additions were made later.

142   The *Midrash Rabbah* includes both early and later midrashic collections based on the Pentateuch and on the five scrolls that are read in the Jewish liturgy. The two earliest *Rabbah* midrashim (by the end of the talmudic period, ca. 500) deal with Gen and Lev. *Gen. Rab.* divides the text into sections and provides a verse-by-verse expositional commentary concerned more with haggadic than with halakic matters. *Lev. Rab.* consists of thematic sermons that expound the first verse of a section. Each section of these two midrashim is introduced by a proem or, in the case of *Lev. Rab.,* a series of proems. A proem begins with a verse remote from the pentateuchal verse and expounds a chain of verses and interpretations which end with the first verse of the pentateuchal section. Such proems are found in other midrashic collections, especially *Pesiqta Rabbati* and *Pesiqta de Rab Kahana,* both of which are cycles of sermons for the major Jewish festivals. Later midrashic collections, such as the *Tanhuma,* the *Yalquts,* and the *Midrash Ha-Gadol,* evolved some new forms and collected a wide variety of earlier exegeses.

143   **(E) Targum** (Hebr "translation, interpretation"). Several of the *targumim* (targums) or Aram transls. of the Hebr Scriptures contain interpretative traditions found elsewhere in rabbinic literature and should be studied along with rabbinic literature. Claims for a 1st-cent. date for some of the targums have led NT scholars to make extensive use of them. However, neither linguistic data nor targumic traditions make an early date obvious, and the targums as we have them stand at the end of a long process of transmission. The use of targums for the study of the 1st cent. is subject to the same cautions proper for rabbinic literature (→ 134 above; also → Texts, 68:103–15).

(TEXTS [in transl.]: *Mishna:* H. Danby [Oxford, 1933]; P. Blackman [7 vols.; London, 1951–56]; J. Neusner [43 vols.; Leiden, 1974–85]. *Tosepta:* J. Neusner [NY, 1977–]. *Palestinian Talmud:* J. Neusner [Chicago, 1982–]. *Babylonian Talmud:* I. Epstein [Soncino ed.; London, 1935–53]; L. Goldschmidt [uncensored with Ger transl.; 9 vols.; Leipzig, 1897–1909]. *Midrash Rabbah:* H. Freedmann and M. Simon [London, 1939]. Other transls. in the Yale Judaica Series and Jewish Publication Society. INTRODUCTIONS: Moore, G. F., *Judaism in the First Centuries of the Christian Era* [3 vols.; Cambridge MA, 1930–32]. Neusner, J., *A History of the Jews in Babylonia* [for Babylonian Talmud; Leiden, 1965–70]; *Judaism in Society* [for Palestinian Talmud; Chicago, 1983]. Saldarini, A. J., "Reconstructions of Rabbinic Judaism," *EJMI* 437–77. Schürer, *HJPAJC* 1. 68–118. Strack, H. and G. Stemberger, *Einleitung in Talmud und Midrasch* [7th ed.; Munich, 1982]. Strack, H., *Introduction to the Talmud and Midrash* [Phl, 1931; from 5th Ger ed.]. Urbach, E. E., *The Sages* [2 vols.; Jerusalem, 1975].)

68

TEXTS
AND VERSIONS

Raymond E. Brown, S.S.   D. W. Johnson, S.J.
Kevin G. O'Connell, S.J. *

BIBLIOGRAPHY

1   General: Best, E. (ed.), *Text and Interpretation* (Fest. M. Black; Cambridge, 1979). Bruce, F. F., *The Books and the Parchments* (4th ed.; Old Tappan, NJ, 1984). Kenyon, F. G., *Our Bible and the Ancient Manuscripts* (5th ed.; NY, 1959); *The Story of the Bible* (rev. ed.; London, 1964). Kenyon, F. G. and A. W. Adams, *The Text of the Greek Bible* (3d ed.; London, 1975). Metzger, *MMGB.* Reumann, J., *The Romance of Bible Scripts and Scholars* (EC, 1965). "Bible IV: Texts and Versions," *NCE* 2. 414–91.

2   Old Testament: Ap-Thomas, D. R., *A Primer of Old Testament Text Criticism* (2d ed.; Oxford, 1964). Barthélemy, D. (ed.), *Critique textuelle de l'Ancien Testament* (OBO 50/1–2; Fribourg, 1982–86); "Text, Hebrew, History of," *IDBSup* 878–84. Childs, B. S., *Introduction to the Old Testament as Scripture* (Phl, 1979) 84–106. Deist, F. E., *Towards the Text of the Old Testament* (Pretoria, 1978). Eissfeldt, *EOTI* 669–721. Kahle, P. E., *The Cairo Geniza* (2d ed.; Oxford, 1959). Klein, R. W., *Textual Criticism of the Old Testament* (Phl, 1974). McCarter, P. K., Jr., *Textual Criticism: Recovering the Text of the Hebrew Bible* (Phl, 1986). Noth, M., *The Old Testament World* (Phl, 1966) 301–63. Roberts, B. J., *The Old Testament Text and Versions* (Cardiff, 1951). Talmon, S., "The Old Testament Text," *CHB* 1. 159–99. Tov, E., "The Text of the Old Testament," in *The World of the Old Testament* (ed. A. S. van der Woude, *et al.; Bible Handbook* 1; GR, 1986) 156–90. Weingreen, J., *Introduction to the Critical Study of the Text of the Hebrew Bible* (Oxford, 1982). Wonneberger, R., *Understanding BHS: A Manual for the Users of Biblia Hebraica Stuttgartensia* (Subsidia Biblica 8; Rome, 1984). Würthwein, E., *The Text of the Old Testament* (4th ed.; GR, 1979). Yeivin, I., *Introduction to the Tiberian Masorah* (SBLMasS 5; Missoula, 1980).

3   New Testament: Aland, *ATNT* (essential). Aland, K. (ed.), *Die alten Übersetzungen des Neuen Testaments, die Kirchenväterzitate, und Lektionare* (ANTF 5; Berlin, 1972). Duplacy, J., *Études de critique textuelle du Nouveau Testament* (ed. J. Delobel; BETL 78; Louvain, 1987); *Où en est la critique textuelle du Nouveau Testament* (Paris, 1959); "Bulletin de critique textuelle," frequently in *RSR* till his death in 1983. Elliott, J. K. (ed.), *Studies in New Testament Language and Text* (Fest. G. D. Kilpatrick; NovTSup 44; Leiden, 1976); *A Survey of Manuscripts Used in Editions of the Greek New Testament* (NovTSup 57; Leiden, 1987). Finegan, J., *Encountering New Testament Manuscripts* (GR, 1974). Greenlee, J. H., *Introduction to New Testament Textual Criticism* (GR, 1964). Gregory, C. R., *The Canon and Text of the New Testament* (NY, 1907). Martini, C. M., "Text, NT," *IDBSup* 884–86. Metzger, B. M., *TCGNT; Chapters in the History of New Testament Textual Criticism* (NTTS 4; Leiden, 1963); *The Early Versions of the New Testament* (Oxford, 1977); *The Text of the New Testament* (2d ed.; NY, 1968). Souter, A., *The Text and Canon of the New Testament* (rev. ed.; Naperville, 1954). Vööbus, A., *Early Versions of the New Testament* (Stockholm, 1954).

4   English Bible: Bruce, F. F., *History of the Bible in English* (3d ed.; NY, 1978). Butterworth, C. C., *The Literary Lineage of the King James Bible 1340–1611* (Phl, 1941). Hammond, G., *The Making of the English Bible* (Manchester, 1982). Kubo, S., and W. F. Specht, *So Many Versions?: Twentieth Century English Versions of the Bible* (2d ed.; GR, 1983). Levi, P., *The English Bible 1534 to 1859* (GR, 1974). Lewis, J. P., *The English Bible from KJV to NIV* (GR, 1982). Robertson, E. H., *The New Translations of the Bible* (London, 1959). Simms, P. M., *The Bible in America* (NY, 1936). Also *McCQ* 19 (May 1966); *RevExp* 76 (Summer 1979); *Austin Sem. Bull.* 96 (May 1981); *BARev* 8 (6, 1982) 56–67. For modern Bibles in various languages, see *CHB* 3.

5   OUTLINE

*Sections 2, 6–147, 153–155 of this article are by K. G. O'Connell; sections 148–152 are by D. W. Johnson. (Both authors preserved what was enduring in the work of their *JBC* predecessors, respectively P. W. Skehan [† 1980] and G. W. MacRae [† 1985].) Sections 1, 3, 4, 156–216 are by R. E. Brown.

INTRODUCTION

6   A detailed understanding of how the different OT and NT books were preserved and transmitted is more possible now than at any time since the initial composition and gradual collection of these books into the Bible as we know it. This is partly due to an unforeseen series of ms. discoveries (including various early Gk papyri, especially since 1920, and the Dead Sea Scrolls since 1947) and partly because printed copies, good photographic reproductions, and critical editions have made textual sources more accessible for scholarly analysis.

7   Knowledge of this history of transmission is important: (1) for a proper appreciation of the care with which the believing community preserved, copied, and sometimes corrected the sacred books over the centuries and thus the substantial integrity of the received text; (2) for an understanding of the growth of the canonical text at the hands of scribes; (3) for an insight into the opportunities and problems that the textual evidence provides for those who translate and explain the Bible; and (4) for an understanding of text-critical questions that are bound to arise in texts which had so long a period of recopying and translation. This knowledge cannot be static, since the analysis of textual evidence continues, and new discoveries may be anticipated. It will always remain incomplete since so much textual evidence is irretrievably lost.

8 For the OT the material to be described consists of textual evidence for the original Hebr and Aram form of most books, for the Gk "Septuagint" or LXX transl. (mostly pre-Christian, and including some books composed or chiefly preserved in Greek), and for various other ancient versions (Jewish Aramaic, Syriac, Latin, Coptic, etc.). The principal textual value of the latter is their evidence as to underlying Hebr or Gk forms of early date. The Jewish Aram renderings (targums) pertain to the OT only; the other versions suppose complete Bibles, and for convenience OT and NT transls. into these languages will be described together.

9 As for the Gk NT, our knowledge of the way in which its books were preserved and transmitted became truly scientific at the end of the 19th cent., somewhat earlier than for the OT. But here also there have been significant 20th-cent. discoveries, especially of early papyrus copies of NT books. Once again the early versions add important evidence that is helpful for determining the type of Gk text from which they were translated. Thus, in both Testaments the science of textual criticism is one that has made rapid progress in our times.

HEBREW TEXT OF THE OLD TESTAMENT

10 No ms. actually written by the author or editor of any OT book is extant; all existing copies are the work of later scribes. Though Jewish tradition, especially in the later period, placed a high value on faithfulness in transmitting both oral and written materials (E. A. Speiser, *IEJ* 7 [1957] 201–16), the antiquity of a particular copy was of no special moment. Indeed, any ms. too worn for continued public use was relegated to a geniza or repository of discarded sacred texts. For modern scholars such materials accidentally recovered from the Cairo Geniza (→ 43 below) were a boon that was neither intended nor desired by those who left them there.

11 Except for the priestly blessing (Num 6:24–26) on silver amulets from *ca.* 600 BC (→ 35 below), no OT book composed wholly or in part before the Babylonian Exile (587–539 BC) has come down to us in even a fragment actually written that early. The oldest extant texts are from cave 4 at Qumran (→ Apocrypha, 67:81), and they represent the period *ca.* 250–175 BC. For such later OT books as Eccl, Dan, and Sir, fragmentary scrolls written only about 100 years after original composition have been recovered (e.g., 4QQoh^a, 4QDan^c, and MasSir). Not so long ago, it would have been impossible to point with assurance to any OT Hebr ms. that was written within 1,000 years after its contents were composed; the most ancient ms. that includes the date of its own preparation is the Cairo Prophets of AD 895 (→ 46 below).

12 We shall now discuss successively the ancient, medieval, and modern periods in the transmission of the OT text. Since we shall speak frequently of the Hebr text, it is perhaps worth noting that the limited portions of the OT transmitted in Aramaic share in all respects the history of the Hebr books of which they form a part. A frequent standard of reference will be the MT. This term refers to the fixed consonantal Hebr and Aram texts established about the end of the 1st cent. AD and carefully transmitted into the medieval period (→ 36–37, 43 below).

13 **(I) Texts from the Ancient Period** (*ca.* 250 BC–AD 135). During this period it was not the practice to give any OT book a separate title or to add the name of its copyist and date. Consequently, apart from general archaeological considerations connected with their discovery, the dating of ancient biblical mss. depends on paleographic analysis. While inevitably approximate, the results for periods of rapid development in writing style can be rather precise, and for the ancient period as a whole they yield relative certainty (with a maximum leeway of about 50 years in difficult cases). The single most significant study is that of F. M. Cross in *BANE* 133–202.

14 **(A) Format and Age of the Mss.** Except for the Nash Papyrus (→ 35 below), the mss. known from this period have all been found since 1947. The writing is in columns and covers only one side of leather skins or, very infrequently, papyrus sheets (see Jer 36); no Hebr codices (books with pages written on both sides) are known before the medieval period. The writing surfaces are ruled (vertically for columns and horizontally for lines) with a dry point. The skins were stitched (and the papyrus sheets were glued) together side by side to form scrolls. The complete Isa scroll from Qumran (1QIsa^a) is an excellent example: 17 strips of well-prepared leather were sewn together to form a scroll that is 24.5 ft. long when unrolled and 10.5 in. high; its text is in 54 cols., with an intentional main division after col. 27 (i.e., after chap. 33, at the middle of the book's 66 chaps.); the cols. average 30 lines of writing each. Columns in other texts from this period contain from 9 to 65 (or more) lines. For papyrus writing, see *Arch* 36 (4, 1983) 31–37.

15 Close to 200 OT mss. from this ancient period have been recovered from various places in the Judean desert: from the caves around Qumran, in the Wadi Murabba'at, and in the Naḥal Ḥever, and from the fortress at Masada (→ Apocrypha, 67:119–23). Oldest are three mss. from cave 4 at Qumran that have been dated as follows by F. M. Cross: 4QExod^f, *ca.* 250 BC; 4QSam^b, *ca.* 200 BC; and 4QJer^a, *ca.* 175 BC. On external grounds, the latest mss. at Qumran are not later than AD 68, those at Masada not later than AD 73, and those from Murabba'at and Ḥever not later than AD 135. Mss. prior to the 1st cent. BC are rare; perhaps most Qumran mss. date from that cent., but the 1st cent. AD is also well represented. The 2d-cent. AD mss. from Murabba'at occupy a place apart and will need to be described separately (→ 36 below).

16 **(B) Qumran Mss.**
(a) ORIGINS, SCRIPTS, ORTHOGRAPHY. The abundant material from Qumran, including approximately 130 fragmentary copies of OT books from cave 4 alone, shows an extraordinary variety in age, format, script, orthography, and textual affiliation. Despite the

evidence for a *scriptorium* at Qumran, it has yet to be proved that any extant biblical ms. was copied there from another surviving ms. Since the group's rules provided for communal ownership of property (→ Apocrypha, 67:107), the Qumran materials probably include many mss. brought by their individual former owners into the community's holdings, but others were probably copied at the site. Thus, e.g., E. C. Ulrich has argued (*BASOR* 235 [1979] 1–25) that 4QSam^c was produced by the same scribe as the Community Rule (1QS), its appendixes (1QSa, 1QSb), and 4QTestim. The age of the scroll fragments spreads over three full centuries, from *ca.* 250 BC to AD 68. Hebr Kgs, Isa, Dan, and Tob (as well as Gk Exod and Lev) are known on papyrus, but almost all OT texts are on leather of varying thickness and quality. Some mss. have wide cols., some narrow; and the number of letters to a line ranges from about 15 to over 70. For the variation in number of lines to the col., → 14 above.

17   At least until the 1st cent. BC, two separate alphabets were used for Hebr mss.: the archaic one now labeled "paleo-Hebrew" (derived from the Canaanite alphabet employed since preexilic times) and various developing forms of the Jewish "Aramaic" script (familiar in its later stages as the square-letter alphabet of printed Hebr bibles). A few OT mss. and a scattering of nonbiblical ones combine the two alphabets by normally employing the square-letter script and changing to the archaic letters either for the sacred name *YHWH* alone or for varying combinations of divine names. This practice, probably not older than Herodian times, also occurs in the latest Qumran period and finds reflection in some Gk OT mss. (see P. W. Skehan, *BIOSCS* 13 [1980] 14–44). Both alphabets represent the standard 22-letter consonantal system of writing Hebrew. In either script, the spelling may be notably sparse, so that the weaker letters—*waw, heh, yod,* and *aleph*—are used rarely to represent vowels. Elsewhere, however, either script may display an expanded orthography in which (as in Syriac) every *o* or *u* vowel, however slight, is represented by a *waw* in the consonantal text, and the ends of words may offer an unexpected *-heh* attached to pronominal suffixes or an extra *aleph* on any word ending in *i, o,* or *u*. When first encountered in the complete Isa scroll, this expanded spelling puzzled scholars, but it is now recognized as an attempt in the last centuries BC to furnish fuller pronunciation guides than did the standard orthography. To some degree, it may also represent a distinctive dialect in the speech of those who used it.

18   Neither script nor orthography seems to have been conditioned by the type of text copied. The paleo-Hebr script is used for 12 mss.; all the books of the Pentateuch are represented (Lev in 4 mss.), but so is Job; there are some possibly nonbiblical fragments in the same script. Of two Exod texts in the archaic script, one is very close to the standard text, while the other is in the fuller "Samaritan" recension (→ 38–39 below) and sometimes has the expanded type of spelling. Some mss. in the more usual Aram script display a conservative spelling, others an expanded one; indeed, the same OT book may be represented both ways in texts that are otherwise closely akin. Detailed final publication may show a trend to less careful copying in mss. with expanded orthography, but this is not yet certain.

19   (b) TEXTUAL CHARACTERISTICS. The Qumran mss. have opened up a new period in the history of the text. However, they are so fragmentary that a ms. providing 10 percent of a biblical book's complete text is counted among the more substantial witnesses. In contrast to the integral Masoretic and Samaritan texts known from the medieval period and to the indirect evidence of the LXX, the Qumran mss. offer a sampling of—and a means of probing into—the antecedents of those other witnesses, rather than a separate basis for future editions of the text.

20   The fact that the sampling is of extraordinary variety even textually does not mean that very many real variants (apart from scribal errors, harmonizations, etc.) have emerged in addition to those previously known. Rather, many alternative readings and expansions for which medieval Hebr mss. in the MT tradition offer no counterpart, but which were often already known from Gk or Samaritan sources, are here found alongside other texts with readings very close to the MT. Also, for the first time it is possible to verify in Hebr mss. what has always been known, both from the nature of the collection as such and from indirect LXX evidence, that *each OT book has its own separate history of transmission.*

21   Let us illustrate from the Qumran mss. how one important type of textual variant, explanatory expansions, developed. Many scribes copying OT texts during this ancient period apparently felt free to embody some results of their own study, whereas in modern times such interpolations would appear as footnotes or cross references. Thus, in the oldest ms. we possess (4QExod^f), Exod 40:17 has "On the first day of the second year *from their leaving Egypt,* the Tabernacle was erected." The reference to leaving Egypt is not in the MT of this verse, but Exod 16:1 and 19:1 do contain it. Although the phrase is found not only in our oldest Qumran witness but also in the Samaritan and Gk texts, it may be an expansion to make the wording clearer and more explicit. Similarly, in a Qumran ms. (4QDeut^n) in the text of the Ten Commandments, the reasons given in the MT for keeping the sabbath day are expanded by the insertion after Deut 5:15 of a related passage (Exod 20:11) with an added reason. Even the Samaritan text of Deut lacks this enlargement, although in the Gk tradition it turns up as an insertion into Deut 5:14 in Codex Vaticanus (only). For a difficult phrase in Isa 34:4 that has been translated "And all the hosts of heaven shall moulder away" (a phrase omitted by the earliest LXX translator), the scroll 1QIsa^a supplies from Mic 1:4 the words "and the valleys split open," presumably because the contexts are similar, but perhaps also because the Hebr letters of the phrase in Isa 34:4 MT could suggest the alternate in Mic 1:4. This type of copying does not indicate that the text was regarded as any less sacred, since the words used to fill out or revise a particular passage are those of the Bible itself, but it is far from a rigid adherence to unalterable consonants of a standardized text. Such an adherence would become the universal rule shortly after AD 70.

22   The full publication of the texts from this ancient period has taken a long time. By 1985 (with the work on 11QpaleoLev by D. N. Freedman and K. A. Mathews) all scrolls and decipherable biblical fragments from major caves 1 and 11 and from minor caves 2–3, 5–10 had been published. The extensive materials found in cave 4 were in generally poor condition and more difficult to treat. The task of preparing the volume on the longer scrolls 4QpaleoExod^l and 4QpaleoExod^m, which had been largely completed in draft form by P. W. Skehan (†1980), was entrusted to E. C. Ulrich. Final publication of thousands of fragments from cave 4 has been slow.

23   A permanent system of reference for the Qumran mss. was developed. Thus, 4QExod^f means that, of all the mss. from the fourth cave at Qumran, the sixth (f) copy of Exod is being referred to. If a text is on papyrus (pap), is in the paleo-Hebr script (paleo), or is a transl. (LXX, tg [= targum]) or interpretation (p

[= *pesher*]), that fact is included before the name of the biblical book (e.g., 4QpaleoExod^m for a ms. in the old script from cave 4; 1QpHab for an interpretation of Hab from cave 1; 4QLXXNum for a ms. of the LXX for Num from cave 4). Other abbreviations identify materials from Masada (Mas), Murabba'at (Mur), and Naḥal Ḥever (Ḥev).

24   (i) *Historical Books.* The 15 fragmentary mss. of Gen found at Qumran show a comparatively uniform text. Readings that coincide with LXX materials do exist, but a high degree of standardization for the Gen text clearly antedates all our evidence. In Exod through Deut, on the other hand, there is great variation in the Qumran witnesses. Sometimes they are very close to the MT; fairly frequently they show regular or sporadic agreement with readings known from the Gk tradition, whether primitive LXX or "proto-Lucianic" (→ 69 below); and at other times they include the systematic expansions found in the Samaritan text (→ 38-39 below). Exod exists in 15 mss., Lev in 9, Num in 6, and Deut in 25. Notable is 4QpaleoExod^m from the early 2d cent. BC; it contains portions of some 40 cols. of text (out of an original 57) in the repetitious expanded form known previously only from Samaritan sources (J. E. Sanderson, *An Exodus Scroll from Qumran: 4QpaleoExod^m and the Samaritan Tradition* [HSS 30; Atlanta, 1986]). On 11QpaleoLev, see K. A. Mathews, *CBQ* 48 (1986) 171-207. The extensively preserved text of 4QNum^b agrees with the Samaritan text in a number of expansions, but it also agrees quite frequently with the earliest strata of LXX texts against the MT, even where Samaritan and MT coincide. Among texts of Deut is a fragment (4QDeut^q) with only the ending (32:37-43) of the Song of Moses (arranged by poetic lines or half-lines); it witnesses to LXX readings supported by no Hebr source previously known. Discussion of this text has shown that similar readings are verifiable at Qumran in the Song's opening and central portions as well (P. W. Skehan, *BASOR* 136 [1954] 12-15).

25   In general, the Palestinian text for these books may be seen as an expanding, harmonizing type, distinct from the received MT, and showing some kinship with the "proto-Lucianic" reworking of the LXX (→ 69 below). An interesting combination of elements occurs in 5Q1, a Deut ms. dated by J. T. Milik to the early 2d cent. BC. So far as preserved, its original text is close to the MT, but about a century later it was "corrected" at four points on the basis of a Hebr text with LXX associations!

26   Qumran mss. for Josh, Judg, and Kgs are comparatively limited in number (two or three mss.) and in the extent of their preserved text; in all cases, there seems to be a definite kinship with LXX sources. For Sam, the four extant mss. are exceptional both for the quantity of text preserved in 4QSam^a (late 1st cent. BC) and for the age of the earliest witness (4QSam^b, late 3d cent. BC). As in the Pentateuch (→ 24 above), at least three types of text are now attested for Sam-Kgs: the Hebr text that lay behind the original LXX translation (→ 68 below); the fuller Hebr text of 4QSam mss. that is reflected in the proto-Lucianic revision of the LXX (→ 69 below); and the Hebr text represented by the present MT, an early form of which served as guide for the *Kaige* or "proto-Theodotionic" revision of the LXX in the 1st cent. AD (→ 70-74 below). It was the Qumran evidence for Sam, along with the Gk Minor Prophets scroll from Naḥal Ḥever (8ḤevXII gr, → 67 below) that provided the key to explain more adequately the complex problems of text transmission long known to be particularly acute in 1-2 Sam.

27   (ii) *Major Prophets.* At Qumran, Isa is represented by two substantial witnesses: 1QIsa^a, a complete scroll from the early part of the 1st cent. BC, and the more fragmentary 1QIsa^b from the latter part of the same century. The complete scroll, the format and unusual orthography of which were described above (→ 14, 17), diverges in many respects from the MT. In the beginning, it gave rise to inflated hopes of providing access to a hitherto unattainably early stage in the book's transmission. Though interesting and instructive, the ms. is textually rather disappointing; it is secondary to the MT in most instances in which the two diverge, and it has no genuine kinship to the Hebr prototype of LXX Isa. In its divergences it is unique among the 18 Qumran mss. of Isa, which otherwise combine to establish that the book's textual tradition was already standardized by the 2d cent. BC to a degree elsewhere observed only for Gen. Similarly overrated at first but for different reasons was 1QIsa^b, regularly said to be quite close to the MT. Sober enough in its spelling, 1QIsa^b is far less faithful in transmitting the narrowly standardized Isa text than is any good medieval Hebr ms. of the book, and such qualities as 1QIsa^b possesses have been appreciated rather by contrast to 1QIsa^a than by any more exacting criteria.

28   In Jer, of which Qumran provides four mss., the significant fact has been the appearance in 4QJer^b of a shorter edition that was previously known only from LXX Jer. Taken in conjunction with the textual variety observable at Qumran in Exod-Deut and Sam (→ 24-26 above), the divided evidence for Jer supports the hypothesis that MT Jer's fuller text represents mainly a reworking, presumably in Palestine, of an older, short edition (see J. G. Janzen, *Studies in the Text of Jeremiah* [HSM 6; Cambridge MA, 1973]). This reworking would have taken place according to the harmonizing and expansionist technique observable in textual witnesses of those other books (→ 21 above) and seen at its fullest in the Samaritan Pentateuch (→ 39 below). Nothing of note has yet emerged from the study of the six Qumran Ezek mss.; if the expansion hypothesis has any merit, it may be that the whole Ezek tradition in Hebrew, Qumran included, represents an expanded and reworked edition of that prophet.

29   (iii) *Minor Prophets.* All parts of the Minor Prophets (including Hab 3) are represented among eight mss. Where different books of the 12 Prophets are extant in the same ms., the Qumran evidence is for the MT order of the books, not that of the LXX. In the Hab commentary from cave 1 (1QpHab, → Apocrypha, 67:89-90), the lemmata, or citations of continuous text, do not always contain the same readings supposed by the discussion that follows them; this type of evidence for divergent texts is frequent enough in later materials in many languages.

30   (iv) *Writings.* The four Job mss. (one in the archaic script) and the two Prov scrolls, all surviving in fragments, exhibit a text that is close to the MT. The Job targum from cave 11 (→ 104 below) witnesses to the standard MT arrangement of chaps., despite the problems of chaps. 23-27 (→ Job, 30:83-96); only in the final chap. 42 does the Aramaic suggest a variant, shorter Hebr form as its base.

31   There are some 30 Pss mss. at Qumran, but many are very limited in the amount of text that survives; 1st-cent. AD 11QPs^a, published by J. A. Sanders (DJD 4), is the most extensive. Its extant text contains parts both of 39 canonical Pss (93, 101-5, 109, 118-19, 121-50) and of other materials. These include LXX Ps 151 (originally two distinct compositions, one also surviving as Syr Ps I); Sir 51:13-30; 1 Sam 23:7; two hymns known earlier as Syr Pss II-III and now as Pss 154-55; three late psalmlike texts ("Plea for Deliverance," "Apostrophe to Zion," and "Hymn to the Creator"); and a prose passage that credits David with 4,050 poetic works. While there are slight indications that the compiler of these materials knew the canonical order of the Psalter, that found in 11QPsa is considerably different. The psalmlike "Apostrophe to Zion" of 11QPsa has also been identified by J. Starcky as one of three nonbiblical pieces (alongside at least three canonical Pss) in 4QPsf. For the rest, though the Pss are often copied in irregular order and show many variants (mostly inferior), our knowledge of the biblical Psalter's textual history will scarcely be increased to any notable degree by these texts.

32   Eight mss. of Dan are known (see *BASOR* 268 [1987] 17–37). The transition from Hebrew into Aramaic and back into Hebrew occurs as in the MT; the portions of LXX Dan that are not in the MT are excluded from the Qumran evidence. Four of the five Megilloth books in the Hebr canon (→ Canonicity, 66:22) are attested (two mss. for Eccl, four each for Ruth, Cant, and Lam); only Esth is missing. Perhaps the Qumran sectarians excluded Esth on principle, because it conflicted with their views about the religious calendar and was meaningful to their Maccabean/Hasmonean enemies (→ Apocrypha, 67:99). Of Ezra and Chr there is one ms. each (and a limited amount of text).

33   (v) *Deuterocanonical Books.* Among these works (→ Canonicity, 66:9–10), Bar is unattested, though a bit of Ep Jer in Greek (Bar 6 in the Vg) was found in cave 7. Wis, Jdt, and 1–2 Macc have not been found; they would all have been ill-matched with the Qumran community's interests. Four mss. of the original Aram text of Tob are known, and one in Hebrew. Their evidence supports the long form of the book in the OL and in the Gk Codex Sinaiticus as primary. Some bits of Sir are written stichometrically (by verse lines) in 2Q18, and fragments of Sir 51:13–30 appear in cols. 21–22 of 11QPsa (see J. A. Sanders, *McCQ* 21 [1968] 284–98). Several Gk OT mss. from cave 4 will be mentioned below (→ 66).

34   **(C) Mss. from Masada and Other Areas.** The Qumran materials are paralleled by ms. discoveries at Masada in 1963/1964 (→ Apocrypha, 67:123). Most notable is the fragmentary scroll of Sir (Y. Yadin, *The Ben Sira Scroll from Masada* [Jerusalem, 1965]) containing parts of seven cols. of text, two hemistichs to the line, from Sir 39:27 to 44:17. Dated paleographically to the early 1st cent. BC, it already shows many recensional differences that also appear in medieval Hebr Sir mss. and in the versions (→ Sirach, 32:5). A copy of Ps 150 from Masada is said to conclude a ms. (similar to the arrangement of the canonical Psalter), and there are also fragments of Gen, Lev, Deut, Ezek, and Pss 81–85.

35   Not strictly a biblical ms., the Nash Papyrus from Egypt (*ca.* 150 BC) contains the Ten Commandments and Deut 6:1ff. Published by S. A. Cook in 1903, only much later was it correctly dated to the Maccabean age by W. F. Albright (*JBL* 56 [1937] 145–76). Also noteworthy are ancient miniature scrolls either to be worn on the person (phylacteries) or to be attached to the doorposts of houses (mezuzas); they contain excerpts from the Pentateuch (sometimes varying from the MT and differing from those specified by later Jewish regulations). Much older (7th/6th-cent. BC script) are two tiny rolled strips of silver discovered in 1979 in a burial chamber (cave 25) on the western slope of the Hinnom Valley in Jerusalem. Presumably originally worn as amulets, they were found by G. Barkay to contain versions of the priestly blessing from Num 6:24–26. The text on one is said to be almost identical to the MT, while the other apparently combines the second and third sentences of the blessing. (See *BARev* 9 [2, 1983] 14–19; *Qad* 17 [1984] 94–108; *BK* 42 [1987] 30–36.)

36   The last group of ancient mss. to be mentioned consists of five from the Wadi Murabba'at, all published, and six or seven more from Naḥal Ḥever (→ Apocrypha, 67:119,121), most unpublished. A Gk ms. of the Minor Prophets from Naḥal Ḥever is discussed with the LXX (→ 67, 70 below). A 1st-cent. AD Hebr Pss ms. from the same site has some variants from the MT, but the other Hebr mss. from there (one of Gen, two or three of Num, and one of Deut) show a text and script similar to those of the Murabba'at mss. The latter were published by P. Benoit and J. T. Milik (DJD 2) and include Gen-Exod-Num (Mur 1), Deut (Mur 2), Isa (Mur 3), a phylactery with parts of Exod and Deut (Mur 4), and the Minor Prophets (Mur 88). The last named is by far the most extensive and contains text from 10 of the 12 Minor Prophets. It is in full accord with the MT tradition and shows only three meaningful variants. The other mss. confirm that the stabilization of the Hebr text, traditionally associated with the Jewish school at Jabneh or Jamnia (→ Canonicity, 66:35) toward the end of the 1st cent. AD, was already decisive for these copies left by refugees of the Second Jewish Revolt in AD 132–35.

37   By the 2d cent. AD, therefore, the consonantal Hebr text had been fixed in the form in which it is still transmitted today. Before that, however, the Qumran (and, for Sir, Masada) evidence shows a period of relative fluidity of text that varied in degree from one OT book to another. Actually the Gk and Samaritan textual evidence, along with the indirect witness of the NT, Philo, and Josephus, have always made it necessary to suppose such a situation.

(For QL bibliography, → Apocrypha 67:78, esp. under [V] for Cross and Milik. Cross, F. M., Jr., "The History of the Biblical Text in the Light of Discoveries in the Judean Desert," *HTR* 57 [1964] 281–99; idem [ed. with S. Talmon], *Qumran and the History of the Biblical Text* [Cambridge MA, 1975]. Eissfeldt, *EOTI* 669–95, 778–83. Goshen-Gottstein, M. H., *Text and Language in Bible and Qumran* [Jerusalem, 1960]. Greenberg, M., "The Stabilization of the Text of the Hebrew Bible," *JAOS* 76 [1956] 157–67. Orlinsky, H. M., "The Textual Criticism of the Old Testament," in *BANE* 113–32. Pisano, S., *Additions or Omissions in the Books of Samuel: The Significant Pluses and Minuses in the Massoretic, LXX and Qumran Texts* [OBO 57; Fribourg, 1984]. Sanders, J. A., "Pre-Masoretic Psalter Texts," *CBQ* 27 [1965] 114–23; "Palestinian Manuscripts 1947–1967," *JBL* 86 [1967] 431–40. Skehan, P. W., "The Scrolls and the Old Testament Text," *McCQ* 21 [1968] 273–83. *Textus: Annual for the Hebrew University Bible Project* 1– [1960–]. Tov, E. [ed.], *The Hebrew and Greek Texts of Samuel* [Proceedings IOSCS; Jerusalem, 1980].)

38   **(II) Texts from the Postbiblical and Medieval Periods** (AD 135–1476).
    (A) Samaritan Pentateuch. This unique survival into the Middle Ages of a Hebr text not subject to the standardization effected by the late-1st-cent. AD Jewish sages was first brought to the notice of European scholars after 1616, when Pietro della Valle obtained a ms. of it in Damascus. It is now represented in European libraries by copies ranging in age from the 12th to the 20th cent. AD. The oldest known exemplar, secondarily reassembled from pieces of varying date, is the "Abisha scroll" that is kept by the Samaritan community at Nablus (→ Biblical Geography, 73:101); its early part is from the 11th cent. AD. The Samaritans maintain that this text was prepared "13 years after the conquest of Canaan by Joshua." Those Western scholars who date the Samaritan schism to the days of Nehemiah in the 5th cent. BC have tended to give this text recension also a 5th-cent. date. However, the form of the script, the nature of the text, and the history of the Samaritans all conspire to make us see in it a developed Palestinian text,

by no means sectarian in origin, that began its separate history among the Samaritans no earlier than the days of John Hyrcanus at the end of the 2d cent. BC. The Qumran ms. 4QpaleoExod^m, which is not sectarian, is from approximately that date. It shows that the Samaritan text tradition has simply appropriated one of the recensional text forms in current (Jewish) usage and has remained remarkably faithful to its pre-Christian recensional prototype (→ 24 above).

39 The harmonizing, expansionist nature of the Samaritan text has been mentioned. It fills out the plague narratives in Exod, so that each time the Lord gives Moses a message for Pharaoh, Moses repeats it word for word before the narrative continues. Similarly, sections of Deut that expand on themes already present in Exod are transposed into the text of Exod; Num undergoes similar harmonizing treatment, as does Deut itself. Such systematic expansions within the framework of the known biblical text are of no special interest; rather this recension is valuable because, often in accord with the LXX, it preserves ancient Palestinian readings of words or phrases that vary from the MT. Where these variants do not just simplify the MT reading or make it more explicit, they need to be evaluated individually. The Samaritan tradition is supported both by Aram targums (→ 112 below) and by the Gk *Samareitikon.* Known fragments of the latter and its Syro-hexaplar transl. show the same expanded text. This expanded recension was occasionally cited in the NT, notably in Acts 7. Traditional Hebr pronunciation among the Samaritans has been exploited with varying degrees of accuracy and success by several scholars seeking light on the pronunciation of Hebrew prior to the work of the Jewish Masoretes (→ 43 below).

(Baillet, M., "La récitation de la loi chez les Samaritans," *RB* 69 [1962] 570–87. Bowman, J., *The Samaritan Problem: Studies in the Relationships of Samaritanism, Judaism, and Early Christianity* [PTMS 4; Pittsburgh, 1975]. Coggins, R. J., *Samaritans and Jews: The Origins of Samaritanism Reconsidered* [Atlanta, 1975]. Giron Blanc, L. F. [ed.], *Pentateuco hebreo-samaritano, Genesis* [Madrid, 1976]. Pérez Castro, F., *Sefer Abiša* [Madrid, 1959; see E. Robertson, *VT* 12 (1962) 228–35]. Pummer, R., "The Present State of Samaritan Studies," *JSS* 21 [1976] 39–61; 22 [1977] 24–47. Purvis, J. D., *The Samaritan Pentateuch and the Origin of the Samaritan Sect* [HSM 2; Cambridge MA, 1968]; "Samaritan Pentateuch," *IDBSup* 772–75; "Samaritans," *IDBSup* 776–77. Sadaqa, A. and R. Sadaqa [eds.], *Jewish and Samaritan Version of the Pentateuch* [Jerusalem, 1965]. Von Gall, A., *Der hebräische Pentateuch der Samaritaner* [5 vols.; Giessen, 1914–18; 1-vol. repr., Berlin 1966].)

40 **(B) Origen's Second Column.** Origen's *Hexapla,* a compilation (usually in six cols.) of Hebr and Gk sources for the study of the OT text, will be discussed in detail below (→ 83). Here we focus on the work's second-col. transliteration (not a translation) of the standardized, 2d-cent. AD Hebr consonantal text into Gk letters. Since the Gk alphabet is not well suited for transcribing Hebr consonants, the result is of limited value. However, it gives scholars an idea of Hebr pronunciation at Origen's time. We shall see in the next section how the Jewish Masoretes of later centuries developed systems to indicate pronunciation. Their native language was not Hebrew, but a developed form of Aramaic, and this influenced their pronunciation. The evidence of Origen's second col. and the earlier materials discovered more recently (→ 17 above) offer Hebr vowel patterns and syllable structures of importance for the history of the language and for an understanding of OT poetic rhythms.

41 The surviving evidence for Origen's second col. is mostly from the Pss and is known best from the original writing on a reused ms. (palimpsest) in the Ambrosian Library in Milan that was identified by Cardinal G. Mercati in 1896 and published by him as *Psalterii hexapli reliquiae* I (Vatican City, 1958). He argued that the orthography of this material was contemporary with Origen's compilation (*ca.* AD 245). It is a shrewd guess (T. W. Manson, followed by P. E. Kahle) that Origen's transliterated text followed an earlier practice of preparing similar materials to train Greek-speaking Jews of the Diaspora for correct public reading from normal Hebr scrolls in synagogues.

42 **(C) Vocalized Medieval Mss.** To the medieval period belong all Hebr OT mss. preserved in libraries and many museums, or by Jewish congregations, from before the spread of printing. Leather scrolls of the text continued to be used for liturgical purposes through medieval into modern times, but codices or books with pages written on both sides (→ 89–90 below) served for private copies. The text could be written in two or three cols. on a page, or it could be the width of the page. The script, wording, paragraphing, and ms. format were so rigidly standardized that paleographical criteria are difficult to apply.

43 The impetus to indicate vowels systematically by adding symbols to the consonantal spelling used for writing Semitic languages, including Hebrew, seems to have arisen in Syria during the 6th and 7th cents. This technique, first applied to the Syr Bible and Muslim Koran, was imitated by Jewish scholars (Masoretes) in both Babylonia and Palestine. The rise of several Masoretic systems (Hebr *massōret* means "tradition") is traceable today mainly on the basis of a late-19th-cent. discovery in Cairo. In the city's oldest quarter is a building that was the Melkite church of St. Michael before AD 969 and that was subsequently purchased by the Karaite (sectarian) Jewish community as its synagogue. Within the building a room was walled off to serve as a geniza (storage place) for sacred mss. that had outlived their usefulness, since Jewish practice forbade their destruction. Between about 1890 and 1898, mss. that had accumulated for centuries in this room were recovered and brought to the West, mainly through the efforts of S. Schechter, then resident in England, later in America (see *BARev* 8 [5, 1982] 38–53). The discovery among these materials of a large part of the original Hebr text of Sir (→ 52 below), which had been lost for centuries, caused a sensation. The geniza also supplied evidence for the history of the protocanonical OT books and of the targums; Kahle's *Cairo* is a good introduction to the various problems involved.

44 On the basis of the several thousand scattered ms. pages from this geniza (now preserved in Cambridge, Oxford, Paris, New York, and elsewhere), Kahle outlined the development in both Babylonia and Palestine of increasingly refined systems to represent the traditional pronunciation of the Hebr text for public recitation in the synagogue. These mss. are also fairly early witnesses for the consonantal text, but they are not so important as the more ancient mss. described above (→ 15–37). The several systems of pronunciation they represent are instructive for the transmission history of the Hebr language and for the details of textual interpretation implicit in the way a text was phrased and read. However, the only system in general use today is that developed by the ben Asher family from Tiberias in Galilee in the 9th and early 10th cents. The other sources are drawn on primarily to supplement and provide a context for the Tiberian apparatus.

45 **(a) MODEL CODICES.** Sometimes designated "crown" (Hebr *keter*) mss., these are models for the study of the text and apparatus as developed by the ben Asher family and are still used as the foundation for critical editions of the printed Hebr Bible.

46 The *Cairo Prophets* (C) was written and provided with its vowel points by Moses ben Asher in AD 895; a concluding copyist's note establishes it as the oldest dated Hebr OT ms. now extant. C contains both the Former Prophets (Josh, Judg, Sam, Kgs) and the Latter Prophets (Isa, Jer, Ezek, and the 12 Minor Prophets) of the Hebr canon. Originally the property of the Karaite Jewish community in Jerusalem, C was seized during the First Crusade and ultimately released by King Baldwin to the Karaites of Cairo. Its apparatus does not show the full development of the Masoretic system as used by Aaron ben Asher in the following generation; it is apparently closer to the rival ben Nefthali tradition than to the later ben Asher texts, though the differences are not great. C was consulted for both *BHK* and *BHS* (→ 56 below) and collated anew for the Hebrew Univ. Bible Project (→ 58 below). Beginning in 1979, C's biblical text and Masora were edited in a series at Madrid under the direction of F. Pérez Castro.

47 The *Aleppo Codex* (A) was originally a complete Hebr OT that had been provided with vowel points and accents (guides to phrasing and inflection in recital) by Aaron ben Moses ben Asher *ca.* 930. It was given first, like C, to the Karaite community in Jerusalem and, while in their keeping, was known and endorsed by Maimonides (d. 1204) as a reliable guide to certain features of the standard text. The presence of A in Aleppo is attested from 1478; but during the anti-Jewish rioting in that city in 1947 it was badly damaged and (for a time) thought lost altogether. In truncated form (lacking the Pentateuch up to Deut 28:1, as well as parts of 2 Kgs, Jer, the Minor Prophets, 2 Chr; Pss 15:1-25:2; Cant 3:11-end; and all of Eccl, Lam, Esth, Dan, Ezra, Neh), it reached Israel by 1958. A photographic edition of the surviving ms. was published (Jerusalem, 1976), and A was employed for the first time as a foundation for the Bible text in the Hebrew Univ. critical edition (→ 58 below; also M. Goshen-Gottstein, *BA* 42 [1979] 145-63).

48 The *Leningrad Codex* (L), dated AD 1009, is a complete OT brought from the Crimea by A. Firkowitsch in 1839. A scribal note at the end says that the ms. was equipped with vowels and other apparatus from mss. corrected and annotated by Aaron ben Moses ben Asher. The vowel points show evidence of early revision in the direction of conformity with the ben Asher standard as known from other sources. This was the best ms. available for *BHK* and *BHS* (→ 56 below), and its readings are being reported again in the Hebrew Univ. undertaking (→ 58 below).

49 (b) Mss. WITH DIVERGENT VOWEL SYSTEMS. Preliminary study and collation of a limited number of geniza OT fragments (→ 43-44 above) with rather rudimentary Palestinian systems of vowel pointing was done by P. E. Kahle, *Masoreten des Westens* (Stuttgart, 1927-30); this work was continued by A. Díez Macho and others.

50 The extensive geniza evidence for two Babylonian vowel systems (one early and more simple, the other later and more complicated) was presented by Kahle in his *Masoreten des Ostens* (Leipzig, 1913), in an album of photographs offered as a supplement to *ZAW* 46 (1928), and in the prefatory matter to *BHK*. In contrast to the MT, the punctuation of these materials from the 8th-10th cents. was supralinear (i.e., its symbols appeared above the consonantal text). The apparatus of *BHK* included variants from some 120 mss. of this group, but they were not reported in such detail in *BHS*. Beginning in 1976, an edition of the Hebr Bible

according to fragments with Babylonian punctuation has been published in Madrid (*Biblia Babilonica*).

51 Certain mss. were ascribed by Kahle to the school of ben Nefthali (rivals of the ben Asher family; → 44 above), but a number of them have divergent features that true ben Nefthali mss. would not share; and so they are probably intermediate between the oldest Palestinian Masora and the full-fledged Tiberian system. They include the *Codex Reuchlinianus* of AD 1105, now in Karlsruhe, and a Pentateuch (G. B. de Rossi's no. 668) and complete OT (de Rossi's no. 2) now preserved in Parma. The reassessment of these mss. has reduced the actual number of differences between the ben Nefthali and ben Asher schools of Masoretes to some 900 points of detail, almost all in the use of a single secondary accent (the *meteg*).

52 (D) Cairo Geniza Mss. of Sirach. It is in keeping with the scattered and fragmentary state of the materials from the Cairo Geniza (→ 43-44 above) that, though the first Hebr Sir leaf identified and published from the source turned up in 1896, one of the five known Sir mss. was not edited until 1931, and stray leaves from two others were not published until 1958 and 1960. A. A. Di Lella's evaluation of these materials (*The Hebrew Text of Sirach* [The Hague, 1966]) concluded that, out of some 1,616 lines of text represented in the LXX for Sir, 1,098 have survived in the five Hebr mss. The Qumran and Masada texts of the book (→ 33-34 above), published between 1962 and 1965, have established conclusively that the text of the Cairo ms. is ancient. Since the actual Cairo copies date from the 11th and 12th cents. AD, they were often dismissed as medieval retroversions into Hebrew from Greek, Syriac, or perhaps even Persian. However, the 1st-cent. BC Sir text from Masada and the book's LXX form combine to show that, when the most elaborate of the medieval mss. (Cairo ms. B) preserves variant readings in its margin, sometimes *both* the text reading *and* the alternative in the margin originated in pre-Christian times. Another feature of Cairo ms. B that is attested as genuinely ancient both by the Masada scroll and by 2Q18 is the copying in verse lines rather than as continuous prose. In contrast, for the alphabetic acrostic poem in Sir 51:13-30, the better text of its first half preserved in 11QPsᵃ (→ 31 above) shows clearly that the medieval form is due to retroversion from the Syriac.

53 (E) Medieval Mss. of Tobit and Judith. The extant medieval texts of Tob and Jdt, in both Hebrew and Jewish Aramaic, are not comparable to the Sir mss.; they are entirely secondary and provide no avenue of approach toward the original form of those two books.

54 (III) Editions from the Modern Period (AD 1477-). Printed editions of the Hebr OT, from the Pss with D. Kimchi's commentary (Bologna, 1477) and the earliest complete OT (Soncino, 1488) up to the year 1525, were based mostly on a limited choice of mss., some no longer extant. Their text varies within the same range as the medieval mss. themselves, and they have been collated in later times (along with the ms. evidence) as more or less independent witnesses, often not very good.

55 (A) Textus Receptus (1525-1929). After the appearance of a first *Biblia rabbinica* (Venice, 1518)— the OT text with Masora, targum, and a selection of Jewish medieval commentators combined on folio pages (Hebr *miqrā'ôt gĕdôlôt*, "large Scriptures")—the same publisher, D. Bomberg, brought out a second rabbinic bible in 1524/25. The editor was Jacob ben Chayim, a careful student of the Masora who was handicapped in his work by the modifications and refinements introduced into the tradition during the six centuries between Aaron ben Asher and his own day. The text that ben Chayim established became, for better or worse, the norm for nearly all printed Hebr bibles until recent years. Its 400-year dominance makes it comparable to the Gk NT *Textus Receptus* (→ 160-61 below).

56   (B) Critical Editions. Produced during the years 1966-1977, *BHS* replaced *BHK* (1929-1937). Both were based on the Leningrad Codex (→ 48 above) and had footnotes that cover a wide range of alternative readings drawn from Hebr mss. and the versions. But *BHS* dropped the distinction made in *BHK* between one apparatus for "slight variants and less important . . . information" and another for "real textual changes and other more significant matter." The number of conjectural readings and retroversions was greatly reduced. Because of these changes, *BHS* became the best available source for a dependable text combined with an indication of the variants suggested by textual criticism, even if its notes needed constant checking and evaluation (as would any textbook). The division of poetic texts into sense lines in *BHS* (as in *BHK*) results from modern editorial judgment; it is not the traditional Jewish presentation from the mss. (where only Exod 15:1-17 and Deut 32:1-43 are always disposed as poetry, and Pss, Prov, and Job more rarely). Though often helpful, such poetic arrangements of the text can also be quite misleading if accepted uncritically. Finally, *BHS* refined the marginal presentation of the Masora Parva ("small Masora") from *BHK* and supplemented it with a new apparatus referring directly to the supporting documentation of the Leningrad (L) Masora Magna ("large Masora") that was published in *BHS* (vol. 2; Stuttgart, 1971) and as the first of several volumes on the *Massorah Gedolah* (Masora Magna; Rome, 1971).

57   Lacking both the hazards and the advantages of *BHK* and *BHS* is the British and Foreign Bible Society's Hebr OT, ed. by N. H. Snaith (London, 1958). The editor based his work on a Lisbon ms. of 1483, but he also took into account a small group of mss. (primarily of Spanish origin) and S. Y. de Norzi's Masoretic studies (1742). Snaith himself noted that his resultant text was quite close to that of *BHK* and its Leningrad prototype. The British edition generally follows the traditional arrangement of the text; it prints Pss, Prov, and Job in double columns, with two half-verse units (hemistichs) to the line.

58   The very important Hebrew Univ. Bible Project began in 1975 with Isa. The basic text for the edition is the Aleppo Codex (→ 47 above) with its own abbreviated Masoretic notes on the right margin and variants in the vowel and accent marks (from a small group of early mss.) on the left. Lower on the page are three other blocks of apparatus: the first cites the evidence of the versions with concise and careful evaluation; the second gives variants from the Qumran scrolls and from rabbinic literature; and the third lists readings from medieval Hebr mss., including the Leningrad Codex (→ 48 above) and the Cairo Prophets (→ 46 above), on a selective basis.

59   **(C) Compilations of Variants.** The basic compilation of consonantal variants from medieval Hebr mss. and early editions is the *Vetus Testamentum hebraicum cum variis lectionibus* of B. F. Kennicott (2 vols.; Oxford, 1776-80). It reproduces the *Textus Receptus* and offers variants from some 600 mss. and 50 editions of the OT or its parts, along with a collation of 16 Samaritan Pentateuch mss. against the text of that recension reprinted from the London Polyglot Bible of 1657. The work had been done over a 10-year period, partly by correspondence with scholars in the various cities of Continental Europe where significant mss. were kept; but its results were so disappointing as to discourage further attempts to resurvey the same or comparable material on any similar basis.

60   A more selective undertaking by G. B. de Rossi entitled *Variae lectiones Veteris Testamenti* (4 vols. and suppl.; Parma, 1784-88, 1798; repr. in 2 vols., Amsterdam, 1969-70) was at the same time more broadly based. De Rossi printed no text, presumed the same collating base as Kennicott, and published evidence only for passages whose existing variants he judged important. He reported variants in vocalization as well as in the consonantal text. To Kennicott's data, which he repeated in detail whenever they bore upon the readings he studied, de Rossi collated an additional 800 mss., some of them noteworthy. He also reported the indirect evidence of the versions. Though its materials need to be reevaluated in the light of later critical studies—and for the versions it can never be cited at face value—this was the most instructive repertory of textual data bearing on the OT before the 20th cent.

61   The work of C. D. Ginsburg (*The Old Testament . . . Diligently Revised* [3 vols. in 4; London, 1908-26]) covered some of the same ground as the two preceding compilations and related the evidence of some 70 mss. and 19 editions to the received Hebr text. It marked no particular advance and was scarcely helpful. Similarly, an Israeli edition ascribed to the studies of M. D. Cassuto was issued by others (1953) after the scholar's death, and there is little to be said in its favor.

(Orlinsky, H. M., "The Masoretic Text: Fact or Fiction?" Prolegomenon [45 pp.] to facsimile reprint of C. D. Ginsburg, *Introduction to the Massoretico-Critical Edition of the Hebrew Bible* [NY, 1966]. Pérez Castro, F., "Estudios masoreticos," *Sef* 25 [1965] 289-317. Roberts, B. J., "The Hebrew Bible Since 1937," *JTS* 15 [1964] 253-64. Yeivin, I., *Introduction to the Tiberian Masorah* [SBLMasS 5; Missoula, 1980].)

GREEK VERSIONS OF THE OLD TESTAMENT

62   **(I) The Septuagint before AD 100.** At the time the foreword of Sir was written, *ca.* 116 BC (→ Sirach, 32:3, 9), the bulk of the OT was already circulating in Greek in the transl. known as the Septuagint (LXX). Beyond its current interest for the history and criticism of the text, the LXX is of great importance for having furnished the cultural milieu and literary vehicle for the preaching of earliest Christianity to the Gentile world. It has been and remains the liturgical OT text used by millions of Eastern Christians throughout the centuries. Not only is the LXX the form in which the OT was most widely circulated in apostolic times, but it also conveys the original text of some (deutero)canonical books (Wis, 2 Macc) and the basic form of others, either in part (Esth, Dan, Sir) or as a whole (Tob, Jdt, Bar, 1 Macc). Indeed, some Catholic scholars have argued that the LXX is directly inspired, at least in what it adds, even in the books of the Hebr canon (but → Inspiration, 65:39).

63   **(A) The Legendary Origin.** How the Pentateuch was translated from Hebrew into Greek is told in the fictitious *Letter of Aristeas to Philocrates,* dating from the 2d cent. BC (→ Apocrypha, 67:32–33). In the story, Demetrius of Phaleron, the librarian of Ptolemy II Philadelphus (285–246 BC), wants to include a copy of the Jewish law in the Egyptian king's famous library at Alexandria. At the royal librarian's urging, Philadelphus requests the high priest in Jerusalem to send to Egypt a band of 72 elders (six from each tribe!) to produce a translation. The work is completed to the satisfaction of all concerned, including the Jewish community of Alexandria. Despite constant repetition in Jewish and Christian circles, only one salient fact can be gleaned from this essentially apologetic propaganda narrative, viz., that the compilation of a full transl. of the Torah was made in the early 3d cent. BC. Yet "Septuagint," reflecting the Latin for 70 and drawn from the (rounded) number of translators in the Aristeas account, has come to designate not only the Pentateuch in Greek but—at least since the 4th cent. in Christian circles—the entire corpus of Gk OT transls. and compositions from the beginnings, possibly before 300 BC, until just prior to the work of Aquila, ca. AD 130 (→ 79–80 below).

64   **(B) Problem of Unified Origin.** The LXX contains transls. that vary enormously in accuracy and style from one book to the next, and sometimes even within a single book. Although the Pentateuch transl. is generally faithful, competent, and idiomatic, various sections come from about six distinct translators. In Gen, differences between the text furnished by the MT and that supposed by the LXX are comparatively limited, and the evidence for Gen shows a high degree of uniformity in the ms. tradition. For Exod through Deut, however, the variations are greater; and the LXX of Exod 35–40 is notably shorter than and arranged differently from the MT and the Samaritan recension. The other historical books of the LXX were developed over a span of at least two centuries. Where Hebr fragments from Qumran can be compared, they tend to support readings from the Greek against those of the MT. But the complexities of textual transmission are many, and each book and passage has to be studied for itself. Thus, the LXX rendering of Isa is good idiomatic Greek and tends to abridge the original (which it does not always understand), but the LXX of Jer is considerably shorter than the MT and gives evidence of being an earlier and better edition (→ 28 above).

65   The differences apparent in various LXX books suggest a question: In 1941 P. E. Kahle began to ask insistently whether what is preserved in our LXX mss. and editions is a single, pre-Christian transl. or an arbitrary, almost random, selection from many oral renderings like the early Palestinian targums (→ 103 below). Kahle pointed to OT quotations in Philo, Josephus, the NT, and such writers as Justin Martyr (d. *ca.* 165) as being incompatible with a straight line of transmission for the Gk text from a unitary origin to the great 4th/5th cent. LXX codices and on to our printed Bibles.

66   **(C) The Earliest LXX and Subsequent Revisions.** Despite the very real difficulties raised by Kahle, which cannot all be resolved on any one basis, the evidence for strict continuity in most OT books between a single pre-Christian rendering and the LXX text extant in our codices is overwhelming. In addition to very early renderings from Greek into Latin, Coptic, and (a little later) Ethiopic, all of which give detailed support to the LXX text we know, there are now various ms. fragments of pre-Christian date with texts in Greek from both Palestine and Egypt that fit into the same textual tradition. They include portions of Exod

(7Q1), Lev (4QLXXLev^a,b), Num (4QLXXNum), Deut (4QLXXDeut, Pap. Rylands Gk 458, Pap. Fuad inv. 266), and Ep Jer (7Q2 = Bar 6 in the Vg). The fragments range in date from the 2d cent. BC down to the turn of the era. (See A. R. C. Leaney, in Elliott (ed.), *Studies* 283–300.)

67   More extensive than these pre-Christian remains are the fragments of a 1st-cent. AD Gk scroll of the Minor Prophets from Naḥal Ḥever in the Judean desert (→ Apocrypha, 67:121), published by D. Barthélemy, in *Les devanciers d'Aquila* (VTSup 10; Leiden, 1963). These fragments (and Barthélemy's study of them) have gone far toward meeting the difficulties raised by Kahle, because they introduce us not to the early Alexandrian LXX of the Minor Prophets but to a 1st-cent. AD *systematic revision* of that rendering. Barthélemy's evidence converges with data from Qumran Hebr mss. of Sam (→ 26 above) studied by F. M. Cross (e.g., *HTR* 57 [1964] 281–99) and E. C. Ulrich (*The Qumran Text of Samuel and Josephus* [HSM 19; Missoula, 1978]). Below we shall follow as a working hypothesis this reconstruction, which in its main lines appears secure. It considerably expands previous historical perspectives on the state of the Gk OT text before and after the work of Origen (d. AD 254).

68   (a) THE LXX IN ALEXANDRIA. The earliest Gk transl. of the OT, done with underlying liturgical and apologetic concerns, employed the somewhat florid Alexandrian Gk idiom. Although the transl. strove in general for word-to-word equivalence, it was indifferent to the presence or absence in the Hebr text of such minor elements as reinforcing particles ("indeed"), signs identifying verbal objects, and resumptive pronouns not required by Gk syntax. The Hebr mss. on which it was based differed in many respects from those later chosen as prototypes for the MT. Good examples of this are available in Deut and Isa (but in either case not in Codex Vaticanus [B] or in editions based on it, since the B text for those books was reworked on the basis of the Hebrew); another good example is Jer. As for Sam–Kgs, since the early version (well represented in B) survives only for two sections (1 Sam 1:1–2 Sam 11:1 and 1 Kgs 2:12–21[MT 20]:43), it may be that the translators' apologetic or edifying purpose was met by presenting only those parts of the Hebr books.

69   (b) EARLIEST PALESTINIAN REVISION: "PROTO-LUCIAN." A subsequent stage, identified for Sam–Kgs by Cross as a result of his work on Qumran Hebr texts, may be labeled "proto-Lucianic." It represents the accommodation of older LXX materials to somewhat more developed Hebr texts (still quite distinct from the MT form) that circulated in the 2d and 1st cents. BC. The revision strove for a choice of terms and phrasing that would more nearly match the Hebrew. For parts of Sam–Kgs, it has actually replaced the earlier Greek in most LXX mss. That the work was done in Palestine is conjectured from the fact that its text type, ascribed subsequently to the patronage of Lucian of Antioch (d. 312), is connected with Syria-Palestine and matches Palestinian Hebr mss. from Qumran. Investigation of this phase of LXX textual transmission calls for much critical sifting of the evidence in various OT books, and the task is still incomplete.

70   (c) FURTHER PALESTINIAN REVISION: "PROTO-THEODOTION." The Minor Prophets scroll referred to above (→ 67) was presented by Barthélemy as evidence of a distinct recensional activity in Palestine, related to rules of textual interpretation formulated by the rabbis around the turn of the era. The revised transl. strove for consistency by developing Gk equivalents for many Hebr lexical items and by representing certain Hebr elements important for exegesis. Barthélemy identified nine features characteristic of the revison that were subsequently adopted by Aquila (→ 79–80 below), as well as a dozen more that Aquila modified or rejected (*Les devanciers* 31–88). The most prominent, Gk *kaige* to represent Hebr *wgm* ("and also"), provided the name *Kaige* recension for the work as a whole.

71	In a later analysis of the *Kaige* recension in Sam–Kgs, J. D. Shenkel proposed 10 further characteristics (*Chronology and Recensional Development in the Greek Text of Kings* [HSM 1; Cambridge MA, 1968] 13–18, 113–16). K. G. O'Connell's study of Exod produced 36 more (*The Theodotionic Revision of the Book of Exodus* [HSM 3; Cambridge MA, 1972] 286–91), and other scholars suggested additional ones (e.g., W. R. Bodine, *The Greek Text of Judges: Recensional Developments* [HSM 23; Chico, 1980] 47–91, 187–89; L. J. Greenspoon, *Textual Studies in the Book of Joshua* [HSM 28; Chico, 1983] 269–377; J. A. Grindel, *CBQ* 31 [1969] 499–513; M. Smith, *Bib* 48 [1967] 443–45).

72	Barthélemy dated the revision to *ca.* AD 30–50 and ascribed it to a Jonathan ben Uzziel mentioned in rabbinic literature in connection with the (Aram) targums. He also equated this Jonathan with the Theodotion to whom a late-2d-cent. AD LXX revision has been attributed. While the need for an earlier predecessor of the later Theodotion is evident from the material at hand, the date suggested by Barthélemy is somewhat less secure — although it is certainly not too late. The proposed identification with Jonathan, however, accounts for an already shadowy figure by fitting him into a garbled legend. Firm conclusions depend on continued examination of all the Gk evidence for Theodotion and the early recension to which he is somehow related.

73	In any case, the important things about the *Kaige* recension are its early date (the Minor Prophets scroll is from the 1st cent. AD), the wide range of texts to which it can be related, and the growing series of criteria by which it can be identified in the ms. tradition of various OT books. For the Minor Prophets, Barthélemy has shown (1) that the ms. did not contain a new transl. but a deliberate reworking of the older Alexandrian LXX in the light of a Hebr text and (2) that the same reworking is evidenced in the citations we have for the *quinta editio* of Origen's *Hexapla* (→ 83 below), as well as in a Gk ms. of the Minor Prophets in the Freer collection in Washington, in the Sahidic Coptic secondary rendering from the Greek, and in the text quoted by Justin Martyr, a native of Neapolis (Nablus) in Palestine (d. *ca.* 165). In printed editions of the Gk OT, the *Kaige* recension provides the "LXX" text of Lam and (probably) of Ruth; it may also have given rise to the "Theodotion" text of Dan (that has replaced the Old Gk form in virtually all LXX witnesses and that is already quoted in the NT and by Clement of Rome at the end of the 1st cent. AD). Yet others have contended that the Dan "Theodotion" is from a different early source that provided a fresh transl. for the Hebr/Aram text: so L. F. Hartman and A. A. Di Lella (*The Book of Daniel* [AB 23; GC, 1977] 81–82), drawing on J. Ziegler (*Susanna, Daniel, Bel et Draco* [LXX 16.2; Göttingen, 1964] 61); and A. Schmitt (*Stammt der sogenannte "θ'"-Text bei Daniel wirklich von Theodotion?* [MSU 9; Göttingen, 1966]). See also S. P. Jeansonne, *The Old Greek Translation of Daniel 7–12* (CBQMS 19; Washington, 1988). The LXX forms of Jer and Job, both shorter than the MT, have been filled out according to the techniques proper to the *Kaige* recension; the supplements appear regularly in the Gk Job and in some mss. and editions of Jer.

74	In Sam–Kgs, the *Kaige* recension supplies 2 Sam 11:2–1 Kgs 2:11, 1 Kgs 22, and all of 2 Kgs in B

and most other LXX mss., as well as in the printed editions. This reworking of Sam–Kgs had already been isolated by H. St. J. Thackeray (*The Septuagint and Jewish Worship* [2d ed.; London, 1923] 16–28, 114–15). Although he did not have the evidence to date the work, he was able to isolate criteria for identifying it.

75	(d) OTHER INDICATIONS OF EARLY REVISION. Once the existence of extensive recensional work on the Gk OT text in the last cent. BC and the 1st cent. AD is recognized, a number of other elements in LXX textual history begin to fall into place. Thus, E. Tov (*The Septuagint Translation of Jeremiah and Baruch* [HSM 8; Missoula, 1976]) has shown that the Old Greek of Jer 29–52 and Bar 1:1–3:8 has been completely replaced by a revision that may date to the late 2d or early 1st cent. BC. The 3d-cent. AD Beatty-Scheide Pap. 967 contains a 1st-cent. AD reworking of LXX Ezek (see J. Ziegler *ZAW* 61 [1945–48] 76–94). Of the five "Scrolls" (Megilloth) in the Hebr canon, only Gk Esth is surely of pre-Christian date in the received form of its text (for Gk Lam and Ruth, → 73 above); Gk Cant has always been thought late, and Gk Eccl is justly ascribed (again by Barthélemy) to 2d-cent. AD Aquila (→ 79–80 below). In all mss., Prov 1–9 includes a number of double renderings and other expansions; and since a secondary rendering of Prov 2:11 was already used by Clement of Rome (*1 Clem.* 14:4), these materials presumably date in general to the 1st cent. AD or earlier. Similarly, the secondary reworking of Gk Sir, found in some LXX mss. and in all the OL evidence, includes a text of Sir 12:1 that is already employed in *Did.* 1:6; once again we have 1st-cent. evidence for a revised text.

76	Through these reworkings of the LXX, when they can be dated approximately, it is possible not only to account historically for many of the difficulties pointed out by Kahle but also to form an idea of the textual situation in the Hebr mss. on which they were based. Though they are often closer to the MT than to the prototypes of the early Alexandrian LXX, it is not in fact the *precise* Hebr consonantal text stabilized at the end of the 1st cent. AD that they presuppose.

77	One may add those cases in which whole books of the Gk OT are present in the mss. in more than one form: two texts of Judg in codices B and A (so different that their common origin is not universally admitted); Alexandrian transls. of Ezra (1 Esdr or Esdr A) and of Dan, which jointly emphasize the late and distinctive origins of both Ezra-Neh (Gk Esdr B; → Apocrypha, 67:38) and the "Theodotionic" Dan (as well as of the similar Gk rendering for 1–2 Chr); and two separate forms of Gk Esth and three of Gk Tob. Thus it is clear that the basic unity of the LXX transl. is subject to many qualifications and that its use as a textual witness, encouraged by indications in the Hebr mss. from Qumran, implies ever more careful and informed study of each individual book. For example, the Gk Psalter appears to be a rather labored patchwork based on an originally inferior rendering. It was not helped at all by becoming the liturgical Psalter known to us in Greek, Latin, or such other languages as Arabic. In Pss, as in the Minor Prophets, Origen's *quinta* text (→ 83 below) was the 1st-cent. "proto-Theodotionic" recension (→ 70–74 above).

78	(II) **Later Renderings and the Work of Origen.** The traditional description of the 2d-cent. AD Jewish OT renderings into Greek, of Origen's 3d-cent. collection of those and other materials into his *Hexapla*, and of the still later activity by Lucian of Antioch (d. 312) needs revision at several points in the light of what has been said above. The stages may now be outlined as follows.

79   **(A) Aquila.** About AD 130, this Jewish proselyte from Pontus revised the "proto-Theodotionic" recension (→ 70–74 above) in the direction of a much more predictable correspondence between the Hebr text and its Gk representation. Single Gk equivalents were chosen for Hebr verbal roots, and then related Gk terms were found (sometimes even created) to represent real or apparent derivatives from the initial Hebr base. This quest for exact equivalence often led to awkward Gk phrases or to renditions that failed to capture the true meaning of a Hebr expression. Gk syntax and idiom were violated to furnish distinct equivalents for incidental Hebr particles. This process had already begun in the *Kaige* recension (where Gk *kaige* represented Hebr [*w*]*gm*, "(and) also," and where Gk *egō eimi*, "I am," two separate words, represented the Hebr pronoun "I" in a longer form ['*nky*] that had become archaic); but Aquila's revision carried it much further. One famous example is the adverbial *syn*, possibly an archaic homonym for the preposition *syn*, "with," that was used repeatedly for the Hebr accusative marker '*t* (presumably because that form resembled the Hebr preposition '*t*, "with"). Since the LXX was used extensively in Christian circles and frequently did not correspond exactly to the closely standardized Hebr mss. of the 2d and later cents., Aquila's recension replaced the LXX as the accepted Gk version of the OT for Jews of the later Roman and Byzantine empires. Because, e.g., it rendered Hebr '*almâ* in Isa 7:14 by *neanis* ("young woman") rather than LXX *parthenos* ("virgin"), Aquila's version entered into Jewish-Christian controversy.

80   Apart from the "LXX" rendering of Eccl, which is really Aquila's, his work has survived only in fragments: parts of Kgs and Pss, marginal readings drawn from Origen's *Hexapla* (→ 83 below) in certain LXX mss., and citations in patristic literature (see J. Reider, *An Index to Aquila,* completed and rev. by N. Turner [VTSup 12; Leiden, 1966]). Aquila's name, transformed into Onqelos, has been associated in Jewish tradition with the Aram targums (→ 106–7 below); but he actually had nothing to do with them. Details about Aquila in Epiphanius (*De mens. et pond.* 14–15) make him a relative of Emperor Hadrian who was converted in Aelia Capitolina (Jerusalem) by Christians from Pella but was later excommunicated. According to these apparently legendary reports, Aquila undertook his OT revision with an explicitly anti-Christian purpose.

81   **(B) Symmachus.** Toward the end of the 2d cent. AD, perhaps during the reign of Commodus (180–192), this writer produced a careful, yet thoroughly idiomatic, Gk rendering of the OT. Although Symmachus worked after Aquila and employed as his base, at least in some books (according to D. Barthélemy), the same 1st-cent. AD recension from which Aquila had worked, he proceeded on entirely different principles. The version is particularly interesting because it served in a number of cases as a lexical and stylistic model for Jerome's OT from the Hebrew. It survives only in Origen's hexaplaric fragments and citations (→ 83 below). In Eccl, where Aquila's version occupied the "LXX" column in Origen's edition, Symmachus stood in Aquila's usual position; faulty attributions of his readings have resulted from this and similar causes. About the author himself, the most likely detail we have is that Origen received the text of his rendering from a certain Juliana, who had it from Symmachus in person. His supposed Samaritan origins (Epiphanius, *De mens. et pond.* 15) and connection with an Ebionite *Gospel of Matthew* (Eusebius, *HE* 6.17; GCS 9/2. 554–56) are highly dubious (→ Apocrypha, 67:59).

82   **(C) Theodotion.** This name covers a large body of 1st-cent. recensional material (→ 70–74 above) that bears on most, if not all, parts of the LXX OT. Irenaeus (*Adv. Haer.* 3.21.1) puts Theodotion before Aquila, and this is the correct order of priority for the bulk of the materials now known. What is left for the traditional late-2d-cent. AD translator Theodotion, a Jewish proselyte supposedly from Ephesus, remains a matter for renewed sifting of the complex and fragmentary data. Since "(proto-)Theodotion" (often = *Kaige* recension) is the ordinary source drawn upon by Origen to fill out correspondences with the Hebr text that were lacking in the older LXX, it is from this recension that printed editions of the Gk OT provide Dan, Lam, Ruth, 2 Sam 11:2–1 Kgs 2:11, 1 Kgs 22 and all of 2 Kgs, possibly Cant, and the extensive supplements in the Greek of Job and (sometimes) of Jer. In Sam–Kgs the recension builds on "proto-Lucian" (→ 69 above); and, wherever they can be compared, "(proto-)Theodotion" is itself built on by Aquila, who carries to an extreme its existing tendencies toward mechanical rendering and imitation of the Hebr word order. Other related materials are the *quinta* recension (→ 83 below) of Pss, a seemingly miniscule text of Judg (*i, r, u, a₂*), the Naḥal Ḥever Minor Prophets (→ 67, 73 above), and most (but not all) known excerpts from the "Theodotion" column of the *Hexapla*. The name Theodotion ("God's gift") can easily be equated with Jonathan ("Yahweh has given"); but that the 1st-cent. Gk recension ascribed to Theodotion was actually done by the Jonathan ben Uzziel of Jewish tradition (→ 72 above) seems hardly susceptible of proof.

83   **(D) Origen's *Hexapla*.** At Caesarea in Palestine before AD 245, Origen put together his famous compilation of Hebr and Gk materials for the study of the OT text. Known as the *Hexapla Biblia* ("Sixfold Books"), the text was arranged in (usually) six vertical cols., of which two pertained to the Hebr text and four to Gk versions, thus: (1) the Hebr consonantal text in the standardized Hebr characters current since the 2d cent.; (2) the same Hebr text transliterated (to the extent possible) into Gk letters; (3) Aquila; (4) Symmachus; (5) the traditional LXX (with elements lacking by comparison with the Hebrew supplied, usually from "Theodotion"); and (6) Theodotion. For some books (e.g., Pss), there were additional forms in Greek beyond the four: a *quinta* (V^a), *sexta* (VI^a), and even *septima* (VII^a) *editio;* in such cases, the number of cols. grew to seven or eight (*quinta* for Pss occupied the usual place of Theodotion, and *septima* may never have been more than marginal notations).

84   The transliterated Hebrew of Origen's col. 2 was described above (→ 40–41). Evidence from the Mercati Ps fragments seems to indicate that col. 5, the LXX col. of the *Hexapla,* did not itself contain the critical markings (for comparison with the Hebrew) that were a special feature of Origen's work. However, when the LXX col. was copied to be circulated separately, it was equipped with the asterisk (⋇) to signal passages lacking in the older LXX that had been supplied (usually from the Greek of "Theodotion") to make the LXX conform to a fuller received Hebr text. The obelus (÷) was introduced before LXX passages for which the Hebrew had no equivalent. At the point where the LXX and the Hebrew began again to coincide, a metobelus (⅄) marked the end of the preceding variant (of either type).

85   Copies of the complete *Hexapla* must always have been scarce, if indeed any were made at all; a *Tetrapla* (the four Gk cols. without the two Hebr ones) is also mentioned. Until about AD 600 the prototype survived in Caesarea in the library founded by the martyr Pamphilus, where it was consulted by Jerome (among others); its ultimate fate is not known. Today we have of the *Hexapla* only fragments from Sam–Kgs and Pss, readings excerpted into the margins of LXX mss., citations by patristic writers in several languages, and extensive portions of the LXX col. with its critical markings in various secondary translations (particularly Syriac and Arabic). Remarkable efforts at reassembling these data were made by F. Field (*Origenis hexaplorum quae supersunt* [2 vols.; Oxford, 1875]) and in the apparatus to the Cambridge and Göttingen editions (→ 100 below).

86 The task of reestablishing exact hexaplaric readings is complicated because the critical markings were frequently misplaced or lost in transmission and because the ascription to one or another col. is sometimes erroneous in our witnesses, either because abbreviations were misunderstood or because even in the prototype the content of a given col. sometimes varied from book to book. Thus, in the portions of Sam–Kgs where "Theodotion" occupied col. 5, the normal LXX col. (2 Sam 11:2–1 Kgs 2:11; 1 Kgs 22; 2 Kgs), the "proto-Lucianic" form went into col. 6; in Eccl, where col. 5 (LXX col.) really contained Aquila, it was Symmachus that appeared in col. 3; in Pss, *quinta* held the place of Theodotion. False citations have resulted in such instances. Abridged extracts of the major work later added to the confusion.

87 **(E) Lucian of Antioch.** In his preface to Vg Chr, written *ca.* 396, Jerome noted that there were in his day three commonly received LXX text traditions: one in Egypt that was connected with the name of Hesychius, a second from Caesarea in Palestine that reflected the work of Origen, and a third (which elsewhere [*Epist.* 106, *Ad Sunniam*] he characterized as the *koinē* ["common"] or vulgate form) that was connected with Antioch and the work of Lucian (d. 312). The character of the text ascribed to Hesychius is now very difficult to determine (see S. Jellicoe, *JBL* 82 [1963] 409–18). As for Lucian (→ 69 above), in Sam–Kgs at least, the text credited to him has been successfully isolated in a group of minuscule mss. (*b, o, c₂, e₂*) that prove on further study to be closely related to the text used by Josephus at the end of the 1st cent. and to the fragmentary Hebr mss. from Qumran. Similar kinship between a group of "Lucianic" mss. and the citations in Josephus and in such Antiochene writers as John Chrysostom is verified also for other OT books. Hence, whatever function may be assigned to Lucian's personal work on the Gk text of the NT (→ 175 below) and however much retouching for stylistic or other reasons the LXX may have received at his hands, the most significant feature regarding the group of Antiochene texts with which he is associated is that they open up for us an approach to the state of the LXX and of the underlying Hebr text in Syria-Palestine *before* the late-1st-cent. AD standardizing of the Hebr consonantal tradition.

88 **(III) Mss. and Editions of the LXX.**
(A) Manuscripts. In addition to the fragmentary texts from before AD 100 now available (→ 66–67 above), there are approximately 1,800 extant LXX mss. of a later period. They are generally divided on the basis of the material used (papyrus and parchment) or of the writing style (uncial and minuscule).

89 Papyrus, made in Egypt, came from a tall reedlike plant (*Cyperus papyrus*). The stem (pith) was sliced lengthwise into strips that were laid side by side to form a layer, and layers were pressed together at right angles to form a sheet. After drying, papyrus made a good, inexpensive writing surface; but it became brittle with age. Papyrus sheets were glued together to form a scroll that could be wound about a stick to constitute a

volume. Since scrolls averaged about 35 ft. in length, they were inconvenient to use. A passage near the beginning of a work could only be consulted by unrolling the entire scroll. Early in the 2d cent. AD, a new book format became popular (apparently for church use in particular); it was the codex, in which sheets were sewn together much as in the modern book. Some of the oldest surviving fragments of Christian works come from papyrus codices.

90 Parchment (or vellum), named after Pergamum, where it was developed in the 2d cent. BC, was a more durable (and more expensive) writing material. It consisted of sheepskin that had been scraped and made smooth. Its durability made it more appropriate for books that would be read over and over, and so the major biblical codices were written on parchment.

91 As for the type of handwriting, although a cursive or "running" hand (where one letter runs into the next) was used for everyday documents, literary works were written in more formal block letters or uncials (large letters separated from one another). Up until the 9th cent. AD, this was the script used for the Gk Bible, but then a script was introduced at Constantinople that employed smaller letters (minuscules) written in a running hand. This reform in handwriting meant that biblical mss. could be copied more swiftly and on a smaller writing space; it greatly increased the number of copies. See *MMGB* 22–29.

92 (a) PAPYRI (2d–9th cents.). Discoveries in Egypt since the 1890s have substantially increased the resources available for knowledge of the LXX as it circulated before or independent of Origen's work. The Chester Beatty collection of papyri, published by F. G. Kenyon (8 vols.; London, 1933–58), includes 2d-cent. AD fragments of Num–Deut and Jer, as well as substantial 3d-cent. parts of Gen and Isa–Ezek–Dan–Esth. The Freer collection in Washington has 33 leaves of a 3d-cent. Minor Prophets. Also of the 3d cent. are portions of Gen, Pss, Prov, Wis, and Sir in Oxford, Geneva, and London. With the 4th cent., extant papyri become more numerous, and some 200 can be counted that are prior to AD 700. References to LXX papyri in the literature suffer from the lack of a uniform method of listing them.

93 (b) GREAT UNCIAL CODICES (4th–10th cents.). These codices, written on vellum, began to make their appearance in the 4th cent. AD; they remain the most complete and often the most careful copies of the LXX. They have been the foundation for almost all printed editions and collations of the ms. evidence, and several have been reproduced in complete photographic facsimile publications; they are usually pandects (complete Bibles). Capital letters, ordinarily roman, are the symbols used to designate the individual uncial mss. Some of these codices contain the NT as well (→ 157 below), but the following are most significant for LXX study.

94 (i) *Codex Vaticanus* (B) is of mid-4th-cent. date. It lacks only Gen 1:1–46:8, some verses in 2 Sam 2, and about 30 Pss; it never contained 1–2 Macc. In a number of OT books, this codex has proved to be in a class by itself as the best single witness to the earliest form of the LXX.

95 (ii) *Codex Sinaiticus* (S or ‬א) also dates from the 4th cent. Some 156 of its leaves are now in the British Museum in London, and 43 others are in Leipzig; but there are some notable lacunae. Its orthography is surprisingly careless; the text to which it witnesses is close to that of B, but in Tob it is the unique Gk witness to the longer and more nearly original text form of the book. It has 1 and 4 Macc, but it never had 2–3 Macc

(H. C. Milne and T. C. Skeat, *Scribes and Correctors of the Codex Sinaiticus* [London, 1979]; *BA* 46 [1983] 54–56).

96   (iii) *Codex Alexandrinus* (A), also in the British Museum, dates from the 5th cent. It has slight lacunae in Gen and 1 Sam, and it also lacks about 30 Pss. Its text is often at variance with B (in Judg strikingly so), and it includes 3–4 Macc as well as the canonical books. "Proto-Lucianic" and hexaplaric influences on its text have been identified.

97   (iv) *Codex Marchalianus* (Q) is a 6th-cent. ms. of the Prophets in the Vatican Library. It is notable especially for marginal citations of later Gk variants from Aquila, Symmachus, and Theodotion.

98   (c) MINUSCULE MSS. (from the 9th cent. on). These mss., about 1,500 in all, occasionally preserve text of great antiquity that is not attested in any uncials, such as the "Lucianic" codices in Sam–Kgs (→ 87 above). Some 300 of these mss. were collated for variants, with differing degrees of accuracy, for the edition of R. Holmes and J. Parsons (*Vetus Testamentum graecum cum variis lectionibus* [5 vols.; Oxford, 1798–1827]). The numbers assigned to various minuscule mss. in that edition were incorporated into the standard list of LXX mss. by A. Rahlfs (*Verzeichnis der griechischen Handschriften des Alten Testaments* [Berlin, 1914]) for reference purposes. For the historical books, however, the Cambridge editors (→ 100 below) followed their own system and employed small letters for the selection of minuscule mss. from which they reported readings.

99   (B) **Printed Editions.**
(a) EDITIONS OF HISTORICAL IMPORT. The two earliest LXX eds. were the Aldine (Venice, 1518), based on minuscule mss., and that in the Complutensian Polyglot from Spain (1521), where the text is largely of the "Lucianic" type. The Council of Trent called for critical texts of the Bible to be published, and for the LXX the result was the Sixtine edition of 1587. This ed. set a significant pattern for later publication and critical study, since it was based largely on Codex B. The Oxford ed. (1707–1720) of J. E. Grabe was a noteworthy ed. based on Codex A. The ed. of Holmes and Parsons (mentioned above) drew on 20 uncials, some 300 minuscules, the evidence of daughter versions from the Greek, and patristic citations. For Prov, Eccl, and Cant, it remains the only substantial repertory of LXX readings even today. A manual ed. of the LXX by C. von Tischendorf (1850) was collated to B and S by E. Nestle (6th ed., 1880). Manual eds. frequently used have been those of H. B. Swete (Cambridge, numerous printings and three eds. since 1894) and A. Rahlfs (Stuttgart, 1935–). The Swete text is that of B where available, A for Gen, and S for the lacuna in Pss, with variants from other uncials. Rahlfs's text is eclectic, and its sources

cannot always be verified; the uncials collated are usually fewer than in Swete. Neither is an adequate critical instrument today. P. de Lagarde projected a Lucianic ed., but the result—a first vol. only (1883)—was not a success and is antiquated.

100   (b) MODERN CRITICAL UNDERTAKINGS. Of these there are three: (1) The larger Cambridge Septuagint of A. E. Brooke, N. McLean, H. St. J. Thackeray, and others, published comprehensive evidence for all the historical books from Gen (1906) through 1–2 Chr (1932) and 1 Esdr–Ezra–Neh (1935), as well as Esth–Jdt–Tob (1940). The collating base is B, even when (Deut, Chr) that ms. is not a good witness. The evidence requires constant interpretation by the user, since the apparatus offers no real guides as to the character of the mss. cited. (2) The *Septuaginta* project of the Göttingen Academy of Sciences (1931–) has a continuous text established by the modern editor (e.g., R. Hanhart, J. Wevers, J. Ziegler); and the mss. are cited by family groups wherever possible. Several volumes have been accompanied by a separate text history. (3) A computer-produced ed., drawing on the first two and on all available data (and conveniently susceptible to further electronic manipulation) is CATSS (Computer Assisted Tools for Septuagint Studies), which in 1986, directed by R. A. Kraft and E. Tov, produced its first vol., *Ruth* (SBLSCS 20; Atlanta). The history and procedures of CATSS are explained there, with accompanying Gk-Hebr and Hebr-Gk concordances to Ruth. It presents in parallel cols. the unvocalized MT of *BHS* (→ 56 above), Rahlfs's LXX text (→ 99 above), and variants from the larger Cambridge Septuagint and the Göttingen eds. (as available).

(*BIOSCS* 1– [1968–]. Devreesse, R., *Introduction a l'étude des manuscrits grecs* [Paris, 1954]. Hatch, E. and H. A. Redpath, *A Concordance to the Septuagint* [2 vols. and Suppl.; Oxford, 1897–1906; repr. in 2 vols., Graz, 1954]. Hyvärinen, K., *Die Übersetzung von Aquila* [ConBOT 10; Lund, 1977]. Jellicoe, S., "Aristeas, Philo, and the Septuagint *Vorlage*," *JTS* 12 [1961] 261–71; *The Septuagint and Modern Study* [Oxford, 1968]; [ed.], *Studies in the Septuagint: Origins, Recensions, and Interpretation* [NY, 1974]. Kahle, P. E., "Die von Origenes verwendeten griechischen Bibelhandschriften," StudP 4 [TU 79; 1961] 107–17. O'Connell, K. G., "Greek Versions [Minor]," *IDBSup* 377–81. Swete, H. B., *An Introduction to the Old Testament in Greek* [rev. ed. 1914; repr. NY, 1968]. Tov, E., *A Computerized Data Base for Septuagint Studies: The Parallel Aligned Text of the Greek and Hebrew Bible* [CATSS 2; *JNSL* Suppl. 1; Stellenbosch, 1986]; *The Text-Critical Use of the Septuagint in Biblical Research* [Jerusalem, 1981]. Tov, E. and R. A. Kraft, "Septuagint," *IDBSup* 807–15. Walters, P., *The Text of the Septuagint* [Cambridge, 1973]. Wevers, J. W., "An Apologia for Septuagint Studies," *BIOSCS* 18 [1985] 16–38. Ziegler, J., *Sylloge: Gesammelte Aufsätze zur Septuaginta* [MSU 10; Göttingen, 1971].)

OTHER ANCIENT VERSIONS OF THE BIBLE

101   (I) **Aramaic and Syriac Versions.**
(A) **The Aramaic Language.** Aramaic is about as close to Hebrew as Spanish is to Italian. In the late 2d millennium BC, it was spoken by pastoral, seminomadic peoples who pressed in upon northern Mesopotamia, the Anatolian foothills, and inner Syria. By the 10th cent. BC, several Aramean states flourished in that region, and the Aram language gradually assumed international importance. The courtiers of Hezekiah, king of Judah, proposed using it in conversations with the Assyrian besiegers of Jerusalem in 701 BC (2 Kgs

18:26). Under the Neo-Babylonian Empire (627–538 BC) and even more under the Persian Empire (538–331 BC), it became first the language of diplomacy and administration and ultimately the native speech of the former Assyro-Babylonian territories (including Syria-Palestine). Aramaic began to displace Hebrew as the vernacular of the Jewish people in the Babylonian Exile after the fall of Jerusalem in 586 BC. In the OT itself, it is employed in Gen 31:47 (2 words); Jer 10:11; Ezra 4:8–6:18; 7:12–26; Dan 2:4–7:28. The use of Hebrew and of the related Phoenician dialects spoken in the nearby coastal cities decreased progressively for some centuries. By AD 135 Hebrew was in effect a dead language, and even before that time it was chiefly limited to Judea, while Galilee, Samaria, and the areas E of the Jordan were of Aram speech.

102 Until after the rise of Islam in the 7th cent. AD, Aramaic remained the dominant vernacular and literary language between the Mediterranean Sea and the Persian Gulf, though under pressure from Greek (especially in the cities). At about the beginning of the Christian era, a dialect split began to make itself felt. As far E as the great bend in the Euphrates, a direct Western Aram successor to the earlier language was used by Christians, Jews, and Samaritans. East of that point, Aram literatures distinguished mainly along religious lines sprang up among the Christians (Syriac), Jews (Babylonian Jewish Aramaic), gnostic sectarians (Mandaean), and pagans of Eastern Aram speech. These eastern dialects all shared a small group of innovations in the forms of the language (and broader differences in diction) that set them apart from the Aramaic of the west.

103 **(B) The Targums.**
(a) ORIGINS. In the last centuries BC, because Hebrew had declined as the spoken language of the Jews not merely in Babylonia (where many remained) but also in Palestine, Hebr OT texts began to be rendered orally into Aramaic during the public reading of the Law and the Prophets in the synagogue liturgy. Either from the start of this practice or at least before the turn of the era, written Aram transls. or targums (Hebr *targûmîm*) were prepared for the purpose, although for some time the rabbis viewed the use of such texts with official disfavor.

104 The Talmud story (b. *Šabb.* 115a) that Rabban Gamaliel I had a targum of Job immured during a 1st-cent. AD building operation on the Temple Mount has been strikingly illustrated by the discovery of a quite literal Job targum at Qumran (11QtgJob) that dates from the middle of the same century. Another bit of targum of Job was recovered from Qumran cave 4, and LXX Job 42:17b also supposes a written Aram Job targum from around the turn of the era. A scrap of Lev 16:12–21 in Aramaic from Qumran (4QtgLev) yields "covering" as the equivalent of *kappōret*, the name of the metal "mercy seat" over the Ark; this sheds new light on an old controversy (→ Pauline Theology, 82:73). While the Aram embellishment of Gen from Qumran (1QapGen; → Apocrypha, 67:93) includes stories foreign to the biblical text, it also has a continuing thread of quite close rendering by which the expansions are strung together.

105 Written targums of Esth and of other books that are alluded to already in the Mishna (*Meg.* 2:1; *Yad.* 4:15) must antedate AD 200; and for some extant elements of Palestinian targums the inference has been drawn that at least their oral formulation must date to the 2d cent. BC. Whenever truly ancient targum materials can be recovered, they are of some value for textual study, but they are even more important for exegetical reasons and for background to the NT and especially to its use of OT texts. Two tendencies in targums, the one to adhere closely to the original text, the other to elaborate and introduce narrative material that goes far beyond the text, are apparently both equally ancient.

106 (b) BABYLONIAN TARGUMS. The targums that have been printed and studied in modern times come mostly from late mss. While the basis for all extant targums was almost certainly provided in Palestine, two principal compilations, *Targum Onqelos to the Pentateuch* and *Targum Jonathan to the* (Former and Latter) *Prophets*, were reworked extensively in the Jewish schools of Babylonia around the 5th cent. AD. The *Targum Onqelos*

was the only targum officially approved by the scholars of the talmudic period (before *ca.* AD 650). In a reworking that adapted it to the details of the received Hebr consonantal text, it lost such midrashic expansions and clues to variant textual readings as it may have had in earlier times. This is true in nearly the same degree of the *Targum Jonathan* to the Prophets (i.e., to Josh, Judg, Sam, Kgs, and the Writing Prophets), which has a similar history. Both targums have been published by A. Sperber in new editions (*The Bible in Aramaic*, vols. I–III [Leiden, 1959–62]) that include variants from several extant mss. and from a number of early printed editions.

107 Where midrashic expansions do survive in the Babylonian targums, they can be of great interest. Thus the targum of Isa 9:5 says of the child who is foretold, "His name has from of old been called Wonderful Counselor, Mighty God, living through the ages, the Messiah, in whose days peace will abound for us." Isa 11:1 and 6 in the same targum are also explicitly messianic (→ OT Thought, 77:158–59). Similarly, a surviving excerpt from the *Jerusalem Targum* (→ 108 below) of Isa 11:3 says, "Behold, the Messiah who is to come shall be one who teaches the Law and will judge in the fear of the Lord." The biblical commentaries from Qumran have a similar tone (i.e., the pesharim; → Apocrypha, 67:89, 117). Onqelos and Jonathan, the traditional authors of the Babylonian targums, are only reflections of the real Aquila and the somewhat more shadowy Theodotion (a name that, like Jonathan, means approximately "God-given"); they produced revisions of Gk (*not* Aram) transls. of the OT (→ 79–80, 82 above).

108 (c) PALESTINIAN TARGUMS. Targum materials directly Palestinian in origin are less easy to come by; but they are ultimately of more significance for textual, literary, and historical purposes. A complete 16th-cent. AD copy of *Targum Yerushalmi to the Pentateuch* was identified (1949) in the codex *Neofiti 1* of the Vatican Library by A. Díez Macho. He announced the discovery in 1956 and produced a five-vol. *editio princeps* (*Neophyti 1: Targum Palestinense* [Madrid-Barcelona, 1968–78]). That the contents of this Jerusalem targum should be uniformly of 2d-cent. AD provenience (with earlier roots but without later contamination), as has been claimed, would be extraordinary; but the targum need not conform fully to such an estimate to be of great value. In the late 11th cent. AD, R. Nathan ben Yehiel used a targum text practically identical to *Neofiti 1* in composing a dictionary called the *Aruk*. Targum fragments from the Cairo Geniza (→ 43 above) that are in essential agreement with *Neofiti 1*, some from the late 7th cent., have been published by Kahle (*Masoreten des Westens* II [→ 49 above] and Díez Macho, *Sef* 15 [1955] 31–39).

109 The "pseudo-Jonathan" targum to the Pentateuch (British Museum Ms. Add. 27031) is based on *Onqelos*, with which patches of older, fulsome Palestinian materials were combined in medieval times to yield a more extensive targum than either *Neofiti 1* (→ 108 above) or the "fragmentary targums" (→ 110 below). A publication of the text was prepared by E. G. Clarke (*Targum Pseudo-Jonathan of the Pentateuch: Text and Concordance* [Hoboken, 1984]).

110 Portions of the fuller Palestinian type of targum to the Pentateuch also survive in medieval mss. of the so-called fragmentary targums (special collections of targum materials for purposes that are no longer clear). A publication, based on five primary sources, is by M. L. Klein (*The Fragment-Targums of the Pentateuch According to their Extant Sources* [2 vols.; AnBib 76; Rome, 1980]). Other evidence from Palestinian targums comes from glosses to *Onqelos* and from 2d–16th cent. rabbinic citations.

111   A critical edition of the major textual authorities for the Palestinian targum to the Pentateuch was
prepared by a team headed by A. Díez Macho († 1984).
A specimen volume (Madrid, 1965) was followed by
vols. on Exod–Deut (Madrid, 1977–80). See also M. L.
Klein, *Genizah Manuscripts of Palestinian Targum to the
Pentateuch* (2 vols.; Cincinnati, 1986).

112   Samaritan targums to the Pentateuch, transmitted in the archaic script used for the Samaritan Hebr
text, also exist; they are in a very fluid state, and no two
mss. yield the same form.

113   The Palestinian targum to the Prophets is
largely unknown. For the "Writings" section of the Hebr
canon of the OT, the known targum materials are both
less systematic and later (8th–9th cents. AD) in their
extant form. Though they offer more suggestions for
underlying Hebr variants than do either *Onqelos* or
Jonathan, it is less certain that their readings have a continuous Aram tradition behind them. The Job targum is
distinct from the Qumran ones (→ 104 above); the
targum of Pss shows conflation and double renderings.
They are both linguistically related to the Chr targum.
The Prov targum is simply the Syr Peshitta (→ 125–27
below) transposed into square-letter script. Dan and
Ezra-Neh, which contain Aram portions in their basic
text, are without targums for any part. For Esth there are
several targums, but only one remains at all close to the
text; the other Esth targums, along with those for the
other four "Scrolls" (Cant, Lam, Eccl, and Ruth), are
very periphrastic and quite late in origin.

114   The *editio princeps* of the Prophets and
Hagiographa in the Aram version and Lat transl. originally prepared by A. de Zamora (and meant for the
Complutensian Polyglot of 1514–1517) has appeared in
the series Bibliotheca Hispana Biblica (ed. L. Díez
Merino; Madrid, 1982–). Targums of Ruth (AnBib 58;
Rome, 1973), Jonah (Jerusalem, 1975), and Lam (Jerusalem, 1976) were edited by E. Levine, and one of Chr
by R. Le Déaut and J. Robert (2 vols.; AnBib 71; Rome
1971); all are based on Codex Vat. Urb. 1. A. Van
Der Heide has edited eight available Yemenite mss. for
the targum of Lam (SPB 32; Leiden, 1981); they differ
from the version in non-Yemenite mss. and may reflect
a lost Babylonian version. Sperber republished the
Berlin ms. of the targum of Chr (first published by M.
F. Beck in 1680), as well as ben Chayim's text of the
Ruth targum and British Museum Ms. Or. 2375 for the
targums of Cant, Lam, Eccl, and Esth (*The Bible in
Aramaic,* vol. IV-A [Leiden, 1968]); he argued that
midrashic elements, simply introduced into the Chr and
Ruth targums, were fused with the transl. in the Cant–
Lam–Eccl targums, while the Esth targum was indis-
tinguishable from midrash. B. Grossfeld (*The First
Targum to Esther according to the Ms Paris Hebrew 110 of the
Bibliothèque Nationale* [NY, 1983]), presents a mid-15th-
cent. ms. that differs from the Esth targum published by
Sperber.

115   A series of critical Eng. transls. of all extant
targums, *The Aramaic Bible (The Targums),* was prepared
under M. McNamara's supervision for publication (19
vols. planned; Wilmington, 1987– 89).

(Bowker, J., *The Targums and Rabbinic Literature* [London, 1969].
Churgin, P., *Targum ketubim* [Hebrew; NY, 1945]. Diaz, R.,
"Ediciones del Targum samaritano," *EstBib* 15 [1956] 105–8.
Díez Macho, A., "The Recently Discovered Palestinian
Targum," *Congress Volume: Oxford 1959* [VTSup 7; Leiden,
1960] 222–45. Grossfeld, B., *A Bibliography of Targum Literature*
[NY, 1972]; *A Bibliography of Targum Literature* II [NY, 1977];
A Critical Commentary on Targum Neofiti I to Genesis [NY, 1978].
Kuiper, G. J., *The Pseudo-Jonathan Targum and Its Relationship to
Targum Onkelos* [Studia Eph. "Augustinianum" 9; Rome, 1972].

Le Déaut, R., "The Current State of Targumic Studies," *BTB* 4
[1974] 1–32. McNamara, M., *Targum and Testament* [Shannon,
1972]; "Targums," *IDBSup* 856–61; *The New Testament and the
Palestinian Targum to the Pentateuch* [2d ed. with Suppl.; AnBib
27A; Rome, 1978]. *Newsletter for Targumic and Cognate Studies*
[Department of Near Eastern Studies, University of Toronto].
Rosenthal, F., *Die aramäistische Forschung* [Leiden, 1937].
Smolar, L., *et al., Studies in Targum Jonathan to the Prophets* [NY,
1978]. Tal, A., *The Samaritan Targum of the Pentateuch* [Tel Aviv,
1980–83]. Van der Ploeg, J. P. M. and A. S. van der Woude, *Le
Targum de Job de la grotte XI de Qumrân* [Leiden, 1971].)

116   (C) Syriac Versions.

(a) ORIGINS.   Translation of the Scriptures
into Syriac had its roots in the developing pre-Christian
Aram targums of OT books brought by 1st/2d-cent. AD
Jewish and Christian preachers from Palestine into the
district of Adiabene (surrounding Irbil in modern Iraq)
and to the neighborhood of Edessa (Urfa in modern
Turkey). The Syr literary dialect of Eastern Aramaic (→
102 above) became standardized during the same period.
Though widely used for a great variety of purposes, this
Aram dialect survives primarily in a copious Christian
religious literature composed between the end of the 2d
and the beginning of the 14th century. It is distinct to
some extent in form, and even more in diction, from the
Western Aramaic of Palestine that was used by Christ
and the apostles. The Syr Bible is in this Eastern dialect,
and its NT is wholly a transl. from the Greek. Claims
that the Syr Gospels are the form in which Jesus spoke
his teaching—claims often made by people who have
every reason to know better—are without foundation.

117   (b) CHURCHES WITH A TRADITION OF SYRIAC.
Syriac remains today the liturgical language for a variety
of churches from Lebanon to the Malabar Coast of
India, most of whose members currently speak Arabic or
(in India) Malayalam; both N and S America have had
substantial numbers of immigrants from these various
communities.

118   They include the Maronites in Lebanon, who
have all been in union with Rome from at least the
Crusades into modern times (and whose tradition denies
that they were Monothelites at an earlier period,
although that is how most historians understand the
matter). The non-Monophysite Melkites in Syria and
Lebanon were deprived of their previous Antiochene
liturgy and of the option to use Aramaic in the 13th
cent.—the Byzantine liturgy in Greek or in Arabic was
substituted. They include both Orthodox and Catholics.

119   There are many "Syrian Orthodox," also
known as West Syrians, Jacobites, or Monophysites, in
Syria, Palestine, and India. Especially around Aleppo
there are a number of Syrians in union with Rome who
follow the same Syro-Antiochene rite as the Orthodox
West Syrians. In Syria, Iraq, Iran, and India there are
East Syrian Christians who have inherited the theological views of Nestorius and call themselves Assyrians;
they share an ancient East Syrian rite with the "Chaldeans" (their counterparts in union with Rome). Among
Christians in India who are united to Rome, the Mala-
barese retain the East Syrian rite, the Malankarese the
West Syrian; similar divisions exist there among the
groups separated from Rome.

120   The dialectal differences between the liturgical
language of the East Syrians and that of the West Syrians
and Maronites are minor and concern divergent vowel
qualities within a uniform language with a common
Bible (the Peshitta). Spoken Western Aramaic (distinct
from the Syr literary tradition) has survived till now at
Ma'lula in the Antilebanon mountains, about 35 mi.
from Damascus; but the primary language of its approximately two thousand speakers is in fact Arabic (A.

Spitaler, *ZDMG* 32 [1957] 299-339). Farther E, several dialects akin to Syriac survive in Syria, Iraq, Iran, and the Asiatic provinces of the USSR; these survivals of Eastern Aram vernaculars are much overlaid with foreign vocabulary from neighboring languages, and some are now nearly unrecognizable as basically Aramaic.

121 (c) BIBLE VERSIONS. In the course of time several different, usually independent, transls. of the OT and the NT circulated in Syriac.

122 (i) *Tatian's Diatessaron* (= "[One] through four"). This was a continuous harmony that wove together material from the four Gospels with a little apocryphal material (from the *History of Joseph the Carpenter* and from a "Hebrew Gospel"). Tatian was a Syrian from Mesopotamia, born *ca.* 110, who lived for years in Rome and was a disciple of Justin Martyr. Charged with exaggerated asceticism of Encratite tendency, Tatian left Rome sometime after 165 and returned to the East. About this time, whether in Rome or in Syria, he composed his harmony. It is uncertain whether he originally wrote it in Greek or in Syriac; if in Greek, it was soon translated into Syriac. The Gk form was lost except for a 3d-cent. fragment, consisting of 14 lines, discovered in 1933 at Dura-Europos on the Euphrates (*ATNT* 58).

123 The *Diatessaron* circulated widely in the Syrian church, seemingly became the official Syrian Gospel text (rather than the four Gospels), and was commented on by Ephraem (d. 373). However, it eventually perished (because opponents like Bishop Theodoret of Cyr [Cyrrhus], who suspected Tatian of heresy, destroyed all available copies), and it was replaced by the four Gospels in Syriac. A useful tool in reconstructing the Syr *Diatessaron* is Ephraem's commentary (long known in an Armenian transl.); about half of the Syr original is available in L. Leloir's publication of C. Beatty ms. 709 (Dublin, 1963). Harmonies similar to the *Diatessaron* or transls. of it have come down in Arabic, Persian, Latin (Codex Fuldensis), medieval Dutch, and Italian. The Armenian and Georgian transls. of the Gospels were influenced by it, and traces may be found in patristic citations. Reconstruction of *Diatessaron* readings is a difficult art, however (→ 183 below). (For editions, see Metzger, *Chapters* 97-120. There is an Eng transl. from the Arabic in the *Ante-Nicene Fathers* 9. 33-138. For the order of passages in the *Diatessaron,* see L. Leloir, CSCO 227, 1-11. Studies by T. Baarda, *Early Transmission of Words of Jesus* [Amsterdam, 1983].)

124 (ii) *Old Syriac Bible.* Of this rendering (OS) for the OT books we know only what survives in incidental citations, plus the evidence of early targumic influence and of Jewish or Judeo-Christian origins that carries over in reworked form into the Peshitta. The separate OS Gospels are known from two 5th-cent. mss.: one is in the British Museum, having been published by W. Cureton in 1842; the other was discovered in the monastery of St. Catherine at Mt. Sinai in 1892 by two British twin sisters, A. Smith Lewis and M. M. Dunlop Gibson, and published in 1910. (It was rephotographed with new methods by J. H. Charlesworth in 1985.) Dependent on the Greek, these Gospels do *not* give direct access to the Aramaic spoken by Jesus (→ 116 above). The two mss. offer divergent forms of one basic Syr text that seems later in origin than the *Diatessaron;* the underlying Greek is an archaic and "Western" type of Gospel text (→ 167, 173 below). Citations from Acts and the Pauline corpus in early writers point to a similar status for those books, but no continuous OS texts are now extant.

125 (iii) *Peshitta Bible.* In both the OT and the NT, the Peshitta is a compilation and careful reworking of earlier materials. It was established firmly enough in the early 5th cent. to remain the Bible of all Syr-language Christians despite the Nestorian and Monophysite movements and the disruption of unity that accompanied them. The Peshitta OT, though basically a translation from the Hebrew, shows distinct secondary influences from the LXX in those books especially (Isa, Pss) that were most used in the liturgy. Its renderings of the various groups of OT books are uneven in quality and were prepared by a number of different hands. Such books as Jdt and Bar were independently translated from the Greek, and Tob was unknown in Syriac until quite late. It is noteworthy that Sir was based on a Hebr text.

126 The name of Rabbula, bishop of Edessa (d. 435), is attached to the production of the Peshitta (particularly of its Gospels) *without warrant.* Though the text existed in his time, he did not himself use it (yet see T. Baarda, *VC* 14 [1960] 102-27). If the Peshitta for the OT shows the persistence of early targumic influences, so its NT (an excellent rendering with an accommodation to the Byzantine type of Gk mss. current about AD 400; → 167, 175 below) shows survivals (e.g., in Acts) of some "Western" readings and other early features. Rev and four smaller epistles (2 Pet, 2-3 John, Jude) were not transmitted in Peshitta mss.; the Syr versions in modern editions are of later origin.

127 For the NT in particular, textual transmission of the Peshitta has been remarkably faithful and precise, and good early mss. exist for both Testaments; those from East Syrian sources tend to have a slightly better text. Beginning in 1961 with a preliminary list of mss., the Peshitta Institute of Leiden has produced in fascicle form (1972-) a critical ed. of the Peshitta OT. For the NT, a British and Foreign Bible Society ed. (London, 1905-1920) approximates critical standards, but no apparatus of ms. variants has been published beyond the Gospels.

128 (iv) *Syro-hexaplar OT.* The Syro-hexapla was produced between about AD 612 or 615 and 617 by a team apparently supervised by Bishop Paul of Tella, the translator of Kgs, in the monastery "at the ninth milestone" (Enaton) outside Alexandria in Egypt. Where it survives, the Syro-hexapla is often our best single extant witness to the content and critical markings of col. 5 in Origen's *Hexapla* (→ 84 above); its apparatus of marginal readings (mainly from Aquila, Symmachus, and Theodotion) was transposed from Greek into a rigid and labored Syriac that reflects the word order, forms, and even incidental particles of the source. The work was transmitted from antiquity in two ms. volumes, but only the second (with Pss, Wisdom books, and Prophets) has come down to the present. Of the lost first volume, numerous excerpts have been found in fragmentary witnesses, and an 11th/12th-cent. pentateuchal ms. discovered in 1964 has been published in facsimile by A. Vööbus (CSCO 369; Subsidia 45; Louvain, 1975); the Pentateuch also survives in a secondary rendering into Arabic.

129 (v) *Harclean NT.* At the same time and place as the Syro-hexaplar OT, a similarly stiff and mechanical rendering of the NT was produced; from its editor, Thomas of Harkel, bishop of Hierapolis (Mabbug) in Syria, it is known as the Harclean NT. This version was based on a revision of the Peshitta done a century earlier (AD 507-508) by one Polycarp, at the instance of Philoxenus, an earlier bishop of Hierapolis. Most of the materials that have been identified as "Philoxenian" are actually from the Harclean version, though it is possible that the texts of the four short epistles and Rev in the

1905-1920 London Peshitta edition come from this intermediate 6th-cent. undertaking. In later centuries, the Harclean NT was used in West Syrian lectionaries, but its text was smoothed out and reworked in the light of the familiar Peshitta. In any form, the Harclean NT is too late to be an important textual witness. (See P. Harb, *OrChr* 64 [1980] 36-47.)

130   (vi) *Syro-Palestinian Bible.* This Western Aram (*not* Syr) version is known to us almost exclusively as a lectionary text for those Melkite Christians (→ 118 above) who followed the liturgies of Antioch and Jerusalem in their native Aramaic rather than in Greek. Though adapted in large measure to the LXX tradition, the Syro-Palestinian OT (of which we know the Pentateuch, Job, Prov, Pss, Isa, and other books in fragmentary form) has its roots in older Syr and (possibly) Jewish Aram texts. A new edition of the Syro-Palestinian OT was begun with a vol. on the Pentateuch and Prophets by M. H. Goshen-Gottstein (Jerusalem, 1973). Extant Syro-Palestinian Gospel lectionaries (from AD 1029 and later) have a text that has been fitted to the usual Byzantine form; but fragmentary evidences of seemingly the same NT version (in 1952-1953 from the abandoned monastery of Castellion, or Khirbet Mird, in the Judean desert; → Apocrypha, 67:118) carry us back to the 6th cent. Its date of origin and textual base remain obscure (see B. M. Metzger in *Neotestamentica et Semitica* [Fest. M. Black; ed. E. E. Ellis and M. Wilcox; Edinburgh, 1969] 209-20).

(Albrektson, B., *Studies in the Text and Theology of the Book of Lamentations,* with a critical ed. of the Peshitta text [Studia Theologica Lundensia 21; Lund, 1963]. Baumstark, A., *Geschichte der syrischen Literatur* [Bonn, 1922]. Duval, R., *La littérature syriaque* [3d ed.; Paris, 1907]. Englert, D. M. C., *The Peshitto of Second Samuel* [SBLMS 3; Phl, 1978; repr. of 1949 ed.]. George, K. A., "The Peshitto Version of Daniel: A Comparison with the Massoretic Text, the Septuagint and Theodotion" [diss.; Hamburg, 1973]. Koster, M. D., *The Peshitta of Exodus: The Development of Its Text in the Course of Fifteen Centuries* [SSN 19; Assen, 1977]. Ortiz de Urbina, I., *Patrologia syriaca* [Rome, 1958]. Rosenthal, F., *Die aramäistische Forschung* [Leiden, 1937], esp. 106-14 on the language of Jesus. Van Puyvelde, C., *DBSup* 6. 834-84. Vööbus, A., *Studies in the History of the Gospel Text in Syriac* [Louvain, 1951]; "Syriac Versions," *IDBSup* 848-54; *The Hexapla and the Syro-Hexapla* [Papers of the Estonian Theological Society in Exile 22; Stockholm, 1971]; "Bible IV: Texts and Versions," *NCE* 2. 433-36. *Die Neue Testament in syrischer Überlieferung* [ed. B. Aland and A. Juckel; ANTF; Berlin, 1986-]. For editions, see Eissfeldt, *EOTI* 699, 783; Metzger, *Text* 68-71.)

131   **(II) Latin Versions.** Except for Jerome's OT from the Hebrew, all early Lat renderings of the OT and NT were made from the Greek. Although some have argued that a Christian idiom arose in Rome in the mid-2d cent. (Metzger, *Early Versions* 289-90), the earliest evidence for the NT in Latin comes later in the century from N Africa. The *Acts of the Scillitan Martyrs* (AD 180) already speaks of a ms. of "the letters of Paul, a just man," presumably in Latin. Not long afterward Tertullian quotes Lat texts for both Testaments, and Cyprian of Carthage (d. 258) directly cites about one-ninth of the NT. The Lat transl. of the letter of Clement of Rome to the Corinthians bears witness to the 2d-cent. use of Lat Scriptures in Europe. The place of origin for the Lat Gospels and, indeed, for many parts of the Old Latin (OL) Bible can no longer be established with certainty; the extant evidence shows an interdependence between N African and European forms of the text, and in Europe both Rome and Gaul have been suggested as early centers for the Lat Scriptures.

132   **(A) Old Latin OT from the Greek.** We no longer possess a complete Lat OT from the Greek done

in this early period, nor can we confidently determine to what extent Jewish translators may have begun this work. Jerome (d. 420) affirmed that in his day there were "as many forms of the text for Latin readers as there are manuscripts" (*Praef. in Josue*), and something of that welter of diverse texts remains to us. The five OT books that we know best in the OL form are those that Jerome intended to exclude from his own undertaking and refused to revise or retranslate, because he judged them noncanonical. Since they were preserved by the church anyway and have become part of the Vg (= deutero-canonical books), we possess for each of them a full text that, in fact, is basically the product of a single translator; their systematic critical study is well advanced. They include 1-2 Macc (ed. D. de Bruyne; Maredsous, 1932), Wis, Sir, and Bar. Both Wis and Sir are clearly African renderings (except for Sir 44-50 and the Prologue to Sir which were put into Latin by two distinct European translators); they have been edited with an apparatus of ms. variants as vol. 12 (1964) of the Benedictine Vulgate project (→ 144 below). Of Bar, four varying forms of the Lat text are known from mss.; they seem to go back through various reworkings to one original translator.

133   Apart from Pss, which has a complicated textual history, the other OT books translated from the Greek survive more or less by accident. Though the OL Pentateuch with Josh and Judg is well known in a single translator's work, much of the rest has had to be pieced together from portions copied into Vg mss., from glosses on Vg mss., and from citations in Christian Lat literature. Already in the 16th cent., the painstaking work of assembling these fragmentary materials was undertaken by F. de Nobili (*Vetus Testamentum sec. LXX,* Rome, 1588) in connection with the LXX Sixtine edition of 1587 (→ 99 above); and the 18th cent. Maurist P. Sabatier later published *Bibliorum sacrorum latinae versionis antiquae . . .* (3 vols.; Rheims, 1739-49; reissued Paris, 1751), a work that for certain books has not been supplanted even today. The extensive files of J. Denk (d. 1927) were entrusted to the archabbey of Beuron, in Germany, where a *Vetus Latina* project directed by B. Fischer published Gen (1951-54) and Wis (1977-85), both with exhaustive support from mss. and patristic sources. (The years between the two OT vols. were devoted to the OL NT; → 142 below.) A. F. J. Klijn (*Der lateinische Text der Apokalypse des Esra* [TU 131; Berlin, 1983]) has provided a new ed. of 4 Ezra 3-14 (based on 10 mss.), in which a 7th-cent. palimpsest is used for the first time. A comprehensive inventory of extant OL mss. and editions of the OT, plus references to all patristic texts that are sources for OL citations, has also been published from Beuron (*Vetus Latina I: Verzeichnis der Sigel,* 1949; rev. ed. 1963, with continuing supplements).

134   Ruth survives only in the 9th/10th-cent. Codex Complutensis (Madrid Univ. ms. 31) and in a few patristic citations. Ezra-Neh and apocryphal 3-4 Esdr are known in full, as are 2 Chr (ed. R. Weber) and Cant (ed. D. de Bruyne). Esth is well represented in the mss., but B. Motzo's edition (1928) does not cover all the sources. Our evidence is especially scarce for Sam-Kgs, 1 Chr, Job, Prov, Eccl, and the Prophets. Some OT books were reworked by Jerome on the basis of hexaplaric materials (→ 83-86 above) before he undertook his more original rendering from the Hebrew; they are said to include 1-2 Chr (only the preface is extant), Prov, Eccl, Cant, and Job (this last is extant). We also know that he revised the Pentateuch, Josh, and Pss (→ 135 below) in the same way. In general, the OL versions, which are still echoed in many liturgical texts, have come down to us in forms that were reworked in the centuries after Jerome's time and in textual traditions that reflect mutual contamination of the Vg and the OL.

135   (B) Latin Psalters. Most of Western Christendom through the centuries has employed in its liturgy and transmitted in its Bibles the so-called *Gallican Psalter,* thus named from the region of its early popularity. This is Jerome's second revision (based on the *Hexapla*) of an OL psalter, completed during the early years of his residence in Bethlehem (before AD 389). It shares the basic limitations of any psalter dependent on the LXX and contributes more of its own. By modern standards it is clumsy and confused, despite the pious associations with which even many of its irrelevancies have been surrounded in the course of time. Contrary to Jerome's intention, it has displaced his rendering from the Hebrew in Vg Bibles. It was edited as vol. 10 (1953) of the Roman Benedictine Commission's Vulgate project (→ 144 below).

136   Older forms of the OL psalter from the Greek are available for convenient study in the edition of R. Weber, *Psalterium Romanum . . .* (CBL 10; Rome, 1953), which summarizes what is known of as many as 14 different text traditions. It is unlikely that any of them can be connected with a first (cursory) revision by Jerome, although this claim has habitually been made for the liturgical psalter used at St. Peter's Basilica in Rome. E. A. Lowe (*Scriptorium* 9 [1955] 177-99) reported on an OL psalter (with an appendix of 18 liturgical canticles from elsewhere in the OL biblical text) that survives in a Mt. Sinai ms. (*slav.* 5), and its variants are recorded in the CCL edition of Augustine's *En. in Ps.* (ser. lat. 38-40; Turnholt, 1956). The psalter publications of T. Ayuso Marazuela (between 1957 and 1962), although notable compilations of mss. and patristic evidence, often do double duty with the editions mentioned and sometimes reflect the Spanish ms. tradition to the exclusion of pertinent materials elsewhere.

137   Jerome's *Psalter from the Hebrew,* one of the earliest results of his decision to produce a new version of the OT, is a somewhat stiff and bookish exercise that draws measurably on Aquila and Symmachus for meanings of uncommon Hebr words. It is not really better suited for liturgical use than the Gallican Psalter itself. The best edition is by H. de Ste. Marie (CBL 11; Rome, 1954).

138   The present survey of Lat versions will not deal with the many 16th-cent. and later renderings of any part of the Bible, but two important exceptions should be made. (1) *Liber Psalmorum cum Canticis* was sanctioned for breviary use by Pope Pius XII in 1945. Prepared by professors at the Pontifical Biblical Institute in Rome, it offers a straightforward rendering of the Hebr text (emended, though with restraint, from other sources) into classical Lat idiom. It has been criticized for failing to preserve in its diction the "Christian Latin" associations of earlier psalters and for being less easily sung; both criticisms are relatively subjective and open to question. In any case, it is desirable that liturgical texts in languages other than Latin should profit by the clarity of Pius XII's psalter, but without being bound even by its conventions of Lat style. (2) Similarly, Pope Paul VI ordered a new ed. of the Lat Vg, not only drawing on scholarly research, but adapted to post-Vatican II revisions in the Roman liturgy, public reading, and chanting in choir. This completed *Nova Vulgata* appeared in one vol. under Vatican imprint in 1979.

139   (C) Vulgate OT from the Hebrew. Beginning about AD 389, Jerome broke with the LXX-OL tradition to provide Western Christendom with a rendering based directly on the Hebr OT text preserved among the Jews. The books of Sam-Kgs, Job, Pss, and the Prophets were done by *ca.* 392; Ezra-Neh by 394; 1-2 Chr by 396; Prov, Cant, and Eccl by 398; and the Pentateuch, Josh, Judg, Ruth, Jdt, Esth, and Tob by *ca.* 405. In part, the progress of the work can be traced by Jerome's own prefaces to the various groups of books. His knowledge of Hebrew was good; of OT Aramaic, somewhat less so. He had oral assistance from Jewish sources and shows familiarity with the exegesis embodied in the various targums. The parts of Esth and Dan not included in the Jewish canon he supplied from the Greek; for Dan, he drew on the book's "Theodotionic" form (→ 73 above), and it also strongly influenced his rendering of the Aram sections. The arrangement of Esth in the Vg, with the parts translated from the Greek placed in a series of appendixes, is a confusing jumble (→ Tobit, 38:50-53). Tob and Jdt were translated on the basis of Aram recensions, now no longer extant, that were rather far removed from the lost originals (Aramaic for Tob, Hebrew for Jdt).

140   The Vg strongly underlines the personal messianic implications of the OT. Thus, *et erit sepulchrum ejus gloriosum* (Isa 11:10) recalls the Constantinian Basilica of the Resurrection; messianic references that go beyond the actual terms of the Hebr text are present in the Vg of Isa 45:8; 62:1-2; Hab 3:18. Although that might nourish Christian piety, it could also limit the apologetic value for dialogue with Jewish scholars desired by Jerome for his version. Be that as it may, the Vg OT bears lasting witness to the inspired word.

141   (D) Latin New Testament.
   (a) VULGATE. From Jerome stems also the Vg recension of the Gospels, prepared in Rome in AD 383-384 at the bidding of Pope Damasus. Basically it was the correction and adaptation of the existing OL text in the light of good Gk mss. Though the remaining NT books in the Vg have often been attributed to Jerome, the extent of his influence on them is unclear. H. J. Frede has suggested that, about the end of the 4th cent., a single editor who was neither Jerome nor Pelagius drew together the Lat texts of Acts to Rev that became the Vg form (on Pelagius, see K. T. Schäfer, *NTS* 9 [1963] 361-66). This composite, late 4th-cent. Lat NT was the goal sought by the critical ed. of J. Wordsworth and H. J. White (3 vols., Oxford, 1898-1954).

142   (b) OLD LATIN. Much scholarly investigation has been necessary, for no ms. contains the entire OL NT. Earlier stages of the Lat NT are represented in the *Vetus Itala* (4 vols.; Berlin, 1938-64; 2d ed., 1970s) where A. Jülicher, A. Matzkow, and K. Aland presented the ms. evidence for pre-Jerome forms of the Gospels. The title *Vetus Itala* comes from a discussion of Lat texts by Augustine, but it does not offer any usable clue to the place of origin of the Lat Gospels. The Beuron *Vetus Latina* has been publishing since 1956 vols. of a critically edited text of the epistles. Two series, the *Old Latin Biblical Texts* (7 vols.; Oxford, 1883-1923) and CBL (14 vols.; Rome, 1912-72) present the evidence of individual mss. Along with its evidence for the received Vg NT, the Wordsworth-White ed. cites much OL evidence and thus replaces the NT of Sabatier's earlier work (→ 133 above) except for patristic citations.

143   As to the origin of the various parts of the OL NT, the corpus of 13 Pauline epistles (exclusive of Heb) goes back to a single, quite early translator. Beneath the varying forms of Acts, there seems to have been one early N African rendering. There are two known renderings for Heb; and there are independent N African and European forms for Rev, to which H. J. Vogels would add a third. The evidence is scanty for the

Catholic Epistles, and for the Gospels it is confused.
Early influences on the OL from Marcion and Tatian
have been suspected, but in neither case is the issue
resolved; the examples cited are textual curiosities of no
doctrinal significance.

144   (E) Later History of the Vulgate. A
Pontifical Commission for the Establishment of the Text
of the Vulgate, set up by Pope Pius X in 1907, was localized in the Abbey of San Girolamo (St. Jerome) in Rome.
Beginning with Gen (1926), the Benedictine editors of
its *Biblia Sacra juxta Latinam Vulgatam Versionem* have
published OT volumes that include most of Jerome's
renderings from the Hebr text, plus his Gallican Psalter
(→ 135 above), as well as Tob, Jdt, Wis, and Sir (of
diverse origins). As was noted above (→ 137), Jerome's
Psalterium juxta Hebraeos is in CBL. The Wordsworth-
White ed. (→ 141 above) provides a suitable NT
counterpart. The entire Vg text has also been edited by
R. Weber, *et al.,* for the Württembergische Bibelanstalt
(2 vols.; 2d ed.; Stuttgart, 1975); the Gallican Psalter and
juxta Hebraeos are printed on facing pages.

145   These attempts to recover the archetypal Vg
form (*ca.* AD 400) are hampered by the lack of sufficiently
early mss. Usually we can recover only a text form
intermediate between the missing archetypes and the
early recensional undertakings of Alcuin (d. 804),
Theodulph of Orléans (d. 821), and the Spanish tradition
centered on the 8th-cent. *Codex Toletanus.* The multiplication of copies in the Middle Ages made further
attempts at standardization necessary, and a developed
text (associated with the Univ. of Paris and accompanied
by several lists of *correctoria*) became the foundation for
the Vg form in most printed Bibles, including the first
(the Gutenberg Bible of 1452-55). This text had a
number of elements not included by Jerome: a series of
excerpts from the OL of 1-2 Sam (e.g., *stravitque Saul in
solario et dormivit,* 1 Sam 9:25) that had been inserted by
the Spanish bishop Peregrinus; the angel stirring the
water at the Pool of Bethesda in John 5:4 (→ John,
61:74); a borrowing into Matt 27:35 from John 19:24;
and the "Johannine Comma" in 1 John 5:7-8 (→
1-3 John, 62:32).

146   The Council of Trent called for an officially
sponsored critical ed. of the Vg (→ Church Pronouncements, 72:11), but (despite serious work toward that
goal over a period of some 30 years in the late 16th cent.)
neither the Sixtine ed. of 1590 nor the (Sixto-)Clemen-
tine texts of 1592-1598 can be considered truly successful fulfillments of that directive. The Clementine text
became the official Catholic Vg, and a one-vol. ed.
(Turin, 1959) has a rather skimpy but useful apparatus
of variants from the reconstituted texts of the St. Jerome
Abbey OT (→ 144 above) and the Wordsworth-White
NT (→ 141 above). A special feature of this ed. is its
parallel presentation of three psalters (Gallican, *juxta
Hebraeos,* and Pius XII).

147   Jerome's OT from the Hebrew is based almost
entirely on the received consonantal Hebr text; its value
in relation to the original is therefore primarily exegetical. The various OL renderings from the Greek, on
the other hand, represent a stage in the transmission of
their prototypes that often cannot be attained directly
through any extant Gk mss. Few even of the earliest Gk
NT papyri (→ 179 below) can claim an antiquity comparable to that of the OL NT renderings, but Lat evidence has to be carefully sifted for later retouchings and
contaminations. For the history of the LXX and the reconstitution of its early text forms, the OL is of special
significance in Sam, Tob, Pss, 1-2 Macc, Wis, and Sir;
and it is instructive wherever it can be recovered in a
relatively early form.

(Berger, S., *Histoire de la Vulgate pendant les premiers siècles du
Moyen Age* [Paris, 1893]. Bogaert, M., "Bulletin de la Bible
latine," *RBén* — continuing bibliography. Botte, B., *DBSup* 5.
178-96. Eissfeldt, *EOTI* 716-19, 785. Fischer, B., *Beiträge zur
Geschichte der lateinischen Bibeltexte* [Vetus Latina; Freiburg,
1986]; *Lateinische Bibelhandschriften im frühen Mittelalter* [Vetus
Latina; Freiburg, 1985]; [ed.], *Novae Concordantiae Bibliorum
Sacrorum Iuxta Vulgatam Versionem Critice Editam* [5 vols.; Stutt-
gart, 1977]. Gribomont, J., "Latin Versions," *IDBSup* 527-32.
Metzger, *Text* 72-79. Peebles, B. M., "Bible IV: Texts and
Versions 13. Latin Versions," *NCE* 2. 436-56. Plater, W. E. and
H. J. White, *A Grammar of the Vulgate* [Oxford, 1926]. Souter,
A., *A Glossary of Later Latin to 600 AD* [Oxford, 1949]. Stramare,
T., "Die Neo-Vulgate: Zur Gestaltung des Textes," *BZ* ns 25
[1981] 67-81. Stummer, F., *Einleitung in die lateinische Bibel*
[Paderborn, 1928]. Thiele, W., "Beobachtungen zu den eusebi-
anischen Sektionen und Kanonen der Evangelien," *ZNW* 72
[1981] 100-11. Trebolle Barrera, J. C., "From the 'Old Latin'
through the 'Old Greek' to the 'Old Hebrew' (2 Kings
10:23-25)," *Textus* 11 [1984] 17-36; "Textos 'kaige' en la *Vetus
Latina* de Reyes (2 Re 10:25-28)," *RB* 89 [1982] 198-209.
Ulrich, E. C., "The Old Latin Translation of the LXX and the
Hebrew Scrolls from Qumran," in *The Hebrew and Greek Texts
of Samuel* [ed. E. Tov; Proceedings IOSCS; Jerusalem, 1980]
121-65.)

148   (III) Coptic Versions.
(A) The Coptic Language. Coptic is the
latest form of the Egyptian language written not in
hieroglyphs or demotic symbols but in the Gk alphabet
augmented by one digraph (*ti*) and by six letters that
represent Egyptian consonantal sounds not found in
Greek. It came into use in the 2d cent. AD and developed
as an almost exclusively Christian language with
numerous Gk loanwords. In fact, by far the greater part
of early Coptic literature consists of transls. from Greek.
The term "Copt" reflects the Arabic name for the Christian inhabitants of Egypt, *qubt,* which is derived from the
Gk *aigyptos.*

149   There are two principal dialects of Coptic
(Sahidic and Bohairic) and several minor ones. Sahidic,
the dialect of Upper, or southern, Egypt was the principal literary dialect until it was supplanted in the 11th
cent. by Bohairic, the dialect of Lower, or northern,
Egypt (the Nile Delta), which has survived as the liturgical language of the Coptic church. The other local
dialects in which biblical books or fragments are known
are: Akhmimic and Subakhmimic, both akin to Sahidic
and at an early date superseded by it; Fayumic, an intermediary between Sahidic and Bohairic spoken in the
Fayum, west of the Nile; and Middle Egyptian, represented by only a few mss., most notably Matt (Codex
Scheide) and Acts (Codex Glazier). Sometimes dialects
are mingled in biblical transls. A good example is the
blend of Sahidic and Akhmimic traits along with various
other elements in an early (4th- or 5th-cent.) version of
Prov published by R. Kasser, *Papyrus Bodmer VI* (CSCO
194-95; Louvain, 1960).

150   (B) Coptic Old Testament. The complete
OT does not survive in any Coptic dialect, although it
may have existed in Sahidic at least. All transls. were
made from individual parts of the Gk Bible and apparently from different recensions of them. The many
extant Coptic versions of separate books and fragments
have their importance for studying the transmission of
the Gk version rather than, directly at least, for studying
the text of the OT. The earliest Coptic versions were
made, however, for the use of the common people who
had no knowledge of Greek, and the translators did not
hesitate to simplify or otherwise alter the texts almost in
the manner of the targums with respect to the Hebr text.
Sometimes they simply misunderstood the Greek. Only
at a later period were attempts made to compare the

versions and to correct them; the Bohairic transl. of Prov stands out for its fidelity to the underlying Greek. Another problem the textual critic must take into account is the peculiar structure of the language itself, the type of construction and circumlocution it uses in rendering Greek. The original wording is often very difficult to recover. Ancient Coptic biblical mss. are fairly numerous but are notoriously difficult to date. In the early dialects there are valuable 4th- and 5th-cent. mss. However it is possible that transls. began to be made as early as the beginning of the 3d cent. Of the Sahidic OT, several historical books (Chr, Ezra, Neh, and Mic) are missing. Of the Bohairic version, some later historical and wisdom books are not represented; and for a few other books it is necessary to rely on quotations in liturgical texts. The minor dialectal versions are very incomplete. In general, the best-attested books are the Pentateuch, Pss, Job, Prov, and the Prophets. *A Critical Edition of the Coptic (Bohairic) Pentateuch* has been published by M. K. H. Peters (Atlanta, 1983-).

151   (C) Coptic New Testament. For the NT the textual critic has at hand complete published versions of the Sahidic and Bohairic NT and a few publications of individual books in all the dialects. But caution is necessary in evaluating their evidence, since for the most part the editions are not critical. Complete mss. in Bohairic are available, but all are late medieval; these were edited by G. Horner from 1898 to 1905. Horner's Sahidic NT, which appeared in 1911-1924, is a mosaic of fragmentary mss. ranging in date over many centuries. Since the completion of Horner's editions a number of very important individual books have come to light in various Coptic collections. More significant publications include a 4th-cent. Subakhmimic version of John published by H. Thompson; Papyrus Bodmer III, which contains John and Gen 1-4:2 in Bohairic in a remarkably early ms. (4th cent; R. Kasser, *Muséon* 74 [1961] 423-33); a Fayumic (or, some think, Middle Egyptian) John from an early 4th-cent. papyrus (Michigan 3521); and early 5th-cent. Sahidic Mark, Luke, and John published by H. Quecke.

152 The various Coptic versions of the NT are potentially of great importance for studying the diffusion of the NT text types in Egypt in the 2d and 3d cents. On the whole, the Coptic NT transls. are fairly literal by contrast with the OT ones, and they tend to reflect the rather standardized Alexandrian text type (→ 167, 172 below). But some mss. provide evidence for the diffusion of the so-called Western recension with its many variants (→ 173 below); a good example is the Middle Egyptian copy of Acts 1-15:3 described by T. C. Petersen in *CBQ* 27 (1964) 225-41. The earliest Coptic NT versions furnish us with independent transls. made from Gk texts older than the Gk mss. upon which our critical NT is based (→ 181 below).

(Bellet, P., "Bible IV: Texts and Versions 14. Coptic Versions," *NCE* 2. 457-58. Botte, B., *DBSup* 6. 818-25. Hallock, F. H., "The Coptic Old Testament," *AJSL* 49 [1932-33] 325-35. Kahle, P. E., *Bala'izah* I [London, 1954] 269-78, for a list of all known Coptic fragments down to the 6th cent. Kammerer, W., *A Coptic Bibliography* [Ann Arbor, 1950]. Schmitz, F.-J. and G. Mink [eds.], *Liste der koptischen Handschriften des Neuen Testaments* [ANTF 8; Berlin, 1986-]. Annual Coptic bibliogs. in *Or*

18ff. [1949-76]; *Enchoria* 1ff. [1971-]. See also Metzger, *Versions* 99-152.)

153   (IV) Other Oriental Versions.
    (A) Ethiopic Version. Ethiopic is a Semitic language, like Hebrew, Aramaic, Assyro-Babylonian, and Arabic; it is closest to Arabic. At the beginning of the Christian era the language of SW Arabia was distinct from that used elsewhere on the peninsula, and it is from this S Arabic branch that the Eth language stems. Its classical biblical and liturgical dialect, no longer spoken, is Ge'ez. The modern Amharic has many features that developed in Africa, but some Eritrean dialects are much closer to the ancient form. Since the days of Athanasius (d. 373) and Frumentius (the first apostle of Ethiopia), the country's church has been bound by close ties to the church of Egypt, which it followed into the Monophysite separatist movement in the 5th cent. The court legend by which Ethiopia's former royal family traced its origins to Solomon and the "queen of Sheba" was fictitious. Some Ethiopians, the Falasha, have been Jewish by religion since the Middle Ages; but theirs is an adopted faith and a borrowed literature.

154 The Eth OT is from the Greek and is sometimes a good witness to the unrevised Alexandrian LXX, especially when it coincides with Gk Codex Vaticanus (→ 94 above) against all later recensions; it also preserves intact the apocryphal books of *1 Enoch* and *Jub.* (→ Apocrypha, 67:9, 17), otherwise known only in fragments. Many scholars date the origin of the Eth NT to the 5th cent. (translated partly from Greek, partly from Syriac); but of some 300 Eth NT mss., very few antedate the 14th cent. (Metzger, *Versions* 223). In the 13th cent., the Eth Gospels were drastically reworked under Arabic influence stemming from Egypt; only two mss. of the unrevised 5th-cent. Gospel rendering are known. Critical studies of the Eth version have been limited in scope.

155   (B) Versions from Western Asia. The early-5th-cent. Armenian transl. depended heavily on pre-Peshitta Syr forms, but it was subsequently reworked from the Greek. A critical ed. of Armenian Deut was published by C. E. Cox (Univ. of Penn. Armenian Texts and Studies 2; Chico, 1981). The Georgian Iberian version had a first period, in the 5th cent., when it was based mainly on Armenian texts with Syr origins; but from the 7th cent. all Georgian texts were conformed to Gk models. The Arabic versions, though of historical interest and serviceable in reconstructing the *Diatessaron* and the Syro-hexaplar OT rendering (→ 122-23, 128 above), are too late to be of much direct text-critical worth. They represent a wide range of prototypes in Greek, Hebrew, Syriac, Coptic, and (for Tob) even Latin.

("Bible IV: Texts and Versions 15. Ethiopic [E. Cerulli]; 16. Armenian, and 17. Georgian [L. Leloir]; 18. Arabic [P. P. Saydon]," *NCE* 2. 458-62. Botte, B. and L. Leloir, *DBSup* 6. 807-18, 825-34. Lyonnet, S., "Contribution récente des littératures arménienne et géorgienne à l'exégèse biblique," *Bib* 39 [1958] 488-96. Macomber, W. F., *Catalogue of Ethiopian Manuscripts* [many vols.; Collegeville, 1975-]. Metzger, *Text* 82-84; *Versions* 153-262. Molitor, J., "Die Bedeutung der altgeorgischen Bibel für die neutestamentliche Textkritik," *BZ* 4 [1960] 39-53. Ullendorff, E., *Ethiopia and the Bible* [London, 1968]. For a catalogue of Armenian biblical mss., see A. Wikgren, *JBL* 79 [1960] 52-56 and references there.)

GREEK TEXT OF THE NEW TESTAMENT

156 We can best study the problem of the text of the Gk NT by seeing its formulation at the end of the 19th cent. and the classical solution then offered. This will enable us to understand what the discoveries of the 20th cent. contributed toward solving the problem. The basic difficulty that arises from the history of the NT text is simple. The NT books accepted as canonical were composed mostly during the 1st cent. AD, and the important collections (Pauline epistles, Gospels; → Canonicity, 66:58, 62) took shape during the 2d cent. However, the oldest copies of the Gk NT available to 19th-cent. scholars were the Great Uncial Codices of the 4th and 5th cents. In some NT passages these codices did not have the same reading. The first problem, then, was to determine which of the codices contained the best extant text of the NT. The second problem was to determine how much alteration had taken place in the 200 to 300 years between the composition and collection of the NT books (*ca.* AD 50-150 for the most important books) and the oldest remaining copies (AD 350). In other words, when one had discovered the "best" text, how faithful was it to the original?

157 (I) Problem of the Best Text. Under this heading we shall treat textual criticism before the 20th cent.

(A) Great Uncial Codices. These have been mentioned in discussing the LXX (→ 93-97 above), for generally such codices contain the whole Bible in Greek. Here we list the four most important for NT study, indicating with each the letter customarily used to designate it and the text type it represents (for these text types, → 167, 171-76 below). For facsimile pages and brief analyses, see *MMGB* 74-79, 86-91.

Codex Vaticanus (B): mid 4th-cent. The oldest of the Great Codices, it has lost the last part of the NT (Heb 9:14 on; Pastorals; Rev). One scribe copied the whole NT, but a later corrector traced over afresh every letter, omitting letters and words he considered incorrect. In origin and in text type it is Alexandrian. In the 14th cent. it was brought by Greeks from Constantinople to the Council of Florence (→ Church Pronouncements, 72:10), probably as a gift to the Pope, whence its presence in the Vatican Library. A photographic facsimile vol. of the NT (1968) was given to each bishop at Vatican Council II. See C. Martini, *Il problema* (→ 179 below); J. Šagi, *DThomP* 75 (1972) 3-29; T. C. Skeat, *JTS* 35 (1984) 454-65.

Codex Sinaiticus (S or ℵ): mid-4th cent. This is the only Great Codex to contain the entire NT, plus *Barn.* and *Herm.* (→ Early Church, 80:41, 43). Of the three scribes from the same school who wrote it, one copied almost all the NT seemingly from dictation. There were spelling mistakes and omissions, and as many as nine correctors between the 4th and the 12th cent. It was discovered by C. von Tischendorf in 1844 at the monastery of St. Catherine in the Sinai Peninsula, taken to Russia, and then sold to the British Museum in 1933. New pages from it were discovered at St. Catherine's in 1975. (See J. Bentley, *Secrets of Mt. Sinai* [GC, 1986]; Reumann, *Romance* 145-62.) The text of S agrees with B (Alexandrian) in Gospels and Acts, although elsewhere it has Western readings. See G. D. Fee, *NTS* 15 (1968-69) 22-44.

Codex Alexandrinus (A): early 5th cent. Although it once contained the whole NT, parts like Matt 1-24; John 7-8; 2 Cor 4-12 have been lost. The codex also contained *1 Clem., 2 Clem.* (now partly lost), and *Pss. Sol.*

(lost). At least two scribes copied it, with several correctors (one contemporary with the original). In the Gospels A has a Byzantine text; in the rest of the NT it is Alexandrian (with B and S); a corrector introduced Western readings. It was sent by the Patriarch of Alexandria as a gift to the English king (arriving in 1627 under Charles I).

Codex Bezae (D): 5th cent. This codex (without OT), written in N Africa or Egypt, contains Matt, John, Luke, Mark, 3 John, and Acts—in Latin and Greek on facing pages. Seemingly, it was copied by one scribe, who blundered in both languages and assimilated the Gk text to the Latin and vice versa. There were as many as nine correctors. It was acquired in 1562 by T. de Bèze (Beza), the French reformer of Geneva, from the loot of the monastery of St. Irenaeus and presented to Cambridge Univ. in 1581. No known NT ms. contains so many peculiar readings; but while mixed, it is the chief representative of the "Western" text-tradition. See C. K. Barrett in Best (ed.), *Text* 15-27; E. J. Epp, *The Theological Tendency of Codex Bezae Cantabrigiensis* (Cambridge, 1966); G. E. Rice, *PRS* 11 (1984) 39-54; J. D. Yoder, *Concordance to the Distinctive Greek Text of Codex Bezae* (NTTS 2; Leiden, 1961).

158 There are also some less important codices with which the student should be familiar. (For a fuller listing, see *ATNT* 102-25.)

Codex Ephraemi Rescriptus (C): 5th cent. As the name implies, this is a palimpsest—an earlier writing washed or scraped off, and the skin reused for a later writing. In this case the later writing consisted of the works of Ephraem, copied in the 12th cent.; the earlier was a 5th-cent. copy of the Gk Bible, with about three-fifths of the NT preserved. There were two correctors, in the 6th and 9th cents. A collection of its NT readings was done in 1716. The text is frequently Byzantine. See R. W. Lyon, *NTS* 5 (1958-59) 266-72; *ATNT* 12.

Codex Washingtonensis I (W): late 4th or early 5th cent. It is the most important biblical ms. in the USA (Smithsonian). Acquired in Egypt in 1906 by C. L. Freer, it contains the four Gospels in the Western order (Matt, John, Luke, Mark). It was copied from several different earlier mss. Its ending of Mark (after 16:14) is peculiar and of importance. See *MMGB* 84-85.

Codex Koridethianus (Θ): 9th cent. Written in a crude hand, it takes its name from the scribe's monastery, Koridethi near the E end of the Black Sea. It contains the Gospels and has significant readings, esp. in Mark. Called to the attention of scholars by H. von Soden in 1906, it has given support to the thesis of a Caesarean textual family. See *MMGB* 100-1.

159 What was the import of these codices for textual study and transl. before modern times? Unfortunately, the oldest and best of the Great Codices (B and S) became available to scholars only in the 19th cent.—S was not known till then; B was not available in accurate copies until the 1867 ed. (photographic facsimile in 1889-90). On the other hand, codices D and A were available since Reformation times, but even these codices were not the backbone of earlier studies of the Gk NT.

160 (B) Textus Receptus. The key to the study of the Gk NT from the 16th to the 19th cent. is the *Textus Receptus* (TR), but to explain its origins we must survey the history of the NT after the writing of the Great Codices. We saw above (→ 91) that there was a revolution in handwriting in the 9th cent. when scribes changed from uncials to minuscules. The practical impact is seen in the fact that, compared with some 260 distinct uncial mss. of the Gk NT which have survived, some 2,800 minuscule mss. are known. Thus, the number of mss. from the 500 years between the change in writing and the invention of printing (in 1450) is more than 10 times larger than the surviving number of mss. from the 500 years before the change. When printing was invented, there were many mss. of the Gk NT available; but the majority of them represented a later and inferior textual tradition (as would become apparent to scholars centuries later).

161 In 1514 Cardinal Ximenes was responsible for the first printing of the Gk NT as part of his Complutensian Polyglot Bible (Hebr–Aram–Gk–Lat in parallel cols.), but it was not published until 1522. The first published printed Gk NT was that of the Dutch Catholic Erasmus in 1516—an edition based on only six or seven mss. and filled with printing errors. Rather than attempting an independent Gk text, Erasmus was offering the reader of the Lat version the opportunity to find out whether it was supported by the Greek (see H. J. de Jonge, *JTS* ns 35 [1984] 394–413). For small parts of the NT where he had no Gk ms., Erasmus simply translated the Vg back into what he thought the Greek might have been! The Protestant printer-editor Robert Estienne, or Stephanus, issued editions of Erasmus from 1546 on, based on a later corrected form, but using more mss. and introducing a critical apparatus to indicate different readings found in various mss. The 1557 ed. was the first to include an enumeration of verses within chaps. The Gk text of Erasmus and Stephanus became the TR on which all the Protestant vernacular transls. were based until the 19th cent. (B. Reicke, *TZ* 22 [1966] 254–65). Luther used the 2d Erasmian ed. of 1519 (see Reumann, *Romance* 55–92). In England the Stephanus 3d ed. (1550) became very popular in scholarly circles.

It is unfortunate that this most influential textual tradition was not based on what today we would consider good mss. Popularized in the minuscule mss., it was a tradition that had become dominant at Constantinople from the 5th cent. on and was used throughout the Byzantine church (whence the name "Byzantine" given to the tradition). It represented a heavily revised NT text wherein scribes had sought to smooth out stylistic difficulties and to conflate variant readings. This means, in the words of the preface to the *RSV,* that the *KJV* NT "was based upon a Greek text that was marred by mistakes, containing the accumulated errors of fourteen centuries of manuscript copying." Curiously, in many passages, particularly in the Gospels, Catholics were better supplied with correct readings than Protestants; for although the Catholic Rheims NT (→ 208 below) was a "second-hand" transl. from the Latin, the Vg Gospels often reflected a better Gk text than that which lay behind the *KJV* (→ 141 above).

162 (C) **Differentiation of Textual Traditions.** The recognition of the limitations of the TR came slowly. When in the next (17th) cent. Codex A became available, it only strengthened the respect for the TR; for, as fate would have it, in the Gospels A was the oldest example of the same inadequate Byzantine text. True, Codex D had a different text, but D was so peculiar that it was looked upon as a freak produced by corruption. T. Beza, the owner of D, published nine eds. of the Gk NT between 1565 and 1604; and although he supplied more textual apparatus than Stephanus, he popularized the TR in the body of his text. It was through Beza's eds. of 1588–89 and 1598 that the TR influenced the *KJV* translators. The brothers Elzevir published a NT taken from Beza's ed., and in the preface to their 1633 ed. they spoke of the "*textum . . . nunc ab omnibus receptum,*" whence the name "*Textus Receptus.*"

163 (a) FIRST ATTEMPTS. A century later in England E. Wells published the first complete Gk NT (1709–19) that abandoned the TR in favor of more ancient mss. His work, that of R. Bentley (1720—who castigated the Stephanus TR as "the Protestant pope"), and that of D. Mace (1729) were bitterly opposed by the supporters of the TR and were soon forgotten. Support of the TR had become a mark of religious orthodoxy!

164 A whole new stage in the textual criticism of the Gk NT opened when it became clear to scholars that there were *traditions* (and not merely mss.) different from what was represented by the TR, and that mss. should be classified as belonging to one or the other tradition. In 1725 the Lutheran J. A. Bengel initiated textual classification by distinguishing between the older African "nation" of documents and the later Asiatic (Constantinopolitan) nation. Bengel's Gk NT (1734) showed in its margin how often the readings of the older mss. were to be preferred to those of the TR. He also standardized NT punctuation and divided the NT into paragraphs. J. J. Wettstein (1751–52) began to use capital roman letters to denote uncial mss.—a system still used. Later in the same century J. S. Semler adapted Bengel's classification to a distinction between an Oriental recension by Lucian of Antioch and a Western or Egyptian recension by Origen (→ 87 above). Ultimately Semler and his student J. J. Griesbach accepted a threefold grouping into Western, Alexandrian, and Constantinopolitan.

165 Indeed, Griesbach (1745–1812) may be said to have put textual criticism on a truly scientific basis and to have laid the foundations for all subsequent work. He offered 15 canons for textual criticism that enabled scholars to decide on the better readings. One such canon was: "The shorter reading [unless it lacks entirely the authority of the ancient and weighty witnesses] is to be preferred to the more verbose." In his threefold classification of traditions he recognized that the Constantinopolitan, represented in the Gospels by Codex A and followed by the TR, was a later compilation from the Alexandrian and Western texts.

166 In the 19th cent. in Germany K. Lachmann published a Gk NT (1831) that broke very clearly with the TR and was constructed directly from ancient mss. The same was true of S. P. Tregelles's NT in England (1857–72). The ms. discoveries by C. von Tischendorf, e.g., Codex S, gave scholars much more to work on, so that Metzger (*Text* 126) does not hesitate to describe Tischendorf as "the man to whom modern textual critics of the New Testament owe most." Tischendorf's own edition of the Gk NT (8th ed., 1869–72) gave great weight to S. (→ NT Criticism, 70:15; I. A. Moir, *NTS* 23 [1976–77] 108–15.)

167 (b) WESTCOTT AND HORT. This progress came to a head in the splendid contribution of the Cambridge scholars B. F. Westcott and F. J. A. Hort (henceforth W-H), a contribution monumentalized in *The New Testament in the Original Greek* (1881–82). With codices B and S now available, W-H were able to classify into four main groups the witnesses to the NT text (for the significance and nomenclature of grouping NT mss., see E. C. Colwell, *NTS* 4 [1957–58] 73–92):

(i) *Neutral,* represented by B, S, and a few minuscules. This was the purest and earliest form of the text, for it had not been systematically revised. It was the common property of the whole Eastern church (the name "neutral" implies that its variants cannot be traced to a particular historical situation or locale).

(ii) *Alexandrian.* The Neutral text, as it was preserved at the Gk literary center of Alexandria, underwent at the hand of scribes a polishing in language and style. This is evident in the scriptural citations of the Alexandrian Fathers (Origen, Cyril), in Codex C, and in the Coptic versions.

(iii) *Western,* represented by D, the OS, and the OL (→ 124, 142 above). This tradition arose very early, perhaps before 150, and was used by Tatian, Marcion, Justin, and the Western Fathers. The scribes of the Western tradition exhibited considerable freedom in both changing and adding. The text arose at a period when the NT was used for edification, and explanation was necessary. Hence explanatory glosses found their way into the text. Readings supported only by the Western tradition are to be rejected.

(iv) *Syrian,* represented by A in the Gospels, by the minuscules, and by the whole Byzantine tradition. This textual form appeared in the late 4th cent. at Antioch, perhaps stemming from the editorial work of Lucian (d. 312; → 87 above). It was taken to Constantinople (by John Chrysostom?) and then disseminated throughout the Byzantine empire. It was heavily marked by conflate readings, i.e., if the Neutral text had one reading and the Western text another, the Syrian combined them. It was the latest of the four textual traditions and the poorest.

168   This theory of W-H represented a head-on challenge to the TR, for the latter quite obviously was a witness of the Syrian tradition. The W-H NT was heavily dependent on B and S and differed from the TR in a great number of verses. The theory was bitterly attacked, but it bore practical fruit in the *Revised Version* (*RV;* → 199 below) of the English Bible. If the King James was a transl. of the TR, the *RV* and the subsequent *RSV* were heavily influenced by principles akin to those of the W-H NT. As Greenlee (*Introduction* 78) puts it, "The textual theory of W-H underlies virtually all subsequent work in NT textual criticism." (See B. M. Metzger, *Cambridge Review* [Nov. 1981] 71–76; G. A. Patrick, *ExpTim* 92 [1981] 359–64.)

169   In Germany Bernhard Weiss edited a Gk NT (1894–1900), also heavily dependent on B; and although his critical methods were his own, the end product was closely akin to W-H. This was important because the popular Nestle pocket ed. (reflecting the work of Eberhard Nestle and subsequently of Erwin Nestle in the first half of the 20th cent.) stemmed from the Tischendorf, W-H, and Weiss eds. and thus from a tradition that rejected the TR—but, notice, a tradition heavily dependent on 19th-cent. scholarship. On the other hand, A. Souter's NT (1910) in England, H. von Soden's (1913) in Germany, and the Catholic edition of H. J. Vogels (1920; 4th ed. 1955) gave more serious consideration to the Syrian text tradition. In particular, von Soden's tremendous work in NT criticism identified three traditions: the Koine text (= Syrian of W-H), the Hesychian text (= Neutral and Alexandrian), and the Jerusalem text (= Western and others); and von Soden often accepted the agreement of any two of the three, thus giving a strong voice to the Koine. Other Catholic critical editions, that of A. Merk (1933; 9th ed. 1964, by C. M. Martini) and that of J. M. Bover (1943; 5th ed. 1968), have been more eclectic but not satisfactory in their critical apparatuses. (J. O'Callaghan revised the Bover text for inclusion in *Nuevo Testamento Trilingüe* [Madrid, 1977].) The reader will notice that in following the history of the TR we have slipped into the 20th cent., the subject of our next section. And yet our treatment was not too much of an anticipation; for, although their critical apparatuses were better, the critical editions published in this century up to 1965 had not yet put into practice the discoveries and insights of our time and

were very much the children of their 19th-cent. forebears. (See K. Aland in *SE* I. 717–31; also in Best, *Texts* 1–14; J. K. Elliott, *Theology* 75 [1972] 338–43; 77 [1974] 338–53; E. J. Epp, *JBL* 93 [1974] 386–414; R. L. Omanson, *BT* 34 [1983] 107–22; F. Pack, *ResQ* 26 [1983] 65–79. Comparative charts in *ATNT* 25–30.)

170   **(II) Problem of the Earliest Text.** If W-H established definitively that in general the "Neutral" tradition of B and S is to be preferred to the Syrian tradition of A (in the Gospels) and of the minuscules, nevertheless, their theory has had to be modified in its assumption that the tradition of B and S is truly neutral and truly the earliest text. This modification has come about through a more detailed study of the grouping of mss. and through a series of new discoveries. And so we come to the second of the two problems we saw at the beginning of this discussion (→ 156 above), the answer to which enables us to survey textual criticism in the 20th cent. (For surveys, see H. H. Oliver, *JBR* 30 [1962] 308–20; B. M. Metzger, *ExpTim* 78 [1976] 324–27, 372–75; E. J. Epp, *HTR* 73 [1980] 131–51; for new critical NT eds., → 187 below.)

171   **(A) Revised Classification of Traditions.** The names given to the ms. groups by W-H have been changed and the groups themselves reevaluated. The work of B. H. Streeter, *The Four Gospels: A Study of Origins* (1924), is extremely important here.

172   (i) *Alexandrian.* The W-H division between Neutral and Alexandrian has been abandoned, and the name "Alexandrian" is preferred for the combined group. No text group has an uncontaminated descent from the originals. There was much editing already in the text represented by B, even though it existed by the end of the 2d cent. S is only partly Alexandrian; for instance, in John 1–8, S has many Western readings. For the possibility of a late Alexandrian text different from that in B, see C. M. Martini, *NTS* 24 (1977–78) 285–96.

173   (ii) *Western.* W-H used this as a catchall for everything that would not fit into the Neutral and the Syrian. The listing of the OS versions here was curious, for it meant that the easternmost text-tradition belonged to the Western group. (This was explained by tracing the Western element in the Syriac version to Tatian [→ 122 above], who had lived in Rome.) But further doubts about the unity of the tradition have been raised by the recognition of Western readings in S, an Egyptian codex, and in P⁶⁶ (→ 179 below), a late-2d-cent. Egyptian papyrus. In a survey of research on the Western text, A. F. J. Klijn (*NovT* 3 [1959] 1–27, 161–73) argued that every Western ms. shows mixture and that there has never been a Western text, although there are Western readings. (See also the doubts in *ATNT* 54–55.) In any case we know that some of the elements that W-H considered Western are just as old and just as at home in Egypt as the Alexandrian tradition. As for antiquity, those who would trace the longer Western text of Acts to Luke himself include M.-É. Boismard and A. Lamouille, *Le texte occidental des Actes des Apôtres* (2 vols.; Paris, 1984–85), and R. S. Mackenzie, *JBL* 104 (1985) 637–50. Yet the W-H preference for some shorter Western readings in the Gospels ("Western Non-Interpolations") has been widely rejected; see K. Snodgrass, *JBL* 91 (1972) 369–79; G. E. Rice in *Luke-Acts: New Perspectives* (ed. C. H. Talbert; NY, 1984) 1–16; yet cf. M. C. Parsons *JBL* 105 (1986) 463–79.

174   (iii) *Caesarean.* This is a new textual family. In 1877 W. H. Ferrar and T. K. Abbott isolated four medieval minuscule Gospel mss. (13, 69, 124, 346), called the Ferrar Group or Family 13, that had a common parentage. In 1902 K. Lake isolated another group of Gospel mss. (1, 118, 131, 209), called the Lake Group or Family 1. In 1906 attention was called to Codex Koridethianus (→ 158 above) as having connection with both families. Streeter argued that all of these were witnesses to a type of Gospel text used by Origen when he was at Caesarea, whence the name given to the tradition. Lake and others (*HTR* 21 [1928] 207-404) corrected Streeter's hypothesis by showing that the text came from Alexandria. They also pointed out that the "Caesarean" text was the basis of the Old Armenian, Old Georgian, and Syro-Palestinian versions (→ 155, 130 above). Subsequently the publication of P⁴⁵ (→ 179 below) added a papyrus to the witnesses for the "Caesarean" text; but this was an Egyptian witness antedating Origen's stay at Caesarea! Many scholars disputed the Streeter-Lake identification of this textual tradition, and in a careful study B. M. Metzger (*Chapters* 42-72) showed that it needs to be modified. The "Caesarean" witnesses may be divided into two groups, one pre-Caesarean from Egypt (the Fayum and Gaza), the other properly Caesarean. (See T. Ayuso, *Bib* 16 [1935] 369-415; K. and S. Lake, *RB* 48 [1939] 497-505; A. Globe, *NTS* 29 [1983] 233-46; *NovT* 26 [1984] 97-127.) The so-called Caesarean text really arose in Egypt in the 2d cent. and was subsequently brought to Caesarea. The mss., versions, and patristic citations that bear witness to it bear witness to a whole process of textual development rather than to a single text. In its characteristics this development lies between the Alexandrian and the Western traditions.

175 (iv) *Byzantine.* This name is somewhat preferable to Syrian, Antiochian, Lucianic, or Constantinopolitan. In 1902 H. von Soden subjected this textual tradition to a minute analysis, revealing how complicated were the relationships among its witnesses (17 subgroups!). In his edition of the Gk NT he gave proportionate weight to this tradition, which he called Koine or "common." The W-H assumption that the Byzantine text was necessarily late because it combined Western and "Alexandrian" readings (in the W-H terminology) has had to be modified by the new appreciation of the antiquity of Western readings and their presence in 2d-cent. Egypt. Chrysostom's link with the Byzantine text is not so simple as once thought, since Chrysostom also preserved some Western readings. Moreover, the work of Lucian of Antioch, thought to be the basis of the Byzantine text, has to be reevaluated in regard to the NT as well as in regard to the LXX (→ 87 above). In many ways the Lucianic work preserved the ancient text used at Antioch in the early 3d cent., as some of the "Byzantine" readings in P⁴⁵ and P⁴⁶ show (→ 179 below). In summation, although the Byzantine text and the TR cannot be preferred in general to the Alexandrian text, some of the Byzantine readings are genuinely ancient (see G. D. Kilpatrick in *The New Testament in Historical and Contemporary Perspective* [ed. by H. Anderson and W. Barclay; Fest. G. H. C. MacGregor; Oxford, 1965] 189-208). In an important article on the Lucianic recension, B. M. Metzger (*Chapters* 39) says, ". . . the general neglect of the Antiochian readings which has been so common among many textual critics is quite unjustified."

176 M.-É. Boismard (*RB* 64 [1957] 365-67) has argued strongly for a 5th classification, at least in the Gospels: the Short Text. This is found chiefly in Tatian's *Diatessaron* (→ 122 above) but is confirmed by the OL, OS, Georgian, Persian, and Ethiopic versions. There are also traces in the Latin of D, and in the Gospel citations of Chrysostom and of Nonnos of Panopolis. As the name indicates, it is characterized by short readings, free of explanatory phrases and words that make the flow of language smoother. Boismard thinks that this Short Text is very ancient, antedating the scribal clarifications

visible in all our codices and papyri. It has many more Western readings than the later Alexandrian text. In a series of articles in *RB* (57 [1950] 388-408; 58 [1951] 161-68) Boismard has defended these shorter readings in John, exemplified in the transl. of *LSB/BJ*. See his *Synopse des Quatre Evangiles: Tome III, Jean* (Paris, 1977). Note that the Short Text is often reconstructed from other languages and patristic citations (→ 184-86 below); it cannot be *consistently* substantiated in any extant Gk ms.

177 The above four or five widely-used classifications are not the only possibilities. (*ATNT* 155-60 classifies mss. in five categories that are only partially similar.) But in the modern efforts to reshuffle the W-H groupings, we find that all the traditions considered have ancient roots, for in the year AD 200 there were in Egypt Gospel mss. with some readings characteristic of each textual tradition. The problem of how such different readings developed between the composition of NT works and 200 finds an answer in what has been learned from the DSS transmission of the OT (→ 37 above), viz., that in the early period there is less uniformity in transmitting a sacred work—only later does a *fixed* text become part of the understanding of sacred text. (See J. A. Sanders, "Text and Canon . . . ," in *Mélanges D. Barthélemy* [ed. P. Casetti, *et al.;* Fribourg, 1981] 375-94.) Also the 2d cent. was a period when the social situation of Christianity favored private copying rather than the more exact work of professional scribes. Thus, *ATNT* (51) describes the 2d cent. as a time when free expansions were permitted, since the NT *text* was still not canonical even when the NT books were becoming canonical. When a great codex was copied in the 4th cent. (in the church after Constantine), educated scribes chose the best available text from that earlier period, e.g., Codex Vaticanus scribes had a P⁷⁵-type text for the Gospels but a freer P⁴⁵⁻⁴⁶-type text for the Pauline epistles, so that by modern standards the Gospel part of the codex is better than the epistle part. (For these papyri text types, → 179 below). In other words, any given 4th-cent. codex or later ms. reflects the textual variations introduced in the early period. But we are anticipating, for we need to discuss the discoveries that made this insight possible.

178 **(B) New Discoveries.** As long as the Great Uncial Codices of the 4th and 5th cents. remained the chief witnesses to textual tradition, the span between the composition/collection of the NT and the earliest available copies was too great to permit much precision about the origin of differences in copies. The chief factors that changed the situation were the discoveries of papyrus mss. of the NT text, reliable analyses of the early versions, and a proper appreciation of patristic citations.

179 (a) PAPYRI. The chance of finding large parchment codices of the NT earlier than B or S is relatively small, since most of the libraries that could have housed them have been combed by scholars. However, Egypt has yielded and continues to yield a remarkable number of papyrus fragments and copies of individual NT books. Since 1890, some 90 papyrus mss. of NT books have been discovered, dating from the 2d to the 8th cent. (See K. Aland, *Repertorium der griechischen christlichen Papyri* [Berlin, 1976]; W. Grunewald [ed.], *Die Neue Testament auf Papyrus* [ANTF 6; Berlin 1986-].) For a full listing of papyri, see *ATNT* 96-101; some of the most important are:

P⁵: (British Museum Papyrus 782), found at Oxyrhynchus in 1896. It consists of two leaves of a 3d-cent. papyrus codex with the text of John 1 and 20. It agrees with B and S.

P⁴⁵: (Chester Beatty Papyrus I), pub. in 1933. It consists of portions of 30 leaves of an early 3d-cent. codex, preserving parts of the Gospels and Acts. Its text is intermediate between the Alexandrian and Western, and in Mark it is closer to the Caesarean.

P⁴⁶: (Chester Beatty Papyrus II), partly in Dublin, partly at the Univ. of Michigan. It consists of 86 leaves of a codex (*ca.* 200) that contained the Pauline epistles, including Heb (following Rom—in order of decreasing length), but not the Pastorals. The text of this papyrus, almost 150 years earlier than B or S, is quite close to the Alexandrian tradition, except in Rom where there are many Western readings. The doxology of Rom (16:25–27) appears at the end of chap. 15! (*MMGB* 64–65; J. D. Quinn, *CBQ* 36 [1974] 379–85).

P⁵²: (Rylands Papyrus 457), pub. in 1935. It consists of a small scrap on which are inscribed four verses of John 18. Its importance is its date of *ca.* 135 — the earliest copy of a NT book yet found, making theories of a late 2d-cent. date for John impossible (*MMGB* 62–63).

P⁶⁶: (Bodmer Papyrus II), pub. in 1956, 1958, and rev. in 1962. It contains considerable portions of John from *ca.* 200; it is a mixture of textual types, but perhaps closest to S (G. D. Fee, *Papyrus Bodmer II* [SD 34; Salt Lake City, 1968]; M. Mees, *BZ* 15 [1971] 238–49; K. Aland, *NTS* 20 [1973–74] 357–81; *MMGB* 66–67).

P⁷²: (Bodmer Papyri VII–VIII), pub. in 1959. Dating from the 3d-4th cent., this papyrus codex contains Jude and 1–2 Pet mixed in with noncanonical works, perhaps reflecting the fact that these epistles had not yet attained canonical status. Apparently prepared for private rather than church usage, it was the work of four scribes. The text agrees with B and the Sahidic Coptic (see F. W. Beare, *JBL* 80 [1961] 253–60).

P⁷⁵: (Bodmer Papyri XIV–XV), pub. in 1961. This papyrus codex from the early 3d cent. contains Luke 2:18–18:18 and Luke 22:4 to John 15:8. It agrees with B and the Sahidic. (See C. L. Porter, *JBL* 81 [1962] 363–76; C. M. Martini, *Il problema della recensionalità del codice B alla luce del papiro Bodmer XIV* [AnBib 26; Rome, 1966]; K. Aland, *NTS* 22 [1975–76] 375–96; S. A. Edwards, *NovT* 18 [1976] 190–212; *MMGB* 68–69; M. C. Parsons, *JBL* 105 [1986] 463–79.)

180   What light have these papyri thrown on the W-H theory? First, they prove that W-H were correct in assuming that the 4th-cent. text found in B really stemmed from a much earlier period. P⁷² and P⁷⁵ are evidence that a text much like that of B was in existence by AD 200 and even earlier. However, a comparison of P⁶⁶ and P⁷⁵ is most instructive. Both are mss. of John from about 200, but whereas P⁷⁵ agrees with B, P⁶⁶ often agrees with S (which in John 1–8 is close to D and the Western tradition). If P⁶⁶ shows the antiquity of some Western readings, P⁴⁵ has been useful in showing the existence and antiquity of Caesarean readings. Thus, in another way, the papyri have also demanded some essential changes in the W-H classification.

181   (b) EARLY VERSIONS. The OS and OL versions of the NT date from the end of the 2d cent.; the Sahidic Coptic version dates from the early 3d cent. Thus these versions antedate the Great Uncial Codices by almost 200 years and are contemporary with many of the papyri. If we can establish the type of Gk NT from which they were translated, they can be useful tools indeed in the quest for the earliest text. Long before the 20th cent., scholars realized the importance of the versions in establishing the text of the Gk NT. The study of the peculiarities of the OL was influential in the first differentiation of textual tradition by Bengel (→ 164 above). But only in the 20th cent. was it possible to use the versions in a truly scientific way. A glance at the discussions of the OS, the OL, and particularly the Coptic above (→ 124, 142, 151) will show that for the most part either the basic discoveries or the publishing of critical editions of these versions belongs to the 20th cent. See, e.g., J. K. Elliott, *NovT* 26 (1984) 225–48 on the use of the OL.

182   The impact of the modern studies of these versions on the W-H theory is interesting. The Sahidic and Bohairic Coptic versions give evidence of readings from various textual traditions. In John, for instance, in general they tend toward Alexandrian usage, agreeing with B and P⁷⁵; but in the early chaps. of John there are also readings that agree with S and thus with a Western tradition. We have already mentioned Western readings in the Middle Egyptian copy of Acts (→ 152 above). The OL, esp. the African mss., tend toward Western readings in agreement with D; but there are certain OL mss., like the Codex Veronensis in John 9:22ff., which in part agree with the Alexandrian tradition. In general the OS tends toward Western readings. The Old Armenian and Georgian versions (→ 155 above), before they were retouched, had many Caesarean readings. Thus, as in the case of the papyri, the evidence of the early versions shows that the Gk texts on which they were based were of different traditions.

183   Particular attention has recently been given to Tatian's *Diatessaron* (→ 123 above). For H. von Soden, Tatian was the source of the corruptions and expansions that existed in the later Gk mss. But Boismard has sought to show that Tatian used a very old Short Text of the Gospel passages and had great influence on the OL and OS. Certainly, should the lost text of Tatian ever be discovered or reliably reconstructed, it may hold the key to why there were such divergent traditions in existence by AD 200; for Tatian comes precisely in between the period of composition/collection and that of our oldest large papyrus mss. But most scholars are less willing than Boismard to depend so heavily on a *Diatessaron* that has to be reconstructed on the contaminated evidence now available. For the dubiety of Diatessaronic readings, see O. C. Edwards, StudP 16 (TU 129; Berlin, 1985) 88–92.

184   (c) PATRISTIC CITATIONS. Many Fathers wrote in the 200 years antedating the Great Uncial Codices, and their citations of the NT are valuable in reconstructing the forms of the Gk text in circulation in this earlier period. Once again, a study of patristic citations of the NT is nothing new. Indeed, since the Fathers were known to have been associated with ancient cities, their use of a specific text has been the greatest single factor in deciding the locale to which a textual tradition should be connected. Thus, the general usage of the Alexandrian Fathers won the name "Alexandrian" for the text represented by Codex B and the Coptic mss. We have seen that Origen's stay at Caesarea gave a somewhat incorrect name to the Caesarean tradition (→ 174 above). The fact that Cyprian was a bishop in North Africa and the text he used was the same as that of the OL Codex Bobbiensis suggested the division of OL mss. into African and European.

185   In the 20th cent., however, there were uncovered pitfalls in discerning the exact Gk text underlying patristic citations. Was the Father citing Scripture by memory, approximation, or allusion; or did he have a written text before him? Even in the latter instance, was his time of textual fluidity before there was a fixed "canonical" text? There is also the danger that in copying a patristic writing a later scribe filled in the Scripture citations from the text available to him (and thus a later text). (This is one way of explaining how the same citation appears in different forms in the same Father's writings.) Often the Fathers commented on Scripture systematically, indicating at the head of a homily or of a chap. the passage on which they were commenting. But later scribes adapted these scriptural headings to the form of Scripture in use in their own times; and only a careful study of the actual homily or commentary will suggest that the Father was not using the exact form of the passage that now stands at the head of his treatment. A many-volume index of patristic Scripture citations has been edited by A. Benoit and P. Prigent (Paris, 1975-). *ATNT* (166-80) gives methodological cautions and a descriptive list of the Gk Church Fathers; a list of Lat and Eastern Fathers is on 210-17.

186   M.-É. Boismard has appealed to patristic citations to bolster his theory of the Short Text of the Gospels (→ 176 above). E.g., Boismard and others argue on the basis of one OL witness and a number of patristic citations that John 1:13 reads "he who was begotten," and not "those who were begotten." This has the effect of making v 13 apply to Christ rather than to the Christian. There is no Gk ms. support for this reading, however; and one may argue that both the version and the patristic evidence sometimes interpret in a free and pastoral way, giving christological meanings to passages that did not have them. There has been considerable criticism of Boismard's use of patristic citations: G. D. Fee, *JBL* 90 (1971) 163-73; *Bib* 52 (1971) 357-94; B. M. Metzger, *NTS* 18 (1971-72) 379-400.

187   We may close this discussion of the Gk NT textual criticism by calling attention to a dominant trend that has produced a new "Standard Text" (*ATNT* 31-36). K. Aland became a major figure in the ongoing Nestle Gk pocket ed. (→ 169 above) *ca.* 1950 and gradually introduced new technology into the collection, classification, and evaluation of mss., centered in the Institute for NT Textual Research directed by him and his wife Barbara at Münster. About the same time (1955) an international committee under the sponsorship of the American, Scottish, and German Bible Societies began work on a critical Gk NT. The Nestle-Aland 25th ed. (1963) and the 1st ed. of the Bible Societies' Gk NT (1966) were in a sense both provisional, and they differed from each other. In subsequent years they moved closer together and farther away from the W-H approach. The Nestle-Aland 26th ed. (1979) and the Bible Societies' 3d ed. (1975) presented the same Gk NT (with different apparatuses). The number and quality of contributors to this standardized text guaranteed wide acceptance, but other scholars pointed out difficulties, even warning of the danger of another *Textus Receptus*. (See H.-W. Bartsch, *NTS* 27 [1980-81] 585-92; J. K. Elliott, *NovT* 20 [1978] 242-77; *JTS* 32 [1981] 19-49; *NovT* 25 [1983] 97-132; *RB* 92 [1985] 539-56.) H. Greeven in revising Huck's *Synopsis of the First Three Gospels* (Tübingen, 1981) printed a divergent Gk text (*ETL* 58 [1982] 123-39). In 1984 the International Greek NT Project, which had been working for over 33 years to prepare a complete critical apparatus to the *Textus Receptus,* finally produced its first vols. (on Luke—*NTS* 29 [1983] 531-38). Obviously, much work remains to be done. See also B. D. Ehrman on group profiles of documents (*JBL* 106 [1987] 465-86).

188   Examples of the rules for textual criticism applied to individual Gk NT verses are offered by Metzger (*Text* 207-46) and *ATNT* (275-92). Metzger's *TCGNT* points out every noteworthy textual problem verse by verse. On the one hand, it is worth noting that the different readings, as numerous as they are, do not touch on any essential questions of Christian faith. In terms of the number of early copies preserved and of fidelity in copying, the NT is remarkable, esp. when compared with the masterpieces of Greco-Roman literature. On the other hand, as we now move to treating Eng Bibles, the practical import of the above discussion of the Gk text may be seen in changes in the *RSV* eds. E.g., in the 1st ed. the eucharistic formula of Luke 22:19c-20 was relegated to a footnote, while the 2d ed. brought it into the text of the Gospel—reflecting the turn of scholarship away from the W-H position.

THE ENGLISH BIBLE

Although a knowledge of the original biblical languages is something to be desired, for most readers the Bible will be familiar in translation. Indeed, one's reaction to new transls. of the Bible is often a test of how well one has understood the implications of modern biblical criticism, textual and literary. For this reason a knowledge of the history of the Eng Bible is important, even beyond all the other reasons of literary and aesthetic nature.

189   **(I) Before Printing.** The Anglo-Saxon period saw many attempts to translate the Bible into the vernacular of the people. Within a century after the conversion of England (AD 600 by Augustine), poetic and prose paraphrases and transls. of the Bible made their appearance (Caedmon, Aldhelm). Bede took care that the Scriptures be delivered to the common people in their own tongue; even on his deathbed (735), he was occupied with the transl. of John. King Alfred (849-901) and the abbot Aelfric (955-1020) are other names associated with Anglo-Saxon transls. The Norman conquest (1066) produced a need for a transl. in Anglo-Norman, and a complete Bible was produced in that tongue.

190   English still remained the language of the people, and by the 14th cent. there was a resurgence of English as the language of all classes. The period 1340-1400, the age of Chaucer, saw the flourishing of Middle English. There is no evidence before 1350 of a transl. of large portions of the Bible into English, but between 1350 and 1400, even apart from the Wycliffite movement, considerable portions of the Bible, especially of the NT, seem to have been translated into various English dialects. (H. Hargreaves, "From Bede to Wyclif: Medieval English Translations," *BJRL* 48 [1965] 118-40.)

191   The first complete transl. of the Bible (Vg) into English is associated with John Wycliffe and dated *ca.* 1382-84. Part of the OT was done by Nicholas Hereford; how much of the rest of the Bible was done by Wycliffe himself (1330-1384) is uncertain, but the whole work emerged from the circle of Wycliffe's supporters. A revision was completed *ca.* 1397 by John Purvey, Wycliffe's secretary. The questions of the priority, status, and acceptability of Wycliffe's Bible have often been discussed in an atmosphere of Catholic-Protestant polemics. Wycliffe, onetime Master of Balliol College, Oxford, has been claimed as the first Eng

Protestant, since he opposed papal taxation and held views considered heretical (Lollard) by the authorities. To the claim that it took a Protestant to produce the first Eng Bible, Catholics have often reacted by insisting on the priority of the transls. mentioned above, of which we have but fragmentary remnants. However, none of these achieved the popularity or status of the Wycliffe transl., which became the vernacular Bible of 15th- and early 16th-cent. England. Thomas More was probably confused in his statement that he had seen Eng Bibles earlier than Wycliffe's. Nor can we support Cardinal Gasquet's attempt (1894) to show that the Wycliffe Bible was really the work of the Eng hierarchy loyal to Rome. On the other hand, the opposition of the hierarchy to Wycliffe's transl. must not be construed as a desire to keep the Scriptures from the people. The provincial council of Oxford in 1408 made it clear that transls. into the vernacular could receive church approval; however, *de facto,* there was a connection both in England and on the Continent between the circulation of vernacular Scriptures and heretical propaganda. Although the transl. in the Wycliffe Bible was reasonably faithful to the Vg and not doctrinally tendentious, the Prologue in Purvey's edition deserved Thomas More's characterization as heretical. In any case, as Kenyon (*Our Bible* 280-81) makes clear, not all the bishops opposed Wycliffe.

192   (II) Printed Bibles: Protestant. The next great era in Englishing the Bible came in the early 16th cent. In 1505 there appeared a text of the Penitential Pss translated from the Vg by John Fisher. However, it was the Reformation movement in England, with its complicated pro-Protestant and Anglican strains, that produced the chain of transls. that were the background of the *King James Version.* We must be content with mentioning the most important.

193   (A) 16th-Century Translations.

(a) TYNDALE'S BIBLE (1525-31). William Tyndale (1490-1536) studied at Oxford. He was already suspected of heresy in 1520, and he left England when the Bishop of London refused to give patronage to his translating effort. In Germany Tyndale was an open partisan of Luther, and there he completed his NT from the Greek, printed at Cologne and Worms in 1525. Although copies were smuggled into England, the virulent anti-Catholicism of the notes and the theological slanting of the transl. made it suspect among the hierarchy. Part of the OT from the Hebrew was published in 1530-31, but Tyndale died a Protestant martyr's death before he could complete the work. The NT was revised in 1534; and since the rupture had now taken place between Henry VIII and Rome, the opposition to this was not so strong as previously. Tyndale's vigorous English left a permanent mark on the history of the Eng Bible. See S. L. Greenslade, *The Work of William Tyndale* (London, 1938); J. F. Mozley, *William Tyndale* (London, 1937).

194   (b) COVERDALE'S BIBLE (1535). The first complete printed Eng Bible was commissioned by Cromwell, Henry VIII's secretary of state; but unlike Tyndale's Bible, it was not entirely from the original languages. The title page says that it was translated from the Dutch (= German, i.e., Luther's transl.) and from Latin; but for the NT, the Pentateuch, and Jonah, much of Tyndale's work was taken over by Miles Coverdale. The rest of the OT was a makeshift rendering from secondary sources. The "Apocrypha" (= deuterocanonical books) were put after the NT as books of lesser value. Printed at Zurich in 1535, it was reprinted in England two years later by the King's permission. (H. Guppy, *BJRL* 19 [1935] 300-28; J. F. Mozley, *Coverdale and His Bibles* [London, 1953].)

195   (c) GREAT BIBLE (1539-41). John Rogers, a friend of Tyndale, under the pseudonym of Thomas Matthew, produced in Antwerp in 1537 an ed. wherein Gen to 2 Chr was filled out from Tyndale's unpublished notes and the rest of the OT was from Coverdale. This ed. was taken in turn and revised by Coverdale on the basis of the Latin. The resultant "Great Bible" was set up in every church in England and thus became the first official church Bible in the vernacular. Its Psalter was the one used in the *Book of Common Prayer.* Some clergymen recognized that by means of the Great Bible Tyndale's work had received approval in England and so remained opposed to it. See Bruce, *History* 72-74, for a comparison of Coverdale, Matthew, and the Great Bible.

196   (d) GENEVA BIBLE (1560). During Mary Tudor's Catholic restoration (1553-1558), Protestant exiles at Geneva produced a revision of Tyndale and the Great Bible, working under the influence of the eminent textual scholar T. Beza. Calvinistic in tone and with controversial and anti-Catholic notes, the Geneva Bible never received authorization for the churches in England, but it did become the Bible commonly used for private reading. In many ways the best of the Bibles before the King James, this was the Bible of Shakespeare, Bunyan, and the Puritans. (B. M. Metzger, *TToday* 17 [1960] 339-52; L. Lupton, *A History of the Geneva Bible* [8 vols.; London, 1966-76].)

197   (e) BISHOPS' BIBLE (1568). Sponsored by Archbishop Matthew Parker of Canterbury and done by many clergymen, this was a revision of the Great Bible in the light of the Geneva Bible. It toned down the Calvinism of the latter (see C. C. Ryrie, *BSac* 122 [1965] 23-30), but the lack of consultation among the revisers produced unevenness, so that it was never so popular as the Geneva Bible. It replaced the Great Bible as the official Bible of the Eng church.

198   (B) King James Tradition.

(a) AUTHORIZED VERSION (King James, 1611). Planned in 1604 and begun in 1607 by a commission appointed by James I, this revision of the Bishops' Bible was the effort of the best scholars in England, working in groups at Westminster, Oxford, and Cambridge. Note that it was not an entirely new transl., and much of the English can be traced to earlier eds., including the Catholic transl. done at Rheims in 1582 (→ 208 below). Although at first there was criticism of the scholarship and some contemporaries thought the English barbarous, this revision was favorably received by the authorities and *authorized* to be read in the churches. In official usage it quickly replaced the Bishops' Bible but waged a 50-year struggle to replace the Geneva Bible in popularity. Gradually the language came to be thought of as classically beautiful, and the *AV* had an important influence on English literature. Among many Protestants the *AV* became so sacrosanct that they felt it blasphemy to change it or to point out the inadequacies of its scholarship in the light of modern criteria. (D. Daiches, *The King James Version of the Bible* [Chicago, 1941].)

A modernization of punctuation, pronouns, and archaic vocabulary appeared as the *New King James Version* in 1979-82.

199   (b) REVISED VERSION (1881-85). Begun in 1870 and done by competent British Protestant scholars (Americans were consulted), the *RV* was the first great revision of the *AV* after over 250 years of use. It aimed to change only where change was imperative because of better textual or biblical knowledge or because of development in the Eng language. The NT, which appeared in 1881, was greatly improved over the *AV* because of the dependence on the W-H Gk text (→ 168 above); the OT, which appeared in 1884, was less satisfactory from the textual viewpoint. The Apocrypha appeared in 1895. The immediate reaction to the *RV,* esp. from the literati, was not favorable; but then the *AV* was too entrenched to perish without a struggle. The *American Standard Version,* i.e., the *RV* with readings preferred by American scholars, appeared in 1901. A conservative revision appeared as the *New American Standard Bible* in 1963–70.

200 (c) REVISED STANDARD VERSION (1946–52; 1990). Authorized by the National Council of Churches, this American work was by far the most important revision of the *AV.* Using modern scholarship and a good sense of English, it nevertheless remained faithful to the *AV* where possible and stated clearly that it was "not a new translation in the language of today." The NT appeared in 1946; the OT in 1952; the Apocrypha in 1957. Minor revisions of the NT took place in 1952, 1959, 1971 (2d ed.); and 3 Macc, 4 Macc, and Ps 151 were added to the Apocrypha in 1976. A major revision of the whole (e.g., abandoning the "thou" prons. and overtly sexist language), which was worked on in the 1980s, produced the *New Revised Standard Version.* The popular *Reader's Digest Bible* (1982, supervised by B. M. Metzger) was an abridgment of the *RSV,* cutting the OT by about 50% and the NT by 25% (see D. J. Harrington, *TBT* 21 [1983] 110–15).

201 The *RSV* received the Catholic *imprimatur* from Cardinal Cushing of Boston in the unaltered form in which the text appears in the *Oxford Annotated Bible* (1966 ed.). In 1965–66 there was an *imprimatur* given to a British Catholic ed. of the *RSV* with some changes made in the NT text, e.g.: the "brethren" of Jesus for the "brothers" (in order to favor the perpetual virginity of Mary—nothing was done about the "sisters" of Jesus); "full of grace" for "favored one" in the angelic salutation to Mary (Luke 1:28). Some American Catholic scholars disapproved of such changes as unscientific—references to doctrines should be made in footnotes, rather than artificially read into the text.

In this general context it should be noted that canon 1400 of the 1918 Code of Canon Law permitted Catholics to read non-Catholic eds. of the Bible even without such approval as given to the *RSV,* if the Catholics were in some way engaged in the study of Scripture and if the eds. were complete and faithful and without notes that constituted an attack on Catholic dogma. Most famous modern non-Catholic Bibles met these requirements. The issue seems to have disappeared after Vatican II, for in the 1983 Code of Canon Law one finds only (825.2) that, with the permission of the Conference of Bishops, Catholic scholars can collaborate with "separated brothers and sisters" in preparing and publishing transls. of the Sacred Scriptures annotated with appropriate explanations. This is virtually an invitation to ecumenical Bibles, which became more frequent in the last part of the 20th cent. For the Vatican guidelines for interconfessional work, see *BT* 19 (1968) 101–10; for the "Common Bible," see W. M. Abbott, *TBT* 37 (1968) 2553–66.

202 **(C) New Translations.** These are myriad and we must confine ourselves to those widely read today. For the *Phillips NT* (1958, rev. 1973), see *JBC* 69:165; Kubo, *So Many* 69–88. (For a comparison of some of these, see *BARev* 9 [6, 1982] 56–67.)

(a) "CHICAGO BIBLE" (1931). E. J. Goodspeed published the NT in 1923; in 1927 an OT was published; the two were combined as *The Bible: An American Translation* in 1931; and Goodspeed's Apocrypha was added in 1939. Goodspeed was an articulate advocate of transl. into modern English, and his NT was important both scientifically and stylistically. The auspices of the Univ. of Chicago gave it its popular name. (E. J. Goodspeed, *The Making of the English New Testament* [Chicago, 1925].)

203 (b) NEW ENGLISH BIBLE (1961–70). As the *RSV* NT was appearing in the USA, the British Protestant churches embarked on a totally new transl. C. H. Dodd was subdirector for the NT, G. R. Driver for the OT (which emerged rather idiosyncratic), and G. D. Kilpatrick for the Apocrypha. The vigorous contemporary British English of the *NEB* evoked hostile comments from those wedded to *KJV* English, some of whom would insist on a literary excellence in transl., even for biblical books that suffered in the original. T. S. Eliot once remarked, "Those who talk of the Bible as a 'monument of English prose' are merely admiring it as a monument over the grave of Christianity." See G. Hunt, *About the New English Bible* (Oxford, 1970); and for evaluation, *The New English Bible Reviewed* (ed. D. Nineham; London, 1965); J. Barr, *HeyJ* 14 (1974) 381–405. Minor changes were made in subsequent eds., and a thorough revision was undertaken in the 1980s, appearing in the 1990s.

204 (c) TODAY'S ENGLISH VERSION—Good News Bible (1966–79). The American Bible Society sponsored this very popular transl. by R. G. Bratcher into contemporary American English (although a British-Usage ed. also appeared). Even freer than the *NEB* and attractively published, this version has won wide following for private reading because of its ready intelligibility, even if there is some truth in the contention that it has made clear some passages that are unclear in the original. There is an edition with an imprimatur (→ 201 above).

205 (d) NEW INTERNATIONAL VERSION (1973–78). Sponsored by the New York International Bible Society and done by scholars of 34 different religious groups working in 20 teams, the *NIV* had the largest first printing ever for an Eng Bible. It has been dubbed a conservative alternative to the *RSV,* e.g., "virgin" in Isa 7:14, not "young woman." Careful, clear, more literal than the *NEB,* the *NIV* avoided the colloquialisms of *TEV.* It is quite useful for study purposes. (K. Barker [ed.], *The NIV* [GR, 1986].)

206 (e) THE LIVING BIBLE (1962–71). This effort of K. A. Taylor, a conservative businessman with a background in the Inter-Varsity Fellowship, was professedly a paraphrase: "A restatement of the author's thought, using different words than he did." Its chatty style made it the best-selling book in the USA in 1972, and free copies were distributed by the Billy Graham Evangelical Association. Taylor's basic guide was the *ASV,* but his theological bias (which he characterized as "a rigid evangelical position") created extraordinary christological readings, e.g., the substitution of Messiah for the Son of Man, and the replacement of "the Word" by Christ in John 1:1. Lewis (*English* 246) expresses the typical scholarly evaluation of this Bible when, using words of Thomas More, he suggests that its errors are as frequent as the water in the sea.

The issue of paraphrasing the Scriptures has arisen also on the liberal side of Christianity in attempts to avoid what some deem racist or sexist language in the established transls., e.g., removing the male references to God. See the lively debate over the *Inclusive Language Lectionary* (Phl, 1983; sponsored by a division of the National Council of Churches) in *BTB* 14 (1984) 28–35.

207 **(III) Printed Bibles: Catholic.** Because the Council of Trent insisted on the Vg as "the authentic edition for public reading, disputations, sermons, and explanations" (→ Church Pronouncements, 72:11), it was standard practice that official Catholic transls. into the vernacular be from the Vg. (For Trent's attitude toward vernacular Bibles, see R. E. McNally, *TS* 27

[1966] 204–27.) Only with the encyclical *DAS* of Pope Pius XII in 1943, 400 years after Trent, was church policy changed and vernacular transls. from the original languages officially encouraged (→ Church Pronouncements, 72:20). Vatican Council II made it possible that such transls. from the original languages be used for pericopes of the vernacular Mass (Instruction of the Congregation of Rites for Interpreting the Constitution of Vatican II on the Sacred Liturgy 1.11.40a). The American Catholic hierarchy approved a transl. from the original languages for use in both the English Mass and the breviary. This history explains why we must distinguish between two types of Catholic transls.

208   (A) From the Vulgate.

(a) DOUAY-RHEIMS (1582–1609). This was done by Gregory Martin, an Oxford-trained scholar in the circle of Eng Catholic exiles on the Continent, under the sponsorship of William (later Cardinal) Allen. The NT appeared at Rheims in 1582; the OT at Douay in 1609. The transl., although competent, exhibited a taste for Latinisms that was not uncommon in Eng writing of the time but seemed excessive in the eyes of later generations. The NT influenced the *AV*.

209   (b) CHALLONER REVISION (1749–63). The official Catholic version underwent revision earlier than its Protestant counterpart, the *AV*. Bishop Richard Challoner, coadjutor in London, revised the NT in 1749 and 1752, and the OT in 1750 and 1763. This was a considerable revision, markedly modernizing the style. For 200 years the Challoner revision remained in almost universal use among English-speaking Catholics.

210   (c) CONFRATERNITY REVISION OF NT (1941). If the need for a Bible revision adapted to the 20th cent. affected Protestantism (→ 200 above), Catholic circles in America and England felt the same need. In America the Episcopal Committee for the Confraternity of Christian Doctrine (whence the *CCD* designation) sponsored a revision of the Rheims-Challoner NT. The footnotes took cognizance of the Gk original; but the text followed the Sixto-Clementine Vg (→ 146 above), even where it was not faithful to Jerome's original Vg. It remained dominant in church usage until Dec. 1964 when the English Mass was introduced employing another transl. A revision of the Douay-Challoner OT was begun, but abandoned after Pius XII permitted and encouraged official transls. from the original languages (→ Church Pronouncements, 72:20).

211   (d) KNOX BIBLE (1944–50). In Britain the Catholic hierarchies approved a new transl. from the Vg. This was the work of Ronald Knox, a distinguished convert who had been trained in the classics at Oxford and was known as an accomplished Eng stylist. Although Knox rendered from the Latin, he took cognizance of the original languages in his footnotes. His command of Greek was far better than his command of Hebrew; and without question the NT (esp. the Pauline epistles), with its lively style, was the better part of the work. (See T. M. Klein, "The Stature of Knox," *AER* 142 [1960] 399–409; R. Knox, *On Englishing the Bible* [London, 1949].)

212   (B) From the Original Languages.

(a) WESTMINSTER VERSION (1935–49). A British project under the editorship of the Jesuit C. Lattey completed the NT in 1935, but left the OT incomplete as of 1949. The scholarship was reasonably scientific, but the style was oppressively stiff and archaic. An unpublished transl. of the NT by J. Bligh appearing in a missal (1961) was identified as a revision of the Westminster Version.

213   (b) KLEIST-LILLY NT (1950–54). In America two priests, J. A. Kleist († 1949) and J. L. Lilly († 1952), with the same intent as Goodspeed (→ 202 above),

reproduced a NT "in a diction that keeps pace with modern developments in the English language." Kleist's style in the Gospels was superbly direct and forceful, better than Lilly's rendering of the Epistles. The critical scholarship was occasionally weak and theologically slanted. (See J. L. McKenzie, *CBQ* 16 [1954] 491–500.)

214   (c) NEW AMERICAN BIBLE (1952–70; 1987). The abandonment of the *CCD* revision of the Douay-Challoner OT in light of *DAS* (→ 210 above) led the Episcopal Committee to project for American Catholics an entirely new, contemporary-language transl. of the whole Bible from the original languages (rather than from the Vg). It began with the OT; and although Gen was choppy and too conservative (and had to be revised for the final publication), overall the OT was very good. T. Meek of the Chicago Bible project (→ 202 above) commented in *CBQ* 18 (1956) 314: "It is much more modern in its English and much truer to the original than the highly vaunted RSV." Some of the NT was carefully done in committee; but the push to have it ready for the English Mass Lectionary produced uneven editing which often was never shown to the scholars who did the translating. Thus, while readable, the NT had major inconsistencies. A totally new transl. of the NT (even if called a revision) appeared in 1987, done with Protestant cooperation even as the *RSV* revision had Catholic cooperation.

215   (d) TRANSLATION OF THE JERUSALEM BIBLE (1966; 1985). In 1948–54, with R. de Vaux as general ed., the Fr Dominicans of Jerusalem produced *La Sainte Bible* (which subsequently underwent revisions). The copious introductions and footnotes made it a landmark of renascent Catholic biblical scholarship after *DAS*. The Eng transl. (1966), made from a one-vol. abbreviation of the Fr work, was guided by A. Jones and became a valuable text for students. Despite its enormous strengths, it had serious defects: in the NT there were idiosyncratic readings influenced by Boismard's theory of the Short Text and patristic citations (→ 176, 186 above); the scholarship of the NT introductions reflected the still quite conservative 1950 situation (e.g., if the Pastorals were not by Paul, they would have to be "forgeries"); the very British style of the English was awkward for public reading in the USA; the Eng transl. was uneven in taking account of the biblical languages and was less scholarly than the French. A new Fr ed. appeared in 1973 heavily revised, and it guided (with much further work) a significantly improved *New Jerusalem Bible* (1985), done with H. Wansbrough as ed. This corrected many defects of the 1966 ed. (See P. Benoit, *RevExp* 76 [1979] 341–49.)

216   (IV) Printed Bibles: Jewish. For American Jews the Bible was translated into English by I. Leeser (1845–53), who drew heavily on Ger scholarship. The Jewish Publication Society, after sponsoring a failed attempt under M. Jastrow in 1892–1903, successfully produced *The Holy Scriptures According to the Massoretic Text* under M. L. Margolis in 1917. Competent and literal, it showed the influence of the *AV*. In 1955, just as with Catholics and Protestants, Jews felt the need of another transl. Sponsored by the Jewish Publication Society, H. M. Orlinsky, H. L. Ginsberg, *et al.*, produced the *New Jewish Publication Society Bible* (*NJPS*, [1962–82]). It is a vigorous, contemporary Eng rendition of high scholarship; textually it remains very close to the MT, with occasional dependence on targumic readings. Thus, by the end of the 20th cent., adherents of the three major biblical faiths had available the Scriptures in very responsible and readable Eng transls., each done without any acrimonious claims over against the others.

69

MODERN
OLD TESTAMENT CRITICISM

Alexa Suelzer, S.P.   *John S. Kselman, S.S.* *

BIBLIOGRAPHY

1   Anderson, G. W. (ed.), *Tradition and Interpretation* (Oxford, 1979). Barton, J., *Reading the Old Testament: A Study in Method* (Phl, 1984). *BHMCS.* Buss, M. J. (ed.), *Encounter with the Text: Form and History in the Hebrew Bible* (Phl, 1979). *CHB.* Clements, R. E., *One Hundred Years of Old Testament Interpretation* (Phl, 1975). Coats, G. W. (ed.), *Saga, Legend, Tale, Fable, Novella* (JSOTSup 35; Sheffield, 1985). Engels, H., *Die Vorfahren Israels in Ägypten* (Frankfurt, 1979). Fogarty, G. P., *American Catholic Biblical Scholarship . . . to Vatican II* (SF, 1989). Grant, R. M. and D. Tracy, *A Short History of the Interpretation of the Bible* (2d ed.; Phl, 1984). Gunneweg, H. J., *Understanding the Old Testament* (Phl, 1978). Hahn, H. F., *The Old Testament in Modern Research* (rev. ed.; Phl, 1966). Harrington, W. J., *The Path of Biblical Theology* (Dublin, 1973). Hasel, G., *Old Testament Theology: Basic Issues in the Debate* (3d ed.; GR, 1982). Hayes, J. H. and F. Prussner, *Old Testament Theology: Its History and Development* (Atlanta, 1985). King, P. J., *American Archaeology in the Mideast* (Phl, 1983). Knight, *HBMI.* Kraeling, E. G., *The Old Testament Since the Reformation* (NY, 1969). Kraus, H.-J., *Die biblische Theologie: Ihre Geschichte und Problematik* (3d ed.; Neukirchen, 1982); *Geschichte der historisch-kritischen Erforschung des Alten Testaments* (3d ed.; Neukirchen, 1982). Krentz, E., *The Historical-Critical Method* (Phl, 1975). Laurin, R. (ed.), *Contemporary Old Testament Theologians* (Valley Forge, 1970). McKane, W., *Studies in the Patriarchal Narratives* (Edinburgh, 1979). Miller, J. M., *The Old Testament and the Historian* (Phl, 1976). Perlitt, L., *Vatke und Wellhausen* (BZAW 94; Berlin, 1965). Reventlow, H. G., *The Authority of the Bible and the Rise of the Modern World* (Phl, 1984); *Problems of Old Testament Theology in the Twentieth Century* (Phl, 1985); *Problems of Biblical Theology in the Twentieth Century* (Phl, 1986). Rogerson, J. W., *Old Testament Criticism in the Nineteenth Century* (Phl, 1985). Smend, R., *Das Mosebild von Heinrich Ewald bis Martin Noth* (BGBE 3; Tübingen, 1959). Spriggs, D. S., *Two Old Testament Theologies: A Comparative Evaluation of the Contributions of Eichrodt and von Rad to Our Understanding of Old Testament Theology* (SBT 30; London, 1974). Stuhlmacher, P., *Historical Criticism and Theological Interpretation of Scripture* (Phl, 1977). Thompson, R. J., *Moses and the Law in a Century of Criticism since Graf* (VTSup 19; Leiden, 1970). Weidmann, H., *Die Patriarchen und ihre Religion im Licht der Forschung seit Julius Wellhausen* (FRLANT 94; Göttingen, 1968).

2   OUTLINE

*Article 70 by A. Suelzer in *JBC* has been revised and brought up to date by J. S. Kselman, to whom all changes and additions are to be credited. Completely new sections include 1, 26, 50, 54, 62–80.

PRECRITICISM TO THE EIGHTEENTH CENTURY

3   (I) Precritical Period.
(A) OT Study before 1650. The modern era of biblical interpretation may be said to have begun *ca.* 1650. Until that date most Christian exegesis viewed the Bible as a heaven-sent collection of writings, a report of events that were independent of their cultural and historical milieux. A narrow view of inspiration neglected the role of the sacred writer in the composition of the books and ignored the possibility of development in OT revelation (→ Inspiration, 65:29–30). The criticism of that era was dogmatic and theological. There were, of course, individuals who questioned one or the other traditional viewpoint, but these isolated scholars failed to capture the attention or interest of their contemporaries.

4   (B) Influential Background Movements. By 1650, however, fresh intellectual currents had gathered sufficient impetus to alter the biblical sciences. The new trends were dependent upon a growing tide of philosophical immanentism that placed the metaphysical absolute no longer in God but in nature and humanity. (Immanentism holds that reality can be explained by the principles of nature itself; once there are successfully formulated scientific laws, we can know reality immediately.) The humanism of the Renaissance had exalted human intellect and senses to a point where philosophy became more concerned with human knowledge of reality (attainable by intellectual and sense impressions) than with reality itself. The shift in emphasis heralded the subsequent replacement of the problem of metaphysics by the problem of knowledge, as in Descartes and Kant.

(a) RATIONALISM AND EMPIRICISM. Exaltation of human knowledge took two forms, namely, rationalism and empiricism, that to some degree tinged all thought during the 17th and 18th cents. The Age of Enlightenment—the *Aufklärung*—throughout the 18th cent. climaxed the development of empiric rationalism. The glorification of reason heralded the dawn of an era in which, it was optimistically anticipated, past darkness would be dispelled and right reason govern all human activity—religious, civil, and artistic. Carried to its logical conclusion, rationalism ended in complete rejection of the supernatural and in pantheism; extreme empiricism terminated in subjectivism and skepticism.

Nevertheless, rationalism and empiricism gave tremendous impetus to the development of various intellectual disciplines during these centuries, including branches of knowledge bearing on biblical studies. Advances in the natural sciences (especially during the early 17th cent.) raised questions about the biblical cosmogony and consequently challenged the inerrancy of Scripture. Historians were discovering sources other than the OT for the chronology of world history. The archaeological investigations that have so profoundly influenced contemporary biblical studies had discernible origins in early travel accounts, and these reports showed an ever-growing concern with scientific presentation of Palestinian geography and topography (→ Biblical Geography, 73:8–9). From the 18th cent. on, new methods in the study and analysis of ancient literatures prepared the way for higher criticism—the analysis of literature in terms of origin as well as of content—and for the subsequent study of the Bible according to the criteria used in the criticism of profane literature.

5   (b) DEISM. Perhaps the most significant consequence of rationalism was the rise of deism, under the tutelage of Lord Herbert of Cherbery (1642), and its spread from England to the Continent. The deists had little to say about the Scriptures, though John Toland (*Christianity Not Mysterious,* 1696) and some others attacked the integrity of the Bible, insisting there is nothing in the Gospel contrary to reason or above it. Deistic emphasis on natural religion, together with a denial of revelation and a rejection of the supernatural, created an atmosphere of biblical study hostile to the traditional interpretation of the Bible. Deist philosophers like Thomas Hobbes (1651) confidently tried their hand at biblical criticism, while Baruch Spinoza (1670) rejected a Bible that is conceived of as an inspired revelation of divine truth, maintaining that it is only a collection of historical books whose content must be examined under the rule of reason.

(Reventlow, *Authority* 289–401. Craigie, P. C., "The Influence of Spinoza in the Higher Criticism of the Old Testament," *EvQ* 50 [1978] 23–32. Sullivan, R. P., *John Toland and the Deist Controversy* [Cambridge MA, 1982].)

6   (II) Beginnings of Modern Criticism.
(A) R. Simon. A convert from Protestantism and a priest of the Oratory, Richard Simon (1638–1712) inaugurated the era of modern biblical criticism with his three-volume *Histoire critique du Vieux Testament* (1678; also → NT Criticism, 70:4). Simon's examination of the Oriental mss. in the Oratorian library in Paris and his work with biblical, rabbinic, and patristic literature enabled him to produce this study of the Bible based on literary and historical analysis. In vol. 1 Simon dealt with the authorship of the various books of the Bible. Particularly significant was his conclusion that Moses was not the only author of the Pentateuch. A history of the chief translations of the Bible, together with rules for textual criticism and for more exact translation, filled vols. 2 and 3. Of prime importance was Simon's recognition that unwritten traditions lie at the base of literary history—a contribution that went unheeded by his contemporaries. Simon's critical study drew fire from other French theologians and exegetes. Bossuet was particularly merciless in his attacks, basing his arguments on theology and refusing to follow Simon into critical realms in which writings were to be judged by grammatical and literary standards. Bossuet was not alone in failing to distinguish between theology and literary criticism as autonomous disciplines and to realize that a theological position does not guarantee the authenticity of a particular biblical passage. The enemies of Simon were temporarily victorious and in 1682 the *Histoire critique* was put on the Index. Simon's work aroused great interest outside France; it was translated into English (London, 1682) and much later into German by J. S. Semler.

(Auvray, P., *Richard Simon (1638–1712)* [Paris, 1974]. Steinmann, J., *Richard Simon et les origines de l'exégèse biblique* [Bruges, 1960].)

7   (B) Textual Criticism.
(a) J. MORINUS AND L. CAPELLUS. A foundation for the textual criticism advocated by Simon had already been laid in the first quarter of the 17th cent. A French Oratorian, Morinus asserted (1633) that the LXX furnishes a better reading and a more fruitful tradition than does the MT; in fact, the MT is so filled with errors that it cannot stand as a norm for biblical studies. Capellus, a French Protestant, showed (*Critica sacra,* first published in 1658) that the vocalization of the MT is late in origin and that its consonantal text is imperfectly preserved. About the same time the Calvinist H. Grotius (1583–1645) pioneered a grammatical-historical

exegesis freed from all dogmatic considerations; he strongly supported the literal interpretation of the Bible, especially of the OT prophetic oracles.

8   (b) J. LECLERC. After the appearance of Simon's epoch-making *Histoire critique,* Leclerc (1657–1736) helped to propagate Simon's historical-literary hypothesis by a masterly review of the *Histoire critique.* Though differing from Simon on many points, Leclerc shared the Oratorian's views about the necessity of textual criticism. His own chief work, *Ars critica* (1697), developed rules for such criticism, especially for the reconstruction of the Hebr text. His work represents a synthesis of critical endeavor on the eve of the Enlightenment.

9   (c) ENGLISH TEXTUAL CRITICISM. During the rest of the 18th cent., English scholars took the lead in textual research, making the MT the chief subject of study. B. F. Kennicott, to mention only one, averred that the Hebr texts are relatively late, but are generally more faithful to the original than are the Gk texts (→ Texts, 68:59; W. McKane, *JTS* 28 [1977] 445–64). Despite the increasing number of textual studies, however, early sanguine expectations of establishing a definitive Hebr text came to nought.

10   (d) A. SCHULTENS AND W. SCHRÖDER. The work of Schultens (1733) utilized the preceding grammatical studies to arrive at the declaration that Hebrew is one of the Semitic languages. By thus challenging the concept of Hebrew as a unique *lingua sacra,* Schultens opened the way to critical scientific exegesis. Schröder (1776) popularized the work of Schultens; he divorced the Hebr language from its arbitrary association with the mechanics of Latin and showed the distinctiveness of the Semitic languages.

11   (e) W. GESENIUS. The labors of Schultens and Schröder were crowned by the achievement of Gesenius (1786–1842). As the climax of two centuries of development of grammatical and philological studies, his work laid the foundation for 19th-cent. exegesis. One of his greatest accomplishments was a comprehensive and masterly presentation of Hebr grammar in its historical development (1817). His Hebr dictionary, first published in 1810, has gone through 17 editions and revisions; it remains a valuable tool, even though modern lexicons have supplemented much of his work. Under rationalistic influences, Gesenius endeavored to separate grammatical research from dogmatic considerations and thus freed Hebrew from the last connotations of being a unique and sacred language.

The successful development of Hebr studies strengthened the tendency toward grammatical exegesis. In one sense this trend was an asset by focusing attention on the literal sense of the sacred texts; it must be admitted, however, that the rationalistic premises of the Enlightenment had a desiccating influence on exegesis and speedily provoked a reaction, as the Enlightenment yielded to romanticism (Rogerson, *Criticism* 50–57).

12   (III) Eighteenth-Century Criticism.
(A) The Rise of Historical Method.
(a) J. D. MICHAELIS. One of the most significant figures in the history of 18th-cent. biblical research, Michaelis (1717–1791) was professor of Oriental languages at Göttingen. Although he was conversant with contemporary trends in rationalism and deism, in the conclusions of his biblical research he deferred to orthodox theology. This tension between theological commitment and scientific scholarship was characteristic of the Enlightenment, in which rationalism challenged orthodoxy. A prolific writer, Michaelis's chief contributions to biblical studies were in the auxiliary sciences, such as philology, Oriental studies,

geography, and archaeology. Nevertheless, he also devoted himself to exegesis; in 1769 he began a translation of the Bible, proposing philological exactness and proper geographic, historical, and theological interpretation as his goal. The 13-volume work was completed in 1786.

13   (b) J. ASTRUC. In 1753, at the height of Michaelis's career, there appeared the *Conjectures* of Jean Astruc, physician at the court of Louis XIV. Astruc observed that the variation in the divine name in Gen indicates two distinct memoirs used as sources; to these he assigned the sigla A and B. The work of the French physician had little effect on his contemporaries, possibly because of Michaelis's unfavorable reaction to the proposed hypothesis. (Forty years later, however, the English Catholic A. Geddes noted the same variations that had caught Astruc's attention. He attributed them not to the juxtaposition of continuous documents but to the amalgamation of numerous fragments.) Astruc's tentative analysis was a landmark in OT studies, since it provided the basis for the elaborated documentary theory that made the Pentateuch a focal point in 19th-cent. scriptural research. (See E. O'Doherty, *CBQ* 15 [1953] 300–4; R. C. Fuller, *Alexander Geddes: 1737–1802* [Sheffield, 1984].)

14   (c) J. S. SEMLER. The tension apparent in Michaelis's work was resolved by Semler, his contemporary (1721–1791). Semler had no use for orthodoxy, which he identified with papist autocracy, nor for the pietism of P. Spener and his school, who opposed to atrophied dogmatism an emotional mysticism. He sought the renovation of Protestant biblical studies in the spirit of a new gnosis; but his reform had little to do with the biblical understanding or goals of Luther or Calvin. Unhampered by the common dogmatic concept of inspiration, Semler's study of the canon and its historical development led him to reject outright the notion of a fixed canon in the primitive church. He made a radical distinction between the divine contents of the Bible and the writings in which the divine truths are expressed. The contents are the word of God, absolute and already realized; but the writings themselves are relatively fallible and passing, a vehicle for the divine message. On the basis of such a distinction, only those books are authoritative that serve human moral betterment at the time; hence, what is "canonical" for one generation can quite properly be rejected by another. Through the use of this theory of accommodation people are able to retain from the Bible the speculative and practical truths that constitute genuine religion.

Semler's insistence in each case on human arbiters of the divine message set the stage for an increasingly anthropocentric, rationalistic approach to the study and interpretation of Scripture. Further, according to Semler's idea of canonicity, the contrast between the OT (narrow, nationalistic, Judaic) and the NT (expansive, universal, eternal) was heightened, and later this tendency led Christians to question the relevance of the OT (→ 21 below; G. Hornig, *Die Anfänge der historisch-kritischen Theologie: Johann Salomo Semlers Schriftverständnis . . .* [Göttingen, 1961]; W. Schmittner, *Kritik und Apologetik in der Theologie J. S. Semlers* [Munich, 1963]).

15   (d) J. G. HAMANN. But even as the Enlightenment reached the peak of its influence, voices of protest were not lacking. A sybilline, obscure genius called "the seer of the North," Hamann (1730–1788) became the opponent of rationalism and the exponent of emotion and intuitive perception as the key to knowledge. His influence was felt chiefly in the field of German literature, but he was also a noteworthy figure in biblical studies. Important in its own right, Hamann's

work took on added significance because of its effect on critics who followed him, particularly the poet Herder. Midway in his career, Hamann discovered the key to the true meaning of the Bible, namely, a realization that God has disclosed himself through human instrumentality in a biblical revelation climaxed by the incarnation of the Son of God. Hamann thus hoped to counter the crass anthropocentrism of Semler by emphasis on a divine economy that employed human beings for the accomplishment of its designs. Although it is proper to speak of Hamann as a humanist, he differed from other humanist scholars of the Enlightenment in that his humanism was rooted in a profound belief in the incarnation. It was Hamann's intent to integrate the humanism of the era into traditional orthodox faith (see R. G. Smith, *J. G. Hamann* [NY, 1960]).

16   (B) Transition to the Nineteenth Century.
(a) J. G. HERDER. Under Hamann's tutelage, Herder (1744–1803) acquired a love for the OT and developed his distinctive "Hebraic humanism." Primarily a poet, Herder, like his contemporary Lessing and his pupil Goethe, did not hesitate to assume the roles of philosopher and theologian. Dissatisfied with Semler's view of the Bible and the concept of the accommodation of the Bible to human needs, Herder found Hamann's view more congenial; nevertheless, he did not espouse Hamann's concept of a distinctive human role in the accomplishment of salvation history. For both Hamann and Herder, human beings are indeed the image of God; but for Herder, it is in human nature apart from Jesus Christ that the secret of the divine resemblance lies.

Herder approached the Bible as an aesthetic work, a rich deposit of literature upon which the educated taste could dwell. Aesthetic interests prompted his initial hermeneutic efforts. A Ger edition of Bishop R. Lowth's literary appreciation of Hebr poetry, *De sacra poesi Hebraeorum* (1753; → Hebrew Poetry, 12:6), brought out by Michaelis in 1780, impressed Herder and led to the inception of his great work on the spirit of Hebr poetry (1782–1783). Herder went beyond Lowth's analysis of form to penetrate the spiritual character of the poetry as an expression of a living religious experience. Given soul by the dynamic vital force behind them, the words of the sacred writer could thus speak to readers of the Bible. The key to Herder's biblical analysis was thus aesthetic empathy with Hebr poetry, a penetration of the ancient biblical world, not through the media of archaeology or of scientific scholarly investigation but through ingenuousness, simplicity of heart, and emotional response. His evaluation of the sacred writings as the expression of Israel's experience of the divine led to his famous dictum that the more humanly one reads the word of God, the closer one approaches its true meaning, for it is a book written by people for people.

Romantic and intuitive, Herder tempered the rationalism of his age by urging a new encounter with the biblical message that would be compatible with the classic, pantheistic, and humanistic spirit of the time. Both orthodox and rationalistic critics hailed Herder's approach as a welcome and needed corrective to the dogmatic and despiritualized treatment of Scripture. Although Herder eschewed grosser rationalism like Semler's, his aesthetic approach to the Bible was one more step toward the position of higher criticism: The study of the Bible as literature is in no way different from that of profane literary works. Following Herder, biblical scholars attempted a similar intuitive interpretation; the dearth of noteworthy scientific exegesis in the second half of the 18th cent. can be attributed in part to Herder's influence. The lasting effects of this influence are seen in the work of Hermann Gunkel (→ 37 below). Called a scientific Herder, Gunkel employed aesthetic appreciation to penetrate the biblical message. In fact, Gunkel's theory of literary forms echoes Herder's assertion that poetry tends to be expressed in forms especially suited to a particular purpose (see A. Baker, *CBQ* 35 [1973] 429–40).

17   (b) J. G. EICHHORN. As already noted, the intellectual ferment of the 17th and 18th cents. had generated tension between orthodoxy and rationalism, between tradition and the Enlightenment. Most apparent in Michaelis, the tension was evident also in the work of Semler and Herder, whose studies were somewhat tentative and groping. It remained for Eichhorn (1752–1827) to synthesize the results of the new trends and to establish the principles of a historical-critical analysis that was to dominate the next two centuries of biblical scholarship. Eichhorn was a pupil of Michaelis at Göttingen, but he soon became independent of his master. He taught Oriental languages at Jena for a time and later became professor of philosophy at Göttingen.

Eichhorn proposed to free himself from every commitment to orthodoxy and to recognize the OT historically as a singular source for the knowledge of antiquity, for he felt that theological preoccupations had severely hindered a true comprehension of the OT. To achieve this end, Eichhorn used both Semler's rationalistic approach to the historical and geographical factors in evaluating the text and Herder's romantic insights into the spiritual value of the doctrine presented. To both men he acknowledged his indebtedness, but it was particularly Herder, his lifelong friend, who influenced his biblical criticism. Eichhorn's famed pioneering work, *Einleitung in das Alte Testament* (1780–83), provided the pattern for general and special introductions that soon became the distinctive feature of historical-critical scholarship. The first volume, a general introduction, examined the contents, redaction, authenticity, and

canonicity of the OT books; the second volume treated the history of the text; and the third furnished special introductory aids for a critical treatment of the OT and discussed individual books.

The name of Eichhorn is chiefly associated with views concerning the Pentateuch. Utilizing Astruc's all but forgotten work, Eichhorn carried the analysis as far as Lev and affirmed the presence of two distinct documents (J and E—later E^1 and E^2), thus successfully proposing a documentary theory. Contrary to the 18th-cent. fashion of denying that Moses ever existed, Eichhorn strongly asserted the Mosaic authorship of the Pentateuch; he insisted, however, that Moses had made extensive use of fixed written sources.

Eichhorn's Pentateuchal work has somewhat overshadowed his contribution to the interpretation of the prophets. His analysis of the prophetic writings was strongly influenced by Herder's understanding of the human characteristics of the prophets and their poetic, mystical bent. Eichhorn was careful to consider the historical milieu and endeavored to transport the readers to ancient times and make them confront prophetical literature in the prophet's own age. A century later Duhm in his work on the Hebr prophets (→ 25 below) acknowledged the influence of Eichhorn, whose intial studies provided the impetus for the achievements of later scholarship. Eichhorn made use of Herder's embryonic insights into Hebr poetry and literary form to determine poetic *Gattungen* (categories, genres, forms). He assumed in part Simon's notion of tradition and enlarged it with the concept of the importance of oral tradition in the transmission of biblical materials. Further, he saw in the mythical elements of primitive history more than poetic adornment or an accommodation to the time; these preliminary studies of myth were of great importance in the work of Gunkel (→ 29, 37 below; E. Sehmsdorf, *Die Prophetenauslegung bei J. G. Eichhorn* [Göttingen, 1971]).

HISTORICAL CRITICISM IN THE NINETEENTH CENTURY

18   **(I) Growth of the Historical Method.**
(A) W. M. L. de Wette. The grammatical-historical exegesis of the day was far from satisfactory to de Wette (1780–1849)—neither grammatical nor historical, scarcely deserving the name of exegesis at all. After a brilliant doctoral dissertation (1805) in which he separated the deuteronomic document in the Hexateuch and Kgs (→ Deuteronomy, 6:3), de Wette turned his attention to the problem of methodology in biblical criticism. He greatly admired the achievements of Eichhorn in the realm of literary criticism, but found even greater incentive for his own research in Eichhorn's consideration of the historical milieu. In his *Manual of Historico-Critical Introduction to the Bible* (1817) de Wette spoke so decisively of the demands of historical criticism that he is deservedly regarded as a founder of this method in biblical studies. The goal to which he directed his efforts was that of understanding the biblical phenomena in their true historical interrelationship. His basic question in biblical analysis was a historical one: What is the Bible and how did it develop? To answer this query de Wette in his *Introduction* treated the events of the Bible as phenomena comparable to other historical phenomena and subject to the same laws of historical research.

De Wette's enthusiasm for history was occasioned in part by the birth and development of critical, scientific, historical scholarship in the early days of the 19th cent., chiefly in Germany. In the name of reason, scholars of the Enlightenment had ignored the religious and social past with its legends and traditions that were regarded as characteristic of a benighted era. Consequently, history was denied value as a factor in human progress. Scholars were mainly concerned with a philosophy of history; and when they did turn their gaze upon alien people or unfamiliar institutions, it was without realizing that any great effort of understanding was necessary. With the dawn of romanticism, however, history—a measured progress from primitive institutions to wise systems—came to be appreciated as a vital factor in civilization.

The historical-critical method as envisaged by de Wette and practiced by his successors combined literary and historical criticism. Literary criticism seeks to establish textual limits and to ascertain the genres and special characteristics of the underlying sources; it studies content under the threefold aspect of language, composition, and origin. Historical criticism attempts to determine the value of the sacred writings as historical documents, both as to facts and as to teaching. This method seeks to reconstruct the writer's life, ideas, and milieu through the use of auxiliary sciences like philology, archaeology, and geography. De Wette's work clarified and strengthened these two critical tendencies current at the beginning of the 19th cent. In the arrangement of his *Introduction,* to achieve the full understanding of the sacred writing, de Wette first used all possible grammatical and rhetorical means to penetrate the biblical message. After this literary analysis he turned to historical investigation of the circumstances that produced the work—the milieu of the author, the thoughts, the views, the hopes and fears he shares with contemporaries.

De Wette often affirmed the irrelevance of dogmatic premises in biblical research, although he was moderate in the midst of the polemic against orthodoxy and tolerated religious judgments that were in accord with the conclusions of his historical method. In fact, he considered the spiritual sensibility of exegetes very important. Exegetes' capabilities will be greater, asserted de Wette, in proportion to the purity and perfection of their religious views—in short, in proportion to the degree to which they are Christian. Consonant with his rejection of dogmatism, de Wette affirmed that for exegesis no fixed theological view was necessary or even possible, since such commitment bars the way to objective analysis. Here de Wette was restoring the rejected premises of the Enlightenment and of romanticism.

As a critic of the psalms de Wette showed the influence of Herder's aesthetic appreciation. Eichhorn had introduced the term *Gattung,* "genre," in reference to the kinds of psalms but had attempted no classification. De Wette divided the psalms into six categories, thus anticipating the more complete analysis of Gunkel (→ 39 below; Rogerson, *Criticism* 28–49).

19   (B) Hegelian Influence.   Even as de Wette was advocating the use of historical criticism in biblical exegesis, the philosopher G. W. F. Hegel (1770–1831) was developing a system of dialectic that had an immediate and invigorating influence as a basis for the interpretation of history. As applied to history, the Hegelian dialectic asserts progress through antagonism and conflict; development takes place because a particular situation (thesis) inevitably produces its opposite (antithesis). The ensuing struggle ends in fusion of the two—a synthesis—that in turn becomes the thesis of the next stage of the struggle. Hegel's *Philosophy of History* (1831) became the final word in metaphysical thinking. After 1850, however, his hypothesis lost ground because of attacks of materialistic science. In two generations the progress of the Enlightenment passed through the dialectic development of Hegel into the evolutionary theory of the second half of the 19th cent. (Thompson, *Moses* 37–41).

20   (a) W. Vatke.   An ardent disciple of Hegel, Vatke (1806–1882) criticized de Wette's conception of historical biblical research as insufficiently dynamic. He regretted de Wette's failure to appreciate the vital role that Hegel's Absolute played in history. In the 1st vol. of his biblical theology, *The Religion of Israel* (1835), Vatke applied the dialectic of Hegel to the study of how religion developed in Israel. Individual historical facts must be related to the eternal truths of reason to form a historical continuum. Religion and history—eternal truth and historical moment—must blend into *Heilsgeschichte,* "salvation history." True religion was revealed slowly through successive stages of simile, allegory, and myth, climaxing in the historical revelation of Jesus Christ.

Vatke held that biblical theology is a historical discipline, not to be determined by dogmatic considerations; it depends solely upon the written word. But since it reflects the dogmatic coloration of a particular age,

biblical theology shares the fate of all historical analysis, changing in accord with the stages of dogmatic development. Since historical events are always mirrored in present consciousness, what appears as history is a continuum of the manifestations of the true religion understood here and now. The biblical writings are more properly called a history of human consciousness rather than a scientific record of past events. Consequently, Vatke concluded, a completely objective biblical theology can never exist. His idealistic concept that historical appearances are only manifestations of the Absolute dissolves the reality of history and of revelation as well (Rogerson, *Criticism* 69–78; Perlitt, *Vatke*).

21   (b) Denigration of the OT.   To Hegel, Christianity is the absolute religion, the final stage of the dialectic process. The religion of the Hebrews (like pagan religions) was but a single necessary moment in the evolution of the Absolute. Because it was transitory, it was valid and useful only for its own period; as religion evolves from the crudest forms of magic to perfect Christianity, OT religion has become empty. Vatke, like Hegel, maintained that the OT was inferior to the NT because Christianity is the culmination of the developmental process. But Vatke opposed paganism to both OT and NT: Heathenism is naturalistic; Judaism is ideal; Christianity raised the idealism of Hebr religion to concrete reality.

This subtle denigration of the OT was accented by Friedrich Schleiermacher (1768–1834), the religious philosopher of romanticism, who held that the gulf between the Hebrew and Christian consciousness is as vast as that between heathen and Christian consciousness. Hence, without rejecting the OT writings, he assigned them a decidedly inferior position, thus anticipating modern questions about the relevance of the OT (→ Hermeneutics, 71:52).

22   (C) H. Ewald.   The historical criticism inaugurated by de Wette and Vatke was carried forward by Ewald (1803–1875), who was professor at Göttingen (where he had been a pupil of Eichhorn) and at Tübingen. Orientalist, philologist, and theologian, Ewald's most influential work was in none of these fields, but in history. His *History of the People of Israel* (1843–55) was the first work in German to deal with Israelite history in a secular spirit. By a painstaking investigation of sources, Ewald succeeded in presenting a complete and coherent picture of Israel's history, though it must be admitted that his work made little use of Near Eastern history and of comparative religion. So popular was Ewald's history that between 1864 and 1868 he brought out a 3d ed. In Ewald's thinking, the core of Hebr history is found in Israel's tireless effort to achieve true and perfect religion, a goal to which the Hebrews alone of all ancient peoples attained. Thus Ewald emphasized that the history of Israel is essentially a religious history. Theoretically, historical-critical scholars conduct their research in an atmosphere of pure objectivity; Ewald's method discloses, however, that this critical historian substituted one commitment for another. Salvation history (→ 20 above) amalgamated revelation and history; in like manner Ewald amalgamated true religion and history.

Ewald regarded the prophets as the spiritual center of Israel's pursuit of true religion, having the power to bring to life the seeds of awareness latent in everyone. Together with the writings of Herder, Ewald's research remained decisive for later 19th-cent. study of the prophets; neither Duhm nor Gunkel could ignore it (→ 25, 37 below; Rogerson, *Criticism* 91–103).

23   (II) Triumphs of the Historical Method. The closely related work of de Wette, Vatke, and Ewald firmly directed OT studies along the path of historical criticism. Yet, concerned though they were with the importance of historical circumstances for understanding the sacred writings, they had formulated no general view of Israelite history. This formulation was to be the significant work of Reuss, Graf, Kuenen, and Wellhausen.

(A) Predecessors of Wellhausen. E. Reuss (1804–1891), professor at Strassbourg, was more influential through his lectures than through his written work; indeed, it was through his classes that many French biblicists became acquainted with biblical scholarship. As early as 1833, Reuss noted that the ritualistic regulations in Lev do not correspond to conditions at the time of the desert wandering and that the prophets have nothing to say of these regulations. Accordingly, Reuss concluded that Israelite cultic law is of late composition. His conclusion simultaneously provided a new picture of Hebr history: The prophets are older than the law and the psalms are younger than both. This view (which Reuss characterized as "my system") was explicated in the work of his successors.

K. H. Graf, Reuss's most distinguished pupil (1815–1869), owed much to the thought of his master in his study *The Historical Books of the Old Testament* (1866). As a forerunner of Wellhausen's studies, Graf's book marked a new phase in the history of OT criticism. He elaborated Reuss's intuitions and in precise terms answered the problem of the historical formulation of the Pentateuch: P is the youngest (postexilic) Pentateuchal document, a proposition more firmly established by the studies of W. H. A. Kosters (1868). Graf profited, too, by the criticism of Abraham Kuenen (1828–1891), a Dutch scholar of great brilliance, who was among the first biblical experts to attempt the diffusion of historical-critical methods among nonspecialists (see S. De Vries, *JBL* 82 [1963] 37–57).

24   (B) J. Wellhausen's Documentary Theory. The stage was now set for a synthesis of historical criticism by Julius Wellhausen (1844–1918). A series of articles on the Hexateuch (1876) and his *Prolegomena to the History of Israel* (1883) enshrined his system. Since his views did not differ radically from those of his immediate predecessors, Wellhausen's success can be traced, at least in part, to his logical and cogent presentation. With Ewald as his teacher at Göttingen, Wellhausen devoted himself to the study of biblical history conceived as a vital process in which Israelite religion grew and matured. For aspects of his literary criticism he was indebted to Reuss, Graf, and H. Hupfeld; for philosophic concepts, to Vatke, and behind him, to Hegel.

Since the Wellhausen documentary theory had repercussions in all fields of biblical research and influenced the course of biblical criticism to the present day, a brief summary of the theory is in order. Wellhausen posited four main documents in the Hexateuch: J, E, D, and P, in that chronological order. The early narrative sections of the J and E he assigned to *ca.* 870 or 770 respectively. Their redaction (*ca.* 680) was followed by Deut (at least the core, chaps. 12–22) and of other D elements which were discovered in 621. The composition of P began with the exile and continued until the final redaction of the Hexateuch during the reforms of Ezra and Nehemiah *ca.* 450 (→ Pentateuch, 1:6).

At the root of this classic exposition lie certain presuppositions, found also in other areas of 19th-cent. scholarship: (1) a general skepticism regarding the historicity of accounts recording noncontemporaneous events; (2) the assumption that the culture and religion of ancient peoples evolved gradually from early primitive forms; (3) an a priori rejection of all supernatural elements in the religion of Israel. There were additional

weaknesses that time would reveal, e.g., a neglect of the influence of Israel's neighbors upon Hebr history and a disregard of archaeological evidence in reconstructing the history of Israel.

These deficiencies, however, did not impede the wide and enthusiastic acceptance of the documentary theory. Assigning the prophetic writings to a period before the composition of the Hexateuch radically changed the concept of the prophets' mission: they became the originators of monotheism, not its renovators. This reversal was a key point in Wellhausen's theory, and its impact was felt in all fields of OT study. As was to be expected, Hexateuchal studies took the center of the scholarly stage. Enthusiastic proponents of the four-source theory conducted further analysis, splitting and resplitting the sources until they were all but atomized (see Perlitt, *Vatke;* also *Semeia* 25 [1982] 1–155).

25   (C) B. Duhm's Studies of the Prophets. If Wellhausen proposed to erect the religious history of Israel upon an investigation of Hexateuchal sources, Bernard Duhm (1847–1928) regarded the theology of the prophets as the basis for tracing the development of OT religion. The work of Wellhausen was of supreme significance for Duhm, for he adopted Wellhausen's chronology, in which the prophetic teaching presupposed the Priestly and deuteronomic legislation. Besides the influential *Theology of the Prophets* (1875), Duhm also published a commentary on Isaiah (1892) and *Israel's Prophets* (1916). In the late 18th cent. J. C. Döderlein (1745–1792) had first questioned the authorship of Isa 40–55 (→ Deutero-Isaiah, 21:2); but Duhm went beyond Döderlein's analysis and identified Trito-Isaiah, chaps. 56–66, assigning the composition to the time of Malachi (→ Deutero-Isaiah, 21:50). He also separated the Servant Songs from Dt-Isa, thus complicating the problem of the Servant of Yahweh (→ Deutero-Isaiah, 21:6).

In an earlier age Herder, Eichhorn, and Ewald had indicated the distinctiveness of the prophetic phenomenon and its relation to historical milieu. Duhm drew on their studies to construct a coherent pattern of religious development in Israel. The achievement of the prophets rested on fresh religious insights that broke the bonds of the ancient naturalistic religion in Israel. This work was not the achievement of a single generation, for the earliest prophets, Duhm said, were still rooted in naturalism. Only with Amos was the new element introduced: emphasis on the action of God. Because of the prophets, the religion of Israel no longer rested on God's dealing with Israel in a naturalistic way; religion was taken out of the realm of nature into a moral sphere. Through the moral guidance of the prophets, the monolatry of the Mosaic age became ethical monotheism.

Morality, then, according to Duhm, was the force behind the development of Hebr religion. Duhm's analysis of the prophets supposed and utilized the Hegelian theory of development of cult. By so stressing the moral influence of prophetic preaching Duhm contributed to a disinterest in cultic and legal elements in Hebr religion. His successors emphasized even more strongly the opposition between the law and prophets; only in recent years have scholars demonstrated that the thesis of the prophetic "rejection" of law and cult has been greatly exaggerated (A. R. Johnson, *The Cultic Prophet in Ancient Israel* [Cardiff, 1962]; R. Murray, "Prophecy and the Cult," *Israel's Prophetic Tradition* [Fest. P. R. Ackroyd; ed. R. Coggins, *et al.;* Cambridge, 1982] 200–16; → 48 below).

26   (D) Wellhausenism in England. Aside from the 1860 publication of the controversial *Essays and Reviews* (a collection of seven essays dealing chiefly with biblical interpretation from a cautiously critical perspective), the pre-1880 situation in English biblical study was marked by resistance to German scholarship on the grounds of its rationalist character. That the situation changed so markedly after 1880 was chiefly the work of S. R. Driver (1846-1914) and W. Robertson Smith (1846-1894). These two outstanding scholars introduced historical-critical study of the OT from the Wellhausenist perspective into England (and thereby indirectly into the English-speaking world) and showed the compatibility of critical study of the Bible with Christian faith. Regius Professor of Hebrew at Oxford from 1883, Driver published in 1891 *An Introduction to the Literature of the Old Testament,* a work still valuable over a century later. Also notable were his work on Hebr lexicography, his commentaries on Deut (1895) in the ICC (for which series he was the British OT editor) and on Gen (1904), and his justly renowned *Notes on the Hebrew Text and Topography of the Books of Samuel* (1890). Smith was a Scottish scholar and professor of OT at the Free Church College of Aberdeen, until his dismissal in 1881 on the grounds of unorthodoxy. He spent his remaining years at Cambridge. His advocacy of the Wellhausenist position was forceful and brilliant in such works as *The Old Testament in the Jewish Church* (1881) and *The Prophets of Israel* (1882). In 1889 he published his most original work, *Lectures on the Religion of the Semites,* applying anthropological and sociological data to ancient Near Eastern religion (an area of renewed interest today; → 73-76 below).

(Bruce, F. F., *ExpTim* 95 [1983-84] 45-49. McHardy, W. D., *ExpTim* 90 [1978-79] 164-67. Riesen, R. A., *Criticism and Faith in Late Victorian Scotland* [Lanham, MD, 1985]. Rogerson, *Criticism,* 273-89; *ExpTim* 90 [1978-79] 228-33.)

27   (III)   *Religionsgeschichte.*
    (A) Development and Importance. The use of the historical-critical method in biblical exegesis had a parallel in the application of the historical method to the study of ancient religion in general. The rationalism that had reached its apogee in the Enlightenment focused attention on religion divorced from theological premises and from all theories of supernatural revelation, but the study of this natural religion was largely speculative and characterized by broad generalizations. About the middle of the 19th cent., however, the impetus given by romanticism to historical research drew scholars to the examination of the historical manifestations of actual religions. This discipline, *Religionsgeschichte* (for which the Eng transl. "history of religion" is inadequate), had a great indirect influence on biblical studies. For the most part the new discipline was conducted on positivist principles, i.e., principles subject to scientific verification. The goal of its research was fact uncolored by philosophical or theological interpretation. Biblical religion, consequently, was investigated on the same plane as other religions, for all religions were conceived to be a product of human culture.

    The recovery of religious literatures of the Near East, as well as rapid advances in archaeology, anthropology, and ethnology, greatly facilitated the progress of the new branch of scientific knowledge. The evolutionary theory of religious development that had succeeded the Hegelian concept of continuous progress found extensive corroboration in the investigation of primitive religions. The task of the historian of religion was to trace the manifestation of religious belief and practice from primitive to highly developed forms. This work was made easier by a comparison of parallel trends in distinct religions and by a determination of mutual influences.

    While the study and comparison of ancient religions were developing, scholars of the Wellhausen school were almost totally occupied with the literary problems of Hexateuchal criticism and generally failed to appreciate and to utilize the conclusions of *Religionsgeschichte.* Nevertheless, the new study would prove to be a valuable corrective to the deficiencies of the Wellhausen formulas. By recognizing the intellectual, cultural, and religious exchange among the peoples of the Near East, including Israel, scholars doing research in primitive religions were able to construct a more accurate picture of Israelite religion on which to base biblical interpretation. Consequently, emphasis on purely literary criticism decreased as the ancient Near East provided fresh materials for investigation and comparison.

28   (B) Application to the Bible.
    (a) PAN-BABYLONIANISM OF H. WINCKLER. As could be expected in the early days of a new science, initial studies exaggerated the universality of the cultural milieu in the Near East. The "pan-Babylonian" theory of Hugo Winckler (1863-1913), for instance, attributed the superior or distinctive elements of Hebr religion, even monotheism, to Assyro-Babylonian influences. Winckler's views were expounded by Friedrich Delitzsch (1850-1922) in lectures published as *Babel und Bibel* (1904). But the pan-Babylonian theory soon faded away for various reasons: Egyptologists could not accept it; the amalgamation of diverse concepts into a single Babylonian pattern of thought was too artificial; and, finally, the theory made no allowance for the undeniable fact of development in Hebr religion. Moreover, modern biblicists are aware that the influences shaping Israelite institutions are far more numerous and complex than originally supposed. The Ugaritic tablets, for example, discovered at Ras Shamra in 1929, have disclosed a strong Canaanite influence. (See H. B. Huffmon, *Michigan Quarterly Review* 22 [1983] 309-20.)

29   (b) SCHÖPFUNG UND CHAOS OF H. GUNKEL. Many biblicists interested themselves in primitive religion on a purely comparative basis, registering similarities and differences. The true practitioner, however, sought to trace the historical traditions of diverse peoples in order to show what distinctive use Israel had ultimately made of the heterogeneous influences exerted on it. Possibly the most balanced and significant biblical work in the field of the history of religion was Gunkel's *Schöpfung und Chaos* (1895; → 37-39 below). This sober investigation of the folk mythology underlying the biblical presentation of the creation and of the end of the world disclosed that the biblical presentation may be derived from ancient Babylonian accounts of the same phenomena. Gunkel went beyond the recording of similarities; he took the Oriental environment into consideration without neglecting Israel's own achievement in the reworking of the materials. What Gunkel had accomplished in his analysis of Gen and Rev, H. Gressmann attempted to do for the prophetic writings, tracing the mythological ideas found in the eschatological sections (→ 41 below).

30   (IV) Reaction to Higher Criticism. Despite the widespread acceptance of the historical method, advocates of the new criticism were not permitted to have things all their own way. Even before the triumph of higher criticism in the theory of Wellhausen, protesting voices had been raised. Both Protestants and Catholics were affronted by the assertions that dogmatic supernaturalism is untenable and that critical canons must be independent of theology. Moreover, the implication that Israel's religious development had been influenced by religious traditions of older cultures was regarded as a challenge to the uniqueness of Hebr religion.

(A) Protestant Reaction.

(a) EARLIER RESPONSES. In attacking rationalistic biblical interpretation, R. Stier (1800–1862) inveighed against the one-sidedness of grammatical-historical exegesis. H. Olshausen (1796–1839) criticized the excesses found in both grammatical and allegorical exegesis; he advocated an interpretation that would employ all the auxiliary sciences and yet would recognize the origin of the inspired text in revelation. Olshausen's work was continued by A. Hahn (1792–1863). Another significant counterattack was that of J. T. Beck (1804–1878). Unlike many biblicists who were content to reiterate traditional dogmatic positions, Beck attempted to find a substitute for verbal inspiration in a theory of the charismatic gifts of expression given to the biblical authors by God. He also asserted that the Bible is an organic whole, a complete system of truth; and so the unity and continuity of the OT are to be found in the thread of salvation history — *heilige Geschichte* was his term — that runs throughout the sacred writings. The most redoubtable opponent of the grammatical-critical and the historical-critical analysis of the OT was E. W. Hengstenberg (1802–1869). A confirmed foe of both rationalism and idealism, he disregarded the authentic history of the OT and interpreted the old dispensation entirely in christological terms (see Rogerson, *Criticism* 79–90).

31 (b) J. VON HOFMANN. This conservative scholar (1810–1877) viewed the OT as *historia sacra* — the history of redemption in and through which God brought salvation to the world. For von Hofmann, revelation is history, not dogma; an event, not a teaching. To assert inspiration dogmatically is not enough; it must be justified by historical means as well. History is the vehicle of divine revelation; the literature of the OT gives knowledge of both the history and the revelation; in fact, the biblical literature is itself a part of that revelation.

32 (c) FRANZ DELITZSCH (1813–1890), father of the Babylonian specialist Friedrich Delitzsch and possibly the most influential of the Protestant exegetes, initially opposed the historical-critical school of research; but in the course of his studies he came to accept many of its conclusions, e.g., Dt-Isa and the late date of P. So great was Delitzsch's influence on teachers and students that his acceptance of certain conclusions of the historical method gave that method entry into some conservative circles. As a convert from Judaism, Delitzsch was more aware than his contemporaries of the need for an encounter with modern Judaism as a means to a fuller understanding of the OT (Rogerson, *Criticism* 104–20).

33 (B) Catholic Biblical Scholarship. During the steady growth of the new criticism in the two centuries after Richard Simon, Catholic biblical scholarship was at low ebb. When one mentions the names of Simon, Astruc, Morinus, Leclerc, and Geddes, the list of influential Catholic biblicists is at an end. Catholic scholars were, of course, engaged in biblical research; but for the most part they directed their studies to side issues and to safe questions, failing to come to grips with the essential biblical problems of the 19th cent. Exegetes had paid little attention to the documentary theory in its original stages; however, faced with Wellhausen's compelling exposition, Catholics began to realize the implications of rationalistic criticism. By and large, they rejected the system; concession was deemed compromise, and no distinction was made between the methods and conclusions of the new criticism and the rationalistic philosophy upon which the system was based. Catholic

opposition merely repeated the old positions. The five-volume *Manuel biblique* (1876) of F. Vigouroux and M. Bacuez was an example of the severely traditional exegesis current among Catholic scholars. The *Cursus Scripturae Sacrae* (1886ff.), ed. by R. Cornely, J. Knabenbauer, and F. von Hummelauer, may also be cited, although certain volumes of this series (especially those of von Hummelauer) showed a willingness to abandon positions that contemporary criticism had demonstrated to be untenable.

34 (a) *DICTIONNAIRE DE LA BIBLE*. The work of Cornely and Vigouroux served, however, to familiarize French Catholics with the results of the new criticism. Vigouroux in 1891 initiated the *Dictionnaire de la Bible,* finally completed in 1912. Cautious and conservative, the work nevertheless marked a step forward in Catholic biblical research. (Current supplements to the dictionary [*DBSup*] are scientifically critical and valuable in scriptural research.) Although almost universally conservative in tone, Catholic biblical publication from around the end of the 19th cent. evinced a growing awareness of modern critical problems in the interpretation of the OT.

35 (b) M.-J. LAGRANGE. Not all Catholic critics remained in a state of siege. The Dominican Marie-Joseph Lagrange (1855–1938) chose to meet the higher criticism on its own grounds. At a Catholic scientific congress held in Fribourg, Switzerland, in 1897, he championed a positive response to the challenges of higher criticism. Limiting himself to Pentateuchal criticism, he questioned the legitimacy and cogency of objections alleged against the investigation of Pentateuchal sources. The new criticism rightly demands, affirmed Lagrange, that critics replace their modern Western concepts with a Semitic view of authorship and historicity. Further, in the testimony of Mosaic authorship furnished by Scripture and tradition, one must distinguish between the literary and the historical testimony; both are valid, but the literary tradition is not so cogent as the historical.

Five years later, Lagrange broadened his field from the Pentateuch to the OT as a whole and entered a plea for criticism according to sound historical method. In his *Historical Criticism and the Old Testament* (1905) he demonstrated the application of such a procedure to the besetting problems of Catholic exegesis: the relation of criticism to dogma, to science, and to history. Lagrange's work was intended to allay the fears of those who were convinced that the use of the historical method would go counter to what they considered the first duty of the Catholic critic — submission to the authority of the church. Lagrange showed, for example, how the exegete, although upholding the immutability of truth, can still deal with the obvious fact of dogmatic development, especially in the OT; though unable to subscribe to the evolutionistic theory of religion, the exegete cannot ignore the growth of doctrine apparent in Scripture. To trace this development one must employ the historical method in the study of Scripture.

In similar fashion Lagrange examined the relation of science to the biblical narrative, reaffirming that scientific instruction is not to be expected in the sacred writings. To those concerned with critical attacks on the historicity of biblical records, Lagrange insisted that the first task in assessing the value of portions having the appearance of history is to analyze their literary genres. Lagrange's initial sketch of literary forms in history was expanded and sanctioned later in Pius XII's *Divino Afflante Spiritu* (→ Church Pronouncements, 72:20–23). Lagrange was not content to propound theory to Catholic biblicists; in his writings in *Revue biblique* (which he established in 1892) he indefatigably applied principles of scientific research to biblical interpretation. Catholic biblical criticism has advanced so far beyond Lagrange that one can easily fail to appreciate both the acumen of his critical views and his courage in expressing them. Had the course he charted been followed, Catholic criticism of the early 20th cent. would have been quite different.

(See R. de Vaux, *The Bible and the Ancient Near East* [London, 1972] 270–84; M.-J. Lagrange, *Père Lagrange: Personal Reflections and Memoirs* [NY, 1985]; A. Paretsky, *Ang* 63 [1986] 509–31. Also → 55, 60 below; NT Criticism, 70:37.)

36   (c) A. VAN HOONACKER.   The research of van Hoonacker (1857–1933), professor at Louvain, is another landmark in the history of Catholic exegesis. He advocated the methodology proposed by Lagrange for OT interpretation, and of particular interest is his historical-critical study of the Hexateuch, *De compositione et de origine Mosaica Hexateuchi* (Bruges, 1949). The ms.

was composed between 1896 and 1906. Considering the progress of biblical studies in the 40 years between the composition and the posthumous publication, it is not surprising that *De compositione* has nothing to say about many questions and methods vital in present-day research. It is surprising, however, that so early a study anticipates the analyses and conclusions of later scholars, far in advance of his age. Van Hoonacker summed up his findings under two headings: (1) the existence of documents and subdocuments in the Hexateuch cannot be doubted; (2) the role of Moses in the composition of the primary sources demands that he be recognized as the author of the substance of the Pentateuch. See J. Lust in *Das Deuteronomium* (ed. N. Lohfink; BETL 68; Louvain, 1985) 13–23. Van Hoonacker also made important contributions to the reconstruction of postexilic Judaism by proposing that Nehemiah preceded Ezra in Jerusalem (*Néhémie et Esdras* [1890]; → History of Israel, 75:121; → Chronicler, 23:82).

RESEARCH IN THE TWENTIETH CENTURY

37   (I) Influence of H. Gunkel's Methods.   As the inadequacies of Wellhausenism became more obvious, even biblicists who harbored no objections on dogmatic grounds began to doubt that Wellhausen's analytic methods were really helping to attain the goals of exegesis. The barrenness of much biblical research in the last years of the 19th cent. made critics wonder if all was said and done when close literary scrutiny had neatly parceled the sacred writings into their component parts.

(A) Gunkel's Contributions.   Of all the reactions to the classic methodology of the 19th cent., the form criticism of Hermann Gunkel (1862–1932) was the most impressive, but its opposition to classic historical-literary analysis should not be exaggerated. Only because he considered the work of literary analysis successfully accomplished did Gunkel assume the tasks proposed in his new method. He had no quarrel with literary criticism as such; yet he regretted that such indispensable literary criticism had limited itself to a critique of the state and origin of the sources, together with their minute philological analysis. This approach to the sacred writings, Gunkel contended, assumes that the critic is dealing with matter transmitted in written form. That present-day critics have taken to heart Gunkel's warning against the exclusiveness of literary criticism is apparent in the work of Otto Eissfeldt, a biblicist distinguished for his literary analysis of the OT; he devoted almost one-fifth of his *EOTI* to a discussion of the preliterary forms of the OT.

38   (a) FORM-CRITICAL METHOD.   Gunkel insisted that exegesis must be founded on recognized separate preliterary and oral traditions, from which the written documents eventually developed. To understand the sacred writers and their work—an accomplishment that Gunkel considered the goal of exegesis—the critic must supplement literary analysis by a thorough study of the history behind the final literary production. Gunkel knew the impossibility of establishing a chronological literary sequence; indeed, he affirmed our ignorance of the dates and authorship of almost the entire OT. But the would-be historian of Israelite literature must separate units of tradition from a secondary context in

the final work and penetrate to the original data behind them. This process does not ignore the role of individual composers; still it must be observed that Hebr religion, conservative in form and content, is more concerned with the typical than with the individual and that it expresses this interest in formal, conventional categories or genres (*Gattungen*). Therefore, according to Gunkel, the history of Israelite literature is the history of Israelite *Gattungen*, and the historian's first task is the determination of the form in which the thought has been clothed. On the basis of stylistic elements, contents, and interest, a particular unit is defined, e.g., taunt song, dirge, or folk legend. To determine the form, it is indispensable to know the particular life situation (the *Sitz im Leben*) that gave rise to it.

Once they have been isolated and placed in a life setting, the original oral data must be followed in their process of developing and merging into larger cycles and finally becoming part of the entity found in the Bible. Tracing this growth is a delicate and tedious process, indispensably assisted by the results of archaeological investigations and by the recovery of the literature of the ancient Near East. Striking extrabiblical parallels to Israelite life and literature have been increasingly utilized in the investigation of Hebr genres, though perhaps not always with due recognition of biblical modifications. In his study of forms, Gunkel worked necessarily with small blocks of tradition; but he never lost sight of the fact that the total effect of the complexes of tradition must be kept in mind if the resulting "book" is to be fully understood. (See M. J. Buss, *ZAW* 90 [1978] 157–70; J. H. Hayes [ed.], *Old Testament Form Criticism* [San Antonio, 1974]; K. Koch, *The Growth of the Biblical Tradition* [NY, 1968].)

To supplement the analysis of 19th-cent. criticism Gunkel proposed an aesthetic, literary approach to the OT (he has been called "a scientific Herder"; → 16 above). True exegesis must do more than furnish an exposition of the text; it must also reveal the varied situations and the complex personalities whose interactions produced the writing in its definitive form. Thus, exegesis for Gunkel was more an art than a science; nevertheless, aesthetic considerations, though important, were secondary for him. The OT forms part of human literary heritage; but it is also the expression of a unique religious experience, which, Gunkel maintained, can best be apprehended by *literary* appreciation. The main tenets of his system were presented in his commentary on Gen (1901), the introduction to which was published separately in English as *The Legends of Genesis*. In *Reden und Aufsätze* (1931), a collection of essays and lectures, he developed and perfected his method. (See P. Gibert, *Une théorie de la legende: Hermann Gunkel*... [Paris, 1979]; W. Klatt, *Hermann Gunkel* [FRLANT 100; Göttingen, 1969].)

Gunkel conceived his method while engaged in religio-historical studies that laid stress on the popular bases of religion, especially as illustrated in folk literature like myths and legends (→ 29 above). Tentative suggestions about myth in the OT had been offered as early as Eichhorn; indeed, 19th-cent. critics who denied scientific historicity to biblical records saw myth everywhere. Gunkel denied, however, that true myth is to be found in the Bible. Although mythic elements abound in the legends, Israelite monotheism rendered them colorless and eliminated their grosser aspects. Present-day criticism questions the definition that considers myth necessarily polytheistic and suggests that myth relates more to the manner of thought than to content (→ OT Thought, 77:23–31; J. W. Rogerson, *Myth in Old Testament Interpretation* [BZAW 134; Berlin, 1974]).

39   (b) PSALM STUDIES. After his analysis of genres in OT prose, Gunkel undertook a similar investigation of poetry. His studies of the psalms became the classic foundation for subsequent research in Hebr poetry. Years of research produced his monumental *Einleitung in die Psalmen* (1928–33), devoted to the problems of literary type, distinctive characteristics, and the historical development of the psalms. Using cultic aspects as a basis, he classified the psalms according to their general subject matter, e.g., thanksgiving, lament, or praise (→ Psalms, 34:8–13). Then, after studying the common characteristics of the psalms in a given category, he arrived at a series of conventional literary forms into which much of religious poetry of the Bible can be fitted. Since the forms gave evidence of a long period of development, Gunkel concluded that many psalms had originated at an early date, even though they did not reach their final form until shortly before the exile. Postexilic psalms, of course, exhibit the final pattern and show no trace of a long period of development (→ Psalms, 34:6). Comparison of the psalms with other ancient literatures also revealed that many forms once thought original with the Hebrews had their counterparts in the religious poetry of Babylon, Egypt, and Ugarit.

(Gunkel's works in Eng: *What Remains of the Old Testament* [NY, 1928]; *The Psalms: A Form-Critical Introduction* [FBBS 19; Phl 1967]; "Israelite Prophecy from the Time of Amos," *Twentieth Century Theology in the Making 1* [ed. J. Pelikan; London, 1969] — transl. of art. in *RGG* [2d ed., 1927–32] 48–75.)

40   (c) EVALUATION OF FORM CRITICISM. It is hardly an exaggeration to say that Gunkel's method of form criticism gave direction to the course of 20th-cent. scriptural scholarship. By emphasis on oral tradition and by the utilization of the archaeological and literary materials of the Near East, it approached closer to the life situation that produced the biblical writings than did static literary criticism. Gunkel anticipated the work of Dibelius and Bultmann in their proposed methodology for the analysis of literary forms in the NT (→ NT Criticism, 70:44–45). Nevertheless, Gunkel's system is not without deficiencies of its own. For example, Gunkel

rightly held that the primitive traditions were oral. But, since oral presentation places limits on the length of a given unit, Gunkel made brevity a criterion of age, holding that the shortest accounts are necessarily the oldest. As the primitive forms developed, affirmed Gunkel, they necessarily lost life and distinctiveness. In accord with his view that it is impossible to write a chronological literary history of Israel, he also stated that objective elements of history are not to be looked for in the sacred writings. Many today would criticize such general stances.

41   (B) Gunkel's Followers.
            (a) H. GRESSMANN. Enthusiastic followers of Gunkel applied the techniques of form criticism to other genres in the OT. As Gunkel's chief collaborator, Gressmann (1877–1927) indefatigably explored the influence of Near Eastern peoples on Israel, especially in the field of religion; and his collection of texts and pictures related to the OT furnished biblicists pertinent materials for comparative studies. In examining Israelite religious development, he placed more emphasis on mythic elements than did Gunkel, averring that they had preserved intact their primitive value. Gressmann also used the techniques of form criticism in his analysis of historical genre. Written biblical history represents the final redaction of many units, all of them dependent on a primitive oral tradition to which the critic must penetrate. As Gressmann's techniques were taken up by others, there was a tendency to reduce the historical books of the OT to fragments.

42   (b) G. VON RAD. In his use of form criticism Gerhard von Rad (1901–1971) became keenly aware of the falsification that can result from preoccupation with individual blocks of tradition. For von Rad, it was as important to know the whole as to differentiate components. Therefore, the critic must examine not only the primitive tradition, but also the import it acquires in the final composition, for the significance of a tradition may be altered when it is built into a more comprehensive theme. Von Rad conceded that analysis is essential — both literary and form-critical. But analysis must be followed by synthesis and herein lies the difficulty: How to explain the coalescence of so much divergent material in the sacred books? Von Rad's solution lay in postulating key traditions, like the exodus, the conquest of the land, and the covenant, which summarized Yahweh's saving acts for Israel. The cultic celebration of these saving acts implemented the original traditions and then transmitted them to succeeding generations. Critics question certain of von Rad's claims, such as the primacy of the tradition of conquest of the land or the role of the Yahwist in the amalgamation of the traditions. Nevertheless, von Rad's emphasis on the process whereby the traditions became literary compositions and his attention to the guiding purposes behind the selection and amalgamation of materials were a healthy reaction against the fragmentation of biblical literature. Von Rad's principles and methodology can be seen in his commentaries (*Genesis* [Phl, 1976]; *Deuteronomy* [Phl, 1966]); *Studies in Deuteronomy* (SBT 9; London, 1953); and *PHOE*. For his work in OT historiography and theology, → 49, 53 below. (See J. L. Crenshaw, *Gerhard von Rad* [Waco, 1978]. F. Moriarty, "Gerhard von Rad's *Genesis*," *BCCT*, 34–45.)

43   (c) M. NOTH. The OT research of Martin Noth (1902–1968) concentrated heavily on the Pentateuch, or, more properly, on the Tetrateuch, since Noth regarded Deut as part of the deuteronomistic history stretching from Deut to 2 Kgs (→ 1–2 Kings, 10:2–3). Noth set for himself the task of determining the history of the traditions behind the biblical documents; this he accomplished by isolating themes and by pushing back to the earliest stages of the tradition. Noth was skeptical about the possibility of reconstructing the primitive history, because Israelite history began only with the tribal settlement in Israel. For Noth, all of Hebr history was bound up with the Israelite tribal federation (the amphictyony; → History, 75:58); see his *Das System der zwölf Stämme Israels* (Stuttgart, 1930). This institution served to connect countless OT elements that an older criticism understood only as a part of an evolutionistic schema. Nevertheless, Noth probably carried his hypothesis too far in giving the tribal federation characteristics of the later Gk amphictyony; surely, too, the Hebr federation was modified more sharply with the passage of time than Noth admitted (→ OT Thought, 77:82). Noth's works include *The Deuteronomistic History* (Sheffield, 1981; Ger 1943); *The Chronicler's History* (Sheffield, 1987; Ger 1943); *A History of Pentateuchal Traditions* (EC, 1972; Ger 1948); *Exodus* (OTL; Phl, 1962); *The Laws in the Pentateuch and Other Essays* (Edinburgh, 1966); → 49 below.

44   (d) A. ALT. Studies in Hebr law also underwent the influence of the form-critical method. Through careful examination of the prescriptions in the Pentateuchal codes, Albrecht Alt (1883–1956) classified biblical legislation according to form, content, and situation in life. The result of his research, published in 1934, contributed to an understanding of the nature and origin of biblical legislation and provided the classic distinction between apodictic laws and casuistic laws (→ OT Thought, 77:87). Because the biblical law codes were amalgamations of independent smaller units, the form-critical technique of studying small literary units has been most successful in the analysis of Hebr law. Research prompted by Alt's pioneering work has continued to establish chronology and to trace the situation in life, which, at least for apodictic law, appears to have been cultic observances in Hebr shrines. See *AEOT* 103–71; on Alt, see R. Smend, *ZTK* 81 (1984) 286–321.

45   (II) The Scandinavian School. In the hands of Scandinavian practitioners Gunkel's methodology underwent great changes. By increased emphasis on oral tradition and by concentration on the cultic aspects of myth, northern biblicists so altered Gunkel's system as to form a separate school.

(A) Prominent Scholars.
(a) J. PEDERSEN; H. S. NYBERG. The first indication of the direction that these scholars were taking was given by Pedersen when he rejected the Wellhausenist documentary theory and accented the sociological factor of the life situation that gave rise to various traditions (see *Israel: Its Life and Culture* [2 vols.; London, 1926, 1940]). A further break with the documentary theory came with Nyberg's assertion of the primacy of oral traditions. His pioneering work, a study of Hos (1935), had for its goal the recovery of the *ipsissima verba* of the prophet by an analysis of their underlying traditions. In Nyberg's theory, the traditions are not rigid; they suffer alteration and deterioration, but they have the advantage of providing the critic with living material, not dead texts. (J. R. Porter, *ExpTim* 90 [1978–79] 36–40.)

46   (b) S. MOWINCKEL. After Wellhausen's dismissal of Hebr cult as a relatively late and unimportant factor in the development of Hebr religion, few biblicists were attracted to cultic studies. The recovery of Near Eastern texts revealed, however, the tremendous significance of cult in ancient religious life. As additional materials were unearthed, Sigmund Mowinckel (1884–1965), one of Gunkel's most brilliant students and a literary critic as well, went far beyond Gunkel in his analysis of the ritual aspects of myth, especially as

found in the Hebr psalms. In his six-volume *Psalmenstudien* (1921–24) he postulated a New Year's enthronement feast in Israel (→ Institutions, 76:139–46; → Psalms, 34:6) like the enthronement of Marduk known in Babylon. Mowinckel's views had great influence on British scholars whose approach to the Bible was anthropological. Members of this "cultic school" — chiefly S. A. Cook and S. H. Hooke — averred that Semitic cult was based on myth common to all peoples of the Near East and that supposedly distinct ritual structures could be reduced to the same schema (S. H. Hooke, *Myth, Ritual and Kingship* [Oxford, 1958]; D. R. Ap-Thomas, *JBL* 85 [1966] 315–25; A. Kapelrud, *ASTI* 5 [1966–67] 4–29). Mowinckel's works include *Prophecy and Tradition* (Oslo, 1946); *He That Cometh* (Oxford, 1959 — on messianism); *The Psalms in Israel's Worship* (NY, 1962).

47   (c) I. ENGNELL. The cultic importance of the king, first suggested in Mowinckel's thesis of an Israelite New Year's feast, was further stressed in *Studies in Divine Kingship in the Ancient Near East* (1943; 2d ed. Oxford, 1967) by Ivan Engnell (1907–1964). He regarded the concept of divine kingship as central to Oriental cult; moreover, he used this same idea to elucidate many portions of the Bible besides the psalms, e.g., explaining the Suffering Servant (→ Deutero-Isaiah, 21:43–46) in terms of divine kingship. Still more radically, Engnell declared the complete inadequacy of literary criticism and even of form criticism insofar as it admits of written sources and redactions. For valid results, Engnell asserted, the critic must work solely with blocks of oral tradition, which are always cultic in origin. The tradition-historical method advocated by Engnell and his compatriots seeks to trace a history of the formation of literature from oral tradition. See his *A Rigid Scrutiny* (Nash, 1969); also J. T. Willis, *TZ* 26 (1970) 385–94.

48   (B) Critique. The chief features of the Scandinavian school — the primacy of oral tradition and of cult — are also its principal weaknesses. Oral tradition, especially as regards stability, can scarcely bear the burden that Scandinavian critics put upon it. Further, if the spoken matter is clearly determined, it constitutes a source resembling the documents spurned by tradition-historical scholars. Their description of Israelite cult sometimes presumes institutions and observances for which there is no cogent proof and at times neglects the peculiar use that Israel made of what it borrowed.

Mowinckel himself, though he has exerted profound influence on the Scandinavian school, differs sharply from the group in regard to the stability of oral transmission and the exclusive validity of the tradition-historical method. Nevertheless, although the assumptions and excesses of the cultic school have been justly censured, its basic premise of the importance of cult is being ever more firmly established. The work of the prophets, for many years considered independent of and even hostile to cult, is now generally viewed in a cultic setting (→ 25 above; → Prophetic Lit., 11:14). Such emphasis on cultic factors has made less significant the 19th-cent. distinction between priests and prophets. The latter did not repudiate cult as such; their attack was directed against the divorce of cult from morality.

(Ahlström, G. W., *HTR* 59 [1966] 69–81. Anderson, G. W., *HTR* 43 [1950] 239–56. Knight, D., *Rediscovering the Traditions of Israel* [SBLDS 9; Missoula, 1975]. Merrill, A. R. and J. R. Spencer, in *In the Shelter of Elyon* [Fest. G. W. Ahlström; ed. W. B. Barrick, *et al.*; Sheffield, 1984] 13–26. Moriarty, F., *Greg* 55 [1974] 721–48.)

49   (III) Trends in History and Theology.
(A) OT Historiography. It has already been noted that 19th-cent. historicism worked on the

principle that ancient narratives are reflections of the era in which they were composed but are unreliable sources for the earlier age they report; hence, accounts like the patriarchal narratives were denied historical worth. Reinforced by the concept of religious evolution, such a view reduced early Hebr religion to a retrojection of later Yahwism. Archaeological discoveries altered this conclusion. Countless texts contemporaneous with Israel's beginnings have provided frames of reference for the historical evaluation of biblical traditions. For example, although archaeological evidence has not confirmed any specific event in the patriarchal narratives, it has furnished parallels and corroborated details, thus showing that some accounts are to be taken seriously as a portrait of institutions in the patriarchal period and that consequently they reflect a plausible or possible memory of the past (→ History, 75:34–41).

(a) M. NOTH; G. VON RAD. Nevertheless, some scholars do not concede that biblical narratives are reliable sources of history. M. Noth, one of the most influential of these critics, agreed that the sacred traditions do contain historical information, but they cannot be credited as a coherent historical narrative. The extent to which they can be taken as historical sources is a problem to be solved only by examination of each separate unit of tradition. Noth valued archaeological discoveries, but their witness is, after all, indirect and therefore cannot determine the historical accuracy of the narratives. (See *NHI.*)

G. von Rad shared Noth's views to a certain extent; but whereas Noth stressed the impossibility of determining historical content, von Rad emphasized the irrelevancy of such determination. A historical kernel is found, to be sure, in many of the biblical accounts, but the genuine historical concern is God's dealing with Israel. Accordingly, said von Rad, the faith of the Hebrews must be explained in terms of what Israel thought of its relation to Yahweh, not by results of studies of Israel's relations to its neighbors nor by historical facts (→ 42–43 above; 53 below).

50   (b) W. F. ALBRIGHT AND HIS STUDENTS. Although agreeing with Noth and his followers that scientific history is not to be found in the biblical records, William Foxwell Albright (1891–1971; → Biblical Archaeology, 74:15) was more sanguine in his appraisal of the biblical narratives as sources of Israelite history, when the biblical records are read in the context provided by archaeology. He never published a full-scale history of Israel, but his views are represented in a number of works (*AP, ARI, BP, FSAC,* and his last book, *Yahweh and the Gods of Canaan* [London, 1968]). A comprehensive history of Israel from the Albright perspective was written by his student John Bright whose *Hist.* (1959) appeared in a 3d ed. in 1981. Two other important works by Albright students on the history of the religion of Israel ought to be mentioned here: F. M. Cross, *Canaanite Myth and Hebrew Epic* (Cambridge MA, 1973) and G. E. Mendenhall, *The Tenth Generation* (Baltimore, 1973). Albright's archaeological work was the focus of G. E. Wright (1909–1974), who trained a generation of Syro-Palestinian archaeologists.

(Freedman, D. N., *The Published Works of William Foxwell Albright* [Cambridge MA, 1975]. Running, L. G. and D. N. Freedman, *William Foxwell Albright* [NY, 1975]. Campbell, E. F. and J. M. Miller, *BA* 42 [1979] 37–47. Dever, W. G., *HTR* 73 [1980] 1–15.)

51   **(B) Old Testament Theology.** While the 19th cent. produced enduring work in the history of Israelite religion, it was the 20th cent. that saw the production of important treatments of OT theology. A

perennial question in the presentation of the theology of the Hebr Scriptures is methodological: What is the principle of organization for such a work? Representative of those who found that principle in the traditional categories of Christian systematic theology was the Belgian Catholic P. van Imschoot. His *Théologie de l'Ancien Testament* (2 vols.; Tournai, 1954–56; the first volume transl. as *Theology of the Old Testament God* [NY, 1965]) arranged OT theology according to the traditional sequence of God in himself and in relationship to the world, esp. Israel (vol. 1); human beings, their nature and destiny, their duties to God and humanity, and sin (vol. 2); and soteriology (which was to be the topic of vol. 3 of van Imschoot's work). See D. A. Hubbard, in Laurin, *Contemporary* 193–215; Harrington, *Path* 81–86.

52   (a) W. EICHRODT. The categories of dogmatic theology were eventually abandoned, and guidelines were sought in the OT itself. Most significant was Walter Eichrodt's *Theology of the Old Testament* (Phl, 1961–67; Ger 1934). By combining historical method with theological interpretation, Eichrodt (1890–1978) attempted to present Hebr religion as an entity whose organic unity can be seen in the central notion of the covenant (→ OT Thought, 77:74ff.). All characteristic features of OT theology stemmed from the basic notion of the alliance with Yahweh that originated in Mosaic times. Eichrodt did not deny that Israel's belief underwent development in the course of the ages, but the orientation of the developmental process had been initially determined by Israel's covenantal relationship to God. In reaction to Eichrodt's classic, some critics have questioned founding the complexities of OT theology upon a single concept, no matter how comprehensive. See Hayes and Prussner, *Old Testament* 179–84.

53   (b) G. VON RAD. An alternative has been offered by von Rad's *Old Testament Theology* (NY, 1962–65; Ger 1957–60), which objected to the notion of a "center." Rather this work focused on the multiple theologies found in the OT by tradition-historical research. The major part of vol. 1 is devoted to the Hexateuch, which developed from short historical creedal statements (Deut 26:5b–10; 6:20–24; Josh 24:2b–13), cultic confessions in which the worshiper rehearsed the sacred story of the ancestors, the deliverance from Egypt, and the settlement in the land. The Sinai traditions had a separate origin and history of transmission, until the Yahwist, reassembling and elaborating this old cultic material, joined the Sinai material to the deliverance and settlement traditions, creating a history marked by the dialectic of law and gospel. Vol. 1 ends with a section on Israel's answer, where von Rad deals with Psalms and Wisdom (magisterially treated in his last book, *Wisdom in Israel* [Nash, 1972]). Vol. 2 is devoted to the prophets.

(Von Rad's seminal ideas were first presented in *PHOE* 1–78; for bibliography, → 42 above. On von Rad's views, see Hayes and Prussner, *Old Testament* 233–39; Spriggs, *Two;* J. P. Hyatt, in *Translating and Understanding the Old Testament* [Fest. H. G. May; ed. H. T. Frank, *et al.;* Nash, 1970] 153–70.)

54   (c) OTHER OT THEOLOGIES. To complete this discussion of 20th-cent. contributions to OT theology, a number of other studies deserve mention. In the tradition of Eichrodt, W. Zimmerli (*Old Testament Theology in Outline* [Atlanta, 1978]) found the dynamic center of the OT in the name of God. S. Terrien (*The Elusive Presence* [NY, 1978]) saw a theology of divine presence as the OT's unifying center, a presence mediated through the proclamation of the divine name and the vision of the divine glory. With Eichrodt, G. E. Wright (→ 50 above) saw the covenant as central and fundamental in OT theology (*The Old Testament and Theology* [NY, 1969] esp. chap. 4), although in an earlier work (*God Who Acts* [SBT 8; London, 1952]) he was closer to some of the characteristic emphases of von Rad, as the subtitle (*Biblical Theology as Recital*) shows (R. L. Hicks, *ATR* 58 [1976] 158-78). C. Westermann organized his presentation of OT theology around the two poles of salvation and blessing. God as Savior is encountered in divine intervention, in acts of liberation and redemption, as in the exodus events. The God who blesses, who providentially maintains and cares for the world, is encountered in creation (*What Does the Old Testament Say About God?* [Atlanta, 1979]; *Elements of Old Testament Theology* [Atlanta, 1982]). Taking up a concern of B. S. Childs (→ 71 below), R. E. Clements advocated closer attention to the canonical form of the OT literature (*Old Testament Theology: A Fresh Approach* [London, 1978]). On a popular level J. L. McKenzie offered *A Theology of the Old Testament* [GC, 1974], and a superb Jewish contribution was provided by J. Levenson, *Sinai and Zion* (Minneapolis, 1985). See G. Hasel, *Old Testament;* also *JSOT* 31 (1985) 31-53; R. Martin-Achard, *TD* 33 (1986) 145-48.

55   (IV) Catholic Biblical Criticism.
    (A) Effects of Modernism. Unfortunately the precautions adopted to combat the heresy of Modernism (→ Church Pronouncements, 72:5) had halted the auspicious beginnings made by Lagrange (→ 35 above) and others. When some of Lagrange's works occasioned a warning from the Sacred Congregation of the Consistory (1912), he gave up OT research and transferred his interests to NT investigation. Just before his death, however, he returned to the OT in an article on Pentateuchal sources (*RB* 47 [1938] 163-83). If the anti-Modernist decrees imposed severe restraints on OT research, on the good side they prevented Catholic scholars from swelling the number of rash and irresponsible critiques spawned by Wellhausenism. Nevertheless, safety was obtained at a high price to scholarship. See H. Wansbrough, "Père Lagrange and the Modernist Crisis," *ClR* 62 (1977) 446-52.

56   (B) Before *Divino Afflante Spiritu.*
    (a) J. TOUZARD. Since critics were emphasizing the Hexateuch during the decades following Wellhausen's statement of the documentary theory, Catholic OT scholars who wished to meet the challenge of higher criticism on its own ground applied themselves to Hexateuchal studies. An important contribution to Catholic research in this area was J. Touzard's "Moïse et Josué" (*DAFC* 3 [1919] 695-755), a comprehensive analysis of the documentary theory. Touzard reiterated Lagrange's appeal for distinction between facts established by literary evidence and the rationalistic system in favor of which the literary data were employed. The views of Touzard were conservative by modern standards, but in his own day the Holy Office censured them as not safe enough to be taught.

57   (b)DIFFUSION OF CATHOLIC SCHOLARSHIP. The founding of periodicals devoted to scriptural research and the institution of series of biblical publications, together with collective translations of the Bible into vernacular languages, provided critics with increased facilities for the expression of their views. In 1920 the Pontifical Biblical Institute inaugurated three periodicals: *Biblica, Orientalia,* and *Verbum Domini,* each concerned with a different aspect of biblical studies. The series Études bibliques, begun by Lagrange in 1902, continued with prestige through the century. Similar biblical series under Catholic auspices made an appearance throughout Europe. In 1935, L. Pirot (succeeded by A. Clamer) began to publish a new Fr transla-

tion of the Bible (*PSBib*). In Germany translations of and commentaries on the OT books entitled *Die heilige Schrift des Alten Testaments,* but popularly known as the *Bonner-Bibel,* were initiated in 1923 by F. Feldmann and H. Herkenne. The quality of these efforts varied, of course, but they accomplished the valuable service of publicizing the new currents in Catholic scriptural studies. In the United States the establishment of *CBQ* (1938), the official organ of the Catholic Biblical Association, gave to American scriptural scholars a publication of their own and acquainted English-speaking Catholics with modern biblical research. See the historical sketch of CBA by F. S. Rossiter in Supplement to *CBQ* 39 (1977) 1-14; also Fogarty, *American.*

58   (c) A. BEA. Many Catholic exegetes remained hostile to the new criticism, even when it had been tempered by the more moderate views adopted by non-Catholic scholars after 1918. A certain tension can be seen in the earlier works of Augustin Cardinal Bea, S.J. His *De Pentateucho* (Rome, 1933) had two concerns: to establish the Mosaic authorship of the Pentateuch and to refute the rationalistic documentary system that denied it. He developed this refutation under three headings: philosophical, critical-literary, and historical-archaeological. Bea's positive exposition of Pentateuchal origins led him to conclude that Moses used many oral and written sources in the composition of the Pentateuch. Although Bea was quite familiar with modern critical methods and became a defender of freedom in Catholic biblical research (especially active at Vatican II), his publications showed caution in dealing with contemporary criticism. He saw in form criticism an ally against rationalistic exegesis; yet the welcome he accorded it was not completely enthusiastic, because, he affirmed, it has been more effective in demolishing old tenets than in proposing new solutions. Furthermore, the excessive attention that the form-critical technique bestows upon individual blocks of tradition has caused a neglect of the personality of the sacred author.

59   (C) After *Divino Afflante Spiritu.*
    (a) J. CHAINE. Phenomenal strides in archaeology and in Oriental linguistics began to exert increasing influence on Catholic criticism after 1930. Not, however, until Pope Pius XII's encyclical on biblical studies, *Divino Afflante Spiritu,* in 1943 and the encouraging reply of the Pontifical Biblical Commission to Cardinal Suhard in 1948 (→ Church Pronouncements, 72:20-23, 31) did Catholic scriptural scholarship move confidently forward. Chaine's translation and commentary, *Le livre de la Genèse* (LD 3; Paris, 1951), revealed the new freedom enjoyed by biblical scholars; for, dispensing with a lengthy and cautious investigation of the classic documentary system, he stated simply that he recognized the presence of three distinct documents in Gen. For the time, Chaine's work was quite liberal, even though he showed a somewhat rigid and mechanical concept of the documents, evincing little concern for the more flexible concept of traditions that had already become a preoccupation of non-Catholic biblicists.

60   (b) JERUSALEM SCHOOL. The École Biblique at Jerusalem, founded by Lagrange, has continued to be a vital center for Catholic OT study, thanks to the research of Dominicans like F.-M. Abel (→ Biblical Geography, 73:13), L.-H. Vincent, and R. de Vaux (→ Biblical Archaeology, 74:12, 18). De Vaux (1903-1971) edited *RB,* directed the school, and presided over the international team of scholars assigned to translate the DSS (→ Apocrypha, 67:80). The fruit of his long years of research is seen in his *AI* and uncompleted *EHI.* The school has shown a respect for tradition combined with the latest archaeological insights, as was apparent in the notes of the monumental translation it sponsored, *La Sainte Bible* [*de Jérusalem*], anglicized as *JB* (2d ed. *NJB* 1985).

61 (c) OTHER CATHOLIC CRITICISM. In France, E. Podechard produced a significant critical study of the Psalms (*Le Psautier* [Lyons, 1949-54]), while the Sulpicians Albert Gelin, André Feuillet, and Henri Cazelles (secretary of the PBC in the 1980s) wrote on various segments of the OT. In Belgium, J. Coppens, van Hoonacker's student and successor at Louvain, ranged over the areas of primitive history, messianism, Josiah's reform, and the history of OT criticism. Catholic American scholars produced the *New American Bible* (1970) from the original languages (→ Texts, 68:214). P. W. Skehan, L. F. Hartman, J. L. McKenzie, B. Vawter, R. E. Murphy, and M. Dahood convinced their Protestant and Jewish colleagues that Catholic OT scholarship had come of age. R. MacKenzie had a similar role on the Canadian scene.

62 **(V) Jewish Biblical Criticism.** With the increasing emphasis on distinguishing (but not divorcing) biblical thought from subsequent religious developments, biblical studies from diverse religious backgrounds have had more in common, using the same methods and tools, as apparent in the interreligious AB commentaries. One cannot hope to give even a brief overview of the work of Jewish scholars in Semitic philology and linguistics, textual criticism, Qumran studies, biblical archaeology, and commentaries. For that we shall have to rely on the bibliographies of the *NJBC*, while here simply calling attention to a few important figures.

63 **(A) Biblical Scholarship in Israel.** While contemporary Israel is represented by many scholars associated with the universities, two figures from the first half of the 20th cent. stand out for special mention.

(a) U. (M. D.) CASSUTO. Born in Florence, Cassuto (1883-1951) taught in the universities of Florence and Rome before being appointed professor of Bible at the Hebrew University in Jerusalem in 1939. His biblical work was marked by opposition to the theories associated with Wellhausen (→ 24 above). In place of the documentary hypothesis, he proposed the evolution of the Pentateuch from oral tradition and a number of ancient poetic epics; in his biblical commentaries he put these theories into practice. Cassuto also realized the importance of the Ugaritic discoveries for the interpretation of the OT and published a number of important studies in this area. His works include *The Documentary Hypothesis* (1961); *A Commentary on the Book of Genesis* (2 vols.; Hebr 1944, 1949; Eng 1961, 1964; on Gen 1:1-13:7); *A Commentary on the Book of Exodus* (Hebr 1951; Eng 1967); *The Goddess Anath* (Hebr 1951; Eng 1971); and 2 vols. of articles, *Biblical and Oriental Studies* (Eng 1973, 1975).

64 (b) Y. KAUFMANN. Born in the Ukraine, Kaufmann (1889-1963) was appointed professor of Bible at the Hebrew University in 1949. Like Cassuto an opponent of Wellhausenism, he attempted to propose an alternative, especially in his great work *Toledot ha'emuna hayyisra'elit* (*History of the Religion of Israel;* Hebr 1937-56; Eng abridgment of parts 1-7 in *The Religion of Israel* [Chicago, 1960]; part 8 in its entirety in *The History of the Religion of Israel IV: From the Babylonian Captivity to the End of Prophecy* [NY, 1977]). In rejecting Wellhausen's evolutionary approach to religion and his understanding of the development of Israel's literature, Kaufmann argued that monotheism, far from being an innovation of the prophets, goes back to the very beginnings of Israel in the Mosaic age. The dominating influence of monotheism in Israel's thought can be seen in Israel's inability to understand paganism and idolatry and in the absence of mythology from the Bible (no OT theogonies or theomachies). Against Wellhausen's history of Israelite literature, Kaufmann proposed that Torah and prophecy were parallel, independent developments of Israel's monotheistic faith. Kaufmann's works include his commentaries on Josh (Hebr 1959) and Judg (Hebr 1962) and *The Biblical Account of the Conquest of Palestine* (1953). These works defend the basic historicity of the biblical portrayals of the conquest and premonarchic periods. (S. Talmon, *Conservative Judaism* 25 [1971] 20-28; J. D. Levenson, ibid. 36 [1982] 36-43.)

65 **(B) Israeli Archaeology.** The important contributions of the many Israeli archaeologists cannot be adequately reviewed here; → Biblical Archaeology, 74. In this section brief mention will be made of two figures who did important archaeological work. Y. Yadin (1917-1984) was active in many areas of public life in Israel, including military and governmental service. His archaeological work included excavations at Hazor (1955-1959, 1968), at Megiddo (1960-1971), and at Masada (1963-1965). Two of these sites were discussed by him in nontechnical books written for the general reader: *Masada: Herod's Fortress and the Zealots' Last Stand* (NY, 1966) and *Hazor: The Rediscovery of a Great Citadel of the Bible* (NY, 1975). Of his many other more technical works, mention should be made of his publications on the Qumran scrolls: → Apocrypha, 67:88, 93, 95. See *BARev* 10 (#5, 1984) 24-29. Another significant figure in Israeli archaeology was Y. Aharoni (1919-1976), who excavated at Arad (1962-1978) and at Lachish (1966-1968). He was the author of such important books as *LBib* and *The Archaeology of the Land of the Bible* (Phl, 1982), as well as an excellent edition of epigraphical finds: *Arad Inscriptions* (Jerusalem, 1981).

66 **(VI) Recent Developments in OT Scholarship.**

(A) Progress in Traditional Areas. In the area of method, the series Forms of OT Literature (GR, 1981-) envisioned a form-critical examination of the whole OT in 24 vols. In OT theology, the single most significant contribution has been the multivolume *TDOT* (Ger 1970- ; Eng 1977-). Also → 54 above; and the work of B. S. Childs (→ 71 below). As for the ever-fruitful production of commentaries, the reader will need to consult the bibliographies of *NJBC*. Two series are of special import: in the Anchor Bible, M. Dahood on Psalms (1966-70), and, in Hermeneia, W. Zimmerli on Ezek (1979-83) illustrate ongoing quality.

This same period has seen as well the emergence of new concerns like feminist interpretation of the OT and new methodologies like rhetorical criticism, structuralism, canonical criticism, and the application of the findings of the social sciences to the OT. It is to these new developments that we will now turn. (Coats, *Saga;* S. Terrien, *BTB* 15 [1985] 127-35.)

67 **(B) Rhetorical Criticism.** In his 1968 presidential address to the SBL, J. Muilenburg (1896-1974) called for renewed attention to the OT as literature; and the methodology for the examination of the final form of the text he termed "rhetorical criticism" (*JBL* 88 [1969] 1-18). To be sure, from Herder on (→ 16 above) there had been scholars who dealt with the stylistics and aesthetics of the biblical text, but the gains of historical-critical research beginning in the 18th cent. were so significant and revolutionary that appreciative study of the OT as literature became a minor discipline. Muilenburg's call brought the literary approach to the text back to the attention of OT scholars, as well as of literary critics who were not professional biblicists.

68 R. Alter fits the second category just mentioned. A highly regarded literary critic rather than a professional biblical scholar, he has made two notable and provocative contributions. In *The Art of Biblical Narrative* (NY, 1981) he studied such material as the Joseph story in Gen and some of the traditions about David in 1–2 Sam with the same tools and techniques ("close reading") that he would use for the study of modern narrative prose fiction. The importance of the book is evident in the responses it has provoked (*JSOT* 27 [1983]), some incisively critical (*BA* 46 [1983] 124–25). Alter's companion volume was *The Art of Biblical Poetry* (NY, 1985). *BR* 31 (1986) was devoted to discussing his theory.

69 Many other scholars (e.g., D. J. A. Clines, J. Fokkelman, D. M. Gunn, C. Conroy) studied Gen and 1–2 Sam from the viewpoint of literary criticism, but their insights pertain to the commentary articles of *NJBC*. The following collections of essays contain diverse studies employing literary techniques in the interpretation of the OT: D. J. A. Clines, *et al.* (eds.), *Art and Meaning* (JSOTSup 19; Sheffield, 1982); J. J. Jackson, *et al.* (eds.), *Rhetorical Criticism* (Fest. J. Muilenburg; Pittsburgh, 1974). A general work is D. Robertson, *The Old Testament and the Literary Critic* (Phl, 1977); see also M. Sternberg, *The Poetics of Biblical Narrative* (Bloomington, 1985). Structuralism with its concern for a synchronic reading of the final text (→ Hermeneutics, 71:61) was slow in making an impact on OT studies. Worthy of mention are D. Jobling, *The Sense of Biblical Narrative* (JSOTSup 7; Sheffield, 1978) and R. Polzin, *Moses and the Deuteronomist* (NY, 1980).

70 **(C) Canonical Criticism.** As in rhetorical criticism, the concern of canonical criticism is the final form of the text. However, this interest is theological rather than literary; the focus is not on the Bible as "literature" but as authoritative Scripture for synagogue and church.

71 (a) B. S. CHILDS. Childs first expressed his dissatisfaction with the results of historical criticism in *Biblical Theology in Crisis* (Phl, 1970), in which he reviewed the failure of the Biblical Theology movement of the mid-20th cent. and proposed in its stead a biblical theology based firmly on the canonical or final form of the text accepted as authoritative for belief and life in the community of faith. Childs did not reject historical-critical research; rather, he proposed a further development with different goals. In *The Book of Exodus* (Phl, 1974) he presented in commentary form an application of his method, which begins with textual and historical-critical study of the text, continues with a history of exegesis, and concludes with a theological reflection on the final canonical form of the text. See also his books *CIOTS* and *Old Testament Theology in a Canonical Context* (Phl, 1986).

72 (b) J. A. SANDERS. In contrast to Childs, Sanders argued that canonical criticism should not focus simply on the end product, the final, stabilized (canonical) form of the text. Rather, in *Torah and Canon* (Phl, 1972), *Canon and Community* (Phl, 1984), and *From Sacred Story to Sacred Text* (Phl, 1987), Sanders has investigated the canonical *process,* by which certain traditions and values became authoritative and thus were preserved by the community of faith, because in some sense the community found its identity and direction for its life-style in them. In this investigation Sanders employed "comparative midrash," the discovery and examination of the reutilization of earlier traditions in new biblical contexts. For the lively discussion that Childs and Sanders have produced, → Hermeneutics, 71:71–74.

73 **(D) The OT and the Social Sciences.** The use of sociology and anthropology as interpretive tools in OT study is not entirely new, as the work of W. Robertson Smith demonstrates (→ 26 above). Since the mid-1970s, however, there has been a marked increase in the study of ancient Israel's history and institutions through the optic of social scientific data and hypotheses.

74 (a) N. K. GOTTWALD. In his massive and boldly conceived study of premonarchic Israel (*The Tribes of Yahweh: A Sociology of the Religion of Liberated Israel, 1250–1050 B.C.E.* [Maryknoll, 1979]), Gottwald adopted the "peasants' revolt" model proposed by G. E. Mendenhall as the explanation for the emergence of Israel in Canaan. In his sociological reconstruction of the origins of Israel, Gottwald understood the internal revolt of indigenous Canaanite peasantry as a rejection of the Canaanite city-state and the replacement of its imperial-feudal values and system with an egalitarian society. Both the revolt hypothesis and Gottwald's amplification of it with Marxist analysis have been questioned by some scholars (→ Biblical Archaeology, 74:82; → History, 75:56).

75 (b) R. R. WILSON. In his first book (*Genealogy and History in the Biblical World* [New Haven, 1977]) Wilson demonstrated the importance of modern anthropology for the understanding of the functions of biblical genealogies. In *Prophecy and Society in Ancient Israel* (Phl, 1980) he provided a thorough analysis of the phenomenon of prophecy in Israel from the perspective of sociology and anthropology. With the use of data gathered by field studies of intermediaries in other societies, Wilson described the Israelite intermediaries (the prophets) and their interaction with society, esp. with those groups in the society that supported, merely tolerated, or actively rejected the intermediaries. He then used the hypothesis of peripheral and central intermediation (i.e., the distance from or closeness to the central religious and civil institutions of the society) to describe the history and development of prophecy in Israel and Judah. G. A. Herion (*JSOT* 34 [1986] 3–33) was critical of both Gottwald and Wilson.

76 (c) OTHER CONTRIBUTIONS. The emergence of the monarchy and associated institutions has been described from an anthropological perspective by J. Flanagan, in a series of important articles, e.g., *JAAR* 47 (1979) 223–44; *JSOT* 20 (1981) 47–73; see *Semeia* 37 (1986) on the monarchy. Also noteworthy is F. S. Frick, *The Formation of the State in Ancient Israel* (Sheffield, 1985). Like Wilson, a number of scholars have concentrated on the study of prophecy with the aid of the social sciences. In *The Roles of Israel's Prophets* (JSOTSup 17; Sheffield, 1981) D. L. Petersen raised questions about whether "ecstasy" (trance or possession behavior) is an appropriate designation for Israelite prophetic activity. While accepting the categories of peripheral and central prophets, he differed from Wilson in their application to OT prophetic figures. R. P. Carroll, in *When Prophecy Failed* (NY, 1979), brought the theory of cognitive dissonance (from the field of social psychology) to bear on the problem of unfulfilled and reinterpreted predictive prophecy in the OT. B. O. Long, M. Buss, and T. W. Overholt have contributed in social scientific investigations of OT prophecy.

(Kselman, J. S., "The Social World of the Israelite Prophets: A Review Article," *RelSRev* 11 [1985] 120–29. Lang, B. [ed.], *Anthropological Approaches to the Old Testament* [Phl, 1985]. Rogerson, J. W., *Anthropology and the Old Testament* [Atlanta, 1979]. Wilson, R. R., *Sociological Approaches to the Old Testament* [Phl, 1984]. Worgul, G. S., "Anthropological Consciousness and Biblical Theology," *BTB* 9 [1979] 3–12. *Semeia* 21 [1981] and *Int* 36 [1982] discuss the use of the social sciences in biblical interpretation.)

77   (E) Feminist OT Studies. In a review of the significant contemporary contributions by women to biblical studies, two approaches are possible. One approach would consider important examples of biblical interpretation produced by women. The other approach, chosen here, concentrates on work (by women and men) that demonstrates the feminist critique of bias in Bible and in biblical scholarship and on work that studies the Bible with a feminist hermeneutic. Not surprisingly, feminist interpretation of the OT uses such recent tools as rhetorical criticism and sociological and anthropological reconstruction of the community behind the biblical text. The hermeneutics of feminism (defined by Phyllis Trible as "a critique of culture in the light of misogyny") alerts us to the countercultural affirmations of the dignity and worth of women even within the assumed and mostly unexamined patriarchy of the biblical tradition. Thus, it has the negative function of exposing the androcentric bias or oppressive intent of the biblical text. But feminist hermeneutics has also the positive function of highlighting the countercultural elements in the tradition, for instance stories that reveal and celebrate the faith, courage, and talents of women. This retrieval of a liberating word for contemporary women in the Bible has been described as the "remnant" strategy. Despite its value, the question posed by feminist scholars is whether such a remnant of text honoring woman is enough to counter the Bible's prevailing androcentrism. In Mary Ann Tolbert's words, "Can feminists remain satisfied with the discovery of the occasional or exceptional in a patriarchal religion?" (*Semeia* 28 [1983] 124). Keeping this question in mind, we now turn to a survey of some of the important feminist contributions to OT study.

78   (a) P. TRIBLE. Employing rhetorical criticism and feminist hermeneutics, P. Trible has produced two important books dealing with the topic of female and male in the OT. In *God and the Rhetoric of Sexuality* (Phl, 1978) she examined such texts as Gen 2–3, the Song of Songs, and Ruth, texts that can speak an affirming and liberating word to women. Gen 2–3 confronts us with a critique of what we have become (a society that oppresses and excludes women, rendering them almost invisible in the biblical tradition) by what we were meant to be (a society of equality and mutuality of female and male). Gen 2–3 makes the point that what God intended was frustrated by human sin, but the preservation in the text of the divine will for equality makes possible the feminist critique of inequality. In the story of Ruth and Naomi we have two of the many "valiant women" in the biblical tradition. However, such stories of joy and celebration must be balanced dialectically with more somber tales of victimized women who endured cruelty and violence, women like Hagar (Gen 16 and 21), Tamar (2 Sam 13), an unnamed concubine (Judg 19), and Jephthah's daughter (Judg 11). Trible eloquently retold their stories in her second book, *Texts of Terror* (Phl, 1984).

79   (b) OTHER CONTRIBUTIONS. J. Cheryl Exum has brought rhetorical criticism to bear on such OT texts as Exod 1:8–2:10, where women act as saviors for the savior Moses (*Semeia* 28 [1983] 63–82). Carol M. Meyers in several important articles used the social sciences to extract a balanced view of women's status in a biblical corpus overwhelmingly patriarchal. She has shown how the results of modern archaeology combined with insights derived from anthropology and sociology can give us entrance into the community of ancient Israel and the possibility of considering the elusive, poorly documented roles and the experience of women in that society (e.g., *BA* 41 [1978] 91–103; *JAAR* 51 [1983] 569–93). Programmatic articles by these and other scholars can be found in the following collections: *JSOT* 22 (1982) 3–77; *Semeia* 28 (1983); Adela Yarbro Collins (ed.), *Feminist Perspectives on Biblical Scholarship* (Chico, 1985); Letty M. Russell (ed.), *Feminist Interpretation of the Bible* (Phl, 1985).

(Bird, P., "Images of Women in the Old Testament," *Religion and Sexism* [ed. R. R. Ruether; NY, 1974] 41–88. Brenner, A., *The Israelite Woman* [Sheffield, 1985]. Johnson, E. A., *TS* 45 [1984] 441–65. Miller, J. W., *CBQ* 48 [1986] 606–19 [a critique of Trible].)

80   (VII) Conclusion. More than 250 years have elapsed since the inauguration of modern biblical research. During this period, the most significant and enduring development was the emergence of the historical-critical method and its increasing application to the biblical material. The early use of historical criticism by 18th-cent. rationalists and deists often involved the denial of the supernatural order and the disparagement of the divine authority of the Bible. In the 19th cent., such towering figures as Vatke and Wellhausen continued and refined OT historical-critical method, introducing the optic of Hegelianism. Accordingly, historical criticism was seen as a threat to faith and was opposed by many in the churches. But from the beginning there were those who understood that the rationalism, deism, and Hegelianism of some of the early advocates of historical criticism were not inherent in the method. In their hands, the historical-critical study of the OT became a tool that could assist the believer in hearing the word of God in the Bible.

The 20th cent. was marked by the development of new methods—form criticism, tradition history, rhetorical criticism, canonical criticism, and several others—and by the light cast on the OT in its ancient Near Eastern context by archaeology. It was marked as well by the emergence of several generations of Roman Catholic biblical scholarship, accepted as a full participant and dialogue partner in the ecumenical task of biblical interpretation. The future holds the promise of continued cooperation by the women and men of the different biblical faiths, whose interpretive efforts will allow the OT to speak to coming generations in a way that is ever new.

70

MODERN NEW TESTAMENT CRITICISM

John S. Kselman, S.S.   Ronald D. Witherup, S.S. *

BIBLIOGRAPHY

1 Anderson, H., *Jesus and Christian Origins* (Oxford, 1964). *Bible de tous les temps* (8 vols.; Paris, 1984–). BHMCS. Boers, H., *What Is New Testament Theology?* (Phl, 1973). CHB. Collins, R. F., *Introduction to the New Testament* (GC, 1983). Doty, W. G., *Contemporary New Testament Interpretation* (EC, 1972). Furnish, V. P., "The Historical Criticism of the New Testament: A Survey of Origins," *BJRL* 56 (1974) 336–70. George, A. and P. Grelot (eds.), *Introduction à la Bible, Édition nouvelle* (Paris, 1976–). Grant, R. M. and D. Tracy, *A Short History of the Interpretation of the Bible* (2d ed.; Phl, 1984). Hasel, G., *New Testament Theology: Basic Issues in the Current Debate* (GR, 1978). Henry, P., *New Directions in New Testament Study* (Phl, 1979). Keegan, T. J., *Interpreting the Bible: A Popular Introduction to Biblical Hermeneutics* (NY, 1985). Kraus, H.-J., *Die biblische Theologie: Ihre Geschichte und Problematik* (Neukirchen, 1970).

Krentz, E., *The Historical-Critical Method* (Phl, 1975). Kümmel, W. G., *The New Testament: The History of the Investigation of Its Problems* (Nash, 1972). Marshall, I. H. (ed.), *New Testament Interpretation: Essays on Principles and Methods* (GR, 1977). Neill, S., *The Interpretation of the New Testament 1861–1986* (2d ed.; Oxford, 1988). NTMI. Noll, M. A., "Review Essay: The Bible in America," *JBL* 106 (1987) 493–509. Rohde, J., *Rediscovering the Teaching of the Evangelists* (Phl, 1968). Smalley, B., *The Study of the Bible in the Middle Ages* (Notre Dame, 1964). Soulen, R. N., *Handbook of Biblical Criticism* (2d ed.; Atlanta, 1981). Stuhlmacher, P., *Historical Criticism and Theological Interpretation of Scripture* (Phl, 1977). Wilder, A. N., "New Testament Studies, 1920–1950," *JR* 64 (1984) 432–51. For other pertinent bibliography, → Jesus, 78:1.

OUTLINE

* Article 41 by J. Kselman in *JBC* has been revised and brought up to date by R. D. Witherup, to whom all changes and additions are to be credited. Completely new material is found in sections 3, 13, 71–84.

(B) Early Catholic Reaction to Critical Study
(§ 36-38)
  (a) M.-J. Lagrange (§ 37)
  (b) A. Loisy (§ 38)
(C) History-of-Religions School (§ 39-41)
  (a) R. Reitzenstein (§ 40)
  (b) W. Bousset (§ 41)
(D) Birth of Form Criticism (§ 42-45)
  (a) K. L. Schmidt (§ 43)
  (b) M. Dibelius (§ 44)
(II) Criticism and Theology: The Work of Rudolf
Bultmann
(A) Bultmann the Form Critic (§ 49)
(B) Bultmann the Theologian (§ 50-52)
  (a) Demythologizing the NT (§ 51)
  (b) Bultmann on John (§ 52)
(III) Reactions to Bultmann
(A) Reaction of Conservative German Scholarship
(§ 55-58)
  (a) K. Barth (§ 56)
  (b) O. Cullmann (§ 57)
  (c) W. Pannenberg (§ 58)
(B) Reaction of British Scholarship (§ 59-63)

  (a) E. Hoskyns (§ 60)
  (b) V. Taylor (§ 61)
  (c) R. H. Lightfoot (§ 62)
  (d) C. H. Dodd (§ 63)
(C) Reaction from Bultmann's School: The Post-
Bultmannians (§ 64-70)
  (a) E. Käsemann (§ 65)
  (b) E. Fuchs (§ 66)
  (c) G. Bornkamm (§ 67)
  (d) H. Conzelmann (§ 68)
  (e) J. M. Robinson (§ 69)
  (f) G. Ebeling (§ 70)
(IV) Emergence of Catholic Critical Scholarship
(A) French (§ 73)
(B) Belgian (§ 74)
(C) German (§ 75)
(D) American (§ 76-77)
(V) Recent Developments in NT Scholarship
(A) Search for NT Communities (§ 79)
(B) Redaction Criticism (§ 80)
(C) Other Forms of Criticism (§ 81)
(D) The NT and Social Sciences (§ 82)
(E) Other Trends (§ 83-84)

PRECRITICISM TO THE NINETEENTH CENTURY

3   (I) Introduction. The application to the
NT of the principles of literary criticism (a study of the
content of the NT) and of historical criticism (a study of
the NT as a historical document) has a history that
ranges from the 2d cent. to the present.

(A) Precritical Period. Although criticism
of the Bible is a distinctly modern undertaking, there
were in the early church scholars who took the first steps
toward scientific study of the NT. The first major figure
was Marcion (*ca.* 150), a heretic who repudiated the OT
and Judaism and produced a truncated NT canon to conform to his teaching. By so doing, he moved the church
to counter his teaching by producing an orthodox NT
canon (→ Canonicity, 66:58, 81). Tatian (*ca.* 175), a
Syrian convert to Christianity, was another 2d-cent.
pioneer who made an attempt at criticism of the NT. His
Diatesseron was the first harmony of the four Gospels,
presented as a single, continuous narrative (→ Texts,
68:122-23).

The greatest ante-Nicene scholar in the church was
Origen (*ca.* 185-254), the head of the famous school of
Alexandria. He made two notable contributions to biblical studies. The first was his *Hexapla,* the earliest Christian attempt at textual criticism of the OT (→ Texts,
68:83). The second was his realization of the importance
of hermeneutics; although excessive, his allegorical
interpretation of the Scriptures was a serious endeavor
to make them relevant and meaningful to his contemporaries (→ Hermeneutics, 71:36; J. W. Trigg, *Origen:
The Bible and Philosophy in the Third-Century Church*
[Atlanta, 1983]).

The first church historian, Eusebius (*ca.* 260-340)
gave much valuable early information about the NT in
his *Ecclesiastical History* (324). He also divided the
Gospels into small numbered sections (still printed in
Nestle's Gk NT) and devised a set of tables to show
parallels between the various Gospels (H. K. McArthur,
CBQ 27 [1965] 250-56).

Augustine (354-430), the great theologian of the
west, laid down in his *De consensu evangelistarum* (400) the
principles that affected the treatment of Synoptic
differences for over a millennium; he was aware that the
order of the Gospel narratives sometimes reflects general

recollection rather than strict chronological history and
that the words of Jesus are often reported with an
accuracy that preserves only their sense, rather than
being given verbatim.

Although the Middle Ages, especially the great
scholastic period, contributed to the better understanding of Scripture (→ Hermeneutics, 71:39-40), the
contributions to real NT criticism were not major. (For
the critical implications of medieval lives of Jesus, see
H. K. McArthur, *The Quest Through the Centuries* [Phl,
1966] 57-84.)

In the 16th cent. the Reformation increased interest in
the Bible, especially in the Reformed churches, though
this interest was more dogmatic than critical. The most
significant figure was Martin Luther (1483-1546),
whose principle of *sola scriptura* became the hallmark of
Protestant biblical interpretation. Despite the polemical
tone of his works, Luther made a significant contribution to NT study. He emphasized the need to study the
Bible in the original languages and to pay careful attention to literary-historical details. Yet, because the Bible
was the medium through which one came to know
Christ, he believed that the Bible should not be
restricted to scholars but should be widely disseminated.
His translation of the Bible from the original languages
into German wielded great influence in his own day and
for centuries thereafter. Another important figure in this
period was A. Osiander (1498-1552), an early Lutheran
reformer, who published in 1537 a harmony of the
Gospels that set the style for Protestant harmonies of the
following centuries. His approach was much more rigid
than Augustine's, and for him minor differences in
sequence or detail meant different events (Kümmel, *New
Testament* 20-39).

**4   (B) Critical Studies before the Nineteenth
Century.** Against the background of rationalism and
the Enlightenment, the 18th cent. saw the rise of the
scientific method. When this method was applied to the
study of history, and particularly to biblical history, the
science of historical criticism of the Bible was born.

(a) R. SIMON. A French Oratorian priest,
Simon (1638-1712) was the first to apply the critical
method to the NT, in the three vols. of his *Histoire critique*

of the NT (1689–92; → OT Criticism, 69:6). J. D. Michaelis (1717–1791) built upon Simon's work to produce the first truly historical and critical introduction to the NT (1750). (→ OT Criticism, 69:12.)

(b) H. S. REIMARUS. As the German title (*Von Reimarus zu Wrede*) of A. Schweitzer's *The Quest of the Historical Jesus* indicates, Reimarus (1694–1768) is a key figure in the history of NT criticism. In 1778 excerpts from his *Von dem Zweck Jesu und seinen Jünger* (*On the Intention of Jesus and His Disciples*) were published posthumously. In this work Reimarus distinguished between the historical Jesus (a Jewish revolutionary who failed in an attempt to establish an earthly messianic kingdom) and the Christ found in the Gospels and preached by the church (a deception created by the disciples who stole the body of Jesus from the tomb and invented the doctrines of the resurrection and parousia). Although prejudiced by rationalism's rejection of the supernatural, Reimarus was the first to try to pierce through the christological dogma of the Gospels to the real historical Jesus, a concern that lost none of its urgency in the 20th cent. See C. H. Talbert (ed.), *Reimarus: Fragments* (Phl, 1970).

5 (II) Birth of Nineteenth-Century Criticism. Starting from the work of their predecessors, the scholars of the 19th cent. continued the study of the NT, pursuing two directions: critically, they were concerned with the question of the historical value of the NT; theologically, they were concerned with its meaning. These two directions shaped the subsequent history of NT criticism.

(A) Tübingen School. Few schools have been so influential in NT interpretations as that which took its name from the University of Tübingen. The questions formulated by the leaders of the Tübingen School and the fundamental insights they provided have been determinative for all later NT criticism. (H. Harris, *The Tübingen School* [Oxford, 1975].)

6 (a) D. STRAUSS. In 1835, Strauss (1808–1874), a student of F. C. Baur, published his *Life of Jesus,* a radical interpretation of the Gospel accounts of Jesus. Previous lives of Christ had been either orthodox interpretations accepting the intervention of the supernatural into human history or rationalist explanations of only apparently supernatural happenings. Strauss added a third alternative, the mythical interpretation: the Gospels give us a basis of historical fact transformed and embellished by the faith of the church. Strauss ended his work by confessing the impossibility of writing a life of Jesus, both because the Gospels refuse to see Jesus simply as a part of history and because the Gospels give us only unconnected fragments, the order being imposed by the evangelists. (R. S. Cromwell, *David Friedrich Strauss and His Place in Modern Thought* [Fairlawn, 1974]; H. Harris, *David Friedrich Strauss and His Theology* [Cambridge, 1973].)

Strauss's work profoundly influenced two other 19th-cent. writers. B. Bauer (1809–1882) removed what historical foundation Strauss had allowed and left only myth, concluding that Jesus and Paul were nonhistorical literary fictions. E. Renan (1823–1892), in his *Life of Jesus* (1863), equated supernatural with unreal and gave his readers a purely human Jesus.

7 (b) F. C. BAUR. One of the most important NT scholars of the 19th cent. and the teacher of Strauss was Baur (1792–1860), undoubtedly the uncontested head of the Tübingen School. Although few of the solutions he proposed are accepted today, the questions he asked are of enduring significance, and he raised NT criticism to a truly scientific level.

According to Baur's Hegelian view, the history of Christianity from *ca.* AD 40 to 160 was one of tension, struggle, and eventual reconciliation. The struggle was between *Pauline libertarianism,* with its message of freedom from the law and the universality of the church's mission, and narrow *Judaic legalism,* represented by the primitive apostles led by Peter, with its insistence on the supposed prerogatives of Judaism. From this thesis–antithesis came the Catholic church and the NT canon, which smoothed away differences by putting Peter and Paul on equal footing, a process we can see in Acts. This synthesis came in the 2d cent. as a result of the gradual cooling of hostilities and the emergent common threat of gnosticism.

The effect of Baur's hypotheses on the formation and dating of the NT was far-reaching. Before 70 only Paul's "authentic" epistles existed (Rom, 1–2 Cor, Gal). The Judaism of Matt was an argument for its priority; the Paulinism of Luke vs. the Judaism of Matt produced Mark as a synthesis; Acts and John were to be dated in the middle of the 2d cent.

The strict application of Hegelian principles and the overemphasis of the influence of Judaism in early Christianity were obvious defects in Baur's work. But the contributions he made to NT studies were estimable. First and most important, he studied the NT as part of the history of Christianity, showing it to be the product of the history of the early church and a witness to the spirit of a definite age. Second, this same historical acumen led him to see that the study of the NT must begin with the earliest evidence, the writings of Paul. Third, he gave deserved prominence to Paul and his theology. Finally, he made a clear distinction between the Synoptic Gospels and John. (P. C. Hodgson, *The Formation of Historical Theology* [NY, 1966]; R. Morgan, *ExpTim* 90 [1978] 4–10.)

8 (B) Reaction to Tübingen. After the critical work of Strauss and Baur there seemed to be only two alternatives: either a naïve sacralization of the Bible and a fundamentalist refusal to subject it to critical study, or an acceptance of German criticism, which seemed to spell the destruction of orthodox Christianity. The task of NT scholarship in the second half of the 19th cent. was to present another alternative: an acceptance of the historical-critical method, but without Baur's presuppositions and conclusions. In England, this task fell to the Cambridge Three; in Germany, to A. von Harnack.

The answer of the three great Cambridge scholars was to attempt a critical commentary on the whole NT, a commentary that was historically and philologically accurate, set against the background of its own era and based on a critically edited Gk NT. Although this proposed commentary was never completed, it would be difficult to overvalue the legacy the Cambridge Three left NT scholarship. (P. C. N. Conder, *Theology* 77 [1974] 422–31; Neill, *Interpretation* 33–76; G. A. Patrick, *ExpTim* 90 [1978] 77–81.)

9 (a) J. B. LIGHTFOOT. Realizing like Baur that a critical study of the NT must begin with Paul, Lightfoot (1828–1889) set himself first to a series of commentaries on the epistles of Paul, of which he completed his commentaries on Gal (1865), Phil (1868), and Col and Phlm (1875). Lightfoot's work on Paul made him acutely aware of the problem of the dating of the NT. Critical NT scholarship had largely accepted the late dates that Baur assigned to the books of the NT. But the Tübingen theories would collapse if one could establish an early date for a body of post-NT literature. Lightfoot found such a starting point in the letters of Ignatius of Antioch and the epistle of Clement of Rome, literature that alludes to most NT books. The results of his labor on Ignatius appeared in 1885, and his edition of Clement was published posthumously in 1890. Because of Lightfoot's careful historical investigation, the date of the epistle of Clement was set at the end of the 1st cent., and the seven authentic letters of Ignatius were assigned to the early 2d cent. Besides giving a fixed point of time from which we can date the NT, this literature gives us a picture of the life of the church in the late 1st and early 2d cent. AD in three great church centers, Antioch, Ephesus (Ignatius), and Rome (Clement). And rather than giving any indication of prolonged and bitter conflict between a Pauline and a Petrine party, both Ignatius and Clement link the names of the two great apostles, a practice which, according to Baur, did not occur until the middle of the 2d cent. (B. N. Kaye, *NovT* 26 [1984] 193–224.)

10 (b) B. F. WESTCOTT. The real exegete of the three was Westcott (1825–1901). His commentary on the Gospel of John, an outstanding blend of criticism and theology, first published in 1880, was republished as recently as 1958. Also *Epistles of St. John* (repub. 1966).

11 (c) F. J. A. HORT. Of the few works Hort (1828–1892) published, two books on the history of the early church are especially noteworthy: *Judaistic Christianity* (1894) and *The Christian Ecclesia* (1897). To the proposed commentary he added only his work on 1 Pet 1:1–2:17 (1898).

However, it is not on the above works that the fame of Westcott and Hort rests but on the great critical edition of the Gk NT that they prepared (→ Texts, 68:167). Previously, NT study had had to rely on the *textus receptus,* substantially the 16th-cent. text of Erasmus, printed in 1516 and based on inadequate ms. evidence (→ Texts 68:160–61). Having formulated a genuinely scientific method of textual criticism, Westcott and Hort published in 1881 the critical text of the NT, with an important introduction on the science of textual criticism.

12 (d) A. VON HARNACK. Perhaps the greatest Protestant theologian of the 19th cent., Harnack (1851–1930) was a universal scholar, proficient in biblical studies, patristics, church history, and systematic theology. Like Baur, Harnack came to the NT documents as a historian of the early church. Unlike Baur, he challenged the new orthodoxy of Tübingen with the cry of "Back to tradition!" This was not a call for the abandonment of historical-critical methods nor a naïve acceptance of the NT merely on the authority of earlier ages in the church. On the contrary, with expert use of the critical method, Harnack examined the evidence and concluded that Baur had rejected overhastily and uncritically the traditional views regarding the origin and growth of the NT.

An illustration of Harnack's method would be his great trilogy on the Lucan writings: *Luke the Physician* (1906), *The Acts of the Apostles* (1908), and *The Date of the Acts and of the Synoptic Gospels* (1911). In these works, Harnack's critical study upheld the traditional view that the author was Luke, companion of Paul, a position that had for 60 years been abandoned because of Baur's criticism. Harnack's most famous work is not one of his many critical studies but a series of popular lectures, published as *What Is Christianity?* (1900), the classical exposition of liberal Protestantism. According to Harnack, the essence of Christianity lay in certain ethical truths preached by Jesus: the fatherhood of God, the brotherhood of humanity, the infinite value of the human soul. It was this position that Schweitzer would attack, with his claim that Jesus preached not a set of timeless principles but the imminent end of his world order. (G. W. Glick, *The Reality of Christianity* [NY, 1967]; R. H. Hiers, *Jesus and Ethics* [Phl, 1968] 11–38.)

13 (e) A. SCHLATTER. A difficult figure to categorize, Schlatter (1852–1938) was influenced by Harnack and by the issues raised by the Tübingen School; yet his approach to the NT represented a unique and independent style. He was at home in both dogmatic and biblical studies. Although his approach was considered conservative for the time, some of his work anticipated later scholarly developments. E.g., his commentary on Matt (*Der Evangelist Matthäus* [1929]) is considered to be most significant despite the fact that it holds to Matthean priority. His frequent reference in the commentary to "the evangelist" demonstrated his awareness of the editorial role of the evangelists in advance of the development of redaction criticism. His understanding of the importance of history in biblical study, his exceptionally broad background in both NT and OT, and his insistence that the Bible leads one to personal faith are all contributions which explain Schlatter's enduring appeal and the continued availability of his works in print: e.g., *Die Geschichte des Christus* (1923), *Die Theologie der Apostel* (1922 — both originally as a one-vol. work, *Die Theologie des Neuen Testaments* [1909/10]), and *Gottes Gerechtigkeit* (1935). (G. Egg, *Adolf Schlatters kritische Position* [Stuttgart, 1968]; P. Stuhlmacher, *NTS* 24 [1978] 433–46.)

THE TRANSITION TO THE TWENTIETH CENTURY

14 (I) Studies in Language and Background. Starting with the insights of Baur and throughout the works of Harnack and the Cambridge Three, the theological question of the religious meaning of the NT loomed ever larger. But before this question could be adequately dealt with, the more prosaic study of the language and background of the NT had to progress.

(A) Language of the NT. In a lecture delivered in 1863, Lightfoot stated that if we could recover letters reflecting the way in which ordinary people of the 1st cent. spoke and wrote, our understanding of the language of the NT would be immeasurably increased. Lightfoot's surmise was prophetic — ancient mss. and papyri, discovered in the second half of the 19th cent., have been of immense benefit.

15 (a) C. VON TISCHENDORF. In 1859, Tischendorf (1815–1874) made one of the most important finds in the history of biblical studies. In a monastery on Mt. Sinai he discovered one of the two oldest biblical mss. we possess, the Codex Sinaiticus, including the complete NT (→ Texts, 68:95, 157). Tischendorf's contribution to the study of the text of the NT ranks in importance with that of Westcott and Hort.

16 (b) (G.) A. DEISSMANN. Late in the 19th cent. papyri were being found in increasing numbers in Egypt, where the dry climate preserved them. These papyri were mostly popular documents — letters, bills, receipts — exactly the sort of material that Lightfoot had spoken of. The documents were written in koine, the common form of the Gk language spoken in NT times.

The pioneer in applying to the NT the new knowledge gained from such discoveries was Deissmann (1866–1937). The subtitle of his *Bible Studies* (Ger 1895; Eng 1901) is a good summary of his work: *Contributions Chiefly from Papyri and Inscriptions to the History of the Language, the Literature, and the Religion of Hellenistic Judaism and Primitive Christianity.* This book was followed by another with the same aim, *Light from the Ancient East* (1908; → NT Epistles, 45:4).

17   (B) Background of the NT. In addition to progress in linguistic studies, NT study profited in this transitional period from the continuing growth of our knowledge of the world from which the NT came, its history, its geography, its government, its religion, its thought forms and literary forms — in short, all those *varia* classified under the rubric of background.

18   (a) E. HATCH. The name of Hatch (1835–1889) will forever be linked with that of H. A. Redpath with whom he produced a monumental concordance to the LXX, published in 1897. But our concern here is with a lesser-known book published in 1889 (and reissued in 1957), whose importance was immediately recognized by Harnack. In this work, titled *The Influence of Greek Ideas on Christianity,* Hatch examined a subject of continuing interest to NT scholars: the question of the interaction of Christianity and its Hellenistic environment and of the distinction between the Semitic and Hellenistic elements in Christian faith and thought. The relevance of this subject can be seen in the impact it made on the history-of-religions school, one of the decisive influences on the thought of R. Bultmann.

19   (b) R. H. CHARLES. Apocalyptic is a literary form somewhat alien to the modern world; but an understanding of it is absolutely necessary for the interpretation of the NT, which came from a world permeated with Jewish apocalyptic thought forms and literature. Charles (1855–1931) was the great student of apocalyptic literature and of Jewish apocryphal literature in particular. He was the editor of and a major contributor to the 2 vols. of *The Apocrypha and Pseudepigrapha of the Old Testament in English* (1913). Charles put his extensive knowledge of apocalyptic to good use when in 1920 he produced for the ICC his important 2-vol. commentary on Rev.

20   (c) W. M. RAMSAY. Archaeologist, historian, and indefatigable explorer of Asia Minor, the early seat of Christianity, Ramsay (1851–1939) is best known for two important books, *St. Paul the Traveller and the Roman Citizen* (1895) and *The Cities of St. Paul* (1907), in which he treats of the historical, political, and geographical background of Acts. Although Ramsay had been skeptical about the historical value of Acts, his historical and archaeological study of Asia Minor as Paul knew and traveled it convinced him of the accuracy and reliability of Luke as a contemporary historian — in the light of archaeological evidence the Lucan writings truly reflect the conditions of the second half of the 1st cent. Ramsay's studies of Paul and the Greco-Roman world in which he moved did much to recreate for us the apostle as a living man. Less well known but significant for the study of Rev is his book *Letters to the Seven Churches of Asia* (1904), which emphasized the importance of the imperial cult as the background for the persecution of the church in proconsular Asia and the influence of historical geography on the picture of the seven churches of Rev 2–3. See W. W. Gasque, *Sir William M. Ramsay* (GR, 1966).

21   (II) Synoptic Gospels: Criticism and Development. There were two interrelated, crucial problems in NT interpretation that the 19th cent. did not adequately consider: the Synoptic question and the

questions connected with the NT accounts of the life and death of Jesus Christ. Both subjects were to engage the attention of 20th-cent. scholars.

(A) The Priority of Mark and the Two-Source Theory. Mark had long been the least examined of the four Gospels in the history of NT interpretation. Augustine had looked upon it as an abbreviation of Matt. In the 19th cent., in response to Strauss's attack on the historical foundation of Christianity, students of the NT began to turn to Mark in an attempt to preserve Christianity as a historical religion, based on a historical figure, Jesus of Nazareth. The historical-critical method was used as an instrument to discover the sources that underlay the NT accounts of Jesus. Important preparation for this quest was the work of J. J. Griesbach (1745–1812), who recognized the difference between John and the first three Gospels. He saw the possibility of arranging Matt, Mark, and Luke in a synopsis, and the impossibility of constructing a harmony, since the evangelists were in all likelihood not concerned with chronological order.

22   (a) K. LACHMANN. A real advance came in 1835, when Lachmann (1793–1851) published "De ordine narrationum in evangeliis synopticis," in which he proposed the literary priority of Mark and claimed that it was closer to the original tradition than the other Gospels, thereby establishing Mark as a basic source for any attempt to get back to the origins of Christianity.

23   (b) C. H. WEISSE. In 1838, Weisse (1801–1866) furthered Lachmann's hypothesis by adding another source, a sayings source common to Matt and Luke (which would eventually be termed the Q source). Thus, by 1838 the main lines of the classic "Two-Source theory" had been proposed (→ Synoptic Problem, 40:12–13).

24   (B) Scientific Source Criticism. Lachmann and Weisse had proceeded by insight. The next task of NT criticism would be to test their theories scientifically.

(a) H. J. HOLTZMANN. In 1863, Holtzmann (1832–1910) published the results of his painstaking study to verify scientifically the Two-Source theory, *Die synoptischen Evangelien.* He concluded that Mark was the original apostolic document and that behind Matt and Luke lay another written document, a very early collection of the sayings and teachings of Jesus, including probably some narratives (e.g., the baptism and temptation accounts).

25   (b) B. H. STREETER. We now turn to the 20th cent. and to the scholar who gave source criticism its classic exposition. Streeter (1874–1937) had two advantages in his work: Westcott and Hort's edition of the NT and the work of Holtzmann. Against a background of nearly universal acceptance of the Two-Source hypothesis, Streeter proposed a refinement of this theory in *The Four Gospels: A Study of Origins* (1924). He theorized thus: If Rome had a cycle of traditions about Jesus enshrined in Mark, written *ca.* 65–70, would it not be likely that the three other great Christian centers of the 1st cent. would also have such local traditions? Working from this hypothesis, Streeter assigned Q (*ca.* 50) to Antioch; the material peculiar to Luke (*ca.* 60) had its origin in Caesarea; and Jerusalem was the home of Matthean special tradition (*ca.* 65). On this basis, Streeter dated Luke in its final form to *ca.* 80, and Matt to *ca.* 85.

Streeter's important contribution was a demonstration that four sources, rather than two, underlie the Synoptic Gospels. What is questionable is his concept of four written documents. Scholars today would tend to speak of cycles of oral tradition rather than of written documents. Streeter's work was the final word on source criticism in two senses, for by the time he had published his book, scholars were turning their attention from source criticism to form criticism. (*ExpTim* 72 [1960-61] 295-99.)

26   (C) Gospel Origins: The Aramaic Question. The interaction of Semitic and Greek influences in the NT is a subject that has continued to hold the attention of critics. Perhaps the greatest indication of this perennial interest is the NT commentary prepared by H. L. Strack and P. Billerbeck from rabbinic sources, the five-vol. *Kommentar zum Neuen Testament aus Talmud und Midrasch* (1922-61); also J. Bonsirven, *Textes rabbiniques des deux premiers siècles chrétiens pour servir à l'intelligence du Nouveau Testament* (Rome, 1955); W. D. Davies, *Paul and Rabbinic Judaism* (2d ed.; London, 1955); and E. P. Sanders, *Paul and Palestinian Judaism* (Phl, 1977).

27   (a) G. DALMAN. Beneath the Greek of the Gospels, source criticism detected much that was of Aram character. The trailblazer in this area was Dalman (1855-1941), a great Aram scholar, representative of the conservative or minimal position regarding Aram influence in the NT. His most important book was *The Words of Jesus* (Ger 1898; Eng 1902). Although the hypothesis of an Aram original underlying the Synoptic tradition was not impossible, Dalman established that Jesus indubitably spoke Aramaic to his disciples; the words of Jesus, as recorded in the Gospels, definitely show Aram influence.

28   (b) C. C. TORREY. The maximal theory of Aram origins found an able defender in Torrey (1863-1956). In two works, *The Four Gospels* (1933) and *Our Translated Gospels* (1936), he argued that the Gospels were transls. of primitive Aram writings. His thesis failed to convince the body of NT scholars.

29   (c) C. F. BURNEY. Burney (1868-1925) focused attention particularly on John, supposedly the most Hellenized Gospel, and did NT studies the service of pointing up its Semitic qualities in *The Aramaic Origin of the Fourth Gospel* (1922). A maximalist like Torrey, he held that John was a transl. of an Aram original.

30   (d) J. JEREMIAS. A student of Dalman, Jeremias (1900-1979) demonstrated the importance of Aramaic as a NT tool in *The Parables of Jesus* (Ger 1947; Eng 1954) and *The Eucharistic Words of Jesus* (Ger 1949; Eng 1955). In both works Jeremias attempted to recover the "ipsissima verba Christi" by reconstructing from the Gk accounts of the primitive church the original Aramaic spoken by Jesus.

31   (e) M. BLACK. In 1946 there appeared his important survey *An Aramaic Approach to the Gospels and Acts* (3d ed., 1967). Black's mediate position modified the extremes of Torrey and Burney: Since Aramaisms are strongest and most frequent in the words of Jesus, an Aram sayings source, oral or written, underlies the Synoptic tradition. Further work by G. Vermes and esp. by J. A. Fitzmyer (*ESBNT, TAG, WA*) has made scholars more cautious about using the Jewish Aramaic of later documents as evidence for the Aramaic of Jesus' time. For a survey up to Black, see S. Brown, *CBQ* 26 (1964) 323-39.

TWENTIETH-CENTURY CRITICISM

32   (I) New Directions. The heritage from the 19th cent. gave a multifaceted aspect to studies in the 20th cent., but historical problems arising from the NT accounts of Jesus remained dominant. To what degree did the early church's confession color or shape the presentation of Jesus? The answer given to this historical question obviously affects the theological meaning and import assigned to the accounts. Form criticism's quest for the "gospel behind the Gospels" was one response of 20th-cent. criticism.

A by-product was that theology came into its own, as indicated by the theological dictionary (*TWNT, TDNT*) begun in 1932 under the editorship of G. Kittel (1888-1948), with every important German NT scholar among its contributors. Although the articles are of uneven quality, the work proved to be one of the great NT theological contributions of the century. (See the 1-vol. abridgment [GR, 1985].) To understand further the alliance of criticism and theology, we begin with some of the prophetic voices raised at the beginning of the century.

33   (A) Abandonment of the Liberal Quest of the Historical Jesus. Strauss's attempt to write a life of Jesus was, by his own admission, a failure, as in his opinion any such attempt must be, in view of the nature of the sources. In an analogy later to be elaborated upon by the form-critical school, Strauss believed that the pericopes, the individual stories and sayings of which our Gospels are composed, are, like a necklace of pearls without a string, fragments that had received an artificial order from the evangelists.

Such skepticism seemed unwarranted later in the 19th cent. First, the discovery and scientific establishment of the Two-Source theory seemed to make available two sources, Mark and Q, which stood very close to the original apostolic tradition. Second, the liberal school, under the leadership of Harnack, believed that, with the use of the historical-critical method, one could cut away the christological dogma that Reimarus had called attention to in the Gospels and get to the historical Jesus behind the Christ of faith proclaimed in the NT. Consequently, the last half of the 19th cent. saw the production of a spate of lives of Jesus based on the established facts of 19th-cent. criticism: two primitive sources that could be stripped of their dogmatic trappings.

34   (a) W. WREDE. The first serious challenge to this presumed factuality came from a 1901 classic by Wrede (1859-1906), *Das Messiasgeheimnis in den Evangelien* (*The Messianic Secret* [Greenwood, SC, 1971]). Using the same critical method employed by the liberals, he demonstrated the unscientific character of the picture of Jesus that they had constructed. He contended further that Mark, like the other Gospels, was not a simple biography but a profound theological interpretation of the meaning of Jesus. Literally from the opening words of his Gospel, the evangelist shows us not a human but a completely divine Jesus. Wrede's thesis on the messiahship runs thus: The historical Jesus never made any claim to be the Messiah. Only after the resurrection did the disciples realize that Jesus was the Christ. They then read back messiahship into the earthly life of Jesus and created the "messianic secret" (Jesus' concealment of his messiahship) to account for the fact that his messiahship was unknown to them and to the Jews at large before his death. The messianic secret was therefore a tradition created by the early Christian community and taken over by Mark, who wrote not as an objective historian but from the viewpoint of Christian faith. Wrede thus dealt the first blow to the liberals' optimistic quest for the Jesus of history. The *coup de grâce* would be administered a few years later by Schweitzer. See J. L. Blevins, *The Messianic Secret in Markan Research 1901-1976* (Washington, 1981); also Boers, *What* 45-60.

35   (b) A. SCHWEITZER. In 1901, Schweitzer (1875-1965) too published a study on the messianic secret entitled *Das Messianitäts- und Leidensgeheimnis* (Eng 1914: *The Mystery of the Kingdom of God*) in which he defended the historicity of the messianic secret, claiming that it was not a creation of the church but a conviction of Jesus. But his most memorable work was *The Quest of the Historical Jesus* (Ger 1906; Eng 1910), an exhaustive survey of the life-of-Jesus research from Reimarus to Wrede. After incisive criticism of the liberal portrait of Jesus, the ethical teacher so attractively presented by Harnack in *What Is Christianity?*, Schweitzer reconstructed what he considered to be the true picture of the historical Jesus. Following the guidelines that J. Weiss proposed in *Jesus' Proclamation of the Kingdom of God* (Ger 1892; Phl, 1971), Schweitzer stressed the eschatological, apocalyptic element in the life and teaching of Jesus, who was a heroic figure, a noble but deluded fanatic convinced that he was the Messiah. He preached an apocalyptic message of the imminent end of the world and went to his death to bring it about.

Although few would accept Schweitzer's reconstruction of the historical Jesus, there is general agreement that his work sounded the death knell for the liberal quest for the Jesus of history and that it pointed up the importance of the apocalyptic background and framework of the teaching of Jesus. (See D. E. Nineham in *Explorations in Theology* 1 [London, 1977] 112-33; L. H. Silberman, *JAAR* 44 [1976] 498-501.)

36   **(B) Early Catholic Reaction to Critical Study.** Up until the 20th cent., biblical criticism had almost no impact on Catholic studies; the critical tradition that had produced Strauss and Baur was looked upon with suspicion. Indifference at best and even overt hostility were the characteristically defensive postures assumed by all but a few pioneers. (Indeed, it was only with Pius XII's encyclical *DAS* in 1943 that Roman Catholic biblicists could begin to take their place in the vanguard of serious NT study; → Church Pronouncements, 72:20-23.)

37   (a) M.-J. LAGRANGE. The greatest of the pioneers in Catholic biblical studies was the Dominican Lagrange (1855-1938; → OT Criticism, 69:35). He had become aware of German critical study while a student of Oriental languages at the University of Vienna. In 1890, with almost no material or financial support, Lagrange founded in Jerusalem the École pratique d'études bibliques (more familiarly known as the École Biblique). The principal aim of the École was to promote study of the Bible not only as the inspired word of God but also as a literary work that could be examined with the aid of the historical-critical method developed in the 19th cent. In 1892 Lagrange founded the *Revue biblique*, the first prominent Catholic journal of biblical studies. In 1902 he launched the *Études bibliques*, a series of biblical commentaries both doctrinal and scientific. In summary, Lagrange's outstanding achievement was that he moved Catholic studies into a field where Protestant scholarship, sometimes rationalistic and skeptical, had dominated, and in so doing he demonstrated that the use of the historical-critical method was not necessarily contrary to faith. See M.-J. Lagrange, *Père Lagrange: Personal Reflections and Memoirs* (NY, 1983); also H. Wansbrough, *ClR* 62 (1977) 446-52.

38   (b) A. LOISY. Another major scholar, whose career unfortunately ended in Modernism, Loisy (1857-1940) was a gifted philologist and exegete. He was an outstanding teacher of Scripture at the Institut Catholique in Paris from 1884 to 1893. He wrote his doctoral dissertation, which he completed in 1890 and in which the impact of criticism could be felt, on the history of the OT canon. Loisy accepted in his work the principles and conclusions of the critical school and soon began to lean toward the hypercritical and skeptical wing of that school. His association with Modernism and consequent clashes with ecclesiastical authority eventually led to his excommunication in 1908. Loisy brought suspicion even on orthodox scholars and loyal churchmen like Lagrange.

Loisy's most important work was *L'Évangile et L'Église* (1902; *The Gospel and the Church* [Phl, 1976]), his answer to Harnack's *What Is Christianity?* In that book Harnack had proposed that, since the essence of Christianity was the interior and individual realization of God in the human soul, Christianity had no need for a church; indeed, a church could become an obstacle to and deformation of genuine Christianity. Against this position Loisy defended the church as an organization that truly mediates God to humanity, but he denied that the church was founded by Christ in the form it later assumed. Although the church developed according to the designs of God, Jesus could never have foreseen what it would become. Loisy developed these ideas further in two later works, *Le Quatrième Évangile* (1903) and *Les Évangiles Synoptiques* (1908), wherein he dissociated the historical Jesus, unconscious of his divinity, and the Christ of faith, and saw the early Christian community as a screen between believer and event. (B. Reardon, *Liberalism and Tradition* [Cambridge, 1975] 249-81.)

39   **(C) History-of-Religions School.** This school (*Religionsgeschichtliche Schule*) applied the principles of comparative religion and saw Christianity as one religious phenomenon among many in the Roman Empire. Parallels like ritual washings, sacred meals, the worship of a dying and rising god, and certainty of eternal life through union with the god suggested a gradual process of syncretism and mutual interpenetration of Christianity and the popular mystery religions from the East. The history-of-religions approach marked NT interpretation especially through the influence it exerted on Bultmann and his school. (K. Müller, *BZ* 29 [1985] 161-92; Neill, *Interpretation* 157-90.)

40   (a) R. REITZENSTEIN. One of the key doctrines of *Religionsgeschichte* found an important expositor in Reitzenstein (1861-1931). In *Die hellenistischen Mysterienreligionen* (1910; *The Hellenistic Mystery Religions* [Pittsburgh, 1978]) Reitzenstein traced this supposed hellenizing process through early Christian history and offered three conclusions affecting NT study: (1) that Hellenistic and Eastern religion exercised a profound influence on NT theology, especially on that of Paul; (2) that the early church's proclamation and cult depended on the mystery religions and gnosticism; (3) that early Christianity's idea of redemption by the death and resurrection of Christ was borrowed from a pre-Christian gnostic redeemer myth.

41   (b) W. BOUSSET. The most influential scholar of the history-of-religions school was undoubtedly Bousset (1865-1920). His great work was *Kyrios Christos* (1913; Eng: Nash, 1970), a sketch of the development of Christian thought up to Irenaeus. Bousset recognized the importance of worship in the early church. According to Bousset, Paul or his successors transformed primitive Christianity into a mystery cult. Many of the early Christian groups in the Hellenistic world had been mystery fellowships, which now simply worshiped a new god, Jesus, as *Kyrios,* a title commonly given to the god-hero in the cult and ritual of the mysteries.

Because of their influence on the Bultmannian school, we shall summarize here the fundamental theses of the *Religionsgeschichtliche Schule.* (1) We have already mentioned the hypothesis of a redeemer myth found in a supposed pre-Christian form of gnosticism. (2) There is posited a distinctly Gentile form of Christianity (*Heidenchristentum*) independent of the traditions of the Jewish church and syncretistically influenced by non-Christian religious groups with which they came in contact. (3) Even in the NT canon one can find evidence of "early Catholicism" (*Frühkatholizismus*), the development of an institutional church as an outward and visible mediator of salvation (*Heilsanstalt*), a process that is viewed as a deformation of genuine Pauline Christianity. (Boers, *What* 60–66.)

42   **(D)   Birth of Form Criticism.**   Source criticism was the signal achievement of 19th-cent. NT study. Among its important contributions were the establishment of the priority of Mark, the identification of Q, and the use of these sources in Matt and Luke. Beyond this, however, source criticism could not go, for by definition it was confined to the study of the documents at hand. Twentieth-century criticism posed a further question: Can we get behind the written documents to the period between the events and the first written records (*ca.* AD 30–60), when the stories of the words and works of Jesus circulated in Aramaic?

This is the aim of form criticism (or *Formgeschichte* = form history), which attempts to investigate and analyze the origin and history of the preliterary, oral tradition behind our written Gospels. The premise is that the Gospels are composed of many smaller pericopes that circulated as separate units in early Christian communities before the Gospels were written. Form criticism is concerned with the forms or patterns of these stories and sayings and the reasons for their preservation in the Gospels. The original impetus for this study came from the great OT scholar H. Gunkel, who had developed techniques in OT interpretation by which he tried to establish the underlying oral traditions behind the documents and the *Sitz im Leben* (life situation) of these traditions (→ OT Criticism, 69:38). New Testament form criticism developed Gunkel's insight, and we may distinguish three levels in the formation and preservation of the Gospel material. (1) The *Sitz im Leben Jesu* (the situation in the life of Jesus) is the context and meaning of an individual story or saying in the earthly life of Jesus whenever such a context is recoverable. (2) The *Sitz im Leben der Kirche* (the situation in the life of the church) is the situation or context of a particular story or saying of Jesus in the life of the early church. What prompted the early community to preserve this particular reminiscence from the life of Jesus and what meaning did the community give to it? (3) The *Sitz im Evangelium* (the situation in the Gospel) is the context of a saying or story of the Lord in the Gospel itself. What did the evangelist mean to teach by recording this particular event in this particular setting? This latter question marks a transition from *Formgeschichte* to *Redaktionsgeschichte* (→ Hermeneutics, 71:28; also → 80 below; E. V. McKnight, *What Is Form Criticism?* [Phl, 1969]).

43   **(a) K. L. Schmidt.**   The form-critical era began in 1919 with the publication by Schmidt (1891–1956) of *Der Rahmen der Geschichte Jesu* (*The Framework of the History of Jesus*). Schmidt's contention was that the Synoptic Gospels were mosaiclike collections of short episodes from the life of Jesus, which had circulated as independent units in the period of oral transmission and

few of which had any indication of time or place of origin. (The one important exception was the passion narrative, which seemed to have existed very early as a continuous, coherent narrative.) Mark supplied a framework of connecting links and "bridge passages" (*Sammelberichte,* generalizing summaries like 1:14–15, 21–22; 2:13, etc.) for these separate, self-contained units. This framework is a product of Marcan theological concerns rather than a picture of the life of Jesus. In form-critical terminology Mark reflects not the *Sitz im Leben Jesu* but more the *Sitz im Leben der Kirche* and the *Sitz im Evangelium.* The early Christian community for which and in which Mark wrote his Gospel preserved and adapted stories relevant for its life, its worship, its pastoral and missionary concerns.

44   **(b) M. Dibelius.**   The year 1919 also saw the publication by Dibelius (1883–1947) of *Die Formgeschichte des Evangeliums* (*From Tradition to Gospel* [rev. ed.; NY, 1965]). Dibelius's starting point was that the missionary activity and needs of the early church were instrumental in shaping the early tradition. In his discussion of the tradition, he advanced two principles that were accepted as axiomatic by later form critics: (1) that the Synoptic Gospels were not literary works in the strict sense of the word but *Kleinliteratur,* literature designed for popular consumption; (2) that the Synoptic evangelists were not true authors but rather compilers of preexisting material. (The first principle has been nuanced by more subtle literary criticism; the second has been challenged by redaction criticism; → 80 below.)

45   The last figure in the great triumvirate of early form critics was R. Bultmann, whose form-critical study of the Synoptic tradition will be discussed below (→ 49). For convenience, however, we shall summarize here the principles on which form criticism generally operates. As was mentioned, the form critics posit a period of oral transmission before the written Gospels, during which time the stories and sayings of the tradition circulated as separate units. These separate units can be discovered in the Gospels and can be classified according to their literary form. The determinative factor in their preservation was to be found in the needs and interests of the Christian community. Such traditions have little historical value. The form critics assumed further that the early Christians were not at all interested in history. Thus, the Gospels are not biographies, giving us a consistent historical picture of the life of Jesus, but reflections of the faith and life of the early church. In fact, history was of so little concern to the early Christian community that they made no great distinction between the earthly history of Jesus and his postresurrectional history and presence with the church, to whom he still spoke by the Spirit. Without the strictures of history and with its assurance of Jesus' presence, the early church could freely adapt and even creatively add to the tradition, if the needs of the church for preaching, apologetics, worship, etc., so required. For a more extensive treatment of these important conclusions of Gospel form criticism, see K. Koch, *The Growth of the Biblical Tradition* (NY, 1968); McKnight, *What* (→ 42 above); and Neill, *Interpretation* 236–91.

46   **(II) Criticism and Theology: The Work of Rudolf Bultmann.**   Certainly Bultmann (1884–1976) was the most influential figure in 20th-cent. NT study, combining immense erudition and scholarship with a profoundly pastoral desire to preach a meaningful and relevant message to his contemporaries in a world where faith is no longer easy. Marburg, the scene of Bultmann's teaching career, became a latter-day Tübingen in the influence it has exerted on Protestant theology. In terms of mere bulk, Bultmann's work extended over a period of almost 50 years and provoked a library of literature pro and con: Boers, *What* 75–84; B. Jaspert, (ed.), *Rudolf Bultmanns Werk und Wirkung* (Darmstadt, 1984); C. W. Kegley (ed.), *The Theology of Rudolf Bultmann* (NY, 1966); N. Perrin, *The Promise of Bultmann* (Phl, 1969).

There are a number of dominant influences distinguishable in Bultmann's thought. From Strauss, Bultmann took the concept of myth as the key to the interpretation of the NT. He accepted Wrede's view of the nonmessianic character of Christ's life and the creative genius of the early Christian community. The history-of-religions school contributed its syncretistic view of Christian origins and the assumption of the pervading influence of gnosticism in the NT world. Form criticism contributed to Butlmann's lack of interest in the historical Jesus. But beneath these diverse elements and bringing them into a basic unity, one can find at the heart of Bultmann's thought and permeating all his work two major influences: a thoroughgoing Lutheranism and the existentialism of M. Heidegger (1889–1976).

47   Lutheranism is a constant in the background and orientation of Bultmann's thought. It can easily be discerned in his strong evangelical emphasis on the preached word. But Bultmann's Lutheranism went deeper, for he understood his own theological enterprise as a logical conclusion of the Reformation doctrine of justification by faith alone. Herein lies the theological reason for Bultmann's lack of interest in the historical Jesus, for to seek a historical basis for faith would be a betrayal of the principle of *sola fide.* Bultmann's distrust of the search for an objective basis for faith thus underlies his deep skepticism concerning the historicity of the Gospel accounts and his consequent dehistoricizing of the kerygma. In his view, the only history that we find in the kerygma is the *Dass,* the bare fact of the existence and death by crucifixion of the man Jesus of Nazareth. The Word that addresses us in the kerygma is therefore the ground, as well as the object, of faith. Bultmann's definition of faith in terms of personal choice and decision, as an act of the will rather than of the intellect, is as much the legacy of Luther as of Heidegger. Bultmann's attenuated concept of the church as little more than the arena in which the word is preached and heard has its roots in Luther's individualism.

48   Heidegger and Bultmann were colleagues at Marburg from 1923 to 1928, and Bultmann readily admitted the influence that Heidegger's thought, particularly as formulated in *Being and Time* (Ger 1927; Eng 1962), had on his theology. An analysis of the impact of Heidegger's existentialism on Bultmann is beyond the scope of this discussion. A good treatment of this subject recommended by Bultmann himself is J. Macquarrie, *An Existentialist Theology: A Comparison of Heidegger and Bultmann* (1955). One example, for the sake of illustration, is Bultmann's interpretation of Pauline theology by Heidegger's concept of the transition from inauthentic to authentic existence. Both Heidegger and Bultmann distinguish inauthentic existence (human life in bondage to the illusory security of a dying world) and authentic existence, which for Heidegger is achieved by personal decision. For Bultmann, authentic existence is a gift of God achieved by abandoning adherence to this world and opening oneself to the word of forgiving grace announced in the kerygma. We note that among Bultmann's disciples Heidegger's philosophy remained a live issue. (See J. M. Robinson and J. Cobb, [eds.], *The Later Heidegger and Theology* [NFT 1; NY, 1963]; → Hermeneutics, 71:54.)

49   **(A) Bultmann the Form Critic.** Working from the conclusions of Schmidt and Dibelius, Bultmann applied the form-critical method in *The History of the Synoptic Tradition* (Ger 1921; Eng 1963). Against the more conservative approach of Dibelius, Bultmann's form-critical investigations are not simply a means of literary classification, but must lead to judgments on the historicity of the stories and the genuineness of the sayings found in the tradition. His skepticism as regards historical reliability is evident in that he assigns most of the tradition to the creative imagination of the early Christian communities. What genuine material there is, he finds chiefly in the sayings of Jesus. But this genuineness does not extend to the contexts of these sayings in the Gospels, the *Sitz im Evangelium,* which is the creation of the later tradition, especially of the evangelists themselves.

50   **(B) Bultmann the Theologian.** Bultmann's most noteworthy theological contribution was in the area of hermeneutics. Although many would disagree violently with his proposed solutions, all admit that Bultmann came to grips with a real problem, viz., the difficulty of communicating the Christian message in the 20th cent. As a theologian, Bultmann's major concern was that the NT message should challenge people rather than prevent them from making an existential decision by its mythological language. (P. J. Cahill, *TS* 38 [1977] 231–74; G. Stanton, *ExpTim* 90 [1979] 324–28.)

51   (a) DEMYTHOLOGIZING THE NT. Bultmann's manifesto, "The New Testament and Mythology," first appeared in 1941, becoming the storm center for a continuing debate, often accompanied by misunderstanding. Two initial observations: (1) By myth, Bultmann does not mean an imaginary story or some sort of fairy tale but the use of imagery to express the otherworldly in terms of this world. (2) One should recognize the profoundly pastoral intent of Bultmann's call for demythologizing, i.e., for interpreting the NT in existentialist terms. For Bultmann, demythologizing is not a reduction of the NT but the only way to make its saving message available today.

Bultmann held that interpretation is necessary because today people find the obsolete mythological world view of the NT incredible. Therefore, if they are to be challenged to decision by the kerygma, the NT must be demythologized; the mythological framework of the NT must be interpreted, to expose the understanding of human life contained in it. Bultmann found in the existentialism of Heidegger a tool suited for such interpretation of the NT. Further, for Bultmann such interpretation is valid not only because the very nature of myth demands it but also because we can see this process starting in the NT itself, especially in Paul and John. One example of such NT demythologizing is John's "realized eschatology," i.e., his emphasis on eternal life here and now, not in some distant future. Finally, the pastoral aspect of demythologizing becomes clear when one realizes that the elimination of the unnecessary stumbling block of mythology helps Bultmann to expose the real stumbling block, the offense of the Gospel which proclaims that the eschatological act of God "for us and for our salvation" took place in the life and death of Jesus Christ.

Perceptive reaction in disagreement with Bultmann (as distinct from fundamentalist reaction) was not directed against the basic need to reinterpret, to decode, to "demythologize" some of the mythical imagery of the NT, but against Bultmann's judgment on what constitutes unacceptable imagery or myth. For instance, resurrection from the dead and the miraculous, which for Bultmann are no longer meaningful for moderns, remain very meaningful in the judgment of other scholars.

(An Eng transl. of "Neues Testament und Mythologie" is available in Bultmann, R., *New Testament and Mythology and Other Basic Writings* [ed. S. M. Ogden; Phl, 1984] 1–43. Johnson, R. A., *The Origins of Demythologizing* [NumenSup 28; Leiden, 1974]. Painter, J., *Theology as Hermeneutics: R. Bultmann's Interpretation of the History of Jesus* [Sheffield, 1986].)

52   (b) BULTMANN ON JOHN. Bultmann wrote on John over an extended period of time, dating from 1923. His masterpiece was his 1941 commentary in the MeyerK series (*The Gospel of John* [Phl, 1971]). With its penetrating critical exegesis, this commentary confirmed Bultmann as a most influential exegete in the history of biblical studies, even though many have disagreed with his conclusions. According to Bultmann, the first step in the formation of John was the work of the *evangelist,* quite possibly a gnostic converted to the Christian faith. He drew his Gospel material from three principal sources independent of one another: (1) a signs-source (*Semeia-Quelle*), a collection of miracles, symbolic rather than historical, attributed to Jesus; (2) revelatory discourses (*Offenbarungsreden*), a collection of poetic discourses of an Oriental gnostic origin; and (3) a passion-resurrection source, parallel to but independent of the Synoptic tradition.

After the death of the evangelist came the work of the *redactor,* or editor, whose work consisted chiefly of organization and harmonization. The organization was necessary because the redactor found the evangelist's work in terrible disorder. He did his best to arrange the material in sequence, but did not totally succeed. Bultmann saw his own attempt to reconstruct the original order of John as a continuation of the work of the redactor. Since the redactor knew the Synoptic tradition, he attempted to harmonize the evangelist's work with this tradition. More important, he had to harmonize the evangelist's work with standard church teaching to make it acceptable to the orthodox church; he did this by adding, e.g., sacramental references to the anti-sacramental work of the evangelist and traditional eschatology to balance and correct the demythologized eschatology of the Gospel. This theological harmonization was necessary because of the gnostic bent of the evangelist who used demythologized gnostic concepts to interpret the meaning of Christ for his contemporaries. The gnostic redeemer myth is demythologized by being attached to the historical person Jesus of Nazareth; gnostic dualism is demythologized by being transformed from a metaphysical to an ethical dualism.

Bultmann heavily stressed Jesus as the Revealer, whose revelation is not the communication of gnostic secrets about the upper world but simply the person of Jesus himself. Thus, the whole point in John is not the salvific action by Jesus but his words: he is truth, he is light, and he has to be accepted. All who *know* him are saved. There is no longer need of salvation history, for Jesus always supplies here and now the opportunity for decision.

(Brown, *BGJ* 1. xxix–xxxiii [sources of John], lii–lvi [gnosticism]. Smith, D. M., *The Composition and Order of the Fourth Gospel* [New Haven, 1965], a lucid analysis of Bultmann's approach to John. For a résumé of the theology of John according to Bultmann, see his *TNT* 2. 3–92.)

53   **(III) Reactions to Bultmann.** One measure of Bultmann's influence on NT studies is the extent of the reactions — both favorable and hostile — caused by his work. These reactions stretch across the whole spectrum of Christian thought, from a fundamentalist conservatism that would reject his work totally to the liberalism represented by F. Buri, who accused Bultmann of not going far enough in demythologizing because he retained the reality of God's act in Christ. In Europe, Catholics like L. Malevez and G. Hasenhüttl became leading authorities on Bultmann's theology.

54   The Scandinavian tradition-historical school in particular supplied important correctives to the negativism of Bultmann's form criticism. The tradition-historical approach was well known in OT studies through the work of scholars like S. Mowinckel (→ OT Criticism, 69:45–46); and the Uppsala school of interpretation began to apply it to the NT, as in the important study of B. Gerhardsson, *Memory and Manuscript: Oral Tradition and Written Transmission in Rabbinic Judaism and Early Christianity* (1961). Gerhardsson contended that the Gospel narratives are the result not of a creative but of a preservative process, through an institution in the early church for the delivery of the Gospel tradition, similar to a contemporary rabbinic institution for the controlled transmission of the written and oral Torah. Gerhardsson's work was a welcome alternative to the negative judgment on historicity characteristic of much form-critical study (J. A. Fitzmyer, *TS* 23 [1962] 442–57). See also Gerhardsson's *The Gospel Tradition* (ConBNT 15; Lund, 1986).

Of wider interest, however, were the alternatives to Bultmann's radicalism proposed by more conservative German and British theologians, as well as the debates carried on in Germany by Bultmann's former students.

55   **(A) Reaction of Conservative German Scholarship.** Bultmann's theology was not without its opponents in Germany, who objected to his excessive skepticism and found the hermeneutical key to the NT not in Heideggerian existentialism but in the Bible itself.

56   (a) K. BARTH. A systematic theologian rather than a NT scholar, Barth (1886–1968) was an early ally of Bultmann. World War I made him see the inadequacy of liberal theology, and he expressed his disenchantment in his memorable and powerful commentary, *The Epistle to the Romans* (Ger 1918; Eng 1933), which focused on the theological significance of Rom, emphasizing the Bible as the word of God. Scientific historical-critical study was at best only a preliminary to the real task of theological, "pneumatic" exegesis. Whereas Bultmann's studies concerned the human side of the relationship between God and humanity (how we can receive revelation), Barth emphasized the divine side (God as the source of revelation). Bultmann was an early defender of Barth, with whom he agreed in principle, if not in methodology. However, Bultmann's demythologizing and existential hermeneutic did not meet with agreement from Barth. (For a bibliography of and on Barth, see his *Faith of the Church* [NY, 1958]. S. W. Sykes [ed.], *Karl Barth* [Oxford, 1979].)

57   (b) O. CULLMANN. At the University of Basel Cullmann (1902–) became the foremost proponent of salvation history (*Heilsgeschichte*) as the key for understanding the NT. He proposed this alternative to the Bultmann school in two important books, *Christ and Time* (Ger 1946; Eng 1951, rev. 1962; cf. *ExpTim* 65 [1953–54] 369–72) and *Salvation in History* (Ger 1965; Eng 1967). The *heilsgeschichtlich* approach views history as a series of redemptive epochs, with the Christ-event as the midpoint of a time line that includes a previous period of preparation, the present stage of the church, and the eschatological future. All biblical history is marked by the permanent tension of promise and fulfillment, the "already" and the "not yet." Against the Bultmannians, Cullmann held that *Heilsgeschichte* is not a Lucan distortion but is rooted in the teaching of Jesus. Salvation history is thus a characteristic of the whole NT, from Jesus himself to John. Cullmann defended the appropriateness of *Heilsgeschichte* as an exegetical tool for arriving at the original meaning of the NT by pointing out that Jesus and the early church were nurtured on the OT and its view of history.

Mention should also be made of Cullmann's important contribution to biblical theology, *The Christology of the New Testament* (Ger 1957; Eng 1959). In this work Cullmann attempted to define the christology of the early church as expressed in the NT, without the developed interpretations of subsequent theology. He examined ten titles applied to Jesus in the NT, referring to Jesus' earthly work, his future eschatological work, his contemporary work in the church, and his preexistence. Cullmann emphasized exclusively the functional aspect of Christology and avoided the static categories of Greco-Roman theology, with its developed notions of person and nature, as beyond the limits of exegesis.

To give an illustration of his method, we can look at the title Lord (*Kyrios*), which Cullmann discusses under the heading of Christ's contemporary work in the church. He admits to Bousset's contention that the church's experience in worship of the presence of Jesus the Lord gave prominence to this title, but against Bousset Cullmann shows that this most advanced christological title has its roots in Palestinian Christianity and is not the result of the church's encounter with the Hellenistic mystery cults. On Cullmann, see Hasel, *New Testament* 111–19.

58   (c) W. PANNENBERG. This scholar has presented another challenge to Bultmann with his *Revelation as History* (Ger 1961; Eng: NY, 1968) and *Jesus—God and Man* (Ger 1964; Eng: 2d ed.; Phl, 1977). Pannenberg proposes an alternative to the lack of interest in history characteristic of Barth's theology of the Word and to Bultmann's relocation of revelation in the kerygma rather than in history. According to Pannenberg, God's self-revelation comes to us not immediately (as Barth and Bultmann hold) nor through a special redemptive history (as Cullmann proposes), but mediately and indirectly, mirrored in the events of history. Since history becomes the locus of revelation, revelation is verifiable by the methods of historical scholarship. And if revelatory history is knowable by reason, then faith does not produce but rather presupposes rational knowledge. Faith does not give us the inner meaning of events of past history, but is trust oriented to the future, to the final end of universal history anticipated in the Christ-event.

(Braaten, C. E., *History and Hermeneutics* [Phl, 1966]. Galloway, A. D., *Wolfhart Pannenberg* [London, 1973]. Neie, H., *The Doctrine of the Atonement in the Theology of Wolfhart Pannenberg* [NY, 1979]. Robinson, J. M. and J. Cobb [eds.], *Theology as History* [NFT 3; NY, 1967].)

59   **(B) Reaction of British Scholarship.** Traditionally more conservative than the Germans in theology and exegesis, British scholarship rejected in the main Bultmann's radical skepticism and his existential hermeneutic. Form criticism, however, received a more sympathetic hearing, and British NT scholars were not slow to put the insights of form criticism to good use.

60   (a) E. HOSKYNS. The man most responsible for bringing German criticism and theology to a British audience was Sir Edwyn Hoskyns (1884–1937). It was he who translated Barth's commentary on Rom into English. In *The Riddle of the New Testament* (1931)

Hoskyns attacked the liberal notion that criticism could arrive at a nontheological picture of Jesus in the earliest tradition. As did the form critics, Hoskyns realized that the crucial problem in the NT, the "riddle," was the relationship between Jesus of Nazareth and the primitive Christian church. But he had more confidence than they in the ability of scientific criticism to reach the historical Jesus behind the Gospels. His greatest work, however, was his commentary on John, edited and published posthumously by F. N. Davey, *The Fourth Gospel* (1940), a commentary in the best British tradition of sound critical study and profoundly theological interpretation.

61   (b) V. TAYLOR. Another scholar no less aware than Hoskyns of the importance of Continental theology, especially of the influence of Bultmann, was Vincent Taylor (1887–1968). Soon after the appearance of Hoskyns's *Riddle,* Taylor published *The Formation of the Gospel Tradition* (1933), his magistral estimate of the values and excesses of form criticism. Still an excellent introduction to the subject, it is an eminently fair treatment, critical of the extremely negative conclusions but willing to accept the positive contributions of form criticism. Taylor saw that form criticism, far from leading inevitably to skepticism, could supply valuable confirmation of the basic historicity of the Gospel tradition. Fully recognizing the theological nature of the Gospels, Taylor was a vigorous defender of the historical trustworthiness of the Gospels as sources for the authentic words and deeds of Jesus.

This confidence is evident in his trilogy on NT christology, *The Names of Jesus* (1953), *The Life and Ministry of Jesus* (1954), and *The Person of Christ in New Testament Teaching* (1958). Although Taylor, like Bultmann, saw the importance of the preached Christ, the exalted Lord of Christian faith, he also recognized the indispensability of the historical Jesus for christology.

Taylor's most famous work was certainly his commentary, *The Gospel According to St. Mark* (1952), wherein he employed the tools of biblical science to offer an alternative to Wrede's skepticism regarding the historicity of Mark. Revised in 1966, this commentary is a standard work in Synoptic studies. For biography and an appraisal of Taylor's work, see his *New Testament Essays* (GR, 1972) 5–30.

62   (c) R. H. LIGHTFOOT. Much more sympathetic to German exegesis than his British confreres in NT studies, Lightfoot (1883–1953) was the champion of form criticism in England. The title of a study published in 1935, *History and Interpretation in the Gospels,* indicates the approach he took, viewing the Gospels as theological interpretation rather than as a biography of Jesus of Nazareth. Lightfoot's approach in *The Gospel Message of St. Mark* (1950) was a significant exception to the traditional British acceptance of the historicity of Mark. He was the author of a commentary on John, *St. John's Gospel,* published posthumously in 1956.

63   (d) C. H. DODD. The concern for relevance in communicating the NT message was not the exclusive preserve of the Bultmann school. As early as the 1930s Dodd (1884–1973) called for an end to the critical atomization of the NT, necessary as such study might have been; and he himself took the first steps toward a synthesis. Although not a member of the form-critical school, Dodd made a contribution to our knowledge of the gospel behind the Gospels in *The Apostolic Preaching and Its Developments* (1936), an investigation of the church's earliest preaching, especially in Acts and Paul. In such primitive apostolic kerygma Dodd found the underlying unity of the NT, and in this he was followed by many Catholic exegetes.

No less influential was his book, *The Parables of the Kingdom* (1935), an attempt, often successful, to get behind the parables as we find them in the Gospels (the *Sitz im Evangelium*) to the parables as originally spoken by Jesus (the *Sitz im Leben Jesu*). Jeremias, in his study of the parables, freely admitted his debt to Dodd's work. Dodd also formulated in this book his widely discussed theory of "realized eschatology," the fact that the kingdom preached by Jesus in the parables was a present rather than a future reality (→ NT Thought, 81:34, 65).

Dodd gave to Johannine studies two brilliant books. The first of these, *The Interpretation of the Fourth Gospel* (1953), is a study of the background, the leading concepts, and the structure of John. One criticism of the book is that Dodd overemphasizes Hellenism as the thought world that produced John, a position that needs serious modification in view of the Qumran discoveries. Ten years later Dodd published *Historical Tradition in the Fourth Gospel* (1963), a study of the relationship between John and the Synoptics and a defense of the reliability of John, which Dodd showed to be based on a tradition parallel to but independent of the Synoptic tradition and deserving of at least as much historical respect. In all his work, Dodd showed a high degree of the historical and theological competence that has become a trademark of the best British NT scholarship. See F. W. Dillistone, *C. H. Dodd* (GR, 1977).

British scholarship continued after the above-named scholars, but the peculiarities of national tones paled in the last third of the 20th cent. Common methods, common tools, and an international society (Societas Novi Testamenti Studiorum) that brought scholars from all nations together annually tended to make distinctiveness less characteristically British, German, etc.

64   (C) Reaction from Bultmann's School: The Post-Bultmannians. The best-known reaction to Bultmannian orthodoxy was certainly that which arose among his own disciples. Despite the individualism of these former students of Bultmann, this reaction was sufficiently well defined to have introduced a new, post-Bultmannian phase in exegesis. Two areas in which the post-Bultmannians built upon Bultmann's work, only to reexamine critically some of his fundamental theses, were the whole question of the historical Jesus and the significance and relevance of Heidegger's later philosophy for exegesis and theology. Because of the complexity of the second question, we shall confine our discussion to the new quest of the historical Jesus, and for the Heideggerian question we refer the reader to the bibliography and discussion in R. E. Brown and P. J. Cahill, *Biblical Tendencies Today: An Introduction to the Post-Bultmannians* (Corpus Papers; Washington, 1969); → Hermeneutics, 71:54.

For Bultmann, the kerygmatic nature of the Gospel precluded any attempt to reach the historical Jesus through the early church's confession of faith in Christ the risen Lord. According to Bultmann, the early church had no biographical interest in the historical Jesus of Nazareth but focused its gaze exclusively on the Christ of faith proclaimed in the kerygma. The historical Jesus was therefore irrelevant to Christian faith.

But for all his theoretical skepticism regarding a historical quest that would go behind the kerygma, in *The History of the Synoptic Tradition* and in *Jesus and the Word* (Ger 1926; Eng 1934) Bultmann went to great lengths to verify the words and deeds of Jesus. It is this direction in Bultmann's own work that the post-Bultmannians claimed to be furthering in their new quest of the historical Jesus. M. Kähler (1835-1912) was an early forerunner of this new quest in *The So-Called Historical Jesus and the Historic Biblical Christ* (Ger 1892;

Eng 1964), a book that was reissued in 1956, during the initial stages of the post-Bultmannian reaction.

65   (a) E. KÄSEMANN. The new quest was formally launched in 1953 by Käsemann (1906-) of Tübingen, in an article entitled "The Problem of the Historical Jesus." Käsemann made three important points in this article. (1) If there is no connection between the glorified Lord of Christian faith and the earthly, historical Jesus, then Christianity becomes a nonhistorical myth. Käsemann strikes here at the danger inherent in Bultmann's dehistoricizing of the kerygma — the danger of a docetic, nonhistorical kerygma. (2) If the early church was so disinterested in the history of Jesus, why were the four Gospels ever written? The evangelists surely believed that the Christ they preached was none other than the earthly, historical Jesus. (3) Although the Gospels are products of Easter faith and it is therefore difficult to get to the historical Jesus, Christian faith requires confidence in the identity of the earthly Jesus and the exalted Lord of the kerygma.

Besides this theoretical defense of the necessity of the new quest, Käsemann gave methodical principles by which the new quest may be carried on. (1) To establish any saying or deed of Jesus as authentic we must eliminate all Gospel material that has a kerygmatic tone. These sayings are not necessarily inauthentic, but since they resemble the church's proclamation they cannot be proved to be authentic utterances of Jesus. Their *Sitz im Leben* could be a post-Easter situation or faith. (2) One must exclude anything that can be paralleled in contemporary Judaism, e.g., in rabbinic tradition or contemporary Jewish apocalyptic, as not demonstrably authentic. (3) An authentic saying of Jesus should reflect Aram features. Käsemann later modified his position somewhat in that he replaced Bultmann's gnosticism with Jewish apocalyptic as the background of primitive Christian theology. After rigorous application of these criteria, Käsemann found in Jesus' teaching elements that unquestionably stem from Jesus himself. His basic ideas on this may be found in his *Essays on New Testament Themes* (SBT 41; London, 1964) and *New Testament Questions of Today* (Phl, 1969). Other significant works include his *Perspectives on Paul* (Phl, 1971) and *Commentary on Romans* (GR, 1980).

(Harrington, D., *Light of All Nations* [Wilmington, 1982] chaps. 1 and 3. Harrisville, R. A., *RelSRev* 11 [1986] 256-58. Scroggs, R., ibid. 260-63. → Canonicity, 66:94-95.)

66   (b) E. FUCHS. In 1956 another of the post-Bultmannians, Fuchs (1903-) of Marburg, published in the *ZTK,* the journal-organ of the post-Bultmannians, an article entitled "The Quest of the Historical Jesus," in which he advanced his canons for the new quest. Fuchs sought in the behavior or conduct (*Verhalten*) of Jesus something that is historical and relevant for faith. Especially in his gracious table fellowship with the outcast, his eating and drinking with sinners, Jesus effectively and authoritatively lived out what he preached in the parables: the present redeeming activity of the near God. This declaration of God's love for sinners was authoritative because in receiving sinners Jesus put himself in God's place, identifying his will with God's. Thus in Jesus' conduct we find the key to his self-understanding of who and what he was: God's eschatological representative. Fuchs's confidence in the historicity of the Gospel reports of Jesus' activity was grounded in the belief that the church would be less likely to change the deeds than the words of Jesus. See his *Studies of the Historical Jesus* (SBT 42; London, 1964); R. N. Soulen, *JAAR* 39 (1971) 467-87; → Hermeneutics, 71:54.

67   (c) G. BORNKAMM. Thirty years after Bultmann's *Jesus and the Word,* Bornkamm (1905–) of
Heidelberg published *Jesus of Nazareth* (Ger 1956; Eng
1960), the first post-Bultmannian study of the historical
Jesus. Like Käsemann and Fuchs, Bornkamm regarded
the unmatched authority of Jesus as historically valid
and relevant for Christian faith. Käsemann found this
authority manifested in the teaching of Jesus; Fuchs, in
his conduct. Bornkamm claimed that the strongest
impression the Gospels make is the immediate, unparalleled authority of Jesus, an authority that is absolute and
present in both the words and the deeds of Jesus. This
authority has its source in the historical Jesus and is not
a product of faith. Although faith acknowledged and
proclaimed it, faith did not create it.

Besides this experience of authority, we can establish
the following facts about the historical Jesus. Jesus was
a Jew, the son of Joseph the carpenter, from Nazareth in
Galilee. He preached in towns along the Lake of Galilee,
healing and doing good works and struggling with
opposition from the Pharisees. Ultimately he was crucified in Jerusalem. More important, however, than these
bare historical facts concerning the ministry of Jesus was
their existential significance—the fact that in the
ministry, the crucial, eschatological hour was present,
calling us to decision. A historical encounter with Jesus
was therefore an eschatological encounter with God. (L.
Keck, *JR* 49 [1969] 1–17; also Bornkamm's *Early Christian Experience* [NY, 1969].)

68   (d) H. CONZELMANN. In *RGG* (3d ed.; 3.
619–53) in 1959 Conzelmann (1915–) offered another
post-Bultmannian Jesus study (*Jesus* [Phl, 1973]). It too
was a rather positive synthesis of what can be known of
the historical Jesus. For Conzelmann, Jesus is humanity's
confrontation with God; in his ministry Jesus' proclamation of the coming reign of God already engages us. His
word is the definitive word of God; his deeds make the
kingdom of God present.

Conzelmann's *Theology of Saint Luke* (Ger 1954; Eng
repr. Phl, 1982) gives an insight into the *Redaktionsgeschichte* practiced by the post-Bultmannians (→ 80
below). Conzelmann argued that Luke had a very
definite theological point of view, in the light of which
he rewrote the history of Jesus and added a supplementary volume dealing with the history of the early church.
According to Conzelmann, the early Christians thought
that the coming of Jesus meant absolutely the end of
history and that therefore the period between the
resurrection-ascension and the parousia would be very
brief. With the delay of the parousia, the early church
had to rethink its whole theology. In this task of
rethinking, Conzelmann contended, Luke deliberately
and radically modified the eschatological perspective of
Jesus and the more primitive sources (e.g., Mark) by
introducing the perspective of *Heilsgeschichte* into early
Christian theology, with Christ's public ministry as an
intermediate period between that of Israel and that of the
church. Conzelmann and the post-Bultmannians in
general view Luke's concept as secondary and erroneous, in fact as a falsification and distortion of the original
Gospel. (It is here that Cullmann takes issue with the
post-Bultmannians, in maintaining that Luke's view of
history is primary and is rooted in the teaching of Jesus,
whose eschatological outlook has been seriously overemphasized by Conzelmann.) His other works included
An Outline of the Theology of the New Testament (NY,
1969); *History of Primitive Christianity* (Nash, 1973).

69   (e) J. M. ROBINSON. An American representative of the post-Bultmannian school, Robinson held
that there are two ways of access to the person of Jesus.
Besides the kerygma, the existential historiography

evolved by the German philosopher W. Dilthey (1833–
1911) and by R. G. Collingwood (1889–1943) in his
posthumously published *The Idea of History* (1946) offers
us the possibility of an encounter with the historical
Jesus, who renounced completely the support of this
present evil world to live only for God. This existential
philosophy of history makes the new quest not only
possible but also legitimate. (J. M. Robinson, *A New
Quest of the Historical Jesus* [SBT 25; London, 1959]; also
P. J. Achtemeier, *An Introduction to the New Hermeneutic*
[Phl, 1969].)

70   (f) G. EBELING. A church historian and systematic theologian, Ebeling (1912–) of Tübingen was
especially concerned with the problem of faith in its
many ramifications: the relevance of the historical Jesus
to faith and theology; the problem of the transition from
the Jesus of history to faith in Jesus the exalted Lord; and
Jesus' teaching about faith. Ebeling distinguished the
following elements in the teaching of Jesus as historical:
the nearness of the kingdom or reign of God as the core
of his message; the identification of his will with God's,
so that he appeals neither to Moses (like the rabbis) nor
even to God (like the prophets) but uses the unprecedented words "Amen *I* say to you"; obedience to the will
of God that liberates humanity from legalism and
casuistry; and a call to conversion and discipleship with
joy. See his *Word and Faith* (London, 1963); *The Nature
of Faith* (London, 1961); *The Problem of Historicity* (Phl,
1967). Also D. W. Hardy, *ExpTim* 93 (1981–82) 68–72.

(Bultmann's reaction to the new quest appears in "The Primitive
Christian Kerygma and the Historical Jesus," *The Historical Jesus
and the Kerygmatic Christ* [ed. C. E. Braaten *et al.;* NY, 1964]
15–42. See also, Harvey, V. A., *The Historian and the Believer*
[NY, 1967] 164–203. Jeremias, J. [→ 30 above], *ExpTim* 69
[1957–58] 333–39. Sobosan, J. G., *Thomist* 36 [1972] 267–92.
Further, → Jesus 78:1.)

**71   (IV) Emergence of Catholic Critical
Scholarship.** The first 40 years of the 20th cent., from
the days of the Modernist crisis and of Lagrange and
Loisy (→ 37, 38 above) to the writing of *DAS* in 1943
(→ Church Pronouncements, 72:20), were dark days for
Catholic biblical scholarship (→ Church Pronounce-
ments, 72:5–6). Significant criticism of the NT reemerged
only after Pius XII's encyclical. For a survey of the
period 1955–1980, see *BHMCS* 211–55; also G. P.
Fogarty, *American Catholic Biblical Scholarship . . . to
Vatican II* (SF, 1989).

Catholic critical scholarship from *DAS* until 1970
was marked by intensive growth. At first, scholarship
on the whole remained right-of-center, much more in
line with Cullmann, Taylor, and Dodd, for instance,
than with the Bultmannian or post-Bultmannian
schools. Yet this new critical approach was looked upon
as shocking by many within the church and only grudgingly received toleration.

Catholic biblical scholars received official church
encouragement through two primary documents, the
PBC's "Instruction on the Historical Truth of the
Gospels" (1964) and Vatican II's *Dei Verbum* (Dogmatic
Constitution on Divine Revelation, 1965). The former
document, in particular, recognized that the Gospels
consisted of several layers of tradition and thus are not
literal or chronological accounts of the life of Jesus. This
position confirmed the results of biblical scholarship
while setting the stage for further developments in the
scientific, critical study of the NT among Catholic
biblical scholars. (→ Church Pronouncements, 72:9, 15,
35; R. E. Brown, *Biblical Reflections on Crises Facing the
Church* [NY, 1975] 3–19.)

72   Moving from a judicious selection and combination of acceptable elements in Protestant scholarship, Catholic NT scholarship increasingly made its own mark in the study of the NT. It succeeded in convincing more intelligent Catholics that the ultraconservative biblical positions of the past were no longer tenable and that the new approaches had values of their own which could feed worship and spirituality. It incorporated the results of scientific NT study into the discussion of issues with dogmatic implications, e.g., the limitations of Jesus' knowledge regarding himself, the future, and the church; qualifications in the reliability of Acts as a guide to how the church historically emerged; the extent of creativity exercised in the formation of the Gospel tradition; the limited historicity of the infancy narratives. By the last decades of the 20th cent., Catholic NT scholarship was no longer seen as a mere stepchild of Protestant NT scholarship. Yet, despite the tremendous advances made since Pius XII's *DAS,* this critical approach to the NT continued to spark much debate and controversy on the part of both liberal and conservative Catholics. (See the assessment in R. E. Brown, *Biblical Exegesis and Church Doctrine* [NY, 1985].)

Before setting forth the contemporary situation, we shall give the briefest survey of some of the more important names in the development of Catholic NT scholarship described above.

73   **(A) French Scholarship.** In the early period French writers were the most productive of all Catholic NT scholars. This was largely due to the heritage of M.-J. Lagrange, the Jerusalem École Biblique, and the *RB* (→ 37 above; → OT Criticism, 69:60). In NT the mantle of Lagrange fell to P. Benoit (1906–1987) and M.-É. Boismard. Benoit published an early cautious but favorable assessment of form criticism in *RB* 53 (1946) 489–512. He became well known for articles on the *sensus plenior* (→ Hermeneutics, 71:49–51), inspiration (→ Inspiration, 65:59), the passion accounts, the eucharist, the resurrection and ascension, and the concept of body in Paul; many of these are gathered in the four-vol. *Exégèse et théologie* (Paris, 1961–82). Boismard worked extensively in the Johannine field, e.g., *St. John's Prologue* (London, 1957), *Du baptême à Cana* (Paris, 1956), and the multi-vol. *Synopse des quatre évangiles.* (For important textual contributions, → Texts, 68:176, 186.) The French Jesuits (both cardinals) J. Daniélou (1905–1974) and H. de Lubac (1896–) made important contributions to the history of the spiritual sense of Scripture (→ Hermeneutics, 71:45–48). In Rome, S. Lyonnet (1902–1986) wrote extensively in the Pauline field, especially on Rom. The French Sulpicians produced a number of notable scholars of the whole Bible (A. Robert [1883–1955], A. Gelin [1902–1960], H. Cazelles). In NT A. Feuillet was outstanding for his studies on the parousia (*DBSup* 6. 1331–1419), *Johannine Studies* (NY, 1965), and *The Apocalypse* (NY, 1964). To some his later works seemed defensively conservative. C. Spicq (1901–) wrote notable commentaries on Heb and the Pastorals in EBib, and a four-vol. investigation of *agapē* in the NT (Paris, 1955–59), which was translated into English in abridged form (St. Louis, 1963–66). Gradually, however, the forefront of Catholic NT scholarship shifted from the French to a broader spectrum. Even though scholars like X. Léon-Dufour and P. Grelot continued in the great tradition, the situation in France in the 1980s was clouded by a reactionary movement spearheaded by C. Tresmontant, J. Carmignac, and R. Laurentin. See R. E. Brown, *USQR* 40 (1985) 99–103.

74   **(B) Belgian Scholarship.** While most Catholicism was still under the shadow of fear cast by the stern repression of Modernism, the University of Louvain preserved its proud tradition in the publications of Msgr. L. Cerfaux (1883–1968). His three vols. of collected essays (*Receuil L. Cerfaux* [Louvain, 1954–62]) showed a broad range of interest and competency, but he is best known for his trilogy on Pauline theology: *ChrTSP, ChTSP,* and *The Christian in the Theology of St. Paul* (NY, 1967). His students carried on the Louvain tradition, e.g., A. Descamps (1916–1980), who was later bishop, rector of the university, and secretary of the Roman PBC. His best-known work was *Les Justes et la Justice* (Louvain, 1950); see M. Giblet, *RTL* 12 (1981) 40–58. I. de la Potterie, a Belgian Jesuit at the Biblical Institute in Rome, wrote extensively on John (see his collected essays with S. Lyonnet, *The Christian Lives by the Spirit* [NY, 1971]; *La Vérité dans Saint Jean* [AnBib 73, 74; Rome, 1977]), as did the Belgian Dominican F.-M. Braun (1893–1980), famous for his *Jean le théologien* (Paris, 1959–72). J. Dupont, a Benedictine prolific in his writings, contributed *Les Béatitudes* (Louvain, 1954–73) and a series of works on Acts: *The Sources of Acts* (NY, 1964); *Le discours de Milet* (Paris, 1962); *The Salvation of the Gentiles* (NY, 1979); *Nouvelles Études sur les Actes des Apôtres* (Paris, 1984). F. Neirynck made significant contributions to the study of the Synoptic Gospels, including *Duality in Mark* (BETL 31; Leuven, 1972); *The Minor Agreements of Matthew and Luke against Mark* (BETL 37; Leuven, 1974); and his collected essays in *Evangelica* (BETL 60; Leuven, 1982).

75   **(C) German Scholarship.** Moved by the example and scholarship of their Protestant counterparts, German Catholics in the 20th cent. produced some excellent NT commentaries. Of particular note are the series RNT and HTKNT. In the former the vols. on the Synoptic Gospels by J. Schmid (1893–1975) were valuable, as well as those on John and Acts by A. Wikenhauser (1883–1960), whose *New Testament Introduction* remained for many years the best Catholic critical introduction to the NT. In HTKNT, R. Schnackenburg, probably the most prominent of German Catholic scholars, produced a major three-vol. commentary, *The Gospel according to St. John* (NY, 1968–82); and R. Pesch wrote two vols. on Mark (Freiburg, 1984). Schnackenburg also was the author of *The Church in the New Testament* (NY, 1965); *God's Rule and Kingdom* (NY, 1963); *Baptism in the Thought of St. Paul* (NY, 1964); *The Moral Teaching of the New Testament* (NY, 1965). Of enduring value are the EKKNT commentaries produced by a cooperative venture between Catholics and Protestants. This joint series is symbolic of the ecumenical progress in biblical studies which was made in the latter half of the 20th cent. (→ 84 below).

76   **(D) American Scholarship.** Across the Atlantic Catholic NT scholarship was initially a question of articles and particular studies which often translated French or German Catholic trends into English. By the late 1950s, however, American Catholic NT scholarship began to find its own identity and to make an impact. Of the many early "pioneers," two deserve particular mention. The Canadian Jesuit D. Stanley wrote many articles in the 1950s which introduced trends from the Continent to English-speaking readers. Stanley encountered early Catholic fundamentalist reaction to new ideas (a reaction that was particularly severe in America in the period 1959–1962). Along with him, E. Siegman (1908–1967) fought bravely in the struggle to introduce modern NT criticism; as editor of the *CBQ* from 1951 to 1958 he put the magazine on a scientific level.

77   At the same time numerous young American Catholic scholars were being trained in critical methods at prestigious institutions both in America (e.g., Johns Hopkins, Harvard, Yale) and abroad. Many of these scholars gained national and international stature and were contributors to the *JBC* (1968). Most noteworthy were R. E. Brown and J. A. Fitzmyer, both of whom became members of the Roman PBC. Brown, a Sulpician who taught at Union Theological Seminary (NY), was the first American Catholic to become president of the prestigious international Societas Novi Testamenti Studiorum. His works included the AB commentaries on John (*BGJ*) and the Johannine Epistles (*BEJ*), as well as a long study of the infancy narratives, *The Birth of the Messiah* (GC, 1977). He had a major impact on the dissemination and acceptance of critical NT scholarship among Catholics through his extensive lectures and popular publications. Fitzmyer, a Jesuit who taught at Catholic University, was noteworthy for his studies of Aramaic (→ 31 above) and for his two-vol. AB commentary on Luke (*FGL*), as well as for editorship of both *JBL* and *CBQ*. See *CBQ* 48 (1986) 375–86.

Although one hesitates to single out names, it is possible to see just how far American Catholic NT scholarship has grown since Vatican II in its continuing ability to produce NT scholars of considerable stature: e.g., J. Donahue, D. Harrington, J. Meier, P. Perkins, D. Senior, among others. In addition to individuals, the Catholic Biblical Association and its professional journal, the *CBQ*, secured the place of American Catholic scholarship on a par with such prestigious societies as the Society of Biblical Literature and the Societas Novi Testamenti Studiorum. In short, American Catholic NT scholarship has demonstrated its vitality and has made its mark internationally. (For other factors in American Catholic biblical scholarship, see R. E. Brown, *The Critical Meaning of the Bible* [NY, 1981].)

78   (V) Recent Developments in NT Scholarship. In the last third of the 20th cent., modern technology, including computerized concordances and bibliographies, accelerated progress in many areas of NT study. In diagnosing the different directions the study has taken, we can offer only a broad survey, giving preference to the newer trends. The reader should be aware, of course, that the standard work of source, form, and tradition criticism continued on lines of development flowing from the earlier part of the century. Significant commentaries continued to be written, e.g., in AB V. Furnish on 2 Cor (1984), and in Herm H. D. Betz on Gal (1979). The two-vol. *Introduction to the New Testament* by H. Koester (Phl, 1982) caused considerable discussion by the audaciousness of many of its positions. A valuable background study was M. Hengel's *Judaism and Hellenism* (Phl, 1981). The publication of *The Nag Hammadi Library in English* (1977) led to a flurry of books relating apocryphal and gnostic works to the NT (→ Apocrypha, 67:56ff), some of them bordering on the sensationalist, e.g., E. Pagels, *The Gnostic Gospels* (NY, 1979). J. D. Crossan, *Four Other Gospels* (Minneapolis, 1985), tried to prove that four noncanonical gospels (three of them fragmentary) were more ancient than the canonical Gospels!

79   (A) Search for NT Communities. Although scholars have always been interested in detecting the thought and life of the Christians written to and about in the NT, a recent development has been the detailed description of 1st-cent. communities. In *History and Theology in the Fourth Gospel* (1968; 2d ed. Nash, 1979) J. L. Martyn described vividly and persuasively how on one level John reflects the trials and defenses of a community being expelled from the synagogue because of the divine claims they made about Jesus. Further work tracing the history of the Johannine

community appeared in Martyn's *The Gospel of John in Christian History* (NY, 1978) and R. E. Brown's *The Community of the Beloved Disciple* (NY, 1979). The history of the Matthean community played a major role in J. P. Meier's several books on Matt, and a considerable literature was generated in strongly dissenting debates about the life situation presupposed by Mark. Was that Gospel written to play down the apostles who were being lionized by Christians with a fixation on Jesus as a wonder-worker? The names T. Weeden, W. H. Kelber, and E. Best, are among the debaters. Related to this search was the study of great Christian centers in a manner different from that of times past (→ 25 above), e.g., R. E. Brown and J. P. Meier, *Antioch and Rome* (NY, 1983), and W. R. Schoedel, *Ignatius of Antioch* (Phl, 1985).

80   (B) Redaction Criticism. The origins of this approach to the NT, which has received much attention, are found in three scholars who wrote earlier in the century: G. Bornkamm, *et al., Tradition and Interpretation in Matthew* (Ger 1948; Phl, 1963); H. Conzelmann, *The Theology of St. Luke* (Ger 1954; NY, 1960); and W. Marxsen, *Mark the Evangelist* (Ger 1956; NY, 1969). Redaction criticism emphasizes the creative role that the evangelists had in shaping the material they inherited. The critic must detect what the evangelist has done to his sources in editing and combining them, since such redactional activity yields clues for the specific concerns of the redactor and the redactor's community. (Thus, redaction criticism has contributed to the search for NT communities.) The technique has also been applied to Acts and Paul. (→ Hermeneutics, 71:28–29; also Rohde, *Rediscovering;* R. H. Stein, *JBL* 88 [1969] 45–56.)

81   (C) Other Forms of Criticism. The *NJBC* article on Hermeneutics (→ 71:53–77) calls the reader's attention to the efflorescence of many different types of "criticism" in the late 20th cent.: literary criticism, structuralism, canonical criticism, rhetorical criticism, etc. The article on OT Criticism (→ 69:67–72) shows how they have been applied to the OT. Bibliographies were given in both articles, and they need not be repeated here; we shall assume the previous discussions and give simply a few outstanding examples. The techniques of modern literary critics were applied to the Gospels with some interesting results in the 1980s (to Mark by D. Rhoads and D. Michie, to John by R. A. Culpepper, to Matt by J. D. Kingsbury). Certainly this approach calls attention to aspects of the biblical book as a whole that would have been overlooked by a purely diachronic analysis. The more complicated structuralist approach, in the judgment of many, has not been strikingly productive, and the arcane terminology has frightened off readers. One area in particular, the passion narrative, received considerable attention by structuralists: e.g., O. Genest, *Le Christ de la passion* (Montreal, 1978) and L. Marin, *The Semiotics of the Passion Narrative* (Pittsburgh, 1980). As for canonical criticism, the main work was done in the OT, but B. S. Childs in *The New Testament as Canon* (Phl, 1985) provoked considerable discussion. It is one thing to consider the meaning a NT book has within the context of the whole Testament or of both Testaments; it is another to let that issue override almost completely what the book meant to the author who wrote it and to the first readers.

82   (D) The NT and Social Sciences. S. J. Case, S. Matthews, and F. Grant were pioneer scholars in using sociology and anthropology in NT study; but this approach gained new life in the early 1970s, as witnessed by J. G. Gager's *Kingdom and Community* (EC, 1975) and G. Theissen's *Sociology of Early Palestinian Christianity* (Phl, 1978). Wisely or not, terms like "the

Jesus movement," "millenarian sectarians," and "wandering charismatics" became facile commonplaces to describe the early Christians. Among outstanding American contributions were J. H. Elliott, *A Home for the Homeless* (Phl, 1981); A. Malherbe, *Social Aspects of Early Christianity* (2d ed.; Phl, 1983); and W. Meeks, *The First Urban Christians* (New Haven, 1983). The first mentioned (a study of the social context of 1 Pet) illustrates the affinity of this research with the search for NT communities (→ 79 above).

(Anderson, B. W., *TToday* 42 [1985] 292–306. Best, T. F., *SJT* 36 [1983] 181–94. Harrington, D. J., *Light of All Nations* 148–61. Kee, H. C., *Christian Origins in Sociological Perspective* [Phl, 1980]. Osiek, C., *What Are They Saying About the Social Setting of the New Testament?* [NY, 1984]. Scroggs, R., *NTS* 26 [1979–80] 164–79. Stambaugh, J. E. and D. L. Balch, *The New Testament in Its Social Environment* [Phl, 1986]. Also *BTB* 16 [1986] 107–15; *Semeia* 35 [1986].)

83   (E) Other Trends.   If scholars became more interested in the social setting of the early Christians who produced and read the NT, some also became interested in contemporary Christians who are reading the NT, as part of a hermeneutics where meaning involves the contemporary reader. The increasing number of women NT scholars (A. Yarbro Collins, B. R. Gaventa, P. Perkins, S. Schneiders, M. A. Tolbert) brought new sensitivities to NT scholarship about oppressive male attitudes, both in antiquity and today. An ambitious attempt at a thoroughgoing feminist critique of NT origins was E. Schüssler Fiorenza's *In Memory of Her* (NY, 1983). Through her optic of a hermeneutics of suspicion, she reconstructed an early egalitarian Jesus movement which existed before the introduction of oppressive male hierarchies. It is debatable, however, whether such a Christianity ever existed and is not a projection of current sensitivities (see W. S. Babcock, *Second Century* 4 [1984] 177–84). Similarly, liberation theologians from South America and elsewhere have written books on the NT (e.g., F. Belo, *A Materialist Reading of the Gospel of Mark* [Maryknoll, 1981]; L. Boff, *Jesus Christ Liberator* [Maryknoll, 1978];

J. Sobrino, *Christology at the Crossroads* [Maryknoll, 1978]). They have discovered elements of liberation and an option for the poor as the dominating elements in the "Jesus movement." Other Third-World interests also entered NT scholarship as trained scholars from India, Japan, and Africa made their contributions. Perhaps the initial decades of the 21st cent. will be able to distinguish between valid reconstruction and exaggerated retrojection in many of the issues raised (Harrington, *Light* [→ 82 above] 186–94).

84   A particularly promising development for the 21st cent. was the flourishing of ecumenical scholarship in the aftermath of Vatican II. Protestant and Catholic scholars, of equal competence and trained with the same methods, were encouraged by church bodies to work together in ecclesiastically sponsored translations of the NT and in commentaries (on EKKNT → 75 above; the French produced *TOB*). In the USA, for dialogue purposes (sponsored by Lutherans and Catholics), ecumenical studies of sensitive subjects were done by bodies of scholars from many churches: *Peter in the New Testament* and *Mary in the New Testament* (ed. R. E. Brown, *et al.;* NY, 1973, 1978); *Righteousness in the New Testament* (ed. J. Reumann, *et al.;* Phl, 1982) — works translated into many other languages. P. J. Achtemeier, a scholar of the Reformed tradition, served as the first non-Catholic president of the Catholic Biblical Association, even as Catholics R. E. Brown amd J. A. Fitzmyer served as presidents of the Society of Biblical Literature. Catholic NT scholars came to teach on the most prominent Protestant graduate faculties, and vice versa. Within the broader context of interreligious NT scholarship an increasing number of Jewish exegetes professionally trained in critical NT approaches have enriched the understanding of documents written by Jews who believed in Jesus. And further enrichment has come from the insistence that doctoral NT studies for Christians must include familiarity with the writings of early Judaism, including midrash and Talmud. Such trends bode well for the future.

71

HERMENEUTICS

Raymond E. Brown, S.S.   *Sandra M. Schneiders, I.H.M.* *

BIBLIOGRAPHY

1 *L'Ancien Testament et les chrétiens* (Paris, 1951). Barr, J., *Old and New in Interpretation* (London, 1966); *Holy Scripture: Canon, Authority, Criticism* (Phl, 1983). Brown, R. E., *The Critical Meaning of the Bible* (NY, 1981). Carson, D. A. and J. D. Woodbridge (eds.), *Hermeneutics, Authority, and Canon* (GR, 1986). Cerfaux, L., J. Coppens and J. Gribomont, *Problèmes et méthode d'exégèse théologique* (Louvain, 1950). Coppens, J., *Les harmonies des deux testaments* (Tournai, 1949). Daniélou, J., *From Shadow to Reality* (Westminster, 1960). De Lubac, H., *L'Écriture dans la tradition* (Paris, 1966). Eagleton, T., *Literary Theory: An Introduction* (Minneapolis, 1983) 1–16. Ferguson, D. S., *Biblical Hermeneutics* (Atlanta, 1986). Funk, R. W., *Language, Hermeneutic, and Word of God* (NY, 1966). Grech, P., *Ermeneutica e Teologia biblica* (Rome, 1986). Harrington, D. J., *Interpreting the New Testament* (NTM 1; Wilmington, 1979); *Interpreting the Old Testament* (OTM 1; Wilmington, 1981). Hayes, J. H. and C. Holladay, *Biblical Exegesis* (rev. ed.; Atlanta, 1986). Keegan, T., *Interpreting the Bible* (NY, 1985). Knight-Tucker (eds.), *HBMI*. Marlé, R., *Introduction to Hermeneutics* (NY, 1967). McKnight, E., *The Bible and the Reader* (Phl, 1985). Miller, D. G. (ed.), *The Hermeneutical Quest* (Fest. J. L. Mays; Allison Park, PA, 1986). Nineham, D. E. (ed.), *The Church's Use of the Bible Past and Present* (London, 1963). Reese, J., *Experiencing the Good News* (Wilmington, 1984). Ricoeur, P., *Interpretation Theory* (Fort Worth, 1976). Russell, D. A., *Criticism in Antiquity* (Berkeley, 1981). Stuhlmacher, P., *Historical Criticism and Theological Interpretation of Scripture* (Phl, 1977). Tuckett, C., *Reading the New Testament* (London, 1987). Vander Goot, H., *Interpreting the Bible in Theology and Church* (NY, 1984).

2   OUTLINE

*Sections 55–70 of this article are by S. M. Schneiders; the remainder of the article is by R. E. Brown.

INTRODUCTION

3   (I) Meaning of Hermeneutics. The Gk word *hermēneia* covered a broad scope of interpretation and clarification—a scope that modern scholars are trying to recapture and expand in their understanding of the hermeneutical task (→ 54 below). First, it can refer to interpretation by *speech* itself, inasmuch as language brings to expression and interprets what is in one's mind (conscious and unconscious)), or even what constitutes one's identity, being, and person. (We should conceive of this process dynamically, not statically; for not only does an established intention or identity find precise expression in language, but in the very act of linguistic communication one's identity and intention can grow or even come into being.) In biblical discussion we must struggle with the added complexity of the capacity of (human) biblical language to bring to expression God's "mind," "will," and "person" (terms used analogously of God; → 7 below). Second, *hermēneia* can refer to the process of *translation* from one language to another—a process that goes beyond the mechanical equivalents of words and enters into the issue of transference from one culture and world view to another. This is pertinent to Bible study because many early Christians knew the OT not in its Hebr original but in LXX Greek, and because the Gospels communicated Jesus' message not in his own Semitic tongue but in Greek. A specific aspect of translation is from an unintelligible language to an intelligible one, e.g., the *hermēneia* of tongues in 1 Cor 12:10 which was a charismatic gift with a revelatory dimension. Third, *hermēneia* can be used for interpretation by *commentary and explanation,* which is a more formal aspect.

4   Textbooks of a previous generation often lost this broad sense of *hermēneia* ("hermeneutic") which covered speech, translation, and commentary. For them "hermeneutics" (Lat pl *hermeneutica*) involved theoretical reflections on meaning, as distinct from "exegesis," an art where the rules detected in hermeneutics were practically applied. Thus understood, the "science" of hermeneutics was customarily divided into three areas: (1) noematics, dealing with the various senses of Scripture; (2) heuristics, explaining how to discover the sense of a passage; (3) prophoristics, offering rules for expounding the sense of a Scripture passage to others. These divisions have been found unwieldy and overspeculative and are rarely used today. Nevertheless, discussions about hermeneutics remain difficult since they involve the philosophy of being, the psychology of language, and sometimes sociology. In particular, there is a disconcerting tendency to attribute new and highly specialized nuances to terms (e.g., to imagination, metonymy, myth, metaphor, narrative) and to distinguish precisely between terms that have been commonly considered synonymous (e.g., between hermeneutic and hermeneutics, speech and language, sign and symbol, author and narrator). Even specialists do not always agree among themselves about the particular significance of such terms, and most readers would not understand them without technical explanations. Unless otherwise indicated, for the sake of intelligibility such terms are used here in their dictionary sense rather than in the esoteric sense proposed by specialists in hermeneutics—a difficult decision that does not in any way reject the need of literary and rhetorical criticism to develop its own vocabulary.

5   (II) General Observations. Although we shall be concerned with the meaning of written biblical *texts,* it is important to realize that initially neither Israel nor the Christian community was a "religion of the book." A set of experiences regarded as a divine deliverance from Egypt, the selection of a people, the formation of a covenant, and the promise of a land gave identity to Israel before there were the written accounts that became the Torah or Pentateuch. A community came to believe in God's eschatological presence and action in Jesus before there were written Gospels. (To be precise, the early Jewish Christians were in an intermediate position: even before they had widely circulated writings of their own composition, the task of relating Jesus to the writings already accepted in Israel [later called OT] was a major hermeneutical issue. Significantly, in facing this issue, they did not write detailed commentaries on OT books [in the manner of the Dead Sea Scroll sectarians; → Apocrypha, 67:89], applying them to Jesus; rather they described and proclaimed Jesus in terminology and imagery drawn from the OT. While there was a mutuality, Jesus was seen as the key to understanding the "book," rather than the "book" as the key to understanding Jesus; → 33 below.) When "books" describing the religious experience did come into existence, some of them quickly became a highly formative factor in the life, practice, and thought respectively of Israel and of the church. Note the word "some," because certain writings achieved sacred status as witnesses to revelation more quickly than did others—the Law and the Prophets in Israel, and the Pauline writings and individual Gospels in Christianity—part of a canon-defining process that extended over centuries. In Christianity a "rule of faith" (not written but also not independent of the first-accepted Scriptures) at times judged which works would be accepted as further Scripture. After the 4th cent. and a relatively finalized NT canon, the written Christian Bible reached a new status in authority for church belief. Even then one can argue that hermeneutics of the "book" never became as directly determinative before 1500 as it did after the Reformation or especially as it has become in the last centuries in fundamentalist strains of American Protestantism.

6   Several other factors complicate hermeneutics applied to the Bible. A canonical Gospel is an authoritative presentation of Jesus to a Christian community and (through the canon) to the whole church. Yet in another sense the authority of the written presentation has never totally replaced the authority of Jesus himself, even if he is largely knowable only through such writings. The written stage of the Christian witness does not dispense with the prewritten stage. Moreover, although we shall emphasize below the enduring importance of what the biblical book conveyed when it was first written, an element in modern literary criticism (→ 63 below) stresses that a text once written assumes a life of its own and may convey meaning or have significance beyond the original author's intention. Thus there is a postwritten stage that cannot be neglected either.

7   Perhaps the unique complication in biblical hermeneutics is the belief that the Bible had a divine as well as a human authorship, so that the written Scriptures are the word of God. This is related to the concept of inspiration (→ Inspiration, 65:67–69). Sometimes this is simplistically understood as if God spoke or dictated words which people wrote down. Speech, however, is a *human* means of communication, and so the words of Scripture were chosen and committed to writing by human beings; the divine contribution is better seen in terms of self-revealing communication which comes to expression in these words. (This has been described as "word of God in words of men," but if "word" is properly understood, "word of God" describes both the human and the divine components.) God as author of Scripture may be understood in terms of the *authority* who gives rise to the biblical books rather than in the sense of *writing* author.

8   Hermeneutics is very actively discussed today, with a concomitant abundance of new literature. The attempt to do elementary justice to current issues in a restricted space causes this article in *NJBC* to omit or curtail drastically issues that needed stress when *JBC* was written (*JBC* 71:54–79; 93–99). One way to treat biblical hermeneutics would be through discussion of the different *forms of research* employed in seeking the meaning of the Scriptures, i.e., the "criticisms": text criticism, historical c., source c., form c., redaction c., canonical c., audience c., sociological c., literary c., structure c. (structuralism, semiotics), narrative c., rhetorical c., etc. However, these approaches are not always understood the same way, and traditionally discussion has centered on the *senses* discovered by the "criticisms," which can conveniently be divided into literal and more-than-literal.

THE LITERAL SENSE OF SCRIPTURE

9   **(I) Definition.** As the term was used in the Middle Ages (Thomas Aq., *Quodl.* 7, q.6, a.14), the *sensus litteralis* was the meaning conveyed by the words (*litterae* or *verba*) of Scripture, as distinct from the sense contained in the "things" of Scripture (the *sensus spiritualis* or typical sense flowing from the *res;* → 47 below). Early church writers on the subject were often not overly aware of the human author or concerned with that author's conscious intent, and so they designated as "literal" whatever the words seemed to convey. On the one hand, this created a famous terminological confusion about the metaphorical: if Christ were designated "the lion of Judah," the literal sense for them would be that he was an animal, whence the occasional rejection of the literal sense of Scripture. On the other hand, church writers interpreted the literal sense of the Bible with great latitude, for they did not have to justify a correspondence between the meaning they found in the text and the author's original intent. The latter outlook has echoes in the sophisticated reaction of some modern literary critics against the historical-critical quest for the author's intent, which they regard as unknowable. For them "literal" refers to the sense perceived in reading, since meaning flows from the dialogue between the text and the reader. Without denigrating the ongoing interpretative possibilities of the biblical text (which some literary critics less confusingly designate as "literary" rather than literal), most exegetes, if we may judge from the commentaries on Scripture, would be working with a definition of the literal sense closely resembling the following: *The sense which the human author directly intended and which the written words conveyed.* The adverb "directly" would distinguish this sense from the ramifications that the human author's words may have taken on later (in the larger context of the Bible or when read in other situations and times) but of which the author was unaware. Two elements in the definition, "author" and "conveyed by words," need careful qualification if we are to keep open the communication between historical critics and literary critics.

10   *Author.* The ancient understanding of author was wider than the popular modern conception of writer. In reference to the biblical books, for instance, the designation "author" covers at least five different relationships between the person whose name is attached to a book and the work attributed to that person (→ Canonicity, 66:89). By modern standards most of the biblical books are anonymous or pseudonymous, with many of them the product of complex growth and collective contribution. None of the writers of canonical Gospels identified himself by name. (The use of male pronouns to refer to final biblical writers need not represent a careless use of sexist language or conscious prejudice; we lack internal and external evidence that would constitute a convincing argument that any of the biblical authors was a woman. — REB) Despite all these complications, the reference to the author's intention in the definition affirms that those who produced the biblical books had in their times a message to convey to their readers and that it is important for us to have this message in mind when we read the texts and ask what they now mean for us. *What the text now means* may well be more abundant, but it should have some relationship to *what the text meant* to the first readers. The quest implied in the definition matches Pius XII's statement in *DAS* (*EB* 550): "Let the interpreters bear in mind that their foremost and greatest endeavor should be to discern and define clearly that sense of the biblical words which is called literal . . . so that the mind of the author may be made clear."

11   We may reject the systematic skepticism of literary critics about ever knowing the intention of a nonpresent author (see E. D. Hirsch, *Validity in Interpretation* [New Haven, 1967] who argues that a charge of "intentional fallacy" is itself a fallacy). Yet common sense suggests that our efforts in this direction will be hampered by our distance from books written 3,000 to 1,900 years ago in ancient languages only imperfectly known today, in world views significantly different from our own, and often in psychological contexts strange to us. Part of the task of critical scholarship is to make not only the reader but also the commentator aware of the differences. (Even astute commentators can unconsciously shape the biblical authors in the image of modern scholarship, by not appreciating sufficiently, for instance, the looser context of oral transmission and remembrance or by imposing organized theological and anthropological approaches on nonsystematic biblical thinkers like Paul.) An intelligent debate centers on how to apply "author" in discussing books where two figures, the substantial writer and the redactor/editor, were separated by considerable distance of time and/or outlook. During the "biblical period" of composition (roughly up to AD 150), we often find considerable redaction of earlier written work. The composition of the book of Isaiah covered a span of at least 200 years

(→ Deutero-Isaiah, 21:2–3); not only were new sections added to the original parts that came from Isaiah's lifetime, but also some additions had the result of modifying the meaning of the original. The last verses of Amos may be an addition; they supply an optimistic conclusion to an otherwise pessimistic book (→ Amos 13:24). In instances like this, the quest for the literal sense includes both the sense that the parts originally had before editing and the sense of the book after editing (→ 28 below).

12 *Conveyed by written words.* This part of the definition of the literal sense gives priority to the text, for the author's intention does not become a sense of Scripture until it is effectively conveyed by writing. (The distinction between the author's thought world and the message he conveys in writing is important in discussing the limits of biblical inerrancy.) In particular it must be noted that, while what Jesus himself intended by his words is important, the intention is not in itself a sense of *Scripture,* for Jesus was not a Gospel writer. Indeed, since most often we do not know the context in which Jesus actually spoke his words, it may be impossible to tell exactly what the words meant when first uttered. The literal sense of a Gospel passage is the meaning attributed to Jesus' words by the individual evangelist, with the result that the same words can have different meanings according to the different contexts in which the evangelists have set them (→ NT Thought, 81:79). In the evangelists' interpretation we have understandings of Jesus' words that the Holy Spirit has inspired for the church—an inspiration that assures believers that even when the evangelists go beyond Jesus' own teaching, they have not seriously distorted Jesus.

13 Implicit in the notion of "conveyed by written words" is the comprehension of the audience/readers envisioned by the author. Reflection on that factor may check overimaginative proposals about what the author meant. Interpretations based on elaborate relationships among widely scattered biblical words and passages (detected through concordances) must be judged on whether the ancient author could have expected his audience, who had no concordance, to make the connections. A debate as to whether the torn veil in Mark 15:38 was the outer or the inner veil of the Temple Holy Place may be enlightened by a query about the makeup of Mark's audience, to whom he had to explain simple Jewish purificatory customs (7:3). Would Mark have expected such an audience to know that there were two veils or where they were placed?

14 **(II) General Problems in Determining the Literal Sense.** We shall not emphasize here the usual rules for determining the sense of any author and book (correct translation of words; attention to phrase and sentence structure; context; peculiar style and usage; etc.). Rather we are concerned with some general issues in approaching the Bible, issues that reflect both the religious and the scholarly situation today.

(A) Different Capabilities for Exegesis. An enthusiasm pushing all to read, know, and understand the Scriptures can quickly founder on the hard fact that determining what an ancient author meant is often no simple task. Although the literal sense is sometimes called the plain sense, it may become plain only after expanded effort. Stock market tables in the newspaper are lucidly clear, but only to those who have taken the effort to learn to read them. Can one think a Bible millennia old is going to be easier to read than the newspaper published this morning? As Pius XII acknowledged in *DAS* (EB 35–36), "The literal sense of a passage is not always as obvious in the speeches and writings of the

ancient authors of the East as it is in the works of our own time." Attempts to minimize or to avoid the necessary steps involved will produce fundamentalist confusion. Nevertheless, reading the Scriptures profitably must not become an elitist privilege for literati. In considering this impasse due respect must be paid to different expectations proportionate to the different capabilities of readers. Let us leave aside formal university requirements for graduate biblical study by future professors who will train teachers and clergy, and let us concentrate on two important groups of Bible students and readers: professional and general.

15 PROFESSIONAL READERS. Those who will preach and teach (clergy, catechists, leaders of Bible classes)—those whose knowledge of the Bible can notably affect how they communicate God's word to others—have to make realistic efforts to grasp what the authors of Scripture were trying to communicate. Otherwise they will impose on the authors grossly anachronistic ideas and conceptions. (The issue here is not the validity of a more-than-literal sense, but the avoidance of a simplistic literalism that presents surface impressions as the literal sense, e.g., as when a pseudo-scientific antievolutionist theory is assumed to conform to the intentions of the author of Genesis, who in fact had no scientific cosmological knowledge and whose conception of creation was so symbolic that it would be equally strange to evolutionists and nonevolutionists.) Extremely useful to those who need a degree of professional knowledge is auxiliary background information about biblical geography, archaeology, and the transmission of biblical texts. Two auxiliaries are especially important: history and language.

A knowledge of the history of the biblical era. The story of God's action in the history of a particular people is largely unintelligible when isolated from Near Eastern history. To seek to divorce God's action from that history and to make it timeless is to distort a fundamental message of the Bible, viz., that God acts only in concrete circumstances and times (such as yours and mine). What we say here is particularly applicable to the historical and the prophetic books of the OT, easily two-thirds of the Bible. Many students, loathe to familiarize themselves with the dates and events of long-dead civilizations, lose through the lack of interest in ancient history the wealth of some of the richest sections of the Bible (→ OT Thought 77:104, 112). Perhaps some of this knowledge of antiquity can be made more palatable to modern tastes when a necessary sociological aspect is added to it—the need to know about not only royal courts, international politics, and wars, but also the very structure of the life of the people involved in the biblical story. In the last third of the 20th cent. sociological studies of the Bible have been frequent. In Israelite history scholars claim to recognize aspects of social struggles known from our own times, e.g., a peasant revolt to gain rights to land (→ OT Criticism, 69:73–76). NT Christianity, alienated from the religious and political society of its time, has been studied in the light of the alienation of modern sectarians (→ NT Criticism, 70:82). While sometimes this sociological analysis is overdone, it helps to underline in a clearly pertinent way the importance of understanding the biblical era in all its aspects.

16 Another important auxiliary is the *knowledge of the biblical languages.* Only a small percentage of those who study the Bible can be experts at Hebrew, Aramaic, and Greek; yet some familiarity with the structure and thought pattern of these languages is essential for a type of professional biblical knowledge. Such a demand is again part of the recognition that God has acted in particular times and places—his message would have taken a different form and nuance had it been expressed in other languages. Unless one has some idea of the latitude of the "tenses" in Hebrew, one has difficulty in understanding the undefined time designations in the words of the prophet, i.e., a lack of temporal precision that opened these prophecies to future as well as present fulfillment. Some of the basic words of biblical theology vocabulary defy adequate translations into English, e.g., *ḥesed* (covenant kindness, mercy) in the OT, *alētheia* (truth) in the NT; modern translations catch only a part of a wider connotation. The frequent plays on similar-sounding words in OT poetry and on words of similar root in NT Greek are lost to the student who takes no interest in the biblical languages. With English as one's only linguistic tool, it is possible to have a good knowledge of the Scriptures but scarcely a professional one.

17   GENERAL READERS, who will not be called on to preach or to teach the Bible but wish to grasp its message for their own lives and for nourishing the faith they share with others, will also be called on to make some effort in their reading. The Judeo-Christian religion is based on a belief that God has communicated with human beings and that the Bible is a privileged vehicle of that communication (see S. M. Schneiders's leaflet, "How to Read the Bible Prayerfully" [Collegeville, 1984]). Biblical communication involves more than a comprehension of the literal sense, for learned scholars who are superbly equipped to detect what a biblical author meant in his time may have no religious appreciation of what the text can mean to their own lives. Moreover, considerable portions of Scripture are easily intelligible to all because they voice universal sentiments, e.g., some of the Psalms and some simple stories of Jesus. Spiritual solace and insight may be drawn from the Bible by those who have no technical knowledge; their appreciation may be based on experience shared with what the Bible narrates. For the ordinary, intelligent Jew or Christian, however, reading the Scriptures should involve a component of understanding what the original author meant, since the message that he directed to his times is certainly part of God's inspired communication. The primary duty of the human author was to be intelligible in his era, writing in a language and a culture far removed from our own. What he wrote communicates meaning to us today, but he did not envision our circumstances or write to us in our times. In an effort to draw from his text a message for our circumstances, there is always the problem of whether we achieve true communication or only an illusion in which we impose on the text what we want to find (eisegesis). A major safeguard consists in establishing an intelligible relationship between what the author meant and what the text now seems to mean—a relationship that is sometimes one of tension or correction. The literal sense constitutes one side of that relationship, and the basic background information enabling the ordinary reader to perceive that sense is not difficult to acquire since scholars write and lecture in order to make commonly accepted views available to the general public.

18   There remains, however, an undercurrent of opposition to the suggestion that general readers should or must make an effort to acquire information in order to profit fully from the Bible. On the one hand, such an undercurrent may reflect a simplistic attitude about scholarly difficulties. One finds the suggestion that if scholars were cooperative, they would make the reading process effortless by rendering the Scriptures into language that is readily intelligible to "the common man." We shall mention below (→ 54) the quest to demythologize and the legitimate desire so to interpret Scripture that its phrasing is not an obstacle. Translations of the Bible into truly contemporary English can to a certain extent give us the equivalent of biblical ideas and facilitate understanding. But much of the biblical imagery cannot be modernized; and if it can be interpreted, it cannot be dispensed with, for it is too integral a part of the biblical message, e.g., the symbolism of Rev. The strangeness of the presentation is an exteriorization of the strangeness of the biblical message, which should be a challenge and should require effort to appropriate. The difference between the world view of the biblical author and our own must involve educating modern readers to understand the ancient mentality so that they can grasp both the message and the modality which that mentality gave to the message.

19   A more frequent assumption behind the thesis of effortlessness in reading Scripture involves God's activity. If he had a guiding role in the composition of Scripture, he will insure that it is meaningful to every interested reader. After all, if the literate but simple folk of the past could read and love Scripture, why cannot the scripturally uneducated do the same today? Yet is God's assistance a cure-all for the different circumstances of people? There is a difference between past generations who often had little education in any field and a present generation that has education (primary or secondary) but not in religion or Scripture. From their general education people consciously or unconsciously bring to the Bible questions that could not have occurred to past generations. For instance, no one who has studied elementary-school textbooks can read the first chapters of Gen without wondering if the world really was created in six days. Biblical information is needed to distinguish between the religious teaching of Gen about creation and the naïve prescientific outlook of the author. Overall, in order to read the Bible with appropriate comprehension, people's biblical education should be proportionate to their general education; then they can deal with issues that arise from that general education. Such a standard implies that the seed which is the word of God does not produce abundantly even on good soil without some patient and generous tilling (Luke 8:11,15).

20   **(B) The Issue of Relevance.** The idea that the Bible is a "classic," even if overdone, means that by common recognition it has a relevance partly independent of the individual reader. Its truth or beauty makes it able to speak to people in all times and cultures. (For the "classic" issue, see D. Tracy, *The Analogical Imagination* [NY, 1981]; K. Stendahl, *JBL* 103 [1984] 3–10.) People read the Bible for a purpose; and, whether they admit it or not, exegetes interpret the Bible for a purpose. A small percentage may be concerned with the Bible for literary appreciation, or for ancient historical information, or as part of comparative religion. The vast majority (even in "neutral" college religion departments) approach the Bible because it is supposed to have religious import for life. Critical exegesis, especially in the 17th and 18th cents., originated in antagonism to a dogmatic theology that imposed later doctrinal issues on biblical texts. An exaggerated ideal developed of a search for objective truth, ruling out the issue of religious relevance. (Note, however, that historical-critical exegesis did *not* find acceptance in this way in 20th-cent. Roman Catholicism; it was encouraged by popes [→ Church Pronouncements, 72:6–9] and was not marked by a desire to be free from dogmatic and ecclesiastical guidance.) This exclusion frustrated the religious interests of those who looked for academic help, thus producing a charge of irrelevancy — a charge often overdone, quite untrue of the Roman Catholic exegesis that developed after Vatican II, and increasingly no longer true of exegesis in general. The search for the literal sense has a descriptive bent, but it is quite appropriate for the search to be religiously sensitive and relevant. The literal sense had a strong religious purpose in the author's own time, and the dynamism of the Bible implies ongoing religious relevance. It is important to distinguish between what a biblical passage meant and what it means, but such meanings are not totally separable or unrelated.

21 Nevertheless, there are problems about the range and immediacy of relevance. In a sense, everything in the Bible can be important and relevant for someone and for some purpose. Frustration occurs when teachers misjudge what is appropriate to the vocation and interest of students, spending undue time on specialized issues more suitable for advanced research. More frequently, students in a quest for instant applicability cannot recognize what they will need by way of biblical knowledge for long-term utility. Working through the text of Scripture in exegesis is not as instantly gratifying as being fed with the synthesized results in terms of biblical themes. Specialized interests on the part of Bible students are quite appropriate unless it is claimed that a particular interest should be the primary rather than the secondary optic, so that general Bible study is deemed irrelevant unless it meets that interest. The biblical authors were not writing for the theologian, the preacher, or the ascetic. The witness to God's revelation that they gave us is not a compendium convenient for our purposes; it is a library of books dealing with relations between God and human beings on the scale of life itself. In particular, the scope of the OT brings into relationship with God not only the spiritual and theological aspects of life but also the secular (→ Wisdom Lit,. 27:5-6ff.; → Canticle, 29:5-8), and the seamy (war, depravity), and the humdrum (political history, bumbling rulers, jaded priests). Selecting from this totality only what seems to us religiously or spiritually useful may deprive Scripture of the possibility of correcting warped attitudes about religion, including the failure to understand that God acts in very ordinary history through ambiguous people. We can recognize how biased were past generations in reading the Scriptures and how they distorted them to their own purposes. We must be careful that the quest for instant relevance does not canonize our biases which we cannot recognize. To pass on to the next generation only what we find relevant in Scripture may be to censor Scripture, for precisely what we do not find relevant to our times may be God's principal word to another generation.

22 In the history of biblical interpretation in the Catholic Church, each time there has been a movement that put emphasis on the primacy of literal exegesis (e.g., Jerome, the school of St. Victor in the Middle Ages, Richard Simon), this movement has been quickly swallowed up in a more attractive movement that stressed the theological or the spiritual aspects of Scripture almost to the exclusion of literal exegesis. And so Origen's spiritual exegesis conquered Jerome's literal exegesis through the efforts of Augustine; the exegesis practiced at St. Victor was swallowed up in the theological and philosophical use of Scripture in later Scholasticism; Bossuet and Pascal outshone R. Simon in popular influence (→ OT Criticism, 69:6). In part this history may warn us that literal exegesis must be careful to be religiously relevant and not only informative on an antiquarian scale. But it should also warn us that it is the duty of those who teach and study Scripture not to allow themselves to be misled into easier paths which in the long run will take them away from the biblical text with all its complexities. The encyclical *DAS,* confirmed by Vatican II, has made a thoroughgoing quest for the literal sense a real possibility for Catholics for the first time in centuries (→ Church Pronouncements, 72:21, 29). It remains to be seen whether this opportunity will be capitalized on or lost.

23 **(C) Establishing Literary Form.** In the quest for the literal sense of any writing, it is important to determine the literary form the author was employing. In a modern library, books are classified according to the type of literature: fiction, poetry, history, biography, drama, etc. Often the classification for individual books is indicated by the dust jacket. The term "classification" should not be misleading, for the issue (and this applies to *all that follows*) is not merely taxonomic: we approach forms of literature with different expectations and we profit from them differently. A history and a novel may treat the same person or event, but we expect different degrees of fact and fiction from them, whereas in regard to poetry the issue of fact and fiction is irrelevant. Nevertheless, all three can convey truth, and sometimes one conveys a truth that the others cannot.

There is a canonical sense in which the Bible as a whole is one book (→ 73 below), but by way of origin it is a library (→ Church Pronouncements, 72:40) — the library of ancient Israel and of the 1st-cent. Christian church. This library has all the diversity we would expect in the literary output of an articulate culture that spanned nearly 2,000 years. In the Bible the library books have been bound together into one, without the advantage of dust jackets. There must be a serious endeavor to classify them according to the type of literature they represent. This is what is meant by determining the literary form (*genus litterarium*) which the author has employed. The encyclical *DAS* and Vatican II have made this approach imperative for all serious Catholic students of the Bible (→ Church Pronouncements, 72:14, 22), so that the first question we must ask in opening any part of the Bible is: What type of literature do we have here? This emphasis on literary form is an offshoot of the German development of form criticism or *Formgeschichte* (→ NT Criticism, 70:42-45; → OT Criticism, 69:38). Classic form criticism has been concerned primarily with the subsections that have gone to make up an individual biblical book; here we are giving primary attention to the literary form of the whole book.

(Berger, K., *Formgeschichte des Neuen Testaments* [Heidelberg, 1984]. Hayes, J. H. [ed.], *Old Testament Form Criticism* [San Antonio, 1974]. McKnight, E. V., *What Is Form Criticism?* [Phl, 1969]. Redlich, E. B., *Form Criticism* [London, 1939]. Tucker, G. M., *Form Criticism of the Old Testament* [Phl, 1971].)

24 In a broad sense, of course, the determination of literary form has been a principle implicitly recognized from a very early period. From the time of Rabbi Gamaliel II (late 1st cent. AD) the Jews have classified the books of the OT as Torah, Prophets, and Writings (→ Canonicity, 66:22, 29); and the Christian division of these books into Pentateuch, Historical, Prophetic, and Sapiential is even closer to a distinction of literary types. Only in modern times, however, with the discovery of the literatures of people contemporary with Israel, have we realized just how many types of literature were current in antiquity. Without attempting to be exhaustive, let us illustrate this from the OT, which is a more varied library than the NT. There are many varieties of poetry in the OT: epic poetry underlies some of the narratives in the Pentateuch and Josh; lyric poetry is found in Pss and Cant; didactic poetry is found in Prov, Sir, and Wis; elements of drama are found in Job. Within the prophetic books there are both prophecy and apocalyptic (→ OT Apocalyptic, 19:5–18). There is not one form of history in the OT but many forms: a factual, penetrating analysis, seemingly by an eyewitness, in the court history of David (2 Sam 11–1 Kgs 2); stylized, abbreviated court records in Kgs and Chr; romanticized and simplified epic history of the national saga in Exod; tales of tribal heroes in Judg; stories of the great men and women of yore in the patriarchal accounts. There is even prehistory in the Gen narratives of the origin of humanity and of evil, narratives that borrow legends from the lore of other nations and make them the vehicles of monotheistic theology (→ Genesis, 2:10–13). In addition, there are fictional tales, parables, allegories, proverbs, maxims, love stories, etc. The combination of literary forms in one complex book may be a transforming factor in interpretation.

25   Once readers have determined the literary form of any biblical book or passage, standards applicable to that form help to clarify what the author meant, i.e., the literal sense. If Jonah is a fictional parable, the reader should recognize that the author is *not* giving a history of the relations of Israel and Assyria and is *not* presenting the story of a prophet in a whale's belly as a factual happening; rather, in an imaginative way the author is communicating a profound truth about God's love for the Gentile nations. If the statement about the sun standing still in Josh 10:13 comes from a fragment of highly poetic description in a victory song, readers will judge it in the light of poetic license rather than according to the rules of strict history. If the Samson narratives are folktales, readers will not give to them the same historical credence allotted to the history of David's court. Many past difficulties about the Bible have stemmed from the failure to recognize the diversity of literary forms that it contains and from the tendency to misinterpret as scientific history pieces of the Bible that are not historical or are historical only in a more popular sense. We have taken examples from the OT, but the same problem exists in the NT. The Gospels are not scientifically historical biographies of Jesus but written accounts of the preaching and teaching of the early church about Jesus, and their accuracy must be judged according to the standards of preaching and teaching (→ Church Pronouncements, 72:35). The infancy narratives may differ in literary form from the rest of Matt and Luke.

26   This approach to exegesis based on detecting the type of literature involved is subject to two common misconceptions. First, some conservatives regard the quest for literary form as an attempt to circumvent the historicity of biblical passages, and therefore they think it dangerous to apply the theory of literary forms to the more sacred sections of the Bible. But every piece of writing can be classified as belonging to one type of literature or another. Factual history is a type of literature; fiction is another; both exist in the Bible, as do almost all the intermediary literary types between the two extremes. If one correctly classifies a certain part of the Bible as fiction, one is not destroying the historicity of

that section, for it never was history; one is simply recognizing the author's intention in writing that section. The second misconception concerns the relation of inspiration to the diversity of biblical literary forms. There is a feeling that somehow the recognition that certain parts of the Bible were written as fiction weakens or challenges their inspiration. The encyclical *DAS* (*EB* 559) gives an answer: God could inspire any type of literature that was not unworthy or deceitful, i.e., not contrary to his holiness and truth (e.g., pornography, lies). Biblical fiction is just as inspired as biblical history.

27   **(D) Literary History and Redaction.** After one has determined the type of literature involved, another step in the quest for the literal sense is to find out the literary history of the book or section one is studying. This is a special problem in biblical study because of the long history of editing (→ 11 above). One must unravel the individual traditions of the Pentateuch, the collections that comprise Isa, the chronological order of Jeremiah's prophecies (different from the present order of the biblical book). In the Gospels it is important to know whether a particular saying of Jesus has come to Luke or Matt from Mark, from Q, or from one of the sources peculiar to the respective evangelist. Such literary history is not investigated in biblical exegesis simply for its own value, which might be largely antiquarian, but for what it tells us about the intention of an author who drew on previous sources in composing his own work. The joining and the adaptation of those sources may be indicative of a theological outlook that reflects on the literal sense of the final composition.

28   Here we touch on the approach to the Bible known as *Redaktionsgeschichte.* If *Formgeschichte* is concerned with the different forms or types of literature in the Bible and the rules germane to them, *Redaktionsgeschichte* is concerned with the way in which these literary pieces are made to serve the general purpose of the writer. For instance Gospel exegetes have done only part of their work when they have classified a story as a particular type of parable and have determined to what extent it conforms to the general rules for that parable type. Why is the parable included in this Gospel and set in this particular context? What meaning does the evangelist attach to it? To answer these questions about aim in composition is to take another step in determining the literal sense of Scripture.

29   After the steps we have described (determining the literary form, the literary history, and the aims of composition), the exegete is then in a position to seek the literal meaning of individual passages and verses. Here the process is the same as for any other ancient work. The literal meaning of some 90–95 percent of the Bible can be determined by a reasonable application of the ordinary rules of interpretation. There are some passages whose meaning eludes us because the text has been corrupted in transmission, because they use rare words, because the author expressed himself obscurely, or because we do not have sufficient knowledge about the context in which they were composed. Continued study constantly casts light even on passages such as these. (See O. Kaiser and W. G. Kümmel, *Exegetical Method: A Student's Handbook* [NY, 1967]; R S. Barbour, *Traditio-Historical Criticism of the Gospels* [London, 1972]; N. Perrin, *What Is Redaction Criticism?* [Phl, 1969].)

MORE-THAN-LITERAL SENSES

30   We now turn to the detection of scriptural meaning that goes beyond the literal — a sense that by definition is not confined to what the human author directly intended and conveyed in his written words. On the one hand, the possibility of such an "excess of meaning" is inherent in *any great work* being read at a later period, for a classic enlarges the horizon of continuing generations of readers. Often the original author did not envision those future readers, but his or her written words keep reaching out in a dialogue confronting new issues — a new "world in front of the text." On the other hand, the issue of more-than-literal meaning is specially pertinent to *Scripture*. First, centuries after he wrote it, the author's book was joined in a collection called the Bible. This new arrangement, which scarcely could have been foreseen by the author, may have seriously modified his intent. (For instance, Luke thought of his Gospel and Acts as a unified book, but the canonical process has divided them. There is no evidence that the author of John with his claim to unique witness would have happily had his work placed alongside and on the same level as other works called Gospels.) The juxtaposition of books provides connections in the Bible that no single author may have made, enlarging the meaning originally intended. Second, even after the canonical collection was stabilized, belief that Scripture had a divine "author" means that the Bible is God's word to audiences of all time. This continuing biblical engagement of readers/hearers with God (with or without the catalyst of preaching) uncovers meaning beyond that envisioned by the human author in his local and limited circumstances.

The recognition of a more-than-literal sense is, as we shall see, as old as Scripture itself and has often had more dynamic influence on people's lives than the literal sense. Nevertheless, it presents a problem of controls. When does the quest cease to be exegesis (the detection of a meaning that arises in the text) and become eisegesis (the imposition upon the text of a meaning alien to it)? When is there a genuine dialogue between the text and current readers, as distinct from the text being merely the occasion of readers talking to themselves about their own preconceptions? To what extent is a responsible relationship between the literal sense and the more-than-literal sense an answer to the issue of controls? The history of more-than-literal exegesis reflects such problems.

31   **(I) History of More-than-literal Exegesis.** While many different approaches will be described, sensitivity toward the issue of deeper meaning is the unifying factor. Difficulties uncovered in this history should not detract from the validity of the goal.

(A) To the End of the New Testament Era. Within the Bible itself we find the author of Wis 11–19 taking the older narratives of the plagues and the deliverance from Egypt and reading out of them a theme of deliverance for his own time. A parallelism between past and present is seen in this type of exegesis. Another example would be the connection that Dt-Isa draws between the exodus from Egypt and the return from Babylon. Such parallelism is based on the thesis that God's actions on behalf of his people follow a pattern of fidelity: he is the same yesterday, today, and forever. It is not based on a cyclic approach to history.

32   In the last centuries BC there was a development that had profound effects on both Jewish and Christian exegesis. Whereas in more ancient times the prophets had been understood primarily as speaking to their own times with a divinely given foreknowledge of God's plan for the immediate and relevant future, now the prophets of old were thought to have predicted the distant future. Apocalyptic (→ OT Apocalyptic, 19:19–21) was an important factor in this change of emphasis, following the pattern of Dan, wherein purportedly a prophet of the 6th cent. had visions of what would happen in the 2d cent. Such an understanding of the prophets, and indeed of other biblical writers like the psalmists, gave birth to the pesher exegesis of Qumran (→ Apocrypha, 67:89), where every line of the ancient books was interpreted in terms of what was happening to the Qumran sect hundreds of years later.

(Brooke, G. J., *Exegesis at Qumran: 4QFlorilegium* [JSOTSup 29; Sheffield, 1985]. Bruce, F. F., *Biblical Exegesis in the Qumran Texts* [Grand Rapids, 1959]. Fitzmyer, J. A., "The Use of Explicit Old Testament Quotations in Qumran Literature and in the New Testament," *NTS* 7 [1960–61] 297–333. Gabrion, H., "L'interprétation de l'Écriture dans la littérature de Qumrân," *ANRW* II/25.1, 779–848. Horgan, M. P., *Pesharim: Qumran Interpretations of Biblical Books* [CBQMS 8; Washington, 1979] esp. 244–59.)

33   Moreover, this understanding of the OT prophets and psalmists explains to some extent the principles according to which the NT authors interpreted the OT. Isa 7:14 could be pictured by Matt 1:23 as foretelling the virgin birth of Jesus; Dt-Isa in the Suffering Servant passages could be pictured as foretelling the sufferings and death of the Messiah (Luke 24:26); the author of Ps 22 could be pictured as foreseeing in detail the passion of Jesus (Matt 27:35,39,43,46). Some would compare this exegesis to the pesher exegesis of Qumran (B. Lindars, *New Testament Apologetic* [Phl, 1961]), but there are important differences. The Qumran interpreters in their systematic commentaries studied the OT to interpret their community's history, but the focal point of the NT authors was Jesus who cast light on the OT. They wrote their "commentaries" on him, so that there were no systematic Christian commentaries on the OT until the late 2d cent., e.g., Hippolytus commenting on Cant and Dan. We have no evidence that the NT writers felt that every line of the OT applied to Jesus or had a Christian meaning — a theory that became popular in patristic times. The NT exegesis of the OT was extraordinarily varied, and any attempt to classify it as one type of exegesis is doomed to failure. It had elements of *sensus plenior,* typology, allegory, and accommodation. A particular feature of this NT exegesis was to read the presence of Jesus back into OT scenes (1 Cor 10:4; see A. T. Hanson, *Jesus Christ in the Old Testament* [London, 1965]).

(Bläser, P., "St. Paul's Use of the Old Testament," *TD* 2 [1954] 49–52. Cerfaux, L., "Simples réflexions à propos de l'exégèse apostolique," *Problèmes et méthode* 33–44; "L'exégèse de l'Ancien Testament par le Nouveau," in *L'Ancien Testament et les chrétiens* 132–48. Ellis, E. E., *Paul's Use of the Old Testament* [GR, 1981]; *Prophecy and Hermeneutic in Early Christianity* [GR, 1978]. Kugel, J. L. and R. A. Greer, *Early Biblical Interpretation* [Phl, 1986] — both Christian and Jewish. Longenecker, R. N., *Biblical Exegesis in the Apostolic Period* [GR, 1975]. Van der Ploeg, J., "L'exégèse de l'Ancien Testament dans l'Épître aux Hébreux," *RB* 54 [1947] 187–228. Venard, L., "Citations de l'Ancien Testament dans le Nouveau Testament," *DBSup* 2. 23–51.)

34   While we shall be concerned in the rest of our brief history with Christian exegesis of the OT, we should note that in pre-Christian Judaism and in post-Christian rabbinic circles the quest for a more-than-literal exegesis was just as common as in Christian circles. The targums (→ Texts, 68:103–5) really supply an exegesis of what they translate, discovering messianic elements in the OT. The midrashim (→ Apocrypha, 67:140) also interpret previous Scripture in application to current problems. The Jewish nonliteral exegesis that had the greatest influence on Christian exegesis was the allegorizing of Philo (→ Apocrypha, 67:125).

(Bonsirven, J., *Exégèse rabbinique et exégèse paulinienne* [Paris, 1939]. Fishbane, M., *Biblical Interpretation in Ancient Israel* [Oxford, 1986]. Gélin, A., "Comment le peuple d'Israel lisait l'Ancien Testament," *L'Ancien Testament et les chrétiens* 117–31. Ginzberg, L., "Allegorical Interpretations," *JE* 1. 403ff. Patte, D., *Early Jewish Hermeneutic in Palestine* (SBLDS 22; Missoula, 1975). Sowers, S. G., *The Hermeneutics of Philo and Hebrews* [Richmond, 1965].)

35   **(B) Patristic Era.** In the early Christian writings of the 2d cent. we find evidence of a very free spiritual exegesis (e.g., *Barn.*). Yet even more restrained exegetes, like Justin and Tertullian, ransacked the OT for proof texts referring to Christ, and they interpreted these passages in a way that went far beyond the literal sense. It was Alexandria that produced the first great Christian school of exegesis; and through men like Clement and Origen, Philo's allegorizing achieved a dominant place in the Christian exegesis of the OT. Clement based his exegesis on the existence of a Christian gnosis, i.e., the secret knowledge of the profoundest truths of the Christian faith, to which the elite were initiated. The key to the gnosis was an allegorical exegesis of the Bible, an exegesis that ran the gamut from typology through accommodation to the Philonic concept of the Bible as a lesson in psychology and cosmology.

36   Origen probably had more influence on patristic exegesis than any other single figure, although later his theological orthodoxy became suspect. Almost every manual states that Origen's exegesis was unrestrainedly allegorical, and he is usually blamed for denying the literal sense of scripture. A. von Harnack spoke of Origen's "biblical alchemy." H. de Lubac, J. Daniélou, and others have modified this picture. Origen did not simply disregard the literal sense (although he did not understand that the metaphorical sense was literal), but he was interested in a sense of Scripture that could make Christians see the OT as their book. A good part of his allegorical exegesis was based on the theory that the OT was christological in many passages. Granting that we should judge Origen more appreciatively and that there is a restrained element in his exegesis (which de Lubac calls spiritual sense, and Daniélou calls typology), this writer does not share the view that Origen's exegesis can really be revived for our time, even though his interests were similar to those exemplified in some modern approaches (→ 45–48, 52 below).

37   The exegetical school of Antioch, Alexandria's rival as a great Christian center, has been too naïvely heroicized as the champion of critical exegesis, in contradistinction to Alexandria's allegorical exegesis. At the end of the 3d cent., Lucian of Samosata laid the foundations of this school, and its representatives included Diodorus of Tarsus (d. 390), Theodore of Mopsuestia (d. 428), and, to some extent, John Chrysostom (d. 407). In the West, Julian, the Pelagian bishop of Aeclanum (d. 454), was the leading adherent to Antiochene principles. The great Antiochenes, then, were not contempo-

raries of Origen but of the later Alexandrians like Athanasius (d. 373) and Didymus the Blind (d. 398). In many ways, Cyril of Alexandria (d. 444) showed a perceptivity in literal exegesis that placed him between the Alexandrian and Antiochene schools. The 4th-cent. Cappadocians (esp. Gregory of Nyssa and Basil), on the other hand, continued very strongly in the Origenist vein.

Little Antiochene exegesis has been preserved. In theory, and to some extent in practice, Antioch did give more attention to the literal sense (with all the limitations of exegesis in the 4th cent.). But Antioch also proposed a more-than-literal exegesis that involved *theōria*, for all practical purposes a close equivalent of Alexandrian *allēgoria*. *Theōria* was an intuition or vision by which the OT prophet could see the future through the medium of his present circumstances. After such a vision it was possible for him to phrase his writing in such a way as to describe both the contemporary meaning of the events and their future fulfillment. (For studies of *theōria*, see A. Vaccari, *Bib* 1 [1920] 3–36; F. Seisdedos, *EstBib* 11 [1952] 31–67; P. Ternant, *Bib* 34 [1953] 135–58, 354–83, 456–86.) The task of the Antiochene exegetes was to find both meanings in the words of the prophets; and in their search for the future meaning of the prophets' words (the product of *theōria*), the Antiochenes took into account the problem of the awareness of the human author more often than did the Alexandrians, who tended to see the future in symbols and events, as well as in the prophetic word.

(On JUSTIN: Prigent, P., *Justin et l'Ancien Testament* [Paris, 1964]. Shotwell, W. A., *The Biblical Exegesis of Justin Martyr* [London, 1965]. On CLEMENT OF ALEXANDRIA: Camelot, T., *RB* 53 [1946] 242–48. Marsh, H. G., *JTS* 37 [1936] 64–80. Mondésert, C., *RSR* 26 [1936] 158–80; *Clément d'Alexandrie* [Paris, 1944]. On ORIGEN: Daniélou, J., *Origène* [Paris, 1948]. De Lubac, H., *Histoire et esprit* [Paris, 1950]. Hanson, R. P. C., *Allegory and Event* [London, 1958]. Nautin, P., *Origène: Sa vie et son oeuvre* [Paris, 1977]. Trigg, J. W., *Origen: The Bible and Philosophy in the Third-Century Church* [Atlanta, 1983]. On THEODORE OF MOPSUESTIA: Devreesse, R., *RB* 53 [1946] 207–41. On CYRIL: Kerrigan, A., *St. Cyril of Alexandria, Interpreter of the Old Testament* [Rome, 1952]. On JULIAN: D'Alès, A., *RSR* 6 [1916] 311–24. On CHRYSOSTOM: Ogara, F., *Greg* 24 [1943] 62–77. For a comparison of Alexandrian and Antiochene exegesis, see J. Guillet, *RSR* 37 [1947] 257–302; also W. Burghardt, "On Early Christian Exegesis," *TS* 11 [1950] 78–116; C. Hay, "Antiochene Exegesis and Christology," *AusBR* 12 [1964] 10–23. On GREGORY OF NYSSA: Canévet, M., *Grégoire de Nysse et l'herméneutique biblique* [Paris, 1983]. Harl, M., *Écriture et culture philosophique dans la pensée de Grégoire de Nysse* [Leiden, 1971]. For the positive value of patristic exegesis, see D. C. Steinmetz, *TToday* 37 [1980] 27–38.)

38   Meanwhile in the West some of the Lat exegetes (e.g., Ambrosiaster, *ca.* 375) showed sobriety in exegesis. However, with Hilary (d. 367), Ambrose (d. 397), and especially Augustine (d. 430), the waves of Alexandrian allegorical exegesis swept into the West. In Hilary's *Tractatus mysteriorum* we find the principle that the OT *in its entirety* is prefigurative of the NT. Tyconius, a Donatist exegete of the late 4th cent. laid down the rule in his *Liber regularum* that every verse in the OT could be interpreted in a Christian way. Augustine epitomized this approach in this principle: "The New Testament lies hidden in the Old; the Old Testament is enlightened through the New" ("*In vetere novum lateat, et in novo vetus pateat*"—*Quaest. in Heptateuchum* 2.73; PL 34. 625).

In his early days Jerome (d. 420) followed Origen's principles, but the commentaries written at the end of Jerome's life betray greater interest in the literal sense. Yet after Jerome's time and the close of the 4th cent., the style of Alexandrian exegesis dominated in the West, and Antiochene exegesis had little lasting influence (see

M. Laistner, *HTR* 40 [1947] 19–31). Indeed, once the Council of Constantinople II (533) blackened the name of Theodore of Mopsuestia, the Antiochene heritage was looked on with suspicion. In the works of some of the great figures of Western exegesis, e.g., Gregory the Great (d. 604) and Bede (d. 735), allegorical exegesis bloomed.

(On LAT EXEGESIS: Kelly, J. N. D. in Nineham (ed.), *Church's Use* 41–56. On AUGUSTINE: Pontet, M., *L'exégèse de S. Augustin prédicateur* [Paris, 1944]. On JEROME: Hartman, L. in *A Monument to St. Jerome* [ed. F. X. Murphy; NY, 1952] 35–81. Kelly, J. N. D., *Jerome* [NY, 1976]. Penna, A., *Principi e carattere dell' esegesi di S. Gerolamo* [Rome, 1950]. Steinmann, J., *St. Jerome and His Times* [Notre Dame, 1959].)

39   (C) Middle Ages. The guiding theoretical principle of medieval exegesis may be said to stem from John Cassian's (d. *ca.* 435) distinction of the four senses of Scripture: (1) the historical or literal, (2) the allegorical or christological, (3) the tropological or moral or anthropological, (4) the anagogical or eschatological. Eventually this division gave rise to the famous couplet:

Littera gesta docet; quid credas allegoria;
moralis quid agas; quo tendas anagogia.

The four senses of Jerusalem, an example supplied by Cassian, illustrates the theory. When Jerusalem is mentioned in the Bible, in its literal sense it is a Jewish city; allegorically, however, it refers to the church of Christ; tropologically Jerusalem stands for the human soul; anagogically it stands for the heavenly city. In such an exegetical climate, the literal sense was considered to have historical importance, while the other senses were essential for belief and behavior. Monastic mysticism, preaching to the faithful, the search for theological material in the schools — these depended more heavily on the more-than-literal senses and gave a dominant nonliteral cast to medieval exegesis. Perhaps we should note that the same love for allegory appears also in the secular literature toward the end of the Middle Ages (e.g., *The Romance of the Rose,* and later *The Faerie Queene*).

40   However, there were moments when the recognition of the importance of the literal sense shone through. Especially influential in this respect was the school at the Abbey of St. Victor in Paris founded in 1110. Hugh of St. Victor attacked the tradition of Gregory and Bede; Andrew of St. Victor revived interest in Hebrew and in the technical tools of exegesis. Since the time of Jerome the Western church had had few men capable of studying the OT in its original languages; and Herbert of Bosham, Andrew's pupil, was the most competent Hebraist in the Christian West in the 1,000 years between Jerome and the Renaissance. Moreover, the development of theology as a discipline separate from strict exegesis enabled scholars to consider christological truths in themselves without basing their discussion on Scripture interpreted allegorically. Thomas Aquinas made it clear that metaphor belonged to the literal sense (→ 9 above) and argued that doctrine should not be based solely on the spiritual sense. His principle was: "Nothing necessary to faith is contained in the spiritual sense [i.e., typical sense or sense of things] that Scripture does not put forward elsewhere in the literal sense" (*Summa* 1.1,10 ad 1). The English Dominican Nicholas Trevet and the Franciscan Nicholas of Lyra (d. 1349) recognized that not all the Pss of them were messianic and gave rules for determining which of them were. Roger Bacon, although theoretically supporting the Alexandrian views on exegesis, showed a fascination for textual criticism and philological apparatus. During the 12th, 13th, and early 14 cents., these tendencies rose

to the surface like islands in the sea, but they did not survive; and the Middle Ages drew to a close with allegory once more dominant in writers like Meister Eckhart (d. 1328), John Gerson (d. 1429), and Denis the Carthusian (d. 1471). The movement to translate the Bible into the vernacular, which, like most efforts at translation, made people think about the literal sense, was often unfortunately tainted with ecclesiastical revolt (→ Texts, 68:191) and thus backfired as a possible corrective to the exaggeration of the spiritual sense.

(*CHB* 2: *The West from the Fathers to the Reformation* [1969]. Chenu, M.-D., "Les deux âges de l'allégorisme scripturaire au Moyen Age," *RTAM* 18 [1951] 19–28. De Lubac, H., *Exégèse médiévale: Les quatre sens de l'Écriture* [4 vols.; Paris, 1959–64]. Evans, G. R., *The Language and Logic of the Bible: The Early Middle Ages* [Cambridge, 1984]. Hailperin, H., *Rashi and the Christian Scholars* [Pittsburgh, 1963]. Leclercq, J., *The Love of Learning and the Desire for God: A Study of Monastic Culture* [2d ed.; NY, 1974] esp. 87–109. McNally, R. E., *The Bible in the Early Middle Ages* [Westminster, 1959]. Oberman, H. A., *The Harvest of Medieval Theology: Gabriel Biel and Late Medieval Nominalism* [GR, 1967] esp. 365–412. Preuss, J. S., *From Shadow to Promise: Old Testament Interpretation from Augustine to the Young Luther* [Cambridge MA, 1969]. Smalley, B., *Medieval Exegesis of Wisdom Literature* [Atlanta, 1986]; *The Study of the Bible in the Middle Ages* [Notre Dame, 1964]. Spicq, C., *Esquisse d'une histoire de l'exégèse latine au Moyen Age* [Paris, 1944]. Torrance, T. F., "Scientific Hermeneutics According to St. Thomas Aquinas," *JTS* 13 [1962] 259–89.)

41   (D) Sixteenth and Seventeenth Centuries. Turning now to the context of the Reformation and its immediate aftermath, we find that, with Cajetan on the Catholic side and Luther and Calvin on the Protestant side, there was a reaction against allegorizing and a stress on the historical background of the biblical works. However, we must not forget that while Luther attacked blatant allegorizing, he remained firmly convinced of the christological character of the OT and, therefore, continued a typological exegesis that would be questioned by many today. Calvin was even less in favor of allegorizing than Luther; yet he too was often more-than-literal. (See R. M. Grant and D. Tracy, *A Short History of the Interpretation of the Bible* [2d ed.; Phl, 1984] 92–99 for the good points and the limits in the Reformers' return to the literal sense.) It is interesting to note that the dissenting sects of the Reform movement, the Anabaptists and the Antitrinitarians, supported spiritual exegesis, often because OT passages were used literally by the more conservative branch of the Reform as scriptural justification for persecuting the sects.

42   The Catholic Counter-Reform had to answer arguments flowing from Protestant literal exegesis by also calling on the literal sense of Scripture. The Jesuit Maldonatus (d. 1583) produced exegetical commentary of substance. However, when the immediacy of the danger from the Reform was over, spiritual exegesis returned, especially under the banners of Jansenism, e.g., Pascal. The Catholic emphasis on the Church Fathers was another strong magnet toward spiritual exegesis; for, if the Fathers were pointed out as the prime example of how to interpret Scripture, their exegesis was more-than-literal. Cornelius a Lapide (d. 1637) filled his commentaries with spiritual exegesis culled from the Fathers. In Protestantism, too, in the Pietism of the 17th cent., typology and accommodation made a comeback as the Scriptures were tapped for ascetic wealth. Cocceius (1603–1669) presented an exegesis impregnated with typology.

But the revival of spiritual exegesis was not to hold the field forever. In this same century lived Richard Simon (d. 1712), a prophet before his time and the first of the modern biblical critics. Rejected by his contemporaries and even by his church, Simon inaugurated a movement that would make literal exegesis supreme.

(CHB 3: *The West from the Reformation to the Present Age* [1963]. Ebeling, G., *Evangelische Evangelienauslegung: Eine Untersuchung zu Luthers Hermeneutik* [Darmstadt, 1962; orig. 1942]. Frei, H. W., *The Eclipse of Biblical Narrative: A Study in Eighteenth and Nineteenth Century Hermeneutic* [New Haven, 1974]. Pelikan, J., *Luther the Expositor* [St. Louis, 1959]. Preuss, J. S. [→ 40 above]. Schwarz, W., *Principles and Problems of Biblical Translation: Some Reformation Controversies and Their Background* [Cambridge, 1955]. Steinmann, J., "Entretien de Pascal et du Père Richard Simon sur les sens de l'Écriture," *VieInt* [March 1949] 239-53.)

43   (E) Recent Past. The 19th and 20th cents. have seen the triumph of the critical and literal exegesis to which R. Simon gave the impetus so long ago. (For the intervening history of critical exegesis, → OT Criticism, 69:6ff.; → NT Criticism, 70:4ff.) Looking back at the hermeneutic just described in §31-42, many exegetes would find an alien thought world where imagination ran riot and where the literal meaning of the Scriptures, even when it was recognized, was constantly submerged beneath a strong tide of symbolism. For instance, a patristic approach that found Christ in every line of the OT would be hard to relate to modern source criticism of the Pentateuch, to an emphasis on the limited perspective of the prophets, and to a recognition of pagan parallels for features in Israel's wisdom books. Research that has become historically conscious distinguishes between the theology of the NT and the theology of the subsequent church, recognizing that the Fathers and the Scholastics had found in the NT theological insights of which the original authors were innocent. Nevertheless, modern emphasis on the literal sense has not wiped out interest in a more-than-literal sense, an interest expressed in a variety of ways in the past 50 years.

44   (a) FUNDAMENTALISM. Before beginning a discussion of recognized scholarly views, we should distinguish this recent more-than-literal interest from the rejection of critical exegesis in what is popularly called fundamentalism. Since some of the early Protestant practitioners of historical-critical exegesis had an antidogmatic bias, conservative Protestant Christians, especially at the beginning of the 20th cent., felt that the fundamentals of the Christian faith were being eroded (esp. creation, the virginal conception, the bodily resurrection). A way to preserve such fundamentals was to insist that "what the Bible says" is always literally factual. In practice, then, the only literary form (→ 23 above) recognized in the Bible was history. This attitude has often been combined with a distorted approach to inspiration whereby God becomes the only author dictating the words of Scripture. With the human author reduced to a recording scribe, the author's limited world view becomes irrelevant in interpreting the Bible. Despite the literalism that has marked this fundamentalist approach to Scripture, it has little to do with the literal sense described in § 9-13 above. The fundamentalist preachers' precritical theology is imposed on Scripture in ways that defy hermeneutical classification. Debate with such fundamentalism belongs more to apologetics than to Scripture studies. The brevity of these remarks cannot disguise, however, that in the USA and surrounding areas fundamentalist use of television and radio have converted millions to this view, not only Protestants but also Catholics and Jews. See J. Barr, *Fundamentalism* (Phl, 1978); *Beyond Fundamentalism* (Phl, 1984).

45   (b) PRESERVING ELEMENTS OF PATRISTIC TYPOLOGY. In connection with the history described

above, we may begin the discussion of recently advocated more-than-literal exegesis with attempts to draw from patristic spiritual exegesis its core-perceptions without embracing the exaggerations and without denigrating the contributions of modern historical-critical exegesis. (Interestingly, an attempt to revive patristic spiritual and symbolic exegesis at the expense of the literal sense was condemned by the Roman PBC in 1941 [→ Church Pronouncements, 72:29].) This movement found its strongest proponents in England and in France in the 1940s through the 1960s, partially in order to preserve a rich heritage, partially in reaction to theological and spiritual sterility in some historical-critical exegesis. Studies of Origen mentioned above (→ 36, 37), such as those written by de Lubac, Daniélou, and Hanson, not only defended the sobriety of much Alexandrian exegesis but also implicitly or explicitly pleaded for the continuing relevance of symbolic interpretations. See also A. G. Hebert, *The Throne of David* (London, 1943); and W. Vischer, *The Witness of the Old Testament to Christ* (London, 1949).

46   A particular form of this movement involved argumentation for the continued validity of the typical sense. The term *typos* is found in Rom 5:14 (Adam was a type of Christ) and in 1 Cor 10:6 (things that happened in the desert to Israel during the exodus are types for Christians). Although interest in biblical "types" flourished in the patristic period, the sense of Scripture involving types was not known as the typical sense until late in the history of exegesis. The Fathers spoke of it as "allegory" or as the "mystical sense"; Thomas Aquinas knew of it as the "spiritual sense." Some recent authors have distinguished sharply between typology and allegory, e.g., typology is based on historical connections, whereas allegory is purely imaginative. Yet we should remember that among the Fathers there was no consciousness that allegory was invalid typology, and they received with equal enthusiasm examples of typology that might be considered invalid today (see Barr, *Old and New* 103-48).

47   A widely accepted definition is: *The typical sense is the deeper meaning of the "things" written about in the Bible when they are seen to have foreshadowed future "things" in God's work of salvation.* (1) The typical sense concerns "things"—an awkward translation of Lat *res,* which includes persons, places, and events. The realities that foreshadow are types; the future realities foreshadowed are antitypes. Some NT examples include types foreshadowing Christ: Jonah in the whale (Matt 12:40), the paschal lamb (John 1:29), the bronze serpent on the pole (John 3:14). The exodus is a type of baptism in 1 Cor 10:2. (2) Although classically there has been a stress that the typical sense pertains to things rather than to words (in order to distinguish it from the literal sense and the *sensus plenior*) the biblical *written* account of those things is the vehicle of the more-than-literal meaning. Melchizedek undoubtedly had parents; but what turns him into a type of Christ according to Heb 7:3 is that his lineage is not recorded in Scripture. (3) Types foreshadow *future* "things." The type and the antitype are on two different levels of time, and only when the antitype appears does the typical sense become apparent. The type is always imperfect; it is a silhouette, not a portrait, of the antitype; and therefore realization is bound to bring surprises. Good typology does not stress the continuity between the Testaments at the price of obliterating important aspects of discontinuity. (4) This foreshadowing is related to God's plan of salvation. The problem of criteria has plagued typology (and other forms of more-than-literal exegesis). How does one distinguish it from relationships constructed by pure fancy of the reader?

One answer has been to appeal to God's intention, or God's plan, or the pattern of divine promise and fulfillment—various ways of recognizing that this sense is related to the Christian belief that the God of Abraham, Isaac, and Jacob was the Father of Jesus Christ, who acted consistently and not haphazardly in his dealings with his people. Consequently, it has long been argued that one needs God's guidance in detecting the connections between type and antitype in order to have some surety. The classical criteria of detecting revelation have often been brought into the discussion: a consensus of the Fathers, liturgical usage, church doctrinal teaching. Advocates of typical exegesis have been more persuasive when the types they proposed could be related to patterns already supported in the Scriptures, e.g., Davidic typology for Jesus, exodus typology for elements of the Christian salvific mysteries. If Heb saw Melchizedek as a type of Christ, it has been argued that liturgy and patristic exegesis were justified in considering Melchizedek's presentation of bread and wine (Gen 14:18) as a type of the Christian eucharistic sacrifice.

(De Lubac, H., "Sens spirituel," *RSR* 36 [1949] 542–76. Daniélou, J., "Qu'est-ce que la typologie?" in *L'Ancien Testament et les chrétiens* 199–205. Goppelt, L., *Typos: The Typological Interpretation of the Old Testament in the New* [GR, 1982]. Lampe, G. W. H. and K. J. Woolcombe, *Essays on Typology* [SBT 22; London, 1957].)

48   Typology in *NJBC* has been treated more briefly than in *JBC* §71–78 and has been placed under the history of the recent past rather than under the contemporary situation. Although the element of typology is still appreciated, the revival of patristic patterns is not so active now; and the discussion has largely been subsumed under the role of metaphor and symbol in literary criticism (→ NT Thought, 81:68–70). An occasional effort to write a modern commentary in almost patristic style has not proved successful (see R. E. Brown's review of J. Mateos and J. Barreto, *El Evangelio de Juan* [Madrid, 1979] in *Bib* 63 [1982] 290–94).

49   (c) THE *SENSUS PLENIOR*. In the period 1925–1970 Roman Catholics were finding another approach to more-than-literal values, an approach less distant from contemporary historical-critical exegesis than were patristic typology and allegory. (For the history, see R. E. Brown, *CBQ* 15 [1953] 141–62; 25 [1963] 262–85.) The term *sensus plenior* (henceforth SPlen) was coined by A. Fernández in 1925; it is best kept in Latin, for the Eng transl. (fuller sense) is used for a wider range of meaning. Related to the NT idea of "fulfilling" the OT, the SPlen permitted its advocates (who included J. Coppens and P. Benoit) to recognize the limited scope of the literal sense of biblical passages and yet to preserve more developed applications of those texts.

50   By definition: *The SPlen is the deeper meaning, intended by God but not clearly intended by the human author, that is seen to exist in the words of Scripture when they are studied in the light of further revelation or of development in the understanding of revelation.* Thus, unlike the typical sense but like the literal sense, the SPlen is concerned primarily with the words of Scripture rather than the "things." Although a few advocates ignored the intent of the human author, the majority, who held that the SPlen lies outside what was clearly intended by that author, distinguished it from the literal sense. The theory of SPlen was formulated when the Scholastic notion of instrumental inspiration was in vogue among Catholics, whence the aspect of divine intention expressed in the biblical words. Less technically, this may be seen as related to the notion of God's plan of salvation, which

was not haphazard and in which Scripture played a role—a notion also relevant to the typical sense. Although more often applied to OT texts as reused in the NT (e.g., the SPlen of Isa 7:14 discoverable in Matt 1:23), the SPlen could cover post-Scriptural reuse of biblical passages by church writers (e.g., Gen 3:15 applied to Mary's participation in Christ's victory over evil). Some of the same criteria appealed to in detecting "valid" typology were involved in discussion of the SPlen (→ 47 above), but the fact that advocacy of the SPlen had its roots in a distrust of excesses in patristic typology and allegory gave SPlen exegesis a more cerebral and cautionary aura. Reasonable homogeneity with the literal sense was insisted on, and the SPlen was relatively seldom invoked even by strong supporters. Those interested in precisions should consult *JBC* 71:56–70; R. E. Brown, *The Sensus Plenior of Sacred Scripture* (Baltimore, 1955).

51   Already by the late 1960s, Brown was recognizing that the interest in more-than-literal meaning implied in the SPlen theory had to find expression in a format less dependent on the Scholastic theory of instrumental relationship between the human and divine authors. He foresaw that the future of the SPlen and also of the typical sense lay in their being revamped as part of a much larger approach to the more-than-literal meaning of the Bible (see *JBC* 71:68, 78). In fact, there has been virtually no discussion of the SPlen since 1970, and its contemporary continuation as the "fuller sense" or "excess of meaning" is in literary criticism related to the new hermeneutic (→ 54 below). J. M. Robinson (*CBQ* 27 [1965] 6–27) perceptively pointed this out, and his point was accepted by Brown (*ETL* 43 [1967] 460–69).

52   (d) CHRISTIAN INTERPRETATION OF THE OT. Since Marcion's time, the problem of what the OT means for a Christian has been with us. If in the recent past Roman Catholics have appealed to a revival of the spiritual sense or to the SPlen in reflection on this issue, another approach had wider currency in the 1950s and 1960s, as distinguished scholars (including G. von Rad, W. Eichrodt, and W. Zimmerli) rejected both the patristic tendency to find Christ in every line of the OT and a historicism that so distanced the Testaments from each other that the Bible was no longer a unity. The issue of the relationship between the Testaments attracted attention especially under the rubric of biblical theology. Works that were particularly significant included S. Amsler, *L'Ancien Testament dans l'Église* (Neuchâtel, 1960); C. Larcher, *L'actualité chrétienne de l'Ancien Testament* (Paris, 1962); P. Grelot, *Sens chrétien de l'Ancien Testament* (Tournai, 1962); *The Old Testament and Christian Faith* (ed. B. W. Anderson; NY, 1963); *Essays on Old Testament Hermeneutics* (ed. C. Westermann; Richmond, 1963). An excellent summary of the literature was given by R. E. Murphy (*CBQ* 26 [1964] 349–59). Some of these scholars did not hesitate to speak of OT predictions of NT events; some were interested in a modified form of typology; but very frequently a relationship of promise/fulfillment was seen to relate the OT to the NT. This pattern was thought to be detectable in the flow of Israel's history, even if that flow did not move smoothly toward Christianity. The reaction of other scholars was hostile, since they thought that an alien concern was being imposed on the Hebr Scriptures (see J. Smart, *The Interpretation of Scripture* [Phl, 1961]; J. Barr, *Old and New*). Moreover, the flow of history was deemed too ambiguous to be invoked: certain streams in messianic expectation actually made it more rather than less difficult for Jews to accept Jesus. An extreme position was expressed by Bultmann (in *The Old Testament*, ed.

Anderson, 31): "To Christian faith the Old Testament is no longer revelation." The vehemence of the debate seemed in one way to slow the progress of this biblical theology approach to a more-than-literal sense, but elements of it have survived in contemporary canonical criticism (→ 71 below).

(Anderson, B. W., "Biblical Theology and Sociological Interpretation," *TToday* 42 [1985] 292–306. Hasel, G. F., "Biblical Theology: Then, Now, and Tomorrow," *HBT* 4 [1982] 61–93. Reventlow, H., *Problems of Biblical Theology in the Twentieth Century* [Phl, 1986]. Terrien, S., "Biblical Theology: The Old Testament [1970–1984]," *BTB* 15 [1985] 127–35. Also for bibliography, → OT Thought, 77:1; → OT Criticism, 69:54 [Terrien and Westermann].)

53   (II) The Contemporary Situation. The line between the recent past and the contemporary situation is somewhat nebulous. Nevertheless, if §43–52 concerned movements that were very much discussed when *JBC* was written but which get less attention now, what follows describes movements beyond the literal sense that have occupied scholars after 1965. These newer movements often involve revision and redirection of interests already apparent in the recent past. This fact should make the proponents of contemporary approaches cautious about claims of offering *the* way to interpret Scripture. Alas, often proponents of one or the other approach to be discussed below reject with equal vigor not only historical-critical emphasis on the literal sense but also other contemporary approaches. Like the quest for the Holy Grail, the quest for the exclusive route in hermeneutics seems to be undying, and past failures only make the questers more optimistic. If in the 21st cent. other editors are brave enough to plan a newer *NJBC*, one can be certain that some of what follows will also have been relegated to the recent past.

54   (A) The New (Heideggerian) Hermeneutic. Already in the period 1950–1965 a hermeneutic related to the role of language was attracting attention among Bible scholars, as reported in *JBC* 71:49–50 and summarized in J. M. Robinson and J. B. Cobb, *The New Hermeneutic* (NFT 2; NY, 1964); and R. E. Brown and P. J. Cahill, *Biblical Tendencies Today: An Introduction to the Post-Bultmannians* (Corpus Papers; Washington, 1969). This issue of language already appeared in German *Sachkritik* (recognizing the applicability of subject matter even when the language in which the matter was objectified was inappropriate), and in R. Bultmann's demythologizing (→ NT Criticism, 70:51), which decoded biblical myth, seeking to state more adequately its meaning by eliminating inadequate mythical conceptualization. In the later philosophical writings of M. Heidegger, hermeneutic came to mean the process of interpreting being, especially through language. Being finds expression in the language of the text even independently of the author's intention. Drawing on the later Heidegger but modifying his ideas, E. Fuchs's programmatic *Hermeneutik* (1954) went beyond Bultmann's hermeneutical principles. For Bultmann, the self-interpretation of the reader is on the level of preunderstanding, subordinate to interpreting the text itself; for Fuchs (→ NT Criticism, 70:66) the text interprets the readers by criticizing their self-understanding. The "hermeneutical principle" is where the text is placed in order to speak to the reader, and for theological exegesis the basic hermeneutic principle is human need—a need that reveals what we mean by God. "Translation" involves finding the place where the biblical text can strike home. G. Ebeling (→ NT Criticism, 70:70), a close friend of Fuchs, carried forward the development of hermeneutic in the direction indicated by the later

Heidegger ("Hermeneutik," *RGG* 3 [1959] 242–62). The role he would attribute to historical criticism is not one of essential interpretation but one of removing all distortions so that the text can effectively speak to readers.

55   (B) Literary Criticism. The discussion of this aspect of biblical hermeneutics is complicated by the fluidity and ambiguity of the terminology, constantly being expanded by new, quasi-technical terms used differently by different authors. *Here "literary criticism" is used as it is in the field of literature, not as it has been used traditionally in the biblical field,* where it refers to the exploration of such historical issues as author, time and place of composition, nature and provenance of sources, and socioreligious implications of literary forms (as, e.g., in Kümmel, *INT*).

56   The study of the Bible as literature has been impeded in the past both by an exaggerated concern for the uniqueness of canonical Scripture and by a narrow restriction of "literature" to self-consciously literary productions, a designation that would apply to relatively little of the OT or the NT. In recent years the growing appreciation of language as mediation of being rather than as system of verbal labels and thus of the intimate relationship of content to form in all texts, including canonical ones, has suggested the possibility of a theologically responsible use of literary-critical methods in biblical interpretation (see A. N. Wilder, *The New Voice* [Cambridge MA, 1971] xi–xxx). Furthermore, literary critics have recognized an ideological prejudice in the narrow restriction of "literature" (Eagleton, *Literary* 1–16) and readily admit that "literature is what we read as literature"(McKnight, *Bible* 9–10), i.e., literature consists of the texts that a society values. Consequently, both theologically and literarily we may treat biblical texts as literary works.

57   (a) FROM HISTORICAL TO LITERARY CRITICISM. D. Robertson (*IDBSup* 547–51) calls the recent emergence of literary criticism in the field of biblical studies a "paradigm shift" in the field. This shift reflects the "turn to language" in both philosophy and the study of literature. However, it developed organically out of the historical approach that has been paradigmatic in the biblical field since the 19th cent. Form and source criticism (→ 23–27 above), esp. in NT studies, eventually focused attention on the literary activity of the "redactor," whose theological concerns governed the production of the final text (→ 28–29 above), e.g., the Gospel of Luke. As N. R. Petersen points out (*Literary Criticism for New Testament Critics* [Phl, 1978]), redaction criticism raised questions about the text as text which neither history nor theology could address. Scholars such as A. N. Wilder, N. Perrin, R. W. Funk, D. Crossan, D. O. Via, and D. Patte, attempting to address these new questions, became the first generation of biblical specialists to join philosophical hermeneutics and literary criticism in a new approach to biblical interpretation that has developed into what McKnight (*Bible* 5) calls "hermeneutic criticism." (For the importance of Wilder's contribution, see J. A. Mirro, *BTB* 10 [1980] 118–23.)

58   Both the Heideggerian ontological tradition (→ 54 above) represented by H.-G. Gadamer (*Truth and Method* [NY, 1975]) and the Husserlian phenomenological tradition represented by P. Ricoeur (*Interpretation*) have contributed philosophically to a language-centered approach to the understanding of texts. (See R. Palmer, *Hermeneutics* [Evanston, 1969] for a history of modern hermeneutical theory since F. Schleiermacher.) Central to contemporary hermeneutical theory is the conviction that all historical (as opposed to mathematical or scientific) understanding is dialogical in nature. The interpretation of texts involves a "dialogue" between reader and text about the subject matter with which the text is concerned (see H. Ott, "Hermeneutics and Personhood," *Interpretation: The Poetry of Meaning* [ed. S. R. Hopper and D. L. Miller; NY, 1967] 14–33). This view of interpretation raises three questions that lead directly into the literary arena: What is the subject matter or referent of the text? How does the text "work" to engage the reader? How does the subjectivity of the reader influence the process of interpretation.?

59   (b) THE PROBLEM OF REFERENCE. In traditional historical criticism the referent of the biblical text was thought to be simply the historical event recounted by the text, e.g., the escape of the Hebrews from Egypt or the crucifixion of Jesus. Later, scholars came to see that the text involved a theological interpretation of events, reflecting the concerns of the communities in which the texts were written. Literary criticism, however, does not view the text as a "window" onto a historical world (the events recounted or the community situation in which the text was composed) but as a "mirror" reflecting a world into which the reader is invited. In other words, the referent of the text as such is not the "real world" of history (e.g., exodus or crucifixion) but the literary world signified by the text. In the case of the biblical texts, the literary world is generated by the theological interpretation of the reality (e.g., escape from Egypt *as* divine liberation for covenant life; the death of Jesus *as* salvific paschal mystery). The concern of the literary biblical interpreter, then, is not the reconstruction of the historical events but the self-transformative understanding, i.e., appropriation, of the subject matter with which the text is concerned. Such an approach does not negate the value of historical inquiry nor lead to an ignoring of the original situation of the text; rather, it expands the concept of meaning beyond any restriction to historical concerns (see McKnight, *Bible* 11–12).

60   (c) NON-CONTEXTUAL APPROACHES. Current literary approaches to texts can be divided roughly into two basic types: non-contextual approaches (text-centered) and contextual approaches (audience-oriented). We begin with the non-contextual.

61   *Structuralism.* This term applies to various methods that view the text as a closed system of signs that have meaning not in themselves or in reference to extratextual reality but only in relation to one another. The model for the understanding of signs, whether minute textual units (e.g., words) or larger units (e.g., parables), is the semiotic model according to which a sign is composed of a signifier (expression) and a signified (content). The form of structural analysis that has been applied most extensively to biblical materials is the method of A. J. Greimas for analyzing narrative. According to Greimas, meaning in a text is the effect of the operation of deep structures or systems of elements, identical for all narratives, which generate individual texts analogously to the way a grammar generates sentences within a language. The aim of structural analysis is to bring to light the deep structures of which the text is a realization. In this way, as Ricoeur (*Interpretation* 82–87) has pointed out, the sense (as opposed to the reference) of a text can be clarified. Structuralism is seen by its practitioners as a scientific method that makes possible comparative studies of texts across cultural and linguistic boundaries. The results of structuralist biblical exegesis have, so far, been relatively meager but as an explanatory method it holds some promise (→ NT Thought, 81:71).

(Histories of formalist and structuralist approaches in McKnight and Eagleton; description and application to Bible in R. M. Polzin, *Biblical Structuralism* [Missoula, 1977]; J. Calloud, *Structural Analysis of Narrative* [Missoula, 1976]; D. C. Greenwood, *Structuralism and the Biblical Text* [Berlin, 1985]; D. Patte, *What Is Structural Exegesis?* [Phl, 1976]; D. O. Via, *Kerygma and Comedy in the New Testament* [Phl, 1975].)

62   *Deconstruction.* This literary theory, associated with J. Derrida (see his *Dissemination* [Chicago, 1981]), turns structuralism against itself by challenging its so-called metaphysics of presence, i.e., its fundamental conviction that the signifier (e.g., the narrative) in a sign (e.g., the Gospel of Mark) manifests a signified (e.g., the narrative world of Mark) which is a determinate referent. The deconstructionist places the emphasis on the signifier, which is such only in relation to other signifiers rather than in relation to a determinate signified, for the signified is itself a signifier within another sign. In other words, the text is a bottomless series of references to other references which never comes to rest in a "real" or determinate referent. Thus, the text itself subverts the very meaning it creates. Perhaps because this theory implies the complete indeterminacy of texts it has not generated wide interest among biblical scholars. See J. I. N. Stewart and J. Cullen, *On Deconstruction* (Ithaca, 1982).

63   (d) CONTEXTUAL APPROACHES. The approaches collected under this rather vague heading have in common that they include the reader in the definition of the literary work and include the context of reader and/or writer in the process of interpretation. The "work" is not the text but comes into being when text and reader interact. The text, therefore, is not an "object" upon which the interpreter performs analytic or investigative procedures (as does a scientist) in order to extract a theoretically univocal intrinsic meaning. Rather, it is a poetic structure that is engaged, from within a concrete situation, by a reader in the process of achieving meaning. Texts, therefore, are intrinsically somewhat indeterminate and open to more than one valid interpretation because meaning is not determined *exclusively* by the author. A text once written is no longer under the author's control and can never be interpreted twice from the same situation.

64   The major problem raised by this understanding of work and interpretation concerns criteria of validity in the face of multiple interpretations. True, an equation of meaning with author's intention (e.g., Hirsch, *Validity* [→ 11 above]) seems to obviate this problem by positing the existence of an ideal univocal meaning, even if such meaning can never be actually attained or verified. But few literary scholars today accept such a notion of meaning. Those who accept neither the total determinacy of meaning by author's intention nor the total indeterminacy of texts in relation to readers can still propose criteria of validity (note, not verification), such as coherence, adequacy to the text, and fullness of meaning. Although no one interpretation is exhaustive and many may be valid, not every interpretation is valid nor are all interpretations equal (see M. A. Tolbert, *Perspectives on the Parables* [Phl, 1979]).

65   *Rhetorical Criticism.* This assumes that all discourse is aimed at influencing a particular audience at a particular time. Therefore, the analysis of the textual strategies by which the communicative aims were achieved in the original situation and are achieved in regard to subsequent readers can give access to the meaning of the text. The basic principle of rhetorical criticism is that texts must reveal the contexts both of the author and of the reader. G. A. Kennedy (*New Testament Interpretation through Rhetorical Criticism* [Chapel Hill,

1984]) describes classical Aristotelian rhetorical criticism, which is primarily concerned with the aims and methods of the writer of the text, and he ably applies this theory to a number of NT texts. For the flourishing development of OT rhetorical studies, → OT Criticism, 69:67–68. See W. Wuellner, "Where is Rhetorical Criticism Taking Us?" *CBQ* 49 (1987) 448–63.

66   Contemporary rhetorical criticism is interested not just in the rules and devices for argumentation used by the writer, but in all the strategies whereby the interests, values, and emotions of readers (both original and later) are engaged. Thus, it is as concerned with the process of interpretation by readers as with the process of creation by the author. A. N. Wilder (*Early Christian Rhetoric* [London, 1964]) has demonstrated the fecundity for the interpretation of NT materials of the rhetorical approach; it has been applied in particular to the interpretation of parables (→ NT Thought, 81:68–70).

67   Narrative criticism (as distinguished from narratology or the structural analysis of story) is the application of rhetorical criticism to stories, whether these be full-length quasi-historical Gospel narratives (D. Rhoads and D. Michie, *Mark as Story* [Phl, 1982]; J. D. Kingsbury, *Matthew as Story* [Phl, 1986]; R. A. Culpepper, *Anatomy of the Fourth Gospel* [Phl, 1983]), shorter narratives such as the raising of Lazarus in John 11, or fictional stories such as Jonah or a parable (R. Funk, *The Poetics of Biblical Narrative* [Sonoma CA, 1988]).

68   *Sociological and Psychoanalytic Criticism.* Both these approaches attend in a particular way to the influence of the reader on the construction of meaning and to the influences, personal or social, on the reader's reception of the work—the current reader not the ancient reader. Audience-oriented sociological criticism (as distinct from historical studies of the social world; → 15 above) seeks to investigate reading as an essentially collective phenomenon in which the individual reader is part of a "reading public" with particular sociohistorical characteristics that influence the process of interpretation. Psychoanalytic criticism emphasizes the influence of personality and personal history on interpretation. (See S. Suleiman, "Introduction: Varieties of Audience-Oriented Criticism," *The Reader in the Text* [ed. S. R. Suleiman and I. Crosman; Princeton, 1980] 3–45, on this and the following section.)

69   *Phenomenological Criticism.* This places the emphasis on the interaction of reader with text in the reading process, by which the text is being actualized or realized by the reader. It implies that "the potential text is infinitely richer than any of its individual realizations" (W. Iser, "The Reading Process: A Phenomenological Approach," *The Implied Reader* [Baltimore, 1974] 280). Ricoeur (*Interpretation*) supplies the philosophical grounding for this approach.

70   (e) CONCLUSION. The variety of literary-hermeneutical approaches to the interpretation of biblical texts precludes any totalitarian claims for any one approach. What all of these recently developed approaches have in common is their operation within the linguistic/literary rather than the historical paradigm. They all deal with the text in its final form rather than with its genesis, and they are concerned with the literary world projected "in front of" the text rather than with the historical world "behind" the text. Their hermeneutical interests are in *present meaning mediated by language through interpretation* rather than in historical meanings uncovered by exegesis which are then inserted into contemporary contexts by a process of application. Most literary-critical biblical scholars recognize the importance, even the necessity, of historical-critical exegesis

for full understanding of biblical texts; but they reject any understanding (or better, misunderstanding) of the historical-critical method as the sole, uniquely authoritative approach to biblical interpretation.

(Alter, R. and F. Kermode [eds.], *The Literary Guide to the Bible* [Cambridge MA, 1987]. Beardslee, W. A., *Literary Criticism of the New Testament* [Phl, 1970]. Fowler, R. M., "Using Literary Criticism on the Gospels," *Christian Century* 99 [1982] 626–29. Gabel, J. B. and C. B. Wheeler, *The Bible as Literature* [Oxford, 1986]. Habel, N., *Literary Criticism of the Old Testament* [Phl, 1971]. Krieger, M. "Literary Analysis and Evaluation—And the Ambidextrous Critic," *Criticism: Speculative and Analytic Essays* [ed. L. S. Dembo; Madison, 1968] 16–36. Lategan, B. C. and W. S. Vorster, *Text and Reality: Aspects of Reference in Biblical Texts* [Phl, 1985]. *Orientation by Disorientation: Studies in Literary Criticism and Biblical Criticism* [Fest. W. A. Beardslee; ed. R. A. Spencer; Pittsburgh, 1980]. Perrin, N., *Jesus and the Language of the Kingdom* [Phl, 1976]. Poland, L., *Literary Criticism and Biblical Hermeneutics* [Chico, 1985]. *Rhetorical Criticism* [Fest. J. Muilenburg; ed. J. J. Jackson and M. Kessler; Pittsburgh, 1974]. Schneiders, S. M., *TS* 39 [1978] 719–36; 43 [1982] 52–68; *CBQ* 43 [1981] 76–92; *TToday* 42 [1985] 353–58—on various aspects of literary criticism. Symposium in *TToday* 44 [1987] 165–221.)

71   (C) **Canonical Criticism.** A major exponent of this has been B. S. Childs of Yale in his works *Introduction to the Old Testament as Scripture* (Phl, 1979) and *The New Testament as Canon: An Introduction* (Phl, 1985). Childs does not dispense with historical criticism, although frequently he regards its results as irrelevant. For Childs what matters is *the final canonical form:* (1) Of the linguistic text. Primary attention should be given not to a Hebr text of the OT reconstructed by scholars who compare mss. and versions but to the text stabilized by Masoretes and known to us in copied traditions of the 10th cent. AD (→ Texts, 68:42–51). (2) Of the individual book. A pentateuchal book may have come together from combining J, E, D, and P traditions; but only the final form is Scripture and should get primary attention, for there the full effect of revelatory history can be perceived. Even if Isa consists of three sections written 250 years apart, the interpretation of the whole will deemphasize the very different life-situations of the parts. (3) Of the collection. The ordering of books in the collected Bible is significant: the Hebr Scriptures become an OT preparatory to a NT; Luke has been separated from Acts and must be treated as a Gospel comparable to three others. Also significant is the larger audience envisaged when we speak of the canon of Israel and the canon of the church. A prophet may have addressed his words to the Israelites of Samaria in 700 BC, but as canonical Scripture his words are now addressed to all Jews and to all Christians. The epistles of John may have been written for that part of the Johannine community remaining after the schism of 1 John 2:19 had taken place, but the limited horizon of the original author can be forgotten since now they are addressed to all Christendom. Only the final canonical form of text, book, and collection is sacred Scripture for a community of faith and practice; and historical criticism has been a distraction with its isolation of individual books, its analysis of sources, and its concentration on the author's intent and circumstances. Childs would be critical of concentration on what Jesus meant by his words, on how the apostles interpreted them when they preached, and on what the evangelists conveyed when they wrote them down. For Childs, "the witness of Jesus Christ has been given its normative shape through an interpretative process of the post-Apostolic Age" (*New Testament* 28).

72   Childs resists the term canonical criticism lest it make the approach just one among many others. The term is acceptable to another exponent, J. A. Sanders (*Torah and Canon: Introduction* [Phl, 1972]; *Canon and Community* [Phl, 1984]), who sees this criticism as having evolved from the other critical disciplines, reflecting back on and informing them. Its unique contribution is in addressing questions of biblical authority by situating the Scriptures as word of God in the matrix of a believing community of readers and interpreters. Sanders differs notably from Childs in resisting an exclusive attention to the final form of a book or the collection. Before that there was an ongoing canonical process or quest ("comparative midrash") where early traditions that were deemed valuable were contemporized and adapted in new situations helping a community to find identity in an otherwise confusing world. Even after the final form, that adaptability of Scripture is continued by hermeneutical techniques. Selectivity is at work in all stages of the process, and a richness of diversity in the canon (diachronically as well as synchronically) prevents later theological constructs from being imposed on the Bible. Despite the attempts of the biblical theology movement (→ 52 above), the Bible cannot be made to speak with one voice. Another advocate of canonical criticism is G. T. Sheppard (*Wisdom as a Hermeneutical Construct* [NY, 1980]). The application of comparative midrash and canonical criticism within Judaism is discussed by J. Neusner (*Ancient Judaism and Modern Category-Formation* [Lanham MD, 1986] 25–53, 83–120, with a response by Sanders in *BTB* 14 [1984] 82–83).

73   A judgment on canonical criticism is complicated by the tone of Childs's claims imperiously dismissing the worth of most recent commentaries. Nevertheless, valuable points should be noted: (1) Too often historical criticism has stopped with reconstructed parts of books, not paying attention to the whole book, which is the only form that has survived. Even then it is a type of fundamentalism to apotheosize an individual book with its peculiarities and to neglect the counterpoint supplied by the total canon. In a very real sense a book is not biblical until it is a part of the Bible. (2) Since the biblical books were written by believers for believers, the believing community is a good (and not necessarily a prejudiced) context for interpretation, provided that this community enters into frank dialogue with its tradition. The enlightenment and enrichment of exegesis by faith cannot be dismissed so easily as "unscientific" (→ 85–87 below). (3) One who believes that the Holy Spirit inspired the writing of these books should recognize that the Spirit could not have become silent once the last book was written and must have been active both in the reception of these books by the ongoing church and in their interpretation.

74   There are also serious problems, as incisively (but perhaps too pejoratively) indicated by Barr (*Holy Scripture*). Most of the objections are directed against Childs's form of the theory: (1) To overemphasize the final form of book and collection is to neglect the continuity of the later believing community with an earlier Israel and a church that existed before there were respectively OT and NT books (→ 5 above). Faith was not controlled by Scripture; Scripture derived from faith. Although neglecting the full value of the canon, historical criticism at its best discovered the faith and community dimensions *within* the Scripture by describing the believing community in the formative stages of the Bible. (2) The contentions of the biblical authors, who were authorities in themselves, cannot be completely overridden by a canonical sense which often would have been foreign to their minds. Moreover, one must take into account the authority of biblical figures (Moses, Jesus) who were not authors of biblical books in the

ordinary sense of writers (→ 6 above). Canonical criticism can have the effect of reinforcing the view that the Bible as a whole is the sole authority in Christianity, a view that many Christians regard as quite inadequate. (3) The canon-forming process was not always so deliberate as might be inferred from the great theological emphasis placed on it by canonical critics. Some books surely perished through historical accident; some books were preserved not because of great theological value but because they were thought to have come from distinguished figures. Even after the completed canon, some books (e.g., Jude) play little or no role in church life. As for textual criticism, versions have often been more influential than canonical forms of the Hebr OT or the Gk NT, e.g., the LXX on the early Christian church, the Vulgate on the Western church, the *KJV* on English Protestantism. Increasingly, critically controlled transls. that depart from both Masoretic Hebrew and *Textus Receptus* Greek (→ Texts, 68:55, 161) become canonical Scripture for most churches. (4) Sanders's thesis that the community found its identity through the canonical process of interpreting traditions has been deemed exaggerated both by Childs and Barr. The latter (*Holy Scripture* 43) observes: "Far from the canon establishing or expressing the self-identity of the church, it is the church that establishes the network of familiar relations within which the scriptures are known and understood." In applying "comparative midrash" to the NT (e.g., *USQR* 33 [1978] 193–96) Sanders at times reverses the hermeneutical process: the first Christians did not discover the identity of Jesus or their identity as believers in Jesus through reflection on the Scriptures of Israel; rather, with their scripturally shaped background they perceived the identity of Jesus through faith and adapted those Scriptures to formulate a description of that identity.

(Barton, J., *Reading the Old Testament* [Phl, 1984]. Betz, H. D. [ed.], *The Bible as a Document of the University* [Chico, 1981]. Bird, P. A., *The Bible as the Church's Book* [Phl, 1982]. Brueggemann, W., *The Creative Word* [Phl, 1982]. Fishbane, *Biblical Interpretation* [→ 34 above]. Fowl, S., *ExpTim* 96 [1984–85] 173–76. Sanders, J. A., *From Sacred Story to Sacred Text* [Phl, 1987]. Also *JSOT* 16 [1980]; *HBT* 2 [1980]; *BTB* 11 [1981] 114–22; *Canon, Theology, and Old Testament Interpretation* [ed. G. Tucker, et al.; Phl, 1988].)

75   (D) Miscellaneous Contributions. The following approaches, which go beyond the literal sense whether or not they admit it, are offered from various perspectives and can be treated only sketchily.

(a) EXEGESIS FOR PERSONAL TRANSFORMATION. After assaulting historical criticism as if it were always divorced from faith and the church, W. Wink (*The Bible in Human Transformation* [Phl, 1973]) stresses the need to interpret the reader of the Bible—a phenomenology of the exegete, an archaeology of the subject. For the Bible to play a religious role in our lives, Wink proposes a psychoanalytically informed critique of the way we read the text. Drawing on the insights of religious depth psychology (C. J. Jung), Wink uses the standard biblical criticism to remove presuppositions about a passage and then asks a number of questions relating the reader to characters and actions in a passage. (See also W. G. Rollins, *Jung and the Bible* [Atlanta, 1983].) For instance, in discussing Mark 2:12, Wink asks, "Who is the 'paralytic' in you?" or "Who is the 'scribe' in you?" Obviously, a text so treated can involve the reader religiously (or spiritually as in the Roman Catholic Ignatian method of using Scripture). Yet the results at times may be quite far from the intention of the original author, who was often addressing community issues. Major areas of biblical concern would scarcely lend themselves to such a concentration on individual conversion. The ecclesiastical, doctrinal, and liturgical dimensions of Scripture, familiar to many Christians, do not emerge in such an approach. Barr (*Holy Scripture* 107) is caustic in his critique of Wink.

76   (b) ADVOCACY EXEGESIS. Liberationist and feminist studies have made recent contributions to the investigation of both Testaments over the full hermeneutical range of what we have called the literal and more-than-literal senses (→ OT Criticism, 69:73–79; → NT Criticism, 70:82–83). An interesting aspect of many of them has been open advocacy that their results be used to change the existing religious or societal situation. Interpretation to support ideologies or meaningful causes is freely defended on the grounds that the biblical writers and writings were not without their own advocacy. For instance, E. Schüssler Fiorenza argues that church history was written primarily as clerical history, because clerics were not only writing but also reading these historical accounts. It is widely recognized that a discernment of bias (conscious or unconscious) in the biblical narrative and a posing of sociological, economic, and political questions that have not been asked by past exegetes may help to fill in the biblical world and to uncover in and beneath the text wealth previously overlooked. But more than that is involved in advocacy exegesis. In order to nurture the faith and vision of Christian communities struggling today for freedom, some would argue that liberation of the oppressed is the only optic through which the Scriptures can be read. Such an optic must be favored by a hermeneutic centered less on texts and more on the people whose story of liberation is remembered in the Bible. For instance, the paradigmatic possibilities of the exodus are freely invoked. Others seek what may be an inspiration for women who are struggling for liberation, upheld by their belief in the God of creation and salvation. If the surface biblical narrative does not offer enough material to support such a feminist cause, maximum usage of the slightest clues is thought to lead to detecting more favorable situations that have been suppressed consciously or unconsciously. To others these advocacy reconstructions seem forced, and the argument is made that one must deal with the possibility that the biblical authors were unconscious of or uninterested in issues that seem important to us. The ancient sociological situation may have been in fact (and not simply through suppression of data) unfavorable to modern causes. Such biblical limitations would not make the modern causes less important but would set them in the context of history. Some issues that mattered to Paul or Matthew (like the Jew-Gentile conversion matter) seem irrelevant to us today (even when interpreted intelligently as to their underlying significance). This fact could constitute a warning that our burning issues may seem irrelevant several decades from now. A Scripture read solely through the modern-issue optic could seem less relevant in the future.

(Brown, R. M., *Unexpected News: Reading the Bible with Third World Eyes* [Phl, 1984]. Clevenot, M., *Materialist Approaches to the Bible* [Maryknoll, 1985]. Gottwald, N., *The Bible and Liberation* [Maryknoll, 1982]. Schottroff, W. and W. Stegemann [eds.], *God of the Lowly* [Maryknoll, 1984]. Schüssler Fiorenza, E., *In Memory of Her* [NY, 1983].)

77   (E) **Final Remarks.** For pedagogical clarity in this article we have discussed first the literal sense and then the more-than-literal senses, at the same time explaining the procedures or types of criticism employed to determine respectively what the text meant and what the text means. While an interpreter can concentrate on one or the other, these are not separable categories; for the total process of explanation and understanding involves the relationship between the two. Most biblical commentaries written up to now have concentrated almost exclusively on the literal sense or the quest for what the text meant. There are at least two reasons for that. First, there is a broad agreement at least in theory on the means (the types of criticism) used to detect the literal sense. Advocates of the importance of a more-than-literal sense are often very divided in the way they approach the text, as indicated by the types of criticism discussed above under the rubric "the contemporary situation." Second, the possibility of engaging the text in order to determine what it now can or should mean to the reader is complicated by the diversity of readership, so that many commentators choose to confine themselves to the task of explanation, expecting that the readers themselves will move to vital understanding. That supposition is a bit optimistic, and commentators cannot rest content with being archaeologists of meaning. Perhaps the situation will be helped when the advocates of the various criticisms that uncover the more-than-literal senses move from theory to practice and begin to write commentaries themselves. That would make some of the discussion less abstract.

RELATED TOPICS

78   (I) **Accommodation.** Beyond the senses *of* Scripture lies accommodation, a sense *given to* Scripture—not the product of exegesis but of eisegesis, even though, admittedly, in a wider understanding of "meaning" the lines between more-than-literal senses and accommodation become blurry. The range of accommodation is immense, running from catechetical application to literary embellishment. Much of the more-than-literal exegesis in the Fathers and in the liturgy is accommodation—a fact that is intelligible when we remember that Scripture was looked upon as the basic text from which a wide span of Christian knowledge was taught. When Gregory the Great told his audience that the Gospel parable of the five talents referred to the five senses, he was accommodating. The liturgy accommodates to the lives of Christian confessor-pontiffs the praise that Sir 44–45 heaps upon the patriarchs of Israel. A very frequent use of accommodation is in sermons, e.g., when preachers eulogized Pope John XXIII by citing John 1:6, "There was sent by God a man whose name was John."
79   Accommodation is inevitable with a book that is as familiar and as respected as the Bible. And, in truth, a certain tolerance can be extended to accommodation when it is done with intelligence, sobriety, and taste. In matters of taste, for instance, it is not unbecoming to apply John 1:6 in eulogy of a beloved and saintly pope; its application to other well-known men named John, not particularly noted for sanctity, is more dubious. But, even when accommodation is handled with a certain sobriety, we must insist that it should be only an occasional use of Scripture and not the principal use. Preachers may find accommodation easy and may resort to it rather than taking the trouble to draw a relevant message from the literal sense of Scripture. They are

then in danger of substituting their own ingenuity for God's word. If it is made clear to the audience that the writer or speaker is accommodating, some of the danger is removed. But, in general, now that we have come to recognize the tremendous wealth of the literal sense of Scripture, a sound exposition of that sense will render far more service than ingenious accommodation.

80   (II) Authoritative Interpretation by the Church. When we discussed the literal sense, we explained the rules of form criticism and redaction criticism, etc., as the best guidelines to the meaning of Scripture. But as Catholics do we not say that the authentic interpretation of Scripture belongs to the church? In the popular understanding there remains a certain confusion about the church's role in exegesis as opposed to "private interpretation." The latter phrase is often an oversimplification of what is regarded as a Protestant position. First of all, it should be stated that in the more traditional Protestant churches there is no suggestion that each individual can authoritatively interpret Scripture. There is church tradition among Protestants, even as there is among Catholics. Moreover, since the correct interpretation of Scripture requires education and effort, the average Protestant is no more capable of picking up the Bible and determining at a glance what the author meant than is the average Catholic. A Protestant's understanding of Scripture comes through Sunday schools, sermons, and church experience, even as the average Catholic's understanding comes from teachers. A truer difference between Protestant and Catholic opinions is not centered on the existence of a traditional interpretation of Scripture but on the binding value given to that tradition.

81   Even in the question of the binding church interpretation of Scripture, however, we must be careful not to oversimplify the Catholic position. A preliminary caution concerns *how* the church has spoken. One must distinguish between truly dogmatic statements and other affirmations that are not on the same level. Examples of the latter include: (1) Prudential decisions made for the common good but which are not infallible guides to truth. For instance, between 1905 and 1915 the Roman PBC issued a series of directives about Scripture. Today, with the approval of the same PBC, most of these directives are regarded as passé by Catholic scholars (→ Church Pronouncements, 72:25). (2) Affirmations that use Scripture only as illustrations. The bull *Ineffabilis Deus* on the Immaculate Conception recalls Gen 3:15, and the bull *Munificentissimus Deus* on the Assumption recalls Rev 12. Few would argue that the respective popes were dogmatically affirming that these texts of Scripture refer in their literal sense to the Marian doctrines. More likely the citations imply no more than that reflection on these scriptural verses aided theologians in understanding the Marian doctrines and thus guided the church to take a dogmatic position. In particular, Pius XII seems to claim no more than that the dogma of the Assumption receives support from Scripture (*AAS* 42 [1950] 767, 769).

82   Another caution concerns the *area about which* the church has spoken. The logic behind claiming church authority over scriptural interpretation is that the church is the custodian of revelation. Since Scripture is a witness to revelation, the church has the power to determine infallibly the meaning of Scripture in matters of faith and morals (DS 1507, 3007). The church claims no absolute or direct authority over matters of biblical authorship, geography, chronology, and many issues of historicity. For that reason the church has not made any *dogmatic* pronouncements in these areas. Similarly, when we come to the actual exegesis of Scripture — something that could be a matter of faith and morals — in regard to 99 percent

of the Bible, the church has not commented officially on what a passage does or does not mean. That task is left to the knowledge, intelligence, and hard work of individual exegetes who claim no more than reasonable conviction for their conclusions. When the church has spoken on a particular verse, most often it has done so in a negative manner, i.e., by rejecting certain interpretations as false because they constitute a threat to faith and morals. The Council of Trent, for instance, condemned the Calvinist interpretation that would reduce the reference to water in John 3:5 (baptismal passage: "Unless one be begotten from above [born again] of water and spirit") to a mere metaphor (DS 1615). Again, it condemned those who would dissociate the power of forgiving sins exercised in the sacrament of Penance from the power accorded in John 20:23 (DS 1703).

83   A third caution concerns the *sense of Scripture* involved in the relatively few instances where the church has spoken affirmatively and authoritatively about a Scripture passage. The church is primarily concerned with what Scripture means to its people; it is not immediately concerned with what Scripture meant to those who wrote it or first heard it — the literal sense. We must remember that the concept of a literal sense established by historical-critical method is very much a modern development. Modern, too, is the emphasis on the distinction between what a text meant to its author and what it has come to mean in subsequent ecclesiastical-theological usage. In the instance cited above, where the Council of Trent condemned a wrong interpretation of John 20:23, did the council fathers wish to imply that the author of John had the sacrament of Penance in mind, or did they not rather wish to insist on the relation of Penance to the forgiveness of sins attested in that verse? If Trent cited Jas 5:14–15 in relation to the sacrament of Anointing of the Sick (DS 1760), did the Council wish to affirm that the author of Jas knew that the healing of the sick was a sacrament, or rather did it not affirm simply that the power of healing described in Jas was an instance of power that later was understood to be exercised in the sacraments? In both instances a knowledge of the history of the development of sacramental theology and belief suggests the second alternative. In other words, the church was not settling a historical question about what was in the mind of the author when he wrote the text, but a religious question about the implications of Scripture for the life of the faithful. (We do not pretend that the council fathers at Trent were necessarily conscious of this distinction; we are merely concerned with the *de facto* import of their decisions.)

84   Are there any instances where the church has spoken authoritatively, positively defining the literal sense of Scripture? Did Trent define the literal sense of Jesus' words of eucharistic institution: "After he had blessed bread and wine, he said in plain, unmistakable words that he was giving them his own body and his own blood. . . . These words have their proper and obvious meaning and were so understood by the Fathers" (DS 1637)? Did Vatican I speak about the literal sense of Matt 16:16–19 and John 21:15–17 when it insisted that Christ gave Peter real primacy among the apostles (DS 3053–55)? Experts in dogmatic theology are not in agreement in answering these questions. V. Betti (*La costituzione dommatica 'Pastor aeternus' del Concilio Vaticano I* [Rome, 1961] 592) states: "The interpretation of these two texts [Matt 16:17–19; John 21:15–17] as proof of the two dogmas mentioned does not fall *per se* under dogmatic definition — not only because no mention is made of them in the canon, but because there is no trace of a desire in the Council to give an authentic interpretation of them in this sense."

85   These few instances of possible church definition (there may be others) and the instances where the
church has condemned a particular interpretation of
Scripture cause much difficulty for Protestants. J. M.
Robinson (*CBQ* 27 [1965] 8–11) protests that if an
exegete by careful use of method comes to a conclusion
about a particular verse of Scripture and then the Magisterium steps in and says the conclusion is wrong, it is a
denial of intellect. He observes: "The invalidation of the
conclusion resulting from the proper application of
method necessarily invalidates the method," and thus in
principle the freedom and scientific quality of Catholic
exegesis is imperiled by the church's action.

In response, three observations should be made.
First, Catholic exegetes would honestly hold that in the
few instances where the church has spoken authoritatively about the literal sense of Scripture (mostly by way
of denying certain interpretations), a plausible exegetical
case can be made for the church's position. The meaning
that the church finds in the verse may not be the only
meaning that one could derive by critical method, but it
is a possible meaning. R. E. Brown (*Biblical Exegesis and
Church Doctrine* [NY, 1985] 36–37) maintains that the
Catholic church insists doctrinally that Jesus was conceived of a virgin without a human father. The historicity of the virginal conception is not the only possible
critical interpretation of Matt 1 and Luke 1, but it is a
possible and even probable interpretation. In accepting
church teaching on this point in interpreting Matt and
Luke, Catholic exegetes are not denying historical-
critical exegesis but supplementing it and moving
beyond its uncertainties. A proper appreciation of the
limited certainty provided by historical-critical investigation is helpful on this point.

86   Second, in interpreting Scripture the Magisterium does not operate independently of and isolated
from reliable Scripture scholarship. The Magisterium
does not come to its conclusion about what a biblical
passage does or does not mean by some sort of mystical
instinct or by direct revelation from on high. Traditional
faith, theological implications, and scholarly contributions all enter into the Magisterial decision. Both Trent
and Vatican I consulted the best Catholic exegetes of the
time. We are close enough to Vatican II to know that
when exegetes pointed out that Scripture was being
misused, such misinterpretation was dropped from the
conciliar documents. In fact, Vatican II affirmed that the
work done by exegetes is a factor in bringing the judgment of the church to maturity (*Dei Verbum* 3:12). It may
be asked if the church has ever spoken against the scholarly opinion of the majority of Catholic exegetes.
Applicable are the words of John Paul II at Catholic
University (Wash. DC) on Oct. 6, 1979: "I want to say
a special word of gratitude, encouragement, and guidance for the theologians. The church needs her theologians. . . . We [the bishops of the church] desire to
listen to you, and we are eager to receive the valued
assistance of your responsible scholarship" (*AAS* 71
[1979] 1263).

87   Third, the role of the church in interpreting
Scripture is a positive hermeneutic contribution and not
simply a curtailment of scientific freedom. "New Hermeneutic" would have the text interpreting the readers by
encountering them and challenging their self-understanding (→ 54 above). Catholics feel very strongly that
the liturgical and doctrinal life of the church constitute a
"hermeneutical place" where Scripture speaks most truly.
The instinctive negative reaction of the Catholic church
to rationalism, liberalism, and modernism was not a
rejection of the scientific method (although unfortunately and accidentally that method was thus brought

into temporary disrepute), but a reflection of the
church's good sense that in such "isms" Scripture was
not speaking truly. One may acknowledge that at times,
because of the weaknesses of those who constitute it, the
church does not immediately or adequately respond to
a meaning of Scripture that is patent to exegetes—
whence the constant need of renewal and reform from
within (→ Canonicity, 66:96). But despite that, the
church remains par excellence the place where Scripture
is heard in its truest and fullest meaning (→ 71–74
above).

88   **(III) Exegetical Authority of the Fathers.**
In almost every Roman document pertaining to scriptural studies there has been a statement about interpreting Scripture in loyalty to the mind of the Fathers
and Doctors of the church. Until recently, as a result of
the Modernist crisis, Catholic exegetes teaching in
seminaries were annually sworn to interpret Scripture
according to the unanimous consent of the Fathers. The
1964 Instruction of the Roman PBC (→ Church Pronouncements, 72:35) continues the insistence: "Let the
Catholic exegete, following the guidance of the church,
derive profit from all the earlier interpreters, especially
the holy Fathers and Doctors of the church."

Yet when one reads the actual exegesis of the Fathers
as we described it above (→ 35–38), it really has little in
common with the methods and results of modern Catholic exegesis. We have recorded a reluctance to return to
the more-than-literal exegesis of the Fathers (→ 48).
What then is the practical import of patristic exegesis as
a guide?

89   First of all, the area in which patristic authority is strongest is that of the dogmatic implications of
Scripture, not that of literal exegesis. For example,
Athanasius was quite aware that no text of Scripture
fully answered the Arian heresy: no single text in its
literal sense irrefutably showed that Jesus was "true God
of true God." But he insisted that in the 4th-cent. controversy the only answer that Scripture could give to the
question which Arius was raising was the answer of
Nicaea ("Letter Concerning the Decrees of the Council
of Nicaea," 5.19–21). Obviously, thus understood,
loyalty to patristic authority is no restriction on the
liberty or scientific quality of modern Catholic exegesis.

Moreover, when it is taken as an absolute norm, the
unanimous consent of the Fathers (morally unanimous
consent, not necessarily numerically unanimous) does
not affect many disputed passages. In a passage where
one might hope for unanimity, e.g., the Petrine application of Matt 16:18, one finds that neither Augustine nor
Chrysostom took the foundation rock to be Peter! In
summary, the church's insistence on the exegetical
authority of the Fathers reflects her desire that Catholic
exegetes should not forget the dogmatic heritage that
comes to them from tradition. The church would challenge modern scholars to emulate the success of the
Fathers in having the Bible nourish the faith, life,
teaching, and preaching of the Christian community.
But in terms of practical guidance in modern literal
exegesis of individual texts, patristic authority is of
restricted importance.

90   **(IV) Popular Communication of Modern
Critical Views.** The 1961 Monitum of the Holy
Office and the 1964 Instruction of the PBC—two
documents from Rome (→ Church Pronouncements,
72:34–35), one restrictive in tendency, the other
liberalizing—both insist on the dangers of scandalizing
the faithful by communicating in the biblical field "vain
or insufficiently established novelties." The PBC Instruction forbids those who publish for the faithful, "led
on by some pernicious itch for newness, to disseminate

any trial solutions for difficulties without a prudent selection and serious discrimination; for thus they perturb the faith of many."

Such warnings have a point. For instance, occasionally preachers enter the pulpit with an itch to shock: "There was no Garden of Eden. There were no magi, etc." Leaving aside the question of the oversimplified and sometimes incorrect tendency of such statements, we must insist that they do not serve to bring the wealth of Scripture to the spiritual and salvific aid of people. (One can preach on a topic like Gen 1–3 or the Matthean infancy narrative in such a way as to respect the historical problems involved but nevertheless to concentrate on the theological message.) An excessively negative popular presentation of the results of biblical criticism is not only dangerous for the faithful but does damage to reputable biblical scholars by popularizing their views without necessary qualifications and in a context where those views were never meant to be presented. The general principle is that one should not leave the audience with problems that the audience is not capable of solving. If one brings in elements of historical criticism, then one should take cognizance of possible implications and head off wrong conclusions.

91   But if we acknowledge the danger of rash popularization, we must firmly accentuate the danger on the other side as well—a danger that unfortunately has not received sufficient attention in church documents. This is the danger that an exaggerated fear of scandal will prevent popularizers from communicating to educated Catholics the more sophisticated understanding of the Bible that they should have. So often we hear about the few that are scandalized, and no voice is raised about the much greater crime of leaving the many in ignorance of modern biblical criticism. Fear of scandal must never lead to a double standard whereby the simple or the young are taught things about the Bible that are false just so that they will not be shocked. Common sense dictates that all education be scaled to the ability of the audience, but this does not mean that elementary biblical instruction should be noncritical. It means that elementary instruction should be critical in an elementary way. From the very first time the story of Gen 1–3 is told to kindergarten children, they should be taught to think of it as a popular story and not as history, even though the teacher may not wish at that level to raise formally the question of historicity. Even beginners can be taught to think of the Gospels as recorded preaching and teaching rather than as biographies of Jesus.

92   Unfortunately too, an exaggerated fear of scandal can hamper scientific research. There are a host of delicate biblical questions that need scientific study and discussion, e.g., the historicity of the infancy narratives, and the human knowledge of Jesus. Yet scholars know that when they write on these subjects even in professional and technical journals, an account, often confused and sometimes hostile, will soon appear in the popular press. In other words, while competent Catholic scholars are urged by the church to keep these matters away from public notice, whether they like it or not, others will popularize their work. The result is that frequently the scholar is accused of being responsible for the scandal and is made the target of recriminations by would-be protectors of the faith. The whole distinction between discussion on a scholarly level and popularization—a distinction sometimes facilely proposed in warnings from Rome—is rapidly dying out; and we should face this problem more frankly and more practically. In the long run more damage has been done to the church by the fact that her scholars have not always been free to discuss delicate problems than by the fact that some of the faithful are scandalized by the dissemination of new ideas. Often more harm is done by the lack of ideas than by the presence of new ideas. Imprudence and occasional scandal are the almost inevitable price that one must pay for the right of free discussion. And indeed such free academic discussion has its own way of crushing errors—a devastating book review in a biblical journal by a competent scholar may be more effective in eradicating nonsense than a warning from church authority that may seem simply to be repressive of freedom.

72

CHURCH PRONOUNCEMENTS

Raymond E. Brown, S.S.   Thomas Aquinas Collins, O.P. *

BIBLIOGRAPHY

1   Ahern, B., "Textual Directives of the Encyclical *Divino Afflante Spiritu*," *CBQ* 7 (1945) 340–47. Brown, R. E., "Rome and the Freedom of Catholic Biblical Studies" in *Search the Scriptures* (Fest. R. T. Stamm; ed. J. M. Myers, *et al.;* Leiden, 1969) 129–50. Cotter, A. C., "The Antecedents of the Encyclical *Providentissimus Deus*," *CBQ* 5 (1943) 117–24. DeFraine, J., "L'encyclique *Humani Generis* et les erreurs concernant l'Écriture Sainte," *ScEccl* 5 (1953) 7–28. Gilbert, M., "Paul VI. In Memoriam," *Bib* 59 (1978) 453–62. Hartdegen, S., "The Influence of the Encyclical *Providentissimus Deus*," *CBQ* 5 (1943) 141–59. Lagrange, M.-J. "A propos de l'encyclique *Providentissimus*," *RB*

4 (1895) 48–64; "Le décret *Lamentabili sane exitu* et la critique historique," *RB* 16 (1907) 542–54; *Personal Reflections and Memories* (NY, 1985; Fr. orig. 1966). Levie, J., *The Bible, Word of God in Words of Men* (NY, 1961). Murphy, R. T., "The Teaching of the Encyclical *Providentissimus Deus*," *CBQ* 5 (1943) 125–40. Rahner, K., "Mysterium Ecclesiae," *CrC* 23 (1973) 183–98.

The two principal collections of church pronouncements are *EB* (cited by section number) and *RSS* (cited by page); see also *MOCT* and *DS* (both cited by section); *The Documents of Vatican II* (ed. W. M. Abbott and J. Gallagher; NY, 1966).

2   **OUTLINE**

Historical Background for Recent Pronouncements (§ 3–9)
   (I) Introduction
      (A) 1870–1900 (§ 4)
      (B) 1900–1940 (§ 5)
      (C) 1941–1965 (§ 6–8)
      (D) 1966–1990 (§ 9)

Summaries of the Pronouncements (§ 10–41)
   (I) Councils of the Church
      (A) Florence (§ 10)
      (B) Trent (§ 11)
      (C) Vatican I (§ 12)
      (D) Vatican II (§ 13–16)
  (II) Encyclical Letters
      (A) *Providentissimus Deus* (§ 17)
      (B) *Pascendi Dominici Gregis* (§ 18)
      (C) *Spiritus Paraclitus* (§ 19)
      (D) *Divino Afflante Spiritu* (§ 20–23)

      (E) *Humani Generis* (§ 24)
  (III) Documents of Roman Commissions
      (A) Early Decrees of the PBC (1905–1933)
         (a) General Historicity (§ 26)
         (b) Old Testament (§ 27)
         (c) New Testament (§ 28)
      (B) More Recent Documents (1941–1990)
         (a) PBC to Italian Hierarchy (§ 29)
         (b) PBC on Biblical Translations (§ 30)
         (c) PBC to Cardinal Suhard of Paris (§ 31)
         (d) PBC on Scripture in Seminaries (§ 32)
         (e) PBC on Biblical Meetings (§ 33)
         (f) Holy Office on Historicity (§ 34)
         (g) PBC on Gospel Historicity (§ 35)
         (h) *Mysterium Ecclesiae* (§ 36)
         (i) PBC 1965–1975 (§ 37)
         (j) PBC Study on Women Priests (§ 38)
         (k) PBC Study on Christology (§ 39)
  (IV) Recent Papal Allocutions (§ 40–41)

---

*Sections 3–9, 13–16, 36–41 are the work of R. E. Brown; 10–12, 17–24 are the work of T. A. Collins; 25–35 were written jointly.

HISTORICAL BACKGROUND FOR RECENT PRONOUNCEMENTS

**3	(I) Introduction.** In what follows we shall present a quick summary of ecclesiastical statements pertaining to the Bible. Some background is necessary for the evaluation of these statements; for, although all demand respect and understanding, not all these statements require equal adherence. Obviously, decrees of the ecumenical councils are more binding than papal encyclicals. In particular, there was a certain temporal character to the binding force of the decrees of the Pontifical Biblical Commission (PBC), for these were prudential decisions on practical problems. They required obedience when issued but were subject to subsequent revision and are in no way to be considered infallible. Moreover, all these documents, conciliar, papal, and curial, must be evaluated in the light of the time in which they were issued and the problems to which they were addressed. A fundamentalism in interpreting them is just as objectionable as a fundamentalism in interpreting Scripture. One must distinguish between the precise truth affirmed and its conceptual or verbal expression, which is determined by historical circumstances (→ 36 below).

With the exception of the decrees of the Councils of Florence and Trent, all the documents to be discussed are dated within the last 125 years, and so it may be helpful to summarize Rome's attitude toward biblical studies during this period in order to show the atmosphere in which the statements must be evaluated.

**4	(A) 1870–1900.** This period saw the first real Catholic encounter with a vigorous Protestant biblical criticism (→ NT Criticism, 70:5ff.; → OT Criticism, 69:23ff.). To religious people accustomed to thinking of Scripture as inspired and inerrant, the new insights raised problems about biblical inerrancy in matters both of natural science and of history (→ Inspiration, 65:38–41). The fact that some non-Catholics were being led by their biblical studies to devalue the religious import of the Scriptures created a certain defensiveness on the part of the church authorities, ever anxious to preserve the Scriptures as God's word. Vatican I gave evidence of this attitude in general questions of theology, but the brevity of this council did not allow a full attitude toward Scripture to be seen. It did little more than repeat the Tridentine statement on canonicity and stress the inspiration of Scripture (→ Inspiration, 65:29). Leo XIII's encyclical *Providentissimus Deus* (1893) is the chief witness to the official ecclesiastical attitude toward biblical studies during this period. It is interesting that despite the dangers of the time, this learned and humanistic pope took a somewhat nuanced stand. The encyclical shows a certain hostility toward higher criticism and the work of non-Catholic scholars: "The sense of Holy Scripture can nowhere be found incorrupt outside the church and cannot be expected to be found in writers who, being without the true faith, only gnaw the bark of Sacred Scripture and never attain its pith" (*EB* 113; *RSS*, p. 17—how far we have come since that time can be seen in the encouragement of Vatican II [*De Rev.* 6:22] to work with non-Catholic scholars on biblical translations!). Nevertheless, the pope showed himself aware of the advantages of scientific linguistic and exegetical studies, and he was attuned to the fact that the views of the biblical authors in questions of science were not invested with scriptural infallibility. Thus, at the start of the 20th cent. the official Catholic attitude toward scriptural advances was one of caution but also of dawning appreciation that boded well for the future.

**5	(B) 1900–1940.** The advent of Modernism, particularly in the writings of A. Loisy, changed the whole situation (→ NT Criticism, 70:38). There was now danger of a virulent heresy, and the saintly Pius X was more interested in protecting the faithful than in the niceties of scientific attitude. In Scripture the Modernists were using the new approaches inaugurated by the German Protestants; and in *Pascendi* and *Lamentabili,* the official Catholic condemnations of Modernism, little distinction was made between the possible intrinsic validity of these approaches and the Modernist theological misuse of them. At the same time the PBC, established by Leo XIII in 1902, began to issue a series of decisions on many fine points of biblical interpretation and authorship. These decrees, issued between 1905 and 1915, were precautionary and, while conservative in tone, were often phrased with perception and nuance. But since they bound Catholic scholars to assent, they gave to the non-Catholic world the unfortunate image of a monolithically conservative Catholic attitude that did not discuss questions on the basis of an exchange of scientific opinion but solved all by mandate from centralized authority.

Even though the decrees of the PBC, when interpreted with juridic insight, allowed a certain room for scholarly investigation, the atmosphere was not conducive to this; and advanced scholars like M.-J. Lagrange (→ OT Criticism, 69:35,55) were virtually silenced on sensitive questions. Well does F.-M. Braun entitle this period in the life of Lagrange "Trials and Struggles" (*The Work of Père Lagrange* [Milwaukee, 1963] 66–100). Levie (*Bible* 73) describes the network of reactionary espionage established to delate to Rome all those whose ideas might show any taint of Modernism, a network so despicable that Pope Benedict XV himself formally censured it. The encyclical *Spiritus Paraclitus* of Benedict XV in 1920 was colored by the difficult period that had preceded it. The pope was more negative in tone in dealing with modern advances than Leo XIII had been and was strongly defensive on the historicity of the Bible. The 1920s saw vigorous ecclesiastical action by the Holy Office under Cardinal Merry del Val against the writings of leading Catholic scholars like J. Touzard, F. Vigouroux, M. Bacuez, and A. Brassac (see Levie, *Bible* 124). The PBC did not issue decrees in these years except for a lone statement on the exegesis of two texts in 1933.

**6	(C) 1941–1965.** This period saw the renaissance of Catholic biblical studies. There were some signs of a change in attitude late in the pontificate of Pius XI, but it is Pius XII who deserves the title of patron of Catholic biblical studies. His pontificate marked a complete about-face and inaugurated the greatest renewal of interest in the Bible that the Roman Catholic Church has ever seen. The signs of this change were visible in the new attitude of the PBC, which in 1941 condemned an overly *conservative* distrust of modern biblical research. The encyclical *Divino Afflante Spiritu* of 1943 was a Magna Charta for biblical progress. Although the pope saluted the encyclicals of his predecessors, he announced that the time for fear was over and that Catholic scholars should use modern tools in their exegesis. The use of the principle of literary forms to solve historical problems and the encouragement to make new translations of the Bible from the original languages (rather than from the Vg) were an invitation to Catholic scholars to begin writing freely again and to catch up with Protestant scholarship, which had greatly outdistanced them during the preceding years of "trials and struggles." The directives of the pope were reinforced by the statements of the PBC in 1948 to Cardinal Suhard on Gen and in 1950 on teaching Scripture in the seminaries. In 1955 the secretary of the PBC took a very brave but most necessary step in stating that now Catholic scholars had complete freedom (*plena libertate*) with regard to the earlier PBC decrees of 1905–1915, except where they touched on faith and morals (and very few of them did). This meant that Catholics were now free to adopt modern positions on authorship and dating.

7   A crisis in the advance of Catholic biblical studies came with the illness and death of Pius XII. In the last year of his pontificate (April 1958) the Congregation of Seminaries expressed displeasure with vol. I of the *Introduction à la Bible* just published under the editorship of A. Robert and A. Feuillet. (Subsequently a 2d ed. was published with virtually no changes and with the indicated approval of the secretary of the PBC and of Cardinal Bea.) At the beginning of the reign of Pope John XXIII, serious attacks were made in Rome on important Catholic biblical scholars like L. Alonso Schökel, J. Levie, S. Lyonnet, and M. Zerwick, and subsequently the latter two were removed from their teaching office at the Pontifical Biblical Institute. The bitter controversy of this difficult period is well reported by J. A. Fitzmyer in *TS* 22 (1961) 426–44. Finally, in 1961 the Holy Office issued a warning against ideas that were calling in question the genuine historical and objective truth of Scripture. The atmosphere of foreboding was increased by reports that the (unpublished) schema "The Sources of Revelation," which was to be presented at the forthcoming Vatican II in the fall of 1962, was negative in its approach to recent biblical advances. However, the pessimism failed to take into account the winds of *aggiornamento* that were sweeping through the window opened by John XXIII. In Nov. 1962 so many of the Council Fathers expressed their displeasure with this schema that Pope John ordered it to be withdrawn and rewritten by a combined commission on which biblical scholars were better represented.

8   The pontificate of Paul VI restored the warmly favorable atmosphere of the days of Pius XII. The above-mentioned professors were restored to their chairs. In April 1964 the PBC issued an "Instruction on the Historical Truth of the Gospels," an encouraging document opening the way to honest biblical criticism in the very delicate field of Gospel historicity. The final form of the schema *De Revelatione* passed by Vatican II in 1965 had much of the tone of the PBC Instruction, giving the official blessing of the church to further progress along the lines laid down by Pius XII.

9   **(D) 1966–1990.** This history of sharp Catholic rejection of modern biblical approaches for the first third of the 20th cent. (period B above) and then sudden acceptance in the second third (period C above) predictably produced unevenness in the last third of the century. First, for the seminaries and colleges there was the task of getting a generation of Catholic scholars educated in depth in the new approaches. Second, for the parishes and schools, priests and teachers trained in the pre-1960 attitudes were shocked to hear an approval of ideas about biblical historicity that they had once been taught to condemn. Third, for ecumenism and dogmatic theology, implications of the contemporary biblical approaches demand a rethinking of old ideas. A small but articulate group of ultraconservatives mounted an unsuccessful attack on noted Catholic biblical scholars, seeking to turn the clock back to 1910. There were occasional liberal abuses of biblical information in popular catechesis and in some theological writings, e.g., facilely denying the virginal conception, the bodily resurrection, miracles, the foundation of the church, and the legitimacy of the ordained ministry. Relatively few Catholic *biblical* scholars, however, adopted such views, so that the main thrust of the biblical movement had remained solidly centrist (see R. E. Brown, *Biblical Exegesis and Church Doctrine* [NY 1985]). The 20-year-old prediction of *JBC* 72:9 has proved true: The modern Catholic biblical movement inaugurated by Pius XII and confirmed by Vatican II is now too much a part of the church to be rejected. In this last third of the 20th cent. there has been no magistral condemnation of any outstanding Catholic biblical scholar. Indeed, some who have annoyed Catholic ultraconservatives have been made members of the Roman PBC (→ 37 below), while recent popes insist on the continued use of biblical criticism by Catholic scholars (→ 40 below).

SUMMARIES OF THE PRONOUNCEMENTS

10   **(I) Councils of the Church.**
    (A) Florence. The Council of Florence (1438–1445) proclaimed the traditional doctrine of the church regarding the canon (→ Canonicity, 66:13) in the *Decree for the Jacobites* (from the bull *Cantate Domino,* Feb. 4, 1441 — *EB* 47). This decree contained a list of inspired books, both protocanonical and deuterocanonical, which is identical with that drawn up at the Council of Hippo in 393, repeated at the 3d and 4th Councils of Carthage in 397 and 419, and found also in "Consulenti tibi," a letter regarding the canon sent by Pope Innocent I in 405 to Exuperius, bishop of Toulouse (*EB* 16–21; → Canonicity, 66:11–12).
11   **(B) Trent.** Major doubts and uncertainties concerning the canon were finally resolved by the Council of Trent (1545–1563) in its fourth session on

Apr. 8, 1546. In this session, the council voted affirmatively on two decrees: (1) concerning the canonical Scriptures (*EB* 57–60), and (2) concerning the edition and use of the sacred books (*EB* 61–64). The first decree, which adopted the canon of Florence, was "the first infallible and effectually promulgated declaration on the Canon of the Holy Scriptures." As H. Jedin observes, it also put a full stop to the 1,000-year-old development of the biblical canon (*History of the Council of Trent* [London, 1961] 91). Henceforth the books of the OT and the NT, protocanonical and deuterocanonical alike, in their entirety and with all their parts, comprise the canon and are held to be of equal authority (→ Canonicity, 66:13, 42–43, 90–91).

    The second decree declares "that the ancient Vulgate edition, which has been approved by the church itself through long usage for so many centuries, should be considered the authentic edition for public reading, disputations, sermons, and explanations" (→ 20 below for the encyclical *DAS,* which would clarify the meaning of this Tridentine decree). The decree goes on to forbid anyone from daring in matters of faith and morals "to distort Scripture to fit meanings of his own that are contrary to the meaning that holy Mother Church has held and now holds, for it is her office to judge about the true sense and interpretation of Scripture. Nor should anyone dare to interpret Scripture contrary to the unanimous agreement of the Fathers" (→ Hermeneutics, 71:88–89). Instructions were given for the publication of the Vg whose text was to be printed as correctly as possible. The result was the Sixto-Clementine Vg (→ Texts, 68:146). For the attitude of Trent toward vernacular Bibles, see R. E. McNally, *TS* 27 (1966) 204–27.

12   (C) Vatican I.   In its third session, on Apr. 24, 1870, Vatican Council I (1869–1870) reaffirmed the decree of Trent concerning the source of revelation (DS 1501) and then clearly stated that the church holds the books of Holy Scripture as sacred and canonical, not because she subsequently approved them, nor because they contain revelation without error, but precisely because "having been written by the inspiration of the Holy Spirit, they have God as their author and, as such, they have been handed down to the church itself" (*EB* 77; → Inspiration, 65:45).

13   (D) Vatican II.   The Dogmatic Constitution on Divine Revelation (*Dei Verbum*), proclaimed Nov. 18, 1965, is a document whose attitude toward modern biblical studies is largely positive but whose statements on disputed subjects reflect careful compromise, stemming from the five revisions through which the document passed between 1962 and 1965 (→ 7 above). We mention here only the most important points relative to biblical studies. Chap. 1 of the constitution discusses revelation. That divine revelation took place both in deeds and in words is emphasized—a view that takes cognizance of the modern biblical emphasis on the "God who acts," along with the traditional emphasis on the "God who speaks." Chap. 2 deals with the disputed theological question of the sources of revelation. Faced with sharply opposed views—two sources (Scripture and Tradition) vs. one source (Scripture alone, as interpreted by Tradition)—the Council does not settle the question. It stresses (2:9) that Tradition and Scripture "in a certain way merge into a unity and tend toward the same end," but "it is not from Sacred Scripture alone that the church draws her certainty about everything that has been revealed." On the relation between the church and Scripture, the council (2:10) insists that the teaching office of the church authentically interprets the word of God but that this teaching office is not above the word of God but serves it.

14   Chap. 3 treats of inspiration and inerrancy. On inspiration it recapitulates traditional teaching and adds little new. Yet the overall focus of *Dei Verbum* on the role of human authors contributed to the post–Vatican II a posteriori approach in Catholic theorizing about inspiration, i.e., concentrating on what we know from the text rather than on speculation about what God might have done (→ Inspiration, 65:3–7, 58). On inerrancy Vatican II made an important qualification as our italics indicate: "The Books of Scripture must be acknowledged as teaching, firmly, faithfully, and without error *that truth which God wanted put into the sacred writings for the sake of our salvation*" (3:11). Some have tried to interpret the italicized phrase to cover everything the human author expressed; but pre-voting debates show

an awareness of errors in the Bible (→ Inspiration, 65:50, 70). Thus, it is proper to take the clause as specifying: Scriptural teaching is truth without error to the extent that it conforms to the salvific purpose of God. Decision about that purpose involves an a posteriori approach in the church, paying attention to literary forms (as in *DAS;* → 22 below) and historical conditioning (→ 36 below).

15   Chap. 4 is devoted to the OT, an indication of the church's desire to call to the attention of clergy and laity this portion of their heritage so poorly known among the Christian people today. The view of the OT in this constitution is heavily christological (4:15—the OT prepares for the NT; it announces the coming of the messianic kingdom through prophecies). In the judgment of many, then, Vatican II does not give sufficient attention to the importance of the OT itself (→ OT Thought, 77:176; → Hermeneutics, 71:21). The NT treatment in chap. 5 largely concerns the Gospels and is drawn from the PBC Instruction of 1964 (→ 35 below). The same three stages in Gospel development are given: Jesus Christ, apostolic preachers, sacred authors. It is recognized (5:19) that the Gospels have selected, synthesized, and explicated what Jesus did and taught, but the council gives no specific norms for determining how much development there was. The distinction between the apostles and the sacred writers would seem to favor the modern opinion that the evangelists were not themselves apostolic eyewitnesses, although earlier the constitution (2:7) resorts to the traditional terminology of "apostles and apostolic men" for the composers of the written record of salvation; and this has been used in times past to distinguish between Matthew and John ("apostles") and Mark and Luke ("apostolic men").

16   Chap. 6 describes the role of the Bible in the life of the church; it provides a wealth of truly pastoral counsel. We note only the following points: A close parallel is drawn between Scripture and the sacraments ("The church has always venerated the divine Scriptures just as she venerates the body of the Lord" [6:21]); there is an insistence that preaching must be nourished and ruled by Scripture; the Bible should be translated *from the original languages* and, where feasible, with the cooperation of non-Catholics (6:22); explicit encouragement is given to biblical scholars to continue their work (6:23—important in the light of the troubles that cast a shadow on biblical scholarship between 1958 and 1962; → 7 above); the study of Scripture is the soul of theology (6:24); the clergy must be well trained in Scripture for preaching and catechizing (6:25); bishops have an obligation to see that the means are provided whereby the people can be instructed in Scripture, by way of both translations and commentaries. For the position of Vatican II toward the translation of Scripture, see L. Legrand, *RB* 64 (1967) 413–22.

(A. Grillmeier in *Commentary on the Documents of Vatican II* [ed. H. Vorgrimler; NY, 1969] 3. 199–246. Baum, G., *TS* 28 [1967] 51–75. Grelot, P., *Études* 324 [1966] 99–113, 233–46. Loretz, O., *TRev* 63 [1967] 1–8. Tavard, G. H., *JES* 3 [1966] 1–35. Zerwick, M., *VD* 44 [1966] 17–42.)

17   (II) Encyclical Letters.
(A) Providentissimus Deus (*EB* 81–134; *RSS,* pp. 1–29).   Issued by Leo XIII on Nov. 18, 1893, this encyclical inaugurated a new era by presenting a plan for Catholic biblical studies. Suitable professors should first teach a sound course in biblical introduction and then proceed to train their students in "a definite and ascertained method of interpretation" (*EB* 103–5; *RSS,* pp. 11–12). The "authentic" Vg version is to be the biblical text used, though other versions, as well as the more

ancient mss., should not be neglected (*EB* 106; *RSS*, p. 13). A biblical text cannot be interpreted against a sense determined by the church or supported by the unanimous consent of the Fathers (*EB* 108; *RSS*, p. 14—for a correct interpretation of this, see *DAS* [*EB* 565; *RSS*, p. 102]). Catholic scholars remain free to pursue their private studies, especially of difficult biblical passages. Such studies "may, in the benignant providence of God, prepare for and bring to maturity the judgment of the church" (*EB* 109; *RSS*, p. 15). In interpreting difficult passages, exegetes must follow the analogy of faith, i.e., they cannot come to an interpretation of the inspired author's meaning that would be a direct and formal contradiction of a dogma taught by the church (→ Pauline Theology, 82:7). They must remember that the supreme law is Catholic doctrine as authoritatively proposed by the church (*EB* 109; *RSS*, p. 15).

The encyclical urges the study of Oriental languages and of the art of criticism (*EB* 118; *RSS*, p. 20). It also calls attention to the dangers of contemporary "higher criticism" (*EB* 119; *RSS*, p. 20). In describing the physical world, the sacred authors did not formally intend to teach natural science. On the contrary, they used terms common at the time, and which, in many instances, are still used even by eminent scientists. God spoke to human beings in the way they could understand—a way to which they were accustomed (*EB* 121; *RSS*, p. 22). These principles will apply to cognate sciences, and especially to history (*EB* 123; *RSS*, p. 23). (The reference to history in this context gave rise to some controversy; → 19 below.) Pope Leo also gave a now-celebrated description of inspiration: By supernatural power God so moved and impelled the human authors to write—he so assisted them when writing—that the things that he ordered and those only they first rightly understood, then willed faithfully to write down, and finally expressed in apt words and with infallible truth. Inspiration, which is incompatible with error, extends to the canonical Scriptures and to all their parts (*EB* 125; *RSS*, p. 24; → Inspiration, 65:41, 42, 45).

18   (B) Pascendi Dominici Gregis (*EB* 257-67; DS 3475-3500). This encyclical was issued on Sept. 8, 1907, by Pius X in refutation of the errors of the Modernists, e.g., on the origin and nature of the sacred books (*EB* 257), on inspiration (*EB* 258-59), on the distinction between the purely human Christ of history and the divine Christ of faith (*EB* 260), on the origin and growth of the Scriptures (*EB* 262-63), and on that faulty apologetics that strives to resolve controversies over religion by historical and psychological investigations (DS 3499). The decree *Lamentabili*, a syllabus of 65 Modernist propositions condemned by the Congregation of the Sacred Inquisition, was issued on July 3, 1907, just prior to the appearance of *Pascendi* (*EB* 190-256). [The reader should be warned that the propositions are condemned *in the sense held by the Modernists*, and the degree of condemnation (from heretical to dangerous) is not specified.]

19   (C) Spiritus Paraclitus (*EB* 440-95; *RSS*, pp. 43-79). This encyclical was issued by Benedict XV on the 15th centenary of St. Jerome's death, Sept. 15, 1920. After a moving tribute to the holy life and biblical labors of the saint, the pope compares modern views with those of Jerome. He briefly commends those who use modern critical methods in their biblical studies (*EB* 453; *RSS*, p. 51). He laments that some scholars have not observed the guidelines of *Providentissimus Deus* and the Fathers (*EB* 454; *RSS*, p. 51). He scores the teaching that limits inspiration to only certain portions of the Scriptures (*EB* 455; *RSS*, p. 52). In treating of the historical portions of Scripture, one cannot apply universally the principle that Leo XIII laid down for judg-

ing biblical statements on scientific matters, viz., that the author spoke only according to appearances (*EB* 456; *RSS*, p. 52). We cannot say that the sacred writers of historical events were ignorant of the truth and simply adopted and handed down false views current at the time (*EB* 459; *RSS*, p. 53). The exegete must avoid a too ready use, or misuse, of those principles governing "implicit quotations" or "pseudohistorical narratives" or "kinds of literature" (*EB* 461; *RSS*, p. 54). As Jerome insisted, all biblical interpretation rests on the literal sense, and one must not think that there is no literal sense merely because a thing is said metaphorically (*EB* 485; *RSS*, p. 67 [→ Hermeneutics, 71:9]). The goal of biblical studies is to learn spiritual perfection, to defend the faith, and to preach the word of God fruitfully (*EB* 482-84; *RSS*, pp. 65-66).

20   (D) Divino Afflante Spiritu (*EB* 538-69; *RSS*, pp. 80-107). Issued by Pius XII on Sept. 30, 1943, *DAS* was to commemorate the 50th anniv. of *Providentissimus Deus* "by ratifying and inculcating all that was wisely laid down by our predecessor . . . and by pointing out what seems necessary in the present day . . ." (*EB* 538; *RSS*, p. 81). Reflecting the complex history of exegesis in those 50 years (→ 4-5 above), *DAS* does, in fact, complete many teachings of *Providentissimus*, e.g., whereas in relation to the Vg *Providentissimus* permitted scholars to pay attention to the original-language texts of Scripture, *DAS* orders them to explain the original texts from which new transls. should be made. There is a similar shift of emphasis on such questions as the relation between the literal and the spiritual sense of Scripture, the binding extent of the unanimous consent of the Fathers, and the interpretation of historical facts in terms of literary forms (Levie, *Word of God* 139-44). *DAS* teaches the great importance of textual criticism and makes specific that the "authenticity" of the Vg (Trent; → 11 above) is primarily juridical (free from error in faith and morals) rather than critical (always an accurate transl.).

**21   The exegete must be principally concerned with the literal sense of the Scriptures (*EB* 550; *RSS*, p. 92); also the theological doctrine (faith and morals) of the individual books or texts must be carefully set forth (*EB* 550; *RSS*, p. 93). The exegete should seek and expound the spiritual sense, provided it is clearly intended by God (*EB* 552; *RSS*, p. 94; → Hermeneutics, 71:78-79). The Church Fathers ought to be studied more assiduously (*EB* 554; *RSS*, p. 95).

**22   In particular, biblical interpreters, with care and without neglecting recent research, ought to endeavor to determine the character and circumstances of the sacred writer, the age in which he lived, his written or oral sources, and the forms of expression he employed (*EB* 557; *RSS*, p. 97). History, archaeology, and other sciences should be employed to understand more perfectly ancient modes of writing (*EB* 558; *RSS*, p. 97); and the study of literary forms cannot be neglected without serious detriment to Catholic exegesis (*EB* 560; *RSS*, p. 99). This emphasis on recognizing different types of literature or different literary forms in the Bible was probably the greatest single contribution of *DAS*, for it offered the Catholic scholar an intelligent and honest way of facing up to the obvious historical problems present in the Bible. Formerly too many books of the Bible were thought to be history in the strict sense; now it could be shown that many of these books were not history at all or were history in a broader and less technical sense. Vatican II gave its approval to the distinction of literary forms (→ 14 above; → Hermeneutics, 71:23-26).

**23   *DAS* urged Catholic exegetes to grapple with

difficult problems, hitherto unsolved, and to arrive at solutions in full accord with the doctrine of the church, as well as in harmony with the indubitable conclusions of profane sciences (*EB* 564; *RSS*, p. 101). This was a refreshing change from the atmosphere after the Modernist crisis when Catholic exegetes deliberately sought out "safe" areas for their biblical research. The pope states that there are but a few texts whose sense has been determined by the authority of the church or about which the teaching of the Holy Fathers is unanimous (*EB* 565; *RSS*, p. 102). This statement counteracts the frequent misunderstanding that Catholics have no freedom in interpreting Scripture. The effects of the very positive encouragement given to biblical scholars by *DAS* (*EB* 565; *RSS*, p. 102) have been mentioned above (→ 6).

24   (E) Humani Generis (*EB* 611–20; *RSS*, pp. 113–15). Issued by Pius XII on Aug. 12, 1950, it instructs exegetes on evolution, polygenism, and OT historical narratives. Liberty for discussing the evolution of the human body is granted, but one should not presume that evolution is completely certain or proved. As for polygenism, "It is in no way apparent how such an opinion can be reconciled" with what has been taught on original sin, viz., that it proceeds from a sin actually committed by an individual Adam. [Note, however, that the pope does not absolutely condemn the theory of polygenism.] The popular type of history found in the OT still enjoyed the charism of inspiration and cannot be considered on a par with myths that are more the product of an extravagant imagination than of a striving for truth (→ OT Thought, 77:31). It is worth noting that in this predominantly monitory encyclical there is virtually no chastisement of biblical scholars. Seemingly to his death Pius XII remained firm in his faith in modern criticism.

25   (III) Documents of Roman Commissions. (A) Early Decrees of the PBC. Decrees issued between 1905 and 1915 and in 1933 are summarized briefly below; this is a difficult task because the decrees were issued in the form of responses to intricate questions (often phrased negatively). Many now have little more than historic interest, being implicitly revoked by later decrees, by *DAS*, and by Vatican II. They must be evaluated according to the 1955 clarification issued in Latin and in German by A. Miller and by A. Kleinhans, secretary and assistant secretary of the PBC (*BenMon* 31 [1955] 49–50; *Antonianum* 30 [1955] 63–65; *CBQ* 18 [1956] 23–29; *RSS*, p. 175—note that the latter mistakenly omits the important clause "with full liberty": *plena libertate; in aller Freiheit*). Miller says: "As long as these [early PBC] decrees propose views that are neither immediately nor mediately connected with truths of faith and morals, the interpreter of Sacred Scripture can pursue his scientific investigations with full liberty and accept the results of these investigations, provided always that he respects the teaching authority of the church."

Ultraconservatives have attempted to salvage the authority of the early PBC decrees by citing the opinion of J. E. Steinmueller (*The Sword of the Spirit* [Waco, 1977] 7) that this clarification was unauthorized and invalid because he heard that Miller and Kleinhans were rebuked by the Holy Office over it (but spared by the intervention of Cardinal Tisserant). An undocumented recollection published much later scarcely constitutes proof, esp. since there was Roman gossip in the other direction as well: Pius XII offered to revoke the PBC decrees officially, but A. Bea persuaded him that the Miller-Kleinhans clarification was sufficient. The clear *fact* is that the clarification was never withdrawn and

Rome has acted consistently in its spirit, never correcting the hundreds of Catholic scholars who have used the "full liberty" to contradict almost *every one* of the early PBC decrees. In the summary below, brackets are used for supplied explanations.

26   (a) GENERAL HISTORICITY.

(i) Against too free a use of the theory of *implicit citations*, i.e., that the biblical author is implicitly citing a noninspired source whose conclusions he does not make his own (Feb. 13, 1905; *EB* 160; *RSS*, p. 117).

(ii) Against too free a recourse to the theory that a book that has been regarded as history is not really history but has only the *appearance of history* (June 23, 1905; *EB* 161; *RSS*, pp. 117–18).

27   (b) OLD TESTAMENT.

(i) *The Pentateuch.* Moses is substantially the author, and there is insufficient evidence that it was compiled from sources posterior to Moses. Moses may have drawn on existing sources; and, as principal author, he may have entrusted composition to others who wrote according to his will. There may have been subsequent modifications, inspired additions, modernizations of language, and even scribal errors in copying (June 27, 1906; *EB* 181–84; *RSS*, pp. 118–19 [→ Pentateuch, 1:5–8].)

(ii) *Genesis.* The literal historical character of Gen 1–3 is defended, esp. with regard to religious fundamentals. These chapters are not fictional narrative, nor purified fables derived from pagan mythologies, nor allegories destitute of foundation in objective reality; nor do they contain edifying legends, partly historical and partly fictional. Yet allowance may be made for metaphor, figurative language, and the scientific naïveté of the author. The word *yôm* [Gen 1:5, 8, etc.] may mean a natural day or a space of time. In particular the PBC insisted on the literal and historical meaning of passages dealing with the following: (1) creation of all things by God at the beginning of time; (2) special creation of man; (3) formation of the first woman from man; (4) unity of the human race; (5) original happiness of our first parents in a state of justice, integrity, and immortality; (6) divine command laid upon man to prove his obedience; (7) transgression of this command at the instigation of the devil in the form of a serpent; (8) fall of our first parents from their primitive state of innocence; (9) promise of a future redeemer (June 30, 1909; *EB* 324–31; *RSS*, pp. 122–24 [→ Genesis, 2:4–5]).

(iii) *Isaiah.* The book contains real prophecies, not simply *vaticinia ex eventu* or shrewd guesses; prophets spoke not only of the immediate future to a contemporary audience but also of things to be fulfilled after many ages. The evidence is insufficient that the book was written by several authors [→ Dt-Isaiah, 21:2–4] living in different centuries (June 28, 1908; *EB* 276–80; *RSS*, pp. 120–22).

(iv) *Psalms.* David is not the sole author, but he is the author of the following Pss: 2, 16(Lat 15), 18(17), 32(31), 69(68), 110(109). The titles of the Pss represent very ancient Jewish tradition, not to be questioned without solid reason. For liturgical purposes, etc., Pss have been divided; others consist of separate pieces welded into one; others have been slightly modified by excision or addition, e.g., 51(50). There is no proof that many of the Pss were composed after the Ezra-Nehemiah period [*ca.* 400]. Some Pss are prophetic and messianic, foretelling the coming and career of the future redeemer (May 1, 1910; *EB* 332–39; *RSS*, pp. 124–26 [→ Psalms, 34:4, 10]).

28   (c) NEW TESTAMENT.

(i) *Matthew.* The apostle Matthew wrote his Gospel before the other Gospels and before the destruction of Jerusalem (AD 70), and not necessarily after Paul

came to Rome [*ca.* 61; → Matthew 42:2–4]. He originally wrote in the dialect used by the Jews in Palestine
[Aramaic or Hebrew], and canonical Gk Matt is identical
in substance with the original Gospel; it is not simply a
collection of sayings and discourses by an anonymous
author. The admitted dogmatic and apologetic purposes
of Matthew and his occasional lack of chronological
order do not permit one to consider as untrue his narrative of the deeds and words of Christ, or to think that
this narrative has been subjected to changes under the
influence of the OT or church development. The historical authenticity of several passages peculiar to Matt is
emphasized; chaps. 1–2; 14:33; 16:17–19; 28:19–20
(June 19, 1911; *EB* 383–89; *RSS*, pp. 126–28). Matt
16:26 (Luke 9:25) refers in a literal sense to the eternal
life of the soul and not only to temporal life (July 1,
1933; *EB* 514; *RSS*, p. 138).

(ii) *Mark, Luke.* The chronological order of
the Synoptics is: original Matt, Mark, Luke—although
Gk Matt may be posterior to Mark and Luke. Mark,
writing according to the preaching of Peter, and Luke,
writing according to that of Paul, are really the authors
of Mark and Luke, which were written before the
destruction of Jerusalem [AD 70]. Luke composed the
Gospel before Acts, which was finished by the end of the
Roman imprisonment of Paul [*ca.* 63; → Canonicity,
66:58, 66]. The evangelists had at their disposal trustworthy sources, oral or written; and their narratives
have a claim to full historical credence. The PBC insists
on the inspiration of certain disputed passages and finds
unconvincing the arguments proposed against their
genuineness and authorship: Mark 16:9–20; Luke 1–2;
and 22:43–44. The Magnificat [Luke 1:46–55] is to be
attributed to Mary, not to Elizabeth as a few textual
witnesses would have it. Liberty is allowed to Catholic
scholars in discussing the Synoptic problem, but they are
not free to advocate the Two-Source theory whereby
Matt and Luke are made to depend on Mark and the
"Sayings of the Lord" ["Q"] (June 26, 1912; *EB* 390–400;
RSS, pp. 129–32).

(iii) *John.* For various reasons given, the
apostle John must be acknowledged as the author [→
John, 61:12]. Differences between John and the Synoptics are open to reasonable solution. The facts narrated
in John were not invented in whole or in part to serve
as allegories or doctrinal symbols; and Jesus' discourses
are properly his and not the theological compositions of
the evangelist (May 29, 1907; *EB* 187–89; *RSS*, pp.
119–20).

(iv) *Acts.* Luke is the sole author, as confirmed by many traditional and critical arguments,
including the "We" passages [→ Acts, 44:2–3]. Composition cannot be placed later than the end of the first
Roman captivity of Paul [*ca.* 63], and the abrupt ending
of Acts need not mean that the author wrote another
volume or intended to. Luke had trustworthy sources
and used them accurately, honestly, and faithfully;
therefore, we may claim complete historical authority
for Luke. The historical authority of Acts is not weakened by the fact that it contains supernatural happenings,
discourses that some consider fabricated, and seeming
discrepancies (June 12, 1913; *EB* 401–6; *RSS*, pp.
132–34).

(v) *Pauline writings.* The Pastorals [1–2 Tim,
Titus], ever counted as genuine and canonical, were
written by Paul himself between his first imprisonment
and his death [*ca.* 63–66]. The genuineness of these
letters is not weakened by arguments, nor by "the fragmentary hypothesis," according to which they were
made up later from Pauline fragments with considerable
additions (June 12, 1913; *EB* 407–10; *RSS*, pp. 134–35

[→ Pastorals, 56:6–8]). Hebrews is canonical and genuinely Pauline; however, the question is left open
whether Paul formed it as it now stands (June 24, 1914;
EB 411–13; *RSS*, pp. 135–36 [→ Hebrews, 60:2–3]).
Problems about the parousia are not solved by asserting
that sometimes the inspired authors expressed their own
human views, possibly erroneous. Paul wrote in harmony with the ignorance of the time of the parousia
proclaimed by Christ himself. 1 Thess 4:15–16 does not
necessarily imply that Paul thought he and his readers
would survive to meet Christ (June 18, 1915; *EB*
414–16; *RSS*, pp. 136–37 [→ Pauline Theology, 82:45]).

29   (B) More Recent Documents. These reflect the growingly progressive attitude toward Catholic
biblical studies since Pius XII.

(a) PBC to Italian Hierarchy (Aug. 20,
1941; *EB* 522–33; *RSS*, pp. 138–47). A response to a
virulent brochure against scientific biblical study written
(anonymously) by Fr. D. Ruotolo (Levie, *Bible* 133),
which minimized the literal sense in favor of a fanciful
spiritual sense and exaggerated the importance of the Vg
vs. textual criticism and the study of Oriental languages.
In correcting these errors, the PBC foreshadowed *DAS*
[→ 20–22 above].

30   (b) PBC on Biblical Translations (Aug. 22,
1943; *EB* 535–37; *RSS*, pp. 148–49). This established
norms for transls. from the original languages which the
bishops might commend to the faithful; but the version
to be read at Mass must conform to the Vg. [Now, as
permitted by Vatican II, the versions approved for the
English Mass are from the original languages.]

31   (c) PBC to Cardinal Suhard of Paris (Jan.
16, 1948; *EB* 577–81; *RSS*, pp. 150–53). As for the
Pentateuch and Gen 1–11: (1) Previous church attitudes
on authorship and historicity (*EB* 161, 181–84, 324–31)
are in no way opposed to further, truly scientific
examination of the problems in accordance with the
results obtained during the last 40 years. Consequently,
no new decrees need to be promulgated. No one today
doubts the existence of written sources and oral traditions in the Pentateuch or refuses to admit a progressive
development of Mosaic laws, a development also manifest in the historical narratives. (2) The literary forms of
Gen 1–11 correspond to none of our classical categories
and cannot be judged in the light of Greco-Roman or
modern literary styles. Though not containing history in
our modern sense, these historical narratives relate in
simple and figurative language the fundamental truths
presupposed for the economy of salvation, as well as the
popular description of the origin of the human race and
of the chosen people [→ Genesis, 2:4–18]. The first task
of the exegete is to collate data from the various sciences
(paleontology, history, epigraphy) to discover better
how the Oriental peoples thought and expressed their
ideas, as well as their very concept of historical thought.

32   (d) PBC on Scripture in Seminaries (May
13, 1950; *EB* 582–610; *RSS*, pp. 154–67). The following points were stressed: (1) the difference between the
training of biblical specialists and that of future shepherds of the Lord's flock (*EB* 583); (2) the Scripture
professor must enjoy the freedom to dedicate himself
entirely to his work and not be compelled to teach other
important subjects at the same time (*EB* 586–90); (3) the
proper method of teaching biblical subjects in seminaries
and religious colleges. Students are to be taught in a
strictly scientific manner and to be made conversant
with current biblical problems (*EB* 593). Difficulties and
obscurities in the OT must be faced squarely and reasonable solutions given (*EB* 600).

33   (e) PBC on Biblical Meetings (Dec. 15,
1955; *EB* 622–33; *RSS*, pp. 168–72). Biblical

associations should be encouraged; there should be meetings, "Scripture days and weeks"; subjects should be properly selected. The jurisdiction of the competent Ordinary over all such gatherings is stressed (*EB* 627-30), and technical and scientific meetings should not be open to outsiders who would be poorly prepared to evaluate and understand what was being said (*EB* 631).

34 (f) HOLY OFFICE ON HISTORICITY (June 20, 1961; *AAS* 53 [1961] 507; *RSS*, p. 174). With the agreement of the PBC cardinals, the Holy Office issued a warning to all who work with Scripture whether orally or in writing. The target of the warning was opinions and affirmations calling in question "the genuine [*germana*] historical and objective truth of Sacred Scripture," not only of the OT but also of the NT, even with regard to the words and actions of Jesus. The document counsels prudence and reverence, for such opinions create anxieties both for pastors and faithful. [J. A. Fitzmyer, *TS* 22 (1961) 443-44, comments on this document, which, being almost wholly negative, temporarily cast a pall on the future of modern criticism in the church.]

35 (g) PBC ON GOSPEL HISTORICITY (Apr. 21, 1964; Latin and English in *CBQ* 26 [1964] 299-312; *AAS* 56 [1964] 712-18; commentary by J. A. Fitzmyer, *TS* 25 [1964] 386-408). This "Instruction on the Historical Truth of the Gospels" begins with praise of biblical scholars as "faithful sons of the church," and repeats Pius XII's command that they be treated with charity by other Catholics. [This was significant in the light of the difficult years between 1958 and 1962, and the above-mentioned Monitum.] The instructions of *DAS* are reiterated, esp. those stressing the concept of different literary forms. In the "Form-critical Method" there are reasonable elements; but there are often inadmissible philosophical and theological principles admixed with this method, at times vitiating the method itself or, at least, conclusions drawn from it.

To judge properly, the interpreter should pay attention to *three stages* by which the doctrine and life of Jesus have come down to us: (1) *Jesus* explained his doctrine, adapting himself to the mentality of his listeners. His chosen disciples saw his deeds, heard his words, and were thus equipped to be witnesses of his life and doctrine. (2) The *apostles* after the resurrection of Jesus clearly perceived his divinity and proclaimed the death and resurrection of the Lord to others. While preaching and explaining his life and words, they took into account the needs and circumstances of their listeners. The faith of the apostles did not deform the message; but rather, with the fuller understanding they now enjoyed, they were able to pass on to their audiences what was really said and done by the Lord. The modes of speaking with which these preachers proclaimed Christ must be distinguished and properly assessed: catecheses, stories, testimonia, hymns, doxologies, prayers, etc. — the literary forms in use at the time. (3) The *sacred authors* committed to writing in four Gospels this primitive instruction that had been passed on orally at first and then in pre-Gospel writings. From the many things handed down, the evangelists "selected some things, reduced others to a synthesis, and still others they explicated, keeping in mind the situation of the churches." They adapted what they narrated to the situation of their readers and to the purpose they themselves had in mind. This adaptation affected the sequence of what is narrated, but truth is not at all affected simply because the words and deeds of the Lord are narrated in different order in different Gospels. And although the evangelists sometimes express the sayings of Jesus not literally but

differently, they nevertheless retain the sense of these sayings. From a study of these three stages it is apparent that the doctrine and life of Jesus were not reported merely for the purpose of being remembered but were preached so as to offer the church a basis of faith and morals.

The advice to the exegete closes with a reminder that he must exercise his skill and judgment in exegesis but always with the disposition to obey the Magisterium [→ Hermeneutics, 71:80-87]. Then short paragraphs of advice are directed to those teaching in seminaries, those preaching to the people, and those writing for the faithful. The people should receive all the benefits of modern biblical science but should not be exposed to insufficiently established novelties or the rash remarks of innovators [→ Hermeneutics, 71:90-92].

36 (h) MYSTERIUM ECCLESIAE (June 24, 1973; *AAS* 65 [1973] 394-408; R. E. Brown, *Biblical Reflections on Crises Facing the Church* [NY, 1975] 116-17). Issued by the Congregation of the Doctrine of the Faith (Holy Office) to refute H. Küng's challenge to infallibility, it extends to dogmatic formulations the idea of historical conditioning that had so marked biblical studies. While insisting on the church's ability to teach infallibly, it acknowledges that in expressing revelation, "difficulties also arise from the historical condition": (1) The meaning of faith pronouncements "depends partly on the power of language used at a certain . . . time." (2) "Some dogmatic truth is at first expressed incompletely (but not falsely) and later . . . receives a fuller and more perfect expression." (3) Pronouncements usually have a limited intention "of solving certain questions or removing certain errors." (4) The truths being taught, while "distinct from the changeable conceptions of a given epoch," are sometimes phrased by the Magisterium "in terms that bear the traces of such conceptions." Accordingly, so as to present more clearly the same truth, the Magisterium, profiting from theological debate, may reformulate them.

37 (i) PBC 1965-1975. Gospel historicity (1964; → 35 above) was the last statement of the PBC as established in 1902 (cardinals as the members; decrees binding Catholics to internal assent). In 1966-1967 the "singularly difficult problem" of the historicity of the infancy narratives (Matt 1-2; Luke 1-2) was submitted in writing to the scholar consultors. (The 1964 historicity statement referred to the Gospel *post-baptismal* ministry when Jesus spoke, acted, and had followers.) No decision was reached or document produced. On June 27, 1971, Paul VI ("Sedula cura," *AAS* 63 [1971] 665-69) reorganized the PBC as a body advisory to the Doctrinal Congregation. The members would be 20 scholars (appointed by the pope for five-year terms) "outstanding for their learning, prudence, and Catholic regard for the Magisterium of the church," with a secretary, meeting annually to discuss topics assigned under the guidance of the cardinal prefect of the Doctrinal Congregation. Included have been: secretaries A. Descamps and H. Cazelles; members P. Benoit, J. Dupont, C. Martini, D. Stanley, and Americans R. E. Brown (1972-78), J. D. Quinn (1978-84), J. A. Fitzmyer (1984-89). American ultraconservatives have criticized the PBC as being dominated by Modernists!

38 (j) PBC STUDY ON WOMEN PRIESTS. In April 1976 the revamped PBC completed a two-year requested study of the Bible as to whether women could be ordained to the priestly ministry of the eucharist. The confidential results were illegally "leaked" to the press (text and comment, see *Women Priests* [ed. L. and A. Swidler; NY, 1977] 25-34, 338-46). Reportedly, PBC member scholars voted 17-0 that the NT does not settle the question in a clear way, once for all; 12–5 that neither Scripture nor Christ's plan alone excluded the possibility. The documentation behind the reasoning was not published.

39   (k) PBC STUDY ON CHRISTOLOGY. In April 1983 the PBC completed a study on biblical christology, which was published (legally this time) in Latin and French; see *Bible et christologie* (ed. H. Cazelles; Paris, 1984). Eng transl. and comment by J. A. Fitzmyer, *Scripture and Christology* (NY, 1986). Long and uneven, Part I surveys 11 approaches to christology, each with advantages and risks; Part II presents a global sketch of the biblical testimony to Christ. Avoiding harmonization, the document recognizes different christologies in the NT (1.2.7.2; 1.2.10), which it interprets generally in accord with the historical-critical method, e.g., the Gospels are not necessarily historical in minute details, nor are Jesus' sayings preserved verbatim (1.2.1.2); Jesus' resurrection "by its very nature cannot be proved in an empirical way" (1.2.6.2); "it is legitimate to begin a historical investigation about Jesus considering him a true human being ... as a Jew" (1.2.7.3).

40   **(IV) Recent Papal Allocutions.** Paul VI, *To OT Experts,* April 19, 1968 (*AAS* 60 [1968] 262–65; *MOCT* 991–1002): Jews, Protestants, and Catholics "can study and venerate these holy books together" (992). "It is your honor that you dedicate yourselves in a professional and scientific way to employ all the means in the literary, historical, and archaeological fields" (993). Paul VI, *Vatican Library Int. Book Year,* March 25, 1972 (*AAS* 64 [1972] 303–7; *MOCT* 1028–42): "The Bible is not just a book; it is a library in itself, a set of books of every different literary genre" (1037). Paul VI, *To PBC,* March 14, 1974 (*AAS* 66 [1974] 235–41; *MOCT* 1046–69): "The NT took shape within the community of God's people. . . . The church has somehow been the matrix of Sacred Scripture" (1048). "Consider the scholarly explorations into the history of traditions, forms, and redactional work (*Tradition-Form-Redaktionsgeschichte*) which We encouraged—with the required methodological correctives" (1050). A "plurality of theologies . . . the varied but complementary ways in which the fundamental themes of the NT are presented"

(1051). Critique of a liberal exegesis which denies the supernatural; against absolutizing one exegetical methodology; the biblical scholar must render service to the ecumenical and missionary church tasks (1056, 1057, 1063). John Paul II, *To the World Catholic Federation for the Biblical Apostolate,* April 7, 1986 (*AAS* 78 [1986] 1217–19): A strong attack on fundamentalism: "Attention must be given to the literary forms of the various biblical books in order to determine the intention of the sacred writers. And it is most helpful, at times crucial, to be aware of the personal situation of the biblical writer, of the circumstances of culture, time, language, etc., which influenced the way the message was presented. . . . In this way, it is possible to avoid a narrow fundamentalism which distorts the whole truth."

41   A final indication of current trends goes beyond papal allocutions. On Jan. 27, 1988 in NYC Joseph Cardinal Ratzinger, prefect of the Sacred Congregation for the Doctrine of the Faith, delivered an address entitled "Biblical Interpretation in Crisis," in which he criticized some of the practice of historical-critical exegesis (unfounded hypotheses, exegeting putative sources rather than the extant text) and some philosophical presuppositions underlying it (specifically those of Bultmann and Dibelius). He rejected, however, fundamentalism or overliteralism as an alternative; in the accompanying press conference he gave praise to moderate critical scholars and specifically resisted an appeal to return to the anti-Modernist attitudes as a corrective. He noted the enduring contributions of modern exegesis which must be preserved, even as those of patristic exegesis. He asked exegetes to practice self-criticism and to develop an exegesis that combined the best of the past with a fuller church context and theological fruitfulness. For the text of the address, see *Biblical Interpretation in Crisis: The Ratzinger Conference on the Bible and the Church* (Encounter Series 9; GR, 1989). For a critique of rationalism and an overemphasis on sources in the critical search for the literal sense, → Hermeneutics, 71:17, 27; for the necessity of moving beyond the literal sense detected by historical criticism to a more-than-literal sense in which patristic exegesis has made a contribution, → 71:30ff.

73

BIBLICAL GEOGRAPHY

Raymond E. Brown, S.S.   Robert North, S.J. *

BIBLIOGRAPHY

1   General. Abel, *GP.* Aharoni, *LBib.* Alon, A., *The Natural History of the Land of the Bible* (GC, 1978). Avi-Yonah, M., *The Holy Land . . . A Historical Geography* (GR, 1977). Baldi, D., *Enchiridion locorum sanctorum* (2d ed.; Jerusalem, 1955). Baly, D., *Geographical Companion to the Bible* (NY, 1963); *The Geography of the Bible* (rev. ed.; NY, 1974). Ben-Arieh, S., "The Geographical Exploration of the Holy Land," *PEQ* 10 (1972) 81–92. Bodenheimer, F. S., *Animal and Man in Bible Lands* (Leiden, 1960). Dalman, G., *Sacred Sites and Ways* (NY, 1934). Du Buit, M., *Géographie de Terre Sainte* (2 vols.; Paris, 1958). Frank, H. T., *Discovering the Biblical World* (Maplewood, 1975). Karmon, Y., *Israel, a Regional Geography* (London, 1971). Keel, O., *et al., Orte und Landschaften der Bibel* (4 vols.; Zurich, 1982–). Kopp, C., *The Holy Places of the Gospels* (NY, 1963). Orni, E. and E. Efrat, *Geography of Israel* (2d ed.; Jerusalem, 1966). Simons, J., *The Geographical and Topographical Texts of the Old Testament* (Leiden, 1958). Smith, G. A., *The Historical Geography of the Holy Land* (repr. of 25th ed.; NY, 1966). Thompson, T. L., *The Settlement of Sinai and the Negev in the Bronze Age* (TAVO B8; Wiesbaden, 1975); *The Settlement of Palestine in the Bronze Age* (TAVO B34; Wiesbaden, 1979). Zohary, M., *Plants of the Bible* (Cambridge, 1982).

2   Atlases. Aharoni, Y. and M. Avi-Yonah, *The Macmillan Bible Atlas* (2d ed.; NY, 1977). Amiran, D., *et al., Atlas of Jerusalem* (Jerusalem, 1973). Baly, D. and A. Tushingham, *Atlas of the Biblical World* (NY, 1971). Bruce, F. F., *Bible History Atlas* (Study ed.; NY, 1982). Cornell, T. and J. Matthews, *Atlas of the Roman World* (NY, 1982). Elster, J., *Atlas of Israel* (Amsterdam, 1970). Gardner, J., *Reader's Digest Atlas of the Bible* (Pleasantville, 1981). Grollenberg, *AtBib;* also *The Penguin Shorter Atlas of the Bible* (London, 1978). *Hammond's Atlas of the Bible Lands* (ed. H. T. Frank; Maplewood, 1984). Lemaire, P. and D. Baldi, *Atlante storico geografico della Bibbia* (Rome, 1955). McEvedy, C., *The Penguin Atlas of Ancient History* (London, 1967). May, H. G. and J. Day, *Oxford Bible Atlas* (3d ed.; NY, 1984). Monson, J. and R. Cleave, *Student Map Manual* (Jerusalem, 1979). Negenman, J. H., *New Atlas of the Bible* (ed. H. H. Rowley; GC, 1969). Pfeiffer, C. F., *Baker's Bible Atlas* (GR, 1979). Rogerson, J., *Atlas of the Bible* (NY, 1985). Wright, G. E. and F. V. Filson, *WHAB.*

3   Guidebooks. *Baedeker's Israel* (ed. O. Garner; EC, ca. 1983). *Carta's Official Guide to Israel* (Jerusalem, 1983). Hoade, E., *Guide to the Holy Land* (Jerusalem, 1978; repr. 1984). Miller, J. M., *Introducing the Holy Land* (Macon, 1986). Murphy-O'Connor, J., *The Holy Land: An Archaeological Guide from Earliest Times to 1700* (2d ed.; Oxford, 1986). Vilnay, Z., *Israel Guide* (Jerusalem, 1982). Evaluation of Guidebooks: *BARev* 11 (6, 1985) 44–58.

Slides: Cleave, R. L. W., *Pictorial Archive* (Near Eastern History; Jerusalem, 1979). Biblical Archeology Society Sets (Washington).

OUTLINE

*Sections 5–31 of this article are the work of R. North; the remainder is by R. E. Brown.

SOURCES AND TOOLS FOR BIBLICAL GEOGRAPHY

We are interested here in biblical geography, not in a purely geographical study of areas that happen to be mentioned in the Bible. Those features and sites that are mentioned are important to an understanding of the Bible; much nonbiblical matter that from a scientific geographical viewpoint might be of more importance has been omitted. Along with details of geology and geography, mixed details from history (even medieval and modern), archaeology, and the "guided tour" of the holy land are included. In short, we discuss whatever can give the reader an appreciation of the country that is the setting of the Bible. Although some of the bibliographical references are to the more scientific works on the subject, there has been a preference for simplified reports and references that the general student can read with profit.

5 **(I) Ancient.** The earliest map of Palestine is a mosaic from AD 560, still partly surviving on the floor of an Orthodox church in Madeba, in Transjordan, near Mt. Nebo (M. Avi-Yonah, *The Madaba Mosaic Map* [Jerusalem, 1954]; R. T. O'Callaghan, *DBSup* 5. 627–704; H. Donner and H. Cüppers, *ZDPV* 83 [1967] 1–33). The only other truly ancient map is the *Tabula Peutingeriana,* a road map of the world reduced to a strip 25 ft. long and 13 in. wide, divided into 12 sections. The original may stem from the 3d cent. AD, but the copy now extant is from 1265. Willed to Konrad Peutinger, the map is in the State Library of Vienna (see K. Miller, *Itineraria romana* [Stuttgart, 1916]; *Arch* 8 [1955] 146–55; 17 [1964] 227–36).

6 What is a map? Basically, it is a listing of cities, though in a spatial rather than in an alphabetical or logical order. In this sense of maps as city lists, the origins of biblical map making are from ancient Egypt; for we possess Egyptian lists of Palestinian cities on fragments of jars, on clay tablets, and on palace walls. About 1900 BC, names of Canaanite cities were written on pottery and smashed as a magic curse; found only *ca.* 1930, these are called Execration Texts. In the period just after 1370 BC many princes of Canaan wrote to the Egyptian Pharaoh asking help for their cities against local marauders called Ḫabiru ('Apiru); these "Amarna Letters," found at the end of the 19th cent. (→ Biblical Archaeology, 74:77), are of great importance for the geographical and political situation in Palestine in the period just before Moses and Joshua. (E. F. Campbell, *BA* 23 [1960] 2–22.) The Pharaohs Ramses II (1290–1224) and Sheshonk (*ca.* 920; = Shishak of 1 Kgs 14:25) left on the palaces of Luxor in southern Egypt important geographical lists (J. Simons, *Handbook for the Study of Egyptian Topographical Lists Relating to Western Asia* [Leiden, 1937]; Aharoni, *LBib*).

7 Next in order come the town lists of the OT itself (cf. Simons, *Geographical*). These supply a genuinely biblical geography since they are expressed in the Bible's own terms and categories. They include Josh 13–21; Gen 10; 2 Chr 11:6–10; and the "Threats against the Nations" in the Major Prophets.

8 Between the OT and our own day there have been various other sources for learning the relation of biblical localities among themselves, which is what a map expresses. First, there are the classic authors, Herodotus, Strabo, Pliny, and the geographer Ptolemy (see M. Cary and E. H. Warmington, *The Ancient Explorers* [Pelican ed.; London, 1963]). The greatest work of early Palestinian topography is the *Onomasticon* of Eusebius, AD 330 (C. U. Wolf, *BA* 27 [1964] 66–96). Observations of postbiblical Judaism are gathered in A. Neubauer, *Géographie du Talmud* (Paris, 1868) and in

Eretz-Israel Annual 2 and *Atlas.* Siftings from the Muslim geographers have been published by G. LeStrange, R. Dussaud, and A. S. Marmardji. The data supplied by pilgrims and the Crusades are important, especially for NT sites (although, unfortunately, pilgrims were often shown localizations that were convenient to main roads rather than those based on real historical memories). See R. North, *A History of Biblical Map Making* (TAVO B32; Wiesbaden, 1979); H. Donner, *Pilgerfahrt ins Heilige Land (4–7 Jahrhundert)* (Stuttgart, 1979); J. Wilkinson, *Pilgrims before the Crusades* (Warminster, 1977).

9 **(II) Modern.** Charting places in Palestine reached a climax in the mid-19th cent. In 1838 E. Robinson, a professor from Union Theological Seminary, NYC, journeying through the Holy Land for three months with the Arabic-speaking missioner Eli Smith, located more Palestinian sites than had been discovered since the time of Eusebius. This success suggested the foundation of the British Palestine Exploration Fund and its *Survey of Western Palestine* (C. R. Conder and H. H. Kitchener [of Khartoum fame] in 6 vols.; London, 1880). For the contributions of Robinson, see *JBL* 58 (1939) 355–87; *BA* 46 (1983) 230–32.

10 The British Survey is the basis of the principal maps in use today. There are four different scales:

(1) The most detailed is the Topocadastral Survey, on 120 sheets, scale 1:20,000. It is an indispensable ultimate, but so sprawling that a single locality might have to be looked up on four sheets rather far apart in enumeration.

(2) Much more usable are the 16 maps (plus 8 for the Negeb) on the scale 1:100,000, reedited by Israel in two forms, either in booklets or on loose sheets preferable for mounting and collating.

(3) The most convenient scale is 1:250,000, of which Israel has prepared a new edition containing on one large sheet the whole of biblical Palestine N of Gaza. To this corresponds an equally large sheet containing only Beersheba and the Negeb. There is a three-sheet edition of the same map that is handier, brighter, and more legible (the northern and central sheets suffice for the ordinary student). The Israel maps include the modern Arab frontiers and territory, everything W of the Jordan, and a fringe also to the E. For Transjordan the British Survey map on the scale of 1:250,000 has been reedited by the Jordanian government in three sheets: Amman/Kerak/Aqabah.

(4) A "Motor Map" on the scale 1:1,000,000, is useful for comparing remote areas. It can serve the average student. It is included with the often-updated Vilnay *Guide.*

An entirely new and vast "survey-of-Israel" project has been issuing folio-sized new maps at a steady rate, some of them on very specialized topics.

11 Besides the great Surveys, noteworthy are the scholarly atlases that have appeared since World War II. (Unfortunately they do not give, even in the margin, the Survey Grid indications which are official for referring to new excavation sites.) A breakthrough began with *WHAB* in 1945, with maps that indicated strikingly reliefs and frontiers, keeping place names to an uncluttered minimum. (These maps have been reproduced in a smaller booklet, in *IDB,* and in *BHI*). Differing strengths are found in the atlases in the bibliography (→ 2 above). The frequently reedited *National Geographic* map of Bible-Lands gives in blue at each modern site a summary of the historic event that made the locality important. This technique has been brilliantly adopted by the Elsevier-Nelson Atlas series of maps: *Mesopotamia* by M. A. Beek; *Christian World* by C. Moorman; and esp.

AtBib. Atlases are compared in *BA* 45 (1982) 61–62; *BARev* 9 (6, 1983) 39–46.

12   A map of Roman Palestine by M. Avi-Yonah shows the roads, milestones, and Lat place names known to nascent Christianity. There is a vivid Geological Map by G. Blake. For Transjordan there is a three-sheet archaeological map indicating numberless mounds, or "tells" (→ Biblical Archaeology, 74:25), though the chief of these are included in more usable fashion on the three-sheet general map (→ 10, part 3 above). Every guide-book contains maps of specialized usefulness; Meistermann's *Guide* (Eng ed.; London, 1928) adds treasures of historical documentation that are not out-of-date as are some of his conclusions.

13   Abel's *GP* contains in vol. 1 a precious mapping of the network of stream beds. In vol. 2 each biblical place-name is given in alphabetical order with a clear indication of the *publication* of the ancient remains excavated or explored at the modern site that allegedly represents the biblical site. The dating of these finds (mostly broken pottery) is an essential basis for deciding whether the spot was occupied at all in the biblical period to which it is ascribed. The type of evidence Père Abel cites must, of course, constantly be brought up to date; and some thorny problems, such as Jericho (→ Biblical Archaeology, 74:80), have not been solved adequately within the framework of his principles. But until a better basis is advocated, such a list must stand as the ultimate justification of all biblical geography and map making.

14   Perhaps we should conclude the treatment of maps with a warning. Every biblical map implicitly involves judgments on the identification of sites and, in particular, on the relation of modern Arabic place-names to the names of ancient sites given in the Bible. No scientific geography of the holy land can dispense with the constant checking of folkloric Arabic place-names. One must be aware of the difficulty that different systems of transliterating Hebr and Arabic names are used in different works.

GEOGRAPHY OF SURROUNDING COUNTRIES

15   As we begin the actual discussion of biblical geography, the readers must understand that the article is written to throw light on places mentioned in the Bible. The only helpful way to do that briefly is to base comments on the face value of the biblical narrative, e.g., what the Bible reports about the travels of Abraham or Moses. Other articles in *NJBC* will make clear that such narratives are not simple history and may reflect very complex combinations of diverse (and perhaps originally contrary) traditions. In particular, the historical character of the patriarchal narratives, about to be discussed geographically below, is very disputed (→ History, 75:29, 34ff.). This warning will not be repeated endlessly, and so readers must remind themselves that a discussion of a geographical description needs to be supplemented with a critical discussion of historicity.

(I) Abraham—The Fertile Crescent. Biblical geography begins not in Palestine but in the Euphrates valley. The earliest identifiable place-names of the Bible are those connected with Abraham in Gen 11:31, viz., Ur and Haran. Ur is near the S, and Haran near the N of a broad arc traced by the Euphrates valley. We can complete the same arc from Haran W toward the Syrian coast, then S as far as Egypt. This gives us a crescent with the tips resting in the Persian and Suez gulfs, and the middle running along the modern border of Turkey. This narrow strip is called the *Fertile Crescent* because it happens to coincide with a fringe of water sources that make food production possible around the edge of a vast desert. The water supply determined not only the "sedentary" or farming centers but also the trade routes used for shuttling back and forth from one of the great export areas to another. We shall find that the movements of Abraham coincide with the major caravan route from Babylonia to Egypt, i.e., from one tip of the Fertile Crescent to the other.

16   At the Babylonian end of the crescent stood *Ur,* which the Bible identifies as Abraham's homeland (Gen 11:28–31). Some scholars have doubted the accuracy of this information, and it is a fact that Ur is not mentioned in the LXX of the Gen passage. But even if Abraham originated at Haran far to the N, it is not improbable that he journeyed S as far as Ur, the heartland of the greatest culture center in antiquity. (L. Woolley, *Ur of the Chaldees* [Pelican ed.; London, 1952; updated ed. by P. R. S. Moorey; Ithaca, 1972].)

This region of the Tigris-Euphrates basin near the Persian Gulf is called in Gen 10:10 the Land of Shinar or Sennaar. This means the land of the Sumerians, the ancient non-Semitic occupants of the region (→ History, 75:11). Near Ur was *Uruk,* the Erech of Gen 10:10 (modern Warka) whose king Gilgamesh (*ca.* 2800 BC) became the hero of a flood story (cf. Gen 6–9). From the excavations of this site have come the earliest known examples of writing, and therefore this momentous cultural advance may have been made in the region.

(For illustrations of Abraham's journeys, see *NatGeog* [Dec. 1966]; for Mesopotamia, *NatGeog* [Jan. 1951]; for Sumer, *BARev* 10 [5, 1984] 56–64.)

17   From *ca.* 2500 on, Semites are found in Mesopotamia under the name of Amorites ("Westerners"). It was formerly agreed that they migrated in successive waves from the SW (Arabian peninsula), but most scholars now locate their origin in the NW (the Syrian desert, N of Palmyra, not far from Ebla, where a Semitic empire was flourishing; → History, 75:16). It is also possible, however, that the Semites were not invaders but coexisted in Sumer as far back as our records go. The greatest of the Semitic dynasties set up in this region was at *Babylon,* some 150 mi. NW of Ur and the site of a famous ziggurat, or temple tower, consisting of receding brick platforms (cf. Gen 11:4–9—the Tower of Babel; *BTS* 35 [1961]). Abraham's presence at Ur has often been associated with the Amorite waves of migration into Sumer, and formerly Abraham was thought to have been a contemporary of Hammurabi, the greatest king of Babylon (*ca.* 1700—wrongly identified as the Amraphel of Gen 14:1). For the problem of the Amorites, → Biblical Archaeology, 74:67.

A millennium later in the biblical story Babylon would once more become prominent in Israel's history when Judah was carried off into captivity to Babylonia (598 and 587 BC; → History, 75:76). From either the earlier or the later contact with this Babylonian region there was a familiarity on the part of Israel with the ancient Sumerian mythology of creation, the *Enuma Elish* epic (*ANET* 60–72), from which some of the imagery of Gen 1–2 may have been borrowed. The Garden of Eden in Gen 2:10–14 is conceived of as a muddy Tigris-Euphrates confluence—perhaps this seemed a paradise to Abraham's dusty, barefoot relatives from the Arabian desert.

18   Much to the E of this area is the mountainous

region of *Persia,* whose king Cyrus would liberate the Jews from Babylonian captivity in 538 (→ History, 75:77). The court-panoply of Persia and its Zoroastrian religion formed a portion of the scenario of later biblical books like Neh, Dan, Esth. (For Persepolis and Susa, see *NatGeog* [Jan. 1968; Jan. 1975]; *BA* 43 [1980] 135-62.)

19 When Abraham journeyed N from Ur, his route lay between *Mari* and *Nuzi.* At each of these two centers excavation during the 20th cent. has revealed thousands of clay documents (→ Biblical Archaeology, 74:71). The history of Mari on the Euphrates is bound up with Hammurabi and gives us the materials entering into disputes about his date (cf. G. Mendenhall, *BA* 11 [1948] 1-19, or *BAR* 2, 3-20). To the E, near the modern Kirkuk oil fields, lies Nuzi. From Nuzi to Haran stretched a region anciently named Mitanni. Its people were called Hurrians, who appear in the Bible under the name Horites (see R. North, *Bib* 54 [1973] 43-62) or possibly as Hivites or Hittites. The business records of the inhabitants, reflecting their commerce with Assyrian merchants, illustrate many biblical customs attested in the patriarchal period.

(On Mari: Malamat, A., *Mari and the Bible* [2d ed.; Jerusalem, 1980]. Parrot, A., *Mari capitale fabuleuse* [Paris, 1974]. Also *BA* 34 [1971] 2-22; 47 [1984] 70-120; *BTB* 5 [1975] 32-55. On Nuzi and the Hurrians: Morrison, M. A., *et al.* [eds.], *Studies on the Civilization and Culture of Nuzi and the Hurrians* [Fest. E. R. Lacheman; Winona Lake, 1981]. *BA* 3 [1940] 1-22; 46 [1983] 155-64. Also → History, 75:23, 27.)

20 *Haran* (Harran), identified in the Bible as the place where Abraham located after he migrated from Ur, is thought by many scholars to have been Abraham's original homeland. The towns of the region bear names that are variants of the names given by Gen 11 to Abraham's relatives: Peleg (v 16), Serug (v 20), Terah and Nahor (v 24), and Haran itself (v 27).

21 The topmost arc of the Fertile Crescent reaches from Haran W to the Euphrates. Where the river cuts the present Turkish frontier is the site of *Carchemish.* It became a last outpost of the Hittite empire about 900 BC, and in 605 it was the scene of Nebuchadnezzar's decisive battle against Assyria.

From here the crescent caravan route turns sharply S, along the line Aleppo-Hama-Damascus-Jerusalem. *Aleppo* was a very ancient city, known already in the Mari records as Iamhad. On the seacoast, W of Aleppo, stood the city-state *Ugarit,* modern Ras Shamra. Archives found there since 1929 show that Ugarit was powerful enough to make treaties with the Hittite empire, a rival of Egypt and Assyria (→ History, 75:23). The language of these texts, Ugaritic, is very important for the study of the earliest form of Hebrew. See P. C. Craigie, *Ugarit and the Old Testament* (GR, 1983); also *BARev* 9 (5, 1983) 54-75. For plans of the site, see R. North, *ZDPV* 89 (1973) 113-60; J.-C. Courtois, *ZDPV* 90 (1974) 77-114. For Ugaritic, *BA* 8 (1945) 41-58; 28 (1965) 102-28.

Farther inland at *Ebla* (Tell Mardikh; → History, 75:16) Italian excavations have yielded tablets datable a millennium earlier than those of Ugarit, thus constituting the earliest attestation of written Semitic (*ca.* 2300 BC). Another powerful city-state, inland farther S, was *Hamath,* now Hama (not to be confused with Homs, the Roman Emesa, which today eclipses Hama). Hamath was also the scene of decisive battles, since it corked the N outlet of the valley between the Lebanon and Antilebanon mountain ranges. This "Hamath approach" was regarded, at times, as the N boundary of the promised land (Num 34:8; see R. North, *MUSJ* 46 [1970] 71-103). Even more ancient and important was *Damascus.* As a well-watered city on the fringe of the desert, it was a

"Last Chance" for caravan supplies. Surprisingly, in describing Abraham's passage (Gen 12:5), the Bible makes no mention of these centers. It skips from Haran to the heart of Canaan, i.e., to what later would be called Samaria. (See C. Thubron, *Mirror to Damascus* [NY, 1967]; *NatGeog* [Apr. 1974; Sept. 1978].)

22 Canaan, the promised land, was small and off to the SW corner of the Fertile Crescent. Yet it was in a strategic midposition between the rival merchant states: Arabia to the S, Egypt to the SW, Hittites to the N, Babylon to the E. Hence, if the lines of traffic and population density are set in proper perspective, Canaan may be considered the "hub" of the whole Fertile Crescent. Indeed, it was the hub of the whole universe known from Abraham's day down to Alexander the Great.

The Abraham clans, migrating from Mesopotamia, made no immediate claim to the land of Canaan. But Abraham personally is portrayed as getting a foothold in Canaan by the important experiences he had at the major centers of worship: Shechem, Bethel, Hebron, and Beersheba (→ Institutions, 76:25-29). In reality, his sojourn in the Holy Land is no more than a nomadic stopover on the route to the natural terminus of the journey, viz., Egypt. (For Abraham and the Negeb, see *BA* 18 [1955] 2-9.)

23 In fact, Abraham does go on immediately to visit Egypt according to Gen 12:10. But the migration to which he has given his name may be justly regarded as taking place in successive waves over several generations. In this light its completion is attained only with the descent of the Jacob tribes to join Joseph in Egypt (Gen 46:7). Thus, the latter part of the Abrahamic migration turns out to be a part of what the historical records outside the Bible recognize as the movement of the Hyksos. "Hyksos" is an Egyptian word meaning "foreign rulers." It refers to Asiatic immigrants who installed themselves in the NE Delta at Avaris and from there ruled Egypt between 1700 and 1560. In the eyes of some modern scholars, they were not an invasion but more a horde of peaceful infiltrators. They were mostly Semites, probably with Hurrians as their ruling caste, who were in turn masterminded by a small, powerful group of "chariot-warriors." It was in the NE Delta, then, in the land that Gen 47:6 calls Goshen, that Joseph's relatives settled. Here at the SW tip of the Fertile Crescent the Bible sets the stage for the exodus. (For historical issues, → History, 75:39-41 on Joseph and the Egyptian sojourn; 75:42-58 on the exodus and the "conquest." As stated above [→ 15], the discussion here explicates the prima facie geographical thrust of the narrative.)

24 **(II) Moses—Egypt and the Exodus Route.** The "People of God" in the Bible, whatever their remoter origins, seem to owe the awareness of their national unity largely to the experiences some of them had within Egypt. From there modern scholars tend to begin the Bible's history and geography properly so called. Abraham's story is looked upon essentially as an account of how Semitic tribes made an encircling migration in order to settle down in Egypt.

Rather than merely "the gift of the Nile," as Herodotus says, the whole of Egypt really *is* the Nile. A five-mile fringe of intense cultivation runs along both sides of the whole length of the river. This region is extremely valuable for biblical research. In the S at the first cataract, *ca.* 500 mi. by air and 700 mi. by water from the Delta (note, the Nile flows N), stood *Elephantine,* the site of a 5th-cent. BC Jewish colony. Aramaic papyri discovered here have thrown light on the period of Ezra-Nehemiah (→ History, 75:125; *BA* 15 [1952] 50-67; 42 [1979] 74-104). Some 100 mi. to the N was *Thebes* (Luxor or Karnak) with its magnificent temples, capital of Egypt under the famous 18th Dynasty

(1570-1310), whose rulers drove out the Hyksos and established Egypt as a world empire. The destruction of this ancient seat of power, deep within Egypt, by the Assyrians in 663 BC stupefied the Jews (Nah 3:8; Thebes in Hebrew = No Amon). As the Nile continues its flow N, about 75 mi. by water from Thebes, in the great bend of the Nile were St. Pachomius's monasteries of Pabau and *Chenoboskion* (near Nag Hammadi), where in 1945 important Coptic gnostic documents were found (→ Apocrypha, 67:56; *NHLE* 10–25; *BA* 42 [1979] 201–56). Roughly another 125 mi. N, the Nile passes the site now called Amarna — ancient *Akhetaton,* capital of monotheist Pharaoh Akhenaton (1364–1347), from whose archives the Amarna Letters came (→ 6 above). On the opposite side of the Nile, still farther N, was *Oxyrhynchus,* where numerous papyri of NT times have been discovered (→ Texts, 68:179). L. Deuel (*Testaments of Time* [NY, 1965] 79–189) tells of these discoveries in an exciting manner.

25 At the vertex of the Delta where the Nile splits into branches (still 100 mi. from the Sea) stood *Memphis* (Moph of Hos 9:6; Noph of Isa 19:13; Jer 2:16; Ezek 30:13), the earliest Egyptian capital. See *Arch* 38 (4, 1985) 25–32. Nearby to the N was On, or *Heliopolis,* home of Joseph's father-in-law (Gen 41:45). Between Memphis and Heliopolis was a great cemetery with deathless pyramids and the sphinx. (Only after the Muslim invasion did Cairo rise here, over a Roman fort named Babylon [hardly = 1 Pet 5:13] and near the place that legend made the terminus of the flight of the Holy Family into Egypt [Matt 2:14].) In the time of Alexander the Great (332) the great metropolis and seaport of *Alexandria* was built in the NW tip of the Delta, and this soon attracted the Jewish colony that produced the LXX. The Rosetta Stone, unlocking the Egyptian language, was discovered near Alexandria in Napoleon's time (1799).

(Fascinating accounts of the exploration of the Nile and of the history that has been lived along the river are given in: *BTS* 53–54 [1963]. Fairservis, W. A., *The Ancient Kingdoms of the Nile* [NY, 1962]. Ludwig, E., *The Nile* [NY, 1937]. Moorehead, A., *The White Nile* [NY, 1960]; *The Blue Nile* [NY, 1962]. *NatGeog* [Dec. 1954; May 1955; Oct. 1963; May 1965; May 1966; May 1969; Mar. 1977; Feb. 1982]. Also Bander, B. [ed.], *The River Nile* [NatGeog book, 1966]; Murnane, W. J., *The Penguin Guide to Ancient Egypt* [London, 1982].)

26 The NE section of the Delta is of interest as the take-off point for the biblical account of the exodus. Ramses II (*ca.* 1290–1224) of the 19th Dynasty cluttered the whole Nile Valley with his building projects. (See K. A. Kitchen, *Pharaoh Triumphant: The Life of Ramesses II* [Warminster, 1982].) His trademark was esp. frequent at *Tanis* (San al-Hagar, and the Zoan of Isa 19:11; Ezek 30:14; Ps 78:12). This site seemingly had been the Hyksos capital of *Avaris* 400 years before; Num 13:22 relates its foundation to that of Hebron. It had been thought that Tanis was also the *Raamses* (Exod 1:11) built by Ramses II or by his father Seti. But excavations by M. Bietak some 20 mi. S at Qantîr-Dab'a have suggested to many that Raamses and its palace were there and that the building stones were later transported to San al-Hagar (where they were found). Others think the two sites constituted a "Greater Raamses," with the palace at one site and the city proper at the other. In this land ("of Goshen": Gen 47:11) surrounding Tanis (and) Raamses (Ps 78:12, 43) the descendants of the patriarchs were enslaved and put to work on building projects. *Pithom* of Exod 1:11 has generally been located 50 mi. SE at Maskhûta in Wadi Tumilat, while *Succoth* of Exod 13:20 was considered either a variant name of the same site or situated at nearby Tell Retâba. Egyptian sources testify that the Wadi Tumilat was a frequent refuge for Asiatics fleeing

from famine or dictatorship. The excavations of J. Holladay, however, seem to show that Maskhûta was not founded before 600 BC; see *BA* 43 (1980) 49–58.

(Bietak, M., *Tell Dab'a II* [Vienna, 1975]; "Avaris and Piramesse," *Proceedings British Academy* 65 [1981] 225–89. Bleiberg, E. L., "The Location of Pithom and Succoth," *Ancient World* 6 [1983] 21–27. Holladay, J., *Tell el Maskhuta* [Malibu, 1982]. North, R., *Archeo-Biblical Egypt* [Rome, 1967]. Roussel, D., "Inscriptions de Ramses . . . vestiges de Tanis" [diss.; Paris, 1984]. Uphill, E. P., "Pithom and Raamses, their Location and Significance," *JNES* 27 [1968] 291–316; 28 [1969] 15–39; *The Temples of Per Ramesses* [Warminster, 1984]. *Varia Aegyptiaca* 3 [1987] 13–24.)

27 The route of the exodus, a much-disputed question, is intimately related to the problem of the location of Mt. Sinai. Sinai and Horeb are not separate peaks, but names for the same place occurring respectively in the J and in the E/D traditions of the Pentateuch. There are at least four candidates for the localization of this holy mountain: (1) In the S of the Sinai Peninsula. The very name given to this peninsula presupposes the correctness of the tradition that the peak Jebel Musa ("Mt. Moses"), at the base of which St. Catherine's Monastery stands, is Sinai. (2) In Arabia. The belching flame and quaking of the mountain described in Exod 19:18 suggest a volcano in eruption, and the nearest volcano is Talat-Badr in modern Arabia, far SE of the Sinai Peninsula. The ancient geographer Ptolemy called this region Modiane, corresponding to Midian of Exod 3:1. Despite these two independent facts favoring Talat-Badr, Arabia seems too far away from Egypt to be the site. (3) In Transjordan. The name Midian fits a long strip of land stretching as far N as Gilead in Transjordan (cf. Judg 6). A candidate for Sinai in this region is Petra (→ 40 below), since its flame-red crags were an object of immemorial religious veneration. There is also an Arab tradition that Aaron was buried there (Num 20:28). This theory, like the preceding one, is not defended today, for it puts Sinai too far E. (4) In the Negeb. A more serious contender against theory (1) is the hypothesis that the Sinai theophany took place at Kadesh-barnea (→ 85 below). In fact, the striking of water from the rock and the murmuring of the people at Meribah during the Kadesh sojourn of Num 20:13 are described in terms identical with the narrative of what happened at Sinai in Exod 17:7. This view of O. Eissfeldt was accepted by W. F. Albright regarding the *route* but not the theophany site, and by M. Noth and H. Cazelles as a *variant* localization preserved within the OT itself. The earliest occupation at Kadesh (Ain Qudeirat), however, as dated by archaeology is 10th cent. — too late for the exodus. For localizing Sinai at Karkom near Kadesh, see *BARev* 11 (4, 1985) 42–57. The works of Thompson (→ 1 above) on the areas that were settled at this period are crucial to the Sinai discussion.

28 Two possible routes for the exodus deserve serious study: the northern route, often corresponding to the localization of Sinai in theory (4); the southern route, corresponding to the localization in theory (1). (Many of the modern biblical critics regard the exodus and the Sinai theophany as two originally independent traditions and hence would discuss the exodus route without reference to the site of Sinai.) First, the theory of the *northern route* suggests that the Israelites came out of Tanis heading E directly across the N part of the "Sinai" Peninsula to Kadesh-barnea. This was the shortest and the natural route from Egypt to Canaan. It is explicitly excluded by Exod 13:17, but in terms involving the Philistines that rouse suspicion of an anachronistic gloss (although the Philistines may have raided the coast of Canaan in the 13th cent., they do not seem to have had firm control of the S Canaan coast before 1180–1150,

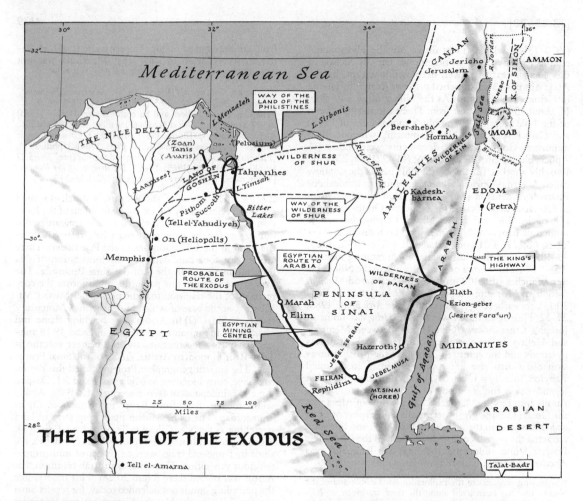

THE ROUTE OF THE EXODUS

long after the exodus). If we try to harmonize the biblical description of sites along the path of the exodus with the theory of the northern route, we must seek to identify the "Reed Sea" of Exod 13:18; 14:22. (This is the usual interpretation of Hebr *sûp;* the "Red Sea" of Eng Bibles stems from a plausible LXX attempt to identify the body of water; another view is that *sûp* is neither red nor reed, but "end," meaning "the sea of extinction.") It might refer to the S extension of Lake Menzaleh or to the shallows of Lake Sirbonis (adjacent to the Mediterranean between Egypt and Canaan); see M. Dothan, *ErIsr* 9 (1969) 47–59; English 135; also *BARev* 10 (4, 1984) 57–63. The Migdol of Exod 14:2 was on the Egyptian side of the sea, and the Hebr text of Ezek 29:10 locates Migdol at the NE extreme of Egypt farthest from Aswan (Syene). Across the shallows from Migdol was Baal-zephon, meaning "Lord of the North." The "north" part of the name is relative and inconclusive, but this name seems to have belonged originally to a towering mountain on the N Syrian coast, Mt. Casius or Amanus. Phoenician soldiers brought the name from their homeland to Egypt and ironically applied it to some low hills to the W of Sirbonis (NE of what is now the Suez Canal), called in classic times Pelusium and now Farama.

29 Other biblical statements are more reconcilable with a *southern route* for the exodus, involving a detour far to the S to a Mt. Sinai as localized in theory (1). (Albright attempts to reconcile both theories by supposing an exodus route that began to the N and switched S; other scholars think of several exoduses, following different routes—a theory also used to explain some archaeological and chronological discrepancies about the exodus and conquest of Palestine; → Biblical

Archaeology, 74:78ff.) Following a southern detour, we find in the south-central Sinai Peninsula inscriptions from *ca.* AD 150 in an Arabic dialect called Nabatean; they attest a religious veneration for the valley Mukattab ("scribbled over") and for the adjacent triangle extending some 20 mi. to Jebel Serbal and to Jebel Musa. Serbal is a majestic saw-toothed ridge that Jerome and even some modern experts identified as the peak of the Sinai theophany; but there is no suitable approach or place of encampment at its foot, as the biblical description would seem to demand. At "traditional Sinai," i.e., Jebel Musa itself, there is a steep precipice named Safsafa towering over the vast plain of er-Raha. The nearness of water and the rugged splendor of the surroundings have convinced most moderns that this is the mountain of Exod 19:2. However, the Gk tradition related to St. Catherine's Monastery focuses attention on the opposite (E) end of the Jebel Musa range. In any case it is sensible to admit that the "proofs" for this localization of Sinai are tenuous.

(Bernstein, B., *Sinai: The Great and Terrible Wilderness* [NY, 1982]. Davies, G. I., *The Way of the Wilderness* [SOTSMS 5; Cambridge, 1979]. Nicholson, E. W., *Exodus and Sinai in History and Tradition* [Oxford, 1973]. *BA* 45 [1982] 9–31; *BARev* 11 [4, 1985] 26–41; *NatGeog* [Jan., 1976]. For the controversial exodus theory of H. Goedicke: *BARev* 7 [5, 1981] 42–54; 7 [6, 1981] 46–53; 11 [4, 1985] 58–69. For a 15th-cent. date: Bimson, J. J., *Redating the Exodus and Conquest* [JSOTSup 5; Sheffield, 1978].)

30 After the Sinai theophany, in a period of about 40 years, the Israelites under Moses are said to have moved on to Transjordan. The route from Mt. Sinai to Edom is indicated twice in the Bible, once with remarkable minuteness in Num 33, and later more briefly in Deut 1. Yet the list of places is in effect unusable, for most of the sites are unknown to us. Paran of Num 12:16; Deut 1:1 recurs importantly as a mountain in Deut 33:2; Hab 3:3; and although its name has undoubtedly survived at the Feiran oasis near Jebel Serbal, the Bible envisions a localization in the wilderness S of the Dead Sea called the Arabah (→ 69 below). The main discrepancy of the two biblical lists concerns Ezion-geber (which 1 Kgs 9:26 places at or near Elath on the shore of the Reed Sea, in the land of Edom; → 69 below). From Deut 2:8 it would appear that the Israelites saw this gulf port only after proceeding from Kadesh-barnea to the Arabah, which constitutes the W fringe of Edom. But Num 33:36 plainly inserts the encampment at Ezion-geber *before* Kadesh and Edom. The exodus refugees may well have touched down twice at so strategic a spot.

31   Below we shall discuss in detail the geography of Transjordan, but it seems wisest to mention here briefly the problem of the continuation of the exodus journey to Mt. Nebo at the NE corner of the Dead Sea, where Moses died and was buried (Deut 34:5). There were three possible routes leading N from Ezion-geber on the Gulf of Aqabah into the Transjordanian mountains E of the Dead Sea: (1) The westernmost route was to go straight N through the Rift Valley of the Arabah, and then just S of the Dead Sea to swing E up into the highlands, passing along the boundary between Edom and Moab. (2) The central and most convenient route was to go NE from the Gulf of Aqabah through the Wadi Yetem (Ithm or Yutm), and then N to join the royal road,

or King's Highway, which proceeded along the top of the mountainous plateau that constituted the backbone of Edom and Moab (see *BTS* 85 [1966]). (3) The easternmost route or desert road was also reached through the Wadi Yetem, but this route continued E into the desert before turning N to flank Edom and Moab on the E.

Route 2, the easiest route, was closed to Israel by the king of Edom (Num 20:14-21). According to the P tradition, Israel seems to have followed route 1, for in Num 33:42 we find the Israelites going N up the Arabah to Punon (apparently the site of the brazen serpent incident in Num 21:6). According to Num 21:10-13, they then seem to have turned E, climbing up through the Zered Valley, passing between Edom and Moab out into the desert. However, Deut (2:8) indicates that Israel did not use the Arabah route but rather route 3. Was the attempt to follow one or the other route abortive? Or were different routes followed by different groups, along the analogy of different routes for the exodus (→ 28-29 above)? An answer to that question involves the extremely difficult historical and archaeological question of the "conquest" of Canaan by Israel (→ History, 75:55-56; → Biblical Archaeology, 74:79ff.; R. E. Brown, *Recent Discoveries and the Biblical World* [Wilmington, 1983] 69-73). At any rate, the Israelites had now come to the land that had been promised to them, after a journey of many centuries that had led them from one end of the Fertile Crescent to the other and then partially back again.

GEOGRAPHY OF PALESTINE

32   **(I) Introduction.** A serious discussion of the land that was center stage in biblical history should begin with a detailed study of its geology and should explain how its natural terrain was formed. This is done admirably by Baly (*Geography* 15-27). Here we shall limit ourselves to only the most basic general observations.

     (A) Size and Features. The land we shall be considering is a narrow strip that measures in length some 200-250 mi. from Dan in the N to the Sinai border in the S (Dan to Kadesh-barnea = 200; Dan to Elath = 250). This measurement includes the vast stretches of the Negeb desert, an area that figured importantly in Israel's history but was not the land of Israel in the proper sense. If one measures the land by the classic dimensions of Dan to Beer-sheba, the length is only 150 mi. The width from the Mediterranean coast to the Rift (Jordan) Valley would be about 30 mi. in the N, and about 50 mi. in the area of the Dead Sea. Strictly speaking, the 20 mi. of Transjordanian mountainous plateau to the E of the Rift Valley would not be considered part of Israel. Thus, Israel proper covered some 7000 sq. mi. and was somewhat smaller than Massachusetts. The biblical story was enacted on a small stage—the capitals of the Divided Monarchy, Samaria in the N and Jerusalem in the S, were less than 35 mi. apart (a shorter distance than that between Baltimore and Washington, cities close enough to share an airport).

33   Here we shall discuss the Negeb and Transjordan, as well as Israel proper. This larger area lends itself to a division of four roughly parallel strips running N to S. From E to W these strips are: (1) the Transjordanian mountains; (2) the Rift Valley; (3) the Palestinian or Cisjordanian mountains; (4) the Mediterranean coastal plain. The two mountain ranges, Transjordanian and Palestinian, are the continuations respectively of the Antilebanon and Palestinian ranges of Syria. Originally

one, these ranges were cleft in two from N to S by the folding of the earth's crust; in the Palestine area this cleft took the form of the great Rift Valley (Arabic: Ghor) through which the Jordan River now flows from above the Huleh Basin in the N to the Dead Sea in the S. This great cleft in the earth, which descends to 1300 ft. below sea level at the Dead Sea, continues S of the sea as the barren valley of the Arabah that opens into the Gulf of Aqabah. (The cleft has left its mark right down into Africa, visible if one follows the line from the Red Sea to Lake Nyassa and the Victoria Falls. See *NatGeog* [Aug. 1965].)

34   It is not certain that any of the Palestinian mountains were ever volcanic (→ 111 below on Mt. Moreh). Considerably to the E of Palestine, the Jebel Druze has left volcanic traces in the lava or basalt that it has spewed over Bashan and the E Transjordanian desert. Underground seething is apparent in the hot springs of Callirrhoe on the NE banks of the Dead Sea. Earthquakes are well attested in antiquity (Amos 1:1; perhaps in Joshua's damming of the Jordan in Josh 3:16; a destruction at the Qumran settlement in 31 BC) and have also occurred in modern times (Safed in 1837; Nazareth, 1900; Jaffa, 1903; Jericho, 1927).

35   **(B) Climate.** The climate varies according to the main natural features of the land: the coast, the mountains, the Rift Valley. Basically there are two seasons: the hot, dry summer and the cool, wet winter. In the USA California weather would probably come closest by comparison. It is helpful to remember that Jerusalem is at the same latitude as Savannah. The Palestinian coast is warm (average: 50s in winter, 80s in summer), and the humid summer heat at Tel Aviv or Haifa approximates that of Washington or St. Louis. The temperature in the Palestinian mountains is about 10° cooler than that of the coast. The summer in the mountains, at Jerusalem for instance, brings hot sunny days (average 85°) and cool nights (65°). Uncomfortable weather in the mountains is not caused by humidity as it is on the coast but by windstorms, whether it is the wind that drives rain in from the Mediterranean or the burning wind (sirocco or khamsin) that sweeps in from the desert in May and Oct. (Isa 27:8; Jer 4:11). Jesus knew of both (Luke 12:54-55); and in the wintertime he circulated in the only porch of the Temple that offered protection from the prevailing wind (John 10:23). The part of the Rift Valley that is far below sea level, e.g., at Jericho, bakes in intense heat in summer (over 100°) but serves as an ideal winter resort—the Palm Springs of Palestine.

36   The rainfall of Palestine also varies according to region. The Mediterranean has had an enormous impact on all the countries that surround it (*NatGeog* [Dec. 1982]). In Palestine the land nearer the Mediterranean tends to get more rain, for the Palestinian mountain range in its higher spots acts as a barrier to storms coming in from the sea, forcing them to dump their water on the W side of the mountains. Correspondingly, the E slopes are much drier. In addition, many other factors cause variation. Beer-sheba in the Negeb averages 8.6 in. of rain a year—like Arizona, but with more dew. Jerusalem gets 35 in.—about the same as London—but almost all of it falls in the months from Dec. to March. A good year is one in which the autumnal or early rain falls in Oct. at seedtime, and the late or spring rain falls in March and Apr. just before harvest. Biblical references to these two rains are numerous: Deut 11:14; Hos 6:3; Jer 5:24; Joel 2:23. Yet one must remember that in general the rain is not concentrated in these early and late periods but in the time in between. The summer months from June to Sept. tend to be very dry except for occasional rainstorms on the coast. (Cf. N. Rosenan, *IEJ* 5 [1955] 137-53.) If the rainfall does not seem very bountiful to westerners, it evidently made an extraordinary impression on the Israelites when they were fresh from Egypt, a land where water comes from the Nile and not from the heavens (Deut 11:10-25). Snow is not unusual in the Palestinian mountains, e.g., in Jerusalem, Bethlehem, or Hebron; and in the Transjordanian mountains snowfalls sometimes block the roads.

37   The seasonal character of the rain means that water has to be stored in cisterns for the dry season, unless a town is fortunate enough to be near a spring and thus have flowing or "living" water (whence the imagery in Ezek 47:1; Zech 13:1; John 4:10-14). Characteristic of Palestine is the wadi, i.e., a valley that is dry in the summer but becomes a channel of flash floods and strong streams in the rainy season. When dry, these wadis serve as roads from the valleys into the mountains. There are far fewer valleys that carry permanent streams.

With this general information we may now turn to each of the four N-S strips already mentioned (→ 33 above). We shall begin with the Transjordanian mountains and trace the geography from S to N, in harmony with the final stage of the exodus that gave Israel its first contact with this region (→ 31 above).

(For a helpful satellite map, see *NatGeog* [Feb. 1984] 244-45. For the Transjordan, older surveys by N. Glueck [→ Biblical Archaeology, 74:17] are constantly being updated and corrected, e.g., surveys of the Jordan Valley [Sauer], Moab [Miller], Edom [Macdonald].

Dornemann, R., *The Archaeology of the Transjordan in the Bronze and Iron Ages* [Milwaukee, 1983]. Glueck, N., *The Other Side of the Jordan* [New Haven, 1940]. Hadidi, A., *Studies in the History and Archaeology of Jordan* [Amman, 1982-]. Harding, G. L., *The Antiquities of Jordan* [London, 1959]. Hoade, E., *East of the Jordan* [Jerusalem, 1954]. Also *BASOR* 263 [1986] 1-26; *NatGeog* [Dec, 1947; Dec, 1952; Dec. 1964]; *Smithsonian* 18 [Nov. 1987] 100-12.)

38   **(II) Transjordan.** The Transjordanian mountains are higher than the Palestinian. They are cut across E-W by a series of tremendous canyons or gorges—radial faulting of the earth fanning out from the great N-S Rift fault, like branches from a tree trunk. These gorges containing perennial streams are from S to N: the *Zered* at the S end of the Dead Sea; the *Arnon,* halfway up the sea; the *Jabbok,* halfway up the Jordan Valley; and the *Yarmuk* at the S end of the Lake of Galilee. Often the gorges supplied the ancient occupants of Transjordan with natural frontiers. The Arnon gorge is only slightly less spectacular than the Grand Canyon of the Colorado (plates 155-57 in *AtBib*).

39   The S Transjordanian mountains, which formed the domain of ancient Edom, begin some 20 mi. NE of Elath (the Gulf of Aqabah). The route from the gulf follows the Wadi Yetem (Ithm or Yutm), which is a pass through the granite mountains of Midian (→ 27 [theory 3] above). Then one crosses the Hasma toward the Edomite mountains. This is truly a fantastic place, more worthy of the lunar than the earthly surface—a broad sandy plain from which sandstone mountains rise as isolated peaks with forbidding precipices. The most famous region of the Hasma is the Wadi Rum (Lawrence-of-Arabia country) where peaks tower one-half mile above the valley floor. When one climbs the southernmost of the Edomite mountains (Ras en-Naqb) and looks back on the Hasma, the view is spectacular and unforgettable.

40   **(A) Edom.** (→ History, 75:68.) The mountainous plateau of Edom, over 5000 ft. in height, is about 70 mi. long (N-S) and about 15 mi. wide. On the W, the mountains are covered with scrub vegetation, watered by the last drops of rain from storms coming in from the Mediterranean. On this side the drop into the Arabah (or continuation of the Rift Valley S of the Dead Sea) offered natural protection. On the E, the mountains slope off into the desert, and this side required protection by forts. For part of its history the N boundary of Edom was the Zered gorge or the Brook of Willows (Isa 15:7), with Moab on the other side (Num 21:12; Deut 2:13). Much of this Edomite highland is red sandstone, soft and easily eroded. In S Edom, *Petra,* the rose-red city carved from the sandstone, the ancient capital of the Arab Nabateans, deserves rank as one of the wonders of the world (on Petra, → Biblical Archaeology, 74:136; *NatGeog* [Dec. 1955]; *BARev* 7 [2, 1981] 22-43; *Arch* 39 [1, 1986] 18-25; I. Browning, *Petra* [2d ed.; London, 1982]).

41   The Edomite plateau is split into two unequal parts by the Punon embayment (on Punon, → 31 above) where the Arabah valley bellies out some 9 mi. into the mountains and pinches the plateau to a very narrow strip. The region S of the Punon embayment is higher, and its Edomite strongholds like *Teman* and *Sela* were almost impregnable. (The location of Sela is disputed; the popular identification with Umm el-Biyara in the center of Petra is questioned; *BA* 19 [1956] 26-36; yet cf. *BTS* 84 [1966].) Passages such as Ps 108:10 and 2 Kgs 14:7-10 reflect the respect of the Israelites for the formidable character of these Edomite strongholds. In N Edom the main cities were *Bozrah* and the rich agricultural settlement of *Tophel* (Deut 1:1). The Bible often groups the northern city Bozrah and the southern city Teman to represent the whole of Edom (Gen 36:33-34; Jer 49:20-22; Amos 1:12).

42   The mountain dwellers of the Edomite plateau, who lived "in the clefts of the rock" (Obad 3), could not support themselves simply by farming or herding flocks. They mined copper from the mountains, and they taxed the caravans that plied the King's Highway, which ran N-S along their plateau (→ 31 [route 2] above). This foreign contact may have given them their reputation for knowledge (Jer 49:7). (N. Glueck, "The Civilization of the Edomites," *BA* 10 [1947] 77–84; "The Boundaries of Edom," *HUCA* 11 [1936] 1–58.)

43   (B) Moab. (→ History, 75:69.) The area of Moab proper seems to have been between the Zered and the Arnon (Deut 2:24; Num 22:36), thus E of the southern half of the Dead Sea. Yet Moab frequently pushed its borders N of the Arnon, so that, as with Edom, one might also speak of S and N Moab with the Arnon as a divider (Jer 48:20 implies that the Arnon was the great geological feature of Moab). In S Moab the chief city was *Kir-hareseth* (modern Kerak), a magnificent natural fortress on an isolated hill. Today it is still surmounted by a Crusader castle, mute testimony that from biblical times to World War I it has been one of the chief military strongholds of the Palestine region. In 2 Kgs 3:25–27 we see this Moabite fortress holding out against the combined forces of Israel and Judah.

44   In N Moab, *Aroer* dominated from the N side the great gorge of the Arnon (2300 ft. deep!). Five miles farther N, *Dibon* (Dhiban) was a principal city; its impressive walls were excavated by ASOR. Farther N in a rich plain was *Medeba* (modern Madeba; Isa 15:2). In a stele erected at Dibon to commemorate his victories (the "Moabite Stone" dating from *ca.* 830 BC; *ANET* 320), Mesha, king of Moab, boasts of having reconquered Medeba from Israel. (For the Madeba mosaic map, → 5 above.) The fortress protecting the northern approaches to Moab was *Heshbon* (Isa 15:4; 16:8–9).

About 5 mi. to the W of Medeba and Heshbon, overlooking the Dead Sea, was the site for Moses' panoramic view of the promised land and for his death, the site called *Nebo* in the P tradition and *Pisgah* in the E tradition (Deut 32:49; 34:1)—perhaps two promontories of the one mountain. In NT times the fortress *Machaerus* stood SW of Nebo near the Dead Sea—an isolated peak made impregnable by the Herods. There JBap met his death (Josephus, *Ant.* 18.5.2 §119). Herod the Great treated his illness at the nearby hot springs of *Callirrhoe* (H. Donner, *ZDPV* 79 [1963] 59–89).

45   As we have mentioned, the Moabite occupation of the area N of the Arnon was often contested, so that, for instance, when Moses led Israel through Transjordan, the Amorites had occupied Heshbon and territory as far S as the Arnon, burning Medeba and ravishing Dibon (Num 21:26–30; → History, 75:20; yet Tell Ḥesbân was not occupied by anyone before 1200 BC; → Biblical Archaeology, 74:122). Subsequently part of N Moab was occupied by the Israelite tribe of Reuben (Num 32:37; Josh 13:9), but this tribe was quickly destroyed by aggressive Moabite expansion that pushed even across the Jordan to Jericho (Judg 3:12ff.; Gen 49:3–4). It should be noted that "the plains of Moab" where the Israelites encamped before crossing to Jericho were not on the Moabite plateau but in the Jordan Valley, just NE of the Dead Sea (→ 66 below).

46   The territory of the Moabite plateau is quite unlike the forbidding reaches of Edom to the S. True, crops like wheat and barley can be planted only in a small area, chiefly in N Moab; but the tableland offers rich grazing for flocks. Even today the black tents of the bedouin dot the land as they pasture their flocks—the economic descendants of Mesha, king of Moab, a sheep breeder, who "had to deliver annually to the king of Israel 100,000 lambs and the wool of 100,000 rams" (2 Kgs 3:4). When Reuben occupied Moabite territory, it was too busy among the sheepfolds to help its Palestinian cousins in time of war (Judg 5:16). The wealth of Moab may have accounted for the pride of which Jer 48:29 and Isa 25:10–11 accuse its inhabitants.

(Van Zyl, A. H., *The Moabites* [Leiden, 1960]. *BA* 44 [1981] 27–35; *BARev* 11 [3, 1986] 50–61; *BASOR* 234 [1979] 43–52; *IDB* 3. 409–19; *IDBSup* 602.)

47   **(C) Ammon.** (→ History, 75:70.) To the immediate N of Medeba and Heshbon lies the long expanse of Gilead, parallel to most of the Rift Valley between the Dead Sea and the Lake of Galilee. Before we consider Gilead, we shall turn aside from our journey N and study Ammon, E of southern Gilead and NE of northern Moab. There, in a poorly defined stretch of land from the Jabbok in the N as far S (at certain times) as the Arnon, the Ammonites may have been expanding at the period when Moses brought the Israelites into Transjordan (Judg 11:13—Ammon seems to have been the weakest of the three kingdoms we have been discussing). To have an idea of the fluctuating border situation, we may note that in attacking the Amorite kingdom of Heshbon (subsequently the territory of Reuben), Israel in its own view was attacking neither Moab nor Ammon, although both peoples laid claim to that territory. (Notice too that Josh 13:25 characterizes the territory of Gad, i.e., S. Gilead, as Ammonite land.)

48   If the frontiers of Ammon were vague, its capital was indisputably Rabbah or *Rabbath Ammon* (in Hellenistic times, Philadelphia in the Decapolis; modern Amman, capital of Jordan). The formidable mountain citadel of this city gave strong resistance to David's army (2 Sam 11:1,14–21; cf. Amos 1:14). In later times, *ca.* 440 BC, Tobiah the Ammonite, the great enemy of Nehemiah (Neh 4:1 [4:7]; 6:1–17; 13:4) seems to have made his headquarters at a stronghold now called *Araq el-Emir*, excavated by ASOR (→ Biblical Archaeology, 74:134). For Neolithic settlement at Ain Ghazal near Amman, → Biblical Archaeology, 74:52.

49   The land of Ammon, caught between the mountains of S Gilead and the great desert to the E, was an area of plateau. The most valuable possession of the Ammonites was the fertile valley of the upper Jabbok, a river that begins near Rabbath Ammon and moves N, before swinging W into the Jordan valley. The Ammonites, who had once seized this region themselves, had constantly to protect it against desert raiders (the woe threatened to the Ammonites in Ezek 25:4–5). Although never very strong, the Ammonites could mount swift attacks against the tribes of Israel (Judg 10:9; 1 Sam 11:1; Amos 1:13; 2 Kgs 24:2; Jer 40:14); yet they needed help when they faced the might of a united Israel (2 Sam 10:6). For long periods Ammon was completely subject to Israel (2 Sam 12:31; 2 Chr 27:5).

(Landes, G. M., "The Material Civilization of the Ammonites," *BA* 24 [1961] 65–86, or *BAR* 2, 69–88; *IDB* 1. 108–14; *IDBSup* 20.)

50   **(D) Gilead.** The Jabbok River, as it comes down from the Transjordanian mountains into the Jordan valley, divides Gilead into two parts. The southern part, conquered from the Amorite king of Heshbon (Deut 2:36; Josh 12:2), was assigned to the Israelite tribe of Gad; the northern, conquered from the king of Bashan (Deut 3:10; Josh 12:5), was assigned to a portion of the Manasseh tribe. See Deut 3:12–13; Josh 13:25,31, although these tribal boundaries in the Bible often represent a historical evolution far more complicated than the narrative conveys.

Gilead's shape is an oval, about 35–40 mi. long (N–S) and 25 mi. wide (E–W). The mountainous plateau here is dome-shaped, rising to a height of 3,300 ft.; and because of its altitude it receives heavy rain from the clouds that sweep in from the Mediterranean in the winter. The limestone hills trap the water, and there are fine springs. In antiquity Gilead, especially N Gilead, had heavy forests (Jer 22:6; Zech 10:10), and even today there is an abundance of scrub oak, carob, and pine. The balm from Gilead's trees was famous (Jer 8:22; 46:11) and was exported both to Phoenicia (Ezek 27:17) and to Egypt (Gen 37:25). Vineyards too flourished in this region. There was some mining, and the forests supplied ample fuel for smelting (→ 65 below; see M. Ottosson, *Gilead* [Lund, 1969]).

51 This was a land subject to warfare both from the Ammonites to the S and E and from the Arameans to the N (→ History, 75:71). In the military campaign of Gideon (Judg 8:4–9), we hear of two important towns of Gilead, Succoth and Penuel, both of which are in the vicinity of the Jabbok. *Succoth* may be Tell Deir Alla, a huge mound at the conjunction of the Jabbok and Jordan valleys. (Excavations of this mound by a Dutch expedition under H. J. Franken suggest an Israelite conquest around 1200 and then later Philistine occupation. Hitherto it had not been realized that the Philistines controlled so much of the Jordan Valley.) *Penuel,* several miles to the E in the Jabbok Valley, was the site of Jacob's wrestling match with the angel (Gen 32:30–31) and seemingly served as a temporary capital of the northern kingdom under Jeroboam I (*ca.* 915; 1 Kgs 12:25). *Mahanaim,* another important center in Gilead (Gen 32:2), S of Jabbok, was the capital-in-exile of Saul's son Ishbaal (= Ishbosheth; 2 Sam 2:8). One of the reasons for locating interim capitals in Gilead was that the terrain gave small forces an advantage over a large army, so that this territory became a place of refuge, e.g., for David when he fled from Absalom (2 Sam 17:24).

52 *Jabesh-gilead,* an important town in N Gilead, seemingly had close relations with Benjamin on the Palestinian side of the Jordan River (Judg 21:5–12; 1 Sam 11). *Ramoth-gilead,* to the E, a levitical city of refuge (Deut 4:43), played an important role in the 9th-cent. wars between Israel and the Arameans of Syria (1 Kgs 22; 2 Kgs 8:28). In NT times *Gerasa* (Jerash), about 5 mi. N of the Jabbok, and *Gadara,* in the NW corner of Gilead, with a spectacular view of the Yarmuk, were important towns of the Decapolis. They are possible sites for the home of the demoniac in Mark 5:1–20 (→ Biblical Archaeology, 74:147). *Pella,* in the Jordan valley at the foot of the mountains of N Gilead, was another Decapolis town and served as a refuge for the Christians of Palestine at the time of the Jewish revolt against the Romans (AD 66–70). See *BA* 21 (1958) 82–96; *RB* 75 (1968) 105–12; *Arch* 26 (4, 1973) 250–56; 34 (5, 1981) 46–53.

53 (E) Bashan. A few miles S of the Yarmuk the mountains of Gilead drop off to a fertile tableland. These are the rich plains of Bashan (also called Hauran) that extend across the Yarmuk. Running parallel to the Lake of Galilee these plains stretch N to the foot of Mt. Hermon, and E to the black volcanic mountains of the Jebel Druze. Volcanic activities made *Hammat Gader,* just N of the Yarmuk and 5 mi. from the Jordan and the Lake of Galilee, one of the largest bathing complexes in the Roman Empire (*BARev* 10 [6, 1984] 22–40). The rainfall is adequate here, for the low hills of Galilee on the Palestinian side permit the storms from the Mediterranean to pass over and to water Bashan. In many areas of the plains the soil is rich volcanic alluvium. The combination of rainfall and fertility makes Bashan the great wheat granary of the region and very good pasture. The Bible speaks of the fatness of the animals in Bashan as proverbial (Ps 22:12; Amos 4:1; Ezek 39:18). In E Bashan, sturdy oaks grew on the slopes of the Jebel Druze, so that Bashan could be grouped with Lebanon for the splendor of its trees (Isa 2:13; Nah 1:4; Ezek 27:6; Zech 11:1–2). The forests of Bashan offered refuge to those in trouble (Ps 68:15, 22; Jer 22:20).

54 The biblical references to specific sites in Bashan are few, for Israel was able to control this area only in the moments of her greatness. One of the cities of Og, king of Bashan, was *Salecah* (Deut 3:10; modern Salkhad) in the Jebel Druze; another was *Edrei* (modern Der'a), which was situated farther W near Gilead. Edrei was the site of Moses' victory over Og (Num 21:33–35). In David's time the Aram kingdom of *Geshur* occupied the section of Bashan near the Lake of Galilee; this kingdom was subject to David and from it he took the princess who was Absalom's mother (2 Sam 3:3; 13:37–38; cf. B. Mazar, *JBL* 80 [1961] 16–28). In the 9th cent. Bashan was a battlefield between Israel and the Syrians of Damascus (2 Kgs 10:32–33). Again in Maccabean times it featured in warfare, as Judas Maccabeus helped Jews in Bosor, Bozrah, and Carnaim (1 Macc 5:24–52).

55 In NT times several towns of the *Decapolis* (Hippos, Dion, Raphana) were in Bashan. *Gaulanitis* (N Bashan) and *Trachonitis* (E Bashan) were part of the tetrarchy of Philip (Luke 3:1). Today the ruins of basalt cities with their black stone buildings rise from the plains of Bashan as funeral monuments to the glory of the past.

56 (III) Rift Valley. In modern Lebanon the twin N–S mountain ranges of the Lebanon and Anti-lebanon are separated by the fertile plain called the Biqa'. Caused by the rift that separated the mountains, this is an upland valley 3000–1600 ft. in elevation. (In the heart of this valley rise the majestic ruins of the Hellenistic temples of Ba'albek; *NatGeog* [Aug. 1965].) The N frontier of Israel is now—as it was in antiquity—marked by the dramatic locale where the Biqa' falls off into the great Palestinian Rift, a drop of 1300 ft. to the Huleh Basin. In antiquity this northernmost territory of Israel belonged to Dan, and the phrase "from Dan to Beer-sheba" stood for the limits of Israel. Dominating the scene is snow-clad Mt. Hermon, the 9100 ft.-high S shoulder of the Antilebanon range—the peak the Arabs call "the Sheikh," because its snowcap (even in summer) resembles a white burnoose. In antiquity it was called Sirion by the Phoenicians and Senir by the Amorites (Deut 3:9); and Israel looked upon it as a sentinel guarding the northern frontiers (Deut 4:48; Cant 4:8).

57 (A) Jordan Tap Waters and the Huleh Basin. In the shadow of Hermon the Jordan is born of four streams fed by the drainage of the Lebanese mountains. Two of the streams, the Bareighit and the Hasbani, cascade from the Biqa', and this beautiful region of waterfalls and turbulent springtime torrents (between modern Merj Ayun and Metulla) is eloquently lyricized in Ps 42:6–7. The two major tributaries, the Liddani and the Banyasi, rise at the foot of Hermon, respectively at the city of *Dan* (modern Tell el-Qadi) and at *Caesarea Philippi* (Baniyas). In Judg 18 we are told how Dan seized this region of woodlands and springs when the tribe moved N from central Palestine. The town of *Laish* (Hebr "lion") mentioned in the story may evoke the local wildlife (Deut 33:22, "Dan is a lion's whelp"). The shrine of Dan, an important religious center since the time of the judges (Judg 18:30; Amos 8:14), was one of the two official shrines of the northern kingdom (1 Kgs 12:29; 2 Kgs 10:29; → Institutions, 76:40; → Biblical Archaeology, 74:119). *Abel of Beth-maacah* in northernmost Dan served as a rallying place for revolutionary sentiment against the southern king (2 Sam 20:14–22). The religious associations of the Dan territory carried over into NT times; for Paneas (whence modern Baniyas) was a center for the worship of the god Pan. The town was rebuilt as Caesarea Philippi (= "Caesar-town" of the Herodian tetrarch Philip to distinguish it from Caesarea Maritima on the coast); Jesus and his disciples visited it, and it was there that Peter acknowledged Jesus as the Messiah

(Mark 8:27). Some have suggested that Mt. Hermon, towering over Caesarea, was the "high mountain" of the transfiguration in the next chapter of Mark (9:2).

58   In antiquity the Huleh Basin, 9 mi. long and 3 mi. wide, saw the convergence of these four streams with some secondary tributaries to form a marshland and a small shallow lake about 3 mi. long. A pestilent source of malaria, this area was effectively drained by Israeli engineers. Two streams entered the lake, called Semechonitis by Josephus, and the Jordan alone emerged. The Huleh Basin offered N–S passage from Palestine into the Biqaʿ of Lebanon, and just S of Huleh passed the E–W road between Palestine and Damascus (Syria). An important stronghold was needed to dominate the strategic spot, and this role was played by *Hazor;* it lay in the mountains just SW of Lake Huleh and was the principal city of N Palestine. After Joshua had conquered central and S Palestine, he naturally turned against Hazor as the key to the conquest of the N (Josh 11; for the important Israeli excavation of Hazor, → Biblical Archaeology, 74:21, 88).

59   In the 10 mi. that separate the former site of Lake Huleh and the Lake of Galilee, the Jordan (whose name means "strongly descending") flows through a narrow basalt gorge whose walls tower 1200 ft. above the stream. The flow is rapid as the river descends from over 200 ft. above sea level at Huleh to emerge at the Lake of Galilee 675 ft. below sea level. High on the W plateau, in the region just before the Jordan reaches the lake, stand the bleak ruins of *Chorazin,* cursed by Jesus for failing to appreciate his miracles (Matt 11:21; *BARev* 13 [5, 1987] 22–36).

60   **(B) Lake of Galilee.** We now come to the center stage of Jesus' ministry and truly one of the most beautiful places in Palestine—the heart-shaped lake, 12–13 mi. long and 7–8 mi. wide at its broadest, called in Hebrew Chinnereth ("harp," whence the plain of Gennesaret in Matt 14:34, the Lake of Gennesaret in Luke 5:1, and the Lake of Gennesar in Josephus). "The Sea of Galilee" is the name given to this body of water by Mark and Matt, but Luke more correctly designates it as a lake. Only John (6:1; 21:1) speaks of it as "Tiberias," the name it took on later in the 1st cent. AD after Herod Antipas had built the town of that name on the SW shore, in flattering homage to the Roman emperor.

The lake's blue waters are framed by cliffs on nearly every side except the N where green plains, especially in the NW, provide an attractive border. Its beauty has never been lost on people: The caves of the NW hills have yielded up some of the earliest prehistoric traces found in Palestine (→ Biblical Archaeology, 74:46), and even today many a tourist or pilgrim finds this the most conducive spot in Palestine for meditation on Him who more than once prayed there himself (Mark 1:35; 6:46). Yet the site has not always been peaceful. At the "Horns of Hattin," a hilly gateway from lower Galilee down to the lake (a site Jesus must have passed as he came down from Nazareth and environs to Capernaum [Luke 4:31; John 2:12]), took place the climactic battle of 1187 where the great Saladin smashed forever the power of the Crusaders in Palestine.

61   Jesus' disciples were fishermen on this lake; more than once he felt the violence of its sudden storms as he traversed it in their boats. (A 1st-cent. boat was found in 1986; see *BARev* 14 [5, 1988] 18–33.) The warm winters of the sheltered lake favored this outdoor preacher, who often lacked shelter (Matt 8:20). He found his audiences in the busy occupants of the commercial towns that dotted its N shores, in the merchants who traversed the road to Syria that ran along the W of the lake, and in the host of government officials who controlled the border crossings along the Jordan, separating Herod's Galilee from Philip's Gentile tetrarchate in Bashan (→ 55 above). *Capernaum* (Tell Hum; → Biblical Archaeology, 74:145) on the NNW shore was Peter's home (according to Mark 1:21,29). This town became Jesus' headquarters, and its synagogue heard his preaching (Luke 4:31; 7:5; John 6:59). Some 4 mi. away, across the Jordan and on the NNE shore, may have stood *Bethsaida,* connected with the multiplication of the loaves (Luke 9:10; John 6:1; but cf. Mark 6:45) and, according to John 1:44; 12:21, the home of Peter, Andrew, and Philip (see *BA* 48 [1985] 196–216). Mary Magdalene, once possessed by seven demons (Luke 8:2), seems to have come from *Magdala* on the W shore of the lake, while the demoniac of Mark 5:1 prowled in tombs on the E shore of the lake (near Gergesa? → 52 above) in the Decapolis region. There is little of OT importance in this area, but at the SW corner of the lake stood the pre-biblical, Early Bronze Age fortress subsequently called Beth-yeraḥ (→ Biblical Archaeology, 74:60). A little farther S at Ubeidiya Paleolithic people settled more than a million years ago (→ Biblical Archaeology, 74:49).

62   **(C) Jordan Valley.** Between the Lake of Galilee and the Dead Sea, a distance of 65 mi., the Jordan falls from 675 ft. below sea level to 1300 ft. below. On both sides the mountains rise 1000 ft. and more above the valley formed by the rift that once tore them apart. This basic Rift Valley, called in Arabic the Ghor, is quite wide in the N (for some 20 mi. down from the Lake of Galilee) and again in the S where it is 20 mi. wide just above the Dead Sea. In the center of the strip we are considering, however, the Rift Valley is constricted into a narrow waist. When water is available in the valley—through rain in the N or through irrigation—the valley floor yields itself to productive cultivation.

(Ben-Arieh, Y., *The Changing Landscape of the Central Jordan Valley* [ScrHier 15; Jerusalem, 1968]. Glueck, N., *The River Jordan* [NY, 1946]. *BA* 41 [1978] 65–75; *NatGeog* [Dec. 1940; Dec. 1944].)

63   Roughly through the center of the Rift Valley runs the Jordan River, a narrow stream only 60–80 ft. wide at the traditional spot for Joshua's crossing to Jericho. Little wonder then that Naaman the Syrian found the rivers of Damascus more impressive (2 Kgs 5:12). As it twists and meanders, especially midway down from the Lake of Galilee and toward the S, the Jordan has worn into the Rift Valley floor a deep bed of its own, called the Zor. In places the Zor is a mile wide and 150 ft. deep. Flooded in springtime when the melting snows of Hermon engorge the Jordan, the Zor is often an impenetrable thicket of shrubs and stunted trees, which in antiquity offered a habitat to wild animals, including lions (Jer 49:19; Zech 11:3). Wisely does Jer 12:5 stress the danger to those who fall down in the jungle of the Jordan (also 49:19). Where the floor of the Rift Valley (the Ghor) breaks away toward the riverbed (the Zor), the ground consists of desert "badlands," i.e., ash-gray marl hills with barren, crumbly soil called *qattara.* The treacherous *qattara* and the junglelike Zor, rather than the width of the stream, were what made the Jordan a divider. In the N where fords were more frequent, there were better communications, not always pleasant, between Palestine and Transjordan, especially Gilead (Judg 8:4; 12:1–6; 21:8–12; 1 Sam 31:11–13).

64   Moving from N to S in the Jordan Valley, we find that the first great tributary from the E is the Yarmuk, which carried as much water as the Jordan itself (and has been the subject for diversionary water projects in the water-war between the Arabs and the Israelis). Near the conjunction of the Yarmuk and the Jordan flourished an important pottery-Neolithic civilization at what is today known as *Sha'ar ha-Golan,* excavated by M. Stekelis. About 12 mi. S of the Lake of Galilee, there is a gap in the western mountains as the Plain of Esdraelon (Jezreel) opens into the Rift Valley. The strategic communication routes into Israel through this opening were controlled by the stronghold of *Beth-shan* (Beisan), a site whose importance is marked by strata of Egyptian, Philistine, and Israelite occupation (→ Biblical Archaeology, 74:89, 96). In Roman times it was called Scythopolis and flourished as an important center both for Jews and for Christians *ca.* AD 400. Opposite the Beth-shan gap, on the Transjordanian side of the valley was Pella; and just to the S where the Brook Cherith (= Wadi Yabes; 1 Kgs 17:3) joins the Jordan, we are in the country of Elijah and near the OT site of Jabesh-gilead (→ 52 above).

65   Still on the E side, where the Rift Valley grows narrow and at the spot where the Wadi Kufrinje joins the Jordan, we come to *Zarethan* (1 Kgs 4:12). This is most probably to be identified with Tell es-Sa'idiyeh, the site of interesting excavations by J. B. Pritchard (*BA* 28 [1965] 10–17; *BTS* 75 [1965]). For Succoth (Tell Deir Alla?), 5 mi. farther S, → 51 above. The E side of the valley between the Wadi Kufrinje and the Jabbok (Nahr ez-Zerqa) was the site of Solomon's smelting activities (1 Kgs 7:45–47), for which the forests of N Gilead on the plateau above offered ready fuel. The distance between Zarethan, at the confluence of the Kufrinje with the Jordan, and *Adam* (Tell ed-Damiyeh), at the confluence of the Jabbok, is 12 mi.; and Josh 3:16 reports that when Joshua stopped the flow of the Jordan, the water backed up from Adam to Zarethan. Historical records confirm that landslides in the Adam area have stopped the Jordan temporarily. On the W side, just opposite this area, the Wadi Far'ah enters the Rift Valley from the Palestinian side, draining the heartland of Samaria. On an isolated peak, dominating the junction of the Far'ah and the Jordan, was the impregnable Herodian fortress called the *Alexandrium;* and indeed in the 15 mi. of the W side that separate the Alexandrium from Jericho, other Herodian fortresses stood at *Phasaelis, Archelais,* and *Dok* (cf. 1 Macc 16:15), protecting the communication routes between the valley and Judea. See *BA* 15 (1952) 26–42; → History, 75:158.

66   About 8 mi. N of the Dead Sea, on the W side set back from the river, stood the pearl of the S Jordan Valley, the city of *Jericho,* one of the oldest cities on earth and the site of extremely important archaeological excavations (→ Biblical Archaeology, 74:19, 51, 80). The fountain near the ruins is suggested as the one purified by Elisha (2 Kgs 2:19–22). The Jericho of NT times was seemingly not at the same site (Tell es-Sultan) but nearby (→ Biblical Archaeology, 74:148). For the road from Jerusalem to Jericho, see *BA* 38 (1975) 10–24. On the E side opposite Jericho, in this region where the valley is very wide, are the *plains of Moab* (Num 22:1), the site of the Israelites' encampment when they came down from the Moabite plateau. N. Glueck has surface-explored this area to identify the various sites mentioned in the Bible, e.g., *Shittim* (Num 25:1; Josh 2:1). These plains are the stage that the Bible gives to the last chapters of Num and the whole of Deut. (Also in this area are the mounds of *Ghassul,* a prebiblical site important for its Chalcolithic pottery and art; → Biblical Archaeology, 74:54.) For the disputed location of *Gilgal,* the first encampment on the W side after crossing (Josh 5:10), see J. Muilenburg, *BASOR* 140 (1955) 11–27; O. Bächli, *ZDPV* 83 (1967) 64–71.

67   **(D) Dead Sea.** The Jordan River comes to an end in the Dead Sea, the most dramatic feature of the Rift Valley. Fringed by mountains on both sides, roughly

50 mi. long by 10 mi. wide, the Dead Sea (Sea of the Arabah, Salt Sea, Lake Asphaltitis) is the lowest point on the earth's surface, 1300 ft. below sea level with a water depth of another 1300 ft. in the N. The Dead Sea, even more than Utah's Salt Lake (*NatGeog* [Dec. 1958] 848–58), can claim to be the world's most unusual body of water. Over 27 percent of its composition is solid chemical matter (salt, chlorides, and bromides); its salt content increases constantly because the seven million tons of water that flow into it daily have no outlet, and the constant evaporation leaves residual solids. The 45 billion tons of chemicals it contains are an attraction for the chemical-extraction industry both in Israel and in Jordan, but even this will not prevent the shallow S end of the sea from being ultimately silted up. (On the Nabatean bitumen industry, see *BA* 22 [1959] 40–48.) No fish can exist in such water—at least until Ezekiel's vision will be fulfilled and a life-giving stream will flow from Jerusalem to sweeten the Dead Sea as far as En-gedi (47:10). Neither the intense heat nor the parched terrain in this area is conducive to large-scale settlement (although the region serves as a winter resort). See *NatGeog* (Feb. 1978); *Scientific American* (Oct. 1983).

68   On the NW shore, near the spring called Ain Feshkha, stand the ruins of *Qumran,* the settlement of the community that produced the Dead Sea Scrolls (→ Apocrypha, 67:79ff.; *NatGeog* [Dec. 1958]). Halfway down on the W shore is the more celebrated water source of *En-gedi* (Cant 1:14), where David sought refuge from Saul (1 Sam 23:29). For Israeli excavations at the En-gedi oasis, see *Arch* 16 (1963) 99–107; also *BA* 34 (1971) 23–39. The isolated mountain fortress of *Masada,* two-thirds of the way down the sea, was the last stronghold in the Jewish struggle against the Romans in AD 73, and the valleys between En-gedi and Masada are dotted with caves that were outposts of Jewish resistance—caves that yielded additional Dead Sea Scrolls (→ Apocrypha, 67:119–23; also Y. Yadin, *Masada* [NY, 1966]). On the S end of the W shore stands the great salt mountain *Jebel Usdum,* whose name recalls biblical Sodom and the pillar of salt that once was Lot's wife (Gen 19:26). It is generally thought that *Sodom* and *Gomorrah* and the three other cities of the plain (Gen 18:16ff.) lie under the waters at the southern end of the sea (*BA* 5 [1942] 17–32; 6 [1943] 41–52; 44 [1981] 87–92; *BARev* 6 [5, 1980] 26–36). This shallow bay glides into the Sebkha or salt marshes that extend for 8 mi. S of the Dead Sea. (W. E. Rast and R. T. Schaub, *Survey of the Southeastern Plain of the Dead Sea* [Jordan, 1974].)

The E shore is marked by precipitous cliffs and the great gorges of the Transjordanian rivers, like the Arnon and the Zered. We have already mentioned the hot springs of Callirrhoe on the N part of this shore (→ 44 above). Two-thirds of the way down the E side is the Lisan ("tongue") peninsula, a gray-marl plateau 9 mi. long protruding into the Dead Sea and cutting its width. In Roman times it was already possible to ford the Dead Sea here. Just to the E of the Lisan peninsula Americans have excavated a series of fascinating Early Bronze Age necropolises at *Bab edh-Dhra'* (→ Biblical Archaeology, 74:64).

69   **(E) Arabah.** Although the OT uses the name Arabah to designate the entire Rift Valley, today the term is most often applied to the southernmost section of the Palestinian Rift, i.e., the 100 mi. from the Sebkha salt marshes to the Gulf of Aqabah. Flanked on both sides by mountains, which are especially high on the E, the valley floor of the Arabah gradually rises, until halfway down at Jebel er-Rishe it reaches 650 ft. above sea level only to descend again toward sea level at Aqabah. The N part of the Arabah is quite wide, especially at the Punon embayment (→ 41 above); the S part is only 6 mi. wide at its broadest. Much of the Arabah is desert area in which only expert irrigationists, like the Nabateans and the modern Israeli, could sustain settlement. The biblical import of the Arabah is centered on two moments in history: (1) It served as one of the routes in Israel's advance from Kadesh-barnea to Transjordan (→ 31 above). (2) It was the focal point of Solomon's copper industry. Copper was mined from the hills and crudely smelted in the valley in order to meet the needs of Israel's greatest builder (*BA* 24 [1961] 59-62), although some of the mines were pre-Solomonic (*BARev* 4 [2, 1978] 16-25). At the S extremity of the Arabah, on the N end of the Gulf of Aqabah, stood the fortress of *Elath* (Eloth), a point of contention between Judah and Edom (2 Kgs 14:22; 16:6). Nearby was *Ezion-geber*, a site that figured in the desert wandering of Israel under Moses (→ 30 above), but most famous as the port built by Solomon for launching his fleet and thus his open door for trade with Somaliland, S Arabia, and points E (1 Kgs 9:26; 10:2). This port was reopened at subsequent periods during the divided monarchy when Israel and Judah were at peace and could work together to rebuild the world trade begun by Solomon (2 Chr 20:36). N. Glueck identified both Elath and Ezion-geber (kept distinct in the Bible) with the site he excavated at Tell el-Kheleifeh, in the center of the N head of the gulf, one-quarter mi. inland, even though he found no remains of port facilities and the strong winds in the region make the site unsuitable as a port. Subsequent archaeology disproved his theory. B. Rothenberg (*PEQ* 94 [1962] 5-71) argued that, while Elath was in this area on the NE end of the gulf (Byzantine Aila, just N of modern Aqabah, and stretching W to Tell el-Kheleifeh), Ezion-geber was on the island of Jeziret Fara'un, off the W shore of the gulf some 8 mi. farther S. This island, where pottery of Solomon's period has been found, provides excellent shelter for ships. Remains of an artificial port are in evidence. G. D. Pratico (*BASOR* 259 [1985] 1-32) has also challenged Glueck's identification of Ezion-geber.

70   (IV) Coastal Plains. Before concentrating on the main geographical area of biblical interest, i.e., the strip of Palestinian mountains between the Mediterranean and the Jordan, we shall turn our attention to the Palestinian coast. From Philistine Gaza in the S to Phoenician Tyre in the N, this coast is about 130 mi. long. For convenience we may divide it into three sections, each 40-45 mi. in length, viz., Philistia, Sharon, and the Dor-Carmel-Asher region.

71   (A) Philistia and the Shephelah. *Ca.* 1200 BC a S strip of the Canaanite coast was invaded from the Mediterranean by the "Sea Peoples," an amalgam of Indo-Europeans from Crete, Cyprus, Sardinia, Sicily, and other islands in the Mediterranean. (Earlier these peoples had invaded the coast farther N, destroying Ugarit [→ 21 above] *ca.* 1230.) The Semites of the land, Canaanite and Israelite, found these uncircumcised foreigners of unintelligible tongue to be formidable adversaries in war, with iron weapons that made them invincible. Within a few years, *ca.* 1170-1150, and probably with Egyptian approval, these people, who became known as Philistines, were in full control of the coast and had formed a pentapolis, or five-city league (1 Sam 6:4), with Gaza, Ashkelon, and Ashdod on the coast (respectively S to N), and Gath and Ekron farther inland (→ Biblical Archaeology, 74:95ff.; → History, 75:67).

72   (a) PHILISTIA. Although the Philistines ultimately controlled much of Canaan, including the Plain of Esdraelon and part of the Jordan Valley, and gave the name "Palestine" to the whole land, Philistia proper was the area of the pentapolis. Along the seashore and up to 2 mi. inland, the coast from Gaza N to Joppa (45 mi.) is marked by sand dunes, sometimes rising to a height of 150 ft. Along this coast ran the main highway, the trunk road, from Egypt toward Syria, and we have suggested (→ 28 above) the possibility that, in part, the biblical description of the exodus followed this route to Canaan.

The Philistine plain is the area between the sand dunes and the foothills, a distance of 5-10 mi. The area is cut crosswise by wadis that drain the hills to the E, and many of the cities command these wadis. Olive groves and grainfields (Judg 15:5) were the agricultural wealth of the Philistines, a bounty marred only by the threefold danger of drought, plague, and war. Especially in the S of Philistia rainfall is light, and the water from the winter storms runs off quickly. Gaza, for instance, stands on the threshold between cultivated land and the desert to the S. Plague, transmitted from Egypt (Deut 7:15; 28:60; Amos 4:10), was not uncommon; and malaria has been a danger in this region until recently. The Bible records that a (bubonic?) plague swept Philistia when the Israelite Ark was held at Ashdod and Ekron (1 Sam 5); and four centuries later Sennacherib's Assyrian army was decimated by plague at Libnah just to the N of Gath (2 Kgs 19:8,35-37). As for war, the tramp of marching armies was well known in Philistia, which served as a passageway in the eternal struggle between Egypt in the S and Syria, Assyria, and Babylon to the N and E along the Fertile Crescent (→ 15 above). (Gaza has also been a sore spot in Egyptian-Israeli relations.) In the heyday of the Philistines (12th-11th cents.), however, it was not international warfare but local battles with the Israelites that made life difficult.

73   (b) THE SHEPHELAH. Between the Philistine plain and the Judean mountains to the E there is a strip of foothills 10-15 mi. wide, 350-1500 ft. in height—the Shephelah ("lowland"). The valleys of the Shephelah were the natural passes from Philistia to the mountains, and they were protected by fortified towns—Debir, Lachish, Libnah, Azekah, Makkedah, Beth-shemesh, and Gezer, a litany that has been immortalized in the biblical accounts of warfare. *Beth-shemesh* has yielded important Philistine artifacts; this shows that these sites were in both Philistine and Israelite zones of influence; → Biblical Archaeology, 74:95. From the beginning to the end of the 20th cent. *Gezer* was the subject of excavations that produced sharp disputes about the dating of its impressive walls and gates; → Biblical Archaeology, 74:14. For the Israeli excavations of Tell Nagila, a Canaanite and Hyksos stronghold some 15 mi. S of Beth-shemesh, see *Arch* 18 (1965) 113-23; *HTR* 64 (1971) 437-48. When Joshua had consolidated his hold in the highlands of central Canaan at Bethel, Ai, and Gibeon, his first great campaign was directed against the cities of the Shephelah (Josh 10:28-40), excavations of some of which attest to destruction *ca.* 1240. When the Philistines came, they used Ekron and Gath as fortresses against Israelite raids from the Judean mountains down through the Shephelah (Samson stories of Judg 15-16). The Davidic victories that definitively broke Philistine power took place in the Shephelah (2 Sam 5:17-25). In short, control of the Shephelah was the deciding factor. In Philistine control the Shephelah wadis were arrows aimed at the heart of the Judean mountains; in Israelite control they were arrows aimed at the Philistine plain. Later on, in the 8th-6th cents., command of these wadis played an important part in the Assyrian and Babylonian campaigns against Judah. Instead of attacking Judah from the N first, Sennacherib and Nebuchadnezzar sent their armies S along the coast to seal off Judah from Egyptian aid and to gain an easy road up into the mountains. *Lachish* was the site of several famous sieges (2 Kgs 18:14; Jer 34:7; → Biblical Archaeology, 74:89, 124–26).

74   Two of the wadis in the N part of the Shephelah deserve special mention. The Vale of *Sorek* was adjacent to the towns of Kiriath-jearim, Beth-shemesh, Timnah, Ekron, and Jabneel. It was the site of the Samson stories (Judg 16) and of the tale of the captivity of the Ark in the late 11th cent. (1 Sam 6; 2 Sam 6). The other wadi, farther to the N, was the Valley of *Aijalon* that climbed past lower and upper Beth-horon, giving access to Bethel and Jerusalem by way of Gibeon. Here Joshua fought the battle against the kings of the S (Josh 10:10–15). The valley played a strategic part in Saul's warfare against the Philistines (1 Sam 14:31) and in the Israeli-Jordanian war of 1948.

75   **(B) Plain of Sharon.** This stretch of 40 mi. runs from Joppa (Jaffa) in the S to the Crocodile River (Shihor-libnath, Josh 19:26) in the N. The Plain of Sharon ("level land"?) is narrower (about 10 mi. wide) than the plain in Philistia; and there is no real Shephelah or foothills, for the plain extends to the base of the mountains. Running from N to S like an island in the midst of the plain is a sandstone elevation. The wadis that drain the mountains are forced to direct their flow around either end of this elevation; and so the clogged mouths of three streams, including the Crocodile, enter the sea at the N end of Sharon; on the S end the mouth of the Yarkon is near Tel Aviv. In OT times the region along both sides of this elevated sandstone was marshland.

76   The obstacles presented by this area's terrain were a deterrent to travel and to settlement. The trunk road hugged the base of the mountains, and the few main towns—Joppa, Lod (Lydda), Aphek, Gilgal, and Socoh—were located along the perimeters of the plain. *Aphek* (Roman Antipatris of Acts 23:31?—at or near modern Rosh ha-Ayin; → Biblical Archaeology, 74:76, 85, 143; *BA* 44 [1981] 75–86) was an important site at the headwaters of the Yarkon, with a control over the route from Joppa to Jerusalem. Aphek is named as the site of a great Israelite defeat at the hands of the Philistines *ca.* 1050 (1 Sam 4:1), although a site farther to the N near Esdraelon seems indicated. *Joppa* ("the beautiful"; Jaffa) was important because it was a port area (although not a very satisfactory one); and seemingly the Lebanese cedars for the Temple were ferried down the coast to Joppa (or more precisely to the excavated site of Qasile just N of the Yarkon; → Biblical Archaeology, 74:102) and then up the Yarkon and overland to Jerusalem (2 Chr 2:16; Ezra 3:7). Tel Aviv (a name reminiscent of Ezek 3:15), a settlement founded by the Jews in 1909 because of the hostility of the Arabs in Jaffa, is a very large city in this area. For this area, see *BA* 35 (1972) 66–95.

77   In NT times Roman roads and bridges made the plain more traversable. We find Peter active in both Lydda and Joppa (Acts 9:32–10:23). Just 10 mi. S of Joppa was *Jabneh* (Jabneel, Jamnia—variant name forms reflecting the underlying Yabneh Yam, "Yabneh by the Sea"), famous for its rabbinic school after the fall of Jerusalem (→ Canonicity, 66:35). On the coast at the N extremity of Sharon, Herod the Great built *Caesarea* (Maritima) and gave the area another badly needed port. We read in Acts 9:30; 18:22; 21:8 that Paul embarked or disembarked there. Caesarea was the center of Roman power in Palestine, the headquarters of the prefect or procurator. The first Palestinian inscription to mention Pontius Pilate was discovered there in 1961 (see plate in *BTS* 57 [1963] 15). The Roman centurion Cornelius of the Italian Cohort lived at Caesarea (Acts 10:1) and was

baptized there by Peter. In AD 58–60 Paul was imprisoned at Caesarea under the Roman governors Felix and Festus (Acts 23:23; 25:12), and both Herod Agrippa I and II are mentioned as coming to Caesarea (12:19; 25:13) in AD 44 and 60 respectively. On Caesarea, → Biblical Archaeology, 74:142.

78   In modern times the Arabs planted flourishing citrus groves in the Plain of Sharon, even before the Israeli occupied and furthered the progress of the region. Although the Bible calls Sharon a place of pasture (1 Chr 5:16; 27:29; Isa 65:10), the lushness of its growth is likened to that of Carmel and Lebanon (Isa 33:9; 35:2). The rose (crocus) of Sharon, a delicate flower in the jungle of underbrush, is used as a comparison in Cant 2:1.

79   **(C) Dor, Carmel, Plain of Asher.**
      (a) DOR. The coastlands of Dor separate Sharon from the great promontory of Carmel, some 20 mi. N of the Crocodile River. In antiquity the marshes that surrounded this river cut Dor off from the S, giving it an orientation toward the northern territory of Asher (Josh 17:11). As in the rest of the N, the coast, only 2 mi. wide, is much narrower than in the S (Sharon or Philistia); and the mountains press close to the sea. This was a region of forest and marshland. The town of *Dor,* which gave its name to the region, was a mediocre harbor. It was not taken by Joshua's invasion (Judg 1:27) and remained in Philistine hands until the 10th cent. (1 Kgs 4:11). In 1 Macc 15:10ff., it is the site of a struggle between the Syrian rulers. The town declined when Herod built Caesarea 8 mi. to the S. See *BARev* 5 (3, 1979) 34–39.

80   (b) CARMEL. The most noticeable natural feature on the Palestinian coast is the great promontory of Carmel jutting out into the sea and forming the large bay that harbors Haifa and Acco. The view from Carmel over Haifa Bay is truly breathtaking, and this very spot is the traditional localization for the dramatic confrontation of Elijah and the priests of Baal (1 Kgs 18:20ff. esp. v 43). Farther SE in caves along the Carmel slope, Stone Age people found a home, particularly in the Wadi Mugharah (→ Biblical Archaeology, 74:46). Although there were ancient settlements in the area of Haifa Bay, *Haifa* itself is not a biblical site; its importance as a port stems from the period of the British Mandate. *Acco* was an ancient city. Under the name Ptolemais (1 Macc 11:22–24; 12:45–48; Acts 21:7), it was famed in Greco-Roman times for the manufacture of glass. It was the port for the Crusaders under the name Saint Jean d'Acre and was their last fortress in the Holy Land after the defeat by Saladin (→ 60 above). Here Francis of Assisi landed to lay the foundations of the Franciscan "Holy Land Custody" of the Christian shrines. On Acco, see *BA* 43 (1980) 35–39.

81   (c) PLAIN OF ASHER. The land between Haifa and Acco is in part a silted bay, with marshes to the E. The tribe of Asher did not take Acco (Judg 1:31) but claimed for its possession the plain from Acco to the "Ladder of Tyre" (Ras en-Naqura) where the Lebanese mountains came down to the coast as a promontory, forming the S border of Phoenicia. This Asher territory was about 12 mi. long and 5 mi. wide, standing between the sea and the mountains. Cut by E-W wadis draining the mountains, the plain was often marshy, and the main settlements were at the base of the mountains. (We follow here the usual theory of the location of Asher's territory. M. Noth would put Asher just SW of Carmel and would give the coastal territory we have described to Zebulun. Cf. Gen 49:13; Deut 33:19, which imply that Zebulun owns the seashore.)

Neither Asher nor its territory was very important in biblical history, although Gen 49:20 speaks of Asher's possessions as rich and providing food for kings (Deut 33:24). In Judg 5:17 Asher is castigated for sitting still at the seacoast while Israel was in danger. Inevitably Asher's poor coastland was overshadowed by Phoenicia to the N, with its great ports of Tyre and Sidon. Asher seems to have been part of the region given up by Solomon to Hiram of Tyre in payment for Phoenician supplies and skills in building the Jerusalem Temple (1 Kgs 9:11).

82   (V) Central Zone of Palestine. As far as biblical history is concerned, this was the most important area of Palestine. The region from the N border of the Negeb to N Galilee was the "essential Israel," from Beer-sheba to Dan. For convenience' sake we shall also treat here the Negeb itself.

(A) Negeb. This is the southernmost area of Palestine—a rough trapezoid formed by Gaza, the Brook of Egypt, Ezion-geber, and Sodom, flanked on the W by the coastal desert, and on the E by the Arabah. The Negeb ("South") is called in the Bible the Wilderness of Zin (Num 20:1; 33:36; perhaps, more precisely, this name refers to the southern part of the Negeb around Kadesh-barnea). Running on a NE–SW slant through the Negeb are two upwarps or thrusts of higher land (the Kurashe and the Kurnub). The W side of these upwarps, particularly the NW, receives some moisture in the form of dew and occasional rains from the Mediterranean; and so it is on this side of the upwarps that the main settlements and oases of the Negeb are found, e.g., Beer-sheba, El Auja, Kadesh-barnea. The modern Israeli have revived the efficient irrigation systems of the Nabateans and once again succeeded in cultivating this area. For climate and cultivation in antiquity, see *BASOR* 185 (1967) 39–43.

83   The E and SE of the upwarps, i.e., facing the Arabah, are barren and desolate, cut by great gorges. The importance of the region stems from the fact that commerce from Transjordan (e.g., from Petra in Nabatean times) or from the Gulf of Aqabah (e.g., from Ezion-geber in Solomon's time; → 69 above) had to pass up these gorges and wadis and go NW through the upwarps in order to reach Beer-sheba and ultimately Palestine proper. The town of *Kurnub* (Roman Mampsis) was situated in a gap in the upwarps through which such caravan routes passed (*PEQ* 101 [1969] 5–14; *EAEHL* 3. 722–35). *Hormah,* which figures in the abortive attempts of the Israelites to invade Canaan from the S (Num 14:39–45; 21:1–3; Deut 1:41–46), was probably in this area, SE of Beer-sheba.

84   In biblical times the Negeb was controlled by the monarchy only at its periods of greatness, and then probably only to the point of keeping open the trade routes to Ezion-geber. For Solomonic fortresses there, see *BARev* 11 (3, 1985) 56–70; 12 (4, 1986) 40–53. Otherwise it was the prey of wandering bedouin who made raids against the settlements in Philistia and Judah and were punished by retaliatory raids, as described in 1 Sam 27:8–12; 30. These accounts of David's raids into the Negeb show that the area was divided into zones of influence. *Ca.* 800 BC *Kuntillat 'Ajrud,* 40 mi. S of Kadesh-barnea, was occupied by people who left inscriptions in Hebrew and Phoenician, plus the disputed "Yahweh-Asherah" drawing (→ Biblical Archaeology, 74:118). After the fall of the monarchy, Edomites moved into the area, whence the name Idumea in Hellenistic times (1 Macc 5:3; Mark 3:8). In 125 BC John Hyrcanus conquered Idumea and brought it under the Hasmonean Jewish state; but the Idumeans eventually had their revenge, for from here came the Herod family that was

to rule in one part of Palestine or the other for nearly a century. The area was again of importance in Byzantine times, as Israeli excavations have shown (e.g., of Avdat or Abda; see A. Negev, *Cities of the Desert* [Tel Aviv, 1966]; *EAEHL* 2. 345–55).

85   The two most important biblical sites in the Negeb are Kadesh-barnea and Beer-sheba. *Kadesh* was the site of a 38–year stop of Moses and the Israelites on their way between Sinai and Transjordan (Deut 1:46; 2:14; for the thesis that Sinai was here, → 27 above). Miriam, Moses' sister, died and was buried here (Num 20:1). Deut 1:2 places Kadesh at the distance of an 11–day journey from Horeb/Sinai; this would agree with the localization of Sinai in the S part of the Sinai Peninsula. The name of Kadesh is preserved in Ain Qudeis on the frontier between the Sinai peninsula and Palestine. Yet Kadesh is supposed to have been the site where Moses brought forth water from the rock to satisfy the whole people (Num 20:2–13), and there must have been abundant water at Kadesh to support the Israelites during a long stay. For this reason scholars do not seek Kadesh at Ain Qudeis, where the supply is sparse, but at nearby Ain Qudeirat (which, however, was not occupied until the 10th cent. BC). See Y. Aharoni in Rothenberg, *God's Wilderness* 121ff.; M. Dothan, *IEJ* 15 (1965) 134–51; also *BA* 39 (1976) 148–51; 44 (1981) 93–107; *BARev* 7 (3, 1981) 20–33.

86   About 50 mi. N of Kadesh-barnea was *Beer-sheba,* of Abraham and Isaac fame (Gen 22:19; 26:33; 46:1–4). About 1000 ft. above sea level, and possessing an excellent water supply, this site sits astride routes from Gaza in the W, from Transjordan in the E, and from Sinai in the S. It was near here in the desert that Hagar wandered with Ishmael (Gen 21:14). At Beersheba Abraham planted a tamarisk tree as a shrine to El Olam (Gen 21:31–34; → OT Thought, 77:16; for Beersheba as a shrine, → Institutions, 76:29; also → Biblical Archaeology, 74:56, 117). About 20 mi. E of Beer-sheba stood *Arad,* one of the northernmost Canaanite cities of the Negeb, whose king resisted the Israelites (Num 21:1–3). When the Israelites destroyed the city, the site was given to their Kenite allies (Judg 1:16; see Josh 12:14). Important Israeli excavations were done at Arad (*BA* 31 [1968] 2–32; *BARev* 6 [1, 1980] 52–56; → Biblical Archaeology, 74:63, 83, 109, 115). However, the mound shows no trace of a Canaanite, pre-Kenite occupation; the excavator, Y. Aharoni, suggests that the Canaanite site was a neighboring mound, a few miles away.

The Negeb or Wilderness of Zin marked the southern border of Israel's domain (Num 34:3; Deut 34:3; Josh 15:1). Sometimes this border is measured from the southern extreme of the Negeb, the Brook of Egypt (Wadi el-Arish: Num 34:5; Josh 15:4); more often it is measured from Beer-sheba in the N of the Negeb (Judg 20:1; 1 Sam 3:20; etc.).

(On the Negeb: Glueck, N., *Rivers in the Desert: A History of the Negev* [NY, 1959]. Rothenberg, B., *God's Wilderness* [NY, 1962]. *Arch* 36 [5, 1983] 30–37; *BA* 22 [1959] 82–97; 40 [1977] 156–66; *BARev* 2 [3, 1976] 25–30; 9 [2, 1983] 28–37.)

87   (B) Territory of the House of Judah.
(a) GENERAL DESCRIPTION. The hill country of Judah or Judea is a strip of mountains or high plateau averaging 10 mi. in width, rising just N of Beer-sheba and continuing to just N of Jerusalem. To the E, where the plateau falls away into the Dead Sea and the Rift Valley, is the barren "Wilderness of Judah" (Josh 15:61; Matt 3:1), a refuge for bandits and those in flight (e.g., David from Saul) and for religious solitaries (JBap; Qumran sectarians; Christian monks, as at Mar Saba).

The barrenness of this wilderness is illustrated by the fact that there is no source of water on the famous span between Jerusalem and Jericho (Luke 10:30). The defense of Judah on this E side could to some extent be entrusted to nature. To the W of Judah, the Shephelah (→ 73 above) flanked the mountains and offered a buffer against Philistine expansion.

88 To the S, the rise of the mountains from Beer-sheba offered a defense, albeit weak, against the Negeb raiders like the Amalekites (1 Sam 15). The Negeb of Judah (1 Sam 27:10) was probably the area of the N Negeb over which Judah tried to maintain some control as a further buffer on her southern flank, whence the occasional inclusion of the Negeb in the delineation of Judah's territory (Josh 15:3-4). The tribe of Judah, which may have entered Palestine from the S rather than from across the Jordan, does seem to have allied itself with a group of southern peoples, like the Kenites, Kenizzites, Calebites, and Jerahmeelites (Josh 14:6-15; 15:13-19; Judg 1:8-20; 1 Chr 2:9,25-27), whom it brought into the Israelite confederacy. Judah also incorporated the rather nebulous territory of Simeon (Josh 19:9), forming a domain quite independent of the Israelite tribes to the N—an independence that remained evident throughout the history of Israel in Palestine.

89 The N frontier of Judah was not well defined; and although Benjamin lay N of Judah, the territory of *Benjamin* was a political rather than a geographical boundary (Josh 15:20-63). By its history and inclination Benjamin was closely related to Ephraim and was not part of the "house of Judah." The area of Benjamin around *Ai* and *Gibeon* was the first foothold in the Palestinian mountains won by Joshua when the Israelites came up from Jericho (Josh 7-9; but → Biblical Archaeology, 74:81, 87 for the dating problem). This area was of strategic importance not only from the E but also from the W, as we see from the fact that Joshua was soon forced to wage war with the Shephelah kings who came up from the W through the Valley of Aijalon to attack Israel (→ 74 above). The Philistines used the same route in an attempt to crush Saul and the Israelite strongholds in the mountains of Benjamin (1 Sam 10:5; 13-14:31). Saul's home and capital was at *Gibeah,* modern Tell el-Ful just N of Jerusalem, the site of interesting ASOR excavations (*BA* 27 [1964] 52-64; 28 [1965] 2-10; → Biblical Archaeology, 74:15, 104).

At the division of the monarchy (*ca.* 922), Benjamin seems to have gone with the N as one of the ten tribes (1 Kgs 11:30) against the two tribes of the S, Judah and the defunct Simeon. But Judah needed Benjaminite territory as a defensive buffer for Jerusalem, a claim mentioned in the glosses in 1 Kgs 12:21, 23 ("all the house of Judah *and the tribe of Benjamin*"). Thus the territorial claims of Judah were made to run from Beer-sheba in the S to Geba in the N; and Geba, about 5 mi. N of Jerusalem, was in Benjamin (2 Kgs 23:8). Judah strenuously resisted the attempt of the northern tribes to push into this area of Benjamin (1 Kgs 15:16-24). The strategic importance of the border fortresses in Benjamin for the defense of Judah from the N is vividly pictured in the imaginative account of how an Assyrian king would attack Jerusalem (Isa 10:28-34), proceeding from Ai (Aiath), 10 mi. N of Jerusalem, to Nob on the Mt. of Olives overlooking Jerusalem. See *BA* 44 (1981) 8-19.

90 (b) CITIES OF JUDAH. *Hebron* was historically the center of Judah's power, as David implicitly bore witness when he was crowned there as Judah's first king (2 Sam 2:1-4; cf. 15:7-10). At 3300 ft. above sea level, this is the highest city in Judah, controlling to the W the roads to the Shephelah cities of Mareshah and Lachish, and to the E the road to En-gedi on the Dead Sea.

Seemingly once called Kiriath-arba (Josh 14:15; 15:13), Hebron was the site where Sarah and Abraham were buried (Gen 23; 25:9). At the nearby shrine of Mamre (modern Ramet el-Khalil; cf. *BTS* 70 [1965]), Abraham received the divine promises and saw God (Gen 13:14-18; 18; → Institutions, 76:28). Isaac also died at Hebron (Gen 35:27). Today the tombs of the patriarchs are venerated under the mosque, once a church, that stands in the middle of Hebron, adjacent to magnificent Herodian remains (see *BARev* 11 [3, 1985] 26-43). The reservoir in Hebron recalls the site of David's punishment of the murderers of Saul's son Ishbaal (2 Sam 4:12). For excavations of Hebron, see *BA* 28 (1965) 30-32; also *BTS* 80 (1966). Maccabean battles were fought in the region just N of Hebron, centered at *Beth-zur,* excavated by Albright (→ Biblical Archaeology, 74:15, 135).

91 *Bethlehem* (or Ephrathah), 15 mi. N of Hebron and 5 mi. S of Jerusalem, was not in itself an important city of Judah (Mic 5:2), but it acquired importance as the ancestral home of David (Ruth 1:1; 4:22; 1 Sam 16; Luke 2:4; Matt 2:5; John 7:42). A church built by Constantine and modified by the Crusaders stands over the grotto traditionally associated with Jesus' birth, and fields E of Bethlehem are most suitable to have been the shepherds' fields of Luke 2:8,15. "Rachel's Tomb," which stands today at the N entry to Bethlehem, represents a confusion based on erroneous glosses in Gen 35:19; 48:7 and on an implicit statement in Matt 2:18; Rachel's burial place in Benjamin (1 Sam 10:2; Jer 31:15) is far more plausible. (*BTS* 42 [1961]; *NatGeog* [Dec. 1926].)

Just SE of Bethlehem stands the truncated-cone hill of *Herodium,* the fortress and castle where Herod the Great was buried—not far from the town whose children he slew, according to Matt 2:16. (→ Biblical Archaeology, 74:141.) From here down to the Dead Sea is the grazing country of the Ta'amireh bedouin who discovered the Dead Sea Scrolls. Nearby was Tekoa, the hometown of the prophet Amos (Amos 1:1).

92 *Jerusalem,* "the holy mountain, fairest of heights, the joy of all the earth" (Ps 48:2), did not come into Judah's possession until David's time (*ca.* 1000). In a stroke of genius, after capturing Jebusite Jerusalem (2 Sam 5:6-10), he moved his capital from the provincial and clearly southern Hebron to this border city with no northern or southern affiliations. We read of its Canaanite prehistory as a shrine of El Elyon and perhaps of Zedek in Gen 14:18 (cf. Josh 10:1; → Institutions, 76:41, 16). Intense archaeological excavations have cast much light on the history of the city (→ Biblical Archaeology, 74:7, 8, 12, 19, 105-7, 109, 138-40, 150-55).

The mount covered by Jerusalem in its era of greatness is set off on three sides by valleys. On the E there is a sharp decline into the Kidron (Cedron), a wadi that has a swift stream when rainfall is plentiful. This valley separates Jerusalem from the higher Mt. of Olives, from which one gains a splendid view of the city (2 Sam 15:23,30; 2 Kgs 23:6; John 18:1). Despite is narrowness, the Kidron is traditionally identified as the Valley of Jehoshaphat where Joel 3:2-12 places the gathering of all nations for judgment. On the W of Jerusalem is the Valley of Hinnom (Josh 15:8; 18:16), swinging around the southern end of the mount to meet the Kidron in the SE at Haceldama (Akeldama of Acts 1:19). This valley (= Ge-Hinnom [Gehenna]) acquired an unpleasant reputation because it was used for the burning of garbage and the worship of pagan gods (1 Kgs 11:7; 2 Kgs 16:3; 23:10), whence the derived meaning of Gehenna as "hell" (Matt 5:22). The mount itself was split into two hills, W and E, by a much shallower valley, scarcely visible today, called the Tyropoeon (Cheese-makers'). The Canaanite (Jebusite) city that fell to David

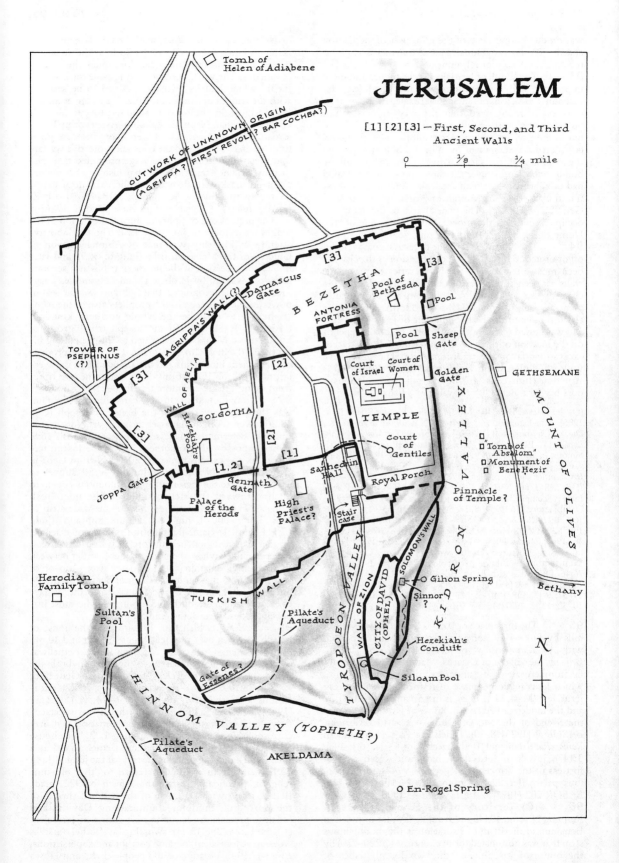

JERUSALEM

[1] [2] [3] — First, Second, and Third Ancient Walls

0   ⅛   ¼ mile

Tomb of Helen of Adiabene

OUTWORK OF UNKNOWN ORIGIN
(AGRIPPA? FIRST REVOLT? BAR COCHBA?)

AGRIPPA'S WALL (?)

Damascus Gate

[3]

BEZETHA

Pool of Bethesda

[3]

Pool

ANTONIA FORTRESS

Pool

Sheep Gate

TOWER OF PSEPHINUS (?)

WALL OF AELIA

[3]

[2]

Court of Israel   Court of Women

Golden Gate

GETHSEMANE

GOLGOTHA

Hezekiah's Pool

[3]

TEMPLE

Court of Gentiles

"Tomb of Absalom"

Monument of Bene Hezir

MOUNT OF OLIVES

[1,2]

[2]

[1]

Sanhedrin Hall

Royal Porch

Joppa Gate

Gennath Gate

High Priest's Palace?

Stair case

Pinnacle of Temple?

Palace of the Herods

Solomon's Wall

Herodian Family Tomb

Gihon Spring

Bethany

TURKISH WALL

Sinnor?

Sultan's Pool

Pilate's Aqueduct

Gate of Essenes?

Hezekiah's Conduit

N

TYROPOEON VALLEY

WALL OF ZION

CITY OF DAVID (OPHEL)

Siloam Pool

KIDRON VALLEY

HINNOM VALLEY (TOPHETH?)

Pilate's Aqueduct

AKELDAMA

O En-Rogel Spring

was on the southern end of the E hill where the Kidron and the Tyropoeon gradually come together to a point, meeting the Valley of Hinnom.

93 The W hill of Jerusalem is the higher and more impressive, and for centuries was identified (e.g., by Josephus) as Zion or ancient Jerusalem. Today it is universally recognized that the city of David and Solomon was on the E hill. (On the inclusion of the W hill in the city, → Biblical Archaeology, 74:140.) David conquered the SE spur of the hill, and Solomon pushed the confines of the city farther N on the E hill by building the Temple over the threshing floor that David had bought from Araunah the Jebusite (2 Sam 24:18) — traditionally the Mt. Moriah of Abraham's sacrifice in Gen 22:2; 2 Chr 3:1. The general area of the Temple is occupied today by the superb Moslem mosque of "the Dome of the Rock" (→ Institutions, 76:42).

94 The N was the one side of Jerusalem not closed off or protected by a valley, and expansion of the city has been most often toward the N. A series of protective walls has been built at various times in the history of the city's expansion, and three of them are prominently mentioned by Josephus (*J.W.* 5.4 § 136ff.). The dispute about the site of the Holy Sepulcher of Jesus (who died and was buried outside the city — John 19:20,42) depends on the location of the wall in Jesus' time. Clearly, recent excavations favor the traditional site. The impressive walls of Old Jerusalem visible today are of Turkish construction (16th cent. AD) on Herodian foundations — possibly Jerusalem's "third wall" (→ History, 75:175).

(ON JERUSALEM: Ben Dov, M., *In the Shadow of the Temple* [NY, 1985]. Join-Lambert, M., *Jerusalem* [NY, 1958]. Kenyon, K., *Digging Up Jerusalem* [NY, 1974]. Mazar, B., *The Mountain of the Lord* [NY, 1975]. Peters, F. E., *Jerusalem* [Princeton, 1985]. Simons, J., *Jerusalem in the Old Testament* [Leiden, 1952]. Wilkinson, J., *Jerusalem as Jesus Knew It* [London, 1978]. Yadin, Y. [ed.], *Jerusalem Revealed* [Jerusalem, 1975]. Also *EAEHL* 2. 579–650; *IDB* 2. 843–66; *IDBSup* 475–77; and *Jerusalem* [Israel Pocket Library, compiled from *EncJud;* Jerusalem, 1973]. ON CITY OF DAVID: *Arch* 33 [6, 1980] 8–17; *BA* 42 [1979] 165–71; 44 [1981] 161–70; *BARev* 5 [4, 1979] 37–49; 7 [4, 1981] 16–43; 11 [6, 1985] 22–38. ON HOLY SEPULCHER: *Arch* 31 [4, 1978] 6–13; *BA* 30 [1967] 74–90; 44 [1981] 21–26; *BARev* 12 [3, 1986] 26–45 [discussing V. Corbo's 3-vol. work in Italian]. ON TEMPLE ARCHITECTURE: → Biblical Archaeology, 74:109; → Institutions, 76:46. ON WALLS AND GATES: *BA* 40 [1977] 11–23; 44 [1981] 108–15; *BARev* 6 [4, 1980] 30–59; 7 [3, 1981] 34–46; 9 [1, 1983] 24–37; 9 [2, 1983] 40–59; 11 [3, 1985] 44–52; 12 [6, 1986] 20–52; 13 [3, 1987] 46–57; *IEJ* 18 [1968] 98–125.)

95 The birthplace of JBap is located in the Judean hills by Luke 1:39; today it is traditionally associated with *Ain Karim* just W of Jerusalem (*BTS* 61 [1964]). *Bethany,* the village of Lazarus, Mary, and Martha, "not far from Jerusalem, just under two miles" (John 11:1,18), which Jesus made his place of residence when visiting Jerusalem (Mark 11:1, 14:3), is the Ananiah of Neh 11:32 and the modern El Azariyeh, just E of Jerusalem around the S end of the Mt. of Olives (see W. F. Albright, *BASOR* 9 [1923] 8–10). Israeli excavations at modern *Ramat Rahel* (ancient Beth-haccherem of Jer 6:1; Neh 3:14?), just S of Jerusalem, have uncovered a royal fortress of the 7th cent. BC, perhaps Jehoiakim's luxurious palace (Jer 22:13–19; see *BA* 24 [1961] 98–118; *BASOR* 202 [1971] 6–16; *EAEHL* 4. 1000–9).

96 **(C) Territory of the House of Joseph.** Running N some 40–45 mi. from the border of Judah in Benjamin to the Plain of Esdraelon is the mountainous strip that was dominated for five centuries (1220–720) by the house of Joseph, i.e., the two Joseph tribes of Ephraim and half of Manasseh (Gen 48). This tribal group was the chief rival of the house of Judah for power

in Israelite Palestine. When in the biblical account the Israelites entered Palestine under Joshua, the strongest tribes, Ephraim and Manasseh, occupied the central mountains. The weaker tribes (leaving aside the house of Judah, which had its own history) had to be satisfied with the fringes of these mountains (e.g., Benjamin, and Dan [original localization]) or with territory to the N in Galilee (Issachar, Naphtali, Zebulun, Asher) or in Transjordan (Reuben, Gad). These were more insecure positions, open to attack; and the constant protective warfare that these lesser tribes had to wage prevented their rise to power. (The "traditional" tribal history that we are reporting masks a much more complicated state of affairs; cf. reconstructions by K. Elliger, *IDB* 4. 701–10; Z. Kallai, *Historical Geography of the Bible* [Leiden, 1986].)

The pretensions of Ephraim during the period of the judges are evident in Judg 8:1; 12:1. The first abortive attempt at kingship was that of Abimelech, son of Gideon, of the Manasseh tribe (Judg 6:15; 9); and later in 922 the secession of the northern tribes as a separate kingdom was led by Jeroboam I, an Ephraimite (1 Kgs 11:26; 12). The recognition that Ephraim was the seat of power in the N is seen in the prophets' use of the name "Ephraim" to describe the whole northern kingdom (Hos 6:4; Isa 11:13). To the Joseph tribal group of Ephraim and Manasseh, described as "prince among his brothers" (Deut 33:16), was granted "the finest produce of the ancient mountains and the abundance of the everlasting hills" (33:15); yet this did not stop the two tribes from being greedy for more (Isa 9:20–21).

97 (a) EPHRAIM. In the early history Ephraim was the dominant tribe in the house of Joseph (Gen 48:20), even though Manasseh was larger. Notice how Ephraim determines Manasseh's territory in Josh 16:9. Ephraim possessed the southern half of the Joseph territory: its possessions ran some 20 mi. N from Geba in Benjamin (the N border of Judah; → 89 above) to Tappuah and to the region where the mountains begin to decline toward the rich plain near Shechem (Josh 17:8–9). The Bible speaks of this 20-mi.-wide strip of hills, 1000–3000 ft. high, as "Mount Ephraim" (Judg 17:1; 1 Sam 1:1). Rainfall is plentiful and the soil is fertile, so that it is a region of fruit orchards and olive trees. Except on the S where there is no natural border between Ephraim and Benjamin (and Judah), the steep drop-off of the Ephraimite plateau to the Plain of Sharon on the W, the Rift Valley on the E, and Manasseh to the N gave Ephraim natural strength and aloofness. The most important cities were Bethel and Shiloh.

98 *Bethel,* which Josh 16:1 gives to the house of Joseph, was just over the Benjaminite border and 10 mi. N of Jerusalem. Once called Luz (Josh 18:13), Bethel was a sanctuary in patriarchal times figuring in both the Abraham and Jacob cycles of narratives (Gen 12:8; 13:3–4; 28:10–22; 35:1–16; → Institutions, 76:27). Excavations at Bethel (*BA* 19 [1956] 36–43; *AASOR* 39 [1968]; *EAEHL* 1. 190–93) show that it was spectacularly destroyed in the 13th cent., information that may correspond with the statement in Judg 1:22: "The house of Joseph went up against Bethel." Bethel served as a shrine and a rallying place in the time of the judges (Judg 20:18); and in an attempt to return to "that old-time religion," Jeroboam I, after the schism of 922, made Bethel, along with Dan, one of the national shrines of the northern kingdom, counteracting Davidic and Judahite pretensions at the upstart shrine of Jerusalem (1 Kgs 12:26–29; 13:11). Worship at Bethel (just as worship at Jerusalem) became corrupt and superstitious; Amos (7:10–17) castigated the people there, and Hosea (4:15; 5:8; see gloss in Josh 7:2) mockingly changed its name from Bethel ("House of God") to Beth-aven

("House of Wickedness"). On nearby Ai, → Biblical Archaeology, 74:81, 87.

99   *Shiloh,* standing on a rocky plain in the heart of Ephraim's territory, had its greatest importance in the period of the judges. It was a place of assembly for the tribes (Josh 22:9,12; Judg 21:19ff.), and the Ark of the Covenant came to rest there in a permanent building (1 Sam 1; 4:4; → Institutions, 76:37). It was destroyed by the Philistines *ca.* 1050 shortly after the battle of Aphek/ Eben-ezer and reduced to ruins (Jer 7:12–14; 26:9). Yet from Shiloh came the prophet who anointed Jeroboam and split Solomon's kingdom (1 Kgs 11:29; → Biblical Archaeology, 74:104).

The prophet-priest Samuel came from *Ramathaim- zophim* (Ramah) in W Ephraim; this place may have been the Arimathea that was the home of Joseph who took Jesus' body and buried it (Luke 23:50–51).

100   (b) MANASSEH (SAMARIA). From the time of the formation of the northern kingdom (922), the area controlled by Manasseh emerged into greater impor- tance. The hill country of Manasseh is lower than Ephraim, with only isolated peaks rising above 2000 ft. In a strip some 15 mi. long and 20 mi. wide, Manasseh runs N of Ephraim to the Plain of Esdraelon. Rich plains and beautiful valleys grace the area; and although the soil is not as fertile as in Ephraim, the climate permits abundant grain production. The natural boundaries of Manasseh were less determinate than those of Ephraim, and so, when the house of Joseph extended its power, expansion was to the W and N of Manasseh, toward the plains of Sharon and Esdraelon respectively. The cities of most interest were Shechem, Tirzah, Samaria, and Dothan.

101   *Shechem.* In S Manasseh, as one descends from Ephraim, the broad plain of Mahneh is singularly beautiful. The W of the plain is hemmed in by the high mountains of Gerizim (2910 ft.) and Ebal (3100 ft.). Between these two mountains, going from E to W, is a valley designed by nature to be the main thoroughfare for traffic from Judah and Ephraim to the N. At the mouth of this valley stood Shechem (Sichem, modern Balatah), the most important Palestinian biblical city after Jerusalem.

Shechem was the first place in Canaan that Abraham visited, and the oak of Moreh was a shrine even then (Gen 12:6; → Institutions, 76:26). When Jacob returned to Canaan from Haran, he settled at Shechem (Gen 33:18–19), and this spot was Jacob's choice gift to the sons of Joseph (Gen 48:22: "one *portion*" = Hebr *šěkem*). Shechem was seemingly in the hands of the Israelites already at the time of Joshua's invasion (perhaps a pre- Joshua conquest lies behind the etiological story in Gen 34); and there, between Ebal and Gerizim, the great covenant of Yahweh with Israel was renewed (Deut 11:29–30; 27; Josh 8:30–35; 24). During the time of the judges there seems to have been a mixed cult at Shechem, as the men of the city backed Abimelech for king with money from the temple of "Baal of the Covenant" or "El of the Covenant" (Judg 9:4,46). It was at Shechem that the northern tribes rejected Rehoboam son of Solomon in favor of Jeroboam I as king (1 Kgs 12:1–25). This king made Shechem his temporary capital; and even when the center of administration and power in the northern kingdom moved to Samaria, Shechem remained the focus of the covenant renewal ceremony (from which Deut drew its legal code). In NT times Jesus stopped at the well of Shechem for a drink and engaged a Samaritan woman in conversation (John 4:4–42). This story reminds us that Mt. Gerizim's slope overlooking Shechem was the holy place of Samaritan worship and the site of the Samaritan temple. Today the Samaritans

survive at Nablus, Roman Neapolis, built 2 mi. farther W in the same valley; and at Passover they proceed to Gerizim's summit to slaughter animals for their celebra- tion—the only remnant of the blood-sacrifice of Israel (*NatGeog* [Jan. 1920]; *BTS* 28 [1960]).

(→ Biblical Archaeology, 74:23, 120, 135. Wright, G. E., *Shechem* [NY, 1965]. *BA* 28 [1965] 18–26; *BASOR* 204 [1971] 2–17; 205 [1972] 20–35; *EAEHL* 4. 1083–94. On Gerizim: *BA* 43 [1980] 217–21. On Ebal: *BARev* 11 [1, 1985] 26–43; 12 [1, 1986] 42–53.)

102   *Tirzah.* If in a journey N from Ephraim, one does not cut W through the Gerizim-Ebal valley but continues to the NE, at the head of the great Wadi Far'ah, which goes off SE to the Jordan valley (→ 65 above), one encounters Tirzah (Tell el-Far'ah, excavated by R. de Vaux; → Biblical Archaeology, 74:18, 113). This town served as capital of the northern kingdom from Jeroboam's time until Omri's time (910–870; 1 Kgs 14:17; 15:21,33; 16:6–23). The site was of strategic importance for the defense of Manasseh from the E, since the Wadi Far'ah was a natural invasion route. (It may have been used by some of the Israelites when they came into Canaan, whence the confusion in passages like Deut 11:30, 27:4; Josh 8:30, which imply that when the Israel- ites crossed the Jordan they soon came to Ebal and Gerizim.)

103   *Samaria.* Retracing our steps and cutting W through the Gerizim-Ebal valley and then swinging N, we find before us the majestic hill of Samaria, Tirzah's successor and the greatest capital of Israel. (We have an idea of the short distances in this area if we realize that Tirzah is 7 mi. NE of Shechem, and Samaria is 7 mi. WNW of Shechem.) King Omri's move from Tirzah to Samaria (*ca.* 870; 1 Kgs 16:24) was in part motivated by political geography. Tirzah, protected at the back by mountains on the W, was open to invasion from the E, in particular from Syria, Omri's chief enemy; Samaria was on the other side of these mountains, which were a barrier against its enemies approaching from the E. On the other hand, Samaria had free access to routes to the NW where Phoenicia, Israel's new ally, was situated with its rich ports and commercial possibilities.

An isolated hill, crowned by the magnificent build- ings of Omri and his son Ahab, Samaria must have been the most beautiful city in Israel: "the proud crown of the drunkards of Ephraim, the fading flower of its glorious beauty which is at the head of a rich valley" (Isa 28:1; → Biblical Archaeology, 74:113–15, 143). For 150 years this city so dominated the northern kingdom that Israel could be called "Samaria," just as Judah was sometimes called "Jerusalem" (Ezek 16:46—thus it is important for the reader of the Bible to distinguish between the city of Samaria and the district of Samaria; the latter means the territory of Manasseh or sometimes the whole northern kingdom). Even after its fall to the Assyrians in 722, the city retained its strategic importance as the capital suc- cessively of an Assyrian province of Samaria, of a Persian province (Ezra 4:17; Neh 3:33–34 [4:1–2]), and of a Syrian district (1 Macc 10:30). Herod the Great rebuilt the city as Sebaste in honor of the emperor Augustus (Gk *sebastos*), but the district retained the name Samaria. Thus the NT references to Samaria are to the district N of Judea (Acts 1:8; 8). In the last centuries BC "Samaritans" came to designate not only the physical inhabitants of Samaria but also the adherents of a deviationist form of Israelite religion centered at Mt. Gerizim. See the anti- Samaritan story in 2 Kgs 17:24–34; also F. M. Cross, *HTR* 59 (1966) 201–11; → History, 75:127.

104   *Dothan.* Continuing into N Manasseh past Samaria, the main route leads to Dothan, a city that guarded the descent from Manasseh into the Plain of Esdraelon. Dothan was excavated by an American expedition under the direction of J. P. Free in 1953 to 1960 (*EAEHL* 1. 337–39). Near Dothan Joseph was sold into slavery by his brothers (Gen 37:17), and Elisha visited Dothan (2 Kgs 6:13).

105   (D) Plain of Esdraelon (Jezreel). The mountains and hills of the house of Joseph were cut off from Galilee, the domain of the northernmost tribes, by a broad valley that runs NW–SE from behind the Bay of Haifa to the Rift Valley. The main part of this valley-plain as its sweeps in from the sea to Mt. Gilboa (technically the 20 mi. from Jokneam to the area of Ibleam and En-gannim [Jennin]) is designated by some geographers as Esdraelon, whereas Jezreel is the name given to the arm that shoots off to the E between Gilboa and the Hill of Moreh through the Beth-shan gap into the Jordan. However, since Esdraelon is simply the Gk form of Jezreel (Hebr *Yizrĕʿeʾl*), it will be convenient to designate here the respective sections of the plain as W and E Esdraelon. See *BARev* 6 (2, 1980) 30–44.

106   (a) West Esdraelon. At some points this part of the Plain of Esdraelon is 20 mi. wide, rising gently from 80 ft. above sea level to 330 ft. near En-gannim. The river Kishon flows through the plain on its way to the sea. This is the broadest expanse of farmland in Palestine. Israelites coming from the desert into the land that was supposed to be flowing with milk and honey must have thought "This is the place," as they looked down from the hills of Manasseh upon the rich valley. Esdraelon had strategic importance on both an international and a national scale.

107   (i) *International importance.* Esdraelon was the plain through which ran the main route between Egypt and Syria. The plain's S side is flanked by the Carmel mountain range, and armies or commerce that came up the coast from Egypt through Philistia and along the fringes of the Plain of Sharon had to pass NE through one of the four passes in the Carmel range to reach the plain. Consequently, four fortresses guarding these passes were built on the southern edge of Esdraelon: Jokneam, Megiddo, Taanach, and Ibleam. The route past *Megiddo* was strategically the most important, as corroborated by an ancient Egyptian report: "The capture of Megiddo is as the capture of a thousand towns" (*ANET* 237). Here in 1468 the greatest of the Egyptian pharaohs, Thutmosis III, reportedly fought the remnants of the Hyksos—a victory that forged a world empire. Solomon and later the kings of the northern kingdom fortified the city magnificently (1 Kgs 9:15; for a detailed account of the archaeology of Megiddo, → Biblical Archaeology, 74:35–43). Here in 609 the good king Josiah, most pious of Judah's kings, died in a vain attempt to block the passage of an Egyptian army (2 Kgs 22:19). Fittingly the visionary of the NT Rev places the assembly for the final world battle at this war-scarred site of "Mount" Megiddo (Hebr *har Mĕgiddô* = Gk *Armagedōn* in Rev 16:16). Few scholars accept W. F. Albright's thesis that settlement alternated between Megiddo and nearby *Taanach* (Judg 5:19, "Taanach by the waters of Megiddo"). For the 1960s excavations of Taanach, see *BA* 30 (1967) 2–27; *RB* 76 (1969) 580–86; *EAEHL* 4. 1138–47; → Biblical Archaeology, 74:13, 63, 75, 120.

108   (ii) *National importance.* Esdraelon was important also on the scale of internal Israelite history. As long as it remained in Canaanite hands (Judg 1:27), the northern tribes (Issachar, Naphtali, Zebulun, and Asher) were cut off from the house of Joseph. Consequently, in the period of the judges, there was a series of battles for control of the plain. In the 12th cent. Deborah and Barak gathered the northern tribes and the Joseph tribes to fight against Sisera and his Canaanites. When the river Kishon flooded the plain and mud made the Canaanite chariots useless, the Israelites won at Taanach (Judg 4:7; 5:20–21). The Philistines' victory over the Israelites at Aphek/Eben-ezer in 1050 (1 Sam 4) gave them control over the plains of Sharon and Esdraelon; and this happened again when they defeated Saul (*ca.* 1000) at Gilboa (1 Sam 29:1; 31).

109   (b) East Esdraelon. The mention of Mt. Gilboa brings us to the strategically important continuation of Esdraelon to the E, sometimes called Jezreel or the Beth-shan Valley. This narrow corridor was a main route for continuing the journey from W Esdraelon into the Jordan Valley and then up into Transjordan and on to Damascus. Running ESE, about 13 mi. long and 2 mi. wide, Esdraelon drops almost 1000 ft. from the entrance between Gilboa and Moreh until it reaches the Jordan Valley.

Since E Esdraelon was a corridor to and from Transjordan, it frequently served as a path for invaders. In the battle between Gideon and the Midianite raiders, Gideon encamped on Mt. Gilboa at Harod on the S side of the entrance to this corridor, while Midian was opposite on the N side at the Hill of Moreh (Judg 6:33; 7:1). Exactly the same positions were taken by Saul and the Philistines (1 Sam 28:3ff.); and we find Saul slipping through the Philistine lines at night to consult the witch at Endor just N of Moreh. As soon as Saul was defeated at Gilboa, the Philistines returned through the corridor and hung his body on the walls of Beth-shan (1 Sam 31:8–10; → 64 above).

110   When Omri and Ahab made Samaria the capital of the northern kingdom, they paid both the beauty and the importance of the Valley of Esdraelon a tribute by keeping a palace at the town of *Jezreel*, standing at the W entrance to the corridor leading to Beth-shan. The tragic incident of Naboth's vineyard and the bloody death of Jezebel took place here (1 Kgs 21:1; 2 Kgs 9:30; 10:11). The prophet Hosea named his son Jezreel as a threat of divine punishment for the crimes committed there: "I will break the bow of Israel in the Valley of Jezreel." Yet, playing on the meaning of the name Jezreel ("May God sow"), Hosea also saw in this name a divine promise of fertility: "The earth shall respond to the grain and wine and oil, and these shall respond to Jezreel, and I will sow him for myself in the land" (Hos 1:4–5; 2:22–23).

111   In NT times Jesus is recorded to have been in the Plain of Esdraelon when he raised to life the son of the widow of *Nain* (Luke 7:11–17), a town on the N slope of the Hill of Moreh. NE of Moreh stands *Mt. Tabor*, solitary and symmetrical. (The closeness of the two made interpreters think that the "Tabor and Hermon" of Ps 89:13 were Tabor and Moreh; this misunderstanding won for Moreh the name "Little Hermon.") Tabor is the hill from which to the NW, the N, and the NE radiated the tribal frontiers of Zebulun, Naphtali, and Issachar. That is probably why Barak gathered his forces on Tabor (Judg 4:6). Tabor controls the entrance from Esdraelon along the main road to the Lake of Galilee, and Jesus must have passed it in his travels from Nazareth. It is the traditional but unlikely site proposed for the "high mountain" of the transfiguration (Mark 9:2).

Basalt is found in the region from Tabor NE along the Lake of Galilee. Some (e.g., F.-M. Abel) would relate this to the lava flow from the Jebel Druze in Transjordan (→ 53 above). But Baly (*Geography* 24) thinks that Moreh may have been a volcano.

112   (E) Galilee. When we cross the Plain of Esdraelon on our journey N, we come to an area which figures surprisingly little in OT history but which for

Christians was to crown the expectations of that history; for on the N side of Esdraelon rise the hills of Galilee, and just 3 mi. into these hills stands Nazareth, the home of Jesus. Situated between Esdraelon and Dan, Galilee extends some 30–40 mi. from S to N, and some 20–25 mi. from E to W. On the W is the coastal Plain of Asher; on the E is the Rift Valley with the Lake of Galilee and the upper reaches of the Jordan. There is a S or lower Galilee and a N or upper Galilee; the division line is an E-W fault running roughly from the direction of Acco (Ptolemais) to just N of the Lake of Galilee. (See *NatGeog* [Dec. 1965; Dec. 1967].)

113 (a) SOUTH GALILEE. This area consists of gentle hills not exceeding 2000 ft. in height; in parts it is rather like the Shephelah of the S (→ 73 above). In OT times the larger part of lower Galilee was occupied by Zebulun, with Asher to the W on the coast (unless we accept Noth's hypothesis; → 81 above), Issachar to the SE, and Naphtali to the N and E. The fact that these surrounding tribes served as a buffer gave Zebulun the best position among the four northern tribes. Nevertheless, Galilee seems to have been outside the mainstream of Israelite life as it is preserved in the biblical records. Galilee fell to the Assyrians after the Syro-Ephraimite war of 735 (2 Kgs 15:29); yet Isaiah (9:1–2), speaking of the land of Zebulun and Naphtali as "Galilee of the Gentiles," promised that the people there who walked in darkness would see a great light (also cf. Matt 4:15–16). In Hellenistic times there was a heavy population of Jews in Galilee (1 Macc 5:9–23). However, during the period of Jesus' ministry when Galilee was ruled by Herod Antipas, it was still treated with disdain by the "pure Jews" of Judea (John 7:52), which was under the control of a Roman governor (Luke 3:1).

114 The terrain of S Galilee is marked by a series of basins watered by drainage from the surrounding hills. The floors of the basins are fertile alluvium and lend themselves to farming, while the towns climb the adjacent hillsides. This was the region described so vividly in Jesus' parables: fields separated by hedgerows and stone fences; flocks pastured on the hills; towns set on mountain tops; etc. Two towns of S Galilee mentioned in the NT, Nazareth and Cana, are built on the sides of rich basins. *Cana* is probably not the now traditional pilgrim site of Kefr Kenna, 3 mi. NE of Nazareth, but rather Khirbet Qana, 9 mi. N of Nazareth (→ Biblical Archaeology, 74:146). *Jotapata,* where Josephus was defeated by the Romans, is close by (→ Apocrypha, 67:127). The main town of the region in NT times was *Sepphoris,* the district capital, on the road from Ptolemais (Acco) to Tiberias. Excavated in the 1980s, it was a large, cosmopolitan city easily visible from Nazareth during Jesus' lifetime (*BA* 49 [1986] 4–19). The postbiblical rabbinical school of *Beth-she'arim* (*BA* 40 [1977] 167–71) in the Plain of Esdraelon ultimately moved to Sepphoris, and there Rabbi Judah the Prince spent the last 17 years of his life (*ca.* AD 200) codifying the Mishna (→ Apocrypha, 67:136). Thus Galilee gave birth both to Christianity and to postbiblical talmudic Judaism (→ Biblical Archaeology, 74:137, 156).

115 (b) NORTH GALILEE. Here the terrain is quite different, much higher (3000–4000 ft.) and truly mountainous. Heavy rainfall and strong winds are characteristic of this region, which is the beginning of the Lebanon mountain chain to the N. This land of Naphtali had little recorded importance in either the OT or the NT, except as a place of refuge where inaccessible heights offered the possibility of resisting stronger armies. *Gischala* was a strong outpost in the Jewish revolt against the Romans; and Josephus's enemy, John, came from there. For the story of this revolt, → History, 75:191–92. *Safed* (Seph or Sephet), on a mountain top (Matt 5:14) with a splendid view reaching to the Lake of Galilee and the Huleh Basin, also figured in the Jewish revolt. It was the center of renewed Jewish colonization *ca.* AD 1500, and here a Jewish school of mystics produced the Shulhan Aruk and some important expositions of the Cabala. Safed mysticism is the most recent flowering of the zeal for God of which this small land of Palestine has been a unique witness for so many centuries.

74

BIBLICAL ARCHAEOLOGY

Robert North, S.J.　　　Philip J. King *

BIBLIOGRAPHY

1　　　Aharoni, *LBib; The Archaeology of the Land of Israel* (Phl, 1982). Albright, *AP.* Amiran, R., *Ancient Pottery of the Holy Land* (Jerusalem, 1969). Avigad, N., *Discovering Jerusalem* (Nash, 1983). Aviram, J. (ed.), *Biblical Archaeology Today* (Jerusalem, 1985). Avi-Yonah, *EAEHL.* Báez-Camargo, G., *Archaeological Commentary on the Bible* (GC, 1986). Beazley, M., *The World Atlas of Archaeology* (London, 1985). Brown, R. E., *Recent Discoveries and the Biblical World* (Wilmington, 1983). De Vaux, *AI.* Dever, W., "Archaeology," *IDBSup* 44–52; "Archaeological Method in Israel: A Continuing Revolution," *BA* 43 (1980) 41–48; "Syro-Palestinian and Biblical Archaeology," in *HBMI* 31–74. Dever, W. and H. D. Lance (eds.), *A Manual for Field Archaeologists* (NY, 1978). Finegan, J., *The Archaeology of the New Testament: Jesus* (Princeton, 1969); *The Archaeology of the New Testament: Early Apostles* (Boulder, 1981). Franken, H. and C. Franken-Battershill, *A Primer of OT Archaeology* (Leiden, 1963). Geraty, L. and L. Herr (eds.), *The Archaeology of Jordan and Other Studies* (Berrien Springs, 1986). Hadidi, A. (ed.), *Studies in the History and Archaeology of Jordan* (Amman, 1982). Harding, G. L., *The Antiquities of Jordan* (London, 1959). Harrison, R. K. (ed.), *Major Cities of the Biblical World* (NY, 1985). Hoppe, L. J., *What Are They Saying About Biblical Archaeology* (NY, 1984). Kenyon, K., *Archaeology in the Holy Land* (4th ed.; London, 1979). King, P. J., *American Archaeology in the Mideast* (Phl, 1983). Lance, H. D., *The OT and the Archaeologist* (Phl, 1981). Lapp, P., *Biblical Archaeology and History* (NY, 1969). Leakey, R. and R. Lewin, *Origins* (NY, 1977). Meyers, E. M. and J. F. Strange, *Archaeology,*

the Rabbis and Early Christianity (Nash, 1981). Moorey. P. R. S., *Excavation in Palestine* (CBW; GR, 1981). Moorey, P. R. S. and P. Parr (eds.), *Archaeology in the Levant* (Fest. K. Kenyon; Warminster, 1978). Murphy-O'Connor, J., *The Holy Land: An Archaeological Guide from Earliest Times to 1700* (2d ed.; Oxford, 1986). North, R., *Stratigraphia Geobiblica: Biblical Near East Archeology and Geography* (3d ed.; Rome, 1970). Saunders, E. W., "Jewish Christianity and Palestinian Archaeology," *RelSRev* 9 (1983) 201–5. Segal, A., "Archaeological Research in Israel 1960–1985," *BTB* 16 (1986) 73–77. Shanks, H. and B. Mazar, *Recent Archaeology in the Land of Israel* (Washington, 1984). Stern, E., *Material Culture of the Land of the Bible in the Persian Period 538–332 BC* (Warminster, 1982). Thomas, D. W. (ed.), *Archaeology and OT Study* (London, 1967). Thompson, H., *Biblical Archaeology* (NY, 1987). Thompson, T. L., *The Settlement of Sinai and the Negev in the Bronze Age* (Tavo BB; Wiesbaden, 1975). Van Beek, G., "Archaeology," *IDB* 1. 195–207. Vogel, E. K., *Bibliography of Holy Land Sites* (2 parts; Cincinnati, 1982). Wilkinson, J., *Jerusalem as Jesus Knew It* (London, 1978). Wright, G. E., "The Phenomenon of American Archaeology in the Near East," *Near Eastern Archaeology in the 20th Century* (Fest. N. Glueck; ed. J. Sanders; GC, 1970) 3–40; "What Archaeology Can and Cannot Do," *BA* 34 (1971) 70–76; *WBA.* On archaeology in Bible dictionaries, see *BA* 48 (1985) 222–37; for a survey of biblical archaeology, see *BA* 45 (1982) 73–107, 201–28.

2　　　　　　　　　　　　**OUTLINE**

* Article 74 by R. North in *JBC* has been thoroughly revised and brought up to date by P. J. King, to whom all changes and additions are to be credited.

GENERAL BACKGROUND

For excavation sites, see the chart (= section 3) on the next page.

4   (I) History of Biblical Excavations. Excavation in Palestine has given an "archaeological slant" to biblical research in our day. The organic growth of the movement may be crystallized about the names of pioneers whose contribution we will describe briefly.

5   Flavius Josephus was a Jew who wrote in Greek in Rome about AD 93 (→ Apocrypha, 67:127). He first used the word *archaiologia* as the title of a book, which is now generally called *Antiquities*. By *archaiologia* he meant "science of the past," or what we would call history. Although the work was lacking in empirical or critical research in the modern sense, it was nevertheless a mine of information diligently compiled. Through the centuries it has focused scholars' minds on "what we can learn about the Bible from outside the Bible." It inspired improved compilations about 1700 by Ugolini and Bochart, and by Keil and Kortleitner down to the present. The sum of this work may be characterized as "a classification of what we can learn about everyday life, especially in its material aspects, from between the lines of the Bible and other books that really aimed at recording political and cultural movements."

6   Heinrich Schliemann in 1873, at Troy in NW Turkey, proved his dream that successive settlements of the past could be dug up out of the ground, one from beneath the other. This was basically an application of excavation techniques inspired by the Italian Renaissance, especially by the rediscovery of Pompeii in 1790. But the digging in Italy and Greece had become largely an irresponsible and destructive search for "museum pieces." This was deplorably the case in Mesopotamia around 1850, as described in Seton Lloyd's *Foundations in the Dust* (London, 1947). Schliemann's "stratification" was naïve. He wrongly imagined each successive "city" sealed off by a mud pack from the ones that preceded and followed it. Schliemann too was at heart a fortune hunter. He financed his digging from a brother's share in the California gold rush and eventually went there himself, after a fling at Mycenae, the Gk homeland of Homer's Agamemnon. His digging at Troy had to be seriously corrected by later German and American expeditions. But Schliemann's audacity and insight deserve much credit for the "stratification principle" that is standard in Palestinian archaeology (→ 26–27 below). See *Arch* 33 (3, 1980) 42–51.

7   Félicien de Saulcy performed the earliest Palestinian excavations in NW Jerusalem in 1863. He discovered "Royal Tombs" containing several sarcophagi, one with an inscription. The burial chambers belonged to a Persian queen, Helen of Adiabene, who embraced the Jewish religion at the time of Christ, rather than to King David and his sons, as de Saulcy thought. Although the pioneering of E. Robinson in 1838 (→ Biblical Geography, 73:9), which had apparently included some casual digging along the Jerusalem North Wall, was of more lasting archaeological significance, de Saulcy and *la belle France* cannot be denied the merit of pioneering the first organized excavation. He also made important contributions to numismatics, the classification of ancient coins.

8   Charles Warren performed at the SE corner of Jerusalem in 1866 the daredevil engineering exploit formerly pictured as frontispiece of *PEQ*. Both the exploit and the periodical were the outcome of a new society or "Fund" established in London the preceding year. Its major achievement was the Survey of Palestine with the help of British army officers, whose work resulted in many important discoveries by digging. Warren's exploit proved that the corner of the Temple retaining wall (questionably the "Pinnacle") went down far deeper than ground level permitted one to see. In this same Kidron Valley, but farther S, Warren discovered the "shaft" leading up from the Gihon water source to the level of the Jebusite citadel.

9   Robert Koldewey meanwhile became a leading figure of the methodical German school of excavation. With W. Andrae he undertook generation-long expeditions at Babylon and Asshur around 1900. At Warka and several other Mesopotamian sites, a model scholarly conscientiousness replaced the "monument snatching" of earlier adventurers. Both in Egypt and at Troy the Koldewey methods were put into practice by W. Dörpfeld. Through Dörpfeld's apprentice G. A. Reisner, the German method later came to dominate the serious entry of Americans into the scene with the Harvard excavation of Samaria in 1908. (An American Palestine Exploration Society had indeed been founded as early as 1870, and the consul Selah Merrill published some of its results; but that particular enterprise did not survive.)

10   Charles Clermont-Ganneau, a Frenchman working with the British Fund, made some of the most important early discoveries in the Holy Land. In 1870 he recovered for the Louvre the stele of King Mesha found by F. A. Klein at Dibon. In 1871 he found the first of two surviving stone inscriptions threatening death to any non-Jew who entered the Temple area. He also found the Gezer boundary stone, and he reported on Ashkelon and other sites in his *Études* (London, 1897). He branded as a forgery the famous "Deuteronomy Scroll" offered by M. W. Shapira to the British Museum; see *BARev* 5 (4, 1979) 12–27.

3   **Chart of Excavations***

Site   *Importance*

Acco   Impt. commercial center and port city on Mediterranean; occup. 2000 BC–AD 324; Philistine domination. → 75, 103.
Ai   (et-Tell); impt. urban center in EB; unoccup. 2400–1220; reoccup. 1220–1050; problem of date of conquest. → 19,
                  63, 81, 87.
Ain Ghazal   Large Neolithic village at entrance to Amman; among oldest human statues ever found. → 52.
Aphek   Occup. from EB; captured by Joshua; here Philistines rallied against Israel; site of Herodian Antipatris. → 76, 85,
                  143.
Arad   Impt. Canaanite fortified city in EB; unoccup. in MB and LB; Israelite citadel and sanctuary; Arad Letters. →63,
                  83, 109, 115, 125.
Ashdod   Founded in MB; Philistine; Ark brought to temple of Dagon; became Azotus in Hell period. →95, 98, 108.
Ashkelon   Occup. from Bronze Age through Crusader period; conquered by Pharaoh Merneptah; major Philistine seaport. →
                  10, 95, 96, 101, 143.
Bab edh-Dhra'   Located in SE Dead Sea plain; EB town with massive cemetery. → 53, 64, 67.
Beer-sheba   Unoccup. before 1200; principal city in N Negeb; a walled fortress in Israelite period; large ashlar horned altar. →
                  56, 117.
Bethel   (Modern Beitin); flourished in MB; impt. in Iron Age (1200–1000); occup. in Hell, Rom, Byz. → 15, 104.
Beth-shan   Occup. from 3500 to Crusader period; conquered by Thutmosis III in 1468, and by Philistines in 1200; named
                  Scythopolis in Hell, Rom, Byz. →16, 89, 95, 96.
Beth-shemesh   Occup. from MB to Byz; prospered during LB; strong Philistine influence (1200–1000); on frontier between Judah
                  and Philistia. →16, 95.
Beth-zur   First occup. at end of 3d millennium; Judahite town fortified by Rehoboam; impt. during Maccabean period. → 15,
                  104, 135.
Caesarea   Seaport on Mediterranean; capital of Roman govt. in Palestine for 600 years; inscription mentioning Pontius Pilate.
                  → 142.
Capernaum   Prominent in Jesus' ministry; synagogue of 4th–5th cent.; earlier synagogue below dates to Jesus' time. →46, 145.
Dan   Occup. from mid-3d millennium; MB rampart and mudbrick gateway with two towers; incense stands and horned
                  altar in Iron II. → 74, 103, 119, 133.
Dor   Occup. from MB to Byz; impt. seaport on Mediterranean; occup. by the Sea Peoples. → 95, 103, 129.
Ebla   In Syria; flourished 2400–2250; spectacular find of more than 10,000 cuneiform tablets. → 61, 72.
Ekron   (Tel Miqne); northernmost of the Philistine cities; largest Iron Age site in Israel; olive oil industry. → 95, 100.
Gerasa   (Jerash in Jordan); Roman provincial city of NT times; reached height in 3d cent. AD.→ 147.
Gezer   Earliest occup. in Chalcolithic period; one of largest Bronze and Iron Age sites in Palestine; massive MB II fortifica-
                  tions. → 10, 14, 41, 62, 76, 115, 135.
Gibeah   (Tell el-Ful); occup. from 1200; site of Saul's fortress; final occup. in Maccabean period. → 15, 104.
Gibeon   (Modern el-Jib); founded about 3000; its zenith in Iron I; a winery here in 8th–7th cents.; jar handles inscribed
                  "Gibeon." → 81, 104.
Hazor   Fortified Canaanite city; occup. in Bronze Age; largest Palestinian city of MB; 13th-cent. destruction; Solomonic
                  walls and gate; gigantic water system. → 21, 39, 41, 74, 79, 88, 109, 120, 129.
Heshbon   In Moab; occup. almost continuously 1200 BC–AD 1456; no occup. before Iron I (1200), so apparently not the city
                  of King Sihon. → 122.
Jericho   Earliest occup. dates to 9000; important Neolithic site; lack of LB city walls raises problem about the date of Joshua's
                  conquest. → 13, 19, 26, 51, 60, 62, 76, 80, 148.
Jerusalem   Occup. from Chalcolithic; bibliography → Biblical Geography, 73:94; three major digs since 1967: Temple Mount,
                  Jewish Quarter, City of David. → 7, 8, 12, 19, 24, 105–7, 109, 115, 138–40, 150–53.
Kadesh-barnea   (Tell el-Qudeirat in NE Sinai; → Biblical Geography, 73:85); associated with exodus, but earliest occup. is 10th
                  cent.; three fortresses (10th–6th cents.). → 118.
Kuntillat 'Ajrud Desert way station in N Sinai; religious center with ancient Hebr and Phoenician inscriptions (9th–8th cent.). → 118.
Lachish   Occup. from Chalcolithic to Persian period; impt. Canaanite and Israelite city; Lachish Letters (590); conquered by
                  Assyrians (701) and Babylonians (586). → 11, 25, 76, 89, 114, 124–27.
Megiddo   Twenty occup. strata; Solomonic gate and casemate city walls; stable complex and water system date to Omride
                  dynasty. → 16, 25, 35–42, 57, 62, 75, 108.
Qasile   Ancient name unknown; one of most impt. sites in Israel for study of Philistine culture; Philistine temple. → 21, 102.
Samaria   Modern Sebastiyeh; abundant ivory decoration; Herod renamed it Sebaste to honor Augustus; Samaria ostraca. → 9,
                  16, 19, 113–15, 129, 143.
Shechem   Twenty-four occup. periods starting in Chalcolithic; impressive sanctuary tradition in MB; religious center of
                  Samaritans from 350 BC. → 13, 23, 24, 75, 120, 135.
Shiloh   Fortified MB II town; LB I occup.; Iron I settlement, ending in destruction; limited Iron II occup. → 76, 104.
Taanach   Earliest city dates from EB (2700–2400); Shishak destruction of city in 918, including cult place. → 13, 36, 63, 75,
                  120.
Timnah   (Tel Batash in Sorek Valley); occup. from MB to Persian period; mentioned in Samson stories; captured by Sen-
                  nacherib in 701. → 103.
Tirzah   (Tell el-Far'ah N); occup. in Bronze Age; destroyed in 1300; reoccup. 1000–600; Israelite four-room houses in well-
                  planned city. → 18, 75, 113, 120.
Tulul el-Alayiq   (Herodian Jericho); in Hasmonean and Herodian periods a royal resort on the banks of Wadi Qelt. → 148.
Ubeidiya   S of the Lake of Galilee, a key site in Lower Paleolithic period; human occup. from 1,600,000. → 49.

* EB = Early Bronze, MB = Middle Bronze, LB = Late Bronze, Hell = Hellenistic, Rom = Roman, Byz = Byzantine.
→ followed by nos. indicates sections in article where site is mentioned

11 **William Flinders Petrie** made the first stratified excavation in Palestine at Tell el-Hesi near Ashkelon in 1890. There he brilliantly exemplified the principle that was to become normative for all Palestine digging: "Broken pottery, even without an inscription, is a sure clue to dating." About halfway down the mound he recognized some fragments of a brownish metal-like jar of the style called "bilbil," which he had seen in some Egyptian tombs alongside inscriptions from *ca.* 1300 BC. Petrie measured the vertical distance from these fragments to the Gk ware at the top of the mound. Then he divided this distance by the number of years and concluded that every foot represented so many years of occupation. This method is often lampooned today as being excessively naïve, especially in ignoring the possibility of interrupted occupation. Still, even the most competent experts of our day, when confronted with two datable objects separated by a yard's depth of earth, will tend to assume a similar "yardstick." Petrie could have better exploited his genius had he paid greater attention to neighboring excavators' results as they came in. Also, he had a tendency to impose on his sites biblical names that are now universally rejected. Thus there is a certain pathos in the titles of his publications, *Hesy — Lachish, Gaza — Ajjul, Jammeh — Gerar, Beth-Pelet — Far'a*, i.e., Tell el-Hesi is not Lachish, etc. Yet no other pioneer took a more important step forward in Palestine excavation. Much of his work was under the auspices of the *Egypt* Exploration Fund; it was in Egypt that his rashly numerous excavations turned up genuinely biblical sites, especially Tanis and Amarna. Petrie's career is described in his autobiography, *Seventy Years in Archaeology* (London, 1931). Also *BARev* 6 (6, 1980) 44–55; *BA* 47 (1984) 220–22.

12 **L.-Hugues Vincent** was only 16 years old when as a Dominican seminarian he joined the École Biblique, just founded by Lagrange in Jerusalem (→ OT Criticism, 69:35, 60). It was within a year of Petrie's epoch-making 1890 excavation. From then until his death in 1960 Père Vincent performed the unique function of interpreting and *correlating* all the excavations that were to be carried on in Palestine. Most of the other excavators were foreign university professors; after "Palestine internship," they would retire to the more congenial homeland atmosphere where they could work up their observations. Thus there would have been lacking in Palestine any permanent scholarly guidance, had it not been so brilliantly supplied by Vincent in *RB*. No less significant were his own original researches at Hebron, Emmaus-Nicopolis, and Jerusalem's Lithostrotos. Most of his massive researches were in collaboration with his geographer confrere F.-M. Abel (*BASOR* 164 [1961] 2–4).

13 **Gottlieb Schumacher** excavated Megiddo in 1903 (→ 36 below) and published for the British Fund important researches on the Gadara region. He was an able surveyor, as was the copublisher of his results, Carl Watzinger, who also worked with Ernst Sellin at Jericho in 1907. Actually it might be fairer to credit Sellin with German pioneering in Palestine, since he excavated also Taanach in 1901 and Shechem in 1913. But the early German expeditions in Palestine tend to show that the principal technical expert on an excavation is the surveyor-architect. If his work is done professionally, the efforts of collaborators to unravel the chronology and to decipher the inscriptions can later be reevaluated.

14 **R. Stewart Macalister** from 1902 to 1909 at Gezer conducted single-handedly the first really major Palestine excavation. The famous Gezer calendar tablet and some other inscriptions were unfortunately dated too late. In addition, there had to be a drastic reassessment of the Solomonic gateway (which Macalister called

Roman) and of his Chalcolithic ware. But the imposing row of rough obelisks that he designated as a place of worship is one of the few discoveries whose cultic diagnosis has held. On Macalister, see *BA* 47 (1984) 33–35. In 1964 G. E. Wright reopened the Gezer excavations under the auspices of the Hebrew Union College. Succeeding Wright as director, W. Dever, assisted by several of Wright's former students, introduced new scientific methods at Gezer (*BA* 30 [1967] 34–70; W. Dever, *Gezer I–IV* [Jerusalem, 1970–85]; also *BA* 47 [1984] 206–18; *BARev* 9 [4, 1983] 30–42; *BASOR* 262 [1986] 9–34).

15 **William F. Albright** in 1920 came to Jerusalem to put some life into ASOR, which had existed since 1900. He was a prodigious linguist and sparked international cooperation, especially through the (Journal of the) Palestine Oriental Society, the early presidents of which included a French Jesuit and an Arab Franciscan. His digging at Gibeah (1922), Bethel (1927), and Beth-zur (1931) was significant. From 1926 to 1932 at Tell Beit Mirsim, S of Hebron, Albright made the excavation that is rated by most experts as a model of economical efficiency and of usefulness in publication (→ 73 below), though Albright's identification of the site as Debir is doubted (cf. M. Kochavi, *Tel Aviv* 1 [1974] 1–32). He was editor of *BASOR* and *AASOR*, author of *FSAC*, a Johns Hopkins Univ. professor, and teacher of many distinguished scholars, including N. Glueck, G. E. Wright, and M. Dahood. Albright exerted much moderate-progressive influence toward infusing archaeological data into exegesis. For debate on his work: *BA* 42 (1979) 37–47; for his bibliography: D. N. Freedman, *The Published Works of William Foxwell Albright* (Cambridge, MA, 1975); for autobiography: Albright, *History, Archaeology, and Christian Humanism* (NY, 1964) 301–27; biography: L. G. Running and D. N. Freedman (NY, 1975).

16 **Clarence Fisher** is an enigmatic figure in the history of Palestine excavation between World War I and II. As a University of Pennsylvania architect, he opened and briefly directed most of the major excavations of that era: Beth-shan, Megiddo, Beth-shemesh, and Samaria. Unfortunately, he seems to have been unable to hold the reins of management or to bring to completion any publication, even the *Corpus of Palestinian Pottery* left at ASOR at his death in 1941.

17 **Nelson Glueck** headed ASOR in the 1930s and 1940s. He added to exploration techniques by his mammoth survey of surface pottery deposits in Transjordan (→ 122 below). In the 1950s he extended this method to the Negeb of Israel, while heading Hebrew Union College of Cincinnati and the branch he built for it in Jerusalem. Glueck's popular books include *The Other Side of the Jordan* (New Haven, 1940); *The River Jordan* (NY, 1946); *Rivers in the Desert* [on the Negeb] (NY, 1959); see also *BA* 22 (1959) 82–108, or *BAR* 1. 1–21.

18 **Roland de Vaux** was director of the Dominican École Biblique, an Assyriologist of renown, and editor of *SBJ* and *RB* (→ OT Criticism, 69:60). From 1946 to 1964 he excavated Omri's capital at Tirzah. From 1952 he headed with dexterity the complex Dead Sea Scrolls research activity: acquiring new manuscripts; guiding the international Scrollery team; and excavating Qumran and Feshka (→ Apocrypha, 67:79–80). His *AI* provides, with the help of archaeological and literary data, an excellent survey of biblical social institutions (→ Institutions, 76). See *BARev* 6 (4, 1980) 14–29.

19 **Kathleen M. Kenyon** contended that excavation should be taught as an independent university discipline. Up to her time it had largely been simply a branch of classics, theology, orientalism, or ethnic history. She also typified the important leadership women have assumed in the field. While she was excavating Samaria (Sebastiyeh) with John and Grace Crowfoot (1930s), other women archaeologists were also at work in Palestine. Judith Marquet-Krause directed the Ai excavation; Dorothy Garrod discovered Natufian and Carmel flint cultures; and Olga Tufnell became the only effectual survivor of the Lachish team. Also, Hetty Goldman's work at Tarsus and Diana Kirkbride's in Transjordan have been conspicuous. Miss Kenyon in 1952 reopened the Jericho *chantier* (→ 80 below) and showed that the brick walls attributed to Joshua by Garstang, Vincent, and Albright were in fact 1000 years older. She established that the Jericho mound called Tell es-Sultan was in an almost complete state of abandonment throughout all dates possible for the major biblical references, from 1500 BC through the periods of Joshua (→ History, 75:55–58) and of Hiel (860 BC; 1 Kgs 16:34). Only *ca.* 800 was the site reoccupied. In compensation she discovered a powerful fortification with a unique early sculpture dating from before 5000 BC. (See K. Kenyon, *Digging up Jericho* [NY, 1957]; *NatGeog* [Dec. 1951; Dec. 1953]). She then turned to clarify the equally muddled state of excavation on Ophel Hill, the Jebusite citadel in the SE corner of Jerusalem (→ see 106 below; cf. *BA* 27 [1964] 34–52; 28 [1965] 22–26; 29 [1966] 27–36; *Digging up Jerusalem* [London, 1974]). On Kenyon, see *BA* 42 (1979) 122–25; *PEQ* 11 (1979) 3–10.

20   Bellarmino Bagatti was the leader of the archaeological activities of the Franciscan Holy Land Custody, which have become prominent since the wars. With S. Saller, V. Corbo, G. Orfali, S. Loffredo, M. Piccirillo, and other confreres, he had an important role in Late Roman-Byzantine excavation. This relates chiefly to churches and mosaics attesting biblical sites such as Nebo, Bethany, Olivet, Nazareth, Ain Karim, Emmaus-Qubeibeh, and the Bethlehem Shepherd's Field. The work is published in FrancP and *SBFLA*.

21   Yigael Yadin was the outstanding representative of the immense boom in archaeological research fostered by the Zionist movement and the State of Israel. He was the son of Eleazar Sukenik, who in the 1930s discovered the Beth Alpha synagogue, the "Jesus son of Joseph" casket-inscription, and Chalcolithic house-shaped burial urns. Sukenik also obtained some of the DSS. Yadin followed in his footsteps by dramatically purchasing the remainder of the cave 1 scrolls for Israel (→ Apocrypha, 67:80). From 1960 he proceeded to sensational explorations of the En-gedi desert and Masada (→ Apocrypha, 67:120–23). But Yadin's major achievement has been the 1955–58 excavation of Hazor with Y. Aharoni, Ruth Amiran, and Jean Perrot—one of the most grandiose digs since Megiddo. It was sponsored by the Hebrew University, the president of which, Benjamin Mazar-Maisler, was himself the excavator of Beth-she'arim, Khirbet el-Kerak (Beth-yerah), and Tel Qasile, and later, of Jerusalem. The University has also been prominent in prehistory, through the work of M. Stekelis, in advancing the cave discoveries of F. Turville-Petre and R. Neuville. The Israel Exploration Society and its journal (*IEJ*), ably coordinated by Joseph Aviram, typify the extent to which "excavation fever" has become a dominant local interest in Israel. On Yadin, see *BARev* 10 (5, 1984) 24–29.

22   Yohanan Aharoni became one of the leading archaeologists of Israel; his excavations and surveys have influenced considerably the archaeology of modern Israel. N. Avigad also deserves special mention among the myriad of Israelis engaging today in field archaeology.

23   G. Ernest Wright was second only to Albright in exercising influence on the archaeology of Palestine. Founder of *BA,* director of the Shechem excavations,

and president of ASOR, Wright was deeply involved in archaeology (→ 38 below). At the same time, he was contributing to the advancement of biblical studies. His influence on the younger generation of scholars was so great that when he died, the vacuum was filled by his own students, e.g., W. Dever, J. Seger, and L. Stager. Today there is hardly an American dig that does not bear the stamp of Wright, either directly or through his students. See *BA* 37 (1974) 83–84; 50 (1987) 5–21.

24   (II) Introductory Notes on Archaeological Method.

(A) Deciding Where to Dig.   The experience of the above pioneers led to steps in organizing an excavation. First, careful study of the Bible and other sources indicates the section of Palestinian surface on which a particular biblical site ought to lie. Next, the British Survey and Israeli maps (→ Biblical Geography, 73:9–10) show whether any traditional Arab name corresponds to the Biblical Hebrew name of a site. Finally, roaming over the general area and picking up pieces of pottery can indicate in advance how deep one will have to dig before encountering the biblical period of interest. Nowadays archaeologists have access to information acquired through aerial photography and land surveys which can be extremely useful in deciding where to dig.

We saw that the pioneers tended to attack first some big center like Jerusalem, whose identity has always been beyond question. Practically, too, the nearer one's dig is to a population center, the fewer are the inconveniences and expenses of lodging and provisioning. But the very fact that such a center has remained important through the centuries makes it more difficult to excavate. Such a settlement has grown by the gradual addition of new buildings. Those of an earlier period either continue in use, or their materials have been transformed into the buildings of later periods. Even debris from the rubbish-heap has been pressed into service or used for fill. The situation is better at cities like Nablus, where the population center has gradually moved off a mile or two, so that a protective layer from 1000 years' disuse has sealed off the biblical settlement of Shechem (→ Biblical Geography, 73:101). There are many such abandoned or sidetracked villages in Palestine, and the name given to them is "tell" (*tell* in Arabic, *tel* in Hebrew).

25   (B) Nature of a Tell.   In Josh 8:28 "tell" is a synonym for the *'ay* (Ai) or "ruin." In English the pl. "tells" seems acceptable, though some use the Arabic pl. *tulul,* or diminutive *tulayl,* pl. *tulaylat* (tuleilat). In some biblical areas the Persian-Turkish words *tepe* or *hüyük* are used for "tell." A tell tends to have a very distinctive truncated-cone shape. Seen from certain angles, the most conspicuous tells are Lachish, nearby Marisa, Megiddo, and Dothan. Also noteworthy is the tell of Homs in Syria (see *ANEP* 224). Erbil in N Mesopotamia is a beautiful example of a tell still crowned by the wall of a city. But in most cases the settlement has disappeared. Such a situation is taken for granted in the definition: The tell is a mound that from successive stages of human occupation has grown up into a truncated cone.

26   At Troy, the successive stages were envisioned as a series of independent cities sitting on top of one another. This romantic notion dominated the early search for Joshua's Jericho. But reflection should have warned that ancient cities simply were not built that way. In ancient Palestine the principal building material was clay. Some wood was used, of course, and a great deal of natural stone. Even many stone buildings had to be finished off with mud "bricks," which were sometimes "fired" to the hardness of stone or pottery. In any case, the vast majority of the houses in a plain or "tell" area were of adobe, i.e., ordinary mud fashioned into chunks about 6–10 in. on a side and laid in rows held together by mortar made of the same mud.

Houses were covered with a roof of branches, which slanted outward and permitted the rather infrequent rain to run off. After every heavy rainfall or similar catastrophe, however, several house walls in a village would topple over. Normally, a wall does not fall over flat as a single unit down to its foundation; the top-heavy part falls, leaving the bottom third almost intact (as with a child's stack of blocks). Such an occurrence was not the end for the Palestinian family. They shivered under reed mats until the rain was over; then with their bare feet trampled the fallen bricks back into the mud of Mother Earth from which they had come. Within a day or two — while the ground was still moist — they could fashion new bricks, let them dry in the sun, and build up their wall again to the desired height.

27   Naturally, every rebuilding involved some improvements, and since materials were constantly being brought in from outside, the ground level of the Palestinian villages gradually rose. If only as little as a quarter inch per year, this rise would amount to 50 ft. in the biblical period alone. It would be far easier for investigators if the growth had been perfectly level and symmetric with each layer sealed off from the next. In reality, however, people remained where they were and, even after the most colossal disasters, continued to use the remains that were sometimes left standing to a considerable height in the very heart of the disaster area. When a city was abandoned for some centuries, new settlers did not find a level surface awaiting them. They huddled at first in sheltered pits or basements, where their debris mingled with that of 1,000 years earlier. Gradually they erected splendid edifices, but often an earlier tower or hilltop villa survived as a landmark above the bulk of their later masonry.

Hence, archaeologists had to adjust to reality their romantic notion of "cities sitting on top of one another." Even the all-important notion of *stratification* borrowed from geology proved too rigid: for, despite terminology like "level," "layer," and "stratum," there is little in a series of successive deposits that is horizontally flat. The interested student should become familiar with the method of excavation in order to appreciate the close relationship between technique and the value of the information reported by the excavator. Improvements in recent years give much more reliability to the results obtained. For an introduction, see Dever and Lance, *Manual*.

28   In the past, archaeologists intent upon studying stratigraphy confined their digging to narrow trenches (usually five-meter squares). This method is still useful for dating events of political history, such as destruction of cities. To understand the ancient environment, however, archaeologists must dig broad, lateral areas. This so-called horizontal approach is helpful for gaining insight into the everyday life of ancient people.

29   A site must always be seen in its setting. In addition to excavating isolated tells, today archaeologists conduct surface surveys and regional studies as means of understanding such phenomena as settlement and trade patterns, population shifts, social structures, ecology, and economics in antiquity. Our own concern for the modern environment has made archaeologists conscious of the ancient environment and the human response to it.

30   To recover as much information as possible, current digs are composed of interdisciplinary staffs; the day when archaeologists worked in isolation is over. Specialists from the natural and social sciences, including geologists, physical and cultural anthropologists, hydrologists, ethnographers, paleoethnobotanists and zoologists, collaborate in the field with archaeologists. The vast reservoir of new evidence amassed through this cooperative effort is extremely useful in reconstructing both the history and the cultural process of past society. At the same time, techniques of retrieval, recording, and analysis have improved substantially.

31   **(C) Pottery and Chronology.** Apart from buildings, the most frequently encountered "artifact" or product of human industry found in Palestine excavation is broken pottery, or "sherds." A rare amulet or brief inscription and fairly numerous flints, stone grinders, bone tools, and seeds are also uncovered. It is natural that clay should be found, whether in the form of unbaked bricks and mortar or in the form of kiln-bricks and pottery. Modern technology has enshrined our homes and offices with complex utensils of varied materials; in biblical times, however, most utensils in an ordinary house were made of clay. Canisters, glasses, and spoons were pottery of various shapes. Bread was baked in the form of a plate, and other food was served on it, so that no table was needed; if company came, a mat served the purpose (biblical šulḥān, Ps 23:5). There was furniture, too, but organic material such as wood is not usually preserved. Blankets and mats were often piled up or spread in various ways and ultimately served as clothing. The source of heat and light was fire often inside a jar. The plumbing and refrigeration were usually a porous jar whose "sweat" evaporation cooled the water inside. But we do have evidence of drains, sewers, and even a toilet (in the City of David).

32   Pottery has a unique value for dating not only because it is so universal but because it is simultaneously the easiest and the most difficult of all things to destroy! It is easily broken in the sense that the complete vessel is smashed and thus loses its form. But to break down the fragments into an unrecognizable, that is, a non-pottery state would be an expensive engineering project even with the machines of today. And from any part of the *rim* or certain other small fragments, the size and shape of the original jar can be very accurately inferred.

Since the broken vessels were easily replaced — virtually with the mud in one's front yard — there was a tremendous turnover. Thus pottery styles were as capricious and fluctuating as fashions in clothes today. Some good gray styles in storage jars or cooking pots were retained unchanged through 1,000 years. But perfume bottles or hip flasks enjoyed a vogue as ephemeral as the tastes of their users. Such ware can sometimes be dated to an interval as exact as 50 years. Even those styles that lasted 300 years overlapped, so that the combination of various styles found at a single site can narrow down the time range. Being so breakable, pottery would not be preserved as a family heirloom or carried along when the family moved to a distant place. Because of this, it is a far better dating criterion than are art objects or even coins (which came in only after 500 BC). For a discussion of Palestinian pottery in biblical times, see Amiran, *Ancient Pottery*.

33   The growth of Palestine archaeology is reflected in the combined achievement of scholars like Petrie, Vincent, Albright, and Mazar in working out the "ceramic clock." By this we mean a table giving pottery types characteristic of each successive 100-year period. Although the major periods have been named after metals (bronze, iron) or predominant cultures, actually the styles of pottery enable us to determine any given period. More recent excavations in Palestine have refined significantly our knowledge of pottery. Not only the shape of the pots but also the composition of the clays is carefully studied. When the source of the clay beds can be located, much is learned about cultural interaction, trade, and commerce. Neutron activation analysis is used today for establishing the provenance of the clay used in particular pottery.

34   Radiocarbon-dating technique was devised by Willard F. Libby at Chicago about 1948. Its point of departure is that all organic compounds (materials that were once alive), as they disintegrate, lose one half of their Carbon 14 isotopes every 5,700 years, more or less. Since the number characteristic of each compound is known, the date of its death can be determined. This is a brilliant discovery that is of great usefulness for archaeological dating, although it has its limitations. Since the material to be tested is completely destroyed in the process, a significant amount must be available. Also the material must never have been contaminated by contact with other organic materials. These conditions are hard to verify. As well as radiocarbon, several other sophisticated dating techniques, such as potassium-argon, thermoluminescence, flourine testing, dendrochronology, and pollen analysis are available today. There seems to be no end to what nuclear and computer sciences can contribute to archaeology.

35   **(III) Example of an Excavation: Megiddo.**
(A) History of the Excavation. Megiddo is a model of the frustrations and achievements of Palestinian excavations. The search for its site in the Plain of Esdraelon was begun by E. Robinson (1838; → Biblical Geography, 73:9), as described in his *Biblical Researches* 3. 117. He stood on the so-called Governor's Mound (Mutesellim) near the E outlet of the strategic pass called Arah leading across Carmel to the sea. "Somewhere near here, Megiddo must have stood," he mused, apparently never suspecting that it was beneath his feet.

36   The architect G. Schumacher (→ 13 above) in 1903–1905 excavated Tell el-Mutesellim for the German Oriental Society. It is claimed that he ignored the decisiveness of broken pottery and used scavenger-trenches, which were not even adequately recorded on his skillfully drafted plans. Nevertheless, the two volumes on Megiddo, as well as Sellin's volume on nearby Taanach in 1904, are important pioneer achievements. The German recording of pottery was at least sufficiently precise to enable Albright to launch his audacious claim that a single perduring community shuttled back and forth, at various dates attested by potsherds, between Taanach and the 5-mi.-distant Megiddo. Schumacher was fully competent and eager to carry on the work after 1920, improving his former techniques; but the Germans had lost the war, and permission to excavate was denied them by the British Mandate.

37   In 1925 James Breasted decided upon the Megiddo mound as the site of an ideal excavation by the Oriental Institute of the University of Chicago. His friend John D. Rockefeller promised a virtually unlimited budget, as well as a spare million for erecting the Palestine Archaeological Museum in Jerusalem. To guard against dangers faced by earlier excavations, such as armed attack, malaria, and boredom, a spacious villa was constructed. Its tennis court and swimming pool alone cost more than Albright's whole excavation of Mirsim! A leisurely 25 years was allotted for peeling off the whole mound layer by layer and for recording every item and aspect of the successive stages. Albright (*AP* 41) commented on the good fortune that this plan proved prohibitively expensive even for a Rockefeller: "The very best technique of today will probably seem primitive a century hence, and . . . it is a sad mistake to exhaust the possibility of any important site like Megiddo. Actually only a fraction of the great mound has been removed [in what looks to the uninitiated like huge trenches!], and there is ample room for correcting chronology and making important discoveries."

38   Twenty separate strata were recognized. The long duration and careful subdivision of these Megiddo strata make them a fine framework for synchronizing Palestine sites of briefer duration. This achievement is not essentially spoiled by the severe criticisms that have been leveled against details of the dating. Serious revisions were suggested by the Albright school because the successors of Fisher (→ 16 above), P. L. Guy and G. Loud, lacked his "experience and flair for pottery." G. E. Wright (→ 23 above) embarked on a clear brief archaeological history of the site, with important alterations in the dating of those periods that most directly concern the Bible. In the 1960s Yadin (→ 21 above) made soundings at Megiddo to clarify some critical stratigraphic problems. As a result, he was satisfied that Stratum V A/IV B, including the six-chamber gateway and the related casemate city walls, is Solomonic. Stratum IV A, incorporating the offset-inset wall and the four-chamber gate, the stable complexes, and the subterranean water system, dates to the Omride dynasty, most likely the reign of Ahab (→ History, 75:92–94).

Most, but not all, Egyptologists maintain that Pharaoh Thutmosis captured Megiddo *ca.* 1482, after a battle that marked the destruction of Stratum IX. To guard against the mistrust that such revisions and uncertainties may provoke, there is in professional discussion a strong secure undertone, "Errors have been made in the past, and even Albright has loyally reorganized his views on many points on which fresh evidence has been discovered; but as of right now everything is under control." A more realistic conclusion would seem to be that the results of excavation are valuable and useful only insofar as their degree of certitude is assessed without exaggeration from the outset. Cf. Wright, "What Archaeology Can and Cannot Do," *BA* 34 (1971) 70–76.

39   **(B) Some Interesting Discoveries.** *The stables.* The most characteristic find at Megiddo was a stone half-column, 3 or 4 ft. high with rectangular faces, repeated in endless rows, as many as 400 in all. Schumacher contended that they had cultic significance. Similar rows of short thick stone pillars, though much less numerous, were left showing on the surface of Hazor by J. Garstang's 1926 sounding there. The Megiddo pillars themselves bear no resemblance at all to the more elongated and tapering steles of the Gezer or Byblos places of worship; what they have in common— a rather curious fact—is that several stand upright in a row. (Indeed, this "uprightness" is the only common feature of the biblical *maṣṣēbôt* or cultic posts which vary in form from natural tree stumps, roughened by weather, to obeliscal shapes in stone or metal. Sometimes these steles have crude indications of human features, either facial or phallic. More often they are formless and in fact are named "asherah" and represent *female* divinities [Ashera = Ishtar], but without the sex-tracing of the numerous Palestine figurines.)

When P. L. Guy came to head the Megiddo enterprise in 1928, he noted that many of the stone posts had a hole pierced diagonally near a corner. He proposed that the Megiddo posts, which also supported wooden beams for the roof, were hitching posts for horses. We know that the town was a district capital of Solomon, who is repeatedly reported as trafficking in horses (1 Kgs 4:12; 9:19; 10:26). (In fact at Jerusalem the masonry-forest under the SE corner of the Temple esplanade has been popularly called "Solomon's Stables," doubtlessly because of a confused combination of two facts: Solomon built some of the masonry, and 2,000 years later the crusaders made a ramp through there to drive their horses right up onto the Temple area!) In many ways the hypothesis of stables at Megiddo is plausible. They are so numerous there as to override any other function the city may have had: we know of Megiddo chiefly as a battle site, and horses were "armaments." Still there is no real proof of the hypothesis, and it has been rejected at Hazor. Pritchard identified the disputed pillared buildings at Megiddo as barracks, while Aharoni thought they functioned as storehouses. Yadin, however, continued to support the "stable" interpretation. At present, the weight of evidence seems to be with Yadin, on the basis of comparable sites in Palestine and beyond. On stables, see J. Holladay, in Geraty, *Archaeology* 103–65.

40   The genuinely cultic remains of Megiddo are described in a separate volume by H. May. The most astounding monument surviving at the site is a huge oval *altar or platform,* dating most likely to EB III (*ca.* 2800–2400). Some 20 ft. in diameter, it was made of unhewn stones but had steps, thus conforming to the law of Exod 20:25 but not to that of Exod 20:26. At the side of this altar-platform was a complex of temples that continued in use with adjustments down to the time of the Israelites' entry into Canaan.

41   *City gates.* The sequence of monumental gates at the N of the Mutesellim mound is instructive. The stone wall of Stratum XVIII (*ca.* 3000 BC) was the most massive fortification ever erected on the site, originally 15 ft. wide, later thickened to an impressive 28 ft. Similarly massive stone fortifications have been found at Jericho, but of an earlier date. An EB Age wall at Beth-yeraḥ was 25 ft. wide, but of mud brick. At Megiddo, too, in the course of the centuries the stone wall was covered over and replaced by one of mud brick. Then in Stratum X (Hyksos period) was erected a gateway of hewn-stone facing, filled in with rubble. This lasted in use through Stratum VII (1300–1150) and was destroyed about 1050. In its place, a small unimposing gate was erected in Stratum VI (1150–25), rebuilt in Stratum V (1050–950), and destroyed probably by David.

In the stratum above, a few yards farther E, was built "the finest fortified gate yet found in Palestine, certainly Solomonic," says Wright, though he claimed that that stratum is not really IV but a combination of the lower part of IV with the upper part of V (*ca.* 950). The gate had four pairs of piers and four entryways, with six chambers between the piers. The correspondence of this gate to the E temple gate of Ezek 40:5 has been maintained by Howie in *BASOR* 117 (1950) 13–17. Yadin showed that the blueprint and measurements of the Solomonic gateway at Megiddo were exactly duplicated both in the gate at Gezer (which had been called Roman) and in the Solomonic gate which he excavated at Hazor.

The stratum *after* Solomon was called III B by the excavators, but IV A (after 900) by Wright. It was only then, allegedly, that the quadruple gate was transformed into a triple gate, presumably by the armed forces of Pharaoh

Sheshonk (Shishak) in occupying the city (though 2 Chr 12:4 mentions only his depredations in Judah). At a still later date, in Stratum III (A) around 800 BC, the triple wall was further reduced to a double one, possibly in the wars with Syrian Ben-hadad (2 Kgs 13:3).

The importance of such city gates far transcends the chronological dilemmas they present. As at Shechem and Lachish, and in Absalom's maneuvers of 2 Sam 15:2, we recognize that the so-called gate was really a tribunal, an archive, and a reception hall; in short, what we might accurately render "courthouse." Naturally, it was a gate as well, and in the interest of defense it contained a maze of passages; but the empty spaces between the doorways could readily be utilized for public business and in fact constituted the forum or heartbeat of the civic life of the town.

42   *Shaft and treasury.* The history of the Megiddo water system, told in a separate volume by R. Lamon, is a saga plagued with stratigraphic problems. Briefly, the water system consisted of a vertical shaft and a horizontal tunnel, which conducted the springwater from a natural cave to the bottom of the vertical shaft. The earliest part of the water system was called the "gallery," leading outside the city to a spring located at the SW slope of the tell. Yadin demonstrated that the gallery was constructed during the reign of Solomon, while the water system dates to the Omride dynasty (9th cent.). The American excavators misdated the construction of shaft and tunnel to the 12th cent. and attributed the gallery to an earlier period. For water tunnels, → 120 below; *BARev* 6 (2, 1980) 8–29.

Another noteworthy feature visible today is the stone bin for grain storage under Jeroboam II (750 BC). Megiddo was doubtless one of the towns used for storage of taxes collected "in kind," as attested by jar handles from all over Palestine bearing the inscription "For the King" (*lmlk*). At an earlier stage in its history (*ca.* 1150), Megiddo held treasures of a different kind, the ivory carvings contemporary to similar Phoenician samples from the Guadalquivir Valley in Spain. At the end of the LB ivory plaques and other luxury items were in use. A cartouche of Ramses III (1182–1151) found on an ivory plaque is further evidence of ivory at Megiddo.

And speaking of treasure, we must note that the Megiddo diggers overlooked a fragment of the cuneiform "Flood Epic" named after its hero Gilgamesh (→ Genesis, 2:12). This was picked up on a debris heap by a shepherd in 1956 and published in Israel's 1958 *Atiqot.* For pictures of Megiddo, see *ANEP* 332, 708, 712, 734, 742; also *EAEHL* 3. 830–56. *BA* 33 (1970) 66–96.

43   **ARCHAEOLOGICAL PERIODS IN PALESTINE**

Paleolithic	1,600,000–18,000		MB II (MB II B)	1800–1650
Lower	1,600,000–120,000		MB III (MB II C)	1650–1550
Middle	120,000–45,000		Late Bronze	1550–1200
Upper	45,000–18,000		LB I	1550–1400
Epipaleolithic (Mesolithic)	18,000–8000		LB II	1400–1200
Neolithic	8000–4500		Iron	1200–539
Prepottery	8000–6000		Early	1200–900
Pottery	6000–4700		Late	900–539
Late	4700–4500		Persian	539–332
Chalcolithic	4500–3200		Hellenistic	332–64
Early Bronze	3200–2000		Roman	64 BC–AD 324
EB I	3200–3000		Early	64 BC–AD 135
EB II	3000–2800		Late	135–324
EB III	2800–2400		Byzantine	324–640
EB IV	2400–2000		Early Islamic	640–1174
Middle Bronze	2000–1550		Crusader	1099–1291
MB I (MB II A)	2000–1800		Late Islamic	1174–1918

The dates in the table are approximate, subject to constant refinement and revision in the light of archaeological evidence and new methods of research. There may be occasional variance between this table and the text because of scholarly disagreement.

In his *AP,* Albright gave us a period-by-period survey of the results established by digging. Building on this basic work by taking into account the extraordinary development in archaeology through virtually nonstop field activities, we present here the scholarly consensus.

44   (I) Prehistory: The Stone Ages. Toolmaking people first appeared upon earth at least two million years ago, perhaps earlier. The day is long past when any serious exegete would seek to harmonize scientific paleontology with the imaginative and theological portrayal of earliest humanity in Gen 1–3. Still, the facts behind the evolutionary theory will continue to hold interest for the exegete. Here we treat primarily of the prehistoric situation in Palestine; for a wider treatment of the prehistoric period in the Near East, → History, 75:6ff.

45   (A) Old Stone Age: Paleolithic. The oldest hominoid fossil remains in the world are those of Ramapithecus, dated to *ca.* seven million years ago. This is the earliest probable ancestor of the modern human species. Fossil remains of *homo erectus,* the genus and species to which modern humanity belongs, are *ca.* 700,000 years old. The term Chellean, signifying the earliest hand-ax culture, has been replaced by the Abbevillian industry, which is closely related to the Acheulean industry. In the caves of Wadi Kharitun, SE of Bethlehem, the French scholar-consul René Neuville found Acheulean flints or perhaps a slightly older type called Tayacian, roughly contemporary with a style later found at Yabrud, N of Damascus. The sequence of Near East Paleolithic cultures is remarkably similar to that known in Europe and Africa.

46   The earliest human skeletal remains date from somewhat later; but they were found in Palestine in such abundance during the 1930s that it was seriously held that human life originated here. We now have much older samples, including Teilhard's Peking man and the bones from Olduvai in Tanzania. Palestinian skeletons are Neanderthal, contemporary with flints of willow-leaf shape called Aurignacian. The six humans discovered by Neuville in a cave at the Qafzeh precipice near Nazareth were at first thought to be Acheulean. Two others were found at the bottom of a long series of prehistoric strata excavated by D. Garrod and T. McCown in "Cave Valley" (Wadi Mugharah) near Atlit, S of Haifa. But the pioneer's crown goes to F. Turville-Petre of Oxford, who in 1925 discovered a youthful Neanderthal skeleton in the "Gypsy Cave" (Mugh009aret ez-Zuttiyeh) of Amud Valley, SW of Capernaum. This was the first recognition of strata in prehistoric Palestine.

47   "Prehistory" is a somewhat fluid term that we may at present conveniently define as "information about human culture, drawn mostly from flints, for the ages preceding the invention of agriculture, pottery, metallurgy, and writing." These four giant strides were not rigidly contemporary, but they are close enough to make this norm practical.

A good 50 years of ardent prehistoric research had preceded Turville-Petre. Quite by chance, this was the branch in which Catholics had taken the lead. In Jerusalem, J. Germer-Durand at the Assumptionist seminary, D. Buzy at the diocesan seminary, and other priests at the White Fathers' Melchite seminary and elsewhere began gathering and classifying earliest flints. These were paralleled on the Phoenician coast by Jesuits Zumoffen and Bovier-Lapierre. Thus in 1917 the German priest Paul Karge had considerable empirical data, which he used accurately to write his history of the Rephaim, or pre-Israelite inhabitants of Palestine. For the Paleolithic period in Palestine, see Aharoni, *Archaeology.*

48   LOWER, MIDDLE, UPPER (1,600,000–18,000). Although much remains to be known, new methods of research combined with new dating techniques are responsible for significant progress in the study of the Paleolithic (Old Stone Age). In many cases, sites investigated earlier have been reexamined. In the Paleolithic period people hunted wild animals and gathered wild plants as a means of subsistence. This era is divided into Lower, Middle (Mousterian), and Upper Paleolithic.

49   The *Lower* Paleolithic was the longest period in prehistory. Ubeidiya, situated W of the Jordan and just S of the Sea of Galilee, is the most prominent site in this period. Its human occupation extended from *ca.* 1,600,000. It is a large site and rich in finds, consisting of simple tools and fragments of human and animal bones. Here were found the most ancient human remains in the Near East, probably to be classified as *homo erectus.* The "Galilee man," found in the Zuttiyeh cave in 1925, has been restudied in the course of new excavations from 1973. The skull, 160,000 years old, is the most ancient human cranial fragment found in Israel and represents the later evolutionary phase of the pre-Neanderthal. The Cave of the Oven (Mughog et et-Tabun), also excavated anew, has the longest stratigraphical sequence yet discovered in Israel.

The *Middle* Paleolithic or Mousterian period dates between 120,000 and 45,000 years ago. The oldest human burials in Israel, found under the floors of caves, are of this period. The worked stone of this period shows noted advancement in technique of manufacture.

The *Upper* Paleolithic, dating *ca.* 45,000–18,000, marks a refinement in flint blades, predecessors of the microlithic tools of the classic Epipaleolithic (Mesolithic).

50   **(B) Later Stone Ages.**
(a) EPIPALEOLITHIC (18,000–8000). This age, still referred to by some as Mesolithic, was a real turning point in human history. In this period those who had been hunters and food-gatherers became farmers and herders; animals were domesticated, and goats and sheep herded. Also there is evidence of small circular enclosures which served as occupation areas. A precursor to the Neolithic was the Natufian (10,000–8000), the principal Epipaleolithic culture in Israel. The name derives from the Wadi Natuf, NW of Jerusalem, where the cave of Shukbah is located. Natufian is defined as the stage of Epipaleolithic that continued the Kebarian, named after the cave of Kebara on Mount Carmel. The advent of the Natufian culture signaled a basic social change. Large, open, permanent settlements are first found in this period. There were circular stone dwellings with burials under the floor. Large Natufian settlements were at Eynan in E Galilee and at Nahal Oren on Mount Carmel, also at Rosh Zin and Rosh Horesha in the Negeb mountains. Grinding tools, microliths, and sickle blades are characteristic. In Israel, art objects are traceable to this period; animal and human figures were carved into bone sickle handles. Many sites in Israel, Jordan, and Syria attest Epipaleolithic artifacts, with extensive remains in the Ras en-Naqb and Humeimah regions of Jordan.

51   (b) NEOLITHIC (8000–4500). Pottery appears for the first time in the middle of the period (*ca.* 5500), so it is customarily divided into Prepottery and Pottery Neolithic. The Neolithic economy was based on food production for the most part. Although Jericho's earliest occupation dates back to the Natufian period, it is a key site of the Neolithic, with both Prepottery Neolithic A (PPNA) and B (PPNB) represented. Other important sites of this era are Nahal Oren, Munhata, Abu Ghosh, and Beisamon. Jordan's most important early Neolithic site is Beidha near Petra, where along with the remains of a flint industry and ground stone artifacts, there are signs of animal domestication.

Characteristic of PPNA culture (8th millennium) are large circular house structures, a lithic industry, and domestication of wheat and barley. In PPNB (from the middle of the 8th millennium until the beginning of the 6th) there was intensive domestication of wheat and barley. The architecture of this period consisted of rectangular-roomed structures.

Some would relate a circular stone tower at PPNA Jericho to a stone wall surrounding the city. The architecture of PPNB at Jericho was more sophisticated, with rooms grouped around courtyards. At Jericho there is no continuity between PPNA and PPNB. From Jericho's PPN came ten human skulls molded with plaster; their lifelike appearance is striking. Similar examples have been found at Beisamon in the Huleh valley. These skulls were probably associated with ancestor worship. For more on Jericho, → 80 below.

52 In 1983 an unexpected cache of human statues made of plaster was uncovered at Ain Ghazal, located on the N entrance to Amman (Jordan). This site, dating to PPNB, is one of the largest Neolithic villages in the Near East. The human statues and busts found there were made of lime plaster formed around a reed core and are similar to those at Jericho. Ain Ghazal apparently was an agricultural community. The tools are of flint for the most part, and the houses are rectangular or square. Ain Ghazal will be useful in reconstructing the social, economic, and religious life of the people who lived in the Near East 8,000 years ago. In 1983 at Naḥal Hemar in the Judean desert, stone masks dating to PPNB were found in a cave, which may have been used for storage or as a pen.

53 The invention of pottery was one of the most important developments in the cultural history of the ancient Near East. Pottery appears in Jordan for the first time at the Late Neolithic site of Dhraʿ, E of Bab edh-Dhraʿ. Hunting continued in this period, but there was also food gathering and tilling of the soil. In Late Neolithic the gazelle was the most hunted animal. Goat and sheep provided meat for the village society. Architecturally there were (defense?) walls and round buildings. Overall the Pottery Neolithic culture was quite inferior to the preceding period, especially with respect to architecture and stone tools. The Stone Age came to an end ca. 4500.

54 (c) CHALCOLITHIC (4500–3200). Coming in time between the Neolithic and Bronze Ages, and roughly coterminous with the 4th millennium, this period is also known as Ghassulian, a name derived from Tuleilat el Ghassul. As the designation "Chalcolithic" suggests, it was the millennium when both stone and copper were used for making tools and weapons. A key site in this period, a series of low mounds called *ghassûl* (soap plant), 4 mi. NE of the Dead Sea, was excavated for the Pontifical Biblical Institute by A. Mallon (1929–1934), R. Koeppel (1936, 1938), and R. North (1960). In the 1970s J. B. Hennessy continued the excavations and found additional wall paintings similar to those known from earlier digs at Ghassul. The complex combination of unusual tools has since appeared at hundreds of other Palestine sites, sometimes followed by earliest Bronze Age remains.

55 There is one important discrepancy. A unique and unimpeachable characteristic of the culture found at Ghassul itself is its polychrome wall-fresco art of an imaginativeness and technical competence not later equaled in Palestine's history. An eight-pointed star, a procession, and a sort of leaping tiger all are accompanied by black masks with great staring eyes, not unlike the necklace-amulets found there in both stone and pottery. This art, which may have belonged to a temple complex, is not found at the other "Ghassulian" sites. A widespread feature of the same culture-complex turned out to be the "house-shaped ossuary" of Hedera (Khudeirah; see sketch in Albright, *AP* 69). Other samples found in 1958 at Azor near Tel Aviv imitate architectural elements even more, but amusingly combine these with traits of the human face.

56 New evidence for the Chalcolithic has been found in several regions, including the Sinai, the Negeb, central Palestine, and the north. Excavation reveals a sophisticated culture with a well-developed technology. The sites share common elements with respect to material culture, agricultural and pastoral economy, and ritual practices. The architecture consists primarily of rectangular structures. The sites were abandoned, but we do not yet understand why.

The N Negeb near Beer-sheba is rich in Chalcolithic sites. There is Beer Matar, with its workshop for making copper tools; Beer es-Safadi, a settlement where ivory and bone were carved and copper tools manufactured; and Horvat Beter. Shiqmim, one of the largest Chalcolithic settlements in Israel, located W of Beer-sheba, shows evidence of metal working, flint tool production, and cult activities. The most recently discovered Chalcolithic site in this area is Neve Noy, a suburb of Beer-sheba and part of Safadi, where various objects associated with the copper industry have come to light. At Gilat in the northern Negeb, a Chalcolithic temple has been discovered. A clay ram with three goblets on its back and a statue of a seated woman with a churn on her head have occasioned much speculation. Found among other ritual implements, the statue is interpreted as a ritual vessel which may have been used in the worship of Ashtaroth. Who she was we do not know.

57 At En-gedi archaeologists have uncovered a Chalcolithic enclosure, probably a central sanctuary for the region's inhabitants (*BA* 34 [1971] 23–39). It bears close resemblance to the Chalcolithic sanctuary at Megiddo. Among the Judean Desert caves (→ Apocrypha, 67:120), the Cave of the Treasure in the Naḥal Mishmar contained an extraordinary residue of pottery, stone vessels, textiles, leather objects, etc. There was also a homogeneous group of more than 400 copper objects wrapped in a straw mat and dating to Chalcolithic. Scholars conjecture that these objects were the ritual equipment used at the En-gedi temple. The central Golan plateau also contains evidence of the Chalcolithic culture. The house plans at these settlements resemble Ghassul. A unique kind of house-god statue has been found in the courtyards of several sites in the Golan. C. Epstein sees here an indication of domestic cult in contrast to centralized religion.

There is continuity in the transition from the Chalcolithic to the Early Bronze. Each period has its own culture, but there is no sharp break in the evolution from one to the other. (For bibliography on the Chalcolithic, see *BA* [1968] 82–108.)

58 **(II) The Bronze Ages.**
(A) Early Bronze Age (3200–2000). Writing was invented about 3200, simultaneously in Iran and at Warka. It was quickly adopted by Semites invading Ur (→ History, 75:17). Thus documented history began. But for 1,000 years more, broken pottery

continues to be our chief source of information about chronology and cultural developments. For a survey of the EB, see *BA* 50 (1987) 20–43.

59 There is a marked improvement in the technology of manufacturing pottery in EB in comparison with the Chalcolithic period. Four periods are distinguished in EB on the basis of ceramic types. Characteristic pottery forms in EB include jars with ledge handles, high loop handles on juglets, flat bases, and shallow bowls. In EB I there is red-burnished ware, "grain wash" (reddish-brown and pink-painted wash), and "line-group" painting. Characteristic of EB II is a graceful elongated jug with squat base. This style is named for Abydos in Egypt, where it was found in abundance along with dating records of Pharaoh Menes of the 1st Dynasty.

60 In EB III the most characteristic pottery was called by Albright "Khirbet Kerak ware," reflecting the Arabic name of Beth-yeraḥ on the SW shore of the Sea of Galilee where it was discovered. It is brittle and fragile, with a special slip and a unique burnish, a shiny red or black, having nothing whatever in common with either the crisscross-slip or the Abydos jug. But the "dead giveaway" style of the EB at any site in Canaan is the ledge handle. The alleged samples at Ghassul should more accurately be called lug handles; they are pinched up out of the clay of the vessel-belly and are often vertical, containing an "eyelet" for inserting a cord. As distinct from these, the Jericho ledge handles are an inch wide and several inches long, almost invariably horizontal. They form a chronological series that develops from simpler into very complex "scallop" or "envelope" forms, rarely perforated.

EB IV, a problematic period, cannot be so easily distinguished because of many uncertainties; no consensus exists concerning terminology and chronology. There is a special need in this period for written evidence to give some clarity to its history and culture (→ 65–67 below).

61 Strangely, the most valuable late EB excavation for biblical study is not in Palestine, but at Mari on the Euphrates. Here, from 1933 André Parrot dug up palaces containing many cuneiform archives and discovered other unique evidence of the Semite immigration waves that flooded over the Tigris Valley. The classic S Mesopotamian excavations too, Ur and Warka and the others, inform us about the period. Mesopotamian EB also furnishes vivid scenes of religion and art on the so-called cylinder seals (*ANEP* 672–702). These, when rolled on soft clay, left a 2 x 4 in. frieze to serve as the owner's signet or signature. Several such seals, dated rather reliably to the "Jemdet Nasr" period around 3000, were found at M. Dunand's excavation of Byblos in Phoenicia and also buried just below the shiny red-black Khirbet el-Kerak ware at Judeideh in the Antioch plain. The EB millennium is also valuably represented at Alaja in central Turkey, a few miles N of Bogazkoy, the later Hittite capital.

Another site bound to illuminate EB is Tell Mardikh, 30 miles S of Aleppo (Syria), where P. Matthiae has uncovered a vast civilization. It has been identified beyond doubt as the ancient city-state of Ebla, a great commercial center in the Near East from the middle of the 3d to the middle of the 2d millennium. The royal palace where the state archives were found dates to *ca.* 2400–2250 (→ History, 75:16).

62 Several Palestinian sites also shed light on EB. Jericho was a walled city in EB and flourished for about six centuries (2900–2300) before being destroyed. Tel Jarmuth in the Shephelah hills, one of the largest EB sites in Israel, is especially important in EB III because of its defense system. Gezer, one of the largest Bronze and Iron Age sites, was occupied through much of EB,

except for a gap from *ca.* 2400 to 2000. Megiddo has immense EB deposits, represented in Strata XIX through XV. In EB I the first of several sanctuaries was situated in the E section of the city. The largest city wall in Megiddo's history dates to EB II. As we have seen, the round altar with a flight of steps dates to EB III. Late in EB III three new temples were erected.

63 Arad, situated in a semiarid region in the E Negeb (→ Biblical Geography, 73:86), has an important lower city pertaining to EB I and II. Characteristic of Arad are the thick city walls with semicircular protective towers, as well as the uniform architecture of its rectangular houses. Arad reached its height in EB II; then it was abandoned. Ai was also an important urban center in EB (3100–2350), when it had a temple and a royal quarter. Then it was destroyed and abandoned. Taanach was first inhabited in EB II–III (*ca.* 2700–2400). With its massive fortifications Taanach was a typical city-state of the period.

64 The most important EB site is Bab edh-Dhraʿ in the SE Dead Sea plain. It was first excavated by Lapp in the 1960s, and since 1975 by Rast and Schaub. In EB I A (3200) nomadic pastoralists used the site to bury their dead; in EB I B (3100) people began to settle permanently. In EB II–III (*ca.* 3000–2400) an enormous stone wall was built around the town; at the end of EB III the town was destroyed. After this destruction there were several phases of EB IV occupation before the settlers departed from the region. At Bab edh-Dhraʿ there is a large cemetery SW of the town, in use from *ca.* 3200 to 2200. In EB I the cemetery had shaft tombs with multiple chambers. Charnel houses constructed of mud brick date to EB II–III. In EB I–II the pottery of this site was handmade; by EB III some pottery was made on a tournette or slow wheel.

Eight miles S of Bab edh-Dhraʿ is Numeira, a settlement occupied in EB III (2450–2350). M. Coogan reports that the fortifications and domestic installations at Numeira resemble Bab edh-Dhraʿ in EB III. Because there is no indication of a cemetery at Numeira, it is assumed that the dead were buried in the charnel houses at Bab edh-Dhraʿ. A significant corpus of EB III ceramics was recovered from storerooms at Numeira. See *BARev* 6 (5, 1980) 26–36.

65 The period following EB III (EB IV–MB I [*ca.* 2400–2000]) continues to be debated by scholars because the pertinent historical information is sparse, and the archaeological evidence is not definitive. The variety of terminology applied to this period indicates the prevailing confusion. Depending on whether archaeologists view this period as more closely related to the preceding (EB) or to the following (MB) or as an intrusion, the terminology they prefer may be EB IV, MB I, Intermediate, or EB–MB. Apart from terminology, the era between *ca.* 2400 and 2000 was a largely nonurban seminomadic phase distinct from the flourishing urban civilization before and after in Palestine. Scholars (Kenyon, Lapp, Kochavi, Cohen) who clearly distinguish this intervening period from both the preceding and the following use the designation "Intermediate."

66 W. Dever, a leading investigator of the late 3d millennium in ancient Palestine, advocates (with Wright, Oren, and others) the EB IV terminology, because he sees continuity with EB on the basis of pottery and other recent evidence in Israel, Jordan, and Syria. EB IV is seen as a transitional period or posturban phase of EB. Dever finds strong support for his position at Beer Resisim, an EB IV settlement in the Negeb-Sinai. Its architecture was one-room curvilinear structures, and the economy was based on herding. Dever also finds confirmation in his excavation at Jebel el-Qaaqir in the Hebron hills where the shaft tombs date to EB IV. Sites in Jordan are also confirmatory: Khirbet Iskander in the Wadi Wala yielded ceramics and lithics of the EB tradition. This town also had a defense wall belonging to EB IV.

67 To explain the socioeconomic changes that took place in this transitional period (2400–2000), scholars offer various suggestions. Lapp spoke of an influx of nonurbanites who dominated Palestine. He interpreted the late 3d-millennium shaft tombs that he excavated at the Dhahr Mirzbaneh cemetery (N of Jericho and similar to that of Bab edh-Dhraʿ) as belonging to invaders who disrupted the urban civilization in EB but failed to establish their own permanent settlements. This invasion hypothesis, however, is now frequently rejected. Dever proposes instead the model of pastoral nomadism to explain the socioeconomic changes in EB IV. Others appeal to a shift between EB III and IV among the populace from urban to nonurban living.

Until recently many scholars have had recourse to the "Amorite invasion" theory to explain cultural modifications that took place during the transitional EB IV period. A fresh analysis of the data, however, does not permit such precision; literary evidence and historical information are too sparse. Consequently, the ethnic identity of the west Semitic people called the "Amorites," as well as their antiquity in Palestine and Transjordan, is uncertain. Without newer models and additional evidence, EB IV will remain one of the more problematic periods in Near Eastern history. (For people at the end of the EB period and the beginning of the MB period, see *BARev* 9 [4, 1983] 16–29.)

68   (B) Middle Bronze Age (2000–1550). This era is usually divided into three parts, but to avoid further confusion in terminology MB will be used to designate the entire first half of the 2d millennium BC. This urban period was the time of greatest power and prosperity in Palestine, characterized by town planning, impressive city walls, new ceramic forms, a simplified alphabet, and international trade. As this era came to an end (*ca.* 1550), every MB site suffered destruction; often a long hiatus in occupation followed. The biblical patriarchs are usually linked to MB (or LB). However, patriarchal chronology is very difficult to determine because the literary traditions embedding them are extremely complex (→ History, 75:29ff.). Egyptian influence in Palestine during this period was pervasive. The presence in Palestine of Asiatics called Hyksos, who ruled Egypt *ca.* 1667–1559, was also keenly felt.

69 Sites both outside and within Palestine provide much information about MB. Also, archaeological evidence is supplemented by literary material. No longer is it necessary to rely exclusively on mute artifacts, although pottery continues to play an important role. New data about MB have surfaced through the accelerated pace of field archaeology in Israel. (With respect to Jordan, major MB sites have yet to be excavated.) In addition to political history, much is being revealed about the life of the MB people, including architecture, trade, cult, and settlement (*BA* 50 [1987] 148–77).

70 The MB period was truly the climax of artistry in Palestine ceramics. Though there was no widespread use of painting or "adventitious" decoration, still the shape of the vessels now possesses an exquisite simplicity and gracefulness of line never later surpassed. The rounded base makes a perfect parabola, then curves upward and in toward the rim at just the right point to give an impression of balance and charm. Similar but more slender vessels are called dippers. In other cases, the flattened base was attached to a delicate low pedestal, and the curve at the belly was replaced by a sharp edge like the keel of a ship, called "carination."

71 Excavations outside Palestine which illuminate the Near East in MB (and LB) cast only indirect light on the Bible. As mentioned, Mari flourished from the mid-3d millennium to the early 18th cent. Famous for its palaces and temples, Mari's archive has been especially useful for understanding the city's ambient history and culture. Mari suffered destruction in 1765. Nuzi in NE Iraq furnishes tables from the second half of the 15th cent. dealing with Hurrian customs, which help in understanding the cultural environment of the Bible. So, too, excavations at sites of the Hyksos (*ca.* 1667–1559), who ruled in Egypt as the 15th and 16th Dynasties, are clarifying the early history of Palestine. The Hyksos stronghold in SW Palestine was at Sharuhen, probably to be located at Tell el-Ajjul, a major Canaanite city in the Bronze Age. Sharuhen was a rich and powerful city in MB, as excavations at Ajjul testify. The city was abandoned, however, in the 12th cent. with the Egyptian decline.

72 The master excavation of this period is Ras Shamra (Ugarit) at the NW seacoast corner of Syria. The whole MB flourishing of the ancient city-state of Ugarit, along with most of LB, was lumped by excavator C. Schaeffer into a single endless "stratum." As often happens outside Palestine, the mute potsherd claimed little attention at Ugarit because it was overshadowed by torrents of artwork and literary documents. The language discovered there, which scholars call Ugaritic, was a NW Semitic dialect very close to biblical Hebrew. The mythology of the Ugaritic epics clarifies many obscure allusions of the Bible. And the diplomatic archives of Ugarit form an indispensable link between the Hittite empire to the N, the Hurrians to the E, and the Canaanite city-states dependent on Egypt to the S.

In addition to Mari and Ras Shamra (Ugarit) in Syria, Tell Mardikh (Ebla; → 61 above) was also of great importance in MB. Its well-examined MB levels demonstrate the city's prosperity as a result of trade. Also, the palaces, temples, and ramparts of this era have been unearthed.

73 At Tell Beit Mirsim, SW of Hebron, Albright established the pottery chronology for Palestine from EB through Iron Age II (*ca.* 3000–600). He classified the stylistic changes in the potsherds and then correlated these data with the stratigraphy of the tell. Later excavations in Palestine and elsewhere helped to refine Albright's pottery chronology. The following are among hundreds of sites in Palestine with significant MB levels; many sites of this period were fortified.

74 At Dan a MB rampart surrounded the city. In 1978 A. Biran uncovered the huge mud brick gateway, consisting of two towers and a mud brick arch completely intact. This well-preserved arch of the gate dates to MB (1900–1700). Hazor was the largest city in Palestine during the MB period. A major fortified city in the Canaanite period, Hazor had extensive architecture in both upper and lower cities in MB and LB. Adorned with temples and palaces, Hazor reached its zenith in the 15th cent. (LB).

75 The earliest excavated city gate at Megiddo dates to MB. Located five mi. from Megiddo, Taanach with its massive fortifications of the Hyksos type (clear traces of contact with Egypt) prospered in MB (1650–1550). Tell el Farʿah, identified with Tirzah, was occupied in MB and LB, until its fall *ca.* 1300. Shechem, too, was an important urban center in MB, when it was surrounded by enormous walls. The oldest fortifications at Acco (Tell el-Fukhar) are MB in date (18th cent.). For MB earthworks, see *BA* 46 (1983) 57–61.

76 The first settlement at Tel Mevorakh, S of Dor, goes back to MB (for this site, see *BA* 40 [1977] 89–91). Gezer reached its zenith as a Canaanite city in

MB, with massive fortifications and a "high place" with ten pillars, which Dever identifies as an open sanctuary. At Aphek (Ras el Ain) on the coastal plain, six strata belonging to the first phase of MB have been uncovered. Shiloh was first occupied in the MB IIB and had massive fortifications in MB IIC. In the MB period Lachish was a Hyksos settlement, fortified with a glacis and a moat. Jericho, too, was a flourishing city with massive walls in MB. Burial caves of the same period discovered at Jericho contain a variety of objects illuminating the daily life of the MB people. Tel Masos, E of Beer-sheba, is one of the largest sites in the N Negeb. In MB and in the Iron Age it played a significant role; in MB Masos and the neighboring site, Tel Malhata, controlled the main roads in the Beer-sheba valley.

77   (C) Late Bronze Age (1550–1200). This is the final stage in the long culture-epoch named "Bronze," but it may more appropriately be called "Canaanite," the term used by Israeli archaeologists. Biblical scholars take a special interest in the eras beginning with LB; from this time on the archaeological evidence has a direct bearing on the Bible. LB is properly called a historical period because of the prevalence of contemporary literary and administrative documents. LB is also the era of Egyptian domination, represented by the 18th and 19th Dynasties of the New Kingdom.

Particularly significant was the Amarna Age, which takes its name from Tell el-Amarna, the modern designation of the capital city constructed by Pharaoh Amenhotep IV (Akhenaton, 1364–1347). In the archives of this city were found letters from Canaanite kings giving a picture of the disorder situation of that land. In Egypt itself the Amarna Age was the center of a twofold reform unique in history. Rejecting the stylized charm of Egyptian art, Akhenaton's court introduced honest realism. Not only was this Pharaoh portrayed with all his physical defects, but he was also shown among his subjects as well as in everyday situations of family life. In addition, in place of the horde of vultures and vipers worshiped as gods at Thebes, there was rigidly enforced at Amarna the worship of only one god. This god was portrayed under the image of the sun-disk, whose rays terminate in tiny hands reaching down to bless the king and his people. The twofold reform was crushed after Akhenaton's death. (See *BARev* 13 [3, 1987] 16–32; D. B. Redford, *Akhenaton* [Princeton, 1984].) Tut-ankh-Amon restored the capital to Thebes and there received the sumptuous burial whose unearthing in 1923 unleashed a worldwide flood of interest in archaeology. Technically, the Amarna effort may not have been monotheism and must certainly have been a movement going far deeper than the weak Pharaoh who consented to act as its spokesman. There is every reason to believe that after it was officially put down, it continued to seethe in sympathetic strata of the population.

78   The exodus event is traditionally placed in the LB period. With respect to a specific date, the following have been suggested: the early 1500s, the mid-1300s, and the early 1200s. Determining the date of the exodus is not simple (→ History 75:42ff.), for the sole source of our knowledge of the exodus is the Hebr Bible. Scriptural testimony to its religious significance and archaeological evidence are quite different sources of knowledge.

79   The Israelite occupation of Canaan, often dated to the 13th cent., is closely related to the exodus and creates the same kinds of problems for the archaeologist. Today, scholars present different models to account for the presence of the Israelites in the land of Canaan, including conquest, immigration, and revolt (→ History, 75:55ff.; *BA* 50 [1987] 84–100)—a situation anticipated by the contradictory accounts already present in Josh and

Judg. Assuming the basic historicity of the biblical account, Albright believed that the Israelites gained their foothold in Canaan by a decisive attack on the chief cities of the land. Hazor provides convincing evidence; its LB city was demolished, then later replaced by a less pretentious Iron I settlement. In addition to Hazor, however, three cities figuring prominently in the biblical narratives of the conquest are Jericho, Ai, and Gibeon, which offer evidence not congenial to the Albright hypothesis, showing no indication of destruction or settlement in the traditional time frame of the conquest.

80   Kenyon dug at Jericho in the 1950s to try to settle the date of the LB city's demise, which some attributed to Joshua. Part of the confusion about the chronology of Jericho was the result of attempts to reconcile the archaeological record and the biblical account. Garstang, an earlier excavator of Jericho, mistook, as we mentioned, two successive EB walls for a LB double wall (thought to have been destroyed by Joshua). Kenyon demonstrated that this "Joshua wall" had been demolished before 2000. Also, evidence of occupation at Jericho between 1400 and 800 was lacking. See J. R. Bartlett, *Jericho* (CBW; 1981).

81   The proposed site of Ai at et-Tell was occupied in EB (*ca.* 3100–2350); the site was then destroyed and abandoned. Only after a hiatus of 1,100 years was Ai resettled in Iron Age I, this time for 200 years; then it was abandoned permanently. (On Ai, see *BA* 39 [1976] 18–30; *BARev* 11 [2, 1985] 58–69.) In view of this evidence, the traditional LB date of the conquest and the biblical record cannot be reconciled. According to archaeological evidence, Gibeon (modern el-Jib) was not settled in LB, despite its prominence in the conquest narrative.

82   Interpreting the conquest accounts in Josh as etiological, Noth and other German scholars espouse the immigration model to explain Israel's entrance into Canaan. The settlement, in their understanding, was a gradual and peaceful infiltration into the unoccupied hill country, followed later by limited military campaigns. According to de Vaux, Malamat, and others, the Israelites settled in Canaan through a combination of peaceful entry and military assault. Mendenhall proposed the model of social revolution to explain the Israelite dominance in Canaan. Gottwald and others, who exclude invasion and immigration, are closer to Mendenhall than to Albright or Noth. Gottwald assumes that the people were already well settled in the land where they had been living as agriculturalists.

83   Archaeological excavation and survey can shed some light on this obscure subject, especially with respect to the unfortified villages of Iron I where the Israelites settled in the premonarchic period. Hundreds of Iron I settlements throughout Palestine, unoccupied in the Bronze Age, were settled peacefully in Iron Age I. Digs at Arad, Beer-sheba, Tel Masos, Tel Ira, and Tel Malhata reveal no remains of Canaanite cities in the N Negeb during LB. Nor does present archaeological evidence support the biblical account of the settlement when it states that Arad and Hormah were two fortified Canaanite cities in the N Negeb.

84   Recently excavated Israelite villages of the Early Iron Age—Masos, Esdar, Izbet Sartah, Giloh, Ai, and Raddana—shed light on the manner of Israelite settlement in Canaan. The architecture and landscaping of these villages reflect a level of sophistication not associated with pastoral nomads. The excavators of Tel Masos, the largest Iron I site in the N Negeb, point out that the Israelite settlers of the latter half of the 13th cent. were people who already had a building tradition dating to the Bronze Age. It is significant that Masos remained unfortified despite its vulnerable location on a low hillock. It would appear that settlement, beginning at the end of the 13th cent. and continuing for two centuries, took place in an era of peace.

85   Izbet Sartah, two mi. E of Aphek-Antipatris, is probably Eben-ezer, where the Israelites mustered their troops against the Philistines encamped at Aphek. At Izbet Sartah, an Early Iron agricultural settlement, excavation has revealed the remains of a four-room house, the largest pillared building of this type in Israel. Among the valuable finds is an ostracon with five lines of incised letters. Dating *ca.* 1200, this inscribed potsherd is the oldest and most complete Proto-Canaanite linear alphabet of 22 letters. Unable to fathom the inscription, epigraphists speculate that it is a writing exercise of a student trying to learn the alphabet. See *BARev* 4 (3, 1978) 23–30.

86   Giloh (not Giloh of Josh 15), an early Israelite settlement SW of Jerusalem, was occupied briefly in Iron I. A. Mazar describes the site as a fortified herdsmen's village. On the basis of evidence unearthed there, he suggests tentatively that the Israelite conquest and settlement date from the late 13th to the mid-12th cent. In that period some Canaanite cities were destroyed and some Israelite settlements established. Yadin always maintained that Galilee was settled after the destruction of the Canaanite city of Hazor.

87   At Ai, after 1220, newcomers established a small village, which was both unfortified and agricultural. As farmers and shepherds, these new occupants were hardly immigrants recently arrived from the desert. Neighboring Raddana shows evidence of intense agricultural activity by settlers experienced in hill-country farming.

88   Hazor, the largest city in Canaan throughout LB, covered an upper tell and a lower rectangular plateau. The upper and lower cities were destroyed *ca.* 1230, the demolition which Yadin attributed to Joshua. The best sequence of Bronze Age temples is at Hazor, where four temples have been uncovered. The most elaborate is the "orthostat temple," so-called from the smooth basalt orthostats which lined the walls of the rooms during the latest phase of the temple. Begun in MB, this temple was rebuilt several times before being destroyed simultaneously with the city. Cult installations (incense altars, libations tables, etc.) were found in connection with these temples. See Y. Yadin, *Hazor* (NY, 1975).

89   Beth-shan, too, had a succession of LB temples built when the city was an Egyptian enclave. At a later day the Philistines transformed these temples and used them to desecrate the memory of their enemy Saul (1 Sam 31:10). Megiddo, Shechem, and Lachish also had temples in the LB era. The series of temples at Lachish was located near the NW corner of the mound, outside the city in the moat, whence the name "fosse temples." The fosse temples were small structures, comprising a cult room with a raised platform against the southern wall. In LB, the city also had a temple on the acropolis of the Canaanite city; its plans, architecture, and equipment reflected Egyptian influence.

90   At Timna, N of Elath, an Egyptian temple was uncovered. It had been built in front of a cliff, near the copper mines of the S Arabah. The temple is an Egyptian shrine dedicated to Hathor, the Egyptian goddess of mining, whose carved figures have been found there. Mining operations were conducted from the beginning of the 13th cent. until the mid-12th, but not during the Israelite monarchy. The recovery of the furnaces, ore, slag, and tools will aid greatly in understanding copper production in the transition between the Bronze and Iron ages.

91   East of the Jordan River, at Tell Deir Alla (Succoth?) the remains of a temple, destroyed by earthquake and fire at the end of LB, were uncovered. Four clay tablets, inscribed with a form of the Cypro-Minoan script, were found in two rooms E of the main sanctuary.

92   The cemetery at Deir el-Balah in the Gaza strip, an Egyptian outpost for the New Kingdom, has contributed a great deal to our knowledge of LB. At this site, T. Dothan unearthed about 40 anthropoid clay coffins, the earliest found in Canaan (14th and 13th cents.). These anthropoid coffins, built in the outline of a body with the lid in the shape of a head with a molded face, were originally used for the interment of Egyptian officials in LB. Borrowing their burial customs from Egypt, the Philistines adopted the anthropoid coffins in the Early Iron Age. At Beth-shan, about 50 anthropoid coffins (13th–11th cents.) have been discovered.

93   Toward the end of MB and at the beginning of LB, so-called bichrome pottery is widely in evidence. Originating in Cyprus, this splendid and distinctive ware is associated especially with Tell el-Ajjul, where it was first discovered. Bichrome jugs and bowls are painted with geometric designs in black and red with bands. Bulls, birds, and fish often adorn these vessels. Megiddo has yielded a large bowl, almost a foot in diameter, called a krater or punch bowl, with painting in two colors. Parallel bands above the belly are divided into squares containing animal and geometric motifs. This style is a snare to the unwary, who are apt to mistake it for the similar Philistine pottery of the next epoch, but close comparison shows recognizable distinctions between the two styles.

94   **(III) The Iron Ages.**
       (A) Early Iron Age (Iron I, 1200–900). This era is called the Iron Age or the Israelite period; both are quite general designations. The transition from bronze to iron tools is not to be fixed precisely at 1200 BC. During the 12th and 11th cents. bronze was commonly used, iron rarely. Nor can the Israelite settlement in Palestine be pinpointed to 1200; it took place over a prolonged period.

95   The Sea Peoples, including the Philistines, settled for the first time in the E Mediterranean basin in the first half of the 12th cent. BC (→ History, 75:67). Philistine culture emerged in Palestine about 1190. Only after a sound defeat at the hands of Ramses III did the Sea Peoples (Philistines) settle in the southern coastal plain of Palestine. This coast and the "pentapolis" (Gaza, Ashkelon, Ashdod on the coast; Gath and Ekron inland; → Biblical Geography, 73:71) were the heartland of Philistine power, although their control extended up the coast at least as far as Dor, and eastward to Beth-shan and Tell Deir Alla in the Jordan Valley. Philistine influence continued through the mid-10th cent., although it did not come to an end at that time.

      The pottery of the Iron Age Philistines, despite the Megiddo resemblances, is one of our clearest norms for dating any mound in SW Palestine. Philistine pottery is painted in black and red ordinarily on a white-slipped background. It is locally made, but strongly influenced by Mycenean III C 1 ware. For Albright, hip flasks, wine kraters, and beer jugs with strainer spouts imaginatively add up to this conclusion: "The Philistines were mighty carousers, as we see from the story of Samson." More inescapably Philistine are ornamental features such as the "backward-looking swan with tired wingspread," painted on a krater with almost vertical loop handles. The swan is sometimes varied by other motifs such as a fish, and each panel is framed with bands and spirals.

      By a fortunate coincidence, the richest deposit of this

style of Aegean origin was encountered by Duncan Mackenzie at Beth-shemesh while he was fresh from his experience at Knossos in Crete. The Aegean parentage has been corroborated also by the excavation of P. Dikaios at Enkomi in Cyprus. Strangely, Beth-shemesh itself is expressly featured in 1 Sam 6:12 as lying *outside* Philistine territory. Either the frontier fluctuated, or wares were traded across the border.

96   Smaller Philistine deposits or stray sherds are found at many mounds W of Beth-shemesh. We know from the story of Saul's death (1 Sam 31:10) that the Philistines had an enclave as far NE as Beth-shan. Coffin lids from there reflect the same Philistine influences as those at Tell el-Far'ah (S). Israeli excavations have been undertaken inland from Ashkelon at a crossroads site named Tel Gath by Israeli authorities in deference to Albright's suggested (but incorrect) identification of the site as Philistine Gath. But here, too, there was a disappointing minimum of Philistine ware. The site was provisionally, in the face of Yadin's opposition, claimed to be the storage city of Mamshith attested by tax receipts at excavations elsewhere in Judah. Today this site is called Tel Erani, based on the Arabic designation Sheikh el-Areini. Tell es-Safi, where many Philistine vessels have been found, seems now to be the best candidate for the pentapolis Philistine city of *Gath*.

97   The influence of Matthew Arnold has made the word "Philistine" a synonym of the crude uncultured boor. But the Bible's contempt for the Philistines is never on the plane of human culture, where excavation shows them to have been far superior to the Israelites. In fact we may safely maintain that the chosen people, while developing their enduring spiritual and ethical worship on the soil of the Holy Land, were content to lag behind or borrow the culture forms of their neighbors. It is interesting that the land shared by the Philistines and the Israelites ultimately came to be named Palestine after the former.

As excavations and surveys continue, much new information on the distribution of Philistine material culture will come to light. More than 40 sites have remains of Philistine culture. This widespread distribution of Philistine pottery, however, does not imply Philistine occupation; it can also be attributed to commercial and military contacts. Our greatest deficiency concerns the Philistine language; no extant texts can be attributed with certainty to them.

(Dohan, T., *The Philistines and Their Material Culture* [New Haven, 1982]. Sanders, N. K., *The Sea Peoples* [London, 1978]. *Arch* 36 [1, 1983] 12–19. *BARev* 8 [4, 1982] 20–44; 8 [6, 1982] 40–54; 10 [2, 1984] 16–28. *NatGeog* [Dec. 1982].)

98   Of the Philistine pentapolis, *Ashdod* is the best known archaeologically. Occupied from EB to the Arab period, Ashdod became, during the 10 cent. BC, one of the largest independent city-states in Philistia. Extensive excavations by M. Dothan in the 1960s revealed Philistine occupation in two levels, dating from the 12th and 11th cents. Ashdod was distinctively Philistine from *ca.* 1175 to 1000. Among the cult objects at Ashdod was the well-known Philistine clay goddess figurine in the shape of a throne, dating to the 12th cent.

99   *Gaza*, the southernmost of the Philistine cities, has been excavated, but not so extensively as Ashdod. More work needs to be done at both sites. Ashdod's harbor has never been found. Because Gaza is buried under the modern city, further digging there is unlikely. The other two cities of the Philistine pentapolis, Ekron and Ashkelon, are less encumbered and more promising sites; excavations requiring a long time were undertaken at both.

100   *Ekron,* the northernmost of the five Philistine cities, is most likely situated at Tel Miqne, the largest Iron Age settlement in Israel. Besides the valuable insights on the Philistines to be gained from digging this site, it should yield data dealing with the historical and cultural relationship among the Canaanites, Israelites, and Assyrians. Occupation at Miqne dates as early as Late Chalcolithic. Assyrian and biblical texts attest that Ekron continued as a Philistine city until the end of the 7th cent. BC, and the pottery confirms this. Both Mycenean III C 1b and Philistine bichrome wares have been found. S. Gitin and T. Dothan have uncovered at Miqne the industrial area for the production of olive oil, which must have been an important export. Over a hundred Iron Age II olive-press installations, consisting of large crushing basins flanked on either side by presses, have been uncovered. Such evidence will elucidate the Philistine material culture and economy, both of which are hardly known. See *BA* 50 (1987) 197–222.

101   In 1985 L. Stager undertook a new phase of excavation at *Ashkelon,* one of the most important ancient seaports in the E Mediterranean and one of the five main cities of the Philistines. Ingeniously, Stager was able to resume digging at the same stratigraphic level where Phythian Adams left off in the early 1920s. As early as 1815, Lady Hester Stanhope "dug" at Ashkelon. When her workers found there a large statue of Zeus, they smashed it, hoping to discover a treasure within. The history of Ashkelon extends from the Bronze Age (*ca.* 2000) through the Crusader period. The Ashkelon project will contribute much to Mediterranean archaeology, as it helps to answer questions about the origins of the Sea Peoples, especially the Philistines. The Egyptian conquest of Ashkelon is recorded on the Merneptah stele and depicted in reliefs at Karnak (Egypt). Already the archaeologists have detected at Ashkelon a 7th-cent. destruction of the Philistine city at the hands of the Babylonians (most likely, Nebuchadnezzar in 605 BC). Underwater archaeology is also in operation at Ashkelon to study the port facilities.

102   One of the most important Philistine sites is Tel Qasile, the ancient name of which is unknown. It is located on the N bank of the Yarkon River within the city of Tel Aviv. The Philistines founded this port city in the first half of the 12th cent. Its city plan is impressive, providing separate areas for cult, residences, and industry. A Philistine temple was found for the first time ever at Tel Qasile (*BA* 40 [1977] 82–87). In fact, A. Mazar uncovered three superimposed Philistine temples, the earliest a one-room structure dating from the 12th cent. The main cult room of the Philistine temples is a "long room" with two wooden pillars reminiscent of the Samson story. Apart from the evidence it yields concerning the Philistines, Tel Qasile has special significance for Israelis: it was the first site excavated by Israeli archaeologists (under the direction of B. Mazar) after the establishment of the modern state.

103   Tel Masos was a prosperous settlement in the Philistine era. This fact led the excavators to believe that this city became part of the commercial and political system of Philistia. Tel Batash in the Sorek Valley (→ Biblical Geography, 73:74) has been identified as Timnah, mentioned in the Samson saga. This site was occupied continuously from MB to the Persian period. A. Mazar began a dig there in 1977 in order to clarify some historical problems dealing with the border region between Philistia and Judah. Philistine artifacts uncovered at Timnah indicate that it flourished in Iron Age I. In the 10th cent. a new town was built upon the ruins of the Philistine city. Dor, one of the largest tells in Israel, was excavated anew in the 1980s (with reports appearing in *IEJ*). Philistine remains were uncovered there, as well as at Zeror, Acco, and Dan.

104 Meanwhile, in those areas of Canaan that were not specifically Philistine, pottery style hit its lowest ebb in the Iron Age, coinciding with Israelite infiltration. The materials are coarse and the shapes are dumpy; the total impression of a collection of Iron Age pottery is that it is the least aesthetic of any period. Several small but important sites near Jerusalem have been excavated by Americans: Albright at Gibeah, Bethel, and Beth-zur; Badè at Tell en-Nasbeh (Mizpah?); Pritchard at Gibeon. (See J. B. Pritchard, *Gibeon: Where the Sun Stood Still* [Princeton, 1962].) Early Iron Age pottery was especially abundant at the excavations of Shiloh. This corroborates the portrayal of Shiloh in 1 Sam 1:3; 4:3 as a center of pilgrimage focused on the ark of the covenant. Saul's capital was at Gibeah, just across the modern road from Samuel's bailiwick at Mizpah (Nasbeh?) and Gibeon, near the tower now called Nebi Samwil, a landmark.

Several years later, other American excavators returned to Gibeah, Bethel, and Beth-zur to clarify and complete the work undertaken earlier by Albright. Because it is almost impossible to declare an excavation complete, these sites will be restudied from time to time, as has happened at Shiloh and Tell en-Nasbeh, to mention only two. Earlier interpretations about Shiloh are being revised. The first settlement there was founded in MB II. The Iron I settlement was destroyed by fire in the mid-11th cent., but followed by a small village in Iron II. The earlier excavators had not recognized the Iron II remains. (See *BARev* 12 [1, 1986] 22–41.)

105 Pliny the Elder called Jerusalem "by far the most renowned city of the East." (→ Biblical Geography, 73:92–94.) Uniquely symbolic, Jerusalem is perhaps the most excavated city in the world. However, it is not so well known archaeologically as other cities in Palestine because continuous occupation from the Bronze Age has impeded intensive excavation. Explorers and pilgrims have been visiting Jerusalem for centuries, but the city became the object of systematic investigation only in the second half of the 19th cent. After establishment in 1865, the British Palestine Exploration Fund sponsored the initial excavations of Jerusalem. Wilson, Warren, Clermont-Ganneau, Bliss, Dickie, Vincent, Weill, Macalister, Duncan, Crowfoot, FitzGerald, and Hamilton were among the earlier investigators of Jerusalem before Kathleen Kenyon (→ 19 above) directed a major dig in the 1960s. Since 1967 Israeli archaeologists have excavated intensively in the Old City: B. Mazar, around the Temple Mount; Avigad, in the Jewish Quarter; Shiloh, at the City of David; Broshi, on Mount Zion and in the Armenian Quarter; Amiran and Eitan, at the Citadel; Netzer and Ben-Arieh, N of the Old City.

106 Kenyon's project, which focused principally on the City of David, inaugurated a new era in the archaeology of Jerusalem. Her purpose was to apply the latest archaeological techniques to the problems raised by earlier excavators, especially the question of the historical topography of Jerusalem. Constituting only a small part of modern Jerusalem, the City of David is situated on the steep slope of the Old City's SE spur. Skilled in stratigraphic technique learned from British archaeologist Mortimer Wheeler, Kenyon excavated in a long, narrow trench from the crest of the hill to the Gihon spring. Although she made some mistakes, she was able to clarify chronology by unraveling the complex stratigraphy of the city's E slope. One of Kenon's important discoveries was the Jebusite wall and adjacent tower surrounding the pre-Israelite city. Until Kenyon's dig, it had been assumed that this wall was located much closer to the crest of the E ridge. Dating as early as 1800 BC, the wall was in use for 1,000 years.

107 Building on Kenyon's work, Y. Shiloh undertook in 1978 further excavation of the City of David. He unearthed 25 occupational strata, spanning the Chalcolithic to medieval times. He opened 12 areas for excavation and succeeded in clarifying several aspects of Jerusalem's history, among them the fortification system of the city from MB to Byzantine; the nature of the dwellings (from EB through Iron II) on the stepped terraces of the E slope; the complex system of the subterranean water installations of the Iron Age. The three interconnected water systems emanating from the Gihon spring are Hezekiah's tunnel, the Siloam channel, and Warren's shaft (named after its discoverer; → 8 above). Anticipating Sennacherib's attack on Jerusalem in 701 BC, Hezekiah brought the waters of the Gihon spring inside Jerusalem by means of a 1,750-ft. tunnel. The Siloam channel serviced reservoirs and provided irrigation water. Warren's shaft, consisting of a vertical shaft and connecting tunnels, enabled the Jerusalemites to draw water from the Gihon spring without exposure to hostile attack. Vincent and other earlier explorers considered Warren's shaft, the earliest of these water systems, to be the ṣinnôr (conduit) of 2 Sam 5, providing David's soldiers access to Jerusalem in their attempt to capture it. Contrary to Vincent, Shiloh has established that this water system dates to the Israelite occupation (10th–9th cents.), not to the pre-Davidic Jebusite period. Shiloh also discovered a hoard of 51 clay bullae used to seal papyri. These sealings were lying in a burnt layer of the "house of the bullae" (area G, at the top of the E slope). Baked by chance during the Babylonian conflagration of Jerusalem, these bullae, dating from the late 7th to the early 6th cent. BC, are well preserved. Of the scores of Hebrew personal names on the bullae, "Gemaryahu ben Shaphan" sounds familiar. A scribe by that name (Jer 36:10–12, 25) served at the court of Jehoiakim (608–597). Shiloh speculates that the "house of the bullae" functioned as the royal archive at the end of the monarchy. Two additional bullae from the First Temple period have come to light. One is of Baruch ben Neriah, the scribe; the other is of Jerahmeel, the king's son. Jer 36 helps in the identification of the two seal-owners. Baruch was the famous secretary and friend of Jeremiah. Jerahmeel was an officer under King Jehoiakim.

108 The spread of David's empire and the building activities of Solomon are archaeologically attested by an innovation called the casemate, i.e., two parallel defense walls partitioned into chambers for storage or lodging. The Solomonic casemate wall and the magnificent city gate with four entryways found at Megiddo were also in use at Hazor and Gezer (1 Kgs 9:15). The prototype of these gateways was found at Ashdod. Other styles attested about this time, especially at Megiddo, are the header-stretcher masonry and the Proto-Aeolic capital. The earliest examples of Israelite monumental architecture are the two Megiddo palaces constructed of ashlar masonry and adorned with Proto-Aeolic stone capitals.

109 Let us summarize here information gathered from excavations elsewhere about the probable structural details of Solomon's Temple (diagram, → Institutions, 76:43–46). The clearest initial approach to envisioning the finished product is the existing complete temple of Edfu in S Egypt. Although this temple was built some 700 years after Solomon, it preserves with utmost conservatism a style that is attested, by partial ruins elsewhere, as far back as 300 years before him. We know that Solomon had not only a marriage alliance but also other close cultural contacts with Egypt, the "arbiter of elegance" for its neighbors. Also instructive is the temple of Baalbek in Lebanon, built about the same time as that of Edfu. Even though it is partially destroyed, incomplete, and shows everywhere garish traces of Greco-Roman interpolations, there is still cogency in the fact that it was built by an architect of the same Phoenician race as the one who drew Solomon's blueprints. At Hazor the main temple of a group of several Bronze Age temples was found to have a recognizable ground plan. The similarity in plan of the Hazor temple to the temple at Alalakh (now Tell Atshana in N Syria), the capital of a Syro-Hittite kingdom, reveals that Hittite styles had an influence on the Temple of Solomon, which was built along the same general lines. See also the design of the 8th-cent. Tainat temple in Syria (→ Institutions, 76:43–46). The remains of these temples show that the innermost "Holy of Holies" was approached from an outer sanctum, which in turn was shielded by an imposing porch.

We cannot ignore the influences of a local Canaanite cult, of course. From the centuries preceding Solomon, important temples were brought to light in the excavations of Lachish, Megiddo, Shechem, and Ai. At Arad in the Negeb, occupied by Kenite clans related to Judah (→ Biblical Geography, 73:86, 88), Israeli excavations have unearthed a temple to Yahweh from the monarchical period. All these temples share common features, but often there are differences in the ground plan. (See BARev 13 [4, 1987] 38–49.) For instance, the Arad structure is a broad-room temple having its entrance on the long side, unlike the Jerusalem Temple, which was a long-room temple with its entrance at the end or short side of the rectangular form.

(For bibliography on the Jerusalem Temple, → Institutions, 77:46. Biran, A. [ed.], Temples and High Places in Biblical Times [Jerusalem, 1981]. Haran, M., Temples and Temple Service in Ancient Israel [Oxford, 1978]. Meyers, C. L., "The Elusive Temple," BA 45 [1982] 33–41.)

110 In 1938 Glueck (→ 17 above) began the excavation of Tell el-Kheleifeh, near the head of the Gulf of Aqabah. He erroneously identified the site as Solomon's seaport of Ezion-geber; there is no evidence there of 10th-cent. pottery to support Glueck's claim (→ Biblical Geography, 73:69).

111 Two recent discoveries pertaining to Iron Age cult have occasioned discussion among biblical scholars. During an archaeological survey, A. Zertal came across an installation on Mt. Ebal which he interprets as a rectangular altar and cult center. The nine-ft.-high structure dates to 1220–1000. Because the altar is constructed of large, unhewn field stones, Zertal made a tentative connection with the altar built by Joshua (Deut 27:1–10; Josh 8:30–35). A. Mazar investigated a one-period site in N Samaria which in his estimation may be an Israelite open-air cult site. A large rectangular stone slab, part of a square incense burner, and some animal bones suggest that the site may have a cultic function. Also, a bronze bull figurine, the largest ever found in Israel, was picked up in the vicinity. This find may help in understanding the cult of the golden calf in the Bible. See, however, BARev 14 (1, 1988) 48–52.

112   (B) Later Iron Age (Iron II, 900–600). The archaeological divisions of the Iron Age are not so uniform as those of the Bronze Age. We may safely regard "Iron II" as coextensive with the divided kingdom (922–586) of Judah-Israel. After the exile (539 on) we find political designations used instead of metals, but it is still the pottery that really affords the basis of division. Excavations, surveys, and inscriptions combine to provide a rather clear picture of Iron II. The material remains, however, are inferior to those of the neighbor-ing people. The highly developed defense system, consisting of fortresses and towers, points to security as a major concern; certainly land, cities, and commerce had to be protected. Providing safe drinking water was another consideration. Typical architecture in this period, as in Iron I, was the pillared house with two to four rooms; the pillars supported a roof or second story. In Iron II the regional geopolitical units were Judah, Israel, Phoenicia, and Philistia; in Transjordan were Moab, Ammon, and Edom (→ History, 75:66ff.).

113 When, under Jeroboam I, Samaria broke off from subjection to the house of David, it had no permanent capital city for a while. In 876 Omri became king at Tirzah on the NE slope of Mt. Ebal (excavated by de Vaux; → 18 above) and soon started to build a palace. However, Omri abruptly changed his plan and moved his capital 10 mi. W. There on the W slope of the mountain range, in view of the Mediterranean, he built an entirely new city under the name of Shomron or Samaria. See A. Parrot, Samaria (SBA 7; London, 1958); G. E. Wright, BA 22 (1959) 67–78, or BAR 2. 248–57; EAEHL 4. 1032–50; → Biblical Geography, 73:103.

114 The excavation of Samaria was begun by G. A. Reisner in 1908–1910 and continued by J. W. Crowfoot in 1931–1935. The city wall, like those of Mirsim and Lachish, seems in Albright's opinion to show the introduction of a new indirect-access gateway of a type still visible today in the entries to old Jerusalem (yet the earlier walls of Nasbeh and of Solomonic Megiddo already exemplify this principle). The most imposing building cleared by Reisner was at the top of the hill, underneath the remains of a Herodian temple to Augustus. (The Roman emperor's honorific appellation in its Gk form Sebastē was given in Herodian times to the whole city and survives in the present Arabic name of the site, Sebastiyeh.) The building of the hilltop palace seems to have been begun by Omri and continued by his son Ahab (869–850), and also by Jeroboam II (786–746). It contained beautifully carved ivories rivaling those of Megiddo from an earlier century (ANEP 332). Similar ones, Phoenician in origin, have been discovered at various points of the Fertile Crescent. The luxury these ivories represent helps us to understand the frequent tirades against social inequalities by the first of the writing prophets, Amos, in whose book we find several contemptuous references to ivory (3:15; 6:4). See BARev 11 (5, 1985) 40–53.

115 Another precious insight into worsening economic maldistribution is afforded by an archive of tax receipts from the Samaria palace. They are in the form of ostraca, i.e., potsherds with writing in ink, dated over a period of some 17 years (BA 45 [1982] 229–39). Seemingly the long reign of Jeroboam II best accommodates this archive.

We should recall here that beginning around the year 1000 we possess several inscriptions in the Phoenician or archaic-Hebr script, translated in ANET 320–21. The oldest is perhaps the Gezer calendar, really too laconic and schoolboyish to warrant any firm inferences about the existence and nature of Hebrew as a separate language at this time. In the 1967 Israeli excavation campaign at Arad a ten-letter ostracon from the 10th cent. was discovered. The long and detailed "stele" inscription of Omri's contemporary, King Mesha of Moab, is considered to be in the Moabite language; and its differences from Hebrew are greater than the differences between Hebrew and Aramaic. From about 700 BC in Jerusalem dates the Siloam tunnel inscription of Hezekiah (715–687), which Albright declares to be "in elegant classical Hebrew . . . but these finds, as well as hundreds of short inscriptions on seals and other objects, pale into insignificance beside the sensational discovery of the Lachish Ostraca." This statement may now need revision, however, in the light of the discovery (1962–1967) of over 200 inscribed ostraca at Arad. According to Y. Aharoni (*BA* 31 [1968] 9–18) over half are in Hebrew and date from the monarchy, while the rest are in Aramaic from *ca.* 400 BC.

116 The following is a catalogue of archaeological projects which provide insights into Iron II. At Ramat Rahel (Beth-haccherem?), S of Jerusalem, a royal citadel (9th or 8th cent.) and an imposing palace belonging to one of the last Judahite kings were excavated. The monumental architecture of these buildings must have been impressive. This site also yielded 145 jar handles with the royal (*lmlk*) stamp. At Khirbet Rabud (Debir?), S of Hebron, excavators uncovered a Judahite city of the 9th cent. A massive wall, 13 ft. wide, surrounded the city. In the En-gedi region near the Dead Sea, an industrial installation of the mid-7th cent. was uncovered at Tel Goren. At Tell el-Hesi in the kingdom of Judah, the 9th-cent. defense installations, surrounding the city with a double rampart, have been unearthed.

117 At Tel Beer-sheba, just E of the modern city, a fortified royal city was founded in the 10th cent. The final destruction of this site dates to Sennacherib's assault in 701. The four stones of a horned altar, dating to the 8th cent., were discovered reused in a wall of a storehouse complex. Three were intact, and the fourth was missing the top part. Contrary to the biblical injunction (Josh 8:31), these stones are well-smoothed ashlar masonry. The horns were the holiest part of the altar: cutting them off was desecration (Amos 3:14); grasping them conferred the right of asylum (1 Kgs 2:28). On Beer-sheba, → Biblical Geography, 73:86; *BA* 35 (1972) 111–27; *BARev* 6 (6, 1980) 12–28. At Tel Masos, E of Beer-sheba, the huge settlement of the 12th and 11th cents. had declined; by the 7th cent. it was reduced to a small fortress. At Aroer, SE of Beer-sheba, the excavators found four phases of Iron II construction (7th–6th cents.). The artifacts found at this fortified desert town indicate that the inhabitants had contact with their Edomite neighbors to the E. Tell Sera (Ziglag?), NW of Beer-sheba, gives evidence of well-planned buildings, including four-room houses, in the 10th–9th cents. This site served later as a fortress for the Assyrian invaders. Tell Jemmeh was also occupied by the Assyrians. The Assyrian governor may have resided at Jemmeh's well-preserved building with its unique brick vaults.

118 Among the small Israelite forts in the Negeb during Iron II, two deserve special mention. Forty miles S of Beer-sheba is the modern site of Ein el-Qudeirat, thought to be Kadesh-barnea, the important Israelite station during the exodus, though there are no remains earlier than the 10th cent. At this site R. Cohen uncovered three fortresses, each built upon the remains of the preceding, dating between the 10th and 6th cents. (→ Biblical Geography, 73:85).

Forty miles S of Ein el-Qudeirat, Z. Meshel excavated Kuntillat 'Ajrud, a remote desert way station. The British explorer E. Palmer discovered this site in 1869. The architecture, consisting of a main rectangular building and a smaller structure, is not the main feature there. The inscriptions are the extraordinary find. There are dedications, requests, prayers, and blessings, in Hebrew and Phoenician, painted on the plaster walls of the building and on two large pithoi (storage jars) or incised on stone vessels. Crude drawings accompany some of the religious inscriptions. The "Yahweh-Asherah" inscription and associated drawing on one pithos have occasioned endless scholarly discussion.

"Asherah," in the opinion of some, is a reference to a sacred tree or cluster of trees, which may have been in the process of being personified, as the prophets feared. In the drawing, two figures are standing and one is seated. The standing figures probably represent the Egyptian demigod Bes; the seated lyre player is simply a musician, not a goddess. On the basis of pottery and scripts, this settlement dates from the late 9th to the early 8th cent. BC. See *BA* 39 (1976) 6–10; *BARev* 5 (2, 1979) 24–35; 10 (6, 1984) 42–51; *TS* 48 (1987) 333–40.

119 There were several important Iron II sites in the N, also. At Tel Dan, a 9th-cent. gate and related fortifications, as well as a sacred area (temenos), have been uncovered (→ Institutions, 76:40). In the sanctuary area a stone horn belonging to a large altar was also found. A. Biran claims that an installation (late 10th-early 9th cent.) found near the temenos was used in a water libation ritual. This installation is composed of a sunken basin flanked by flat basalt slabs, sloping away from the basin; at the end of each slab is a sunken jar. Others identify the installation as an olive press. Because olive oil was used for ritual purposes in biblical times, it would not be incongruous to find an oil press in a sacred area. (For the excavations, see *BA* 37 [1974] 26–51; 43 [1980] 168–82; 44 [1981] 139–44; *BARev* 7 [5, 1981] 20–37; 10 [6, 1984] 52–58; 13 [4, 1987] 12–25.)

120 Hazor, rebuilt in the Solomonic era, continued to function until its demise in 732. The gigantic water system at Hazor, dating to Omri (9th cent.), was similar to Megiddo's. It consisted of three main sections: shaft, sloping tunnel, and entrance structure. In Iron II the fortified city of Achzib, near the coast in the N, reached its zenith as a most important Phoenician settlement. Taanach was destroyed about the end of the 12th cent. Reoccupied in the 10th cent., it was leveled by Shishak in 918. A mass of cultic materials was uncovered in Taanach's 10th-cent. sanctuary. The best-known artifact is the baked-clay cultic stand with reliefs of animals and a winged sun disk. Shechem was fairly prosperous in Iron II after Jeroboam I moved the capital to Tirzah (→ Biblical Geography, 73:102). The Assyrians destroyed Israelite Shechem in 722, and it was abandoned until the 4th cent. BC.

121 Near the coastal city of Yabneh Yam there is a fortress on the site of Meṣad Hashavyahu. Conquered by Josiah, it was subsequently destroyed in 609 by Neco's Egyptian army (→ History, 75:111). This site is famous for the discovery of a 14-line ostracon, which is a letter of a harvest worker, complaining that his garment had been unjustly confiscated (Exod 22:25; Deut 24:12). This ostracon, dating to the second half of the 7th cent., is an important nonbiblical document dealing with everyday life in Judah during the preexilic period.

122 During Iron II and the Persian era Ammon, Moab, and Edom flourished (→ History, 75:68–70; → Biblical Geography, 73:40–49). The whole region E of the Jordan River has now been extensively surveyed; consequently, much more is known today about Transjordan than at any other time. Glueck's surveys were informative, but his successors have generated far more data, while correcting some of his conclusions. The Ammonites, occupying N-central Jordan, had their capital at Amman. Written evidence about the Ammonites (including the Tell Siran bronze bottle inscription, the Amman citadel inscription, the Amman theater inscription, and numerous seals) supplements excavation and survey. The Moabites, located in central Jordan, had Kerak and Dibon as their capitals. Iron II fortifications were excavated at Dibon (modern Dhiban), where the Moabite Stone (Mesha stele), describing relations between Moab and Israel in the 9th cent., was discovered in 1868. Modern Ḥesbân, once reputed to be Heshbon, had no Bronze Age remains and little Early Iron. Late Iron II is well represented, however. In addition to the defense wall, ostraca from the 7th and 6th cents. have been uncovered. The Edomites were located in S Jordan, with Bozrah (modern Buseirah) as their capital. Several Iron II sites have been excavated in the S, including Buseirah, Umm el-Biyara, Tawilan, and Tell el-Kheleifeh. At Buseirah the fortifications and a major temple or palace have been found. However, no major Edomite inscriptions have come to light.

123 Tell Deir Alla in the Jordan Valley is usually identified with Succoth (→ Biblical Geography, 73:51), but the excavator H. Franken has suggested Gilgal. In addition to the LB clay tablets inscribed in a linear script, an important religious text has been recovered. Written in red and black ink on a wall of an 8th-cent. building, and perhaps in old Aram dialect, the inscription refers to "Balaam, son of Beor" (Num 22–24). See *BA* 39 (1976) 11–17; *BARev* 11 (5, 1985) 26–39.

Another Aram inscription was found in 1979 near Tell Fakhariyah in E Syria. Dating to the mid-9th cent. BC, it is bilingual with Akkadian as the second language and was inscribed on the skirt of a life-size black basalt statue of a governor.

124 **(IV) From the Fall of Jerusalem to Herod. (A) Babylonian and Persian Periods (600–332).** After Jerusalem, Lachish was the most important fortified city in Judah. It sheds great light on the Assyrian assault against Judah under Sennacherib, as well as the later Babylonian invasion of the southern kingdom under Nebuchadnezzar. Lachish is the extensive site named Tell ed-Duweir (not Tell el-Hesi, which Petrie thought to be Lachish; → 11 above). The Duweir site had already been suggested by Albright even before the name Lachish itself was dug up by the excavation of J. Starkey in 1932–1938. Of note is that the most vivid excavated information about Lachish did not come from Duweir at all, but from faraway Nineveh in northern Assyria. From there came the British Museum frieze of Sennacherib (*ANEP* 372) showing how he overcame the resistance of Lachish during his invasion of Palestine in 701. The maneuvers of Judah's king Hezekiah, obscurely described in 2 Kgs 18:14, averted a subjugation similar to that of Samaria. But one century later, there arose in S Babylonia the new military machine of Nebuchadnezzar. It inflicted a decisive defeat upon the Egyptians at Carchemish in 605, then launched a full-scale invasion of Palestine in 598 and 589. Both times the citadel of Lachish bore the brunt of the attack on the open country outside Jerusalem. See *BARev* 14 (2, 1988) 42–47.

125 Within one room of the city gate of Duweir, Starkey found in 1936 some 20 jar fragments with messages in ink from a military official to his regional captain (*ANET* 321–22). One of these "ostraca" bemoans the fact that a hostile army is advancing so relentlessly that the signals of nearby Azekah have already been extinguished, although those of Lachish are still visible. These sherds were found in a narrow level between two destruction-layers of ash. It seemed natural to ascribe these two layers to the two destructions inflicted by Nebuchadnezzar within 10 years of each other (598 and 589). But Starkey was killed shortly afterward in an ambush, and a reexamination of the facts by their publisher Olga Tufnell made it seem that the earlier ash-layer may have been Sennacherib's (701). Meanwhile, however, the content of the messages proves to the satisfaction of all experts that they were composed around 590. Mention of a Coniah, son of Elnathan, recalls the Elnathan of Jer 26:22; 36:12. The appeals to

Egypt, and the frantic activity of Jeremiah during the black moments of the deportation, seem also reflected in the Lachish Letters. (See reference to Lachish and Azekah in Jer 34:7.) One of the Arad ostraca, seemingly to be dated on paleographic grounds to the end of the monarchy, mentions the coming of the Edomites. Y. Aharoni would relate this to an Edomite assault on the Negeb just before Nebuchadnezzar's final campaign against Judah (*ca.* 600).

126 In 1973 D. Ussishkin began a new phase of excavations near Lachish. Besides digging the LB temple and other installations, he concentrated on the Iron Age city-gate complex near the SW corner of the tell. Consisting of several superimposed gates that were destroyed successively, this complex caused serious dating problems which Ussishkin wanted to resolve. The date of Stratum III has been the subject of scholarly dispute for a long time. Like Tufnell, Ussishkin concluded on the basis of stratigraphic evidence that Stratum III marks the destruction by Sennacherib in 701. Likewise, Stratum II represents the Babylonian conquest by Nebuchadnezzar in 588–586. Starkey wanted to date the Stratum III destruction to the Babylonian assault of 597, but the sharp difference in pottery forms found in Strata III and II required, in Ussishkin's estimation, more than a 10-year interval to account for such typological changes. Most, but not all, archaeologists concur with Ussishkin's dating of the city-gate complex. The Assyrians attacked Lachish at the SW corner of the city precisely because it was so vulnerable; everywhere else the city was protected by deep valleys. There the Assyrians constructed their siege ramp of earth and stone and threw it up against the city wall, as depicted on the Sennacherib reliefs. The defenders of Lachish responded by building their own counter-ramp inside the city wall, opposite the Assyrian ramp. (On Lachish: *BA* 40 [1977] 71–76; *BARev* 5 [6, 1979] 16–39; 10 [2, 1984] 48–77; 13 [1, 1987] 18–39; for sites at the end of the kingdom, see *BA* 38 [1975] 26–54.)

127 The Babylon to which a certain proportion of Judeans was deported has been brought magnificently to light by the German excavation of Nebuchadnezzar's palace and Ishtar temple. Numerous other excavations in the Tigris-Euphrates valley give incidental insights regarding the life of the exiles described in Ezek and Dan 1. Farther E, in Iran, excavations such as Susa and Persepolis give ample detail on the mode of government of Cyrus and Darius (late 6th cent.) reflected in Dt-Isa and Esth.

Within devastated Judah itself, excavation may show that daily life was interrupted by the deportation but cannot settle the debate as to how large a percentage of the population was left behind. At Lachish, on the very top of the mound, a large palace that had served the local ruler since 900 was transformed into a different style during the exile. Tufnell accepted the judgment of Watzinger that the innovations were Syro-Hittite. But Albright claimed them to be Persian, "strongly reminiscent in plan and detail of such early Parthian buildings as the small palace at Nippur in Babylonia, where we have a similar use of courts and columns."

128 Our knowledge of Palestine's material culture in the Persian period, when the Jews returned from Babylonian exile, is increasing rapidly because of renewed interest in this era. Digs, surveys, epigraphic evidence, coins, figurines, and underwater archaeology are illuminating this once little-known period. The distribution of settlements and populations in the Persian period are now much better understood. Israeli archaeologist E. Stern, a specialist in the Persian period, is making a significant contribution by his own excavations and by coordinating results from other sites. Hazor, Shiqmona, Tel Megadim, Tel Mevorakh, En-gedi, Tell el-Hesi, and several other sites have much to teach about the Persian period. Stern concludes that Palestine in the Persian period was divided into two regions: the first was the hilly area of Judea, Jordan, and Samaria, reflecting the "eastern" culture of Assyria, Babylonia, and Egypt; the second was Galilee and the Mediterranean coast, reflecting the "western" culture of Greece and Cyprus.

129 Stratum II of the upper city at Hazor is ascribed to the Persian period. The citadel built by the Assyrians in an earlier period continued to be used in the Persian age. In the coastal town of Shiqmona, a fortress and residential quarter have been excavated. At Tel Megadim on the coast, there are remains of a well-preserved Persian town, quadrangular in shape, with a street paralleling the city wall. Objects found at the site indicate that the city's wealth accrued from commerce and agriculture. The abundance of Attic pottery there is evidence of trade with Greece. Tel Mevorakh in the Sharon plain has three phases of the Persian period, with evidence of an administrative center or large estate. On Tel Goren in the En-gedi area is a large Persian building which had been used as a dwelling. A rich hoard of potsherds from the Persian period and two Aramaic ostraca were also uncovered. In the Persian levels at Tell el-Hesi a significant amount of building took place. Hesi had strong affinities with Tell Jemmeh and Tell el-Far'ah (S) in this period; all were large grain storage areas. (For a report on excavations at Hesi, see *BA* 41 [1978] 165–82.)

Other sites will help to illuminate the Persian period, but several are either not yet published or the digs are in progress. Dor on the coast was an important Phoenician city in the Persian period. It was surrounded by a city wall constructed of large limestone blocks. The principal city in the Persian era was Samaria, the seat of the Persian governor. Unfortunately, only scanty remains of the period have survived.

130 The caves of Wadi ed-Daliyeh, concealed in a remote area N of Jericho, contained 27 papyri and many fragments of others. Commercial and legal in nature, the Wadi ed-Daliyeh documents, written in Aramaic, are dated 375–335 BC. These are the oldest legal papyri of Palestinian origin. Besides the papyri, 300 skeletons were found in the caves. F. Cross speculates that these were the remains of unfortunate Samaritans who rebelled against Alexander the Great. Escaping from Samaria when Macedonian troops destroyed the city in 331, these victims sought refuge in the Daliyeh caves. Discovering them, the soldiers ignited the mouth of the cave and suffocated them.

131   (B) Greek and Hasmonean Periods (332–1 BC). In 330 Alexander the Great brought Greek armies to Palestine, which in the following centuries was flooded with the good and bad features of Greek culture. The strong resistance to the encroachments of Hellenism ultimately led to the revolutionary reactions of the Maccabees in 167. But with Pompey's invasion of Palestine in 63 BC, the Roman Empire began to serve as a framework to bring Judea to a greater power and extension than it had known since David, e.g., under Herod the Great and Herod Agrippa I.

132 One of the pioneering excavations at Marisa (Tell Sandahanna), W of Hebron, by F. Bliss in 1898 yielded the imposing ground plan of a 2d-cent. BC Hellenistic city. The tombs of Marisa excavated in 1902 and still visible are among our earliest Hellenistic monuments. They contained Greek inscriptions and color frescoes of a Hellenistic bawdiness.

133 Anafa, a wealthy Hellenistic town in Upper Galilee, flourished from the mid-2d cent. to about 80 BC. This settlement represented the transition from Hellenistic to Roman. Artifacts attesting to the affluence of the town are molded glass vessels and terra sigillata (red-glazed bowls and plates rouletted on the interior and the rim). A dedicatory bilingual inscription in Greek and Aramaic was found at Dan. Dating to the first half of the 2d cent. BC, this votive inscription refers to "the god who is in Dan."

134 From about 175 BC survives an imposing structure in the lonely region of Araq el-Emir, W of Amman. Once it was thought to have been a mausoleum; but three campaigns of excavation (1961–1962) convinced P. Lapp that it was a temple. If there is a basis for calling the monumental building a temple, it would be architectural typology. It belonged to a certain Tobiah, a dynastic political leader prominent in Josephus (*Ant.* 12.5.1 §240) and seemingly descended from Tobiah the Ammonite, prominent in Neh (→ History, 75:130). After making a stone-by-stone architectural study of the building, French archaeologists undertook a total reconstruction and restoration.

135 On the road to Hebron an important citadel was excavated at Tubeiqa by Albright and O. Sellers in 1931. It seems to have been Beth-zur, center of Maccabean troubles during what is the only recorded biblical observance of the sabbath year (1 Macc 6:49, but see North's reservations in *Bib* 34 [1953] 501). In 165 BC Judas Maccabeus defeated Lysias, the Syrian regent, at Beth-zur. Later, numerous coins, catalogued there, helped to determine the date of Beth-zur's demise in the 70s BC. When Sellers resumed excavation at this site in 1957, he was able to shed further light on the defense of the city, as well as on other questions left unanswered during the first campaign. The Shechem excavation, as reopened by Wright in 1956, also brought to light a noteworthy Hellenistic city (*ca.* 330–107), relating to the Samaritan temple on Mt. Gerizim. Tell er-Ras, the northernmost peak of Mt. Gerizim, produced valuable Hellenistic and Roman remains. R. Bull discovered the foundation of a Greek-style temple. Dedicated to Zeus Hypsistos, it was erected by Hadrian in the 2d cent. AD. This Roman temple most likely was built over the Samaritan sanctuary which John Hyrcanus destroyed in 128 BC. The monumental gate at Gezer, dated to this period by Macalister (→ 14 above), has been shown by Yadin to be Solomonic in origin, but rebuilt in this period.

136 The Roman occupation of Palestine began in 67 BC, and from this time Rome's allies in Edom (Idumea) became steadily more powerful; in fact, Antipater and his son Herod the Great came from Idumean stock. The Edomites or Idumeans were cousins of the Jews (Gen 25:25), closely linked with both Midianites and Arameans (1 Chr 1:36,42; Num 24:21). Since their center was SE of the Dead Sea, they are to be associated with the Nabateans ruling Petra as Roman allies, whom Josephus loosely but not improbably calls Arabs. Apparently the Edomites traveled W of Wadi Arabah where they became the Idumeans of the Hellenistic and Early Roman era. At the same time the Nabateans, speaking a dialect of Aramaic, settled in the vicinity of Petra.

Petra is today one of the wonders of the world (I. Browning, *Petra* [2d ed.; London, 1982]). This immense red sandstone ghost town consists almost entirely of tomb façades 100 ft. high, carved out of the living rock. Most of them date from the centuries preceding and following Herod. From this period there is also a "high place" with obelisks, a late but important sample of the style of worship constantly reprobated by the prophets. Near it is a high-relief "horned altar" of the kind found freestanding at Megiddo and Luxor, and presumed in Exod 27:2. The rare hewn stone used by the Nabateans has a diagonal combing, conspicuous in a palace at Dibon. Scarcely less enchanting than their redstone structures is the Nabateans' eggshell-thin pottery with exquisite red painting, which may still be picked up not only at Petra but at SW Palestinian sites like Abda. The Nabateans ruled as far N as Damascus under Aretas IV (9 BC–AD 40; → Paul, 79:8, 20).

137 Pella in the N Jordan Valley, a city of the Decapolis in Roman times, had been revitalized in the Hellenistic period. During the First Jewish Revolt (AD 66–70) Christian refugees from Jerusalem fled to Pella for safety. Beginning in 1979 intense excavations were undertaken at Pella by an American and an Australian team, but little evidence of everyday life at Pella during the Early Roman period has surfaced. Sepphoris (Sippori) in Lower Galilee was the administrative center for the Galilee area during the Hasmonean era. Excavations of this large Jewish city were conducted in the 1930s and the 1980s (*BA* 49 [1986] 4–19; *BARev* 14 [1, 1988] 30–33).

The excavation of Qumran by R. de Vaux from 1951 to 1956 provides the best archaeological evidence of the last pre-Christian century (→ Apocrypha, 67:79). In fact, the corpus of pottery he found there marks the beginning of an effort (collated in *Palestinian Ceramic Chronology* [1961] by P. Lapp) to use pottery as a chronological indicator for the several centuries before and after Christ with the same reliability as in other periods of Palestine history.

138 Herodian Jerusalem was the scene of intensive excavation after 1967 when Israel annexed the Old City (E Jerusalem). B. Mazar conducted one of the major projects there. Working close to the retaining walls of the Temple Mount, he concentrated on the area S and SW of the temenos where he recovered remains spanning the Iron Age to the Arab period. The Herodian era produced the largest number of finds, all attesting to the splendor of that period. Before rebuilding the Temple, Herod doubled the size of the Temple Mount and constructed a far more extensive enclosure wall. The resultant podium measured 36 acres. Mazar also uncovered the entrances to the Temple Mount on the S side; they consisted of a double and a triple gate, together forming the Hulda gates. The royal stoa (portico) which towered over the S court of the Temple was the object of considerable study. Modeled on a Roman basilica, it was composed of 160 columns supporting the roof. Mazar also clarified "Robinson's arch," which juts out near the SW corner of the enclosure wall. Robinson thought this arch supported a bridge across the Tyropoeon Valley. In fact, the arch supported a monumental staircase leading from the Temple Mount to the street below.

139 N. Avigad excavated in the center of the Jewish Quarter, an area never before investigated. This project illuminated the everyday life of Jerusalem's residents during the Herodian period, an era of considerable affluence. Beautiful stone objects, including tables, bowls, cups, and purification jars (reminiscent of the wedding feast at Cana), have been recovered. Stone vessels were popular among observant Jews because they were not susceptible to uncleanness. Colorful mosaics, painted plaster, and exquisite frescoes were also unearthed. The destruction of Jerusalem in AD 70 brought this luxury to an abrupt end.

140 Resolving a longstanding dispute among archaeologists, Avigad demonstrated that as early as the 8th cent. BC the Western Hill (Upper City) was an integral part of Jerusalem (see *BARev* 4 [2, 1978] 10–15

for the population of that hill). This area is probably the Mishneh and Machtesh of Zeph 1:10–11. Avigad also shed light on Byzantine Jerusalem by uncovering the *cardo maximus*. This "main street," 75 ft. wide, was paved with flagstones and flanked by a colonnaded portico, exactly as portrayed on the Madeba map (6th cent. AD). The vaulted foundation of the Nea (New Church), built by Justinian in 543, was also uncovered. The Jerusalem excavations underscore the value of Josephus (→ 5 above) as source for the topography and history of the city in the Herodian period. For the Herodian water supply to Jerusalem, see *BARev* 10 (3, 1984) 49ff.

141 Archaeological legacies from the energetic building activity of Herod the Great (→ History, 75:158) include the fortresses he left on isolated mountain peaks; not all have been adequately excavated. Masada on the shore of the Dead Sea fell to the Romans in AD 73. Its impressive remains span three periods: the Herodian (37–4 BC), the revolt of the Jews (66–73), and the Byzantine (5th–6th cents.). The Herodium, a magnificent palace-fortress, was built in 23 BC on the top of a natural hill in the Judean wilderness. V. Corbo excavated the upper Herodium (palace-fortress) in the 1960s; E. Netzer later dug the lower Herodium (a complex of buildings associated with the Herodium; see *BARev* 9 [3, 1983] 30–51). Often referred to as "the Masada of the north," Gamla on the Golan heights was one of the first Jewish strongholds to succumb to the Romans in AD 67 (*BARev* 5 [1, 1979] 12–27).

142 The "Roman capital of Judea," built by Herod at seacoast Caesarea, has yielded extremely interesting ruins. Most are of Late Roman date, perhaps connected with the flourishing Christian center at Caesarea. However, in 1961, among the remains of Caesarea appeared our first record of the name of Pontius Pilate inscribed on stone. R. Bull began digging at Caesarea in 1971 and has made further significant discoveries, including the *cardo maximus* and *decumani* ("side streets"). More important, he discovered the only Mithraeum yet known in Palestine. It was housed in a barrel-vault warehouse near the Caesarea harbor, where the Roman military could worship Mithra, the Persian warrior-deity of light and truth.

(*Arch* 3 [2, 1981] 56–60; *BA* 38 [1975] 2–10; 46 [1983] 133–43; *BARev* 8 [3, 1982] 24–47; *NatGeog* [Feb. 1987]; L. I. Levine, *Roman Caesarea* [Jerusalem, 1975]; *Caesarea under Roman Rule* [SJLA 7; Leiden, 1975].)

143 Herod's birthplace, Ashkelon, never became incorporated into his kingdom. He enriched it with public buildings, however, of which mostly scattered stones were encountered by past digging; recent excavations may be more productive. Aphek at the source of the Yarkon River was named Antipatris after the father of Herod the Great when in 9 BC the latter rebuilt the city. When Herod rebuilt Samaria (*ca.* 30 BC) after its destruction by John Hyrcanus, he renamed it Sebaste in honor of Augustus.

144 **(V) New Testament Period.** Interest in the sites of the life of Jesus has been understandably great. Unfortunately, in many instances there are rival claimants for sites, two or even three, with alleged archaeological evidence. Supporting the incarnation and nativity sites of *Nazareth* and *Bethlehem* is the virtual absence of any rival claimant. The earliest monumental remains in the basilicas erected over these sites go back to approximately 300 years after the event they commemorate. *Nain* (Luke 7:11) too is an uncontested little hamlet, and a few tombs there have been traced back to NT times. *Caesarea Philippi* (Matt 16:13) is uncontested, but near the Lake of Galilee are three possible sites for *Bethsaida* (*BA* 48 [1985] 207–16).

145 Tell Hum on the NNW shore of the Sea of Galilee has been identified as *Capernaum*. The date of the synagogue, not the site, is in dispute. When the Franciscans (→ 20 above) renewed excavation of the synagogue, they dated the structure to the 4th or 5th cent. AD on the basis of coins found beneath the pavement. Yet Israeli archaeologists prefer a date in the late 2d or 3d cent. AD. The final word has not been said, but the Franciscans have a strong argument. Meanwhile, all agree that this most famous limestone synagogue of Galilee is a magnificent structure. The ruins of a more ancient basalt building lying beneath are probably of the synagogue where Jesus preached. In the 5th cent. an octagonal church was constructed over the site in the Franciscan section traditionally thought to mark the location of St. Peter's house. In view of this constant tradition, the identity of this site deserves serious consideration. The contiguous section of Capernaum owned by the Greek Orthodox Church continues the history unfolded at the Franciscan site, which came to an end in the 7th cent. (see *BA* 46 [1983] 198–204; *BARev* 8 [6, 1982] 26–37; 9 [4, 1983] 50–53; *TBT* 22 [4, 1984] 233–35).

146 *Cana* (John 2:1) is contested; geographical and phonological reasons favor Khirbet Qana, 9 mi. N of Nazareth, even though tourists go to Kefr Kenna 3 mi. NE of Nazareth. The excavated remains of the "pious nonscientific" site of Kenna are in fact far nearer to the time of Jesus than any at Qana. But they also relate to the private Jewish shrine of a certain Tanhum, which, if anything, diminishes the likelihood that this was a focus of Christian veneration.

147 The Greeks established a number of Hellenistic cities E of the Jordan, two of which are Gerasa and Gadara. Most imposing of all excavated monumental sites of the NT world is the provincial Roman city *Gerasa* (Jerash). It was a chief city of the Decapolis (→ Biblical Geography, 73:52) and may have witnessed the visit of Jesus, recorded in Mark 7:31. Its forum, colonnaded avenues, and two theaters give us a good idea of the Greco-Roman culture that was trying to absorb Palestine. Gerasa also possesses 13 (by most recent count) churches affording some of our earliest examples of Christian architecture and mosaic. Gerasa is undergoing limited excavation (an estimated 90 percent of the site still lies underground) and extensive restoration (*Arch* 38 [1, 1985] 18–25; I. Browning, *Jerash* [London, 1982]). Some 30 mi. NW of Gerasa, close enough to be considered part of its district, the *Gadara* of Roman times survives in some important ruins of Umm Qeis, high on the precipitous S bank of the Yarmuk River in view of the Sea of Galilee. The pig owners of Matt 8:28 are called by some manuscripts Gadarene and by others Gerasene. Starting in 1973, excavation and restoration were undertaken at Umm Qeis under auspices of the German Evangelical School.

148 Beginning in 1950 Americans excavated Tulul (Abu) el-Alayiq, which extends to both sides of the Wadi Qelt, 2 mi. SW of OT Jericho (Tell es-Sultan; see *NatGeog* [Dec. 1951]). In the 1970s E. Netzer renewed excavations at this site, sometimes called "NT Jericho," but more accurately "Herodian Jericho"; he corrected some earlier interpretations and also expanded the project. In the 2d cent. BC the Hasmonean kings, descendants of the Maccabees, chose Jericho for their winter palaces. When Herod the Great succeeded the Hasmoneans in 37 BC, he enlarged the resort, at the same time making it more luxurious with a sunken garden, pool, citadel, amphitheater, and hippodrome to pamper his guests. The whole royal complex was abandoned before AD 70. For the necropolis nearby, see *BA* 43 (1980) 235–40; *BARev* 5 (4, 1979) 28–35; 9 (1, 1983) 44–53.

149 The site commemorating Jesus' baptism at the Jordan near Jericho, not really claimed to be authentic, is located at the most conveniently accessible point *near* a site supported by an ancient tradition. Just about here would be the Beth-arabah of Josh 15:6, a name easily recognizable in "Bethabara," which some manuscripts of John 1:28 give instead of "Bethany." North would suggest that the presence at Qumran of a penitential baptizing sect (→ Apocrypha, 67:106) tends both to reinforce the Bethabara tradition and to render almost inescapable that JBap was in fairly close communication with the Qumran votaries.

150 Concerning *Jerusalem* the chief observation of an archaeologist would be that much of the energy spent in wrangling or recrimination over unproved sites ought rather to be constructively expended in rejoicing that the Temple area is so uncontested. Here took place a large number of the most important events in the life of Jesus, from his presentation and finding, down through his public ministry to the evening before his death. The Mt. of Olives is similarly important and undisputed. Caskets for bones (ossuaries) found on the Olivet slope called Dominus Flevit bear 1st-cent. Jewish names and are claimed to be our earliest record of the Judeo-Christian community. As for the ascension site, the minority opinion of Vincent, preferring Eleona to Imbomon, implies a minuteness of localization that is unimportant when compared with the momentousness of "Olivet's upper slope" in general for various incidents of the Jerusalem ministry.

151 The ancient tradition of localizing Calvary in the Church of the Holy Sepulchre has shown itself strong enough to rise above both its own legendary accretions and a concerted 19th-cent. attack in favor of a less congested spot; → Biblical Geography, 73:94. (See *BARev* 12 [2, 1986] 40–57 on Gordon's "Garden Tomb," which, as the burial place of Jesus, is based on fantasy, not evidence.) An important issue concerning Gospel topography is the Praetorium with the Lithostrotos (John 19:13; "Pavement"), traditionally identified with the Antonia Fortress built by Herod the Great. Upon it depends the validity of the basic arrangement of the Way of the Cross (which, however, is founded on devotion more than on history). Vincent (→ 12 above) favored the Antonia Fortress, at the NW corner of the Temple area, as the place where Pilate condemned Jesus to death. A large stone pavement near the Ecce Homo arch has often been identified as the Lithostrotos. The alternative site on the other side of Jerusalem is Herod's citadel excavated by C. Johns for the British Mandate authorities and more recently by Israeli archaeologists. P. Benoit and others maintain that the Praetorium where Pilate condemned Jesus was located there. Excavations have shown that the stone pavement was not related to the Antonia (the ruins of which have never been located) but was part of a small Roman forum contemporary with Hadrian's Aelia Capitolina (2d cent. AD). The Ecce Homo arch may have been a city gate at the time of Herod Agrippa I (AD 37–44). See *BA* 40 (1977) 11–17.

152 Despite the fact that thousands of crucifixions took place in Palestine, pertinent archaeological evidence was discovered for the first time in 1968. In the Jewish tombs at Givat ha-Mivtar, NE of Jerusalem, were the remains of a crucified man, a Jew in his twenties who had lived in Jerusalem before AD 70. The analysis in *BA* 48 (1985) 190–91 suggests that the man's wrists were tied to the crossbeam; his legs straddled the upright, with a nail attaching each heel to the side of the cross. The victim would die slowly from asphyxia.

153   The pool of Bethesda (Bethzatha), mentioned in John 5:2, has been discovered and excavated in Jerusalem on the property of the White Fathers, near St. Anne church. Trapezoidal in form and divided by a central partition, the pool had colonnades on the four sides and the partition—thus John's "five porticoes."

154   Vincent located *Emmaus* (Luke 24:13) at Nicopolis. Although many still accept his view, the imposing remains of the early churches he excavated there are just what we would expect from a bishopric as populous as Nicopolis, some 160 stadia (20 mi.) from Jerusalem. At a more suitable 60 stadia (8 mi.) is an "alternative Emmaus," called Qubeibeh, with less imposing excavated finds. Neither it nor Abu Ghosh (also 60 stadia) seems to have been identified as Emmaus before Crusader times. Wilkinson (*Jerusalem* 161–64) argues for Motza or Ammasa (renamed Colonia) some 4 mi. from Jerusalem. Emmaus may set a record for claimants to the title!

155   (VI) Period after New Testament. The Judean Desert caves, inhabited during the Bar Cochba War (AD 132–135), have yielded letters and artifacts adding enormously to our knowledge of the Second Jewish War against the Romans. Also, underground hiding complexes located in the Judean Shephelah have shed further light on the Bar Cochba War. As mentioned above (→ 140, 151) excavations are uncovering Jerusalem of the period after this war—both the Aelia Capitolina of Hadrian and the Byzantine period.

156   Many synagogues, especially in Upper Galilee, have been excavated in an effort to date the earliest synagogues and to determine their architectural styles. (Literary sources have shed little light on the dates and architecture of synagogues.) Four synagogues thus excavated in Galilee are Khirbet Shema, Meiron, Gush Halav (Giscala), and Khirbet en-Nabratein. At Khirbet Shema, the first broad-house synagogue (with the focal point on the long wall) in Galilee was uncovered. The remains of the early synagogue at this site date to the late 3d cent. AD; the second, built over the ruins of the first, was completed by the mid-4th cent., then destroyed by an earthquake at the beginning of the 5th cent. The synagogue at Meiron (late 3d cent. AD) was a standard basilica type (rectangular with two rows of columns dividing the structure into nave and two side aisles). The basilical synagogue at Gush Halav was constructed *ca.* AD 250 and continued to function until the 6th cent. The synagogue at Khirbet en-Nabratein (Nevorraya) had three phases, spanning the 2d to the 6th cent. At this site a part of the aedicula or Torah shrine (the Holy Ark), dating to the 3d cent. AD, was uncovered in a secondary use. The study of these synagogues is providing a clearer understanding of Jewish life in the towns of Galilee during the Late Roman and Byzantine periods.

(Levine, L. I., *Ancient Synagogues Revealed* [Detroit, 1982]. Saunders, E. W., "Christian Synagogues and Jewish Christianity in Galilee," *Explor* 3 [1977] 70–78. Shanks, H., *Judaism in Stone* [NY, 1979]. *BA* 43 [1980] 97–108; 44 [1981] 237–43; 51 [1988] 69–96. *BARev* 4 [2, 1978] 32–42; 7 [6, 1981] 24–39; 10 [3, 1984] 32–44.)

157   To close, we mention an archaeological site where the Jewish and Christian heritages came together in the postbiblical period—Dura Europos, far NE of Palestine in the great bend of the Euphrates River. It was excavated by a French expedition under F. Cumont in 1922–1925 and then, with the support of Yale University, in 1928–1937. The publication of the rich finds was concluded in 1967 by C. Kraeling. Founded under the Gk Seleucid dynasty *ca.* 300 BC, Dura Europos became a Roman commercial and military outpost on the trade routes with the East. In AD 170 a small Jewish synagogue was built; in an enlargement in 240, the walls were covered with impressive frescoes of biblical subjects. This unique treasury of Jewish art was preserved because, as part of the defense against a Parthian invasion in 256, the wall frescoes were buried under an earthwork intended to strengthen the adjacent outer wall of the city. A Christian house-chapel with a painted baptistry, from the same period, has also been discovered at Dura. Literary evidence from cities like Antioch and Constantinople shows that in the 3d to the 5th cents. synagogue and church had little use for each other; one can only wonder how the citizens who attended the two cultic sites at Dura Europos regarded each other. See A. Perkins, *The Art of Dura-Europos* (Oxford, 1973); C. Hopkins, *The Discovery of Dura-Europos* (New Haven, 1979); *BA* 47 (1984) 166–81.

75

A HISTORY OF ISRAEL

Addison G. Wright, S.S.   Roland E. Murphy, O.Carm.
Joseph A. Fitzmyer, S.J. *

BIBLIOGRAPHY

1   **General Bibliography.** Albrektson, B., *History and the Gods* (Lund, 1967). Avi-Yonah, *EAEHL.* Bickermann, E. and M. Smith, *The Ancient History of Western Civilization* (NY, 1976). Braidwood, R. J., *Prehistoric Men* (8th ed.; Glenview, 1974). *CAH.* Childe, V. G., *New Light on the Most Ancient East* (4th ed.; NY, 1969). Drioton, E. and J. Vandier, *L'Egypte* (5th ed.; Paris, 1975). Frankfort, H., *The Birth of Civilization in the Near East* (NY, 1956); *Kingship and the Gods* (Chicago, 1948). Frankfort, H., *et al., The Intellectual Adventure of Ancient Man* (7th ed.; Chicago, 1977). Gelb, I. J., *A Study of Writing* (2d ed.; Chicago, 1963). Gray, J., *The Canaanites* (NY, 1964). Gurney, O. R., *The Hittites* (2d ed.; Harmondsworth, 1969). Hallo, W. W. and W. K. Simpson, *The Ancient Near East* (NY, 1971). Jacobsen, T., *The Treasures of Darkness: A History of Mesopotamian Religion* (New Haven, 1976). Kramer, S. N., *The Sumerians* (Chicago, 1963). Macqueen, J. C., *The Hittites* (rev. ed.; London, 1986). Mazar, *VBW* and *WHJP.* Morenz, S., *Egyptian Religion* (Ithaca, 1973). Moscati, S., *The Face of the Ancient Orient* (NY, 1962). Nissen, H. J., *Grundzüge einer Geschichte der Frühzeit des Vorderen Orients* (Darmstadt, 1983). Oates, J., *Babylon* (rev. ed.; London, 1986). Oppenheim, A. L., *Ancient Mesopotamia* (2d ed.; Chicago, 1977). Perrot, J., "Préhistoire Palestinienne," *DBSup* 8. 286–446. Pritchard, *ANET, ANEP, ANE.* Ringgren, H., *Religions of the Ancient Near East* (Phl, 1973). Roux, G., *Ancient Iraq* (2d ed.; London, 1980). Starr, C., *A History of the Ancient World* (3d ed.; NY, 1983). Steindorff, G. and K. C. Seele, *When Egypt Ruled the East* (2d ed.; Chicago, 1963). Trigger, B. G., *et al., Ancient Egypt: A Social History* (Cambridge, 1983). Van der Woude, A. S. (ed.), *The World of the Bible* (GC, 1986). Van Seters, J., *In Search of History* (New Haven, 1983). Woolley, L., *The Beginnings of Civilization* (NY, 1965). Yadin, Y., *The Art of Warfare in Biblical Lands* (London, 1963). Also *Or* 49 (1980).

2   **Bibliography for OT Times.** Aharoni, *LBib.* Albright, *BP.* Bright, *BHI.* Cazelles, H., *Histoire politique d'Israël* (Paris, 1982). De Vaux, R., "Israël," *DBSup* 4. 729–77; *EHI.* Donner, H., *Geschichte des Volkes Israel und seiner Nachbarn in Grundzügen* (2 vols.; ATD 4; Göttingen, 1984–86). Gottwald,

N., *The Tribes of Yahweh* (Maryknoll, 1979); review of *BHI* in *BARev* 8 (4, 1982) 56–61. Grant, M., *The History of Ancient Israel* (NY, 1984). Gunneweg, A. H. J., *Geschichte Israels bis Bar Kochba* (TW 2; 5th ed.; Stuttgart, 1984). Hayes, *IJH.* Herrmann, S., *A History of Israel in Old Testament Times* (2d ed.; Phl, 1981). Jagersma, H., *A History of Israel in the Old Testament Period* (Phl, 1983). Lemaire, *HPH.* Lemche, N. P., *Early Israel* (VTSup 37; Leiden, 1985). Mazar, B., *The Early Biblical Period* (Jerusalem, 1986). Miller, J. M. and J. H. Hayes, *A History of Ancient Israel and Judah* (Phl, 1986). Noth, *NHI.* Rowley, H. H., *Men of God* (London, 1963). Smith, M., *Palestinian Parties and Politics That Shaped the Old Testament* (NY, 1971). Soggin, *HAI.* Weber, M., *Ancient Judaism* (Glencoe, 1952).

3   **Bibliography for NT Times.** Abel, F.-M., *Histoire de la Palestine depuis la conquête d'Alexandre jusqu'à l'invasion arabe* (EBib; Paris, 1952) 1. 224–505; 2. 1–104. *ANRW* II/19.1, 646–875; 19.2, 1–101; 25.1, 3–890. Avi-Yonah, M. (ed.), *A History of the Holy Land* (NY, 1969) 109–71; "Palaestina," *PWSup* 13 (1973) 321–454, esp. cols. 369–404. Barrett, *NTB.* Bruce, F. F., *New Testament History* (GC, 1972). Ehrlich, E. L., *A Concise History of Israel* (London, 1962). Foerster, W., *Palestinian Judaism in New Testament Times* (Edinburgh, 1964). Grant, M., *The Jews in the Roman World* (NY, 1973). Hayes, *IJH* 605–77. Jeremias, J., *Jerusalem in the Time of Jesus* (Phl, 1969). Jones, A. H. M., *The Cities of the Eastern Roman Provinces* (2d ed.; Oxford, 1971) 226–92. Kee, H. C., *The Origins of Christianity: Sources and Documents* (EC, 1973). Leaney, A. R. C., *The Jewish and Christian World 200 BC and AD 200* (Cambridge, 1984). Lohse, E., *The New Testament Environment* (Nash, 1976). Malina, B. J., *The New Testament World* (Phl, 1981). Mor, M. and U. Rappaport, "A Survey of 25 Years (1960–85) of Israeli Scholarship on Jewish History in the Second Temple Period," *BTB* 16 (1986) 56–72. Safrai, S. and M. Stern (eds.), *The Jewish People in the First Century* (2 vols.; CRINT; Phl, 1974–76). Schürer, *HJPAJC.* Sherwin-White, A. N., *Roman Society and Roman Law in the New Testament* (Oxford, 1963). Zeitlin, S., *The Rise and Fall of the Judaean State* (3 vols.; Phl, 1962–78).

---

* Sections 5–25 of this article are by A. G. Wright; 26–144 are by R. E. Murphy; 145–93 are by J. A. Fitzmyer.

4   OUTLINE

BEFORE ABRAHAM WAS

5   Up to 200 years ago our only sources for a
knowledge of the ancient Near East were the Bible and
Herodotus. During the past two centuries, through the
science of archaeology and related fields, we have learned
a vast amount about the history of the human race and
of Israel's predecessors and neighbors, and this information has revolutionized our understanding of human
origins, of the course of early history, and of many
aspects of the Bible. Some knowledge of these recently
acquired data will be useful to situate the events of the
biblical period in the larger context of human history.
This knowledge is also of exegetical value in helping us
to come to a proper understanding of the kind of literature we possess in the prehistory of Gen 1–11. In the
space allotted we can give only the most general outline
of prehistory and of the political and cultural history of
the ancient Near East; for this reason we refer the interested student to the more detailed treatments in the
bibliography. (Also → Biblical Archaeology, 74:44ff.)
The dates given below for the various Stone and Bronze
Ages are all approximate.
6   **(I) The Stone Ages (Before 3200 BC).** The
various stages of human existence on earth are distinguished and named according to the material most commonly used for basic tools and weapons at the respective
period. Since change from one material to another did

not occur instantaneously, the designations are always
approximate as to both the beginning and the end of the
period. Stone (Gk *lithos*) was the oldest material, copper
(*chalkos*) or bronze came next.
7   **(A) Old Stone Age or Paleolithic.** Our
planet is about 4.5 billion years old. Simple forms of life
first appeared on it about a billion years later, and more
complex forms of life began leaving a fossil record about
600 million years ago. In Africa fossils of primates who
habitually walked upright can be traced back to 7 to 5
million years ago, and from 2.5 million years ago stone
tools have been found associated with some of these
remains, indicating incipient stages of human intelligence. This early stage of human development (*australo-
pithecus; homo habilis*) was followed by *homo erectus*
(possessing a larger brain, and the ability to control fire
and to make more advanced stone tools). Evidence of this
stage has been found in Africa dating from over 1.5
million years ago, and other fossils of this type have been
found in India, China, Java, and probably Southern
Europe. This stage lasted to about 350,000 years ago.
Thereafter came transitional types (archaic *homo sapiens?*)
such as finds at Swanscombe in England and Steinheim
in Germany (250,000) and then the Neanderthals
(125,000–30,000), and beginning about 40,000 years
ago the first traces of fully modern skeletons (*homo*

sapiens) appear (Cro-Magnon, Combe-Capelle, Grimaldi, etc.).

In early Paleolithic, people were hunters and food gatherers living in the open in the summer and in caves and other natural shelters in the winter. Life was characterized by a mobility dictated by food supply and seasonal changes. There is evidence that around 40,000 BC people began to settle down more, restricting themselves in their wanderings and learning to utilize a far greater variety of resources within a given locality. This is sometimes described as a transition to food collecting (i.e., more purposeful and specialized than food gathering). Perhaps by 40,000 years ago people had spread to Australia by sea, and a little less than 30,000 years ago migrations began across the Bering Strait into the Western Hemisphere. For our early ancestors, see *NatGeog* (Dec. 1976; Nov. 1985); *Arch* 34 (4, 1981) 20-29.

8   (B) Middle Stone Age, Mesolithic, or Epipaleolithic (18,000–8000 BC). Mesolithic culture is characterized by a further intensification of the food-collecting process and a gradual transition to food production (the planting of crops and the domestication of animals). This first really basic change in human living (the second in a sense being the Industrial Revolution of the past 200 years) took place in the Near East around 10,000–8000 BC (Natufian in Palestine; → Biblical Archaeology, 74:50). From there it rippled out to Europe and India (7000–5000 BC) and occurred again independently in Mesoamerica (7000 BC) and a little later in SE Asia. (Yet there are still a few primitive peoples in out-of-the-way parts of the world whom the revolution has not affected and who remain in the food-gathering or food-collecting stage.) In the Near East the center of the Mesolithic change was the region of the hilly flanks of rain-watered grassland (2,000–5,000 ft. elevation), which build up to the high mountain ridges of Iran, Iraq, Turkey, Syria, and Palestine; sites reflecting this incipient era of cultivation and animal domestication have been discovered at Beldibi in Turkey, at Karim Shahir, M'lefaat, and Zawi Chemi in Iraq, at Mt. Carmel, Jericho, and elsewhere.

9   (C) New Stone Age or Neolithic (8000–4500 BC in the Near East). This is the stage of Stone Age culture in which people became full-fledged food producers. Food collectors, i.e., hunters, fishers, berry and nut gatherers, had lived in small groups and bands for they had to be ready to move whenever an area no longer supplied sufficient food. There was not enough food to store nor was it the kind that could be stored for long. Clothing probably consisted of animal skins. There were no breakable utensils, no pottery, no time to think of much of anything except food and protection. But the food producer lived a more sedentary life. If one were to plant, one had to remain in the same place for the harvest. One lived in a house—it was worthwhile to build one. In a given area enough food could be grown for many people. Hence villages became common, and with them came informal customs and rules. There was more time to modify nature in other areas than food production (e.g., the production of pottery and textiles), and probably some people began to specialize in such crafts, work full time at them, and trade their goods for food. Seventh-millennium sites of such primary farming villages have been found among other places at Jarmo in Iraq, Ras Shamra in Syria, Çatal Hüyük in Turkey, and at Jericho; and later sites have been found at Fayum in Egypt and throughout the Fertile Crescent.

10   (D) Copper-Stone Age or Chalcolithic (4500–3200 BC in the Near East). In the period following the Neolithic, agriculture was vastly improved and expanded; this made possible the support of an increasing density of population, and here also we find a similar progress in culture. In *Upper Mesopotamia* small groups began to move down from the highlands to sites adjacent to the mud flats of the rivers (e.g., at Baghouz and Samarra) to establish farming villages with increased craft specialization. Painted pottery (a hallmark of Chalcolithic) began to appear. Soon all of Upper Mesopotamia was rather densely settled and Chalcolithic villages became fairly numerous in Palestine as well.

11   But nowhere was the progress more brilliant than in *Lower Mesopotamia,* for here the first experiment in civilization took place. Without attempting to define "civilization" let us simply describe it as urbanization. There are cities, a formal political setup (kings or governing bodies), formal laws enacted by the government, formalized projects (roads, harbors, irrigation canals, and the like), some sort of army or police force, new and different art forms, and usually writing. (We say "usually" because the Incas had everything that goes to make up a civilization except writing, and there is no reason to say they were not civilized.) The Mesopotamian experiment in civilization took place in the alluvial land of the lower Tigris and Euphrates, and in the 4th millennium the first city-states appeared in Lower Mesopotamia (Eridu, Al-Ubaid, Warka [Erech], Ur, etc.). No doubt there had been riverbank food collectors in the area long before and perhaps isolated villages, but the fertile yet rainless land could not be placed under intensive cultivation until the techniques necessary for providing irrigation had been mastered. Once the rich bottom land was gradually made available, settlers must have flocked in by the thousands. The irrigation required by the area demanded common effort and an increasing complexity of organization. It encouraged technological, political, social, and moral advances and was certainly a factor in the development of civilization here and in Egypt. And development was very fast. Among the advances in culture was the invention of writing (about 3200 BC), and before the end of the period there were links of trade and cultural exchange between Mesopotamia and Palestine and predynastic Egypt.

The creators of civilization in Lower Mesopotamia were the Sumerians, a people unknown to us a century ago and who still constitute one of the major mysteries of history. We are not sure of what race they were; their language is unaffiliated with any other known language living or dead; the time and manner of their arrival in Mesopotamia are uncertain, but it is clear that they were present in Mesopotamia by the middle of the 4th millennium, and since the earliest texts known to us are in Sumerian, we assume that it was they who introduced the pictographic (cuneiform) system of writing.

12   In *Egypt,* too, great strides were made in the development of agriculture and irrigation, where again the necessary cooperative effort helped in the formation of political units (nomes). Probably by the second half of the 4th millennium the various local nomes were united into two sizable kingdoms, one in Upper Egypt and one in Lower Egypt. Copper was in use, its source being either Sinai or the eastern desert. Writing in hieroglyphic script was invented. Egypt was in touch with Palestine and Mesopotamia and apparently even then with the cedar port of Byblos, with which it maintained contact for centuries to come.

13   (II) The Bronze Ages (3200–1550 BC). With this period we leave the realm of prehistory and enter the era of history properly speaking, for here we are dealing with a period that is documented by numerous contemporary inscriptions. The terminology for Egyptian, Palestinian, and Mesopotamian chronology is different for each, and there is no standard terminology covering all three areas. For simplicity we have adopted the Syrian-Palestinian terms of Early Bronze (EB) and Middle Bronze (MB) and have grouped under each period the corresponding history in Egypt and Mesopotamia. The Late Bronze (LB: 1550–1200 BC) is not treated in the present discussion (→ Biblical Archaeology, 74:77–93).

14   (A) Early Bronze Age (3200–2000 BC in the Near East).

(a) MESOPOTAMIA. During the Sumerian Age (2900–2360) Mesopotamia was organized into a system of city-states most of which were quite small. The city-state usually consisted of a walled city, dominated by its temple precinct and surrounded by small villages and hamlets. In theory the entire domain belonged to its main deity; the temple was his house; the city was viewed as his estate and the people as workers on the estate. In practice, however, most of the land belonged to private individuals, and in many respects the economy was free and uncontrolled. Originally, government was by city assembly; later, kingship developed, first as an emergency measure and then as a permanent institution, the head of state being seen as the viceroy of the god. To judge from the fortifications, there were in this period increased threats of danger from war or from raids from bandits, but, despite this, economic life flourished as well as trade (begun in prehistoric times) with the Iranian plateau and the NW. Improved agriculture permitted the support of an increased population; urban life in turn fostered a greater specialization of the arts and crafts, and the scribal schools produced a vast body of literature.

15   Early Mesopotamian political development existed in a kind of tension between the concept of the independent city-state and recurrent attempts to forge a greater unity between the cities. In the early 3d millennium lower Mesopotamia may have enjoyed a measure of unity under the hegemony of Kish in a loose league of equals. A religious center for the cities seems to have existed at Nippur. Subsequently other rival cities successively achieved hegemony (Erech, Ur, Adab, Lagash, and Umma), often in the role of defenders of the frontiers against incursions from the E and NW, and for a brief period Hamazi, a kingdom in the Iranian plateau, gained control. Our sources of information on the period have been meager and our understanding of the cooperative political and economic endeavors of Mesopotamian society is therefore sketchy.

16   Even more scanty has been our information on Syria to the NW, the least excavated area of the ancient Near East. Mari was known as a prominent participant in Mesopotamian life and probably a guardian of the northern frontier, but beyond there to the NW the history of the area was largely unknown. That some urbanization had taken place in central Syria was clear from excavations, but little was known about it. When Sargon later extended his empire into Syria (→ 17 below), a text from the period described it as a conquest of Iarmuti and Ebla, and the description of his grandson's expedition into the same area speaks of it as the conquest of Arman, Ebla, and Ullis. The location of these sites was unknown, but the texts suggested that there were several significant political units or confederations in 3d-millennium Syria.

In 1964 excavations began at Tell Mardikh, SW of Aleppo in Syria, and subsequently the site was identified as that of ancient Ebla. Since 1974 over 16,000 fragments of tablets have been unearthed. The tablets, containing political, commercial, literary, and lexical texts, are the largest 3d-millennium archive discovered to date, the oldest state archive, and the first written texts from

central Syria. They indicate that Syria in this period after 2500 already had an advanced culture of its own, and that Ebla was indeed a sizable kingdom and a commercial center dealing in foodstuffs, metals, various artifacts, and especially textiles. The city had commercial ties with many other cities in Palestine, Anatolia, Cyprus, Syria, and Mesopotamia, and dealt as an equal with such cities as Mari, Ashur, Akkad, and even with Hamazi on the Iranian plateau. The texts indicate a greater degree of urbanization in Syria and Palestine than hitherto thought and may also indicate the existence of commercial centers other than Ebla of possibly equal significance. The tablets will make possible for the first time the detailed study of the life of a late-3d-millennium community. They will also yield information on the early population of Syria, on activities transpiring elsewhere, and on the directions and extent of cultural influence in the Fertile Crescent. The bilingual Sumerian-Eblaite texts discovered will contribute to our understanding of those and related languages. In addition, because of their geographical and linguistic proximity to Palestine, these texts will surely provide some comparative materials for the study of various aspects of early Israelite traditions. (On Ebla in general, see C. Bermant and M. Weitzman, *Ebla: A Revelation in Archaeology* [NY, 1979]; P. Matthiae, *Ebla: An Empire Rediscovered* [NY, 1981]; G. Pettinato, *The Archives of Ebla* [NY, 1981]. Also *BA* 47 [1984] 6–32, with bibliography; and *NatGeog* [Dec. 1978].)

17   Since the earliest times there had undoubtedly been nomads on the western fringes of the Euphrates valley, and since the 4th millennium they had pressed in, in increasing numbers, and by the 3d millennium constituted an appreciable portion of the population. These people were Semites and are known as *Akkadians.* They intermingled with the Sumerian population, adopted and modified their culture, and even became rulers in some city-states. In the 24th cent. a dynasty of these Semitic rulers seized power and created the first true empire in world history, the Akkadian Empire (2360–2180). The founder, Sargon, rose to power in Kish, subdued all Sumer to the Persian Gulf, moved his capital to Akkad or Agade (near later Babylon), and he and his sons then extended their rule over Upper Mesopotamia to the Mediterranean (including Ebla), with military expeditions into Asia Minor, SE Arabia, and trade contacts with the Indus Valley. However, Akkadian power soon waned and was brought to an end by the onslaught of a barbarian people from the Zagros Mountains called the Guti, who held sway over Mesopotamia for 100 years.

18   (b) EGYPT. For protodynastic Egypt, see *BA* 48 (1985) 240–53. The oldest known Egyptian temple, from *ca.* 3350–3200 BC, has been excavated at Hierakonopolis in Upper Egypt (SW of Karnak or Thebes). This town is associated with King Narmer (identifiable with Menes?) who at the end of the 4th millennium is said to have joined the two predynastic kingdoms into a unified nation with the capital at Memphis, and Egypt entered upon the period known as the Old Kingdom (29–23 cents.). With the rise of the 3d Dynasty (*ca.* 2600) Egypt began the age of its classical flowering and period of creative genius, by which time all significant features of its culture had assumed a form ever thereafter to be normative. This was the age of the pyramids, and it was a period of development in literature, architecture, sculpture, painting, and the minor arts. The organization of the state in Egypt differed vastly from that of contemporary Mesopotamia. The pharaoh was not a viceroy of the god; he was a god. All Egypt was his property and was managed by a complex bureaucracy headed by the vizier. No law code was ever developed; the word of the god-king sufficed.

19   Beginning with the 5th Dynasty the power of the state began to disintegrate, and by the 22d cent., as the Guti were destroying Akkadian power, Egypt entered a period of disorder and depression known as the *First Intermediate* (22d–21st cents.). There was internal disunity with rival pharaohs claiming the throne and many officials seizing power locally. The situation was further aggravated by the infiltration of seminomads into the Delta. Confusion reigned, law and order broke down, and trade languished.

20   (c) PALESTINE. Here in EB we find the establishment of many city-states—Jericho (rebuilt *ca.* 3200 after a gap of centuries), Beth-shan, Ai, Shechem, Gezer, Lachish, etc., a number of them being built for the first time. By the mid-3d millennium sedentary occupation had reached to the southern end of Transjordan. Palestine never developed a material culture comparable to that found in Mesopotamia and Egypt, nor was any political unity established. The population was predominantly Canaanite, a Semitic people who had probably inhabited Palestine in the 4th millennium and before. Late in the 3d millennium, life in Palestine suffered a major disruption at the hands of seminomadic invaders. City after city was destroyed, some with incredible violence. Towns were abandoned and the land, particularly in the interior areas, was left without settled population; in Transjordan sedentary occupation came virtually to an end. A traditional view, now widely challenged, is that the newcomers were an offshoot of a people called the Amorites, a NW-Semitic element that was pressing in on all parts of the Fertile Crescent at this time. The Semites infiltrating Egypt in the First Intermediate were thought to have been of similar stock. (For other interpretations, → Biblical Archaeology, 74:65–67.)

21   (B) Middle Bronze Age (2000–1550 BC).
              (a) MESOPOTAMIA. The king of Erech broke the grip of the Guti over Mesopotamia; and he in turn was speedily overthrown by Ur-Nammu of Ur, who with the succeeding kings of the *3d Dynasty of Ur* (2060–1950) gained control probably over most of the Mesopotamian plain and brought about a brief renaissance of Sumerian culture. Ur-Nammu is noted not only for his many buildings and for the literary activity that marked his reign but above all for his law code, the oldest so far known. But Sumerian culture had come to the end of the road. The Sumerian language was dying and Akkadian was superseding it as the vernacular. Sumerians and Semites had become completely intermingled by this time, and the latter had become the predominant element. So a whole culture and civilization had come into being, run a magnificent course over 1,500 years and played itself out before Israel had even come upon the scene. Some of the important contributions of the Sumerians, in addition to city-state government, a fully developed legal system, and the invention of pictographic (cuneiform) writing mentioned above, were the lunar calendar; water clock; sundial; the chariot and military phalanx; the potter's wheel; the use of the vault, arch, dome, column, and tower in architecture; plus a highly developed polytheistic religion that had an enormous influence on all the later civilizations of the ancient world.

22   As the central authority of Ur deteriorated, the city-states of Mesopotamia one by one regained independence. According to the traditional theory there was a numerous, ethnically identifiable Semitic people called *Amorites* (but → Biblical Archaeology, 74:67), who had been pressing in on the Fertile Crescent since late in the 3d millennium and had overrun Palestine and turned Upper Mesopotamia into an Amorite land. They flooded into all parts of Mesopotamia and took over state after state, so that by the 18th cent. virtually every state in

Mesopotamia was ruled by Amorites. Gradually a three-way power struggle materialized for control of Mesopotamia between Assyria, Mari, and Babylon. Beginning even before the fall of Ur and continuing down into the 18th cent., *Assyria* (so named from the city of Asshur) had pursued a policy of commercial expansion in Asia Minor, witnessed by the Cappadocian Texts, business documents in Old Assyrian found at Kultepe in Asia Minor. Infiltrated by Amorites, who finally took over, Assyria then entered upon a brief period of conquest—Upper Mesopotamia from the Mediterranean to the Zagros Mountains. However, Assyria could not hold its gains, and within a very few years *Mari* succeeded Assyria briefly in the 18th cent. as the dominant power in Mesopotamia. It is from this period that the bulk of the famous Mari texts comes—letters, and economic, juridical, and administrative texts, which among other things describe nomadic tribal groups of the period and thus provide material useful for studying the early tribal society of Israel. But victory in the struggle for power went to *Babylon* under Hammurabi (1728–1686). Seizing control of most of Lower Mesopotamia, he brought Mari and Assyria under subjection, introducing an era of peace and cultural flowering to the Mesopotamian plain (the Old Babylonian Empire). From this period there has come a wealth of texts, especially copies of ancient epics (e.g., the Babylonian accounts of creation and the flood) and Hammurabi's famous law code, which shed light on the culture of the times and provide comparative material for many biblical texts.

23   The Babylonian Empire was subjected to various pressures because new peoples were pushing into all parts of the Fertile Crescent. In the N were the *Hurrians,* whose original home seems to have been the mountains of Armenia. They had been present in N Mesopotamia in small numbers since the 24th cent., but in the 17–16th cents. there was a tremendous influx of Hurrians into Upper Mesopotamia, Asia Minor, Syria, and even Palestine. Across Upper Mesopotamia there was established the kingdom of Mitanni; it had Indo-Aryan rulers but a population basically Hurrian, and this kingdom further reduced Assyria to a mere petty state. The Hurrians were the transmitters of Sumero-Akkadian culture to the Hittites and other peoples of Asia Minor, and tablets dating from the 15–14th cents. found at the Hurrian city of Nuzi are a valuable source of information on social customs associated with the biblical patriarchs. From the E there were incursions of *Kassites* from Luristan into parts of the Babylonian Empire. And in Asia Minor there was the presence of an increasingly powerful Hittite kingdom. By 2000 BC the population of Asia Minor had been infiltrated by various groups of Indo-Europeans, the most influential of whom called themselves *Hittites*. These had gradually unified the land and by the mid-16th cent. a strong Hittite kingdom existed in eastern and central Asia Minor and was pressing southward into Syria. In a daring thrust down the Euphrates the Hittites sacked Babylon *ca.* 1530. It was only a raid, for, beleaguered by Hurrian pressure from the E and beset with internal problems, Hittite power then retreated into Asia Minor for over a century, but in Babylon the Kassites seized control and held power for some 400 years plunging Mesopotamia into a dark age. For Hittites in the Bible, see *BARev* 5 (5, 1979) 20–45.

24   (b) EGYPT. As the 2d millennium began, Egypt was preparing to enter a new period of prosperity under the pharaohs of the *Middle Kingdom* (21st–18th cents.). The country was again united; there were economic prosperity and political expansion with sporadic control over Nubia, Libya, Palestine, and Phoenicia; and it was a golden age of Egyptian culture. However, in the

18th cent. Egyptian power rapidly declined through internal disintegration, and Egypt entered upon the *Second Intermediate Period* (18–16th cents.). It was at this time that the Hyksos (probably Canaanite or Amorite princes from Palestine and southern Syria) pressed in upon the land, establishing themselves at first in the Delta and then mastering for about 100 years all Egypt and an empire reaching to N Syria. In a bitter fight for freedom the Egyptians finally expelled the Hyksos (*ca.* 1580–1550), and Egypt began to revive and enter upon the period of the *New Kingdom* and the empire.

25   (c) PALESTINE.   At the end of EB the country had been thrown into upheaval by the (possibly) Amorite

invasions, but beginning in the 19th cent. a rapid recovery took place in W Palestine and N Transjordan with many new towns being built as the seminomads settled in and assimilated the language and culture of Canaan. Nevertheless, large areas, especially in the central mountain range, continued to be very thinly settled. Gradually the city-state system, characteristic of Palestine down into the Israelite period, evolved; and under the Hyksos Palestine attained a prosperity that it seldom knew in ancient times. The MB period is generally thought to be the context for the beginnings of the history of the people whom the Bible presents as Hebrews and then as Israel.

FROM ABRAHAM TO POMPEY

26   (I) **Introduction.** The biblical narratives were not composed in order to provide a "history of Israel." That concept is a creation of modern historical standards and methods, the product of evaluation of sources and the use of evidence from archaeology and other sciences. These approaches have been applied to the OT, esp. to the period from the patriarchs to the settlement in Canaan, and several hypothetical reconstructions have resulted. This is inevitable from the nature of the biblical sources. The early traditions were written only at a much later time, although oral tradition could have preserved some valid historical memories. There is also the perspective of unity in which the data has been synthesized: "all Israel" (Deut 1:1; 5:1) is involved in the exodus events; the "whole land" (Josh 11:16,23) is conquered; the tribal traditions of the fathers are unified by the "generations" (*tôlēdôt;* → Genesis, 2:3, 16). How does one deal with genealogies that are built on geographical and commercial considerations? Moreover, the biblical record itself preserves enough data to show that the global synthesis is an oversimplification: not all the tribes were involved in a primal exodus event (was there more than one exodus?); the description of the conquest in Judg 1 differs from that in Josh 1–12. Indeed, modern historians have something to learn from the easy tolerance that the biblical traditions display (e.g., the disinclination to harmonize differences in the Pentateuch). Mindful of these problems, scholars have drawn on archaeology and anthropology, as well as literary analysis (form and redaction criticism), in an effort to reconstruct a history which the Bible only imperfectly suggests.

27   How certainly can one draw historical conclusions from purely literary analysis? This is particularly true when the firmness with which the Pentateuchal J and E traditions have been distinguished and dated is now in question. What can be concluded from the presence of ancient social practices (e.g., of Nuzi; → 23 above) in the patriarchal traditions? One can point to the Nuzi slave adoption rule as applicable to Gen 16:1–4, or the legal treatment of a slave wife and her child as applicable to Gen 21:10ff. Presumably these are traits that would not ordinarily be found in a biblical narrative created much later. But now the pertinence and validity of many parallels are being questioned (e.g., the pertinence of the Nuzi household gods as signs of inheritance claims in Gen 31:19–42).

28   Since Wellhausen the narratives of the patriarchs and of the exodus/conquest have illustrated the range of scholarly uncertainties about historicity

(summaries in *IJH* 53–148, 213–84; M. Weippert, *The Settlement of the Israelite Tribes* [SBT 21; London, 1971]). With Albright at one end and T. Thompson and J. van Seters at the other, the spectrum runs from the cautious to the radical (with Bright, de Vaux, Mendenhall, Gottwald, Alt, Noth, and Soggin somewhere in between; see S. Herrmann on de Vaux in *VT* 23 [1973] 117–26). The complexity and paucity of material lead to honest differences. The scope of the problems can be illustrated by a brief survey of the period from the patriarchs to the judges (12th cent.).

29   *Patriarchal period.* This cannot be securely dated. The relationship of father-son-grandson seems contrived and explicable in the style of biblical genealogies that are built on social and commercial relationships (cf. Table of the Nations in Gen 10:1–32), as much as on blood ties. The patriarchal narratives are characterized by promises of descendant(s) and land—open-ended promises as later interpreted for "all Israel." The incidents are chiefly theophanies at shrines, such as Beersheba, Hebron, Bethel, Penuel (→ Institutions, 76:27–29), formulated perhaps in the light of later cult. Did the groups associated with the eponymous ancestors come from Mesopotamia (Gen 11:31) or from the Arameans (Deut 26:5)?

30   *Egyptian experience.* The Bible portrays this from the later "all Israel" perspective. The exodus and Sinai traditions seem to have been carried by the Joseph tribes (Ephraim, Manasseh) and perhaps Benjamin. The other tribes, such as the sons of Leah (Reuben, Simeon, Levi, Judah, Issachar, and Zebulun) and still other groups (see Josh 24:14–15), seem to have adopted the Israelite traditions at a later date. The liberation from Egypt and guidance in the desert are central to the exodus experience, but the details and the groups concerned are difficult to determine. The Sinai experience is made up of a theophany, a covenant with the community, and a law (in later perspective detectable as several law codes in Exod 19–Num 10).

31   *Settlement of Canaan.* The narratives schematize basic events that are difficult to correlate with archaeological data. Stories in Josh and Judg, which may have originally involved only individual tribes (see Judg 1:1–36), describe the settlement in terms of a smashing victory (Josh 1–12). But Judg 1 suggests a different scenario. The nature and growth of the tribal federation that exists in this period are unclear.

32   In summary, neuralgic points are: (1) the dating and historical nature of the patriarchal narratives; (2) the dating and the details of the exodus experience and the Sinai encounter (e.g., who participated); (3) the nature of "Israel's" occupation of Canaan and the origins and unity of the "tribes." In the face of such difficulties, the following "history" of the patriarchs and early Israel *will not propose another reconstruction, but will follow the biblical description* while alerting the reader to problems.

33 Not surprisingly, biblical chronology remains quite uncertain for the early period. In the monarchy there are several dates that can be trusted, through synchronization of the kings of Judah and Israel and absolute dating obtained from extrabiblical sources. But even here different chronologies have been worked out (see Jagersma, *History* 268–69). For the sake of convenience the dates of Albright (*BP* 116–17) will be followed (→ 88 below) for dating the kings of the divided monarchy.

34 **(II) The Patriarchal Period (*ca.* 2000–1700 BC).** The dubiety concerning dating is illustrated by de Vaux's conclusion that no exact dates can be given to the beginning or to the end of the patriarchal period (*EHI* 266). He is inclined to the first half of the 2d millennium because of patriarchal names, which can be shown to go back that far, and because of an alleged connection of the patriarchs with the Amorite migrations in this early period.

35 **(A) Abraham, Isaac, and Jacob.** *Abram* (see Gen 17:5) is presented as an emigrant from Mesopotamia. His settling in Palestine had been associated with the penetration of both Mesopotamia and Palestine by the Amorites (→ 22 above; yet → Biblical Archaeology, 74:65–67) by those who favor an early date. He lived an unsettled, if not seminomadic, existence in Palestine, pasturing his flocks in the pattern of transhumance; but the memory of a more permanent residence attached itself to the Mamre-Hebron area. The primary characteristics of the patriarchs were wandering and theophanies at the sanctuaries in Palestine: Shechem (Gen 12:6), Bethel (Gen 28:19; 35:1), and Penuel (Gen 32:23–33). The name Abram has been found in Babylonian texts dating from the 16th century; and the Mari texts mention the name Nahor (Gen 11:22; 24:10) as a town near Haran, subject to an Amorite leader. Similarly, the name Jacob appears in an 18th-cent. Mesopotamian text, designating a Hyksos ruler (Ya'qob-har). Names identical with those of some of Jacob's sons are to be found in the Mari texts, e.g., Benjamin and Levi. The relationship of the patriarchal customs to legal practice in the ancient Near East is disputed; for a cautious assessment see M. Morrison, *BA* 46 (1983) 155–64.

36 The call of Abraham (Gen 12:1–3) involves the promise of a land and a people. The episodes related concerning him gravitate about the theme of the promised birth of an heir and his relationship to his nephew Lot. Sarah's sterility, the endangering of the mother of the heir (Gen 12:10–20 and par.), the rejection of Ishmael—these events build up the suspense to the point where finally the child of promise is born, only to be offered as a sacrificial victim (Gen 22). The Abraham-Lot cycle affords an opportunity to contrast the two men (in favor of Abraham) and to introduce the events of Sodom-Gomorrah as well as the enigmatic expedition of Gen 14. The purchase of Machpelah (P account in Gen 23) is, as it were, a first installment on the fulfillment of the promise of a land.

37 *Isaac.* A relatively shadowy figure, he serves chiefly as a link between Abraham and Jacob. He is associated with Beer-sheba (Gen 26:23–33), although archaeology has yielded no evidence of Bronze Age remains there (*LBib* 191–92).

Jacob. Two main cycles make up his family history: Jacob-Esau, which highlights the theme of election even

of unworthy persons, and Jacob-Laban, which reflects patriarchal relationship with the Arameans. Unless the Arameans are an anachronism at this time (so de Vaux, *EHI* 200–9), the events of Gen 29–31 suggest a late dating for the patriarchs (Herrmann, *History* 45). The scene is laid in Aram-naharaim, in the upper courses of the Euphrates, but the Arameans were not settled there until the end of the 2d millennium.

38 The religion of the patriarchs is not what one would expect from a late document. (Baal worship, so prominent in later times, and illustated from the early Ugaritic myths, is absent.) The God of Abraham, Isaac, and Jacob is a "God of the Fathers" (→ OT Thought, 77:15). The deity is unnamed, but identified with reference to the ancestor who worshiped him; thus, the God of Abraham, the Fear (or Kinsman) of Isaac (Gen 31:42), and the Mighty One of Jacob (Gen 49:24). The "God of the Father" is thus associated with the patriarch or father with whom he has established a special relationship; he is the patron of the patriarch's family or clan and guides them in their history. He is not just a local deity, attached to a shrine, for epithets such as "Olam" (the Eternal, Gen 21:33) were attributed to this God (El or Elohim). It is likely that the concept of El, the high God of the Ugaritic pantheon, has influenced the development of the notion of the "God of the Father" (*CMHE* 3–75; C. L'Heureux, "Searching for the Origins of God," in *Traditions in Transformation* [Fest. F. M. Cross; ed. B. Halpern; Winona Lake, 1981] 33–57). Thus there is continuity between the God of the Fathers and Yahweh, the God of Moses (Exod 3:3–15 and 6:2–3 insist on this); but the historical development escapes us.

39 **(B) The Joseph Story.** Gen 37–50 is one of the biblical masterpieces, marked by the providence motif (Gen 45:5–8; 50:20). The suspense in Joseph's dealing with his brothers (42–45) is sustained with great literary skill (cf. von Rad's analysis of it as a "wisdom" story, in *SAIW* 439–47). A traditional date for Joseph's rise to power is the Hyksos period (1720–1550), but there is nothing in the Joseph story to demand it (see S. Herrmann, *Israel in Egypt* [SBT 27; London, 1973] 1–37). Historicity has been vigorously disputed, even if the narrative displays a fair knowledge of Egyptian life (J. Vergote, *Joseph en Egypte* [Louvain, 1959]). On the whole, de Vaux (*EHI* 291–320) has an optimistic view of the historical character of the Joseph tradition, compared with Herrmann, *History* 56–57, or Soggin, *HAI* 113–15.

40 More problematical, however, is the question, Who is the "Israel" or the tribes actually in Egypt? Certainly the tradition of the sojourn in Egypt is to be associated with the "sons of Joseph"—Ephraim, Manasseh, and also with Benjamin. It is possible that various Semitic groups could have entered Egypt. M. Weippert has argued that the patriarchs came from the nomadic Shasu population of Canaan (*Bib* 55 [1974] 265–80, 427–33). Another hypothesis associates the Hebrews with the (Egyptian) 'Apiru or (Akkadian) Ḥabiru, mentioned throughout the ancient Near East (Egypt, Amarna Letters, Alalakh, Nuzi, Ugarit, Mari). Their identity is not clear. The debate centers on whether they are a sociological or an ethnic unit (see H. Cazelles in *POTT* 1–28, but see de Vaux, *EHI* 216). Strikingly, the term "Hebrews" is used in Gen and Exod when an Israelite speaks to an Egyptian, or when a distinction is made between Israelites and Egyptians (e.g., Gen 39:17; 43:32; Exod 2:13). Overall the identity of Hebrew and 'Apiru remains disputed.

41 The uncertainty surrounding the date of the patriarchal period attaches also to the sojourn of "Israel" in Egypt. The biblical data yield conflicting results. The 430 years of Exod 12:40–41 is modified in the LXX to include the patriarchal period. According to Gen 21:5; 25:26; 47:28 one can calculate 307 years from the birth of Abraham to the death of Jacob, but the chronology is admittedly artificial. It is no longer possible to be certain (see Albright, *BP* 10-11) that the sojourn in Egypt goes as far back as the Hyksos period (1720-1550). What remains is only the historical plausibility of the entrance of Semitic groups into Egypt at several historical periods. We know that there was such a people as Israel already present in Canaan by 1220 (→ 42 below), but the historical background of the Egyptian sojourn cannot be reconstructed.

(Cazelles, H., "Patriarches," *DBSup* 7. 82-156. De Vaux, R., *EHI* 161-287; *IJH* 70-148; *WHJP II: Patriarchs*. Millard, A. and D. Wiseman (eds.), *Essays on the Patriarchal Narratives* [Leicester, 1980]. Miller, J. M., *The Old Testament and the Historian* [Phl, 1976]. Sarna, N. M., "Abraham in History," *BARev* 3 [4, 1977] 5-9. Thompson, T., *The Historicity of the Patriarchal Narratives* [BZAW 133; Berlin, 1974]. Van Seters, J., *Abraham in History and Tradition* [New Haven, 1975]. ON JOSEPH: Coats, G., *From Canaan to Egypt* [CBQMS 4; Washington, 1975]; Redford, D. B., *A Study of the Biblical Story of Joseph* [VTSup 20; Leiden, 1970].)

42   (III) The Exodus and the Conquest (ca. 1300-1050 BC). This complex of events seems to belong to the latter part of the Late Bronze Age (→ Biblical Archaeology, 74:78-93). If the king who "knew not Joseph" (Exod 1:8) cannot be identified, there is some reason to regard the "pharaoh of the oppression" (and exodus) as Ramses II (1290-1224). The strongest argument is the mention of Israelites working at the store-cities, Pithom and Raamses (Exod 1:1-11). Ramses was well known for his building activities (which also involved the mysterious 'Apiru as laborers!) in the Nile Delta where the Hebrews settled "in the land of Goshen" (→ Biblical Geography, 73:26). The implication is that the exodus occurred in the 13th cent. — a conclusion supported by the stele of Ramses' successor, Merneptah, which mentions a people "Israel" existing in Canaan about 1220 (*ANET* 375-78). The exodus then can be dated about 1250. But there is no viable explanation for the number involved (over 600,000: Num 1:46; 26:51). There is no reference in Egyptian records to the sojourn of Israel in Egypt.

43   (A) Moses. Evaluating this figure is a difficult task for the historian (H. Schmid, *Mose: Überlieferung und Geschichte* [BZAW 110; Berlin, 1968]). There is a certain legendary quality to Moses' birth (cf. the story of Sargon, *ANET* 119); and the text of Exod 1-15 is a conflation of sources, e.g., his commission according to JE in Exod 3-4, and according to P in 6-7. He is presented as an "adopted" Egyptian bearing an Egyptian name (cf. Thutmoses), but at the same time he is associated with the Midianites, to whom he fled after perpetrating a murder. In the desert he is confronted by the Lord and commissioned to lead God's people out of Egypt. This occurs through the instrumentality of the plagues, culminating in the death of the firstborn on the occasion of the "passover" (for the origin and historicization of this feast, see de Vaux, *AI* 484-93; → Institutions, 76:127).

44   The Lord reveals himself to Moses as "I am who I am" (→ OT Thought, 77:11-13), the God of the Fathers, thus assuring the continuity of the promise and salvation history. Was *yhwh* a god that was known before this? The theory that made Yahweh a god of the Midianite tribe of Kenites (H. H. Rowley, *From Joseph to Joshua* [London, 1950]) has not found many advocates. Herrmann (*History* 76-77) is inclined to recognize *yhwh* in the designation of an Edomite group, the Shasu of

yhw', who are mentioned in Egyptian texts (*ANET* 259) as being on the move in the area. But *yhw'* here designates the land, not the divinity. Dubious is the alleged presence of a divine name Ya (= Yahweh) in the Ebla texts from about 2400 (G. Pettinato, *BA* 39 [1976] 44-52, lists *Mi-ka-Ya*, "Who is like Ya?"; → 16 above). Thus far there is no clear evidence for a god *yhwh* before the time of Moses. Certainly, however, the monotheism of Moses was practical, not theoretical (see Exod 15:11; Ps 89:7-9).

45   (B) The Plagues. The number of 10 plagues is reached by a combination of several variant traditions, especially J and P (→ Exodus, 3:17-22). It is irrelevant to explain the plagues as natural phenomena verifiable in Egyptian life (e.g., the changing of water into blood has been associated with the annual flooding of the Nile). For the biblical writer these are not usual catastrophes but "signs" and "wonders" wrought by God through Moses. Neither are they "miracles" or events outside the laws of nature — a modern, not a biblical, category (→ NT Thought, 81:92-94). The plagues serve to emphasize the tension of the context between God and pharaoh, Israel and Egypt, which leads up to the climax in the 10th plague and the Passover.

46   (C) The Crossing. The literary sources describing the exodus from Egypt, the *yām sûp* (perhaps "Reed Sea"), and the route followed are too complex to yield firm conclusions (→ Biblical Geography, 73:26-31, with map). De Vaux (*EHI* 363-87) has pointed out the double tradition of "flight" (associated with the nine plagues) and "expulsion" (associated with the 10th plague); he connects them with two exoduses. The exodus-expulsion went the northern route (Kadesh and entry into Canaan from the south) whereas the exodus-flight went east, involving pursuit from the Egyptians, the crossing, the Sinai event, and the entry into Canaan from Transjordan. This is in line with the J tradition of a northern route (by way of Baal-zephon, Exod 14:2), as opposed to the E tradition which is by "way of the wilderness" to the east and the south. Perhaps the Leah tribes took to the north, and the Rachel tribes, under Moses' leadership, went south to Sinai. This is a hypothesis to account for the various traditions in Exod. De Vaux's analysis of Exod 14:10-31 follows a recognition of two sources: one emphasizes the destruction of the Egyptians by the Lord (14:13, 30; cf. 15:21); the other emphasizes the marvelous crossing by the partition of the waters (14:21-22). In any case, it is the Lord, the "warrior" (Exod 15:3), who saves the Hebrews.

47   (D) The Desert Experience. Famous episodes, viz., murmuring and revolt, intercession by Moses, providential care of the people (manna, quail, water), and 40 years of "wandering," are provided by various traditions (JEP). Uncertainty about the exodus route attaches also to the location of Sinai, or Horeb, "the mountain of God" (see de Vaux, *EHI* 426-39). Some modern scholars agree with the traditional (Byzantine) localization in the southern Sinai peninsula. Others would locate the mountain near Kadesh or Kadesh-barnea (the area of Ain Qudeirat, some 50 mi. S of Beer-sheba). For other localizations, → Biblical Geography, 73:27.

48   Most important: What happened at Sinai? The Pentateuch associates everything from Exod 19 to Num 11 with "the wilderness of Sinai": the covenant, the Decalogue, and the entire Torah. Since the seminal study of G. Mendenhall (*Law and Covenant in the Ancient Near East* [Pittsburgh, 1955]; *BAR* 3. 3-53) covenant has been interpreted in the light of the discoveries of ancient Near Eastern treaties, especially the suzerainty treaties of the Hittites. This has been a profitable comparison for understanding Deut, which does use the genre of the treaty covenant. But D. J. McCarthy (*Treaty and Covenant* [AnBib 21A; Rome, 1978]) has shown that "the treaty analogy for the relation of Yahweh and Israel is thus a flowering of a development, not a root from which covenant ideas grow" (293). Specifically, the Sinai tradition (Exod 19:1-24:11) is not marked by the treaty genre, which admittedly has influenced covenant language and concept in *later* traditions. Exod 24 points to a covenant ritual, a sacred meal, as "Israel" becomes the people of God. This idea is not incompatible with a vassal relationship, but legalism is to be avoided. Covenant is not the same as contract, but treaty (with attendant stipulations) is a good analogy to express the relationship of commitment signified by covenant (→ OT Thought, 77:75-98). While the theology of covenant developed over centuries, its origin in the Sinai experience should not be denied (*pace* L. Perlitt, *Bundestheologie im Alten Testament* [WMANT 36; Neukirchen, 1969]).

49   The Code of the Covenant (Exod 20:22-23:33) presupposes a settled people (in Palestine), and doubtless dates from a later period than the Sinai experience. The Decalogue in its present form (Exod 20:1-17; cf. Deut 5:6-21) certainly contains elements that go back to the origins of Mosaic religion: the exclusive claim to worship an imageless God (the first two commandments), and the other commandments seem general and universal enough (perhaps even the Sabbath observance?) to have defined the life style of the Hebrews.

50   Von Rad (*PHOE* 1-78) has argued that the Sinai tradition was originally independent of the Exodus tradition. The former was a cultic legend of the covenant feast, deriving from Shechem, and the latter a cultic legend of a feast at Gilgal which commemorated the entry into Palestine. His arguments are purely literary: the absence of Sinai in several key texts such as the "credo" in Deut 26:5-9. Such an argument from silence is not enough to counter the fact that the traditions exist together in the oldest narrative of the Pentateuch (JE; cf. de Vaux, *EHI* 401-19).

51   The P tradition occupies the central block of the Pentateuch (Exod 25-Num 10), and thus the entire priestly legislation is attributed to Moses. For a discussion of the desert "tabernacle," etc., and the apparently old traditions in the priestly description of these various articles, → Institutions, 76:30-34.

52   The "wandering in the desert," interpreted as a penalty for the failure to follow the lead of Joshua and Caleb (Num 14:26-35), is portrayed as lasting a generation, with Kadesh-barnea probably being the center of activity (but cf. R. Cohen in *BA* 44 [1981] 93-107). The attempt to enter Palestine through the Negeb is unsuccessful (Num 14:39-45). Yet in Num 21:1-3 a victory over "Canaanites" at Hormah is recorded; and this seems to tie in with Judg 1:16-17, indicating that there was a successful penetration of some groups (Simeon, Judah) from the south (see Aharoni, *LBib* 201-2; 214-18). The penetration of the Moses group was by way of Transjordan (→ Biblical Geography, 73:38-49) where the kingdoms of Edom, Moab, and Ammon were settled (see Num 20:14-21:10-35; Aharoni, *LBib* 204-6). The victories over the kings Sihon and Og, which took place N of the Arnon and N of the Jabbok respectively, became traditional in Israel (see Num 21:21-35; Ps 136:17-20). Transjordan appeared open to the invaders. Near the plains of Moab, after the utterance of Balaam's oracles (→ Numbers, 5:44-51), Moses died on Mt. Nebo. His failure to enter the promised land is cloaked in mystery and gave rise to several explanations in the traditions (Num 20:12; Deut 1:37). The infidelity of Israel with the

Baal of Peor (Num 25) was already an omen of its life in Canaan.

53   **(E) The Land of Canaan.** The end of the 13th century was a propitious time for a settlement in Canaan. The Fertile Crescent was alive with movement, thanks especially to the Sea Peoples. More important, it was not dominated by a single power as was so often true in previous centuries when Egyptians, Hittites, Mitanni, and Assyrians had vied for control over Palestine. The Egyptians' domination was about to end, although their presence in the fortress cities of Megiddo, Beth-Shan, and Gezer is attested into the 12th cent. The Hittite empire in Asia Minor came to an end with the invasions of the Sea Peoples and others. Independent small kingdoms were able to establish themselves in Edom, Moab, and Ammon. Arameans (Ahlamu) from the NE, despite wars with Assyria, were poised to enter Palestine. A political vacuum had created possibilities of settlement for the Hebrews and many other small groups. The biblical phrase, "Canaanites, Hittites, Hivites, Perizzites, Girgashites, Amorites, and Jebusites" (e.g., Josh 3:10) aptly describes the maelstrom of peoples (see G. Mendenhall, *The Tenth Generation* [Baltimore, 1973] 142-73). The political structure was characterized by the existence of city-states. For centuries this situation had been countenanced by Egypt, which exercised the dominant control. The kinglets were "loyal" to the pharaoh to whom they paid tribute, but the Amarna letters of the 14th cent. tell us of their trials, particularly with the 'Apiru (*DOTT* 38-45; E. Campbell, *BA* 23 [1960] 2-22).

54   Egyptian influence on Canaan extended to things cultural; but Canaanite religion was a relatively independent development, as the religious texts from Ugarit illustrate. The pantheon dwelt on a mountain in the N (Saphon, the later *mons Casius*, 25 mi. NE of Ugarit). El was the head of these divinities, but was outshone by Baal (Hadad). The three principal goddesses were Asherah (*qnyt ilm,* perhaps "creatress of the gods," and of a strongly sexual stamp), Astarte (Ashtoreth), and Anath (the "virgin," and of warlike nature) whose exploits are well known from the Ugaritic texts. Canaanite worship was marked by fertility rites, which involved sacred prostitution.

(*ARI* 68-94. Gray, J., *The Legacy of Canaan* [VTSup 5; Leiden, 1957] 113-59. Craigie, P., *Ugarit and the Old Testament* [GR, 1983].)

55   **(F) Conquest.** The biblical narrative of the "conquest" has telescoped the actual events in the manner of an epic. Everything is attributed to Joshua, just as all the laws are attributed to Moses. The conquest is schematized in three campaigns: the capture of Jericho and of Ai in the central hill country; then the victories in the S after the alliance with the Gibeonites; and finally, the thrust to the N in which Hazor fell. There was no total liquidation of the Canaanites, despite the ideal of *ḥerem* or "doom" war, a feature of ancient Near Eastern culture that Israel shared with its neighbors (*ANET* 320). The text makes clear that the fortified cities (Megiddo, etc.) were not taken, and many pockets of Canaanites remained; "explanations" of this are given in Judg 2:21-23; 3:2.

56   In modern times more than one scenario of the conquest has been offered. Albright and others (e.g., J. Bright) concentrated on the data in Josh 1-12 and correlated the conquest with the archaeological evidence of the destruction of cities mentioned in the biblical record. The archaeological evidence, however, presents more problems than it solves: if it shows that some of the cities mentioned in the Bible were destroyed, it does not necessarily tell us that Israelites destroyed them; and it seems to indicate that other cities that according to the Bible were destroyed were not even occupied at this time (Jericho, Ai, Gibeon; → Biblical Archaeology, 74:79ff.). The so-called immigration model, associated with the names of Alt, Noth, and M. Weippert, postulated a relatively peaceful infiltration of various tribes. Although skirmishes were not lacking, the "conquest" of Josh 1–12 is seen mainly as a composite of etiologies, i.e., stories that give the reason for the present situation (why is Ai a "ruin"?). Mendenhall has similarly denied that there was any "real conquest," and explained the settlement socio-politically as a "peasant's revolt" against Canaanite city-states. Those involved, among whom are to be counted the Hebrews, "withdrew" from the city-state network, and were ultimately united by the ensuing tribal federation established by the Mosaic groups. Gottwald has approximated this position, but emphasized the aspect of revolution, involving the transition from an oppressed proletariat to a relatively egalitarian society in which power is shared. Obviously, there is no scholarly consensus on the nature of the "conquest."

(*AEOT* 175–221. Aharoni, *LBib* 191–285. Albright, *BP* 24–34. *BHI* 129–43. Gottwald, N., *The Tribes of Yahweh* [Maryknoll, 1979], esp. 191–233. Mendenhall, G., "The Hebrew Conquest of Palestine," *BA* 25 [1962] 66–87; repr. in *BAR* 3. 100–20. *NHI* 53–84. *Palestine in Transition* (eds. D. N. Freedman and D. Graf; Sheffield, 1983]. Soggin, *HAI* 138–71. See also *BA* 39 [1976] 55–76, 152–57.)

57 Hence it is difficult to determine the identity of "Israel" at this period. The virtually peaceful take-over of Shechem (Josh 24:1–18, implying the whole area of Ephraim and Manasseh) suggests that the newcomers met here one or several tribes that were related to them (→ Biblical Geography, 73:101). Significantly, the Shechem excavations show that the city was *not* destroyed in the 13th cent. (*BAR* 2. 258–300). Moreover, the Shechem covenant celebration (Josh 24:14–15) presupposes that Israel incorporated other groups (Canaanites) into itself. The Hebrews are described as a "crowd of mixed ancestry" (Exod 12:38; cf. Num 11:4), which was led out of Egypt. Presumably many others had associated themselves with them in Goshen. It is also reasonable to suppose that there had long been a movement of Hebrews to Palestine during the previous centuries, or that even many Hebrews had remained in Palestine without ever going to Egypt (Albright, *BP* 32). Gradually, then, the traditions of those who had shared the exodus experience became the traditions of all, as various ethnic groups (Calebites, etc.) became absorbed.

58 The term "amphictyony," of Gk derivation, was first employed by Noth (*NHI* 85–137) to designate the nature of the tribal federation. It means a sacral confederation of tribes united around a central sanctuary, analogous to the Gk organizations. Although this view has dropped out of favor (cf. de Vaux, *EHI* 695–715; C. de Geus, *The Tribes of Israel* [Assen, 1976]), some kind of tribal federation, however loose, existed. If it did not exist since the Sinai experience, that event soon became the focus around which the tribes in Canaan united. The tradition of lineal descent of the 12 tribes from a common ancestor must be interpreted broadly: The genealogy expresses cultural rather than biological connections; i.e., it reflects relationships based on geography, trade, and other considerations. The unity created by the tribal federation was religious, not political, as may be inferred from the highly individualistic conduct of the tribes in the period of the judges. The center of worship seems to have changed residence several times in this early period: Shechem, Bethel, Shiloh (eventually destroyed by the

Philistines in the time of Samuel). The tribes are named in two different forms in the lists that have been preserved. The older form includes Levi (Gen 29:31–30:24; 49:1–27) and presents Joseph (Ephraim and Manasseh) as one tribe; in the later form Levi is omitted and Ephraim and Manasseh are separate (Num 26:4–51). The union of the 12 was not simply created by a covenant; behind it was a complicated historical process which escapes us (see de Vaux, *EHI* 717–49, 775–824).

59 **(G) The Judges.** The period of the judges is commonly dated in the Early Iron Age from about 1200 to 1050. (For a discussion of the schematic chronology of 410 years, see de Vaux, *EHI* 689–93). We do not have a continuous history within this period; but a series of separate incidents, largely local in scope, illustrate the thesis set down clearly in Judg 2:10–3:26, involving a sequence of sin, oppression, conversion, and deliverance (and echoing the deuteronomic theology of history). Yet the vignettes throw some light on the history of the period. Mostly the tribes operated individualistically in meeting the attacks of their neighbors, e.g., the Song of Deborah scores several tribes for their lack of cooperation (Judg 5:15–17). The geographical situation increased the individualism of the separate groups. The tribes in Galilee were separated from the central area by the Plain in Esdraelon (→ Biblical Geography, 73:105–11); the central mountain area was itself divided into pockets by the many valleys. Finally, the Jordan Valley served to cut off the West from the East.

60 Moreover, the Israelites themselves were in the process of settling down and changing to new ways of life, particularly farming. The assimilation of Canaanite culture was beginning, and this extended also to the veneration of the Baals and Astartes worshiped in the many Canaanite "high places" remaining in the land. Baal was already in possession of the land — a god of fertility, who needed to be propitiated. Yahweh was the God of history, who had saved Israel; but now there was the practical matter of ensuring fertility and abundant crops. Yahweh took on the features of Baal, and syncretism was the result. In contrast to an occasional pilgrimage to the sanctuary at Shiloh, the Canaanite high places were closer and the rites attractive (see J. L. McKenzie, *The World of the Judges* [EC, 1966] 34–44).

61 The origin and function of the judge (*šōpēt*) is difficult to determine (see de Vaux, *EHI* 751–73). The judge seems to be primarily a charismatic military leader, a "deliverer" (Judg 2:16; 3:9). The tribes were exposed to attack from every quarter and from any group that could hope to succeed. The invasion by Cushan-rishathaim of "Aram of the two rivers" (if Aram rather than Edom is to be read) was successfully resisted by Othniel, whom the tradition identifies as the one who had conquered Debir for Judah (Judg 1:11–16). The daring exploit of the left-handed Ehud in slaying Eglon of Moab precipitated a successful campaign against the Moabites that kept them E of the Jordan. Deborah inspired Barak and several northern tribes to do battle in the Plain of Jezreel against Canaanites, led by Sisera. The advantage of the Canaanite chariots was wiped out by rainstorms that flooded the river Kishon (Judg 4:15; 5:20–21) and made possible an Israelite victory. The event cannot be dated (*pace* Bright, *BHI* 179, following Albright), but it gave rise to one of the earliest Hebrew poems in the OT (→ Judges, 8:26).

62 The razzias made upon the central highlands by camel-riding bands of Midianites, Amalekites, and desert Arabs ("Qedemites") were met by Gideon (Jerubbaal). The details of his campaigns betray the expansion and literary embellishments characteristic of these early tales of victory (e.g., the fleece episode, Judg 6:36–40).

His victory at Ain Harod was followed by pursuit across the Jordan and the slaying of Zebah and Zalmunna (Ps 83:12). Already the ascendancy of the tribe of Ephraim appears (8:1; cf. the Shibboleth episode in 12:1-6)—an omen of the later division into N and S. There was a premature movement toward monarchy when, after Gideon had refused (?) the offer of kingship, his son Abimelech succeeded in establishing a precarious "kingdom" for a short time (Judg 9). He seems to have united the Canaanites of Shechem and the neighboring Israelites under his dominion—living in Arumah but governing Shechem through a regent.

63 Despite his origins and life as an outlaw in Transjordan, Jephthah was asked by the men of Gilead to give aid against the Ammonites. His success bound him to fulfill his savage vow to sacrifice his own daughter. The raw moral conditions of the tribes are illustrated by this incident, and also by the appendixes (in Judg 17-21). Samson's colorful exploits are indicative of the desperate situation in Judah, for his own compatriots delivered him to the Philistines (15:12-14). But his astonishing deeds of strength and bravery lived on among a subjugated tribe as tales of hope, which were handed down as a satire on the Philistines.

Very few details have been preserved concerning the so-called minor judges, whose activity may have been more judicial than military; it is possible that some of them were not Israelite. Shamgar's exploit against the Philistines is reminiscent of Samson. His name, "son of Anath," witnesses to the influences of the Canaanite (Ugaritic) divinities in the land.

64 (IV) The Monarchy and the Exile (ca. 1020-539 BC). The establishment of a monarchy under Saul was in response to the people's demand to be "like other nations" (2 Sam 8:20). The "other nations" are the bordering states, such as Edom, Moab, the Arameans, and of course Egypt and the peoples of the Tigris-Euphrates valley. It is impossible to grasp the flow of Israelite history without a brief sketch of Israel's neighbors and the super-powers. The major developments will be indicated here by treating the various groups separately.

(Hallo, W. and W. Simpson, *The Ancient Near East* [NY, 1971]. Moscati, S., *The Face of the Ancient Orient* [GC, 1962]. Oppenheim, A. L., *Ancient Mesopotamia* [Chicago, 1964]. Wiseman, D. [ed.], *Peoples of Old Testament Times* [Oxford, 1973]. See also "Cities and Lands of Israel's Neighbors" in *BAR* 2. 3-188, and the appropriate entries in *IDB, IDBSup,* and *DBSup.*)

65 (A) The Nations. CANAANITES. This term is used loosely to describe various peoples who inhabited the land of "Canaan" which the Israelites entered. It is important as a cultural designation of the various influences which impinged upon Israel. Thus, the Phoenicians in the North, along with ancient Ugarit (Ras Shamra; → Biblical Archaeology, 74:72), play a large role in the development of the religion of Baal which figures so prominently in the Bible. In the biblical period enclaves of Canaanite settlements persisted for centuries, thereby promoting the religious syncretism against which the prophets inveighed.

66 PHOENICIANS. Their colonies in Tyre, Sidon, and Byblos became famous for seagoing prowess (for Tyre, see *BA* 42 [1979] 23-24). It was with Hiram of Tyre that Solomon formed a fleet of Tarshish ships at Ezion-geber (1 Kgs 10:22). The religious influence is illustrated by the marriage between King Ahab and Jezebel (daughter of Ethbaal of Sidon), who promoted the worship of Baal-Melqart in Samaria (1 Kgs 16:31). Although the Phoenicians "invented" the alphabet, there are no significant literary remains except for the

documents from Ugarit of the 14th cent. BC, which had enormous influence upon biblical study (*ANET* 129-55; P. Craigie, *Ugarit and the Old Testament* [GR, 1983]; D. B. Harden, *The Phoenicians* [NY, 1962]; S. Moscati, *The World of the Phoenicians* [London, 1968]).

67 PHILISTIA. The mention of "Philistines" in the patriarchal period is generally considered an anachronism; perhaps these were Aegean settlements. The Philistines, who gave their name to Palestine, were part of the invading Sea Peoples from the Mediterranean who were finally repulsed from Egypt by Ramses III about 1200. The (proximate) origins for the Philistines are given as Caphtor (Crete) in Amos 9:7. After their defeat by Egypt they settled in the SW coastal region, where their pentapolis (Gaza, Ashkelon, Ashdod, Gath, and Ekron) was established. Their expansion (even to Gilboa in the N, where Saul died in battle against them) is recorded in Judg and 1-2 Sam. David finally broke their power (2 Sam 5:17-18; 8:1), without incorporating them into his kingdom. There is sporadic mention of Philistine activity (at Gibbethon, 1 Kgs 16:15-17; Hezekiah's campaign, 2 Kgs 18:8), but they practically disappear from the biblical record. The end of the Philistines comes with the Assyrian and Babylonian invasions. Gaza, Ashkelon, and Ashdod (cf. Isa 20:1) were savaged by the Assyrians, and the Philistine area served as a buffer for them against Egypt (→ Biblical Archaeology, 74:95-104).

68 EDOM. Edom, Moab, and Ammon were in the Transjordan at the entry of the Hebrews (→ Biblical Geography, 73:38-49). Commercial and political issues were behind the eventual subjugation of Edom by David and Solomon. But the split of the kingdom provided the occasion for sporadic independence. In Assyrian ascendancy, Edom, along with Moab, paid regular tribute to Assyria (*ANET* 281-82). Although reputed for "wisdom" (Jer 49:7; Obad 1:8), Edom is remembered in the OT more for its rejoicing over the fall of Jerusalem (Obad 1:12-13; Ps 137:7). Edom eventually yielded to the Nabatean kingdom, but preserved a kind of identity in the Idumea of the Negeb in later times (→ Biblical Geography, 73:84; *BARev* 14 [2, 1988] 28-41).

69 MOAB is remembered in early Israelite history for Balaam's connivance with King Balak to curse Israel (Num 23-24) and for Ehud's slaying of King Eglon (Judg 3:15-20). David incorporated Moab into the empire, but the conquest was superficial. The famous stele of King Mesha (*ANET* 320-21) witnesses to the oppression of Moab under Omri and a successful revolt at Ahab's death (2 Kgs 3:4). But Moab was unable to resist the onslaught of Assyria.

70 AMMON is bitterly satirized, along with Moab, in Gen 19:30-38; and there are frequent references to battles in early history (Jephthah in Judg 10-11; Saul in 1 Sam 11; David in 2 Sam 10:1-4 and 12:26-31). With the fall of Rabbath-Ammon, Ammon was incorporated into the Davidic kingdom; and when David fled to Mahanaim during Absalom's revolt, he was cared for by "Shobi, the son of Nahash from Rabbah of the Ammonites" (2 Sam 17:27). The Ammonites appear to have become independent after Solomon's reign and are mentioned as in league with other countries resisting the Assyrians at Qarqar (853 BC; *ANET* 279). For Ammonite kings, see *BA* 48 (1985) 169-72. But Assyrian power eventually prevailed, and Ammon was reduced to a vassal state of Assyria. The Ammonites revolted against Chaldean domination (see Jer 27:3) and even played a role in the death of Gedaliah (Jer 40:14; 41:15). They disappeared as a state in the 6th cent., and the territory became part of the Persian Empire. A Jewish enclave in Ammon was led by a certain Tobiah (Neh 2:10), from whom came the important Tobiad family (→ 130 below).

71   ARAMEANS. By the time of David, Aramean tribes had been established in S Syria: the petty kingdoms of Aram-Zobah, Tob, and Maakah. But David conquered them under the reign of King Hadadezer of Zobah (2 Sam 10). The next Aramean kingdom to appear gave the Israelites real trouble. Already in the aftermath of the division of the monarchy, Ben-hadad of Aram-Damascus was invoked by Asa of Judah against Baasha of Israel (1 Kgs 15:18-20), and he stripped E Galilee from the northern kingdom. The relationship between the Arameans of Damascus and the Israelites was one of inter-mittent warfare. Although they united to face the Assyrian threat at Qarqar (853), they were soon at war at Ramoth-gilead (1 Kgs 22). Despite the ever constant threat of Assyria, Damascus under Hazael grew more powerful until it took over Transjordan as far as the Arnon (2 Kgs 10:22-33) and even forced Judah to pay tribute (2 Kgs 12:17-18). But with Adad-nirari III the tide turned, and Aram-Damascus paid heavy tribute to the Assyrians. Joash of Israel ("Ia-'a-su of Samaria," as he is named in the Tell Al-Rimāḥ inscription; A. Cody, CBQ 32 [1970] 325-40) struck against the Arameans three times (2 Kgs 13:24-25), recovering cities that had been lost to Hazael. Under Jeroboam II Transjordan was re-covered by Israel. The efforts of Rezin of Damascus and Pekah of Israel to control Judah in the Syro-Ephraimite war (Isa 7) turned out to be a dying gasp, since Tiglath-pileser III crushed the Arameans once and for all in 732. Henceforth they were absorbed into Assyrian provinces, as also happened to a great part of Israel after the Assyrian campaign of 733 (2 Kgs 15:29-30).

72   EGYPT. Solomon married the daughter of a pharaoh (probably Siamun); nevertheless, asylum was granted by Egypt to the rebel Jeroboam. Shortly after the death of Solomon, Shishak (Sheshonk) plundered Jeru-salem and (according to the inscription in the Amon temple of Karnak) invaded both the Negeb and the N. Over 150 place-names are recorded (for analysis, see Y. Aharoni, LBib 323-30). But Egypt was not strong enough to restore the old hegemony over Palestine. It did not figure prominently again until the decline of the Assyrian empire, when Pharaoh Neco attempted to prop up the faltering Assyria against the onrush of Babylonia. He slew Josiah at Megiddo (609) when the latter opposed him and put his brother Jehoiakim on the throne as a vassal to Egypt (2 Kgs 23:29-35). The defeat of Neco at Carchemish by the Babylonian army of Nebuchadnezzar (605) ended Egyptian pretensions. Egypt did not play a role in Jewish history until the division of the empire of Alexander the Great, when the Ptolemies took control of Palestine during the 3d century.

73   ASSYRIA. Assyria experienced a resurgence of military might under Ashurnasirpal II (ca. 883-859), whose plundering expeditions consolidated Assyrian power along the Tigris and Euphrates. Plunder gave way to conquest with Shalmaneser III, a contemporary of Ahab, who began pounding at the N Syrian city-states (Carchemish, Adini, etc.). This threat induced the S Syrian states (Hamath, Damascus) to persuade other smaller powers to league against Shalmaneser at the battle of Qarqar on the Orontes River (853). Although the Assyrian annals claimed victory (ANET 278-79), the situation was rather a stalemate. Shalmaneser's next cam-paigns did not range so far, and meantime Israel and Damascus returned to fighting with each other (1 Kgs 22). But Assyrian domination was inevitable, and the campaigns continued until in 841 Shalmaneser success-fully reduced Israel to tribute (King Jehu). When other military concerns in the E eventually led to the loss of Assyrian power in the W, Hazael of Damascus attacked Israel and even Judah (capturing Gath, 2 Kgs 12:18).

Hence the Bible is able to regard Adad-nirari III as a savior (2 Kgs 13:5), when he conquered Damascus in 805. His power extended to the Mediterranean, and Israel ("the land of Omri") was among the nations who had to pay him tribute (ANET 381).

74   Palestine was spared further depredations for the next 50 years, as Assyria's military fortunes declined. Accordingly, there were prosperous reigns in Judah (Azariah) and Israel (Jeroboam II). Then a new king, a usurper, appeared on the throne, Tiglath-pileser III (745-727, called "Pul," 2 Kgs 15:19), who inaugurated a series of successful campaigns. In 743 Menahem of Israel paid tribute, and soon Israel was at bay. The Syro-Ephraimite war was one result. Rezin of Damascus and Pekah of Israel were not able to persuade Ahaz to join a coalition against Tiglath-pileser; and the latter "accepted" Ahaz's appeal for help, not without taking tribute from Ahaz. He dismembered Israel (2 Kgs 15:29), reducing it to a vassal state, replacing Pekah with Hoshea.

Under Shalmaneser V, the successor of Tiglath-pileser, Hoshea became involved with the anti-Assyrian factions led by Egypt, and another campaign resulted. Samaria was besieged for three years (2 Kgs 17:5), and fell in 722-721, perhaps to Sargon (ANET 284-85), Shalmaneser's successor. Sargon had considerable diffi-culty with Merodach-baladan of Babylon (2 Kgs 20:12), who was finally defeated by Sennacherib.

75   Sennacherib's biblical fame derives from the siege of Jerusalem in 701 under Hezekiah (2 Kgs 18:13-19:36; Isa 36:1-37:37; 2 Chr 32:1-22). Although there remains the problem of one or two sieges (→ 1-2 Kings, 10:65-66). Sennacherib boasted of having Hezekiah "like a bird in a cage" (ANET 288), and of receiving tribute, but fortunately Jerusalem was deliv-ered. Sennacherib went on to crush Babylon, before being succeeded by Esarhaddon. Despite the latter's invasion of Egypt against Pharaoh Tirhakah (2 Kgs 19:9) and the destruction of Thebes (Nah 3:8-10), the power of Assyria began to wane. The forces of Ashurbanipal (668-629) were driven from Egypt under Pharaoh Psammetichus. Nevertheless, Manasseh's long reign (687-642) in Jerusalem was still under complete Assyrian domination. With the death of Ashurbanipal, Josiah of Judah could extend his reform (and control) into the area of the former kingdom of Israel (2 Kgs 23; 2 Chr 34-35). It is ironic that, when Nineveh finally fell to the Chaldeans in 612 (cf. Nahum), Egypt was taking the side of the Assyrians in an effort to prop them up against the rising power of the Neo-Babylonians. See A. C. Brockman, The Luck of Nineveh (NY, 1978).

76   BABYLONIANS. "Babylon" refers to the city Babel (S of modern Baghdad) and can refer to the area at the S end of the Tigris-Euphrates plain, the home of the great cultures of ancient Sumer and Akkad. The influ-ence of Babylonian civilization upon the Bible is clear from the Gilgamesh Epic, the Code of Hammurabi, and many other sources. The view of Gen 11:27-31 is that Abraham came from this area, "Ur of the Chaldees" (→ Biblical Geography, 73:15-19). The Neo-Babylonian Empire figures in Israel's historical period. The Babylo-nians were dominated by the Assyrians from 900-700; but by the time of Hezekiah, Merodach-baladan of Babylon was intriguing with Judah and others against the Assyrians (2 Kgs 20:12-15). The rise of Nabopolassar (626) established the supremacy of Baby-lon in the Fertile Crescent. He prepared the way for the hectic events leading to the Babylonian destruction of Jerusalem by Nebuchadnezzar's army in 587, 10 years after the successful siege of Jerusalem in 597 and the first exile of Jewish leaders (→ 112-14 below). The Babylo-nian Exile of the people of Judah came to an end as Cyrus of Anshan allowed them to return to Jerusalem (→ 117 below) after the capture of Babylon in 539.

77 PERSIANS. The Persians of the biblical period were the people ruled by the Achaemenid line of kings in the territory more or less identical with modern Iran. Two dominant tribes, Medes and Persians, had settled below Lake Urmia in the 1st millennium. The Medes opposed the Assyrian power for over a century, but it was only in 612 that they combined with Babylon to destroy Nineveh. Their glory was short-lived, for Cyrus ("the Great") of Anshan united Persia and then conquered the Median capital of Ecbatana *ca.* 550. The mighty Persian empire (539–331) was on its way to the eventual conquest of Babylon, Egypt, Asia Minor, and, almost, Greece (for a list of the rulers → Daniel, 25:3). Cyrus went on to take Babylon in 539, allowing the Jews to return in accordance with a policy of toleration. The period of Jewish restoration, from Darius to Artaxerxes (520–445), records the Persian involvement in Palestine (→ 117–25 below). But from Nehemiah (445) to Alexander (333) the Persian period is a dark age. The victories of Alexander the Great over Darius III at Granicus and Gaugamela led to the Greek period (→ 126–44 below).

78 (B) Saul (*ca.* 1020). In the 11th cent. the greatest single threat to Israel's existence was the Philistines (→ 67 above), who had established their five city-states in a pocket of the coastal plain. The Samson stories (Judg 13–16) illustrate their domination of Judah. Their monopoly in iron (1 Sam 13:19–22) put the Israelites at a severe disadvantage. Their victory at Aphek gave them entry to the northern area (1 Sam 4; several tribes seem to be represented in this battle, and the Ark was captured by the Philistines).

In this crisis two figures emerged: a "prophet," Samuel, and the first king, Saul. Because of the varied nature of the narratives that deal with his birth, vocation, and activities, Samuel appears as an ambiguous personality. His youth is said to have been spent in the Nazirite manner (1 Sam 1:11; Num 6) as a servant of the Shiloh sanctuary under the tutelage of the priest, Heli. He is portrayed as a seer and prophet who stood for the old tribal rights against Saul, the new king. At this time, and associated with Samuel, there appear the bands of ecstatics, who resemble the Canaanite prophets. Finally, Samuel is also described as the last of the judges (1 Sam 7:2–17), exercising his office at Bethel, Gilgal, and Mizpah. It is in this context of a schematized report relating him to the judges that Samuel's victory over the Philistines (7:10–14) is reported, and it must be evaluated accordingly. The one who bore the brunt of the Philistine oppression was Saul.

79 The Philistine threat united the tribes under a king in the face of a common enemy. The introduction of kingship in Israel has been preserved in two traditions, one favorable to monarchy (1 Sam 9:1–10:16; 11), the other hostile (8; 10:17–27; 12). The first is the story of young Saul searching for lost asses and finding a kingdom when he was anointed by Samuel at Ramah. The second narrative portrays the end of an era, as Samuel, the "last judge," yields to the people's plea to be like the other nations. Saul seems to have been viewed as continuing the charismatic strain of the judges; it may be questioned if at first his leadership was viewed in the light of royalty. He is said to have been appointed *nāgîd* (1 Sam 9:16; 10:1; also of David, 2 Sam 7:8), not *melek*, or king. The nuance of *nāgîd* remains unknown (military commander? crown prince?). Certainly he could boast of no impressive court or administration.

Saul was helped considerably by his initial successes, such as that against the Ammonites who had besieged Jabesh-gilead (1 Sam 11)—a military venture with which the Philistines did not interfere. He also obtained a local victory over the Philistines at Michmash, thanks to his son Jonathan (1 Sam 14). But he quarreled with Samuel (two accounts in 1 Sam 13 and 15) and became subject to fits of depression and envious rage that mark the well-known narratives concerning his dealings with David. His eventual downfall was sealed by his slaughter of the priests at Nob, and he presents a pathetic figure in the episode of the "witch of Endor." Meanwhile the Philistines were exerting even greater pressure culminating in the devastating defeat at Gilboa, where both Saul and his son Jonathan were slain (David's dirge in 2 Sam 1:17–27).

80 (C) David (1000–962). Two major narratives have been recognized in the story of David: his "rise to power" (1 Sam 16:14–2 Sam 5:25) and the so-called succession narrative (2 Sam 9–20 and 1 Kgs 1–2, also called the "court history"). See J. Flanagan, *JBL* 91 (1972) 172–81.

There are variant traditions concerning his introduction to Saul: 1 Sam 16:14–23; 17:1–11,32–53 (minstrel and military aide of Saul) and 17:12–30; 17:33–18:2 (the young brother who brings provisions to the front lines). The later chaps. dealing with court life and outlaw days also seem to have many doublets (twice David spares Saul's life; twice Saul tries to pin David to the wall; etc.). His ability as a warrior made him rise at court (marriage with Saul's daughter, Michal)—and fall just as quickly as Saul strove to kill him. Fleeing to the Judean wilderness, David gathered about him a band of some 400 outlaws like himself and bided his time. He succeeded even in turning his delicate relationship with the Philistine king of Gath to his own political profit, and he emerged as vassal chief of Ziklag before Saul met his death at Gilboa.

81 David immediately became king of Judah in Hebron (2 Sam 2:1–4)—a coup assisted by his tribal origins and his marriages to Judahites (Abinoam, Abigail). At Mahanaim in Transjordan Saul's kingdom was continued by his son Ishbaal (or Ishbosheth as the scribes wrote the name), supported by Abner, the general of Saul's army. There was intermittent, but not very significant, war (the duel at the pool of Gibeon, 2 Sam 2:12–17) until Abner defected to David. David showed a sense of political realities in proving himself completely innocent of Ishbaal's assassination and of Joab's brutal murder of Abner. The way was now open to David's being anointed as "king over Israel" when the elders of Israel came to Hebron, where he had reigned seven years, and accepted him (2 Sam 5:1–5). The kingship remained twofold—over Judah and Israel—even though one speaks of the "united" kingdom.

82 David went on to extend his kingdom in the N at the expense of the Arameans; he incorporated Zobah (victory over the Aramean Hadadezer) and the territory of Damascus (→ 71 above). Profitable treaties with Hamath and Tyre were concluded. In Transjordan there were victories over Ammon and Edom, and a vassal king was set up in Moab. Thus, David's kingdom reached from Ezion-geber on the Gulf of Aqabah to Homs, from the Mediterranean to the Euphrates (2 Sam 8:3). The Canaanite enclaves still existing in Palestine were gradually incorporated (e.g., Megiddo). Such an empire had never before been achieved in this area, which had always been Egypt's domain; it was possible only because Egypt was on the wane and Assyria had not yet awakened. David also broke the power of the Philistines, seemingly with a string of successes, although the data are sparse (2 Sam 5:17–25; 21:15–17). The Philistine pentapolis was reduced to vassal status.

83 David's master stroke was the choice of Jerusalem as the capital (→ Biblical Geography, 73:92–94).

By his capture of this Jebusite city he made it a "royal city," i.e., his own (just as later he made a personal appearance at the capture of Rabbah in Ammon so that his "name be proclaimed over it" (2 Sam 12:28). Politically a neutral site acceptable to both N and S, Jerusalem presented distinct advantages for defense, since it was surrounded by valleys except on the N. It is certain that the "city of David," or Ophel, occupied the southern spur on the E side of the mountain (→ Biblical Archaeology, 74:106-7). The transfer of the Ark of the Covenant gave the city a religious importance that it was never to lose. How much of the Jebusite liturgy and ideology entered into Israelite thought is hard to determine, but the "priesthood according to the order of Melchizedek" seems to be one such element (Ps 110:4; → Institutions, 76:15-17).

The political organization was modeled on Egyptian institutions: herald (*mazkîr*), army general, etc. (see de Vaux, *AI* 129-32). In his own bodyguard David had various groups of foreign mercenaries, e.g., the Cherethites and Pelethites. One can imagine the crisis precipitated within Israel by this radical change, which involved moving from tribal federation to a monarchy with a complex administration, a standing army, and the inevitable taxation—all of which tended to wipe out the old tribal individualism (2 Sam 8:15-18; 20:23-26).

84   The "court history" has been analyzed in various fashions. R. N. Whybray has classified it as a specimen of wisdom literature (*The Succession Narrative* [SBT 9; Naperville, 1968]). Von Rad (*PHOE* 176-89) agreed with L. Rost (1926, 1965; also *The Succession to the Throne of David* [Sheffield, 1982]) in emphasizing the suspense concerning the succession to David's throne. Would the dynastic principle really work? As the court history unfolds, Ammon is eliminated, Absalom's revolt ends in his death, Adonijah loses out to Solomon. The theme of succession runs through many scenes, within the court and without, and on both sides of the Jordan. There is also a wide range of characters: David, passionate and with a blind love for his sons; the generals Joab and Amasa; the priests Zadok and Abiathar; the commoners Ziba and Barzillai; the rebels Shimei and Sheba; the women Tamar, Bathsheba, and the widow of Tekoa. The ineluctable connection between sin and punishment is present in the stories of Ammon, Absalom, and especially of David. Only rarely is a direct positive theological judgment expressed (2 Sam 11:27; 12:24; 17:14); God is at work behind the scenes.

Absalom's revolt against David is less revealing, from a political point of view, than the later revolt of Sheba (2 Sam 20). This was precipitated by jealousy over David's overtures to the leaders of Judah, the very people who had supported Absalom's revolt. David's move caused some of the northern tribes to rally to Sheba. Led by the redoubtable Joab (who had murdered Amasa, David's own replacement for Joab) David's troops quickly ended this schism, but it was an omen of the division to come.

85   The real credit for consolidating the Israelite kingdom lies with David. The greater prosperity under Solomon came at the expense of the solidity that David had achieved. Several stories suggest that David possessed considerable personal charm (the loyalty of his foreign mercenary, Ittai of Gath—2 Sam 15:18-22; the episode of the drink of water from Bethlehem—2 Sam 23:13-17). But his crowning importance was due to the dynastic principle that became incarnate in him through the prophetic oracle of Nathan (2 Sam 7). This prophecy (the Magna Charta of royal messianism; → OT Thought, 77:152-63) contributed to the general stability of the

royal house in Judah, in contrast to the instability in the northern kingdom after the division.

(*AEOT* 225-309. Aharoni, *LBib* 286-320. Carlson, R., *David, The Chosen King* [Stockholm, 1964]. Grønbaek, J., *Die Geschichte vom Aufstieg Davids (1 Sam 15-2 Sam 5)* [Copenhagen, 1971]. Gunn, D., *The Story of King David* [JSOTSup 6; Sheffield, 1978]; *The Fate of King Saul* [JSOTSup 14; Sheffield, 1980]. Sinclair, L., *TRE* 8. 378-84.)

86   **(D) Solomon (961-922).** In Israelite tradition the glory of Solomon's reign became proverbial. He first secured his position by political alliances: marriage with the pharaoh's daughter, which brought to him Gezer as a dowry; commercial arrangements with Hiram of Tyre, which opened up possibilities of export. Trading reached a new high: e.g., commerce in the Gulf of Aqabah, thanks to a merchant fleet at Ezion-geber; trade for gold and valuables with Arabia (the Queen of Sheba, 1 Kgs 10:1-10) and with Ophir (Somaliland in Africa, or perhaps the lower part of the Arabian peninsula); a profitable exchange of horses and chariots between Egypt and Cilicia (1 Kgs 10:28, corrected text). Military establishments were set up to support a standing army with chariotry (→ Biblical Archaeology, 74:39).

Solomon's reputation as a builder (→ Biblical Archaeology, 74:108-10) rests not only on the Temple, which was built in the Phoenician tradition, but also on an elaborate palace complex (see *BA* 36 [1973] 78-105). Moreover, he was the patron of wisdom and the arts (→ Wisdom Lit., 27:7-8), and the JE traditions of the Pentateuch may have taken form during his reign—the "period of enlightenment," as it has been called (von Rad). The deuteronomic editor angrily emphasizes the care with which Solomon provided for the worship of other gods at the whim of his harem (1 Kgs 11:1-8). A pattern for syncretism and outright idolatry even in Jerusalem was thus created. Each succeeding king is judged by deuteronomic standards, i.e., his attitudes toward idolatry and toward worship on the "high places" (which was doubtless nominally Yahwistic)—the latter standard is really anachronistic, for centralization of worship only gradually became the ideal because of the reforms of Hezekiah and Josiah in the late 8th and 7th cents. (→ Institutions, 76:53-55).

87   Solomon's reorganization of the kingdom into 12 districts that did not strictly agree with tribal boundaries was a strong move toward centralization of government; and it made possible an efficient system of heavy taxation in order to meet royal expenses. One must consider the great transformation in Israelite society that is implied in the reigns of Solomon and David. In a few generations there was a transition from tribal federation to "empire" status; the agricultural and pastoral life yielded to urban life with a corresponding growth of social inequalities. Albright (*BP* 56) estimates a possible Israelite population of 800,000 in this period.

But not everything was peace and light in Solomon's days. There was the partial loss of Edom and of Damascus (1 Kgs 11:14ff.). An unsuccessful attempt at revolt was led by Jeroboam, who fled to Egypt only to return under Rehoboam and inaugurate the northern kingdom of Israel. The institution of forced labor or corvee added to the general dissatisfaction. This discontent was imprudently disregarded by Solomon's son Rehoboam, and the division of the young kingdom was at hand.

88   **(E) Israel and Judah (922-842).** Significantly, it was at an old religious center, Shechem (Josh 24), that the rebellion of the northern tribes took place. Here Rehoboam (922-915) was to have been acknowledged as king by "all Israel." But when he failed

KINGS OF THE DIVIDED MONARCHY

Judah				Israel
Rehoboam	922–915	922–901		**Jeroboam I**
Abijah (Abijam)	915–913	901–900		Nadab
Asa	913–873	900–877		Baasha
		877–876		Elah
		876		Zimri
		876–869		**Omri**
Jehoshaphat	873–849	869–850		**Ahab**
		850–849		Ahaziah
Jehoram (Joram)	849–842	849–842		Jehoram (Joram)
Ahaziah	842			
Queen Athaliah	842–837	842–815		**Jehu**
Jehoash (Joash)	837–800	815–801		Jehoahaz (Joahaz)
Amaziah	800–783	801–786		Jehoash (Joash)
Uzziah (*Azariah)	783–742	786–746		**Jeroboam II**
[Regency of Jotham	750–742]	746–745		Zechariah
		745		Shallum
		745–738		Menahem
Jotham	742–735	738–737		Pekahiah
		737–732		Pekah
Ahaz (Jehoahaz I)	735–715	732–724		Hoshea
		721		FALL OF SAMARIA
Hezekiah	715–687			
Manasseh	687–642			
Amon	642–640			
Josiah	640–609			
Jehoahaz II (*Shallum)	609			
Jehoiakim (*Eliakim)	609–598			
Jehoiachin (*Jeconiah)	597			
Zedekiah (*Mattaniah)	597–587			
FALL OF JERUSALEM	587			

EXPLANATION: The names of the most important kings are in boldface. Variant or alternative names are put in parentheses; an asterisk marks possible birth names of kings whose regnal names are given first. In the list of Israel the shifting back and forth of the column indicates new dynasties, e.g., Omri and the next three names belong to one dynasty, while Jehu begins a new dynasty. The dates are those suggested by Albright, *BP* 116–17; other scholars will suggest other dates. (See also E. R. Thiele, *The Mysterious Numbers of the Hebrew Kings* [3d ed.; GR, 1983].) It is impossible to reconcile perfectly the biblical information supplied by 1–2 Kgs and 2 Chr, for sometimes the information is contradictory. In part the dating is affected by when the civil year began. For most of the period it seems to have begun in the fall (Tishri); but certainly after the time of Josiah (609), when Babylonian influence became dominant, there was a shift to a spring New Year (Nisan). This may have been a religious custom even earlier.

Moreover there is the problem of antedating and postdating. In antedating (an Egyptian practice, followed during most of the monarchy), the months between the king's accession and the next New Year are counted as the first year of his reign, even if only a few days are involved. In postdating (a Babylonian practice followed by, at least, the last kings of Judah), the first year of the king's reign begins with the New Year's day following his accession. The intervening period is not counted.

This chart was supplied by R. E. Brown.

---

to heed the advice of elder statesmen and pledged "scorpions" for Solomon's "whips," the old desert cry of revolt was sounded, "To your tents, O Israel!" Only Benjamin went with Judah, because Rehoboam occupied it at once (2 Chr 11:12). More grief awaited Solomon's son, for Palestine was invaded by Sheshonk (Shishak) of Egypt, who plundered Jerusalem. His report indicates that he ravaged the N and S kingdoms and also the Negeb (cf. Aharoni, *LBib* 325). The kingdom of David and Solomon dissolved as the Philistines regained power and the Arameans obtained independence. Very quickly the Moabites and Ammonites followed suit.

89 It was relatively easy for the northern tribes to return to the charismatic principle and recognize a new leader. Jeroboam I (922–901), already a symbol of revolt, was favored by the prophet Ahijah (who was later to forsake him). Acclaimed as king, he took up residence in Shechem, Penuel, and finally in Tirzah (→ Biblical Geography, 73:102). In order to insure the loyalty of his people and to offset the attraction that the Jerusalem Temple might still hold for them, Jeroboam established royal temples in Dan and Bethel, sites already famous as ancient sanctuaries (Amos 7:13; 8:14; → Institutions, 76:27, 40). Here he set up a golden bull, presumably as a pedestal on which the invisible Yahweh was enthroned

(Albright, *FSAC* 299–301). The danger of syncretism and of crass identification of Yahweh with the bull image was only too real, as later events proved. Jeroboam's act became known in deuteronomic parlance as "the sin of Jeroboam," although his unifying the tribes against the Jerusalem Temple doubtless was dictated by political realism.

90 The deuteronomic historian, author of 1–2 Kgs, has written the story of the divided kingdoms within a rigid framework of chronology, synchronization of reigns, and religious evaluation from the point of view of the Jerusalem Temple. Even though he is composing a confession of guilt and thus offering a justification for the catastrophes of 721 and 587, he indicates many sources (about 16 references to the "Book of the Chronicles of the Kings of Israel" and 14 to the "Book of the Chronicles of the Kings of Judah"); and he incorporates many disparate tales, such as those from the prophetic cycles of Elijah and Elisha. (On the deuteronomistic historian(s), see *CMHE* 274–89; van Seters, *In Search* 249–362.)

91 For the next 50 years, from Jeroboam I (922) to Omri (876), there was little stability on the Israelite throne, which lacked the dynastic promise given to David. Civil war between the N and S raged intermittently. During this time Jeroboam's son Nadab, after reigning less than two years, was assassinated by Baasha, whose son and successor Elah was assassinated by Zimri, who in turn committed suicide in the face of the successful army revolt led by Omri. The civil war between Asa of Judah (913–873) and Baasha of Israel (900–877) was resolved when Asa made a mutual assistance treaty with Ben-hadad of Damascus (→ 71 above). The resultant invasion of Israel by the Syrians from Damascus cost Baasha part of N Galilee (1 Kgs 15:18ff.).

92   Omri (876–869) was an outstanding king of Israel, but in the Bible he is dismissed in a few verses because of the particular interest of the deuteronomic editor. He left a mark in history that even the Assyrians acknowledged as late as the time of Sargon II (*ca.* 700) by speaking of Israel as the "land" and "house of Omri." If his dealings with the Arameans ended unsuccessfully (1 Kgs 20:34), he did succeed in subjecting Moab to tribute (Mesha stele, *ANET* 320f.). He pursued a peaceful policy with Judah, and his alliance with the Phoenicians was sealed by the marriage of his son Ahab to Jezebel, daughter of Ethbaal (Ittobaal) of Tyre. He established a new capital at Samaria (→ Biblical Geography, 73:103; → Biblical Archaeology, 74:113–15). For a full appreciation of the role of Samaria, see Alt, *KlS* 3. 258–302.

93   Most of the reign of Omri's son, Ahab (869–850), was occupied with wars against the Arameans of Damascus. But in 853 both united in the league against the Assyrian armies of Shalmaneser III in the famous battle of Qarqar (W. Hallo, *BAR* 2. 152–62; → 73 above). The inscription of the Assyrian king specifies that Ahab contributed 2,000 chariots and 10,000 footmen to the fray (*ANET* 278f.). The Assyrians' claim to victory rings hollow; they did not press their alleged advantage and seem to have withdrawn for a time. The revolt of Moab against Ahab was successful, but contrary to the boast of the Mesha stele, Israel was not destroyed forever (*ANET* 320, lines 6–7; J. Liver, *PEQ* 99 [1967] 14–31).

94   The religious policy of Ahab is illustrated by the stories of the Elijah cycle (1 Kgs 17–19, 21). Ahab appears to have been an indifferent Yahwist and easily influenced by his wife Jezebel, who was intent upon establishing the worship of Baal (probably the Tyrian god Melqart). A temple to Baal was built in Samaria (1 Kgs 16:32), doubtless as a concession to the large Canaanite population in Israel. This constituted official recognition of Baalism. The seriousness of the threat to Yahwism is illustrated by the fact that in the dramatic incident on Mt. Carmel Elijah confronted 450 prophets of Baal and 400 prophets of Asherah (1 Kgs 18:19). Elijah's victory saved the traditional religion at a critical moment, although he had to flee Jezebel's wrath. Ahab himself met death in battle against the Arameans at Ramoth-gilead (→ 1–2 Kings, 10:41).

95   During this period the kings of Judah were eclipsed by Omri and his son, and Judah was in fact little more than a vassal state of Israel. Jehoshaphat of Judah (873–849), to whom 2 Chr 19:4–11 attributes a judicial reform, was allied with Ahab of Israel at Ramoth-gilead, and apparently with Jehoram (Joram) of Israel in the war against Moab (1 Kgs 22; cf. 2 Chr 20). Although Jehoshaphat subjugated Edom and was credited by the Chronicler with a victory over Moab, he failed to renew the Ophir trade (→ 86 above). The reigns of Jehoram (Joram; 849–842) and Ahaziah (842) of Judah were dominated by the queen mother, Athaliah, the daughter of Ahab. Edom and Libnah revolted against Jehoram, and 2 Chr 21:8–20 describes further misfortunes. When in 842 Ahaziah of Judah was killed as a by-product of Jehu's revolt in Israel, Athaliah made her move and

obtained the throne (842–837), slaying the royal heirs, except for Jehoash (Joash), who was hidden. The low ebb of Yahwism in official circles is illustrated by the position held by a certain Mattan, "priest of Baal" (2 Kgs 11:18). But Athaliah met an inglorious end in the bloodless revolution engineered by Jehoiada the priest, who put Joash on the throne.

96   The brief reign in Israel of Ahab's son and successor, Ahaziah (850–849), saw the end of Elijah's activity (2 Kgs 1); and the stories of the Elisha cycle (2 Kgs 2–9) are set mostly in the reign of Jehoram (849–842), another son of Ahab. In this period the Moabites were successful in their fight for independence (→ 69 above), and the Arameans of Syria made further inroads. Within Israel itself the bands of ecstatic prophets encouraged revolution, which came when one of their number anointed Jehu, an army general, king (→ 1–2 Kings, 10:50–52).

(ON ELIJAH: Fohrer, G., *Elia* [2d ed.; Zurich, 1968]. Gunkel, H., *Elias, Jahve und Baal* [Tübingen, 1906]. Hentschel, G., *Die Elia-erzählungen* [Leipzig, 1977]. Smend, R., in *Congress Volume: Edinburgh 1974* [VTSup 28; Leiden, 1975] 167–84. Steck, O., *Überlieferung und Zeitgeschichte in den Elia-Erzählungen* [WMANT 26; Neukirchen, 1968]. ON ELISHA: Miller, J. M., *JBL* 85 [1966] 441–55. Schmitt, H.-C., *Elisa* [Gütersloh, 1972].)

97   **(F) The Dynasty of Jehu (842–746).** The revolt of Jehu (842–815) touched off a bloody purge; he did away with King Jehoram of Israel, who was recovering from wounds sustained in battle fought against the Syrian Hazael at Ramoth-gilead, and also killed Ahaziah of Judah, who was visiting the king of Israel. His execution of the redoubtable Jezebel is a dramatic scene. Jehu demanded the heads of the 70 "sons" of Ahab in Samaria and even slew 42 representatives from the Jerusalem court ruled by relatives of Ahaziah. The final touch was the slaughter of the Baal prophets and sympathizers in Samaria, where Jehu destroyed the temple of Baal. The triumph of Yahweh over Baal was in effect secured by this ruthless king, whose brutality was condemned by the prophet Hosea (1:4–5).

But Jehu was much less successful in external political affairs. He has been immortalized on the famous Black Obelisk of Shalmaneser III (*ANE* 192, plate 100), where he is called "son of Omri," and where he is shown kneeling and paying tribute of silver and gold to the Assyrian monarch. This occurred about 841 at the beginning of his reign. But greater misfortune came at the hands of Hazael of Damascus, whom Shalmaneser III of Assyria had not been able to liquidate (→ 73 above). Hazael took Transjordan from Israel during Jehu's reign (2 Kgs 10:32) and bedeviled both Israel and Judah for a half century (even exacting tribute from Joash of Jerusalem, 2 Kgs 12:18).

98   The "savior" (2 Kgs 13:5) of Israel was probably the Assyrian Adad-nirari (810–783), who made several campaigns against the Arameans, finally subduing Damascus in 802 (*ANET* 281). The son of Jehu, Jehoahaz of Israel (815–801), bore the brunt of the Aramean wars (2 Kgs 13:7), but his successor Jehoash (801–786) was able to recoup the losses at the expense of Hazael's successor, Ben-hadad (mentioned perhaps in the Zakir stele, *DOTT* 242–50; *ANET* 655–56).

99   With the accession of Jeroboam II (786–746) to the throne of Israel, a new era began. He succeeded in restoring Israel "from the entrance of Hamath as far as the sea of the Arabah" (2 Kgs 14:25), and archaeological excavations bear witness to his fortifications at Samaria (→ Biblical Archaeology, 74:114). His long and prosperous reign set the stage for the gross social and religious conditions that provoked the tirades of the prophets Amos and Hosea. These were not from the ecstatic bands, such as those associated with Elijah and Elisha (Amos 7:14); rather, Amos and Hosea viewed their call as a direct mission from the Lord (→ Prophetic Lit., 11:6–10). Neither king nor people were spared as these prophets condemned social evils, luxury and immorality, insincere worship and outright idolatry. They were not innovators but reformers, passing judgment on the contemporary scene in light of older Israelite traditions. Amos, from Judah, proclaimed that the Day of the Lord, which was expected to be a triumph, would instead be a day of darkness and gloom. In and through his own marital misfortunes Hosea understood and expressed the corresponding experience of Yahweh with his faithless people (→ Hosea, 14:4, 8). The short-lived ascendancy of Israel was about to end, both for the internal reasons indicated by these two prophets and for the political reason that Assyria's Tiglath-pileser III had now begun his campaigns to the W (→ Hosea, 14:2–3).

100   As we saw, the revolt of Jehu found an echo in the southern kingdom. A successful palace revolt against Athaliah placed a child on the Jerusalem throne, Joash (837–800), whose adviser (perhaps regent) was the priest Jehoiada. The Arameans of Syria continued to have the upper hand, and tribute had to be paid to Hazael, but Joash instituted the restoration of the Temple. His long mediocre reign ended in assassination, which was avenged by his son, Amaziah (800–783). The new king of Judah succeeded in conquering the Edomites, thus opening up the old commercial routes. But he foolishly (see 2 Chr 25 for the motivation) challenged Joash of Israel to a war; and he would not be put off by the latter's warning, couched in a fable (2 Kgs 14:9–10). The battle ended disastrously with Joash plundering the Temple. Like his father, Amaziah of Judah was slain in a palace conspiracy and was succeeded by his son Azariah (Uzziah).

101   The material success of the reign of Jeroboam II of Israel was matched by that of his southern contemporary, Azariah (783–742). He restored the Solomonic commercial center at Elath (Ezion-geber), fortified Jerusalem, and engaged in strong military operations and surveillance to the E, S, and W (2 Chr 26:6ff.) But leprosy curtailed Azariah's career and he gave over the throne of Judah to Jotham (750?–735), whose building and military record has been preserved in 2 Chr 27:1–9. Azariah is probably not to be identified with the Azriau of Judah whose opposition to Tiglath-pileser III (about 743?) is noted in the Assyrian annals (*ANET* 282; cf. N. Na'aman, *BASOR* 114 [1974] 25–39).

102   (G) The Last Years of Israel (746–721). Despite the political success of the long reign of Jeroboam II, the fall of the northern kingdom was rapid. One reason was the appearance of a new Assyrian conqueror, Tiglath-pileser III (745–727), who conducted a series of campaigns in the W that were designed for conquest and not merely tribute (*ANET* 282–84; → 74 above; *LBib* 368–79; *IJH* 415–34). Another reason was the political anarchy that swept over Israel in the decade following the death of Jeroboam II (Hos 7:3–16). His son Zechariah was murdered by Shallum after a reign of only six months. Within a month Shallum was slain by Menahem (745–738). Menahem's reign was marked by heavy tribute to Tiglath-pileser III (the "Pul" of 2 Kgs 15:18; see his inscription concerning Menahem, *ANET* 283). (The Assyrian policy is described in M. Cogan, *Imperialism and Religion* [SBLMS 19; Missoula, 1974].)

103   Menahem's son and successor, Pekahiah (738–737), was murdered by Pekah (737–732), apparently a usurper ("son of Remaliah," as Isaiah calls him in 7:4). This seizure of power represented an attempt to throw off Assyrian domination, for Pekah united with Rezin of Damascus to form a coalition against Tiglath-pileser. Their attempt to pressure Judah into this alliance led to the so-called Syro-Ephraimite war. Judah refused to join—it was having trouble with Edom (2 Kgs 16:6)—and was attacked by the alliance from the N, which threatened to put on the Davidic throne a certain Ben Tabeel (probably an Aramean of Transjordan; W. F. Albright, *BASOR* 140 [1955] 34–35). According to Isa 7, Ahaz refused to rely on Yahweh and called on the Assyrians for help. Tiglath-pileser mounted a campaign and in 733-732 he destroyed Damascus and stripped Israel of a large portion of its territory (Galilee and Transjordan). Israel, now a small state and vassal to Assyria, was left under rule of Hoshea (732-724).

104   With the death of the Assyrian monarch, however, Hoshea defected to Egypt and sent envoys to the court at Sais (we correct 2 Kgs 17:4 in the light of *BASOR* 171 [1963] 64–66). He thus incurred the wrath of the new Assyrian king, Shalmaneser V, who apparently imprisoned him; Hosea's end is glossed over in the biblical narrative. The siege of Samaria (724-721) began. Sargon describes the victory in his annals, inscribed at his new royal city Dur Sharrukin (= Khorsabad): "I beseiged and conquered Samaria (Sa-me-ri-na), led away as booty 27,290 inhabitants of it" (*ANET* 284–85). The customary policy of displacing and reallocating captive peoples was followed; the remaining people assimilated with groups from the other side of the Fertile Crescent, and the area became a province of the empire, with an Assyrian governor (→ Biblical Geography, 73:103). The text of 2 Kgs 17 is a many-sided theological meditation on this event. Lemaire (*HPH* 51–52) sums up the historical reasons why Israel survived alongside Judah for only two centuries: The only thing they had in common was their religious tradition, for there was no longer one capital and one Temple. Nor were their political institutions the same: Israel experienced at least eight *coups d'etat*. There royal authority was more sharply opposed by the prophets (Ahab confronted by Elijah) than in Judah. Finally, the territory of Israel was exposed to the invasions of the Arameans and the Assyrians.

105   (H) Ahaz (735-715) and Hezekiah (715-687). The usual deuteronomic judgment on Ahaz acquires more substance when we learn of his child sacrifice to Molech (2 Kgs 16:3) and his cynical reaction to Isaiah (Isa 7:1ff.). His recourse to Assyria in the crisis of the Syro-Ephraimite war did not exempt him from paying tribute to Tiglath-pileser (*ANET* 282). The religious significance of his subjection to Assyria is spelled out by his adoption of an Assyrian-style altar for the Jerusalem Temple (2 Kgs 16:10–16). Both Isaiah (3:13–15; 5:8–13) and Micah (2:1–10) give vivid descriptions of social injustices during his reign.

106   Hezekiah receives full praise from the Deuteronomist because his religious reforms underscored centralization of worship. This reform was probably guided more by political motives (national unity) than by theological (such as the religious ideal of the Ark shrine that existed in the days of the judges). The Chronicler (2 Chr 30:1ff.) describes Hezekiah's bold invitation to the people of Israel remaining in Ephraim and Manasseh to come to Jerusalem and celebrate the Passover. We are not able to judge if this relatively ineffectual move to extend influence over the N caught the attention of the Assyrian overlords. But it is true that the spiritual awakening induced by the reform was accompanied by a heightened nationalism. Unity in cult reinforced social and political unity.

107   It is difficult to ascertain the precise details of Hezekiah's relationship to Assyria. He certainly flirted with revolt in 713-711 when Ashdod and Gaza rebelled against Sargon. Edom and Moab were also involved (*ANET* 286–87); but Egypt stayed at a distance, despite the negotiations scored in Isa 18:1–7. It is to this period that Isa 20 refers, and the symbolic act of the prophet concerning the fall of Egypt was a clear warning to Judah to remain clear of political entanglement. The far-reaching building program of Hezekiah's reign was probably linked to his military aspirations. The text of 2 Kgs 20:20 (cf. 2 Chr 32:3–5,30) mentions a tunnel built by him to provide water within the city walls during siege. The famous Siloam inscription was found here (*ANET* 321; → Biblical Archaeology, 74:115).

108 The greatest danger arose when Ashkelon and Ekron revolted in 704 (now with a promise of help from Egypt, which was to be defeated ignominiously at Eltekeh; *cf.* Isa 30:1–7; 31:1–3). Sennacherib came to the Assyrian throne (704) and quashed the rebellion of Merodach-baladan in Babylon (perhaps the visit of the Babylonian envoys to Jerusalem took place shortly before this; see 2 Kgs 20:12–19; Isa 39). He then scourged the Phoenician coast, which had also joined in the revolt, and came S to the Philistine cities to settle the score. The people of Ekron had handed over to Hezekiah their own king, Padi, who had shown loyalty to Assyria; hence Judah was deeply involved. As Sennacherib describes it, he took 46 of Judah's cities and shut up Hezekiah in Jerusalem "like a bird in a cage" (*ANET* 288; *DOTT* 67). The ensuing events are dramatically recorded in 2 Kgs 18:13–19:34 (Isa 36–37), where probably two versions of the same events have been strung together (instead of 18:17ff. being the record of a later revolt in 688; but cf. *BHI* 298–309). Despite the intervention of the Lord, Judah was ravaged (Isa 1:4–9) and faced a long period of subjection to Assyria (see B. S. Childs, *Isaiah and the Assyrian Crisis* [SBT 2d ser. 3; London, 1967]).

109 (I) Manasseh (687–642) and Josiah (640–609). During the long reign of Manasseh Judah was subject politically to Assyria (see the annals of Esarhaddon and Ashurbanipal, *ANET* 291, 294). In 2 Chr 33:11ff. we are told of his temporary imprisonment at Babylon—perhaps in connection with the revolt of Ashurbanipal's brother around 650—and the apocryphal Prayer of Manasseh was composed later to commemorate his "conversion" (→ Apocrypha, 67:37). But no conversion (if it took place) could succeed in changing the idolatrous trend of his reign. The centralization of cult inaugurated by Hezekiah was undone, and the fertility cults associated with high places were once more in vogue. Even in the Temple there were altars in honor of the astral gods venerated by Assyria, and also sacred prostitution. The situation does not seem to have changed in the brief reign of his son, Amon (642–640), whose assassination brought the eight-year-old Josiah to the throne.

110 Josiah became king on the eve of a propitious turn of events. Assyria was beginning to weaken, and the Medes and the Babylonians were in the ascendancy (→ 76–77 above). From 626, when Nabopolassar of Babylon revolted, to 612, when Nineveh was destroyed, Assyria declined. This was the opportunity for Josiah to assert independence, both politically and religiously. His thoroughgoing religious reform is known as the deuteronomic reform, since it followed the program of Deut. At the very least, the "Book of the Law," which was discovered in the Temple in 621, must have contained Deut 12–26. The deuteronomic ideals of centralization of worship and condemnation of idolatry were those of Josiah's reform (→ Institutions, 76:54). The reform attempted to renew the covenant spirit; and the insistent, hortatory tone of Deut is in keeping with the revival that characterized Josiah's activities. He renewed the Passover

feast, inviting the people of the N to take part—a move that had political as well as religious overtones. However, to judge from Jer, it appears that this reform eventually succumbed to formalism; and the tragic death of Josiah at Megiddo probably contributed to the dissolution of the reform movement. Josiah's son Jehoahaz succeeded to the throne, but international politics swept Judah into a vortex that led to its downfall.

111 With the fall of Nineveh in 612, Assyria fought a losing battle against the Babylonians and retreated to Haran, which was finally taken by the Babylonian army in 610. Egypt intervened in favor of its former enemy in order to preserve the balance of power, and Neco II (609–593) led an army through Palestine to help Assyria reconquer Haran. When Josiah resisted, he was slain in battle at Megiddo in 609; and Neco continued on to the Euphrates. Although the Egyptian's mission was unsuccessful, he returned through Palestine and replaced Jehoahaz with another son of Josiah, Eliakim, whose name he changed to Jehoiakim, indicating that the king of Judah was now a vassal of Egypt (→ Jeremiah, 18:2–5; for a list of the rulers of the Neo-Babylonian Empire [605–539], → Daniel, 25:3).

112 (J) The Last Years of Judah (609–587). The ineffectual and irreligious reign of Jehoiakim (609–598) is well illustrated in many episodes of the life of Jeremiah (e.g., Jer 36). Whatever good the deuteronomic reform had accomplished was undone (Jer 7:16–20; Ezek 8). Judah was caught in a power play of Egypt versus Babylon. We now know from the Babylonian Chronicles the details of the ascendancy of Babylon (see *ANET* 563–64, with bibliog.). Nebuchadnezzar administered a severe defeat to Egypt at Carchemish in 605 (Jer 46:2–12); but Neco was able to fight back and defeat him in 601, a defeat that was doubtless a factor in Jehoiakim's disloyalty to Babylon. The seesaw turn of events mirrors the split in Jerusalem politics between the pro-Babylonian and pro-Egyptian parties. When Jehoiakim finally revolted against Babylon, there was speedy retaliation. The Babylonian Chronicles (*ANET* 564) relate the surrender of Jerusalem on the 2d of the month of Adar, i.e., mid-March 597. Jehoiakim had already died, perhaps by assassination; and his young son Jehoiachin, who had reigned only a few months, was now taken prisoner to Babylon, along with a large group of exiles. The Weidner tablets (*ANET* 308; Albright, *BAR* 1. 106–12) testify to the mild treatment given to this ill-fated king, who became the true representative of the Davidic dynasty for the exiles (Ezekiel dates his prophecies by the years of Jehoiachin).

113 Zedekiah (597–587), the last king of Judah, was no match for the political maneuverings of his era. Zedekiah's dealings with Jeremiah illustrate his vacillating character (Jer 32–38). He finally yielded to the Egyptian party, whose hopes were fanned by the pharaohs Psammetichus II and Hophra (Apries). The retaliation was swift and sure. Nebuchadnezzar besieged Jerusalem in 589 and devastated the rest of the Judean strongholds until only Azekah and Lachish remained (Lachish letters in *ANET* 322; → Biblical Archaeology, 74:125.) Although the siege was lifted temporarily by the advance of Egyptian forces (Jer 37), Jerusalem was doomed. The walls were breached and the city fell in July 587. Zedekiah was apprehended in flight and brought to Riblah, where he was blinded after having been forced to watch the execution of his own sons. By order of Nebuchadnezzar, Jerusalem was destroyed, and large-scale deportations ensued. Gedaliah, son of the Ahikam who had defended Jeremiah, was appointed governor with headquarters at Mizpah. But he was soon slain by a certain

Ishmael, of royal blood; and this indication of revolutionary spirit may have led to further repressive measures by Babylon (perhaps the third deportation of 582; Jer 52:30). Those who had supported Gedaliah failed to apprehend Ishmael, and they determined to flee to Egypt, forcing Jeremiah to come with them (Jer 42). For the destruction of Jerusalem, see *BARev* 9 (6, 1983) 66–72.

114   (K) The Exile (587–539). The state of Judah was apparently incorporated into the Babylonian province of Samaria; but there was no importation of Gentiles, as there had been when the northern kingdom was defeated in 721. The land was desolate (Albright, *BP* 85–86; Aharoni, *LBib* 408–11), although not totally depopulated. Besides the devastation wrought by Nebuchadnezzar's army, there was also the plundering by Judah's neighbors, esp. by Edom (Obad 11), which seems to have occupied the S and by Ammon (Ezek 25:1–4).

But the heart of the nation was in exile; the exiles were numbered at 4,600 (probably adult males) in Jer 52:28–30. The book of Ezekiel throws light on the situation of those settled at Tel-abib in Babylonia, who were not enslaved but were permitted to move about. The community of Jews prospered at Nippur (see M. Coogan, *BA* 37 [1974] 6–12). The Diaspora had begun. Gradually the Jews reconciled themselves to their situation; their religious practices, e.g., circumcision and sabbath observance, became their source of unity (also → Institutions, 76:118–21).

115   Despite the shattering blow to their beliefs in the inviolability of Zion and the covenant with Yahweh, the Jews held to their faith tenaciously. Indeed, a period of intense religious activity began: Israel's traditions were gathered and committed to writing. The Torah was given form by the P (Priestly) school, which collected old desert traditions and codified the practice of the Jerusalem Temple (see *CMHE* 293–325). A definitive law was taking shape that would be the base of the new theocratic community of Judah. The Deuteronomic History (Joshua–Kings) was edited, and the writings of the prophets were collected. Ezekiel had pointed to the future resurrection of the nation (chap. 37); but it remained for an unknown prophet and his followers, whose oracles are contained in Isa 40–66, to spark Israel to return. The preaching of this "Second Isaiah" (→ Deutero-Isaiah, 21:5–6) is marked by deep theological insights and by an ability to ransom the time. He understood that Israel's punishment was at an end and that Cyrus of Persia was the "anointed" (or messiah) of the Lord who would secure Israel's return. Yahweh alone was God and had the power to save his people; once more he would save them—in a new exodus (43:14–21; 48:20–21; 52:11–12).

116   Cyrus, king of Anshan, from the Achaemenid line, took control of Media in 553 (Ecbatana) and then of Lydia, the land of Croesus, in Asia Minor in 546. By about 550 he posed a threat to Babylon and became a symbol of hope to the exiles. Finally, in 539 he took over Babylon intact from Nabonidus, after defeating the Babylonian army at the Tigris. The religious tolerance of Cyrus is known from the so-called Cyrus cylinder (*ANET* 315–16). In 538 he issued a decree allowing the exiles to return to Palestine. (For a list of the rulers of the Persian Empire [539–331], → Daniel, 25:3).

(Ackroyd, P., *Exile and Restoration* [London, 1968]; *Israel Under Babylon and Persia* [Oxford, 1970]; "Archaeology, Politics and Religion: The Persian Period," *IR* 39 [1982] 5–24. Freedman, D. N., "'Son of Man, Can These Bones Live?'" *Int* 29 [1975] 171–86. Hanson, P., *The Dawn of Apocalyptic* [Phl, 1975]. Kaufmann, Y., *History of the Religion of Israel: IV, From the*

Babylonian Captivity to the End of Prophecy [NY, 1977]. Schottroff, W., "Zur Sozialgeschichte Israel in der Perserzeit," *VF* 27 [1982] 46–68.)

117   (V) The Early Postexilic Period (539–333 BC).
    (A) The Restoration. The edict of Cyrus (Ezra 1:2–4; 6:3–5) permitted the exiles to rebuild the Temple at state expense and to restore the sacred vessels plundered by Nebuchadnezzar. The first wave of returning exiles was led by Sheshbazzar, "the prince of Judah," probably a son of Jehoiachin (see 1 Chr 3:18; to be identified with Shenazzar?). He was governor (*peḥâ*), but responsible to Persian overlords of the land. We are ill-informed about the return, although we know that the exiles were largely from Judah and Benjamin. It is Sheshbazzar's nephew(?), Zerubbabel, whose exploits are detailed in Ezra 3–6. The impetus of the newly arrived exiles led to the rebuilding of the altar and to the beginning of the Temple foundations, but not until 520 did serious work on the Temple begin. Spurred on by the prophets Haggai and Zechariah, the building was completed by 515 under Zerubbabel and Joshua/Jeshua the high priest. The two prophets also supported a renewal of the messianic hope in the Davidic dynasty (Hag 2:20–23; Zech 3:8; 6:9–15). Perhaps Zerubbabel became politically suspect in the eyes of the Persians; at any rate he quietly disappeared from history. If these hopes rose in connection with the troubles of the Persian Empire upon the death of Cambyses (522), they were quickly dashed by the effective leadership given the empire by Darius the Great (522–486). Yet Darius was not harsh with the Jews. When Tattenai, the Persian governor of the satrapy "Beyond the River" (Abar-nahara), questioned the right of the Jews to rebuild the Temple, Darius reaffirmed the authorization Cyrus had given (Ezra 5–6).

118   By 520 the community may have numbered 20,000 (Albright, *BP* 87), but many factors slowed its progress: economic problems, divided opinion, and especially the hostility of its neighbors in Samaria, who (as followers of Yahweh) claimed the old territory of Judah. When Zerubbabel rejected their offer of help to rebuild the Temple (Ezra 4:1–5), the seed was sown for the classical enmity between Jews and Samaritans which continued in the next century (→ 119, 127 below). The events from 515 to 450 are almost completely unknown to us, although Ezra 4 describes difficulties. From the conditions reflected in Malachi and from the reforms judged necessary by Ezra and Nehemiah, it would seem that the situation went from bad to worse.

119   (B) Nehemiah and Ezra. Nehemiah, a Jewish eunuch and cupbearer of Artaxerxes I in the Persian court at Susa, was informed about 445 of the lamentable situation in Jerusalem. He had himself appointed governor of Judah (thus making Judah independent of Samaria) with his first task the rebuilding of the walls of Jerusalem (see Neh 2–4). He had to overcome not only the lethargy of the people but also the opposition of two powerful men: Sanballat and Tobiah. Sanballat was the governor of the province of Samaria and a worshiper of Yahweh, as the names of his sons, Delaiah and Shelemiah, suggest. Tobiah was governor of the Transjordan province of Ammon. There was also a third enemy, Geshem, who was governor of the Arabian province. These men could count on many influential people in Judah who opposed the social reforms urged by Nehemiah. Undaunted by their deceit and harassment, Nehemiah resolutely carried out his plans (Neh 5:1–6:14).

120   The province of Judah was small, extending from Bethel to Beth-zur, with a population of about

50,000. The census list in Neh 7:6-38 (= Ezra 2; see *LBib* 413-19) shows the diverse origin of those who had settled by the mid-5th cent. Albright's analysis (*BP* 92) indicates two chief groups: the returnees, many of them with foreign names (Bigvai, Elam), and others of N Judah (from places like Ramah and even Bethel) who had either never left or had returned before 538. The political and economic situation was hardly viable without the resolution and ability of Nehemiah, whose extreme measures preserved the province. He returned to Persia about 433; but his 12-year residence had not been sufficient to realize his plan, and after a short time he was back in Jerusalem. The conditions had become intolerable, and there was great need of religious reform. Tobiah (Neh 13:4ff.) had been given a room in the Temple itself by the high priest, Eliashib. Nehemiah ejected Tobiah and his belongings from the Temple, regulated the tithes for the Levites, stopped trade on the sabbath, and legislated against mixed marriages (Neh 13). We do not know how long his second term as governor lasted. Although hard and severe, he was primarily responsible for the reestablishment of the community. His personal apologia (Neh 5:14-19) shows another side of his character.

121 The date of Ezra remains a moot question. Ezra 7:7 describes his activity in the seventh year of a king Artaxerxes. The seventh year of Artaxerxes I would be 458, therefore, before Nehemiah in 445. The seventh year of Artaxerxes II would be 398, which seems too late. (There is no textual evidence for the 37th year [Albright's emendation of 7:7] of Artaxerxes I, which would be 428, contemporary with Nehemiah's second mission to Jerusalem.) It may be that the original memoirs of both Ezra and Nehemiah failed to mention these two men together (R. de Vaux, *DBSup* 765-66) and that the Chronicler creatively combined their respective religious and political roles.

(Surveys of literature on the date of Ezra: Kellerman, U., *ZAW* 80 [1968] 55-87. *SLOE* 117-49. See also *BHI* 391-402. Cross, F. M., *JBL* 94 [1975] 4-18. Talmon, S., *IDBSup* 317-28. Widengren, G., *IJH* 503-9.)

122 In contradistinction to Nehemiah, Ezra was primarily a religious leader. He was a priest and was given the official title "scribe of the law of the God of heaven." This means that he was a sort of secretary for Jewish affairs, empowered (Ezra 7:12-26) by Persian authorities to teach and enforce the law among the Jews in the province "Beyond the River." He led a group of Jews back to Palestine, and seemingly his first public act was to read aloud the law (some part of the Pentateuch) on the new year feast (Ezra 7; Neh 8). He directed a dramatic ritual of penitence (Ezra 10), deciding to divorce foreign wives; and this grim measure was resolutely carried out. Nehemiah 9 and 10 give information about a final moving confession and covenant renewal. There were to be no more mixed marriages, sabbath infractions, or neglect of the Temple.

123 The figure of Ezra was magnified in later legend as another Moses, as the man who determined the Hebr canon, etc. (→ Apocrypha, 67:38-42; → Canonicity, 66:33). It must be conceded that he oriented the people to an emphasis on the law that characterized subsequent Judaism. But Ezra's connection with the Pentateuch is not at all clear; possibly he worked with the Torah in its finished and present form. There is no evidence that Ezra is the Chronicler (*pace* Albright, *BP* 95). The Chronicler's role seems to be less creative than reflective, for his peculiar point of view is representative of the postexilic theocracy of which he was a faithful member. His preoccupation was legitimacy—the association of the present practices of the community with the leading figures of

old, such as Moses and David (D. N. Freedman, *CBQ* 23 [1961] 436-42; W. Rudolph, *VT* 4 [1954] 401-9). Rudolph is right in assessing the intent of the Chronicler's work as the presentation of realized theocracy in Israel. Yet it is helpful as a historical source for an otherwise dark period of Jewish history (4th cent). Now Judah and Jerusalem saw themselves separated from the nations, chosen by God to survive the disaster of the exile and reconstitute the people of God. The kingdom of God is concentrated in Judah, and the Chronicler presents the people of God in zealous worship at the Temple, secure behind the walls that are rebuilt, separated from all that is alien (expulsion of foreign wives).

(Davies, W. D. and L. Finkelstein [eds.], *CHJ: I, The Persian Period* [1984]. Kippenberg, H., *Religion und Klassenbildung im antiken Judäa* [SUNT 14; Göttingen, 1978]. McEvenue, S., "The Political Structure in Judah from Cyrus to Nehemiah," *CBQ* 43 [1981] 353-64. Stone, M. E. and D. Satran [eds.], *Emerging Judaism* [Phl, 1988]. Welch, A., *Post Exilic Judaism* [London, 1935].)

124 **(C) The Persian Era.** The political history of the Persian "province" of Judah is largely unknown. On the basis of the Samaria papyri discovered in 1962, F. Cross has succeeded in establishing the sequence of governors in Samaria (descendants of Sanballat; → 119 above) in the 5th cent. (*BA* 26 [1963] 110-21; *New Directions in Biblical Archaeology* [ed. D. N. Freedman and J. C. Greenfield; GC, 1971] 45-69). His reconstruction (including the date of Ezra in 458) of the list of Jewish high priests awaits wider acceptance (F. M. Cross, "A Reconstruction of the Judean Restoration," *JBL* 94 [1975] 4-18; cf. Widengren, *IJH* 506-9). Judah may have had a part in the Phoenician rebellion of King Tennes of Sidon against Artaxerxes III about 350 (the evidence is discussed, and rejected, by Widengren, *IJH* 500-2). We know that the Persians allowed the Jews to mint coins; several bearing the Hebrew letters *yhd* (Judah) have been found (U. Rappaport, *JJS* 32 [1981] 1-17).

The religious situation can be inferred from the writings of the period (Mal, the Chronicler, etc.). Worship was carried out in the Temple under the leadership of the priests and Levites. The three traditional feasts and the Day of Atonement were the high points of the year (→ Institutions, 76:122-38, 147-50). Israel developed its intense devotion to the law. It was a theocracy ruled by a high priest who supposedly could trace his lineage to David's priest, Zadok (→ Chronicler 23:20).

125 The 5th-cent. Elephantine papyri (discovered at the beginning of the 20th cent.) have thrown light on a particular brand of Yahwism that flourished in a Diaspora community (A. Cowley, *Aramaic Papyri of the Fifth Century B.C.* [Oxford, 1923]; E. Kraeling, *The Brooklyn Museum Aramaic Papyri* [New Haven, 1953]). Jewish mercenaries, employed by the Egyptian pharaoh for protection against the Ethiopians at Syene (modern Aswan), lived for over a century on an island in the Nile, Elephantine (Yeb), and developed their own form of Yahwism. Contrary to centralization of worship (e.g., Deut 12:13-14), they erected a temple to *yhw* (*yahu*); and their worship betrays Canaanite influence, for they associated the Lord with Anath. Names in this literature (Eshembethel, Herembethel, Anathbethel) have been interpreted by Albright as hypostatizations of the Lord under the titles "Name of the House of God," "Sacredness of the House of God," and "Sign of the House of God" (*FSAC* 373). The Elephantine Jews were not bothered by Cambyses when the Persian king conquered Egypt (*ca.* 525). Indeed, the Persian leaders extended some patronage to them, e.g., Darius II gave instructions to the governor Arsames concerning the feast of the Azymes in 419.

By 410, however, the situation had changed. A certain Persian official, Widrang (or Vidaranag), had replaced Arsames, and he abetted the destruction of the temple by the Egyptians. Some of the Elephantine letters (nos. 30 and 32) deal with Jewish efforts to have the temple rebuilt, throwing light on the otherwise unknown years of the late 5th cent. They wrote to Johanan, a son of the Eliashib mentioned in Neh 12:23 (and perhaps 13:28), who was high priest in Jerusalem, enlisting his support for the rebuilding of the temple. Understandably, he did not answer (a temple outside Jerusalem was of course anomalous); and so they had recourse to the Persian governor of Judah, Bagoas, and even to the sons of Sanballat, Delaiah and Shelemiah (*ANET* 492), who were governors in Samaria. This time there was an answer and help may have been forthcoming, for the project was actually carried out. But it was probably short-lived in view of the successful overthrow of the Persian yoke by the Egyptians toward 400.

(Couroyer, B., "Le temple de Yaho et l'orientation dans les papyrus araméens d'Eléphantine," *RB* 75 [1968] 80–85. Meyer, E., *Der Papyrusfund von Elephantine* [2d ed.; Leipzig, 1912]. Porter, B., *Archives from Elephantine* [Berkeley, 1968]. Van Hoonacker, A., *Une communauté judéo-araméenne à Eléphantine* [Schweich Lectures 1914; London, 1915]. Vincent, A., *La religion des Judéo-araméens d'Eléphantine* [Paris, 1937].)

126   (VI) The Greek Era (333–63 BC).
(A) From Alexander to Seleucid Domination (333–175). We are better informed about the Persian adventures in Greece (Herodotus, Livy) than we are about Israel's history in the Persian period. But these very adventures contributed to the downfall of Persia. Greek unity was achieved by Philip of Macedon, and his son Alexander extended the kingdom across the Hellespont. He defeated the Persians at Granicus River and took Asia Minor. The battle of Issus (333) gave the Greeks access to Syria; and in a passage that raises problems Josephus (*Ant.* 11.8.2 § 304ff.) tells of Alexander's passage through Jerusalem. In 331 he founded the storied city of Alexandria in Egypt and returned N to inflict a final defeat on the Persians at Arbela on the other side of the Tigris. He went on past the Indus and returned to Babylon, where he died in 323, having forged a vast empire.

(Abel, F.-M., *Histoire de la Palestine depuis la conquête d'Alexandre* [Paris, 1952]. Bartlett, J. R., *Jews in the Hellenistic World* [Cambridge, 1985]. Bickermann, E., *Der Gott der Makkabäer* [Berlin, 1937]. Hengel, M., *Jews, Greeks and Barbarians* [London, 1980]; *Judaism and Hellenism* [2 vols.; Phl, 1974]. Oesterley, W., *The Jews and Judaism During the Greek Period* [London, 1941]. Schalit, A., "The Hellenistic Age," *WHJP* 1. 6. Tcherikover, V., *Hellenistic Civilization and the Jews* [Phl, 1955].)

127   Alexander is associated with the Samaritans and their temple by Josephus (*Ant.* 11.8.3–7 § 313–47; see summary by H. H. Rowley, *BJRL* 38 [1955] 166–98). When was the Samaritan temple built on Mt. Gerizim? There is a wide consensus that the breach between the Jews and the Samaritans was a gradual one (R. Coggins). It was aggravated by Jewish exclusivism (e.g., Ezra and Nehemiah) and sealed by the building of the temple. Archaeological excavations suggest that this should be dated after the Persian period (an alleged Hellenistic Age altar is the evidence). Inscriptions on the island of Delos (3d–2d cents. BC) describe Samaritans as "Israelites who make offerings on hallowed Gerizim."

The Samaria papyri from the Wadi ed-Daliyeh provide the basis for some association between Alexander and the Samaritans. The initial welcome given to the Greeks by the Samaritans (according to Josephus) seems to have been followed by a revolt against the prefect whom Alexander appointed. Upon his return from Egypt Alexander seemingly quelled the revolt and destroyed the city. Archaeological evidence suggests that Samaria was rebuilt in the Gk manner (Hellenistic round towers) and settled with Macedonians. On the other hand, Shechem was also reestablished at this time, by the Samaritans who fled Alexander's wrath. Those who did not reach Shechem seem to have been slaughtered in the Wadi ed-Daliyeh, where the remnants of their possessions have been discovered.

(Bull, R., "The Excavation of Tell er-Ras on Mt. Gerizim," *BA* 31 [1968] 58–72. Coggins, R., *Samaritans and Jews* [Atlanta, 1975]. Cross, F. M., "Aspects of Samaritan and Jewish History in Late Persian and Hellenistic Times," *HTR* 59 [1966] 201–11; "Papyri of the Fourth Century B.C. from Daliyeh," *New Directions in Biblical Archaeology* [ed. D. N. Freedman and J. C. Greenfield; GC, 1971] 45–69. Pummer, R., *The Samaritans* [Leiden, 1987]. Purvis, J., *The Samaritan Pentateuch and the Origin of the Samaritan Sect* [HSM 2; Cambridge MA, 1968]. Also *BA* 47 [1984] 41–46; and [on Daliyeh] *BARev* 4 [1, 1978] 16–27.)

128   After Alexander's death, several successors (Diadochoi) were ineffectual, and finally a fourfold division of the empire took place. Biblical history is concerned with two of these kingdoms that were rivals for the control of Palestine: the Egyptian kingdom founded by Ptolemy, son of Lagus, and the Asian kingdom ruled by Seleucus. (The Seleucid era, according to which 1–2 Macc date events, began in 312/11 when Seleucus solidified his power in Babylon.) For a partial list of the successors of Alexander, → Daniel, 25:3).

129   From *ca.* 300 to 200 the Jews fell under the paternalistic aegis of the Ptolemaic dynasty. Several events of this century are indicated in the summary in Dan 11:5–45. The large number of Jews in the Diaspora, esp. in Alexandria, created a need for the translation of the OT into Greek (→ Texts, 68:63). In Palestine the fundamental nature of the Jewish community remained unchanged; it was primarily a religious association headed by the high priest, who combined civil and religious authority in his own person. The council of elders, or *gerousia*, served as a ruling board with him. Judea proper remained a relatively small, self-contained area having only loose contact with the rest of Palestine; yet everywhere a process of Hellenization was taking place. The most concrete evidence of the cultural change was the existence in this period of the *polis* or Hellenistic city — in the Philistine plain (Gaza, Ashdod, Ashkelon), on the coast (Joppa, Ptolemais), and inland (Samaria, Scythopolis [= Beth-shan]), even in Transjordan (Gadara, Philadelphia [= Rabbah of Ammon]). Gk fashions and ways, which were eventually to enter Jerusalem itself (1 Macc 1:13–15; 2 Macc 4:10–15), began to pose a threat to the Jewish way of life (Sirach is an indirect protest). The Jews themselves were divided; many became openly Hellenistic, while the *ḥăsîdîm*, or Hasideans (1 Macc 2:42), were fanatically devoted to the law.

130   The important Tobiad family exemplifies the ties that bound many Jews to the new ways. Descendants of the enemy of Nehemiah (Neh 2:10), they resided in the old Ammonite territory at Araq el-Emir (*BASOR* 171 [1963] 8ff.). Already in the 3d cent. they were governors of the area, as the Zeno papyri indicate. Josephus (*Ant.* 12.4.1ff. § 154ff.) informs us of Joseph who won the favor of Ptolemy III (246–221) and was made tax collector in Palestine. Ruthless in this post, he succeeded in enriching himself. His son (or perhaps grandson) Hyrcanus rebuilt (Josephus says, simply, built) the famous fortress at Araq el-Emir, NE of Heshbon; and he is mentioned as possessing treasure kept in the Temple

(2 Macc 3:11). With the Maccabean revolt, however, the Tobiads lost their power; Antiochus IV Epiphanes confiscated their possessions (Tcherikover, *Hellenistic Civilizations* 153-74; 201-3; B. Mazar, "The Tobiads," *IEJ* 7 [1957] 137-45, 229-38).

131   In 200 BC the Seleucid king Antiochus III defeated the troops of Ptolemy V at Paneas near the sources of the Jordan, and Palestine passed from the Ptolemaic to the Seleucid aegis. According to Josephus (*Ant.* 12.3.3 § 138-44, although the authenticity of the decree has been contested), Antiochus was very gracious to Jerusalem, ordering the repair of the damages suffered in the recent past and providing an allowance for the Temple expenses, while the framework of the local government (high priest, etc.) was continued and certain tax exemptions were given. When Antiochus intervened in international affairs, he had Rome to contend with; and he paid a bitter price in the treaty of Apamea (188) when he was forced to evacuate Asia Minor and pay a severe indemnity. The need for money led him into more campaigns; he died in Elam in 187. He was succeeded by his son Seleucus IV (187-175), while a younger son, Antiochus (the future Epiphanes), was held as hostage in Rome in lieu of full payment of the indemnity. It was during Seleucus's reign that his chancellor Heliodorus came to the Jerusalem Temple to obtain more funds (2 Macc 3). This same Heliodorus killed Seleucus, only to provide Antiochus IV, released from Rome, with the opportunity of taking over royal power. Antiochus came to adopt the title of Epiphanes or Manifest, for the Olympian Zeus was manifest in him; his subjects were not slow to counter with the nickname Epimanes, or madman! His policy was one of unity (therefore, the Hellenization of all his subjects) and of expansion, and this meant the appropriation of large sums of money.

132   **(B) The Maccabean Revolt (175-135).** The episode of Heliodorus in Jerusalem was an ill omen of future Seleucid policy, and the venality of the Oniad family of priests provided Antiochus Epiphanes with a precious opportunity. The Oniads belonged to the family of a certain Yohanan (Honi; Gk form, Onias), father of the high priest Simon II, who is so fervently praised in Sir 50:1-21. Simon's son, Onias III (the anointed of Dan 9:26?), was high priest when Antiochus IV ascended the throne; but he was the victim of his own brother Jason, a Hellenist, who set out to buy the office from the Seleucid authorities. At Antioch, Antiochus IV deposed Onias in favor of Jason (174-171). A full-scale Hellenization of Jerusalem itself was begun, and the possibility of becoming citizens of Antioch was now offered to the inhabitants (2 Macc 4:9-16). Many Jews remained loyal to the traditions, esp. the Hasideans (1 Macc 2:42; 7:13; → Apocrypha, 67:97). Jason was in turn deceived by a certain Menelaus, to whom Antiochus gave the office of high priest in 171, while Jason fled to Transjordan. Menelaus pushed on with the Hellenization and conspired to have Onias III murdered (→ 1-2 Maccabees, 27:62-66).

133   Although Antiochus executed the murderer Andronicus, everything was building up toward a revolt, as repressive measures increased. On his return from his first campaign in Egypt (169), Antiochus, abetted by Menelaus, entered and plundered the Temple. The unsuccessful attempt of Jason to take possession of Jerusalem was another indication of unrest, and so the citadel in Jerusalem (the "Akra": 1 Macc 1:33) was staffed with a Syrian garrison (*BASOR* 176 [1964] 10-19). On his return from his 2d Egyptian campaign (168, when Popilius of Rome delivered the famous ultimatum to get out of Egypt immediately), Antiochus took further repressive measures. An official persecution began;

sacrifice and Jewish practices like circumcision were proscribed under penalty of death; and eventually the "abomination of desolation," an altar (rather than an image) to the Olympian Zeus, was erected in the Temple. (The chronology followed in this report is based on that of J. Starcky and F. Abel, *Les Livres des Maccabées* [SBJ; Paris, 1961], esp. 46-49; see also the chronology table in J. Goldstein, *1 Maccabees* [AB 41; GC, 1976] 161-74.)

134   Many Jews were ready to lay down their lives to preserve their faith—2 Macc tells of Eleazar and of the mother of the seven sons (6:18-7:42). The Hasideans did not waver in observing the law, as their refusal to fight on the sabbath indicates (1 Macc 2:29-38). Of such courage and conviction were the groups who rallied to the Maccabee family of Modin when in 167 they issued the summons to revolt. The courageous father of this family, Mattathias, died in 166; and the leadership passed to **Judas Maccabeus** (this name is usually, but probably incorrectly, taken to mean "the hammer"—the family itself was of the priestly lineage of Joarib [1 Macc 2:1]). Despite formidable odds, Judas whipped into shape a guerrilla force that conquered the Gk Seleucid armies. At the very outset there was a series of important Maccabean victories. The defeat of Apollonius yielded the storied sword (1 Macc 3:12) used by Judas; another army, led by Seron, was cut down at Beth-horon. Even in the face of more determined opposition, the successes continued. Judas attracted many Jews to his cause, for he seems to have been an inspiring leader (1 Macc 3:4). During this time, too, Dan 7-12 was written, portraying the ultimate victory of God's people over oppressive kingdoms and providing inspirational stories about heroes who trusted in God and resisted kings—a resistance literature.

135   Finally Antiochus, who had to fight the Parthians in the E, appointed Lysias as regent to quell the revolt; and Lysias dispatched three generals, Ptolemy, Nicanor, and Gorgias. But Judas had been solidifying a loyal group at Mizpah, N of Jerusalem; and so again there were victories: at Emmaus against the army of Gorgias; and the following year at Beth-zur against Lysias himself, who was forced to return to Antioch. Then in 164 Judas boldly cleansed the Temple of the "abomination of desolation"—within sight of the Akra garrison. The Hanukkah feast wiped out the three years of blasphemy (→ Institutions, 76:151-54), and the regaining of the Temple fired a determination to cap the victories with further independence. There remained Jewish minority groups throughout Palestine and Transjordan, esp. those in the Gk cities. Moving in Idumea, Ammon, Gilead, Galilee, and the Philistine plain, Judas skirmished with the heathen in order to help his fellow Jews, many of whom he brought back to Jerusalem. Meanwhile his brother Simon was doing the same in Galilee. The purpose was also to solidify and to extend Maccabean power.

136   With the death of Antiochus Epiphanes, Lysias became the effective leader and regent of the young ruler, Antiochus V. He replied to Judas's bold siege of the Jerusalem Akra in 163 by defeating him at Beth-zechariah (the dramatic death of Eleazar: 1 Macc 6:43- 46); and Lysias would have taken Jerusalem had he not been forced to return to Antioch to preserve his own political authority. He had to settle for a treaty granting the Jews freedom to "follow their own laws" (1 Macc 6:59). The initial purpose of the Maccabean revolt had been achieved, for the oppression inaugurated by Antiochus IV was over. But the perspective of even more independence and political power tempted the Maccabees.

The Hellenistic Jews opposed Judas and had recourse to the new king, Demetrius I (Soter), for protection

against him. The king appointed their candidate Alcimus
to the high priesthood. The split among the Jews was
never so clear as at this point. The Hasideans and the
scribes (*grammateis*) supported Alcimus because he was of
priestly descent, even though he was favored by the
Hellenists. But Judas opposed him, and Alcimus's
murder of the Hasideans proved him right. Finally
Nicanor was dispatched from Antioch at the head of an
army. Judas defeated him at Capharsalama and later
thoroughly routed him at the battle of Beth-horon and
Adasa on the 13th of Adar (March 28, 160); and so "the
day of Nicanor" became a recurrent feast (1 Macc 7:49).
But Judas was unable to capitalize on this victory; for in
retaliation Demetrius sent Bacchides at the head of a
strong army, and they routed the Jews in the area of
Beroea and Elasa N of Jerusalem (1 Macc 9:4-5). Judas
himself was slain when reprisals against the Maccabean
party began.

137   His brother **Jonathan** (160-143) took his
place and was at least able to stand off Bacchides at
Bethbasi. But Jonathan's forays were modest; he was
content to establish himself in the style of one of the
ancient "judges" (1 Macc 9:73) at Michmash during a
period of relative peace (159-152) and to wait for
developments. A splendid opportunity presented itself
when Alexander Balas landed at Ptolemais and challenged Demetrius I. Demetrius authorized Jonathan to
muster an army, but Alexander offered him the office of
the high priesthood, which had been vacant since
Alcimus's death. Jonathan acted upon both offers but
eventually supported Alexander, who triumphed over
Demetrius to become king in 150. Jonathan received further honors when he attended the wedding of Alexander
and Cleopatra, daughter of Ptolemy; he was clothed in
purple and was made general and governor of Judea (cf.
1 Macc 10:65).

138   A new phase in the development of Maccabean
power was beginning. The Jewish leader was able to play
the Seleucid kings against one another. In 148 Demetrius
II attempted to gain the throne, and Apollonius, governor of Coele-Syria, supported him. Apollonius was
defeated by Jonathan, who remained loyal to Alexander;
and in reward the city of Ekron was given to the Jews.
Even when Demetrius came to the throne in 145 after the
slaying of Alexander, Jonathan was strong enough to
make demands for exemption from tribute; and Ephraim,
Lydda, and Ramathaim were given over to Judea. Demetrius even promised to hand over the Akra, the citadel of
Syrian control in Jerusalem, if Jonathan would help him
put down a revolt in Antioch (1 Macc 11:42). Although
Demetrius was able to renege on this promise, his time
was running out. A new claimant to the throne appeared,
Antiochus VI, who was supported by a certain Trypho.
Jonathan threw his support behind them and engaged in
several battles that strengthened his own hand (Ashkelon, Gaza, Beth-zur). Moreover, he entered into
political exchanges with Rome and Sparta (1 Macc
12:1-23). All this did not pass unnoticed, and Trypho
decided that Jonathan was too dangerous; he tricked him
and imprisoned him in Ptolemais (143).

139   The Jewish reaction was immediate. The third
Maccabee brother, **Simon** (143-134), stepped in and
prepared for attack by appropriating the city of Joppa.
But he could not prevent the murder of Jonathan, who
was eventually buried in the Maccabean home town of
Modin. Now Simon turned to the support of Demetrius
II in return for the recognition of Jewish independence;
and in 142 "the yoke of the heathen was lifted from
Israel" (1 Macc 13:41), as Simon was recognized as high
priest, governor, and commander. The Maccabean
claims to rulership and high priesthood were finally

legitimized by the Jews themselves (14:41) "until a true
prophet should appear." Simon captured the Seleucid
garrison of Gazara and finally succeeded in forcing the
Akra in Jerusalem to surrender, and some years of peace
ensued. A new claimant to the Seleucid throne then
appeared, Antiochus Sidetes. Simon refused to honor his
demands, and Simon's sons were victorious in the subsequent battle against Antiochus's general, Cendebaeus, in
138 (1 Macc 16). But Simon himself was slain treacherously by his son-in-law, Ptolemy, at the fortress of Dok
near Jericho; and Simon's son, John Hyrcanus, succeeded
him in office. Here 1 Macc ends its account; for the reign
of Hyrcanus and his successors we must depend largely
upon Josephus. Christian writers tend to use the name
"Hasmonean" to describe Hyrcanus's line of descendants, whereas Jewish writers, following in the pattern of
Josephus and of the Talmud, include Hyrcanus's predecessors, the Maccabee brothers, under this title as well.
We are not certain of the real derivation of the name, but
traditionally it is related to Asamōnaios (Hebr: *Ḥašmôn*)
whom Josephus (*Ant.* 12.6.1 § 265) identifies as the
great-grandfather of Mattathias (the father of Judas
Maccabee).

140   **(C) The Hasmonean Rulers (134-63).**
Simon's son, *John Hyrcanus I* (134-104), escaped Ptolemy's murderous designs because he had been at Gazara
at the time of the murder. He succeeded his father as high
priest and ruler and tried unsuccessfully to punish
Ptolemy, who finally fled to Transjordan. The first years
of Hyrcanus's reign were unhappy. Almost immediately
Antiochus VII Sidetes besieged Jerusalem after laying
waste Judea. But unexpectedly, because of pressure from
Rome, he came to terms with Hyrcanus and raised the
siege. The indemnities were relatively light but for the
next few years Hyrcanus served Antiochus, helping him
in a campaign against the Parthians. Events now took a
favorable turn. In 128 Demetrius II succeeded to the
throne when Antiochus was slain in battle, and he
became involved in civil war. This enabled Hyrcanus to
recover the cities in Judea and beyond. After a long siege
he took Medeba in Transjordan and subdued the Idumeans in the Negeb, imposing circumcision and the
Torah upon them. He also destroyed the Samaritan
temple on Mt. Gerizim (→ Biblical Archaeology,
74:135). These military victories were effected with the
help of foreign mercenaries (an indication of the people's
apathy). During this time the power of the Seleucids
deteriorated because of inner conflicts, and Hyrcanus
was left with a free hand to consolidate his gains. By 107,
despite the intervention of the Seleucid king, Antiochus
IX (Cyzicenus), Samaria had fallen to Jewish forces
under the sons of Hyrcanus, Aristobulus and Antigonus.
The most significant development within Judaism at this
time was the emergence of the two parties of the Pharisees and Sadducees (→ 146-50 below).

141   John's eldest son *Aristobulus* (104-103) succeeded his father by force, imprisoning his mother (who
might have ruled) and three brothers. With Antigonus
(whose death he eventually brought about), he continued
the course of conquest, extending his power into N
Galilee, which he Judaized. (The Judaizing of Galilee
proved to be relatively lasting, even into the Christian
era.) The inroad of Hellenization is apparent from the Gk
name he bore (although known by "Judah" on his coins)
and the title "king" (instead of ethnarch), which he
affected and which was retained by his successors until 63.
But the general moral deterioration of the Hasmonean
line can be said to have continued. Aristobulus died after
only a one-year reign; and his widow, Salome Alexandra,
a remarkable woman, freed the brothers and married one

THE HASMONEAN FAMILY

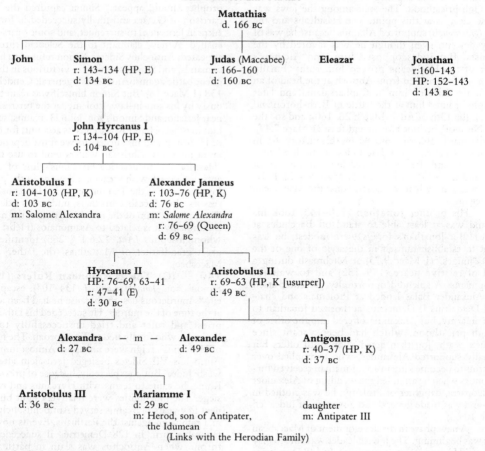

Mattathias
d. 166 BC

| John | Simon
r: 143–134 (HP, E)
d: 134 BC | Judas (Maccabee)
r: 166–160
d: 160 BC | Eleazar | Jonathan
r:160–143
HP: 152–143
d: 143 BC |

John Hyrcanus I
r: 134–104 (HP, E)
d: 104 BC

Aristobulus I
r: 104–103 (HP, K)
d: 103 BC
m: Salome Alexandra

Alexander Janneus
r: 103–76 (HP, K)
d: 76 BC
m: *Salome Alexandra*
r: 76–69 (Queen)
d: 69 BC

Hyrcanus II
HP: 76–69, 63–41
r: 47–41 (E)
d: 30 BC

Aristobulus II
r: 69–63 (HP, K [usurper])
d: 49 BC

Alexandra   – m –   Alexander
d: 27 BC   d: 49 BC

Antigonus
r: 40–37 (HP, K)
d: 37 BC

Aristobulus III
d: 36 BC

Mariamme I
d: 29 BC
m: Herod, son of Antipater,
the Idumean

daughter
m: Antipater III

(Links with the Herodian Family)

d = died; m = married; r = ruled
E = Ethnarch; HP = High Priest; K = King

of them, Alexander Janneus, who now succeeded to the "throne" and office of high priest.

142 The reign of *Alexander Janneus* (103–76) was marked by wars that eventually brought all Palestine under his control. He fought Ptolemy IX Lathyrus unsuccessfully for Ptolemais and would have lost Palestine if Ptolemy had not been pressured by Egypt to return to Cyprus, to which he had been banished. In central Transjordan he besieged and captured Gadara and Amathus on the Jordan. Janneus plundered and burned Gaza on the seacoast but had to return to reconquer Amathus; also he became involved with the Nabateans to the N. The Nabatean king, Obedas, nearly caught him in ambush, but he escaped and returned to Jerusalem, which itself now revolted against him. Thanks to his mercenaries, he held out against the rebels. But when the Pharisees brought the Seleucid king, Demetrius III Eukairos, against him at Shechem, Janneus was nearly dethroned (about 88 BC). He found supporters among Jewish patriots (some 6,000) and then proceeded to wreak vengeance upon the Jews who had turned against him; this was the famous scene of the crucifixion that seems to be referred to in a Qumran document (4QpNah; → Apocrypha, 67:90; F. M. Cross, *The Ancient Library of Qumran* [Anchor ed.; GC, 1961] 122–26). When Aretas became king of the Nabateans, he marched into Judea and defeated Janneus, withdrawing only after due concessions. Janneus now turned his attention to Transjordan, and during the campaign of

84–81 BC he acquired Pella, Gerasa, Golan, and other cities. When his dissolute life came to an end, he was engaged in besieging Ragaba in Transjordan. By that time the territory of Judea had expanded considerably: in a sense the old boundaries of the Davidic kingdom were now realized, and the Gk cities had been Judaized.

143 Janneus's widow, *Salome Alexandra* (76–69), reigned at his death, leaving the office of high priest to the ineffectual elder son, Hyrcanus II. She was reconciled to the Pharisees, who enjoyed great power in these years, and she succeeded in keeping the state intact without wars. But her death left Judea to be fought over by Hyrcanus and the ambitious younger son Aristobulus.

144 *Aristobulus II* (69–63), who was supported by the Sadducees, quickly attained a victory over Hyrcanus at Jericho and imprisoned him in Jerusalem; and so Aristobulus became king and high priest. However, the governor of Idumea, Antipater, conspired in favor of Hyrcanus. In a daring move he persuaded Hyrcanus to seek "refuge" with Aretas, king of the Nabateans, and accompanied him to the royal city at Petra. A deal was made: Hyrcanus was to be restored if he ceded to the Nabateans certain cities in Moab. The Nabateans marched into Judea and locked Aristobulus in Jerusalem; they would have been successful in restoring Hyrcanus had not Rome intervened. Both parties sought the favor of M. Aemilius Scaurus, legate of Pompey in Syria, and Roman power called off the siege. It was up to Pompey to decide the fate of the wrangling brothers. He moved into Damascus in 63, and finally to Jerusalem, where he was forced to besiege the Temple when Aristobulus failed to hand it over to him. Some 1,200 Jews were said to have been killed. Then he imprisoned Aristobulus,

accepting Hyrcanus II as high priest; and Palestine became part of the Roman province of Syria, governed by Scaurus (→ 152 below). The independence won for the Jews by the Maccabee family was at an end.

FROM POMPEY TO BAR COCHBA

145 **(I) Jewish Movements in Palestine.** The NT period coincided in part with the Roman occupation of Palestine. When Pompey became "the first Roman to subdue the Jews and set foot in their Temple by right of conquest" (Tacitus, *Hist.* 5.9), this act symbolized the beginning of the Roman domination of the land, a domination that continued throughout the NT period. At this time Palestinian Jews, for all their national and religious solidarity, were not a united people. In their attitude to the law and the Temple, differences existed among them, which were often compounded by varying political allegiances and intrigues. Josephus (*Ant.* 13.5.9 § 171) mentions three "sects" (*haireseis*) among the Jews: Pharisees, Sadducees, and Essenes. In Palestine there were also Samaritans (→ 127, 140 above).

146 **(A) Pharisees.** By name (Gk *pharisaioi*, Aram *pĕrîšāyê*, Hebr *pĕrûšîm*) they were the "Separated Ones," probably so dubbed by opponents because of their professed strict avoidance of Gentiles, of unclean persons, of sinners, and of Jews less observant of the Torah (for an attempt to explain their name differently, see A. I. Baumgarten, *JBL* 102 [1983] 411-28: "specifiers"). Though this group had its roots in lay "scribes" (lawyers) who emerged in the postexilic Hellenistic period, it first appeared as an organized movement under Jonathan *ca.* 150 BC, shortly before the time of John Hyrcanus I. They seem to have been related to the Hasideans (Gk *asidaioi*, Hebr *ḥăsîdîm*, "Pious Ones," 1 Macc 2:42), who supported the Maccabean revolt until it became too political and secular (1 Macc 7:12-25; → 132 and 134 above).

The Pharisees were chiefly a lay group that accepted as normative not only the written Torah (*tôrâ še-biktab*) but also the oral Torah (*tôrâ še-bĕ-ʿal-peh;* see Josephus, *Ant.* 13.10.6 § 297). The latter came to include elaborate interpretations of the former as propounded by scribes probably since Ezra's time. Such "Sayings of the Fathers" (*Pirqê ʾAbôt;* cf. Gal 1:14; Mark 7:3) were designed to be "a fence around the law," and were eventually codified in the Mishna (→ Apocrypha, 67:134, 136). Influenced by Hellenistic ideas about the value of *paideia*, the Pharisees regarded education in the Torah and in its dos and don'ts as a guarantee of pious conduct. To be a holy nation, sacred and dedicated to Yahweh, was the goal of all Jews; but to achieve this by education, knowledge, and a strict interpretation of the Torah was peculiarly Pharisaic (Josephus, *J.W.* 2.8.14 § 162; cf. E. Bickermann, *The Maccabees* [NY, 1947] 92-97). This attitude more than anything else separated the Pharisees from the *ʿam hāʾāres*, "the people of the land," the "rabble that knows not the law" (John 7:49). A meticulous observance of the sabbath, ritual purity regulations, and tithing, as points of ancestral pride, characterized them. Yet because of such emphasis on oral interpretation, the Pharisees were able to adjust to new contingencies and manifested a vitality and flexibility that made them the "liberals" of the time. Since the inspiration of this movement was fundamentally religious, the Pharisees exerted a great influence on other Jews through their learning and piety, even though they probably never numbered more than

6,000 (*Ant.* 17.2.4 § 42). In addition to their interpretation of the Torah, they believed in a certain human freedom under the control of divine providence, in the general resurrection, in angels (*Ant.* 13.5.9 § 172; cf. Acts 23:8), in the coming of a "Messiah" (*Pss. Sol.* 17:21-18:12), and in the ingathering of Israel and its tribes at the end (ibid.).

147 Though basically a religious movement, in time Pharisaism became involved in politics. Pharisees opposed the secular attitude of the Hasmonean priest-king John Hyrcanus I, desiring him to give up the high priesthood. The king retaliated by abrogating legislation that favored Pharisaic teachings and withdrew his royal favor (*Ant.* 13.10.5 § 288-98). In reality, he feared their influence on the people. Under Alexander Janneus (103-76 BC) Pharisees numbered among the 800 Jews put to death for opposing him (*Ant.* 13.14.2 § 380; → 142 above). They regained favor under Queen Alexandra (76-69 BC) and once again became the spiritual leaders of the people. They often opposed the Sadducees, who had capitalized on the disfavor shown to them. The strife between them was acute when Pompey arrived in Palestine. The Pharisee Sameas persuaded the Jewish sanhedrin to accept Herod's rule (*Ant.* 14.9.4 § 172-74), but Pharisee influence diminished somewhat from his accession until the destruction of Jerusalem.

148 The fundamental religious outlook of the Pharisees enabled them to make a permanent mark on Judaism. After the destruction of Jerusalem, when Temple cult was no longer possible, Pharisees rallied the Jews. Their tradition developed into rabbinic Judaism and persists to some extent in orthodox Judaism of today. The degree to which one can use the rabbinic writings to assess the Pharisaism of pre-70 Judaism remains a problem. The separatism of the group induced an attitude that caused Jesus of Nazareth to castigate them, at least as he is presented in Matt (chap. 23). But the gospel evaluation of the Pharisees, committed to writing in the last third of the 1st cent., emerged in an apologetic context and is far too negative; it does not give the Pharisees sufficient credit for being the constructive force in Jewish spirituality that they really were.

(Finkelstein, L., *The Pharisees and the Men of the Great Synagogue* [NY, 1950]. Neusner, J., "The Rabbinic Traditions about the Pharisees before A.D. 70: The Problem of Oral Transmission," *IJS* 22 [1971] 1-18; "The Use of the Later Rabbinic Evidence for the Study of First-Century Pharisaism," *Approaches to Ancient Judaism: Theory and Practice* [ed. W. S. Green; Missoula, 1978] 215-28. Rivkin, E., *A Hidden Revolution: The Pharisees' Search for the Kingdom Within* [Nash, 1978]. Simon, M., *Jewish Sects at the Time of Jesus* [Phl, 1967].)

149 **(B) Sadducees.** This group was mainly a priestly and aristocratic movement among Palestinian Jews, and their name (Gk *saddoukaioi*, Aram *ṣadduqāyê*, Hebr *ṣaddûqîm*) supports their claim to be descended from the old priestly Zadokite family (*Ṣādôq*, 1 Kgs 1:26). As such they should have been Temple ministers in the spirit of the "sons of Zadok" (Ezek 40:46; 44:15; 48:11).

To their number belonged most of the priests of Jerusalem, "the party of the high priest" (Acts 5:17). However, not a few priests were Pharisees; and the Sadducees included hangers-on from other influential Jewish families. Josephus (*Ant.* 13.10.6 § 298) depicts them as influential among the rich, but with little influence among the people at large (cf. *Ant.* 18.1.4 § 16–17). The first reference to them as a formed group comes from the time of John Hyrcanus I (134–104 BC). Jonathan, the second Maccabee brother, had begun his rule simply as a charismatic leader; in time he assumed the role of high priest (→ 137 above). As "sons of Zadok," the Sadducees should have opposed this Hasmonean usurper of the high priesthood; instead, they supported the Hasmonean priest-kings, probably to ensure their own influence. This influence fluctuated, depending on the favor they enjoyed with ruling princes. It was strong in the time of John Hyrcanus I, whom they won over after his breach with the Pharisees. Again under Aristobulus II (69–63) they enjoyed prestige.

150   No less than the Pharisees, the Sadducees were affected, unconsciously perhaps, by the enlightenment of Hellenistic philosophy and culture. Their sympathy with the foreign occupying power had its roots in the Persian and Seleucid periods, when Jewish priests had to bear the burden of political responsibility vis-à-vis the foreign ruler. The "party" that emerged in Hasmonean times was conservative and tended to guard its priestly prerogatives. It opposed the Pharisees and their oral tradition of the fathers (Josephus, *Ant.* 13.10.6 § 297), mainly because it resented lay intrusion in what it regarded as a priestly area. The Sadducees' attitude rejecting any development or modernization of the Torah came in part from their secular outlook and a general lack of interest in religious questions. Josephus (*J.W.* 2.8.14 § 165) ascribes to them a denial of divine providence and insistence on absolute responsibility for human conduct, along with the denial of reward or punishment of the soul in afterlife. The NT frequently depicts them as Jesus' opponents, along with the scribes and Pharisees; it attributes to them disbelief in the general resurrection and in angels or spirits (Mark 12:18; Acts 23:8), thus pitting them against the Pharisees. After AD 70 the Sadducees disappear from the pages of history.

(Le Moyne, J., *Les Sadducéens* [EBib; Paris, 1972]. Mantel, H. D., "The Sadducees and the Pharisees," in *Society and Religion in the Second Temple Period* [ed. M. Avi-Yonah and Z. Baras; WHJP 1/8; Jerusalem, 1977].)

151   **(C) Essenes.** This third group of Palestinian Jews (Gk *essēnoi, essaioi,* possibly = Aram *ḥāsayyā',* "Pious Ones," or more likely *'āsayyā',* "Healers") may have been related to the Hasideans (→ 132 above) or possibly represented a group of Jews who returned to Palestine from Babylonia about the mid-2d cent. BC, having heard about the Maccabean revolt. They seem to have emerged as a group *ca.* 150. Pliny the Elder (*Nat. Hist.* 5.17.4 § 73) locates them on the western shore of the Dead Sea between Jericho and En-gedi. The only area he could have meant is Khirbet Qumran. Though the identification of them with the Qumran sect is not without some problems, this identification is admitted by the majority of scholars today. (For more on the origin and history of this Qumran Essene movement, → Apocrypha, 67:96–105). The Essenes are not mentioned in the NT, possibly because their aloofness brought them less into contact with nascent Christianity, and possibly because some of their ideas were less definitely opposed to it.

(Adam, A., *Antike Berichte über die Essener* [KIT 182; 2d ed.; Berlin, 1972]. Murphy-O'Connor, J., "The Essenes and Their

History," *RB* 81 [1974] 215–44. Vermes, G., *The Dead Sea Scrolls: Qumran in Perspective* 2d ed.; Phl, 1981].)

152   **(II) Roman Palestine before Jesus' Lifetime (63–4 BC).** The years 63–37 saw the definitive establishment of Roman power in Palestine and the end of the Hasmoneans. The story of the downfall of this dynasty and of its replacement by the Herodians is complicated and marked by intrigues. Only the barest outline can be given here.

(A) Pompey, Julius Caesar, Mark Antony. Having taken Jerusalem, Pompey incorporated Palestine into the reorganized province of Syria, ruled over by a Roman legate. Pompey kept the weak Hyrcanus II as high priest, limiting his religious authority to areas where Jews who actually recognized him were dwelling (Jerusalem, Judea, Perea, Galilee, the southern tip of Samaria, and northern Idumea). The coastlands and the rest of Samaria were made dependent directly on the Roman governor of Syria. This reorganization brought peace and renewed welfare to the Jews. The only dark spot in the next few years of Roman domination was the plundering of the province by M. Licinius Crassus, who had been triumvir in 60 BC. He robbed the treasury of the Jerusalem Temple in 53; the Jewish community rebelled, but the revolt was eventually put down by the quaestor, C. Cassius Longinus.

153   In the year 49 Julius Caesar crossed the Rubicon, with significant consequences for subsequent Roman history. His rival, Pompey, withdrew to the East with his followers. At first Hyrcanus II and his Idumean friend, Antipater II, courted the favor of Pompey, whom they expected to be ruler of the East. But when Pompey was defeated at Pharsalus in the Egyptian Delta (48 BC), they quickly shifted their allegiance to Caesar. Hyrcanus even sent troops to help Caesar, putting Antipater in command. They conquered Pelusium for him, and Hyrcanus succeeded in persuading the Alexandrian Jews to support Caesar. When the latter came to Syria in 47, he rewarded Hyrcanus with the title of ethnarch (ruler of a racial group within a province). His high priesthood was confirmed; he and his descendants were declared *socii populi Romani.* The scheming Antipater was also rewarded—with Roman citizenship and the influential post of prefect of Judea. Two of his sons were appointed governors (*stratēgoi*), Phasael over Jerusalem, and Herod over Galilee. The next years were marked by continual intrigues of Jewish leaders trying to win or preserve the favor of the Roman governor.

154   On the Ides of March 44 J. Caesar was assassinated, and none of Rome's subject peoples lamented his death as much as the Jews (Suetonius, *Caesar* 84). When the assassins fled to the East, L. Cassius came to Syria and seized control of the province and its legions. Antipater I and his son Herod distinguished themselves in raising 700 talents in Judea and Galilee to support him. But in 43 Antipater was poisoned by Hyrcanus's cupbearer. In order to cement the relations between his Hasmonean family and its Idumean rivals, Hyrcanus II offered his granddaughter Mariamme in marriage to Herod, Antipater's son; the engagement took place in 42, and the marriage in 37.

155   Meanwhile, Cassius, after exploiting the province, withdrew in 42 and was finally defeated by Mark Antony and Octavian at Philippi. Since Roman control of the province of Syria was weak at this time, the Parthians, successors of the Persians of old, invaded in 40. They supported Antigonus (son of Aristobulus II and nephew of Hyrcanus II) who now became high priest and king for three years (40–37). He captured Phasael, Herod's brother, and Hyrcanus by a ruse; the former

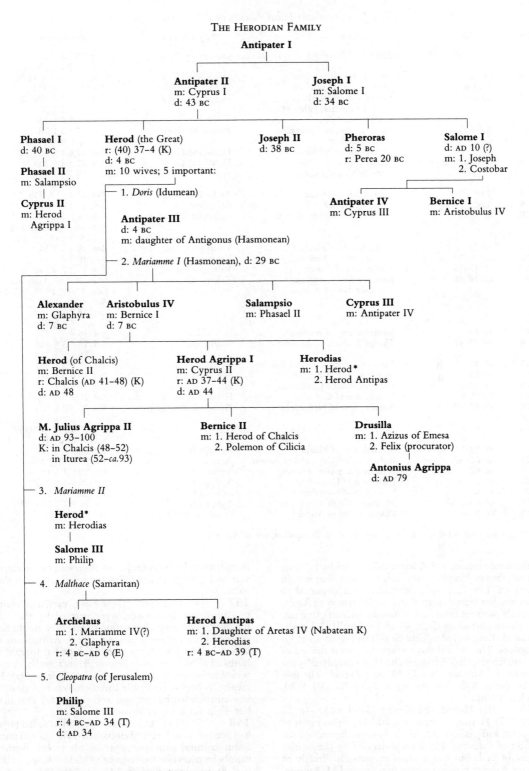

The Herodian Family

Antipater I

Antipater II
m: Cyprus I
d: 43 BC

Joseph I
m: Salome I
d: 34 BC

Phasael I
d: 40 BC

Phasael II
m: Salampsio

Cyprus II
m: Herod
Agrippa I

Herod (the Great)
r: (40) 37–4 (K)
d: 4 BC
m: 10 wives; 5 important:

— 1. *Doris* (Idumean)

Antipater III
d: 4 BC
m: daughter of Antigonus (Hasmonean)

— 2. *Mariamme I* (Hasmonean), d: 29 BC

Joseph II
d: 38 BC

Pheroras
d: 5 BC
r: Perea 20 BC

Salome I
d: AD 10 (?)
m: 1. Joseph
2. Costobar

Antipater IV
m: Cyprus III

Bernice I
m: Aristobulus IV

Alexander
m: Glaphyra
d: 7 BC

Aristobulus IV
m: Bernice I
d: 7 BC

Salampsio
m: Phasael II

Cyprus III
m: Antipater IV

Herod (of Chalcis)
m: Bernice II
r: Chalcis (AD 41–48) (K)
d: AD 48

Herod Agrippa I
m: Cyprus II
r: AD 37–44 (K)
d: AD 44

Herodias
m: 1. Herod*
2. Herod Antipas

M. Julius Agrippa II
d: AD 93–100
K: in Chalcis (48–52)
in Iturea (52–*ca*.93)

Bernice II
m: 1. Herod of Chalcis
2. Polemon of Cilicia

Drusilla
m: 1. Azizus of Emesa
2. Felix (procurator)

Antonius Agrippa
d: AD 79

— 3. *Mariamme II*

Herod*
m: Herodias

Salome III
m: Philip

— 4. *Malthace* (Samaritan)

Archelaus
m: 1. Mariamme IV(?)
2. Glaphyra
r: 4 BC–AD 6 (E)

Herod Antipas
m: 1. Daughter of Aretas IV (Nabatean K)
2. Herodias
r: 4 BC–AD 39 (T)

— 5. *Cleopatra* (of Jerusalem)

Philip
m: Salome III
r: 4 BC–AD 34 (T)
d: AD 34

d = died; m = married; r = ruled
E = Ethnarch; HP = High Priest; K = King; T = Tetrarch   *Called by some "Herod Philip."

THE TWENTY-EIGHT HIGH PRIESTS IN HERODIAN TIMES

No.	Dates	Name	Appointed by	References
1	37, 35 BC	Ananel (of Babylon)	Herod the Great	*Ant.* 15.2.4 § 22; 3.1 § 39–41
2	36 BC	Aristobulus III	Herod the Great	*Ant.* 15.3.1–3 § 41,56
3	?–23 BC	Jesus, son of Phiabi	Herod the Great	*Ant.* 15.9.3 § 322
4	23–6 BC	Simon, son of Boethus (of Alexandria; father of Mariamme II)	Herod the Great	*Ant.* 15.9.3 § 320–22 17.4.3 § 78 18.5.4 § 136
5	6–5 BC	Matthias, son of Theophilus (of Jerusalem)	Herod the Great	*Ant.* 17.4.3 § 78 6.4 § 164–67
6	? (1 day)	Joseph, son of Ellemus	Herod the Great	*Ant.* 17.6.4 § 165–67
7	5–4 BC; 3 BC–AD 6	Joazar, son of Boethus (br. of Herod's wife)	Herod the Great	*Ant.* 17.6.4 § 165 18.1.1 § 3 2.1 § 26
8	4 BC	Eleazar, br. of Joazar	Archelaus	*Ant.* 17.13.1 § 339, 341
9	4 BC	Jesus, son of Seë	Archelaus	*Ant.* 17.13.1 § 341
10	AD 6–15	Ananus (Annas), son of Seth	P. Sulpicius Quirinius	Luke 3:2; John 18:13,24; Acts 4:6; *Ant.* 18.2.1–2 § 26–34; etc.
11	AD 15	Ishmael, son of Phiabi	Valerius Gratus	*Ant.* 18.2.2 § 34
12	AD 16–17	Eleazar, son of Ananus	Valerius Gratus	*Ant.* 18.2.2 § 34
13	AD 17–18	Simon, son of Camith	Valerius Gratus	*Ant.* 18.2.2 § 34
14	AD 18–36	Joseph, called Caiaphas (son-in-law of Annas)	Valerius Gratus	Matt 26:3,57; Luke 3:2; John 11:49; 18:13,14,24,28; Acts 4:6; *Ant.* 18.2.2 § 35 4.3 § 95
15	AD 37	Jonathan, son of Ananus*	L. Vitellius	*Ant.* 18.4.3 § 95
16	AD 37–41	Theophilus, son of Ananus*	L. Vitellius	*Ant.* 18.5.3 § 123 19.6.4 § 313
17	AD 41	Simon Cantheras, son of Boethus	Herod Agrippa I	*Ant.* 19.6.2 § 297
18	AD 43(?)	Matthias, son of Ananus	Herod Agrippa I	*Ant.* 19.6.4 § 316
19	AD 44(?)	Elioneus, son of Cantheras	Herod Agrippa I	*Ant.* 19.8.1 § 342
20	AD 45(?)	Joseph, son of Camith	Herod of Chalcis	*Ant.* 20.1.3 § 16
21	AD 47–59	Ananias, son of Nedebaeus	Herod of Chalcis	*Ant.* 20.5.2 § 103 6.2 § 131 9.2–4 § 205ff. Acts 23:2; 24:1
22	AD 59–61	Ishmael, son of Phiabi	Agrippa II	*Ant.* 20.8.8 § 179
23	AD 61–62	Joseph, called Cabi, son of Simon	Agrippa II	*Ant.* 20.8.11 § 196
24	AD 62 (3 mos.)	Ananus (II), son of Ananus	Agrippa II	*Ant.* 20.9.1 § 197
25	AD 62–63	Jesus, son of Damneus	Agrippa II	*Ant.* 20.9.1 § 203
26	AD 63(?)–65	Jesus, son of Gamaliel	Agrippa II	*Ant.* 20.9.4 § 213
27	AD 65(?)–67	Matthias, son of Theophilus	Agrippa II	*Ant.* 20.9.7 § 223
28	AD 67–	Phannias, son of Samuel	People in revolt	*Ant.* 20.10.1 § 227

*These are probably one person: Jonathan, called Theophilus, son of Ananus.

committed suicide, and Antigonus had the latter's ears cut off, thus making him incapable of continuing as high priest (cf. Lev 21:17–23). Hyrcanus was deported to Babylon, but Herod escaped and made his way to Rome, where he won the favor first of Antony, then of Octavian. By a *senatusconsultum* (Dec. 40 BC [= AUC 714]) he was declared "King of Judea," but he still had to conquer his kingdom. This he did three years later with the aid of Roman troops, after Antigonus had been executed by the Romans in Antioch. (See E. M. Smallwood, *The Jews under Roman Rule from Pompey to Diocletian* [SJLA 20; Leiden, 1976].)

156   (B) Herod the Great (37–4 BC). In 37 (AUC 717) Herod, a vigorous athlete, unscrupulous schemer, and passionate autocrat, became the undisputed master of Palestine. He did not depend on the nearby legate of Syria but was a vassal responsible directly to Rome. A clever politician, he at first favored M. Antony; but after the latter's defeat at Actium in 31, Herod hastily visited Octavian on the island of Rhodes, removed his crown in the victor's presence, and explained his attitude. Octavian restored the crown and confirmed his kingship by decree (*J.W.* 1.20.2 § 392). Herod became *rex socius* of Rome, enjoying full domestic autonomy and freedom

from tribute, but was subject to the *princeps* in matters of war and foreign policy. Herod's reign falls into three parts.

157   (1) 37–25 BC. These early years, used mainly to consolidate his power, were marked by the cold-blooded, systematic elimination of any who might have contested his authority (among others, Aristobulus III, whom he had previously made high priest; Joseph, the husband of his own sister Salome; Hyrcanus II; his own wife Mariamme I; his mother-in-law, Alexandra). His cruelty, rooted in insatiable ambition, was notorious; he was surrounded by intrigue and conspiracy that made him fight for his very existence.

158   (2) 25–13 BC. Once opposition to his power had been removed, Herod embarked on lavish and munificent cultural improvements in his realm, financed mainly by taxes (for the remains of his buildings, → Biblical Archaeology, 74:138, 141–43, 148, 151). He supported emperor worship; to enhance its quadrennial celebration he saw to the building of emperor-temples, theaters, hippodromes, gymnasia, baths, and even new cities. At Jerusalem he erected a theater, an amphitheater, parks and gardens, fountains, a royal palace, and the Fortress Antonia. In the 18th year of his reign (*ca.* 20 BC,

Ant. 15.11.1 § 380) Herod began a magnificent restoration of the Second Temple. The Temple proper was soon finished, but the reconstruction of its precincts continued long after him, being completed *ca.* AD 63 (*Ant.* 20.9.7 § 219), a mere seven years before its destruction. (See A. Parrot, *The Temple of Jerusalem* [London, 1957].) Outside Jerusalem Herod carried on similar construction. Samaria was rebuilt and renamed Sebaste (fem. Gk equivalent of "Augustus"), in honor of the emperor; in it a temple to Augustus was erected (see A. Parrot, *Samaria* [SBA 7; NY, 1958]). Strato's Tower on the coast became an important harbor city, Caesarea Maritima. Mamre, sacred to the memory of Abraham, was enclosed with massive "Herodian" masonry. Fortresses were constructed or fortified anew throughout the land (Cyprus, Alexandrium, Herodium, Hyrcania, Machaerus, Masada, etc.); in some cases they were fitted out with royal apartments. Jericho became Herod's favorite dwelling place, adorned with a theater, racecourse, gymnasium, and tower.

Herod was influenced by the cultural advances of the Augustan age and surrounded himself with Gk philosophers and rhetors as advisors. Most famous of these was Nicolas of Damascus, scientist, (Aristotelian) philosopher, and historian, on whose annals Josephus depended (→ Apocrypha, 67:128). But Herod had little interest in Judaism, being at heart a Hellenist; though a king of the Jews, he was not a Jewish king. He never succeeded in gaining the support of the Jews, who really hated him (*Ant.* 15.1.2 § 9–10, where Strabo's testimony is quoted). Being an Idumean, he was to them a "half Jew" (*Ant.* 14.15.2 § 403). He removed and appointed at will high priests who were no longer Sadducees (because of their Hasmonean leanings) but men steeped in Hellenistic culture and philosophy. These were accordingly most unacceptable to the Pharisees. Twice the latter refused to swear allegiance to Herod and the emperor (*Ant.* 15.10.4 § 369–70; 17.2.4 § 41–42). Hence Herod resorted to violence to hold the Jews in check, and fortresses were constructed throughout the land.

159 (3) 13–4 BC. Domestic strife marked the last years of Herod's reign. He had married 10 wives (*J.W.* 1.28.4 § 562) and repudiated some of them as well as their children. Real trouble came from the two eldest sons born to Mariamme I, Alexander and Aristobulus IV (whom he finally slew in 7 BC), and from Antipater III (whom he executed five days before his own death). During his last illness two Jewish lawyers incited followers to tear down the golden eagle from the gate of the Herodian Temple in Jerusalem. Herod retaliated by ordering them burned alive (*J.W.* 1.33.2–4 § 648–55). Josephus (*Ant.* 17.8.1 § 191; *J.W.* 1.33.8 § 665) records that Herod died 37 years "from the date he was appointed king by the Romans" (AUC 714) and 34 years "after he assumed control of the state" (AUC 717)—thus (shortly before Passover) in AUC 750 = 4 BC. (E. L. Martin, *The Birth of Christ Recalculated* [2d ed.; Pasadena, 1980] has argued for 1 BC; but cf. P. M. Bernegger, *JTS* 34 [1983] 526–31; also O. Edwards, *PEQ* 114 [1982] 29–42.) A great funeral procession accompanied his corpse from Jericho to Herodium, a few miles SE of Bethlehem, where he was buried (→ Biblical Geography, 73:91).

(Grant, M., *Herod the Great* [NY, 1971]. Gross, W. J., *Herod the Great* [Baltimore, 1962]. Jones, A. H. M., *The Herods of Judaea* [Oxford, 1938] 35–155. Perowne, S., *The Life and Times of Herod the Great* [Nash, 1959]. Sandmel, S., *Herod: Profile of a Tyrant* [Phl, 1967]. Schalit, A., *König Herodes: Der Mann und sein Werk* [St Jud 4; Berlin, 1969].)

160 (III) Roman Palestine in Jesus' Lifetime (4 BC–AD 30).

(A) Birth of Jesus. Luke (1:5; 2:1) records Jesus' birth in the days of Herod and of the emperor Augustus (cf. Matt 2:1). Though the year is not reckoned with certainty, the birth did not occur in AD 1. The Christian era, supposed to have had its starting point in the year of Jesus' birth, is based on a miscalculation introduced *ca.* 533 by Dionysius Exiguus, a Scythian monk, "abbot" of a Roman monastery, who objected to the prevailing system of dating according to the era of Diocletian, the "impious persecutor," and decided to use the incarnation for the years of "the Lord" (*Ep. ad Petron.* 61; PL 67. 487). Equating *annum Domini* with AUC 754, he erred by about four years; how he did this is not certain. Dionysius may have been aware of a tradition (preserved by Clement of Alexandria, *Strom.* 1.21.145; GCS 15. 90), according to which Augustus reigned 43 years. On the basis of Luke 3:1,23 Jesus' 30th year, the beginning of his public ministry, was equated with the 15th year of Tiberius's reign. Hence, Jesus would have lived 15 years during Augustus's reign and been born in the latter's 28th year. Reckoning the 28th year from AUC 727, one arrives at AUC 754, which became AD 1. However, seemingly Herod died in AUC 750 (→ 159 above), and so Dionysius's reckoning would mean that Jesus was born four years *after* Herod's death. (See BBM 547–55; H. U. Instinsky, *Das Jahr der Geburt Christi* [Munich, 1957].) Martin (*Birth* [→ 159 above]) would have Jesus born on Sept. 11, 3 BC; many more scholars prefer a date *ca.* 6 BC.

161 After the conquest of Pompey, the province of Syria was ruled by Roman legates (listed in Schürer, *HJPAJC* 1. 244–66). Luke 2:2 mentions P. Sulpicius Quirinius. How does he fit into the succession of legates about the time of Jesus' birth? The succession seems to have been:

M. Vipsanius Agrippa	23–13 BC
M. Titius	*ca.* 10 BC
( )	
S. Sentius Saturninus	*ca.* 9–6 BC
P. Quinctilius Varus	7/6–4 BC
(?) L. Calpurnius Piso	*ca.* 4–1 BC
C. Julius Caesar	1 BC–AD 4 (?)
L. Volusius Saturninus	AD 4–5
P. Sulpicius Quirinius	AD 6–7 (?)
Q. Caecilius Metellus Creticus Silanus	AD 12–17

That Quirinius was legate in AD 6–7 (= AUC 759) and took up a census in that year is certain (37 years after the battle of Actium [31 BC = AUC 723]; *Ant.* 17.13.5 § 355; 18.1.1 § 1–2; 18.2.1 § 26; *J.W.* 2.8.1 § 118; 7.8.1 § 253; cf. Acts 5:37). If Luke's mention of the "first" census were significant, then that of AD 6–7 might be a second one. But when was the "first" census? And in what sense did Luke write of the "first" census? The legates during the last few years of Herod's life (from 9 to 4 BC) are known with certainty, even if some hesitation surrounds the beginning or end of their terms. If Quirinius is known to have been consul in 12 BC (Tacitus, *Ann.* 3.48), he was most likely a proconsular legate shortly thereafter (and as such could have waged war against the Homonadensians in Cilicia [Tacitus, ibid.; Strabo, *Geogr.* 12.6.5]). But there is no clear evidence that he was ever legate in Syria in the last years of Herod. Though Tertullian (*Adv. Marc.* 4.19) notes that Jesus' birth occurred at the time of a census taken up under S. Sentius Saturninus, it is far from clear that Quirinius enjoyed an *imperium maius* in Syria at that time—a problematic thesis often proposed. It would make the birth of Jesus very early. Rather, Luke is giving only a general indication of time, placing the edict of enrollment roughly in the days of Herod and Augustus, without any further specification; cf. Acts 11:28 for a similar generalization.

(*FGL* 1. 392–417. Gabba, E., *Iscrizioni greche e latine per lo studio della Bibbia* [Turin, 1958] 52–61. Schürer, *HJPAJC* 1. 399–472. Syme, R., "The Titulus Tiburtinus," *Akten des vi. internationalen Kongresses für griechische und lateinische Epigraphik* [Munich, 1973] 585–601.)

162   (B) Caesar Augustus (27 BC–AD 14). NT times proper began under Augustus. On the death of Julius Caesar two of his relatives vied for power, Mark Antony and Octavian (originally named C. Octavius; later, Gaius Iulius Caesar Octavianus). The latter finally won out, defeating Antony at Actium in Sept. 31 BC. He soon became the sole master of the Roman world; two years later at his triumph the doors of the Roman temple of Janus were closed for the first time in 200 years, symbolizing the peace restored. In 27 BC the senate conferred on Octavian the title *Augustus,* "the venerable," in recognition of his distinguished service to Rome. Thus began the custom of Roman emperors using this title (see Acts 25:21,25 [of Nero]). It is also customary to date the beginning of the Roman Empire from this occasion. Augustus's rule was a principate, i.e., a benign dictatorship; yet *pax Augusta* reigned, with peace and prosperity prevailing in most of the Mediterranean world for centuries.

(Charles-Picard, G., *Augustus and Nero: The Secret of Empire* [NY, 1965]. Ehrenberg, V. and A. H. M. Jones, *Documents Illustrating the Reigns of Augustus & Tiberius* [2 ed.; Oxford, 1976]. Gardthausen, V., *Augustus und seine Zeit* [6 vols.; repr. Aalen, 1964]. Jones, A. H. M., *Augustus* [NY, 1970]. Millar, F. and E. Segal (eds.), *Caesar Augustus: Seven Aspects* [Oxford, 1984]. Reinhold, M., *The Golden Age of Augustus* [Toronto, 1978].)

163   (C) Herod's Heirs. A codicil to Herod's will divided his kingdom among three of his sons, Archelaus, Herod Antipas, and Philip. Family intrigue continued, and Jewish hatred for Herod the Great evoked opposition to the succession of his sons as rulers. Delegations from all sides were sent to Rome; in the end Augustus respected Herod's will.

164   (a) ARCHELAUS (4 BC–AD 6), the elder son of Malthace, inherited half of the kingdom (Judea, Samaria, Idumea). Herod wanted him to have the title of king, but Rome granted him only the rank of ethnarch. He was the least liked of the sons, mainly because of his high-handed, autocratic ways. Archelaus arbitrarily deposed high priests. Despite an extensive building program and considerable munificence to the country, he so aroused the Jews that they sent a delegation of leading men from Jerusalem and Samaria to Rome to complain against his misgovernment. This brought an end to his nine-year reign; he was exiled to Vienne (southern Gaul) in AD 6. Rome used the occasion to make Judea, Samaria, and Idumea into a Roman province.

165   (b) HEROD ANTIPAS (4 BC–AD 39), the younger son of Malthace, inherited Galilee and Perea as a tetrarch (a petty prince who ruled over a fourth part of a territory; so Luke 3:2,19; Matt 14:1; but Mark 6:14 calls him "king"). He built for himself a magnificent capital at Tiberias on the W shore of the Lake of Galilee, naming it in honor of the emperor. Herod Antipas had some of his father's traits: he was vainglorious, indolent, hostile, and crafty (Luke 13:32 "that fox"); yet he knew how to court Rome's favor. After marrying the daughter of the Nabatean king Aretas IV, he repudiated her in favor of Herodias, the wife of his half brother Herod, the son of Mariamme II (*Ant.* 18.5.4 § 136; cf. Luke 3:19). In Matt 14:3; Mark 6:17 Herodias appears as the wife of a "Philip." Since this cannot be Philip the tetrarch, whose wife was Salome III, daughter of Herodias and Herod, commentators often suppose that Herod, the husband of Herodias, had the surname Philip (a supposition not

otherwise attested). John the Baptist was executed by Herod Antipas (cf. Mark 6:17–29; *Ant.* 18.5.2 § 117–19). The repudiation of King Aretas's daughter brought warfare to Herod Antipas's land; when the Roman legate of Syria, L. Vitellius (AD 35–39), failed to help him, Herod was defeated by Aretas in AD 37. The emperor Caligula finally exiled him to Lyons (AD 39) after 43 years of reign.

166   (c) PHILIP (4 BC–AD 34), the son of Cleopatra of Jerusalem, became tetrarch of the regions E and N of the Lake of Galilee, Auranitis, Batanea, Gaulanitis, Paneas, Trachonitis (*Ant.* 17.8.1 § 189; 17.11.4 § 319; *J.W.* 2.6.3 § 95; Luke 3:2 mentions only Trachonitis and Iturea). These were buffer areas against the Nabateans and the Parthians, where the population was largely non-Jewish. Philip was a good ruler; he was often praised for his benevolence and justice. Sometime before 2 BC he transformed the fishing village Bethsaida (on the N coast of the Lake of Galilee) into his capital, renaming it Julias in honor of Augustus's daughter Julia. At the sources of the Jordan River he rebuilt the old Gk town Paneas, renaming it Caesarea Philippi (cf. Mark 8:27; Matt 16:13). After 37 years of rule he died without an heir *ca.* AD 34, and his territory formally became part of the Roman province of Syria.

(Harlowe, V. E., *The Destroyer of Jesus* [Oklahoma City, 1953]. Hoehner, H. W., *Herod Antipas* [SNTSMS 17; Cambridge, 1972]. Perowne, S., *The Later Herods* [Nash, 1958]. Stern, M., "The Status of *provincia judaea* and Its Governors in the Roman Empire under the Julio-Claudian Dynasty," *Zalman Shazar Volume* [ErIsr 10; Jerusalem, 1971] 274–82.)

167   (D) The Procurators. After the banishment of Archelaus (AD 6), his territory of Judea, Samaria, and Idumea was "reduced to a province, and Coponius, a Roman of equestrian order, was sent out as governor (*epitropos*), entrusted with full authority by the emperor, even with the power of capital punishment" (*J.W.* 2.8.1 § 117). Thus the main part of Herod the Great's vassal kingdom was no longer ruled by ethnarchs (except for the brief span of AD 41–44), but rather by Roman governors. ("Prefect" was the governor's title until the time of Claudius, who changed it to "procurator"; cf. A. H. M. Jones, "Procurators and Prefects in the Early Principate," *Studies in Roman Government and Law* [Oxford, 1960] 115–25.) The *praefecti* or *procuratores* were financial and military administrators who ruled the imperial province, dwelt in Herod's palace at Caesarea or Jerusalem, and could call on the legate of Syria for help, if needed. They collected the tribute for the emperor and maintained public order. When the new province was set up, the legate of Syria, P. Sulpicius Quirinius, was commissioned to take up a census (→ 161 above). This occasioned a minor revolt of the Palestinian Jews against Rome, sparked by Judas the Galilean (Acts 5:37), who upbraided his compatriots for cowardice and for admitting mortal masters when in reality Yahweh was their true Lord. Little is known about most of the prefects/procurators except their names (given by Josephus, *Ant.* 18.2.2 § 29–35 to 20.9.5 § 215):

Coponius	AD 6–9	C. Cuspius	
		Fadus	AD 44–46
M. Ambivius	9–12(?)	Tiberius Julius	
		Alexander	46–48
Annius Rufus	12–15(?)	Ventidius	
		Cumanus	48–52
Valerius Gratus	15–26	M. Antonius	
		Felix	52–60(?)
Pontius Pilatus	26–36	Porcius Festus	60–62(?)
Marcellus	36–37	Lucceius Albinus	62–64
Marullus	37–41(?)	Gessius Florus	64–66

168   (E) Pontius Pilate (AD 26–36). The best known prefect of Judea was Pontius Pilate (Luke 3:1). A dedicatory inscription discovered at Caesarea Maritima from a building called the *Tiberieum,* erected in honor of the emperor, attests Pilate's presence there in the time of Tiberius. It gives him the title *praefectus Iudaeae* (not *procurator,* as in Tacitus, *Ann.* 15.44.2 [see J. Vardaman, *JBL* 81 (1962) 70–71]). Appointed to office by Sejanus, Tiberius's anti-Jewish advisor, Pilate was a high-handed, stern ruler who never went out of his way to ingratiate himself with the Jews. Writing to Caligula, Herod Agrippa I described Pilate as "inflexible by nature and cruel because of stubbornness" and accused him of "graft, insults, robberies, assaults, wanton abuse, constant executions without trial, unending grievous cruelty" (Philo, *Embassy* 38 § 301–2). On his arrival in Judea, Pilate smuggled into Jerusalem by night military standards bearing medallions of the emperor. The Jews, whose customs forbade such images, implored Pilate to remove them. When he refused, they stood about his residence in Caesarea in silent protest for five days. He had them surrounded by soldiers with drawn swords, ready to kill them if they continued to protest. Rather than tolerate such a violation of the Decalogue, the Jews bared their necks, preferring to die. Amazed at the sight, Pilate ordered the removal of the standards (*J.W.* 2.9.2–3 § 169–74; *Ant.* 18.3.1 § 55–59; probably the incident recorded in Philo, *Embassy* 38 § 299–305). When the Jews again opposed Pilate because he used money from the Temple treasury (*korbōnas,* cf. Matt 27:6) to build a much-needed, but profane, aqueduct, he had his soldiers mix with the demonstrators and cudgel them. Many died from the blows or the crush of the mob (*J.W.* 2.9.4 § 175–77). Luke 13:1 preserves a cryptic notice about a violent act, otherwise unattested, committed by Pilate against Galileans, "whose blood he mingled with their sacrifices," presumably as they brought offerings to Jerusalem.

Pilate's attitude toward the people of the province was his undoing. In AD 35 he attacked, imprisoned, or slaughtered some credulous Samaritans gathered on Mt. Gerizim to witness the "discovery" of sacred vessels, allegedly buried by Moses on their holy mountain. The Samaritans had made their pilgrimage to Mt. Gerizim without any revolutionary intent. They complained of Pilate's attack on them to the legate of Syria, L. Vitellius, who eventually sent Pilate to Rome to account for his deeds before the emperor (*Ant.* 18.4.1–2 § 85–89). What happened to Pilate after that is unknown. Later legends tell of his suicide under Caligula (Eusebius, *HE* 2.7), or of his execution under Nero (John of Antioch, *Fragm. hist. graec.* 4.574). Tertullian (*Apol.* 21.24) believed that he was at heart a Christian.

(Blinzler, J., *The Trial of Jesus* [Westminster, 1959] 177–84. Lémonon, J.-P., *Pilate et le gouvernement de la Judée* [EBib; Paris, 1981]. Morison, F., *And Pilate Said* [NY, 1940]. Winter, P., *On the Trial of Jesus* [StJud 1; 2d ed.; Berlin, 1974] 70–89.)

169   (F) John the Baptist. During the prefecture of Pilate and the rule of Herod Antipas, John "the Baptist" appeared in the desert of Judah and the valley of the Jordan, "preaching a baptism of repentance for the forgiveness of sins" (Luke 3:3). Luke (3:1) dates his appearance in the 15th regnal year of Tiberius, which probably began on Aug. 19 or Sept. 17, AD 28 (= AUC 781). Possibly John, the son of Zechariah, a Temple priest, was in the desert because of some early connection with the Qumran Essenes, from whom he broke off, when "a message from God came to him" (Luke 3:3), to go forth to preach to all who would hear him. Such a hypothesis, though plausible (see J. A. T. Robinson, *HTR* 50 [1957]

175–81), has no proof pro or con. According to Josephus, John was "a good man, who exhorted the Jews to live upright lives, in dealing justly with one another and in submitting devoutly to God, and to join in baptism" (*Ant.* 18.5.2 § 117). John gathered disciples (John 1:35–37; Matt 9:14; Luke 7:18), who were subsequently found even in Alexandria and Ephesus (Acts 18:24–25). He was imprisoned by Herod Antipas because of his influence on the people and because he criticized Herod for marrying Herodias (→ 165 above). After confinement in the fortress of Machaerus on the E shore of the Dead Sea, he was put to death (*Ant.* 18.5.2 § 119; cf. Mark 6:17–28). In the NT John is depicted as a forerunner of Jesus, announcing the coming of "one stronger than I am" (Mark 1:7), a reformer to come in the likeness of Elijah (Matt 11:3,10–14; cf. Mal 3:1; 4:5).

(Becker, J., *Johannes der Täufer und Jesus von Nazareth* [Neukirchen, 1972]. Finegan, J., *Handbook of Biblical Chronology* [Princeton, 1964] 259–80. Hoehner, H. W., *Chronological Aspects of the Life of Christ* [GR, 1977]. Schütz, R., *Johannes der Täufer* [ATANT 50; Zurich, 1967]. Scobie, C., *John the Baptist* [London, 1964]. Steinmann, J., *Saint John the Baptist and the Desert Tradition* [NY, 1958].)

170   (G) Ministry and Death of Jesus. Sometime before the imprisonment of JBap, Jesus of Nazareth began his ministry in Palestine—at a date not determinable with certainty but possibly the same year as that of his appearance (AD 28–29). Yet John 2:20 suggests that Jesus' ministry was already under way in the 46th year of the Herodian Temple (begun *ca.* 20 BC), hence AD 26. At any rate, Jesus, like John, gathered to himself followers whom he trained. The main sphere of Jesus' activity was at first Galilee, the territory of Herod Antipas. As he moved about, he preached as a Jewish religious leader of early 1st-cent. Palestine. At times he disagreed with current views of other religious teachers who professed to be interpreting the Scriptures for the people. He announced a new way of salvation, but his influence with the people naturally created opposition.

171   In time, a negative reaction to Jesus crystallized. When he transferred his sphere of activity to Jerusalem, on the occasion of a Passover celebration (the date of which cannot be pinpointed; perhaps AD 30), steps were taken against him. With the aid of one of his own followers, Judas Iscariot, he was arrested and arraigned before the sanhedrin. Whether that session constituted a formal trial or a sort of grand-jury investigation can no longer be determined, nor even whether a formal sentence was passed by it. Mark 14:64 mentions an accusation of blasphemy. Since the sanhedrin's powers were apparently limited in capital cases (John 18:31), Jesus was handed over to the Roman prefect, P. Pilate (Mark 15:1), who enjoyed supreme judicial authority in Judea, including that of capital punishment (*J.W.* 2.8.1 § 117). Tacitus (*Ann.* 15.44.2) recorded: "Christ had been executed in Tiberius' reign by Pontius Pilate, the procurator [of Judea]." Pilate, not understanding the religious issue, suspected that a political issue affecting Rome was involved. Learning that Jesus was a Galilean, he sent him to the ruler of Galilee, Herod Antipas, who had come to Jerusalem for the Passover (Luke 23:6–12). Herod refused to go along with the scheme and sent Jesus back to Pilate, who eventually yielded to the demands of the leaders and crowd (Mark 15:15). Jesus was crucified by Roman soldiers outside the city walls of Jerusalem and buried; two days later his tomb was found empty. Before long, appearances of him as alive were reported by his followers. The latter had banded together and on the following feast of Pentecost began to proclaim that "the whole house of Israel must know for sure that God has made this Jesus whom you crucified both Lord and Messiah" (Acts 2:36). They called for faith in him as the risen Son of God and the only means of salvation now available to human beings. The religious movement that Jesus of Nazareth had initiated in his lifetime became known in time as the Christian church (Acts 11:26). (For a bibliography and a detailed treatment of the Jesus of history, → Jesus, 78.)

172 **(IV) Roman Palestine after Jesus' Lifetime (AD 30–135).**

(A) Spread of the Christian Church. The primitive Christian community gradually became more conscious of its mission to proclaim "the gospel of Jesus Christ" (Mark 1:1). After initial success in converting Palestinian Jews (Acts 2:41,47; 6:7) apostolic preachers turned to the metropolitan centers of the Roman Empire. The "good news" spread from Jerusalem to "the end of the earth" (Acts 1:8), addressed first of all to the Jews of the Diaspora and then to Gentiles.

Possibly in AD 36 amid the disruption when Pilate was sent back to Rome and a new prefect, Marcellus, was named, "a great persecution of the church" (Acts 8:1) took place, in which Stephen was martyred and Saul of Tarsus "breathed [his] murderous threats" (Acts 9:1–2). For relating Saul's conversion to this time, → Paul, 79:13, 20.

173 **(B) Herod Agrippa I (37–44).** When Tiberius died on March 16, AD 37, the legate of Syria, L. Vitellius, was still in Jerusalem, trying to soothe the feelings of the Jews who had been outraged by Pilate. When news came of the new emperor, Gaius Caligula (37–41), the Jews were the first of the nationalities of Syria to pledge their allegiance to him and hailed his regime, which was peaceful and quiet for the first 18 months. Whereas Tiberius had eschewed emperor worship, Caligula now insisted on it. He wanted images of himself as *divus* erected in all shrines and temples (including synagogues) in the empire.

Caligula was not long on the imperial throne before he granted his friend Herod Agrippa I, the brother of Herodias and the grandson of Herod the Great, the territory of Philip's tetrarchy in N Transjordan (→ 166 above). With this grant went the title of king. On his way back to Palestine, King Herod stopped at Alexandria. His brief sojourn there became the occasion of a serious defamatory outburst against him and against local Jews. This was tolerated by the Roman prefect A. Avilius Flaccus (Philo, *Flaccus* 5 § 25–75), and there ensued a violent anti-Jewish persecution (AD 38). In protest the Jews of Alexandria sent a legation to the emperor in AD 40 to plead their cause. A noted member of it was Philo (→ Apocrypha, 67:124), but the emissaries had little success (*Ant.* 18.8.1 § 257; Philo, *Embassy*).

174 When Herod Antipas was exiled in AD 39, his territory (Galilee and Perea) was added to the domain of Herod Agrippa I. The latter, who had been insulted by the Roman prefect of Egypt, was more successful in influencing the legate of Syria, P. Petronius, sent out by Caligula in 39. King Herod urged him not to press the issue of emperor worship; so Petronius delayed, as far as Jerusalem was concerned. But when pagan inhabitants of Jamnia erected a crude altar to the emperor, it was torn down by local Jews. The incident was reported to the emperor, who retaliated by ordering the immediate erection of a colossal statue of himself in the Jerusalem Temple (Philo, *Embassy* 30 § 203). Petronius procrastinated, trying to get the Jewish leaders to accept the order with good grace. Horrified, the Jews gathered in Ptolemais, where Petronius was quartered, and begged him not to erect the statue. Petronius wrote to Caligula, only to bring down imperial wrath upon himself; the emperor commanded him to commit suicide. Herod Agrippa

visited Caligula, hoping to have him rescind the order. The whole issue, however, was resolved by the murder of Caligula on Jan. 24, AD 41.

175 When Claudius (AD 41–54) became emperor by the acclamation of Roman troops, his reign began with an edict of toleration in favor of the Jews (*Ant.* 19.5.2–3 § 279–91). Claudius rewarded Herod Agrippa for his support of Roman rule, extending his territory to include that of the ethnarchy of Archelaus (Judea, Samaria, Idumea). Until his death Herod Agrippa ruled over a territory almost as vast as that of Herod the Great. He undertook to build Jerusalem's "third wall," which, if completed, would have made the city impregnable (*J.W.* 2.11.6 § 218). But before it could be finished, Claudius, who had been warned by Marsus, the legate of Syria, forbade any further work on it (*Ant.* 19.7.2 § 326–27). The location of this wall is disputed (→ Biblical Geography, 73:94; *BARev* 13 [3, 1987] 46–57).

176 Herod Agrippa I was an insignificant but pious king, whose passing was mourned by the people. Although abroad he liberally advocated Hellenistic culture, contributing much to pagan institutions at Berytus (modern Beirut), at home he supported Pharisaism. Not surprisingly, then, he persecuted Christians (Acts 12:1–19), putting James, son of Zebedee, to the sword (ca. AD 44). Herod Agrippa died suddenly at Caesarea in 44, after attending the *Vicennalia,* games in honor of the emperor (Acts 12:19–23; *Ant.* 19.8.2 § 343–50).

177 **(C) Agrippa II to the First Revolt.** On the death of Herod Agrippa I, Claudius again reorganized the country into a Roman province, to be ruled by procurators. The last of the Herodian family to enjoy partial rule was Marcus Julius Agrippa II, son of Herod Agrippa I, who like most of his family had been brought up in Rome and was a youth of 17 when his father died. He did not immediately inherit his father's realm; but when his uncle, Herod of Chalcis, died (AD 48), he became the ruler of this small territory on the slopes of the Antilebanon. He subsequently relinquished this realm (ca. 52) and received from Claudius the old tetrarchy of Philip, to which Nero later added parts of Galilee and Perea. His relations with his sister Bernice (probably incestuous) caused scandal in Rome (*Ant.* 20.7.3 § 145; Juvenal, *Sat.* 6.156ff.). The prisoner Paul explained his case before Agrippa and Bernice (Acts 25:23–26:32). After Jerusalem fell, Agrippa II went to Rome and lived there with Bernice; he was a praetor for a while and died between 93 and 100. While ruling in Palestine, he had little influence on the Jewish population; he was opposed constantly by the priests and arbitrarily nominated and deposed high priests. The end of the Herodian dynasty was not glorious.

178 Under the procurator T. Julius Alexander (46–48), Judea and other parts of the Mediterranean world suffered a severe famine (→ Paul, 79:11). Queen Helen of Adiabene, a convert to Judaism, aided the stricken Palestinian populace with grain brought from Egypt (*Ant.* 20.5.2 § 101). Shortly thereafter occurred the Jerusalem "Council," probably in 49 (→ Paul, 79:25–33).

179 The real rulers of Palestine were now the procurators, who made no attempt to understand the Jews, made little allowance for popular manifestations, and rather looked for the chance to harass them. The period was marked by a succession of minor uprisings (*Ant.* 20.5.1 § 97–98; 20.5.3 § 106–12; *HE* 2.11.2–3). The most notorious procurator was M. Antonius Felix (ca. 52–60), who married into the Herodian family, becoming the second husband of Drusilla, sister of Agrippa II (Acts 24:24). Under him the uprisings developed into open hostility. He had been sent to Palestine by the emperor at the request of a deposed high priest, then living in Rome. Tacitus wrote of Felix: "In the spirit of a slave he carried out the royal duties with all sorts of cruelty and lust" (*Hist.* 5.9; cf. Acts 24:24–26; *Ant.* 20.7.2 § 142). The years preceding his arrival in Palestine saw the rise of Jewish "bandits" (*lēstai*), and Josephus records that Felix crucified countless numbers (*J.W.* 2.13.2 § 253) in an effort to rid the country of them. "Sicarii" (nationalists armed with short daggers, *sicae,* and dedicated to the removal of opponents by quiet assassination, often at public functions) arose at this time (*J.W.* 2.13.3 § 254–55). Political murders occurred almost daily; their first victim was Jonathan the high priest, whom Felix was happy to have out of the way. There arose still other groups of villains, "with cleaner hands but more wicked intentions" (*J.W.* 2.13.4 § 258), who aroused the people to a wild enthusiasm against Rome and claimed a divine mission. To this period probably belongs the exploit of the Egyptian impostor of Acts 21:38. This Jewish false prophet led people to the Mt. of Olives, promising that at his word Jerusalem's walls would fall so that they could enter the city and wrest it from the Romans. Felix met him with heavily armed infantry; the Egyptian escaped, but most of his force was either captured or killed. In the midst of Felix's term Claudius died (Oct. 13, AD 54), and Nero succeeded him as emperor (54–68). In the last two years of Felix's procuratorship Paul lay in prison in Caesarea (Acts 23:33–24:27).

180 Nero sent out Porcius Festus (*ca.* 60–62) to succeed Felix; he sincerely tried to be an honest administrator (even showing favor to the Jews, cf. Acts 24:27). But the tinderbox situation that had developed under Felix was beyond the point of any lasting solution. Soon after Festus's arrival a dispute arose between the Jewish and Syrian inhabitants of Caesarea; it was decided by an imperial rescript in favor of the Syrians. This embittered the Jews still more. It was Festus who finally sent Paul to Rome, when as a Roman citizen he used his right to appeal to the emperor for justice (Acts 25:11ff.). The situation was not improved under the next procurator, L. Albinus (62–64): "There was no form of crime that he failed to perform" (*J.W.* 2.14.1 § 272).

(Marsh, F. B., *The Reign of Tiberius* [NY, 1959]. Momigliano, A., *Claudius: The Emperor and His Achievement* [NY, 1961]. Smallwood, E. M., *Documents Illustrating the Principates of Gaius Claudius and Nero* [Cambridge, 1967].)

181   (D) First Revolt (AD 66–70). The last of the Roman procurators was Gessius Florus (64–66), who by comparison made his predecessor seem like a "paragon of virtue" (*J.W.* 2.14.1 § 277). He openly plundered the land, robbed individuals, sacked towns, and took bribes. About this time arose the Zealots (Gk *zēlōtai,* Aram *qannānāyê*), chauvinists fanatically opposed to Rome occupation. The Jews were greatly humiliated in Caesarea, when Nero decided to grant the Gentiles superior civic rights and the "Hellenes" obstructed access to the synagogue by building shops before its entrance. They appealed to Florus, but he did nothing to correct the situation. Later, when he took 17 talents from the Temple treasury, the Jerusalem Jews could contain themselves no longer. With supreme sarcasm they passed around their community a basket to take up a collection for "indigent" Florus (*J.W.* 2.14.6 § 293–95). He took revenge on them for the insult and turned part of the city over to his soldiers for plunder. Since the priests tried to control the Jews during these incidents and counseled the people to patience, the meek attitude of the people, who did not react against the soldiers, was interpreted by the latter as scorn. Slaughter ensued, but the Jews withdrew to the Temple precincts and soon cut off the portico passageway between the Temple and the Fortress Antonia. Florus, momentarily not strong enough to

check the rebels, was forced to withdraw to Caesarea. The revolt against Rome thus became formal.

182 The Jews were led by Eleazar, aided by Menahem, a son of the Zealot leader Judas of Galilee. The land was organized for battle. The sanhedrin entrusted Galilee to Joseph, son of Matthias (= the historian Josephus; → Apocrypha, 67:127). He was, however, suspected of disloyalty by John of Gischala, leader of the Galilean Zealots; for Josephus spent more time in curbing insurgents than in organizing them. At first the Jews succeeded in routing Florus's troops, and even those of C. Cestius Gallus, the legate of Syria, whose aid had been summoned. Nero then sent out an experienced field commander, Vespasian, who began operations in Antioch in the winter of 66–67 and soon moved against Galilee. Within a year it fell with the surrender of Josephus at Jotapata (*J.W.* 3.7.3 § 339).

183 Northern Palestine was once again subject to Rome. Two legions, the Fifth and the Fifteenth, wintered at Caesarea (67–68), while the Tenth was quartered in Scythopolis (Beth-shan). Meanwhile, the Jews sought aid from Idumea, but the Idumeans soon realized that the situation was hopeless and withdrew. Apparently at this time Jerusalem Christians fled to Perea, settling mostly in Pella (Eusebius, *HE* 3.5.3).

184 In the spring of 68 Vespasian moved toward Jerusalem via the Jordan Valley, seizing and burning rebel quarters en route (Samaria, Jericho, Perea, Machaerus, Qumran). He would have proceeded directly to Jerusalem, had Nero not died on June 9, 68. Vespasian halted his activities and watched developments in Rome. Meanwhile, civil war broke out in Jerusalem (spring 68). Simon bar Giora had been riding through the land with bands, plundering what the Romans had left. When he turned toward Jerusalem, the people, tired of the tyranny of John of Gischala, welcomed the new leader. John and his party withdrew to the Temple and closed themselves in, while Simon ruled the city.

185   (E) Siege of Jerusalem (69–70). It was the Year of the Four Emperors: Galba succeeded Nero in Rome but was murdered in Jan. 69. Otho became emperor, but was soon replaced by Vitellius. The latter reigned only until Dec. 69. Since Vespasian had moved against Jerusalem in June 69, the Roman troops acclaimed him *imperator* on July 1; he returned to Rome, leaving his son Titus to continue the attack on Jerusalem.

186 The siege proper began in the spring of 70, before Passover. Because the city was accessible only from the N (deep valleys flanked it on the W, S, and E), Titus encamped to the NE on Mt. Scopus. At Passover riots took place within the city in the sight of the Romans, but the Jews united to face the common enemy. Titus threw up circumvallation and in plain view of the defenders crucified all who tried to flee from the besieged city. Hunger and thirst began to tell, so that in July the Fortress Antonia was entered by the Romans and razed. From this stronghold Titus was able to move toward the Temple. Fire was set to the gates on the 8th of Ab (August), and entry was made the next day. Titus wanted to spare the Temple (*J.W.* 6.4.3 § 140–41), demanding surrender as the price. The people refused; when further fighting ensued on the 10th, a soldier cast a blazing brand into one of the Temple chambers. Confusion frustrated Titus's attempt to extinguish the fire. Before the Holy of Holies was consumed, Titus and some of his officers managed to enter it to inspect it (*J.W.* 6.4.6–7 § 254–66). Roman standards were soon set up opposite the east gate, and the soldiers "with the loudest of shouts acclaimed Titus *imperator*" (*J.W.* 6.6.1 § 316).

187 Jews were slaughtered. John of Gischala had withdrawn to Herod's palace in the upper city, and once more siege was set. By Sept. 70 the city was finally taken, plundered, and razed; its walls were torn down, with only a few sections left standing. A Roman garrison was stationed in the city. John, Simon, and the seven-branched candlestick taken from the Temple formed part of Titus's triumphal procession in Rome in 71. Pockets of rebels still had to be conquered throughout the land (at Herodium, Masada, Machaerus); the last stronghold, Masada, did not yield until 74 (→ Apocrypha, 67:123).

188   *Iudaea capta* was inscribed on the coins struck for the Roman province thereafter. It expressed a truth with which Jewish people had to live for centuries. Except for a brief time during the "Liberation of Jerusalem" by Simon ben Kosibah (→ 191 below), when Temple sacrifice may have been restored, the destruction of Jerusalem in AD 70 meant much more than the mere leveling of the holy city. It brought an end to the ancient tradition according to which sacrifice was offered to Yahweh only in Jerusalem, making it the center of the world for Jews. Now the Temple was no more; Rome dominated the land. The fall of Jerusalem represented a decisive break with the past; from now on Judaism would take a different form. The Christian community was also affected by this destruction. To the Romans they were a subject people like the Jews; to the Jews eventually they were *mînîm*, "heretics." Palestinian Christian refugees carried to the Diaspora reminiscences of the life of Jesus and of Palestinian conditions found in the Gospels.

189   (F) Between the Revolts (71–132). After Titus left Jerusalem in ruins, the Roman garrison maintained military control, and the lot of the Jews was not easy. Roman colonists were settled in Flavia Neapolis (modern Nablus); 800 veterans were given property in Emmaus. In Jerusalem itself old inhabitants, both Jews and Christians, returned to live side by side with the Romans, as ossuaries and tombs of the period attest. Titus claimed the entire land of Judea as his private property.

The Jewish community, used to paying a half-shekel tax for the Temple of Yahweh, now had to contribute the same to the *fiscus iudaicus* for the Roman temple of Jupiter Capitolinus. Religious practice shifted to forms of synagogue worship, to a more intensive study of the Torah. With the destruction of the Temple, the influence of the Jerusalem sanhedrin, headed by the high priest, waned. An academic sanhedrin of 72 elders (or rabbis) in Jamnia, under the leadership of Yoḥanan ben Zakkai and later under Gamaliel II, took over the authoritative position in the Jewish community. Though Judea was ruled by Romans, this *Yeshiva* enjoyed a certain autonomy. It fixed the calendar and functioned as a court of law (→ Canonicity, 66:35; cf. J. Neusner, *First Century Judaism in Crisis* [Nash, 1975]).

190   Both in Palestine and in the Diaspora a yearning for "the restoration of Israel" was fed by the recollection of how restoration followed the destruction of Jerusalem in 587 BC. While Trajan (AD 98–117) was occupied toward the end of his reign with a Parthian threat, revolts of Jews occurred in various parts of the empire (Cyrene, Egypt, Cyprus, Mesopotamia) *ca.* 115–116. These uprisings stemmed in part from oppression, but also from messianic expectations current among the Jews. The general who finally put down the Mesopotamian revolt was a Romanized Moor, Lusius Quietus, subsequently rewarded with the governorship of Judea.

191   (G) Second Revolt (132–135). The unsettled conditions in Judea finally came to a head in the so-called Second Revolt. Its causes are not certain. Dio Cassius (*Rom. Hist.* 69.12.1–2) records that it was sparked by Hadrian's attempt to build a Greco-Roman city, Aelia Capitolina, on the site of Jerusalem and to erect a shrine to Jupiter on the ruins of the Temple. The

Vita Hadriani 14.2 cites rather an imperial edict forbidding circumcision as the cause. Hadrian (117–138) had previously prohibited castration, but about this time renewed the prohibition and understood it to include circumcision. Though the edict was not directed specifically against Jews, it affected them in an important religious issue. Both causes may have been at work.

Again the Jews of Judea rose up against the Romans. Coins struck by them labeled the uprising the "Liberation of Jerusalem" and the "Redemption of Israel." Their intellectual leader was R. Aqiba, their spiritual leader, the priest Eleazar, and their military commander, Simon ben Kosibah (also known by the name he bears in Christian documents, Bar Cochba [Kochba, Cocheba]). The latter also administered the land politically from headquarters probably in liberated Jerusalem. He preserved the elaborate administrative machinery and division of Judea into toparchies that the Romans had set up. Judea was now his private property, and the tenant farmers paid their rent into his treasury. His tactics against the Romans were those of guerrilla warfare, launched from villages and outposts throughout the land (Herodium, Tekoa, En-gedi, Mĕṣad Ḥăsîdîn [= Khirbet Qumran]).

192   At the beginning of the revolt the Roman governor, Tineius Rufus, was helpless, even though he had Roman troops in the land. The legate of Syria, Publicius Marcellus, came to his aid; but eventually Hadrian had to send his best general, Sextus Julius Severus, recalling him from Britain. Severus put down the revolt, only after a long process of starving out Jews who had taken refuge in strongholds and desert caves. In the wadis of Murabbaʿat, Ḥever, and Ṣeʾelim caves were used by families who fled there with household belongings, biblical scrolls, and family archives. Officers from En-gedi fled to the Ḥever caves, taking with them letters of their commander Simon (→ Apocrypha, 67:119–22). When Jerusalem fell to the Romans, Simon made his last stand at Beth-ter (modern Bittir, 6 mi. WSW of Jerusalem). In Hadrian's 18th regnal year (134–135), after a siege, Beth-ter was finally taken. Then Hadrian razed Jerusalem to build Aelia Capitolina. He decreed "that the whole [Jewish] nation should be absolutely prohibited from that time on from entering even the district around Jerusalem, so that not even from a distance could it see its ancestral home" (Eusebius, *HE* 4.6.3).

(Fitzmyer, J. A., "The Bar Cochba Period," *ESBNT* 305–54. Fulco, W. J., "The Bar Kokhba Rebellion," *TBT* 64 [1973] 1041–45. Yadin, Y., *Bar-Kokhba* [London, 1971].)

193   Very little is known about Christianity in Judea in this period during which the break between the synagogue and church took place. When Christians returned to Jerusalem after 70, the church was presided over by Simeon, son of Clopas, who was bishop until his martyrdom in 107. (Some would identify him with Simon, the "brother" of Jesus [Mark 6:3], so that a succession of Jesus' relatives would have ruled the Jerusalem church, in the manner of a "caliphate." With less evidence [*Apost. Const.* 7.46], B. H. Streeter [*The Primitive Church* (NY, 1929)] identified Judas or Jude, the "brother" of Jesus, as the third bishop.) After Simeon, 13 other Jewish Christian bishops ruled the Jerusalem church until the time of Hadrian: Justus, Zacchaeus, Tobias, Benjamin, John, Matthias, Philip, Seneca, Justus, Levi, Ephres, Joseph, Judas (*HE* 4.5.3). Eusebius further records that by the martyrdom of Simeon, "many thousands of the circumcision had come to believe in Christ" (*HE* 3.35).

(Baus, K., *From the Apostolic Community to Constantine* [History of the Church 1; NY, 1980] 70–158. Bihlmeyer, K. and H. Tüchle, *Church History 1: Christian Antiquity* [Westminster, 1958] 33–102.)

76

RELIGIOUS INSTITUTIONS OF ISRAEL

John J. Castelot   Aelred Cody, O.S.B. *

BIBLIOGRAPHY

1   **General:** Albright, *ARI, FSAC.* De Vaux, *AI.* Haran, M., *Temples and Temple-Service in Ancient Israel* (Oxford, 1977; repr. Winona Lake, 1985). Kraus, H.-J., *Worship in Israel* (Richmond, 1966). Miller, P. D., *et al.* (eds.), *Ancient Israelite Religion* (Fest. F. M. Cross; Phl, 1987). Ringgren, H., *Israelite Religion* (Phl, 1966). Rowley, H. H., *Worship in Ancient Israel* (London, 1967).
2   **Priesthood:** Cody, A., *A History of Old Testament Priesthood* (AnBib 35; Rome, 1969). Gunneweg, A. H. J., *Leviten und Priester* (FRLANT 89; Göttingen, 1965). Haran, M., *et al., EncJud* 13. 1069–91. Levine, B. A., *IDBSup* 687–90.
3   **Places of Worship:** Biran, A. (ed.), *Temples and High Places in Biblical Times* (Jerusalem, 1981). Clements, R. E., *God and Temple* (Oxford, 1965). Fritz, V., *Tempel und Zelt* (WMANT 47; Neukirchen, 1977). Ottosson, M., *Temples and Cult Places in Palestine* (Uppsala, 1980). For the Near Eastern ideological and architectural context of the Temple: Nelson, H. H., *et al., BA* 7 (1944) 41–88 (= *BAR* 1, 145–200). Kuschke, A., "Tempel,"

Biblisches Reallexikon (HAT 1/1; 2d ed.; Tübingen, 1977) 333–42.
4   **Altars and Sacrifices:** De Vaux, R., *Studies in Old Testament Sacrifice* (Cardiff, 1964). Gray, G. B., *Sacrifice in the Old Testament* (Oxford, 1925; repr. NY, 1971, with a prolegomenon by B. A. Levine). Levine, B. A., *In the Presence of the Lord* (SJLA 5; Leiden, 1974). Milgrom, J., *Cult and Conscience* (SJLA 18; Leiden, 1976); *Studies in Cultic Theology and Terminology* (SJLA 36; Leiden, 1983). Rainey, A. F., "The Order of Sacrifice in Old Testament Ritual Texts," *Bib* 51 (1970) 485–98. Reichert, A., "Altar," *Biblisches Reallexikon* (HAT 1/1; 2d ed.; Tübingen, 1977) 5–10. Rendtorff, R., *Studien zur Geschichte des Opfers im Alten Israel* (WMANT 24; Neukirchen, 1967).
5   **Feasts and Special Days:** Andreasen, N. E., *The Old Testament Sabbath* (SBLDS 7; Cambridge MA, 1972). Gaster, T. H., *Purim and Hanukkah in Custom and Tradition* (NY, 1950). Goudoever, J. van, *Biblical Calendars* (2d ed.; Leiden, 1964). Milgrom, J., "Day of Atonement," *EncJud* 5. 1376–87.

6   OUTLINE

---

* Article 76 by J. J. Castelot in *JBC* has been revised and brought up to date by A. Cody, to whom all changes and additions are to be credited. Completely redone sections include 7–24, 58–64, 76–78, 139–46.

THE PRIESTHOOD

7 **(I) The Word "Priest."** An Israelite priest is called in Hebrew *kōhēn,* a sympathetic word also used of priests who were not Israelites. Cognates of *kōhēn* exist in Ugaritic, Phoenician, and some Aram languages; the Arabic cognate may be borrowed from one of those NW Semitic languages. The pejorative word *kĕmārîm,* found in the OT only in its pl. form, designates priests of Baalistic or idolatrous cults. Recourse to etymology in the hope of finding the original idea of what a *kōhēn* was obtains no certain results. Some proposed etymologies have had to be abandoned in the face of advances made in comparative Semitic philology. The Syr vb. *kahhen* in its sense of "to make prosperous" presents no such difficulties, but has the Syriac retained a meaning integral to the original NW Semitic concept of a *kōhēn?* The Arabic cognate, *kāhin,* which in ancient Arabia meant "soothsayer," evokes the oracular function of an Israelite priest, but the distribution of cultic functions in Arabia was different from that in Israel. In order to see what an Israelite priest was, we have to see what his functions were and how their combination changed in the course of priesthood's evolution in Israel.

8 **(II) Priestly Functions.** A synchronic view of priestly responsibilities and functions was not available until the pentateuchal P's provisions had been put into effect after the exile, with a clear division of work between priests and levites (→ 19-24 below). In the following paragraphs the major responsibilities and activities of priests will be taken separately, and the historical evolution of each will be traced.

(A) Care of the Sanctuary. Throughout the biblical period an Israelite priest was fundamentally a man attached to a sanctuary or temple, the house of God, where he took care of the direct service of the deity and provided certain services for society which only a person enabled to approach God more closely might provide. In the ancient Near Eastern religious view, priests waited upon a god resident in his temple, with his presence focused in a mysterious, quasi-sacramental manner in his image or on a sacred object, even as earthly courtiers and retainers waited upon a king resident in his palace. This idea lies behind some of the cultic practices still evident in the OT. The priestly groups at Shiloh (1 Sam 1-3) and at Nob (1 Sam 21-22) existed because of the sanctuaries in those places; the bread that the priests set before Yahweh in the sanctuary of Nob, like sacrificial victims offered to God, had its historical roots in the ancient idea of offering food to a god in the sanctuary that was his house. In the relatively primitive narrative of Judg 17-18, Micah needed a man fit to be a priest for his household sanctuary with its images, and so did the Danites, who took away both the sacred images and the priest for the temple they were going to build in the north. Images of Yahweh were forbidden in orthodox Israelite religion, but Yahweh's presence was focused on the Ark. The Ark was attended by priests in the sanctuaries of Shiloh (1 Sam 1:3) and Jerusalem (1 Kgs 6:9; 8:1-9) or by a man set apart for that purpose at Kiriath-jearim (1 Sam 7:1). When the Ark was moved, it had to be carried by priests (1 Sam 4:4,11; 2 Sam 6:6-7; 15:24-29) or, according to P and Chr and deuteronomistic editors, by levites.

Until the use of priestly ritual was limited to Jerusalem (→ 54-55 below) priests served God in sanctuaries throughout the land. In Jerusalem, their administrative functions came to the fore in their management of the complex operations of the Temple. It is significant in this respect that the priests (*khnm*) mentioned in Ugaritic texts and Phoenician inscriptions were clearly responsible for the administration and upkeep of temples and for the supervision of their temple staffs, although in the published Ugaritic texts no direct involvement in cultic acts happens to be attested for them (see J.-M. de Tarragon, *Le culte à Ugarit* [CahRB 19; Paris, 1980] 113, 134-35). When the Israelite temple personnel became structurally diversified, the hierarchically supreme administrative class was that of the priests.

9   (B) Manifestation of the Divine Mind.
(a) ORACULAR CONSULTATION. In earlier OT times, the activity primarily associated with priests was oracular consultation, an activity which, through a somewhat complex process, evolved into responsibility for the law. Early Israelite priests consulted God (in Hebrew "asked" God) by using objects called Urim and Thummim inside an ephod. The literary evidence for the appearance of the ephod is ambiguous: on the one hand, it was an article of clothing, perhaps a sort of apron, worn when one was in a sanctuary or near the Ark (1 Sam 2:18; 2 Sam 6:14), retained later in ornate form as a symbolic rather than functional hieratic vestment (Exod 29:5; Lev 8:7); on the other hand, it was a cultic object of some sort (Judg 8:27; 17:5; 18:14,17,20; 1 Sam 2:28; 14:3; 23:6,9; 30:7) which was kept in a sanctuary (1 Sam 21:20). Words cognate to ephod in Ugaritic and in Old Akkadian designate some kind of garment; an Israelite ephod too was probably something which could be worn strapped to the body but which had metallic components (see Judg 8:26-27) making it stiff enough to conceal an object placed behind it (see 1 Sam 21:20). There is no way of knowing precisely what the Urim and Thummim looked like. Like the stylized ephod, some form of Urim and Thummim were part of the postexilic high priest's vesture, worn in connection not with his ephod, however, but with his breastplate (Exod 28:30).

Those who wished to ask God what course of action to take went to a priest, who used the Urim and Thummim to manifest the divine mind in the form of a Yes or a No; a "this one" rather than any alternative. In a given case, an answer could be withheld; and, if the case required, written lots making possible more than a binary answer may have been used (H. B. Huffmon, "Priestly Divination in Israel," in *WLSGF* 355-59). This could be done at the sanctuary to which the priest was attached (Judg 18:5-7; 1 Sam 22:10,13,15) or at a distance from the sanctuary, as it was when the priest accompanied a military expedition (1 Sam 14:18-19, 36-42 [best preserved in the LXX]; 23:9-12; 30:7-8). In this early period a priest was characterized as one who carried the ephod (1 Sam 14:3; 22:18); and to carry the ephod was still a characteristic of a priest somewhat later, when the altar and sacrificial work had already been introduced into the idea of a priest's typical functions (1 Sam 2:28). The Urim and Thummim are still mentioned as hallmarks of a priest in Ezra 2:63/Neh 7:65, but by then their actual use was surely a thing of the past.

10   (b) TÔRÂ. In the Blessing of Moses for Levi (Deut 33:8-11), the Urim and Thummim are still characteristic of a priest in an earlier part (vv 8-9a,11); but in a later part (vv 9b-10, perhaps of the early 8th cent. BC) God's ordinances or decisions and God's *tôrâ* are mentioned, along with sacrifice. *Tôrâ* probably should not yet be understood as "law" (a meaning that later evolved). The result of an early priest's consultation of God through the Urim and Thummim may itself have been called *tôrâ*, since the result of certain acts of divination in Mesopotamia were called *têrtu*, an Akkadian word etymologically akin to the Hebr *tôrâ*. In the Israelite royal

period, the divine answers produced by priestly lot-casting developed into priestly pronouncements on questions of the separation of the holy from the profane (J. Begrich, *Werden und Wesen des Alten Testaments* [BZAW 66; Berlin, 1936] 63-88). A clear example of this is still found in the early postexilic Hag 2:11-13.

Meanwhile, already in the royal period, the Israelite sense of holiness itself had been refined in such a way that it encompassed not only matters of the spatial and material separation of the holy from the profane but also ethical, moral questions affecting the propriety of approach to God in his holy place (Pss 15:2-5; 24:4; Isa 33:14-17). By the mid-8th cent., priestly *tôrâ* was also linked to priestly knowledge (Hos 4:6), and some priestly *tôrâ* had been committed to writing (Hos 8:12). Accordingly, we suspect that the evolution of *tôrâ* toward its later sense of "law" began with the gathering of written priestly decisions (*tôrôt*) on sacral issues, both ritual and ethical, into collections or quasi codes like the Law of Holiness (Lev 17-26), and that the word *tôrâ* was subsequently extended to collections of divinely sanctioned law more generally (→ OT Thought, 77:86-87), whether the objects of its provisions were in themselves religious or secular. With *tôrâ* in Deut 31:9, the Deuteronomic Code is surely in mind, as divinely entrusted to the care of the priests and the elders—representing both the religious and the secular sides of society. No distinction of sacral and civil competences seems to be implied in Deut 17:8-13, although both levitical priests and a lay judge are mentioned. In Deut 21:5 and Ezek 44:24 priests alone have competence in handling all disputes, both religious and secular (see R. R. Wilson, *JQR* 74 [1983-84] 242). In Lev 10:10-11 they are "to distinguish between the sacred and the profane and between the impure and the pure [which is *tôrâ* in the older and narrower sense], and hand down . . . all the statutes which Yahweh, God, spoke through Moses [which is *tôrâ* in the newer and broader sense]." *Tôrâ* had by then begun to designate the Mosaic law but had not ceased to imply the expression of God's mind—the Mosaic law, whether dealing with secular or religious concerns, was the expression of the will of God, and new jurisprudence based on it was entrusted to priests.

11   (c) TEACHING AND PREACHING? It has been said that *tôrâ* was instruction and that priests, because they gave it, were teachers. Evidence has been cited from the very end of the royal period, in Jer 18:18: "*Tôrâ* shall not depart from the priest, nor counsel from the wise man, nor the word from the prophet." Yet above we saw that *tôrâ* in various periods never meant what we might properly call instruction, and that a priest dealing with it could not properly be said to be teaching. It has also been suggested that in the postexilic period levites were preachers (G. von Rad, in *Fest. Otto Procksch* [ed. A. Alt, et al.; Leipzig, 1934] 113-24; repr. in G. von Rad, *Gesammelte Studien* [TBü; Munich, 1961] 248-61). Yet the passages in Chr that can be called sermons are never said to have been given by levites. The texts taken as signs that levites gave sermons seem rather to be evidence that Temple singers absorbed into the levitical ranks sang sacred texts in the Temple and perhaps provided the kind of interpretation that eventually received literary form as targum (→ Texts, 68:103). In the Hellenistic period, the scribes (who could be priests, although few of them were) became the learned persons in Jewish Palestine, studying the Law and the Prophets and the Writings with erudition and wisdom (Sir 39:1-11; → History, 75:146). They were the jurists and theologians who interpreted the law, while the priests remained responsible for making statutes and legal judgments (the components of living *tôrâ*) known to the people (Sir 45:14–17).

12   (C) Sacrifice. In earlier times, individual sacrifices and family sacrifices did not need to be made at a sanctuary, and as long as they were not made at a sanctuary there was nothing priestly about them. The patriarchs (Gen 4:3–5; 8:20; 22:12; 31:34; 46:1), Gideon (Judg 6:25–26) and Manoah (Judg 13:16–23), who were not priests, sacrificed, as did the men of Beth-shemesh (1 Sam 6:14–15) and David's ambitious son Adonijah (1 Kgs 1:9); but all of them did so on natural altars unrelated to any sanctuary (→ 58–59 below). If a sacrifice was made at a sanctuary, however, some involvement of the priest of that sanctuary could be expected (1 Sam 2:12–17). The sacrificial role of priests increased during the royal period, as the sense of the holiness of God's house was extended to the altar of holocausts in the courtyard outside the house. Contact with the altar came to be reserved to priests, by their office endowed with a degree of ritual holiness greater than that of the rest of the people (→ 22 below). King Ahaz's sacrifice on an altar, already viewed negatively in 2 Kgs 16:22–23, is later represented as idolatrous in 2 Chr 28:23.

As a consequence of this development, the sacrificial prescriptions in P still allow a nonpriestly Israelite to slaughter his victim (Lev 1:5; 3:2,8,13; 4:24,29,33); but the blood rites (Exod 33:10; Lev 17:11,14) and all the other sacrificial actions have to be performed by a priest, because they entail contact with the altar or close approach to it. Already in Deut 33:10 (a relatively late addition to the Blessing of Moses, with mention of the altar) sacrifice is claimed as a priestly prerogative, and in Jer 33:18 priests are characterized as persons who make the holocaust rise and the vegetable offering smoke and who offer the daily sacrifice. By the end of the royal period, and throughout the time of the Second Temple, sacrifice was considered something it had not always been: an activity characteristic of priests.

13   (III) The Making of a Priest. We do not find in Israel the idea that a person was divinely called to be a priest. If a family had rights to priesthood at a sanctuary, a son might become a priest there because he was of that family. A priest in earlier times could be engaged by a person or by a group of persons, thus becoming a priest "to" him or them: to Micah (Judg 17:5,10,12), to the tribe of Dan (Judg 18:4,19,30), to the king (2 Sam 20:26). David had sons who were priests in his service (2 Sam 8:18), as Ahijah had been a priest in Saul's service (1 Sam 14:3,18).

We know almost nothing about any ritual acts used in inaugurating a priest in the earlier periods of Israelite history. The idiomatic expression "to fill the hand" often denotes entrance into priestly office (Exod 28:41; 29:9, 33,35; Lev 8:3; 16:32; 21:10; Num 3:3; Judg 17:5,12; 1 Kgs 13:33), but it is also used of acquiring gain (Ps 26:10) or of having one's just vengeance (Ps 48:11). It does not appear to represent a ritual gesture actually used in making someone a priest. In 2d-millennium texts from Mari in upper Mesopotamia the expression is used of taking, and even killing, captives. This connotation, combined with that of priestly inauguration, is evident in the use of the expression in the account of a violent intervention undertaken by the levites out of zeal for Yahweh in Exod 32:29, which is meant to show how the levites acquired their priestly rights. In Exod 29, closely paralleled by Lev 8, we see the postexilic (and most probably late preexilic) ritual for inaugurating new priests and high priests. The ceremonies, distributed over a week's period during which the new priests were not to leave the sacred space of the Temple precincts, consisted of a clothing with the priestly vestments,

followed by a complex series of sacrificial actions. At least some of the components of this ritual are late. The inaugural anointing of a high priest (Exod 29:7; Lev 8:12) was not a custom until after the exile, when the former royal anointing was transferred to the high priest. The anointing of ordinary priests (Exod 28:41; 30:30; 40:12–15; Lev 7:35–36; 10:7; Num 3:3) was a custom introduced still later.

14   When the men of Kiriath-jearim installed Eleazar, whom they had chosen as the person to tend the Ark, they are said simply to have "hallowed him" or "made him holy" (1 Sam 7:1). This vb., *qiddēš*, was used of making a priest in later texts also (Exod 29:1; Lev 8:12): to make someone a priest was to make him holy. Holiness was not in itself a moral quality. It was primarily an attribute of God, marking his transcendent separation from all creatures. It was secondarily an attribute of those persons and things set apart from the ordinary affairs of the created world in order that they might be more intensely in touch with God—thus they participated in God's holiness (Lev 21:6–8). To make someone a priest was to set him apart from profane activity so that he might be God's personal servant, properly in a sanctuary, God's house, but elsewhere too where God's presence was focused in the created world, as it was on the Ark. A priest was made holy so that he could with propriety draw near to God and handle communication between God and the people, as courtiers handle communication between an earthly lord and his people. A priest's holiness was thus the basis of his role as mediator between God and the people at large.

15   (IV) The Priests of Jerusalem. We have been examining the activities of priests in narratives of the judges, of Samuel and David. Information on priests outside Jerusalem is scarce during the royal period because of the limited interests of our extant sources. When they are mentioned after David's time, they tend to be mentioned negatively, because of the deuteronomistic editorial idea that priests should not function outside Jerusalem or because they fall within the view of prophets who are denouncing abuses in society. We are best informed about the priests of Israelite Jerusalem in the royal period and afterward.

16   (A) Zadok and His "Sons." Before David became king in Jerusalem, his oracle priest was Abiathar, a descendant of Eli the priest of Shiloh and thus of levitical origin (→ 18 below). After David's accession to kingship in the new capital, Abiathar is always mentioned together with another priest, Zadok, whose name is consistently put before Abiathar's (2 Sam 8:17; 15:24–29; 17:15; 19:12). In the contest for the succession to David's throne, Abiathar supported Adonijah (1 Kgs 1:5–48), whereas Zadok supported Solomon (1:7,19,25; 2:22). When Solomon had won the throne, he banished Abiathar from Jerusalem (2:26–27), leaving Zadok in sole possession of the royal priesthood (4:2). Whether the priests of Jerusalem in the centuries following were all descendants of Zadok or not, they claimed him as the founder of their priestly lineage, and so any question of the origins of that lineage necessarily involves the obscure origins of Zadok.

According to one hypothesis, Zadok was the chief priest of Jebusite Jerusalem before the city was taken by David (H. H. Rowley, *JBL* 58 [1939] 113–41; also A. Bentzen, *ZAW* 51 [1933] 173–76; C. E. Hauer, *JBL* 82 [1963] 89–94). This would explain why Israelite sources give no genealogical information on Zadok, not even where such information is provided for others (2 Sam 8:16–18; 20:23–26). It would also explain why Abiathar, the descendant of Eli who had been David's priest in earlier years, supported Adonijah, a full-blooded

Israelite born in Hebron (2 Sam 3:4), whereas Zadok, if he was a Jebusite, supported Solomon, born in Jerusalem of Bathsheba, whose first husband, Uriah, was a Hittite (2 Sam 12:24; 1 Kgs 1:11). If Zadok remained a faithful Jebusite until the Israelite capture of Jerusalem had been completed, David's appointing him to serve as priest together with the Israelite Abiathar could be seen as a political move made in the hope of gaining the favor of the new capital's Jebusite inhabitants. To this hypothesis it can be objected that for David to take such a step to conciliate the Jebusite population would be for him to risk the alienation of his own Israelites. When the Ark had been brought to Jerusalem, the altar for Israelite worship was erected not at one of the existing Jebusite sanctuaries but in the space of Arauna's threshing floor (2 Sam 24:18-25); this suggests that in David's reign Jebusite religious institutions, including Jebusite priesthood, were not readily assimilated by the Israelites and indeed were avoided.

According to another hypothesis Zadok was not a Jebusite but an Israelite, and indeed a member of a particular group of levites known as Aaronides, who claimed the right to function at certain sanctuaries in southern and central Palestine, while his associate and rival, Abiathar, was of a different group of levites known as Mushites, who vindicated priestly claims in N and far S Palestine (F. M. Cross, *CMHE* 195-215). "Mushite" would indicate relation to Moses, and the rivalry between Zadok and Abiathar would thus be one important element in a pattern of conflict between Aaron and Moses visible in pentateuchal narratives (Exod 32; Num 12; 25:6-15). In 1 Chr 12:27-29, Zadok is mentioned as an aide to a commander of Aaronide troups who rallied around David in Hebron in his struggle against Saul. Now Hebron in the list of levitical cities is attributed to the Aaronide subgroup of Kohathites (Judg 21:9-12; 1 Chr 6:39-41 [54-56]). Zadok, then, would have been a levitical priest of the Aaronide group in Hebron, until he went to Jerusalem to be one of David's priests there. This hypothesis sets the tension between Zadok and Abiathar into a broader issue of priestly group rivalry. One can pose objections: that Aaron's priestly traits developed in tradition much later than Zadok's day, that the priests of Jerusalem were advancing their claims as sons of Zadok without any mention of Aaron at all as late as Ezekiel's day, that the division of the levitical cities into an Aaronide subgroup is perhaps much later than the list of cities itself, that in the old list of levitical clans (one of them Mushite) in Num 26:58 none is called Aaronide although one is called Hebronite, that the information on Zadok in Hebron (1 Chr 12) is historically suspect unless the Chronicler can be verified from another source. Yet the hypothesis of Zadok as a levite from Hebron could be held independently, apart from the question whether a group of levites claiming Aaron as their eponymous ancestor existed so early. In any case, the complete lack of early reliable information on Zadok's origins means that the question may never be solved.

17   (B) Organization; Relation to the King. The four occurrences of the title high priest in preexilic contexts are probably anachronisms due to a late editor, for the title did not become current until after the exile. In the royal period, the head of the priests in Jerusalem was called simply "the priest" (1 Kgs 4:2; 2 Kgs 11:9-11; 12:8; 16:10-12; 22:12,14; Isa 8:2) or "the chief priest" (2 Kgs 25:18). Next in the hierarchy was a "second priest" (2 Kgs 23:4; 25:18; Jer 52:24), who was probably responsible for the maintenance of order in the Temple precincts. Mentioned after him in the same texts are the "keepers of the threshold," whose duties were certainly

greater than their title would indicate (cf. 2 Kgs 12:10; 22:4). These priests of the royal establishment were naturally likely to be somewhat subservient to the king. So were those of the royal sanctuary of Bethel in the northern kingdom, to judge from Amos 7:10-15. We are not told what the priests of the establishment did when Manasseh built altars for Baal in Jerusalem (2 Kgs 21:3); but we do know from 2 Kgs 11 that, while Queen Athalia had her priest of Baal (11:11), it was the priest Jehoiada, zealous for Yahweh, who led the way in overthrowing her. On the other hand, a king might intervene when the priests of the establishment were shirking their administrative responsibilities for the Temple (2 Kgs 12).

18   (V) Priests and Levites. The levites in early tradition were members of the tribe of Levi, which had no territory of its own but claimed the cities, with their pasturelands, listed in Josh 21:9-42; 1 Chr 6:39-66 (54-81). Scholars differ in dating the lists and in deciding whether the claim itself is based on some historical situation or not (see Soggin, *HAI* 151-53). Evaluation of the levites' tribal status depends partly on the position one takes on the history and sociology of the Israelite tribes generally. Levites were particularly desirable as priests (Judg 17-18); but a nonlevite might be made priest, in the period of the judges (Judg 17:5; 1 Sam 7:1), and in the early royal period, when Ira (2 Sam 20:26) and sons of David (2 Sam 8:18) were priests. When the late genealogical constructions in Chr are left aside, the members of the priestly family of Eli at the sanctuary of Shiloh are, not unambiguously, said to have been levites. (Even if the unnamed ancestor mentioned in 1 Sam 2:27 were Moses rather than Levi, Moses figured in tradition as a member of the tribe of Levi.) The old genealogical data in 1 Sam 4:19-22; 14:3; 22:9; 22:20, when taken together, show Ahimelech, priest at Nob, and Abiathar, one of David's priests, to have been descendants of Eli, and thus, implicitly, levites. Whether David's other priest in Jerusalem, Zadok, was a levite or not is disputed (→ 16 above). Of the two royal sanctuaries of the northern kingdom, Dan at least had a levitical priesthood according to Judg 18:30, but it is not clear from 1 Kgs 12:31 whether the priests of Bethel were among those nonlevitical priests whom Jeroboam I appointed to sanctuaries in the northern kingdom or not. By the middle of the royal period levites were basing their tribal identity on a claim that they exercised priestly functions by divine right (Deut 33:8-11; see Exod 32:25-29). We are justified in presuming that there were persons rejecting that claim. By the end of the exile, the claim was both accepted and rejected in the shaping of the reconstituted Temple personnel: from that time on, all priests were reckoned as levitical, but there were new Temple clergy called as a class "levites," who had no hope of advancement to priesthood.

19   This dichotomy of priestly class and nonpriestly levitical class was the result of a contest for the right to function at a sanctuary, a contest which became acute when the principle that there should be a single sanctuary for all Israel was put into effect to the advantage of the priesthood in Jerusalem. No one could function as a priest except in Jerusalem, once all the other sanctuaries of Yahweh had been abolished, as they were definitively at the end of the royal period, in Josiah's reign (2 Kgs 23:5,8-9,15-20). In the Deuteronomic Code the principle of a single sanctuary is promoted. Promoted too in the final form of the Code are the principles that legitimately functioning priests should be levites and that levites from outside Jerusalem could be admitted to function as priests in the city, with those not succeeding in gaining admission commended to the charitable attention of the people (Deut 12:12,18–19; 14:27,29; 16:11,14; 26:11–13). In more recent parts of the Code there is a tendency to write "levitical priest" instead of "priest." In 18:1–8, we find the simple "priest" in a list of rights that is probably old (vv 3–4), "levite" in a provision for those not actually functioning as priests (v 6), and "levitical priest" heading the section (v 1), which is primarily meant for those actually functioning as priests.

In Ezek's exilic program for the future restoration of worship in Jerusalem, the priests of the Temple, the "sons of Zadok," are said to be levitical (Ezek 40:46; 43:19; 44:15). They alone have the right to officiate at the altar and to receive those offerings which are the priest's (40:46; 43:19; 44:15–17,29–30). All other members of the Temple staff are put in a subordinate position; once, in 40:45 (probably one of the earlier texts in Ezek's program), they are called "priests," but elsewhere in 40–48 they are called "levites." For the exilic situation, see N. Allan, *HeyJ* 23 (1982) 259–69.

20   In P and Chr this class distinction receives genealogical justification (and divine sanction) through the principle that the necessary ancestor of all legitimate priests is Moses' brother Aaron. Within the family of Levi in P's genealogies, priesthood is limited to descendants of Aaron through the two lines of Eleazar and Ithamar, and to them the other levites, denied Aaronide ancestry, are made subordinate (e.g., Num 3:1–10). In 1 Chr 24:1–6 the Zadokites of Jerusalem are made descendants of Eleazar, through his son Phinehas according to 5:27–41(6:1–14), while other priests are made descendants of Ithamar. The Zadokites are given numerical preponderance. The proposal has been made that the dichotomy between priests claiming Aaron as their ancestor and non-Aaronide levites excluded from priesthood was made in a P existing already by the late 8th cent. in the priestly circle of Jerusalem, that it was originally aimed at levitical priests of the recently fallen northern kingdom (since all the levitical cities attributed to Aaron in Josh 21:9–40 are in the south), and that it was put into effect briefly in the short-lived centralization of worship accomplished by Hezekiah (2 Kgs 18:4, 22; see M. Haran, *JBL* 100 [1981] 321–33, and his *Temples, passim*). In that case, Deut, with its particular attitudes toward levites and priesthood, would have been independent of such an early P, whereas Ezek would reflect it, and it would have become normative when Ezra promulgated P to the postexilic community at large. In any case, certainly from Ezra's time on the dichotomy was completely effective, with simple levites a class subordinated to the priestly class, but with all priests reckoned as descendants of Aaron the levite.

21   (VI) Duties of Postexilic Priests and Levites.   In the postexilic period we find, at last, enough material to assemble a fairly complete list of the duties of priests and of the levites distinct from priests. The material is furnished by the pentateuchal P, and somewhat later by Chr, Ezra, and Neh, which allow us to see that the provisions of P had actually been put into effect, with some minor alterations. In P, the prescriptions for "the sons of Aaron" are those intended for the priests generally, whereas the prescriptions for Aaron alone are those intended for the high priest.

22   (A) Grades of Holiness.   An Israelite priest had always been a holy person apt for dealing with holy spaces and objects (→ 14 above). In the postexilic period, the distinctions of hierarchical rights and duties correspond to degrees in the holiness of different sacred spaces and objects (see K. Koch, *Die Priesterschrift von Exodus 25 bis Leviticus 16* [FRLANT 71; Göttingen, 1959] 101–2). In consonance with this coordinated

system, the Israelite laity, a holy people (Deut 7:6; 14:2, 21; 26:19; 28:9) because Yahweh's people, might enter the Temple courtyard, from which pagans were excluded (Num 1:51,53; 3:10,38). Because priests and levites were endowed with holiness greater than that of the people as a whole (cf. Lev 21:1–22:9 with Lev 22:10–46), only they could enter the Temple building, from which the laity were excluded (2 Chr 23:6; 35:5). The holiness of priests was higher than that of levites (Num 4:4–15; 18:3), and so the priests, but not the levites, might come in contact with the objects that were "most holy": the altars of holocaust (Exod 29:37; 40:10) and of incense (Exod 30:10). The holiest space of all was the Debir of the Temple building, where God's presence on earth was most intensely concentrated on the *kappōret:* into this space the high priest alone might enter, for the annual expiatory rites of the Day of Atonement (Lev 16:2–3, 15,32–34).

23   (B) Priestly Duties.   In the actual division between priests and levites, the priests did all that required contact with the altars and with the offerings after they had passed from the common, secular sphere to that of the holy: the burning of offerings on the altars, the slaughter of birds on the altar of holocaust, the libations, and the sacrificial blood rites (Lev 1–7; 10:16–20; 16; 17). In rites of purification or expiation priests were involved because the sacrifices and sacrificial blood were integral parts of such rituals. As the experts on all questions of distinction or separation between the holy and the profane, the pure and the impure, they were also asked for pronouncements (*tôrōt:* → 10 above) deciding such questions, which determined whether a purification rite was needed or not (Lev 11–16; 17–26). In the archaic rite of purification with the lustral waters prepared with the ashes of a red heifer (Num 19), the priest's role was retained, justified by superficial assimilation of some aspects of the ritual to those of a sacrificial sin offering (vv 4,9,17; see J. Milgrom, *VT* 31 [1981] 62–72). Priests had to mix the ritual spices (1 Chr 9:30), presumably for the incense and the holy oil (Exod 30:22–38), although only the incense actually burned on the altar of incense was "most holy" (30:36), and hence to be handled only by priests, in P's view. As particularly qualified mediators between God and the people, the priests blessed the people (Num 6:22–27; so already Deut 10:8; 21:5). In the 2d cent. BC priests were still characterized as men who offered sacrifice and incense, who performed rites of expiation, who blessed the people and made known to them *tôrâ* in the form of statutes and legal pronouncements (Sir 45:6–26).

24   (C) Levitical Duties.   The postexilic levites were responsible for the liturgies of praise and thanksgiving twice daily and on special days; the ritual purifications of objects with a minor degree of holiness; the making of the ritual bread; and the care of the Temple's courtyards and supply rooms (1 Chr 9:26–32; 23:25–32). In sacrificial rites, they proffered to the priests the blood which was to be sprinkled (2 Chr 30:16), and they could help priests prepare a holocaust by flaying the victim (2 Chr 29:34; 35:11)—something that according to P the lay offerer himself was to do (Lev 1:6). The levites also worked, under the priests, in the administration of the Temple and its finances and in overseeing construction work in the Temple precincts (2 Chr 24:5–6; 34:9,12–13). Although in documents retained in Ezra and Neh the Temple gatekeepers (Ezra 2:42,70; 7:24; 10:24; Neh 7:45; 10:29; 11:19) and the Temple singers (Ezra 2:41; Neh 7:44) are distinct from the category of levites (and seem still to be so in 2 Chr 35), they were being assimilated into the levitical category or class (1 Chr 15:16–23; 25:1–31; 26:1–9; 2 Chr 5:12;

29:25-26,30). In addition, the postexilic levites may have engaged in considerable scribal activity and functioned as interpreters of the Scriptures (→ 11 above; see A. Jepsen, *VT* 31 [1981] 318-23). For the question whether some of the leviticized cultic singers might have been "cultic prophets," see A. R. Johnson, *The Cultic Prophet in Ancient Israel* (2d ed.; Cardiff, 1962) 69-75.

On the political role of the high priest in the Persian and Hellenistic periods, → History, 75:124, 139, 149-50.

PLACES OF WORSHIP

25   (I) The Patriarchal and Mosaic Period. The patriarchs, Abraham, Isaac, and Jacob, are said to have founded several sanctuaries throughout Canaan. These sanctuaries usually marked places where God had manifested himself to the patriarchs. In many instances it was a case of taking over already established Canaanite shrines and dedicating them to the one true God.
26   (A) Shechem. A case in point is Shechem, Abraham's first stop in Canaan (Gen 12:6-7). It is called a *māqôm*, which in this context is virtually a technical term for a sanctuary, although the basic meaning of the word is simply "place." Here stood the terebinth (oak?) of Moreh, apparently where pagan oracles were delivered, for it was called the "Terebinth of the Teacher or Soothsayer." Here God manifested himself to Abraham, and the patriarch built an altar to commemorate the event. And this seems to have been the normal pattern in the establishment of a sanctuary: divine manifestation, divine communication, setting up of an altar.

Shechem also figures prominently in the story of Jacob. Returning from a long sojourn with his uncle Laban, Jacob set up camp on the outskirts of Shechem, bought camping ground, and erected an altar (Gen 33:18-20). The idolatrous images that his wives had smuggled out of their homeland he ceremoniously buried beneath the terebinth as a sign of definitive rejection of heathen cult and of wholehearted dedication to the one true God. At the end of the patriarchal age, Joseph's remains were brought to Shechem from Egypt for burial (Josh 24:32).

In the period of the judges, the people solemnly renewed the Sinaitic covenant at Shechem and set up a stele in memory of the event "under the oak that was in the sanctuary of the Lord" (Josh 24:25-28). Other events associated with this shrine were the proclamation of Abimelech as king (Judg 9:6) and the meeting of Solomon's son Rehoboam with delegates of the northern tribes (1 Kgs 12:1-19). Some scholars think that, during the period of Israel's monarchy, Shechem was the site of yearly covenant ceremonies that were the source of the legal tradition preserved in Deut (→ OT Thought, 77:77ff.). Excavation has revealed within the city an area occupied *ca.* 1650-1100 (with perhaps a break *ca.* 1550-1450) by a temple, remodeled or replaced at various times (J. Toombs and G. E. Wright, *BASOR* 169 [Feb. 1963] 25-32). This temple in its last phase may have been the house of Baal-berith (Judg 9:4) or of El-berith (Judg 9:46), a deity explicitly related to covenant (*běrît*).
27   (B) Bethel. As for the patriarchal connection with Bethel, the data of the various traditions are confusing. The J tradition of Gen attributes the establishment of this sanctuary to Abraham (12:8), but the (J-)E tradition would indicate that Jacob founded it (28:10-22). In the E account, Jacob stopped at the sanctuary en route to Mesopotamia and during the night had his well-known vision of the ladder or stairway connecting heaven and earth. When he awoke, he realized that he was in a truly sacred place, a *bêt 'El* (house of God).

He took the stone that he had used as a pillow, set it upright, and poured oil over it as a sign of consecration. He promised God that if his venture in Haran prospered, he would build a shrine at Bethel and support it out of his possessions. (This picture from the E tradition of Gen is complicated somewhat by being intermingled with J's narrative of an appearance of Yahweh in which he reconfirmed the promises he had made to Abraham [28:13-15].) Then E completes the story by telling how Jacob, after his return from Haran, went from Shechem to Bethel, where he built an altar and set up a sacred stone (35:1-9,14-15 – repeating 28:18-19). Apparently Jacob did at Bethel what Abraham had done at Shechem; he took over an already existing Canaanite shrine and dedicated it to the one true God. Just as in the description of Shechem in Gen 12:6, the word *māqôm*, "place," seems to be applied to Bethel in the sense of "sacred place," "sanctuary."
28   (C) Mamre. We are told: "Abram moved his tent and came to dwell by the terebinth of Mamre which was at Hebron; and he built an altar there to the Lord" (Gen 13:18). Although Mamre is frequently mentioned in Gen as the dwelling place of Abraham, Isaac, and Jacob, or as a point of reference for locating the burial cave in which their bodies and those of their wives were laid to rest, there is only this one reference to its being a place of worship. In fact, no biblical book apart from Gen mentions Mamre at all. This is strange considering that it had figured so prominently in the patriarchal stories and that in later centuries it became a popular place of pilgrimage. The explanation may lie in the fact that the cult carried out there subsequently became tainted by the infiltration of pagan practices. For this reason, the later editors of the sacred books may have refused to mention it and may have altered any traditional references so as to make its localization uncertain. See Gen 13:18; 23:19; 35:27, where it is identified with Hebron.
29   (D) Beer-sheba. This sanctuary is associated in a special way with the name of Isaac. God appeared to him here and repeated the promises previously made to Abraham. As a memorial of the theophany, Isaac built an altar (Gen 26:23-25 – again the constants in the establishment of a sanctuary: divine appearance, divine message, construction of an altar). Subsequently Jacob offered a sacrifice here and God appeared to him (46:1-4). A later addition to the text (21:33) traces the establishment of this shrine all the way back to Abraham, who is said to have planted a tamarisk tree there and "called on the name of the Lord, the everlasting God." The phrase here translated "everlasting God" is in all likelihood the proper name of the Canaanite divinity formerly worshiped at this spot: El Olam (→ OT Thought, 77:16). The patriarchs would have appropriated his title, quite fittingly, to their God. Beer-sheba continued to be a popular Israelite shrine for centuries. Yet the worship there became tainted with idolatry, and in the 8th cent. we find Amos proscribing it along with other sanctuaries of the same type (Amos 5:5; 8:14).

30   (E) The Tent or Tabernacle. After the descendants of Jacob escaped from Egypt and made their way back to the land of the patriarchs, other shrines came into prominence. During the exodus, however, the Israelites had a portable sanctuary: the Tabernacle or Tent. In the earliest traditions, it was a place where Moses consulted Yahweh to learn his will (Exod 33:7, 11; Num 12:8). This role appears in the later tradition as well, but there a new word, *miškān,* is preferred to the ordinary word for tent, *'ōhel.* This new term emphasizes the abiding presence of Yahweh among his people. The older tradition (E) represents God's arrival and departure under the figure of a descending and lifting cloud (Exod 33:9; Num 12:4-10). But the P tradition has the cloud settling over the Abode at the moment it was fully constructed and remaining there, even when the Tent was in transit (Exod 40:34-35,36-38; Num 9:15-23). The two traditions vary also on the matter of the location of the Tent. In the earlier texts (E) it was outside the camp; in the later (P) it was in the center of the encampment.

**31   ** It is very difficult to say with assurance just what the desert Tent looked like, for the oldest traditions offer no information. The P tradition seems to give an idealized reconstruction, making the Tent a sort of portable scale model of the Temple of Solomon, which was the center of worship when this tradition was on its way to definitive formulation. Twice the P editors describe the Tent in detail: first, when Yahweh gives the specifications for its construction (Exod 26), and again when Moses has it built (36:8-38). According to this description, the Tent itself consisted of a rectangular wooden framework, 45 ft. x 15 ft. x 15 ft., which was covered over, except for the eastern entrance, with two long strips of a delicate fabric joined together with an intricate system of hooks and eyes. This fabric was adorned with embroidered cherubim. Then came another covering of more durable goatskin and finally a red covering of dyed ram skins and other light leathers. A curtain closed off the eastern entry, and another curtain of more precious material was placed 15 ft. from the western end. This separated the Holy Place from the Holy of Holies, thus making the Holy of Holies a perfect 15-ft. cube. Here was kept the Ark of the Covenant. In the Holy Place were the seven-branched candlestick and the table for the loaves of proposition. Outside the entrance were the altar and the laver used for ritual purification. The Tent was surrounded by a large courtyard, 150 ft. x 75 ft., marked off by a system of bronze posts to which were affixed silver rods, and from these hung linen drapes. (For a description of the Tent, see F. M. Cross, *BA* 10 [1947] 45-68.) It is significant that the dimensions of the Tent as reconstructed by the P editors are exactly half of those of the Temple. This fact, plus the evident idealistic elements of the descriptions, points to the conclusion that the Tent (as conceived in P) was reconstructed with the Temple as a model rather than vice versa, or at least that an ancient description of the Tent was modified in P so that it resembled the Temple more closely. It has been proposed, however, that the description of the Tent in P is based on an old description of the tent built by David to house the Ark in Jerusalem, when the Temple had not yet been built (F. M. Cross, in Biran (ed.), *Temples* 169-80).

Still one may conclude to a basic truth: There was a Tent that served as a center of worship during the sojourn in the desert. Such a Tent has parallels in ancient and modern Arabian institutions, specifically the *qubba.* The latter was a small tent of red leather used to protect the tribal idols; it had a prominent place in the camp, adjacent to the tent of the chief; to it came members of the tribe seeking oracular pronouncements. Thus, the *qubba*

and the Israelite Tent had in common both appearance (red outer covering of Tent) and function (a place for the giving of oracles). Modern bedouin tribes have a similar small tent that goes with them on camelback wherever they wander. It is thought to possess some sort of supernatural power and accompanies them when they engage in battle. At times, the bedouin offer sacrifice to the divinity whose abode it is thought to be. From these parallels as well as from the constant biblical tradition, we think it probable that the movable sanctuary of Israel's desert wanderings was fashioned like the people's own tents. The last clear mention of it occurs in Num 25:6, which tells of the Tent's being put up in the plains of Moab, the last stop before the invasion of Canaan. Once the Israelites had settled in the promised land and were no longer living in tents themselves, the Ark, too, would have been housed in a more permanent abode (the one described in the P tradition?). The sanctuary at Shiloh was a building of some sort (1 Sam 1:7,9; 3:15), and later traditions that speak of the "Tent" of Shiloh (Josh 18:1; 19:51; Ps 78:60) do so by a sort of poetic archaism (→ 37 below). When David brought the Ark to Jerusalem, he housed it in a tent, but this was not the Tent, in spite of the gloss in 1 Kgs 8:4. It was a temporary arrangement meant to recall the days of wandering in the desert (2 Sam 6:17). See de Vaux, *BANE* 136-51; but also R. E. Friedman, *BA* 43 (1980) 241-48.

32   (F) The Ark. What the Tent was to shelter (Exod 26:33; 40:21) was called in Hebrew *'ărôn hā'ēdût,* "Ark of the Testimony," because the two "tables of the testimony" given at Sinai (31:18) were kept inside it (25:16; 40:20). According to 25:10-22; 37:1-9, the Ark was a box 4 ft. x 2.5 ft. x 4 ft. made of acacia wood, gold-plated without, and furnished with rings through which poles were passed when it had to be transported. On top was a plate of gold called the *kappōret,* variously translated "propitiatory" or "mercy seat." "Propitiatory" (from Lat *propitiatorium*) is based on the Gk *hilastērion,* used to render *kappōret* in the LXX; "mercy seat" is based on the idea that from the *kappōret,* on which he was enthroned, God dispensed mercy to his people. In etymological fact, *kappōret* is derived from the verb *kippēr,* which has to do not with covering over (as has often been claimed) but with wiping away (*HALAT* 470) and, in a cultic context, with wiping away sin from the sinner or from the object contaminated by personal offense (see Levine, *Presence* 55-77, 123-27; and more recently his remarks in *Mesopotamien und seine Nachbarn* [ed. H.-J. Nissen and J. Renger; BBVO 1; Berlin, 1982] 2. 523-25). At either end of the *kappōret* was a cherub with outstretched wings. It was in the Second Temple that the *kappōret* had great significance (→ 35 below; → Pauline Theology, 82:73).

In Deut 10:1-5 only the acacia wood and the tablets of the Decalogue are mentioned. In 10:8 we are told that only the levites could carry the Ark, here called *'ărôn habbĕrît,* Ark of the Covenant. Later on in Deut we read that the scroll containing the deuteronomic version of the law was given an honored place alongside the Ark (31:9,26). We are informed by Num 10:33-36 that the Ark preceded the Israelites when they left Sinai and indicated where they were to stop and pitch camp. Num 14:44 points out significantly that when the people defied Moses' orders and attacked the Canaanites, the Ark remained in the camp.

All this information comes from different traditions. The P tradition is represented in the first set of these texts (those from Exod); and its reconstruction of the Ark, like its description of the Tent, is colored by actual knowledge of the Ark as it was in the Temple (1 Kgs 8:6). The deuteronomic tradition attempts no description except that the Ark was made of acacia wood. The old text in Num is more concerned with the function of the Ark than with its appearance. Its information, however, ties in nicely with what Josh 3–6 tells us of the part played by the Ark during the invasion of Canaan.

33 The Ark was the center of Israelite worship during the wandering in the desert, and it continued to be such until the destruction of the Temple in 587. After the entrance into the promised land, it was kept at Gilgal (Josh 7:6), then at Bethel (Judg 20:27), then at Shiloh (1 Sam 3:3). Carried into that of Aphek (1 Sam 4:3ff.), it was captured by the Philistines (4:11). After causing havoc among the Philistines and being shunted from town to town, it was eventually returned to the Israelites and was kept at Kiriath-jearim (5:5–7:1). Eventually David had it brought to Jerusalem, where it was kept in a tent until Solomon built the Temple and installed it in the Holy of Holies (2 Sam 6; 1 Kgs 6:19; 8:1–9). This is the last we hear of it, except for the apocryphal tradition mentioned in 2 Macc 2:4ff.

34 Of much more interest and importance than the appearance and history of the Ark is its theological meaning. When all the data of the texts are sifted, they yield two dominant evaluations of the Ark: it was considered to be (1) the place of divine presence (God's throne or footstool) and (2) a sort of archive where the law was kept.

First, the Ark was the locus of God's presence in Israel. The awe felt for it is reflected in the alarm expressed by the Philistines when the Israelites brought the Ark into the battle camp: "God has come into their camp!" (1 Sam 4:7); and when the Ark was captured, the disaster was interpreted as God's departure from their midst (1 Sam 4:22; see A. Bentzen, *JBL* 67 [1948] 37–53). An even older appreciation is reflected in Num 10:35 (cf. Ps 132:8): When the Ark left the desert camp, it was Yahweh who was leading the way. The Ark wreaked havoc among the Philistines while they had it in their territory (1 Sam 5), and 70 men of Beth-shemesh were struck dead for not rejoicing at its reappearance (1 Sam 6:19). Uzzah was similarly affected when he dared touch it, even though innocently (2 Sam 6:7; see also Num 4:5,15; Exod 25:15; 1 Kgs 8:8). A very common epithet applied to the Ark reveals its significance for the Israelites: God's "footstool." The earliest occurrence of this notion is in 1 Sam 4:4, where there is a reference to "the Ark of Yahweh Sabaoth who sits above the cherubim" (see 2 Sam 6:2; 2 Kgs 19:15). The designation as a footstool persisted as long as the Ark (and the Temple) existed (1 Chr 28:2; Pss 99:5; 132:7; Lam 2:1; Isa 66:1). Some confusion arises for us from the fact that the Ark was referred to both as God's footstool and as his throne; both, however, are poetic figures for the place of the divine presence and should not be pressed too literally.

The Ark was also a depository for the tablets of the Decalogue, and Deut 10:1–5 seems to suggest that this is all it was. The Ark was accordingly the "Ark of the Covenant"; the P tradition has a similar designation, "Ark of the Testimony" (Exod 25:16; 40:20). Far from being contradictory, the two notions—throne of God and depository of his law—are complementary. Egyptian and Hittite documents testify that customarily covenants and treaties were deposited at the feet of the gods. Studies on the Hittite suzerainty treaties make this especially clear, one of the stipulations being that a copy of the treaty had to be preserved in a temple at the feet of an idol. The parallels between these suzerainty treaties and the Sinaitic covenant, at least as far as external form is concerned, are most striking (→ OT Thought, 77:79–80).

35 **(G) The Postexilic** *kappōret.* When the Second Temple was built after the Babylonian exile, the ancient Ark was gone—presumably, but not demonstrably, as a result of the Babylonian destruction in Jerusalem. No new Ark was constructed. In Jer 3:16–17 the people were told not to preoccupy themselves with the absence of the historical Ark, Yahweh's throne. They were not to build another one, for the new Jerusalem in its entirety would be Yahweh's throne. Nevertheless, a *kappōret,* which according to Exod 25:17–22; 37:6–9 (perhaps secondary to P's description of the Ark itself) was to be on top of the Ark (→ 32 above), was installed in the new Debir, the Holy of Holies, of the Second Temple. In historical reality this may have been a substitute for the Ark when the latter was no longer in existence (J.-M. de Tarragon, *RB* 88 [1981] 5–12). In 1 Chr 28:11, the Holy of Holies is called not the room of the Ark but the "house of the *kappōret.*" God's mysterious presence, once intensely focused on the Ark, would thenceforth be focused on the *kappōret,* which in the postexilic period figured in so awesome a manner in the annual ritual of the Day of Atonement (→ 147–50 below). The requirements of that ritual perhaps best explain why there was a *kappōret* in the Second Temple even though there was no Ark—despite the lack of ease with God's spatially restricted presence which one finds esp. in deuteronomic texts (→ 51 below).

36 **(II) Israelite Sanctuaries from the Conquest to the Temple.**

(A) Gilgal. After the Israelites had completed their exodus and had settled in Canaan, they established several new sanctuaries. The first was in Gilgal, between the Jordan and Jericho. The name refers to the circle of stones that marked the site of the shrine, which was probably used by the Canaanites before its adoption by the Israelites. It was here that the Ark was placed after the crossing of the Jordan (Josh 4:19; 7:6); here, too, the men of Israel indicated their acceptance of the covenant by being circumcised (5:2–9) and celebrated the Passover for the first time in the promised land. Samuel later came to Gilgal to judge the people (1 Sam 7:16), and the locale played an important part in the career of Saul, who was here proclaimed king "before the Lord" (11:15). Gilgal was the site of Saul's repudiation by Samuel (13:7–15; cf. 10:8; 15:12–33) on the occasion of his unauthorized offering of sacrifice. The tribe of Judah welcomed David here when he returned from Transjordan (2 Sam 19:16,41). The shrine later came under censure (Hos 4:15; Amos 4:4; 5:5); apparently the worship had become contaminated by pagan practices.

37 **(B) Shiloh.** After the conquest Shiloh soon displaced Gilgal as Israel's center of worship. We cannot ascertain just when or how the transfer was made, but it had been effected by the time of the judges. A political as well as religious center, Shiloh was a meeting place for all the tribes (Josh 18:1; 21:2; 22:9,12), and seven of the tribes were allotted their territories here (18:8). A later, questionable tradition places the Tent here (18:1; 19:51). It is quite certain that the Ark was kept here, and Elkanah, Samuel's father, made an annual trip to Shiloh to offer sacrifice (1 Sam 1:3). There was also a type of annual pilgrimage called a *ḥag* (Judg 21:19–21). The Ark was kept in a building, referred to variously as a "house of Yahweh" (1 Sam 1:7,24; 3:15), a "palace" of Yahweh (3:3), and a "house of God" (Judg 18:31). Here, too, the epithet "Sabaoth, who sits above the cherubim" was first applied to Yahweh (1 Sam 1:3; 4:4; → OT Thought, 77:14). Not long after the Shiloh shrine came into prominence in the biblical story, it made a most dramatic exit. Shortly after 1050 BC the Ark was taken from there to ensure Yahweh's military presence in the battle of Aphek, where it was captured by the Philistines. When the Ark was recovered, it was never taken back to Shiloh. Jer 7:12–14; 26:6 have been taken as evidence that Shiloh itself was ravaged by the Philistines and lay in ruins throughout the following centuries, but corrective excavations in 1963 have shown that it was occupied through the period of the Israelite monarchy (see M. L. Buhl and S. Holm-Nielsen, *The Danish Investigations at Tall Sailūn, Palestine* [Copenhagen, 1969]). Although no remains identifiable as a temple have been found, we may take it for granted that Shiloh ceased to be a place of Israelite pilgrimage as soon as it ceased to be the place where the Ark was kept. Among the pilgrims to Jerusalem just after the fall of the monarchy in Judah were pilgrims from Shiloh (Jer 41:4–10).

38   (C) Mizpah. In Benjamin there was another cultic center during the period of the judges, for at Mizpah the Israelites convened to take a solemn oath before Yahweh (Judg 20:1,3; 21:1,5,8). In the time of Samuel, the Israelites gathered there to worship Yahweh, pouring out libations and offering sacrifice (1 Sam 7:5–12). Mizpah was another stop on Samuel's rounds of the country to "judge" the people (7:16). One of the variant traditions concerning Saul's selection as king places the event at Mizpah (10:17–24). The next mention of this site as a shrine occurs in 1 Macc 3:46–54, some 850 years later.

39   (D) Ophrah. Two accounts of the establishment of the shrine of Ophrah are given in Judg 6, one immediately following the other. According to the first (6:11–24), the angel of Yahweh appeared to Gideon and commissioned him to rescue the Israelites from Midianite marauders. At the time of the apparition, Gideon was treading corn on a rock. He had stopped for lunch, and the angel directed that the meal be offered in sacrifice on the rock. Gideon then built an altar there. According to the second account (6:25–32), it was Yahweh who spoke to Gideon in a dream and commanded him to break up the altar his fathers had erected in honor of Baal, to cut up the pagan *asherah* (sacred post), to build an altar to Yahweh, and to burn a sacrifice, using the wood of the *asherah* for the fire. The execution of this command caused some consternation among the people, but Joash came to his son's defense.

These two accounts have to do with the same shrine. It was a sanctuary venerated by the clan of Joash, Gideon's father, and two traditions were passed down in the family relating how it had been converted into a Yahwistic shrine. The older of the two (the first) recalled a peaceful transition; the second seems to have been colored by later conflicts between Baal worship and Yahweh worship. The only subsequent incident related in connection with this shrine reflects these two tendencies. After his victory, Gideon made an ephod — destined for the honor of Yahweh — for the sanctuary as part of its cultic furnishing; but the deuteronomic editor interpreted it as an object of idolatrous worship (Judg 8:22–27; → 9 above).

40   (E) Dan. The sanctuary of Dan had strange beginnings (Judg 17–18). A man named Micah stole some silver from his mother but returned it later; she then used some of it to have an idol made. Micah placed it in a shrine together with an ephod and some teraphim (household gods). He appointed his son priest of the sanctuary until a levite happened by. Then a group from the tribe of Dan, which was migrating to the north, pilfered everything from the shrine including the levite. When they arrived at Laish, they killed off the inhabitants, renamed it Dan, and erected their stolen sanctuary.

At first glance this story of idolatry and violence does not seem to refer to a Yahwistic shrine, and indeed the deuteronomic editor tells the story to give the impression that Jeroboam I's shrine at Dan was corrupt from the very start. However, truly it was Yahweh who was worshiped there, even though in quite unorthodox fashion. It was to him that Micah's mother dedicated the silver, and it was he who blessed Micah for giving it back to her. As soon as a levite came along, Micah engaged him, for he knew that the levitical priesthood was more acceptable to Yahweh (→ 18 above). The Danites used the ephod to consult God, and they were answered. The levite in the story was a grandson of Moses named Jonathan, and his descendants continued to serve the sanctuary until the Assyrian invasion. When Jeroboam I set up the northern kingdom of Israel, he chose two religious centers as rivals to the Temple, one at either end of his realm, Dan in the north and Bethel in the south. In each of them he installed a golden calf (→ 53 below). Excavation of Dan has revealed the city's sacred area. Within it, from roughly the time of Jeroboam I in the late 10th cent., there was a stone platform (a *bāmâ*? → 60 below), enlarged in the first half of the 9th cent. and fitted with stairs to its upper surface in the 8th cent. The architectonic relation of this platform to the golden calf is not known. See A. Biran, *BA* 37 (1974) 40–43; *Temples* 142–51; → Biblical Archaeology, 74:119.

41   (F) Jerusalem. Jerusalem was, of course, the greatest of Israel's shrines. The city itself did not come under Israelite control until the time of David, who effected its capture and made it his capital. He brought the Ark from Kiriath-jearim (2 Sam 6) in a procession that was marked by most dramatic incidents and installed it under a tent in the spot chosen for it. (This narrative may have been colored by Pss 24:7–10 and 132, if they were sung on the anniversary of the occasion.) David later erected an altar on the site of the future Temple. This story, as told in 2 Sam 24:16–25 (see 1 Chr 21:15–22:1), contains all the conventional features of foundation accounts: celestial apparition, divine message, erection of the altar, offering of sacrifice.

One other conventional feature, however, is missing here. Rather consistently in the patriarchal period and not infrequently during the period of the judges, Israelite shrines were established on the sites of already existing pagan sanctuaries. There was undoubtedly such a shrine in Jerusalem: Melchizedek, its king during the patriarchal period, is introduced as priest of El Elyon, a well-known Canaanite deity (Gen 14:18–20). However, everything in the passages dealing with the establishment of the Israelite sanctuary indicates rather clearly that, if there were such a shrine, it was not taken over by David. The Ark was housed in a tent, not in an already existing structure; and the site chosen for the altar and, eventually, for the Temple had no religious associations. It had been a threshing floor belonging to a native Jebusite named Araunah (2 Sam 24:18–20). However, it is tenuously possible that the editors purposely omitted from their narrative anything that might suggest that the Temple had pagan antecedents (→ 16 above).

42   (III) The Temple of Jerusalem.
(A) Location. According to 2 Chr 3:1, Solomon built the Temple on the site selected and purchased by David; this was a rocky eminence N of Ophel, the eastern hill to which the city was then confined. The site has been occupied continuously ever since and is now occupied by the Mosque of Omar and the so-called Dome of the Rock. Whereas the general area is easily identifiable, there has been question as to the Temple's exact position. That its entrance faced E seems certain,

SOLOMON'S TEMPLE

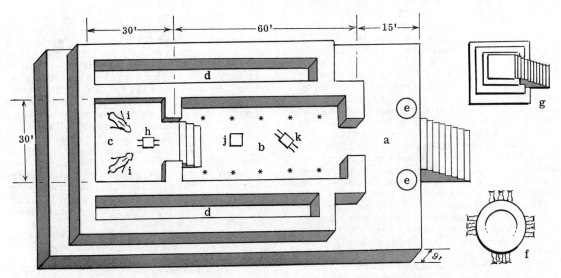

I. GROUND PLAN

a. Vestibule or Porch *('ûlām)*
b. Holy Place or Sanctuary *(hêkāl)*, 60′ × 30′ × 40′
c. Holy of Holies *(děbîr)*, 30′ × 30′ × 30′
d. Side Chambers—three stories, each level 1.5′ wider than the lower story
e. Two Free-standing Pillars of Jachin and Boaz
f. Bronze Sea

g. Bronze Altar (with straight steps of Albright–Wright)
h. Ark of the Covenant
i. Cherubim
j. Altar of Incense
k. Table for Loaves of Proposition
* Ten Candlesticks—five on each side

II. FRONTAL VIEW

d. Side Chambers: Treasury
e. Jachin and Boaz (40′ high)
f. Bronze Sea (15′ diameter)
g. Bronze Altar (Garber's ziggurat)
h. Flat Roof (Garber's Egyptian cornice) (Albright shows crenelations)

N.B.: No towers.

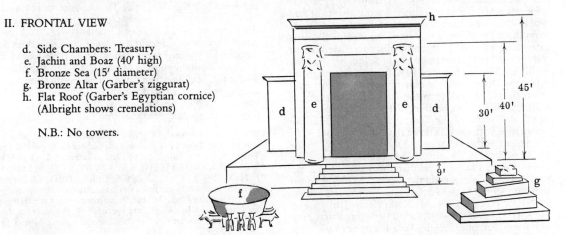

III. FLOOR PLAN OF A PHOENICIAN CHAPEL

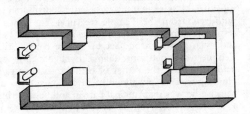

This 8th-cent. Phoenician chapel of the kings of Hattina (Tell Tainat), in Syria, was two-thirds the size of Solomon's Temple.

and explorations suggest that the Sanctuary stood about 50 yards N of the Dome of the Rock (*BARev* 9 [2, 1983] 40–59; → Biblical Geography, 73:92–93).

43   (B) Interior and Exterior. It took approximately seven years to build Solomon's Temple (1 Kgs 6:37–38; → Biblical Archaeology, 74:109). The timber and skilled labor were obtained from Hiram, king of Tyre; the stone and unskilled labor came from the environs of Jerusalem (1 Kgs 5:15–31). The biblical description of the Temple is clear in its general lines, but in details it leaves much to be desired (1 Kgs 6–7; 2 Chr 3–4). We are not told, for instance, how thick the walls were, how the façade was ornamented, or what kind of roof was used. Many scholars draw on later information supplied in Ezekiel's vision in order to fill out what is lacking in 1 Kgs. For instance, Ezek 41:5 speaks of Temple walls that are 9 ft. thick, and Ezek 40:49; 41:8 describe the Temple as standing on a platform 9 ft. high.

The *interior* was divided into three sections: the Ulam or vestibule; the Hekal (palace; temple), later called the Holy Place or Sanctuary; and the Debir (back room), later called the Holy of Holies. The most sacred part was the Holy of Holies, for in it was kept the Ark of the Covenant. The interior measurements were as follows: the building was 30 ft. wide throughout; the Ulam was 15 ft. long, the Hekal 60 ft., and the Debir 30 ft. The text does not make it clear how these sections were partitioned off, but there must have been a wall between the Ulam and the Hekal. And while 1 Kgs 6:2 speaks of the Hekal and the Debir as a unit, 6:16–17 suggests that they were separated, for it gives the length of each. De Vaux's suggested emendation of 6:16 would throw further light on the subject: Solomon "used cedar planks to build the twenty cubits [= 30 ft.] from the back of the Temple, from the ground to the rafters, and (these twenty cubits) 'were set apart' from the Temple for the Debir." There would then have been a transverse partition different from the cedar paneling that lined the inner walls. It is interesting that in the recently discovered temple to Yahweh at Arad (a contemporary of Solomon's Temple; → Biblical Archaeology, 74:109), the area that might be called the Debir is only a cella projecting off the main room that is equivalent to the Hekal.   According to 6:20, the Debir was a perfect 30-ft. cube, but according to 6:2 the height of the Temple building, presumably comprising both the Hekal and the Debir, was not 30 ft. (the height of that cube) but 45 ft. (or, according to the LXX, 37.5 ft.). This may be because the floor of the Debir was on a higher level than that of the Hekal, but some scholars, interpreting the Debir as a cubic wooden structure set inside the Temple at its W end (H. Schult, *ZDPV* 80 [1964] 46–54; M. Noth, *Könige* [BKAT 9/2; Neukirchen, 1965] 99–100, 119–21), distinguish the top of the wooden cube from the Temple's stone roof several feet higher.

44   *Exterior.* Directly in front of Solomon's Temple stood two bronze pillars, flanking the entrance; they were not an integral part of the façade, but stood free of it. Symbolic rather than functional, they may have been vestiges of the old Canaanite *masseboth* or sacred steles. Each had a name: one was Jachin, the other was Boaz (1 Kgs 7:21). The precise significance of these names is still not certain. One popular explanation takes them together and translates: "He (Yahweh) will establish with strength." Many other conjectures have been made, but one of the most interesting is that they represent the satisfied exclamations of the artisan: *Yākîn* (It is solid!) and *Bōʿaz* (With strength!). See R. B. Y. Scott, *JBL* 58 (1939) 143–49. The Arad temple also had two pillars flanking the entrance to the main room.

**45   ** According to 1 Kgs 6:5–10, a structure of

three low stories surrounded the three sides of the Debir and the two sides of the Hekal. Apparently only one such story, 7.5 ft. high, was in the original plan. Later it proved inadequate as a place for storage; and two more stories were added, each 1.5 ft. wider than the other, and were fitted into the existing recesses in the outer wall of the Temple. We are not certain where the entrance to these storerooms was, but it may have been at the right corner (1 Kgs 6:8). Access to the second and third stories was by means of trap doors. The existence of recesses in the outer walls is explained by the manner in which those walls were constructed. According to 1 Kgs 6:36; 7:12, the walls of the courts and of the palace had three courses of dressed stone and one of timber, and the Temple walls were probably built up in the same fashion (see Ezra 6:14). The timber course would have served as a framework for the brick superstructure that topped the stonework, and each course of stone would have been lighter and narrower than the one on which it rested, thus forming the recesses.

Surrounding the Temple was the "inner court" (1 Kgs 6:36). This was later extended to include an upper and a lower court (2 Chr 20:5; 2 Kgs 21:5; Jer 36:10).

46   (C) Furniture. The interior appointments of Solomon's Temple were as follows. Inside the Debir or Holy of Holies was the Ark of the Covenant, near or on top of which were two gold-plated wooden cherubim whose extended wings reached from wall to wall. The figures themselves rose halfway to the ceiling (1 Kgs 6:23–28; 2 Chr 3:10–13; see 1 Kgs 8:6–7; 2 Chr 5:7–8). In the Hekal or Sanctuary were the altar of incense, the table for the loaves of proposition, and ten candlesticks (1 Kgs 7:48–49). In the court in front of the Temple, off to one side of the entrance steps, was the altar of bronze (8:64; 9:25; 2 Kgs 16:14); on the opposite side was the "Sea" of bronze. This was a capacious laver resting on the backs of twelve statues of bulls (1 Kgs 7:23–26). Ranged on either side of the entrance were ten tables on top of which were bronze basins. These tables could be wheeled about the court as needed (7:27–29). The priests used the "Sea" for their own ritual purifications; the smaller basins were used for the purification of the victims (2 Chr 4:6). On the *kappōret* in the Second Temple, which had no Ark, → 35 above.

(For the architecture and plan of Solomon's Temple, see: T. Busink, *Der Tempel von Jerusalem von Salomo bis Herodes 1: Der Tempel Salomos* [Leiden, 1970]; P. L. Garber, *BA* 14 [1951] 2–24; J. Ouelette, *RB* 76 [1969] 365–78; *JBL* 89 [1970] 338–43; *JNES* 31 [1972] 187–91; G. E. Wright, *BA* 4 [1941] 17–31; *BA* 18 [1955] 41–44. For temples similar in structure elsewhere, → Biblical Archaeology, 74:109. Reconstructions of the Temple by Garber and by Wright are the basis of the diagram that accompanies this article. For the lampstand, see *BARev* 5 [5, 1979] 46–57.)

47   (D) Status. It has been suggested, rather disparagingly, that Solomon's Temple was merely a royal chapel. True, it was one of many buildings in the palace compound and was of relatively modest proportions. It is also true that the king dedicated it and richly subsidized it, and that his successors contributed to and withdrew from the Temple treasury. The kings were responsible for the upkeep of the Temple (→ 17 above) and even had a throne set up in the court. Still, the Temple was much more than a royal chapel: it was the national shrine, the center of orthodox worship. If the king figured so prominently in its operation, it was because he was its principal patron and because his role as Yahweh's vice-regent gave him a character—if not strictly priestly, at least sacred—that he was free to exercise on occasion.

48   **(E) History of First and Second Temples.**
The First or Solomonic *Temple* suffered all the
vicissitudes of the nation itself. It was altered, defiled,
restored, and eventually reduced to rubble. The two
upper stories may have been added to the outer building
by Asa (1 Kgs 15:15). Jehoshaphat extended the court
(2 Chr 20:5). The resulting upper and lower courts were
connected by a gate during the rule of Jotham (2 Kgs
15:35; cf. Jer 26:10; 36:10). All the successors of
Solomon were anointed in the Temple court, and the
rebellion against Athaliah and the subsequent anointing
of Joash took place there (2 Kgs 11). Ahaz had Solomon's
bronze altar dismantled and erected a new one on the
pattern of one in Damascus (16:10–16). He also confiscated the movable basins and removed the bronze
bulls from beneath the great "Sea," probably because he
needed money to pay tribute to his Assyrian overlord
(16:17). Manasseh erected idolatrous altars and an image
of Asherah (21:4–5,7).

In times of religious fervor and reform, these
abominations were removed and the Temple was refur-
bished. Such were the times of Hezekiah (2 Kgs 18:4)
and especially of Josiah (23:4–12). However, these
reforms remained largely external and were not able to
effect a lasting and general change of attitude among the
people. With official encouragement, the people repeatedly returned to their old syncretistic ways, and Ezek 8
portrays graphically the situation just before the Babylonians leveled Solomon's Temple in 587.

49   *The Second Temple.*   When, in 538, the Jews
returned from the exile, they brought with them Persian
authorization to rebuild the Temple. Cyrus restored to
them the precious utensils that Nebuchadnezzar had
pilfered. But the work of reconstruction proceeded at a
snail's pace. The first repatriates erected a new altar (Ezra
3:2–6) and began to rebuild the Temple (5:16). They had
hardly removed the rubble from the area when they
were interrupted by the hostile tactics of the Samaritans
(4:1–5). Another reason is suggested by Hag 1:2, viz.,
their own discouragement and flagging enthusiasm.
Work was resumed in 520 under the energetic direction
of Zerubbabel and Joshua, and with the urging of
Haggai and Zechariah (Ezra 4:24–5:2; Hag 1:1–2,9;
Zech 4:7–10). The task was completed in 515.

Unfortunately, we are poorly informed about the
appearance of the postexilic Temple. In all likelihood it
was built on the same lines and was of the same proportions as the Temple of Solomon. The old people who
remembered Solomon's Temple are said to have shed
tears at the sight of the reconstruction (Ezra 3:12–13;
Hag 2:3). However, these texts refer to the new Temple
as it was in the process of construction. The finished
product, although not so glittering as its predecessor,
was substantial and worthy of its high purpose.

50   In time its splendor increased; and when
Antiochus Epiphanes plundered it in 169, his booty was
noteworthy: the golden altar and candelabrum, the table
of offerings, the veil that hung at the entrance, gold
plate, sacred utensils, and treasures (1 Macc 1:21–24;
2 Macc 5:15–16; see 2 Macc 3). Further profanation
occurred when, in 167, legitimate sacrifice was proscribed and supplanted by the cult of Zeus Olympios
(1 Macc 1:44–59; 2 Macc 6:1–6). In 164, after the Maccabean victories, the sacred precincts were purified, the
stolen furnishings restored, and the Temple rededicated
(1 Macc 4:36–59). In 20 BC Herod the Great undertook
the complete rebuilding of the Temple (→ Biblical
Archaeology, 74:138).

51   **(F) Theological Import.**   The Temple
played an important part in the life of Israel, fundamentally because the Temple was considered God's own
house in the midst of his people. At the entrance of the
Ark into Solomon's new Temple, God symbolically
took possession of his house; and according to 1 Kgs
8:10, a cloud signifying the divine presence filled the
Temple (Exod 33:9; 40:34–35; Num 12:4–10). There is
reference to the idea of divine dwelling in Solomon's
dedication speech (1 Kgs 8:13); see also 1 Kgs 8:12;
2 Kgs 19:14; Pss 27:4; 84; Amos 1:2; Isa 2:2–3; 6:1–4;
Jer 14:21. The prophets, however, realized that God's
presence among his people was a favor that could be
withdrawn if they proved unworthy of it. Jeremiah was
outspoken against those compatriots who looked upon
the Temple as a sort of good luck charm that would
protect them against hostile forces, whether or not they
lived so as to deserve protection (Jer 7:1–15; 26:1–15;
see Exod 8–10).

As theological notions became refined and the transcendence of Yahweh came to be realized more precisely,
an uneasiness manifested itself. Could the transcendent
God be confined within the physical limits of the Holy
of Holies? This conflict is reflected in the prayer that the
deuteronomic editor puts on the lips of Solomon: "But
is God really to dwell with people on earth? The
heavens, even the highest heavens, cannot contain him,
much less this house which I have built" (1 Kgs 8:27). In
the next verses (30–40) he gives the answer: God lives
in heaven, but he hears the prayers that are addressed to
him in the Temple. His transcendence was safeguarded
further by the notion that his "Name" dwelt in the
Temple (1 Kgs 8:17,29; Deut 12:5,11). This was an
ingenious compromise, for among the Semites there was
an intrinsic connection between person and name (→
OT Thought, 77:6). Where Yahweh's Name was, there
he was, too, in a special but not an exclusive way. Other
biblical documents stress that God's "Glory" dwelt in the
Temple (2 Chr 5:14; Ezek 10:4; 43:5).

52   In addition to being a sign of God's presence,
or perhaps because it was, the Temple was also a symbol
of his choice of Israel as his very own people. Even more
specifically, it signified his predilection for Jerusalem
(2 Sam 24:16; 2 Chr 3:1; Pss 68:17; 78:68). This notion
is rooted ultimately in Yahweh's choice of David and the
promise of perpetuity to the Davidic dynasty (1 Kgs
8:16; 11:13,32; 2 Chr 6:5–6; 2 Kgs 19:34; Isa 37:35; →
OT Thought, 77:155). In 701 when the holy city was
saved from destruction by Sennacherib's army, the
people were persuaded that the Temple itself afforded
them protection against whatever forces might assail
them. This conviction was shaken by the catastrophe of
587, but it revived in moderated form after the return
from the exile and the reconstruction of the Temple.

53   **(G) Oneness of Sanctuary.**   We have been
speaking of the Temple as the center of legitimate worship, indeed as the only place of worship in Israel; and
it is true that eventually it was recognized as such. Yet,
in the beginning, as we have seen, there were many
shrines throughout the land, particularly during the
period of the judges; and indeed Exod 20:24–26
recognized the legitimacy of these several altars and of
the sacrifices offered thereon, provided that they had
been erected with divine sanction. This sanction would
have been indicated by a theophany at the place in question. However, not all of these sanctuaries were of equal
importance. During the period of the judges, whenever
the tribes met for communal worship, it was always at
the shrine where the Ark was kept, particularly at Shiloh
and later at Gibeon.

David's installation of the Ark in Jerusalem was the
beginning of this city's prestige; yet Gibeon was still the
"greatest high place" in Solomon's day (1 Kgs 3:4–15).
But with the building of the Temple, Jerusalem became

the focal point of divine worship, attracting thousands of pilgrims from all over the country. Then came the split of the kingdom: the ten northern tribes seceded and formed the kingdom of Israel with Jeroboam as their first king. Fearing that continued religious allegiance to Jerusalem would weaken his people's political allegiance to the new kingdom, he set up rival sanctuaries at Bethel and Dan (1 Kgs 12:27–30). Even though he installed gold-plated bullocks in these shrines, he did not mean to reject Yahweh. Like the cherubim atop the Ark, these figures were conceived of as thrones of God, not as gods themselves. Unfortunately, however, the bull was a popular symbol for the Canaanite god Baal and was associated with the gross fertility cults of which the Canaanites were so passionately fond. The step to a syncretism bordering on idolatry was a short one, and the violent reactions of the prophets indicate that the step was all too nimbly taken (1 Kgs 12:32; 14:9; 19:18; 2 Kgs 10:29; 17:22; Hos 8:5–6; 10:5; 13:2). In spite of the fulminations of the prophets, the sanctuaries of Dan and Bethel, Beer-sheba (Amos 5:5; 8:14), Gilgal (4:4; 5:5; Hos 4:15), and other unnamed places continued to flourish (Amos 7:9; Ezek 7:24). The excavations at Arad in the Negeb (→ Biblical Archaeology, 74:109) have uncovered a temple that was in use during the whole period of the monarchy; however, its altar of holocausts seems to have disappeared about King Hezekiah's time—perhaps a mark of the reform to be mentioned below. Nevertheless, Jerusalem kept its prestige, and even after it had been destroyed, groups of pilgrims came from all over the devastated country to worship there (Jer 41:5).

54   Before the fall of the city, there had been two notable attempts to make its Temple not only the central place for worship but the only legitimate sanctuary. Hezekiah took the first steps in this direction, *ca.* 715–705, by proscribing the "high places" (2 Kgs 18:4,22; Isa 36:7). But his successor, Manasseh, undid his reform by reopening the suppressed shrines (2 Kgs 21:3). Josiah renewed the efforts made by Hezekiah on a more solemn and ambitious scale. The international situation was in his favor; for he was able to liberate his country from Assyrian domination, and the extirpation of foreign intrusions into the cult of Yahweh took on a patriotic allure. He again suppressed the local shrines and summoned all the priests of Judah to Jerusalem (23:5,8–9). The weakening of the Assyrian hegemony allowed him to move into what had once been the northern kingdom and put the shrine at Bethel out of operation. Finally, Josiah gathered all the people to a national celebration of the Passover in Jerusalem. This was in the year 621, the year of the finding of the "Book of the Law" in the Temple (probably the core of Deut; → Deuteronomy, 6:4).

This discovery was literally a godsend for Josiah, for one of the central preoccupations of the book was

precisely unity of sanctuary (Deut 12). Since the deuteronomic redaction of the law originated in the northern kingdom, originally it may have had in mind a northern shrine (Shechem?) as the one legitimate place of worship. According to one theory, refugee levites brought the book to Jerusalem after the fall of Samaria in 721, and Hezekiah applied the principle of unity of sanctuary to the Temple. After Hezekiah's time, the "Book of the Law" fell into disuse during Manasseh's long and evil reign, only to be rediscovered under Josiah. An attractive alternative theory is the following: The law of unity of sanctuary may have been the result of, rather than the stimulus for, Hezekiah's reform. After all, in connection with Hezekiah's reform no appeal was made to an earlier law that would justify one sanctuary; but by the time of Josiah such a law was on the books. The phraseology of the law in reference to "the place chosen by Yahweh that his Name shall dwell there" is characteristic of the theology of the Jerusalem Temple and can only with difficulty be explained as a secondary application of a designation once applied to a northern sanctuary.

55   At any rate, after the death of Josiah in 609, the reform deteriorated until the Temple was finally destroyed in 587. After the return from the exile, however, the deuteronomic ideal that Josiah had so zealously espoused became a reality. From 515 BC to AD 70, when the Romans destroyed the Temple once and for all, it was the unique place of worship for all Judah. Outside of Judah we know of two Jewish temples in Egypt, one at Elephantine, the other at Leontopolis. Both were looked upon with open disfavor by orthodox Palestinian Jewry (→ History, 75:125). Within Palestine itself there was the Samaritan temple on Mt. Gerizim, but this was even less an Israelite institution. The accounts of its establishment are conflicting and unreliable, yet it was certainly in existence before 167 BC, when Antiochus Epiphanes hellenized it. John Hyrcanus, of the Hasmonean line, destroyed it in 129 (→ History, 75:127, 140).

56   **(IV) Synagogues.** Synagogues do not figure in the OT literature, and there is a great diversity of opinion about when they came into existence. As the Gk root of their name indicates (*syn* = "together"; *agein* = "to lead, bring"), they were meetinghouses—places where people gathered not for sacrifice but for prayer, devout reading, meditation, and instruction. They certainly existed in the postexilic period, and the most popular hypothesis is that they arose as an institution during the exile when the people were cut off from the Temple. However, there is no substantial evidence for this theory; other scholars, with no stronger evidence in their favor, feel that they sprang up in Palestine itself after the exile. Some few opine that they originated before the exile as a result of Josiah's suppression of the local shrines. (See J. Gutmann [ed.], *The Synagogue* [NY, 1975].)

ALTARS AND SACRIFICES

57   Altar and sacrifice are correlative terms; the mention of the one immediately suggests the other. Indeed, the Hebr word for altar, *mizbēaḥ,* includes in its connotation the very notion of sacrifice, for it is derived from a verb meaning "to slaughter." Apparently, victims were originally slaughtered on the altar, although in a later period the altar was used only for the act of offering. Consequently, *mizbēaḥ* assumed the general meaning of

a place where sacrifice was offered, whether the victim was an (already slaughtered) animal, cereals, or incense.

58   **(I) The Typology of Altars.** Archaeological investigation of ancient Palestine and its neighboring regions has revealed altars built of earth or unbaked brick, or of uncut stone; it has also revealed natural outcroppings of rock with cuttings which have led some to suspect that they were used as altars, although that is very difficult to establish. (See F. L. Stendebach, *BZ* 20 [1976] 180–96.) Altars of wood, known from a few texts, disintegrated long before they could be uncovered by the archaeologist's spade. The majority of ancient altars found in Palestine itself are altars hewn from a single block of stone, rather typically with protrusions (called "horns" in the OT) rising from each of the four corners of the upper surface. Such altars differ in size according to their function. Smaller altars were apt for incense offered by burning or for offerings of food or drink laid out on the altar as on a table, without being burned. These smaller altars could easily stand inside a temple building, since the materials offered on them were consumed by a small smoldering fire or were not consumed by fire at all. (For such purposes, terra-cotta stands, often found in the ruins of ancient sanctuaries, would also do.) Larger altars were apt for sacrifices in which large or entire animal portions were burned. Because of the amount of fire necessary for such sacrifices and the resultant smoke, these larger altars normally stood in the open, outside a temple building.

59 The Bible shows that in early Israelite Palestine a natural outcropping of rock or a large stone did serve as an altar. Gideon was ordered to place his offerings on a rock (Judg 6:19–23; see also 13:19–20). When the Ark was sent back to Israel by the Philistines, the cows, along with the cart they drew, were burned as sacrifice on a large stone (1 Sam 6:14). In Exod 20:24–26 (early legislation in the Code of the Covenant), both unbaked bricks and stone are allowed as materials for the building of an altar, with the provision (supposed by Deut 27:5; Josh 8:30–31) that stone should be uncut by tools when used for building an altar. This provision may reflect a religious idea that an object as holy as an altar should be built of materials in their natural state, unworked by the hands of creatures (see Exod 20:25). A similar concern may be the basis of the law forbidding steps rising from the ground to the top of the altar (Exod 20:26). Modesty has been given as the reason for this provision: when the only garment worn by a sacrificing priest was a type of loincloth, the priest ran the risk of indecent exposure in ascending a flight of steps. More likely the original reason for the prohibition is that artificially constructed steps, trodden upon, would have suppressed the separation of the holy altar from what was profane.

60 (II) The *bāmâ*. The *bāmâ,* conventionally translated "high place," was an open-air place of worship whose precise appearance has not been determined, but which seems to have been a platform of rather large dimensions. The *bāmâ* itself was not a temple or sanctuary, the house of a god; as a sacral construction it is best understood as analogous to an open-air altar. Like the altars independent of any sanctuary, it was a place where sacrificial offerings could be made without the intervention of a priest, although when a *bêt bāmâ* (some type of sanctuary building) was built, the service of a priest was required (1 Kgs 12:31). Sacrificial meals at a *bāmâ* (1 Sam 9:13,19,22–24) were eaten in a hall (*liškâ,* 9:22). Prophets (10:5) or a seer (9:11–21) might be active at a *bāmâ.* In these early texts, the *bāmâ* is a legitimate cultic place. The later deuteronomistic editorial comments on the *bāmâ,* and on any priest who functioned at a sanctuary connected with a *bāmâ,* are negative, doubtless because of the view that one temple should be the sole legitimate place of all worship requiring priestly service. (See W. B. Barrick, *SEA* 45 [1980] 50–57; P. H. Vaughan, *The Meaning of 'Bāmâ' in the Old Testament* [SOTSMS 3; Cambridge, 1974]; P. Welten, *ZDPV* 88 [1972] 19–37; Biran (ed.), *Temples* 31–37, 142–51.)

61 (III) **Altars of the Jerusalem Temple.** Biblical descriptions of the altars of the desert Tabernacle have been affected by the appearance of the Temple altars and so constitute a major source of our knowledge of the latter. In the courtyard before the Temple building stood the *altar of holocausts* (Exod 40:6,29), strangely omitted from the detailed description of Solomon's Temple in 1 Kgs 6–7 but mentioned in 1 Kgs 8:22,54,64; 9:25. According to Exod 27:1–8; 38:1–7 (a description related to the desert Tabernacle), the altar of holocausts, 7.5 ft. x 7.5 ft. x 4.5 ft., was made of acacia wood plated with bronze. It was hollow with a bronze grill, presumably on top. Nothing is said about how the sacrificial fire was kept from destroying an altar so constructed, or whether there were steps to facilitate access to the top. One detail in this description corresponds to the only preserved descriptive detail of Solomon's altar (1 Kgs 8:64; 2 Kgs 16:14–15), built in the late 10th cent.: it was of bronze. This altar was replaced 200 years later with one patterned on an altar that King Ahaz of Judah had seen in Damascus (2 Kgs 16:10–16).

62 References to the *altar of incense* in Solomon's Temple are sufficient to establish its existence; however, the obscurity of the texts has caused some to doubt this fact. This altar's proper place was in the Hekal of the Temple, in front of the Debir containing the Ark. Its appearance can be estimated from the description of an altar of incense for the desert Tabernacle in Exod 30:1–5; 37:25–28: an altar 1.5 ft. square and 3 ft. high, made of acacia wood plated with gold, with a hornlike projection at each of the four upper corners. This is the "altar of gold" mentioned in 1 Kgs 7:48. In Isaiah's inaugural vision, a seraph is described taking a live coal from an altar inside the Temple (Isa 6:6) — an altar that can only be the altar of incense (see also 2 Chr 26:16).

63 Of the altars in the Second Temple we have little reliable information. The visionary description of the altar of holocausts in Ezek 43:13–17 shows Babylonian traits, and there is no evidence that the altar of holocausts actually built for the Second Temple was in close conformity with it. Historically reliable is the information that Antiochus Epiphanes removed the altar of incense (the "golden altar") and the table for the bread of the Presence from the Second Temple in 169 BC (1 Macc 1:21–22) and profaned the altar of holocausts in 167 by superimposing on it an altar to Olympian Zeus (1 Macc 1:54,59; 2 Macc 6:2,5) — the "abomination of desolation" (1 Macc 1:54; Dan 9:27). New altars and a new table were put in place after the Maccabean victories (1 Macc 4:44–47,49–51; 2 Macc 10:3).

64 (IV) **Significance of the Altar.** Like the Temple, the altar had deep religious significance for the Israelites, much of it received from ancient Near Eastern cultures but modified conceptually to bring it into harmony with the theological views of orthodox Israelite religion. Temples in the ancient Near East had always been regarded as the houses of the gods on earth, and from this it was easy to derive a sense of a larger altar as the god's hearth. In Israel, this idea is implicit in the law requiring that a fire always be kept burning on the altar (Lev 6:5–6 [12–13]). In the ancient Near East, food offered to a god was the god's meal. This concept appears rarely in the Bible and is ridiculed in the relatively late story of Bel and the Dragon (Vg Dan 14:1–22); but Ezek 41:21–22 speaks of "the table" of the bread of the Presence, and in Mal 1:7 the altar (of holocausts) is itself called "the table of Yahweh" (see also Ezek 44:15–16; Mal 1:12). The altar was also a sign of the divine presence. As such, both the altar of holocausts (Exod 29:37; 40:10) and the altar of incense (Exod 30:10, 36) were particularly holy and could be served only by priests (Lev 21:6; Num 17:5; 1 Chr 23:13). The altar of holocausts had to be consecrated before it could be used (Exod 29:36-37; Lev 8:15), and in later times it was purified annually on the Day of Atonement (Lev 16:18-19). The numinous presence in an altar could be marked by its receiving a divine name, e.g., "El, God of Israel" of the altar erected by Jacob at Shechem (Gen 33:20), or "Yahweh is my battle-standard" of the one erected by Moses after his victory over the Amalekites (Exod 17:15-16).

65 The "horns" of the altar—the projections rising from the four corners of its upper surface—were considered to be especially sacred. As part of the ritual of expiation when the altar was consecrated, the blood of sacrificial victims was rubbed on them (Exod 29:12; 30:10; Ezek 43:20), and the same thing was done in other rites of expiation or purification (Lev 4; 8:15; 9:9; 16:18). A person seeking asylum rushed to take hold of the horns (1 Kgs 2:28). Their precise signification is uncertain; suggestions include the following: that the horn is a symbol of strength and power; or that the horns symbolize those of the sacrificial victims; or again that they are vestiges of the *masseboth* or steles which in ancient Palestine were common symbols of a divinity (→ Biblical Archaeology, 74:39).

66 (V) Sacrifices. The central act of Israelite worship, sacrifice, took different specific forms. There is often a disconcerting lack of precision in the designations of sacrifices, and later practices are interpolated into descriptions or prescriptions from an earlier time, which makes it difficult to trace historical development clearly. In Lev 1-7, though, we find the various types of sacrifice as they were carried out in the postexilic Temple. Sporadically we find other texts which are parallel to a section in Lev 1-7, but which differ in detail.

67 (A) Holocaust or Burnt Offering. The most solemn of the Israelite sacrifices was the holocaust, or burnt offering. In it, the victim was completely burned, as *holocauston* (used for it in Jewish Greek) indicates. The technical Hebr word, *'ōlâ*, is derived from the root meaning "to go up," probably because the flame and smoke went up toward heaven (so Judg 13:20). It is also called *kālîl*, a word meaning "complete" (Deut 33:10; 1 Sam 7:9; Ps 51:21).

According to the prescriptions of Lev, the victim of a holocaust had to be an unblemished male animal or bird (turtledove or pigeon). The one making the offering laid his hand on the victim's head to signify that the sacrifice was to be offered in his name and for his benefit. The gesture did not signify that the victim was a substitute for the offerer or that the sins of the offerer were transferred to it for expiation. The offerer then slit the throat of the victim, and the priest poured its blood around the altar—blood, considered the seat of life, belonged to God in a special way. After the animal had been skinned and quartered, the pieces were washed and placed on the altar to be consumed in the flames. If the victim was a bird, the one making the offering simply handed it over to the priest, who performed the ritual directly on the altar. Such offerings were usually made by the poor, who could not afford to offer animals (Lev 5:7; 12:8).

In the latest development of the holocaust ritual, the law called for an accompanying gift (*minḥâ*) of flour mixed with oil and a libation of wine. The flour was burned and the wine poured out at the base of the altar. According to Lev 23:18, this requirement had to be satisfied only during the feast of Weeks; Exod 29:38-42 extends it to the daily holocaust, and Num 15 further extends it to all holocausts.

The holocaust, as an act by which Yahweh's power and might were acknowledged (Judg 13:16,19-20), is often found in a context in which his power is compared with the inferior power of other gods (Exod 18:10; Judg 6:26, 28; 1 Kgs 18:38). It was offered on particularly solemn occasions, even by a king (1 Kgs 3:4), with a communion sacrifice (peace offering, *šĕlāmîm*) often accompanying it (2 Sam 6:17-18; 1 Kgs 8:64; 9:25). Ezekiel, in his program for the postexilic future, programmed a holocaust to be provided by the prince, with his communion sacrifices, on sabbath days and days of new moon (Ezek 46:1-2,4); but by the later royal period a holocaust was already a daily act in the Temple (2 Kgs 16:15; 1 Chr 16:40). In the postexilic period, its importance in the religious consciousness of Israel was overshadowed by the expiatory sin offering (→ 72-78 below).

68 (B) Communion Sacrifice or Peace Offering. A union between God and the donor was effected by a thanksgiving offering called *zebaḥ šĕlāmîm*, *zebaḥ* alone, or *šĕlāmîm* alone. This sacrifice has frequently been called, under the influence of the LXX, a "peace offering" or "welcome offering," but "communion sacrifice" best describes its essential nature. There were three types of communion sacrifice: the *tôdâ* or sacrifice of praise (Lev 7:12-15; 22:29-30); the *nĕdābâ* or freewill sacrifice, made out of pure devotion and not in fulfillment of a precept or a vow (7:16-17; 22:18-23); and the *neder* or votive offering, made in fulfillment of a vow (7:16-17; 22:18-23).

The ritual of the communion sacrifice is described in Lev 3, and its characteristic feature is that the victim is shared, with portions going to God, to the priest, and to the offerer. The laws about the victims are slightly different from those governing the victims for holocausts: birds are not allowed; the animal may be male or female; and, according to Lev 22:23, the animal may be slightly blemished when the offering is of the freewill type. The imposition of hands, the slaughtering, and the pouring out of blood take place just as in the holocaust.

Yahweh's portion was burned on the altar; it consisted of the fat surrounding the intestines, the kidneys, the liver, and the fat of the sheep's tail. (Fat, like blood, was looked upon as life-giving [Lev 3:16-17; 7:22-24].) The priest received two parts: the breast and the right leg (7:28-34; 10:14-15). The remaining portion went to the one making the offering, who shared it with family and guests. The victim of a *tôdâ* had to be eaten the same day it was offered (7:15), and this sacrifice had to include also an offering of unleavened cakes and wafers and of leavened loaves. One of the cakes was offered to Yahweh and constituted part of the priest's share. The victim of a freewill or a votive sacrifice could be eaten on the morrow of the offering, but if any of it was left on the third day it had to be burned (7:16-17). On the *tôdâ* as a communitarian celebration and on the Passover sacrifice as *tôdâ*, see G. Couturier, *EgThéol* 13 (1982) 5-34.

69 This type of sacrifice was common in Israel from the earliest days, and the early texts often call it simply *zebah* (Josh 22:26-29; 1 Sam 1:21; 2:13,19; 3:14; 2 Sam 15:12; 1 Kgs 8:22; 12:27; 2 Kgs 5:17; 10:24; Isa 1:11; 19:21; Jer 7:22; Hos 3:4; 4:19; Amos 4:4; Exod 23:18; 34:15,25). Frequently it is designated as *šĕlāmîm* (Judg 20:26; 21:4; 1 Sam 13:9; 2 Sam 6:17,18; 24:25; 1 Kgs 3:15; 9:25; 2 Kgs 16:13; Exod 20:24; 32:6; Ezek 43:27; 45:15,17; 46:12). The compound *zebaḥ šĕlāmîm* is almost exclusively used in P and in the Law of Holiness (Lev 17:1-26:46), which is slightly earlier than P and originally had an independent existence. In texts earlier yet, viz., Exod 24:5 and 1 Sam 11:15, the plurals of the two nouns are juxtaposed, as *zĕbāḥîm šĕlāmîm;* but grammar suggests that one of the two words was inserted secondarily as an explanatory gloss when the two words, and the sacrificial realities which they designated, were becoming closely associated or confused. Refined literary study has led to the conclusion that a *zebaḥ* — basically a private offering, made typically on occasions of private devotion or of importance to a family, with a sacrificial meal as the central act — was originally distinct from the *šĕlāmîm* — a public offering, perhaps with a dedicatory function, made on great occasions, with a blood rite as its central act. The two types coalesced in the time of the Law of Holiness and of P, with the main interest then placed in sprinkling the blood and burning the fat on the altar — actions reserved to priests, which meant that the *zebaḥ šĕlāmîm* could thenceforth be offered only at the Temple. (See Rendtorff, *Studien* 119-68, 237-38; Levine, *Presence* 45-52). *Zebaḥ* is itself a generic word for slaughtering, or for sacrifice involving slaughtering, whereas *šĕlāmîm* is a more specific word. There is much difference of opinion on the precise meaning of *šĕlāmîm* (Levine, *Presence* 3-45), but it seems to connote a tribute offered to God with a view to maintaining or reestablishing amicable relations with him (cf. *šālôm*, "peace"). For that reason, perhaps, it was at times used in covenant making. The theory that it was a sacrifice meant for that specific purpose (R. Schmid, *Das Bundesopfer in Israel* [SANT 9; Munich, 1964]) has been criticized both for exaggerating the place of covenant renewal in the Israelite sacrificial system and for limiting the place of the *šĕlāmîm* within that system.

70 We have little information about the ritual followed in the ancient communion sacrifice. That it varied until it was fixed after the exile seems to be indicated in several texts. If the corrected reading of 1 Sam 9:24 actually represents the original, the lay participants ate the fat of a sheep's tail; yet the law of Lev 3:9; 7:3 reserves this for God. At Shiloh the priest had to take pot luck: he stuck a fork into the pot while the meat was boiling and was entitled to whatever he drew forth (1 Sam 2:13-14); yet according to Deut 18:3, he was entitled to the shoulder, jaws, and stomach (Lev 7:34 improved his lot and gave him the uncooked breast and the right leg).

71 How far back can we trace holocausts and communion sacrifices in the history of Israel? Do they date from the period of the exodus, as the pentateuchal laws would lead one to believe? For a direct answer, one might turn to Amos 5:25, where Yahweh asks: "Did you bring me sacrifices and offerings for forty years in the desert, O house of Israel?" In Jer 7:22, Yahweh speaks in a similar strain: "In speaking to your fathers on the day I brought them out of the land of Egypt, I gave them no command concerning holocaust or sacrifice." Still, both Amos and Jeremiah were familiar with the most ancient traditions, J and E, concerning sacrifices offered during the exodus (Exod 3:18; 5:3,8,17; 10:25; 18:12; 32:6,8). And when read in their respective contexts, the two passages from the Prophets are not really so categorical as they seem when taken in isolation. Amos and Jeremiah were preachers, not legalists or historical critics. They were objecting to the empty, formalistic sacrifices offered in their day and were holding up the desert days as the ideal — days when sacrifices were offered with the proper interior dispositions. We must allow for prophetic license in their unqualified statements.

We are justified in assuming that, like other ancient Near Eastern seminomads, the Israelites of the desert wanderings offered animal sacrifices. We must confess, though, that it is impossible, with the data at our disposal, to speak with any certainty of the ritual practice that they followed in doing so. The most primitive ritual elements preserved in our extant texts seem to be those of that particular *zebaḥ* which was the Passover sacrifice.

72   **(C) Sacrifices of Expiation.** These receive a major share of the attention given to sacrifices in the ritual code of the postexilic Temple. There are two: the sin offering and the guilt offering.

(a) SIN OFFERING. The Hebr noun *ḥaṭṭā't* means "sin," and so, when used to designate a particular type of sacrifice, it is usually translated "sin offering." Yet just as the piel of the corresponding denominative vb. has the sense of "to free from sin" (GKC §52h), the noun may signify a sacrifice freeing or purifying from sin (see J. Milgrom, *JAOS* 103 [1983] 250). The ritual texts governing a *ḥaṭṭā't* are found in Lev 4:1-5:13; 6:17-23 ([24-30] → Leviticus, 4:9-10, 15). Some of the details in 5:1-6 are distinctive characteristics of the Mesopotamian apotropaic *šurpu* ritual (M. Geller, *JSS* 25 [1980] 181-92). The dignity of the one making the offering determined the victim to be sacrificed. The high priest was required to offer a bull; similarly, a bull had to be sacrificed when there was question of a collective sin of the whole people. The sin of a prince (*nāsî'*) could be expiated only by the sacrifice of a he-goat, but a private person could offer a she-goat or a sheep. If one was very poor, two turtledoves or pigeons sufficed; one of them was offered as a sacrifice for sin, the other as a holocaust. As an alternative, the poor could offer some flour.

73 The distinguishing characteristics of these sacrifices were the use made of the blood and the disposal of the victim's flesh. When expiation was made for the high priest or for the people as a whole, the sacrificing priest first gathered the blood, went into the sanctuary, and sprinkled the blood seven times on the veil before the Holy of Holies; then he rubbed blood on the horns of the altar of incense and finally poured out what remained at the base of the altar of holocausts. If a prince or a private individual was making atonement, the priest did not enter the sanctuary, but rubbed blood on the horns of the altar of holocausts and poured out the rest at its base. The importance of the blood of the victim in these sacrifices is obvious (see Lev 17:11; Heb 9:22).

Just as in communion sacrifices, all the fat of the victim was burned; but in the sacrifice for sin, the guilty person received no flesh, for the priest took it all. Furthermore, when this sacrifice was offered for the high priest or the community, no one shared in the flesh of the victim; it was taken away and thrown on the refuse heap. A popular theory is that the sin of the guilty party was thought to be transferred to the victim and destroyed along with it. However, the fat of the victim was burned rather as a pleasing sacrifice to God; and in the private sacrifices just mentioned, the priests partook of the flesh of the victims "since it is most sacred" (Lev 6:22 [29]; see 2 Cor 5:21).

74 The description of the sin offering in Num 15:15-31 differs noticeably from the prescription in Lev 4. In the Num passage no provision is made for the sin of a high priest or of a prince. Inadvertent faults committed by the community as a whole may be expiated by the sacrifice of a bull as a holocaust and of a he-goat as a sin offering; such faults committed by an individual may be wiped out by the sacrifice of a she-goat as a sin offering. The ritual details of the sacrifices are not given. According to Num 15:31, no sacrifice can satisfy for a deliberate sin. (See J. Milgrom, in *WLSGF* 211-15.)

75 (b) GUILT OFFERING. The noun *'āšām* designates several related things: offense, the means of repairing an offense, and the type of sacrifice with which we are dealing here, viz., the "guilt offering" or "sacrifice of reparation." The ritual texts governing this sacrifice are found in Lev 5:14-26 (5:14-6:7); 7:1-10 (→ Leviticus,

4:11, 16). Although the ritual is much the same as that of a sin offering, the guilt offering was offered only for private individuals, and the only victim mentioned is a ram. In some instances, in addition to the sacrifices offered, a fine had to be paid (Lev 5:14–16,21–26; Num 5:5–8); but the fine was distinct from the sacrifice itself.

76 (c) PURPOSES OF THESE SACRIFICES. The distinction between the *ḥaṭṭā't* and the *'āšām* is by no means evident. The *ḥaṭṭā't* might seem applicable to sins in general, and the *'āšām* might seem restricted to those sins which required some kind of restitution or redressing of injured rights; but the extant texts do not admit so clear a distinction. In Lev 5:6–7 the two terms even appear to overlap. The problem is made more complex by the fact that the pertinent texts are not all of a piece and have been reworked editorially before reaching their present form in Lev. This lack of consistently clear distinction between the function and purposes of the *ḥaṭṭā't* and those of the *'āšām* in our extant biblical texts suggests that the final editors of the sacrificial prescriptions and descriptions were codifying expiatory sacrifices received in traditional practice as distinct, with the original grounds for their distinction no longer fully perceived and understood.

77 From the surviving evidence, *'āšām* has been interpreted as an adaptation of what was originally an offering in the form of silver or other objects of value, secondarily commuted to an altar sacrifice. *Ḥaṭṭā't* has been interpreted as a coalition of two originally distinct types of sacrifice: one eaten by the priests, which was meant to expiate certain offenses of the people and their leaders, and another not eaten but consumed by burning, which was meant to preserve the sanctuary and its priests from contamination with the unholy, profane, or ritually impure, thus reckoning with impurity as a dynamic force capable of contaminating persons and objects by a sort of contagion (Levine, *Presence* 91–114).

Levine's distinction of the two types of *ḥaṭṭā't* on the basis of the two ways in which the sacrificial parts are consumed has also been made by J. Milgrom (*VT* 26 [1976] 333–37; *RB* 83 [1976] 390–99; *JAOS* 103 [1983] 249–54) but with a different explanation based on the degree of impurity that each type expiated. According to Milgrom, the *ḥaṭṭā't* was always a sacrifice of purification, and so it should never be called a "sin offering." Furthermore, it expiated not persons but objects or places in the Temple, holy in various degrees because of the varying intensity of the divine presence and subject to contamination by correspondingly varying impurity. The *ḥaṭṭā't* eaten by the priests, then, would be one by which the altar of holocausts in the Temple courtyard was purified from a relatively low, less contagious impurity arising from sins of inadvertence committed by an individual Israelite. The burned *ḥaṭṭā't* was either (a) one by which the Hekal within the Temple building itself was purified from a greater impurity resulting from those sins of inadvertence committed by the high priest or by the entire community, or (b) one carried out annually on the Day of Atonement, by which God's throne (the *kappōret;* → 32, 35 above) and the rest of the Temple, including the altar of holocausts, were purified from the greatest impurity: that resulting from sins of willful, unrepented presumption.

78 As for the *'āšām*, Milgrom (*Cult*) develops the thesis that it was a sacrifice made when someone had violated an oath, although with time its need was extended to any case in which a prohibition of the law had been violated. Repentance had to accompany an *'āšām*, and so did confession of one's wrong, if the violation was deliberate (Lev 5:1–6; 16:21; Num 5:6–8).

79 (D) The *minḥâ*. The victim in the sacrifices so far discussed was an animal, but the Israelites also commonly offered various cereals. This offering was known by the generic name *minḥâ*, "gift," and several kinds are listed in Lev 2. There was one of fine wheaten flour mixed with oil; the ritual called for an offering of incense as part of this sacrifice. A handful of the prepared flour and all the incense were burned on the altar, and the priests got the remaining flour (2:1–2; 6:7–11 [14–18]; 7:10). In another sacrifice the same mixture of flour and oil was first baked. A part of the loaf was burned, and the rest went to the priests (2:4–10; 7:9). No leaven was used, but salt was required (2:11–13). Lastly, there was the offering of firstfruits in the form of roasted ears of grain or baked bread, together with oil and incense. Part of the grain and oil and all the incense were burned (2:14–16).

80 The part of the *minḥâ* that was burned was called *'azkārâ*, the precise meaning of which in this context is not certain. It could mean "memorial" (from the vb. *zākar*, "to remember"), in the sense that the offering reminded God of the one who made it. Or it could mean "pledge," in the sense that the part actually offered to God was a token of the donor's willingness to offer his all.

In some cases the cereal alone was offered without oil or incense, as in the high priest's daily offering; and in this instance the entire offering was burned (Lev 6:13–16 [20–23]). Again, when a *minḥâ* was offered by a poor person as a sacrifice for sin (5:11–13), and when it was offered as a "sacrifice for jealousy" (Num 5:15), it consisted of only flour. When the *minḥâ* accompanied a holocaust or a communion sacrifice, a libation of wine was added to the ritual (Exod 29:40; Lev 23:13; Num 15:1–12).

Cereal offerings can be traced to the period before the exile. It has been contended that the word *minḥâ* in preexilic texts is used in its generic sense of "gift" or "offering" to apply to any type of sacrifice. This is not quite true; *minḥâ* is distinguished from *zebaḥ* in 1 Sam 2:29; 3:14; Isa 19:21; from *'ōlâ* in Jer 14:12; Ps 20:4; and from *šelem* in Amos 5:22. In these texts it is a technical term for the cereal offering. The showbread, analogous to the *minḥâ*, is mentioned in 1 Sam 21:3–7.

81 (E) The Showbread. Related to the cereal offerings was the showbread, which is called in Hebrew *leḥem happānîm*, "the bread of the face" (of God) or "the bread of the Presence," and *leḥem hamma'āreket*, "the showbread." This consisted of 12 cakes of fine wheaten flour arranged in two rows on a table before the Holy of Holies; fresh cakes were put on the table every sabbath (Lev 24:5–9). The priests consumed the old cakes at the time of the renewal, and the incense that had been placed alongside each row was burned on the altar of incense. The 12 loaves were a perpetual reminder or pledge of the covenant between Yahweh and the 12 tribes (→ OT Thought, 77:76ff.). The presence of the incense on the table with the loaves gave them something of the character of a sacrifice, even though it was only the incense that was burned on the altar.

82 (F) Perfume Offerings. Incense played a large part in the sacrificial ritual of Israel. The word *qĕṭōret* has the generic meaning of "that which goes up in smoke" and in this wide sense may be applied to anything burned on an altar. In the liturgy, it refers to perfumed offerings, the full expression for which is *qĕṭōret sammîm*. The specific word for incense is *lĕbōnâ*, but incense was only one of several aromatics of which the perfumed mixture was compounded. The others were storax, onyx, and galbanum, which were to be mixed with incense in four equal parts (Exod 30:34–38).

The recipes grew more complicated as time went on, and the rabbinic writings mention one containing 16 ingredients.

The manner of offering was as follows. A priest scooped live coals from the altar of holocausts with a small shovel and sprinkled the aromatic mixture on the coals. He then placed the shovel's contents on the altar of incense. This offering was made every morning and evening (Exod 30:7–8). On the Day of Atonement (→ 148 below) the coals and incense were carried within the Holy of Holies to be burned before the Ark (Lev 16:12–13). Pure unmixed incense (lĕbōnâ) was used when it accompanied a minḥâ or was placed on the table of the showbread.

83 In tracing the history of perfume offerings, we find that the word qĕṭōret, which acquired a restrictive technical meaning after the exile, was used only in its generic sense of "that which goes up in smoke" in pre-exilic texts (1 Sam 2:28; Isa 1:13; see 2 Kgs 16:13,15). Yet, although the terminology did not exist before the exile, the custom of offering incense certainly did. The "incense that comes from Sheba" is used in parallelism with "your holocausts" in Jer 6:20 (see 17:26). Solomon's Temple had an altar of incense (→ 62 above), and the deuteronomic editor of 1 Kgs 3:3 condemned the offering of incense elsewhere than at the Temple. Incense was used quite commonly in the liturgies of other ancient Near Eastern nations; it would be rather surprising if the custom did not exist in Israel (see M. Haran, VT 10 [1960] 113–29).

In the early days censers may have been used for burning incense instead of the stationary altar, as in the story of Nadab and Abihu (Lev 10:1ff.) and in that of Korah in Num 16:1ff. The first certain mention of an altar of incense is in the description of Solomon's Temple. In the early stages of the ritual, pure unmixed incense was used. It formed part of the minḥâ (Lev 2:1ff.), firstfruits (2:15), and the showbread, all of which were preexilic. After the exile, with the further development of the ritual, the four-part mixture alluded to above came into use.

84 **(VI) The Origin of Israelite Sacrifice.** All the postexilic sacrifices of Israelite religion, then, had preexilic antecedents. Some were more ancient than others, and at times one predominated over another, with a subsequent shift in emphasis as the ritual developed. It would be surprising if development had not taken place over such a long span. The fact that we are best informed about the latest stage should not blind us to the fact that the development began centuries before. This brings us to the question of the origin of Israelite ritual.

Without going into an extended discussion of the sacrificial system of Mesopotamia, we can say that the evidence at our disposal does not warrant looking to that area for the source of Israel's rites. Contacts with Mesopotamian ritual are rare and superficial; the differences are fundamental. Blood played little or no part in the Mesopotamian sacrifices, and the two basic forms of Israelite sacrifice, the holocaust and the communion sacrifice, were not in use in Mesopotamia.

The sacrificial system of Arabia was closer to that of Israel, to judge from the meager information at our disposal. Blood was used for libations and domestic animals were slaughtered and eaten; perfume offerings were common in southern Arabia. However, the absence of similarities in essentials prevents our concluding that Israel borrowed from Arabia. The burning of the victim, in whole or in part, was of the essence of the Israelite sacrifice. In Arabia the animal was simply slaughtered and eaten. The few similarities between the two systems can be explained by the distant common origin of the two peoples, by the pastoral life that Israel and Arabia once shared, and by cultural and commercial contacts.

85 It is a different story when we consider Canaan. The biblical information about Canaanite ritual shows it to be similar to Israelite ritual, at least materially. The Canaanite wives of Solomon offered incense and sacrifices to their gods (1 Kgs 11:8). According to 2 Kgs 5:17, Naaman the Syrian offered holocausts and communion sacrifices; and when Elijah had his contest with the prophets of Baal, both he and they prepared their sacrifices in the same fashion (1 Kgs 18). Other passages confirm this evidence; and the biblical condemnation of Canaanite worship is not because of the form that such worship took but because it was offered to idols or performed in proscribed sanctuaries. The terminology of Canaanite ritual, as it is known from Punic and Phoenician inscriptions, was not altogether consistent, but it contains some interesting points of contact with Israelite terminology. The much earlier Ugaritic texts of the 14th cent. BC from Ras Shamra (→ Biblical Archaeology, 74:72) furnish little reliable information beyond a few ritual terms corresponding to those used by Israel. When all the available evidence is assembled, however, there is a definite similarity between Canaanite and Israelite ritual. There were holocausts, communion sacrifices, cereal and perfume offerings in Canaanite ritual, but no particular importance seems to have been attached to blood in the animal sacrifices.

Given the similarities between these two systems, what historical relationship existed between them? Sacrifices in which victims were wholly or partially burned on the altar were common in Canaan before the coming of the Israelites. However, the Israelites do not seem to have offered such sacrifices in the desert days. Rather, something similar to the Passover ritual would have been normal during that pastoral, seminomadic period: The victim was not burned, even in part; but its blood had ritual significance, and the flesh was shared by the participants. (This was precisely the type of sacrifice practiced by nomads in ancient Arabia.) Then when the Israelites came into Canaan, they took over the Canaanite practice of burnt offerings and integrated it gradually into their own system. From that point on the two rituals, Canaanite and Israelite, followed their own lines of development. There is nothing certain about this reconstruction, but it does justice to the available data.

86 **(VII) Human Sacrifice.** When Israelites sacrificed human beings, they incurred the divine wrath evident in Jer 7:31; Ezek 20:25–26,31. Sacrifice of children by Israelites to a god Molech is mentioned in Lev 18:21; 20:2–5; 2 Kgs 23:10; Jer 32:35. Such sacrifices, with burning, took place in the Valley of Hinnom near Jerusalem, according to 2 Kgs 23:10; Jer 32:35. The same kind of sacrifice is mentioned in Deut 12:31; 2 Kgs 16:3; 17:31; 21:6; Jer 7:31; 19:5; Ezek 23:39 without mention of Molech's name. Although the various Israelite attitudes toward the sacrifice of children in the monarchical period may be open to discussion, the OT texts that have come down to us reflect an attitude of strong condemnation of what they regarded as a foreign practice.

87 Since children were sacrificed in the Punic colonies, it can be surmised, but not proved, that the practice existed in Phoenicia, the Punic colonies' motherland and Israel's neighbor. In Punic, the word molk was apparently a technical term designating child sacrifice. The similarity of Punic molk and the OT Molech (Hebr mōlek) has raised the question whether Molech was itself originally a sacrificial term. Scholarly opinion tends to favor the view that both Molech and Punic molk are divine names and that the shift of molk's meaning to that of a technical term is peculiar to Punic. (For surveys of scholarship on human sacrifice and Molech, see H. Cazelles, *DBSup* 5. 1337–46; A. R. W. Green, *The Role of Human Sacrifice in the Ancient Near East* [ASOR Diss. Series 1; Missoula, 1975]; G. C. Heider, *The Cult of Molek* [JSOTSup 43; Sheffield, 1985].)

88 **(VIII) The Meaning of Sacrifice in Israel.** Holocausts, communion sacrifices, sin offerings, guilt offerings: What did all these signify? What was the essential meaning of sacrifice in Israel? Several answers to such questions have been given.

89 **(A) Unsatisfactory Theories.** According to one hypothesis, Israelite sacrifice was a gift of appeasement to a cruel and demanding deity. There is no evidence to support such a position. A more subtle suggestion is that sacrifice was a sort of bilateral contract in which people gave a gift to God and God reciprocated by granting some boon. There is an element of truth in this (→ 93 below), but it implies that God was in much need of a human gift—an idea foreign to Israelite thought.

90 In another theory, sacrifice is pictured as a quasi-magic act by which a person enters into union with God. This theory takes two forms. In the first form, a person achieves union by eating a divine victim. This assumes that Israelite sacrifice was basically totemistic, a view of sacrifice inherited from remote ancestors in Arabia. By eating the animal representing the deity (the totem) the person absorbs a share of the life of the deity. There is no evidence, however, that such a notion really prevailed among the ancient Arabs or that when a totem was eaten it was thought to effect any communication of divine life. In the second form of the theory, the Israelite was supposed to have entered into union with God by immolating a victim that substituted for and represented the donor. The pouring of the victim's blood at the base of the altar is interpreted as an effective symbol bringing the life of the sacrificer into contact with the deity whom the altar represented. Such an interpretation is highly dubious. While the pouring out of the blood around the altar did symbolize the immediate and direct offering of the victim's life to God, it carried with it no connotation of effecting a vital union between the offerer and God.

91 Another fairly widespread theory is that the Israelites, like their Mesopotamian and Canaanite neighbors, considered sacrifice to be a meal prepared for a hungry God. Those who hold this theory point to those passages in which the altar is called God's table and the showbread called God's loaves (→ 8, 64 above), as well as to God's being said to have "smelled the sweet odor" of Noah's holocausts (Gen 8:21). Admittedly, there are certain elements of Israelite sacrifice that suggest the sharing of a meal with Yahweh, especially in the communion sacrifice (the peace offering). Such Israelite practices as the offering of cakes, oil, and wine to Yahweh may have had this meaning in the Canaanite ritual from which they were probably borrowed. But the attitude of authentic Yahwism is expressed quite unequivocally in Ps 50:12–13: "If I were hungry, I would not tell you; for mine are the world and its fullness. Do I eat the flesh of strong bulls, or is the blood of goats my drink?"

92 **(B) Distinctive Understanding of Sacrifice.** What, positively, was the Israelite notion of sacrifice? The answer must begin with an appreciation of Israel's notion of God. He was unique, transcendent, all-powerful, supremely self-sufficient, personal; and because he was personal, he called for a response on the part of his people. This response had to be correspondingly personal, rational. Sacrifice, then, was the external expression of a personal response to a personal God. It

was not a mechanical, magic gesture with an efficacy unrelated to the interior dispositions of the one offering it. If sacrifice was not motivated by sincere interior dispositions, it was empty formalism, a mocking of true divine–human relationship. A failure to recognize this fundamental truth is the basic weakness of the hypotheses rejected above.

It is true that some elements of Israelite ritual and sacrificial vocabulary are rooted in customs antedating the formation of Israel as a nation. However, material similarity is not an indication of real identity with these customs or the primitive theology they reflected. Certain ancient forms were retained but were used as vehicles of new concepts. The same observation holds good for ritual borrowings from neighboring religions; the adoption of pagan ritual does not necessarily indicate adoption of pagan religious thought. Ritual is relatively neutral; it is given specific meaning by the religion that employs it, and the religion of Israel was quite different from and infinitely superior to that of Canaan. Israelite sacrifice, then, was distinctive and difficult to define. Sacrifice was not a simple concept: it was not uniquely the offering of a *gift* to God to acknowledge his dominion, nor uniquely a *means of effecting union* with him, nor uniquely an *act of expiation*. Simultaneously it was all three and more. Let us now study one by one its varied aspects.

93 Sacrifice was a *gift,* but a gift to which God had an imperative right, since anything that people could offer had first come from the bountiful divine hand. "The Lord's are the earth and its fullness; the world and those who dwell in it" (Ps 24:1; also 50:9–13; 1 Chr 29:14). In returning a part of God's property to him, people symbolically acknowledged God's right to it all, and thereby acquired a right to use the rest of it, under God, for their own purposes. This was the idea behind the offering of the firstfruits and the firstborn. From another point of view, since the offerings were staples (meat and vegetables) by which people sustained their lives, the victims represented the life and being of the one offering. In sacrificing, a person symbolically surrendered to God; and God, by accepting, bound himself in some way. It was not a *quid pro quo* notion (→ 89 above), since God had no need of the gift and there could be no proportion between the gift and God's favor.

The essence of the sacrifice did not consist in the destruction of the victim. In fact, in the case of animal sacrifices, the slaughter of the victim was only a preparatory rite and was performed by the offerer, not by the priest. One reason for the destruction of the offering, whether animal or vegetable, was that it made the gift irrevocably definitive and withdrew it completely from ordinary use. Also, it rendered the victim invisible and thereby symbolically sent it into the invisible sphere of the divine. The word for holocaust, *'ōlâ,* means basically "that which goes up." The ritual served to symbolize this idea of "giving," of "sending up" to God. The altar was the symbol of God's presence; and the victim's blood, the most sacred element, was brought into direct contact with this symbol. In every sacrifice, the blood was poured out at the base of the altar; in expiatory sacrifices it was rubbed on the horns of the altar; in sin offerings it was sprinkled on the veil that concealed God's special presence in the Holy of Holies. On the Day of Atonement it was taken inside the Holy of Holies and sprinkled on the propitiatory, God's throne. The combustible parts of the victim were burned and, in a sense, spiritualized as they rose heavenward in the form of smoke.

94 The sacrifice, then, served as a gift expressing the Israelite sense of dependence on God, but it also indicated the *desire for union with God.* The Israelites never entertained a crassly physical notion of this union (→ 90 above); theirs was a more subtle attitude, in harmony with the sublime spiritual transcendence of Yahweh. When God had received his share of the victim, the ones who had presented it ate the remainder in a sacrificial meal. The fact that the one victim had both been offered to God and eaten by the worshipers brought the two parties together in a spiritual communion, establishing and consolidating the covenant bond between the two. This was a joyful occasion and in the early days the communion sacrifice was the most popular in the ritual.

95 Every sacrifice implied at least some notion of *expiation*. The making of the offering necessarily entailed self-denial, and the reestablishment or maintenance of amicable relations with God implied that these relations had been disturbed. The author of 1 Sam 3:14 wrote that "neither sacrifice nor offering will ever wipe out the sin of Eli." The use of blood gave all animal sacrifices expiatory overtones (Lev 17:11), in addition to the specific sacrifices of expiation for various faults (→ 72–78 above).

96 **(IX) Condemnations of Sacrifice.** Given the central importance of sacrifice in Israelite religion, it is surprising to find some harsh condemnations of it in the OT. But an unbiased study of these condemnatory passages reveals implicitly that sacrifice was held in high esteem in Israel and was not a mere external rite of magic efficacy, but an externalization of noble religious sentiments, without which sacrifice was a mockery. Particularly vehement are the attacks of the preexilic prophets (Isa 1:11–17; Jer 6:20; 7:21–22; Hos 6:6; Amos 5:21–27; Mic 6:6–8). These passages have often been interpreted as condemnations of sacrifice in any shape or form, for their language is direct and unconditional. But we must recall that in Hebrew an absolute statement or a direct contrast is often made where we would use a comparison. The wording of Hos 6:6 is a splendid example of this type of expression: "For it is love that I desire, not sacrifice, and knowledge of God rather than holocausts." The laws of parallelism require that we understand the first phase in the same comparative sense as it is expressed in the second: "For it is love that I desire rather than sacrifice." Examples of this manner of speaking can be multiplied many times over, even in the NT (cf. Luke 14:26 and Matt 10:37).

One of the earliest prophets, Samuel, expressed the prophets' attitude toward sacrifice clearly: "Does the Lord desire holocausts and victims, and not rather that the voice of the Lord should be obeyed? For it is better to obey than to sacrifice, and to hearken rather than to offer the fat of rams" (1 Sam 15:22). What the prophets were condemning was formalistic, merely external worship without the proper dispositions. Such "worship" was only an empty rigmarole bordering on superstition.

97 **(X) Other Ritual Acts.** Sacrifice was the central, but not the only, act of Israelite worship. There were also public prayers and various rites of purification and consecration.

(A) Prayer. The fundamental expression of religious sentiment is prayer, that turning of the mind and heart to God which establishes immediate personal contact between a human being and the divinity. Sacrifice is prayer in act. We are concerned here, however, not with private, personal devotion, but with prayer as an element of cult, i.e., liturgical prayer.

The Bible does give formulas for blessing (Num 6:22–27) and for cursing (Deut 27:14–26). It prescribes a formula to be used in the rite of the "bitter water" (Num 5:21–22) and in the situation resulting from the nonapprehension of a murderer (Deut 21:7–8). It gives the formulas to be used in the offering of the firstfruits (Deut 26:1–10) and in the payment of the tithe that was

due every three years (Deut 26:13–15). It specifies the scriptural reading for the Passover celebration (Deut 6:20–25; see Exod 12:26–27).

Although the ritual does not contain any prescription for the prayer formulas to be used during the offering of sacrifices, such formulas certainly existed and were in common use. They are found in every religious ritual throughout the world. Amos (5:23) refers to the singing of the hymns to instrumental accompaniment, but only in a general way. We may assume that the development of liturgical chant kept pace with that of the ritual and of the increasingly specialized priesthood. There were official chanters in Solomon's Temple from the beginning; and the importance of this group grew steadily until, in the postexilic Temple, it enjoyed great prestige. The official hymnbook of the new Temple was the Psalter, and several of its clearly liturgical hymns had already been in use during the royal period.

98 The ideal place for prayer was the Temple precincts, with one's face turned toward the Holy Place (Pss 5:8; 28:2; 138:2). When exile or absence made this ideal an impossibility, the expatriates did the best they could by facing in the direction of Jerusalem (1 Kgs 8:44,48; Dan 6:11). The synagogues of the postexilic period (→ 56 above) were constructed so that the faithful would be able to direct their prayers to the Holy Place.

Information about the times for official prayer services is scanty. Appropriate evening and morning prayers are found in Pss 4 and 5 respectively. Judith timed her prayer to coincide with the evening incense offering in the Temple (Jdt 9:1); and Daniel followed what seems to have been the general custom of praying three times a day, evening, morning, and noon (Dan 6:11; Ps 55:18). But the reference in these texts is to private, individual prayer. During the period in which they were written there were only two daily services in the Temple, one in the morning and the other in the evening.

99 An erect, standing posture seems to have been usual for prayer during the OT period. Solomon, however, is said to have knelt down (2 Chr 6:13), and in Neh 9:3–5 there is an interesting analogy to the *Flectamus Genua–Levate* procedure of the Latin liturgy. In this penitential rite the people stood for the reading; then they fell to their knees for the confession of sins and remained in this position until the levites cried: *qûmû* (*levate*). External body posture is intended to express one's internal dispositions, and one's usual disposition before God is humble submission. In Ps 95:6 we read: "Come, let us bow down in worship; let us kneel before the Lord who made us" (Invitatory for Matins in the Roman Breviary). It is not surprising, then, to read of people kneeling in prayer (1 Kgs 8:54; Isa 45:23; Dan 6:11) with arms raised toward heaven (1 Kgs 8:22,54; Isa 1:15; Lam 2:19). Other texts suggest the Muslim custom of falling to the knees and pressing the forehead to the ground (Pss 5:8; 99:5; also MT of 99:9, "to his holy mountain").

100 **(B) Purifications.** Modern minds find strange the OT concepts of "cleanness" and "uncleanness," especially when "uncleanness" is described as the result of contact with the sacred. In the minds of the Israelites, certain things, both profane and sacred, possessed mysterious qualities that communicated themselves to any who came into contact with them and set these people in a class apart from the ordinary. In order to return to the everyday world and activity, they had to be "purified." Undoubtedly this attitude reflected primitive mentality and customs; but the resulting legislation served a sublime purpose by putting Israel in a class apart. The pagans might touch this or that and eat anything with impunity, but not the people of Israel.

They belonged to an all-pure, transcendent God and had to reflect his holiness. Several different rites were used to restore an "unclean" person to normalcy.

101   (a) SACRIFICES AND RITUAL WASHING. Following childbirth a woman was required to offer a holocaust and a sin offering (Lev 12:1–8). For people who considered marriage something sacred, childbirth the greatest of blessings, and sterility a curse, a new mother was certainly not, by the very fact of her motherhood, in a "state of sin." But she had come into contact with, as it were, the creative power of God and consequently had to be "purified" in the ritual sense before resuming normal activities. Analogously, the church, which considers matrimony a sacrament and reveres motherhood, has a ceremony of "churching" after childbirth — with this same idea in mind.

102   When "lepers" were declared healed, they had to offer a sacrifice of reparation or a sin offering and a holocaust (Lev 14:10–32). Here again, there is no question of moral guilt, for the same sacrifices were required of a man or woman who had contacted the types of ritual irregularity described in Lev 15:14–15,29–30. A Nazirite who touched a corpse had to offer a sacrifice for sin, a holocaust, and a sacrifice for reparation (Num 6:9–12). The same three sacrifices were required at the expiration of the term of his vow (Num 6:13–20).

103   Sometimes ritual washing accompanied sacrifices of purification; sometimes it was a distinct rite. A priest washed himself ritually before exercising sacred functions (Exod 29:4; 30:17–21; Lev 8:6; 16:4). Utensils, clothing, or people had to be washed if they had come into contact with a legally unclean person or object (Lev 11:24–25,28,32,40; 15; 22:6) or even with something sacred. The metal pot in which sacrificial meat had been cooked had to be washed thoroughly afterward; if an earthenware vessel had been used, the law prescribed that it be subsequently broken (Lev 6:21). After the high priest came out of the Holy of Holies on the Day of Atonement, he had to change clothes and wash himself from head to toe. The man who drove the scapegoat into the desert and burned the sin-offering victims had to do the same (Lev 16:23–28). This prescription also bound those who participated in the ritual of the red heifer (Num 19:7–10,21). A seven-day period of purification was prescribed for soldiers who had engaged in a holy war and for all their garments (Num 31:16–24).

104   (b) RITUAL OF THE RED HEIFER. If the booty from a holy war was of metal, it had to be washed in special water called *mê middâ*, "purifying water" (Num 31:22–23). The preparation of the water is described in Num 19:1–10. An unblemished red heifer that had never been yoked was slaughtered outside the town by a layman, while a priest looked on. It was then completely burned, and while it was burning, the priest tossed into the pyre cedarwood, hyssop, and scarlet yarn. The resulting ashes were gathered up and stored to be used in the preparation of lustral water. Some of the ashes were put into a receptacle into which water coming directly from a spring or stream was poured. If all this smacks of magic, it may be because the rite was originally pagan and was taken over and sanctified by the Israelites. Red is considered apotropaic (i.e., empowered to turn away evil) by many, and purifying powers are attributed to the ashes of burned animals and running water. This water was sprinkled on anyone who had come into contact with a corpse, bones, or a tomb, and on the house and furnishings of the dead (Num 19:11–22). Apart from these instances and the one mentioned in Num 31:22–23, ordinary water was used for ritual ablutions.

105   (c) RITUAL FOR LEPROSY. The Hebr word translated as "leprosy," *ṣāraʿat*, does not refer to Hansen's disease, which is what we normally mean by leprosy. The biblical disease was noticeably less serious, for it was curable and its symptoms were those of a number of relatively superficial skin diseases (Lev 13:1–44). The disease, when so diagnosed by a priest, rendered people ritually unclean. They then had to move to a safe distance from town until cured (2 Kgs 7:3). It was for the priest to determine that the cure had taken place (Lev 14:3) and to perform the rite of purification.

106   This rite is described in Lev 14, which is apparently a fusion of two rituals, one primitive and the other more recent. In the primitive rite a vessel was filled with "living" water and over this a bird was slaughtered so that its blood ran into the water. A live bird was then plunged into the water, and cedarwood, scarlet yarn, and hyssop were added. Finally, the bird was allowed to fly away. Lepers were sprinkled with this water and declared pure; but it was not until seven days later, after having shaved their whole body, washed their clothes, and bathed that they were definitively clean (Lev 14:2–9). This rite contained vestiges of very ancient superstitions. Unsightly skin diseases were considered to be caused by a devil, who must be expelled. As in the case of the red heifer, the reddened water was used for its apotropaic qualities; and the escaping bird symbolized the fleeing demon.

In the more recent ritual (Lev 14:10–32) the cured person offered a sacrifice for reparation, a sin offering, and a holocaust. With blood from the first sacrifice the priest daubed the subject's right ear, right thumb, and right big toe; he then anointed the same members with oil and poured oil on the former leper's head. This anointing is paralleled in the Mesopotamian and Canaanite ceremony accompanying the freeing of a slave.

107   Especially strange is the notion of "leprosy" in clothes, textiles, and even houses. Here the "disease" was some sort of mildew or fungus growth. If the affected article did not respond to washing, it had to be burned. If it did respond, it was washed again and declared clean (Lev 13:47–59). In the case of houses, the discolored stones were removed and the walls scraped. If the condition continued spreading, the house was torn down; if it stopped, the house was declared clean. In either case, the same ritual of expiation had to be performed as that described in Lev 14:29. Archaic and mysterious though these notions and rites may be, they turn up only in postexilic texts. A consciousness of guilt that was heightened by the exile and a stress on God's transcendence in the theology of the P tradition brought about a preoccupation with cleanness and uncleanness that amounted to almost an obsession in P legislation. The legislators adduced instance after instance of possible uncleanness and even reached back into the dim past in their desire for completeness.

108   (d) CONSECRATION RITES. Purification expressed a negative aspect of holiness by removing a legal obstacle to contact with the divine. Consecration was the positive side; it readied a person or an object for such contact or even resulted from the contact. It consisted fundamentally in removing people or things from the realm of the profane and dedicating them to a sacred purpose. This dedication did not always require a distinct ceremony; any entrance into the realm of the sacred effected a consecration. For example, soldiers who fought in a holy war and the prizes they captured were automatically dedicated to God; priests were consecrated by the simple fact of their service of the sanctuary. Such consecration imposed obligations. The priests had to observe strict regulations safeguarding their purity (Lev 21:1-8); the soldiers in the holy war had to remain continent for the duration (1 Sam 21:6; 2 Sam 11:11), and the booty they took could be used for no one's personal advantage (Josh 6:18ff.; 1 Sam 15:18-19).

109 We have been discussing examples of automatic consecration. As the ritual developed, specific ceremonies appeared. In the postexilic period, the high priest was consecrated by an elaborate rite involving purification, investiture, and anointing. Similarly, the sanctuary, the altar, and sacred objects had to be anointed (Exod 30:26-29; 40:9-11; Lev 8:10). In the preexilic period it was the king who was the "anointed one" (→ OT Thought, 77:155), and as a sign of his sacred character he wore the *nēzer* or crown (2 Sam 1:10; 2 Kgs 11:12; Ps 89:40). The postexilic high priest wore a similar ornament, a golden flower (*ṣîṣ*) as part of his headdress (Exod 39:30; Lev 8:9). The root meaning of the verb *nāzar* is "to set apart" and hence "to place under interdict" or "to consecrate." The derived noun, *nāzîr,* signifies a dedicated person. Allied to this root is *ndr,* and from it comes the noun *neder,* a vow.

110 **(C) Vows.** A vow in OT thought was a conditioned promise to dedicate a person or thing to God. If God granted a certain request, the beneficiary would fulfill a promise. It was a special type of prayer in which a person not only asked for a favor but strengthened the request by promising to give something in return. Not all vows were conditional, although this seems to have been the case in the early days. As time went on, simple disinterested promises became more of a rule than an exception.

The taking of a vow imposed a solemn obligation, but the law ruled out certain vows, whether because the thing promised already belonged to God, like the first-born of cattle (Lev 27:26), or because it was unworthy of him, like the proceeds of sacred prostitution (Deut 23:19). Women were restricted in the matter of vows; e.g., a father could cancel a vow taken by his unmarried daughter; a husband could annul his wife's vow. A widow or divorcee, however, could assume full responsibility for a vow (Num 30:4-17). In later legislation, people were allowed to substitute a sum of money for the specific objects promised (Lev 27:1-25).

111 *Nazirites.* Not only some object but even one's own person could be consecrated to God for a specific length of time. One thus became a Nazirite (Num 6:1-21). During the specified time, the person had to abstain from all alcoholic drink, even wine, to leave his hair uncut, and to shun all contact with a corpse. This last prescription was interpreted quite strictly; if anyone died while a Nazirite was present, the latter was defiled and had to begin again by shaving his head and offering various sacrifices (6:9-12). When he had completed the term of his vow, he offered a holocaust, a sin offering, and a communion sacrifice; he shaved his head and burned the hair as part of the communion sacrifice (6:18). He then returned to normal life.

These prescriptions seem to be an adapted mitigation of an ancient custom according to which Nazirite consecration was for life and was more charismatic than entirely voluntary (see Amos 2:11-12). In the story of Samson we see a consecration begun while he was still in his mother's womb (Judg 13:4-5,7,13-14). The element of uncut hair seems to have been the characteristic feature of the Nazirite. Soldiers who fought in a holy war did not cut their hair (Judg 5:2; see Deut 32:42); and when Samuel's mother dedicated him to God's service, she promised that his head would never be shaved (1 Sam 1:11). Samson's long hair, the sign of his lifelong consecration, was the source of his extraordinary strength (Judg 16:17).

PREEXILIC ISRAELITE FEASTS

112 **(I) Daily Services.** The Israelites observed several important holy days each year; but before we discuss them, it would be helpful to see something of the everyday Temple services. According to Exod 29:38-42 and Num 28:2-8, two lambs were to be offered daily as holocausts, one in the morning and the other in the evening. Along with the holocausts went an offering of flour mixed with oil, a libation of wine, and an incense offering (Exod 30:7-8). This daily ritual was introduced after the exile, although Chr characteristically speaks of it as existing during the royal period (1 Chr 16:40; 2 Chr 13:11; 31:3). The preexilic ritual is reflected in Ezek 46:13-15, where no mention is made of an evening holocaust. During the monarchy there was a morning holocaust and an afternoon cereal offering (*minḥâ;* see 2 Kgs 16:15; Ezra 9:4-5; Dan 9:21). The postexilic custom of two holocausts continued into NT times, but the hour of the second shifted from twilight to midafternoon. On the sabbath the same ritual was observed, but in each holocaust two lambs were offered rather than one as on ordinary days (Num 28:9-10). On the first day of each month, the day of the new moon, there was a special ritual calling for a holocaust of two bulls, a ram, and seven lambs, together with offerings and libations, and the sacrifice of a goat as a sin offering (Num 28:11-15).

113 **(II) Liturgical Calendars.** The more important feast days, of course, had to be indicated by a liturgical calendar. Several such calendars are given in the OT, and it will be necessary to consider them separately. (See also van Goudoever, *Biblical Calendars.*)

The Elohist Code gives the simplest and most succinct calendar (Exod 23:14-17). It prescribes a *ḥag* or pilgrimage (cf. Muslim *ḥajj*) three times a year: the pilgrimage of the unleavened bread in the month of Abib (March-April), the pilgrimage of the grain harvest (late spring), and the pilgrimage of the fruit harvest (autumn).

114 *The Yahwist Code* (Exod 34:18-23) is the same as the Elohist Code but with slight variations, e.g., calling the pilgrimage of the grain harvest the "feast of Weeks" and the fruit harvest "at the turn of the year." This latter phrase is, however, synonymous with the Elohist Code's "at the close of the year." And the vagueness of both terms indicates that the prescribed pilgrimages took place not on fixed dates but according to the variable agricultural seasons. Before the centralization of worship each locale determined its own dates within the prescribed general seasons, since the people made the pilgrimage to a local shrine.

115 *The Deuteronomic Code* (Deut 16:1-17) introduces only slight changes, the most significant of which is the specification of the place of pilgrimage: "in the place which he (Yahweh) will choose." The three annual feasts are: (1) the Passover, joined to the feast of

Unleavened Bread of the earlier codes; (2) the feast of Weeks, with the explanation that it takes place seven weeks after the beginning of the grain harvest; and (3) the feast of Tabernacles or Tents (sukkôt), corresponding to the fruit harvest festival of the earlier codes. No explanation is offered for this new term.

116   *The Priestly Collection* (Lev 23). This has more precision in the matter of dates, along with a new calendar (the Babylonian), according to which the year begins in the spring instead of in the autumn. But we also find a problem, for Lev 23 gives clear evidence of being a conflation of two different sources: it has two titles (vv 2 and 4), two endings (vv 37 and 44), two sets of prescriptions for the feast of Tabernacles (vv 34–36 and 39–43). In the view of R. de Vaux, one of these sources is the Holiness Code from the end of the royal period (→ Leviticus, 4:3, 35), and the other is made up of exilic and postexilic additions. To the royal period would belong these verses: 4–8, dealing with the Passover, to be celebrated on the 14th of Nisan (the old Abib) and to be followed by the ancient week-long feast of Unleavened Bread; 16–21a, dealing with the feast of Weeks, to be celebrated fifty days after the feast of Unleavened Bread; 34b–36, dealing with the feast of Tabernacles, to begin on the 15th of Tishri (September–October) and to last for seven days, followed by a solemn day of rest; and 37–38, the conclusion. Postexilic additions would be these verses: 3, dealing with the sabbath; 10–15, dealing with the feast of the First Sheaf; 24–25, dealing with the celebration of the 1st of Tishri; 27–32, dealing with the Day of Atonement (10th of Tishri); 39–43, giving a different ritual for the feast of Tabernacles; and 44, a new conclusion (→ Leviticus, 4:43–48).

117   Ezek 45:18–25 gives a type of liturgical calendar, seemingly an idealization similar to the prophet's view of the new Temple. There is no evidence that Ezekiel's calendar was ever followed; the calendar which prevailed was that of the Priestly Collection (Lev 23), which can be supplemented by the table of the sacrifices to be offered on specific days found in Num 28–29. These are the passages that provide the calendar of observance after the exile, in the Second Temple.

Now we shall consider individually the more important Israelite religious festivals.

118   **(III) The Sabbath.**

(A) Origin. Our Eng word is virtually a transcription of Hebr *šabbāt,* which, in turn, is seemingly a derivative, albeit irregular, of the vb. *šābat,* "to cease," and, by extension, "to cease working, to rest." At least this is the popular etymology of the word given in Gen 2:2–3, but the scientific derivation is not totally clear, nor is the origin of the religious institution itself. All attempts to prove that the Hebrews (*via* Ezekiel) borrowed it from the Babylonians fail completely. Such attempts are based chiefly on the similarity between *šabbāt* and the Akkadian word *šappattu,* signifying the middle day of the month, the day of the full moon. However, the only admissible similarity is etymological; and from this point of view, the common denominator would be the meaning of "bringing to a halt": the *šappattu* brought a month to a halt; the Hebr sabbath marked the end of a week. As for the suggestion that Ezekiel (20:12,20; 46:1) adapted Babylonian customs to Israelite life, the fact is that, far from introducing the sabbath, he presents it as a long-standing institution to which his compatriots have been unfaithful (20:13; 22:26; 23:38). Others think that the origin of the sabbath may lie culturally in regularly occurring market days, although in that case the theologized observance of the sabbath as a day of rest in Israel would have put an end to the very purpose for which it was originally observed. Still

others seek the origins in the ancient custom of prolonging important events, celebrations, mourning, for seven days—a phenomenon widespread in the ancient Near East. None of these directions has led to any supported conclusions on the origin of the Israelite sabbath. (See B. E. Shafer, *IDBSup* 760–62.)

119   Exod 16:22–30 suggests that the sabbath existed before the Sinaitic covenant, and Gen 2:2–3 traces it to the time of creation itself. Such claims are not based on any real historical memory; yet the sabbath is mentioned in all the traditions that make up the Pentateuch: in the Elohist Code (Exod 23:12), in the Yahwist Code (Exod 34:21), in the two versions of the Decalogue (Deut 5:12–14 and Exod 20:8–10), and in the Priestly Collection (Exod 31:12–17). The Israelite observance of the sabbath is surely ancient. More than this we cannot say at present.

120   **(B) Significance.** The role that the sabbath played in Israelite life and thought made it quite unique. It was not just a holiday on which to rest up for another week of work. It was related to the covenant that God had made with his people and was a day consecrated to him in a special way. Initially, the law of the sabbath rest was simply stated; later forms of the law added motives that betray two different theological perspectives. First, in Deut 5:14b–15 humanitarian factors are stressed: one cannot work without the proper rest. But at the same time, the religious aspect is not neglected: the sabbath will serve as a memorial of God's liberation of his people from slave labor in Egypt and bringing them into a "resting place" (12:9; see Ps 95:11). Second, Exod 20:11 expresses a motive that reflects the attitude of the Priestly school: "In six days the Lord made the heaven and the earth, the sea and all that is in them, but on the seventh day he rested. That is why the Lord has blessed the sabbath day and made it holy" (see Gen 2:2–3; Exod 31:12–17).

Both motives are an expression of covenant theology; only the points of view are different. The deuteronomic view focuses on one of the parties to the covenant, the people; the Priestly view focuses on the other party, God. The latter outlook prevailed and gave the sabbath its predominantly religious tone (Lev 23:3,28; Exod 20:11; 31:15). As the postexilic period began, Israelites observing the sabbath were made conscious of celebrating the lordship of Yahweh over all creation; see F. Götz, *TBei* 9 (1978) 243–56.

121   **(C) Observance.** As a sign of the covenant, observance of the sabbath indicated fidelity to the covenant and was an assurance of salvation (Isa 58:13–14; Jer 17:19–27); nonobservance was tantamount to apostasy (Exod 31:14; 35:2; Num 15:32–36). If the people as a whole neglected the sabbath, God would punish them severely (Ezek 20:13; Neh 13:17–18).

In the early days, however, the sabbath was a joyful, relaxed holiday, predominantly religious but not overly restrictive. Manual labor and business were suspended, but the people could move about freely. They made pilgrimages to nearby sanctuaries (Isa 1:13; Hos 2:13) or went to consult their prophets (2 Kgs 4:23). Then during the exile, when celebration of the other feasts was impossible, the sabbath came into prominence as the distinctive sign of the covenant. After the exile, although the sabbath continued to be a day of pleasurable relaxation, it was subject to tighter restrictions. All business and travel were forbidden (Isa 58:13); the people could not carry anything from their homes or do any work (Jer 17:21–22, a postexilic addition). During his second visit to Jerusalem, Nehemiah reacted vigorously to the people's neglect of the sabbath laws by ordering the city gates closed and extracting a promise of future fidelity from the people (Neh 10:32; 13:15-16,19-22). As time went on, the restrictions were multiplied until, by NT times, they were meticulous.

122   (IV) Passover and the Feast of Unleavened Bread. As we have seen, the important holy days in the calendar of ancient Israel were the three pilgrimage feasts (Unleavened Bread, Weeks, and Tabernacles) and the Passover. The Passover and the feast of Unleavened Bread were later combined. Information about the Passover, which is not abundant and not always clear, is contained in two sets of texts, the liturgical and the historical.

123   (A) History—Liturgical Texts. These texts come from different pentateuchal traditions, formulated at different times; thus it is possible to use them as guides in tracing the development of the great Jewish feasts.

(a) PRIESTLY TRADITION. By the time this latest of the pentateuchal traditions was formulated, the celebration of the Passover had been joined to that of the feast of Unleavened Bread. The pertinent texts are: Lev 23:5-8; Num 28:16-25 (see 9:1-4); Exod 12:1-20, 40-51. From them we learn that the Passover was to be celebrated in conjunction with the full moon of the first month of the year (March–April). On the tenth of this month each family was to select an unblemished, male, one-year-old lamb. At twilight on the 14th (Exod 12:6: "between the two evenings"), the lamb was slaughtered and the blood sprinkled on the lintels and doorposts of the house. During this night of the full moon the lamb was roasted and eaten; not one of its bones could be broken, and whatever was left over after the meal had to be burned. Unleavened bread and bitter herbs were eaten also, and those who partook of the meal had to be dressed as if ready for a journey. In case a family was too small to consume a whole lamb, it joined some neighbors. Slaves and resident aliens (gērîm) could take part, so long as they were circumcised.

On the 15th of the month, the week-long feast of Unleavened Bread began. All leftover leavened bread had to be destroyed and for the following week only unleavened bread could be eaten. The first and seventh days of the festival were holidays on which religious gatherings took place. The same ritual for the Passover-Unleavened Bread feasts is reflected in Ezek 45:21, in Ezra 6:19-22, and in the "Passover Papyrus" from Elephantine (→ History, 75:125). This papyrus, from 419 BC, insists on the dates to be observed, an indication that the dates are an innovation for these colonists.

124   (b) DEUTERONOMIC TRADITION. Let us go back to an earlier stage in the celebration of the two feasts. The pertinent text, Deut 16:1-8, is an artificial welding of two distinct rituals, one referring to the Passover and the other to the feast of Unleavened Bread. Deut 16:1,2,4b-7 deals with the Passover, which was to be celebrated during the month of Abib (March–April); no specific dates are given. The victim could be a calf or a sheep or a goat; it was to be slaughtered at sundown, cooked, and eaten that same night. But all this was to take place at the Temple, and the next morning all were to go home. Deut 16:3,4a,8 deals with the feast of Unleavened Bread, when for seven days the people were to eat the unleavened "bread of affliction." The seventh day was to be a day of rest and of religious convocation. These two rituals imply a distinction between the two festivals, marked by the departure, on the evening after the Passover, of all who had taken part in that solemnity.

The deuteronomic ritual for Passover was followed under Josiah (2 Kgs 23:21-23; → 126 below), and the text does not even mention the feast of Unleavened Bread. However, the author takes pains to point out that this Passover was something new. The Chronicler also describes Josiah's Passover celebration (2 Chr 35:1-18) but inserts into his description practices followed later. He mentions the feast of Unleavened Bread as in Deut 16:7-8, but he also mentions the novelty of Josiah's Passover ritual (2 Chr 35:18). For an idea of the newness of the deuteronomic ritual we must compare it with what the older calendars tell us.

125   (c) ANCIENT LITURGICAL CALENDARS. The two oldest calendars (Exod 23:15; 34:18) mention the feast of Unleavened Bread but not the Passover. They prescribe that unleavened bread be eaten for a week during the month of Abib; this festival was one of the three pilgrimage (ḥag) feasts (Exod 23:14,17; 34:23). The Passover is mentioned in Exod 34:25, but this verse does not deal with the pilgrimages nor does Exod 23:18. Yet the word ḥag is used in both these verses; therefore they must have been edited after Deut had classified the Passover as a pilgrimage feast. It is this that seems to constitute the novelty of the deuteronomic Passover ritual observed in the central sanctuary. Formerly Passover had been a local, family affair (Exod 12:21-23; Deut 16:5), distinct from the Unleavened Bread pilgrimage. But since both occurred in the same month and shared several features, it is not surprising that they were finally joined together. This combination had not taken place before Josiah's day (ca. 620), and the first reference to them as one festival is in Ezek 45:21 (during the exile, after 587) and in the Priestly ritual. The Chronicler's description of Hezekiah's solemn Passover (2 Chr 30) is clearly anachronistic (yet see F. L. Moriarty, CBQ 27 [1965] 404-6).

126   (B) History—Josiah's Passover. Was the deuteronomic Passover celebrated under Josiah really new or was it rather a return to an older, long-neglected custom? Some passages (2 Kgs 23:22; 2 Chr 35:18) would seem to support the latter view. Two questions are involved, however: the joining of the Passover with the feast of Unleavened Bread and the restriction of the celebration of the Passover to Jerusalem. It has often been alleged that Josh 5:10-12 points to an original combination of the two feasts. This passage tells how, when the Israelites pitched camp at Gilgal, they celebrated the Passover on the evening of the 14th and on that same day (according to the better reading) "they ate of the produce of the land in the form of unleavened bread and parched grain." But it is difficult to see any real resemblance between this eating of unleavened cakes on the day of the Passover celebration and the seven-day festival that is mentioned in the liturgical texts. As far as can be determined, the two feasts were still separate when the deuteronomic legislation was promulgated. The celebration of the Passover under Josiah, which was inspired by Deut, did not include the feast of Unleavened Bread.

On the other hand the restriction of the Passover celebration to Jerusalem was a deuteronomic innovation. Before the monarchy, Passover may have been celebrated at a central tribal shrine (2 Kgs 23:22; 2 Chr 35:18); before the settlement in Canaan it had been a tribal feast. But with the disintegration of tribal unity that followed upon this settlement, Passover became a family feast. This may be why it was not mentioned in Exod 23 and 24 and also why the Yahwist ritual of Exod 12:21-23 was so detailed: individual families would have needed clear instructions. The feast of Unleavened Bread remained a group festival, a pilgrimage to a local sanctuary. With the eventual deuteronomic insistence on Jerusalem as the only legitimate locale for both feasts, they were brought into conjunction.

127   (C) Origin of Passover. Etymology is of little help here. The popular explanation given in Exod

12:13,23,27 links the name of the feast (*pesaḥ*) with the fact that the destroying angel "jumped over, passed by" (*psḥ*) the homes of the Hebrews during the execution of the tenth plague; but this is popular, not scientific, etymology. The Akkadian word *pašâḫu*, to "appease," does not apply, for the Passover was not an expiatory feast. More recently it has been suggested that the Hebrew is a transcription of an Egyptian word meaning "a stroke, a blow," and the reference was to the blow that Yahweh struck at Egypt; but this is hardly tenable.

Looking to the rite itself, we find it characteristically pastoral, and no other Israelite rite resembles so closely those of the ancient nomadic Arabs. Passover required no priest, no altar, and the blood of the victim played an important role. Originally a young animal was sacrificed to obtain fertility for the whole flock, and the blood was put on the tentpoles to drive away evil powers (see Exod 12:23: the Destroyer). This ritual has all the appearance of a rite celebrated when the tribe broke camp to head for the fresh spring pastures. The nomadic character of Passover is further suggested by several features: the victim was roasted; the meat was eaten with unleavened bread and bitter (wild, not cultivated) herbs; and the participants were to be dressed for immediate departure, with their shepherd's crooks in hand. The later texts that fix the dates for the celebration of the Passover reflect the pastoral, nomadic origin of the feast. They specify the 14th–15th of the first month (Abib: later Nisan; our March–April), precisely at the time of the full moon. In the desert life, a brightly lit night would be the logical choice for such a festival. All the evidence, therefore, points to the fact that the Passover went back to the days when the Israelites were leading a seminomadic existence, even to the time before the exodus. This may be the feast that the Israelites, while still in Egypt, wanted to celebrate in the desert (Exod 5:1), permission for which was refused by the Pharaoh.

128 (D) Origin of Unleavened Bread (*maṣṣôt* or matzoth). This feast marked the beginning of the barley harvest. For the first seven days of the harvest the only bread eaten was with flour from the new grain, prepared without leaven. Containing nothing of the "old year," it symbolized a fresh start. Furthermore, there was an offering to Yahweh from the new crops, but this was merely an anticipation of the more formal offering of firstfruits on the feast of Weeks that marked the end of the grain harvesting season, 50 days after the beginning of the barley harvest. Since the feast of Unleavened Bread was an agricultural feast and was not celebrated until after settlement in Canaan (Lev 23:10), the Israelites may have borrowed it from the Canaanites. However, they made it an Israelite feast, reckoning it from sabbath to sabbath and fixing the main harvest feast (Weeks) seven weeks later (neither the sabbath nor the week was known outside Israel—see de Vaux, *AI* 186–88). Since it was an agricultural feast, determined by the readiness of the barley harvest, it could be dated no more precisely than within the month in which this harvest normally occurred, Abib.

129 The deuteronomic legislation and the reform of Josiah brought about some precision in this matter, causing complications in the process. The Passover became a pilgrimage feast, and its proximity to the feast of Unleavened Bread led to an eventual combination of the two sometime between the reform of Josiah (621) and the exile (587–539). Whereas the date of the Passover was determined by the full moon, the feast of Unleavened Bread had depended on the harvest and was supposed to begin and end on a sabbath. As it turned out, the Passover took precedence: On whatever day it occurred, the feast of Unleavened Bread began on the next day and lasted a week. Moreover, the two feasts took on a profound new meaning as commemorations of God's deliverance of his people from Egypt, which had taken place at the same time of the year.

(Le Déaut, R., *La nuit pascale* [AnBib 22; Rome, 1963]. Segal J. B., *The Hebrew Passover* [London, 1963]. For the Passover rite of the earliest rabbinic period: Bokser, B. M., *The Origins of the Seder* [Berkeley, 1984].)

130 (V) Feast of Weeks—Pentecost. This feast is called the Harvest feast in Exod 23:16, the feast of the Wheat Harvest in Exod 34:22. In the latter passage it is called also the feast of Weeks, but this may be a gloss added to identify it with the pilgrimage of the weeks mentioned in Deut 16:9–10. Here we learn that the feast was to be celebrated seven weeks after the beginning of the barley harvest (the feast of Unleavened Bread). The term "feast of Weeks" turns up in Num 28:26 also, along with "feast of the Firstfruits"; for the token offering of firstfruits at the beginning of the barley harvest had been only an anticipation of this, the definitive firstfruit offering.

Like all harvest feasts, it was a joyful occasion (Deut 16:11; Isa 9:2). The complete ritual for its celebration is given in Lev 23:15–21. Counting seven full weeks from the day following the sabbath on which the first barley sheaf was offered to God, we arrive at the day following the seventh sabbath, exactly fifty days later. (Thus the feast ultimately came to be known as Pentecost, from the Gk word for "fiftieth" [2 Macc 12:31–32; Tob 2:1].) The ceremony consisted in offering two leavened loaves made from the new wheaten flour. The use of unleavened bread at the beginning of the harvest, 50 days before, had marked a fresh start; but now that the harvest was over, normal customs were resumed. There was thus a sort of organic unity between the feast of Weeks and the earlier feast of Unleavened Bread, and through the latter, with the Passover.

131 Since the feast of Weeks presumed an agricultural economy, the Israelites began to celebrate it only after the entrance into Canaan, probably adopting it from the Canaanites. There was at first no fixed date for its celebration (Exod 23:16; 34:22). Deut 16:9–10 adds precision in relating the feast of Weeks to the feast of Unleavened Bread; but the date of the latter feast was itself still rather flexible. Finally, when the Passover and the feast of Unleavened Bread were joined and given definite dates, the feast of Weeks also acquired a fixed place in the calendar. Not all accepted this dating without demur, however. In the calendar given by *Jubilees* and followed at Qumran (→ Apocrypha, 67:18, 99), the feasts fell on the same days of the week each year. According to this reckoning, the offering of the first sheaf, which was to take place "on the day after the sabbath," occurred not on the Sunday following the Passover, but a week later, on the 26th of the month. This put the feast of Weeks on the 15th of the third month.

132 Although originally an agricultural feast, Pentecost later acquired even deeper religious significance by being related to the exodus. According to Exod 19:1, the Israelites arrived at Sinai in the third month after their departure from Egypt. Since this departure had taken place in the middle of the first month, the feast of Weeks was seen to coincide with the date of their arrival at Sinai and took on added stature as a commemoration of the Sinaitic covenant. This connection is mentioned explicitly in *Jubilees*. At Qumran, too, the renewal of the covenant was celebrated on the feast of Weeks, the most important feast in the Qumran calendar (B. Noack, *ASTI* 1 [1962] 72–95). Many detect in Acts

2 the Sinai covenantal background of Pentecost. Among Jews in general, however, it retained only a secondary importance. In the rabbinic period it was considered a feast on which the theophany on Sinai and the giving of the law were commemorated (J. Potin, *La fête juive de la Pentecôte* [LD 65; Paris, 1971]).

133 (VI) Feast of Tents—Tabernacles. The Hebr name of the third great pilgrimage feast is *sukkôt*, variously translated as Tabernacles, Booths, Tents, and Huts. None of these translations is completely acceptable, although "Huts" comes closest. However, we shall use the conventional "feast of Tents," with the reminder that the feast never called for the setting up of tents of any sort. We first meet the name *sukkôt* in the later liturgical calendars (Deut 16:13,16; Lev 23:34) and in texts dependent on these calendars (Ezra 3:4; Zech 14:16,18). But while the name may be relatively new, the feast is old; it is the "feast of the Ingathering" (*'āsîp*) mentioned in the two most ancient calendars (Exod 23:16 and 34:22).

Of the three annual pilgrimage feasts, this was the most important and the best attended. It is called "the feast of Yahweh" in Lev 23:39 (see Num 29:12); and Ezek 45:25 calls it simply "*the* feast," as does 1 Kgs 8:2,65. It is also to be identified with "the yearly feast of Yahweh at Shiloh" (Judg 21:19). Zechariah, foretelling a worldwide annual pilgrimage of all nations to the Temple, chose this feast as the occasion of the pilgrimage (Zech 14:16). And Josephus referred to it as "the holiest and greatest of Hebrew feasts" (*Ant.* 8.4.1 § 100).

134 (A) History. (See G. W. MacRae, *CBQ* 22 [1960] 251–76.) Like the feasts of Unleavened Bread and of Weeks, the feast of Tents was an agricultural feast, indeed the climax of the agricultural year. It marked the ingathering of all the produce of the fields (Exod 23:16), the products of the threshing floors and of the wine and oil presses (Deut 16:13). When the earth had yielded all its bounty for the current year, and that bounty had been gathered and stored, the people gave joyful thanks to God (the analogy with our Thanksgiving Day is obvious). There was dancing, singing, and general merriment (Judg 21:19–21), including, apparently, a generous sampling of the new wine (1 Sam 1:14–15).

135 As for the ritual of the feast, the earliest texts are not too detailed. Later the feast is called *sukkôt* as in Deut 16:13–15, but no explanation of the name is offered. It is described as a pilgrimage to the Temple, and the duration is given as seven days. More precise information is found in Lev 23:33–43, but this passage is not a literary unit and must be studied *per partes*. The vague prescriptions of Deut 16:13–15 are repeated in Lev 23:34–36, with the added mention of an eighth day, one of rest and of assembly for worship. We learn from Num 29:12–34 what sacrifices were offered during the seven days of the festival, and Num 29:35–38 prescribes the sacrifices for the eighth day. This eighth day seems to be an addition to the original ritual, a day of transition, of catching one's breath, before returning to normal activities.

A second stage in the redaction of Lev 23 is reflected in the account of the celebration of the feast under Ezra in Neh 8:13–18; for 8:14 depends on Lev 23:42–43, where we read that for seven days the people are to live in huts in memory of how the Israelites lived after their liberation from Egypt. When the people to whom the law was being read heard this, they hurried off and collected branches to fashion lean-tos, which they put on roofs, in the courts of the Temple, and in the city squares. Neh 8:17 remarks: "The Israelites had never done the like since the days of Joshua." Certainly this cannot refer to the building of the improvised huts, for the name *sukkôt* goes back to a period before Deut. The fact that this took place in Jerusalem is probably the novelty.

The final stage in the redaction of Lev 23 is represented by vv 40–41, which direct that the people "shall gather foliage from majestic trees, branches of palms, and boughs of myrtles and of valley poplars" and "make merry before the Lord." The word translated "foliage" means literally "good fruit." There is no mention of this in the text from Neh; the fruit had no connection with the building of huts. Later historical texts make it clear that the foliage was carried in procession, as in the Catholic Palm Sunday ceremony. According to 2 Macc 10:6–8, the dedication of the Temple was celebrated "like the feast of Tents": For eight days the Jews held triumphal processions carrying thyrsus, green branches, and palms. And Josephus (*Ant.* 13.13.5 § 372) tells how the despised monarch Alexander Janneus (→ History, 75:142) was bombarded with fruit carried by the people during the feast of Tents.

136 (B) Date. According to Exod 23:16, the feast of Tents was to be celebrated at the close of the year (in autumn); according to Exod 34:22, at the turn of the year. The texts, taken together, indicate that no definite date had yet been fixed for the celebration, which depended on the condition of the crops. In Deut 16:13 the date is given as dependent on the progress of the harvest work. When the harvest was finished, the feast was to be celebrated. The offhand references to the celebration of the feast in Kgs cause complications; see de Vaux, *AI* 498–99. Actually, the date was not definitely fixed before the period reflected in Lev 23:34 (see Num 29:12), which puts it on the 15th day of the seventh month (the month, Sept.-Oct., is counted from the beginning of the year in spring). The feast is to last seven days and come to a conclusion on the eighth. The same dating is given in Ezek 45:25.

137 (C) Origin. There have been abortive attempts to connect the feast of Tents with the vintage time celebration in honor of Bacchus and with the feast of Adonis-Osiris, in which an arbor was set up over the bier of Adonis. Both explanations are completely devoid of foundation. Another, more popular hypothesis is based on the primitive idea that evil powers were especially active at the turn of the year and attacked houses. To escape this malevolent influence the people moved out of their houses and lived in makeshift dwellings until the danger passed. The Israelites, it is claimed, would have been particularly susceptible to such superstitions during their first years of sedentary living in Canaan, when the feast of Tents would have been introduced. Actually, there is no trace of such notions in the biblical texts, which offer a more satisfactory and less strained explanation. The feast began as a harvest festival, as its earliest name (*'āsîp* or Ingathering) suggests, and as the ancient texts (Exod 23:16; 34:22) indicate. Even after it had taken on a name inspired by an accidental part of the ritual (*sukkôt* or Huts), it remained essentially an agricultural feast. If we seek its origin outside of Israel, the logical place is in Canaan, as was true for the feasts of Unleavened Bread and of Weeks.

138 But how did the rite of the *sukkôt* come into such prominence? It had its roots in a very common Palestinian custom: during the harvest time the people built shelters in the orchards and vineyards. These improvised huts afforded some protection from the sun during periods of rest. Since the feast of the Ingathering was celebrated outdoors where these little huts were so much a part of the harvest scene, it is not difficult to see how it could come to be known as the feast of Huts (*sukkôt*). While retaining the name and allowing the custom,

Deut 16:13–15 insisted that the people go to Jerusalem for the sacrifices. Finally, the *sukkôt* were set up in the Holy City itself and became a permanent fixture of the ritual (Lev 23:42; Neh 8:16).

As in the case of the Passover and the feast of Weeks (→ 129, 132 above), the feast of Tents was later given a deeper religious significance by being related to an event in the exodus. The *sukkôt* were interpreted as a memorial of the *sukkôt* in which the Israelites had lived after their liberation from Egypt (Lev 23:43). Actually, they did not live in huts, but in tents during the desert sojourn; so the association is liturgical, not historical.

139   (VII) An OT New Year Feast?   When the new calendar year began in Judah and in Israel is not totally clear, but it began in the autumn in Judah during most of the royal period. By the time of the exile, however, and in the postexilic period, it began in the springtime, with the Babylonian month Nisan (March–April). There is no mention of a new year feast in the OT. *Rōʾš haššānâ* in Ezek 40:1 refers not to a festival but to the time of year. In Lev 23:23–25 and Num 29:1–6, both of which suppose a calendar year beginning with Nisan, the first day of the seventh month, which would be Tishri (Sept.–Oct) was a day of *těrûʿâ* ("blowing of trumpets"? → Leviticus, 4:46), to be observed in clearly more solemn manner than the first day of the other months. We read in Neh 8:2 that Ezra chose the same first day of the seventh month, Tishri, for his solemn reading of the law. The importance of the first of autumnal Tishri in these early postexilic texts, when the year began in the springtime, has been taken as evidence that there had been a new year feast in the preexilic period, when the new year—in Judah at least—began in the autumn. The occurrence of both the Day of Atonement and the feast of Tents within the month of Tishri in the postexilic period would have been determined by the importance Tishri had had as the first month of the year in the royal period. Such texts of the royal period as 1 Kgs 8:2–3; 12:32–33 (in the light of 12:26–27) might have been alluding to an autumnal feast, perhaps the feast of Ingathering, with a strongly royal religious character. Hypothetically, such a feast would have celebrated the divine kingship of Yahweh as Lord of all creation, in which the earthly king participated. Some would add that this participation of the earthly king in divine kingship was felt to have consequences for the welfare of nature in the ebb and flow of the forces of the universe—a religious ideology of royalty thus being combined with elements of classical Canaanite nature religion. By the postexilic period, the feast would have been suppressed because of opposition to elements of old Canaanite nature religion and because of opposition to monarchy as such.

140   The existence of such a feast in the autumnal beginning of the year in the royal period of Judah can only be suspected by induction from accumulated data difficult to assess. If such a feast existed, with significant participation of the earthly king, and with Yahweh's kingship at its ideological center, that would help us to understand certain OT passages, especially in the Psalms (→ Psalms, 34:6). It could explain why the Jewish feast of the calendar new year, *Rōʾš haššānâ*, even when it first appeared in the Mishna in the 2d cent. AD, was a feast in which God's kingship figured and was celebrated in autumn on the 1st of Tishri, despite the occurrence of the calendar new year in the springtime in postexilic Judah. If there was such a preexilic feast at the autumnal beginning of the year, it may have been a single festival of a week (see Deut 16:13,15), eventually separated into the solemnity of the 1st of Tishri, the Day of Atonement on the 10th, and the feast of Tents from the 15th to the

22d (Mowinckel, *Psalmenstudien* 2. 83–89), as there took place a shift of festive emphasis to the public celebration of Passover in the springtime. Such changes in the religious institutions of Israel may have reflected changes of theological attitude (see T. N. D. Mettinger, *The Dethronement of Sabaoth* [ConBOT 18; Lund, 1982] 67–79).

141   (VIII) A Feast of the Enthronement of Yahweh?   Some who held the theory just described went further: they saw the central act of such a new year feast as a ritual enthronement of Yahweh, meant to renew annually the mythic victory of Yahweh over his enemies, with real consequences for the renewal of the works of creation. For this, the following lines of reasoning have been proposed:

142   (A) Arguments from Comparative Religion.   In Babylon, during the first twelve days of Nisan, the new year festival was celebrated. Its extant ritual (*ANET* 331–34) is incomplete and very late (from the Seleucid period), but the feast itself and presumably many of its component elements were much older. Among its elements were the reading of the Mesopotamian epic of creation, *Enuma Elish* (*ANET* 60–72), before the image of Babylon's national god Marduk, a procession to a festival chapel (the *akītu*) outside the city, a ritual representation of Marduk's victory over the gods of chaos, and a proclamation of the divine kingship with the formula "Marduk is king." The king of Babylon had a certain ritual role to play. Among the Hittites of an earlier period, the king had a still more important role in a new year festival; and the feast of the Pharaoh's coronation in Egypt was considered the beginning of a new year, though not of the civil new year.

In Canaanite mythology, the victory of Baal over the forces of chaos and of death, represented by Yamm and by Mot (*ANET* 129–42), was parallel to the victory of Marduk over Tiamat and the gods of chaos in the Babylonian epic of creation. In Canaanite religious practice, there was a rite of sacred marriage, which Hellenistic authors called *hieros gamos*. The myth of Tammuz, cyclically dying and springing to life again like the green plants, had its religious expression in both Canaan and Mesopotamia (see, for Palestine and the littoral regions, N. Robertson, *HTR* 75 [1982] 313–60).

These elements in the religious systems of the ancient Near East have been used to reconstruct an Israelite new year feast of Yahweh's enthronement—in a most eclectic and extreme manner by what came to be known as the Myth and Ritual school. S. H. Hooke (*The Origins of Early Semitic Ritual* [London, 1938] 45–68) appealed to a "pattern" of religious concepts and practices valid everywhere in the ancient Near East (to some extent *mutatis mutandis*). On the basis of this "pattern," he and other adherents of the school saw an Israelite feast of Yahweh's enthronement whose ritual included an enactment of battle between Yahweh and the forces of chaos with Yahweh victorious, a dramatic representation of divine death and resurrection, a *hieros gamos*, a reading of a mythic account of creation, and a procession to the Temple for the rite of Yahweh's enthronement. Hooke's "pattern" was worked out in greater detail, with more inclusion of biblical and later Jewish material, by Widengren (*Sakrales Königtum*). Few today would admit that the official, orthodox worship of Israel at any time included a *hieros gamos* or was influenced by the myth of a dying and rising god. (That the latter was applied to Marduk in Babylon has been disproved by W. von Soden, *ZA* 51 [1955] 130–66.) Yet some of the Babylonian and other ideological and mythic parallels to divine kingship in Israel are surely valid.

143   (B) Arguments from the OT. The hypothesis of a feast of Yahweh's enthronement in Judah's royal period would hardly have been formulated without the Babylonian parallels mentioned in the preceding section. But in the first place it was an attempt to find the vital setting of certain psalms that led to the hypothesis and to the mustering of Babylonian parallels. The idea of an Israelite new year feast had already been advanced by P. Volz, when Mowinckel (*Psalmenstudien*, vol. 2) established a category of "enthronement psalms" for several psalms celebrating God's kingship. Mowinckel proposed a cultic setting as part of a ritual for a new year feast of Yahweh's enthronement, which he described by analogies with the Babylonian new year festival, combined with information on the Jewish new year drawn from rabbinic sources and with what he took to be OT allusions to ritual elements of the feast. He insisted that an important aspect of the feast was ritual "creative drama," by which the ancients thought that effects were produced in reality. In this view, the Israelites would have thought that the annual performance of a ritual representation of Yahweh's mythic victory over his enemies and the forces of chaos, with his ritual enthronement as its climax, actually effected the renewal of creation. Even Israel itself, the culmination of creation, would have been renewed through a dramatization of the exodus, with a renewal of Israel's covenant with God. An almost sacramental role of the earthly king in the renewal of created nature was stressed for the first time in OT studies.

144   (C) Assessment of Arguments. Mowinckel's arguments have not stood the test of critical scrutiny very well. Although an Israelite enthronement feast and the validity of the Babylonian parallels were at first accepted, without the excesses of "patternism," by some reputable Assyriologists like F. M. T. de Liagre Böhl, refinement has since taken place in the interpretation of the Babylonian new year festival. It was indeed a feast in which Marduk was honored as the principal god of Babylon, supreme god of all gods and ruler of all creation; but it was not specifically or primarily a festival of Marduk's enthronement. Nor did the king of Babylon have any glorious role to play; in fact, his only central role in the sacral proceedings entailed a ritual humiliation (see A. L. Oppenheim, *Ancient Mesopotamia* [Chicago, 1964] 122). The concept of a god's kingship had ancient roots in Canaan itself (O. Eissfeldt, *ZAW* 46 [1928] 81–105). Serious critics of "patternism" have shown that one cannot validly construct ritual or calendar infused with mythic elements in Israel by simple intuitive analogy with those elements elsewhere. It remains true, nevertheless, that Marduk's divine kingship was celebrated in the Babylonian new year festival and that Yahweh's divine kingship was celebrated in the Jewish new year, according to evidence later than the OT.

145   A crucial point in the hypothesis of a feast of Yahweh's enthronement lies in the exclamation *Yahweh mālak* (Pss 93:1; 96:10; 97:1; 99:1), understood as "Yahweh has become king" and interpreted as an enthronement formula (→ Psalms, 34:109). Whether in a given case that means "Yahweh reigns/is king" or "Yahweh has become king" (just now? or long ago with permanent effects not subject to renewal?) has to be determined from a given context, about which disagreement remains possible (see J. H. Ulrichsen, *VT* 17 [1977] 361–74). *Yahweh mālak* does not correspond to the form of what seems to have been the typical Israelite public acclamation upon a king's accession. The acclamation "Marduk is king" in the proceedings of the Babylonian new year festival was not used with the idea of a renovation of Marduk's kingship in mind. Ps 47 contains details in vv 6,9 (→ Psalms, 34:63) that might be taken as allusions to a divine enthronement rite, but those details have received other equally plausible explanations and do not, of themselves, justify the acceptance of a feast specifically "of Yahweh's enthronement."

146   (D) Modified Views of the Feast. Some scholars, rejecting Mowinckel's hypothesis of an enthronement feast, have accepted his idea of an autumnal feast, along with some elements of his reconstructed ritual, and have given them a different interpretation. A. Weiser (*The Psalms* [Phl, 1962] 23–52) interpreted the feast as a feast of covenant. H. J. Kraus (*Die Königsherrschaft Gottes im Alten Testament* [Tübingen, 1951]), with more hesitation in later publications, interpreted it as a royal feast celebrating the divine election of David's dynasty and Zion, in which the renewal was not of creation but of covenant.

(Böhl, F. M. T. de Liagre, *Opera minora* [Groningen, 1953] 263–81. Cazelles, H., "Nouvel an IV: Le nouvel an en Israël," *DBSup* 6. 620–45. Clines, D. J. A., "The Evidence for an Autumnal New Year in Pre-exilic Israel Reconsidered," *JBL* 93 [1974] 22–40. Hooke, S. H. (ed.), *Myth, Ritual and Kingship* [Oxford, 1958]. Johnson, A. R., *Sacral Kingship in Ancient Israel* [2d ed.; Cardiff, 1967]. Mowinckel, S., *Psalmenstudien* [Kristiania, 1922] vol. 2. Snaith, N., *The Jewish New Year Festival* [London, 1947]. Volz, P., *Das Neujahrsfest Jahwes* [Tübingen, 1912]. Welten, P., "Königsherrschaft Jahwes und Thronbesteigung," *VT* 32 [1982] 297–310. Widengren, G., *Sakrales Königtum im Alten Testament und im Judentum* [Stuttgart, 1955].)

LATER OLD TESTAMENT FEASTS

147   (I) The Day of Atonement. Yom Kippur is one of the better-known Jewish feasts. In NT times it had achieved such prestige as to be called simply "The Day," and it is under this title (*Yoma*) that the Mishna treats of it. Ever since its institution, it has been celebrated on the same date, the 10th of Tishri (September–October), the seventh month (Lev 23:27–32; Num 29:7–11).

148   (A) Ritual. This is given in detail in Lev 16. *The ritual of expiation.* The Day of Atonement was a day of complete rest, penance, and fasting. In a solemn assembly at the Temple, special sacrifices were offered in atonement for the sanctuary, the clergy, and the people. There seems to be a combination of two distinct rituals in Lev 16. According to the first or levitical ritual, the high priest offered a bull as a sacrifice for his own sins and those of the whole Aaronic priesthood. Then he went into the Holy of Holies to incense the *kappōret* (→ 32, 35 above) and to sprinkle it with blood from the bull (16:11–14). This was the only day during the year that he entered this holiest of places. Next, he sacrificed a goat for the sins of the people; he also took some of its blood into the Holy of Holies to sprinkle it on the *kappōret* (16:15). Blood was rubbed and sprinkled on the altar too (16:16–19).

149   *The goat for Azazel.* Interwoven in the levitical ritual is another that reflects a different mentality. The community presented two goats, and lots were cast to determine their fate: one was chosen for Yahweh, the other "for Azazel." The parallelism of "for Yahweh" and "for Azazel" indicates that Azazel is a proper name, probably of a demon. It is so interpreted by the Syr version of Lev, by the Targum, and by *1 Enoch,* which identifies Azazel as the prince of devils who was banished to the desert. This would agree with the notion that devils dwelt in the desert (Isa 13:21; 34:11–14; see Tob 8:3; Matt 12:43). The goat chosen for Yahweh was sacrificed for the sins of the people. The high priest then imposed hands on the goat for Azazel; by this symbolic gesture he transferred to the goat all the sins of the community. This goat was sacrificed neither to Yahweh nor to the demon. It was led into the desert, and with it were removed the sins of the people (Lev 16:8–10,20–22).

This ritual recalls what was done in Babylon annually on the 5th of Nisan. A chanter, intoning incantations, purified the sanctuaries of Bel and Nabu with water, oil, and perfumes. Then another man decapitated a sheep and rubbed the corpse against the temple of Nabu to purify it. Next the two of them carried the head and body of the sheep to the Euphrates and threw them in. Then they retired to the country and could not return until the 12th of Nisan, when the new year festival came to an end. There are undeniable similarities between this ceremony and that of the scapegoat on Yom Kippur; but there are differences, too—especially the use of the scapegoat in Israel to carry away the sins of the people. Other peoples had similar rites, and there is an analogy for the scapegoat within Israelite ritual in the bird that was released in the ritual for cleansing from leprosy (→ 106 above).

150   (B) Institution. Certainly there are very ancient elements in the ritual for the feast of Atonement, elements that were combined with levitical customs and adapted to orthodox religious ideas. Such a combination is evident in the ritual of a red heifer and of the purification of a leper (→ 104–7 above). But there is no allusion to the feast in any preexilic text. In Ezekiel's prophecy of the future Temple he envisioned a ceremony to take place on the 1st and 7th of the first month. On the 1st a bull would be sacrificed and its blood used to purify the Temple and the altar; on the 7th a similar sacrifice would take place for the indeliberate sins of the people (Ezek 45:18–20). In spite of a fundamental similarity, this is not the Day of Atonement, which fell on the 10th of the seventh month; and Ezekiel does not mention the ceremony of the scapegoat. The books of Ezra and Neh make no mention of the feast. All the available evidence points to a relatively late date for the feast of Atonement, but it is impossible to determine that date with any precision.

151   (II) Feast of Hanukkah—Dedication. Hebr *ḥanukkâ* as rendered in Greek (*ta enkainia*) signifies "inauguration" or "renewal." The usual Eng transl. for the title of the feast is Dedication; Josephus gives it another name, the feast of Lights.

(A) Origin and History. The origin of the feast of Hanukkah is described in 1 Macc 4:36–59. The tyrant Antiochus Epiphanes had desecrated the Temple and its altar and had put up on the site of the altar of holocausts a pagan altar. This was the Abomination of Desolation (1 Macc 1:54; Dan 9:27; 11:31); upon it he offered the first sacrifice to Zeus Olympios on the 25th of Kisleu (Dec.) 167 BC. Just three years later, on this same date, Judas Maccabeus purified the sanctuary, erected a new altar, and dedicated it (2 Macc 10:5). It was agreed that the event be commemorated annually (1 Macc 4:59), yet for the next twelve years or so the feast could not have been observed with any regularity because of the military situation (→ History, 75:135–37).

Once freedom was definitively won and Jonathan became high priest in 152, the regular observance of the feast was resumed. It is mentioned in John 10:22 and in Josephus (*Ant.* 12.7.7 § 323–26).

152   (B) Ritual. The feast lasted eight days beginning on the 25th of Kisleu and was characterized by an atmosphere of great rejoicing. Sacrifices were offered in the Temple; and thyrsus, green branches, and palms were carried in procession, while appropriate hymns were sung (2 Macc 10:6–8; see 1 Macc 4:54). Ps 30, entitled "A song for the dedication of the Temple," was most likely one of these hymns, but the principal hymns were the Hallel psalms (113–18). We learn from the Mishna and rabbinic writings that the people lighted lamps in front of their houses, adding one each day for the duration of the feast. This is a later development, for the lighting of lamps referred to in 1 Macc 4:50 indicates the restoration of the candelabra in the Temple. However, 2 Macc 1:8 does refer to the lighting of lamps—but again in the Temple; and Ps 118:27 reads: "The Lord is God, and he has given us light. Join in procession with leafy boughs up to the horns of the altar." At any rate, the use of lights became a traditional feature of the feast, and this continued to be the case even after the destruction of the Temple in AD 70. This explains Josephus's "feast of Lights."

153   The similarity between the rituals of Hanukkah and Tents is obvious; 2 Macc stresses it quite explicitly (1:9; 10:6). Possibly Judas Maccabeus patterned the ritual after that of Tents, for it was in connection with the Tents that Solomon's Temple (1 Kgs 8:2,65) and the postexilic altar (Ezra 3:4) had been dedicated. Both feasts lasted eight days, and in both palms were carried in procession. There were differences, too: the Hallel psalms were probably sung first at Hanukkah and later extended to Passover, Pentecost, and Tents; and during Hanukkah no huts were erected. The lights that figured so prominently in Hanukkah are quite distinctive.

154   (C) Influences. In spite of the clear account of the origin of the feast and of its connection with a specific historical event, some scholars insist that Hanukkah is actually a Jewish version of the pagan feast of the winter solstice and that there is a clear connection between Hanukkah and Enoch, whose life span of 365 years coincided perfectly with the number of days in a solar year (Gen 5:23). Others equate Hanukkah with the Roman feast of *Sol Invictus* (Dec. 25). Still others observe that when Antiochus Epiphanes was in control, he made the Jews wear ivy crowns and march in a procession honoring Bacchus (2 Macc 6:7) and that he imported an Athenian (2 Macc 6:1) to instruct them in the ritual. Finally, others see in the lighting of a new lamp each night a symbol of the lengthening of the days after the winter solstice.

Such influences are not likely. If pagan customs affected the choice of the date for Hanukkah, they did so only indirectly. Judas Maccabeus selected the date to erase the memory not only of the profanation of the altar, which had occurred on the 25th of Kisleu, but also of the pagan sacrifice offered every month on the 25th day, which was Antiochus's birthday (2 Macc 6:7). Carrying branches in a procession honoring Yahweh may also have been a reaction against the pagan custom which the Jews had been forced to follow in the worship of Bacchus. Lighting lamps in front of houses may have been intended to replace the burning of incense at the doors of houses ordered by Antiochus (1 Macc 1:55). It is not clear why one more lamp each day was lighted, but this sort of thing is not uncommon in folk customs and in liturgy (cf. the Catholic customs with the Advent wreath and in the former Tenebrae service). The feast of

Hanukkah was essentially a commemoration of the purification of the Temple, and all its rites may be explained as reactions to the temporary pagan abominations in Jerusalem.

155   (III) Feast of Purim.

(A) Date and Ritual. According to Josephus, this feast was celebrated on the 14th and 15th of Adar (Feb.–March) in memory of the victory of the Jews of Persia over their would-be exterminators. For the ritual we must turn to the rabbinic writings. The 13th of Adar was a fast day; in the evening lamps were lighted in all the houses, and the people went to the synagogue. The next two days were festive days. All attended the synagogue for the reading of the book of Esther and the congregation would interrupt the reading with curses against the villain Aman and his ilk. The meeting closed with a solemn blessing of Mordecai, of Esther, and of the Israelites in general. The feast of Purim was the occasion for the exchange of gifts and the distribution of alms; but apart from these expressions of piety and charity, it was the most worldly of the Jewish festivals — a sort of carnival, with the wearing of masks and other disguises. The rabbis laid down a rule that one had to stop drinking when he could no longer distinguish between "Cursed be Aman!" and "Blessed be Mordecai!"

156   (B) Book of Esther. The story of Esther gave this feast its existence and its name. According to 3:7 and 9:24 Aman cast lots (*pûrîm*) to determine the fate of the Jews, which was to be extermination. This he had done on the 14th of Adar, but his scheme boomeranged and he himself was hanged. Now *pûr* is neither Hebrew nor Persian, but Akkadian; and it is strange both that the lots play such an insignificant role in the story itself and that there is no reference to them in the feast to which they have given a name. In fact, 3:7 has all the earmarks of an interpolation, and 9:20–32 is an account of a letter that Mordecai wrote to his fellow Jews urging them to observe the feast. One suspects that the two passages were interpolated to make the feast acceptable to the Jews as a whole and to fix its name as Purim. The whole book, in fact, seems designed as a justification for the feast. Everything in the story converges on the celebra-

tion that took place the day after the massacre of the Persians, and the final verses (9:16–19) are an attempt to explain why the feast lasted two days (14th and 15th of Adar). Yet there may have been some historical basis for the story that was freely expanded into the legend of a feast (de Vaux, *AI* 515; see also W. W. Hallo, *BA* 46 [1983] 19–29).

157   (C) Origin of the Feast. If Esth were a truly historical book, the answer to this question would be as easy as the answer to the question of the origin of Hanukkah. But Esth is not historical; it is a story designed, among other things, to justify a rather peculiar feast. The name of the God of Israel is not even mentioned in the Hebr (protocanonical) form of the book. Purim itself was not a particularly religious festival: it was not specifically related to salvation history, nor did it contain elements of worship. It was clearly a foreign feast, but its precise origins are not easy to determine. Attempts to trace it to Babylonia and to translate it entirely into terms of Babylonian mythology (Mordecai-Esther = Marduk-Ishtar; Aman-Vashti = Aman-Mashti) are quite unconvincing. The authentic Persian flavor of Esth points rather to a Persian origin for the feast; yet the Babylonian correspondences between Mordecai and Marduk and between Esther and Ishtar are hardly coincidental. Moreover, the word *pûru* is definitely Akkadian. The feast, then, must have had roots in several cultures.

At any rate, it originated in the Eastern Jewish Diaspora and probably commemorated a projected genocide from which the Jews narrowly escaped. It also had many of the elements of a pagan new year festival (amusements, banquets, exchange of gifts, etc.) and was probably patterned after such a Persian festival. If it came to Palestine by way of Mesopotamia, it could have picked up some Babylonian features en route, specifically, the name Purim. The first mention of the feast in a Palestinian milieu is in 2 Macc 15:36, where it is called the "Day of Mordecai" and is dated the 14th of Adar; Josephus is the next to mention it (*Ant.* 11.6.13 § 295). Only by stretching categories can we include this feast under the religious institutions of Israel. But it does have its roots, however tenuous, in a book of the OT.

77

ASPECTS OF
OLD TESTAMENT THOUGHT*

John L. McKenzie

BIBLIOGRAPHY

1 Alt, *AEOT*. Childs, B. S., *Old Testament Theology in a Canonical Context* (Phl, 1985). Clements, R. E., *Old Testament Theology* (Atlanta, 1978). De Vries, S. J., *The Achievements of Biblical Religion* (NY, 1983). Eichrodt, *ETOT*. Fohrer, G., *History of Israelite Religion* (Nash, 1972); *Theologische Grundstrukturen des Alten Testaments* (Berlin, 1972). Gese, H., *Essays on Biblical Theology* (Minneapolis, 1981). Gottwald, N. K., *The Tribes of Yahweh* (Maryknoll, 1979). Hanson, P. D., *The Diversity of Scripture* (OBT 11; Phl, 1982). Hasel, G. F., *Old Testament Theology* (rev. ed.; GR, 1975); "Major Recent Issues in Old Testament Theology, 1978–1983," *JSOT* 31 (1985) 31–53. Hayes, J. H. and F. Prussner, *Old Testament Theology: Its History and Development* (Atlanta, 1985). *HBT* 6 (1984) 1–80. Jacob, E., *Theology of the Old Testament* (NY, 1958). Kaiser, W. C., *Toward an Old Testament Theology* (GR, 1978); *Toward Old Testament Ethics* (GR, 1983). Kaufmann, Y., *The Religion of Israel* (Chicago, 1958). Knight, D. A., (ed.), *Tradition and Theology in the Old Testament* (Phl, 1977). Köhler, L., *Old Testament Theology* (Phl, 1957).

Lang, B. (ed.), *Anthropological Approaches to the Old Testament* (IRT; Phl, 1985). Léon-Dufour, *DBT*. McKenzie, J. L., *A Theology of the Old Testament* (GC, 1974). Martin-Achard, R., *Permanence de l'Ancien Testament* (Geneva, 1984); "Théologies de l'Ancien Testament et confessions de foi," *RTP* 117 (1985) 81–91; Eng *TD* 33 (1986) 145–48. Miller, P., *et al.* (eds.), *Ancient Israelite Religion* (Fest. F. M. Cross; Phl, 1987). Pedersen, J., *Israel* (2 vols.; London, 1926–40). Renckens, H., *The Religion of Israel* (NY, 1966). Reventlow, H. G., *Problems of Old Testament Theology in the Twentieth Century* (Phl, 1985). Ringgren, H., *Israelite Religion* (Phl, 1966). Rogerson, J., *Anthropology and the Old Testament* (Oxford, 1978). Schmidt, W., *The Faith of the Old Testament* (Phl, 1983). Terrien, S., *The Elusive Presence* (NY, 1978). Von Rad, *OTT*. Vriezen, *OOTT*. Westermann, C., *Elements of the Old Testament Theology* (Phl, 1974); *What Does the Old Testament Say about God?* (Atlanta, 1979). Wolff, H.-W., *Anthropology of the Old Testament* (Phl, 1974). Zimmerli, W., *Old Testament Theology in Outline* (Atlanta, 1978).

2

OUTLINE

---

*Sections 152–163 of this article were composed and added by R. E. Brown.

THE GOD OF ISRAEL

3   (I) Introduction. Although biblical theology as a formal discipline is now nearly 200 years old, there is still wide disagreement on its object, principles, and methods (→ OT Criticism, 69:51–54). Something should be said about the limitations of biblical theology as it is understood in this essay. Biblical theology is a part of theology as a whole; it cannot claim to present a synthesis of the whole of revealed doctrine, and in particular OT theology cannot make this claim. Biblical theology does not lend itself to a synthesis like the synthesis of speculative theology created by Thomas Aq.; the treatment adopted here is a collection of essays on topics or themes, with no attempt to integrate them into a single whole. (This contribution is not a complete collection of theological themes; it contains only those themes that in the judgment of the writer were most deserving of inclusion.) Biblical theology does not follow the categories of speculative theology; it must create its own categories drawn from biblical thought itself, and it is precisely here that an area of disagreement among scholars is found.

4   Biblical theology must be historical in its methods and exposition. The revelation of the Bible is enmeshed in the historic experience of Israel, and it is impossible to fix it at any one point that recapitulates the entire experience. Limitations of space have not permitted the full exposition of this factor here. Biblical theology, at best, is an aid to understanding the Bible; it does not communicate an understanding. The themes stated theologically here were originally uttered in a concrete historical situation of urgency, usually with a depth of conviction and even of passion that matched the urgency. Understanding the Bible requires that one senses the urgency as much as one comprehends the intelligible content of the utterance. Biblical theology can show that these utterances fall into the structure of Israelite faith; but the impact of that faith is perceived only when one hears it announced by its own spokesmen. Biblical theology is not a substitute for exegesis but presupposes it (→ Hermeneutics, 71:21).

5   **(II) Names of God.** The object of theology is the knowledge of God. Theological knowledge of God is understood to be an elaboration and a synthesis of concepts formed by combining the data of revealed theological sources with the conclusions of dialectical reasoning. In the OT this type of thinking does not appear. Israelite thought in the biblical era lacked the discursive reasoning developed by Gk philosophy (→ 23–24 below) and was incapable of general and abstract speculation. In Hebrew "to know God" is to encounter a personal reality; and a person is not known unless his name is known.

6   In Hebr speech there is a peculiar association of the person and the name foreign to our idiom. "Name" is used in contexts where modern language uses "person" or "self." To have no name is to have no existence in reality; when one's name is blotted out, one ceases to exist. To give a name is to confer identity and not merely to distinguish from other individuals or species; when God creates (Gen 1), he gives a name to each object of his creation. Conferring a name is an act of power and an assertion of ownership or some other form of control. A change of name indicates a change of state or condition, the beginning of a new existence. To know the name is to know the reality named. For this reason the OT reflects the love of etymologies which, if analyzed linguistically, are fanciful. The name is pregnant with meaning; a connection by paronomasia with a characteristic or deed of a person reveals the person more fully. Hence, the knowledge of God is disclosed in his name.

7   **(A) El, Elohim, Eloah.** EL transliterates the Hebr form of the common word for deity in the Semitic languages. In polytheistic belief '*ēl* is the word for a member of the divine species, just as "man" has served as the word for an individual member of the human species. ELOHIM has no cognate in the other Semitic languages; it is probably related to El. Grammatically '*ĕlōhîm* is a Hebr pl.; this is often taken to reflect the polytheistic thinking current among the ancestors of Israel. "Elohim" is applied either to the one God worshiped by Israel or to the gods of other peoples; in the second usage it can be pl. in meaning as well as in form. When it is used of the God of Israel, "Elohim," despite its pl. form, is sg. in meaning and grammatical agreement, except in a few passages where the polytheistic reminiscences of the narrative from which the Bible borrowed still shine through, e.g., Gen 1:26: "God said, 'Let *us* . . . in the *image of God* he created them—*male and female.*'" (This passage may be a reminiscence of a heavenly pantheon of "elohim," male and female.) "El" appears as a personal divine name borne by the head of the pantheon of Ugarit. Possibly the Ugaritic usage is the only remaining trace of an earlier and more widely diffused theology in which the name El was a proper name before it became a common name. ELOAH ('*ĕlôah*), which also lacks a cognate in other languages, appears only in poetry and seems to be no more than a poetic variant. Hebrew has no feminine word for deity. (Cf. P. Trible, *God and the Rhetoric of Sexuality* [Phl, 1978.])

8   There is no generally accepted etymological explanation of the meaning of the names El and Elohim. Most scholars connect the names with a word meaning "power," and it is not unlikely that power was the fundamental and essential note of deity in the ancient Semitic world. Even if this is the proper explanation, "power" is not reflected in the Hebr usage. If the Israelite idea of the essential note of deity can be summed up in one word, it is the word "holy," felicitously paraphrased by R. Otto as "wholly other"; the essential note is that God is totally unlike any of his creatures. Hebrew exhibits a number of adjectival uses of the names El and Elohim in which a person or a thing is said to be identical with or to belong to El or Elohim. These attributions raise the object so designated above the ordinary level of human or terrestrial being and locate it on a higher level that is most properly called superhuman. The object is raised because in some such quality as size, strength, or sheer wonder it exceeds the normal. In ancient Semitic usage there was no sharp line that divided the gods from other superhuman beings: the world of El-Elohim was the world of being and power superior to human beings. But in the Bible when Yahweh is called El or Elohim, he is necessarily raised above even this superhuman world to a level that belongs to him alone.

9 **(B) Shaddai.** According to the E and P sources (→ Pentateuch, 1:5, 7), the divine name Yahweh was not known before Moses—a genuine historical tradition—and in the P source Shaddai is the name by which the patriarchs invoke God. The name is attested also in some older poems outside the P source (Num 24:4,16; Gen 49:25). The meaning of this name, which appears only in the Bible, is not certain; it was rendered in the LXX by *pantokratōr,* "Almighty." Many scholars follow the suggestion of W. F. Albright that the name means "The One of the Mountain." The name thus interpreted reflects the common ancient Semitic belief that the home of the gods lay on "the mountain of the north," mentioned in some passages of the OT (Isa 14:13; Ps 48:3; → History, 75:54).

10 **(C) Baal, Adonai, Melek.** These three titles convey the idea of the power to rule. BAAL, "owner," is rarely used of Yahweh because it was a conventional title of the most popular god of the Canaanites. Often, however, when Baal is a component of an Israelite name (e.g., son of Saul = Ishbaal; son of Jonathan = Meribbaal: 1 Chr 8:33–34), we may suspect that the child was given a Yahweh/baal name, rather than being named after the pagan god. Later OT writers took a dim view of the use of "baal" in a name and often changed it to "bosheth" (Hebr "shame"). Thus in 2 Sam 2:8 and 9:6, the names of the two men just cited appear as Ishbosheth and Mephibosheth. ADONAI (*'ădōnāy,* "my lord"—this pronunciation is used only of Yahweh) is the same word as *'ădōnî,* by which the king was usually addressed. MELEK, "king," is used frequently of Yahweh. Kingship was an attribute of many gods of the ancient Semitic peoples, but the Israelite development of the idea follows its own way. Yahweh is the king of Israel, king of all nations, king in virtue of creation, king savior who delivers Israel, the eschatological king who establishes his universal reign in the end of history (→ 75, 165–166 below). It is not possible to determine which of these aspects was primary; but the view of the covenant as a vassal–overlord relationship (→ 81–82 below) suggests that the kingship of Yahweh was not a later development of Israelite thought. The functions of the ancient king were war and law, and Yahweh exercises both of these functions for Israel. He is the savior who fights the battles of Israel, the lawmaker who imposes a code of conduct, and the judge who sanctions the code that he imposes.

11 **(D) Yahweh.** This is the personal name of the God of Israel. The pronunciation "Yahweh" has been recovered in recent times. In the Hebr Bible the name is written with the four consonants (Tetragrammaton) YHWH and the vowels of the word *'ădōnāy (adonai =* "lord"—at some time in the late pre-Christian centuries Jews ceased to pronounce the sacred name out of reverence, and said instead *Adonai*). This combination produced the non-word Jehovah that appeared in the *AV.* (G. H. Parke-Taylor, *Yahweh* [Waterloo, Canada, 1975]; M. Rose, *Jahwe* [ThStud 122; Zurich, 1978].)

12 The meaning of the name is uncertain, and the explanations that have been suggested are too numerous to cite. The text of Exod 3:13–14 is not an explanation and is extremely difficult to translate. The Hebr Bible has the name in the first person, *'ehyeh 'ăšer 'ehyeh.* The LXX

rendered the name as "I am the existent [*ho ōn* = he who is]"; the Vg as "I am who am." Following P. Haupt, many have suggested that the formula was originally in the third person and read *yahweh 'ăšer yahweh.* Most modern scholars would connect the form *'ehyeh* or *yahweh* with the verb *hāwâ,* the archaic form of the verb "to be." In particular, W. F. Albright and F. M. Cross insist that *yahweh* is from the causative conjugation of this verb and means "he causes to be."

As a name, "Yahweh" is for Albright a fragment of a longer name that he reconstructs as *yahweh-'ăšer-yihweh,* "he who brings into being whatever comes into being" (*FSAC* [2d ed.] 15–16, 259–61). The name so explained identifies Yahweh as the creator. F. M. Cross (*HTR* 55 [1962] 256) has a variation on this thesis, for he thinks of "Yahweh" as part of a liturgical title for El, e.g., *'ēl 'ăšer* [or *dū,* an older relative] *yahweh ṣĕbā'ôt* = "El who brings into being the hosts" (→ 14 below). On the other hand, if some explanation similar to the translations of the LXX and Vg is accepted and more emphasis is put on existence, then the name signifies that Yahweh is the one who really is—possibly the one who really is *elohim,* God. (However, this emphasis should not be carried into the philosophical sphere as if the Bible were telling us that the essence of God is existence.) But perhaps all this speculation on the etymology of Yahweh is deceptive; for even if we knew with certainty the original meaning of the name, we would have no assurance that the Hebrews understood the name correctly (most etymologies in the Bible are popular and scientifically incorrect). The usage of the name Yahweh in the Bible shows no awareness of any etymology, and there is no evidence in the OT of a theology being built around the meaning of the name. The name occurs over 6,700 times and is the usual designation of God, more frequently than all other designations combined. It is also a frequent component of personal names: those that begin with Je/Jehu/Jeho and those that end with iah/jah (Adonijah, Elijah, Jeremiah, Isaiah, Jehoshaphat, Jehoiachin). It is, so to speak, the Israelite name for God by which the association of Yahweh and Israel is mutually accepted and proclaimed.

13 The revelation of the name to Moses in Exod 3:13–14 is attributed to the E tradition, and the P tradition of Exod 6:3 affirms that the name was not known to the patriarchs. Although the J tradition uses the name from the beginning of its narrative in Gen 2, this should not be understood as a contradiction of the E and P traditions, but as unawareness of it. In the theology of the name explained above (→ 6), the revelation of the name Yahweh to Israel through Moses represented a new and fuller revelation of the personal reality of Yahweh. This is reflected in the exodus traditions whereby the name of Yahweh is associated with the origin of the covenant (→ 81ff. below; → History, 75:44). Israel knows its God by this name, and no further definition or qualification is needed. By this name he is proclaimed as the personal divine being who has revealed himself to Israel, who has vindicated himself by the saving acts of the exodus and has established a covenant relationship with the people he has made. The distinctive name "Yahweh" indicates that he is a personal being whose essence and attributes can be shared by no other being.

14 **(E) Yahweh Sebaoth.** This title, "Yahweh (God) of Hosts," does not occur in Gen through Judg and is particularly associated with the shrine built for the Ark of the Covenant at Shiloh from which the Ark was led out to battle (1 Sam 1:3; 4:4). It appears frequently in the prophets (Isa 1–39, Jer, Amos, Hag, Zech). The identification of the "hosts" is difficult. Scholars propose the armies of Israel, or "the hosts of heaven" (the heavenly bodies or even the angels), or "the hosts of heaven and earth" (the created universe). The prophetic contexts of the title do not recommend identification of the "hosts" with the armies of Israel; but the usage in 1 Sam does, and possibly this was the earliest sense. The third proposal is most in harmony with the prophetic usage; the title would then designate Yahweh as "lord of creation."

15   (F) Patriarchal Names for God. As A. Alt (*AEOT* 1–100) has shown, one form under which the patriarchs worshiped God can be classified as "the God of the Fathers." The God who had dealings with the patriarch was identified as "the God of Abraham" (or "of Isaac," or "of Jacob"). This God of Abraham was worshiped by Abraham and his clan and was to some extent a tribal God. Perhaps the God of each patriarch had a special title, e.g., the Shield of Abraham (Gen 15:1); the Fear of Isaac (or perhaps Kinsman — Gen 31:42,53); the Mighty One of Jacob (Gen 49:24). Worshiping the god of one special figure is customary only among nomadic people. The earliest example is in the 18th cent. BC in Cappadocia, perhaps contemporary with the patriarchal period. Settled people can worship a national god associated with a particular region, but nomads need a personal or clan god who goes with them. The theological strain of "the God of the Fathers" is important in biblical religion because it involves a personal relationship between God and the patriarch (and the clan) and thus works against formalism in religion. It supplies the background of the future covenantal relationship between God and Israel and also is a deterrent against any thought that God is found in only one place. (→ History, 75:38.)

16   Another form under which the patriarchs worshiped God was as El with various qualifying words: El Elyon (Gen 14:18); El Olam (Gen 21:33); El Shaddai (Gen 17:1; → 9 above); etc. F. M. Cross (→ 12 above) has shown that these qualifying words are not names of individual gods (i.e., the god Elyon, Shaddai, or Olam) but are adjectival titles of the one God El. When the patriarchs came into the land, they found that the Canaanites worshiped the supreme God El at various sanctuaries, under various titles. Thus, El Elyon (God Most High) was worshiped at Jerusalem; El Olam (God Eternal) was worshiped at Beer-sheba; El Berith (God of the Covenant) was worshiped at Shechem. (For these sanctuaries, → Institutions, 76:26, 29, 41.) The Bible portrays the patriarchs worshiping El under these titles at the respective sanctuaries. Comparing this to what we have said about "the God of the Fathers," we find that apparently the patriarchs did not see any contradiction in combining the worship of a God who had revealed himself to them in a particular way with the worship of a universal God already known in Canaan. Thus, Gen 49:25 puts "the God of your Father" in parallelism with El Shaddai. The El-worship of the patriarchs added a universal aspect not found in worship of the God of the Fathers, and thus both the God of nature (El) and the God of history (the God of Abraham) played a role in pre-Mosaic religion. When the God of history revealed himself to Moses as Yahweh, he was continuing the tradition of the God of the Fathers (Exod 3:15), but the Bible does not hesitate to apply to him the designations of El as Elyon, Shaddai, and Olam.

17   (III) The One God. Israelite thought is neither discursive nor speculative. The speculative questions of the existence of God and his unicity could not be considered in the OT, for the Israelites had no patterns of thought in which questions like this could be asked and answered. In the ancient Near East the existence of divine beings was universally accepted without question. As for unicity, in Israel there is no clear and unambiguous denial of the existence of gods other than Yahweh before Dt-Isa in the 6th cent. BC. (However,

Deut 32:39 has the same emphasis as Dt-Isa, and some scholars would date this Song of Moses to a considerably earlier period; → Deuteronomy, 6:57.) The absence of such a denial does not mean that the Israelites shared in some mitigated way the polytheistic beliefs of other ancient peoples; rather, they rejected these beliefs, but couched their rejection in other than philosophical terms.

If we pose these questions and answer them in biblical terms, we may say that whether or not there are many elohim ("god," "gods"; → 7 above), there is only one Yahweh (see C. J. Labuschagne, *The Incomparability of Yahweh in the Old Testament* [Leiden, 1966]). No matter what one understands by "elohim," Yahweh is elohim in a way in which no other being is. The question was not whether there is only one elohim, but whether there is any elohim like Yahweh. To the question put in this way the Israelites never gave any answer except a categorical denial. We observe, then, that in its early phases the Israelite vocabulary cannot adequately express Israelite belief.

18   In the first instance, the fact that there is only one Yahweh is clear from his name, which belongs to no one else. It is clear also from his unique relationship to Israel, which is shared with no other. The relationship is one of election and covenant that imposes upon Israel demands made by no other god upon his people. The most striking demand is that Israel shall worship no god but Yahweh. This is a violent departure from the cult patterns of the ancient Semitic world. Among the neighbors of Israel no god is conceived of as being so entirely and solely the benefactor and the judge of his worshipers that reverence for other gods is excluded — the cosmos is not the province of any single god. For the Israelites there is nothing they can ask from any other god and nothing to fear from any other god. This is not an explicit profession of monotheism, but it is to treat other gods as negligible.

19   The prohibition of not having other gods does not imply merely that Israel is Yahweh's peculiar possession from which he has excluded the action of competitors. Rather, wherever human beings and nature are found, there is the domain of Yahweh. He alone creates, and he alone directs the operations of natural forces — a concept that is peculiarly significant against the background of ancient nature deities. Theogony, the myth of the origin of the gods, is found everywhere else in the ancient Near East. It is highly important that the Israelites ask neither about the origin of Yahweh nor about the origin of other gods. To ask about the origin of Yahweh would be to deny that he is wholly other (→ 8 above), and to ask about the origin of other gods would be to admit their reality.

20   The unique nature of Yahweh is further demonstrated by the prohibition of images. We know of no other ancient Near Eastern god who was not visually represented. Their images were anthropomorphic, except in Egypt, where, for reasons obscure even to the Egyptians, some gods were represented theriomorphically (i.e., by animal images) or symbolically, as in the eccentric cult of Aton, which used the sun-disk (→ Biblical Archaeology, 74:77). The prohibition of representing Yahweh in image is even more striking in contrast with the biblical habit of speaking of Yahweh in human terms (→ 21 below). The prohibition (Exod 20:4; Deut 5:8) forbids the worship of anything in the heavens above, the earth beneath, or the water under the earth. This is intended to be a comprehensive enumeration of the entire visible world, and the commandment denies that Yahweh resembles anything in the universe. He is above and beyond it, and thereby has no resemblance to any elohim known to the Israelites.

Archaeology has illustrated the observance of this commandment. Although hundreds of divine images have been found in Israelite sites, nothing that could be called an image of Yahweh has been discovered. (But → Biblical Archaeology, 74:118, for the debate about the "Yahweh-Asherah" inscription and drawing at Kuntillat 'Ajrud in the Negeb.) Of course, the OT mentions perversions of the cult of Yahweh; but modern scholars have shown that even such a prominent instance as the bull or calf image set up at Bethel and at Dan did not involve a representation of Yahweh himself, for the bull was thought of as a pedestal upon which the invisible Yahweh stood (→ Institutions, 76:53).

A common epithet of Yahweh is "the living God"; this designation is by way of contrast with other gods who are sometimes identified with their images. Positively the epithet affirms that Yahweh possesses life, power, and personality: he is alert, attentive, and responsive. As the living God, he is also contrasted with mortal humanity— Yahweh gives and sustains life. From these ideas it was not a difficult step to the affirmation that Yahweh alone is elohim. If the gods of other peoples were ineffective, they had not the reality of elohim, and therefore no reality at all—they were only lifeless and manufactured images. (See O. Keel [ed.], *Monotheismus im Alten Israel und seiner Umwelt* [BibB 14; Fribourg, 1980]; B. Lang [ed.], *Der einzige Gott* [Munich, 1981]; D. Patrick, *The Rendering of God in the Old Testament* [OBT 10; Phl, 1981]; E. Zenger, *Der Gott der Bibel* [Stuttgart, 1979].)

21   (IV) Anthropomorphism. The attribution of human features and behavior to nonhuman beings (along with anthropopathism—the attribution of human feelings) is common in both religious and profane literature of all cultures. What makes anthropomorphism worthy of special attention in the OT is the difficulty of reconciling it with the prohibition of images and the explicit denials that Yahweh is like any created being. The fear of a plastic image of Yahweh is in marked contrast to the lack of restraint in employing verbal images. Yahweh has a countenance, eyes, ears, mouth, nostrils, hands, feet. He speaks, hears, smells, laughs, hisses, whistles, strikes, writes, walks. He feels delight, joy, anger, hatred, love, disgust, regret, compassion (see, e.g., T. E. Fretheim, *The Suffering of God* [OBT 14; Phl, 1984]). The OT never speaks of Yahweh without attributing human traits to him. There is scarcely any OT anthropomorphism that cannot be paralleled in other ancient Semitic literature; for the gods of other ancient Semitic peoples were personifications of natural forces or social realities to whom were attributed human features and behavior.

Some explicit restraints placed on anthropomorphism in the OT are not so easily paralleled elsewhere. When the OT says that Yahweh is not humanly changeable or infirm of purpose (Num 23:19), that he is elohim and not human (Hos 11:9), that he is spirit and not flesh, it is apparent that the authors were aware that figures of speech have limitations. In the context of ancient speech and religious beliefs, anthropomorphisms certainly made it difficult to understand the transcendence of Yahweh. Furthermore, they might have been an obstacle to the development of a truly spiritual idea of God. Yet an understanding of God is possible through anthropomorphisms that cannot be gained through a more refined and abstract discourse. After all, human speech cannot enunciate the ineffable reality of God by any means.

22 Through anthropomorphic description, the personality of Yahweh, the "living God," is constantly emphasized. The election of Israel, the formation of the covenant, and the saving acts by which Yahweh made Israel a people are acts of favor arising from personal benevolence. The law that is imposed upon Israel in the covenant is the externalization of a vital personal will. The response of Yahweh to love or to disobedience is a personal response of love or anger. His relations with Israel can be represented as the relations of the father to his children or of the husband to his wife. The personal relation of Yahweh to Israel demands a personal response and not merely an official or a cultic posture toward him. It becomes almost a commonplace in the prophetic books that cult without personal commitment is vain and hypocritical. The total demands of Yahweh can be met only by total surrender. Personal communication becomes possible: Yahweh speaks to Israel, and Israel can speak to Yahweh. The reality of his involvement in the history of Israel cannot be doubted. In prayer the speech of the OT attains through anthropomorphism an intimacy and an urgency that are scarcely paralleled elsewhere and cannot be achieved in any other way. The risk of humanizing God is accepted in order that the danger of thinking of him as an abstraction or an impersonal force may be avoided.

23   (V) Mythopoeic Thinking. The ancient civilizations of Mesopotamia and Egypt had an extensive mythology that has been largely recovered. The mythology of Canaan has been partly known since 1929 through the documents of ancient Ugarit, which illuminate many OT allusions (M. Coogan, *Stories from Ancient Canaan* [Phl, 1978]; P. Craigie, *Ugarit and the Old Testament* [GR, 1983]). Studies of these documents brought out the differences between the mythological thinking of ancient peoples and the thinking of Israel; and for many years a large number of scholars have agreed that the OT has no mythology. But to deny all mythology in the OT leaves a number of passages without a satisfactory explanation. Moreover, recently it has become clear that the denial of mythology in the OT implies a questionable definition of myth as essentially polytheistic and false.

(A) Definition of Myth. Modern analyses of the nature of myth suggest that it is not, by definition, polytheistic and false. Many myths express a polytheistic or an essentially distorted view of the universe; but this view is not necessarily due to mythological thinking itself, any more than philosophical or theological errors are due to the nature of philosophical and theological thinking. Most critics of myth have measured it against the standards of discursive logic and found it wanting; but in cultures without a developed discursive thought, mythological thinking is the only way in which the mind can approach certain problems that lie beyond sensible experience. These problems involve some of the most important questions that one can ask: the origin of the world and of the human race; the nature of deity; humanity's relations to nature and to deity; the origins of society and of social institutions; the ultimate validation of moral principles; the purpose and direction of human existence. These problems can also be approached by discursive reasoning with its own methods and principles. Myth does not really solve these problems, but it expresses an attitude in the presence of mystery; it is questionable whether discursive reasoning achieves any more. See Reventlow (*Problems* 154–67), who speaks of "a revolution in the assessment of myth" (155).

24 Myth is defined by E. Cassirer (*Language and Myth* [NY, 1946] 8ff.) as a symbolic form of expression together with art, language, and science. Each of these produces and posits a world of its own. Myth is an intuition and an act of belief. It seeks to impose intelligible form upon the realities that transcend experience. Myth does not attempt the paradox of knowing the unknowable; these realities can be expressed only by symbolic representation created from the data of experience. The symbol easiest to employ and to grasp is the symbol of personal activity, and in the world of myth impersonal causes do not appear.

Myth is couched in narrative, but the narrative is not historical and it is not intended to be historical. The event of myth is not the singular event located in time and space, but the recurring event of *the eternal Now,* as M. Eliade has called it. Myth presents in a story the constant reality of the universe. It does not pretend that the symbol is the reality, but it proposes the symbol as that which affords an insight into a reality beyond understanding. The goal of mythopoeic thinking is truth, not falsehood; and the fact that myth sometimes exhibits contradictory approaches to the reality it seeks is not in opposition to its quest for truth. In the world of discursive thought, the laws of being and of thought demand rigorous consistency. Myth allows that reality cannot be adequately apprehended and concedes the validity of more than one avenue of approach. These several avenues may lead to contradictory expressions, but myth admits contradictions on the assumption that their resolution lies beyond the insight that it conveys.

25   **(B) OT Mythopoeic Thought.** The use of mythical language and imagery in the OT has long been recognized; and since the discovery of the mythological literature of the ancient Near East, it has been possible to identify the sources of many mythological allusions in the OT. The following allusions can be adduced as examples, although not all of them are equally forceful: the personalization of natural phenomena (the sun, Ps 19:5–7; the morning star, Isa 14:12ff.; the rainbow, Gen 9:12ff.); the eschatological period described as a return to the conditions of the primeval period (Isa 11:6–9); etiological stories or stories composed to explain an existing situation, e.g., the stories of the creation of woman from the rib of man (Gen 2:21ff.) and of the origin of human toil and the pains of childbirth (Gen 3:16ff.); the union of the sons of Elohim and the daughters of men (Gen 6:4); the world catastrophe as a reversal of creation and a return to chaos (Isa 17:12ff.; 24:19; Jer 4:23); the enthroned Yahweh (Isa 6) and the chariot of Yahweh (Ezek 1); some features of the Day of Yahweh (Joel 2:10ff.; 3:3ff.); the assembly of the holy ones (Ps 89:18); Jerusalem as the mountain of the north, the mountain of assembly (Ps 48:3); the imagery of the theophany (Exod 19; 33:19–23; Judg 5:4; Heb 3; → 57 below). The poetic employment of imagery drawn from mythology is not of itself sufficient to establish a pattern of mythopoeic thought; but when these images are viewed in conjunction with other passages of the OT, a pattern that can be called mythopoeic begins to emerge. In these passages imagery drawn from mythology is not mere poetic embellishment, but is employed in a serious effort to express in words an intuition of transcendent reality.

26   Where the OT touches upon problems that in other cultures were the objects of mythopoeic thought, a comparison between Israelite treatment of these problems and the mythologies of other ancient peoples is possible. There is scarcely any mythology without a myth of ORIGINS OR CREATION. Since the discovery of the Mesopotamian myth of creation, *Enuma Elish (ANET* 60–72), it has been evident that Gen 1 exhibits the same superficial and unscientific view of the structure of the visible universe as the Mesopotamian myth (→ Genesis, 2:2, 4). The differences are striking: The Israelite account contains nothing of the origin of the gods or of a cosmic conflict between gods—elements that in the Mesopotamian myth were a vital part of the process of creation.

Nothing is left but a tranquil act of creation by word that makes clear the effortless supremacy of the creative deity. The OT account is openly polemic against the Mesopotamian myth, or rather against the conception of creation that is represented in the Mesopotamian myth; but it does not replace the myth with history or science, of which it has none, nor with theological reasoning, unless this term is used very loosely. The Mesopotamian myth is replaced by another myth; the difference lies in the conception of the deity.

27   The OT contains no account of a COSMIC CONFLICT from which creation arises—a common motif in mythology. But the allusions to a victory of Yahweh over the monster of chaos are numerous (→ 51 below), an indication that oral tradition probably contained an account of creation in which Yahweh was the victor in a combat. This combat was found in the myths of both Mesopotamia and Canaan and perhaps was transferred to Yahweh from these sources, thus becoming an example of mythopoeic thinking transformed by the character of Yahweh. It has been noticed above (→ 24) that a feature of mythopoeic thought is to permit several diverse avenues of approach; the allusions to a combat are a diverse approach to creation from that of Gen 1. It is also characteristic of myth that the "event" is not a contingent historical event but a constant in reality, an eternal Now; the allusions to the creative victory of Yahweh treat it as a present and enduring reality. Were Yahweh to relax his domination over the monster, the world would relapse into chaos.

28   The story of the DELUGE exhibits another example of the revision of a foreign myth. No OT passage has so many and such clear literary affinities with extrabiblical literature as the flood story; its dependence on this earlier myth is manifest (*ANET* 42–44, 93–95; → Genesis, 2:12). The Mesopotamian myth is an effort to face the problem of natural catastrophes, accompanied by random destruction. It attributes them to the capricious anger of the gods; for divine anger, like human anger, can be irrational and human beings can do nothing except submit to superior power. To the Israelites this was an erroneous conception of the deity. The error was corrected not by eliminating the story but by rewriting it in such a way that the anger of Yahweh is intelligibly motivated by human wickedness. In natural catastrophe the Israelites saw the righteous judgment of God on sin, and they expressed this insight by retelling an existing story. This is mythopoeic thinking and, again, the transforming element is the conception of God.

29   There is no ancient myth parallel to the account of the ORIGIN AND FALL OF ADAM AND EVE found in Gen 2–3, but biblical details echo features of ancient mythology. These details have been woven into a conception of human origins and destiny that is one of the most profound and creative pieces of literature in the entire OT. Here the conception of God is balanced by a conception of humanity that differs in a striking way from what is found elsewhere in the ancient Near East. In narrative form the story describes the condition of human beings: their dignity and their fall, their mortality, their relations with God and with the material universe, moral responsibility, the origin and meaning of sex. Notable is the polemic of the story against the myth and ritual of fertility. To present these profound insights the author uses such mythopoeic symbols as the trees, the serpent, the garden, and the rib. A parallel account of the first man, found in Ezek 28:12–16 (→ Ezekiel, 20:71), suggests that this story was told in variant forms in Israel; and the form found in Ezek, which is even richer in mythological imagery, may be one of the elements from which Gen 2–3 was composed.

30   Mythopoeic thought in the OT or elsewhere is not deliberately chosen in preference to logical discourse. Myth arises in cultures in which logical discourse has not been achieved. But myth is never entirely expelled even in advanced cultures. It remains the most apt form for the expression of transcendental reality, too large and too profound for scientific observation and philosophical analysis. For this reason, the mythopoeic thought of the OT retains not only its charm but also its validity in the history of Christian belief and theology. The history of thought shows that as thinking demythologized, it is proportionately secularized. Mythopoeic thought sees the transcendent reality as pervading the visible universe. In Mesopotamia the origin of kingship was explained by its descent from heaven. Philosophical thought seeks an explanation in processes that can be submitted to logical investigation and analysis. In expelling myth we run the risk of expelling the divine also. We have not always succeeded in replacing the intuitions of mythopoeic thought with intuitions of a higher order.

31   Pius XII (*Humani Generis, EB* 618) echoed a warning uttered by many earlier exegetes when he said that OT beliefs must not be reduced to the level of the mythology of other peoples. It is more accurate to speak of mythopoeic thought in the OT rather than of its myths or mythology. We have alluded in the preceding paragraphs to the factor that makes Israelite mythopoeic thought unique in the ancient Near East and is the ultimate basis of its validity, viz., the Israelite conception of the reality of God—the personal character of Yahweh. This insight into the divine reality the Israelites themselves attributed to revelation, to a personal encounter with the God who spoke to them, their savior and their judge. To present this insight no forms of thought and speech were available to them except those forms that were common in the ancient Near East. The transcendental reality of Yahweh breaks through the forms of mythology as it breaks through the forms of science and metaphysics; but we cannot reject any of these forms in an effort to grasp more firmly a truth whose comprehension ever eludes us.

32   **(VI) The Spirit of God.**
      (A) Concept of Spirit. The same Hebr word serves to signify both *wind* and *spirit*. The wind is the breath of God; it is a sensible manifestation of the divine presence and power. It moves suddenly and unpredictably; we can neither foretell nor control its direction or its strength. We cannot determine its source or its destination (John 3:8). It is subtle, verges on the immaterial in its nature, and is universal and irresistible in its scope. Hence, the wind is an extremely apt symbol of the divine.

33   In the OT the spirit is not a personal being. It is a principle of action, not a subject. It belongs properly to Yahweh alone; it is communicated to living beings, but it never becomes a part of the structure of the living being in such a way that the living being possesses the spirit as its own. The spirit is said to clothe (Judg 6:34; 1 Chr 12:19; 2 Chr 24:20), to be poured out (Isa 29:10; 44:3; Ezek 39:29; Joel 2:28), to leap upon (Judg 14:6,19; 15:14; 1 Sam 10:10; 11:6). One is filled with the spirit (Exod 31:3), or Yahweh puts his spirit into one (Isa 63:11; Ezek 36:27; Num 11:25,29). The spirit can also be taken from a person (Ps 51:13) or can depart (1 Sam 16:14). Elisha asked for a double portion of the spirit of Elijah (2 Kgs 2:9). The phrases used in these contexts treat the spirit as a subtle substance or liquid; more clearly, they emphasize the impersonal nature of the spirit. The quality that is most evident in the spirit is power.

34   The spirit is not often mentioned as a creative force. In Gen 1:2 the wind "broods" over the waters of chaos; the movement of the wind is the first sign of the creative activity about to break forth. In Ps 33:6 the word of Yahweh and his breath are creative forces; the power by which Yahweh expels an utterance is the power felt in the wind. The wind is also a destructive force; it is the breath of the nostrils of Yahweh, his anger (Ps 18:16), which dries up the springs (Hos 13:15) and is an instrument of his judgment (Isa 30:27–28).

      The breath of Yahweh is the principle of life for all living beings; they survive by the communication of his spirit. This thought appears in a number of passages (Gen 2:7; 6:17; 7:15; Job 33:4; Eccl 3:19,21). The breath of life is communicated by inspiration (Gen 2:7), and the living being dies when Yahweh takes away his spirit (Ps 104:29), which then returns to Yahweh (Eccl 12:7).

35   **(B) The Spirit in the History of Israel.** The spirit is more frequently represented as a principle of those activities that affect the people of Israel precisely as the people of Yahweh. In the period of the judges and of the early monarchy we meet the spirit as a mysterious divine impulse that moves a man to deeds above his known capacity and habits of behavior—deeds of delivering Israel from its enemies (Judg 3:10; 6:34; 11:29; 13:25; 14:6,19; 15:14). Similarly, Saul is moved by the spirit to deliver the city of Jabesh-gilead (1 Sam 11:6,13). Here also the spirit appears primarily as a principle of power. The movement of the spirit is the distinctive mark of the person whom Max Weber called the "charismatic leader." In normal times the loose organization of the tribes of Israel needed no more than the simple government of clan and village elders. When the peace of Israel was threatened by external enemies, this leadership was not enough, and it was supplanted by the leader who demonstrated the possession of the spirit by the deeds of the spirit. During the period of the judges, the spirit of the charismatic leader was a passing phenomenon: the spirit came upon the leaders during the emergency, impelled them to a mission, and departed after the mission was accomplished (→ Judges, 8:8). The king, on the contrary, was a permanent charismatic officer, as signified by the anointing at which the spirit was conferred (1 Sam 10:10). When David was anointed, the spirit passed to him from Saul (16:13). Once the idea was established that the spirit reposed permanently upon the king, there was less frequent mention of the spirit in the narratives about the king; and extraordinary actions in the manner of the judges were not attributed to the kings after Saul.

36   The spirit that impels to action may be an evil spirit "from Yahweh" or "of Elohim" (never "of Yahweh"). An evil spirit causes dissension at Shechem (Judg 9:23), moves Saul to attempt to murder David (1 Sam 19:9), and Yahweh sends a lying spirit into the mouth of false prophets (1 Kgs 22:23). This usage illustrates the idea of spirit as a universally pervasive divine power. In the very simple and unsophisticated thinking of early Israel, human actions that are unexpected or inexplicable indicate the activity of a power greater than that possessed by the individual. This power can be attributed to no other than Yahweh, who through his spirit enables actions beyond the usual capacity. The spirit itself is morally neutral; the moral responsibility for such actions lies upon the agents.

37   The operations of the spirit in prophecy are somewhat ambiguous. Prophecy is not attributed to the spirit by Amos, Hosea, Isaiah, and Jeremiah. (The passage Mic 3:8, where the prophet speaks of himself as full of the spirit of Yahweh, is not certainly original with this prophet.) Yet in earlier prophecy the spirit is frequently associated with prophetic utterance (Num 11:17,25; 24:2; 1 Sam 10:10; 19:20–24).

The idea of prophecy passed through a notable development between the early monarchy and the prophets of the 8th cent. (→ Prophetic Lit., 11:7–8). In the period of the early monarchy the prophets were often ecstatic rather than inspired speakers. "The sons of the prophets" seem to have been cultic groups that practiced a worship of song and dance, often in an unrestrained manner; such exaltation was a sign of the activity of the spirit. The references to prophetic speech in Num (given above) occur in contexts of ecstatic utterance. In the stories of Elijah and Elisha the spirit is an agent that transports the prophet from place to place (1 Kgs 18:12; 2 Kgs 2:16) or a power that enables the prophet to work wonders (2 Kgs 2:15). In the classical period of prophecy, beginning with Amos, *ca.* 750 BC—a period when the prophet speaks the word of Yahweh (→ 45 below)—the spirit is not an inspiring agent. In the exilic and postexilic periods the spirit does appear as an inspiring agent (Ezek 2:2; 3:24; 11:5; Zech 7:12; Neh 9:30). Here we notice that Ezekiel, in contrast with the prophets of the 8th and 7th cents., frequently employs vision and ecstasy as media of expression. These are the areas of the activity of the spirit.

38 As a principle of activity, the spirit, morally neutral, is manifested in a large variety of operations both good and bad. There is a spirit of lying (1 Kgs 22:22), of knowledge of a craft (Exod 31:3), of jealousy (Num 5:14), of judgment (Isa 4:4), of confusion (Isa 19:14), of deep sleep (Isa 29:10), of fornication (Hos 4:12), of compassion and supplication (Zech 12:10), a willing spirit (Ps 51:14), a spirit of princes (a haughty spirit, Ps 76:13). It is difficult to synthesize such uses as these, and it seems better not to seek perfect consistency in Hebr thought and language about the spirit. The common element in these uses, if one is to be found, seems to be the unusual or the extraordinary degree in which skill, fornication, confusion, compassion, and other things are exhibited. Behavior surpassing the normal is, again, the area in which spirit is manifested.

39 In the messianic era (→ 152ff. below) the spirit breaks out in a new fullness. "Messianic" persons such as the king (Isa 11:1), the servant of Yahweh (42:1), and the prophet who announces the messianic salvation (61:1) receive the spirit; in the messianic king, the operations of the spirit demonstrate his messianic character. The spirit is poured upon the whole people (Isa 32:15; 44:3; Ezek 39:29; Joel 3:28); combined with a new heart, the spirit is a principle of moral regeneration (Ezek 36:26). Later prophets attribute the deliverance of Israel in the exodus to the spirit (Isa 63:11,14). The individual Israelite may ask for a portion of the spirit (Ps 51:12; 143:10). The spirit becomes a power for righteous conduct.

This may appear to be a conventionalizing of older usage so that the idea of spirit is weakened; but the messianic regeneration is not conceived of as the achievement of merely conventional morality—it is a revolution in human conduct. The tremendous development of the idea of spirit in the NT flows easily from the conception of the spirit as the vivifying, energizing power of God in the messianic fullness. In the NT all the OT lines of development are brought together in the revelation of the personal reality of the Spirit.

(Heron, A. I. C., *The Holy Spirit* [Phl, 1983]. Lys, D., *"Rûach": Le souffle dans l'Ancien Testament* [Paris, 1962]. Neve, L., *The Spirit of God in the Old Testament* [Tokyo, 1972].)

40 (VII) The Word of God.
(A) Concept of Word. In the ancient Near East the spoken word was conceived of as a distinct entity laden with power. This was eminently true of the divine word. In both Egypt and Mesopotamia the divine word was a creative force educing the world into existence. In Mesopotamia, the divine decree determining the various fates was the power that moved and directed the course of events. The divine word partook of the power and the eternity of the gods themselves, and people could not resist or alter it.

Similarly, the human word was a being endowed with power, but in a lesser degree—a power most clearly manifested in solemn utterances such as blessings and curses, contracts, promises, and other processes that were intended to stabilize human relations. The word of the king was more powerful than the word of a commoner, but even a commoner possessed the fearful power of blessing and cursing (on *dābār*, "word," see *TDOT* 3. 84–125).

41 In magic, as distinct from other forms of speech, the power resides in the word itself and not in the person; this is in contrast to the Israelite conception of the spoken word (→ 42 below). The operative factor in magical rites is the rigidly correct formula, a set arrangement of words properly pronounced. Since the power resides in the formula, that must be kept occult; anyone who knows the formula possesses the power. The magical conception of the power of the word is actually a perversion of the older conception.

42 The concept of the power of the word probably arises, at least in part, from the importance given to the spoken formula in cultures that use little or no writing. In such utterances as blessings and curses, promises, threats, wishes, commands, and contracts, the word has a reality that endures into the future; indeed, the effect of the spoken word may outlive the speaker. The word posits a reality, and it is, in itself, the reality that it posits. The reality exists first in the heart or desire, then passes into speech, and finally effective speech brings into existence the reality that it signifies.

The power of the word is rooted in the power of the person. By speaking, one externalizes oneself (G. van der Leeuw) or releases psychic energy (J. Pedersen). The permanence and energy of personal volition reach the external world through the spoken word, and the spoken word retains these qualities of permanence and energy. Such respect for and even fear of the spoken word are not frequently encountered in cultures where important utterances must be recorded in writing for validity. In these cultures a fear of the document is more likely.

43 Instances of the word's power are numerous in the OT. In the deception of Isaac by Jacob (Gen 27) and the deception of Jacob by Laban (Gen 29:20–27), an error concerning the person does not invalidate the solemn spoken word; for the word by its emission has become a reality that cannot be recalled. Isaac can give Esau another, inferior blessing, but he cannot cancel the blessing he mistakenly gave to Jacob. When Micah's mother curses the thief who, unknown to her, is her own son (Judg 17:1–2), she cannot withdraw the curse but can send a blessing to follow it and counteract it. David's pronunciation of a sentence of death upon the man in the parable of Nathan (2 Sam 12:1–18) is unwittingly directed at himself; the prophet assures him that it will be diverted, but it falls upon David's child born of Bathsheba. The woman accused of adultery must consume an oath of execration by drinking water into which the written words of a curse have been immersed (Num 5:12–31); nothing but innocence will neutralize the fatal effects of the curse.

44 Correlative with the dynamic aspect of the word is its dianoetic aspect (O. Procksch), i.e., its ability to render things intelligible. This is the function of the word as name (→ 6 above). To know the name is to experience the dynamism of the word in the reverse direction; as the power of the person determines reality by conferring the name, so the power of the person apprehends reality by knowing the name.

45   (B) The Word in the History of Israel. The OT conception of "the word of Yahweh" must be understood against the above background. Most occurrences of "the word of Yahweh" designate the prophetic word; the word is the specific charism of the prophet, as *tôrâ* (law) is the charism of the priest, and counsel the charism of the sage (Jer 18:18). The prophetic word is misunderstood if one thinks of it as merely the experience of hearing; it is the reception of a positive dynamic reality that arises from the power of the person of Yahweh and compels the prophet to speak (Amos 3:8). The reception of the word is compared in Ezek 2:9–3:3 to the eating of a scroll. The word of Yahweh is a joy and a delight (Jer 15:16), a burning fire shut up in the bones of the prophet (20:7–9), a fury that he must pour out (6:11).

The prophetic word partakes of the dynamism of Yahweh himself; it is fulfilled or established when the reality of which it speaks comes into existence. The relation of the prophetic word to the event is more than the relation of prediction and fulfillment; the word is an entity endowed with power that effects the thing signified by the word. The word of Yahweh placed in the mouth of Jeremiah gives the prophet power to uproot and to tear down, to destroy and to ruin, to build and to plant (Jer 1:9–10); the prophet accomplishes these things by uttering the word. The word of Yahweh does not return to him empty (Isa 45:23; 55:10–11) nor does he take it back (31:2). Were it to return without fulfilling its destiny, the personal dynamism of Yahweh himself would be frustrated. This word partakes of Yahweh's eternity (40:8); its dynamism may be delayed, but its fulfillment is inevitable (9:8).

46   The word of Yahweh is the essential operative agent in the history of Israel from the first act of the creative process (Gen 1:3) to the rebuilding of Jerusalem by the decree of Cyrus (Isa 44:28). The utterance of Yahweh brings about the call of Abraham and of Moses, the exodus of Israel from Egypt, the conquests of Joshua, the call of Samuel, the establishment of the monarchy, the election of David, the division of the kingdom, the fall of the house of Omri, the invasions of the Assyrians and the Chaldeans, the fall of the kingdom of Israel and of the kingdom of Judah.

The word of Yahweh is also a creative agent (Gen 1; Isa 40:26; 48:13; Pss 33:6,9; 147:15–18). In the comprehensive concept of the OT, creation by word is combined with other ideas that are perhaps older (e.g., creation by work; → 54 below). However, modern critics regard this development as late; both Dt-Isa and Gen 1 come from exilic and postexilic literature.

47   (VIII) God and Nature. Our idea of nature has an incalculable effect on our idea of the deity; yet to an extent the two ideas should be independent. The relations of nature with a transcendental deity who is not included in the ambit of nature do not depend on the constitution of nature. But when one identifies the deity with nature, either in the mythological polytheism of the ancient Near East, or in the scientism of modern thought, the deity is given the form of nature itself, and the idea of the deity consequently undergoes substantial modifications.

48   (A) Concept of Nature. The OT idea of nature has more in common with the prevailing ideas of the ancient Near East than it has with the modern scientific and philosophical outlook; and the difference has often been an obstacle to the incorporation of the biblical idea of the relations of God and nature into modern systems of thought. In this area philosophy and science have sometimes dictated the terms to theology. Classically, nature has been conceived of as an impersonal and objective unity with regular and predictable behavior governed by "laws." The idea of nature as a unity first appeared as *kosmos* in Gk thought, and early Gk philosophers devoted most of their efforts to formulating a principle of the unity that they perceived in nature. The entire development of modern science rests upon the conviction of the unity and the regularity of nature. However, in the ancient Near East there is not even a word that can be translated "nature." The phenomena of the visible world are regarded neither as constituting a unity nor as impersonal. The conflicting diversity of natural forces is what first impresses the unsophisticated observer; and because of the conflict the observer is more impressed by irregularity than by the recurrence of basic patterns. The forces of nature exhibit the kind of unpredictability that we associate with human behavior, and so are endowed in prephilosophical thought with the qualities of the human person. But since the forces of nature are so vast in power and scope, they are magnified as persons and thus become gods. Cosmic order is achieved by compromise, by the unsteady balance of the mutual agreement of many powerful wills, by a recurring conflict in which no single force ever emerges supreme. Cosmic order is conceived of as political; it is maintained in the universe as it is maintained in the state. Beneath this order there is always the potential of anarchy that would reduce nature to chaos. If the course of nature is to be maintained in harmony with our goals, we must keep these personal forces benevolently disposed.

The resultant concept of deity lacks perfect unity and is as fluid as nature itself. The gods are not simply identified with the forces and phenomena of nature; and in addition to the gods there are demons, either beneficent or maleficent, to whom belong many lesser areas of natural phenomena. Demons are met not by cult but by magic. In the areas of demonic operations, nature is seen at its most unpredictable and irrational; but even in the areas governed by the gods one is never assured that the divine will is not arbitrary and capricious. Finally, the resultant idea of the divine will does not really arise above the level of nature; the gods are not a kind of being totally different either from people or from the phenomena of the visible world.

49   The OT shares the ancient conception of nature as diversified and personal. There is no Hebr word for "nature," and the unity that the OT sees in nature is not mechanical unity but the unity of a personal will. Yet the Israelites do not attribute personality to the distinct forces of nature, and there are no separate gods to correspond to the separate natural forces. The divine personal reality of Yahweh does not lie within nature; Yahweh is identified neither with nature as a whole nor with any of its parts. The absence of sexual characteristics and functions in Yahweh is a striking illustration of the unique OT conception of God. (In Hebr thought, male gender is attributed to the angels or "sons of God" who are members of the heavenly court—this reflects the distant origins of the heavenly court as a polytheistic pantheon with male and female gods who were the children of a supreme god. The angels impregnate women in Gen 6:2 [cf. 1 Cor 11:10], and in some Jewish legends they are circumcised.) Sex as the source of life is vitally involved in the mythology of other ancient Near Eastern peoples; and much of their myth and ritual is intended to communicate to the worshipers the sexual energy of the gods. For Israel Yahweh is the source of life but not through sexual processes.

50   (B) Creation. There is nothing in the beliefs of other ancient Near Eastern peoples that corresponds to Yahweh as creator, in spite of the fact that the OT exhibits several ways of conceiving the creative process. These ways, no doubt, represent different phases of development. It happens that the most explicit texts about creation are exilic or later, and several modern scholars have concluded that the idea of creation was either unimportant or missing in early Israelite belief. That it was missing entirely is highly improbable; other religions dealt with creation formally and at length. Nor was the idea unimportant; but its importance must be viewed in the entire context of Israelite thought and not as a detached article of belief. In the OT, creation is the beginning of history—the first of the saving deeds of Yahweh. The Israelites do not ask questions about creation for its own sake; creation and nature are integrated in the history of the salvation wrought by Yahweh. (Note that in the Israelite "credos" Yahweh is not proclaimed as God the creator—as in the Christian creed—but as the God who was active in the history of the patriarchs [Deut 6:20–25; 26:5–10; Josh 24:2–13].) It is in this historical context that the several approaches to creation must be seen. See B. W. Anderson [ed.], *Creation in the Old Testament* (IRT 6; Phl, 1984); N. Young, *Creator, Creation and Faith* (Phl, 1976).

51   *Creation as combat.* Probably the oldest approach to creation, now reflected only in some OT allusions, related it to a combat between Yahweh and an adversary representing chaos. In Mesopotamia, creation is achieved by the victory of Marduk over the monster Tiamat. In the Canaanite myths of Ugarit, Aleyan Baal engages in combat with an adversary Mot, with another called Sea or River, and with another named Leviathan or Shalyat of the seven heads. Leviathan appears in the OT (Isa 27:1). Such a combat is reflected in Pss 74:13–15; 89:10–11; Isa 27:1; 51:9; Job 9:13; 26:12; 38:8–11. None of these passages is certainly early, and the allusions are most frequently explained as poetic imagery borrowed from foreign mythology. Yet there is no reason to suppose that this primitive conception, so evidently reflecting the mythology of other peoples, was not the earliest and the most unsophisticated account of creation in Israel. With the progress of belief in Yahweh, this account was suppressed in favor of other more advanced explanations until it survived only in poetic allusions. The survival exhibits a basic conception of nature that Israel shared with other peoples, the conception that cosmic order is not mechanical. Cosmic order is maintained by Yahweh's power over the forces of chaos, which he can release (→ 55 below). See J. Day, *God's Conflict with the Dragon and the Sea* (Cambridge, 1985).

52   *Creation according to Gen.* The allusions to creation in the OT are numerous, but the passages in which the theme is treated explicitly and at length are few: Gen 1:1–2:4a; Ps 104. The story in Gen 2:4b–25 is not a creation account in the same sense. It treats of human origins, or more precisely of the origin of sex; and the creation of the material world is mentioned merely by allusion. Gen 2:4b–25 (J) is older than Gen 1:1–2:4a (P), but the concept of creation exhibited by P is older than its present literary form (→ Genesis, 2:4). Even in Gen 1:1 we are probably not dealing with creation from nothing or creation in the strictest sense, but with God's ordering of chaos into a fixed universe. Creation from nothing does not appear clearly in the Bible until the Gk period when philosophical notions are current (2 Macc 7:28).

The structure of the material universe seen in Gen 1 and in almost all allusions to creation and to the material world (see Job 38:4–38) is the structure seen also in Mesopotamian creation accounts. The universe exists in three levels: heavens, earth, and subterranean abyss of waters. The earth is a flat disk that floats upon the waters, and the heavens above are the divine dwelling. The entire structure rests on pillars. The heavenly bodies move across the sky; and rain, snow, hail, and wind are stored in chambers above the sky. The enumeration of eight works in Gen 1:1ff. is intended to be complete; it covers every item in the structure so conceived and affirms expressly that Elohim has made each item. The account is framed in such a way that it is a counterposition to the Mesopotamian myth of creation (→ 26 above). Items like the abyss and the heavenly bodies, which in Mesopotamia were personified and deified, are here depersonalized. There is nothing prior to the creative word, and in particular no combat. The concept of the material universe is not altered, but the relations of the universe to the creative deity are completely different.

53   *Creation according to Ps 104.* This creation poem shows certain literary relations to the Aton hymn produced in 14th-cent. Egypt in the reign of Akhenaton (*ANET* 368–71; → Biblical Archaeology, 74:77). It is difficult to determine whether these relationships arise from similarity of subject or from the Israelite poet's knowledge of the Egyptian work. In any case, the conception of Ps 104 is wholly Israelite. The dominant theme is the care of the creator for living beings, both animals and humans. Natural phenomena are almost entirely represented in relation to the sustenance of life. The poem is very optimistic, although in this it does not differ substantially from the other creation accounts. In all of them the work of creation is seen as good in its origin, without defect or any element hostile to humanity. By the removal of the theme of the cosmic combat Israelite thought removes the dualism implicit in other creation accounts.

54   Through these poems and other allusions to creation there runs a double conception of the creative act; creation by work and creation by word. Although creation by work is especially evident in older passages such as Gen 2, creation by word (→ 46 above) is not necessarily recent. Creation by word appears in the Egyptian theology of Memphis, which is placed by Egyptologists about 2700 BC, much earlier than any OT document (*ANET* 4–6). Both creation by work and creation by word appear in Gen 1. The original naïve anthropomorphism (→ 21 above) involved in creation by work is seen in Gen 2, where Yahweh "forms" humans and animals—a word used of the work of the potter, which is the image intended. The same image appears in Egypt and in Mesopotamia. Other words such as "build" or "make" are common in allusions to creation. A refinement is seen in the use of the word that we translate "create" (Hebr *bārā'*), which is never used except with Yahweh as its subject; it is the kind of production of which only Yahweh is capable. More refined still is the creation by word, in which the command is followed by the execution with no further action. The two conceptions are mingled in the same passage—an illustration of the multiplicity of mythopoeic thinking (→ 24 above).

55   **(C) Continued Creation.** The creation account of Gen 1 suggests that the Israelites thought of creation as finished with the six days. In other accounts, creation is represented as a continuing process that endures as long as the world itself endures. The victory of Yahweh over the monster of chaos is sometimes spoken of as a victory that constantly recurs; the monster is said to be bound or restrained rather than killed (Pss 89:10; 104:6–8; Job 26:12; 38:8–11). Thus Yahweh sustains and defends the material universe against the forces of disintegration; without the uninterrupted exercise of his saving power, the world will relapse into chaos. This Israelite conception escapes the dualism of pagan cosmic mythology by denying to the forces of disintegration any power that matches the power of Yahweh. In the dualism of the pagan cosmic myth the balance of order and chaos is so close that a cyclic conflict is inevitable.

Similarly, each manifestation of Yahweh's dominion can be represented as a reenactment of his victory over chaos. The heavenly bodies are marshaled by him daily and appear in obedience to his call (Isa 40:26; 45:12; 48:13). Yahweh makes dawn and darkness (Amos 4:13; 5:8), measures the waters in the hollow of his hand (Isa 40:12), gives breath and spirit to those who walk the earth (42:5). The creative acts of Ps 104 recur each day.

56   The continuing creative activity of Yahweh is emphasized in the area of *fertility*. Throughout the ancient Near East, there was a ritual reenactment of the myth of creation, in which fertility was annually restored through the death and resurrection of the god of fertility and his union with his consort. Against this belief the OT contains a vigorous polemic. Yahweh, and not the Baal, bestows the fruits of the soil (Hos 2:10ff.); he blesses the progeny of humans and of animals and the fruit of the soil (Deut 7:13; Jer 31:12). He gives and withholds rain (Isa 30:23; Lev 26:4; Deut 11:13–15; Jer 5:24). Unlike the gods of fertility, Yahweh bestows the blessings of fertility without himself being involved in the process.

57   In some conceptions the involvement of Yahweh in nature seems closer. The OT sees nature as personal, but not as the activity of a number of personal beings. The one natural phenomenon with which Yahweh is most frequently associated is *the storm*. OT poetry in which he is represented as the lord of the storm has obvious affinities with the literature and art of other ancient Near Eastern peoples; the number and vivid coloring of allusions to Yahweh and the storm have persuaded a number of scholars that Yahweh was originally a storm god like Adad or Hadad (Pss 29:3–9; 77:17–21; 107:25–29; Isa 30:27,30; Nah 1:3,5; Job 38:25,35,37). This opinion is now generally abandoned, but the connection between Yahweh and the storm is too common to be merely coincidental.

The presentation of Yahweh in *the theophany* of the storm is striking (Pss 18:8–16; 68:8–10; Hab 3:3–15; Judg 5:4–5; Exod 19:16,19; Ezek 1). The elements of the theophanies suggest not only the storm but also earthquake and possibly volcanic eruption. The theophany is an Israelite confession of the power of Yahweh in nature; but this power is not seen as blind, irrational force. Most frequently Yahweh appears in the theophany as the savior of his people from their enemies. In the theophany of Sinai, Yahweh comes as the deliverer who makes a covenant with Israel; his power in nature is a warrant of his power and will to save Israel. According to later biblical developments (→ 60 below) the power of Yahweh in nature is also manifested as a power of judgment, an act of his moral will that affects all evildoers, whether they be Israelites or others.

58   In Israelite belief the unpredictability of nature (→ 48 above) is modified by the conception of an order in nature, an order founded on the wisdom of Yahweh. Being wise, Yahweh is not capricious, and nature is not fundamentally irrational. The allusions to the wisdom of Yahweh in nature are numerous (Prov 3:19; Isa 28:23–29);

his relations with nature are called a covenant (Hos 2:18; Job 5:23). Several poems extol the wisdom of Yahweh in creation (Prov 8:22ff.; Ps 104). Job 38–39 sees Yahweh's wisdom in the production of paradoxes in nature; his directive intelligence maintains order and harmony among diverse and conflicting agents. Nature becomes dependable according to the dependability of the moral will of Yahweh; its order is the order of righteousness.

Hence, when nature strikes with disaster, it is no chance occurrence; nature is the weapon of Yahweh's anger (Amos 4:7; Joel 2:1–11; Jer 5:24; Hos 8:7; 9:14; → 99–102 below). Hebr language and thought do not distinguish between "physical" and "moral" evil; the moral evil of sin inevitably has cosmic repercussions in nature because Yahweh withholds his blessings and employs nature as the executor of his judgments. This is the thought expressed in the OT rewriting of the Mesopotamian myth of the deluge (→ 28 above) and in the curses laid on the man and the woman of Gen 3:16ff. "Disorder" in nature is not really disorder but a higher order, the order of righteous judgment.

59   Nature as a personal activity is a wonder to the Israelites, and the word wonder here is equivalent to mystery rather than to miracle. Until recent times apologetics had elaborated a concept of miracle that presupposed a closed system of nature governed by fixed laws. This concept of miracle is not found in the OT because the presupposition is missing (→ NT Thought, 81:93). Creation itself is as emphatically a wonder as any extraordinary phenomenon in nature (Job 4:8–10; 9:5–10; 26:5–14; 36:26–37:18; 38:1–41:26). When the events of the exodus or other saving deeds of Yahweh are called wonders, the element of wonder does not lie precisely in Yahweh's work in nature, which is always wonderful, but rather in his saving will. This is the supreme wonder—both mystery and miracle—of Israelite faith and history. Into this saving will all the phenomena of nature and the events of history (→ 113ff. below) are integrated.

60   The supreme manifestation of the power of Yahweh in nature is eschatological (→ 167 below). Nature as the instrument of judgment finds expression in the expectation of the Day of Yahweh, i.e., the cataclysmic encounter of Yahweh with the powers of evil (→ 137 below). The annihilating judgment of Yahweh will reduce the earth to the primitive chaos that it was before the creative action (Jer 4:23–26). The structure of the earth and sky and their supporting pillars will totter (Isa 13:3,10; 24:3,19,23; Joel 3:3; Amos 8:8; 9:5). In the past the deluge was a return to chaos, according to the P version (Gen 7:11).

Eschatological chaos is the necessary condition for a new creation (Isa 65:17). The hostile desert will be transformed and watered (Isa 32:15; 35:1ff.; 41:18–20). Fertility of the land, the gift of Yahweh, will be granted in superabundance (Ezek 36:6–12; Joel 4:18; Amos 9:13). The alternation of the seasons, the annual token of the uncertainty of nature, and even the alternation of day and night will cease (Zech 14:6). The struggle for life in the animal world will be ended (Isa 11:6–9). Israelite eschatology demands such a goal or terminus for nature. The withdrawal of Yahweh's anger and the bestowal of his blessings without restraint must bring about a new creation—a witness to the righteousness and power of Yahweh demanded by his holiness. Yahweh is the supreme lord of nature, and his power must be demonstrated in salvation and blessing just as it is demonstrated in judgment.

ISRAEL—GOD'S COVENANTED PEOPLE

61   (I) Human Nature. The OT has no consistent psychology. Its language and vocabulary concerning human actions and the components of human nature are altogether popular and difficult to translate into modern terms. The usual Hebr word for "man" (modern Eng "humanity") as a species (*'ādām*) is an instance; it does not designate a species but a group (like the English word sheep), and an individual member of the group is distinguished by being called a "son" or a "daughter" of man. The group is seen as an existent reality rather than as an abstract essence; and so the Israelites neither asked nor enunciated a definition of the metaphysical human essence. They were more concerned with the relations of the collective group to the deity and to the world in which the group lives than they were with the inner constitution of the species.

62   The OT is profoundly aware of the paradoxical and the mysterious in human nature, as is evident in the *J* account of creation (Gen 2). Human beings are made of clay and are therefore mortal and feeble, but the clay is vitalized by the spirit given by Yahweh (→ 34 above). Human dignity, however, does not rest only on the communication of the spirit, which is the principle of animal life as well. Superior to the animals and therefore able to give them names, the human being finds none of them a fit helper or associate. Human personal relations are with Yahweh who creates a garden in which the first humans dwell.

63   The *P* account of creation (Gen 1) is more explicit in affirming human dignity. The human being is made in the image and likeness of Elohim (Gen 1:26–27). The precise meaning of this phrase is disputed, but seemingly the divine image and likeness are associated with human dominion over the lower animals (1:28–30). Dominion over creation is proper to God; correspondingly, the conferring of dominion on human beings raises them above the lower creatures and implies the possession of godlike qualities not shared by beasts. Ps 8 makes the human being ("son of man") "a little less than Elohim," crowned with glory and honor, and empowered to rule all lower living creatures.

64   The image of Elohim constitutes the human mystery or paradox: this eminent dominion is combined with an element of weakness generally termed "flesh" (*bāśār*). Flesh is the natural human condition; it is opposed to spirit, the element associated with God (Isa 31:3; → 33 above). The OT does not always clearly distinguish physical weakness and mortality from moral weakness; the association between the two is assumed rather than consciously elaborated. In Gen 3 humanity's loss of dominion over nature and of the prospect of immortality is the result of moral failure. In the OT, flesh is not yet the seat of concupiscence or earth-oriented tendencies which it becomes in the Pauline writings (→ Pauline Theology, 82:103), nor is "flesh" always used in a pejorative sense. Yet flesh is what human beings have in common with animals; it is the unstable and perishable.

65   According to Gen 2, human creation is in two sexes. This is not explicitly considered in any ancient Near Eastern mythology, where sex is assumed as a primary principle in the divine world just as in the created world. In contrast with these mythologies (as well as with the patterns of thought reflected in almost the whole OT) we read in Gen 2:18–25 that woman is the object of a distinct creative act, the only living being who is a fit partner and companion of the male. The female has the same dignity as the male and is therefore not a depressed or subhuman species.

66   In spite of the use of such words as flesh, spirit, and soul, the OT conceived of the human being as a unity and not as a composite of different principles. H. Wheeler Robinson observed in a classic remark that the Greeks thought of an incarnate spirit and the Israelites thought of an animated body. The Hebr language does not distinguish a seat of intellectual operations; these are located in the heart—in Hebrew the heart is the organ of thought rather than of feeling. The Hebr *nefesh* (*nepeš*) has usually been mistranslated "soul"—introducing an idea that is foreign to the OT. Actually, the use of the word *nefesh* is too fluid to permit any synthesis. When Yahweh breathes the spirit, the human being becomes a living *nefesh* (Gen 2:7). "Person" or "self" may be the basic, if not the primitive, meaning of the word. The blood is sometimes said to be the seat of the *nefesh*; in such instances the *nefesh* is not the self or the person, but rather life, which is poured out with the blood. The *nefesh* is often associated with the psychic processes of desire, and in these contexts the word can often be translated by "will" or "appetite."

In none of these instances, taken singly or together, is there anything resembling the "soul" of Gk and modern thought. This difference has important corollaries in the biblical idea of survival after death (→ 170 below). The usage of the word *nefesh* shows the failure of OT thought to arrive at any real analysis of the principles of human nature. It is seen as an existing totality, and words that refer to anything except parts of the anatomy designate the totality of conscious life in some way. Indeed, even when particular parts of the anatomy such as the loins, the bowels, the eye, the hand, or the heart are made the subject and the seat of vital acts, the total person is identified with the organ, in which the sum of psychic energy comes to focus.

(Köhler, L., *Hebrew Man* [Nash, 1956]. Mork, W., *The Biblical Meaning of Man* [Milwaukee, 1967]. Also *TDOT* articles on respective Hebr terms; and the works on anthropology by Lang, Rogerson, and Wolff [→ 1 above].)

67   (II) Human Community. The relations of the individual to the social group in the OT, as in the rest of the ancient world, are notably different from these relations in the modern world. The differences have led to extensive discussions among scholars, but not a consensus. The discussion has often been set within the framework of an antithesis between collectivism and individualism: early Israel has been said to exhibit an exaggerated collectivism, and later Israel an exaggerated individualism. This is an improper frame of reference. Collectivism and individualism are modern ideas (with complicating emotional overtones) that have no correspondents in Israelite thought.

68   The social groups found in the OT are of two kinds: real or fictitious kinship groups, which include the family, the clan, and the tribe; and political groups, which include the village, the city, and the kingdom. The kinship group is conceived and spoken of as "one flesh" rather than "one blood"; the difference seems slight, but it is significant when the group is considered as a single person (→ 69 below). The unity of village and city resembles the unity of kinship rather than political unity; these ancient communities were small enough and usually, as in the modern Near Eastern village, had such a network of interrelationships between families that the analogy of kinship was easily applied. See R. R. Wilson, *Sociological Approaches to the Old Testament* (Phl, 1984) 40–53.

The only genuine political society in the OT is the monarchy; here the principle of unity is the person of the king, who incorporates in himself the people whom he rules. Both in the political society and in the kinship group the unity is ultimately personal, reposing on the father, the patriarch, or the king. The unity of the group is both horizontal and vertical: horizontally it extends to all the members of a contemporary generation, and vertically it extends through all earlier generations. Even though hundreds of years separate the prophets from Moses, they often address their own generation as those whom Yahweh has brought up from Egypt, guided through the desert, and given the land of Canaan. "Israel" is a continuing reality, contemporary to all the events of its past history and subject to all the responsibilities that this history has laid upon it.

69   The personification of a group is universal in human speech and would not of itself establish anything distinctive in Israelite thought. However, there is a distinctive element in Israelite personification. H. W. Robinson (*Corporate Personality in Ancient Israel* [1931; repr. Phl, 1984]) has explained it thus: Corporate personality is fluid; it may designate the individual person or the group, yet neither without reference to the other. This is illustrated in the patriarchal stories of Gen. The patriarchs in their personal characters and experiences exhibit those traits that were thought to be peculiarly Israelite and foreshadow the adventures of the group that was descended from them. Jacob in relation to Esau and to Laban clearly reflects Israel in relation to Edom and to the Arameans. The covenant relation of Israel with Yahweh is retrojected into a covenant of Abraham with Yahweh in which Abraham is the ideal covenant partner (→ 78 below). The acquisition of the land of Canaan effected before the monarchy is initiated in the movements of Abraham, Isaac, and Jacob.

The king also is such a corporate personality; here Israelite thought patterns do not differ substantially from the ideas of other ancient Near Eastern peoples. In the relations of Israel with Yahweh, however, the position of the Israelite king does not correspond to the position that Egyptian, Mesopotamian, and Canaanite kings had in the cult. The difference lies in the transcendental superiority of Yahweh; the king is as much Yahweh's subject as any other Israelite. The Israelite king cannot be a visible manifestation of Yahweh's majesty, for this would be to represent Yahweh by image (→ 20 above). The king is a charismatic person (→ 35 above), but no more. With these reservations, the king incorporates in himself the fortunes and the destiny of Israel.

70   The corporate personality thus synthesized in the leader can be conceived apart from the leader. Because the group is a single personality, the history of the rebellion of Israel from its beginnings to the present can be reviewed by Ezek 20—the sins of the fathers are visited upon the children (20:5). Amos addresses his contemporaries as the family that Yahweh brought out of Egypt (Amos 3:1). The generation of Jeremiah is the faithless bride of Yahweh (Jer 2:2). Hosea sees in his contemporaries the deviousness of Jacob, their eponymous ancestor (Hos 12:2–4), the child who has grown into an ungrateful adult (11:1–7). The group must answer for what it is historically, even as the individual must answer; neither can entirely escape the past except by a complete reversal of character. Similarly, the messianic

future of Israel is the future of Israel as a group and not as individual persons.

71   The need for security was a highly important factor in determining the relation of the individual to the group. In the ancient world once one went beyond the limits of the village or the city, one entered into a lawless wilderness. Even under the Israelite monarchy perfect security could not be guaranteed beyond the limits of the settlements. The monarchy sanctioned law and organized defense against external enemies, but it could not police its territory effectively. The individual who had no group affiliations was defenseless and helpless. The vindication of the life, integrity, and property of the individual was the responsibility of the kinship group, which through the custom of blood vengeance effectively threatened retaliation for attack on its members.

The price that the individual person paid for security was complete integration in the group and complete acceptance of its ways and its decisions. The solidarity that maintained a defense against external aggression left no room for individual deviations. As the group protected the individual even at its own risk (since a threat to any individual member was a threat to the whole group), so it could demand of the member a total dedication. Such a way of life left no room for anything like the modern ideal of individual personal development or personal career; in fact it left no room even for personal privacy. It must be understood that few, if any, felt oppressed or deprived in this way of life. Human life simply was group life, and no other way of life was conceivable or desirable.

72   There are indications in the OT that important group decisions were reached through wide participation, at least of the representative persons, such as heads of families and clans. Seventy of the elders of Israel ratify the covenant of Israel with Yahweh (Exod 24). "The people" accept a covenant to serve Yahweh imposed by Joshua (Josh 24). Gideon deals with 77 elders of Succoth (Judg 8). In the several accounts of the institution of the monarchy (1 Sam 8–10) the initiative comes from the people. The elders of Israel accept David as king (2 Sam 5:1ff.).

T. Jacobsen has shown that in early Mesopotamia the government of the state was conducted by an assembly of elders and a popular assembly; to this structure he gave the name "Primitive Democracy" (*JNES* 2 [1943] 166ff.; reinforced by G. Evans, *JAOS* 78 [1958] 1ff.). We have no evidence that popular sovereignty was formalized by institutions in Israel, but many details suggest that there were ample channels for the expression of the popular will. This feature of Israelite society warns us against speaking too easily of the opposition between collectivism and individualism in Israel. Individuals expressed themselves through the group and readily accepted decisions that they had helped to formulate.

73   Religious activities were as much determined by society as were any other activites. We do not find in the ancient Semitic world any clear instance of a purely religious group that is not also a social group; the position of Israel here is unique, but Israel is not a purely religious group. It is against this background that we should consider the problems raised by Jer 31:29–35 and by Ezek 18 together with 33:1–20. No relation of the individual to the deity was known except the relation of membership in a cult group identified with the social group. The collapse of the Israelite political society in the time of Jeremiah and Ezekiel left no relationship of the individual Israelite with Yahweh. In the ancient world a god without a people simply vanished. Jeremiah and Ezekiel were not exactly the creators of personal religion, as many scholars have called them, although one cannot deny that they made statements about personal responsibility that have no parallel in earlier OT literature. Rather, the emphasis of their statements is an assurance that Yahweh has not ceased to exist and that Israel is still his people. Faith in the enduring power of Yahweh is also faith in the resurgence of Israel from its downfall. In the absence of the collapsing traditional religious and social group of Israel, individuals must now become aware that they will meet personal demands of a type not made on the individual in the organized society under the monarchy. A purely individual religion, however, is not in the mind of either Jeremiah or Ezekiel (→ Jeremiah, 18:88; → Ezekiel, 20:51–52).

74   (III) The Covenant. The relationship of Yahweh and Israel is unique in the religions of the ancient world. In other ancient religions the deity is identified either with nature (→ 47–48 above) or with the society that worships the deity. The relation is, therefore, in a sense natural, since in the mind of ancient peoples both physical nature and human society are primary data with which the human being is essentially involved. On the contrary, the relation of Yahweh and Israel is, like the created universe, the result of a positive action of Yahweh; and the relation of Yahweh and Israel is completed by a positive response of Israel. The relation is not a given necessary component of human existence but a freely instituted community of persons.

75   (A) Analogies for the Relationship of God to Israel. The OT uses a number of analogies to designate this relationship. The analogy of *father–son* may appear to be primarily a natural relationship; but when it is seen in the context of other analogies and the character of the parent–child relationship is examined, it becomes evident that even here it is the freely associated community of persons that is meant. Yahweh is never called the physical progenitor of Israel; he "begets" Israel by forming a people for himself. The attitudes that appear in the father–son analogy are the personal attitudes of love, devotion, and obedience, and not the relations of carnal kinship. The sonship of Israel is adoptive, not natural.

The analogy of *marriage* shows the personal relations even more clearly, and in particular highlights the initiative of Yahweh, since in ancient marriage it was always the man who chose his wife. In Hos and Jer the matrimonial analogy is presented with emphasis on the relation of love; the fidelity of Israel is a work of love, and the infidelity of Israel is a personal offense against Yahweh.

The analogy of *shepherd and flock* is less common and does not so explicitly present the mutual personal relationship. But a shepherd is bound to a flock by a devotion to which corresponds the confidence of the sheep. This analogy shows Yahweh as the protector of Israel.

The analogy of *kinsman* also appears. Yahweh is called the "avenger" of Israel ("redeemer" in many English versions). This title alludes to the custom of blood revenge, by which the next of kin is obliged at any risk to defend the life, person, or property of his kinsman and to execute punishment upon any aggressor. In this analogy Yahweh acts not only as the protector and the security of Israel but also as a kinsman (*gōʾēl*). Here again the suggestion of a natural relationship is not to be pressed, since the obligation of the avenger is freely assumed by Yahweh.

The analogy of *king and subject* is not frequently explicit, but is reflected in the divine title "Lord" (→ 10 above) and is implicit in the analogy of covenant. The king–subject relationship carries less of the intimacy so obvious in the analogies of father–son and husband–wife, but it should not be conceived of in the patterns of ancient Egypt and Mesopotamia or of more recent royalty. Theoretically, the Israelite king could be approached by any of his subjects, and some episodes in the lives of David and Saul suggest that this was the practice in the early monarchy. Where the title of king is given to Yahweh, it emphasizes his power and will to save (→ 140–41 below).

76   Most modern writers now take the analogy of *covenant* as the basic key to the others. A covenant was originally a verbal agreement in a culture that did not keep written records. Mutual agreements and obligations were solemnly professed in the presence of witnesses and with imprecatory oaths and sacrificial rites. Fidelity was ensured less by the memory of the witnesses (which substituted for the written instrument) than by the threat of vengeance by the deity invoked as a witness and by a belief in the power of the spoken word (→ 40 above).

77   (B) Covenant Forms. In the OT, covenants cover all social transactions. They are not always strictly bilateral, for the stronger can impose a covenant on the weaker. A covenant settles a dispute about a well (Gen 21:32; 26:38) and the quarrel of Jacob and Laban (31:44); a covenant designates an alliance of Abraham and his neighbors (14:13) and the alliance of Gibeon and Israel (Josh 9:15); a covenant designates the agreement of Abner and David that terminates the civil war and assures the allegiance of Israel to David (2 Sam 3:12–19).

78   The covenant of Yahweh and Israel dominates the last four books of the Pentateuch and recurs in the historical books. The traditions concerning the covenant are obscure and complex; but Moses' connection with the establishment of the covenant is so deeply embedded in the several traditions that one cannot remove him (→ History, 75:48). The existence of a covenant between Yahweh and Abraham (the E and P traditions) is less clearly indicated and is very probably a retrojection of the patterns of later Israelite belief into the story of Abraham. (See R. E. Clements, *Abraham and David* [SBT NS 5; London, 1967].) The covenant with Noah in the P tradition is obviously such a retrojection. Even the Mosaic covenant is so heavily overlaid with later material that a historical reconstruction of the course of events is beyond present possibilities. The basic account, found in Exod 19–24, is compiled from several sources that cannot be analyzed clearly; the account in Exod 33, now edited so that it has become a renewal of the covenant, is probably a parallel account. Deut 4–5 depends on Exod 19–24. The covenant mediated by Joshua (Josh 24) demands special treatment; → 80 below.

79   G. E. Mendenhall has argued that the Israelite covenant follows the form of the suzerainty treaty of the late 2d millennium BC (*BA* 17 [1954] 49–76). This treaty formula is known chiefly through Hittite treaties, but it is the formula that was generally employed in international relations of the period. The suzerainty treaty is distinguished from the parity treaty, which is made between two equal powers, for the suzerainty treaty is imposed upon a vassal by an overlord and is not bilateral. The vassal is obliged by the treaty; the overlord is not strictly obliged by the promises he makes.

Mendenhall adopted V. Korošec's analysis of six elements in the suzerainty treaty: (1) The preamble identifies the overlord and gives his genealogy and titulary. (2) The historical prologue sets forth the previous relations between the two parties and is principally a recital of the benefits conferred upon the vassal by the overlord; the "I–Thou" form of address is used. (3) The stipulations imposed upon the vassal: prohibition of other foreign relations, maintenance of peace and existing conditions among vassals, military assistance to be rendered to the overlord, full confidence in the overlord, no asylum to fugitives from the overlord, annual appearance before the overlord. (4) Provision for the deposit of the treaty in the temple and for periodic public reading. (5) List of gods who witness the treaty. (6) Curses and blessings for violation or fulfillment of the treaty. Mendenhall added: (7) Vassal's oath of obedience. (8) Solemn ceremony of oath. (9) Procedure against rebellious vassal.

80   In the existing OT literature, Mendenhall found a close parallel to the treaty form only in Josh 24, which contains an introductory formula, a historical prologue in the "I–Thou" form of address, the stipulation to renounce other gods, a reference to the people themselves as witnesses, and a provision for the writing and deposit of the covenant in the sanctuary—the curses and blessings are absent. (For this Shechem covenant, see J. L'Hour, *RB* 69 [1962] 5–36, 161–84, 350–68.) The elements of the treaty formula, however, are found scattered through the covenant narratives of the Pentateuch. The enumeration of Yahweh's titles is illustrated in Exod 34:6. The recital of the saving deeds of Yahweh is common (Exod 19:4; 20:2; Josh 24:2–13); indeed the entire composition of the Pentateuch sets the laws of Israel in a narrative framework that relates Yahweh's deliverance of Israel. In the existing text the stipulations are the laws themselves, and the original stipulations are not easily determined. They included the prohibition of the worship of other gods and very probably the prohibition of the cult of images. Beyond this the Decalogue itself is most probably to be understood as the original stipulation (for the relation of covenant and law, → 88 below). The relations between vassals are parallel to the relations of the Israelite tribes with each other; and exhortations to trust Yahweh correspond to the obligation of trust in the overlord. The annual appearance before the overlord is provided for in the three great annual festivals consisting of a pilgrimage to a sanctuary of Yahweh (→ 91 below). The tradition that the stone tablets of the Decalogue were preserved in the Ark of the Covenant corresponds to the preservation of the treaty in the sanctuary (1 Kgs 8:9; → Institutions, 76:34). The provision for regular reading of the covenant is not found explicitly but is assumed by most modern scholars even without reference to the treaty formula; e.g., Alt (*AEOT* 162–64) has suggested that the ceremony of Deut 27 is intended as a regular act and not as a single event. Blessings and curses appear in Lev 26 and Deut 27–28.

81   (C) Covenant and the History of Israel. The covenant is initiated by Yahweh through an act that is often called election, especially in Deut. Israel is the people of Yahweh through the choice of Yahweh. The saving acts of Yahweh—the deliverance of the people from Egypt and the gift of the land of Canaan—establish Israel as a people and give Israel the identity and stability that the word "people" denotes. The election made by Yahweh is an act of love (Deut 4:37ff.; 7:6ff.) and is not because of the greatness or the merits of Israel (7:7; 9:4ff.). The election of Israel imposes upon Israel the responsibility of recognizing Yahweh alone as God (4:39) and of keeping his commandments (4:40; 7:9ff.; 10:16ff.). The treaty formula brings out more clearly the fact that the election of Israel is an election to responsibility and obligation, not merely to a position of privilege. The OT does not conceive of election as an act of favoritism. (P. D. Hanson, *The People Called* [SF, 1986].)

82   Recent studies have shown that the covenant was the principle of Israel's unity as a people. It is clear that the Israel of the period of the judges and the monarchy included a number of groups of diverse origins, most of whom had not shared the experience of the exodus and the settlement (→ Biblical Archaeology, 74:79–88; →History, 75:55–58). These were joined to the original group of Israel by accepting the covenant of Yahweh with Israel. The traditions of Yahweh's saving acts became the traditions of the entire group; and the obligations of the covenant, in particular the obligation of worshiping Yahweh alone, became normative. Israel was primarily a religious and not an ethnic unity. The covenant account of Josh 24 has been interpreted by M. Noth as describing a ceremony in which such diverse groups were pledged to observe the covenant. He related the resultant grouping in Israel to the amphictyony of classical Greece: a league of cities or tribes organized to maintain and defend a common central shrine. Many scholars have reacted against this terminology and interpretation (→ History, 75:58) but have thus underestimated the very genuine similarities between the two situations. In Noth's interpretation of Israel, the tribes were vassals of Yahweh and had to maintain peace with each other; they could form no alliance with other peoples or with other gods. But before the monarchy there was no central government; tribal and local affairs were in the hands of tribal and local authorities, and the political unification under the monarchy issued from political needs, not from the theology of the covenant. Rather, in the quest for undergirding, the monarchy had to devise a new theology.

83   When one considers the evident fundamental importance of the idea of covenant in early Israelite history and belief, it is surprising that the word occurs rarely in the writings of the classical prophets of the 8th cent. (Amos, Hosea, Isaiah, Micah). This rarity does not indicate any substantial change in the idea of the relations of Yahweh and Israel; these prophets emphasized the basic themes of the covenant theology—the sovereignty of Yahweh, his saving deeds, Israel's unique position as the people of Yahweh, and its unique obligations to him. Several scholars have plausibly suggested that the prophets did not use the word because in the popular mind it had become perverted into a false idea of privilege and security: Yahweh, it was wrongly thought, was obligated to Israel, whatever Israel might do. As a corrective, Amos (3:2) made the "knowledge" (= election) of Israel a reason why Yahweh would punish Israel.

84   Mendenhall has suggested another reason why the prophets could not use the idea. In the kingdom of Judah the covenant of Israel had been largely supplanted by the covenant of Yahweh with the house of David (→ 155 below). Plainly, the secessionist Israelites of the North felt no guilt about a breach of the Davidic covenant; but even in Judah the covenant with David became a pledge to the dynasty of David rather than to the people of Israel. In the early traditions Yahweh had made no such commitment; and prophets avoided the word covenant lest the reality of Israel be conditioned on the survival of the dynasty of David.

85   With Jer the word covenant reappears; and this was probably because of the emphasis on covenant in Deut, which must be placed in the same period (→ Jeremiah, 18:7). The covenant in Deut is conceived of as a source of obligation and of blessing conditioned on its observance. Yahweh is no more than faithful to his covenant if he punishes Israel for violation. Jeremiah himself conceives of the future of Israel in terms of a new covenant (31:31–34; → 146 below). The novelty of this covenant lies in the personal relationship that it establishes between Yahweh and the individual Israelite; just as Israel was the people of Yahweh, so the individual person is related to Yahweh (→ 73 above). For the theme of the prophetic lawsuit, → Jeremiah, 18:15.

In the P tradition of the Pentateuch the covenant becomes identified with law. The external sign of the covenant is circumcision. The entire history of the saving deeds of Yahweh is represented in P as a series of covenants that go back to Noah.

(Baltzer, K., *The Covenant Formulary in the Old Testament* [Phl, 1971]. Buis, P., *La notion d'Alliance dans l'Ancien Testament* [LD 88; Paris, 1976]. Hillers, D. R., *Treaty-Curses and the Old Testament Prophets* [BibOr 16; Rome, 1964]. Kalluveettil, P., *Declaration and Covenant* [AnBib 88; Rome, 1982]. McCarthy, D. J., *Old Testament Covenant* [Atlanta, 1972]; *Treaty and Covenant* [rev. ed.; AnBib 21A; Rome, 1978]. McComiskey, T. E., *The Covenants of Promise: A Theology of Old Testament Covenants* [GR, 1985]. Mendenhall, G., *The Tenth Generation* [Baltimore, 1973]. Nicholson, E., *God and His People* [Oxford, 1986]. Riemann, P., *IDBSup* 192-97. Weinfeld, M., *IDBSup* 188-92.)

86   (IV) Covenant and Law.

(A) Law Codes and Formulations. The Pentateuch in Exod through Deut contains vast collections of laws. Critics now recognize that these laws come from diverse origins and dates; very few of the laws can be attributed to Moses himself. Several distinct collections can be distinguished. The collections are often called codes, but the word is inaccurate. The collections are not codified in the usual sense of the term; none of the collections or all taken together constitute a complete corpus of Israelite law.

The Decalogue, given in Exod 20:1-17 and Deut 5:6-21, and representing the basic stipulations of Yahweh's covenant with Israel, is not included under the collections (→ Exodus, 3:34), although it gives tone and spirit to all subsequent collections. The earliest of the collections, possibly antedating the monarchy, is the Book of the Covenant (Exod 20:22-23:19; → Exodus, 3:34-44). The deuteronomic Book of the Law contains a parenetic restatement of the law (Deut 12-26; → Deuteronomy, 6:6). The Holiness Code of Lev 17-26 is generally thought to be earlier than the exile (→ Leviticus, 4:35). All the other laws are lumped under the designation of the Priestly Collection, which is exilic or later; but a large number of the individual laws must be earlier than the exile (→ Pentateuch, 1:6→7). No collection contains civil and criminal law exclusively; the Holiness code is chiefly religious, and the Priestly Collection is chiefly ceremonial.

87

Alt (*AEOT* 103-71) has distinguished two principal formulations of Israelite law: (1) The casuistic laws (the "decrees" or judgments, the *mišpāṭîm,* the "if" laws), where the conditional clause sets forth the case, usually a civil matter, and the apodosis tells how to handle it. Casuistic laws are common in the Book of the Covenant (e.g., Exod 21:2-6) and in Deut. These laws, much like English Common Law, reflect previous legal decisions that have set a precedent. This style of casuistic law is found in the jurisprudence of the ancient Near East, and undoubtedly many casuistic laws were part of Israel's heritage from the civilizations that surrounded her.

(2) The apodictic laws. There are two types: (a) The statutes (*huqqîm*) that establish penalties, frequently death penalties (Exod 21:12,15-17), e.g., "Whoever strikes a man so that he dies shall be put to death." Curses on evildoers also come under this grouping. These laws may also spring from ancient decisions on cases, but on very fundamental cases in a simple society. As now phrased they are tantamount to basic statements of morality and are treated as edicts of divine authority. (b) The imperatives or commands (*miṣwôt*), which may be positive or negative. These are generally stated in the second person sg. ("You shall [not] . . .") and give no specific penalty (Lev 18:7-17). Unlike the casuistic laws, they deal primarily with religious questions and bind all regardless of individual circumstances. The Decalogue

consists of apodictic imperatives, mostly prohibitive, and thus comes under this last classification, even though the Bible refers to the Decalogue as "words" rather than as "commands."

Since apodictic law is moral and religious and the speaker of the imperative is thought to be the deity, it is this formulation that is considered most properly as "covenant law." And indeed the Near Eastern parallels for the apodictic imperatives are not in law codes but precisely in covenants. The Hittite treaties mentioned above (→ 79) laid down the stipulations for the vassal in the form "You [thou] shall not. . . ." It is just such parallelism that has made some scholars willing to accept the Decalogue as the original stipulations of the covenant between God and Israel. (See F.-L. Hossfeld, *Der Dekalog* [OBO 45; Fribourg, 1982].)

88   (B) Covenant Law.

To use the word "law" of the original covenant stipulations is somewhat misleading. The Decalogue, for instance, is not law in the usual sense, either in the ancient Near East or in modern society; the Decalogue is a basis of law. The original covenant stipulation is primarily the revealed moral will of Yahweh, who is the custodian of the moral order and also its author and expositor. In the community of the covenant, the will of the God of the covenant is the supreme authority to which every human authority is subordinate. The moral will of Yahweh in the covenant stipulations establishes a distinctively Israelite way of life sanctioned by curse and blessing.

The expansion and interpretation of the revealed moral will of Yahweh led to incorporating into the covenant the corpus of Israelite law. All law was thought to contribute to the definition of the Israelite way of life imposed by the revealed will of Yahweh. This development cannot be traced before Deut; but that does not prove that it was original with Deut. In this book of the 7th cent. BC, there was a patent effort to organize Israelite life on the basis of covenant law precisely as such. The law of Deut was a reform measure calculated to avert the threat to Israelite security being offered by habitual and widespread violations of the covenant. The Israelite way of life, it was felt, needed that definition and precision that only a written code could give. The prophets who are echoed in Deut spoke of the moral imperative of the will of Yahweh and of certain flagrant abuses, but they did not elaborate legal prescriptions that would remove uncertainty in the interpretation of the will of Yahweh. The code of Deut, although not a complete corpus of law, represents those legal prescriptions thought to be vital to the preservation of the covenant and of Israel. (H. J. Boeker, *Law and the Administration of Justice in the Old Testament* [Minneapolis, 1980].)

89

After the exile, the Jewish community of Jerusalem made itself a people of the law. The contents of the law that Ezra promulgated cannot be determined precisely (→ Chronicler, 23:95; → Canonicity, 66:24), but again the contents are less important than the spirit in which the law was declared and accepted. Postexilic Judaism accepted the law of the Pentateuch as a complete codification of the revealed moral will of Yahweh and developed an oral law to interpret in detail the written law and to protect it against violation (→ Apocrypha, 67:134). Thus the community felt that the covenant relationship was assured. The development was not altogether wholesome, and in parts of the NT the issue between law and gospel is sharply drawn (→ Pauline Theology, 82:89-100).

90   (V) Covenant and Cult.

Cult in every religion is an encounter of the community with the deity and a profession of belief. This meaning is not always apparent to those who engage in the cult; cultic symbolism often grows so archaic that few of those who participate understand its significance, and the ritual degenerates into mere rote or something worse. In the luxuriant ritual of the Priestly Collection, Israelite cult exhibits some features of degeneration; but it was not thus from the beginning, and the cult should not be judged on its least attractive features. For cult, as for law, the covenant is the article of faith that confers basic meaning.

Our knowledge of the ancient Near East shows that many details of the Israelite cult are not peculiar to Israel. The basic elements of cult are myth and ritual. By myth is meant the recital of the saving event, and by ritual, its symbolic reenactment. Through these two elements of cult the society establishes and maintains communion with the deity. Such recital and the reenactment appear in Israelite cult with one essential difference: the saving event that is recited is not the mythological event in nature but the saving deeds of Yahweh in history (→ 31 above), viz., the actions by which he delivered Israel from Egypt and established Israel as the people of his covenant in the promised land. In the recital Yahweh reveals himself anew as the God of Israel. Apparently the narratives of the Pentateuch had much of their origin in such ritual recitals.

91 The major festivals of the Israelite calendar— Passover, Unleavened Bread, Weeks, and Tents—have both an agricultural and a historical significance; they are harvest festivals, but they also commemorate events in the history of Israel. The Israelite festivals are not the pure nature festivals found in other ancient Near Eastern religions. In their historical significance they are reenactments of Yahweh's saving deeds, and by their celebration the saving power and will of Yahweh are experienced anew (→ Institutions, 76:122–38).

92 Scholars have long found it mysterious that the OT Israelite calendar of festivals contains no festival that is properly and formally a covenant festival. In the Judaism of the 1st cent. AD, the feast of Weeks was celebrated as the anniversary of the revelation of the law (→ Institutions, 76:132). If this is a genuinely ancient interpretation of the feast, we still have no biblical information on the manner in which this theme was celebrated. Scattered allusions in the OT have led a number of recent scholars to postulate some kind of covenant festival that included a recital of the covenant terms and a public pledge by Israel of its fidelity to the covenant. These reconstructions have not been generally accepted, but the principle behind them seems sound; and it is probably by sheer chance that no account of the covenant festival has been preserved.

Several scholars associate the covenant festival with the new year (→ Institutions, 76:139–46). The new year festival in Mesopotamia was a reenactment of creation achieved anew each year with the return of the cycle of fertility. Israel accepts no such fertility cult, which cannot be incorporated into the worship of Yahweh. When Israel celebrates the agricultural festivals, it recognizes in fertility the creative power and the blessing of Yahweh. The saving power and will of Yahweh exhibited in the history of Israel are also exhibited in the bounty of the land. By the fruits of the soil Yahweh fulfills the covenant promise of blessing; and by thanking him Israel attests its own fidelity to the covenant, a fidelity that is approved by God's blessing. The fertility of nature is incorporated into the moral will of Yahweh (→ 56 above). In its basic features, then, the Israelite cult fulfills the description of cult as an encounter of the community with the deity and a profession of faith. More than any other element of Israelite religion, it communicated to the people the intimate awareness of the presence and activity of Yahweh as the God of Israel by his covenant.

93 **(VI) Righteousness.** Certain moral attributes of Yahweh are closely associated with the covenant. Here we find ourselves in the area of anthropomorphism (→ 21–22 above); but there is a clear distinction drawn between the qualities in Yahweh and the same qualities in human beings. In morality, as in everything else, Yahweh is wholly different.

"Righteous" and "righteousness" are the customary Eng transls. of the Hebr words *ṣedeq* and *ṣĕdāqâ*, which only with difficulty can be translated into any modern language. Another translation as "just" and "justice" is inadequate, but not simply because of juridical or forensic connotation (in fact, very often *ṣĕdāqâ* is predicated of Yahweh or of a human person as judge). Rather, "just" and "justice" presuppose a whole juridical order that does not exist in Israelite thinking. There is no abstract idea of justice in Israelite thought.

"Righteous" describes one who is judicially declared innocent or who has a claim judicially vindicated. This is probably the primary meaning from which other uses of the word are derived: a righteous weight (Lev 19:36, an accurate weight); righteous sacrifices (Deut 33:19, sacrificed according to the correct ritual prescriptions); righteous paths (Ps 23:3, paths that lead in the right direction). A person is righteous not only by a judicial verdict but also because the person has a just claim or is innocent. A righteous judge is a judge who awards the verdict to the righteous litigant. In early usage the word is employed in an extremely simple and unsophisticated sense; the righteous claim is simply my claim, and the righteous judge is the judge who renders a verdict in my favor. This forensic background of the word does not imply that righteousness is merely an extrinsic denomination; the reality of personal innocence or a personal claim is present, but it cannot be an effective reality until it is juridically recognized. (See L. Epsztein, *La justice sociale dans le Proche-Orient Ancien et le Peuple de la Bible* [Paris, 1983].)

94 The idea of righteousness cannot be transferred to Yahweh without difficulty. The earliest use of the term, it seems, occurs in the Song of Deborah (Judg 5:11), where the "righteous acts" of Yahweh are his saving deeds in behalf of Israel. The judge and lord who vindicates Israel against its enemies, Yahweh is called righteous because he is on the side of Israel. Obviously, such a conception is remote from any abstract idea of justice. Righteousness is primarily a saving attribute, apparently often synonymous with salvation. The development toward a more objective conception comes with the realization that the righteousness which defends the righteous against the wicked can take a reverse direction if Israel itself is unrighteous.

Righteousness conceived as a purely covenantal attribute is, therefore, subject to certain limitations. The OT approaches most nearly to an abstract, universal idea of justice when Israel perceives that the righteousness of Yahweh is rooted in the divine reality itself. Yahweh cannot act unrighteously; if he could, there would be no genuine righteousness at all. The measure of righteousness, therefore, is not simply the covenant and its stipulations but the actions of Yahweh. There is no righteousness that is not created and maintained by him. His righteousness is not measured by human standards, but human standards are measured by him.

95 **(VII) Covenant Love.** The Hebr word *hesed* has been a more severe problem to translators of the Bible than the word *ṣedeq,* "righteous." The traditional translation "mercy" goes back to the Gk and Lat Bibles. "Loving-kindness" is a better but still inadequate effort. The somewhat clumsy "covenant love," suggested by N. Glueck and adopted here, places in the translation itself the dominant themes implied in the usage of the word. The translation is defective in its failure to indicate that *ḥesed* is not only the love exhibited in virtue of the covenant but also the movement of the will that initiates the covenant. In common usage *ḥesed* includes kinship love as well as covenant love.

Ḥesed is a normal part of good human relations, but it has its proper place within members of a group, even if the association is as temporary as the relation of host and guest. *Ḥesed* is a kindness that is above and beyond the minimum duties imposed by the association, but the maintenance of good human relations demands that people do go beyond the minimum duties.

96 The meaning of covenant love is more clearly understood through the words with which it is most frequently associated. It is often joined with "fidelity" (*'ĕmet* or *'ĕmûnâ*), the attribute by which Yahweh fulfills his covenant and his promises (Exod 34:6; cf. John 1:14). Indeed, the two words are united closely in the noun pair "steadfast covenant love" (*ḥesed we'ĕmet*). Love is also joined with judgment (→ 136 below); covenant love in the judge is his readiness to save. Covenant love, fidelity, judgment, and righteousness are the attributes of the ideal ruler (Isa 16:5); together they designate the will to save. Covenant love is also associated frequently with "salvation."

97 Covenant love is an emotional complex. Yahweh exhibits it to Israel, his bride (Jer 2:2), and will show it again when he restores Israel after its fall (Jer 31:2; Hos 2:21). The anthropopathism implicit in the word is most clearly exhibited by Hosea and Jeremiah, who employ the analogy of the marriage of Yahweh and Israel with extraordinarily profound feeling. *Ḥesed* is most frequently associated with the covenant. It is a fruit of the covenant itself (Exod 20:6; 34:6), and indeed the formation of the covenant is an act of covenant love (Isa 55:3). Breach of the covenant is a sufficient reason for Yahweh to withdraw his covenant love, but it would be out of character for him to do so. His covenant love is more enduring than human good will, and it is a forgiving attribute as well as a benevolent attitude to which Israel can appeal when it has sinned against the covenant (Exod 34:6; Num 14:19; Jer 3:12).

98 Covenant love is broader than the covenant itself. It is the movement of the will of Yahweh that initiates and continues the history of Israel (Isa 54:10; 63:7; Jer 31:3; Mic 7:20). Indeed, the entire history of the encounter of Israel with Yahweh—and this is the history of Israel—can be summed up as one act of covenant love. In the OT this attribute is the dominating motive of the acts of Yahweh; it gives singleness of purpose and ultimate intelligibility to his dealings, including anger and judgment. More than any other attribute, this love is the attribute that gives Yahweh personal identity; it is the key to understanding his character. (K. Sakenfeld, *The Meaning of Ḥesed in the Hebrew Bible* [HSM 17; Missoula, 1978]; *Faithfulness in Action* [Phl, 1985]. Also L. Morris, *Testaments of Love* [GR, 1981].)

ASPECTS OF THE RELATIONS BETWEEN GOD AND ISRAEL

99 **(I) Anger.** Of all the anthropopathisms applied to God, anger is perhaps the most difficult to apprehend with sympathy. Yet anger is as much a human emotion as love, and each is a human way of conceiving and speaking of the deity. Each emotion denotes a reality that must not be omitted in any attempt to describe the relations of God and human beings, along with the divine nature from which these relations arise. Our difficulty in conceiving of anger in God was not felt by the writers of the OT; the anger of Yahweh is mentioned more frequently than human anger.

100 To some extent the idea of divine anger was a part of the cultural inheritance of Israel from the ancient Near East. Where nature was mythologically understood as the area of diverse and conflicting personages (→ 27, 51 above), natural catastrophe was easily understood as the effects of divine anger. Ancient Mesopotamian peoples were unable to conceive of the divine anger without an element of caprice: the motivation escaped human understanding, and indeed the divine anger was often regarded as irrational and unmotivated.

Such an idea of divine anger is rejected by Israelite belief; the anger of Yahweh is always associated with his righteousness, his judgments, his holiness, his covenant. There is a direct connection between the anger of Yahweh and sin; if the connection is not perceived, it must be presumed to exist. The Israelites are ready to admit that divine anger, like divine wisdom, is more profound than human anger and is elicited where human anger would not be. If this happens, the righteous judgment of Yahweh must be accepted. There is another element, pointed out by W. Eichrodt, that plays a role in moderating the Israelite fear of Yahweh's anger—the realization that anger is not the habitual attitude of Yahweh. Habitually Yahweh is inclined to show covenant love, and his anger is the exceptional eruption. Yahweh's anger endures only for a moment; his covenant love endures for life (Ps 30:6).

101 Anger in the OT occupies the place that justice occupies in modern thinking about the deity. The difference between the two approaches is the difference between the personal and the impersonal. Although it is easier for us to think of God as the author and defender of a juridical order, in Israelite thought Yahweh is personally offended by breaches of the covenant, and he responds not only with authority and power but also with a personal revulsion against the offender. This is part of the pattern of the Israelite conception of the living God (→ 22 above) and of the malice of sin. Were Yahweh not angered by sin, he would not take it seriously.

The object of the anger of Yahweh mentioned most frequently is the people of Israel, motivated by their unbelief, distrust, rebellion, and worship of false gods. Yahweh's anger is excited by inhumanity and human pride and by refusal to observe his laws. Other nations also are the objects of his anger because of their pride and arrogance, particularly when they attack Israel; such attacks are an implicit denial of the power of Yahweh to protect his people. Certain heinous crimes also arouse his anger, such as the crimes that preceded the deluge and the destruction of Sodom and Gomorrah.

102 In contrast to ethically motivated instances of Yahweh's anger are other instances that approach the irrational. To the Israelite these outbursts are aroused by offenses against the holiness of Yahweh, the very essence of his divinity, which is unfathomable. Such are the attacks of Yahweh against Jacob (Gen 32:23ff.) and Moses (Exod 4:24ff.), the anger excited by too near an approach to Yahweh or by the sight of his countenance (Exod 19:9–25; 33:20; Judg 13:22; Isa 6:5), or by contact with sacred objects (1 Sam 6:19; 2 Sam 6:7). The anger of Yahweh is veiled in the mystery of his holiness and cannot be submitted to human calculation; it is never unrighteous, but it is sometimes unintelligible.

Yahweh's anger is often a blazing consuming fire (Jer 17:4; Isa 30:27; 65:5) or a furious storm (Jer 30:23; Isa 30:30). It is a liquid that can be poured out (Hos 5:10; Jer 6:11; Ezek 7:8; Ps 69:25), a bitter poisonous drink that makes men stagger (Jer 25:15; Isa 51:17,22). The anger of Yahweh annihilates unless it is restrained (Deut 7:4; Num 16:21; Isa 30:28; Jer 4:23–26). It is restrained by his covenant love, which can be reached by intercession (Exod 32:11ff.; Num 11:1ff.; 14:11–20). But Yahweh's anger can reach a pitch where intercession is no longer effective (Jer 14:11–12; Ezek 14:14). However, this anger never exceeds due bounds and never reaches the fullness that the objects of anger deserve. (On anger, see *TDOT* 1. 348–60.)

103   **(II) Revelation.** The conviction that Yahweh is a God of revelation is fundamental to OT belief. Yahweh as a personal being cannot be known except through revelation; persons can reveal themselves to others only by speech. The acts of Yahweh are forms of revelation, just as the acts of any person manifest the reality of the person; but the meaning of the acts of Yahweh can be understood only through the interpretation of Yahweh himself. The will of Yahweh cannot be ascertained by the arts of divination universally practiced in the ancient Near East. (Actually in the religions of Israel's neighbors there was no expectation that divination would disclose the character of the gods whose will was being investigated. A knowledge of the character of these gods was not regarded as necessary, for their will did not exhibit any moral pattern.)

104   **(A) Nature of Revelation.** Yahweh's revelation of himself occurs in history and is an event that the OT locates in time and place. This does not mean that revelation is a single incident. The revelation of Yahweh, inasmuch as it is the revelation of a person, is a developing process; for no person can be known through a single encounter. Insight into the character of Yahweh grows in depth through the successive periods of Israelite history. One should not expect to find the same understanding of Yahweh in the period of the judges or in the early monarchy that one finds in the era of the 8th-cent. prophets. Nor is the process entirely unilinear. Students of the OT have observed that the understanding of Yahweh found in the postexilic literature frequently fails to attain the clarity of vision that is found in such earlier sources as Hos, Isa, and Dt-Isa. Any particular passage or writing of the OT must be studied in its historical context, determined as precisely as possible; for the revelation found in each writing is a response to a determined historical situation (→ Hermeneutics, 71:15). The OT does not deal in generalities.

105   The OT has its own terminology of revelation, which can be misleading if it is not distinguished from more recent terminology. In the OT the response to revelation is not "faith" but "knowledge." These two terms do not mean what they mean in modern theology. The knowledge of Yahweh that is communicated by his speech is not speculative but experiential. The words and the deeds of Yahweh give Israel a personal experience of him that is like the experience of other persons. This is not purely intellectual knowledge, but the complex of experience, feeling, and desire that a personal encounter elicits. In some contexts to know Yahweh is to do his revealed will (Jer 22:16). In other contexts to know him is to recognize him in the character in which he has revealed himself, as in the frequent phrase "They shall know that I am Yahweh." The OT conception of revela-

tion includes the word spoken by Yahweh and the knowledge that issues from the word. That which Yahweh reveals is himself, not propositions. The OT relates the encounter of Yahweh and Israel: the manifestation of Yahweh and the response of Israel.

106   The personal reality of Yahweh is not thought to lie within human comprehension. Yahweh is mysterious, wonderful in counsel and excellent in wisdom (Isa 28:29). His thoughts are not our thoughts, and his ways are not our ways (Isa 55:8–9). To make Yahweh comprehensible would be to reduce him to the level of creatures; to challenge him is to speak what one does not understand (Job 42:3). Before this mystery the only proper position is submission, for the manifestation of Yahweh makes human self-assertion ridiculous.

107   **(B) Channels of Revelation.** Yahweh reveals himself through inspired representatives called *prophets*. The first in the line of Israel's spokesmen, Moses, is not called a prophet in the earlier sources (but cf. Deut 18:18; Num 12:6–8); he stands outside the line because of his uniquely close association with Yahweh. The prophet has the charisma of the word of Yahweh (→ 45 above); the prophetic mystical experience is normally described by the analogy of speech and hearing. Prophecy appears through the history of Israel from the early monarchy into the postexilic period, when it loses its vigor and finally disappears (although some vital features of prophecy survive in apocalyptic; → OT Apocalyptic, 19:18). Through this period the prophet is the conscience of Israel, its admonitor in public and private morality, in its internal administration and external politics. There is no sphere of life in which the word of Yahweh is irrelevant (→ Prophetic Lit., 11:25).

108   *Wisdom* is not, like prophecy, represented as an experience of hearing the word of Yahweh. Yet, at least in the postexilic period, true wisdom is a gift of Yahweh and cannot be achieved by merely human investigation, for Yahweh alone has true wisdom (→ Wisdom Lit., 27:15–16). Wisdom is the skill by which one manages one's life and affairs; without the communication of Yahweh's wisdom no one can hope to achieve success and prosperity even in private affairs. Wisdom moves on a lower level than prophecy; but it applies the revealed will of Yahweh to the business of daily life and shows the permanent importance of personal decision even in affairs of purely personal significance.

109   As the creator of Israel, Yahweh has revealed himself in the institutions of Israel. The weight of his revealed will enforces the *law* of Israel (→ 88 above). Israelite tradition is also an expression of his voice; and hence the priests have the office of interpreting his will in *tôrâ*, instruction. The instruction given by the priests deals primarily with cultic questions; but to an undetermined extent they are also the spokesmen of Yahweh in the interpretation of Israelite morality (→ Institutions, 76:10).

110   Yahweh reveals himself in *nature* (→ 55–60 above); but to the Israelite this is an inarticulate revelation. The nations fail to recognize the divine reality of Yahweh in nature and worship false gods. Israel knows Yahweh because he has spoken to Israel, and therefore Israel can recognize him in his creative works. The activity of Yahweh in nature is not distinguished from his activity in history; his power is always directed to salvation and judgment (→ 136ff., 140ff. below). Once known, his activity is apparent in every detail of nature; to the Israelite the normal phenomenon is as much a sign of Yahweh's personal intervention as the abnormal.

111   **(III) Lord of History.** Finally, Yahweh reveals himself chiefly in *history*. The idea of history as a unified series of events is not found in the ancient Near

East. The records preserved from the civilizations of this area are annals and chronicles in which events are listed according to year and summed up for regnal periods. We have no instances of any attempts to establish a pattern in events, to show a development in the life and the culture of a people. For these peoples their own beginnings and the beginnings of institutions are the object of mythology, not of history (→ 23 above). The event of myth is the constant event that recurs in a cyclic rhythm; it is the annual return of the seasons, the celestial revolutions, the cycle of day and night, the perpetual conflict between order and chaos. In opposition to the mythical event is the contingent historical event, singular and irreversible. Life is lived against the cycle of myth and ultimately returns to its beginning, whence the process is resumed once more. In this thinking, history was merely an epiphenomenon in nature. Ancient Near Eastern peoples sought no issue from the cycle of myth and hoped for no issue.

Even the Greeks, who were responsible for the beginnings of modern historical thought, did not rise above the cyclical ideal of history. At the risk of reading something into the mind of Gk thinkers, one may see in the cyclical conception of history an effort to synthesize the unchanging world of intelligible reality and the flux of contingent events. Events could be made intelligible in Gk thought only by constraining them into recurring cycles that the mind can grasp. In the cycle, events follow a set and predictable pattern of origin, rise, decline, and fall. The pattern of history visible in Herodotus's account of the Persian wars and Thucydides' history of the Peloponnesian war shows the same sense of inevitability that is the motif of Gk tragedy.

112   (A) The Old Testament as History. In the ancient world the OT is a unique collection of historical documents. A historical framework dominates the entire collection; H. W. Robinson has said that the OT is a history into which other kinds of literature have been incorporated (*Inspiration and Revelation in the Old Testament* [Oxford, 1946] 123). The Pentateuch presents the history of the origins of Israel and, in the complex of the history, the laws and the institutions that are attributed to this period. With the historical books from Josh through Chr belongs the prophetic collection: the separate prophetic books can be understood only if it is recognized that they are responses to the events of history, many of which are mentioned. Those portions of the OT that seem most timeless are the wisdom and poetic books; these also are included in the collection dominated by history, if not incorporated in the strict sense of the term. Many of the titles of the Pss offer a curious example of historical thinking on the part of the compilers of the OT: attempts, often by sheer conjecture, to find an occasion in the life of David when the psalm was written (→ Psalms, 34:4–5).

113   The OT collection of the literary remains of Israel is properly a history of Israel, although not in the modern sense of the term. The OT is a theological statement and an interpretation of history. For Israel its history is its encounter with Yahweh. The very idea that history is a process with beginning, middle, and end is original with Israel. It is the will and purpose of Yahweh that unifies the process. The historic career of Israel is directed by the will of Yahweh to fulfill his designs. These designs are not revealed in their full clarity at any stage of the process; e.g., the insight into the designs of Yahweh in history that appears in the J tradition of the Pentateuch (probably from the reign of David; → Pentateuch, 1:6–7) is more elementary than the insight manifested in Dt-Isa. The serene confidence characteristic of J rests on the assurance that history is not the

chance collision of blind forces without meaning or purpose nor an epiphenomenon of the eternally recurring cycles of nature; it is the execution of an intelligent plan. But in J, as in the entire OT, the acceptance of history as the execution of the designs of Yahweh demands an act of faith. The saving and judging will of Yahweh gives to history both intelligibility and morality. It gives intelligibility, for it defines both the origin and the end of the human experience in history and the process by which the two are joined. It gives morality, for it shows that history is governed by a supremely powerful and entirely incorruptible moral will. The fulfillment of the process is conditioned neither by human success nor by human failure. Human achievement is not the agent that brings about the fulfillment of history and destiny, and human sin does not block the accomplishment of the purpose of history.

114   In the J tradition the activity of Yahweh begins with the creation of man and woman; in the E tradition, with the call of Abraham; and in the P tradition, with the creation of the world. The point of origin differs; what the traditions have in common is the conviction that the act of Yahweh initiates the historical process. Thereafter, each turn in the history of Israel is the result of a decisive intervention of Yahweh. He manifests himself to the descendants of Abraham, sends Joseph to Egypt to prepare a place for his people; and when they are oppressed by the Egyptians, he intervenes in a brilliantly new fashion by revealing himself to Moses, liberating his people from Egypt, and forming a covenant with them. With his guidance and assistance they take possession of the land of Canaan. There they are assailed by various enemies, from whom Yahweh delivers them by the charismatic leadership of the judges. When the Philistine crisis proves too severe for a politically unorganized group, the kingship is instituted to meet this threat. Although the traditions of the institution of the monarchy are variant both in details and in the conception of kingship (→ 1–2 Samuel, 9:11–16), they agree that kingship is from Yahweh.

The monarchy is the period of prophecy, and the spokesmen of Yahweh reveal and interpret the acts of Yahweh in history: the schism of the kingdom, the fall of the dynasty of Omri, and above all the collapse of the kingdoms of Israel and Judah under the attacks of the great powers. The entire series of events is woven into a unity by the deuteronomic historians to exhibit the judgment of Yahweh on the infidelity of Israel (→ 1–2 Kings, 10:3). After the exile the reestablishment of a Jewish community under the law is another great saving act of Yahweh. The history of Israel throughout attests the wholly consistent and righteous deeds of Yahweh, revealed in his holiness.

115   The Israelite consciousness of history is attested in such "credos" or professions of faith as Deut 6:20–25; 26:5–10; Josh 24:2–13. Similar recitals are found in Pss 77; 78; 105; 106. These credos are liturgical. The cult was formed around the historic memory of the deeds of Yahweh (→ 90 above). When Israel wished to profess its belief in Yahweh, its "knowledge" of him, it recited his deeds in history. From these deeds Israel developed a consciousness of itself as a historical reality with an origin and a destiny. So deep was Israel's awareness of its place in history that, alone of the contemporary peoples in the ancient world, it exhibited a sense of its history as a career with a determined finality.

116   (B) Determinism and Universality. Two further questions arise from the consideration of the Israelite conception of history. The first is the question of *determinism:* If Yahweh is the lord of history, as Israel believed him to be, are people truly free and responsible agents in history? It has been noticed above (→ 111) that Gk thought, dominated by the logic of Parmenides, saw reality and intelligibility only in one unchanging being. Hence it reduced the contingent events of history to cycles of necessity, thus obtaining intelligibility by effectively denying contingency and human liberty. Does Israelite thought escape the inner necessity of logic only to fall into a necessity imposed by a supremely powerful will that controls events absolutely?

The OT never proposes this speculatively, and it does not appear to have been a problem for the Israelites. The OT affirms both the sovereignty of Yahweh and the freedom and responsibility of human beings. Were people not responsible agents, they would not be objects of judgment. When the prophets charge Israel with sin, they do not fail to warn that Israel can escape the imminent judgment by conversion—until a point of cumulative malice is reached at which conversion can assure only survival, but not the reversal of the course of history and judgment. The prophets show no awareness of any conflict between the sovereignty of Yahweh and human freedom; the theological concept of history demands that neither of these beliefs be maintained at the expense of the other.

117   The second question concerns the *universal scope of history:* What is the place of other nations in the historical process dominated by the will of Yahweh? Here, as much as anywhere, one can trace development in the insights of Israel. For early Israel other peoples are either enemies or irrelevant. If they are enemies of Israel, they are hostile to the purpose of Yahweh in history, and he removes them. With the rise of prophecy and a deeper awareness of the totally demanding moral will of Yahweh, the foreign nations take their place in the historical process as the weapons of Yahweh's judgment on Israel. Outside of this they are irrelevant; unlike Israel, they have no destiny in history. Hence, much of the preexilic literature is parochial in its treatment of other peoples. During the exile and afterward Israel perceives that the universal lordship of Yahweh cannot be vindicated unless he is recognized as Yahweh by all peoples. If all peoples are to know him, then they will share the religious gift originally conferred on Israel; and ultimately the differences between Israel and other peoples must and will be obliterated. Yahweh had not made the world a chaos; he made it to be inhabited, and everyone must confess at last that Yahweh alone is God (Isa 45:18–24). The glory that belongs to Yahweh is not manifested unless he is universally recognized in the fullness in which he has made himself known to Israel. The function of Israel in history then becomes the function of mediating the knowledge of Yahweh to the nations. (See W. Vogels, *God's Universal Covenant* [Ottawa, 1979].)

118   **(IV) Morality.** That the morality of the OT rises notably above the morality of other ancient Near Eastern religious documents is no longer seriously questioned. Yet it is not easy to point out precisely where the differences lie, and it is still less easy to trace the development of OT morality. Earlier critics commonly made monotheism the decisive factor in the formation of OT morality, and they attributed both monotheism and a deeper moral consciousness to the prophets of the 8th cent. More recent scholarship has found this explanation oversimplified (→ Prophetic Lit., 11:20–21). Both monotheism and a sharper conscience must be dated earlier than the 8th cent., and certain limitations in the moral insight of the OT appear after this date.

Association of religion and morality appears in the ancient Near East outside Israel. In other ancient religions the gods are the guardians of morality; the language in which this belief is uttered may often seem conventional, but there is no reason to think that a genuine belief does not lie behind the conventions. The difference between these ancient beliefs and Israelite beliefs can be summed up under two heads: (1) for other religions the gods are not the sources of moral principles nor of moral obligation; and (2) the gods themselves exhibit no moral character. Morality, therefore, becomes ultimately conventional, and moral obligation becomes merely the social pressure of the community rejecting behavior that is socially intolerable. In spite of the explicit association of religion and morality in the literature, the morality of the other ancient Near Eastern peoples does not rise above humanism.

119   In Israel the association between religion and morality reposes on the historical and the revelational character of Yahweh. For Israel's polytheistic neighbors, the gods alone possess true freedom, which consists in release from all moral restraint. On the one hand, Israel does not believe that Yahweh is restrained or bound by a higher moral law, for all moral law is imposed by his will. On the other hand, for an Israelite it would be incomprehensible that Yahweh would indulge in vice: he exhibits in the supreme degree the morality that his will imposes upon his creatures. The moral will of Yahweh is revealed in the covenant, and the stipulations of the covenant oblige Israel to a peculiarly Israelite way of life governed by that will (→ 88 above). Failure to meet these obligations is faithlessness and treachery. Through observance of these duties the Israelites attain the "holiness" that is proper to the people of Yahweh. Holiness in the OT is more than a moral attribute; it is the essence of divinity itself, with which Israel can communicate by meeting the standards of conduct imposed by Yahweh.

120   This conviction does not imply that all or most of Israel's moral principles are directly and formally revealed by Yahweh. Israel has its folk morality that is the immediate source of its public and private morality. Folk morality creates the Israelite way of life; conduct opposed to this way is "folly in Israel" or "not done in Israel" (Gen 34:7; Josh 7:15; Judg 19:23; 20:6,10; 2 Sam 13:12; Jer 29:23). Here it must be noted that folk morality in Israel rises not merely from an ethnic community, but from a community of faith; it is the folk morality of the covenanted people of Yahweh. Hence, the development of Israelite morality is always substantially affected by Israel's conviction about the moral character of Yahweh.

(Gilbert, M., *et al.,* *Morale et Ancien Testament* [LSV 1; Louvain, 1976]. Salm, C. L., *Readings in Biblical Morality* [EC, 1966]. Smend, R., *TRE* 10. 423–35. Wright, C. J. H., *Living as the People of God* [Leicester, 1983].)

121   This influence can be suggested in two areas: the morality of sex and the humanity of Israelite law. The *morality of sex* is far more rigorous in Israel than among its neighbors. It is not merely fanciful to see in this a reflection of the character of Yahweh himself in contrast to the gods and goddesses of the fertility cults. Sexual license profanes the holiness of a God who is above all sexual processes. The *humanity of Israelite law* is exhibited in a singular respect for the honor and the dignity of the human person. This respect appears in the treatment of slaves, in the rarity of the capital penalty as compared with other ancient laws, in the absence of torture and mutilation as penalties, and in insistence on the equal legal rights of all members of the community. Humanity is extended also to foreigners resident in Israel. The respect for the dignity of the human person, it seems, should be connected with Israelite belief about human nature and relations with Yahweh (→ 63 above). It is true that neither sexual morality nor humanity in Israelite laws is without limitations (→ 123 below), but even then there is perceptible superiority over other moral systems, which, therefore, cannot be the sources of Israelite morality.

122 It is also peculiarly Israelite that the emphasis lies on *the heart* as the principle of morality. The heart in Hebr idiom is not the seat of the emotions, as it is in modern speech; the "heart" is more nearly synonymous with our word "mind." But whatever the translation, the insistence on the heart means that morality must be interior, must be rooted in conviction and desire. Genuine morality is not exterior demeanor nor conformity to social manners. The contrast is explicit in Isa 29:13. It is probably too much to say that the OT reaches the idea that morality is itself something interior; for the idea remains that actions and words, not thoughts and desires, determine moral character. But it is recognized that words and actions are not honest unless they come from the heart.

123 The morality of the OT shows both growth and limitations. At the beginning of the *growth*, the historical books from Gen through Kgs show Israelite heroes and heroines frequently acting on a low moral level. One should not too quickly take the absence of moral judgments in the narratives as instances of tacit approval; for Israelite authors were capable of expressing moral judgments in a subtle way, as one can see in the stories of Jacob and the family history of David. However, these early biblical figures are often only lightly touched by what we have pointed out as the distinctive features of Israelite morality. The high moral passion of Amos and Isaiah does not appear in early Israel, but the conviction that the will of Yahweh is the urgent motive of moral obligation does appear. In the postexilic conception of the law as the compendium of morality there is a certain relaxation from the level of the writings of the prophets; the code of morality is more refined, but morality itself has been systemized to the point where external observance may become more important than the morality of the heart—a complaint made in the Gospels (Matt 23:28).

The *limitations* of Israelite morality have often been pointed out; they include the acceptance of slavery, polygamy, and divorce, the double standard of sexual morality (stricter on women), a remarkably intense hatred of foreigners, inhumanity in war, and a certain laxness in regard to mendacity and theft. In these instances Israelite morality fails to rise entirely above that of its world, though even in these areas it is somewhat superior. A more refined moral insight should not be demanded as if morality could be produced instantly; Israelite morality was not the creation of a few intellectuals but the code of behavior of an entire people, a folk morality in its development as in its origins. The remarkable feature of Israelite morality is that it contained the principles by which its limitations could be overcome. (See P. C. Craigie, *The Problem of War in the Old Testament* [GR, 1978]; P. Trible, *Texts of Terror* [Phl, 1984].)

124 Personal morality in the OT is principally the concern of the wisdom literature (→ Wisdom Lit., 27:5). The maxims of wisdom, often paralleled in other ancient wisdom literatures, instruct the young man on how to manage his life. The morality of the sages has often been called pedestrian, and to a degree it is; the sages deal with the situations of everyday life, and they have no occasion to teach a morality of crisis or to propose heroism. Their motivation at times appears less than noble, although it is not positively ignoble; moral conduct is recommended because it assures success and happiness. Against this eudaemonism must be measured the conviction of the sages that morality is wisdom, and vice is folly; the essence of wisdom is the fear of Yahweh. The belief that moral conduct will assure worldly success is too simple and needs further refinement; but the sages do not believe that one can ever advance one's success by wrongdoing. Only by righteous conduct can one be certain of "peace," the state of well-being with God and with one's fellows. Peace is a gift of Yahweh, and he does not grant it to the wicked (Isa 57:21). The wisdom literature, except for Job and Eccl, does not meet the problem of the righteous person who suffers; and traditional wisdom really lacked the resources to meet this problem. But the principles of wisdom demand that the problem shall not be met by abandoning righteousness. The "peace" of the wicked is neither genuine nor lasting.

125 **(V) Sin.** The biblical concept of sin is expressed by a number of Hebr words; a survey of four of the most important words shows the multiple OT approach to the idea. In modern moral theology sin is defined as the voluntary transgression of a divine law; there is no Hebr word that can be so defined. The basic word usually translated by "sin," *ḥaṭṭāʾt*, means a missing of the mark, a failure. One who "sins" fails to meet what is expected in relation to another person. In the cognate languages the same word is used to designate the rebellion of a vassal against an overlord. Another word, *ʿāwōn*, means a twisted or distorted condition: one who sins is crooked or deformed, deviating from the standard. This word is usually translated "guilt"; it designates the permanent damage that is done to the person by the sinful act. Still another term, *pešaʿ*, means rebellion. When used of interpersonal relations, it designates the violation of the rights of others; when used of the sins of Israel, it connotes infidelity to the obligations of the covenant. Finally, *maʿal* means infidelity, the breach of an obligation freely undertaken. Sin is also called a lie, the act that denies the reality of one's professions, an abandonment of the truth. Thus, sin is an attack on reality. Sin is folly, which in Hebrew does not mean an intellectual error but the choice of a course of action that is stupid because it is disastrous. (For further information about sin and its expiation, → Institutions, 76:72–78.)

126 The OT is aware of the universality of sin, although less aware than the writers of the NT, esp. Paul (→ Pauline Theology, 82:82–88). Emphasis in the OT falls on the sins of Israel, a people of unclean lips, unworthy of seeing Yahweh (Isa 6:5). Jeremiah sees no innocent person in Jerusalem and Judah (Jer 5:1–6; 8:10); there is none who does not sin (1 Kgs 8:46). No one can survive if Yahweh reckons iniquities (Ps 130:3). No one is righteous or innocent before God (Job 4:17; 15:14). The consciousness of the universality of sin grows with Israel's historic experience; the shattering events of the fall of the Israelite monarchies and of the exile leave the survivors of early Judaism with a sense of sinfulness that is almost excessive. Where Yahweh punishes so severely, guilt must be great indeed.

127 The universality of sin rises from evil inclinations within oneself. The thoughts of the heart are evil from youth (Gen 6:5). Jeremiah frequently alludes to the evil inclinations of the heart (Jer 16:12; 18:12), which is treacherous and sick (17:9). No serious effort is made in the OT to investigate further this condition or its origins; but it is the belief of both J and P that this is not the original human condition. In P, human beings are made in the image and likeness of Elohim and, like other creatures, are very good (Gen 1:31). In J, the man and woman perceive that they are naked only after they have sinned (Gen 3:7); this verse implies that disorderly sexual appetite did not exist in the original creation.

128   The longest and most explicit treatment of sin is found in the J account of Gen 3–11. Gen 3 should not be interpreted apart from the chapters that follow; the paradise story contains an account of the first sin, and the following chapters relate the spread of sin until it reaches the point where Yahweh can no longer tolerate it. The first sin is followed by the first murder, polygamous marriage, the invention of weapons, the first cry of vengeance, and the growth of wickedness to the degree where Yahweh repents his creation of the race, which he wipes out by the deluge. The family of one innocent man is spared, and the evil propensity that led to the doom of human beings (6:5) becomes a motive of Yahweh's kindly tolerance (8:21). But the race that rises after the deluge falls into intoxication, into unnatural vice, and finally into the pride that erects the tower of Babel. The panorama of wickedness drawn by J is vast and impressive, and it sets the background for the story of the saving acts and judgments of Yahweh that follows. Here, more clearly than elsewhere in the OT, the universality of sin is set forth; and at the same time the response of Yahweh to sins is revealed.

The paradise story of Gen 3 is an account of the first sin and of its consequences, viz., the curse of those processes of fertility by which human life is sustained, and death as the inevitable end of the struggle for survival. But the paradise story is also a splendid psychological study of the sinful act, unparalleled elsewhere in the OT. In a brief, simple dialogue the writer traces with masterful art the self-deception of the sinner, the rationalization of the action in one's own mind, the desire to be something greater than one really is, and the sinful choice made under the personal pressure of another. Almost every Hebr word for sin is illustrated in the steps by which the man and the woman rebel against the restraint of the will of Yahweh. It has long been a puzzle that this powerful narrative has no explicit echo in the other books of the OT before the Gk period, but the narrative is entirely in harmony with the OT attitude toward sin.

129   GUILT.   Correlative with sin is guilt; and the peculiarity of this conception in the OT is best seen in the fact that there is no distinct Hebr word for guilt. The words for sin, in particular *ḥaṭṭā't* and *'āwōn*, in some contexts can be translated only by guilt; they designate a permanent condition that is produced by the sinful act and is sometimes described in most realistic terms. Guilt is a burden that can be laid upon one (Num 12:11), that must be borne (Gen 4:13), that can be passed from father to son (Lev 26:39). It is a crack in a wall that will fall suddenly upon the guilty (Isa 30:13). It falls upon the head of the evildoer (Isa 3:9; Jer 7:19; Ezek 22:31). It is like water kept cool in a cistern (Jer 6:7), like rust corroding a metal vessel (Ezek 24:6ff.). These examples show how the OT pictures sin as an enduring evil, present and active in the world; the sinful act remains, doing damage beyond repair. (On retribution and consequences, see J. Barton, *JTS* 30 [1979] 1–12; K. Koch, in *Theodicy in the Old Testament* [ed. J. Crenshaw; IRT 4; Phl, 1983] 57–87; also → Wisdom Lit., 27:12–13.)

130   This guilt can extend through an entire social group (→ 70 above); indeed, the prophets usually address the entire community of Israel. All humankind perishes in the flood; the entire cities of Sodom and Gomorrah perish in fire from heaven. More difficult for the modern mind is the collective guilt that lies at the base of such stories as those of Achan (Josh 7) and of the descendants of Saul (2 Sam 21). This idea of group responsibility is understood only in the framework of

Israelite thinking about society as a kinship relationship (→ 68 above). But the idea illustrates the profound Israelite belief in the reality of guilt and of its power to wreak harm far beyond the individual person who commits the sin. Guilt is a disease, an infection that corrupts the entire group in which the sin is committed.

In some OT episodes there is a more primitive conception of guilt as something mechanical and independent of personal responsibility. The guilt in such stories is less an abiding malice than a certain material infection that can be contracted even by the innocent. Thus, the kings who in ignorance take the wives of the patriarchs are punished with illness in their households (Gen 20:3ff.; 26:10); Jonathan's unknowing contravention of his father's vow is a mortal offense (1 Sam 14); Uzzah dies when he touches the Ark (2 Sam 6). The punishment that comes is an impersonal, almost demonic effect evoked by the material act. In such a primitive concept of guilt the idea of personal malice and responsibility, and with it the moral will of Yahweh, is obscured. The spiritual growth of Israel would involve rising above this primitive way of thinking.

131   The words of the prophets, in contrast, emphasize sin as a rupture of personal relations with Yahweh. In respect to Yahweh, human sin is pride (Amos, Isa), adultery (Hos, Jer, Ezek), filial disobedience, and ingratitude (Isa, Jer). The classical prophets all dwell on the fact that sin is a deliberate choice made with full knowledge; sin is contempt of Yahweh, a profanation of his holiness and effectively a denial of his divinity. They emphasize also the personal response of Yahweh. The anger of Yahweh is a concept totally opposed to the mechanical conception of guilt and punishment (→ 100 above). When Yahweh punishes sin, he is personally involved. His anger is not blind rage; it is directed by judgment (→ 138 below), and the judgments of Yahweh are not impersonal.

132   **(VI) Forgiveness.**   The removal of sin and guilt is a matter of vital concern in the religion of the OT. Community with Yahweh is life itself; and if community with Yahweh is sundered, there is no hope of security. If community is to be restored, the anger of Yahweh must be appeased. There is no belief that human beings can restore community with Yahweh. As the community was a free gift of grace in the first instance, so the restoration of community cannot be achieved by merit. People must commit themselves to the mercy and the forgiveness of Yahweh. The system of cultic expiation that is found in Lev–Num is not directed to the ritual obtaining forgiveness. For sins committed "with a high hand" (Num 15:30; cf. 1 Sam 3:14) there is no ritual expiation. The "sin" and "guilt" for which sacrifices are offered are not malicious acts; they are inadvertent failures to meet ritual prescriptions. One may judge from the words of the prophets that the Israelites frequently regarded their sacrificial ritual as a mechanical atonement that was automatically effective (Jer 7:9). This is not the idea that governs the ritual prescriptions, and the prophets attack this idea as gross superstition (→ Institutions, 76:92).

133   Expiation of formal sins is achieved only by bearing the punishment that follows the guilt; indeed, guilt and punishment sometimes seem almost to be identified. When Nathan announces to David that Yahweh has forgiven David's sin, he says that David will not die (2 Sam 12). But the guilt is a present and active reality; and although the life of David is spared, the penalty of death falls upon the child of David and Bathsheba. The entire account that follows in 2 Sam 13–20 relates the disasters that fall upon David and his house after his crime. Without explicitly moralizing, the writer shows that the fortunes of David are reversed by this crisis in his life. The moral impact of the story is no less massive than the impact of the J account of the origin and spread of sin in Gen 3–11 (→ 128 above).

134   To obtain forgiveness *conversion* is necessary. Conversion is usually expressed by the Hebr word that means "turn" (the vb. *šûb*), frequently used in prophetic admonitions addressed to Israel. Eichrodt (*ETOT* 2. 465) has assembled numerous phrases that fill out the idea of conversion: to seek Yahweh, to ask for him, to humble oneself, to direct one's heart to Yahweh, to seek good, to hate evil and to love good, to learn to do good, to obey, to acquire a new heart, to circumcise one's heart, to plow a new furrow, to wash oneself from wickedness. The abundance of these metaphors shows that conversion is conceived of as a genuine interior change of attitude that issues in a revolution in personal conduct.

The assurance of forgiveness reposes on the forgiving character of Yahweh, which is often attested (Amos 7:2ff.; Hos 11:8ff.; Pss 78:38; 103:3). Yahweh desires not that the wicked man die but that he be converted from his evil ways and live (Ezek 18:23). Confession of Yahweh's forgiveness is frequent in Isa 40–55. In the exile, Israel has atoned for its former wickedness; its community with Yahweh is restored and he is ready to fulfill his promises. The prophet sees in Yahweh the father, the shepherd, the avenging kinsman, the savior (→ 75 above).

135   There is a large amount of anthropomorphism (→ 21–22 above) in the conception of the motives that prompt Yahweh's forgiveness. Israel appeals to his covenant love and his fidelity; and in spite of the faithlessness of Israel to the covenant, there is an assurance that the good will of Yahweh is not limited by covenant stipulations. Israel appeals to the promises of Yahweh and to oaths sworn to the patriarchs, which should not be frustrated even by the failure of Israel to measure up to the stature of the patriarchs. Yahweh has promised an eternal seed and must find a way to keep this promise. He does not punish under compulsion and is free to relax the standards that he himself has set. Israel appeals to the name of Yahweh and to his honor. If in anger he allows his own people to become the prey of foreign nations, these nations will blaspheme his name by saying that Yahweh cannot protect his own. Israel appeals to the kindness of Yahweh: it is more consistent with his character to forgive than to punish, and he prefers to forgive. He should tolerate some degree of sin because people's evil instincts make it impossible for them to overcome sin entirely. Frail and mortal, they should not be tested rigorously. In Hos there are eloquent appeals to the love of Yahweh: Israel is his spouse, and Yahweh cannot entirely suppress affection for his beloved even when she is faithless and perverse. This book represents the tension between punishment and forgiveness as an emotional conflict in Yahweh — though he punishes Israel, his saving love is not frustrated by the sins of his people (→ Hosea, 14:4, 30).

These motives of forgiveness are not all of equal value, and some of the anthropomorphisms are naïve. But the motives illustrate the many facets under which Israel has known Yahweh, and they merge into a conception of his forgiveness which expresses Israel's assurance that Yahweh can surely find a way to overcome sin. Ultimately the idea of forgiveness leads into eschatology. If Yahweh's forgiveness is to be exercised in a way that suits his character, it must find an outlet in some act that lies outside history (→ 165–66 below). The final achievement of Yahweh's forgiveness must be a reconciliation that renders further forgiveness unnecessary.

136   **(VII) Judgment.** The words "judge" and "judgment" in the OT have connotations somewhat different from those in modern speech. In the early writings of the OT the judge is primarily one to whom a person appeals for the defense of rights, and a judgment is a vindication. When the judgment of Yahweh is invoked, his assistance is asked; and when he grants judgment, it is a saving act.

137   In the older view the "Day of Yahweh" is the day on which Yahweh judges the enemies of Israel. The appearance of Yahweh in the theophany (→ 57 above) is no doubt to be connected with this imagery. The earliest occurrence of the phrase "Day of Yahweh" is in Amos 5:18–20: Hitherto the Israelites have been looking upon the Day of Yahweh as a day of victory and deliverance, but Amos inverts the idea and affirms that it is a day of judgment on Israel. Israel is no less under judgment than the foreign nations cited in 1:3–2:3, and Yahweh's sentence of doom is pronounced on Israel as well as on the Ethiopians, the Philistines, and the Arameans (9:7–10). A day in which Yahweh acts against all that is proud and lofty is described in Isa 2:10–17; this judgment is universal, and Israel, although not mentioned, is not excluded. Zeph 1 has a much more elaborate poem on the day of Yahweh that may not be of a single origin. The Day of Yahweh is not only universal but even cosmic in scope, suggesting later apocalyptic conceptions (→ 139 below); yet the judgment is also focused on Judah and Jerusalem. The usage of the phrase suggests a "day," an event; whether this needs some modification is discussed below.

138   For the preexilic prophets the judgment of Yahweh is accomplished in history. Amos (5:18–20, 26–27; 7:1–9; 9:1–8a) speaks of the coming downfall both of foreign nations and of Israel; nothing suggests that he is thinking of anything other than the historical factors as the weapons of Yahweh's judgment. Hosea (4:8–14; 8:7–10; 13:4–14:1) speaks less clearly of a day or even of an event; but the doom of Israel is clearly announced and surely threatened. The judgments of Yahweh are much more prominent in Isaiah's thought (1:2–9; 5:26–30; 10:5–19). They are against both Israel and Judah and against various social classes, particularly against those in power. The language of Isa rarely if ever suggests a cosmic catastrophe; Isa 30:27ff. is the language of the theophany. The agent of Yahweh's judgment is the contemporary historical reality of Assyria, which will bring disaster not only on the Israelite monarchies but also on all the people of the area. Assyria is also under judgment, to be accomplished in Yahweh's good time; but so long as Assyria acts as the rod of Yahweh's anger, it is irresistible. The older portions of the book of Micah (1:2–16), Isaiah's contemporary, portray the judgment on Israel and Judah as an imminent event to be accomplished by historical forces. Other and probably later passages take a view of the judgment more in harmony with subsequent conceptions.

Jeremiah and Ezekiel, contemporaries of the fall of Jerusalem, are perhaps preeminently the prophets of judgment. They are certain of an imminent judgment and of its justice, and they present the totality of the judgment in an impressive manner. Their assurance comes not only from their awareness of the threatening power of the Chaldeans, but also from their conviction of the deep collective guilt of Judah — not even the most worthy intercessors can avert the punishment that such guilt demands (Jer 14:11; Ezek 14:12–20). Even in this picture of inevitable and terrifying judgment, the idea of judgment as a saving act does not disappear entirely. Each step in the judgment is a warning as well as a punishment; if Israel learns that its sins excite the anger of

Yahweh and turns from them, Israel may survive. This is not a promise of mechanical forgiveness; when evil has advanced to the degree that the prophets describe, repentance alone is not enough to reverse the course of events. But Israel can retain its community with Yahweh even in such a judgment if Israel will but listen. In fact, it is only after the catastrophe that Israel becomes aware that the judgment was necessary to preserve the people of Yahweh as such. Its own wickedness would destroy Israel as the people of Yahweh; but if Israel is purged by judgment, it can continue to exist as the people of Yahweh, even if only as a sorry remnant.

139   Reference has been made above to another concept of judgment that appears in later OT books; to this type of literature the name "apocalyptic" is given. Strictly speaking, the name does not fit many specific OT passages (→ Apocalyptic, 19:3), but the type of literature thus designated has its roots in the OT. A world catastrophe that is the work of the judgment of Yahweh is seen in Isa 13; 24; Joel 2-3; and in much of Dan. Ezek 38-39 with its vision of the war against Gog is closer to these passages than to the preexilic prophets. In such passages there is no reference to a judgment on Israel or on any particular nation that can surely be identified; the apocalyptic judgment is a judgment on humanity and even on the material universe. This is an extension of the judgment of Israel; just as the genuine Israel could survive only if the historical Israel perished in the judgment, so the world and humanity can be united with Yahweh only if the existing world passes through a consuming judgment. The old world must be removed to make room for the new world to be created by Yahweh (→ 60 above). In apocalyptic description the judgment is not explicitly an event in history, as in the preexilic prophets; this raises the problem of eschatology (→ 164 below).

140   **(VIII) Salvation.**   The OT idea of salvation is complex and exhibits a historical development that is extremely difficult to synthesize. We treat here passages in which no individual savior appears (for the Messiah, → 152ff. below).

(A) Yahweh's Saving Deeds.   The Hebr word *yĕšûʿâ,* which we translate "salvation," often occurs in contexts where it refers to deliverance by military means; in these contexts the word can be translated "victory." In such uses "salvation" is parallel to the "righteous deeds" or the "judgments" of Yahweh in behalf of Israel (→ 94, 136 above). Salvation also signifies deliverance from any threat to life or integrity of person. In the ancient world the king was always the king savior, to whom his people looked for salvation against external enemies through war, or for salvation from injustice within the community through his judgment and the administration of law.

141   Yahweh is celebrated as king-savior, particularly in Pss 47; 93; 96-99. These are often called "the Enthronement Psalms" in modern scholarship because of the hypothesis that these psalms were used in a cult festival celebrating the enthronement of Yahweh as king (→ Institutions, 76:141-46; → Psalms, 34:6, 63, 109). In these psalms Yahweh as king is hailed as creator and lord of nature, and it is on a cosmic scale that his saving deeds are done. His salvation is manifested to all the world. The association of Yahweh's kingly saving power with creation and with the revelation of his power in nature is also prominent in Isa 40-55.

142   The first saving deed of Yahweh in the history of Israel and the exemplar to which other saving deeds are likened is the deliverance from Egypt. This is an act of creation, for Israel becomes a people—the people of Yahweh—by this deliverance. It is the basis of the claims

of Yahweh in the covenant; it is also that saving act to which Israel most frequently appeals when it asks for deliverance from threats to its national welfare.

The subsequent history of Israel is a recital of the saving acts of Yahweh: the passage of Israel, the victories giving Israel the land of Canaan, deliverance in Canaan through the judges from the attacks of enemies, and the culminating saving act of the early period—the establishment of the monarchy and the deliverance from the Philistines. The recital of the saving deeds is interspersed with the recital of the infidelities of Israel; these arouse the anger of Yahweh, but they do not alter his will to save Israel. The historians of Israel know that the strokes of Yahweh's anger are also saving acts, for they teach Israel that a revolt from Yahweh will bring Israel to a condition where salvation can be achieved only through a tremendous judgment that will reduce the nation to a mere remnant.

143   This theme of salvation through judgment becomes dominant in the period of the monarchy in the words of the preexilic prophets. Amos says almost nothing of the saving will of Yahweh (the conclusion of Amos [9:8b-15] is the work of a later hand). Salvation in Hos is postponed to a distant future to be achieved by means that are hidden from the insight of the prophet. In Isa the assurance of salvation is deeper, but the theme of judgment is no less prominent than it is in Amos and Hos. In Jer and Ezek the salvation of historic Israel has become impossible; salvation now means a restoration, but not of historical Israel as it existed under the monarchy. Restoration becomes the dominant theme in Dt-Isa—of all OT works the one that elaborates the theme of salvation with greatest richness, frequently alluding to the creative power of Yahweh in connection with salvation. The restoration of Israel is a new act of creative power scarcely less impressive than Yahweh's creation of Israel at the exodus. Whereas Yahweh's work of salvation in the exodus was manifested to the Egyptians, the restoration of Israel is manifested to the entire world. The author of Dt-Isa echoes the theme of the new exodus almost as much as he echoes that of the new creation.

144   **(B) Nature of Salvation.**   The varied character of salvation can be seen from an enumeration of some of its expressions. The oracles of Balaam (Num 23-24) must be regarded as among the older portions of the OT, perhaps 10th cent. (→ Numbers, 5:48-52). Salvation in the oracles of Balaam consists in the blessing of Yahweh, which makes Israel a people set apart from other nations, assured of victory over their enemies, of peaceful dwelling in their own land, and of abundant prosperity. The tone of salvation is predominantly but not exclusively militant. The large place that material blessings hold in these oracles is never entirely lost in the further development of the idea of salvation; indeed, the prosperity included in salvation is sometimes described extravagantly (Isa 60; 65; Amos 9:13-15). The idea of victory over enemies is explicitly political, and this element likewise does not disappear. The Zion poems of Isa 49-52; 60-62 locate salvation in a restored Jerusalem that receives as tribute the wealth of the nations. Political salvation means not only deliverance from enemies, but final victory and the submission of the nations to the rule of Israel.

145   Salvation seems to be conceived in more elevated terms when seen as the era of universal peace (Isa 2:1ff.). Salvation means the elimination of injustice and the establishment of that security that comes from government administered in righteousness and judgment (Isa 32). In Jer and Ezek salvation is stated in the formula of the covenant union, "You shall be my people and I will be your God"; by this statement is promised the restoration of the communion with Yahweh that was destroyed by the faithlessness of Israel. Salvation is Yahweh dwelling in the midst of his people. In the new Israel of Ezek 40–48 the Temple becomes the center of the land, a focus of holiness from which the power of Yahweh radiates. The restoration of Judah described in Jer 30–31 contains all the elements of victory over enemies and of a life of material prosperity; but the defeat of enemies is not emphasized as it is elsewhere (in contrast, for instance, with Isa 63:1ff.) — material prosperity is depicted in moderate terms, and the dominant ideas are peace and joy.

146 In all these conceptions of salvation it is at least implicitly supposed that the Israel which is saved is a new Israel — not only a new creation but also new in the sense that it is purified of the vices that corrupted the historical Israel. This purification is quite explicit in Jer and Ezek. Salvation for Jer (31:31ff.) is a new covenant written on the heart; the terms of the covenant, the revealed will of Yahweh, will be embedded in the interior dispositions of each person and will govern life. Salvation is not merely membership in the people of salvation; it is a total acceptance of Yahweh on the part of each individual. In such a saved community Yahweh will not deal through the established human mediators and teachers of the historical Israel but will reveal himself to each Israelite as he revealed himself to Moses in the original covenant (→ Jeremiah, 18:89). Ezek (36:26) sees the heart of stone replaced by a heart of flesh, sensitive and responsive to the will of Yahweh. Israel receives a new spirit, the spirit of Yahweh, that will impel Israel to obedience. This interior regeneration is the basis of the peace and prosperity that are promised.

147 Salvation at times is seen as broader than the salvation of Israel. The revelation and instruction of Yahweh shall go out from Zion to all nations, who shall then achieve universal peace (Isa 2:1ff.). The mission of Israel as a medium of salvation is clear in Dt-Isa: through Israel Yahweh will reveal himself to the nations, who, once they know him, will give the obedience that will save them (Isa 45:18–25). Israel is Yahweh's witness to the nations. The universal scope of salvation is implied also in the return of paradise (Isa 11:6–9; 65:25) and in the creation of new heavens and a new earth (Isa 65:17ff.), as well as in the frequent allusions to the transformation of the material universe and to the marvelous prosperity of the era of salvation.

148 Zech 1–8 contains a compact account of salvation as it was conceived in 520–518 BC in Jerusalem. The earth is at peace; Israel is restored to its land; the oppressors of Israel have disappeared; the Israelites dwell in peace, joy, security, and moderate prosperity; the land is purged of gross crimes and vices; and it is expected that many nations will come and worship Yahweh. Compared to some other postexilic writings this concept of salvation is plain and simple; yet one cannot reckon it among the most elevated ideas of the OT. One may say that Zech is on the way to the "realized salvation" of the P tradition (→ Pentateuch, 1:7), in which salvation is scarcely more than the existence of Israel united to Yahweh through the cult.

149 **(C) Reign of God.** The multiple developments of the idea of salvation are best summed up, if they can be summed up at all, in the idea of the reign (kingdom) of Yahweh, although this phrase is rare in the OT. Yet it was a phrase apt enough to be used in Jewish literature and in the Gospels (→ NT Thought, 81:44–45, 53) as a designation of the expected salvation that needed no further definition. The reign of Yahweh is the acceptance of his will by all. This cannot happen until all know him, and they can know only by perceiving his revelation of himself to Israel. The universal knowledge of Yahweh must work a revolutionary change in humankind; and since the struggle against nature arises from human insubmissiveness to God, there must be a corresponding revolution even in material nature. The revelation of Yahweh will be no more willingly accepted by others than it was accepted by Israel; and hence, like Israel, all must pass through a process of judgment, which is a saving act. Resistance to Yahweh must yield before his matchless power. In such a world, people will be secure from threat and free to lead the life that becomes human beings. (See J. Gray, *The Biblical Doctrine of the Reign of God* [Edinburgh, 1979].)

150 An attempt is made in the preceding paragraph to enunciate the idea, scarcely found in so many words in the OT, that lies at the base of the Israelite hope of salvation; and it is within the framework of this idea that certain more difficult elements such as material blessings and political salvation are to be understood.

First, material blessings. The OT Israelites are material-minded, by which is meant that their literature exhibits no abstract and generalized thinking. Furthermore, they have no idea of a spiritual reality in the modern sense of the term. It is clear from the passages summarized above that salvation is not conceived of without the supreme spiritual achievement, which is total submission to God issuing in a human perfection that reflects the image of God. The Israelites find the enumeration of virtues less convincing than the consideration of the concrete changes that submission to Yahweh will achieve in human existence. The most obvious change will be the cessation of certain definite obstacles to the good life, in particular, those obstacles that the Palestinian peasant knows best: the danger of war and of crop failure. Salvation will be achieved if these two threats to security are removed, and it is doubtful that one could appreciate any more elevated ideal. Add to these two blessings freedom from debt and debt-slavery and freedom from the oppression of rapacious magnates and landlords, and the Israelite is content to sit under his vine and fig tree with none to terrify him (Mic 4:4). If human malice is removed, what limit can one put to the fertility of the soil? For the importance to Israel of the land, see W. Brueggemann, *The Land* (OBT; Phl, 1977).

These material blessings are not merely symbols of spiritual blessings; they are the effect of spiritual blessings. In general, the OT shows no awareness of an afterlife (yet → 172 below); the only good life that Israel knows is conceived of in terms of concrete experienced existence. This existence is transformed by perfect community with Yahweh, who dwells among his people. Life is good where there is no resistance to his saving will.

151 Second, political salvation. For the reason that life is conceived of in terms of concrete experience, the good life is represented in political terms. Salvation, like life itself, is experienced in community and not by isolated individuals (→ 73 above). The only ordered society that the OT Israelite knows is a monarchy administered with justice and competence. Salvation is not a return to a more primitive life, but a perfection of the form of social life that offers the best possibilities for salvation. If monarchy fails because of the unrighteousness of its rulers, salvation does not consist in the elimination of rulers but in the installation of righteous rulers (→ 158 below).

Political salvation is sometimes seen as the rule of Israel over defeated nations. This limited insight must be combined with the other insights mentioned above in which salvation is extended to the entire world. But even the political supremacy of Israel is not a purely secular form of salvation. Israel is the people of Yahweh, and only through Israel will Yahweh reveal himself to the nations. In the simple thinking of the ancient world, the people whose god is the most powerful obtains supremacy over other nations. The OT hope of salvation rarely rises to an idea of salvation simply for human beings; it sees the salvation of peoples, of Israel first and then of others. Had Yahweh not been the God of Israel,

his reality would have been less clearly perceived; but further development was necessary before it could be seen that he was the God of Israel in an affirmative sense that made him no less the God of peoples who did not worship him. It is only in the NT that the renewed Israel, the people of God, is seen to include equally all children of God, all who are willing to be included.

Our discussion of salvation has brought us into the area of God's future plans for his people.

GOD'S FUTURE PLANS FOR HIS PEOPLE

152   (I) The Messiah. The figure of the Messiah ultimately came to have an important place in Israel's understanding of God's plans for its future. This discussion, necessarily brief, is dependent implicitly on the exegesis of important but disputed OT texts; for details the reader is referred to commentary on the individual OT books. The treatment here (§ 152-63) has been added to this article by R. E. Brown.

(A) The Term "Messiah." The Eng word is from Aram *mĕšîḥā'*, *reflecting Hebr māšîaḥ,* "anointed"; the Gk word is *christos,* whence "Christ." In this discussion a distinction will be made between "Messiah" (capitalized) and "messiahs" or salvific figures. Judaism knew of a gallery of figures who were expected to appear at the time of God's definitive intervention in behalf of Israel, e.g., Elijah, the Prophet-like-Moses, perhaps the Son of Man, the Anointed Priest, etc. These figures can loosely be called messianic. But the capitalized term "Messiah" is best confined to a precisely delineated concept, viz., the anointed king of the Davidic dynasty who would establish in the world the definitive reign of Yahweh (→ 149 above). Such a notion of Messiah is the product of a long development sketched below.

153   The expectation of the Messiah appears in post-exilic Judaism (although in the OT "Messiah" is not used as a title in the sense we are using it). From the frequency and spontaneity with which the question of the Messiah appears in the NT (Mark 8:29; 14:61; John 1:20; 4:25; etc.) and also from the evidence of early Jewish writings (→ Apocrypha, 67:48), we are safe in assuming that the expectation of the Messiah became common in inter-testamental Judaism and could perhaps be called a national hope. However, not all Jews expected the Messiah. In the 1st cent. AD many had lost faith in the Davidic dynasty, which had not ruled for 500 years; and there are Jewish books that treat of eschatological questions without ever mentioning the Messiah (→ Apocrypha, 67:49). Moreover, often the expectation of the Messiah was accompanied by some of the other expectations mentioned above; at Qumran the sectarians awaited the coming of the Prophet, of the Davidic Messiah, and of the Anointed Priest (→ Apocrypha, 67:115-117).

154   Indeed there may have been an amalgamation of the figure of the Messiah with other salvific figures, e.g., the Suffering Servant, or the Son of Man, into one composite figure. Certainly this happened in the Christian description of Jesus, but the evidence is quite uncertain for determining whether this happened in pre-Christian Judaism (→ Apocrypha, 67:15). For instance, no pre-Christian work ever describes a suffering Messiah. The Christian reader must beware of an instinctive tendency to interpret the Jewish expectation of the Messiah in the light of Jesus' career and person. Actually, the Jewish concept of the Messiah had to undergo considerable modification before it could be applied to Jesus,

whence Jesus' reluctance to accept the title without qualification (→ 178 below; → NT Thought, 81:13-15).

In particular, while the Jewish hope of the Messiah was highly idealized almost to the point of making the Messiah a figure of superhuman abilities, there was no expectation of a divine Messiah in the sense in which Jesus is professed as Son of God. Moreover, nationalistic coloring was never absent from any stage of the pre-Christian development of messianic thought, any more than the OT concept of salvation itself was devoid of materialistic and nationalistic aspects (→ 150-51 above). It is inaccurate and unjust to say that the Jews of Jesus' time had corrupted the idea of the Messiah as a spiritual savior by making it secular and nationalistic and that Jesus restored the concept to its pristine meaning. The Christian understanding of a spiritual Messiah represented a change rather than a restoration—a change that we believe brought the development of the idea to a rich fruition, but a change nevertheless.

155   (B) Development of Royal Messianism. That God sent saviors to deliver his people (Moses, the judges, Nehemiah, Ezra) is a commonplace in Israel's theological understanding of its history. But messianism, as we shall discuss it, is involved with the salvific role of men in the framework of an institution, the monarchy.

(a) THE FIRST STAGE OF DEVELOPMENT. In the first days of the Davidic monarchy in Judah every anointed king (messiah) was looked on as a savior sent by God to his people. There is no record in the OT of a similar sublimation of the kingship in northern Israel. It is altogether probable that the first literary record of the messianic character of the dynasty of David is found in the oracle of Nathan, preserved in three forms (2 Sam 7; Ps 89; 1 Chr 17). Scholars do not agree on which is the most primitive; none of them appears to preserve the original oracle unmodified (J. L. McKenzie, *TS* 8 [1947] 187-218). In Ps 89:20-38 the following elements may be distinguished: the election of David by Yahweh; promises of victory and wide dominion; adoption of David and his successors as sons; covenant of Yahweh with David and his house; promise of an eternal dynasty, not conditioned on the fidelity of the successors of David to Yahweh. This oracle is also echoed in Ps 132. The oracle does not speak of any individual successor, nor does it look into the eschatological future. It is a simple assurance that the dynasty will endure as the chosen human agent of the salvation of Yahweh wrought in history (→ 142 above). The salvation to be accomplished by David and his house does not here go beyond the political salvation to be achieved by the king.

156   The Blessing of Judah by Jacob (Gen 49:9-12) probably comes from the early monarchy and alludes implicitly to the reign of David. However this blessing is to be construed, it seems to assure the permanence of the dynasty of David. Fertility is assured so long as the chosen king savior reigns.

157 The "Royal Psalms" (in particular Pss 2; 72; 110; → Psalms, 34:10, 21, 88, 126) should also be considered in this first stage of messianism. Scholars have abandoned the notion that they were composed by David himself (even though they may be of 10th-cent. origin), who was singing of one future Messiah — such an expectation did not exist at this period. Rather, these psalms were compositions applicable to any Davidic monarch, and they may have been recited on important occasions in the life of the monarch, like the coronation. The references to a divine begetting of the king (110:3) and divine sonship (2:7) — once thought to be literal references to Jesus — were part of the symbolic court language (*Hofstil*) used to describe the king as Yahweh's representative. The eternal priesthood "according to the order of Melchizedek" (110:4) promised to the king was probably part of the hereditary titulature of the Canaanite kings of Jerusalem, exemplified in the priest king Melchizedek of Gen 14 (→ Genesis, 2:23; → Institutions, 76:16). The eternal and universal reign of the king — formerly thought to be a literal reference to Jesus — was partly an optimistic wish for long life and many victories, and partly a reflection of the permanent greatness promised the Davidic dynasty.

Ps 72 may be taken as the clearest expression of the idea of the king savior. The king governs with the justice that becomes a ruler; he is the savior of the poor and the needy. He is victorious over his enemies, who are also the enemies of his people; he is the savior of his people from external danger. During his reign the blessing of Yahweh brings fertility to the land. Nowhere in the Ps is the king presented as a future eschatological deliverer. He is the reigning successor of David and the heir to the covenantal promises made to David.

158 (b) THE SECOND STAGE OF DEVELOPMENT. In the writings of the 8th cent. there is a development in royal messianism. Wicked and inept kings like Ahaz had dimmed the glory of the Davidic line and the optimistic hope that each king would be a savior of his people. Isaiah, in particular, gives voice to a more nuanced expectation: there would be an inbreak of the power of Yahweh that would revive the dynasty and ensure its permanence. Yahweh would soon raise up a successor of David who would be worthy of the name of Davidic king; he would be an example of charismatic power, just as David had been when the royal line was instituted (→ Isaiah, 15:19, 22). Isa 7:14-17 and 9:1ff. grow rhapsodical in their description of the heir to the throne to be born in Isaiah's time (735 BC), perhaps the son of the wicked Ahaz and of a well-known maiden of the court (the "virgin" of Isa 7:14 — an inaccurate translation of the Hebrew). The child would be a sign that God was still with his people (Emmanuel) in the person of the Davidic king. The heir would establish justice, build a vast empire and bring peace to it, and be worthy of the traditional courtly titles of the monarch (9:5). Although Isaiah may have believed that his expectations were fulfilled in the good king Hezekiah, Ahaz's successor, the Isaian passages are describing an ideal for restoration rather than a reality; and this permitted them to be used by later generations who also looked forward to a divine renewal of the monarchy.

159 The passage in Isa 11:1ff. may be later than Isaiah; scholars are divided. It looks into a more remote future than the passages we have just discussed. The charismatic power of the expected ideal ruler is clearly affirmed (→ 35 above), for the spirit will rest upon him and bestow on him the qualities of an ideal ruler. He will save the kingdom from internal injustice and external threat. In comparison with the undisputed writings of

Isa, the novel element in Isa 11:1ff. is the return of the conditions of paradise that the reign of this king will bring to pass. Universal peace under his reign is cosmic; and peace rests upon the universal "knowledge of Yahweh," the experience of the personal reality of Yahweh through his revelation of himself (→ 105 above). This knowledge can be communicated to the world only through Israel. These two ideas, the restoration of the dynasty of David and the universal and religious scope of the salvation of which the dynasty of David is the medium, probably appear here for the first time in the OT.

160 That the hope for a resurgence of the dynasty under a new and ideal ruler was not confined to Isaiah is seen from Mic 5:1-6. Micah, a contemporary of Isaiah, sees a new David coming from Bethlehem to give his people security against the Assyrian threat. Mic 5:3 sees a restoration of the unity of Israel and Judah under this new David; the schism that occurred under Rehoboam will be healed.

Other and later allusions to the restoration of the dynasty of David echo these passages with little modification. The "branch" or "shoot" of Jer 23:5 will be the king-savior whose name will affirm the righteousness of Yahweh; righteousness here means saving will (→ 94 above). The restoration of the dynasty appears also in Jer 30:9,21. The dynasty of David is the sprig of cedar that Ezek sees planted by Yahweh (Ezek 17:22), and in the new Israel David will once more be king (Ezek 34:23; 37:24). Ezekiel does not, however, emphasize the function of the king as savior; this hesitancy may reflect the historical events of which he was a contemporary, viz., the fall of the nation and the exile of the Davidic king. The monarchy appears in Ezek simply because the monarchy is an Israelite institution without which the prophet cannot conceive Israel. Several interpreters have asked whether a return of David in person is not implied in these passages of Ezek; but such an implication is not immediately obvious, for the name may designate the dynasty.

161 (c) THE THIRD STAGE OF DEVELOPMENT. The postexilic development of messianism is difficult to trace because of the lack of written evidence; in part we must reconstruct its history from the end product, viz., the expectation of the Messiah in the latest pre-Christian period. The fact that the Davidic line no longer ruled after the exile (or at least after the governorship of Zerubbabel, to the best of our knowledge) made a profound difference in messianism. Before the exile the ideal king who would restore the vigor of the Davidic line could always be thought of in terms of the next generation of a reigning dynasty. But now there could be no ideal king until the indefinite future when the Davidic throne would be restored. Thus the expectations began to move toward the indefinite future; and rather than centering on one monarch in a continuing line of rulers, these expectations came to center on one supreme king who would represent Yahweh's definitive intervention to save his people. It is in this period that we may begin to speak of *the Messiah* in the strict sense. Earlier Scripture (Royal Pss; Isa) was now reread with this new messianic understanding in mind.

162 If the definitive character of the Messiah's action is clear, the eschatological character is less clear. There is no clear evidence that the Messiah was thought of as a transcendental figure whose mission would go beyond the realities of history. True, his work would be a terminal manifestation of the power of Yahweh that would make any further saving act of Yahweh unnecessary. This saving act would not be the work of ordinary historical forces, but the kind of visible inbreak of

Yahweh's power into history that had been seen in the exodus. Yet, so far as we know, the inbreak was expected to be accomplished in historical circumstances, even if at times the anticipation of the Messiah may have taken on some of the trappings of apocalyptic.

In certain passages the concept of the king-savior (→ 140 above) has undergone an interesting transformation. In Zech 9:9ff. (4th cent.?; → Haggai, 22:39) his reign will bring universal peace and all warlike traits will have disappeared. He is the instrument of Yahweh's salvation, but the salvation is the work of Yahweh himself with no human agent. The king has even lost the trappings of royalty. Yet this is not a universally accepted view of the Messiah, for in the much later (1st cent. BC) *Pss. Sol.* (→ Apocrypha, 67:48) there is a strong mixture of the political and the spiritual in picturing a Messiah who would bring the Gentiles under his yoke.

The advent of the Messiah was also a cause of speculation in early Judaism. How would people know him? In some passages (Matt 2:4–6; John 7:42) we can see the popular expectation that he would be born at Bethlehem, David's city, and that his birth would be known to all Israel. But in other passages (John 7:27; Mark 8:29) we see the thought that the Messiah would be hidden; for people would not know where he would come from, and he could stand in their midst without their knowing it (see *BGJ* 1. 53).

163 In summation, in the course of 1,000 years Israelite messianism developed to the point where the expectation of the Messiah embodied one of the principal hopes for Yahweh's intervention to save his people. While this king-savior, almost by definition, would be a political savior, he would be a savior in virtue of the charisma and power of Yahweh, and so his saving acts would never be merely political. In his reign, the Messiah would bring to Israel the ideal rule of Yahweh himself. That the salvation mediated by the Messiah would have a scope outside Israel is less frequently mentioned and is often viewed chauvinistically. Yet granting the origins of the concept of anointed king, we may be surprised that the wider view occurs as often as it does.

(Becker, J., *Messianic Expectation in the Old Testament* [Phl, 1980]. Cazelles, H., *Le Messie de la Bible* [Paris, 1978]. Coppens, J., *L'attente du Messie* [RechBib 6; Bruges, 1953]; *Le messianisme royal* [LD 54; Paris, 1968]; *La relève apocalyptique du messianisme royal* [3 vols.; BETL 50, 55, 61; Louvain, 1979–83). Grelot, P., *L'espérance juive à l'heure de Jésus* [Paris, 1978]. Klausner, J., *The Messianic Idea in Israel* [London, 1956]. Landman, L., *Messianism in the Talmudic Era* [NY, 1979]. Mettinger, T. N. D., *King and Messiah* [ConBOT 8; Lund, 1976]. Mowinckel, S., *He That Cometh* [Nash, 1964].)

164 (II) Eschatology. The question of eschatology in the OT was not formally answered in our discussions of judgment, salvation, and messianism. In recent scholarship the question has been argued whether there is any eschatology in the OT at all *earlier than the exile*. Much of the discussion is obscured by the ambiguity of the term eschatology. Literally, eschatology means "the doctrine of the last things"; and if one compares the OT with the much fuller eschatology of Christianity, it appears that the early books of the OT have no eschatology (→ NT Thought, 81:25–56).

The problem can be approached by noticing those books and passages of the OT that no one would deny are eschatological. These passages are called "apocalyptic" (→ OT Apocalyptic, 19:3–4). In them certain standard themes appear: a final cosmic struggle between God and the powers of the world or the powers of evil; a cosmic catastrophe that includes the collapse of the visible world as well as of human institutions; the defeat and

judgment of the powers opposed to God; the beginning of a new world and a new age in which God reigns supreme. These themes are here merely outlined; no biblical literature has such luxuriant, even exaggerated, imagery as apocalyptic literature. The final battle, the collapse of the visible universe, the judgment, the bliss of the new world of the kingdom of God are described in great and usually fanciful detail. The imagery grows more extravagant in those apocalyptic books produced in Judaism but not included among the canonical Scriptures (→ Apocrypha, 67:13, 41, 44, 45). In the OT, apocalyptic literature is found in Dan 2; Dan 7–12; Isa 24 (probably also 13 and 65–66); Joel; and probably Ezek 38–39. See P. D. Hanson, *Old Testament Apocalyptic* (Nash, 1987).

The absence of these themes in earlier literature leads many scholars to deny that there is an early Israelite eschatology (Mowinckel, *He That Cometh* 125–54). In preexilic thought the saving and judging acts of Yahweh are entirely accomplished in history and through historical processes. The enemies of Yahweh are definite historical peoples; the judgment is a historic act such as the fall of Israel or of Assyria; and the salvation expected is the peaceful existence of Israel in its own land. Eschatology, Mowinckel affirms, arises when Israel no longer has any historical hope. If Yahweh is now to establish his supremacy, it has to be done by an act that comes from outside history and puts an end to history. This interpretation has much to recommend it. It takes account of the differences between the early prophets and the apocalyptic writers; it sedulously avoids reading later ideas into earlier literature. Certain features that resemble some details of apocalyptic eschatology are explained as part of the traditional theophany (→ 57 above) or as derived from cultic festivals (Mowinckel).

165 At the same time, there are elements of Israelite thought that this interpretation does not incorporate. Hence, other scholars (von Rad, *OTT* 2. 114–25; Eichrodt, *ETOT* 1. 385–91; Jacob, *Theology* 319–22) affirm the existence not only of preexilic eschatology but even of prophetic eschatology. Vriezen (*OOTT* 350–72) places the beginning of eschatology with Isaiah. Mowinckel's rejoinder has been that to include earlier utterances is to make the word eschatology so broad as to deprive it of all meaning; in earlier passages, he says, we should speak of "a hope of the future," not of eschatology. The problem may appear to be merely a question of semantics, and perhaps it is. Yet to deny early eschatology in Israel seems to carry the implication that Israel had no idea of history that was really different from the ideas of other peoples (→ 113 above). A hope of the future that leads to nothing definitive is scarcely a hope for more than a continuation of the present. In early Israel it was hoped that in the course of history Yahweh would actively intervene in the future as he had intervened in the past, and that he would preserve Israel through his judgments and his saving acts. Whether this hope was eschatological is a question that the early Israelites could have neither asked nor answered. But there were implications in the active intervention of Yahweh in history, implications that history was governed by his moral will with supreme power. Could Yahweh be the lord of history if history were to continue indefinitely? If the conflict between Yahweh and the forces of chaos were not to be resolved by a victory, Yahweh would lack truly divine power, and Israelite belief would fall into the cyclic dualism that governed the thought of the ancient Near East. Since eschatology in its simplest form means at least the belief that history has an end, then the early Israelite hope of the future is implicitly eschatological. The idea of the end of history need not be proposed in apocalyptic imagery. It is true that both salvation and judgment in the preexilic prophets do not appear in terms that transcend the historical world in which Israel lives. But if this historical world is established in a permanent condition of peace by an act of Yahweh, it has arrived at a term that is not produced by historical forces.

166 The Israelite conviction, expressed by the earlier as well as the later prophets, is that history must issue in the universal reign of Yahweh. This hope is not equally clear at all stages of its development. When it is expressed (as in the oracle of Nathan; → 155 above) in terms of the world-wide reign of the king-messiah of Israel, it appears in perhaps its most primitive form. What at one period is seen as a term of history may be later recognized as a step that demands further resolution—in such a development, the principle of eschatology is accepted, but the eschatological term has not been fully defined. The concept of eschatology is not so rigid in its structure that its form and content are not capable of further development. The early faith of Israel is not yet a transcendent eschatology; and if transcendentalism is an essential part of an eschatological faith, then early Israelite faith should not be called eschatological.

167 Apocalyptic imagery is as full of mythopoeic thinking and language as any portion of the OT (→ 25 above), and here mythopoeic thought performs a function that no other type of thinking could have performed. The eschatological event lies not only outside experience but also outside history; yet, at the same time, the judgments of Yahweh in history are exhibitions of his power that can be incorporated into the eschatological picture. The eschatological battle and the collapse of world empires are portrayed in terms drawn from the historic experience of Israel. To these elements are added the reversal of the mythology of creation; the world returns to primeval chaos, as it returned in the deluge. From this chaos by a new and final creative act Yahweh produces a new heaven and a new earth with the features of paradise; but in this new heaven and new earth there will be no rebellion against his saving will. Paradoxically a crassly literal interpretation of the mythopoeic imagery of eschatology obscures the reality of the divine acts of salvation and judgment.

168 **(III) Life after Death.** It is generally held by scholars that no hope of individual survival after death is expressed in the OT before some of its latest passages, which were probably written in the 2d cent. BC. Even though this thesis will be modified below (→ 172), the general lack of OT belief in an afterlife is somewhat surprising, since belief in the resurrection of the body was so important both in Pharisaic Judaism and in Christianity. Here ancient Israel was much closer to the beliefs of Mesopotamia and Canaan than it was to the beliefs of Egypt.

The Egyptian idea of the afterlife, exhibited in the well-preserved tombs of Egypt and in Egyptian literature, conceives of survival after death as a two-dimensional continuation of earthly human existence and not as a genuinely new and different state. The joys of the world beyond the grave are the carnal joys of normal experience. People share the life of the gods, but in a purely human way; survival is not an attainment of destiny, but rather an evasion of destiny. The literature called "The Book of the Dead" presents entrance into bliss as contingent on successfully passing an examination on one's moral conduct (*ANET* 32-36), but success depends more on knowing the correct answers rather than on one's moral character. There is no idea that anyone would or should be excluded from bliss; if life after death is merely a continuation of earthly life, no moral qualification should be demanded any more for one than for the

other. Thus, Egyptian belief in survival is really a stout affirmation of the goodness of human life on earth and of the impossibility and the undesirability of a change of state. (For variations in Egyptian thought, → Wisdom Lit., 27:26.)

The Egyptian idea is incompatible with basic Israelite beliefs about Yahweh and about humanity. The Egyptian afterlife is not a world dominated by the personal divine presence and will, but is really a thoroughly secularized world. That the Egyptian idea leaves people in their present condition is not of itself in opposition to early Israelite belief, for the Israelites of this period make no affirmations about a high destiny in another life. But the Egyptians explicitly affirm that human beings reach full stature in the joys of earthly existence, and for the Israelites such unconcealed faith in the material world is intolerable. (Perhaps Israel's failure to reach an idea of survival after death was partly due to revulsion for Egypt's unmitigated secularism.)

169 In Mesopotamia, on the contrary, there is explicitly no hope of survival. Arallu, the world of the dead, is a vast tomb where the bodies of the dead lie inert, no more than semiconscious at best (*ANET* 87, 107); and a description of the underworld is cause for one to sit and weep (*ANET* 98). Mesopotamian literature faces death with a deep pessimism. The gods reserve life for themselves and allot death as the human portion; therefore, people should enjoy the pleasures that life affords, for they have no other hope (*ANET* 90). Thus, unlike the Egyptians, the Mesopotamians face death as the end of life. Like the Egyptians, they see no moral discrimination in death, which comes, like birth, to all alike; nor do they even face the problem of premature death, which is raised in the OT. The fact of death is utterly without religious or moral significance. If people could reach the food of life and the water of life (*ANET* 96, 101-102), they would share in the immortality of the gods; but the gods withhold immortality. The difference between Mesopotamian belief and Israelite belief is patent here; in Gen 2-3 the food of life is withheld not from jealousy, but because of a moral fault (also → Wisdom Lit., 27:27-31).

170 The moral significance of death is vital in Israelite belief; but the Israelite attitude toward the possibility of life after death shows no appreciable difference from Mesopotamian beliefs. The death that comes to the first human being as a consequence of sin is the termination of life on this earth, and no wider horizon appears. The constitution of human nature, as understood in Israelite thought, reveals no principle of survival. Neither "soul" nor "spirit" is a component entity that survives death. The human person is an animated body (→ 66 above), and no other form of human life is conceived of. The underworld of the OT (Sheol) is mentioned many times, and sometimes described vividly (Isa 14). These descriptions show that Sheol, like the Arallu of Mesopotamia, is no more than a vast tomb where the bodies of the dead lie inert (Job 10:21; 17:13-16). Sheol is not a form of survival but a denial of survival; all come to Sheol and the good and evil of life cease there.

(Grelot, P., *De la mort à la vie eternelle* [LD 67; Paris, 1971]. Tromp, N., *Primitive Conceptions of Death and the Netherworld in the Old Testament* [BibOr 21; Rome, 1969].)

171 The OT does not often exhibit the pessimism toward death that can be seen in Mesopotamian literature (→ Wisdom Lit., 27:30-31), except for passages like Job, the song of Hezekiah (Isa 38) and a few Pss (30; 88). Job (3:11-19) expresses the cynical bitterness of an unfulfilled life, which might seem to make death and Sheol appear desirable; cf. also Jer 20:14-18. In general, however, the Israelites look upon death as the normal term of life, asking only that they be allowed to fill out their days in peace—and the normal portion of days was 70 years. An early death or a sudden or painful death is for the wise men of Israel a punishment of wickedness. But apart from these reflections on untimely death, the penal character of death, so clearly seen in the J narrative of Gen 3, is not observed elsewhere in the OT.

It is very probable that the Israelites' idea of society had much to do with their attitude toward death. An Israelite man lives on in his sons who bear his name and in the people of Israel of which he is a member. If Israel continues to live, the deceased members of Israel have not entirely perished. Such a collective immortality is not entirely foreign even to modern thought, despite our emphasis on the dignity and the importance of the individual person. People have always been concerned, and they are now concerned, with the fortunes of their children or of others who are under their care; they live after their death in the influence that they have had on their juniors.

172 For whatever value they may have, we should also consider those passages of the OT that seem to express a striving for some form of afterlife. Some Pss contain petitions for life or expressions of thanksgiving for the bestowal of life; the context, not only of these Pss but also of Israelite thought, suggests that the psalmist speaks of preservation from a particular danger to life. M. Dahood (*Psalms 1–50* [AB 16; NY, 1966] xxxvi) argued that there is much more thought about immortality and resurrection in Pss than previously thought: the "Foe" the psalmist opposes is often death (7:6; 13:3; 18:4; etc.). But cf. B. Vawter, *JBL* 91 (1972) 158–71.

Let us consider in particular Pss 49 and 73, where the psalmist faces the problem of the universality of death, which overtakes the righteous as well as the wicked. Since both righteous and wicked are mortal, what comfort is it to the righteous to be assured that death is a punishment for the wicked? In this context, when the psalmist expresses his faith that Yahweh will deliver him from death, the deliverance can scarcely mean preservation that will distinguish the righteous from some particular danger; it must be a preservation that will distinguish the righteous from the wicked. Should these psalms express such a hope, it must be noticed that the hope, while sure, is vague and formless in the extreme, reposing on the assurance of communion with Yahweh that is so often expressed in the Pss. Communion with Yahweh is life, and surely communion with a kindly and righteous God ought not be destroyed except by deliberate rebellion. Yahweh must have some way in which communion with him can be preserved for those who are faithful to him; otherwise there would be no ultimate difference between righteousness and wickedness.

173 The obstacle to any more explicit statement of this hope is the Israelite conception of human nature and of human life, which knows of no principle that could survive death. When the hope is finally expressed, it takes the only possible form that it can take in Israelite thought: the resurrection of the body. The hope of the resurrection is not really expressed in the vision of the dry bones of Ezek 37; under the image of the resurrection, the prophet expresses his faith that Israel will survive its national extinction in 587 BC. A hope that the Servant of Yahweh will triumph over death seems to be expressed in Isa 53:10–12; but the unique character and mission of the Servant do not permit the extension of this hope, if indeed it is expressed, to any apart from the Servant himself. The first clear expression of the hope of resurrection occurs in the Maccabean period in Dan 12:2. See also Isa 26:19 in the relatively late part of Isa known

as "the Isaian Apocalypse" (→ Isaiah, 15:48–49)—unless this passage simply expresses faith in Israel's survival.

There is no history of the development of the idea. Attempts to trace the belief to Iranian influence have not been successful. If the considerations mentioned above have any value, they indicate that this distinctively Israelite idea arises from the Israelite conception of God and of the human being. Resurrection is not, like the Egyptian form of survival, merely a resumption of terrestrial existence; it involves an eschatological new life in a new world. Nor is there merely a resurrection of the righteous; the dignity of the human person is such that it resists extinction, even in the wicked.

174 Another form of belief in survival appears in Wis, probably written in Alexandria in the 1st cent. BC (→ Wisdom, 33:6). In this book the influence of Gk philosophy is apparent, and the writer may have accepted the Gk doctrine of the immortality of the soul. This idea, as we have seen, is not part of the Israelite understanding of the constitution of human nature (→ 66 above). It does not take deep root in the thought of Judaism or in the NT, although the Essenes may have believed in immortality (Josephus, *Ant.* 18.1.5 §18), and certain NT passages *may* refer to immortality—see J. Barr, *Old and New in Interpretation* (London, 1966) 52ff.

175 **(IV) Promise and Fulfillment.** The Christian theological study of the OT is truncated unless the relation of the OT to the NT is considered. In the Gospels, Jesus presents himself as fulfillment of the hope and the destiny of Israel, and the early church follows him in this. Such a presentation implies certain principles of interpretation and raises a number of detailed problems; only the principles are considered here, and the problems of detail are left to articles on separate books and passages.

The NT affirmation that Jesus is the Messiah (→ 178 below) implies the unity of history under a single divine plan of salvation. In Jesus the Acts of God related in the OT converge and reach their fullness; in him the OT idea of history and the OT hope of the future are brought to a term. Israel has no further destiny to which it can look—in Jesus the saving and judging acts of God are accomplished.

176 The unity and continuity of the plan and the history of salvation do not imply that the OT is meaningless without Jesus Christ. It was the theory of Origen and many of his followers that the true meaning of the OT was not intelligible unless one interpreted every word of the OT as referring to Christ in some way (→ Hermeneutics, 71:36, 38). Such an interpretation is possible only by a kind of allegorizing that goes far beyond the meaning of the text. Moreover, such a view fails to recognize the intrinsic value of the OT. Even from a Christian viewpoint, if there never had been a NT, the Hebr Scriptures would retain value because they were a vehicle through which God revealed himself. The literature of the OT was meaningful to those who produced it and to those for whom it was produced; it had a contemporary significance and force that could be grasped by those who were unaware of the precise form that the historical development of salvation would take. In modern interpretation the first (but not the only) task of the interpreter is considered to be the apprehension of that contemporary Israelite meaning (→ Hermeneutics, 71:22).

177 The unity of the plan and of the history of salvation does imply a unity of the basic theological themes of OT and NT. Many OT themes have been considered in this survey, and there is scarcely one that does not find its development in the NT. It is a misunderstanding to consider the themes in the NT as if they had no origin and growth in the OT from which the NT writers themselves took their point of departure. The heresy of Marcion in the 2d cent. AD denied the relevance of the OT for Christian revelation, and in particular, the unity of the concept of God in OT and NT. But when Jesus spoke of his Father, he meant the God of whom all Jews knew, the Yahweh whose encounter with Israel is related in the OT. He could speak to them of Yahweh as one who was revealed to them in their history, and expound for them the fullness of the revelation of that Yahweh. The character of Yahweh, his attributes, his providence, and his government of history could be recognized in the proclamation of Jesus.

The unity of themes is manifest in the unity of vocabulary exhibited in the two Testaments. Almost every key theological word of the NT is derived from some Hebr word that had a long history of use and development in the OT. Jesus and the apostles used familiar terms. Obviously this does not imply that these terms underwent no further development in the NT, but the theological language that Jesus and the apostles used was the language available to them and to their listeners. The creation of such a theological language was not the work of a day. Without a background of the OT and Israelite beliefs and traditions, the message of Jesus would have been unintelligible. Contemporary scholarship has given much attention to the study of the theological vocabulary of the NT and to its roots in the OT (e.g., *TDNT*), and the value of these studies is universally recognized.

178 Yet the unity of themes is accompanied by a development that must not be missed or minimized. Although there is scarcely any key theological word that is not common to both OT and NT, there is likewise scarcely any key word that has not been enriched in the NT. The novelty of the Christian fact becomes more apparent from a close study of the development of the vocabulary; the Christian fact rises in Judaism, but it is not derived from Judaism. The Christian fact is the newest and the most radical of the saving acts of God; it initiates a permanent revolution that affects Judaism as much as it affects the world at large.

The novelty of the Christian revolution is not well perceived in a scheme of interpretation that sees the relation of OT and NT as prediction and fulfillment (→ Hermeneutics, 71:52). Without denying the unity of history and of themes, we maintain that the concrete historical reality of Jesus Christ is literally predicted nowhere in the OT. Jesus exceeds the limits of the OT knowledge of God; for, in his own words, one cannot put new wine into old wineskins. The radical novelty of his person and mission can be seen in the very designation Messiah/Christ (→ NT Thought, 81:12-24). The early church proclaimed Jesus as the Messiah, well aware that no figure like him can be found in the OT. He is the Messiah and is recognized as such not because he can be identified with any particular prediction or with a number of predictions taken together, but because he unifies in his person all the ideas that are called messianic. The unification transforms some of these ideas profoundly (→ 154 above).

Similar developments can be pointed out in other key ideas. The idea of fulfillment, often mentioned in the NT, is not of necessity the fulfillment of a prediction. Hope or destiny can be fulfilled; promise can be fulfilled, and promise is a more accurate word to designate the relation of OT and NT. The promise is fulfilled with an abundance that is not predicted because it could not have been predicted; it could not have been understood. The religious growth of Israel was necessary in order that Jesus Christ, when he came, could be recognized by at least a few for what he was. He is indeed the key to the understanding of the OT. For further discussion of the relation of the two Testaments, → Hermeneutics, 71:30ff.

78

JESUS

John P. Meier

BIBLIOGRAPHY

1 For older works, see survey of research on historical Jesus (→ NT Criticism, 70:3–13, 33ff.); for works on christology, → NT Thought, 81:1). Anderson, C., *Critical Quests of Jesus* (GR, 1969); *The Historical Jesus: A Continuing Quest* (GR, 1972). Aulén, G., *Jesus in Contemporary Historical Research* (Phl, 1976). Bornkamm, G., *Jesus of Nazareth* (NY, 1960). Braaten, C. and R. Harrisville (eds.), *The Historical Jesus and the Kerygmatic Christ* (Nash, 1964). Braun, H., *Jesus of Nazareth* (Phl, 1979). Breech, J., *The Silence of Jesus* (Phl, 1983). Bultmann, R., *Jesus and the Word* (London, 1934); *TNT* 1. 3–32. Charlesworth, J., *Jesus within Judaism* (GC, 1987). Conzelmann, H., *Jesus* (Phl, 1973). Cook, M., *The Jesus of Faith* (NY, 1981). Dibelius, M. and W. Kümmel, *Jesus* (Berlin, 1966). Dodd, C. H., *The Founder of Christianity* (London, 1971). Dulles, A., "Jesus as the Christ," *Thought* 39 (1964) 359–79. Dunn, J. D. G., *The Evidence for Jesus* (Phl, 1985). Feneberg, R. and W. Feneberg, *Das Leben Jesu im Evangelium* (QD 88; Freiburg, 1980). Fuchs, E., *Studies of the Historical Jesus* (SBT 42; London, 1964). Goppelt, L., *Theology of the New Testament 1: The Ministry of Jesus* (GR, 1981). Grant, M., *Jesus* (NY, 1977). Grech, P., "Recent Developments in the Jesus of History Controversy," *BTB* 1 (1971) 190–213. Harvey, A. E., *Jesus and the Constraints of History* (Phl, 1982). Jeremias, *JNTT*. Käsemann, E., "The Problem of the Historical Jesus," *ENTT* 15–47; "Blind Alleys in the 'Jesus of History' Controversy," *NTQT* 23–65. Keck, L., *A Future for the Historical Jesus* (Nash, 1971). Kertelge, K. (ed.), *Rückfrage nach Jesus* (QD 63; Freiburg, 1974). Kümmel, W., *Promise and Fulfillment* (SBT 23; 3d ed.; London, 1961); "Jesusforschung," *TRu* 40 (1975); 41 (1976); 43 (1978); 45 (1980); 46 (1981); 47 (1982); collected as *Dreissig Jahre Jesusforschung* (BBB 60; Bonn, 1985). Léon-Dufour, X., *The Gospels and the Jesus of History* (NY, 1968). Lohfink, G., *Jesus and Community* (Phl, 1984). Mackey, J., *Jesus the Man and the Myth* (NY, 1979). Marshall, I. H., *I Believe in the Historical Jesus* (GR, 1977). Meyer, B., *The Aims of Jesus* (London, 1979). Perrin, N., *Rediscovering the Teaching of Jesus* (London, 1967); *Jesus and the Language of the Kingdom* (Phl, 1976). Reumann, J., *Jesus in the Church's Gospels* (Phl, 1968). Ristow, H. and K. Matthiae, *Der historische Jesus und der kerygmatische Christus* (Berlin, 1962). Robinson, J. M., *A New Quest of the Historical Jesus* (SBT 25; London, 1959). Roloff, J., *Das Kerygma und der irdische Jesus* (Göttingen, 1970). Sanders, E. P., "Jesus, Paul and Judaism," *ANRW* II/25.1, 390–450; *Jesus and Judaism* (Phl, 1985). Schubert, K., (ed.), *Der historische Jesus und der Christus unseres Glaubens* (Vienna, 1962). Schweizer, E., *Jesus* (London, 1971). Smith, M., *Jesus the Magician* (SF, 1978). Stauffer, E., "Jesus, Geschichte und Verkündigung," *ANRW* II/25.1, 3–130. Thompson, W., *The Jesus Debate* (NY, 1985). Vermes, G., *Jesus the Jew* (Phl, 1981). *Jesus and the World of Judaism* (Phl, 1984). Wilcox, M., "Jesus in the Light of His Jewish Environment," *ANRW* II/25.1, 129–95. Wilson, I., *Jesus: The Evidence* (SF, 1984).

OUTLINE

METHOD

3   (I) Scope and Definitions. The sole focus of this article is the "Jesus of history" or the historical Jesus — *that Jesus who is knowable or recoverable by the means of modern historical-critical research.* Since scientific historical research arose only in the 18th cent., the quest for the historical Jesus is a peculiarly modern endeavor with its own tangled history. The "Jesus of history" is a modern theoretical reconstruction — a fragmentary, tentative portrait painted by modern scholars — and is not to be identified naively with the full reality of the Jesus who actually lived in the 1st cent. AD (the "real Jesus"). In a sense, this distinction between "historical" and "real" holds true for any figure of ancient history. There was more to the real Socrates or Nero than what we can know today. This is a fortiori true of Jesus, not only because of our fragmentary sources but also because of the depth of the mystery involved. The historical Jesus should also be distinguished from the "earthly Jesus," i.e., Jesus as *portrayed* during his life on earth. The Gospels purport to depict the earthly Jesus; they do not aim at depicting the historical Jesus, though they are the chief sources for our modern reconstructions. German authors often distinguish between the historical (*historisch*) Jesus and the historic (*geschichtlich*) Christ, a distinction made famous by M. Kähler (*The So-Called Historical Jesus and the Historic Biblical Christ* [Phl, 1964]). The former refers to a scientifically reconstructed figure; the latter, to the object of Christian faith and worship, which has had an impact on Christianity through the ages. However, the distinction between *historisch* and *geschichtlich* is not observed even by all German critics. Some recent scholars (e.g., Perrin, *Rediscovering* 234-38) prefer a three-part distinction: (1) descriptive historical knowledge about Jesus; (2) those aspects of such historical knowledge that can become significant to us today (as can be true of other ancient figures, e.g., Socrates); (3) faith-knowledge of Jesus as Lord and Christ. This article is directly concerned only with the first type of knowledge, though this first level naturally leads to the second and third levels. For methodological reasons the quest for the historical Jesus prescinds from what is known by faith, *but by no means denies it.*

4   (II) Sources. The major sources are the canonical Gospels — and therein lies the major problem. While the Gospels certainly contain historical facts about Jesus, the Gospels as a whole are suffused with the Easter faith of the early church. (For formal Catholic acknowledgment of this, → Church Pronouncements, 72:35.) To distinguish original event or saying from later interpretation can be very difficult, at times impossible (cf. the treatment of methodological problems in D. Hill, *NT Prophecy* [Atlanta, 1979] 160-85; and M. Boring, *NTS* 29 [1983] 104-12). The fact that all four Gospels are faith-documents reflecting later theology means, however, that John is not to be rejected automatically in favor of the Synoptics (*contra* Braun, *Jesus* 17). Although the sayings tradition in John has

undergone massive reworking, some individual data preserved in John seem even more reliable than parallel material in the Synoptics. Judgments must be made on the merits of the individual cases. The rest of the NT yields few data about the historical Jesus, and the apocryphal gospels may yield at most some sayings (→ Apocrypha, 67:58; →Canonicity, 66:64).

5   *Jewish sources.* Ca. 93-94 Josephus wrote of "James, the brother of Jesus, the so-called Christ" in *Ant.* 20.9.1 § 200. This passing reference to the brother of *Jesus* (not the Christian formula "brother of the *Lord*") is hardly the work of a Christian scribe; hence, it is usually accepted as authentic. The vital point here is that Josephus presupposes that his readers know who this Jesus-called-Christ is. This should be remembered as we approach Josephus's other possible mention of Jesus, *Ant.* 18.3.3 § 63-64, the famous *Testimonium Flavianum.* As it now stands, the *Testimonium* betrays signs of Christian interpolation, but many scholars think that some simpler reference to Jesus lies behind the present text (see S. Brandon, *The Trial of Jesus* [NY, 1968] 151-52; L. Feldman, "Flavius Josephus Revisited," *ANRW* II/21.2, 822-35; Smith, *Magician* 45-46; P. Winter, *Journal of Historical Studies* 1 [1968] 289-302; also E. Bammel, *ExpTim* 85 [1973-74] 145-47). The scattered references to Jesus in later rabbinic literature are often polemical and garbled; they add nothing to our knowledge of the historical Jesus (see J. Klausner, *Jesus of Nazareth* [NY, 1925] 18-54; Smith [*Magician* 46-50] is more confident; → Apocrypha, 67:134).

6   *Pagan sources.* The historian Tacitus, *ca.* AD 110, mentions the origin of Christianity in Christ, "who was put to death during the reign of Tiberius by the procurator [*sic*] Pontius Pilate" (*Ann.* 15.44). Writing roughly around the same time, Suetonius possibly refers to Christ as the source of tumult among Jews in Rome under Claudius, but the allusion is uncertain (*Claudius* 25; see W. Wiefel, in *The Romans Debate* [ed. K. Donfried; Minneapolis, 1977] 100-19; R. E. Brown, *Antioch and Rome* [NY, 1983] 100-2; → Paul, 79:10). Pliny the Younger, writing *ca.* AD 111-113, describes how Christians "sing a hymn to Christ as to a god" (*Ep.* 10.96). At most, then, non-Christian authors of the 1st and early 2d cents. give independent witness to the existence of Jesus Christ, his crucifixion by Pilate, and subsequent worship of him.

7   (III) Criteria. Since scholars are thrown back on the canonical Gospels, they must devise criteria (or indices) for judging what in them comes from Jesus himself, as distinct from early Christian tradition. As with most judgments about ancient history, the best one can hope for is varying degrees of probability. Five criteria may be distilled from the many suggested: (1) The criterion of *embarrassment* focuses on actions or sayings of Jesus that would have embarrassed the early church and so have tended to be softened or suppressed in later stages of the tradition (e.g., the baptism of Jesus or his ignorance of the day of judgment). (2) The most controversial criterion, that of *discontinuity* or *dissimilarity*, focuses on those words or deeds of Jesus that cannot be derived from Judaism before him or Christianity after him (e.g., prohibition of oaths and of fasting). This criterion must be used with care, however, since Jesus was a 1st-cent. Jew from whom flowed the early Christian movement. A total rupture with history before and after him is a priori unlikely. Hence, one must be careful about insisting on what is "unique" to Jesus. Since we are ill-informed about popular Jewish-Aramaic religious practices and vocabulary in early 1st-cent. AD Galilee, it is wiser to speak of what is "strikingly characteristic" of Jesus (e.g., "Abba," "Amen, I say to you"). Similarly, in dealing with the deeds of Jesus, it is better to speak of the "sort of things Jesus did" rather than to claim that a particular narrative describes exactly what Jesus did at one particular time. (3) The criterion of *multiple attestation* or *multiple sources* focuses on the material witnessed by a number of independent streams of early Christian tradition, often in variant forms (e.g., Jesus' prohibition of divorce in Mark, Q, and 1 Cor 7; the institution of the eucharist in Mark 14 and 1 Cor 11). (4) The criterion of *coherence* or *consistency* comes into play after a certain amount of historical material has been isolated by the previous criteria. Other sayings and deeds of Jesus that fit in well with the preliminary "data base" have a good chance of being historical (e.g., sayings reflecting the imminent coming of the kingdom). Yet it is possible that Jesus' sayings did not form a totally coherent pattern. Elements of teaching about God and morality may not have fit in perfectly with Jesus' eschatological message, but may have rather reflected Israel's wisdom traditions. Again, caution is needed. (5) The criterion of the *rejection* and *execution* of Jesus does not tell us directly what is historical, but directs our attention to those deeds and words that would explain why Jesus met a violent end at the hands of Jewish and Roman authorities. A bland Jesus, a mere symbol-maker who spun riddles and who therefore did not radically threaten people, especially the powers that be, could not be historical. Needless to say, all these criteria must be used in tandem as mutually self-correcting.

(Lentzen-Deis, F., in Kertelge, *Rückfrage* 78–117. Meyer, *Aims* 76–94. Perrin, *Rediscovering* 15–53. Sanders, *Jesus and Judaism* 1–58. Schillebeeckx, *Jesus* 77–100.)

8   (IV) Legitimacy and Purpose of the Quest. Strange to say, fundamentalists and strict followers of R. Bultmann find themselves united in opposing a quest for the historical Jesus. Both groups would stress the sufficiency of the Gospels, but for opposite reasons. Fundamentalists naively and uncritically equate the Christ of the Gospels with the historical Jesus, allowing no place for the development and reinterpretation of Jesus-traditions in the early church. Bultmann, on the contrary, postulates a yawning chasm between the historical Jesus and the Christ of faith (→ NT Criticism, 70:46–52). Although something can be known about Jesus' preaching, one cannot (and should not try to) know much about the historical Jesus. Otherwise, one is guilty of trying to prove faith by reason; one is unwilling to accept the self-authenticating word of God apart from the works of human scholarship.

9   The fundamentalist position is rendered untenable by the contrasting and even conflicting forms of Gospel traditions (e.g., the different forms of the words of eucharistic institution; Jesus' ignorance in Mark and his omniscience in John). The Bultmannian approach has been abandoned even by some post-Bultmannians (→ NT Criticism, 70:64–70), since there is simply too much historical and theologically relevant Gospel information about Jesus for scholars to ignore it. Moreover, Bultmann's rejection of the quest as theologically illegitimate springs from debatable theological principles. The quest for the historical Jesus, properly understood, does not seek to prove faith. Faith is a grace-filled act that assents to God's revealing word on the authority of God alone; it therefore enjoys a unique type of certitude. The quest for the historical Jesus is part of empirical, historical research and can therefore generate only varying degrees of probability. Both believers and nonbelievers can engage in the quest, even if their interpretation of the results and their integration of the results into their whole worldview will differ. For the believer, the Jesus of history is not and cannot be the direct object of Christian faith. A millennium and a half of believing Christians never heard of the historical Jesus. Moreover, how could a present-day Christian make the historical Jesus the object of faith when the portrait varies so radically from scholar to scholar and from one generation to the next? Yet, insofar as theology is faith seeking understanding, the quest for the historical Jesus can and must form a part of a modern Christian's theological reflection, which is necessarily marked by an explicit historical consciousness unknown to former ages.

10   The quest for the historical Jesus helps give concrete content to our christological statements and thus does play a useful role in theology. Against any tendency to evaporate Jesus into a timeless gnostic or mythic symbol, the quest reaffirms the scandal of the Word made flesh, the shocking identification of the fullness of God's revelation with a particular Jew of 1st-cent. Palestine (→ Church Pronouncements, 72:39). The quest performs a similar function with regard to mystical or docetic tendencies among staunch Christians who think they are preserving the faith by emphasizing Christ's divinity to the detriment of his true humanity. The nonconformist Jesus who associated with the religious and social "lowlife" of Palestine also serves as a corrective to a Christianity that is ever tempted to become respectable by this world's standards. Yet the historical Jesus must not be naively coopted by the social revolutionary. The fact is that the historical Jesus escapes all our neat categories and programs; he subjects them all to question and judgment by unmasking their limitations. In this he is indeed "eschatological." While at first glance attractively relevant, the historical Jesus will always strike the careful inquirer as strange, disturbing, even offensive. The exact opposite of the Jesus of the "liberal lives" (who served as a clear pool into which scholars gaze to see themselves), he frustrates all attempts to turn Christian faith into relevant ideology, right or left, and is a constant catalyst for renewing theological thought and church life.

(Fuller, R. H., *Thomist* 48 [1984] 368–82. Johnson, E., ibid. 1–43. Schnackenburg, R., in Kertelge, *Rückfrage* 194–220.)

JESUS OF HISTORY: ORIGINS AND MINISTRY

11   (I) Origins.
        (A) Birth. The name Jesus (Gk *Iēsous;* Hebr
Yēšûaʿ [*yhwh* helps or saves], often shortened to *Yēšûʿ*
[BDF 53.2b]) was common at the turn of the era among
Jews. Jesus of Nazareth was born near the end of the
reign of Herod the Great (37-4 BC), hence *ca.* 6-4 BC.
(For this dating, → History, 75:160.) His mother was
Mary, his putative father Joseph. No more can be stated
with certitude about his origins according to the scientific
limits described in section 3 above, since the Gospel
infancy narratives (Matt 1-2; Luke 1-2) reflect strongly
later theology. Chap. 1 of each affirms that Jesus was
conceived through the Holy Spirit without a human
father—information not found elsewhere in the NT. The
claim of liberal scholars that this is purely a theological
creation is dubious, but for the believer surety about the
virginal conception comes from church teaching rather
than from scientific exegesis (see *BBM* 517-33; *CBQ* 48
[1986] 476-77, 675-80). Chap. 2 of each has Jesus born
at Bethlehem, a detail again not affirmed elsewhere in the
NT and one symbolically related to Jesus' status as royal
Davidic Messiah. Of questionable historicity are the
very different genealogies in Matt 1:2-16 and Luke
3:23-38 (see *BBM* 84-95). Yet very early NT creeds
(Rom 1:3-4 and 2 Tim 2:8) proclaim Jesus to be "of the
seed of David" in a context of resurrection faith. An
early interpretation of the resurrection in terms of the
enthronement of the royal Son of David—by no means
an obvious or necessary interpretation—may have been
facilitated by the fact that Jesus did come from an
obscure collateral branch of the house of David (see
BBM 513-16, 505-12). In any event, his Davidic lineage
is traced through his legal father, Joseph. The only NT
indication about Mary (Luke 1:5,36) points to levitical
descent (*MNT* 154, 260-61).
12   (B) Status as a Layman. Jesus was considered a layman during his earthly life (true in a Christian as well as in a Jewish view of him; see Heb 8:4).
This helps to account for his slighting reference to both
priest and Levite in the parable of the Good Samaritan
(Luke 10:30-37, something of an anticlerical joke; see J.
Crossan, *Semeia* 2 [1974] 82-112). More important, it
helps to explain why only once in the Synoptic tradition
is Jesus presented in dialogue exclusively with Sadducees (the largely priestly party), with hostility obvious
on both sides (Mark 12:18-27 par.). Most important, it
helps to explain why the priestly and lay aristocracy in
Jerusalem (i.e., the Sadducees) was most prominent in
bringing Jesus before Pilate. The mortal struggle
between Jesus and his opponents has elements not only
of Galilean versus Judean, of the poor versus the rich, of
the charismatic versus the institutional, of the eschatological versus the this-worldly, but also of the laity
versus the priests.
13   (C) Formative Years. Jesus spent about 30
years of his life in Nazareth, an obscure hill town in S
Galilee. We know almost nothing about this period. He
was by profession a *tektōn* (Mark 6:3), most likely a
carpenter, though the term covers any artisan working
or building with hard materials. Jesus' legal father,
Joseph, does not appear during the public ministry;
presumably, he had died. In contrast, his mother, Mary,
is mentioned, as well as his brothers, James, Joses (=
Joseph), Judas (= Jude), and Simon (Mark 6:3; Matt
13:55). Sisters also are mentioned, but unnamed. (From
patristic times controversy has raged about the precise

relationship of these figures [siblings, children of Joseph
by a previous marriage, cousins]; for mariological import, see *MNT* 65-72.) Most Gospel references indicate
that the relatives of Jesus did not follow him during the
public ministry (Mark 3:21,31-35; John 7:5; though cf.
John 2:12). This stands in marked contrast to their influential position later on in the Jerusalem church. A passing
reference of Paul in 1 Cor 9:4 indicates that Jesus'
brothers were married. Nothing explicit is ever said in
the NT about Jesus' marital status. However, in the face
of various references to his father, mother, brothers, and
sisters, the total silence about a wife may be taken as an
indication that Jesus remained unmarried (*contra* W.
Phipps, *Was Jesus Married?* [NY, 1970]). His unusual
celibate status—and the jibes it occasioned—may be the
original setting for the stray logion about eunuchs (Matt
19:12). Vermes (*Jesus the Jew* 99-102) thinks that a prophetic vocation might have been understood to include
celibacy, but most of his evidence comes from centuries
later (Mishna and Talmud; yet see Jer 16:1). Qumran is
also invoked as a parallel, but Qumran celibacy is a complex question (→ Apocrypha, 67:108).
14   We know nothing of Jesus' formal education.
His enemies in John 7:15 wonder how Jesus can know
Scripture when he never formally studied—though they
are probably referring to technical training in the law
such as scribes would receive by studying under a
recognized teacher. Jesus was addressed honorifically as
"Rabbi," but the title in pre-AD 70 Judaism was more
loosely used than later on (cf. its application to JBap in
John 3:26; see *BGJ* 74-75; M. Hengel, *The Charismatic
Leader and His Followers* [NY, 1981] 42-50). Luke
4:16-21 presupposes that Jesus could read and understand Biblical Hebrew. Ordinarily Jesus would have
used Aramaic in conversation and discourses, since this
was the common language of Galilean peasants (Fitzmyer, *WA* 29-56). Greek would have been used at times
by Jewish peasants in Galilee for commercial purposes,
and Jesus may have known some. That he regularly used
it in his teaching, however, is unlikely. All in all, there
was nothing in his early life or educational background
that prepared his fellow townspeople for the startling
career he was soon to undertake: hence the shock and
scandal that greeted him when he returned home after a
preaching tour (Mark 6:1-6a par.).
15   (II) Beginnings of the Ministry. Sometime *ca.* AD 28-29, during the reign of the emperor
Tiberius (14-37), Jesus emerged from obscurity to
receive baptism from JBap, a figure also known from
Josephus (*Ant.* 18.5.2 § 116-19; → History, 75:169-70).
A stern ascetic with traits of the OT prophets, esp.
Elijah, JBap called a sinful Israel to repentance and to a
once-and-for-all cleansing (baptism) in view of the imminent, fiery judgment of God. In this limited sense,
JBap's message and imagery were "apocalyptic." The
very fact that Jesus submitted to JBap's baptism, a fact
increasingly played down by the embarrassed evangelists (e.g., Matt 4:14-15), indicates that Jesus basically
accepted JBap's mission and message. It is esp. this
matrix of Jesus' own mission that renders present-day
attempts to eliminate or soften the element of future
eschatology in Jesus' preaching highly suspect (e.g., N.
Perrin, *Jesus and Language* 15-88). Correctly opposing
these tendencies is Sanders (*Jesus and Judaism* 90-156).
Some of Jesus' first and closest disciples were apparently
JBap's former disciples (Peter, Andrew, Philip, and

Nathanael in John 1:35–51). We do not know whether JBap ever acknowledged Jesus as a special figure. JBap may not have anticipated any further agent in the eschatological drama except God himself (the "coming one"?).

(On JBap: Hollenbach, P., *ANRW* II/25.1, 196–219 [highly imaginative]. Koester, *INT* 71–73. Meier, J. P., *JBL* 99 [1980] 383–405 [esp. nn. 1, 8 on bibliog.]. Merklein, H., *BZ* 25 [1981] 29–46.)

16   When Jesus set out on his own, he initially imitated JBap by baptizing (John 3:22; 4:1; but cf. the embarrassed final redactor in 4:2). This may have occasioned some rivalry between the JBap and Jesus groups, at least for the period when the ministries of the two leaders overlapped (John 3:22–30; but Mark 1:14 par. schematize by having Jesus' ministry begin only after JBap's arrest). Although Jesus continued JBap's eschatological message, there was a major shift in emphasis. JBap had stressed the fearful imminent judgment and punishment to be inflicted on sinners; the promise of salvation was muted and implicit. Jesus emphasized instead the joy of salvation, even now impinging and soon to be fulfilled.

17   **(III) Basic Message of Jesus.**
    (A) Kingdom of God. Jesus proclaimed this joyful news in terms of the coming of God's kingdom and the consequent need for all Israel to repent (*pace* Sanders [*Jesus and Judaism* 106–19]). Especially against the heritage of 19th-cent. liberal Protestantism, it is vital to understand that Jesus addressed his kingdom preaching to Israel as a whole and not just to isolated individuals (*contra* G. Klein, *EvT* 30 [1970] 642–70). It is almost impossible to define what Jesus meant by the kingdom (better: rule or reign) of God, since, as N. Perrin points out, it is a "tensive symbol" with many allusive resonances, rather than a clearly defined doctrine or abstract concept. The kingdom of God refers to an action: "God is ruling powerfully as king." The symbol is primarily dynamic rather than spatial—kingly rule rather than kingdom as territory—though spatial imagery is also used to explicate it. The poetic, allusive nature of the symbol does not mean that it conveys no intelligible content (rightly Sanders *contra* Perrin). It presumes the truth that God has always been king of Israel and of the universe. But God's rebellious creation (and Israel in particular) has fallen away from his righteous rule and come under domination by Satan and sin. Faithful to his promises and prophecies in the covenant, God is now beginning to assert his rightful claim over his rebellious creatures and will soon establish his rule fully and openly by gathering a scattered Israel back into one holy people. Yet, although the kingdom of God ("kingdom of heaven," a pious Semitic periphrasis to avoid God's name, is unique to the Matthean tradition) is central to Jesus' message, Jesus does not dwell on the image of God as a fearsome, remote, or all-powerful king. At the heart of Jesus' "good news" is the proclamation that the divine king delights in revealing himself as a loving father, a father who rejoices over regaining his lost children (e.g., the core material behind Luke 15:1–32).

(From section 1 above, see Perrin, *Jesus and Language;* Sanders, *Jesus and Judaism* 125–26, 222–41. Also Beasley-Murray, G., *Jesus and the Kingdom of God* [GR, 1985]. Chilton, B. [ed.], *The Kingdom of God* [Phl, 1984]. Merklein, H., *Die Gottesherrschaft als Handlungsprinzip* [FB 34; Würzburg, 1978]; *Jesu Botschaft von der Gottesherrschaft* [SBS 111; Stuttgart, 1983]. Mitton, C. L., *Your Kingdom Come* [GR, 1978]. Schnackenburg, R., *God's Rule and Kingdom* [NY, 1963].)

18   **(B) Parables.** A skilled speaker and teacher, Jesus used many forms of speech from the wisdom and prophetic traditions of Israel to hammer home his message (beatitudes, woes, oracles, etc.). Most prominent was his use of "parables" (Hebr *māšāl,* pl. *měšālîm*). In the OT, "parable" is an extremely elastic form of wisdom speech that includes short proverbs, metaphors, taunt-songs, bywords of reproach, and prophetic oracles. Enigmatic allegories, arising out of a historical matrix and with an eschatological thrust, come to the fore esp. in Ezek. Continuing this tradition, Jesus uses parables in their manifold forms (including proverbs, maxims, and aphorisms) to call a sinful Israel to decision in this critical final period. He employs these mysterious sayings and stories to tease the minds of his audience, to knock his cocky hearers off balance, destroying false security and opening their eyes. With a tone of urgency the parables warn that delay is dangerous, for any moment may be too late. His audience must risk all on a decision to accept Jesus' message. No sacrifice is too great, for soon the present conditions of this sinful world will be reversed (a message esp. clear in the primitive form of the Beatitudes; see L. Schottroff, *EvT* 38 [1978] 298–313). The sorrowful will be made happy by God, but the smug and self-satisfied will be made miserable. Far from pleasant stories, Jesus' parables were at times violent verbal attacks on the whole religious world presumed by his audience. They promised a radical reversal of values, bringing in a new world, in a revolution wrought by God, not humans. Indeed, the parables did not simply speak about this new world of the kingdom; they already communicated something of the kingdom to those who allowed themselves to be challenged by and drawn into Jesus' parabolic message. This "turnaround" or conversion in people's lives was jarring yet salvific. Thus, the parables themselves were part of the eschatological drama (→ NT Thought, 81:64–66).

19   **(IV) Deeds of Jesus.**
    (A) Table Fellowship. The loving embrace of a God welcoming sinners home was acted out in Jesus' own life. He delighted in associating and eating with the religious low-life of his day, the "toll collectors and sinners" (not to be confused with the *'ammê hā'āreș,* the common people, another audience Jesus cultivated). This practice of associating with the religiously "lost" or marginalized put Jesus in a constant state of ritual impurity, as far as the stringently law-observant were concerned. Jesus' insistence on offering admission to the kingdom to "sinners" (Jews who were considered to have departed from the covenant) without demanding that they employ the usual mechanism of Jewish repentance and sacrifice was probably a major reason why zealously pious Jews opposed this nonconformist preacher. Jesus' message was one of joy that the eschatological banquet was at hand, a banquet anticipated in the meals he shared with these sinners. In keeping with this festive mood, he did not practice voluntary fasting; nor did he enjoin it on his disciples (Mark 2:18–20 par.), for the time of penitential preparation was over. His non-ascetic ways not only distinguished him from JBap but also exposed him to ridicule from the more conventionally devout. In their eyes he was a bon vivant, an "eater and wine-drinker" (Matt 11:29 par.; see J. Donahue, *CBQ* 33 [1971] 39–61).

20   **(B) Miracles.** It is in this context of giving eschatological joy, of liberating from evil, and of making Israel whole again that Jesus' miracles must be understood. Extraordinary deeds of Jesus not easily explained by human means, esp. exorcisms and cures, were never denied in antiquity, even by his enemies, who referred his miracles to the power of the devil (Mark 3:20–30 par.) and, in later polemics, to magic. Jesus and his disciples, of course, referred them to the Spirit of God (Mark 3:29–30; Matt 12:28). Bultmann and others would dismiss the miracles as propaganda invented in a world that expected prodigies of religious figures. But as N. Perrin pointed out, the early form critics were wrong to relegate exorcisms and cures to a late stage of the tradition. Nothing is more certain about Jesus than that he was viewed by his contemporaries as an exorcist and a healer. In becoming entranced by supposed pagan parallels (e.g., Apollonius of Tyana), one can lose the overall context of Jesus' miracles in his Jewish life and eschatological teaching (a danger in the approach of M. Smith and Petzke). Jesus' miracles were not simply kind deeds done to aid individuals; they were concrete ways of proclaiming and effecting God's triumph over the powers of evil in the final hour. The miracles were signs and partial realizations of what was about to come fully in the kingdom. Commentators who accept all this nevertheless often seek to explain the exorcisms and cures in terms of psychological suggestion, while dismissing the more intractable nature miracles. Such a judgment is based not on historical exegesis but on a philosophical a priori about what God can and cannot do in this world—an a priori rarely if ever defended with rigorous logic. Instead, appeal is made to "modern man," who looks suspiciously like 18th-cent. Enlightenment man.

(→NT Thought, 81:89; also Hollenbach, P., *JAAR* 49 [1981] 567–88. Petzke, G., *Die Traditionen über Apollonius von Tyana und das Neue Testament* [Leiden, 1970]; *NTS* 22 [1975–76] 180–204.)

21   (C) Coherence of Words and Deeds. Methodologically, it is incorrect to focus primarily either on the teaching (Bultmann) or on the deeds (M. Smith, Sanders) of Jesus, with slight attention paid to the other. The two coalesce into a whole, one half of which cannot simply be deduced from the other half. Taken together, Jesus' words and deeds affirmed that the kingdom was in a sense both future and yet already present in and through his ministry. The future-oriented sayings of Jesus cannot be totally deleted; nor can sayings that affirm salvation now be evaporated into timeless existential philosophy (so rightly Sanders [*ANRW* II/25.1, 419], who, however, plays down the presence of salvation in Jesus' ministry). For all his eclectic use of apocalyptic imagery, Jesus did not provide an exact timetable for the eschatological drama. Thus, he was not a thoroughgoing apocalypticist, presenting a detailed scenario and cosmology. Indeed, Jesus affirmed that he was ignorant of the time of the final judgment (Mark 13:32 par.)—a saying that is difficult to dismiss as an expression of the church's faith in its risen Lord (→ 35 below).

22   (V) Moral Teaching and the Law.
(A) Radicalization of the Law. In the light of the coming judgment and of God's free offer of forgiveness and salvation in this final hour, Jesus specified how those who experienced conversion should live. Jesus the Jew basically affirmed the Mosaic law as God's will, but he rejected any casuistic fragmentation of God's will into countless petty commandments and ritual observances. Reflecting the apocalyptic idea that end-time corresponds to primordial time, Jesus sought to radicalize the law by reaching back to God's will in creation and his original purpose in giving the law. At the same time, Jesus sought to internalize the law by reaching into the human heart to purify the font of all action. Sometimes this radicalization simply deepened or broadened the thrust of the law (e.g., the equation of angry words with murder or of impure thoughts with

adultery, Matt 5:21–22,27–28). Sometimes this radicalization reached the point of rescinding the letter of the law (prohibition of divorce, Luke 16:18; prohibition of oaths, Matt 5:32), perhaps even the rescinding of food laws (Mark 7:15; see J. Lambrecht, *ETL* 53 [1977] 25–82). What is remarkable here is that Jesus did not ground his startling commands and teaching in the authenticating claim of the OT prophets ("The word of the Lord came to me, saying . . .") or in scribal appeals to earlier authorities ("Rabbi X said in the name of Rabbi Y") or in contorted arguments from a string of Scripture texts. Jesus claimed to know directly, intuitively, and without the usual organs that mediate authority, what the will of God was in any given situation—a claim summed up in his solemn affirmation ("Amen, I say to you." This form of speech ("Amen" not as a response but as an introduction to a new statement) was characteristic of Jesus and does not seem to have been common before his time—though it was imitated by the Gospel tradition and the evangelists (J. Jeremias, *ZNW* 64 [1973] 122–23, *contra* K. Berger, *Die Amen-Worte Jesu* [Berlin, 1970] and V. Hasler, *Amen* [Zurich, 1969]).

(Banks, R., *Jesus and the Law in the Synoptic Tradition* [NY, 1975]. Berger, K., *Die Gesetzesauslegung Jesu I* [Neukirchen, 1972]. Davies, W. D., *The Setting of the Sermon on the Mount* [Cambridge, 1966]. Dupont, J., *Les Béatitudes* [3 vols.; Paris, 1969–73]. Gundry, R., *The Sermon on the Mount* [Waco, 1982]. Hoffmann, P. and V. Eid, *Jesus von Nazareth und ein christliche Moral* [QD 66; Freiburg, 1975]. Hübner, H., *Das Gesetz in der synoptischen Tradition* [Witten, 1973]. Kertelge, K. [ed.], *Ethik im Neuen Testament* [QD 102; Freiburg, 1984]. Meier, J., *Law and History in Matthew's Gospel* [Rome, 1976]. Moo, D., "Jesus and the Authority of the Mosaic Law," *JSNT* 20 [1981] 3–49. Piper, J., *'Love Your Enemies'* [Cambridge, 1979].)

23   (B) Unrestricted Love and Mercy. Positively, Jesus emphasized unrestricted love of God and neighbor (Mark 12:28–34 par.; Luke 10:25–37; Matt 5:38–42; 7:12 par.), indeed, even love of enemies (Luke 6:27–28,32–36 par.; see R. Fuller [ed.], *Essays on the Love Commandment* [Phl, 1978]). Actually the word "love" does not occur frequently in the authentic sayings of Jesus. But if one joins together all the authentic sayings that deal with mercy, compassion, forgiveness, and similar obligations toward others, the results portray a Jesus who stressed the need to show mercy without measure, love without limits. Such fierce moral demands made sense and were possible only in the context of the eschatological message Jesus proclaimed and the eschatological reality he claimed to bring. Such commands were doable only for those who had experienced through Jesus God's merciful forgiveness and unconditional acceptance. Radical demand flowed from radical grace. If religion became a matter of grace, then ethics became a matter of gratitude. This morality was eschatological not in the sense that its validity depended on the view that there was just a short time before the end of the world (A. Schweitzer's interim ethic), but in the sense that the future kingdom had already invaded and transformed the lives of those accepting the good news of its coming. Thus, the future-yet-present kingdom, the miracles as signs of the kingdom's power and presence, and eschatological morality formed a coherent whole. To play down Jesus' moral teaching or to detach it from his miraculous activity does violence to the meaningful whole that the ministry of Jesus formed (*contra* Smith, *Magician*).

24   (C) Jesus and Jewish Parties. With regard to Jesus' attitude toward the law, attempts have been made to identify Jesus with almost every movement in contemporaneous Judaism (→ History, 75:145–51). He has been identified by various authors as a Pharisee (sometimes following Shammai, sometimes Hillel), or a "non-conforming Pharisee" akin to a ḥāsîd (Wilcox, "Jesus" 185), or a firm Hillelite (H. Falk, *Jesus the Pharisee* [NY, 1985]). Others identify him as a Sadducee (rejecting the normative value of the Pharisees' oral tradition), an Essene (gathering together the true Israel of the new covenant in the last days) or a revolutionary (announcing the end of the present order and the triumph of the poor). The truth is that Jesus the Jew had points of contact with almost every branch of Judaism, but is totally identifiable with none, since he envisioned a radically new situation for Israel. This new situation, the coming of the kingdom, accounts for the fact that Jesus did not directly address and take stands on most of the burning political and social questions of the day. He did not propose the reform of contemporary society; he announced its end. Nevertheless, his "liberating" praxis vis-à-vis the law and religious outcasts could not help but have certain social overtones and implications. Contrary to the revolutionaries, for example, Jesus taught the love of enemies and did not denounce the payment of taxes to Rome. This example, by the way, shows that to paint Jesus as a nationalist or a revolutionary sympathizer is a misguided attempt to make him "relevant" to liberation movements today (see M. Hengel, *Victory over Violence* [Phl, 1973] 45–59; *Christ and Power* [Phl, 1977] 15–22; E. Bammel and C. F. D. Moule (eds.), *Jesus and the Politics of His Day* [Cambridge, 1985]; contrast J. L. Segundo, *The Historical Jesus of the Synoptics* [Maryknoll, 1985]; J. Sobrino, *Jesus in Latin America* [NY, 1984]).

25   (VI) The Disciples of Jesus and Their Mission.

(A) Literal Following. Some people accepted Jesus' message of the kingdom and the challenge he presented in a stark, literal way by leaving their families and ordinary livelihood to travel with Jesus, receive his teaching at length, assist his needs, and share his ministry. At least some were directly called to do so by Jesus (Mark 1:16–20 par.; 2:14; Matt 9:18–22 par.; John 1:43). Noteworthy is the radical summons, "Let the dead bury their dead" (Matt 8:21–22 par.), which is not paralleled in the Judaism of Jesus' day and is another example of Jesus' call to contravene certain commandments of the law for the sake of the kingdom. Similarly, that the master should initiate the call and attach his disciples permanently to his person was contrary to ordinary rabbinic practice, though some partial parallels can be found in philosophers (e.g., Cynics) of the Greco-Roman period (see Hengel, *Charismatic Leader* 50–57; V. Robbins, *Jesus the Teacher* Phl, 1984] 75–123; M. Pesce, "Discepolato gesuano e discepolato rabbinico," *ANRW* II/25.1, 351–89). Also strikingly different were Jesus' easy approach to women, his inclusion of women in his traveling entourage, and his willingness to teach them (Luke 8:1–3; 10:38–42; John 4:7–42; 11:1–44; Mark 15:40–41 par.)—again, practices contrary to common rabbinic custom.

26   (B) The Twelve. Out of these literal "followers" Jesus formed a special inner group called the Twelve (→ NT Thought, 81:137–48). Although the names vary slightly in the NT lists, the most prominent members remain the same: Peter, Andrew, James, John, and Judas Iscariot. The facts that Jesus' betrayer was remembered as one of the Twelve (an embarrassing truth that had to be explained by apologetic appeal to prophecy) and that the Twelve soon faded from view in the early church argue in favor of their having been created by the historical Jesus instead of their being a retrojection of church structures into his life. Jesus' choice of precisely twelve men symbolized his mission to gather and reconstitute the twelve tribes of Israel in

the end-time, thus fulfilling the hopes of OT prophets and apocalypticists (Luke 22:29–30 par.; see Lohfink, *Jesus* 7–73). It is noteworthy that Jesus did not symbolize this restored Israel by choosing eleven men and making himself the twelfth member of the group. In some sense Jesus stood above and over against the nucleus he was creating. It was not Jesus' intention to found a new sect separated from Israel. Rather he sought to make his circle of disciples the exemplar, nucleus, and concrete realization of what he was calling all Israel to be: the restored people of God in the last days. Within this context, Jesus' sending out of his disciples on a limited mission to their fellow Israelites makes perfect sense and is witnessed to by both Mark and Q (Mark 6:7–13; Luke 9:1–6; 10:1–16 par.). Despite modern theorizing, there is no contradiction between Jesus' eschatological perspective and his assignment of specific roles to certain followers in renewing Israel—cf. detailed organization plus apocalyptic vision in the Jewish community of Qumran.

27   (C) The Wider Circle. Not all who accepted Jesus' message engaged in the literal discipleship of following the itinerant Jesus on his journeys. We hear of disciples or sympathizers who retained their ordinary forms of living while implementing Jesus' message in their daily lives and giving him support (Luke 10:38–42; Mark 14:3–9 par.; 14:12–16 par.). The last two citations remind us that Jesus could count on disciples resident in and around Jerusalem for hospitality, a point that supports John's presentation of Jesus' visiting Jerusalem a number of times throughout a multiyear ministry. (Granted Jesus' desire to regather the whole people of God, it would have been strange indeed if he had not visited the capital of the nation often.) The existence of such disciples also helps to explain both the rapid gravitation of church leadership to Jerusalem after Easter and the peculiar nature of the Johannine tradition (see O. Cullmann, *The Johannine Circle* [Phl, 1976]; R. E. Brown, *The Community of the Beloved Disciple* [NY, 1979]). The Marcan presentation of a ministry solely in and around Galilee, with only one visit to Jerusalem at the end of the ministry is a Marcan construct—often taken over uncritically by scholars. Moreover, John may likewise be correct in supposing that the ministry of Jesus lasted at least two or three years (see the Passovers in 2:13; 6:4; 12:1).

28   (D) Jesus and the Gentiles. The fact that Jesus saw his own mission in terms of regathering Israel explains why he undertook no programmatic mission to the Gentiles or the Samaritans. Yet he did not avoid all contact with these groups and was willing at times to perform exorcisms or miracles for them (Mark 5:1–20 par.; 7:24–30 par.; Matt 8:5–13 par.; Luke 17:11–19). In his woes on the unbelieving towns of Galilee, Jesus claimed that the fate of Gentiles on the day of judgment would compare favorably with that of unbelieving Israel (Matt 1:20–24 par.). In fact, in the great eschatological reversal, Gentiles would be included in the eschatological banquet with the patriarchs, while unbelieving Israelites would be shut out (Luke 13:28–30 par.). How exactly the Gentiles would be included in God's saving plan remains unclear in the teaching of Jesus. Perhaps he thought in terms of the pilgrimage of the nations to Mt. Zion in the last days, as prophesied in Isa 2:1–4 (see J. Jeremias, *Jesus' Promise to the Nations* [SBT 24; London, 1967]).

29   (VII) The Identity of Jesus.

(A) The Problem. The center and focus of Jesus' message and ministry were the coming kingdom of God, the triumph of the Father in mercy and judgment, and the regathering of the people of God in the end-time. In other words, Jesus was totally other-directed; he did not make himself the direct object of his proclamation. Jesus had a direct *theo*-logy (God as object of his preaching), which involved an indirect or implicit *christo*-logy (Jesus as final agent of God). Thus, Jesus' identity was absorbed into and defined by his mission. He gives no indication of suffering an identity crisis or of a desperate need to define himself. He seems to have been quite sure of who he was.

Unfortunately, no one else was. As the whole of the NT, Josephus, rabbinic writings, and pagan literature attest, friends and foes alike groped toward understanding him by using various categories and titles, but without complete satisfaction. The reason for this confusion lies in a basic paradox Jesus presented. Though he rarely spoke about his status, he implicitly made himself *the* pivotal figure in the eschatological drama he announced and inaugurated. It was through *his* preaching and healing that the kingdom was breaking in even now. His hearers would be judged on the last day according to how they reacted to Jesus' words in the present moment of decision (Matt 7:24–27 par.; Luke 9:26 par.; 12:8 par.). Whether or not Jesus spoke of himself as the judge on the last day, he spoke and acted on the presumption that he would be the criterion used for the final judgment. That alone involved a monumental claim to a unique status and role at the climax of Israel's history. How, more precisely, did Jesus intimate this role—if he did? A couple of approaches can be taken.

30   (B) God as Father. Many emphasize the *Abba*-experience of Jesus as a major source of his message and manner of life (see R. Hamerton-Kelly, *Concilium* 143 [3, 1981] 95–102; J. Jeremias, *Abba* [Göttingen, 1966] 15–67; Schillebeeckx, *Jesus* 256–71). This approach stresses that Jesus enjoyed a deep experience of God as his own father. He dared to address God with the intimate but reverent Aram '*Abbā*' ("my own dear Father"), a religious usage—as far as we know—unknown and probably offensive to pious Jews of his day. A word used in addressing human fathers, it was not addressed to God in the liturgy of the synagogue. Jesus also taught his disciples to imitate his intimate relationship to God as *Abba*. From this total confidence in and abandonment to God as Father sprang Jesus' startling praxis and teaching.

31 Caution, however, is required here (see Conzelmann, *Jesus* 49–50; J. A. Fitzmyer, in *À cause de l'Evangile* [Fest. J. Dupont; LD 123; Paris, 1985] 15–38). Some passages in which Jesus uses "Father" for God are probably secondary, as a comparison of parallels and redactional tendencies (esp. of Matt and John) indicates. Moreover, in the four Gospels *Abba* occurs only in Mark 14:36 (where Jesus is alone!) and might be explained as a retrojection of early Christian practice (Gal 4:6; Rom 8:15). Still, Jesus' use of the father image enjoys multiple attestation (Mark, Q, special Matthean and Lucan traditions, and John). It coheres well with the rest of Jesus' teaching and praxis. The "Father-prayer" of Luke 11:2–4 is usually held to be fairly close to what Jesus taught his disciples to pray. The peculiar Gk *ho patēr* (nom. plus def. art.) used as a vocative probably reflects the emphatic Aram form '*Abbā*' (so Mark 14:36). Moreover, sayings judged authentic on other grounds (e.g., Luke 22:29–30; → 26 above) present Jesus speaking of "my Father." In the light of all this, the tradition history of *Abba* probably runs from the historical Jesus to the Christian use echoed in Paul, rather than vice versa. Otherwise, we would have to invent another origin for the early Christian use of *Abba*, after ignoring the obvious one. It is wise, however, to avoid claiming that no other Jew had ever used *Abba* in prayer to God. We know next to

nothing of the private popular piety of Aramaic-speaking Galilean Jews of the 1st cent. AD, and a partial parallel to Jesus' usage can be found in a much later rabbinic source (see Vermes, *Jesus the Jew* 210–11). On the whole, though, one is justified in claiming that Jesus' striking use of *Abba* did express his intimate experience of God as his own father and that this usage did make a lasting impression on his disciples. This special relationship to God as Father gives more definite contours to Jesus' view of himself. A sketch of Jesus, however, should not be based on this datum alone.

32   (C) Categories and Titles. Can we be more specific in placing Jesus in certain religious categories of the time? Did he ever use definite categories or titles of himself? In a spirit of skepticism, some critics would prefer to waive the complex question of titles or relegate it to a brief appendix (Bornkamm, *Jesus* 226–31; Sanders, *Jesus and Judaism* 324). But the vast and complicated data refuse to be dismissed so easily (for a general survey, see R. Leivestad *ANRW* II/25.1, 220–64). The remarkable thing is that Jesus fits into many categories, but no one category fits exactly and exhaustively. As Schweizer says (*Jesus* 13–51), Jesus is "the man who fits no formula," though many formulas converge on him. We should remember that 1st-cent. Jewish eschatological expectations varied widely and that no one portrait of *the* eschatological agent of God was normative. Indeed, in some groups, no such agent was expected.

33 (a) PROPHET. At the very least Jesus acted like a prophet. He was by no means the only Palestinian Jew to assume that role around the turn of the era, as Josephus demonstrates (Vermes, *Jesus the Jew* 86–102). But Jesus went further; he behaved like an eschatological prophet, empowered by God's spirit to proclaim to Israel its final chance for repentance. Although the concept of *the* eschatological prophet may not have been widespread in Judaism at the time (R. Horsley, *CBQ* 47 [1985] 435–63), some such figure does appear in the Qumran writings and is presupposed in John 6:14. As far as the title, Jesus refers to himself only indirectly as a prophet, and esp. in a context of rejection (Mark 6:4 par.; Luke 4:24; John 4:44; Luke 13:33; 13:34–35 par.; 11:32). Since in his time there was a growing Jewish theology concerning rejected and martyred prophets, Jesus' implicit assumption of a prophetic role carried consequences for his possible fate. Nevertheless, prophet is an inadequate category to explain the full phenomenon of Jesus (so Smith, *Magician* 158–64).

34 (b) MESSIAH. The title and image of Messiah are esp. difficult to discuss, since there was no one concept of what a/the Messiah should be. Indeed, some Jewish eschatological expectations dispensed entirely with a Messiah; the word meant only "anointed one." In the OT, priests and sometimes prophets were anointed as well as kings; hence, messiah did not necessarily connote a royal son of David. Qumran awaited both a priestly Messiah of Aaron and a royal Messiah of Israel, as well as an eschatological prophet (→ Apocrypha, 67:114–17). If Jesus saw himself as the eschatological prophet anointed with the Spirit, as promised by Isa 61:1–3 (cf. Luke 4:16–21; 7:22 par.), then in that sense he would be a Messiah: the prophetic Messiah or messianic prophet of the end-time. There is no proof that Jesus ever directly described himself as Messiah in the royal Davidic sense; nor is there any proof that categorically or clearly he rejected the title. When Peter confessed Jesus as Messiah (Mark 8:29; Luke 9:20; contrast Matt 16:16–19), Jesus reacted with great reserve (retained even in Matt 16:20). At times, outsiders may have spoken to or about Jesus as "Son of David" (Mark

10:47-48), but Jesus did not directly take over the title (cf., however, the possible veiled reference in Mark 12:35-37 parr.). Despite Jesus' reserve, his disciples, even during his earthly life, seem to have thought of their master as in some sense the Davidic Messiah. Otherwise, their early post-Easter identification of Jesus as the Davidic Messiah, enthroned at the resurrection, makes no sense (Rom 1:3-4; Acts 2:36; 2 Tim 2:8). To say that the resurrection caused his disciples to call Jesus the Davidic Messiah explains nothing, since at the time there was no common Jewish belief concerning an earthly Davidic Messiah who must die and rise again within ongoing history. The resurrection could act as a catalyst and could be interpreted as the enthronement of the Son of David only if the disciples already harbored some idea of Jesus as Davidic Messiah. That Jesus' actions and claims were interpreted in some royal messianic sense even by his adversaries during his lifetime seems confirmed by the charge on which he was brought before Pilate: being "King of the Jews" (see N. A. Dahl, *The Crucified Messiah and Other Essays* [Minneapolis, 1974]).

35   (c) THE SON OR SON OF GOD. The possibility that Jesus spoke of himself as the Son or the Son of God in a messianic or eschatological context is often dismissed out of hand with the claim that Son of God was not a messianic title at the time of Jesus. That may well be. Yet the fragmentary 4QpsDan A[a] from Qumran speaks of a mysterious royal figure in an eschatological context as the Son of God and the Son of the Most High (cf. Luke 1:32,35; J. Fitzmyer, *JBL* 99 [1980] 14-15). Admittedly, very few "Son-words" have a chance of going back to the historical Jesus. Yet Mark 13:32 does give pause. The church would not likely have created a saying emphasizing the ignorance of its risen Lord about the time of his own parousia, nor have gone out of its way to insert the exalted title Son into an authentic saying of Jesus that stressed his ignorance. Still, the case is not clear-cut, since the church might have introduced the title by way of compensation, to balance the affirmation of ignorance. (Yet a much simpler solution would have been to suppress the embarrassing logion. The introduction of the Son-title vis-à-vis the Father would only have exacerbated the problem.) In the light of his use of *Abba* for God, Jesus might at times have alluded correlatively to himself as the Son, precisely in reference to the future consummation.

36   A second candidate for an authentic "Son-word" is the parable of the evil tenants of the vineyard (Mark 12:1-12 parr.). Discernible under heavy redaction are the outlines of a parable that ended simply with the death of the son, with no note of reversal, vindication, or resurrection (so J. Jeremias, *The Parables of Jesus* [London, 1963] 72-73). Such a parable would be a strange invention of the post-Easter church, but perfectly understandable in the mouth of Jesus as he clashed with his opponents for the last time in Jerusalem. The son in the parable stands very much in the line of the rejected and martyred prophets; hence, the message coheres neatly with Jesus' view of himself as eschatological prophet. The idea that the son is the last in the line of the prophets also serves to remind us that, if Jesus did use "Son" of himself, it must be understood in a functional, salvation-historical sense and not in the ontological sense hammered out in later patristic controversy. Indeed, Vermes (*Jesus the Jew* 192-222) considers it possible that Jesus was called Son of God during his lifetime in a "Jewish sense" (pious miracle worker and exorcist). M. Hengel (*The Son of God* [Phl, 1976]) strongly rejects the idea that the title came to Christianity from pagan religions.

37   A third but highly debated candidate for an authentic "Son-word" is Matt 11:27 par., where Jesus claims mutual and exclusive knowledge between the Father and himself, the Son. The meshing of wisdom and apocalyptic motifs in this verse is not impossible in the mouth of Jesus, who presents himself here more as mediator than as content of revelation. The saying was preserved in Q, but Q does not elsewhere speak of Jesus as "the Son." Indeed, this absolute use ("*the* Son," as opposed to "my Son" or "Son of God") occurs in only three separate cases (Matt 11:27 par.; Mark 13:32 par.; Matt 28:19). Moreover, this absolute usage may point more in the direction of Son of Man than Son of God. Yet, in the view of many critics, the thought content of Matt 11:27, akin as it is to Matt 16:17-19, fits better in a post-Easter situation than in the mouth of the historical Jesus.

38   (d) THE SON OF MAN. The most widely debated and confusing title (or designation) applied to Jesus is Son of Man (in Aramaic, *bar ('e)nāšā'*). The questions whether the historical Jesus used the title and, if so, in what sense he used it have received every answer imaginable (see W. G. Kümmel, *TRu* 45 [1980] 50-84; C. C. Caragounis, *The Son of Man* [WUNT 39; Tübingen, 1986]). Some claim that Jesus used Son of Man in all three senses found in the Synoptics: earthly ministry, death-resurrection, future exaltation or coming judgment (so O. Cullmann, *The Christology of the NT* [Phl, 1959] 152-64; S. Kim, *The 'Son of Man' as the Son of God* [WUNT 30; Tübingen, 1983]; more guardedly, Schweizer, *Jesus* 19-21). Others accept only one or two senses of the title as authentic, e.g., *JNTT* (257-99) accepts the passion and exaltation sayings. A. Higgins (*The Son of Man in the Teaching of Jesus* [Cambridge, 1980]) accepts only the future sayings, though like many he allows that Jesus used *bar ('e)nāšā'* in the sense of "someone," "anyone," or "a man" for his present state on earth. R. Fuller (*Thomist* 48 [1984] 375-76) accepts some present and suffering sayings. Still others, like R. Bultmann, (*Theology* 1. 26-32) and H. Tödt (*The Son of Man in the Synoptic Tradition* [London, 1965]) favor the idea that Jesus used Son of Man when speaking of some eschatological figure other than himself. The general tendency today, however, is to see all sayings employing the title Son of Man as coming from the midrashic activity of the early church or from the theology of the redactors (for a survey, see W. Walker, *CBQ* 45 [1983] 584-607). A mediating view allows that Jesus used Son of Man not as a title but as a modest circumlocution, referring to himself as a member of a larger group or simply as a man. (Various nuances: Vermes, *Jesus the Jew* 160-91; *Jesus and the World* 89-99; B. Lindars, *Jesus Son of Man* [GR, 1983]; P. Casey, *ExpTim* 96 [1985] 233-36.) The early church then interpreted this circumlocution as a title referring to Jesus at the parousia.

39   There are, however, difficulties. If, as is commonly supposed today (*contra* A. Higgins), Son of Man did not exist as a title in Judaism before the time of Jesus and the early church, what caused the church to invent this title and apply it to Jesus? Why does it occur almost exclusively on the lips of Jesus in the NT? Why is it represented in so many different strata of gospel tradition (triple tradition, double tradition, special Matthean, special Lucan, and Johannine traditions), yet almost nowhere else outside of the Gospels? Why do the Son-of-Man sayings that may be authentic show no distinction between resurrection and parousia? More specifically, why does belief in the Son of Man never appear in primitive creedal statements, liturgical formulas, and summaries of Christian preaching? No other title applied to Jesus by the early church displays such a strange tradition history. The answers suggested by W. Walker do not entirely meet these objections.

Hence, it seems likely that the peculiar Son-of-Man locution goes back in some way to Jesus, however much it was developed later by the church. The problem with the explanation that Jesus used the phrase in the sense of "I" or "a man in my situation" is that we lack firm proof that *bar ('e)nāšā'* carried such a meaning at the time of Jesus (Fitzmyer, *WA* 143–60; J. Donahue, *CBQ* 48 [1986] 484–98). Also, it is difficult to read the sense of "a man in my situation" into some of the earthly Son-of-Man sayings, e.g., the two-part parallel description in Matt 11:18–19 par. of JBap and Jesus as the two final envoys of divine wisdom sent to Israel. Jesus is a specific figure here; hence, a generic sense for Son of Man will not do. Both the slur on Jesus in v 19 and the relegation of him to a status more or less equivalent to that of JBap make it unlikely that this saying was created by the church. Why should the early church have inserted a title connected with the parousia into a context where Jesus is called a glutton and a drunkard? Seemingly, then, Jesus the parable maker used the enigmatic, parablelike designation Son of Man to refer in a paradoxical way to himself as the lowly, disreputable messenger of the powerful kingdom of God.

40 Whether Jesus also used the designation to allude to his future vindication, with a glance at Dan 7:13–14 ("one like a son of man") is more difficult to say. As Tödt affirms (*Son of Man* 32–112), sayings like Mark 8:38 par. and Luke 12:8–9 may have the best chance of reflecting authentic eschatological statements of Jesus about the Son of Man. What strains credulity, though, is Tödt's claim that Jesus is referring to someone else when he speaks of the Son of Man. No such apocalyptic figure can be proved to have existed in Jewish thought before the time of Jesus, and Jesus gives no indication that he sees himself as the forerunner of anyone except God. Moreover, the scene of final judgment portrayed in these sayings collects all the significant actors involved in the apocalyptic drama: God, the angels, the confessors, the deniers, and the Son of Man. Conspicuous by his absence is Jesus, the very criterion of judgment—unless the Son of Man *is* the vindicated and exalted Jesus. Thus, Jesus may have used the riddlelike Son of Man for his own paradoxical situation: a lowly, increasingly rejected messenger at the present moment, yet with vindication assured in the near future. This may be the reason why Son of Man does not occur in the kingdom-of-God sayings: Son of Man and kingdom of God are two alternate "tensive symbols" for the same paradox of already/not yet.

41 The appearance of "Son of Man" in the passion predictions is more problematic. The lack of such statements in Q and their clearly schematic arrangement in Mark 8, 9, and 10 may indicate that we have here a secondary use of Son of Man in the early church (so even the conservative E. Stauffer, *ANRW* II/25.1, 96). In particular, the lengthy prediction in Mark 10:33–34 par. looks like a literary summary of the passion narrative that follows. More likely candidates for historicity would be the short, *māšāl*-like statements of Luke 9:44 ("the Son of Man will be delivered into the hands of

men"), Mark 14:41 ("the Son of Man is being delivered into the hands of sinners"), and Mark 14:21 ("the Son of Man goes his way as it is written of him; but woe to that man through whom the Son of Man is delivered up"). These sayings do not attribute an explicit soteriological significance to Jesus' death. It is simply part of his mission as willed by the Father. In addition, some of these sayings may reflect a wordplay in Aramaic (Son of Man—sons of men). Such laconic *logia* might be viewed as extensions of the earthly-Son-of-Man sayings, moving in the direction of the explicit passion predictions. But whether they come from Jesus or the church cannot be determined with certainty. It remains questionable whether Jesus used Son of Man in reference to his approaching death (→ 45–50 below). Worth noting is that the three predictions of the fate of the Son of Man in John 3:14; 8:28; 12:32–34 have him being "lifted up" without further specification of the details of death.

42 (e) LORD. There is no problem in maintaining that Jesus was addressed as Lord during his earthly life, if one remembers that the Aram *mārē'*, like the Gk *kyrios*, had a wide spectrum of meanings, extending from a polite "sir" to a title for God (Fitzmyer, *WA* 115–42; Vermes, *Jesus the Jew* 103–28). Various people who met the historical Jesus and saw in him a teacher, healer, eschatological prophet, or a mysterious person transcending these categories could have all addressed him as *mārē'*; yet each person could have intended a different degree of reverence. The title therefore provided a living link between the circle of disciples around its rabbi Jesus and the post-Easter church worshiping its risen Lord.

43 (f) CHARISMATIC HOLY MAN. Another category that ties in with the titles and designations already treated is the Jewish holy man, *ḥāsîd*, or charismatic, known in Palestine around the time of Jesus. Vermes (*Jesus the Jew* 58–85) points out that alongside the professional scribes and the pious Pharisees there existed holy men—in some cases, from Galilee—famous for miracles or exorcisms. They were products of popular folk religion rather than academic theology. Among them were Honi the Circle-Drawer (1st cent. BC), who practically forced God to give rain, importuning him as a son importunes a father, and Hanina ben Dosa (1st cent. AD), who could heal from a distance, banish demons, and control nature, and who was noted for his poverty and his lack of interest in legal and ritual affairs, concentrating instead on moral questions. There seems to have been some tension between these charismatic, Elijah-like "men of deeds," with their highly individual, nonconformist piety, and the developing Judaism of the Pharisees and the rabbis. The evidence, however, for such charismatic figures is later, drawn from the Mishna and the Talmud; and so their relevance to a critical treatment of the historical Jesus must remain questionable. At the least, we are reminded that Jesus may have reflected a particular type of popular, charismatic Galilean piety that would inevitably clash with the more institutional forms of Judaism at home in Jerusalem (see S. Freyne, *Galilee from Alexander the Great to Hadrian* [Wilmington, 1980] 329–34; Hengel, *Charismatic Leader* [→ 14 above] 44: "eschatological charismatic").

JESUS OF HISTORY: PASSION AND RESURRECTION

44 (I) Last Days in Jerusalem.
(A) Triumphal Entry; Temple Cleansing.
In the spring of AD 30 (or 33), Jesus journeyed with his

disciples from Galilee to Jerusalem for the last time. Two events connected with his arrival (triumphal entry and cleansing of the Temple) are problematic, and not all accept their historicity. If some event—however modest in reality—lies behind the triumphal entry, Jesus apparently chose to make a symbolic claim to messianic status as he entered the ancient Davidic capital. The cleansing of the Temple (independently attested by John but placed at the beginning of the ministry) made a further claim to authority, this time over the central cultic institution of the Jewish religion. Although the event may not have been so public and sweeping as the Gospels portray, necessarily Jesus would have been challenging the corrupt and unpopular hierarchy in Jerusalem. Indeed, the "cleansing" may not have been a call for reform, but rather an ominous prophetic sign that the present Temple was about to be destroyed to make way for a new and perfect one.

These two symbolic actions of Jesus the prophet, actions redolent of the OT prophets, may have been the reasons why the priestly aristocracy chose to strike at Jesus during this particular visit to Jerusalem, as opposed to his earlier stays. Thus, Jesus himself had chosen to press the issue, forcing the capital of Israel to make a decision for or against him, the final prophet of its history. However, to interpret these two events as signs of Jesus' sympathy with Jewish revolutionaries is to go beyond the data.

(On Temple-cleansing: Catchpole, D. in Bammel and Moule, *Jesus* (→ 24 above) 319–34. Jeremias, J., "Zwei Miszellen," *NTS* 23 [1976–77] 177–80. Müller, K., "Jesus und die Sadduzäer," *Biblische Randbemerkungen* [Fest. R. Schnackenburg; ed. H. Merklein, *et al.;* Würzburg, 1974] 3–24. Roloff, J. *Das Kerygma* 89–110. Sanders, *Jesus and Judaism* 61–76. Schnackenburg, R., *Schriften zum Neuen Testament* [Munich, 1971] 155–76.)

45   (B) Jesus' Attitude toward Death. In the context of Jesus' last days in Jerusalem, the question arises as to how Jesus understood and faced his death. Some claim that Jesus did not speak of his death and so we simply do not know whether or not Jesus broke down in the face of it. Thus Bultmann, *Jesus* 150–52; for him such a question need not concern the believer. Others (V. Howard, *CBQ* 39 [1977] 515–27; X. Léon-Dufour, *NRT* 100 [1978] 802–21; H. Schürmann in *Begegnung mit dem Wort* [Fest. H. Zimmermann; ed. J. Zmijewski; BBB 53; Bonn, 1980] 273–309) hold that we can know something of Jesus' attitude and that this attitude is of significance for Christian faith. The latter opinion seems more in keeping with the data. First, though, an a priori general principle: As a person lives, so that person dies. Although there can be sudden reversals, more commonly one's manner of dying flows from and interprets one's manner of living. Jesus' message and praxis consisted of radical love for God and neighbor, of humble service and sacrifice for others, even for enemies. This message was based on total confidence in and surrender to the God who was coming in his kingdom as Father. Jesus' acts of healing, exorcising, pursuing the lost sheep, eating with sinners, declaring sins forgiven, teaching the crowds, and disputing with opponents were all concrete expressions of his service of love. Jesus was indeed the "man for others" whose whole life interprets his death—and vice versa.

46   Moving to the a posteriori data, we must ask: (a) Did Jesus foresee the possibility of a violent death? (b) If so, how did he understand it?

(a) In view of the mounting opposition against him, esp. among the aristocratic priests and laity in Jerusalem, Jesus would have had to be a simpleton not to have foreseen the possibility of a violent death when visiting the capital at Passover. Negative signs were already on the horizon. Despite his efforts, whole cities had rejected his message (Matt 11:20–24 par.). Herod Antipas, Pontius

Pilate, the high priest and the Sadducean party, the scribes, and the pious lay movement of Pharisees all had their varied reasons for being opposed to Jesus—and, unlike the Pharisees, the other individuals or groups had ways of getting rid of him legally. Moreover, in the great festal crowds of Passover, there was always the possibility of lynch-mob justice or assassination.

More to the point, Jesus saw himself as the eschatological prophet, and Jewish piety increasingly viewed the OT prophets as rejected figures and often as martyrs (J. Jeremias, *Heiligengräber in Jesu Umwelt* [Göttingen, 1958] 61–63; O. Steck, *Israel und das gewaltsame Geschick der Propheten* [Neukirchen, 1967] 40–58). Consequently, Jesus would have had to reckon with the prospect of martyrdom and its meaning. Among 1st-cent. Jews, the blood of martyrs was thought to have an atoning power for sinful Israel (e.g., 4 Macc 6:28–29; 17:22). More concretely, the martyrdom of JBap by Herod turned this theology into a real possibility for Jesus. To move beyond possibility, though, one must look at the relevant sayings that have a claim to authenticity.

47   (b) Did Jesus indicate how he understood his possible death? Here esp. one must beware of prophecies after the fact, retrojected into the life of Jesus. Therefore, for methodological reasons, one should exclude those sayings that include the title Son of Man or a clear reference to the resurrection. This is not to say that such sayings are necessarily later creations; the exclusion is a tactical one, to isolate data that are as reliable as possible. There are some sayings in which Jesus speaks in general terms of his approaching death and uses the image of the martyred prophet or servant of God, images that cohere well with the self-understanding of the historical Jesus. Although these sayings, discussed below, are scattered throughout the public ministry in the Gospels, their proper place—if they be authentic—may be during the final clash of Jesus with the authorities in Jerusalem. (There is no reason to think that Jesus expected a violent end from the beginning of his ministry; so L. Oberlinner, *Todeserwartung und Todesgewissheit Jesu* [SBB 10; Stuttgart, 1980].)

48   (1) In a Q saying (Matt 23:37–39 par.), Jesus excoriates the Jerusalem that has rejected him, rebuking the city with the reminder that it has a history of killing the prophets. The possibility that Jerusalem might do the same to Jesus the prophet remains a muted suggestion (positive on historicity: Kümmel and Jeremias). (2) In special Lucan material preceding this Q saying, Jesus brushes off a warning that Herod Antipas may try to kill him in Galilee with an ironic, perhaps bitter, remark (Luke 13:31–33; see *FGL* 2. 1028–33; positive: Ruppert and Bornkamm; negative: Steck). The remark ends with a general truth drawn from the theology of the martyred prophets: "But it is impossible that a prophet perish [note the indefinite noun and vb.] outside Jerusalem [actually, Jesus does perish outside the gates of Jerusalem]."

49   (3) When James and John, sons of Zebedee, seek special places in the kingdom, Jesus asks whether they are prepared to share his suffering and death (Mark 10:35–40 par.). The suffering and death are spoken of in general OT terms (cup and baptism, the second being so unusual that Matt omits it). Jesus does not have the power to grant places in the kingdom, but he does promise both brothers a share in his passion and death. The vague reference to Jesus' sufferings, the affirmation of Jesus' impotence to grant places in the kingdom, and the bad light in which James the protomartyr among the Twelve is placed argue in favor of historicity. (4) Peter rebelled against the idea of Jesus' *suffering* and Jesus had to rebuke Peter in the strongest terms: "Get behind me, Satan!" (Mark 8:32–33 par.). This is not likely a saying created by the early church.

50   If historicity is granted to some of these sayings (also the primitive form of the evil tenants parable
[→ 36 above] and the laconic Son-of-Man sayings [→41
above]), Jesus did contemplate the martyrdom that the
final prophet must undergo as part of God's mysterious
plan for the salvation of Israel. None of these sayings,
however, assigns a more detailed theological meaning to
the death: no vicarious sacrifice; no tying of death to
resurrection to form *the* apocalyptic event—indeed, no
explicit idea of vindication. For more clarity on how
Jesus might have understood his death, we must turn to
his Last Supper.

51   (C) The Last Supper. On Thursday evening as the 14th of Nisan (the Day of Preparation) began,
Jesus celebrated a final meal with his disciples at the
home of a Jerusalem sympathizer. The historicity of such
a final meal is supported by Marcan, special Lucan,
Johannine, and pre-Pauline traditions. The meal was not
the official Passover meal, which was to be held on the
next evening, beginning the 15th of Nisan. Jesus,
apparently sensing his imminent fate and perhaps
already suspecting betrayal by one of his own, may have
purposely given the meal some Passover touches, since
he would not be able to share the regular Passover with
his disciples. At the beginning and the end of the meal
respectively, Jesus used bread and wine to represent his
coming death, which he accepted as part of God's mysterious will for bringing in the kingdom (*contra* Braun
[*Jesus* 56–57], who rejects the historicity of Jesus' ritual
actions with the bread and wine). Jesus' words over the
bread and wine are recorded in four different versions
(1 Cor 11:23–26; Mark 14:22–25; Matt 26:26–29; Luke
22:15–20), representing two major traditions (Pauline
and Marcan). Each version shows some liturgical and
redactional influences, and so no one version can claim
to be the exact formulation of Jesus. There is also John
6:51: "The bread . . . is my flesh," which may reflect more
literally a Semitic original (see also eucharistic bread as
flesh in Ign. *Rom.* 7:3; *Phld.* 4:1). Probably Jesus' words
ran something like, "This is my flesh [body]," and "This
[cup?] is [= contains, mediates] the covenant [sealed] by
my blood" (cf. the echo of Exod 24:8). Jesus therefore
interpreted his death as the (sacrificial? atoning?) means
by which God would restore the covenant with Israel at
Sinai. Even to his death, Jesus saw his mission as the
regathering and saving of all Israel in the final hour of its
history. Jesus also saw this supper as the *last*—the last in
a whole series of meals he had shared with his disciples
and sinners alike during his life, meals that had proleptically communicated God's forgiveness and salvation. This
last meal was a pledge that, despite the apparent failure
of his mission, God would vindicate Jesus even beyond
death and bring him and his followers to the eschatological banquet (see the eschatological note struck in Mark
14:25 and 1 Cor 11:26). Hence Jesus insists that the
disciples all share his one cup rather than drink from
their own cups. They are to hold fast to their fellowship
with him as he dies, so that they may share this triumph
in the kingdom.

(Jeremias, J., *The Eucharistic Words of Jesus* [London, 1966].
Marshall, I. H., *Last Supper and Lord's Supper* [GR, 1980]. Pesch,
R., *Das Abendmahl und Jesu Todesverständnis* [QD 80; Freiburg,
1978]. Reumann, J., *The Supper of the Lord* [Phl, 1985] 1–52.
Schweitzer, A., *The Problem of the Lord's Supper* [ed. J. Reumann;
Macon, 1982]. Schweizer, E., *The Lord's Supper According to the
NT* [FBBS 18; Phl, 1967].)

52   (II) Passion and Death.
     (A) Gethsemane and Arrest. After the
supper, Jesus led his disciples to a small plot of land on
or at the foot of the Mt. of Olives (Gethsemane = olive

press or oil vat). While he was praying there, he was
arrested by an armed band assisted by Judas, one of the
Twelve. Since it is unlikely that a member of the Twelve
would be gratuitously defamed by a story that created
theological difficulties for the early church, Judas's
betrayal should be judged a historical fact. The arresting
group was probably under the control of the high priest,
though John mentions a "cohort" (*speira*) and a "tribune"
(*chiliarchos*), possibly signs of Roman participation
(against this possibility, see O. Betz, *ANRW* II/25.1,
564–647, esp. 613). Indeed, one would expect the
priestly authorities to have kept Pilate informed of what
they were planning for the Galilean troublemaker. Faced
with arrest, Jesus rejected armed resistance, and his
disciples fled in ignominious disarray.

53   (B) Trial(s). From this point until the trial
before Pilate, matters are obscure for three reasons: the
disagreements of the Gospels among themselves, the uncertainty about Jewish and Roman law at the time, and
religious apologetics that are with us to this day. Three
major scenarios are possible: (1) A night trial before the
sanhedrin was presided over by the high priest Caiaphas
(AD 18–36); this session either lasted till dawn or was
followed by a brief session at dawn (Mark-Matthew; so
Blinzler and Betz). (2) Only an early morning session of
the sanhedrin was held (Luke; so Catchpole). (3) An informal hearing was held, probably at night, by some
Jewish official, perhaps by the father-in-law of Caiaphas,
Annas, who had been high priest from AD 6 to 15 (John;
so Winter, Brandon, Smith). Against the first possibility
stand many prescriptions of the Mishna tractate *Sanhedrin,* prescriptions flouted by the trial recorded in
Mark-Matthew. The Mishna, however, written down
only at the end of the 2d cent. AD, presents rabbinic
(closer to Pharisaic), not Sadducean, rules and may depict an idealized picture that never fully existed prior to
AD 70. (There is little support for the contention of S.
Zeitlin and E. Rivkin that there were two sanhedrins at
this time, one political and priestly, the other religious
and Pharisaic—Jesus being tried by the former. See O.
Betz, *ANRW* II/25.1, 646–47.) Luke's depiction offends
less against the Mishna, but whether it reflects an independent source or imaginative redaction of Mark is still
debated. John's narrative presents the least difficulty, but
also fits well into John's theology. The best we can say
is that between the arrest and the trial before Pilate, Jesus
was held in custody by the Temple authorities. At least
a hearing and perhaps a trial resulted in formal charges
that were presented to Pilate. The theological accusations brought against Jesus during the Jewish hearing or
trial (threats against the Temple? teaching contrary to
the law? leading the people astray as a false prophet?
claiming transcendent status?) could probably have been
summed up under the vague label of blasphemy, broadly
understood. During the Jewish proceedings, Peter, who
had followed the arrested Jesus at a distance, was confronted by some underlings of the priestly officials and
in a panic denied his relationship to Jesus. The historicity
of this embarrassing event is much more likely than its
invention in the early church as anti-Peter propaganda
(*contra* G. Klein, *Rekonstruktion und Interpretation* [BEvT
50; Munich, 1969] 49–98).

54   Pontius Pilate, prefect of Judea (AD 26–36),
would have been interested only in political crimes, and
so theological concerns were translated by the Temple
authorities into *lèse majesté* (an easy task in a country
where there was no firm line between politics and
religion). Jesus was represented as a revolutionary, a
false claimant to the Jewish throne. "King of the Jews"
was the charge on which Jesus was tried and condemned
before Pilate, as the *titulus crucis,* the charge placed on a

placard above Jesus' head on the cross, proclaimed. (Braun [*Jesus* 34] is almost alone in denying the historicity of the *titulus*.) This *titulus* translated into a political category something in Jesus' teaching and praxis that was open to a messianic interpretation. Whether or not the Temple authorities *had* to have recourse to Pilate to have Jesus executed is hotly debated. The evidence is unclear, but it seems more likely that John 18:31 is correct: the sanhedrin had lost its power to put criminals to death (Blinzler, Catchpole; Winter's counterarguments are not convincing). Also disputed is whether the Barabbas incident and the supposed custom underlying it are historical or the creation of Christian tradition.

(Betz, O., *ANRW* II/25.1, 564–647. Blinzler, J., *Der Prozess Jesu* [4th ed.; Regensburg, 1969]; Eng *The Trial of Jesus* [Westminster, 1959]. *BGJ* 2. 791–802. Catchpole, D., *The Trial of Jesus* [SPB 18; Leiden, 1971]. Hengel, M., *Crucifixion* [Phl, 1977]. Kuhn, H.-W., *ANRW* II/25.1, 648–793. Merritt, R., *JBL* 104 [1985] 57–68. Rivkin, E., *What Crucified Jesus?* [Nash, 1984]. Sherwin-White, A., *Roman Society and Roman Law in the NT* [GR, 1963] 24–47. Winter, P., *On the Trial of Jesus* [StJud 1; 2d ed.; Berlin, 1974].)

55   (C) Crucifixion and Death. At the end of the Roman trial Jesus was condemned to death by crucifixion and received the preliminary scourging (a cruel mercy, intended to hasten death). So weakened was Jesus that he could not carry his crossbeam. The soldiers pressed into service one Simon from Cyrene to carry the beam. He and his sons, Alexander and Rufus, apparently became prominent members of the early church (Mark 15:21). Thus, there was at least one eyewitness at the crucifixion who later became a Christian. The crucifixion took place outside the city walls at Golgotha (Skull Place), possibly an abandoned quarry. Whether Jesus was tied or nailed to the cross is not specified, although nails are mentioned in the resurrection appearances (Luke 24:39; John 20:20,25,27) and are consistent with recent archaeological findings (see *TAG* 125–46; but also modifying reappraisal in *BA* 48 [1985] 190–91). Two robbers (*lēstai*, possibly insurrectionists) were crucified along with Jesus; the edifying repentance of the "good thief" is probably Lucan redaction. Mockery and abuse, narrated at various points during the trial, were also hurled at Jesus as he hung on the cross. Whether he responded verbally to this abuse and to his sufferings cannot be said. The "words from the cross," including the so-called cry of dereliction (Ps 22:2), may come from later Christian interpretation of Christ's death. Besides Simon of Cyrene, the only sympathetic witnesses on Calvary were some female disciples from Galilee. The placing of Jesus' mother and the beloved disciple at the cross may be Johannine symbolism.

56   Although the crucified sometimes lingered for days, Jesus' death occurred relatively quickly; hence, there was no need to hasten his death by breaking his legs, as was done in the case of the two robbers. Haste was important, since at sundown (the beginning of Saturday, the 15th of Nisan), Passover would coincide with the sabbath that year. The special solemnity of the feast reinforced the general Jewish rule that corpses were not to be left hanging overnight, lest the Holy Land be defiled (Deut 21:22–23). In the absence of close relatives, Jesus' corpse might have been disposed of unceremoniously in a common grave (a possibility left open by Braun [*Jesus* 35]). But Joseph of Arimathea, an influential Jewish official, interceded with Pilate and obtained the body for (temporary?) burial in a tomb he owned nearby. Some of the Galilean women witnessed the preparations for burial. The only constant name at both cross and tomb is Mary Magdalene. The account of setting a guard at the sealed tomb must be judged a later creation of Jewish-Christian debates (Matt 27:62–66; cf. 28:11–15). On the Shroud of Turin, see R. E. Brown, *Biblical Exegesis and Church Doctrine* (NY, 1985) 147–55; on the burial, R. E. Brown, *CBQ* 50 (1958) 233–45.

57   (III) Resurrection. Since the Jesus of history is by definition the Jesus who is open to empirical investigation by any and all observers, the risen Jesus lies outside the scope of such investigation (as now stated formally by the PBC; → Church Pronouncements, 72:39). This does not mean that the resurrection is not real, but rather that the resurrection is an event that in itself transcends time and space (hence the term "metahistorical") as Jesus enters into eternal life in his Father's presence. Certain claimed effects of the resurrection (the empty tomb and the resurrection appearances) do belong to our world of time and space but are more properly treated in a history of the early church. Suffice it to say that the empty-tomb traditions should not be dismissed automatically as "late legends." Mark and John preserve two different versions of a story that in its outline seems to belong to some stream of early Christian tradition (see W. Craig, *NTS* 31 [1985] 67 n. 88, for a list of exegetes affirming some form of historicity; but I. Broer [*Die Urgemeinde und das Grab Jesu* (SANT 31; Munich, 1972)] hesitates on whether the early Jerusalem church knew the grave of Jesus). That there were witnesses known by name who claimed that the risen Jesus appeared to them (1 Cor 15:5–8), that these witnesses included disciples of the historical Jesus who had deserted him out of fear and then did a remarkable *volte face* after his disgraceful death, that these disciples were not demented incompetents but people capable of intelligent propagation of a new movement, and that some of these disciples laid down their lives for the truth of their resurrection-experiences—are all historical facts. How people react to these facts and to the historical Jesus brings one beyond empirical investigation into the sphere of religious decision, of belief and unbelief.

79

PAUL

Joseph A. Fitzmyer, S.J.

BIBLIOGRAPHY

1 Bornkamm, G., *Paul* (NY, 1971) 1–106. Brown, R. E. and J. P. Meier, *Antioch and Rome* (NY, 1982). Cadbury, H. J., *The Book of Acts in History* (London, 1955) 123–33. Campbell, T. H., "Paul's 'Missionary Journeys' as Reflected in His Letters," *JBL* 74 (1955) 80–87. Deissmann, A., *St. Paul, a Study in Social and Religious History* (London, 1912; repr. Magnolia MA, 1972). Dockx, S., "Chronologie de la vie de Saint Paul, depuis sa conversion jusqu'à son séjour à Rome," *NovT* 13 (1971) 261–304; *Chronologies néotestamentaires et vie de l'église primitive* (Gembloux, 1976) 45–128. Gunther, J. J., *Paul: Messenger and Exile* (Valley Forge, 1972). Hengel, M., *Acts and the History of Earliest Christianity* (Phl, 1979). Hurd, J. C., "Pauline Chronology and Pauline Theology," *Christian History and Interpretation* (Fest. J. Knox; ed. W. R. Farmer, *et al.;* Cambridge, 1967) 225–48; "Paul the Apostle," *IDBSup* 648–51; "The Sequence of Paul's Letters," *CJT* 14 (1968) 189–200. Hyldahl, N., *Die paulinische Chronologie* (AThD 19; Leiden, 1986). Jewett, R., *A Chronology of Paul's Life* (Phl, 1979). Knox, J., *Chapters in a Life of Paul* (NY, 1950); "'Fourteen Years Later': A Note on the Pauline Chronology," *JR* 16 (1936) 341–49; "The Pauline Chronology," *JBL* 58 (1939) 15–39. Lüdemann, G., *Paul, Apostle to the Gentiles: Studies in Chronology* (Phl, 1984). Murphy-O'Connor, J., "Pauline Missions before the Jerusalem Conference," *RB* 89 (1982) 71–91; *St. Paul's Corinth: Texts and Archaeology* (Wilmington, 1983). Ogg, G., *The Chronology of the Life of Paul* (London, 1968). Riddle, D. W., *Paul, Man of Conflict* (Nash, 1940). Rigaux, B., *The Letters of St. Paul* (Chicago, 1969) 40–99. Sherwin-White, A. N., *Roman Society and Roman Law in the New Testament* (Oxford, 1969) 144–71. Suhl, A., *Paulus und seine Briefe* (SNT 11; Gütersloh, 1975).

OUTLINE

INTRODUCTION

3 **(I) Paul's Name.** In his letters the apostle calls himself *Paulos,* the name also used in 2 Pet 3:15 and from Acts 13:9 on. Prior to that in Acts he is called *Saulos* (7:58; 8:1,3; 9:1, etc.), the Gk form of *Saoul.* The latter spelling is found only in the conversion accounts (9:4,17; 22:7,13; 26:14) and stands for the Hebr *Šā'ûl,* the name of the first king of ancient Israel (e.g., 1 Sam 9:2,17; cf. Acts 13:21). It means "asked" (of God *or* of

Yahweh). Acts 13:9 marks the transition from "Saul" to "Paul" (except for the later *Saoul*): *Saulos de kai Paulos,* "Saul, also known as Paul." The name *Paulos* is the Gk form of the well-known Roman cognomen (family name), *Paul(l)us,* used by the Aemilian gens, the Vettenii, and the Sergii. One can only conjecture how Paul got such a Roman name. It is pure coincidence that Saul begins to be called Paul in the account in Acts where the

Roman proconsul Sergius Paulus is converted (13:7–12); for it is hardly likely that Paul assumed the name of this illustrious Roman convert from Cyprus (*pace* Jerome, *In Ep. ad Philem.* 1; PL 26. 640; H. Dessau, *et al.*). More likely the apostle was called *Paulos* from birth, and *Saoul* was the *signum* or *supernomen* (added name) used in Jewish circles. Many Jews of the period had two names, one Semitic (Saul) and the other Greek or Roman (Paul); cf. Acts 1:23; 10:18; 13:1. The names were often chosen for their similarity of sound. There is no evidence that "Saul" was changed to "Paul" at the time of his conversion; indeed, *Saulos* is used in Acts even after this event. The change in 13:9 is probably due to different sources of Luke's information. *Paulus* in Latin means "small," "little," but it had nothing to do with Paul's stature or modesty.

(Dessau, H., *Hermes* 45 [1910] 347–68. Harrer, G. H., *HTR* 33 [1940] 19–33. On *supernomen:* Lambertz, M., *Glotta* 4 [1913] 78–143.)

4   (II) Sources and Chronology of Paul's Life.
What little is known about Paul comes to us from two main sources: (1) passages in his genuine letters, principally 1 Thess 2:1–2,17–18; 3:1–3a; Gal 1:13–23; 2:1–14; 4:13; Phil 3:5–6; 4:15–16; 1 Cor 5:9; 7:7–8; 16:1–9; 2 Cor 2:1,9–13; 11:7–9,23–27,32–33; 12:2–4, 14,21; 13:1,10; Rom 11:1c; 15:19b,22–32; 16:1; and (2) Acts 7:58; 8:1–3; 9:1–30; 11:25–30; 12:25; 13:1–28:31. (Details in the Deutero-Pauline and Pastoral Epistles are of dubious value and can be used only to support what is known from the other two sources.)
5   The two sources mentioned, however, are not of equal value. In the reconstruction of Paul's life, preference must be given to what Paul has told us about himself, for Luke's story of Paul's missionary activity is colored by his pronounced literary tendencies and theological concerns. Recent writers such as J. Knox, D. W. Riddle, R. Jewett, G. Lüdemann, J. Murphy-O'Connor, *et al.* have tried to work out a "life" of Paul or a chronology of his letters either solely or mainly on the basis of his own writings, often expressing a reluctance to admit information from Acts. Yet, puzzling enough, such writers at times admit details that Luke alone recounts —details that they *need* for their varying solutions (e.g., the appearance of Paul before Gallio [18:12], Paul's 18-month sojourn in Corinth [18:11], or the Lystran origin of Timothy [16:2–3])! In the following reconstruction of Paul's career I shall use caution and a critical sense and admit further details for which Acts is the sole source, provided that they do not contradict or conflict with Pauline data. (The reader will note that my account uses the past tense for Pauline data, but the present tense for data from Acts.)
6   Years ago T. H. Campbell ("Paul's 'Missionary Journeys'") showed that in the Pauline passages mentioned above there is a sequence of Paul's movements from his conversion to the arrival in Rome that parallels the more detailed movements in Acts. In the Sequence Chart on the next page I adapt his fundamental study, making use of more recent discussions of the data and adding references to Paul's collaborators.
7   Differences in the Sequence Chart of Paul's movements are to be noted: (1) Luke's failure to mention Paul's withdrawal to "Arabia" (Gal 1:17b); (2) Luke's grouping of Paul's missionary activities in three blocks (I: 13:1–14:28; II: 15:36–18:22; III: 18:23–21:16). Some critics think that Mission I is a completely Lucan fabrication; but no little part of the problem is the question of sources in this part of Acts (→ Acts, 44:10). (3) Luke's occasion for Paul's escape from Damascus: a plot made by Jews (Acts 9:23; contrast 2 Cor 11:32). (4) Luke's

depiction of Paul "consenting" to the death of Stephen (Acts 7:58–8:1; cf. 22:20), whereas Paul himself speaks only of persecuting "the church of God" (Gal 1:13) or "the church" (Phil 3:6) and never mentions Stephen.
8   The Sequence Chart yields at best only a relative chronology. In Paul's own letters the only incident that can be dated extrabiblically is his Damascus escape (2 Cor 11:32–33): the ethnarch of King Aretas closed off the city to take Paul captive, but he escaped by being let down in a basket through a window in the city wall (cf. Acts 9:24–25). That occurred at the end of Paul's three years in Damascus (Gal 1:17c–18). Since Damascus was apparently under Roman rule until Tiberius's death (March 16, AD 37; cf. Josephus, *Ant.* 18.5.3 § 124) and the Nabatean Aretas IV Philopatris (9 BC–AD 39) was given control over it by the emperor Gaius Caligula, Paul's escape must have occurred between AD 37 and 39, probably in AD 39 (see PW 2/1 [1895] 674). Paul's conversion was about three years earlier, probably in AD 36.
9   As for Acts, extrabiblical data are found for five events in Paul's career. In *descending* order of importance, these are:
    (1) The proconsulate of L. Junius Gallio Annaeus in Achaia, before whom Paul is haled in Corinth (Acts 18:12). This is the "one link between the Apostle's career and general history that is accepted by all scholars" (Murphy-O'Connor, *Corinth* 141), even though it is reported solely by Luke. Gallio's proconsulate is mentioned in a Gk inscription set up in a temple of Apollo and discoverd by E. Bourguet at Delphi in 1905 and 1910. It is fragmentary, and the full publication of all the fragments (by A. Plassart) took place only in 1970. It is a copy of a letter sent by Claudius to the city of Delphi about its depopulation problems.

[1]Tiber[ius Claudius Caes]ar Au[gust]us Ge[rmanicus, invested with tribunician po]wer [2][for the 12th time, acclaimed Imperator for t]he 26th time, F[ather of the Fa]ther[land . . . sends greetings to . . .]. [3]For a l[ong time I have been not onl]y [well disposed toward t]he ci[ty] of Delph[i, but also solicitous for its [4]pro]sperity, and I have always guar[ded th]e cul[t of t]he [Pythian] Apol[lo. But] [5]now [since] it is said to be desti[tu]te of [citi]zens, as [L. Jun]ius [6]Gallio, my fri[end] an[d procon]sul, [recently reported to me, and being desirous that Delphi] [7]should continue to retain [inta]ct its for[mer rank, I] ord[er you (pl.) to in]vite [well born people also from [8]ot]her cities [to Delphi as new inhabitants and to] [9]all[ow] them [and their children to have all the] privi[leges of Del]phi [10]as being citi[zens on equal and like (basis)]. For i[f] so[me . . .] [11]were to trans[fer as citi]zens [to these regions, . . . (The rest is inconsequential; my translation follows Oliver's text, and brackets enclose restorations.)

From this text we may deduce that Gallio was proconsul in Achaia in the 12th year of the reign of Claudius, after the latter's 26th acclamation as "imperator." Whereas the tribunician power, with which the emperor was invested each year, marked his regnal years, acclamation as imperator was sporadic, being accorded to him after triumphs or important military victories. To date an event by it, one must know when the specific acclamation occurred. From other inscriptions one knows that the 22d–25th acclamations took place in Claudius's 11th regnal year and that the 27th occurred in his 12th year, before Aug. 1, AD 52 (CIL 6. 1256; Frontinus, *De Aquis* 1.13). The 26th acclamation could have occurred before winter in AD 51 or in the spring of AD 52. But the 12th regnal year began on Jan. 25, 52, and a Carian inscription combines the 26th acclamation with the 12th regnal year (*dēmarchikēs exousias to dōdekaton . . . autokratora to eikoston kai hekaton, BCH* 11 [1887] 306–7; A. Brassac, *RB* 10 [1913] 44; cf. CIL 8. 14727).

Letters	Acts
Conversion near Damascus (implied in Gal 1:17c)	Damascus (9:1–22)
To Arabia (Gal 1:17b)	
Return to Damascus (1:17c): 3 yrs.	
Flight from Damascus (2 Cor 11:32–33)	Flight from Damascus (9:23–25)
To Jerusalem (Gal 1:18–20)	To Jerusalem (9:26–29)
"The regions of Syria and Cilicia" (Gal 1:21–22)	Caesarea and Tarsus (9:30)
	Antioch (11:26a)
	(Jerusalem [11:29–30; 12:25]; → 25 below)
	Mission I: Antioch (13:1–4a)
	Seleucia, Salamis, Cyprus (13:4b–12)
	South Galatia (13:13–14:25)
Churches evangelized before Macedonian Philippi (Phil 4:15)	
	Antioch (14:26–28)
"Once again during 14 years I went up to Jerusalem" (for "Council," Gal 2:1)	Jerusalem (15:1–12)
Antioch Incident (Gal 2:11–14)	Antioch (15:35); Mission II
	Syria and Cilicia (15:41)
	South Galatia (16:1–5)
Galatia (1 Cor 16:1) evangelized for the first time (Gal 4:13)	Phrygia and North Galatia (16:6)
	Mysia and Troas (16:7–10)
Philippi (1 Thess 2:2 [= Macedonia, 2 Cor 11:9])	Philippi (16:11–40)
Thessalonica (1 Thess 2:2; cf. 3:6; Phil 4:15–16)	Amphipolis, Apollonia, Thessalonica (17:1–9)
	Berea (17:10–14)
Athens (1 Thess 3:1; cf. 2:17–18)	Athens (17:15–34)
Corinth evangelized (cf. 2 Cor 1:19; 11:7–9)	Corinth for 18 months (18:1–18a)
Timothy arrives in Corinth (1 Thess 3:6), probably accompanied by Silvanus (1 Thess 1:1)	Silas and Timothy come from Macedonia (18:5)
	Paul leaves from Cenchreae (18:18b)
	Leaves Priscilla and Aquila at Ephesus (18:19–21)
Apollos (in Ephesus) urged by Paul to go to Corinth (1 Cor 16:12)	Apollos dispatched to Achaia by Priscilla and Aquila (18:17)
	Paul to Caesarea Maritima (18:22a)
	Paul to Jerusalem (18:22b)
	In Antioch for a certain amount of time (18:22c)
Northern Galatia, second visit (Gal 4:13)	Mission III: North Galatia and Phrygia (18:23)
Ephesus (1 Cor 16:1–8)	Ephesus for 3 yrs. or 2 yrs., 3 mos. (19:1–20:1; cf. 20:31)
Visit of Chloe, Stephanas, *et al.* to Paul in Ephesus (1 Cor 1:11; 16:17), bringing letter (7:1)	
Paul imprisoned (? cf. 1 Cor 15:32; 2 Cor 1:8)	
Timothy sent to Corinth (1 Cor 4:17; 16:10)	
Paul's 2nd "painful" visit to Corinth (2 Cor 13:2); return to Ephesus	
Titus sent to Corinth with letter "written in tears" (2 Cor 2:13)	
(Paul's plans to visit Macedonia, Corinth, and Jerusalem/Judea, 1 Cor 16:3–8; cf. 2 Cor 1:15–16)	(Paul's plans to visit Macedonia, Achaia, Jerusalem, Rome, 19:21)
Ministry in Troas (2 Cor 2:12)	
To Macedonia (2 Cor 2:13; 7:5; 9:2b–4); arrival of Titus (2 Cor 7:6)	Macedonia (20:1b)
Titus sent on ahead to Corinth (2 Cor 7:16–17), with part of 2 Cor	
Illyricum (Rom 15:19)?	
Achaia (Rom 15:26; 16:1); Paul's third visit to Corinth (2 Cor 13:1)	3 mos. in Greece (Achaia) (20:2–3)
	Paul starts to return to Syria (20:3), but goes via Macedonia and Philippi (20:3b–6a)
	Troas (20:6b–12)
	Miletus (20:15c–38)
	Tyre, Ptolemais, Caesarea (21:7–14)
	Jerusalem (21:15–23:30)
(Plans to visit Jerusalem, Rome, Spain [Rom 15:22–27])	Caesarea (23:31–26:32)
	Journey to Rome (27:1–28:14)
	Rome (28:15–31)

Achaia was a senatorial province, governed by a pro-consul appointed by the Roman senate. Such a provincial governor was normally in office for a year and was expected to take his post by June 1 (Dio Cassius, *Rom. Hist.* 57.14.5) and to leave for it by mid-April (ibid., 60.11.6; 60.17.3). Claudius's letter mentions that Gallio had reported to him about conditions in Delphi. Hence Gallio was already in Achaia and had reported in the late spring or early summer of AD 52. This could have been toward the end of Gallio's proconsular year (June 51 to May 52) or at the beginning of such a year (June 52 to May 53). Since Seneca, Gallio's younger brother, says that Gallio developed a fever in Achaia and "took ship at once" (*Ep.* 104.1), it seems that Gallio cut short his stay in Achaia and hurried home. That suggests that Gallio had been there in the late spring and summer of 52 and left it not later than the end of Oct. (before *mare clausum,* when sea travel became impossible). Hence, Paul would have been haled before Gallio sometime in the summer or early fall of 52. Having been in Corinth for 18 months, Paul would have arrived there in early 51 (see Acts 18:11).

(Bourguet, E., *De rebus delphicis imperatoriae aetatis capita duo* [Montpellier, 1905]. Brassac, A., *RB* 10 [1913] 36–53, 207–17. Murphy-O'Connor, *Corinth* 141–52, 173–76. Oliver, J. H., *Hesperia* 40 [1970] 239–40. Plassart, A., *REG* 80 [1967] 372–78; *Les inscriptions du temple du IV siècle* [Fouilles de Delphes III/4; Paris, 1970] § 286.)

10   (2) The expulsion of Jews from Rome by the emperor Claudius (Acts 18:2c), related by Luke to the arrival of Aquila and Priscilla in Corinth, with whom Paul eventually stays. Suetonius (*Claudius* 25) reports: *Iudaeos impulsore Chresto assidue tumultuantes Roma expulit,* "He expelled from Rome Jews who were making constant disturbances at the instigation of *Chrestus.*" If "at the instigation of Chrestus" (which in Suetonius's day would have been pronounced *Christos*) is a garbled way of referring to disputes over whether Jesus was Christ, Suetonius would be reporting strife at Rome between Jews and Jewish Christians. A 5th-cent. Christian historian, P. Orosius (*Hist. adv. pag.* 7.6.15–16; *CSEL* 5. 451), quotes Suetonius's text and dates the expulsion in the 9th regnal year of Claudius (Jan. 25, AD 49 to Jan. 24, AD 50). But because Orosius says that Josephus tells of this expulsion, whereas the Jewish historian says nothing of

it, his testimony has appeared suspect to some scholars. No one knows where Orosius got his information about the 9th year. This date of the expulsion, however, remains the most likely (see E. M. Smallwood, *The Jews under Roman Rule* [SJLA 20; Leiden, 1976] 211–16; Jewett, *Chronology* 36–38; G. Howard, *ResQ* 24 [1981] 175–77). But some scholars have tried rather to interpret Suetonius's testimony as a reference to a decision made by Claudius in his first regnal year (AD 41) reported by Dio Cassius (*Rom. Hist.* 60.6.6). The emperor, noting the increasing number of Roman Jews, "did not drive them out," but rather ordered them "not to hold meetings" (see Lüdemann, *Paul* 165–71; Murphy-O'Connor, *Corinth* 130–40). This, however, is unconvincing, since Dio Cassius says explicitly that Claudius did *not* expel the Jews (at that time). He may well have expelled *some* Jews later on, as Suetonius affirms. (Dio Cassius's history for AD 49 exists only in epitomes.) However, one must pre-scind from the Lucan hyperbole, "all the Jews" (Acts 18:2), and ask how "recently" Aquila and Priscilla would have come from "Italy" (not specifically Rome). If the Claudian expulsion was an event in the 9th regnal year, Paul's arrival in Corinth would have been sometime after that.

11   (3) The famine in the reign of Claudius (Acts 11:28b) is not easily dated. It apparently affected the whole eastern Mediterranean area for several years; some evidence suggests that it occurred in Judea about the beginning of the procuratorship of T. Julius Alexander (AD 46–48; cf. Josephus, *Ant.* 20.5.2 § 101; → History, 75:178). On its relation to the so-called Famine Visit, → 25, 27 below.

12   (4) Porcius Festus succeeded Felix as procurator of Judea (Acts 24:27). The precise date of this succession is difficult to establish, but it may have occurred *ca.* AD 60 (see *HJPAJC* 1. 465–66; *HBC* 322–24). On the arrival of Festus, Paul appealed to Caesar for a trial (25:9–12).

13   (5) The recall of Pontius Pilate to Rome in AD 36 to answer for his conduct (see Josephus, *Ant.* 18.4.2 § 89; → History, 75:168). The removal of Pilate and the arrival of the new prefect, Marcellus, may be a plausible occasion for the lynching of Stephen (Acts 7:58–60) and the beginning of the persecution of the Jerusalem church (Acts 8:1). Paul's conversion may be related to these events.

PAUL'S CAREER

14   **(I) Youth and Conversion.**
    (A) Paul's Youth. The date of Paul's birth is unknown. He called himself an "old man" (*presbytēs*) in Phlm 9 (→ Philemon, 52:10), i.e., someone between 50 and 56 years of age (*TDNT* 6. 683); this would mean that he was born in the first decade AD. Luke depicts Saul as a "youth" (*neanias*) standing at the stoning of Stephen, i.e., as between 24 and 40 (cf. Diogenes Laertius 8.10; Philo, *De cher.* 114).

15   Paul never tells us where he was born, but his name, Paulos, would connect him with some Roman town. He boasted of his Jewish background and traced his lineage to the tribe of Benjamin (Rom 11:1; Phil 3:5; 2 Cor 11:22). He was an "Israelite" (ibid.), "a Hebrew, born of Hebrews . . . , as to the law a Pharisee" (Phil 3:6), one "extremely zealous for the traditions of my fathers" and one who excelled his peers "in Judaism" (Gal 1:14). In calling himself a "Hebrew" (*Hebraios*), he may have

meant that he was a Greek-speaking Jew who could also speak Aramaic (see C. F. D. Moule, *ExpTim* 70 [1958–59] 100–2) and could read the OT in the original. Paul's letters, however, reveal that he knew Greek well and could write it and that in addressing Gentile churches he usually quoted the OT in Greek. Traces of Stoic rhetorical diatribe in his letters (→ Pauline Theology, 82:12) show that he had a Gk education.

16   Luke also presents Paul as "a Jew," as "a Pharisee" born in Tarsus, a Hellenistic town of Cilicia (Acts 22:3,6; 21:39), as having a sister (23:16), and as a Roman citizen from birth (22:25–29; 16:37; 23:27). If Luke's information about Paul's origins is correct, it helps explain both the Hellenistic and the Jewish background of Paul. Tarsus is first attested as *Tarzi* on the 9th-cent. BC Black Obelisk of Shalmaneser III (l.138; cf. D. D. Luckenbill, *ARAB* 1. 207). In the 4th cent., Xenophon (*Anab.* 1.2.23) called it "a great and prosperous city," and

Gk coins from the 5th and 4th cents. reveal its early Hellenization. It was heavily hellenized by Antiochus IV Epiphanes (175–164), who also established a colony of Jews there (*ca.* 171) to foster commerce and industry. See W. M. Ramsay, *ExpTim* 16 (1904–5) 18–21; cf. Philostratus, *Life of Apol.* 6.34; Sherwin-White, *Roman Society* 144–93.

17   In Pompey's reorganization of Asia Minor in 66 BC, Tarsus became the capital of the province of Cilicia. Later on, freedom, immunity, and citizenship were granted to the town by Mark Antony, and Augustus confirmed these rights, which may explain Paul's Roman connections. Tarsus was a well-known center of culture, philosophy, and education. Strabo (*Geogr.* 14.673) knows of its schools as surpassing those of Athens and Alexandria and of its students as native Cilicians, not foreigners. Athenodorus Cananites, a Stoic philosopher and teacher of the emperor Augustus, retired there in 15 BC and was given the task of revising the city's democratic and civic processes. Other philosophers, Stoic and Epicurean, also settled and taught there. Famous Romans visited Tarsus: Cicero, Julius Caesar, Augustus, Mark Antony, and Cleopatra. Hence the Lucan Paul can boast that he is a "citizen of no mean town" (21:39).

(Böhlig, H., *Die Geisteskultur von Tarsus* [Göttingen, 1913]. Welles, C. B., "Hellenistic Tarsus," *MUSJ* 38 [1942] 41–75. Jones, A. H. M., *The Cities of the Eastern Roman Provinces* [Oxford, 1971] 192–209.)

18   The Lucan Paul also boasts of being "brought up in this city of Jerusalem and educated at the feet of Gamaliel" (Acts 22:3), i.e., Gamaliel I, the Elder, whose *floruit* in Jerusalem was *ca.* AD 20–50 (see W. C. van Unnik, *Tarsus or Jerusalem: The City of Paul's Youth* [London, 1962]). Though the Lucan picture of Paul's youth spent in Jerusalem may explain his Semitic training and mode of thought, Paul himself never utters a word about this feature of his youth. Moreover, it creates a difficulty: Paul's writings never suggest that he encountered or had any personal acquaintance with the Jesus of the public ministry (see 2 Cor 5:16; 11:4, which need not mean that he had, even though some commentators so understand 5:16)—if he spent his youth in Jerusalem, would he have escaped such an encounter? Though Paul's mode of argumentation and use of the OT resemble those of contemporary learned Palestinian Jews, his dependence on rabbinical traditions is more alleged than proved (see E. P. Sanders, *Paul and Palestinian Judaism* [Phl, 1977], but cf. J. Neusner, *HR* 18 [1978] 177–91). In the long run the only evidence that Paul was trained by a rabbinical figure such as Gamaliel is the statement of Acts.

19   According to J. Jeremias (*ZNW* 25 [1926] 310–12; *ZNW* 28 [1929] 321–23), at his conversion Paul was not merely a rabbinical disciple (*talmîd ḥākām*), but a recognized teacher with the right to make legal decisions. This authority would have been presupposed in his going to Damascus to arrest Christians (Acts 9:1–2; 22:4–5; 26:12) and his voting against Christians as a member of the sanhedrin (26:10). From this Jeremias concluded that, since 40 was the age required for rabbinical ordination, Paul would have been converted in middle age and have been married, since marriage was also required of rabbis. Jeremias harmonizes the foregoing Lucan data with Pauline material in interpreting 1 Cor 7:8 ("I say to the unmarried and the widowed, 'It is good for them to remain as I am'") to mean that Paul was classing himself with the widowed (*chērai*) rather than with the unmarried (*agamoi*; → 1 Corinthians, 49:36). Again, 1 Cor 9:5 would mean that Paul had not remarried. But almost every point in this intriguing view

is dubious: questionable harmonization, Paul's age, the late date of the rabbinical evidence used, Paul's status. See further E. Fascher, *ZNW* 28 (1929) 62–69; G. Stählin, *TDNT* 9. 452 n. 109.

20   **(B) Paul's Conversion.** Paul wrote of the crucial turn in his life in Gal 1:16: "God was pleased to reveal his son to/in me so that I might preach him among the Gentiles." This revelation followed upon a career in Judaism and a persecution of "the church of God" (1:13; cf. Phil 3:6 and A. J. Hultgren, *JBL* 95 [1976] 97–111). After it he withdrew to "Arabia" and then "returned" to Damascus (Gal 1:17). That the conversion took place near Damascus is inferred from the vb. "returned." Three years later he escaped from Damascus (*ca.* AD 39; → 8 above) and went up to Jerusalem (1:18). Thus *ca.* 36 Paul the former Pharisee became a Christian and an "apostle to the Gentiles" (Rom 11:13). (Depending on how long one reckons Aretas's control over Damascus, the dates of Paul's conversion and flight are differently estimated: Lüdemann dates the conversion in 30 or 33, the flight in 33 or 36; Jewett dates the conversion in 34, the flight in 37.)

21   Paul clearly regarded the experience near Damascus as the turning point in his life and in that sense a "conversion." It was for him an encounter wth the risen Lord (*Kyrios*) that he never forgot. When his apostolate was subsequently challenged, he was wont to expostulate, "Am I not an apostle? Have I not seen Jesus our Lord?" (1 Cor 9:1; cf. 15:8). As a result of that "revelation of Jesus Christ" (Gal 1:12), he became "a servant of Christ" (Gal 1:10), someone with a compulsion (*anankē*, 1 Cor 9:16) to preach the gospel of Christ, and for it he became "all things to all human beings" (1 Cor 9:22).

22   Paul's conversion should not be regarded as the result of the human condition described in Rom 7:7–8:2, as if that were an autobiographical account of his own experience. Paul as a Christian looked back on his Jewish career with a robust conscience: "As for righteousness under the law, I was blameless" (Phil 3:6b). He was not crushed by the law. The psychological origins of Paul's experience remain largely inaccessible to us, but in any case there was a "reversal or transvaluation of values" (J. G. Gager) that led to a new self-understanding of himself as an apostle of the gospel among the Gentiles and to an interpretation of the Christ-event under different images. (For the meaning of Paul's conversion, → Pauline Theology, 82:13–15.)

23   Luke also associates Paul's conversion with a persecution of the church—in Jerusalem, because of which (Hellenist Jewish) Christians scattered to Judea and Samaria (Acts 8:1–3) and farther (9:2; 11:19). Luke recounts the Damascus experience three times in Acts: once in a narrative that depicts Paul eventually sojourning for several days in Damascus (9:3–19—but with no mention of a withdrawal to Arabia); and twice in speeches, before a crowd in Jerusalem (22:6–16) and before Festus and King Agrippa (26:12–18). Each of these accounts stresses the overwhelming and unexpected character of the experience which occurred during Paul's persecution of Christians. Puzzling, however, are the variant details in the accounts: whether Paul's companions stand by speechless or fall to the ground; whether or not they hear the heavenly voice; though Jesus addresses Paul "in the 'Hebrew' language," he quotes a Gk proverb (26:14). The failure to harmonize such details reflects Luke's lack of concern for consistency. Yet in each account the essential message is conveyed to Paul: "Saul, Saul, why do you persecute me?"—"Who are you, Sir?"—"I am Jesus (of Nazareth) whom you are persecuting."

(On the "conversion": Bornkamm, G., in *Reconciliation and Hope* [Fest. L. L. Morris; ed. R. J. Banks; GR, 1974] 90–103. Dupont, J., in *Apostolic History and the Gospel* [Fest. F. F. Bruce; ed. W. W. Gasque and R. P. Martin; GR, 1970] 176–94. Gager, J. G., *NTS* 27 [1980–81] 697–704. Menoud, P. H., *Int* 7 [1953] 131–41. Stanley, D. M., *CBQ* 15 [1953] 315–38. Wood, H. G., *NTS* 1 [1954–55] 276–82. Also Meinardus, O. F. A., "The Site of Paul's Conversion at Kaukab," *BA* 44 [1981] 57–59.)

24   (II) Paul's Visits to Jerusalem. According to Paul's letters he visited Jerusalem twice after his conversion, once after three years (Gal 1:18) and "once again during fourteen years" (Gal 2:1). In Rom 15:25 he planned another visit, before going to Rome and Spain.
25   According to Acts, however, Paul visits Jerusalem after his conversion five or possibly six times: (1) 9:26–29, after his flight from Damascus; cf. 22:17; (2) 11:29–30, Barnabas and Saul bring a collection from Antioch to the brethren of Judea—related by Luke to the famine in the days of Claudius (→ 11 above); (3) 12:25, Barnabas and Saul go up to Jerusalem (again? some mss. rather read "from" [Jerusalem], which would mean their return to Antioch after the foregoing visit; but *eis,* "to," is the preferred reading; → Acts 44:67); (4) 15:1–2, the visit of Paul and Barnabas at the "Council"; (5) 18:22, after Mission II, Paul goes up and greets the church before going down to Antioch; (6) 21:15–17, the visit at the end of Mission III, when Paul is arrested.

The correlation of the Pauline and Lucan data about the visits to Jerusalem after the conversion is the most difficult aspect of any reconstruction of Paul's life. The best solution is to equate the Lucan visit 1 with Gal 1:18 and to regard Lucan visits 2, 3, and 4 as references to the same event, the "Council" (= Gal 2:1–10). Luke has undoubtedly historicized and made separate visits out of references to one visit found in different sources. The Lucan visit 5 creates no problem, and visit 6 is that planned by Paul in Rom 15:25.
26   Thus, after Paul escaped from Damascus in AD 39, he came to Jerusalem for the first time *historēsai Kēphan* (Gal 1:18), the meaning of which is debated: "to get information from Cephas" or "to visit Cephas" (→ Galatians, 47:16). During his 15 days there he met James, "the Lord's brother," but none of the other apostles; he was otherwise personally unknown to the churches of Judea. According to the Lucan version of this visit 1, Barnabas introduces Paul to the "apostles" and tells them how he has preached boldly in Damascus in the name of Jesus. Paul circulates in Jerusalem among them, continuing to preach boldly and provoking the Hellenists, who seek to kill him (Acts 9:27–29).
27   After the 15 days in Jerusalem, according to Gal 1:21 Paul retired to Syria and Cilicia—for how long he does not say. About this time he must have had the vision to which he refers in 2 Cor 12:2–4; it occurred 14 years before 2 Cor was written but is scarcely to be equated with the conversion experience. According to Acts 22:17–21 Paul has an ecstasy while praying in the Jerusalem Temple during visit 1. It is the danger presented by the provoked Hellenists that leads the brethren to bring Paul from Jerusalem to Caesarea and to send him off to Tarsus (Acts 9:30). Acts does not specify how long Paul stays in this city of Cilicia, but the sequence makes a number of years not improbable (perhaps AD 40–44). The stay ends with a visit from Barnabas, who brings him back to Antioch where he remains a whole year (11:25–26), engaged in evangelization. Luke relates visit 2 to Jerusalem, the "Famine Visit," to this period. See W. A. Meeks and R. Wilken, *Jews and Christians in Antioch* (Missoula, 1978).
28   (III) Pauline Missions. Acts organizes Paul's missionary activity into three segments; but "if

you had stopped Paul on the streets of Ephesus and said to him, 'Paul, which of your missionary journeys are you on now?' he would have looked at you blankly without the remotest idea of what was in your mind" (Knox, *Chapters* 41–42). Yet the trouble is not solely Lucan; it stems from the way we read Acts, since Luke does not distinguish Mission I, II, or III, as moderns tend to count them. Yet we have seen (→ 6 above [chart]) that there is a certain correlation in the Pauline and Lucan data for Paul's missionary journeys, apart from the first. His journeys cover roughly AD 46–58, the most active years of his life, as he evangelized Asia Minor and Greece.
29   (A) Mission I (AD 46–49). The story of this pre-"Council" mission is recounted solely by Acts (13:3–14:28) and is confined to essentials to suit Luke's literary purpose (cf. 2 Tim 3:11). Paul has given us no details about his missionary activity in the pre-"Council" period of 14 years (Gal 2:1). For a time he was in "the areas of Syria and Cilicia" (1:21) and was "preaching the faith" (1:23) "among the Gentiles" (2:2). When later he wrote Phil, he recalled that "at the beginning of the evangelization, no church except you shared with me in the matter of giving and receiving, when I left Macedonia" (4:15). As he left Macedonia, then (*ca.* AD 50; → 39 below), there were other churches, presumably evangelized by Paul. Where were they? Since he passed to Philippi in Macedonia from Asia Minor, he could be referring to churches of S Galatia in the account of Mission I (Acts 13:13–14:25)—or less likely to those of N Galatia, Mysia, or Troas at the beginning of Mission II (→ 38 below). In any case, Macedonia was scarcely the first area evangelized by Paul (*pace* M. J. Suggs, *NovT* 4 [1960] 60–68), and the account of Mission I in Acts does not contradict the sparse Pauline details.
30   Moved by the Spirit, Antiochene prophets and teachers impose hands on Barnabas and Saul and send them forth in the company of John Mark, Barnabas's cousin (Col 4:10). They depart from Seleucia, the port of Syrian Antioch, head for Cyprus, and pass through the island from Salamis to Paphos. There the proconsul Sergius Paulus is converted (13:7–12). From Paphos the missionaries sail for Perga in Pamphylia (on the S coast of central Asia Minor), where John Mark deserts Barnabas and Paul and returns to Jerusalem. Barnabas and Paul make their way to towns in S Galatia: to Pisidian Antioch, Iconium, Lystra, and Derbe. In Antioch Paul preaches first to Jews in their synagogue; and when he encounters resistance, Paul announces his turning henceforth to the Gentiles (13:46). After evangelizing the area and meeting opposition from Jews in various towns (even stoning in Iconium), Paul and Barnabas retrace their steps from Derbe through Lystra, Iconium, and Pisidian Antioch to Perga and sail from Attalia for Syrian Antioch, where Paul spends "no little time" with Christians (14:28). One of the issues that surfaces in Mission I is the relation of the new faith to Judaism, and more specifically the relation of Gentile Christians to older Jewish converts. Are the Gentile converts to be circumcised and required to observe the Mosaic law? See Ogg, *Chronology* 58–71.
31   (B) "Council" Visit (AD 49). According to Luke, during Paul's stay in Antioch (end of Mission I) converts from Judea arrive and begin to insist on circumcision as necessary for salvation (15:1–3). When this leads to a dispute between them and Paul and Barnabas, the Antiochene church sends Paul, Barnabas, and others up to Jerusalem to consult the apostles and elders about the status of Gentile converts. This visit results in the so-called Council of Jerusalem.
32   In Gal 2:1–10 Paul told of this visit; he went up to Jerusalem with Barnabas and Titus "once again

during 14 years" (to be reckoned from his conversion, i.e., in the year 49-50). Paul spoke of this visit as the result of "a revelation" (2:2), and he laid before "those of repute" in Jerusalem the gospel that he had been preaching to the Gentiles, and they "added nothing" to it. James, Cephas, and John realized the grace given to Paul and Barnabas and extended to them the right hand of fellowship—uninfluenced by the "false brethren" who had slipped in to spy out the freedom (from the law) gained in Christ and to whom Paul had not yielded "so that the truth of the gospel might be preserved" (2:4-5). The issue settled on this occasion was circumcision: It was not obligatory for salvation; and Titus, though a Greek, was not forced to be circumcised. (On Gal 2:7-8, → Galatians, 47:17.)

33 The first part of Acts 15 (vv 4-12) deals with this same doctrinal issue. Those whom Paul labeled "false brethren" are here identified as "some believers from the sect of the Pharisees" (15:5). When the matter is debated by the apostles and elders, Peter's voice seemingly prevails; and the assembly acquiesces in his decision (based on his own experience in Acts 10:1-11:18). The Jerusalem "Council" thus frees the nascent church from its Jewish roots and opens it to the world apostolate then confronting it. Paul's position is vindicated.

34 **(C) Antioch Incident (AD 49).** After the Jerusalem "Council" Paul went down to Antioch, and before long Peter followed. At first both of them ate with Gentile Christians, but soon "some people from James" (Gal 2:12), i.e., Christians with pronounced Jewish leanings, arrived and criticized Peter for eating with Gentile converts. Yielding to their criticism, Peter separated himself; and his action led other Jewish Christians, even Barnabas himself, to do the same. Paul protested and opposed Peter to his face, because he was "not walking according to the truth of the gospel" (2:11). It may be implied that Paul was successful in his criticism, but even so the disciplinary question of Jewish dietary regulations for Gentile converts was now posed. See Brown and Meier, *Antioch and Rome* 28-44.

35 **(D) Jerusalem Decree on Dietary Matters.** Paul's opposition to Peter did not solve the dietary problem at Antioch. Emissaries seem to have been sent again to Jerusalem, presumably after Paul's and Peter's departure from Antioch. James convenes the apostles and elders again, and their decision is sent as a letter to the local churches of Antioch, Syria, and Cilicia (Acts 15:13-19). Paul himself says nothing about this decision, and even in Acts he is only subsequently informed about it by James on his arrival in Jerusalem after Mission III (21:25).

36 Acts 15 is a problematic and composite chapter, in which Luke has undoubtedly telescoped two incidents that were distinct in subject and time. To be noted: (1) Vv 1-2 are a literary suture joining information from different sources. (2) V 34 is missing in the best Gk mss., but added in the Western textual tradition to explain where Silas was at the beginning of Mission II. (If v 34 be omitted, Silas's location becomes a problem: When does he join Paul on Mission II?) (3) Simeon (15:14), who is usually identified as Simon Peter (and has to be so understood in Luke's telescoped story), was probably someone else in the source used. Elsewhere in Acts Peter is called *Petros* (15:7) or *Simōn Petros* (10:5; 18:32), but never *Symeōn*. In Luke's source the Simeon of 15:14 may well have been Simeon Niger, one of the prophets or teachers of Antioch (13:1); he is probably sent as one of the emissaries to James of Jerusalem about the dietary regulations. (4) Peter's speech about circumcision and about the Mosaic law (15:7-11) scarcely coincides with the topic discussed by James (15:14-21).

37 As a result of the consultation James sends a letter to Antioch, Syria, and Cilicia (15:22-29), recommending that Gentile Christians in such mixed communities abstain from meat sacrificed to idols, from blood, from the meat of strangled animals, and from illicit sexual unions. It would have been sent with Judas Barsabbas and Silas (15:22) to Antioch and to Paul and Barnabas presumed to be still there. Acts 15:35-36 mentions Paul and Barnabas preaching in Antioch; but this should be understood of their sojourn immediately following the "Council," after which Paul would have left Antioch for Mission II. Paul learns about the letter later (21:25; → Acts 44:110).

(On relating Acts 15 to Gal 2 and the problem of Paul's visits to Jerusalem: Benoit, P., *Bib* 40 [1959] 778-92. Dupont, J., *RSR* 45 [1957] 42-60. Funk, R. W., *JBL* 75 [1956] 130-36. Giet, S., *RevScRel* 25 [1951] 265-69; *RSR* 39 [1951] 203-20; *RSR* 41 [1953] 321-47; *RevScRel* 31 [1957] 329-42. Parker, P., *JBL* 86 [1967] 175-82. Rigaux, *Letters* 68-99. Strecker, G., *ZNW* 53 [1962] 62-77.)

38 **(E) Mission II (AD 50-52).** According to Acts 15:37-39 Paul refuses to take John Mark with him on Mission II because of his earlier defection. Instead Silas accompanies Paul, and setting out from Antioch they make their way through Syria and Cilicia to the towns of S Galatia, Derbe and Lystra (where Paul takes Timothy as a companion, having had him circumcised, Acts 16:1-3!). From there he passes through Phrygia to N Galatia (Pessinus, Ancyra, and Tavium) and founds new churches. Hindered from moving to Bithynia, he goes on from Galatia into Mysia and Troas. Here he seems to have been joined by Luke—or at least data from Luke's diary begin at this point (Acts 16:10-17, the first of the "We-Sections"; → Acts, 44:2).

39 In response to a dream-vision Paul passes over to Neapolis, the port of Philippi, and the latter becomes the site of his first Christian church in Europe (→ 6 above [chart]). After imprisonment and flogging at Philippi for having exorcised a slave girl who had been the source of much gain for her masters, he passes on to Thessalonica via Amphipolis and Apollonia (Acts 17:1-9). His short stay in Thessalonica is occupied by evangelization and controversy with Jews; it ends with his flight to Beroea (17:10), and eventually to Athens (17:15). Here Paul tries to interest Athenians, renowned for their love of novel ideas, in the gospel of the risen Christ (17:22-31). But he fails: "We'll listen to you on this topic some other time" (17:32). After this disappointment Paul moves on to Corinth (AD 51), at that time one of the most important towns in the Mediterranean world. (For a collection of ancient descriptive texts about Corinth and a report of archaeological work, see Murphy-O'Connor, *Corinth*.) Here he lives with Aquila and Priscilla (18:2-3), Jewish Christians recently come from Italy (→ 10 above) and tentmakers by trade like Paul (see R. F. Hock, *JBL* 97 [1978] 555-64). During his stay in Corinth, which lasts for 18 months, he converts many Jews and Greeks and founds a vigorous, predominantly Gentile Christian church. In AD 51 Paul wrote his first letter to the THESSALONIANS. Near the end of his stay (AD 52; → 9 above), Paul is haled before the proconsul L. Junius Gallio, who dismisses the case as a matter of words, names, and Jewish law (18:15). Some time later Paul withdraws from Corinth, sailing from its port of Cenchreae for Ephesus and Caesarea Maritima. After paying a visit to the Jerusalem church (18:22), he goes to Antioch, where he stays well over a year (possibly from late autumn of 52 until the spring of 54).

(Davies, P. E., "The Macedonian Scene of Paul's Journeys," *BA* 26 [1963] 91-106. Ogg, *Chronology* 112-26.)

40   (F) Mission III (AD 54–58). Leaving Antioch (Acts 18:23), Paul travels overland once again through N Galatia and Phrygia to Ephesus. The capital of the province of Asia becomes the center of his missionary activity for the next three years (Acts 20:31), and for "two years" he lectures in the hall of Tyrannus (19:10). Shortly after his arrival in Ephesus, Paul wrote GALATIANS (*ca.* 54). To this missionary period also belong the letter to the PHILIPPIANS and possibly that to PHILEMON (*ca.* 56–57). Acts says nothing of an imprisonment of Paul at Ephesus, but see 1 Cor 15:32; 2 Cor 1:8–9; cf. Phil 1:20–26. Some of the problems that Paul experienced and has described in 2 Cor 11:24–27 may well have happened to him in this period of missionary activity.

41   During this time reports came to Paul about the situation of the Corinthian church. To cope with the situation there—doubts, factions, resentment toward Paul himself, scandals—he wrote at least five letters to Corinth, of which only two survive (one of which is composite; → 2 Corinthians, 50:2–3). One letter preceded 1 Cor (see 1 Cor 5:9), warning the Corinthians about associating with immoral Christians (and probably also recommending a collection for the poor of Jerusalem, a question about which the Corinthians sent a subsequent inquiry [see 1 Cor 16:1]). Then, to comment on reports and to answer questions sent to him, Paul wrote 1 CORINTHIANS shortly before Pentecost (probably in 57). This letter, however, was not well received, and his relations with the faction-torn church of Corinth worsened. The situation called forth a hasty visit to Corinth (2 Cor 12:14; 13:1–2; 2:1 ["a painful visit"]; 12:21), which really accomplished nothing. On his return to Ephesus, Paul wrote to the Corinthians a third time, a letter composed "with many tears" (2 Cor 2:3–4,9; 7:8,12; 10:1,9). This letter may have been taken by Titus, who visited the Corinthians personally in an attempt to smooth out relations.

42   Probably during Titus's absence the revolt of the Ephesian silversmiths occurs (Acts 19:23–20:1). Paul's preaching of the new Christian "Way" incites Demetrius, a maker of miniature shrines of Artemis of Ephesus, to lead a riotous mob into the theater in protest against Paul and the spread of Christianity.

43   This experience prompted Paul to leave Ephesus and go to Troas (2 Cor 2:12) to work. Not finding Titus there, he decided to go on to Macedonia (2:13). Somewhere in Macedonia (possibly at Philippi) he met Titus and learned from him that a reconciliation between Paul and the Corinthians had been worked out. From Macedonia, Paul wrote to Corinth his fourth letter (the Letter A of 2 CORINTHIANS; → 50:4) in the autumn of 57. It is not possible to say whether Paul proceeded immediately to Corinth or went first from Macedonia into Illyricum (cf. Rom 15:19), whence he may have written 2 Cor 10–13 (Letter B). Eventually, Paul did arrive in Corinth, on his third visit there, probably in the winter of 57 and stayed for three months in Achaia (Acts 20:2–3; cf. 1 Cor 16:5–6; 2 Cor 1:16).

44   By this time Paul had been thinking of returning to Jerusalem. Mindful of the injunction of the "Council" that the poor should be remembered (Gal 2:10), he saw to it that his Gentile churches took up a collection for the poor of Jerusalem. This was done in the churches of Galatia, Macedonia, and Achaia (1 Cor 16:1; Rom 15:25–26). Paul planned to take the collection to Jerusalem and thus terminate his evangelization of the eastern Mediterranean world. He wanted to visit Rome (Rom 15:22–24) and from there go on to Spain and the West. During the three-month stay in Achaia Paul wrote the letter to the ROMANS (probably from Corinth, or its port Cenchreae [Rom 16:1]) at the beginning of 58. See further Brown and Meier, *Antioch and Rome* 105–27.

45   When spring arrives, Paul decides to sail from Corinth (Acts 20:3) for Syria. But as he is about to embark, a plot against him is hatched by some Jews; and he resolves to travel overland, by way of Macedonia. Disciples from Beroea, Thessalonica, Derbe, and Ephesus accompany him. They spend Passover of 58 in Philippi (where Luke rejoins him—Acts 20:5, a "We-Section"). After the feast they leave by ship for Troas and journey overland to Assos, where they take ship again for Mitylene. Skirting the coast of Asia Minor, Paul sails from Chios to Samos, then to Miletus, where he addresses the elders of Ephesus summoned there (Acts 20:17–35). He is not deterred by their prediction of his coming imprisonment, but sails on to Cos, Rhodes, Patara in Lycia, Tyre in Phoenicia, Ptolemais, and Caesarea Maritima. An overland journey brings him to Jerusalem, which he has been hoping to reach by Pentecost of 58 (20:16; 21:17). See Ogg, *Chronology* 133–45.

46   (IV) Paul's Last Imprisonment. For the rest of Paul's career we are dependent solely on the Lucan information in Acts; it covers several years after 58, during which Paul endures a long captivity.

47   (A) Last Visit to Jerusalem and Arrest (AD 58). Arriving in Jerusalem, Paul and his companions pay their respects to James in the presence of the elders of that church (Acts 21:18). James immediately realizes that Paul's presence in Jerusalem might cause a disturbance among Jewish Christians. So he counsels Paul to join four men who are about to go through the Nazirite vow ceremony and to pay the expenses for them as a gesture of goodwill toward Jewish Christians. Paul consents, and the seven-day ceremonial period is almost over when he is seen in the Temple precincts by Jews from the province of Asia. They accuse him of advocating violation of the Mosaic law and of defiling the sanctity of the Temple by bringing a Greek into it. They set upon him, drag him from the Temple, and try to kill him. He is saved, however, by the tribune of the Roman cohort stationed in the Fortress Antonia. The tribune eventually puts Paul under protective arrest (22:27) and brings him before the sanhedrin. But fear of the Jews makes the tribune send Paul to the procurator of Judea, Antonius Felix, residing in Caesarea Maritima (23:23–33). Felix, who expects Paul to bribe him (24:26), keeps Paul in prison for two years (58–60; → History, 75:179).

48   (B) Appeal to Caesar; Journey to Rome (AD 60). When the new procurator, Porcius Festus, arrives (possibly *ca.* 60; → 12 above), Paul "appeals to Caesar," i.e., requests trial in Rome (25:11), in virtue of his Roman citizenship. Festus has to grant this request. See Sherwin-White, *Roman Society* 48–70.

Escorted by a Roman centurion (and probably by Luke, as the "We-Sections" indicate), he sets sail from Caesarea Maritima for Sidon and passes Cyprus to come to Myra in Lycia. In the late autumn of 60 (27:9) they leave Myra on an Alexandrian ship bound for Italy, expecting bad weather. Their route takes them first to Cnidus (on the S coast of Asia Minor), then southward "under the lee of Crete off Salmone" as far as Fair Havens, near the Cretan town of Lasea (27:7–8). When they try to reach the harbor of Phoenix, a northeaster blows up and carries them for days across the Adriatic to Malta, where they are finally shipwrecked (28:1).

49   After spending the winter on Malta, Paul and his escort sail for Syracuse in Sicily, then for Rhegium (modern Reggio di Calabria), and lastly for Puteoli (modern Pozzuoli, near Naples). Their overland journey to Rome takes them through Appii Forum and Tres Tabernae (28:15). Paul arrives in the capital of the empire in the spring of 61 and for two years is kept in house arrest (61–63) with a soldier to guard him. This situation, however, does not deter him from summoning Roman Jews to his quarters and evangelizing them (28:17–28). Traditional interpretation ascribes Paul's writing of PHILEMON, COLOSSIANS, and EPHESIANS to this imprisonment; but → Philemon, 52:5; Colossians, 54:7; Ephesians, 55:13. See Sherwin-White, *Roman Society* 108–19; R. E. Brown, *The Churches the Apostles Left Behind* (NY, 1984) 47–60.

50   (C) End of Paul's Life. Acts ends with the brief account of Paul's house arrest. His arrival in Rome and his unhindered preaching of the gospel there form the climax of the story of the spread of the word of God from Jerusalem to the capital of the civilized world of the time—Rome symbolizing "the end of the earth" (Acts 1:8). But this was not the end of Paul's life. The mention of "two whole years" (28:30) does not imply that he died immediately thereafter, no matter what interpretation is given to the enigmatic end of Acts.

51   The PASTORAL LETTERS (Titus; 1–2 Tim) have often been regarded as genuine writings of Paul and have been considered as composed by him after his Roman house arrest. Indeed, they suggest that he visited the East again (Ephesus, Macedonia, and Greece). According to them Paul would have set up Titus as the head of the Cretan church and Timothy as the head of the Ephesian church. 2 Tim purports to be Paul's last will and testament, written as he was about to face death. It suggests that he may have been arrested at Troas (4:13) and brought to Rome again (1:17), where this letter would have been written from prison. But these letters are usually regarded today as pseudepigraphical, possibly written by a disciple of Paul (→ Pastorals, 56:6–8; cf. Brown, *Churches* [→ 49 above] 31–46).

52   For other details about the end of Paul's life we are dependent on later ecclesiastical traditions, which became heavily laced with legend. Did Paul ever visit Spain? Perhaps little more than a historicization of plans expressed in Rom 15:24,28 is involved; subsequent tradition tells of Paul, freed after two years of house arrest, going to Spain. Clement of Rome (*I Cor.* 5:7) records that Paul "taught the whole world uprightness and traveled to the extreme west [*epi to terma tēs dyseōs elthōn*]. And after he had borne witness before the authorities, he was taken from this world and went to the holy place, having proved himself the greatest model of endurance." Clement's testimony (*ca.* 95) suggests the visit to Spain, another trial, and martyrdom. *Ca.* 180 the Muratorian Fragment (lines 38–39; *EB* 4) implies that the last part of Acts, recounting "the departure of Paul from the City [Rome] as he set out for Spain," has been lost.

53   Eusebius (*HE* 2.22.3) is the first to mention Paul's second imprisonment in Rome and his martyrdom under Nero: "After defending himself, [Paul] was again sent on the ministry of preaching, and coming a second time to the same city suffered martyrdom under Nero. During this imprisonment he wrote the second epistle to Timothy, indicating at the same time that his first defense had taken place and that his martyrdom was at hand." Eusebius further quotes Dionysius of Corinth (*ca.* 170), who stated that Peter and Paul "were martyred at the same time" (*HE* 2.25.8). Tertullian (*De praescr.* 36) compares Paul's death with that of John (the Baptist), i.e., by beheading.

The Eusebian testimony about Paul's death in the persecution of Nero is widely accepted. This persecution lasted, however, from the summer of AD 64 to the emperor's death (June 9, 68); and it is hard to pinpoint the year of Paul's martyrdom. The notice of Dionysius of Corinth that Peter and Paul "were martyred at the same time" (*kata ton auton kairon*) has often been understood to mean in the same year, but the preferred year for the death of Paul is 67, toward the end of Nero's persecution, as Eusebius's account seems to suggest. This chronology, however, is not universally accepted and is not without its difficulties.

54   Paul is said to have been buried on the Via Ostiensis, near the site of the modern basilica of San Paolo fuori le Mura. In 258, when Christian tombs in Rome were threatened with desecration during the persecution of Valerian, Paul's remains were transferred for a time to a place called *Ad Catacumbas* on the Appian Way. Later they were returned to their original resting place, over which Constantine built his basilica.

(Meinardus, O. F. A., "Paul's Missionary Journey to Spain: Tradition and Folklore," *BA* 41 [1978] 61–63. Perigo, L. P., "Paul's Life after the Close of Acts," *JBL* 70 [1951] 277–84.)

80

EARLY CHURCH

Raymond E. Brown, S.S.   Carolyn Osiek, R.S.C.J.
Pheme Perkins *

BIBLIOGRAPHY

1   **General Bibliography.** Bauer, W., *Orthodoxy and Heresy in Earliest Christianity* (Phl, 1971; Ger 1934). Becker, J., *Die Anfänge des Christentums* (Stuttgart, 1987). Callan, T., *Forgetting the Root: The Emergence of Christianity from Judaism* (NY, 1986). Chadwick, H., *The Early Church* (Pelican Hist. of the Church 1; London, 1967). Chadwick, H. and H. von Campenhausen, *Jerusalem and Rome* (Facet Hist. Series 4; Phl, 1966). Conzelmann, H., *History of Primitive Christianity* (Nash, 1973). Davies, J. G., *The Early Christian Church: A History of the First Five Centuries* (GC, 1967). Frend, W. H. C., *The Rise of Christianity* (Phl, 1984). Goppelt, L., *Apostolic and Post-apostolic Times* (GR, 1977). Harnack, A. von, *The Mission and Expansion of Christianity in the First Three Centuries* (NY, 1961; Ger 2d ed. 1906). Hinson, E. G., *The Evangelization of the Roman Empire* (Macon, 1981). Kümmel, W. G., "Das Urchristentum," *TRu* 48 (1983) 101–28; 51 (1986) 239–68; cont. Lietzmann, H., *A History of the Early Church* (2 vols.; London, 1961; Ger 1932–44). Lüdemann, G., *Das frühe Christentum nach den Traditionen der Apostelgeschichte* (Göttingen, 1987). Manns, F., *Bibliographie du Judéo-Christianisme* (Studia Biblica Franciscana Analecta 13; Jerusalem, 1979). Neusner, J., *Judaism in the Beginning of Christianity* (Phl, 1984). Ramsay, W. M., *The Church in the Roman Empire before AD 170* (London, 1893). Schneemelcher, W., *Das Urchristentum* (Stuttgart, 1981). Snyder, G. F., *Ante Pacem: Archaeological Evidence of Church Life before Constantine* (Macon, 1985). Turner, H. E. W., *The Pattern of Christian Truth* (London, 1954 – see D. L. Hawkin, *Churchman* 99 [1985] 51–56). Von Campenhausen, H., *Ecclesiastical Authority and Spiritual Power in the Church of the First Three Centuries* (Stamford, 1969; Ger 1953). Weiss, J., *Earliest Christianity: A History of the Period AD 30–150* (2 vols.; NY, 1959; Ger 1914). Wilken, R. L., *The Christians as the Romans Saw Them* (New Haven, 1984); *The Myth of Christian Beginnings* (GC, 1971).

2   **Bibliography for Church in NT.** *Aux origines de l'Église* (RechBib 7; Brouwer, 1965). *Catholicity and Apostolicity,* issue of *One in Christ* 6 (1970) 242–483. *Le ministère et les ministères selon le Nouveau Testament* (ed. J. Delorme; Paris, 1974). Brown, R. E., *Biblical Exegesis and Church Doctrine* (NY, 1985) 114–34; *The Churches the Apostles Left Behind* (NY, 1984); *The Community of the Beloved Disciple* (NY, 1979). Brown, R. E. and J. P. Meier, *Antioch and Rome* (NY, 1983). Cazelles, H., *La naissance de l'Église, secte juive rejetée* (Lire la Bible 3; 2d ed.; Paris, 1983). Cwiekowski, F. J., *The Beginnings of the Church* (NY, 1988). Fiorenza, F. S., *Foundational Theology: Jesus and the Church* (NY, 1984). Goppelt, L., *Theology of the New Testament 2: Variety and Unity of the Apostolic Witness* (GR, 1982). Hahn, F., *et al.,* The *Beginnings of the Church in the New Testament* (Minneapolis, 1970); *Einheit der Kirche* (QD 84; Freiburg, 1979). Harrington, D. J., *God's People in Christ* (Phl, 1980); *Light of All Nations* (Wilming-

ton, 1982). Holmberg, B., *Paul and Power: The Structure of Authority in the Primitive Church* (ConBNT 11; Lund, 1978). Kee, H. C., *Christian Origins in Sociological Perspective* (Phl, 1980). Küng, H., *The Church* (NY, 1967). Lemaire, A., *Les ministères aux origines de l'Église* (LD 68; Paris, 1971). Lohfink, G., *Jesus and Community* (Phl, 1984). MacDonald, M. Y., *The Pauline Churches* (SNTSMS 60; Cambridge, 1988). Meeks, W. A., *The First Urban Christians* (New Haven, 1983). Meyer, B. F., *The Early Christians* (Wilmington, 1986). Perkins, P., *Ministering in the Pauline Churches* (NY, 1982). Rowland, C., *Christian Origins* (Minneapolis, 1985). Schnackenburg, R., *The Church in the New Testament* (NY, 1965). Schüssler Fiorenza, E., *In Memory of Her* (NY, 1983). Schweizer, E., *Church Order in the New Testament* (SBT 32; London, 1961). Vögtle, A., *Die Dynamik des Anfangs* (Freiburg, 1988).

SPECIAL TOPICS: *Baptism in the New Testament* (ed. A. Grail; London, 1964). Brown, R. E. (on ministry, priesthood, episcopate), *Priest and Bishop* (NY, 1970); *The Critical Meaning of the Bible* (NY, 1981) 96–146. Brown, R. E., *et al., PNT.* Delling, G., *Worship in the New Testament* (London, 1962). Gerhardsson, B., *The Ethos of the Bible* (Phl, 1981). Hahn, F., *The Worship of the Early Church* (Phl, 1973). Hengel, M., *Property and Riches in the Early Church* (Phl, 1974). Koenig, J., *New Testament Hospitality* (OBT 17; Phl, 1985). Léon-Dufour, X., *Le partage du pain eucharistique selon le Nouveau Testament* (Paris, 1983). Malherbe, A. J., *Social Aspects of Early Christianity* (2d ed.; Phl, 1983). Marshall, I. H., *Last Supper and Lord's Supper* (GR, 1980). Reumann, J., *The Supper of the Lord* (Phl, 1985).

3   **Bibliography for 2d-Cent. Church Writers.** Altaner, B., *Patrology* (5th ed.; NY, 1961). Burghardt, W., "Literature of Christian Antiquity," *TS* 45 (1984) 275–306. Goodspeed, E. J., *A History of Early Christian Literature* (rev. ed. R. M. Grant; Chicago, 1966). Grant, R. M., *After the NT* (Phl, 1967). Halton, T. P. and R. D. Sider, "A Decade of Patristic Scholarship 1970–1979," *Classical World* 76 (1982) 313–83. KINT 2. Lake, K., *The Apostolic Fathers* (2 vols.; LCL; NY, 1912–13). Quasten, J., *Patrology* 1 (Westminster, 1975). Sparks, J. (ed.), *The Apostolic Fathers* (Nash, 1978).

4   **Bibliography for Gnosticism.** Scholer, D., *Nag Hammadi Bibliography* (NHS 1; Leiden, 1971); annual supplements in *NovT.* TEXTS: *Facsimile Edition of the Nag Hammadi Codices* (Leiden, 1972–79). Individual codices and tractates with Coptic texts and transls. published in NHS series (Eng; Leiden) and Bibliothèque copte "Textes" (Fr; Quebec). Cameron, R. and A. Dewey, *Cologne Mani Codex* (SBLTT 15; Missoula, 1979). Foerster, W., *Gnosis* (2 vols.; Oxford, 1972–74). Layton, B., *The Gnostic Scriptures* (GC, 1987). Robinson, *NHLE.* Schmidt, C. and V. MacDermot, *The Books of Jeu and the Untitled Text in the Bruce Codex* (NHS 13; Leiden, 1978); *Pistis Sophia* (NHS 9; Leiden, 1978).

---

* Sections 3, 34–63 of this article are by C. Osiek; sections 4, 64–82 are by P. Perkins; the remainder is by R. E. Brown.

STUDIES: Aland, B., ed., *Gnosis* (Fest. Hans Jonas; Göttingen, 1978). Brown, P., "The Diffusion of Manichaeism" *JRS* 49 (1969) 92–103. Green, H. A., *Economic and Social Origins of Gnosticism* (SBLDS 77; Atlanta, 1985). Hedrick, C. W. and R. Hodgson, *Nag Hammadi, Gnosticism and Early Christianity* (Peabody MA, 1986). Hoffmann, R. J., *Marcion* (AAR Academy Ser 46; Chico, 1984). Jonas, H., *Gnostic Religion* (2d ed.; Boston, 1963). Korschorke, K., *Die Polemik der Gnostiker gegen das Kirchliche Christentum* (NHS 12; Leiden, 1978). Layton, B., ed. *Rediscovery of Gnosticism* (2 vols; NumenSup 41; Leiden 1980–81). Lüdemann, G., "Zur Geschichte des ältesten Christentums in Rom," *ZNW* 70 (1979) 86–114. MacRae, G. W., *Studies in the New Testament and Gnosticism* (GNS 26; Wilmington, 1987). Pearson, B. A., "Jewish Sources in Gnostic Literature," in *Jewish Writings of the Second Temple Period* (ed. M. Stone; CRINT 2.2; Leiden, 1984) 443–81. Pelikan, J., *Emergence of the Catholic Tradition (100–600)* (Chicago, 1971). Perkins, P., *The Gnostic Dialogue* (NY, 1980). Rudolph, K., *Gnosis* (SF, 1983). Stroumsa, G. A., *Another Seed* (NHS 24; Leiden, 1984). Vallé, G., *A Study in Antignostic Polemics* (Waterloo, 1981). Van den Broek, R., "The Present State of Gnostic Studies," *VC* 37 (1983) 41–71. Also *The New Testament and Gnosis* (Fest. R. McL. Wilson; ed. A. H. B. Logan, *et al.;* Edinburgh, 1983).

5   OUTLINE

6   The church is not the central topic of any NT writing, although Col/Eph direct attention to the church as body of Christ, and 1 Tim/Tit discuss local church structure. The joining of those who accepted the proclamation of Jesus into churches sharing *koinōnia* and the gradual separation of Christians from the Jewish synagogues have to be reconstructed from scattered references. The references stemming from the period AD 30–95 are in works that were eventually accepted into the canon of the NT. But from AD 95–150 there is an overlapping between the last NT works to be canonized (often hard to date; → Canonicity, 66:55) and noncanonical writings. Some of the latter (e.g., the Apostolic Fathers, the Apologists) have offered theological guidance to the church of subsequent centuries. Others are classified as NT Apocrypha (→ Apocrypha, 67:53), sometimes embodying theology that would later be designated as heretical (gnostic, docetic). After AD 150, by which time the last of the eventually canonized works had been composed, the mixed trends of the preceding era became more sharply delineated, until with Irenaeus in the late 2d cent. the patristic period may be said to have begun. To understand the Christianity of the NT period, a knowledge of the 2d cent. is important since certain lines of development that are very faintly evidenced in the NT are more completely documented later. This article, besides describing the church in NT times, will supply the reader with an outline of the basic 2d-cent. church writings, along with a discussion of gnosticism and its sources.

CHURCH IN THE NEW TESTAMENT

7   In the four Gospels *ekklēsia,* "church," "community," appears on Jesus' lips only twice. Since Matt 18:17 clearly refers to the local community, only once in Jesus remembered to have spoken about the church in the larger sense: "Upon this rock I will build my church" (Matt 16:18). Despite such slender terminological basis in Jesus' recorded ministry, within a half century Eph 5:25 claims: "Christ loved the church and gave himself up for her." Some 30 years later (*ca.* 110) Bishop Ignatius of Antioch can refer to "the catholic church" (*hē katholikē ekklēsia; Smyrn.* 8:2); and by the end of the 2d cent. the opponent of Christianity, Celsus, knows of "the great church" (Origen, *Contra Celsum* 5.59) distinct from the gnostic conventicles. Let us consider some elements in that line of development.

8   **(I) Jesus' Public Ministry.** How can we best describe the situation of those who accepted Jesus' proclamation of the kingdom during the period between the baptism by John and the crucifixion? The older blueprint supposition by which Jesus had the church clearly in mind and had already planned its structure, sacraments, etc., has little or no textual support; for the very few passages to which appeal may be made (e.g., Matt 16:18 [above]; Luke 22:19: "Do this in commemoration of me") have no parallel in the other Gospels and probably represent postresurrectional understandings specifying Jesus' intentions. In what are commonly accepted as historical memories from Jesus' ministry (for method, → Jesus, 78:4–7) he is singularly silent on foundational or structural issues. This is understandable if we see Jesus interested not in founding a separate religion but in renewing Israel, which already had worship, priests, sacrifices—Jesus did not need to plan such structures. The choice of the Twelve (surely a historical feature; → Jesus, 78:26) is no exception to this image, for they represent the 12 patriarchs at the beginning of Israel and function eschatologically sitting "on thrones judging the twelve tribes of Israel" (Matt 19:28; Luke 22:30—Jesus' only recorded words about his purpose in choosing the Twelve). In the tradition of Jesus' precrucifixion sayings there is never a reference to a mission outside Israel; indeed, in Matt 10:5 he instructs his disciples, "Go nowhere among the Gentiles and enter no town of the Samaritans." Of course, his vision of the renewed Israel included the Gentiles' *coming* (Matt 8:11) as did the vision of the prophets of Israel (Isa 2:2–3; 49:12); but that is quite different from a mission going to them (→ Jesus, 78:28). Again, Matt 28:19, which is clearly postresurrectional, represents a specification in the light of church experience guided by the Spirit; see Acts 11:1–4,12.

9   In reaction to the oversimplified notion of a church already existing in Jesus' lifetime or his immediate planning, some prefer to speak sociologically of a "Jesus movement" during the ministry or the early decades thereafter. This designation is not satisfactory for several reasons. It evokes a modern parallel of people leaving their former affiliation to attach themselves to a religious guru. Although some did leave their work (fishing, tax collecting) or home to follow Jesus during his ministry and be with him, many who accepted his proclamation of the kingdom seemed to have remained where they were without a visible or distinctive movement in their lifestyle (→ Jesus, 78:27). In regard to those who did follow him about, the earliest Gospel descriptions are not Jesus-centered. In the Synoptics, Jesus talks about God and not himself; only in passing is the explicit identity of Jesus an issue (→ Jesus, 78:29ff.). The requirements imposed by the Synoptic Jesus on those who are interested in his proclamation (Mark 10:17–22) include no overt stance about his identity. Only in the postresurrectional period will the confession of "the name of Jesus" be required (and the Gospel of John sees the ministry in this light). If scholars have difficulty in identifying Jesus as belonging to a known sect of the Jews (Pharisees, Sadducees, Essenes, Zealots; → Jesus, 78:24), it is not surprising that those who during his lifetime accepted his proclamation of the kingdom of God—a much more accurate designation than "Jesus movement"—do not fit easily into a recognized historical or sociological pattern.

10   **(II) The Apostolic Period: *ca.* 30–66.**
    (A) The Community and Its Life.   Granted that Jesus showed little interest in a formally distinct society, it is remarkable how quickly the Christians became community-minded. Although Acts 19:1–5 indicates that there were followers of Jesus who had not received Christian baptism, the unanimity of Matt, Acts, Paul, and John suggests that this baptism very quickly became a standard feature of Christian life. As a visible action it helped to designate those who "belonged"—a verifiable indication singularly absent from Jesus' ministry. The wide distribution of the term *koinōnia*,

"community," "communion," in the NT shows that those who were baptized felt very strongly that they had much in common (→ 11–14 below). Indeed, *koinōnia* may reflect in Greek an early Semitic name for the Christian group, like the Qumran self-designation as *Yaḥad,* "the oneness," "unity," (→ Apocrypha 67:83). Another early name may have been "the Way," e.g., Acts 24:14: "According to the Way . . . I worship the God of our Fathers" (also Acts 9:2; 19:9,23; 22:4; 24:22; cf. 16:17; 18:25–26). This was also a Qumran self-designation: "When these people join the community [*Yaḥad*] in Israel, they . . . go into the wilderness to prepare the way of the Lord" (1QS 8:12–14). Followers of JBap who came to believe in Jesus may have brought along this ideology associated with their master's movement (all four Gospels), which in turn reflected the idealism of the return of Israel from exile (Isa 40:3), the second exodus, when Israel came along the way prepared by God to his promised land. The designation that became the most popular, i.e., *ekklēsia,* "church," plausibly reflects the first exodus, in which Israel came into being, for in Deut 23:2 the LXX rendered *qāhāl,* "assembly," by *ekklēsia* to describe Israel in the desert as "the church of the Lord." Paul would use "the church of God" to remind regional Christian communities that they were patterned on and imitative of the church in Judea. Thus, just as in the case of "the Twelve," so also the various terms of early Christian self-understanding reflect continuity with Israel. And that may be the original symbolism of the Pentecost theme in Acts 2 as well, because we know that among some Jews this feast (Weeks) celebrated the renewal of the Sinai covenant; and at Qumran it was the occasion of the entry of new members into the community. The tradition reflected in Acts portrays that, amid Sinai-like wind and fire, God renewed his covenant for Israel, a covenant now intimately based on what he had done in Jesus of Nazareth.

11   The life pattern of the Christian *koinōnia* also showed a strong heritage from Israel. Acts 2:42 mentions some features. (1) *Prayer:* Jews who came to believe in Jesus continued to say prayers they had known previously. When Mark (12:29) wrote, the primacy of the basic Jewish prayer, the *Shema* ("Hear O Israel, the Lord our God, the Lord is one"), was still being inculcated, even for Gentiles. Early Christian hymns such as the Magnificat and the Benedictus (Luke 1:46–55,68–79) were very similar to the Qumran hymns as a pastiche of OT references. Indeed, while the Benedictus celebrates what God has now done ("the daystar has dawned from on high to give light to those who sit in darkness"), the context speaks of David, Abraham, and the prophets, rather than christologically of Jesus as do the later hymns (Phil 2:5–11; Col 1:15–20; John 1:1–18). The Lord's Prayer also echoes petitions of synagogue prayers.

12   (2) *Breaking bread:* Acts portrays early Christians like Peter and John as going frequently, or even daily, to the Temple to pray at the regular hours (2:46; 3:1; 5:12,21). There seems little reason to doubt this information, which implies that the first Jews to believe in Jesus saw no rupture in their ordinary worship pattern. The "breaking of bread," presumably the eucharist, was in addition to and not in place of the sacrifices and worship of Israel. Paul, writing in the mid-50s (1 Cor 11:23–26), mentions a eucharistic pattern that was handed on to him (presumably, therefore, from the 30s) and says, "As often as you eat this bread and drink this cup, you proclaim the Lord's death until he comes." The recalling of the Lord's death *may* echo the Jewish Passover re-presentation (Hebr *zikkārôn,* Gk *anamnēsis*), making present again the great salvific act, now shifted from the exodus to the crucifixion/resurrection. The "until he comes" also echoes a Jewish outlook. In the sacred meal at Qumran there was a place left vacant for the messiah in case God should raise him up during the meal (→ Apocrypha, 67:84). (The dynamism of the "new" among these "old" elements may be the relation of the eucharist to the meals at which the *risen* Jesus showed himself present [Luke 24:30,41; John 21:9-13; Mark 16:14], so that they recognized him in the breaking of the bread [Luke 24:35].) Indeed, a Jewish pattern may also have affected the time of the Christian eucharist. Undoubtedly, the discovery of the empty tomb early Sunday morning helped to fix the Christian attention on what by the end of the 1st cent. would be known as "the Lord's Day" (*Did.* 14:1; *Gos. Pet.* 12:50); but the Sunday motif may have been aided by the pattern of the Jewish sabbath, which ended at sundown on Saturday. Before sundown Jews who believed in Jesus did not have extensive freedom of motion, but when the sabbath was over (Saturday evening) they would have been free to come a distance to assemble in the house of another believer to break the bread. This may explain why the ancient Christian memory is of a celebration on the night between Saturday and Sunday.

13 (3) *Teaching (Didachē) of the apostles:* Authoritative for all Jews were the Scriptures, in particular the Law and the Prophets (→ Canonicity, 66:22-29); this would have been true for the first followers of Jesus as well. Thus, early Christian teaching would for the most part have been Jewish teaching (a fact often overlooked by those who search out NT theology or ethics: the points of unique importance mentioned in the NT are like the tip of an iceberg, the bulk of which is the unmentioned, presupposed teaching of Israel). Points where Jesus modified or differed from the law or from the Pharisee interpretation of the law were remembered and became the nucleus of a special teaching. As they passed this on, the Christian preachers would have made their own application to situations that Jesus had not encountered; and the Jesus content in the teaching would have been expanded by apostolic teaching. (See the example of two instructions on marriage, one from the Lord and one from Paul, in 1 Cor 7:10,12; and the expansion of Jesus' Temple saying in Mark 14:58: "Made with hands . . . not made with hands"—absent from pars.) This teaching of Jesus and of the apostles, while secondary to the teaching of the Jewish Scriptures, was more authoritative in regard to the restricted points it touched. When such teaching was eventually committed to writing, those writings had within themselves the possibility of becoming a second set of sacred Scriptures (the NT). This canon-forming process was especially sharp in the late 2d cent. (→ Canonicity, 66:58, 65). In a sense, a similar process in Judaism produced the Mishna, a second teaching alongside the Scriptures (→ Apocrypha, 67:136), so that by the end of the 2d cent. both those who believed in Jesus and Jews who did not had written supplements to the Law and the Prophets. The different characters of the two writings reflect essential differences in the respective religious focus.

14 (4) *Common goods:* An important aspect of koinōnia in Acts 2:44-45; 5:1-6 was a voluntary sharing of goods among the members of the community. While Lucan idealism probably exaggerates in referring to "all goods," the fact that there were common goods at Qumran shows that the picture is plausible for an eschatologically-minded Jewish community. Moreover, shared goods among Jerusalem Christians is indirectly confirmed by the Pauline references to the poor in Jerusalem for whom he was collecting money (Rom 15:26; Gal 2:10; 1 Cor 16:1-3). This idealism of common goods had some important ramifications. It increased intracommunity dependence, making defection less likely. It also bound communities together, as one had to support the other. A Christian ethic developed of giving up goods for the poor and of condemning wealth as an obstacle (Luke 1:53; 6:24; Mark 10:23; 2 Cor 8:9; Jas 5:1). Finally, a competent and just administration of (common) goods would be an issue in Christian communities and, later, a requirement imposed on Christian community leaders (1 Pet 5:2; 1 Tim 3:4-5).

15 **(B) Diversity within the Community.** Indeed, administration of common goods was the occasion of the first recorded dispute within the Christian community, i.e., between the Hebrews and the Hellenists in Acts 6:1-6, a scene that surely has a historical substratum since it runs against Luke's tendency to stress one-mindedness (Acts 4:32). While not overly clear, the Acts' designation Hellenists (Greek-like) and the Gk names of the seven Hellenist leaders (6:5) suggest that these were Jews (or in one case a proselyte) who spoke (only?) Greek and were raised acculturated to the Greco-Roman civilization. The Hebrews, then, would have spoken Aramaic or Hebrew as well and have been more traditionally Jewish in outlook. (Paul considered himself a Hebrew [2 Cor 11:22; Phil 3:5] in his strict preconversion behavior as a Jew, whether or not the designation "Hebrew" meant the same for him as for Luke.) Jews of both Hebrew and Hellenist backgrounds had come to believe in Jesus and were now quarreling, perhaps because the Hellenists rejected Temple worship (Acts 7:48-50), whereas the Hebrews, who included the Twelve, were very faithful to the Temple (→ 12 above). In any case, the Hebrews were attempting to force the Hellenists to conformity by shutting off common funds from the Hellenist widows, who presumably were totally dependent on these for support. The description of the meeting that dealt with the question (the "multitude" convened by the Twelve) corresponds very well to the Qumran community meeting of the "many" and the 12 (plus three representing the priestly families; → Apocrypha, 67:110). The sociological situation (increase in Christian numbers [Acts 6:1], disputes among Christians) was certain to make the outcome of this meeting highly significant for the future. Pluralism was accepted, since the Hellenists were neither forced into conformity nor expelled from the koinōnia. Implicitly, cultural and theological differences that existed between the Hebrews and the Hellenists must have been deemed less important than their common belief in Jesus (→ 18 below for other confirmations of this picture). True to their symbolic role for all Israel (→ 8 above), the Twelve refused to get involved in the administration of goods (6:2). Rather, the Hellenists were given their own administrators, i.e., the seven (who are not to be considered deacons—their function would be closer to that of the later presbyter-bishops). Probably administrators also emerged in the Hebrew Christian community at the same time; for in subsequent references in Acts (12:17; 15:4,22; 21:18) James the brother of the Lord and the elders are portrayed as authorities in Jerusalem. While it is difficult to know whether Acts is historical in all these details, surely administrative structure emerged as an answer to problems like divisions and increased numbers—a development that in NT thought was no contradiction to seeing such structure as part of God's guidance through the Spirit for the church in response to prayer (6:6).

16 The decision to preserve pluralism within the Christian koinōnia affected the missionary thrust of the group. Acts 5:34-40 indicates that, although at first the Twelve were persecuted by the Sanhedrin authorities, eventually they won a grudging tolerance (esp. in the eyes of the Pharisees personified by Luke in the famous Gamaliel [the elder]). This picture gets indirect confirmation from Paul, who seems to have been able to go to Jerusalem in the 30s and in the 40s and find James and Peter there without any hint of persecution. Presumably, the fact that there were different sects of the Jews in pre-70 Palestine as indicated by Josephus (→ History, 75:145–51) enabled the Christians to find a certain tolerance even if they did not consider themselves a sect (Acts 24:14). In any case, in Jerusalem between the mid-30s and the mid-60s (when James was killed) the only recorded overall persecution of Christians by Jews who did not believe in Jesus was under Herod Agrippa I in the early 40s (12:1–5), a short interval when Judea was no longer ruled by Roman prefects. The persecution that broke out over Stephen (*ca.* 36?) described in 7:54–8:1 was a selective persecution of Hellenists, not of Hebrew Christians, and therefore presumably was motivated less by belief in Jesus than by Stephen's attack on the Temple. (There is nothing historically implausible in this, for the Jerusalem priests had a history of intolerance toward those who threatened the Temple.) This persecution caused the Hellenists to leave Jerusalem for Samaria (where they converted many Samaritans: Acts 8:4–5) and for Antioch (where they converted Gentiles: 11:19–20). The picture in Acts whereby there was no outgoing Christian mission till the expulsion of the Hellenists from Jerusalem is probably too simple; indeed, 9:2 implies that there were Christians in Damascus even before the expulsion. Nevertheless, in some details, the Acts picture is plausible, e.g., that the widespread mission resulted from unforeseen circumstances rather than from a blueprint plan of going to the whole world, that the acceptance to the *koinōnia* of non-Jews (Samaritans and Gentiles) provoked concern and even dissent among the Christians of Jerusalem (8:14; 11:2–3), and that ultimately the debate about the conversion of whole groups of Gentiles brought a showdown among the most famous Christian spokesmen. These included Cephas/Peter, the first among the Twelve; James, the brother of the Lord and the main authority in the Jerusalem community; and Paul, the apostle to the Gentiles (→ Paul, 79:31–37 for the Jerusalem debate). By the late 40s, the Gentile issue had produced at least four different attitudes within the Christian *koinōnia*, reflecting theological differences—attitudes attested in various NT witnesses.

17   (1) There may have been Jewish Christians so insistent on the importance of being observant Jews that they wished no Gentile converts. But the NT attests rather a willingness of the very conservative (Christian Pharisees or the circumcision party: Acts 11:2; 15:5) to convert Gentiles to Christianity provided they first became Jews, i.e., the males were circumcised. Their missionaries moved outside Jerusalem (15:1,24; Gal; Phil 3), often causing trouble for missionaries like Paul who did not demand circumcision for conversion. Perhaps they appealed to the example of Jesus, who never spoke against circumcision, and surely they argued from the example of Abraham, who was required to submit to circumcision as part of receiving the covenant. (2) Peter (Acts 10:47–48; 15:6–11) and James (15:13–29) agreed with Paul that the Gentiles should be converted without circumcision, but (at least on occasion) they insisted on Gentile observance of certain Jewish purity laws, esp. with regard to food (15:20,29; Gal 2:12). Seemingly, this stance prevailed in the churches of the Palestine-Syria area (Acts 15:23). (3) Paul bitterly resisted this imposition of demands of the law on Christian Gentiles as impugning the freedom of the gospel (Gal 2:14–21) and had no such requirement in the churches he had founded, like Corinth (1 Cor 8:1–13). It is important, however, to note that Paul's statements rejecting the imposition of circumcision and the food laws pertain to *Gentile* converts; nowhere does he express his views of the demands to be made on Jews who believe in Jesus. Acts 16:3 has Paul insist on the circumcision of Timothy, who had a Jewish mother and thus could be considered Jewish. According to Acts 20:16; 21:26; 24:11 Paul kept the feast of Pentecost/Weeks and went to the Jerusalem Temple. If these details are accurate, Paul may have allowed the possibility that for Jewish believers in Jesus there was enduring religious value in the Jewish cult—an outlook at least consonant with Rom 9–11, e.g., 9:4. (4) The Hellenist opposition to the Temple expressed in Stephen's speech (Acts 7:47–51) at least incipiently implies a break with the institutions of Judaism more severe than what is demonstrable in the attitudes of Jesus or of Paul. After AD 65, this radicalism came to fruition in the outlook of Heb, which regards the levitical priesthood and the sacrifices as no longer meaningful: the new covenant has rendered the first obsolete and ready to vanish (Heb 8:13). Much of the same attitude is found in John, where Jesus is the spokesman of alienation from Judaism (15:25: "their law"). Inevitably this led to overt hostility toward Judaism (8:44; Rev 3:9).

18   The four different outlooks listed above (and different tonalities within them) could be found among Jews who believed in Jesus in the period before 65. Since all these Jews made Gentile converts, the oft-used designation Jewish Christianity and Gentile Christianity does not effectively differentiate attitudes toward the Jewish law and cult in this period. On the whole, Gentile Christians would have shared the attitude of the respective Jewish Christians who converted them. (Of course, after a while, Gentile converts might develop Christian strains of their own in the light of their peculiar background; but the stance taken on the relationship between belief in Jesus and the observance of the Jewish law was not simply a matter of Gentile vs. Jew.) It is remarkable that the Christian *koinōnia* seems to have withstood this wide range of differences. Acts 6 bears witness that the Hellenists were not expelled from the *koinōnia* even if given their own administrators; Acts 8:14 has the Twelve in Jerusalem (who were Hebrews) showing concern for the Hellenist mission. Even though Paul demeans James and Cephas/Peter as so-called pillars who were of no importance to him (Gal 2:6,9), they certainly showed concern about his views and mission. After dispute, they extended to him and Barnabas the right hand of *koinōnia* (2:9). If subsequently Paul opposes Peter and the men from Jerusalem face to face for the truth of the gospel (2:11–14), this rhetoric does not imply broken *koinōnia;* for two or three years later in the context of Corinthian Christians forming separate parties, Paul cites Cephas and James, declaring solidarity with them about the gospel: "Whether it was I or they, so we preach, and so you believed" (1 Cor 15:5,7,11; see also the solidarity implied in 9:5). We have already mentioned Paul's collection of money for the Jerusalem church of James to stress the *koinōnia* of his Gentile churches with the churches of God in Palestine, which they are encouraged to imitate (1 Thess 2:14). It is not apparent in this early period that even group 1 (→ 17 above) was expelled from the *koinōnia* despite Paul's anathema against proclaimers of another gospel (Gal 1:9) and rhetoric against "false brothers" (2:4). They were present at the Jerusalem meeting in AD 49, and part of the reason for Paul's description of that meeting in Gal 2 is that they were claiming unanimity with James and Peter. Moreover, a chain of references from *1 Clem.* 5:2–7 through Ign. *Rom.* 4:3 to 2 Pet 3:15 shows no memory of a permanent break of *koinōnia* between Peter and Paul. One can scarcely dismiss all this evidence as later harmonizing idealism.

19   The picture given thus far of Christianity before 65 is highly apostolic (a term wider than the Twelve; → NT Thought, 81:154), for the Gospels, Acts, and Paul all indicate the importance of apostles as a group or as individuals in this formative period. Was there a wider early Christianity not influenced by the apostles known to us? In fact, we have little evidence about whole areas reached by the Christian mission. Who first brought Christianity to Damascus (Acts 9:2), to Alexandria (Acts 18:24–25), to Rome (Rom 1:8), and to all the points lying E of Jerusalem? Does Acts 2:9–11 retain a memory of a Jerusalem-church mission (as distinct from the Antioch-church missions known to us in Paul and in Acts 13ff.)? Despite the lack of evidence, scholars have posited a Galilean Christianity distinct from Jerusalem Christianity, and bands of wandering preachers proclaiming Jesus in less-structured situations than those evidenced in Acts and Paul. Texts like Mark 9:38–41 and Acts 19:1–3 indicate that there was a proclamation of Jesus beyond what is known to us directly in the NT books. Good sense, however, warns against elevating this unknown Christianity as the norm and seeing the NT as a conspiracy to eliminate memories of a purer following of Jesus.

20   Above (→ 15) we saw one account of the emergence of structure through the appointment of Hellenist administrators (Acts 6:5). Once again, working more on suspicion than on evidence, scholars have painted a picture of an early egalitarian "Jesus movement" gradually becoming more patriarchally authoritative in developing churches. That there was a development in articulating structure cannot be denied. Moreover, Jesus' proclamation of the kingdom of God certainly broke down some of the social and religious barriers of his time for those who accepted the proclamation. Yet his nonstructural approach (→ 8 above) implies a disinterestedness in overthrowing existing institutions rather than a plan to construct egalitarian groups (an idea closer to the French Revolution than to the NT). Paul, too, saw Christianity breaking down barriers between Jew and Greek, slave and free, male and female (Gal 3:28); but at the same time his first letter (1 Thess 5:12: the oldest preserved Christian document) has a demand to respect "those who are over you in the Lord"—scarcely an egalitarian designation. There was a diversity of functions in the early Pauline churches (Phil 1:1: "overseers and deacons"; 1 Cor 12:28: numerous charisms) but nothing to support an egalitarianism where anybody or everybody could play any or every role. The nondifferentiation of Gal 3:28 is in relation to baptismal newness of life in the eyes of God (cf. 1 Cor 12:13); it did not lead to nondifferentiation in church and family (1 Cor 11; 12:4–11). Evidently the first Christians did not interpret equality as many today would interpret equality; however, that does not prevent a development in the Christian understanding and appreciation of equality.

21   **(III) The Subapostolic and Postapostolic Periods: after 65.**   The above survey of the church in the period AD 30–65 is necessarily sketchy; but many issues discussed there took a notably different turn in the last third of the 1st cent. (subapostolic period) and the early 2d cent. (postapostolic).

(A) The Great Transition.   By AD 65 the three best-known figures of the early church (James, Peter, and Paul) had died as martyrs respectively in Jerusalem and Rome. Our documentation for the years 65–100 gives few new names for Christian leaders.

Rather, there is a tendency to wear the mantle of the deceased apostles and to speak in their name (whence "subapostolic"), indicating implicitly what they would have said to a new generation. For instance, if Col, Eph, and the Pastorals were written after Paul's death, each writer continues to speak in Paul's name. The oldest Gospel bears no name but by the 2d cent. there was a tradition attributing it to (John) Mark, a companion of Peter and Paul, with the contention that it reflects Peter's preaching. It is doubtful that Matthew, one of the Twelve, or Luke, a disciple of Paul, wrote the Gospels attributed to them; but these Gospels preserve apostolic tradition. The Fourth Gospel specifically claims to contain eyewitness tradition from the unnamed disciple whom Jesus loved—a disciple who is presented as outpointing even the Peter lionized by so many late 1st-cent. Christians. The epistles of Jas, Pet, and Jude may also be examples of subapostolic trajectories (→ Canonicity, 66:71–72, 74–75). The ecclesiastical thrust of the subapostolic period is now less missionary (fishing) and more pastoral (shepherding), as the care for the ongoing communities founded between the 30s and the 60s becomes a major concern. This development is illustrated in an emphasis on shepherd imagery for Peter and Paul (1 Pet 5:1–4; John 21:15–17; Acts 20:28–30).

22   Another internal transition in Christianity was from Jewish to Gentile dominance. Before 65, known leaders were Jews. After 100, when new names become prominent (Ignatius, Polycarp) seemingly many of them were not. In the 65–100 period, probably the majority in Christianity changed from Jews to Gentiles. The destruction of Jerusalem by the Romans had the side effect that the Jerusalem church no longer had its pre-65 central role evident in Acts and even in Paul (Gal 1–2; the collection). If Acts 15:23 describes Jerusalem in AD 49 as speaking to the Christians of Antioch, Syria, and Cilicia, by the late 1st cent. the church of Rome speaks to the Christians of N Asia Minor and Corinth (1 Pet 1:1; *1 Clem.*) and is preeminent in love (Ign. *Rom.* Preface). While there were large Jewish colonies in Rome and other major Christian centers such as Antioch and Ephesus, none of these cities personified Judaism in the way Jerusalem had. Accordingly, less attention was given to converting Jews to belief in Christ, at least in the documentation preserved. If in the late 50s Paul (Rom 11:11–16) could have hoped for the full inclusion of Israel ("my fellow Jews"), in the 80s or 90s the Paul of Lucan memory proclaims as his last words that this people shall understand nor perceive; rather, salvation has been sent to the Gentiles who will listen (Acts 28:25–28). There is still an occasional voice of idealism that the wall of hostility has been broken down (Eph 2:13–16), but increasingly dominant is a polemic against "the synagogue of Satan" (Rev 2:9; 3:9) and the Jews whose father is the devil (→ 17 above, under [4]).

23   This was not simply an internal Christian development; Judaism had also undergone a transition. The Jewish revolt against Rome in the late 60s (→ History, 75:181–184) did not get uniform support within Judaism, for the Pharisees were more reluctant to engage in violence than the Zealots. *Seemingly* the Jewish Christians refused entirely to join the revolt and withdrew across the Jordan to Pella (M. Simon, "La migration à Pella: Légende ou réalité?" in *Judéo-Christianisme* [Fest. J. Daniélou; Paris, 1972] 37–54). One can surmise that such a dissociation from the national cause furthered alienation between Jews who did not believe in Jesus and Jews who did. The threat to Jewish religious identity caused by the destruction of the Temple and the end of priestly sacrifices served to limit Jewish pluralism. The Essenes of Qumran and their settlement perished in the war (→ Apocrypha, 67:104); the Sadducee priest leaders suffered a loss of status. While it is generally affirmed that the Pharisees became the rabbis of Jamnia (→ History, 75:189), that may be too simple a picture. By etymology a Pharisee was a sectarian separatist (→ History, 75:146); and the pre-70 period saw sharp hostility among the Jewish sectarians to the point of the high priest's killing Pharisees and seeking to kill the Essene leader, and extreme vituperation of the Jerusalem priests by the Essenes. If after 70 the general Pharisee respect for the oral law (→ Apocrypha, 67:134) had become victorious among the rabbis of Jamnia, the sectarian separatism of the Pharisees was gone; and there was an internal pluralism for debating the law *within the rabbinic guidelines* (see S. J. D. Cohen, *HUCA* 55 [1984] 27–53). The Essenes and the Sadducees were relegated to unpleasant memories.

24   Sometime between 85 and 130 the rabbinic distaste for sectarians (*mînîm*) was enshrined by a curse against them introduced into synagogue prayer (the expanded 12th of the Eighteen Benedictions). Since Jewish Christians were considered among the *mînîm*, gradually they were excluded from synagogue worship. Often this is erroneously portrayed as an excommunication edict from Jamnia; in fact it must have been a spreading practice dependent on how numerous and assertive, and thus apparently sectarian, the Jewish Christians were in a given local synagogue. The Johannine community with its proclamation of Jesus as "my Lord and my God" (John 20:28) may have been among the first to provoke exclusion by the synagogue authorities, to whom this proclamation would have sounded as if a human being were being elevated to a status that challenged the only "creed" of Israel: "The Lord our God is one" (Deut 6:4). The Johannine answer was that Jesus was not a man who was being "made" God (John 5:16–19; 10:33–38) but rather a Son whom the Father loved and to whom the Father gave all things (5:20–23), to the point that whoever saw him saw the Father (14:9). This answer would scarcely have satisfied the synagogue authorities. They were disciples of Moses, and the Christians were the disciples of Jesus; the synagogue authorities knew God had spoken to Moses, and they did not know where "that fellow" came from (9:28–29). Accordingly, those Johannine Christians who confessed Jesus were thrown out of the synagogue (9:22,34; 12:42), with the result that the Johannine Christians understood themselves as being killed (16:2). Was this a direct killing of Christians by Jewish authorities or indirect in the sense that, without the umbrella of the synagogue and being acknowledged as Jews (who were excused from the duty of Roman civil worship of the gods), the expelled Christians were now exposed to Roman investigation and persecution for being atheists? Certainly the latter situation is apparent in *Letter 96* of Pliny, a governor in Bithynia (*ca.* AD 112), writing shortly after John.

25   With its adherents made unwelcome in synagogues and gradually becoming more Gentile by percentage, Christianity now more clearly appeared as a new religion. The religious institutions of Israel were regarded as finished (in themselves and for Christians). What was permanently worthwhile was simply taken over as pertaining to Christians, not to "unbelieving Jews." 1 Pet 2:9–10 tells Gentile Christian readers: "You are a chosen race, a royal priesthood, a holy nation, God's own people"—titular privileges of Israel in the OT. By the end of the 1st cent. the eucharist was beginning to take the place of the sacrifices of Israel—a Christian pure oblation magnifying God's name among the Gentiles as "foretold" by Mal 1:11 (*Did.* 14:3). *1 Clem.* 40:5; 42 compares the high priest, priest, and levite to

Christ, the bishop, and the deacon. *Barn.* 4:6–7 states that the covenant is "ours not theirs"; they lost it; indeed Christians are God's new people (7:5). The ultimate in replacing Judaism will be Marcion in mid-2d cent., who will reject the Jewish Scriptures and their God and accept as his Scriptures only those Christian writings that he can interpret as repudiating the OT (10 Pauline letters; Luke—without the infancy narrative). His views will be rejected by the larger church as extreme to the point of heresy (→ 81 below).

26   Yet there were also Jewish believers in Jesus who did not go this route of alienation. The Christian Pharisee strain (→ 17 above) did not disappear with the destruction of Jerusalem; indeed, it is possible that the movement to Pella (→ 23 above) helped to preserve a vibrant element of Jewish Christianity. In the literature of AD 65–95, Matt is a Gospel that moves from the earthly Jesus' mission involving only the lost sheep of the house of Israel (10:6) to the risen Jesus' mission to all nations (28:19). Yet the Matthean Jesus is remembered as stressing every "jot and tittle" of the law (5:18) and the observance of what the Pharisees and the scribes say because they "sit on the chair of Moses" (23:2–3)—an indication that the Christian Pharisee mindset was still a factor with a voice. Paul stood against the imposition of the law on Gentile Christians: "A human being is justified by faith apart from the works of the Law" (Rom 3:28). But Jas 2:24 shows how Jewish Christians would correct this slogan (perhaps misrepresented to them): "A human being is justified by works and not by faith alone." Even if "faith" and "works" do not have the same meaning in the two affirmations, a different outlook is obvious. The best evidence for an ongoing Christianity loyal to the institutions of Judaism is found in the *Pseudo-Clementines*, a 4th-cent. work with 2d-cent. sources (see F. S. Jones, *Second Century* 2 [1982] 1–33, 63–96). The 2d-cent. element reflects the Christianity of those who claim that their belief in Jesus as the prophet whom Moses predicted and as the eternal Messiah is the *only* "difference between us who believe in Jesus over against the Jews who do not believe" (*Recog.* 1.43.1–2). For them Paul was an enemy responsible for the failure of the mission to the Jews (1.71.3–5), whereas "our James" (the brother of the Lord) was ordained by the Lord himself (1.43.2) and was "bishop of bishops who rules Jerusalem, the holy church of the Hebrews, and the churches everywhere" (*Letter from Clement to James*). When one looks at the extreme anti-Jewish developments (or distortions) of the Pauline trajectory and the extreme anti-Pauline elements of the James trajectory, it is interesting that Peter is portrayed as a friend to each group (e.g., 2 Pet 3:15–16; *Pseudo-Clem., passim*). If in his lifetime Peter stood somewhere between Paul and James and was criticized by both as not sufficiently purist (Gal 2:11–14), the Petrine trajectory in the 2d cent. carried on the image of a bridge figure.

27   **(B) Different Emphases in Late NT Ecclesiology.** We have seen that the passing of the great apostles in the 60s, the destruction of Jerusalem, and the increasing separation from Judaism produced various Christian reactions. Now let us turn to some specific attitudes in the subapostolic and postapostolic periods that would enduringly shape later ecclesiology. Space requirements confine what follows to description, not evaluation. (For the latter see Brown, *Churches*.)

(a) REGULARIZED CHURCH STRUCTURE. Although there was incipient church structure in the pre-65 period (→ 15, 20 above), it was neither uniform nor greatly emphasized. The post-Pauline Pastorals make it a leitmotif. In a setting where the apostle is disappearing from the scene (2 Tim 4:6–7) and false teachers are making an appearance (1 Tim 4:1ff.; Tit 1:10–13; 2 Tim 3:1–9; 4:3–4), the remedy is regularized church order. *Presbyteroi* (presbyters, elders) are to be appointed in every town and they are to have the *episkopos* function (bishop, overseer, supervisor). Certainly that includes checking the religious and ethical behavior of community members, caring for the needy out of common goods, and above all ensuring sound doctrine. They are to hold on to what they received (Tit 1:5–9), correcting false teachers. Thus they constitute a chain preserving apostolic teaching and authority. The virtues demanded of the presbyter/bishops are "institutional" (to be sensible, dignified, temperate), so as to make them both models for the community (able to manage their own household; married no more than once; having well-behaved Christian children; not recent converts) and examples of respectability to outsiders (not drunken, nor violent, nor lovers of money). Deacons are also part of the structure, subject to most of the same requirements; yet we are not clear as to what deacons did as distinct from presbyters. As for women, seemingly there were women deacons (not simply the wives of male deacons: 1 Tim 3:11) and an official class of widows (1 Tim 5:3–16). It is not clear whether there were women presbyters (see Brown, *Critical Meaning* 141). Yet one of the most important functions of the presbyter/bishops was to rule and teach (1 Tim 5:17–18), and no woman was permitted to have authority over or to teach men (1 Tim 2:12).

28 While the post-Pauline Pastorals have Titus, an apostolic delegate and Pauline companion, appointing presbyter/bishops (Tit 1:5), almost contemporaneously *Did.* 15:1–2 urges Christians, "Appoint for yourselves bishops and deacons" to take the place of the older charismatic structure of apostles, prophets, and teachers (cf. 1 Cor 12:28). Itinerant prophets and apostles have become a source of trouble and are unverifiable (*Did.* 11:1–12), and so a more regulated and controllable structure is needed. (See also a distrust in the 90s of false apostles and prophets in Rev 2:2,20.) *1 Clem.* 42 canonizes the regularity of presbyter/bishops and deacons by giving them a very clear pedigree: God sent Jesus Christ; Jesus Christ sent the apostles; the apostles appointed their first converts to be bishops and deacons; and these functionaries appointed other bishops and deacons to succeed them in the ministry (44:1). Accordingly, such ministers were not to be removed (44:3). Although *1 Clem.* speaks of liturgy and sacrifices with relation to the episcopate, sacramental activity for this regularized clergy becomes clear in the writings of Ignatius, *ca.* 110. He insists that only the bishop or his appointee is to celebrate the eucharist and to baptize (*Smyrn.* 8). Another development in Ignatius is a threefold ministry so that in each church there is only one bishop, and under him presbyters and deacons, whereas in the previous examples discussed above there was a twofold ministry of presbyter/bishops and deacons. We do not know how the practice of having only one bishop developed, but Ignatius's insistence suggests that it may have been a recent innovation not universally accepted. By exception he does not mention a sole bishop in writing to Rome, and plausibly that practice did not develop in the church of Rome before AD 140–150 (see *Herm. Vis.* 2.4.2; *Sim.* 9.27.2). A slower acceptance of the monepiscopate would be consonant with Rome's reluctance about innovations (see Brown, *Antioch and Rome* 214). In any case, by the end of the 2d cent., the threefold structure became universal in the church. Writing in that circumstance, Irenaeus (*Adv. Haer.* 3.3.3) gives a list of the "bishops" of Rome, anachronistically using his understanding of the designation for figures of the earlier period who were probably the most prominent among the plurality of presbyter/bishops, e.g., Clement. The term "priest" began to be used for the 2d-cent. bishop because he presided at the eucharist (→ 25 above), and with that term some of the OT ideology of the Israelite priesthood was reinstated in Christianity (see Brown, *Priest* 16–19).

29 (b) IDEALIZING THE CHURCH. We have seen (→ 10 above) that the early Jewish Christians understood themselves as the renewal of Israel, so that there was a unified concept at the beginning. Nevertheless, in the period 35–65 the most frequent use of *ekklēsia* was for a local church, sometimes in a region (1 Cor 1:2; 16:1,19), sometimes in a house when there were several house-churches in a region (Rom 16:5,14,15). Yet a passage like 1 Cor 12:28 indicates that there was a more universal usage as well. In the last third of the cent., this universal usage becomes very frequent; see Acts 9:31; Matt 16:18; and the female symbols in Rev 12:4–5; 19:7; 21:9. Nowhere is it more apparent than in Col and Eph, where it dominates completely. For Eph 2:19–20 the church is "the household of God built upon the foundation of apostles and prophets with Christ Jesus himself being the chief cornerstone." The church is the kingdom of God's beloved Son free from the dominion of darkness, in which Christians share the inheritance of the holy ones in light (Col 1:12–13). Most often the church is identified with the body of Christ (Col 1:18,24; Eph 4:15–16), "the fullness of him who fills all in all" (Eph 1:22–23). The church is the spotless bride whom Christ loved and for whom he gave himself (Eph 5:23–27). Col 1:24 has "Paul" continue this: "What is lacking in Christ's afflictions I complete in my flesh for the sake of his body which is the church." Clearly, the church has moved to center stage in Christian activity and thought. Christ has made known "the plan of the mystery hidden for ages in God who created all things, that through the church the manifold wisdom of God might now be made known" (Eph 3:9–10; → Pauline Theology, 82:134–35).

30 (c) THE SPIRIT GUIDING THE CHURCH. Acts places little emphasis on church structure and does not identify the church as the body of Christ. Rather, it offers a view of history in which God's Spirit promised by Jesus (1:4–5) guides the Christian community every step of the way. Peter and Paul and other human actors in the decisions of Christian history are but instruments of the Spirit. The crucial Pentecost scene employs the creational image of the wind as the Spirit of God (Gen 1:2) to describe a renewal of the covenant that will now affect all peoples. Receiving the Spirit is part of the baptismal entry into the *koinōnia* of believers (Acts 2:38; 8:15–17; 9:17; 15:8; 19:5–6). The Spirit directs new steps in the mission as Samaritans and Gentiles are converted (8:29,39; 10:38,44–47; 11:12,15; 13:2,4). When the great decision pertinent to the Gentiles is taken at Jerusalem in the presence of Paul, Peter, and James, that decision is phrased thus: "It has seemed good to the Holy Spirit and to us" (15:28). In steps significant for the spread of Christianity, the Spirit prevents Paul from taking a detour that would have delayed his planting Christianity in Europe (16:6–7); Paul's decision that he must go to Rome is a resolve in the Spirit (19:21); and when Paul bids farewell to Asia, the Holy Spirit has been provident by making presbyters who are overseers (bishops) of the flock (20:28). Thus, every essential step in the Acts' story of how witness was borne to Christ from Jerusalem to the end of the earth is guided by the Spirit, whose presence becomes obvious at the great moments where human agents would otherwise be hesitant or choose wrongly.

31   (d) DISCIPLESHIP ANIMATED BY CHRIST. In the subapostolic period, constitutive imagery of Jesus as the builder, founder, or cornerstone of the church is frequent (Matt 16:18; Eph 2:20; 1 Pet 2:4–8). Such imagery is singularly absent from John, which favors animated imagery like the vine and the branches (15:2–6) to portray Jesus not as a past founder, but as a living presence, still "alive and well" among Christians. Nor are there instituting formulas about baptism and the eucharist comparable to the parting statements of Jesus in Matt 28:19 and Luke 22:19. Rather, baptismal and eucharistic hints are associated with the signs of Jesus' ministry like the opening of the eyes of the blind (John 9) and the multiplication of the loaves (John 6), and conversations of Jesus about water (3:5; 4:10,13–14). For John, during Jesus' lifetime, those signs and conversations had to be understood not only of earthly, visible data but primarily of heavenly realities that he had brought to earth. After the ministry, Jesus continues to make present these realities in the church through the water and bread signs of baptism and the eucharist. As God's Son he has God's life (6:57); he gives that life to all who believe in him in a birth of water and Spirit, and he nourishes that life through the food and drink of his flesh and blood. (If for Paul the eucharist instituted at the Last Supper recalls the death of the Lord until he comes [1 Cor 11:23–26], for John the eucharist, never mentioned at the Last Supper, is primarily the food of eternal life.)

32   The gift of life is the really important element for Christians; John shows no interest in a diversity of church functions or charisms. On the vine all are branches if they get life. If one thinks of a Christian structure of apostles, prophets, and teachers (1 Cor 12:28), neither Johannine Gospel nor Epistles mention apostles or true prophets, and there is a specific denial of the need of teachers (1 John 2:27). In Johannine thought, all are disciples and primacy is constituted by the closeness to Jesus; there is no mention of an authority of supervision. The greatest figure for John (consistently contrasted with Peter, the most prominent of the Twelve) is the disciple whom Jesus loved—the sole male figure who never abandons him even at the crucifixion and who is the first to believe after the resurrection (John 19:26; 20:8). If in other Christian documents a shepherd's authority over the sheep becomes an image for the presbyter/bishops' authority over Christians (1 Pet 5:1–2; Acts 20:28; *1 Clem.* 44:3), in John 10 Jesus is the Good Shepherd contrasted with all others, who are thieves and bandits; and his shepherding involves not power over the sheep but knowledge of each by name and a love of the sheep to the point of dying for them. (If in a later Johannine strain exemplified in John 21:15–19, Simon Peter is given the shepherding role of feeding the sheep, that comes only if he loves Jesus and with the demand that he lay down his life for the sheep, which still belong

to Jesus and not to him.) No chain of human teachers is ever suggested to preserve the message of Jesus. That is the work of the Paraclete—a form of the Spirit that is the enduring presence of Jesus in each believer—who guides the Christian in the way of truth (16:13–15). If not teachers, Christians can be witnesses through whom the Paraclete bears witness (15:26–27).

Such a heady ecclesiology did not offer a solution for situations where Johannine Christians disagreed among themselves, each group claiming to be guided by the Paraclete-Spirit. Accordingly, 1 John (1:3; 2:19), written after John, offers the first specific evidence of breaking the *koinōnia*. A schism has occurred; and since the writer cannot claim the authority of an apostolic teacher or presbyter/bishop (2:27), his only answer to the schismatics who claim to have the Spirit has to be: "Do not believe every Spirit; rather put these Spirits to the test to see which belongs to God. . . . Anyone who does not belong to God refuses to listen to us. That is how we can know the Spirit of Truth from the Spirit of Deceit" (4:1,6). Communion with the author's chain of witnesses is part of the test (1:1–4). The pains of Johannine Christianity in coming to grips with the need for church structure may be seen in 3 John 9 (the battle over "Diotrephes who likes to be first among them") and John 21:15–19 (Peter as a shepherd).

33   **(C) The Postapostolic Period.** The above treatment of diverse subapostolic emphases in NT ecclesiology is a selection (Pastorals, Col/Eph, Acts, John). To be complete one would need to treat Matt, Heb, the other Catholic Epistles, Rev, etc., but the selection gives a sufficient sampling of the range of Christian ecclesiology—a diversity for the most part, not a dichotomy. Already in a discussion of the diverse views, noncanonical works of the late 1st cent. and early 2d cent. had to be mentioned, not only because chronologically some of them were contemporaneous with the NT books, but also because the trajectory of almost any view could be plotted only by including observations from the postapostolic literature. "Postapostolic" here refers to the age after 95/100, when instead of attempting to wear the apostolic mantle, writers began to use their own names (Ignatius, Polycarp). That there is no sharp delineation may be seen from the fact that canonical 2 Pet uses Peter's name in the early or mid-2d cent., and the apocryphal gospels use apostles' names throughout the 2d cent. and even later. The postapostolic works not only follow outlines of development already prominent in the 1st cent. but develop new ones. Moreover, as mentioned above (→ 6), the division between ideas becomes sharper and more exclusive, so that later some works of this period will be considered orthodox and some heterodox. The following major sections of the article discuss both sides of 2d-cent. Christian literature and some of the ideas contained therein.

SECOND-CENTURY CHURCH WRITERS

34   The overlapping between canonical and noncanonical works in the postapostolic period has been stressed in the previous section. The struggle for Christianity's self-identification over against its theological parent, Judaism (→ 21–26 above), continued well into the 2d cent. Another major 2d-cent. struggle involved self-definition amid Christian diversity as exemplified by struggles with the gnostic systems (→ 70 below) and Marcion (→ 81 below). There was also the need for

Christians to explain themselves to the Roman governing powers. These situations produced a remarkable amount of Christian literature of many types, only some of which has been preserved. While complete texts of hitherto lost 2d-cent. works are still occasionally discovered (e.g., of Melito), the rest is known to us primarily through fragmentary books and allusions in the *Ecclesiastical History* of Eusebius of Caesarea (*ca.* 324). For texts and transls. of the works discussed below, in

addition to information given in the pertinent section, →
3 above.

35   (I) Apostolic Fathers. Since the 17th cent.
it has been customary to collect under this title a group
of rather diverse writings from the immediate post-NT
period (*ca.* AD 90–150 with the earliest overlapping the
late NT writings). They are so called because they were
thought to be closest to the apostolic age and because
some were considered Scripture by ancient authors.
They reveal the concerns, thought patterns, and emerging theology of a Christianity moving toward the end of
its first 100 years of existence.

36   (A) Letters and Homilies. The memory of
Paul remained vivid among many of the churches with
which he was associated. Already in the later NT
writings, his authority as apostle and letter writer was
drawn upon (Pastoral Epistles; 2 Pet 3:15–16). Once his
letters began to be collected and circulated, those in a
position to write official letters to descendants of Paul's
congregations did so with conscious awareness of continuing his legacy (*1 Clem.* 47:1; Ign. *Eph.* 12:2; Pol. *Phil.*
3:2; 9:1; 11:3), sometimes in connection with the
memory of Peter (*1 Clem.* 5:3–7; Ign. *Rom.* 4:3; *Trall.*
3:3). Likewise the tradition of presenting a written
homily or treatise as an epistle was carried over from the
NT (→ NT Epistles, 45:16) into later writing (*2 Clem.*,
Barn.)—an enduring tribute to the impact of the letter or
epistle form on Christian literary heritage.

37   (a) 1 CLEMENT. This persuasive letter-treatise
was from the church of Rome to the church of Corinth.
No internal evidence identifies the author, but Dionysius
of Corinth *ca.* 170 attributed it to Clement, a key figure
(presbyter?) in the collegial presbyteral government of
the late-1st-cent. Roman church (→ 28 above). The
letter (known and used by Polycarp) is generally dated
to the 90s, because of oblique references to troubles
thought to be a persecution under Domitian, mixed with
memories of one by Nero 30 years before (e.g., 1:1;
6:1–2; 7:1). Thus, it may antedate some of the late NT
books. Until 1875 *1 Clem.* was known only in an incomplete ms. as part of the 5th-cent. biblical Codex
Alexandrinus, but since then also in a complete Gk ms.
of 1056 and in several ancient versions.

The purpose of *1 Clem.* is to persuade the Corinthians
to remedy their situation, in which presbyters responsible for church government have been deposed by a
faction of young upstarts. Understandably, then, *1 Clem.*
stresses traditional authority and is the first evidence of
the joining together of the memories of Peter and Paul
in the early years of Roman Christianity (chap. 5). It sets
forth the idea of a succession of authority (42) in which
the gospel was given by God to Christ, who gave it to
the apostles, who appointed *episkopoi* and *diakonoi*
("bishops" and "deacons"; → 27–28 above) to be succeeded by others when they died. This, the memory of
the apostles, esp. of Paul, and an impressive list of OT
examples are mustered to demonstrate that envy and
jealousy are destructive of God's work and that it is not
right to eject validly appointed ministers from their
office (44). We have no evidence about the success of
Clement's letter or the outcome of the Corinthian crisis
except for the statement of Dionysius some 80 years
later that Clement's letter was still read occasionally at
Corinth with appreciation (Eusebius, *HE* 4.23.11). *Text:*
Jaubert, A., SC 167 (1971); Eng: Sparks, 15–34. See
Brown, *Antioch and Rome* 159–83; J. Fuellenbach, *Ecclesiastical Office and the Primacy of Rome* (Washington, 1980).

38   (b) 2 CLEMENT. This follows *1 Clem.* in
Codex Alexandrinus and was already attributed to
Clement at the time of Eusebius, who, however, doubted
its authenticity as not being on his list of books used in

the first Christian generations (→ Canonicity, 66:7,
83–84). It is not a letter but a homily or treatise (see
17:3), differing markedly in style from *1 Clem.* Even if
anonymous, it is a useful piece of early Christian literature, written in the late 1st or early 2d cent., perhaps
either at Corinth or Rome, where it could have been
readily associated with the memory of Clement. K.
Donfried (*HTR* 66 [1973] 487–501; *The Setting of Second
Clement in Early Christianity* [NovTSup 38; Leiden,
1974]) has by form-critical analysis confirmed that the
work is a treatise—possibly composed by the reinstated
Corinthian presbyters and thus associated with *1 Clem.*
in the Corinthian archives. A use of sports imagery (7)
is reminiscent of 1 Cor 9; both may echo the Isthmian
games held every two years near Corinth. The principal
themes are repentance and leading a good life. There are
quotes of sayings of Jesus (4:5; 5:2–4; 12:2) found elsewhere only in apocryphal gospels or not at all, and use
(11:2–3) of an unknown prophetic writing which also
appears in *1 Clem.* 23:3–4 (→ Canonicity, 66:64). *Text:*
Bihlmeyer, K. and W. Schneemelcher, *Die Apostolischen
Väter* (Tübingen, 1956); Eng: Sparks, 57–70.

39   (c) LETTERS OF IGNATIUS. This bishop of
Syrian Antioch was arrested, condemned to death, and
brought as a convicted criminal under guard from Syria
to Rome. He was executed *ad bestias* at the games there
under Trajan, probably about AD 110. On the way,
Ignatius was visited at stopping points in Asia Minor by
representatives of neighboring Christian communities.
What we have as a result are five letters written back to
those communities (*Eph.*, *Magn.*, and *Trall.* from Smyrna;
Phld. and *Smyrn.* from Troas), and one back to Polycarp
(from Troas). In addition, he wrote from Smyrna an
advance letter to the Romans. This list of seven (Eusebius, *HE* 3.36.10) is accepted as authentic over against
several editions of spurious addenda, interpolations, and
abbreviations. (A longer list of Ignatian letters once
widely accepted, continues to be defended occasionally.)
Ignatius is our earliest proponent of church government
headed by a sole bishop, backed up by a college of
presbyters and deacons. This form of three-tiered
church organization was new in Asia Minor at the time
and seemingly had not yet arrived in Rome (→ 28
above). The purpose of Ignatius's insistence on strong
episcopal authority was defense against heresy and
schism. Ignatius did not wish the Roman Christians to
obtain his freedom, which they were apparently trying
to do. Here his mystique of martyrdom comes through
(*Rom.* 1–2; 4; 6:3), an important link between Pauline
conformity to Christ's sufferings (→ Pauline Theology,
82:113, 120) and the martyrdom literature that would
arise in the next generation. There are traces of early
Christian creeds in his affirmations of sound teaching
(e.g., *Eph.* 7:2; *Trall.* 9:1–2), and a strong and highly
developed eucharistic spirituality (see *Eph.* 20:2) which
is integrated into his spirituality of martyrdom and
theology of the episcopate as well (*Smyrn.* 7:1; *Rom.* 4:1;
Phld. 4; *Magn.* 7:1–2). His is the first use of the expression *hē katholikē ekklēsia*, "the catholic church" (*Smyrn.*
8:2), describing the intercity network of Christians in
communion with one another. *Text:* Camelot, P.-Th.,
SC 10 (4th ed., 1969); Eng: Schoedel, W. R. (Hermeneia;
Phl, 1985).

40   (d) LETTER OF POLYCARP to the Philippians.
This was probably written as a cover letter for a collection of Ignatius's letters that he was sending (13:2).
There is much to commend the suggestion of P. N. Harrison that it is composite and that chap. 13 and perhaps
14 were written soon after Ignatius's visit to Smyrna (for
he seems still alive at 13:1–2), and chaps. 1–12 quite a bit
later when Ignatius was grouped with the martyrs (9:1).

Polycarp is an important link in the 2d-cent. network of relationships: he was closely associated with Ignatius and according to Irenaeus (Eusebius, *HE* 5.20.6) was a disciple of John; in turn Irenaeus, originally from Asia Minor, was a disciple of Polycarp (*HE* 5.20.5–8). *Text:* Camelot, SC 10; Eng: Sparks, 116–19.

41   (e) LETTER OF BARNABAS (Pseudo-Barnabas). Despite ancient attribution to the companion of Paul and inclusion in Codex Sinaiticus as part of the NT (→ Texts, 68:157), this was a treatise of the early 2d cent. In chaps. 1–17 it uses the allegorical method of interpretation typical of the Alexandrian tradition (→ Hermeneutics, 69:35) to argue that the Jewish law was meant to be interpreted not literally but figuratively and to be fulfilled in the church. Chaps. 18–21 form a parenetic instruction on ethical life by means of the literary form of the Two Ways, the way of light and the way of darkness. Some of the material in this section derives from a source similar to that used in the *Did.* (cf. *Barn.* 19:9–10 with *Did.* 4:5,7). The christology of *Barn.* emphasizes the redemptive suffering and death of the Son of God, who came in the flesh (5). The allusion to the rebuilding of the Temple by its enemies (16:3–4) suggests a date near 130, when Hadrian was erecting a temple of Zeus on the Jerusalem site of the destroyed Temple. *Text:* Kraft, R. A., SC 172 (1971); Eng: Sparks, 263–301. See F. Manns, *SBFLA* 31 (1981) 105–46; P. Richardson and M. B. Shukster, *JTS* ns 34 (1983) 31–35 (who date *Barn.* to *ca.* 98).

42   **(B) Parenesis and Church Order.**
(a) DIDACHE. Despite ancient references, this work became available only after being discovered in 1875 in a codex of 1057. Under its full name, "The Teaching of the Twelve Apostles," or "The Teaching of the Lord through the Twelve Apostles to the Nations," it was the basis for many later church-order texts. Coming from late 1st- or early 2d-cent. Syria, *Did.* is probably a composite work. Chaps. 1–6 develop ethical instruction under the form of the Two Ways (→ 41 above for *Barn.*); chaps. 7–10 and 14 give regulations regarding baptism, fasting, and eucharist, including a liturgical blessing to be used for eucharistic celebration; chaps. 11–13 give regulations for receiving itinerant apostles and prophets into a community; chap. 15 reflects the changing form of church leadership from apostles and prophets to bishops and deacons (→ 28 above); chap. 16 is a mini-apocalypse admonishing to watchfulness. *Did.* is of enormous importance for tracing the development of early church law. *Text:* Audet, J.-P. (Paris, 1958); Eng: Sparks, 305–19.

43   (b) SHEPHERD OF HERMAS. This document from early 2d-cent. Rome contains revelation given to one Hermas in the form of an apocalypse consisting of visions, mandates, and similitudes. *Vis.* 1–4 features a feminine figure of the church as revelatory agent and warns of an impending tribulation. *Vis.* 5 through *Mand.* 12 puts more emphasis on parenesis; the 10 *Similitudes* reveal and instruct through images and parables. In the latter two sections the revealer is a shepherd, from whom the work gets its title. The author's major concern is a call to repentance from doublemindedness, compromise with pagan lifestyle, and social insensitivity. He proclaims the possibility of a second forgiveness of sin in the light of imminent crisis — either persecution or, more likely, the warning of God's imminent apocalyptic judgment. The Clement of *Vis.* 2.4.3 is usually thought to be the author of *1 Clem.;* the Muratorian Fragment (late 2d cent.? → Canonicity, 66:84) identifies the author Hermas as brother of Pius, bishop of Rome in the mid-2d cent. It is generally thought that *Vis.* 1–4 is earlier than the rest of the work. Composite authorship

is likely. Like *Barn., Hermas* was included in the NT section of Codex Sinaiticus. *Text:* Whittaker, M., GCS 48/2 (1967); Eng: Sparks, 155–259.

44   **(II) Apologists.**   In the early 2d cent., as the church began to take into account the intellectual and philosophical currents of the time, the apology or reasoned exposition and explanation of one's position was adapted to Christian usage. Reflective of the growing level of Christian culture, the apologies were ostensibly addressed to nonbelievers, often even dedicated to the emperor or some other prominent pagan. Nevertheless, their primary function was probably to expound *for believers* how Christianity too is a true "philosophy" or a coherent and lofty way of life. Thus, they seek to ground Christian belief and practice in reason and ancient traditions, esp. the Scriptures, and to demonstrate on these grounds the superiority of Christianity over paganism and Judaism.

45   **(A) Early Apologists.**   The earliest example is a document known as *The Preaching of Peter,* probably from early 2d-cent. Egypt, which survives only in fragmentary quotes, mostly by Clement of Alexandria. The first Christian writer to be identified as author of an apology is *Quadratus,* who addressed his work to Hadrian (Eusebius, *HE* 4.3.1–2), perhaps as early as 125. Of his work only a short quote has survived, and we know nothing else about him. He is not to be identified with the later bishop of Athens of the same name, as Jerome thought. *Ca.* 140 *Aristo* from Pella (Transjordan; → 23 above) was the first Christian to use the literary form of the dialogue to shape his apology. His *Dialogue of Jason and Papiscus,* a conversation between a Jew and a Christian, is known only from mentions in later writers.

46   *Aristides* of Athens addressed an apology to Antoninus Pius *ca.* 140. It was known only through Eusebius's brief reference (*HE* 4.3.3) until the discovery of an Armenian fragment in 1878 and a Syriac transl. in 1889. This made possible the recognition and retrieval of large parts of it from the 7th-cent. Gk romance *Barlaam and Joasaph.* It offers philosophical proofs for the existence of God and the nonexistence of pagan gods, argues that Jews misunderstood true worship, gives the basic elements of Christian belief, and closes with an exposition of Christian moral standards and practices. *Text:* Harris, J. R. and J. A. Robinson, TextsS 1.1 (1893); Gk fragment: Milne, H. J. M., *JTS* 25 (1924) 73–77; Eng: ANF 9. 263–79.

47   **(B) The "Golden Age" of Christian Apology.**   This literary medium flourished after 150.
(a) JUSTIN MARTYR, the greatest apologist, was a Gentile from Flavia Neapolis (ancient Shechem, modern Nablus), and thus a Palestinian like Aristo (→ 45 above). He had run the gamut of Gk philosophies of his time before settling on Christianity. He moved from Palestine to Ephesus and later established himself as a teacher in Rome, where he met a martyr's death about 165 (→ 57 below). Of eight works attributed to Justin, only *Apology 1* and *2* and the *Dialogue with Trypho* have survived, though some 12 spurious works have also been erroneously assigned to him. Justin saw himself as a Christian philosopher; he is one of the first to attempt systematically to bridge the gap between Christianity and the intellectual world of Neoplatonism. His christology of the incarnate Logos subordinate to the Father was influential in the christological controversies of the following century.

48   *Apology 1,* addressed to Antoninus Pius, protests the unjust prosecution of Christians. Because of their high moral principles, they are really the best of citizens. Similarities between Christianity and paganism are to be explained by demons inspiring pagan devotees to imitate Christian practices. Chaps. 65–67 contain an invaluable description of liturgical customs at baptism, the eucharist connected with it, and the Sunday assembly in mid-2d-cent. Rome. Appended to the text is a rescript of Hadrian from approximately 125 specifying that Christians are only to be tried for statutory crimes, and that correct legal procedure is to be followed. *Apology 2* is generally thought to have been originally an addition to the first. It follows the same general themes.

49 The *Dialogue* is ostensibly a conversation between Justin and an important Jewish scholar of the day. It assesses Judaism more positively than did *Barn.* (perhaps in reaction to Marcion?), but Judaism was a temporary arrangement until the coming of the true chosen people in Christ. Extensive supporting arguments are given from the Hebr Scriptures. Chap. 47 contains important information about various Christian attitudes and customs in regard to the Mosaic law in Justin's day. While the *Dialogue* would seem to be aimed at a Jewish audience, it has also been argued that it is directed to a Gentile pagan audience to help them distinguish between Judaism and Christianity. The first part of the ms. and a large part of chap. 74 have not survived. *Text:* Otto, J. C. T. (3d ed.; repr. Wiesbaden, 1969–71: orig. Jena, 1876); Eng: Falls, T. B., FC 6 (1948).

50 (b) TATIAN. If Justin tried to make Christianity acceptable in Greco-Roman intellectual circles, his student Tatian went in the opposite direction. From Syria or Assyria, he too embraced Christianity after a long philosophical search, probably in Rome. Soon after Justin's martyrdom, around 167, he returned to Syria and there wrote in Greek his *Oration to the Greeks,* less an apology than a bitter denunciation of Gk culture in favor of the "barbarian" (i.e., non-Gk, esp. Eastern) heritage of culture and Christianity. He developed increasingly heterodox and ascetical (Encratite) leanings. As with Justin, many lost writings are attributed to Tatian; but his most famous work was the *Diatessaron* ("through four"), the first harmony of the four canonical Gospels (→ Texts, 68:122–23, 183), using John as a structural basis. Intended for liturgical use, it was written in either Greek or Syriac and is nearly completely recoverable from fragments and transls. into Latin, Arabic, and Middle Dutch. Nearly simultaneous with Irenaeus's identification of the same four Gospels for church use, the *Diatessaron* is one of the earliest witnesses to their acceptance for lectionary use. *Text* and Eng: Whittaker, M. (Oxford, 1982).

51 (c) ATHENAGORAS, said to be a Christian philosopher from Athens, wrote his *Plea* (*presbeia*) *on Behalf of Christians* between 176 and 180, addressed to Marcus Aurelius and Commodus. (In the ancient church, only Methodius, *ca.* 300, alludes to it.) In polished rhetorical style he offers a defense against three accusations frequently leveled against Christians: atheism, cannibalism, and incest (3:1). With Justin, Athenagoras holds a Logos christology and gives evidence of a surprisingly well-developed trinitarian theology (10). His other surviving work, the treatise *On the Resurrection,* is a demonstration from reason of the credibility of bodily resurrection and the necessary integrity of body and soul. *Text* and Eng: Schoedel, W. R. (Oxford, 1972).

52 (d) THEOPHILUS, bishop of Antioch but of Mesopotamian origin, wrote his three-part apology *To Autolycus* (a pagan friend) soon after 180, the only extant work of many attributed to him. He argues the futility of paganism and the truth of Christianity, the superiority of the Scriptures over pagan religion, and the baselessness of charges of immorality against Christians. He speaks of the triad (*trias*) of God, Word, and Wisdom (not to be identified completely with the Trinity, since a fourth, Humanity, is immediately added: 2:15). He gives evidence of solid classical and biblical education and is the first writer to quote explicitly a passage from the NT by author: John 1:1–3 (2:22). Traces of his influence are probably to be found in quite a number of later Christian writers, beginning already with Irenaeus. *Text* and Eng: Grant, R. M. (Oxford, 1970).

53 (e) MELITO was bishop of Sardis *ca.* 170. Of nearly 20 works attributed to him by Eusebius, only fragments of an *Apology* to Marcus Aurelius had survived until 1931, when new discoveries enabled the identification of his *On the Pasch,* probably a homily for a festive occasion. It develops a theology of the passion in the light of the theology of Passover, representing the Asia Minor tradition of Quartodecimanism, or celebration of Christ's death and resurrection beginning on the 14th of Nisan according to the Jewish calendar. The polished rhetorical style may have been influenced by the contemporary popularity of the Second Sophistic in Asia Minor and is thought in turn to have influenced Tertullian and Clement of Alexandria. *Text* and Eng: Hall, S. G. (Oxford, 1979).

54 (f) LETTER TO DIOGNETUS. From a single, now-destroyed medieval ms. comes this anonymous work, addressee unknown, unless intended to be the tutor of Marcus Aurelius by the same name. In florid style it argues the superiority of Christianity over paganism and Judaism and proposes the analogy that "what the soul is to the body, so are Christians in the world" (6:1). The last two chaps. are really a homily for a special occasion, perhaps Epiphany (11:5). Although the attribution to Justin found in the ms. has been rejected, the suggestion of P. Andriessen (1946–47) that the letter is the lost apology of Quadratus (→ 45 above) has not been generally accepted. *Text:* Marrou, H. I., SC 33 (1952); Eng: Kleist, J. A., ACW 6, 125–47.

55 (III) Acts of Martyrs. Before the emperor Decius (249–251) it is not clear to what extent professing Christianity was a capital offense. Yet there is indisputable evidence that in isolated instances earlier Christians were tried and condemned to death. Here we are concerned only with the literature of martyrdom and its place in Christian theology and spirituality.

56 The *Martyrdom of Polycarp* (→ 40 above) recounts the death of the venerable bishop sometime between 155 and 166, the last of a number of martyrs at Smyrna (chap. 1). Though he accepted advice to go into hiding, he was betrayed and discovered, after being warned in a dream that he would be burned alive (chaps. 5–7). The explicit passion theology and miraculous elements of the narrative are complemented by the homey and surely authentic details of Polycarp's behavior. When urged to renounce Christ, he uttered his famous question: How could he now renounce the one who had not wronged him in 86 years of service (9:3). The end section of the ms. evidences several stages of copying from an original in the possession of Irenaeus (chap. 22). The present text may also represent several stages of redaction, as argued by von Campenhausen.

57 The *Acts of Justin* and the *Acts of the Scillitan Martyrs* represent a different kind of martyrdom account, one either based on or imitating official court records of an interrogation. Justin (→ 47 above) and six companions, perhaps his students, were martyred in Rome under the urban prefect Q. Junius Rusticus between 163 and 168. Three recensions of the text are preserved, all in medieval mss. It is now generally conceded that recension A, the simplest, is the original, from which B and C were embellished. (See G. A. Bisbee, *Second Century* 3 [1983] 129–57.) The 12 Scillitan martyrs were beheaded at Carthage on July 17, 180—the punishment usually reserved for Roman citizens. This text is generally thought to be the most authentic account preserved of a martyrs' trial and is the earliest surviving Latin Christian document.

58   The *Acts of the Martyrs of Lyons and Vienne* are quoted in full by Eusebius, our only source. They are actually a letter from the Christians of Gaul to their home churches in Asia Minor narrating the events of 177. A number of this Greek-speaking community in a Latin-speaking environment were the victims of mob violence and eventually were executed in cruel ways during games in the amphitheater. The document features a good amount of drama and theological reflection, which may be part of the original or later redaction but is based on an undoubtedly authentic account. The biblical allusions and passion motifs in this story and that of Polycarp reveal the direction in which the theology of martyrdom was already developing. *Text* and *Eng* of all Acts: Musurillo, H., *The Acts of the Christian Martyrs* (Oxford, 1972).

59   **(IV) Historians and Antiheretical Writers.**
(A) Early Writers. *Papias* of Hierapolis in the early 2d cent. wrote five books of *Interpretations of the Sayings of the Lord* based on the oral tradition he had compiled from those who had known the companions of Jesus. Unfortunately, only fragments survive, mostly in Irenaeus and Eusebius. Papias is the source of our earliest information about the origins of Mark and Matthew (Eusebius, *HE* 3.39.15–16), and he is described by Eusebius as a man of limited intelligence (3.39.13), probably because he was a millenarian. Eng: Kleist, J., ACW 6, 105–24; for Armenian remnants, see *NTS* 27 (1980–81) 605–14. A major study is J. Kürzinger, *Papias von Hierapolis und die Evangelien des Neuen Testaments* (Regensburg, 1983).

60   *Hegesippus* traveled in the mid-2d cent. from the E via Corinth to Rome in search of the tradition of apostolic teaching in contrast to gnosticism. In Rome, he ascertained an authentic tradition running from the beginning to his own day. On his return he wrote five books of *Memoirs,* of which only fragments survive, mostly in Eusebius. From him we get accounts of the martyrdom of James and of the grandsons of Jude. Eng: ANF 8. 762–65.

61   **(B) Irenaeus.** The greatest theologian and antiheretical writer of the late 2d cent. came from Asia Minor (where he had known Polycarp as a child) to Gaul. As a presbyter of the church of Lyons, he was sent to a meeting about Montanism in Rome about 177. Upon his return to Lyons he was elected to succeed bishop Pothinus, who had perished in the persecution (→ 58 above). Nothing more is known of Irenaeus's life. He wrote *Proof of the Apostolic Preaching* (extant only in an Armenian version discovered in 1904), a synthesis of orthodox teaching at the end of the 2d cent. But his

major work was his five-book refutation of gnosticism, *Adversus Haereses* (completed *ca.* 190), extant completely only in a literal Lat transl., but also in large fragments of Greek, Syriac, and Armenian. His major sources were lost works of Hegesippus, Justin, and Valentinus and other gnostic writers.

62   On the basis of reason, apostolic tradition, Scripture, and belief in the resurrection, Irenaeus attacks and refutes principally Valentinian gnostic teaching. He argues that the tradition of apostolic teaching is the foundation of continuing truth, and that therefore the churches with the most reliable apostolic tradition, notably Rome, are the major sources of authentic teaching. His christology, heavily influenced by Col and Eph, is centered on the doctrine of *anakephalaiōsis* (Eph 1:10), whereby all human history is summed up and renewed in Christ and all human destiny takes its future direction from him. Partly in reaction to gnostic docetism and rejection of the body, but also largely because of his own innate theological sense, Irenaeus insists on the fleshly reality of Christ. The transformation of Christ's flesh in the resurrection is the model of all human transformation to be accomplished through the saving reality of the redemption. Thus, the human person of Christ is the summation not only of the past but of the future as well, the focal point of salvation history. With Tatian, Irenaeus is one of the first to acknowledge four canonical Gospels (3.11.8) and one of the earliest sources of a canonical list of NT books (→ Canonicity, 66:63, 65, 67).

(Apostolic Preaching: *Text:* Froidevaux, L., SC 62 [1971]; Eng: Smith, J. P., ACW 16 [Westminster, 1952]. Adversus Haereses: *Text:* Rousseau, A. and L. Doutreleau, SC 100, 152–53, 210–11, 263–64, 293–94 [1969–82]; Eng: Ante-Nicene Christian Library 5.9 [Edinburgh, 1868–69]; or ANF 1. 309–567. Donovan, M. A., "Irenaeus in Recent Scholarship," *Second Century* 4 [1984] 219–41.)

63   *Conclusion.* The 2nd cent. saw the continuation of directions begun in the NT, viz., the search for the church's self-understanding through deepened awareness of christology and ecclesiology in the light of growing diversity of teaching and the threat of resistance from outside forces. The need for consolidation was recognized early by the authors of that literature known as the Apostolic Fathers. The need for serious interaction with the political and intellectual world was first met by the Apologists. At the same time, the experience of persecution provoked a continuation of the theology of suffering, begun in the NT, in the form of a literature and theology of martyrdom. With Irenaeus, the concept of orthodoxy as an ancient and established tradition over against gnostic heterodoxy became prominent, and the age of the great patristic syntheses had begun. Let us turn now to the other side of the 2d-cent. picture: the gnostic movements that so disturbed Irenaeus and later church writers.

GNOSTICISM

64   **(I) Description of Gnosticism.** The conference at Messina (*CBQ* 28 [1966] 322–33) attempted to bring some order into terminological confusion by coming to a consensus about a distinction between gnosis ("knowledge of divine mysteries reserved for the elite") and gnosticism (described through a coherent series of characteristics from the developed 2d-cent. gnostic systems). This solution, however, has been strongly criticized by others, e.g., K. Rudolph and M.

Smith. Elements are presented below which are essential to any description of gnosticism.
(A) The Gnostic Phenomenon. "Gnosticism" (from Gk *gnōsis,* "knowledge") refers to a group of religious movements that arose in the eastern part of the Roman Empire and in the section of E Syria and Babylonia that lay in the Sassanid empire. Information about gnostic sects is found beginning with the 2d cent. AD in the antignostic writings of Christian apologists and in

Coptic codices. Diverse finds of Manichean material stem from the 4th to the 10th cent., and we also have writings of the Mandeans, who continue to exist in S Iraq. Gnostic sects spread among Christians in the major cities of Asia Minor, Alexandria, Carthage, Rome, and S France. But by the 6th cent., Manicheism (→ 76 below), the last of these sects to challenge Christianity, was in decline. This decline reflects the convergence of several factors: (1) ecclesiastical opposition; (2) development of monasticism and mystical traditions within orthodox Christianity, which had absorbed intellectual and spiritual interests that had been prominent in gnostic sects; (3) the decline of the merchants and traders who had carried many of these movements; and (4) the consolidation of local Christian churches around the bishops. Manicheism continued to exist in central Asia, whence it again spread west during the Crusades to spawn new movements such as the Bogomils and Cathars. Portuguese traders report followers of the "religion of venerable light" in S China during the 17th cent.

65 The details of gnostic mythological systems, cultic practices, ethical injunctions, appropriation of religious and philosophical symbols, and sectarian organization vary widely; yet gnostic sects also share common features. Salvation depends on "awakening" to a revealed knowledge of the soul's identity with a heavenly realm of light. This realm is the true "divine" order, often spoken of as the "fullness" (plēroma) and characterized by an elaborate hierarchy of emanations from the true God. The various powers and levels have abstract names or those of Semitic angelic beings. Some gnostic sects use the Neoplatonic ascent of the mind to union with the One as a framework for their description. Others refer to baptismal rites and elaborate ritual sounds that accompany ascent.

66 The peculiar monism of the gnostic vision of the divine undercuts the pantheism of pagan religion, the ordered cosmos of Stoic speculation, the progressive ascent of the soul in Platonism, and the Jewish and Christian vision of the cosmos as divine creation. It often expresses hostility toward the powers that rule the created world, a place of violence, ignorance, passion, and disorder. Some forms of gnostic mythology begin with a principle of evil and darkness that has succeeded in entrapping part of the divine light (e.g., Hippolytus, Ref. 5.6.3–11.1 [Naasenes]; 5.12.1–17.13 [Peratae]; 5.19.1–22.1 [Sethians]; Paraph. Shem; Mani; Mandeans). Most other examples of gnostic cosmology begin with a "descent" or "fall" of a being in the light world—often a female Wisdom figure who desires to create or emanate without a consort, just as the great Unknown God did in generating the light world. The result is a defective creature to be cast out of the light world and hidden from its view (e.g., Sethian mythologies such as Ap. John; Orig. World; Irenaeus, Adv. Haer. 1.29 and 30; also Valentinian speculation). This creature is the "god" of the lower world, often identified with the creator of the OT, who ignorantly thinks he is supreme and whose powers work to keep humanity entrapped in the lower realm (e.g., Apoc. Adam).

67 Awakened by the call of the heavenly revealer, the gnostic knows that such powers and authorities are arrogant and contemptuous. Many sects concluded that gnostics had to free themselves from the passions and desires of the body, which the evil archon had created to entrap the light. Cultic rites and ascetic practices, esp. rejection of sexuality and the "works of femaleness," are the practical expression of this view. It is difficult to assess the reports of patristic opponents that other gnostic groups drew the opposite conclusion and flaunted social and sexual conventions in bizarre rituals involving sex

and ritual consumption of the semen and menses (e.g., Epiphanius, Pan. 25 and 26: Epiphanius claims that as a young man he was seduced by a woman belonging to one of these sects). The NHL, a monastic collection, gives no indication of such a libertine form of gnosis.

68 **(B) Social Location of Gnostic Sects.** The revolt against this world and its powers (esp. evident in gnostic interpretations of the OT) seems to require a sectarian mentality that is "parasitic" in a larger religious culture whose pretensions it claims to "unmask." It is also difficult to imagine the elaboration of gnostic mythology without the Greco-Roman use of writing to collect philosophic and religious traditions. Consequently, many scholars think that the primary audience for gnostic speculation was the growing class of literate bureaucrats and their families in the urban areas of the Greco-Roman world. Such persons did not belong to the aristocratic elite, with its literary and philosophic heritage; rather, they were intellectually and perhaps even physically dislocated from their ancestral religious roots. Gnosis makes them the true elite, the "generation without a king," the "immovable race," as many of the gnostic writings put it. (Unless otherwise indicated, the English of the gnostic works cited below can be found in NHLE; for sources, → 72–74 below).

69 Since many gnostic mythologies assign a prominent role in the emergence of the world and in its redemption to the feminine Wisdom figure, and since the pleroma is often described as populated by androgynous spiritual beings, many interpreters think that gnostic sects were particularly attractive to women. Mary Magdalene is often portrayed among Jesus' disciples as a woman whose insight and understanding are equal or superior to those of Jesus' male disciples (e.g., Gos. Mary; Pistis Sophia; Gos. Thom. 114; Dial. Sav.). On the other hand, the weak, ignorant, passion-driven soul is imaged as a female who must be rescued and returned to virginity by her male heavenly consort (e.g., Exeg. Soul). The gnostic ascetic must flee "the works of femaleness" (Thom. Cont. 144.8–10; Dial. Sav. 144.12–21). Irenaeus claims that a certain Marcellina was propagating the doctrines of the Carpocratian sect in Rome (Adv. Haer. 1.26.6). He condemns the gnostic Marcus for seducing wealthy women, claiming to endow them with his prophetic spirit and permitting them to celebrate the eucharist (Adv. Haer. 1.13.1–4). Ptolemy's gnostic letter of instruction is addressed to a wealthy woman in Rome, Flora. However, most of the gnostic teachers and disciples known to us appear to have been men. The situation in gnostic sects may not have been much different from that in the early spread of Christianity. Gnostic teachers and groups might find patrons in wealthy women, who in turn may have been somewhat freer to assume teaching and cultic roles in gnostic sects than they were in Christian groups. In the latter, as the Pastoral Epistles suggest, an earlier crisis of deviant teaching and gnosticizing asceticism had been met by formalization of the requirements for bishops and the exclusion of women from any role in public worship or teaching. However, gnostic sects do not appear to be particularly devoted to the equality of women.

70 **(C) Organization of Gnostic Groups.** We know very little about the organization of gnostic groups. The "bishops and deacons" of the orthodox community are criticized as "dry canals" who claim divine authority and for a time rule over and persecute the gnostic elect (Apoc. Pet. 79.22–80.7). In mid-2d-cent. Rome, Justin Martyr, Marcion, and the gnostic teachers Valentinus and Ptolemy seem to have functioned as private teachers of a "higher Christianity." Each gathered disciples who studied his teaching. Ptolemy's

Letter to Flora (Epiphanius, *Pan.* 33.3.1–33.7.10) explains the tripartite division of the Mosaic law: pure legislation fulfilled by the savior; legislation symbolic of the savior's coming, such as the religious festivals; and legislation mixed with baseness, which was destroyed by the savior's coming. The law was not given by the good God represented by the savior; nor was it the work of the devil, but of the intermediate demiurge who fashioned this world. Ptolemy's explanation may even be directed against Marcion's total rejection of the OT. He argues that his view reflects Jesus' and Paul's own teaching about the law. A similar teacher/disciples picture of Christianity and gnostic sects appears to have been the case in Alexandria with Theodotos, Basilides, Isidore, and the Christian teachers Clement of Alexandria and Origen. *Testim. Truth* criticizes the lack of ascetic renunciation among orthodox Christians and among gnostic groups such as the Valentinians, Basilides, his disciple Isidore, and the Simonians, (56.1–58.6).

71   Many gnostic groups engaged in cultic rituals, such as baptisms, anointings, eucharistic meals, prayers to accompany the ascent of the soul into the pleroma, and rites for the ascent of the soul of the deceased. A Valentinian rite of the "bridal chamber" enacts the union of the soul with its heavenly counterpart (*Gos. Phil.* 67.27–30; 69.1–71.15; 72.29–73.8; 74.13–25; 77.2–15). Clearly, persons within the sect must have officiated at such rites (e.g., *Gos. Phil.* 77.2–6). Gnostic cosmologies have the summons of the heavenly Wisdom which awakens Adam cast in what appears to be a formula for baptismal initiation (e.g., *Ap. John* II 31.5–25; *Trim. Prot.* 44.29–45.20). Irenaeus lists the sacramental rites and formulas of Marcosian gnostics (*Adv. Haer.* 1.21.2–5). The formula that he gives for the ascent of the soul at death is repeated in *1 Apoc. Jas.* 33.15–34.20. *Gos. Eg.* contains the baptismal prayers that accompanied the initiate's heavenly baptism and transition to immortality as a being of light (e.g., III 65.20–68.1). Some of the gnostic hymns found in the *Odes of Solomon* were used in a 3d-cent. gnostic account of the heavenly realm and repentance of Wisdom, *Pistis Sophia*. The original composition of the *Odes* may have occurred in Syria (ca. AD 100) in a Jewish-Christian baptismal sect, a milieu that would spawn a number of gnostic sects in the 2d and 3d cents. The tradition of psalms and hymns is continued in Manichean and Mandean writings.

72   **(D) Gnostic Sources.** Our information about gnostic sects in the 2d to the 3d cent. is based on a number of codices that contain the Coptic transls. of gnostic writings, on church fathers who wrote against gnostic teachers, and on surviving Manichean and Mandean material that has been preserved in various languages. There are also writings that express a gnosticizing spirituality, though they may not have been produced by a gnostic sect, e.g., the *Odes of Solomon*, the apocryphal acts, and the Hermetic writings. As a group, the Hermetic writings reflect a form of occult wisdom from Alexandria in the 2d and 3d cents. AD, which taught a rebirth of the soul through mystic ecstasy. The first work in the *Corpus Hermeticum*, *Poimandres*, recounts a gnostic vision, which includes a dualistic cosmogony that draws upon Gen as well as popular philosophical writings. Other Hermetic writings have been found among the gnostic treatises of Codex VI (*Disc. 8–9; Asclepius; Pr. Thanks.*). *Asclepius* is an excerpt from a work previously known only in Latin, with a few Gk fragments. Since the concluding section of Codex VI which contains the Hermetica includes a gnosticized excerpt from Plato's *Republic* (588B–589B), the scribe may have been using excerpts to fill out the codex.

73   The Askew and Bruce codices were acquired

by the British Museum and Bodleian Library in the 18th cent. and first published in the late 19th cent. They contain what appear to be gnostic writings from the 3d cent. The *Pistis Sophia* consists of three lengthy books recounting the repentances of Sophia and interpreting psalm texts in the light of gnostic myth. A fourth book contains a second revelation dialogue between Jesus and his disciples. The Bruce codex contains two tracts which *Pistis Sophia* had referred to as "the two books of Jeu" and a third untitled work. They describe the heavenly light world and show affinities to the type of gnostic speculation known to us from the 2d-cent. writers. Examples of 2d-cent. gnostic speculation have been known since the end of the 19th cent. (though not published until the middle of the 20th cent.) in the Berlin Codex 8502. In addition to a fragment of an apocryphal act of Peter, it contains three gnostic writings, *Ap. John*, *Soph. Jes. Chr.*, and *Gos. Mary*. Gk fragments of the last two confirm that their original language was Greek. The cosmogonic system of *Ap. John* is so close to that attributed to the Barbelo gnostics in *Adv. Haer.* 1.29 that Irenaeus would appear to have used an epitome of a gnostic system.

74   Additional versions of *Ap. John* and *Soph. Jes. Chr.* were found among the spectacular collection of Coptic gnostic codices discovered by peasants near Nag Hammadi in Egypt *ca.* 1945 and completely published only in 1977 (→ Apocrypha, 67:56). This collection of writings from 13 different codices has provided scholars with some 50 different writings, comprising some 1,153 pages out of an original 1,257, though some of the codices are extremely fragmentary. (For detail, see G. W. MacRae, *IDBSup* 613–19.) The treatises in the collection reflect the wide diversity of gnostic speculation. Some can be associated with known groups, like the Valentinians. Others seem to belong to a general pattern of gnostic mythologizing which links the gnostic race to Seth; reinterprets Gen to demote its god to the arrogant ruler of the lower world; speaks of the fall of the heavenly Wisdom figure, and the coming of redemption through the activity of the heavenly Seth or heavenly Adam, a figure also associated with Christ. Many scholars describe this type of gnosis as "Sethian." Valentinian speculation seems to have drawn on its mythology. In addition, we find writings which use the terminology of Middle-Platonic and Neoplatonic speculation and which are related to gnostics who had found their way into Plotinus's circles in Rome and against whom that philosopher wrote a treatise (*Ennead* 2.9). These writings are *Allogenes*, *Zost.*; also *Marsanes*, and *Steles Seth*.

75   The antignostic heresiologists tended to construct elaborate genealogies of gnostic sects, connecting teachers with one another, emphasizing their odd speculations and myriad numbers, and tracing them back to heresiarchs like Simon Magus. It has been impossible to fit the Nag Hammadi material into the sectarian genealogies constructed by Justin, Irenaeus, Hippolytus, and Epiphanius. Scholars now treat their information as secondary to the extensive primary sources in the Coptic codices. However, there are some important "primary sources" that are preserved only in the heresiologists: Ptolemy's *Letter to Flora* (*Pan.* 33.3.1–33.7.10); *Excerpta ex Theodoto* (Clement of Alexandria, *Strom.* 7.5); fragments of Heracleon's commentary on John, (Origen, *Comm. in Jo.*). The account in Hippolytus of the Sethians, which claims to use a "Paraphrase of Seth" (*Ref.* 5.19.1–22), appears to be a later christianization of the non-Christian cosmogony of *Paraph. Shem*. Hippolytus may have had similar paraphrases for his account of Basilides (*Ref.* 7.20.1–27); of the gnostic Justin (*Ref.* 5.26–27), and of Simon's *Megale Apophasis* (*Ref.* 6.9.4–6.18.7). The *Acts of Thomas* (108–13) contains an important hymnic expression of Eastern gnosis, the *Hymn of the Pearl.*

76   (II) Gnostic Origins. Scholars have been sharply divided over what factor was most influential in giving rise to gnosticism. Was it a Hellenization of Christianity? Or a Hellenization of Jewish wisdom speculation? Or an offshoot of Eastern religious myth, esp. from Iran? Or a combination of Gk philosophy and Oriental mythology? The following are some of the originating strains that must be considered.

(A) Gnosticism and Heterodox Judaism. In Mesopotamia Mani started an Eastern sect of gnosis that was to become a worldwide missionary effort and an opponent of Christianity in the 4th–5th cents. He and his father had belonged to a Jewish Christian baptismal sect, the Elkesai, which had originated *ca.* AD 100 in Syria. Mani's biography confirms for the 3d cent. what scholars suspect was already the case for gnostic speculation at the beginning of the 2d cent. AD, viz., origins in heterodox Jewish speculation. Study of the mythological traditions in the NHL confirm this impression. While many of the treatises have a very superficial link with Christianity (gnosis is revealed by the risen Lord, or Christ is identified with one of the beings of the pleroma), speculation about the origins of the lower world and the plight of humanity cannot be excised from their attachment to heterodox Judaism.

77   The legends of the fallen angels and the daughters of men that appear in *1 Enoch* 6–10 (cf. Gen 6:1–2) are reflected not only in Mani's *Kephalia* but also in gnostic legends of the seduction (actual or attempted) of Eve and her offspring by the evil powers of the lower god (e.g., *Ap. John* 26.16–20; 19.20–23; 29.30–30.2; *Orig. World* 123.4–15). *Ap. John*'s version of the tradition adds the theme that the powers appeared like the women's husbands (cf. *T. Reuben* 5:5–7) and links this episode with the creation of the "imitation spirit." Gnostic exegesis displays a particular animosity toward the arrogance and pride of the OT God and his servants (e.g., *Testim. Truth* 45.30–46.2, a midrash on Gen 3:1; 69.32–70.24, associating David and Solomon with demons). The angelic tetrad, Armozel, Oriel, Daveith and Eleleth, appears to be associated with the four throne beings of Ezek 1:4–21 and perhaps the archangels of *1 Enoch* 9–10. Other scholars propose that the name of the feminine manifestation of the highest god, Barbelo, is a word play on the tetragrammaton, *barba''elo*, "in the form of God." The frequent comparison of heavenly Wisdom's offspring to an "abortion" could derive from a wordplay, *nĕpālîm*, "abortions," and *nĕpîlîm*, "fallen ones." We also meet the female counterpart of Seth, Norea, in *Hyp. Arch.* (91.34– 92.31), who is clearly linked to the Naamah of Jewish legends (sometimes Noah's wife).

78   Other parallels can be found between heavenly journeys such as *Zost.* and *2 Enoch* (e.g., *2 Enoch* 9–11; *Zost.* 128.15–18) and between the Adam testament in *Apoc. Adam* and *Adam and Eve.* In some cases, form and redaction criticism may provide clues to the development of gnostic speculation. For example, the polemic against false views of the savior in *Apoc. Adam* 77.18– 82.19, which is directed also against false views of salvation, may consider the 13th kingdom in a series to be christianizing gnostics. *Melch.* may reflect three stages of editing: (1) a Jewish substratum that contained speculation about the angelic Melchizedek; (2) a christianizing in which Jesus is identified with Melchizedek; and (3) the incorporation of Sethian gnostic material. While these examples make evident a role of heterodox Judaism in the origins of gnostic sects, they also show that no "straight"-line developmental account of gnostic origins is likely to be possible.

79   (B) Gnosticism and Christianity. The NHL provides sufficient evidence of superficial christianization of gnostic materials to indicate that gnosticism emerged in the same milieu, perhaps, but independently of Christianity. We know far too little about the development of the traditions represented in our 2d-cent. gnostic writings to determine whether or not the image of Jesus as revelation of the Father in John, for example, might have been influenced by gnostic descriptions and discourses of a heavenly revealer, though *Thund.* and other gnostic writings use the "I Am" style of discourse for the revealer. A common fund of religious symbols and expressions may adequately account for the parallels between gnostic writings and the NT.

80   However, the heresiologists may not be completely wrong to suggest that gnostic sects found their strongest base in Christian circles. There the revolt against a Jewish construction of the world and the quest for a higher, esoteric knowledge of God found a sympathetic ear. There the heavenly revealer was not just a mythic figure from the Urgeschichte but was concretized in Jesus, even though a gnostic would never grant that the heavenly revealer actually died on the cross. Just as the revealer descended into Jesus at baptism, so the revealer departed leaving the powers to crucify an empty shell (e.g., *Apoc. Pet.* 81.3–83.15). Christianity also provided the missionary impulse to convert others, which is reflected in some of the gnostic writings (e.g., *Gos. Mary; Ep. Pet. Phil.*). Later, Mani would deliberately take the model of the apostle to represent his own effort at founding a universal religion to link East and West.

81   (III) Marcion. The heresiologists consider Marcion a gnostic teacher (e.g., Justin, *Apol.* 1.26.3–8; Irenaeus, *Adv. Haer.* 3.3.4; Epiphanius, *Pan.* 42.1.7–2.8; Tertullian, *Marcion* 1.2), and link him with gnostic descendants, Cerdo and Apelles. Though Marcion's teaching exploited the contradictions between the OT and the NT to argue that Jesus revealed the true God, who is not the god of the OT, Marcion's teaching does not contain peculiarly gnostic features. Rather than allegorize the OT, Marcion rejected it as the "law," which Paul had shown was ended in Christ. Marcion (→ Canonicity, 66:65) did not expound his views in esoteric treatises but sought to define an appropriate Christian "canon" in edited versions of Luke and the Pauline epistles (excluding the Pastorals). Whatever the cause of his break with the Christian church at Rome, Marcion's response was to undertake a missionary effort to establish a church that was hierarchically ordered. Not concerned with esoteric teaching, he baptized in the name of the Trinity, used water rather than wine at the eucharist, and accepted martyrdom. His movement continued in parts of Syria along the Euphrates frontier into the 4th cent. An inscription (*ca.* AD 318) from Lebada, near Damascus, reads "synagogue of the Marcionites." Many Marcionites may have been absorbed by Manicheism.

82   Though Marcion was not a gnostic, his teaching provides important clues about the success of gnostic speculation among Christians. Christians were not certain about their Jewish heritage. Both Marcion and gnostic teachers provided ways to transcend that heritage. But, lacking a Christian canon, something would have to replace the discredited or devalued "Scriptures" on which Christians had relied. Marcion turned to the 1st-cent. heritage of Christians Luke and Paul. The gnostics turned to an open-ended syncretism of sacred writings and esoteric exegesis. The difference may reflect a more profound split. The gnostics were content to operate as an esoteric sect; Marcion understood that the gospel required founding a church.

81

ASPECTS OF
NEW TESTAMENT THOUGHT

Raymond E. Brown, S.S.   John R. Donahue, S.J.
Donald Senior, C.P.   Adela Yarbro Collins *

GENERAL OUTLINE

CHRISTOLOGY

BIBLIOGRAPHY

1   Items in the important bibliography on Jesus (→ 78:1) will not be repeated here. Brown, R. E., *Jesus God and Man* (NY, 1972); "Who Do Men Say that I Am?" *Biblical Reflections on Crises Facing the Church* (NY, 1975) 20–37. Chouinard, L., "Gospel Christology: A Study of Methodology," *JSNT* 30 (1987) 21–37. Cullmann, O., *The Christology of the New Testament* (London, 1963). Dunn, J. D. G., *Unity and Diversity in the New Testament* (London, 1977); *Christology in the Making* (Phl, 1980). Dupont, J. (ed.), *Jésus aux Origines de la Christologie* (BETL 40; Louvain, 1973). Dwyer, J. C., *Son of Man & Son of God* (NY, 1983). Ernst, J., *Anfänge der Christologie* (SBS 57; Stuttgart, 1972). Fitzmyer, J. A., *A Christological Catechism* (NY, 1982); *Scripture and Christology* (NY, 1986). Fuller, R. H., *The Foundations of New Testament Christology* (NY, 1965); "The Conception/Birth of Jesus as a Christological Moment," *JSNT* 1 (1978) 37–52; "Pre-Existence Christology: Can We Dispense with It?" *Word & World* 2 (1982) 29–33. Fuller, R. H. and P. Perkins, *Who Is This Christ?* (Phl, 1983). Goergen, D. J., *The Mission and Ministry of Jesus* (Wilmington, 1986). Hahn, F., *The Titles of Jesus in Christology* (London, 1969). Hiers, R. H., *Jesus and the Future* (Atlanta, 1981). Holladay, C. H., *Theios Aner in Hellenistic Judaism* (SBLDS 40; Missoula, 1977). Kasper, W., *Jesus the Christ* (NY, 1976). Kingsbury, J. D., *Jesus Christ in Matthew, Mark, and Luke* (Phl, 1981). Longenecker, R. N., *The Christology of Early Jewish Christianity* (SBT ns 17; London, 1970). Marshall, I. H., *The Origins of New Testament Christology* (London, 1976). Moule, C. F. D., *The Origin of Christology* (Cambridge, 1977). O'Collins, G., *What Are They Saying about Jesus?* (NY, 1977); *Interpreting Jesus* (London, 1983). O'Grady, J. F., *Lord, Jesus and Christ* (NY, 1972). Pannenberg, W., *Jesus—God and Man* (Phl, 1968). Thompson, W. M., *The Jesus Debate* (NY, 1985). Van Beeck, F. J., *Christ Proclaimed: Christology as Rhetoric* (NY, 1979). Also *Semeia* 30 (1984), *Christology and Exegesis: New Approaches* (ed. R. Jewett).

* R. E. Brown is the author of the articles "Christology," "The Resurrection of Jesus," and "The Twelve and the Apostolate"; J. R. Donahue wrote "The Parables of Jesus"; D. Senior wrote "The Miracles of Jesus"; A. Yarbro Collins wrote "Eschatology and Apocalypticism."

2   Outline.

3   In a narrow sense christology would involve speaking about Jesus as the *christos* (Messiah), but the term is used more widely to cover the various ways in which those who followed or believed in Jesus evaluated him. The issue is raised explicitly in the Gospel question "Who do people say that I am?" with a response given in terms of JBap, Elijah, one of the prophets, the Messiah, the Son of God (Mark 8:26–30; Matt 16:13–20; Luke 9:18–22; cf. John 6:68–69; 11:27). This means that in the NT period one way to evaluate Jesus was in terms of the entitled roles recognizable from the OT or intertestamental Jewish literature. In *JBC* (78:2–61) there was an excellent treatment of "Titles of Christ"; in *NJBC* these titles are treated in other articles (→ Jesus, 78:32–43; → Pauline Theology, 82:48–54; → Johannine Theology, 83:35–49). Such an approach, while important, does not cover all NT christology.

4   (I) Survey of Modern Christological Analyses. How was the evaluation of Jesus in NT writings related to Jesus' evaluation of himself? E.g., did Jesus himself adopt or accept the titles given to him in the NT? Did others use them of him; and, if so, did he accept such appellations? Included in this survey will be not only scholarly views but also nonscholarly views, i.e., outlooks current among many Christians even if not defended by publishing scholars.

5   (A) Nonscholarly Conservatism. This view identifies the christology of NT writings with the christology of Jesus himself. Even though the Gospels were written some 30 to 70 years after the ministry of Jesus, such a conservatism maintains that there has been no significant christological development. E.g., Matt 16:13–20 is accepted as pure history whereby Jesus acknowledges enthusiastically Peter's confession that he is the Messiah, the Son of the living God—despite the fact that in Mark 8:27–30 (held by most to be earlier) Peter's confession and Jesus' reaction are quite different. Again, John 8:58; 17:5 are treated as accurate history in which Jesus speaks as a preexistent divine figure—despite the fact that there is no indication of that in the Synoptic tradition. Some hold such a conservative position in reaction to more liberal views; others hold it because they are unfamiliar with any more liberal views. Catholics are usually in the latter class and are equally uninformed of the official teaching of the church that the Gospels are *not* necessarily literal accounts of the words and deeds of Jesus (→ Church Pronouncements, 72:35).

6   (B) Nonscholarly Liberalism. At the opposite end of the spectrum is the view that there is no continuity between Jesus' self-evaluation and the exalted christology of the NT documents. Such liberalism dismisses NT christology as unimportant. Already in the late 18th cent. there were attempts to eliminate the doctrinal sections of the NT to preserve the view of Jesus as a gentle moralizer who never spoke in a way that would imply he was more than an ordinary man. His overenthusiastic followers were regarded as the source of all higher evaluations moving toward divinity.

7   (C) Scholarly Liberalism. We turn now from such extreme views to more nuanced positions held by reputable scholars. Scholarly liberalism differs from nonscholarly liberalism in several important ways. It recognizes that the NT is shot through with christology from beginning to end and that its authors claimed far more than that Jesus was a moralizer. Nevertheless, it is liberalism because it regards the theology of the NT as a mistaken evaluation of Jesus which does not stand in real continuity with his self-evaluation. Scholarly liberals have traced the creative process in NT christology with careful methodology, and we owe to them some of the first detailed schemas of the growth of NT thought. They stressed the possibility of growth from the distinctive theological viewpoints proper to the Palestinian communities of Aramaic-/Hebrew-speaking Jewish Christians, to the Syrian communities of Greek-speaking Jewish Christians, to the Greek-speaking Gentile Christians of the churches of Asia Minor and Greece, and finally to communities influenced by individual geniuses such as Paul and John. In the late 19th cent., scholarship thought it had the linguistic and historical data necessary for detecting exactly such phases of Christian development. (But some 20th-cent. discoveries actually overthrew some of the 19th-cent. hypotheses.) A classic example was W. Bousset, *Kyrios Christos,* which appeared in 1913 (Nash, 1970; → NT Criticism, 70:41). A frequent claim in liberal analyses of developing christology would be that titles such as Lord and Son of God were applied to Jesus in a divine sense only in the Hellenistic Christian mission—either they did not exist at an earlier Jewish-Christian stage or were used in a much humbler sense of Master and Messiah. One got the impression of a linear development toward a "higher christology," i.e., a christology which utilized titles more clearly evocative of divinity. This linear development would have moved from the Jewish world to the Hellenistic world, from an earlier period to a later period. The invented high christology was often treated as a *felix culpa* because only through such divinization was the memory of Jesus preserved. The historical Jesus was a preacher of stark ethical demand who challenged the religious institutions and the false ideas of his time. His ideals and insights were not lost because the community imposed on its memory of him a christology that turned him into the heavenly Son of Man, the Lord and Judge of the world, indeed, into a God. But if in centuries past such a christological crutch was necessary to keep the memory of Jesus operative, in the judgment of the liberal scholars that crutch could now be discarded. Modern scholarship could detect the real Jesus and hold onto him without the christological trappings.

8   (D) Bultmannian Existentialism. Scholarly liberalism flourished in the optimistic period antedating World War I: a period marked by an appreciation of the achievements of modern technology and of human ability to learn a correct way to live. The war showed that humanity was more adept in learning a way to die and led to a new appreciation of a more traditional Christian emphasis on the need of salvation by God in Jesus. Spokesmen of this reaction included K. Barth in systematic theology and R. Bultmann in NT study (→ NT Criticism, 70:46–52). Because Bultmann was radical in his approach to the NT, sometimes he has falsely been described as liberal when in fact he categorically rejected the liberalism of the prewar period. Of course, he continued to accept the methodology developed by liberal scholars in classifying stages in the development of NT christology and indeed sought to refine the method more precisely. He remained almost agnostic about the relationship between NT christology and the self-evaluation of Jesus, but he did not think that the christology distorted the import of Jesus. Rather, there was a *functional equivalence* between the NT christological proclamations and Jesus' proclamation of the kingdom of God. This functional equivalence was worked out in terms of an existentialism. Humanity needs to escape from the vicious circle of futile existence, and that can come only through the delivering action of God. Jesus came proclaiming that God was acting decisively in his own ministry and challenged people to accept this divine action. The church demanded that people accept Jesus as Messiah and Lord and by so doing was equivalently offering the same existential challenge that Jesus offered. For this reason it would be disastrous to dispense with the christology of the NT as liberals had advocated, because that would be tantamount to dispensing with the challenge that is the core of Christianity, a challenge based on what God has done for us rather than on what we can do for ourselves. Bultmann's greatest influence on christology was in the period from the 1920s to the 1950s.

9   (E) Moderate Conservatism. In the second half of the 20th cent. there was a shift to a more conservative position than that of Bultmann in terms of a discernible continuity between the evaluation of Jesus during the ministry and the evaluation of him in NT writings. Some of the scholars listed below might be surprised to have themselves classified under a conservatism; but when their positions are compared to those of liberalism and existentialism, that designation is not too inappropriate, for they clearly posit a christology in the ministry of Jesus himself. They would be divided on whether that christology was *explicit* or *implicit*. Explicit christology would have been a self-evaluation in which Jesus employed titles or designations already known in Jewish circles. Implicit christology would relegate the titles and designations to early church usage attested in the NT but would attribute to Jesus himself attitudes and actions that implied an exalted status which was made explicit after his death. Among the earlier advocates of explicit christology one might list O. Cullmann, C. H. Dodd, J. Jeremias, V. Taylor, and many Roman Catholic writers in the pre–Vatican II period. Among those who tended toward implicit christology may be listed F. Hahn, R. H. Fuller, N. Perrin, and some of the post-Bultmannians in Germany (→ NT Criticism, 70:64–70). Explicit christology, which seemed to be fading, was revived in the late 20th cent. because of the Qumran discoveries, which gave new impetus to the contention that Jesus might very well have used titles like Son of God, and Lord, since they were current in an exalted meaning in Palestine in his time. For the positions of J. P. Meier and J. A. Fitzmyer pertaining to titles, → Jesus, 78:35, 39; → Pauline Theology, 82:49, 51, 52.

"Son of Man" remains one title that many scholars think Jesus used of himself. "Messiah" remains a title that others may have used of him during his lifetime. It is quite inaccurate to say that Jesus rejected the title Messiah, even though a comparison of Gospels and a critical evaluation of passages in which it occurs would indicate that he may never have fully accepted the designation. (Acceptance in Matt 16:16–17 and Mark 14:61–62 is balanced by qualification in the parallels Mark 8:29–30; and Matt 26:63–64. John 4:25–26 is modified by the peculiar sense "Messiah" might have in a Samaritan context.) The strongest elements in implicit christology are Jesus' use of *Abba*, his prefacing his statements with *Amen*, his teaching with authority as if he had the right to speak for God (without any indica-

tion that the word of God had come to him—he seemed already to possess it), and his assumption that what he said and did (by way of healing, etc.) was bringing the rule or kingdom of God into this world (→ Jesus, 78:19–23, 30–31).

**10   ** A peculiar aspect of the issue of Jesus' self-evaluation involves the range of *Jesus' knowledge*—a subject discussed particularly by Catholics. An ultra-conservatism (nonscholarly) claims that since Jesus was the divine Son, the Second Person of the Trinity, he knew, even as a human, all that God knows. Some with scholarly pretensions defend this by the argument that the person is the subject of knowledge and there was only one person in Jesus. In fact, however, this approach was unacceptable to the greatest of the scholastic theologians. Thomas Aq. (*Summa Theologiae* 3, q.9, a.1, ad 1) observed: "If there had not been in the soul of Christ some other knowledge besides his divine knowledge, he would not have known anything. Divine knowledge cannot be an act of the human soul of Christ; it belongs to another nature." For the Scholastics, knowledge comes through nature, and God and human beings know in different ways: God's knowledge is immediate and nonconceptual; human knowledge is through abstraction and is conceptual. Therefore, divine knowledge is not simply transferable to a human mind. Precisely because of that limitation, Scholastics posited special aids to the human nature of Jesus, so that he would know more than other people, e.g., beatific vision, infused knowledge. Current systematic theologians of various tendencies (K. Rahner, B. Lonergan, H. U. von Balthasar, J. Galot) deny the presence of such aids and/or recognize that Jesus did not have unlimited human knowledge. Appeal may be made to the teaching of Chalcedon (DS 301, based on Heb 4:15) which made Jesus consubstantial with human beings in all things except sin—note that the exception to his human limitations was sin, not ignorance. Indeed, Cyril of Alexandria, the orthodox archfoe of Nestorianism (two persons or powers in Christ) said of Christ: "We have admired his goodness in that for love of us he has not refused to descend to such a low position as to bear all that belongs to our nature, included in which is ignorance" (PG 75. 369). From the viewpoint of doctrine or of systematic theology, accepting a limited human knowledge for Jesus does not deny that he was God; it acknowledges that he was truly human. From the viewpoint of biblical studies, accepting a limited human knowledge for Jesus means doing justice to passages like Mark 5:30–32; 10:17–18; 13:32; Luke 2:40,52; Heb 4:15; 5:8–9.

**11   ** A particular facet of the issue of Jesus' self-evaluation and self-knowledge is sometimes studied under the question "Did he know he was God?" That is an unfortunate phrasing because sometimes it creates confusion with the wider issue of whether Jesus knew his own identity. It would be perfectly possible to assume that Jesus knew who he was (and no page of the NT ever indicates self-doubt; → Jesus, 78:29) and yet to think that he could not have formulated that identity in the terminology of later theology. Some passages in the NT call Jesus God (Heb 1:8–9; John 1:1; 20:28; cf. Rom 9:5; 1 John 5:20; Tit 2:13), but they do not solve the issue of Jesus' self-appellation. "God" for a Jew at the beginning of the 1st cent. would refer to the Father in heaven. The person who asks the question "Did Jesus know he was God?" almost always has a trinitarian interpretation of God and so is not asking, "Did Jesus know he was the Father in heaven?" The term might not have been applicable to Jesus in his lifetime (Mark 10:17–18) but might have become perfectly applicable to him later on because reflection on Jesus changed the notion of "God," so that it could refer not only to the Father in heaven but also to the Son on earth. Such a development need not mean that Christians were trying to change the true identity of Jesus; it could mean that they began to adapt human language to express that identity. An understanding of such a process of adaptation in Christian thought and language underlies much of what follows (see Brown, *Jesus;* also *BTB* 15 [1985] 74–79).

12   (II) Development in the NT Understanding of Jesus. The survey given above of different attitudes toward NT christology centered on efforts to relate evaluations of Jesus in the NT writings to his self-evaluation. Now let us leave aside Jesus' self-evaluation in order to analyze differences in NT evaluations. While some have done this under the rubric of titles (→ 3 above), another helpful procedure is to study how evaluations were associated by NT writers with different aspects of Jesus' career. We may use the term "christological moments," i.e., scenes in the life of Jesus which became the vehicle for *giving expression* to postresurrectional christology. This term is not meant to include the issue of whether revelation took place at a "moment" such as the baptism of Jesus by JBap, but only the extent to which the NT writers communicated christology in describing that moment. If one consults NT thought chronologically, beginning with the earliest evidence (some of it antedating the earliest writings) and moving toward the later evidence, one can trace a peculiar "backwards" pattern. The earlier evidence interpreted scenes at the end of Jesus' life christologically; the later evidence interpreted scenes at the beginning of his life christologically. That observation may be useful but requires *caution:* the evidence is slim and far from complete; development of thought is rarely linear; at any given moment, surely, different views coexisted. Liberal scholars in the early 20th cent. (→ 7 above) sought to trace a pattern such as the one given below, but did so with the supposition that developments gave to Jesus and his life a christological meaning that they never had historically. Here we are accepting the self-understanding of the NT writers who thought that they were vocalizing and appreciating a reality that was already there. The development involved a growing Christian understanding about the identity of Jesus, not the creation *ex nihilo* of a new identity.

13   (A) Second-Coming Christology. An expectation of the parousia was strong throughout the NT period. We are concerned here only with statements that attach a christological evaluation to the moment of Jesus' second coming. The antiquity of these statements is plausible but not certain. E.g., it is notoriously difficult to distinguish from Lucan interpretation in the 70s or 80s a nucleus of what may be truly ancient in the sermons Luke reports in Acts. Some christological statements in those sermons do not resemble typical Lucan christology; but Luke may have been archaizing, imagining how early Christians spoke and thought. In Acts 3:19–21 the Lucan Peter posits an interval of repentance before the parousia. That event will involve God's sending the appointed Messiah, Jesus, whom heaven must welcome until the time for establishing all that God spoke by the prophets. This could be read to mean that only when Jesus comes back will he be the Messiah. A strong strain in Jewish messianic expectation would have the Davidic anointed king setting up a monarchy centered on Jerusalem, where the Gentiles would come to worship; the Messiah would bring victory, peace, and prosperity to Israel on earth. In fact, Jesus did none of that, but the Jewish expectations could be kept intact and still applied to Jesus if one hoped that when Jesus came

back he would do everything that Judaism expected. Similarly, the prayer *maranatha,* "Our Lord, come!" (1 Cor 16:22; cf. Rev 22:20; → Pauline Theology, 82:53), *may* be early and may have arisen among the first Aramaic-speaking Christians. It may have implied that when Jesus came then he would be Lord ruling the earth. Some scholars maintain that future sayings with Jesus returning from heaven as the Son of Man in order to judge the world were the earliest Son-of-Man usage (→ Jesus, 78:38–40). Note that the relatively few statements which attach titles primarily to the parousia do not represent the dominant christology of the works that include them; and so future christology may have enjoyed relatively short preeminence. See J. A. T. Robinson, *JTS* 7 (1956) 177–89; Fuller, *Foundations* 143–47, 184–85; R. F. Zehnle, *Peter's Pentecost Discourse* (SBLMS 15; Nash, 1970) 57–59, 92–93.

14   (B) Resurrection Christology. The christology of some epistolary statements that have a likelihood of pre-Pauline origin, as well as the dominant christology of the sermons attributed to Peter and Paul in Acts, is related not to a future but to a present moment: the resurrection. Jesus is Messiah, Lord, and Son of God in the Father's presence in heaven, and he has achieved this status by being raised up. Acts 2:32,36: "This Jesus God raised up.... God has made him both Lord and Messiah, this Jesus whom you crucified." Acts 5:31: "God exalted him at His right hand as Leader and Savior." Acts 13:32–33: "What God promised to the Fathers, He has fulfilled for us their children by raising Jesus, as it is written in Ps 2: 'You are my son; today I have begotten you.'" Rom 1:3–4: "Born of the seed of David according to the flesh; designated Son of God in power according to the Holy Spirit [Spirit of Holiness] as of resurrection from the dead." Phil 2:8–9: "[Jesus] became obedient unto death, even death on the cross. Therefore God has exalted him and bestowed on him the name [i.e., 'Lord'] which is above every name." In some of these texts the resurrection was originally contrasted with a public ministry of lowliness, so that through the resurrection Jesus became greater than he had been in the ministry. (This is what scholars mean by a "two-step" christology. Of course, they are speaking about the christology of the individual quotations, not the christology of the works in which they are preserved.) The origins of such a christology may lie in the fact that through the resurrection the first disciples learned aspects of Jesus that they had not known clearly before—an insight translated into terms of God *making* Jesus Lord and Messiah, *begetting* him as his Son, or *giving* him an exalted name. Resurrection christology would have required a greater change in the Jewish expectations of the Messiah than did second-coming christology, for now the victory, peace, prosperity, and divine worship are all transferred to heaven from the earth of Jewish expectation. It is understandable that resurrection christology may have had a greater preeminence than parousia christology because in the balance, while Christianity remains a religion of hope in what God has yet to do through Jesus, it is much more strongly a religion of what God has already done through Jesus.

15   (C) Ministry Christology. By the time of preserved Christian writings (after AD 50; → Canonicity, 66:56), moments of Jesus' earthly existence before his death and resurrection were being interpreted christologically. All the canonical Gospels (written between 65 and 100) present a Jesus who was clearly Messiah, Son of Man, and Son of God (and sometimes specifically Lord) during his public ministry. The Gospel reader is made party to a revelation connected to the baptism of Jesus by JBap where God points out his Son (Mark 1:11;

Matt 3:17; Luke 3:22; cf. John 1:33–34). In two-step christology (→ 14 above) the ministry from the baptism to the cross could easily be one of lowliness (Phil 2:7: "the form of a servant") since exaltation came only with resurrection; but in ministry christology, where exalted status and lowly service coexist, there is inevitable tension. Interestingly, a resurrection christology passage, such as Acts 13:33, can apply Ps 2:7 to the risen Jesus without qualification: "You are my son; today I have begotten you." Yet the Synoptic baptismal texts just cited modify Ps 2:7 by combining it with words (italicized here) from the description of the Suffering Servant of Isa (42:1): "You are my *beloved* son; *with you I am well pleased.*" To understand Jesus as the messianic king during his public ministry one must recognize that he was simultaneously the Suffering Servant without beauty, pierced for our offences, bearing the guilt of all (Isa 53). Jews who did not accept Christian claims might well point out that a Messiah whose life terminated in suffering was a drastic change of the concept of the expected anointed Davidic king. Christians would reply that Jesus threw light on the whole of the Scriptures and showed how once separate passages should be combined.

16   In describing the ministry of Jesus, individual NT writings treat differently the tension between the exalted Messiah/Son image and the lowly servant, and this difference contributed to the distinctiveness of each of the four Gospels. *Mark* preserves the greatest amount of lowliness by describing a precrucifixion ministry in which no human being acknowledges Jesus' Sonship—a "secret" (→ Mark, 41:4) known to the reader and to the demons. Mark 8:27–33 shows how little even Peter, the most prominent disciple, has understood Jesus. Only after Jesus' death do we finally have a believing acknowledgment of him as Son of God (15:39). The Marcan picture of Jesus as not knowing certain things and being treated rudely by his disciples reflects a ministry of lowliness. With *Matt* some of the tension in the ministry is resolved in favor of exaltation breaking through lowliness, for christological insights (presumably of post-resurrectional origin) are gained by Jesus' disciples (Matt 14:33; 16:16–17). This leads to a portrayal of Jesus where limitations are avoided and the disciples are more reverent (cf. Matt 8:25 with Mark 4:38; Matt 9:22 with Mark 5:30–33). The situation in *Luke* is complicated because the author has a second book (Acts) in which Peter can vocalize postresurrectional christology. (By comparison, Matthew has written his "Acts of the Apostles" by superimposition on the Gospel narrative.) Consequently, Luke does not increase the intensity of Marcan christological confession during the ministry in the way Matt does; yet Luke is even more sensitive than Matt in refusing to portray the human limitations of Jesus or irreverence toward him on the part of disciples, e.g., on the Mt. of Olives there is no extreme agitation of Jesus nor a flight of his disciples. In *John* the tension is largely dissolved, for the glory of Jesus (revealed by exception at the transfiguration in the Synoptics) is manifested to the disciples in Jesus' first miraculous sign (John 2:11). His disciples know his titles (Messiah, King of Israel, Son of God) in the first days of the ministry, only to be told they shall see greater things (1:41,49,50). Jesus makes clear divine claims (10:30,36; 14:9); his opponents reject them (5:18; 10:33; 19:7); but Thomas is led to confess him as Lord and God (20:28). The Johannine Jesus has no real human limitations: he knows all things (6:5–6,71); he does not need to ask the Father for anything because of their unity (11:41–42; 12:27–28); and he is in complete control even of his death (10:17–18,39; 18:6; 19:30).

17   **(D) Boyhood Christology.** Mark identifies

Jesus as the Son of God at his baptism, without raising the question of whether Jesus was Son of God before the ministry. But the other three Gospels, as well as some Pauline passages, associate an exalted christological identity with preministry moments in Jesus' career. It is not illogical that Christians would wonder whether the solemn pronouncements and miraculous power of the postbaptismal Jesus were apparent during his "private life" at Nazareth before his baptism. Because the Gospels report that during his public career Jesus was a relatively unknown figure among his townspeople (Mark 6:1–6 par.), they are discreet about a marvelous preministry awareness. Luke 2:49 has Jesus at age 12 (the first time his speech is recorded) conscious that God is his Father and that he has a special task; but Luke 2:50–51 adds that Jesus was obedient to parents who did not understand and so, presumably, did not proclaim his identity in an open manner while he was growing up. The Cana miracle in John may originally have been an in-family, preministry miracle (cf. 2:1–2,12; R. E. Brown, *The Community of the Beloved Disciple* [NY, 1978] 193–95) where again Jesus had to deal with a mother who did not understand him. The extracanonical tradition is less restrained, and in the *Infancy Gospel of Thomas* (→ Apocrypha, 67:65) Jesus does miracles at ages 5 through 12, producing some of the same reactions that his miracles produce in the canonical Gospel accounts of the ministry.

18   **(E) Conception Christology.** Matt 1:20–25; Luke 1:34–35; and *Prot. Jas.* 11–14 associate Jesus' christological identity as Emmanuel, the Holy One, and the Son of God with the moment of his conception through the Spirit without a human father. This identity is made known through an angel to Joseph or Mary. Others (magi, shepherds) who also receive the revelation are carefully removed from the scene after they honor the child (Matt 2:12; Luke 2:20). Presumably, then, the two evangelists used the idea of a family secret to explain how Jesus was unknown when he began his ministry even though he had such auspicious beginnings. In any case, Matt and Luke omit Marcan references to Jesus' relatives as not understanding him (see Mark 3:21; 6:4 ["among his own relatives"]). The idea of a virginal conception of the Messiah was completely unknown to Judaism; nevertheless, reflection on Jesus' conception threw light on the potentialities of the LXX of Isa 7:14: "The virgin shall conceive and bear a son and name him Emmanuel." Although not yet the christology of Nicaea, where Jesus is identified with the eternal divine Son, the idea that the Son of God was conceived without a human father certainly corrected any idea that Jesus was a human being adopted by God as his Son at the baptism. Conception christology appeared in writing first *ca.* the 80s, but the agreement of Matt and Luke on this point in their infancy narratives, when almost everything else differs, suggests that it was an early pre-Gospel insight.

19   **(F) Preexistence Christology.** Thus far, the moments discussed as vehicles for vocalizing the Christian understanding of Jesus were moments within his earthly career. But certain NT passages indicate that early Christians understood the story of God's Son to have had a prehistory before that career. In what follows it is not always easy to distinguish between a precise notion of the preexistence of the divine Son and a plan of preparation in God's "mind" for the coming of the Son.

Preexistence in the Moses and Abraham Periods. In 1 Cor 10:4 Paul states that "our fathers" who accompanied Moses in the desert-wandering all drank the same spiritual drink: "They drank from the spiritual rock that was following them and the rock was Christ." This is closer to preexistence than is John 3:14, which also uses desert-wandering imagery for Jesus. Matt 1:1 starts the story of the birth or genesis of Jesus with Abraham begetting Isaac. This is closer to preexistence than is Gal 3:16, where Paul contends that Jesus is the descendant or seed of Abraham. In John 8:56 Jesus says: "Abraham rejoiced to see my day; he saw it and was glad." When "the Jews" object that this was impossible, given Jesus' age of less than 50, Jesus insists "Before Abraham came to be, I am" (8:58).

20 *Preexistence in the Adam Period.* The Lucan genealogy (3:23,38) identifies Jesus as son of Adam, Son of God. The pre-Pauline hymn of Phil 2:6 *may* be interpreted as describing Jesus coexistent with and parallel to Adam—two figures in the image of God, one grasping at being equal to God and falling (Gen 3:5,15-19), the other not grasping at being equal to God but emptying himself voluntarily and therefore being raised by God to equality (Phil 2:9-11). This would be closer to preexistence than the parallel between Jesus and Adam in Rom 5:12-17 (cf. also G. Howard, *CBQ* 40 [1978] 368-87).

21 *Creational Preexistence.* 1 Cor 8:6 speaks of everything being made through Jesus Christ. Col 1:15-20 (which may have antedated the letter) is part of a hymn making God's Son the firstborn of all creation, through whom all things were created (cf. Sir 24:9). The hymn in John 1:1-2 makes clearer that the Son (see 1:18) existed *before* creation. Only John is precise about an incarnation in which this divine Word becomes flesh and dwells among us as Jesus Christ, although some would interpret Phil 2:6-7 to mean that. Clearer for some notion of incarnation in Pauline thought is 2 Cor 8:9. That the preexistence of Jesus as God's Son is not merely hymnic figurative language or poetic license is clear from John 17:5, where Jesus speaks literally and consciously of having had a glorified existence with the Father before the world began (see also 16:28; 3:16; 5:19; 8:27,58).

22 *Eternal Preexistence.* No NT passage states precisely that the Son coexisted from all eternity with the Father. No earlier NT "moment" is found than "In the beginning was the Word" of John 1:1. In the 4th cent., Arius was content with the idea that the Word had a beginning before the creation of the world; but Athanasius led the Council of Nicaea in condemning Arius by insisting that the Word had no beginning: Begotten not made; there never was a time when he was not. The fact that such specifications were not found in the NT did not refute Athanasius, for he recognized that Arius was raising a question not specifically asked in NT times and which therefore could not be answered by quoting the NT. The all-important issue for him was whether the necessary postbiblical specification was loyal to the direction of the NT: "If the expressions are not in so many words in the Scriptures, yet they contained the sense of the Scriptures" ("Letters concerning the Decrees of the Council of Nicaea" 5.19-21 [NPNF 2.4. 162-64]).

23 **(G) Overview.** The variation in insights discussed above is intelligible as a reaction against a temporal limitation to christology. It is and remains true that Jesus will be the Messiah at the parousia—the formula becomes problematic only if by limitation it signals that he was and is not the Messiah before the parousia. Resurrection christology avoids such a misunderstanding by insisting that he is already Messiah, Lord, and Son of God through the resurrection—an insight that becomes problematical only when by limitation Christians might think that he did not have that identity before the resurrection. Similarly for ministry, boyhood, and conception christology. Of course, "moment christology" (even that of Nicaea) has the drawback of using time categories to phrase what lies outside time. Preexistence may be a more exalted category than thinking of Jesus' becoming God's Son in time, but from another viewpoint there is no "pre" in the timeless realm of God. From the most orthodox viewpoint no human language has expressed Jesus' identity perfectly, and the best that Christians have been able to do is to reject limitations that become obvious.

24 An underlying difficulty is that christology is a struggle to describe *God's* presence and action in and through Jesus, and the human never comprehends the divine totally. That realization may show how superficial is the complaint that Jesus spoke about God and the church erroneously spoke about Jesus. In speaking about Jesus the church was speaking about how God made his kingdom present. Inadequate, too, is the distinction proposed by E. Schillebeeckx (*Jesus* [NY, 1979] 545-50) that in the earlier stages there was only a "theology of Jesus of Nazareth" (a first-order assertion that in Jesus the man God saves human beings) while in the later stages there was a "christology" (a second-order assertion about the identity of Jesus). Even though Schillebeeckx confirms that the first-order assertion leads necessarily to the second-order assertion, he is content with the notion that one is already a Christian in entertaining the former. The *NJBC* article on Jesus (→ 78) indicates that there were affirmations by Jesus, titles applied to him in his lifetime, and peculiar silences (e.g., no statement that the word of God came to Jesus, possibly implying that the divine was already intimate to him), so that "christology" may be a more appropriate (even if inadequate) term than a "theology of Jesus of Nazareth." NT christology was primarily functional, indicating what role Jesus played in effecting God's salvation of human beings (*pro nobis*); but in so doing, it reflects much about what Jesus was in himself (*in se*). The Pauline affirmation that God was in Christ reconciling the world to himself (2 Cor 5:19), John's affirmation that the Word was God (1:1), and Nicaea's confession of true God of true God show an increasing movement from the functional to the ontological—but the earliest affirmation was not without its ontological implications, and the latest had a very functional origin and goal.

ESCHATOLOGY AND APOCALYPTICISM

BIBLIOGRAPHY

25   Allison, D. C., *The End of the Ages Has Come* (Phl, 1985). Beker, J. C., *Paul's Apocalyptic Gospel* (Phl, 1982); *Paul the Apostle* (Phl, 1980). Bultmann, R., *Jesus and the Word* (NY, 1958); *TNT.* Collins, J. J. (ed.), *Apocalypse* (Semeia 14 [1979]); *The Apocalyptic Imagination* (NY, 1984). Cullmann, O., *Christ and Time* (London, 1951); *Salvation in History* (NY, 1967). Dodd, C. H., *The Parables of the Kingdom* (2d ed.; NY, 1961). Hellholm, D. (ed.), *Apocalypticism in the Mediterranean World and the Near East* (Tübingen, 1983). Hoekema, A. A., *The Bible and the Future* (GR, 1979). Horsley, R. A. and J. S. Hanson, *Bandits, Prophets* *and Messiahs* (NY, 1985). Jeremias, J., *The Parables of Jesus* (8th ed.; NY, 1972). Käsemann, E., "The Beginnings of Christian Theology" and "On the Subject of Primitive Christian Apocalyptic," *NTQT* 82–107, 108–137. Koch, K., *The Rediscovery of Apocalyptic* (SBT ns 22; Naperville, 1972). Kümmel, W. G., *Promise and Fulfillment* (SBT 23; London, 1957). Ladd, G. E., *The Presence of the Future* (GR, 1974). Lambrecht, J. (ed.), *L'Apocalypse johannique et l'Apocalyptique dans le Nouveau Testament* (BETL 53; Gembloux, 1980). Otto, R., *The Kingdom of God and the Son of Man* (rev. ed.; London, 1938). Perrin, N., *Jesus and the Language of the Kingdom* (Phl, 1976). Rowland, C., *The Open Heaven* (NY,

1982). Sanders, E. P., *Jesus and Judaism* (Phl, 1985). Schweitzer, A., *The Mysticism of Paul the Apostle* (NY, 1968; Ger 1930). Snyder, G. F., "The Literalization of the Apocalyptic Form in the New Testament Church," *BR* 14 (1969) 5–18. Vawter, B., "Levitical Messianism and the New Testament" and "'And He Shall Come Again With Glory': Paul and Christian Apocalyptic," *The Path of Wisdom* (Wilmington, 1986) 257–80, 315–23. Wilder, A. N., *Jesus' Parables and the War of Myths* (Phl, 1982). Yarbro Collins, A., *Crisis and Catharsis* (Phl, 1984); (ed.), *Early Christian Apocalypticism* (*Semeia* 36 [1986]).

26   Outline.

27   (I) Terminology and Modern Scholarship. This is a field in which terminology has been disputed, and scholars have had very divergent interpretations of the evidence.

(A) "Eschatology" and "Apocalypticism." The term "eschatology," from the Gk *eschatos*, "last," was coined in Germany in the early 19th cent. when it was used primarily for that branch of systematic theology which dealt with the last things: death, judgment, heaven and hell. The emphasis was on the destiny of the individual. In the 20th cent., literary and historical perspectives overshadowed the dogmatic. The term has been redefined to take more into account the actual content of biblical and related writings, to include the ultimate destiny of the Israelite or Jewish nation (national eschatology) and of the world in general (cosmic eschatology), as well as the destiny of the individual (personal eschatology). In place of concern for the future of the nation, some texts express hope for a righteous remnant or for the church (collective eschatology).

28   One of the debated issues relating to eschatology has been whether the term should be used only for events and states of being beyond history or also for events within salvation history. One step toward resolving this debate is the distinction between prophetic and apocalyptic eschatology. The eschatology of the prophets includes the expectation of decisive turning points in history due to divine intervention, and so it focuses on the fate of Israel and Judah (→ OT Apocalyptic, 19:3). The eschatology of the apocalypses focuses more on the heavenly world, personal afterlife, and a new cosmic creation. The term thus may be used appropriately for events both within and beyond history.

29   "Apocalypticism" is a modern scholarly term, based on the preface to the NT book of Revelation (the Apocalypse), which describes the content of the work as an *apokalypsis*, "revelation." Scholars have defined a literary genre "apocalypse," which includes Dan and other writings similar in form and content to Rev (→ OT Apocalyptic, 19:4). Apocalyptic eschatology consists of the interpretation of past and present and especially the hopes for the future found in these works. Similar ideas

and hopes are found in writings that are not themselves apocalypses in literary form.

30   (B) Scholarship and Early Christian Eschatology. In 19th-cent. Germany, liberal theologians overlooked the eschatological element in the traditions about Jesus and interpreted the kingdom of God as an inner and spiritual change within human hearts (S. Neill, *The Interpretation of the New Testament 1861–1961* [NY, 1966] 111–12). Similarly, American proponents of the "social gospel" held that the kingdom of God in the teaching of Jesus was the expression of an ideal social order (H. J. Cadbury, *The Peril of Modernizing Jesus* [London, 1962] 88–93).

31   In explicit opposition to the liberal interpretation of Jesus, especially that of A. Ritschl, J. Weiss argued in 1892: "The Kingdom of God as Jesus thought of it is never something subjective, inward, or spiritual, but is always the objective messianic Kingdom, which usually is pictured as a territory into which one enters, or as a land in which one has a share, or as a treasure which comes down from heaven" (*Jesus' Proclamation of the Kingdom of God* [Phl, 1971] 133). Weiss believed that such an objective, cosmic eschatology was incompatible with the modern world view. He proposed (135–36) that preaching and instruction inculcate a modern approximation of Jesus' attitude: "The world will further endure, but we, as individuals will soon leave it. . . . We do not await a Kingdom of God which is to come down from heaven to earth and abolish this world, but we do hope to be gathered with the church of Jesus Christ into the heavenly *basileia* [kingdom]."

32   A. Schweitzer (→ NT Criticism, 70:35), building on the work of Weiss, argued in 1906 that Jesus joined the movement of repentance begun by JBap and proclaimed that the harvest ripening on earth was the last. He sent out his disciples to make known what was about to happen. He did not expect to see them back in the present age (Matt 10:23). Before they completed their missionary journey, the Son of Man would appear from heaven, an event identical with the dawn of the kingdom of God. But the disciples returned to him and the Son of Man did not appear, i.e., Jesus was not revealed as the Son of Man. From the first, Jesus' preaching about the kingdom of God included the expectation of suffering, death, and resurrection, not as the special mission of Jesus but as the tribulation that all the elect would suffer in the final struggle with the evil powers. When the prediction of Matt 10:23 failed to come to pass, Jesus concluded that the premessianic tribulation was to be concentrated on himself alone. He must suffer that the kingdom might come, and so he set out for Jerusalem to die there. Jesus laid hold of the wheel of the world to set it moving on its last revolution, which would bring history to a close. When it refused to turn, he threw himself upon it. Then it turned and crushed him. His mangled body is hanging on it still. "That is His victory and His reign" (*The Quest of the Historical Jesus* [NY, 1968; Ger 1906] 350–97; esp. 371). According to Schweitzer (399), "Jesus means something to our world because a mighty spiritual force streams forth from Him and flows through our time also." The essential difference between Jesus' world view and the modern one is that Jesus' spirit was world-negating, whereas the modern spirit is world-affirming. Rather than our twisting Jesus' words to make them conform to modern values, the spirit of Jesus should be recovered in all its strangeness and allowed to challenge modern individuals by calling for a personal rejection of the world (401–2). Schweitzer's point of view was that Jesus' eschatology was primarily oriented to the future; there was no fulfillment or decisive turning point in his lifetime. This position is called consistent or thoroughgoing eschatology.

33 In 1926 R. Bultmann (→ NT Criticism, 70:46–52) in his *Jesus* developed a position along the same lines as Weiss and Schweitzer from the historical point of view. Theologically, however, he argued that, whereas the kingdom of God is itself entirely future in the message of Jesus, it is a power which determines the present by calling for human decision (see Perrin, *Jesus* 35–37).

34 C. H. Dodd (→ NT Criticism, 70:63) in 1935 interpreted the eschatology of Jesus in explicit opposition to Schweitzer. He argued, on the basis of Mark 1:15 and Matt 12:28/Luke 11:20, that Jesus proclaimed the kingdom of God to have come in his ministry. The parables imply, according to Dodd, that the eschatological crisis, the coming of the kingdom of God, was present in the activity of Jesus. This position is known as realized eschatology.

35 J. Jeremias (→ NT Criticism, 70:30) contended that Weiss, Schweitzer, and Bultmann were one-sided in arguing that Jesus' eschatology was purely future and that Dodd was one-sided in arguing that it was purely present. Each position had some justification. Jeremias' own summary of Jesus' teaching was that it was an eschatology in the process of realization (→ 66 below; Perrin, *Jesus* 39). Many scholars followed Jeremias in concluding that for Jesus the kingdom of God was both present and future (Kümmel, *Promise*; N. Perrin, *The Kingdom of God in the Teaching of Jesus* [Phl, 1963]; also, *Jesus* 39–40). In his later work, Perrin questioned the propriety of thinking about the kingdom of God in terms of present and future. Rather, he argued that kingdom of God is a tensive symbol that cannot be related simply to space and time (*Jesus* 45; → Jesus, 78:17).

36 One of the strengths of Weiss's and Schweitzer's reconstructions was that they interpreted the life and teaching of Jesus in the context of contemporary Jewish eschatology. Since Dodd, the tendency has been either to ignore that context or to overemphasize the differences between Jesus' teaching and Jewish eschatological literature. Recently Sanders (*Jesus*) has offered an interpretation which preserves some of the valid insights of Weiss and Schweitzer, but in a form which takes into account the results of historical-critical study of the Gospels in the meantime. His thesis is that Jesus was an eschatological prophet who taught a form of Jewish restoration (national) eschatology. Allison's position (*End*) is developed along similar lines.

37 **(C) Scholarship and Early Jewish Eschatology.** A phrase often used to express the older consensus about the kingdom of God being both present and future for Jesus (and Paul) was "already and not yet." This partially realized eschatology often was said to be unique to Jesus and the early Christians; Jewish eschatology was described as completely future-oriented (so, e.g., E. Schüssler Fiorenza, in *Apocalypticism* [ed. D. Hellholm] 302, 311–12). In fact, Jewish apocalyptic and eschatological texts of the 1st cents. BC and AD did not always present themselves as merely "proleptic" revela-

tion of a future reality. In many of them, the kingdom of God or its equivalent is a present reality, fully manifest in heaven and making its influence felt to some degree on earth. The hope for the future (and sometimes imminent expectation) is that this heavenly reality will determine fully all earthly circumstances.

38 The *Psalms of Solomon* constitute a collection similar in form and content to the canonical Pss and to the hymns from Qumran (→ Apocrypha, 67:46, 86). Produced by a group of devout Jews in Jerusalem in response to the conquest of Jerusalem by the Romans in 63 BC, *Pss. Sol.* date to the period between 63 and 45 BC. In several passages God is proclaimed as king in the heavens (at the present time), whose kingship is felt in the present through blessings and punishments (2:30–32; 17:1–3,46). The hope for the future is deliverance from foreign rule (chap. 7), the gathering of the dispersion of Israel (8:28; 11:2–6), and the raising up of an ideal king, the son of David, who will rule wisely over Israel and the nations (17:21–46; 18:5–9). The eschatology of this work is primarily national and earthly. There is recognition, however, that not all in Israel are faithful (*Pss. Sol.* 4; 8:1–22; 17:15–20). In addition to earthly blessings, the eschatology of this work includes eternal rewards and punishments beyond earth and history (3:11–12; 14:9–10).

39 The *Testament* (or *Assumption*) *of Moses* is Moses' farewell address to Joshua based on Deut 31–34. Although probably composed in the 2d cent. BC, it was revised and updated in the period between 3 BC and AD 30 (→ Apocrypha, 67:49). This revision was made in response to the political and social turmoil that followed Herod's death. The text portrays God as king seated on his royal throne in heaven (10:3). The hope for the future is that God will make his kingship effective on earth by punishing the Gentiles and destroying their idols (10:3–7). The eschatology is national, concerned with Israel's triumph over its enemies (10:8; see A. Yarbro Collins, *HTR* 69 [1976] 179–86). But it is heavenly as well as earthly; the people of Israel will be exalted to heaven (10:9).

40 Apart from (Jewish-) Christian literature, the clearest example of a partially realized eschatology among Jews of this period is found in the Dead Sea Scrolls (→ Apocrypha, 67:113–17). The Essenes who settled at Qumran apparently understood their leading priest and the guardian of the camp as partial fulfillments of the hoped-for Messiahs of Aaron and Israel. The hymns describe the present life of members of the group in terms of resurrection and exaltation to heaven (see Collins, *Apocalyptic* 122–40).

41 The texts discussed above were produced by members of an at least somewhat educated stratum of society, whose primary expressions of eschatological hope were probably writing and teaching. There was another stratum of society whose hopes were expressed in a more "activist," even "revolutionary" manner. The two types (writers and activists) may have worked together, but the present state of the evidence does not permit drawing that conclusion. The eschatological writings provide a context in which to understand Jesus' teaching. The historical reports about the "activists" shed light at least on how Jesus' activities probably were perceived by his contemporaries, if not on his self-understanding. The reports about the eschatological "activists" are found in the historical writings of Josephus. Of the numerous groups or movements he described, two are particularly relevant for Jesus: popular kings and eschatological prophets. After the death of Herod the Great in 4 BC, three men independently claimed kingship for themselves, supported by those who longed for an end to Roman domination and the reestablishment of an ideal native monarchy, probably Davidic (Horsley and Hanson, *Bandits* 110–17). These groups arose out of the same situation that produced the revision of *As. Mos.* Two other messianic pretenders found a following during the Jewish revolt of AD 66–70 (ibid., 118–27).

42 Some popular prophets led the people in activities that promised to be new eschatological re-enactments of the great historical acts of redemption of the past. Under Pontius Pilate a Samaritan prophet presented himself as a new Moses. About AD 45, a certain Theudas led a large group of people to the Jordan, which he expected to divide for their crossing. An Egyptian Jewish prophet led another crowd to the Mt. of Olives and promised that the walls around Jerusalem would fall, allowing them to get control of the city (ibid., 161–72). Other prophets spoke oracles and interpreted omens and signs of the eschatological judgment of God. JBap was one of these, although his baptism may also be interpreted as an eschatological activity or event. It is notable that the majority of these prophets were executed by the Romans (see R. MacMullen, *Enemies of the Roman Order* [Cambridge MA, 1966]).

After the fall of Jerusalem in AD 70, some Jewish eschatological and apocalyptic literature continued to focus on the national hopes of Israel (4 Ezra, *2 Apoc. Bar.;* → Apocrypha, 67:41–44). Other texts expressed a universal perspective (*Sib. Or.* 4; see J. J. Collins in *OTP* 1. 381–89; → Apocrypha, 67:51–52). Some returned to early apocalyptic themes like description of cosmic secrets, the heavens, and angels (*2 Enoch;* → Apocrypha, 67:8), or to personal afterlife, including the eternal rewards of the righteous and punishment of sinners (*T. Abraham;* see N. Turner in *AOT* 393–421).

43 **(II) NT Eschatology before AD 65.** The mid or late 60s are often looked on as a convenient dividing line in Christian experience, both because of the death in the 60s of major known figures like Peter, Paul, and James the brother of the Lord and because of the impact of the Jewish war against Rome and the resulting destruction of the Temple. At least we can use the date as a convenient point of organization.

(A) John the Baptist. Born of priestly descent in a town of the Judean hill country sometime before Jesus' birth (C. H. H. Scobie, *John the Baptist* [Phl, 1964] 204), JBap was one of a number of popular prophets in the 1st cent. AD (→ 42 above). His rite of baptism had affinities with the ritual washings of other ascetic individuals and groups in Syria-Palestine in the period (Scobie, *John* 33–40). Unlike most other ritual washings of the time, JBap's baptism seems to have been an act once and for all, rather than repeated. It was apparently a symbol of repentance in preparation for the manifestation of God's kingdom on earth (Matt 3:1–2,7–10; Luke 3:7–9). According to a text composed about 50 years after JBap's activity, in the last days humanity would become very wicked, so that God in wrath would destroy the human race by fire. This judgment could be averted, however, if people would repent and be baptized (*Sib. Or.* 4:152–70).

44 **(B) Jesus.** When one allows for the attempts of later Christian writers to relate and subordinate JBap to Jesus, one can infer from the Gospels that Jesus recognized JBap as an agent of God and was baptized by him (Mark 1:9; Matt 11:2–19 par.). The clear eschatological character of JBap's activity and teaching suggests that Jesus ought to be interpreted in the same context. Since the Gospels reflect the post-Easter faith and concerns of various Christian communities, they can be used only indirectly to reconstruct the life and teaching of Jesus (→ NT Criticism, 70:33–35, 65; → Church

Pronouncements, 72:35; → Jesus, 78:3, 7–10). On the methods for this reconstruction, see Jeremias, *Parables;* N. Perrin, *Rediscovering the Teaching of Jesus* [NY, 1967]; and Sanders, *Jesus*).

It is likely that Jesus, like the *Pss. Sol.* and other Jewish texts and teachers of the time, pictured God reigning in heaven as king in the present. The kingly power of God could be perceived most fundamentally in his ongoing work of creating and sustaining (this is probably one level of meaning of certain parables and sayings, e.g., Mark 4:26–29; 4:30–32 par.; Matt 6:25–33 par.). The joy communicated by Jesus, the imagery of weddings and feasting, and the mighty deeds of healing are evidence that the kingdom of God was active or manifest in Jesus' activity in a special way in both his self-understanding and in the response of many people to him (Mark 2:19; Matt 11:2–6,16–19; 13:16–17 par.).

45 It is unlikely that these present or realized aspects constitute the totality of Jesus' eschatology. When he prayed and taught his disciples to pray "Thy kingdom come," he probably referred to some objective manifestation of God's rule on earth that was more complete than any experienced so far, even in his own activity. Jesus may have been intentionally reticent about what form this coming of the kingdom would take and when it would occur (a reticence maintained, e.g., in Mark 13:32–37; 1 Thess 5:1–11). But it would be difficult to explain the apocalypticism of many of the earliest Christian communities if Jesus had been non- or anti-apocalyptic.

46 **(C) Apostolic Preaching.** It was once widely held that the speeches of Peter in the first part of Acts represent the preaching of the Christian community in Jerusalem at an early date. That opinion has been called into question, because these speeches make use of the Gk transl. of the OT and thus reflect "Hellenistic Christianity," i.e., Greek-speaking and writing Christian communities (E. Haenchen, *The Acts of the Apostles* [Phl, 1971] 185). Most of the available evidence for earliest Christianity is in Gk form. Occasionally, however, an earlier Aram stage of the tradition is discernible. For example, Paul preserves the ecstatic prayer *Abba* ("Father") addressed to God (Rom 8:15–16) and the prayerful cry *maranatha* (Our Lord, come!), presumably addressed to Christ (1 Cor 16:22; cf. 1 Thess 1:10; 4:14–17; → Pauline Theology, 82:53). The Aram prayer *maranatha* indicates that at least some of the early Aramaic-speaking Christians' faith was eschatological. The hope for the coming (full earthly manifestation and effectiveness) of the kingdom of God in the teaching of Jesus had been replaced by or transformed into the hope for the parousia (appearance, coming) of the exalted Jesus Christ from heaven (→ 13 above).

47 **(D) Paul.** Before Paul's conversion to faith in Jesus Christ, he was a Pharisee (Phil 3:5; → Paul, 79:15–19; → Pauline Theology, 82:10–11). The Pharisaic "party" had accepted certain apocalyptic ideas—at least the hope for resurrection and an interest in angelic beings (Acts 23:6–10). Whether Paul was eschatologically oriented before his conversion or not, he certainly was afterward. Eschatological thinking shaped his interpretation of history; he was also imbued with imminent expectation.

48 Paul's view of salvation history is not expounded systematically but may be inferred from various remarks in his letters. The original creation before sin was a time in which nature and humanity shared in the glory of God. Then came the sin of Adam (and Eve), which led to the subjection of nature to decay and humanity to death (Rom 5:12–14; 8:18–22). During this period, God made a covenant with Abraham and promised to bless all nations through him (Gal 3:6–9, 14–18). Next came the period or dispensation of the law, the time from Moses to Christ (= the Messiah — Gal 3:17–29; Rom 5:14,20–21; 7:7–12; 2 Cor 3:6–11). The transition from the age of the law to the age of the Messiah was for Paul the death and resurrection of Jesus Christ. This event inaugurated the age of Christ, or of the Spirit (which were equivalent for Paul; see 2 Cor 3:17–18; Gal 3:23–29; 4:1–7; 5:1; 2 Cor 3:6–11; Rom 3:21–26). This is the age of the church in which Christians live as children of God, possessing the Spirit as the "down payment" of future glory (2 Cor 1:22; 5:5) and leading ethically transformed lives (Rom 6). The transition from the age of Christ to the final age, the time of fulfillment, involves the return of Christ from heaven and the resurrection, i.e., the defeat of the final enemy, Death (1 Thess 4:15–17; 1 Cor 15:20–26). The time of fulfillment is the age when God will be "everything to everyone" (1 Cor 15:28), the time when those who are called will be united in love with God and Christ and will participate in the glory of God as Adam (and Eve) did before they sinned (Rom 8:18–25,28–30,38–39).

49   In some passages, it is evident that Paul expected to be alive at the return of Christ from heaven (1 Thess 4:15,17; 1 Cor 15:15–52). In these passages, he emphasizes resurrection at the return of Christ as the point at which individual hope for salvation is fulfilled (cf. Rom 4:5; Phil 3:10–11). In other passages, Paul reckons with the possibility that he, as well as others, may die before the parousia of Christ. In these passages, he seems to expect the individual to enjoy at least some of the benefits of salvation immediately after death, such as union with Christ (Phil 1:23) and the gift of a "spiritual body" (2 Cor 5:1–5; cf. 1 Cor 15:35–44). The tension between these two sets of passages may be explained in several ways. One is to say that Paul's statements about the future and about personal afterlife are symbolic statements and that symbolic expressions do not have the same coherence and consistency as doctrinal or systematic theological statements. Another possibility is to argue that Paul's thought changed over time (→ Pauline Theology, 82:9, 45; B. F. Meyer [*TS* 47 (1986) 363–87] argues to the contrary).

50   A third approach, which is actually a more precise form of the first, is to conclude that the ambiguity in Paul's statements is due to the vacillation in Jewish and Christian eschatology between temporal and spatial imagery. The Hebr word *'ôlām* and the Gk word *aiōn* could both be translated either "age" or "world." Thus, the expressions *'ôlām habbā'* and *ho aiōn ho erchomenos* could be translated either "the age to come" or "the world to come." The temporal aspect of the image points to the cosmic future: the age to come. The spatial aspect, however, often appears in contexts which reveal the conviction that this "world" to come already exists; it is the heavenly world, the eternal realm of the divine (see H. Sasse, "aiōn," *TDNT* 1. 204–7; U. Fischer, *Eschatologie und Jenseitserwartung im hellenistischen Diasporajudentum* [BZNW 44; Berlin, 1978] 53–62). Thus, those who die "in Christ" are united with him in heaven after their personal deaths and live in a glorified state; they also will share in the resurrection at the parousia. Paul may well have shifted in his emphasis from the temporal to the spatial over time or may have emphasized different aspects in different contexts. But there was no fundamental change in perspective.

51   **(III) NT Eschatology after AD 65.** While the works considered below contain earlier traditions, in the view of most scholars they were written after 65 (→ Canonicity, 66:61)

(A) Mark. Like Paul and the community at Qumran, the author of Mark believed that the promises of the Scriptures (our OT) were being fulfilled in and for his believing community. Mark opens with the proclamation that ancient prophecy had been fulfilled in the mission of JBap, who prepared the way for the work of Jesus. The message of Jesus is presented as eschatological; the kingdom of God is at hand (1:14–15). The activity of Jesus, in which exorcisms play a major role, is presented as a cosmic, eschatological struggle with Satan and his demonic allies, the powers of evil (J. M. Robinson, *The Problem of History in Mark* [SBT 21; London, 1957]). A major title of Christ in Mark is Son of Man. The origin and development of this title is one of the most debated issues in NT studies (→ Jesus, 78:38–41). In Mark, Jesus' role as Son of Man has three phases: (1) his activity on earth prior to the passion (2:10,28); (2) the suffering and dying Son of Man who was to rise again (8:31; 9:9,12,31; 10:33,45; 14:21,41); (3) the exalted Son of Man who would return on the clouds and exercise judgment (8:38; 13:26; 14:62). The eschatological hope of Mark centers on the coming Son of Man. The death of Christ in Mark is an eschatological event because it makes possible the liberation of humanity from the power of Satan (10:45). The resurrection is not itself a major focal point; it demonstrates the effectiveness of Jesus' death, his vindication, and is a sign of the salvation of believers to come (8:34–35). But if the Gospel ended with 16:8, as seems likely (→ Mark, 41:108), the resurrection of Jesus is not significantly the fulfillment of eschatological hope. It is a preparation for the second coming, an event for which Mark expresses imminent expectation (9:1; 13:24–37).

52   **(B) Matthew.** This Gospel has preserved the eschatological material in Mark and added more from other sources (e.g., 10:23; 13:24–30,37–40; 25:1–13). It has heightened the visionary or theophanic elements in several passages of Mark, elements associated with apocalypticism (17:2,6; 27:51; 28:2–4). Although Matt retains the hope for the return of the Son of Man (24:29–25:46), its eschatology puts more emphasis on fulfillment than does Mark's. The death of Jesus is more clearly presented as an eschatological event (Allison, *End* 40–50). More important, the resurrection of Jesus plays a larger role. In Mark the emphasis is on awaiting the Son of Man. In Matt the risen Lord is present to the Christian community (18:20; 28:20). Those who believe in Christ and keep his commandments are "the sons (and daughters) of the kingdom" (13:37–38). In the postresurrection period the world is the kingdom of the Son of Man (cf. 13:38 with 41). But that kingship will not be exercised until "the close of the age," when the general judgment will occur (cf. 13:30 with vv 40–43).

53   **(C) Luke-Acts.** Luke has preserved much of the eschatological material in Mark and added more to it, notably eschatological and apocalyptic sayings from the sayings source (Q; → Synoptic Problem, 40:13–20) and other sources (e.g., 12:49–50). An eschatological speech attributed to Jesus in Luke begins with the claim that "the kingdom of God is not coming with signs to be observed" (17:20). This statement is a criticism of a particular type of apocalypticism, but by no means a rejection of apocalypticism as such. Its point, in the context of Luke, is not that there will be no objective, cosmic manifestation of God's rule in the future, but that this rule will arrive suddenly and entirely, like the flood in Noah's time and the fire that destroyed Sodom (17:24,26–30). The kingdom of God will be manifest in the revelation of the Son of Man (cf. v 20 with vv 24 and 30). Like Matt, Luke places more emphasis on the presence of the risen Lord with the Christian communities than does Mark. The Emmaus story suggests that this presence is perceived especially when the community gathers for its common meal (24:30–31). Like Mark, however, the 2-vol. work of Luke-Acts portrays the resurrection not as an end in itself but as a step toward a more important event. In Mark that event is the parousia. In Luke-Acts it is the sending of the Spirit (Acts 1:4–8; 2:32–33). This gift is an important aspect of the fulfillment of the eschatological promises; in fact, it is referred to as "the promise" (Acts 1:4; 2:39). But this double work looks forward to the fulfillment of other aspects as well (Acts 3:18–21).

54   (D) John.   Mark is the Gospel most oriented to the future; John is the one most oriented to the present (→ Johannine Theology, 83:50–54). The eschatological judgment of God has occurred already in the sending of the incarnate Word into the world and the human response to him. Those who believe are acquitted; those who do not are condemned (3:18–19). This claim, however, does not mean that there will be no cosmic, general judgment on the last day. It means that the primary function of that judgment will be to ratify what has already taken place (12:48). Like the letters of Paul, John combines temporal and spatial eschatology. The believer looks forward to resurrection "on the last day" (6:39–40,54; cf. 5:28–29). But, in the meantime, when the faithful die, they have a place prepared for them in the Father's house, i.e., heaven (14:1–3). Thus future, cosmic, objective eschatology is not eliminated in John. But the emphasis has shifted to the life of Jesus, as shown above, and, as in Luke, to the postresurrectional life of the Christian community. In the farewell discourse the tradition of the second coming is reinterpreted to refer to the resurrection appearances of Jesus (cf. 14:18–29 and 16:16–24 with 20:18,19–23). Major results of the death and exaltation of Jesus are: (1) a new relationship of believers with the Father (14:12–14; 15:7–8); and (2) the sending of the Paraclete or Holy Spirit (14:16–17,25–26; 16:7–15). The presence of the Spirit shapes the life of the Christian community (14:25–26; 16:12–15; 20:22–23).

55   (E) The Book of Revelation.   In recent times, the delay of the parousia has been an important concept in the reconstruction of early Christian history (see Kümmel, *INT* 144–45, 170–71, 386; Koester, *KINT* 2. 113–14, 242–46, 278, 295–97). However, this notion should not be pressed into the service of an evolutionary theory which implies that Christian faith involved imminent expectation at its earliest stage but that this hope gradually disappeared, to be replaced by theologies of history and eschatological doctrine. Rev is evidence that intense and imminent eschatological expectation was still a major factor in the 90s (Yarbro Collins, *Crisis* 54–77). *Did.* and *Barn.* are also relatively late works which still manifest such expectation. The attempt has been made to interpret Rev as an example of realized eschatology, but the results are not convincing (G. B. Caird, *A Commentary on the Revelation of St. John the Divine* [NY, 1966]). Spatial dualism is prominent in Rev. God is enthroned in heaven (chap. 4), but Satan rules the earth (12:12; 13:3–4, 7–8). The faithful who die have a heavenly dwelling place (6:9–11). Christ reigns as king in heaven (1:5; 3:21; cf. chap. 5). Temporal dualism is also important. In the present the opponents of God are dominant (12:12; 13:5– 7); but in the near future the reign of Christ will be manifest on earth (1:1,3; 19:11–21; 22:6–7,20). This extension of Christ's reign will mean the punishment of the wicked (chaps. 17–18) and the vindication of the innocent sufferers (6:9–11; 20:4–6). It also includes a new cosmic creation and an eternal intimate relationship between God, Christ, and the faithful (21:1–22:5).

56   *Conclusion.*   Eschatology has posed enormous problems for Christian life and theology throughout history including the 20th cent. Although its powerful symbols and images are difficult to reconcile with modern critical theories of astronomy and history, they speak from depth to depth about the flawed character of the universe, human responsibility, and the unfinished work of creation.

THE PARABLES OF JESUS

BIBLIOGRAPHY

57   Bailey, K. E., *Poet and Peasant; Through Peasant Eyes* (2 vols. in 1; GR, 1984). Boucher, M., *The Parables* (NTM 7; Wilmington, 1981). Breech, J. E., *The Silence of Jesus* (Phl, 1983). Carlston, C., *The Parables of the Triple Tradition* (Phl, 1975). Crossan, J. D., *In Parables: The Challenge of the Historical Jesus* (NY, 1973). Dodd, C. H., *The Parables of the Kingdom* (NY, 1961; 1st ed. 1935). Donahue, J. R., *The Gospel in Parable* (Phl, 1988). Drury, J., *The Parables in the Gospels* (NY, 1985). Eichholz, G., *Gleichnisse der Evangelien* (Neukirchen, 1984). Funk, R., *Language, Hermeneutic, and Word of God* (NY, 1966); *Parables and Presence* (Phl, 1982). Hendrickx, H., *The Parables of Jesus* (SF, 1987). Hermaniuk, M., *La parabole évangélique* (Louvain, 1937). Jeremias, J., *The Parables of Jesus* (8th ed.; NY, 1972). Jones, G. V., *The Art and Truth of the Parables* (London, 1964). Kingsbury,

J., *The Parables of Jesus in Matthew 13* (Richmond, 1969). Kissinger, W. S., *The Parables of Jesus: A History of Interpretation and Bibliography* (Metuchen NJ, 1979). Lambrecht, J., *Once More Astonished: The Parables of Jesus* (NY, 1981). Linnemann, E., *Jesus of the Parables* (NY, 1966). McFague, S., *Speaking in Parables: A Study in Metaphor and Theology* (Phl, 1975). Perkins, P., *Hearing the Parables of Jesus* (NY, 1981). Perrin, N., *Jesus and the Language of the Kingdom* (Phl, 1976). Sabourin, L., "The Parables of the Kingdom," *BTB* 6 (1976) 115–60. Scott, B., *Jesus, Symbol-Maker for the Kingdom* (Phl, 1981). Stein, R. H., *An Introduction to the Parables of Jesus* (Phl, 1981). Tolbert, M. A., *Perspectives on the Parables* (Phl, 1979). Via, D. O., *The Parables: Their Literary and Existential Dimension* (Phl, 1967). Wilder, A., *The Language of the Gospel* (NY, 1964); *Jesus' Parables and the War of Myths* (Phl, 1982).

58   Outline.

59   (I) Nature of Parable.   "Parable" is from the Gk *parabolē* (the root meaning involves the placing of things side by side for the sake of comparison); it was a technical term for a figure of speech in ancient oratory.

Two most basic figures of speech are simile and metaphor. In a *simile* one thing is compared to another of a different kind and the similarity is expressed by "like" or "as," e.g., Jesus sends out his disciples "as lambs in the midst of wolves" (Luke 10:3). In *metaphor* (from the Gk *metapherein*, "carry over"), a more literary figure, the qualities of one thing are directly ascribed to another without an explicit point of comparison, e.g., "You are the salt of the earth" (Matt 5:13) or "Beware of the leaven of the Pharisees" (Mark 8:15). In general parable is a developed simile, where the story, while fictitious, is true to life (in contrast to fable). In the Gospel parables the introductory formula of the parables is often, "The kingdom of heaven is like . . ." (frequently in Matt with 10 kingdom parables in contrast to Mark and Luke with two each). Yet the object of a parable's comparison is often not the single word that follows, but the total situation envisioned. The kingdom is not like the king who wished to settle accounts (Matt 18:23–35), but involves generous forgiveness; nor is the kingdom like the net (Matt 13:47), but like the catch of fish and the separation of the good from the bad. Allegory is a developed metaphor or series of metaphors, less clear and more allusive than parable. In allegory each detail or character is significant, often with a hidden meaning (e.g., Mark 4:13–20).

60   The use of *parabolē* in the LXX is a caution against a too narrow understanding of parable. Here it normally translates the Hebr *māšāl*, which embraces various literary forms: proverbs (1 Sam 10:12; Prov 1:1, 6; 26:7–9), riddles (Judg 14:10–18), taunt-songs (Mic 2:4; Hab 2:6), oracles (Num 23:7,18), metaphors and allegories (Isa 5:1–7; Ezek 17:2–24). The term also embraces didactic historical recital (Ps 78), as well as long revelatory discourses such as the "similitudes" in the second section of *1 Enoch* (37–71; → Apocrypha, 67:10). The Synoptic Gospels use *parabolē* with the same wide range as *māšāl*, comprising proverbs (Luke 4:23), examples (Luke 12:16–21), similitudes (Luke 5:36–39), similes (Matt 23:27), allegory (Matt 25:1–13), as well as the more familiar narrative parables (→ Jesus, 78:18). John, though rich in imagery, symbolism, and allegory (e.g., 10:1–17), uses *paroimia* (16:25) rather than *parabolē*. Outside the Gospels (only in Heb 9:9; 11:19) *parabolē* means "symbol" or "prefiguration."

(Polk, T., "Paradigms, Parables and *Měšālîm*: On Reading the *Māšāl* in Scripture," *CBQ* 45 [1983] 564–83. Stewart, R. A., "The Parable Form in the Old Testament and the Rabbinic Literature" *EvQ* 36 [1964] 133–47. Westermann, C., *Vergleiche und Gleichnisse im Alten und Neuen Testament* [Stuttgart, 1984].)

61   **(II) History of Parable Exegesis.** In the NT itself (Mark 4:13–20; Matt 13:36–43) and in patristic and medieval exegesis, the parables were generally treated as allegories. In his rather forced exegesis of the parable of the Good Samaritan (Luke 10:29–37), Augustine identified the man who went down from Jerusalem to Jericho as Adam; Jerusalem is the state of original happiness; Jericho represents human mortality; the Samaritan is Christ; the inn is the church; the innkeeper is Paul, etc. (Dodd, *Parables* 1–2). Such allegorical exegesis interpreted details independent of their literary and historical context.

(For history of research, see W. Harnisch (ed.), *Gleichnisse Jesu* [WF 366; Darmstadt, 1982]. Harrington, W. J., *BTB* 2 [1972] 219–41. Jones, *Art* 3–54. Kümmel, W. G., *TRu* 43 [1978] 120–42; 47 [1982] 348–83. Perrin, *Jesus* 89–193.)

62   **(A) From Jülicher to Jeremias.** With the rise of historical criticism, allegorical interpretation faded, especially because of the influence of A. Jülicher,

whose 2-vol. study (*Die Gleichnisreden Jesu* [1888, 1899]) marked a new era in parable research. From an understanding of *parabolē* as found in Gk rhetoric (→ 59 above), Jülicher argued that parables are simple moralizing stories with no admixture of allegory. Every parable is composed of an image (the *Bild*) and the "reality part" (the *Sache*) to which the image points. The focus of Jülicher's position is that each parable has only *one point* of comparison (the *punctum* or *tertium comparationis*). The individual details or characters in a parable have no meaning outside the parable (e.g., the Father does not stand for God, nor the elder brother for the Pharisees, Luke 15:11–32) and the point of comparison is one of the widest possible moral application. Jülicher then interpreted the parables in the light of Jesus' instruction on the kingdom of God and the defense of his ministry; but Jülicher's 19th-cent. understanding of the kingdom was "a fellowship of brothers and sisters under the protection of their Father," and a fellowship in which "spiritual effort and endeavour is demanded of all its members" (as cited by Perrin, *Jesus* 96).

63   Subsequent examination of the form, images, and the content of rabbinic parables (which, though from later *texts,* may embody oral traditions contemporaneous with the NT; → Apocrypha, 67:134–135) forced a modification of Jülicher's positions. The rabbinic parables are not clear illustrations of religious truth, but often a collection of enigmatic sayings and images that puzzle and challenge the hearer. They employ standard images such as a king for God and servants for those summoned to follow the law of God. Thus, study of rabbinic parables, as well as other uses of *māšāl* in the OT, will continue to undermine the rigid division between parable and allegory. In assessing this division one must distinguish (a) interpreting an allegory, which itself is a rich literary form; (b) allegorical interpretation of non-allegorical material; (c) mixed forms of parabolic and allegorical elements in a Semitic context unaware of precise definitions (e.g., Mark 12:1–12); (d) and the valid or invalid use of allegory itself as a method of interpretation.

(On rabbinic parables: Feldman, A., *The Parables and Similes of the Rabbis, Agricultural and Pastoral* [Cambridge, 1927]. Fiebig, P., *Die Gleichnisreden Jesu im Lichte der rabbinischen Gleichnisse des neutestamentlichen Zeitalters* [Tübingen, 1912]. Flusser, D., *Die rabbinischen Gleichnisse und der Gleichniserzähler Jesus* [Frankfurt, 1981]. Neusner, J., "Types and Forms in Ancient Jewish Literature: Some Comparisons," *HR* 11 [1972] 354–90. On parable and allegory: Brown, R. E., *New Testament Essays* [NY, 1982; orig. art. 1962] 254–64. Klauck, H.-J., *Allegorie und Allegorese in synoptischen Gleichnistexten* [NTAbh 13; Münster, 1978].)

64   Though the kingdom proclamation has remained the main key to the meaning of the parables, the understanding of kingdom has shifted radically. Under the influence of J. Weiss and A. Schweitzer, the kingdom was viewed not as a timeless truth of human history or a hidden power at work in human hearts, but as the eschatological reign of God, the irruption into human history of God's rule, the victory of God over evil, and the offer of mercy and forgiveness to sinners (→ 30–32 above; → Jesus, 78:15–17). Kingdom is less a definable concept than a symbol of God's directing Israel's history and continuing to act in the life and teaching of Jesus (Perrin, *Jesus*, esp. 29–32).

65   Research in the 20th cent. alternated then between concern for parable as a literary form and for parable as an entrée to the kingdom proclamation and, later, to the self-understanding of Jesus. Dodd (→ 34 above) argued that Jesus offered a "realized eschatology"; i.e., the goal of God's intervention in history was reached in Jesus' life and teaching. (Dodd interpreted Mark 1:15 as the kingdom of God has "arrived.") The reign of God causes a change and crisis in all human history. Dodd argued that in those parables which seemed to deal with the future (e.g., Matt 25:1–30) the point of comparison is the crisis evoked by the kingdom rather than its futurity.

66 The most influential mid-century study was J. Jeremias, *The Parables* (1947). With almost unparalleled knowledge of 1st-cent. Palestine, Jeremias shed light on the details of daily life that provided the material for the parables. More significant, he carefully analyzed the changes the parables underwent, moving from the life of Jesus through the missionary proclamation of the early church to final incorporation in the Gospels. For example, parables are allegorized (Mark 4:13–20; Matt 13:36–43); life situations are changed (parables originally addressed to opponents are directed to church leaders, e.g., Luke 15:1–7; Matt 18:10–14); details are embellished; and OT allusions are added. Presenting a full-scale study of the message of Jesus, Jeremias rejected "realized eschatology" and proposed "inaugurating eschatology," i.e., in the process of realization (*sich realisierende Eschatologie*; → 35 above). The definitive revelation of God's reign has begun in Jesus; its full effect lies in the future. Jeremias's view was widely accepted as a faithful exegesis of Jesus' parables and of Christian eschatology in general (cf. Paul's tension between the "already" and the "not yet"; → Pauline Theology, 82:45–47).

67   (B) Parable Study since Jeremias. Along with concern for the parables as the key to the teaching of Jesus, the other major focus of parable research has been their literary nature. This owes much to Dodd's inductive description (*Parables* 5) of parable "as a metaphor or simile drawn from nature or common life, arresting the hearer by its vividness or strangeness and leaving the mind in sufficient doubt about its precise application to tease it into active thought." Metaphoric language, realism, paradox, and open-ended summons to personal engagement became the focus for subsequent discussion.

68 A major turning point in parable research occurred in the mid 60s with the seminal works of Wilder and Funk, who viewed parables primarily as *poetic* rather than *rhetorical* forms, where an appreciation of metaphor provided a key to a new vision of the parables (Funk, *Language* 133–62; Wilder, *Language* 79–96). By the often surprising equation of dissimilar elements (e.g., "The eye is the lamp of the body" [Matt 6:22]), metaphor produces an impact on the imagination that cannot be conveyed by discursive speech. Metaphorical predication leads beyond the expressive power of language, so that logically "interpretation of parables should take place in parables" (Funk, *Language* 196). Metaphor has thus moved from literary trope or figure to a theological and hermeneutical category, especially suited to expressing the two necessary qualities of all religious language, immediacy and transcendence. A religious experience (a sense of awe in the face of the holy or of being grasped by mystery) is immediate and personal and, in great religious literature, is expressed in concrete, physical imagery. As metaphors, the parables of Jesus use concrete and familiar images which touch people in their everyday lives, but which point to a reality (God's reign or kingdom) that transcends definition or literal description.

(Harnisch, W. (ed.), *Die neutestamentliche Gleichnisforschung im Horizont von Hermeneutik und Literaturwissenschaft* [WF 575; Darmstadt, 1982]. McFague, S., *Metaphorical Theology* [Phl, 1982]. Weder, H., *Die Gleichnisse Jesu als Metaphern* [FRLANT 120; Göttingen, 1978].)

69 The parables of Jesus are more exactly "meta-

phoric" rather than metaphors. Metaphor involves the combination of two distinct images joined in a *single sentence,* whereas the Gospel parables are generally extended *narratives.* They combine narrative form and metaphorical process (P. Ricoeur, "Biblical Hermeneutics" *Semeia* 4 [1975] 27–148). Reflection on the narrative quality of the parables became another major direction in the literary study of the parables. Again, Wilder was a leader, arguing that in telling about God's reign "in story," Jesus continued the narrative legacy of biblical revelation. In reading the stories of Jesus, a Christian realizes that life is "a race, a pilgrimage, in short, a story" (*Language* 65).

70 A major impetus in this direction was Via, who offered a "dramatic" reading of the longer narrative parables. By studying the plot of the parables and by using the categories of "tragedy" and "comedy"— in the classical sense of a dramatic change from good fortune to evil, or the reverse—Via argued that the parables confront the reader with the same tragic or salvific possibilities as the drama. Readers can, like the unmerciful servant (Matt 18:23–35), remain untouched by unmerited forgiveness, attempting to maintain an order of strict justice with their neighbors, and thus end in tragedy. Readers can also look at the picaresque or roguish unjust steward (Luke 16:1–8) and be aware that God can summon us to live by our wits when faced with a crisis.

71 Subsequent to Via's work there was a brief but intense flurry of studies devoted to the "semiotic" or structuralist analysis of narrative parables (see essays in *Semeia* 1–2 [1974]). Setting aside the historical referent of the parables and the historical development of the traditions behind them, these studies, through analysis of the "synchronic" structure, attempted to uncover the deep structures of meaning behind an individual parable. Too complicated and diffuse for general adoption, the method itself called attention to issues such as identification of the central character(s) in a parable, the narrative dynamics, and the dramatic tension that unfolds. In her judicious assessment and appropriation of aspects of this method, Tolbert noted the difference between "narrated discourse" and "direct discourse." Most often the central thrust of the parable emerges at the shift from narrative to direct dialog (*Perspectives,* esp. 73–78).

72   (III) Characteristics of Jesus' Parables. Jesus used realistic images from daily life that caught his hearers' attention by their vividness and narrative color. Yet his parables have a surprising twist; the realism is shattered and the hearers know that something more is at stake than a homey illustration to drive home a point. The parables raise questions, unsettle the complacent, and challenge the hearers to reflection and inquiry.

(A) Illustrations from Daily Life. In the parables of Jesus the life of ordinary people from a distant time and culture comes alive in a way true of little ancient literature. Jesus was familiar with a rural Galilean milieu: outdoor scenes of farming and shepherding, and domestic scenes in a simple one-room house (Luke 11:5–8). The homes of the rich are seen only through the kitchen door—the view of servants and slaves. The farming is hill-country farming, done in small patches with stone fences and briars (Mark 4:4–7), not that of the broad lowland plains. There are donkeys, sheep, wolves, and birds; seeds, wheat, and harvests; lilies of the field and fruit trees; patched wineskins and household lamps; children quarreling in the market place and shady merchants. People are threatened by drought and flood, and the din of war is never distant. Jesus sees life through the eyes of the "anawim," the poor and humble of the land. This creates an obstacle for the modern urban reader and poses challenges to historians and archeologists to help us understand better the cultural context of the parables. The realism of the parables means also that Jesus places the point of contact between God and humans within the everyday world of human experience. Jesus does not proclaim the kingdom in "God language" but summons his hearers to realize that their destinies are at stake in their "ordinary, creaturely existence, domestic, economic, social" (Wilder, *Language* 82).

73 The details of ordinary life are woven into vivid narratives of varying length, and the reader should be aware of techniques of popular story telling that are employed. One of these is the "rule of three," viz., that in popular stories (and jokes) it is customary to have three characters with the point or punch line coming in the third instance. Three servants are entrusted with talents; three men pass the victim who fell among robbers. Another technique is the "soliloquy," where the reader is made privy to the devious plans of the wicked tenants (Mark 12:7), the dire straits of the younger son (Luke 15:17), or the hopeful plans of the unjust steward (Luke 16:3–4). One character holds the stage at a time; and confrontations between the characters unfold in measured pace, e.g., in the laborers in the vineyard (Matt 20:1–16) and the talents (Matt 25:14–30). The parables often lack conclusions or resolutions—we do not know whether the man who was left half-dead recovered (Luke 10:37) nor whether the two brothers were reconciled (Luke 15:32). There is an economy of detail, and the parables show little interest in psychological motivation. (For "narrative laws" of parables, see Bultmann, *HST* 187–92.)

74 **(B) Novelty and Paradox.** The realism of the parables is but one side of the coin. The novel twists in Jesus' stories make his hearers take notice. The harvest is not only bountiful but also extravagant (Mark 4:8); wealthy hosts ordinarily do not react to the absence of invited guests by substituting the poor, blind, and lame (Luke 14:21). The payment *first* by the vineyard owner of those hired *last* (Matt 20:8) makes the audience suspect something strange is about to happen. A major key to the "meaning" of a given parable appears when the realism begins to break down.

75 Crossan and Ricoeur, especially, underscore the paradoxical aspect of parables, a seeming absurdity that conceals a deeper truth. Their fundamental message is that things are not as they seem; you must have your tidy image of reality shattered. The Good Samaritan is not primarily an illustration of compassion and loving-kindness to the suffering, but a challenge to see as "good" those we would call enemy. The strange and paradoxical character of the parables is a counterpart of Jesus' association with and offer of mercy and grace to tax collectors and sinners, those thought to be beyond the pale of God's concern. Similarly, Ricoeur notes that parables operate in a pattern of orientation, disorientation, and reorientation. Their hyperbolic and paradoxical language presents an extravagance that interrupts our normal way of viewing things and presents the extraordinary within the ordinary. The parables dislocate our project of trying to make a tight pattern of our lives, which Ricoeur feels is akin to the Pauline "boasting" or justification by works (*Semeia* 4 [1975] 112–28). The parables comprise a "poetics of faith" by summoning us to openness and trust in the face of the unexpected.

(Crossan, J. D., *Cliffs of Fall: Paradox and Polyvalence in the Parables of Jesus* [NY, 1980]. Brown, F. B. and E. S. Malbon, "Parabling as a *Via Negativa*: A Critical Review of the Work of John Dominic Crossan," *JR* 64 [1984] 530–38.)

76 **(C) An Open-Ended Challenge.** In transmission the parables received different applications and interpretations. Appended to the enigmatic parable of the Unjust Steward is a parade of interpretations, joined mainly by catchwords (Luke 16:8b–13; see Fitzmyer, *ESBNT* 161–84). Other parables have appended sayings that are found in a number of different contexts (e.g., Matt 25:13 = Mark 13:35; and Matt 25:29 = Mark 4:25; Matt 13:12; Luke 8:18). In their original form the parables of Jesus may have ended at the narrative conclusion (e.g., Matt 13:30; 18:34) or with a challenge or question (Mark 4:9; Matt 20:15; 21:31a). The meaning of a given parable is often elusive: e.g., is the point of the parable of the pearl (Matt 13:45–46) the search, the joy of finding, or the willingness to risk all? Both in the early church and in subsequent history, the parables are "polyvalent." They demand and receive different interpretation from different audiences. Though exegesis may determine the perimeters of incorrect interpretation for a given parable, it can scarcely exhaust the potentialities for fruitful interpretation and application.

77 A major reason for the polyvalence of parables is their dialogic quality. Whether spoken to confront opponents or to encourage disciples, the parables take up the world of the hearer. Linnemann (*Jesus* 27–30) has described this phenomenon as "interlocking." The audience recognizes its own values and ethos and can identify with the situation and characters; yet the familiar values are transformed. The parable of the two debtors "works" with Simon the Pharisee (Luke 7:40–43) because the Pharisees had reflected on mercy and forgiveness. Parables are often like traps that catch us unawares. Contemporary readers who smugly reject the piety of the Pharisee (Luke 18:11, "I am not like other people") may themselves be "pharisaical."

78 Parables are open-ended invitations waiting for a response. The parable is not effective until it is freely appropriated. The response of the reader completes the meaning of the parable. Parable is a form of religious discourse that appeals not only to the imagination or to the joyous perception of paradox or surprise but also to the most basic of human qualities, freedom. In couching his message in parable Jesus challenged people to a free response and risked rejection.

79 **(IV) Parables in the Gospels.** In the traditions prior to the Gospels and in the Gospels themselves, the parables form different settings and groupings. Though Jesus may have narrated his parables by pairs (Mark 2:21–22; Luke 14:28–32), the evangelists often group topically parables that were probably uttered on different occasions. In Mark 4 there are three seed parables; Matt 13 has seven parables referring to the kingdom of heaven; Matt 24:32–25:46 has seven parousia parables; Luke 14:7–24 has three banquet parables; Luke 15 has three parables on regaining what was lost. The evangelists not only transmit the parables; through editorial changes, literary context, and by the addition of parabolic material from their own traditions, each evangelist stamps them with his own theological perspective.

(→ 57 above, esp. Carlston, Drury, Kingsbury, Lambrecht; also Goulder, M., "Characteristics of the Parables in the Several Gospels," *JTS* 19 [1968] 51–69.)

80 **(A) Mark.** Commentators generally list six Marcan parables: the sower (4:3–9), the seed growing secretly (4:26–29), the mustard seed (4:30–32), the wicked husbandmen (12:1–11), the fig tree (13:28–29), and the doorkeeper (13:34–37). Mark contains also a large number of parabolic sayings, such as the sons of the bridechamber (2:19–20), the patched garment and the old wineskins (2:21–22), the Beelzebul parables (3:23–27, called explicitly *parabolai* in Mark 3:23), the riddle about things that defile (7:1–23, also called a *parabolē,* 7:17), and the sayings of Mark 4:21–25. Two parables are explicitly called kingdom parables (4:26–29, 30–32) and all of Mark's parables except the seed growing secretly (4:26–29) are taken over by Matthew and Luke. The world of the Marcan parables is that of village, farming, and the processes of nature. Mark has only one dramatic parable (i.e., where characters interact, 12:1–11), and it does not stand in one of the two great blocks of teaching material (chap. 4 and chap. 13).

81   In one of the most discussed NT passages (Mark 4:10–12) Jesus says to the disciples, "To you has been given the mystery of the kingdom of God, but to those outside all things happen in parables that 'they may indeed see but not perceive and may indeed hear but not understand; lest they should turn again and be forgiven'" (citing Isa 6:9–10). This saying is a summation of the *result* of the proclamation of the kingdom by Jesus and of the crucified one by the church rather than its purpose, and it likely reflects early Christian apologetics that sought in the OT an explanation for the suffering and rejection of Jesus. It also reflects the theology of Mark, who wants the readers to view it in relation to the parables of 3:23–27, the despoiling of Satan's kingdom. The disciples are meant to "see" what blinds outsiders: viz., that, though Jesus is the stronger one who defeats Satan (Mark 1:7, 21–27), Satan can still hinder God's kingdom (4:15) and that the power of Jesus, though seemingly hidden and insignificant, will ultimately prevail.

(Boucher, M., *The Mysterious Parable: A Literary Study* [CBQMS 6; Washington, 1977]. Brown, S., "The Secret of the Kingdom of God," *JBL* 92 [1973] 60–74. Marcus, J., *The Mystery of the Kingdom of God* [SBLDS 90; Atlanta, 1986].)

82   The important Marcan themes of christology and discipleship (→ Mark 41:4) are conveyed in parable. The first group of parables (3:23–27) concludes the christological tableau of the beginning of the Gospel, where Jesus is proclaimed as the herald of God's reign and the "stronger one" who will despoil Satan of his power. The following parables of chap. 4 contrast appearance and reality (e.g., three failed sowings, an extravagant harvest; the smallest of the seeds, a great bush) and further the Marcan theme of the messianic secret. They also encourage faithful discipleship in the face of failure. By the (probable) addition of the sending of the "beloved son" (12:6, cf. 1:11; 9:7) Mark turns the parable of the wicked tenants into an allegory of the rejection of Jesus. The eschatological discourse of Mark 13 concludes with the parable of the absent householder (13:33–37), which warns the community to be vigilant in the face of the delay of the parousia.

83   **(B) Matthew.** In contrast to Mark's relatively few parables, which deal mainly with the world of agriculture, Matthew has a great number: 5 from Mark (omitting only the seed growing secretly, Mark 4:26–29); extensive parabolic sayings and longer narrative parables from Q, e.g., lost sheep (18:12–14), marriage feast (22:1–10), the wise and faithful servants (24:45–51), and the talents (25:14–30); along with important parables either from his own special material (M) or due to his own composition, e.g., the wheat and the tares (13:24–30), the unmerciful servant (18:23–35), laborers in vineyard (20:1–16), the ten virgins (25:1–13), and the sheep and the goats (25:31–46).

84   Matt's parables manifest common traits. Many are dramatic parables where human actions and human decisions engage the hearers. Matt shows a love of extravagance. Mark's shrub (Mark 4:32) becomes a tree (Matt 13:32); the treasure and the pearl exceed all value (Matt 13:44–46); the debt of the servant exceeds the

taxes from Syria, Phoenicia, Judea, and Samaria (Matt 18:24); and the talents given to the servants equal wages for 30, 60, or 150 years (Matt 25:15). Matt also exhibits stark contrasts and reversals. Its parables contain more allegorical elements than those of Mark or Luke and exhibit a fondness for apocalyptic imagery to underscore the crisis occasioned by the teaching of Jesus. The stakes are heaven or hell, outer darkness, weeping and gnashing of teeth (13:42–43; 22:13; 25:30). This combination of dramatic interaction, imaginative language, and religious awe stamps the Gospel as a whole.

85   The parables also reflect Matt's theological perspective (→ Matthew, 42:6, 84). Whereas Mark emphasizes the mighty deeds of Jesus, Matt stresses the authoritative teaching: Jesus is a messiah of deed and word. Matt enlarges the two major Marcan discourses of Jesus (chaps. 4 and 13) by the addition of considerable parabolic material (chaps. 13, 24–25). Matt's parables in their present form reflect conflicts between the early church and Jewish leaders; they are used as warnings to the community. The lost sheep becomes an exhortation to care for the straying little ones in the community (18:10); the unmerciful servant, a paradigm of unlimited forgiveness which is to characterize community leaders (e.g., Peter, 18:21–22); those to whom the vineyard is given must produce fruit (21:34,41; cf. 7:16–20); and an invitation to the banquet after the rejection of those first invited is no assurance of entrance (22:11–14). In Matt the parables of Jesus become allegories of the summons to discipleship that is to be proclaimed between Jesus' resurrection and return (28:16–20).

86   **(C) Luke.** This extensive collection of parables contains classic statements of the teaching of Jesus such as the Good Samaritan, the Prodigal Son, and the Rich Man and Lazarus. Their atmosphere and tone differ from those of Mark and Matt. While taking over Mark's nature parables, Luke centers the drama less in the mystery of nature than in the mystery of human interaction. By the frequent use of soliloquy Luke invites us to become participants in the parables. Luke eschews allegory; its stories are realistic. Luke's parables very often serve as shocking examples of the behavior that is to characterize the followers of Jesus. Most of Luke's parables and a preponderance of those unique to this Gospel occur in the journey section (9:51–19:27), where Jesus on his way to Jerusalem teaches the way of Christian discipleship to his community.

87   The parables reflect distinct Lucan themes and theology. In Zechariah's hymn of praise, the coming of the "dawn from on high" (Jesus) is due to the "merciful compassion" of God (1:78); and "compassion" is important in Luke's parables (10:33; 15:20). Mary speaks of God who sends the rich away empty (1:53); Jesus announces good news to the poor (4:18–19); and Luke contains significant parables on the dangers of wealth (12:13–21; 16:19–31). In the Lucan parables the defenseless are vindicated (7:40–43; 18:1–7) and the complacent are challenged (18:9–14). More than the other Gospels Luke presents the demands of *daily* Christian existence and understands discipleship as following Jesus' example. In his parables and by his deeds the Lucan Jesus becomes the paradigm of Christian life.

88   The parables of Jesus received new interpretations when addressed to a new audience in the context of a Gospel. Today the parables occur very often in the liturgical context of the Sunday Gospels. Preachers, even as they attempt to make the parables a contemporary message, should be aware of their original contexts, especially in the kingdom proclamation of Jesus and in the theology of the Gospels. The parables should not be moralized as if they were isolated units. Attention to these original settings as well as to the images of the parables, their metaphoric power and dramatic quality,

enables the parables again to surprise and challenge people with gospel power.

THE MIRACLES OF JESUS

BIBLIOGRAPHY

89   Borgen, P., "Miracles of Healing in the New Testament: Some Observations," *ST* 35 (1981) 91–106. Brown, C., *Miracles and the Critical Mind* (GR, 1984). Brown, R. E., "The Gospel Miracles," *New Testament Essays* (NY, 1982; orig. art. 1962) 168–91. Bultmann, *HST* 209–44. Douglas, M., *Purity and Danger* (London, 1966). Dunn, J. D. G., *Jesus and the Spirit* (Phl, 1975) 69–76. Empereur, J. L., *Prophetic Anointing* (Message of the Sacraments 7; Wilmington, 1982) 141–201. Fridrichsen, A., *The Problem of Miracle in Primitive Christianity* (Minneapolis, 1972). Fuller, R. H., *Interpreting the Miracles* (London, 1963). Harvey, A. E., *Jesus and the Constraints of History* (Phl, 1982) 98–119. Jervell, J., *The Unknown Paul* (Minneapolis, 1984) 77–95. Kasper, W., *Jesus the Christ* (NY, 1976) 89–99. Kee, H. C., *Miracle in the Early Christian World* (New Haven, 1983). Léon-Dufour, X. (ed.), *Les Miracles de Jesus* (Parole de Dieu; Paris, 1977). Malina, B., *The New Testament World* (Atlanta,

1981) 122–52. Moule, C. F. D. (ed.), *Miracles* (London, 1965). Mussner, F., *The Miracles of Jesus* (Notre Dame, 1968). Pesch, R., *Jesu Ureigene Taten?* (QD 52; Freiburg, 1970). Praeder, S. M., *Miracle Stories in Christian Antiquity* (Phl, 1987). Ramsey, I. T., *et al., The Miracles and the Resurrection* (SPCK Theol. Coll. 3; London, 1964). Sabourin, L., "The Miracles of Jesus, I, II, III" *BTB* 1 (1971) 59–80; 4 (1974) 115–75; 5 (1975) 146–200. Seybold, K. and U. Mueller, *Sickness & Healing* (Biblical Encounter Series; Nash, 1981). Suhl, A. (ed.), *Der Wunderbegriff im Neuen Testament* (WF 295; Darmstadt, 1980). Theissen, G., *The Miracle Stories of the Early Christian Tradition* (Phl, 1983). Tiede, D. L., *The Charismatic Figure as Miracle Worker* (SBLDS 1; Missoula, 1972). Van der Loos, H., *The Miracles of Jesus* (Leiden, 1965). Vermes, G., *Jesus the Jew* (NY, 1973) 58–82. Wilms, F. E., *Wunder im Alten Testament* (Regensburg, 1979). Also *Semeia* 11 (1978).

90   Outline.

(I) Biblical Notion of Miracle (§ 91–95)
(II) Modern Criticism of Gospel Miracles
   (A) Form-critical Approach (§ 97–102)
     (a) Pronouncement Miracle Stories (§ 98)
     (b) Miracle Stories Proper
       (i) Healing Miracles (§ 100)
       (ii) Nature Miracles (§ 101)
     (c) Summaries of Miracles (§ 102)
   (B) Evaluation of the Form-critical Approach (§ 103–109)
   (C) Other Approaches to the Miracle Stories (§ 110)
(III) Meaning of Miracles in the Gospels
   (A) Synoptics (§ 112–114)
   (B) John (§ 115–116)
   (C) Acts (§ 117)

91   (I) Biblical Notion of Miracle. From the time that Quadratus made use of the Gospel miracles in his *Apology to Hadrian* (*ca.* AD 125), the significance of the miracles of Jesus seems to have been inextricably bound up with apologetics. Vatican Council I (DS 3034) anathematized anyone who would say there could be no miracles, or that all biblical miracles were to be reduced to the level of fable or myth, or that miracles could not be known with certainty and used to prove the divine origin of the Christian religion. This wedding of the study of the Gospel miracles with apologetics has been somewhat unfortunate, however, for it has emphasized an aspect of the miracle that (legitimate though it may be) was not primary in the career of Jesus nor in the Gospels. The Gospels take for granted the possibility of the miraculous, and so we shall not concern ourselves with that philosophical question in our descriptive study. Moreover, we shall not raise the question of how miracles can be used to show the reasonableness of faith (apologetics). We are concerned here with the significance of the miracles in the mission of Jesus and in the Gospels.

92   It has been traditional to define miracles either, with Augustine, as actions beyond the *ordinary* laws of nature, or, even more demandingly with Thomas, as actions surpassing the power of *all* nature. (C. Brown, *Miracles* 11–12). Theologians themselves are becoming quite discontent with such an understanding that divorces miracles from the climate of faith (Kasper, *Jesus* 89–99; J. Donahue, *Way* 18 [1978] 252–62). In any case,

the biblical approach to the miraculous is different on several scores.

93   *First,* the Bible does not view nature as a closed system of laws. The ordinary workings of nature are often attributed directly to God: e.g., storm, famine, and plague are looked upon as divine visitations and punishments. There is little sensitivity to secondary causality, and the distinction between the natural and the supernatural is frequently tenuous. The biblical notion of the miraculous includes acts that are explicable on the level of human interaction as well as those that are not; thus, it includes actions that would not be miracles under either apologetic definition given above. If there are OT stories of stupendous incidents like the raising of the dead and the stopping of the sun in its path (→ Hermeneutics, 71:25), the principal OT miracle is the deliverance of Israel from Egypt, in itself an action governed by historical forces. But the biblical authors look upon such a historical event with the eyes of faith and see in it the miraculous action of God on Israel's behalf (Sabourin, *BTB* 1 [1971] 60–64; → Exodus, 3:17).

94   *Second,* if the Bible sees as direct divine actions events that are not outside the realm of nature or history, then we must recognize that the element of the marvelous, which is so much a part of the traditional understanding of miracles, is not overly prominent in the Bible. This is seen in the terms used for miracles. The Eng word "miracle" comes from Lat *miraculum,* "something to be wondered at," but this word does not even occur in the Vg NT. The Hebr words that are translated into English as "miracle" are *môpēt,* "symbolic act," and *'ôt,* "sign," neither of which need refer to anything marvelous (Ezek 12:1–6). When something extraordinary is described, then *niplā'ôt,* the pl. word for marvels, is added. In the LXX the element of the prodigious becomes stronger, for *môpēt* is translated by *teras,* "wonder."

    In the NT the Synoptic word for miracles is *dynamis,* "act of power," and John uses *sēmeion,* "sign," or *ergon,* "work." *Teras,* "wonder," is used only once, in Acts 2:22, to refer to the miracles of Jesus (in conjunction with "signs" and "acts of power"; B. Gerhardsson, *SEA* 44 [1979] 122–33). Thus, in neither Testament does the vocabulary of the original texts give real emphasis to the marvelous.

95   *Third,* from apologetics we are accustomed to think of miracles as actions performed for individuals, e.g., healings, raising of the dead, calming of dangerous storms. It is worth noting that in the OT, although there are divine interventions on behalf of Israel, miracles performed for individual needs and purposes are found with frequency only in the Elijah and Elisha cycles (→ 1-2 Kings, 10:29-31, 43-48). The parallel between Jesus' miracles and those narrated in the two cycles caused him to be thought of as another Elijah and even another Elisha (see B. Lindars in Moule (ed.), *Miracles* 61-79; R. E. Brown, *Perspective* 12 [1971] 85-104; D. G. Bostock, *ExpTim* 92 [1980] 39-41).

96   **(II) Modern Criticism of Gospel Miracles.** In the 19th cent., rationalist or liberal studies of miracles generally took either of two directions. The one approach accepted the fact that healings were performed by Jesus but explained them as ordinary cures (faith healings, special medical techniques ahead of his time, hypnosis). Similar natural explanations were offered for other miracles like raising the dead (coma, not real death) and the nature miracles (walking on marshland instead of on the water). The second approach judged the miracle stories to be fictional, stemming from overzealous evangelistic exaggeration or from primitive Christian credulity and misunderstanding. Conservative apologetic manuals offered a response to every such explanation or combination of explanations. At the present time, although the rationalistic or liberal approach to the miracles of Jesus still has some following, it is not triumphant. On the one hand, many conservative exegetes have come to recognize that *some* Gospel stories may involve ordinary cures and that occasionally popular imagination and theological interpretation color the Gospel picture of a miracle. On the other hand, some less conservative critics are willing to admit that the rationalistic or liberal approach cannot adequately explain the early faith in Jesus' miracles found in the Gospels. It is recognized that the empirical, scientific model of reality dominant in Western culture, while having its own validity, is not the only or solely valid approach to interpreting reality. Greater attention to the cultural context of the 1st-cent. Hellenistic world has also demonstrated the importance of ecstatic religious experience in the Jewish, Greco-Roman, and, therefore, early Christian world (see Kee, *Miracle;* Dunn, *Jesus;* Vermes, *Jesus the Jew* 58-82). Modern biblical criticism, therefore, has now taken a somewhat different approach to the miracles of Jesus.

97   **(A) Form-critical Approach.** We shall study this area particularly as exemplified in the thought of R. Bultmann, one of the pioneers of the form-critical method (→ NT Criticism, 70:49). He works on the presupposition that miracles are impossible. Therefore, although it is credible that Jesus may have healed a few people by natural means, the origins of the miracle stories of the Gospels must be sought in circumstances other than the historical career of Jesus. As we have noted, there are few OT parallels for the miracles that Jesus worked for individuals. Bultmann, therefore, does not seek in the OT the origins of the portrait of Jesus as a wonder-worker; rather, such a portrait has been colored by the fact that Judaism attributed marvelous deeds to Palestinian rabbis and the Hellenistic world attributed them to professional wonder-workers like Apollonius of Tyana (see Theissen, *Miracle* 265-76; Kee, *Miracle*). The general thesis is that Christianity could not have converted a world, whether Jewish or Gentile, that gave credence to such miracles unless Jesus was presented as an equal, at least, in miraculous power. Specifically, Bultmann distinguishes two types of miracle narratives:

98   (a) PRONOUNCEMENT MIRACLE STORIES. These miracles are attached to important sayings of Jesus and are recalled primarily for the sake of the pronouncement. (Such units are called apophthegms by Bultmann, *HST* 11-16.) Thus, in Mark 3:1-6 the center of interest is not the healing of the man with the withered hand, but Jesus' attitude toward the sabbath (also Luke 13:10-17; 14:1-6). In judging the historicity of such miracles, some would suggest that only the pronouncement authentically comes from Jesus and that the miracle is an illustration created by the Palestinian community in its debates with the Pharisees.

99   (b) MIRACLE STORIES PROPER. Here the miracle itself is the center of interest. The narratives are subdivided into the healing miracles (including the expulsion of demons) and nature miracles.

100   (i) *Healing miracles* have a fixed format:
Setting: A description, sometimes detailed, of the illness of the sick person and of past failure to cure that person (Mark 5:25; 9:17-22). Often this is accompanied by doubts about the healer's ability or scorn on the part of the bystanders (Mark 5:40; 9:18,22-23). But the person who is ill or a relative expresses belief in the healer (Bultmann stresses that this is merely trust in a wonder-worker and not true faith).
Cure: The intervention of the healer is usually immediately effective. Most of the time the healing is brought about by a simple word of Jesus (Mark 5:41; 7:34). Sometimes the technique involves physical touching (Mark 1:31,41; 5:41; 7:33) and three times spittle (Mark 7:33; 8:23; John 9:6). On occasion Jesus prays (Mark 7:34; John 11:41).
Result: The reality of the cure is attested by the patient's response. A disabled person walks away (Mark 2:12); a blind man describes what he sees (8:24-25); a possessed or insane man acts normally (5:15); a dead person becomes active (5:42). The divine nature of the intervention that brought the healing is recognized, often by the crowd in chorus (1:27; 5:20,42; Luke 7:16).

Bultmann points out that the miracles attributed to the Gk wonder-workers have exactly the same format. The healing stories for him, then, are embellishments added to the Gospel narrative in the Greek-speaking churches and form no integral part of the original good news of salvation.

101   (ii) *Nature miracles* include calming the storm (Mark 4:35-41), walking on the sea (6:45-52), multiplication of the loaves (6:33-44; 8:1-9), blighting the fig tree (11:12-14), finding a coin in a fish's mouth (Matt 17:24-27), arranging a large catch of fish (Luke 5:1-11; John 21:1-14), and changing water to wine (John 2:1-11). Not only for Bultmann but even for some more conservative scholars the nature miracles are not genuine historical tradition about Jesus but reflect later theological interpretation by the early community and the evangelists.

102   (c) SUMMARIES OF MIRACLES. Besides the two main classes of miracle stories given above, there are in the Gospels summary paragraphs mentioning many healings (Mark 1:32-34; 3:10-12; 6:54-56). The language of these summary paragraphs resembles that of the individual miracle stories, and the summaries are generalizations based on the individual stories rather than memories of numerous miracles really worked by Jesus.

103   **(B) Evaluation of the Form-critical Approach.** The above observations obviously have some value in suggesting ways in which the miracle stories were shaped and passed on in the early church. A knowledge, for instance, of the standard format of a healing may enable the exegete to detect in an individual narrative unique features that need explanation. But there are a number of points on which Bultmann's approach needs refinement or correction. The following observations are in order:

104   *First,* the literary analysis of the form may be inadequate and need further nuance, for the data that Bultmann examined were too narrow. In particular, the parallels he detected between Gospel miracles and the miracles of rabbis or Hellenistic wonder-workers need circumspection, as suggested by J.-M. van Cangh, *RTL* 15 (1984) 28–53; L. Sabourin, *BTB* 2 (1972) 281–307. On the issue of greater form-critical subtlety, see H. D. Betz, *Semeia* 11 (1978) 69–81; R. Funk, *Semeia* 12 (1978) 57–96. Moreover, Theissen (*Miracle*) and others attempt to go beyond the "archaeological" approach of Bultmann, in which the development of the miracle form is seen as the accumulation of successive layers of tradition. Using the insights of modern structuralism, Theissen identifies some 33 literary motifs common to a wide range of Christian, Jewish, and Greco-Roman healing stories. He suggests that various combinations of these motifs are given prominence according to the setting and function of the miracle story within a particular milieu and religious system.

105   *Second,* the miracle stories are an integral part of the Gospel narrative. Almost half of Mark's account of the public ministry (200 of 425 verses of Mark 1–10) is concerned with the miraculous. If the miracles are proposed as subsequent embellishments of the original Gospel preaching, one wonders what deeds of Jesus the original preaching contained. Moreover, a theory of the miracles as later additions fits none of the evidence of Gospel sources; for the oldest hypothetical sources, including "Q" and the Petrine kerygma (Acts 2:22; 10:38), mention miracles. This was conceded by a form critic contemporary with Bultmann; see Fridrichsen, *Problem.* Paul seems to take for granted the working of miracles within the church (e.g., 1 Cor 12:28), and he himself was endowed with this charismatic gift (2 Cor 12:11–12), a point sometimes neglected in assessments of Paul (Jervell, *Unknown* 77–95). G. H. Boobyer (Ramsey [ed.], *Miracles* 40) concludes: "Detailed analysis of the oral and literary stages through which the contents of the gospels passed before reaching their present literary form has now been in progress for more than a century, but no scholar would claim to have unearthed an early layer of narrative traditions which contained no miracles or allusions to miracles."

106   *Third,* there are some faulty leaps of logic in judging the origin of the miracle stories. To start with a presupposition that miracles are impossible and that therefore the miracles of Jesus cannot be authentic is circular argumentation and represents a secularist approach to reality. The whole Gospel conviction is that the kingdom (or dominion) of God was making its presence felt in an *extraordinary* way in the ministry of Jesus. Another difficulty is the attempt to establish the origin of the biblical healing narratives on the basis of their similarity in form to pagan healing narratives. In giving either a fictional or a real account of a healing, how else could the story be told than by describing the sickness, the cure, and the reaction? Such similarities of form are quite predictable and tell us nothing of origin or veracity. The fact that healing was an important religious phenomenon in the 1st-cent. Mediterranean world does not argue against the fact that Jesus of Nazareth was an authentic miracle worker. The assumption that noting parallels between the Gospel miracles and other religious systems is equivalent to explaining their origin is a fallacy of the history-of-religions approach (Kee, *Miracle* 1–41).

107   *Fourth,* the sharp distinction between healing and nature miracles is convenient but has no real justification within the biblical viewpoint. The evangelists show no more amazement at nature miracles than at healings, nor any more difficulty in accepting them. In a world view where not only sickness and death but also natural catastrophe represent the power of Satan, the intervention of the kingdom of God would require a demonstration of power in the realm of nature as well as in that of human existence.

108   *Fifth,* if the Gospel miracles had been created by a desire to give Jesus the reputation of a wonder-worker, the element of the prodigious would have been more prominent than it is now. Even though more miracle stories are attributed to Jesus than to any other figure from antiquity, there is a noticeable restraint in the Gospel accounts concerning the magnitude and manner of his healing activity (Harvey, *Jesus* 98–114). Consistently, Jesus is presented as refusing to work miracles to show off his power (Matt 4:5–7; Luke 23:6–12; Mark 8:11–13; Matt 12:38–42; Mark 15:31–32). Mark in particular has Jesus attempting to avoid the attention attracted by his miracles (7:33; 8:23; 9:25). Some Marcan interpreters have suggested that a major purpose of the Gospel was to discourage a portrayal of Jesus based too exclusively on his role as wonder-worker; rather, Mark wants to shift the reader's emphasis toward the death of Jesus (see R. Tannehill, *Semeia* 16 [1979] 71). Jesus cautions people about the danger of prodigies that can deceive even holy people (Mark 13:22–23), and he insists that even the greatest of wonders cannot force faith (Luke 16:31). Only in a later stratum of Gospel material does there seem to be some amplification of the marvelous element in the miracle stories. For example, in the miracle summaries (→ 102 above) Matt and Luke prefer to report that Jesus healed *all* the sick, rather than Mark's *many* (Mark 3:10; Matt 12:15; Luke 6:19); more impressive details appear in Matt's narratives (the fig tree dries up immediately in 21:19, rather than the next day as in Mark 11:20). Only in a rare miracle, however, like the finding of a coin in the fish's mouth (Matt 17:24–27), do we have the miraculous performed for self-convenience in a manner that approximates the style of a Hellenistic wonder-worker; and even here the real intent of the story may be symbolic and didactic (→ 113–14 below; see *PNT* 101–5).

109   *Sixth,* the faith in Jesus that is mentioned in the miracle stories cannot be written off as mere trust in a wonder-worker. The Gospels are narrated from the perspective of resurrection faith, and the response to Jesus within the healing stories illustrates a faith directed to the power of God active within the ministry of one who became the risen Christ. The miracle stories reflect a christological estimate of Jesus as one through whom God's power touches humanity. This is evident in the fact that suppliants in the healing stories address Jesus with full christological titles such as "Son of David" (Mark 10:47) or "Lord" (Luke 18:41) or cry out to him with prayer forms of the early church (Matt 8:25: "Save, Lord, we are perishing!").

110   **(C) Other Approaches to the Miracle Stories.**   The form-critical and historical approaches to the miracles, while important and valid, are not the only means of interpreting the Gospel miracles. Contemporary biblical criticism, along with its attempt to refine form-critical methodology, has used a variety of other methodologies to plumb the meaning of these stories. Redaction criticism (→ NT Criticism, 70:80) and literary or narrative criticism (→ Hermeneutics, 71:55, 67) have demonstrated that each evangelist integrated the miracles into his overall theological perspective and literary presentation, adding new dimensions to the stories themselves (→ 114 below; J. Donahue, *Way* 18 [1978] 252–62; Kee, *Miracle* 174–251; D. Stanley, *Way* 18 [1978] 272–86). Using the tools of cultural anthropology and sociology has led to new awareness of the symbolic dimensions of the body and of the taboos connected with illness (and healing) within the ancient world (see Douglas, *Purity;* Malina, *New Testament* 122–52; J. Pilch, *BTB* 11 [1981] 108–13; 15 [1985] 142–50). The healings of the leper in Mark 1:40–45 or of the woman bent double in Luke 13:10–17, for instance, involve not only a visible demonstration of Jesus' power but illustrate the inclusive nature of his mission. Phenomena such as demon possession and exorcism can have a social and political meaning as well as an explicitly religious one. In the exorcism of the Gerasene demoniac (Mark 5:1–20), the man possessed and dehumanized by "Legion" (a word that may originally have connoted the powerlessness of the people under Roman occupation) is fully empowered as a follower of Jesus and a proclaimer of the gospel (P. W. Hollenbach, *JAAR* 49 [1981] 567–88). Attention to the psychological and social dynamics of illness has also been instructive in interpreting the significance of the healing stories. Illness highlights the isolation of human beings and the boundaries that often stand between life and death, clean and unclean, insider and outsider (P. Borgen, *ST* 35 [1981] 91–106; Seybold and Mueller, *Sickness* 9–13; Empereur, *Prophetic* 141–201). In the miracles both suppliant and healer assault the boundaries of the "possible" and "rational" to reveal a new reality achievable through the power of God (Theissen, *Miracle* 300–2). It is not by accident that some miracle stories involve Jesus' contact with Gentiles and were probably used in the early church to bolster the Jewish-Christian community in its struggle to reach out to the Gentile world (see Mark 7:24–30; Matt 8:5–13; Luke 8:26–39). Because the miracles were revelatory, such actions of Jesus were seen not only as past events but as a divine mandate for the universal mission of the church.

111   (III) Meaning of Miracles in the Gospels. There is no doubt that many of the miracle stories have a certain apologetic interest in that they wish to affirm the extraordinary power and mission of Jesus (D. Dennison, *BTB* 6 [1976] 190–202). But Jesus' miracles were not only or primarily external confirmations of his message; rather the miracle was the vehicle of the message. They are "revelation stories" (Theissen, *Miracle* 291–301; Pesch, *Jesu*). Side by side, word and miraculous deed gave expression to the advent of God's redemptive power.

112   (A) Synoptics. The many facets of exorcisms and healings are apparent in the Synoptic Gospels. The description of Jesus' ministry includes both preaching and healings or exorcisms (Mark 3:7–12; Matt 4:23; Acts 10:36–38). This ministry, centered on the establishment of God's imminent reign (kingdom), involves the destruction of Satan's rule over the world; for since the entry of sin and death into the world, Satan had maintained a certain dominion over nature and humanity. The miracles were Jesus' chief weapon in the struggle with Satan (Mark 3:22–27), defeating the power of evil and liberating humanity; that is why a miracle is a *dynamis* or "act of power." The expulsion of demons is the most obvious example of the use of miracles to destroy Satan's power: "If it is by the Spirit of God that I cast out demons, then the kingdom of God has come upon you" (Matt 12:28; Luke 11:20). Along with the direct expulsion of demons, the cure of sickness is another aspect of the war against Satan (Luke 13:32), for sickness was part of the dark realm of Satan (Kasper,

Jesus 95–99). In raising the dead and even in conquering natural disasters like storms (notice in Mark 4:39 Jesus addresses the wind as if it were a demon), Jesus is showing God's power over the demonic (Sabourin, *BTB* 14 [1974] 115–75).

113   Besides giving primary emphasis to miracles as the means of establishing God's reign (kingdom), the Synoptists also portray Jesus as occasionally attaching other symbolic meaning to his miraculous actions. The answer given to the disciples of JBap (Matt 11:4–6) shows that the miracles fulfilled Isaiah's prophecies of the days to come (Isa 61:1–3; 35:5–6; 26:19); the multiplication of the loaves fulfilled Ezekiel's promise (Ezek 34:11; Mark 6:34) that God would be a shepherd pasturing his flock; the large catch of fish (Luke 5:1–11) was a prophetic symbolic action of how God's word would attract human beings; the miraculous withering of the fig tree (Mark 11:12–14,20–25) is presented by Mark as a sign of judgment against the Jerusalem Temple (J. Senior, *The Passion of Jesus in the Gospel of Mark* [Wilmington, 1984] 24–28).

114   In some instances Jesus himself may have used his powerful deeds as prophetic signs (M. Trautmann, *Zeichenhafte Handlungen Jesu: Ein Beitrag zur Frage nach dem geschichtlichen Jesu* [FB 37; Würzburg, 1980]), but undoubtedly much of this symbolic use of the miracles can be traced to the early church and to the evangelists themselves. Thus, in Mark 8:22–26 Jesus' opening of the eyes of the blind becomes for Mark a discipleship story in which Bartimaeus's newly gained sight is a metaphor for authentic faith in Jesus (P. Achtemeier, *Semeia* 11 [1978] 115–45; → Mark, 41:54). Not only does Matt's account of the stilling of the storm reveal Jesus' divine power over the chaos of the sea, but by means of special Petrine material the evangelist also reflects on his special theme of "little faith" (Matt 14:22–33; H. J. Held, "Matthew as Interpreter of the Miracle Stories," in G. Bornkamm, *et al., Tradition and Interpretation in Matthew* [Phl, 1963] 204–6; *PNT* 80–83). In Luke's version of the call of the first disciples (Luke 5:1–11), the miraculous catch of fish that precedes the invitation to Simon expresses Luke's theology, in which the power of Jesus' words and deeds draws people to him (P. Achtemeier, in C. H. Talbert [ed.], *Perspectives on Luke-Acts* [Danville VA, 1978]). Each Synoptic Gospel, therefore, uses the revelatory "sign" potential in the miracle stories as a vehicle for communicating the evangelist's reflections on the identity of Jesus and the meaning of Christian life.

115   (B) John. Although fewer than those of the Synoptics, John's miracles (only some seven in detail and comparatively few summaries) are thoroughly integrated into that Gospel's overall theological perspective. There is little overt emphasis on the miracles as overcoming Satan (no exorcisms) and establishing the kingdom of God, since the latter motif is virtually absent in Johannine theology. Yet the fact that the Johannine Jesus refers to his miracles as *erga*, "works" (5:36; etc.), shows that the miracles are an integral part of the work given to Jesus by the Father (5:17; 14:10), and indeed a continuation of the "works" of God in the OT, like creation (Gen 2:2) and the exodus (Exod 34:10; Ps 66:5).

116   The narrator and other characters in John refer to Jesus' miracles as *sēmeia*, "signs" (→ Johannine Theology, 83:55–57); and indeed the symbolic element of the miracle, which was secondary in the Synoptics, becomes primary in John. Physical miracles are used to signify spiritual truth. Some have suggested that John incorporated a "signs source" (a collection of the miracles of Jesus; → John, 61:2) into his Gospel, reinterpreting stories that originally were intended to demonstrate the messianic identity of Jesus so that they now affirmed John's higher christology, which proclaimed Jesus the unique revealer of God. While the hypothesis of a signs source continues to be debated, there is little doubt that the miracle stories are put at the service of John's christology. The miraculous abundance of the wine—the first of Jesus' "signs"—at Cana reveals Jesus' "glory" to the disciples (John 2:11). The raising of Lazarus illustrates Jesus' identity as the "resurrection and the life" (11:25–26). The life given to the royal official's son (4:50,51,53) is a symbol of the life of the Spirit that will be given through the death and resurrection of Jesus (5:21–24). The conversation in 9:35–41 shows that the primary interest is not in the blind man's having regained physical sight but in his coming to the spiritual insight of faith, an insight made possible by Jesus, the "light of the world" (John 9:5; see BGJ 525–32). The background of John's use of the term "signs" may be found in that designation of Moses' miracles (Exod 10:1; Num 14:11,22) and in the frequent use of symbolic actions by the prophets. Thus, pace Bultmann, there is some OT background for the Gospel concept of miracles (D. Stanley, *Way* 18 [1978] 272–86).

117   (C) Acts. The miracles described in Acts do not lie within the scope of this article. We would simply mention that the miracles of Peter, Paul (those of Paul seem to be somewhat patterned on Peter's), and other apostles are of the same genre as the miracles worked by Jesus, e.g., healing the disabled and the sick, bringing the dead to life, etc. They are worked in the name of Jesus (Acts 3:6), and they represent the continuing power of the reign of God inaugurated by Jesus (→ Acts, 44:29; see F. Neirynck in *Les Actes des Apôtres* [ed. J. Kremer; BETL 48; Gembloux, 1979] 169–213; R. F. O'Toole, *The Unity of Luke's Theology* [GNS 9; Wilmington, 1984] 51–53).

THE RESURRECTION OF JESUS

BIBLIOGRAPHY

118   Anderson, H., *Jesus and Christian Origins* (NY, 1964) 185–240. Bartsch, H.-W., *Das Auferstehungszeugnis* (Hamburg, 1965). Brown, R. E., *The Virginal Conception and Bodily Resurrection of Jesus* (NY, 1973). Craig, W. L., *The Historical Argument for the Resurrection of Jesus during the Deist Controversy* (Lewiston, NY, 1985). De Haes, P., *La résurrection de Jésus dans l'apologétique des cinquante dernières années* (AnGreg 59; Rome, 1953). Descamps, A., "La structure des récits évangéliques de la résurrection," *Bib* 40 (1959) 726–41. Dhanis, E. (ed.), *Resurrexit* (Vatican, 1974)—with bibliography (1920–1973) by G. Ghiberti. Dodd, C. H., "The Appearances of the Risen Christ: An Essay in Form-Criticism of the Gospels," *More New Testament Studies* (GR, 1968) 102–33. Durrwell, F. X., *The Resurrection: A Biblical Study* (NY, 1960). Fuller, D. P., *Easter Faith and History* (GR, 1965). Fuller, R. H., *The Formation of the Resurrection Narratives* (NY, 1971). Ghiberti, G., *RivB* 23 (1975) 424–40—continuation of bibliography in Dhanis (above); *La risurrezione di Gesù* (Brescia, 1982). Grass, H., *Ostergeschehen und Osterberichte* (3d ed.; Göttingen, 1964). Grelot, P., "La resurrection de Jésus et l'histoire," *Quatres Fleuves* 15–16 (1982) 145–79. Greshake, G. and J. Kremer, *Resurrectio Mortuorum . . . Leibliche Auferstehung* (Darmstadt, 1986). Hendrickx, H. H., *The Resurrection Narratives of the Synoptic Gospels* (2d ed.; London, 1984). Kessler, H., *Sucht den Lebenden nicht bei den Toten: Die Auferstehung Jesu Christi* (Düsseldorf, 1985). Kremer, J., *Das älteste Zeugnis von der Auferstehung Christi* (SBS 17; Stuttgart, 1966); *Die Osterevangelien* (Stuttgart, 1977). Lake, K., *The Historical Evidence for the Resurrection of Jesus* (London, 1907). Léon-Dufour, X., *Resurrection and the Message of Easter* (NY, 1975). Martini, C. M., *Il problema storico della risurrezione negli studi recenti* (AnGreg 104; Rome, 1959). Marxsen, W., *The Resurrection of Jesus of Nazareth* (Phl, 1970). Morison, F., *Who Moved the Stone?* (London, 1930). Niebuhr, R., *Resurrection and Historical Reason* (NY, 1957). O'Collins, G., *The Resurrection of Jesus Christ* (Valley Forge, 1974); *Jesus Risen* (NY, 1987). Osborne, G. R., *The Resurrection Narratives: A Redactional Study* (GR, 1984). Pannenberg, W., "Did Jesus Really Rise from the Dead?" *Dialog* 4 (1965) 128–35. Perkins, P., *Resurrection* (NY, 1984). Rengstorf, K. H., *Die Auferstehung Jesu* (5th ed.; Witten, 1967). Rigaux, B., *Dieu l'a ressuscité* (Gembloux, 1973). Schmitt, J., "Résurrection de Jésus," *DBSup* 10. 487–582. Stanley, D. M., *Christ's Resurrection in Pauline Soteriology* (AnBib 13; Rome, 1961). Swete, H. B., *The Appearances of Our Lord After the Passion* (London, 1907).

119   Outline.
(I) Reality of the Resurrection (§ 120–126)
(II) Differences in the Resurrection Narratives (§ 127–130)
(III) Special Problems
   (A) The Lost Ending of Mark? (§ 131)
   (B) Matthean Expansions (§ 132)
   (C) Jesus Raised or Risen? (§ 133)
   (D) The Resurrection/Ascension (§ 134)

120   (I) Reality of the Resurrection. The raising of Jesus from the dead was unlike all the other restorations to life mentioned in the Bible. In the NT Lazarus, Jairus's daughter, and the son of the widow of Nain are described as returning to ordinary human existence; there is no suggestion that they were glorified or that they would not have to die again. But Jesus is portrayed as conquering death, as returning immortal in glory and power. The resurrection of Jesus was the supreme intervention of God in human existence, the supreme miracle. No wonder then that, on the one hand, the resurrection has become a principal apologetic argument for the truth of Christianity and that, on the other hand, the reality of the resurrection has been questioned.

As with the miracles, however, the constant interplay of apologetics in the study of the resurrection has had bad effects (→ 91 above). The impression has been given that the chief importance of the resurrection was probative, whereas salvation was completed on the cross. Scholars like Durrwell and Stanley have sought to reclaim the salvific import of the resurrection as its principal role. The passion, death, resurrection, and ascension of Jesus constitute one indissoluble action for human salvation, as Paul implicitly recognized in Rom 4:25 when he said that Jesus "was put to death for our sins and raised for our justification." The life to which Jesus was restored through the resurrection is eternal life that he now can share with those who believe in him. It was with this theological understanding, and not primarily with apologetic intent, that Paul exclaimed, "If Christ has not been raised, then our preaching is in vain, and your faith is in vain" (1 Cor 15:14; → Pauline Theology, 82:58–60; see Kessler, *Sucht,* on the resurrection as a theological topic).

121   Nevertheless, once it is put into proper secondary focus, the question of the apologetic value of the resurrection cannot be bypassed. The NT does not claim that anyone saw the resurrection and makes no attempt to describe it, as does the *Gospel of Peter* (→ Apocrypha, 67:72). Therefore, the reality of the bodily resurrection hinges on the missing body or the empty tomb and, above all, on the validity of the experiences of those who claimed they saw Jesus risen. The rationalistic or liberal criticism of the last century tried to discredit the resurrection stories as demonstrative either of apostolic *fraud* (the apostles invented the stories; they stole the body) or of apostolic *credulity* and confusion (he was not dead but in a coma; the tombs were confused; hallucinations were mistaken for real appearances). We refer the reader to the painstaking refutation of these attacks in standard apologetic books (see Morison, *Who Moved*).

It is of interest here to point out that some of these attacks were already current in the 1st cent. and have left their mark on the later layers of the NT resurrection accounts that sought to answer the attacks. The assertion that the apostles were lying in claiming to have seen the risen Jesus when others did not see him is implicit in Peter's explanation in Acts 10:41. The charge that the apostles stole the body is attributed to the priests and Pharisees in Matt 28:13 (cf. 27:64), and Matthew refutes it with the story of the guards at the tomb. The suggestion that the apostles were credulous probably prompted the constant reminder that at first they did not believe that Jesus was truly risen (Matt 28:17; Luke 24:11,37; Mark 16:11,14; John 20:25). An apologetic stress on the corporeal and tangible qualities of the risen Jesus lies behind the insistence that he ate food (Luke 24:41-43; Acts 10:41) and that his wounds could be verified by the apostles (Luke 24:39; John 20:24-28). Seemingly, the empty tomb played little direct role in NT apologetics, although it is the background for the Easter morning stories. According to John (20:2), the brute fact of the empty tomb suggests to Mary Magdalene only that the body has been stolen. There are possible indications that the idea of the empty tomb was implicit in the early preaching, e.g., in the mention of burial in 1 Cor 15:4; in the comparison hinted at in Acts 2:29-31.

(For a defense of the antiquity and importance of the memory of the empty tomb, see R. H. Fuller, *BR* 4 [1960] 8-24; W. Nauck, *ZNW* 47 [1956] 243-67; H. F. von Campenhausen, *Tradition and Life in the Church* [Phl, 1968] 42-89; W. L. Craig, *NTS* 31 [1985] 39-67.)

122   In the early part of the 20th cent., under the impact of S. Reinach's *Orpheus* of 1909, a new assault was mounted on the reality of the resurrection through the study of comparative religions (→ NT Criticism, 70:39). It was proposed that the early Christians, either consciously or unconsciously, had conformed the story of Jesus to the pagan legends and mystery cults surrounding the dying and rising gods (Attis, Adonis, Osiris, Dionysus). But the apologists were quick to point out that while Jesus may have risen in the spring, his death and resurrection had nothing to do with the natural cycle of winter dormancy and spring flowering that lay behind the suggested parallels. For details on the history of the apologetics of the resurrection, see the works of De Haes, Martini, and Craig in the bibliography.

123   Another attempt (e.g., H. Grass) to explain the resurrection in terms other than real bodily restoration is centered on the theory that the genuine faith of the Jewish Christians in Jesus' victory over death could be expressed by a Hebr mind only in terms of corporeal resurrection, for the resurrection of the body was the only form of immortality known to the disciples. Truly Jesus was glorified; and since spiritual happiness was inconceivable without one's body, Jesus' glorification was described as a resurrection. Thus the resurrection of the body becomes a symbol of a spiritual truth.

In fact, however, bodily resurrection was not the only way in Judaism to express victory over death; see G. W. E. Nickelsburg, *Resurrection, Immortality, and Eternal Life in Intertestamental Judaism* (HTS 26; Cambridge MA, 1972); R. Martin-Achard, *DBSup* 10. 437-87, esp. 471ff.; Perkins, *Resurrection* 37-66. Moreover, the great subtlety supposed on the part of the disciples in the theory just mentioned and the difficulty of reconciling this theory with the very early insistence that people did *see* the risen Jesus have made some critical scholars wary of a purely symbolic approach to the resurrection. It is obvious that Paul believed not only that he himself had seen the risen Jesus (Gal 1:12,16) but that many others had seen Jesus (1 Cor 15:5-8). This has led to a suggested distinction between the experience of "seeing" Jesus and the interpretation of that experience as the resurrection of Jesus (e.g., Marxsen).

124   Pannenberg has made some interesting points that militate against a cavalier attitude toward the historicity of the resurrection. He insists that there is no question here of a simple revivification of a corpse. Not only is there the physical fact that immediately after death irreversible processes of dissolution begin, but — and this is more to the point — the NT authors are thinking of transformation rather than revivification. Paul, who draws a close analogy between the resurrection of Jesus and the future resurrection of the dead (1 Cor 15:12), stresses heavily the characteristics of the transformation that takes place in resurrection. What died was perishable, weak, and mortal; what rises is imperishable, glorious, and immortal (15:42-43,52-54). In short, "It is sown a physical body; it is raised a spiritual body" (15:44; see M. E. Dahl, *The Resurrection of the Body* [SBT 36; London, 1962]). Nevertheless, if the NT stresses that what was seen was a radically transformed Jesus, it was *Jesus* who was seen. True, the story of the empty tomb seems to represent a layer of tradition different from that of the stories of Jesus' appearances; but the disciples' preaching of the resurrection (and therefore their understanding of the resurrection) supposes that the tomb was empty (→ 121 above). This preaching would have been quickly refuted if there were any tradition of a tomb where Jesus' corpse still lay. Even the Jews who sought to refute the followers of Jesus never suggested that the tomb was not empty. And this concept of an empty tomb helps to confirm the continuity between the Jesus of the earthly ministry and the transformed Jesus seen by the disciples.

125   Pannenberg ("Did Jesus" 135) writes: "Something happened in which the disciples in these appearances were confronted with a reality which also in our language cannot be expressed in any other way than by the symbolic and metaphorical expression of the hope beyond death, the resurrection from the dead. Please understand me correctly: Only the name we give to this event is symbolic, metaphorical, but not the reality of the event itself. The latter is so absolutely unique that we have no other name for this than the metaphorical expression of the apocalyptic expectation. In this sense, the resurrection of Jesus is an historical event, an event that really happened at that time."

We shall leave to theologians the task of evaluating what is analogical and what is literal in the general concepts of "life" after death and the resurrection of a body.

(For examples, see W. Pannenberg, *Jesus — God and Man* [Phl, 1968] 66-114; F. S. Fiorenza, *Foundational Theology* [NY, 1984] 5-55; J. P. Galvin, *TS* 49 [1988] 25-44; Perkins, *Resurrection* 391-452.)

126   As far as the biblical evidence is concerned, on the one hand, according to the NT the disciples were claiming to have seen the Jesus who had been crucified and buried. (In this light, we think it biblically irresponsible to claim that Christian faith in the resurrection is independent of the question of whether or not Jesus still lies buried in Palestine—Christian faith in the resurrection is in continuity with apostolic faith in the resurrection, and there is no evidence that the first witnesses took such a stance of indifference toward the body in the tomb.) On the other hand, there is reiteration in the NT that the risen Jesus was different ("in another form"—Mark 16:12) and somewhat unrecognizable (Luke 24:16; John 20:14; 21:4). Any solution to the problem must take into account the element of continuity and the element of change and spiritualization, if that solution is to be guided by the biblical evidence.

127 (II) Differences in the Resurrection Narratives. In the passion narrative each of the Gospels presents a continuous story, the general sequence of which is singularly parallel in all four. (This has been a reason for assuming that the passion narrative was one of the earliest portions of Gospel tradition to take shape.) But the resurrection tradition consists of isolated appearances with little agreement among the various Gospels on circumstances and details. A close study of the chart on the next page shows how numerous the variations are. In the chart we make two basic critical assumptions: First, that Mark 16:9-20 is not by Mark but is a later compilation, partly from material similar to Luke, added to the Gospel—the "Marcan Appendix" (→ Mark, 41:109; see W. R. Farmer, *The Last Twelve Verses of Mark* [NY, 1974]; J. C. Thomas, *JETS* 26 [1983] 407-19). Second, that John 21, although composed within the Johannine school, may not have been by the same writer as the rest of John, so that, despite a redactional attempt to make John 20 and 21 consecutive, it represents independent traditions about the appearances of Jesus. (See R. E. Brown, "John 21 and the First Appearance of the Risen Jesus to Peter," in Dhanis [ed.], *Resurrexit* 246-65.)

128 Let us concentrate on the narratives of the appearances to the Twelve. It is clear that there are traditions attached to two different localities. Appearances in *Jerusalem* are attested by Luke, John 20, and the Marcan Appendix; appearances in *Galilee* are attested by Matt, John 21, and presumably by Mark (cf. 16:7; 14:28). That such a double tradition also exists in the apocryphal gospels and in other documents has been argued by E. Lohmeyer, *Galiläa und Jerusalem* (Göttingen, 1936) 6-7. (On Lohmeyer's thesis of a special Galilean Christianity, see G. Stemberger, in W. D. Davies, *The Gospel and the Land* [Berkeley, 1974] 409-38; also S. Freyne, *Galilee* [Wilmington, 1980] 344-91.)

Neither of the two traditions shows any awareness of a tradition of appearances in the other locale. The *Jerusalem accounts* leave little or no room for subsequent appearances in Galilee. Luke 24:50 portrays the departure of Jesus from his disciples as taking place at Bethany, just outside Jerusalem, on Easter night, and the Marcan Appendix has the same picture. A study of how Luke 24:6 changes the import of Mark 16:7 would seem to indicate a desire on Luke's part to avoid mention of appearances in Galilee. True, in Acts 1:3 there is evidence of Lucan awareness of a longer period of postresurrectional appearances; but there is no mention of Galilee, and the ascension takes place in the Jerusalem area (1:12). In John we have postresurrectional appearances over an eight-day period (20:19,26), and then the Gospel comes to an end (20:30-31).

The *Galilean accounts* seem to rule out prior Jerusalem appearances to the Twelve. The angel's directive in Mark 16:7 and Matt 28:7 bids the disciples to go to Galilee to see Jesus—a command that would make little sense were they to see him first in Jerusalem. When Jesus does appear to the disciples on the mountain in Galilee (Matt 28:16-17), they express doubt; and the other Gospels associate this hesitancy with initial appearances (Luke 24:37; John 20:25; Mark 16:13,14). There would be little reason for doubt if they had already seen him in Jerusalem. The editor who added John 21 made it seem that the Galilean appearances followed the Jerusalem ones by inserting verses that sew the two accounts together (21:1,14). But it is quite apparent from the story itself of the Galilean appearance (21:4,7) that the disciples are seeing Jesus for the first time.

129 Writers of harmonistic lives of Jesus have imposed their own sequence on the Gospel evidence: Jesus first appeared to the Twelve in Jerusalem for a week; then, for some inexplicable reason, they went to Galilee where he appeared to them at the seashore and on the mountain; and finally they returned to Jerusalem where Jesus appeared to them before ascending. Such a sequence does violence to the Gospel evidence, as Bishop Descamps ("Structure" 737-39) has shown. *If* one must venture beyond the evidence to establish a sequence, then (after the discovery of the empty tomb in Jerusalem and perhaps after appearances of Jesus to the women in Jerusalem and to "minor" disciples on the road to Emmaus) one might place the appearances to them in Galilee before the appearances to them in Jerusalem—a sequence that is not ruled out in the Galilean accounts. The Lucan and Johannine attempt to have the main appearance to the Twelve take place on Easter day is probably a construction dictated by theological rather than historical interests.

But the more biblical answer is to recognize that the evidence does not permit us to establish a sequence with any assurance. Each tradition in the Gospels centers on an all-important appearance to the Twelve in which they are commissioned for their future task (Matt 28:19; Luke 24:47-49; Mark 16:15; John 20:21; 21:15-17 and the symbolism of the catch of fish). Each tradition gives the impression that Jesus is appearing to them for the first time, whence the doubt and reassurance. Thus, Descamps is correct in maintaining that in a certain way, *as far as substance is concerned*, all the Gospels are narrating the same appearance to the Twelve.

130 How did it arise that an evangelist recorded appearances only in Jerusalem or in Galilee and that there was no attempt to make a sequence of all the postresurrectional appearances of Jesus? Taylor (*FGT* 59-62) makes an interesting suggestion. In preaching the resurrection, what was essential was a testimony that a well-known apostolic witness had seen Jesus. There was no chain of related events in the resurrection as there was in the passion. Thus, in Paul's primitive kerygma of the resurrection (1 Cor 15:5-7) only the names of those to whom Jesus appeared are listed, and no locale is mentioned. Each community would preserve the memory of an appearance of Jesus to figures known to that community. The important Palestinian Christian communities of Jerusalem and of Galilee would retain the memory of appearances with local associations, or perhaps, if Descamps' theory is correct, would have adapted to the respective local setting the tradition of a basic appearance to the Twelve. The individual evangelists drew on one or the other of these local traditions available to them, perhaps in ignorance of the existence of other traditions.

131 (III) Special Problems. Here we must be highly selective, only suggesting the direction of the answer.

(A) The Lost Ending of Mark? It is often supposed that Mark once ended with an appearance in Galilee similar to that recounted in Matt, and that unfortunately this ending was lost. There are difficulties,

The Variant Accounts of Resurrection Appearances

		Mark 16:1–8	Matt 28:1–20	Luke 24	Mark 16:9–20	John 20
AT TOMB	TIME	very early 1st day of week; sun risen	1st day of week dawning or drawing on	1st day of week; early dawn	early; 1st day of week;	early; 1st day of week; still dark
	WOMEN	Mary Magdalene; Mary, mother of James; Salome	Mary Magdalene; other Mary	Mary Magdalene; Mary, mother of James; Joanna; others	Mary Magdalene	Mary Magdalene another? ("we" in v. 2)
	PURPOSE	brought spices; came to anoint	came to see tomb	spices from Friday; took spices along		
	VISUAL PHENOMENON	stone rolled back; youth sitting inside on right	earthquake; angel descended; he rolled back stone; sat on it (outside)	stone rolled back; two men standing (inside); angels (v. 23)	Jesus	stone rolled away; (later) two angels sitting inside
	CONVERSATION	Youth said: Not to fear; Jesus risen; tell disciples he is going to Galilee	Angel said: Not to fear; Jesus risen; tell disciples he is going to Galilee	Men asked question; Why seek living among dead? recalled prophecy made in Galilee		(Later) angels asked: Why do you weep? She thought body stolen
	REACTION OF THE WOMEN	fled trembling; told no one	went away quickly with fear to tell disciples	returned; told Eleven and the rest	went and told followers	went and told Peter and "other disciple"
APPEARANCES OF JESUS			Jesus met them; they took his feet; he repeated message about Galilee		Jesus appeared first to Mary Magdalene	(Later Jesus appeared to Mary Magdalene. She clutched him; he spoke of ascending)
				[Peter ran to tomb; saw burial clothes went home.] Lord appeared to Simon (v. 34)		Peter and the disciple ran to tomb; saw burial clothes; the disciple went home believing
						Mary returned and saw Jesus as described above in parentheses
COUNTRY ROAD				Jesus appeared to two disciples on road to Emmaus	Jesus appeared to two of them walk- ing into country	
JERUSALEM				Appeared to Eleven at meal Easter night	Afterward to Eleven at table	Appeared to disciples minus Thomas at meal Easter night
						week later, to disciples with Thomas
GALILEE			To Eleven on a mountain			**John 21** To seven disciples at Sea of Tiberias

however; e.g., the fact that Luke shows no awareness of Galilean appearances may mean that the form of Mark available to him was already without the supposed ending. Lohmeyer has suggested that Mark had no resurrection appearances and that the promise that the disciples would see Jesus in Galilee (16:7) referred to the parousia (a thesis rightly rejected in the commentaries on Mark of Taylor [p. 608], Haenchen [p. 546], and Schweizer [p. 366]). Yet, even if one thinks that Mark must have believed in postresurrectional appearances, in harmony with all the early kerygmatic strains of the NT, it is possible that Mark ended without narrating a specific appearance—just with the general assurance that the Lord was truly risen. After all, despite the angelic order to go to Galilee (v 7—which may be secondary), 16:8 insists that the women did not transmit this order—a failure that may be related to the theme of the Marcan secret and the failure of the disciples to understand.

(For a survey of research: Trompf, G. W., *AusBR* 21 [1973] 15–26. For the thesis that Mark intentionally ended with 16:8: Boomershine, T. E., *JBL* 100 [1981] 193–223; Petersen, N. R., *Int* 34 [1980] 151–66.)

132   (B) Matthean Expansions. In Mark 16:4 and Luke 24:2 the women find the stone rolled back from the tomb, and at the site they encounter a (heavenly) man or men. The implication that the heavenly visitor(s) moved the stone is spelled out in Matt 28:1–4, which has the women present when the angel of the Lord comes down and rolls back the stone, frightening guards who have been placed at the tomb. These guards (Matt 27:62–66; 28:4,11–15) are absent from the other Gospels and are difficult to reconcile with narratives in Mark and Luke—why would the women come to the tomb with spices, expecting to roll back the stone (Mark 16:3) if there were guards whose express purpose was to keep people out? Elsewhere Matt seems to draw on traditions dramatized in popular circles (the magi and the star, Herod and the children, the suicide of Judas, the dream of Pilate's wife, Pilate washing his hands, the resurrection of the saints at Jesus' death)—stories to which Matt, as here, may give an apologetic function. The earthquake, the guards, and the angel(s) appear in a more elaborate form in *Gos. Pet.* For a discussion of the guard at the tomb, see W. L. Craig, *NTS* 30 (1984) 273–81.

133   (C) Jesus Raised or Risen? In about 19 passages, chiefly in the Pauline writings, the NT makes absolutely clear that God the Father (subject) raised Jesus (object) from the dead (e.g., 1 Thess 1:10; 1 Cor 6:14; Gal 1:1). Thus, the earliest tradition that we know attributes

the agency in the resurrection to the Father. The vb. that appears in the Gospel narratives (Mark 16:6; Matt 28:6, 7; Luke 24:6,34) is *ēgerthē*, an aor. pass. form that would normally be translated, "He was raised up"—see C. F. D. Moule, *Idiom Book of New Testament Greek* (2d ed.; Cambridge, 1963) 26. However, such passive forms in Koine Greek can be translated intransitively with an active nuance: "He is risen"—see J. H. Moulton and N. Turner, *A Grammar of New Testament Greek* (London, 1963) 3. 57. The latter transl., which shifts the agency in the resurrection to Jesus, has been common in Catholic Bibles translated from the Vg because Jerome rendered *ēgerthē* by *surrexit*, an active form. However, the translation "He was raised" is probably to be preferred in the Synoptics as less christologically tendentious and as a literal translation in harmony with the early theological outlook. In John the theology has developed to the point where it is realized that Jesus and the Father act by the same divine power (John 10:30) and that therefore one may say that Jesus rose by his own power (10:17–18). Thus the *ēgerthē* of 2:22 is probably to be translated, "When he had risen from the dead. . . ."

134   (D) The Resurrection/Ascension. "Ascension" normally evokes the image of Jesus' being lifted up to heaven on a cloud after 40 days (Acts 1:3,9). Such an understanding presents several difficulties: 40 is a symbolic number in the Bible and not always to be taken literally; other passages imply an ascension on Easter (Luke 24:51; John 20:17; Mark 16:19); the notion of ascending to heaven implies figurative language, for heaven is not really to be thought of as above the earth. P. Benoit (*Jesus and the Gospel* [NY, 1973] 1. 209–53) has made a very important distinction in the concept of ascension which helps to solve the problem. If one is speaking of the terminus of the risen Jesus' frequent appearances, this took place some time (contrast the 40 days of Acts with the longer period envisioned in 1 Cor 15:8) after the resurrection, perhaps in the symbolic form of a levitation as Acts describes. If one is speaking of ascension theologically, i.e., as a return to the Father or as a glorification in heaven at God's right hand, this exaltation was an integral part of the resurrection. Jesus rose from the dead to glory, and he appeared after the resurrection as one already glorified with supreme power (Matt 28:18; Luke 24:26). The intimate and immediate connection between the resurrection and the ascension so understood is spelled out in John 20:17ff. and is implicit in many other NT texts (Acts 5:30–31; Eph 4:10; 1 Pet 3:21–22; Heb 4:14; 1 Tim 3:16). See J. A. Fitzmyer, *TS* 45 (1984) 409–40.

THE TWELVE AND THE APOSTOLATE

BIBLIOGRAPHY

135   Agnew, F. H., "On the Origin of the Term *Apostolos*," *CBQ* 38 (1976) 49–53; "The Origin of the NT Apostle-Concept," *JBL* 105 (1986) 75–96. Barrett, C. K., *The Signs of an Apostle* (Phl, 1972). Brown, R. E., *The Critical Meaning of the Bible* (NY, 1981) 121–46. Cerfaux, L., "L'unité du corps apostolique dans le Nouveau Testament," *Recueil* 2. 227–37; "Pour l'histoire du titre *Apostolos* dans le Nouveau Testament," *Recueil* 2. 185–200. Culver, R. D., "Apostles and the Apostolate in the New Testament," *BSac* 134 (1977) 131–43. Ehrhardt, A., *The Apostolic Succession in the First Two Centuries of the Church* (London, 1953). Gerhardsson, B., *Die Boten Gottes und die Apostel Christi* (Lund, 1962). Giles, K., "Apostles before and after Paul," *Churchman* 99 (1985) 241–56. Hahn, F., "Der Apostolat in Urchristentum,"

KD 20 (1974) 56–77. Herron, R. W., "The Origin of the New Testament Apostolate," *WTJ* 45 (1983) 101–31. Käsemann, E., "Die Legitimität des Apostels," *ZNW* 41 (1942) 33–71. Kertelge, K., "Das Apostelamt des Paulus," *BZ* 14 (1970) 161–81. Kirk, J. A., "Apostleship since Rengstorf," *NTS* 21 (1974–75) 249–64. Klein, G., *Die Zwölf Apostel* (FRLANT 59; Göttingen, 1961). Kraft, H., "Die Anfänge des geistlichen Amts," *TLZ* 100 (1975) 81–98. Kredel, E. M., "Der Apostelbegriff in der neueren Exegese," *ZKT* 78 (1956) 169–93, 257–305. Lightfoot, J. B., *Saint Paul's Epistle to the Galatians* (10th ed.; London, 1910) 92–101. Mosbech, H., "*Apostolos* in the New Testament," *ST* 2 (1948) 166–200. Munck, J., "Paul, the Apostles, and the Twelve," *ST* 3 (1950) 96–110. Rengstorf, K., "*Apostolos*," *TDNT*

1. 407–47. Roloff, J., *Apostolat-Verkündigung-Kirche* (Gütersloh, 1965). Schmithals, W., *The Office of Apostle in the Early Church* (Nash, 1969). Schnackenburg, R., "Apostolicity, the Present Position of Studies," *One in Christ* 6 (1970) 243–73. Stuhlmacher, P., "Evangelium-Apostolat-Gemeinde," *KD* 17 (1971) 28–45. Villegas, B., "Peter, Philip and James of Alphaeus," *NTS*

33 (1987) 292–94. Vogelstein, H., "The Development of the Apostolate in Judaism and Its Transformation in Christianity," *HUCA* 2 (1925) 99–123. Von Campenhausen, H., *Ecclesiastical Authority and Spiritual Power in the Church of the First Three Centuries* (Stamford, 1969) 12–54.

136   Outline.

(I) The Twelve
  (A) Identity of the Twelve (§ 137–146)
    (a) First Group of Four:
      Simon and Andrew (§ 138)
      James and John (§ 139)
    (b) Second Group of Four:
      Philip, Bartholomew, Thomas (§ 140)
      Matthew/Levi (§ 141)
    (c) Third Group of Four:
      James, Judas (Jude), "brothers" of Jesus
      (§ 142–143)
      Simon (§ 144)
      Judas Iscariot (§ 145)
      Lebbaeus/Thaddaeus/Judas (§ 146)
  (B) Role of the Twelve (§ 147–148)
(II) The Apostles
  (A) Origin of the Term (§ 149–152)
  (B) Some Corollaries (§ 153–157)
    (a) Apostle: A Postresurrectional Title (§ 153)
    (b) Apostles Other Than the Twelve (§ 154)
    (c) The Twelve as Apostles (§ 155–157)

137   (I) The Twelve.   The NT gives four lists of 12 men whom Jesus chose during his ministry to be with him: Mark 3:16–19; Matt 10:2–4; Luke 6:14–16; Acts 1:13 (without Iscariot). John gives no list but mentions "the Twelve" (6:67; 20:24).

(A) Identity of the Twelve.   The following table gives the names found in the four lists and indicates the sequence in which they occur. Note that they break down into three groups of four. The order within the groups varies, but a name never passes from one group to another. Perhaps the grouping was a mnemonic device.

	Mark	Matt	Luke	Acts
Simon Peter	1	1	1	1
James of Zebedee	2	3	3	3
John of Zebedee	3	4	4	2
Andrew brother of Peter	4	2	2	4
Philip	5	5	5	5
Bartholomew	6	6	6	7
Matthew	7	8	7	8
Thomas	8	7	8	6
James of Alphaeus	9	9	9	9
Thaddaeus	10	10		
Lebbaeus		10*		
Judas (Jude) of James			11	11
Simon the Zealot	11	11	10	10
Judas Iscariot	12	12	12	

*In some Western mss.

138   (a) First Group of Four.   The first apostle mentioned is always SIMON whose name was changed to Peter (Gk *Petros* is from *petra*, "rock," the translation of Aram *kêpā'* — John 1:42; Matt 16:18), a change that took place early, since Paul refers to him as Cephas, not as Simon. Discussions of Peter have been influenced consciously or unconsciously by Catholic–Protestant debates over the papacy, but *PNT* offers ecumenical scholarly evaluation of all pertinent NT texts. (Also R. Pesch, *Simon-Petrus* [Stuttgart, 1980]; *TAG* 112–24.) Helpful is the distinction between Peter's role in his lifetime (before 65), and the development of his image in the NT works written after his death — the Petrine

trajectory. Closely associated with Peter in the Gospels is his brother ANDREW (John 1:40–41). Bethsaida is identified as the city of Andrew and Peter in John 1:44, but the Synoptics place Peter's house at Capernaum (Matt 8:14). Simon and Andrew were fishermen on the Sea of Galilee (Mark 1:16). According to John 1:40, Andrew (and seemingly Peter too — also Acts 1:22) was a disciple of JBap (P. M. Peterson, *Andrew, Brother of Simon Peter* [NovTSup 1; Leiden, 1958]).

139   JAMES and JOHN were also Galilean fishermen, as was Zebedee their father (Mark 1:19). An implausibly complicated comparison persuades some that "the mother of the sons of Zebedee" (Matt 27:56) was Salome (Mark 15:40), who was the sister of Jesus' mother (John 19:25), all of which would make James and John cousins of Jesus. The mother figures in Matt 20:20 (cf. Mark 10:35). The two brothers were known as Boanerges, "the sons of thunder" (Mark 3:17) and seem to have been of fiery character (Luke 9:54). This James, known as "the Greater" or "the Elder" by contrast with the other James(es) of the Gospel (→ 143 below), was put to death by Herod Agrippa I between AD 41 and 44 (Acts 12:1–2) and thus was presumably the first martyr among the Twelve. John of Zebedee is not mentioned by name in the Fourth Gospel (cf. 21:2); few scholars today would identify the Beloved Disciple who was the source of the Fourth Gospel's tradition (19:35; 21:20,24) with this John. Neither should he be confused with the prophet John of Rev 1:1–3; 22:7–8, who lived for a while in Asia Minor on Patmos.

Peter, James, and John figure as a special group of three who were especially close to Jesus. They witnessed the transfiguration (Mark 9:2) and the raising of Jairus's daughter (5:37); they were near Jesus at Gethsemane (14:33). Andrew makes it a foursome in 1:29 and 13:3. Peter and John are closely associated in Acts 3:1; 4:13; 8:14.

140   (b) SECOND GROUP OF FOUR. PHILIP was from Bethsaida and seems to have been a close friend of Andrew (John 1:44; 6:5–8; 12:22). Nothing is known of BARTHOLOMEW (= son [*bar*] of Talmai). However, John (1:45–46; 21:2) mentions Nathanael, a native of Cana brought to Jesus by Philip; and by the 9th cent. AD, Nathanael was being identified with Bartholomew because Bartholomew's name follows Philip's in three of the lists. But it is far more likely that Nathanael was not one of the Twelve (so Augustine, Gregory the Great). THOMAS is called "the Twin," Didymus, in John 11:16; 20:24. An early apocryphal legend makes him the twin of Jesus, as also in the Syrian tradition of Judas Thomas (→ 143, 146 below).

141   MATTHEW is found in all lists, but only the Matthean list calls him a tax collector. The call of Levi, son of Alphaeus, a tax collector, is found in Mark 2:14; Luke 5:27, while Matt 9:9 gives a parallel description of the call of Matthew and never mentions Levi. No connection between Levi the tax collector and Matthew one of the Twelve is made in Mark and Luke. Perhaps the tradition of Matt had more information than the other Gospels, and thus Matt's implied identification of Levi with Matthew may be historical. However, Origen (*Contra Celsum* 1.62) said that Levi was not one of the Twelve, and Matt may simply be exhibiting the tendency to make all the early followers of Jesus members of the Twelve. (If Levi and Matthew were both tax collectors, confusion was possible.) We see this same tendency at work in scribal attempts to identify Levi with James, another of the Twelve; for instead of reading "Levi son of Alphaeus," some Western witnesses read in Mark 2:14 "James son of Alphaeus." Perhaps still another example can be found in the name Lebbaeus that appears in some Western readings of the list in Mark 3:18 and Matt 10:3 (→ 146 below), if Westcott and Hort are correct in thinking that Lebbaeus is a form of Levi (through the Latin?). See B. Lindars, *NTS* 4 (1957–58) 220–22.

142   (c) THIRD GROUP OF FOUR. Popular tradition would identify two of the Twelve, JAMES of Alphaeus (all lists) and JUDAS (Jude) of James (Lucan lists), with two of the four "brothers" of Jesus: James, Joses or Joseph, Simon, Judas.

The Greek of the passage that mentions these brothers of Jesus (and also sisters: Mark 6:3; Matt 15:55–56) uses the normal word for blood or uterine brothers. Were there not an ecclesiastical tradition to the contrary, one might assume that they were Mary's children born after Jesus, especially since they are mentioned together with her (also Mark 3:31–35 and par.). But a strong tradition (accepted also by Luther, Calvin, and Zwingli) portrays Mary as "ever virgin." The 2d-cent. *Prot. Jas.* identifies these men as children of the aged Joseph by a previous marriage (thus explaining also why Mary would raise and accompany them); in the 4th cent. Jerome (an ardent defender of Joseph's virginity) contended that they were cousins of Jesus, born of a parent who was related to Joseph or Mary. (In that direction some would identify "Mary the mother of James and Joses [Joseph]" of Mark 15:40 and Matt 27:56 with "his mother's sister, Mary [the wife] of Clopas" of John 19:25.) *Because of the ecclesiastical teaching,* one can argue plausibly that "brothers" in the Gk NT is a (overliteral) rendition of Hebr 'āḥ or Aram 'aḥā', covering a wide range of relationship, including brothers, cousins, and half-brothers. Clearly, the exact identity of these figures is a post-NT, not a biblical, problem. See J. Blinzler, *Die Brüder und Schwestern Jesu* (SBS 21; Stuttgart, 1967); *MNT* 65–72; 273–75; J. Gilles, *Les "frères et soeurs" de Jésus* (Paris, 1979).

In any case, it is most doubtful that James and Judas (Jude) or any of "the brothers of Jesus" were members of the Twelve. "The brothers" did not follow Jesus during the ministry (John 7:5; Mark 3:21 where presumably "his relatives" are "the mother and brothers" of 3:31). Passages like Acts 1:13–14; 1 Cor 15:5–7 distinguish between the Twelve and "the brothers," and this distinction is implied in Mark 3:13–19 compared with 3:31. In particular, James the brother of Jesus, if he is the son of Clopas, is clearly not that member of the Twelve identified as James the son of Alphaeus (of whom we know nothing), despite Jerome's attempt to identify Clopas and Alphaeus.

143   Thus, among Jesus' acquaintances we seem to have three men named James: (1) James son of Zebedee, "the Greater," one of the Twelve (→ 139 above); (2) James son of Alphaeus, one of the Twelve; (3) James, presumably son of Clopas, "the Less" (Mark 15:40 = the smaller or younger), a "brother" of Jesus, later presiding (anachronistically "bishop") at Jerusalem, traditional author of an epistle, an apostle in the broad sense of the word (Gal 1:19?), but not one of the Twelve (P. Gächter, *ZKT* 76 [1954] 126–69).

There also seem to have been three men named Judas or Jude: (1) Judas Iscariot, one of the Twelve (→ 145 below); (2) Judas son of James of whom we know nothing; the translation found in some Bibles, "Judas brother of James," is a tendentious attempt to identify him with the next-mentioned Judas and is unwarranted by ordinary Gk grammar (BDF 162.2); (3) Judas "brother"

of Jesus and brother of the third James above (Jude 1:1), traditional author of an epistle, dubiously the third "bishop" of Jerusalem after James and Simon (his other brother? → History, 75:193), but not one of the Twelve.

144   Returning to the lists of the Twelve, we find a SIMON, called *zēlōtēs* in the Lucan lists and *kananaios* in Mark/Matt. The latter does not mean that he is from Cana or a Canaanite, but reflects Aram *qan'ānā'*, "zeal." By the 60s a Zealot was a member of the extreme nationalist, anti-Roman party that had supporters in Galilee (→ History, 75:179); but earlier it may have described someone "zealous for God" like Phinehas (Num 25:13).

145   JUDAS ISCARIOT was son of Simon (John 12:4; interestingly, the best readings of 6:71 and 13:26 would seem to describe Simon as the Iscariot, thus: "Judas, son of Simon the Iscariot"). The surname of Judas appears as *Iskariōth, Iskariōtēs* (or as *Skariōth, Skariōtēs* in Western mss.) and *apo Karyōtou* (in some witnesses of the verses in John). The meaning is uncertain, but many take it to reflect Hebr 'îš Qerîyôt, i.e., a man from Kerioth, a town in southern Judea, an interpretation that would make Judas the only known non-Galilean member of the Twelve. Others interpret the name as reflecting *sicarius*, "dagger man," a Lat name for a member of a nationalist Jewish group related to the Zealots (→ History, 75:179). O. Cullmann (*RHPR* 42 [1962] 133–40) accepts this opinion and suggests that the troublesome "other" Judas of the Lucan lists of the Twelve was really Judas the Zealot and thus was the same as Judas Iscariot (even though different fathers are named—James and Simon respectively!). See W. Vogler, *Judas Iskarioth* (Berlin, 1982).

146   The lists show a lack of agreement on the identity of one member of the Twelve, for in the 10th or 11th place three names appear: (1) LEBBAEUS in some important Western textual witnesses of Matt 10:3—"Lebbaeus" in Mark 3:18 has less support; (2) THADDAEUS in Mark 3:18 and in the better witnesses of Matt 10:3; (3) JUDAS (Jude) son—not brother—of James in the two Lucan lists. Origen maintained that these were three different names for the one man. Others think that Lebbaeus is Levi (→ 141 above). John 14:22 mentions among the followers of Jesus "a Judas not the Iscariot." The Coptic of this verse reads "Judas the Zealot"; the Syriac reads "Judas Thomas"—obviously attempts to identify this Judas with one of the Twelve in the lists, either with Simon the Zealot or with Thomas. It seems more probable that Thaddaeus, Lebbaeus, and Jude (all Semitic names) do not refer to the same person, but rather the difference of names means that by the time the Gospels were written the historical memory of who among the disciples of Jesus belonged to the Twelve was already hazy.

147   (B) Role of the Twelve. According to Mark 3:14–15, Jesus chose the Twelve to be with him, to be sent out to preach, and to have authority over demons; John 20:19ff. describes Jesus as appearing to 10 of the Twelve after the resurrection and sending them out; Acts 1:13 with 2:1 makes them recipients of the Pentecostal Spirit; Acts 6:2 shows them active in deciding questions of government in the Jerusalem church; Rev 21:14 makes the Twelve Apostles the foundations of the heavenly Jerusalem. Thus, the prima facie evidence of the NT (or of parts of the NT, at least) is that the Twelve, carefully selected by Jesus, became (with the exception of Judas Iscariot) his chief representatives in the church. A critical examination of the evidence, however, shows that the picture was somewhat more complicated.

148   Early critics, like F. Schleiermacher and F. C. Baur, challenged the thesis that Jesus really chose twelve men and suggested that the concept of the Twelve came from the church's patterning itself on the twelve sons of Jacob and the twelve-tribe pattern of the OT. Schmithals (*Office* 58ff.) has argued that the Twelve had no connection with the historical Jesus, for the claim of their having been chosen by Jesus was advanced only to substantiate their position as authoritative interpreters of the Jesus-tradition. Two questions are involved in considering such objections: (1) Were the men mentioned in the lists truly companions of the historical Jesus? (2) Was the idea of *Twelve* part of Jesus' ministry? The first question must be answered affirmatively in regard to the better-known figures, like Peter, James, and John. They are too much a part of the Gospel structure of the ministry for their names to have been added later without great protest in the primitive church. Indeed, it seems most probable that all those mentioned in the lists were in fact companions of Jesus, for the very confusion over the lesser names in the lists (→ 146 above) indicates that by the time the lists were being copied the memory of these men was growing dim. As a teacher, Jesus certainly attracted disciples, and it takes much imagination to propose that the names of all his original followers were forgotten and totally new names put in their place (Gerhardsson, *Boten* 101–3).

The second question is more difficult: Granted that Jesus had companions whose names were preserved, did he separate exactly twelve very close friends or was the specification of *the Twelve* a later idea? We present the evidence for Jesus' choice of the Twelve but cannot prove it definitively. Not only the Gospels attribute the institution of the Twelve to Jesus himself; it is also implicit in the story about the choice of Matthias in Acts 1:15–26 (admittedly an intrusive passage, but taken seriously by P.-H. Menoud, *RHPR* 37 [1957] 71–80). In 1 Cor 15:5 Paul mentions that one of the first postresurrectional appearances was to the Twelve, so that seemingly he saw nothing anachronistic in supposing that the Twelve were in existence by the end of Jesus' life. We note that the Qumran community, steeped in eschatological expectation, had a council of twelve men (1QS 8:1; → Apocrypha, 67:110), so that the thought of patterning an elect community on the twelve-tribe system of Israel was already current in Jesus' time. The differences of names in the four lists of the Twelve probably mean that the institution of the Twelve was not a recent development at the time of Gospel composition (AD 60–85); rather, the Twelve had been more active in the early days of the church, and now the identity of some had faded away beyond verification. The question of the career of the Twelve after the earthly ministry of Jesus leads us into the problem of the apostles.

149   (II) The Apostles. What constituted an apostle in NT times has been bitterly argued in the years since Lightfoot's 1st ed. in 1865 of *Saint Paul's Epistle to the Galatians* (see Kredel, "Apostelbegriff").

(A) Origin of the Term. Secular Gk *apostolos,* from *apostellein,* "to send," is not a frequent term. It refers to a fleet or army sent on an expedition; the command of an expedition; a colonist sent to settle; a bill or an invoice. These meanings are not helpful as the background of the NT concept. *Apostolos* occurs once in the LXX (1 Kgs 14:6) as a transl. of the pass. ptc. šālûaḥ (root šlḥ, "send"), used of Ahijah as one sent by God with a message.

150   This LXX usage has led some to connect the origin of the NT apostolate with the rabbinic institution of the *sheluhim* or *sheluhin* (Hebr šālûaḥ, pl. šĕlûḥîm; Aram šālîaḥ, pl. šĕlûḥîn: "a commissioned emissary"). This thesis was defended by Vogelstein and Rengstorf. The legal institution of the *sheluhim* took on a distinctive character in the religious Jewish circles of the 2d cent. AD or even the late 1st cent., when the Palestinian authorities commissioned or sent out rabbis to represent them and act for them with full power. Those sent were often ordained by the laying on of hands. Sometimes the task of these emissaries was to conduct financial business, collecting tithes or Temple taxes; other times it was to act with religious authority and to proclaim religious truths. When acting within their commission, the *sheluhim* had all the authority of the sender. Those who would trace the NT apostolate to this background cite as parallels John 20:21 ("As the Father has sent me, so do I send you") and Luke 9:48 ("Whoever receives me receives him who sent me"). They contend that Jesus is the *shaluah (shaliah)* or apostle of the Father (Heb 3:1), and the apostles are his *sheluhim.* See also John 13:16; 2 Cor 8:23.

151   While very popular, the derivation of the NT apostolate from the rabbinic institution of the *sheluhim* was rejected by many scholars in the mid-20th cent. There is no evidence that such an institution existed before or during NT times. Klein and others traced the apostolate to Paul's missionary experience, regarding the apostolate of the Twelve as a later intrusion. Schmithals traced the apostolate to gnostic groups in Syria who thought of a redeemer sent from heaven and of men who were sent to bring the heavenly gnosis to others. Such theories run up against the fact that Paul recognizes the existence of apostles from the time of the postresurrectional appearances (1 Cor 15:7) and speaks of "those who were apostles before me" (Gal 1:17 — in Palestine, not in Syria). Paul never gives the slightest indication of creating the concept of apostolate or of borrowing it from gnostic groups; rather he struggles to have himself accepted as an apostle in the face of an established ideal of an apostle that existed before his conversion. His argument in Gal 2:7–10 is that he is entitled to be thought of as an apostle, even as Peter is an apostle (→ Pauline Theology, 82:13).

152   After the *sheluhim* proposal and its subsequent rejection, a third phase of 20th-cent. scholarship revived the proposal of Jewish background in a more nuanced way (see Agnew, "The Origin"). Forms from the verbal root šlḥ (rendered some 700 times in the LXX by [*ex*]*apostellein*) are frequent in the OT, often to describe a religious mission with God as the sender. (Gerhardsson has developed this point.) For instance, this verb was used for the mission of the OT prophets. The supporters of the *sheluhim* proposal had cited these texts but had no satisfactory answer for the objection that the OT does not use the cognate substantive *shaluah* for Moses and the great prophets, as do the rabbinic writings. A plausible thesis is that from the OT usage involving šlḥ in a religious sense came both the rabbinic institution of the *sheluhim* and the NT apostolate as parallel, independent developments.

In this approach a key step in the Christian development of the *apostolos* ("one sent") would be Jesus' sending to preach those who could bear witness to his victory over death (Luke 24:47–48; Matt 28:19–20; John 20:21; Acts 1:8; Mark 16:15). This sending would involve not only those who had known Jesus during his ministry (the Twelve, James, etc.) but also Paul. Among various constituents in Paul's notion of an "apostle of Jesus Christ," the two main ones seem to have been: (1) a vision of the risen Jesus — whence Paul's stress that he saw Jesus (1 Cor 9:1; 15:7–9) near Damascus (Gal 1:17); (2) a commission by Jesus to preach. Such an understanding of what constitutes apostleship shows the resemblance between the OT prophet and the NT apostle (implicit comparison in 2 Pet 3:2; Luke 11:49). The OT prophet began his career by being introduced in vision into the heavenly court before God, and then he was sent to preach God's will to the people. The same vision and sending constitute a NT apostle. In particular, Paul *the* apostle closely resembles Jeremiah the greatest of the prophets, even in his career as apostles as one who suffers for others (Rengstorf, "Apostolos" 439–41). The importance of the apostle in the church is seen in the first rank given to apostleship in 1 Cor 12:28; Eph 4:11.

153   (B) Some Corollaries.
(a) APOSTLE: A POSTRESURRECTIONAL TITLE. J. Dupont has argued persuasively that the disciples were not known as apostles during the ministry (*L'Orient Syrien* 1 [1956] 267–90, 425–44). Therefore, the lone reference to "apostles" in Mark 6:30 and Matt 10:2 is anachronistic, as is also Luke's more persistent use in five passages (6:13; 9:10; 17:5; 22:14; 24:10). Luke 11:49 is the only passage that puts "apostle" on the lips of Jesus during the ministry, and this passage refers to the future (cf. parallel in Matt 23:34). It is true that the Gospels present the Twelve as being *sent* out during the ministry (Mark 6:7; see 3:14), and in this mission they were to some extent Jesus' *sheluhim*. But the definitive sending that constitutes the Christian apostolate came after the resurrection. The analogy between the two missions may be what attracted the evangelists to use the name "apostle" even during the ministry. In talmudic circles the disciples of the rabbis often became their *sheluhim;* so also the disciples of Jesus.

154   (b) APOSTLES OTHER THAN THE TWELVE. As Lightfoot established in 1865, "apostle" was originally a much wider term than "the Twelve." This is the implication in 1 Cor 15:5–7. The following are called apostles in the NT, yet were not members of the Twelve: James the "brother" of the Lord (Gal 1:19?); Paul (1 Cor 1:1; etc.); Barnabas (Acts 14:14?; 1 Cor 9:6 with 4:9; Gal 2:9); probably Andronicus and Junias (Rom 16:7 – Chrysostom and others think Junias was a woman – a view that a study of the name Junia makes plausible [B. Brooten, in *Women Priests* (ed. L. and A. Swidler; NY, 1977) 141–44]). The very existence of false apostles (Rev 2:2; 2 Cor 11:13) suggests a wider use of "apostles." If "apostle" was used for the many who met the two conditions given above (→ 152), was the title even more broadly used for those who had not seen the risen Jesus but who had joined themselves to the mission of those who had? This may be indicated if Andronicus and Junias are really called apostles in Rom 16:7, or if the "we . . . apostles" of 1 Thess 2:6 includes Sylvanus and Timothy (see Acts 17:4,14), or if 1 Cor 4:9 refers to the Apollos of 4:6. Cerfaux ("L'histoire" 191–94) argues for this wider extension, and certainly *Did.* 11:3–6 uses "apostle" in a very broad sense.

155   (c) THE TWELVE AS APOSTLES. We hold to the thesis that the Twelve were members of the apostolate from the first postresurrectional days, a thesis denied by many (Harnack, Munck, Lohse, Klein, Schmithals). The Twelve were the first important group to see the risen Jesus (1 Cor 15:5); indeed theirs was a place of honor for they had been witnesses of Jesus "from the baptism of John until the day when Jesus was taken up" (Acts 1:22). Therefore the Twelve had a special role in authenticating tradition about Jesus and in making decisions affecting the Christian community (implied in Gal 1:18–2:10; Acts 6:2–6; 15:2ff.). The Twelve played their role in Jerusalem (Acts 8:1,14; 15:2), although it is to be noted that James, the head of the Jerusalem church, was *not* one of the Twelve – perhaps his relationship to Jesus gave him special importance. The Twelve were not replaceable; for once Judas Iscariot's place, vacated by desertion, had been filled by Matthias, elected by divine choice to keep the number at Twelve (Acts 1:26), the membership was set permanently. Thus, when James of Zebedee was martyred (Acts 12:2), there was no attempt to replace him. This is probably because the Twelve were understood as unique: they were representatives of the renewed Israel who would play an eschatological role seated on the twelve thrones of judgment (Matt 19:28; Luke 22:30 – this Q-tradition saying is the only preserved word of Jesus on why he chose the Twelve).

The Twelve functioned as apostles or those "sent" by Jesus (→ 152 above) by proclaiming him in Jerusalem. Acts (8:5; 11:19–20) describes Hellenists like Philip as first organizing a mission outside Jerusalem, going as far as Cyprus and Antioch. It was Paul, however, who brought to the fore the traveling missionary aspect of the apostolate. Whether the Twelve did undertake a traveling apostolate is not clear from the NT, although after the first two decades (*ca.* AD 50) some probably did scatter from Jerusalem. Only Peter is specifically pictured as ministering outside Palestine (1 Pet 1:1; Acts 12:17; perhaps 1 Cor 1:12). Whether through death or missionary travels afar, most of the individual members of the Twelve had faded from the known Christian scene by AD 60 and were seemingly but names in lists. Only the memories of Peter and John drew attention in the NT works of the last third of the century.

156   It was as a group that the Twelve retained importance in Christian thought even after the individual members were long dead. Thus Rev 21:14, one of the last NT works, pictures the Twelve as the essential foundations of the city of God. For theological purposes of church constitution and order we should concentrate on the collegiate concept of the Twelve as a body (Cerfaux, "L'unité"). Most of the traditions connecting members of the Twelve with specific Christian churches are not well founded precisely because the NT does not tell us whether the Twelve had a traveling role. Once again Peter is the exception, for archaeology and history do support the tradition that he went to Rome. However, to be honest, it must be admitted that the NT never shows Peter or any other member of the Twelve appointing a successor. Paul is reported to have appointed Timothy and Titus as legates with the task of establishing presbyter-bishops in every town (esp. Tit 1:5); and Acts 14:23 has Paul and Barnabas appointing presbyters in every church (see also the presbyter-bishops of Ephesus in Acts 20:17,28). The bishops became the successors of the apostles by taking over the pastoral care of the churches the traveling apostles had established – this is the most verifiable understanding of "apostolic succession." The contention that all early bishops had hands laid on them by the Twelve or even by apostles understood in a broader sense is unverifiable and unnecessary for the validity of apostolic succession.

157   The continuing importance of the concept of the Twelve and the importance of the Twelve among the apostles led the later NT works to simplify the picture of the apostolate and to speak of "the Twelve Apostles" as if they were the only apostles. Klein has argued strongly that Luke was the prime mover in this direction. We have seen that unlike the other Gospels Luke insistently speaks of the Twelve during the ministry as "apostles." Throughout Acts, with the exception of 14:4, "apostles" always refers to the Twelve; and even in 14:4 Codex Bezae has a reading that does not refer to Paul and Barnabas as apostles. (Klein argues [*Zwölf* 114–201] that Luke was deliberately refusing the title "apostle" to all others, including Paul – an argument to the contrary would be suggested by the emphasis that Luke places on Paul's missionary activity and the way in which the figure of Paul is assimilated in sermon and deed to that of Peter, one of the Twelve Apostles.) The tendency to identify the Twelve as *the* apostles is also seen in Matt 10:2; Rev 21:14; and, of course, this tendency grew in post-NT writings (*Barn.* 8:3). As Klein (*Zwölf* 65–113) has shown, however, the concept of a wider apostolate also survived (*Herm. Sim.* 9.15,4; Irenaeus, *Adv. Haer.* 2.21.1).

82

PAULINE THEOLOGY

Joseph A. Fitzmyer, S.J.

BIBLIOGRAPHY

1 Barrett, C. K., *Essays on Paul* (Phl, 1982). Beker, J. C., *Paul the Apostle: The Triumph of God in Life and Thought* (Phl, 1980); *Paul's Apocalyptic Gospel: The Coming Triumph of God* (Phl, 1982). Bornkamm, G., *Paul* (NY, 1971). Brox, N., *Understanding the Message of Paul* (Notre Dame, 1968). Bruce, F. F., *Paul, Apostle of the Heart Set Free* (Exeter, 1977). Bultmann, R., *TNT* 1. 185–352. Dahl, N. A., *Studies in Paul* (Minneapolis, 1977). Dodd, C. H., *The Meaning of Paul for Today* (NY, 1972). Drane, J. W., *Paul, Libertine or Legalist?* (London, 1975). Giblin, C. H., *In Hope of God's Glory* (NY, 1970). Hanson, A. T., *Studies in Paul's Technique and Theology* (London, 1974). Käsemann, E., *Perspectives on Paul* (Phl, 1971). Kuss, O., *Paulus: Die Rolle des Apostels in der theologischen Entwicklung der Urkirche* (Regensburg, 1971). Longenecker, R. N., *Paul: Apostle of Liberty* (NY, 1964). Lyonnet, S. and L. Sabourin, *Sin, Redemption, and Sacrifice* (AnBib 48;

Rome, 1970). Meeks, W. A., *The First Urban Christians: The Social World of the Apostle Paul* (New Haven, 1983); *The Writings of St. Paul* (NY, 1972). Rengstorf, K. H. (ed.), *Das Paulusbild in der neueren deutschen Forschung* (WF 24; 2d ed.; Darmstadt, 1969). Ridderbos, H. N., *Paul: An Outline of His Theology* (GR, 1975). Rigaux, B., *The Letters of St. Paul* (Chicago, 1968). Sandmel, S., *The Genius of Paul* (Phl, 1979). Schoeps, H. J., *Paul* (Phl, 1961). Schütz, J. H., *Paul and the Anatomy of Apostolic Authority* (SNTSMS 26; Cambridge, 1975). Smyth, B. T., *Paul: Mystic and Missionary* (Maryknoll, 1980). Stendahl, K., *Paul among Jews and Gentiles and Other Essays* (Phl, 1976). Suhl, A., *Paulus und seine Briefe* (SNT 11; Gütersloh, 1975). Taylor, M. J. (ed.), *A Companion to Paul: Readings in Pauline Theology* (Staten Island, 1975). Whiteley, D. E. H., *The Theology of St. Paul* (2d ed.; Oxford, 1974). Also *IDBSup* 648–51. *DBSup* 7. 279–387.

OUTLINE

INTRODUCTION

AIMS, LIMITS, PROBLEMS

3   A sketch of Pauline theology must take into account the character of the apostle's writings, which do not offer a systematic presentation of his thought. Most of what Paul wrote was composed *ad hoc*—to handle concrete problems by letters. In them he developed certain topics and exhorted his churches to the practice of a more intense Christian life. Almost every extant letter exemplifies this twofold purpose. This also explains how he could mingle elements of revelation, fragments of the primitive kerygma, teachings of Christ, interpretations of the OT, a personal understanding of the Christ-event, and even his own private opinions. Any attempt, therefore, to sketch Pauline "theology" must try to reckon with the varied nuances of the apostle's thought and expression.

Moreover, a presentation of "Pauline" theology is an admission that Paul's view of the Christian experience is but one among several theologies in the NT. It is imperative to respect Paul's theology and not confuse it with John's, Luke's, or any other's. It must be studied in and for itself. This caution is not meant to imply that a NT theology is impossible or that contradictions are to be expected between Paul and other NT writers. The NT as a whole bears witness to a faith in one Lord, one baptism, one God and Father of all (Eph 4:5-6), and a theology explaining that one faith is not an impossibility. But such a presentation will be the richer if nuances of individual NT writers are respected (→ Canonicity, 66:93-97).

4   A sketch of Pauline theology is a systematization of the apostle's thought in a form in which he himself did not present it. If such a systematization forces his thought into categories foreign to it or attempts merely to line up "proofs" for a theological system born of another inspiration, it has little value. The effort to synthesize Paul's thought must respect his categories as far as possible, with due allowance for the unequal degree of his affirmations and the diversity of the formative contexts. The guiding principle of such a sketch, therefore, cannot be an extrinsic one, be it Aristotelian, Thomistic, Hegelian, or Heideggerian.

5   Though the primary aim is a descriptive presentation of Paul's view of Christian faith, this sketch also intends to be a normative theological presentation. It aims above all at determining what Paul meant when he wrote to the Christians whom he immediately addressed, but it also aims at ascertaining what his theology means for Christians of today. This sketch is not merely a study of Paul's thought as a historian of religion (agnostic or believer) might present it; it does not attempt merely to determine what Paul taught, what influenced him, or how his teachings fit into the general history of Hellenistic, Jewish, or Christian ideas. Paul's theology is an exposition of the inspired biblical heritage of early Christians, and the word of God proposed in his exposé still has an existential meaning for the faith of people of today. In this way, Paul's theology is a *part* of normative biblical theology, just as biblical theology itself is only a part of normative theology as such. There are two poles in biblical theology, one descriptive, the other normative.

6   The "meaning for the faith of people of today" cannot be something completely other than the meaning intended by Paul for his contemporaries. Any attempt to understand him that fails to recognize a radical homogeneity between his meaning "now" and "then" fails to bring *his* inspired message to people of today. A valid sketch of Pauline theology must, therefore, ascertain first of all what Paul meant, and in this sense must be descriptive. The means to achieving this are not the logic or metaphysics of some philosophical system foreign to him, however legitimate or fruitful such a transposition might be for other purposes. The means are rather those of philological, historical, and literary criticism, joined to an empathy of Christian faith. In other words, those who sketch Paul's theology in a descriptive presentation share with Paul the same faith and seek through it to determine his meaning for today. Although biblical theologians, in trying to discover what Paul meant, employ the same tools of interpretation used by historians of religion—or, for that matter, by interpreters of any ancient document—they also affirm that through Paul "the one Lord . . . the one God and Father of us all" is communicating an inspired message to them and the people of their time. The fundamental presupposition is the inspired character of the Pauline corpus, a matter of *faith*. Paul's exposé and understanding of Christian faith are sketched in a way that is meaningful and relevant for Christians of a later age (→ Hermeneutics, 71:10, 21).

7   This empathy of Christian faith is sometimes expressed in terms of the "analogy of faith," a phrase derived ultimately from Paul himself (Rom 12:6). It may not be used to insist that the totality of Christian faith has to be found in Paul or even that his thought *must* be interpreted according to the sense of later dogmatic progress, with its precisions and specific nuances. If a seminal notion formulated by Paul has in time undergone further dogmatic development because of a polemical situation or a conciliar decision in the church, then that seminal notion must be recognized as such. It may be that the seminal notion is expressed by Paul in a vague, "open" fashion; and, thus formulated, it could conceivably (by philological criteria) have developed in one way or another. But the further dogmatic development may have removed that *openness* of formulation, so far as Christian tradition is concerned. Yet this does not mean that the historian of dogma or the dogmatic theologian can insist that this later development is the precise meaning of a text of Paul. Such scholars have no charism whereby they can read more in an "open" Pauline text than can the exegete or biblical theologian. To understand the "analogy of faith" in such a way as to read back into Paul a later meaning would be false to him and to the inspired autonomy of his conception and formulation. Rather, that analogy must be understood in terms of the total Pauline biblical faith. Obviously, the biblical theologian is not content merely with the interpretation of individual passages in their immediate context (i.e., with exegesis). One seeks to express the total Pauline message, which transcends the contextual situation and embraces also the relational meaning of Pauline utterances.

Though normative biblical theology is only a part of the larger complex of Christian theology, it does enjoy its own autonomy of formulation and conception. While inceptive, for it cannot be regarded as the full answer to theological problems of today, it is privileged: It attempts to formulate systematically what the witnesses of the early Christian tradition were inspired to set down in their own way. It deals immediately and exclusively with a form of Christian tradition that alone enjoys the distinctive divine charism of inspiration. True, for a Christian, the continued guidance of the Spirit has guarded the authentic dogmatic developments of later times from contradicting the seminal formulations and conceptions. But such protection does not mean that the full flower is already present in the seed. Hence the need to respect Pauline theology for what it is (→ Hermeneutics, 71:83).

(Barr, J., "Biblical Theology," IDBSup 104–11. Käsemann, E., "The Problem of a New Testament Theology," NTS 19 [1972–73] 235–45. Merk, O., "Biblische Theologie: II. Neues Testament," TRE 6.455–77. Richardson, A., "Historical Theology and Biblical Theology," CJT 1 [1955] 157–67. Stendahl, K., "Biblical Theology, Contemporary," IDB 1. 418–32. Strecker, G., [ed.], Das Problem der Theologie des Neuen Testaments [WF 367; Darmstadt, 1975].)

8   This sketch of Pauline theology reckons with seven uncontested letters of the Pauline corpus: 1 Thess, Gal, Phil, 1–2 Cor, Rom, and Phlm. Today three letters of that corpus, 2 Thess, Col, and Eph, are disputed and often considered to be Deutero-Pauline (i.e., written by a disciple of Paul). The three "Pastoral Letters" (Titus, 1–2 Tim) create a still greater problem; their relation to the two foregoing groups of letters is at best pseudepigraphical (→ NT Epistles, 45:12; → Canonicity, 66:87–89). Following other modern Catholic interpreters, we shall omit the data from the Pastorals. References to the Deutero-Paulines, when called for, will be set in parentheses. The theology of Heb is a problem

apart and is not treated as Pauline (→ Hebrews, 60:2). Material in Acts related to Paul's teaching can at best be used for comparative purposes, since it really forms part of the Lucan portrait of Paul and more properly belongs to Lucan theology.

9   Can one detect any development in Paul's teaching? This is a debated issue. Those who in the past admitted a development were often reckoning with a corpus of 10 or more Pauline letters; and so, for instance, it was not difficult to detect a development in Paul's ecclesiological teaching, as one moved from the uncontested letters to Col and Eph, and then on to the Pastorals. But that alleged development is precisely part of the reason why one distinguishes the Pauline letters as in § 8 above. The majority view today queries whether a development can be detected in the seven letters that constitute the uncontested group (see W. G. Kümmel, NTS 18 [1971–72] 457–58). Yet one can note at times differences in issues (often of minor importance) that reveal some development. For instance, in the early letter, 1 Thess 4:14, one finds only an extrinsic connection between Christ's resurrection and the glorious resurrection of Christians: Through Jesus, God will lead with him those who have died. It is thus set forth in an apocalyptic description of the eschaton, reflecting the primitive eschatology of the early church. Later on one notes a more intimate connection between the passion, death, and resurrection of Christ and human beings who find salvation in him. Christ has become a "power," producing new life in Christian believers which eventually ensures their resurrection and life "with Christ" (see Phil 3:10–11; cf. Rom 6:4). Again, Paul's treatment of the role of the Mosaic law in human life develops from Gal to Rom (→ 95 below).

(Allo, E.-B., "L''Evolution' de l'évangile de Paul," VP 1 [1941] 48–77, 165–93. Buck, C. and G. Taylor, Saint Paul: A Study of the Development of His Thought [NY, 1969]. Dodd, C. H., "The Mind of Paul, I and II," New Testament Studies [Manchester, 1953] 67–128. Hurd, J. C., The Origin of I Corinthians [London, 1965] 8–12. Lester-Garland, L. V., "The Sequence of Thought in the Pauline Epistles," Theology 33 [1936] 228–38. Lowe, J., "An Examination of Attempts to Detect Development in St. Paul's Theology," JTS 42 [1941] 129–42.)

PAUL'S BACKGROUND

Five factors that influenced Paul's theology may be considered; not all of them are of equal importance.

10   **(I) Pharisaic, Jewish Background.** The polemical passages in which Paul reacts against the Mosaic law should not be allowed to obscure the fact that even the Christian Paul looked back with pride on his life as a Jew of the Pharisaic tradition (Phil 3:5–6; Gal 1:14; 2 Cor 11:22). This strong Jewish background accounts for the fact that he thinks and expresses himself in OT categories and images. It also accounts for his abundant use of the OT, which he cites explicitly almost 90 times (yet never in 1 Thess, Phil, or Phlm). Though his use of the OT is often similar to that of the authors of Qumran and other intertestamental Jewish literature, he usually quotes it according to the LXX. At times, he accommodates the OT text or gives new meaning to passages he cites (e.g., Hab 2:4 in Rom 1:17 or Gal 3:11; Gen 12:7 in Gal 3:16; Exod 34:34 in 2 Cor 3:17); he may allegorize a text (Gen 16:15; 17:16 in Gal 4:21–25) or wrest it from its original context (Deut 25:5 in 1 Cor 9:9). Paul's use of the OT does not conform to our modern ideas of quoting Scripture, but it does conform

to the contemporary Jewish way of interpreting and must be judged in that light. That he was inspired by the Spirit to interpret it in this fashion does not mean that his interpretation always reveals a hidden, deeper (literal) sense otherwise unsuspected. Yet his Jewish background makes him quote the OT to stress the unity of God's action in both dispensations and often as announcing the Christian gospel (Rom 1:2) or preparing for Christ (Gal 3:24). Even if he contrasts the "letter (of the law) and the Spirit" (2 Cor 3:6; Rom 2:29; 7:6), the OT is still for him a means through which God speaks to humanity (1 Cor 9:10; 2 Cor 6:16–17; cf. Rom 4:23; 15:4). Indeed, most of his theology (in the narrow sense, teaching about God) and his anthropology (teaching about human beings) clearly reveal this Jewish background.

11   Luke depicts Paul as trained by a rabbi in Jerusalem (→ Paul, 79:18), but Paul himself never says anything about his "rabbinical" background. Though he has identified himself as a former Pharisee (Phil 3:5), as a member of the Jewish group out of which came the later rabbinic tradition, one must use discernment in appealing to such literature to illustrate his Jewish background, since the vast majority of it was not put in writing until the time of Rabbi Judah the Prince at the beginning of the 3d cent. AD (→ Apocrypha, 67:133-35).

(Bring, R., "Paul and the Old Testament," *ST* 25 [1971] 21-60. Byrne, B., *'Sons of God'—'Seed of Abraham'* [AnBib 83; Rome, 1979]. Davies, W. D., "Paul and the Dead Sea Scrolls: Flesh and Spirit," in *The Scrolls and the New Testament* [ed. K. Stendahl; NY, 1957] 157-82. Ellis, E. E., *Paul's Use of the Old Testament* [GR, 1981]. Espy, J. M., "Paul's 'Robust Conscience' Re-examined," *NTS* 31 [1985] 161-88. Fitzmyer, J. A., "The Use of Explicit Old Testament Quotations in Qumran Literature and in the New Testament," *ESBNT* 3-58. Murphy-O'Connor, J. [ed.], *Paul and Qumran* [Chicago, 1968]. Sanders, E. P., *Paul and Palestinian Judaism* [Phl, 1977]. On the rabbinic issue: Daube, D., *The New Testament and Rabbinic Judaism* [London, 1956]. Davies, W. D., *Jewish and Pauline Studies* [Phl, 1984]; *Paul and Rabbinic Judaism* [Phl, 1980].)

12   (II) Hellenistic Background. Despite Paul's heavily Jewish way of thinking, factors such as his use of a Roman name, his appeal to the OT in Greek, and his composition of letters in Greek reveal him to have been a Diaspora Jew. Though he does not write literary Koine, his style betrays a good Gk education (→ Paul, 79:16-17). Attempts to detect Aramaisms in Paul's Greek (see W. C. van Unnik, *Sparsa collecta* [NovTSup 29; Leiden, 1973] 129-43) have not been successful, even though Paul, in calling himself a "Hebrew" (Phil 3:5), may mean that he also spoke Aramaic, a Semitic language widely used in his day in Syria and Asia Minor.

Even if Paul had not been trained as a professional *rhētōr*, his mode of composition and expression often reveals the influence of Gk rhetoric. See H. D. Betz's analysis of Gal according to Greco-Roman rhetoric and epistolography (*Galatians* [Hermeneia; Phl, 1979] 14-25). Traces are found in his letters of the Cynic-Stoic mode of argumentation called *diatribē*, a mode of discourse conducted in familiar, conversational style and developed by lively debate with an imaginery interlocutor; its sentence structure is often short, and questions are interjected; antitheses and parallel phrases often punctuate the development (see J. Nélis, *NRT* 70 [1948] 360-87). Good examples of this style are found in Rom 2:1-20; 3:1-9; 9:19; 1 Cor 9. It was once fashionable to ascribe to Paul's Hellenistic background such terms as "Lord," "Son of God," "flesh and spirit," and "mystery" and to ascribe to Hellenistic gnosticism his use of "Adam" and "Man," a redeemer myth, preexistence, instrumentality in creation, etc. But many of these terms and notions have been shown to have been at home in 1st-cent. Judaism, even in Palestine itself, which in the last pre-Christian centuries had come to grips with Hellenistic influence and the use of the OT in Greek.

Whereas Jesus' illustrations often reflect the agrarian life of Galilee, Paul frequently uses images derived from city culture, esp. Hellenistic. He uses Gk political terminology (Phil 1:17; 3:20), alludes to Gk games (Phil 2:16; 1 Cor 9:24-27), employs Gk commercial terms (Phlm 18) or legal terminology (Gal 3:15; 4:1-2; Rom 7:1), and refers to Hellenistic slave trade (1 Cor 7:22; Rom 7:14) or Hellenistic celebrations in honor of a visiting emperor (1 Thess 2:19). He employs the Hellenistic ideas of *eleutheria*, "freedom" (Gal 5:1,13), and *syneidēsis*, "conscience" (1 Cor 8:7,10,12; 10:25-29; 2 Cor 5:11; Rom 2:15), and the Stoic ideas of *autarkeia*, "sufficiency, contentment" (2 Cor 9:8), and *physis*, "nature" (Rom 2:14). Note especially the Hellenistic vocabulary in Phil 4:8: *prosphilēs*, "amiable," *euphēmos*, "well-sounding," *aretē*, "moral excellence," and *epainos*, "something praiseworthy." In 1 Cor 15:33 he even quotes Menander, *Thais*, frg. 218. This Hellenistic

influence is detected more in Paul's ethical teaching than in his theology proper.

(Betz, H. D., *Der Apostel Paulus und die sokratische Tradition* [BHT 45; Tübingen, 1972]. Broneer, O., "Paul and the Pagan Cults at Isthmia," *HTR* 64 [1971] 169-87. Bultmann, R., *Der Stil der paulinischen Predigt und die kynisch-stoische Diatribe* [FRLANT 13; Göttingen, 1910]. De Witt, N. W., *St. Paul and Epicurus* [Minneapolis, 1954]. Hugedé, N., *Saint Paul et la culture grecque* [Geneva, 1966]. Koester, H., "Paul and Hellenism," *The Bible in Modern Scholarship* [ed. P. J. Hyatt; NY, 1965] 187-95. Pfitzner, V. C., *Paul and the Agon Motif* [NovTSup 16; Leiden, 1967]. Stowers, S. K., *The Diatribe and Paul's Letter to the Romans* [SBLDS 57; Chico, 1981].)

13   (III) The Revelation to Paul. Paul's theology was influenced most of all by his experience near Damascus and by his faith in the risen Christ as the Son of God that developed from that experience. Today NT scholars are less prone than those of former generations to look on that experience merely as a psychological "conversion" to be explained in terms of Paul's Jewish background or of Rom 7 understood as a biographical account. Paul himself speaks of that experience as a revelation of the Son accorded him by the Father (Gal 1:16); in it he "saw Jesus the Lord" (1 Cor 9:1; cf. 1 Cor 15:8). The revelation of the crucified "Lord of glory" (1 Cor 2:8) not only turned Paul the Pharisee into an apostle but also made him the first Christian theologian. The only difference between that experience, in which Christ appeared to him (1 Cor 15:8), and the experience of the official witnesses of the resurrection (1 Cor 15:5-7) was that his vision occurred much later. It put him on an equal footing with the Twelve and others who had seen the Lord. He spoke of it as an event in which he had been "seized" by Christ Jesus (Phil 3:12) and in which a "necessity" had been laid upon him to preach the gospel to the Gentiles (1 Cor 9:16; cf. Gal 1:16b). He compared that experience to God's creation of light: "For God who said, 'Let light shine out of darkness,' has shone in our hearts to give the light of the knowledge of God's glory on the face of Christ" (2 Cor 4:6). The compulsion of divine grace pressed him into the service of Christ. His response was one of vivid faith, in which he confessed with the early church that "Jesus is Lord" (1 Cor 12:3; cf. Rom 10:9; Phil 2:11). In a creative act that experience illumined Paul's mind and gave him an insight into what a disciple later called "the mystery of Christ" (Eph 3:4).

14   That "revelation" (Gal 1:12,16) impressed Paul, *first*, with the unity of divine action for the salvation of all humanity, which is manifest in both the old and new dispensations. As a result of the encounter with the risen Christ, Paul did not become a Marcionite, rejecting the OT. The Father who revealed his Son to Paul was the same God that Paul the Pharisee had always served. He was the creator, the lord of history, the God who continually saved his people Israel, and who proved to be a faithful lord of the covenant despite Israel's infidelities. Probably because he had been a Pharisee preoccupied with the minutiae of the law, Paul never manifested a profound understanding of that "covenant," so infrequently does he speak of it. Yet his experience near Damascus did not alter his fundamental commitment to the "one God."

Second, that vision taught him the soteriological value of the death and resurrection of Jesus the Messiah in God's salvific plan. If his basic *theology* did not change, his christology did. As a Jew, Paul had shared the messianic expectations of his people (see Dan 9:25; 1QS 9:11), looking forward to the coming of a messiah (of some sort). But the vision of the risen Christ taught him that God's Anointed One had already come, that he was

"Jesus our Lord, who was handed over for our offenses and raised up for our justification" (Rom 4:25). Before his experience near Damascus, Paul certainly knew that Jesus of Nazareth had been crucified, "hung on a tree," and hence "cursed" in the sense of Deut 21:23 (see Gal 1:13; 3:13). This was undoubtedly one of the reasons why he as a Pharisee could not accept Jesus as the Messiah. Jesus was "a stumbling block" (1 Cor 1:23), one "cursed" by the very law that Paul so zealously observed (Gal 3:13; cf. 1:14). But that revelation impressed him emphatically with the messianic, soteriological, and vicarious value of the death of Jesus of Nazareth in a way that he never suspected before. With a logic that only a Pharisee could appreciate, Paul saw Christ Jesus taking upon himself the law's curse and transforming it into its opposite, so that he became the means of freeing humanity from malediction. The cross, which had been the stumbling block to Jews, became in his eyes the "power and the wisdom of God" (1 Cor 1:24). Henceforth, he would understand that crucified "Lord of glory" (1 Cor 2:8) as his exalted Messiah.

Third, that revelation impressed Paul with a new vision of salvation history. Before the encounter with the Lord, Paul saw human history divided into three great periods: (1) from Adam to Moses (the period without the law); (2) from Moses to the Messiah (the period of the law); (3) the messianic age (the period when the law would be perfected or fulfilled). The experience near Damascus taught him that the messianic age had already begun, thus introducing a new perspective into salvation history. The *eschaton,* "end-time," so avidly awaited before, had already started (1 Cor 10:11), although a definitive stage of it was still to be realized (as was hoped, not too far in the future). The Messiah had come, but not yet in glory. Paul realized that he (with all Christians) found himself in a double situation: one in which he looked back upon the death and resurrection of Jesus as the inauguration of the new age, and another in which he still looked forward to his coming in glory, his parousia (→ NT Thought, 81:13).

15   Far more than his Pharisaic background, therefore, or even his Hellenistic cultural roots, that revelation of Jesus gave Paul an ineffable insight into the "mystery of Christ." It enabled him to fashion his "gospel," to preach the fundamental good news of salvation in a form that was distinctively his own. However, Paul did not immediately understand all the implications of the vision accorded him. It provided only a basic insight that was to color all that he was to learn about Jesus and his mission among human beings, not only from the early church's tradition but also from his own apostolic experience in preaching "Christ crucified" (1 Cor 1:23).

Beker, *Paul the Apostle* 3–10. Jeremias, J., "The Key to Pauline Theology," *ExpTim* 76 [1964] 27–30. Menoud, P.-H., "Revelation and Tradition: The Influence of Paul's Conversion on His Theology," *Int* 7 [1953] 131–41. Munck, J., *Paul and the Salvation of Mankind* [Richmond, 1959] 11–35. Rigaux, *Letters* 40–67. Stob, H. "The Doctrine of Revelation in Paul," *CTJ* 1 [1966] 182–204. Wood, H. G., "The Conversion of St. Paul," *NTS* 1 [1954–55] 276–82.)

16   **(IV) Paul, Jesus, and Early Tradition.** If the main inspiration of Paul's theology was the revelation granted near Damascus, that event was not the only source of his knowledge about Christ and the Christian movement. Paul was not the founder of the movement but joined after missionary activity had already been begun by those who were apostles before him (Gal 1:17). It is a priori likely, then, that Paul inherited from the pioneer tradition of the church at least some ideas about Christ. At first this observation might seem to contradict

what he himself says in Gal about the origin of his gospel, that he was not taught it and that it came to him rather through a revelation of Jesus Christ (1:11,15–17; 2:6). Yet here especially we must be sensitive to the nuances of Paul's expression: these passages in Gal were written in the heat of controversy. Paul had been under attack, accused of not being a real apostle and of preaching only a watered-down version of the gospel because of his attitude toward the law of Moses and Jewish practices. When he wrote Gal, Paul was at pains, therefore, to emphasize his divine, direct, and undelegated apostolic commission and the heavenly origin of his gospel (→ NT Thought, 81:151–52).

Yet this emphasis must not be allowed to obscure what is found elsewhere in his letters clearly indicating a dependence on the apostolic tradition of the early church—on its kerygma, liturgy, hymns, confessional formulas, theological terminology, and parenesis. Fragments of the primitive kerygma are found in Paul's letters: 1 Thess 1:10; Gal 1:3–4; 1 Cor 15:2–7; Rom 1:3–4; 4:25; 8:34; 10:8–9. He has incorporated elements of the liturgy into them: the eucharistic formula (of Antiochene origin? 1 Cor 11:23–25); prayers like "Amen" (1 Thess 3:13[?]); Gal 6:18; cf. 1 Cor 14:16; 2 Cor 1:20), "*Maranatha*" (1 Cor 16:22), "*Abba,* Father" (Gal 4:6; Rom 8:15); doxologies (Gal 1:5; Phil 4:20; Rom 11:36; 16:27[?]), and hymns (Phil 2:6–11; [cf. Col 1:15–20; Eph 5:14]). His confessional formulas also echo church usage: "Jesus is Lord" (1 Cor 12:3; Rom 10:9), "Jesus Christ" (1 Cor 3:11), or "the Messiah" (Rom 9:5). He inherited as well a number of theological terms, e.g., the titles "Lord," "Son of God"; the word "apostle"; the expressions *baptizō eis,* "church of God," etc. Finally, certain hortatory parts of his letters which employ stereotyped terminology suggest that Paul is incorporating parenetic or catechetical material drawn from common usage (1 Thess 4:1–12; 1 Cor 6:9–10; Gal 5:19–21; [Eph 5:5]).

17   At times Paul explicitly calls attention to the fact that he is "handing on" (*paradidonai*) what he has "received" (*paralambanein*); see 1 Cor 11:2,23; 15:1,3. He thus uses the Gk equivalents of the technical vocabulary of tradition paralleled in the rabbinic schools: *māsar lĕ-,* "pass on to"; *qibbēl min,* "receive from." He appeals also to the customs of the churches (1 Cor 11:16) and recommends fidelity to tradition (1 Thess 2:13; Phil 4:9; 1 Cor 11:2; 15:2; Rom 6:17; [cf. 2 Thess 2:15; 3:6]). O. Cullmann (*RHPR* 30 [1950] 12–13) found it surprising that Paul applied such a discredited notion to the normative doctrinal and moral precepts of the primitive community, when one recalls how Jesus reacted precisely to the *paradosis* of the Jews (Mark 7:3–13; Matt 15:2). Obviously, Paul saw something different here; it was for him not merely "the tradition of human beings" (Mark 7:8). Cf. 1 Thess 2:13.

18   Another aspect of Paul's dependence on early church tradition is seen in his acquaintance with what Jesus did and taught. Paul gives no evidence of having known Jesus personally in his earthly ministry (→ Paul, 79:18); not even 2 Cor 5:16 need imply that he did. Nor should it be imagined that Paul was granted a cinematic view of that ministry at the time of his Damascus experience. It is remarkable how little his letters betray knowledge of Jesus of Nazareth or even of what is recorded about him in the Gospels. One reason for this is that Paul wrote his letters before the Gospels took the form that we know. Yet an even more important reason is that Paul, not having been an eyewitness, emphasizes the salvific effects of the passion, death, and resurrection of Christ, which for him transcend the data of the historical ministry of Jesus. His interest lies in these climactic events of Jesus' career rather than in the minutiae of Jesus' manner of life, his ministry, his personality, or even his message. He may allude to or quote a saying of Jesus occasionally (1 Thess 4:2,15; 5:2,13,15; 1 Cor 7:10–11 [cf. 25]; 9:14; 11:23–25; 13:2; Rom 12:14,17; 13:7; 14:13,14; 16:19), and such allusions or quotations reveal that sayings of Jesus were already being handed on in the early church in addition to the kerygma. But these sayings are invariably referred to by Paul as utterances of "the Lord" (*Kyrios*), a title that immediately reveals the transcendent aspect under which Paul regarded them. He was not interested in Jesus as a teacher, a prophet, or as the chronological source of such transmission. Rather, he was interested in the exalted, risen Lord, who became the real agent of the tradition developing in the bosom of the apostolic church. That is why he attributed to the *Kyrios* what in reality he had derived from the early community. The *Kyrios* is at work in that transmission, and as such he is regarded as "the end of the law" and a replacement of the *paradosis* of the Jews.

19 Paul alludes to remarkably few events of the life of Jesus: he was born of a woman under the law (Gal 4:4), instituted the eucharist (1 Cor 11:23), was betrayed (1 Cor 11:23), was crucified (Gal 2:20; 3:1; Phil 2:8; 1 Cor 2:2,8), died (1 Cor 15:3), was buried (1 Cor 15:4), was raised from the dead (1 Cor 15:5), and taken up to heaven (Rom 10:6 [cf. Eph 4:9]). Yet even these events are not narrated for their own sake or in the manner of the evangelists; they are, instead, recorded in contexts of a peculiarly theological or kerygmatic character. Paul may have learned the outline of Jesus' last days from the early church, but probably some of the details were already known to him before his conversion and were related to his persecution of "the church of God" (Gal 1:13).

20 Such features as these suggest that Paul had derived information from the traditions of early churches (Jerusalem, Damascus, Antioch). Moreover, his visit to Jerusalem, when he spent 15 days with Cephas (Gal 1:18), would support this (→ Galatians, 47:16). But such information was always transformed by Paul's personal vision and insight.

(Baird, W., "What Is the Kerygma?" *JBL* 76 [1957] 181–91. Bruce, F. F., "Paul and the Historical Jesus," *BJRL* 56 [1973–74] 317–35. Cullmann, O., "'Kyrios' as Designation for the Oral Tradition Concerning Jesus," *SJT* 3 [1950] 180–97. Dungan, D. L., *The Sayings of Jesus in the Churches of Paul* [Phl, 1971]. Gerhardsson, B., *Memory and Manuscript* [ASNU 22; Lund, 1961] 262–323; *Tradition and Transmission in Early Christianity* [ConNT 20; Lund, 1964]. Hunter, A. M., *Paul and His Predecessors* [Phl, 1981]. Kuss, *Paulus* 440–51. Ridderbos, H. N., *Paul and Jesus: Origin and General Character of Paul's Preaching of Christ* [Phl, 1958]. Stanley, D. M., "'Become Imitators of Me': The Pauline Conception of Apostolic Tradition," *Bib* 40 [1959] 859–77; "Pauline Allusions to the Sayings of Jesus," *CBQ* 23 [1961] 26–39.)

21 **(V) Paul's Apostolic Experience.** Another factor in the development of Paul's theology was his experience as an apostle and a missionary proclaiming the gospel and founding churches throughout Asia Minor and Europe. How much did his practical experience and concrete contacts with Jews and Gentiles mold his view of Christianity? Would he have written as he did on justification or on the relation of the gospel to the law, if it were not for the Judaizing problem that he encountered? The real meaning of the universal scope of Christian salvation probably dawned on Paul as he worked continually with Jews who failed to accept his

message and with Gentiles who did heed him. From his earliest letters he reveals an awareness of the privileged position of his fellow Jews in the divine plan of salvation (1 Thess 2:13–14; cf. Rom 1:16; 2:9–10). He wrestled in Rom 9–11 with the problem of the role of Israel in the Father's new plan of salvation by grace and through faith in Christ Jesus. But he was keenly aware that he had been called to preach to the Gentiles (Gal 1:15–16); he calls himself the "apostle of the Gentiles" (Rom 11:13). He admits that he is "indebted to Greeks and to Barbarians" (Rom 1:14). Moreover, the church as the "body" of Christ (1 Cor 12:27–28) is almost certainly the result of his understanding of the Christian *ekklēsia* in the light of the contemporary Greco-Roman understanding of the state as the body politic (→ 122 below). (The tendency manifested here is carried further by the disciples of Paul who in Col and Eph unite the themes of church, body, and head in a view of the risen Christ as the lord of the *kosmos* and employ the notion of *plērōma*, "fullness.") The problems that Paul himself encountered in founding and governing individual churches were almost certainly responsible for his gradual awareness of what the "church" meant in a transcendent, universal sense. To his apostolic experience must also be attributed a number of references to the Hellenistic world, which are met in various developments of his teaching (see 1 Cor 8:5; 10:20–21; 12:2; Gal 4:9–10).

22 Was part of Paul's apostolic experience a contact with gnostics? This is a highly debated question today. That Paul speaks of *gnōsis*, "knowledge," in a special sense and pits over against his "story of the cross" (1 Cor 1:18) a worldly knowledge is clear. But that he is coping with some form of gnosticism that was invading his communities is another question. Here no little part of the problem is what is meant by "gnosticism." That full-blown gnosticism was already current in the time of Paul is very difficult to admit. There may be elements in Pauline teaching that eventually fed into its full-blown form in the 2d cent. AD (→ Early Church, 80:64–80), but they are at most proto-gnostic elements in his letters. Despite all the claims about gnosticism as a pre-Christian phenomenon, no real evidence of a *pre-Christian* redeemer figure or of such a myth of the primal man has been adduced.

(Cook, R. B., "Paul . . . Preacher or Evangelist?" *BT* 32 [1981] 441–44. Holtz, T., "Zum Selbstverständnis des Apostels Paulus," *TLZ* 91 [1966] 321–30. Kertelge, K., "Das Apostelamt des Paulus, sein Ursprung und seine Bedeutung," *BZ* 14 [1970] 161–81. Lüdemann, G., *Paulus, der Heidenapostel: II. Antipaulinismus im frühen Christentum* [FRLANT 130; Göttingen, 1983]. Seidensticker, P., *Paulus der verfolgte Apostel Jesu Christi* [SBS 8; Stuttgart, 1965].

Chadwick, H., "Gnosticism," *OCD* 470–71. Dupont, J., *Gnosis: La connaissance religieuse dans les épîtres de S. Paul* [Louvain, 1960]. Pagel, E. H., *The Gnostic Paul: Gnostic Exegesis of the Pauline Letters* [Phl, 1975]. Ridderbos, *Paul* 27–29, 33–35. Schmithals, W., *Gnosticism in Corinth* [Nash, 1971]; *Paul and the Gnostics* [Nash, 1972]. Yamauchi, E. M., *Pre-Christian Gnosticism: A Survey of the Proposed Evidences* [GR, 1973].)

23 Whatever Paul inherited from his Jewish background, from his contacts with Hellenism, and whatever he later derived from the tradition of the early church and his own missionary activity were all uniquely transformed by his insight into the mystery of Christ accorded to him near Damascus. Other NT writers could claim a Jewish background and Hellenistic contacts, but none of them have Paul's profundity in understanding the Christ-event, except possibly John.

DOMINANT PERSPECTIVES

PAUL'S CHRISTOCENTRIC SOTERIOLOGY

24   (I) The Key to Pauline Theology.   There
has been a constant effort to formulate the key to Pauline
theology, its essence, its core, or its center. Since the
Reformation Lutherans and Calvinists, with varying
nuances, have found it in justification by faith—a view
still held by many today (e.g., E. Käsemann, W. G. Kümmel). In the 19th cent. F. C. Baur, using Hegelian philosophy, sought to explain the core in terms of the antithesis
between "flesh" (human) and "Spirit" (divine). Subsequently, liberal Protestant interpreters introduced a
more rational, ethical view of the antithesis, expressing
it in terms of the (human) spirit and (sensual) flesh.
Eventually, W. Wrede, though he belonged to the same
movement, sought to find the essence of Pauline Christianity in Christ and his redemptive work. The history-
of-religions school, using varied data from the mystery
cults of the eastern Mediterranean world, depicted Paul's
"religion" in terms of a mystical communion with the
crucified and risen Lord through the cultic acts of baptism and eucharist. These 19th-cent. views were eventually analyzed by A. Schweitzer, for whom Paul's
theology was rather to be summed up as an eschatological
Christ-mysticism. For him Paul's eschatology differed
from the consistent eschatology that Schweitzer claimed
was that of Jesus, because with the death and resurrection
of Jesus the *eschaton* had actually begun for Paul.
Believers then shared mystically in the eschatological
mode of being of the risen Christ. Forms of these earlier
explanations have persisted beyond the 19th cent.

25   In the 20th cent., R. Bultmann insisted that NT
theology "begins with the *kerygma* of the earliest Church
and not before" (*TNT* 1. 3), i.e., it has little to do with
the Jesus of history. He also demythologized that *kerygma*
and cast it in terms of Heideggerian philosophy so that
faith, the response to the *kerygma*, becomes an existential
"decision," by which human beings embark on a new
way of life that is fully authentic. As for Paul, his "basic
position is not a structure of theoretical thought . . . but
it lifts the knowledge inherent in faith itself into the clarity of conscious knowing" (ibid. 1. 190). Thus Bultmann
has, in effect, returned to a nuanced (existentialist)
understanding of the antithesis used by F. C. Baur mentioned above and has reduced Paul's theology to an
"anthropology," an interpretation of human existence.
    Bultmann's exposé of Pauline theology has two main
parts: Man Prior to the Revelation of Faith, and Man
under Faith. In the first part (Man Prior to Faith) he
discusses Paul's anthropological concepts (body, soul,
spirit, life, mind and conscience, heart), his treatment of
"flesh, sin, and world" (creation, the human condition as
sarx, "flesh," its relation to the universality of sin, the
world, and the law). In the second part (Man under Faith)
Bultmann treats the Pauline ideas of God's righteousness, human righteousness as a present reality and gift
from God, reconciliation, grace (as an event coming
from Christ's salvific death and resurrection), the Word,
church, and sacraments; faith (its structure, place in life,
and relation to the *eschaton*); freedom (from sin
[= walking in the Spirit], law, and death). This justly
praised exposé of Paul's teaching is marked by Bultmann's sustained effort to present it in genuinely biblical
categories.

26   Such an approach to Paul's teaching is, how

ever, too exclusively a development of Paul's ideas in
Rom, to which all else seems to have been made subservient. The reduction of Pauline theology to an anthropology has, in effect, minimized Christ's role (cf. Rom
7:24–8:2), since the salvific events of the first Good
Friday and Easter Sunday have been demythologized to
the point of being dehistoricized. Again, Christ's role in
the life of the individual called to such an existential decision of faith has been maximized to the neglect of his role
in the corporate and cosmological view of salvation
history (cf. Rom 9–11, which Bultmann does not sufficiently consider). This minimizing of the role of Christ
stems from a reluctance to admit the "content sense" of
Paul's theology, the historical "objective phase" of
human redemption, and a concern to recast Pauline
teaching in phenomenological terminology. A certain
amount of demythologizing the NT is needed to bring
its message to the people of today, but one still has to
reckon with the way Paul himself looked upon the
Christ-event in the effort to formulate the key to his
theology.

27   More recently, J. C. Beker has coped with the
same problem, recognizing both the contingent character of Paul's teaching and its coherent center. The latter
he regards as "a symbolic structure in which a primordial
experience (Paul's call) is brought into language in a particular way," viz., in "the apocalyptic language of
Judaism, in which he [Paul] lived and thought." Thus he
delineated "the Christ-event in its meaning for the apocalyptic consummation of history, that is, in its meaning
for the triumph of God" (*Paul the Apostle* 15–16). It
would have been better if Beker had written of the
"eschatological" consummation of history rather than of
its "apocalyptic" consummation. Similarly, "the triumph
of God" is too un-Pauline an expression to be the goal
of Pauline teaching; it is redolent of E. Käsemann. This
has to be said, even when one recognizes the centrality
of Christ in Beker's view of the core of Pauline teaching.

28   The key to Pauline theology, however, should
be formulated in terms of what the apostle stated over
and over again in various ways: "It pleased God to save
those who would believe through the folly of the gospel
message (*kērygma*). For whereas Jews demand signs and
Greeks look for philosophy, we proclaim a Christ who
has been crucified, a stumbling block to Jews and an
absurdity to Gentiles. But to those who have been called,
whether Jews or Greeks, he is Christ, the power of God
and the wisdom of God" (1 Cor 1:21–25; cf. Rom 1:16;
2 Cor 4:4). This "story of the cross" (1 Cor 1:18) thus
puts Christ himself at the center of soteriology (God's
new mode of salvation), and all else in Paul's teaching has
to be oriented to this christocentric soteriology.

29   If Paul's theology is predominantly a christology, one must insist on its functional character (→ NT
Thought, 81:24). Paul was little concerned to explain the
intrinsic constitution of Christ *in se;* he preached "Christ
crucified," Christ as significant for humanity: "You are
God's children through your union with Christ Jesus
who became for us wisdom from God, our uprightness,
our sanctification, our redemption" (1 Cor 1:30). This
"Christ crucified," though described in figures derived
from contemporary Jewish or Hellenistic backgrounds
and even embellished with myth, still has relevance for

people of our times. To understand what Paul meant and
still means for people today one does not merely
demythologize his ideas; rather, a certain remythologi-
zation of the modern mind may be needed. In any case,
what is needed is not a subtractive but an interpretative
demythologization.

(Dahl, N., "Rudolf Bultmann's *Theology of the New Testament*,"
The Crucified Messiah and Other Essays [Minneapolis, 1974]
90–128, esp. 112–22. Fuller, R. H., *The New Testament in Current
Study* [NY, 1962] 54–63. Käsemann, *NTQT* 13–15.)

30   In our attempt to give a genetic development
of Paul's theology, we shall begin with the term that he
himself used to describe his message about Christ, his
"gospel." From such a starting point we can move on to
various aspects of the content of his message.

31   (II) Paul's Gospel. *Euangelion* as "the good
news of Jesus Christ" is a specifically Christian meaning
of the word, and as such almost certainly developed
by Paul within the early Christian community (see W.
Marxsen, *Mark the Evangelist* [Nash, 1969] 117–50). Paul
uses the word more frequently than does any other NT
writer: 48 times in his uncontested letters (it occurs 8
times in the Deutero-Paulines, and 4 times in the
Pastorals). In general, it designates Paul's own personal
presentation of the Christ-event.

Euangelion sometimes denotes the activity of
evangelization (Gal 2:7; Phil 4:3,15; 1 Cor 9:14b,18b;
2 Cor 2:12; 8:18), as does the verb *euangelizesthai* (used
by Paul 19 times; it occurs twice also in the Deutero-
Paulines). Normally, however, it denotes the content of
his apostolic message — what he preached, proclaimed,
announced, spoke about (see J. A. Fitzmyer, *TAG* 160
n. 5). Paul realized that his message had its origin in God
himself: "God's gospel" (1 Thess 2:2,8–9; 2 Cor 11:7;
Rom 1:1; 15:16). Succinctly, its content was for him "the
gospel of Christ" (1 Thess 3:2; Gal 1:7; Phil 1:27) or "the
gospel of his Son" (Rom 1:9), wherein the genitive is
normally understood as objective, i.e., the good news
about Christ, even though in some instances one may
detect a nuance of Christ as the originator of the gospel
(2 Cor 5:20; Rom 15:18–19). More specifically, the
gospel is "the good news of the *glory* of Christ" (2 Cor
4:4), i.e., the message about the risen Christ: "We proclaim not ourselves, but Christ Jesus as Lord!" (2 Cor
4:5), giving to Christ the title par excellence for his risen
status. Sometimes, the content is expressed simply as
"the faith" (Gal 1:23), "the word" (1 Thess 1:6), "the
word of God" (2 Cor 2:17).

32   *Euangelion* became Paul's personal way of summing up the meaning of the Christ-event (→ 67 below),
the meaning that the person and lordship of Jesus of
Nazareth had and still has for human history and existence. Hence Paul could speak of "my gospel" (Rom 2:16),
"the gospel that I preach" (Gal 2:2; cf. 1:8,11), or "our
gospel" (1 Thess 1:5; 2 Cor 4:3; cf. 1 Cor 15:1), because
he was aware that "Christ did not send me to baptize, but
to preach the gospel" (1 Cor 1:7). Though patristic
writers (Irenaeus, *Adv. Haer.* 3.1.1; Tertullian, *Adv. Marc.*
4.5 [CSEL 47. 431]; Origen in Eusebius, *HE* 6.25.6
[GCS 9/2. 576]; Eusebius himself, *HE* 3.4.7 [GCS 9/1.
194]) sometimes interpreted these Pauline expressions to
mean the Lucan Gospel, which they regarded as a digest
of Paul's preaching (as the Marcan Gospel was supposed
to be of Peter's), nothing so specific as a Gospel-like narrative is meant by these expressions. Paul was fully
aware that his commission to preach the good news of
God's Son among the Gentiles (Gal 1:16) was not a
message wholly peculiar to himself or different from that
preached by those "who were apostles before me" (Gal

1:17); "whether it was I or they, so we preach and so you
came to believe" (1 Cor 15:11). Paul recognized himself
as the "servant" of the gospel (*doulos,* Phil 2:22), conscious
of a special grace of apostolate. He thought of himself as
set apart like the prophets of old (Jer 1:5; Isa 49:1) from
his mother's womb for this task (Gal 1:15; Rom 1:1),
being "entrusted" with the gospel as some prized possession (1 Thess 2:4; Gal 2:7). He experienced a "compulsion" (*ananke,* 1 Cor 9:16) to proclaim it and considered
his preaching of it to be a cultic, priestly act offered to
God (Rom 1:9; 15:16). He was never ashamed of the
gospel (Rom 1:16); even imprisonment because of it was
for him a "grace" (Phil 1:7,16).

33   Various characteristics of the gospel in Paul's
sense may be singled out: (1) Its *revelatory* or *apocalyptic*
nature. God's salvific activity for his people is now made
known in a new way through the lordship of Jesus
Christ (Rom 1:17); thus the gospel reveals the reality of
the new age, the reality of the *eschaton.* To this apocalyptic nature of the gospel must be related Paul's view of it
as *mystērion,* "mystery, secret," hidden in God for long
ages and now revealed — a new revelation about God's
salvation. In the best mss. of 1 Cor 2:1–2, Paul equates
"God's mystery" with "Jesus Christ . . . crucified" (see
app. crit.), just as he had equated his "gospel" with "Christ
crucified" in 1 Cor 1:17,23–24. Paul viewed himself as
a "steward," dispensing the wealth of this mystery (1 Cor
4:1). It now reveals to Christians the plan conceived by
God and hidden in him from all eternity (1 Cor 2:7) to
bring humanity, Gentiles as well as Jews, to share in the
salvific inheritance of Israel, now realized in Christ Jesus.
Even the partial insensibility of Israel belongs to this
mystery (Rom 11:25). In presenting the gospel as "mystery," Paul is implying that it is never fully made known
by ordinary means of communication. As something
revealed, it is apprehended only in faith; and even when
revealed, the opacity of divine wisdom is never completely dispelled. *Mystērion* is an eschatological term
derived from Jewish apocalyptic sources; its application
to the gospel gives the latter a nuance that *euangelion*
alone would not have had, i.e., something fully comprehended only in the *eschaton.*

34   In thus coming to speak of the gospel as
mystery, Paul is using a word already familiar in contemporary Gk mystery religions. However, the comprehension that he gives to it and the mode in which he uses
it reveal that he depended not so much on Hellenistic
sources as on the OT and Jewish apocalyptic writings of
the intertestamental period. Its OT roots are found in
Hebr *sôd* and in Aram *rāz,* "mystery," "secret" (Dan
2:18–19,27–30,47; 4:6). The latter is a Persian loanword,
used in Aramaic to designate the revelation made to
Nebuchadnezzar in his dreams. QL also offers abundant
parallels to the Pauline use of "mystery" (e.g., 1QpHab
7:5; 1QS 3:23), showing that its real roots are in Palestinian Judaism rather than in the Hellenism of Asia
Minor. As in QL, "mystery" is a carrier-idea for Paul; it
conveys for him the content of his gospel, whereas in QL
it conveys the hidden meaning of OT passages.

35   (2) Its *dynamic* nature. Though "the story of the
cross" is not recounted by Paul in narrative form, as it is
by the evangelists, the gospel for him is not an abstraction. It is "the power of God," a salvific force (*dynamis*)
unleashed in the world of human beings for the salvation
of all (Rom 1:16). The gospel may, indeed, announce a
proposition, "Jesus is Lord" (1 Cor 12:3; Rom 10:9), to
which human beings are called to assent; but it involves
more, for it proclaims "a Son whom God has raised from
the dead, Jesus, who *is delivering* us from the coming
wrath" (1 Thess 1:10). It is thus a gospel that comes "not
in words alone, but with power and the holy Spirit"

(1 Thess 1:5); it is "the word of God, which is at work (*energeitai*) among you who believe" (1 Thess 2:13; cf. 1 Cor 15:2).

36   (3) Its *kerygmatic* character. Paul's gospel is related to the pre-Pauline kerygmatic tradition: "I passed on to you above all what I received" (1 Cor 15:1–2); and he is careful to stress the "form" or the "terms" (*tíni logō*) in which he "evangelized" the Corinthians. In vv 3–5 there follows a fragment of the kerygma itself, and v 11 asserts the common origin of Paul's gospel.

(4) Its *normative* role in Christian life. For Paul the gospel stands critically over Christian conduct, church officials, and human teaching. It tolerates no rival; that there is no "other gospel" (Gal 1:7) is affirmed by Paul in the context of the Judaizing problem in the early churches, when certain Jewish practices were being foisted on Gentile Christians (circumcision, dietary and calendaric regulations). Human beings are called to welcome the gospel (2 Cor 11:4), obey it (Rom 1:5), and listen to it (Rom 10:16–17). It is to be accepted as a guide for life: "Let your manner of life be worthy of the gospel of Christ" (Phil 1:27). Even Cephas, a pillar of the church (Gal 2:9), was rebuked publicly by Paul in Antioch, when he was found to be not "walking straight according to the truth of the gospel" (Gal 2:14). Yet for Paul the normative character of the gospel was also liberating, for he mentions "the truth of the gospel" in connection with "the freedom that we have in Christ Jesus" (Gal 2:4), which has to be preserved in the face of the opposition of "false brethren" seeking to undermine it. Hence, though normative, it also liberates from legalisms devised by humans.

(5) Its *promissory* nature. The gospel continues the promises made by God of old: "promised beforehand through the prophets in the holy Scriptures" (Rom 1:1; cf. Isa 52:7). See further Gal 3:14–19; 4:21–31; Rom 4:13–21; 9:4–13. (This characteristic is more fully formulated in Eph 1:13; 3:6).

(6) Its *universal* character. The gospel is God's power for the salvation of "everyone who has faith, the Jew first and also the Greek" (Rom 1:16; cf. 10:12).

(Bring, R., "The Message to the Gentiles: A Study to the Theology of Paul the Apostle," *ST* 19 [1965] 30–46. Brown, R. E., *The Semitic Background of the Term "Mystery" in the New Testament* [FBBS 21; Phl, 1968]. Fitzmyer, J. A., "The Gospel in the Theology of Paul," *TAG* 149–61. Friedrich, G., "*Euangelizomai*, etc.," *TDNT* 2. 707–37. Johnson, S. L., Jr., "The Gospel that Paul Preached," *BSac* 128 [1971] 327–40. O'Brien, P. T., "Thanksgiving and the Gospel in Paul," *NTS* 21 [1974–75] 144–55. Schlier, H., "*Euangelion* in Römerbrief," in *Wort Gottes in der Zeit* [Fest. K. H. Schelkle; ed. H. Feld and J. Nolte; Düsseldorf, 1973] 127–42. Strecker, G., "*Euangelizō*" and "*Euangelion*," *EWNT* 2. 173–86. Stuhlmacher, P., *Das paulinische Evangelium: I. Vorgeschichte* [FRLANT 95; Göttingen, 1968]; "Das paulinische Evangelium," *Das Evangelium und die Evangelien: Vorträge von Tübinger Symposium 1982* [ed. P. Stuhlmacher; WUNT 28; Tübingen, 1983] 157–82.)

37   **(III) God and His Plan of Salvation History.** The nuance of mystery added by Paul to his idea of the gospel opens up a broad perspective: he saw the gospel as part of a plan, gratuitously conceived by God for a new form of human salvation, to be revealed and realized in his Son. The author of this plan was God (*ho theos*, 1 Cor 2:7), whom Paul had worshiped as a Pharisee, the God of "the covenants" (Rom 9:4) of old. What Paul teaches about God is not a theology (in the strict sense) independent of his christocentric soteriology, for this God is the "Father of our Lord Jesus Christ" (2 Cor 1:3; Rom 15:6), and what he says about God is usually asserted in contexts dealing with his salvific activity. "It pleased God to save those who believe through the folly

of the gospel message (*kērygma*)" (1 Cor 1:21). Even when Paul speaks of the qualities or attributes of God, they almost always depict God as such and such *for us, on our behalf*. Thus he acknowledges God as Creator: the "one God, the Father, from whom are all things and for whom we exist" (1 Cor 8:6); he is "the living and true God" (1 Thess 1:9); "the God who said, 'Let light shine out of darkness' (cf. Gen 1:3), who has shone in our hearts" (2 Cor 4:6); he is the one who "calls into being what does not exist"—so depicted in Paul's use of the Abraham story (Rom 4:19). Paul speaks of God's "eternal power and divinity" (Rom 1:20), his "truth" (1:25), his "wisdom and knowledge" (11:33).

38   Three qualities of God, however, have to be singled out in particular. (1) "The Wrath of God" (*orgē theou*, Rom 1:18; cf. 1 Thess 1:10; 2:16; 5:9; Rom 2:8; 3:5; 4:15; 5:9; 9:22; [Col 3:6; Eph 5:6]). This quality is inherited by Paul from the OT (see Ps 78:31; cf. Isa 30:27–28), where it expresses not so much a divine emotion as God's reaction to evil and sin. God may seem to be portrayed anthropomorphically with an angry frame of mind, but "the wrath of God" is not meant to express his malicious hatred or jealous caprice (→ OT Thought, 77:99–102). It is the OT way of expressing God's steadfast reaction as a judge to Israel's breach of the covenant relation (Ezek 5:13; 2 Chr 36:16) or the nations' oppression of his people (Isa 10:5–11; Jer 50[LXX 28]:11–17). Related to "the Day of Yahweh" (Zeph 1:14–18), wrath was often conceived of as God's eschatological retribution. For Paul it is either already "manifested" (Rom 1:18) or still awaited (2:6–8).

(MacGregor, G. H. C., "The Concept of the Wrath of God in the New Testament," *NTS* 7 [1960–61] 101–9. Pesch, W., "*Orgē*," *EWNT* 2. 1293–97. Wilckens, U., *Der Brief an die Römer* [EKKNT 6/1–3; Einsiedeln, 1978–82] 101–2.)

39   (2) In contrast to "God's wrath" there stands "the uprightness" or "the righteousness of God," appearing as a quality in Rom 1:17; 3:5,21–22,25–26; 10:3. (In 2 Cor 5:21 it is rather conceived of as a gift given to human beings; cf. Phil 3:9.) This quality of God is also inherited by Paul from the OT, even though the phrase itself is not found as such. The closest one comes to the Pauline phrase is *ṣidqat Yhwh*, "the just decrees of the Lord" (Deut 33:21 *RSV*; cf. LXX, *dikaiosynēn Kyrios epoiēsen*, "the Lord has wrought righteousness") or *ṣidqôt Yhwh*, "the triumphs of the Lord" (Judg 5:11 *RSV*; cf. LXX, *ekei dōsousin dikaiosynas Kyriō*, "there they will grant the Lord righteous acts"). The exact equivalent of the Pauline phrase, however, is found in QL (1QM 4:6, *ṣedeq ʾEl*), revealing its pre-Christian Palestinian usage. In the early books of the OT *ṣedeq* or *ṣĕdāqâ* expresses the quality by which Yahweh, depicted as involved in a lawsuit (*rîb*) with his rebellious people, judges Israel and displays his "righteousness" (Isa 3:13; Jer 12:1; Hos 4:1–2; 12:3; Mic 6:2). It describes his legal or judicial activity; he judges with "righteousness" (Ps 9:9; 96:13; 98:9). In this context "the triumphs of the Lord" should be understood as his legal triumphs (cf. Mic 6:5; 1 Sam 12:7). At times OT scholars try to claim that Yahweh's righteousness has a cosmic dimension, that creation and all that he has done in the OT may be attributed to this divine quality. Appeal is made to Dan 9:14 or Jer 31:35–36 (see H. H. Schmid, *Gerechtigkeit als Weltordnung* [BHT 40; Tübingen, 1968]; H. G. Reventlow, *Rechtfertigung im Horizont des Alten Testaments* [BEvT 58; Munich, 1971]). To do this they have to empty the quality of its legal or judicial aspect—creation and the regulating of world order are scarcely judicial acts. In the postexilic period, however, *ṣedeq* as a quality of God acquires an added nuance; it becomes the quality whereby he acquits his people, manifesting toward them his gracious salvific activity in a just judgment (see Isa 46:13 [where "my righteousness" and "my salvation" stand in parallelism]; 51:5,6,8; 56:1; 61:10; Ps 40:9–10). Similarly, in the LXX *dikaiosynē* is used to translate other (nonjudicial) covenant qualities of God: his '*ĕmet,* "fidelity" (Gen 24:49; Josh 24:14; 38:19); his *hesed,* "steadfast mercy" (Gen 19:19; 20:13; 21:23) — a mode of translating that reflects more the postexilic nuance of *sedeq* than its original denotation. In virtue of this OT understanding of "God's uprightness" Paul sees God providing a new mode of salvation for humanity as justification by grace through faith in Christ Jesus — as a part of his plan of salvation history. E. Käsemann has also insisted on Paul's notion of God's righteousness as his "saving activity" and as a manifestation of God's power: "God's sovereignty over the world revealing itself eschatologically in Jesus . . . , the rightful power with which God makes his cause triumph in the world which has fallen away from him and which yet, as creation, is his inviolable possession" ("'The Righteousness of God,'" 180). This can be said, but once again one must guard against the emptying out of the legal or judicial denotation that is basic to the quality. Käsemann, however, rightly insists on the aspect of "power" in God's righteousness.

(On the righteousness of God: Berger, K., *ZNW* 68 [1977] 266–75. Brauch, M. T., in Sanders, *Paul* [→ 11 above] 523–42. Bultmann, R., *JBL* 83 [1964] 12–16. Hübner, H., *NTS* 21 [1974–75] 462–88. Käsemann, *NTQT* 168–82. Kertelge, K., "*Rechtfertigung" bei Paulus* [NTAbh ns 3; Münster, 1967]. Lyonnet, S., *VD* 25 [1947] 23–34, 118–21, 129–44, 193–203, 257–63. Schlatter, A., *Gottes Gerechtigkeit* [3d ed.; Stuttgart, 1959] 116–22. Schmid, H. H., in *Rechtf* 403–14. Stuhlmacher, P., *Gerechtigkeit Gottes bei Paulus* [FRLANT 87; Göttingen, 1965]. Williams, S. K., *JBL* 99 [1980] 241–90.)

40   (3) "The Love of God." Though this divine quality does not appear as often as "God's uprightness," it is an important concept for Paul, pervading the second section of the doctrinal part of Rom. It "is poured out into our hearts" (Rom 5:5; cf. 5:8; 8:31–39; 2 Cor 13:11,13; [2 Thess 3:5]). In virtue of this quality Paul sees Christians chosen as "brethren beloved by God" (1 Thess 1:4). For him it is the basis of the divine plan of salvation history.

(Levie, J., "Le plan d'amour divin dans le Christ selon saint Paul," in *L'Homme devant Dieu* [Fest. H. de Lubac; Théologie 56–58; Paris, 1963–64] 1. 159–67. Romaniuk, K., *L'Amour du Père et du Fils dans la sotériologie de Saint Paul* [AnBib 15; Rome, 1961]. Schneider, G., "*Agapē,*" *EWNT* 1. 19–29.)

41   That Paul thinks in terms of a divine plan of salvation history can be seen in his references to God's "purpose" (*prothesis,* Rom 8:28; 9:11), or his "will" (*thelēma,* Gal 1:4; 1 Cor 1:1; 2 Cor 1:1; 8:5; Rom 1:10; 15:32), or his "predestination" (*proorizein,* Rom 8:28–30); cf. "the fullness of time" (Gal 4:4); God's "appointed time" (*kairos,* 1 Cor 7:29–32); the period "from Adam to Moses" (Rom 5:14); the meeting of "the ends of the ages" (1 Cor 10:11), the approach of "the day" of the Lord (Rom 13:11–14); "now is the day of salvation" (1 Cor 6:2). In virtue of this plan God chooses or calls human beings to salvation (1 Thess 5:9; Rom 1:16; 11:11) or to glory (Rom 8:29–31). "All this comes from God who has reconciled us to himself through Christ" (2 Cor 5:18).

Not all commentators are sure that Paul thinks in terms of a divine plan of salvation history, despite the elements listed above to support it. S. Schulz (*ZNW* 54 [1963] 104) has maintained that "the Hellenist Luke is the creator of salvation history." That would imply that such a view was not found among NT writers prior to Luke. In reply, however, Kümmel ("Heilsgeschichte") not only

reasserted the Pauline view of salvation history but listed many interpreters of Paul who have recognized this as a valid aspect of his theology (Bultmann, Dibelius, Feine, Holtzmann, *et al.*). "Salvation history" cannot be applied in a univocal sense to NT writers; Luke and Paul, in particular, have their own view of it. Indeed, in Paul's view of such history, one may ask about the sense in which its first and second stages are "salvific" (if the first was lawless and the second, though under the law that was destined to bring "life" [Lev 18:5], failed to achieve it). Again, though Paul reckons with the meeting of the ages (1 Cor 10:11), the third stage is for him the *eschaton,* even if it is still part of human "history" (→ NT Thought, 81:47–48). In any case, the Pauline view of this salvific plan manifests historical, corporate, cosmic, and eschatological dimensions.

42   (1) The historical dimension of the divine plan is seen in its embrace of all phases of human history, from creation to its consummation. Being rooted in the intervention of Christ Jesus in that history "in the fullness of time" (Gal 4:4), it gives that history a meaning that is not otherwise apparent in it. This dimension leads to a periodization of God's plan of salvation. Most likely Paul derived his three-stage view of salvation history from his Jewish education, for it makes sense only against such a background — Paul views human history through Jewish spectacles. The first period was the time "from Adam to Moses" (Rom 5:13–14; cf. Gal 3:17), the law-less period, when human beings did evil indeed, but when there was no imputation of transgressions (Rom 5:13–14). The second period was the time from Moses to the Messiah, when "the law was added" (Gal 3:19; cf. Rom 5:20), when humanity "was imprisoned, held in custody under the law until" it reached maturity (Gal 3:23); then the law reigned, and human sin was imputed as a transgression of it. The third period is the time of the Messiah, of "Christ," who is "the end of the law" (Rom 10:4), when human beings find themselves "justified by faith" (Gal 3:24), which "works itself out through love" (Gal 5:6), "the fulfillment of the law" (Rom 13:10). Paul realized that the time in which he lived followed upon that when warnings were written in the law (such as Exod 32:1–6 or Num 25:1–18), "composed for our instruction upon whom the ends of the ages have met" (1 Cor 10:11). Here the "ends" refer to the last end of the second period and the opening end of the third, that of "the last Adam," or the Adam of the *eschaton* (1 Cor 15:45). Whether Paul's three-stage view of human history is related to a similar division of the world's duration found in later rabbinic tradition (*b. Sanh.* 97b; *b. 'Abod. Zar.* 9b; *j. Meg.* 70d), as I once held (*JBC,* art. 79, § 41), may be questioned.

43   (2) The corporate dimension of the divine plan is seen in the role played by Israel. Privileged of old through God's promises to Abraham and to his posterity, Israel became the chosen instrument by which salvation would reach all human beings: "All nations will be blessed in you" (Gal 3:8; cf. Rom 4:16; Gen 18:18; 12:3). All the divine preparations for the Christ were thus made within the nation of the Jews: "To them belong filial adoption, God's glorious presence, the covenants, the legislation, the Temple cult, the promises, the patriarchs, and even the Messiah according to the flesh" (Rom 9:4–5). But though descended from Abraham, Israel rejected (Rom 11:15) Jesus as the Messiah and thereby apparently excluded itself from the salvation offered in Jesus the Christ whom Paul preached. It might seem that the divine plan had failed in its most crucial moment (Rom 9:6). Paul insists, however, that it has not, for this infidelity of Israel was foreseen by God and was part of the plan itself. It is not contrary to God's direction of history, since both the infidelity of the Jews and the call of the Gentiles have been announced in the OT (Rom 9:6–32). Israel's infidelity proceeds from its own refusal to accept him in whom a new mode of uprightness is now open to all humanity. It is only a partial infidelity (Rom 11:1–10), because "a remnant chosen by (God's) grace" (Rom 11:5) has accepted Jesus as the Christ. And it is only temporary, for through Israel's false step "salvation has gone to the Gentiles to make Israel jealous. But if their false step means riches for the world, and if their failure means riches for the Gentiles, how much more will the addition of their full number mean!" (Rom 11:11–12). Indeed, "only partial insensibility has come upon Israel, to last until all the Gentiles have come in, and then all Israel will be saved" (Rom 11:25). This corporate aspect envisages the effects of the Christ-event on "the Israel of God" (Gal 6:16; cf. Rom 9:6). One must stress this aspect of the salvific plan, since it dominates many passages in Paul's writings, such as Rom 5:12–21; Rom 9–11 (cf. Eph 1:3–12; 2:4–16). It warns us against interpreting Paul's teaching too narrowly or exclusively in an individualistic sense, or as some I-Thou relationship between the Christian and God or, less sophisticatedly, as an individual, personal piety or an exaggerated anthropology. This corporate aspect appears above all in the incorporation of both Jewish and Gentile Christians into Christ and his church.

44   (3) The cosmic dimension of the divine plan is seen in Paul's relating the entire created *kosmos* to human salvation: "God has put all things in subjection under the feet" of the risen Christ (1 Cor 15:27; cf. Ps 8:7; Phil 3:21). This is why Paul views physical creation itself "eagerly awaiting" its share in the freedom from bondage to decay and in "the glorious freedom of the children of God" (Rom 8:19–21), proleptically attained in the redemption wrought by Christ Jesus. Again, Paul also views the *kosmos* sharing in the reconciliation of sinful humanity achieved by Christ (2 Cor 5:18–21; cf. Rom 11:15). But significantly, he never relates "justification" to this cosmic dimension. (In Col and Eph Paul's disciples develop the cosmic dimension still further in depicting the cosmic role of Christ himself: "All things have been created through him and for him" [Col 1:16]; "that he might be preeminent in all things" [Col 1:18; cf. Eph 1:19–23; 2:11–18].)

45   (4) The eschatological dimension of the divine plan is also important, since the first two periods of salvation history (Adam to Moses, Moses to Christ) have been brought to a close, and Christians are already living in the last period. If the *eschaton* has thus been inaugurated, from another point of view the "end" has not yet come (1 Cor 15:24 [according to a most probable interpretation of that verse]). Christ the Lord of the *kosmos* does not yet reign supreme; he has not yet handed the kingdom over to the Father. All this is related to the "parousia of the Lord" (1 Thess 2:19; 3:13; 4:15; 5:23; 1 Cor 15:23). It is scarcely to be denied that Paul expected it in the near future. However, we find him at times gradually reconciling himself to his own imminent death (Phil 1:23) and to an intermediate phase between his death and his "appearance before the tribunal of Christ" (2 Cor 5:1–10). In either case, there is a future aspect in his salvation history, whether its term be near or far off, and Paul's one hope is "to make his home with the Lord" (2 Cor 5:8), for "to be with the Lord" is the way Paul conceives of the destiny of all Christians (1 Thess 4:17; Phil 1:23). The undeniable elements of his futurist eschatology are the parousia (1 Thess 4:15), the resurrection of the dead (1 Thess 4:16; 1 Cor 15:13–19), the judgment (2 Cor 5:10; Rom 2:6–11; 14:10), and the glory of the justified believer (Rom 8:18,21; 1 Thess 2:12). Some commentators would even regard this

perspective as "apocalyptic" (Käsemann, *NTQT* 133; cf. J. L. Martyn, *NTS* 31 [1985] 410–24; L. E. Keck, *Int* 38 [1984] 234); → 33 above; → NT Thought, 81:49.

But along with this future aspect there is also the present aspect, according to which the *eschaton* has already begun and human beings are already in a sense saved. "Now is the acceptable time, now is the day of salvation" (2 Cor 6:2). The "firstfruits" (Rom 8:23) and the "pledge" (2 Cor 1:22; 5:5; [Eph 1:14]) are already the possession of Christian believers. Christ has already "glorified" us (Rom 8:30; cf. 2 Cor 3:18; Phil 3:20; [in Eph 2:6 and Col 2:12 this is formulated in terms of Christ's having already transferred us to the heavenly realm]). At times Paul speaks as if Christians have already been "saved" (Rom 8:24 [where he adds, "in hope"]; cf. 1 Cor 15:2; 1:18; 2 Cor 2:15); yet at other times he intimates that they are still to be saved (1 Cor 5:5; 10:33; Rom 5:9,10; 9:27; 10:9,13).

This difference of viewpoint is owing in part to a development of Paul's thought about the imminence of the parousia. In 1 Thess there are future references; but with the passage of time, and especially after an experience that Paul had in Ephesus when he came close to death (1 Cor 15:32; 2 Cor 1:8) and the parousia had not yet occurred, his understanding of the Christian situation developed. (This development is further seen in the full-blown vision of the Father's plan that emerges in Col and Eph.)

46   The double aspect of Pauline eschatology has been variously explained. Some, like C. H. Dodd and R. Bultmann, would label the predominant aspect "realized eschatology." This expression is partly acceptable, but care must be had in defining it. For Bultmann, Paul is not interested in the history of the nation of Israel or of the world, but only in the "historicity of man, the true historical life of the human being, the history of which every one experiences for himself and by which he gains his real essence. This history of the human person comes into being in the encounters which man experiences, whether with other people or with events, and in the decisions he takes in them" (*The Presence of Eternity: History and Eschatology* [NY, 1957] 43). In other words, the future elements in Paul's eschatology are only a symbolic mode of expressing human self-realization, as one is freed from self by the grace of Christ and continually asserts oneself as a free individual in decisions for God. In such acts one continually stands "before the tribunal of Christ." Bultmann would thus write off the future elements of Paul's eschatology listed above; they would be vestiges of an apocalyptic view of history, which is meaningless for the people of today. Indeed, he thinks, Paul would have already reinterpreted it in terms of his anthropology. "The Pauline view of history is the expression of his view of man" (ibid. 41).

Such an interpretation has the advantage of emphasizing the "critical" moment that the Christ-event brings into the life of everyone: a challenge of faith is presented by it. But this interpretation of Paul's eschatology denies, in effect, some major elements of his view of salvation history. Although truly "the history into which Paul looks back is the history not of Israel only, but of all mankind" (ibid. 40), it hardly seems accurate to say that Paul "does not see it as the history of the nation with its alternations of divine grace and the people's obstinacy, of sin and punishment, of repentance and forgiveness" (ibid.). Such a view of Pauline history is too much dominated by the polemics of Rom and Gal and actually minimizes the problem that Paul tried to face in composing Rom 9–11. Israel's history and role in human destiny are factors in Paul's whole theology; they are scarcely theologoumena that one can simply relegate to the realm of myth. Moreover, even if Paul calls Christ "the end of the law" (Rom 10:4), he is not saying that "history has reached its end" (ibid. 43). Rather, he would seem to be saying that a new phase of salvation history has begun because "the ends of the ages have met" (1 Cor 10:11).

47 An alternative to such a "realized eschatology" is to interpret Paul's teaching as an "inaugurated eschatology," or even as a "self-realizing eschatology" (with "self" referring to the *eschaton*). For, in Paul's view, Christians live in the *eschaton*, in the age of the Messiah. This is an age of dual polarity; it looks back to the first Good Friday and Easter Sunday and forward to a final glorious consummation, when "we shall always be with the Lord" (1 Thess 4:17). This age has initiated a status of union with God previously unknown and one destined to a final union with him in glory. This is the basis of Christian hope and patience (Rom 8:24-25).

Such a view of Paul's eschatology reckons with an objective mode of existence in which Christians find themselves through faith, a mode of existence inaugurated by Christ, which will find its perfection in an event that Paul refers to as the parousia of the Lord. Such an interpretation, however, does not commit one to a naïve credulity that fails to reckon with the apocalyptic paraphernalia and stage props used by Paul to describe the forms of the parousia, resurrection, judgment, and glory — see 1 Thess 4:16-17; 1 Cor 15:51-54 (cf. 2 Thess 2:1-10).

(Allan, J. A., "The Will of God: III. In Paul," *ExpTim* 72 [1960-61] 142-45. Barrett, C. K., *From First Adam to Last* [London, 1962]. Benoit, P., "L'Evolution du langage apocalyptique dans le corpus paulinien," in *Apocalypses et théologie de l'espérance* [LD 95; ed. L. Monloubou; Paris, 1977] 299-335. Dietzfelbinger, C., *Heilsgeschichte bei Paulus?* [TEH ns 126; Munich, 1965]. Dinkler, E., "Prädestination bei Paulus," in *Festschrift für Günther Dehn* [ed. W. Schneemelcher; Neukirchen, 1957] 81-102. Goppelt, L., "Paulus und die Heilsgeschichte," *NTS* 13 [1966-67] 31-42. Kümmel, W. G., "Heilsgeschichte im Neuen Testament?" in *Neues Testament und Kirche* [Fest. R. Schnackenburg; ed. J. Gnilka; Freiburg, 1974] 434-57. Scroggs, R., *The Last Adam: A Study in Pauline Anthropology* [Phl, 1966].

Baird, W., "Pauline Eschatology in Hermeneutical Perspective," *NTS* 17 [1970-71] 314-27. Gager, J. G., Jr., "Functional Diversity in Paul's Use of End-Time Language," *JBL* 89 [1970] 325-37. Longenecker, R. N., "The Nature of Paul's Early Eschatology," *NTS* 31 [1985] 85-95. Mayer, B., "*Elpis*, etc." *EWNT* 1. 1066-75.)

48 (IV) Christ's Role in Salvation History. Against the background of the gospel, the mystery, and the Father's plan of salvation, we must now try to depict the role of Christ himself as seen by Paul. For although Abraham and Israel play roles in the execution of that plan and the church is deeply involved in it, Christ's role is central to Paul's thought. Only rarely does Paul refer to "Jesus" solely by his proper name (1 Thess 1:10; 4:14; Gal 6:17; Phil 2:10; 1 Cor 12:3 [probably a quoted slogan]; 2 Cor 4:5 [see *app. crit.*],10,11,14; 11:4; Rom 8:11), in contrast to an abundant use of titles for Jesus, with one even as his second name (→ 51 below). This immediately indicates the primary interest of Paul in the significance of Christ Jesus, or, in our terms, *christology*.

49 (A) Preexistent Son. Paul calls Jesus "the Son of God" (Gal 2:20; 3:26; 2 Cor 1:19) or "his [i.e., the Father's] Son" (1 Thess 1:10 [in a kerygmatic fragment]; Gal 1:16; 4:4,6; 1 Cor 1:9; Rom 1:3,9; 5:10; 8:3,29,32 ["his own Son"]; [cf. Col 1:13; Eph 4:13]). What did he mean by the title "Son of God"? Given its long history in the ancient Near East, the title could imply many things. Egyptian pharaohs were looked on as "sons of God," because the sun-god Rê was regarded as their father (C. J. Gadd, *Ideas of Rule in the Ancient East*

[London, 1948] 45-50). Its use is attested also in references to Assyrian and Babylonian monarchs. In the Greco-Roman world it was used of the ruler, especially in the phrase *divi filius* or *theou huios* applied to the Roman emperor (see A. Deissmann, *LAE* 350-51). It was also given to mythical heroes and thaumaturges (sometimes called *theioi andres*) and even to historical persons such as Apollonius of Tyana, Pythagoras, and Plato (see G. P. Wetter, *Der Sohn Gottes* [FRLANT 26; Göttingen, 1916]). The basis of the Hellenistic attribution of this title was apparently the conviction that such persons had divine powers. Although some have maintained that the application of this title to Jesus stems entirely from such a Hellenistic background (since it could scarcely have been used by Jesus himself or even applied to him by the early Palestinian community [Schoeps, *Paul* 158]), that contention is by no means clear (→ Jesus, 78:35-37).

50 In the OT, "son of God" is a mythological title given to angels (Job 1:6; 2:1; 38:7; Ps 29:1; Dan 3:25; Gen 6:2); a title of predilection for the people of Israel collectively (Exod 4:22; Deut 14:1; Hos 2:1; 11:1; Isa 1:2; 30:1; Jer 3:22; Wis 18:13); a title of adoption for a king on the Davidic throne (2 Sam 7:14; Ps 2:7; 89:27); for judges (Ps 82:6); for the upright individual Jew (Sir 4:10; Wis 2:18). It is often said to have been a messianic title, but there is no clear evidence of such usage in preChristian Palestinian Judaism; not even Ps 2:7 is clearly to be interpreted as messianic. "Son of God" and "Son of the Most High" are attested in QL (4Q246 2:1) even if the subject of attribution is lost because of the fragmentary state of the text (see Fitzmyer, *WA* 90-94). One also hesitates about the use of "son" in 4QFlor (= 4Q174) 1:11, which cites 2 Sam 7:14 in a context that some claim is messianic. See further 1QSa 2:11-12, where God's begetting the Messiah seems to be mentioned (*JBL* 75 [1956] 177 n. 28; cf. J. Starcky, *RB* 70 [1963] 481-505; → Apocrypha, 67:84, 92). None of these texts is unequivocal. The identification of the Messiah and the Son of God is made in the NT (Mark 14:61; Matt 16:16), and Cullmann may be right in thinking that the fusion of the two titles "Son of God" and "Messiah" first takes place in reference to Jesus. The dominant idea underlying the use of "Son of God" in the Jewish world was that of divine election for a God-given task and the corresponding obedience to such a vocation. The Hebraic notion of sonship is at the root of the NT application of the title to Christ.

Paul is scarcely the creator of this title for Christ; he inherits it from the early church. It is found in fragments of the kerygma that he incorporates into his letters (e.g., Rom 1:3, "God's gospel concerning his Son" [see Conzelmann, *OTNT* 77]). But the term does not always have the same connotation. When Paul says that Jesus was "set up as a Son of God in power with a spirit of holiness as of the resurrection from the dead" (Rom 1:4), he uses the title in the Hebraic sense. It expresses the role of Jesus endowed with a life-giving spirit for the salvation of human beings (1 Cor 15:45). Elsewhere Paul presupposes, if he does not allude to, the preexistence of Christ. "God sent his Son, born of a woman, subject to the law, to redeem those who were under the law" (Gal 4:4); cf. "his own Son" (Rom 8:3,32). Theoretically, one could say that this "sending" refers to nothing more than a divine commission. But is that all that Paul implies? The ambiguity seems to be removed by Phil 2:6, "Who, though of divine status" (*en morphē theou hyparchōn*); cf. 2 Cor 8:9. The status that the Son enjoyed was one of "being equal to God" (*to einai isa theō*; → Philippians, 48:19). (In Col 1:15,17; 2:9 reference is made to Jesus as the Son, who was "the image of the invisible God, the firstborn of all creation.") In 1 Cor 15:24-25,28 Paul further speaks of Christ as "the Son" in a way that may even transcend functional christology, for he treats there of the end of the salvific plan, when "the Son himself" will be subjected to him (the Father) who has put all things under his feet. Christ with his role brought to completion is "the Son," related to the Father.

51   (B) Christos.   In the LXX *christos* is the Gk transl. of Hebr *māšîaḥ,* "anointed (one)," a title often used for historical kings of Israel (e.g., 1 Sam 16:6; 24:7,11; 26:16), rarely for a high priest (Lev 4:5,16), and once even for a pagan king (Cyrus, Isa 45:1). Because it was often used of David, when the Davidic line was carried off into Babylonian captivity (Jer 36:30) and the promise of a future "David" to be raised up by God emerged in Israel (Jer 30:9; cf. 23:5), the title was eventually transferred to that figure (see Dan 9:25, "to the coming of a Messiah, a prince"). Thus arose the messianic expectation in Israel (→ OT Thought, 77:152-63). The title denoted an anointed agent of Yahweh awaited by the people for their deliverance. This expectation of a coming Messiah developed further among the Essenes of Qumran: "until the coming of a prophet and the Messiahs of Aaron and Israel" (1QS 9:11; → Apocrypha, 67:29, 114-17).

The title was applied to Jesus of Nazareth very quickly after his death and resurrection, evoked among his followers undoubtedly by the title that Pilate had affixed to his cross, "King of the Jews" (Mark 14:26; cf. Dahl, *Crucified* 23-33; note that the kerygmatic fragment preserved in Acts 2:36 hints at the same application). What is striking about the Pauline use of *Christos* is not its frequency (266 times in his uncontested letters [81 in the Deutero-Paulines; 32 in the Pastorals]), but its having practically become Jesus' second name: "Jesus Christ" (e.g., 1 Thess 1:1,3) or "Christ Jesus" (e.g., 1 Thess 2:14; 5:18). Only in Rom 9:5 does he clearly use *Christos* in a titular sense; even then it is not a generic title but refers to the one Messiah, Jesus. Dahl (*Crucified* 40, 171) would detect "messianic connotations" in the use of *Christos* in 1 Cor 10:4; 15:22; 2 Cor 5:10; 11:2-3; Phil 1:15,17; 3:7; Rom 1:2-4; but each of these instances is debatable. What is, therefore, important is to realize that for Paul *Christos* meant what Christians had come to understand about the former Jewish title. Paul came to faith through "a revelation of Jesus Christ" (Gal 1:12), a revelation in which "the Father revealed his Son to/in me" (Gal 1:16), that he might preach him among the Gentiles. Whereas before the Damascus experience Paul persecuted "the churches of Christ" (Gal 1:22) and their faith in Jesus as the Messiah, the revelation of Jesus as God's Son not only brought an abrupt break with his past but corrected his own messianic belief. That belief became, as it were, second nature to Paul, and the title soon became Jesus' second name.

(Dahl, *The Crucified Messiah* [→ 29 above]. Hahn, F., *The Titles of Jesus in Christology* [London, 1969] 136-222. Kramer, W., *Christ, Lord, Son of God* [SBT 1/50; London, 1966].)

52   (C) Kyrios.   Perhaps an even more important Pauline title for Jesus, esp. as the risen Christ, is *Kyrios,* "Lord." Paul uses it not as often as *Christos* but more often than "Son" or "Son of God."

Paul employs *Kyrios* for Yahweh of the OT, esp. in passages where he quotes or explains OT texts (1 Thess 4:6; 1 Cor 2:16; 3:20; 10:26; 14:21; Rom 4:8; 9:28,29; 11:3,34; 12:19; 15:11; cf. L. Cerfaux, *ETL* 20 [1943] 5-17). In these instances the absolute or unmodified (*ho*) *Kyrios* occurs. Whence comes this absolute usage, even for Yahweh? It is found in the great mss. of the LXX, but they are Christian copies, and *Kyrios* might be the substitution of later Christian copyists. That the usage could have come to NT-era Christians from contem-

porary Gk transls. of the OT is often denied because "(the) Lord" was an unusual designation for God in Judaism—indeed, according to Bultmann, "unthinkable" (*TNT* 1. 51). In Gk transls. of the OT made for Jews and by Jews the tetragram (*YHWH*) was actually written in Hebr characters, or sometimes as *IAO* (see Conzelmann, *OTNT* 83-84). However, there is now evidence that Palestinian Jews in the last pre-Christian centuries were beginning to call their God "the Lord" (absolutely). Thus, Hebr *'ādôn* is found in Ps 114:7 ("Tremble, O earth, before the Lord, before the God of Jacob"), perhaps also in Ps 151, as it is quoted in 11QPs^a 28:7-8 ("Who can recount the deeds of the Lord?"—a contested reading; see P. Auffret and J. Magne, *RevQ* 9 [1977-78] 163-88, 189-96). The Aram *mārêh* is found in 11QtgJob 24:6-7 ("Now will God really prove faithless, and [will] the Lord [distort judgment]?" = MT Job 34:12). The emphatic *māryā',* "the Lord," occurs in 4QEn^b 1 iv 5: "[To Gabriel] the [L]ord said" (= *1 Enoch* 10:9, and the Gk version has *ho Ks*). Moreover, Gk *Kyrios* is used twice by Josephus (*Ant.* 20.4.2 § 90, in a prayer of King Izates, a convert to Judaism; *Ant.* 13.3.1. § 68, quoting Isa 19:9 in a letter of Onias the high priest). Such evidence shows that Palestinian Jews, speaking Hebrew, Aramaic, or Greek, were beginning (at least) to refer to God as "the Lord."

53   Paul's absolute use of (*ho*) *Kyrios* for the risen Christ is often attributed to his Hellenistic background (e.g., W. Bousset, *Kyrios Christos* [Nash, 1970] 119-52; Bultmann, *TNT* 1. 124; Conzelmann, *OTNT* 82-84), since the absolute use of *kyrios* is well attested in the Hellenistic world of the Roman Empire (see W. Foerster in *TDNT* 3. 1046-58). In religious texts from Asia Minor, Syria, and Egypt, gods and goddesses such as Isis, Osiris, and Serapis were often called simply *kyrios* or *kyria.* Paul himself was aware of this: though there are many "lords," yet for us there is only one Lord, Jesus Christ (1 Cor 8:5-6). *Kyrios* was also a sovereign title for the Roman emperor (Acts 25:26, where the *RSV* has added "my," which is not in the Greek). Though denoting primarily the emperor's political and judicial sovereignty, it also carried the nuance of his divinity, esp. in the eastern Mediterranean area. When the primitive Christian kerygma was carried out of Palestine, it would have encountered this Hellenistic usage—it is argued—and would have adopted this title for the risen Christ. But this argument needs scrutiny, esp. in the light of the evidence for the Palestinian Jewish religious usage presented above.

Paul himself inherited the title from the Palestinian Jewish Christian community in Jerusalem, where "Hebrews" and "Hellenists" (Acts 6:1-6) had already fashioned the creedal formula "Jesus is Lord" (1 Cor 12:3; Rom 10:9) and probably even made it a kerygmatic proclamation. Indeed, the title forms the climax of the pre-Pauline (probably Jewish-Christian) hymn to Christ used in Phil 2:6-11: "Let every tongue confess to the glory of God the Father that Jesus Christ is Lord" (retroverted into Aram: *wĕkol liššān yitwaddê dî mārê' Yēšûa' mĕšîḥā' liqār 'Elāhā' 'abbā'*). (Compare Col 2:6, "You have received by tradition [*parelabete*] Christ Jesus as the Lord.") Even when writing to a Greek-speaking community (1 Cor 16:22) Paul preserved *maranatha,* "Our Lord, come," a liturgical formula related to *Kyrios.* Though no longer the absolute form, it betrays an early Palestinian origin, for it reflects Aram *māránā' thā'* (cf. Rev 22:20: "Come, Lord Jesus!"; *Did.* 10:6). It was an eschatological prayer invoking the parousiac Lord, probably derived from a eucharistic liturgy considered as a foretaste of that coming (see 1 Cor 11:26). Such evidence suggests, then, that Paul derived the use of "Lord" for the risen Christ from the early Jewish-Christian community of Jerusalem itself.

54 What did the title *Kyrios* mean for Paul? It was, first, a way of referring to the risen status of Jesus the Christ. "Am I not an apostle? Have I not seen Jesus our Lord?" (1 Cor 9:1). So exclaimed Paul in relating his claim to apostleship to his vision of the risen Christ. Second, it expressed for him, as it did for the Jewish Christians before him, that this exalted Christ (Phil 2:9) was worthy of the same adoration as Yahweh himself, as the allusion to Isa 45:23 in Phil 2:10 suggests. Third, both the use of *maranatha* (1 Cor 16:22) and Paul's interpretation of the eucharist ("As often as you eat this bread and drink this cup, you proclaim the death of the Lord Jesus until he comes," 1 Cor 11:26) seem to suggest that *Kyrios* was originally applied to the parousiac Christ and then gradually retrojected to other, earlier phases of Jesus' existence (→ NT Thought, 81:13). Fourth, though in itself *Kyrios* does not mean "God" or assert the divinity of Christ, the fact that Paul (and early Jewish Christians before him) used of the risen Christ the title that Palestinian Jews had come to use of Yahweh, puts him on the same level with Yahweh and implies his transcendent status. He is in reality something more than human. (In this regard, one should recall here that only in Rom 9:5 does Paul possibly call Jesus Christ *theos*, "God," and that is a highly controverted text; → Romans, 51:94). Fifth, the title expresses Jesus' dominion over people precisely in his glorious, risen condition as an influence affecting their lives even in the present. It is a title by which Christians acknowledge their relation to Christ as the Lord of "the living and the dead" (Rom 14:9). In acknowledging this lordship, Christians along with Paul admit that they are his *douloi*, "servants" (1 Cor 7:22; cf. Rom 1:1; Gal 1:10).

(In Col and Eph the lordship of Christ, developed as "the mystery of Christ," is further explained. As *Kyrios* of the *kosmos*, he has disarmed "the principalities and powers" [Col 2:15]; in him, the "one Lord" [Eph 4:5], the church finds its unity.)

(Boismard, M.-É., "La divinité du Christ d'après Saint Paul," *LumVie* 9 [1953] 75–100. Cerfaux, L., "Kyrios," *DBSup* 5. 200–28. Conzelmann, *OTNT* 76–86. Fitzmyer, J. A., "*Kyrios, kyriakos*," *EWNT* 2. 811–20; "New Testament Kyrios and Maranatha and Their Aramaic Background," *TAG* 218–35; "The Semitic Background of the New Testament *Kyrios*-Title," *WA* 115–42; also "The Aramaic Background of Philippians 2:6–11," *CBQ* 50 [1988] 470–83.)

55 **(D) Passion, Death, and Resurrection.** The decisive moment of the divine plan of salvation was reached in the passion, death, and resurrection of Jesus, the Christ. The unity of these phases must be retained in Paul's view of this plan. Unlike the Johannine view, which tends to make of the ignominious raising of Jesus on the cross a majestic elevation to glory (John 3:14; 8:28; 12:34) so that the Father seems to glorify the Son on Good Friday itself (John 12:23; 17:1–5), Paul's view sees the passion and death as a prelude to the resurrection. All three phases make up "the story of the cross" (1 Cor 1:18); for it was the "Lord of glory" who was crucified (1 Cor 2:8). Though he was humiliated and subjected to powers controlling this age, his resurrection meant his victory over them as Lord (Phil 2:10–11; 2 Cor 13:4). "He who died" is also "he who was raised up" (Rom 8:34). Although his assuming the "form of a slave" (Phil 2:7), i.e., becoming human (2 Cor 8:9), is part of the salvific process, Paul is not as interested in it apart from the passion, death, and resurrection. For in the last phases of Jesus' earthly existence Paul sees Jesus' filial obedience really displayed (Phil 2:8; Rom 5:19). Paul often traces the redemption of humanity to the gracious

initiative of the Father, but he also makes clear the free, loving cooperation of Christ in the execution of the Father's plan (Gal 2:20; Rom 3:23). It is "our Lord Jesus Christ who gave himself for our sins to rescue us from the present evil age" (Gal 1:4).

56 The early church recorded the memory of Jesus as the Son of Man who said that he had come not to be served but to serve and to give his life as a ransom for many (Mark 10:45). Paul nowhere alludes to such a saying of Jesus, except perhaps in his use of the eucharistic formula in 1 Cor 11:24. Yet he does emphasize Christ's vicarious suffering and death for humanity. His teaching depends on the early church's kerygma (1 Cor 15:3: "Christ died for our sins"), echoed often in one form or another (1 Cor 1:13, "for you"; Rom 14:15; Gal 1:4; 3:13; 2 Cor 5:14,21; "Christ died for us godless people," Rom 5:6). One may debate whether it should be "for us" or "instead of us"; in either case the basic Pauline idea is present. If at times Paul seems to stress the death of Christ for human salvation (1 Thess 5:10; Gal 2:20; Rom 3:25; 5:6,9–10) without mentioning the resurrection, he does so to emphasize the cost that this experience on behalf of human beings demanded of Christ. "You have been bought for a price" (1 Cor 6:20). Thereby Paul stresses that it was no small thing that Christ Jesus did for them.

57 At times Paul hints that Jesus' death was a form of sacrifice that he underwent on behalf of human beings. This notion is alluded to in 1 Cor 5:7, where Christ is depicted as the passover lamb. A more specific nuance of "covenant sacrifice" is found in the eucharistic passage of 1 Cor 11:24–25. (For the sacrificial interpretation of the disputed passage in 2 Cor 5:21, see the lengthy discussion of L. Sabourin in Lyonnet, *Sin* 185–296.) Bultmann (*TNT* 1. 296) may be right in saying that this view of Christ's death is not characteristically Pauline but represents a tradition that originated in the early church. (The view is explicitly formulated in Eph 5:2, where it is linked to the love of Christ and where allusions are made to Ps 40:7 and Exod 29:18, "As Christ loved you and gave himself up for you as a fragrant offering and sacrifice [*prosphoran kai thysian*] to God.")

58 What is much more characteristic of Paul is the linking of Christ's death and resurrection as the salvific event. The cardinal text in this regard is Rom 4:25: "Jesus our Lord . . . was handed over to death for our transgressions and was raised for our justification." See also 1 Thess 4:14; Phil 2:9–10; 1 Cor 15:12,17,20–21; 2 Cor 5:14–15; 13:4; Rom 8:34; 10:9–10. Most of these texts leave no doubt about the soteriological value of the first Easter. Rom 4:25 is not an empty pleonasm or only an instance of *parallelismus membrorum*. It expresses, rather, the double effect of the salvation-event: the wiping away of human transgressions (on the negative side) and the instituting of a status of uprightness (on the positive side). Christ's resurrection was not a purely personal by-product of his passion and death. Rather, it contributed as much as these did in a causal way to the objective redemption of humanity. "If Christ has not been raised, then . . . you are still in your sins" (1 Cor 15:17; →NT Thought, 81:120). That Christian faith may be salvific, human lips must acknowledge that "Jesus is Lord," and human hearts must believe "that God raised him from the dead" (Rom 10:9).

59 Note how Paul speaks of the resurrection. Only in 1 Thess 4:14 does he say that "Jesus died and rose again" (as if by his own power). Elsewhere the efficiency of the resurrection is attributed to the Father, the gracious author of the salvific plan: "God the Father raised him from the dead" (Gal 1:1; cf. 1 Thess 1:10; 1 Cor 6:14; 15:15; 2 Cor 4:14; Rom 4:24; 8:11; 10:9;

[Col 2:12; Eph 1:20]). Christ's loving generosity is expressed in his being handed over to death, but God's act of prevenient favor is emphasized when Paul attributes the resurrection to the Father. "By the power of God he is alive" (2 Cor 13:4). Indeed, in Rom 6:4 we learn that the power of "the Father's glory" has brought about Christ's resurrection. This *doxa* exalted Christ to his glorious state (Phil 2:10); this heavenly exaltation is his *anabasis,* his ascent to the Father, just as his death on the cross expressed the depths of his humiliation and his *katabasis.* Like many in the early church Paul saw the resurrection-ascension as a single phase of the glorious exaltation of "the Lord" (→ NT Thought, 81:134). (In Col 2:15 a disciple of Paul views this exaltation as a triumphant victory-ascent over death and the spirit-rulers of this world. God's "surpassing might and strength" were "exerted in raising Christ from the dead and seating him at his right hand in the heavenly realm, far above all principalities, authorities, powers, and dominions and above every name that could be named. . ." [Eph 1:19–21].)

60 For Paul the resurrection brought Christ into a new relationship with people who had faith. As a result of it he was "set up by the Father as the Son of God in power with [lit., "according to"] a spirit of holiness" (Rom 1:4). The "glory" that he received from the Father became *his* power, a power to create new life in those believing in him. At the resurrection he thus became the "last Adam," the first being of the *eschaton* (1 Cor 15:45: "The first man Adam became a 'living being'; the last Adam became a life-giving Spirit"; → 79 below). In virtue of this dynamic principle, Paul realizes that it is not he who now lives, but that the risen Christ lives in him (Gal 2:20). As a "life-giving Spirit," Christ brings about the justification of believers and saves them from wrath on the day of the Lord (1 Thess 1:10). Paul even prays "to know Christ and the power of his resurrection" (Phil 3:10), realizing that the Lord is possessed of a power, derived from the Father and capable of bringing about the resurrection of Christians.

(Dhanis, E. [ed.], *Resurrexit: Actes du symposium international sur la résurrection de Jésus* [Rome, 1974]. Durrwell, F. X., *The Resurrection: A Biblical Study* [NY, 1960]. Fitzmyer, J. A., "'To Know Him and the Power of His Resurrection' (Phil 3:10)," *TAG* 202–17. Feuillet, A., "Mort du Christ et mort du chrétien d'après les épîtres pauliniennes," *RB* 66 [1959] 481–513. Güttgemanns, E., *Der leidende Apostel und sein Herr* [FRLANT 90; Göttingen, 1966]. Luz, U., "Theologia crucis als Mitte der Theologie im Neuen Testament," *EvT* 34 [1974] 116–41. Ortkemper, F.-J., *Das Kreuz in der Verkündigung des Apostels Paulus* [SBS 24; Stuttgart, 1967]. Schade, H.-H., *Apokalyptische Christologie bei Paulus* [GTA 18; Göttingen, 1981]. Schweizer, E., "Dying and Rising with Christ," *NTS* 14 [1967–68] 1–14. Stanley, D. M., *Christ's Resurrection in Pauline Soteriology* [AnBib 13; Rome, 1961]. Tannehill, R. C., *Dying and Rising with Christ* [BZNW 32; Berlin, 1967]. Weder, H., *Das Kreuz Jesu bei Paulus* [FRLANT 125; Göttingen, 1981].)

61 **(E) The Lord and the Spirit.** Before considering the various effects that Paul attributes to what Christ has done for humanity, we must devote some attention to the relation of the Lord to the Spirit in the Father's plan of salvation. We have already seen that Paul called Christ "the power of God and the wisdom of God" (1 Cor 1:24). Like the term "spirit of God," these epithets are ways of expressing God's outgoing activity (cf. Wis 7:25); for the "spirit of God" in the OT, see Gen 1:2; Ps 51:13; 139:7; Isa 11:2; 61:1; Ezek 2:2. It expresses God's creative, prophetic, or renovating presence to human beings or to the world at large; through it God is provident for Israel or the world (→ OT Thought, 77:32–39). Though Paul comes to identify Christ with the power and wisdom of God, he never calls him explicitly "the spirit of God."

In several places, however, Paul does not clearly distinguish the Spirit from Christ. In Rom 8:9–11 the terms "Spirit of God," "the Spirit of Christ," "Christ," and "the Spirit of him who raised Jesus from the dead" are used interchangeably in Paul's description of God dwelling in the Christian. Related to this ambiguity is the designation of Christ as the "last Adam" since the resurrection, when he became "a life-giving Spirit" (1 Cor 15:45), one "set up as the Son of God in power with [lit., "according to"] a spirit of holiness" (Rom 1:4). Indeed, Paul speaks of a sending of the "Spirit of the Son" (Gal 4:6), of "the Spirit of Jesus Christ" (Phil 1:19), and of Jesus as "the Lord, the Spirit" (2 Cor 3:18). Finally, he even goes so far as to say, "The Lord is the Spirit" (2 Cor 3:17; → 2 Corinthians, 50:17).

There are, however, triadic texts in Paul's letters that line up God (or the Father), Christ (or the Son), and the Spirit in a parallelism that becomes the basis for the later dogma of the three distinct persons in the Trinity (2 Cor 1:21–22; 13:13; 1 Cor 2:7–16; 6:11; 12:4–6; Rom 5:1–5; 8:14–17; 15:30). In Gal 4:4–6 there is a double sending of the "Son" and the "Spirit of his Son," and even though one may at first hesitate about the distinction of the Spirit and the Son here, the text probably echoes the distinct sending of the Messiah and of the Spirit in the OT (e.g., Dan 9:25; Ezek 36:26). Moreover, 1 Cor 2:10–11, attributing to the Spirit a comprehensive knowledge of God's profound thoughts, may even imply its divine character.

62 This double set of texts manifests Paul's lack of clarity in his conception of the relation of the Spirit to the Son. Normally, he uses "Spirit" in the OT sense, without the later theological refinements (nature, substance, and person). His lack of clarity should be respected; he provides only the starting point of later theological developments.

63 As in his christology, so too in his references to the Spirit, Paul is interested in the functional role played by the latter in human salvation. If Christ opened up to human beings the possibility of a new life, to be lived in him and for God, it is more accurately the "Spirit of Christ" that is the mode of communicating this dynamic, vital, and life-giving principle to human beings.

64 The Spirit is for Paul an "energizer," a Spirit of power (1 Cor 2:4; Rom 15:13) and the source of Christian love, hope, and faith. It frees human beings from the law (Gal 5:18, cf. Rom 8:2), from "the cravings of the flesh" (Gal 5:16), and from all immoral conduct (Gal 5:19–24). It is the gift of the Spirit that constitutes adoptive sonship (Gal 4:6; Rom 8:14), that assists Christians in prayer ("pleading along with us with inexpressible yearnings," Rom 8:26), and that makes Christians especially aware of their relation to the Father. The power of the Spirit is not something distinct from the power of the risen Christ: Christians have been "washed, consecrated, and have become upright in the name of our Lord Jesus Christ and in the Spirit of our God" (1 Cor 6:11).

65 Commentators on Paul have at times tried to distinguish between the "Holy Spirit" (*pneuma* with capital P) and the "effects" of the indwelling Spirit (with a small *p*)—see E.-B. Allo, *Première épître aux Corinthiens* (Paris, 1934) 93–94. Should not one at times prefer one meaning to the other? Thus Paul might be providing the basis for the later theological distinction between the created gift (grace) and the uncreated gift (the Spirit). But this distinction is not really Paul's; the Spirit for him is God's gift of his creative, prophetic, or renovative presence to human beings or the world, and it is better left in this undetermined state.

66   Related to the foregoing question is the use of *charis*, "grace." For Paul it most frequently designates God's "favor," the gratuitous aspect of the Father's initiative in salvation (Gal 2:21; 2 Cor 1:12) or of Christ's own collaboration (2 Cor 8:9). Thus it characterizes the divine prevenience in the promise to Abraham (Rom 4:16), in the apostolic call (Gal 1:6,15; 1 Cor 15:10; Rom 1:4), in election (Rom 11:5), in the justification of human beings (Rom 3:24; 5:15,17,20-21). Moreover, it characterizes the dispensation that supersedes the law (Rom 6:14-15; 11:6). But at times Paul speaks of *charis* as something that is given or manifested (Gal 2:9; 1 Cor 1:4; 3:10; 2 Cor 6:1; 8:1; 9:14; Rom 12:3,6; 15:15). It accompanies Paul or is in him (Phil 1:7; 1 Cor 15:10). One may debate whether this is to be conceived of as something produced or not. In any case this last group of texts led in time to the medieval idea of "sanctifying grace." Even though to read this notion into such Pauline passages would be anachronistic, one must remember that the Pauline teaching about the Spirit as an energizing force is likewise the basis of that later teaching.

(On Spirit: Benjamin, H. S., *BTB* 6 [1976] 27-48. Brandenburger, E., *Fleisch und Geist: Paulus und die dualistische Weisheit* [WMANT 29; Neukirchen, 1968]. Hermann, I., *Kyrios und Pneuma* [SANT 2; Munich, 1961]. Ladd, G. E., in *Current Issues in Biblical and Patristic Interpretation* [Fest. M. C. Tenney; ed. G. Hawthorne; GR, 1975] 211-16. Luck, U., *TLZ* 85 [1960] 845-48. Stalder, K., *Das Werk des Geistes in der Heiligung bei Paulus* [Zurich, 1962].
On grace (*charis*): Arichea, D. C., *BT* 29 [1978] 201-6. Berger, K., *EWNT* 3. 1095-1102. Cambe, M., *RB* 70 [1963] 193-207. De la Potterie, I., in *Jesus und Paulus* [Fest. W. G. Kümmel; ed. E. E. Ellis and E. Grässer; Göttingen, 1975] 256-82. Doughty, D. J., *NTS* 19 [1972-73] 163-80.)

67   **(V) Effects of the Christ-Event.** The term "Christ-event" is a short way of referring to the complex of decisive moments of the earthly and risen life of Jesus Christ. Above we considered three of them, his passion, death, and resurrection; but in reality one should also include Jesus' burial, exaltation, and heavenly intercession, for Paul sees significance in these moments as well. We have already noted how little interest Paul shows in the life of Jesus prior to his passion (→ 18 above). What was more important for him was this complex of six decisive moments. When Paul looked back at these moments, he realized what Christ Jesus had accomplished for humanity, and he spoke of the effects of that accomplishment (the "objective redemption," as it has often been called) under ten different images: justification, salvation, reconciliation, expiation, redemption, freedom, sanctification, transformation, new creation, and glorification. For each of these images expresses a distinctive aspect of the mystery of Christ and his work. If the Christ-event be conceived of as a decahedron, a 10-sided solid figure, one can understand how Paul, gazing at one panel of it, would use one image to express an effect of it, whereas he would use another image when gazing at another panel. Each one expresses an aspect of the whole. The multiple images have been derived from his Hellenistic or Jewish backgrounds and have been applied by him to that Christ-event and its effects. In each case one has to consider its (1) origin or background, (2) meaning for Paul, and (3) occurrences.
68   **(A) Justification.** The image most frequently used by Paul to express an effect of the Christ-event is "justification" (*dikaiōsis, dikaioun*). (1) It is drawn from Paul's Jewish background, being an OT image expressive of a relationship between God and human beings or between human beings themselves, whether as kings and commoners, or brothers and sisters, or neighbors. But it denotes a societal or judicial relationship,

either ethical or forensic (i.e., related to law courts; see Deut 25:1; cf. Gen 18:25). Though Noah is described as "a righteous man" before God (Gen 6:9, said in a pre-Mosaic law context), the *dikaios*, "righteous, upright (person)," came to denote normally one who stood acquitted or vindicated before a judge's tribunal (Exod 23:7; 1 Kgs 8:32). Its covenantal nuance was expressive of the status of "righteousness" or "uprightness" to be achieved in the sight of Yahweh the Judge by observing the statutes of the Mosaic law (see Pss 7:9-12; 119:1-8). The OT also noted constantly how difficult a status it was to achieve (Job 4:17; 9:2; Ps 143:2; Ezra 9:15). Whereas Josephus could imagine nothing "more righteous" than obeying the statutes of the law (*Ag.Ap.* 2.41 § 293), the Essene of Qumran sang of his sinfulness and sought justification only from God: "As for me, I belong to wicked humanity, to the assembly of perverse flesh; my iniquities, my transgressions, my sins together with the wickedness of my heart belong to the assembly doomed to worms and walking in darkness. No human being sets his own path or directs his own steps, for to God alone belongs the judgment of him, and from his hand comes perfection of way. . . . If I stumble because of a sin of the flesh, my judgment is according to the righteousness of God" (1QS 11:9-12; cf. 1QH 9:32-34; 14:15-16). Here we find an awareness of sin and of God as the source of human uprightness that are somewhat similar to Paul's ideas, but they are not as developed as his would eventually become. Though Paul, even as a Christian, could look back on his own experience as a Pharisee and assert that "as to righteousness under the law" he had been "blameless" (Phil 3:6), his experience near Damascus impressed him with the sinfulness of all human beings and with the role of Christ Jesus in repairing that situation (see Rom 3:23). (2) When, then, Paul says that Christ has "justified" human beings, he means that by his passion, death, etc. Christ has brought it about that they now stand before God's tribunal acquitted or innocent—and this apart from deeds prescribed by the Mosaic law. For "God's uprightness" (→ 39 above) now manifests itself toward human beings in a just judgment that is one of acquittal, since "Jesus our Lord was handed over to death for our trespasses and raised for our justification" (Rom 4:25). (3) Paul clearly affirms the gratuitous and unmerited character of this justification of all humanity in Rom 3:20-26, which ends with the assertion that God has displayed Jesus in death ("by his blood") "to show forth at the present time that he [God] is upright himself and justifies [= vindicates] the one who has faith in Jesus" (3:26; cf. 5:1; Gal 2:15-21). The process of justification begins in God who is "upright" and who "justifies" the godless sinner as a result of what Christ has done for humanity. The sinner becomes *dikaios* and stands before God as "upright," "acquitted." For this reason Paul also speaks of Christ as "our uprightness" (1 Cor 1:30), since through his obedience many are "made upright" (*dikaioi katastathēsontai hoi polloi*, Rom 5:19; cf. 1 Cor 6:11; Rom 5:18). Paul insists on the utter gratuity of this status before God because "all have sinned and fall short of the glory of God" (Rom 3:23). He even brings himself to admit that in all of this "we become the righteousness of God" (2 Cor 5:21), a bold assertion that states that God's righteousness is communicated to us. This is "righteousness from God" (Phil 3:9); it is not our own (Rom 10:3).
69   This effect of the Christ-event was undoubtedly recognized by early Christians even before Paul; at least 1 Cor 6:11 and Rom 4:25 are often looked upon as pre-Pauline affirmations about Christ's role in justification. The distinctive Pauline contribution, however, is his teaching that such justification comes about "by grace as a gift" (Rom 3:24) and "through faith" (Rom 3:25).

Though it is unlikely that the Judaizing problem in the early church, which Paul combatted so vigorously, gave rise to this way of viewing the Christ-event, that problem undoubtedly helped Paul to sharpen his own view of the matter.

70   The action whereby God "justifies" the sinner has been the subject of no little debate. Does the verb *dikaioun* mean "to declare upright" or "to make upright?" One might expect that *dikaioun*, like other Gk verbs ending in *-oō*, would have a causative, factitive meaning, "to make someone *dikaios*" (cf. *douloun*, "enslave"; *nekroun*, "mortify"; *dēloun*, "make clear"; *anakainoun*, "renew"). But in the LXX *dikaioun* seems normally to have a declarative, forensic meaning (G. Schrenk, *TDNT* 2. 212–14; cf. D. R. Hillers, *JBL* 86 [1967] 320–24). At times this seems to be the sense in Paul's letters (e.g., Rom 8:33), but many instances are ambiguous. From patristic times on, the effective sense of *dikaioun*, "make upright," has been used (see John Chrysostom, *In ep. ad rom. hom.* 8.2 [PG 60. 456]; *In ep. II ad Cor. hom.* 11.3 [PG 61. 478]; Augustine, *De Spir. et litt.* 26.45 [CSEL 60. 199]. Indeed, this sense seems suggested by Rom 5:19, "by one man's obedience many will be made upright" (*katastathēsontai*). Moreover, if E. Käsemann's emphasis on "God's uprightness" as "power" is correct, this sense of *dikaioun* acquires an added nuance, and the OT idea of God's word as effective (Isa 55:10–11) would support it. This debate about the forensic/declarative or effective sense of *dikaioun* has been acute ever since the time of the Reformation. Yet it might be well to recall that even Melanchthon admitted that "Scripture speaks both ways" (*Apol.* 4.72).

(On justification: Betz, O., in *Rechtf* 17–36. Conzelmann, H., *EvT* 28 [1968] 389–404. Daalen, D. H. van, *SE VI* 556–70. Donfried, K. P., *ZNW* 67 [1976] 90–110. Gyllenberg, R., *Rechtfertigung und Altes Testament bei Paulus* [Stuttgart, 1973]. Jeremias, J., *The Central Message of the New Testament* [London, 1965] 51–70. Keck, L. E., in *Rechtf* 199–209. Kertelge, *"Rechtfertigung"* [→ 39 above]. Kuyper, L. J., *SJT* 30 [1977] 233–52. Reumann, J., *"Righteousness" in the New Testament* [Phl, 1982]. Strecker, G., in *Rechtf* 479–508. Wilckens, U., *Rechtfertigung als Freiheit: Paulusstudien* [Neukirchen, 1974]. Wolter, M., *Rechtfertigung und zukünftiges Heil* [BZNW 43; Berlin, 1978]. Ziesler, J. A., *The Meaning of Righteousness in Paul* [SNTSMS 20; Cambridge, 1972].)

71   **(B) Salvation.** A fairly common way for Paul to express an effect of the Christ-event is "salvation" (*sōtēria, sōzein*). (1) This image is most probably derived by Paul from the OT expression of Yahweh's delivering his people Israel, either as its savior (*môšîa'*, Isa 45:15; Zech 8:7; cf. Ps 25:5; Mic 7:7) or by "saviors" whom he raised up for them (Judg 3:9,15; 6:36; 2 Kgs 13:5; Isa 19:20; → OT Thought, 77:140–48). It is, however, not impossible that Paul has been influenced by the use of *sōtēr*, "savior," in the contemporary Greco-Roman world, where Zeus, Apollo, Artemis, or Asclepius were often called *theos sōtēr*, a cultic epithet used in time of need (illness, sea storms, travail). This title was also applied to kings, emperors, and town councils (see H. Volkmann, "Soter, Soteria," *DKP* 5. 289–90). (2) The image expresses deliverance or rescue from evil or harm, whether physical, psychic, national, cataclysmic, or moral. (3) In using it, Paul recognizes that Christians "are being saved" by the cross of Christ (1 Cor 1:18,21; cf. 15:2; 2 Cor 2:15), i.e., rescued from evil (moral and otherwise). Strikingly enough, he uses this image, and not "justification," in the very thesis of Rom 1:16, where he identifies "the gospel" as "the power of God for the salvation of everyone who believes." Only in Phil 3:20 does Paul call Jesus *sōtēr*, and he is such as one still "awaited," for although Paul looks on this effect of the

Christ-event as already achieved, he realizes that its end result is still something of the future, with an eschatological aspect (see 1 Thess 2:16; 5:8–9; 1 Cor 3:15; 5:5; Rom 5:9–10; 8:24 ["In hope we have been saved"!]; 10:9–10,13). Related to this future is the role of intercession ascribed to the risen Christ in heaven (Rom 8:34). This, too, is why Paul can recommend to the Philippians, "work out your own salvation in fear and trembling" (Phil 2:12), adding, however, immediately, "for God is the one working in you, both to will and to work for his good pleasure" (2:13)—lest anyone might think that salvation can be achieved without God's grace. Likewise related is Paul's insistence that all human beings must one day "appear before the tribunal of Christ so that each one may receive good or evil for what one has done in the body" (2 Cor 5:10; cf. Rom 2:6–11). This future aspect of Pauline teaching has to be kept in mind against the broader backdrop of what God has already graciously achieved for humanity in the cross and resurrection of Christ Jesus.

(Noteworthy is the development in Eph, where Christ is again called "Savior" [5:23] and where all the characteristic Pauline terminology associated with justification now appears with salvation: "By grace you have been *saved* through faith; and this is not of your own doing, but is a gift of God—not because of deeds, lest anyone begin to boast. For we are his workmanship, created in Christ Jesus for good deeds, which God prepared in advance that we might walk in them" [2:8–10]. By the time that Eph is written, the Judaizing problem has abated, and the role of grace and faith has been shifted to more generic salvation. See A. T. Lincoln, *CBQ* 45 [1983] 617–30.)

(On salvation: Brox, N., *EvT* 33 [1973] 253–79. Cullmann, O., *The Christology of the New Testament* [rev. ed.; Phl, 1963] 238–45. Dornseiff, F., *PW* 2/III.1. 1211–21. Lyonnet and Sabourin, *Sin* 63–78. Packer, J. I., *BSac* 129 [1972] 195–205, 291–306. Schelkle, K. H., *EWNT* 3. 781–84, 784–88.)

72   **(C) Reconciliation.** Another image that Paul uses to describe an effect of the Christ-event is "reconciliation" (*katallagē, katallassein* [Col and Eph use *apokatallassein*]). (1) This image is derived by Paul from his Greco-Roman background, since there is no Hebr or Aram word to express the idea in the OT. The LXX uses *diallassein*, which has the same meaning, about a Levite who became angry with his concubine and went to talk to her "to reconcile her to himself" (Judg 19:3); but the Hebrew says "to cause her to return to him" (see *RSV*). Cf. 1 Sam 29:4, where the Hebrew reads, "He will make himself acceptable." In Hellenistic Greek, however, the verbs *katallassein, diallassein* are found abundantly (see Dupont, *La réconciliation* 7–15). The words are compounds of the root *all-*, meaning "other"; they denote a "making otherwise," in both a secular and a religious sense. In a secular sense, they denote a change in relations between individuals, groups, or nations and pertain to relations in the social or political sphere. They mean a change from anger, hostility, or alienation to love, friendship, or intimacy; feelings may accompany that change, but they are not essential (see Matt 5:23–24; 1 Cor 7:11). In a religious sense, Gk literature uses the verbs of the reconciliation of gods and humans (e.g., Sophocles, *Ajax* 744). 2 Macc 1:5 speaks of God being reconciled to Jews (cf. 7:33; 8:29); and Josephus (*Ant.* 6.7.4 § 143) similarly tells of God being reconciled to Saul. (2) When Paul applies this image to the Christ-event, he speaks always of God or Christ reconciling human beings, enemies or sinners, to himself. The initiative is with God, who through Christ brings it about that human sinners are brought from a status of enmity to friendship (see 2 Cor 5:18-19). "If, while we were enemies, we were reconciled to God by the death of his Son, much more, now that we are reconciled, shall we be saved by his life. Not only so, but we also rejoice in God through our Lord Jesus Christ, through whom we have now received our reconciliation" (Rom 5:10-11). (3) What is striking in this instance is Paul's extension of this effect of the Christ-event from human beings to the *kosmos* itself: "In Christ God was reconciling the world to himself" (2 Cor 5:19; cf. Rom 11:15). Reconciliation has not only an anthropological dimension, but a cosmic dimension too. (In Col and Eph this effect is further developed in that it is related to the overall cosmic role of the risen Christ [Col 1:20-22, and esp. Eph 2:11-19]. The reconciliation is described both "horizontally," in that Gentiles and Jews are brought near as Christians, and "vertically," in that both Gentile and Jewish Christians have been reconciled to God through Christ, who is "our peace.")

This idea of reconciliation is the same as "atonement," when that word is understood rightly as *at-one-ment*. Unfortunately, atonement has often been misunderstood and confused with "expiation" (e.g., by Käsemann, in *Future* 50)—and, worse still, with "propitiation." Reconciliation/atonement has nothing to do *per se* with cult or sacrifice; it is an image derived from relationships within the social or political sphere.

(On reconciliation: Büchsel, F., *TDNT* 1. 251-59. Dupont, J., *La réconciliation dans la théologie de Saint Paul* [ALBO 3/32; Bruges, 1953]. Fitzmyer, J. A., *TAG* 162-85. Furnish, V. P., *CurTM* 4 [1977] 204-18. Hahn, F., *EvT* 33 [1973] 244-53. Hengel, M., *The Atonement* [Phl, 1981]. Käsemann, E., in *The Future of Our Religious Past* [Fest. R. Bultmann; ed. J. M. Robinson; NY, 1971] 49-64. Lührmann, D., *ZTK* 67 [1970] 437-52. Merkel, H., *EWNT* 2. 644-50.)

73   (D) Expiation. Another effect of the Christ-event is expressed by Paul under the image of "expiation" (*hilastērion*). (1) Despite attempts to relate this image to Paul's Hellenistic background, it has been derived by him from the OT, i.e., from the LXX transl. of Hebr *kappōret*, the lid made of fine gold erected over the top of the ark of the covenant in the Holy of Holies, which served as the base for the two cherubim of Yahweh's throne (see Exod 25:17-22). *Kippēr* in Hebrew basically means "smear over," "wipe away" (see *HALAT* 470), and the lid was called *kappōret* because it was smeared with sacrificial blood by the high priest, who entered the Holy of Holies once a year for this purpose on *Yom hakkippûrîm* (Lev 16:14-20). The first time that *kappōret* occurs in the OT it is translated in the LXX by *hilastērion epithema* (Exod 25:17), "expiating cover/lid," but thereafter simply as *to hilastērion* (e.g., Exod 25:18-22 with the art. as in the MT), a noun signifying "means of expiation." In the Lat Vg *kappōret* was rendered in most cases as *propitiatorium* (whence the translation "propitiatory" in some older Eng Bibles). Luther translated it as *Gnadenstuhl,* and in imitation the *KJV* rendered it as "mercy seat." (2) Paul uses this image as an effect of the Christ-event only in Rom 3:25, where he reflects its OT relation to the Day of Atonement ritual in Lev 16: "God displayed him [Christ] as *hilastērion* with [or, "in"] his blood for the remission of bygone sins. . . ." Thus, Christ by his death or the shedding of his blood has achieved for humanity once and for all what the Day of Atonement ritual symbolized each year for Israel of old; he has become the new "mercy seat." *Hilastērion* could, in fact, be understood as an adj.: "displayed Christ as expiating"; but, given the more common LXX use, it is preferably interpreted as a noun, "displayed Christ as a means of expiation," i.e., a means whereby human sin is wiped

out, smeared away. (3) Some commentators have tried to relate *hilastērion* to the Gk vb. *hilaskesthai,* which was often used in the Hellenistic period with a god or hero as its object and meant "to propitiate," "placate," "appease" such an angry being. This might suggest that Paul was saying that Christ was so displayed with his blood in order to placate the Father's wrath (see Morris, "The Meaning"). This is, however, far from certain. In the LXX God is at times the object of *hilaskesthai* (Mal 1:9; Zech 7:2; 8:22); but in these three places there is no question of an appeasement of his wrath (see the *RSV*). More frequently *hilaskesthai* is used either of expiating sins (i.e., removing them or their guilt, Ps 65:4; Sir 5:6; 28:5) or of expiating some object, person, or place (i.e., purifying from defilement, Lev 16:16,20,33; Ezek 43:20,26; etc.). It frequently translates *kippēr,* which even has God sometimes as its subject, not its object (see Lyonnet, "The Terminology"). One should not invoke such passages as 1 Thess 1:10; Rom 5:9 to suggest that the shedding of Christ's blood has actually appeased the Father's wrath: we have explained "the wrath of God" (→ 38 above), and it is reserved for human sin. Expiation, however, wipes away human sin, and Paul sees this achieved once and for all in Jesus' death on the cross.

74   A fuller meaning of the public manifestation of Christ "in his blood" (Rom 3:25) is understood only when contemporary Jewish ideas are recalled that "there is no expiation of sins without blood" (Heb 9:22; cf. *Jub.* 6:2,11,14). It was not that blood shed in sacrifice pleased Yahweh; nor that the shedding of the blood and ensuing death were a recompense or price to be paid (→ Institutions, 76:89-95). Rather, the blood was shed either to purify and cleanse objects ritually dedicated to Yahweh's service (Lev 16:15-19) or to consecrate objects or persons to that service (i.e., by removing them from the profane and uniting them intimately with Yahweh, as it were, in a sacred pact; cf. Exod 24:6-8). On the Day of Atonement the high priest sprinkled the *kappōret* with blood "because of the uncleanness of the Israelites and their transgressions in all their sins" (Lev 16:16). The underlying reason is found in Lev 17:11: "The life of the flesh is in the blood; for it is the blood that expiates by reason of the life (*bannepeš*)." Cf. Lev 17:14; Gen 9:4; Deut 12:33. Blood was identified with life itself because the *nepeš,* "breath," was thought to be in the blood. When it ran out of a being, the *nepeš* left. The blood shed in sacrifice was not, then, a vicarious punishment meted out on an animal instead of on the person who immolated it. Rather, the "life" of the animal was consecrated to God (Lev 16:8-9); it was a symbolic dedication of the life of the person who sacrificed to Yahweh. It cleansed people of faults in Yahweh's sight and associated them once more with Yahweh. Christ's blood, shed in expiation of human sin, removed the sins that alienated human beings from God. Paul insists on the gracious and loving initiative of the Father and on the love of Christ himself in this action. He often says of Christ that he "gave himself" for us or for our sins (Gal 1:4; 2:20) and that he "loved us" (Gal 2:20; Rom 8:35,37). Through the death of Christ, Paul (along with all Christians) has been crucified with Christ so that he "may live for God" (Gal 2:19). It is *not* Pauline teaching that the Father willed the death of his Son to satisfy the debts owed to God or to the devil by human sinners. Lest Paul's statements, which are at times couched in juridical terminology, be forced into rigid categories after the fashion of some patristic and scholastic commentators, one has to insist on the love of Christ involved in this activity. Paul did not theorize about the Christ-event, as did later theologians. He offers us "not theories but vivid metaphors, which can, if we will let them operate in our imagination, make real to us the saving truth of our redemption by Christ's self-offering on our behalf. . . . It is an unfortunate kind of sophistication which believes that the only thing to do with metaphors is to turn them into theories" (*RITNT* 222-23).

(Dodd, C. H., *The Bible and the Greeks* [London, 1935] 82-95. Fitzer, G., "Der Ort der Versöhnung nach Paulus," *TZ* 22 [1966] 161-83. Fitzmyer, J. A., "The Targum of Leviticus from Qumran Cave 4," *Maarav* 1 [1978-79] 5-23. Garnet, P., "Atonement Constructions in the Old Testament and the Qumran Scrolls," *EvQ* 46 [1974] 131-63. Lyonnet, S., "The Terminology of 'Expiation' . . . ," *Sin* 120-66. Manson, T. W., "*Hilastērion*," *JTS* 46 [1945] 1-10. Moraldi, L., *Espiazione sacrificale e riti espiatori nell'ambiente biblico e nell'Antico Testamento* [AnBib 5; Rome, 1956] 182-221. Morris, L., "The Biblical Use of the Term 'Blood,'" *JTS* 3 [1952] 216-27; "The Meaning of *hilastērion* in Romans iii.25," *NTS* 2 [1955-56] 33-43. Roloff, J., "*Hilastērion*," *EWNT* 2. 455-57.)

75   (E) Redemption. Yet another image employed by Paul to describe an effect of the Christ-event is "redemption" (*apolytrōsis; agorazein, exagorazein*). (1) It is not easy to say whence this image is derived by Paul. It has been related to sacral manumission of slaves in the Gk world (BAGD 12; *LAE* 320-23: more than 1,000 Delphic inscriptions record that "Pythian Apollo purchased So-and-So for freedom"). That Paul is aware of a social institution of emancipation is clear from 1 Cor 7:21, even though he otherwise counsels Christians to remain "in the state in which one has been called," for a slave is a "freedman of the Lord" (7:20,22). But Paul's Gk vocabulary is notably different from that found in the Delphic inscriptions, where the verb is *priasthai*, "purchase," not the Pauline *(ex)agorazein*, which never appears in sacral-manumission texts. Nor is the freed slave ever considered "a slave of Apollo" or "a freedman of Apollo" (see Bartchy, *Mallon* 121-25; Lyonnet, "L'Emploi"). The only term used in common is *timē*, "price" (1 Cor 6:20; 7:23). For this reason it is better to explain the background of Paul's image mainly in the light of LXX terminology. There the verb *apolytroun* is used for the "redeeming" of a slave (Exod 21:8); *apolytrōsis* occurs (Dan 4:34); and the simple forms *lytron*, "ransom," and *lytroun*, "redeem," are found abundantly (e.g., Exod 6:6; 15:13-16; 21:30; 30:12). Paul uses *exagorazein*, "buy," a rare word, never used in the LXX in a context of emancipation of a slave or in extrabiblical texts of sacral manumission. But it is used by Diodorus Siculus (*Hist.* 36.2) for buying a slave (as a possession) and again (*Hist.* 15.7) for setting free an enslaved person by purchase—though *lytron* is not mentioned, such a purchase was in effect a "ransom." (2) When Paul sees "redemption" as an effect of the Christ-event, he acknowledges that Christ's passion, death, etc. were a ransom to set sinners free from bondage and enslavement. Behind the Pauline image lies the OT idea of Yahweh as Israel's *gô'ēl*, "redeemer," the kinsman who had the duty of buying back an enslaved or captive relative (Isa 41:14; 43:14; 44:6; 47:4; Ps 19:15; 78:35). It referred at first to the freeing of Israel from Egyptian bondage (Deut 6:6-8; Ps 111:9), when Yahweh "acquired" a people as a possession for himself (Exod 15:16; 19:5; Mal 3:17; Ps 74:2); later on, to the return of Israel from Babylonian Captivity (Isa 51:11; 52:3-9). In time, it acquired an eschatological nuance: what God would do for Israel at the end of days (Hos 13:14; Isa 59:20; Ps 130:7-8). (3) Paul never calls Christ *lytrōtēs*, "redeemer" (a term used of Moses in Acts 7:35); nor does he ever speak of *lytron*, "ransom." But he does call Christ "our redemption" (*apolytrōsis*, 1 Cor 1:30). "Through the redemption which is in Christ Jesus" (Rom 3:24), human beings are freed and justified. Though this has already

been achieved by Christ, there is still a future, eschatological aspect, for Christians "await the redemption of the body" (Rom 8:23)—even a cosmic aspect, since all "creation" (8:19-22) is groaning in expectation of it. When Paul speaks of Christians as having been "bought for a price" (1 Cor 6:20; 7:23), he is stressing the onerous burden of what Christ did for humanity. He never specifies to whom the price was paid (whether to God or to the devil, as later commentators often theorized).

(In Col and Eph "the forgiveness of sins" [*aphesis hamartiōn*] is related to the effect of redemption [Col 1:14; Eph 1:7]. This effect of the Christ-event is never found in Paul's uncontested letters, unless one argues that *paresis* in Rom 3:25 carries the meaning of "remission," which is not unlikely. Moreover, Eph 1:14 explicitly mentions "the redemption of acquisition," echoing the OT idea; in 4:30 the indwelling Spirit is already a pledge of "the day of redemption.")

(Bartchy, S., *Mallon Chrēsai: First-Century Slavery and the Interpretation of 1 Corinthians 7:21* [SBLDS 11; Missoula, 1973]. Börner, F., *Untersuchungen über die Religion der Sklaven in Griechenland und Rom* [4 vols.; Mainz, 1957-63] 2. 133-41. Elert, W., "Redemptio ab hostibus," *TLZ* 72 [1947] 265-70. Gibbs, J. G., "The Cosmic Scope of Redemption according to Paul," *Bib* 56 [1975] 13-29. Kertelge, K., "*Apolytrōsis*," *EWNT* 1. 331-36; "*Lytron*," ibid. 2. 901-5. Lyonnet, S., "L'Emploi paulinien de *exagorazein* au sens de 'redimere' est-il attesté dans la littérature grecque?" *Bib* 42 [1961] 85-89; "Redemptio cosmica secundum Rom 8,19-23," *VD* 44 [1966] 225-42; "The Terminology of Liberation," *Sin* 79-119. Marshall, I. H., "The Development of the Concept of Redemption in the New Testament," in *Reconciliation and Hope* [Fest. L. L. Morris; ed. R. J. Banks; GR, 1974] 153-69.)

76   (F) Freedom. Related to the image of redemption is another used by Paul, viz., "freedom" (*eleutheria, eleutheroun*). (1) Though "freedom" sometimes carries the nuance of "redemption/ransom" (→ 75 above), it is more properly related to the Greco-Roman idea of freedom as the social status of citizens in a Gk *polis* or a Roman *municipium* (see *OCD* 703, 851-52). (The root *eleuthero-* occurs in the LXX, but it is found for the most part in the deuterocanonical and apocryphal Gk writings.) The secular use of the adj. *eleutheros* is found in 1 Cor 7:21-22. (2) Paul applies this image to the Christ-event, meaning thereby that Christ Jesus has set human beings free, has given them the rights of citizens of a free city or state. As a result, "our commonwealth (*politeuma*) is in heaven" (Phil 3:20); and while here on earth we are already a colony of free heavenly citizens. (3) Paul's principle is found in 2 Cor 3:17: "Where the Spirit of the Lord is, there is freedom." That is why he insists with the Galatians: "For freedom Christ has set us free; so stand fast and be not encumbered again with a yoke of slavery" (Gal 5:1). The slavery to which he refers is that of "sin and death," "self," and "the law" (see Rom 5-7; esp. 7:3; 8:1-2). "When you were slaves of sin, you became free for uprightness" (Rom 6:20; cf. 6:18). The allegory of Sarah and Hagar (Gal 4:21-31) teaches that all Christians are children of the "free woman." In his struggle with the Judaizers Paul became aware of the "false brethren" who had "slipped in to spy out the freedom that we have in Christ Jesus" (Gal 2:4). This effect of the Christ-event also has its eschatological aspect, since it is associated with the destiny of the Christian in "glory" (Rom 8:21). Paul, however, realizes that the Christian has not yet fully achieved that destiny and insists, "You were called to freedom; but do not use your freedom as an opportunity for the flesh" (Gal 5:13a-b). Freedom is not license; but "through love become servants of one another" (5:13c).

(On freedom: Betz, H. D., *SEA* 39 [1974] 145-60. Cambier, J., *SE II* 315-53. Krentz, E., *CTM* 40 [1969] 356-68. Lyonnet, S., *The Bridge* 4 [1962] 229-51. Mussner, F., *Theologie der Freiheit nach Paulus* [QD 75; Freiburg, 1976]. Nestle, D., *Eleutheria: Studien zum Wesen der Freiheit bei den Griechen und im Neuen Testament* [HUT 16; Tübingen, 1967]. Niederwimmer, K., *EWNT* 1. 1052-58. Schlier, H., *Das Ende der Zeit* [Freiburg, 1971] 216-33. Schnackenburg, R., *Present and Future: Modern Aspects of New Testament Theology* [Notre Dame, 1966] 64-80.)

77   (G) Sanctification. Another image used by Paul for an effect of the Christ-event is "sanctification" (*hagiasmos, hagiazein*). (1) Though things and persons were often said in the Gk world to be *hagios*, "holy," or dedicated to the gods (Herodotus, *Hist.* 2.41.44; Aristophanes, *Birds* 522), Paul's image is mainly derived from the OT. There Hebr *qādôš* and Gk *hagios* were often used to characterize things (e.g., the ground, Exod 3:5; Jerusalem, Isa 48:2; the Temple, Isa 64:10; its inner sanctuary, Exod 26:33) or persons (e.g., the people of Israel, Exod 19:14; Lev 19:2; Isa 62:12; priests, 1 Macc 2:54; prophets, Wis 11:1). This term did not express an inner, ethical piety or outward sanctimony, but rather the dedication of things or persons to the awesome service of Yahweh. It was a cultic term that marked off from the secular or the profane such persons or things for this service. (2) For Paul God made Christ Jesus "our sanctification" (1 Cor 1:30), i.e., the means whereby human beings were dedicated anew to God and oriented to serving him with awe and respect. (3) To this status "God has called us" (1 Thess 4:7), and we have been "made holy" or "sanctified" by Christ Jesus (1 Cor 1:2; 6:11) or by his "holy Spirit" (Rom 15:16; cf. 6:22). So true is this for Paul that *hagioi*, "saints," becomes a common designation for Christians in his uncontested letters, except 1 Thess and Gal: they are "called to be saints" (Rom 1:7; 1 Cor 1:2). (As in Job 5:1; Tob 8:15; 11:14; 12:15; Ps 89:6,8, *hagioi* sometimes refers to heavenly beings, angels; it may so appear in Col 1:12; cf. 1QS 3:1; 11:7-8.)

(Balz, H., "*Hagios*, etc.," *EWNT* 1. 38-48. Delehaye, P., *Sanctus* [Subsidia hagiographica 17; Brussels, 1927]. Jones, O. R., *The Concept of Holiness* [NY, 1961]. Procksch, O. and K. G. Kuhn, "*Hagios*, etc." *TDNT* 1. 88-115. Wolff, R., "La sanctification d'après le Nouveau Testament," *Positions luthériennes* 3 [1955] 138-43.)

78   (H) Transformation. Another effect of the Christ-event is presented by Paul under the image of "transformation" (*metamorphōsis, metamorphoun* [he uses only the vb.]). (1) This image is derived from Greco-Roman mythology, which even developed in Hellenistic times a literary form, viz., collections of legends about transformation—of snakes into stones (Homer, *Iliad* 2.319), of Niobe into a rock on Mt. Sipylon (Pausanias 1.21.3), of Lucian into an ass (Apuleius, *Golden Ass*); cf. Nicander, *Heteroioumena;* Ovid, *Metamorphoses*. This mythological image was quite current in Paul's day, and he did not hesitate to borrow it and apply it to the Christ-event. (2) In so doing, Paul sees Christ Jesus gradually reshaping human beings, "who turn to the Lord." The creator God through the risen Christ shines creative light anew in human lives, which transforms them. (3) Paul clearly uses this image in 2 Cor 3:18: "All of us, with unveiled face, behold the glory of the Lord and are being transformed into a likeness of him from one degree of glory to another." Related to this verse is 2 Cor 4:6, which explains how the face of the risen Christ acts as a mirror to reflect the glory that comes from the creator God: "It is the God who said, 'Let light shine out of darkness,' who has shone in our hearts to give us the light of the knowledge of God's glory on the face of Christ." This is one of the most sublime Pauline descrip-

tions of the Christ-event. Phil 3:21 uses another vb. *metaschēmatizein* to express a similar idea: "Christ Jesus . . . will change our lowly body to be like his glorious body." Cf. Rom 12:2 (in a hortatory context). (From this image Gk patristic writers derived the later idea of *theōsis* or *theopoiēsis*, the gradual "divinization" of the Christian—their practical equivalent for "justification.")

(Behm, J., "*Metamorphoō*," *TDNT* 4. 755-59. Fitzmyer, J. A., "Glory Reflected on the Face of Christ (2 Cor 3:7-4:6) and a Palestinian Jewish Motif," *TS* 42 [1981] 630-44. Hermann, R., "Über den Sinn des *morphousthai Christon en hymin* in Gal. 4,19," *TLZ* 80 [1955] 713-26. Liefeld, W. L., "*Metamorphoō*," *NIDNTT* 3. 861-64. Nützel, J. M., "*Metamorphoō*," *EWNT* 2. 1021-22.)

79   (I) New Creation. Another Pauline image, related to the foregoing, is "new creation" (*kainē ktisis*). (1) Paul has derived this image from the OT references to God's creation of the world and of human beings (LXX Gen 14:19,22; Ps 89:48; 104:1-30; Sir 17:1). (2) In applying it to the Christ-event, Paul means that God in Christ has created humanity anew, giving it "newness of life" (Rom 6:4), i.e., a life in union with the risen Christ (Gal 2:20: "Christ lives in me"), a life destined to share in "the glory of God" (Rom 3:23b). (3) "New creation" is found in Gal 6:15, where its worth is contrasted with circumcision and the lack of circumcision; and in 2 Cor 5:17, where its source is "being in Christ." This is why Paul calls the risen Christ "the last Adam" (1 Cor 15:45), i.e., he has become the Adam of the *eschaton* through his life-giving Spirit. He is thus the head of a new humanity, just as the first Adam was the beginning of life for physical humanity. For this reason too Christ is "the firstborn among many brethren" who have been "predestined to be conformed to his image" (Rom 8:29)—the newness of life that Christ has brought is a share in his own risen life (1 Cor 6:14; 2 Cor 4:14; Rom 6:4-5; 8:11). This is, in effect, the Pauline sense of "eternal life" (Gal 6:8; Rom 5:21; 6:23).

(On [new] creation: Baumbach, G., *Kairos* 21 [1979] 196-205. Foerster, W., *TDNT* 3. 1000-35, esp. 1033-35. Petzke, O., *EWNT* 2. 803-8. Sjöberg, E., *ST* 9 [1955] 131-36. Stuhlmacher, P., *EvT* 27 [1967] 1-35.)

80   (J) Glorification. The last image used by Paul to describe an effect of the Christ-event is "glorification" (*doxa, doxazein*). (1) This image is derived from the OT *kābôd* or *doxa*, "glory," "splendor," an expression of the presence of God or of the resplendent manifestation of that presence, esp. in the theophanies of the exodus (e.g., Exod 24:17; 40:34; Num 14:10; Tob 12:15). (2) We have already seen how Paul related "glory" to the creator God (→ 78); he is now playing on another aspect of that transforming power of the risen Christ. It is depicted as "glorifying" Christians, i.e., giving them in advance a share in the glory that he, as one raised from the dead, now enjoys with the Father. (3) Paul speaks of this effect in Rom 8:30: "Those whom he predestined he also called; and those whom he called he also justified; and those whom he justified he also glorified" (*edoxasen*). Cf. 1 Thess 2:12; 1 Cor 2:7; Rom 8:18,21. (In the Deutero-Paulines this idea is given another formulation: "God has transferred us to the kingdom of his Son" [Col 1:13]; "he has raised us up with him and made us sit with him in the heavenly places" [Eph 2:6]. "Buried with him in baptism . . . you were also raised with him through faith in the action of God who raised him from the dead" [Col 2:12]. "You have been raised with Christ" [Col 3:1]. In none of these Deutero-Pauline passages does *doxa* occur.)

(On glory [*doxa*]: Brockington, L. H., in *Studies in the Gospels*

[Fest. R. H. Lightfoot; ed. D. E. Nineham; Oxford, 1957] 1–8. Dupont, J., *RB* 56 [1949] 392–411. Forster, A. H., *ATR* 12 [1929–30] 311–16. Hegermann, H., *EWNT* 1. 832–41, 841–43. Schlier, H., *SPC* 1. 45–56.)

PAUL'S ANTHROPOLOGY

81   **(I) Humanity before Christ.** What effect does the Christ-event actually have on the lives of human beings? Having sketched the objective aspects of Christ's salvific role, we now discuss the ways in which Paul saw humanity sharing in the effects listed above. To understand Paul's view of the Christian experience from the human side, however, we must inquire first into the way he regarded the human condition prior to Christ's coming. Paul's anthropology (his teaching about human-ity) is at once individual and corporate; we sketch the latter first because it is more closely related to salvation history than his view of the individual. For Paul often contrasts what the situation of humanity was with what it is "now" in the Christian dispensation (see Gal 4:8–9; 1 Cor 6:11; Rom 3:21; 6:22; 7:6).

82   **(A) Sin.** In the period before Christ, human beings were all sinners who, despite their striving to live uprightly, never achieved that goal and never reached the destiny of glory intended by the creator for them; they failed to "hit the mark," as the basic meaning of *hamarta-nein,* "to sin," implies (see Rom 3:23; cf. 3:9,20). In his teaching on this pervasive influence of sin in humanity, Paul depends on the OT itself (Gen 6:5; 1 Kgs 8:46; Isa 64:5–7; Job 4:17; 15:14–16; Qoh 7:20; Sir 8:5). The tendency to sin is with one from birth: "I was brought forth in iniquity; in sin my mother conceived me" (Ps 51:5; cf. Jer 16:12). Human sin is contagious; the people of Judah "have followed their own hearts in stubborn-ness and have gone after the Baals, as their fathers taught them" (Jer 9:14; cf. 3:25). Such sin creates a solidarity of sinners, of contemporaries (Gen 11:1–9; 2 Sam 24:1–17; Num 16:22) and of successive generations (Ps 79:8; Exod 20:5; 34:7). This conviction about the universality of sin among human beings was born of experience, observa-tion, and corporate attestation: "No one has power to re-tain the spirit (i.e., not to die) or authority over the day of death; there is no relief from war, and wickedness will not deliver those who are given to it. All this I have observed, in applying my mind to all that is done under the sun" (Qoh 8:8–9; cf. 7:29). See further 1QH 4:29–30; Philo, *De vita Mos.* 2.29 § 147.

83   The etiological narrative of Gen 2–3 sought to explain how this sinful condition began. Its rich sym-bolism portrays ʾ*Adām,* "Man," and *Ḥawwāh,* "Eve" (ex-plained as ʾ *ēm kol ḥay,* "mother of all living [beings]"), as having brought sin into the world. The story teaches that sin did not originate with God, but began with human beings and that it has been around as long as they have been. Through it they lost their trusted intimacy with God and incurred death and all human misery (hard labor, pangs of travail, experience of evil). The cursing of the serpent symbolizes the lasting enmity that is to ensue between humanity and all evil. The notion of in-heritance of such a condition through the centuries is introduced in that the woman's offspring will always be confronted by evil; generation after generation of human beings will be seduced by the temptation to become like God, as were their forebears, Adam and Eve.

84   Strikingly enough, this etiological story has produced almost no echo in any protocanonical book of the OT. In these books Adam appears only in the open-ing genealogy of 1 Chr 1:1. In the so-called Lament over

the King of Tyre (Ezek 28:11–19) an allusion to Gen 3 is clear; but Adam is not named, and the transgression is identified as violence-filled "abundance of trade" (28:16), not the eating of fruit. Cf. Job 15:7. Only in the late deuterocanonical books and in intertestamental literature does the story of Eden reemerge, with notable emphases. In Tob 8:6 allusion is made to the creation of Adam and Eve as the origin of humanity; they are looked upon as models of married life. In Sir 36(33):10 the creation of "all human beings" is related to the creation of Adam from the dust. In Sir 40:1 the author alludes to the yoke of heavy toil laid on the children of Adam, and in Sir 49:16 the Hebr text speaks explicitly of "Adam's glory," as he is listed among the "famous men" of old (Sir 44:1). In contrast to this benign treatment of Adam stands Sir 25:24, "Sin began with a woman, and because of her we all die." The origin of sin is traced to Eve, and a causal connection is asserted between it and all human death. Death affects all her descendants because of what she did. Similarly, in *Jub.* 2–5 the story of Gen 2–3 is embellished, and two details are noteworthy: (1) at Adam's expulsion from Eden "the mouth of all beasts was closed . . . so that they could no longer speak" (3:28); and (2) the depravity of humanity that develops is traced not to Adam's trans-gression, but to the daughters of mankind seduced by the angels (5:1–4). The blessings bestowed by God on Adam are later recalled (19:27), as he is singled out and regarded as one of the patriarchs of Israel. In Wis Adam is not named, but he is clearly referred to as "child of the earth, the first-formed" (7:1). Indeed, Wisdom herself "pro-tected the first-formed father of the world, . . . delivered him from his transgression, and gave him strength to rule over all things" (10:1–2). In this late pre-Christian Jewish literature there is thus the tendency to exalt Adam and to trace "the glory of Adam" (1QS 4:22–23; CD 3:20–4:2; 1QH 17:13–15; cf. 4QpPsᵃ 1,3–4 iii 1–2) to his having been created (according to the P document of Gen 1:27) in the image of God. "God created man for incorruption and made him the image of his own eter-nity, but through the devil's envy death came into the world" (Wis 2:23–24). But whereas Adam is thus ex-tolled, sin, death, and evil are traced to Eve: "I created for him a wife that death should come to him by his wife" (*2 Enoch* 30:17); "Adam said to Eve, 'What have you done to us in bringing on us the great wrath [death], which rules over our whole race?'" (*Apoc. Mos.* 14). Cf. *Apoc. Mos.* 32:1; 2 Esdr. 3:7. In this late literature only the *Life of Adam and Eve* 44:2 may ascribe the "transgression and sin of all our generations" to "our parents" (in the pl.).

85   Paul, however, breaks with this late pre-Christian Jewish tradition about Adam's glory and returns to the earlier tradition of Gen 2–3 itself, ascribing not only death but even sin itself to Adam. In 1 Cor 15:21–22 he ascribes death to "one man": "As in [or, "through"] Adam all die, so too all shall be made alive in Christ." In that context death is contrasted with resur-rection to life (eternal), and Paul is thus thinking of total death, spiritual as well as physical. However, in Rom 5:12 he goes further, ascribing to Adam a causal connec-tion that brings not only death, but sin itself into human life: "Just as through one man Sin entered the world, and through that Sin, Death, and in this way Death spread to all human beings, since all have sinned." There follows a notorious anacoluthon (→ Romans, 51:53) because of a break in Paul's thought, as he feels obligated to explain his ascription of *sin* to Adam. Thus Paul attributes to Adam not only the condition of total death that affects every human being, but even the contagion of sin that is ratified by personal sins. This sense of Rom 5:12 does not depend on the vb. *hēmarton*, "all have sinned," being understood of some "habitual" sin, nor on the prep. phrase *eph' hō* understood as connoting some incorporation of all human beings in Adam (→ Romans, 51:56). Rather, the context of vv. 13-14 indicates such a causal connection, and esp. 5:19, "Just as through one man's disobedience the mass of mankind were made sinners, so by one man's obedience will the mass of them be made upright." The contrast of antitype and type, Christ and Adam, demands that the sinful condition of all human beings be attributable to Adam, just as their condition of uprightness is attributable to Christ alone.

86 Paul's indictment of the ungodliness and wickedness of Gentiles, who have suppressed the truth in their lives, is severe (Rom 1:18-23). He finds that they have no excuse for not honoring God as a result of what they have known about him from his creation (apart from his revelation of himself in the OT). "In not knowing God," the Gentiles "were in bondage to beings that were no gods . . . and were slaves to elemental spirits" (Gal 4:8-9). Their condition of servitude did not enlighten them about their degraded conduct (Rom 1:24-32; cf. 1 Cor 6:9-10). But the picture is not entirely negative, since Paul admits that Gentiles do at times fulfill some prescriptions of the Mosaic law (Rom 2:14), "being a law unto themselves," i.e., being aware through their consciences of some of what the Mosaic law positively prescribed for the Jews.

87 As for the Jews, who gloried in the possession of the Mosaic law as a manifestation of Yahweh's will and as a guide for their conduct (Rom 2:17-20; 3:2), Paul's indictment of them is equally telling. They may have the law, but they do not keep it (Rom 2:21-24). Not even their practice of circumcision or their possession of the oracles of salvation can save them from the wrath befitting sin (Rom 3:3-8). Without the gospel the whole human race, "all, both Jews and Greeks, are under the power of sin" (Rom 3:9). They find themselves in a condition of hostility toward God (2 Cor 5:19; Rom 5:10; 8:5-7), being dedicated neither to his honor and service (Rom 1:18) nor to honoring his name (Rom 2:24). (In the Deutero-Paulines their condition is depicted as an estrangement from God and bondage to Satan [Eph 2:2; 6:11-12; Col 1:13], which is a form of "death" [Eph 2:1,5; Col 2:13].)

88 Paul refers at times to sin in such a way that one might consider it a "debt" to be remitted (*paresis,* Rom 3:25), but more frequently he treats it as a force or power that has invaded human beings and is abetted by all their natural and fleshly inclinations. The individual wrongful deeds of human beings are "transgressions" (Gal 3:19; Rom 2:23; 4:15), "trespasses" (Gal 6:1; Rom 5:15-18,20), "sins" (*hamartēmata,* Rom 3:25). But Paul often personifies both Death and Sin, depicting them as actors on the stage of human history. *Hamartia* is thus an active evil force that pervades human existence. It "dwells" in humanity (Rom 7:17,23), deceives it, and kills it (Rom 7:11).

(On sin: Barrosse, T. A., *CBQ* 15 [1953] 438-59. Fiedler, P., *EWNT* 1. 157-65. Lyonnet and Sabourin, *Sin* 3-30, 46-57. Malina, B. J., *CBQ* 31 [1969] 18-34. Weder, H., *NTS* 31 [1985] 357-76.)

89   **(B) The Law and the Spirits.** The human condition before Christ was not only bondage to Sin and Death, but also an enslavement to the "spirits" of this world and to the law. Paul writes to former pagans of Galatia, "In not knowing God, you were enslaved to beings that were no gods" (4:8). It is debated whether these "gods" are to be identified with the "weak and beggarly elements" (4:9), the "elements of the world" (4:3), often interpreted as spirits controlling the world elements. See also 1 Cor 2:12. Paul further envisages the possibility of "angels" or "principalities" being hindrances to the love of God poured out on our behalf in Christ Jesus (Rom 8:38-39) or as announcing another gospel different from that which he preached (Gal 1:18). Indeed, angels are conceived of as promulgators of the law of Moses, which held humans in bondage; they thus symbolize its inferiority to the promises that God himself made to the patriarchs of old (Gal 3:19). For Paul such beings were not always evil; they may have been good or at least neutral (1 Cor 11:10; Gal 4:14). Yet if they have held sway over humanity until now, their rule has been broken by the coming of the *Kyrios,* Jesus Christ, because of whom Christians are even to judge the angels (1 Cor 6:3). Paul speaks of Satan only twice (2 Cor 11:14; 12:7), in contexts related to his own personal experience of opposition or suffering. He never speaks of the devil. (In this regard one notes a significant difference in the Deutero-Paulines: Christ's cosmic role includes a victor's place over all "thrones, dominations, principalities, and authorities" [Col 1:16; Eph 1:21], the "elements of the world" [Col 2:20] — or "whatever title is given to them" [Eph 1:21]. Whereas the sinful condition of former pagans resulted from a following of "the course of this world, the prince of the power of air, and the spirit at work in the children of disobedience" [Eph 2:2], Christians are now exhorted to put on the armor of God to stand firm against the wiles of the devil, because they "are contending not with flesh and blood, but with principalities, powers, the world-rulers of the present darkness, and evil spiritual hosts" [Eph 6:12]. Such a view is scarcely envisaged in Paul's uncontested letters.)

90 For Paul, however, human beings, especially Israel of old, were also enslaved to the law (Gal 3:23-24). Paul's attitude toward the law (*nomos*) has been called "the most intricate doctrinal issue in his theology" (Schoeps, *Paul* 168). His discussion of it is restricted to Gal, Phil, 1-2 Cor, and Rom (in the Deutero-Paulines reference to it is made only in Eph 2:15, where it is said to be "abolished"). Yet even in these few letters, which reflect the Judaizing problem that confronted Paul, *nomos* carries different connotations. (1) At times Paul uses it in a generic sense, "a law," (Gal 5:23, "against such [fruits of the Spirit] there is no law"; Rom 4:15b, "where there is no law, there is no transgression"; 5:13, "sin is not counted where there is no law"; 7:1a, "to those who know what law is"[?]). (2) Sometimes he uses *nomos* in a figurative sense: as a "principle" (Rom 3:27a; 7:21,23a), as a way of referring to "sin" (Rom 7:23c,25b) or "sin and death" (Rom 8:2b), as "human nature" (Rom 2:14d); indeed, even as a way of referring to "faith" (Rom 3:27b) or to "Christ" (Gal 6:2), or to the "Spirit" (Rom 8:2a) — speaking in the last three instances with oxymoron. (3) On a few occasions Paul uses *nomos* when he refers to the OT, either the Psalms (Rom 3:19a), the Prophets (1 Cor 14:21), or esp. the Torah (Gal 3:10b; 1 Cor 9:9, the only place where he speaks of the "law of Moses"; 14:34[?]; Rom 3:31b). (4) As for the rest, about 97 times in all, he uses *nomos* (with or without the article) to refer to the law of Moses (cf. Bultmann, *TNT* 1. 259-60).

91 In discussing Paul's attitude toward the law of Moses, one has to recall his three-stage view of human history (→ 14, 42 above), perceived through solely

Jewish spectacles. He sees it as a stage on which certain figures perform as actors. Among these struts *Anthrōpos*, "Human Being" (Rom 7:1), also called at times *Egō*, "I" (Rom 7:9), confronted not only by *Hamartia*, "Sin," *Thanatos*, "Death" (Rom 5:12), and *Nomos* (Rom 7:1), all personified as actors, but also by *Charis*, "Grace" (Rom 5:21). The roles of these figures come from Paul's own personification of them, attributing to them human acts: they "enter," "dwell," "reign," "revive," etc.

92   The intricate role that *Nomos* plays brings an anomaly into human life. As an actor on the stage of human life, *Nomos* is depicted as good: "The law is holy; the commandment is holy, upright, and good" (Rom 7:12), "noble" (*kalos*, 7:16), and "spiritual" (7:14), i.e., belonging to the sphere of God and not to that of this-worldly humanity. For it is "the law of God" (7:22,25b; 8:7), having come from him and destined to lead *Anthrōpos* to "life," i.e., to communion with God (7:10). In Gal 3:12 Paul even quotes Lev 18:5, constrained to admit that it formulates the purpose of the law: "The one who does them (i.e., the law's prescriptions) shall live by them," i.e., find "life" through them. Again, in Rom 9:4 Paul concedes that the giving of the law was one of the prerogatives of Israel, privileged by God with this means of knowing his will. It was addressed by God to all those who are under its authority and acknowledge it (Rom 3:19). Even when human beings reject the law, it continues to be good; for it is in a sense "God's oracles" (Rom 3:2) entrusted to privileged Israel.

Despite this God-given aid whereby Israel might find "life," Paul recognized that his "kinsmen by race" (Rom 9:3) were as much sinners as the law-less Gentiles (Rom 2:17–24 and 1:18–32); for "all have sinned and fall short of the glory of God" (Rom 3:23). Given this situation, Paul formulates the anomaly that the law creates in human life, boldly stating it when he quotes Ps 143:2 and makes a daring addition to it: "No human being shall be justified in the sight of God—*by observing the law*," lit., "by the deeds of the law." Whereas *Nomos* was supposed to lead *Anthrōpos* to life, as Lev 18:5 had promised, it proved incapable of doing so. Thus Paul states the *negative* role of the law in human history: "what the law could not do" (*to adynaton tou nomou*, Rom 8:3). It was incapable of giving life because it was an external norm expressing only dos and don'ts and possessed itself no life-giving force.

93   Paul went still further in depicting *Nomos* playing a *positive* role in human history. Arriving on the stage in the second act (from Moses to the Messiah), when it "was added" to the promises already made to Abraham in the first act, it is said to have been added "for the sake of transgressions" (Gal 3:19). "The law came in to increase transgression" (Rom 5:20). Though good in itself, it entered the scene to become the henchman or tool of another actor, *Hamartia*: The law thus became instead the very "force of sin" itself (1 Cor 15:56). Since the law supplied no *dynamis*, "force," whereby *Anthrōpos* could find life in obeying it, it ironically became the instrument of Sin, thus unleashing God's wrath on humanity: "For the law brings wrath" (Rom 4:15). Not sinful in itself, it aided sin: "What then shall we say? That the law is sin? By no means! Yet if it had not been for the law, I would not have known sin," because "in the absence of law sin was dead" (Rom 7:7–8). Paul depicts this positive role of the law as played in three ways.

94   (1) The law acted as an occasion (*aphormē*) for sin, instructing humanity in the material possibility of doing evil, either by forbidding what was indifferent (e.g., the eating of certain animals, Lev 11:2–47; Deut 14:4–21—cf. 1 Cor 8:8) or by arousing desires or annoying the conscience with external regulations about "forbidden fruit." Paul speaks of this role in Rom 7:5,8,11:

The *Egō* would not have known "what it is to covet, if the law had not said, 'You shall not covet'" (7:7).

(2) The law also acted as a moral informer; it gave humanity "a real knowledge of sin" (*epignōsis hamartias*, Rom 3:20), i.e., it revealed the true character of moral disorder as a rebellion against God, as a transgression of his will, and as an infidelity to the covenant with its stipulated regulations (e.g., the Decalogue). Paul admits, indeed, that "sin was in the world before the law was given; but sin is not registered where there is no law" (Rom 5:13). He would not have denied that human beings were evil during the first period, from Adam to Moses; but in that law-less period their sins were not booked against them as open rebellion or transgression. Human beings had sinned, but it was not "like the transgression of Adam" (Rom 5:14), who had violated a command of God (Gen 2:17; 3:6,11). Hence Paul could write generically, "Where there is no law, there is no transgression" (Rom 4:15). "Apart from the law Sin lies dead; I was once alive apart from the law, but when the commandment came, Sin revived, and I died" (Rom 7:8b–9a). So Paul depicts humanity first in the law-less period and then in the period of Torah.

(3) The law also laid a curse on the human beings under its authority. Paul derived this idea from Deut 27:26, quoted in Gal 3:10: "Cursed be everyone who abides not by all the things written in the book of the law and does them not!" In this way the law brought *Anthrōpos* "under condemnation" (Rom 8:1), because it was really a "dispensation of death" (2 Cor 3:7), a "dispensation of condemnation" (3:9). To formulate the anomaly pointedly, Paul exclaims, "Did that which is good, then, bring death to me?" (Rom 7:13). Did the God-given *Nomos* bring humanity into the clutches of *Thanatos*? Paul's answer: "Yes," and it so happened that the true colors of *Hamartia* might be shown up, "that sin might be shown to be sin" (Rom 7:13). All of this reveals the anomalous situation that *Anthrōpos* is in as a result of the law. But how could this be?

95   Paul has two different explanations: one in Gal and one in Rom—a difference that is not always duly noted.

(1) In Gal Paul sets forth an extrinsic explanation, ascribing to the law of Moses a temporary role in salvation history: "Now before faith came, we were held in custody under the law, imprisoned until faith was to be revealed; so the law was our custodian (*paidagōgos*) until Christ came that we might be justified by faith" (3:23–24). *Nomos* is depicted as the slave who in the Hellenistic world kept the school-age boy in tow, conducted him to and from classes, and supervised his study and conduct. The law thus disciplined humanity until the coming of Christ, during the period of *Anthrōpos'* minority. This provisional role of the law is seen also in its being added 430 years after the promises made to Abraham (3:17). Paul's chronology may be off by several centuries; but his point is that the law appeared on the stage *later*, and its inferiority to the promises is also manifest in that it was promulgated by angels (3:19; cf. Deut 33:2 LXX) and through a mediator (3:20, Moses). This temporary role of the law and its inferior status in salvation history did not nullify the "covenant previously ratified by God so as to make the promise void" (3:18).

(2) When Paul came to write Rom, he probably realized that the explanation of the anomaly set forth in Gal was not very satisfactory, not coming to grips with the inability of *Anthrōpos* to observe the God-given law. In composing Rom 7:13–8:4, Paul abandoned the extrinsic explanation and used a more intrinsic one, i.e., a philosophical explanation of the human predicament. In Rom

he shows that the difficulty is not with the law, but with humanity in its this-worldly condition of *sarx,* "flesh," alienated from God and hostile to him. Because of this condition *Anthrōpos* or *Egō* is weak and dominated by indwelling *Hamartia:* "I am carnal (*sarkinos*), sold under Sin" (7:14). The evil force, *Hamartia,* introduced into the world of human existence by Adam's transgression, has kept *Anthrōpos* in bondage because he is basically "carnal." Though he recognizes God's law with his "mind," he recognizes another principle at work in him that is at war with it: "It is no longer I that do it, but Sin that dwells in me" (7:17). Though the *Egō* "serves the law of God with the mind, it serves the law of Sin with the flesh" (7:25), i.e., the human mind acknowledges God's law for what it is, but its weak human condition as flesh is in bondage to Sin, which Paul even figuratively calls *nomos,* "the law of sin," an appositional genitive.

96 Paul has a solution for this anomaly created by the Mosaic law in human existence. For the observance of it Paul substituted faith in Christ Jesus, "who was handed over for our trespasses and raised up for our justification" (Rom 4:25). Yet once again his solution is proposed in two ways.

(1) In Gal, Paul emphasizes that in the third period of salvation history *Anthrōpos* has come of age and reached majority—no longer under the custodian, no longer "under guardians and trustees" and awaiting "the date set by the father" (4:2). That date has been reached; "in the fullness of time" Christ Jesus was sent by the Father to ransom us from bondage and free us from the law. As a result, the believer is no longer a school-age boy in tow, but a son in the full sense, who cries out *"Abba,* Father" and has become the heir of the promises made to Abraham, who himself found uprightness in God's sight not by observing the law but by faith (3:16-22; 4:3-6; cf. Gen 15:16). To be noted again is the temporal aspect of the solution that Paul presents in Gal; it corresponds to the temporal, extrinsic explanation of the anomaly. True, Paul does introduce an intrinsic element into Gal, when he speaks of the Spirit "sent into our hearts" (4:6), enabling us to cry *"Abba,* Father" and revealing our adoptive sonship. But even that adoption is still only in terms of a new stage in salvation history.

(2) In Rom, however, the solution is proposed in terms of the intrinsic anomaly itself. In 7:24 Paul exclaims, "Wretched being that I am, who will rescue me from this doomed body?" His answer: "Thanks be to God, (it is done) through Jesus Christ our Lord!" (→ Romans, 51:78). His answer is further explained in 8:1-4: "Now, then, there is no condemnation for those who are in Christ Jesus, for the law of the Spirit of life in Christ Jesus has freed me from the law of sin and death. For God has done what the law, weakened by the flesh, could not do; he sent his own Son in the likeness of sinful flesh and because of sin; he has condemned sin in the flesh in order that the just requirement of the law might be achieved in us who walk not according to the flesh but according to the Spirit." Here Paul's solution to the anomaly is not sought in terms of salvation history or the temporal character of the law. Rather, "God's love has been poured into our hearts through the holy Spirit that has been given to us" (5:5). This "Spirit of life in Christ Jesus" (8:2) brings it about that *Anthrōpos* now stands before God's tribunal as "justified," i.e., acquitted, through the cross and resurrection of Christ Jesus. Thus a human being achieves the status before God that the observance of the law of Moses was supposed to achieve. What the law could not achieve (8:3), God himself has brought about in Christ Jesus.

97 Such a solution of the anomaly of the law in human existence has to cope with the highly contested verse in Rom 10:4, where Paul speaks of Christ as *telos nomou,* the "end of the law." That expression might seem to allude to the "end" of the period of the Torah. But *telos* can mean either "end," "termination" or "goal," "purpose," "finis" (→ Romans, 51:101). In the former sense Christ would be the end of the law as the termination of all human striving to achieve uprightness in God's sight through the observance of the law. Whereas this sense might fit the temporal perspective of Gal, is it suitable for Rom? Unfortunately, the second sense of the phrase as a final or purposive expression has often been related to the "custodian" of Gal 3:24, understood as a teacher who trained the schoolboy for life. The law would have been schooling humanity for Christ. But the ancient *paidagōgos* was not a pedagogue or teacher in our modern sense, nor does *eis Christon* (Gal 3:24) have a final sense; it is temporal (see E. Käsemann, *Romans* [GR, 1980] 282). Ultimately, however, the final sense of *telos nomou* is preferable because of the Rom context; it is logically related to the metaphor of the chase or race in 9:31-33: "Gentiles who were not pursuing uprightness" actually achieved it (through faith in Christ Jesus), whereas "Israel that was pursuing the law of uprightness" did not "attain (that) law." This metaphor clearly involves a goal, and in v 32 Paul explains the reason of Israel's failure: it did not pursue that goal "through faith, but as if (it were based) on works," and so it tripped over the Isaian stumbling block (Isa 28:16; 18:14-15). Though Paul commends Israel's "zeal for God" (Rom 10:2), misconceived though it was, he depicts Israel "seeking to set up its own uprightness," instead of submitting to "the uprightness of God," i.e., to a process that begins in God who is himself *ṣaddîq* (Jer 12:1; Ps 11:7), or possibly even an "uprightness from God that depends on faith" (Phil 3:9). Such a pursuit implies a goal; hence the preference for *telos* as "goal" in 10:4. What Israel sought to attain has now been achieved through faith in Christ. Even Rom 3:21, "apart from (the observance of) the law" (*chōris nomou*), does not militate against this interpretation, because what was the goal of the law (uprightness in God's sight) is achieved through Christ and not by mere observance of the law. Similarly, 8:2-3 does not demand the translation of *telos* in 10:4 as "termination," since 8:4 makes it clear that "the just requirement of the law is fulfilled in us who walk not according to the flesh, but according to the Spirit." In other words, through grace and faith in Christ, God has brought it about that humanity fulfills what the law requires.

98 There is, however, yet another aspect of the law that is the key to the fuller understanding of Christ as the goal of the law in Rom. In Gal 5:6 Paul speaks of the sole validity of *pistis di' agapēs energoumenē,* "faith working itself out through love." He never explains this phrase in Gal; but one can find an explanation in Rom 13:8-10, where he speaks of the Mosaic law and strikingly regards love not only as something owed to others, but even as "the fulfillment of the law." Even if one were to insist that "fulfillment" is not necessarily the same as *telos,* the final sense of the latter term becomes clear when Paul says, "Love does no wrong to a neighbor; hence love is the fulfillment of the law." Faith in the Christian sense, introduced into human history by the death and resurrection of Christ Jesus, when it works itself out through love, is understood by Paul as accomplishing what the law was intended to accomplish. Only Paul has such a christological understanding of the law of Moses among NT writers.

99 With such an understanding of the law, Paul can even say, "I through the law died to the law that I might live for God" (Gal 2:19; for the understanding of this difficult verse, → Galatians, 47:20). Paul thinks of

the Christian as co-crucified with Christ, and what
Christ accomplished through his death and resurrection
is something in which Christians share so that they now
live for God. But how has this been accomplished by a
death to the law through the law? In Gal 3 Paul explains
how the curse that was leveled on those who had to live
under the law has been removed by Christ, who "redeemed us from the curse of the law, by becoming a
curse for us" (3:13). Here one cannot make use of
Aristotelian logic, for Paul's argument depends on two
different senses of the term "curse." In v 10 the "curse"
meant is that of Deut 27:26, whereas the "curse" in v 13
is rather that of Deut 21:23, "Cursed be everyone who
hangs upon a tree," a curse formulated against the dead
body of an executed criminal hanged from a tree as a
deterrent to further crime. It was not to be allowed to
hang beyond sundown, lest it defile the land. In late pre-
Christian Palestinian Judaism that curse was applied to
crucified persons: their dead bodies were not to be permitted to hang overnight (see *TAG* 125–46). Such a
curse was pronounced over the crucified body of Jesus;
and by becoming a "curse" in that sense, Paul argues,
Christ removed the "curse" of the law (Deut 27:26) from
those who were under it. This does not mean, however,
that the relation of human beings to God is completely
removed from the realm of law, but that that relation,
though still judicial and forensic, finds a mode of
achievement or fulfillment other than through "deeds of
the law." In this way Rom 7:4,6 are to be understood.

100   A final comment: Paul often uses the expression *erga nomou*, "deeds/works of the law," i.e., deeds
prescribed by the Mosaic law (Gal 2:16; 3:2,5,10; Rom
2:15; 3:20,27,28). One even gets the impression that this
phrase was a sort of slogan current in his day. Yet it is
never found as such either in the OT or in later rabbinic
literature (see *TDNT* 2. 646; Str-B 3. 160–62). It is used,
however, in QL (*ma'ăśê tôrâ*, "deeds of the law," 4QFlor
[= 4Q*174*] 1–2 i 7; cf. 1QS 6:18; 1QpHab 7:11). At
times Paul shortens the phrase and uses merely *erga*,
"deeds" (Rom 4:2,6; 9:11,32; 11:6). From this shortening
stems the difficulty that his slogan later encountered,
when his teaching about justification by grace through
faith, apart from works, was being heard in a different
Christian context. Recall the correction (not of his
teaching, but of a caricature of it) that is found in Jas
2:14–26; see Reumann, *"Righteousness"* [→ 70 above], §
270–75, 413.

(On the Law: Benoit, P., *Jesus and the Gospel* [London, 1974] 2.
11–39. Bruce, F. F., *BJRL* 57 [1974–75] 259–79. Cranfield,
C. E. B., *SJT* 17 [1964] 43–68. Dülmen, A. von, *Die Theologie
des Gesetzes bei Paulus* [SBM 5; Stuttgart, 1968]. Fitzmyer, J. A.,
TAG 186–201. Gundry, R. H., *Bib* 66 [1985] 1–38. Hahn, F.,
ZNW 67 [1976] 29–63. Hübner, H., *Law in Paul's Thought*
[Edinburgh, 1984]. Lang, F., in *Rechtf* 305–20. Larsson, E., *NTS*
31 [1985] 425–36. Räisänen, H., *Paul and the Law* [WUNT 29;
Tübingen, 1983]. Sanders, E. P., *Paul, the Law, and the Jewish
People* [Phl, 1983]. Schäfer, P., *ZNW* 65 [1974] 27–42.
Wilckens, U., *NTS* 28 [1982] 154–90.)

101   (C) Human Beings. Part of Paul's picture
of humanity before Christ's coming is the makeup of a
human being (*anthrōpos*). Inability to observe the Mosaic
law stems in part from the carnal condition of a human
being as *sarkinos*. What does Paul mean by this? To explain, we must try to ascertain what he means by *sōma*,
"body," *sarx*, "flesh," *psychē*, "soul," *pneuma*, "spirit," *nous*,
"mind," and *kardia*, "heart." Paul does not describe a
human being *in se;* he rather hints at different relations of
humanity vis-à-vis God and the world in which he or
she lives. These terms, then, do not designate parts of
human beings, but rather aspects of the person as seen

from different perspectives (→ OT Thought, 77:66).

102   A popular, common conception of the human
being as made up of two elements is found at times in
Paul's writings (1 Cor 5:3; 7:34; 2 Cor 12:2–3). The visible, tangible, biological part made up of members is
called *sōma*, "body" (Rom 12:4; 1 Cor 12:14–26).
Though Paul seems at times to mean by it only the flesh,
blood, and bones (Gal 1:16; 1 Cor 13:3; 2 Cor 4:10;
10:10; Rom 1:24), he normally means far more. A human
being does not merely have a *sōma*; one is *sōma*. It is a way
of saying "self" (Phil 1:20; Rom 6:12–13; cf. 1 Cor 6:15
and 12:27). It denotes a human being as a whole, complex, living organism, even as a person, esp. when he or
she is the subject to whom something happens or is the
object of one's own action (1 Cor 9:27; Rom 6:12–13;
8:13; 12:1; cf. Bultmann, *TNT* 1. 195). A corpse is not
a *sōma*, but there is no form of human existence for Paul
without a body in its full sense (see Phil 3:21; 1 Cor
15:35–45; but cf. 2 Cor 5:2–4; 12:2–3; 5:6–8). When
Paul uses *sōma* in a pejorative sense, speaking of its
"desires or passions" (Rom 6:12; 8:13), of the "body of
sin" (Rom 6:6), of the "body of humiliation" (Phil 3:21),
or of "the body of death" (Rom 8:3), he really means the
human being under the sway of some power like sin
(Rom 7:14,18,23; 8:13). In these cases, the "body" is the
sin-ruled self (Rom 7:23), the human condition before
the coming of Christ—or even after that coming for
those who do not live in Christ.

103   In the OT the word *bāśār* expresses the idea of
both "body" and "flesh." Paul reflects this OT notion
when he uses *sarx* as a synonym for *sōma* (1 Cor 6:16,
quoting Gen 2:24; 2 Cor 4:10–11; cf. Gal 4:13; 6:17). In
these cases "flesh" means the physical body. The phrase
"flesh and blood" denotes a human being (Gal 1:16;
1 Cor 15:50), connoting natural frailty. It is a late OT expression (Sir 14:18; 17:31). But *sarx* alone can denote the
whole human being, human nature (Rom 6:19). However, the more typically Pauline use of flesh connotes
natural, material, and visible human existence, weak and
earthbound, the human creature left to itself: "No flesh
can boast of anything before God" (1 Cor 1:29). "People
controlled by the flesh think of what pertains to the
flesh" (Rom 8:5); they cannot please God (Rom 8:8). The
"deeds of the flesh" are set forth in Gal 5:19–21, and it
should be superfluous to note that for Paul "flesh" is not
restricted to the area of sex. He identifies the *egō* and *sarx*
and finds no good in them (Rom 7:18). This notion is
prominent in the Pauline contrast of "flesh" and "Spirit,"
which compares a human being subject to earthly tendencies with a human being under the influence of God's
Spirit (Gal 3:3; 4:29; Rom 8:4–9,13). For the OT idea of
flesh, → OT Thought, 77:64.

104   Similarly, *psychē* is not just the vital principle of
biological activity, but as in the OT, it denotes a "living
being, living person" (Hebr *nepeš;* 1 Cor 15:45). It expresses the vitality, consciousness, intelligence, and volition of a human being (1 Thess 2:8; Phil 2:30; 2 Cor
12:15; Rom 11:3; 16:4). Even when it seems to mean
nothing more than "self" (2 Cor 1:23; Rom 2:9; 13:1), it
connotes the conscious, purposeful vitality of the self.
Still it is only the earthly, natural aspect of a living
human being. Normally, Paul does not use *psychē* in a
derogatory sense; but it is clearly the life of *sarx*, not the
life dominated by the Spirit. Hence he calls the one who
lives without the Spirit of God *psychikos*, "material"
(1 Cor 2:14), not "spiritual" (*pneumatikos*). For the OT
idea of *nepeš*, → OT Thought, 77:66.

105   In 1 Thess 5:23 Paul lines up a threesome: *sōma*,
psychē, and *pneuma*. In this case, *pneuma* does not
designate the holy Spirit (cf. Rom 8:16; 1 Cor 2:10–11).
Joined to *sōma* and *psychē*, which denote the whole human

being under different aspects, *pneuma* would seem to be yet another aspect. But it is not always easy to distinguish *pneuma* in this sense from *psychē* (cf. Phil 1:27; 2 Cor 12:18). If anything, *pneuma* suggests the knowing and willing self and, as such, the aspect that is particularly apt to receive the Spirit of God. Sometimes, however, it is a mere substitute for the personal pronoun (Gal 6:18; 2 Cor 2:13; 7:13; Rom 1:9; Phlm 25). For the OT idea of spirit, → OT Thought, 77:32-34.

106   *Nous*, "mind," for Paul seems to describe a human being as a knowing and judging subject; it designates a capacity for intelligent understanding, planning, and decision (cf. 1 Cor 1:10; 2:16; Rom 14:5). In Rom 7:23 it is the understanding self that hears God's will addressed to it in the law, agrees with God's will, and accepts it as its own. It is the capacity to recognize what can be known about God from his creation (Rom 1:20): the *nooumena* are the things that the *nous* can grasp. There is really little difference in Paul's use of *nous* and *kardia,* "heart," which, as in the OT, often means "mind." If anything, *kardia* would connote the more responsive and emotional reactions of the intelligent, planning self. For it "loves" (2 Cor 7:3; 8:16), "grieves" (Rom 9:2), "plans" (1 Cor 4:5), "lusts" (Rom 1:24), and "suffers" (2 Cor 2:4). It doubts and believes (Rom 10:6-10), is hardened (2 Cor 3:14), and is impenitent (Rom 2:5); but it can be strengthened (1 Thess 3:13; Gal 4:6; 2 Cor 1:22). For the relation of "mind" and "conscience," → 144 below.

107   All these aspects of human existence are summed up in *zōē,* "life," a gift of God that expresses the concrete existence of a human being as the subject of his or her own actions. Yet life before the coming of Christ is one lived "according to the flesh" (Rom 8:12; cf. Gal 2:20). With all the capacities for conscious, intelligent, and purposeful planning of one's life, a human being without Christ remains one who has not been able to achieve the destined goal. Of this situation Paul can only say, "All have sinned and fall short of the glory of God" (Rom 3:23), the latter being for him Christian destiny (cf. Rom 8:18-23). This sketch of the human condition before the coming of Christ has at times hinted at the difference that Christ's coming has made for humanity; a fuller description of that difference now follows.

(Gundry, R. H., *Sōma in Biblical Theology with Emphasis on Pauline Anthropology* [SNTSMS 29; Cambridge, 1976]. Jewett, R., *Paul's Anthropological Terms* [AGJU 10; Leiden, 1971]. Kümmel, W. G., *Man in the New Testament* [rev. ed.; London, 1963]. Robinson, J. A. T., *The Body: A Study in Pauline Theology* [SBT 5; London, 1952]. Sand, A., *Der Begriff "Fleisch" in den paulinischen Hauptbriefen* [BU 2; Regensburg, 1967]. Stacey, W. D., *The Pauline View of Man in Relation to Its Judaic and Hellenistic Background* [London, 1956].)

108   **(II) Humanity in Christ.** Christ's salvific activity has brought about a new union of humanity with God. Paul calls it a "new creation" (→ 79 above), since it has introduced a new mode of existence into human history in which Christ and the Christian enjoy, as it were, a symbiosis. Human beings share in this new life by faith and baptism, which incorporate them into Christ and his church; this incorporation finds a unique expression in the eucharist. To such elements of Pauline theology, often regarded as aspects of the subjective redemption, we now turn.

109   **(A) Faith and Love.** The experience whereby a human being begins to apprehend the effects of the Christ-event is for Paul *pistis,* "faith." This experience is a reaction to the gospel, to the "preached word" (Rom 10:8). Paul's most elaborate treatment is found in Rom 10, a chapter that must be studied in detail. The experience begins with a "hearing" (*akoē,* 10:17) of the gospel

or of the "word" about Christ and his salvific role. This hearing results in an assent of the mind, which acknowledges that "Jesus is Lord" in one's existence (10:9). It ends, however, as *hypakoē pisteōs,* usually translated as the "obedience of faith" (1:5; 16:26), but which really means "a hearing-under" and connotes for Paul the "submission" or the "commitment" of the whole person to God in Christ. "If with your lips you acknowledge that Jesus is Lord and with your heart you believe that God raised him from the dead, you will be saved" (10:9). Thus the faith that one is asked to put in God or Christ (1 Thess 4:14; 1 Cor 1:21-23; Rom 4:24) is not a mere intellectual assent to the proposition that "Jesus is Lord." It is a vital, personal commitment, engaging the whole person to Christ in all his or her relations with God, other human beings, and the world. It is thus an awareness of the difference the lordship of Christ has made in human history. This awareness underlies the statement of Paul, "It is no longer I who live, but Christ who lives in me; and even now the physical life I am living (lit., what I now live in the flesh) I live through faith in the Son of God who loved me and gave himself for me" (Gal 2:20). Such a faith far transcends the OT idea of fidelity. As *hypakoē,* it is a full acceptance of Christian dedication (Rom 6:16-17; 16:19), to the exclusion of all reliance on self or on what Paul calls "boasting" (3:27). The basis of this experience is a new union with God in Christ, an ontological reality that is not immediately perceived by human consciousness but must be allowed to pervade the psychological level of existence so that one's conscious activity is guided by it. This is the integrated Christian life that Paul envisages (Gal 2:20; 2 Cor 10:5).

110   Such faith is a gift of God, just as is the whole salvific process (Rom 3:24-25; 6:14; 11:6; 12:3). This is the underlying notion in the whole discussion of Abraham's faith in Rom 4. (In the Deutero-Pauline passage of Eph 2:8 this idea becomes explicit: "It is by his [Christ's] favor that you have been saved through faith; and this does not come from you; it is the gift of God.") But since God accosts a human being as a responsible person, that person can accept or reject his gracious call. Faith is thus only the acceptance or the response on the part of the human being who realizes that the initiative rests with God. The one who does not respond is regarded by Paul as disobedient and committed to "the god of this age" (2 Cor 4:4), hence culpable and "perishing."

111   In the polemical contexts in which Paul rejects the "deeds of the law" as a means to justification, he stresses that this justification comes through "faith" (Gal 2:16; Rom 3:28; cf. Phil 3:9). However, the full sense of that faith demands that the Christian manifest it in conduct through deeds of love. "In union with Christ Jesus neither circumcision nor the lack of it means anything, but only faith working itself out through love" (Gal 5:6). This is why Paul continually exhorts his Christian converts to the practice of all sorts of good deeds, why he includes a hortatory section in almost every one of his letters. Christian faith is not only a freedom from the law, from sin, and from the *sarx*-self, but also a freedom to serve others in love or charity (Gal 5:13). For Paul love (*agapē*) is an openness, an outgoing concern and respect of one person for another/others in concrete acts that result in the diminution of the lover's "self." See Phlm 9-12; Gal 5:13; Rom 12:9-13. It is a way of Christian life that is extraordinary (*kath' hyperbolēn,* 1 Cor 12:31), surpassing even all the charismatic manifestations of the Spirit. Interpreters may debate about the character of 1 Cor 13, whether it is hymnic or a rhetorical description (→ 1 Corinthians, 49:61), but one finds there Paul's praise of love in Christian life: its indispensability, its 11 characteristics (positive and negative), and its perdurance and superiority. But love is also for Paul the summation of the law (Rom 13:8–10; Gal 5:14). In other words, the person motivated by a faith that works itself out through love is not in reality concerned about "the deeds of the law," but finds himself or herself doing all that the law has required. In this way faith for Paul turns out to be more than a mere assent to monotheism (cf. Jas 2:14–26). The root of such love is the Spirit (Gal 5:22) and ultimately the love of the Father; for the "love of God" is poured out into our hearts (Rom 5:5; 8:28), and thus it is just as much a grace of God as faith itself. Such service of others is not accomplished without the activity of God in human beings: "God is at work in you both to will and to work for his good pleasure" (Phil 2:13). This is why Paul formulated the hymn to the love of God made manifest in Christ Jesus (Rom 8:31–39), and speaks of the controlling love of Christ in Christian life (2 Cor 5:14).

(On faith: Barth, G., *EWNT* 3. 216–31. Binder, H., *Der Glaube bei Paulus* [Berlin, 1968]. Bultmann, R. and A. Weiser, *TDNT* 6. 174–228. Daalen, D. H. van, *ExpTim* 87 [1975–76] 83–85. Kuss, O., *Auslegung und Verkündigung* [Regensburg, 1963] 1. 187–212. Lohse, E., *ZNW* 68 [1977] 147–63. Lührmann, D., *Glaube im frühen Christentum* [Gütersloh, 1976]. Michel, O., *NIDNTT* 1. 587–606. Walter, N., *NTS* 25 [1978–79] 422–42.
  On love: Bornkamm, G., *Early Christian Experience* [NY, 1969] 180–93. Descamps, A., *RDTour* 8 [1953] 123–29, 241–45. Furnish, V. P., *The Love Command in the New Testament* [Nash, 1972] 91–131. Lyonnet, S., *Foi et salut selon Saint Paul* (*Epître aux Romains 1,16*) [AnBib 42; Rome, 1970] 211–31. Navone, J. J., *Worship* 40 [1966] 437–44. Perkins, P., *Love Commands in the New Testament* [NY, 1982]. Sanders, J. T., *Int* 20 [1966] 159–87. Spicq, C., *Agape in the New Testament* [3 vols.; St. Louis, 1963–66] 2. 1–341. Wischmeyer, O., *ZNW* 74 [1983] 222–36.)

112   (B) Baptism. Paul's stress on the role of faith in the human response to the Christ-event is, however, adequately understood only when it is linked to his teaching on baptism. This initiatory rite, which incorporates human beings into Christ and the church, already existed in pre-Pauline Christianity; but Paul developed its significance. The formulas he uses (Rom 10:9; 1 Cor 12:3) possibly echo primitive baptismal creeds; yet it is Paul who teaches that the condition of Christians as "sons of God through faith" is owing to their baptism "into Christ" (Gal 3:26–27). Christians so washed have been "sanctified and made upright" (1 Cor 6:11). They have "put on Christ," as if they were putting on a new garment (an allusion to the robe worn in the baptismal ceremony?). (In Eph 5:26 a disciple of Paul may allude to the rite itself, in speaking of a "washing of water" and a "word" [= formula?].)

113   Through baptism the Christian is actually identified with the death, burial, and resurrection of Christ. The early church preserved a recollection that Jesus referred to his own death as a "baptism" (Mark 10:38; Luke 12:50). But Paul's view of the effects of the Christ-event led him to identify, as it were, Christians with the very phases of Christ's salvific activity; "one died for all, therefore all died" (2 Cor 5:14). Prima facie, this may seem like a mere assertion of the vicarious nature of Christ's death, but it must be understood in the light of the following: "Through baptism we have been buried with him in death, so that just as Christ was raised from the dead through the Father's glory, so we too might have a new life. For if we have grown into union with him by undergoing a death like his, so we shall do by being raised to life like him" (Rom 6:4–5). Paul's comparison of baptism with the death, burial, and resurrection of Christ is often thought to allude to the rite of immersion. Though this mode of baptism may be difficult

to certify for the 1st cent. AD, Paul's symbolism is sufficiently preserved if the baptized person is thought of as somehow under the water. Identified with Christ in death, the Christian dies to the law and to sin (Gal 2:19; Rom 6:6,10; 7:4). Identified with Christ in his resurrection, one shares a new life and the very vitality of the risen Christ and his Spirit (1 Cor 6:17). The Christian "has grown together" with Christ through this likeness of his death, burial, and resurrection (Rom 6:5). The one who dies in baptism becomes a "new creation" (Gal 6:15; 2 Cor 5:17). (The Deutero-Paulines will express it in terms of the Christian already enjoying a new "heavenly" existence [Col 2:12–13]. "Though we were dead because of our offenses, God has made us live again with Christ. By his grace we are saved, and he has raised us up with Christ Jesus and made us sit down with him in the heavenly realm" [Eph 2:5–6].)

114   This is no mere individualistic experience for Christians, but a corporate one, for through baptism a special union of Christians is formed. "We have all, Jews or Greeks, slaves or free men, been baptized in one spirit to form one body" (1 Cor 12:13; cf. Gal 3:28). Human beings, therefore, attain salvation by identification with a salvific community (*Heilsgemeinde*), by incorporation into the "body of Christ." This is why Paul compares baptism to Israel's passage through the waters of the Reed Sea (1 Cor 10:1–2); in the waters of baptism the new "Israel of God" (Gal 6:16) is formed.

115   Paul never quotes a primitive baptismal formula such as Matt 28:19; yet he seems to echo an early trinitarian theologoumenon on baptism: "You have been washed, sanctified, and made upright in the name of the Lord Jesus Christ and in the Spirit of our God" (1 Cor 6:11). The baptized Christian becomes a "temple of the holy Spirit" (1 Cor 6:19), an adopted child of the Father in virtue of the communication of the Spirit (Gal 4:6; Rom 8:9,14–17). The Spirit so received is the constitutive principle of filial adoption and the dynamic source of Christian life and conduct. "All who are led by God's Spirit are children of God" (Rom 8:14). Such passages are the basis of the later teaching about the relation of the baptized Christian to the persons of the Trinity. Only indirectly does Paul make use of a baptismal formula, "in the name of" (*eis to onoma tou . . .* , 1 Cor 6:11; 1:13,15). Though it expresses proprietorship and suggests that the baptized person becomes the property of Christ, Paul prefers to speak of the person as baptized "into Christ" (Rom 6:3; Gal 3:27), i.e., symbolically plunged into Christ himself.

(Beasley-Murray, G. R., *Baptism in the New Testament* [London, 1962]. Bieder, W., "*Baptizō*, etc." *EWNT* 1. 459–69. Bornkamm, *Early Christian* [→ 111 above] 71–86. Delling, G., *Die Zueignung des Heils in der Taufe* [Berlin, 1961]. Dunn, J. D. G., *Baptism in the Holy Spirit* [Naperville, 1970]. Frankemölle, H., *Das Taufverständnis des Paulus* [SBS 47; Stuttgart, 1970]. Hartman, L., "'Into the Name of Jesus,'" *NTS* 20 [1973–74] 432–40. Iacono, V., "Il battesimo in S. Paolo," *RivB* 3 [1955] 348–62. Kaye, B. N., "*Baptizein eis* with Special Reference to Romans 6," *SE VI* 281–86. Kuss, O., "Zur vorpaulinischen Tauflehre im Neuen Testament," *Auslegung und Verkündigung* [→ 111 above] 1. 98–120; "Zur paulinischen und nachpaulinischen Tauflehre im Neuen Testament," ibid. 121–50. Lampe, G. W. H., *The Seal of the Spirit* [2d ed.; London, 1967]. Schnackenburg, R., *Baptism in the Thought of St. Paul* [Oxford, 1964]. Voss, G., "Glaube und Taufe in den Paulusbriefen," *US* 25 [1970] 371–78.)

116   (C) Incorporation into Christ. To appreciate the effects of faith and baptism as seen by Paul, we turn to his ideas on this intimate union of Christ and Christians, expressed by pregnant prepositional phrases and by the figure of the "body of Christ."
117   (a) PREPOSITIONAL PHRASES. Paul uses mainly

four prepositions with "Christ" as their object to suggest different facets of Christ's influence on the life of the Christian. The use of each of them is varied and often rich with nuances. We can indicate here only some of the most important implications. The four prepositions are *dia, eis, syn,* and *en.*

118   The prep. *dia,* "through," normally expresses the mediation of Christ in a statement of which the subject is the Father. It may denote the mediation of Christ in some activity of his earthly ministry (1 Thess 5:9), of his present status as Lord (Rom 1:5), or of his eschatological role (1 Thess 4:14). It is a phrase that opens up, as it were, the path that leads to the Christian's experience *en Christō,* and eventually *syn Christō.*

119   The prep. *eis,* "into," esp. in the phrase *eis Christon,* has at times been taken as an abridgment of *eis to onoma Christou,* "into the name of Christ." With the vb. *baptizein* this is possible (→ 115 above). But *eis Christon* is used also with *pisteuein,* "believe." In fact, the phrase is found mainly in these two contexts: belief or baptism in Christ. It pregnantly expresses the movement toward Christ that these initial experiences imply, the beginning of the Christian's condition *en Christō* (see 1 Cor 10:2). Torn from one's original condition ("in Adam," 1 Cor 15:22), from one's natural inclinations ("in the flesh," Rom 7:5), and from one's ethnic background ("under the law," 1 Cor 9:20), one is solemnly introduced "into Christ" in faith and baptism. *Eis Christon* denotes, then, the movement of incorporation.

120   The prep. *syn,* "with," not only is used with the object "Christ" but also is compounded with verbs and adjectives and can in these constructions express a double relation of the Christian to Christ. Either it suggests an identification of the Christian with the preeminently salvific acts of the Christ-event, or else it denotes an association of the Christian with Christ in eschatological glory. On the one hand, the identification is seen above all in the compounds of *syn-.* Aside from generic expressions like *symmorphos,* "formed with him," *symphytos,* "grown together with him," *synklēronomos,* "heir with him," these words refer to some phase of Christ's existence from his passion and death on: *sympaschein,* "suffer with," *systaurousthai,* "be crucified with," *synapothnēskein,* "die with," *synthaptesthai,* "be buried with," *syndoxazesthai,* "be glorified with," *synzan,* "live with." (In the Deutero-Paulines one also finds *synegeirein,* "raise with.") By contrast, the Christian is never said to be born with Christ, to be baptized with him, or to be tempted with him. Such events of the life of Jesus were not significant for Paul's soteriology (→ 18 above). On the other hand, *syn Christō* expresses the association of the Christian with Christ in eschatological glory; one is destined to be "with Christ" (1 Thess 4:17 [significantly, *syn Kyriō*]; Rom 6:8; 8:32; 2 Cor 4:14). Hence *syn* pregnantly expresses two poles of the Christian experience, identification with Christ at its beginning, and association with him at its term. In the meantime the Christian is *en Christō.*

121   The prep. *en,* "in," with the object "Christ" occurs 165 times in Paul's letters (including *en Kyriō,* "in the Lord," and *en autō,* "in him"). Since the studies of A. Deissmann, the prep. has often been interpreted in a local, spatial sense, and *Christos* has been understood mystically of the glorified Lord identified with the Spirit as some spiritual atmosphere in which Christians are bathed. This is supposed to be Paul's mysticism. But subsequent studies of E. Lohmeyer, A. Schweitzer, F. Büchsel, *et al.* have brought out other aspects of the phrase (metaphysical, eschatological, dynamic, etc.). A detailed summary is impossible here, but several distinctions should be noted. (1) With the object *Kyrios* the phrase usually occurs in greetings, blessings, exhortations

(often with imperatives) and formulations of Paul's apostolic plans and activity. The title *Kyrios* denotes, then, the influence of the risen Lord in practical and ethical areas of Christian conduct. *En Kyriō* hardly ever reflects Jesus' historical, earthly activity or his eschatological function; it implies rather his present, sovereign dominion in the life of the Christian. Paul tells the Christian to become "in the Lord" what one really is "in Christ." (2) With the object *Christos* the phrase frequently has an instrumental sense, when it refers to the historical, earthly activity of Jesus (Gal 2:17; 2 Cor 5:19; Rom 3:24; [Col 1:14; Eph 2:10]). In this sense the phrase is often close in meaning to *dia Christou.* (3) The most common use of *en Christō* is to express the close union of Christ and the Christian, an inclusion that connotes a symbiosis of the two. "If anyone is in Christ, one is a new creature" (2 Cor 5:17). This vital union, however, can also be expressed as "Christ in me" (Gal 2:20; 2 Cor 13:5; Rom 8:10; [Col 1:27; Eph 3:17]). The result is that one belongs to Christ (2 Cor 10:7) or is "of Christ"—a "mystical" genitive expressing the same idea (Rom 16:16). The phrase should not be limited to a spatial dimension, for it often connotes a dynamic influence of Christ on the Christian who is incorporated into him. The Christian so incorporated becomes a member of the whole Christ, of the body of Christ. Needless to say, at times one hesitates about the precise nuance (instrumental? inclusive?).

(Bouttier, M., *En Christ* [Paris, 1962]. Büchsel, F., "'In Christus' bei Paulus," *ZNW* 42 [1949] 141–58. Deissmann, A., *Die neutestamentliche Formel "in Christo Jesu"* [Marburg, 1892]. Dupont, J., *Syn Christo: L'Union avec le Christ suivant Saint Paul* [Bruges, 1952]. Elliger, W., "*Eis*," "*En*," "*Syn*," *EWNT* 1. 965–68, 1093–96; 3. 697–99. Hess, A. J., "*Dia*," *EWNT* 1. 712–13. Kuss, O., *Der Römerbrief* [Regensburg, 1957–78] 319–81. Lohmeyer, E., "*Syn Christo*," in *Festgabe für Adolf Deissmann* [Tübingen, 1927] 218–57. Neugebauer, F., *In Christus:* En Christō: *Eine Untersuchung zum paulinischen Glaubensverständnis* [Göttingen, 1961]. Schweitzer, A., *The Mysticism of Paul the Apostle* [NY, 1931]. Schweizer, E., "Dying and Rising with Christ," *NTS* 14 [1967–68] 1–14. Wikenhauser, A., *Pauline Mysticism* [NY, 1961].)

122   (b) BODY OF CHRIST. Paul uses the expression *sōma Christou,* "body of Christ," in various senses: of his historical, crucified body (Rom 7:4), of his eucharistic body (1 Cor 10:16; cf. 11:27), and of the church (1 Cor 12:27–28; [cf. Col 2:17; Eph 4:12]). In the last sense it is a figurative way of expressing the corporate identity of Christians with Christ. Absent from his early letters (1 Thess, Gal, Phil) the term appears in 1 Cor, the letter wherein Paul copes with divisive Christian factions. Christ is not divided, he tells them, formulating a teaching about the unity of all believers in Christ. The symbol of unity is the figure of the body with its members. The origin of the figure is disputed (see Robinson, *The Body* 55–58; Bultmann, *TNT* 1. 299; Hill, "The Temple"). But it is probably derived by Paul from contemporary Hellenistic notions about the state as the body politic. This idea is found as early as Aristotle (*Polit.* 5.2.7 [1302b, 35–36]) and became part of Stoic philosophy (see Cicero, *Or. Philip.* 8.5.15; Seneca, *Ep.mor.* 95.52; Plutarch, *Coriolanus* 6.3–4). In *Moralia* 426A, Plutarch recalls the ideas of the Stoic Chrysippus and asks, "Is there not often in this world of ours a single body (*sōma hen*) composed of disparate bodies, such as an assembly (*ekklēsia*) or an army or a chorus, each one of which happens to have a faculty of living, thinking, and learning . . . ?" (The collocation of *sōma* and *ekklēsia* here is important.) In this case the philosophical figure expresses the moral unity of members (citizens, soldiers) conspiring together to achieve a common goal (e.g., peace, prosperity, and well-being). In Cor 12:12–27 the figure as used by Paul scarcely transcends this idea of a moral union of the members: the spiritual gifts enjoyed by the Corinthians (wisdom, faith, healing, prophecy, tongues, etc.) are to be used "for the common good" (12:7), not for its disruption. As all the members and limbs of the body conspire for its well-being, so it is with the body of Christ. The usage is similar in the hortatory context of Rom 12:4–5.

123   But more is suggested elsewhere by Paul. In 1 Cor 6:15 he warns against the defilement of the human body by sexual license: "Don't you know that your bodies are members of Christ? Am I to take away the members of Christ and make them members of a harlot? No indeed! Or don't you know that a man who has to do with a harlot makes one body with her? For 'the two,' Scripture says, 'shall become one flesh.'" The union implied here is more than moral; somehow Christ and the Christians share in a union that connotes "one flesh." Recall what was said above (→ 102–3) about the meaning of *sōma* and *sarx* as designations, not of the physical body as something distinct from the soul, but as equivalents of the whole person under different aspects. In speaking of the "body of Christ" Paul is not speaking merely of members of a society governed by a common objective, but of members of Christ himself; their union is not only corporate, but somehow corporal. A similar conclusion is suggested by 1 Cor 10:16–17, where Paul insists on the union of all Christians achieved by their share in the one eucharistic bread and cup: "Because there is one loaf, we, many as we are, are one body, for we all share the one loaf." The unity of Christians is thus derived from their physical consumption of the one loaf; the oneness implied transcends a mere extrinsic union effected by cooperation to attain a common goal. (The figure of marriage in Eph 5:22–23 also points to the same transcendent union.)

124   And yet Christians and Christ are not physically united like the yolk and the albumen of an egg. Hence theologians later called the union "mystical," an adj. that Paul does not use. The ontological reality that is the basis of the union is the possession of the Spirit of Christ: "We have all been baptized in one Spirit to form one body" (1 Cor 12:13; cf. Rom 8:9–11). The possession of this Spirit springs from the incorporation of believers through faith and baptism; it is, as it were, the term of Paul's christocentric soteriology.

125   However, Paul rarely speaks in 1 Cor and Rom explicitly of the church as the body of Christ; the closest one comes to this identification is 1 Cor 12:27–28. (In the Deutero-Paulines, where, when the cosmic significance of Christ has dawned, a disciple of Paul links the themes of body and church, which have often appeared separately in the uncontested letters. Now the church is explicitly identified as the body of Christ in various formulations: "He [Christ] is the head of the body, the church" [Col 1:18; cf. 1:24]; God "made him the supreme head of the church, which is his body" [Eph 1:23]. In Eph there is great emphasis on the unity of the church: Christ has broken down the barrier between Jew and Greek; all now share one salvation, for he has "reconciled both in one body to God through the cross" [2:16]. "There is only one body and one Spirit, just as there is only one hope in the calling you have received: one Lord, one faith, one baptism, one God and Father of us all" [4:4]. And yet with all this stress on unity and the oneness of Christians in Christ, there is no mention of *mia ekklēsia*, "one church." Is this just fortuitous? Part of the answer appears below in the discussion of "church" [→ 133–37]. In the Pastoral Letters, otherwise so

preoccupied with church interests, the "body of Christ" makes no appearance.

126   Intimately related to the body theme in the Deutero-Paulines is that of the head: Christ is "the head of the body, the church" [Col 1:18; cf. Eph 1:23]. It may seem that this is a mere extension of the body theme. Having portrayed the union of Christ and Christians by the analogy of the body and its parts, the disciple of Paul would have concluded that Christ must be its head because the head is the most important part of the body, as can be illustrated in contemporary Hellenistic medical writers [see Benoit, *Jesus* 73]. But Paul himself had used the head theme independently of the body theme in his uncontested letters, not as a figure of unity but as one of subordination. In 1 Cor 11:3–9 Paul argues that women should wear a head-covering in liturgical assemblies because, among other reasons, the order of creation in Gen seems to call for the subordination of woman to husband—the head-covering would be a sign of this status: "Christ is the head of every man, while a woman's head is her husband, and Christ's head is God" [11:3]. Paul plays on two senses of "head": the physical head, which must be covered, and the figurative head, like "head" of a department. In 1 Cor 11, however, there is no mention of "body." There is another instance of this sense of "head" in Col 2:10, where Christ is said to be "the head of every principality and power." In the Deutero-Paulines the body theme and head theme are joined in the picture of the church; and the analogy is exploited with details drawn from contemporary medical teaching: "Let us rather hold to the truth with love; thus we shall fully grow up into union with him who is head, Christ. For in dependence on him the whole body is bonded and knit together" [Eph 4:15–16]. Another aspect of this subordination of Christians to Christ underlies the comparison of Christian marriage and the church: "Just as the church is in subjection to Christ, so too should wives be subject to their husbands" [Eph 5:24].

127   The Christian experience, then, rooted in the historical reality of the physical body of Christ, becomes a living, dynamic union with the individual *risen body* of the *Kyrios*. The corporate union of all Christians must grow to fill out the whole Christ, the *plērōma* of the cosmic Christ [Eph 1:23]. In the lives of individual Christians this means apostolic suffering that fills up what was lacking in Christ's tribulations on behalf of the church [Col 1:24]. This does not mean that apostolic suffering adds anything to the redemptive value of the cross; rather, such suffering on behalf of the church continues in time that which Christ began, but did not finish in time. It must continue until the cosmic dimensions of the church are achieved.)

(On the body of Christ: Benoit, *Jesus and the Gospel* [→ 100 above] 2. 51–92. Daines, B., *EvQ* 50 [1978] 71–78. Harrington, D. J., *God's People in Christ* [Phl, 1980]. Havet, J., in *Littérature et théologie pauliniennes* [ed. A. Descamps; RechBib 5; Bruges, 1960] 185–216. Hegermann, H., *TLZ* 85 [1960] 839–42. Hill, A. E., *JBL* 99 [1980] 437–39. Käsemann, *Perspectives* 102–21. Meeks, W. A., in *God's Christ and His People* [Fest. N. A. Dahl; ed. J. Jervell and W. A. Meeks; Oslo, 1977] 209–21. Ramaroson, L., *ScEs* 30 [1978] 129–41. Robinson, *The Body* [→ 107 above]. Schweizer, E., *EWNT* 3. 770–79. Weiss, H.-F., *TLZ* 102 [1977] 411–20. Worgul, G. S., *BTB* 12 [1982] 24–28.)

128   **(D) Eucharist.**   As mentioned above (→ 122–23), Paul uses "body of Christ" also to mean his eucharistic body. "As for the bread that we break, is it not a participation in the body of Christ?" (1 Cor 10:16). In the eucharistic body Paul finds a source not only of the union of Christians with Christ, but also of Christians among themselves. The earliest account of the institution of the eucharist in the NT is found in 1 Cor 11:23-25. Though it may be related in origin to the Lucan account (22:15-20) and differs somewhat from that of Mark (14:22-25) and Matt (26:26-29), it is an independent record of that institution, possibly derived from the liturgy of the Antiochene church. Paul passes it on as a tradition (→ 16 above). His account is not so much an eyewitness's report as a quotation of a liturgical recitation of what the "Lord" did at the Last Supper, even with its directive rubric, "Do this in memory of me" (11:24). Paul does not recount the event in and for itself, but alludes to it in discussing other problems. He mentions this meal of the Lord as part of his criticism of the abuses that had crept into Corinthian community suppers associated with the eucharist (1 Cor 11) or in the course of his remarks on the eating of meat sacrificed to idols (1 Cor 10).

129 For Paul the eucharist is above all the "Lord's Supper" (1 Cor 11:20), the repast at which the new people of God eats its "spiritual food" and consumes its "spiritual drink" (1 Cor 10:3-4). In this act it manifests itself as the community of the "new covenant" (1 Cor 11:25; cf. Jer 31:31; Exod 24:8), as it shares in "the table of the Lord" (1 Cor 10:21; cf. Mal 1:7,12). The communion of this people denotes not only its union with Christ and with one another, but also a proclamation of the Christ-event itself and its eschatological character.

130 Three aspects in particular reveal Paul's understanding of the eucharist as the source of Christian unity. (1) It is the ritual act whereby Christ's presence with his people is concretized. Paul quotes, in effect, the rite of liturgical celebration and comments on its meaning in the immediate context (1 Cor 11:27-32): Christ's body and blood are identified with the bread and the wine so consumed by the community. Any "unworthy" sharing in that repast brings judgment on the Christian, for one would be "profaning the body and blood of the Lord" (11:27). Since the Lord is identified with such food, those who partake of it may not violate its sacred character and his presence by abuses of individualism, of disregard of the poor, or of idol-worship. One cannot argue away the realism of the identity of Christ with the eucharistic food in Paul's teaching, even if Paul does not explain how this identity is achieved. Through this presence the eucharistic Christ alone *brings about* unity of believers in Paul's view.

131 (2) As a memorial and proclamation of Christ's sacrificial death, the eucharist is a rallying point. "As often as you eat this bread and drink this cup, you proclaim the death of the Lord until he comes" (1 Cor 11:26). The community is to do this "in memory of" him (11:24). The repetition of this ritual act, in which the Lord's body and blood are made present to nourish his people, becomes a solemn proclamation of the Christ-event itself (it is "the death of the Lord"—"for you") announcing to those who share in the meal the salvific effect of that death. A sacrificial aspect is proclaimed through reference to covenant blood (11:25): The eucharistic cup is the blood of the "new covenant" (Jer 31:31), an allusion to Moses' sealing of the covenant of old with the blood of sacrificed animals (Exod 24:8). This allusion invests the shedding of Christ's blood with an efficacy analogous to that of the sacrifice sealing the covenant of Sinai (cf. 1 Cor 10:14-21).

132 (3) There is also an eschatological aspect to the eucharist, for the proclamation of the Lord's death must continue "until he comes" (a reference to the parousia). Thus, only Christ in his risen, glorious status fully accomplishes the salvation of those who partake of the table of the Lord. From such a view of the eucharist

undoubtedly comes the ancient acclamation *maranatha*, "Our Lord, come!" (1 Cor 16:22; → 53 above).

(Boismard, M.-E., "The Eucharist according to Saint Paul," in *The Eucharist in the New Testament: A Symposium* [ed. J. Delorme; Baltimore, 1964] 123-39. Bornkamm, *Early Christian* [→ 111 above]. Chenderlin, F., *"Do This as My Memorial"* [AnBib 99; Rome, 1982]. Delling, G., "Das Abendmahlsgeschehen nach Paulus," *KD* 10 [1964] 61-77. Hahn, F., *The Worship of the Early Church* [Phl, 1973]. Jeremias, J., *The Eucharistic Words of Jesus* [Phl, 1977] 101-5. Käsemann, E., "The Pauline Doctrine of the Lord's Supper," *ENTT* 108-35. Kilmartin, E. J., *The Eucharist in the Primitive Church* [EC, 1965]. Marxsen, W., *The Lord's Supper as a Christological Problem* [FBBS 25; Phl, 1970]. Neuenzeit, P., *Das Herrenmahl* [SANT 1; Munich, 1960]. Reumann, J., *The Supper of the Lord* [Phl, 1985] 1-52. Schweizer, E., *The Lord's Supper according to the New Testament* [FBBS 18; Phl, 1967].)

133 **(E) The Church.** For all its rarity in the Gospels (Matt 16:18; 18:17), the word *ekklēsia* is found frequently in the Pauline corpus. In Acts it does not occur in the first four chapters and thereafter is found in the sense of "church" only once (5:11, in a Lucan comment) before the story of Paul begins (8:1); after that 21 times. In Paul's uncontested letters it is found 44 times (in the Deutero-Paulines 15 times; in the Pastorals 3 times). This situation seems to suggest that it took some time before early Christians became aware of their union in Christ as *ekklēsia*. The abundant use of the term in Paul's letters does not really contradict this. Incidentally, in the three accounts of Paul's conversion in Acts, where the heavenly voice says, "Saul, Saul, why are you persecuting me? I am Jesus whom you are persecuting" (9:4-5; 22:7-8; 26:14-15), the "church" is never explicitly mentioned. Consequently, one should hesitate to include as an element of Paul's experience near Damascus an awareness of the Christian community either as "church" or as "the body of Christ." The latter is a Pauline way of conceiving of the Christian community; it is not Lucan. Hence the "me" of Acts 9:4; 22:7; 26:14 is not to be associated with the body-of-Christ notion in Pauline theology.

134 The data in Paul's letters also reveal a certain development in his thinking about the "church." In 1 Thess, Paul uses *ekklēsia* both to designate a local church (1:1; cf. 2 Thess 1:1) and in the phrase "church of God" (1 Thess 2:14). In the first sense it denotes the unity of the Thessalonians developed from their common faith and worship; in the second it is given by Paul as a title of predilection to the primitive Judean communities. In the LXX *ekklēsia* was used to translate Hebr *qāhāl*, the term given to the assembly of the Israelites, particularly in their desert wanderings. They were "the *ekklēsia* of the Lord" (Deut 23:2) or "the *ekklēsia* of the people of God" (Judg 20:2; cf. Acts 7:38). It also designated the Israelites in liturgical gatherings (1 Kgs 8:55; 1 Chr 29:10). However, Paul's expression *ekklēsia tou theou* is unique (except possibly for Neh 13:1, where Sinaiticus reads *Kyriou* against all other mss.); but its exact equivalent is found in QL (1QM 4:10, where "congregation of God" is to be inscribed on one of the standards to be borne into the eschatological war). Given such a Palestinian Jewish background for the phrase, it probably became an apt designation for the primitive communities of Judea, the first units formed in Christian history and peculiarly linked through their Jewish roots with the Israelite "congregation" of old.

135 In Paul's great letters the same double sense of *ekklēsia* is found again, designating both the local churches of Galatia, Judea, Macedonia, and Cenchreae (Gal 1:2,22; 2 Cor 8:1; Rom 16:1) and the primitive communities of Judea as "church of God" (1 Cor 11:16). The latter titular use, however, is now applied also to the church of Corinth (1 Cor 1:2; 2 Cor 1:1). According to Cerfaux (*ChTSP* 113), this titular usage does not designate the "universal church" as manifested at Corinth, but is rather a Pauline way of flattering a church with which he has had such stormy relations, now that they are being smoothed out. He accords to the Corinthian community the title that he has previously used of the mother churches of Palestine (cf. 1 Cor 10:32). But in this extension of the titular usage one also detects a broadening of Paul's understanding of *ekklēsia;* it is beginning to denote the Christian community as transcending local barriers. This is the seed of Paul's teaching about the universality of the church. Precisely in 1 Cor one detects the planting of this seed, since when Paul warns the Corinthians against submitting ordinary matters of dispute for settlement to the judgment of "people who are nothing in the church" (1 Cor 6:4), one can seriously query whether he means merely the local church. Similarly, in 1 Cor 14:5,12 he speaks of "doing the church some good." *Per se,* these could be references to the local community, but one senses in the term at least the beginnings of a more general sense (cf. 1 Cor 12:28). Strangely enough, in Rom, the letter often regarded as the most representative of Paul's theology, *ekklēsia* is absent, save for five instances in chap. 16, all of which refer to local churches (vv 1,4,5,16,23). Part of the problem is that this chapter in Rom has a character quite different from the rest of Rom, even if one admits that it is integral to the letter (→ Romans, 51:10).

136   (In the Deutero-Paulines, *ekklēsia* plays an important role as a crucial part of the "mystery of Christ." The barrier between Jew and Greek has been broken down, and all human beings have been reconciled to God in Christ's "body, the church" [Col 1:17]. According to the view of Paul's disciple, the cosmic Christ is now the head of the church, which is his body; he is preeminent in all creation. For God "has put all things under his feet and made him the supreme head of the church, which is his body, the fullness of him who is filled out, all in all"

[Eph 1:22-23]. In this passage the church is said to be "the fullness" [*plērōma*] of Christ; contrast Col 1:19; 2:9. It is given cosmic dimensions, and even the spirits, who are not members of the church, are said to learn about the Father's plan of salvific activity in Christ through the church [Eph 3:9-11]. Note the order in the praise given by Paul's disciple to the Father for his wisdom "through the church and through Christ Jesus" [Eph 3:21] – the church becomes so important that it seems to take precedence over Christ!)

137   For Paul himself the "church" represents a development in his thinking about Christ's role in salvation. It is the concrete manifestation among human beings who have been baptized "in one Spirit to form one body" (1 Cor 12:13). The unity of these believers in one body, i.e., the church that transcends all local barriers, is Paul's great contribution to Christian theology. It is a unity that is derived from the single purpose of the divine plan for the salvation of human beings in Christ Jesus. Paul came eventually to look on the "church of God" as a unit transcending both Jews and Greeks, yet incorporating them both when they became believers (1 Cor 10:32).

(On the church: Berger, K., *ZTK* 73 [1976] 167-207. Best, E., *One Body in Christ* [London, 1955]. Cerfaux, *ChTSP.* Coenen, L., *NIDNTT* 1. 291-307. Gärtner, B., *The Temple and the Community in Qumran and the New Testament* [SNTSMS 1; Cambridge, 1965]. Hainz, J., *Ekklesia: Strukturen paulinischer Gemeinde-Theologie und Gemeinde-Ordnung* [MTS 9; Regensburg, 1972]. Holmberg, B., *Paul and Power: The Structure of Authority in the Primitive Church as Reflected in the Pauline Epistles* [ConBNT 11; Lund, 1978]. Käsemann, *NTQT* 252-59. Lanne, E., *Irénikon* 50 [1977] 46-58. Minear, P. S., *Images of the Church in the New Testament* [2d ed.; Phl, 1975]. Pfammatter, J., *Die Kirche als Bau* [AnGreg 110; Rome, 1960]. Roloff, J., *EWNT* 1. 998-1011. Schlier, H., *Christus und die Kirche im Epheserbrief* [BHT 6; Tübingen, 1930]. Schmidt, K. L., *TDNT* 3. 501-36. Schnackenburg, R., *The Church in the New Testament* [NY, 1965]; also in *Ortskirche Weltkirche* [Fest. J. Döpfner; Würzburg, 1973] 32-47. Schweizer, E., *TLZ* 86 [1961] 161-74.)

PAUL'S ETHICS

138   **(I) Dual Polarity of Christian Life.** No sketch of Pauline theology would be adequate without a discussion of Paul's ethical teaching. All his letters not only teach fundamental truths about the Christ-event (his christocentric soteriology) but also exhort Christians to upright ethical conduct. And it is not simply a matter of the hortatory sections of his letters, for exhortations are found elsewhere as well. There is, however, a certain tension between his theology and his ethics: Does it make a difference what justified, reconciled, or redeemed Christians do in their lives? On the one hand, Paul insists that Christians have become a "new creation" (Gal 6:15), in whom Christ really lives (Gal 2:20). We have already mentioned the integral Christian life that this elicits (→ 109). Christians have been justified by grace through faith in Christ Jesus (Rom 3:24-25) so that they are no longer "under law, but under grace" (Rom 6:15). On the other hand, even they still have to be delivered "from the present wicked world" (Gal 1:14; cf. 1 Cor 7:26,29-31). You must "not be conformed to this world, but be transformed by the renewal of your mental attitude so that you may assess the will of God – what is good, pleasing to him, and perfect" (Rom 12:2). Paul still

tells the Christian who has experienced the effects of the Christ-event: "Work out your own salvation in fear and trembling" (Phil 2:12c); "for we must all appear before Christ's judgment-seat so that each one may receive good or evil for what one has done in the body" (2 Cor 5:10). Yet Paul knows that "God is the one working in you, both to will and to work for his good pleasure" (Phil 2:13; → 71). The Christian, then, lives a life of dual polarity.

139   The dual polarity that characterizes Christian life is the reason why Paul insists that the Christian energized by the Spirit of God (Rom 8:14) can no longer sin or live a life bound by a merely natural, earthly horizon. One is no longer *psychikos,* "material," but *pneumatikos,* "spiritual"; one must fasten, then, one's gaze on the horizon of the Spirit that comes from God (1 Cor 2:11). Whereas the material person does not welcome what comes from the Spirit, the spiritual person is alive to everything, does not stifle the Spirit or disregard its promptings, but tests all things and holds on to what is good (1 Thess 5:19-22). This dual polarity also explains Christian freedom, in which Paul's Galatian converts are exhorted to stand firm (5:1): freedom from the law, freedom from sin and death, freedom from the self (Rom 6:7–11,14; 7:24–8:2). But that freedom is not an antinomian license. Paul vigorously rejects the idea that Christians should blatantly sin in order to give God more scope for his mercy and gracious justification (Rom 6:1; cf. 3:5–8). The "law of Christ" (Gal 6:2), when scrutinized, is seen to be a "law of love," explained in terms of bearing one another's burdens (in a context of fraternal correction). Even more explicitly, Paul repeats commandments 5, 6, 7, and 8 of the Decalogue, summing them up as "You must love your neighbor as you do yourself" (Rom 13:8–10) and concluding, "So love fully satisfies the law." This is precisely "the law of the Spirit" (Rom 8:2), so that Christ has not simply substituted another legal code for the law of Moses. The "law of the Spirit" may be a reflection of Jer 31:33, but it is more likely that Paul has coined the phrase to describe the Spirit's activity in terms of *nomos,* about which he had just been speaking. The Spirit's law of love is the new inner source and guide of the life by which the *pneumatikos* lives; it is the ontic principle of new vitality, whence springs the love that must interiorize the Christian's entire ethical conduct. And yet it is to such spiritual persons that Paul addresses his varied exhortations to virtuous conduct. We can only single out here a few of his characteristic exhortations, but before doing so we must say a few more words about the relation of Paul's ethics to his theology.

140   (II) Pauline Ethics and Theology. Patristic writers, medieval scholastics, and Reformation and Post-Tridentine theologians had often used Paul's ethical teachings in treatises on moral theology, but it was only in 1868 that H. Ernesti made the first attempt to synthesize his ethics. (Part of the reason for the neglect of the latter stemmed from the way earlier theologians viewed the relation between revelation and natural law, between philosophical and Christian ethics.) Ernesti's starting point was that human beings were called to a status of righteousness before God, to an obedience to God's will, which is the absolute and unconditioned norm of Christian morality. He emphasized the freedom of the Christian in ethical conduct because of the gift of the Spirit. From the outset the study of Pauline ethics was dominated by vestiges of the Reformation debate about justification by faith and freedom from the law (see Furnish, *Theology* 242–79). In the early part of the 20th cent. A. Schweitzer sought to free the discussion of Pauline ethics from the doctrine of justification and emphasized rather the eschatological aspect of such teaching. Paul's ethics have an interim, temporary character and are grounded in his "mysticism," i.e., the Christians' share in the dying and rising of Christ. Being "in Christ," Christians are in possession of the Spirit, the life-principle of the new existence on which they have embarked. Later on (1924) R. Bultmann again related Paul's ethics to his doctrine of (forensic) justification by faith and introduced a distinction between the Pauline *indicative* (you are a justified Christian) and the Pauline *imperative* (then live like a Christian): "*Because* the Christian is freed from sin through justification, he ought to wage war against sin." Yet the righteousness of the Christian is an eschatological phenomenon, since it does not depend on human accomplishment, moral or otherwise, but solely on the event of God's grace, an otherworldly phenomenon. This righteousness is not an "ethical" quality; it involves no change in the moral character of a human being. Faith is obedience, and human ethical acts do not bring about righteousnes; they are rather the expressions of the radical obedience to which humans are called. Still later, C. H. Dodd (1927) introduced the distinction between *kērygma* and *didachē,*

which roughly corresponded for him to "theology" and "ethics," or to "gospel" and "law." A new age has dawned (realized eschatology), and Paul is the promulgator of its new law, a Christian pattern for conduct to which a Christian is obliged to conform, "the law of Christ" (Gal 6:2). Reverting to an emphasis of A. Schweitzer, of H. D. Wendland, and of others, V. P. Furnish (1968) considered eschatology to be "the heuristic key" to Pauline theology, the lever to organize the other elements in his teaching, including the ethical. His understanding of Pauline eschatology differs from Schweitzer's and is nuanced enough to be acceptable (→ 47 above); and certainly eschatology is important in Pauline ethics (see Phil 2:12; 2 Cor 5:10; Rom 2:6–11). Yet it is not the heuristic key to the whole (see my review, *PSTJ* 22 [1969] 113–15). The best way to explain the relation of Paul's ethics to his theology, in my opinion, is to see the former as a detailed, concrete explanation of the love that is the way for Christian faith to work itself out. In other words, Gal 5:6 ("faith working itself out through love") again proves its importance in Pauline thinking, for it is the link between Pauline theology and ethics.

(On ethics: Austgen, R. J., *Natural Motivation in the Pauline Epistles* [2d ed.; Notre Dame, 1969]. Bultmann, R., *ZNW* 23 [1924] 123–40; *Exegetica* [Tübingen, 1967] 36–54. Corriveau, R., *The Liturgy of Life: A Study of the Ethical Thought of St. Paul in His Letters to the Early Christian Communities* [Montreal, 1970]. Enslin, M. S., *The Ethics of Paul* [Nash, 1957]. Ernesti, H., *Die Ethik des Apostels Paulus in ihren Grundzügen dargestellt* [Göttingen, 1868]. Furnish, V. P., *Theology and Ethics in Paul* [Nash 1968]. Glaser, J. W., *TS* 31 [1970] 275–87. Gnilka, J., in *Mélanges bibliques* [Fest. B. Rigaux; ed. A. Descamps, *et al.;* Gembloux, 1970] 397–410. Hasenstab, R., *Modelle paulinischer Ethik* [Tübingen theologische Studien 11; Mainz, 1977]. Merk, O., *Handeln aus Glauben: Die Motivierungen der paulinischen Ethik* [MarTS 5; Marburg, 1968]. Moule, C. F. D., in *Christian History and Interpretation* [Fest. J. Knox; ed. W. R. Farmer, *et al.;* Cambridge, 1967] 389–406. Romaniuk, K., *NovT* 10 [1968] 191–207. Schnackenburg, R., *The Moral Teaching of the New Testament* [NY, 1965] 261–306; *Die sittliche Botschaft des Neuen Testaments* [HTKNT Suppl.; Freiburg, 1986–]. Strecker, G., *NTS* 25 [1978–79] 1–15. Watson, N. M., *NTS* 29 [1983] 209–21. Westerholm, S., *NTS* 30 [1984] 229–48.)

141   (III) Christian Life and Its Demands. Paul's ethical teaching, in its specific and concrete recommendations, echoes at once his Pharisaic, Jewish background (→ 10–11) and his Hellenistic background (→ 12). When Paul exhorts his readers to proper Christian conduct, his recommendations fall under various headings. Some, which have been analyzed form-critically, are the generic ethical lists of virtues and vices (and *Haustafeln*). Others are more specific.

142   (A) Ethical Lists. In his uncontested letters Paul incorporates catalogues of virtues and vices that should or should not characterize Christian life (Gal 5:19–23; 1 Cor 5:10–11; 6:9–10; 2 Cor 6:6–7; 12:20; Rom 1:29–31; 13:13 [Col 3:5–8,12–14; Eph 5:3–5]). The eschatological reference in these catalogues is often evident: "People who do such things will not inherit the kingdom of God" (Gal 5:21). Since "kingdom of God" is hardly an operative element in Pauline teaching (occurring elsewhere only in 1 Thess 2:12; 1 Cor 4:20; 6:9–10; 15:24,50; Rom 14:17), the association of it with these catalogues seems to mark them as elements of pre-Pauline catechetical instruction, which he has inherited and made use of. These lists have been compared with similar ones found in Hellenistic (esp. Stoic) philosophical writings and in Palestinian Jewish texts (e.g., of the Essenes; cf. 1QS 4:2–6,9–11).

(Easton, B. S., "New Testament Ethical Lists," *JBL* 51 [1932] 1–12. Kamlah, E., *Die Form der katalogischen Paränese im Neuen*

Testament [WUNT 7; Tübingen, 1964]. Segalla, G., "I cataloghi dei peccati in S. Paolo," *SPat* 15 [1968] 205-28. Vögtle, A., *Die Tugend- und Lasterkataloge im Neuen Testament* [NTAbh 16/4-5; Münster, 1936]. Wibbing, S., *Die Tugend- und Lasterkataloge im Neuen Testament und ihre Traditionsgeschichte unter besonderer Berücksichtigung der Qumran-Texte* [BZNW 25; Berlin, 1959].)

143   (In the Deutero-Paulines [Col 3:18-4:1; Eph 5:21-6:9] and in the Pastoral Letters [1 Tim 2:8-15; Titus 2:1-10] one finds another literary list, the so-called *Haustafel* (a term from Luther's *Deutsche Bibel* that has become a standard designation even in English). Roughly it would mean a "domestic bulletin board," for it lists the Christian obligations or duties of members of the household, i.e., the *familia* of the Greco-Roman world: husbands and wives, parents and children, and masters and slaves. These lists show a Pauline disciple coping with social ethical problems of his day, although they list little more than generalities.)

(Crouch, J. E., *The Origin and Intention of the Colossian Haustafel* [FRLANT 109; Göttingen, 1973]. Schrage, W., "Zur Ethik der neutestamentlichen Haustafeln," *NTS* 21 [1974-75] 1-22. Weidinger, K., *Die Haustafeln: Ein Stück urchristlicher Paränese* [UNT 14; Leipzig, 1928].)

144   (B) **Conscience.** We might well have included this element of Paul's teaching under "Human Beings" above (→ 101-7), but prefer to treat it here because of the relation to his ethics. "Conscience" is the capacity to judge one's actions either in retrospect (as right and wrong) or in prospect (as a guide for proper activity). Paul's word for it is *syneidēsis* (= Lat *con-scientia*). It is related to *nous*, "mind" (Rom 7:23,25), but is best treated separately. It has no counterpart in the MT or in QL, but enters the Judaic tradition in the LXX (Job 27:6; Qoh 10:20; cf. Sir 42:18; Wis 17:10). The claim that it was derived by Paul from Stoic philosophy is debatable; more likely it is from the popular Hellenistic philosophy of his day. Initially *syneidēsis* denoted "consciousness" (of human activity in general); eventually it was applied to consciousness of moral aspects, at first as "bad conscience," then as "conscience" in general. Of the 30 NT occurrences, 14 are found in 1-2 Cor and Rom (and 6 in the Pastorals): 1 Cor 8:7,10,12; 10:25,27,28,29bis; 2 Cor 1:12; 4:2; 5:11; Rom 2:15; 9:1; 13:5. Three passages are particularly important: (1) Rom 2:14-15, where Paul recognizes that by means of "conscience" Gentiles perform some of the prescriptions of the Mosaic law and are thus a "law" unto themselves. (2) 1 Cor 8:7-12, where Paul calls upon the Christian to respect the weak conscience of a fellow Christian troubled about eating food consecrated to idols. (3) 1 Cor 10:23-29, where Paul discusses a similar problem. In 2 Cor 1:12 Paul relates the conscience to the problem of boasting; in Rom 8:16; 9:1 he relates it to the gift of the Spirit. Paul's teaching on the subject has often been compared to that in later rabbinic texts about the *yēṣer hārāʿ* and *yēṣer haṭṭôb*, "evil impulse" and "good impulse."

(Coune, M., "Le problème des idolothytes et l'éducation de la syneidêsis," *RSR* 51 [1963] 497-534. Davies, W. D., "Conscience," *IDB* 1. 671-76. Jewett, *Anthropological Terms* [→ 107 above] 402-46. Maurer, C., "Synoida, Syneidēsis," *TDNT* 7. 899-919. Pierce, C. A., *Conscience in the New Testament* [SBT 15; London, 1955]. Stelzenberger, J., *Syneidēsis im Neuen Testament* [Abh. z. Moraltheologie 1; Paderborn, 1961]. Stendahl, K., "The Apostle Paul and the Introspective Conscience of the West," *HTR* 56 [1963] 199-215. Therrien, G., *Le discernement dans les écrits pauliniens* [EBib; Paris, 1973] 263-301. Thrall, M. E., "The Pauline Use of *syneidēsis*," *NTS* 14 [1967-68] 118-25.)

145   (C) **Natural Law.** Related to the question of "conscience" in Paul's teaching is that of the so-called

natural law. Because it is a debated issue, we have not included it under Paul's view of the law of Moses (→ 89-100 above), which is complicated enough. Moreover, Pauline teaching that bears on it is better related to his ethics. The issue arises mainly because of Rom 2:14-15, "When Gentiles who do not have the law do by nature (*physei*) what the law prescribes, they are a law (*nomos*) to themselves, even though they do not have the law. They show that the deed prescribed by the law is written on their hearts, while their conscience also bears witness and their conflicting thoughts accuse or perhaps excuse them." The *nomos* of v 14 has been related to "another law" or to "the law of my mind" in Rom 7:23, probably wrongly since the prime analogate there is the Mosaic law. In Rom 2:14 we have one of the figurative uses of *nomos* (→ 90). Though in 1 Cor 11:14 Paul does argue from "nature" (*physis*), in Rom 2:14 he may merely be quoting a contention of others (perhaps one should set quotation marks about "by nature" in Rom 2:14). Also, in speaking of a law written on the heart, Paul may only be echoing Jer 31:33 or Isa 51:7. And so it is difficult to be certain about his views of the "natural law," an idea more at home in Gk philosophy. Perhaps the most that should be admitted is that the idea should be regarded as the *sensus plenior* of Paul's teaching (in view of the patristic tradition about it; → Hermeneutics, 71:49-51).

(On natural law: Dodd, *New Testament Studies* [→ 9 above] 129-42. Flückiger, F., *TZ* 8 [1952] 17-42. Greenwood, D., *BTB* 1 [1971] 262-79. Lyonnet, S., *VD* 41 [1963] 238-42. McKenzie, J. L., *BR* 9 [1964] 1-13.)

146   (D) **Prayer and Asceticism.** These are prime considerations of Christian life, because one sees Paul himself not only engaged in them, but also speaking about them in a reflex manner. For Paul "prayer" is the explicit recollection of the Christian that one lives in the presence of God and has the duty of communing with him in adoration, praise, thanksgiving, and supplication. Paul's letters are permeated with expressions of prayer; the formal thanksgiving in each letter, except Gal and 2 Cor, is an integral part of his writing—and not merely conformity with an epistolary custom. The object of his prayer is at times himself (1 Thess 3:11; 2 Cor 12:8-9), his converts (1 Thess 3:9-10,12-13; Phil 1:9-11; 2 Cor 13:7-9), or his former coreligionists, the Jewish people (Rom 10:1). Paul often exhorts his readers to pray (1 Thess 5:16-18; Phil 4:6; Rom 12:11-12); it is the mark of the mature Christian disciple, who prays to God as *Abba* (Gal 4:1-6). The ground of Christian prayer is the Spirit (Rom 8:15-16,26-27), who aids Christians in praying, interceding on their behalf (8:28-30). Paul prays to the Father (*theos*) through Christ and in the Spirit (Rom 1:8; 7:25). Examples of his prayers: doxologies (2 Cor 11:31; Phil 4:21; Rom 1:25; 11:33-36 [Eph 3:20-21]); intercessory petitions (1 Thess 3:11-13; 5:23-24); benedictional confessions (2 Cor 1:3-7 [Eph 1:3-14]); thanksgivings (1 Thess 1:3-4; Phil 1:3-11; 1 Cor 1:4-9; Rom 1:8-12). Paul could even consider his preaching of the gospel a form of worship (Rom 15:16-17).

Linked to such prayer and worship is Paul's ascetical attitude. Though he never speaks of *askēsis*, he does regard *enkrateia*, "self-control, self-discipline," as a fruit of the Spirit (Gal 5:23). This attitude is owing not simply to the imminence of the parousia (1 Cor 7:29-31), but to his view of life as a struggle (1 Thess 5:6-8; 2 Cor 10:3-4; 4:7-11 [suffering as a passive asceticism]) or as an athletic competition (Phil 3:12-14; 1 Cor 9:24-27, where the asceticism is active). Paul freely renounced his right to recompense for preaching the gospel (1 Cor 9:1,4-18) lest he be tempted to boast. Specific forms of asceticism are recommended by him: the use of material abundance to help those in need (2 Cor 8:8–15); temporary abstinence from the marital act "to devote oneself to prayer" (1 Cor 7:5–6).

(Campenhausen, H. von, "Early Christian Asceticism," *Tradition and Life in the Church* [Phl, 1968] 90–122. Cerfaux, L., "L'Apôtre en présence de Dieu: Essai sur la vie d'oraison de saint Paul," *Recueil* 2. 469–81. Giardini, F., "Conversione, ascesi e mortificazione nelle lettere di S. Paolo," *RAM* 12 [1967] 197–225. Niederwimmer, K., "Zur Analyse der asketischen Motivation in 1. Kor. 7," *TLZ* 99 [1974] 241–48. Quinn, J., "Apostolic Ministry and Apostolic Prayer," *CBQ* 33 [1971] 479–91. Stanley, D. M., *Boasting in the Lord* [NY, 1973]. Wiles, G. P., *Paul's Intercessory Prayers* [SNTSMS 24; Cambridge, 1974].)

147   (E) Marriage, Celibacy, and Widowhood. Paul considers marriage, celibacy (or virginity), and widowhood, along with slavery and civic freedom, as conditions of life in which Christians find themselves. The principle that governs his view of them is expressed in 1 Cor 7:17, "Let each one walk in the lot that the Lord has assigned to him and in which God has called him." 1 Cor 7 spells out various details of such ways of life. For Paul, both marriage and celibacy are God-given charisms (7:7b). He recommends monogamous marriage, with its mutual rights and obligations, because "there is so much immorality" (*dia tas porneias*, 7:2) and because "it is better to marry than to burn with passion" (7:9b). But Paul clearly recognizes the salvific character of marriage, the influence of one spouse on the other and on the children born of them (7:12,14–16), even when the marriage involves a Christian and a non-Christian. He repeats as a charge "from the Lord" the absolute prohibition of divorce (and subsequent marriage, 7:10–11). But in saying that "the wife should not separate from her husband," Paul's formulation is already adapted to a Greco-Roman setting, where divorce instituted by a woman was possible (cf. the Palestinian setting in the formulation of Luke 16:18). But when the marriage is "mixed" (i.e., between a Christian and a non-Christian), Paul—not the Lord—tolerates separation or divorce, if the two cannot live in peace (7:15), whence develops later the so-called Pauline privilege. In 1 Cor 7 Paul never tries to justify marriage in terms of a purpose of procreation; nor does he show any concern there for the Christian family. (This will be remedied by the *Haustafeln* of the Deutero-Paulines.) Paul echoes the contemporary view of women in the society of his day, when he speaks of the "husband" as "the head of the wife" (1 Cor 11:3; see further 11:7–12; 14:34–35 [probably a non-Pauline interpolation!]). But one has to recall that the same Paul writes in Gal 3:28, "There is neither Jew nor Greek, neither slave nor free, neither male nor female, for you are all one in Christ Jesus."

(One finds in Eph 5:21–33 a different and somewhat more exalted view of Christian marriage. The author begins by asserting the mutual subjection of all "out of reverence for Christ." Then he immediately says, "Wives, be subject to your husbands, as to the Lord" [5:22]—a subordinate role of wives, echoing 1 Cor 11:3, that is tempered by the instruction to husbands, "Love your wives" [5:25]. Here the author is trying to cope with the psychological difference between husbands and wives, as he insists on the *mutual* obligation that they have to each other. But he does it in the only—time-conditioned—way that he knows: the wife must be subject, and the husband must love. He never implies that the wife is an inferior being. As a model for the husband's love, he cites the love of Christ for the church [5:25]. Finally, in quoting Gen 2:24, "For this reason a man leaves father and mother and clings to his wife, and the

two become one flesh," the author reveals a "secret" [*mystērion*] hidden in that verse of Gen centuries before, i.e., that the fundamental union of marriage established by God long ago was a prefigured "type" of the union of Christ and his church. This view of the sublimity of marriage has colored much of the Christian tradition throughout the centuries.)

148   As for celibacy, Paul states his preference gradually in 1 Cor 7. Celibacy is his own opinion, "not a command of the Lord" (7:25), even though he thinks that he is as attuned to the Spirit in this matter as anyone else (7:40). At first, there is no comparison, "It is good for a man not to touch a woman" (7:1); but his preference emerges in 7:7a, "I wish that all were as I myself am." Again, "to the unmarried and the widows I say, It is good for them to remain as I am" (7:8)—an unclear statement usually understood as meaning that Paul aligns himself with the "unmarried" (but → Paul, 79:19). Paul gives two reasons for his preference: (1) "because of the impending distress" (7:26, i.e., the imminent parousia; cf. 7:29; 1 Thess 4:15,17; Rom 13:11); and (2) because one is thus freed from "worldly cares" (7:28) and "divided interests" (i.e., the concern for a husband or a wife) so that one can give "undivided devotion to the Lord" (7:32–35). Here a comparison between the married and the unmarried is implied, and Paul recommends celibacy in view of apostolic service. At the end of the chapter he introduces the comparison explicitly in the difficult passage about the marrying of one's "virgin" (daughter, ward, fiancée?): "The man who marries her does what is right, but he who does not does even better" (*kreisson poiēsei*, 7:38). As for widows, Paul recognizes their right to marry again, but he judges that they will be happier if they remain widows.

(Allmen, J. J. von, *Pauline Teaching on Marriage* [London, 1963]. Baltensweiler, H., *Die Ehe im Neuen Testament* [Zurich, 1967]. Crouzel, H., *L'Eglise primitive face au divorce* [Théologie historique 13; Paris, 1971]. Dulau, P., "The Pauline Privilege," *CBQ* 13 [1951] 146–52. Elliott, J. K., "Paul's Teaching on Marriage in 1 Corinthians," *NTS* 19 [1972–73] 219–25. Greeven, H., "Ehe nach den Neuen Testament," *NTS* 15 [1968–69] 365–88. Grelot, P., *Man and Wife in Scripture* [NY, 1964]. Matura, T., "Le célibat dans le Nouveau Testament d'après l'exégèse récente," *NRT* 107 [1975] 593–604. Niederwimmer, K., "*Gameō*, etc.," *EWNT* 1. 564–71. Pesch R., *Freie Treue: Die Christen und die Ehescheidung* [Freiburg, 1971]. Swain, L., "Paul on Celibacy," *ClR* 51 [1966] 785–91.)

149   **(F) Society, State, and Slavery.** Paul recognizes differences both in human and in Christian society. He recognizes that both Jews and Greeks have been called to become children of God through faith and baptism and their oneness in the church, the body of Christ. Though he does not obliterate all distinctions, he recognizes their lack of value in Christ Jesus. "By one Spirit we were all baptized into one body, Jews or Greeks, slaves or free; and all were made to drink of the same Spirit" (1 Cor 12:13; cf. Gal 3:28). Yet he can also say, "Let each one walk in the lot to which the Lord has assigned him . . . ; everyone should remain in the state in which one was called" (1 Cor 7:17–20). For Paul's basic attitude is expressed in 1 Cor 9:19–23: "I have become all things to all that I may save some." Hence he reckons with Jews and Greeks, slaves and free, men and women, rich and poor, married and celibate, the weak in conviction and the strong, those material and those spiritual in Christian society.

150   Paul is also aware that the Christian must live in civil and political society that is not wholly oriented to the same goals as the Christian community. Christians may in reality be citizens of another, a heavenly, "commonwealth" (Phil 3:20), but they do have obligations of another sort in this earthly life. These Paul treats in Rom 13:1–7, and indirectly in 1 Cor 6:1–8; 2:6–8. One can agree with E. Käsemann that Paul does not really have an "ethic" of the state ("Principles," 196), or even a well-formulated systematic understanding of it. Rom 13:1–7 has been suspected of being an interpolation, but it stands today as part of the hortatory section of that letter. In it Paul recognizes that Christians must "subject themselves to the authorities," who are most likely human state officials, even though some have tried to identify them as angelic beings (→ Romans, 51:119). Christians are to recognize their place in the structure of human society. Paul's motivating reasons are mainly three: (1) eschatological (the danger of facing "judgment" [13:2] and "wrath" [13:5]); (2) the dictate of "conscience" itself (13:5); and (3) "the (common) good" (13:4). For the same reasons Paul insists that Christians must not only "pay taxes" and "revenue" (13:6–7a), but accord the authorities "honor" and "respect" (13:7b). Underlying Paul's discussion is the conviction that "there is no authority except from God and those that exist have been set up by God" (13:1). In writing to the Romans, Paul is implicitly recognizing the God-given character of the authority of the Roman Empire in which he himself was living. The trouble with his teaching in this passage is that he never envisages the possibility that human authorities could be evil or do evil; it does no good to try to save Paul in this matter by invoking angelic authorities. His teaching is limited; and even his reference to "the (common) good" (13:4a) can scarcely be invoked in defense of civil disobedience.

151   Lastly, Paul's counsel to slaves in 1 Cor 7:21–22 is always a difficult teaching to cope with. Paul did not seek to change the social system in which he lived. This is undoubtedly the reason why he returns the runaway slave Onesimus to his master Philemon (Phlm 8–20). Yet in the latter passage we may detect what he really thinks about the matter; for he sends Onesimus back as "more than a slave, as a 'brother'" (16), i.e., suggesting that Philemon recognize him as a fellow Christian, and possibly even hinting that he should emancipate him (though the latter is far from certain). Paul was in this instance more concerned with interiorizing the existing social situation than with changing it, realizing that even a slave in civil society could have freedom in Christ Jesus (Gal 3:28). (Cf. Col 3:22–4:1; Eph 6:5–9.)

(Bartchy, *Mallon Chrēsai* [→ 75 above]. Borg, M., "A New Context for Romans xiii," *NTS* 19 [1972–73] 205–18. Broer, I., "*Exousia*," *EWNT* 2. 23–29. Coleman-Norton, P. R., "The Apostle Paul and the Roman Law of Slavery," *Studies in Roman Economic and Social History* [Princeton, 1951] 155–77. Cook, W. R., "Biblical Light on the Christian's Civil Responsibility," *BSac* 127 [1970] 44–57. Cullmann, O., *The State in the New Testament* [NY, 1956]. Hutchinson, S., "The Political Implications of Romans 13:1–7," *Biblical Theology* 21 [1971] 49–59. Käsemann, E., "Principles of the Interpretation of Romans 13," *NTQT* 196–216. Lyall, F., "Roman Law in the Writings of Paul—The Slave and the Freedman," *NTS* 17 [1970–71] 73–79. Murphy-O'Connor, J., "The Christian and Society in St. Paul," *New Blackfriars* 50 [1968–69] 174–82. Pagels, E. H., "Paul and Women: A Response to Recent Discussion," *JAAR* 42 [1974] 538–49. Scroggs, R., "Paul and the Eschatological Woman," *JAAR* 40 [1972] 283–301; cf. *JAAR* 42 [1974] 432–37.)

CONCLUSION

152   Paul has instructions for Christian conduct in other areas as well, which cannot be included in this brief sketch. We conclude our remarks on Paul's theology and ethics by insisting on its christocentrism. As Christ was "the image of God" (2 Cor 4:4), so human beings are destined to be "the image of the heavenly man" (1 Cor 15:49; cf. Rom 8:29). It is growth in Christ that Paul recommends to his readers, contemporary and modern. In this way the Christian lives his or her life "for God" (Gal 2:19). Thus, for all his emphasis on Christ, Paul once again refers Christian existence ultimately to the Father—through Christ.

83

JOHANNINE THEOLOGY

Francis J. Moloney, S.D.B.

BIBLIOGRAPHY

1 For commentaries, → John, 61:1; → 1–3 John, 62:1. Ashton, J. (ed.), *The Interpretation of John* (London, 1986). Barrett, C. K., *Essays on John* (London, 1982). Beutler, J., "Literarische Gattungen im Johannesevangelium. Ein Forschungsbericht," *ANRW* II/25.3, 2506–68. Borgen, P., *Logos was the True Light and Other Essays on the Gospel of John* (Relieff 9; Trondheim, 1983). Brown, R. E., *The Community of the Beloved Disciple* (NY, 1979). Bultmann, *TNT* 2. 3–92. Culpepper, R. A., *Anatomy of the Fourth Gospel* (Phl, 1983). De Jonge, M., *Jesus: Stranger from Heaven and Son of God* (SBLSBS 11; Missoula, 1977). De la Potterie, I., *La Vérité dans Saint Jean* (2 vols.; AnBib 73–74; Rome, 1977). Dodd, C. H., *The Interpretation of the Fourth Gospel* (Cambridge, 1953). Hartman, L. and B. Olsson (eds.), *Aspects on the Johannine Literature* (ConBNT 18; Uppsala, 1987).

Käsemann, E., *The Testament of Jesus* (Phl, 1968). Kysar, R. *The Fourth Evangelist and His Gospel* (Minneapolis, 1975); "The Fourth Gospel: A Report on Recent Research," *ANRW* II/25.3, 2389–2480. Martyn, J. L., *History and Theology in the Fourth Gospel* (2d ed.; Nash, 1979). Meeks, W. A., *The Prophet-King* (NovTSup 14; Leiden, 1967). Moloney, F. J., *The Johannine Son of Man* (Biblioteca di Scienze Religiose 14; Rome, 1978). Painter, J., *John: Witness and Theologian* (London, 1975). Pancaro, S., *The Law in the Fourth Gospel* (NovTSup 42; Leiden, 1975). Schillebeeckx, E., *Christ* (London, 1980) 305–432. Smalley, S. S., *John: Evangelist and Interpreter* (London, 1986). Smith, D. M., *Johannine Christianity* (Univ. of S. Carolina, 1984). Thüsing, W., *Die Erhöhung und Verherrlichung Jesu im Johannesevangelium* (NTAbh 21/1–2; Münster, 1970).

OUTLINE

COMPONENTS IN JOHANNINE THEOLOGY

3 The Fourth Gospel (henceforth John) fell into disfavor as the 19th-cent. search for the "real Jesus" (→ NT Criticism, 70:6, 33) discovered Mark as the "historical" Gospel. The contemporary interest in the theologies of the earliest church, however, has restored John to center stage. (E. Haenchen, *John* [Herm; Phl, 1984] 1.20–39.) Already in the 2d cent. Clement of Alexandria was able to call John "the Spiritual Gospel"

(Eusebius, *HE* 6.14.7), and the 4th-cent. Fathers spoke of "John the Theologian." The uniqueness of its theological viewpoint is a major feature of John.

4 **(I) The Structure of John.**
The saying that John is like a magic pool in which an infant can paddle and an elephant can swim is verifiable in so many ways. The language of John is generally uncomplicated; the vocabulary and syntax are

simple; and yet it presents one of the most profound and moving portraits of Jesus of Nazareth and his message found in the NT. (C. K. Barrett, *The Gospel according to St John* [2d ed.; London, 1978] 5–15.)

5   (A) Overall Structure.   The issue of simplicity and profundity affects the comprehension of the structure of John. Whatever debates there may be about the structure of the Synoptic Gospels, there is wide agreement that John can be divided into a clearly designed theological prologue (1:1–18), followed by two long sections. The first (1:19–12:50) is devoted to the public life of Jesus until he withdraws from the crowds (12:36b) — a section John closes solemnly with concluding reflections (12:37–50). The second (13:1–20:31) is devoted entirely to Jesus' presence with his "own" disciples, leading up to his glorification through the hour of the cross, resurrection, and return to the Father. The final chap. (21) is seemingly an addendum, which apparently originated in the same Johannine background as the Gospel proper, but was added at a final stage (no ancient ms. lacks it) to deal with further issues of concern to the Johannine church (→ John, 61:4; for a contrary view, see P. S. Minear, *JBL* 102 [1983] 85–98).

6   There is less agreement among scholars as to the care and deliberation given by the evangelist to more detailed *internal* structures. On the positive side, the narratives of the man born blind (John 9), the raising of Lazarus (John 11), and the passion (esp. 18:28–19:16) indicate an author who wrote with considerable skill. Detailed analyses have shown beyond reasonable doubt that John is the end product of considerable literary and theological activity.

7   (B) Problems.   One might believe that clear overall structure and careful literary shaping, conditioned by an obviously theological point of view, should make the identification and description of Johannine theology an easy task. Yet there are structural and literary problems that have puzzled interpreters for centuries, centered on difficult sequences in John's logic, geography, and time line. E.g., the solemn conclusion of Jesus' discourse to his disciples in 14:31 ("Rise, let us go hence") leads beautifully into 18:1, the opening verse of the passion narrative ("When Jesus had spoken these words, he went forth with his disciples across the Kidron valley"). However, without any explanatory indication of time or space, these two affirmations are separated by chaps. 15–17! Chaps. 5 and 6 of John seem to many scholars to have been reversed. Moreover, passages like 3:31–36 and 12:44–50 are strangely situated; there is some confusion over Caiaphas and Annas in chap. 18; etc.

8   Such illogicalities in an otherwise well-structured Gospel have led to different theories, e.g., that the Gospel as we have it is "unfinished" (D. M. Smith, *The Composition and Order of the Fourth Gospel* [New Haven, 1965] 238–40) or that it has come down to us out of sequence, and we must attempt to reconstruct its original order (R. Bultmann; → NT Criticism, 70:52). The most popular approach to this problem, however, has been the attempt to recognize the various "layers" of tradition in the Gospel from a tradition-history point of view (expertly done in the commentaries of R. Schnackenburg and R. E. Brown). Recent Johannine scholarship is asking a further important question: Is it possible to trace (behind this blending of ancient, more recent, and exclusively Johannine elements) the experience of the Johannine community? An attempt to answer that question positively stands at the center of a great deal of Johannine scholarship today (surveyed by F. J. Moloney, "Revisiting John," *ScrB* 11 [Summer 1980] 9–15; → John, 61:13–15).

9   (II) The Johannine Community.   The rediscovery of the faith journey of the Johannine community is of great importance for a proper appreciation of the Gospel's theology (→ John, 61:9–11).

(A) History of the Community.   In John the first days of Jesus are marked by a series of questions framed in terms of Jewish messianic expectations. Religious authorities come from Jerusalem and ask whether JBap is the Messiah, Elijah, or the Prophet (1:19–28). JBap, the one "who came for testimony, to bear witness to the light" (1:7), points away from himself toward Jesus: the Lamb of God who takes away the sin of the world, the Son of God (1:29, 34–35). Eventually he sends two of his disciples to "follow" Jesus (v 37). They call Jesus Rabbi and spend some time with him (vv 38–39). Eventually they bring other disciples, announcing: "We have found" the Messiah, the Christ, the one of whom Moses in the law and also the prophets wrote (vv 41 and 45). These confessions finally lead Nathanael to proclaim: "Rabbi, you are the Son of God! The King of Israel!" (v 49). This procession of christological titles is seen by many commentators as gradually leading to a final, fully Johannine confession of faith from Nathanael. However, difficulties appear in v 50, where Jesus himself is unhappy with this profession of faith, which is inspired by the mere miracle of Jesus' knowledge that Nathanael had been under a fig tree. Jesus promises the sight of "greater things": the opening of the heavens and the ascent and descent of the angels of God upon the Son of Man (vv 50–51).

10   This passage (and many similar passages throughout John) uses a whole gamut of christological categories, which can be traced back to various stages in the faith journey of the early church (→ NT Thought, 81:12–24). We find references to a messianic precursor (Elijah or the Prophet), and to Jesus as an authoritative teacher (Rabbi), as Christ (Messiah), and the one who fulfills the Scriptures, arriving finally at Nathanael's belief that Jesus is the Son of God (in Jewish messianic terms, interpreting 2 Sam 7:14 and Ps 2:7) and the King of Israel. There is a progression from the earliest and simplest terms for the messianic precursor through to the most elevated Jewish expectations of a messianic King of Israel. But then there are three further confessions that cannot be contained within those categories: the Lamb of God, the Son of God (in the full Johannine sense), and the Son of Man (also in the Johannine sense). Is this confusion? Is it a juxtaposition of traditions that are not well matched? Perhaps the apparent multiplicity of christological categories found in 1:19–51 reflects a christological journey within the community itself.

11   This community had its beginnings in the earliest days of Christianity. It has had close contacts with a primitive Jewish-Christian understanding of Jesus as the Mosaic Prophet and the fulfillment of the Scriptures. Dialogue with Judaism would have eventually led to the more developed, fully Jewish confessions of Jesus as Messiah, King of Israel, and Son of God. The earliest years of the community would have been lived in close contact with Judaism and its traditions. Gradually, this closeness to Judaism seems to have broken down, and the first step in this breakdown would probably have come with the introduction of non-Jewish and even anti-Temple elements into the Johannine community. The concentration on the mission to the Samaritans in chap. 4 is a strong indication of this direction (esp. the implications of 4:20–24). Certainly the introduction of non-Jewish elements caused much of the theological development of the early church. (One need only think of elements in Paul and Matthew.) There can be little doubt that Samaritans, Hellenists, etc. would have caused the Johannine community to look again at their understanding and their preaching of the person of Jesus of Nazareth. A shift in meaning of the term "Son of God" may have been unacceptable to an original Jewish audience, and the use of the "I am" expression to refer to Jesus would meet similar opposition.

12 A mounting tension between the Johannine community and the synagogue seems to have led eventually to the complete expulsion of the community from the synagogue. The evidence for this final rift is found in the description of the experience of the man born blind in chap. 9, where his growing faith in Jesus (9:11: "the man called Jesus"; v 17: "He is a prophet"; v 33: "If this man were not from God"; vv 35–38: confession of Jesus as the Son of Man) finally leads to his being "cast out" (v 34). Already John has used the parents of the man born blind to explain the background for such a dismissal. They refused to speak for their son because "they feared the Jews, for the Jews had already agreed that if any one should confess him to be the Christ, he was to be put out of the synagogue" (9:22; see also 12:42; 16:2). It appears that this final rift between church and synagogue, reflected in John, is to be linked with the decision gradually taken by Judaism (sometime after AD 85) to exclude from the synagogue sectarians, including those who believed that Jesus of Nazareth was the Christ (see W. D. Davies, *The Setting of the Sermon on the Mount* [Cambridge, 1966] 256–315; R. Kimelman, in *Jewish and Christian Self-Definition 2* [ed. E. P. Sanders, et al.; Phl, 1981] 226–44; → Early Church, 80:24).

13 Once the Johannine community had been forcibly cut away from its Jewish roots, further modifications of Johannine theology seem to have taken place. An originally Jewish-Christian community now had a developing hostility to official Judaism (the reason for the negative use of the term "the Jews" throughout the Gospel) and a growing openness to the strange world within which it now had both to live and to preach its unique form of Christianity. Contact with the syncretistic Hellenistic religions and some early form of what eventually became gnosticism (→ Early Church, 80:64–82) would have been part of this new world. The community made it clear that true Johannine Christians could not possibly remain in the synagogue (see 12:43–44). Gradually they developed an independent understanding of a primacy of love rather than of authority (the reason for the continual "upstaging" of Peter by the Beloved Disciple: see esp. 13:21–26 and 20:2–10). The Johannine community became more aggressive in its gradual development of a new and higher christology (Jesus as the Logos, the Son of God, "sent" by the Father from "above" to "below" in a way quite unknown to the Synoptic Gospels), a unique Paraclete pneumatology, and an ethic based on a law of love, without emphasizing the restrictions of a final, end-of-time judgment on behavior (there is no Johannine scene to parallel Matt 25:31–46).

14 That this was a risky process is indicated by the Johannine letters. There we have traces of the further history of a Johannine community irrevocably divided into at least two factions. There the group who "went out from us" (1 John 2:19)—to go by the author's description of their heresies (and we unfortunately are not able to hear their defense)—seemed to be moving into a more gnostic form of Christianity through their understanding of the Jesus of the Gospel. The community portrayed by the letters themselves seems to be drawing back into a more "controllable" Christianity, where the importance of the person of Jesus of Nazareth and of the historical, physical experience of his suffering and his death is spelled out without any ambiguity (1 John

4:2–3; 5:6; 2 John 7). Similarly, the quality of life that should be lived by his followers is given a more practical treatment than in the Gospel itself (see, e.g., 1 John 1:6; 2:4,6,9). Yet both groups—those represented by the letters and those attacked by them—could justifiably claim to be basing their christology, ecclesiology, pneumatology, and ethics on the traditions and theological heritage of the Beloved Disciple and his Gospel. The community behind the letters appears to have taken the Gospel message with them into a form of church that eventually became the "greater church," while the teachings of the ex-members of the community attacked by the letters are in many ways close to 2d-cent. gnosticism.

(Brown, R. E., *BEJ* 47–115; *Community.* Langbrandtner, W., *Weltferner Gott oder Gott der Liebe* [BBET 6; Frankfurt, 1977]. Martyn, J. L., *The Gospel of John in Christian History* [NY, 1978]. Meeks, W. A., "'Am I a Jew?' Johannine Christianity and Judaism," *Christianity, Judaism and Other Greco-Roman Cults* [Fest. M. Smith; ed. J. Neusner; SJLA 12; Leiden, 1975] 1. 163–86. Müller, U. B., *Die Geschichte der Christologie in der johanneischen Gemeinde* [SBS 77; Stuttgart, 1975]. Richter, G., "Zum gemeindebildenden Element in den johanneischen Schriften," *Kirche im Werden* [Fest. G. Richter; ed. J. Hainz; Munich, 1976] 252–92.)

15 **(B) Theological Significance.** Our rapid sketch is of necessity speculative, a synthesis based on the work of contemporary Johannine scholarship. It is proposed, however, to indicate that contemporary Johannine studies, rather than being limited to a variety of redactional theories to explain the internal tensions of the Gospel, now look to the growth of a particular early Christian community for such an explanation (→ NT Criticism, 70:79). Behind this growing tradition stands the figure of the Beloved Disciple (whether he was John the son of Zebedee or not need not be decided here). His charismatic and sensitive appreciation of Jesus of Nazareth stands at the beginnings of the Johannine tradition. His ability to reread and reteach that tradition, without ever betraying the fundamental elements of the Christian message, also stands behind the growth already outlined. He challenged his community in his own time. After the death of the Beloved Disciple (see 21:21–23), that same community was prepared to face their new situation and go on looking at their faith in Jesus and its expression.

16 The tensions in the text of John are obviously present; yet both the overall organization and much of the internal structure show a clear and well-organized mind. This phenomenon indicates the skill of an evangelist who produced a theological unity as he worked creatively in the real-life situation of his community. John is an attempt to preserve and to instruct by making the older traditions understandable to a new Christian generation. The evangelist was telling an "old story" in a new way. It was inevitable that many of the experiences of the community, in which he had heard the story told and retold it himself, would shape the way in which it was narrated. There are important theological issues at stake here. As J. L. Martyn has written: "The Evangelist has extended the *einmalig* [actual events from his tradition concerning the historical life of Jesus], not because he discovered additional information about what the earthly Jesus did on this [or that] occasion, but rather because he wishes to show how the Risen Lord continues his earthly ministry in the work of his servant, the Christian preacher" (*History and Theology* 29–30).

17 In a study of Johannine theology such reflections are of real theological importance. The "story of Jesus" as we now have it told in John is the result of the journey of faith of a particular Christian community in the second half of the 1st cent. The experience of the Johannine community and the rich theological vision it has produced indicate that this particular early Christian community committed itself seriously to "the problem of relating the givenness of the past with the exhilarating experience of the present" (M. D. Hooker, "In His own Image," *What about the New Testament?* [Fest. C. Evans; ed. M. D. Hooker, *et al.;* London, 1975] 41). John is not just a hotchpotch of contradicting traditions.

GOD AND JESUS

18   (I) Theology. John is the story of Jesus of Nazareth, written to communicate belief in him and in his saving life, death, and resurrection. One could come to that conclusion by reading the christological prologue (1:1-18) and then the concluding words: "These things are written that you may believe that Jesus is the Christ, the Son of God, and that believing you may have life in his name" (20:31). Yet, despite appearances, John really is not a story about Jesus but a story about what God has done in Jesus (→ 1-3 John, 62:5).

19   (A) Telling God's Story. The Prologue is a christological confession but also more than that. The Logos exists from all time, turned in loving union toward God (1:1-2); and the significance of this is not only christological. The rest of the Prologue tells of the inbreak of the Logos as "life" and "light" (vv 3-5,9), "flesh" (v 14), "the fullness of a gift which is truth" (vv 14, 16-17), "the only Son" (vv 14, 18), "Jesus Christ" (v 17). The evangelist begins from a presupposition shared by many of his contemporaries that "the world" is caught in darkness (1:5), unable to "see" or "know" the mystery of God. Of old, God was made known in a limited but fundamentally important way through the law given to Moses. Now that "gift" has been replaced by the fullness of the gift of God, i.e., the Truth revealed through Jesus Christ (1:16-17). No one has ever seen God, but Jesus Christ, the unique Son of that God, has told the story of God in his life (v 18). Thus, this hymn tells the reader a great deal about Jesus but does more. The purpose of the "enfleshing" of the Logos in Jesus is to tell the story of God; and the Gospel's account of that story will reflect the Johannine understanding of God and his relationship to Jesus, to the world, and to those in the world (→ John, 61:16-17).

(De la Potterie, I., "Structure du Prologue de Saint Jean," *NTS* 30 [1984] 354-81. Käseman, *NTQT* 138-67. Moloney, F. J., "'In the Bosom of' or 'Turned towards' the Father," *AusBR* 31 [1983] 63-71. Panimolle, S. A., *Il dono della Legge e la Grazia della Verità* [Rome, 1973].)

20   (B) What Sort of God? 1 John 4:8 affirms "God is love" (see also 4:16). Coming at the end of decades of reflection, this expression attempts to encapsulate God's caring, saving action in the gift of his Son. It was drawn from the experience of Jesus. Nevertheless, it is the closest the NT comes to telling us about the "being" of God, and it provides a starting point for a consideration of Johannine theology (see R. Schnackenburg, *Die Johannesbriefe* [HTKNT 13/3; Freiburg, 1979] 231-39; also *BEJ* 542-67).

**21   The section of John (3:16-17) that contains the first use of the vb. "to love" (*agapaō*) has been called "a miniature Gospel." We learn there that the earthly presence of the Son flows from the fact that God loved the world so much that he gave his Son so that the world might be saved, and that those who are in the world might have a chance for eternal life. The Son has been loved by God, his Father, from before all time (17:24). The love that has existed between the Father and the Son from all time has broken into history, as the Father, who loves the Son, has given all things into his hands (3:35; 5:19-30). Without use of love terminology, the opening verses of the Prologue have the same message, telling of a unique union between the Logos and God which reaches out into the darkness to bring an invincible light (1:1-5). A logical conclusion to this "story of God" is that the presence of the Son in the world is a challenge to recognize in him the Father who has loved in this way (8:42; 14:9-10,23; 15:9). To reveal a God of love to the world can be seen as the purpose of Jesus' presence. In his final prayer to the Father, the Son prays that the love which initiated and infused his mission be repeated in the lives of "his own" (17:11) and in the lives of all those who would come to believe in the Son through the preaching of his disciples (17:20,23,26). Thus a God who is love will continue to be proclaimed in the world, as those who believe in Jesus are sent into the world, just as Jesus was sent into the world (17:17-19).

**22   At the beginning of Jesus' ministry, as the disciples wonder about Jesus' presence to the Samaritan woman, he announces: "My food is to do the will of him who sent me, and to accomplish his work" (4:34). This constitutes a major statement: Jesus is to fulfill the purpose of the one who sent him (the vb. *pempō* here, whereas in other places *apostellō* is used), to bring to perfection (*teleioō*) the work (*to ergon*) entrusted to him. As the public ministry unfolds, Jesus again proclaims the centrality of the will of his Father: "I seek not my own will, but the will of him who sent me" (5:30), repeating that this can only be done by performing the "works which the Father has granted me to accomplish; these very works which I am doing, bear witness that the Father has sent me" (5:36). These themes run through the Gospel: Jesus is the "sent one" of the Father (*pempō:* 4:34; 5:23-24,30,36-37; 6:38,39,44; 7:16-18,28-29,33; 8:16, 18,26,28-29; 9:4; 12:44-45,49-50; 13:20; 14:24; 15:21; 16:5; *apostellō:* 3:17,34; 5:36; 6:29,57; 7:29; 8:42; 9:7; 10:36; 17:3,8,18,21,23,25), accomplishing, "bringing to perfection" (*teleioō:* 4:34; 5:36; 17:4; 19:28; *teleō:* 19:28,30) the "work" which the Father gave him to do (*to ergon:* 4:34; 6:29; 17:4).

**23   John is, in some ways, a story of what Jesus has done for God. This is made particularly clear in Jesus' final prayer to his Father and his final cry from the cross. He opens his prayer with the claim: "I glorified you on earth, having accomplished the work (*to ergon teleiōsas*) which you gave me to do" (17:4). "Lifted up" on the cross, he proclaims in his moment of death: "It has been accomplished" (*tetelestai,* 19:30). It is in the moment of death that Jesus himself can proclaim that he has brought to perfection the task which the Father gave him to do. In some way, the life (where Jesus does the "works" of the Father: 5:20,36; 6:28; 7:3; 9:3,4; 10:25,32,37,38; 14:10-12) and death of Jesus are the realization of the work of God. In this life and death God is made known.

(Barrett, "Christocentric or Theocentric?" *Essays* 1-18. Borgen, "God's Agent in the Fourth Gospel," *Logos* 121-32. Buhner, J. A., *Der Gesandte und sein Weg im 4. Evangelium* [WUNT 2/2; Tübingen, 1977]. Haenchen, E., "Der Vater, der mich gesandt hat," *NTS* 9 [1962-63] 208-16. Loader, W. R. G., "The Central

Structure of Johannine Christology," *NTS* 30 [1984] 188–216. Miranda, J. P., *Der Vater, der mich gesandt hat* [EHS 23/7; Frankfurt, 1972]; *Die Sendung Jesu im vierten Evangelium* [SBS 87; Stuttgart, 1977].)

24   (II) Christology. John's story about God, then, is inextricably bound up with the life, death, resurrection, and return to the Father of Jesus the Son. If the revelation of a God who loves makes this Gospel "theological," such a theology is made possible through a "christology" (→ John, 61:16–17).

25   (A) Jesus the Glory of God. In 1:43–51, the first disciples come to a belief that they have found one "of whom Moses and the prophets wrote" (v 45), "Rabbi, Son of God and King of Israel" (v 49). Jesus warns them that they have come to this belief merely on the basis of his knowledge that Nathanael had been under a fig tree. This is only a beginning. They will see "greater things" as they will see the revelation of the heavenly in the Son of Man (1:50–51) beginning in the first miracle at Cana where Jesus "manifested his glory" (2:11). The reader has met the term "glory" (*doxa*) in the Prologue: 1:14 claims that the enfleshing of the preexistent Word produces a situation where "we" (the members of the community) can "behold" the glory, a unique glory because it is the glory of the only begotten Son of God who dwells among us. This theme is essential to the Johannine story of Jesus, who tells the story of God.

26   In the OT, various authors used a term to speak of the felt presence of a loving, saving, and guiding God among his people. Whether it was the opening of the Reed Sea, the pillar of fire, the manna from heaven, the ark of the covenant, the Temple, or (among the poets) the beauty of the heavens, the biblical authors used the same term: *kĕbôd YHWH,* the glory of Yahweh (see Exod 16:7–10; 24:16–17; Lev 9:26; Num 14:21; 2 Chr 5:14; Ps 19:2; Isa 40:5). Strangely, the LXX rendered this as *doxa tou theou;* for the normal Gk meaning of *doxa* was not "glory," but "esteem," "honor," "earthly success," covering a range of ideas connected with achievements humanly measured by culture and history (LSJ 444). Once this odd translation choice was made, the word *doxa* passed into the biblical vocabulary, rendering an important OT concept expressed through Hebr *kābôd.* (See G. Kittel and G. von Rad, *TDNT* 2. 232–55; W. Grossouw, in *L'Évangile de Jean* [RechBib 3; Bruges, 1958] 131–33.)

27   (B) The Cross and the Glory of God. More fully, then, 1:14, "We have beheld his glory (*tēn doxan autou*), glory as of the only Son from the Father," implies that in the enfleshed Logos, the loving, saving presence of God himself is made visible. We must look at the story of Jesus to see how this glory is made visible, how Jesus is glorified, and how God is glorified in him. John indicates on three occasions that the activity of Jesus reflects the glory of God: at Cana (2:11) and twice within the context of the raising of Lazarus (11:4,40). Already in 11:4 there are strong indications that the ultimate moment of glorification lies elsewhere: "This illness is not unto death; it is for the glory of God, so that the Son of God may be glorified by means of it."

28   There are two issues here: the revelation of the glory of God in the raising of Lazarus to life (see also 11:40), and then the further glorification of the Son generated by this event. The "hour of Jesus" is set in motion by the Lazarus event. The presence of the power of God in the miracle itself is a revelation of the "glory" of God (see 11:21–27), but there is more to it. In John's story line this miracle leads to the decision that Jesus must die for the nation—and not for the nation only, but to gather into one the children of God who are scattered abroad (see 11:49–52). To this point in John, the death of

Jesus has never been explicitly mentioned. It has been referred to through the use of the important Johannine themes of the "lifting up" (3:14; 8:28) and "the hour" (2:4; 4:21,23; 7:30; 8:20), but the first reference to Jesus' destiny in explicit terms of "death" (using the vb. *apothnēskō*) is found in 11:16. In chaps. 11–12, as Jesus moves from his public ministry into his "hour of glory" (chaps. 13–20), such references abound (11:16,50,51; 12:24,33).

29   The link between the raising of Lazarus—in itself an event that reveals "the glory of God" (11:40)—and the further moment of the glorification of the Son (11:4) becomes important. The sister of Lazarus anoints Jesus for death (12:1–8). Jesus enters Jerusalem (12:12–16), surrounded by people who come to see Lazarus and by "the chief priests" who are planning the death of both Jesus and Lazarus (12:9–11,17–19). The Pharisees declare, "Look, the world has gone after him" (12:19). The prophecy of Caiaphas and John's explanation of it as a death not only for the nation but also to gather into one the children of God scattered abroad, are being fulfilled (11:49–52). As some Greeks come to see Jesus (12:20–22), he can announce the arrival of a turning point in his story: "The hour has come for the Son of Man to be glorified" (12:23).

30   Thus far in the Gospel "the hour" has not yet come (2:4; 7:6,30; 8:20); but now we find that it has come (12:23; see further 13:1; 17:1; 19:27) and that in it the Son of Man will be glorified. There is a connection between the hour, the glorification, and the death of Jesus in 12:31–32: "Now is the judgment of this world, now shall the ruler of this world be cast out; and I, when I am lifted up from the earth, will draw all to myself." The theme of the "gathering" of all people around a Jesus who dies, "lifted up" on a cross, begun in 11:49–52 and carried further in 12:19, is now fully explained: the cross of Jesus is the place where the glory of God will shine forth, drawing all to himself. This is made abundantly clear in the redactional 12:33: "He said this to show by what death he was to die" (see also 18:32). John presents the cross as the climactic moment in the revealing activity of Jesus. Jesus makes this clear during his ministry: "When you have lifted up the Son of Man, then you will know that I am he, and that I do nothing on my own authority, but speak thus as the Father taught me" (8:28). The evangelist spells it out again in his final comment on the death of Jesus: "They shall look on him whom they have pierced" (19:37).

(*BGJ* 1. 503–4. De Jonge, M., "Jesus as Prophet and King in the Fourth Gospel," *ETL* 49 [1973] 160–79. Forestell, J. T., *The Word of the Cross* [AnBib 57; Rome, 1974]. Meeks, *Prophet-King* 61–81. Müller, U. B., "Die Bedeutung des Kreuzestodes Jesu im Johannesevangelium," *KD* 21 [1975] 49–71.)

31   (C) Dualism. John did not invent this message of a loving God, revealed through the gift of his Son (3:16–17) in a supreme act of love (13:1; 15:13), for the life and death of Jesus constituted the foundational story of Christianity. Yet there are unique elements in John's form of the story, e.g., its dualistic world view, which have no parallel in the Synoptic tradition. A form of dualism was part of 1st-cent. Judaism, steeped in ideas of a sovereign Lord of creation and a world trapped by forces opposing the divine way only to be finally overcome in the messianic appearance (see C. Rowland, *Christian Origins* [London, 1985] 87–97). This dualism of the present evil age resolved by the rule of God in the age to come is replaced in John with another form of dualism. A traditional temporal dualism has been (partly) replaced by a cosmic dualism. Underlying the Gospel story are a series of contrasts: e.g., light and darkness (1:5), above and below (8:23), spirit and flesh (3:6), life and death (3:36), truth and falsehood (8:44-45), heaven and earth (3:31), God and Satan (13:27). These opposing forces do not simply coexist but are locked in conflict: "The light shines in the darkness, and the darkness has not overcome it" (1:5); "Now is the judgment of this world, now shall the ruler of this world be cast out" (12:31); → John 61:6.

32 The origin of this dualism is difficult to define. Bultmann has regarded John as a christianization of early gnostic schemes (*TNT* 2. 15-32). Käsemann argued that a drift into a naïve, incipient docetism is evident (*Testament* 4-26). There are indications that this form of dualism was not foreign to 1st-cent. Jewish thinking (see J. H. Charlesworth, *John and Qumran* [London, 1972] 76-106) or to the syncretistic religions that flowered in the latter part of the 1st cent. It was central to gnosticism in the 2d cent. Is John a product of the Hellenistic or the Jewish world? The answer is probably that it is neither, but both. John built bridges out of the Judaism of its birth into the new world of Hellenistic syncretism.

(Barrett, "Paradox and Dualism," *Essays* 98-115. Baumbach, G., "Gemeinde und Welt im Johannes-evangelium," *Kairos* 14 [1972] 121-36. Böcher, O., *Der johanneische Dualismus im Zusammenhang des nachbiblischen Judentums* [Gütersloh, 1965]. Onuki, T., *Gemeinde und Welt im Johannesevangelium* [WMANT 56; Neukirchen, 1984]. Schillebeeckx, *Christ* 331-49. Schottroff, L., *Der Glaubende und die feindliche Welt* [WMANT 37; Neukirchen, 1970]. Stemberger, G., *La symbolique du bien et du mal selon saint Jean* [Paris, 1970].)

33 Against this background the categories of Johannine christology can be understood. Fundamental to the whole of the Gospel is the origin of Jesus: the fact that the preexistent Logos (1:1-2) has become flesh and dwelt among us in the person of Jesus (1:14-18). Throughout the Gospel the question of "origins" is raised: at Cana (2:9), with the Samaritan woman (4:11), by "the Jews" (9:29), by the crowd at the feast of Tabernacles (7:27; 8:14) and even by Pilate (19:9). If the origin of Jesus is turned toward God as the Logos (1:1), then his presence in history will be the result of his being the "sent one" of the Father.

34 The evangelist believes that no one has ever seen God, but that there is one person who is able to reveal him to us: the one who comes from the Father (1:18; 6:46). Given, however, the dualistic presentation of God and "the world," of "above" and "below," such a mission involves the descent of the revealer from above (3:13) and his subsequent ascent to where he was before (6:62; 17:5; 20:17). The Johannine Jesus comes from the Father, reveals him in a unique way as his Son, and returns to the Father, to have again the glory that was his before the world was made (17:1-5). Again we find ourselves in touch with categories of revelation and redemption that can be found at both poles of the Johannine experience: Judaism and Hellenistic syncretism. (See Schillebeeckx, *Christ* 321-31; C. H. Talbert, *NTS* 22 [1975-76] 418-40.)

35 (D) Son of God. Central to the revealing task of Jesus is his being the Son of God. John is not the first to use this term to speak of Jesus. It can be found in one of the earliest christological confessions in the NT (Rom 1:3-4) and in the earliest of the Gospels (see Mark 1:1,11; 9:7; 15:39). There is every indication that the concept, so important to the NT as a whole, had its origins in the relationship which existed between Jesus of Nazareth and the God of Israel, a relationship which Jesus summed up by his use of the term "*abba*" (→ Jesus, 78:30-31, 35-37). Yet the Johannine use of "the Son" is bolder than its earlier uses to interpret the person and significance of Jesus. Again we seem to find the evan-

gelist leading his community on their journey from the earlier use of christological terminology into a new vision which could be grasped (even if not accepted) by the world the community was leaving. In the new world, both evangelist and commmunity would live and preach Jesus of Nazareth, the unique once-for-all revelation of his God, whom he claimed was his Father (see 5:17-18).

36 The absolute use of the term "the Son" appears only 3 times in the Synoptic Gospels (Matt 11:27, par. Luke 10:22; Mark 13:32, par. Matt 24:36; Matt 28:19); once in Paul (1 Cor 15:28); and 5 times in Hebrews (Heb 1:2,8; 3:6; 5:8; 7:28). In John, Jesus speaks of his sonship 20 times (3:16,17,18; 5:18 [twice], 20,21,22,23 [twice], 25,26; 6:40; 8:35-36; 10:36; 11:4; 14:13; 17:1 [twice]); additionally, it appears 4 times as a Johannine comment (3:35,36 [twice], 20:31), once in the Prologue (1:18), and 4 times on the lips of others (1:34: JBap; 1:49: Nathanael; 11:27: Martha; 19:7: "the Jews"). There is also a series of "sonship" passages where Jesus refers to God as his Father (see R. Schnackenburg, *The Gospel according to St John* [3 vols.; NY, 1968-82] 2. 174-77). These sayings almost always express a relationship between God and Jesus (e.g., 1:18,34; 3:16; 5:19-26; 6:40; 14:13). This title of honor is not ultimately about Jesus, but about God and God's relationship to the world and those who dwell in the world but are not of the world (3:16-17; 17:14-16). "The Johannine Son-Christology is essentially the doctrine of salvation for believers, i.e., not a doctrine about Jesus Christ in isolation but taking in the human race, with Jesus as God's emissary revealing and mediating salvation" (Schnackenburg, *St John* 2. 185). This is made clear in 3:16-21,34-36, passages that argue fundamental Johannine themes. Jesus' mission is explained in terms of God's having so loved the world that he sent his only son (v 16) in order that the world may have the opportunity to accept or refuse the light and truth (vv 19-21,35-36) found in him (vv 18,36). Salvation or condemnation is already made possible through the acceptance or refusal of that life available in the revelation of God in the Son (vv 17,36; see esp. 5:24-25).

37 The close link that exists between the glorification of the Son and the event of the cross is expressed in 11:4,40 (see also 14:13). The glory spoken of in 11:4 is the glory that the Son will have when he returns to the presence of his Father (14:13; 17:1,5), but this glory will be his as a result of the cross. Although the glory of God shines through all the words and deeds of Jesus, it is on the cross where he reveals love (13:1; 15:13); there is the place where God's saving revelation in his Son shines forth. Jesus claims that he is the Son of God and that because of his Sonship he has authority to reveal what he has seen with his Father and thus bring eternal life to those who believe in him. The preexistent Word of God has become flesh, dwelling among us as God's Son, revealing the truth or (as John would say) making visible the glory as of the only Son of the Father (1:14). The evangelist has written a Gospel so that his readers may come to an ever-deeper belief in this revelation, confess Jesus as the Son, and thus come to eternal life (20:31).

(Dodd, *Interpretation*, 250-62. Moloney, F. J., "The Johannine Son of God," *Salesianum* 38 [1976] 71-86. Schillebeeckx, *Christ* 427-32.)

38 (E) Son of Man. This Son-of-God christology is dominant as a God who loves is revealed to the world in an act of love as the Son freely lays down his life (10:11,17-18; 12:27; 13:1; 15:13). However, John has its own view of the cross, not as a moment of humiliation (see Phil 2:5-11; Mark 15:33-39) but as Jesus' consummation of his life's journey and purpose, the place where he returns to the glory that was his and where he glorifies his Father by bringing to perfection the task given to him (4:34; 11:4; 13:31–32; 17:4; 19:30). One of the techniques used by the evangelist to make this point is the Gk vb. *hypsōthēnai*, which has a double meaning: "to lift up physically," and "to exalt" (3:14). It is clear that the event of the cross is simultaneously the lifting up of Jesus on a cross and the exaltation of Jesus (Thüsing, *Erhöhung* 3–49; cf. G. C. Nicholson, *Death as Departure* [SBLDS 63; Chico, 1983]). It is important to notice further that this very important Johannine play on words is always associated with another title which had been used of Jesus in the Synoptic Gospels (→ Jesus, 78:38–41), and which is developed here: the Son of Man (3:13–14; 8:28; 12:23,32–34).

39 In part John reaches back into early Christian tradition. After the initial promise that the believer will see the revelation of the heavenly in the Son of Man (1:51), the same title is consistently used in association with the "lifting up" on the cross, reflecting the Marcan use of the title "the Son of Man" in the passion predictions (Mark 8:31; 9:31; 10:33–34). However, again John has gone his own way. The Synoptic tradition also used this term to speak of Jesus as a human figure who has a unique authority and who will eventually return as universal judge (Mark 2:10,27–28; 8:38; 13:26; 14:21,40; Matt 13:37; 16:13,28; 24:29–30,39; Luke 6:22; 9:58; 11:30; 17:22,24,26,30; 21:36). Because, for John, the presence of Jesus is the revelation of God among men and women, this presence also brings judgment (3:16–21,31–36; 5:24–25; 12:44–50). Thus, we can say that John is able to fuse the two Synoptic uses, drawing the judgment theme back into the historical encounter with Jesus (John 5:27; 9:35–39; 12:24–36). It should also be noticed that a future judgment is not totally excluded in John; this is most clear in 5:28–29 in the context of the Johannine presentation of Jesus, the Son of Man, as judge (5:27).

40 Further Son-of-Man sayings in John indicate that Jesus is the unique giver of life (6:27,53). These sayings also seem to be linked to the cross, the fulfillment of the "work of God" (see 6:28–29). It appears that John uses a traditional term to present the earthly ministry of Jesus—and especially the "lifting up" on the cross—as "the place" where the man Jesus, the Son of Man, reveals God and thus brings life and judgment. However, in perfect agreement with the rest of Johannine christology, such an understanding of Jesus, the Son of Man, is possible only because he comes from the Father and will return to the Father (3:13; 6:62). The cross, the focal point of the human revelation of God in the Johannine scheme of things, is never very far from the Son-of-Man sayings. It is not surprising that the final Son-of-Man passage (placed in the context of the hour that has come) points to the imminent revelation of the glory of the Father and the subsequent glorification of the Son. But here the language used is not Father/Son, but God/Son of Man: "Now is the Son of Man glorified, and in him God is glorified; if God is glorified in him, God will also glorify him in himself, and glorify him at once" (13:31–32). The language used differs, as the evangelist wishes to throw the human event of the cross into greater relief; but the underlying theology is the same.

(Coppens, J., "Le fils de l'homme dans l'évangile johannique," *ETL* 52 [1976] 28–81. Lindars, B., *Jesus Son of Man* [London, 1983] 145–57. Maddox, R. "The Function of the Son of Man in the Gospel of John," *Reconciliation and Hope* [Fest. L. L. Morris; ed. R. J. Banks; Exeter, 1974] 186–204. Meeks, W. A., "The Man from Heaven in Johannine Sectarianism," *JBL* 91 [1972] 44–72. Moloney, *Son of Man*. Smalley, S. S., "The Johannine Son of Man Sayings," *NTS* 15 [1968–69] 278–301.)

41   (F) "I Am He." Another unique feature of John's presentation of the person and function of Jesus of Nazareth is the "I am" (Gk *egō eimi*) sayings. These sayings are generally grouped into three forms exhibiting different grammatical structures.

(i) *No Predicate Complement* or absolute use. 8:24: "You will die in your sins unless you believe that *I am* [*he*]"; 8:28: "When you have lifted up the Son of Man, then you will know that *I am* [*he*]"; 8:58: "Before Abraham was, *I am*"; 13:19: "So that when it does take place you may believe that *I am* [*he*]." Although there are many examples of the use of "I am" in the syncretistic religions of antiquity (e.g., mystery religions, Hermetic literature and Mithraic liturgies), a comparison shows that the Johannine use of the absolute *egō eimi* has no parallel in such literature.

42 There is now widespread agreement that the most likely background for the Johannine sayings is the OT. Many have looked to Exod 3:14, where the name YHWH is revealed as "I am who I am" (Hebr *'ehyĕh 'ăšer 'ehyĕh*), but this is not very helpful; the LXX does not translate the passage with a finite verb but with the participle *ho ōn*, "the existing one." A more likely background is the prophetic literature, and esp. Dt-Isa. One of the main concerns of this prophet was to assert the authoritative word of the unique God of Israel, YHWH, against the claims of the "other Gods." He did this through the use of two Hebr expressions (*'ănî hû'* and *'ănî yhwh*): Isa 43:10: "You are my witnesses . . . and my servant whom I have chosen that you may know and believe that *I am He* [*'ănî hû'*]"; 45:18: "*I am the Lord* [*'ănî yhwh*] and there is no other." In these and other passages (Isa 41:4; 43:13; 46:4; 48:12; Deut 32:39), the Hebrew for "I am He" and "I am the Lord" is translated in the LXX by *egō eimi*.

43 As in Dt-Isa YHWH revealed himself through these formulas, so also with John: Jesus reveals his uniqueness not by speaking of his divine "being" but by taking over a formula used by YHWH, through his prophet, to reveal himself to his people. Thus, the Johannine Jesus carries on the task of revelation: he reveals God, his Father, and identifies his task with God's will (see 17:3–4).

> If a translation of *egō eimi* in these verses (8:24,28) is sought I should be inclined to offer the colloquial English, "I'm the one," that is, "It is at me, to me, that you must look, it is I whom you must hear." This corresponds well with John's view of the person of Jesus, and harmonizes well with such passages as Isaiah 45:18–25. The sense would be not, "Look at me because I am identical with the Father," but "Look at me for I am the one by looking at whom you will see the Father (14:9), since I make him known" (1:18).
> (Barrett, *Essays* 13)

44   (ii) *Understood Predicate Complement*. An example of this form of "I am" saying is John 6:20: the frightened disciples see someone coming to them across the waters, but Jesus assures them, "*Egō eimi*, do not be afraid." This may simply mean, "It is only I, so you need not worry." A similar use is found in 18:5, where Jesus presents himself to the arresting party who have come for him, saying, "*Egō eimi*." Once again, this may mean only, "I am the one you are looking for." In these cases, however, contexts are important. After the bread miracle and the attempts of the crowd to make him King, Jesus escapes (6:15), only to reveal himself as something more than a messianic pretender who has come to bring the second manna (see 2 Apoc. Bar. 29:8–30:1). Similarly, the collapse of the arresting party before the word of Jesus (18:6) shows that something more than "Jesus of Nazareth" is present.

45   These passages should be understood in the light of the OT use of "I am YHWH" in theophanies. Sometimes such revelations are used to reassure men and women and are often accompanied by an exhortation not to fear (Gen 26:24; Isa 51:12). On other occasions this revelatory statement is given as an indication of the authority of God's revelation (Exod 6:6; 20:1,5; Lev 18:6; Isa 52:6). There is a revelation of God in these two Johannine encounters with Jesus: one is to comfort and strengthen (6:20) and the other is a revelation that leaves all prostrate with fear before the revealer (18:5–6).

46   (iii) *Expressed Predicate Complement.* While the above forms of "I am" sayings are closely linked to the revelation of God in and through Jesus, this final form is more closely associated with Jesus' function: 6:51: "I am the bread of life"; 8:12; 9:5: "I am the light of the world"; 10:7,9: "I am the door (of the sheep)"; 10:11,14: "I am the good shepherd"; 11:25: "I am the resurrection and the life"; 14:6: "I am the way, the truth, and the life"; 15:1,5: "I am the (true) vine."

47   Some have argued that these sayings are polemical statements against the claims of other revealer figures as life, light, truth; and thus they are "strongly stressed and always contrasted with false or pretended revelation" (R. Bultmann, *The Gospel of John* [Phl, 1971] 226). Although there is a measure of truth in this insight, there is no need to go to gnostic revealer figures (as does Bultmann) to find the contrasts. These strong affirmations of the uniqueness of Jesus are much better understood within the context of a past (the manna given by Moses, the light at the feast of Tabernacles, the way of the Torah, etc.) which has now been replaced by Jesus.

48   Even here, however, these sayings are not primarily concerned with defining or describing Jesus in himself. All the predicates indicate what Jesus is in relation to women, men, and the world. In his mission he is the source of eternal life for all (vine, life, resurrection), the means through which all find life (way, gate), the one who leads all to life (shepherd) as he reveals the truth (light, truth) which can nourish their life (bread from heaven). These sayings reveal the divine commitment involved in the Father's sending his Son. It is possible for Jesus to make these claims only because he and the Father are one (10:30), and thus he possesses the life-giving power of the Father (10:21).

49   There is a difference between the "I am" sayings without an expressed predicate, which are directly concerned with the presentation of Jesus as the revealer and the revelation of God, and these sayings. Even here, however, the theme of revelation is present. Jesus, who is one with the Father, is able to reveal the Father in a unique way. Only because this is true can he be described as the vine, the life, the resurrection, the way, the gate, the good shepherd, the truth, and the bread of life—the unique saving revelation of God among men and women. Schnackenburg (*St John* 2. 88) states: "The Johannine *egō eimi* sayings are completely and utterly expressions of John's christology (Son, Son of Man) but have the particular advantage of making the saving character of Jesus' mission visible in impressive images and symbols."

(*BGJ* 1. 533–38. Harner, P. B., *The "I Am" of the Fourth Gospel* [FBBS 26; Phl, 1970]. Feuillet, A.,"Les *Egō eimi* christologiques du quatrième évangile," *RSR* 54 [1966] 5–22, 213–40. Schnackenburg, *St John* 2. 79–89. Zimmermann, H., "Das Absolute *egō eimi* als die neutestamentliche Offenbarungsformel," *BZ* 4 [1960] 54–69, 266–76.)

50   (G) Eschatology and the Spirit.   Reflecting John's claims about origin, destiny, and oneness with the Father's will, Jesus is presented during his earthly mission as the unique once-for-all revelation of God. This leads to the conviction of the evangelist that the moment of judgment is "now." The revelation of God in Jesus is the place where one must look upon a God who has revealed himself to us "now." One must make one's decisions "now" (see 3:16–21,35–36; 4:23; 5:24–25; 6:46–47; 9:39–41; 12:31,44–46). This so-called present (realized) eschatology is often seen as the only possible eschatology that could flow from the Johannine christology, dominated by Jesus' claim: "The Father and I are one" (10:30). Throughout the Gospel, however, there is mention of future resurrection and judgment (see 5:28–29; 6:39–40,54; 12:25,48; 14:3,18,28). The last discourse (esp. chaps. 15–16) makes frequent reference to the tribulations that will mark the coming of the messianic age. Thus, despite the centrality of a "present eschatology" in John, there are also many indications of a "future eschatology." If a "present eschatology" was the result of the sort of christology involved in the oneness between God and Jesus expressed in 10:30, then the "future eschatology" could claim to be the result of a christology reflected in another Johannine word of Jesus: "The Father is greater than I" (14:28).

51   These apparently contradictory elements can be best understood if we read John as a story of God, told through the life, death, resurrection, and return of Jesus to the Father. In such a Gospel story the evangelist is intensely interested in Jesus, but Jesus is not the end of the story. Only through revelation in and by Jesus can God become known; but as Jesus himself tells his disciples: "I have yet many things to say to you, but you cannot bear them now" (16:12). Although the historical appearance of Jesus is central to John's story, it is not final. In this, John is true to tradition. The Synoptic Gospels used a "future eschatology" to convey this message: the reigning presence of God is seen and experienced in Jesus' person and actions, but is still to come in power and glory. Thus the Synoptic Gospels are able to hold Jesus at the center of their story, but still look forward to the coming of the Son of Man (see esp. Matt 23:31–46, but the theme abounds in the Synoptic tradition). Attempts either to remove the "future" elements from John as the mistaken attempts of a later redactor (esp. Bultmann, *John* 218–21; *TNT* 2. 38) or to see one theme as a later Johannine rereading of an earlier version (e.g., M. E. Boismard, *RB* 68 [1961] 507–24) do not entirely answer the question of what the Johannine Gospel itself means. No matter what the history of the traditions may have been, our present text made sense to someone. What was that sense?

52   The Johannine community, at the end of the 1st cent. could not "look upon" and "hear" the historical Jesus. They were living in another stage—the stage of the Holy Spirit, an outflow of living water that would be received by those who believed in Jesus, but only after he had been glorified (7:39). There was something more to come, *after* the ministry of Jesus. This has been more fully worked out in the Paraclete sayings in the last discourse. The tension between the revealing presence of Jesus and the coming period of the Spirit is most explicitly expressed in 14:25–26: "These things I have spoken to you while I am still with you. But the Paraclete, the Holy Spirit, whom the Father will send in my name, he will teach you all things, and bring to your remembrance all that I have said to you." All the verbs in this passage are in the fut. tense (see also 16:13–15). The relationship between God and Jesus (a Father who sends a Son) is repeated in the relationship that will exist between the Paraclete and the Father. Yet the sending of the Paraclete depends on the departure of the Son (16:7). The Johannine community experienced the revelation of the Father through the action of the Spirit, not through direct contact with Jesus himself. However, it is still the story of Jesus telling the story of God that they are to hear, since the Paraclete does not bring a new revelation. That has taken place only once—in Jesus—but the Paraclete applies and elucidates what was already present in Jesus and his words (see BGJ 2. 1135–44). The Gospel exists because of that very truth: "Blessed are those who have not seen [the historical events of the story of Jesus] and yet believe" (20:29; also 17:20).

53   The life story of Jesus is not the end of God's revelation of himself. The experience of life and death within the community itself had to be dealt with. John was written at the end of the 1st cent., when death was surely one of the community's serious problems (and the death of the Beloved Disciple himself indicates that this was the case [21:20–23]). Is it possible that such a Gospel would have had no interest in "the other side of death"? Over the years of their journey—both physical and spiritual—members of the Johannine community had died and were still dying. "The one who hears my word and believes him who sent me has eternal life" (5:24) was not the whole answer, and this evangelist returned to earliest Christian tradition to find his answer in a "future eschatology" which did not deny the truth of the important "present eschatology."

54   There is no contradiction between 10:30 and 14:28 then. The life story of Jesus of Nazareth is not the end of the story of God. However, it is vital for John that the reader be fully aware that the God revealed in Jesus was truly God. Jesus is not revealing some secondary

God. "Yet he is *Deus revelatus;* not the whole abyss of Godhead, but God known" (Barrett, *Essays* 12). The community living after the glorification of Jesus at Easter, in the presence of the Spirit, is aware of this. Schillebeeckx (*Christ* 426–27) has summarized it well:

> The "now already" and the "not yet" are preserved, but in a community which lives in the present of the Easter grace. The tension is reproduced in what is clearly an authentic Johannine text: "I am the resurrection and the life; he who believes in me *though he die,* yet shall he live, and whoever lives and believes in me *shall never die*" (11:25). It is at this very point that we find the Johannine paradox of the eternal life of the Christian which has already begun; since Easter he is "from God" (like Jesus), and nevertheless still knows that he is to be raised at the last day—a grain of wheat, like Jesus!

(Betz, O., *Der Paraklet* [AGJU 2; Leiden, 1963]. Blank, J., *Krisis* [Freiburg, 1964]. Burge, G. M., *The Anointed Community: The Holy Spirit in the Johannine Tradition* [GR, 1986]. De la Potterie, I., "Parole et Esprit dans S. Jean," *L'Évangile de Jean* [ed. M. de Jonge; BETL 44; Gembloux, 1977] 177–201. Franck, E., *Revelation Taught: The Paraclete* [ConBNT 14; Lund, 1985]. Johnston, G., *The Spirit-Paraclete in the Gospel of John* [SNTSMS 12; Cambridge, 1970]. Kysar, R., "The Eschatology of the Fourth Gospel—A Correction of Bultmann's Hypothesis," *Perspective* 13 [1972] 23–33. Müller, U. B., "Die Parakletenvorstellung im Johannesevangelium," *ZTK* 71 [1974] 31–77. Porsch, F., *Pneuma und Wort* [FrFS 16; Frankfurt, 1974]. Richter, G., "Präsentische und futurische Eschatologie im vierten Evangelium," in *Gegenwart und kommendes Reich* [ed. P. Fiedler and D. Zeller; Stuttgart, 1975] 117–52. Schnackenburg, R., "Die johanneische Gemeinde und ihre Geisterfahrung," *Die Kirche des Anfangs* [Fest. H. Schürmann; ed. R. Schnackenburg, *et al.;* Leipzig, 1977] 277–306.)

THE BELIEVERS' RESPONSE

55   **(I) Signs and Faith.** Significantly, to characterize the response of faith John uses only the vb. *pisteuein* (98 times), never the noun *pistis.* The Johannine community is on a journey of faith, and perhaps nowhere is this better reflected than in the choice of a dynamic "doing-word" to speak of that journey. John's narrative unfolds between two passages explicitly aimed at the readers. In 1:1–18 the reader is given the solutions to the mystery of Jesus. The "story" that follows, however, is the story of various groups and individuals who have not read 1:1–18. Only the reader has read the Prologue. Thus, the people in the story frequently "misunderstand" Jesus (see Culpepper, *Anatomy* 151–65). They have only the signs and his words to go by, and often they are not able to penetrate into the mystery of Jesus, where he comes from (7:40–42; 8:23–24,42–44; 9:29,33), who he is (1:38,41,45,49; 3:2; 4:19,25–26; 6:25), or what he has come to do (2:19–20; 3:11–12; 4:13–15; 6:32–34,51–52). At the end of this story of "misunderstanding," the readers are informed that it has been told so that *they* may grow deeper in their faith in Jesus Christ as the Son of God and might have life in his name (20:31). This Gospel is not written to tell us about the faith experience of the people "in the story" but to challenge the faith of the people who are "reading the story" (Culpepper, *Anatomy* 15–49), who are to ask, "Where do I stand?"

56   Throughout John, various stages of faith are presented in the experience of different characters who meet Jesus and are called to a decision by his word and person. This appears to be a central theme in that section of John 2:1–4:54 which runs from Cana to Cana (*BGJ* 1. cxlii; F. J. Moloney, *Salesianum* 40 [1978] 817–43). In the two Cana miracles respectively the mother of Jesus and

a royal official entrust themselves to the efficacy of Jesus' word, whatever the cost (2:4–5; 4:48–50). Their faith leads to a "sign," and the first steps of faith in others (2:6–11; 4:51–53). Between these two accounts there are six other examples of faith. By means of these examples the evangelist challenges his readers. Those who do not accept the "word" of Jesus (e.g., "the Jews" [2:12–22] and the Samaritan woman at first [4:1–15]) must be judged as not believing. There is a further difficulty in the journey of faith for anyone who stops at the externals of the signs, understanding them within the categories determined by culture and history (e.g., Nicodemus [3:1–21] and the Samaritan woman in a second instance [4:16–26]). This "stage of faith" must be understood as partial. It is not the end of the story, as the subsequent journey of Nicodemus shows (see 7:50–52; 19:38–42). As the examples of the mother of Jesus and the royal official indicate, true faith is an unconditional commitment to "the word," i.e., the revelation of God in the word and person of Jesus (e.g., JBap [3:22–36] and the Samaritan villagers [4:39–42]). Examples could be multiplied, but this should suffice to show that the evangelist calls his readers to make their own journey from no faith, through partial faith, into full faith.

57   As for the complicated issue of the "signs," on several occasions the Johannine Jesus appears to be critical of a faith based on signs (2:23–25, and the subsequent example of Nicodemus, with the limitations of a "signs faith" expressed in 3:2; → John 61:45). Yet the Gospel ends with the evangelist declaring that he has written a book which tells the story of the "signs" of Jesus to lead people further into faith (20:31). This difficulty has often been explained by arguing that the evangelist was using an old source containing Synoptic-type miracle stories, and that there is still a certain conflict between the source and the Johannine use of the source, leading to seeming contradictions. While it is quite probable that the evangelist did use a "signs-source," there is no need to conclude that he used it poorly (see R. T. Fortna, *The Gospel of Signs* [SNTSMS 11; Cambridge, 1970]; W. Nicol, *The Semeia in the Fourth Gospel* [NovTSup 27; Leiden, 1972]). What must be grasped is that while the "signs" are important for John, they are what he calls them—signs. When believers base their faith on signs alone, that faith is insufficient. It is an incipient faith which may well lead them into true faith (Nicodemus), but it is also possible that the signs will take them no farther (esp. 6:26: "You seek me not because you saw signs, but because you ate your fill of the loaves"). Signs that become ends in themselves and do not lead the believer into a deeper recognition of the revelation of God in the word and person of Jesus are useless. However, signs can lead the believer beyond the sign to a recognition that Jesus Christ is the Son of God; then one may have life in his name (20:30–31).

(*BGJ* 1. 525–32. Baron, M., "La progression des confessions de foi dans les dialogues de S. Jean," *BVC* 82 [1968] 32–44. Giblin, C. H., "Suggestion, Negative Response, and Positive Action in St. John's Portrayal of Jesus," *NTS* 26 [1979–80] 197–211. Hahn, F., "Sehen und Glauben im Johannesevangelium," *Neues Testament und Geschichte* [Fest. O. Cullmann; ed. H. Baltensweiler, et al.; Tübingen, 1972] 125–41. Painter, *John* 71–85. Schnackenburg, *St John* 1. 558–75. Walter, L., *Foi et incredulité selon S. Jean* [Lire la Bible 43; Paris, 1976].)

58   (II) Sacraments. Tension between the revealing presence of God in Jesus "now" and the need to look to some future moment emerges again in allusions to the community's sacramental life. Some scholars argue for a strong presence of sacramental allusions (esp. O. Cullmann, *Early Christian Worship* [SBT 10; London, 1953]). Others claim that such references have been added by a later ecclesiastical redactor in an attempt to make the original "word-Gospel" conform more closely to the ways of the early church (esp. Bultmann, *John* 138–40, 300, 324–25, 677–78; *TNT* 2. 3–14). No matter what their origin, clear references to eucharist and baptism are found in 3:5; 6:51c–58; 19:34; and 1 John 5:8. Is it possible to understand these references as a coherent part of the Johannine theology (→ John, 61:50–51)?

59   At the end of the 1st cent., John proclaims that a God who loves has sent his only Son into the world (3:16–17). This Son, Jesus Christ, had a task (*ergon*) to bring to completion (esp. 4:34; 17:4). That task was to make God known, so that women and men could come to eternal life (17:2–3). He performed this task in many ways: through his discourses (*logos* and *rhēmata*), through his "signs" (*sēmeia*), and through the supreme act of love, when he is "lifted up" on the cross (3:13–14; 8:28; 12:32; 13:1; 15:13; 19:30). Jesus not only "speaks" and "gives signs" of his oneness with a Father who loves (10:30), but he reveals this Father by loving in a consummate fashion. John demands that believers "look upon" Jesus the unique revealer of God (esp. 1:18; 3:13; 6:46; 8:38) to see the revelation of the Father. This is promised in the programmatic 1:51: "You *will see* the heavens opened"; and it is repeated like an antiphon through the whole Gospel (see 1:18; 4:45; 5:37; 6:2,36; 8:38,57; 9:37; 11:40; 14:7,9; 15:24; 16:16–17; 19:22,35) climaxing in the final words of the scene at the cross: "They *shall look* on him whom they have pierced" (19:37; C. Traets, *Voir Jésus et*

le Père en Lui selon l'Évangile de Saint Jean [AnGreg 159; Rome, 1967]).

60   Such teaching is very clear, but for the Johannine community at the end of the 1st cent. Jesus was no longer present. As noted earlier, the absence of the physical revelation of the glory of God in the person of Jesus posed a problem for the community. Jesus' presence is assured throughout the last discourse (esp. 13:31–14:31) and in his final prayer (esp. 17:9–19), but how is he present? No doubt the proclamation of Jesus as "the Word" was a large part of the answer, but another part is reflected in the Johannine community's experience of sacraments. The two need not contradict each other. Throughout 6:25–58 a single theme is spelled out several times, but most clearly in 6:40: "For this is the will of my Father, that everyone who sees the Son and believes in him should have eternal life," and in 6:46–48: "Not that anyone has seen the Father except him who is from God; he has seen the Father. Truly, truly I say to you, the one who believes has eternal life." One could understand the reaction of the Johannine community faced with this teaching: "But where is he, that we may see him, and thus come to know the Father and possess eternal life?" The answer to that question is given in 6:51c–58: in Jesus' flesh and blood at their eucharistic celebrations. The eucharist for the Johannine community was the presence of the absent one (see F. J. Moloney, *DRev* 93 [1975] 243–51).

61   The same technique is used in 19:34. The whole of the passion account has culminated in the exaltation of Jesus as king upon his cross (19:17–21). There he has founded his church (19:25–27) and brought to perfection the task that his Father had given him (19:28–30). Such is the Johannine understanding of a past event, but how is it to become part of the present experience of the community? The answer is found in 19:34 as the blood and water, the life-giving sacraments of eucharist and baptism, are described as flowing down upon the nascent church from the king lifted up on his throne. In both sacraments, then, the Johannine community can find the presence of the absent one.

(On sacraments: Barrett, *Essays* 80–97. Brown, R. E., *New Testament Essays* [NY, 1982; orig. essay 1962] 51–76; *BGJ* 1. cxi–cxiv. Klos, H., *Die Sakramente im Johannesevangelium* [SBS 46; Stuttgart, 1970]. Léon-Dufour, X., *NTS* 27 [1980–81] 439–56. Matsunaga, K., *NTS* 27 [1980–81] 516–24. Moloney, F. J., *AusBR* 30 [1982] 10–33. Schnackenburg, R., in *SP* 2. 235–54. Tragan, P. R. (ed.), *Segni e Sacramenti nel Vangelo di Giovanni* [SAns 66; Rome, 1977], esp. E. Malatesta, pp. 165–81; S. M. Schneiders, pp. 221–35.)

62   (III) Conclusion. John brings the reader to a point of decision, as stated in the express goal of writing: "that you may believe that Jesus is the Christ, the Son of God, and that believing you may have life in his name." Knowing no middle course, John presents only two possibilities: to perish or to have eternal life (3:16). Humankind is inexorably faced with these alternatives, caught in a struggle between cosmic forces. On one side is darkness (blindness, evil, this world, the Prince of this world) and on the other is light (sight, the Spirit, life). To choose darkness means death, but the possibility of light and life has now been revealed in Jesus Christ. We judge ourselves by our own free decision for or against the revelation of God revealed in and through Jesus Christ. We can gaze upon him and be saved (3:13–14; 8:28; 12:32; 19:37).

SUGGESTED
BASIC BIBLIOGRAPHY

Each article in this commentary contains extensive bibliographies. Amid this profusion of references, the following limited list will aid students in selecting the basic books *in English* (where possible) that they may wish to consult or purchase.

GENERAL

ENGLISH BIBLES (for classroom and study purposes):

The New Oxford Annotated Bible with the Apocrypha: Expanded Edition (NY: Oxford, 1977). This employs the *RSV* with useful footnotes and excellent maps.
The New Jerusalem Bible (GC: Doubleday, 1985). Helpful notes.
The New American Bible (Saint Joseph ed.; NY: Catholic Book Publishing Co., 1970).
The *NAB* has also been published by other companies. In 1987 *The New Testament: Revised Edition* (Saint Joseph ed.; NY: Catholic Publishing Co.) appeared. The translation is the product of the labors of members of the Catholic Biblical Association of America.

DICTIONARIES:

Achtemeier, P. J. (ed.), *Harper's Bible Dictionary* (SF: Harper & Row, 1985).
Buttrick, G. A. (ed.), *The Interpreter's Dictionary of the Bible* (4 vols.; Nash: Abingdon, 1962).
An important *Supplementary Volume* (ed. K. Crim) was published in 1976.

ATLASES:

May, H. G. (ed.), *Oxford Bible Atlas* (3d ed.; NY: Oxford, 1985). The maps of this atlas are used in the *New Oxford Annotated Bible* (see above).
Rogerson, J. (ed.), *Atlas of the Bible* (NY: Facts on File, 1985).
Pritchard, J. B. (ed.), *The Harper Atlas of the Bible* (NY: Harper & Row, 1987).

BIBLIOGRAPHY:

Fitzmyer, J. A., *An Introductory Bibliography for the Study of Scripture* (Subsidia biblica 3; Rome: Biblical Institute, 1981).

North, R. (ed.), *Elenchus of Biblica* (Rome: Biblical Institute). This annual was formerly known as *Elenchus bibliographicus biblicus* and supplies an enormous amount of bibliographical material.
Also helpful are *BL, NTA, OTA*.

HISTORY OF TEXTS AND VERSIONS:

Kenyon, F. and A. W. Adams, *Our Bible and the Ancient Manuscripts* (NY: Harper, 1958).
Metzger, B. M., *The Early Versions of the New Testament: Their Origin, Transmission and Limitations* (Oxford: Clarendon, 1977).
Aland, K. and B., *The Text of the New Testament* (GR: Eerdmans, 1987).
Würthwein, E., *The Text of the Old Testament* (rev. ed.; GR: Eerdmans, 1979).

GEOGRAPHY:

Baly, D., *The Geography of the Bible* (rev. ed.; NY: Harper, 1974).

ARCHAEOLOGY:

Avi-Yonah, M., *et al.* (eds.), *Encyclopedia of Archaeological Excavations in the Holy Land* (4 vols.; EC: Prentice Hall, 1975–78).

CONCORDANCES:

Whitaker, R. W. (ed.), *Eerdmans Analytical Concordance to the Revised Standard Version* (GR: Eerdmans, 1988).
Ellison, J. W. (ed.), *Nelson's Complete Concordance of the Revised Standard Version of the Bible* (2d ed.; NY: Nelson, 1984).
Hartdegen, S. (ed.), *Nelson's Complete Concordance of the New American Bible* (Collegeville, MN: Liturgical, 1977).

PERIODICALS:

The Catholic Biblical Quarterly, Interpretation, The Journal of Biblical Literature, Biblical Theology Bulletin

OLD TESTAMENT

BACKGROUND:

Anderson, B. W., *Understanding the Old Testament* (4th ed.; EC: Prentice Hall, 1986).
Boadt, L., *Reading the Old Testament: An Introduction* (NY: Paulist, 1984). Popular.
De Vaux, R., *Ancient Israel* (NY: McGraw-Hill, 1961).
Eissfeldt, O., *The Old Testament: An Introduction* (NY: Harper, 1965). A standard reference work.
Miller, J. M. and J. H. Hayes, *A History of Ancient Israel and Judah* (Phl: Westminster, 1986).
Herrmann, S., *A History of Israel in Old Testament Times* (2d ed.; Phl: Fortress, 1981).
Rendtorff, H., *The Old Testament: An Introduction* (Phl: Fortress, 1986).
Reventlow, H., *Problems of Old Testament Theology in the Twentieth Century* (Phl: Fortress, 1985).

HEBREW AND ARAMAIC BIBLE:

Introductory Works:
Johns, A. F., *A Short Grammar of Biblical Aramaic* (Berrien Springs: Andrews University, 1966).
Lambdin, T. O., *Introduction to Biblical Hebrew* (NY: Scribner, 1971).

Weingreen, J., *A Practical Grammar for Classical Hebrew* (2d ed.; Oxford: Clarendon, 1959).

Text:
Biblia hebraica stuttgartensia (Stuttgart: Deutsche Bibelgesellschaft, 1977).

Dictionary:
Brown, F., S. R. Driver, and C. A. Briggs, *A Hebrew and English Lexicon of the Old Testament* (corrected impression; Oxford: Clarendon, 1952).

Grammar:
Gesenius, W. and E. Kautzsch, *Gesenius' Hebrew Grammar* (tr. A. E. Cowley; Oxford: Clarendon, 1910).

Concordance:
Mandelkern, S., *Veteris Testamenti concordantiae hebraicae et chaldaicae* (9th ed.; Jerusalem: Schocken, 1971).

SEPTUAGINT:

Text:
Rahlfs, A., *Septuaginta* (2 vols.; 3d ed.; Stuttgart: Württembergische Bibelanstalt, 1949).
The Septuagint Version of the Old Testament and Apocrypha, with an English Translation (London: Bagster; NY: Harper, 1900). Not a critical text, but convenient.

Concordance:
Hatch, E. and H. Redpath, *A Concordance to the Septuagint* (2 vols.; Graz: Akademische Verlags-anstalt, 1954).

NEW TESTAMENT

BACKGROUND:

Kümmel, E. G., *Introduction to the New Testament* (rev. H. C. Kee; Nash: Abingdon, 1975).
Perkins, P., *Reading the New Testament* (2d ed.; NY: Paulist, 1988). Popular.

GREEK NEW TESTAMENT:

Introductory Works:
Gignac, F. T., *An Introductory New Testament Greek Course* (Chicago: Loyola University, 1973).

Text:
Aland, K., *et al.* (eds.), Nestle-Aland: *Greek English New Testament* (26th ed.; Stuttgart: Deutsche Bibelgesellschaft; NY: United Bible Societies, 1979).

Dictionary:
Bauer, W., *A Greek-English Lexicon of the New Testament* (ed. W. F. Arndt, *et al.;* 2d ed.; Chicago: University of Chicago, 1979).

Grammar:
Blass, F. and A. Debrunner, *A Greek Grammar of the New Testament* (ed. R. W. Funk; Chicago: University of Chicago, 1961).

Concordances:
Moulton, W. F. and A. S. Geden, *A Concordance to the Greek Testament* (5th ed.; Edinburgh: Clark, 1978).
Aland, K., *et al., Vollständige Konkordanz zum griechischen Neuen Testament* (2 vols.; Berlin/NY: De Gruyter, 1975–83).

Parallel Gospel Texts:

Synoptics:
Huck, A. and H. Greeven, *Synopse der drei ersten Evangelien mit Beigabe der johanneischen Parallel-stellen—Synopsis of the First Three Gospels with the Addition of the Johannine Parallels* (13th ed.; Tübingen: Mohr [Siebeck], 1981).

Four Gospels:
Aland, K., *Synopsis of the Four Gospels: Greek English Edition of the Synopsis Quattuor Evangeliorum with the Text of the Revised Standard Version* (Stuttgart/NY: United Bible Societies, 1972).

RELATED AREAS

Vermes, G., *The Dead Sea Scrolls in English* (3d ed.; London/NY: Penguin, 1987).
Charlesworth, J. (ed.), *The Old Testament Pseudepigrapha* (2 vols.; GC: Doubleday, 1983–85).
Sparks, H. F. D. (ed.), *The Apocryphal Old Testament* (Oxford: Clarendon, 1984).
Hennecke, E. and W. Schneemelcher, *New Testament Apocrypha* (ed. R. M. Wilson; 2 vols.; Phl: Westminster, 1964).
Robinson, J. M. (director), *The Nag Hammadi Library in English* (NY: Harper & Row, 1977).

INDEX

INDEX

INDEX

The references in the index are to article and section numbers: thus, 70:18,22 refers to sections 18 and 22 in article 70 (Modern New Testament Criticism). References in boldface indicate principal treatment of a subject. The index covers both subjects and persons. The bibliographies are not indexed. The attention of the reader is also called to the helpful outlines provided in each article.

MEMORANDA

MEMORANDA

MEMORANDA

MEMORANDA

MEMORANDA

MEMORANDA

MEMORANDA

MEMORANDA

MEMORANDA

THE WORLD OF THE NEW TESTAMENT
ROME AND THE EASTERN MEDITERRANEAN

Boundary of the Roman Empire — Provincial boundaries — + Seven Churches of Asia

0   100   200   300   400   500 miles